Bill James presents. . .

STATS™
All-Time
Baseball Sourcebook

Edited by Bill James, John Dewan, Neil Munro and Don Zminda

Jim Callis, Associate Editor

Ethan D. Cooperson, Kevin Fullam, Jim Henzler,
Chuck Miller, Tony Nistler and Mat Olkin, Assistant Editors

STATS
PUBLISHING

Published by STATS Publishing
A Division of Sports Team Analysis & Tracking Systems, Inc.

Cover by Walter Lis and Ron Freer

First Edition: August, 1998

Printed in the United States of America

ISBN 1-884064-53-1

Acknowledgments

Many people had a hand in compiling the information contained in the *STATS All-Time Baseball Sourcebook*. We'd like to take this opportunity to thank them.

We'll begin with Associate Editor Jim Callis, who took care of most of the details involved in putting the book together. It was a huge task, and Jim handled it magnificently. Thanks, Jim.

Chuck Miller did the designs for the various sections of the book, with some timely assistance from Kevin Fullam. Mat Olkin wrote many of the prose sections of the book, including the vast majority of the team capsules, and he also handled numerous other details involved in producing the final manuscript. Jim Henzler of the Publications Department programmed several sections of the book and wrote numerous data-entry and checking programs. Ethan D. Cooperson coordinated much of the data entry needed to produce the All-Star Game and postseason sections, and Tony Nistler coordinated data entry for the manager and umpire sections. Dan Ford's expert knowledge of old-time ballplayers, particularly the Negro Leaguers, was invaluable in helping us select many of the STATS Awards winners.

A number of programmers worked on various sections of the book: Dave Carlson, Mike Hammer, Stefan Kretschmann, David Pinto, Jeff Schinski and Allan Spear. Kevin Thomas helped on a number of the data-entry programs during the early stages of production. Thanks, guys. Thanks also go to STATS Chief Operating Officer Marty Gilbert, who was an enormous help in coordinating the programming resources for this book, and to Assistant Director of Information Services Mike Canter, who was always able to find a way to fit the numerous programming tasks into the Systems Department schedule.

Tips of the hat also should go to Walter Lis, who designed the cover for this book; to Marc Elman, who worked tirelessly at getting this book (and the *All-Time Handbook*) into bookstores; and to Steve Byrd, for his efforts in promoting all our products and services, including this book.

Thanks also to the other STATS employees: Doug Abel, Arthur Ashley, Andrew Bernstein, Grant Blair, Derek Boyle, Jim Capuano, Jeff Chernow, Brian Cousins, Sue Dewan, Steve Drago, Scott Enslen, Drew Faust, Mark Hong, Michael Janosi, Sherlinda Johnson, Antoinette Kelly, Jason Kinsey, Greg Kirkorsky, Kenneth Li, Tracy Lickton, Jennifer Manicki, Bob Meyerhoff, Betty Moy, Jim Musso, Jim Osborne, Brent Osland, Mary Owen, Oscar Palacios, Doug Palm, Dean Peterson, Pat Quinn, Corey Roberts, Eric Robin, Mike Sarkis, John Sasman, Carol Savier, Taasha Schroeder, Heather Schwarze, Stephanie Seburn, Matt Senter, Leena Sheth, Scott Spencer, Nick Stamm, Bill Stephens, Devin Tuffy, Joe Weindel and Susan Zamechek. We also want to thank part-timers Thom Henninger, Chad Huebner and Randy Lakeman for their great help with data entry, research and fact-checking. Part-timers Josephine Mallari, Sydney Moy and Jason Raidbard also contributed to the project.

Finally, a number of people outside STATS helped us compile the information you see in this book. Bill wanted to thank Greg Mount, Rob Neyer and John Sickels, three of his former assistants, for their research contributions over the years. Neil singled out Frank Williams, John Schwartz, Bob Davids and the many members of the Society for American Baseball Research who assisted him in tracking down a lot of the more out-of-the-way information. Bill Carle has supplied us with biographical information (birth and death dates) for a number of years. Although he works for a nominal competitor, Pete Palmer has been very generous in sharing information with Neil, as Neil does with him, to the benefit of the entire baseball community. David Rawnsley's amateur draft database also proved helpful.

Several other SABR members were particularly helpful in supplying research material for the *Sourcebook*. Bill Deane researched missing data for a number of sections of the book, especially the awards section. Bob Tiemann helped us fill in the gaps in our month-by-month and home-road data, as well as information on pennant-clinching dates and days in first place. Ray Nemec also provided us with difficult-to-find data.

Another huge help was Retrosheet and especially David Smith, who helped us fill in the blanks in our box scores of baseball's greatest games. Their play-by-play information is available free of charge and is copyrighted by Retrosheet, which can be contacted at 20 Sunset Road, Newark, DE 19711.

Our deep appreciation to all of you.

— Bill James, John Dewan, Neil Munro and Don Zminda

To my wife Ann and sons A.J. and Ryan,
who bring me so much joy
and make each new day the best of my life.

—Jim Callis

Table of Contents

Introduction by Bill James

Sooner or later, it was inevitable that baseball encyclopedias would outgrow a single volume.

While this is intended to be a fun book, entirely on its own, it is also intended to be a companion to a book we published a few months ago, the *All-Time Handbook*. The *Handbook* has the most complete batting, pitching, and fielding records ever compiled for all players who have ever played in the major leagues—and almost nothing else.

Those of us who put this book together absolutely love baseball reference books, perhaps to a degree that is not entirely healthy. We publish a lot of reference books, and we had talked for ten years about doing an encyclopedia, so when we sat down to revive the project, about eighteen months ago, there was a lot of history behind us. We had all come up with things that we wanted to do in an encyclopedia—lots of things. Hundreds of things; millions. OK, so it wasn't a million; it seemed like it.

As a base line, we wanted to publish a book that included all of the "little" stats that the other encyclopedias leave out—GDP, pitcher's hitting stats, sacrifice hits and flies, hit by pitch and hit batsmen, intentional walks, batters facing pitcher, home runs at home and on the road, etc., etc. We did that in the *All-Time Handbook*, but we had a million other things that we wanted to do, some of which had been done before in other reference books, but just not lately, and some of which had never been done at all, perhaps because nobody had ever thought of them, but more likely because only the advent of the computer age had made it practical to undertake the research.

I'll give you an example: what's the record for the lowest opponents' on-base percentage by a rookie pitcher? That record is in here (it's .199, by Guy Hecker in 1882), but do you want to try researching that without a computer? You do? OK, hold on a minute, I've got a hundred more here. . .

There's a lot of things you can know now that it just was not possible to know fifteen years ago. I can't tell you that all of that stuff is interesting, but some of it is *really* interesting. It is kind of fun to know who drove in the most runs through age 29, who drove in the most runs at age 29, and who drove in the most runs after age 29. It is fun to see the all-time leaders in GDP or wild pitches. There are hundreds of lists in this book which, as far as we know, have never been published before.

But in truth, most of the things which make up this book *have* been published before, somewhere, sometime, in some form, God knows where. There's a section in this book that gives the won-lost record for each major league team in each month of its history—what the August and September records of the White Sox, Twins, Tigers and Red Sox were, for example, as they battled for the pennant in 1967. That's probably been published before, somewhere. Most of it. It was a substantial research effort to put it all together.

There is a section in this book that gives box scores and accounts of every postseason game in the 20th century. That's all been published before. I mean, we didn't have a reporter at the 1912 World Series; we got the information second-hand from somewhere. But it's never been brought together before, anywhere that you could find it all.

There is a section in this book which has box scores of the games that people still talk about 20 years later, like Harvey Haddix' 12 perfect innings and the 26-inning game and the 26-23 game and the time Mark Whiten went nuclear. All of those box scores have been published before, somewhere.

Some of the things in this book have been published in media guides, if you have a collection of those. Some of them have been published by *The Sporting News*, in the *Dope Book* (which hasn't been published in more than ten years) or *Daguerreotypes* (but leaving out a few categories). Some of them were published in SABR publications in the 1970s.

To acquire all of those books, you can spend any amount of money. I spend hundreds of dollars a year on my baseball library, and have for many years, and I still don't have all of it. And I lose a couple of hours every day trying to find the information I want in the books that I have.

So when we sat down to outline what we wanted to have in a comprehensive baseball reference, I had some things I wanted to include, Don Zminda had some things, John Dewan had some things, Neal Munro had some things, and a lot of other people had their own ideas, some of which were nutty. We asked the same questions about everything—how many pages is that, how many hours of work would be required to pull it together, how many people would want the information once we had it? As it turned out, getting the information together was never really a problem, never a big enough problem that we couldn't get past it if we cared about the information. The problem was the pages. When we first outlined our encyclopedia, we had. . . I forget how many thousands of pages it was. We had a lot more than we could possibly get into one volume. For that matter, we had a lot more than we could possibly get into two volumes. One volume is the player's records, the *All-Time Handbook*. This volume is the most interesting stuff that was left on the list.

This book is just a collection of things that you want to know sometimes, if you're a baseball fan, brought together in a place where you can find it, where you can revel in it, where you can roll around in it until you forget what it was that you were looking for. Baseball exists to be enjoyed. We only hope that this book helps you to love the game.

The Evolution of Baseball Statistics

by Neil Munro

While many casual fans have come to believe that there are innumerable baseball statistics, the most commonly used ones can be summarized in three distinct categories. These include the counting statistics, percentages and analysis statistics. This outline will only attempt to deal with the first two categories. The analysis statistics have been primarily developed by members of The Society for American Baseball Research (SABR) in recent times, but they have actually been added to baseball's lore by many dedicated fans, sportswriters and managers for more than a century. Some of the more exotic ones may gradually evolve into those as recognizable as the RBI or ERA, but their time for this recognition has not yet arrived.

The Counting Statistics— Batting and Baserunning

Since 1876, when the National League was organized as a professional sport with permanent teams, player contracts and a season-long schedule of games, the following batting statistical categories have not really changed to the present day. The number of times a player batted (at-bats), struck out, walked (given his base on balls)—along with the number of base hits, two-base hits (doubles), three-base hits (triples) and home runs he collected—have remained fairly consistent even if they were not always dutifully or accurately recorded. One small exception to this list centers on home runs hit—particularly for the case in which a batter drove in the game-winning run(s) with a homer in the bottom of the last inning. In the years before 1920, a player received credit for only enough bases to account for the winning run. For example, if he hit a bases-loaded home run in the bottom of the ninth inning when his team trailed by one run, he would only get credit for a double and two runs driven in (the runs needed to win the game). From 1920 to the present, the batter would get a home run and four RBI in this situation.

In addition, the number of strikes and balls needed for a strikeout or a walk varied for baseball's first 15 years. A batter struck out on three strikes between 1876 and 1886, and again from 1888 to the present. In the 1887 season, four strikes were required. In addition, the rules governing foul balls and called strikes have been modified several times during those years when three strikes constituted a strikeout. Strikeouts are not available for batters for the years from 1897 to 1909 in the NL, and for the years 1901 to 1912 in the American League. This batting statistic is also unavailable for the American Association from 1882 to 1888, for the Union Association for 1884 (its one year of existence) and for the Federal League in 1914 and 1915 . The rules did not change for this period; the data is simply incomplete for batters (it is complete for pitchers' strikeouts, however).

The number of balls needed for a batter to be credited with a walk has changed over the same period of time to an even greater extent. Between 1876 and 1879, nine balls were necessary for a walk. The rule was revised for 1880 and 1881 so that eight balls were required, then it became seven balls for 1882 and 1883, then six balls for 1884 and 1885, then back to seven for 1886, then changed again to five for 1887 and 1888 and finally to our present-day four in 1889. For the 1887 season only, a batter received credit for a base hit (and was charged with a time at bat) when he received a base on balls. This rule was changed retroactively by Major League Baseball so that the walks are now recorded for 1887 in the same fashion as in every other season. Earlier guides and encyclopedias do not always reflect this revision of baseball statistical history, though.

The number of times that a batter received an intentional walk (IBB) was officially recorded for the first time in 1955. Hence the statistic is shown only from 1955 to the present (for batters and pitchers). However, this category has been researched to a small extent for some of the more noteworthy batters who played before 1955.

The number of runs batted in by a batter became an official baseball statistic for the first time in the 1920 season. Prior to that time, the RBI concept had been advocated by many of the game's most noteworthy scribes, in particular by Ernie Lanigan. The RBI was originally referred to as "the number of runs responsible for" (RRF) in the baseball guides from 1920 to 1928. Lanigan actually published his own tabulations of RBI totals for the 1907 through 1919 seasons. Most of the RBI totals for the years before 1907 were compiled by Informations Concepts, Inc. (ICI), which was commissioned to carry out the historical research that became the basis for much of the statistical data appearing in the player register section of the first Macmillan *Baseball Encyclopedia* published in 1969. Some of this data was taken from earlier guides and from the personal statistical collections of baseball historians Lee Allen and John Tattersall. Most were compiled from reconstructing the play-by-play accounts of baseball games from newspaper articles and box scores. Even today, we are still missing the complete RBI data for a few 19th century seasons (the UA in 1884 and the AA from 1882 to 1884). For a few years after the RBI became an official statistic (1920 to 1939), a batter was credited with an RBI when a teammate scored as a batter grounded into a double play.

The game-winning RBI (GWRBI) made a very brief appearance as an official baseball statistic from 1980 to 1988, but was then just as suddenly dropped from the batters' records. Some GWRBI data was tabulated by several teams for many years before 1980, and STATS, Inc. has continued to record GWRBI data in its own play-by-play accounts since the official demise of this batting statistic.

The stolen base was first recorded for the 1886 season. However, between the years 1886 and 1897, a baserunner was credited with a stolen base if he advanced an extra base on a hit or an out made by a teammate, as in the case of a runner going from first to third on a single. For this reason, the number of stolen bases accumulated by players before the 1898 season is significantly higher than those since that time, when a stolen base has essentially been described in the same fashion as our modern rule. A runner is not credited with a stolen base on a double steal attempt if the other baserunner has been retired in his steal attempt.

The flip-side to the stolen-base statistic, namely when the runner has been caught stealing (CS), has had a much shorter run as an official baseball stat. The CS totals were first officially recorded in the 1920 season (both in the AL and NL), but after 1925, the NL stopped recording CS data until the 1951 season when it appeared once more, this time for good. The AL dropped the CS category only for the 1927 season; otherwise it has been recorded every year from 1920 to the present for that league. This was one more statistic that Ernie Lanigan had championed, and he kept a tabulation of some CS data for certain seasons between 1912 and 1920. As a result of finding some of Lanigan's published work from this period, and also from the painstaking play-by-play research on a few players like Max Carey, Bob Davids, the founder of SABR, has given us some spotty caught-stealing data from 1912 through 1919. In particular, we have complete CS records for 1915 for both leagues, 1914 for the AL only and 1916 for players with 20 or more stolen bases. Yet another SABR committee has researched the CS data for the 1927 AL season, and some work has been done in researching the CS data for the Dodgers and Giants in the 1940s. This explains why the caught stealing data will appear and then disappear for several players between 1912 and 1950.

The concept of the sacrifice has changed to an even greater extent since it was first introduced for the 1889 season. Before that time, the players and writers certainly described a batter as having sacrificed himself to advance a teammate, but the category of the sacrifice (SH) was listed periodically in the guides as one more batting statistic beginning in 1889. However, a batter was given a sacrifice almost any time he advanced another teammate on the basepaths by making an out. This was to have included only bunt attempts, but many players did get credit for a sacrifice for a flyball or a groundball out. As a consequence, the number of sacrifices accumulated by some players was significantly higher before 1894 than anything since. In addition, from 1889 to 1893, the batter was charged with an at-bat on the sacrifice play, and hence it was used as part of the divisor in calculating his batting average. Beginning in the 1894 season, a player was credited with a sacrifice (recorded as an SH in the batting tables) only for advancing a baserunner when he laid down a bunt to essentially give up an out for the extra base. This SH did not count as an

at-bat for the batter, but was instead recorded as a separate plate appearance which was not used in determining his batting average. This change was to have occurred for the 1893 season, but was not really begun until 1894, and then it was done in a most inconsistent manner until 1897.

Beginning in 1908, a player was also given a SH (and not charged with an at-bat) if he made a flyball out which allowed another baserunner to score. This sacrifice fly, as we would categorize it today, was actually listed as a separate category from the sacrifice bunt in the box scores, but the two figures were combined in the player's SH total for the year-end official batting statistics. This practice continued through the 1925 season, but the box scores dropped most references to sacrifice flies by 1920. From 1926 to 1930, the sacrifice fly component of the SH stat was modified so that a batter was given credit for a sacrifice when he advanced a teammate by making a flyball out. Then for the 1931 season, the rule governing SH was changed back to the same method which had been in use from 1894 to 1907; that is, a batter received an SH only for a sacrifice bunt, and his run-scoring flyball outs reverted back to count as at-bats (although the batter still got an RBI, as had always been the case). The best illustration of the effect of these frequent sacrifice rule changes can be seen in the SH figures which Babe Ruth accumulated as a Yankee slugger from 1920 to 1934.

Year	1920	'21	'22	'23	'24	'25	'26	'27	'28	'29	'30	'31	'32	'33	'34
SH	5	4	4	3	6	6	10	14	8	13	21	0	0	0	0

It is pretty clear that the Bambino was not laying down that many bunts in 1930.

From 1931 until 1938, the SH category again counted only sacrifice bunts, but surprisingly, the 1939 season saw the rule change back once more so that run-scoring sacrifice flies, as well as sacrifice bunts, were also counted in the SH totals. This change lasted only for that one season, and once again, from 1940 to 1953, SH included only bunts. Beginning in 1954, a new category, the sacrifice fly (SF), was added to the official baseball statistics for those run-scoring flyball outs that Major League Baseball was unable to record in a consistent fashion for more than 45 years. Since 1954, sacrifices have been recorded as SH (bunts) and SF (fly balls) and have not been charged as official times at bat for the batter.

The category of batters hit by a pitch (HBP) has also varied somewhat over time. Before the 1887 season in the NL (and the 1884 season in the AA), a batter was awarded first base after being plunked by the pitcher, but he was charged with a time at bat (and it was also scored as an error on the pitcher). From that time until the present, the batter was allowed to take first base after being hit, provided that he did not deliberately attempt to get in the way of the pitch. Also, this HBP did not count as a time at bat, and was not used in determining his batting average. However, the HBP did not become an official batting statistic until the 1917 season in the NL, and the 1920 season in the AL. This statistic was recorded in box scores to some extent and the full tabulation of batters' HBP has now been completed (including the 1890 Players' League season and the 1914-1915 Federal League seasons) thanks to the diligent research of various SABR committees and members over a long period of time. In the 19th century, a batter was given a base on balls if he was hit by a pitch on what would otherwise have been ball four. For this reason, Hughie Jennings has been listed with 49 HBP in 1896 in some sources, while others credit him with 51.

The grounding-into-double-play category (GIDP) has also had a rather brief history as an official batting statistic. The NL first compiled this category in its official year-end statistics in 1933, but from 1933 to 1938, the category was actually listed as HIDP (hit into a double play) and it included cases in which a batter caused a double play by lining out or hitting a fly ball. From 1939 to the present time (for both leagues), this category became the GIDP, and counted only for cases when the batter hit a ground ball. The AL did not actually include the GIDP category in its official 1939 statistics in the Baseball Guide, but did record the GIDP figures on the individual players' day-by-day statistical sheets kept by the league office, so these are available to us. No GIDP data exists for the AL from 1933 to 1938.

Another batting category is the number of times that a batter has been awarded first base because of interference by the catcher (usually tipping the catcher's mitt with his bat while swinging at a pitch). It is believed that this play was first called in 1905 but for many years it was only described in the box scores on an inconsistent basis. It was not regularly listed in the baseball guides (nor on the official league player sheets) until the early 1960s. It has been researched by STATS, Inc. for the 1950s and some instances have been found in box scores for years before that time. However, this play takes place very rarely, occurring perhaps 20 times at most in a league in a year. In fact, there are some years in which not even a single incidence was found to occur, and we can probably estimate the total number of times that catcher's interference was called from 1905 to 1949 was less than 100. When it does occur, a batter is not charged with an official time at bat, and this statistic is not used for any percentage calculation, even though it might seem reasonable to count it when determining a player's on-base percentage.

Also recorded in a similar fashion to catcher's interference is obstruction by a defensive player which results in the batter being awarded first base and not being charged with an official time at bat. However this play is extremely rare indeed, being called perhaps just once per decade.

Four other counting statistics, which could be classified as analysis data because they are calculated directly from the number of base hits, doubles, triples and home runs, are also listed here because they are required for some percentage calculations. The first of these is the number of total bases, in which a single counts as one base, a double as two, a triple as three and a home run as four. Second is the number of extra bases (beyond a

one-base hit) and this time a double counts as one base, a triple as two and a home run as three bases. The number of long hits (or extra-base hits) is simply the sum of the number of doubles, triples and home runs hit by a batter. Finally, the number of total plate appearances (TPA) is found by taking the sum of times at bat, bases on balls, hit by pitch, sacrifice hits, sacrifice flies and the number of times in which a batter has been awarded first base because of interference or obstruction.

The final batting category here is games played by a batter (or fielder). This category now includes the total number of games in which a player makes an appearance as a batter (including as a designated hitter), a defensive replacement, a pinch hitter or a pinch runner. However, before 1907 in the AL (and 1912 in the NL), a player was usually not given credit for a game played if he only appeared as a defensive replacement or as a pinch runner. This category was still recorded in an inconsistent fashion by the major leagues before the 1920 season. Baseball now keeps official records for the batting statistics accumulated as designated hitters (since its inception in 1973 in the AL) and as pinch hitters.

The Percentages— Batting

There are three official categories in which baseball now calculates percentage statistics. These include batting average (hits divided by at-bats), slugging average or percentage (total bases divided by at-bats) and on-base percentage. On-base percentage first appeared as an official statistic in the baseball guides in 1984, although it can easily be calculated for all other seasons throughout major league history. It is the sum of base hits, bases on balls and hit by pitch, divided by the sum of official at-bats, bases on balls, hit by pitch and sacrifice flies. Readers should note that this formula cannot be used for exact comparisons between players over time because of variations in the way at-bats and sacrifices were handled.

One other percentage calculation will be described here, although it is not recorded officially by Major League Baseball. Bill James developed the concept of "isolated power" some years ago, and defined this statistic as extra bases divided at-bats. In fact, some earlier baseball analysts and writers, including Branch Rickey, used a similar method for comparing a batter's ability as a power hitter once Babe Ruth had demonstrated how important this offensive aspect of the game could be to a team's success.

The Counting Statistics— Pitching

Most of the counting statistics for pitching have been recorded in exactly the same fashion and for the same duration as have been the corresponding batting statistics. These include: games pitched, base hits allowed, bases on balls and intentional bases on balls given up, home runs surrendered, sacrifice hits and flies allowed and opposing batters hit. However, the full hit-batter record for pitchers is still incomplete for most seasons in the 19th century because this data can only be obtained from game-by-game research through newspaper accounts of box scores. In addition, this category was actually recorded as an error on the pitcher before 1887 in the NL (1884 in the AA). The same problem with availability of data also exists for the number of sacrifice hits allowed. This data is only partially complete for most years up to 1912 in the NL and to 1920 in the AL. Just a few instances have been tabulated for the FL seasons of 1914 and 1915. The number of strikeouts which pitchers recorded is known for all major league seasons since 1876, and even for the National Association before that (from 1871 to 1875). Up until very recent times, the number of doubles and triples allowed by pitchers had never been officially recorded. For most seasons before 1907, the number of games pitched for several players had been inaccurate because this number did not include many brief outings in relief. The correct numbers have now been fairly well determined from research through box scores.

The number of earned runs allowed by pitchers has been officially tabulated since the 1912 season in the NL and the 1913 season in the AL. However, research from the ICI project and from work by SABR members has provided a complete record of earned runs allowed for years before 1913. In some seasons, the baseball guides actually listed the number of earned runs allowed for most pitchers, and for a few years, the total number of earned runs has been estimated from partial data. Some difficulty still exists with accurate historical comparisons of earned runs (and consequently of earned run averages) because this category did not always include runs which scored as a result of wild pitches, hit batters or stolen bases, and sometimes included those which scored because of fielding errors committed by pitchers. The current rule governing the recording of earned runs came into effect in 1917.

The numbers of games started (GS), games finished (GF) and complete games pitched (CG) have been officially listed for both leagues since 1920. The statistics in these categories have been determined for all pitchers before 1920 from research by members of SABR and in work done for STATS, Inc. It is possible that the number of games started and finished will be greater than the actual number of games pitched for some players in the 19th century. This occurs because a few pitchers switched positions with other fielders for an inning or two and then returned to the mound later in the same contest to finish the game that they had started. The number of shutouts pitched has been listed in the guides or on official league sheets for most seasons since 1903 in the NL (1908 in the AL). The remaining data for this category has also been completed from the same research sources which are mentioned above. However, many discrepancies and unreliable data have frequently been entered for all of the above statistical categories and these figures continue to be revised from time to time as more accurate information is uncovered.

The save statistic became official for the first time in the 1969 season, but the definition of a save has changed a few times since then. It was first advocated and recorded by *The Sporting News* in 1960. However, historical research has provided the full tabulation of saves for all pitchers since 1876 using the rules which are currently in effect. Since this data has been compiled retroactively, it has not been consistently cataloged, and thus this save data varies from source to source.

The number of innings pitched has been available for every season since 1876. In most years in the 19th century, and for some seasons before 1920, the number of fractions of innings pitched (in thirds) has been accurately recorded. This practice was generally not followed in either league from 1920 through 1981 as far as season totals go, but fractions of innings have always been given on the official league sheets on a game-by-game basis. Hence, innings pitched can be given in fractions for all years.

The number of wild pitches allowed by pitchers has also always been listed in box scores, but it has not been consistently tabulated in the official league records before 1903 in the NL and 1908 in the AL. Before 1887, wild pitches were also counted as errors by pitchers and the practice continued after that to some extent. Box score research by SABR members and STATS, Inc. has yielded the complete record for wild pitches for most years since 1876, but some data is still missing here. The same is also true for the number of balks charged against pitchers. This statistical data has not been completed for the following seasons: 1876 to 1880 in the NL, 1882 to 1891 in the AA, 1890 in the PL and 1884 in the UA. In some of these years, the figure is available for a few pitchers of note.

The number of wins and losses is now recorded for all pitchers in major league history from several sources. However, the rules used for determining the winning and losing pitcher in each game have varied somewhat over time. After 1920, the leagues required the official scorer to designate the winning and losing pitcher for the game, but there were some years before then that the AL specifically refrained from designating won-lost records for pitchers (AL founding president Ban Johnson believed that it was the team that should be charged with the loss and not an individual player). Beginning in 1950, the rules governing the winning and losing pitcher became officially specified by the NL and AL.

Two counting statistics for pitchers that are closely related are the number of at-bats by the pitchers' opponents and the total number of batters faced by pitchers. This number of at-bats corresponds exactly to the batters' at-bat statistic given above, but much of this data is incomplete for the years from 1901 to 1907 in the AL and for the years from 1890 to 1902 in the NL. It is also incomplete for most AA seasons (1882 to 1891), for the UA (1884), the PL (1890) and the FL (1914-1915). The figures that are listed for these years have been primarily compiled by the research carried out for STATS, Inc. The AL compiled opponents' at-bats for the years from 1908 through 1973, and the NL from 1903 to 1911. After these years (beginning in 1974 in the AL and 1912 in the NL) the leagues adopted the BFP statistic in place of the opponents' at-bats. BFP corresponds to total plate appearances by batters, and is the sum of at-bats, bases on balls, hit batters, sacrifice hits and flies and the times batters were awarded first base for interference or obstruction. Of course, for the seasons in which some of these statistics did not exist (for example sacrifice flies before 1954) the BFP calculation does not consider those categories in the sum.

Hence BFP has been compiled for all years before 1974 in the AL and before 1912 in the NL, when all of the necessary components for its calculation are available. On the other hand, the opponents' at-bats figures have been calculated for the years after 1974 (in the AL) and 1911 (in the NL) by finding the difference between the BFP figure and the other components used in its sum. The BFP data for the Federal League (1914 and 1915) is generally unknown because most SH data and some opponents' at-bats are still missing. This league recorded opponents' at-bats rather than BFP, as did the AL at the time. The one statistic that has been ignored in the calculation of BFP or opponents' at-bats for all years before 1985 has been the number of times that the pitchers' opponents have been awarded first base because of interference or obstruction. These instances occur infrequently today, and were in fact extremely rare before 1950, so the actual error obtained in calculating at-bats or BFP is almost negligible, but must at least be acknowledged here.

The Percentages— Pitching

There are also three official categories in which baseball now calculates pitching percentage statistics. These are opponents' batting average (hits divided by at-bats), pitcher's winning percentage (number of wins divided by the sum of wins and losses) and earned run average per nine innings pitched (ERA). ERA is found by multiplying the number of earned runs by nine, and dividing this figure by the number of innings pitched. The data for the latter two percentages are fully available, but the data for opponents' batting average is available only when at-bats have been recorded (or can be calculated from BFP).

The Counting Statistics— Fielding

Throughout major league history, the usual fielding statistics that have been recorded are the number of put-outs, assists and errors made. These are completely available for all fielding positions played by all players. Pitchers were originally given credit for an assist on a strikeout for the years 1885 through 1888, but the category has been adjusted to reflect the current practice. The category of errors has been adjusted from the way it was originally done from 1876 to 1888, when wild pitches and hit batters were often included as errors on pitchers, and passed balls were counted as errors on catchers. This is in keeping with the practice advocated by Major League Baseball today in compiling historical fielding data. Baseball only began to record the number of double plays participated in (DP) as an official statistic in the 1922 season. However, the box scores always listed the players who had participated in each double play in the notes accompanying the game, and hence the full DP data has been reconstructed for years before 1922, largely from ICI research.

Major league catchers have also had the additional fielding statistics of passed balls recorded since the 1880s in the NL and since 1925 in the AL. Again, this statistic was listed in the box scores in all other years before those previously mentioned, so this data has also been fully compiled. This work was largely carried out by members of SABR. The guides and box scores have also listed the number of triple plays participated in by all fielders, but this statistic has not been provided in the records given here.

Two other fielding counting statistics, which are merely the sum of statistics already given above, will also be mentioned here. The first is the number of successful chances accepted (putouts plus assists) and the second is the total number of chances attempted (putouts plus assists plus errors). These categories are also complete for all fielders in all years.

The Percentages— Fielding

While many analysis fielding statistics, such as range factors and zone ratings, are used in modern times, baseball generally has recorded the fielding average as the only percentage statistic in this category. It is found by determining the successful number of chances accepted, and dividing by the total number of chances attempted.

Runs Created

A hitter's job is a mirror image of a pitcher's job. A pitcher's job is to prevent runs from scoring. A hitter's job is to cause runs to score.

The best hitter, therefore, is not the hitter with the highest batting average, nor the hitter with the most home runs, nor the hitter with the most total bases or the highest total average. The best hitter is the hitter who creates the most runs. But how can we know how many runs any hitter has created? We have his runs scored and RBI counts, but those are heavily influenced by his surrounding hitters. How can we measure how many runs he has created, as an individual?

Over the years, I have introduced several sets of formulas to measure how many runs a hitter creates. The basic runs created formula is (Hits Plus Walks), Times Total Bases, Divided by (At-Bats Plus Walks). If you apply this simple formula to any modern team, any team since World War II, it will predict how many runs the team should have scored with a fair degree of accuracy.

There are, however, other versions of the formula which have even greater accuracy. These formulas, which attempt to deal with every little nook and cranny of the record book, are called Technical Runs Created Formulas.

As one stumbles through baseball history, one is confronted by a constantly changing surface of information. Prior to 1939, for example, there are no records of how many double plays each player grounded into. For a few years before then there are some comparable records in the National League only, records of how many times a player hit into a double play, even if he may have hit a fly ball to the outfield which resulted in two outs. Those records go back to 1933; before that, there's nothing.

There are dozens of changes like that in the available data. The last time I introduced a set of Technical Runs Created Formulas was in 1984, when I first published the *Historical Baseball Abstract*. At that time I introduced 14 different Technical Runs Created Formulas, each intended to deal with a different set of available data.

Since then, the search for more accurate runs created methods has moved forward a significant distance. The runs created formulas used for this book are different from the methods introduced in 1984 in essentially six ways:

1. Since 1988, STATS has kept track of every plate appearance and every event in major league baseball, yielding a vast array of new information about contemporary seasons. We have used some of this information to yield more accurate runs created estimates for players from those seasons.

2. We have developed formulas which deal with the negative effect of strikeouts as opposed to other outs.

3. In the *Historical Abstract*, I wrestled with the data back to 1900, but basically threw up my arms at the start of

the nineteenth century, and said, "I can't do anything with this mess." On the doorstep of the twenty-first century, we have accepted the challenge of dealing with nineteenth century information to make accurate runs created estimates for nineteenth century players.

4. The runs created for each individual are now figured in a "theoretical team" context, rather than assuming, as I did before, that an individual's offensive contributions interacted with one another.

5. We have added a stage of reconciling the total runs created by the players on a team with the number of runs actually scored by that team.

6. The existence of modern computers, the development of large, organized data bases, and the blessing of being able to work with Stefan Kretschmann, has enabled us to test and re-test and re-test runs created formulas for groups of hundreds of teams, thereby enabling us to achieve a level of accuracy which I could only dream of in 1984.

When I did this in 1984, there were 14 runs created formulas. Now, there are 24, all of them new.

For the players since 1988, we make two after-the-fact adjustments to the runs created estimate which emerges from the formula. Those are:

1. If a player hit well with runners in scoring position, we credit him with extra runs created for each extra hit that he has gotten with a runner in position.

2. If a player has hit more than his share of home runs with men on base (and less with the bases empty), we credit him with one extra run created for each additional home run with men on base.

I am sure there is much more which could be done with this data, but these two adjustments substantially reduce the standard error of the team runs created estimates since 1988.

The lion's share of the increase in Technical Runs Created Formulas (from 14 to 24) is created by the effort to deal with the nineteenth century data. The statisticians of a hundred years ago would change the scoring rules every year or two. From 1886 to 1897, for example, stolen bases were sometimes credited to runners who went from second to third on a ground ball. Each significant redefinition of the rules forces us to form a new data group, and find a new Technical Runs Created Formula for that data group. All of these formulas are found in the appendix on page 2690.

In calculating runs created for the *Historical Abstract*, I acted as if the individual player was a microcosm of a team—in other words, as if his own walks were interacting with his home runs. This is also how the runs created estimates in *Total Baseball* were calculated, in the manner that I prescribed at that time.

But, of course, this is a false assumption; a player's walks do not interact with his home runs. What each player does interacts with eight other players.

In making the runs created estimates in this book, we placed each player in a theoretical team context consisting of players with average skills and eight times as many plate appearances as the subject. We then figured two things: the number of runs created in that context *with* the player added, and the number of runs created by that context without him. The difference between those two figures is the runs created by the individual.

This creates significantly lower runs created estimates for the best players. The guys like Babe Ruth, Mickey Mantle, Ted Williams and Frank Thomas, who had both very high on-base percentages and great power, may wind up with many fewer runs created, in this method, than they would have had with the old method.

Finally, we reconciled runs created, after the fact, with the runs actually scored by the team. Suppose, for example, that the individual runs created estimates for the members of a team were to total up to 500, but the team actually scored 700 runs. This would be an extraordinary thing, and I don't think such a discrepancy has ever actually happened. We're ordinarily talking about an adjustment in the range of 20 runs per team, or two runs per player. But if it did happen, we would then increase the runs created for each individual on the team by 40%, since 700 divided by 500 is 1.4. We don't know who created these extra runs, but somebody on the team certainly did. The best we can do is to distribute them among the hitters proportional to their accomplishments.

Thus, if you go through this book and pick out all the runs created by all of the individuals on any one team, those should total up to the runs actually scored by that team, with the exception of a rounding error. If a team scored 827 runs, the individuals on that team should be credited with 827 runs created.

There is a similar adjustment for league outs per game in the "RC/27" figure, or Runs Created per 27 outs. If, within a league, we can account for 27.000 outs per team game (and often we are very close to that), then we would multiply the runs created by 27 in figuring the runs created per 27 outs.

If, however, we could account for only 25.41 outs per team game (which is sometimes true in early baseball, where the records have gaps), then we would multiply the runs created by 25.41 in figuring the runs created per 27 outs. Some of the outs aren't accounted for, so we distribute them as best we can among the players who may have been responsible for them.

In some cases, the end result of this process will be a runs created estimate substantially different from previously published results. Such adjustments are not made lightly. These changes can be interpreted as an admission that I didn't know what I was talking about the last time I wrote about this subject.

But a search for objective knowledge cannot be static. It must lead to steadily improving methods. I am confident that these are the best runs created estimates yet devised.

— Bill James

Component ERA (ERC)

For each pitcher in this book in each season, there is a figure called "ERC", or Component ERA. This is a new statistic, which is introduced here for the first time; we would have used the acronym CERA, except that we were already using that for something else.

The Component ERA is an evaluation of a pitcher's "other" stats—his hits per nine innings, walks and hit batsmen and home runs allowed—in the form of an equivalent ERA. There is a formula in the appendix. In 1997 Roger Clemens allowed 204 hits in 264 innings, walked 68, gave up nine home runs and hit 12 batters. What is the ERA that one would normally expect of a pitcher who had these statistics? The formula is designed to answer this question, and the answer is 2.17. A pitcher with those rates of hits, walks and home runs allowed would normally post an ERA about 2.17—a few points higher than Clemens actual ERA, 2.05.

The Component ERA formula is, essentially, a runs created formula; it's a little different, but it's a lot the same. The basic runs created formula is (Hits Plus Walks), times Total Bases, divided by (At-Bats Plus Walks). We have all of that information for pitchers except Total Bases. If you know how many hits a pitcher has allowed and how many home runs he has allowed, you can estimate how many total bases he has allowed with a great degree of accuracy by multiplying the home runs times four and the hits which aren't home runs by 1.255.

A Runs Created formula for a pitcher does not have the importance of runs created by a hitter because, of course, we have the actual number of runs that the pitcher has allowed. We don't really know how many runs any hitter has put on the scoreboard over the course of a season, so we have to estimate that. For a pitcher, we know.

But while the Earned Run Average of a pitcher is an extremely valuable stat, one of the most reliable and most useful of all baseball statistics, it is nonetheless an imperfect stat. There are things that can happen which cause a pitcher's ERA, in some cases, to misstate how well he has pitched; I'm sure you are all as aware of that as we are. It was our thinking that because the ERA is not a perfect assessment of how well the pitcher has pitched, it would be worthwhile to take another look at the pitcher's performance—his control, his batting average allowed, etc.—and combine those into a stat which was parallel to ERA, but independent of it.

In most cases, as you will see, the ERC figure tracks ERA exceptionally well, if a pitcher pitches more than 100 innings. For a pitcher to have a Component ERA of 4.50 but an actual ERA of 3.50 (in 100 or more innings)—that happens for about two pitchers per season. For a pitcher to have a Component ERA two full runs different from his actual ERA has never happened in the history of baseball, for a pitcher pitching 100 or more innings, although it is common for pitchers pitching less than 20 innings.

We have people on our editorial staff who feel that the Component ERA provides a better measure of how a pitcher has pitched than does his actual ERA. We have other people on staff who disagree. If a pitcher's ERA is significantly better than his ERA components, there are really two possibilities. Either the pitcher was just lucky that more runs didn't score, or else the pitcher has a special skill which is not reflected in the Component ERA. He could have an exceptional pickoff move, for example, that takes 15 runners a year off base, or he could get an unusual number of ground balls, which will mean an unusual number of double plays, or he could be a pitcher who has an unusual ability to pitch his way out of trouble, perhaps because he saves his best stuff for the emergency room.

As to which of these possibilities may apply in a particular case, I would say that the more innings are involved, the more seriously one should consider the possibility of a hidden talent. Bob Buhl, for example, had a Component ERA of 3.87 for his career; he gave up about 100 walks and 20 homers a year, regular as winter. But his actual ERA was 3.55, in a career of more than 2,500 innings. Obviously, he must have had a special skill, which made him more effective than he ought to have been with his other numbers.

On the other hand, Sammy Stewart posted a 2.32 ERA in 1981, Rod Scurry had a 1.74 ERA in 1982, Doug Sisk was at 2.24 ERA in 1983, Frank Williams at 2.30 in 1987, and Chuck McElroy was at 1.95 in 1991, in all cases with Component ERAs a run or more higher. Those guys obviously just had a run of good luck, which caught up with them the next year or the year after.

Another thing that is interesting about Component ERA is that unlike the Runs Created formula, the same formula works for all of baseball history. The basic Runs Created formula doesn't work in the nineteenth century, because the large number of errors led to additional runs, which the formula doesn't account for. But the extra runs are unearned, so the Component ERA formula still works. When we don't have data on the number of batters faced by the pitcher we have to patch in with another formula to estimate that, but it still works. We don't want to try to make more of it than it is, but for those of you who own baseball encyclopedias so that you can play around with the numbers. . . well, here's something else that you can play around with.

—Bill James

Seasons

Standings, Leaders

For each year, we provide the standings for the league, including the days spent in first place by each club. We also provide a home-road breakdown not only for each team's won-lost record, but also the runs and home runs by the team and its opponents, and calculate each ballpark's effect on scoring and homers. Team's records also are provided by month, from March/April through September/October, as well as against each of its rivals. Bob Tiemann was essential in filling out our data for many of the teams from the 19th century. Where available, we list 24 batting, 24 pitching and eight fielding statistics for each team. The leaders in these categories are listed in bold. In some cases, the batting and pitching statistics in a league do not match perfectly. We have researched these discrepancies as thoroughly as possible.

For individual players, we show the league leaders in 24 batting and 24 pitching categories. For percentage-based statistics, we used the qualifying rules of the day, when they were clear, and recognized consensus champions who didn't qualify under the rules. In all other cases, we used common sense:

Batting Champions

1876-1888: There were basically no formal rules during this period, so we used the modern criteria of 3.1 plate appearances per scheduled game.

1889-1944: Minimum 100 games played.

1945-1956: Minimum 400 at-bats.

1957-present: Minimum 3.1 plate appearances per scheduled game, or 3.1 plate appearances per game played by the player's team in a strike-shortened season.

There have been a few cases since 1889 when the player with the highest average according to the above criteria was not recognized as the champion. These are:

1910 AL: This was one of the strangest batting races in major league history. Detroit's Ty Cobb went into the last day of the season with a solid lead over Cleveland's Napoleon Lajoie. Lajoie went 7-for-8 in his season-ending doubleheader against the St. Louis Browns with some considerable help from the opposing manager, who ordered his third baseman to play deep and allow Lajoie to bunt for hits. That closed the gap, but when American League officials went over their figures, Cobb still prevailed by a point, .385 to .384. That seemed to settle the matter, but decades later, a game-by-game review of the 1910 season conducted by Pete Palmer unearthed the fact that one of Cobb's games had inadvertently (we assume) been entered twice. Remove that game, in which Cobb had gone 2-for-3, and Cobb's average dips to .383, one point behind Lajoie. Despite that, we decided that Cobb deserved to be recognized as the champion, mostly because of the last-day chicanery on behalf of Lajoie and also because baseball still

considers him the official winner of the batting race. We list Cobb first at .383 and Lajoie second at .384.

1914 AL: Cobb again. This time he batted .368 but appeared in only 97 games, three fewer than the standard of the day. The leading qualifier, Philadelphia's Eddie Collins, hit .344, and Cobb would have won the title even if he'd gone 0-for-7 in each of those three missing games. The AL sensibly anointed Cobb as the champ.

1938 AL. By the 100-game standard, the batting champion would have been Washington rookie Taffy Wright with a .350 average. But Wright had only 263 at-bats, so Boston's Jimmie Foxx (.349 in 585 at-bats) was recognized as the leader. The *Reach Guide* of 1939 claimed after the fact that the AL standard for winning the batting title in 1938 was 400 at-bats, so it may have been a moot point. Either way, the league recognized Foxx as the champ.

1996 NL. San Diego's Tony Gwynn hit .353, but didn't have the minimum 3.1 plate appearances per scheduled game. However, there's an addendum to the qualifying rules that says a non-qualifier should be recognized as the champion if his average still would have been the best after being given enough imaginary hitless plate appearances to reach the qualifying standard. So Gwynn won the title over Colorado's Ellis Burks, who batted .344. This is a formalized definition of the rationale for making Cobb the AL champion in 1914.

ERA Champions

ERA was not an official statistic until 1912, when the National League first adopted it. The AL followed suit a year later. Until 1950, a pitcher needed to work 10 complete games to qualify for the title; and since then the standard has been one inning pitched per scheduled game. We used the latter qualifier in selecting ERA champions for the seasons prior to 1912, and used the same criteria the leagues used since then. As with the batting titles, there were a couple of instances where the rules were overridden and a very weird case in 1981 where the rule should have been overridden but wasn't.

1927 AL. New York rookie Wilcy Moore worked 213 innings, which was quite obviously a full season of pitching. He also had a 2.28 ERA, which was lower than any qualifier that year. But Moore was used primarily in relief and had only six complete games, four fewer than the 10 needed to qualify for the ERA crown. Using common sense, the AL awarded Moore the title.

1940 AL. Another Yankees rookie, Tiny Bonham, bettered all ERA qualifiers with a 1.91 mark and had 10 complete games. But he only pitched in 12 games and worked 99 1/3 innings. As in 1927, the league used common sense and decided that Bonham simply hadn't pitched enough to be recognized as the ERA leader. They gave the crown to Cleveland's Bob Feller, who had a 2.62 ERA in 320 innings.

1981 AL. Baltimore's Sammy Stewart allowed 29 earned runs in 112 1/3 innings for an ERA of 2.32, while Oakland's Steve McCatty permitted 48 earned runs in 185 2/3 innings for an ERA of 2.33. Back then, the leagues rounded off thirds of an inning in their official statistics and they used the rounded totals in compiling ERAs. With Stewart rounded down to 112 innings, his ERA rose to 2.33. McCatty's ERA improved to 2.32 when his innings were rounded up to 186. The rounding, not McCatty's pitching, gave him the crown. This was unfair, but the AL nonetheless awarded the title to McCatty. The fiasco convinced the leagues to begin reporting thirds of an inning beginning in 1982, and ERAs have been figured using the thirds ever since then. This book lists thirds of innings when applicable for all pitchers in all years, and we have compiled our ERAs based on the exact number of innings pitched. We list McCatty as the leader at 2.33 and Stewart second at 2.32, based on their official standing according to the league.

In addition to the various league leaders, we also list players who won the Triple Crown, pitched a no-hitter that lasted nine or more innings, hit three or more home runs in a game, batted for the cycle or turned an unassisted triple play. We also provide the official choices for Most Valuable Player, Cy Young Award, Rookie of the Year and Manager of the Year, and choose our own when baseball didn't. Additionally, we pick an all-star team for each league for each season. Finally, we include managerial records for each team's skippers, as well as postseason results.

Team Rosters

Teams are listed in order by finish by year. We provide 14 statistics for each hitter and 13 for each pitcher, as well as their age and how they bat (hitters) or throw (pitchers). The hitters who played the most games at each of the eight non-pitching positions are listed (including the top three outfielders rather than one left, center and right fielder), followed by reserves in order of plate appearances. As for pitchers, starters are listed in order of games started, followed by relievers in order of appearances. A starter is defined as someone who started in at least half his appearances that season. The start of each new league is indicated by a ». Players who played more than three positions in one season are asterisked and have their additional positions listed at the bottom of the team entry. Players who played with more than one team in a season are indicated with a †.

Abbreviations & Formulas

A complete list of team and statistical abbreviations are listed in the back of the book, along with an appendix explaining formulas and the availability of certain statistics.

1876 National League Standings

Team	Overall					Home Games						Road Games						Park Index		Record by Month					
	W	L	Pct	GB	DIF	W	L	R	OR	HR	OHR	W	L	R	OR	HR	OHR	Run	HR	M/A	May	June	July	Aug	S/O
Chicago	52	14	.788	—	153	25	6	352	143	3	1	27	8	272	114	5	5	145	45	3-0	10-3	11-2	11-2	7-5	10-2
St. Louis	45	19	.703	6.0	0	24	6	150	58	1	1	21	13	236	171	1	2	58	76	1-2	9-4	9-4	8-4	8-3	10-2
Hartford	47	21	.691	6.0	5	23	9	220	107	0	0	24	12	209	154	2	2	101	0	1-1	10-2	11-2	3-5	8-5	14-6
Boston	39	31	.557	15.0	5	19	17	253	200	5	3	20	14	218	250	4	4	91	94	2-2	7-5	5-8	8-4	8-3	9-9
Louisville	30	36	.455	22.0	0	15	16	149	154	6	3	15	20	131	190	0	0	107	—	0-3	6-7	6-7	6-7	7-5	5-7
New York	21	35	.375	26.0	0	13	20	143	207	2	7	8	15	117	205	0	1	76	627	1-1	4-9	5-8	5-6	5-3	1-8
Philadelphia	14	45	.237	34.5	1	10	24	259	309	4	0	4	21	119	225	3	2	121	59	1-1	4-9	4-9	2-7	2-12	1-7
Cincinnati	9	56	.138	42.5	2	6	24	119	243	2	2	3	32	119	336	2	7	93	52	2-1	1-12	1-12	2-10	1-10	2-11

Clinch Date—Chicago 9/26.

Team Batting

Team	G	AB	R	OR	H	2B	3B	HR	TB	RBI	TBB	IBB	SO	HBP	SH	SF	SB	CS	SB%	GDP	Avg	OBP	Slg
Chicago	66	2748	624	257	926	131	32	8	1145	441	70	—	45	—	—	—	—	—	—	—	.337	.353	.417
Boston	70	2722	471	450	723	96	24	9	894	281	58	—	98	—	—	—	—	—	—	—	.266	.281	.328
Hartford	69	2664	429	261	711	96	22	2	857	265	39	—	78	—	—	—	—	—	—	—	.267	.277	.322
St. Louis	64	2478	386	229	642	73	27	2	775	264	59	—	63	—	—	—	—	—	—	—	.259	.276	.313
Philadelphia	60	2387	378	534	646	79	35	7	816	249	27	—	36	—	—	—	—	—	—	—	.271	.279	.342
Louisville	69	2570	280	344	641	68	14	6	755	191	24	—	98	—	—	—	—	—	—	—	.249	.256	.294
New York	57	2180	260	412	494	39	15	2	569	161	18	—	35	—	—	—	—	—	—	—	.227	.233	.261
Cincinnati	65	2372	238	579	555	51	12	4	642	132	41	—	136	—	—	—	—	—	—	—	.234	.247	.271
NL Total	520	20121	3066	3066	5338	633	181	40	6453	1984	336	—	589	—	—	—	—	—	—	—	.265	.277	.321
NL Avg Team	65	2515	383	383	667	79	23	5	807	248	42	—	74	—	—	—	—	—	—	—	.265	.277	.321

Team Pitching

Team	G	CG	ShO	Rel	Sv	IP	H	R	ER	HR	SH	SF	HB	TBB	IBB	SO	WP	Bk	H/9	SO/9	BB/9	OAvg	OOBP	ERA
St. Louis	64	63	16	1	0	577.0	472	229	78	3	—	—	—	39	—	103	34	—	7.4	1.6	0.6	.210	.224	1.22
Hartford	69	69	11	0	0	624.0	570	261	116	2	—	—	—	27	—	114	15	—	8.2	1.6	0.4	.227	.235	1.67
Louisville	69	67	5	2	0	643.0	605	344	121	3	—	—	—	38	—	125	25	—	8.5	1.7	0.5	.229	.240	1.69
Chicago	66	58	9	9	4	592.1	608	257	116	6	—	—	—	29	—	51	3	—	9.2	0.8	0.4	.247	.256	1.76
Boston	70	49	3	21	7	632.0	732	450	176	7	—	—	—	104	—	77	46	—	10.4	1.1	1.5	.268	.295	2.51
New York	57	56	2	1	0	530.0	718	412	173	8	—	—	—	24	—	37	3	—	12.2	0.6	0.4	.302	.309	2.94
Philadelphia	60	53	1	7	2	550.0	783	534	197	2	—	—	—	41	—	22	33	—	12.8	0.4	0.7	.310	.321	3.22
Cincinnati	65	57	0	9	0	591.0	850	579	238	9	—	—	—	34	—	60	28	—	12.9	0.9	0.5	.313	.322	3.62
NL Total	520	472	47	50	13	4739.1	5338	3066	1215	40	—	—	—	336	—	589	187	—	10.1	1.1	0.6	.265	.277	2.31
NL Avg Team	65	59	6	6	2	592.1	667	383	152	5	—	—	—	42	—	74	23	—	10.1	1.1	0.6	.265	.277	2.31

Team Fielding

Team	G	PO	A	E	TC	DP	PB	Pct
St. Louis	64	1734	732	268	2734	33	57	.902
Chicago	66	1777	731	282	2790	33	31	.899
Hartford	69	1874	786	337	2997	27	31	.888
Louisville	69	1930	850	397	3177	44	45	.875
Boston	70	1895	826	442	3163	42	62	.860
Cincinnati	65	1772	708	469	2949	45	81	.841
Philadelphia	60	1657	724	456	2837	32	109	.839
New York	57	1591	638	473	2702	18	37	.825
NL Total	520	14230	5995	3124	23349	274	453	.866

Team vs. Team Records

	Bos	ChN	Cin	Har	Lou	NYM	PhN	StL	Won
Bos	—	1	10	2	5	8	9	4	39
ChN	9	—	10	6	9	7	7	4	52
Cin	0	0	—	1	2	1	3	2	9
Har	8	4	9	—	9	4	9	4	47
Lou	5	1	8	1	—	5	6	4	30
NYM	2	1	7	4	3	—	3	1	21
PhN	1	1	5	1	2	4	—	0	14
StL	6	6	7	6	6	6	8	—	45
Lost	31	14	56	21	36	35	45	19	

1876 National League Batting Leaders

Games		At-Bats		Runs		Hits		Doubles		Triples	
J. Manning, Bos	70	G. Wright, Bos	335	R. Barnes, ChN	126	R. Barnes, ChN	138	P. Hines, ChN	21	R. Barnes, ChN	14
J. O'Rourke, Bos	70	J. Remsen, Har	324	G. Wright, Bos	72	J. Peters, ChN	111	D. Higham, Har	21	G. Hall, PhN	13
G. Wright, Bos	70	R. Barnes, ChN	322	J. Peters, ChN	70	C. Anson, ChN	110	R. Barnes, ChN	21	L. Pike, StL	10
H. Schafer, Bos	70	J. Peters, ChN	316	J. Burdock, Har	66	C. McVey, ChN	107	L. Pike, StL	19	L. Meyerle, PhN	8
4 tied with	69	2 tied with	312	D. White, ChN	66	D. White, ChN	104	2 tied with	18	3 tied with	7

Home Runs		Total Bases		Runs Batted In		Walks		Intentional Walks		Strikeouts	
G. Hall, PhN	5	R. Barnes, ChN	190	D. White, ChN	60	R. Barnes, ChN	20	Statistic unavailable		J. Ryan, Lou	23
C. Jones, Cin	4	G. Hall, PhN	146	P. Hines, ChN	59	J. O'Rourke, Bos	15			L. Brown, Bos	22
8 tied with	2	C. Anson, ChN	139	C. Anson, ChN	59	J. Burdock, Har	13			R. Snyder, Cin	19
		P. Hines, ChN	134	R. Barnes, ChN	59	J. Glenn, ChN	12			C. Jones, Cin	17
		2 tied with	133	C. McVey, ChN	53	C. Anson, ChN	12			J. O'Rourke, Bos	17

Hit By Pitch	Sac Hits	Sac Flies	Stolen Bases	Caught Stealing	GDP
Statistic unavailable	Statistic unavailable	Statistic unavailable	Statistic unavailable	Statistic unavailable	Statistic unavailable

Runs Created		Runs Created/27 Outs		Batting Average		On-Base Percentage		Slugging Percentage		OBP+Slugging	
R. Barnes, ChN	113	R. Barnes, ChN	17.46	R. Barnes, ChN	.429	R. Barnes, ChN	.462	R. Barnes, ChN	.590	R. Barnes, ChN	1.052
J. O'Rourke, Bos	78	G. Hall, PhN	12.54	G. Hall, PhN	.366	G. Hall, PhN	.384	G. Hall, PhN	.545	G. Hall, PhN	.929
C. Anson, ChN	78	C. Anson, ChN	11.14	C. Anson, ChN	.356	C. Anson, ChN	.380	L. Pike, StL	.472	C. Anson, ChN	.830
G. Hall, PhN	75	J. O'Rourke, Bos	10.56	J. Peters, ChN	.351	D. White, ChN	.358	C. Anson, ChN	.450	L. Pike, StL	.813
G. Wright, Bos	73	L. Pike, StL	10.42	C. McVey, ChN	.347	J. O'Rourke, Bos	.358	L. Meyerle, PhN	.449	L. Meyerle, PhN	.797

1876 National League Pitching Leaders

Wins		Losses		Winning Percentage		Games		Games Started		Complete Games	
A. Spalding, ChN	47	J. Devlin, Lou	35	A. Spalding, ChN	.797	J. Devlin, Lou	68	J. Devlin, Lou	68	J. Devlin, Lou	66
G. Bradley, StL	45	B. Mathews, NYM	34	J. Manning, Bos	.783	G. Bradley, StL	64	G. Bradley, StL	64	G. Bradley, StL	63
T. Bond, Har	31	D. Dean, Cin	26	T. Bond, Har	.705	A. Spalding, ChN	61	A. Spalding, ChN	60	B. Mathews, NYM	55
J. Devlin, Lou	30	L. Knight, PhN	22	G. Bradley, StL	.703	B. Mathews, NYM	56	B. Mathews, NYM	56	A. Spalding, ChN	53
B. Mathews, NYM	21	2 tied with	20	C. Cummings, Har	.667	T. Bond, Har	45	T. Bond, Har	45	T. Bond, Har	45

Shutouts		Saves		Games Finished		Batters Faced		Innings Pitched		Hits Allowed	
G. Bradley, StL	16	J. Manning, Bos	5	J. Manning, Bos	13	J. Devlin, Lou	2568	J. Devlin, Lou	622.0	B. Mathews, NYM	693
A. Spalding, ChN	8	G. Zettlein, PhN	2	J. Borden, Bos	6	B. Mathews, NYM	2327	G. Bradley, StL	573.0	J. Devlin, Lou	566
T. Bond, Har	6	C. McVey, ChN	2	C. McVey, ChN	5	G. Bradley, StL	2269	A. Spalding, ChN	528.2	A. Spalding, ChN	542
J. Devlin, Lou	5	4 tied with	1	G. Zettlein, PhN	4	A. Spalding, ChN	2219	B. Mathews, NYM	516.0	G. Bradley, StL	470
C. Cummings, Har	5			C. Fisher, Cin	4	T. Bond, Har	1623	T. Bond, Har	408.0	D. Dean, Cin	397

Home Runs Allowed		Walks		Walks/9 Innings		Strikeouts		Strikeouts/9 Innings		Strikeout/Walk Ratio	
B. Mathews, NYM	8	J. Borden, Bos	51	G. Zettlein, PhN	0.2	J. Devlin, Lou	122	T. Bond, Har	1.9	T. Bond, Har	6.77
C. Fisher, Cin	6	G. Bradley, StL	38	C. Fisher, Cin	0.2	G. Bradley, StL	103	J. Devlin, Lou	1.8	C. Fisher, Cin	4.83
A. Spalding, ChN	6	J. Devlin, Lou	37	T. Bond, Har	0.3	T. Bond, Har	88	G. Bradley, StL	1.6	J. Devlin, Lou	3.30
J. Borden, Bos	4	L. Knight, PhN	34	B. Mathews, NYM	0.4	A. Spalding, ChN	39	J. Borden, Bos	1.4	G. Bradley, StL	2.71
2 tied with	3	J. Manning, Bos	32	D. Williams, Cin	0.4	B. Mathews, NYM	37	C. Fisher, Cin	1.1	D. Williams, Cin	2.25

Earned Run Average		Component ERA		Hit Batsmen	Wild Pitches		Opponent Average		Opponent OBP	
G. Bradley, StL	1.23	G. Bradley, StL	1.45	Statistic unavailable	G. Bradley, StL	34	G. Bradley, StL	.211	G. Bradley, StL	.224
J. Devlin, Lou	1.56	T. Bond, Har	1.53		L. Knight, PhN	23	T. Bond, Har	.220	T. Bond, Har	.227
C. Cummings, Har	1.67	J. Devlin, Lou	1.67		J. Borden, Bos	21	J. Devlin, Lou	.224	J. Devlin, Lou	.235
T. Bond, Har	1.68	C. Cummings, Har	2.02		D. Dean, Cin	17	C. Cummings, Har	.239	C. Cummings, Har	.251
A. Spalding, ChN	1.75	A. Spalding, ChN	2.20		J. Manning, Bos	16	A. Spalding, ChN	.247	A. Spalding, ChN	.256

1876 National League Miscellaneous

Managers		
Boston	Harry Wright	39-31
Chicago	Al Spalding	52-14
Cincinnati	Charlie Gould	9-56
Hartford	Bob Ferguson	47-21
Louisville	Jack Chapman	30-36
New York	Bill Craver	21-35
Philadelphia	Al Wright	14-45
St. Louis	Mase Graffen	39-17
	George McManus	6-2

Awards

STATS Most Valuable Player	Ross Barnes, 2b, ChN
STATS Cy Young	Al Spalding, ChN
STATS Rookie of the Year	Charley Jones, of, Cin
STATS Manager of the Year	Al Spalding, ChN

STATS All-Star Team

C	Deacon White, ChN	.343	1	60
1B	Cal McVey, ChN	.347	1	53
2B	Ross Barnes, ChN	.429	1	59
3B	Cap Anson, ChN	.356	2	59
SS	John Peters, ChN	.351	1	47
OF	George Hall, PhN	.366	5	45
OF	Paul Hines, ChN	.331	2	59
OF	Jim O'Rourke, Bos	.327	2	43
P	Al Spalding, ChN	47-12	1.75	39 K

Postseason

None

Outstanding Performances

No-Hitters
George Bradley, StL vs. Har on July 15

1877 National League Standings

Team	Overall					Home Games						Road Games						Park Index		Record by Month					
	W	L	Pct	GB	DIF	W	L	R	OR	HR	OHR	W	L	R	OR	HR	OHR	Run	HR	M/A	May	June	July	Aug	S/O
Boston	42	18	.700	—	79	27	5	260	110	0	1	15	13	159	153	4	4	104	11	—	6-2	7-4	7-9	10-2	12-1
Louisville	35	25	.583	7.0	40	21	9	219	172	7	3	14	16	120	117	2	1	165	333	—	5-5	7-5	9-2	6-8	8-5
Hartford	31	27	.534	10.0	2	19	8	167	92	2	1	12	19	174	219	2	1	76	115	—	4-3	8-4	5-11	8-3	6-6
St. Louis	28	32	.467	14.0	26	20	10	177	124	0	1	8	22	108	194	1	1	100	50	—	6-4	5-6	8-4	5-6	4-12
Chicago	26	33	.441	15.5	2	17	12	206	156	0	4	9	21	160	219	0	3	99	138	—	4-7	5-6	4-6	7-4	6-10
Cincinnati	15	42	.263	25.5	0	12	17	157	201	4	1	3	25	134	284	2	3	83	97	—	3-7	0-7	5-6	1-14	6-8

Clinch Date—Boston 9/27.

Team Batting

Team	G	AB	R	OR	H	2B	3B	HR	TB	RBI	TBB	IBB	SO	HBP	SH	SF	SB	CS	SB%	GDP	Avg	OBP	Slg
Boston	61	2368	419	263	700	91	37	4	877	291	65	—	121	—	—	—	—	—	—	—	.296	.314	.370
Chicago	60	2273	366	375	633	79	30	0	772	248	57	—	111	—	—	—	—	—	—	—	.278	.296	.340
Hartford	60	2358	341	311	637	63	31	4	774	201	30	—	97	—	—	—	—	—	—	—	.270	.279	.328
Louisville	61	2355	339	288	659	75	36	9	833	248	58	—	140	—	—	—	—	—	—	—	.280	.297	.354
Cincinnati	58	2135	291	485	545	72	34	6	703	224	78	—	110	—	—	—	—	—	—	—	.255	.282	.329
St. Louis	60	2178	284	318	531	51	36	1	657	198	57	—	147	—	—	—	—	—	—	—	.244	.263	.302
NL Total	360	13667	2040	2040	3705	431	204	24	4616	1410	345	—	726	—	—	—	—	—	—	—	.271	.289	.338
NL Avg Team	60	2278	340	340	618	72	34	4	769	235	58	—	121	—	—	—	—	—	—	—	.271	.289	.338

Team Pitching

Team	G	CG	ShO	Rel	Sv	IP	H	R	ER	HR	SH	SF	HB	TBB	IBB	SO	WP	Bk	H/9	SO/9	BB/9	OAvg	OOBP	ERA
Boston	61	61	7	0	0	548.0	557	263	131	5	—	—	—	38	—	177	20	—	9.1	2.9	0.6	.249	.261	2.15
Louisville	61	61	4	0	0	559.0	617	288	140	4	—	—	—	41	—	141	20	—	9.9	2.3	0.7	.270	.283	2.25
Hartford	60	59	4	1	0	544.0	572	311	140	2	—	—	—	56	—	99	18	—	9.5	1.6	0.9	.253	.271	2.32
St. Louis	60	52	1	8	0	541.0	582	318	160	2	—	—	—	92	—	132	52	—	9.7	2.2	1.5	.262	.291	2.66
Chicago	60	45	3	16	3	534.0	630	375	200	7	—	—	—	58	—	92	45	—	10.6	1.6	1.0	.274	.292	3.37
Cincinnati	58	48	1	10	1	515.0	747	485	240	4	—	—	—	61	—	85	47	—	13.1	1.5	1.1	.318	.335	4.19
NL Total	360	326	20	35	4	3241.0	3705	2040	1011	24	—	—	—	346	—	726	202	—	10.3	2.0	1.0	.271	.289	2.81
NL Avg Team	60	54	3	6	1	540.0	618	340	169	4	—	—	—	58	—	121	34	—	10.3	2.0	1.0	.271	.289	2.81

Team Fielding

Team	G	PO	A	E	TC	DP	PB	Pct
Louisville	61	1677	824	267	2768	37	60	.904
St. Louis	60	1622	708	281	2611	29	58	.892
Boston	61	1644	674	290	2608	36	48	.889
Hartford	60	1632	783	313	2728	32	38	.885
Chicago	60	1602	754	313	2669	43	74	.883
Cincinnati	58	1554	711	394	2659	33	81	.852
NL Total	360	9731	4454	1858	16043	210	359	.884

Team vs. Team Records

	Bos	ChN	Cin	Har	Lou	StL	Won
Bos	—	10	11	7	8	6	42
ChN	2	—	8	4	4	8	26
Cin	1	3	—	3	5	3	15
Har	5	8	7	—	6	5	31
Lou	4	8	7	6	—	10	35
StL	6	4	9	7	2	—	28
Lost	18	33	42	27	25	32	

1877 National League Batting Leaders

Games		At-Bats		Runs		Hits		Doubles		Triples	
9 tied with	61	G. Wright, Bos	290	J. O'Rourke, Bos	68	D. White, Bos	103	C. Anson, ChN	19	D. White, Bos	11
		J. Latham, Lou	278	G. Wright, Bos	58	C. McVey, ChN	98	J. Manning, Cin	16	C. Jones, 2tm	10
		J. Burdock, Har	277	C. McVey, ChN	58	J. O'Rourke, Bos	96	T. York, Har	16	L. Brown, Bos	8
		T. Carey, Har	274	J. Start, Har	55	J. Cassidy, Har	95	G. Wright, Bos	15	G. Hall, Lou	8
		A. Leonard, Bos	272	2 tied with	53	J. Start, Har	90	G. Hall, Lou	15	6 tied with	7

Home Runs		Total Bases		Runs Batted In		Walks		Intentional Walks		Strikeouts	
L. Pike, Cin	4	D. White, Bos	145	D. White, Bos	49	J. O'Rourke, Bos	20	Statistic unavailable		L. Brown, Bos	33
O. Shaffer, Lou	3	C. McVey, ChN	121	J. Peters, ChN	41	C. Jones, 2tm	15			J. Devlin, Lou	27
P. Snyder, Lou	2	J. O'Rourke, Bos	118	E. Sutton, Bos	39	A. Booth, Cin	12			C. Jones, 2tm	25
C. Jones, 2tm	2	G. Hall, Lou	118	C. Jones, 2tm	38	G. Hall, Lou	12			T. Larkin, Har	23
D. White, Bos	2	J. Cassidy, Har	115	T. York, Har	37	D. Force, StL	11			J. Blong, StL	22

Hit By Pitch	Sac Hits	Sac Flies	Stolen Bases	Caught Stealing	GDP
Statistic unavailable	Statistic unavailable	Statistic unavailable	Statistic unavailable	Statistic unavailable	Statistic unavailable

Runs Created		Runs Created/27 Outs		Batting Average		On-Base Percentage		Slugging Percentage		OBP+Slugging	
D. White, Bos	75	D. White, Bos	12.73	D. White, Bos	.387	J. O'Rourke, Bos	.407	D. White, Bos	.545	D. White, Bos	.950
J. O'Rourke, Bos	65	C. McVey, ChN	10.71	J. Cassidy, Har	.378	D. White, Bos	.405	C. Jones, 2tm	.471	J. O'Rourke, Bos	.852
C. McVey, ChN	65	J. O'Rourke, Bos	10.64	C. McVey, ChN	.368	C. McVey, ChN	.387	J. Cassidy, Har	.458	J. Cassidy, Har	.844
J. Cassidy, Har	59	J. Cassidy, Har	10.47	J. O'Rourke, Bos	.362	J. Cassidy, Har	.386	C. McVey, ChN	.455	C. McVey, ChN	.842
C. Anson, ChN	56	C. Anson, ChN	9.17	C. Anson, ChN	.337	C. Anson, ChN	.360	J. O'Rourke, Bos	.445	C. Jones, 2tm	.824

1877 National League Pitching Leaders

Wins		Losses		Winning Percentage		Games		Games Started		Complete Games	
T. Bond, Bos	40	T. Larkin, Har	25	T. Bond, Bos	.702	J. Devlin, Lou	61	J. Devlin, Lou	61	J. Devlin, Lou	61
J. Devlin, Lou	35	J. Devlin, Lou	25	J. Devlin, Lou	.583	T. Bond, Bos	58	T. Bond, Bos	58	T. Bond, Bos	58
T. Larkin, Har	29	G. Bradley, ChN	23	T. Larkin, Har	.537	T. Larkin, Har	56	T. Larkin, Har	56	T. Larkin, Har	55
G. Bradley, ChN	18	T. Nichols, StL	23	J. Blong, StL	.526	G. Bradley, ChN	50	G. Bradley, ChN	44	G. Bradley, ChN	35
T. Nichols, StL	18	T. Bond, Bos	17	2 tied with	.439	T. Nichols, StL	42	T. Nichols, StL	39	T. Nichols, StL	35

Shutouts		Saves		Games Finished		Batters Faced		Innings Pitched		Hits Allowed	
T. Bond, Bos	6	C. McVey, ChN	2	G. Bradley, ChN	7	J. Devlin, Lou	2328	J. Devlin, Lou	559.0	J. Devlin, Lou	617
T. Larkin, Har	4	J. Manning, Cin	1	J. Manning, Cin	6	T. Bond, Bos	2165	T. Bond, Bos	521.0	T. Bond, Bos	530
J. Devlin, Lou	4	A. Spalding, ChN	1	C. McVey, ChN	6	T. Larkin, Har	2132	T. Larkin, Har	501.0	T. Larkin, Har	510
G. Bradley, ChN	2			A. Booth, Cin	4	G. Bradley, ChN	1719	G. Bradley, ChN	394.0	G. Bradley, ChN	452
4 tied with	1			J. Blong, StL	4	T. Nichols, StL	1484	T. Nichols, StL	350.0	T. Nichols, StL	376

Home Runs Allowed		Walks		Walks/9 Innings		Strikeouts		Strikeouts/9 Innings		Strikeout/Walk Ratio	
T. Bond, Bos	5	T. Larkin, Har	53	T. Bond, Bos	0.6	T. Bond, Bos	170	B. Mitchell, Cin	3.7	T. Bond, Bos	4.72
G. Bradley, ChN	4	T. Nichols, StL	53	J. Devlin, Lou	0.7	J. Devlin, Lou	141	T. Bond, Bos	2.9	B. Mitchell, Cin	3.73
J. Devlin, Lou	4	J. Devlin, Lou	41	C. Cummings, Cin	0.8	T. Larkin, Har	96	J. Blong, StL	2.5	J. Devlin, Lou	3.44
4 tied with	2	G. Bradley, ChN	39	G. Bradley, ChN	0.9	T. Nichols, StL	80	J. Devlin, Lou	2.3	C. McVey, ChN	1.82
		J. Blong, StL	38	T. Larkin, Har	1.0	G. Bradley, ChN	59	T. Nichols, StL	2.1	T. Larkin, Har	1.81

Earned Run Average		Component ERA		Hit Batsmen		Wild Pitches		Opponent Average		Opponent OBP	
T. Bond, Bos	2.11	T. Bond, Bos	2.25	Statistic unavailable		G. Bradley, ChN	39	T. Larkin, Har	.245	T. Bond, Bos	.261
T. Larkin, Har	2.14	T. Larkin, Har	2.28			J. Blong, StL	29	T. Bond, Bos	.249	T. Larkin, Har	.264
J. Devlin, Lou	2.25	J. Devlin, Lou	2.71			T. Nichols, StL	22	J. Blong, StL	.262	J. Devlin, Lou	.283
T. Nichols, StL	2.60	T. Nichols, StL	2.79			J. Devlin, Lou	20	T. Nichols, StL	.263	G. Bradley, ChN	.286
J. Blong, StL	2.74	G. Bradley, ChN	2.92			2 tied with	18	G. Bradley, ChN	.269	T. Nichols, StL	.289

1877 National League Miscellaneous

Managers

Boston	Harry Wright	42-18
Chicago	Al Spalding	26-33
Cincinnati	Lip Pike	3-11
	Bob Addy	5-19
	Jack Manning	7-12
Hartford	Bob Ferguson	31-27
Louisville	Jack Chapman	35-25
St. Louis	George McManus	28-32

Awards

STATS Most Valuable Player	Deacon White, 1b, Bos
STATS Cy Young	Tommy Bond, Bos
STATS Rookie of the Year	Terry Larkin, p, Har
STATS Manager of the Year	Harry Wright, Bos

STATS All-Star Team

C	Cal McVey, ChN	.368	0	36
1B	Deacon White, Bos	.387	2	49
2B	Joe Gerhardt, Lou	.304	1	35
3B	Cap Anson, ChN	.337	0	32
SS	John Peters, ChN	.317	0	41
OF	John Cassidy, Har	.378	0	27
OF	Charley Jones, 2tm	.313	2	38
OF	Jim O'Rourke, Bos	.362	0	23
P	Tommy Bond, Bos	40-17	2.11	170 K

Postseason

None

Outstanding Performances

None

Team	Overall					Home Games						Road Games						Park Index		Record by Month					
	W	L	Pct	GB	DIF	W	L	R	OR	HR	OHR	W	L	R	OR	HR	OHR	Run	HR	M/A	May	June	July	Aug	S/O
Boston	41	19	.683	—	86	23	7	171	104	1	3	18	12	127	137	1	3	104	100	—	6-3	8-4	12-3	11-3	4-6
Cincinnati	37	23	.617	4.0	62	25	8	190	126	4	2	12	15	143	155	1	0	87	491	—	11-3	4-8	7-7	9-4	6-1
Providence	33	27	.550	8.0	0	17	13	182	170	4	2	16	14	171	167	4	3	104	86	—	3-6	6-5	8-6	8-6	8-4
Chicago	30	30	.500	11.0	8	17	13	226	210	2	2	13	12	145	121	1	2	117	95	—	4-9	10-3	12-3	2-10	2-5
Indianapolis	24	36	.400	17.0	0	10	17	106	115	1	1	14	19	187	213	2	2	68	61	—	7-7	6-6	3-12	6-7	2-4
Milwaukee	15	45	.250	26.0	0	7	18	127	177	1	0	8	27	129	209	1	3	126	35	—	5-8	2-10	2-13	4-10	2-4

Clinch Date—Boston 9/12.

Team Batting

Team	G	AB	R	OR	H	2B	3B	HR	TB	RBI	TBB	IBB	SO	HBP	SH	SF	SB	CS	SB%	GDP	Avg	OBP	Slg
Chicago	61	2333	371	331	677	91	20	3	817	284	88	—	157	—	—	—	—	—	—	—	.290	.316	.350
Providence	62	2298	353	337	604	107	30	8	795	250	50	—	218	—	—	—	—	—	—	—	.263	.279	.346
Cincinnati	61	2281	333	281	629	67	22	5	755	225	58	—	141	—	—	—	—	—	—	—	.276	.294	.331
Boston	60	2220	298	241	535	75	25	2	666	194	35	—	154	—	—	—	—	—	—	—	.241	.253	.300
Indianapolis	63	2300	293	328	542	76	15	3	657	198	64	—	197	—	—	—	—	—	—	—	.236	.256	.286
Milwaukee	61	2212	256	386	552	65	20	2	663	177	69	—	214	—	—	—	—	—	—	—	.250	.272	.300
NL Total	368	13644	1904	1904	3539	481	132	23	4353	1328	364	—	1081	—	—	—	—	—	—	—	.259	.279	.319
NL Avg Team	61	2274	317	317	590	80	22	4	726	221	61	—	180	—	—	—	—	—	—	—	.259	.279	.319

Team Pitching

Team	G	CG	ShO	Rel	Sv	IP	H	R	ER	HR	SH	SF	HB	TBB	IBB	SO	WP	Bk	H/9	SO/9	BB/9	OAvg	OOBP	ERA
Cincinnati	61	61	6	0	0	548.0	546	281	112	2	—	—	—	63	—	220	43	—	9.0	3.6	1.0	.248	.269	1.84
Boston	60	58	9	2	0	544.0	595	241	140	6	—	—	—	38	—	184	17	—	9.8	3.0	0.6	.272	.284	2.32
Indianapolis	63	59	2	4	1	578.0	621	328	149	3	—	—	—	87	—	182	30	—	9.7	2.8	1.4	.262	.288	2.32
Chicago	61	61	1	0	0	551.0	577	331	145	4	—	—	—	35	—	175	38	—	9.4	2.9	0.6	.253	.265	2.37
Providence	62	59	6	0	0	556.0	609	337	147	5	—	—	—	86	—	173	58	—	9.9	2.8	1.4	.265	.291	2.38
Milwaukee	61	54	1	7	0	547.0	589	386	158	3	—	—	—	55	—	147	50	—	9.7	2.4	0.9	.255	.272	2.60
NL Total	368	352	25	17	1	3324.0	3537	1904	851	23	—	—	—	364	—	1081	236	—	9.6	2.9	1.0	.259	.278	2.30
NL Avg Team	61	59	4	3	0	554.0	590	317	142	4	—	—	—	61	—	180	39	—	9.6	2.9	1.0	.259	.278	2.30

Team Fielding

Team	G	PO	A	E	TC	DP	PB	Pct
Boston	60	1630	801	228	2659	48	45	.914
Cincinnati	61	1642	780	269	2691	37	56	.900
Indianapolis	63	1725	830	290	2845	37	65	.898
Providence	62	1661	902	311	2874	42	75	.892
Chicago	61	1652	836	304	2792	37	103	.891
Milwaukee	61	1641	780	376	2797	32	99	.866
NL Total	368	9951	4929	1778	16658	233	443	.893

Team vs. Team Records

	Bos	ChN	Cin	Ind	Mil	Prv	Won
Bos	—	8	6	10	11	6	41
ChN	4	—	2	8	10	6	30
Cin	6	10	—	4	8	9	37
Ind	2	4	8	—	8	2	24
Mil	1	2	4	4	—	4	15
Prv	6	6	3	10	8	—	33
Lost	19	30	23	36	45	27	

1878 National League Batting Leaders

Games		At-Bats		Runs		Hits		Doubles		Triples	
N. Williamson, Ind	63	J. Start, ChN	285	D. Higham, Prv	60	J. Start, ChN	100	D. Higham, Prv	22	T. York, Prv	10
R. McKelvy, Ind	63	D. Higham, Prv	281	J. Start, ChN	58	A. Dalrymple, Mil	96	L. Brown, Prv	21	C. Jones, Cin	7
S. Flint, Ind	63	J. Quest, Ind	278	T. York, Prv	56	P. Hines, Prv	92	O. Shaffer, Ind	19	J. O'Rourke, Bos	7
O. Shaffer, Ind	63	A. Dalrymple, Mil	271	C. Anson, ChN	55	B. Ferguson, ChN	91	T. York, Prv	19	3 tied with	6
J. Clapp, Ind	63	C. McVey, Cin	271	A. Dalrymple, Mil	52	2 tied with	90	J. O'Rourke, Bos	17		

Home Runs		Total Bases		Runs Batted In		Walks		Intentional Walks		Strikeouts	
P. Hines, Prv	4	P. Hines, Prv	125	P. Hines, Prv	50	T. Larkin, ChN	17	Statistic unavailable		W. White, Cin	41
C. Jones, Cin	3	J. Start, ChN	125	L. Brown, Prv	43	J. Remsen, ChN	17			R. McKelvy, Ind	38
R. McKelvy, Ind	2	T. York, Prv	125	C. Anson, ChN	40	O. Shaffer, Ind	13			L. Brown, Prv	37
C. McVey, Cin	2	O. Shaffer, Ind	121	C. Jones, Cin	39	J. Clapp, Ind	13			F. Hankinson, ChN	36
12 tied with	1	D. Higham, Prv	117	B. Ferguson, ChN	39	C. Anson, ChN	13			M. Golden, Mil	35

Hit By Pitch	Sac Hits	Sac Flies	Stolen Bases	Caught Stealing	GDP
Statistic unavailable	Statistic unavailable	Statistic unavailable	Statistic unavailable	Statistic unavailable	Statistic unavailable

Runs Created		Runs Created/27 Outs		Batting Average		On-Base Percentage		Slugging Percentage		OBP+Slugging	
O. Shaffer, Ind	65	P. Hines, Prv	10.15	P. Hines, Prv	.358	B. Ferguson, ChN	.375	P. Hines, Prv	.486	P. Hines, Prv	.849
P. Hines, Prv	61	O. Shaffer, Ind	10.14	A. Dalrymple, Mil	.354	C. Anson, ChN	.372	T. York, Prv	.465	O. Shaffer, Ind	.824
T. York, Prv	59	T. York, Prv	8.71	B. Ferguson, ChN	.351	O. Shaffer, Ind	.369	O. Shaffer, Ind	.455	J. Start, ChN	.794
J. Start, ChN	58	J. Start, ChN	8.61	J. Start, ChN	.351	A. Dalrymple, Mil	.368	L. Brown, Prv	.453	T. York, Prv	.793
D. Higham, Prv	56	B. Ferguson, ChN	8.50	C. Anson, ChN	.341	P. Hines, Prv	.363	C. Jones, Cin	.441	A. Dalrymple, Mil	.789

1878 National League Pitching Leaders

Wins		Losses		Winning Percentage		Games		Games Started		Complete Games	
T. Bond, Bos	40	S. Weaver, Mil	31	T. Bond, Bos	.678	T. Bond, Bos	59	T. Bond, Bos	59	T. Bond, Bos	57
W. White, Cin	30	T. Larkin, ChN	26	M. Ward, Prv	.629	T. Larkin, ChN	56	T. Larkin, ChN	56	T. Larkin, ChN	56
T. Larkin, ChN	29	T. Nolan, Ind	22	W. White, Cin	.588	W. White, Cin	52	W. White, Cin	52	W. White, Cin	52
M. Ward, Prv	22	W. White, Cin	21	T. Larkin, ChN	.527	S. Weaver, Mil	45	S. Weaver, Mil	43	S. Weaver, Mil	39
T. Nolan, Ind	13	T. Bond, Bos	19	T. Nolan, Ind	.371	T. Nolan, Ind	38	T. Nolan, Ind	38	2 tied with	37

Shutouts		Saves		Games Finished		Batters Faced		Innings Pitched		Hits Allowed	
T. Bond, Bos	9	T. Healey, 2tm	1	M. Golden, Mil	4	T. Bond, Bos	2159	T. Bond, Bos	532.2	T. Bond, Bos	571
M. Ward, Prv	6			R. McKelvy, Ind	3	T. Larkin, ChN	2105	T. Larkin, ChN	506.0	T. Larkin, ChN	511
W. White, Cin	5			S. Weaver, Mil	2	W. White, Cin	1939	W. White, Cin	468.0	W. White, Cin	477
5 tied with	1			7 tied with	1	S. Weaver, Mil	1589	S. Weaver, Mil	383.0	S. Weaver, Mil	371
						T. Nolan, Ind	1469	T. Nolan, Ind	347.0	T. Nolan, Ind	357

Home Runs Allowed		Walks		Walks/9 Innings		Strikeouts		Strikeouts/9 Innings		Strikeout/Walk Ratio	
T. Bond, Bos	5	T. Nolan, Ind	56	S. Weaver, Mil	0.5	T. Bond, Bos	182	B. Mitchell, Cin	5.7	T. Bond, Bos	5.52
T. Larkin, ChN	4	W. White, Cin	45	T. Larkin, ChN	0.6	W. White, Cin	169	H. Wheeler, Prv	3.6	T. Larkin, ChN	5.26
M. Ward, Prv	3	M. Ward, Prv	34	T. Bond, Bos	0.6	T. Larkin, ChN	163	W. White, Cin	3.3	S. Weaver, Mil	4.52
T. Healey, 2tm	2	M. Golden, Mil	33	T. Nichols, Prv	0.7	T. Nolan, Ind	125	T. Nolan, Ind	3.2	W. White, Cin	3.76
S. Weaver, Mil	2	T. Bond, Bos	33	W. White, Cin	0.9	M. Ward, Prv	116	M. Ward, Prv	3.1	M. Ward, Prv	3.41

Earned Run Average		Component ERA		Hit Batsmen		Wild Pitches		Opponent Average		Opponent OBP	
M. Ward, Prv	1.51	M. Ward, Prv	1.92	Statistic unavailable		W. White, Cin	40	B. Mitchell, Cin	.223	S. Weaver, Mil	.247
J. McCormick, Ind	1.69	S. Weaver, Mil	1.93			T. Larkin, ChN	37	M. Ward, Prv	.231	M. Ward, Prv	.251
W. White, Cin	1.79	B. Mitchell, Cin	2.07			M. Ward, Prv	26	S. Weaver, Mil	.237	T. Larkin, ChN	.257
S. Weaver, Mil	1.95	T. Larkin, ChN	2.17			S. Weaver, Mil	25	T. Larkin, ChN	.246	B. Mitchell, Cin	.265
T. Bond, Bos	2.06	W. White, Cin	2.32			M. Golden, Mil	24	W. White, Cin	.252	W. White, Cin	.269

1878 National League Miscellaneous

Managers		
Boston	Harry Wright	41-19
Chicago	Bob Ferguson	30-30
Cincinnati	Cal McVey	37-23
Indianapolis	John Clapp	24-36
Milwaukee	Jack Chapman	15-45
Providence	Tom York	33-27

Awards	
STATS Most Valuable Player	Paul Hines, of, Prv
STATS Cy Young	Tommy Bond, Bos
STATS Rookie of the Year	Will White, p, Cin
STATS Manager of the Year	Cal McVey, Cin

STATS All-Star Team

C	Lew Brown, Prv	.305	1	43
1B	Joe Start, ChN	.351	1	27
2B	Jack Burdock, Bos	.260	0	25
3B	Cal McVey, Cin	.306	2	25
SS	Bob Ferguson, ChN	.351	0	39
OF	Cap Anson, ChN	.341	0	40
OF	Paul Hines, Prv	.358	4	50
OF	Orator Shaffer, Ind	.338	0	30
P	Tommy Bond, Bos	40-19	2.06	182 K

Postseason

None

Outstanding Performances

Triple Crown
Paul Hines, Prv   .358-4-50
Unassisted Triple Plays
Paul Hines, Prv   on May 8

1879 National League Standings

Team	W	L	Pct	GB	DIF	W	L	R	OR	HR	OHR	W	L	R	OR	HR	OHR	Run	HR	M/A	May	June	July	Aug	S/O
								Home Games						**Road Games**				**Park Index**				**Record by Month**			
Providence	59	25	.702	—	50	34	8	323	143	9	4	25	17	289	212	3	5	93	163	—	10-5	9-5	10-8	16-3	14-4
Boston	54	30	.643	5.0	6	29	13	308	165	11	2	25	17	254	183	9	7	108	81	—	7-8	8-6	12-6	16-3	11-7
Buffalo	46	32	.590	10.0	0	23	16	223	204	1	0	23	16	167	161	1	3	130	25	—	6-9	8-5	13-4	8-6	11-8
Chicago	46	33	.582	10.5	103	29	13	264	191	2	0	17	20	173	219	1	5	102	29	—	14-1	9-3	11-8	8-9	4-12
Cincinnati	43	37	.538	14.0	9	21	16	215	196	8	6	22	21	270	268	0	5	89	325	—	8-7	3-9	11-7	8-6	13-8
Cleveland	27	55	.329	31.0	0	15	27	167	236	2	1	12	28	155	225	2	3	101	57	—	3-12	5-7	6-12	7-10	6-14
Syracuse	22	48	.314	30.0	0	11	22	115	200	1	2	11	26	160	257	4	2	85	56	—	8-7	3-10	6-12	4-15	1-4
Troy	19	56	.253	35.5	0	12	27	191	263	3	6	7	29	130	281	1	7	102	104	—	4-11	6-6	2-14	2-17	5-8

Clinch Date—Providence 9/26.

Team Batting

Team	G	AB	R	OR	H	2B	3B	HR	TB	RBI	TBB	IBB	SO	HBP	SH	SF	SB	CS	SB%	GDP	Avg	OBP	Slg
Providence	85	3392	612	355	1003	142	55	12	1291	405	91	—	172	—	—	—	—	—	—	—	.296	.314	.381
Boston	84	3217	562	348	883	138	51	20	1183	393	90	—	222	—	—	—	—	—	—	—	.274	.294	.368
Cincinnati	81	3085	485	464	813	127	53	8	1070	364	66	—	207	—	—	—	—	—	—	—	.264	.279	.347
Chicago	83	3116	437	411	808	167	32	3	1048	293	73	—	294	—	—	—	—	—	—	—	.259	.276	.336
Buffalo	79	2906	394	365	733	105	54	2	952	279	78	—	314	—	—	—	—	—	—	—	.252	.272	.328
Cleveland	82	2987	322	461	666	116	29	4	852	229	37	—	214	—	—	—	—	—	—	—	.223	.232	.285
Troy	77	2841	321	543	673	102	24	4	835	206	45	—	182	—	—	—	—	—	—	—	.237	.249	.294
Syracuse	71	2611	276	462	592	61	19	5	706	188	28	—	238	—	—	—	—	—	—	—	.227	.235	.270
NL Total	642	24155	3409	3409	6171	958	317	58	7937	2357	508	—	1843	—	—	—	—	—	—	—	.255	.271	.329
NL Avg Team	80	3019	426	426	771	120	40	7	992	295	64	—	230	—	—	—	—	—	—	—	.255	.271	.329

Team Pitching

Team	G	CG	ShO	Rel	Sv	IP	H	R	ER	HR	SH	SF	HB	TBB	IBB	SO	WP	Bk	H/9	SO/9	BB/9	OAvg	OOBP	ERA
Providence	85	73	3	12	2	776.0	765	355	188	9	—	—	—	62	—	329	46	—	8.9	3.8	0.7	.243	.258	2.18
Boston	84	80	13	5	0	753.0	757	348	183	9	—	—	—	46	—	230	24	—	9.0	2.7	0.5	.251	.262	2.19
Cincinnati	81	79	4	3	0	726.0	756	464	185	11	—	—	—	81	—	246	57	—	9.4	3.0	1.0	.248	.267	2.29
Buffalo	79	78	8	1	0	713.0	698	365	185	3	—	—	—	47	—	198	25	—	8.8	2.5	0.6	.242	.254	2.34
Chicago	83	82	6	1	0	744.0	762	411	203	5	—	—	—	57	—	211	24	—	9.2	2.6	0.7	.244	.258	2.46
Cleveland	82	79	3	3	0	741.0	818	461	218	4	—	—	—	116	—	287	56	—	9.9	3.5	1.4	.265	.292	2.65
Troy	77	75	3	2	0	695.0	840	543	216	13	—	—	—	47	—	210	67	—	10.9	2.7	0.6	.275	.286	2.80
Syracuse	71	64	5	7	0	649.0	775	462	230	4	—	—	—	52	—	132	64	—	10.7	1.8	0.7	.277	.290	3.19
NL Total	642	610	45	34	2	5797.0	6171	3409	1608	58	—	—	—	508	—	1843	363	—	9.6	2.9	0.8	.255	.271	2.50
NL Avg Team	80	76	6	4	0	724.0	771	426	201	7	—	—	—	64	—	230	45	—	9.6	2.9	0.8	.255	.271	2.50

Team Fielding

Team	G	PO	A	E	TC	DP	PB	Pct
Boston	84	2257	1103	319	3679	58	84	.913
Buffalo	79	2142	1056	331	3529	62	74	.906
Providence	85	2327	1188	382	3897	41	82	.902
Chicago	83	2232	1181	381	3794	52	69	.900
Cleveland	82	2222	1016	406	3644	42	122	.889
Cincinnati	81	2181	1055	454	3690	48	109	.877
Troy	77	2094	1127	460	3681	44	150	.875
Syracuse	71	1943	779	398	3120	37	86	.872
NL Total	642	17398	8505	3131	29034	384	776	.892

Team vs. Team Records

	Bos	Buf	ChN	Cin	Cle	Prv	Syr	Try	Won
Bos	—	9	4	7	10	4	9	11	54
Buf	3	—	6	7	8	6	5	11	46
ChN	8	6	—	3	8	5	8	8	46
Cin	5	3	8	—	8	2	8	9	43
Cle	2	4	4	4	—	4	4	5	27
Prv	8	6	7	10	8	—	10	10	59
Syr	3	3	1	4	7	2	—	2	22
Try	1	1	3	2	6	2	4	—	19
Lost	30	32	33	37	55	25	48	56	

1879 National League Batting Leaders

Games			At-Bats			Runs			Hits			Doubles			Triples		
P. Hines, Prv		85	P. Hines, Prv		409	C. Jones, Bos		85	P. Hines, Prv		146	C. Eden, Cle		31	B. Dickerson, Cin		14
M. McGeary, Prv		85	G. Wright, Prv		388	P. Hines, Prv		81	J. O'Rourke, Prv		126	A. Dalrymple, ChN		25	N. Williamson, ChN		13
G. Wright, Prv		85	J. Peters, ChN		379	G. Wright, Prv		79	K. Kelly, Cin		120	P. Hines, Prv		25	K. Kelly, Cin		12
3 tied with		84	M. McGeary, Prv		374	K. Kelly, Cin		78	C. Jones, Bos		112	T. York, Prv		25	J. O'Rourke, Bos		11
			P. Hotaling, Cin		369	B. Dickerson, Cin		73	D. White, Cin		110	S. Houck, Bos		24	4 tied with		10

Home Runs			Total Bases			Runs Batted In			Walks			Intentional Walks			Strikeouts		
C. Jones, Bos		9	P. Hines, Prv		197	J. O'Rourke, Bos		62	C. Jones, Bos		29	Statistic unavailable			W. White, Cin		56
J. O'Rourke, Bos		6	C. Jones, Bos		181	C. Jones, Bos		62	N. Williamson, ChN		24				P. Galvin, Buf		56
D. Brouthers, Try		4	K. Kelly, Cin		170	B. Dickerson, Cin		57	T. York, Prv		19				M. Mansell, Syr		45
C. Eden, Cle		3	J. O'Rourke, Prv		166	C. McVey, Cin		55	H. Richardson, Buf		16				S. Flint, ChN		44
8 tied with		2	J. O'Rourke, Bos		165	2 tied with		52	R. Barnes, Cin		16				D. Eggler, Buf		41

Hit By Pitch	Sac Hits	Sac Flies	Stolen Bases	Caught Stealing	GDP
Statistic unavailable	Statistic unavailable	Statistic unavailable	Statistic unavailable	Statistic unavailable	Statistic unavailable

Runs Created			Runs Created/27 Outs			Batting Average			On-Base Percentage			Slugging Percentage			OBP+Slugging		
P. Hines, Prv		98	J. O'Rourke, Bos		11.12	P. Hines, Prv		.357	J. O'Rourke, Prv		.371	J. O'Rourke, Bos		.521	J. O'Rourke, Bos		.877
C. Jones, Bos		94	C. Jones, Bos		10.84	J. O'Rourke, Prv		.348	P. Hines, Prv		.369	C. Jones, Bos		.510	C. Jones, Bos		.877
K. Kelly, Cin		85	K. Kelly, Cin		10.58	K. Kelly, Cin		.348	C. Jones, Bos		.367	K. Kelly, Cin		.493	K. Kelly, Cin		.855
J. O'Rourke, Prv		85	P. Hines, Prv		10.44	J. O'Rourke, Bos		.341	K. Kelly, Cin		.363	P. Hines, Prv		.482	P. Hines, Prv		.851
J. O'Rourke, Bos		83	J. O'Rourke, Prv		10.09	D. White, Cin		.330	J. O'Rourke, Bos		.357	J. O'Rourke, Prv		.459	J. O'Rourke, Prv		.829

1879 National League Pitching Leaders

Wins			Losses			Winning Percentage			Games			Games Started			Complete Games		
M. Ward, Prv		47	J. McCormick, Cle		40	M. Ward, Prv		.712	W. White, Cin		76	W. White, Cin		75	W. White, Cin		75
W. White, Cin		43	G. Bradley, Try		40	T. Bond, Bos		.694	M. Ward, Prv		70	P. Galvin, Buf		66	P. Galvin, Buf		65
T. Bond, Bos		43	H. McCormick, Syr		33	B. Mathews, Prv		.667	P. Galvin, Buf		66	T. Bond, Bos		64	J. McCormick, Cle		59
P. Galvin, Buf		37	W. White, Cin		31	F. Hankinson, ChN		.600	T. Bond, Bos		64	M. Ward, Prv		60	T. Bond, Bos		59
T. Larkin, ChN		31	P. Galvin, Buf		27	W. White, Cin		.581	J. McCormick, Cle		62	J. McCormick, Cle		60	M. Ward, Prv		58

Shutouts			Saves			Games Finished			Batters Faced			Innings Pitched			Hits Allowed		
T. Bond, Bos		11	M. Ward, Prv		1	M. Ward, Prv		10	W. White, Cin		2906	W. White, Cin		680.0	W. White, Cin		676
P. Galvin, Buf		6	B. Mathews, Prv		1	C. Foley, Bos		4	P. Galvin, Buf		2436	P. Galvin, Buf		593.0	G. Bradley, Try		590
H. McCormick, Syr		5				H. McCormick, Syr		4	M. Ward, Prv		2425	M. Ward, Prv		587.0	P. Galvin, Buf		585
W. White, Cin		4				B. Purcell, 2tm		3	J. McCormick, Cle		2325	T. Bond, Bos		555.1	J. McCormick, Cle		582
T. Larkin, ChN		4				2 tied with		2	T. Bond, Bos		2189	J. McCormick, Cle		546.1	M. Ward, Prv		571

Home Runs Allowed			Walks			Walks/9 Innings			Strikeouts			Strikeouts/9 Innings			Strikeout/Walk Ratio		
G. Bradley, Try		12	J. McCormick, Cle		74	T. Bond, Bos		0.4	M. Ward, Prv		239	B. McGunnigle, Buf		4.7	M. Ward, Prv		6.64
W. White, Cin		10	W. White, Cin		68	P. Galvin, Buf		0.5	W. White, Cin		232	B. Mathews, Prv		4.3	T. Bond, Bos		6.46
T. Bond, Bos		8	B. Mitchell, Cle		42	G. Bradley, Try		0.5	J. McCormick, Cle		197	B. Mitchell, Cle		4.2	G. Bradley, Try		5.12
M. Ward, Prv		5	M. Ward, Prv		36	T. Larkin, ChN		0.5	T. Bond, Bos		155	M. Ward, Prv		3.7	T. Larkin, ChN		4.73
T. Larkin, ChN		5	2 tied with		31	M. Ward, Prv		0.6	T. Larkin, ChN		142	J. McCormick, Cle		3.2	P. Galvin, Buf		4.39

Earned Run Average			Component ERA			Hit Batsmen			Wild Pitches			Opponent Average			Opponent OBP		
T. Bond, Bos		1.96	M. Ward, Prv		2.00	Statistic unavailable			W. White, Cin		49	B. McGunnigle, Buf		.235	T. Larkin, ChN		.250
W. White, Cin		1.99	P. Galvin, Buf		2.03				G. Bradley, Try		43	W. White, Cin		.238	M. Ward, Prv		.250
M. Ward, Prv		2.15	B. McGunnigle, Buf		2.05				B. Purcell, 2tm		34	M. Ward, Prv		.239	P. Galvin, Buf		.253
H. Salisbury, Try		2.22	T. Larkin, ChN		2.07				H. McCormick, Syr		31	T. Larkin, ChN		.240	W. White, Cin		.256
P. Galvin, Buf		2.28	T. Bond, Bos		2.12				J. McCormick, Cle		30	P. Galvin, Buf		.243	T. Bond, Bos		.259

1879 National League Miscellaneous

Managers

Boston	Harry Wright	54-30
Buffalo	John Clapp	46-32
Chicago	Cap Anson	41-21
	Silver Flint	5-12
Cincinnati	Deacon White	9-9
	Cal McVey	34-28
Cleveland	Jim McCormick	27-55
Providence	George Wright	59-25
Syracuse	Mike Dorgan	17-26
	Bill Holbert	0-1
	Jimmy Macullar	5-21
Troy	Horace Phillips	12-34
	Bob Ferguson	7-22

Awards

STATS Most Valuable Player	Monte Ward, p, Prv
STATS Cy Young	Monte Ward, Prv
STATS Rookie of the Year	John O'Rourke, of, Bos
STATS Manager of the Year	George Wright, Prv

STATS All-Star Team

C	Deacon White, Cin	.330	1	52
1B	Joe Start, Prv	.319	2	37
2B	Jack Farrell, 2tm	.295	1	26
3B	King Kelly, Cin	.348	2	47
SS	George Wright, Prv	.276	1	42
OF	Paul Hines, Prv	.357	2	52
OF	Charley Jones, Bos	.315	9	62
OF	John O'Rourke, Bos	.341	6	62
P	Monte Ward, Prv	47-19	2.15	239 K

Postseason

None

Outstanding Performances

None

1880 National League Standings

Team	Overall					Home Games						Road Games						Park Index			Record by Month				
	W	L	Pct	GB	DIF	W	L	R	OR	HR	OHR	W	L	R	OR	HR	OHR	Run	HR	M/A	May	June	July	Aug	S/O
Chicago	67	17	.798	—	150	37	5	284	148	1	0	30	12	254	169	3	8	102	9	—	14-2	16-1	11-6	11-3	15-5
Providence	52	32	.619	15.0	5	31	12	210	116	4	2	21	20	209	183	4	5	79	64	—	8-7	11-6	9-8	11-3	13-8
Cleveland	47	37	.560	20.0	2	23	19	182	168	2	1	24	18	205	169	5	3	94	38	—	9-6	9-8	10-5	6-10	13-8
Troy	41	42	.494	25.5	0	20	21	204	257	5	6	21	21	188	181	0	2	128	563	—	7-9	5-9	10-7	11-4	8-13
Worcester	40	43	.482	26.5	11	24	17	247	186	5	6	16	26	165	184	3	7	127	113	—	9-7	7-10	8-7	6-10	10-9
Boston	40	44	.476	27.0	0	25	17	213	190	14	1	15	27	203	265	6	1	86	214	—	7-9	9-8	7-10	6-8	11-9
Buffalo	24	58	.293	42.0	3	13	29	173	233	1	1	11	29	159	269	2	9	90	17	—	5-12	6-10	6-11	4-10	3-15
Cincinnati	21	59	.263	44.0	0	14	25	163	216	5	8	7	34	131	256	2	2	103	342	—	4-11	2-13	5-12	4-11	6-12

Clinch Date—Chicago 9/15.

Team Batting

Team	G	AB	R	OR	H	2B	3B	HR	TB	RBI	TBB	IBB	SO	HBP	SH	SF	SB	CS	SB%	GDP	Avg	OBP	Slg
Chicago	86	3135	538	317	876	164	39	4	1130	378	104	—	217	—	—	—	—	—	—	—	.279	.303	.360
Providence	87	3196	419	299	793	114	34	8	999	278	89	—	186	—	—	—	—	—	—	—	.248	.268	.313
Boston	86	3080	416	456	779	134	41	20	1055	313	105	—	221	—	—	—	—	—	—	—	.253	.278	.343
Worcester	85	3024	412	370	699	129	52	8	956	278	81	—	278	—	—	—	—	—	—	—	.231	.251	.316
Troy	83	3007	392	438	755	114	37	5	958	253	120	—	260	—	—	—	—	—	—	—	.251	.280	.319
Cleveland	85	3002	387	337	726	130	52	7	981	273	76	—	237	—	—	—	—	—	—	—	.242	.261	.327
Buffalo	85	2962	331	502	669	104	37	3	856	240	90	—	327	—	—	—	—	—	—	—	.226	.249	.289
Cincinnati	83	2895	296	472	649	91	36	7	833	209	75	—	267	—	—	—	—	—	—	—	.224	.244	.288
NL Total	680	24301	3191	3191	5946	980	328	62	7768	2222	740	—	1993	—	—	—	—	—	—	—	.245	.267	.320
NL Avg Team	85	3038	399	399	743	123	41	8	971	278	93	—	249	—	—	—	—	—	—	—	.245	.267	.320

Team Pitching

Team	G	CG	ShO	Rel	Sv	IP	H	R	ER	HR	SH	SF	HB	TBB	IBB	SO	WP	Bk	H/9	SO/9	BB/9	OAvg	OOBP	ERA
Providence	87	75	13	12	2	799.0	663	299	146	7	—	—	—	51	—	286	26	—	7.5	3.2	0.6	.215	.228	1.64
Cleveland	85	83	7	2	1	759.2	685	337	160	4	—	—	—	98	—	289	31	—	8.1	3.4	1.2	.228	.253	1.90
Chicago	86	80	8	8	3	775.0	622	317	166	8	—	—	—	129	—	367	33	—	7.2	4.3	1.5	.209	.242	1.93
Worcester	85	68	7	18	5	762.2	709	370	192	13	—	—	—	97	—	297	33	—	8.4	3.5	1.1	.233	.257	2.27
Cincinnati	83	79	3	4	0	713.1	785	472	193	10	—	—	—	88	—	208	45	—	9.9	2.6	1.1	.259	.280	2.44
Troy	83	81	4	2	0	738.0	760	438	225	8	—	—	—	112	—	169	37	—	9.3	2.1	1.4	.255	.282	2.74
Boston	86	70	4	17	0	744.2	840	456	255	2	—	—	—	86	—	187	39	—	10.2	2.3	1.0	.276	.296	3.08
Buffalo	85	72	6	13	1	739.0	879	502	254	10	—	—	—	78	—	186	50	—	10.7	2.3	0.9	.279	.297	3.09
NL Total	680	608	52	76	12	6031.1	5943	3191	1591	62	—	—	—	739	—	1989	294	—	8.9	3.0	1.1	.245	.267	2.37
NL Avg Team	85	76	7	10	2	753.1	743	399	199	8	—	—	—	92	—	249	37	—	8.9	3.0	1.1	.245	.267	2.37

Team Fielding

Team	G	PO	A	E	TC	DP	PB	Pct
Chicago	86	2327	1113	329	3769	41	108	.913
Providence	87	2386	1221	357	3964	53	73	.910
Cleveland	85	2279	1051	330	3660	52	86	.910
Worcester	85	2288	1114	355	3757	49	61	.906
Boston	86	2232	1112	367	3711	54	93	.901
Troy	83	2217	1061	366	3644	58	123	.900
Buffalo	85	2217	1103	408	3728	55	135	.891
Cincinnati	83	2158	952	437	3547	49	74	.877
NL Total	680	18104	8727	2949	29780	411	753	.901

Team vs. Team Records

	Bos	Buf	ChN	Cin	Cle	Prv	Try	Wor	Won
Bos	—	9	3	7	5	5	7	4	40
Buf	3	—	1	5	3	2	1	9	24
ChN	9	11	—	10	8	9	10	10	67
Cin	5	5	2	—	3	2	1	3	21
Cle	7	9	4	9	—	3	9	6	47
Prv	7	10	3	10	9	—	7	6	52
Try	5	11	2	10	3	5	—	5	41
Wor	8	3	2	8	6	6	7	—	40
Lost	44	58	17	59	37	32	42	43	

1880 National League Batting Leaders

Games		At-Bats		Runs		Hits		Doubles		Triples	
E. Gross, Prv	87	A. Dalrymple, ChN	382	A. Dalrymple, ChN	91	A. Dalrymple, ChN	126	F. Dunlap, Cle	27	H. Stovey, Wor	14
7 tied with	86	P. Hines, Prv	374	H. Stovey, Wor	76	C. Anson, ChN	120	A. Dalrymple, ChN	25	A. Dalrymple, ChN	12
		F. Dunlap, Cle	373	K. Kelly, ChN	72	G. Gore, ChN	116	C. Anson, ChN	24	J. Hornung, Buf	11
		J. O'Rourke, Bos	363	J. O'Rourke, Bos	71	P. Hines, Prv	115	G. Gore, ChN	23	J. O'Rourke, Bos	11
		J. Peters, Prv	359	G. Gore, ChN	70	R. Connor, Try	113	J. O'Rourke, Bos	22	B. Phillips, Cle	10

Home Runs		Total Bases		Runs Batted In		Walks		Intentional Walks		Strikeouts	
H. Stovey, Wor	6	A. Dalrymple, ChN	175	C. Anson, ChN	74	B. Ferguson, Try	24	Statistic unavailable		P. Galvin, Buf	57
J. O'Rourke, Bos	6	H. Stovey, Wor	161	K. Kelly, ChN	60	G. Gore, ChN	21			H. Stovey, Wor	46
C. Jones, Bos	5	F. Dunlap, Cle	160	R. Connor, Try	47	J. O'Rourke, Bos	21			G. Bradley, Prv	38
F. Dunlap, Cle	4	J. O'Rourke, Bos	160	G. Gore, ChN	47	J. Clapp, Cin	21			4 tied with	37
4 tied with	3	R. Connor, Try	156	J. O'Rourke, Bos	45	B. Crowley, Buf	19				

Hit By Pitch	Sac Hits	Sac Flies	Stolen Bases	Caught Stealing	GDP
Statistic unavailable	Statistic unavailable	Statistic unavailable	Statistic unavailable	Statistic unavailable	Statistic unavailable

Runs Created		Runs Created/27 Outs		Batting Average		On-Base Percentage		Slugging Percentage		OBP+Slugging	
A. Dalrymple, ChN	83	G. Gore, ChN	10.74	G. Gore, ChN	.360	G. Gore, ChN	.399	G. Gore, ChN	.463	G. Gore, ChN	.862
G. Gore, ChN	82	C. Anson, ChN	8.92	C. Anson, ChN	.337	C. Anson, ChN	.362	R. Connor, Try	.459	R. Connor, Try	.816
C. Anson, ChN	78	A. Dalrymple, ChN	8.75	R. Connor, Try	.332	R. Connor, Try	.357	A. Dalrymple, ChN	.458	A. Dalrymple, ChN	.793
H. Stovey, Wor	72	R. Connor, Try	8.32	A. Dalrymple, ChN	.330	A. Dalrymple, ChN	.335	H. Stovey, Wor	.454	C. Anson, ChN	.781
R. Connor, Try	70	T. Burns, ChN	7.51	T. Burns, ChN	.309	T. Burns, ChN	.333	J. O'Rourke, Bos	.441	J. O'Rourke, Bos	.756

1880 National League Pitching Leaders

Wins		Losses		Winning Percentage		Games		Games Started		Complete Games	
J. McCormick, Cle	45	W. White, Cin	42	F. Goldsmith, ChN	.875	L. Richmond, Wor	74	J. McCormick, Cle	74	J. McCormick, Cle	72
L. Corcoran, ChN	43	P. Galvin, Buf	35	L. Corcoran, ChN	.754	J. McCormick, Cle	74	M. Ward, Prv	67	M. Welch, Try	64
M. Ward, Prv	39	L. Richmond, Wor	32	G. Bradley, Prv	.636	M. Ward, Prv	70	L. Richmond, Wor	66	M. Ward, Prv	59
M. Welch, Try	34	M. Welch, Try	30	M. Ward, Prv	.619	M. Welch, Try	65	M. Welch, Try	64	W. White, Cin	58
L. Richmond, Wor	32	T. Bond, Bos	29	J. McCormick, Cle	.616	2 tied with	63	W. White, Cin	62	2 tied with	57

Shutouts		Saves		Games Finished		Batters Faced		Innings Pitched		Hits Allowed	
M. Ward, Prv	8	L. Richmond, Wor	3	L. Richmond, Wor	9	J. McCormick, Cle	2669	J. McCormick, Cle	657.2	J. McCormick, Cle	585
J. McCormick, Cle	7	L. Corcoran, ChN	2	C. Foley, Bos	8	L. Richmond, Wor	2410	M. Ward, Prv	595.0	M. Welch, Try	575
L. Richmond, Wor	5	F. Corey, Wor	2	G. Bradley, Prv	7	M. Welch, Try	2387	L. Richmond, Wor	590.2	T. Bond, Bos	559
P. Galvin, Buf	5	5 tied with	1	F. Corey, Wor	6	M. Ward, Prv	2351	M. Welch, Try	574.0	W. White, Cin	550
4 tied with	4			T. Bond, Bos	6	W. White, Cin	2217	L. Corcoran, ChN	536.1	L. Richmond, Wor	541

Home Runs Allowed		Walks		Walks/9 Innings		Strikeouts		Strikeouts/9 Innings		Strikeout/Walk Ratio	
W. White, Cin	9	L. Corcoran, ChN	99	G. Bradley, Prv	0.3	L. Corcoran, ChN	268	L. Corcoran, ChN	4.5	G. Bradley, Prv	9.00
M. Welch, Try	7	M. Welch, Try	80	P. Galvin, Buf	0.6	J. McCormick, Cle	260	F. Goldsmith, ChN	3.9	M. Ward, Prv	5.11
L. Richmond, Wor	7	J. McCormick, Cle	75	M. Ward, Prv	0.7	L. Richmond, Wor	243	L. Richmond, Wor	3.7	F. Goldsmith, ChN	5.00
L. Corcoran, ChN	6	L. Richmond, Wor	74	S. Wiedman, Buf	0.7	M. Ward, Prv	230	T. Keefe, Try	3.7	P. Galvin, Buf	4.00
F. Corey, Wor	6	W. White, Cin	56	F. Goldsmith, ChN	0.8	W. White, Cin	161	J. McCormick, Cle	3.6	J. McCormick, Cle	3.47

Earned Run Average		Component ERA		Hit Batsmen		Wild Pitches		Opponent Average		Opponent OBP	
T. Keefe, Try	0.86	T. Keefe, Try	1.25	Statistic unavailable		W. White, Cin	35	T. Keefe, Try	.187	G. Bradley, Prv	.217
G. Bradley, Prv	1.38	G. Bradley, Prv	1.37			L. Richmond, Wor	29	L. Corcoran, ChN	.199	T. Keefe, Try	.222
M. Ward, Prv	1.74	L. Corcoran, ChN	1.52			M. Welch, Try	26	G. Bradley, Prv	.210	M. Ward, Prv	.232
F. Goldsmith, ChN	1.75	M. Ward, Prv	1.56			P. Galvin, Buf	24	M. Ward, Prv	.217	L. Corcoran, ChN	.236
J. McCormick, Cle	1.85	J. McCormick, Cle	1.79			T. Bond, Bos	24	F. Corey, Wor	.219	F. Corey, Wor	.239

1880 National League Miscellaneous

Managers		
Boston	Harry Wright	40-44
Buffalo	Sam Crane	24-58
Chicago	Cap Anson	67-17
Cincinnati	John Clapp	21-59
Cleveland	Jim McCormick	47-37
Providence	Mike McGeary	8-7
	Monte Ward	18-13
	Mike Dorgan	26-12
Troy	Bob Ferguson	41-42
Worcester	Frank Bancroft	40-43

Awards	
STATS Most Valuable Player	George Gore, of, ChN
STATS Cy Young	Larry Corcoran, ChN
STATS Rookie of the Year	Larry Corcoran, p, ChN
STATS Manager of the Year	Cap Anson, ChN

STATS All-Star Team

C	John Clapp, Cin	.282	1	20
1B	Cap Anson, ChN	.337	1	74
2B	Fred Dunlap, Cle	.276	4	30
3B	Roger Connor, Try	.332	3	47
SS	Tom Burns, ChN	.309	0	43
OF	Abner Dalrymple, ChN	.330	0	36
OF	George Gore, ChN	.360	2	47
OF	Harry Stovey, Wor	.265	6	28
P	Larry Corcoran, ChN	43-14	1.95	268 K

Postseason

None

Outstanding Performances

Perfect Games
Lee Richmond, Wor vs. Cle on June 12
Monte Ward, Prv vs. Buf on June 17

No-Hitters
Larry Corcoran, ChN vs. Bos on August 19
Pud Galvin, Buf @ Wor on August 20

1881 National League Standings

Team	Overall					Home Games						Road Games						Park Index		Record by Month					
	W	L	Pct	GB	DIF	W	L	R	OR	HR	OHR	W	L	R	OR	HR	OHR	Run	HR	M/A	May	June	July	Aug	S/O
Chicago	56	28	.667	—	131	32	10	309	186	7	6	24	18	241	194	5	8	114	100	1-0	12-6	12-4	8-8	11-4	12-6
Providence	47	37	.560	9.0	0	23	20	209	194	4	2	24	17	240	232	7	3	81	57	—	8-10	6-10	9-7	11-5	13-5
Buffalo	45	38	.542	10.5	7	25	16	241	206	2	0	20	22	199	242	10	9	104	11	—	11-8	9-6	8-7	8-8	9-9
Detroit	41	43	.488	15.0	0	23	19	252	213	14	4	18	24	188	216	3	4	115	257	—	8-11	8-8	11-5	6-9	8-10
Troy	39	45	.464	17.0	0	24	18	222	196	4	9	15	27	177	232	1	2	102	433	0-1	5-12	10-6	6-10	7-8	11-8
Boston	38	45	.458	17.5	0	19	22	151	180	2	4	19	23	197	230	3	5	79	77		9-9	5-11	8-8	10-6	6-11
Cleveland	36	48	.429	20.0	0	20	22	190	185	3	4	16	26	201	229	4	5	87	78	0-1	9-9	6-10	9-6	6-10	6-12
Worcester	32	50	.390	23.0	25	19	22	240	253	7	4	13	28	170	239	0	7	121	157	1-0	10-7	7-8	4-12	3-12	7-11

Clinch Date—Chicago 9/16.

Team Batting

Team	G	AB	R	OR	H	2B	3B	HR	TB	RBI	TBB	IBB	SO	HBP	SH	SF	SB	CS	SB%	GDP	Avg	OBP	Slg
Chicago	84	3114	550	379	918	157	36	12	1183	400	140	—	224	—	—	—	—	—	—	—	.295	.325	.380
Providence	85	3077	447	426	780	144	37	11	1031	322	146	—	214	—	—	—	—	—	—	—	.253	.287	.335
Buffalo	83	3019	440	447	797	157	50	12	1090	349	108	—	270	—	—	—	—	—	—	—	.264	.289	.361
Detroit	84	2995	439	429	780	131	53	17	1068	351	136	—	250	—	—	—	—	—	—	—	.260	.293	.357
Worcester	83	3093	410	492	781	114	31	7	978	277	121	—	169	—	—	—	—	—	—	—	.253	.281	.316
Troy	85	3046	399	429	754	124	31	5	955	255	140	—	240	—	—	—	—	—	—	—	.248	.281	.314
Cleveland	85	3117	392	414	796	120	39	7	1015	282	132	—	224	—	—	—	—	—	—	—	.255	.286	.326
Boston	83	2916	349	410	733	121	27	5	923	252	110	—	193	—	—	—	—	—	—	—	.251	.279	.317
NL Total	672	24377	3426	3426	6339	1068	304	76	8243	2488	1033	—	1784	—	—	—	—	—	—	—	.260	.290	.338
NL Avg Team	84	3047	428	428	792	134	38	10	1030	311	129	—	223	—	—	—	—	—	—	—	.260	.290	.338

Team Pitching

Team	G	CG	ShO	Rel	Sv	IP	H	R	ER	HR	SH	SF	HB	TBB	IBB	SO	WP	Bk	H/9	SO/9	BB/9	OAvg	OOBP	ERA
Providence	85	76	7	9	0	757.2	756	426	202	5	—	—	—	138	—	264	58	0	9.0	3.1	1.6	.243	.275	2.40
Chicago	84	81	9	3	0	744.2	722	379	201	14	—	—	—	122	—	228	38	1	8.7	2.8	1.5	.243	.273	2.43
Detroit	84	83	10	1	0	744.2	785	429	219	8	—	—	—	137	—	265	34	0	9.5	3.2	1.7	.257	.289	2.65
Cleveland	85	82	2	3	0	760.0	737	414	226	9	—	—	—	126	—	240	36	0	8.7	2.8	1.5	.244	.274	2.68
Boston	83	72	6	11	3	730.2	763	410	220	9	—	—	—	143	—	199	72	1	9.4	2.5	1.8	.258	.292	2.71
Buffalo	83	72	5	12	0	742.1	881	447	234	9	—	—	—	89	—	185	44	1	10.7	2.2	1.1	.281	.301	2.84
Troy	85	85	8	0	0	770.0	813	429	254	11	—	—	—	159	—	207	24	0	9.5	2.4	1.9	.265	.301	2.97
Worcester	83	80	5	3	0	737.1	882	492	290	11	—	—	—	120	—	196	37	1	10.8	2.4	1.5	.288	.315	3.54
NL Total	672	631	52	42	3	5987.1	6339	3426	1846	76	—	—	—	1034	—	1784	343	4	9.5	2.7	1.6	.260	.290	2.77
NL Avg Team	84	79	7	5	0	748.1	792	428	231	10	—	—	—	129	—	223	43	1	9.5	2.7	1.6	.260	.290	2.77

Team Fielding

Team	G	PO	A	E	TC	DP	PB	Pct
Troy	85	2310	1113	311	3734	70	61	.917
Chicago	84	2234	1140	309	3683	54	67	.916
Boston	83	2190	1038	325	3553	54	132	.909
Detroit	84	2234	1027	338	3599	80	49	.906
Cleveland	85	2278	1014	348	3640	68	93	.904
Worcester	83	2212	1086	353	3651	50	76	.903
Providence	85	2273	1078	390	3741	66	81	.896
Buffalo	83	2227	1133	408	3768	48	106	.892
NL Total	672	17958	8629	2782	29369	490	665	.905

Team vs. Team Records

	Bos	Buf	ChN	Cle	Det	Prv	Try	Wor	Won
Bos	—	4	2	8	4	5	7	8	38
Buf	8	—	5	7	9	7	3	6	45
ChN	10	7	—	6	7	9	8	9	56
Cle	4	5	6	—	5	3	6	7	36
Det	8	3	5	7	—	4	7	7	41
Prv	7	5	3	9	8	—	6	9	47
Try	5	9	4	6	5	6	—	4	39
Wor	3	5	3	5	5	3	8	—	32
Lost	45	38	28	48	43	37	45	50	

1881 National League Batting Leaders

Games		At-Bats		Runs		Hits		Doubles		Triples	
10 tied with	85	C. Foley, Buf	375	G. Gore, ChN	86	C. Anson, ChN	137	K. Kelly, ChN	27	J. Rowe, Buf	11
		J. Cassidy, Try	370	K. Kelly, ChN	84	A. Dalrymple, ChN	117	P. Hines, Prv	27	B. Phillips, Cle	10
		R. Connor, Try	367	A. Dalrymple, ChN	72	B. Dickerson, Wor	116	H. Stovey, Wor	25	4 tied with	9
		B. Dickerson, Wor	367	J. O'Rourke, Buf	71	3 tied with	114	F. Dunlap, Cle	25		
		A. Dalrymple, ChN	362	J. Farrell, Prv	69			D. White, Buf	24		

Home Runs		Total Bases		Runs Batted In		Walks		Intentional Walks		Strikeouts	
D. Brouthers, Buf	8	C. Anson, ChN	175	C. Anson, ChN	82	J. Clapp, Cle	35	Statistic unavailable		P. Galvin, Buf	70
C. Bennett, Det	7	F. Dunlap, Cle	156	C. Bennett, Det	64	J. Farrell, Prv	29			J. Denny, Prv	44
J. Farrell, Prv	5	K. Kelly, ChN	153	K. Kelly, ChN	55	B. Ferguson, Try	29			F. Hankinson, Try	41
T. Burns, ChN	4	A. Dalrymple, ChN	150	3 tied with	53	T. York, Prv	29			S. Flint, ChN	39
2 tied with	3	B. Dickerson, Wor	149			2 tied with	27			C. Bennett, Det	37

Hit By Pitch	Sac Hits	Sac Flies	Stolen Bases	Caught Stealing	GDP
Statistic unavailable	Statistic unavailable	Statistic unavailable	Statistic unavailable	Statistic unavailable	Statistic unavailable

Runs Created		Runs Created/27 Outs		Batting Average		On-Base Percentage		Slugging Percentage		OBP+Slugging	
C. Anson, ChN	94	C. Anson, ChN	12.25	C. Anson, ChN	.399	C. Anson, ChN	.442	D. Brouthers, Buf	.541	C. Anson, ChN	.952
K. Kelly, ChN	73	D. Brouthers, Buf	9.19	J. Start, Prv	.328	T. York, Prv	.362	C. Anson, ChN	.510	D. Brouthers, Buf	.902
A. Dalrymple, ChN	72	K. Kelly, ChN	8.20	F. Dunlap, Cle	.325	D. Brouthers, Buf	.361	C. Bennett, Det	.478	C. Bennett, Det	.819
3 tied with	67	T. York, Prv	8.17	A. Dalrymple, ChN	.323	F. Dunlap, Cle	.358	F. Dunlap, Cle	.444	F. Dunlap, Cle	.802
		G. Gore, ChN	7.92	K. Kelly, ChN	.323	G. Gore, ChN	.354	K. Kelly, ChN	.433	T. York, Prv	.790

1881 National League Pitching Leaders

Wins		Losses		Winning Percentage		Games		Games Started		Complete Games	
J. Whitney, Bos	31	J. Whitney, Bos	33	O. H. Radbourn, Prv	.694	J. Whitney, Bos	66	J. Whitney, Bos	63	J. Whitney, Bos	57
L. Corcoran, ChN	31	J. McCormick, Cle	30	L. Corcoran, ChN	.689	J. McCormick, Cle	59	J. McCormick, Cle	58	J. McCormick, Cle	57
G. Derby, Det	29	T. Keefe, Try	27	F. Goldsmith, ChN	.649	G. Derby, Det	56	G. Derby, Det	55	G. Derby, Det	55
P. Galvin, Buf	28	G. Derby, Det	26	P. Galvin, Buf	.538	P. Galvin, Buf	56	P. Galvin, Buf	53	L. Richmond, Wor	50
J. McCormick, Cle	26	L. Richmond, Wor	26	M. Welch, Try	.538	L. Richmond, Wor	53	L. Richmond, Wor	52	P. Galvin, Buf	48

Shutouts		Saves		Games Finished		Batters Faced		Innings Pitched		Hits Allowed	
G. Derby, Det	9	B. Mathews, 2tm	2	M. Ward, Prv	5	J. Whitney, Bos	2301	J. Whitney, Bos	552.1	J. Whitney, Bos	548
J. Whitney, Bos	6	J. Morrill, Bos	1	O. H. Radbourn, Prv	4	J. McCormick, Cle	2145	J. McCormick, Cle	526.0	L. Richmond, Wor	547
F. Goldsmith, ChN	5			B. Purcell, Buf	4	G. Derby, Det	2101	G. Derby, Det	494.2	P. Galvin, Buf	546
P. Galvin, Buf	5			B. Mathews, 2tm	4	P. Galvin, Buf	2037	P. Galvin, Buf	474.0	G. Derby, Det	505
3 tied with	4			4 tied with	3	L. Richmond, Wor	1992	L. Richmond, Wor	462.1	J. McCormick, Cle	484

Home Runs Allowed		Walks		Walks/9 Innings		Strikeouts		Strikeouts/9 Innings		Strikeout/Walk Ratio	
L. Corcoran, ChN	10	J. Whitney, Bos	90	P. Galvin, Buf	0.9	G. Derby, Det	212	G. Derby, Det	3.9	P. Galvin, Buf	2.96
M. Welch, Try	7	G. Derby, Det	86	S. Wiedman, Det	0.9	J. McCormick, Cle	178	L. Corcoran, ChN	3.4	G. Derby, Det	2.47
L. Richmond, Wor	7	J. McCormick, Cle	84	F. Goldsmith, ChN	1.2	J. Whitney, Bos	162	M. Ward, Prv	3.2	L. Richmond, Wor	2.29
J. Whitney, Bos	6	T. Keefe, Try	81	L. Richmond, Wor	1.3	L. Richmond, Wor	156	O. H. Radbourn, Prv	3.2	M. Ward, Prv	2.25
4 tied with	4	2 tied with	78	J. McCormick, Cle	1.4	L. Corcoran, ChN	150	J. McCormick, Cle	3.0	S. Wiedman, Det	2.17

Earned Run Average		Component ERA		Hit Batsmen		Wild Pitches		Opponent Average		Opponent OBP	
S. Wiedman, Det	1.80	S. Wiedman, Det	2.04	Statistic unavailable		J. Whitney, Bos	46	O. H. Radbourn, Prv	.235	S. Wiedman, Det	.258
M. Ward, Prv	2.13	J. McCormick, Cle	2.11			M. Ward, Prv	32	J. McCormick, Cle	.235	J. McCormick, Cle	.265
G. Derby, Det	2.20	O. H. Radbourn, Prv	2.27			P. Galvin, Buf	31	S. Wiedman, Det	.238	O. H. Radbourn, Prv	.270
L. Corcoran, ChN	2.31	M. Ward, Prv	2.35			L. Corcoran, ChN	27	L. Corcoran, ChN	.242	F. Goldsmith, ChN	.271
P. Galvin, Buf	2.37	F. Goldsmith, ChN	2.37			2 tied with	24	M. Ward, Prv	.242	M. Ward, Prv	.271

1881 National League Miscellaneous

Managers		
Boston	Harry Wright	38-45
Buffalo	Jim O'Rourke	45-38
Chicago	Cap Anson	56-28
Cleveland	Mike McGeary	4-7
	John Clapp	32-41
Detroit	Frank Bancroft	41-43
Providence	Jack Farrell	24-27
	Tom York	23-10
Troy	Bob Ferguson	39-45
Worcester	Mike Dorgan	24-32
	Harry Stovey	8-18

Awards	
STATS Most Valuable Player	Cap Anson, 1b, ChN
STATS Cy Young	Larry Corcoran, ChN
STATS Rookie of the Year	Jim Whitney, p, Bos
STATS Manager of the Year	Jim O'Rourke, Buf

STATS All-Star Team

C	Charlie Bennett, Det	.301	7	64
1B	Cap Anson, ChN	.399	1	82
2B	Fred Dunlap, Cle	.325	3	24
3B	Jim O'Rourke, Buf	.302	0	30
SS	Tom Burns, ChN	.278	4	42
OF	Dan Brouthers, Buf	.319	8	45
OF	King Kelly, ChN	.323	2	55
OF	Tom York, Prv	.304	2	47
P	Larry Corcoran, ChN	31-14	2.31	150 K

Postseason

None

Outstanding Performances

None

Team	Overall					Home Games						Road Games						Park Index		Record by Month					
	W	L	Pct	GB	DIF	W	L	R	OR	HR	OHR	W	L	R	OR	HR	OHR	Run	HR	M/A	May	June	July	Aug	S/O
Chicago	55	29	.655	—	35	35	10	360	140	9	8	20	19	243	213	6	5	95	134	—	9-9	12-6	12-5	6-7	16-2
Providence	52	32	.619	3.0	108	30	12	247	172	6	6	22	20	216	184	5	6	105	109	—	13-6	9-8	12-7	9-4	9-7
Boston	45	39	.536	10.0	1	27	15	263	191	8	7	18	24	209	220	7	3	106	150	—	9-11	11-7	9-8	9-4	7-9
Buffalo	45	39	.536	10.0	1	26	13	286	184	5	7	19	26	214	278	13	9	110	63	—	9-9	7-10	10-8	8-5	11-7
Cleveland	42	40	.512	12.0	0	21	19	175	170	6	7	21	21	227	240	14	15	78	47	—	7-12	10-8	9-8	10-4	6-8
Detroit	42	41	.506	12.5	21	24	18	221	238	14	10	18	23	186	252	5	9	102	167	—	12-6	11-7	8-10	4-9	7-9
Troy	35	48	.422	19.5	0	22	20	238	217	7	2	13	28	192	305	5	11	89	55	—	11-10	7-9	7-10	5-8	5-11
Worcester	18	66	.214	37.0	0	12	30	216	338	9	15	6	36	163	314	7	6	116	185	—	6-13	3-15	3-14	2-12	4-12

Clinch Date—Chicago 9/28.

Team Batting

Team	G	AB	R	OR	H	2B	3B	HR	TB	RBI	TBB	IBB	SO	HBP	SH	SF	SB	CS	SB%	GDP	Avg	OBP	Slg
Chicago	84	3225	604	353	892	209	54	15	1254	451	142	—	262	—	—	—	—	—	—	—	.277	.307	.389
Buffalo	84	3128	500	461	858	146	47	18	1152	383	116	—	228	—	—	—	—	—	—	—	.274	.300	.368
Boston	85	3118	472	414	823	114	50	15	1082	368	134	—	244	—	—	—	—	—	—	—	.264	.294	.347
Providence	84	3104	463	356	776	121	53	11	1036	322	102	—	255	—	—	—	—	—	—	—	.250	.274	.334
Troy	85	3057	430	522	747	116	59	12	1017	313	109	—	298	—	—	—	—	—	—	—	.244	.270	.333
Detroit	86	3144	407	488	724	117	44	19	986	271	122	—	308	—	—	—	—	—	—	—	.230	.259	.314
Cleveland	84	3009	402	411	716	139	40	20	995	297	122	—	261	—	—	—	—	—	—	—	.238	.268	.331
Worcester	84	2984	379	652	689	109	57	16	960	279	113	—	303	—	—	—	—	—	—	—	.231	.259	.322
NL Total	676	24769	3657	3657	6225	1071	404	126	8482	2684	960	—	2159	—	—	—	—	—	—	—	.251	.279	.342
NL Avg Team	85	3096	457	457	778	134	51	16	1060	336	120	—	270	—	—	—	—	—	—	—	.251	.279	.342

Team Pitching

Team	G	CG	ShO	Rel	Sv	IP	H	R	ER	HR	SH	SF	HB	TBB	IBB	SO	WP	Bk	H/9	SO/9	BB/9	OAvg	OOBP	ERA
Chicago	84	83	7	1	0	763.2	667	353	188	13	—	—	—	102	—	279	30	0	7.9	3.3	1.2	.221	.246	2.22
Providence	84	80	10	4	1	752.0	690	356	190	12	—	—	—	87	—	273	36	0	8.3	3.3	1.0	.228	.250	2.27
Cleveland	84	81	4	3	0	751.2	743	411	230	22	—	—	—	132	—	232	39	0	8.9	2.8	1.6	.249	.280	2.75
Boston	85	81	4	4	0	749.0	738	414	233	10	—	—	—	77	—	352	44	0	8.9	4.2	0.9	.248	.277	2.80
Detroit	86	82	7	4	0	793.0	808	488	263	19	—	—	—	129	—	354	25	0	9.2	4.0	1.5	.248	.277	2.98
Troy	85	81	6	4	0	757.0	837	522	259	13	—	—	—	168	—	189	28	0	10.0	2.2	2.0	.268	.305	3.08
Buffalo	84	79	3	5	0	737.0	778	461	266	16	—	—	—	114	—	287	32	1	9.5	3.5	1.4	.254	.280	3.25
Worcester	84	75	0	9	0	738.1	964	652	308	21	—	—	—	151	—	195	76	0	11.8	2.4	1.8	.294	.325	3.75
NL Total	676	642	41	34	1	6041.2	6225	3657	1937	126	—	—	—	960	—	2161	310	1	9.3	3.2	1.4	.251	.279	2.89
NL Avg Team	85	80	5	4	0	755.2	778	457	242	16	—	—	—	120	—	270	39	0	9.3	3.2	1.4	.251	.279	2.89

Team Fielding

Team	G	PO	A	E	TC	DP	PB	Pct
Boston	85	2249	933	314	3496	42	77	.910
Buffalo	84	2183	1003	315	3501	37	104	.910
Cleveland	84	2242	1150	358	3750	71	124	.905
Providence	84	2275	1090	371	3736	67	78	.901
Chicago	84	2265	1061	376	3702	54	68	.898
Detroit	86	2353	961	396	3710	44	63	.893
Troy	85	2257	1121	432	3810	70	78	.887
Worcester	84	2210	1147	468	3825	66	89	.878
NL Total	676	18034	8466	3030	29530	451	681	.897

Team vs. Team Records

	Bos	Buf	ChN	Cle	Det	Prv	Try	Wor	Won
Bos	—	7	6	7	8	6	4	7	45
Buf	5	—	6	6	5	6	6	11	45
ChN	6	6	—	9	8	8	9	9	55
Cle	5	6	3	—	4	4	9	11	42
Det	4	7	4	7	—	3	8	9	42
Prv	6	6	4	8	9	—	9	10	52
Try	8	6	3	2	4	3	—	9	35
Wor	5	1	3	1	3	2	3	—	18
Lost	39	39	29	40	41	32	48	66	

1882 National League Batting Leaders

Games		At-Bats		Runs		Hits		Doubles		Triples	
L. Knight, Det	86	A. Dalrymple, ChN	397	G. Gore, ChN	99	D. Brouthers, Buf	129	K. Kelly, ChN	37	R. Connor, Try	18
F. Pfeffer, Try	85	J. Hornung, Bos	388	A. Dalrymple, ChN	96	C. Anson, ChN	126	C. Anson, ChN	29	G. Wood, Det	12
J. Hornung, Bos	85	B. Purcell, Buf	380	H. Stovey, Wor	90	5 tied with	117	P. Hines, Prv	28	F. Corey, Wor	12
20 tied with	84	P. Hines, Prv	379	K. Kelly, ChN	81			J. Glasscock, Cle	27	5 tied with	11
		P. Hotaling, Bos	378	B. Purcell, Buf	79			N. Williamson, ChN	27		

Home Runs		Total Bases		Runs Batted In		Walks		Intentional Walks		Strikeouts	
G. Wood, Det	7	D. Brouthers, Buf	192	C. Anson, ChN	83	G. Gore, ChN	29	Statistic unavailable		S. Flint, ChN	50
M. Muldoon, Cle	6	R. Connor, Try	185	D. Brouthers, Buf	63	N. Williamson, ChN	27			P. Galvin, Buf	49
D. Brouthers, Buf	6	P. Hines, Prv	177	N. Williamson, ChN	60	O. Shaffer, Cle	27			J. Denny, Prv	46
4 tied with	5	C. Anson, ChN	174	H. Richardson, Buf	57	N. Hanlon, Det	26			T. Keefe, Try	46
		A. Dalrymple, ChN	167	K. Kelly, ChN	55	2 tied with	24			S. Wise, Bos	45

Hit By Pitch	Sac Hits	Sac Flies	Stolen Bases	Caught Stealing	GDP
Statistic unavailable	Statistic unavailable	Statistic unavailable	Statistic unavailable	Statistic unavailable	Statistic unavailable

Runs Created		Runs Created/27 Outs		Batting Average		On-Base Percentage		Slugging Percentage		OBP+Slugging	
C. Anson, ChN	95	C. Anson, ChN	11.74	D. Brouthers, Buf	.368	D. Brouthers, Buf	.403	D. Brouthers, Buf	.547	D. Brouthers, Buf	.950
D. Brouthers, Buf	94	D. Brouthers, Buf	11.62	C. Anson, ChN	.362	C. Anson, ChN	.397	R. Connor, Try	.530	C. Anson, ChN	.897
R. Connor, Try	86	R. Connor, Try	10.08	R. Connor, Try	.330	J. Whitney, Bos	.382	J. Whitney, Bos	.510	J. Whitney, Bos	.892
G. Gore, ChN	85	J. Whitney, Bos	10.00	J. Start, Prv	.329	G. Gore, ChN	.369	C. Anson, ChN	.500	R. Connor, Try	.884
P. Hines, Prv	83	G. Gore, ChN	9.33	J. Whitney, Bos	.323	R. Connor, Try	.354	P. Hines, Prv	.467	P. Hines, Prv	.794

1882 National League Pitching Leaders

Wins		Losses		Winning Percentage		Games		Games Started		Complete Games	
J. McCormick, Cle	36	L. Richmond, Wor	33	L. Corcoran, ChN	.692	J. McCormick, Cle	68	J. McCormick, Cle	67	J. McCormick, Cle	65
O. H. Radbourn, Prv	33	J. McCormick, Cle	30	O. H. Radbourn, Prv	.623	O. H. Radbourn, Prv	55	O. H. Radbourn, Prv	52	O. H. Radbourn, Prv	51
F. Goldsmith, ChN	28	T. Keefe, Try	26	F. Goldsmith, ChN	.622	P. Galvin, Buf	52	P. Galvin, Buf	51	P. Galvin, Buf	48
P. Galvin, Buf	28	P. Galvin, Buf	23	M. Ward, Prv	.613	J. Whitney, Bos	49	J. Whitney, Bos	48	J. Whitney, Bos	46
L. Corcoran, ChN	27	J. Whitney, Bos	21	B. Mathews, Bos	.559	L. Richmond, Wor	48	L. Richmond, Wor	46	F. Goldsmith, ChN	45

Shutouts		Saves		Games Finished		Batters Faced		Innings Pitched		Hits Allowed	
O. H. Radbourn, Prv	6	M. Ward, Prv	1	F. Corey, Wor	7	J. McCormick, Cle	2412	J. McCormick, Cle	595.2	J. McCormick, Cle	550
M. Welch, Try	5			O. H. Radbourn, Prv	3	O. H. Radbourn, Prv	1948	O. H. Radbourn, Prv	474.0	L. Richmond, Wor	525
4 tied with	4			6 tied with	2	P. Galvin, Buf	1900	P. Galvin, Buf	445.1	P. Galvin, Buf	476
						L. Richmond, Wor	1876	J. Whitney, Bos	420.0	O. H. Radbourn, Prv	429
						J. Whitney, Bos	1743	2 tied with	411.0	J. Whitney, Bos	404

Home Runs Allowed		Walks		Walks/9 Innings		Strikeouts		Strikeouts/9 Innings		Strikeout/Walk Ratio	
J. McCormick, Cle	14	J. McCormick, Cle	103	B. Mathews, Bos	0.7	O. H. Radbourn, Prv	201	B. Mathews, Bos	4.8	B. Mathews, Bos	6.95
L. Richmond, Wor	11	L. Richmond, Wor	88	P. Galvin, Buf	0.8	J. McCormick, Cle	200	G. Derby, Det	4.5	J. Whitney, Bos	4.39
S. Wiedman, Det	10	G. Derby, Det	81	F. Goldsmith, ChN	0.8	G. Derby, Det	182	L. Corcoran, ChN	4.3	S. Wiedman, Det	4.13
G. Derby, Det	8	T. Keefe, Try	81	S. Wiedman, Det	0.9	J. Whitney, Bos	180	O. Daily, Buf	4.1	P. Galvin, Buf	4.05
P. Galvin, Buf	8	O. Daily, Buf	70	J. Whitney, Bos	0.9	L. Corcoran, ChN	170	J. Whitney, Bos	3.9	O. H. Radbourn, Prv	3.94

Earned Run Average		Component ERA		Hit Batsmen		Wild Pitches		Opponent Average		Opponent OBP	
L. Corcoran, ChN	1.95	L. Corcoran, ChN	1.58	Statistic unavailable		J. Whitney, Bos	29	L. Corcoran, ChN	.200	L. Corcoran, ChN	.234
O. H. Radbourn, Prv	2.09	O. H. Radbourn, Prv	1.86			L. Richmond, Wor	26	O. H. Radbourn, Prv	.226	B. Mathews, Bos	.246
J. McCormick, Cle	2.37	F. Goldsmith, ChN	2.01			O. H. Radbourn, Prv	23	B. Mathews, Bos	.232	O. H. Radbourn, Prv	.246
F. Goldsmith, ChN	2.42	B. Mathews, Bos	2.03			F. Corey, Wor	23	M. Ward, Prv	.232	S. Wiedman, Det	.253
T. Keefe, Try	2.50	J. Whitney, Bos	2.06			2 tied with	22	O. Daily, Buf	.234	F. Goldsmith, ChN	.254

1882 National League Miscellaneous

Managers

Boston	John Morrill	45-39
Buffalo	Jim O'Rourke	45-39
Chicago	Cap Anson	55-29
Cleveland	Jim McCormick	0-4
	Fred Dunlap	42-36
Detroit	Frank Bancroft	42-41
Providence	Harry Wright	52-32
Troy	Bob Ferguson	35-48
Worcester	Freeman Brown	9-32
	Tommy Bond	2-4
	Jack Chapman	7-30

Awards

STATS Most Valuable Player	Dan Brouthers, 1b, Buf
STATS Cy Young	Jim McCormick, Cle
STATS Rookie of the Year	Mike Muldoon, 3b, Cle
STATS Manager of the Year	Cap Anson, ChN

STATS All-Star Team

C	Charlie Bennett, Det	.301	5	51
1B	Dan Brouthers, Buf	.368	6	63
2B	Hardy Richardson, Buf	.271	2	57
3B	Ned Williamson, ChN	.282	3	60
SS	King Kelly, ChN	.305	1	55
OF	Abner Dalrymple, ChN	.295	1	36
OF	George Gore, ChN	.319	3	51
OF	Paul Hines, Prv	.309	4	34
P	Jim McCormick, Cle	36-30	2.37	200 K
P	Jim Whitney, Bos	24-21	2.64	180 K

Postseason

None

Outstanding Performances

No-Hitters

Larry Corcoran, ChN vs. Wor on September 20

Cycles

Curry Foley, Buf on May 25

1882 American Association Standings

Team	W	L	Pct	GB	DIF	W	L	R	OR	HR	OHR	W	L	R	OR	HR	OHR	Run	HR	M/A	May	June	July	Aug	S/O
		Overall						**Home Games**						**Road Games**				**Park Index**			**Record by Month**				
Cincinnati	55	25	.688	—	110	31	11	270	130	0	5	24	14	219	138	5	2	101	65	—	8-8	12-2	11-4	11-6	13-5
Philadelphia	41	34	.547	11.5	40	21	18	236	220	3	11	20	16	166	166	2	2	127	323	—	10-5	7-9	10-3	9-10	5-7
Louisville	42	38	.525	13.0	0	26	13	215	129	0	0	16	25	230	229	9	6	79	0	—	6-7	9-5	7-8	12-7	8-11
Pittsburgh	39	39	.500	15.0	1	17	18	185	172	12	3	22	21	237	241	6	1	92	263	—	6-5	5-10	7-8	11-11	10-5
St. Louis	37	43	.463	18.0	5	24	20	253	262	7	2	13	23	150	236	4	5	109	82	—	10-7	11-5	4-13	7-12	5-6
Baltimore	19	54	.260	32.5	0	9	25	138	225	2	7	10	29	134	287	2	8	99	103	—	3-11	0-13	7-10	6-10	3-10

Clinch Date—Cincinnati 9/16.

Team Batting

Team	G	AB	R	OR	H	2B	3B	HR	TB	RBI	TBB	IBB	SO	HBP	SH	SF	SB	CS	SB%	GDP	Avg	OBP	Slg
Cincinnati	80	**3007**	**489**	268	**795**	95	47	5	999	—	102	—	204	—	—	—	—	—	—	—	**.264**	.289	.332
Louisville	80	2806	443	352	728	**110**	28	9	921	—	**128**	—	193	—	—	—	—	—	—	—	.259	**.292**	.328
Pittsburgh	79	2904	428	418	730	**110**	59	18	**1012**	—	90	—	183	—	—	—	—	—	—	—	.251	.274	**.348**
Philadelphia	75	2707	406	389	660	89	21	5	806	—	125	—	164	—	—	—	—	—	—	—	.244	.277	.298
St. Louis	80	2865	399	496	663	87	41	11	865	—	112	—	**226**	—	—	—	—	—	—	—	.231	.260	.302
Baltimore	74	2583	273	515	535	60	24	4	655	—	72	—	215	—	—	—	—	—	—	—	.207	.229	.254
AA Total	468	16872	2438	2438	4111	551	220	52	5258	—	629	—	1185	—	—	—	—	—	—	—	.244	.271	.312
AA Avg Team	78	2812	406	406	685	92	37	9	876	—	105	—	198	—	—	—	—	—	—	—	.244	.271	.312

Team Pitching

Team	G	CG	ShO	Rel	Sv	IP	H	R	ER	HR	SH	SF	HB	TBB	IBB	SO	WP	Bk	H/9	SO/9	BB/9	OAvg	OOBP	ERA
Cincinnati	80	**77**	11	3	0	721.1	609	268	132	7	—	—	—	125	—	165	—	—	**7.6**	2.1	1.6	**.214**	**.247**	**1.65**
Louisville	80	73	6	7	0	693.1	637	352	156	6	—	—	—	112	—	240	—	—	8.3	3.1	1.5	.228	.258	2.03
Pittsburgh	79	**77**	2	2	0	696.2	694	418	216	4	—	—	—	82	—	**252**	—	—	9.0	**3.3**	**1.1**	.243	.264	2.79
St. Louis	80	75	3	5	1	688.1	729	496	223	7	—	—	—	103	—	225	—	—	9.5	2.9	1.3	.254	.280	2.92
Philadelphia	75	72	2	3	0	663.0	682	389	219	13	—	—	—	99	—	190	—	—	9.3	2.6	1.3	.249	.275	2.97
Baltimore	74	64	1	12	0	646.1	760	515	279	15	—	—	—	108	—	113	—	—	10.6	1.6	1.5	.275	.302	3.88
AA Total	468	438	25	32	1	4109.0	4111	2438	1225	52	—	—	—	629	—	1185	—	—	9.0	2.6	1.4	.244	.271	2.68
AA Avg Team	78	73	4	5	0	684.0	685	406	204	9	—	—	—	105	—	198	—	—	9.0	2.6	1.4	.244	.271	2.68

Team Fielding

Team	G	PO	A	E	TC	DP	PB	Pct
Cincinnati	80	**2161**	1091	332	3584	41	68	**.907**
Philadelphia	75	1985	1094	361	3440	36	74	.895
Louisville	80	2075	**1132**	385	**3592**	57	114	.893
Pittsburgh	79	2088	1093	397	3578	40	86	.889
St. Louis	80	2065	1043	446	3554	41	**136**	.875
Baltimore	74	1938	1047	490	3475	41	107	.859
AA Total	468	12312	6500	2411	21223	256	585	.886

Team vs. Team Records

	Bal	Cin	Lou	Phi	Pit	STL	Won
Bal	—	2	3	4	7	3	**19**
Cin	14	—	11	10	10	10	**55**
Lou	13	5	—	5	10	9	**42**
Phi	7	6	11	—	6	11	**41**
Pit	7	6	6	10	—	10	**39**
STL	13	6	7	5	6	—	**37**
Lost	54	25	38	34	39	43	

Seasons: Standings, Leaders

1882 American Association Batting Leaders

Games		At-Bats		Runs		Hits		Doubles		Triples	
J. Sommer, Cin	80	J. Sommer, Cin	354	E. Swartwood, Pit	86	H. Carpenter, Cin	120	E. Swartwood, Pit	18	M. Mansell, Pit	16
H. Carpenter, Cin	80	H. Carpenter, Cin	351	J. Sommer, Cin	82	P. Browning, Lou	109	M. Mansell, Pit	18	B. Taylor, Pit	13
5 tied with	79	B. Gleason, STL	347	H. Carpenter, Cin	78	E. Swartwood, Pit	107	P. Browning, Lou	17	E. Swartwood, Pit	11
		M. Mansell, Pit	347	P. Browning, Lou	67	J. Sommer, Cin	102	B. Taylor, Pit	16	H. Wheeler, Cin	11
		H. Wheeler, Cin	344	J. Birchall, Phi	65	B. Gleason, STL	100	N. Cuthbert, STL	16	C. Wolf, Lou	8

Home Runs		Total Bases		Runs Batted In		Walks		Intentional Walks		Strikeouts	
O. Walker, STL	7	E. Swartwood, Pit	159	Statistic unavailable		J. Gleason, STL	27	Statistic unavailable		Statistic unavailable	
P. Browning, Lou	5	M. Mansell, Pit	152			P. Browning, Lou	26				
E. Swartwood, Pit	4	H. Carpenter, Cin	148			J. Sommer, Cin	24				
4 tied with	3	P. Browning, Lou	147			J. Reccius, Lou	23				
		B. Taylor, Pit	135			E. Swartwood, Pit	21				

Hit By Pitch	Sac Hits	Sac Flies	Stolen Bases	Caught Stealing	GDP
Statistic unavailable	Statistic unavailable	Statistic unavailable	Statistic unavailable	Statistic unavailable	Statistic unavailable

Runs Created		Runs Created/27 Outs		Batting Average		On-Base Percentage		Slugging Percentage		OBP+Slugging	
P. Browning, Lou	82	P. Browning, Lou	12.54	P. Browning, Lou	.378	P. Browning, Lou	.430	P. Browning, Lou	.510	P. Browning, Lou	.940
H. Carpenter, Cin	79	E. Swartwood, Pit	9.55	H. Carpenter, Cin	.342	E. Swartwood, Pit	.370	E. Swartwood, Pit	.489	E. Swartwood, Pit	.859
E. Swartwood, Pit	76	H. Carpenter, Cin	9.37	E. Swartwood, Pit	.329	H. Carpenter, Cin	.360	B. Taylor, Pit	.452	H. Carpenter, Cin	.782
J. Sommer, Cin	69	J. Sommer, Cin	7.50	C. Wolf, Lou	.299	J. Sommer, Cin	.333	M. Mansell, Pit	.438	B. Taylor, Pit	.749
M. Mansell, Pit	63	C. Wolf, Lou	7.25	P. Snyder, Cin	.291	C. Wolf, Lou	.318	H. Carpenter, Cin	.422	M. Mansell, Pit	.729

1882 American Association Pitching Leaders

Wins		Losses		Winning Percentage		Games		Games Started		Complete Games	
W. White, Cin	40	D. Landis, 2tm	28	W. White, Cin	.769	T. Mullane, Lou	55	T. Mullane, Lou	55	W. White, Cin	52
T. Mullane, Lou	30	T. Mullane, Lou	24	S. Weaver, Phi	.634	W. White, Cin	54	W. White, Cin	54	T. Mullane, Lou	51
S. Weaver, Phi	26	J. McGinnis, STL	18	D. Driscoll, Pit	.591	J. McGinnis, STL	45	J. McGinnis, STL	45	J. McGinnis, STL	43
J. McGinnis, STL	25	H. Salisbury, Pit	18	J. McGinnis, STL	.581	D. Landis, 2tm	44	D. Landis, 2tm	41	S. Weaver, Phi	41
H. Salisbury, Pit	20	S. Weaver, Phi	15	H. McCormick, Cin	.560	S. Weaver, Phi	42	S. Weaver, Phi	41	H. Salisbury, Pit	38

Shutouts		Saves		Games Finished		Batters Faced		Innings Pitched		Hits Allowed	
W. White, Cin	8	E. Fusselback, STL	1	J. Reccius, Lou	3	Statistic unavailable		W. White, Cin	480.0	D. Landis, 2tm	425
T. Mullane, Lou	5			D. Landis, 2tm	3			T. Mullane, Lou	460.1	T. Mullane, Lou	418
J. McGinnis, STL	3			H. Myers, Bal	3			J. McGinnis, STL	388.1	W. White, Cin	411
H. McCormick, Cin	3			H. Wheeler, Cin	3			S. Weaver, Phi	371.0	J. McGinnis, STL	391
S. Weaver, Phi	2			T. Nichols, Bal	3			D. Landis, 2tm	358.0	S. Weaver, Phi	374

Home Runs Allowed		Walks		Walks/9 Innings		Strikeouts		Strikeouts/9 Innings		Strikeout/Walk Ratio	
D. Landis, 2tm	8	T. Mullane, Lou	78	G. Hecker, Lou	0.4	T. Mullane, Lou	170	H. Salisbury, Pit	3.6	G. Hecker, Lou	6.60
S. Weaver, Phi	6	W. White, Cin	71	D. Driscoll, Pit	0.5	H. Salisbury, Pit	135	H. Arundel, Pit	3.5	D. Driscoll, Pit	4.92
B. Sweeney, Phi	4	J. McGinnis, STL	53	S. Weaver, Phi	0.8	J. McGinnis, STL	134	T. Mullane, Lou	3.3	H. Salisbury, Pit	3.65
T. Mullane, Lou	4	D. Landis, 2tm	47	H. Salisbury, Pit	1.0	W. White, Cin	122	J. McGinnis, STL	3.1	S. Weaver, Phi	2.97
H. McCormick, Cin	4	2 tied with	42	D. Landis, 2tm	1.2	S. Weaver, Phi	104	J. Reccius, Lou	2.9	J. McGinnis, STL	2.53

Earned Run Average		Component ERA		Hit Batsmen		Wild Pitches		Opponent Average		Opponent OBP	
D. Driscoll, Pit	1.21	G. Hecker, Lou	1.17	Statistic unavailable		Statistic unavailable		G. Hecker, Lou	.188	G. Hecker, Lou	.199
G. Hecker, Lou	1.30	D. Driscoll, Pit	1.44					H. McCormick, Cin	.206	D. Driscoll, Pit	.218
H. McCormick, Cin	1.52	W. White, Cin	1.82					D. Driscoll, Pit	.206	H. McCormick, Cin	.243
W. White, Cin	1.54	H. McCormick, Cin	1.83					E. Geis, Bal	.220	W. White, Cin	.250
T. Mullane, Lou	1.88	H. Salisbury, Pit	2.10					W. White, Cin	.221	H. Salisbury, Pit	.253

1882 American Association Miscellaneous

Managers		
Baltimore	Henry Myers	19-54
Cincinnati	Pop Snyder	55-25
Louisville	Denny Mack	42-38
Philadelphia	Juice Latham	41-34
Pittsburgh	Al Pratt	39-39
St. Louis	Ned Cuthbert	37-43

Awards	
STATS Most Valuable Player	Pete Browning, 2b, Lou
STATS Cy Young	Will White, Cin
STATS Rookie of the Year	Pete Browning, 2b, Lou
STATS Manager of the Year	Pop Snyder, Cin

STATS All-Star Team

C	Jack O'Brien, Phi	.303	3	37
1B	Guy Hecker, Lou	.276	3	—
2B	Pete Browning, Lou	.378	5	—
3B	Hick Carpenter, Cin	.342	1	62
SS	Bill Gleason, STL	.288	1	—
OF	Joe Sommer, Cin	.288	1	29
OF	Ed Swartwood, Pit	.329	4	—
OF	Chicken Wolf, Lou	.299	0	—
P	Tony Mullane, Lou	30-24	1.88	170 K
P	Will White, Cin	40-12	1.54	122 K

Postseason

None

Outstanding Performances

No-Hitters

Tony Mullane, Lou   @ Cin on September 11
Guy Hecker, Lou   @ Pit on September 19

1883 National League Standings

Team	Overall					Home Games						Road Games						Park Index		Record by Month					
	W	L	Pct	GB	DIF	W	L	R	OR	HR	OHR	W	L	R	OR	HR	OHR	Run	HR	M/A	May	June	July	Aug	S/O
Boston	63	35	.643	—	20	41	8	391	190	21	3	22	27	277	267	13	8	107	114	—	7-12	17-5	9-11	14-4	16-3
Chicago	59	39	.602	4.0	30	36	13	410	254	11	6	23	26	269	287	2	15	119	100	—	15-6	8-11	13-6	11-10	12-6
Providence	58	40	.592	5.0	75	34	15	330	186	10	5	24	25	304	250	11	7	93	83	—	12-8	18-5	11-9	8-10	9-8
Cleveland	55	42	.567	7.5	36	31	18	248	203	0	4	24	24	227	240	8	3	95	36	—	13-6	13-8	14-6	9-11	6-11
Buffalo	52	45	.536	10.5	0	36	13	355	241	3	4	16	32	258	335	5	8	98	53	—	8-9	9-12	13-8	12-9	10-7
New York	46	50	.479	16.0	3	28	19	292	262	20	15	18	31	238	315	4	4	104	456	—	6-12	12-10	9-13	12-7	7-8
Detroit	40	58	.408	23.0	1	23	26	264	280	12	9	17	32	260	371	1	13	86	150	—	12-8	5-18	8-10	10-10	5-12
Philadelphia	17	81	.173	46.0	0	9	40	224	439	0	1	8	41	222	449	3	19	99	5	—	4-16	5-18	3-17	2-17	3-13

Clinch Date—Boston 9/27.

Team Batting

Team	G	AB	R	OR	H	2B	3B	HR	TB	RBI	TBB	IBB	SO	HBP	SH	SF	SB	CS	SB%	GDP	Avg	OBP	Slg
Chicago	98	3658	679	540	1000	277	61	13	1438	467	129	—	399	—	—	—	—	—	—	—	.273	.298	.393
Boston	98	3657	669	456	1010	209	86	34	1493	515	123	—	423	—	—	—	—	—	—	—	.276	.300	.408
Providence	98	3685	636	436	1001	189	59	21	1371	449	149	—	309	—	—	—	—	—	—	—	.272	.300	.372
Buffalo	98	3729	614	576	1058	184	59	8	1384	427	147	—	342	—	—	—	—	—	—	—	.284	.311	.371
New York	98	3524	530	577	900	139	69	24	1249	371	127	—	297	—	—	—	—	—	—	—	.255	.281	.354
Detroit	101	3726	524	650	931	164	48	13	1230	367	166	—	378	—	—	—	—	—	—	—	.250	.282	.330
Cleveland	100	3457	476	443	852	184	38	8	1136	303	139	—	374	—	—	—	—	—	—	—	.246	.276	.329
Philadelphia	99	3576	437	887	859	181	48	3	1145	298	141	—	355	—	—	—	—	—	—	—	.240	.269	.320
NL Total	790	29012	4565	4565	7611	1527	468	124	10446	3197	1121	—	2877	—	—	—	—	—	—	—	.262	.290	.360
NL Avg Team	99	3627	571	571	951	191	59	16	1306	400	140	—	360	—	—	—	—	—	—	—	.262	.290	.360

Team Pitching

Team	G	CG	ShO	Rel	Sv	IP	H	R	ER	HR	SH	SF	HB	TBB	IBB	SO	WP	Bk	H/9	SO/9	BB/9	OAvg	OOBP	ERA
Cleveland	100	92	5	8	2	879.0	818	443	217	7	—	—	—	217	—	402	50	0	8.4	4.1	2.2	.237	.282	2.22
Providence	98	88	4	10	1	871.0	827	436	229	12	—	—	—	111	—	376	59	0	8.5	3.9	1.1	.238	.262	2.37
Boston	98	89	6	9	3	860.0	853	456	244	11	—	—	—	90	—	538	54	0	8.9	5.6	0.9	.243	.262	2.55
Chicago	98	91	5	8	1	862.0	942	540	266	21	—	—	—	123	—	299	30	1	9.8	3.1	1.3	.260	.284	2.78
New York	98	87	5	11	0	866.0	907	577	283	19	—	—	—	170	—	323	81	0	9.4	3.4	1.8	.253	.287	2.94
Buffalo	98	90	5	9	2	859.1	971	576	317	12	—	—	—	101	—	362	43	0	10.2	3.8	1.1	.268	.288	3.32
Detroit	101	89	5	12	2	894.1	1026	650	356	22	—	—	—	184	—	324	34	0	10.3	3.3	1.9	.270	.303	3.58
Philadelphia	99	91	3	9	0	864.2	1267	887	513	20	—	—	—	125	—	253	54	0	13.2	2.6	1.3	.318	.338	5.34
NL Total	790	717	38	76	11	6956.1	7611	4565	2425	124	—	—	—	1121	—	2877	405	1	9.8	3.7	1.5	.262	.290	3.14
NL Avg Team	99	90	5	10	1	869.1	951	571	303	16	—	—	—	140	—	360	51	0	9.8	3.7	1.5	.262	.290	3.14

Team Fielding

Team	G	PO	A	E	TC	DP	PB	Pct
Cleveland	100	2652	1233	389	4274	69	85	.909
Providence	98	2604	1309	419	4332	75	97	.903
Boston	98	2580	1132	409	4121	58	168	.901
Buffalo	98	2605	1221	445	4271	52	128	.896
Detroit	101	2673	1246	470	4389	77	98	.893
New York	98	2564	1181	468	4213	52	100	.889
Chicago	98	2569	1364	543	4476	76	107	.879
Philadelphia	99	2594	1270	639	4503	62	125	.858
NL Total	790	20841	9956	3782	34579	521	908	.891

Team vs. Team Records

	Bos	Buf	ChN	Cle	Det	NYG	Phi	Prv	Won
Bos	—	7	7	10	10	7	14	8	63
Buf	7	—	5	7	9	8	9	7	52
ChN	7	9	—	6	9	9	12	7	59
Cle	4	7	8	—	9	7	12	8	55
Det	4	5	5	5	—	8	11	2	40
NYG	7	5	5	6	6	—	12	5	46
Phi	0	5	2	2	3	2	—	3	17
Prv	6	7	7	6	12	9	11	—	58
Lost	35	45	39	42	58	50	81	40	

1883 National League Batting Leaders

Games		At-Bats		Runs		Hits		Doubles		Triples	
J. Farrell, Det	101	J. Hornung, Bos	446	J. Hornung, Bos	107	D. Brouthers, Buf	159	N. Williamson, ChN	49	D. Brouthers, Buf	17
M. Powell, Det	101	J. Farrell, Det	444	G. Gore, ChN	105	R. Connor, NYG	146	D. Brouthers, Buf	41	J. Morrill, Bos	16
S. Houck, Det	101	P. Hines, Prv	442	J. O'Rourke, Buf	102	J. O'Rourke, Buf	143	T. Burns, ChN	37	R. Connor, NYG	15
3 tied with	100	G. Wood, Det	441	E. Sutton, Bos	101	E. Sutton, Bos	134	C. Anson, ChN	36	E. Sutton, Bos	15
		J. O'Rourke, Buf	436	P. Hines, Prv	94	G. Wood, Det	133	3 tied with	34	2 tied with	13

Home Runs		Total Bases		Runs Batted In		Walks		Intentional Walks		Strikeouts	
B. Ewing, NYG	10	D. Brouthers, Buf	243	D. Brouthers, Buf	97	T. York, Cle	37	Statistic unavailable		P. Galvin, Buf	79
J. Denny, Prv	8	J. Morrill, Bos	212	J. Burdock, Bos	88	N. Hanlon, Det	34			S. Wise, Bos	74
J. Hornung, Bos	8	R. Connor, NYG	207	E. Sutton, Bos	73	M. Powell, Det	28			S. Flint, ChN	69
M. Ward, NYG	7	E. Sutton, Bos	201	J. Morrill, Bos	68	G. Gore, ChN	27			J. Morrill, Bos	68
J. Morrill, Bos	6	J. Hornung, Bos	199	C. Anson, ChN	68	O. Shaffer, Buf	27			L. Corcoran, ChN	62

Hit By Pitch	Sac Hits	Sac Flies	Stolen Bases	Caught Stealing	GDP
Statistic unavailable	Statistic unavailable	Statistic unavailable	Statistic unavailable	Statistic unavailable	Statistic unavailable

Runs Created		Runs Created/27 Outs		Batting Average		On-Base Percentage		Slugging Percentage		OBP+Slugging	
D. Brouthers, Buf	115	D. Brouthers, Buf	11.71	D. Brouthers, Buf	.374	D. Brouthers, Buf	.397	D. Brouthers, Buf	.572	D. Brouthers, Buf	.969
R. Connor, NYG	103	R. Connor, NYG	10.61	R. Connor, NYG	.357	R. Connor, NYG	.394	J. Morrill, Bos	.525	R. Connor, NYG	.900
G. Gore, ChN	101	G. Gore, ChN	10.48	G. Gore, ChN	.334	G. Gore, ChN	.377	R. Connor, NYG	.506	J. Morrill, Bos	.868
J. Morrill, Bos	98	J. Morrill, Bos	9.65	J. Burdock, Bos	.330	F. Dunlap, Cle	.361	E. Sutton, Bos	.486	G. Gore, ChN	.849
E. Sutton, Bos	98	E. Sutton, Bos	9.48	J. O'Rourke, Buf	.328	J. Burdock, Bos	.353	B. Ewing, NYG	.481	E. Sutton, Bos	.836

1883 National League Pitching Leaders

Wins		Losses		Winning Percentage		Games		Games Started		Complete Games	
O. H. Radbourn, Prv	48	J. Coleman, Phi	48	J. McCormick, Cle	.700	O. H. Radbourn, Prv	76	P. Galvin, Buf	75	P. Galvin, Buf	72
P. Galvin, Buf	46	P. Galvin, Buf	29	O. H. Radbourn, Prv	.658	P. Galvin, Buf	76	O. H. Radbourn, Prv	68	O. H. Radbourn, Prv	66
J. Whitney, Bos	37	O. H. Radbourn, Prv	25	C. Buffinton, Bos	.641	J. Coleman, Phi	65	J. Coleman, Phi	61	J. Coleman, Phi	59
L. Corcoran, ChN	34	S. Wiedman, Det	24	J. Whitney, Bos	.638	J. Whitney, Bos	62	J. Whitney, Bos	56	J. Whitney, Bos	54
J. McCormick, Cle	28	M. Welch, NYG	23	L. Corcoran, ChN	.630	L. Corcoran, ChN	56	L. Corcoran, ChN	53	L. Corcoran, ChN	51

Shutouts		Saves		Games Finished		Batters Faced		Innings Pitched		Hits Allowed	
P. Galvin, Buf	5	J. Whitney, Bos	2	M. Ward, NYG	9	P. Galvin, Buf	2741	P. Galvin, Buf	656.1	J. Coleman, Phi	772
C. Buffinton, Bos	4	S. Wiedman, Det	2	O. H. Radbourn, Prv	8	J. Coleman, Phi	2546	O. H. Radbourn, Prv	632.1	P. Galvin, Buf	676
O. Daily, Cle	4	7 tied with	1	J. Whitney, Bos	5	O. H. Radbourn, Prv	2540	J. Coleman, Phi	538.1	O. H. Radbourn, Prv	563
O. H. Radbourn, Prv	4			S. Wiedman, Det	5	J. Whitney, Bos	2101	J. Whitney, Bos	514.0	J. Whitney, Bos	492
M. Welch, NYG	4			2 tied with	4	L. Corcoran, ChN	2041	L. Corcoran, ChN	473.2	L. Corcoran, ChN	483

Home Runs Allowed		Walks		Walks/9 Innings		Strikeouts		Strikeouts/9 Innings		Strikeout/Walk Ratio	
J. Coleman, Phi	17	O. Daily, Cle	99	J. Whitney, Bos	0.6	J. Whitney, Bos	345	J. Whitney, Bos	6.0	J. Whitney, Bos	9.86
F. Goldsmith, ChN	14	L. Corcoran, ChN	82	P. Galvin, Buf	0.7	O. H. Radbourn, Prv	315	C. Buffinton, Bos	5.1	O. H. Radbourn, Prv	5.63
M. Welch, NYG	11	S. Wiedman, Det	72	O. H. Radbourn, Prv	0.8	P. Galvin, Buf	279	W. Sawyer, Cle	4.9	P. Galvin, Buf	5.58
P. Galvin, Buf	9	M. Welch, NYG	66	J. Coleman, Phi	0.8	L. Corcoran, ChN	216	O. H. Radbourn, Prv	4.5	M. Ward, NYG	3.90
2 tied with	8	J. McCormick, Cle	65	F. Goldsmith, ChN	0.9	C. Buffinton, Bos	188	L. Corcoran, ChN	4.1	C. Buffinton, Bos	3.69

Earned Run Average		Component ERA		Hit Batsmen		Wild Pitches		Opponent Average		Opponent OBP	
J. McCormick, Cle	1.84	O. H. Radbourn, Prv	1.77	Statistic unavailable		J. Whitney, Bos	37	W. Sawyer, Cle	.217	O. H. Radbourn, Prv	.244
O. H. Radbourn, Prv	2.05	J. Whitney, Bos	2.00			O. H. Radbourn, Prv	36	O. H. Radbourn, Prv	.227	J. Whitney, Bos	.251
J. Whitney, Bos	2.24	J. McCormick, Cle	2.17			T. O'Neill, NYG	33	J. McCormick, Cle	.233	P. Galvin, Buf	.265
W. Sawyer, Cle	2.36	W. Sawyer, Cle	2.24			P. Galvin, Buf	28	C. Sweeney, Prv	.237	M. Ward, NYG	.267
O. Daily, Cle	2.42	M. Ward, NYG	2.32			M. Welch, NYG	27	J. Whitney, Bos	.238	J. McCormick, Cle	.268

1883 National League Miscellaneous

Managers		
Boston	Jack Burdock	30-24
	John Morrill	33-11
Buffalo	Jim O'Rourke	52-45
Chicago	Cap Anson	59-39
Cleveland	Frank Bancroft	55-42
Detroit	Jack Chapman	40-58
New York	John Clapp	46-50
Philadelphia	Bob Ferguson	4-13
	Blondie Purcell	13-68
Providence	Harry Wright	58-40

Awards

STATS Most Valuable Player	Jim Whitney, p, Bos
STATS Cy Young	Old Hoss Radbourn, Prv
STATS Rookie of the Year	Ch. Buffinton, of, Bos
STATS Manager of the Year	John Morrill, Bos

STATS All-Star Team

C	Buck Ewing, NYG	.303	10	41
1B	Dan Brouthers, Buf	.374	3	97
2B	Jack Burdock, Bos	.330	5	88
3B	Ezra Sutton, Bos	.324	3	73
SS	Tom Burns, ChN	.294	2	67
OF	George Gore, ChN	.334	2	52
OF	Jim O'Rourke, Buf	.328	1	38
OF	George Wood, Det	.302	5	47
P	Old Hoss Radbourn, Prv	48-25	2.05	315 K
P	Jim Whitney, Bos	37-21	2.24	345 K

Postseason

None

Outstanding Performances

No-Hitters
O. H. Radbourn, Prv @ Cle on July 25
One Arm Daily, Cle @ Phi on September 13

1883 American Association Standings

Team	Overall					Home Games						Road Games						Park Index		M/A	Record by Month				
	W	L	Pct	GB	DIF	W	L	R	OR	HR	OHR	W	L	R	OR	HR	OHR	Run	HR		May	June	July	Aug	S/O
Philadelphia	66	32	.673	—	141	37	13	402	258	9	8	29	19	318	289	11	14	104	65	—	18-3	9-8	12-7	14-7	13-7
St. Louis	65	33	.663	1.0	12	35	14	298	197	5	3	30	19	251	211	2	4	107	133	—	11-10	14-4	16-6	14-6	10-7
Cincinnati	61	37	.622	5.0	6	37	13	378	163	29	13	24	24	279	250	5	4	98	448	—	12-8	10-7	14-8	13-8	12-6
New York	54	42	.563	11.0	0	30	18	273	189	3	4	24	24	225	216	3	8	109	66	—	13-9	5-12	13-7	14-7	9-7
Louisville	52	45	.536	13.5	2	29	19	282	229	4	0	23	26	282	334	10	7	85	24	—	11-8	13-5	11-11	7-14	10-7
Columbus	32	65	.330	33.5	0	18	29	198	283	5	8	14	36	276	376	10	8	78	77	—	5-17	8-9	6-15	7-14	6-10
Pittsburgh	31	67	.316	35.0	0	18	31	292	321	10	3	13	36	231	405	3	18	96	62	—	7-13	7-11	6-16	6-15	5-12
Baltimore	28	68	.292	37.0	1	18	31	300	395	4	6	10	37	173	342	1	6	129	137	—	6-15	4-14	6-14	8-12	4-13

Clinch Date—Philadelphia 9/28.

Team Batting

Team	G	AB	R	OR	H	2B	3B	HR	TB	RBI	TBB	IBB	SO	HBP	SH	SF	SB	CS	SB%	GDP	Avg	OBP	Slg
Philadelphia	98	3712	720	547	974	149	50	20	1283	—	200	—	268	—	—	—	—	—	—	—	.262	.300	.346
Cincinnati	98	3669	662	413	961	122	74	34	1333	—	139	—	261	—	—	—	—	—	—	—	.262	.289	.363
Louisville	98	3553	564	562	892	114	64	14	1176	—	141	—	304	—	—	—	—	—	—	—	.251	.280	.331
St. Louis	98	3495	549	409	891	118	46	7	1122	—	124	—	240	—	—	—	—	—	—	—	.255	.280	.321
Pittsburgh	98	3607	525	728	892	120	58	13	1167	—	164	—	345	—	—	—	—	—	—	—	.247	.280	.324
New York	97	3534	498	405	883	111	58	6	1128	—	142	—	259	—	—	—	—	—	—	—	.250	.279	.319
Columbus	97	3553	476	659	854	101	79	15	1158	—	134	—	409	—	—	—	—	—	—	—	.240	.268	.326
Baltimore	96	3532	471	742	870	125	49	5	1108	—	164	—	331	—	—	—	—	—	—	—	.246	.280	.314
AA Total	780	28655	4465	4465	7217	960	478	114	9475	—	1208	—	2417	—	—	—	—	—	—	—	.252	.282	.331
AA Avg Team	98	3582	558	558	902	120	60	14	1184	—	151	—	302	—	—	—	—	—	—	—	.252	.282	.331

Team Pitching

Team	G	CG	ShO	Rel	Sv	IP	H	R	ER	HR	SH	SF	HB	TBB	IBB	SO	WP	Bk	H/9	SO/9	BB/9	OAvg	OOBP	ERA
St. Louis	98	93	9	5	1	879.1	729	409	218	7	—	—	—	150	—	325	—	—	7.5	3.3	1.5	.211	.244	2.23
Cincinnati	98	96	8	2	0	866.2	766	413	218	17	—	—	—	168	—	215	—	—	8.0	2.2	1.7	.222	.258	2.26
Philadelphia	98	92	1	6	0	873.0	921	547	279	22	—	—	—	95	—	347	—	—	9.5	3.6	1.0	.254	.273	2.88
New York	97	97	6	0	0	874.0	751	405	282	12	—	—	—	123	—	490	41	—	7.7	5.0	1.3	.225	.253	2.90
Louisville	98	96	7	2	0	873.2	987	562	340	7	—	—	—	110	—	269	—	—	10.2	2.8	1.1	.267	.289	3.50
Columbus	97	90	4	7	0	840.1	980	659	370	16	—	—	—	211	—	222	—	—	10.5	2.4	2.3	.274	.314	3.96
Baltimore	96	86	1	11	0	844.2	943	742	383	12	—	—	—	190	—	290	—	—	10.0	3.1	2.0	.265	.302	4.08
Pittsburgh	98	82	1	18	1	867.2	1140	728	445	21	—	—	—	151	—	271	—	—	11.8	2.8	1.6	.298	.325	4.62
AA Total	780	732	37	51	2	6919.1	7217	4465	2535	114	—	—	—	1198	—	2429	—	—	9.4	3.2	1.6	.252	.282	3.30
AA Avg Team	98	92	5	6	0	864.1	902	558	317	14	—	—	—	150	—	304	—	—	9.4	3.2	1.6	.252	.282	3.30

Team Fielding

Team	G	PO	A	E	TC	DP	PB	Pct
St. Louis	98	2636	1221	388	4245	62	76	.909
Cincinnati	98	2595	1071	383	4049	57	90	.905
New York	97	2618	1100	391	4109	45	79	.905
Louisville	98	2621	1112	478	4211	67	131	.886
Pittsburgh	98	2598	1260	504	4362	55	159	.884
Columbus	97	2520	1195	535	4250	69	26	.874
Philadelphia	98	2614	1138	522	4336	40	122	.865
Baltimore	96	2528	1139	624	4291	44	213	.855
AA Total	780	20730	9236	3887	33853	439	896	.885

Team vs. Team Records

	Bal	Cin	Col	Lou	NY	Phi	Pit	STL	Won
Bal	—	3	6	6	3	3	5	2	28
Cin	11	—	11	10	4	9	8	8	61
Col	7	3	—	5	3	1	10	3	32
Lou	8	4	9	—	7	7	11	6	52
NY	10	10	11	6	—	5	9	3	54
Phi	11	5	13	7	9	—	12	9	66
Pit	9	6	4	3	5	2	—	2	31
STL	12	6	11	8	11	5	12	—	65
Lost	68	37	65	45	42	32	67	33	

1883 American Association Batting Leaders

Games		At-Bats		Runs		Hits		Doubles		Triples	
C. Wolf, Lou	98	J. Birchall, Phi	449	H. Stovey, Phi	110	E. Swartwood, Pit	147	H. Stovey, Phi	31	P. Smith, Col	17
B. Gleason, STL	98	J. Reilly, Cin	437	J. Reilly, Cin	103	J. Reilly, Cin	136	E. Swartwood, Pit	24	B. Kuehne, Col	14
A. Latham, STL	98	H. Carpenter, Cin	436	H. Carpenter, Cin	99	H. Carpenter, Cin	129	J. Hayes, Pit	23	J. Reilly, Cin	14
J. Reilly, Cin	98	S. Brady, NY	432	L. Knight, Phi	98	H. Stovey, Phi	127	L. Knight, Phi	23	F. Mann, Col	13
J. Battin, Pit	98	L. Knight, Phi	429	2 tied with	95	C. Nelson, NY	127	2 tied with	21	M. Mansell, Pit	13

Home Runs		Total Bases		Runs Batted In		Walks		Intentional Walks		Strikeouts	
H. Stovey, Phi	14	J. Reilly, Cin	212	Statistic unavailable		E. Stearns, Bal	34	Statistic unavailable		Statistic unavailable	
C. Jones, Cin	10	H. Stovey, Phi	212			C. Nelson, NY	31				
J. Reilly, Cin	9	E. Swartwood, Pit	196			M. Moynahan, Phi	30				
T. Brown, Col	5	C. Jones, Cin	184			J. Gleason, 2tm	29				
C. Fulmer, Cin	5	B. Gleason, STL	167			J. Clinton, Bal	27				

Hit By Pitch	Sac Hits	Sac Flies	Stolen Bases	Caught Stealing	GDP
Statistic unavailable	Statistic unavailable	Statistic unavailable	Statistic unavailable	Statistic unavailable	Statistic unavailable

Runs Created		Runs Created/27 Outs		Batting Average		On-Base Percentage		Slugging Percentage		OBP+Slugging	
H. Stovey, Phi	119	H. Stovey, Phi	11.13	E. Swartwood, Pit	.356	E. Swartwood, Pit	.391	H. Stovey, Phi	.504	E. Swartwood, Pit	.866
J. Reilly, Cin	105	P. Browning, Lou	10.44	P. Browning, Lou	.338	P. Browning, Lou	.378	J. Reilly, Cin	.485	H. Stovey, Phi	.846
E. Swartwood, Pit	100	E. Swartwood, Pit	10.34	J. Clinton, Bal	.313	J. Clinton, Bal	.357	E. Swartwood, Pit	.475	P. Browning, Lou	.842
M. Moynahan, Phi	100	M. Moynahan, Phi	9.93	J. Reilly, Cin	.311	M. Moynahan, Phi	.356	C. Jones, Cin	.471	J. Reilly, Cin	.810
C. Jones, Cin	94	J. Reilly, Cin	9.59	M. Moynahan, Phi	.308	C. Nelson, NY	.353	P. Browning, Lou	.464	C. Jones, Cin	.799

1883 American Association Pitching Leaders

Wins		Losses		Winning Percentage		Games		Games Started		Complete Games	
W. White, Cin	43	F. Mountain, Col	33	T. Mullane, STL	.700	T. Keefe, NY	68	T. Keefe, NY	68	T. Keefe, NY	68
T. Keefe, NY	41	H. Henderson, Bal	32	B. Mathews, Phi	.698	W. White, Cin	65	W. White, Cin	64	W. White, Cin	64
T. Mullane, STL	35	T. Keefe, NY	27	G. Bradley, Phi	.696	F. Mountain, Col	59	F. Mountain, Col	59	F. Mountain, Col	57
B. Mathews, Phi	30	G. Hecker, Lou	23	W. White, Cin	.662	T. Mullane, STL	53	G. Hecker, Lou	50	G. Hecker, Lou	49
J. McGinnis, STL	28	2 tied with	22	J. McGinnis, STL	.636	G. Hecker, Lou	51	T. Mullane, STL	49	T. Mullane, STL	49

Shutouts		Saves		Games Finished		Batters Faced		Innings Pitched		Hits Allowed	
J. McGinnis, STL	6	B. Barr, Pit	1	B. Taylor, Pit	9	Statistic unavailable		T. Keefe, NY	619.0	F. Mountain, Col	546
W. White, Cin	6	T. Mullane, STL	1	T. Mullane, STL	4			W. White, Cin	577.0	G. Hecker, Lou	509
T. Keefe, NY	5			4 tied with	3			F. Mountain, Col	503.0	T. Keefe, NY	486
F. Mountain, Col	4							T. Mullane, STL	460.2	W. White, Cin	473
S. Weaver, Lou	4							G. Hecker, Lou	451.0	S. Weaver, Lou	468

Home Runs Allowed		Walks		Walks/9 Innings		Strikeouts		Strikeouts/9 Innings		Strikeout/Walk Ratio	
W. White, Cin	16	F. Mountain, Col	123	B. Mathews, Phi	0.7	T. Keefe, NY	361	T. Keefe, NY	5.2	B. Mathews, Phi	6.55
B. Mathews, Phi	11	W. White, Cin	104	S. Weaver, Lou	0.8	B. Mathews, Phi	203	B. Mathews, Phi	4.8	J. Lynch, NY	4.76
J. Neagle, 3tm	10	T. Keefe, NY	98	J. Lynch, NY	0.9	T. Mullane, STL	191	J. Lynch, NY	4.2	T. Keefe, NY	3.68
F. Mountain, Col	8	H. Henderson, Bal	87	G. Bradley, Phi	0.9	F. Mountain, Col	159	T. Mullane, STL	3.7	S. Weaver, Lou	3.05
2 tied with	7	T. Mullane, STL	74	D. Driscoll, Pit	1.0	G. Hecker, Lou	153	H. Henderson, Bal	3.6	B. Barr, Pit	2.89

Earned Run Average		Component ERA		Hit Batsmen		Wild Pitches		Opponent Average		Opponent OBP	
W. White, Cin	2.09	T. Keefe, NY	1.59	Statistic unavailable		Statistic unavailable		T. Keefe, NY	.209	T. Keefe, NY	.242
T. Mullane, STL	2.19	T. Mullane, STL	1.63					T. Mullane, STL	.211	T. Mullane, STL	.242
R. Deagle, Cin	2.31	J. McGinnis, STL	1.83					W. White, Cin	.213	W. White, Cin	.249
J. McGinnis, STL	2.33	W. White, Cin	1.83					J. McGinnis, STL	.217	J. McGinnis, STL	.252
T. Keefe, NY	2.41	R. Deagle, Cin	2.17					B. Emslie, Bal	.225	G. Bradley, Phi	.256

1883 American Association Miscellaneous

Managers		
Baltimore	Billy Barnie	28-68
Cincinnati	Pop Snyder	61-37
Columbus	Horace Phillips	32-65
Louisville	Joe Gerhardt	52-45
New York	Jim Mutrie	54-42
Philadelphia	Lon Knight	66-32
Pittsburgh	Al Pratt	12-20
	Ormond Butler	17-36
	Joe Battin	2-11
St. Louis	Ted Sullivan	53-26
	Charlie Comiskey	12-7

Awards	
STATS Most Valuable Player	Harry Stovey, 1b, Phi
STATS Cy Young	Will White, Cin
STATS Rookie of the Year	Steve Brady, 1b, NY
STATS Manager of the Year	Lon Knight, Phi

STATS All-Star Team

C	Ed Whiting, Lou	.292	2	—
1B	Harry Stovey, Phi	.302	14	—
2B	Pop Smith, Col	.262	4	—
3B	Hick Carpenter, Cin	.296	3	—
SS	Mike Moynahan, Phi	.308	1	—
OF	Pete Browning, Lou	.338	4	—
OF	Charley Jones, Cin	.294	10	—
OF	John O'Rourke, NY	.270	2	—
P	Tim Keefe, NY	41-27	2.41	361 K
P	Will White, Cin	43-22	2.09	141 K

Postseason
None

Outstanding Performances

Cycles

Lon Knight, Phi	on July 30
John Reilly, Cin	on September 12
John Reilly, Cin	on September 19

1884 National League Standings

Team	W	L	Pct	GB	DIF	W	L	R	OR	HR	OHR	W	L	R	OR	HR	OHR	Run	HR	M/A	May	June	July	Aug	S/O
		Overall						**Home Games**						**Road Games**				**Park Index**				**Record by Month**			
Providence	84	28	.750	—	101	45	11	329	164	4	6	39	17	336	224	17	20	88	27	—	20-4	14-8	13-7	17-1	20-8
Boston	73	38	.658	10.5	53	40	16	328	181	14	4	33	22	356	288	22	26	78	37	—	21-4	14-7	13-8	10-6	15-13
Buffalo	64	47	.577	19.5	0	37	18	409	311	23	20	27	29	292	314	16	26	121	104	—	11-14	14-7	14-6	11-7	14-13
Chicago	62	50	.554	22.0	0	39	17	498	312	131	66	23	33	336	334	11	17	121	704	—	9-15	11-11	14-6	7-13	21-5
New York	62	50	.554	22.0	19	34	22	378	261	8	4	28	28	315	362	15	24	94	31	—	17-8	12-11	11-8	10-9	12-14
Philadelphia	39	73	.348	45.0	4	19	37	281	388	1	1	20	36	268	436	13	37	95	4	—	8-17	7-17	5-15	7-9	12-15
Cleveland	35	77	.313	49.0	0	22	34	264	348	4	6	13	43	194	368	12	29	109	24	—	8-15	11-11	4-18	8-11	4-22
Detroit	28	84	.250	56.0	0	18	38	228	347	14	16	10	46	215	389	17	20	95	81	—	3-20	6-17	7-13	2-16	10-18

Clinch Date—Providence 9/27.

Team Batting

Team	G	AB	R	OR	H	2B	3B	HR	TB	RBI	TBB	IBB	SO	HBP	SH	SF	SB	CS	SB%	GDP	Avg	OBP	Slg
Chicago	113	4182	**834**	647	**1176**	162	50	**142**	**1864**	658	264	—	469	—	—	—	—	—	—	—	.281	.324	.446
Buffalo	115	**4197**	700	626	1099	163	**69**	39	1517	533	215	—	458	—	—	—	—	—	—	—	.262	.298	.361
New York	116	4124	693	623	1053	149	67	23	1405	497	249	—	492	—	—	—	—	—	—	—	.255	.298	.341
Boston	116	4189	684	468	1063	**179**	60	36	1470	467	207	—	660	—	—	—	—	—	—	—	.254	.289	.351
Providence	114	4093	665	**388**	987	153	43	21	1289	404	**300**	—	469	—	—	—	—	—	—	—	.241	.293	.315
Philadelphia	113	3998	549	824	934	149	39	14	1203	343	209	—	512	—	—	—	—	—	—	—	.234	.272	.301
Cleveland	113	3934	458	716	934	147	49	16	1227	329	170	—	576	—	—	—	—	—	—	—	.237	.269	.312
Detroit	114	3970	445	736	825	114	47	31	1126	297	207	—	**699**	—	—	—	—	—	—	—	.208	.247	.284
NL Total	914	32687	5028	5028	8071	1216	424	322	11101	3528	1821	—	4335	—	—	—	—	—	—	—	.247	.287	.340
NL Avg Team	114	4086	629	629	1009	152	53	40	1388	441	228	—	542	—	—	—	—	—	—	—	.247	.287	.340

Team Pitching

Team	G	CG	ShO	Rel	Sv	IP	H	R	ER	HR	SH	SF	HB	TBB	IBB	SO	WP	Bk	H/9	SO/9	BB/9	OAvg	OOBP	ERA
Providence	114	107	**16**	8	**2**	1036.1	825	**388**	185	**26**	—	—	—	172	—	639	68	0	**7.2**	5.5	1.5	**.209**	**.242**	**1.61**
Boston	116	109	14	7	**2**	**1037.0**	932	468	285	30	—	—	—	**135**	—	**742**	52	0	8.1	**6.4**	**1.2**	.226	.250	2.47
Buffalo	115	108	14	6	1	1001.0	1041	626	328	46	—	—	—	189	—	534	62	0	9.4	4.8	1.7	.254	.286	2.95
Chicago	113	106	9	**9**	0	997.1	1028	647	336	83	—	—	—	231	—	472	60	0	9.3	4.3	2.1	.250	.290	3.03
New York	116	**111**	4	5	0	1014.0	1011	623	351	28	—	—	—	326	—	567	101	1	9.0	5.0	2.9	.245	.300	3.12
Detroit	114	109	3	5	0	984.2	1097	736	370	36	—	—	—	245	—	488	44	0	10.0	4.5	2.2	.262	.302	3.38
Cleveland	113	107	7	6	0	994.2	1046	716	379	35	—	—	—	269	—	482	94	2	9.5	4.4	2.4	.256	.302	3.43
Philadelphia	113	106	3	7	1	981.0	1090	824	428	38	—	—	—	254	—	411	**126**	0	10.0	3.8	2.3	.261	.304	3.93
NL Total	914	863	70	53	6	8046.0	8070	5028	2662	322	—	—	—	1821	—	4335	607	3	9.0	4.8	2.0	.247	.287	2.98
NL Avg Team	114	108	9	7	1	1005.0	1009	629	333	40	—	—	—	228	—	542	76	0	9.0	4.8	2.0	.247	.287	2.98

Team Fielding

Team	G	PO	A	E	TC	DP	PB	Pct
Boston	116	**3124**	1393	**384**	4901	46	86	**.922**
Providence	114	3121	1324	398	4843	50	77	.918
Buffalo	115	3001	1383	462	4846	71	105	.905
Cleveland	113	2980	1478	512	4970	75	136	.897
New York	116	3014	1379	514	4907	69	99	.895
Philadelphia	113	2921	1337	536	4794	67	**200**	.888
Detroit	114	2953	1344	550	4847	62	108	.887
Chicago	113	2987	**1620**	595	**5202**	**107**	138	.886
NL Total	914	24101	11258	3951	39310	547	949	.899

Team vs. Team Records

	Bos	Buf	ChN	Cle	Det	NYG	Phi	Prv	Won
Bos	—	9	10	14	12	8	13	7	**73**
Buf	6	—	10	14	12	5	11	6	**64**
ChN	6	6	—	8	11	12	14	5	**62**
Cle	2	2	8	—	9	5	6	3	**35**
Det	4	4	5	7	—	2	5	1	**28**
NYG	8	11	4	11	14	—	11	3	**62**
Phi	3	5	2	10	11	5	—	3	**39**
Prv	9	10	11	13	15	13	13	—	**84**
Lost	38	47	50	77	84	50	73	28	

1884 National League Batting Leaders

Games		At-Bats		Runs		Hits		Doubles		Triples	
A. McKinnon, NYG	116	A. Dalrymple, ChN	521	K. Kelly, ChN	120	J. O'Rourke, Buf	162	P. Hines, Prv	36	B. Ewing, NYG	20
R. Connor, NYG	116	J. Hornung, Bos	518	J. Hornung, Bos	119	E. Sutton, Bos	162	J. O'Rourke, Buf	33	D. Brouthers, Buf	15
J. Hornung, Bos	115	P. Hines, Prv	490	J. O'Rourke, Buf	119	A. Dalrymple, ChN	161	C. Anson, ChN	30	J. Rowe, Buf	14
5 tied with	114	M. Ward, NYG	482	A. Dalrymple, ChN	111	K. Kelly, ChN	160	J. Manning, Phi	29	A. McKinnon, NYG	12
		R. Connor, NYG	477	C. Anson, ChN	108	C. Anson, ChN	159	3 tied with	28	B. Phillips, Cle	12

Home Runs		Total Bases		Runs Batted In		Walks		Intentional Walks		Strikeouts	
N. Williamson, ChN	27	A. Dalrymple, ChN	263	C. Anson, ChN	102	G. Gore, ChN	61	Statistic unavailable		S. Wise, Bos	104
F. Pfeffer, ChN	25	C. Anson, ChN	258	F. Pfeffer, ChN	101	K. Kelly, ChN	46			F. Meinke, Det	89
A. Dalrymple, ChN	22	F. Pfeffer, ChN	240	K. Kelly, ChN	95	P. Hines, Prv	44			J. Morrill, Bos	87
C. Anson, ChN	21	K. Kelly, ChN	237	N. Williamson, ChN	84	N. Williamson, ChN	42			3 tied with	80
D. Brouthers, Buf	14	N. Williamson, ChN	231	R. Connor, NYG	82	2 tied with	40				

Hit By Pitch	Sac Hits	Sac Flies	Stolen Bases	Caught Stealing	GDP
Statistic unavailable	Statistic unavailable	Statistic unavailable	Statistic unavailable	Statistic unavailable	Statistic unavailable

Runs Created		Runs Created/27 Outs		Batting Average		On-Base Percentage		Slugging Percentage		OBP+Slugging	
K. Kelly, ChN	122	K. Kelly, ChN	11.28	K. Kelly, ChN	.354	K. Kelly, ChN	.414	D. Brouthers, Buf	.563	D. Brouthers, Buf	.941
C. Anson, ChN	121	D. Brouthers, Buf	11.18	J. O'Rourke, Buf	.347	G. Gore, ChN	.404	N. Williamson, ChN	.554	K. Kelly, ChN	.938
P. Hines, Prv	120	J. O'Rourke, Buf	10.53	E. Sutton, Bos	.346	J. O'Rourke, Buf	.392	C. Anson, ChN	.543	C. Anson, ChN	.916
J. O'Rourke, Buf	119	C. Anson, ChN	10.34	C. Anson, ChN	.335	E. Sutton, Bos	.384	K. Kelly, ChN	.524	N. Williamson, ChN	.898
E. Sutton, Bos	116	E. Sutton, Bos	10.23	D. Brouthers, Buf	.327	D. Brouthers, Buf	.378	F. Pfeffer, ChN	.514	J. O'Rourke, Buf	.872

1884 National League Pitching Leaders

Wins		Losses		Winning Percentage		Games		Games Started		Complete Games	
O. H. Radbourn, Prv	59	J. Harkins, Cle	32	O. H. Radbourn, Prv	.831	O. H. Radbourn, Prv	75	O. H. Radbourn, Prv	73	O. H. Radbourn, Prv	73
C. Buffinton, Bos	48	C. Ferguson, Phi	25	C. Buffinton, Bos	.750	P. Galvin, Buf	72	P. Galvin, Buf	72	P. Galvin, Buf	71
P. Galvin, Buf	46	F. Meinke, Det	23	C. Sweeney, Prv	.680	C. Buffinton, Bos	67	C. Buffinton, Bos	67	C. Buffinton, Bos	63
M. Welch, NYG	39	L. Corcoran, ChN	23	P. Galvin, Buf	.676	M. Welch, NYG	65	M. Welch, NYG	65	M. Welch, NYG	62
L. Corcoran, ChN	35	2 tied with	22	M. Welch, NYG	.650	L. Corcoran, ChN	60	L. Corcoran, ChN	59	L. Corcoran, ChN	57

Shutouts		Saves		Games Finished		Batters Faced		Innings Pitched		Hits Allowed	
P. Galvin, Buf	12	J. Morrill, Bos	2	J. Morrill, Bos	6	O. H. Radbourn, Prv	2672	O. H. Radbourn, Prv	678.2	P. Galvin, Buf	566
O. H. Radbourn, Prv	11	C. Ferguson, Phi	1	F. Meinke, Det	4	P. Galvin, Buf	2554	P. Galvin, Buf	636.1	O. H. Radbourn, Prv	528
C. Buffinton, Bos	8	C. Sweeney, Prv	1	4 tied with	3	C. Buffinton, Bos	2383	C. Buffinton, Bos	587.0	M. Welch, NYG	528
L. Corcoran, ChN	7	O. H. Radbourn, Prv	1			M. Welch, NYG	2370	M. Welch, NYG	557.1	C. Buffinton, Bos	506
J. Whitney, Bos	6	J. O'Rourke, Buf	1			L. Corcoran, ChN	2180	L. Corcoran, ChN	516.2	L. Corcoran, ChN	473

Home Runs Allowed		Walks		Walks/9 Innings		Strikeouts		Strikeouts/9 Innings		Strikeout/Walk Ratio	
L. Corcoran, ChN	35	M. Welch, NYG	146	J. Whitney, Bos	0.7	O. H. Radbourn, Prv	441	J. Clarkson, ChN	7.8	J. Whitney, Bos	10.00
P. Galvin, Buf	23	L. Corcoran, ChN	116	P. Galvin, Buf	0.9	C. Buffinton, Bos	417	J. Whitney, Bos	7.2	P. Galvin, Buf	5.86
B. Serad, Buf	21	B. Serad, Buf	111	C. Buffinton, Bos	1.2	P. Galvin, Buf	369	M. Dorgan, NYG	7.2	C. Buffinton, Bos	5.49
O. H. Radbourn, Prv	18	J. Harkins, Cle	108	C. Sweeney, Prv	1.2	M. Welch, NYG	345	C. Getzien, Det	6.5	C. Sweeney, Prv	5.00
J. McCormick, Cle	16	E. Begley, NYG	99	J. Coleman, Phi	1.3	L. Corcoran, ChN	272	C. Buffinton, Bos	6.4	O. H. Radbourn, Prv	4.50

Earned Run Average		Component ERA		Hit Batsmen	Wild Pitches		Opponent Average		Opponent OBP	
O. H. Radbourn, Prv	1.38	C. Sweeney, Prv	1.28	Statistic unavailable	J. Harkins, Cle	48	C. Sweeney, Prv	.187	C. Sweeney, Prv	.215
C. Sweeney, Prv	1.55	J. Whitney, Bos	1.55		J. McElroy, Phi	46	C. Getzien, Det	.204	J. Whitney, Bos	.223
C. Getzien, Det	1.95	O. H. Radbourn, Prv	1.59		B. Serad, Buf	42	O. H. Radbourn, Prv	.205	O. H. Radbourn, Prv	.234
P. Galvin, Buf	1.99	C. Getzien, Det	1.61		M. Welch, NYG	39	J. Whitney, Bos	.207	C. Getzien, Det	.237
J. Whitney, Bos	2.09	C. Buffinton, Bos	1.83		O. H. Radbourn, Prv	34	J. Clarkson, ChN	.208	C. Buffinton, Bos	.244

1884 National League Miscellaneous

Managers			Awards		Postseason	
Boston	John Morrill	73-38	STATS Most Valuable Player	O. H. Radbourn, p, Prv	World Series	Providence (NL) 3 vs. NY (AA) 0
Buffalo	Jim O'Rourke	64-47	STATS Cy Young	Old Hoss Radbourn, Prv		
Chicago	Cap Anson	62-50	STATS Rookie of the Year	A. McKinnon, 1b, NYG		
Cleveland	Charlie Hackett	35-77	STATS Manager of the Year	Frank Bancroft, Prv		
Detroit	Jack Chapman	28-84				

Outstanding Performances

New York	Jim Price	56-42	STATS All-Star Team				
	Monte Ward	6-8	C	Jack Rowe, Buf	.315	4	61
Philadelphia	Harry Wright	39-73	1B	Dan Brouthers, Buf	.327	14	79
Providence	Frank Bancroft	84-28	2B	Fred Pfeffer, ChN	.289	25	101
			3B	Ned Williamson, ChN	.278	27	84
			SS	Jack Glasscock, Cle	.249	1	22
			OF	Paul Hines, Prv	.302	3	41
			OF	King Kelly, ChN	.354	13	95
			OF	Jim O'Rourke, Buf	.347	5	63
			P	Pud Galvin, Buf	46-22	1.99	369 K
			P	Old Hoss Radbourn, Prv	59-12	1.38	441 K

No-Hitters
Larry Corcoran, ChN vs. Prv on June 27
Pud Galvin, Buf @ Det on August 4

Three-Homer Games
Ned Williamson, ChN on May 30
Cap Anson, ChN on August 6
Jack Manning, Phi on October 9

Cycles
Jim O'Rourke, Buf on June 16

1884 American Association Standings

Team	Overall					Home Games						Road Games						Park Index		Record by Month					
	W	L	Pct	GB	DIF	W	L	R	OR	HR	OHR	W	L	R	OR	HR	OHR	Run	HR	M/A	May	June	July	Aug	S/O
New York	75	32	.701	—	106	42	9	370	179	11	4	33	23	364	244	11	11	99	75	—	17-6	12-7	18-5	10-5	18-9
Columbus	69	39	.639	6.5	4	38	16	282	207	23	14	31	23	303	252	17	8	88	148	—	14-9	13-7	16-3	14-6	12-14
Louisville	68	40	.630	7.5	51	41	14	278	145	4	2	27	26	295	280	13	7	71	29	—	18-5	9-7	15-8	11-7	15-13
St. Louis	67	40	.626	8.0	20	38	15	383	256	6	10	29	25	275	281	5	6	117	148	—	13-9	15-4	13-8	9-11	17-8
Cincinnati	68	41	.624	8.0	0	40	16	439	233	31	20	28	25	315	279	5	7	107	402	—	12-8	14-6	15-8	9-11	18-8
Baltimore	63	43	.594	11.5	2	42	13	371	224	21	8	21	30	264	292	11	8	99	142	—	12-10	13-4	5-13	14-5	19-11
Philadelphia	61	46	.570	14.0	2	38	16	438	268	12	4	23	30	262	278	14	12	128	60	—	15-8	8-11	14-9	12-6	12-12
Toledo	46	58	.442	27.5	0	28	25	270	267	3	2	18	33	193	305	5	10	104	32	—	6-17	6-13	9-12	9-10	16-6
Brooklyn	40	64	.385	33.5	0	23	26	263	265	9	8	17	38	213	379	7	12	100	100	—	10-11	8-12	6-15	9-9	7-17
Richmond	12	30	.286	30.5	0	5	15	96	142	3	8	7	15	98	153	4	6	104	121	—	—	—	3-12		9-18
Pittsburgh	30	78	.278	45.5	0	18	37	225	350	1	4	12	41	182	375	1	21	99	22	—	8-15	4-16	8-13	3-14	7-20
Indianapolis	29	78	.271	46.0	0	16	39	244	377	13	15	13	39	219	378	7	16	99	100	—	3-17	7-13	6-14	7-14	6-20
Washington	12	51	.190	11.0	1	10	20	137	181	3	4	2	31	111	300	3	17	85	39	—	4-17	5-14	2-19	1-1	—

Clinch Date—New York 10/08.

Team Batting

Team	G	AB	R	OR	H	2B	3B	HR	TB	RBI	TBB	IBB	SO	HBP	SH	SF	SB	CS	SB%	GDP	Avg	OBP	Slg
Cincinnati	112	4090	754	512	1037	109	96	36	1446	—	154	—	409	52	—	—	—	—	—	—	.254	.289	.354
New York	112	4012	734	423	1052	155	64	22	1401	—	203	—	315	35	—	—	—	—	—	—	.262	.304	.349
Philadelphia	108	3959	700	546	1057	167	100	26	1502	—	153	—	434	40	—	—	—	—	—	—	.267	.301	.379
St. Louis	110	3952	658	539	987	151	60	11	1291	—	172	—	339	39	—	—	—	—	—	—	.250	.288	.327
Baltimore	108	3845	636	515	896	133	84	32	1293	—	211	—	545	64	—	—	—	—	—	—	.233	.284	.336
Columbus	110	3759	585	459	901	107	96	40	1320	—	196	—	629	59	—	—	—	—	—	—	.240	.288	.351
Louisville	110	3957	573	425	1004	152	69	17	1345	—	146	—	408	34	—	—	—	—	—	—	.254	.286	.340
Brooklyn	109	3763	476	644	845	112	47	16	1099	—	179	—	417	16	—	—	—	—	—	—	.225	.263	.292
Toledo	110	3712	463	571	859	153	48	8	1132	—	157	—	545	26	—	—	—	—	—	—	.231	.268	.305
Indianapolis	110	3813	462	755	890	149	62	20	1203	—	125	—	561	22	—	—	—	—	—	—	.233	.262	.315
Pittsburgh	110	3689	406	725	777	105	50	2	988	—	143	—	411	41	—	—	—	—	—	—	.211	.248	.268
Washington	63	2166	248	481	434	61	24	6	561	—	100	—	377	16	—	—	—	—	—	—	.200	.241	.259
Richmond	46	1469	194	294	326	40	33	7	453	—	53	—	282	24	—	—	—	—	—	—	.222	.261	.308
AA Total	1318	46186	6889	6889	11065	1574	833	243	15034	—	1992	—	5672	468	—	—	—	—	—	—	.240	.278	.326
AA Avg Team	101	3553	530	530	851	121	64	19	1156	—	153	—	436	36	—	—	—	—	—	—	.240	.278	.326

Team Pitching

Team	G	CG	ShO	Rel	Sv	IP	H	R	ER	HR	SH	SF	HB	TBB	IBB	SO	WP	Bk	H/9	SO/9	BB/9	OAvg	OOBP	ERA
Louisville	110	101	6	9	0	989.2	836	425	239	9	—	—	30	97	—	470	—	—	7.6	4.3	0.9	.216	.241	2.17
New York	112	110	9	1	0	985.0	802	423	269	15	—	—	25	115	—	628	—	—	7.3	5.7	1.1	.209	.237	2.46
St. Louis	110	99	8	11	0	987.0	881	539	293	16	—	—	42	172	—	477	—	—	8.0	4.3	1.6	.226	.266	2.67
Columbus	110	102	8	8	1	962.1	815	459	287	22	—	—	27	172	—	526	—	—	7.6	4.9	1.6	.217	.256	2.68
Baltimore	108	105	8	3	1	955.2	869	515	288	16	—	—	31	219	—	635	—	—	8.2	6.0	2.1	.226	.273	2.71
Toledo	110	103	9	6	1	946.0	885	571	322	12	—	—	53	169	—	501	—	—	8.4	4.8	1.6	.233	.275	3.06
Cincinnati	112	111	11	1	0	983.2	956	512	364	27	—	—	78	181	—	308	—	—	8.7	2.8	1.7	.244	.291	3.33
Philadelphia	108	105	5	3	0	948.2	920	546	360	16	—	—	39	127	—	530	—	—	8.7	5.0	1.2	.237	.269	3.42
Brooklyn	109	105	6	4	0	948.2	996	644	400	20	—	—	26	163	—	378	—	—	9.4	3.6	1.5	.254	.288	3.79
Washington	63	62	3	1	0	543.2	643	481	242	21	—	—	20	110	—	235	—	—	10.6	3.9	1.8	.273	.311	4.01
Indianapolis	110	107	2	3	0	937.2	1001	755	438	30	—	—	28	199	—	479	—	—	9.6	4.6	1.9	.255	.295	4.20
Pittsburgh	110	108	4	2	0	943.1	1059	725	456	25	—	—	56	216	—	338	—	—	10.1	3.2	2.1	.265	.312	4.35
Richmond	46	45	1	0	0	370.1	402	294	186	14	—	—	17	52	—	167	—	—	9.8	4.1	1.3	.257	.288	4.52
AA Total	1318	1263	80	52	3	11501.2	11065	6889	4144	243	—	—	472	1992	—	5672	—	—	8.7	4.4	1.6	.240	.278	3.24
AA Avg Team	101	97	6	4	0	884.2	851	530	319	19	—	—	36	153	—	436	—	—	8.7	4.4	1.6	.240	.278	3.24

Team Fielding

Team	G	PO	A	E	TC	DP	PB	Pct
Louisville	110	2967	1436	426	4829	84	145	.912
Cincinnati	112	2944	1351	430	4725	82	92	.909
Columbus	110	2882	1390	433	4705	74	127	.908
New York	112	2952	1328	441	4721	42	92	.907
Philadelphia	108	2845	1328	457	4630	63	129	.901
Toledo	110	2830	1376	469	4675	67	191	.900
St. Louis	110	2955	1436	490	4881	65	102	.900
Baltimore	108	2867	1257	461	4585	61	130	.899
Brooklyn	109	2840	1340	520	4700	68	169	.889
Pittsburgh	110	2825	1369	523	4717	71	139	.889
Indianapolis	110	2804	1308	515	4627	45	175	.889
Richmond	46	1108	540	239	1887	27	63	.873
Washington	63	1630	786	400	2816	40	102	.858
AA Total	1318	34449	16245	5804	56498	789	1656	.897

Team vs. Team Records

	Bal	Bro	Cin	Col	Ind	Lou	NY	Phi	Pit	Ric	STL	Tol	WaD	Won
Bal	—	5	4	6	9	6	5	3	9	4	5	5	2	63
Bro	5	—	2	3	7	3	1	3	4	3	2	4	3	40
Cin	6	8	—	3	9	5	4	4	8	4	4	7	6	68
Col	4	7	7	—	8	5	4	5	9	2	5	8	5	69
Ind	1	3	1	2	—	1	2	4	4	1	3	3	4	29
Lou	4	6	5	5	9	—	3	6	8	4	5	9	4	68
NY	5	9	6	5	8	7	—	8	9	2	5	5	6	75
Phi	7	6	6	6	6	3	2	—	8	2	3	6	7	61
Pit	0	6	1	1	6	1	2	1	—	1	1	5	4	30
Ric	0	2	0	2	2	1	0	4		—	1	0	0	12
STL	5	7	6	5	6	5	4	7	9	3	—	5	5	67
Tol	5	4	3	1	6	1	4	3	5	4	5	—	5	46
WaD	1	1	0	1	2	1	2	1	1	0	1	1	—	12
Lost	43	64	41	39	78	40	32	46	78	30	40	58	51	

Seasons: Standings, Leaders

1884 American Association Batting Leaders

Games		At-Bats		Runs		Hits		Doubles		Triples	
B. McPhee, Cin	112	C. Wolf, Lou	486	H. Stovey, Phi	124	D. Orr, NY	162	S. Barkley, Tol	39	H. Stovey, Phi	23
D. Esterbrook, NY	112	S. Brady, NY	485	C. Jones, Cin	117	J. Reilly, Cin	152	P. Browning, Lou	33	J. Reilly, Cin	19
S. Brady, NY	112	L. Knight, Phi	484	A. Latham, STL	115	P. Browning, Lou	150	D. Orr, NY	32	F. Mann, Col	18
C. Jones, Cin	112	J. Sommer, Bal	479	J. Reilly, Cin	114	D. Esterbrook, NY	150	D. Esterbrook, NY	29	J. Peltz, Ind	17
C. Nelson, NY	111	D. Esterbrook, NY	477	C. Nelson, NY	114	C. Jones, Cin	148	F. Lewis, STL	25	C. Jones, Cin	17

Home Runs		Total Bases		Runs Batted In	Walks		Intentional Walks	Strikeouts
J. Reilly, Cin	11	D. Orr, NY	247	Statistic unavailable	C. Nelson, NY	74	Statistic unavailable	Statistic unavailable
H. Stovey, Phi	10	J. Reilly, Cin	247		B. Geer, Bro	38		
D. Orr, NY	9	H. Stovey, Phi	244		C. Jones, Cin	37		
F. Mann, Col	7	C. Jones, Cin	222		J. Macullar, Bal	36		
C. Jones, Cin	7	P. Browning, Lou	211		J. Richmond, Col	35		

Hit By Pitch		Sac Hits	Sac Flies	Stolen Bases	Caught Stealing	GDP
E. Swartwood, Pit	15	Statistic unavailable	Statistic unavailable	Statistic unavailable	Statistic unavailable	Statistic unavailable
J. Reilly, Cin	14					
J. Clinton, Bal	13					
3 tied with	12					

Runs Created		Runs Created/27 Outs		Batting Average		On-Base Percentage		Slugging Percentage		OBP+Slugging	
C. Jones, Cin	142	J. Reilly, Cin	12.30	D. Orr, NY	.354	C. Jones, Cin	.376	J. Reilly, Cin	.551	J. Reilly, Cin	.918
J. Reilly, Cin	137	C. Jones, Cin	11.64	J. Reilly, Cin	.339	C. Nelson, NY	.375	H. Stovey, Phi	.545	H. Stovey, Phi	.913
D. Orr, NY	125	D. Orr, NY	11.22	P. Browning, Lou	.336	H. Stovey, Phi	.368	D. Orr, NY	.539	D. Orr, NY	.901
H. Stovey, Phi	125	H. Stovey, Phi	11.00	H. Stovey, Phi	.326	F. Fennelly, 2tm	.366	F. Fennelly, 2tm	.480	F. Fennelly, 2tm	.847
C. Nelson, NY	111	F. Fennelly, 2tm	10.89	D. Esterbrook, NY	.314	J. Reilly, Cin	.366	P. Browning, Lou	.472	C. Jones, Cin	.846

1884 American Association Pitching Leaders

Wins		Losses		Winning Percentage		Games		Games Started		Complete Games	
G. Hecker, Lou	52	L. McKeon, Ind	41	T. O'Neill, STL	.733	G. Hecker, Lou	75	G. Hecker, Lou	73	G. Hecker, Lou	72
J. Lynch, NY	37	F. Sullivan, Pit	35	E. Morris, Col	.723	T. Mullane, Tol	67	T. Mullane, Tol	65	T. Mullane, Tol	64
T. Keefe, NY	37	A. Terry, Bro	35	G. Hecker, Lou	.722	L. McKeon, Ind	61	L. McKeon, Ind	60	L. McKeon, Ind	59
T. Mullane, Tol	36	B. Barr, 2tm	34	D. Foutz, STL	.714	A. Terry, Bro	57	T. Keefe, NY	57	T. Keefe, NY	56
2 tied with	34	H. O'Day, Tol	28	J. Lynch, NY	.712	T. Keefe, NY	57	A. Terry, Bro	56	A. Terry, Bro	55

Shutouts		Saves		Games Finished		Batters Faced		Innings Pitched		Hits Allowed	
T. Mullane, Tol	7	O. Burns, Bal	1	P. Reccius, Lou	7	G. Hecker, Lou	2649	G. Hecker, Lou	670.2	G. Hecker, Lou	526
W. White, Cin	7	H. O'Day, Tol	1	B. Caruthers, STL	6	T. Mullane, Tol	2364	T. Mullane, Tol	567.0	F. Sullivan, Pit	496
G. Hecker, Lou	6	F. Mountain, Col	1	T. Brown, Col	4	L. McKeon, Ind	2185	L. McKeon, Ind	512.0	L. McKeon, Ind	488
3 tied with	5			T. O'Neill, STL	3	A. Terry, Bro	2046	J. Lynch, NY	496.0	A. Terry, Bro	487
				6 tied with	2	J. Lynch, NY	2002	A. Terry, Bro	485.0	T. Mullane, Tol	481

Home Runs Allowed		Walks		Walks/9 Innings		Strikeouts		Strikeouts/9 Innings		Strikeout/Walk Ratio	
L. McKeon, Ind	20	H. Henderson, Bal	116	G. Hecker, Lou	0.8	G. Hecker, Lou	385	H. Henderson, Bal	7.1	J. Lynch, NY	6.95
W. White, Cin	16	F. Sullivan, Pit	96	J. Lynch, NY	0.8	H. Henderson, Bal	346	D. Davis, STL	6.5	G. Hecker, Lou	6.88
F. Sullivan, Pit	15	L. McKeon, Ind	94	E. Dugan, Ric	0.8	T. Mullane, Tol	325	E. Morris, Col	6.3	E. Morris, Col	5.92
B. Barr, 2tm	11	T. Mullane, Tol	89	J. McGinnis, STL	0.9	T. Keefe, NY	317	B. Mathews, Phi	6.0	B. Mathews, Phi	5.84
3 tied with	10	B. Emslie, Bal	88	B. Mathews, Phi	1.0	L. McKeon, Ind	308	T. Keefe, NY	5.9	A. Atkinson, Phi	4.43

Earned Run Average		Component ERA		Hit Batsmen		Wild Pitches	Opponent Average		Opponent OBP	
G. Hecker, Lou	1.80	G. Hecker, Lou	1.43	W. White, Cin	35	Statistic unavailable	T. Keefe, NY	.203	G. Hecker, Lou	.226
D. Foutz, STL	2.18	E. Morris, Col	1.52	T. Mullane, Tol	32		G. Hecker, Lou	.204	E. Morris, Col	.234
E. Morris, Col	2.18	T. Keefe, NY	1.60	G. Shallix, Cin	26		E. Morris, Col	.204	J. Lynch, NY	.236
T. Keefe, NY	2.26	J. Lynch, NY	1.66	F. Sullivan, Pit	20		F. Mountain, Col	.209	T. Keefe, NY	.240
F. Mountain, Col	2.45	F. Mountain, Col	1.89	4 tied with	18		D. Foutz, STL	.212	D. Foutz, STL	.255

1884 American Association Miscellaneous

Managers			Awards		Postseason	
Baltimore	Billy Barnie	63-43	STATS Most Valuable Player	Guy Hecker, p, Lou	World Series	New York (AA) 0 vs. Prv (NL) 3
Brooklyn	George Taylor	40-64	STATS Cy Young	Guy Hecker, Lou		
Cincinnati	Will White	44-27	STATS Rookie of the Year	Dave Orr, 1b, NY		
	Pop Snyder	24-14	STATS Manager of the Year	Jim Mutrie, NY	**Outstanding Performances**	
Columbus	Gus Schmelz	69-39			**No-Hitters**	
Indianapolis	Jim Gifford	25-60			Al Atkinson, Phi	vs. Pit on May 24
	Bill Watkins	4-18	**STATS All-Star Team**		Ed Morris, Col	@ Pit on May 29
Louisville	Mike Walsh	68-40	C	Jim Keenan, Ind	.293	3	—	Frank Mountain, Col	@ WaD on June 5
New York	Jim Mutrie	75-32	1B	John Reilly, Cin	.339	11	—	Sam Kimber, Bro	vs. Tol on October 4
Philadelphia	Lon Knight	61-46	2B	Sam Barkley, Tol	.306	1	—		
Pittsburgh	Denny McKnight	4-8	3B	Pete Browning, Lou	.336	4	—		
	Bob Ferguson	11-31	SS	Frank Fennelly, 2tm	.311	4	—		
	Joe Battin	6-7	OF	Charley Jones, Cin	.314	7	—		
	George Creamer	0-8	OF	Fred Lewis, STL	.323	0	—		
	Horace Phillips	9-24	OF	Chief Roseman, NY	.298	4	—		
Richmond	Felix Moses	12-30							
St. Louis	Jimmy Williams	51-33	P	Guy Hecker, Lou	52-20	1.80	385 K		
	Charlie Comiskey	16-7	P	Tim Keefe, NY	37-17	2.26	317 K		
Toledo	Charlie Morton	46-58							
Washington	Holly Hollingshead	12-50							
	Bickerson	0-1							

1884 Union Association Standings

Team	Overall W	L	Pct	GB	DIF	Home Games W	L	R	OR	HR	OHR	Road Games W	L	R	OR	HR	OHR	Park Index Run	HR	Record by Month M/A	May	June	July	Aug	S/O
St. Louis	94	19	.832	—	183	50	6	461	179	10	4	44	13	426	250	22	5	96	53	6-0	18-1	14-3	15-5	18-2	23-8
Milwaukee	8	4	.667	35.5	0	8	4	53	34	0	1	0	0	0	0	0	0	—	—	—	—	—	—	—	8-4
Cincinnati	69	36	.657	21.0	10	35	17	382	239	18	12	34	19	325	241	8	5	112	235	5-2	14-7	5-7	10-10	11-7	24-3
Baltimore	58	47	.552	32.0	2	29	21	372	312	12	16	29	26	304	318	5	8	121	237	7-2	8-10	12-3	13-5	9-6	9-21
Boston	58	51	.532	34.0	1	34	23	346	260	7	5	24	28	290	297	12	12	94	46	6-2	10-7	6-8	10-7	13-7	13-20
Chicago	34	39	.466	40.0	0	20	14	177	159	2	2	14	25	183	252	8	9	89	27	2-3	11-9	8-9	8-11	5-7	—
Washington	47	65	.420	46.5	0	36	27	382	318	4	10	11	38	192	362	0	6	98	181	2-7	4-14	6-8	11-9	9-10	15-17
Pittsburgh	7	11	.389	39.5	0	1	4	22	29	0	1	6	7	56	42	0	0	135	—	—	—	—	—	1-4	6-7
Philadelphia	21	46	.313	50.0	0	13	21	223	249	4	1	8	25	192	296	3	6	94	54	2-6	4-16	4-12	9-10	2-2	—
St. Paul	2	6	.250	39.5	0	0	0	0	0	0	0	2	6	24	57	0	1	—	—	—	—	—	—	—	2-6
Altoona	6	19	.240	44.0	0	6	12	73	156	0	2	0	7	17	60	2	1	116	26	0-8	6-11	—	—	—	—
Kansas City	16	63	.203	61.0	0	11	23	150	205	3	6	5	40	159	414	3	8	82	108	—	—	3-8	1-20	3-18	9-17
Wilmington	2	16	.111	44.5	0	1	6	16	46	1	4	1	10	19	68	1	0	112	786	—	—	—	—	1-9	1-7

Clinch Date—St. Louis 9/11.

Team Batting

Team	G	AB	R	OR	H	2B	3B	HR	TB	RBI	TBB	IBB	SO	HBP	SH	SF	SB	CS	SB%	GDP	Avg	OBP	Slg
St. Louis	113	4285	887	429	1251	259	41	32	1688	—	181	—	542	—	—	—	—	—	—	—	.292	.321	.394
Cincinnati	105	3786	703	466	1027	118	63	26	1349	—	147	—	482	—	—	—	—	—	—	—	.271	.299	.356
Baltimore	106	3883	662	627	952	150	26	17	1205	—	144	—	652	—	—	—	—	—	—	—	.245	.272	.310
Boston	111	3940	636	558	928	168	32	19	1217	—	128	—	787	—	—	—	—	—	—	—	.236	.260	.309
Washington	114	3926	572	679	931	120	26	4	1115	—	118	—	558	—	—	—	—	—	—	—	.237	.259	.284
Philadelphia	67	2518	414	545	618	108	35	7	817	—	103	—	405	—	—	—	—	—	—	—	.245	.275	.324
Chicago	74	2564	360	411	601	99	19	10	768	—	100	—		—	—	—	—	—	—	—	.234	.263	.300
Kansas City	82	2802	311	618	557	104	15	6	709	—	123	—	529	—	—	—	—	—	—	—	.199	.232	.253
Altoona	25	899	90	216	223	30	6	2	271	—	22	—	130	—	—	—	—	—	—	—	.248	.266	.301
Pittsburgh	18	648	78	71	141	28	7	0	183	—	19	—		—	—	—	—	—	—	—	.218	.240	.282
Milwaukee	12	395	53	34	88	25	0	0	113	—	20	—	70	—	—	—	—	—	—	—	.223	.260	.286
Wilmington	18	521	35	114	91	8	8	2	121	—	22	—	123	—	—	—	—	—	—	—	.175	.208	.232
St. Paul	9	272	24	57	49	13	1	0	64	—	7	—	47	—	—	—	—	—	—	—	.180	.201	.235
UA Total	854	30439	4825	4825	7457	1230	279	125	9620	—	1134	—	4325	—	—	—	—	—	—	—	.245	.272	.316
UA Avg Team	66	2341	371	371	574	95	21	10	740	—	87	—	333	—	—	—	—	—	—	—	.245	.272	.316

Team Pitching

Team	G	CG	ShO	Rel	Sv	IP	H	R	ER	HR	SH	SF	HB	TBB	IBB	SO	WP	Bk	H/9	SO/9	BB/9	OAvg	OOBP	ERA
St. Louis	113	104	8	9	6	993.0	838	429	216	9	—	—	—	110	—	550	—	—	7.6	5.0	1.0	.214	.235	1.96
Milwaukee	12	12	3	0	0	104.0	49	34	26	1	—	—	—	13	—	139	—	—	4.2	12.0	1.1	.132	.161	2.25
Cincinnati	105	95	11	8	1	914.1	831	466	242	17	—	—	—	90	—	503	—	—	8.2	5.0	0.9	.226	.245	2.38
Pittsburgh	18	18	1	0	0	157.0	139	71	46	1	—	—	—	26	—	119	—	—	8.0	6.8	1.5	.222	.253	2.64
Boston	111	100	5	9	1	953.1	885	558	286	17	—	—	—	110	—	753	—	—	8.4	7.1	1.0	.230	.252	2.70
Chicago	74	68	5	6	0	646.2	604	411	197	11	—	—	—	111	—	560	—	—	8.4	7.8	1.5	.231	.263	2.74
Baltimore	106	92	4	14	0	946.2	1002	627	317	24	—	—	—	177	—	628	—	—	9.5	6.0	1.7	.254	.286	3.01
Wilmington	18	15	0	2	0	142.0	165	114	48	4	—	—	—	18	—	113	—	—	10.5	7.2	1.1	.272	.293	3.04
St. Paul	9	7	1	2	0	71.0	72	57	25	1	—	—	—	27	—	44	—	—	9.1	5.6	3.4	.247	.310	3.17
Washington	114	94	5	20	0	953.2	992	679	364	16	—	—	—	168	—	684	—	—	9.4	6.5	1.6	.251	.282	3.44
Kansas City	82	70	0	12	0	702.2	862	618	317	14	—	—	—	127	—	334	—	—	11.0	4.3	1.6	.283	.312	4.06
Philadelphia	67	64	1	3	0	593.1	726	545	304	7	—	—	—	105	—	310	—	—	11.0	4.7	1.6	.283	.311	4.61
Altoona	25	20	0	5	0	219.2	292	216	114	3	—	—	—	52	—	93	—	—	12.0	3.8	2.1	.300	.336	4.67
UA Total	854	759	44	90	8	7397.1	7457	4825	2502	125	—	—	—	1134	—	4830	—	—	9.1	5.9	1.4	.245	.272	3.04
UA Avg Team	66	58	3	7	1	569.1	574	371	192	10	—	—	—	87	—	372	—	—	9.1	5.9	1.4	.245	.272	3.04

Team Fielding

Team	G	PO	A	E	TC	DP	PB	Pct
Pittsburgh	18	470	216	66	752	—	13	.912
Milwaukee	12	312	125	53	490	4	25	.892
St. Louis	113	2973	1418	554	4945	79	107	.888
Cincinnati	105	2742	1241	532	4515	45	137	.882
Chicago	74	1938	823	393	3154	—	101	.875
Baltimore	106	2838	1383	616	4837	53	156	.873
St. Paul	9	211	109	47	367	6	5	.872
Washington	114	2857	1278	625	4760	55	176	.869
Boston	111	2851	1312	633	4796	39	170	.868
Altoona	25	658	316	156	1130	4	49	.862
Kansas City	82	2107	1102	520	3729	51	125	.861
Wilmington	18	424	213	104	741	10	43	.860
Philadelphia	67	1778	880	501	3159	36	188	.841
UA Total	854	22159	10416	4800	37375	382	1295	.872

Team vs. Team Records

	Alt	Bal	Bos	C/P	Cin	KC	Mil	Phi	STL	STP	Was	Wil	Won
Alt	—	1	1	0	0	0	0	1	0	0	3	0	**6**
Bal	3	—	10	6	3	10	1	10	2	0	12	1	**58**
Bos	1	6	—	4	5	8	2	8	8	0	12	4	**58**
Chi/Pit	0	5	8	—	7	12	0	3	2	0	4	0	**41**
Cin	3	11	11	8	—	10	0	8	2	3	10	3	**69**
KC	0	2	4	4	0	—	0	0	1	1	4	0	**16**
Mil	0	3	2	0	0	0	—	0	0	0	3	0	**8**
Phi	3	2	3	6	0	4	0	—	0	0	3	0	**21**
STL	8	13	13	14	14	10	0	8	—	2	13	4	**94**
STP	0	0	0	0	0	1	0	0	1	—	0	0	**2**
Was	1	4	4	8	6	8	1	8	3	0	—	4	**47**
Wil	0	0	0	0	1	0	0	0	0	0	1	—	**2**
Lost	19	47	51	50	36	63	4	46	19	6	65	16	

Seasons: Standings, Leaders

1884 Union Association Batting Leaders

Games		At-Bats		Runs		Hits		Doubles		Triples	
H. Moore, Was	111	D. Rowe, STL	485	F. Dunlap, STL	160	F. Dunlap, STL	185	O. Shaffer, STL	40	D. Burns, Cin	12
J. McCormick, 2tm	109	E. Seery, 2tm	467	O. Shaffer, STL	130	O. Shaffer, STL	168	F. Dunlap, STL	39	D. Rowe, STL	11
T. Evers, Was	109	O. Shaffer, STL	467	E. Seery, 2tm	115	H. Moore, Was	155	D. Rowe, STL	32	O. Shaffer, STL	10
D. Rowe, STL	109	H. Moore, Was	461	Y. Robinson, Bal	101	E. Seery, 2tm	146	T. O'Brien, Bos	31	5 tied with	8
4 tied with	106	J. McCormick, 2tm	452	D. Rowe, STL	95	D. Rowe, STL	142	J. Gleason, STL	30		

Home Runs		Total Bases		Runs Batted In		Walks		Intentional Walks		Strikeouts	
F. Dunlap, STL	13	F. Dunlap, STL	279	Statistic unavailable		Y. Robinson, Bal	37	Statistic unavailable		Statistic unavailable	
E. Crane, Bos	12	O. Shaffer, STL	234			O. Shaffer, STL	30				
C. Levis, 3tm	6	D. Rowe, STL	208			F. Dunlap, STL	29				
8 tied with	4	E. Crane, Bos	193			B. Harbidge, Cin	25				
		E. Seery, 2tm	192			J. Gleason, STL	23				

Hit By Pitch	Sac Hits	Sac Flies	Stolen Bases	Caught Stealing	GDP
Statistic unavailable	Statistic unavailable	Statistic unavailable	Statistic unavailable	Statistic unavailable	Statistic unavailable

Runs Created		Runs Created/27 Outs		Batting Average		On-Base Percentage		Slugging Percentage		OBP+Slugging	
F. Dunlap, STL	160	F. Dunlap, STL	16.46	F. Dunlap, STL	.412	F. Dunlap, STL	.448	F. Dunlap, STL	.621	F. Dunlap, STL	1.069
O. Shaffer, STL	133	O. Shaffer, STL	12.08	O. Shaffer, STL	.360	O. Shaffer, STL	.398	O. Shaffer, STL	.501	O. Shaffer, STL	.899
E. Seery, 2tm	115	H. Moore, Was	10.12	H. Moore, Was	.336	H. Moore, Was	.363	D. Burns, Cin	.457	J. Gleason, STL	.802
H. Moore, Was	114	J. Gleason, STL	9.77	J. Gleason, STL	.324	J. Gleason, STL	.361	E. Crane, Bos	.451	H. Moore, Was	.777
E. Crane, Bos	104	E. Seery, 2tm	9.73	E. Seery, 2tm	.313	E. Seery, 2tm	.342	J. Gleason, STL	.441	D. Burns, Cin	.773

1884 Union Association Pitching Leaders

Wins		Losses		Winning Percentage		Games		Games Started		Complete Games	
B. Sweeney, Bal	40	J. Bakely, 3tm	30	J. McCormick, Cin	.875	B. Sweeney, Bal	62	B. Sweeney, Bal	60	B. Sweeney, Bal	58
O. Daily, 3tm	28	O. Daily, 3tm	28	B. Taylor, STL	.862	O. Daily, 3tm	58	O. Daily, 3tm	58	O. Daily, 3tm	56
B. Taylor, STL	25	B. Sweeney, Bal	21	H. Boyle, STL	.833	B. Wise, Was	50	J. Bakely, 3tm	45	J. Bakely, 3tm	43
G. Bradley, Cin	25	A. Voss, 2tm	20	C. Sweeney, STL	.774	J. Bakely, 3tm	46	B. Wise, Was	41	G. Bradley, Cin	36
C. Sweeney, STL	24	B. Wise, Was	18	B. Sweeney, Bal	.656	G. Bradley, Cin	41	D. Burns, Cin	40	D. Shaw, Bos	35

Shutouts		Saves		Games Finished		Batters Faced		Innings Pitched		Hits Allowed	
J. McCormick, Cin	7	B. Taylor, STL	4	A. Voss, 2tm	8	Statistic unavailable		B. Sweeney, Bal	538.0	B. Sweeney, Bal	522
D. Shaw, Bos	5	H. Boyle, STL	1	Y. Robinson, Bal	8			O. Daily, 3tm	500.2	O. Daily, 3tm	446
O. Daily, 3tm	5	L. Sylvester, Cin	1	B. Wise, Was	8			J. Bakely, 3tm	394.2	J. Bakely, 3tm	443
B. Sweeney, Bal	4	F. Dunlap, STL	1	L. Sylvester, Cin	5			B. Wise, Was	364.1	B. Wise, Was	383
B. Wise, Was	4	L. Brown, Bos	1	J. Murphy, 2tm	5			G. Bradley, Cin	342.0	G. Bradley, Cin	350

Home Runs Allowed		Walks		Walks/9 Innings		Strikeouts		Strikeouts/9 Innings		Strikeout/Walk Ratio	
B. Sweeney, Bal	13	J. Bakely, 3tm	81	C. Sweeney, STL	0.4	O. Daily, 3tm	483	D. Shaw, Bos	8.8	C. Sweeney, STL	14.77
O. Daily, 3tm	11	B. Sweeney, Bal	74	J. McCormick, Cin	0.6	B. Sweeney, Bal	374	O. Daily, 3tm	8.7	J. McCormick, Cin	11.50
W. Burke, Bos	10	O. Daily, 3tm	72	H. Boyle, STL	0.6	D. Shaw, Bos	309	C. Geggus, Was	7.9	T. Bond, Bos	9.14
D. Burns, Cin	7	B. Wise, Was	60	G. Bradley, Cin	0.6	B. Wise, Was	268	W. Burke, Bos	7.1	H. Boyle, STL	8.80
G. Bradley, Cin	7	J. Brown, 3tm	50	J. Murphy, 2tm	0.6	W. Burke, Bos	255	J. McCormick, Cin	6.9	D. Shaw, Bos	8.35

Earned Run Average		Component ERA		Hit Batsmen		Wild Pitches		Opponent Average		Opponent OBP	
J. McCormick, Cin	1.54	J. McCormick, Cin	1.25	Statistic unavailable		Statistic unavailable		D. Shaw, Bos	.188	J. McCormick, Cin	.202
B. Taylor, STL	1.68	D. Shaw, Bos	1.31					J. McCormick, Cin	.188	C. Sweeney, STL	.207
H. Boyle, STL	1.74	C. Sweeney, STL	1.32					C. Sweeney, STL	.197	D. Shaw, Bos	.212
D. Shaw, Bos	1.77	H. Boyle, STL	1.47					H. Boyle, STL	.202	H. Boyle, STL	.215
C. Sweeney, STL	1.83	P. Werden, STL	1.65					P. Werden, STL	.205	P. Werden, STL	.235

1884 Union Association Miscellaneous

Managers		
Altoona	Ed Curtis	6-19
Baltimore	Bill Henderson	58-47
Boston	Tim Murnane	58-51
Chicago	Ed Hengle	34-39
Cincinnati	Dan O'Leary	20-15
	Sam Crane	49-21
Kansas City	Harry Wheeler	0-4
	Matt Porter	3-13
	Ted Sullivan	13-46
Milwaukee	Tom Loftus	8-4
Philadelphia	Fergy Malone	21-46
Pittsburgh	Joe Ellick	6-6
	Joe Battin	1-5
St. Louis	Ted Sullivan	28-3
	Fred Dunlap	66-16
St. Paul	Andrew Thompson	2-6
Washington	Mike Scanlon	47-65
Wilmington	Joe Simmons	2-16

Awards

STATS Most Valuable Player	Fred Dunlap, 2b, STL	
STATS Cy Young	Jim McCormick, Cin	
STATS Rookie of the Year	Harry Moore, of, Was	
STATS Manager of the Year	Fred Dunlap, STL	

STATS All-Star Team

C	Eddie Fusselback, Bal	.284	1	—
1B	Jumbo Schoeneck, 3tm	.308	2	—
2B	Fred Dunlap, STL	.412	13	—
3B	Jack Gleason, STL	.324	4	—
SS	Jack Glasscock, Cin	.419	2	—
OF	Buster Hoover, Phi	.364	0	—
OF	Harry Moore, Was	.336	1	—
OF	Orator Shaffer, STL	.360	2	—
P	Jim McCormick, Cin	21-3	1.54	161 K
P	Billy Taylor, STL	25-4	1.68	154 K

Postseason

None

Outstanding Performances

No-Hitters

Dick Burns, Cin	@ KC on August 26
Ed Cushman, Mil	vs. Was on September 28

1885 National League Standings

Team	W	L	Pct	GB	DIF	W	L	R	OR	HR	OHR	W	L	R	OR	HR	OHR	Run	HR	M/A	May	June	July	Aug	S/O
			Overall					Home Games						Road Games				Park Index				Record by Month			
Chicago	87	25	.777	—	129	43	14	458	269	47	27	44	11	377	200	7	10	122	420	0-1	14-5	21-2	18-6	15-4	19-7
New York	85	27	.759	2.0	40	45	10	362	178	7	6	40	17	329	192	9	5	107	96	—	17-4	15-5	18-7	18-3	17-8
Philadelphia	56	54	.509	30.0	0	29	26	277	244	7	7	27	28	236	267	13	11	104	58	—	14-8	7-14	9-14	11-11	15-7
Providence	53	57	.482	33.0	2	30	24	203	218	3	1	23	33	239	313	3	17	79	21	—	13-7	14-6	12-11	7-13	7-20
Boston	46	66	.411	41.0	0	21	35	245	283	7	5	25	31	283	306	15	21	90	33	—	8-12	7-14	8-17	10-10	13-13
Detroit	41	67	.380	44.0	7	29	23	294	228	13	8	12	44	220	355	12	10	98	103	—	4-16	4-17	15-9	3-16	15-9
Buffalo	38	74	.339	49.0	0	19	38	265	406	13	13	19	36	229	355	10	18	111	90	—	4-15	8-14	8-17	13-7	5-21
St. Louis	36	72	.333	49.0	1	23	33	215	262	6	4	13	39	175	332	2	11	87	71	1-0	6-13	9-13	8-15	3-16	9-15

Clinch Date—Chicago 10/06.

Team Batting

Team	G	AB	R	OH	H	2B	3B	HR	TB	RBI	TBB	IBB	SO	HBP	SH	SF	SB	CS	SB%	GDP	Avg	OBP	Slg
Chicago	113	4093	834	470	1079	184	75	54	1575	604	340	—	429	—	—	—	—	—	—	—	.264	.320	.385
New York	112	4029	691	370	1085	150	82	16	1447	464	221	—	312	—	—	—	—	—	—	—	.269	.307	.359
Boston	113	3950	528	589	915	144	53	22	1231	375	190	—	522	—	—	—	—	—	—	—	.232	.267	.312
Detroit	108	3773	514	582	917	149	66	25	1273	387	216	—	451	—	—	—	—	—	—	—	.243	.284	.337
Philadelphia	111	3893	513	511	891	156	35	20	1177	326	220	—	401	—	—	—	—	—	—	—	.229	.270	.302
Buffalo	112	3900	495	761	980	149	50	23	1298	365	179	—	380	—	—	—	—	—	—	—	.251	.284	.333
Providence	110	3727	442	531	820	114	30	6	1012	292	265	—	430	—	—	—	—	—	—	—	.220	.272	.272
St. Louis	111	3758	390	593	829	121	21	8	1016	278	214	—	412	—	—	—	—	—	—	—	.221	.263	.270
NL Total	890	31123	4407	4407	7516	1167	412	174	10029	3091	1845	—	3337	—	—	—	—	—	—	—	.241	.284	.322
NL Avg Team	111	3890	551	551	940	146	52	22	1254	386	231	—	417	—	—	—	—	—	—	—	.241	.284	.322

Team Pitching

Team	G	CG	ShO	Rel	Sv	IP	H	R	ER	HR	SH	SF	HB	TBB	IBB	SO	WP	Bk	H/9	SO/9	BB/9	OAvg	OOBP	ERA
New York	112	109	16	3	1	994.0	758	370	190	11	—	—	—	265	—	516	77	1	6.9	4.7	2.4	.205	.258	1.72
Chicago	113	108	14	5	4	1015.2	868	470	252	37	—	—	—	202	—	458	29	0	7.7	4.1	1.8	.221	.259	2.23
Philadelphia	111	108	10	3	0	976.0	860	511	259	18	—	—	—	218	—	378	63	3	7.9	3.5	2.0	.224	.266	2.39
Providence	110	108	8	3	0	960.2	912	531	289	18	—	—	—	235	—	371	85	0	8.5	3.5	2.2	.235	.278	2.71
Detroit	108	105	6	3	1	954.1	966	582	305	18	—	—	—	224	—	475	41	0	9.1	4.5	2.1	.249	.290	2.88
Boston	113	111	10	2	0	981.0	1045	589	330	26	—	—	—	188	—	480	71	2	9.6	4.4	1.7	.261	.294	3.03
St. Louis	111	107	4	4	0	965.1	935	593	361	15	—	—	—	278	—	337	71	1	8.7	3.1	2.6	.245	.296	3.37
Buffalo	112	107	4	5	1	956.0	1175	761	456	31	—	—	—	234	—	320	99	0	11.1	3.0	2.2	.289	.328	4.29
NL Total	890	863	72	28	7	7803.0	7519	4407	2442	174	—	—	—	1844	—	3335	536	7	8.7	3.8	2.1	.241	.284	2.82
NL Avg Team	111	108	9	4	1	975.0	940	551	305	22	—	—	—	231	—	417	67	1	8.7	3.8	2.1	.241	.284	2.82

Team Fielding

Team	G	PO	A	E	TC	DP	PB	Pct
New York	112	3001	1359	331	4691	85	91	.929
St. Louis	111	2887	1452	398	4737	67	107	.916
Philadelphia	111	2908	1368	447	4723	66	104	.905
Chicago	113	3033	1606	496	5135	80	104	.903
Providence	110	2875	1411	459	4745	70	80	.903
Detroit	108	2881	1354	463	4698	61	74	.901
Boston	113	2938	1431	478	4847	79	113	.901
Buffalo	112	2869	1364	464	4697	65	97	.901
NL Total	890	23392	11345	3536	38273	573	770	.908

Team vs. Team Records

	Bos	Buf	ChN	Det	NYG	Phi	Prv	StL	Won
Bos	—	10	2	7	3	7	9	8	46
Buf	6	—	0	11	1	5	3	12	38
ChN	14	16	—	15	6	11	11	14	87
Det	9	5	1	—	4	7	6	9	41
NYG	13	15	10	12	—	11	12	12	85
Phi	9	11	5	9	5	—	8	9	56
Prv	7	13	5	9	4	7	—	8	53
StL	8	4	2	4	4	6	8	—	36
Lost	66	74	25	67	27	54	57	72	

1885 National League Batting Leaders

Games			At-Bats			Runs			Hits			Doubles			Triples		
N. Williamson, ChN	113		A. Dalrymple, ChN	492		K. Kelly, ChN	124		R. Connor, NYG	169		C. Anson, ChN	35		J. O'Rourke, NYG	16
A. Dalrymple, ChN	113		J. O'Rourke, NYG	477		J. O'Rourke, NYG	119		D. Brouthers, Buf	146		D. Brouthers, Buf	32		R. Connor, NYG	15
5 tied with	112		F. Pfeffer, ChN	469		G. Gore, ChN	115		C. Anson, ChN	144		J. Rowe, Buf	28		G. Gore, ChN	13
			C. Anson, ChN	464		A. Dalrymple, ChN	109		J. O'Rourke, NYG	143		A. Dalrymple, ChN	27		C. Bennett, Det	13
			E. Sutton, Bos	457		R. Connor, NYG	102		E. Sutton, Bos	143		J. Mulvey, Phi	25		2 tied with	12

Home Runs			Total Bases			Runs Batted In			Walks			Intentional Walks			Strikeouts		
A. Dalrymple, ChN	11		R. Connor, NYG	225		C. Anson, ChN	108		N. Williamson, ChN	75		Statistic unavailable			C. Bastian, Phi	82
K. Kelly, ChN	9		D. Brouthers, Buf	221		K. Kelly, ChN	75		C. Anson, ChN	68					J. Morrill, Bos	78
4 tied with	7		A. Dalrymple, ChN	219		F. Pfeffer, ChN	73		J. Morrill, Bos	64					S. Wise, Bos	61
			C. Anson, ChN	214		T. Burns, ChN	71		R. Connor, NYG	51					C. Bassett, Prv	60
			J. O'Rourke, NYG	211		2 tied with	65		2 tied with	47					N. Williamson, ChN	60

Hit By Pitch	Sac Hits	Sac Flies	Stolen Bases	Caught Stealing	GDP
Statistic unavailable	Statistic unavailable	Statistic unavailable	Statistic unavailable	Statistic unavailable	Statistic unavailable

Runs Created			Runs Created/27 Outs			Batting Average			On-Base Percentage			Slugging Percentage			OBP+Slugging		
R. Connor, NYG	129		R. Connor, NYG	11.96		R. Connor, NYG	.371		R. Connor, NYG	.435		D. Brouthers, Buf	.543		D. Brouthers, Buf	.951
G. Gore, ChN	124		G. Gore, ChN	10.85		D. Brouthers, Buf	.359		D. Brouthers, Buf	.408		R. Connor, NYG	.495		R. Connor, NYG	.929
C. Anson, ChN	118		D. Brouthers, Buf	9.96		M. Dorgan, NYG	.326		G. Gore, ChN	.405		B. Ewing, NYG	.471		G. Gore, ChN	.858
A. Dalrymple, ChN	117		C. Anson, ChN	9.78		H. Richardson, Buf	.319		N. Hanlon, Det	.372		C. Anson, ChN	.461		C. Anson, ChN	.819
2 tied with	107		K. Kelly, ChN	9.10		G. Gore, ChN	.313		C. Anson, ChN	.357		H. Richardson, Buf	.458		C. Bennett, Det	.812

1885 National League Pitching Leaders

Wins			Losses			Winning Percentage			Games			Games Started			Complete Games		
J. Clarkson, ChN	53		J. Whitney, Bos	32		M. Welch, NYG	.800		J. Clarkson, ChN	70		J. Clarkson, ChN	70		J. Clarkson, ChN	68
M. Welch, NYG	44		C. Buffinton, Bos	27		J. Clarkson, ChN	.768		M. Welch, NYG	56		M. Welch, NYG	55		M. Welch, NYG	55
T. Keefe, NYG	32		D. Shaw, Prv	26		J. McCormick, 2tm	.750		C. Buffinton, Bos	51		E. Daily, Phi	50		J. Whitney, Bos	50
O. H. Radbourn, Prv	28		G. Getzien, Det	25		T. Keefe, NYG	.711		J. Whitney, Bos	51		C. Buffinton, Bos	50		3 tied with	49
2 tied with	26		2 tied with	24		O. H. Radbourn, Prv	.571		E. Daily, Phi	50		J. Whitney, Bos	50			

Shutouts			Saves			Games Finished			Batters Faced			Innings Pitched			Hits Allowed		
J. Clarkson, ChN	10		F. Pfeffer, ChN	2		H. Boyle, StL	3		J. Clarkson, ChN	2487		J. Clarkson, ChN	623.0		J. Whitney, Bos	503
T. Keefe, NYG	7		N. Williamson, ChN	2		C. Ferguson, Phi	3		M. Welch, NYG	1963		M. Welch, NYG	492.0		J. Clarkson, ChN	497
M. Welch, NYG	7		L. Baldwin, Det	1		F. Pfeffer, ChN	3		J. Whitney, Bos	1887		O. H. Radbourn, Prv	445.2		C. Buffinton, Bos	425
D. Shaw, Prv	6		M. Welch, NYG	1		P. Wood, Buf	2		O. H. Radbourn, Prv	1841		J. Whitney, Bos	441.1		O. H. Radbourn, Prv	423
C. Buffinton, Bos	6		P. Galvin, Buf	1		N. Williamson, ChN	2		C. Buffinton, Bos	1838		E. Daily, Phi	440.0		M. Welch, NYG	372

Home Runs Allowed			Walks			Walks/9 Innings			Strikeouts			Strikeouts/9 Innings			Strikeout/Walk Ratio		
J. Clarkson, ChN	21		M. Welch, NYG	131		J. Whitney, Bos	0.8		J. Clarkson, ChN	308		L. Baldwin, Det	6.8		J. Whitney, Bos	5.41
J. Whitney, Bos	14		C. Buffinton, Bos	112		P. Galvin, Buf	1.2		M. Welch, NYG	258		T. Keefe, NYG	5.2		L. Baldwin, Det	4.82
E. Daily, Phi	12		T. Keefe, NYG	103		J. Clarkson, ChN	1.4		C. Buffinton, Bos	242		C. Buffinton, Bos	5.0		J. Clarkson, ChN	3.18
P. Conway, Buf	10		H. Boyle, StL	100		L. Baldwin, Det	1.4		T. Keefe, NYG	230		M. Welch, NYG	4.7		P. Galvin, Buf	2.51
C. Buffinton, Bos	10		D. Shaw, Prv	99		C. Sweeney, StL	1.6		J. Whitney, Bos	200		J. Clarkson, ChN	4.4		C. Ferguson, Phi	2.43

Earned Run Average			Component ERA			Hit Batsmen			Wild Pitches			Opponent Average			Opponent OBP		
T. Keefe, NYG	1.58		L. Baldwin, Det	1.47		Statistic unavailable			E. Daily, Phi	40		L. Baldwin, Det	.197		L. Baldwin, Det	.228
M. Welch, NYG	1.66		J. Clarkson, ChN	1.69					M. Welch, NYG	39		T. Keefe, NYG	.201		J. Clarkson, ChN	.239
J. Clarkson, ChN	1.85		T. Keefe, NYG	1.71					B. Serad, Buf	38		M. Welch, NYG	.203		T. Keefe, NYG	.254
L. Baldwin, Det	1.86		M. Welch, NYG	1.73					T. Keefe, NYG	35		J. Clarkson, ChN	.208		D. Shaw, Prv	.254
O. H. Radbourn, Prv	2.20		C. Ferguson, Phi	1.93					O. H. Radbourn, Prv	34		D. Shaw, Prv	.209		E. Daily, Phi	.256

1885 National League Miscellaneous

Managers		
Boston	John Morrill	46-66
Buffalo	Pud Galvin	7-17
	Jack Chapman	31-57
Chicago	Cap Anson	87-25
Detroit	Charlie Morton	7-31
	Bill Watkins	34-36
New York	Jim Mutrie	85-27
Philadelphia	Harry Wright	56-54
Providence	Frank Bancroft	53-57
St. Louis	Fred Dunlap	21-29
	Alex McKinnon	6-32
	Fred Dunlap	9-11

Awards	
STATS Most Valuable Player	John Clarkson, p, ChN
STATS Cy Young	John Clarkson, ChN
STATS Rookie of the Year	Ed Daily, p, Phi
STATS Manager of the Year	Cap Anson, ChN

STATS All-Star Team

C	Buck Ewing, NYG	.304	6	63
1B	Roger Connor, NYG	.371	1	65
2B	Hardy Richardson, Buf	.319	6	44
3B	Ezra Sutton, Bos	.313	4	47
SS	Sam Wise, Bos	.283	4	46
OF	Abner Dalrymple, ChN	.274	11	61
OF	George Gore, ChN	.313	5	57
OF	King Kelly, ChN	.288	9	75
P	John Clarkson, ChN	53-16	1.85	308 K
P	Mickey Welch, NYG	44-11	1.66	258 K

Postseason	
World Series	Chicago (NL) 3 vs. StL (AA) 3 (1 tie)

Outstanding Performances

No-Hitters
John Clarkson, ChN @ Prv on July 27
Charlie Ferguson, Phi vs. Prv on August 29
Cycles
George Wood, Det on June 13
Mox McQuery, Det on September 28

1885 American Association Standings

Team	Overall W	L	Pct	GB	DIF	Home Games W	L	R	OR	HR	OHR	Road Games W	L	R	OR	HR	OHR	Park Index Run	HR	M/A	Record by Month May	June	July	Aug	S/O
St. Louis	79	33	.705	—	153	44	11	319	160	6	5	35	22	358	301	11	7	75	63	6-3	16-2	13-10	16-5	13-8	15-5
Cincinnati	63	49	.563	16.0	9	35	21	358	269	17	17	28	28	284	307	9	7	106	213	5-4	14-8	10-11	12-9	12-8	10-9
Pittsburgh	56	55	.505	22.5	1	37	20	342	242	3	3	19	35	206	295	2	11	110	44	4-5	15-7	10-11	14-6	8-11	5-15
Philadelphia	55	57	.491	24.0	2	33	23	449	330	18	9	22	34	315	362	12	9	115	193	5-4	5-16	14-7	9-13	9-9	13-8
Louisville	53	59	.473	26.0	0	37	19	334	259	16	4	16	40	228	339	3	9	105	167	3-6	13-8	9-12	16-6	7-13	5-14
Brooklyn	53	59	.473	26.0	2	36	22	386	308	9	14	17	37	238	342	5	13	111	119	5-3	6-14	10-11	6-15	14-5	12-11
New York	44	64	.407	33.0	0	28	24	262	212	10	5	16	40	265	476	11	31	69	38	3-6	6-15	8-12	5-15	7-9	15-7
Baltimore	41	68	.376	36.5	7	29	25	360	296	11	2	12	43	182	388	6	10	117	83	4-4	7-12	11-11	7-16	5-12	7-13

Clinch Date—St. Louis 9/12.

Team Batting

Team	G	AB	R	OR	H	2B	3B	HR	TB	RBI	TBB	IBB	SO	HBP	SH	SF	SB	CS	SB%	GDP	Avg	OBP	Slg
Philadelphia	113	4142	764	691	1099	169	76	30	1510	536	223	—	410	45	—	—	—	—	—	—	.265	.310	.365
St. Louis	112	3972	677	461	979	132	57	17	1276	449	234	—	282	49	—	—	—	—	—	—	.246	.297	.321
Cincinnati	112	4050	642	575	1046	108	77	26	1386	451	153	—	420	51	—	—	—	—	—	—	.258	.294	.342
Brooklyn	112	3943	624	650	966	121	65	14	1259	431	238	—	324	42	—	—	—	—	—	—	.245	.295	.319
Louisville	112	3969	564	598	986	126	83	19	1335	416	152	—	448	25	—	—	—	—	—	—	.248	.281	.336
Pittsburgh	111	3975	547	539	955	123	79	5	1251	371	189	—	537	44	—	—	—	—	—	—	.240	.282	.315
Baltimore	110	3820	541	683	837	124	59	17	1130	380	279	—	529	42	—	—	—	—	—	—	.219	.280	.296
New York	108	3731	526	688	921	123	57	21	1221	363	217	—	428	35	—	—	—	—	—	—	.247	.295	.327
AA Total	890	31602	4885	4885	7789	1026	553	149	10368	3397	1685	—	3378	333	—	—	—	—	—	—	.246	.292	.328
AA Avg Team	111	3950	611	611	974	128	69	19	1296	425	211	—	422	42	—	—	—	—	—	—	.246	.292	.328

Team Pitching

Team	G	CG	ShO	Rel	Sv	IP	H	R	ER	HR	SH	SF	HB	TBB	IBB	SO	WP	Bk	H/9	SO/9	BB/9	OAvg	OOBP	ERA
St. Louis	112	111	11	1	0	1002.0	879	461	272	12	—	—	43	168	—	378	54	—	7.9	3.4	1.5	.228	.268	2.44
Louisville	112	109	3	4	1	1002.0	927	598	298	13	—	—	40	217	—	462	65	—	8.3	4.1	1.9	.232	.278	2.68
Pittsburgh	111	104	8	7	0	1011.0	918	539	328	14	—	—	36	201	—	454	59	—	8.2	4.0	1.8	.232	.275	2.92
Philadelphia	113	105	5	8	0	1003.1	1038	691	360	11	—	—	45	212	—	506	95	—	9.3	4.5	1.9	.254	.298	3.23
Cincinnati	112	102	7	10	1	999.1	998	575	362	24	—	—	72	250	—	330	76	—	9.0	3.0	2.3	.253	.309	3.26
Brooklyn	112	110	3	2	1	991.2	955	650	381	27	—	—	28	211	—	436	80	—	8.7	4.0	1.9	.240	.283	3.46
Baltimore	110	103	2	7	4	971.0	1059	683	421	12	—	—	48	222	—	395	115	—	9.8	3.7	2.1	.270	.317	3.90
New York	108	103	2	6	0	937.0	1015	688	432	36	—	—	21	204	—	408	92	—	9.7	3.9	2.0	.262	.303	4.15
AA Total	890	847	41	45	7	7917.1	7789	4885	2854	149	—	—	333	1685	—	3369	636	—	8.9	3.8	1.9	.246	.292	3.24
AA Avg Team	111	106	5	6	1	989.1	974	611	357	19	—	—	42	211	—	421	80	—	8.9	3.8	1.9	.246	.292	3.24

Team Fielding

Team	G	PO	A	E	TC	DP	PB	Pct
St. Louis	112	3002	1384	381	4767	64	123	.920
Pittsburgh	111	3026	1370	422	4818	77	141	.912
Cincinnati	112	2997	1325	423	4745	86	99	.911
Brooklyn	112	2971	1416	434	4821	56	132	.910
Baltimore	110	2911	1298	418	4627	71	159	.910
Louisville	112	3003	1371	460	4834	75	179	.905
Philadelphia	113	3008	1408	483	4899	79	144	.901
New York	108	2805	1304	452	4561	62	99	.901
AA Total	890	23723	10876	3473	38072	570	1076	.909

Team vs. Team Records

	Bal	Bro	Cin	Lou	NY	Phi	Pit	STL	Won
Bal	—	7	6	7	7	6	6	2	41
Bro	9	—	5	10	8	11	6	4	53
Cin	10	11	—	8	10	9	9	6	63
Lou	9	6	8	—	9	8	6	7	53
NY	6	8	6	7	—	5	8	4	44
Phi	10	5	7	8	11	—	10	4	55
Pit	10	10	7	10	7	6	—	6	56
STL	14	12	10	9	12	12	10	—	79
Lost	68	59	49	59	64	57	55	33	

1885 American Association Batting Leaders

Games		At-Bats		Runs		Hits		Doubles		Triples	
13 tied with	112	C. Jones, Cin	487	H. Stovey, Phi	130	P. Browning, Lou	174	H. Larkin, Phi	37	D. Orr, NY	21
		H. Stovey, Phi	486	H. Larkin, Phi	114	C. Jones, Cin	157	P. Browning, Lou	34	B. Kuehne, Pit	19
		A. Latham, STL	485	C. Jones, Cin	108	H. Stovey, Phi	153	D. Orr, NY	29	F. Fennelly, Cin	17
		C. Wolf, Lou	483	P. Browning, Lou	98	D. Orr, NY	152	H. Stovey, Phi	27	C. Wolf, Lou	17
		J. Reilly, Cin	482	C. Nelson, NY	98	H. Larkin, Phi	149	2 tied with	23	C. Jones, Cin	17

Home Runs		Total Bases		Runs Batted In		Walks		Intentional Walks		Strikeouts	
H. Stovey, Phi	13	P. Browning, Lou	255	F. Fennelly, Cin	89	C. Nelson, NY	61	Statistic unavailable		Statistic unavailable	
F. Fennelly, Cin	10	D. Orr, NY	241	H. Larkin, Phi	88	J. Macullar, Bal	49				
P. Browning, Lou	9	H. Larkin, Phi	238	D. Orr, NY	77	P. Hotaling, Bro	49				
H. Larkin, Phi	8	H. Stovey, Phi	237	H. Stovey, Phi	75	H. Stovey, Phi	39				
D. Orr, NY	6	C. Jones, Cin	225	P. Browning, Lou	73	2 tied with	38				

Hit By Pitch		Sac Hits		Sac Flies		Stolen Bases		Caught Stealing		GDP	
B. Gleason, STL	15	Statistic unavailable		Statistic unavailable		Statistic unavailable		Statistic unavailable		Statistic unavailable	
B. Phillips, Bro	11										
C. Roseman, NY	10										
C. Jones, Cin	9										
2 tied with	8										

Runs Created		Runs Created/27 Outs		Batting Average		On-Base Percentage		Slugging Percentage		OBP+Slugging	
H. Stovey, Phi	132	P. Browning, Lou	11.16	P. Browning, Lou	.362	P. Browning, Lou	.393	D. Orr, NY	.543	P. Browning, Lou	.923
P. Browning, Lou	128	H. Larkin, Phi	11.09	D. Orr, NY	.342	H. Larkin, Phi	.372	P. Browning, Lou	.530	D. Orr, NY	.901
H. Larkin, Phi	126	H. Stovey, Phi	10.61	H. Larkin, Phi	.329	H. Stovey, Phi	.371	H. Larkin, Phi	.525	H. Larkin, Phi	.897
C. Jones, Cin	117	C. Jones, Cin	9.49	C. Jones, Cin	.322	T. Brown, Pit	.366	H. Stovey, Phi	.488	H. Stovey, Phi	.858
F. Fennelly, Cin	104	D. Orr, NY	9.25	H. Stovey, Phi	.315	B. Phillips, Bro	.364	C. Jones, Cin	.462	C. Jones, Cin	.824

1885 American Association Pitching Leaders

Wins		Losses		Winning Percentage		Games		Games Started		Complete Games	
B. Caruthers, STL	40	H. Henderson, Bal	35	B. Caruthers, STL	.755	E. Morris, Pit	63	E. Morris, Pit	63	E. Morris, Pit	63
E. Morris, Pit	39	E. Morris, Pit	24	D. Foutz, STL	.702	H. Henderson, Bal	61	H. Henderson, Bal	61	H. Henderson, Bal	59
H. Porter, Bro	33	G. Hecker, Lou	23	B. Mathews, Phi	.638	H. Porter, Bro	54	H. Porter, Bro	54	H. Porter, Bro	53
D. Foutz, STL	33	3 tied with	21	E. Morris, Pit	.619	B. Caruthers, STL	53	B. Caruthers, STL	53	B. Caruthers, STL	53
2 tied with	30			H. Porter, Bro	.611	G. Hecker, Lou	53	G. Hecker, Lou	53	G. Hecker, Lou	51

Shutouts		Saves		Games Finished		Batters Faced		Innings Pitched		Hits Allowed	
E. Morris, Pit	7	O. Burns, Bal	3	P. Corkhill, Cin	7	E. Morris, Pit	2321	E. Morris, Pit	581.0	H. Henderson, Bal	539
B. Caruthers, STL	6	A. Terry, Bro	1	O. Burns, Bal	4	H. Henderson, Bal	2268	H. Henderson, Bal	539.1	E. Morris, Pit	459
J. McGinnis, STL	3	P. Corkhill, Cin	1	J. Coleman, Phi	4	H. Porter, Bro	2035	B. Caruthers, STL	482.1	G. Hecker, Lou	454
8 tied with	2	P. Reccius, Lou	1	D. Orr, NY	3	G. Hecker, Lou	1988	H. Porter, Bro	481.2	B. Caruthers, STL	430
		J. Sommer, Bal	1	C. Eden, Pit	3	B. Caruthers, STL	1948	G. Hecker, Lou	480.0	H. Porter, Bro	427

Home Runs Allowed		Walks		Walks/9 Innings		Strikeouts		Strikeouts/9 Innings		Strikeout/Walk Ratio	
J. Lynch, NY	17	H. Henderson, Bal	117	J. Lynch, NY	1.0	E. Morris, Pit	298	B. Mathews, Phi	6.1	B. Mathews, Phi	5.02
H. Porter, Bro	11	H. Porter, Bro	107	G. Hecker, Lou	1.0	B. Mathews, Phi	286	E. Cushman, 2tm	5.5	J. Lynch, NY	4.21
A. Terry, Bro	9	E. Morris, Pit	101	B. Caruthers, STL	1.1	H. Henderson, Bal	263	E. Morris, Pit	4.6	G. Hecker, Lou	3.87
W. White, Cin	9	D. Foutz, STL	92	B. Mathews, Phi	1.2	G. Hecker, Lou	209	H. Henderson, Bal	4.4	E. Cushman, 2tm	3.40
D. Foutz, STL	8	N. Baker, Lou	69	J. McGinnis, STL	1.5	H. Porter, Bro	197	J. Harkins, Bro	4.3	B. Caruthers, STL	3.33

Earned Run Average		Component ERA		Hit Batsmen		Wild Pitches		Opponent Average		Opponent OBP	
B. Caruthers, STL	2.07	E. Morris, Pit	1.67	W. White, Cin	27	H. Henderson, Bal	55	E. Morris, Pit	.208	E. Morris, Pit	.247
G. Hecker, Lou	2.17	B. Caruthers, STL	1.98	B. Mathews, Phi	20	J. Harkins, Bro	39	A. Mays, Lou	.219	B. Caruthers, STL	.260
E. Morris, Pit	2.35	J. McGinnis, STL	2.09	B. Caruthers, STL	19	E. Cushman, 2tm	34	H. Porter, Bro	.223	G. Hecker, Lou	.265
B. Mathews, Phi	2.43	B. Mathews, Phi	2.19	H. Henderson, Bal	19	J. Lynch, NY	28	J. McGinnis, STL	.225	E. Cushman, 2tm	.266
D. Foutz, STL	2.63	G. Hecker, Lou	2.20	2 tied with	18	H. Porter, Bro	26	D. Foutz, STL	.227	B. Mathews, Phi	.267

1885 American Association Miscellaneous

Managers

Baltimore	Billy Barnie	41-68
Brooklyn	Charlie Hackett	15-22
	Charlie Byrne	38-37
Cincinnati	Ollie Caylor	63-49
Louisville	Jim Hart	53-59
New York	Jim Gifford	44-64
Philadelphia	Harry Stovey	55-57
Pittsburgh	Horace Phillips	56-55
St. Louis	Charlie Comiskey	79-33

Awards

STATS Most Valuable Player	Bob Caruthers, p, STL
STATS Cy Young	Bob Caruthers, STL
STATS Rookie of the Year	Norm Baker, p, Lou
STATS Manager of the Year	Charlie Comiskey, STL

STATS All-Star Team

C	Fred Carroll, Pit	.268	0	30
1B	Harry Stovey, Phi	.315	13	75
2B	Sam Barkley, STL	.268	3	53
3B	Hick Carpenter, Cin	.277	2	61
SS	Frank Fennelly, Cin	.273	10	89
OF	Pete Browning, Lou	.362	9	73
OF	Charley Jones, Cin	.322	5	35
OF	Henry Larkin, Phi	.329	8	88
P	Bob Caruthers, STL	40-13	2.07	190 K
P	Ed Morris, Pit	39-24	2.35	298 K

Postseason

World Series	St. Louis (AA) 3 vs. ChN (NL) 3 (1 tie)

Outstanding Performances

Cycles

Dave Orr, NY	on June 12
Henry Larkin, Phi	on June 16

Team	Overall					Home Games						Road Games						Park Index		Record by Month					
	W	L	Pct	GB	DIF	W	L	R	OR	HR	OHR	W	L	R	OR	HR	OHR	Run	HR	M/A	May	June	July	Aug	S/O
Chicago	90	34	.726	—	59	52	10	539	275	45	34	38	24	364	281	8	15	126	343	—	18-4	14-6	18-8	17-6	23-10
Detroit	87	36	.707	2.5	108	48	12	441	255	37	10	39	24	388	283	16	10	109	190	—	20-4	15-4	20-6	10-13	22-9
New York	75	44	.630	12.5	6	47	12	327	195	10	4	28	32	366	363	11	19	73	47	—	15-8	16-5	16-9	14-8	14-14
Philadelphia	71	43	.623	14.0	0	45	14	333	215	13	12	26	29	287	283	13	17	90	78	—	9-12	13-6	17-7	13-9	19-9
Boston	56	61	.479	30.5	0	32	25	354	280	15	8	24	36	303	379	9	25	98	71	—	6-17	10-11	13-10	12-10	15-13
St. Louis	43	79	.352	46.0	0	27	34	288	313	13	10	16	45	260	399	17	24	91	56	—	10-15	5-15	6-19	13-10	9-20
Kansas City	30	91	.248	58.5	0	19	42	301	456	9	4	11	49	193	420	10	23	121	39	—	5-12	4-17	6-19	8-16	7-27
Washington	28	92	.233	60.0	1	19	42	245	372	13	12	9	50	200	420	10	22	96	76	—	4-15	4-17	3-21	4-19	13-20

Clinch Date—Chicago 10/09.

Team Batting

Team	G	AB	R	OR	H	2B	3B	HR	TB	RBI	TBB	IBB	SO	HBP	SH	SF	SB	CS	SB%	GDP	Avg	OBP	Slg
Chicago	126	4378	900	555	1223	198	87	53	1754	673	460	—	513	—	—	—	213	—	—	—	.279	.348	.401
Detroit	126	4501	829	538	1260	176	81	53	1757	635	374	—	426	—	—	—	194	—	—	—	.280	.335	.390
New York	124	4298	692	558	1156	175	68	21	1530	527	237	—	410	—	—	—	155	—	—	—	.269	.307	.356
Boston	118	4180	657	661	1085	151	59	24	1426	503	250	—	537	—	—	—	156	—	—	—	.260	.301	.341
Philadelphia	119	4072	621	498	976	145	66	26	1331	424	282	—	516	—	—	—	226	—	—	—	.240	.289	.327
St. Louis	126	4250	547	712	1001	183	46	30	1366	406	235	—	656	—	—	—	156	—	—	—	.236	.276	.321
Kansas City	126	4236	494	872	967	177	48	19	1297	370	269	—	608	—	—	—	96	—	—	—	.228	.274	.306
Washington	125	4082	445	791	856	135	51	23	1162	332	265	—	582	—	—	—	143	—	—	—	.210	.258	.285
NL Total	990	33997	5185	5185	8524	1340	506	249	11623	3870	2372	—	4248	—	—	—	1339	—	—	—	.251	.300	.342
NL Avg Team	124	4250	648	648	1066	168	63	31	1453	484	297	—	531	—	—	—	167	—	—	—	.251	.300	.342

Team Pitching

Team	G	CG	ShO	Rel	Sv	IP	H	R	ER	HR	SH	SF	HB	TBB	IBB	SO	WP	Bk	H/9	SO/9	BB/9	OAvg	OOBP	ERA
Philadelphia	119	110	10	9	2	1045.2	923	498	285	29	—	—	—	264	—	540	60	0	7.9	4.6	2.3	.224	.271	2.45
Chicago	126	116	8	10	3	1097.2	988	555	310	49	—	—	—	262	—	647	53	0	8.1	5.3	2.1	.232	.277	2.54
Detroit	126	122	8	4	0	1103.2	995	538	350	20	—	—	—	270	—	592	62	0	8.1	4.8	2.2	.231	.276	2.85
New York	124	119	3	5	1	1062.0	1029	558	338	23	—	—	—	280	—	588	95	0	8.7	5.0	2.4	.246	.294	2.86
St. Louis	126	118	6	8	0	1077.1	1050	712	388	34	—	—	—	392	—	501	127	3	8.8	4.2	3.3	.246	.309	3.24
Boston	118	116	3	2	0	1029.0	1049	661	371	33	—	—	—	298	—	511	95	0	9.2	4.5	2.6	.252	.302	3.24
Washington	125	115	4	6	0	1041.0	1147	791	497	34	—	—	—	379	—	500	102	1	9.9	4.3	3.3	.271	.331	4.30
Kansas City	126	117	4	6	0	1066.2	1345	872	574	27	—	—	—	246	—	442	95	0	11.3	3.7	2.1	.295	.331	4.30
NL Total	990	933	46	50	6	8523.0	8526	5185	3113	249	—	—	—	2391	—	4321	689	4	9.0	4.6	2.5	.251	.300	3.29
NL Avg Team	124	117	6	6	1	1065.0	1066	648	389	31	—	—	—	299	—	540	86	1	9.0	4.6	2.5	.251	.300	3.29

Team Fielding

Team	G	PO	A	E	TC	DP	PB	Pct
New York	124	3183	1496	359	5038	70	127	.929
Detroit	126	3301	1504	373	5178	82	76	.928
Philadelphia	119	3125	1454	393	4972	46	95	.921
St. Louis	126	3216	1581	452	5249	92	166	.914
Chicago	126	3289	1644	475	5408	82	144	.912
Washington	125	3096	1532	458	5086	69	109	.910
Kansas City	126	3183	1676	482	5341	79	135	.910
Boston	118	3095	1341	465	4901	63	122	.905
NL Total	990	25488	12228	3457	41173	583	974	.916

Team vs. Team Records

	Bos	ChN	Det	KCN	NYG	Phi	StL	WaN	Won
Bos	—	6	6	11	6	3	11	13	56
ChN	12	—	11	17	10	10	13	17	90
Det	11	7	—	16	11	10	15	17	87
KCN	6	1	2	—	3	2	5	11	30
NYG	11	8	7	15	—	8	15	11	75
Phi	10	7	7	14	8	—	12	13	71
StL	6	4	2	12	3	6	—	10	43
WaN	5	1	1	6	3	4	8	—	28
Lost	61	34	36	91	44	43	79	92	

1886 National League Batting Leaders

Games		At-Bats		Runs		Hits		Doubles		Triples	
E. Seery, StL	126	H. Richardson, Det	538	K. Kelly, ChN	155	H. Richardson, Det	189	D. Brouthers, Det	40	R. Connor, NYG	20
N. Hanlon, Det	126	C. Anson, ChN	504	G. Gore, ChN	150	C. Anson, ChN	187	C. Anson, ChN	35	G. Wood, Phi	15
J. Cahill, StL	125	S. Thompson, Det	503	D. Brouthers, Det	139	D. Brouthers, Det	181	K. Kelly, ChN	32	D. Brouthers, Det	15
H. Richardson, Det	125	E. Sutton, Bos	499	H. Richardson, Det	125	K. Kelly, ChN	175	P. Hines, WaN	30	S. Thompson, Det	13
C. Anson, ChN	125	N. Hanlon, Det	494	C. Anson, ChN	117	R. Connor, NYG	172	2 tied with	29	3 tied with	12

Home Runs		Total Bases		Runs Batted In		Walks		Intentional Walks		Strikeouts	
D. Brouthers, Det	11	D. Brouthers, Det	284	C. Anson, ChN	147	G. Gore, ChN	102	Statistic unavailable		E. Seery, StL	82
H. Richardson, Det	11	C. Anson, ChN	274	F. Pfeffer, ChN	95	K. Kelly, ChN	83			J. Morrill, Bos	81
C. Anson, ChN	10	H. Richardson, Det	271	S. Thompson, Det	89	N. Williamson, ChN	80			J. Lillie, KCN	80
J. Denny, StL	9	R. Connor, NYG	262	J. Rowe, Det	87	D. Brouthers, Det	66			J. Cahill, StL	79
P. Hines, WaN	9	K. Kelly, ChN	241	M. Ward, NYG	81	P. Radford, KCN	58			G. Wood, Phi	75

Hit By Pitch	Sac Hits	Sac Flies	Stolen Bases		Caught Stealing	GDP
Statistic unavailable	Statistic unavailable	Statistic unavailable	E. Andrews, Phi	56	Statistic unavailable	Statistic unavailable
			K. Kelly, ChN	53		
			N. Hanlon, Det	50		
			H. Richardson, Det	42		
			P. Radford, KCN	39		

Runs Created		Runs Created/27 Outs		Batting Average		On-Base Percentage		Slugging Percentage		OBP+Slugging	
K. Kelly, ChN	156	K. Kelly, ChN	14.63	K. Kelly, ChN	.388	K. Kelly, ChN	.483	D. Brouthers, Det	.581	D. Brouthers, Det	1.026
C. Anson, ChN	152	D. Brouthers, Det	12.61	C. Anson, ChN	.371	D. Brouthers, Det	.445	C. Anson, ChN	.544	K. Kelly, ChN	1.018
D. Brouthers, Det	150	C. Anson, ChN	12.41	D. Brouthers, Det	.370	G. Gore, ChN	.434	R. Connor, NYG	.540	C. Anson, ChN	.977
H. Richardson, Det	141	R. Connor, NYG	11.08	R. Connor, NYG	.355	C. Anson, ChN	.433	K. Kelly, ChN	.534	R. Connor, NYG	.945
R. Connor, NYG	134	H. Richardson, Det	10.46	H. Richardson, Det	.351	R. Connor, NYG	.405	H. Richardson, Det	.504	H. Richardson, Det	.906

1886 National League Pitching Leaders

Wins		Losses		Winning Percentage		Games		Games Started		Complete Games	
L. Baldwin, Det	42	S. Wiedman, KCN	36	J. Flynn, ChN	.793	T. Keefe, NYG	64	T. Keefe, NYG	64	T. Keefe, NYG	62
T. Keefe, NYG	42	J. Whitney, KCN	32	C. Ferguson, Phi	.769	M. Welch, NYG	59	M. Welch, NYG	59	O. H. Radbourn, Bos	57
J. Clarkson, ChN	36	D. Shaw, WaN	31	L. Baldwin, Det	.764	O. H. Radbourn, Bos	58	O. H. Radbourn, Bos	58	M. Welch, NYG	56
M. Welch, NYG	33	O. H. Radbourn, Bos	31	J. McCormick, ChN	.738	L. Baldwin, Det	56	L. Baldwin, Det	56	L. Baldwin, Det	55
J. McCormick, ChN	31	J. Kirby, StL	26	C. Getzien, Det	.732	J. Clarkson, ChN	55	J. Clarkson, ChN	55	J. Clarkson, ChN	50

Shutouts		Saves		Games Finished		Batters Faced		Innings Pitched		Hits Allowed	
L. Baldwin, Det	7	C. Ferguson, Phi	2	J. Ryan, ChN	5	T. Keefe, NYG	2173	T. Keefe, NYG	540.0	S. Wiedman, KCN	549
D. Casey, Phi	4	J. Devlin, NYG	1	E. Daily, Phi	4	O. H. Radbourn, Bos	2162	O. H. Radbourn, Bos	509.1	O. H. Radbourn, Bos	521
C. Ferguson, Phi	4	J. Flynn, ChN	1	D. Richardson, NYG	4	M. Welch, NYG	2151	M. Welch, NYG	500.0	M. Welch, NYG	514
4 tied with	3	J. Ryan, ChN	1	H. Richardson, Det	4	L. Baldwin, Det	1936	L. Baldwin, Det	487.0	T. Keefe, NYG	478
		N. Williamson, ChN	1	2 tied with	3	S. Wiedman, KCN	1924	J. Clarkson, ChN	466.2	J. Whitney, KCN	465

Home Runs Allowed		Walks		Walks/9 Innings		Strikeouts		Strikeouts/9 Innings		Strikeout/Walk Ratio	
J. Clarkson, ChN	19	M. Welch, NYG	163	J. Whitney, KCN	1.3	L. Baldwin, Det	323	B. Stemmeyer, Bos	6.2	J. Clarkson, ChN	3.64
O. H. Radbourn, Bos	18	B. Stemmeyer, Bos	144	C. Ferguson, Phi	1.6	J. Clarkson, ChN	313	J. Clarkson, ChN	6.0	L. Baldwin, Det	3.23
J. McCormick, ChN	18	J. Kirby, StL	134	J. Clarkson, ChN	1.7	T. Keefe, NYG	291	L. Baldwin, Det	6.0	C. Ferguson, Phi	3.07
M. Welch, NYG	13	E. Healy, StL	118	T. Keefe, NYG	1.7	M. Welch, NYG	272	E. Healy, StL	5.4	J. Whitney, KCN	3.04
D. Shaw, WaN	12	S. Wiedman, KCN	112	L. Baldwin, Det	1.8	B. Stemmeyer, Bos	239	J. Flynn, ChN	5.1	T. Keefe, NYG	2.91

Earned Run Average		Component ERA		Hit Batsmen	Wild Pitches		Opponent Average		Opponent OBP	
H. Boyle, StL	1.76	L. Baldwin, Det	1.65	Statistic unavailable	B. Stemmeyer, Bos	63	L. Baldwin, Det	.202	L. Baldwin, Det	.243
C. Ferguson, Phi	1.98	C. Ferguson, Phi	1.74		M. Welch, NYG	51	C. Ferguson, Phi	.210	C. Ferguson, Phi	.244
L. Baldwin, Det	2.24	J. Flynn, ChN	1.99		J. Kirby, StL	43	J. Flynn, ChN	.210	J. Flynn, ChN	.257
J. Flynn, ChN	2.24	H. Boyle, StL	2.11		E. Healy, StL	40	B. Stemmeyer, Bos	.218	H. Boyle, StL	.261
J. Clarkson, ChN	2.41	T. Keefe, NYG	2.11		T. Keefe, NYG	40	H. Boyle, StL	.220	J. Clarkson, ChN	.264

1886 National League Miscellaneous

Managers

Boston	John Morrill	56-61
Chicago	Cap Anson	90-34
Detroit	Bill Watkins	87-36
Kansas City	Dave Rowe	30-91
New York	Jim Mutrie	75-44
Philadelphia	Harry Wright	71-43
St. Louis	Gus Schmelz	43-79
Washington	Mike Scanlon	13-67
	John Gaffney	15-25

Awards

STATS Most Valuable Player	King Kelly, of, ChN
STATS Cy Young	Lady Baldwin, Det
STATS Rookie of the Year	Jocko Flynn, p, ChN
STATS Manager of the Year	Bill Watkins, Det

STATS All-Star Team

C	Buck Ewing, NYG	.309	4	31
1B	Cap Anson, ChN	.371	10	147
2B	Fred Pfeffer, ChN	.264	7	95
3B	Tom Burns, ChN	.276	3	65
SS	Jack Glasscock, StL	.325	3	40
OF	George Gore, ChN	.304	6	63
OF	King Kelly, ChN	.388	4	79
OF	Hardy Richardson, Det	.351	11	61
P	Lady Baldwin, Det	42-13	2.24	323 K
P	John Clarkson, ChN	36-17	2.41	313 K
P	Tim Keefe, NYG	42-20	2.53	291 K

Postseason

World Series	Chicago (NL) 1 vs. St. Louis (AA) 5

Outstanding Performances

Three-Homer Games

Dan Brouthers, Det   on September 10

Cycles

Fred Dunlap, StL   on May 24

Jack Rowe, Det   on August 21

1886 American Association Standings

Team	Overall					Home Games						Road Games						Park Index		Record by Month					
	W	L	Pct	GB	DIF	W	L	R	OR	HR	OHR	W	L	R	OR	HR	OHR	Run	HR	M/A	May	June	July	Aug	S/O
St. Louis	93	46	.669	—	162	52	18	546	286	13	7	41	28	398	307	7	6	116	152	9-3	13-10	16-8	17-8	18-5	20-12
Pittsburgh	80	57	.584	12.0	0	46	29	423	272	2	3	34	28	386	373	14	7	76	20	4-7	15-8	12-10	12-13	19-6	18-13
Brooklyn	76	61	.555	16.0	6	43	25	453	364	9	7	33	36	379	462	7	10	99	96	6-4	11-9	14-10	13-11	11-14	21-13
Louisville	66	70	.485	25.5	7	37	34	484	402	19	9	29	40	348	395	1	7	123	360	6-5	10-15	12-11	18-7	14-9	6-23
Cincinnati	65	73	.471	27.5	0	40	31	472	380	32	16	25	42	406	484	13	9	90	206	4-8	11-13	12-14	16-9	9-14	13-15
Philadelphia	63	72	.467	28.0	6	37	32	434	468	13	11	26	40	337	472	8	24	107	72	7-4	10-9	7-13	9-17	12-13	18-16
New York	53	82	.393	38.0	0	30	33	336	352	10	9	23	49	290	415	8	14	112	99	2-8	8-11	12-10	7-18	6-16	18-19
Baltimore	48	83	.366	41.0	4	30	31	320	315	2	2	18	52	298	560	6	23	85	16	6-5	8-11	6-15	8-17	7-19	13-16

Clinch Date—St. Louis 9/28.

Team Batting

Team	G	AB	R	OR	H	2B	3B	HR	TB	RBI	TBB	IBB	SO	HBP	SH	SF	SB	CS	SB%	GDP	Avg	OBP	Slg
St. Louis	139	5009	944	592	1365	206	85	20	1801	655	400	—	425	52	—	—	336	—	—	—	.273	.333	.360
Cincinnati	141	4915	883	865	1225	145	95	45	1695	666	374	—	633	65	—	—	185	—	—	—	.249	.311	.345
Louisville	138	4921	833	805	1294	182	88	20	1712	564	410	—	558	26	—	—	202	—	—	—	.263	.323	.348
Brooklyn	141	5053	832	832	1261	196	80	16	1665	572	433	—	523	18	—	—	248	—	—	—	.250	.311	.330
Pittsburgh	140	4854	810	647	1171	186	96	16	1597	564	478	—	713	38	—	—	260	—	—	—	.241	.314	.329
Philadelphia	139	4856	772	942	1142	192	82	21	1561	510	378	—	697	41	—	—	284	—	—	—	.235	.296	.321
New York	137	4683	628	766	1047	108	72	18	1353	426	330	—	578	33	—	—	120	—	—	—	.224	.279	.289
Baltimore	139	4639	625	878	945	124	51	8	1195	417	379	—	603	36	—	—	269	—	—	—	.204	.269	.258
AA Total	1114	38930	6327	6327	9450	1339	649	164	12579	4374	3182	—	4730	309	—	—	1904	—	—	—	.243	.305	.323
AA Avg Team	139	4866	791	791	1181	167	81	21	1572	547	398	—	591	39	—	—	238	—	—	—	.243	.305	.323

Team Pitching

Team	G	CG	ShO	Rel	Sv	IP	H	R	ER	HR	SH	SF	HB	TBB	IBB	SO	WP	Bk	H/9	SO/9	BB/9	OAvg	OOBP	ERA
St. Louis	139	134	14	5	2	1229.1	1087	592	340	13	—	—	26	329	—	583	—	—	8.0	4.3	2.4	.227	.281	2.49
Pittsburgh	140	137	15	3	1	1226.0	1130	647	385	10	—	—	34	299	—	515	—	—	8.3	3.8	2.2	.235	.285	2.83
Louisville	138	131	5	7	2	1209.2	1109	805	412	16	—	—	26	432	—	720	—	—	8.3	5.4	3.2	.230	.297	3.07
Brooklyn	141	138	6	3	0	1234.2	1202	832	469	17	—	—	34	464	—	540	—	—	8.8	3.9	3.4	.243	.312	3.42
New York	137	134	5	3	0	1186.1	1148	766	462	23	—	—	31	386	—	559	—	—	8.7	4.2	2.9	.243	.305	3.50
Philadelphia	139	134	4	6	0	1218.2	1308	942	538	35	—	—	61	388	—	513	—	—	9.7	3.8	2.9	.259	.319	3.97
Baltimore	139	134	5	7	0	1206.2	1197	878	547	25	—	—	53	403	—	805	—	—	8.9	6.0	3.0	.244	.308	4.08
Cincinnati	141	129	3	14	0	1247.2	1267	865	580	25	—	—	48	481	—	495	—	—	9.1	3.6	3.5	.255	.327	4.18
AA Total	1114	1071	57	48	5	9759.0	9448	6327	3733	164	—	—	313	3182	—	4730	—	—	8.7	4.4	2.9	.243	.305	3.44
AA Avg Team	139	134	7	6	1	1219.0	1181	791	467	21	—	—	39	398	—	591	—	—	8.7	4.4	2.9	.243	.305	3.44

Team Fielding

Team	G	PO	A	E	TC	DP	PB	Pct
Pittsburgh	140	3668	1703	487	5858	90	162	.917
St. Louis	139	3692	1615	494	5801	96	108	.915
Baltimore	139	3613	1651	523	5787	93	135	.910
New York	137	3550	1738	544	5832	81	153	.907
Cincinnati	141	3734	1811	582	6127	122	131	.905
Louisville	138	3621	1748	593	5962	89	203	.901
Brooklyn	141	3701	1786	610	6097	87	150	.900
Philadelphia	139	3647	1729	637	6013	99	176	.894
AA Total	1114	29226	13781	4470	47477	723	1218	.906

Team vs. Team Records

	Bal	Bro	Cin	Lou	NY	Phi	Pit	STL	Won
Bal	—	6	5	7	8	8	7	7	48
Bro	14	—	13	13	10	11	8	7	76
Cin	13	7	—	10	13	10	7	5	65
Lou	12	7	10	—	11	9	7	10	66
NY	9	9	7	8	—	8	8	4	53
Phi	10	7	10	11	12	—	8	5	63
Pit	12	12	13	12	12	11	—	8	80
STL	13	13	15	9	16	15	12	—	93
Lost	83	61	73	70	82	72	57	46	

Seasons: Standings, Leaders

1886 American Association Batting Leaders

Games		At-Bats		Runs		Hits		Doubles		Triples	
G. Pinckney, Bro	141	G. Pinckney, Bro	597	A. Latham, STL	152	D. Orr, NY	193	H. Larkin, Phi	36	D. Orr, NY	31
B. Phillips, Bro	141	B. McClellan, Bro	595	B. McPhee, Cin	139	T. O'Neill, STL	190	B. McClellan, Bro	33	F. Fennelly, Cin	17
B. McClellan, Bro	141	B. Phillips, Bro	585	H. Larkin, Phi	133	H. Larkin, Phi	180	C. Welch, STL	31	B. Kuehne, Pit	17
B. McPhee, Cin	140	T. O'Neill, STL	579	B. McClellan, Bro	131	A. Latham, STL	174	S. Barkley, Pit	31	J. Coleman, 2tm	17
2 tied with	139	2 tied with	578	G. Pinckney, Bro	119	B. Phillips, Bro	160	P. Browning, Lou	29	H. Larkin, Phi	16

Home Runs		Total Bases		Runs Batted In		Walks		Intentional Walks	Strikeouts
B. McPhee, Cin	8	D. Orr, NY	301	T. O'Neill, STL	107	G. Pinckney, Bro	70	Statistic unavailable	Statistic unavailable
D. Orr, NY	7	T. O'Neill, STL	255	P. Corkhill, Cin	97	E. Swartwood, Bro	70		
H. Stovey, Phi	7	H. Larkin, Phi	254	C. Welch, STL	95	R. Mack, Lou	68		
3 tied with	6	C. Welch, STL	221	D. Orr, NY	91	J. Kerins, Lou	66		
		B. McPhee, Cin	221	J. Reilly, Cin	79	4 tied with	64		

Hit By Pitch		Sac Hits	Sac Flies	Stolen Bases		Caught Stealing	GDP
F. Fennelly, Cin	18	Statistic unavailable	Statistic unavailable	H. Stovey, Phi	68	Statistic unavailable	Statistic unavailable
Y. Robinson, STL	15			A. Latham, STL	60		
C. Welch, STL	14			C. Welch, STL	59		
F. Mann, Pit	11			Y. Robinson, STL	51		
J. Gleason, Phi	11			B. McClellan, Bro	43		

Runs Created		Runs Created/27 Outs		Batting Average		On-Base Percentage		Slugging Percentage		OBP+Slugging	
H. Larkin, Phi	138	D. Orr, NY	9.52	P. Browning, Lou	.340	H. Larkin, Phi	.390	D. Orr, NY	.527	D. Orr, NY	.890
T. O'Neill, STL	138	H. Larkin, Phi	9.49	D. Orr, NY	.338	P. Browning, Lou	.389	H. Larkin, Phi	.450	H. Larkin, Phi	.839
D. Orr, NY	136	T. O'Neill, STL	9.39	T. O'Neill, STL	.328	T. O'Neill, STL	.385	P. Browning, Lou	.441	P. Browning, Lou	.830
A. Latham, STL	122	P. Browning, Lou	9.02	H. Larkin, Phi	.319	H. Stovey, Phi	.377	T. O'Neill, STL	.440	T. O'Neill, STL	.826
B. McPhee, Cin	120	H. Stovey, Phi	8.97	A. Latham, STL	.301	E. Swartwood, Bro	.377	H. Stovey, Phi	.440	H. Stovey, Phi	.817

1886 American Association Pitching Leaders

Wins		Losses		Winning Percentage		Games		Games Started		Complete Games	
D. Foutz, STL	41	M. Kilroy, Bal	34	D. Foutz, STL	.719	M. Kilroy, Bal	68	M. Kilroy, Bal	68	M. Kilroy, Bal	66
E. Morris, Pit	41	J. Lynch, NY	30	B. Caruthers, STL	.682	T. Ramsey, Lou	67	T. Ramsey, Lou	67	T. Ramsey, Lou	66
T. Ramsey, Lou	38	A. Mays, NY	28	E. Morris, Pit	.672	E. Morris, Pit	64	E. Morris, Pit	63	E. Morris, Pit	63
T. Mullane, Cin	33	T. Ramsey, Lou	27	N. Hudson, STL	.615	T. Mullane, Cin	63	D. Foutz, STL	57	D. Foutz, STL	55
B. Caruthers, STL	30	T. Mullane, Cin	27	A. Atkinson, Phi	.595	D. Foutz, STL	59	T. Mullane, Cin	56	T. Mullane, Cin	55

Shutouts		Saves		Games Finished		Batters Faced		Innings Pitched		Hits Allowed	
E. Morris, Pit	12	N. Hudson, STL	1	T. Mullane, Cin	7	T. Ramsey, Lou	2477	T. Ramsey, Lou	588.2	T. Mullane, Cin	501
D. Foutz, STL	11	D. Foutz, STL	1	7 tied with	2	M. Kilroy, Bal	2469	M. Kilroy, Bal	583.0	J. Lynch, NY	485
M. Kilroy, Bal	5	J. Strauss, Lou	1			T. Mullane, Cin	2258	E. Morris, Pit	555.1	M. Kilroy, Bal	476
A. Terry, Bro	5	B. Ely, Lou	1			E. Morris, Pit	2252	T. Mullane, Cin	529.2	P. Galvin, Pit	457
T. Ramsey, Lou	3	E. Morris, Pit	1			D. Foutz, STL	2091	D. Foutz, STL	504.0	E. Morris, Pit	455

Home Runs Allowed		Walks		Walks/9 Innings		Strikeouts		Strikeouts/9 Innings		Strikeout/Walk Ratio	
A. Atkinson, Phi	11	T. Ramsey, Lou	207	P. Galvin, Pit	1.6	M. Kilroy, Bal	513	M. Kilroy, Bal	7.9	M. Kilroy, Bal	2.82
T. Mullane, Cin	11	M. Kilroy, Bal	182	E. Morris, Pit	1.9	T. Ramsey, Lou	499	T. Ramsey, Lou	7.6	E. Morris, Pit	2.76
M. Kilroy, Bal	10	T. Mullane, Cin	166	B. Caruthers, STL	2.0	E. Morris, Pit	326	E. Morris, Pit	5.3	T. Ramsey, Lou	2.41
J. Lynch, NY	10	D. Foutz, STL	144	J. McGinnis, 2tm	2.3	D. Foutz, STL	283	C. Miller, Phi	5.3	D. Foutz, STL	1.97
2 tied with	8	A. Mays, NY	140	A. Atkinson, Phi	2.3	T. Mullane, Cin	250	A. Terry, Bro	5.1	B. Caruthers, STL	1.93

Earned Run Average		Component ERA		Hit Batsmen		Wild Pitches	Opponent Average		Opponent OBP	
D. Foutz, STL	2.11	E. Morris, Pit	1.86	A. Atkinson, Phi	22	Statistic unavailable	T. Ramsey, Lou	.198	E. Morris, Pit	.258
B. Caruthers, STL	2.32	T. Ramsey, Lou	1.95	J. McGinnis, 2tm	21		M. Kilroy, Bal	.210	B. Caruthers, STL	.263
T. Ramsey, Lou	2.45	B. Caruthers, STL	1.96	M. Kilroy, Bal	19		E. Morris, Pit	.214	T. Ramsey, Lou	.269
E. Morris, Pit	2.45	D. Foutz, STL	2.14	T. Mullane, Cin	18		D. Foutz, STL	.216	D. Foutz, STL	.274
P. Galvin, Pit	2.67	M. Kilroy, Bal	2.20	A. Terry, Bro	16		B. Caruthers, STL	.217	M. Kilroy, Bal	.274

1886 American Association Miscellaneous

Managers

Baltimore	Billy Barnie	48-83
Brooklyn	Charlie Byrne	76-61
Cincinnati	Ollie Caylor	65-73
Louisville	Jim Hart	66-70
New York	Jim Gifford	5-12
	Bob Ferguson	48-70
Philadelphia	Lew Simmons	41-55
	Bill Sharsig	22-17
Pittsburgh	Horace Phillips	80-57
St. Louis	Charlie Comiskey	93-46

Awards

STATS Most Valuable Player	B. Caruthers, p-of, STL
STATS Cy Young	Dave Foutz, STL
STATS Rookie of the Year	Matt Kilroy, p, Bal
STATS Manager of the Year	Horace Phillips, Pit

STATS All-Star Team

C	Fred Carroll, Pit	.288	5	64
1B	Dave Orr, NY	.338	7	91
2B	Bid McPhee, Cin	.268	8	70
3B	Arlie Latham, STL	.301	1	47
SS	Frank Fennelly, Cin	.249	6	72
OF	Pete Browning, Lou	.340	2	68
OF	Tip O'Neill, STL	.328	3	107
OF	Harry Stovey, Phi	.294	7	59
P	Bob Caruthers, STL	30-14	2.32	166 K
P	Dave Foutz, STL	41-16	2.11	283 K
P	Ed Morris, Pit	41-20	2.45	326 K

Postseason

World Series	St. Louis (AA) 5 vs. Chicago (NL) 1

Outstanding Performances

No-Hitters
Al Atkinson, Phi	vs. NY on May 1
Adonis Terry, Bro	vs. STL on July 24
Matt Kilroy, Bal	@ Pit on October 6

Three-Homer Games
Guy Hecker, Lou	on August 15

Cycles
Pete Browning, Lou	on August 8
Jim McGarr, Phi	on September 23

1887 National League Standings

Team	W	L	Pct	GB	DIF	W	L	R	OR	HR	OHR	W	L	R	OR	HR	OHR	Run	HR	M/A	May	June	July	Aug	S/O
		Overall						**Home Games**						**Road Games**				**Park Index**				**Record by Month**			
Detroit	79	45	.637	—	162	43	17	502	306	25	20	36	28	467	405	30	32	99	77	3-0	18-7	12-8	11-11	15-9	20-10
Philadelphia	75	48	.610	3.5	0	37	23	438	321	25	22	38	25	453	380	22	26	96	103	1-2	14-11	9-13	13-10	16-7	22-5
Chicago	71	50	.587	6.5	1	44	18	540	347	67	44	27	32	278	372	13	11	130	440	0-1	11-14	15-5	16-8	11-10	18-12
New York	68	55	.553	10.5	2	36	27	439	340	21	8	32	28	378	377	27	19	98	60	2-1	14-11	14-9	11-11	13-9	14-14
Boston	61	60	.504	16.5	5	39	21	466	322	29	17	22	39	367	471	24	38	96	75	2-0	17-8	11-12	10-10	9-13	12-17
Pittsburgh	55	69	.444	24.0	3	31	34	336	336	6	4	24	35	285	421	14	35	86	19	1-0	9-14	9-12	9-16	11-11	16-16
Washington	46	76	.377	32.0	0	27	32	329	349	29	19	19	44	271	466	18	32	98	111	0-2	8-13	9-12	11-11	9-16	9-22
Indianapolis	37	89	.294	43.0	0	24	39	349	456	19	28	13	50	278	507	14	32	103	102	0-3	6-19	7-15	9-13	7-16	8-23

Clinch Date—Detroit 10/04.

Team Batting

Team	G	AB	R	OR	H	2B	3B	HR	TB	RBI	TBB	IBB	SO	HBP	SH	SF	SB	CS	SB%	GDP	Avg	OBP	Slg
Detroit	127	4689	969	714	1404	213	126	55	2034	818	352	—	258	38	—	—	267	—	—	—	.299	.353	.434
Philadelphia	128	4630	901	702	1269	213	89	47	1801	702	385	—	346	52	—	—	355	—	—	—	.274	.337	.389
Boston	127	4531	831	792	1255	185	94	53	1787	649	340	—	392	37	—	—	373	—	—	—	.277	.333	.394
New York	129	4516	816	723	1259	167	93	48	1756	651	361	—	326	47	—	—	415	—	—	—	.279	.339	.389
Chicago	127	4350	813	716	1177	178	98	80	1791	655	407	—	400	20	—	—	382	—	—	—	.271	.336	.412
Indianapolis	127	4368	628	965	1080	162	70	33	1481	488	300	—	379	44	—	—	334	—	—	—	.247	.302	.339
Pittsburgh	125	4414	621	750	1141	183	78	20	1540	479	319	—	381	38	—	—	221	—	—	—	.258	.314	.349
Washington	126	4314	601	818	1039	149	63	47	1455	457	269	—	339	41	—	—	334	—	—	—	.241	.292	.337
NL Total	1016	35812	6180	6180	9624	1450	711	383	13645	4899	2733	—	2821	317	—	—	2681	—	—	—	.269	.326	.381
NL Avg Team	127	4477	773	773	1203	181	89	48	1706	612	342	—	353	40	—	—	335	—	—	—	.269	.326	.381

Team Pitching

Team	G	CG	ShO	Rel	Sv	IP	H	R	ER	HR	SH	SF	HB	TBB	IBB	SO	WP	Bk	H/9	SO/9	BB/9	OAvg	OOBP	ERA
Chicago	127	117	4	12	3	1126.0	1156	716	433	55	—	—	53	338	—	510	86	0	9.2	4.1	2.7	.257	.317	3.46
Philadelphia	128	119	7	10	1	1132.2	1173	702	437	48	—	—	34	305	—	435	56	0	9.3	3.5	2.4	.259	.311	3.47
New York	129	123	5	6	1	1113.2	1096	723	442	27	—	—	38	373	—	415	84	1	8.9	3.4	3.0	.250	.314	3.57
Detroit	127	122	3	5	1	1116.1	1172	714	490	52	—	—	34	344	—	337	51	0	9.4	2.7	2.8	.264	.322	3.95
Pittsburgh	125	123	4	2	0	1108.2	1287	750	507	39	—	—	33	246	—	248	41	0	10.4	2.0	2.0	.281	.322	4.12
Washington	126	124	3	2	0	1090.1	1216	818	508	47	—	—	43	299	—	396	65	0	10.0	3.3	2.5	.272	.323	4.19
Boston	127	123	4	4	1	1100.2	1226	792	539	55	—	—	43	396	—	254	64	0	10.0	2.1	3.2	.273	.338	4.41
Indianapolis	127	118	4	7	1	1088.0	1289	965	634	60	—	—	44	431	—	245	97	1	10.7	2.0	3.6	.284	.352	5.24
NL Total	1016	969	34	51	8	8876.1	9615	6180	3990	383	—	—	322	2732	—	2840	544	2	9.8	2.9	2.8	.269	.326	4.05
NL Avg Team	127	121	4	6	1	1109.1	1202	773	499	48	—	—	40	342	—	355	68	0	9.8	2.9	2.8	.269	.326	4.05

Team Fielding

Team	G	PO	A	E	TC	DP	PB	Pct
Detroit	127	3271	1563	394	5228	92	44	.925
Pittsburgh	125	3326	1596	425	5347	70	99	.921
New York	129	3317	1650	431	5398	83	112	.920
Chicago	127	3352	1683	472	5507	99	115	.914
Philadelphia	128	3380	1515	471	5366	76	96	.912
Indianapolis	127	3243	1701	479	5423	105	126	.912
Washington	126	3265	1593	483	5341	77	129	.910
Boston	127	3302	1677	522	5501	94	90	.905
NL Total	1016	26456	12978	3677	43111	696	811	.915

Team vs. Team Records

	Bos	ChN	Det	Ind	NYG	Phi	Pit	WaN	Won
Bos	—	6	7	11	7	9	11	10	61
ChN	9	—	10	13	11	12	5	11	71
Det	11	8	—	14	10	10	13	13	79
Ind	7	5	4	—	3	1	7	10	37
NYG	10	6	8	15	—	7	12	10	68
Phi	9	6	8	17	10	—	12	13	75
Pit	7	12	4	11	6	6	—	9	55
WaN	7	7	4	8	3	3	9	—	46
Lost	60	50	45	89	55	48	69	76	

Seasons: Standings, Leaders

1887 National League Batting Leaders

Games		At-Bats		Runs		Hits		Doubles		Triples	
M. Ward, NYG	129	S. Thompson, Det	545	D. Brouthers, Det	153	S. Thompson, Det	203	D. Brouthers, Det	36	S. Thompson, Det	23
5 tied with	127	M. Ward, NYG	545	J. Rowe, Det	135	M. Ward, NYG	184	J. Denny, Ind	34	R. Connor, NYG	22
		H. Richardson, Det	543	H. Richardson, Det	131	H. Richardson, Det	178	K. Kelly, Bos	34	D. Johnston, Bos	20
		J. Rowe, Det	537	K. Kelly, Bos	120	J. Rowe, Det	171	C. Anson, ChN	33	D. Brouthers, Det	20
		J. Denny, Ind	510	2 tied with	118	D. Brouthers, Det	169	2 tied with	32	G. Wood, Phi	19

Home Runs		Total Bases		Runs Batted In		Walks		Intentional Walks		Strikeouts	
B. O'Brien, WaN	19	S. Thompson, Det	311	S. Thompson, Det	166	J. Fogarty, Phi	82	Statistic unavailable		J. Morrill, Bos	86
R. Connor, NYG	17	D. Brouthers, Det	281	R. Connor, NYG	104	R. Connor, NYG	75			E. Seery, Ind	68
F. Pfeffer, ChN	16	H. Richardson, Det	263	C. Anson, ChN	102	N. Williamson, ChN	73			T. Brown, 2tm	65
G. Wood, Phi	14	J. Denny, Ind	256	D. Brouthers, Det	101	E. Seery, Ind	71			N. Williamson, ChN	57
2 tied with	12	R. Connor, NYG	255	J. Denny, Ind	97	D. Brouthers, Det	71			M. Sullivan, ChN	53

Hit By Pitch		Sac Hits		Sac Flies		Stolen Bases		Caught Stealing		GDP	
P. Smith, Pit	13	Statistic unavailable		Statistic unavailable		M. Ward, NYG	111	Statistic unavailable		Statistic unavailable	
J. Fogarty, Phi	10					J. Fogarty, Phi	102				
S. Farrar, Phi	10					K. Kelly, Bos	84				
J. Glasscock, Ind	10					N. Hanlon, Det	69				
3 tied with	9					J. Glasscock, Ind	62				

Runs Created		Runs Created/27 Outs		Batting Average		On-Base Percentage		Slugging Percentage		OBP+Slugging	
S. Thompson, Det	152	D. Brouthers, Det	11.60	S. Thompson, Det	.372	D. Brouthers, Det	.426	S. Thompson, Det	.571	D. Brouthers, Det	.988
D. Brouthers, Det	149	S. Thompson, Det	11.46	C. Anson, ChN	.347	C. Anson, ChN	.422	D. Brouthers, Det	.562	S. Thompson, Det	.987
J. Fogarty, Phi	130	K. Kelly, Bos	10.14	D. Brouthers, Det	.338	S. Thompson, Det	.416	R. Connor, NYG	.541	C. Anson, ChN	.939
K. Kelly, Bos	129	C. Anson, ChN	10.13	M. Ward, NYG	.338	O. Schomberg, Ind	.397	S. Wise, Bos	.522	R. Connor, NYG	.933
R. Connor, NYG	124	S. Wise, Bos	9.95	S. Wise, Bos	.334	K. Kelly, Bos	.393	C. Anson, ChN	.517	S. Wise, Bos	.913

1887 National League Pitching Leaders

Wins		Losses		Winning Percentage		Games		Games Started		Complete Games	
J. Clarkson, ChN	38	E. Healy, Ind	29	C. Getzien, Det	.690	J. Clarkson, ChN	60	J. Clarkson, ChN	59	J. Clarkson, ChN	56
T. Keefe, NYG	35	H. Boyle, Ind	24	C. Ferguson, Phi	.688	T. Keefe, NYG	56	T. Keefe, NYG	56	T. Keefe, NYG	54
C. Getzien, Det	29	O. H. Radbourn, Bos	23	D. Casey, Phi	.683	O. H. Radbourn, Bos	50	O. H. Radbourn, Bos	50	O. H. Radbourn, Bos	48
D. Casey, Phi	28	J. McCormick, Pit	23	T. Keefe, NYG	.648	P. Galvin, Pit	49	P. Galvin, Pit	48	P. Galvin, Pit	47
P. Galvin, Pit	28	E. Morris, Pit	22	J. Clarkson, ChN	.644	J. Whitney, WaN	47	J. Whitney, WaN	47	J. Whitney, WaN	46

Shutouts		Saves		Games Finished		Batters Faced		Innings Pitched		Hits Allowed	
D. Casey, Phi	4	8 tied with	1	J. Cahill, Ind	5	J. Clarkson, ChN	2183	J. Clarkson, ChN	523.0	J. Clarkson, ChN	513
K. Madden, Bos	3			M. Tiernan, NYG	4	T. Keefe, NYG	1981	T. Keefe, NYG	478.2	O. H. Radbourn, Bos	505
E. Healy, Ind	3			J. Ryan, ChN	4	O. H. Radbourn, Bos	1915	P. Galvin, Pit	440.2	P. Galvin, Pit	490
J. Whitney, WaN	3			C. Ferguson, Phi	4	P. Galvin, Pit	1897	O. H. Radbourn, Bos	425.0	T. Keefe, NYG	447
6 tied with	2			2 tied with	3	J. Whitney, WaN	1718	J. Whitney, WaN	404.2	J. Whitney, WaN	430

Home Runs Allowed		Walks		Walks/9 Innings		Strikeouts		Strikeouts/9 Innings		Strikeout/Walk Ratio	
E. Healy, Ind	24	O. H. Radbourn, Bos	133	J. Whitney, WaN	0.9	J. Clarkson, ChN	237	M. Baldwin, ChN	4.4	J. Whitney, WaN	3.48
C. Getzien, Det	24	K. Madden, Bos	122	P. Galvin, Pit	1.4	T. Keefe, NYG	186	F. Gilmore, WaN	4.4	C. Ferguson, Phi	2.66
M. Baldwin, ChN	23	M. Baldwin, ChN	122	C. Ferguson, Phi	1.4	M. Baldwin, ChN	164	C. Buffinton, Phi	4.3	J. Clarkson, ChN	2.58
3 tied with	20	D. Casey, Phi	115	J. Clarkson, ChN	1.6	C. Buffinton, Phi	160	G. Van Haltren, ChN	4.2	C. Buffinton, Phi	1.74
		H. O'Day, WaN	109	H. Boyle, Ind	1.9	J. Whitney, WaN	146	J. Clarkson, ChN	4.1	T. Keefe, NYG	1.72

Earned Run Average		Component ERA		Hit Batsmen		Wild Pitches		Opponent Average		Opponent OBP	
D. Casey, Phi	2.86	T. Keefe, NYG	2.57	K. Madden, Bos	20	M. Baldwin, ChN	41	P. Conway, Det	.235	J. Clarkson, ChN	.281
P. Conway, Det	2.90	J. Clarkson, ChN	2.67	M. Baldwin, ChN	17	E. Healy, Ind	39	T. Keefe, NYG	.240	J. Whitney, WaN	.284
C. Ferguson, Phi	3.00	P. Conway, Det	2.76	G. Van Haltren, ChN	16	T. Keefe, NYG	37	D. Casey, Phi	.246	T. Keefe, NYG	.286
J. Clarkson, ChN	3.08	C. Ferguson, Phi	2.86	J. Whitney, WaN	16	H. O'Day, WaN	31	J. Clarkson, ChN	.246	C. Ferguson, Phi	.289
T. Keefe, NYG	3.10	J. Whitney, WaN	2.90	E. Healy, Ind	15	2 tied with	25	M. Baldwin, ChN	.248	P. Galvin, Pit	.299

1887 National League Miscellaneous

Managers

Boston	King Kelly	49-43
	John Morrill	12-17
Chicago	Cap Anson	71-50
Detroit	Bill Watkins	79-45
Indianapolis	Watch Burnham	6-22
	Fred Thomas	11-18
	Horace Fogel	20-49
New York	Jim Mutrie	68-55
Philadelphia	Harry Wright	75-48
Pittsburgh	Horace Phillips	55-69
Washington	John Gaffney	46-76

Awards

STATS Most Valuable Player	Sam Thompson, of, Det
STATS Cy Young	John Clarkson, ChN
STATS Rookie of the Year	Billy O'Brien, 1b, WaN
STATS Manager of the Year	Bill Watkins, Det

STATS All-Star Team

C	Jack Clements, Phi	.280	1	47
1B	Dan Brouthers, Det	.338	12	101
2B	Hardy Richardson, Det	.328	8	94
3B	Jerry Denny, Ind	.324	11	97
SS	Sam Wise, Bos	.334	9	92
OF	King Kelly, Bos	.322	8	63
OF	Sam Thompson, Det	.372	11	166
OF	George Wood, Phi	.289	14	66
P	Dan Casey, Phi	28-13	2.86	119 K
P	John Clarkson, ChN	38-21	3.08	237 K
P	Tim Keefe, NYG	35-19	3.10	186 K

Postseason

World Series	Detroit (NL) 10 vs. St. Louis (AA) 5

Outstanding Performances

Cycles

Fred Carroll, Pit	on May 2

1887 American Association Standings

Team		Overall						Home Games						Road Games					Park Index			Record by Month				
	W	L	Pct	GB	DIF	W	L	R	OR	HR	OHR	W	L	R	OR	HR	OHR	Run	HR	M/A	May	June	July	Aug	S/O
St. Louis	95	40	.704	—	159	58	15	679	381	26	16	37	25	453	372	13	3	109	223	7-3	21-2	14-9	16-7	21-5	16-14
Cincinnati	81	54	.600	14.0	10	45	26	517	386	24	16	36	28	376	360	13	12	111	144	6-4	11-14	14-10	16-8	15-11	19-7
Baltimore	77	58	.570	18.0	10	42	21	500	328	16	6	35	37	470	536	15	10	94	101	6-3	13-9	16-5	10-14	11-16	21-11
Louisville	76	60	.559	19.5	3	46	23	561	409	14	15	30	37	394	450	13	16	112	97	6-4	13-12	10-12	17-8	16-8	14-16
Philadelphia	64	69	.481	30.0	0	41	27	502	404	18	11	23	42	387	492	11	18	99	96	5-3	13-12	9-14	9-13	13-13	15-14
Brooklyn	60	74	.448	34.5	14	36	38	514	470	18	14	24	36	398	448	7	13	94	130	6-2	9-13	12-10	10-15	12-16	11-18
New York	44	89	.331	50.0	0	25	34	322	398	10	10	19	55	425	693	11	29	81	63	0-9	6-15	8-14	12-12	8-19	10-20
Cleveland	39	92	.298	54.0	0	22	37	375	481	2	7	17	55	354	619	12	27	107	28	1-9	6-15	7-16	5-18	10-18	10-16

Clinch Date—St. Louis 9/17.

Team Batting

Team	G	AB	R	OR	H	2B	3B	HR	TB	RBI	TBB	IBB	SO	HBP	SH	SF	SB	CS	SB%	GDP	Avg	OBP	Slg
St. Louis	138	5048	1131	761	1550	261	78	39	2084	862	442	—	340	67	—	—	581	—	—	—	.307	.371	.413
Baltimore	141	4825	975	861	1337	202	100	31	1832	765	469	—	334	68	—	—	545	—	—	—	.277	.349	.380
Louisville	139	4916	956	854	1420	194	98	27	1891	728	436	—	356	40	—	—	466	—	—	—	.289	.352	.385
Brooklyn	138	4913	904	918	1281	200	82	25	1720	689	456	—	365	51	—	—	409	—	—	—	.261	.330	.350
Philadelphia	137	4954	893	890	1370	231	84	29	1856	661	321	—	388	51	—	—	476	—	—	—	.277	.327	.375
Cincinnati	136	4797	892	745	1285	179	102	37	1779	678	382	—	366	56	—	—	527	—	—	—	.268	.329	.371
New York	138	4820	754	1093	1197	193	66	21	1585	549	439	—	463	50	—	—	305	—	—	—	.248	.318	.329
Cleveland	133	4649	729	1112	1170	178	77	14	1544	562	375	—	463	46	—	—	355	—	—	—	.252	.314	.332
AA Total	1100	38922	7234	7234	10610	1638	687	223	14291	5494	3320	—	3075	429	—	—	3664	—	—	—	.273	.337	.367
AA Avg Team	138	4865	904	904	1326	205	86	28	1786	687	415	—	384	54	—	—	458	—	—	—	.273	.337	.367

Team Pitching

Team	G	CG	ShO	Rel	Sv	IP	H	R	ER	HR	SH	SF	HB	TBB	IBB	SO	WP	Bk	H/9	SO/9	BB/9	OAvg	OOBP	ERA
Cincinnati	136	129	11	6	1	1182.2	1202	745	471	28	—	—	59	396	—	330	—	—	9.1	2.5	3.0	.257	.322	3.58
St. Louis	138	132	6	5	2	1199.1	1254	761	503	19	—	—	52	323	—	334	—	—	9.4	2.5	2.4	.258	.311	3.77
Louisville	139	133	3	4	1	1205.2	1274	854	512	31	—	—	42	357	—	544	—	—	9.5	4.1	2.7	.260	.316	3.82
Baltimore	141	132	8	9	0	1220.0	1288	861	524	16	—	—	53	418	—	470	—	—	9.5	3.5	3.1	.262	.326	3.87
Brooklyn	138	132	3	6	3	1185.1	1348	918	589	27	—	—	42	454	—	332	—	—	10.2	2.5	3.4	.281	.348	4.47
Philadelphia	137	131	5	6	1	1186.1	1227	890	605	29	—	—	71	433	—	417	—	—	9.3	3.2	3.3	.259	.331	4.59
Cleveland	133	127	2	6	1	1136.0	1472	1112	630	34	—	—	61	533	—	332	—	—	11.7	2.6	4.2	.308	.384	4.99
New York	138	132	1	9	0	1180.1	1545	1093	693	39	—	—	50	406	—	316	—	—	11.8	2.4	3.1	.308	.365	5.28
AA Total	1100	1048	39	51	9	9495.2	10610	7234	4527	223	—	—	430	3320	—	3075	—	—	10.1	2.9	3.1	.273	.337	4.29
AA Avg Team	138	131	5	6	1	1186.2	1326	904	566	28	—	—	54	415	—	384	—	—	10.1	2.9	3.1	.273	.337	4.29

Team Fielding

Team	G	PO	A	E	TC	DP	PB	Pct
St. Louis	138	3592	1694	481	5767	86	110	.917
Cincinnati	136	3547	1699	484	5730	106	115	.916
Baltimore	141	3654	1742	549	5945	66	145	.908
Philadelphia	137	3555	1608	528	5691	95	167	.907
Brooklyn	138	3547	1804	562	5913	88	117	.905
Louisville	139	3614	1751	574	5939	83	135	.903
Cleveland	133	3401	1701	576	5678	97	120	.899
New York	138	3532	1834	632	5998	102	102	.895
AA Total	1100	28442	13833	4386	46661	723	1011	.906

Team vs. Team Records

	Bal	Bro	Cin	Cle	Lou	NY	Phi	STL	Won
Bal	—	10	11	17	7	15	14	3	77
Bro	9	—	7	13	8	9	10	4	60
Cin	9	13	—	11	8	17	11	12	81
Cle	3	6	6	—	8	11	4	1	39
Lou	11	12	12	11	—	12	11	7	76
NY	4	9	3	8	8	—	7	5	44
Phi	6	8	9	14	8	11	—	8	64
STL	16	16	6	18	13	14	12	—	95
Lost	58	74	54	92	60	89	69	40	

1887 American Association Batting Leaders

Games		At-Bats		Runs		Hits		Doubles		Triples	
O. Burns, Bal	140	A. Latham, STL	627	T. O'Neill, STL	167	T. O'Neill, STL	225	T. O'Neill, STL	52	6 tied with	19
B. Purcell, Bal	140	B. Gleason, STL	598	A. Latham, STL	163	P. Browning, Lou	220	D. Lyons, Phi	43		
G. Pinckney, Bro	138	T. Poorman, Phi	585	M. Griffin, Bal	142	D. Lyons, Phi	209	P. Browning, Lou	35		
3 tied with	137	G. Pinckney, Bro	580	T. Poorman, Phi	140	A. Latham, STL	198	A. Latham, STL	35		
		D. Lyons, Phi	570	C. Comiskey, STL	139	O. Burns, Bal	188	J. Reilly, Cin	35		

Home Runs		Total Bases		Runs Batted In		Walks		Intentional Walks	Strikeouts
T. O'Neill, STL	14	T. O'Neill, STL	357	T. O'Neill, STL	123	P. Radford, NY	106	Statistic unavailable	Statistic unavailable
J. Reilly, Cin	10	P. Browning, Lou	299	P. Browning, Lou	118	Y. Robinson, STL	92		
O. Burns, Bal	9	D. Lyons, Phi	298	J. Davis, Bal	109	H. Nicol, Cin	86		
3 tied with	8	O. Burns, Bal	286	D. Foutz, STL	108	R. Mack, Lou	83		
		J. Reilly, Cin	263	C. Welch, STL	108	F. Fennelly, Cin	82		

Hit By Pitch		Sac Hits	Sac Flies	Stolen Bases		Caught Stealing	GDP
T. Tucker, Bal	29	Statistic unavailable	Statistic unavailable	H. Nicol, Cin	138	Statistic unavailable	Statistic unavailable
Y. Robinson, STL	17			A. Latham, STL	129		
F. Mann, 2tm	15			C. Comiskey, STL	117		
J. Reilly, Cin	15			P. Browning, Lou	103		
J. McTamany, Bro	12			B. McPhee, Cin	95		

Runs Created		Runs Created/27 Outs		Batting Average		On-Base Percentage		Slugging Percentage		OBP+Slugging	
T. O'Neill, STL	192	T. O'Neill, STL	16.99	T. O'Neill, STL	.435	T. O'Neill, STL	.490	T. O'Neill, STL	.691	T. O'Neill, STL	1.180
P. Browning, Lou	163	B. Caruthers, STL	13.03	P. Browning, Lou	.402	P. Browning, Lou	.464	B. Caruthers, STL	.547	P. Browning, Lou	1.011
D. Lyons, Phi	154	P. Browning, Lou	12.88	D. Lyons, Phi	.367	B. Caruthers, STL	.463	P. Browning, Lou	.547	B. Caruthers, STL	1.010
O. Burns, Bal	153	D. Lyons, Phi	11.02	B. Caruthers, STL	.357	Y. Robinson, STL	.445	D. Lyons, Phi	.523	D. Lyons, Phi	.943
A. Latham, STL	138	O. Burns, Bal	10.89	D. Foutz, STL	.357	D. Lyons, Phi	.421	O. Burns, Bal	.519	O. Burns, Bal	.933

1887 American Association Pitching Leaders

Wins		Losses		Winning Percentage		Games		Games Started		Complete Games	
M. Kilroy, Bal	46	A. Mays, NY	34	B. Caruthers, STL	.763	M. Kilroy, Bal	69	M. Kilroy, Bal	69	M. Kilroy, Bal	66
T. Ramsey, Lou	37	B. Crowell, Cle	31	S. King, STL	.727	T. Ramsey, Lou	65	T. Ramsey, Lou	64	T. Ramsey, Lou	61
E. Smith, Cin	34	P. Smith, Bal	30	M. Kilroy, Bal	.708	P. Smith, Bal	58	G. Weyhing, Phi	55	P. Smith, Bal	54
S. King, STL	32	G. Weyhing, Phi	28	D. Foutz, STL	.676	G. Weyhing, Phi	55	P. Smith, Bal	55	G. Weyhing, Phi	53
T. Mullane, Cin	31	T. Ramsey, Lou	27	E. Smith, Cin	.667	E. Seward, Phi	55	3 tied with	52	E. Seward, Phi	52

Shutouts		Saves		Games Finished		Batters Faced		Innings Pitched		Hits Allowed	
M. Kilroy, Bal	6	A. Terry, Bro	3	A. Terry, Bro	5	M. Kilroy, Bal	2492	M. Kilroy, Bal	589.1	M. Kilroy, Bal	585
T. Mullane, Cin	6	6 tied with	1	P. Corkhill, Cin	4	T. Ramsey, Lou	2430	T. Ramsey, Lou	561.0	A. Mays, NY	551
E. Smith, Cin	3			P. Smith, Bal	3	P. Smith, Bal	2204	P. Smith, Bal	491.1	T. Ramsey, Lou	544
E. Seward, Phi	3			C. Stricker, Cle	3	G. Weyhing, Phi	2042	E. Seward, Phi	470.2	B. Crowell, Cle	541
5 tied with	2			6 tied with	2	A. Mays, NY	2002	G. Weyhing, Phi	466.1	P. Smith, Bal	526

Home Runs Allowed		Walks		Walks/9 Innings		Strikeouts		Strikeouts/9 Innings		Strikeout/Walk Ratio	
M. Morrison, Cle	13	M. Morrison, Cle	205	G. Hecker, Lou	1.6	T. Ramsey, Lou	355	T. Ramsey, Lou	5.7	T. Ramsey, Lou	2.13
G. Weyhing, Phi	12	P. Smith, Bal	176	B. Caruthers, STL	1.6	M. Kilroy, Bal	217	M. Morrison, Cle	4.5	E. Smith, Cin	1.40
A. Mays, NY	11	G. Weyhing, Phi	167	J. Lynch, NY	1.7	P. Smith, Bal	206	A. Terry, Bro	3.9	A. Terry, Bro	1.39
T. Mullane, Cin	11	T. Ramsey, Lou	167	D. Foutz, STL	2.4	G. Weyhing, Phi	193	P. Smith, Bal	3.8	M. Kilroy, Bal	1.38
A. Terry, Bro	10	M. Kilroy, Bal	157	M. Kilroy, Bal	2.4	E. Smith, Cin	176	G. Weyhing, Phi	3.7	J. Lynch, NY	1.25

Earned Run Average		Component ERA		Hit Batsmen		Wild Pitches	Opponent Average		Opponent OBP	
E. Smith, Cin	2.94	E. Smith, Cin	2.45	G. Weyhing, Phi	37	Statistic unavailable	E. Smith, Cin	.230	E. Smith, Cin	.286
M. Kilroy, Bal	3.07	B. Caruthers, STL	2.68	T. Mullane, Cin	32		T. Ramsey, Lou	.242	B. Caruthers, STL	.287
T. Mullane, Cin	3.24	T. Ramsey, Lou	2.88	E. Seward, Phi	24		E. Seward, Phi	.244	T. Ramsey, Lou	.299
B. Caruthers, STL	3.30	E. Seward, Phi	2.90	M. Morrison, Cle	22		B. Caruthers, STL	.247	M. Kilroy, Bal	.306
T. Ramsey, Lou	3.43	M. Kilroy, Bal	2.99	3 tied with	20		M. Kilroy, Bal	.253	D. Foutz, STL	.306

1887 American Association Miscellaneous

Managers		
Baltimore	Billy Barnie	77-58
Brooklyn	Charlie Byrne	60-74
Cincinnati	Gus Schmelz	81-54
Cleveland	Jimmy Williams	39-92
Louisville	Honest John Kelly	76-60
New York	Bob Ferguson	6-24
	Dave Orr	3-5
	Ollie Caylor	35-60
Philadelphia	Frank Bancroft	26-29
	Charlie Mason	38-40
St. Louis	Charlie Comiskey	95-40

Awards	
STATS Most Valuable Player	Tip O'Neill, of, STL
STATS Cy Young	Matt Kilroy, Bal
STATS Rookie of the Year	Mike Griffin, of, Bal
STATS Manager of the Year	Billy Barnie, Bal

STATS All-Star Team

C	Kid Baldwin, Cin	.253	1	57
1B	Charlie Comiskey, STL	.335	4	103
2B	Yank Robinson, STL	.305	1	74
3B	Denny Lyons, Phi	.367	6	102
SS	Oyster Burns, Bal	.341	9	99
OF	Pete Browning, Lou	.402	4	118
OF	Dave Foutz, STL	.357	4	108
OF	Tip O'Neill, STL	.435	14	123
P	Bob Caruthers, STL	29-9	3.30	74 K
P	Matt Kilroy, Bal	46-19	3.07	217 K
P	Elmer Smith, Cin	34-17	2.94	176 K

Postseason	
World Series	St. Louis (AA) 5 vs. Detroit (NL) 10

Outstanding Performances

Triple Crown	
Tip O'Neill, STL	.435-14-123

Cycles	
Tip O'Neill, STL	on April 30
Tip O'Neill, STL	on May 7
Dave Orr, NY	on August 10
Bid McPhee, Cin	on August 26

Team	Overall					Home Games						Road Games						Park Index		Record by Month					
	W	L	Pct	GB	DIF	W	L	R	OR	HR	OHR	W	L	R	OR	HR	OHR	Run	HR	M/A	May	June	July	Aug	S/O
New York	84	47	.641	—	79	44	23	313	182	21	9	40	24	347	296	34	18	74	55	5-3	12-9	13-11	18-5	16-8	20-11
Chicago	77	58	.570	9.0	88	43	27	438	336	50	44	34	31	294	323	27	19	116	190	6-2	15-7	14-8	10-14	12-13	20-14
Philadelphia	69	61	.531	14.5	0	37	29	313	268	6	12	32	32	222	241	10	14	122	73	2-7	11-7	13-10	9-15	15-9	19-13
Boston	70	64	.522	15.5	17	36	30	365	315	23	16	34	34	304	305	33	20	115	76	9-0	11-13	12-11	5-17	16-6	17-17
Detroit	68	63	.519	16.0	8	40	26	400	279	24	18	28	37	321	350	27	26	100	78	3-5	14-8	16-6	14-10	5-16	16-18
Pittsburgh	66	68	.493	19.5	4	37	30	280	234	0	1	29	38	254	346	14	22	86	3	5-3	7-13	5-15	13-9	16-9	20-19
Indianapolis	50	85	.370	36.0	0	31	35	328	302	27	40	19	50	270	426	7	24	95	226	2-6	8-14	7-14	13-11	6-21	14-19
Washington	48	86	.358	37.5	0	26	38	260	318	17	25	22	48	222	410	13	25	100	121	1-7	7-14	9-14	11-12	10-14	10-25

Clinch Date—New York 10/03.

Team Batting

Team	G	AB	R	OR	H	2B	3B	HR	TB	RBI	TBB	IBB	SO	HBP	SH	SF	SB	CS	SB%	GDP	Avg	OBP	Slg
Chicago	136	4616	734	659	1201	147	95	77	1769	569	290	—	563	28	—	—	287	—	—	—	.260	.308	.383
Detroit	134	4849	721	629	1275	177	72	51	1749	571	307	—	396	46	—	—	193	—	—	—	.263	.313	.361
Boston	137	4834	669	619	1183	167	89	56	1696	535	282	—	524	32	—	—	293	—	—	—	.245	.291	.351
New York	138	4747	659	479	1149	130	76	55	1596	487	270	—	456	29	—	—	314	—	—	—	.242	.287	.336
Indianapolis	136	4623	603	731	1100	180	33	34	1448	427	236	—	492	43	—	—	350	—	—	—	.238	.281	.313
Philadelphia	132	4528	535	509	1021	151	46	16	1312	418	268	—	485	51	—	—	246	—	—	—	.225	.276	.290
Pittsburgh	139	4713	534	580	1070	150	49	14	1360	392	194	—	583	46	—	—	287	—	—	—	.227	.264	.289
Washington	136	4546	482	731	944	98	49	30	1230	373	246	—	499	43	—	—	331	—	—	—	.208	.255	.271
NL Total	1088	37456	4937	4937	8943	1200	509	333	12160	3772	2093	—	3998	318	—	—	2301	—	—	—	.239	.285	.325
NL Avg Team	136	4682	617	617	1118	150	64	42	1520	472	262	—	500	40	—	—	288	—	—	—	.239	.285	.325

Team Pitching

Team	G	CG	ShO	Rel	Sv	IP	H	R	ER	HR	SH	SF	HB	TBB	IBB	SO	WP	Bk	H/9	SO/9	BB/9	OAvg	OOBP	ERA
New York	138	133	20	4	1	1208.0	907	479	263	27	—	—	37	307	—	726	65	0	6.8	5.4	2.3	.199	.256	1.96
Philadelphia	132	125	16	6	3	1167.0	1072	509	309	26	—	—	25	196	—	519	50	2	8.3	4.0	1.5	.236	.271	2.38
Boston	137	134	7	3	0	1225.1	1104	619	355	36	—	—	46	269	—	484	66	0	8.1	3.6	2.0	.232	.280	2.61
Pittsburgh	139	135	13	3	0	1203.1	1190	580	357	23	—	—	30	223	—	367	47	0	8.9	2.7	1.7	.249	.287	2.67
Detroit	134	130	10	4	1	1199.0	1115	629	365	44	—	—	28	183	—	522	60	1	8.4	3.9	1.4	.234	.266	2.74
Chicago	136	123	13	12	1	1186.1	1139	659	390	63	—	—	59	308	—	588	81	1	8.6	4.5	2.3	.246	.301	2.96
Washington	136	133	6	3	0	1179.1	1157	731	464	50	—	—	46	298	—	406	58	1	8.8	3.1	2.3	.248	.300	3.54
Indianapolis	136	132	6	5	0	1187.2	1260	731	503	64	—	—	42	308	—	388	87	1	9.5	2.9	2.3	.263	.313	3.81
NL Total	1088	1045	91	40	6	9556.0	8944	4937	3006	333	—	—	313	2092	—	4000	514	6	8.4	3.8	2.0	.239	.285	2.83
NL Avg Team	136	131	11	5	1	1194.0	1118	617	376	42	—	—	39	262	—	500	64	1	8.4	3.8	2.0	.239	.285	2.83

Team Fielding

Team	G	PO	A	E	TC	DP	PB	Pct
Pittsburgh	139	3594	1694	416	5704	88	94	.927
Chicago	136	3551	1742	417	5710	112	105	.927
New York	138	3632	1609	432	5673	76	128	.924
Philadelphia	132	3463	1651	424	5538	70	78	.923
Indianapolis	136	3544	1717	449	5710	84	96	.921
Detroit	134	3570	1663	463	5696	83	41	.919
Boston	137	3651	1797	494	5942	91	89	.917
Washington	136	3492	1651	494	5637	69	94	.912
NL Total	1088	28497	13524	3589	45610	673	725	.921

Team vs. Team Records

	Bos	ChN	Det	Ind	NYG	Phi	Pit	WaN	Won
Bos	—	7	10	11	8	9	10	15	70
ChN	12	—	10	14	11	8	9	13	77
Det	8	10	—	11	7	11	10	11	68
Ind	9	6	8	—	5	4	6	12	50
NYG	12	8	11	14	—	14	10	15	84
Phi	10	10	7	13	5	—	14	10	69
Pit	8	11	10	14	7	6	—	10	66
WaN	5	6	7	8	4	9	9	—	48
Lost	64	58	63	85	47	61	68	86	

1888 National League Batting Leaders

Games		At-Bats		Runs		Hits		Doubles		Triples	
B. Kuehne, Pit	138	D. Johnston, Bos	585	D. Brouthers, Det	118	J. Ryan, ChN	182	J. Ryan, ChN	33	D. Johnston, Bos	18
D. Hoy, WaN	136	D. Richardson, NYG	561	J. Ryan, ChN	115	C. Anson, ChN	177	D. Brouthers, Det	33	R. Connor, NYG	17
5 tied with	135	J. Ryan, ChN	549	D. Johnston, Bos	102	D. Johnston, Bos	173	D. Johnston, Bos	31	B. Nash, Bos	15
		B. O'Brien, WaN	528	C. Anson, ChN	101	D. Brouthers, Det	160	J. Denny, Ind	27	B. Ewing, NYG	15
		E. Andrews, Phi	528	R. Connor, NYG	98	D. White, Det	157	P. Hines, Ind	26	2 tied with	14

Home Runs		Total Bases		Runs Batted In		Walks		Intentional Walks		Strikeouts	
J. Ryan, ChN	16	J. Ryan, ChN	283	C. Anson, ChN	84	R. Connor, NYG	73	Statistic unavailable		J. Denny, Ind	79
R. Connor, NYG	14	D. Johnston, Bos	276	B. Nash, Bos	75	D. Hoy, WaN	69			P. Smith, Pit	78
D. Johnston, Bos	12	C. Anson, ChN	257	J. Rowe, Det	74	D. Brouthers, Det	68			E. Seery, Ind	73
J. Denny, Ind	12	D. Brouthers, Det	242	N. Williamson, ChN	73	N. Williamson, ChN	65			N. Williamson, ChN	71
C. Anson, ChN	12	R. Connor, NYG	231	3 tied with	71	E. Seery, Ind	64			B. O'Brien, WaN	70

Hit By Pitch		Sac Hits		Sac Flies		Stolen Bases		Caught Stealing		GDP	
S. Farrar, Phi	13	Statistic unavailable		Statistic unavailable		D. Hoy, WaN	82	Statistic unavailable		Statistic unavailable	
D. Brouthers, Det	12					E. Seery, Ind	80				
D. Hoy, WaN	11					B. Sunday, Pit	71				
F. Carroll, Pit	10					F. Pfeffer, ChN	64				
2 tied with	9					J. Ryan, ChN	60				

Runs Created		Runs Created/27 Outs		Batting Average		On-Base Percentage		Slugging Percentage		OBP+Slugging	
J. Ryan, ChN	132	C. Anson, ChN	9.49	C. Anson, ChN	.344	C. Anson, ChN	.400	J. Ryan, ChN	.515	C. Anson, ChN	.899
D. Brouthers, Det	122	J. Ryan, ChN	9.46	J. Ryan, ChN	.332	D. Brouthers, Det	.399	C. Anson, ChN	.499	J. Ryan, ChN	.892
C. Anson, ChN	122	R. Connor, NYG	8.95	K. Kelly, Bos	.318	R. Connor, NYG	.389	R. Connor, NYG	.480	R. Connor, NYG	.869
R. Connor, NYG	116	D. Brouthers, Det	8.86	D. Brouthers, Det	.307	J. Ryan, ChN	.377	K. Kelly, Bos	.480	D. Brouthers, Det	.862
D. Johnston, Bos	106	K. Kelly, Bos	8.77	B. Ewing, NYG	.306	D. Hoy, WaN	.374	D. Johnston, Bos	.472	K. Kelly, Bos	.848

1888 National League Pitching Leaders

Wins		Losses		Winning Percentage		Games		Games Started		Complete Games	
T. Keefe, NYG	35	H. O'Day, WaN	29	T. Keefe, NYG	.745	E. Morris, Pit	55	E. Morris, Pit	55	E. Morris, Pit	54
J. Clarkson, Bos	33	C. Getzien, Det	25	P. Conway, Det	.682	J. Clarkson, Bos	54	J. Clarkson, Bos	54	J. Clarkson, Bos	53
P. Conway, Det	30	P. Galvin, Pit	25	B. Sanders, Phi	.655	T. Keefe, NYG	51	T. Keefe, NYG	51	P. Galvin, Pit	49
E. Morris, Pit	29	L. Shreve, Ind	24	G. Krock, ChN	.641	P. Galvin, Pit	50	P. Galvin, Pit	50	T. Keefe, NYG	48
C. Buffinton, Phi	28	E. Healy, Ind	24	C. Titcomb, NYG	.636	M. Welch, NYG	47	M. Welch, NYG	47	M. Welch, NYG	47

Shutouts		Saves		Games Finished		Batters Faced		Innings Pitched		Hits Allowed	
B. Sanders, Phi	8	G. Wood, Phi	2	G. Van Haltren, ChN	6	J. Clarkson, Bos	2029	J. Clarkson, Bos	483.1	E. Morris, Pit	470
T. Keefe, NYG	8	G. Van Haltren, ChN	1	J. Ryan, ChN	5	E. Morris, Pit	2002	E. Morris, Pit	480.0	J. Clarkson, Bos	448
C. Buffinton, Phi	6	L. Twitchell, Det	1	7 tied with	2	P. Galvin, Pit	1809	P. Galvin, Pit	437.1	P. Galvin, Pit	446
P. Galvin, Pit	6	E. Crane, NYG	1			T. Keefe, NYG	1723	T. Keefe, NYG	434.1	C. Getzien, Det	411
2 tied with	5	J. Tyng, Phi	1			M. Welch, NYG	1710	M. Welch, NYG	425.1	H. O'Day, WaN	359

Home Runs Allowed		Walks		Walks/9 Innings		Strikeouts		Strikeouts/9 Innings		Strikeout/Walk Ratio	
L. Shreve, Ind	23	J. Clarkson, Bos	119	B. Sanders, Phi	1.1	T. Keefe, NYG	333	T. Keefe, NYG	6.9	C. Getzien, Det	3.74
G. Krock, ChN	20	H. O'Day, WaN	117	P. Galvin, Pit	1.1	J. Clarkson, Bos	223	C. Titcomb, NYG	5.9	B. Sanders, Phi	3.67
H. O'Day, WaN	19	M. Welch, NYG	108	G. Krock, ChN	1.2	C. Getzien, Det	202	M. Baldwin, ChN	5.6	T. Keefe, NYG	3.66
J. Clarkson, Bos	17	M. Baldwin, ChN	99	C. Getzien, Det	1.2	C. Buffinton, Phi	199	G. Van Haltren, ChN	5.1	G. Krock, ChN	3.58
G. Van Haltren, ChN	15	L. Shreve, Ind	93	K. Madden, Bos	1.3	H. O'Day, WaN	186	C. Getzien, Det	4.5	C. Buffinton, Phi	3.37

Earned Run Average		Component ERA		Hit Batsmen		Wild Pitches		Opponent Average		Opponent OBP	
T. Keefe, NYG	1.74	T. Keefe, NYG	1.56	H. O'Day, WaN	16	J. Clarkson, Bos	33	T. Keefe, NYG	.195	P. Conway, Det	.243
B. Sanders, Phi	1.90	C. Buffinton, Phi	1.67	K. Madden, Bos	15	L. Shreve, Ind	24	C. Titcomb, NYG	.201	T. Keefe, NYG	.243
C. Buffinton, Phi	1.91	P. Conway, Det	1.74	E. Healy, Ind	15	C. Getzien, Det	23	M. Welch, NYG	.207	C. Buffinton, Phi	.244
M. Welch, NYG	1.93	C. Titcomb, NYG	1.75	M. Welch, NYG	14	H. Boyle, Ind	22	P. Conway, Det	.208	H. Gruber, Det	.249
B. Sowders, Bos	2.07	B. Sanders, Phi	1.86	3 tied with	13	2 tied with	21	C. Buffinton, Phi	.213	C. Titcomb, NYG	.253

1888 National League Miscellaneous

Managers

Boston	John Morrill	70-64
Chicago	Cap Anson	77-58
Detroit	Bill Watkins	49-44
	Bob Leadley	19-19
Indianapolis	Harry Spence	50-85
New York	Jim Mutrie	84-47
Philadelphia	Harry Wright	69-61
Pittsburgh	Horace Phillips	66-68
Washington	Walter Hewett	10-29
	Ted Sullivan	38-57

Awards

STATS Most Valuable Player	Cap Anson, 1b, ChN
STATS Cy Young	Tim Keefe, NYG
STATS Rookie of the Year	Dummy Hoy, of, WaN
STATS Manager of the Year	Jim Mutrie, NYG

STATS All-Star Team

C	King Kelly, Bos	.318	9	71
1B	Cap Anson, ChN	.344	12	84
2B	Fred Pfeffer, ChN	.250	8	57
3B	Jerry Denny, Ind	.261	12	63
SS	Ned Williamson, ChN	.250	8	73
OF	Dick Johnston, Bos	.296	12	68
OF	Jimmy Ryan, ChN	.332	16	64
OF	Mike Tiernan, NYG	.293	9	52
P	Charlie Buffinton, Phi	28-17	1.91	199 K
P	Tim Keefe, NYG	35-12	1.74	333 K
P	Mickey Welch, NYG	26-19	1.93	167 K

Postseason

World Series	New York (NL) 6 vs. St. Louis (AA) 4

Outstanding Performances

Three-Homer Games
Roger Connor, NYG   on May 9

Cycles
Jimmy Ryan, ChN   on July 28
Mike Tiernan, NYG   on August 25

1888 American Association Standings

Team	W	L	Pct	GB	DIF	W	L	R	OR	HR	OHR	W	L	R	OR	HR	OHR	Run	HR	M/A	May	June	July	Aug	S/O
		Overall						Home Games						Road Games				Park Index				Record by Month			
St. Louis	92	43	.681	—	104	60	21	525	284	22	13	32	22	264	215	14	6	113	117	5-3	14-5	16-7	15-12	18-3	24-13
Brooklyn	88	52	.629	6.5	48	53	20	451	267	18	10	35	32	307	312	7	5	106	214	7-5	18-4	14-9	12-11	8-14	29-9
Philadelphia	81	52	.609	10.0	3	54	20	505	253	20	8	27	32	320	338	11	6	92	131	7-4	7-11	19-4	12-11	16-6	20-16
Cincinnati	80	54	.597	11.5	34	55	24	467	317	24	5	25	30	277	311	8	14	93	92	8-3	15-6	9-13	16-7	12-9	20-16
Baltimore	57	80	.416	36.0	2	30	26	285	276	7	11	27	54	361	503	12	12	94	108	6-4	7-11	12-13	9-16	7-17	16-19
Cleveland	50	82	.379	40.5	0	34	28	374	326	8	12	16	54	278	513	4	26	100	75	2-9	9-11	6-15	12-13	7-12	14-22
Louisville	48	87	.356	44.0	0	27	30	324	303	1	4	21	57	362	567	3	24	92	18	4-7	5-16	7-15	13-10	8-14	11-25
Kansas City	43	89	.326	47.5	0	23	34	330	392	15	10	20	55	249	502	4	22	126	127	2-6	5-16	7-14	8-17	11-12	10-24

Clinch Date—St. Louis 10/03.

Team Batting

Team	G	AB	R	OR	H	2B	3B	HR	TB	RBI	TBB	IBB	SO	HBP	SH	SF	SB	CS	SB%	GDP	Avg	OBP	Slg
Philadelphia	136	4828	827	594	1209	183	89	31	1663	624	303	—	473	77	—	—	434	—	—	—	.250	.305	.344
St. Louis	137	4755	789	501	1189	149	47	36	1540	591	410	—	521	50	—	—	468	—	—	—	.250	.316	.324
Brooklyn	143	4871	758	584	1177	172	70	25	1564	574	353	—	439	56	—	—	334	—	—	—	.242	.300	.321
Cincinnati	137	4801	745	628	1161	132	82	32	1553	571	345	—	555	60	—	—	469	—	—	—	.242	.301	.323
Louisville	139	4881	689	870	1177	183	67	14	1536	543	322	—	604	69	—	—	318	—	—	—	.241	.297	.315
Baltimore	137	4656	653	779	1068	162	70	19	1427	455	298	—	479	58	—	—	326	—	—	—	.229	.284	.306
Cleveland	135	4603	651	839	1076	128	59	12	1358	475	315	—	559	75	—	—	353	—	—	—	.234	.294	.295
Kansas City	132	4588	579	896	1000	142	61	19	1321	431	288	—	604	57	—	—	257	—	—	—	.218	.273	.288
AA Total	1096	37983	5691	5691	9057	1251	545	188	11962	4264	2634	—	4234	502	—	—	2959	—	—	—	.238	.297	.315
AA Avg Team	137	4748	711	711	1132	156	68	24	1495	533	329	—	529	63	—	—	370	—	—	—	.238	.297	.315

Team Pitching

Team	G	CG	ShO	Rel	Sv	IP	H	R	ER	HR	SH	SF	HB	TBB	IBB	SO	WP	Bk	H/9	SO/9	BB/9	OAvg	OOBP	ERA
St. Louis	137	132	12	5	0	1212.2	939	501	282	19	—	—	—	225	—	517	—	—	7.0	3.8	1.7	.206	.244	2.09
Brooklyn	143	138	9	5	0	1286.1	1059	584	333	15	—	—	—	285	—	577	—	—	7.4	4.0	2.0	.215	.258	2.33
Philadelphia	136	133	13	3	0	1208.2	988	594	324	14	—	—	—	324	—	596	—	—	7.4	4.4	2.4	.215	.267	2.41
Cincinnati	137	132	10	5	2	1237.2	1103	628	375	19	—	—	—	310	—	539	—	—	8.0	3.9	2.3	.230	.277	2.73
Louisville	139	133	6	6	0	1231.1	1264	870	444	28	—	—	—	281	—	599	—	—	9.2	4.4	2.1	.256	.296	3.25
Cleveland	135	131	6	4	1	1171.0	1235	839	484	38	—	—	—	389	—	500	—	—	9.5	3.8	3.0	.261	.318	3.72
Baltimore	137	130	3	9	0	1200.1	1162	779	504	23	—	—	—	419	—	525	—	—	8.7	3.9	3.1	.245	.307	3.78
Kansas City	132	128	4	4	0	1157.2	1306	896	552	32	—	—	—	401	—	381	—	—	10.2	3.0	3.1	.275	.331	4.29
AA Total	1096	1057	63	41	3	9705.2	9056	5691	3298	188	—	—	—	2634	—	4234	—	—	8.4	3.9	2.4	.238	.288	3.06
AA Avg Team	137	132	8	5	0	1213.2	1132	711	412	24	—	—	—	329	—	529	—	—	8.4	3.9	2.4	.238	.288	3.06

Team Fielding

Team	G	PO	A	E	TC	DP	PB	Pct
St. Louis	137	3634	1614	430	5678	73	98	.924
Cincinnati	137	3708	1792	456	5956	100	96	.923
Baltimore	137	3597	1703	461	5761	88	118	.920
Philadelphia	136	3620	1747	475	5842	73	132	.919
Brooklyn	143	3850	1771	502	6123	88	98	.918
Cleveland	135	3511	1752	488	5751	87	129	.915
Kansas City	132	3468	1954	507	5929	95	114	.914
Louisville	139	3691	1770	609	6070	75	131	.900
AA Total	1096	29079	14103	3928	47110	679	916	.917

Team vs. Team Records

	Bal	Bro	Cin	Cle	KC	Lou	Phi	STL	Won
Bal	—	8	6	10	11	11	5	6	57
Bro	12	—	14	16	11	13	12	10	88
Cin	14	6	—	10	15	17	10	8	80
Cle	9	4	7	—	10	9	7	4	50
KC	8	9	4	9	—	6	3	4	43
Lou	9	7	3	8	12	—	5	4	48
Phi	14	8	10	13	14	15	—	7	81
STL	14	10	10	16	16	16	10	—	92
Lost	80	52	54	82	89	87	52	43	

1888 American Association Batting Leaders

Games		At-Bats		Runs		Hits		Doubles		Triples	
G. Pinckney, Bro	143	C. Comiskey, STL	576	G. Pinckney, Bro	134	T. O'Neill, STL	177	H. Collins, 2tm	31	H. Stovey, Phi	20
D. Foutz, Bro	140	G. Pinckney, Bro	575	H. Collins, 2tm	133	J. Reilly, Cin	169	H. Larkin, Phi	28	E. McKean, Cle	15
M. Griffin, Bal	137	A. Latham, STL	570	H. Stovey, Phi	127	E. McKean, Cle	164	C. Wolf, Lou	28	O. Burns, 2tm	15
P. Corkhill, 2tm	137	D. Foutz, Bro	563	C. Welch, Phi	125	H. Collins, 2tm	162	J. Reilly, Cin	28	J. Reilly, Cin	14
C. Comiskey, STL	137	P. Corkhill, 2tm	561	A. Latham, STL	119	P. Corkhill, 2tm	160	2 tied with	27	D. Foutz, Bro	13

Home Runs		Total Bases		Runs Batted In		Walks		Intentional Walks		Strikeouts	
J. Reilly, Cin	13	J. Reilly, Cin	264	J. Reilly, Cin	103	Y. Robinson, STL	116	Statistic unavailable		Statistic unavailable	
H. Stovey, Phi	9	H. Stovey, Phi	244	H. Larkin, Phi	101	F. Fennelly, 2tm	72				
H. Larkin, Phi	7	T. O'Neill, STL	236	D. Foutz, Bro	99	J. McTamany, KC	67				
5 tied with	6	E. McKean, Cle	233	T. O'Neill, STL	98	H. Nicol, Cin	67				
		O. Burns, 2tm	230	P. Corkhill, 2tm	93	G. Pinckney, Bro	66				

Hit By Pitch		Sac Hits		Sac Flies		Stolen Bases		Caught Stealing		GDP	
C. Welch, Phi	29	Statistic unavailable		Statistic unavailable		A. Latham, STL	109	Statistic unavailable		Statistic unavailable	
J. Faatz, Cle	21					H. Nicol, Cin	103				
T. Tucker, Bal	18					C. Welch, Phi	95				
J. Reilly, Cin	18					T. McCarthy, STL	93				
R. Mack, Lou	15					H. Stovey, Phi	87				

Runs Created		Runs Created/27 Outs		Batting Average		On-Base Percentage		Slugging Percentage		OBP+Slugging	
H. Stovey, Phi	128	T. O'Neill, STL	9.37	T. O'Neill, STL	.335	Y. Robinson, STL	.400	J. Reilly, Cin	.501	J. Reilly, Cin	.864
T. O'Neill, STL	125	J. Reilly, Cin	9.14	J. Reilly, Cin	.321	T. O'Neill, STL	.390	H. Stovey, Phi	.460	T. O'Neill, STL	.836
J. Reilly, Cin	124	H. Stovey, Phi	8.94	H. Collins, 2tm	.307	H. Collins, 2tm	.373	T. O'Neill, STL	.446	H. Stovey, Phi	.825
G. Pinckney, Bro	112	D. Lyons, Phi	8.22	E. McKean, Cle	.299	H. Stovey, Phi	.365	O. Burns, 2tm	.435	H. Collins, 2tm	.796
C. Welch, Phi	111	H. Collins, 2tm	7.88	D. Lyons, Phi	.296	D. Lyons, Phi	.363	E. McKean, Cle	.425	O. Burns, 2tm	.780

1888 American Association Pitching Leaders

Wins		Losses		Winning Percentage		Games		Games Started		Complete Games	
S. King, STL	45	H. Porter, KC	37	N. Hudson, STL	.714	S. King, STL	66	S. King, STL	65	S. King, STL	64
E. Seward, Phi	35	J. Bakely, Cle	33	E. Chamberlin, 2tm	.694	J. Bakely, Cle	61	J. Bakely, Cle	61	J. Bakely, Cle	60
B. Caruthers, Bro	29	T. Ramsey, Lou	30	S. King, STL	.682	E. Seward, Phi	57	E. Seward, Phi	57	E. Seward, Phi	57
G. Weyhing, Phi	28	B. Cunningham, Bal	29	B. Caruthers, Bro	.659	H. Porter, KC	55	H. Porter, KC	54	H. Porter, KC	53
L. Viau, Cin	27	2 tied with	21	L. Viau, Cin	.659	B. Cunningham, Bal	51	B. Cunningham, Bal	51	B. Cunningham, Bal	50

Shutouts		Saves		Games Finished		Batters Faced		Innings Pitched		Hits Allowed	
S. King, STL	6	B. Gilks, Cle	1	S. Stratton, Lou	5	Statistic unavailable		S. King, STL	585.2	H. Porter, KC	527
E. Seward, Phi	6	P. Corkhill, Cin	1	O. Burns, Bal	4			J. Bakely, Cle	532.2	J. Bakely, Cle	518
E. Smith, Cin	5	T. Mullane, Cin	1	D. Foutz, Bro	4			E. Seward, Phi	518.2	S. King, STL	437
N. Hudson, STL	5			9 tied with	2			H. Porter, KC	474.0	B. Cunningham, Bal	412
5 tied with	4							B. Cunningham, Bal	453.1	E. Seward, Phi	388

Home Runs Allowed		Walks		Walks/9 Innings		Strikeouts		Strikeouts/9 Innings		Strikeout/Walk Ratio	
H. Porter, KC	16	B. Cunningham, Bal	157	S. King, STL	1.2	E. Seward, Phi	272	A. Terry, Bro	6.4	S. King, STL	3.39
J. Bakely, Cle	14	P. Smith, 2tm	147	B. Caruthers, Bro	1.2	S. King, STL	258	T. Ramsey, Lou	6.0	T. Ramsey, Lou	2.65
T. Ramsey, Lou	10	J. Bakely, Cle	128	N. Hudson, STL	1.6	T. Ramsey, Lou	228	E. Chamberlin, 2tm	5.1	B. Caruthers, Bro	2.64
B. Crowell, 2tm	9	E. Seward, Phi	127	J. Ewing, Lou	1.6	J. Bakely, Cle	212	P. Smith, 2tm	4.9	J. Ewing, Lou	2.56
T. Mullane, Cin	9	H. Porter, KC	120	G. Hecker, Lou	1.7	G. Weyhing, Phi	204	E. Seward, Phi	4.7	T. Mullane, Cin	2.48

Earned Run Average		Component ERA		Hit Batsmen		Wild Pitches		Opponent Average		Opponent OBP	
S. King, STL	1.64	S. King, STL	1.44	Statistic unavailable		Statistic unavailable		A. Terry, Bro	.191	S. King, STL	.224
E. Seward, Phi	2.01	E. Seward, Phi	1.67					S. King, STL	.197	B. Caruthers, Bro	.248
A. Terry, Bro	2.03	B. Caruthers, Bro	1.86					E. Seward, Phi	.199	E. Seward, Phi	.248
M. Hughes, Bro	2.13	E. Chamberlin, 2tm	1.88					G. Weyhing, Phi	.204	N. Hudson, STL	.256
E. Chamberlin, 2tm	2.19	M. Hughes, Bro	1.89					M. Hughes, Bro	.206	A. Terry, Bro	.257

1888 American Association Miscellaneous

Managers

Baltimore	Billy Barnie	57-80
Brooklyn	Bill McGunnigle	88-52
Cincinnati	Gus Schmelz	80-54
Cleveland	Jimmy Williams	20-44
	Tom Loftus	30-38
Kansas City	Dave Rowe	14-36
	Sam Barkley	21-36
	Bill Watkins	8-17
Louisville	Honest John Kelly	10-29
	Mordecai Davidson	1-2
	John Kerins	3-4
	Mordecai Davidson	34-52
Philadelphia	Bill Sharsig	81-52
St. Louis	Charlie Comiskey	92-43

Awards

STATS Most Valuable Player	Silver King, p, STL
STATS Cy Young	Silver King, STL
STATS Rookie of the Year	Mickey Hughes, p, Bro
STATS Manager of the Year	Charlie Comiskey, STL

STATS All-Star Team

C	Jim Keenan, Cin	.233	1	40
1B	John Reilly, Cin	.321	13	103
2B	Yank Robinson, STL	.231	3	53
3B	Denny Lyons, Phi	.296	6	83
SS	Ed McKean, Cle	.299	6	68
OF	Pete Browning, Lou	.313	3	72
OF	Tip O'Neill, STL	.335	5	98
OF	Harry Stovey, Phi	.287	9	65
P	Bob Caruthers, Bro	29-15	2.39	140 K
P	Silver King, STL	45-21	1.64	258 K
P	Ed Seward, Phi	35-19	2.01	272 K

Postseason

World Series	St. Louis (AA) 4 vs. New York (NL) 6

Outstanding Performances

No-Hitters

Adonis Terry, Bro	vs. Lou on May 27
Henry Porter, KC	@ Bal on June 6
Ed Seward, Phi	vs. Cin on July 26
Gus Weyhing, Phi	vs. KC on July 31

Cycles

Harry Stovey, Phi	on May 15
Sam Barkley, KC	on June 13

1889 National League Standings

Team	Overall					Home Games						Road Games						Park Index		Record by Month					
	W	L	Pct	GB	DIF	W	L	R	OR	HR	OHR	W	L	R	OR	HR	OHR	Run	HR	M/A	May	June	July	Aug	S/O
New York	83	43	.659	—	29	47	15	513	311	18	15	36	28	422	396	34	23	104	60	3-1	14-11	12-7	15-10	18-9	21-5
Boston	83	45	.648	1.0	134	48	17	455	272	24	14	35	28	371	352	18	27	97	82	2-2	18-4	14-9	15-10	14-10	20-10
Chicago	67	65	.508	19.0	0	37	30	450	398	54	52	30	35	416	417	25	19	99	234	2-3	11-14	11-12	16-10	15-12	12-14
Philadelphia	63	64	.496	20.5	13	43	24	467	347	27	12	20	40	274	402	17	21	108	92	2-1	17-9	8-15	16-9	10-14	10-16
Pittsburgh	61	71	.462	25.0	2	40	28	388	307	6	2	21	43	337	492	36	40	79	10	4-2	8-16	10-11	9-16	17-14	13-12
Cleveland	61	72	.459	25.5	0	33	35	353	341	8	13	28	37	302	379	17	23	97	50	3-4	14-9	17-7	9-15	7-19	11-18
Indianapolis	59	75	.440	28.0	1	32	36	495	478	50	54	27	39	325	416	12	19	127	326	3-3	7-17	9-11	10-17	16-13	14-14
Washington	41	83	.331	41.0	0	24	29	302	323	12	10	17	54	330	569	13	27	93	74	0-3	6-15	7-16	10-13	11-17	7-19

Clinch Date—New York 10/05.

Team Batting

Team	G	AB	R	OR	H	2B	3B	HR	TB	RBI	TBB	IBB	SO	HBP	SH	SF	SB	CS	SB%	GDP	Avg	OBP	Slg
New York	131	4671	935	708	1319	208	77	52	1837	742	538	—	386	27	—	—	292	—	—	—	.282	.360	.393
Chicago	136	4849	867	814	1274	184	66	79	1827	705	518	—	516	30	—	—	243	—	—	—	.263	.338	.377
Boston	133	4628	826	626	1251	196	54	42	1681	667	471	—	450	41	—	—	331	—	—	—	.270	.343	.363
Indianapolis	135	4879	819	894	1356	228	35	62	1840	662	377	—	447	44	—	—	252	—	—	—	.278	.335	.377
Philadelphia	130	4695	742	748	1248	215	52	44	1699	605	393	—	353	35	—	—	269	—	—	—	.266	.327	.362
Pittsburgh	134	4748	726	801	1202	209	65	42	1667	596	420	—	467	44	—	—	231	—	—	—	.253	.320	.351
Cleveland	136	4673	656	720	1167	131	59	25	1491	523	429	—	417	38	—	—	237	—	—	—	.250	.318	.319
Washington	127	4395	632	892	1105	151	57	25	1445	488	466	—	456	43	—	—	232	—	—	—	.251	.329	.329
NL Total	1062	37538	6203	6203	9922	1522	465	371	13487	4988	3612	—	3492	302	—	—	2087	—	—	—	.264	.334	.359
NL Avg Team	133	4692	775	775	1240	190	58	46	1686	624	452	—	437	38	—	—	261	—	—	—	.264	.334	.359

Team Pitching

Team	G	CG	ShO	Rel	Sv	IP	H	R	ER	HR	SH	SF	HB	TBB	IBB	SO	WP	Bk	H/9	SO/9	BB/9	OAvg	OOBP	ERA
Boston	133	121	10	12	4	1166.0	1152	626	435	41	—	—	—	413	—	497	31	0	8.9	3.8	3.2	.248	.309	3.36
New York	131	118	6	13	3	1151.0	1073	708	444	38	—	—	—	523	—	558	51	0	8.4	4.4	4.1	.239	.318	3.47
Cleveland	136	132	6	5	1	1191.2	1182	720	485	36	—	—	—	519	—	435	79	0	8.9	3.3	3.9	.251	.325	3.66
Chicago	136	123	6	13	2	1237.0	1313	814	512	71	—	—	—	408	—	434	50	0	9.6	3.2	3.0	.263	.319	3.73
Philadelphia	130	106	4	27	2	1153.1	1288	748	513	33	—	—	—	428	—	443	47	0	10.1	3.5	3.3	.274	.334	4.00
Pittsburgh	134	125	5	9	1	1130.2	1296	801	566	42	—	—	—	374	—	345	63	0	10.3	2.7	3.0	.282	.336	4.51
Washington	127	113	1	16	0	1103.0	1261	892	573	37	—	—	—	527	—	388	55	1	10.3	3.2	4.3	.278	.353	4.68
Indianapolis	135	109	3	29	2	1174.1	1365	894	633	73	—	—	—	420	—	440	44	0	10.5	3.1	3.2	.282	.339	4.85
NL Total	1062	947	41	124	15	9307.0	9930	6203	4161	371	—	—	—	3612	—	3508	420	1	9.6	3.4	3.5	.264	.329	4.02
NL Avg Team	133	118	5	16	2	1163.0	1241	775	520	46	—	—	—	452	—	439	53	0	9.6	3.4	3.5	.264	.329	4.02

Team Fielding

Team	G	PO	A	E	TC	DP	PB	Pct
Cleveland	136	3562	1780	365	5707	108	84	.936
Pittsburgh	134	3513	1679	385	5577	94	77	.931
Boston	133	3503	1694	413	5610	105	46	.926
Indianapolis	135	3489	1762	420	5671	102	73	.926
Chicago	136	3734	1843	463	6040	91	92	.923
New York	131	3418	1574	437	5429	90	51	.920
Philadelphia	130	3437	1597	466	5500	92	59	.915
Washington	127	3299	1613	519	5431	91	54	.904
NL Total	1062	27955	13542	3468	44965	773	536	.923

Team vs. Team Records

	Bos	ChN	Cle	Ind	NYG	Phi	Pit	WaN	Won
Bos	—	10	12	10	8	13	16	14	83
ChN	7	—	11	13	5	9	10	12	67
Cle	8	9	—	9	4	10	7	14	61
Ind	10	7	10	—	7	4	10	11	59
NYG	6	13	14	13	—	12	12	13	83
Phi	6	10	9	13	7	—	9	9	63
Pit	3	9	13	10	7	9	—	10	61
WaN	5	7	3	7	5	7	7	—	41
Lost	45	65	72	75	43	64	71	83	

1889 National League Batting Leaders

Games		At-Bats		Runs		Hits		Doubles		Triples	
H. Duffy, ChN	136	H. Duffy, ChN	584	M. Tiernan, NYG	147	J. Glasscock, Ind	205	K. Kelly, Bos	41	W. Wilmot, WaN	19
P. Tebeau, Cle	136	J. Glasscock, Ind	582	H. Duffy, ChN	144	D. Brouthers, Bos	181	J. Glasscock, Ind	40	J. Fogarty, Phi	17
P. Radford, Cle	136	J. Denny, Ind	578	J. Ryan, ChN	140	J. Ryan, ChN	177	S. Thompson, Phi	36	R. Connor, NYG	17
C. Stricker, Cle	136	J. Ryan, ChN	576	G. Gore, NYG	132	H. Duffy, ChN	172	J. O'Rourke, NYG	36	M. Tiernan, NYG	14
T. Burns, ChN	136	C. Stricker, Cle	566	J. Glasscock, Ind	128	G. Van Haltren, ChN	168	H. Richardson, Bos	33	J. Ryan, ChN	14

Home Runs		Total Bases		Runs Batted In		Walks		Intentional Walks		Strikeouts	
S. Thompson, Phi	20	J. Ryan, ChN	287	R. Connor, NYG	130	M. Tiernan, NYG	96	Statistic unavailable		P. Smith, 2tm	68
J. Denny, Ind	18	J. Glasscock, Ind	272	D. Brouthers, Bos	118	R. Connor, NYG	93			J. Denny, Ind	63
J. Ryan, ChN	17	S. Thompson, Phi	262	C. Anson, ChN	117	P. Radford, Cle	91			J. Ryan, ChN	62
R. Connor, NYG	13	R. Connor, NYG	262	J. Denny, Ind	112	C. Anson, ChN	86			S. Wise, WaN	62
H. Duffy, ChN	12	M. Tiernan, NYG	248	S. Thompson, Phi	111	F. Carroll, Pit	85			2 tied with	60

Hit By Pitch		Sac Hits		Sac Flies		Stolen Bases		Caught Stealing		GDP	
D. Brouthers, Bos	14	Statistic unavailable		Statistic unavailable		J. Fogarty, Phi	99	Statistic unavailable		Statistic unavailable	
F. Carroll, Pit	11					K. Kelly, Bos	68				
J. Faatz, Cle	10					T. Brown, Bos	63				
E. Seery, Ind	10					M. Ward, NYG	62				
P. Smith, 2tm	10					J. Glasscock, Ind	57				

Runs Created		Runs Created/27 Outs		Batting Average		On-Base Percentage		Slugging Percentage		OBP+Slugging	
M. Tiernan, NYG	145	D. Brouthers, Bos	11.80	D. Brouthers, Bos	.373	D. Brouthers, Bos	.462	R. Connor, NYG	.528	D. Brouthers, Bos	.969
J. Ryan, ChN	145	M. Tiernan, NYG	11.36	J. Glasscock, Ind	.352	M. Tiernan, NYG	.447	D. Brouthers, Bos	.507	R. Connor, NYG	.955
R. Connor, NYG	141	R. Connor, NYG	10.82	M. Tiernan, NYG	.335	R. Connor, NYG	.426	J. Ryan, ChN	.498	M. Tiernan, NYG	.944
D. Brouthers, Bos	138	J. Ryan, ChN	9.45	J. O'Rourke, NYG	.321	G. Gore, NYG	.416	M. Tiernan, NYG	.497	J. Ryan, ChN	.886
J. Glasscock, Ind	133	C. Anson, ChN	9.25	E. McKean, Cle	.318	C. Anson, ChN	.414	S. Thompson, Phi	.492	J. Glasscock, Ind	.857

1889 National League Pitching Leaders

Wins		Losses		Winning Percentage		Games		Games Started		Complete Games	
J. Clarkson, Bos	49	H. Staley, Pit	26	J. Clarkson, Bos	.721	J. Clarkson, Bos	73	J. Clarkson, Bos	72	J. Clarkson, Bos	68
C. Buffinton, Phi	28	H. Boyle, Ind	23	M. Welch, NYG	.692	H. Staley, Pit	49	H. Staley, Pit	47	H. Staley, Pit	46
T. Keefe, NYG	28	C. Getzien, Ind	22	T. Keefe, NYG	.683	C. Buffinton, Phi	47	H. Boyle, Ind	45	D. O'Brien, Cle	39
M. Welch, NYG	27	J. Bakely, Cle	22	O. H. Radbourn, Bos	.645	T. Keefe, NYG	47	T. Keefe, NYG	45	M. Welch, NYG	39
P. Galvin, Pit	23	2 tied with	19	C. Buffinton, Phi	.636	H. Boyle, Ind	46	C. Getzien, Ind	44	3 tied with	38

Shutouts		Saves		Games Finished		Batters Faced		Innings Pitched		Hits Allowed	
J. Clarkson, Bos	8	B. Sowders, 2tm	2	A. Rusie, Ind	11	Statistic unavailable		J. Clarkson, Bos	620.0	J. Clarkson, Bos	589
P. Galvin, Pit	4	B. Bishop, ChN	2	K. Gleason, Phi	7			H. Staley, Pit	420.0	H. Staley, Pit	433
4 tied with	3	M. Welch, NYG	2	M. Sullivan, WaN	6			C. Buffinton, Phi	380.0	H. Boyle, Ind	422
		9 tied with	1	3 tied with	5			H. Boyle, Ind	378.2	B. Sanders, Phi	406
								M. Welch, NYG	375.0	C. Getzien, Ind	395

Home Runs Allowed		Walks		Walks/9 Innings		Strikeouts		Strikeouts/9 Innings		Strikeout/Walk Ratio	
C. Getzien, Ind	27	J. Clarkson, Bos	203	P. Galvin, Pit	2.1	J. Clarkson, Bos	284	T. Keefe, NYG	5.2	J. Clarkson, Bos	1.40
P. Galvin, Pit	19	D. O'Brien, Cle	167	H. Boyle, Ind	2.3	T. Keefe, NYG	209	E. Crane, NYG	5.1	C. Getzien, Ind	1.39
A. Gumbert, ChN	16	T. Keefe, NYG	151	O. H. Radbourn, Bos	2.3	H. Staley, Pit	159	A. Rusie, Ind	4.4	T. Keefe, NYG	1.38
J. Tener, ChN	16	M. Welch, NYG	149	F. Dwyer, ChN	2.3	C. Buffinton, Phi	153	E. Healy, 2tm	4.3	O. H. Radbourn, Bos	1.38
J. Clarkson, Bos	16	G. Keefe, WaN	143	B. Sanders, Phi	2.5	C. Getzien, Ind	139	J. Clarkson, Bos	4.1	H. Staley, Pit	1.37

Earned Run Average		Component ERA		Hit Batsmen		Wild Pitches		Opponent Average		Opponent OBP	
J. Clarkson, Bos	2.73	T. Keefe, NYG	2.56	Statistic unavailable		H. Staley, Pit	30	T. Keefe, NYG	.216	J. Clarkson, Bos	.296
J. Bakely, Cle	2.96	J. Clarkson, Bos	2.88			D. O'Brien, Cle	27	J. Clarkson, Bos	.234	T. Keefe, NYG	.299
M. Welch, NYG	3.02	M. Welch, NYG	3.23			J. Bakely, Cle	24	D. Casey, Phi	.243	E. Morris, Pit	.299
C. Buffinton, Phi	3.24	H. Staley, Pit	3.23			3 tied with	18	M. Welch, NYG	.245	C. Getzien, Ind	.305
T. Keefe, NYG	3.31	J. Bakely, Cle	3.27					E. Morris, Pit	.251	H. Staley, Pit	.311

1889 National League Miscellaneous

Managers		
Boston	Jim Hart	83-45
Chicago	Cap Anson	67-65
Cleveland	Tom Loftus	61-72
Indianapolis	Frank Bancroft	25-43
	Jack Glasscock	34-32
New York	Jim Mutrie	83-43
Philadelphia	Harry Wright	63-64
Pittsburgh	Horace Phillips	28-43
	Fred Dunlap	7-10
	Ned Hanlon	26-18
Washington	John Morrill	13-38
	Arthur Irwin	28-45

Awards

STATS Most Valuable Player	John Clarkson, p, Bos
STATS Cy Young	John Clarkson, Bos
STATS Rookie of the Year	Patsy Tebeau, 3b, Cle
STATS Manager of the Year	Jim Hart, Bos

STATS All-Star Team

C	Buck Ewing, NYG	.327	4	87
1B	Dan Brouthers, Bos	.373	7	118
2B	Hardy Richardson, Bos	.304	6	79
3B	Jerry Denny, Ind	.282	18	112
SS	Jack Glasscock, Ind	.352	7	85
OF	Jimmy Ryan, ChN	.307	17	72
OF	Sam Thompson, Phi	.296	20	111
OF	Mike Tiernan, NYG	.335	10	73
P	Charlie Buffinton, Phi	28-16	3.24	153 K
P	John Clarkson, Bos	49-19	2.73	284 K
P	Mickey Welch, NYG	27-12	3.02	125 K

Postseason

World Series	New York (NL) 6 vs. Brooklyn (AA) 3

Outstanding Performances

Cycles

Jack Glasscock, Ind	on August 8
Larry Twitchell, Cle	on August 15

1889 American Association Standings

Team	Overall					Home Games						Road Games						Park Index		Record by Month					
	W	L	Pct	GB	DIF	W	L	R	OR	HR	OHR	W	L	R	OR	HR	OHR	Run	HR	M/A	May	June	July	Aug	S/O
Brooklyn	93	44	.679	—	46	50	18	488	297	28	19	43	26	510	417	19	14	86	145	3-7	18-7	15-8	15-6	20-8	22-8
St. Louis	90	45	.667	2.0	134	51	18	581	317	45	28	39	27	372	367	13	11	116	291	11-2	16-10	14-7	16-9	14-8	19-9
Philadelphia	75	58	.564	16.0	5	46	22	506	347	16	13	29	36	380	440	27	22	99	57	8-2	10-13	16-7	9-11	16-11	16-14
Cincinnati	76	63	.547	18.0	0	47	26	543	362	37	19	29	37	354	407	15	16	108	163	4-8	17-9	10-10	14-11	13-12	18-13
Baltimore	70	65	.519	22.0	2	41	23	436	314	10	4	29	42	355	481	10	23	100	47	7-3	9-14	17-7	13-9	15-10	9-22
Columbus	60	78	.435	33.5	1	36	33	407	350	13	11	24	45	376	573	23	22	80	53	2-8	10-14	10-13	9-17	10-16	19-10
Kansas City	55	82	.401	38.0	4	35	35	523	518	8	17	20	47	329	512	10	34	118	54	7-4	11-13	7-15	6-16	12-16	12-18
Louisville	27	111	.196	66.5	0	18	47	330	473	10	18	9	64	302	617	12	25	98	85	2-10	6-17	2-24	9-12	4-23	4-25

Clinch Date—Brooklyn 10/15.

Team Batting

Team	G	AB	R	OR	H	2B	3B	HR	TB	RBI	TBB	IBB	SO	HBP	SH	SF	SB	CS	SB%	GDP	Avg	OBP	Slg
Brooklyn	140	4815	995	706	1265	188	79	47	1752	761	550	—	401	49	—	—	389	—	—	—	.263	.344	.364
St. Louis	141	4939	957	680	1312	211	64	58	1825	743	493	—	477	55	—	—	336	—	—	—	.266	.339	.370
Cincinnati	141	4844	897	769	1307	197	96	52	1852	696	452	—	511	60	—	—	462	—	—	—	.270	.340	.382
Philadelphia	138	4868	880	787	1339	239	65	43	1837	680	534	—	496	62	—	—	252	—	—	—	.275	.354	.377
Kansas City	139	4947	852	1031	1256	162	76	18	1624	621	430	—	626	66	—	—	472	—	—	—	.254	.322	.328
Baltimore	139	4756	791	795	1209	155	68	20	1560	618	418	—	536	82	—	—	311	—	—	—	.254	.325	.328
Columbus	140	4816	779	924	1247	171	95	36	1716	617	507	—	609	42	—	—	304	—	—	—	.259	.335	.356
Louisville	140	4955	632	1091	1249	170	75	22	1635	503	320	—	521	41	—	—	203	—	—	—	.252	.303	.330
AA Total	1118	38940	6783	6783	10184	1493	618	296	13801	5239	3704	—	4177	457	—	—	2729	—	—	—	.262	.333	.354
AA Avg Team	140	4868	848	848	1273	187	77	37	1725	655	463	—	522	57	—	—	341	—	—	—	.262	.333	.354

Team Pitching

Team	G	CG	ShO	Rel	Sv	IP	H	R	ER	HR	SH	SF	HB	TBB	IBB	SO	WP	Bk	H/9	SO/9	BB/9	OAvg	OOBP	ERA
St. Louis	141	121	7	20	3	1237.2	1166	680	413	39	—	—	—	413	—	617	—	—	8.5	4.5	3.0	.242	.301	3.00
Cincinnati	141	114	3	27	8	1243.0	1270	769	484	35	—	—	—	475	—	562	—	—	9.2	4.1	3.4	.257	.322	3.50
Philadelphia	138	130	9	8	1	1199.1	1200	787	470	35	—	—	—	509	—	479	—	—	9.0	3.6	3.8	.253	.325	3.53
Baltimore	139	128	10	12	1	1192.0	1168	795	471	27	—	—	—	424	—	540	—	—	8.8	4.1	3.2	.249	.311	3.56
Brooklyn	140	120	10	20	1	1212.2	1205	706	487	33	—	—	—	400	—	471	—	—	8.9	3.5	3.0	.251	.309	3.61
Kansas City	139	128	0	11	2	1204.1	1373	1031	583	51	—	—	—	457	—	447	—	—	10.3	3.3	3.4	.278	.339	4.36
Columbus	140	114	9	27	4	1199.0	1274	924	585	33	—	—	—	551	—	610	—	—	9.6	4.6	4.1	.264	.340	4.39
Louisville	140	127	2	13	1	1226.1	1529	1091	656	43	—	—	—	475	—	451	—	—	11.2	3.3	3.5	.296	.356	4.81
AA Total	1118	982	50	138	21	9714.1	10185	6783	4149	296	—	—	—	3704	—	4177	—	—	9.4	3.9	3.4	.262	.326	3.84
AA Avg Team	140	123	6	17	3	1214.1	1273	848	519	37	—	—	—	463	—	522	—	—	9.4	3.9	3.4	.262	.326	3.84

Team Fielding

Team	G	PO	A	E	TC	DP	PB	Pct
Brooklyn	140	3636	1751	421	5808	92	87	.928
Cincinnati	141	3724	1781	440	5945	121	112	.926
St. Louis	141	3710	1705	438	5853	100	110	.925
Philadelphia	138	3597	1792	465	5854	120	75	.921
Columbus	140	3596	1796	497	5889	92	131	.916
Baltimore	139	3565	1663	536	5764	104	95	.907
Louisville	140	3674	1987	584	6245	117	151	.906
Kansas City	139	3607	1865	611	6083	109	110	.900
AA Total	1118	29109	14340	3992	47441	855	871	.916

Team vs. Team Records

	Bal	Bro	Cin	CoC	KC	Lou	Phi	STL	Won
Bal	—	8	8	12	11	16	8	7	70
Bro	12	—	15	11	16	19	12	8	93
Cin	11	5	—	11	14	18	9	8	76
CoC	8	8	9	—	9	13	7	6	60
KC	7	4	6	11	—	13	8	6	55
Lou	4	1	2	7	7	—	5	2	27
Phi	11	7	11	12	12	14	—	8	75
STL	12	11	12	14	14	18	9	—	90
Lost	65	44	63	78	82	111	58	45	

1889 American Association Batting Leaders

Games			At-Bats			Runs			Hits			Doubles			Triples		
O. Beard, Cin	141		T. McCarthy, STL	604		M. Griffin, Bal	152		T. Tucker, Bal	196		C. Welch, Phi	39		L. Marr, CoC	15	
S. Fuller, STL	140		C. Comiskey, STL	587		H. Stovey, Phi	152		D. Orr, CoC	183		H. Stovey, Phi	38		O. Beard, Cin	14	
T. McCarthy, STL	140		J. Burns, KC	579		D. O'Brien, Bro	146		B. Holliday, Cin	181		D. Lyons, Phi	36		M. Griffin, Bal	14	
3 tied with	139		E. Daily, CoC	578		B. Hamilton, KC	144		T. O'Neill, STL	179		T. O'Neill, STL	33		3 tied with	13	
			H. Long, KC	574		H. Collins, Bro	139		B. Shindle, Bal	178		H. Long, KC	32				

Home Runs			Total Bases			Runs Batted In			Walks			Intentional Walks			Strikeouts		
B. Holliday, Cin	19		H. Stovey, Phi	292		H. Stovey, Phi	119		Y. Robinson, STL	118		Statistic unavailable			C. Duffee, STL	81	
H. Stovey, Phi	19		B. Holliday, Cin	280		D. Foutz, Bro	113		J. McTamany, CoC	116					F. Fennelly, Phi	78	
C. Duffee, STL	16		T. Tucker, Bal	255		T. O'Neill, STL	110		M. Griffin, Bal	91					D. O'Brien, Bro	76	
J. Milligan, STL	12		T. O'Neill, STL	255		L. Bierbauer, Phi	105		B. Hamilton, KC	87					J. Hornung, Bal	72	
2 tied with	9		D. Orr, CoC	250		B. Holliday, Cin	104		L. Marr, CoC	87					B. Greenwood, CoC	71	

Hit By Pitch			Sac Hits			Sac Flies			Stolen Bases			Caught Stealing			GDP		
T. Tucker, Bal	33		Statistic unavailable			Statistic unavailable			B. Hamilton, KC	111		Statistic unavailable			Statistic unavailable		
C. Welch, Phi	19								D. O'Brien, Bro	91							
J. Reilly, Cin	18								H. Long, KC	89							
D. O'Brien, Bro	16								H. Nicol, Cin	80							
H. Larkin, Phi	16								A. Latham, STL	69							

Runs Created			Runs Created/27 Outs			Batting Average			On-Base Percentage			Slugging Percentage			OBP+Slugging		
T. Tucker, Bal	158		T. Tucker, Bal	12.32		T. Tucker, Bal	.372		T. Tucker, Bal	.450		H. Stovey, Phi	.525		T. Tucker, Bal	.934	
D. O'Brien, Bro	151		T. O'Neill, STL	10.69		T. O'Neill, STL	.335		H. Larkin, Phi	.428		B. Holliday, Cin	.497		H. Stovey, Phi	.918	
B. Hamilton, KC	149		B. Hamilton, KC	10.31		D. Lyons, Phi	.329		D. Lyons, Phi	.426		T. Tucker, Bal	.484		T. O'Neill, STL	.897	
T. O'Neill, STL	147		D. O'Brien, Bro	9.82		D. Orr, CoC	.327		T. O'Neill, STL	.419		T. O'Neill, STL	.478		D. Lyons, Phi	.895	
H. Stovey, Phi	146		H. Stovey, Phi	9.79		B. Holliday, Cin	.321		B. Hamilton, KC	.413		D. Lyons, Phi	.469		B. Holliday, Cin	.869	

1889 American Association Pitching Leaders

Wins			Losses			Winning Percentage			Games			Games Started			Complete Games		
B. Caruthers, Bro	40		M. Baldwin, CoC	34		B. Caruthers, Bro	.784		M. Baldwin, CoC	63		M. Baldwin, CoC	59		M. Kilroy, Bal	55	
S. King, STL	34		J. Ewing, Lou	30		E. Chamberlin, STL	.681		M. Kilroy, Bal	59		M. Kilroy, Bal	56		M. Baldwin, CoC	54	
J. Duryea, Cin	32		R. Ehret, Lou	29		S. King, STL	.680		S. King, STL	56		G. Weyhing, Phi	53		G. Weyhing, Phi	50	
E. Chamberlin, STL	32		P. Swartzel, KC	27		J. Stivetts, STL	.650		B. Caruthers, Bro	56		S. King, STL	53		S. King, STL	47	
G. Weyhing, Phi	30		M. Kilroy, Bal	25		T. Lovett, Bro	.630		G. Weyhing, Phi	54		E. Chamberlin, STL	51		B. Caruthers, Bro	46	

Shutouts			Saves			Games Finished			Batters Faced			Innings Pitched			Hits Allowed		
B. Caruthers, Bro	7		T. Mullane, Cin	5		T. Mullane, Cin	9		Statistic unavailable			M. Baldwin, CoC	513.2		P. Swartzel, KC	481	
M. Baldwin, CoC	6		16 tied with	1		R. Ehret, Lou	7					M. Kilroy, Bal	480.2		M. Kilroy, Bal	476	
M. Kilroy, Bal	5					W. Widner, CoC	7					S. King, STL	458.0		S. King, STL	462	
F. Foreman, Bal	5					E. Smith, Cin	7					G. Weyhing, Phi	449.0		M. Baldwin, CoC	458	
G. Weyhing, Phi	4					4 tied with	6					B. Caruthers, Bro	445.0		B. Caruthers, Bro	444	

Home Runs Allowed			Walks			Walks/9 Innings			Strikeouts			Strikeouts/9 Innings			Strikeout/Walk Ratio		
P. Swartzel, KC	21		M. Baldwin, CoC	274		B. Caruthers, Bro	2.1		M. Baldwin, CoC	368		J. Stivetts, STL	6.7		J. Stivetts, STL	2.10	
E. Chamberlin, STL	18		G. Weyhing, Phi	212		J. Conway, KC	2.4		M. Kilroy, Bal	217		M. Baldwin, CoC	6.4		M. Kilroy, Bal	1.53	
B. Caruthers, Bro	16		E. Chamberlin, STL	165		S. King, STL	2.5		G. Weyhing, Phi	213		A. Terry, Bro	5.1		S. King, STL	1.50	
G. Weyhing, Phi	15		J. Ewing, Lou	147		T. Lovett, Bro	2.6		E. Chamberlin, STL	202		J. Sowders, KC	5.1		A. Terry, Bro	1.48	
S. King, STL	15		M. Kilroy, Bal	142		P. Swartzel, KC	2.6		S. King, STL	188		H. Gastright, CoC	4.6		J. Duryea, Cin	1.44	

Earned Run Average			Component ERA			Hit Batsmen			Wild Pitches			Opponent Average			Opponent OBP		
J. Stivetts, STL	2.25		J. Stivetts, STL	2.29		Statistic unavailable			Statistic unavailable			J. Stivetts, STL	.205		J. Stivetts, STL	.271	
J. Duryea, Cin	2.56		F. Foreman, Bal	2.58								A. Terry, Bro	.227		J. Duryea, Cin	.288	
M. Kilroy, Bal	2.85		A. Terry, Bro	2.73								E. Chamberlin, STL	.227		J. Conway, KC	.293	
G. Weyhing, Phi	2.95		J. Duryea, Cin	2.79								G. Weyhing, Phi	.229		E. Chamberlin, STL	.298	
E. Chamberlin, STL	2.97		B. Caruthers, Bro	2.96								M. Baldwin, CoC	.231		A. Terry, Bro	.298	

1889 American Association Miscellaneous

Managers

Baltimore	Billy Barnie	70-65
Brooklyn	Bill McGunnigle	93-44
Cincinnati	Gus Schmelz	76-63
Columbus	Al Buckenberger	60-78
Kansas City	Bill Watkins	55-82
Louisville	Dude Esterbrook	2-8
	Chicken Wolf	14-51
	Dan Shannon	10-46
	Jack Chapman	1-6
Philadelphia	Bill Sharsig	75-58
St. Louis	Charlie Comiskey	90-45

Awards

STATS Most Valuable Player	Tommy Tucker, 1b, Bal
STATS Cy Young	Bob Caruthers, Bro
STATS Rookie of the Year	Jesse Duryea, p, Cin
STATS Manager of the Year	Bill McGunnigle, Bro

STATS All-Star Team

C	Jocko Milligan, STL	.366	12	76
1B	Tommy Tucker, Bal	.372	5	99
2B	Lou Bierbauer, Phi	.304	7	105
3B	Denny Lyons, Phi	.329	9	82
SS	Herman Long, KC	.275	3	60
OF	Bug Holliday, Cin	.321	19	104
OF	Tip O'Neill, STL	.335	9	110
OF	Harry Stovey, Phi	.308	19	119
P	Bob Caruthers, Bro	40-11	3.13	118 K
P	Elton Chamberlin, STL	32-15	2.97	202 K
P	Jesse Duryea, Cin	32-19	2.56	183 K

Postseason

World Series	Brooklyn (AA) 3 vs. New York (NL) 6

Outstanding Performances

Cycles
Pete Browning, Lou   on June 7

1890 National League Standings

Team	Overall					Home Games						Road Games						Park Index		Record by Month					
	W	L	Pct	GB	DIF	W	L	R	OR	HR	OHR	W	L	R	OR	HR	OHR	Run	HR	M/A	May	June	July	Aug	S/O
Brooklyn	86	43	.667	—	70	58	16	547	303	27	9	28	27	337	318	16	18	96	79	4-3	14-9	16-9	19-8	18-7	15-7
Chicago	84	53	.613	6.0	5	48	24	506	369	55	29	36	29	340	323	12	12	119	316	5-3	10-11	13-11	15-13	18-9	23-6
Philadelphia	78	54	.591	9.5	57	54	22	554	378	14	10	24	32	269	329	9	12	115	84	4-3	16-9	14-11	21-6	10-14	13-11
Cincinnati	77	55	.583	10.5	36	50	23	470	323	19	25	27	32	283	309	8	16	108	148	4-4	14-8	19-6	12-15	15-8	13-14
Boston	76	57	.571	12.0	7	43	23	435	284	20	11	33	34	328	308	11	16	115	117	5-4	10-13	17-8	21-7	16-8	7-17
New York	63	68	.481	24.0	0	37	27	361	272	8	2	26	41	347	424	17	12	86	36	3-6	13-10	9-16	11-17	13-11	14-8
Cleveland	44	88	.333	43.5	0	30	37	357	355	13	8	14	51	268	476	8	25	93	62	3-5	7-12	7-18	6-23	8-15	13-15
Pittsburgh	23	113	.169	66.5	5	14	25	225	261	3	5	9	88	373	971	17	47	90	31	4-4	5-17	4-20	5-21	1-27	4-24

Clinch Date—Brooklyn 9/26.

Team Batting

Team	G	AB	R	OR	H	2B	3B	HR	TB	RBI	TBB	IBB	SO	HBP	SH	SF	SB	CS	SB%	GDP	Avg	OBP	Slg
Brooklyn	129	4419	884	620	1166	184	75	43	1629	691	517	—	361	41	—	—	349	—	—	—	.264	.346	.369
Chicago	139	4891	847	692	1271	147	60	67	1739	653	516	—	514	46	—	—	329	—	—	—	.260	.336	.356
Philadelphia	133	4707	823	707	1267	220	78	23	1712	632	522	—	403	64	—	—	335	—	—	—	.269	.350	.364
Boston	134	4722	763	593	1220	175	62	31	1612	580	530	—	515	69	—	—	285	—	—	—	.258	.342	.341
Cincinnati	134	4644	753	633	1203	150	120	27	1674	563	433	—	377	51	—	—	312	—	—	—	.259	.329	.360
New York	135	4832	713	698	1250	208	89	25	1711	563	350	—	479	51	—	—	289	—	—	—	.259	.315	.354
Cleveland	136	4633	630	832	1073	132	59	21	1386	492	497	—	474	42	—	—	152	—	—	—	.232	.312	.299
Pittsburgh	138	4739	597	1235	1088	160	43	20	1394	426	408	—	458	64	—	—	208	—	—	—	.230	.299	.294
NL Total	1078	37587	6010	6010	9538	1376	586	257	12857	4600	3773	—	3581	428	—	—	2259	—	—	—	.254	.329	.342
NL Avg Team	135	4698	751	751	1192	172	73	32	1607	575	472	—	448	54	—	—	282	—	—	—	.254	.329	.342

Team Pitching

Team	G	CG	ShO	Rel	Sv	IP	H	R	ER	HR	SH	SF	HB	TBB	IBB	SO	WP	Bk	H/9	SO/9	BB/9	OAvg	OOBP	ERA
Cincinnati	134	124	9	10	1	1190.2	1097	633	369	41	—	—		407	—	488	48	1	8.3	3.7	3.1	.238	.300	2.79
Boston	134	132	13	2	1	1187.0	1132	593	387	27	—	—		354	—	506	60	1	8.6	3.8	2.7	.244	.298	2.93
Brooklyn	129	115	6	14	2	1145.0	1102	620	389	27	—	—		401	—	403	56	1	8.7	3.2	3.2	.246	.308	3.06
New York	135	115	6	20	1	1177.0	1029	698	400	14	—	—		607	—	612	68	0	7.9	4.7	4.6	.228	.320	3.06
Chicago	139	126	6	13	3	1237.1	1103	692	446	41	—	—		481	—	504	67	0	8.0	3.7	3.5	.232	.302	3.24
Philadelphia	133	122	9	12	2	1194.2	1210	707	441	22	—	—		486	—	507	45	2	9.1	3.8	3.7	.255	.325	3.32
Cleveland	136	129	2	8	0	1184.1	1322	832	544	33	—	—		462	—	306	49	0	10.0	2.3	3.5	.274	.338	4.13
Pittsburgh	138	119	3	20	0	1176.1	1520	1235	780	52	—	—	76	573	—	381	115	0	11.6	2.9	4.4	.297	.376	5.97
NL Total	1078	982	54	99	10	9492.1	9515	6010	3756	257	—	—		3771	—	3707	508	5	9.0	3.5	3.6	.254	.322	3.56
NL Avg Team	135	123	7	12	1	1186.1	1189	751	470	32	—	—		471	—	463	64	1	9.0	3.5	3.6	.254	.322	3.56

Team Fielding

Team	G	PO	A	E	TC	DP	PB	Pct
Brooklyn	129	3427	1598	320	5345	92	58	.940
Chicago	139	3665	1698	344	5707	89	72	.940
Boston	134	3545	1576	359	5480	77	34	.934
Cincinnati	134	3567	1698	382	5647	106	68	.932
Cleveland	136	3523	1772	405	5700	108	59	.929
Philadelphia	133	3572	1615	398	5585	122	57	.929
New York	135	3507	1709	449	5665	104	96	.921
Pittsburgh	138	3482	1726	607	5815	94	77	.896
NL Total	1078	28288	13392	3264	44944	792	521	.927

Team vs. Team Records

	Bos	Bro	ChN	Cin	Cle	NYG	Phi	Pit	Won
Bos	—	6	8	11	13	11	11	16	76
Bro	11	—	11	9	17	10	10	18	86
ChN	11	9	—	12	13	13	9	17	84
Cin	8	7	8	—	13	14	11	16	77
Cle	7	3	7	4	—	6	5	12	44
NYG	8	8	6	6	12	—	6	17	63
Phi	9	8	10	9	14	11	—	17	78
Pit	3	2	3	4	6	3	2	—	23
Lost	57	43	53	55	88	68	54	113	

1890 National League Batting Leaders

Games		At-Bats		Runs		Hits		Doubles		Triples	
W. Wilmot, ChN	139	C. Carroll, ChN	582	H. Collins, Bro	148	S. Thompson, Phi	172	S. Thompson, Phi	41	J. Reilly, Cin	26
T. Burns, ChN	139	J. Cooney, ChN	574	C. Carroll, ChN	134	J. Glasscock, NYG	172	H. Collins, Bro	32	B. McPhee, Cin	22
C. Anson, ChN	139	W. Wilmot, ChN	571	B. Hamilton, Phi	133	M. Tiernan, NYG	168	J. Glasscock, NYG	32	M. Tiernan, NYG	21
D. Miller, Pit	138	E. Burke, 2tm	554	M. Tiernan, NYG	132	C. Carroll, ChN	166	B. Myers, Phi	29	O. Beard, Cin	15
4 tied with	136	2 tied with	553	B. McPhee, Cin	125	J. Reilly, Cin	166	D. O'Brien, Bro	28	2 tied with	14

Home Runs		Total Bases		Runs Batted In		Walks		Intentional Walks		Strikeouts	
W. Wilmot, ChN	13	M. Tiernan, NYG	274	O. Burns, Bro	128	C. Anson, ChN	113	Statistic unavailable		P. Smith, Bos	81
M. Tiernan, NYG	13	J. Reilly, Cin	261	C. Anson, ChN	107	B. Allen, Phi	87			B. Hutchison, ChN	63
O. Burns, Bro	13	S. Thompson, Phi	243	S. Thompson, Phi	102	E. McKean, Cle	87			J. Denny, NYG	62
H. Long, Bos	8	W. Wilmot, ChN	237	W. Wilmot, ChN	99	H. Collins, Bro	85			C. Bennett, Bos	56
6 tied with	7	J. Glasscock, NYG	225	D. Foutz, Bro	98	B. Hamilton, Phi	83			2 tied with	54

Hit By Pitch		Sac Hits		Sac Flies		Stolen Bases		Caught Stealing		GDP	
T. Tucker, Bos	25	Statistic unavailable		Statistic unavailable		B. Hamilton, Phi	102	Statistic unavailable		Statistic unavailable	
S. LaRoque, Pit	12					H. Collins, Bro	85				
S. Brodie, Bos	11					B. Sunday, 2tm	84				
C. Zimmer, Cle	11					W. Wilmot, ChN	76				
B. Myers, Phi	10					M. Tiernan, NYG	56				

Runs Created		Runs Created/27 Outs		Batting Average		On-Base Percentage		Slugging Percentage		OBP+Slugging	
M. Tiernan, NYG	130	G. Pinckney, Bro	10.02	J. Glasscock, NYG	.336	C. Anson, ChN	.443	M. Tiernan, NYG	.495	M. Tiernan, NYG	.880
G. Pinckney, Bro	129	B. Hamilton, Phi	9.94	B. Hamilton, Phi	.325	B. Hamilton, Phi	.430	J. Reilly, Cin	.472	C. Anson, ChN	.844
B. Hamilton, Phi	128	C. Anson, ChN	9.52	S. Thompson, Phi	.313	G. Pinckney, Bro	.411	O. Burns, Bro	.464	G. Pinckney, Bro	.842
H. Collins, Bro	128	H. Collins, Bro	9.05	J. Knight, Cin	.312	E. McKean, Cle	.401	J. Burkett, NYG	.461	J. Glasscock, NYG	.834
C. Anson, ChN	127	M. Tiernan, NYG	8.79	C. Anson, ChN	.312	J. Glasscock, NYG	.395	S. Thompson, Phi	.443	B. Hamilton, Phi	.829

1890 National League Pitching Leaders

Wins		Losses		Winning Percentage		Games		Games Started		Complete Games	
B. Hutchison, ChN	42	A. Rusie, NYG	34	T. Lovett, Bro	.732	B. Hutchison, ChN	71	B. Hutchison, ChN	66	B. Hutchison, ChN	65
K. Gleason, Phi	38	E. Beatin, Cle	30	K. Gleason, Phi	.691	A. Rusie, NYG	67	A. Rusie, NYG	63	A. Rusie, NYG	56
T. Lovett, Bro	30	B. Hutchison, ChN	25	P. Luby, ChN	.690	K. Gleason, Phi	60	K. Gleason, Phi	55	K. Gleason, Phi	54
A. Rusie, NYG	29	T. Vickery, Phi	22	B. Caruthers, Bro	.676	E. Beatin, Cle	54	E. Beatin, Cle	54	E. Beatin, Cle	53
B. Rhines, Cin	28	2 tied with	19	E. Stein, Cin	.667	K. Nichols, Bos	48	K. Nichols, Bos	47	K. Nichols, Bos	47

Shutouts		Saves		Games Finished		Batters Faced		Innings Pitched		Hits Allowed	
K. Nichols, Bos	7	K. Gleason, Phi	2	J. Burkett, NYG	7	Statistic unavailable		B. Hutchison, ChN	603.0	E. Beatin, Cle	518
B. Rhines, Cin	6	D. Foutz, Bro	2	J. Sharrott, NYG	6			A. Rusie, NYG	548.2	B. Hutchison, ChN	505
K. Gleason, Phi	6	B. Hutchison, ChN	2	A. Rusie, NYG	5			K. Gleason, Phi	506.0	K. Gleason, Phi	479
B. Hutchison, ChN	5	4 tied with	1	K. Gleason, Phi	5			E. Beatin, Cle	474.1	A. Rusie, NYG	436
3 tied with	4			B. Hutchison, ChN	5			K. Nichols, Bos	424.0	T. Vickery, Phi	405

Home Runs Allowed		Walks		Walks/9 Innings		Strikeouts		Strikeouts/9 Innings		Strikeout/Walk Ratio	
B. Hutchison, ChN	20	A. Rusie, NYG	289	C. Young, Cle	1.8	A. Rusie, NYG	341	A. Rusie, NYG	5.6	K. Nichols, Bos	1.98
T. Lovett, Bro	14	B. Hutchison, ChN	199	J. Duryea, Cin	2.0	B. Hutchison, ChN	289	K. Nichols, Bos	4.7	J. Duryea, Cin	1.80
J. Clarkson, Bos	14	E. Beatin, Cle	186	C. Getzien, Bos	2.1	K. Nichols, Bos	222	A. Terry, Bro	4.5	C. Getzien, Bos	1.71
L. Viau, 2tm	12	T. Vickery, Phi	184	K. Nichols, Bos	2.4	K. Gleason, Phi	222	B. Hutchison, ChN	4.3	B. Rhines, Cin	1.61
3 tied with	11	K. Gleason, Phi	167	B. Rhines, Cin	2.5	A. Terry, Bro	185	J. Sharrott, NYG	4.1	B. Hutchison, ChN	1.45

Earned Run Average		Component ERA		Hit Batsmen		Wild Pitches		Opponent Average		Opponent OBP	
B. Rhines, Cin	1.95	B. Rhines, Cin	2.22	Statistic unavailable		A. Rusie, NYG	36	A. Rusie, NYG	.212	B. Rhines, Cin	.275
K. Nichols, Bos	2.23	K. Nichols, Bos	2.45			K. Nichols, Bos	30	T. Mullane, Cin	.221	B. Hutchison, ChN	.283
T. Mullane, Cin	2.24	B. Hutchison, ChN	2.47			B. Hutchison, ChN	27	B. Hutchison, ChN	.221	K. Nichols, Bos	.286
A. Rusie, NYG	2.56	P. Luby, ChN	2.52			A. Terry, Bro	27	B. Rhines, Cin	.221	P. Luby, ChN	.289
K. Gleason, Phi	2.63	A. Rusie, NYG	2.69			T. Vickery, Phi	23	P. Luby, ChN	.222	J. Duryea, Cin	.289

1890 National League Miscellaneous

Managers

Boston	Frank Selee	76-57
Brooklyn	Bill McGunnigle	86-43
Chicago	Cap Anson	84-53
Cincinnati	Tom Loftus	77-55
Cleveland	Gus Schmelz	21-55
	Bob Leadley	23-33
New York	Jim Mutrie	63-68
Philadelphia	Harry Wright	14-8
	Jack Clements	13-6
	Al Reach	4-7
	Bob Allen	25-10
	Harry Wright	22-23
Pittsburgh	Guy Hecker	23-113

Awards

STATS Most Valuable Player	Oyster Burns, of, Bro
STATS Cy Young	Bill Hutchison, ChN
STATS Rookie of the Year	Billy Rhines, p, Cin
STATS Manager of the Year	Cap Anson, ChN

STATS All-Star Team

C	Jack Clements, Phi	.315	7	74
1B	Cap Anson, ChN	.312	7	107
2B	Hub Collins, Bro	.278	3	69
3B	George Pinckney, Bro	.309	7	83
SS	Jack Glasscock, NYG	.336	1	66
OF	Oyster Burns, Bro	.284	13	128
OF	Sam Thompson, Phi	.313	4	102
OF	Mike Tiernan, NYG	.304	13	59
P	Kid Gleason, Phi	38-17	2.63	222 K
P	Bill Hutchison, ChN	42-25	2.70	289 K
P	Billy Rhines, Cin	28-17	1.95	182 K

Postseason

World Series	Brooklyn (NL) 3 vs. Lou (AA) 3 (1 tie)

Outstanding Performances

Cycles

Tom Burns, Bro	on August 1
John Reilly, Cin	on August 6

1890 American Association Standings

Team	W	L	Pct	GB	DIF	W	L	R	OR	HR	OHR	W	L	R	OR	HR	OHR	Run	HR	M/A	May	June	July	Aug	S/O
		Overall						**Home Games**						**Road Games**				**Park Index**				**Record by Month**			
Louisville	88	44	.667	—	101	57	13	513	275	8	8	31	31	307	304	7	10	114	83	7-2	10-12	12-11	20-4	15-4	24-11
Columbus	79	55	.590	10.0	9	47	22	453	246	9	8	32	33	377	369	7	12	88	84	4-6	11-12	16-8	9-16	15-5	24-8
St. Louis	77	58	.570	12.5	1	44	25	551	396	42	31	33	33	313	341	6	7	139	537	7-3	9-14	13-10	17-6	13-9	18-16
Toledo	68	64	.515	20.0	0	40	27	422	316	17	11	28	37	316	374	7	12	104	143	1-8	14-7	9-13	10-14	17-4	17-18
Rochester	63	63	.500	22.0	29	40	22	348	252	13	4	23	41	361	458	18	15	76	53	7-2	14-10	12-11	11-12	7-12	12-16
Baltimore	15	19	.441	24.0	0	8	11	117	115	1	0	7	8	65	77	1	3	129	20	—	—	—	—	1-3	14-16
Syracuse	55	72	.433	30.5	1	30	30	321	320	2	4	25	42	373	501	12	24	82	19	3-6	10-13	9-14	12-12	6-13	15-14
Philadelphia	54	78	.409	34.0	66	36	36	453	452	16	6	18	42	240	493	8	11	103	96	6-3	16-7	15-9	9-17	5-14	3-28
Brooklyn	26	72	.265	45.0	0	15	22	220	252	4	3	11	50	272	481	9	18	103	43	2-7	6-15	7-17	8-15	3-18	—

Clinch Date—Louisville 10/05.

Team Batting

Team	G	AB	R	OR	H	2B	3B	HR	TB	RBI	TBB	IBB	SO	HBP	SH	SF	SB	CS	SB%	GDP	Avg	OBP	Slg
St. Louis	139	**4800**	870	736	1308	178	73	48	1776	634	474	—	490	**95**	—	—	307	—	—	—	.273	**.350**	**.370**
Columbus	140	4741	831	617	1225	159	77	16	1586	620	**545**	—	557	46	—	—	353	—	—	—	.258	.341	.335
Louisville	136	4687	819	588	**1310**	156	65	15	1641	608	410	—	460	51	—	—	341	—	—	—	**.279**	.344	.350
Toledo	134	4575	739	689	1152	152	**108**	24	1592	512	486	—	**558**	67	—	—	**421**	—	—	—	.252	.332	.348
Rochester	133	4553	709	711	1088	131	64	31	1440	528	446	—	538	55	—	—	310	—	—	—	.239	.314	.316
Philadelphia	132	4490	702	945	1057	**181**	51	24	1412	508	475	—	540	87	—	—	305	—	—	—	.235	.320	.314
Syracuse	128	4469	698	831	1158	151	59	14	1469	487	457	—	482	35	—	—	292	—	—	—	.259	.333	.329
Brooklyn	100	3475	492	733	769	116	47	13	1018	328	328	—	456	31	—	—	182	—	—	—	.221	.294	.293
Baltimore	38	1213	182	192	278	34	16	2	350	119	125	—	152	28	—	—	101	—	—	—	.229	.316	.329
AA Total	1080	37003	6042	6042	9345	1258	560	187	12284	4344	3746	—	4233	495	—	—	2612	—	—	—	.253	.329	.332
AA Avg Team	120	4111	671	671	1038	140	62	21	1365	483	416	—	470	55	—	—	290	—	—	—	.253	.329	.332

Team Pitching

Team	G	CG	ShO	Rel	Sv	IP	H	R	ER	HR	SH	SF	HB	TBB	IBB	SO	WP	Bk	H/9	SO/9	BB/9	OAvg	OOBP	ERA
Louisville	136	114	13	20	7	1206.0	1120	588	345	18	—	—	56	293	—	587	58	—	8.4	4.4	**2.2**	.239	.292	**2.57**
Columbus	140	120	**14**	**22**	3	**1214.2**	976	617	403	20	—	—	—	471	—	624	—	—	**7.2**	4.6	3.5	**.214**	**.287**	2.99
Toledo	134	**122**	4	14	2	1159.1	1122	689	459	23	—	—	—	429	—	533	—	—	8.7	4.1	3.3	.247	.312	3.56
Rochester	133	**122**	5	12	2	1161.2	1115	711	460	19	—	—	—	530	—	477	—	—	8.6	3.7	4.1	.245	.324	3.56
St. Louis	139	118	4	20	1	1195.1	1127	736	488	38	—	—	—	447	—	**733**	—	—	8.5	**5.5**	3.4	.242	.308	3.67
Baltimore	38	36	1	2	0	315.1	307	192	140	3	—	—	—	123	—	134	—	—	8.8	3.8	3.5	.248	.316	4.00
Brooklyn	100	96	0	4	0	879.0	1011	733	460	21	—	—	—	421	—	230	—	—	10.4	2.4	4.3	.280	.355	4.71
Syracuse	128	115	5	12	0	1089.2	1158	831	603	28	—	—	—	518	—	454	—	—	9.6	3.7	4.3	.265	.342	4.98
Philadelphia	132	119	3	14	2	1132.0	1405	945	657	17	—	—	—	514	—	461	—	—	11.2	3.7	4.1	.296	.364	5.22
AA Total	1080	962	49	120	17	9353.0	9341	6042	4015	187	—	—	3746	4233	—	4233	—	—	9.0	4.1	3.6	.253	.322	3.86
AA Avg Team	120	107	5	13	2	1039.0	1038	671	446	21	—	—	416	470	—	470	—	—	9.0	4.1	3.6	.253	.322	3.86

Team Fielding

Team	G	PO	A	E	TC	DP	PB	Pct
Louisville	136	3613	1722	380	5715	79	84	**.934**
Columbus	140	**3640**	**1746**	396	**5782**	**101**	90	.932
Baltimore	38	945	451	**109**	1505	21	17	.928
Rochester	133	3486	1700	416	5602	95	51	.926
Syracuse	128	3266	1540	391	5197	90	85	.925
Toledo	134	3476	1664	419	5559	75	**107**	.925
Philadelphia	132	3393	1657	452	5502	93	65	.918
St. Louis	139	3574	1613	478	5665	93	60	.916
Brooklyn	100	2630	1399	404	4433	92	52	.909
AA Total	1080	28023	13492	3445	44960	739	611	.923

Team vs. Team Records

	Bal	Brk	CoC	Lou	Phi	Roc	STL	Syr	Tol	Won
Bal	—	0	2	1	2	5	2	1	2	**15**
Brk	0	—	5	2	2	3	4	5	5	**26**
CoC	4	5	—	10	11	10	12	10	13	**79**
Lou	2	13	8	—	17	11	9	14	14	**88**
Phi	2	10	9	3	—	7	7	10	6	**54**
Roc	1	10	9	6	12	—	8	11	6	**63**
STL	5	9	8	11	13	12	—	10	9	**77**
Syr	2	12	7	5	7	4	9	—	9	**55**
Tol	3	9	7	6	14	11	7	11	—	**68**
Lost	19	72	55	44	78	63	58	72	64	

1890 American Association Batting Leaders

Games		At-Bats		Runs		Hits		Doubles		Triples	
M. Lehane, CoC	140	H. Lyons, Roc	584	J. McTamany, CoC	140	C. Wolf, Lou	197	C. Childs, Syr	33	P. Werden, Tol	20
C. Reilly, CoC	137	F. Weaver, Lou	557	T. McCarthy, STL	137	T. McCarthy, STL	192	D. Lyons, Phi	29	S. Johnson, CoC	18
J. Sneed, 2tm	137	H. Taylor, Lou	553	S. Fuller, STL	118	S. Johnson, CoC	186	C. Wolf, Lou	29	B. Alvord, Tol	16
J. Gerhardt, 2tm	136	T. McCarthy, STL	548	J. Sneed, 2tm	117	C. Childs, Syr	170	3 tied with	28	J. Sneed, 2tm	15

Home Runs		Total Bases		Runs Batted In		Walks		Intentional Walks		Strikeouts	
C. Campau, STL	9	C. Wolf, Lou	260	S. Johnson, CoC	113	J. McTamany, CoC	112	Statistic unavailable		Statistic unavailable	
E. Cartwright, STL	8	T. McCarthy, STL	256	C. Wolf, Lou	98	J. Crooks, CoC	96				
J. Stivetts, STL	7	S. Johnson, CoC	248	C. Childs, Syr	89	E. Swartwood, Tol	80				
D. Lyons, Phi	7	C. Childs, Syr	237	J. Knowles, Roc	84	T. Scheffler, Roc	78				
						P. Werden, Tol	78				

Hit By Pitch		Sac Hits		Sac Flies		Stolen Bases		Caught Stealing		GDP	
C. Welch, 2tm	34	Statistic unavailable		Statistic unavailable		T. McCarthy, STL	83	Statistic unavailable		Statistic unavailable	
C. Roseman, 2tm	29					T. Scheffler, Roc	77				
E. Swartwood, Tol	17					B. Van Dyke, Tol	73				
T. Scheffler, Roc	14					C. Welch, 2tm	72				

Runs Created		Runs Created/27 Outs		Batting Average		On-Base Percentage		Slugging Percentage		OBP+Slugging	
T. McCarthy, STL	136	C. Wolf, Lou	9.95	C. Wolf, Lou	.363	E. Swartwood, Tol	.444	C. Childs, Syr	.481	C. Childs, Syr	.915
C. Wolf, Lou	134	T. McCarthy, STL	9.82	T. McCarthy, STL	.350	C. Childs, Syr	.434	C. Wolf, Lou	.479	C. Wolf, Lou	.900
S. Johnson, CoC	130	C. Childs, Syr	9.63	S. Johnson, CoC	.346	T. McCarthy, STL	.430	T. McCarthy, STL	.467	T. McCarthy, STL	.898
C. Childs, Syr	121	S. Johnson, CoC	9.49	C. Childs, Syr	.345	C. Wolf, Lou	.421	S. Johnson, CoC	.461	E. Swartwood, Tol	.887
P. Werden, Tol	113	E. Swartwood, Tol	9.26	E. Swartwood, Tol	.327	S. Johnson, CoC	.409	P. Werden, Tol	.456	S. Johnson, CoC	.870

1890 American Association Pitching Leaders

Wins		Losses		Winning Percentage		Games		Games Started		Complete Games	
S. McMahon, 2tm	36	J. Keefe, Syr	24	S. Stratton, Lou	.708	S. McMahon, 2tm	60	S. McMahon, 2tm	57	S. McMahon, 2tm	55
S. Stratton, Lou	34	B. Barr, Roc	24	H. Gastright, CoC	.682	B. Barr, Roc	57	B. Barr, Roc	54	B. Barr, Roc	52
H. Gastright, CoC	30	C. McCullough, 2tm	23	E. Chamberlin, 2tm	.682	J. Stivetts, STL	54	S. Stratton, Lou	49	S. Stratton, Lou	44
B. Barr, Roc	28	D. Casey, Syr	22	R. Ehret, Lou	.641	S. Stratton, Lou	50	J. Stivetts, STL	46	E. Healy, Tol	44
J. Stivetts, STL	27	4 tied with	21	2 tied with	.632	H. Gastright, CoC	48	E. Healy, Tol	46	2 tied with	41

Shutouts		Saves		Games Finished		Batters Faced		Innings Pitched		Hits Allowed	
E. Chamberlin, 2tm	6	H. Goodall, Lou	4	J. Easton, CoC	8	Statistic unavailable		S. McMahon, 2tm	509.0	S. McMahon, 2tm	498
H. Gastright, CoC	4	F. Knauss, CoC	2	J. Stivetts, STL	8			B. Barr, Roc	493.1	B. Barr, Roc	458
R. Ehret, Lou	4	R. Ehret, Lou	2	G. Meakim, Lou	7			S. Stratton, Lou	431.0	J. Stivetts, STL	399
S. Stratton, Lou	4	9 tied with	1	4 tied with	5			J. Stivetts, STL	419.1	S. Stratton, Lou	398
4 tied with	3							H. Gastright, CoC	401.1	D. Casey, Syr	365

Home Runs Allowed		Walks		Walks/9 Innings		Strikeouts		Strikeouts/9 Innings		Strikeout/Walk Ratio	
J. Stivetts, STL	14	B. Barr, Roc	219	S. Stratton, Lou	1.3	S. McMahon, 2tm	291	T. Ramsey, STL	6.6	S. Stratton, Lou	3.39
F. Smith, Tol	13	J. Stivetts, STL	179	R. Ehret, Lou	2.0	J. Stivetts, STL	289	J. Stivetts, STL	6.2	T. Ramsey, STL	2.52
T. Ramsey, STL	10	S. McMahon, 2tm	166	T. Ramsey, STL	2.6	T. Ramsey, STL	257	G. Meakim, Lou	5.8	R. Ehret, Lou	2.20
J. Keefe, Syr	9	D. Casey, Syr	165	F. Smith, Tol	2.8	E. Healy, Tol	225	E. Chamberlin, 2tm	5.5	G. Meakim, Lou	1.95
2 tied with	8	J. Keefe, Syr	148	S. McMahon, 2tm	2.9	B. Barr, Roc	209	E. Healy, Tol	5.2	E. Healy, Tol	1.77

Earned Run Average		Component ERA		Hit Batsmen		Wild Pitches		Opponent Average		Opponent OBP	
S. Stratton, Lou	2.36	S. Stratton, Lou	2.13	Statistic unavailable		Statistic unavailable		F. Knauss, CoC	.219	S. Stratton, Lou	.265
R. Ehret, Lou	2.53	H. Gastright, CoC	2.38					E. Chamberlin, 2tm	.220	R. Ehret, Lou	.293
F. Knauss, CoC	2.81	F. Knauss, CoC	2.50					H. Gastright, CoC	.220	H. Gastright, CoC	.297
E. Chamberlin, 2tm	2.83	E. Healy, Tol	2.64					J. Easton, CoC	.223	E. Healy, Tol	.308
E. Healy, Tol	2.89	R. Ehret, Lou	2.74					E. Healy, Tol	.232	S. McMahon, 2tm	.313

1890 American Association Miscellaneous

Managers

Baltimore	Billy Barnie	15-19
Brooklyn	Jim Kennedy	26-72
Columbus	Al Buckenberger	39-41
	Gus Schmelz	38-13
	Pat Sullivan	2-1
Louisville	Jack Chapman	88-44
Philadelphia	Bill Sharsig	54-78
Rochester	Pat Powers	63-63
St. Louis	Tommy McCarthy	11-11
	John Kerins	9-8
	Chief Roseman	7-8
	Count Campau	26-14
	Tommy McCarthy	4-1
	Joe Gerhardt	20-16
Syracuse	George Frazer	31-40
	Wally Fessenden	4-7
	George Frazer	20-25
Toledo	Charlie Morton	68-64

Awards

STATS Most Valuable Player	Chicken Wolf, of, Lou
STATS Cy Young	Scott Stratton, Lou
STATS Rookie of the Year	Cupid Childs, 2b, Syr
STATS Manager of the Year	Jack Chapman, Lou

STATS All-Star Team

C	Jack O'Connor, CoC	.324	2	66
1B	Perry Werden, Tol	.295	6	72
2B	Cupid Childs, Syr	.345	2	89
3B	Denny Lyons, Phi	.354	7	73
SS	Phil Tomney, Lou	.277	1	58
OF	Spud Johnson, CoC	.346	1	113
OF	Tommy McCarthy, STL	.350	6	69
OF	Chicken Wolf, Lou	.363	4	98
P	Sadie McMahon, 2tm	36-21	3.27	291 K
P	Jack Stivetts, STL	27-21	3.52	289 K
P	Scott Stratton, Lou	34-14	2.36	207 K

Postseason

World Series	Louisville (AA) 3 vs. Bro (NL) 3 (1 tie)

Outstanding Performances

No-Hitters

C. Titcomb, Roc	vs. Syr on September 15

Cycles

Bill Van Dyke, Tol	on July 5
Jumbo Davis, Brk	on July 18
Farmer Weaver, Lou	on August 12

1890 Players League Standings

Team	Overall					Home Games						Road Games						Park Index		Record by Month					
	W	L	Pct	GB	DIF	W	L	R	OR	HR	OHR	W	L	R	OR	HR	OHR	Run	HR	M/A	May	June	July	Aug	S/O
Boston	81	48	.628	—	149	48	21	602	383	42	38	33	27	386	384	12	11	111	302	7-2	14-9	14-11	13-9	17-10	16-7
Brooklyn	76	56	.576	6.5	5	46	19	564	410	20	7	30	37	398	480	14	19	114	84	4-4	17-9	10-15	18-10	17-7	10-11
New York	74	57	.565	8.0	0	47	19	628	404	35	21	27	38	389	477	31	16	117	117	2-6	15-8	11-13	18-9	15-9	13-12
Chicago	75	62	.547	10.0	11	46	23	504	345	18	12	29	39	381	425	13	15	104	106	4-3	11-11	15-10	14-14	14-14	17-10
Philadelphia	68	63	.519	14.0	3	35	30	482	418	20	15	33	33	465	434	29	18	102	76	3-4	13-12	15-10	15-12	13-12	9-13
Pittsburgh	60	68	.469	20.5	0	37	28	435	356	21	15	23	40	398	535	14	17	82	113	4-4	6-15	17-8	8-14	9-16	16-11
Cleveland	55	75	.423	26.5	0	31	30	416	403	10	15	24	45	433	623	17	30	88	60	3-5	9-11	10-13	12-15	8-17	13-14
Buffalo	36	96	.273	46.5	9	23	42	425	498	7	20	13	54	367	698	13	47	89	46	4-3	5-15	5-17	6-21	9-17	7-23

Clinch Date—Boston 9/29.

Team Batting

Team	G	AB	R	OR	H	2B	3B	HR	TB	RBI	TBB	IBB	SO	HBP	SH	SF	SB	CS	SB%	GDP	Avg	OBP	Slg
New York	132	4913	1018	875	1393	204	97	66	1989	793	486	—	364	31	—	—	231	—	—	—	.284	.352	.405
Boston	130	4626	992	767	1306	223	76	54	1843	773	652	—	435	43	—	—	412	—	—	—	.282	.376	.398
Brooklyn	133	4887	964	893	1352	186	93	34	1826	748	502	—	369	42	—	—	272	—	—	—	.277	.349	.374
Philadelphia	132	4855	941	855	1350	187	113	49	1910	761	431	—	321	51	—	—	203	—	—	—	.278	.343	.393
Chicago	138	4968	886	770	1311	200	95	31	1794	705	492	—	410	43	—	—	276	—	—	—	.264	.335	.361
Cleveland	131	4804	849	1027	1370	213	94	27	1852	701	509	—	345	49	—	—	180	—	—	—	.285	.360	.386
Pittsburgh	128	4577	835	892	1192	168	113	35	1691	652	569	—	375	54	—	—	249	—	—	—	.260	.349	.369
Buffalo	134	4795	793	1199	1249	180	64	20	1617	630	541	—	367	96	—	—	160	—	—	—	.260	.347	.337
PL Total	1058	38425	7278	7278	10523	1561	745	316	14522	5763	4182	—	2986	409	—	—	1983	—	—	—	.274	.351	.378
PL Avg Team	132	4803	910	910	1315	195	93	40	1815	720	523	—	373	51	—	—	248	—	—	—	.274	.351	.378

Team Pitching

Team	G	CG	ShO	Rel	Sv	IP	H	R	ER	HR	SH	SF	HB	TBB	IBB	SO	WP	Bk	H/9	SO/9	BB/9	OAvg	OOBP	ERA
Chicago	138	124	5	14	2	1219.1	1238	770	459	27	—	—	38	503	—	460	53	—	9.1	3.4	3.7	.253	.327	3.39
Boston	130	105	6	26	4	1137.1	1291	767	479	49	—	—	—	467	—	345	—	—	10.2	2.7	3.7	.274	.339	3.79
Brooklyn	133	111	4	22	7	1184.0	1334	893	519	26	—	—	53	570	—	377	59	—	10.1	2.9	4.3	.270	.352	3.95
Philadelphia	132	118	4	14	2	1154.1	1292	855	520	33	—	—	—	495	—	361	—	—	10.1	2.8	3.9	.271	.340	4.05
New York	132	111	3	23	6	1172.1	1216	875	543	37	—	—	—	569	—	449	—	—	9.3	3.4	4.4	.256	.336	4.17
Pittsburgh	128	121	7	7	0	1116.2	1267	892	523	32	—	—	32	334	—	318	—	—	10.2	2.6	2.7	.275	.329	4.22
Cleveland	131	115	1	16	0	1143.2	1386	1027	537	45	—	—	—	571	—	325	—	—	10.9	2.6	4.5	.287	.363	4.23
Buffalo	134	125	2	9	0	1141.0	1499	1199	775	67	—	—	—	673	—	351	—	—	11.8	2.8	5.3	.304	.387	6.11
PL Total	1058	930	32	131	21	9268.2	10523	7278	4355	316	—	—	—	4182	—	2986	—	—	10.2	2.9	4.1	.274	.347	4.23
PL Avg Team	132	116	4	16	3	1158.2	1315	910	544	40	—	—	—	523	—	373	—	—	10.2	2.9	4.1	.274	.347	4.23

Team Fielding

Team	G	PO	A	E	TC	DP	PB	Pct
New York	132	3512	1708	450	5670	94	70	.921
Boston	130	3410	1730	460	5600	109	46	.918
Chicago	138	3655	1817	492	5964	107	46	.918
Buffalo	134	3417	1771	491	5679	116	63	.914
Philadelphia	132	3459	1688	510	5657	118	55	.910
Brooklyn	133	3542	1759	531	5832	114	50	.909
Pittsburgh	128	3346	1658	512	5516	80	52	.907
Cleveland	131	3428	1761	533	5722	103	85	.907
PL Total	1058	27769	13892	3979	45640	841	467	.913

Team vs. Team Records

	Bos	Bro	Buf	Chi	Cle	NY	Phi	Pit	Won
Bos	—	11	14	12	12	12	10	10	81
Bro	7	—	12	10	12	7	14	14	76
Buf	6	6	—	5	7	3	4	5	36
Chi	8	9	15	—	13	9	10	11	75
Cle	8	8	9	7	—	8	8	7	55
NY	8	10	17	9	11	—	5	14	74
Phi	6	6	16	10	11	12	—	7	68
Pit	5	6	13	9	9	6	12	—	60
Lost	48	56	96	62	75	57	63	68	

Seasons: Standings, Leaders

1890 Players League Batting Leaders

Games		At-Bats		Runs		Hits		Doubles		Triples	
H. Duffy, Chi	138	H. Duffy, Chi	596	H. Duffy, Chi	161	H. Duffy, Chi	191	P. Browning, Cle	40	J. Beckley, Pit	22
T. O'Neill, Chi	137	L. Bierbauer, Bro	589	T. Brown, Bos	146	M. Ward, Bro	189	J. Beckley, Pit	38	J. Visner, Pit	22
B. Joyce, Bro	133	B. Shindle, Phi	584	H. Stovey, Bos	142	B. Shindle, Phi	188	J. O'Rourke, NY	37	B. Shindle, Phi	21
L. Bierbauer, Bro	133	T. O'Neill, Chi	577	M. Ward, Bro	134	P. Browning, Cle	184	H. Duffy, Chi	36	J. Fields, Pit	20
2 tied with	132	M. Ward, Bro	561	R. Connor, NY	133	H. Richardson, Bos	181	D. Brouthers, Bos	36	B. Joyce, Bro	18

Home Runs		Total Bases		Runs Batted In		Walks		Intentional Walks		Strikeouts	
R. Connor, NY	14	B. Shindle, Phi	281	H. Richardson, Bos	146	B. Joyce, Bro	123	Statistic unavailable		T. Brown, Bos	84
H. Richardson, Bos	13	H. Duffy, Chi	280	D. Orr, Bro	124	Y. Robinson, Pit	101			B. Joyce, Bro	77
H. Stovey, Bos	12	J. Beckley, Pit	276	J. Beckley, Pit	120	D. Brouthers, Bos	99			J. Fields, Pit	52
B. Shindle, Phi	10	H. Richardson, Bos	274	J. O'Rourke, NY	115	D. Hoy, Buf	94			M. Baldwin, Chi	51
G. Gore, NY	10	R. Connor, NY	265	H. Larkin, Cle	112	2 tied with	88			J. Fogarty, Phi	50

Hit By Pitch		Sac Hits		Sac Flies		Stolen Bases		Caught Stealing		GDP	
C. Mack, Buf	20	Statistic unavailable		Statistic unavailable		H. Stovey, Bos	97	Statistic unavailable		Statistic unavailable	
D. White, Buf	19					T. Brown, Bos	79				
D. Brouthers, Bos	18					H. Duffy, Chi	78				
B. Joyce, Bro	12					N. Hanlon, Pit	65				
H. Larkin, Cle	12					M. Ward, Bro	63				

Runs Created		Runs Created/27 Outs		Batting Average		On-Base Percentage		Slugging Percentage		OBP+Slugging	
R. Connor, NY	155	R. Connor, NY	12.99	P. Browning, Cle	.373	D. Brouthers, Bos	.466	R. Connor, NY	.548	R. Connor, NY	.998
H. Duffy, Chi	153	D. Orr, Bro	11.61	D. Orr, Bro	.373	P. Browning, Cle	.459	D. Orr, Bro	.537	P. Browning, Cle	.976
B. Shindle, Phi	143	P. Browning, Cle	11.53	J. O'Rourke, NY	.360	R. Connor, NY	.450	J. Beckley, Pit	.535	D. Orr, Bro	.952
M. Ward, Bro	140	D. Brouthers, Bos	11.31	R. Connor, NY	.349	H. Larkin, Cle	.420	P. Browning, Cle	.517	J. O'Rourke, NY	.925
2 tied with	135	J. O'Rourke, NY	11.30	J. Ryan, Chi	.340	D. Hoy, Buf	.418	J. O'Rourke, NY	.515	D. Brouthers, Bos	.921

1890 Players League Pitching Leaders

Wins		Losses		Winning Percentage		Games		Games Started		Complete Games	
M. Baldwin, Chi	34	G. Haddock, Buf	26	B. Daley, Bos	.720	M. Baldwin, Chi	59	M. Baldwin, Chi	57	M. Baldwin, Chi	54
G. Weyhing, Bro	30	H. Staley, Pit	25	O. H. Radbourn, Bos	.692	S. King, Chi	56	S. King, Chi	56	S. King, Chi	48
S. King, Chi	30	J. Bakely, Cle	25	P. Knell, Phi	.667	G. Weyhing, Bro	49	H. Staley, Pit	46	H. Staley, Pit	44
O. H. Radbourn, Bos	27	B. Cunningham, 2tm	24	A. Gumbert, Bos	.657	H. Gruber, Cle	48	G. Weyhing, Bro	46	H. Gruber, Cle	39
A. Gumbert, Bos	23	M. Baldwin, Chi	24	G. Weyhing, Bro	.652	H. Staley, Pit	46	H. Gruber, Cle	44	G. Weyhing, Bro	38

Shutouts		Saves		Games Finished		Batters Faced		Innings Pitched		Hits Allowed	
S. King, Chi	4	G. Hemming, 2tm	3	G. Hemming, 2tm	10	Statistic unavailable		M. Baldwin, Chi	501.0	M. Baldwin, Chi	498
H. Staley, Pit	3	H. O'Day, NY	3	B. Daley, Bos	8			S. King, Chi	461.0	H. Gruber, Cle	464
G. Weyhing, Bro	3	4 tied with	2	H. O'Day, NY	7			G. Weyhing, Bro	390.0	S. King, Chi	420
5 tied with	2			E. Crane, NY	7			H. Staley, Pit	387.2	G. Weyhing, Bro	419
				4 tied with	6			H. Gruber, Cle	383.1	2 tied with	412

Home Runs Allowed		Walks		Walks/9 Innings		Strikeouts		Strikeouts/9 Innings		Strikeout/Walk Ratio	
A. Gumbert, Bos	18	M. Baldwin, Chi	249	H. Staley, Pit	1.7	M. Baldwin, Chi	211	J. Ewing, NY	4.9	H. Staley, Pit	1.96
G. Haddock, Buf	15	E. Crane, NY	210	B. Sanders, Phi	1.8	S. King, Chi	185	B. Daley, Bos	4.2	B. Sanders, Phi	1.55
H. Gruber, Cle	15	H. Gruber, Cle	204	P. Galvin, Pit	2.0	G. Weyhing, Bro	177	G. Weyhing, Bro	4.1	J. Ewing, NY	1.39
M. Kilroy, Bos	14	B. Cunningham, 2tm	201	E. Morris, Pit	2.2	H. Staley, Pit	145	W. McGill, Cle	4.0	S. King, Chi	1.13
3 tied with	13	G. Weyhing, Bro	179	O. H. Radbourn, Bos	2.6	J. Ewing, NY	145	G. Haddock, Buf	3.8	T. Keefe, NY	1.04

Earned Run Average		Component ERA		Hit Batsmen		Wild Pitches		Opponent Average		Opponent OBP	
S. King, Chi	2.69	H. Staley, Pit	2.77	Statistic unavailable		Statistic unavailable		S. King, Chi	.234	H. Staley, Pit	.293
H. Staley, Pit	3.23	S. King, Chi	2.80					T. Keefe, NY	.237	S. King, Chi	.304
M. Baldwin, Chi	3.31	T. Keefe, NY	3.19					E. Crane, NY	.247	T. Keefe, NY	.304
O. H. Radbourn, Bos	3.31	O. H. Radbourn, Bos	3.25					G. Hemming, 2tm	.251	O. H. Radbourn, Bos	.312
T. Keefe, NY	3.38	M. Baldwin, Chi	3.76					P. Nell, Phi	.253	P. Galvin, Pit	.320

1890 Players League Miscellaneous

Managers

Boston	King Kelly	81-48
Brooklyn	Monte Ward	76-56
Buffalo	Jack Rowe	22-58
	Jay Faatz	9-24
	Jack Rowe	5-14
Chicago	Charlie Comiskey	75-62
Cleveland	Henry Larkin	34-45
	Patsy Tebeau	21-30
New York	Buck Ewing	74-57
Philadelphia	Jim Fogarty	7-9
	Charlie Buffinton	61-54
Pittsburgh	Ned Hanlon	60-68

Awards

STATS Most Valuable Player	Roger Connor, 1b, NY
STATS Cy Young	Silver King, Chi
STATS Rookie of the Year	Bill Joyce, 3b, Bro
STATS Manager of the Year	King Kelly, Bos

STATS All-Star Team

C	Buck Ewing, NY	.338	8	72
1B	Roger Connor, NY	.349	14	103
2B	Lou Bierbauer, Bro	.306	7	99
3B	Patsy Tebeau, Cle	.300	5	74
SS	Monte Ward, Bro	.337	4	60
OF	Pete Browning, Cle	.373	5	93
OF	Jim O'Rourke, NY	.360	9	115
OF	Hardy Richardson, Bos	.326	13	146
P	Mark Baldwin, Chi	34-24	3.31	211 K
P	Silver King, Chi	30-22	2.69	185 K
P	Old Hoss Radbourn, Bos	27-12	3.31	80 K

Postseason

None

Outstanding Performances

Cycles

Roger Connor, NY   on July 21

Team	W	L	Pct	GB	DIF	W	L	R	OR	HR	OHR	W	L	R	OR	HR	OHR	Run	HR	M/A	May	June	July	Aug	S/O
			Overall					**Home Games**						**Road Games**				**Park Index**				**Record by Month**			
Boston	87	51	.630	—	22	51	20	527	328	34	33	36	31	320	330	19	18	124	171	6-2	11-13	13-12	15-7	17-9	25-8
Chicago	82	53	.607	3.5	111	43	22	467	343	39	30	39	31	366	387	21	23	116	169	5-3	15-8	13-12	17-9	16-9	16-12
New York	71	61	.538	13.0	37	39	28	377	302	28	14	32	33	377	409	18	12	84	136	3-5	13-10	17-6	10-11	12-11	16-18
Philadelphia	68	69	.496	18.5	0	35	34	372	350	8	9	33	35	384	423	13	20	88	51	5-3	12-13	11-13	10-13	17-7	13-20
Cleveland	65	74	.468	22.5	11	40	28	484	426	4	6	25	46	352	462	18	18	117	29	5-3	13-13	12-13	12-13	7-17	16-15
Brooklyn	61	76	.445	25.5	1	41	31	438	383	11	19	20	45	327	438	12	21	97	82	2-6	10-14	16-10	8-13	11-13	14-20
Cincinnati	56	81	.409	30.5	0	26	41	296	328	19	17	30	40	350	463	21	23	80	85	2-6	10-15	10-14	13-13	7-17	14-16
Pittsburgh	55	80	.407	30.5	0	32	34	379	316	14	9	23	46	300	428	15	22	100	65	4-4	12-10	6-18	10-16	11-15	12-17

Clinch Date—Boston 10/01.

Team Batting

Team	G	AB	R	OR	H	2B	3B	HR	TB	RBI	TBB	IBB	SO	HBP	SH	SF	SB	CS	SB%	GDP	Avg	OBP	Slg
Boston	140	4956	**847**	658	1264	181	81	53	**1766**	707	533	—	537	82	—	—	289	—	—	—	.255	**.337**	.356
Cleveland	141	**5074**	835	888	**1295**	183	88	22	1720	673	519	—	464	46	—	—	242	—	—	—	.255	.330	.339
Chicago	137	4873	832	730	1231	159	88	**60**	1746	684	526	—	457	50	—	—	238	—	—	—	.253	.332	.358
Brooklyn	137	4748	765	820	1233	**200**	69	23	1640	603	465	—	435	36	—	—	**337**	—	—	—	.260	.330	.345
Philadelphia	138	4929	756	773	1244	180	51	21	1589	617	482	—	412	58	—	—	232	—	—	—	.252	.326	.322
New York	136	4833	754	711	1271	189	72	46	1742	630	438	—	394	36	—	—	224	—	—	—	**.263**	.329	**.360**
Pittsburgh	137	4794	679	744	1148	148	71	29	1525	524	427	—	503	50	—	—	205	—	—	—	.239	.308	.318
Cincinnati	138	4791	646	790	1158	148	**90**	40	1606	537	414	—	439	44	—	—	244	—	—	—	.242	.308	.335
NL Total	1104	38998	6114	6114	9844	1388	610	294	13334	4975	3804	—	3641	402	—	—	2011	—	—	—	.252	.325	.342
NL Avg Team	138	4875	764	764	1231	174	76	37	1667	622	476	—	455	50	—	—	251	—	—	—	.252	.325	.342

Team Pitching

Team	G	CG	ShO	Rel	Sv	IP	H	R	ER	HR	SH	SF	HB	TBB	IBB	SO	WP	Bk	H/9	SO/9	BB/9	OAvg	OOBP	ERA
Boston	140	**126**	9	15	**6**	1241.2	1223	658	381	51	—	—	—	364	—	525	43	0	8.9	3.8	**2.6**	.248	**.300**	2.76
Pittsburgh	137	122	7	16	2	1197.2	1160	744	384	31	—	—	—	465	—	446	56	0	8.7	3.4	3.5	.245	.313	2.89
New York	136	117	**11**	21	3	1204.0	**1098**	711	400	26	—	—	—	593	—	**651**	65	1	**8.2**	**4.9**	4.4	**.234**	.320	2.99
Chicago	137	114	6	24	3	1220.2	1207	730	471	53	—	—	—	475	—	477	63	1	8.9	3.5	3.5	.249	.316	3.47
Cleveland	141	118	1	25	3	**1244.0**	1371	888	484	**24**	—	—	—	466	—	400	56	0	9.9	2.9	3.4	.270	.331	3.50
Cincinnati	138	125	6	13	1	1218.2	1234	790	481	40	—	—	—	465	—	393	59	0	9.1	2.9	3.4	.253	.318	3.55
Philadelphia	138	105	3	**34**	5	1229.1	1279	773	510	29	—	—	—	507	—	342	49	1	9.4	2.5	3.7	.258	.327	3.73
Brooklyn	137	121	8	16	3	1204.2	1272	820	516	40	—	—	—	459	—	407	59	0	9.5	3.0	3.4	.261	.325	3.86
NL Total	1104	948	51	164	26	9760.2	9844	6114	3627	294	—	—	—	3794	—	3641	450	3	9.1	3.4	3.5	.252	.319	3.34
NL Avg Team	138	119	6	21	3	1220.2	1231	764	453	37	—	—	—	474	—	455	56	0	9.1	3.4	3.5	.252	.319	3.34

Team Fielding

Team	G	PO	A	E	TC	DP	PB	Pct
Boston	140	3722	1679	**358**	5759	96	36	**.938**
New York	136	3611	1731	384	5726	104	**73**	.933
Chicago	137	3652	1828	397	5877	**119**	63	.932
Cincinnati	138	3653	**1896**	409	5958	101	61	.931
Philadelphia	138	3681	1801	443	5925	108	53	.925
Brooklyn	137	3610	1635	432	5677	73	36	.924
Cleveland	141	**3728**	1856	485	**6069**	86	55	.920
Pittsburgh	137	3587	1693	475	5755	76	64	.917
NL Total	1104	29244	14119	3383	46746	763	441	.928

Team vs. Team Records

	Bos	Bro	ChN	Cin	Cle	NYG	Phi	Pit	Won
Bos	—	15	7	11	11	15	12	16	**87**
Bro	5	—	7	9	11	8	12	9	**61**
ChN	13	13	—	14	16	5	9	12	**82**
Cin	9	10	6	—	7	5	9	10	**56**
Cle	9	9	4	13	—	6	10	14	**65**
NYG	5	11	13	13	13	—	9	7	**71**
Phi	7	8	10	11	10	10	—	12	**68**
Pit	3	10	6	10	6	12	8	—	**55**
Lost	51	76	53	81	74	61	69	80	

1891 National League Batting Leaders

Games		At-Bats		Runs		Hits		Doubles		Triples	
C. Childs, Cle	141	E. McKean, Cle	603	B. Hamilton, Phi	141	B. Hamilton, Phi	179	M. Griffin, Bro	36	H. Stovey, Bos	20
E. McKean, Cle	141	H. Long, Bos	577	H. Long, Bos	129	E. McKean, Cle	170	G. Davis, Cle	35	J. Beckley, Pit	19
T. Tucker, Bos	140	G. Davis, Cle	570	C. Childs, Cle	120	M. Tiernan, NYG	166	H. Stovey, Bos	31	B. McPhee, Cin	16
B. Nash, Bos	140	J. McAleer, Cle	565	A. Latham, Cin	119	G. Davis, Cle	165	M. Tiernan, NYG	30	J. Ryan, ChN	15
2 tied with	139	B. McPhee, Cin	562	H. Stovey, Bos	118	J. O'Rourke, NYG	164	2 tied with	29	J. Virtue, Cle	14

Home Runs		Total Bases		Runs Batted In		Walks		Intentional Walks		Strikeouts	
M. Tiernan, NYG	16	H. Stovey, Bos	271	C. Anson, ChN	120	B. Hamilton, Phi	102	Statistic unavailable		H. Stovey, Bos	69
H. Stovey, Bos	16	M. Tiernan, NYG	268	B. Nash, Bos	95	C. Childs, Cle	97			M. Baldwin, Pit	67
W. Wilmot, ChN	11	H. Long, Bos	235	H. Stovey, Bos	95	R. Connor, NYG	83			H. Collins, Bro	63
4 tied with	9	G. Davis, Cle	233	J. O'Rourke, NYG	95	H. Long, Bos	80			B. Hutchison, ChN	62
		J. Beckley, Pit	232	R. Connor, NYG	94	F. Pfeffer, ChN	79			C. Bennett, Bos	61

Hit By Pitch		Sac Hits	Sac Flies	Stolen Bases		Caught Stealing	GDP
T. Tucker, Bos	29	Statistic unavailable	Statistic unavailable	B. Hamilton, Phi	111	Statistic unavailable	Statistic unavailable
C. Carroll, ChN	15			A. Latham, Cin	87		
A. Latham, Cin	11			M. Griffin, Bro	65		
S. Brodie, Bos	10			H. Long, Bos	60		
J. Reilly, Cin	10			2 tied with	57		

Runs Created		Runs Created/27 Outs		Batting Average		On-Base Percentage		Slugging Percentage		OBP+Slugging	
B. Hamilton, Phi	156	B. Hamilton, Phi	11.84	B. Hamilton, Phi	.340	B. Hamilton, Phi	.453	H. Stovey, Bos	.498	M. Tiernan, NYG	.882
H. Stovey, Bos	134	M. Tiernan, NYG	9.13	B. Holliday, Cin	.319	R. Connor, NYG	.399	M. Tiernan, NYG	.494	B. Hamilton, Phi	.874
M. Tiernan, NYG	130	H. Stovey, Bos	9.03	P. Browning, 2tm	.317	C. Childs, Cle	.395	B. Holliday, Cin	.473	H. Stovey, Bos	.870
H. Long, Bos	127	R. Connor, NYG	8.47	J. Clements, Phi	.310	P. Browning, 2tm	.395	R. Connor, NYG	.449	B. Holliday, Cin	.848
C. Childs, Cle	123	C. Childs, Cle	8.20	M. Tiernan, NYG	.306	M. Tiernan, NYG	.388	J. Ryan, ChN	.434	R. Connor, NYG	.848

1891 National League Pitching Leaders

Wins		Losses		Winning Percentage		Games		Games Started		Complete Games	
B. Hutchison, ChN	44	S. King, Pit	29	J. Ewing, NYG	.724	B. Hutchison, ChN	66	B. Hutchison, ChN	58	B. Hutchison, ChN	56
A. Rusie, NYG	33	M. Baldwin, Pit	28	B. Hutchison, ChN	.698	A. Rusie, NYG	61	A. Rusie, NYG	57	A. Rusie, NYG	52
J. Clarkson, Bos	33	T. Mullane, Cin	26	H. Staley, 2tm	.649	C. Young, Cle	55	J. Clarkson, Bos	51	M. Baldwin, Pit	48
K. Nichols, Bos	30	B. Rhines, Cin	24	K. Nichols, Bos	.638	J. Clarkson, Bos	55	M. Baldwin, Pit	50	J. Clarkson, Bos	47
C. Young, Cle	27	3 tied with	22	J. Clarkson, Bos	.635	2 tied with	53	K. Nichols, Bos	48	K. Nichols, Bos	45

Shutouts		Saves		Games Finished		Batters Faced	Innings Pitched		Hits Allowed	
A. Rusie, NYG	6	K. Nichols, Bos	3	K. Gleason, Phi	9	Statistic unavailable	B. Hutchison, ChN	561.0	B. Hutchison, ChN	508
K. Nichols, Bos	5	J. Clarkson, Bos	3	C. Young, Cle	8		A. Rusie, NYG	500.1	J. Clarkson, Bos	435
J. Ewing, NYG	5	C. Young, Cle	2	B. Hutchison, ChN	8		J. Clarkson, Bos	460.2	C. Young, Cle	431
B. Hutchison, ChN	4	J. Thornton, Phi	2	4 tied with	6		M. Baldwin, Pit	437.2	K. Gleason, Phi	431
3 tied with	3	16 tied with	1				T. Mullane, Cin	426.1	K. Nichols, Bos	413

Home Runs Allowed		Walks		Walks/9 Innings		Strikeouts		Strikeouts/9 Innings		Strikeout/Walk Ratio	
B. Hutchison, ChN	26	A. Rusie, NYG	262	K. Nichols, Bos	2.2	A. Rusie, NYG	337	A. Rusie, NYG	6.1	A. Rusie, NYG	2.33
J. Clarkson, Bos	18	M. Baldwin, Pit	227	H. Staley, 2tm	2.2	B. Hutchison, ChN	261	K. Nichols, Bos	5.1	H. Staley, 2tm	1.74
K. Nichols, Bos	15	T. Mullane, Cin	187	P. Galvin, Pit	2.3	K. Nichols, Bos	240	J. Ewing, NYG	4.6	B. Hutchison, ChN	1.47
H. Staley, 2tm	15	B. Hutchison, ChN	178	O. H. Radbourn, Cin	2.6	M. Baldwin, Pit	197	B. Hutchison, ChN	4.2	J. Ewing, NYG	1.31
T. Mullane, Cin	15	K. Gleason, Phi	165	B. Hutchison, ChN	2.9	S. King, Pit	160	M. Baldwin, Pit	4.1	A. Rusie, NYG	1.29

Earned Run Average		Component ERA		Hit Batsmen	Wild Pitches		Opponent Average		Opponent OBP	
J. Ewing, NYG	2.27	A. Rusie, NYG	2.67	Statistic unavailable	B. Hutchison, ChN	25	A. Rusie, NYG	.207	H. Staley, 2tm	.289
K. Nichols, Bos	2.39	J. Ewing, NYG	2.69		M. Baldwin, Pit	24	M. Baldwin, Pit	.228	B. Hutchison, ChN	.290
A. Rusie, NYG	2.55	B. Hutchison, ChN	2.84		S. King, Pit	22	J. Ewing, NYG	.228	K. Nichols, Bos	.295
H. Staley, 2tm	2.58	K. Nichols, Bos	2.91		L. Viau, Cle	21	B. Hutchison, ChN	.233	J. Ewing, NYG	.298
M. Baldwin, Pit	2.76	H. Staley, 2tm	2.91		T. Lovett, Bro	21	T. Mullane, Cin	.235	J. Clarkson, Bos	.300

1891 National League Miscellaneous

Managers

Boston	Frank Selee	87-51
Brooklyn	Monte Ward	61-76
Chicago	Cap Anson	82-53
Cincinnati	Tom Loftus	56-81
Cleveland	Bob Leadley	34-34
	Patsy Tebeau	31-40
New York	Jim Mutrie	71-61
Philadelphia	Harry Wright	68-69
Pittsburgh	Ned Hanlon	31-47
	Bill McGunnigle	24-33

Awards

STATS Most Valuable Player	Billy Hamilton, of, Phi
STATS Cy Young	Bill Hutchison, ChN
STATS Rookie of the Year	Bill Dahlen, 3b, ChN
STATS Manager of the Year	Frank Selee, Bos

STATS All-Star Team

C	Jack Clements, Phi	.310	4	75
1B	Cap Anson, ChN	.291	8	120
2B	Cupid Childs, Cle	.281	2	83
3B	Arlie Latham, Cin	.272	7	53
SS	Herman Long, Bos	.282	9	75
OF	Billy Hamilton, Phi	.340	2	60
OF	Harry Stovey, Bos	.279	16	95
OF	Mike Tiernan, NYG	.306	16	73
P	Bill Hutchison, ChN	44-19	2.81	261 K
P	Kid Nichols, Bos	30-17	2.39	240 K
P	Amos Rusie, NYG	33-20	2.55	337 K

Postseason

None

Outstanding Performances

No-Hitters
Tom Lovett, Bro   vs. NYG on June 22
Amos Rusie, NYG   vs. Bro on July 31

Cycles
Jimmy Ryan, ChN   on July 1

Team	Overall W	L	Pct	GB	DIF	Home Games W	L	R	OR	HR	OHR	Road Games W	L	R	OR	HR	OHR	Park Index Run	HR	Record by Month M/A	May	June	July	Aug	S/O
Boston	93	42	.689	—	148	51	17	518	299	37	22	42	25	507	379	15	20	91	166	11-6	16-9	13-7	18-5	18-5	17-10
St. Louis	85	51	.625	8.5	10	52	21	604	390	42	30	33	30	348	341	16	20	125	173	11-8	17-9	16-8	13-6	14-10	14-10
Milwaukee	21	15	.583	22.5	0	16	5	172	82	11	5	5	10	56	74	2	1	140	381	—	—	—	—	3-4	18-11
Baltimore	71	64	.526	22.0	11	44	24	481	354	13	8	27	40	367	442	17	25	102	49	12-4	13-10	10-12	13-8	11-13	12-17
Philadelphia	73	66	.525	22.0	0	43	26	465	366	29	9	30	40	354	427	26	26	108	74	5-11	14-11	10-12	12-9	16-9	16-14
Columbus	61	76	.445	33.0	0	34	29	309	263	4	8	27	47	395	512	16	21	74	38	7-12	13-12	11-12	12-8	8-18	10-14
Cincinnati	43	57	.430	32.5	0	24	20	290	282	21	9	19	37	250	354	7	11	121	212	8-12	13-12	11-9	5-16	6-8	—
Louisville	54	83	.394	40.0	19	39	32	388	331	7	6	15	51	309	540	10	27	79	33	13-7	7-19	8-15	2-20	8-10	16-12
Washington	44	91	.326	49.0	1	28	40	389	519	18	18	16	51	300	547	6	26	106	95	4-11	6-17	9-13	9-12	7-14	9-24

Clinch Date—Boston 9/25.

Team Batting

Team	G	AB	R	OR	H	2B	3B	HR	TB	RBI	TBB	IBB	SO	HBP	SH	SF	SB	CS	SB%	GDP	Avg	OBP	Slg
Boston	139	4889	1028	675	1341	163	100	52	1860	775	651	—	499	66	—	—	447	—	—	—	.274	.367	.380
St. Louis	141	5005	976	753	1330	169	51	58	1775	738	625	—	440	87	—	—	283	—	—	—	.266	.357	.355
Baltimore	139	4771	850	798	1217	142	99	30	1647	643	551	—	553	111	—	—	342	—	—	—	.255	.346	.345
Philadelphia	143	5039	817	794	1301	182	123	55	1894	649	447	—	548	74	—	—	149	—	—	—	.258	.329	.376
Louisville	141	4833	713	890	1247	130	69	17	1566	557	443	—	473	70	—	—	230	—	—	—	.258	.329	.324
Columbus	138	4697	702	777	1113	154	61	20	1449	547	529	—	530	37	—	—	280	—	—	—	.237	.319	.308
Washington	139	4715	691	1067	1183	147	84	19	1555	536	468	—	485	76	—	—	219	—	—	—	.251	.328	.330
Cincinnati	102	3574	549	643	838	105	58	28	1143	407	428	—	385	36	—	—	164	—	—	—	.234	.324	.320
Milwaukee	36	1271	227	156	332	58	15	13	459	165	107	—	114	29	—	—	47	—	—	—	.261	.333	.361
AA Total	1118	38794	6553	6553	9902	1250	660	292	13348	5017	4249	—	4027	586	—	—	2161	—	—	—	.255	.338	.344
AA Avg Team	124	4310	728	728	1100	139	73	32	1483	557	472	—	447	65	—	—	240	—	—	—	.255	.338	.344

Team Pitching

Team	G	CG	ShO	Rel	Sv	IP	H	R	ER	HR	SH	SF	HB	TBB	IBB	SO	WP	Bk	H/9	SO/9	BB/9	OAvg	OOBP	ERA
Milwaukee	36	35	3	1	0	309.2	291	156	86	6	—	—	—	120	—	137	—	—	8.5	4.0	3.5	.241	.309	2.50
Boston	139	108	9	34	7	1219.2	1158	675	410	42	—	—	—	497	—	524	—	—	8.5	3.9	3.7	.242	.314	3.03
St. Louis	141	103	8	38	5	1222.2	1106	753	444	50	—	—	—	576	—	621	—	—	8.1	4.6	4.2	.234	.317	3.27
Baltimore	139	118	6	21	2	1217.0	1238	798	464	33	—	—	—	472	—	408	—	—	9.2	3.0	3.5	.255	.321	3.43
Cincinnati	102	86	2	18	1	902.0	921	643	344	20	—	—	—	446	—	331	—	—	9.2	3.3	4.4	.256	.338	3.43
Columbus	138	118	6	21	0	1213.1	1141	777	505	29	—	—	—	588	—	502	—	—	8.5	3.7	4.4	.241	.324	3.75
Philadelphia	143	135	3	7	0	1233.2	1274	794	550	35	—	—	—	520	—	533	—	—	9.3	3.9	3.8	.258	.329	4.01
Louisville	141	128	9	12	1	1226.0	1353	890	582	33	—	—	—	464	—	485	—	—	9.9	3.6	3.4	.271	.333	4.27
Washington	139	123	2	17	2	1181.0	1420	1067	634	44	—	—	—	566	—	486	—	—	10.8	3.7	4.3	.288	.361	4.83
AA Total	1118	954	48	169	18	9725.0	9902	6553	4019	292	—	—	—	4249	—	4027	—	—	9.2	3.7	3.9	.255	.329	3.72
AA Avg Team	124	106	5	19	2	1080.0	1100	728	447	32	—	—	—	472	—	447	—	—	9.2	3.7	3.9	.255	.329	3.72

Team Fielding

Team	G	PO	A	E	TC	DP	PB	Pct
Columbus	138	3634	1823	379	5836	126	59	.935
Boston	139	3656	1870	392	5918	115	59	.934
Philadelphia	143	3696	1693	389	5778	109	63	.933
Louisville	141	3671	1770	458	5899	113	98	.922
Milwaukee	36	927	444	116	1487	20	12	.922
St. Louis	141	3663	1691	468	5822	91	73	.920
Baltimore	139	3646	1745	503	5894	103	58	.915
Cincinnati	102	2704	1356	389	4449	68	45	.913
Washington	139	3538	1765	589	5892	95	73	.900
AA Total	1118	29135	14157	3683	46975	840	540	.922

Team vs. Team Records

	Bal	Bos	Cin	CoC	Lou	Mil	Phi	STL	Was	Won
Bal	—	8	7	12	14	3	9	7	11	71
Bos	12	—	8	15	14	5	13	8	18	93
Cin	5	5	—	8	7	0	4	5	9	43
CoC	7	5	7	—	12	0	9	9	12	61
Lou	6	3	9	8	—	1	8	9	10	54
Mil	3	2	0	5	3	—	3	1	4	21
Phi	10	7	8	11	12	5	—	10	10	73
STL	12	10	14	11	11	0	10	—	17	85
Was	9	2	4	6	10	1	10	2	—	44
Lost	64	42	57	76	83	15	66	51	91	

1891 American Association Batting Leaders

Games			At-Bats			Runs			Hits			Doubles			Triples		
B. Hallman, Phi	141		T. Brown, Bos	589		T. Brown, Bos	177		T. Brown, Bos	189		J. Milligan, Phi	35		T. Brown, Bos	21	
D. Hoy, STL	141		B. Hallman, Phi	587		D. Hoy, STL	136		H. Duffy, Bos	180		T. Brown, Bos	30		D. Brouthers, Bos	19	
C. Comiskey, STL	141		S. Fuller, STL	586		G. Van Haltren, Bal	136		G. Van Haltren, Bal	180		C. Duffee, CoC	28		J. Canavan, 2tm	18	
5 tied with	139		C. Comiskey, STL	580		H. Duffy, Bos	134		T. McCarthy, STL	179		T. O'Neill, STL	28		P. Werden, Bal	18	
			T. McCarthy, STL	578		T. McCarthy, STL	127		D. Brouthers, Bos	170		H. Larkin, Phi	27		3 tied with	15	

Home Runs			Total Bases			Runs Batted In			Walks			Intentional Walks			Strikeouts		
D. Farrell, Bos	12		T. Brown, Bos	276		H. Duffy, Bos	110		D. Hoy, STL	119		Statistic unavailable			T. Brown, Bos	96	
D. Lyons, STL	11		G. Van Haltren, Bal	251		D. Farrell, Bos	110		J. Crooks, CoC	103					J. McTamany, 2tm	92	
J. Milligan, Phi	11		D. Brouthers, Bos	249		D. Brouthers, Bos	109		J. McTamany, 2tm	101					P. Gilbert, Bal	77	
4 tied with	10		H. Duffy, Bos	243		J. Milligan, Phi	106		P. Radford, Bos	96					M. Lehane, CoC	77	
			T. McCarthy, STL	236		P. Werden, Bal	104		B. Johnson, Bal	89					G. Weyhing, Phi	65	

Hit By Pitch			Sac Hits			Sac Flies			Stolen Bases			Caught Stealing			GDP		
C. Welch, Bal	36		Statistic unavailable			Statistic unavailable			T. Brown, Bos	106		Statistic unavailable			Statistic unavailable		
P. Gilbert, Bal	28								H. Duffy, Bos	85							
D. Brouthers, Bos	24								G. Van Haltren, Bal	75							
D. Lyons, STL	18								D. Hoy, STL	59							
2 tied with	15								P. Radford, Bos	55							

Runs Created			Runs Created/27 Outs			Batting Average			On-Base Percentage			Slugging Percentage			OBP+Slugging		
T. Brown, Bos	160		D. Brouthers, Bos	12.45		D. Brouthers, Bos	.350		D. Brouthers, Bos	.471		D. Brouthers, Bos	.512		D. Brouthers, Bos	.983	
D. Brouthers, Bos	152		D. Lyons, STL	10.64		H. Duffy, Bos	.336		D. Lyons, STL	.445		J. Milligan, Phi	.505		J. Milligan, Phi	.903	
D. Hoy, STL	144		H. Duffy, Bos	10.40		T. Brown, Bos	.321		D. Hoy, STL	.424		D. Farrell, Bos	.474		D. Lyons, STL	.900	
H. Duffy, Bos	143		T. Brown, Bos	10.36		T. O'Neill, STL	.321		H. Duffy, Bos	.408		T. Brown, Bos	.469		T. Brown, Bos	.865	
G. Van Haltren, Bal	141		G. Van Haltren, Bal	9.46		G. Van Haltren, Bal	.318		T. O'Neill, STL	.402		L. Cross, Phi	.458		H. Duffy, Bos	.861	

1891 American Association Pitching Leaders

Wins			Losses			Winning Percentage			Games			Games Started			Complete Games		
S. McMahon, Bal	35		K. Carsey, Was	37		C. Buffinton, Bos	.763		J. Stivetts, STL	64		S. McMahon, Bal	58		S. McMahon, Bal	53	
G. Haddock, Bos	34		P. Knell, CoC	27		G. Haddock, Bos	.756		S. McMahon, Bal	61		J. Stivetts, STL	56		G. Weyhing, Phi	51	
J. Stivetts, STL	33		S. McMahon, Bal	24		B. Sanders, Phi	.688		P. Knell, CoC	58		K. Carsey, Was	53		P. Knell, CoC	47	
G. Weyhing, Phi	31		F. Dwyer, 2tm	23		C. Griffith, 2tm	.609		K. Carsey, Was	54		P. Knell, CoC	52		K. Carsey, Was	46	
C. Buffinton, Bos	29		E. Chamberlin, Phi	23		G. Weyhing, Phi	.608		G. Weyhing, Phi	52		G. Weyhing, Phi	51		E. Chamberlin, Phi	44	

Shutouts			Saves			Games Finished			Batters Faced			Innings Pitched			Hits Allowed		
S. McMahon, Bal	5		B. Daley, Bos	2		C. Griffith, 2tm	13		Statistic unavailable			S. McMahon, Bal	503.0		K. Carsey, Was	513	
G. Haddock, Bos	5		D. O'Brien, Bos	2		D. O'Brien, Bos	9					P. Knell, CoC	462.0		S. McMahon, Bal	493	
P. Knell, CoC	5		14 tied with	1		B. Daley, Bos	8					G. Weyhing, Phi	450.0		G. Weyhing, Phi	428	
3 tied with	3					J. Stivetts, STL	8					J. Stivetts, STL	440.0		F. Dwyer, 2tm	424	
						W. Mains, 2tm	6					K. Carsey, Was	415.0		E. Chamberlin, Phi	397	

Home Runs Allowed			Walks			Walks/9 Innings			Strikeouts			Strikeouts/9 Innings			Strikeout/Walk Ratio		
K. Carsey, Was	17		J. Stivetts, STL	232		S. Stratton, Lou	1.8		J. Stivetts, STL	259		J. Meekin, Lou	5.7		S. Stratton, Lou	1.53	
J. Stivetts, STL	15		P. Knell, CoC	226		B. Sanders, Phi	2.3		P. Knell, CoC	228		J. Stivetts, STL	5.3		S. McMahon, Bal	1.47	
S. McMahon, Bal	13		E. Chamberlin, Phi	206		S. McMahon, Bal	2.7		S. McMahon, Bal	219		W. McGill, 2tm	5.0		G. Weyhing, Phi	1.36	
D. O'Brien, Bos	13		W. McGill, 2tm	168		R. Ehret, Lou	2.9		G. Weyhing, Phi	219		E. Chamberlin, Phi	4.5		C. Buffinton, Bos	1.32	
2 tied with	12		2 tied with	161		C. Griffith, 2tm	2.9		E. Chamberlin, Phi	204		P. Knell, CoC	4.4		J. Meekin, Lou	1.27	

Earned Run Average			Component ERA			Hit Batsmen			Wild Pitches			Opponent Average			Opponent OBP		
E. Crane, Cin	2.45		C. Buffinton, Bos	2.38		Statistic unavailable			Statistic unavailable			C. Buffinton, Bos	.219		C. Buffinton, Bos	.281	
G. Haddock, Bos	2.49		P. Knell, CoC	2.55								P. Knell, CoC	.239		C. Griffith, 2tm	.319	
C. Buffinton, Bos	2.55		G. Haddock, Bos	2.64								W. McGill, 2tm	.240		G. Weyhing, Phi	.323	
S. McMahon, Bal	2.81		J. Stivetts, STL	2.96								J. Stivetts, STL	.243		B. Sanders, Phi	.328	
J. Stivetts, STL	2.86		S. McMahon, Bal	3.01								E. Chamberlin, Phi	.255		W. McGill, 2tm	.331	

1891 American Association Miscellaneous

Managers

Baltimore	Billy Barnie	71-64
Boston	Arthur Irwin	93-42
Cincinnati	King Kelly	43-57
Columbus	Gus Schmelz	61-76
Louisville	Jack Chapman	54-83
Milwaukee	Charlie Cushman	21-15
Philadelphia	Bill Sharsig	6-11
	George Wood	67-55
St. Louis	Charlie Comiskey	85-51
Washington	Sam Trott	4-7
	Pop Snyder	23-46
	Dan Shannon	15-34
	Sandy Griffin	2-4

Awards

STATS Most Valuable Player	Dan Brouthers, 1b, Bos
STATS Cy Young	George Haddock, Bos
STATS Rookie of the Year	Jim Canavan, ss, Cin
STATS Manager of the Year	Billy Barnie, Bal

STATS All-Star Team

C	Jocko Milligan, Phi	.303	11	106
1B	Dan Brouthers, Bos	.350	5	109
2B	Jack Crooks, CoC	.245	0	46
3B	Duke Farrell, Bos	.302	12	110
SS	Paul Radford, Bos	.259	0	65
OF	Tom Brown, Bos	.321	5	71
OF	Hugh Duffy, Bos	.336	9	110
OF	Tip O'Neill, STL	.321	10	95
P	George Haddock, Bos	34-11	2.49	169 K
P	Sadie McMahon, Bal	35-24	2.81	219 K
P	Jack Stivetts, STL	33-22	2.86	259 K

Postseason

None

Outstanding Performances

No-Hitters
Ted Breitenstein, STL vs. Lou on October 4

Cycles
Abner Dalrymple, Mil on September 12

1892 National League Standings

Team	W	L	Pct	GB	DIF	W	L	R	OR	HR	OHR	W	L	R	OR	HR	OHR	Run	HR	M/A	May	June	July	Aug	S/O
		Overall						**Home Games**						**Road Games**				**Park Index**				**Record by Month**			
Boston	102	48	.680	—	—	54	**21**	490	344	20	27	48	**27**	372	**305**	14	**14**	123	168	11-2	16-7	18-9	15-10	14-11	28-9
Cleveland	93	56	.624	8.5	—	54	24	483	281	4	4	39	32	372	332	**22**	24	99	16	7-4	11-13	14-10	17-11	20-5	24-13
Brooklyn	95	59	.617	9.0	—	51	24	485	340	14	8	44	35	**450**	393	16	18	103	68	9-3	12-10	18-10	21-8	13-13	22-15
Philadelphia	87	66	.569	16.5	—	**55**	26	**512**	322	**34**	8	32	40	348	368	16	16	104	117	5-8	12-11	22-5	16-11	12-14	20-17
Cincinnati	82	68	.547	20.0	—	45	32	440	352	29	21	37	36	326	379	15	18	107	144	9-6	12-10	13-10	18-11	12-14	18-17
Pittsburgh	80	73	.523	23.5	—	52	34	477	363	32	14	28	39	325	433	6	**14**	86	179	9-4	11-14	11-16	11-13	16-10	22-16
Chicago	70	76	.479	30.0	—	37	31	292	**278**	9	9	33	45	343	457	17	26	82	48	3-10	19-3	5-18	10-16	14-11	19-18
New York	71	80	.470	31.5	—	42	36	452	382	26	12	29	44	359	444	13	20	97	108	6-6	11-12	10-17	12-13	10-14	22-18
Louisville	63	89	.414	40.0	—	37	31	309	286	7	**3**	26	58	340	518	11	23	86	36	9-3	7-16	10-19	8-19	15-10	14-22
Washington	58	93	.384	44.5	—	34	36	404	379	23	22	24	57	327	490	14	18	111	163	4-7	9-14	17-13	11-15	6-20	11-24
St. Louis	56	94	.373	46.0	—	37	36	379	380	32	32	19	58	324	542	13	15	92	241	2-10	10-14	13-11	9-18	12-14	10-27
Baltimore	46	101	.313	54.5	—	28	46	472	486	13	14	18	55	307	534	17	37	112	49	1-12	8-14	7-20	12-15	8-16	10-24

Team Batting

Team	G	AB	R	OR	H	2B	3B	HR	TB	RBI	TBB	IBB	SO	HBP	SH	SF	SB	CS	SB%	GDP	Avg	OBP	Slg
Brooklyn	158	**5485**	**935**	733	**1439**	183	105	30	1922	**719**	**629**	—	506	54	—	—	**409**	—	—	—	.262	**.344**	.350
Boston	152	5301	862	649	1324	203	51	34	1731	668	526	—	492	**62**	—	—	338	—	—	—	.250	.325	.327
Philadelphia	155	5413	860	690	1420	**225**	95	**50**	**1985**	693	528	—	515	54	—	—	216	—	—	—	.262	.334	**.367**
Cleveland	153	5412	855	**613**	1375	196	96	26	1841	687	552	—	536	40	—	—	225	—	—	—	.254	.328	.340
New York	153	5291	811	826	1326	173	85	39	1786	645	510	—	474	34	—	—	301	—	—	—	.251	.320	.338
Pittsburgh	155	5469	802	796	1288	143	108	38	1761	600	435	—	453	44	—	—	222	—	—	—	.236	.297	.322
Baltimore	152	5296	779	1020	1342	160	**111**	30	1814	628	499	—	480	**62**	—	—	227	—	—	—	.253	.325	.343
Cincinnati	155	5349	766	731	1288	155	75	44	1725	604	503	—	474	38	—	—	270	—	—	—	.241	.311	.322
Washington	153	5204	731	869	1245	149	78	37	1661	562	529	—	553	39	—	—	276	—	—	—	.239	.314	.319
St. Louis	155	5259	703	922	1187	138	53	45	1566	553	607	—	491	52	—	—	209	—	—	—	.226	.312	.298
Louisville	154	5334	649	804	1208	133	61	18	1517	509	433	—	508	46	—	—	275	—	—	—	.226	.290	.284
Chicago	147	5063	635	735	1188	149	92	26	1599	492	427	—	482	36	—	—	233	—	—	—	.235	.299	.316
NL Total	1842	63876	9388	9388	15630	2007	1010	417	20908	7360	6178	—	5964	561	—	—	3201	—	—	—	.245	.317	.327
NL Avg Team	154	5323	782	782	1303	167	84	35	1742	613	515	—	497	47	—	—	267	—	—	—	.245	.317	.327

Team Pitching

Team	G	CG	ShO	Rel	Sv	IP	H	R	ER	HR	SH	SF	HB	TBB	IBB	SO	WP	Bk	H/9	SO/9	BB/9	OAvg	OOBP	ERA
Cleveland	153	140	11	12	2	1336.0	1178	**613**	358	28	—	—	—	413	—	472	35	0	7.9	3.2	**2.8**	.227	**.284**	2.41
Boston	152	142	**15**	11	1	1336.0	**1156**	649	424	41	—	—	—	460	—	514	52	0	**7.8**	3.5	3.1	**.224**	.288	2.86
Philadelphia	155	131	10	24	**5**	1379.0	1297	690	449	**24**	—	—	—	492	—	502	41	0	8.5	3.3	3.2	.239	.302	2.93
Pittsburgh	155	130	3	22	1	1347.1	1300	796	464	28	—	—	—	537	—	455	46	0	8.7	3.0	3.6	.244	.313	3.10
Chicago	147	133	6	13	1	1298.0	1269	735	456	35	—	—	—	424	—	518	40	0	8.8	3.6	2.9	.246	.303	3.16
Cincinnati	155	130	8	25	2	1377.1	1327	731	485	39	—	—	—	535	—	437	55	0	8.7	2.9	3.5	.243	.311	3.17
Brooklyn	158	132	12	26	**5**	**1405.2**	1285	733	507	26	—	—	—	600	—	597	59	1	8.2	3.8	3.8	.234	.309	3.25
New York	153	139	5	13	1	1322.2	1165	826	484	32	—	—	—	635	—	**650**	**78**	0	7.9	**4.4**	4.3	.227	.313	3.29
Louisville	154	**147**	9	7	0	1346.0	1358	804	499	26	—	—	—	447	—	430	31	0	9.1	2.9	3.0	.252	.309	3.34
Washington	153	129	5	**26**	3	1315.1	1293	869	506	40	—	—	—	556	—	479	61	0	8.8	3.3	3.8	.247	.319	3.46
St. Louis	155	139	4	22	1	1344.2	1466	922	628	47	—	—	—	543	—	478	49	0	9.8	3.2	3.6	.267	.333	4.20
Baltimore	152	131	2	22	2	1298.2	1537	1020	618	51	—	—	—	536	—	437	56	0	10.7	3.0	3.7	.283	.348	4.28
NL Total	1842	1623	90	223	24	16106.2	15631	9388	5878	417	—	—	—	6178	—	5969	603	1	8.7	3.3	3.5	.245	.311	3.28
NL Avg Team	154	135	8	19	2	1342.2	1303	782	490	35	—	—	—	515	—	497	50	0	8.7	3.3	3.5	.245	.311	3.28

Team Fielding

Team	G	PO	A	E	TC	DP	PB	Pct
Brooklyn	158	**4214**	1992	398	6604	98	71	**.940**
Cincinnati	155	4131	2084	402	6617	**140**	56	.939
Philadelphia	155	4132	1917	**393**	6442	128	43	.939
Cleveland	153	3995	1868	407	6270	95	30	.935
Chicago	147	3898	1891	424	6213	85	41	.932
Boston	152	4001	1969	454	6424	127	54	.929
St. Louis	155	4030	1912	452	6394	100	53	.929
Louisville	154	4031	2051	471	6553	133	81	.928
Pittsburgh	155	4032	**2110**	483	**6625**	113	62	.927
Washington	153	3939	2004	547	6490	122	59	.916
New York	153	3965	1911	565	6441	97	**145**	.912
Baltimore	152	3889	1993	584	6466	100	59	.910
NL Total	1842	48257	23702	5580	77539	1338	754	.928

Team vs. Team Records

	Bal	Bos	Bro	ChN	Cin	Cle	Lou	NYG	Phi	Pit	StL	Was	Won
Bal	—	0	2	4	4	2	6	5	4	5	8	6	**46**
Bos	13	—	9	10	8	8	12	11	6	7	7	11	**102**
Bro	12	5	—	10	6	8	9	7	9	10	9	10	**95**
ChN	7	4	4	—	6	3	5	10	5	7	7	12	**70**
Cin	10	5	8	7	—	5	7	8	5	5	12	10	**82**
Cle	11	6	6	9	9	—	13	8	10	7	8	6	**93**
Lou	7	2	5	9	6	1	—	4	4	8	9	8	**63**
NYG	9	3	7	4	6	5	10	—	5	4	9	9	**71**
Phi	10	7	5	9	9	4	10	9	—	8	7	9	**87**
Pit	9	6	4	7	9	6	10	6	—	10	6	**80**
StL	6	7	5	5	2	5	5	4	7	4	—	6	**56**
Was	7	3	4	2	3	8	6	4	5	8	8	—	**58**
Lost	101	48	59	76	68	56	89	80	66	73	94	93	

1892 National League Batting Leaders

Games		At-Bats		Runs		Hits		Doubles		Triples	
R. Connor, Phi	155	T. Brown, Lou	660	C. Childs, Cle	136	D. Brouthers, Bro	197	R. Connor, Phi	37	E. Delahanty, Phi	21
S. Brodie, StL	154	L. Bierbauer, Pit	649	B. Hamilton, Phi	132	S. Thompson, Phi	186	H. Long, Bos	33	H. Long, Bos	20
S. Thompson, Phi	153	H. Long, Bos	646	H. Duffy, Bos	125	H. Duffy, Bos	184	E. Delahanty, Phi	30	D. Brouthers, Bro	20
T. Brown, Lou	153	D. Miller, Pit	623	R. Connor, Phi	123	B. Hamilton, Phi	183	D. Brouthers, Bro	30	B. Dahlen, ChN	19
9 tied with	152	A. Latham, Cin	622	D. Brouthers, Bro	121	H. Long, Bos	181	C. Zimmer, Cle	29	J. Beckley, Pit	19

Home Runs		Total Bases		Runs Batted In		Walks		Intentional Walks		Strikeouts	
B. Holliday, Cin	13	D. Brouthers, Bro	282	D. Brouthers, Bro	124	J. Crooks, StL	136	Statistic unavailable		T. Brown, Lou	94
R. Connor, Phi	12	B. Holliday, Cin	270	S. Thompson, Phi	104	C. Childs, Cle	117			J. Virtue, Cle	68
J. Beckley, Pit	10	S. Thompson, Phi	263	J. Beckley, Pit	96	R. Connor, Phi	116			L. Whistler, 2tm	67
J. Ryan, ChN	10	R. Connor, Phi	261	O. Burns, Bro	96	T. McCarthy, Bos	93			G. Weyhing, Phi	67
S. Thompson, Phi	9	H. Duffy, Bos	251	H. Larkin, Was	96	3 tied with	86			2 tied with	61

Hit By Pitch		Sac Hits		Sac Flies		Stolen Bases		Caught Stealing		GDP	
T. Tucker, Bos	26	Statistic unavailable		Statistic unavailable		M. Ward, Bro	88	Statistic unavailable		Statistic unavailable	
C. Welch, 2tm	17					T. Brown, Lou	78				
D. Brouthers, Bro	16					A. Latham, Cin	66				
J. Beckley, Pit	14					B. Dahlen, ChN	60				
2 tied with	11					D. Hoy, Was	60				

Runs Created		Runs Created/27 Outs		Batting Average		On-Base Percentage		Slugging Percentage		OBP+Slugging	
D. Brouthers, Bro	149	D. Brouthers, Bro	10.01	D. Brouthers, Bro	.335	C. Childs, Cle	.443	E. Delahanty, Phi	.495	D. Brouthers, Bro	.911
C. Childs, Cle	138	C. Childs, Cle	9.52	B. Hamilton, Phi	.330	D. Brouthers, Bro	.432	D. Brouthers, Bro	.480	R. Connor, Phi	.883
R. Connor, Phi	135	B. Hamilton, Phi	9.00	C. Childs, Cle	.317	B. Hamilton, Phi	.423	B. Ewing, NYG	.473	E. Delahanty, Phi	.855
H. Duffy, Bos	131	R. Connor, Phi	8.91	O. Burns, Bro	.315	R. Connor, Phi	.420	R. Connor, Phi	.463	O. Burns, Bro	.849
B. Hamilton, Phi	127	B. Ewing, NYG	8.82	B. Ewing, NYG	.310	J. Crooks, StL	.400	O. Burns, Bro	.454	B. Ewing, NYG	.845

1892 National League Pitching Leaders

Wins		Losses		Winning Percentage		Games		Games Started		Complete Games	
B. Hutchison, ChN	37	G. Cobb, Bal	37	C. Young, Cle	.750	B. Hutchison, ChN	75	B. Hutchison, ChN	70	B. Hutchison, ChN	67
C. Young, Cle	36	B. Hutchison, ChN	36	M. Sullivan, Cin	.750	A. Rusie, NYG	64	A. Rusie, NYG	61	A. Rusie, NYG	58
K. Nichols, Bos	35	A. Rusie, NYG	31	A. Terry, 2tm	.692	F. Killen, Was	60	M. Baldwin, Pit	53	K. Nichols, Bos	49
J. Stivetts, Bos	35	M. Baldwin, Pit	27	G. Haddock, Bro	.690	G. Weyhing, Phi	59	F. Killen, Was	52	C. Young, Cle	48
G. Weyhing, Phi	32	F. Killen, Was	26	H. Staley, Bos	.688	M. Baldwin, Pit	56	K. Nichols, Bos	51	3 tied with	46

Shutouts		Saves		Games Finished		Batters Faced		Innings Pitched		Hits Allowed	
C. Young, Cle	9	G. Weyhing, Phi	3	G. Weyhing, Phi	10	Statistic unavailable		B. Hutchison, ChN	622.0	B. Hutchison, ChN	571
E. Stein, Bro	6	J. Duryea, 2tm	2	F. Killen, Was	7			A. Rusie, NYG	532.0	G. Cobb, Bal	495
G. Weyhing, Phi	6	19 tied with	1	K. Carsey, Phi	7			G. Weyhing, Phi	469.2	F. Killen, Was	448
3 tied with	5			D. Foutz, Bro	7			F. Killen, Was	459.2	M. Baldwin, Pit	447
				5 tied with	6			2 tied with	453.0	S. McMahon, Bal	430

Home Runs Allowed		Walks		Walks/9 Innings		Strikeouts		Strikeouts/9 Innings		Strikeout/Walk Ratio	
G. Cobb, Bal	21	A. Rusie, NYG	267	S. Stratton, Lou	1.8	B. Hutchison, ChN	312	B. Kennedy, Bro	5.1	B. Hutchison, ChN	1.64
F. Killen, Was	15	M. Baldwin, Pit	194	F. Dwyer, 2tm	2.0	A. Rusie, NYG	288	A. Rusie, NYG	4.9	K. Nichols, Bos	1.55
K. Nichols, Bos	15	B. Hutchison, ChN	190	B. Sanders, Lou	2.1	G. Weyhing, Phi	202	E. Stein, Bro	4.5	C. Young, Cle	1.42
S. King, NYG	15	E. Crane, NYG	189	C. Young, Cle	2.3	E. Stein, Bro	190	B. Hutchison, ChN	4.5	G. Davies, Cle	1.38
2 tied with	12	F. Killen, Was	182	R. Ehret, Pit	2.4	K. Nichols, Bos	187	E. Crane, NYG	4.3	S. Stratton, Lou	1.33

Earned Run Average		Component ERA		Hit Batsmen		Wild Pitches		Opponent Average		Opponent OBP	
C. Young, Cle	1.93	C. Young, Cle	2.02	Statistic unavailable		E. Crane, NYG	31	T. Mullane, Cin	.201	C. Young, Cle	.265
T. Keefe, Phi	2.36	T. Keefe, Phi	2.39			K. Nichols, Bos	24	A. Rusie, NYG	.203	J. Duryea, 2tm	.281
J. Clarkson, 2tm	2.48	A. Terry, 2tm	2.40			A. Rusie, NYG	24	A. Terry, 2tm	.205	S. Stratton, Lou	.281
N. Cuppy, Cle	2.51	T. Mullane, Cin	2.42			G. Haddock, Bro	21	J. Duryea, 2tm	.212	R. Ehret, Pit	.283
A. Terry, 2tm	2.57	E. Stein, Bro	2.49			S. King, NYG	21	C. Young, Cle	.214	T. Mullane, Cin	.283

1892 National League Miscellaneous

Managers

Baltimore	George Van Haltren	1-10
	John Waltz	2-6
	Ned Hanlon	43-85
Boston	Frank Selee	102-48
Brooklyn	Monte Ward	95-59
Chicago	Cap Anson	70-76
Cincinnati	Charlie Comiskey	82-68
Cleveland	Patsy Tebeau	93-56
Louisville	Jack Chapman	21-33
	Fred Pfeffer	42-56
New York	Pat Powers	71-80
Philadelphia	Harry Wright	87-66
Pittsburgh	Al Buckenberger	15-14
	Tom Burns	27-32
	Al Buckenberger	38-27
St. Louis	Jack Glasscock	1-3
	Cub Stricker	6-17
	Jack Crooks	27-33
	George Gore	6-9
	Bob Caruthers	16-32
Washington	Billy Barnie	0-2
	Arthur Irwin	46-60
	Danny Richardson	12-31

Awards

STATS Most Valuable Player	Dan Brouthers, 1b, Bro
STATS Cy Young	Cy Young, Cle
STATS Rookie of the Year	Nig Cuppy, p, Cle
STATS Manager of the Year	Patsy Tebeau, Cle

STATS All-Star Team

C	Jack Doyle, 2tm	.297	6	69
1B	Dan Brouthers, Bro	.335	5	124
2B	Cupid Childs, Cle	.317	3	53
3B	Bill Joyce, Bro	.245	6	45
SS	Bill Dahlen, ChN	.291	5	58
OF	Oyster Burns, Bro	.315	4	96
OF	Ed Delahanty, Phi	.306	6	91
OF	Billy Hamilton, Phi	.330	3	53
P	Kid Nichols, Bos	35-16	2.84	187 K
P	Jack Stivetts, Bos	35-16	3.03	180 K
P	Cy Young, Cle	36-12	1.93	168 K

Postseason

World Series	Boston (NL) 5 vs. Cle (NL) 0 (1 tie)

Outstanding Performances

No-Hitters

Jack Stivetts, Bos	vs. Bro on August 6
Ben Sanders, Lou	vs. Bal on August 22
Bumpus Jones, Cin	vs. Pit on October 15

1893 National League Standings

Team	Overall					Home Games						Road Games						Park Index		Record by Month					
	W	L	Pct	GB	DIF	W	L	R	OR	HR	OHR	W	L	R	OR	HR	OHR	Run	HR	M/A	May	June	July	Aug	S/O
Boston	86	43	.667	—	81	49	15	557	350	48	41	37	28	451	445	17	25	103	215	1-1	16-11	17-6	20-9	20-5	12-11
Pittsburgh	81	48	.628	5.0	15	54	19	593	417	25	8	27	29	377	349	12	21	107	77	0-2	18-7	8-18	20-6	16-11	19-4
Cleveland	73	55	.570	12.5	27	47	22	579	440	10	9	26	33	397	399	22	26	109	34	2-0	10-9	14-12	16-10	14-16	17-8
Philadelphia	72	57	.558	14.0	0	43	22	559	351	45	13	29	35	452	490	35	17	95	110	1-1	19-6	15-12	12-14	12-14	11-13
New York	68	64	.515	19.5	0	49	20	571	390	48	19	19	44	370	455	13	17	106	204	1-1	12-15	12-12	12-14	19-7	12-15
Cincinnati	65	63	.508	20.5	1	37	27	424	375	19	21	28	36	335	439	10	17	103	148	2-2	12-14	10-12	14-14	13-11	14-10
Brooklyn	65	63	.508	20.5	13	43	24	393	348	24	17	22	39	382	497	21	24	77	83	1-1	16-9	17-8	7-20	13-13	11-12
Baltimore	60	70	.462	26.5	0	36	24	451	404	16	9	24	46	369	489	11	20	116	94	1-2	13-13	10-12	10-18	15-12	11-13
Chicago	56	71	.441	29.0	0	38	34	538	471	20	15	18	37	291	403	12	11	111	116	2-2	8-14	13-15	10-18	13-8	—
St. Louis	57	75	.432	30.5	9	40	30	424	405	7	14	17	45	321	424	3	24	99	69	2-1	11-13	8-15	16-12	10-19	10-15
Louisville	50	75	.400	34.0	0	24	28	329	367	3	14	26	47	430	575	16	24	97	60	1-2	2-13	8-16	14-14	15-16	10-14
Washington	40	89	.310	46.0	3	21	27	281	298	8	7	19	62	441	734	15	47	83	41	2-1	11-14	11-13	7-20	6-21	3-20

Clinch Date—Boston 9/20.

Team Batting

Team	G	AB	R	OR	H	2B	3B	HR	TB	RBI	TBB	IBB	SO	HBP	SH	SF	SB	CS	SB%	GDP	Avg	OBP	Slg
Philadelphia	133	5151	1011	841	1553	246	90	80	2219	865	468	—	335	71	—	—	202	—	—	—	.301	.368	.431
Boston	131	4678	1008	795	1358	178	50	65	1831	828	561	—	292	46	—	—	243	—	—	—	.290	.372	.391
Cleveland	129	4747	976	839	1425	222	98	32	1939	833	532	—	229	30	—	—	252	—	—	—	.300	.374	.408
Pittsburgh	131	4834	970	766	1447	176	127	37	1988	816	537	—	274	62	—	—	210	—	—	—	.299	.377	.411
New York	136	4858	941	845	1424	182	101	61	1991	768	504	—	281	56	—	—	299	—	—	—	.293	.366	.410
Chicago	128	4664	829	874	1299	186	93	32	1767	682	465	—	262	36	—	—	255	—	—	—	.279	.348	.379
Baltimore	130	4651	820	893	1281	164	86	27	1698	665	539	—	323	70	—	—	233	—	—	—	.275	.359	.365
Brooklyn	130	4511	775	845	1200	173	83	45	1674	644	473	—	296	40	—	—	213	—	—	—	.266	.341	.371
Cincinnati	131	4617	759	814	1195	161	65	29	1573	615	532	—	256	48	—	—	238	—	—	—	.259	.342	.341
Louisville	126	4566	759	942	1185	177	73	19	1565	616	485	—	306	54	—	—	203	—	—	—	.260	.338	.343
St. Louis	135	4879	745	829	1288	152	98	10	1666	616	524	—	251	63	—	—	250	—	—	—	.264	.343	.341
Washington	130	4742	722	1032	1258	180	83	23	1673	608	523	—	237	63	—	—	154	—	—	—	.265	.346	.353
NL Total	1570	56898	10315	10315	15913	2197	1047	460	21584	8556	6143	—	3342	639	—	—	2752	—	—	—	.280	.356	.379
NL Avg Team	131	4742	860	860	1326	183	87	38	1799	713	512	—	279	53	—	—	229	—	—	—	.280	.356	.379

Team Pitching

Team	G	CG	ShO	Rel	Sv	IP	H	R	ER	HR	SH	SF	HB	TBB	IBB	SO	WP	Bk	H/9	SO/9	BB/9	OAvg	OOBP	ERA
St. Louis	135	114	3	22	4	1207.0	1292	829	545	38	—	—	—	542	—	301	45	0	9.6	2.2	4.0	.266	.340	4.06
Pittsburgh	131	104	8	29	2	1167.0	1232	766	529	29	—	—	—	504	—	280	32	1	9.5	2.2	3.9	.263	.335	4.08
Cleveland	129	110	2	21	2	1140.1	1361	839	532	35	—	—	—	356	—	242	48	0	10.7	1.9	2.8	.288	.338	4.20
New York	136	111	6	26	4	1211.1	1271	845	578	36	—	—	—	581	—	395	60	0	9.4	2.9	4.3	.262	.341	4.29
Boston	131	114	2	20	2	1163.2	1314	795	573	66	—	—	—	402	—	253	30	1	10.2	2.0	3.1	.277	.333	4.43
Cincinnati	131	97	4	34	5	1172.0	1305	814	592	38	—	—	—	549	—	258	46	0	10.0	2.0	4.2	.274	.349	4.55
Brooklyn	130	109	3	23	3	1154.0	1262	845	583	41	—	—	—	547	—	297	52	0	9.8	2.3	4.3	.270	.347	4.55
Philadelphia	133	107	4	28	2	1189.0	1357	841	618	30	—	—	—	521	—	283	34	0	10.3	2.1	3.9	.279	.348	4.68
Chicago	128	101	4	31	5	1117.1	1278	874	597	26	—	—	—	553	—	273	41	0	10.3	2.2	4.5	.279	.357	4.81
Baltimore	130	104	1	26	2	1123.2	1325	893	621	29	—	—	—	534	—	275	67	1	10.6	2.2	4.3	.285	.359	4.97
Washington	130	110	2	20	0	1139.0	1485	1032	704	54	—	—	—	574	—	292	39	3	11.7	2.3	4.5	.306	.379	5.56
Louisville	126	113	4	12	1	1080.0	1431	942	708	38	—	—	—	479	—	190	29	0	11.9	1.6	4.0	.310	.374	5.90
NL Total	1570	1294	43	292	32	13864.1	15913	10315	7180	460	—	—	—	6142	—	3339	523	6	10.3	2.2	4.0	.280	.350	4.66
NL Avg Team	131	108	4	24	3	1155.1	1326	860	598	38	—	—	—	512	—	278	44	1	10.3	2.2	4.0	.280	.350	4.66

Team Fielding

Team	G	PO	A	E	TC	DP	PB	Pct
Philadelphia	133	3564	1774	318	5656	121	28	.944
Cincinnati	131	3513	1788	321	5622	138	43	.943
Pittsburgh	131	3496	1792	347	5635	112	45	.938
Louisville	126	3237	1666	330	5233	111	40	.937
Boston	131	3486	1680	353	5519	118	32	.936
St. Louis	135	3618	1683	398	5699	110	56	.930
Brooklyn	130	3459	1662	385	5506	88	31	.930
Cleveland	129	3419	1778	395	5592	92	50	.929
Baltimore	130	3366	1633	384	5383	95	44	.929
New York	136	3632	1834	432	5898	95	77	.927
Chicago	128	3345	1616	421	5382	92	38	.922
Washington	130	3411	1763	497	5671	96	46	.912
NL Total	1570	41546	20669	4581	66796	1268	530	.931

Team vs. Team Records

	Bal	Bos	Bro	ChN	Cin	Cle	Lou	NYG	Phi	Pit	StL	Was	Won
Bal	—	2	10	5	4	8	5	4	5	1	9	7	60
Bos	10	—	8	8	6	7	10	8	8	4	10	7	86
Bro	2	4	—	7	4	5	7	6	6	8	8	8	65
ChN	7	3	3	—	5	4	6	7	6	3	3	9	56
Cin	8	6	8	7	—	6	6	6	1	3	7	7	65
Cle	4	5	7	8	5	—	6	6	3	9	9	11	73
Lou	5	2	5	4	6	3	—	5	4	4	4	8	50
NYG	8	4	6	5	6	6	7	—	7	4	8	7	68
Phi	7	4	5	6	9	9	8	5	—	7	4	8	72
Pit	11	6	4	9	9	3	8	8	5	—	9	9	81
StL	3	6	4	9	5	3	8	4	8	3	—	8	57
Was	5	5	3	3	4	1	4	5	4	2	4	—	40
Lost	70	43	63	71	63	55	75	64	57	48	75	89	

1893 National League Batting Leaders

Games		At-Bats		Runs		Hits		Doubles		Triples	
E. Burke, NYG	135	S. Thompson, Phi	600	H. Long, Bos	149	S. Thompson, Phi	222	S. Thompson, Phi	37	P. Werden, StL	29
J. Quinn, StL	135	B. Hallman, Phi	596	H. Duffy, Bos	147	E. Delahanty, Phi	219	E. Delahanty, Phi	35	G. Davis, NYG	27
R. Connor, NYG	135	E. Delahanty, Phi	595	J. Burkett, Cle	145	H. Duffy, Bos	203	J. Beckley, Pit	32	E. McKean, Cle	24
M. Ward, NYG	135	M. Ward, NYG	588	E. Delahanty, Phi	145	G. Davis, NYG	195	P. Tebeau, Cle	32	E. Smith, Pit	23
G. Davis, NYG	133	T. Dowd, StL	581	C. Childs, Cle	145	M. Ward, NYG	193	3 tied with	29	J. Beckley, Pit	19

Home Runs		Total Bases		Runs Batted In		Walks		Intentional Walks		Strikeouts	
E. Delahanty, Phi	19	E. Delahanty, Phi	347	E. Delahanty, Phi	146	J. Crooks, StL	121	Statistic unavailable		T. Daly, Bro	65
J. Clements, Phi	17	S. Thompson, Phi	318	E. McKean, Cle	133	C. Childs, Cle	120			T. Brown, Lou	63
M. Tiernan, NYG	15	G. Davis, NYG	304	S. Thompson, Phi	126	P. Radford, Was	105			G. Treadway, Bal	50
B. Lowe, Bos	14	E. Smith, Pit	272	B. Nash, Bos	123	J. McGraw, Bal	101			J. Kelley, Bal	44
3 tied with	11	2 tied with	258	B. Ewing, Cle	122	J. Burkett, Cle	98			P. Radford, Was	42

Hit By Pitch		Sac Hits		Sac Flies		Stolen Bases		Caught Stealing		GDP	
E. Burke, NYG	25	Statistic unavailable		Statistic unavailable		T. Brown, Lou	66	Statistic unavailable		Statistic unavailable	
J. Beckley, Pit	20					T. Dowd, StL	59				
T. Tucker, Bos	20					A. Latham, Cin	57				
J. McGraw, Bal	16					E. Burke, NYG	54				
S. Brodie, 2tm	14					S. Brodie, 2tm	49				

Runs Created		Runs Created/27 Outs		Batting Average		On-Base Percentage		Slugging Percentage		OBP+Slugging	
E. Delahanty, Phi	163	J. Burkett, Cle	11.68	S. Thompson, Phi	.370	C. Childs, Cle	.463	E. Delahanty, Phi	.583	E. Delahanty, Phi	1.007
J. Burkett, Cle	149	T. McCarthy, Bos	11.41	E. Delahanty, Phi	.368	J. Burkett, Cle	.459	G. Davis, NYG	.554	G. Davis, NYG	.964
S. Thompson, Phi	149	E. Delahanty, Phi	11.32	H. Duffy, Bos	.363	J. McGraw, Bal	.454	S. Thompson, Phi	.530	E. Smith, Pit	.960
H. Duffy, Bos	147	E. Smith, Pit	10.78	G. Davis, NYG	.355	E. Smith, Pit	.435	E. Smith, Pit	.525	S. Thompson, Phi	.954
G. Davis, NYG	142	H. Duffy, Bos	10.75	J. Burkett, Cle	.348	D. Lyons, Pit	.430	B. Ewing, Cle	.496	J. Burkett, Cle	.951

1893 National League Pitching Leaders

Wins		Losses		Winning Percentage		Games		Games Started		Complete Games	
F. Killen, Pit	36	D. Esper, Was	28	H. Gastright, 2tm	.750	A. Rusie, NYG	56	A. Rusie, NYG	52	A. Rusie, NYG	50
C. Young, Cle	34	T. Breitenstein, StL	24	F. Killen, Pit	.720	F. Killen, Pit	55	F. Killen, Pit	48	K. Nichols, Bos	43
K. Nichols, Bos	34	S. Stratton, Lou	24	K. Nichols, Bos	.708	C. Young, Cle	53	C. Young, Cle	46	C. Young, Cle	42
A. Rusie, NYG	33	B. Hutchison, ChN	24	C. Young, Cle	.680	K. Nichols, Bos	52	K. Gleason, StL	45	B. Kennedy, Bro	40
B. Kennedy, Bro	25	2 tied with	22	H. Staley, Bos	.643	T. Mullane, 2tm	49	2 tied with	44	3 tied with	38

Shutouts		Saves		Games Finished		Batters Faced		Innings Pitched		Hits Allowed	
A. Rusie, NYG	4	F. Donnelly, ChN	2	T. Mullane, 2tm	10	Statistic unavailable		A. Rusie, NYG	482.0	A. Rusie, NYG	451
R. Ehret, Pit	4	F. Dwyer, Cin	2	J. Taylor, Phi	9			K. Nichols, Bos	425.0	S. Stratton, Lou	451
6 tied with	2	M. Baldwin, 2tm	2	M. Sullivan, Cin	9			C. Young, Cle	422.2	C. Young, Cle	442
		T. Mullane, 2tm	2	G. Hemming, Lou	8			F. Killen, Pit	415.0	D. Esper, Was	442
		23 tied with	1	8 tied with	7			2 tied with	382.2	K. Gleason, StL	436

Home Runs Allowed		Walks		Walks/9 Innings		Strikeouts		Strikeouts/9 Innings		Strikeout/Walk Ratio	
H. Staley, Bos	22	A. Rusie, NYG	218	C. Young, Cle	2.2	A. Rusie, NYG	208	A. Rusie, NYG	3.9	C. Young, Cle	0.99
K. Gleason, StL	18	T. Mullane, 2tm	189	K. Nichols, Bos	2.5	B. Kennedy, Bro	107	J. Meekin, Was	3.3	A. Rusie, NYG	0.95
J. Stivetts, Bos	17	K. Gleason, StL	187	N. Cuppy, Cle	2.8	T. Breitenstein, StL	102	P. Hawley, StL	2.9	K. Nichols, Bos	0.80
F. Dwyer, Cin	17	W. McGill, ChN	181	H. Staley, Bos	2.8	C. Young, Cle	102	A. Terry, Pit	2.8	H. Staley, Bos	0.75
A. Maul, Was	17	G. Hemming, Lou	176	S. Stratton, Lou	2.9	G. Weyhing, Phi	101	B. Hawke, 2tm	2.7	P. Hawley, StL	0.71

Earned Run Average		Component ERA		Hit Batsmen		Wild Pitches		Opponent Average		Opponent OBP	
T. Breitenstein, StL	3.18	F. Killen, Pit	3.10	Statistic unavailable		T. Mullane, 2tm	29	A. Rusie, NYG	.240	F. Killen, Pit	.306
A. Rusie, NYG	3.23	T. Breitenstein, StL	3.13			A. Rusie, NYG	26	T. Breitenstein, StL	.241	C. Young, Cle	.313
C. Young, Cle	3.36	C. Young, Cle	3.25			E. Stein, Bro	17	F. Killen, Pit	.246	T. Breitenstein, StL	.313
R. Ehret, Pit	3.44	E. Stein, Bro	3.29			S. McMahon, Bal	17	B. Kennedy, Bro	.250	K. Nichols, Bos	.316
D. Clarkson, StL	3.48	K. Nichols, Bos	3.29			K. Gleason, StL	16	E. Stein, Bro	.250	E. Stein, Bro	.319

1893 National League Miscellaneous

Managers

Baltimore	Ned Hanlon	60-70
Boston	Frank Selee	86-43
Brooklyn	Dave Foutz	65-63
Chicago	Cap Anson	56-71
Cincinnati	Charlie Comiskey	65-63
Cleveland	Patsy Tebeau	73-55
Louisville	Billy Barnie	50-75
New York	Monte Ward	68-64
Philadelphia	Harry Wright	72-57
Pittsburgh	Al Buckenberger	81-48
St. Louis	Bill Watkins	57-75
Washington	Jim O'Rourke	40-89

Awards

STATS Most Valuable Player	Ed Delahanty, of, Phi
STATS Cy Young	Cy Young, Cle
STATS Rookie of the Year	Heinie Reitz, 2b, Bal
STATS Manager of the Year	Frank Selee, Bos

STATS All-Star Team

C	Jack Clements, Phi	.285	17	80
1B	Roger Connor, NYG	.305	11	105
2B	Cupid Childs, Cle	.326	3	65
3B	George Davis, NYG	.355	11	119
SS	Ed McKean, Cle	.310	4	133
OF	Ed Delahanty, Phi	.368	19	146
OF	Billy Hamilton, Phi	.380	5	44
OF	Sam Thompson, Phi	.370	11	126
P	Frank Killen, Pit	36-14	3.64	99 K
P	Kid Nichols, Bos	34-14	3.52	94 K
P	Cy Young, Cle	34-16	3.36	102 K

Postseason

None

Outstanding Performances

No-Hitters

Bill Hawke, Bal   vs. Was on August 16

Team	Overall					Home Games						Road Games						Park Index		Record by Month					
	W	L	Pct	GB	DIF	W	L	R	OR	HR	OHR	W	L	R	OR	HR	OHR	Run	HR	M/A	May	June	July	Aug	S/O
Baltimore	89	39	.695	—	92	52	15	626	378	13	9	37	24	545	442	20	22	93	48	5-3	12-6	20-6	10-14	22-7	20-3
New York	88	44	.667	3.0	0	49	17	477	362	29	21	39	27	463	427	14	16	94	167	3-5	13-11	15-8	18-7	20-8	19-5
Boston	83	49	.629	8.0	48	44	19	672	519	77	70	39	30	550	483	26	19	126	358	6-2	14-9	18-8	16-9	15-10	14-11
Philadelphia	71	57	.555	18.0	1	48	20	674	398	26	31	23	37	469	568	14	31	91	112	6-3	12-7	11-12	11-14	19-10	12-11
Brooklyn	70	61	.534	20.5	0	42	24	512	452	22	15	28	37	509	555	20	26	89	79	3-5	12-10	18-5	9-15	14-14	14-12
Cleveland	68	61	.527	21.5	33	35	24	511	411	8	18	33	37	421	485	29	36	121	47	6-2	13-7	9-14	18-11	9-15	13-12
Pittsburgh	65	65	.500	25.0	4	46	28	559	475	26	11	19	37	396	497	22	28	88	56	4-4	18-5	13-13	9-16	8-16	13-11
Chicago	57	75	.432	34.0	0	35	30	625	513	26	13	22	45	416	553	39	30	121	58	1-8	9-12	8-17	16-9	15-12	8-17
St. Louis	56	76	.424	35.0	8	34	32	429	438	30	16	22	44	342	516	24	32	101	82	6-2	9-13	10-15	10-17	9-13	12-13
Cincinnati	55	75	.423	35.0	4	38	28	512	515	43	45	17	47	398	570	18	40	103	147	4-4	7-13	12-13	16-11	7-19	9-15
Washington	45	87	.341	46.0	1	32	30	476	463	35	20	13	57	406	659	24	39	100	99	2-7	4-19	10-15	8-16	13-14	8-16
Louisville	36	94	.277	54.0	1	24	37	317	366	16	7	12	57	375	635	26	32	76	45	4-5	6-14	4-22	13-15	5-18	4-20

Clinch Date—Baltimore 9/25.

Team Batting

Team	G	AB	R	OR	H	2B	3B	HR	TB	RBI	TBB	IBB	SO	HBP	SH	SF	SB	CS	SB%	GDP	Avg	OBP	Slg
Boston	133	5011	1220	1002	1658	272	94	103	2427	1043	535	—	261	47	64	—	241	—	—	—	.331	.401	.484
Baltimore	129	4799	1171	819	1647	271	150	33	2317	976	516	—	200	98	151	—	324	—	—	—	.343	.418	.483
Philadelphia	129	4967	1143	966	1732	252	131	40	2366	981	496	—	245	57	119	—	273	—	—	—	.349	.414	.476
Chicago	135	4960	1041	1066	1555	265	86	65	2187	895	496	—	298	36	75	—	327	—	—	—	.314	.380	.441
Brooklyn	134	4816	1021	1007	1507	228	130	42	2121	866	466	—	294	34	100	—	282	—	—	—	.313	.378	.440
Pittsburgh	132	4676	955	972	1458	222	124	48	2072	803	434	—	208	68	163	—	256	—	—	—	.312	.379	.443
New York	137	4806	940	789	1446	197	96	43	1964	789	476	—	217	32	80	—	319	—	—	—	.301	.368	.409
Cleveland	130	4764	932	896	1442	241	90	37	1974	790	471	—	301	24	77	—	220	—	—	—	.303	.368	.414
Cincinnati	132	4671	910	1085	1374	224	67	61	1915	772	508	—	252	41	60	—	215	—	—	—	.294	.368	.410
Washington	132	4581	882	1122	1317	218	118	59	1948	762	617	—	375	71	56	—	249	—	—	—	.287	.381	.425
St. Louis	133	4610	771	953	1320	171	113	54	1879	650	442	—	289	39	112	—	190	—	—	—	.286	.354	.408
Louisville	130	4482	692	1001	1206	173	88	42	1681	560	350	—	364	54	93	—	217	—	—	—	.269	.330	.375
NL Total	1586	57143	11678	11678	17662	2734	1287	627	24851	9887	5807	—	3304	601	1150	—	3113	—	—	—	.309	.379	.435
NL Avg Team	132	4762	973	973	1472	228	107	52	2071	824	484	—	275	50	96	—	259	—	—	—	.309	.379	.435

Team Pitching

Team	G	CG	ShO	Rel	Sv	IP	H	R	ER	HR	SH	SF	HB	TBB	IBB	SO	WP	Bk	H/9	SO/9	BB/9	OAvg	OOBP	ERA
New York	137	111	5	30	1	1212.0	1292	789	516	37	—	—	—	539	—	395	50	0	9.6	2.9	4.0	.271	.344	3.83
Cleveland	130	106	6	28	1	1124.1	1390	896	621	54	—	—	—	435	—	254	40	0	11.1	2.0	3.5	.301	.361	4.97
Baltimore	129	97	1	36	11	1116.1	1371	819	620	31	—	—	—	472	—	275	31	0	11.1	2.2	3.8	.299	.365	5.00
St. Louis	133	114	2	24	0	1161.0	1418	953	682	48	—	—	—	500	—	319	39	0	11.0	2.5	3.9	.298	.365	5.29
Boston	133	108	3	25	2	1166.0	1529	1002	701	89	—	—	—	411	—	262	41	0	11.8	2.0	3.2	.313	.367	5.41
Louisville	130	113	2	17	1	1096.2	1462	1001	664	39	—	—	—	475	—	258	36	0	12.0	2.1	3.9	.317	.381	5.45
Washington	132	101	0	35	4	1107.0	1573	1122	678	59	—	—	—	446	—	190	46	0	12.8	1.5	3.6	.331	.388	5.51
Brooklyn	134	105	3	30	5	1162.1	1447	1007	712	41	—	—	—	555	—	285	70	1	11.2	2.2	4.3	.302	.375	5.51
Pittsburgh	132	106	2	29	0	1164.2	1552	972	725	39	—	—	—	457	—	304	21	0	12.0	2.3	3.5	.317	.375	5.60
Philadelphia	129	102	3	33	4	1125.2	1482	966	704	62	—	—	—	469	—	262	36	0	11.8	2.1	3.7	.314	.376	5.63
Chicago	135	117	0	18	0	1148.0	1561	1066	725	43	—	—	—	557	—	281	38	1	12.2	2.2	4.4	.321	.391	5.68
Cincinnati	132	110	4	21	3	1147.1	1585	1085	763	85	—	—	—	491	—	219	35	0	12.4	1.7	3.9	.325	.386	5.99
NL Total	1586	1290	31	326	36	13731.1	17662	11678	8111	627	—	—	—	5807	—	3304	483	2	11.6	2.2	3.8	.309	.373	5.32
NL Avg Team	132	108	3	27	3	1144.1	1472	973	676	52	—	—	—	484	—	275	40	0	11.6	2.2	3.8	.309	.373	5.32

Team Fielding

Team	G	PO	A	E	TC	DP	PB	Pct
Baltimore	129	3347	1630	293	5270	105	29	.944
Pittsburgh	132	3486	1675	354	5515	106	41	.936
Philadelphia	129	3373	1521	338	5232	111	45	.935
Cleveland	130	3367	1587	344	5298	107	31	.935
Brooklyn	134	3483	1557	390	5430	85	32	.928
Boston	133	3488	1649	415	5552	120	35	.925
Cincinnati	132	3437	1773	423	5633	119	18	.925
New York	137	3627	1721	443	5791	101	47	.924
St. Louis	133	3476	1641	426	5543	109	40	.923
Louisville	130	3418	1620	428	5466	130	31	.922
Chicago	135	3437	1625	452	5514	113	30	.918
Washington	132	3316	1631	499	5446	81	36	.908
NL Total	1586	41255	19630	4805	65690	1287	415	.927

Team vs. Team Records

	Bal	Bos	Bro	ChN	Cin	Cle	Lou	NYG	Phi	Pit	StL	Was	Won
Bal	—	4	8	9	10	9	10	6	6	6	10	11	89
Bos	8	—	6	7	8	9	10	6	6	8	6	9	83
Bro	4	6	—	6	6	6	8	5	5	7	8	9	70
ChN	3	5	6	—	6	2	8	1	7	6	6	7	57
Cin	2	4	6	6	—	3	7	5	3	5	7	7	55
Cle	3	3	5	10	8	—	8	3	7	4	9	8	68
Lou	2	2	4	4	4	3	—	0	3	3	6	4	36
NYG	6	6	7	11	7	9	12	—	5	8	7	10	88
Phi	4	6	7	5	8	5	8	7	—	8	5	8	71
Pit	4	4	5	6	7	8	9	4	4	—	6	8	65
StL	2	6	4	6	6	5	6	5	7	6	—	6	56
Was	1	3	3	5	5	4	8	2	4	4	6	—	45
Lost	39	49	61	75	75	61	94	44	57	65	76	87	

1894 National League Batting Leaders

Games		At-Bats		Runs		Hits		Doubles		Triples	
G. Van Haltren, NYG	137	B. Lowe, Bos	613	B. Hamilton, Phi	192	H. Duffy, Bos	237	H. Duffy, Bos	51	H. Reitz, Bal	31
E. Burke, NYG	136	W. Wilmot, ChN	597	W. Keeler, Bal	165	B. Hamilton, Phi	220	J. Kelley, Bal	48	S. Thompson, Phi	27
M. Ward, NYG	136	W. Keeler, Bal	590	J. Kelley, Bal	165	W. Keeler, Bal	219	W. Wilmot, ChN	45	G. Treadway, Bro	26
3 tied with	133	P. Donovan, Pit	576	H. Duffy, Bos	160	B. Lowe, Bos	212	3 tied with	39	R. Connor, 2tm	25
		T. Corcoran, Bro	576	B. Lowe, Bos	158	S. Brodie, Bal	210			D. Brouthers, Bal	23

Home Runs		Total Bases		Runs Batted In		Walks		Intentional Walks		Strikeouts	
H. Duffy, Bos	18	H. Duffy, Bos	374	H. Duffy, Bos	145	B. Hamilton, Phi	126	Statistic unavailable		T. Brown, Lou	73
B. Lowe, Bos	17	B. Lowe, Bos	319	S. Thompson, Phi	141	J. Kelley, Bal	107			G. Treadway, Bro	43
B. Joyce, Was	17	W. Keeler, Bal	305	E. Delahanty, Phi	131	C. Childs, Cle	107			E. Cartwright, Was	43
B. Dahlen, ChN	15	J. Kelley, Bal	305	W. Wilmot, ChN	130	J. McGraw, Bal	91			J. Bannon, Bos	42
6 tied with	13	J. Stenzel, Pit	303	2 tied with	128	B. Nash, Bos	91			T. Daly, Bro	42

Hit By Pitch		Sac Hits		Sac Flies		Stolen Bases		Caught Stealing		GDP	
H. Jennings, Bal	27	P. Donovan, Pit	26	Statistic unavailable		B. Hamilton, Phi	98	Statistic unavailable		Statistic unavailable	
J. Beckley, Pit	19	S. Brodie, Bal	24			J. McGraw, Bal	78				
W. Keeler, Bal	18	J. Beckley, Pit	22			W. Wilmot, ChN	74				
T. Tucker, Bos	17	B. Hallman, Phi	22			T. Brown, Lou	66				
2 tied with	13	2 tied with	20			B. Lange, ChN	65				

Runs Created		Runs Created/27 Outs		Batting Average		On-Base Percentage		Slugging Percentage		OBP+Slugging	
H. Duffy, Bos	204	H. Duffy, Bos	16.77	H. Duffy, Bos	.440	B. Hamilton, Phi	.523	H. Duffy, Bos	.694	H. Duffy, Bos	1.196
B. Hamilton, Phi	187	B. Hamilton, Phi	14.49	E. Delahanty, Phi	.407	J. Kelley, Bal	.502	J. Kelley, Bal	.602	J. Kelley, Bal	1.104
J. Kelley, Bal	173	J. Kelley, Bal	13.57	B. Hamilton, Phi	.404	H. Duffy, Bos	.502	E. Delahanty, Phi	.585	E. Delahanty, Phi	1.063
J. Stenzel, Pit	153	E. Delahanty, Phi	12.52	J. Kelley, Bal	.393	E. Delahanty, Phi	.478	J. Stenzel, Pit	.580	B. Hamilton, Phi	1.050
B. Lowe, Bos	153	J. Stenzel, Pit	11.48	L. Cross, Phi	.386	C. Childs, Cle	.475	B. Dahlen, ChN	.566	J. Stenzel, Pit	1.022

1894 National League Pitching Leaders

Wins		Losses		Winning Percentage		Games		Games Started		Complete Games	
A. Rusie, NYG	36	P. Hawley, StL	27	J. Meekin, NYG	.786	T. Breitenstein, StL	56	T. Breitenstein, StL	50	T. Breitenstein, StL	46
J. Meekin, NYG	33	J. Menefee, 2tm	25	S. McMahon, Bal	.758	A. Rusie, NYG	54	A. Rusie, NYG	50	A. Rusie, NYG	45
K. Nichols, Bos	32	W. Mercer, Was	23	A. Rusie, NYG	.735	P. Hawley, StL	53	J. Meekin, NYG	48	C. Young, Cle	44
T. Breitenstein, StL	27	T. Breitenstein, StL	23	K. Nichols, Bos	.711	J. Meekin, NYG	52	C. Young, Cle	47	J. Meekin, NYG	40
E. Stein, Bro	27	F. Dwyer, Cin	22	E. Stein, Bro	.659	C. Young, Cle	52	K. Nichols, Bos	46	K. Nichols, Bos	40

Shutouts		Saves		Games Finished		Batters Faced		Innings Pitched		Hits Allowed	
N. Cuppy, Cle	3	T. Mullane, 2tm	4	W. Mercer, Was	10	Statistic unavailable		T. Breitenstein, StL	447.1	T. Breitenstein, StL	497
K. Nichols, Bos	3	W. Mercer, Was	3	P. Hawley, StL	10			A. Rusie, NYG	444.0	C. Young, Cle	488
A. Rusie, NYG	3	B. Hawke, Bal	3	N. Cuppy, Cle	10			J. Meekin, NYG	409.0	K. Nichols, Bos	488
3 tied with	2	5 tied with	2	D. Esper, 2tm	10			C. Young, Cle	408.2	P. Hawley, StL	481
				2 tied with	9			K. Nichols, Bos	407.0	F. Dwyer, Cin	471

Home Runs Allowed		Walks		Walks/9 Innings		Strikeouts		Strikeouts/9 Innings		Strikeout/Walk Ratio	
J. Stivetts, Bos	27	A. Rusie, NYG	200	C. Young, Cle	2.3	A. Rusie, NYG	195	A. Rusie, NYG	4.0	C. Young, Cle	1.02
F. Dwyer, Cin	27	T. Breitenstein, StL	191	J. Menefee, 2tm	2.5	T. Breitenstein, StL	140	B. Hawke, Bal	3.0	A. Rusie, NYG	0.98
K. Nichols, Bos	23	J. Meekin, NYG	171	K. Gleason, 2tm	2.5	J. Meekin, NYG	133	J. Wadsworth, Lou	3.0	K. Nichols, Bos	0.93
K. Carsey, Phi	22	E. Stein, Bro	171	H. Staley, Bos	2.6	P. Hawley, StL	120	J. Meekin, NYG	2.9	B. Hawke, Bal	0.87
T. Breitenstein, StL	21	G. Hemming, 2tm	159	K. Nichols, Bos	2.7	K. Nichols, Bos	113	E. Chamberlin, Cin	2.9	J. Menefee, 2tm	0.85

Earned Run Average		Component ERA		Hit Batsmen		Wild Pitches		Opponent Average		Opponent OBP	
A. Rusie, NYG	2.78	A. Rusie, NYG	3.39	Statistic unavailable		P. Hawley, StL	21	A. Rusie, NYG	.250	J. Meekin, NYG	.328
J. Meekin, NYG	3.70	J. Meekin, NYG	3.49			B. Kennedy, Bro	21	J. Meekin, NYG	.256	A. Rusie, NYG	.329
W. Mercer, Was	3.76	J. Clarkson, Cle	4.04			J. Meekin, NYG	21	E. Stein, Bro	.277	C. Young, Cle	.334
C. Young, Cle	3.94	C. Young, Cle	4.11			D. Daub, Bro	17	T. Breitenstein, StL	.279	J. Clarkson, Cle	.336
J. Taylor, Phi	4.08	J. Taylor, Phi	4.20			E. Stein, Bro	17	J. Clarkson, Cle	.285	K. Nichols, Bos	.339

1894 National League Miscellaneous

Managers		
Baltimore	Ned Hanlon	89-39
Boston	Frank Selee	83-49
Brooklyn	Dave Foutz	70-61
Chicago	Cap Anson	57-75
Cincinnati	Charlie Comiskey	55-75
Cleveland	Patsy Tebeau	68-61
Louisville	Billy Barnie	36-94
New York	Monte Ward	88-44
Philadelphia	Arthur Irwin	71-57
Pittsburgh	Al Buckenberger	53-55
	Connie Mack	12-10
St. Louis	Doggie Miller	56-76
Washington	Gus Schmelz	45-87

Awards

STATS Most Valuable Player	Hugh Duffy, of, Bos
STATS Cy Young	Amos Rusie, NYG
STATS Rookie of the Year	Jimmy Bannon, of, Bos
STATS Manager of the Year	Ned Hanlon, Bal

STATS All-Star Team

C	Wilbert Robinson, Bal	.353	1	98
1B	Dan Brouthers, Bal	.347	9	128
2B	Bobby Lowe, Bos	.346	17	115
3B	Bill Joyce, Was	.355	17	89
SS	Bill Dahlen, ChN	.357	15	107
OF	Hugh Duffy, Bos	.440	18	145
OF	Billy Hamilton, Phi	.404	4	87
OF	Sam Thompson, Phi	.407	13	141
P	Sadie McMahon, Bal	25-8	4.21	60 K
P	Jouett Meekin, NYG	33-9	3.70	133 K
P	Amos Rusie, NYG	36-13	2.78	195 K

Postseason

World Series	New York (NL) 4 vs. Baltimore (NL) 0

Outstanding Performances

Triple Crown
Hugh Duffy, Bos   .440-18-145
Four-Homer Games
Bobby Lowe, Bos   on May 30
Three-Homer Games
Frank Shugart, StL   on May 10
Bill Joyce, Was   on August 20
Cycles
Lave Cross, Phi   on April 24
Bill Hassamaer, Was on June 13
Sam Thompson, Phi   on August 17
Tom Parrott, Cin   on September 28

1895 National League Standings

Team	W	L	Pct	GB	DIF	W	L	R	OR	HR	OHR	W	L	R	OR	HR	OHR	Run	HR	M/A	May	June	July	Aug	S/O
		Overall						**Home Games**						**Road Games**				**Park Index**				**Record by Month**			
Baltimore	87	43	.669	—	56	54	12	581	293	10	8	33	31	428	353	15	23	109	46	4-2	11-9	15-8	14-12	23-5	20-7
Cleveland	84	46	.646	3.0	32	47	13	423	274	5	10	37	33	494	446	24	23	87	37	5-4	14-9	14-10	19-11	19-6	13-6
Philadelphia	78	53	.595	9.5	2	51	21	653	455	42	16	27	32	415	502	19	20	99	122	2-4	15-8	11-12	14-10	18-11	18-8
Chicago	72	58	.554	15.0	3	43	26	477	439	32	23	29	32	389	415	23	15	101	128	4-5	16-9	15-11	13-14	9-11	15-8
Brooklyn	71	60	.542	16.5	2	43	22	444	334	22	20	28	38	423	500	17	21	86	112	3-3	9-14	16-8	13-12	17-10	13-13
Boston	71	60	.542	16.5	25	48	19	537	363	50	38	23	41	370	463	4	18	103	382	3-3	12-9	17-6	10-15	16-12	13-15
Pittsburgh	71	61	.538	17.0	51	44	21	422	334	9	3	27	40	389	453	17	14	93	40	7-2	15-9	12-11	14-11	11-16	12-12
Cincinnati	66	64	.508	21.0	7	42	22	528	404	8	7	24	42	375	450	28	32	117	26	5-4	15-9	9-11	16-11	9-15	12-14
New York	66	65	.504	21.5	0	40	27	424	376	14	8	26	38	428	458	18	26	86	48	3-3	12-12	11-12	15-9	14-14	11-15
Washington	43	85	.336	43.0	0	31	34	523	521	39	33	12	51	314	527	16	22	120	184	3-3	9-16	10-12	3-16	7-19	11-19
St. Louis	39	92	.298	48.5	0	25	41	411	491	26	35	14	51	336	541	12	29	101	147	3-6	8-16	6-18	11-16	5-17	6-19
Louisville	35	96	.267	52.5	1	19	38	328	447	14	12	16	58	370	643	20	28	99	70	3-6	2-18	3-20	10-15	8-20	9-17

Clinch Date—Baltimore 9/28.

Team Batting

Team	G	AB	R	OR	H	2B	3B	HR	TB	RBI	TBB	IBB	SO	HBP	SH	SF	SB	CS	SB%	GDP	Avg	OBP	Slg
Philadelphia	133	5037	1068	957	1664	272	73	61	2265	930	463	—	262	69	120	—	276	—	—	—	.330	.394	.450
Baltimore	132	4725	1009	646	1530	235	89	25	2018	828	355	—	243	106	125	—	310	—	—	—	.324	.384	.427
Cleveland	131	4658	917	720	1423	194	67	29	1838	772	472	—	361	49	87	—	187	—	—	—	.305	.375	.395
Boston	132	4715	907	826	1369	197	57	54	1842	753	500	—	236	51	126	—	199	—	—	—	.290	.365	.391
Cincinnati	132	4684	903	854	1395	235	105	36	1948	766	414	—	249	36	56	—	326	—	—	—	.298	.359	.416
Brooklyn	133	4717	867	834	1330	189	77	39	1790	715	397	—	318	63	66	—	183	—	—	—	.282	.346	.379
Chicago	133	4708	866	854	1401	171	85	55	1907	727	422	—	344	42	80	—	260	—	—	—	.298	.361	.405
New York	132	4605	852	834	1324	191	90	32	1791	699	454	—	292	30	38	—	292	—	—	—	.288	.355	.389
Washington	132	4577	837	1048	1314	207	101	55	1888	713	518	—	396	52	68	—	237	—	—	—	.287	.366	.412
Pittsburgh	134	4645	811	787	1349	190	89	26	1795	673	376	—	299	65	106	—	257	—	—	—	.290	.352	.386
St. Louis	135	4781	747	1032	1344	155	88	38	1789	629	384	—	279	28	64	—	205	—	—	—	.281	.338	.374
Louisville	133	4724	698	1090	1320	171	73	34	1739	574	346	—	323	76	58	—	156	—	—	—	.279	.339	.368
NL Total	1592	56576	10482	10482	16763	2407	994	484	22610	8779	5101	—	3602	667	994	—	2888	—	—	—	.296	.361	.400
NL Avg Team	133	4715	874	874	1397	201	83	40	1884	732	425	—	300	56	83	—	241	—	—	—	.296	.361	.400

Team Pitching

Team	G	CG	ShO	Rel	Sv	IP	H	R	ER	HR	SH	SF	HB	TBB	IBB	SO	WP	Bk	H/9	SO/9	BB/9	OAvg	OOBP	ERA
Baltimore	132	104	10	30	4	1134.1	1216	646	479	31	—	—	—	430	—	244	23	0	9.6	1.9	3.4	.270	.334	3.80
Cleveland	131	108	6	25	3	1143.2	1272	720	497	33	—	—	—	346	—	326	36	1	10.0	2.6	2.7	.278	.328	3.91
Pittsburgh	134	106	4	29	6	1171.2	1263	787	527	17	—	—	—	500	—	382	44	0	9.7	2.9	3.8	.271	.342	4.05
Boston	132	116	4	18	4	1175.1	1364	826	558	56	—	—	—	363	—	370	31	0	10.4	2.8	2.8	.286	.337	4.27
New York	132	115	6	18	1	1147.1	1359	834	575	34	—	—	—	415	—	409	32	1	10.7	3.2	3.3	.290	.348	4.51
Chicago	133	119	3	14	1	1150.2	1422	854	597	38	—	—	—	432	—	297	34	0	11.1	2.3	3.4	.299	.358	4.67
Cincinnati	132	97	2	35	6	1147.1	1451	854	613	39	—	—	—	362	—	245	27	0	11.4	1.9	2.8	.304	.353	4.81
Brooklyn	133	103	5	29	6	1150.2	1360	834	632	41	—	—	—	395	—	216	36	0	10.6	1.7	3.1	.290	.345	4.94
Washington	132	99	0	37	5	1101.2	1507	1048	646	55	—	—	—	465	—	258	24	0	12.3	2.1	3.8	.321	.382	5.28
Philadelphia	133	106	2	29	7	1161.0	1467	957	705	36	—	—	—	485	—	330	41	1	11.4	2.6	3.8	.304	.367	5.47
St. Louis	135	105	1	30	1	1152.1	1562	1032	738	64	—	—	—	439	—	280	20	0	12.2	2.2	3.4	.319	.375	5.76
Louisville	133	104	1	34	1	1117.1	1520	1090	732	40	—	—	—	470	—	245	48	1	12.2	2.0	3.8	.320	.381	5.90
NL Total	1592	1282	46	328	45	13753.1	16763	10482	7299	484	—	—	—	5102	—	3602	396	4	11.0	2.4	3.3	.296	.355	4.78
NL Avg Team	133	107	4	27	4	1146.1	1397	874	608	40	—	—	—	425	—	300	33	0	11.0	2.4	3.3	.296	.355	4.78

Team Fielding

Team	G	PO	A	E	TC	DP	PB	Pct
Baltimore	132	3392	1623	288	5303	108	20	.946
Brooklyn	133	3451	1698	325	5474	96	20	.941
Cleveland	131	3428	1679	348	5455	77	47	.936
Boston	132	3514	1661	364	5539	104	45	.934
Philadelphia	133	3480	1659	369	5508	93	28	.933
Cincinnati	132	3436	1668	377	5481	112	27	.931
Pittsburgh	134	3511	1727	392	5630	95	39	.930
St. Louis	135	3451	1594	380	5425	94	25	.930
Chicago	133	3446	1707	401	5554	113	38	.928
New York	132	3438	1728	438	5604	106	41	.922
Washington	132	3297	1656	447	5400	96	29	.917
Louisville	133	3348	1638	477	5463	104	31	.913
NL Total	1592	41192	20038	4606	65836	1198	390	.930

Team vs. Team Records

	Bal	Bos	Bro	ChN	Cin	Cle	Lou	NYG	Phi	Pit	StL	Was	Won
Bal	—	10	7	8	8	5	10	9	8	7	6	9	87
Bos	2	—	4	7	5	6	9	8	5	7	9	9	71
Bro	5	7	—	6	5	2	11	9	5	7	9	5	71
ChN	4	5	6	—	5	6	9	4	6	8	10	9	72
Cin	4	7	7	7	—	6	6	4	4	4	9	8	66
Cle	6	6	10	5	6	—	10	7	7	7	11	9	84
Lou	1	3	1	3	6	2	—	3	2	2	6	6	35
NYG	3	4	3	8	8	5	9	—	3	4	11	8	66
Phi	4	7	7	6	8	5	10	8	—	8	7	8	78
Pit	5	5	5	4	8	5	10	8	4	—	9	8	71
StL	6	3	3	2	3	1	6	1	5	3	—	6	39
Was	3	3	7	2	2	3	6	4	4	4	5	—	43
Lost	43	60	60	58	64	46	96	65	53	61	92	85	

1895 National League Batting Leaders

Games		At-Bats		Runs		Hits		Doubles		Triples	
J. Quinn, StL	134	W. Keeler, Bal	565	B. Hamilton, Phi	166	J. Burkett, Cle	225	E. Delahanty, Phi	49	K. Selbach, Was	22
B. Everitt, ChN	133	E. McKean, Cle	565	W. Keeler, Bal	162	W. Keeler, Bal	213	S. Thompson, Phi	45	M. Tiernan, NYG	21
J. Boyle, Phi	133	J. Boyle, Phi	565	H. Jennings, Bal	159	S. Thompson, Phi	211	H. Jennings, Bal	41	S. Thompson, Phi	21
6 tied with	132	D. Cooley, StL	563	J. Burkett, Cle	153	H. Jennings, Bal	204	J. Stenzel, Pit	38	D. Cooley, StL	20
		3 tied with	550	E. Delahanty, Phi	149	B. Hamilton, Phi	201	M. Griffin, Bro	38	3 tied with	19

Home Runs		Total Bases		Runs Batted In		Walks		Intentional Walks		Strikeouts	
S. Thompson, Phi	18	S. Thompson, Phi	352	S. Thompson, Phi	165	B. Joyce, Was	96	Statistic unavailable		T. Brown, 2tm	60
B. Joyce, Was	17	E. Delahanty, Phi	296	J. Kelley, Bal	134	B. Hamilton, Phi	96			B. Joyce, Was	54
J. Clements, Phi	13	J. Burkett, Cle	288	S. Brodie, Bal	134	M. Griffin, Bro	93			T. Daly, Bro	52
E. Delahanty, Phi	11	J. Kelley, Bal	283	H. Jennings, Bal	125	E. Delahanty, Phi	86			B. Dahlen, ChN	51
5 tied with	10	E. McKean, Cle	283	E. McKean, Cle	119	J. Kelley, Bal	77			C. LaChance, Bro	48

Hit By Pitch		Sac Hits		Sac Flies		Stolen Bases		Caught Stealing		GDP	
H. Jennings, Bal	32	H. Jennings, Bal	28	Statistic unavailable		B. Hamilton, Phi	97	Statistic unavailable		Statistic unavailable	
J. Beckley, Pit	21	F. Genins, Pit	23			B. Lange, ChN	67				
T. Tucker, Bos	19	W. Keeler, Bal	21			J. McGraw, Bal	61				
3 tied with	14	H. Long, Bos	21			J. Kelley, Bal	54				
		J. Boyle, Phi	20			2 tied with	53				

Runs Created		Runs Created/27 Outs		Batting Average		On-Base Percentage		Slugging Percentage		OBP+Slugging	
J. Burkett, Cle	169	E. Delahanty, Phi	13.99	J. Burkett, Cle	.409	E. Delahanty, Phi	.500	S. Thompson, Phi	.654	E. Delahanty, Phi	1.117
B. Hamilton, Phi	160	J. Burkett, Cle	13.08	E. Delahanty, Phi	.404	B. Hamilton, Phi	.490	E. Delahanty, Phi	.617	S. Thompson, Phi	1.085
E. Delahanty, Phi	159	B. Hamilton, Phi	12.65	S. Thompson, Phi	.392	J. Burkett, Cle	.486	B. Lange, ChN	.575	B. Lange, ChN	1.032
J. Kelley, Bal	158	B. Lange, ChN	12.29	B. Lange, ChN	.389	B. Lange, ChN	.456	J. Kelley, Bal	.546	J. Burkett, Cle	1.009
S. Thompson, Phi	154	S. Thompson, Phi	12.03	B. Hamilton, Phi	.389	J. Kelley, Bal	.456	J. Stenzel, Pit	.539	J. Kelley, Bal	1.003

1895 National League Pitching Leaders

Wins		Losses		Winning Percentage		Games		Games Started		Complete Games	
C. Young, Cle	35	T. Breitenstein, StL	30	B. Hoffer, Bal	.838	P. Hawley, Pit	56	P. Hawley, Pit	50	T. Breitenstein, StL	46
B. Hoffer, Bal	31	W. Mercer, Was	23	C. Young, Cle	.778	T. Breitenstein, StL	54	T. Breitenstein, StL	50	P. Hawley, Pit	44
P. Hawley, Pit	31	A. Rusie, NYG	23	A. Maul, Was	.667	A. Rusie, NYG	49	A. Rusie, NYG	47	K. Nichols, Bos	42
4 tied with	26	P. Hawley, Pit	22	B. Rhines, Cin	.655	3 tied with	47	K. Nichols, Bos	42	A. Rusie, NYG	42
		2 tied with	21	3 tied with	.650			C. Griffith, ChN	41	C. Griffith, ChN	39

Shutouts		Saves		Games Finished		Batters Faced		Innings Pitched		Hits Allowed	
B. Hoffer, Bal	4	E. Beam, Phi	3	J. Malarkey, Was	12	Statistic unavailable		P. Hawley, Pit	444.1	K. Carsey, Phi	460
P. Hawley, Pit	4	T. Parrott, Cin	3	B. Kissinger, 2tm	10			T. Breitenstein, StL	429.2	T. Breitenstein, StL	458
C. Young, Cle	4	K. Nichols, Bos	3	T. Parrott, Cin	10			A. Rusie, NYG	393.1	P. Hawley, Pit	449
S. McMahon, Bal	4	8 tied with	2	3 tied with	9			K. Nichols, Bos	379.2	C. Griffith, ChN	434
A. Rusie, NYG	4							C. Young, Cle	369.2	W. Mercer, Was	430

Home Runs Allowed		Walks		Walks/9 Innings		Strikeouts		Strikeouts/9 Innings		Strikeout/Walk Ratio	
W. Mercer, Was	17	T. Breitenstein, StL	178	C. Young, Cle	1.8	A. Rusie, NYG	201	A. Rusie, NYG	4.6	K. Nichols, Bos	1.63
T. Breitenstein, StL	16	A. Rusie, NYG	159	D. Clarke, NYG	1.9	P. Hawley, Pit	142	W. McGill, Phi	4.3	C. Young, Cle	1.61
K. Nichols, Bos	15	B. Hart, Pit	135	K. Nichols, Bos	2.0	K. Nichols, Bos	140	B. Foreman, Pit	3.5	A. Rusie, NYG	1.26
J. Stivetts, Bos	15	A. Terry, ChN	131	H. Staley, StL	2.2	T. Breitenstein, StL	127	J. Stivetts, Bos	3.4	J. Stivetts, Bos	1.25
K. Carsey, Phi	14	B. Hutchison, ChN	129	J. Taylor, Phi	2.2	C. Young, Cle	121	K. Nichols, Bos	3.3	P. Hawley, Pit	1.16

Earned Run Average		Component ERA		Hit Batsmen		Wild Pitches		Opponent Average		Opponent OBP	
A. Maul, Was	2.45	C. Young, Cle	2.70	Statistic unavailable		M. McDermott, Lou	16	B. Foreman, Pit	.245	C. Young, Cle	.289
P. Hawley, Pit	3.18	P. Hawley, Pit	3.03			E. Stein, Bro	15	B. Hoffer, Bal	.246	A. Maul, Was	.306
B. Hoffer, Bal	3.21	A. Maul, Was	3.13			B. Hutchison, ChN	14	C. Young, Cle	.249	P. Hawley, Pit	.307
B. Foreman, Pit	3.22	B. Foreman, Pit	3.15			K. Carsey, Phi	13	A. Rusie, NYG	.252	K. Nichols, Bos	.311
C. Young, Cle	3.24	B. Hoffer, Bal	3.16			K. Nichols, Bos	11	A. Maul, Was	.257	B. Hoffer, Bal	.316

1895 National League Miscellaneous

Managers		
Baltimore	Ned Hanlon	87-43
Boston	Frank Selee	71-60
Brooklyn	Dave Foutz	71-60
Chicago	Cap Anson	72-58
Cincinnati	Buck Ewing	66-64
Cleveland	Patsy Tebeau	84-46
Louisville	John McCloskey	35-96
New York	George Davis	16-17
	Jack Doyle	32-31
	Harvey Watkins	18-17
Philadelphia	Arthur Irwin	78-53
Pittsburgh	Connie Mack	71-61
St. Louis	Al Buckenberger	16-34
	Chris Von Der Ahe	1-0
	Joe Quinn	11-28
	Lew Phelan	11-30
Washington	Gus Schmelz	43-85

Awards	
STATS Most Valuable Player	H. Jennings, ss, Bal
STATS Cy Young	Cy Young, Cle
STATS Rookie of the Year	Bill Hoffer, p, Bal
STATS Manager of the Year	Cap Anson, ChN

STATS All-Star Team

C	Jack Clements, Phi	.394	13	75
1B	Ed Cartwright, Was	.331	3	90
2B	Bid McPhee, Cin	.299	1	75
3B	Bill Joyce, Was	.312	17	95
SS	Hughie Jennings, Bal	.386	4	125
OF	Jesse Burkett, Cle	.409	5	83
OF	Ed Delahanty, Phi	.404	11	106
OF	Sam Thompson, Phi	.392	18	165
P	Pink Hawley, Pit	31-22	3.18	142 K
P	Bill Hoffer, Bal	31-6	3.21	80 K
P	Cy Young, Cle	35-10	3.24	121 K

Postseason

World Series	Cle (NL) 4 vs. Bal (NL) 1

Outstanding Performances

Cycles

Tommy Dowd, StL	on August 16
Ed Cartwright, Was	on September 30

1896 National League Standings

Team	Overall					Home Games						Road Games						Park Index		Record by Month					
	W	L	Pct	GB	DIF	W	L	R	OR	HR	OHR	W	L	R	OR	HR	OHR	Run	HR	M/A	May	June	July	Aug	S/O
Baltimore	90	39	.698	—	71	49	16	528	310	8	4	41	23	467	352	15	18	101	36	5-6	17-7	15-6	18-8	19-7	16-5
Cleveland	80	48	.625	9.5	35	43	19	445	315	9	4	37	29	395	335	19	23	111	33	4-5	16-6	15-7	20-12	10-12	15-6
Cincinnati	77	50	.606	12.0	35	51	15	450	292	6	1	26	35	333	328	14	26	104	16	6-4	16-10	18-8	21-7	8-11	8-10
Boston	74	57	.565	17.0	1	42	24	510	371	23	39	32	33	350	390	13	18	117	197	7-4	13-10	14-8	10-17	15-10	15-8
Chicago	71	57	.555	18.5	3	42	24	470	427	19	16	29	33	345	372	15	14	118	113	6-5	12-14	14-12	20-7	12-10	7-9
Pittsburgh	66	63	.512	24.0	18	35	31	369	335	5	2	31	32	418	406	22	16	82	18	8-2	10-12	12-13	16-12	13-10	7-14
New York	64	67	.489	27.0	0	39	26	438	371	21	14	25	41	391	450	19	19	98	94	1-10	13-11	10-12	10-16	18-10	12-8
Philadelphia	62	68	.477	28.5	19	42	27	530	448	30	24	20	41	360	443	19	15	108	140	8-3	15-11	8-15	9-16	13-12	9-11
Brooklyn	58	73	.443	33.0	5	35	28	298	298	13	19	23	45	394	466	15	20	75	99	6-5	10-13	13-11	9-17	14-10	6-17
Washington	58	73	.443	33.0	6	38	29	462	395	30	12	20	44	356	525	15	12	93	149	6-5	10-13	11-8	8-21	9-18	14-8
St. Louis	40	90	.308	50.5	1	27	34	322	374	25	18	13	56	271	555	12	22	95	143	6-5	5-19	4-20	12-14	7-16	6-16
Louisville	38	93	.290	53.0	0	25	37	326	471	24	38	13	56	327	526	13	10	104	300	1-10	7-18	3-17	10-16	6-18	11-14

Clinch Date—Baltimore 9/12.

Team Batting

Team	G	AB	R	OR	H	2B	3B	HR	TB	RBI	TBB	IBB	SO	HBP	SH	SF	SB	CS	SB%	GDP	Avg	OBP	Slg
Baltimore	132	4719	995	662	1548	207	100	23	2024	854	386	—	201	120	98	—	441	—	—	—	.328	.393	.429
Philadelphia	130	4680	890	891	1382	234	84	49	1931	778	438	—	297	60	95	—	191	—	—	—	.295	.363	.413
Boston	132	4717	860	761	1416	175	74	36	1847	736	414	—	274	51	118	—	241	—	—	—	.300	.363	.392
Cleveland	135	4856	840	650	1463	207	72	28	1898	712	436	—	316	37	106	—	175	—	—	—	.301	.363	.391
New York	133	4661	829	821	1383	159	87	40	1836	720	439	—	271	53	72	—	274	—	—	—	.297	.364	.394
Washington	133	4639	818	920	1328	179	79	45	1800	702	516	—	365	61	99	—	258	—	—	—	.286	.365	.388
Chicago	132	4582	815	799	1311	182	97	34	1789	660	409	—	290	35	92	—	332	—	—	—	.286	.349	.390
Pittsburgh	131	4701	787	741	1371	169	94	27	1809	667	387	—	286	57	108	—	217	—	—	—	.292	.353	.385
Cincinnati	128	4360	783	620	1283	204	73	20	1693	648	382	—	226	42	127	—	350	—	—	—	.294	.357	.388
Brooklyn	133	4548	692	764	1292	174	87	28	1724	557	344	—	269	39	94	—	198	—	—	—	.284	.340	.379
Louisville	134	4588	653	997	1197	142	80	37	1610	520	371	—	427	45	53	—	195	—	—	—	.261	.322	.351
St. Louis	131	4520	593	929	1162	134	78	37	1563	487	332	—	300	35	101	—	185	—	—	—	.257	.313	.346
NL Total	1584	55571	9555	9555	16136	2166	1005	404	21524	8041	4854	—	3522	635	1163	—	3057	—	—	—	.290	.354	.387
NL Avg Team	132	4631	796	796	1345	181	84	34	1794	670	405	—	294	53	97	—	255	—	—	—	.290	.354	.387

Team Pitching

Team	G	CG	ShO	Rel	Sv	IP	H	R	ER	HR	SH	SF	HB	TBB	IBB	SO	WP	Bk	H/9	SO/9	BB/9	OAvg	OOBP	ERA
Cleveland	135	113	9	24	5	1195.2	1363	650	460	27	—	—	—	280	—	336	24	0	10.3	2.5	2.1	.285	.324	3.46
Cincinnati	128	105	12	26	4	1108.0	1240	620	452	27	—	—	—	310	—	219	23	0	10.1	1.8	2.5	.281	.328	3.67
Baltimore	132	115	9	17	1	1168.1	1281	662	477	22	—	—	—	339	—	302	25	0	9.9	2.3	2.6	.277	.326	3.67
Boston	132	110	6	24	3	1155.2	1254	761	485	57	—	—	—	397	—	277	35	0	9.8	2.2	3.1	.275	.333	3.78
Brooklyn	133	97	3	38	1	1144.0	1353	764	540	39	—	—	—	400	—	259	36	0	10.6	2.0	3.1	.292	.348	4.25
Pittsburgh	131	108	8	26	1	1159.1	1286	741	554	18	—	—	—	439	—	362	42	1	10.0	2.8	3.4	.279	.342	4.30
Chicago	132	118	2	15	1	1161.0	1302	799	569	30	—	—	—	467	—	353	28	0	10.1	2.7	3.6	.281	.347	4.41
New York	133	104	1	30	2	1136.2	1303	821	574	33	—	—	—	403	—	312	50	1	10.3	2.5	3.2	.286	.344	4.54
Washington	133	106	2	29	3	1136.2	1435	920	582	24	—	—	—	435	—	292	47	0	11.4	2.3	3.4	.306	.365	4.61
Louisville	134	108	1	29	4	1148.2	1398	997	654	48	—	—	—	541	—	288	53	1	11.0	2.3	4.2	.298	.371	5.12
Philadelphia	130	107	3	25	2	1117.0	1473	891	645	39	—	—	—	387	—	243	21	1	11.9	2.0	3.1	.315	.368	5.20
St. Louis	131	115	1	18	1	1130.2	1448	929	669	40	—	—	—	456	—	279	28	0	11.5	2.2	3.6	.309	.370	5.33
NL Total	1584	1306	57	301	28	13761.2	16136	9555	6661	404	—	—	—	4854	—	3522	412	4	10.6	2.3	3.2	.290	.347	4.36
NL Avg Team	132	109	5	25	2	1146.2	1345	796	555	34	—	—	—	405	—	294	34	0	10.6	2.3	3.2	.290	.347	4.36

Team Fielding

Team	G	PO	A	E	TC	DP	PB	Pct
Cincinnati	128	3320	1584	252	5156	107	19	.951
Cleveland	135	3581	1816	288	5685	117	28	.949
Baltimore	132	3500	1619	296	5415	114	33	.945
Brooklyn	133	3429	1707	297	5433	104	17	.945
Pittsburgh	131	3470	1624	317	5411	103	26	.941
Philadelphia	130	3344	1626	313	5283	112	27	.941
St. Louis	131	3387	1701	345	5433	73	29	.936
Boston	132	3463	1732	368	5563	94	41	.934
Chicago	132	3478	1662	366	5506	115	25	.934
New York	133	3404	1647	365	5416	90	43	.933
Washington	133	3400	1686	398	5484	99	32	.927
Louisville	134	3442	1754	475	5671	110	29	.916
NL Total	1584	41218	20158	4080	65456	1238	349	.938

Team vs. Team Records

	Bal	Bos	Bro	ChN	Cin	Cle	Lou	NYG	Phi	Pit	StL	Was	Won
Bal	—	5	6	7	10	3	10	9	12	9	9	10	90
Bos	7	—	10	3	5	5	8	7	7	7	8	7	74
Bro	6	2	—	6	2	5	8	4	8	6	7	4	58
ChN	4	9	6	—	4	2	9	5	4	11	9	8	71
Cin	2	6	10	6	—	6	9	6	8	5	12	7	77
Cle	8	7	7	9	5	—	8	7	6	4	10	9	80
Lou	2	4	4	3	3	3	—	4	7	2	3	3	38
NYG	3	5	8	7	6	5	8	—	3	4	9	6	64
Phi	0	5	4	8	4	6	5	8	—	6	8	8	62
Pit	2	5	5	1	7	8	10	8	6	—	8	6	66
StL	3	4	5	3	0	2	9	3	3	3	—	5	40
Was	2	5	8	4	4	3	9	6	4	6	7	—	58
Lost	39	57	73	57	50	48	93	67	68	63	90	73	

1896 National League Batting Leaders

Games		At-Bats		Runs		Hits		Doubles		Triples	
7 tied with	133	J. Burkett, Cle	586	J. Burkett, Cle	160	J. Burkett, Cle	240	E. Delahanty, Phi	44	T. McCreery, Lou	21
		B. Everitt, ChN	575	W. Keeler, Bal	153	W. Keeler, Bal	210	D. Miller, Cin	38	G. Van Haltren, NYG	21
		P. Donovan, Pit	573	B. Hamilton, Bos	152	H. Jennings, Bal	209	J. Kelley, Bal	31	J. Kelley, Bal	19
		E. McKean, Cle	571	J. Kelley, Bal	148	E. Delahanty, Phi	198	B. Dahlen, ChN	30	B. Dahlen, ChN	19
		G. Van Haltren, NYG	562	B. Dahlen, ChN	137	G. Van Haltren, NYG	197	2 tied with	29	F. Clarke, Lou	18

Home Runs		Total Bases		Runs Batted In		Walks		Intentional Walks		Strikeouts	
B. Joyce, 2tm	13	J. Burkett, Cle	317	E. Delahanty, Phi	126	B. Hamilton, Bos	110	Statistic unavailable		T. McCreery, Lou	58
E. Delahanty, Phi	13	E. Delahanty, Phi	315	H. Jennings, Bal	121	B. Joyce, 2tm	101			B. Clingman, Lou	51
S. Thompson, Phi	12	J. Kelley, Bal	282	H. Duffy, Bos	113	C. Childs, Cle	100			B. Lush, Was	49
R. Connor, StL	11	G. Van Haltren, NYG	272	E. McKean, Cle	112	J. Kelley, Bal	91			T. Brown, Was	49
2 tied with	9	W. Keeler, Bal	270	2 tied with	106	M. Tiernan, NYG	77			2 tied with	48

Hit By Pitch		Sac Hits		Sac Flies		Stolen Bases		Caught Stealing		GDP	
H. Jennings, Bal	51	D. Hoy, Cin	33	Statistic unavailable		J. Kelley, Bal	87	Statistic unavailable		Statistic unavailable	
B. Joyce, 2tm	22	B. Ely, Pit	28			B. Lange, ChN	84				
J. Sullivan, 2tm	20	B. Dahlen, ChN	27			B. Hamilton, Bos	83				
S. Brodie, Bal	18	F. Tenney, Bos	21			D. Miller, Cin	76				
J. Beckley, 2tm	15	2 tied with	20			J. Doyle, Bal	73				

Runs Created		Runs Created/27 Outs		Batting Average		On-Base Percentage		Slugging Percentage		OBP+Slugging	
E. Delahanty, Phi	162	E. Delahanty, Phi	13.61	J. Burkett, Cle	.410	B. Hamilton, Bos	.477	E. Delahanty, Phi	.631	E. Delahanty, Phi	1.103
J. Kelley, Bal	160	J. Kelley, Bal	12.24	H. Jennings, Bal	.401	H. Jennings, Bal	.472	B. Dahlen, ChN	.553	J. Kelley, Bal	1.013
J. Burkett, Cle	156	B. Hamilton, Bos	11.75	E. Delahanty, Phi	.397	E. Delahanty, Phi	.472	T. McCreery, Lou	.546	J. Burkett, Cle	1.002
B. Hamilton, Bos	155	H. Jennings, Bal	11.43	W. Keeler, Bal	.386	B. Joyce, 2tm	.470	J. Kelley, Bal	.543	B. Dahlen, ChN	.990
H. Jennings, Bal	144	J. Burkett, Cle	11.39	M. Tiernan, NYG	.369	J. Kelley, Bal	.469	J. Burkett, Cle	.541	B. Joyce, 2tm	.988

1896 National League Pitching Leaders

Wins		Losses		Winning Percentage		Games		Games Started		Complete Games	
F. Killen, Pit	30	B. Hart, StL	29	B. Hoffer, Bal	.781	F. Killen, Pit	52	F. Killen, Pit	50	F. Killen, Pit	44
K. Nichols, Bos	30	B. Hill, Lou	28	D. Esper, Bal	.737	C. Young, Cle	51	C. Young, Cle	46	C. Young, Cle	42
C. Young, Cle	28	C. Fraser, Lou	27	G. Hemming, Bal	.714	P. Hawley, Pit	49	W. Mercer, Was	45	W. Mercer, Was	38
J. Meekin, NYG	26	T. Breitenstein, StL	26	F. Foreman, Cin	.714	K. Nichols, Bos	49	3 tied with	43	4 tied with	37
3 tied with	25	2 tied with	24	F. Dwyer, Cin	.686	D. Clarke, NYG	48				

Shutouts		Saves		Games Finished		Batters Faced		Innings Pitched		Hits Allowed	
F. Killen, Pit	5	C. Young, Cle	3	C. Fisher, Cin	11	Statistic unavailable		F. Killen, Pit	432.1	C. Young, Cle	477
C. Young, Cle	5	B. Hill, Lou	2	J. Hughey, Pit	9			C. Young, Cle	414.1	F. Killen, Pit	476
5 tied with	3	C. Fisher, Cin	2	L. German, 2tm	8			P. Hawley, Pit	378.0	J. Taylor, Phi	459
		21 tied with	1	D. Clarke, NYG	8			K. Nichols, Bos	372.1	W. Mercer, Was	456
				4 tied with	7			W. Mercer, Was	366.1	D. Clarke, NYG	431

Home Runs Allowed		Walks		Walks/9 Innings		Strikeouts		Strikeouts/9 Innings		Strikeout/Walk Ratio	
J. Stivetts, Bos	20	C. Fraser, Lou	166	C. Young, Cle	1.3	C. Young, Cle	140	B. Briggs, ChN	3.9	C. Young, Cle	2.26
J. Taylor, Phi	17	P. Hawley, Pit	157	D. Clarke, NYG	1.5	P. Hawley, Pit	137	A. Pond, Bal	3.4	A. Pond, Bal	1.40
B. Hill, Lou	14	B. Hill, Lou	155	F. Dwyer, Cin	1.9	F. Killen, Pit	134	D. McJames, Was	3.3	C. Griffith, ChN	1.16
K. Nichols, Bos	14	B. Hart, StL	141	N. Cuppy, Cle	1.9	T. Breitenstein, StL	114	P. Hawley, Pit	3.3	N. Cuppy, Cle	1.15
3 tied with	12	D. Friend, ChN	139	C. Griffith, ChN	2.0	J. Meekin, NYG	110	C. Young, Cle	3.0	F. Killen, Pit	1.13

Earned Run Average		Component ERA		Hit Batsmen		Wild Pitches		Opponent Average		Opponent OBP	
B. Rhines, Cin	2.45	B. Rhines, Cin	2.59	Statistic unavailable		C. Fraser, Lou	27	B. Rhines, Cin	.238	B. Rhines, Cin	.300
K. Nichols, Bos	2.83	B. Hoffer, Bal	3.12			D. McJames, Was	24	P. Hawley, Pit	.261	N. Cuppy, Cle	.311
N. Cuppy, Cle	3.12	N. Cuppy, Cle	3.23			P. Hawley, Pit	17	M. Sullivan, NYG	.261	C. Young, Cle	.313
F. Dwyer, Cin	3.15	K. Nichols, Bos	3.30			4 tied with	13	D. Friend, ChN	.263	K. Nichols, Bos	.314
C. Young, Cle	3.24	D. Esper, Bal	3.33					B. Hoffer, Bal	.264	F. Dwyer, Cin	.315

1896 National League Miscellaneous

Managers			Awards		Postseason	
Baltimore	Ned Hanlon	90-39	STATS Most Valuable Player	H. Jennings, ss, Bal	World Series	Bal (NL) 4 vs. Cle (NL) 0
Boston	Frank Selee	74-57	STATS Cy Young	Kid Nichols, Bos		
Brooklyn	Dave Foutz	58-73	STATS Rookie of the Year	Gene DeMontreville, ss, Was		
Chicago	Cap Anson	71-57	STATS Manager of the Year	Ned Hanlon, Bal	**Outstanding Performances**	
Cincinnati	Buck Ewing	77-50				
Cleveland	Patsy Tebeau	80-48			**Four-Homer Games**	
Louisville	John McCloskey	2-17			Ed Delahanty, Phi	on July 13
	Bill McGunnigle	36-76	**STATS All-Star Team**		**Cycles**	
New York	Arthur Irwin	36-53	C	Deacon McGuire, Was	.321	2	70	Herman Long, Bos	on May 9
	Bill Joyce	28-14	1B	Jack Doyle, Bal	.339	1	101	Bill Joyce, Was	on May 30
Philadelphia	Billy Nash	62-68	2B	Cupid Childs, Cle	.355	1	106		
Pittsburgh	Connie Mack	66-63	3B	Bill Joyce, 2tm	.333	13	94		
St. Louis	Harry Diddlebock	7-10	SS	Hughie Jennings, Bal	.401	0	121		
	Arlie Latham	0-3	OF	Jesse Burkett, Cle	.410	6	72		
	Chris Von Der Ahe	0-2	OF	Ed Delahanty, Phi	.397	13	126		
	Roger Connor	8-37	OF	Joe Kelley, Bal	.364	8	100		
	Tommy Dowd	25-38	P	Bill Hoffer, Bal	25-7	3.38	93 K		
Washington	Gus Schmelz	58-73	P	Kid Nichols, Bos	30-14	2.83	102 K		
			P	Cy Young, Cle	28-15	3.24	140 K		

Team	Overall					Home Games							Road Games							Park Index		Record by Month					
	W	L	Pct	GB	DIF	W	L	R	OR	HR	OHR	W	L	R	OR	HR	OHR	Run	HR	M/A	May	June	July	Aug	S/O
Boston	93	39	.705	—	77	54	12	573	307	26	26	39	27	452	358	19	13	109	163	1-6	19-6	21-2	15-10	19-10	18-5
Baltimore	90	40	.692	2.0	76	51	15	470	293	4	7	39	25	494	381	15	11	85	41	7-1	16-7	14-9	15-9	21-6	17-8
New York	83	48	.634	9.5	0	51	19	495	347	16	12	32	29	400	348	15	14	98	84	2-5	13-8	18-8	14-10	20-7	16-10
Cincinnati	76	56	.576	17.0	8	49	18	444	345	4	3	27	38	319	360	18	15	113	21	6-1	17-10	11-6	17-10	11-16	14-13
Cleveland	69	62	.527	23.5	0	49	16	477	306	8	11	20	46	296	374	8	21	119	67	2-5	15-9	10-13	16-9	10-15	15-11
Brooklyn	61	71	.462	32.0	2	38	29	456	412	11	19	23	42	346	433	13	15	108	104	3-6	13-10	10-13	8-17	13-15	14-10
Washington	61	71	.462	32.0	0	40	26	434	372	28	13	21	45	347	421	8	14	105	186	2-4	7-17	13-11	7-18	17-10	15-11
Pittsburgh	60	71	.458	32.5	2	38	27	354	363	10	5	22	44	322	472	15	17	92	48	3-2	15-10	8-16	11-15	9-17	14-11
Chicago	59	73	.447	34.0	0	36	30	444	405	16	15	23	43	388	489	22	15	97	84	2-6	9-16	10-13	12-13	13-12	9-14
Philadelphia	55	77	.417	38.0	14	32	34	381	357	17	6	23	43	371	435	23	22	92	51	8-1	9-16	11-13	12-14	9-17	6-16
Louisville	52	78	.400	40.0	6	34	31	343	402	26	23	18	47	326	457	14	16	95	163	5-1	10-15	6-17	16-16	11-13	4-16
St. Louis	29	102	.221	63.5	0	18	41	273	467	20	41	11	61	315	616	11	13	97	310	2-5	4-23	5-17	11-18	4-19	3-20

Clinch Date—Boston 9/30.

Team Batting

Team	G	AB	R	OR	H	2B	3B	HR	TB	RBI	TBB	IBB	SO	HBP	SH	SF	SB	CS	SB%	GDP	Avg	OBP	Slg
Boston	135	4937	1025	665	1574	230	83	45	2105	885	423	—	262	47	114	—	233	—	—	—	.319	.378	.426
Baltimore	136	4872	964	674	1584	243	66	19	2016	821	437	—	256	115	72	—	401	—	—	—	.325	.394	.414
New York	137	4844	895	695	1449	188	84	31	1898	759	404	—	327	66	45	—	328	—	—	—	.299	.361	.392
Chicago	138	4803	832	894	1356	189	97	38	1853	681	430	—	317	49	103	—	264	—	—	—	.282	.347	.386
Brooklyn	136	4810	802	845	1343	202	72	24	1761	644	351	—	255	58	115	—	187	—	—	—	.279	.336	.366
Washington	135	4636	781	793	1376	194	77	36	1832	674	374	—	348	67	72	—	208	—	—	—	.297	.358	.395
Cleveland	132	4604	773	680	1374	192	88	16	1790	663	435	—	344	38	98	—	181	—	—	—	.298	.364	.389
Cincinnati	134	4524	763	705	1311	219	69	22	1734	617	380	—	218	65	131	—	194	—	—	—	.290	.353	.383
Philadelphia	134	4756	752	792	1392	213	83	40	1891	633	399	—	299	42	97	—	163	—	—	—	.293	.353	.398
Pittsburgh	135	4590	676	835	1266	140	108	25	1697	575	359	—	334	67	98	—	170	—	—	—	.276	.337	.370
Louisville	134	4520	669	859	1197	160	70	40	1617	564	370	—	453	66	101	—	195	—	—	—	.265	.329	.358
St. Louis	132	4642	588	1083	1277	149	67	31	1653	494	354	—	314	73	80	—	172	—	—	—	.275	.336	.356
NL Total	1618	56538	9520	9520	16499	2319	964	367	21847	8010	4716	—	3727	753	1126	—	2696	—	—	—	.292	.354	.386
NL Avg Team	135	4712	793	793	1375	193	80	31	1821	668	393	—	311	63	94	—	225	—	—	—	.292	.354	.386

Team Pitching

Team	G	CG	ShO	Rel	Sv	IP	H	R	ER	HR	SH	SF	HB	TBB	IBB	SO	WP	Bk	H/9	SO/9	BB/9	OAvg	OOBP	ERA
New York	137	118	8	19	3	1187.1	1214	695	458	26	—	—	66	486	—	456	56	2	9.2	3.5	3.7	.263	.342	3.47
Baltimore	136	118	3	20	0	1197.2	1296	674	473	18	—	—	75	382	—	361	28	0	9.7	2.7	2.9	.274	.338	3.55
Boston	135	115	8	21	7	1194.1	1273	665	485	39	—	—	45	393	—	329	23	2	9.6	2.5	3.0	.271	.333	3.65
Cleveland	132	111	6	20	0	1119.1	1297	680	491	32	—	—	45	289	—	277	29	1	10.4	2.2	2.3	.288	.337	3.95
Washington	135	102	7	30	6	1148.0	1383	793	512	27	—	—	81	400	—	348	44	0	10.8	2.7	3.1	.296	.362	4.01
Cincinnati	134	100	4	38	2	1156.2	1375	705	525	18	—	—	57	329	—	270	16	0	10.7	2.1	2.6	.293	.347	4.09
Louisville	134	114	2	20	0	1138.0	1363	859	569	39	—	—	88	459	—	267	42	0	10.8	2.1	3.6	.295	.369	4.50
Chicago	138	131	2	7	1	1197.0	1485	894	603	30	—	—	64	433	—	361	32	1	11.2	2.7	3.3	.302	.366	4.53
Brooklyn	136	114	4	22	2	1194.2	1417	845	611	34	—	—	52	410	—	256	22	1	10.7	1.9	3.1	.293	.354	4.60
Philadelphia	134	115	4	19	2	1155.1	1415	792	591	28	—	—	54	364	—	253	33	0	11.0	2.0	2.8	.299	.356	4.60
Pittsburgh	135	112	2	24	2	1153.1	1397	835	599	22	—	—	65	318	—	342	31	1	10.9	2.7	2.5	.297	.350	4.67
St. Louis	132	109	1	25	1	1127.1	1584	1083	778	54	—	—	73	453	—	207	40	0	12.6	1.7	3.6	.329	.395	6.21
NL Total	1618	1359	51	268	26	13969.0	16499	9520	6695	367	—	—	765	4716	—	3727	396	8	10.6	2.4	3.0	.292	.354	4.31
NL Avg Team	135	113	4	22	2	1164.0	1375	793	558	31	—	—	64	393	—	311	33	1	10.6	2.4	3.0	.292	.354	4.31

Team Fielding

Team	G	PO	A	E	TC	DP	PB	Pct
Boston	135	3579	1675	272	5526	80	31	.951
Baltimore	136	3587	1731	277	5595	110	39	.950
Cleveland	132	3355	1583	261	5199	74	17	.950
Cincinnati	134	3461	1565	273	5299	100	14	.948
Philadelphia	134	3463	1568	296	5327	72	25	.944
Pittsburgh	135	3453	1587	346	5386	70	23	.936
Brooklyn	136	3581	1721	364	5666	99	28	.936
Washington	135	3437	1710	369	5516	103	20	.933
St. Louis	132	3377	1816	375	5568	84	23	.933
Chicago	138	3582	1824	393	5799	111	29	.932
New York	137	3556	1733	397	5686	109	33	.930
Louisville	134	3413	1792	395	5600	84	44	.929
NL Total	1618	41844	20305	4018	66167	1096	326	.939

Team vs. Team Records

	Bal	Bos	Bro	ChN	Cin	Cle	Lou	NYG	Phi	Pit	StL	Was	Won
Bal	—	6	9	9	6	8	10	5	10	9	10	9	90
Bos	6	—	9	8	9	7	9	8	10	10	10	7	93
Bro	3	3	—	6	7	5	5	3	6	7	7	6	61
ChN	3	4	6	—	5	4	6	5	5	6	8	7	59
Cin	6	3	5	7	—	7	9	7	8	5	11	8	76
Cle	4	5	5	8	5	—	5	3	9	6	11	8	69
Lou	1	3	7	6	3	7	—	6	3	4	8	4	52
NYG	7	4	9	7	5	9	6	—	7	8	12	9	83
Phi	2	2	6	7	4	3	9	5	—	5	8	4	55
Pit	3	2	5	6	7	6	8	3	7	—	8	5	60
StL	2	2	5	4	1	1	3	0	4	4	—	3	29
Was	3	5	5	5	4	4	8	3	8	7	9	—	61
Lost	40	39	71	73	56	62	78	48	77	71	102	71	

1897 National League Batting Leaders

Games		At-Bats		Runs		Hits		Doubles		Triples	
T. McCreery, 2tm	138	DeMontreville, Was	566	B. Hamilton, Bos	152	W. Keeler, Bal	239	J. Stenzel, Bal	43	H. Davis, Pit	28
J. Ryan, ChN	136	F. Tenney, Bos	566	W. Keeler, Bal	145	F. Clarke, Lou	202	N. Lajoie, Phi	40	N. Lajoie, Phi	23
F. Jones, Bro	135	D. Cooley, Phi	566	M. Griffin, Bro	136	E. Delahanty, Phi	200	E. Delahanty, Phi	40	B. Wallace, Cle	21
6 tied with	134	W. Keeler, Bal	564	F. Jones, Bro	134	J. Burkett, Cle	198	B. Wallace, Cle	33	W. Keeler, Bal	19
		G. Van Haltren, NYG	564	H. Jennings, Bal	133	N. Lajoie, Phi	197	J. Ryan, ChN	33	2 tied with	17

Home Runs		Total Bases		Runs Batted In		Walks		Intentional Walks		Strikeouts	
H. Duffy, Bos	11	N. Lajoie, Phi	310	G. Davis, NYG	136	B. Hamilton, Bos	105	Statistic unavailable		Statistic unavailable	
G. Davis, NYG	10	W. Keeler, Bal	304	J. Collins, Bos	132	J. McGraw, Bal	99				
N. Lajoie, Phi	9	E. Delahanty, Phi	285	H. Duffy, Bos	129	M. Griffin, Bro	81				
J. Beckley, 2tm	8	F. Clarke, Lou	276	N. Lajoie, Phi	127	K. Selbach, Was	80				
2 tied with	7	H. Duffy, Bos	265	J. Kelley, Bal	118	B. Joyce, NYG	78				

Hit By Pitch		Sac Hits		Sac Flies		Stolen Bases		Caught Stealing		GDP	
H. Jennings, Bal	46	T. McCreery, 2tm	30	Statistic unavailable		B. Lange, ChN	73	Statistic unavailable		Statistic unavailable	
F. Clarke, Lou	24	F. Tenney, Bos	27			J. Stenzel, Bal	69				
B. Joyce, NYG	17	D. Hoy, Cin	23			B. Hamilton, Bos	66				
D. Padden, Pit	16	D. Miller, Cin	21			G. Davis, NYG	65				
J. Warner, NYG	16	B. Shindle, Bro	21			W. Keeler, Bal	64				

Runs Created		Runs Created/27 Outs		Batting Average		On-Base Percentage		Slugging Percentage		OBP+Slugging	
W. Keeler, Bal	153	F. Clarke, Lou	11.64	W. Keeler, Bal	.424	J. McGraw, Bal	.471	N. Lajoie, Phi	.569	W. Keeler, Bal	1.003
F. Clarke, Lou	144	W. Keeler, Bal	11.59	F. Clarke, Lou	.390	J. Burkett, Cle	.468	W. Keeler, Bal	.539	F. Clarke, Lou	.994
B. Hamilton, Bos	138	B. Hamilton, Bos	10.46	J. Burkett, Cle	.383	W. Keeler, Bal	.464	E. Delahanty, Phi	.538	E. Delahanty, Phi	.981
H. Duffy, Bos	135	J. Burkett, Cle	10.09	E. Delahanty, Phi	.377	H. Jennings, Bal	.463	F. Clarke, Lou	.533	N. Lajoie, Phi	.960
G. Davis, NYG	133	G. Davis, NYG	9.96	J. Kelley, Bal	.362	F. Clarke, Lou	.462	G. Davis, NYG	.509	J. Burkett, Cle	.944

1897 National League Pitching Leaders

Wins		Losses		Winning Percentage		Games		Games Started		Complete Games	
K. Nichols, Bos	31	R. Donahue, StL	35	F. Klobedanz, Bos	.788	R. Donahue, StL	46	W. Mercer, Was	42	R. Donahue, StL	38
A. Rusie, NYG	28	B. Hart, StL	27	J. Nops, Bal	.769	C. Young, Cle	46	R. Donahue, StL	42	F. Killen, Pit	38
F. Klobedanz, Bos	26	D. McJames, Was	23	J. Corbett, Bal	.750	F. Killen, Pit	46	F. Killen, Pit	41	C. Griffith, ChN	38
J. Corbett, Bal	24	F. Killen, Pit	23	K. Nichols, Bos	.738	W. Mercer, Bos	45	B. Kennedy, Bro	40	K. Nichols, Bos	37
T. Breitenstein, Cin	23	3 tied with	20	A. Rusie, NYG	.737	2 tied with	44	K. Nichols, Bos	40	B. Kennedy, Bro	36

Shutouts		Saves		Games Finished		Batters Faced		Innings Pitched		Hits Allowed	
D. McJames, Was	3	K. Nichols, Bos	3	R. Ehret, Cin	11	Statistic unavailable		K. Nichols, Bos	368.0	R. Donahue, StL	484
W. Mercer, Was	3	6 tied with	2	L. German, Was	9			R. Donahue, StL	348.0	F. Killen, Pit	417
12 tied with	2			B. Rhines, Cin	9			C. Griffith, ChN	343.2	C. Griffith, ChN	410
				5 tied with	7			B. Kennedy, Bro	343.1	W. Mercer, Was	395
								F. Killen, Pit	337.1	B. Hart, StL	395

Home Runs Allowed		Walks		Walks/9 Innings		Strikeouts		Strikeouts/9 Innings		Strikeout/Walk Ratio	
R. Donahue, StL	16	C. Seymour, NYG	164	C. Young, Cle	1.3	D. McJames, Was	156	C. Seymour, NYG	4.8	K. Nichols, Bos	1.87
F. Klobedanz, Bos	13	B. Kennedy, Bro	149	J. Tannehill, Pit	1.5	C. Seymour, NYG	149	D. McJames, Was	4.3	C. Young, Cle	1.80
A. Orth, Phi	12	B. Hart, StL	148	K. Nichols, Bos	1.7	J. Corbett, Bal	149	J. Corbett, Bal	4.3	J. Tannehill, Pit	1.67
T. Lewis, Bos	11	D. McJames, Was	137	N. Cuppy, Cle	1.7	A. Rusie, NYG	135	A. Rusie, NYG	3.8	A. Rusie, NYG	1.55
C. Fraser, Lou	11	C. Fraser, Lou	133	F. Killen, Pit	2.0	K. Nichols, Bos	127	K. Nichols, Bos	3.1	J. Nops, Bal	1.33

Earned Run Average		Component ERA		Hit Batsmen		Wild Pitches		Opponent Average		Opponent OBP	
A. Rusie, NYG	2.54	K. Nichols, Bos	2.68	W. Mercer, Was	28	C. Fraser, Lou	22	C. Seymour, NYG	.242	K. Nichols, Bos	.290
K. Nichols, Bos	2.64	A. Rusie, NYG	2.96	J. Taylor, Phi	28	D. McJames, Was	21	K. Nichols, Bos	.254	A. Rusie, NYG	.308
J. Nops, Bal	2.81	N. Cuppy, Cle	3.27	P. Hawley, Pit	27	J. Taylor, Phi	16	A. Rusie, NYG	.254	N. Cuppy, Cle	.313
J. Corbett, Bal	3.11	J. Nops, Bal	3.37	C. Fraser, Lou	24	J. Meekin, NYG	15	B. Hill, Lou	.268	J. Nops, Bal	.319
J. Powell, Cle	3.16	T. Breitenstein, Cin	3.45	F. Klobedanz, Bos	23	B. Hart, StL	15	J. Corbett, Bal	.269	C. Young, Cle	.321

1897 National League Miscellaneous

Managers			Awards		Postseason	
Baltimore	Ned Hanlon	90-40	STATS Most Valuable Player	George Davis, ss, NYG	World Series	Baltimore (NL) 4 vs. Boston (NL) 1
Boston	Frank Selee	93-39	STATS Cy Young	Kid Nichols, Bos		
Brooklyn	Billy Barnie	61-71	STATS Rookie of the Year	Chick Stahl, of, Bos		
Chicago	Cap Anson	59-73	STATS Manager of the Year	Frank Selee, Bos	**Outstanding Performances**	
Cincinnati	Buck Ewing	76-56			**No-Hitters**	
Cleveland	Patsy Tebeau	69-62			Cy Young, Cle	vs. Cin on September 18
Louisville	Jim Rogers	17-24			**Three-Homer Games**	
	Fred Clarke	35-54			Tom McCreery, Lou	on July 12
New York	Bill Joyce	83-48			Jake Beckley, Cin	on September 26
Philadelphia	George Stallings	55-77				
Pittsburgh	Patsy Donovan	60-71				
St. Louis	Tommy Dowd	6-22				
	Hugh Nicol	8-32				
	Bill Hallman	13-36				
	Chris Von Der Ahe	2-12				
Washington	Gus Schmelz	9-25				
	Tom Brown	52-46				

STATS All-Star Team

C	Deacon McGuire, Was	.343	4	53
1B	Nap Lajoie, Phi	.361	9	127
2B	Cupid Childs, Cle	.338	1	61
3B	Jimmy Collins, Bos	.346	6	132
SS	George Davis, NYG	.353	10	136
OF	Fred Clarke, Lou	.390	6	67
OF	Billy Hamilton, Bos	.343	3	61
OF	Willie Keeler, Bal	.424	0	74
P	Joe Corbett, Bal	24-8	3.11	149 K
P	Kid Nichols, Bos	31-11	2.64	127 K
P	Amos Rusie, NYG	28-10	2.54	135 K

1898 National League Standings

Team	W	L	Pct	GB	DIF	W	L	R	OR	HR	OHR	W	L	R	OR	HR	OHR	Run	HR	M/A	May	June	July	Aug	S/O
	Overall					**Home Games**						**Road Games**						**Park Index**		**Record by Month**					
Boston	102	47	.685	—	58	62	15	510	272	45	22	40	32	362	342	8	15	104	272	6-5	17-8	15-10	18-7	15-11	31-6
Baltimore	96	53	.644	6.0	20	58	15	505	268	4	1	38	38	428	355	8	16	103	22	6-2	11-11	17-11	16-10	18-6	28-13
Cincinnati	92	60	.605	11.5	113	58	28	521	423	2	3	34	32	310	317	17	13	116	13	9-2	18-5	13-16	22-6	11-14	19-17
Chicago	85	65	.567	17.5	7	58	31	520	378	10	4	27	34	308	301	8	13	101	46	6-3	11-15	19-8	14-14	14-14	21-15
Cleveland	81	68	.544	21.0	0	37	19	268	212	5	1	44	49	462	471	13	25	85	26	7-5	17-7	12-12	18-9	12-13	15-22
Philadelphia	78	71	.523	24.0	2	49	31	452	371	13	9	29	40	371	413	20	14	91	56	5-4	9-13	13-12	14-14	12-13	25-15
New York	77	73	.513	25.5	0	45	28	423	322	18	10	32	45	414	478	16	11	88	109	3-6	16-9	10-16	18-9	16-9	14-24
Pittsburgh	72	76	.486	29.5	0	39	34	314	308	6	3	33	42	320	386	8	11	91	49	6-6	13-11	14-11	12-16	11-16	16-16
Louisville	70	81	.464	33.0	1	43	34	410	368	24	25	27	47	318	465	8	8	95	294	3-9	9-16	9-17	11-16	14-11	24-12
Brooklyn	54	91	.372	46.0	2	30	41	319	367	10	15	24	50	319	444	7	19	94	100	4-4	8-15	12-15	9-18	9-13	12-26
Washington	51	101	.336	52.5	0	34	44	418	471	29	17	17	57	286	468	7	12	112	230	3-6	6-18	15-13	7-19	9-16	11-29
St. Louis	39	111	.260	63.5	0	20	44	285	424	8	15	19	67	286	505	5	17	120	140	2-8	8-15	11-19	3-24	8-17	7-28

Clinch Date—Boston 10/11.

Team Batting

Team	G	AB	R	OR	H	2B	3B	HR	TB	RBI	TBB	IBB	SO	HBP	SH	SF	SB	CS	SB%	GDP	Avg	OBP	Slg
Baltimore	154	5242	933	623	1584	154	77	12	1928	757	519	—	316	159	79	—	250	—	—	—	.302	.382	.368
Boston	152	5276	872	614	1531	190	55	53	1990	761	405	—	303	32	134	—	172	—	—	—	.290	.344	.377
New York	157	5349	837	800	1422	190	86	34	1886	712	428	—	372	69	61	—	214	—	—	—	.266	.328	.353
Cincinnati	157	5334	831	740	1448	207	101	19	1914	688	455	—	300	59	136	—	165	—	—	—	.271	.335	.359
Chicago	152	5219	828	679	1431	175	84	18	1828	656	476	—	394	71	113	—	220	—	—	—	.274	.343	.350
Philadelphia	150	5118	823	784	1431	238	81	33	1930	706	472	—	382	69	120	—	182	—	—	—	.280	.348	.377
Cleveland	156	5246	730	683	1379	162	56	18	1707	605	545	—	306	45	125	—	93	—	—	—	.263	.337	.325
Louisville	154	5193	728	833	1389	150	71	32	1777	601	375	—	429	66	141	—	235	—	—	—	.267	.325	.342
Washington	155	5257	704	939	1423	177	80	36	1868	591	370	—	386	70	88	—	197	—	—	—	.271	.327	.355
Brooklyn	149	5126	638	811	1314	156	66	17	1653	563	328	—	314	65	91	—	130	—	—	—	.256	.309	.322
Pittsburgh	152	5087	634	694	1313	140	88	14	1671	520	336	—	343	75	141	—	107	—	—	—	.258	.314	.328
St. Louis	154	5214	571	929	1290	149	55	13	1588	470	383	—	402	84	117	—	104	—	—	—	.247	.309	.305
NL Total	1842	62661	9129	9129	16955	2088	900	299	21740	7630	5092	—	4247	864	1346	—	2069	—	—	—	.271	.334	.347
NL Avg Team	154	5222	761	761	1413	174	75	25	1812	636	424	—	354	72	112	—	172	—	—	—	.271	.334	.347

Team Pitching

Team	G	CG	ShO	Rel	Sv	IP	H	R	ER	HR	SH	SF	HB	TBB	IBB	SO	WP	Bk	H/9	SO/9	BB/9	OAvg	OOBP	ERA
Chicago	152	137	13	15	0	1342.2	1357	679	422	17	—	—	82	364	—	323	27	3	9.1	2.2	2.4	.261	.319	2.83
Baltimore	154	138	12	15	0	1323.0	1236	623	426	17	—	—	61	400	—	422	30	1	8.4	2.9	2.7	.246	.309	2.90
Boston	152	127	9	26	8	1340.0	1186	614	443	37	—	—	66	470	—	432	41	1	8.0	2.9	3.2	.236	.310	2.98
Cleveland	156	142	9	15	0	1334.0	1429	683	475	26	—	—	57	309	—	339	26	0	9.6	2.3	2.1	.272	.320	3.20
Pittsburgh	152	131	10	22	3	1323.2	1400	694	501	14	—	—	65	346	—	330	18	1	9.5	2.2	2.4	.270	.323	3.41
New York	157	141	9	15	1	1353.2	1359	800	517	21	—	—	88	587	—	558	63	1	9.0	3.7	3.9	.260	.344	3.44
Cincinnati	157	131	10	27	2	1385.1	1484	740	538	16	—	—	74	449	—	294	24	0	9.6	1.9	2.9	.272	.336	3.50
Philadelphia	150	129	10	22	0	1288.1	1440	784	533	23	—	—	82	399	—	325	27	2	10.1	2.3	2.8	.281	.342	3.72
Brooklyn	149	134	1	17	0	1298.2	1446	811	579	34	—	—	57	476	—	294	31	0	10.0	2.0	3.3	.280	.347	4.01
Louisville	154	137	4	19	0	1334.0	1457	833	629	33	—	—	94	470	—	271	26	3	9.8	1.8	3.2	.276	.346	4.24
Washington	155	129	0	27	1	1307.0	1577	939	657	29	—	—	80	450	—	371	40	1	10.9	2.6	3.1	.296	.360	4.52
St. Louis	154	133	0	26	2	1324.1	1584	929	667	32	—	—	86	372	—	288	30	1	10.8	2.0	2.5	.295	.350	4.53
NL Total	1842	1609	87	246	17	15954.2	16955	9129	6387	299	—	—	892	5092	—	4247	383	14	9.6	2.4	2.9	.271	.334	3.60
NL Avg Team	154	134	7	21	1	1329.2	1413	761	532	25	—	—	74	424	—	354	32	1	9.6	2.4	2.9	.271	.334	3.60

Team Fielding

Team	G	PO	A	E	TC	DP	PB	Pct
Cleveland	156	3999	1985	301	6285	95	20	.952
Boston	152	4014	1875	310	6199	102	46	.950
Cincinnati	157	4150	2012	325	6487	128	20	.950
Baltimore	154	3962	1836	326	6124	105	35	.947
Brooklyn	149	3890	2035	334	6259	125	25	.947
Pittsburgh	152	3969	1969	340	6278	105	24	.946
St. Louis	154	3968	2052	388	6408	97	26	.939
Louisville	154	3995	1907	382	6284	114	30	.939
Philadelphia	150	3862	1808	379	6049	102	27	.937
Chicago	152	4022	2020	412	6454	149	24	.936
New York	157	4053	2099	447	6599	113	56	.932
Washington	155	3914	1866	443	6223	119	16	.929
NL Total	1842	47798	23464	4387	75649	1354	349	.942

Team vs. Team Records

	Bal	Bos	Bro	ChN	Cin	Cle	Lou	NYG	Phi	Pit	StL	Was	Won
Bal	—	5	8	9	8	8	9	10	10	10	12	7	96
Bos	7	—	11	9	9	6	8	10	10	9	12	11	102
Bro	5	2	—	4	3	6	2	3	6	9	7	7	54
ChN	5	5	10	—	6	7	9	9	6	7	10	11	85
Cin	6	4	11	8	—	9	8	9	6	7	12	12	92
Cle	6	7	7	7	5	—	9	6	7	5	10	12	81
Lou	5	6	10	5	5	5	—	6	4	4	10	10	70
NYG	3	4	11	5	8	8	8	—	6	5	10	9	77
Phi	3	4	6	7	7	7	10	7	—	6	9	12	78
Pit	4	5	5	4	2	8	9	9	8	—	9	9	72
StL	2	2	6	4	2	3	4	3	5	4	—	4	39
Was	7	3	6	3	5	2	4	4	2	5	10	—	51
Lost	53	47	91	65	60	68	81	73	71	76	111	101	

1898 National League Batting Leaders

Games		At-Bats		Runs		Hits		Doubles		Triples	
G. Van Haltren, NYG	156	G. Van Haltren, NYG	654	J. McGraw, Bal	143	W. Keeler, Bal	216	N. Lajoie, Phi	43	J. Anderson, 2tm	22
B. Wallace, Cle	154	D. Cooley, Phi	629	H. Jennings, Bal	135	J. Burkett, Cle	213	E. Delahanty, Phi	36	D. Hoy, Lou	16
B. Clingman, Lou	154	J. Burkett, Cle	624	G. Van Haltren, NYG	129	G. Van Haltren, NYG	204	J. Collins, Bos	35	G. Van Haltren, NYG	16
T. Corcoran, Cin	153	T. Corcoran, Cin	619	W. Keeler, Bal	126	N. Lajoie, Phi	197	B. Dahlen, ChN	35	3 tied with	15
3 tied with	152	P. Donovan, Pit	610	D. Cooley, Phi	123	2 tied with	196	J. Anderson, 2tm	33		

Home Runs		Total Bases		Runs Batted In		Walks		Intentional Walks		Strikeouts	
J. Collins, Bos	15	J. Collins, Bos	286	N. Lajoie, Phi	127	J. McGraw, Bal	112	Statistic unavailable		Statistic unavailable	
H. Wagner, Lou	10	N. Lajoie, Phi	280	J. Collins, Bos	111	B. Joyce, NYG	88				
B. Joyce, NYG	10	G. Van Haltren, NYG	270	J. Kelley, Bal	110	B. Hamilton, Bos	87				
J. Anderson, 2tm	9	J. Anderson, 2tm	257	H. Duffy, Bos	108	E. Flick, Phi	86				
E. McKean, Cle	9	D. Cooley, Phi	256	D. McGann, Bal	106	H. Jennings, Bal	78				

Hit By Pitch		Sac Hits		Sac Flies		Stolen Bases		Caught Stealing		GDP	
H. Jennings, Bal	46	C. Ritchey, Lou	31	Statistic unavailable		E. Delahanty, Phi	58	Statistic unavailable		Statistic unavailable	
D. McGann, Bal	39	K. Douglass, Phi	25			B. Hamilton, Bos	54				
B. Dahlen, ChN	23	T. O'Brien, 2tm	24			G. DeMontreville, Bal	49				
D. Harley, StL	22	H. Blake, Cle	23			C. Dexter, Lou	44				
4 tied with	19	J. McCarthy, Pit	21			J. McGraw, Bal	43				

Runs Created		Runs Created/27 Outs		Batting Average		On-Base Percentage		Slugging Percentage		OBP+Slugging	
E. Delahanty, Phi	137	B. Hamilton, Bos	12.54	W. Keeler, Bal	.385	B. Hamilton, Bos	.480	J. Anderson, 2tm	.494	B. Hamilton, Bos	.933
J. McGraw, Bal	136	J. McGraw, Bal	10.08	B. Hamilton, Bos	.369	J. McGraw, Bal	.475	J. Collins, Bos	.479	E. Delahanty, Phi	.880
G. Van Haltren, NYG	132	E. Delahanty, Phi	9.49	J. McGraw, Bal	.342	H. Jennings, Bal	.454	N. Lajoie, Phi	.461	E. Flick, Phi	.878
H. Jennings, Bal	131	H. Jennings, Bal	9.15	E. Smith, Cin	.342	E. Flick, Phi	.430	E. Delahanty, Phi	.454	H. Jennings, Bal	.876
J. Ryan, ChN	131	E. Smith, Cin	8.94	J. Burkett, Cle	.341	E. Delahanty, Phi	.426	B. Hamilton, Bos	.453	J. McGraw, Bal	.871

1898 National League Pitching Leaders

Wins		Losses		Winning Percentage		Games		Games Started		Complete Games	
K. Nichols, Bos	31	J. Taylor, StL	29	T. Lewis, Bos	.765	J. Taylor, StL	50	J. Taylor, StL	47	J. Taylor, StL	42
B. Cunningham, Lou	28	W. Sudhoff, StL	27	A. Maul, Bal	.741	K. Nichols, Bos	50	C. Seymour, NYG	43	B. Cunningham, Lou	41
D. McJames, Bal	27	G. Weyhing, Was	26	K. Nichols, Bos	.721	C. Young, Cle	46	4 tied with	42	D. McJames, Bal	40
P. Hawley, Cin	27	J. Hughey, StL	24	P. Hawley, Cin	.711	3 tied with	45			C. Young, Cle	40
T. Lewis, Bos	26	2 tied with	22	C. Griffith, ChN	.706					K. Nichols, Bos	40

Shutouts		Saves		Games Finished		Batters Faced		Innings Pitched		Hits Allowed	
W. Piatt, Phi	6	K. Nichols, Bos	4	B. Dammann, Cin	13	Statistic unavailable		J. Taylor, StL	397.1	J. Taylor, StL	465
J. Powell, Cle	6	C. Hickman, Bos	2	W. Donovan, Was	10			K. Nichols, Bos	388.0	G. Weyhing, Was	428
J. Hughes, Bal	5	B. Dammann, Cin	2	C. Gettig, NYG	9			C. Young, Cle	377.2	C. Young, Cle	387
J. Tannehill, Pit	5	T. Lewis, Bos	2	T. Lewis, Bos	8			D. McJames, Bal	374.0	B. Cunningham, Lou	387
K. Nichols, Bos	5	J. Tannehill, Pit	2	K. Nichols, Bos	8			B. Cunningham, Lou	362.0	B. Kennedy, Bro	360

Home Runs Allowed		Walks		Walks/9 Innings		Strikeouts		Strikeouts/9 Innings		Strikeout/Walk Ratio	
J. Taylor, StL	14	C. Seymour, NYG	213	C. Young, Cle	1.0	C. Seymour, NYG	239	C. Seymour, NYG	6.0	C. Young, Cle	2.46
F. Klobedanz, Bos	13	V. Willis, Bos	148	F. Dwyer, Cin	1.6	D. McJames, Bal	178	V. Willis, Bos	4.6	K. Nichols, Bos	1.62
B. Kennedy, Bro	12	B. Magee, Lou	129	B. Cunningham, Lou	1.6	V. Willis, Bos	160	D. McJames, Bal	4.3	D. McJames, Bal	1.58
W. Sudhoff, StL	11	B. Kennedy, Bro	123	J. Tannehill, Pit	1.7	K. Nichols, Bos	138	E. Doheny, NYG	4.1	C. Griffith, ChN	1.52
2 tied with	10	T. Breitenstein, Cin	123	C. Griffith, ChN	1.8	W. Piatt, Phi	121	W. Piatt, Phi	3.6	J. Tannehill, Pit	1.48

Earned Run Average		Component ERA		Hit Batsmen		Wild Pitches		Opponent Average		Opponent OBP	
C. Griffith, ChN	1.88	K. Nichols, Bos	1.99	C. Seymour, NYG	32	C. Seymour, NYG	19	K. Nichols, Bos	.217	K. Nichols, Bos	.267
A. Maul, Bal	2.10	A. Maul, Bal	2.14	V. Willis, Bos	30	E. Doheny, NYG	19	V. Willis, Bos	.229	A. Maul, Bal	.275
K. Nichols, Bos	2.13	C. Griffith, ChN	2.53	C. Fraser, 2tm	29	K. Nichols, Bos	15	T. Lewis, Bos	.229	C. Young, Cle	.285
D. McJames, Bal	2.36	D. McJames, Bal	2.53	W. Sudhoff, StL	27	D. McJames, Bal	13	A. Maul, Bal	.232	C. Griffith, ChN	.294
N. Callahan, ChN	2.46	C. Young, Cle	2.59	J. Taylor, StL	25	A. Rusie, NYG	13	D. McJames, Bal	.234	D. McJames, Bal	.297

1898 National League Miscellaneous

Managers			Awards		Postseason	
Baltimore	Ned Hanlon	96-53	STATS Most Valuable Player	Billy Hamilton, of, Bos	None	
Boston	Frank Selee	102-47	STATS Cy Young	Kid Nichols, Bos		
Brooklyn	Billy Barnie	15-20	STATS Rookie of the Year	Elmer Flick, of, Phi	**Outstanding Performances**	
	Mike Griffin	1-3	STATS Manager of the Year	Tom Burns, ChN		
	Charlie Ebbets	38-68			**No-Hitters**	
Chicago	Tom Burns	85-65			Ted Breitenstein, Cin vs. Pit on April 22	
Cincinnati	Buck Ewing	92-60	**STATS All-Star Team**		Jim Hughes, Bal vs. Bos on April 22	
Cleveland	Patsy Tebeau	81-68			Red Donahue, Phi vs. Bos on July 8	
Louisville	Fred Clarke	70-81			W. Thornton, ChN vs. Bro on August 21	
New York	Bill Joyce	22-21				

STATS All-Star Team

C	Mike Grady, NYG	.296	3	49	
1B	Dan McGann, Bal	.301	5	106	
2B	Nap Lajoie, Phi	.324	6	127	
3B	John McGraw, Bal	.342	0	53	
SS	Hughie Jennings, Bal	.328	1	87	
OF	Ed Delahanty, Phi	.334	4	92	
OF	Elmer Flick, Phi	.302	8	81	
OF	Billy Hamilton, Bos	.369	3	50	
P	Clark Griffith, ChN	24-10	1.88	97 K	
P	Doc McJames, Bal	27-15	2.36	178 K	
P	Kid Nichols, Bos	31-12	2.13	138 K	
P	Cy Young, Cle	25-13	2.53	101 K	

Managers (continued):

	Cap Anson	9-13
	Bill Joyce	46-39
Philadelphia	George Stallings	19-27
	Bill Shettsline	59-44
Pittsburgh	Bill Watkins	72-76
St. Louis	Tim Hurst	39-111
Washington	Tom Brown	12-26
	Jack Doyle	8-9
	Deacon McGuire	21-47
	Arthur Irwin	10-19

1899 National League Standings

Team	Overall					Home Games						Road Games						Park Index		Record by Month					
	W	L	Pct	GB	DIF	W	L	R	OR	HR	OHR	W	L	R	OR	HR	OHR	Run	HR	M/A	May	June	July	Aug	S/O
Brooklyn	101	47	.682	—	146	61	16	510	315	13	18	40	31	382	343	14	14	105	102	7-6	21-5	17-7	15-10	16-8	25-11
Boston	95	57	.625	8.0	2	53	26	460	346	32	33	42	31	398	299	7	11	107	334	7-6	17-7	15-9	14-11	18-10	24-14
Philadelphia	94	58	.618	9.0	4	58	25	503	353	11	3	36	33	413	390	20	14	89	34	10-4	11-12	16-7	14-12	21-10	22-13
Baltimore	86	62	.581	15.0	4	50	25	473	343	4	2	36	37	354	348	13	11	113	24	7-6	14-11	12-9	17-10	16-9	20-17
St. Louis	84	67	.556	18.5	37	50	33	480	446	38	33	34	34	339	293	9	8	120	342	9-2	15-12	12-13	14-9	15-17	19-14
Cincinnati	83	67	.553	19.0	0	57	29	543	416	2	7	26	38	313	354	11	19	107	22	7-5	13-11	9-13	16-13	17-8	21-17
Pittsburgh	76	73	.510	25.5	2	49	34	475	381	12	8	27	39	359	384	15	19	92	47	2-8	13-13	13-11	17-11	12-15	19-15
Chicago	75	73	.507	26.0	3	44	39	429	415	14	14	31	34	383	348	13	6	90	115	9-6	15-9	13-9	9-16	13-17	16-16
Louisville	75	77	.493	28.0	0	33	28	369	306	23	17	42	49	458	469	17	16	109	181	5-5	7-21	10-14	16-8	12-15	25-14
New York	60	90	.400	42.0	0	35	38	394	394	7	6	25	52	352	469	16	13	100	47	4-8	11-14	15-10	16-13	6-16	14-25
Washington	54	98	.355	49.0	0	34	44	415	448	30	15	20	54	328	535	17	20	95	115	4-9	8-18	6-17	16-13	6-16	14-25
Cleveland	20	134	.130	84.0	0	9	33	152	293	3	5	11	101	377	959	9	38	89	45	1-7	7-19	3-22	4-26	4-26	1-34

Clinch Date—Brooklyn 10/07.

Team Batting

Team	G	AB	R	OR	H	2B	3B	HR	TB	RBI	TBB	IBB	SO	HBP	SH	SF	SB	CS	SB%	GDP	Avg	OBP	Slg
Philadelphia	154	5353	916	743	1613	241	83	31	2113	787	441	—	341	75	117	—	212	—	—	—	.301	.363	.395
Brooklyn	150	4937	892	658	1436	178	97	27	1889	723	477	—	263	125	75	—	271	—	—	—	.291	.368	.383
Boston	153	5290	858	645	1517	178	90	39	1992	741	431	—	269	43	133	—	185	—	—	—	.287	.345	.377
Cincinnati	156	5225	856	770	1439	194	105	13	1882	699	485	—	295	66	133	—	228	—	—	—	.275	.345	.360
Pittsburgh	154	5450	834	765	1574	196	121	27	2093	700	384	—	345	63	143	—	179	—	—	—	.289	.343	.384
Louisville	155	5307	827	775	1484	192	68	40	1932	647	436	—	375	77	160	—	233	—	—	—	.280	.343	.364
Baltimore	152	5073	827	691	1509	204	71	17	1906	649	418	—	383	122	94	—	364	—	—	—	.297	.365	.376
St. Louis	155	5304	819	739	1514	172	88	47	2003	699	468	—	262	33	108	—	210	—	—	—	.285	.347	.378
Chicago	152	5148	812	763	1428	173	82	27	1846	661	406	—	342	64	148	—	247	—	—	—	.277	.338	.359
Washington	155	5256	743	983	1429	162	87	47	1906	613	350	—	341	87	90	—	176	—	—	—	.272	.328	.363
New York	152	5092	734	863	1431	161	65	23	1791	607	387	—	360	45	61	—	234	—	—	—	.281	.337	.352
Cleveland	154	5279	529	1252	1333	142	50	12	1611	454	289	—	280	65	57	—	127	—	—	—	.253	.299	.305
NL Total	1842	62714	9647	9647	17707	2193	1007	350	22964	7980	4972	—	3856	865	1319	—	2666	—	—	—	.282	.343	.366
NL Avg Team	154	5226	804	804	1476	183	84	29	1914	665	414	—	321	72	110	—	222	—	—	—	.282	.343	.366

Team Pitching

Team	G	CG	ShO	Rel	Sv	IP	H	R	ER	HR	SH	SF	HB	TBB	IBB	SO	WP	Bk	H/9	SO/9	BB/9	OAvg	OOBP	ERA
Brooklyn	150	121	9	30	9	1269.1	1320	658	458	32	—	—	53	463	—	331	33	3	9.4	2.3	3.3	.268	.338	3.25
Boston	153	138	13	17	4	1348.0	1273	645	489	44	—	—	69	432	—	385	34	1	8.5	2.6	2.9	.250	.317	3.26
Baltimore	152	132	10	21	4	1304.1	1403	691	480	13	—	—	71	349	—	294	31	2	9.7	2.0	2.4	.275	.330	3.31
St. Louis	155	134	7	23	1	1340.2	1476	739	500	41	—	—	54	321	—	331	25	2	9.9	2.2	2.2	.279	.327	3.36
Chicago	152	147	8	5	1	1331.1	1433	763	499	20	—	—	82	330	—	313	18	5	9.7	2.1	2.2	.275	.328	3.37
Louisville	155	134	5	22	2	1351.2	1509	775	518	33	—	—	66	323	—	287	16	7	10.0	1.9	2.2	.282	.331	3.45
Philadelphia	154	129	15	26	2	1333.1	1398	743	514	17	—	—	83	370	—	281	38	6	9.4	1.9	2.5	.270	.328	3.47
Pittsburgh	154	117	9	39	4	1364.0	1464	765	545	27	—	—	68	437	—	334	22	6	9.7	2.2	2.9	.274	.337	3.60
Cincinnati	156	130	8	28	5	1361.0	1484	770	559	26	—	—	76	370	—	360	18	7	9.8	2.4	2.4	.277	.333	3.70
New York	152	138	4	14	0	1278.1	1454	863	610	19	—	—	100	628	—	397	59	7	10.2	2.8	4.4	.286	.375	4.29
Washington	155	131	3	20	0	1300.1	1649	983	713	35	—	—	78	422	—	328	27	4	11.4	2.2	3.8	.309	.368	4.93
Cleveland	154	138	0	18	0	1264.0	1844	1252	894	43	—	—	109	527	—	215	40	10	13.1	1.5	3.8	.339	.409	6.37
NL Total	1842	1589	91	271	32	15846.1	17707	9647	6779	350	—	—	909	4972	—	3856	361	60	10.1	2.2	2.8	.282	.344	3.85
NL Avg Team	154	132	8	23	3	1320.1	1476	804	565	29	—	—	76	414	—	321	30	5	10.1	2.2	2.8	.282	.344	3.85

Team Fielding

Team	G	PO	A	E	TC	DP	PB	Pct
Boston	153	4042	1941	303	6286	124	24	.952
Baltimore	152	3908	1862	308	6078	96	28	.949
Brooklyn	150	3803	1936	314	6053	125	19	.948
Cincinnati	156	4076	1938	339	6353	111	25	.947
Pittsburgh	154	4090	2099	361	6550	98	31	.945
Philadelphia	154	3989	1977	379	6345	110	40	.940
Louisville	155	4050	2067	394	6511	101	13	.939
St. Louis	155	4016	2147	397	6560	117	23	.939
Cleveland	154	3779	2000	388	6167	121	26	.937
Chicago	152	3988	2178	428	6594	145	15	.935
Washington	155	3895	1871	403	6169	99	33	.935
New York	152	3830	2107	433	6370	140	38	.932
NL Total	1842	47466	24123	4447	76036	1387	322	.942

Team vs. Team Records

	Bal	Bos	Bro	ChN	Cin	Cle	Lou	NYG	Phi	Pit	StL	Was	Won
Bal	—	7	6	9	4	12	6	10	6	9	8	9	86
Bos	7	—	6	5	10	11	9	12	5	10	8	12	95
Bro	8	8	—	8	7	14	11	10	8	8	8	11	101
ChN	5	7	5	—	8	13	7	7	5	6	8	4	75
Cin	9	4	6	6	—	14	8	9	4	10	5	8	83
Cle	2	3	0	1	0	—	4	1	2	2	1	4	20
Lou	7	5	3	7	6	10	—	7	7	6	5	12	75
NYG	4	2	2	6	5	13	7	—	4	6	4	7	60
Phi	7	9	6	9	10	12	6	10	—	6	7	12	94
Pit	3	4	2	7	3	12	8	7	6	—	7	11	76
StL	6	6	4	6	8	13	9	10	7	7	—	8	84
Was	4	2	3	9	6	10	2	7	2	3	6	—	54
Lost	62	57	47	73	67	134	77	90	58	73	67	98	

Seasons: Standings, Leaders

1899 National League Batting Leaders

Games		At-Bats		Runs		Hits		Doubles		Triples	
B. Freeman, Was	155	D. Hoy, Lou	633	W. Keeler, Bro	140	E. Delahanty, Phi	238	E. Delahanty, Phi	55	J. Williams, Pit	27
M. Cross, Phi	154	J. Williams, Pit	617	J. McGraw, Bal	140	J. Burkett, StL	221	H. Wagner, Lou	43	B. Freeman, Was	25
D. Hoy, Lou	154	J. Quinn, Cle	615	R. Thomas, Phi	137	J. Williams, Pit	219	D. Holmes, Bal	31	C. Stahl, Bos	19
J. Williams, Pit	152	T. Dowd, Cle	605	E. Delahanty, Phi	135	W. Keeler, Bro	216	H. Long, Bos	30	F. Tenney, Bos	17
B. Lowe, Bos	152	G. Van Haltren, NYG	604	J. Williams, Pit	126	F. Tenney, Bos	209	H. Duffy, Bos	29	J. McCarthy, Pit	17

Home Runs		Total Bases		Runs Batted In		Walks		Intentional Walks		Strikeouts	
B. Freeman, Was	25	E. Delahanty, Phi	338	E. Delahanty, Phi	137	J. McGraw, Bal	124	Statistic unavailable		Statistic unavailable	
B. Wallace, StL	12	B. Freeman, Was	331	B. Freeman, Was	122	R. Thomas, Phi	115				
J. Williams, Pit	9	J. Williams, Pit	328	J. Williams, Pit	116	C. Childs, StL	74				
S. Mertes, ChN	9	C. Stahl, Bos	284	H. Wagner, Lou	113	G. Van Haltren, NYG	74				
E. Delahanty, Phi	9	H. Wagner, Lou	282	B. Wallace, StL	108	2 tied with	72				

Hit By Pitch		Sac Hits		Sac Flies		Stolen Bases		Caught Stealing		GDP	
D. McGann, 2tm	37	B. Ely, Pit	29	Statistic unavailable		J. Sheckard, Bal	77	Statistic unavailable		Statistic unavailable	
S. Brodie, Bal	23	J. McCarthy, Pit	27			J. McGraw, Bal	73				
H. Jennings, 2tm	19	M. Cross, Phi	26			E. Heidrick, StL	55				
J. Sheckard, Bal	18	H. Long, Bos	25			D. Holmes, Bal	50				
B. Freeman, Was	18	R. Thomas, Phi	23			F. Clarke, Lou	49				

Runs Created		Runs Created/27 Outs		Batting Average		On-Base Percentage		Slugging Percentage		OBP+Slugging	
E. Delahanty, Phi	165	J. McGraw, Bal	13.79	E. Delahanty, Phi	.410	J. McGraw, Bal	.547	E. Delahanty, Phi	.582	E. Delahanty, Phi	1.046
J. Williams, Pit	148	E. Delahanty, Phi	11.95	J. Burkett, StL	.396	E. Delahanty, Phi	.464	B. Freeman, Was	.563	J. McGraw, Bal	.994
C. Stahl, Bos	146	J. Burkett, StL	10.01	J. McGraw, Bal	.391	J. Burkett, StL	.463	J. Williams, Pit	.532	J. Burkett, StL	.963
J. Burkett, StL	137	C. Stahl, Bos	9.61	W. Keeler, Bro	.379	R. Thomas, Phi	.457	J. Burkett, StL	.500	J. Williams, Pit	.949
J. McGraw, Bal	134	J. Williams, Pit	9.23	J. Williams, Pit	.355	C. Stahl, Bos	.426	H. Wagner, Lou	.494	B. Freeman, Was	.925

1899 National League Pitching Leaders

Wins		Losses		Winning Percentage		Games		Games Started		Complete Games	
J. McGinnity, Bal	28	J. Hughey, Cle	30	J. Hughes, Bro	.824	S. Leever, Pit	51	B. Carrick, NYG	43	B. Carrick, NYG	40
J. Hughes, Bro	28	B. Carrick, NYG	27	A. Orth, Phi	.824	J. McGinnity, Bal	48	J. Powell, StL	43	J. Powell, StL	40
V. Willis, Bos	27	S. Leever, Pit	23	V. Willis, Bos	.771	J. Powell, StL	48	C. Young, StL	42	C. Young, StL	40
C. Young, StL	26	C. Knepper, Cle	22	N. Hahn, Cin	.742	B. Carrick, NYG	44	J. McGinnity, Bal	41	J. Taylor, ChN	39
J. Tannehill, Pit	24	2 tied with	21	R. Donahue, Phi	.724	C. Young, StL	44	2 tied with	39	J. McGinnity, Bal	38

Shutouts		Saves		Games Finished		Batters Faced		Innings Pitched		Hits Allowed	
V. Willis, Bos	5	S. Leever, Pit	3	S. Leever, Pit	11	Statistic unavailable		S. Leever, Pit	379.0	B. Carrick, NYG	485
8 tied with	4	5 tied with	2	T. Sparks, Pit	10			J. Powell, StL	373.0	J. Powell, StL	433
				B. Bernhard, Phi	9			C. Young, StL	369.1	G. Weyhing, Was	414
				J. McGinnity, Bal	7			J. McGinnity, Bal	366.1	J. Hughey, Cle	403
				6 tied with	6			B. Carrick, NYG	361.2	B. Cunningham, Lou	385

Home Runs Allowed		Walks		Walks/9 Innings		Strikeouts		Strikeouts/9 Innings		Strikeout/Walk Ratio	
J. Powell, StL	15	C. Seymour, NYG	170	C. Young, StL	1.1	N. Hahn, Cin	145	C. Seymour, NYG	4.8	C. Young, StL	2.52
C. Knepper, Cle	11	E. Doheny, NYG	156	N. Cuppy, StL	1.4	C. Seymour, NYG	142	N. Hahn, Cin	4.2	N. Hahn, Cin	2.13
B. Kennedy, Bro	11	B. Carrick, NYG	122	J. Tannehill, Pit	1.5	S. Leever, Pit	121	E. Doheny, NYG	3.9	N. Garvin, ChN	1.64
K. Nichols, Bos	11	S. Leever, Pit	122	W. Woods, Lou	1.8	V. Willis, Bos	120	D. McJames, Bro	3.4	K. Nichols, Bos	1.32
3 tied with	10	D. McJames, Bro	122	D. Phillippe, Lou	1.8	E. Doheny, NYG	115	V. Willis, Bos	3.2	G. Weyhing, Was	1.26

Earned Run Average		Component ERA		Hit Batsmen		Wild Pitches		Opponent Average		Opponent OBP	
V. Willis, Bos	2.50	N. Hahn, Cin	2.41	E. Doheny, NYG	37	E. Doheny, NYG	21	V. Willis, Bos	.222	C. Young, StL	.275
C. Young, StL	2.58	C. Young, StL	2.48	V. Willis, Bos	30	C. Fraser, Phi	17	J. Hughes, Bro	.232	N. Hahn, Cin	.290
J. McGinnity, Bal	2.68	V. Willis, Bos	2.54	J. McGinnity, Bal	28	D. McJames, Bro	16	N. Hahn, Cin	.242	K. Nichols, Bos	.299
N. Hahn, Cin	2.68	K. Nichols, Bos	2.79	G. Weyhing, Was	28	C. Seymour, NYG	14	C. Seymour, NYG	.245	V. Willis, Bos	.303
J. Hughes, Bro	2.68	J. Hughes, Bro	2.88	2 tied with	24	V. Willis, Bos	12	S. Leever, Pit	.247	F. Kitson, Bal	.304

1899 National League Miscellaneous

Managers		
Baltimore	John McGraw	86-62
Boston	Frank Selee	95-57
Brooklyn	Ned Hanlon	101-47
Chicago	Tom Burns	75-73
Cincinnati	Buck Ewing	83-67
Cleveland	Lave Cross	8-30
	Joe Quinn	12-104
Louisville	Fred Clarke	75-77
New York	John Day	29-35
	Fred Hoey	31-55
Philadelphia	Bill Shettsline	94-58
Pittsburgh	Bill Watkins	7-15
	Patsy Donovan	69-58
St. Louis	Patsy Tebeau	84-67
Washington	Arthur Irwin	54-98

Awards

STATS Most Valuable Player	Ed Delahanty, of, Phi
STATS Cy Young	Vic Willis, Bos
STATS Rookie of the Year	Jimmy Williams, 3b, Pit
STATS Manager of the Year	Bill Shettsline, Phi

STATS All-Star Team

C	Mike Grady, NYG	.334	2	54
1B	Jake Beckley, Cin	.333	3	99
2B	Nap Lajoie, Phi	.378	6	70
3B	John McGraw, Bal	.391	1	33
SS	Bobby Wallace, StL	.295	12	108
OF	Jesse Burkett, StL	.396	7	71
OF	Ed Delahanty, Phi	.410	9	137
OF	Buck Freeman, Was	.318	25	122
P	Jim Hughes, Bro	28-6	2.68	99 K
P	Joe McGinnity, Bal	28-16	2.68	74 K
P	Vic Willis, Bos	27-8	2.50	120 K
P	Cy Young, StL	26-16	2.58	111 K

Postseason

None

Outstanding Performances

No-Hitters
D. Phillippe, Lou	vs. NYG on May 25
Vic Willis, Bos	vs. Was on August 7

1900 National League Standings

	Overall					Home Games						Road Games						Park Index		Record by Month					
Team	W	L	Pct	GB	DIF	W	L	R	OR	HR	OHR	W	L	R	OR	HR	OHR	Run	HR	M/A	May	June	July	Aug	S/O
Brooklyn	82	54	.603	—	117	43	26	452	394	15	15	39	28	364	328	11	15	119	112	6-3	12-11	17-5	14-10	12-10	21-15
Pittsburgh	79	60	.568	4.5	0	42	28	359	315	14	7	37	32	374	297	12	17	99	71	4-6	16-10	9-12	14-10	13-10	23-12
Philadelphia	75	63	.543	8.0	61	45	23	434	353	13	7	30	40	376	439	16	22	99	54	7-3	15-7	11-13	10-13	9-14	23-13
Boston	66	72	.478	17.0	0	42	29	507	420	40	43	24	43	271	319	8	16	148	326	2-7	9-11	16-9	11-14	13-10	15-21
Chicago	65	75	.464	19.0	2	45	30	337	329	12	5	20	45	394	422	21	16	80	40	4-6	13-11	9-13	14-9	10-14	15-22
St. Louis	65	75	.464	19.0	4	40	31	382	316	23	13	25	44	362	432	13	24	85	95	6-4	12-10	5-15	11-13	14-12	17-21
Cincinnati	62	77	.446	21.5	2	27	34	255	309	12	9	35	43	448	436	21	19	82	67	6-4	6-16	14-9	11-15	12-9	13-24
New York	60	78	.435	23.0	0	38	31	393	375	13	8	22	47	320	448	10	18	100	75	3-5	8-15	8-13	11-12	11-15	19-18

Clinch Date—Brooklyn 10/06.

Team Batting

Team	G	AB	R	OR	H	2B	3B	HR	TB	RBI	TBB	IBB	SO	HBP	SH	SF	SB	CS	SB%	GDP	Avg	OBP	Slg
Brooklyn	142	4860	816	722	1423	199	81	26	1862	676	421	—	272	81	78	—	274	—	—	—	.293	.359	.383
Philadelphia	141	4969	810	792	1439	187	82	29	1877	694	440	—	374	72	113	—	205	—	—	—	.290	.356	.378
Boston	142	4952	778	739	1403	163	68	48	1846	676	395	—	278	45	107	—	182	—	—	—	.283	.342	.373
St. Louis	142	4877	744	748	1420	141	81	36	1831	602	406	—	318	81	80	—	243	—	—	—	.291	.356	.375
Pittsburgh	140	4817	733	612	1312	185	100	26	1775	602	327	—	321	63	110	—	174	—	—	—	.272	.327	.368
New York	141	4724	713	823	1317	177	61	23	1685	564	369	—	343	56	80	—	236	—	—	—	.279	.338	.357
Cincinnati	144	5026	703	745	1335	178	83	33	1778	591	333	—	408	50	108	—	183	—	—	—	.266	.318	.354
Chicago	146	4907	635	751	1276	202	51	33	1679	519	343	—	383	64	130	—	189	—	—	—	.260	.317	.342
NL Total	1138	39132	5932	5932	10925	1432	607	254	14333	4924	3034	—	2697	512	806	—	1686	—	—	—	.279	.339	.366
NL Avg Team	142	4892	742	742	1366	179	76	32	1792	616	379	—	337	64	101	—	211	—	—	—	.279	.339	.366

Team Pitching

Team	G	CG	ShO	Rel	Sv	IP	H	R	ER	HR	SH	SF	HB	TBB	IBB	SO	WP	Bk	H/9	SO/9	BB/9	OAvg	OOBP	ERA
Pittsburgh	140	114	11	30	1	1229.0	1232	612	418	24	—	—	67	295	—	415	28	1	9.0	3.0	2.2	.261	.313	3.06
Chicago	146	137	9	9	1	1271.0	1375	751	456	21	—	—	81	324	—	357	25	2	9.7	2.5	2.3	.275	.330	3.23
Boston	142	116	8	29	2	1240.1	1263	739	513	59	—	—	52	463	—	340	36	4	9.2	2.5	3.4	.264	.335	3.72
St. Louis	142	117	12	26	0	1217.1	1373	748	507	37	—	—	43	299	—	325	23	2	10.2	2.4	2.2	.284	.331	3.75
Cincinnati	144	118	9	28	1	1274.2	1383	745	543	28	—	—	60	404	—	399	31	1	9.8	2.8	2.9	.276	.338	3.83
Brooklyn	142	104	8	40	4	1225.2	1370	722	530	30	—	—	72	405	—	300	22	2	10.1	2.2	3.0	.282	.346	3.89
New York	141	113	4	31	0	1207.1	1423	823	531	26	—	—	94	442	—	277	32	4	10.6	2.1	3.3	.293	.363	3.96
Philadelphia	141	116	7	28	3	1248.2	1506	792	572	29	—	—	67	402	—	284	23	2	10.9	2.0	2.9	.298	.357	4.12
NL Total	1138	935	68	221	12	9914.0	10925	5932	4070	254	—	—	536	3034	—	2697	220	16	9.9	2.4	2.8	.279	.339	3.69
NL Avg Team	142	117	9	28	2	1239.0	1366	742	509	32	—	—	67	379	—	337	28	2	9.9	2.4	2.8	.279	.339	3.69

Team Fielding

Team	G	PO	A	E	TC	DP	PB	Pct
Boston	142	3720	1815	273	5808	86	49	.953
Brooklyn	142	3672	1849	303	5824	102	29	.948
Philadelphia	141	3744	1955	330	6029	125	57	.945
Cincinnati	144	3822	2029	341	6192	120	46	.945
Pittsburgh	140	3685	1832	322	5839	106	32	.945
St. Louis	142	3648	1834	331	5813	73	32	.943
Chicago	146	3808	1980	418	6206	98	38	.933
New York	141	3617	2029	439	6085	124	37	.928
NL Total	1138	29716	15323	2757	47796	834	331	.942

Team vs. Team Records

	Bos	Bro	ChN	Cin	NYG	Phi	Pit	StL	Won
Bos	—	4	12	13	11	9	5	12	66
Bro	16	—	10	15	10	10	8	13	82
ChN	8	10	—	9	12	9	8	9	65
Cin	7	4	11	—	7	9	12	12	62
NYG	7	10	8	13	—	7	9	6	60
Phi	11	8	11	11	13	—	9	12	75
Pit	15	11	12	8	11	11	—	11	79
StL	8	7	11	8	14	8	9	—	65
Lost	72	54	75	77	78	63	60	75	

1900 National League Batting Leaders

Games			At-Bats			Runs			Hits			Doubles			Triples		
J. Collins, Bos		142	J. Collins, Bos		586	R. Thomas, Phi		132	W. Keeler, Bro		204	H. Wagner, Pit		45	H. Wagner, Pit		22
5 tied with		141	J. Slagle, Phi		574	J. Slagle, Phi		115	J. Burkett, StL		203	N. Lajoie, Phi		33	C. Hickman, NYG		17
			G. Van Haltren, NYG		571	J. Barrett, Cin		114	H. Wagner, Pit		201	E. Flick, Phi		32	J. Kelley, Bro		17
			G. Beaumont, Pit		567	G. Van Haltren, NYG		114	E. Flick, Phi		200	E. Delahanty, Phi		32	E. Flick, Phi		16
			W. Keeler, Bro		563	H. Wagner, Pit		107	J. Beckley, Cin		190	G. Van Haltren, NYG		30	C. Stahl, Bos		16

Home Runs			Total Bases			Runs Batted In			Walks			Intentional Walks		Strikeouts	
H. Long, Bos		12	H. Wagner, Pit		302	E. Flick, Phi		110	R. Thomas, Phi		115	Statistic unavailable		Statistic unavailable	
E. Flick, Phi		11	E. Flick, Phi		297	E. Delahanty, Phi		109	B. Hamilton, Bos		107				
M. Donlin, StL		10	J. Burkett, StL		265	H. Wagner, Pit		100	J. McGraw, StL		85				
C. Hickman, NYG		9	W. Keeler, Bro		253	J. Collins, Bos		95	B. Dahlen, Bro		73				
B. Sullivan, Bos		8	J. Beckley, Cin		242	J. Beckley, Cin		94	2 tied with		72				

Hit By Pitch			Sac Hits			Sac Flies		Stolen Bases			Caught Stealing		GDP	
D. McGann, StL		24	J. Slagle, Phi		27	Statistic unavailable		P. Donovan, StL		45	Statistic unavailable		Statistic unavailable	
J. McGraw, StL		23	S. Mertes, ChN		22			G. Van Haltren, NYG		45				
H. Jennings, Bro		20	G. Beaumont, Pit		21			J. Barrett, Cin		44				
C. Hickman, NYG		17	C. Childs, ChN		20			W. Keeler, Bro		41				
E. Flick, Phi		16	3 tied with		19			2 tied with		38				

Runs Created			Runs Created/27 Outs			Batting Average			On-Base Percentage			Slugging Percentage			OBP+Slugging		
H. Wagner, Pit		150	H. Wagner, Pit		11.61	H. Wagner, Pit		.381	R. Thomas, Phi		.451	H. Wagner, Pit		.573	H. Wagner, Pit		1.007
E. Flick, Phi		145	E. Flick, Phi		10.55	E. Flick, Phi		.367	B. Hamilton, Bos		.449	E. Flick, Phi		.545	E. Flick, Phi		.986
B. Hamilton, Bos		126	B. Hamilton, Bos		9.14	J. Burkett, StL		.363	E. Flick, Phi		.441	N. Lajoie, Phi		.510	J. Burkett, StL		.904
K. Selbach, NYG		125	K. Selbach, NYG		8.99	W. Keeler, Bro		.362	H. Wagner, Pit		.434	J. Kelley, Bro		.485	K. Selbach, NYG		.885
J. Burkett, StL		120	J. Kelley, Bro		8.43	J. Beckley, Cin		.340	J. Burkett, StL		.429	C. Hickman, NYG		.482	J. Kelley, Bro		.882

1900 National League Pitching Leaders

Wins			Losses			Winning Percentage			Games			Games Started			Complete Games		
J. McGinnity, Bro		28	B. Carrick, NYG		22	J. McGinnity, Bro		.778	B. Carrick, NYG		45	B. Carrick, NYG		41	P. Hawley, NYG		34
D. Phillippe, Pit		20	E. Scott, Cin		20	J. Tannehill, Pit		.769	J. McGinnity, Bro		44	P. Hawley, NYG		38	B. Dinneen, Bos		33
B. Dinneen, Bos		20	N. Hahn, Cin		20	C. Fraser, Phi		.625	E. Scott, Cin		42	4 tied with		37	4 tied with		32
J. Tannehill, Pit		20	C. Jones, StL		19	D. Phillippe, Pit		.606	B. Kennedy, Bro		42						
B. Kennedy, Bro		20	C. Young, StL		19	B. Kennedy, Bro		.606	2 tied with		41						

Shutouts			Saves			Games Finished			Batters Faced		Innings Pitched			Hits Allowed		
N. Hahn, Cin		4	F. Kitson, Bro		4	H. Howell, Bro		10	Statistic unavailable		J. McGinnity, Bro		343.0	B. Carrick, NYG		415
C. Griffith, ChN		4	B. Bernhard, Phi		2	F. Kitson, Bro		9			B. Carrick, NYG		341.2	P. Hawley, NYG		377
C. Young, StL		4	6 tied with		1	D. Newton, Cin		8			P. Hawley, NYG		329.1	E. Scott, Cin		370
K. Nichols, Bos		4				6 tied with		7			C. Young, StL		321.1	J. McGinnity, Bro		350
5 tied with		3									B. Dinneen, Bos		320.2	N. Callahan, ChN		347

Home Runs Allowed			Walks			Walks/9 Innings			Strikeouts			Strikeouts/9 Innings			Strikeout/Walk Ratio		
F. Kitson, Bro		12	J. McGinnity, Bro		113	C. Young, StL		1.0	N. Hahn, Cin		132	R. Waddell, Pit		5.6	C. Young, StL		3.19
B. Dinneen, Bos		11	B. Kennedy, Bro		111	D. Phillippe, Pit		1.4	R. Waddell, Pit		130	N. Garvin, ChN		3.9	R. Waddell, Pit		2.36
V. Willis, Bos		11	V. Willis, Bos		106	J. Tannehill, Pit		1.7	C. Young, StL		115	N. Hahn, Cin		3.8	D. Phillippe, Pit		1.79
T. Lewis, Bos		11	B. Dinneen, Bos		105	C. Griffith, ChN		1.9	B. Dinneen, Bos		107	D. Newton, Cin		3.4	S. Leever, Pit		1.75
K. Nichols, Bos		11	D. Newton, Cin		100	S. Leever, Pit		1.9	N. Garvin, ChN		107	S. Leever, Pit		3.2	N. Garvin, ChN		1.70

Earned Run Average			Component ERA			Hit Batsmen			Wild Pitches			Opponent Average			Opponent OBP		
R. Waddell, Pit		2.37	R. Waddell, Pit		2.31	J. McGinnity, Bro		41	E. Scott, Cin		11	R. Waddell, Pit		.225	R. Waddell, Pit		.287
N. Garvin, ChN		2.41	D. Phillippe, Pit		2.64	E. Doheny, NYG		22	B. Bernhard, Phi		11	N. Garvin, ChN		.243	C. Young, StL		.288
J. Taylor, ChN		2.55	N. Garvin, ChN		2.73	N. Callahan, ChN		22	B. Dinneen, Bos		11	K. Nichols, Bos		.248	D. Phillippe, Pit		.290
S. Leever, Pit		2.71	C. Young, StL		2.73	W. Mercer, NYG		20	S. Leever, Pit		10	B. Dinneen, Bos		.250	N. Garvin, ChN		.304
D. Phillippe, Pit		2.84	S. Leever, Pit		2.92	P. Hawley, NYG		20	E. Doheny, NYG		10	D. Phillippe, Pit		.257	C. Griffith, ChN		.306

1900 National League Miscellaneous

Managers

Boston	Frank Selee	66-72
Brooklyn	Ned Hanlon	82-54
Chicago	Tom Loftus	65-75
Cincinnati	Bob Allen	62-77
New York	Buck Ewing	21-41
	George Davis	39-37
Philadelphia	Bill Shettsline	75-63
Pittsburgh	Fred Clarke	79-60
St. Louis	Patsy Tebeau	42-50
	Louie Heilbroner	23-25

Awards

STATS Most Valuable Player	Honus Wagner, of, Pit
STATS Cy Young	Joe McGinnity, NYG
STATS Rookie of the Year	Jimmy Barrett, of, Cin
STATS Manager of the Year	Ned Hanlon, Bro

STATS All-Star Team

C	Ed McFarland, Phi	.305	0	38
1B	Jake Beckley, Cin	.341	2	94
2B	Nap Lajoie, Phi	.337	7	92
3B	John McGraw, StL	.344	2	33
SS	George Davis, NYG	.319	3	61
OF	Jesse Burkett, StL	.363	7	68
OF	Elmer Flick, Phi	.367	11	110
OF	Honus Wagner, Pit	.381	4	100
P	Bill Dinneen, Bos	20-14	3.12	107 K
P	Joe McGinnity, Bro	28-8	2.94	93 K
P	Deacon Phillippe, Pit	20-13	2.84	75 K
P	Jesse Tannehill, Pit	20-6	2.88	50 K

Postseason

World Series	Brooklyn (NL) 3 vs. Pittsburgh (NL) 1

Outstanding Performances

No-Hitters

Noodles Hahn, Cin   vs. Phi on July 12

1901 American League Standings

Team	Overall W	L	Pct	GB	DIF	Home Games W	L	R	OR	HR	OHR	Road Games W	L	R	OR	HR	OHR	Park Index Run	HR	M/A	May	June	July	Aug	S/O
Chicago	83	53	.610	—	122	49	21	441	285	14	11	34	32	378	346	18	16	95	69	4-2	20-7	13-11	17-9	13-13	16-11
Boston	79	57	.581	4.0	14	49	20	383	252	21	16	30	37	376	356	16	17	84	109	1-3	10-11	20-5	16-12	17-14	15-12
Detroit	74	61	.548	8.5	26	42	27	438	369	15	10	32	34	303	325	14	12	123	92	5-1	15-11	10-14	15-11	13-14	16-10
Philadelphia	74	62	.544	9.0	0	42	24	410	352	15	9	32	38	395	409	20	11	101	82	1-3	12-14	8-15	13-10	22-10	18-10
Baltimore	68	65	.511	13.5	3	40	25	430	367	10	11	28	40	330	383	14	10	117	92	2-2	11-10	14-8	16-12	13-16	12-17
Washington	61	72	.459	20.5	6	31	35	333	375	17	36	30	37	349	396	16	15	96	174	4-0	10-11	11-11	7-18	15-17	14-15
Cleveland	54	82	.397	29.0	0	28	39	321	399	0	13	26	43	346	432	12	9	95	64	2-4	6-18	11-12	10-15	14-14	11-19
Milwaukee	48	89	.350	35.5	0	32	37	342	373	15	14	16	52	299	455	11	18	93	99	1-5	11-13	7-18	11-18	8-17	10-18

Clinch Date—Chicago 9/23.

Team Batting

Team	G	AB	R	OR	H	2B	3B	HR	TB	RBI	TBB	IBB	SO	HBP	SH	SF	SB	CS	SB%	GDP	Avg	OBP	Slg
Chicago	137	4725	819	631	1303	173	89	32	1750	656	475	—	337	62	127	—	280	—	—	—	.276	.350	.370
Philadelphia	137	4882	805	761	1409	239	87	35	1927	665	301	—	344	53	78	—	173	—	—	—	.289	.337	.395
Baltimore	135	4589	760	750	1348	179	111	24	1821	633	369	—	377	52	97	—	207	—	—	—	.294	.353	.397
Boston	138	4866	759	608	1353	183	104	37	1855	632	331	—	282	47	105	—	157	—	—	—	.278	.330	.381
Detroit	136	4676	741	694	1303	180	80	29	1730	611	380	—	346	54	131	—	204	—	—	—	.279	.340	.370
Washington	138	4772	682	771	1282	191	83	33	1738	560	356	—	340	51	80	—	127	—	—	—	.269	.313	.364
Cleveland	138	4833	667	831	1311	197	68	12	1680	523	243	—	326	48	75	—	125	—	—	—	.271	.313	.348
Milwaukee	139	4795	641	828	1250	192	66	26	1652	513	325	—	384	46	122	—	176	—	—	—	.261	.314	.345
AL Total	1098	38138	5874	5874	10559	1534	688	228	14153	4793	2780	—	2736	413	815	—	1449	—	—	—	.277	.333	.371
AL Avg Team	137	4767	734	734	1320	192	86	29	1769	599	348	—	342	52	102	—	181	—	—	—	.277	.333	.371

Team Pitching

Team	G	CG	ShO	Rel	Sv	IP	H	R	ER	HR	SH	SF	HB	TBB	IBB	SO	WP	Bk	H/9	SO/9	BB/9	OAvg	OOBP	ERA
Chicago	137	110	11	28	2	1218.1	1250	631	403	27	—	—	52	312	—	394	32	1	9.2	2.9	2.3	.263	.315	2.98
Boston	138	123	7	15	1	1217.0	1178	608	411	33	—	—	42	294	—	396	12	0	8.7	2.9	2.2	.251	.301	3.04
Detroit	136	118	8	20	2	1188.2	1328	694	436	22	—	—	47	313	—	307	18	0	10.1	2.3	2.4	.279	.330	3.30
Baltimore	135	115	4	21	3	1158.0	1313	750	480	21	—	—	48	344	—	271	29	0	10.2	2.1	2.7	.282	.338	3.73
Philadelphia	137	124	6	14	1	1200.2	1346	761	534	20	—	—	59	374	—	350	40	0	10.1	2.6	2.8	.280	.340	4.00
Milwaukee	139	107	3	34	4	1218.0	1383	828	549	32	—	—	63	395	—	376	34	0	10.2	2.8	2.9	.283	.344	4.06
Washington	138	118	8	20	2	1183.0	1396	771	538	51	—	—	63	284	—	308	13	0	10.6	2.3	2.2	.290	.338	4.09
Cleveland	138	122	7	19	4	1182.1	1365	831	541	22	—	—	73	464	—	334	43	4	10.4	2.5	3.5	.286	.358	4.12
AL Total	1098	937	54	171	19	9566.0	10559	5874	3892	228	—	—	447	2780	—	2736	221	5	9.9	2.6	2.6	.277	.333	3.66
AL Avg Team	137	117	7	21	2	1195.0	1320	734	487	29	—	—	56	348	—	342	28	1	9.9	2.6	2.6	.277	.333	3.66

Team Fielding

Team	G	PO	A	E	TC	DP	PB	Pct
Washington	138	3542	1794	323	5659	97	15	.943
Boston	138	3649	1877	337	5863	104	23	.943
Philadelphia	137	3600	1903	337	5840	93	23	.942
Cleveland	138	3531	1740	324	5595	99	35	.942
Chicago	137	3653	1856	345	5854	100	23	.941
Milwaukee	139	3650	1886	393	5929	106	30	.934
Detroit	136	3558	1928	410	5896	127	16	.930
Baltimore	135	3472	1560	401	5433	76	20	.926
AL Total	1098	28655	14544	2870	46069	802	185	.938

Team vs. Team Records

	Bal	Bos	ChA	Cle	Det	Mil	Phi	Was	Won
Bal	—	9	4	11	9	12	12	11	68
Bos	9	—	12	12	9	15	10	12	79
ChA	14	8	—	13	10	16	12	10	83
Cle	8	7	7	—	6	11	6	9	54
Det	10	11	10	14	—	13	7	9	74
Mil	8	4	4	9	7	—	6	10	48
Phi	8	10	8	14	9	14	—	11	74
Was	8	8	8	9	11	8	9	—	61
Lost	65	57	53	82	61	89	62	72	

1901 American League Batting Leaders

Games		At-Bats		Runs		Hits		Doubles		Triples	
I. Waldron, 2tm	141	I. Waldron, 2tm	598	N. Lajoie, Phi	145	N. Lajoie, Phi	232	N. Lajoie, Phi	48	J. Williams, Bal	21
B. Hallman, Mil	139	T. Dowd, Bos	594	F. Jones, ChA	120	J. Anderson, Mil	190	J. Anderson, Mil	46	B. Keister, Bal	21
6 tied with	138	J. Anderson, Mil	576	J. Williams, Bal	113	J. Collins, Bos	187	J. Collins, Bos	42	S. Mertes, ChA	17
		J. Collins, Bos	564	D. Hoy, ChA	112	I. Waldron, 2tm	186	J. Farrell, Was	32	C. Stahl, Bos	16
		D. Fultz, Phi	561	J. Barrett, Det	110	S. Dungan, Was	179	5 tied with	28	J. Collins, Bos	16

Home Runs		Total Bases		Runs Batted In		Walks		Intentional Walks		Strikeouts	
N. Lajoie, Phi	14	N. Lajoie, Phi	350	N. Lajoie, Phi	125	D. Hoy, ChA	86	Statistic unavailable		Statistic unavailable	
B. Freeman, Bos	12	J. Collins, Bos	279	B. Freeman, Bos	114	F. Jones, ChA	84				
M. Grady, Was	9	J. Anderson, Mil	274	J. Anderson, Det	99	J. Barrett, Det	76				
3 tied with	8	B. Freeman, Bos	255	S. Mertes, ChA	98	H. McFarland, ChA	75				
		J. Williams, Bal	248	J. Williams, Bal	96	J. McGraw, Bal	61				

Hit By Pitch		Sac Hits		Sac Flies		Stolen Bases		Caught Stealing		GDP	
J. McGraw, Bal	14	D. Nance, Det	24	Statistic unavailable		F. Isbell, ChA	52	Statistic unavailable		Statistic unavailable	
D. Hoy, ChA	14	F. Parent, Bos	21			S. Mertes, ChA	46				
N. Lajoie, Phi	13	C. Stahl, Bos	20			C. Seymour, Bal	38				
B. Clarke, Was	12	S. Mertes, ChA	20			F. Jones, ChA	38				
D. Casey, Det	10	J. McCarthy, Cle	19			2 tied with	36				

Runs Created		Runs Created/27 Outs		Batting Average		On-Base Percentage		Slugging Percentage		OBP+Slugging	
N. Lajoie, Phi	169	N. Lajoie, Phi	13.99	N. Lajoie, Phi	.426	N. Lajoie, Phi	.463	N. Lajoie, Phi	.643	N. Lajoie, Phi	1.106
J. Collins, Bos	120	B. Freeman, Bos	9.21	M. Donlin, Bal	.340	F. Jones, ChA	.412	B. Freeman, Bos	.520	B. Freeman, Bos	.920
B. Freeman, Bos	118	S. Seybold, Phi	8.92	B. Freeman, Bos	.339	M. Donlin, Bal	.409	S. Seybold, Phi	.503	S. Seybold, Phi	.901
D. Hoy, ChA	117	M. Donlin, Bal	8.61	S. Seybold, Phi	.334	D. Hoy, ChA	.407	J. Williams, Bal	.495	M. Donlin, Bal	.883
J. Anderson, Mil	116	J. Williams, Bal	8.05	J. Collins, Bos	.332	B. Freeman, Bos	.400	J. Collins, Bos	.495	J. Williams, Bal	.883

1901 American League Pitching Leaders

Wins		Losses		Winning Percentage		Games		Games Started		Complete Games	
C. Young, Bos	33	P. Dowling, 2tm	26	C. Griffith, ChA	.774	J. McGinnity, Bal	48	J. McGinnity, Bal	43	J. McGinnity, Bal	39
J. McGinnity, Bal	26	B. Carrick, Was	22	C. Young, Bos	.767	P. Dowling, 2tm	43	C. Young, Bos	41	C. Young, Bos	38
C. Griffith, ChA	24	H. Howell, Bal	21	S. Wiltse, Phi	.722	C. Young, Bos	43	B. Carrick, Was	37	R. Miller, Det	35
R. Miller, Det	23	3 tied with	20	N. Callahan, ChA	.652	B. Carrick, Was	42	C. Fraser, Phi	37	C. Fraser, Phi	35
C. Fraser, Phi	22			C. Patten, Was	.643	R. Patterson, ChA	41	R. Miller, Det	36	B. Carrick, Was	34

Shutouts		Saves		Games Finished		Batters Faced		Innings Pitched		Hits Allowed	
C. Griffith, ChA	5	B. Hoffer, Cle	3	N. Garvin, Mil	10	Statistic unavailable		J. McGinnity, Bal	382.0	J. McGinnity, Bal	412
C. Young, Bos	5	N. Garvin, Mil	2	B. Husting, Mil	8			C. Young, Bos	371.1	B. Carrick, Was	367
C. Patten, Was	4	12 tied with	1	D. Gear, Was	8			R. Miller, Det	332.0	B. Reidy, Mil	364
E. Moore, Cle	4			P. Dowling, 2tm	7			C. Fraser, Phi	331.0	R. Patterson, ChA	345
R. Patterson, ChA	4			3 tied with	6			B. Carrick, Was	324.0	C. Fraser, Phi	344

Home Runs Allowed		Walks		Walks/9 Innings		Strikeouts		Strikeouts/9 Innings		Strikeout/Walk Ratio	
W. Lee, Was	14	C. Fraser, Phi	132	C. Young, Bos	0.9	C. Young, Bos	158	N. Garvin, Mil	4.3	C. Young, Bos	4.27
B. Reidy, Mil	14	P. Dowling, 2tm	118	D. Gear, Was	1.2	R. Patterson, ChA	127	C. Patten, Was	3.9	R. Patterson, ChA	2.05
T. Lewis, Bos	14	E. Moore, Cle	107	W. Lee, Was	1.5	P. Dowling, 2tm	124	C. Young, Bos	3.8	D. Gear, Was	1.59
B. Carrick, Was	12	R. Miller, Det	98	C. Griffith, ChA	1.7	N. Garvin, Mil	122	R. Patterson, ChA	3.7	J. Cronin, Det	1.48
R. Patterson, ChA	11	J. McGinnity, Bal	96	J. Cronin, Det	1.7	C. Fraser, Phi	110	P. Dowling, 2tm	3.6	C. Patten, Was	1.47

Earned Run Average		Component ERA		Hit Batsmen		Wild Pitches		Opponent Average		Opponent OBP	
C. Young, Bos	1.62	C. Young, Bos	1.87	C. Fraser, Phi	32	E. Plank, Phi	13	C. Young, Bos	.232	C. Young, Bos	.256
N. Callahan, ChA	2.42	N. Callahan, ChA	2.53	J. McGinnity, Bal	21	E. Moore, Cle	13	N. Callahan, ChA	.239	N. Callahan, ChA	.290
J. Yeager, Det	2.61	G. Winter, Bos	2.81	P. Dowling, 2tm	21	N. Garvin, Mil	13	E. Moore, Cle	.246	C. Griffith, ChA	.300
C. Griffith, ChA	2.67	C. Griffith, ChA	2.90	B. Carrick, Was	20	C. Fraser, Phi	11	T. Lewis, Bos	.247	G. Winter, Bos	.300
G. Winter, Bos	2.80	E. Plank, Phi	2.93	C. Patten, Was	18	2 tied with	10	G. Winter, Bos	.248	T. Lewis, Bos	.304

1901 American League Miscellaneous

Managers		
Baltimore	John McGraw	68-65
Boston	Jimmy Collins	79-57
Chicago	Clark Griffith	83-53
Cleveland	Jimmy McAleer	54-82
Detroit	George Stallings	74-61
Milwaukee	Hugh Duffy	48-89
Philadelphia	Connie Mack	74-62
Washington	Jimmy Manning	61-72

Awards	
STATS Most Valuable Player	Nap Lajoie, 2b, Phi
STATS Cy Young	Cy Young, Bos
STATS Rookie of the Year	Socks Seybold, of, Phi
STATS Manager of the Year	Clark Griffith, ChA

STATS All-Star Team

C	Ossee Schreckengost, Bos	.304	0	38
1B	Buck Freeman, Bos	.339	12	114
2B	Nap Lajoie, Phi	.426	14	125
3B	Jimmy Collins, Bos	.332	6	94
SS	Kid Elberfeld, Det	.308	3	76
OF	Mike Donlin, Bal	.340	5	67
OF	Fielder Jones, ChA	.311	2	65
OF	Socks Seybold, Phi	.334	8	90
P	Clark Griffith, ChA	24-7	2.67	67 K
P	Roscoe Miller, Det	23-13	2.95	79 K
P	Roy Patterson, ChA	20-16	3.37	127 K
P	Cy Young, Bos	33-10	1.62	158 K

Postseason

None

Outstanding Performances

Triple Crown		
Nap Lajoie, Phi	.426-14-125	
Cycles		
Harry Davis, Phi	on July 10	
Nap Lajoie, Phi	on July 30	

1901 National League Standings

Team	Overall					Home Games						Road Games						Park Index		Record by Month					
	W	L	Pct	GB	DIF	W	L	R	OR	HR	OHR	W	L	R	OR	HR	OHR	Run	HR	M/A	May	June	July	Aug	S/O
Pittsburgh	90	49	.647	—	127	45	24	372	255	15	8	45	25	404	279	14	12	93	90	3-3	13-11	17-9	16-9	13-9	28-8
Philadelphia	83	57	.593	7.5	0	46	23	349	247	11	6	37	34	319	296	13	13	100	67	4-4	13-9	13-13	16-9	17-12	20-10
Brooklyn	79	57	.581	9.5	7	43	25	400	303	13	6	36	32	344	297	19	12	110	61	4-3	10-12	16-11	14-13	18-9	17-9
St. Louis	76	64	.543	14.5	2	40	31	392	338	21	19	36	33	400	351	18	20	94	102	5-3	8-14	18-10	17-10	12-14	16-13
Boston	69	69	.500	20.5	5	41	29	297	298	17	17	28	40	234	258	11	12	117	144	3-3	8-11	14-11	14-15	14-16	16-13
Chicago	53	86	.381	37.0	1	30	39	293	357	6	10	23	47	285	342	12	17	105	56	3-6	9-14	7-20	15-15	12-12	7-19
New York	52	85	.380	37.0	23	30	38	255	350	8	11	22	47	289	405	11	13	88	80	2-3	13-6	12-12	7-20	8-20	10-24
Cincinnati	52	87	.374	38.0	22	27	43	279	409	23	33	25	44	282	409	15	18	98	167	4-3	12-9	7-18	10-18	10-12	9-27

Clinch Date—Pittsburgh 9/27.

Team Batting

Team	G	AB	R	OR	H	2B	3B	HR	TB	RBI	TBB	IBB	SO	HBP	SH	SF	SB	CS	SB%	GDP	Avg	OBP	Slg
St. Louis	142	5039	792	689	1430	187	94	39	1922	657	314	—	540	90	122	—	190	—	—	—	.284	.337	.381
Pittsburgh	140	4913	776	534	1407	182	92	29	1860	636	386	—	493	50	116	—	203	—	—	—	.286	.335	.379
Brooklyn	137	4879	744	600	1399	206	93	32	1887	633	312	—	449	39	80	—	178	—	—	—	.287	.335	.387
Philadelphia	140	4793	668	543	1275	194	58	24	1657	552	430	—	549	62	124	—	199	—	—	—	.266	.334	.346
Chicago	140	4844	578	699	1250	153	61	18	1579	481	314	—	532	52	68	—	204	—	—	—	.258	.310	.326
Cincinnati	142	4914	561	818	1232	173	70	38	1659	476	323	—	584	42	113	—	137	—	—	—	.251	.303	.338
New York	141	4839	544	755	1225	167	46	19	1541	458	303	—	575	44	73	—	133	—	—	—	.253	.303	.318
Boston	140	4746	531	556	1180	135	36	28	1471	449	303	—	519	34	136	—	158	—	—	—	.249	.298	.310
NL Total	1122	38967	5194	5194	10398	1397	550	227	13576	4342	2685	—	4241	413	832	—	1402	—	—	—	.267	.321	.348
NL Avg Team	140	4871	649	649	1300	175	69	28	1697	543	336	—	530	52	104	—	175	—	—	—	.267	.321	.348

Team Pitching

Team	G	CG	ShO	Rel	Sv	IP	H	R	ER	HR	SH	SF	HB	TBB	IBB	SO	WP	Bk	H/9	SO/9	BB/9	OAvg	OOBP	ERA
Pittsburgh	140	119	15	21	4	1244.2	1198	534	357	20	—	—	60	244	—	505	21	2	8.7	3.7	1.8	.252	.297	2.58
Philadelphia	140	125	15	16	2	1246.2	1221	543	397	19	—	—	50	259	—	480	24	2	8.8	3.5	1.9	.255	.300	2.87
Boston	140	128	11	13	0	1263.0	1196	556	407	29	—	—	38	349	—	558	29	2	8.5	4.0	2.5	.249	.304	2.90
Brooklyn	137	111	7	26	5	1213.2	1244	600	424	18	—	—	51	435	—	583	28	1	9.2	4.3	3.2	.264	.333	3.14
Chicago	140	131	2	9	0	1241.2	1348	699	460	27	—	—	53	324	—	586	33	2	9.8	4.2	2.3	.275	.327	3.33
St. Louis	142	118	5	29	5	1269.2	1333	689	519	39	—	—	57	332	—	445	37	1	9.4	3.2	2.4	.268	.322	3.68
New York	141	118	11	23	1	1232.0	1389	755	530	24	—	—	62	377	—	542	49	3	10.1	4.0	2.8	.283	.341	3.87
Cincinnati	142	126	4	18	0	1265.2	1469	818	587	51	—	—	68	365	—	542	31	0	10.4	3.9	2.6	.289	.344	4.17
NL Total	1122	976	70	155	17	9977.0	10398	5194	3681	227	—	—	439	2685	—	4241	252	13	9.4	3.8	2.4	.267	.321	3.32
NL Avg Team	140	122	9	19	2	1247.0	1300	649	460	28	—	—	55	336	—	530	32	2	9.4	3.8	2.4	.267	.321	3.32

Team Fielding

Team	G	PO	A	E	TC	DP	PB	Pct
Philadelphia	140	3734	1759	262	5755	65	37	.954
Boston	140	3785	1750	282	5817	89	15	.952
Pittsburgh	140	3728	1748	287	5763	97	23	.950
Brooklyn	137	3636	1661	281	5578	99	31	.950
St. Louis	142	3808	1912	305	6025	108	29	.949
Chicago	140	3724	1812	336	5872	87	30	.943
New York	141	3691	1884	348	5923	81	48	.941
Cincinnati	142	3791	1806	355	5952	102	13	.940
NL Total	1122	29897	14332	2456	46685	728	226	.947

Team vs. Team Records

	Bos	Bro	ChN	Cin	NYG	Phi	Pit	StL	Won
Bos	—	10	13	11	14	7	5	9	69
Bro	10	—	13	14	11	11	11	9	79
ChN	6	7	—	10	11	3	6	10	53
Cin	8	6	10	—	8	4	7	9	52
NYG	6	6	9	12	—	8	4	7	52
Phi	13	9	17	16	12	—	7	9	83
Pit	15	8	14	13	16	13	—	11	90
StL	11	11	10	11	13	11	9	—	76
Lost	69	57	86	87	85	57	49	64	

Seasons: Standings, Leaders

1901 National League Batting Leaders

Games		At-Bats		Runs		Hits		Doubles		Triples	
O. Krueger, StL	142	J. Burkett, StL	601	J. Burkett, StL	142	J. Burkett, StL	226	E. Delahanty, Phi	38	J. Sheckard, Bro	19
J. Burkett, StL	142	W. Keeler, Bro	595	W. Keeler, Bro	123	W. Keeler, Bro	202	T. Daly, Bro	38	E. Flick, Phi	17
5 tied with	140	J. Beckley, Cin	580	G. Beaumont, Pit	120	J. Sheckard, Bro	196	H. Wagner, Pit	37	4 tied with	16
		DeMontreville, Bos	577	F. Clarke, Pit	118	H. Wagner, Pit	194	J. Beckley, Cin	36		
		K. Bransfield, Pit	566	J. Sheckard, Bro	116	E. Delahanty, Phi	192	B. Wallace, StL	34		

Home Runs		Total Bases		Runs Batted In		Walks		Intentional Walks		Strikeouts	
S. Crawford, Cin	16	J. Burkett, StL	306	H. Wagner, Pit	126	R. Thomas, Phi	100	Statistic unavailable		Statistic unavailable	
J. Sheckard, Bro	11	J. Sheckard, Bro	296	E. Delahanty, Phi	108	T. Hartsel, ChN	74				
J. Burkett, StL	10	E. Delahanty, Phi	286	S. Crawford, Cin	104	L. Davis, 2tm	66				
3 tied with	8	H. Wagner, Pit	271	J. Sheckard, Bro	104	E. Delahanty, Phi	65				
		2 tied with	270	2 tied with	91	B. Hamilton, Bos	64				

Hit By Pitch		Sac Hits		Sac Flies		Stolen Bases		Caught Stealing		GDP	
D. McGann, StL	23	B. Hallman, Phi	29	Statistic unavailable		H. Wagner, Pit	49	Statistic unavailable		Statistic unavailable	
O. Krueger, StL	13	DeMontreville, Bos	24			T. Hartsel, ChN	41				
H. Jennings, Phi	12	W. Keeler, Bro	22			S. Strang, NYG	40				
D. Padden, StL	11	D. Harley, Cin	21			D. Harley, Cin	37				
4 tied with	10	2 tied with	20			G. Beaumont, Pit	36				

Runs Created		Runs Created/27 Outs		Batting Average		On-Base Percentage		Slugging Percentage		OBP+Slugging	
J. Burkett, StL	153	J. Burkett, StL	10.60	J. Burkett, StL	.376	J. Burkett, StL	.440	J. Sheckard, Bro	.534	E. Delahanty, Phi	.955
J. Sheckard, Bro	135	J. Sheckard, Bro	9.80	E. Delahanty, Phi	.354	R. Thomas, Phi	.437	E. Delahanty, Phi	.528	J. Burkett, StL	.949
H. Wagner, Pit	133	E. Delahanty, Phi	9.61	J. Sheckard, Bro	.354	E. Delahanty, Phi	.427	S. Crawford, Cin	.524	J. Sheckard, Bro	.942
E. Delahanty, Phi	132	H. Wagner, Pit	9.55	H. Wagner, Pit	.353	H. Wagner, Pit	.416	J. Burkett, StL	.509	H. Wagner, Pit	.910
T. Hartsel, ChN	126	T. Hartsel, ChN	8.83	W. Keeler, Bro	.340	T. Hartsel, ChN	.414	E. Flick, Phi	.500	S. Crawford, Cin	.903

1901 National League Pitching Leaders

Wins		Losses		Winning Percentage		Games		Games Started		Complete Games	
W. Donovan, Bro	25	L. Taylor, NYG	27	S. Leever, Pit	.737	L. Taylor, NYG	45	L. Taylor, NYG	43	N. Hahn, Cin	41
J. Harper, StL	23	L. Hughes, ChN	23	J. Chesbro, Pit	.677	W. Donovan, Bro	45	N. Hahn, Cin	42	L. Taylor, NYG	37
D. Phillippe, Pit	22	J. Powell, StL	21	J. Harper, StL	.657	J. Powell, StL	45	C. Mathewson, NYG	38	C. Mathewson, NYG	36
N. Hahn, Cin	22	N. Hahn, Cin	19	D. Phillippe, Pit	.647	N. Hahn, Cin	42	W. Donovan, Bro	38	W. Donovan, Bro	36
J. Chesbro, Pit	21	J. Taylor, ChN	19	J. Tannehill, Pit	.643	C. Mathewson, NYG	40	2 tied with	37	4 tied with	33

Shutouts		Saves		Games Finished		Batters Faced		Innings Pitched		Hits Allowed	
J. Chesbro, Pit	6	J. Powell, StL	3	W. Sudhoff, StL	11	Statistic unavailable		N. Hahn, Cin	375.1	L. Taylor, NYG	377
V. Willis, Bos	6	D. Phillippe, Pit	2	J. Chesbro, Pit	8			L. Taylor, NYG	353.1	N. Hahn, Cin	370
A. Orth, Phi	6	F. Kitson, Bro	2	J. Powell, StL	8			W. Donovan, Bro	351.0	B. Phillips, Cin	364
3 tied with	5	W. Sudhoff, StL	2	W. Donovan, Bro	7			J. Powell, StL	338.1	J. Powell, StL	351
		4 tied with	1	4 tied with	6			C. Mathewson, NYG	336.0	J. Taylor, ChN	341

Home Runs Allowed		Walks		Walks/9 Innings		Strikeouts		Strikeouts/9 Innings		Strikeout/Walk Ratio	
J. Powell, StL	14	W. Donovan, Bro	152	A. Orth, Phi	1.0	N. Hahn, Cin	239	L. Hughes, ChN	6.6	N. Hahn, Cin	3.46
N. Hahn, Cin	13	L. Hughes, ChN	115	D. Phillippe, Pit	1.2	W. Donovan, Bro	226	R. Waddell, 2tm	6.2	J. Tannehill, Pit	3.28
A. Stimmel, Cin	10	L. Taylor, NYG	112	J. Tannehill, Pit	1.3	L. Hughes, ChN	225	C. Mathewson, NYG	5.9	A. Orth, Phi	2.88
4 tied with	9	J. Hughes, Bro	102	B. Duggleby, Phi	1.3	C. Mathewson, NYG	221	W. Donovan, Bro	5.8	D. Phillippe, Pit	2.71
		J. Harper, StL	99	J. Powell, StL	1.3	R. Waddell, 2tm	172	N. Hahn, Cin	5.7	J. Powell, StL	2.66

Earned Run Average		Component ERA		Hit Batsmen		Wild Pitches		Opponent Average		Opponent OBP	
J. Tannehill, Pit	2.18	A. Orth, Phi	2.00	D. Newton, 2tm	21	C. Mathewson, NYG	23	J. Townsend, Phi	.223	A. Orth, Phi	.264
D. Phillippe, Pit	2.22	D. Phillippe, Pit	2.27	W. Sudhoff, StL	18	J. Harper, StL	19	V. Willis, Bos	.228	D. Phillippe, Pit	.271
A. Orth, Phi	2.27	J. Chesbro, Pit	2.31	L. Hughes, ChN	17	L. Hughes, ChN	16	C. Mathewson, NYG	.229	J. Chesbro, Pit	.279
V. Willis, Bos	2.36	V. Willis, Bos	2.32	L. Taylor, NYG	16	R. Waddell, 2tm	11	J. Chesbro, Pit	.236	V. Willis, Bos	.283
J. Chesbro, Pit	2.38	J. Tannehill, Pit	2.37	J. Harper, StL	16	3 tied with	10	A. Orth, Phi	.237	J. Tannehill, Pit	.283

1901 National League Miscellaneous

Managers		
Boston	Frank Selee	69-69
Brooklyn	Ned Hanlon	79-57
Chicago	Tom Loftus	53-86
Cincinnati	Bid McPhee	52-87
New York	George Davis	52-85
Philadelphia	Bill Shettsline	83-57
Pittsburgh	Fred Clarke	90-49
St. Louis	Patsy Donovan	76-64

Awards	
STATS Most Valuable Player	Honus Wagner, ss, Pit
STATS Cy Young	Deacon Phillippe, Pit
STATS Rookie of the Year	C. Mathewson, p, NYG
STATS Manager of the Year	Fred Clarke, Pit

STATS All-Star Team

C	Deacon McGuire, Bro	.296	0	40
1B	Joe Kelley, Bro	.307	4	65
2B	Tom Daly, Bro	.315	3	90
3B	Otto Krueger, StL	.275	2	79
SS	Honus Wagner, Pit	.353	6	126
OF	Jesse Burkett, StL	.376	10	75
OF	Ed Delahanty, Phi	.354	8	108
OF	Jimmy Sheckard, Bro	.354	11	104
P	Wild Bill Donovan, Bro	25-15	2.77	226 K
P	Noodles Hahn, Cin	22-19	2.71	239 K
P	Al Orth, Phi	20-12	2.27	92 K
P	Deacon Phillippe, Pit	22-12	2.22	103 K

Postseason

None

Outstanding Performances

No-Hitters
C. Mathewson, NYG @ StL on July 15
Cycles
Fred Clarke, Pit   on July 23

1902 American League Standings

Team	Overall					Home Games						Road Games						Park Index		Record by Month					
	W	L	Pct	GB	DIF	W	L	R	OR	HR	OHR	W	L	R	OR	HR	OHR	Run	HR	M/A	May	June	July	Aug	S/O
Philadelphia	83	53	.610	—	62	56	17	477	330	19	12	27	36	298	306	19	21	115	67	3-3	16-10	7-14	15-8	21-11	21-7
St. Louis	78	58	.574	5.0	11	49	21	350	289	16	14	29	37	269	318	13	22	103	81	3-4	11-11	13-10	15-11	18-12	18-10
Boston	77	60	.562	6.5	4	43	27	348	284	21	15	34	33	316	316	21	12	96	104	3-4	16-11	12-12	14-12	17-8	15-13
Chicago	74	60	.552	8.0	77	48	19	371	238	5	2	26	41	304	364	9	28	91	19	4-2	14-10	15-5	11-17	16-15	14-11
Cleveland	69	67	.507	14.0	0	40	25	357	257	15	7	29	42	410	410	18	19	91	65	3-5	8-18	13-12	14-13	17-10	14-9
Washington	61	75	.449	22.0	4	40	28	407	341	36	38	21	47	300	449	11	18	100	255	4-3	10-17	13-11	13-12	12-16	9-16
Detroit	52	83	.385	30.5	18	35	33	312	286	13	8	17	50	254	371	9	12	94	99	3-2	15-12	8-14	9-16	6-21	11-18
Baltimore	50	88	.362	34.0	0	32	31	391	369	16	18	18	57	324	479	17	12	113	140	3-3	13-14	10-13	11-13	8-22	5-23

Clinch Date—Philadelphia 9/24.

Team Batting

Team	G	AB	R	OR	H	2B	3B	HR	TB	RBI	TBB	IBB	SO	HBP	SH	SF	SB	CS	SB%	GDP	Avg	OBP	Slg
Philadelphia	137	4762	775	636	1369	235	67	38	1852	673	343	—	293	38	118	—	201	—	—	—	.287	.340	.389
Baltimore	141	4760	715	848	1318	202	107	33	1833	598	417	—	429	54	115	—	189	—	—	—	.277	.342	.385
Washington	138	4734	707	790	1338	261	66	47	1872	606	329	—	296	44	81	—	121	—	—	—	.283	.335	.395
Cleveland	137	4840	686	667	1401	248	68	33	1884	582	308	—	356	35	118	—	140	—	—	—	.289	.336	.389
Chicago	138	4654	675	602	1248	170	50	14	1560	537	411	—	381	36	154	—	265	—	—	—	.268	.332	.335
Boston	138	4875	664	600	1356	195	95	42	1867	572	275	—	375	42	100	—	132	—	—	—	.278	.322	.383
St. Louis	140	4736	619	607	1254	208	61	29	1671	520	373	—	327	38	104	—	137	—	—	—	.265	.312	.353
Detroit	137	4644	566	657	1167	141	55	22	1484	488	359	—	287	52	83	—	130	—	—	—	.251	.312	.320
AL Total	1106	38005	5407	5407	10451	1660	569	258	14023	4576	2815	—	2744	339	873	—	1315	—	—	—	.275	.331	.369
AL Avg Team	138	4751	676	676	1306	208	71	32	1753	572	352	—	343	42	109	—	164	—	—	—	.275	.331	.369

Team Pitching

Team	G	CG	ShO	Rel	Sv	IP	H	R	ER	HR	SH	SF	HB	TBB	IBB	SO	WP	Bk	H/9	SO/9	BB/9	OAvg	OOBP	ERA
Boston	138	123	6	16	1	1238.0	1217	600	416	27	—	—	40	326	—	431	16	1	8.8	3.1	2.4	.258	.311	3.02
Cleveland	137	116	16	23	3	1204.1	1199	667	439	26	—	—	48	411	—	361	37	1	9.0	2.7	3.1	.260	.327	3.28
Philadelphia	137	114	5	25	2	1216.1	1292	636	444	33	—	—	63	368	—	455	29	4	9.6	3.4	2.7	.273	.334	3.29
St. Louis	140	120	7	22	2	1244.0	1273	607	461	36	—	—	45	343	—	348	20	1	9.2	2.5	2.5	.266	.321	3.34
Chicago	138	116	11	22	0	1221.2	1269	602	463	30	—	—	50	331	—	346	31	0	9.3	2.5	2.4	.269	.323	3.41
Detroit	137	116	9	22	3	1190.2	1267	657	471	20	—	—	44	370	—	245	29	1	9.6	1.9	2.8	.273	.333	3.56
Baltimore	141	119	3	22	1	1210.1	1531	848	582	30	—	—	37	354	—	258	26	0	11.4	1.9	2.6	.309	.359	4.33
Washington	138	130	2	8	1	1207.2	1403	790	585	56	—	—	51	312	—	300	22	2	10.5	2.2	2.3	.291	.341	4.36
AL Total	1106	954	59	160	13	9733.0	10451	5407	3861	258	—	—	378	2815	—	2744	210	10	9.7	2.5	2.6	.275	.331	3.57
AL Avg Team	138	119	7	20	2	1216.0	1306	676	483	32	—	—	47	352	—	343	26	1	9.7	2.5	2.6	.275	.331	3.57

Team Fielding

Team	G	PO	A	E	TC	DP	PB	Pct
Chicago	138	3659	1850	257	5766	125	23	.955
Boston	138	3710	1877	263	5850	101	24	.955
St. Louis	140	3728	1890	274	5892	122	27	.953
Philadelphia	137	3646	1819	270	5735	75	13	.953
Cleveland	137	3609	1877	287	5773	96	29	.950
Washington	138	3622	1827	316	5765	70	22	.945
Detroit	137	3523	1854	332	5709	111	15	.942
Baltimore	141	3622	1763	357	5742	109	26	.938
AL Total	1106	29119	14757	2356	46232	809	179	.949

Team vs. Team Records

	Bal	Bos	ChA	Cle	Det	Phi	StL	Was	Won
Bal	—	4	8	9	10	6	2	11	50
Bos	16	—	12	6	11	9	15	8	77
ChA	11	8	—	12	12	10	9	12	74
Cle	11	14	7	—	8	8	9	12	69
Det	10	7	7	10	—	4	5	9	52
Phi	13	11	10	12	16	—	9	12	83
StL	18	5	9	10	15	10	—	11	78
Was	9	11	7	8	11	6	9	—	61
Lost	88	60	60	67	83	53	58	75	

1902 American League Batting Leaders

Games			At-Bats			Runs			Hits			Doubles			Triples		
B. McCormick, StL		139	F. Parent, Bos		567	T. Hartsel, Phi		109	C. Hickman, 2tm		193	H. Davis, Phi		43	J. Williams, Bal		21
F. Parent, Bos		138	B. Freeman, Bos		564	D. Fultz, Phi		109	L. Cross, Phi		191	E. Delahanty, Was		43	B. Freeman, Bos		19
C. LaChance, Bos		138	H. Davis, Phi		561	S. Strang, ChA		108	B. Bradley, Cle		187	B. Bradley, Cle		39	H. Ferris, Bos		14
B. Freeman, Bos		138	L. Cross, Phi		559	B. Bradley, Cle		104	E. Delahanty, Was		178	L. Cross, Phi		39	E. Delahanty, Was		14
J. Burkett, StL		138	J. Burkett, StL		553	E. Delahanty, Was		103	B. Freeman, Bos		174	B. Freeman, Bos		38	C. Hickman, 2tm		13

Home Runs			Total Bases			Runs Batted In			Walks			Intentional Walks	Strikeouts
S. Seybold, Phi		16	C. Hickman, 2tm		288	B. Freeman, Bos		121	T. Hartsel, Phi		87	Statistic unavailable	Statistic unavailable
B. Bradley, Cle		11	B. Bradley, Cle		283	C. Hickman, 2tm		110	S. Strang, ChA		76		
C. Hickman, 2tm		11	B. Freeman, Bos		283	L. Cross, Phi		108	J. Barrett, Det		74		
B. Freeman, Bos		11	E. Delahanty, Was		279	S. Seybold, Phi		97	J. Burkett, StL		71		
E. Delahanty, Was		10	S. Seybold, Phi		264	2 tied with		93	G. Davis, ChA		65		

Hit By Pitch			Sac Hits			Sac Flies	Stolen Bases			Caught Stealing	GDP
D. Harley, Det		12	D. Fultz, Phi		35	Statistic unavailable	T. Hartsel, Phi		47	Statistic unavailable	Statistic unavailable
K. Elberfeld, Det		11	D. Green, ChA		24		S. Mertes, ChA		46		
B. Gilbert, Bal		9	F. Isbell, ChA		23		D. Fultz, Phi		44		
D. Padden, StL		9	M. Cross, Phi		22		3 tied with		38		
3 tied with		8	3 tied with		20						

Runs Created			Runs Created/27 Outs			Batting Average			On-Base Percentage			Slugging Percentage			OBP+Slugging		
E. Delahanty, Was		130	E. Delahanty, Was		11.35	E. Delahanty, Was		.376	E. Delahanty, Was		.453	E. Delahanty, Was		.590	E. Delahanty, Was		1.043
T. Hartsel, Phi		115	S. Seybold, Phi		7.90	C. Hickman, 2tm		.361	P. Dougherty, Bos		.407	C. Hickman, 2tm		.539	C. Hickman, 2tm		.926
S. Seybold, Phi		112	C. Hickman, 2tm		7.89	P. Dougherty, Bos		.342	J. Barrett, Det		.397	B. Bradley, Cle		.515	B. Bradley, Cle		.890
C. Hickman, 2tm		107	T. Hartsel, Phi		7.52	L. Cross, Phi		.342	K. Selbach, Bal		.393	S. Seybold, Phi		.506	S. Seybold, Phi		.881
L. Cross, Phi		107	L. Cross, Phi		7.35	B. Bradley, Cle		.340	F. Jones, ChA		.390	B. Freeman, Bos		.502	J. Williams, Bal		.861

1902 American League Pitching Leaders

Wins			Losses			Winning Percentage			Games			Games Started			Complete Games		
C. Young, Bos		32	B. Dinneen, Bos		21	B. Bernhard, 2tm		.783	C. Young, Bos		45	C. Young, Bos		43	C. Young, Bos		41
R. Waddell, Phi		24	S. Wiltse, 2tm		19	R. Waddell, Phi		.774	B. Dinneen, Bos		42	B. Dinneen, Bos		42	B. Dinneen, Bos		39
J. Powell, StL		22	A. Orth, Was		18	C. Young, Bos		.744	J. Powell, StL		42	J. Powell, StL		39	J. Powell, StL		36
R. Donahue, StL		22	W. Mercer, Det		18	B. Husting, 2tm		.700	S. Wiltse, 2tm		38	A. Orth, Was		37	A. Orth, Was		36
B. Dinneen, Bos		21	3 tied with		17	R. Donahue, StL		.667	A. Orth, Was		38	S. Wiltse, 2tm		35	2 tied with		33

Shutouts			Saves			Games Finished			Batters Faced	Innings Pitched			Hits Allowed		
A. Joss, Cle		5	J. Powell, StL		3	C. Shields, 2tm		8	Statistic unavailable	C. Young, Bos		384.2	S. Wiltse, 2tm		397
E. Moore, Cle		4	W. Sudhoff, StL		2	6 tied with		5		B. Dinneen, Bos		371.1	A. Orth, Was		367
W. Mercer, Det		4	12 tied with		1					J. Powell, StL		328.1	C. Young, Bos		350
5 tied with		3								A. Orth, Was		324.0	B. Dinneen, Bos		348
										R. Donahue, StL		316.1	B. Carrick, Was		344

Home Runs Allowed			Walks			Walks/9 Innings			Strikeouts			Strikeouts/9 Innings			Strikeout/Walk Ratio		
A. Orth, Was		18	E. Moore, Cle		101	A. Orth, Was		1.1	R. Waddell, Phi		210	R. Waddell, Phi		6.8	R. Waddell, Phi		3.28
J. Townsend, Was		12	B. Husting, 2tm		99	C. Young, Bos		1.2	C. Young, Bos		160	J. Powell, StL		3.8	C. Young, Bos		3.02
J. Powell, StL		12	B. Dinneen, Bos		99	B. Bernhard, 2tm		1.5	J. Powell, StL		137	C. Young, Bos		3.7	A. Orth, Was		1.90
3 tied with		11	G. Mullin, Det		95	E. Siever, Det		1.5	B. Dinneen, Bos		136	A. Joss, Cle		3.5	E. Plank, Phi		1.75
			J. Powell, StL		93	E. Plank, Phi		1.8	E. Plank, Phi		107	W. Piatt, ChA		3.5	B. Bernhard, 2tm		1.57

Earned Run Average			Component ERA			Hit Batsmen			Wild Pitches			Opponent Average			Opponent OBP		
E. Siever, Det		1.91	B. Bernhard, 2tm		1.69	E. Plank, Phi		18	G. Mullin, Det		13	B. Bernhard, 2tm		.216	B. Bernhard, 2tm		.254
R. Waddell, Phi		2.05	E. Siever, Det		2.03	C. Griffith, ChA		16	R. Patterson, ChA		11	R. Waddell, Phi		.223	E. Siever, Det		.273
B. Bernhard, 2tm		2.15	R. Waddell, Phi		2.11	A. Joss, Cle		13	A. Joss, Cle		11	A. Joss, Cle		.224	R. Waddell, Phi		.276
C. Young, Bos		2.15	C. Young, Bos		2.23	J. Townsend, Was		13	S. Wiltse, 2tm		10	E. Siever, Det		.237	C. Young, Bos		.277
N. Garvin, ChA		2.21	A. Joss, Cle		2.24	C. Young, Bos		13	J. Townsend, Was		10	G. Winter, Bos		.238	A. Joss, Cle		.286

1902 American League Miscellaneous

Managers		
Baltimore	John McGraw	26-31
	Wilbert Robinson	24-57
Boston	Jimmy Collins	77-60
Chicago	Clark Griffith	74-60
Cleveland	Bill Armour	69-67
Detroit	Frank Dwyer	52-83
Philadelphia	Connie Mack	83-53
St. Louis	Jimmy McAleer	78-58
Washington	Tom Loftus	61-75

Awards	
STATS Most Valuable Player	Ed Delahanty, of, Was
STATS Cy Young	Cy Young, Bos
STATS Rookie of the Year	P. Dougherty, of, Bos
STATS Manager of the Year	Connie Mack, Phi

STATS All-Star Team

C	Ossee Schreckengost, 2tm	.327	2	52
1B	Charlie Hickman, 2tm	.361	11	110
2B	Nap Lajoie, 2tm	.378	7	65
3B	Lave Cross, Phi	.342	0	108
SS	George Davis, ChA	.299	3	93
OF	Ed Delahanty, Was	.376	10	93
OF	Buck Freeman, Bos	.309	11	121
OF	Socks Seybold, Phi	.316	16	97
P	Bill Bernhard, 2tm	18-5	2.15	58 K
P	Red Donahue, StL	22-11	2.76	63 K
P	Rube Waddell, Phi	24-7	2.05	210 K
P	Cy Young, Bos	32-11	2.15	160 K

Postseason

None

Outstanding Performances

No-Hitters
Nixey Callahan, ChA vs. Det on September 20

Seasons: Standings, Leaders

1902 National League Standings

Team	Overall					Home Games						Road Games						Park Index		Record by Month					
	W	L	Pct	GB	DIF	W	L	R	OR	HR	OHR	W	L	R	OR	HR	OHR	Run	HR	M/A	May	June	July	Aug	S/O
Pittsburgh	103	36	.741	—	170	56	15	410	207	9	2	47	21	365	233	9	2	99	96	8-2	22-4	11-6	20-8	22-8	20-8
Brooklyn	75	63	.543	27.5	2	45	23	277	210	9	2	30	40	287	309	10	8	84	63	5-7	12-12	16-8	16-13	11-13	15-10
Boston	73	64	.533	29.0	0	42	27	283	230	13	11	31	37	289	286	1	5	88	394	5-6	10-13	13-8	14-10	13-15	18-12
Cincinnati	70	70	.500	33.5	0	35	35	353	305	11	8	35	35	280	261	7	7	122	136	3-7	10-15	9-10	15-12	17-12	16-14
Chicago	68	69	.496	34.0	6	31	38	228	249	1	3	37	31	302	252	5	4	85	44	6-3	17-9	8-12	13-17	11-14	13-14
St. Louis	56	78	.418	44.5	0	28	38	262	336	3	6	28	40	255	359	7	10	100	55	2-7	11-14	8-14	17-11	10-15	8-17
Philadelphia	56	81	.409	46.0	0	29	39	264	351	1	6	27	42	220	298	4	6	120	71	6-5	8-15	14-11	7-19	9-14	12-17
New York	48	88	.353	53.5	1	24	44	214	297	5	6	24	44	187	293	1	10	106	100	7-5	8-16	5-15	7-19	12-14	9-19

Clinch Date—Pittsburgh 9/03.

Team Batting

Team	G	AB	R	OR	H	2B	3B	HR	TB	RBI	TBB	IBB	SO	HBP	SH	SF	SB	CS	SB%	GDP	Avg	OBP	Slg
Pittsburgh	142	4926	775	440	1410	189	95	18	1843	660	372	—	446	64	118	—	222	—	—	—	.286	.344	.374
Cincinnati	141	4908	633	566	1383	188	77	18	1779	531	297	—	465	39	98	—	131	—	—	—	.282	.328	.362
Boston	142	4728	572	516	1178	142	39	14	1440	452	398	—	481	43	131	—	189	—	—	—	.249	.313	.305
Brooklyn	141	4845	564	519	1242	147	49	19	1544	476	319	—	489	60	118	—	145	—	—	—	.256	.310	.319
Chicago	141	4802	530	501	1200	131	40	6	1429	423	353	—	565	44	153	—	222	—	—	—	.250	.307	.298
St. Louis	140	4751	517	695	1226	116	37	10	1446	402	273	—	438	52	108	—	158	—	—	—	.258	.306	.304
Philadelphia	138	4615	484	649	1139	110	43	5	1350	389	356	—	481	31	122	—	108	—	—	—	.247	.305	.293
New York	139	4571	401	590	1088	147	34	6	1321	337	252	—	530	35	106	—	187	—	—	—	.238	.283	.289
NL Total	1124	38146	4476	4476	9866	1170	414	96	12152	3670	2620	—	3895	368	954	—	1362	—	—	—	.259	.312	.319
NL Avg Team	141	4768	560	560	1233	146	52	12	1519	459	328	—	487	46	119	—	170	—	—	—	.259	.312	.319

Team Pitching

Team	G	CG	ShO	Rel	Sv	IP	H	R	ER	HR	SH	SF	HB	TBB	IBB	SO	WP	Bk	H/9	SO/9	BB/9	OAvg	OOBP	ERA
Chicago	141	132	17	9	2	1275.1	1235	501	313	7	—	—	44	279	—	437	26	1	8.7	3.1	2.0	.254	.301	2.21
Pittsburgh	142	131	21	10	3	1264.2	1142	440	323	4	—	—	61	250	—	564	19	1	8.1	4.0	1.8	.241	.288	2.30
Boston	142	124	14	18	4	1259.2	1233	516	365	16	—	—	46	372	—	523	29	0	8.8	3.7	2.7	.256	.316	2.61
Cincinnati	141	130	9	13	1	1239.0	1228	566	368	15	—	—	55	352	—	430	23	0	8.9	3.1	2.6	.259	.317	2.67
Brooklyn	141	131	14	10	3	1256.0	1113	519	376	10	—	—	37	363	—	536	27	0	8.0	3.8	2.6	.238	.298	2.69
New York	139	118	11	21	1	1226.1	1193	590	384	16	—	—	54	332	—	501	32	2	8.8	3.7	2.4	.255	.312	2.82
St. Louis	140	112	7	29	4	1227.2	1399	695	474	16	—	—	37	338	—	400	19	0	10.3	2.9	2.5	.287	.337	3.47
Philadelphia	138	118	8	21	3	1211.0	1323	649	471	16	—	—	57	334	—	504	31	3	9.8	3.7	2.5	.278	.333	3.50
NL Total	1124	996	101	131	21	9959.2	9866	4476	3074	96	—	—	391	2620	—	3895	206	7	8.9	3.5	2.4	.259	.313	2.78
NL Avg Team	141	125	13	16	3	1244.2	1233	560	384	12	—	—	49	328	—	487	26	1	8.9	3.5	2.4	.259	.313	2.78

Team Fielding

Team	G	PO	A	E	TC	DP	PB	Pct
Boston	142	3775	1812	240	5827	90	14	.959
Pittsburgh	142	3790	1791	247	5828	87	20	.958
Brooklyn	141	3766	1717	275	5758	79	20	.952
Philadelphia	138	3628	1764	305	5697	81	16	.946
Chicago	141	3823	1923	327	6073	111	20	.946
Cincinnati	141	3703	1853	322	5878	118	27	.945
St. Louis	140	3677	1939	336	5952	107	17	.944
New York	139	3675	1814	330	5819	104	26	.943
NL Total	1124	29837	14613	2382	46832	777	160	.949

Team vs. Team Records

	Bos	Bro	ChN	Cin	NYG	Phi	Pit	StL	Won
Bos	—	8	11	11	16	11	6	10	73
Bro	12	—	12	12	10	13	6	10	75
ChN	9	8	—	12	10	10	7	12	68
Cin	9	8	8	—	14	13	5	13	70
NYG	3	10	10	6	—	6	6	7	48
Phi	9	6	10	7	12	—	2	10	56
Pit	14	14	13	15	13	18	—	16	103
StL	8	9	5	13	13	10	4	—	56
Lost	64	63	69	70	88	81	36	78	

1902 National League Batting Leaders

Games		At-Bats		Runs		Hits		Doubles		Triples	
C. Dolan, Bro	141	C. Dolan, Bro	592	H. Wagner, Pit	105	G. Beaumont, Pit	193	H. Wagner, Pit	30	S. Crawford, Cin	22
S. Crawford, Cin	140	J. Farrell, StL	565	F. Clarke, Pit	103	W. Keeler, Bro	186	F. Clarke, Pit	27	T. Leach, Pit	22
E. Gremminger, Bos	140	W. Keeler, Bro	559	G. Beaumont, Pit	100	S. Crawford, Cin	185	D. Cooley, Bos	26	H. Wagner, Pit	16
6 tied with	138	S. Crawford, Cin	555	T. Leach, Pit	97	H. Wagner, Pit	176	B. Dahlen, Bro	25	F. Clarke, Pit	14
		D. Cooley, Bos	548	S. Crawford, Cin	92	J. Beckley, Cin	175	J. Beckley, Cin	23	E. Gremminger, Bos	12

Home Runs		Total Bases		Runs Batted In		Walks		Intentional Walks	Strikeouts
T. Leach, Pit	6	S. Crawford, Cin	256	H. Wagner, Pit	91	R. Thomas, Phi	107	Statistic unavailable	Statistic unavailable
J. Beckley, Cin	5	H. Wagner, Pit	247	T. Leach, Pit	85	B. Lush, StL	76		
J. Sheckard, Bro	4	J. Beckley, Cin	227	S. Crawford, Cin	78	F. Tenney, Bos	73		
T. McCreery, Bro	4	G. Beaumont, Pit	226	B. Dahlen, Bro	74	J. Sheckard, Bro	57		
8 tied with	3	T. Leach, Pit	219	2 tied with	69	2 tied with	53		

Hit By Pitch		Sac Hits		Sac Flies	Stolen Bases		Caught Stealing	GDP
H. Wagner, Pit	14	F. Tenney, Bos	29	Statistic unavailable	H. Wagner, Pit	43	Statistic unavailable	Statistic unavailable
F. Clarke, Pit	14	J. Dobbs, 2tm	26		J. Slagle, ChN	40		
P. Carney, Bos	12	DeMontreville, Bos	26		P. Donovan, StL	34		
C. Irwin, Bro	11	W. Keeler, Bro	25		G. Beaumont, Pit	33		
H. Jennings, Phi	11	2 tied with	21		H. Smith, NYG	32		

Runs Created		Runs Created/27 Outs		Batting Average		On-Base Percentage		Slugging Percentage		OBP+Slugging	
H. Wagner, Pit	117	H. Wagner, Pit	8.33	G. Beaumont, Pit	.357	R. Thomas, Phi	.414	H. Wagner, Pit	.463	H. Wagner, Pit	.857
G. Beaumont, Pit	106	F. Clarke, Pit	8.22	S. Crawford, Cin	.333	F. Tenney, Bos	.409	S. Crawford, Cin	.461	F. Clarke, Pit	.850
S. Crawford, Cin	103	G. Beaumont, Pit	7.61	W. Keeler, Bro	.333	G. Beaumont, Pit	.404	F. Clarke, Pit	.449	S. Crawford, Cin	.848
F. Clarke, Pit	101	S. Crawford, Cin	7.14	H. Wagner, Pit	.330	F. Clarke, Pit	.401	J. Beckley, Cin	.428	G. Beaumont, Pit	.822
F. Tenney, Bos	93	F. Tenney, Bos	6.66	J. Beckley, Cin	.330	H. Wagner, Pit	.394	T. Leach, Pit	.426	J. Beckley, Cin	.804

1902 National League Pitching Leaders

Wins		Losses		Winning Percentage		Games		Games Started		Complete Games	
J. Chesbro, Pit	28	S. Yerkes, StL	21	J. Chesbro, Pit	.824	V. Willis, Bos	51	V. Willis, Bos	46	V. Willis, Bos	45
T. Pittinger, Bos	27	D. White, Phi	20	E. Doheny, Pit	.800	T. Pittinger, Bos	46	T. Pittinger, Bos	40	T. Pittinger, Bos	36
V. Willis, Bos	27	V. Willis, Bos	20	J. Tannehill, Pit	.769	S. Yerkes, StL	39	S. Yerkes, StL	37	N. Hahn, Cin	35
N. Hahn, Cin	23	R. Evans, 2tm	19	E. Poole, 2tm	.750	5 tied with	36	N. Hahn, Cin	36	D. White, Phi	34
J. Taylor, ChN	23	H. Iburg, Phi	18	S. Leever, Pit	.696			D. White, Phi	35	J. Taylor, ChN	33

Shutouts		Saves		Games Finished		Batters Faced	Innings Pitched		Hits Allowed	
C. Mathewson, NYG	8	V. Willis, Bos	3	R. Evans, 2tm	8	Statistic unavailable	V. Willis, Bos	410.0	V. Willis, Bos	372
J. Chesbro, Pit	8	S. Leever, Pit	2	B. Wicker, StL	6		T. Pittinger, Bos	389.1	T. Pittinger, Bos	360
T. Pittinger, Bos	7	11 tied with	1	E. Murphy, StL	6		J. Taylor, ChN	324.2	S. Yerkes, StL	341
J. Taylor, ChN	7			B. Duggleby, Phi	6		N. Hahn, Cin	321.0	M. O'Neill, StL	297
N. Hahn, Cin	6			2 tied with	5		D. White, Phi	306.0	H. Iburg, Phi	286

Home Runs Allowed		Walks		Walks/9 Innings		Strikeouts		Strikeouts/9 Innings		Strikeout/Walk Ratio	
E. Murphy, StL	7	T. Pittinger, Bos	128	D. Phillippe, Pit	0.9	V. Willis, Bos	225	D. White, Phi	5.4	D. Phillippe, Pit	4.69
V. Willis, Bos	6	W. Donovan, Bro	111	J. Tannehill, Pit	1.0	D. White, Phi	185	C. Mathewson, NYG	5.2	J. Tannehill, Pit	4.00
4 tied with	4	V. Willis, Bos	101	J. Menefee, ChN	1.2	T. Pittinger, Bos	174	W. Donovan, Bro	5.1	S. Leever, Pit	2.77
		R. Evans, 2tm	91	J. Taylor, ChN	1.2	W. Donovan, Bro	170	V. Willis, Bos	4.9	D. White, Phi	2.57
		D. Newton, Bro	87	S. Leever, Pit	1.3	C. Mathewson, NYG	159	B. Wicker, StL	4.6	N. Hahn, Cin	2.45

Earned Run Average		Component ERA		Hit Batsmen		Wild Pitches		Opponent Average		Opponent OBP	
J. Taylor, ChN	1.33	J. Taylor, ChN	1.73	J. Chesbro, Pit	21	C. Mathewson, NYG	16	J. McGinnity, NYG	.212	J. Taylor, ChN	.254
N. Hahn, Cin	1.77	J. McGinnity, NYG	1.87	H. Thielman, 2tm	19	V. Willis, Bos	13	D. Newton, Bro	.217	J. McGinnity, NYG	.265
J. Tannehill, Pit	1.95	J. Tannehill, Pit	1.93	T. Pittinger, Bos	16	C. Fraser, Phi	11	J. Taylor, ChN	.221	J. Tannehill, Pit	.266
C. Lundgren, ChN	1.97	N. Hahn, Cin	2.07	3 tied with	15	J. Taylor, ChN	9	W. Donovan, Bro	.226	N. Hahn, Cin	.270
D. Phillippe, Pit	2.05	D. Newton, Bro	2.18			J. Hughes, Bro	9	J. Chesbro, Pit	.227	D. Phillippe, Pit	.272

1902 National League Miscellaneous

Managers		
Boston	Al Buckenberger	73-64
Brooklyn	Ned Hanlon	75-63
Chicago	Frank Selee	68-69
Cincinnati	Bid McPhee	27-37
	Frank Bancroft	9-7
	Joe Kelley	34-26
New York	Horace Fogel	18-23
	Heinie Smith	5-27
	John McGraw	25-38
Philadelphia	Bill Shettsline	56-81
Pittsburgh	Fred Clarke	103-36
St. Louis	Patsy Donovan	56-78

Awards	
STATS Most Valuable Player	Honus Wagner, of, Pit
STATS Cy Young	Jack Taylor, ChN
STATS Rookie of the Year	Homer Smoot, of, StL
STATS Manager of the Year	Fred Clarke, Pit

STATS All-Star Team

C	Johnny Kling, ChN	.285	0	57
1B	Jake Beckley, Cin	.330	5	69
2B	Heinie Peitz, Cin	.315	1	60
3B	Tommy Leach, Pit	.278	6	85
SS	Bill Dahlen, Bro	.264	2	74
OF	Ginger Beaumont, Pit	.357	0	67
OF	Fred Clarke, Pit	.316	2	53
OF	Honus Wagner, Pit	.330	3	91
P	Jack Chesbro, Pit	28-6	2.17	136 K
P	Noodles Hahn, Cin	23-12	1.77	142 K
P	Jesse Tannehill, Pit	20-6	1.95	100 K
P	Jack Taylor, ChN	23-11	1.33	83 K

Postseason
None

Outstanding Performances
None

1903 American League Standings

Team	W	L	Pct	GB	DIF	W	L	R	OR	HR	OHR	W	L	R	OR	HR	OHR	Run	HR	M/A	May	June	July	Aug	S/O
	Overall					**Home Games**						**Road Games**						**Park Index**		**Record by Month**					
Boston	91	47	.659	—	118	49	20	395	266	35	12	42	27	313	238	13	11	120	196	4-6	15-9	19-7	16-9	18-9	19-7
Philadelphia	75	60	.556	14.5	10	44	21	323	238	17	8	31	39	274	281	15	12	109	100	6-4	13-12	16-9	17-9	8-17	15-9
Cleveland	77	63	.550	15.0	0	49	25	364	256	12	5	28	38	275	323	19	11	92	51	2-3	15-12	14-11	13-13	19-11	14-13
New York	72	62	.537	17.0	0	41	26	301	269	10	6	31	36	278	304	8	13	98	76	4-4	11-14	10-10	14-12	14-12	19-10
Detroit	65	71	.478	25.0	13	37	28	279	222	5	7	28	43	288	317	7	12	90	69	5-1	12-16	9-12	15-10	14-15	10-17
St. Louis	65	74	.468	26.5	0	38	32	250	228	7	15	27	42	250	297	5	11	86	136	1-4	16-10	9-13	9-18	17-14	13-15
Chicago	60	77	.438	30.5	32	41	28	284	244	5	2	19	49	232	369	2	21	87	23	3-3	16-12	10-11	8-18	14-17	9-16
Washington	43	94	.314	47.5	1	29	40	275	349	15	24	14	54	162	342	2	14	122	240	4-4	6-19	5-19	12-15	9-18	7-19

Clinch Date—Boston 9/16.

Team Batting

Team	G	AB	R	OR	H	2B	3B	HR	TB	RBI	TBB	IBB	SO	HBP	SH	SF	SB	CS	SB%	GDP	Avg	OBP	Slg
Boston	141	4919	708	504	1336	222	113	48	1928	609	262	—	561	36	147	—	141	—	—	—	.272	.313	.392
Cleveland	140	4773	639	579	1265	231	95	31	1779	550	259	—	595	40	151	—	175	—	—	—	.265	.308	.373
Philadelphia	137	4673	597	519	1236	227	68	32	1695	502	268	—	513	32	101	—	157	—	—	—	.264	.309	.363
New York	136	4565	579	573	1136	193	62	18	1507	474	332	—	465	65	129	—	160	—	—	—	.249	.309	.330
Detroit	137	4582	567	539	1229	162	91	12	1609	451	292	—	526	45	170	—	128	—	—	—	.268	.318	.351
Chicago	138	4670	516	613	1152	176	49	14	1468	436	325	—	537	38	142	—	180	—	—	—	.247	.301	.314
St. Louis	139	4639	500	525	1133	166	68	12	1471	408	271	—	539	26	111	—	101	—	—	—	.244	.290	.317
Washington	140	4613	437	691	1066	172	72	17	1433	372	257	—	463	39	81	—	131	—	—	—	.231	.277	.311
AL Total	1108	37434	4543	4543	9553	1549	618	184	12890	3802	2266	—	4199	321	1032	—	1173	—	—	—	.255	.303	.344
AL Avg Team	139	4679	568	568	1194	194	77	23	1611	475	283	—	525	40	129	—	147	—	—	—	.255	.303	.344

Team Pitching

Team	G	CG	ShO	Rel	Sv	IP	H	R	ER	HR	SH	SF	HB	TBB	IBB	SO	WP	Bk	H/9	SO/9	BB/9	OAvg	OOBP	ERA
Boston	141	123	20	18	4	1255.0	1142	504	358	23	54	—	36	269	—	579	18	1	8.2	4.2	1.9	.244	.290	2.57
Cleveland	140	125	20	15	1	1243.2	1161	579	377	16	127	—	35	271	—	521	27	0	8.4	3.8	2.0	.245	.291	2.73
Detroit	137	123	15	15	2	1196.1	1169	539	366	19	116	—	29	336	—	554	21	0	8.8	4.2	2.5	.256	.311	2.75
St. Louis	139	124	12	16	3	1222.1	1220	525	376	26	125	—	37	237	—	511	22	0	8.8	3.8	1.7	.258	.299	2.77
Philadelphia	137	112	10	28	1	1207.1	1124	519	400	20	94	—	71	315	—	728	38	2	8.4	5.4	2.3	.249	.309	2.98
Chicago	138	114	9	26	4	1235.0	1233	613	414	23	133	—	53	287	—	391	22	1	9.0	2.8	2.1	.260	.309	3.02
New York	136	111	7	26	2	1201.1	1171	573	411	19	117	—	41	245	—	463	22	1	8.8	3.5	1.8	.253	.297	3.08
Washington	140	122	6	18	3	1223.2	1333	691	519	38	136	—	41	306	—	452	25	1	9.8	3.3	2.3	.277	.326	3.82
AL Total	1108	954	99	162	20	9784.2	9553	4543	3221	184	889	—	343	2266	—	4199	195	6	8.8	3.9	2.1	.255	.304	2.96
AL Avg Team	139	119	12	20	3	1223.2	1194	568	403	23	111	—	43	283	—	525	24	1	8.8	3.9	2.1	.255	.304	2.96

Team Fielding

Team	G	PO	A	E	TC	DP	PB	Pct
Philadelphia	137	3618	1613	217	5448	66	20	.960
Boston	141	3761	1832	239	5832	86	26	.959
Washington	140	3668	1772	260	5700	86	12	.954
St. Louis	139	3661	1827	268	5756	94	12	.953
New York	136	3602	1785	264	5651	87	21	.953
Detroit	137	3586	1710	281	5577	82	19	.950
Chicago	138	3698	1758	297	5845	85	30	.949
Cleveland	140	3730	1911	322	5963	99	24	.946
AL Total	1108	29324	14300	2148	45772	685	164	.953

Team vs. Team Records

	Bos	ChA	Cle	Det	NYA	Phi	StL	Was	Won
Bos	—	14	12	10	13	13	14	15	91
ChA	6	—	10	10	7	6	9	12	60
Cle	8	10	—	9	14	9	11	16	77
Det	9	9	11	—	10	11	6	9	65
NYA	7	11	6	9	—	10	15	14	72
Phi	6	14	11	9	8	—	11	16	75
StL	6	11	9	14	5	8	—	12	65
Was	5	8	4	10	5	3	8	—	43
Lost	47	77	63	71	62	60	74	94	

Seasons: Standings, Leaders

1903 American League Batting Leaders

Games			At-Bats			Runs			Hits			Doubles			Triples		
H. Ferris, Bos	141		P. Dougherty, Bos	590		P. Dougherty, Bos	106		P. Dougherty, Bos	195		S. Seybold, Phi	45		S. Crawford, Det	25	
C. LaChance, Bos	141		H. Bay, Cle	579		B. Bradley, Cle	101		S. Crawford, Det	184		N. Lajoie, Cle	41		B. Bradley, Cle	22	
B. Freeman, Bos	141		B. Freeman, Bos	567		J. Barrett, Det	95		F. Parent, Bos	170		B. Freeman, Bos	39		B. Freeman, Bos	20	
3 tied with	140		F. Parent, Bos	560		W. Keeler, NYA	95		H. Bay, Cle	169		B. Bradley, Cle	36		F. Parent, Bos	17	
			L. Cross, Phi	559		H. Bay, Cle	94		B. Bradley, Cle	168		J. Anderson, StL	34		J. Collins, Bos	17	

Home Runs			Total Bases			Runs Batted In			Walks			Intentional Walks			Strikeouts		
B. Freeman, Bos	13		B. Freeman, Bos	281		B. Freeman, Bos	104		J. Barrett, Det	74		Statistic unavailable			Statistic unavailable		
C. Hickman, Cle	12		S. Crawford, Det	269		C. Hickman, Cle	97		B. Lush, Det	70							
H. Ferris, Bos	9		B. Bradley, Cle	266		N. Lajoie, Cle	93		O. Pickering, Phi	53							
S. Seybold, Phi	8		N. Lajoie, Cle	251		L. Cross, Phi	90		J. Burkett, StL	52							
2 tied with	7		P. Dougherty, Bos	250		S. Crawford, Det	89		E. Flick, Cle	51							

Hit By Pitch			Sac Hits			Sac Flies			Stolen Bases			Caught Stealing			GDP		
K. Elberfeld, 2tm	15		B. Lush, Det	34		Statistic unavailable			H. Bay, Cle	45		Statistic unavailable			Statistic unavailable		
W. Keeler, NYA	13		W. Keeler, NYA	27					O. Pickering, Phi	40							
J. Ganzel, NYA	12		J. Gochnauer, Cle	26					P. Dougherty, Bos	35							
J. Yeager, Det	9		3 tied with	25					D. Holmes, 2tm	35							
2 tied with	8								W. Conroy, NYA	33							

Runs Created			Runs Created/27 Outs			Batting Average			On-Base Percentage			Slugging Percentage			OBP+Slugging		
P. Dougherty, Bos	109		N. Lajoie, Cle	7.88		N. Lajoie, Cle	.344		J. Barrett, Det	.407		N. Lajoie, Cle	.518		N. Lajoie, Cle	.896	
B. Freeman, Bos	103		P. Dougherty, Bos	6.89		S. Crawford, Det	.335		N. Lajoie, Cle	.379		B. Bradley, Cle	.496		S. Crawford, Det	.855	
S. Crawford, Det	100		J. Barrett, Det	6.80		P. Dougherty, Bos	.331		B. Lush, Det	.379		B. Freeman, Bos	.496		B. Bradley, Cle	.844	
B. Bradley, Cle	100		S. Crawford, Det	6.67		J. Barrett, Det	.315		D. Green, ChA	.375		S. Crawford, Det	.489		B. Freeman, Bos	.823	
N. Lajoie, Cle	100		B. Bradley, Cle	6.67		B. Bradley, Cle	.313		P. Dougherty, Bos	.372		C. Hickman, Cle	.466		S. Seybold, Phi	.815	

1903 American League Pitching Leaders

Wins			Losses			Winning Percentage			Games			Games Started			Complete Games		
C. Young, Bos	28		P. Flaherty, ChA	25		C. Young, Bos	.757		E. Plank, Phi	43		E. Plank, Phi	40		W. Donovan, Det	34	
E. Plank, Phi	23		C. Patten, Was	22		L. Hughes, Bos	.741		G. Mullin, Det	41		R. Waddell, Phi	38		R. Waddell, Phi	34	
4 tied with	21		A. Orth, Was	22		B. Bernhard, Cle	.700		P. Flaherty, ChA	40		G. Mullin, Det	36		C. Young, Bos	34	
			J. Powell, StL	19		E. Moore, Cle	.679		J. Chesbro, NYA	40		D. White, ChA	36		3 tied with	33	
			H. Wilson, Was	18		B. Dinneen, Bos	.618		C. Young, Bos	40		J. Chesbro, NYA	36				

Shutouts			Saves			Games Finished			Batters Faced			Innings Pitched			Hits Allowed		
C. Young, Bos	7		G. Mullin, Det	2		H. Howell, NYA	10		E. Plank, Phi	1378		C. Young, Bos	341.2		P. Flaherty, ChA	338	
G. Mullin, Det	6		B. Dinneen, Bos	2		W. Henley, Phi	7		G. Mullin, Det	1354		E. Plank, Phi	336.0		A. Orth, Was	326	
B. Dinneen, Bos	6		J. Powell, StL	2		J. Townsend, Was	7		J. Chesbro, NYA	1354		J. Chesbro, NYA	324.2		E. Plank, Phi	317	
L. Hughes, Bos	5		A. Orth, Was	2		F. Owen, ChA	6		C. Young, Bos	1335		R. Waddell, Phi	324.0		C. Patten, Was	313	
W. Sudhoff, StL	5		C. Young, Bos	2		D. Dunkle, 2tm	6		R. Waddell, Phi	1307		G. Mullin, Det	320.2		J. Chesbro, NYA	300	

Home Runs Allowed			Walks			Walks/9 Innings			Strikeouts			Strikeouts/9 Innings			Strikeout/Walk Ratio		
C. Patten, Was	11		G. Mullin, Det	106		C. Young, Bos	1.0		R. Waddell, Phi	302		R. Waddell, Phi	8.4		C. Young, Bos	4.76	
J. Powell, StL	11		W. Donovan, Det	95		B. Bernhard, Cle	1.1		W. Donovan, Det	187		W. Donovan, Det	5.5		R. Waddell, Phi	3.55	
P. Flaherty, ChA	9		R. Waddell, Phi	85		R. Donahue, 2tm	1.1		E. Plank, Phi	176		E. Moore, Cle	5.4		A. Joss, Cle	3.24	
F. Kitson, Det	8		C. Patten, Was	80		A. Joss, Cle	1.2		C. Young, Bos	176		J. Powell, StL	5.0		J. Tannehill, NYA	3.12	
A. Orth, Was	8		2 tied with	74		J. Tannehill, NYA	1.3		G. Mullin, Det	170		G. Mullin, Det	4.8		J. Powell, StL	2.91	

Earned Run Average			Component ERA			Hit Batsmen			Wild Pitches			Opponent Average			Opponent OBP		
E. Moore, Cle	1.74		A. Joss, Cle	1.70		C. Bender, Phi	25		R. Waddell, Phi	9		E. Moore, Cle	.214		A. Joss, Cle	.250	
C. Young, Bos	2.08		E. Moore, Cle	1.83		E. Plank, Phi	23		C. Wright, 2tm	8		A. Joss, Cle	.217		C. Young, Bos	.257	
B. Bernhard, Cle	2.12		C. Young, Bos	1.89		D. White, ChA	14		E. Plank, Phi	8		W. Donovan, Det	.222		E. Moore, Cle	.267	
D. White, ChA	2.13		B. Bernhard, Cle	2.02		P. Flaherty, ChA	14		E. Moore, Cle	8		C. Young, Bos	.230		B. Bernhard, Cle	.272	
A. Joss, Cle	2.19		W. Donovan, Det	2.17		W. Henley, Phi	12		4 tied with	7		R. Waddell, Phi	.230		W. Sudhoff, StL	.276	

1903 American League Miscellaneous

Managers		
Boston	Jimmy Collins	91-47
Chicago	Nixey Callahan	60-77
Cleveland	Bill Armour	77-63
Detroit	Ed Barrow	65-71
New York	Clark Griffith	72-62
Philadelphia	Connie Mack	75-60
St. Louis	Jimmy McAleer	65-74
Washington	Tom Loftus	43-94

Awards

STATS Most Valuable Player	Nap Lajoie, 2b, Cle
STATS Cy Young	Cy Young, Bos
STATS Rookie of the Year	Charlie Carr, 1b, Det
STATS Manager of the Year	Jimmy Collins, Bos

STATS All-Star Team

C	Harry Bemis, Cle	.261	1	41
1B	Charlie Hickman, Cle	.295	12	97
2B	Nap Lajoie, Cle	.344	7	93
3B	Bill Bradley, Cle	.313	6	68
SS	Freddy Parent, Bos	.304	4	80
OF	Sam Crawford, Det	.335	4	89
OF	Patsy Dougherty, Bos	.331	4	59
OF	Buck Freeman, Bos	.287	13	104
P	Bill Dinneen, Bos	21-13	2.26	148 K
P	Earl Moore, Cle	19-9	1.74	148 K
P	Eddie Plank, Phi	23-16	2.38	176 K
P	Cy Young, Bos	28-9	2.08	176 K

Postseason

World Series	Boston (AL) 5 vs. Pittsburgh (NL) 3

Outstanding Performances

Cycles

Patsy Dougherty, Bos	on July 29
Bill Bradley, Cle	on September 24

1903 National League Standings

Team	Overall					Home Games						Road Games						Park Index		Record by Month					
	W	L	Pct	GB	DIF	W	L	R	OR	HR	OHR	W	L	R	OR	HR	OHR	Run	HR	M/A	May	June	July	Aug	S/O
Pittsburgh	91	49	.650	—	112	46	24	393	327	18	5	45	25	400	286	16	4	105	115	9-4	16-12	17-3	17-9	18-9	14-12
New York	84	55	.604	6.5	42	41	27	368	296	9	10	43	28	361	271	11	10	110	94	8-3	17-8	12-10	11-15	21-10	15-9
Chicago	82	56	.594	8.0	11	45	28	345	285	2	7	37	28	350	314	7	7	84	57	7-4	21-7	10-13	16-14	13-8	15-10
Cincinnati	74	65	.532	16.5	0	41	35	440	389	12	7	33	30	325	267	16	7	116	68	2-9	15-12	10-7	19-15	14-8	14-14
Brooklyn	70	66	.515	19.0	1	40	33	359	361	8	9	30	33	308	321	7	9	99	92	5-6	15-12	9-9	12-15	14-13	15-11
Boston	58	80	.420	32.0	1	31	35	283	314	11	19	27	45	295	385	14	11	96	131	7-6	9-13	8-16	12-11	10-16	12-18
Philadelphia	49	86	.363	39.5	0	25	33	250	298	9	6	24	53	367	440	3	15	90	111	4-9	7-17	6-14	12-17	4-13	16-16
St. Louis	43	94	.314	46.5	1	22	45	248	393	6	13	21	49	257	402	2	12	102	142	6-7	4-23	11-11	12-15	5-22	5-16

Clinch Date—Pittsburgh 9/18.

Team Batting

Team	G	AB	R	OR	H	2B	3B	HR	TB	RBI	TBB	IBB	SO	HBP	SH	SF	SB	CS	SB%	GDP	Avg	OBP	Slg
Pittsburgh	141	4988	793	613	1429	208	110	34	1959	650	364	—	—	50	109	—	172	—	—	—	.286	.341	.393
Cincinnati	141	4857	765	656	1399	228	92	28	1895	652	403	—	—	30	96	—	144	—	—	—	.288	.346	.390
New York	142	4741	729	567	1290	181	49	20	1629	569	379	—	—	91	185	—	264	—	—	—	.272	.338	.344
Chicago	139	4733	695	599	1300	191	62	9	1642	548	422	—	—	50	118	—	259	—	—	—	.275	.340	.347
Brooklyn	139	4534	667	682	1201	177	56	15	1535	539	522	—	—	53	124	—	273	—	—	—	.265	.348	.339
Philadelphia	139	4781	617	738	1283	186	62	12	1629	500	338	—	—	39	155	—	120	—	—	—	.268	.322	.341
Boston	140	4682	578	699	1145	176	47	25	1490	479	398	—	—	59	99	—	159	—	—	—	.245	.312	.318
St. Louis	139	4689	505	795	1176	138	65	8	1468	403	277	—	—	34	103	—	171	—	—	—	.251	.297	.313
NL Total	1120	38005	5349	5349	10223	1485	543	151	13247	4340	3103	—	—	406	989	—	1562	—	—	—	.269	.331	.349
NL Avg Team	140	4751	669	669	1278	186	68	19	1656	543	388	—	—	51	124	—	195	—	—	—	.269	.331	.349

Team Pitching

Team	G	CG	ShO	Rel	Sv	IP	H	R	ER	HR	SH	SF	HB	TBB	IBB	SO	WP	Bk	H/9	SO/9	BB/9	OAvg	OOBP	ERA
Chicago	139	117	6	24	6	1240.1	1182	599	382	14	—	—	37	354	—	451	23	0	8.6	3.3	2.6	.250	.307	2.77
Pittsburgh	141	117	16	26	5	1251.1	1215	613	405	9	—	—	44	384	—	454	28	1	8.7	3.3	2.8	.255	.316	2.91
New York	142	115	8	29	8	1262.2	1257	567	413	20	—	—	40	371	—	628	32	1	9.0	4.5	2.6	.259	.336	3.07
Cincinnati	141	126	11	16	1	1230.0	1277	656	420	14	—	—	63	378	—	480	24	0	9.3	3.5	2.8	.274	.336	3.07
Boston	140	125	8	15	1	1228.2	1310	699	456	30	—	—	53	460	—	516	39	0	9.6	3.8	3.4	.278	.349	3.34
Brooklyn	139	118	11	23	4	1221.1	1276	682	467	18	—	—	68	377	—	438	35	1	9.4	3.2	2.8	.276	.339	3.44
St. Louis	139	111	4	29	2	1212.1	1353	795	494	25	—	—	44	430	—	419	32	2	10.0	3.1	3.2	.284	.349	3.67
Philadelphia	139	126	5	13	3	1212.1	1347	738	533	21	—	—	62	425	—	381	38	1	10.0	2.8	3.2	.285	.352	3.96
NL Total	1120	955	69	175	30	9859.0	10217	5349	3570	151	—	—	411	3179	—	3767	251	6	9.3	3.4	2.9	.269	.332	3.26
NL Avg Team	140	119	9	22	4	1232.0	1277	669	446	19	—	—	51	397	—	471	31	1	9.3	3.4	2.9	.269	.332	3.26

Team Fielding

Team	G	PO	A	E	TC	DP	PB	Pct
New York	142	3802	1743	287	5832	87	15	.951
Pittsburgh	141	3753	1942	295	5990	100	25	.951
Brooklyn	139	3636	1825	284	5745	98	11	.951
Philadelphia	139	3618	1762	300	5680	76	20	.947
Cincinnati	141	3687	1804	312	5803	84	31	.946
Chicago	139	3695	1775	338	5808	78	9	.942
St. Louis	139	3637	1956	354	5947	111	19	.940
Boston	140	3672	1840	361	5873	89	32	.939
NL Total	1120	29500	14647	2531	46678	723	162	.946

Team vs. Team Records

	Bos	Bro	ChN	Cin	NYG	Phi	Pit	StL	Won
Bos	—	9	7	7	8	10	5	12	58
Bro	11	—	8	10	7	11	9	14	70
ChN	13	12	—	9	8	12	12	16	82
Cin	13	10	11	—	12	12	4	12	74
NYG	12	12	12	8	—	15	10	15	84
Phi	8	8	6	8	5	—	4	10	49
Pit	15	11	8	16	10	16	—	15	91
StL	8	4	4	7	5	10	5	—	43
Lost	80	66	56	65	55	86	49	94	

1903 National League Batting Leaders

Games			At-Bats			Runs			Hits			Doubles			Triples		
G. Browne, NYG		141	G. Beaumont, Pit		613	G. Beaumont, Pit		137	G. Beaumont, Pit		209	H. Steinfeldt, Cin		32	H. Wagner, Pit		19
G. Beaumont, Pit		141	G. Browne, NYG		591	M. Donlin, Cin		110	C. Seymour, Cin		191	S. Mertes, NYG		32	M. Donlin, Cin		18
E. Gremminger, Bos		140	C. Seymour, Cin		558	G. Browne, NYG		105	G. Browne, NYG		185	F. Clarke, Pit		32	T. Leach, Pit		17
3 tied with		139	D. Cooley, Bos		553	J. Slagle, ChN		104	H. Wagner, Pit		182	3 tied with		30	3 tied with		15
			S. Barry, Phi		550	S. Strang, Bro		101	M. Donlin, Cin		174						

Home Runs			Total Bases			Runs Batted In			Walks			Intentional Walks			Strikeouts		
J. Sheckard, Bro		9	G. Beaumont, Pit		272	S. Mertes, NYG		104	R. Thomas, Phi		107	Statistic unavailable			Statistic unavailable		
6 tied with		7	C. Seymour, Cin		267	H. Wagner, Pit		101	B. Dahlen, Bro		82						
			H. Wagner, Pit		265	J. Doyle, Bro		91	J. Slagle, ChN		81						
			M. Donlin, Cin		256	T. Leach, Pit		87	F. Chance, ChN		78						
			J. Sheckard, Bro		245	H. Steinfeldt, Cin		83	2 tied with		75						

Hit By Pitch			Sac Hits			Sac Flies			Stolen Bases			Caught Stealing			GDP		
C. Babb, NYG		22	D. McGann, NYG		30	Statistic unavailable			F. Chance, ChN		67	Statistic unavailable			Statistic unavailable		
B. Gilbert, NYG		20	B. Gilbert, NYG		26				J. Sheckard, Bro		67						
D. Gessler, Bro		12	H. Wolverton, Phi		23				H. Wagner, Pit		46						
D. McGann, NYG		12	4 tied with		20				S. Strang, Bro		46						
2 tied with		11							S. Mertes, NYG		45						

Runs Created			Runs Created/27 Outs			Batting Average			On-Base Percentage			Slugging Percentage			OBP+Slugging		
H. Wagner, Pit		126	R. Bresnahan, NYG		10.52	H. Wagner, Pit		.355	R. Thomas, Phi		.453	F. Clarke, Pit		.532	F. Clarke, Pit		.946
J. Sheckard, Bro		124	F. Chance, ChN		9.97	F. Clarke, Pit		.351	R. Bresnahan, NYG		.443	H. Wagner, Pit		.518	M. Donlin, Cin		.936
M. Donlin, Cin		120	H. Wagner, Pit		9.58	M. Donlin, Cin		.351	F. Chance, ChN		.439	M. Donlin, Cin		.516	R. Bresnahan, NYG		.936
G. Beaumont, Pit		118	M. Donlin, Cin		9.34	R. Bresnahan, NYG		.350	J. Sheckard, Bro		.423	R. Bresnahan, NYG		.493	H. Wagner, Pit		.931
F. Chance, ChN		116	F. Clarke, Pit		9.12	C. Seymour, Cin		.342	M. Donlin, Cin		.420	H. Steinfeldt, Cin		.481	J. Sheckard, Bro		.899

1903 National League Pitching Leaders

Wins			Losses			Winning Percentage			Games			Games Started			Complete Games		
J. McGinnity, NYG		31	T. Pittinger, Bos		22	S. Leever, Pit		.781	J. McGinnity, NYG		55	J. McGinnity, NYG		48	J. McGinnity, NYG		44
C. Mathewson, NYG		30	J. McGinnity, NYG		20	D. Phillippe, Pit		.735	C. Mathewson, NYG		45	C. Mathewson, NYG		42	C. Mathewson, NYG		37
D. Phillippe, Pit		25	C. McFarland, StL		19	J. Weimer, ChN		.714	T. Pittinger, Bos		44	T. Pittinger, Bos		39	T. Pittinger, Bos		35
S. Leever, Pit		25	V. Willis, Bos		18	C. Mathewson, NYG		.698	H. Schmidt, Bro		40	O. Jones, Bro		36	N. Hahn, Cin		34
2 tied with		22	N. Garvin, Bro		18	B. Wicker, 2tm		.690	2 tied with		38	H. Schmidt, Bro		36	J. Taylor, ChN		33

Shutouts			Saves			Games Finished			Batters Faced			Innings Pitched			Hits Allowed		
S. Leever, Pit		7	C. Lundgren, ChN		3	C. Currie, 2tm		8	Statistic unavailable			J. McGinnity, NYG		434.0	T. Pittinger, Bos		396
H. Schmidt, Bro		5	R. Miller, NYG		3	J. Cronin, 2tm		8				C. Mathewson, NYG		366.1	J. McGinnity, NYG		391
N. Hahn, Cin		5	8 tied with		2	R. Miller, NYG		7				T. Pittinger, Bos		351.2	H. Schmidt, Bro		321
O. Jones, Bro		4				4 tied with		6				O. Jones, Bro		324.1	C. Mathewson, NYG		321
D. Phillippe, Pit		4										J. Taylor, ChN		312.1	O. Jones, Bro		320

Home Runs Allowed			Walks			Walks/9 Innings			Strikeouts			Strikeouts/9 Innings			Strikeout/Walk Ratio		
T. Pittinger, Bos		12	T. Pittinger, Bos		143	D. Phillippe, Pit		0.9	C. Mathewson, NYG		267	C. Mathewson, NYG		6.6	D. Phillippe, Pit		4.24
C. Currie, 2tm		8	H. Schmidt, Bro		120	N. Hahn, Cin		1.4	J. McGinnity, NYG		171	W. Piatt, Bos		5.0	N. Hahn, Cin		2.70
C. Fraser, Phi		8	J. McGinnity, NYG		109	J. Taylor, ChN		1.6	N. Garvin, Bro		154	N. Garvin, Bro		4.7	C. Mathewson, NYG		2.67
T. F. Brown, StL		7	J. Weimer, ChN		104	C. McFarland, StL		1.9	T. Pittinger, Bos		140	J. Weimer, ChN		4.1	N. Garvin, Bro		1.83
L. Taylor, NYG		6	F. Mitchell, Phi		102	S. Leever, Pit		1.9	J. Weimer, ChN		128	V. Willis, Bos		4.0	W. Piatt, Bos		1.64

Earned Run Average			Component ERA			Hit Batsmen			Wild Pitches			Opponent Average			Opponent OBP		
S. Leever, Pit		2.06	J. Taylor, ChN		2.10	H. Schmidt, Bro		21	C. Mathewson, NYG		18	J. Weimer, ChN		.226	D. Phillippe, Pit		.263
C. Mathewson, NYG		2.26	D. Phillippe, Pit		2.13	F. Mitchell, Phi		19	F. Mitchell, Phi		17	C. Mathewson, NYG		.232	J. Taylor, ChN		.273
J. Weimer, ChN		2.30	S. Leever, Pit		2.26	J. McGinnity, NYG		19	T. Pittinger, Bos		14	J. Taylor, ChN		.235	S. Leever, Pit		.282
J. McGinnity, NYG		2.43	C. Mathewson, NYG		2.37	E. Doheny, NYG		19	C. McFarland, StL		9	J. McGinnity, NYG		.237	C. Mathewson, NYG		.288
D. Phillippe, Pit		2.43	J. McGinnity, NYG		2.45	2 tied with		17	N. Garvin, Bro		9	S. Leever, Pit		.238	J. McGinnity, NYG		.291

1903 National League Miscellaneous

Managers		
Boston	Al Buckenberger	58-80
Brooklyn	Ned Hanlon	70-66
Chicago	Frank Selee	82-56
Cincinnati	Joe Kelley	74-65
New York	John McGraw	84-55
Philadelphia	Chief Zimmer	49-86
Pittsburgh	Fred Clarke	91-49
St. Louis	Patsy Donovan	43-94

Awards	
STATS Most Valuable Player	Honus Wagner, ss, Pit
STATS Cy Young	C. Mathewson, NYG
STATS Rookie of the Year	Jake Weimer, p, ChN
STATS Manager of the Year	John McGraw, NYG

STATS All-Star Team

C	Johnny Kling, ChN	.297	3	68
1B	Frank Chance, ChN	.327	2	81
2B	Claude Ritchey, Pit	.287	0	59
3B	Harry Steinfeldt, Cin	.312	6	83
SS	Honus Wagner, Pit	.355	5	101
OF	Roger Bresnahan, NYG	.350	4	55
OF	Fred Clarke, Pit	.351	5	70
OF	Mike Donlin, Cin	.351	7	67
P	Sam Leever, Pit	25-7	2.06	90 K
P	Christy Mathewson, NYG	30-13	2.26	267 K
P	Joe McGinnity, NYG	31-20	2.43	171 K
P	Deacon Phillippe, Pit	25-9	2.43	123 K

Postseason	
World Series	Pittsburgh (NL) 3 vs. Boston (AL) 5

Outstanding Performances

No-Hitters
Chick Fraser, Phi   @ ChN on September 18
Cycles
Fred Clarke, Pit   on May 7

1904 American League Standings

Team	Overall					Home Games						Road Games						Park Index		Record by Month					
	W	L	Pct	GB	DIF	W	L	R	OR	HR	OHR	W	L	R	OR	HR	OHR	Run	HR	M/A	May	June	July	Aug	S/O
Boston	95	59	.617	—	132	49	30	325	240	17	18	46	29	283	226	9	13	105	151	10-2	15-8	12-11	15-12	17-10	26-16
New York	92	59	.609	1.5	39	46	29	321	288	22	25	46	30	277	238	5	4	120	529	5-5	14-10	15-7	16-11	17-10	25-16
Chicago	89	65	.578	6.0	7	50	27	297	226	0	2	39	38	303	256	14	11	94	8	7-6	12-11	18-8	16-10	12-14	24-16
Cleveland	86	65	.570	7.5	2	44	31	329	242	14	2	42	34	318	240	13	8	104	77	4-6	14-11	19-12	19-10	14-13	25-17
Philadelphia	81	70	.536	12.5	5	47	31	308	235	19	8	34	39	249	268	12	5	98	149	6-4	14-11	11-11	15-12	16-7	19-25
St. Louis	65	87	.428	29.0	0	32	43	231	288	2	14	33	44	250	316	8	11	94	86	5-4	10-14	11-10	8-17	10-20	21-22
Detroit	62	90	.408	32.0	3	34	40	237	295	3	4	28	50	268	332	8	12	93	37	6-6	6-15	11-13	10-16	14-13	15-27
Washington	38	113	.252	55.5	0	23	52	221	350	3	2	15	61	216	393	7	17	95	21	0-10	6-16	4-19	8-19	8-21	12-28

Clinch Date—Boston 10/10.

Team Batting

Team	G	AB	R	OR	H	2B	3B	HR	TB	RBI	TBB	IBB	SO	HBP	SH	SF	SB	CS	SB%	GDP	Avg	OBP	Slg
Cleveland	154	5152	647	482	1340	225	90	27	1826	553	307	—	714	46	169	—	178	—	—	—	.260	.308	.354
Boston	157	5231	608	466	1294	194	105	14	1776	522	347	—	570	51	145	—	101	—	—	—	.247	.301	.340
Chicago	156	5027	600	482	1217	193	68	14	1588	519	373	—	586	41	197	—	216	—	—	—	.242	.300	.316
New York	155	5220	598	526	1354	195	91	27	1812	499	312	—	548	57	133	—	163	—	—	—	.259	.308	.347
Philadelphia	155	5088	557	503	1266	197	77	31	1710	486	313	—	605	41	137	—	137	—	—	—	.249	.298	.336
Detroit	162	5321	505	627	1231	154	69	11	1556	431	344	—	635	35	154	—	112	—	—	—	.231	.282	.292
St. Louis	156	5291	481	604	1266	153	53	10	1555	406	332	—	609	56	122	—	150	—	—	—	.239	.291	.294
Washington	157	5149	437	743	1170	171	57	10	1485	348	283	—	759	59	132	—	150	—	—	—	.227	.275	.288
AL Total	1252	41479	4433	4433	10138	1482	610	156	13308	3764	2611	—	5026	386	1189	—	1207	—	—	—	.244	.295	.321
AL Avg Team	157	5185	554	554	1267	185	76	20	1664	471	326	—	628	48	149	—	151	—	—	—	.244	.295	.321

Team Pitching

Team	G	CG	ShO	Rel	Sv	IP	H	R	ER	HR	SH	SF	HB	TBB	IBB	SO	WP	Bk	H/9	SO/9	BB/9	OAvg	OOBP	ERA
Boston	157	148	21	9	1	1406.0	1208	466	331	31	131	—	31	233	—	612	22	1	7.7	3.9	1.5	.232	.269	2.12
Cleveland	154	141	20	15	0	1356.2	1273	482	335	10	126	—	36	285	—	627	36	1	8.4	4.2	1.9	.246	.290	2.22
Chicago	156	134	26	22	3	1380.0	1161	482	353	13	116	—	47	303	—	550	37	2	7.6	3.6	2.0	.226	.275	2.30
Philadelphia	155	136	26	20	0	1361.1	1149	503	355	13	124	—	63	366	—	887	23	2	7.6	5.9	2.4	.227	.287	2.35
New York	155	123	15	33	1	1380.2	1180	526	394	29	122	—	42	311	—	684	41	0	7.7	4.5	2.0	.232	.282	2.57
Detroit	162	143	15	21	2	1430.0	1345	627	440	16	164	—	70	433	—	556	37	1	8.5	3.5	2.7	.252	.316	2.77
St. Louis	156	135	13	22	1	1410.0	1335	604	443	25	174	—	62	333	—	577	25	0	8.5	3.7	2.1	.253	.305	2.83
Washington	157	137	7	20	4	1359.2	1487	743	547	19	184	—	63	347	—	533	39	2	9.8	3.5	2.3	.281	.333	3.62
AL Total	1252	1097	143	162	12	11084.1	10138	4433	3198	156	1141	—	414	2611	—	5026	260	9	8.2	4.1	2.1	.244	.296	2.60
AL Avg Team	157	137	18	20	2	1385.1	1267	554	400	20	143	—	52	326	—	628	33	1	8.2	4.1	2.1	.244	.296	2.60

Team Fielding

Team	G	PO	A	E	TC	DP	PB	Pct
Chicago	156	4136	2163	238	6537	95	20	.964
Boston	157	4217	1987	242	6446	83	19	.962
St. Louis	156	4225	2179	267	6671	78	19	.960
Detroit	162	4288	2177	273	6738	92	21	.959
Philadelphia	155	4080	1835	250	6165	67	21	.959
Cleveland	154	4037	1963	255	6255	86	14	.959
New York	155	4141	2102	275	6518	90	17	.958
Washington	157	4077	2049	314	6440	97	13	.951
AL Total	1252	33201	16455	2114	51770	688	144	.959

Team vs. Team Records

	Bos	ChA	Cle	Det	NYA	Phi	StL	Was	Won
Bos	—	13	9	16	12	13	12	20	95
ChA	9	—	14	14	12	8	14	18	89
Cle	13	8	—	14	9	11	13	18	86
Det	6	8	8	—	7	10	11	12	62
NYA	10	10	11	15	—	12	16	18	92
Phi	9	14	10	12	9	—	11	16	81
StL	10	8	9	11	6	10	—	11	65
Was	2	4	4	8	4	6	10	—	38
Lost	59	65	65	90	59	70	87	113	

1904 American League Batting Leaders

Games			At-Bats			Runs			Hits			Doubles			Triples		
J. Barrett, Det	162		P. Dougherty, 2tm	647		P. Dougherty, 2tm	113		N. Lajoie, Cle	208		N. Lajoie, Cle	49		J. Cassidy, Was	19	
C. Stahl, Bos	157		J. Collins, Bos	631		E. Flick, Cle	97		W. Keeler, NYA	186		J. Collins, Bos	33		C. Stahl, Bos	19	
C. LaChance, Bos	157		T. Jones, StL	625		B. Bradley, Cle	94		B. Bradley, Cle	183		B. Bradley, Cle	32		B. Freeman, Bos	19	
B. Freeman, Bos	157		J. Barrett, Det	624		N. Lajoie, Cle	92		P. Dougherty, 2tm	181		4 tied with	31		D. Murphy, Phi	17	
3 tied with	156		B. Bradley, Cle	609		2 tied with	85		E. Flick, Cle	177					E. Flick, Cle	17	

Home Runs			Total Bases			Runs Batted In			Walks			Intentional Walks			Strikeouts		
H. Davis, Phi	10		N. Lajoie, Cle	302		N. Lajoie, Cle	102		J. Barrett, Det	79		Statistic unavailable			Statistic unavailable		
D. Murphy, Phi	7		E. Flick, Cle	260		B. Freeman, Bos	84		J. Burkett, StL	78							
B. Freeman, Bos	7		B. Bradley, Cle	249		B. Bradley, Cle	83		T. Hartsel, Phi	75							
6 tied with	6		B. Freeman, Bos	246		J. Anderson, NYA	82		B. Lush, Cle	72							
			2 tied with	245		2 tied with	77		K. Selbach, 2tm	72							

Hit By Pitch			Sac Hits			Sac Flies			Stolen Bases			Caught Stealing			GDP		
D. Padden, StL	18		F. Jones, ChA	36		Statistic unavailable			H. Bay, Cle	38		Statistic unavailable			Statistic unavailable		
J. Stahl, Was	15		N. Callahan, ChA	33					E. Flick, Cle	38							
K. Elberfeld, NYA	13		B. Lush, Cle	30					E. Heidrick, StL	35							
B. Freeman, Bos	12		M. McIntyre, Det	28					G. Davis, ChA	32							
3 tied with	9		F. Parent, Bos	28					W. Conroy, NYA	30							

Runs Created			Runs Created/27 Outs			Batting Average			On-Base Percentage			Slugging Percentage			OBP+Slugging		
N. Lajoie, Cle	129		N. Lajoie, Cle	9.55		N. Lajoie, Cle	.376		N. Lajoie, Cle	.413		N. Lajoie, Cle	.546		N. Lajoie, Cle	.959	
E. Flick, Cle	111		E. Flick, Cle	6.83		W. Keeler, NYA	.343		W. Keeler, NYA	.390		H. Davis, Phi	.490		H. Davis, Phi	.840	
C. Stahl, Bos	101		H. Davis, Phi	6.56		H. Davis, Phi	.309		E. Flick, Cle	.371		E. Flick, Cle	.449		E. Flick, Cle	.820	
B. Bradley, Cle	90		C. Stahl, Bos	5.96		E. Flick, Cle	.306		C. Stahl, Bos	.366		D. Murphy, Phi	.440		W. Keeler, NYA	.799	
2 tied with	88		W. Keeler, NYA	5.89		B. Bradley, Cle	.300		J. Burkett, StL	.363		C. Hickman, 2tm	.437		C. Stahl, Bos	.782	

1904 American League Pitching Leaders

Wins			Losses			Winning Percentage			Games			Games Started			Complete Games		
J. Chesbro, NYA	41		J. Townsend, Was	26		J. Chesbro, NYA	.774		J. Chesbro, NYA	55		J. Chesbro, NYA	51		J. Chesbro, NYA	48	
E. Plank, Phi	26		L. Hughes, 2tm	24		J. Tannehill, Bos	.656		J. Powell, NYA	47		R. Waddell, Phi	46		G. Mullin, Det	42	
C. Young, Bos	26		B. Jacobson, Was	23		F. Smith, ChA	.640		R. Waddell, Phi	46		J. Powell, NYA	45		C. Young, Bos	40	
R. Waddell, Phi	25		G. Mullin, Det	23		B. Bernhard, Cle	.639		G. Mullin, Det	45		G. Mullin, Det	44		R. Waddell, Phi	39	
3 tied with	23		C. Patten, Was	23		B. Dinneen, Bos	.622		C. Patten, Was	45		E. Plank, Phi	43		J. Powell, NYA	38	

Shutouts			Saves			Games Finished			Batters Faced			Innings Pitched			Hits Allowed		
C. Young, Bos	10		C. Patten, Was	3		E. Walsh, ChA	10		J. Chesbro, NYA	1778		J. Chesbro, NYA	454.2		C. Patten, Was	367	
R. Waddell, Phi	8		9 tied with	1		W. Clarkson, NYA	9		G. Mullin, Det	1597		J. Powell, NYA	390.1		G. Mullin, Det	345	
G. Mullin, Det	7					C. Bender, Phi	8		J. Powell, NYA	1572		R. Waddell, Phi	383.0		J. Powell, NYA	340	
E. Plank, Phi	7					3 tied with	6		R. Waddell, Phi	1548		G. Mullin, Det	382.1		J. Chesbro, NYA	338	
D. White, ChA	7								C. Patten, Was	1507		C. Young, Bos	380.0		C. Young, Bos	327	

Home Runs Allowed			Walks			Walks/9 Innings			Strikeouts			Strikeouts/9 Innings			Strikeout/Walk Ratio		
J. Powell, NYA	15		G. Mullin, Det	131		C. Young, Bos	0.7		R. Waddell, Phi	349		R. Waddell, Phi	8.2		C. Young, Bos	6.90	
B. Dinneen, Bos	8		J. Townsend, Was	100		J. Tannehill, Bos	1.1		J. Chesbro, NYA	239		C. Bender, Phi	6.6		R. Waddell, Phi	3.84	
W. Sudhoff, StL	8		W. Donovan, Det	94		R. Patterson, ChA	1.3		J. Powell, NYA	202		E. Moore, Cle	5.5		J. Tannehill, Bos	3.52	
4 tied with	7		E. Killian, Det	93		A. Joss, Cle	1.4		E. Plank, Phi	201		E. Plank, Phi	5.1		A. Joss, Cle	2.77	
			J. Powell, NYA	92		N. Altrock, ChA	1.4		C. Young, Bos	200		F. Glade, StL	4.9		J. Chesbro, NYA	2.72	

Earned Run Average			Component ERA			Hit Batsmen			Wild Pitches			Opponent Average			Opponent OBP		
A. Joss, Cle	1.59		J. Chesbro, NYA	1.56		B. Pelty, StL	20		J. Townsend, Was	19		J. Chesbro, NYA	.205		J. Chesbro, NYA	.248	
R. Waddell, Phi	1.62		F. Owen, ChA	1.70		C. Patten, Was	20		E. Moore, Cle	13		F. Owen, ChA	.214		C. Young, Bos	.249	
D. White, ChA	1.78		C. Young, Bos	1.73		W. Henley, Phi	19		F. Smith, ChA	12		F. Smith, ChA	.216		F. Owen, ChA	.261	
J. Chesbro, NYA	1.82		A. Joss, Cle	1.82		E. Plank, Phi	19		J. Powell, NYA	12		N. Gibson, Bos	.216		A. Joss, Cle	.265	
F. Owen, ChA	1.94		R. Waddell, Phi	1.98		E. Killian, Det	17		W. Donovan, Det	11		R. Waddell, Phi	.217		B. Dinneen, Bos	.270	

1904 American League Miscellaneous

Managers		
Boston	Jimmy Collins	95-59
Chicago	Nixey Callahan	23-18
	Fielder Jones	66-47
Cleveland	Bill Armour	86-65
Detroit	Ed Barrow	32-46
	Bobby Lowe	30-44
New York	Clark Griffith	92-59
Philadelphia	Connie Mack	81-70
St. Louis	Jimmy McAleer	65-87
Washington	Mal Kittridge	1-16
	Patsy Donovan	37-97

Awards

STATS Most Valuable Player	Jack Chesbro, p, NYA
STATS Cy Young	Jack Chesbro, NYA
STATS Rookie of the Year	Fred Glade, p, StL
STATS Manager of the Year	Fielder Jones, ChA

STATS All-Star Team

C	Joe Sugden, StL	.267	0	30
1B	Harry Davis, Phi	.309	10	62
2B	Nap Lajoie, Cle	.376	5	102
3B	Bill Bradley, Cle	.300	6	83
SS	Freddy Parent, Bos	.291	6	77
OF	Elmer Flick, Cle	.306	6	56
OF	Willie Keeler, NYA	.343	2	40
OF	Chick Stahl, Bos	.290	3	67
P	Jack Chesbro, NYA	41-12	1.82	239 K
P	Eddie Plank, Phi	26-17	2.17	201 K
P	Rube Waddell, Phi	25-19	1.62	349 K
P	Cy Young, Bos	26-16	1.97	200 K

Postseason

None

Outstanding Performances

Perfect Games
Cy Young, Bos   vs. Phi on May 5
No-Hitters
Jesse Tannehill, Bos @ ChA on August 17

1904 National League Standings

Team	Overall					Home Games						Road Games						Park Index		Record by Month					
	W	L	Pct	GB	DIF	W	L	R	OR	HR	OHR	W	L	R	OR	HR	OHR	Run	HR	M/A	May	June	July	Aug	S/O
New York	106	47	.693	—	168	56	26	397	258	23	30	50	21	347	218	8	6	100	328	9-2	16-9	19-5	18-8	22-8	22-15
Chicago	93	60	.608	13.0	9	49	27	303	240	6	10	44	33	296	277	16	6	96	74	5-5	19-6	13-10	16-12	15-13	25-14
Cincinnati	88	65	.575	18.0	8	49	27	409	295	12	7	39	38	286	252	9	6	133	128	8-6	18-6	9-11	17-14	15-13	21-15
Pittsburgh	87	66	.569	19.0	1	48	30	338	286	5	2	39	36	337	306	10	11	93	32	4-7	12-12	15-9	18-8	17-11	21-19
St. Louis	75	79	.487	31.5	0	39	36	298	280	14	15	36	43	304	315	10	8	98	170	6-5	11-12	10-15	19-11	14-16	14-22
Brooklyn	56	97	.366	50.0	0	31	44	234	287	3	11	25	53	263	327	12	16	92	52	6-5	9-18	10-15	7-21	8-15	16-23
Boston	55	98	.359	51.0	0	34	45	269	363	13	10	21	53	222	386	11	15	97	83	5-7	8-15	11-16	9-19	11-17	11-24
Philadelphia	52	100	.342	53.5	1	28	43	269	348	7	7	24	57	302	436	16	15	95	52	2-8	4-19	7-16	9-20	11-20	19-17

Clinch Date—New York 9/22.

Team Batting

Team	G	AB	R	OR	H	2B	3B	HR	TB	RBI	TBB	IBB	SO	HBP	SH	SF	SB	CS	SB%	GDP	Avg	OBP	Slg
New York	158	5150	744	476	1347	202	65	31	1772	564	434	—	—	79	166	—	283	—	—	—	.262	.328	.344
Cincinnati	157	5231	695	547	1332	189	92	21	1768	561	399	—	—	49	140	—	179	—	—	—	.255	.313	.338
Pittsburgh	156	5160	675	592	1333	164	102	15	1746	522	391	—	—	47	124	—	178	—	—	—	.258	.316	.338
St. Louis	155	5104	602	595	1292	175	66	24	1671	456	343	—	—	46	131	—	199	—	—	—	.253	.306	.327
Chicago	156	5210	599	517	1294	157	62	22	1641	470	298	—	—	48	141	—	227	—	—	—	.248	.295	.315
Philadelphia	155	5103	571	784	1268	170	54	23	1615	469	377	—	—	40	119	—	159	—	—	—	.248	.305	.316
Brooklyn	154	4917	497	614	1142	159	53	15	1452	390	411	—	—	42	129	—	205	—	—	—	.232	.297	.295
Boston	155	5135	491	749	1217	153	50	24	1542	394	316	—	—	42	101	—	143	—	—	—	.237	.287	.300
NL Total	1246	41010	4874	4874	10225	1369	544	175	13207	3826	2969	—	—	393	1051	—	1573	—	—	—	.249	.306	.322
NL Avg Team	156	5126	609	609	1278	171	68	22	1651	478	371	—	—	49	131	—	197	—	—	—	.249	.306	.322

Team Pitching

Team	G	CG	ShO	Rel	Sv	IP	H	R	ER	HR	SH	SF	HB	TBB	IBB	SO	WP	Bk	H/9	SO/9	BB/9	OAvg	OOBP	ERA
New York	158	127	21	29	15	1396.2	1151	476	337	36	—	—	35	349	—	707	29	3	7.4	4.6	2.2	.223	.277	2.17
Chicago	156	139	18	17	6	1383.2	1150	517	354	16	—	—	36	402	—	618	24	4	7.5	4.0	2.6	.224	.285	2.30
Cincinnati	157	142	12	15	2	1392.2	1256	547	362	13	—	—	55	343	—	502	33	4	8.1	3.2	2.2	.241	.295	2.34
St. Louis	155	146	7	8	2	1368.0	1286	595	401	23	—	—	40	319	—	529	22	2	8.5	3.5	2.1	.238	.286	2.64
Brooklyn	154	135	12	20	2	1337.1	1281	614	401	27	—	—	56	414	—	453	28	3	8.6	3.0	2.8	.256	.320	2.70
Pittsburgh	156	133	15	25	1	1348.1	1273	592	433	13	—	—	53	379	—	455	30	5	8.5	3.0	2.5	.248	.306	2.89
Philadelphia	155	131	10	25	2	1339.1	1418	784	505	22	—	—	70	425	—	469	32	8	9.5	3.2	2.9	.267	.330	3.39
Boston	155	136	13	20	0	1348.1	1405	749	514	25	—	—	52	500	—	544	50	4	9.4	3.6	3.3	.272	.343	3.43
NL Total	1246	1089	108	159	30	10914.1	10220	4874	3307	175	—	—	397	3131	—	4277	248	33	8.4	3.5	2.6	.249	.309	2.73
NL Avg Team	156	136	14	20	4	1364.1	1278	609	413	22	—	—	50	391	—	535	31	4	8.4	3.5	2.6	.249	.309	2.73

Team Fielding

Team	G	PO	A	E	TC	DP	PB	Pct
New York	158	4176	2147	294	6617	93	14	.956
Pittsburgh	156	4043	2072	291	6406	93	19	.955
Chicago	156	4140	2039	298	6477	89	25	.954
Cincinnati	157	4161	2028	301	6490	81	27	.954
St. Louis	155	4079	2036	307	6422	83	20	.952
Boston	155	4020	2078	353	6451	91	27	.945
Brooklyn	154	3995	1924	343	6262	87	13	.945
Philadelphia	155	4012	1989	403	6404	93	18	.937
NL Total	1246	32626	16313	2590	51529	710	163	.950

Team vs. Team Records

	Bos	Bro	ChN	Cin	NYG	Phi	Pit	StL	Won
Bos	—	9	9	7	2	11	8	9	55
Bro	13	—	5	8	3	13	7	7	56
ChN	13	17	—	13	11	15	9	15	93
Cin	15	14	8	—	10	16	11	14	88
NYG	20	19	11	12	—	17	12	15	106
Phi	10	9	7	6	4	—	9	7	52
Pit	14	14	13	11	10	13	—	12	87
StL	13	15	7	8	7	15	10	—	75
Lost	98	97	60	65	47	100	66	79	

Seasons: Standings, Leaders

1904 National League Batting Leaders

Games		At-Bats		Runs		Hits		Doubles		Triples	
C. Ritchey, Pit	156	G. Beaumont, Pit	615	G. Browne, NYG	99	G. Beaumont, Pit	185	H. Wagner, Pit	44	H. Lumley, Bro	18
E. Abbaticchio, Bos	154	G. Browne, NYG	596	G. Beaumont, Pit	97	J. Beckley, StL	179	S. Mertes, NYG	28	H. Wagner, Pit	14
G. Beaumont, Pit	153	K. Gleason, Phi	587	H. Wagner, Pit	97	H. Wagner, Pit	171	J. Delahanty, Bos	27	J. Tinker, ChN	13
K. Gleason, Phi	153	P. Geier, Bos	580	M. Huggins, Cin	96	G. Browne, NYG	169	C. Seymour, Cin	26	C. Seymour, Cin	13
J. Evers, ChN	152	2 tied with	579	2 tied with	92	C. Seymour, Cin	166	B. Dahlen, NYG	26	J. Kelley, Cin	13

Home Runs		Total Bases		Runs Batted In		Walks		Intentional Walks	Strikeouts
H. Lumley, Bro	9	H. Wagner, Pit	255	B. Dahlen, NYG	80	R. Thomas, Phi	102	Statistic unavailable	Statistic unavailable
D. Brain, StL	7	H. Lumley, Bro	247	H. Lumley, Bro	78	M. Huggins, Cin	88		
4 tied with	6	C. Seymour, Cin	233	S. Mertes, NYG	78	A. Devlin, NYG	62		
		G. Beaumont, Pit	230	H. Wagner, Pit	75	H. Wagner, Pit	59		
		J. Beckley, StL	222	T. Corcoran, Cin	74	C. Ritchey, Pit	59		

Hit By Pitch		Sac Hits		Sac Flies	Stolen Bases		Caught Stealing	GDP
D. McGann, NYG	18	K. Gleason, Phi	35	Statistic unavailable	H. Wagner, Pit	53	Statistic unavailable	Statistic unavailable
B. Gilbert, NYG	17	S. Shannon, StL	29		S. Mertes, NYG	47		
F. Chance, ChN	16	J. Evers, ChN	23		B. Dahlen, NYG	47		
C. Babb, Bro	11	G. Beaumont, Pit	23		F. Chance, ChN	42		
J. Burke, StL	10	4 tied with	22		D. McGann, NYG	42		

Runs Created		Runs Created/27 Outs		Batting Average		On-Base Percentage		Slugging Percentage		OBP+Slugging	
H. Wagner, Pit	128	H. Wagner, Pit	10.11	H. Wagner, Pit	.349	H. Wagner, Pit	.423	H. Wagner, Pit	.520	H. Wagner, Pit	.944
R. Thomas, Phi	95	M. Donlin, 2tm	7.66	M. Donlin, 2tm	.329	R. Thomas, Phi	.416	M. Grady, StL	.474	M. Grady, StL	.850
S. Mertes, NYG	94	F. Chance, ChN	7.39	J. Beckley, StL	.325	M. Donlin, 2tm	.382	M. Donlin, 2tm	.457	M. Donlin, 2tm	.839
F. Chance, ChN	93	M. Grady, StL	6.93	M. Grady, StL	.313	F. Chance, ChN	.382	C. Seymour, Cin	.439	F. Chance, ChN	.812
C. Seymour, Cin	93	R. Bresnahan, NYG	6.86	C. Seymour, Cin	.313	R. Bresnahan, NYG	.381	F. Chance, ChN	.430	R. Bresnahan, NYG	.791

1904 National League Pitching Leaders

Wins		Losses		Winning Percentage		Games		Games Started		Complete Games	
J. McGinnity, NYG	35	O. Jones, Bro	25	J. McGinnity, NYG	.814	J. McGinnity, NYG	51	C. Mathewson, NYG	46	J. Taylor, StL	39
C. Mathewson, NYG	33	V. Willis, Bos	25	H. Wiltse, NYG	.813	C. Mathewson, NYG	48	J. McGinnity, NYG	44	V. Willis, Bos	39
J. Harper, Cin	23	C. Fraser, Phi	24	C. Mathewson, NYG	.733	O. Jones, Bro	46	V. Willis, Bos	43	O. Jones, Bro	38
L. Taylor, NYG	21	J. Cronin, Bro	23	J. Harper, Cin	.719	V. Willis, Bos	43	O. Jones, Bro	41	J. McGinnity, NYG	38
K. Nichols, StL	21	T. Pittinger, Bos	21	P. Flaherty, Pit	.679	C. Fraser, Phi	42	J. Taylor, StL	39	2 tied with	35

Shutouts		Saves		Games Finished		Batters Faced	Innings Pitched		Hits Allowed	
J. McGinnity, NYG	9	J. McGinnity, NYG	5	T. Fisher, Bos	9	Statistic unavailable	J. McGinnity, NYG	408.0	O. Jones, Bro	387
J. Harper, Cin	6	H. Wiltse, NYG	3	H. Camnitz, Pit	8		O. Jones, Bro	376.2	V. Willis, Bos	357
4 tied with	5	R. Ames, NYG	3	H. Wiltse, NYG	8		C. Mathewson, NYG	367.2	K. Wilhelm, Bos	316
		B. Briggs, ChN	3	W. Kellum, Cin	7		J. Taylor, StL	352.0	J. McGinnity, NYG	307
		2 tied with	2	J. McGinnity, NYG	7		V. Willis, Bos	350.0	C. Mathewson, NYG	306

Home Runs Allowed		Walks		Walks/9 Innings		Strikeouts		Strikeouts/9 Innings		Strikeout/Walk Ratio	
J. Cronin, Bro	10	T. Pittinger, Bos	144	N. Hahn, Cin	1.1	C. Mathewson, NYG	212	H. Wiltse, NYG	5.7	D. Phillippe, Pit	3.15
H. Wiltse, NYG	8	J. Sutthoff, 2tm	114	D. Phillippe, Pit	1.4	V. Willis, Bos	196	C. Mathewson, NYG	5.2	N. Hahn, Cin	2.80
K. Wilhelm, Bos	8	V. Willis, Bos	109	K. Nichols, StL	1.4	J. Weimer, ChN	177	J. Weimer, ChN	5.2	C. Mathewson, NYG	2.72
J. McGinnity, NYG	8	C. Fraser, Phi	100	W. Kellum, Cin	1.8	T. Pittinger, Bos	146	V. Willis, Bos	5.0	K. Nichols, StL	2.68
4 tied with	7	J. Weimer, ChN	97	C. McFarland, StL	1.9	J. McGinnity, NYG	144	D. Phillippe, Pit	4.4	C. McFarland, StL	1.98

Earned Run Average		Component ERA		Hit Batsmen		Wild Pitches		Opponent Average		Opponent OBP	
J. McGinnity, NYG	1.61	T. F. Brown, ChN	1.60	T. Walker, Cin	18	E. McNichol, Bos	12	T. F. Brown, ChN	.199	T. F. Brown, ChN	.253
N. Garvin, Bro	1.68	J. McGinnity, NYG	1.71	O. Jones, Bro	17	J. Harper, Cin	12	J. Weimer, ChN	.204	J. McGinnity, NYG	.258
T. F. Brown, ChN	1.86	K. Nichols, StL	1.83	M. Lynch, Pit	15	V. Willis, Bos	11	J. McGinnity, NYG	.208	K. Nichols, StL	.260
J. Weimer, ChN	1.91	J. Weimer, ChN	1.90	F. Corridon, 2tm	15	C. Mathewson, NYG	10	L. Taylor, NYG	.214	N. Hahn, Cin	.262
K. Nichols, StL	2.02	N. Hahn, Cin	1.90	2 tied with	14	T. Pittinger, Bos	10	N. Garvin, Bro	.218	L. Taylor, NYG	.270

1904 National League Miscellaneous

Managers		
Boston	Al Buckenberger	55-98
Brooklyn	Ned Hanlon	56-97
Chicago	Frank Selee	93-60
Cincinnati	Joe Kelley	88-65
New York	John McGraw	106-47
Philadelphia	Hugh Duffy	52-100
Pittsburgh	Fred Clarke	87-66
St. Louis	Kid Nichols	75-79

Awards

STATS Most Valuable Player	Honus Wagner, ss, Pit
STATS Cy Young	Joe McGinnity, NYG
STATS Rookie of the Year	Harry Lumley, of, Bro
STATS Manager of the Year	John McGraw, NYG

STATS All-Star Team

C	Mike Grady, StL	.313	5	43
1B	Frank Chance, ChN	.310	6	49
2B	Miller Huggins, Cin	.263	2	30
3B	Art Devlin, NYG	.281	1	66
SS	Honus Wagner, Pit	.349	4	75
OF	Mike Donlin, 2tm	.329	3	52
OF	Harry Lumley, Bro	.279	9	78
OF	Cy Seymour, Cin	.313	5	58
P	Jack Harper, Cin	23-9	2.30	125 K
P	Christy Mathewson, NYG	33-12	2.03	212 K
P	Joe McGinnity, NYG	35-8	1.61	144 K
P	Kid Nichols, StL	21-13	2.02	134 K

Postseason

None

Outstanding Performances

Cycles

Duff Cooley, Bos	on June 20
Sam Mertes, NYG	on October 4

1905 American League Standings

Team	Overall W	L	Pct	GB	DIF	Home Games W	L	R	OR	HR	OHR	Road Games W	L	R	OR	HR	OHR	Park Index Run	HR	Record by Month M/A	May	June	July	Aug	S/O
Philadelphia	92	56	.622	—	82	50	23	337	247	12	12	42	33	286	245	12	9	113	117	7-4	12-11	15-8	15-12	20-9	23-12
Chicago	92	60	.605	2.0	24	50	29	300	207	3	2	42	31	312	244	8	9	84	27	7-5	14-9	14-7	15-12	15-12	27-15
Detroit	79	74	.516	15.5	2	45	30	267	275	5	5	34	44	245	327	8	6	99	74	5-6	13-11	11-13	14-13	11-17	25-14
Boston	78	74	.513	16.0	0	44	32	296	281	21	20	34	42	283	283	8	13	102	195	3-10	12-9	10-9	14-15	17-11	22-20
Cleveland	76	78	.494	19.0	73	40	37	290	284	5	13	36	41	277	303	13	10	99	78	6-5	16-6	14-10	17-14	8-18	15-25
New York	71	78	.477	21.5	10	40	35	316	303	15	15	31	43	270	319	8	11	104	156	7-4	7-18	9-9	16-10	16-12	16-25
Washington	64	87	.424	29.5	6	33	42	289	340	10	4	31	45	270	283	12	8	115	71	7-6	9-14	6-16	9-18	16-11	17-22
St. Louis	54	99	.353	40.5	1	34	42	250	267	5	7	20	57	261	341	11	12	87	53	5-7	10-15	7-14	10-16	9-22	13-25

Clinch Date—Philadelphia 10/06.

Team Batting

Team	G	AB	R	OR	H	2B	3B	HR	TB	RBI	TBB	IBB	SO	HBP	SH	SF	SB	CS	SB%	GDP	Avg	OBP	Slg
Philadelphia	152	5146	623	492	1310	256	51	24	1740	511	376	—	644	34	165	—	190	—	—	—	.255	.310	.338
Chicago	158	5114	612	451	1213	200	55	11	1556	487	439	—	613	58	241	—	194	—	—	—	.237	.305	.304
New York	152	4957	586	622	1228	163	61	23	1582	480	360	—	537	67	158	—	200	—	—	—	.248	.307	.319
Boston	153	5049	579	564	1179	165	69	29	1569	488	486	—	553	37	137	—	131	—	—	—	.234	.305	.311
Cleveland	155	5166	567	587	1318	211	72	18	1727	482	286	—	712	55	148	—	188	—	—	—	.255	.301	.334
Washington	154	5015	559	623	1121	193	68	22	1516	483	298	—	824	54	165	—	169	—	—	—	.224	.274	.302
Detroit	154	4971	512	602	1209	190	54	13	1546	421	375	—	583	40	181	—	129	—	—	—	.243	.302	.311
St. Louis	156	5204	511	608	1205	153	49	16	1504	415	362	—	639	52	151	—	130	—	—	—	.232	.288	.289
AL Total	1234	40622	4549	4549	9783	1531	479	156	12740	3767	2982	—	5105	397	1346	—	1331	—	—	—	.241	.299	.314
AL Avg Team	154	5078	569	569	1223	191	60	20	1593	471	373	—	638	50	168	—	166	—	—	—	.241	.299	.314

Team Pitching

Team	G	CG	ShO	Rel	Sv	IP	H	R	ER	HR	SH	SF	HB	TBB	IBB	SO	WP	Bk	H/9	SO/9	BB/9	OAvg	OOBP	ERA
Chicago	158	131	15	32	0	1427.0	1163	451	315	11	—	—	35	329	—	613	39	0	7.3	3.9	2.1	.225	.276	1.99
Philadelphia	152	117	19	37	0	1383.1	1137	492	337	21	—	—	63	409	—	895	40	4	7.4	5.8	2.7	.226	.293	2.19
St. Louis	156	134	10	22	2	1384.2	1245	608	421	19	—	—	62	389	—	633	41	0	8.1	4.1	2.5	.243	.304	2.74
Detroit	154	124	17	31	1	1348.0	1226	602	424	11	—	—	51	474	—	578	19	1	8.2	3.9	3.2	.245	.316	2.83
Boston	153	124	14	30	1	1356.1	1198	564	428	33	—	—	44	292	—	652	25	1	7.9	4.3	1.9	.239	.287	2.84
Cleveland	155	140	16	15	0	1363.1	1251	587	431	23	—	—	64	334	—	555	32	0	8.3	3.7	2.2	.246	.301	2.85
Washington	154	118	12	40	1	1362.1	1250	623	434	12	—	—	63	385	—	539	32	1	8.3	3.6	2.5	.246	.307	2.87
New York	152	88	16	75	4	1353.2	1235	622	441	26	—	—	44	396	—	642	46	1	8.2	4.3	2.6	.245	.306	2.93
AL Total	1234	976	119	282	9	10978.2	9705	4549	3231	156	—	—	426	3008	—	5107	274	8	8.0	4.2	2.5	.241	.298	2.65
AL Avg Team	154	122	15	35	1	1372.2	1213	569	404	20	—	—	53	376	—	638	34	1	8.0	4.2	2.5	.241	.298	2.65

Team Fielding

Team	G	PO	A	E	TC	DP	PB	Pct
Chicago	158	4247	2234	217	6698	95	19	.968
Cleveland	155	4075	1893	233	6201	84	24	.962
Philadelphia	152	4101	1746	265	6112	64	21	.957
Detroit	154	4010	1861	267	6138	80	19	.957
St. Louis	156	4148	2182	296	6626	78	20	.955
Boston	153	4034	1913	296	6243	75	26	.953
New York	152	4047	1767	293	6107	88	23	.952
Washington	154	4127	2043	318	6488	76	11	.951
AL Total	1234	32789	15639	2185	50613	640	163	.957

Team vs. Team Records

	Bos	ChA	Cle	Det	NYA	Phi	StL	Was	Won
Bos	—	6	14	10	13	7	15	13	78
ChA	16	—	13	11	15	9	14	14	92
Cle	8	9	—	12	12	7	14	14	76
Det	12	11	10	—	13	9	13	11	79
NYA	8	7	10	8	—	8	15	15	71
Phi	15	12	15	13	11	—	15	11	92
StL	7	7	8	9	7	7	—	9	54
Was	8	8	8	11	7	9	13	—	64
Lost	74	60	78	74	78	56	99	87	

1905 American League Batting Leaders

Games		At-Bats		Runs		Hits		Doubles		Triples	
B. Wallace, StL	156	G. Stone, StL	632	H. Davis, Phi	93	G. Stone, StL	187	H. Davis, Phi	47	E. Flick, Cle	18
G. Stone, StL	154	H. Davis, Phi	607	F. Jones, ChA	91	S. Crawford, Det	171	S. Crawford, Det	38	H. Ferris, Bos	16
T. Turner, Cle	154	F. Parent, Bos	602	H. Bay, Cle	90	H. Davis, Phi	171	S. Seybold, Phi	37	T. Turner, Cle	14
S. Crawford, Det	154	B. Wallace, StL	587	T. Hartsel, Phi	88	W. Keeler, NYA	169	C. Hickman, 2tm	37	G. Stone, StL	13
3 tied with	153	L. Cross, Phi	583	W. Keeler, NYA	81	H. Bay, Cle	164	2 tied with	34	J. Burkett, Bos	13

Home Runs		Total Bases		Runs Batted In		Walks		Intentional Walks	Strikeouts
H. Davis, Phi	8	G. Stone, StL	259	H. Davis, Phi	83	T. Hartsel, Phi	121	Statistic unavailable	Statistic unavailable
G. Stone, StL	7	H. Davis, Phi	254	L. Cross, Phi	77	F. Jones, ChA	73		
5 tied with	6	S. Crawford, Det	247	J. Donahue, ChA	76	K. Selbach, Bos	67		
		C. Hickman, 2tm	232	S. Crawford, Det	75	J. Burkett, Bos	67		
		E. Flick, Cle	229	T. Turner, Cle	72	G. Davis, ChA	60		

Hit By Pitch		Sac Hits		Sac Flies	Stolen Bases		Caught Stealing	GDP
J. Stahl, Was	17	W. Keeler, NYA	42	Statistic unavailable	D. Hoffman, Phi	46	Statistic unavailable	Statistic unavailable
K. Elberfeld, NYA	16	G. Davis, ChA	40		D. Fultz, NYA	44		
B. Bradley, Cle	15	H. Hill, Was	36		J. Stahl, Was	41		
I. Rockenfield, StL	14	F. Parent, Bos	35		3 tied with	36		
J. Yeager, NYA	13	H. Bay, Cle	30					

Runs Created		Runs Created/27 Outs		Batting Average		On-Base Percentage		Slugging Percentage		OBP+Slugging	
T. Hartsel, Phi	105	E. Flick, Cle	7.02	E. Flick, Cle	.306	T. Hartsel, Phi	.411	E. Flick, Cle	.462	E. Flick, Cle	.844
G. Stone, StL	103	T. Hartsel, Phi	6.83	W. Keeler, NYA	.302	E. Flick, Cle	.382	S. Crawford, Det	.430	S. Crawford, Det	.786
H. Davis, Phi	98	F. Huelsman, Was	6.17	H. Bay, Cle	.298	W. Keeler, NYA	.357	H. Davis, Phi	.418	T. Hartsel, Phi	.758
S. Crawford, Det	96	S. Crawford, Det	6.14	S. Crawford, Det	.297	S. Crawford, Det	.357	G. Stone, StL	.410	G. Stone, StL	.756
E. Flick, Cle	96	G. Stone, StL	5.89	G. Stone, StL	.296	K. Selbach, Bos	.355	C. Hickman, 2tm	.405	H. Davis, Phi	.750

1905 American League Pitching Leaders

Wins		Losses		Winning Percentage		Games		Games Started		Complete Games	
R. Waddell, Phi	27	F. Glade, StL	25	R. Waddell, Phi	.730	R. Waddell, Phi	46	G. Mullin, Det	41	G. Mullin, Det	35
E. Plank, Phi	24	C. Patten, Was	22	J. Tannehill, Bos	.710	G. Mullin, Det	44	E. Plank, Phi	41	E. Plank, Phi	35
E. Killian, Det	23	H. Howell, StL	22	A. Coakley, Phi	.692	C. Patten, Was	42	F. Owen, ChA	38	H. Howell, StL	35
N. Altrock, ChA	23	G. Mullin, Det	21	E. Plank, Phi	.667	F. Owen, ChA	42	J. Chesbro, NYA	38	E. Killian, Det	33
J. Tannehill, Bos	22	2 tied with	20	N. Altrock, ChA	.657	2 tied with	41	3 tied with	37	F. Owen, ChA	32

Shutouts		Saves		Games Finished		Batters Faced	Innings Pitched		Hits Allowed	
E. Killian, Det	8	R. Waddell, Phi	4	C. Griffith, NYA	17	Statistic unavailable	G. Mullin, Det	347.2	G. Mullin, Det	303
R. Waddell, Phi	7	C. Griffith, NYA	3	B. Hogg, NYA	13		E. Plank, Phi	346.2	C. Patten, Was	300
A. Orth, NYA	6	J. Buchanan, StL	2	C. Bender, Phi	12		F. Owen, ChA	334.0	E. Plank, Phi	287
J. Tannehill, Bos	6	B. Wolfe, Was	2	J. Powell, 2tm	12		R. Waddell, Phi	328.2	F. Owen, ChA	276
2 tied with	5	8 tied with	1	R. Waddell, Phi	11		H. Howell, StL	323.0	N. Altrock, ChA	274

Home Runs Allowed		Walks		Walks/9 Innings		Strikeouts		Strikeouts/9 Innings		Strikeout/Walk Ratio	
N. Gibson, Bos	9	G. Mullin, Det	138	C. Young, Bos	0.8	R. Waddell, Phi	287	R. Waddell, Phi	7.9	C. Young, Bos	7.00
W. Sudhoff, StL	8	F. Smith, ChA	107	A. Joss, Cle	1.4	E. Plank, Phi	210	C. Young, Bos	5.9	R. Waddell, Phi	3.19
A. Orth, NYA	8	E. Killian, Det	102	F. Owen, ChA	1.5	C. Young, Bos	210	C. Bender, Phi	5.6	A. Joss, Cle	2.87
B. Dinneen, Bos	7	3 tied with	101	B. Bernhard, Cle	1.8	H. Howell, StL	198	H. Howell, StL	5.5	E. Plank, Phi	2.80
J. Tannehill, Bos	7			N. Altrock, ChA	1.8	F. Smith, ChA	171	B. Hogg, NYA	5.5	F. Owen, ChA	2.23

Earned Run Average		Component ERA		Hit Batsmen		Wild Pitches		Opponent Average		Opponent OBP	
R. Waddell, Phi	1.48	C. Young, Bos	1.49	E. Plank, Phi	24	O. Hess, Cle	18	R. Waddell, Phi	.198	C. Young, Bos	.239
D. White, ChA	1.76	R. Waddell, Phi	1.66	E. Moore, Cle	18	B. Hogg, NYA	14	F. Smith, ChA	.208	R. Waddell, Phi	.261
C. Young, Bos	1.82	D. White, ChA	1.86	J. Townsend, Was	15	F. Smith, ChA	13	C. Young, Bos	.213	A. Joss, Cle	.266
A. Coakley, Phi	1.84	F. Owen, ChA	1.92	5 tied with	13	C. Bender, Phi	12	D. White, ChA	.218	F. Owen, ChA	.267
N. Altrock, ChA	1.88	A. Joss, Cle	1.98			2 tied with	10	H. Howell, StL	.221	D. White, ChA	.270

1905 American League Miscellaneous

Managers		
Boston	Jimmy Collins	78-74
Chicago	Fielder Jones	92-60
Cleveland	Nap Lajoie	37-21
	Bill Bradley	20-21
	Nap Lajoie	19-36
Detroit	Bill Armour	79-74
New York	Clark Griffith	71-78
Philadelphia	Connie Mack	92-56
St. Louis	Jimmy McAleer	54-99
Washington	Jake Stahl	64-87

Awards

STATS Most Valuable Player	Rube Waddell, p, Phi	
STATS Cy Young	Rube Waddell, Phi	
STATS Rookie of the Year	George Stone, of, StL	
STATS Manager of the Year	Connie Mack, Phi	

STATS All-Star Team

C	Ossee Schreckengost, Phi	.272	0	45
1B	Harry Davis, Phi	.282	8	83
2B	Danny Murphy, Phi	.278	6	71
3B	Jimmy Collins, Bos	.276	4	65
SS	George Davis, ChA	.278	1	55
OF	Sam Crawford, Det	.297	6	75
OF	Elmer Flick, Cle	.306	4	64
OF	George Stone, StL	.296	7	52
P	Nick Altrock, ChA	23-12	1.88	97 K
P	Ed Killian, Det	23-14	2.27	110 K
P	Eddie Plank, Phi	24-12	2.26	210 K
P	Rube Waddell, Phi	27-10	1.48	287 K

Postseason

World Series	Philadelphia (AL) 1 vs. NYG (NL) 4

Outstanding Performances

No-Hitters

Weldon Henley, Phi	@ StL on July 22
Frank Smith, ChA	@ Det on September 6
Bill Dinneen, Bos	vs. ChA on September 27

Team	W	L	Pct	GB	DIF	W	L	R	OR	HR	OHR	W	L	R	OR	HR	OHR	Run	HR	M/A	May	June	July	Aug	S/O
			Overall					Home Games						Road Games				Park Index				Record by Month			
New York	105	48	.686	—	174	54	21	377	234	33	19	51	27	403	271	6	6	94	451	8-3	22-6	17-10	20-6	16-9	22-14
Pittsburgh	96	57	.627	9.0	4	49	28	362	287	4	1	47	29	330	283	18	11	104	17	8-4	15-13	17-9	18-8	21-9	17-14
Chicago	92	61	.601	13.0	1	54	25	365	212	7	5	38	36	302	230	5	9	102	80	7-6	13-15	17-7	16-12	17-10	22-11
Philadelphia	83	69	.546	21.5	7	39	36	353	314	8	9	44	33	355	288	8	12	106	87	5-5	16-11	18-8	14-14	10-17	20-14
Cincinnati	79	74	.516	26.0	0	50	28	438	330	12	2	29	46	297	368	15	20	111	38	3-8	12-15	10-17	11-19	10-17	12-20
St. Louis	58	96	.377	47.5	0	32	45	245	342	13	10	26	51	290	392	7	18	86	92	5-7	9-17	5-21	10-20	10-18	12-20
Boston	51	103	.331	54.5	0	29	46	234	344	14	14	22	57	234	389	3	22	98	118						
Brooklyn	48	104	.316	56.5	0	29	47	273	379	16	16	19	57	233	428	13	8	99	152	6-9	9-19	3-20	10-14	9-18	11-24

Clinch Date—New York 9/30.

Team Batting

Team	G	AB	R	OR	H	2B	3B	HR	TB	RBI	TBB	IBB	SO	HBP	SH	SF	SB	CS	SB%	GDP	Avg	OBP	Slg
New York	155	5094	780	505	1392	191	88	39	1876	642	517	—	—	90	138	—	291	—	—	—	.273	.351	.368
Cincinnati	155	5205	735	698	1401	160	101	27	1844	611	434	—	—	52	174	—	181	—	—	—	.269	.332	.354
Philadelphia	155	5243	708	602	1362	187	82	16	1761	567	406	—	—	44	174	—	180	—	—	—	.260	.318	.336
Pittsburgh	155	5213	692	570	1385	190	91	22	1823	564	382	—	—	36	159	—	202	—	—	—	.266	.320	.350
Chicago	155	5108	667	442	1249	157	82	12	1606	522	448	—	—	61	193	—	267	—	—	—	.245	.313	.314
St. Louis	154	5066	535	734	1254	140	85	20	1624	446	391	—	—	43	110	—	162	—	—	—	.248	.307	.321
Brooklyn	155	5100	506	807	1255	154	60	29	1616	430	327	—	—	41	136	—	186	—	—	—	.246	.297	.317
Boston	156	5190	468	733	1217	148	52	17	1520	387	302	—	—	54	86	—	132	—	—	—	.234	.284	.293
NL Total	1240	41219	5091	5091	10515	1327	641	182	13670	4169	3207	—	—	421	1170	—	1601	—	—	—	.255	.315	.332
NL Avg Team	155	5152	636	636	1314	166	80	23	1709	521	401	—	—	53	146	—	200	—	—	—	.255	.315	.332

Team Pitching

Team	G	CG	ShO	Rel	Sv	IP	H	R	ER	HR	SH	SF	HB	TBB	IBB	SO	WP	Bk	H/9	SO/9	BB/9	OAvg	OOBP	ERA
Chicago	155	133	23	22	2	1407.1	1135	442	319	14	—	—	51	385	—	627	21	2	7.3	4.0	2.5	.225	.287	2.04
New York	155	117	18	42	15	1370.0	1160	505	364	25	—	—	31	364	—	760	58	3	7.6	5.0	2.4	.229	.284	2.39
Philadelphia	155	119	12	42	5	1398.2	1303	602	437	21	—	—	66	411	—	516	27	1	8.4	3.3	2.6	.253	.316	2.81
Pittsburgh	155	113	12	47	6	1382.2	1270	570	440	12	—	—	59	389	—	512	36	1	8.3	3.3	2.5	.248	.308	2.86
Cincinnati	155	119	12	39	2	1365.2	1409	698	457	22	—	—	54	439	—	547	32	1	9.3	3.6	2.9	.272	.335	3.01
Boston	156	139	14	18	0	1383.0	1390	733	541	36	—	—	28	433	—	533	30	3	9.0	3.5	2.8	.265	.324	3.52
St. Louis	154	135	10	19	2	1347.2	1431	734	537	28	—	—	49	367	—	411	31	2	9.6	2.7	2.5	.279	.333	3.59
Brooklyn	155	125	7	33	3	1347.0	1416	807	562	24	—	—	64	476	—	556	18	1	9.5	3.7	3.2	.274	.343	3.76
NL Total	1240	1000	106	262	35	11002.0	10514	5091	3657	182	—	—	402	3264	—	4462	253	14	8.6	3.7	2.7	.255	.316	2.99
NL Avg Team	155	125	13	33	4	1375.0	1314	636	457	23	—	—	50	408	—	558	32	2	8.6	3.7	2.7	.255	.316	2.99

Team Fielding

Team	G	PO	A	E	TC	DP	PB	Pct
Chicago	155	4207	2021	248	6476	99	24	.962
Pittsburgh	155	4115	2089	255	6459	112	25	.961
New York	155	4108	2057	258	6423	93	24	.960
Philadelphia	155	4161	1930	275	6366	99	13	.957
St. Louis	154	4042	2024	274	6340	83	17	.957
Cincinnati	155	4084	2150	310	6544	122	36	.953
Boston	156	4093	2138	325	6556	89	42	.950
Brooklyn	155	4022	2012	408	6442	101	21	.937
NL Total	1240	32832	16421	2353	51606	798	202	.954

Team vs. Team Records

	Bos	Bro	ChN	Cin	NYG	Phi	Pit	StL	Won
Bos	—	11	7	8	3	5	9	8	51
Bro	11	—	6	4	7	3	7	10	48
ChN	15	16	—	12	10	12	10	17	92
Cin	14	18	10	—	5	13	9	10	79
NYG	19	15	12	16	—	14	12	17	105
Phi	17	18	9	9	8	—	6	16	83
Pit	13	14	12	13	10	16	—	18	96
StL	14	12	5	12	5	6	4	—	58
Lost	103	104	61	74	48	69	57	96	

1905 National League Batting Leaders

Games		At-Bats		Runs		Hits		Doubles		Triples	
S. Magee, Phi	155	E. Abbaticchio, Bos	610	M. Donlin, NYG	124	C. Seymour, Cin	219	C. Seymour, Cin	40	C. Seymour, Cin	21
E. Courtney, Phi	155	K. Gleason, Phi	608	R. Thomas, Phi	118	M. Donlin, NYG	216	J. Titus, Phi	36	S. Magee, Phi	17
J. Slagle, ChN	155	M. Donlin, NYG	606	M. Huggins, Cin	117	H. Wagner, Pit	199	H. Wagner, Pit	32	S. Mertes, NYG	17
K. Gleason, Phi	155	T. Corcoran, Cin	605	H. Wagner, Pit	114	S. Barry, 2tm	182	M. Donlin, NYG	31	H. Smoot, StL	16
R. Cannell, Bos	154	S. Magee, Phi	603	2 tied with	100	S. Magee, Phi	180	C. Ritchey, Pit	29	M. Donlin, NYG	16

Home Runs		Total Bases		Runs Batted In		Walks		Intentional Walks		Strikeouts	
F. Odwell, Cin	9	C. Seymour, Cin	325	C. Seymour, Cin	121	M. Huggins, Cin	103	Statistic unavailable		Statistic unavailable	
C. Seymour, Cin	8	M. Donlin, NYG	300	S. Mertes, NYG	108	J. Slagle, ChN	97				
H. Lumley, Bro	7	H. Wagner, Pit	277	H. Wagner, Pit	101	R. Thomas, Phi	93				
M. Donlin, NYG	7	S. Magee, Phi	253	S. Magee, Phi	98	F. Chance, ChN	78				
B. Dahlen, NYG	7	J. Titus, Phi	239	J. Titus, Phi	89	J. Titus, Phi	69				

Hit By Pitch		Sac Hits		Sac Flies		Stolen Bases		Caught Stealing		GDP	
D. McGann, NYG	19	K. Gleason, Phi	43	Statistic unavailable		A. Devlin, NYG	59	Statistic unavailable		Statistic unavailable	
F. Chance, ChN	17	J. Tinker, ChN	29			B. Maloney, ChN	59				
D. Gessler, Bro	14	E. Courtney, Phi	26			H. Wagner, Pit	57				
A. Devlin, NYG	13	S. Barry, 2tm	25			S. Mertes, NYG	52				
3 tied with	12	F. Clarke, Pit	22			S. Magee, Phi	48				

Runs Created		Runs Created/27 Outs		Batting Average		On-Base Percentage		Slugging Percentage		OBP+Slugging	
C. Seymour, Cin	147	C. Seymour, Cin	10.18	C. Seymour, Cin	.377	F. Chance, ChN	.450	C. Seymour, Cin	.559	C. Seymour, Cin	.988
H. Wagner, Pit	136	H. Wagner, Pit	9.82	H. Wagner, Pit	.363	C. Seymour, Cin	.429	H. Wagner, Pit	.505	H. Wagner, Pit	.932
M. Donlin, NYG	130	F. Chance, ChN	9.54	M. Donlin, NYG	.356	H. Wagner, Pit	.427	M. Donlin, NYG	.495	M. Donlin, NYG	.908
J. Titus, Phi	116	M. Donlin, NYG	8,31	G. Beaumont, Pit	.328	R. Thomas, Phi	.417	J. Titus, Phi	.436	F. Chance, ChN	.883
S. Magee, Phi	115	J. Titus, Phi	7.74	R. Thomas, Phi	.317	M. Donlin, NYG	.413	M. Grady, StL	.434	J. Titus, Phi	.834

1905 National League Pitching Leaders

Wins		Losses		Winning Percentage		Games		Games Started		Complete Games	
C. Mathewson, NYG	31	V. Willis, Bos	29	S. Leever, Pit	.800	T. Pittinger, Phi	46	I. Young, Bos	42	I. Young, Bos	41
T. Pittinger, Phi	23	H. McIntire, Bro	25	C. Mathewson, NYG	.775	J. McGinnity, NYG	46	V. Willis, Bos	41	V. Willis, Bos	36
R. Ames, NYG	22	O. Overall, Cin	23	R. Ames, NYG	.733	I. Young, Bos	43	O. Overall, Cin	39	C. Fraser, Bos	35
J. McGinnity, NYG	21	K. Wilhelm, Bos	23	C. Lundgren, ChN	.722	C. Mathewson, NYG	43	J. McGinnity, NYG	38	J. Taylor, StL	34
4 tied with	20	4 tied with	21	H. Wiltse, NYG	.714	O. Overall, Cin	42	3 tied with	37	2 tied with	32

Shutouts		Saves		Games Finished		Batters Faced		Innings Pitched		Hits Allowed	
C. Mathewson, NYG	8	C. Elliott, Cin	6	C. Chech, Cin	13	Statistic unavailable		I. Young, Bos	378.0	H. McIntire, Bro	340
I. Young, Bos	7	H. Wiltse, NYG	4	H. Wiltse, NYG	12			V. Willis, Bos	342.0	V. Willis, Bos	340
E. Reulbach, ChN	5	J. McGinnity, NYG	3	M. Lynch, Pit	10			C. Mathewson, NYG	338.2	I. Young, Bos	337
D. Phillippe, Pit	5	3 tied with	2	5 tied with	8			T. Pittinger, Phi	337.1	C. Fraser, Bos	320
B. Briggs, ChN	5							C. Fraser, Bos	334.1	T. Pittinger, Phi	311

Home Runs Allowed		Walks		Walks/9 Innings		Strikeouts		Strikeouts/9 Innings		Strikeout/Walk Ratio	
B. Duggleby, Phi	10	C. Fraser, Bos	149	D. Phillippe, Pit	1.5	C. Mathewson, NYG	206	R. Ames, NYG	6.8	C. Mathewson, NYG	3.22
C. Fraser, Bos	8	O. Overall, Cin	147	T. F. Brown, ChN	1.6	R. Ames, NYG	198	H. Wiltse, NYG	5.5	D. Phillippe, Pit	2.77
K. Wilhelm, Bos	7	M. Lynch, Pit	107	I. Young, Bos	1.7	O. Overall, Cin	173	O. Overall, Cin	5.5	I. Young, Bos	2.20
V. Willis, Bos	7	V. Willis, Bos	107	C. Mathewson, NYG	1.7	B. Ewing, Cin	164	O. Overall, Cin	4.9	E. Reulbach, ChN	2.08
4 tied with	6	R. Ames, NYG	105	J. McGinnity, NYG	2.0	I. Young, Bos	156	D. Scanlan, Bro	4.9	B. Ewing, Cin	2.08

Earned Run Average		Component ERA		Hit Batsmen		Wild Pitches		Opponent Average		Opponent OBP	
C. Mathewson, NYG	1.28	C. Mathewson, NYG	1.54	H. McIntire, Bro	20	R. Ames, NYG	30	E. Reulbach, ChN	.201	C. Mathewson, NYG	.245
E. Reulbach, ChN	1.42	E. Reulbach, ChN	1.68	E. Reulbach, ChN	18	O. Overall, Cin	18	C. Mathewson, NYG	.205	E. Reulbach, ChN	.266
B. Wicker, ChN	2.02	D. Phillippe, Pit	1.93	F. Corridon, Phi	16	V. Willis, Bos	12	H. Wiltse, NYG	.219	T. F. Brown, ChN	.271
B. Briggs, ChN	2.14	B. Wicker, ChN	1.93	T. Pittinger, Phi	16	H. Wiltse, NYG	10	C. Lundgren, ChN	.220	D. Phillippe, Pit	.274
T. F. Brown, ChN	2.17	T. F. Brown, ChN	2.06	C. Case, Pit	15	3 tied with	9	B. Wicker, ChN	.221	B. Wicker, ChN	.276

1905 National League Miscellaneous

Managers		
Boston	Fred Tenney	51-103
Brooklyn	Ned Hanlon	48-104
Chicago	Frank Selee	37-28
	Frank Chance	55-33
Cincinnati	Joe Kelley	79-74
New York	John McGraw	105-48
Philadelphia	Hugh Duffy	83-69
Pittsburgh	Fred Clarke	96-57
St. Louis	Kid Nichols	5-9
	Jimmy Burke	34-56
	Matt Robison	19-31

Awards	
STATS Most Valuable Player	C. Mathewson, p, NYG
STATS Cy Young	C. Mathewson, NYG
STATS Rookie of the Year	Ed Reulbach, p, ChN
STATS Manager of the Year	Hugh Duffy, Phi

STATS All-Star Team

C	Roger Bresnahan, NYG	.302	0	46
1B	Frank Chance, ChN	.316	2	70
2B	Miller Huggins, Cin	.273	1	38
3B	Ernie Courtney, Phi	.275	2	77
SS	Honus Wagner, Pit	.363	6	101
OF	Mike Donlin, NYG	.356	7	80
OF	Cy Seymour, Cin	.377	8	121
OF	John Titus, Phi	.308	2	89
P	Red Ames, NYG	22-8	2.74	198 K
P	Christy Mathewson, NYG	31-9	1.28	206 K
P	Deacon Phillippe, Pit	20-13	2.19	133 K
P	Ed Reulbach, ChN	18-14	1.42	152 K

Postseason

World Series	New York (NL) 4 vs. Phi (AL) 1

Outstanding Performances

No-Hitters
C. Mathewson, NYG @ ChN on June 13

1906 American League Standings

Team	Overall W	L	Pct	GB	DIF	Home Games W	L	R	OR	HR	OHR	Road Games W	L	R	OR	HR	OHR	Park Index Run	HR	Record by Month M/A	May	June	July	Aug	S/O
Chicago	93	58	.616	—	45	54	23	275	180	2	1	39	35	295	280	5	10	76	19	7-6	8-13	19-10	16-13	21-4	22-12
New York	90	61	.596	3.0	48	53	23	398	294	14	8	37	38	246	249	3	13	138	136	5-8	18-5	14-11	17-10	13-14	23-13
Cleveland	89	64	.582	5.0	22	47	30	351	229	3	8	42	34	312	253	9	8	101	64	6-5	15-8	16-13	14-12	11-14	27-12
Philadelphia	78	67	.538	12.0	78	48	23	285	211	21		30	44	276	331	11	5	85	163	8-5	16-8	14-12	18-8	9-18	13-16
St. Louis	76	73	.510	16.0	0	40	34	272	225	13	10	36	39	286	273	7	4	90	212	6-7	14-11	12-14	13-13	15-11	16-17
Detroit	71	78	.477	21.0	0	42	34	315	317	4	5	29	44	203	282	6	9	125	58	6-7	12-10	17-12	11-15	9-15	16-19
Washington	55	95	.367	37.5	6	33	41	260	288	7	5	22	54	258	376	19	10	89	42	7-6	7-17	8-17	11-16	13-15	9-24
Boston	49	105	.318	45.5	0	22	54	230	364	10	22	27	51	233	342	3	15	106	182	6-7	4-22	6-17	9-22	13-13	11-24

Clinch Date—Chicago 10/03.

Team Batting

Team	G	AB	R	OR	H	2B	3B	HR	TB	RBI	TBB	IBB	SO	HBP	SH	SF	SB	CS	SB%	GDP	Avg	OBP	Slg
Cleveland	157	5425	663	482	1514	240	73	12	1936	548	330	—	—	41	190	—	203	—	—	—	.279	.325	.357
New York	155	5095	644	543	1354	166	77	17	1725	528	331	—	—	47	191	—	192	—	—	—	.266	.316	.339
Chicago	154	4925	570	460	1133	152	52	7	1410	444	453	—	—	51	227	—	214	—	—	—	.230	.302	.286
Philadelphia	149	4883	561	543	1206	213	49	32	1613	489	385	—	—	43	157	—	165	—	—	—	.247	.308	.330
St. Louis	154	5030	558	498	1244	145	60	20	1569	456	366	—	—	47	171	—	221	—	—	—	.247	.304	.312
Washington	151	4956	518	664	1180	144	65	26	1532	433	306	—	—	49	144	—	233	—	—	—	.238	.289	.309
Detroit	151	4930	518	599	1195	154	64	10	1507	409	333	—	—	34	175	—	206	—	—	—	.242	.295	.306
Boston	155	5168	463	706	1223	160	75	13	1572	408	298	—	—	41	134	—	99	—	—	—	.237	.284	.304
AL Total	1226	40412	4495	4495	10049	1374	515	137	12864	3715	2802	—	—	353	1389	—	1533	—	—	—	.249	.303	.318
AL Avg Team	153	5052	562	562	1256	172	64	17	1608	464	350	—	—	44	174	—	192	—	—	—	.249	.303	.318

Team Pitching

Team	G	CG	ShO	Rel	Sv	IP	H	R	ER	HR	SH	SF	HB	TBB	IBB	SO	WP	Bk	H/9	SO/9	BB/9	OAvg	OOBP	ERA
Cleveland	157	133	27	27	4	1412.2	1197	482	328	16	—	—	49	365	—	530	23	1	7.6	3.4	2.3	.233	.290	2.09
Chicago	154	117	32	43	3	1375.1	1212	460	326	11	—	—	32	255	—	543	33	1	7.9	3.6	1.7	.240	.281	2.13
St. Louis	154	133	17	21	5	1357.2	1132	498	336	14	—	—	61	314	—	558	38	2	7.5	3.7	2.1	.230	.284	2.23
Philadelphia	149	107	19	51	4	1322.0	1135	543	382	9	—	—	57	425	—	749	30	1	7.7	5.1	2.9	.235	.304	2.60
New York	155	99	18	68	5	1357.2	1236	543	419	21	—	—	45	351	—	605	36	2	8.2	4.0	2.3	.246	.301	2.78
Detroit	151	128	7	25	4	1334.1	1398	599	454	14	—	—	58	389	—	469	24	0	9.4	3.2	2.6	.273	.331	3.06
Washington	151	115	13	47	1	1322.2	1331	664	478	15	—	—	44	451	—	558	34	1	9.1	3.8	3.1	.265	.331	3.25
Boston	155	124	6	35	6	1382.0	1360	706	524	37	—	—	43	285	—	549	27	3	8.9	3.6	1.9	.260	.304	3.41
AL Total	1226	956	139	317	32	10864.1	10001	4495	3247	137	—	—	389	2835	—	4561	245	11	8.3	3.8	2.3	.249	.303	2.69
AL Avg Team	153	120	17	40	4	1358.1	1250	562	406	17	—	—	49	354	—	570	31	1	8.3	3.8	2.3	.249	.303	2.69

Team Fielding

Team	G	PO	A	E	TC	DP	PB	Pct
Cleveland	157	4241	2153	217	6611	111	22	.967
Chicago	154	4134	2257	243	6634	80	19	.963
Detroit	151	4014	2000	260	6274	86	10	.959
New York	155	4063	1969	272	6304	69	18	.957
Philadelphia	149	3941	1728	267	5936	86	17	.955
Washington	151	3965	1922	279	6166	78	20	.955
St. Louis	154	4073	1973	290	6336	80	20	.954
Boston	155	4109	2126	335	6570	84	31	.949
AL Total	1226	32540	16128	2163	50831	674	157	.957

Team vs. Team Records

	Bos	ChA	Cle	Det	NYA	Phi	StL	Was	Won
Bos	—	4	8	10	5	8	5	9	49
ChA	18	—	12	11	12	12	13	15	93
Cle	14	10	—	14	10	12	14	15	89
Det	12	11	8	—	11	6	9	14	71
NYA	17	10	11	11	—	13	13	15	90
Phi	14	9	10	13	8	—	9	15	78
StL	17	7	8	13	8	11	—	12	76
Was	13	7	7	6	7	5	10	—	55
Lost	105	58	64	78	61	67	73	95	

1906 American League Batting Leaders

Games		At-Bats		Runs		Hits		Doubles		Triples	
E. Flick, Cle	157	E. Flick, Cle	624	E. Flick, Cle	98	N. Lajoie, Cle	214	N. Lajoie, Cle	48	E. Flick, Cle	22
C. Stahl, Bos	155	N. Lajoie, Cle	602	T. Hartsel, Phi	96	G. Stone, StL	208	H. Davis, Phi	40	G. Stone, StL	20
G. Stone, StL	154	F. Parent, Bos	600	W. Keeler, NYA	96	E. Flick, Cle	194	E. Flick, Cle	33	S. Crawford, Det	16
J. Donahue, ChA	154	H. Chase, NYA	597	H. Davis, Phi	94	H. Chase, NYA	193	T. Turner, Cle	27	H. Ferris, Bos	13
C. Hemphill, StL	154	C. Stahl, Bos	595	G. Stone, StL	91	W. Keeler, NYA	180	G. Davis, ChA	26	2 tied with	12

Home Runs		Total Bases		Runs Batted In		Walks		Intentional Walks	Strikeouts
H. Davis, Phi	12	G. Stone, StL	291	H. Davis, Phi	96	T. Hartsel, Phi	88	Statistic unavailable	Statistic unavailable
C. Hickman, Was	9	N. Lajoie, Cle	280	N. Lajoie, Cle	91	F. Jones, ChA	83		
G. Stone, StL	6	E. Flick, Cle	274	G. Davis, ChA	80	E. Hahn, 2tm	72		
S. Seybold, Phi	5	H. Davis, Phi	253	J. Williams, NYA	77	B. Wallace, StL	58		
3 tied with	4	H. Chase, NYA	236	H. Chase, NYA	76	M. McIntyre, Det	56		

Hit By Pitch		Sac Hits		Sac Flies	Stolen Bases		Caught Stealing	GDP
H. Schlafly, Was	14	T. Jones, StL	40	Statistic unavailable	E. Flick, Cle	39	Statistic unavailable	Statistic unavailable
E. Hahn, 2tm	11	J. Donahue, ChA	36		J. Anderson, Was	39		
R. Hartzell, StL	10	B. Coughlin, Det	36		D. Altizer, Was	37		
K. Elberfeld, NYA	10	W. Keeler, NYA	35		F. Isbell, ChA	37		
J. Yeager, NYA	9	F. Isbell, ChA	31		J. Donahue, ChA	36		

Runs Created		Runs Created/27 Outs		Batting Average		On-Base Percentage		Slugging Percentage		OBP+Slugging	
G. Stone, StL	127	G. Stone, StL	8.41	G. Stone, StL	.358	G. Stone, StL	.417	G. Stone, StL	.501	G. Stone, StL	.918
E. Flick, Cle	108	N. Lajoie, Cle	6.72	N. Lajoie, Cle	.355	N. Lajoie, Cle	.392	N. Lajoie, Cle	.465	N. Lajoie, Cle	.857
N. Lajoie, Cle	105	E. Flick, Cle	6.29	H. Chase, NYA	.323	E. Flick, Cle	.372	H. Davis, Phi	.459	H. Davis, Phi	.815
H. Davis, Phi	96	H. Davis, Phi	6.23	B. Congalton, Cle	.320	S. Seybold, Phi	.367	E. Flick, Cle	.439	E. Flick, Cle	.811
2 tied with	87	S. Seybold, Phi	5.69	S. Seybold, Phi	.316	T. Hartsel, Phi	.363	C. Hickman, Was	.421	S. Seybold, Phi	.786

1906 American League Pitching Leaders

Wins		Losses		Winning Percentage		Games		Games Started		Complete Games	
A. Orth, NYA	27	J. Harris, Bos	21	E. Plank, Phi	.760	J. Chesbro, NYA	49	J. Chesbro, NYA	42	A. Orth, NYA	36
J. Chesbro, NYA	23	C. Young, Bos	21	D. White, ChA	.750	A. Orth, NYA	45	G. Mullin, Det	40	G. Mullin, Det	35
B. Rhoads, Cle	22	C. Falkenberg, Was	20	A. Joss, Cle	.700	O. Hess, Cle	43	A. Orth, NYA	39	O. Hess, Cle	33
F. Owen, ChA	22	B. Dinneen, Bos	19	B. Rhoads, Cle	.688	R. Waddell, Phi	43	3 tied with	36	B. Rhoads, Cle	31
2 tied with	21	2 tied with	18	F. Owen, ChA	.629	F. Owen, ChA	42			2 tied with	30

Shutouts		Saves		Games Finished		Batters Faced	Innings Pitched		Hits Allowed	
E. Walsh, ChA	10	C. Bender, Phi	3	C. Griffith, NYA	15	Statistic unavailable	A. Orth, NYA	338.2	A. Orth, NYA	317
A. Joss, Cle	9	O. Hess, Cle	3	J. Eubank, Det	12		O. Hess, Cle	333.2	G. Mullin, Det	315
R. Waddell, Phi	8	8 tied with	2	W. Clarkson, NYA	10		G. Mullin, Det	330.0	J. Chesbro, NYA	314
4 tied with	7			3 tied with	9		J. Chesbro, NYA	325.0	F. Owen, ChA	289
							B. Rhoads, Cle	315.0	C. Young, Bos	288

Home Runs Allowed		Walks		Walks/9 Innings		Strikeouts		Strikeouts/9 Innings		Strikeout/Walk Ratio	
J. Tannehill, Bos	9	C. Falkenberg, Was	108	C. Young, Bos	0.8	R. Waddell, Phi	196	R. Waddell, Phi	6.5	C. Young, Bos	5.60
G. Winter, Bos	8	G. Mullin, Det	108	N. Altrock, ChA	1.3	C. Falkenberg, Was	178	C. Bender, Phi	6.0	C. Bender, Phi	3.31
W. Clarkson, NYA	6	B. Rhoads, Cle	92	A. Joss, Cle	1.4	E. Walsh, ChA	171	E. Walsh, ChA	5.5	E. Walsh, ChA	2.95
6 tied with	5	R. Waddell, Phi	92	D. White, ChA	1.6	O. Hess, Cle	167	C. Falkenberg, Was	5.4	D. White, ChA	2.50
		J. Dygert, Phi	91	B. Jacobson, StL	1.6	C. Bender, Phi	159	J. Powell, StL	4.9	A. Joss, Cle	2.47

Earned Run Average		Component ERA		Hit Batsmen		Wild Pitches		Opponent Average		Opponent OBP	
D. White, ChA	1.52	D. White, ChA	1.52	O. Hess, Cle	24	C. Falkenberg, Was	14	B. Pelty, StL	.206	A. Joss, Cle	.247
B. Pelty, StL	1.59	A. Joss, Cle	1.60	B. Pelty, StL	19	H. Eells, Cle	11	D. White, ChA	.207	D. White, ChA	.249
A. Joss, Cle	1.72	E. Walsh, ChA	1.69	G. Mullin, Det	15	A. Joss, Cle	11	A. Joss, Cle	.214	E. Walsh, ChA	.263
J. Powell, StL	1.77	B. Pelty, StL	1.70	E. Plank, Phi	15	G. Mullin, Det	11	E. Walsh, ChA	.215	B. Pelty, StL	.268
B. Rhoads, Cle	1.80	J. Powell, StL	1.95	C. Falkenberg, Was	13	2 tied with	10	R. Waddell, Phi	.221	J. Powell, StL	.275

1906 American League Miscellaneous

Managers

Boston	Jimmy Collins	35-79
	Chick Stahl	14-26
Chicago	Fielder Jones	93-58
Cleveland	Nap Lajoie	89-64
Detroit	Bill Armour	71-78
New York	Clark Griffith	90-61
Philadelphia	Connie Mack	78-67
St. Louis	Jimmy McAleer	76-73
Washington	Jake Stahl	55-95

Awards

STATS Most Valuable Player	George Stone, of, StL
STATS Cy Young	Al Orth, NYA
STATS Rookie of the Year	C. Rossman, 1b, Cle
STATS Manager of the Year	Clark Griffith, NYA

STATS All-Star Team

C	Ossee Schreckengost, Phi	.284	1	41
1B	Harry Davis, Phi	.292	12	96
2B	Nap Lajoie, Cle	.355	0	91
3B	Frank LaPorte, NYA	.264	2	54
SS	George Davis, ChA	.277	0	80
OF	Elmer Flick, Cle	.311	1	62
OF	Socks Seybold, Phi	.316	5	59
OF	George Stone, StL	.358	6	71
P	Addie Joss, Cle	21-9	1.72	106 K
P	Al Orth, NYA	27-17	2.34	133 K
P	Bob Rhoads, Cle	22-10	1.80	89 K
P	Doc White, ChA	18-6	1.52	95 K

Postseason

World Series	Chicago (AL) 4 vs. Chicago (NL) 2

Outstanding Performances

None

1906 National League Standings

Team	Overall					Home Games						Road Games						Park Index		Record by Month					
	W	L	Pct	GB	DIF	W	L	R	OR	HR	OHR	W	L	R	OR	HR	OHR	Run	HR	M/A	May	June	July	Aug	S/O
Chicago	116	36	.763	—	147	56	21	345	214	7	6	60	15	360	167	13	6	103	67	10-6	19-9	17-5	20-8	26-3	24-5
New York	96	56	.632	20.0	25	51	24	309	239	9	8	45	32	316	271	6	5	96	159	12-3	14-12	16-8	16-9	16-11	22-13
Pittsburgh	93	60	.608	23.5	7	49	27	325	232	4	8	44	33	298	238	8	5	105	94	9-5	15-10	18-5	16-12	19-10	16-18
Philadelphia	71	82	.464	45.5	3	37	40	226	270	2	5	34	42	302	294	10	13	82	30	8-8	18-10	8-16	8-17	13-14	16-17
Brooklyn	66	86	.434	50.0	0	31	44	191	287	11	5	35	42	305	338	14	10	76	68	4-12	10-15	11-12	13-14	8-17	20-16
Cincinnati	64	87	.424	51.5	0	36	40	316	333	10	10	28	47	217	249	6	4	137	197	6-13	11-14	9-14	15-12	10-18	13-16
St. Louis	52	98	.347	63.0	0	28	48	241	313	6	10	24	50	229	294	4	7	103	142	6-7	14-15	5-21	11-17	9-16	7-22
Boston	49	102	.325	66.5	8	28	47	218	329	11	16	21	55	190	320	5	8	109	210	7-8	5-21	11-14	8-18	9-21	9-20

Clinch Date—Chicago 9/19.

Team Batting

Team	G	AB	R	OR	H	2B	3B	HR	TB	RBI	TBB	IBB	SO	HBP	SH	SF	SB	CS	SB%	GDP	Avg	OBP	Slg
Chicago	155	5018	705	381	1316	181	71	20	1699	539	448	—	—	45	147	—	283	—	—	—	.262	.328	.339
New York	153	4768	625	510	1217	182	53	15	1530	513	563	—	—	70	147	—	288	—	—	—	.255	.343	.321
Pittsburgh	154	5030	623	470	1313	164	67	12	1647	497	424	—	—	41	189	—	162	—	—	—	.261	.324	.327
Cincinnati	155	5025	533	582	1198	140	71	16	1528	454	395	—	—	59	170	—	170	—	—	—	.238	.302	.304
Philadelphia	154	4911	528	564	1183	197	47	12	1510	444	432	—	—	36	143	—	180	—	—	—	.241	.307	.307
Brooklyn	153	4897	496	625	1156	141	68	25	1508	407	432	—	—	36	164	—	175	—	—	—	.236	.297	.308
St. Louis	154	5075	470	607	1195	137	69	16	1500	362	361	—	—	38	119	—	110	—	—	—	.235	.291	.296
Boston	152	4925	408	649	1115	136	43	16	1385	330	356	—	—	52	119	—	95	—	—	—	.226	.286	.281
NL Total	1230	39649	4388	4388	9693	1258	489	126	12307	3546	3367	—	—	377	1286	—	1463	—	—	—	.244	.310	.310
NL Avg Team	154	4956	549	549	1212	157	61	16	1538	443	421	—	—	47	161	—	183	—	—	—	.244	.310	.310

Team Pitching

Team	G	CG	ShO	Rel	Sv	IP	H	R	ER	HR	SH	SF	HB	TBB	IBB	SO	WP	Bk	H/9	SO/9	BB/9	OAvg	OOBP	ERA
Chicago	155	125	30	33	10	1388.1	1018	381	270	12	—	—	53	446	—	702	20	4	6.6	4.6	2.9	.207	.280	1.75
Pittsburgh	154	116	27	42	2	1358.0	1234	470	333	13	—	—	42	309	—	532	26	0	8.2	3.5	2.0	.245	.294	2.21
New York	153	105	19	55	18	1334.1	1207	510	369	13	—	—	25	394	—	639	24	2	8.1	4.3	2.7	.240	.299	2.49
Philadelphia	154	108	21	52	5	1354.1	1201	564	388	13	—	—	64	436	—	500	33	2	8.0	3.3	2.9	.234	.302	2.58
Cincinnati	155	126	12	31	5	1369.2	1248	582	409	14	—	—	49	470	—	567	34	3	8.2	3.7	3.1	.250	.320	2.69
St. Louis	154	118	4	37	2	1354.0	1246	607	458	17	—	—	58	479	—	559	35	3	8.3	3.7	3.2	.246	.318	3.04
Brooklyn	153	119	22	36	11	1348.2	1255	625	469	15	—	—	38	453	—	476	18	2	8.4	3.2	3.0	.249	.316	3.13
Boston	152	137	10	16	0	1334.1	1291	649	465	24	—	—	56	436	—	562	26	2	8.7	3.8	2.9	.259	.325	3.14
NL Total	1230	954	145	302	53	10841.2	9700	4388	3161	126	—	—	385	3423	—	4537	216	18	8.0	3.8	2.8	.244	.311	2.62
NL Avg Team	154	119	18	38	7	1355.2	1213	549	395	16	—	—	48	428	—	567	27	2	8.0	3.8	2.8	.244	.311	2.62

Team Fielding

Team	G	PO	A	E	TC	DP	PB	Pct
Chicago	155	4160	1935	194	6289	100	14	.969
Pittsburgh	154	4092	1974	228	6294	109	26	.964
New York	153	3984	2120	233	6337	84	26	.963
Cincinnati	155	4063	1988	262	6313	97	21	.958
St. Louis	154	4055	2071	272	6398	92	38	.957
Philadelphia	154	4013	1827	271	6111	83	13	.956
Brooklyn	153	4020	1950	283	6253	73	16	.955
Boston	152	3978	2093	337	6408	102	23	.947
NL Total	1230	32365	15958	2080	50403	740	177	.959

Team vs. Team Records

	Bos	Bro	ChN	Cin	NYG	Phi	Pit	StL	Won
Bos	—	9	5	11	6	6	3	9	49
Bro	13	—	6	8	9	8	9	13	66
ChN	17	16	—	18	15	19	16	15	116
Cin	10	14	4	—	5	11	8	12	64
NYG	15	13	7	16	—	15	11	19	96
Phi	16	13	3	11	7	—	8	13	71
Pit	19	13	5	14	11	14	—	17	93
StL	12	8	6	9	3	9	5	—	52
Lost	102	86	36	87	56	82	60	98	

1906 National League Batting Leaders

Games			At-Bats			Runs			Hits			Doubles			Triples		
S. Shannon, 2tm		156	P. Bennett, StL		595	F. Chance, ChN		103	H. Steinfeldt, ChN		176	H. Wagner, Pit		38	W. Schulte, ChN		13
J. Nealon, Pit		154	S. Shannon, 2tm		589	H. Wagner, Pit		103	H. Wagner, Pit		175	S. Magee, Phi		36	F. Clarke, Pit		13
M. Doolan, Phi		154	C. Seymour, 2tm		576	J. Sheckard, ChN		90	C. Seymour, 2tm		165	K. Bransfield, Phi		28	J. Nealon, Pit		12
S. Magee, Phi		154	D. Casey, Bro		571	J. Nealon, Pit		82	S. Magee, Phi		159	H. Steinfeldt, ChN		27	H. Lumley, Bro		12
J. Evers, ChN		154	B. Maloney, Bro		566	3 tied with		81	M. Huggins, Cin		159	J. Sheckard, ChN		27	2 tied with		11

Home Runs			Total Bases			Runs Batted In			Walks			Intentional Walks		Strikeouts	
T. Jordan, Bro		12	H. Wagner, Pit		237	J. Nealon, Pit		83	R. Thomas, Phi		107	Statistic unavailable		Statistic unavailable	
H. Lumley, Bro		9	H. Steinfeldt, ChN		232	H. Steinfeldt, ChN		83	R. Bresnahan, NYG		81				
C. Seymour, 2tm		8	H. Lumley, Bro		231	C. Seymour, 2tm		80	J. Titus, Phi		78				
W. Schulte, ChN		7	S. Magee, Phi		229	T. Jordan, Bro		78	B. Dahlen, NYG		76				
2 tied with		6	W. Schulte, ChN		223	2 tied with		71	A. Devlin, NYG		74				

Hit By Pitch			Sac Hits			Sac Flies		Stolen Bases			Caught Stealing		GDP	
W. Alperman, Bro		14	J. Sheckard, ChN		40	Statistic unavailable		F. Chance, ChN		57	Statistic unavailable		Statistic unavailable	
H. Smoot, 2tm		14	J. Tinker, ChN		36			S. Magee, Phi		55				
H. Steinfeldt, ChN		14	B. Ganley, Pit		35			A. Devlin, NYG		54				
R. Bresnahan, NYG		14	W. Schulte, ChN		31			H. Wagner, Pit		53				
D. McGann, NYG		13	K. Gleason, Phi		31			J. Evers, ChN		49				

Runs Created			Runs Created/27 Outs			Batting Average			On-Base Percentage			Slugging Percentage			OBP+Slugging		
H. Wagner, Pit		117	H. Wagner, Pit		8.58	H. Wagner, Pit		.339	S. Strang, NYG		.423	H. Lumley, Bro		.477	H. Wagner, Pit		.875
F. Chance, ChN		112	F. Chance, ChN		8.36	H. Steinfeldt, ChN		.327	F. Chance, ChN		.419	H. Wagner, Pit		.459	H. Lumley, Bro		.864
H. Steinfeldt, ChN		106	S. Strang, NYG		7.40	H. Lumley, Bro		.324	R. Bresnahan, NYG		.418	S. Strang, NYG		.435	S. Strang, NYG		.857
S. Magee, Phi		94	H. Steinfeldt, ChN		6.95	S. Strang, NYG		.319	H. Wagner, Pit		.416	H. Steinfeldt, ChN		.430	F. Chance, ChN		.849
H. Lumley, Bro		94	H. Lumley, Bro		6.87	F. Chance, ChN		.319	A. Devlin, NYG		.396	F. Chance, ChN		.430	H. Steinfeldt, ChN		.825

1906 National League Pitching Leaders

Wins			Losses			Winning Percentage			Games			Games Started			Complete Games		
J. McGinnity, NYG		27	G. Dorner, 2tm		26	E. Reulbach, ChN		.826	J. McGinnity, NYG		45	I. Young, Bos		41	I. Young, Bos		37
T. F. Brown, ChN		26	I. Young, Bos		25	T. F. Brown, ChN		.813	I. Young, Bos		43	J. Weimer, Cin		39	B. Pfeffer, Bos		33
V. Willis, Pit		23	V. Lindaman, Bos		23	S. Leever, Pit		.759	B. Duggleby, Phi		42	J. McGinnity, NYG		37	4 tied with		32
C. Mathewson, NYG		22	B. Pfeffer, Bos		22	C. Lundgren, ChN		.739	T. Sparks, Phi		42	T. Sparks, Phi		37			
S. Leever, Pit		22	H. McIntire, Bro		21	J. Pfiester, ChN		.714	3 tied with		41	3 tied with		36			

Shutouts			Saves			Games Finished			Batters Faced		Innings Pitched			Hits Allowed		
T. F. Brown, ChN		9	G. Ferguson, NYG		7	G. Ferguson, NYG		19	Statistic unavailable		I. Young, Bos		358.1	I. Young, Bos		349
L. Leifield, Pit		8	H. Wiltse, NYG		6	H. Wiltse, NYG		12			J. McGinnity, NYG		339.2	J. McGinnity, NYG		316
7 tied with		6	E. Stricklett, Bro		5	B. Duggleby, Phi		11			V. Willis, Pit		322.0	V. Lindaman, Bos		303
			5 tied with		3	3 tied with		9			T. Sparks, Phi		316.2	V. Willis, Pit		295
											V. Lindaman, Bos		307.1	G. Dorner, 2tm		280

Home Runs Allowed			Walks			Walks/9 Innings			Strikeouts			Strikeouts/9 Innings			Strikeout/Walk Ratio		
I. Young, Bos		7	D. Scanlan, Bro		127	D. Phillippe, Pit		1.1	F. Beebe, 2tm		171	R. Ames, NYG		6.9	D. Phillippe, Pit		3.46
D. Scanlan, Bro		5	J. Lush, Phi		119	S. Leever, Pit		1.7	B. Pfeffer, Bos		158	F. Beebe, 2tm		6.7	J. Pfiester, ChN		2.43
G. Dorner, 2tm		5	B. Pfeffer, Bos		114	T. Sparks, Phi		1.8	R. Ames, NYG		156	J. Pfiester, ChN		5.5	B. Ewing, Cin		2.42
B. Duggleby, Phi		5	B. Brown, StL		112	B. Ewing, Cin		1.9	J. Pfiester, ChN		153	O. Overall, 2tm		5.1	T. F. Brown, ChN		2.36
6 tied with		4	G. Dorner, 2tm		107	J. McGinnity, NYG		1.9	2 tied with		151	J. Lush, Phi		4.8	H. Wiltse, NYG		2.16

Earned Run Average			Component ERA			Hit Batsmen			Wild Pitches			Opponent Average			Opponent OBP		
T. F. Brown, ChN		1.04	T. F. Brown, ChN		1.53	G. Dorner, 2tm		17	B. Brown, StL		12	E. Reulbach, ChN		.175	T. F. Brown, ChN		.252
J. Pfiester, ChN		1.51	J. Pfiester, ChN		1.63	B. Pfeffer, Bos		16	B. Ewing, Cin		10	J. Pfiester, ChN		.197	T. Sparks, Phi		.257
E. Reulbach, ChN		1.65	E. Reulbach, ChN		1.68	J. Lush, Phi		16	L. Richie, Phi		9	T. F. Brown, ChN		.202	J. Pfiester, ChN		.260
V. Willis, Pit		1.73	T. Sparks, Phi		1.75	3 tied with		14	I. Young, Bos		9	F. Beebe, 2tm		.209	D. Phillippe, Pit		.276
L. Leifield, Pit		1.87	B. Ewing, Cin		2.13				3 tied with		8	T. Sparks, Phi		.211	E. Reulbach, ChN		.278

1906 National League Miscellaneous

Managers		
Boston	Fred Tenney	49-102
Brooklyn	Patsy Donovan	66-86
Chicago	Frank Chance	116-36
Cincinnati	Ned Hanlon	64-87
New York	John McGraw	96-56
Philadelphia	Hugh Duffy	71-82
Pittsburgh	Fred Clarke	93-60
St. Louis	John McCloskey	52-98

Awards	
STATS Most Valuable Player	Frank Chance, 1b, ChN
STATS Cy Young	T. F. Brown, ChN
STATS Rookie of the Year	Jack Pfiester, p, ChN
STATS Manager of the Year	Frank Chance, ChN

STATS All-Star Team

C	Roger Bresnahan, NYG	.281	0	43
1B	Frank Chance, ChN	.319	3	71
2B	Sammy Strang, NYG	.319	4	49
3B	Harry Steinfeldt, ChN	.327	3	83
SS	Honus Wagner, Pit	.339	2	71
OF	Harry Lumley, Bro	.324	9	61
OF	Sherry Magee, Phi	.282	6	67
OF	Roy Thomas, Phi	.254	0	16
P	Three Finger Brown, ChN	26-6	1.04	144 K
P	Joe McGinnity, NYG	27-12	2.25	105 K
P	Jack Pfiester, ChN	20-8	1.51	153 K
P	Vic Willis, Pit	23-13	1.73	124 K

Postseason	
World Series	Chicago (NL) 2 vs. Chicago (AL) 4

Outstanding Performances

No-Hitters

Johnny Lush, Phi @ Bro on May 1
Mal Eason, Bro @ StL on July 20

1907 American League Standings

Team	Overall					Home Games						Road Games						Park Index		Record by Month					
	W	L	Pct	GB	DIF	W	L	R	OR	HR	OHR	W	L	R	OR	HR	OHR	Run	HR	M/A	May	June	July	Aug	S/O
Detroit	92	58	.613	—	32	50	27	373	265	3	5	42	31	321	267	8	3	103	69	8-5	12-9	12-12	19-9	19-9	22-14
Philadelphia	88	57	.607	1.5	45	50	20	324	235	14	6	38	37	258	276	8	7	112	143	10-4	9-14	16-8	16-10	18-10	19-11
Chicago	87	64	.576	5.5	102	48	29	316	222	0	5	39	35	272	252	5	8	99	37	6-7	19-7	14-10	15-13	14-13	17-15
Cleveland	85	67	.559	8.0	1	46	31	267	226	6	3	39	36	263	299	5	5	85	88	6-7	19-7	14-10	15-13	14-12	17-18
New York	70	78	.473	21.0	6	33	40	331	372	10	7	37	38	274	293	5	6	127	159	8-5	11-11	8-14	15-16	12-16	16-16
St. Louis	69	83	.454	24.0	2	36	40	261	262	6	11	33	43	281	293	4	6	91	170	4-11	11-13	12-13	9-16	11-15	22-15
Boston	59	90	.396	32.5	2	34	41	249	270	12	11	25	49	215	288	6	11	102	133	5-9	7-17	10-13	13-14	17-16	7-21
Washington	49	102	.325	43.5	0	27	47	228	310	2	3	22	55	278	381	10	7	85	31	4-9	6-14	8-14	10-20	7-21	14-24

Clinch Date—Detroit 10/05.

Team Batting

Team	G	AB	R	OR	H	2B	3B	HR	TB	RBI	TBB	IBB	SO	HBP	SH	SF	SB	CS	SB%	GDP	Avg	OBP	Slg
Detroit	153	5204	694	532	1383	179	75	11	1745	551	315	—		—	44	162	—	192	—	—		.266	.313	.335
New York	152	5044	605	665	1258	150	67	15	1587	497	474	—		—	53	181	—	206	—	—	.249	.302	.315
Chicago	157	5070	588	474	1205	149	33	5	1435	474	421	—		—	48	176	—	175	—	—	.238	.302	.283
Philadelphia	150	5010	582	511	1276	220	44	22	1650	485	384	—		—	27	176	—	137	—	—	.255	.311	.329
St. Louis	155	5224	542	555	1324	154	63	10	1634	433	370	—		—	39	121	—	144	—	—	.253	.308	.313
Cleveland	158	5068	530	525	1221	182	68	11	1572	433	335	—		—	56	187	—	193	—	—	.241	.295	.310
Washington	154	5112	506	691	1243	134	57	12	1527	414	390	—		—	59	141	—	223	—	—	.243	.304	.299
Boston	155	5235	464	558	1224	154	48	18	1528	405	305	—		—	35	135	—	125	—	—	.234	.281	.292
AL Total	1234	40967	4511	4511	10134	1322	455	104	12678	3692	2824	—		—	361	1228	—	1395	—	—	.247	.302	.309
AL Avg Team	154	5121	564	564	1267	165	57	13	1585	462	353	—		—	45	154	—	174	—	—	.247	.302	.309

Team Pitching

Team	G	CG	ShO	Rel	Sv	IP	H	R	ER	HR	SH	SF	HB	TBB	IBB	SO	WP	Bk	H/9	SO/9	BB/9	OAvg	OOBP	ERA
Chicago	157	112	17	53	9	1406.1	1279	474	347	13	151	—	22	305	—	604	31	1	8.2	3.9	2.0	.245	.289	2.22
Cleveland	158	127	20	36	5	1392.2	1253	525	350	8	163	—	58	362	—	513	46	1	8.1	3.3	2.3	.243	.301	2.26
Detroit	153	120	15	35	7	1370.2	1281	532	355	8	144	—	53	380	—	512	20	1	8.4	3.4	2.5	.250	.308	2.33
Philadelphia	150	106	27	65	6	1354.2	1106	511	353	13	129	—	67	378	—	789	36	1	7.3	5.2	2.5	.222	.286	2.35
Boston	155	100	17	70	7	1414.0	1222	558	385	22	159	—	40	337	—	517	28	4	7.8	3.3	2.1	.237	.289	2.45
St. Louis	155	129	15	28	9	1381.1	1254	555	401	17	179	—	52	352	—	463	22	1	8.2	3.0	2.3	.247	.303	2.61
New York	152	93	10	67	5	1333.2	1327	665	449	13	135	—	48	428	—	511	30	2	9.0	3.4	2.9	.257	.319	3.03
Washington	154	106	12	57	5	1351.1	1383	691	467	10	169	—	48	344	—	570	53	2	9.2	3.8	2.3	.263	.315	3.11
AL Total	1234	893	133	411	53	11004.2	10105	4511	3107	104	1229	—	388	2886	—	4479	266	13	8.3	3.7	2.4	.247	.302	2.54
AL Avg Team	154	112	17	51	7	1375.2	1263	564	388	13	154	—	49	361	—	560	33	2	8.3	3.7	2.4	.247	.302	2.54

Team Fielding

Team	G	PO	A	E	TC	DP	PB	Pct
Chicago	157	4207	2419	233	6859	101	24	.966
Cleveland	158	4164	2199	264	6627	137	30	.960
St. Louis	155	4132	2143	266	6541	97	13	.959
Detroit	153	4106	1951	260	6317	79	26	.959
Boston	155	4197	2174	274	6645	100	23	.959
Philadelphia	150	4046	1959	263	6268	67	14	.958
Washington	154	4046	1937	310	6293	69	25	.951
New York	152	3958	1974	334	6266	79	24	.947
AL Total	1234	32856	16756	2204	51816	729	179	.957

Team vs. Team Records

	Bos	ChA	Cle	Det	NYA	Phi	StL	Was	Won
Bos	—	10	8	6	8	8	10	9	59
ChA	11	—	10	13	12	10	16	15	87
Cle	13	11	—	11	15	8	12	15	85
Det	16	9	11	—	13	11	14	18	92
NYA	12	10	7	8	—	10	8	15	70
Phi	14	12	14	8	9	—	14	17	88
StL	12	6	10	8	14	6	—	13	69
Was	12	6	7	4	7	4	9	—	49
Lost	90	64	67	58	78	57	83	102	

1907 American League Batting Leaders

Games		At-Bats		Runs		Hits		Doubles		Triples	
J. Donahue, ChA	157	J. Donahue, ChA	609	S. Crawford, Det	102	T. Cobb, Det	212	H. Davis, Phi	37	E. Flick, Cle	18
E. Hahn, ChA	156	B. Ganley, Was	605	D. Jones, Det	101	G. Stone, StL	191	S. Crawford, Det	34	S. Crawford, Det	17
G. Stone, StL	155	T. Cobb, Det	605	T. Cobb, Det	97	S. Crawford, Det	188	N. Lajoie, Cle	30	T. Cobb, Det	15
T. Jones, StL	155	C. Hemphill, StL	603	T. Hartsel, Phi	93	B. Ganley, Was	167	3 tied with	29	B. Unglaub, Bos	13
2 tied with	154	G. Stone, StL	596	E. Hahn, ChA	87	E. Flick, Cle	166			G. Stone, StL	13

Home Runs		Total Bases		Runs Batted In		Walks		Intentional Walks	Strikeouts
H. Davis, Phi	8	T. Cobb, Det	286	T. Cobb, Det	119	T. Hartsel, Phi	106	Statistic unavailable	Statistic unavailable
T. Cobb, Det	5	S. Crawford, Det	268	S. Seybold, Phi	92	E. Hahn, ChA	84		
D. Hoffman, NYA	5	G. Stone, StL	243	H. Davis, Phi	87	F. Jones, ChA	67		
S. Seybold, Phi	5	H. Davis, Phi	232	S. Crawford, Det	81	E. Flick, Cle	64		
3 tied with	4	E. Flick, Cle	226	B. Wallace, StL	70	D. Jones, Det	60		

Hit By Pitch		Sac Hits		Sac Flies	Stolen Bases		Caught Stealing	GDP
B. Hinchman, Cle	15	B. Bradley, Cle	46	Statistic unavailable	T. Cobb, Det	49	Statistic unavailable	Statistic unavailable
J. Delahanty, 2tm	14	S. Nicholls, Phi	34		W. Conroy, NYA	41		
D. Hoffman, NYA	13	F. Jones, ChA	34		E. Flick, Cle	41		
K. Elberfeld, NYA	13	C. Rossman, Det	28		B. Ganley, Was	40		
2 tied with	12	B. Ganley, Was	27		D. Altizer, Was	38		

Runs Created		Runs Created/27 Outs		Batting Average		On-Base Percentage		Slugging Percentage		OBP+Slugging	
T. Cobb, Det	133	T. Cobb, Det	8.53	T. Cobb, Det	.350	T. Hartsel, Phi	.405	T. Cobb, Det	.473	T. Cobb, Det	.853
S. Crawford, Det	117	S. Crawford, Det	7.51	S. Crawford, Det	.323	G. Stone, StL	.387	S. Crawford, Det	.460	S. Crawford, Det	.826
E. Flick, Cle	103	E. Flick, Cle	6.76	G. Stone, StL	.320	E. Flick, Cle	.386	E. Flick, Cle	.412	E. Flick, Cle	.798
G. Stone, StL	99	T. Hartsel, Phi	6.70	E. Flick, Cle	.302	T. Cobb, Det	.380	G. Stone, StL	.408	G. Stone, StL	.795
T. Hartsel, Phi	97	G. Stone, StL	6.18	S. Nicholls, Phi	.302	S. Crawford, Det	.366	H. Davis, Phi	.399	T. Hartsel, Phi	.771

1907 American League Pitching Leaders

Wins		Losses		Winning Percentage		Games		Games Started		Complete Games	
A. Joss, Cle	27	B. Pelty, StL	21	W. Donovan, Det	.862	E. Walsh, ChA	56	E. Walsh, ChA	46	E. Walsh, ChA	37
D. White, ChA	27	A. Orth, NYA	21	J. Dygert, Phi	.714	G. Mullin, Det	46	G. Mullin, Det	42	G. Mullin, Det	35
E. Killian, Det	25	C. Smith, Was	20	A. Joss, Cle	.711	D. White, ChA	46	E. Plank, Phi	40	A. Joss, Cle	34
W. Donovan, Det	25	G. Mullin, Det	20	D. White, ChA	.675	R. Waddell, Phi	44	A. Joss, Cle	38	E. Plank, Phi	33
2 tied with	24	E. Walsh, ChA	18	2 tied with	.667	2 tied with	43	2 tied with	37	C. Young, Bos	33

Shutouts		Saves		Games Finished		Batters Faced		Innings Pitched		Hits Allowed	
E. Plank, Phi	8	E. Walsh, ChA	4	T. Pruiett, Bos	15	E. Walsh, ChA	1663	E. Walsh, ChA	422.1	G. Mullin, Det	346
D. White, ChA	7	B. Dinneen, 2tm	4	B. Keefe, NYA	14	G. Mullin, Det	1493	G. Mullin, Det	357.1	E. Walsh, ChA	341
R. Waddell, Phi	7	6 tied with	3	J. Dygert, Phi	12	E. Plank, Phi	1390	E. Plank, Phi	343.2	E. Killian, Det	286
A. Joss, Cle	6			E. Walsh, ChA	10	A. Joss, Cle	1332	C. Young, Bos	343.1	C. Young, Bos	286
C. Young, Bos	6			L. Hughes, Was	10	C. Young, Bos	1328	A. Joss, Cle	338.2	E. Plank, Phi	282

Home Runs Allowed		Walks		Walks/9 Innings		Strikeouts		Strikeouts/9 Innings		Strikeout/Walk Ratio	
B. Dinneen, 2tm	8	F. Smith, ChA	111	D. White, ChA	1.2	R. Waddell, Phi	232	R. Waddell, Phi	7.3	D. White, ChA	3.71
E. Plank, Phi	5	G. Mullin, Det	106	N. Altrock, ChA	1.3	E. Walsh, ChA	206	J. Dygert, Phi	5.2	C. Bender, Phi	3.29
R. Glaze, Bos	4	E. Killian, Det	91	C. Young, Bos	1.3	E. Plank, Phi	183	E. Plank, Phi	4.8	R. Waddell, Phi	3.18
C. Morgan, 2tm	4	H. Howell, StL	88	C. Bender, Phi	1.4	J. Dygert, Phi	151	C. Bender, Phi	4.6	C. Young, Bos	2.88
J. Powell, StL	4	E. Walsh, ChA	87	A. Joss, Cle	1.4	C. Young, Bos	147	E. Walsh, ChA	4.4	E. Walsh, ChA	2.37

Earned Run Average		Component ERA		Hit Batsmen		Wild Pitches		Opponent Average		Opponent OBP	
E. Walsh, ChA	1.60	G. Winter, Bos	1.75	B. Pelty, StL	19	E. Walsh, ChA	14	J. Dygert, Phi	.213	C. Bender, Phi	.254
E. Killian, Det	1.78	C. Bender, Phi	1.76	J. Dygert, Phi	18	B. Rhoads, Cle	14	G. Winter, Bos	.215	A. Joss, Cle	.261
A. Joss, Cle	1.83	A. Joss, Cle	1.80	E. Plank, Phi	17	C. Falkenberg, Was	13	C. Bender, Phi	.221	C. Young, Bos	.264
H. Howell, StL	1.93	C. Young, Bos	1.85	R. Waddell, Phi	16	J. Dygert, Phi	12	E. Plank, Phi	.224	G. Winter, Bos	.266
C. Young, Bos	1.99	E. Walsh, ChA	1.86	2 tied with	15	F. Smith, ChA	12	E. Walsh, ChA	.224	E. Walsh, ChA	.270

1907 American League Miscellaneous

Managers

Boston	Cy Young	3-3
	George Huff	2-6
	Bob Unglaub	9-20
	Deacon McGuire	45-61
Chicago	Fielder Jones	87-64
Cleveland	Nap Lajoie	85-67
Detroit	Hughie Jennings	92-58
New York	Clark Griffith	70-78
Philadelphia	Connie Mack	88-57
St. Louis	Jimmy McAleer	69-83
Washington	Joe Cantillon	49-102

Awards

STATS Most Valuable Player	Ty Cobb, of, Det
STATS Cy Young	Addie Joss, Cle
STATS Rookie of the Year	Glenn Liebhardt, p, Cle
STATS Manager of the Year	Hughie Jennings, Det

STATS All-Star Team

C	Nig Clarke, Cle	.269	3	33
1B	Harry Davis, Phi	.266	8	87
2B	Nap Lajoie, Cle	.299	2	63
3B	Jimmy Collins, 2tm	.279	0	45
SS	Kid Elberfeld, NYA	.271	0	51
OF	Ty Cobb, Det	.350	5	119
OF	Sam Crawford, Det	.323	4	81
OF	Elmer Flick, Cle	.302	3	58
P	Wild Bill Donovan, Det	25-4	2.19	123 K
P	Addie Joss, Cle	27-11	1.83	127 K
P	Ed Killian, Det	25-13	1.78	96 K
P	Ed Walsh, ChA	24-18	1.60	206 K

Postseason

World Series	Det (AL) 0 vs. ChN (NL) 4 (1 tie)

Outstanding Performances

None

1907 National League Standings

Team	W	L	Pct	GB	DIF	W	L	R	OR	HR	OHR	W	L	R	OR	HR	OHR	Run	HR	M/A	May	June	July	Aug	S/O
			Overall					Home Games						Road Games				Park Index				Record by Month			
Chicago	107	45	.704	—	151	54	19	282	198	2	5	53	26	290	192	11	6	108	45	13-2	16-7	18-7	20-8	22-8	18-13
Pittsburgh	91	63	.591	17.0	0	47	29	330	258	7	3	44	34	304	252	12	9	109	49	7-3	12-12	15-10	21-8	14-16	22-14
Philadelphia	83	64	.565	21.5	4	45	30	265	247	2	4	38	34	247	229	10	9	103	30	8-5	13-10	12-11	13-12	19-13	18-13
New York	82	71	.536	25.5	25	45	30	317	250	19	19	37	41	257	260	4	6	114	395	11-3	17-7	8-11	18-13	15-14	13-23
Brooklyn	65	83	.439	40.0	0	37	38	223	232	9	10	28	45	223	290	9	6	86	123	1-11	10-16	12-11	18-13	14-14	10-18
Cincinnati	66	87	.431	41.5	5	43	36	287	227	3	5	23	51	239	292	12	11	91	33	4-10	11-12	14-13	8-17	13-17	16-18
Boston	58	90	.392	47.0	4	31	42	253	304	14	20	27	48	249	348	8	8	96	218	6-7	10-15	10-10	11-19	6-24	15-15
St. Louis	52	101	.340	55.5	0	31	47	223	289	8	10	21	54	196	317	11	10	96	82	3-12	7-17	6-22	5-24	14-11	17-15

Clinch Date—Chicago 9/23.

Team Batting

Team	G	AB	R	OR	H	2B	3B	HR	TB	RBI	TBB	IBB	SO	HBP	SH	SF	SB	CS	SB%	GDP	Avg	OBP	Slg
Pittsburgh	157	4957	634	510	1261	133	78	19	1607	485	469	—	—	46	178	—	264	—	—	—	.254	.325	.324
New York	155	4874	574	510	1222	160	48	23	1547	475	516	—	—	69	165	—	205	—	—	—	.251	.331	.317
Chicago	155	4892	574	390	1224	162	48	15	1521	450	435	—	—	48	195	—	158	—	—	—	.247	.304	.318
Cincinnati	156	4966	526	519	1226	126	90	15	1577	443	372	—	—	34	196	—	158	—	—	—	.236	.304	.318
Philadelphia	149	4725	512	476	1113	162	65	12	1441	424	424	—	—	41	130	—	154	—	—	—	.243	.304	.305
Boston	152	5020	502	652	1222	142	61	22	1552	395	413	—	—	57	131	—	118	—	—	—	.243	.308	.309
Brooklyn	153	4895	446	522	1135	142	63	18	1457	380	336	—	—	40	197	—	121	—	—	—	.232	.287	.298
St. Louis	155	5008	419	608	1163	121	51	19	1443	331	312	—	—	42	156	—	125	—	—	—	.232	.283	.288
NL Total	1232	39337	4187	4187	9566	1148	504	141	12145	3383	3277	—	—	377	1348	—	1380	—	—	—	.243	.308	.309
NL Avg Team	154	4917	523	523	1196	144	63	18	1518	423	410	—	—	47	169	—	173	—	—	—	.243	.308	.309

Team Pitching

Team	G	CG	ShO	Rel	Sv	IP	H	R	ER	HR	SH	SF	HB	TBB	IBB	SO	WP	Bk	H/9	SO/9	BB/9	OAvg	OOBP	ERA
Chicago	155	114	32	45	8	1373.1	1054	390	264	11	—	—	38	368	—	586	25	1	6.9	3.8	2.6	.216	.281	1.73
Pittsburgh	157	111	24	51	5	1363.0	1207	510	348	12	—	—	46	368	—	497	20	1	8.0	3.3	2.4	.241	.299	2.30
Brooklyn	153	125	20	29	1	1356.1	1218	522	359	16	—	—	39	463	—	479	21	0	8.1	3.2	3.1	.249	.319	2.38
Cincinnati	156	118	10	39	2	1351.1	1223	519	362	16	—	—	66	444	—	481	11	0	8.1	3.2	3.0	.251	.322	2.41
Philadelphia	149	110	21	46	4	1299.1	1095	476	351	13	—	—	52	422	—	499	20	1	7.6	3.5	2.9	.253	.327	2.43
New York	155	109	22	63	13	1371.0	1219	510	373	25	—	—	40	369	—	655	41	3	8.0	4.3	2.4	.239	.295	2.45
St. Louis	155	127	19	29	2	1365.2	1212	608	408	20	—	—	48	500	—	594	49	3	8.0	3.9	3.3	.242	.317	2.69
Boston	152	121	9	38	2	1338.2	1324	652	496	28	—	—	68	458	—	426	20	2	8.9	2.9	3.1	.270	.341	3.33
NL Total	1232	935	157	340	37	10818.2	9552	4187	2961	141	—	—	397	3426	—	4217	207	10	8.0	3.5	2.9	.243	.310	2.46
NL Avg Team	154	117	20	43	5	1352.2	1194	523	370	18	—	—	50	428	—	527	26	1	8.0	3.5	2.9	.243	.310	2.46

Team Fielding

Team	G	PO	A	E	TC	DP	PB	Pct
Chicago	155	4110	2071	211	6392	110	6	.967
Cincinnati	156	4042	1880	227	6149	118	14	.963
New York	155	4089	1893	232	6214	75	19	.963
Boston	152	3970	2114	249	6333	128	25	.961
Pittsburgh	157	4078	1922	256	6256	75	24	.959
Brooklyn	153	4053	2013	262	6328	94	17	.959
Philadelphia	149	3883	1875	256	6014	104	20	.957
St. Louis	155	4077	2115	340	6532	105	25	.948
NL Total	1232	32302	15883	2033	50218	809	147	.960

Team vs. Team Records

	Bos	Bro	ChN	Cin	NYG	Phi	Pit	StL	Won
Bos	—	12	5	9	9	8	9	6	58
Bro	7	—	5	15	10	8	6	14	65
ChN	17	15	—	17	16	14	12	16	107
Cin	13	7	5	—	9	8	10	14	66
NYG	13	12	6	13	—	11	10	17	82
Phi	11	13	8	13	10	—	14	14	83
Pit	13	16	10	12	12	8	—	20	91
StL	16	8	6	8	5	7	2	—	52
Lost	90	83	45	87	71	64	63	101	

1907 National League Batting Leaders

Games		At-Bats		Runs		Hits		Doubles		Triples	
M. Huggins, Cin	156	S. Shannon, NYG	585	S. Shannon, NYG	104	G. Beaumont, Bos	187	H. Wagner, Pit	38	W. Alperman, Bro	16
S. Shannon, NYG	155	G. Beaumont, Bos	580	T. Leach, Pit	102	H. Wagner, Pit	180	S. Magee, Phi	28	J. Ganzel, Cin	16
H. Steinfeldt, ChN	152	M. Huggins, Cin	561	H. Wagner, Pit	98	T. Leach, Pit	166	H. Steinfeldt, ChN	25	G. Beaumont, Bos	14
J. Evers, ChN	151	B. Byrne, StL	559	F. Clarke, Pit	97	S. Magee, Phi	165	C. Seymour, NYG	25	H. Wagner, Pit	14
3 tied with	150	2 tied with	558	F. Tenney, Bos	83	M. Mitchell, Cin	163	D. Brain, Bos	24	F. Clarke, Pit	13

Home Runs		Total Bases		Runs Batted In		Walks		Intentional Walks		Strikeouts	
D. Brain, Bos	10	H. Wagner, Pit	264	S. Magee, Phi	85	M. Huggins, Cin	83	Statistic unavailable		Statistic unavailable	
H. Lumley, Bro	9	G. Beaumont, Bos	246	E. Abbaticchio, Pit	82	R. Thomas, Phi	83				
R. Murray, StL	7	S. Magee, Phi	229	H. Wagner, Pit	82	S. Shannon, NYG	82				
H. Wagner, Pit	6	T. Leach, Pit	221	C. Seymour, NYG	75	F. Tenney, Bos	82				
G. Browne, NYG	5	D. Brain, Bos	214	H. Steinfeldt, ChN	70	G. Anderson, Pit	80				

Hit By Pitch		Sac Hits		Sac Flies		Stolen Bases		Caught Stealing		GDP	
A. Devlin, NYG	15	O. Knabe, Phi	40	Statistic unavailable		H. Wagner, Pit	61	Statistic unavailable		Statistic unavailable	
F. Chance, ChN	13	A. Devlin, NYG	36			S. Magee, Phi	46				
W. Alperman, Bro	12	J. Sheckard, ChN	35			J. Evers, ChN	46				
B. Maloney, Bro	10	D. Casey, Bro	32			T. Leach, Pit	43				
2 tied with	9	T. Leach, Pit	29			A. Devlin, NYG	38				

Runs Created		Runs Created/27 Outs		Batting Average		On-Base Percentage		Slugging Percentage		OBP+Slugging	
H. Wagner, Pit	121	H. Wagner, Pit	8.76	H. Wagner, Pit	.350	H. Wagner, Pit	.408	H. Wagner, Pit	.513	H. Wagner, Pit	.921
S. Magee, Phi	104	S. Magee, Phi	7.60	S. Magee, Phi	.328	S. Magee, Phi	.396	S. Magee, Phi	.455	S. Magee, Phi	.852
F. Clarke, Pit	92	F. Chance, ChN	6.43	G. Beaumont, Bos	.322	F. Chance, ChN	.395	H. Lumley, Bro	.425	G. Beaumont, Bos	.790
G. Beaumont, Bos	89	F. Clarke, Pit	6.25	T. Leach, Pit	.303	S. Strang, NYG	.388	G. Beaumont, Bos	.424	F. Clarke, Pit	.772
T. Leach, Pit	89	S. Strang, NYG	5.97	C. Seymour, NYG	.294	F. Clarke, Pit	.383	D. Brain, Bos	.420	S. Strang, NYG	.770

1907 National League Pitching Leaders

Wins		Losses		Winning Percentage		Games		Games Started		Complete Games	
C. Mathewson, NYG	24	S. McGlynn, StL	25	E. Reulbach, ChN	.810	J. McGinnity, NYG	47	S. McGlynn, StL	39	S. McGlynn, StL	33
O. Overall, ChN	23	I. Young, Bos	23	T. F. Brown, ChN	.769	S. McGlynn, StL	45	B. Ewing, Cin	37	B. Ewing, Cin	32
T. Sparks, Phi	22	F. Beebe, StL	19	O. Overall, ChN	.742	B. Ewing, Cin	41	V. Willis, Pit	37	C. Mathewson, NYG	31
V. Willis, Pit	21	E. Karger, StL	19	T. Sparks, Phi	.733	C. Mathewson, NYG	41	C. Mathewson, NYG	36	E. Karger, StL	28
2 tied with	20	B. Ewing, Cin	19	C. Lundgren, ChN	.720	2 tied with	40	J. McGinnity, NYG	34	V. Willis, Pit	27

Shutouts		Saves		Games Finished		Batters Faced		Innings Pitched		Hits Allowed	
O. Overall, ChN	8	J. McGinnity, NYG	4	J. McGinnity, NYG	11	Statistic unavailable		S. McGlynn, StL	352.1	S. McGlynn, StL	329
C. Mathewson, NYG	8	O. Overall, ChN	3	J. Boultes, Bos	10			B. Ewing, Cin	332.2	J. McGinnity, NYG	320
C. Lundgren, ChN	7	T. F. Brown, ChN	3	L. Richie, Phi	10			C. Mathewson, NYG	315.0	I. Young, Bos	287
5 tied with	6	4 tied with	2	H. Camnitz, Pit	10			J. McGinnity, NYG	310.1	B. Ewing, Cin	279
				3 tied with	9			E. Karger, StL	310.0	L. Leifield, Pit	270

Home Runs Allowed		Walks		Walks/9 Innings		Strikeouts		Strikeouts/9 Innings		Strikeout/Walk Ratio	
V. Lindaman, Bos	10	S. McGlynn, StL	112	D. Phillippe, Pit	1.5	C. Mathewson, NYG	178	R. Ames, NYG	5.6	C. Mathewson, NYG	3.36
S. McGlynn, StL	6	F. Beebe, StL	109	C. Mathewson, NYG	1.5	B. Ewing, Cin	147	F. Beebe, StL	5.3	T. F. Brown, ChN	2.67
H. McIntire, Bro	6	V. Lindaman, Bos	108	T. F. Brown, ChN	1.5	R. Ames, NYG	146	C. Mathewson, NYG	5.1	C. Mathewson, NYG	2.07
J. Weimer, Cin	6	R. Ames, NYG	108	J. McGinnity, NYG	1.7	F. Beebe, StL	141	O. Overall, ChN	4.7	E. Karger, StL	2.06
J. McGinnity, NYG	6	2 tied with	101	T. Sparks, Phi	1.7	O. Overall, ChN	141	E. Reulbach, ChN	4.5	O. Overall, ChN	2.04

Earned Run Average		Component ERA		Hit Batsmen		Wild Pitches		Opponent Average		Opponent OBP	
J. Pfiester, ChN	1.15	J. Pfiester, ChN	1.67	J. Weimer, Cin	23	R. Ames, NYG	20	C. Lundgren, ChN	.185	C. Mathewson, NYG	.251
C. Lundgren, ChN	1.17	C. Mathewson, NYG	1.67	V. Lindaman, Bos	15	F. Beebe, StL	15	J. Pfiester, ChN	.207	T. F. Brown, ChN	.262
T. F. Brown, ChN	1.39	C. Lundgren, ChN	1.68	G. Dorner, Bos	15	S. McGlynn, StL	11	O. Overall, ChN	.208	J. Pfiester, ChN	.263
S. Leever, Pit	1.66	T. F. Brown, ChN	1.70	J. McGinnity, NYG	15	N. Rucker, Bro	10	H. Camnitz, Pit	.211	E. Karger, StL	.265
O. Overall, ChN	1.68	O. Overall, ChN	1.84	I. Young, Bos	13	O. Overall, ChN	10	C. Mathewson, NYG	.216	O. Overall, ChN	.268

1907 National League Miscellaneous

Managers

Boston	Fred Tenney	58-90
Brooklyn	Patsy Donovan	65-83
Chicago	Frank Chance	107-45
Cincinnati	Ned Hanlon	66-87
New York	John McGraw	82-71
Philadelphia	Billy Murray	83-64
Pittsburgh	Fred Clarke	91-63
St. Louis	John McCloskey	52-101

Awards

STATS Most Valuable Player	Honus Wagner, ss, Pit
STATS Cy Young	Orval Overall, ChN
STATS Rookie of the Year	Mike Mitchell, of, Cin
STATS Manager of the Year	Frank Chance, ChN

STATS All-Star Team

C	Roger Bresnahan, NYG	.253	4	38
1B	Frank Chance, ChN	.293	1	49
2B	Ed Abbaticchio, Pit	.262	2	82
3B	Dave Brain, Bos	.279	10	56
SS	Honus Wagner, Pit	.350	6	82
OF	Fred Clarke, Pit	.289	2	59
OF	Tommy Leach, Pit	.303	4	43
OF	Sherry Magee, Phi	.328	4	85
P	Three Finger Brown, ChN	20-6	1.39	107 K
P	Christy Mathewson, NYG	24-12	2.00	178 K
P	Orval Overall, ChN	23-8	1.68	141 K
P	Tully Sparks, Phi	22-8	2.00	90 K

Postseason

World Series	ChN (NL) 4 vs. Det (AL) 0 (1 tie)

Outstanding Performances

No-Hitters
Big Jeff Pfeffer, Bos   vs. Cin on May 8
Nick Maddox, Pit   vs. Bro on September 20
Cycles
Johnny Bates, Bos   on April 26

1908 American League Standings

	Overall					Home Games						Road Games						Park Index		Record by Month					
Team	W	L	Pct	GB	DIF	W	L	R	OR	HR	OHR	W	L	R	OR	HR	OHR	Run	HR	M/A	May	June	July	Aug	S/O
Detroit	90	63	.588	—	85	44	33	315	300	6	6	46	30	332	247	13	6	105	62	3-9	17-7	14-13	23-6	11-13	22-15
Cleveland	90	64	.584	0.5	17	51	26	305	223	8	6	39	38	263	234	10	10	106	70	8-5	11-13	18-8	12-17	17-10	24-11
Chicago	88	64	.579	1.5	19	51	25	271	184	1	4	37	39	266	286	2	7	82	56	7-7	10-12	19-9	16-13	14-11	22-12
St. Louis	83	69	.546	6.5	29	46	31	292	234	12	2	37	38	252	249	8	5	102	105	9-6	12-12	17-8	18-12	11-12	16-19
Boston	75	79	.487	15.5	3	37	40	273	249	9	9	38	39	291	264	5	9	94	129	7-7	8-17	11-12	17-14	13-12	19-17
Philadelphia	68	85	.444	22.0	5	46	30	294	272	11	5	22	55	192	290	10	5	119	108	8-7	12-11	11-13	13-15	14-11	10-28
Washington	67	85	.441	22.5	0	43	32	249	237	2	8	24	53	230	302	6	8	94	73	5-9	12-11	5-20	13-15	13-11	19-19
New York	51	103	.331	39.5	38	30	47	234	352	11	16	21	56	225	361	2	10	100	225	8-5	11-10	10-22	3-23	6-19	13-24

Clinch Date—Detroit 10/06.

Team Batting

Team	G	AB	R	OR	H	2B	3B	HR	TB	RBI	TBB	IBB	SO	HBP	SH	SF	SB	CS	SB%	GDP	Avg	OBP	Slg
Detroit	154	5115	647	547	1347	199	86	19	1775	520	320	—	—	42	189	—	165	—	—		.263	.312	.347
Cleveland	157	5108	568	457	1221	188	58	18	1579	458	364	—	—	55	228	—	177	—	—		.239	.297	.309
Boston	155	5048	564	513	1239	117	88	14	1574	444	289	—	—	69	172	—	167	—	—		.245	.295	.312
St. Louis	155	5151	544	483	1261	173	52	20	1598	447	343	—	—	35	223	—	126	—	—		.245	.296	.310
Chicago	156	5027	537	470	1127	145	41	3	1363	430	463	—	—	62	236	—	209	—	—		.224	.298	.271
Philadelphia	157	5065	486	562	1131	183	50	21	1477	392	368	—	—	37	177	—	116	—	—		.223	.281	.292
Washington	155	5041	479	539	1186	132	74	8	1490	378	368	—	—	43	194	—	170	—	—		.235	.293	.296
New York	155	5047	459	713	1190	142	50	13	1471	372	288	—	—	45	188	—	231	—	—		.236	.283	.291
AL Total	1244	40602	4284	4284	9702	1279	499	116	12327	3441	2803	—	—	388	1607	—	1361	—	—		.239	.294	.304
AL Avg Team	156	5075	536	536	1213	160	62	15	1541	430	350	—	—	49	201	—	170	—	—		.239	.294	.304

Team Pitching

Team	G	CG	ShO	Rel	Sv	IP	H	R	ER	HR	SH	SF	HB	TBB	IBB	SO	WP	Bk	H/9	SO/9	BB/9	OAvg	OOBP	ERA
Cleveland	157	108	18	62	5	1424.1	1172	457	319	16	—	—	32	328	—	548	23	1	7.4	3.5	2.1	.228	.279	2.02
St. Louis	155	107	11	61	5	1397.0	1151	483	333	7	—	—	63	387	—	607	22	0	7.4	3.9	2.5	.230	.294	2.15
Chicago	156	107	23	62	10	1414.0	1165	470	349	11	—	—	28	284	—	623	30	3	7.4	4.0	1.8	.225	.269	2.22
Boston	155	102	12	65	7	1380.1	1200	513	349	18	—	—	47	364	—	624	41	5	7.8	4.1	2.4	.248	.307	2.28
Washington	155	106	15	60	7	1391.2	1236	539	362	16	—	—	41	348	—	649	48	4	8.0	4.2	2.3	.240	.293	2.34
Detroit	154	119	15	39	5	1374.1	1313	547	367	12	—	—	60	318	—	553	33	1	8.6	3.6	2.1	.255	.306	2.40
Philadelphia	157	102	23	73	4	1400.1	1194	562	398	10	—	—	53	410	—	741	46	1	7.7	4.8	2.6	.235	.298	2.56
New York	155	90	11	75	3	1366.0	1293	713	479	26	—	—	64	458	—	585	34	0	8.5	3.9	3.0	.252	.321	3.16
AL Total	1244	841	132	497	46	11148.0	9724	4284	2956	116	—	—	388	2897	—	4930	277	13	7.8	4.0	2.3	.239	.296	2.39
AL Avg Team	156	105	17	62	6	1393.0	1216	536	370	15	—	—	49	362	—	616	35	2	7.8	4.0	2.3	.239	.296	2.39

Team Fielding

Team	G	PO	A	E	TC	DP	PB	Pct
Chicago	156	4238	2348	232	6818	82	13	.966
St. Louis	155	4174	2127	237	6538	97	23	.964
Cleveland	157	4250	2185	257	6692	95	22	.962
Washington	155	4128	2117	275	6520	89	15	.958
Philadelphia	157	4158	1886	272	6316	68	20	.957
Boston	155	4135	2115	297	6547	71	22	.955
Detroit	154	4136	2075	305	6516	95	7	.953
New York	155	4096	2000	337	6433	78	14	.948
AL Total	1244	33315	16853	2212	52380	675	136	.958

Team vs. Team Records

	Bos	ChA	Cle	Det	NYA	Phi	StL	Was	Won
Bos	—	6	10	11	12	10	15	11	75
ChA	16	—	8	9	16	13	11	15	88
Cle	12	14	—	13	16	16	11	8	90
Det	11	13	9	—	15	14	12	16	90
NYA	10	6	6	7	—	8	5	9	51
Phi	12	9	6	8	14	—	8	11	68
StL	7	10	11	10	17	13	—	15	83
Was	11	6	14	5	13	11	7	—	67
Lost	79	64	64	63	103	85	69	85	

1908 American League Batting Leaders

Games			At-Bats			Runs			Hits			Doubles			Triples		
N. Lajoie, Cle		157	S. Crawford, Det		591	M. McIntyre, Det		105	T. Cobb, Det		188	T. Cobb, Det		36	T. Cobb, Det		20
T. Jones, StL		155	G. Stone, StL		588	S. Crawford, Det		102	S. Crawford, Det		184	C. Rossman, Det		33	J. Stahl, 2tm		16
G. McBride, Was		155	G. Schaefer, Det		584	G. Schaefer, Det		96	M. McIntyre, Det		168	S. Crawford, Det		33	S. Crawford, Det		16
J. Freeman, Was		154	T. Cobb, Det		581	F. Jones, ChA		92	N. Lajoie, Cle		168	N. Lajoie, Cle		32	D. Gessler, Bos		14
3 tied with		153	N. Lajoie, Cle		581	G. Stone, StL		89	G. Stone, StL		165	G. Stovall, Cle		29	2 tied with		13

Home Runs			Total Bases			Runs Batted In			Walks			Intentional Walks			Strikeouts		
S. Crawford, Det		7	T. Cobb, Det		276	T. Cobb, Det		108	T. Hartsel, Phi		93	Statistic unavailable			Statistic unavailable		
B. Hinchman, Cle		6	S. Crawford, Det		270	S. Crawford, Det		80	F. Jones, ChA		86						
H. Niles, 2tm		5	C. Rossman, Det		219	H. Ferris, StL		74	M. McIntyre, Det		83						
G. Stone, StL		5	M. McIntyre, Det		218	N. Lajoie, Cle		74	J. Clarke, Cle		76						
H. Davis, Phi		5	N. Lajoie, Cle		218	C. Rossman, Det		71	H. Davis, Phi		61						

Hit By Pitch			Sac Hits			Sac Flies			Stolen Bases			Caught Stealing			GDP		
J. Stahl, 2tm		23	B. Bradley, Cle		60	Statistic unavailable			P. Dougherty, ChA		47	Statistic unavailable			Statistic unavailable		
E. Hahn, ChA		13	B. Ganley, Was		52				C. Hemphill, NYA		42						
B. Bradley, Cle		13	G. Schaefer, Det		43				G. Schaefer, Det		40						
A. McConnell, Bos		11	H. Lord, Bos		36				T. Cobb, Det		39						
D. Gessler, Bos		11	T. Jones, StL		34				J. Clarke, Cle		37						

Runs Created			Runs Created/27 Outs			Batting Average			On-Base Percentage			Slugging Percentage			OBP+Slugging		
T. Cobb, Det		113	D. Gessler, Bos		7.31	T. Cobb, Det		.324	D. Gessler, Bos		.394	T. Cobb, Det		.475	T. Cobb, Det		.842
S. Crawford, Det		104	T. Cobb, Det		7.26	S. Crawford, Det		.311	M. McIntyre, Det		.391	S. Crawford, Det		.457	D. Gessler, Bos		.817
M. McIntyre, Det		102	M. McIntyre, Det		6.44	D. Gessler, Bos		.308	C. Hemphill, NYA		.374	D. Gessler, Bos		.423	S. Crawford, Det		.812
N. Lajoie, Cle		90	S. Crawford, Det		6.32	C. Hemphill, NYA		.297	T. Hartsel, Phi		.371	C. Rossman, Det		.418	M. McIntyre, Det		.775
D. Gessler, Bos		87	P. Dougherty, ChA		5.84	M. McIntyre, Det		.295	P. Dougherty, ChA		.367	M. McIntyre, Det		.383	C. Rossman, Det		.748

1908 American League Pitching Leaders

Wins			Losses			Winning Percentage			Games			Games Started			Complete Games		
E. Walsh, ChA		40	J. Lake, NYA		22	E. Walsh, ChA		.727	E. Walsh, ChA		66	E. Walsh, ChA		49	E. Walsh, ChA		42
E. Summers, Det		24	J. Chesbro, NYA		20	W. Donovan, Det		.720	R. Vickers, Phi		53	D. White, ChA		37	C. Young, Bos		30
A. Joss, Cle		24	R. Vickers, Phi		19	A. Joss, Cle		.686	J. Chesbro, NYA		45	R. Waddell, StL		36	A. Joss, Cle		29
C. Young, Bos		21	G. Winter, 2tm		19	E. Summers, Det		.667	L. Hughes, Was		43	F. Smith, ChA		35	H. Howell, StL		27
R. Waddell, StL		19	H. Howell, StL		18	B. Dinneen, StL		.667	R. Waddell, StL		43	A. Joss, Cle		35	G. Mullin, Det		26

Shutouts			Saves			Games Finished			Batters Faced			Innings Pitched			Hits Allowed		
E. Walsh, ChA		11	E. Walsh, ChA		6	R. Vickers, Phi		17	Statistic unavailable			E. Walsh, ChA		464.0	E. Walsh, ChA		343
A. Joss, Cle		9	L. Hughes, Was		4	R. Manning, NYA		15				A. Joss, Cle		325.0	G. Mullin, Det		301
4 tied with		6	R. Waddell, StL		3	E. Walsh, ChA		15				H. Howell, StL		324.1	H. Howell, StL		279
			7 tied with		2	E. Cicotte, Bos		13				R. Vickers, Phi		317.0	E. Summers, Det		271
						J. Chesbro, NYA		13				E. Summers, Det		301.0	J. Chesbro, NYA		271

Home Runs Allowed			Walks			Walks/9 Innings			Strikeouts			Strikeouts/9 Innings			Strikeout/Walk Ratio		
C. Morgan, Bos		7	J. Dygert, Phi		97	A. Joss, Cle		0.8	E. Walsh, ChA		269	R. Waddell, StL		7.3	E. Walsh, ChA		4.80
J. Lake, NYA		6	C. Morgan, Bos		90	B. Burns, Was		1.0	R. Waddell, StL		232	J. Dygert, Phi		6.2	A. Joss, Cle		4.33
J. Chesbro, NYA		6	R. Waddell, StL		90	E. Walsh, ChA		1.1	L. Hughes, Was		165	W. Johnson, Was		5.6	C. Young, Bos		4.05
3 tied with		4	R. Manning, NYA		86	C. Young, Bos		1.1	J. Dygert, Phi		164	L. Hughes, Was		5.4	B. Burns, Was		3.06
			G. Liebhardt, Cle		81	E. Summers, Det		1.6	W. Johnson, Was		160	W. Donovan, Det		5.2	W. Johnson, Was		3.02

Earned Run Average			Component ERA			Hit Batsmen			Wild Pitches			Opponent Average			Opponent OBP		
A. Joss, Cle		1.16	A. Joss, Cle		1.23	E. Summers, Det		20	E. Cicotte, Bos		14	A. Joss, Cle		.197	A. Joss, Cle		.218
C. Young, Bos		1.26	E. Walsh, ChA		1.38	R. Manning, NYA		18	W. Johnson, Was		13	F. Smith, ChA		.203	E. Walsh, ChA		.232
E. Walsh, ChA		1.42	C. Young, Bos		1.48	H. Howell, StL		17	L. Hughes, Was		13	E. Walsh, ChA		.203	C. Young, Bos		.241
E. Summers, Det		1.64	F. Smith, ChA		1.58	E. Willett, Det		14	R. Vickers, Phi		12	W. Johnson, Was		.211	F. Smith, ChA		.256
W. Johnson, Was		1.65	W. Johnson, Was		1.66	J. Chesbro, NYA		14	G. Mullin, Det		12	C. Young, Bos		.213	B. Burns, Was		.257

1908 American League Miscellaneous

Managers

Boston	Deacon McGuire	53-62
	Fred Lake	22-17
Chicago	Fielder Jones	88-64
Cleveland	Nap Lajoie	90-64
Detroit	Hughie Jennings	90-63
New York	Clark Griffith	24-32
	Kid Elberfeld	27-71
Philadelphia	Connie Mack	68-85
St. Louis	Jimmy McAleer	83-69
Washington	Joe Cantillon	67-85

Awards

STATS Most Valuable Player	Ed Walsh, p, ChA
STATS Cy Young	Ed Walsh, ChA
STATS Rookie of the Year	Ed Summers, p, Det
STATS Manager of the Year	Jimmy McAleer, StL

STATS All-Star Team

C	Boss Schmidt, Det	.265	1	38
1B	Claude Rossman, Det	.294	2	71
2B	Nap Lajoie, Cle	.289	2	74
3B	Hobe Ferris, StL	.270	2	74
SS	Germany Schaefer, Det	.259	3	52
OF	Ty Cobb, Det	.324	4	108
OF	Sam Crawford, Det	.311	7	80
OF	Doc Gessler, Bos	.308	3	63
P	Addie Joss, Cle	24-11	1.16	130 K
P	Ed Summers, Det	24-12	1.64	103 K
P	Ed Walsh, ChA	40-15	1.42	269 K
P	Cy Young, Bos	21-11	1.26	150 K

Postseason

World Series	Detroit (AL) 1 vs. Chicago (NL) 4

Outstanding Performances

Perfect Games

Addie Joss, Cle	vs. ChA on October 2

No-Hitters

Cy Young, Bos	@ NYA on June 30
Bob Rhoads, Cle	vs. Bos on September 18
Frank Smith, ChA	vs. Phi on September 20

Cycles

Otis Clymer, Was	on October 2

1908 National League Standings

Team	Overall					Home Games						Road Games						Park Index		Record by Month					
	W	L	Pct	GB	DIF	W	L	R	OR	HR	OHR	W	L	R	OR	HR	OHR	Run	HR	M/A	May	June	July	Aug	S/O
Chicago	99	55	.643	—	90	47	30	294	264	9	15	52	25	330	197	10	5	106	160	8-3	15-10	14-10	18-13	16-11	28-8
Pittsburgh	98	56	.636	1.0	53	42	35	227	255	12	4	56	21	358	214	13	12	84	64	7-4	11-12	22-8	16-12	14-11	28-9
New York	98	56	.636	1.0	44	52	25	343	235	10	11	46	31	309	221	10	15	109	84	8-6	10-9	19-12	16-10	16-8	29-11
Philadelphia	83	71	.539	16.0	0	43	34	251	213	0	3	40	37	229	232	11	5	96	19	7-7	14-10	15-14	14-16	10-14	15-21
Cincinnati	73	81	.474	26.0	0	40	37	260	272	9	7	33	44	229	272	5	12	106	94	5-6	14-10	15-14	14-16	10-14	15-21
Boston	63	91	.409	36.0	2	35	42	295	328	13	20	28	49	242	294	4	9	116	254	7-7	10-12	10-18	13-15	10-15	13-24
Brooklyn	53	101	.344	46.0	0	27	50	179	243	16	3	26	51	198	273	12	14	90	73	6-8	7-14	9-17	11-17	10-15	10-30
St. Louis	49	105	.318	50.0	0	28	49	185	295	9	11	21	56	186	331	8	5	93	154	3-10	12-15	9-15	7-20	11-14	7-31

Clinch Date—Chicago 10/08.

Team Batting

Team	G	AB	R	OR	H	2B	3B	HR	TB	RBI	TBB	IBB	SO	HBP	SH	SF	SB	CS	SB%	GDP	Avg	OBP	Slg
New York	157	5006	652	456	1339	182	43	20	1667	562	494	—	—	75	250	—	181	—	—	—	.267	.342	.333
Chicago	158	5085	624	461	1267	196	56	19	1632	492	418	—	—	40	270	—	212	—	—	—	.249	.311	.321
Pittsburgh	155	5109	585	469	1263	162	98	25	1696	496	420	—	—	40	184	—	186	—	—	—	.247	.309	.332
Boston	156	5131	537	622	1228	137	43	17	1502	426	414	—	—	54	194	—	134	—	—	—	.239	.303	.293
Philadelphia	155	5012	504	445	1223	194	68	11	1586	400	334	—	—	53	213	—	200	—	—	—	.244	.298	.316
Cincinnati	155	4879	489	544	1108	129	77	14	1433	398	372	—	—	44	214	—	196	—	—	—	.227	.288	.294
Brooklyn	154	4897	377	516	1044	110	60	28	1358	306	323	—	—	28	166	—	113	—	—	—	.213	.266	.277
St. Louis	154	4959	371	626	1105	134	57	17	1404	301	282	—	—	45	164	—	150	—	—	—	.223	.271	.283
NL Total	1244	40078	4139	4139	9577	1244	502	151	12278	3381	3057	—	—	379	1655	—	1372	—	—	—	.239	.299	.306
NL Avg Team	156	5010	517	517	1197	156	63	19	1535	423	382	—	—	47	207	—	172	—	—	—	.239	.299	.306

Team Pitching

Team	G	CG	ShO	Rel	Sv	IP	H	R	ER	HR	SH	SF	HB	TBB	IBB	SO	WP	Bk	H/9	SO/9	BB/9	OAvg	OOBP	ERA
Philadelphia	155	116	22	43	6	1393.0	1167	445	325	8	—	—	43	379	—	476	26	1	7.5	3.1	2.4	.234	.294	2.10
Pittsburgh	155	100	24	71	9	1402.1	1142	469	331	16	—	—	52	406	—	468	19	1	7.3	3.0	2.6	.223	.287	2.12
Chicago	158	108	29	60	12	1433.2	1137	461	341	20	—	—	39	437	—	668	34	1	7.1	4.2	2.7	.221	.287	2.14
New York	157	95	25	76	18	1411.0	1214	456	336	26	—	—	35	288	—	656	18	1	7.7	4.2	1.8	.233	.277	2.14
Cincinnati	155	110	17	50	8	1384.0	1218	544	365	19	—	—	42	415	—	433	20	2	7.9	2.8	2.7	.243	.307	2.37
Brooklyn	154	118	20	43	4	1369.0	1165	516	375	17	—	—	60	444	—	535	24	0	7.7	3.5	2.9	.238	.309	2.47
St. Louis	154	97	13	72	4	1368.0	1217	626	401	16	—	—	45	430	—	528	34	3	8.0	3.5	2.8	.232	.296	2.64
Boston	156	92	14	77	1	1404.2	1262	622	436	29	—	—	57	423	—	416	25	3	8.1	2.7	2.7	.239	.302	2.79
NL Total	1244	836	164	492	62	11165.2	9522	4139	2910	151	—	—	373	3222	—	4180	200	12	7.7	3.4	2.6	.239	.300	2.35
NL Avg Team	156	105	21	62	8	1395.2	1190	517	364	19	—	—	47	403	—	523	25	2	7.7	3.4	2.6	.239	.300	2.35

Team Fielding

Team	G	PO	A	E	TC	DP	PB	Pct
Chicago	158	4292	2057	205	6554	76	12	.969
Pittsburgh	155	4201	1904	226	6331	74	8	.964
Philadelphia	155	4157	2071	238	6466	75	19	.963
Boston	156	4160	2224	253	6637	90	10	.962
New York	157	4218	2088	250	6556	79	23	.962
Brooklyn	154	4074	2039	247	6360	66	13	.961
Cincinnati	155	4083	1915	255	6253	72	21	.959
St. Louis	154	4039	2059	348	6446	68	24	.946
NL Total	1244	33224	16357	2022	51603	600	130	.961

Team vs. Team Records

	Bos	Bro	ChN	Cin	NYG	Phi	Pit	StL	Won
Bos	—	12	6	8	6	10	7	14	63
Bro	10	—	4	6	6	5	9	13	53
ChN	16	18	—	16	11	9	10	19	99
Cin	14	16	6	—	8	10	8	11	73
NYG	16	16	11	14	—	16	11	14	98
Phi	12	17	13	12	6	—	9	14	83
Pit	15	13	12	14	11	13	—	20	98
StL	8	9	3	11	8	8	2	—	49
Lost	91	101	55	81	56	71	56	105	

1908 National League Batting Leaders

Games		At-Bats		Runs		Hits		Doubles		Triples	
A. Devlin, NYG	157	E. Grant, Phi	598	F. Tenney, NYG	101	H. Wagner, Pit	201	H. Wagner, Pit	39	H. Wagner, Pit	19
J. Tinker, ChN	157	J. Hummel, Bro	594	H. Wagner, Pit	100	M. Donlin, NYG	198	S. Magee, Phi	30	H. Lobert, Cin	18
C. Seymour, NYG	156	R. Murray, StL	593	T. Leach, Pit	93	R. Murray, StL	167	F. Chance, ChN	27	S. Magee, Phi	16
F. Tenney, NYG	156	M. Donlin, NYG	593	J. Evers, ChN	83	H. Lobert, Cin	167	O. Knabe, Phi	26	T. Leach, Pit	16
2 tied with	155	C. Seymour, NYG	587	F. Clarke, Pit	83	K. Bransfield, Phi	160	M. Donlin, NYG	26	2 tied with	15

Home Runs		Total Bases		Runs Batted In		Walks		Intentional Walks		Strikeouts	
T. Jordan, Bro	12	H. Wagner, Pit	308	H. Wagner, Pit	109	R. Bresnahan, NYG	83	Statistic unavailable		Statistic unavailable	
H. Wagner, Pit	10	M. Donlin, NYG	268	M. Donlin, NYG	106	F. Tenney, NYG	72				
R. Murray, StL	7	R. Murray, StL	237	C. Seymour, NYG	92	J. Evers, ChN	66				
J. Tinker, ChN	6	H. Lobert, Cin	232	K. Bransfield, Phi	71	F. Clarke, Pit	65				
M. Donlin, NYG	6	T. Leach, Pit	222	J. Tinker, ChN	68	2 tied with	62				

Hit By Pitch		Sac Hits		Sac Flies		Stolen Bases		Caught Stealing		GDP	
D. McGann, Bos	19	O. Knabe, Phi	42	Statistic unavailable		H. Wagner, Pit	53	Statistic unavailable		Statistic unavailable	
A. Devlin, NYG	14	M. Donlin, NYG	33			R. Murray, StL	48				
J. Titus, Phi	14	C. Seymour, NYG	33			H. Lobert, Cin	47				
J. Kane, Cin	12	H. Lobert, Cin	32			S. Magee, Phi	40				
S. Magee, Phi	11	H. Steinfeldt, ChN	32			J. Evers, ChN	36				

Runs Created		Runs Created/27 Outs		Batting Average		On-Base Percentage		Slugging Percentage		OBP+Slugging	
H. Wagner, Pit	131	H. Wagner, Pit	8.89	H. Wagner, Pit	.354	H. Wagner, Pit	.415	H. Wagner, Pit	.542	H. Wagner, Pit	.957
M. Donlin, NYG	102	J. Evers, ChN	6.85	M. Donlin, NYG	.334	J. Evers, ChN	.402	M. Donlin, NYG	.452	M. Donlin, NYG	.816
H. Lobert, Cin	95	M. Donlin, NYG	6.16	L. Doyle, NYG	.308	R. Bresnahan, NYG	.401	S. Magee, Phi	.417	J. Evers, ChN	.777
J. Evers, ChN	83	R. Bresnahan, NYG	5.68	K. Bransfield, Phi	.304	J. Titus, Phi	.365	H. Lobert, Cin	.407	S. Magee, Phi	.776
S. Magee, Phi	81	H. Lobert, Cin	5.65	J. Evers, ChN	.300	M. Donlin, NYG	.364	R. Murray, StL	.400	R. Bresnahan, NYG	.760

1908 National League Pitching Leaders

Wins		Losses		Winning Percentage		Games		Games Started		Complete Games	
C. Mathewson, NYG	37	B. Raymond, StL	25	E. Reulbach, ChN	.774	C. Mathewson, NYG	56	C. Mathewson, NYG	44	C. Mathewson, NYG	34
T. F. Brown, ChN	29	K. Wilhelm, Bro	22	C. Mathewson, NYG	.771	G. McQuillan, Phi	48	G. McQuillan, Phi	42	K. Wilhelm, Bro	33
E. Reulbach, ChN	24	J. Pastorius, Bro	20	T. F. Brown, ChN	.763	B. Raymond, StL	48	H. Wiltse, NYG	38	G. McQuillan, Phi	32
4 tied with	23	H. McIntire, Bro	20	N. Maddox, Pit	.742	E. Reulbach, ChN	46	V. Willis, Pit	38	N. Rucker, Bro	30
		2 tied with	19	S. Leever, Pit	.682	2 tied with	44	B. Raymond, StL	37	H. Wiltse, NYG	30

Shutouts		Saves		Games Finished		Batters Faced		Innings Pitched		Hits Allowed	
C. Mathewson, NYG	11	T. F. Brown, ChN	5	G. Ferguson, Bos	16	Statistic unavailable		C. Mathewson, NYG	390.2	C. Mathewson, NYG	285
T. F. Brown, ChN	9	C. Mathewson, NYG	5	J. McGinnity, NYG	14			G. McQuillan, Phi	359.2	H. Wiltse, NYG	266
4 tied with	7	J. McGinnity, NYG	5	S. Leever, Pit	14			N. Rucker, Bro	333.1	K. Wilhelm, Bro	266
		O. Overall, ChN	4	B. Malarkey, NYG	13			K. Wilhelm, Bro	332.0	N. Rucker, Bro	265
		B. Ewing, Cin	3	T. F. Brown, ChN	12			H. Wiltse, NYG	330.0	G. McQuillan, Phi	263

Home Runs Allowed		Walks		Walks/9 Innings		Strikeouts		Strikeouts/9 Innings		Strikeout/Walk Ratio	
J. McGinnity, NYG	8	N. Rucker, Bro	125	C. Mathewson, NYG	1.0	C. Mathewson, NYG	259	O. Overall, ChN	6.7	C. Mathewson, NYG	6.17
J. Boultes, Bos	7	E. Reulbach, ChN	106	T. F. Brown, ChN	1.4	N. Rucker, Bro	199	C. Mathewson, NYG	6.0	T. F. Brown, ChN	2.51
V. Lindaman, Bos	7	B. Raymond, StL	95	T. Sparks, Phi	1.7	O. Overall, ChN	167	N. Rucker, Bro	5.4	O. Overall, ChN	2.14
3 tied with	6	G. McQuillan, Phi	91	B. Ewing, Cin	1.7	B. Raymond, StL	145	H. Camnitz, Pit	4.5	H. Camnitz, Pit	1.71
		2 tied with	90	B. Campbell, Cin	1.8	E. Reulbach, ChN	133	G. Ferguson, Bos	4.2	J. Pfiester, ChN	1.67

Earned Run Average		Component ERA		Hit Batsmen		Wild Pitches		Opponent Average		Opponent OBP	
C. Mathewson, NYG	1.43	T. F. Brown, ChN	1.31	H. McIntire, Bro	20	B. Raymond, StL	9	F. Beebe, StL	.193	C. Mathewson, NYG	.225
T. F. Brown, ChN	1.47	C. Mathewson, NYG	1.34	N. Rucker, Bro	19	B. Foxen, Phi	8	T. F. Brown, ChN	.195	T. F. Brown, ChN	.232
G. McQuillan, Phi	1.53	G. McQuillan, Phi	1.64	G. Dorner, Bos	15	J. Lush, StL	8	C. Mathewson, NYG	.200	V. Willis, Pit	.262
H. Camnitz, Pit	1.56	V. Willis, Pit	1.82	B. Raymond, StL	14	4 tied with	7	G. McQuillan, Phi	.207	G. McQuillan, Phi	.263
A. Coakley, 2tm	1.78	B. Raymond, StL	1.83	2 tied with	12			B. Raymond, StL	.207	F. Beebe, StL	.267

1908 National League Miscellaneous

Managers

Boston	Joe Kelley	63-91
Brooklyn	Patsy Donovan	53-101
Chicago	Frank Chance	99-55
Cincinnati	John Ganzel	73-81
New York	John McGraw	98-56
Philadelphia	Billy Murray	83-71
Pittsburgh	Fred Clarke	98-56
St. Louis	John McCloskey	49-105

Awards

STATS Most Valuable Player	C. Mathewson, p, NYG
STATS Cy Young	C. Mathewson, NYG
STATS Rookie of the Year	G. McQuillan, p, Phi
STATS Manager of the Year	John McGraw, NYG

STATS All-Star Team

C	Roger Bresnahan, NYG	.283	1	54
1B	Frank Chance, ChN	.272	2	55
2B	Johnny Evers, ChN	.300	0	37
3B	Hans Lobert, Cin	.293	4	63
SS	Honus Wagner, Pit	.354	10	109
OF	Fred Clarke, Pit	.265	2	53
OF	Mike Donlin, NYG	.334	6	106
OF	Sherry Magee, Phi	.283	2	57
P	Three Finger Brown, ChN	29-9	1.47	123 K
P	Nick Maddox, Pit	23-8	2.28	70 K
P	Christy Mathewson, NYG	37-11	1.43	259 K
P	Ed Reulbach, ChN	24-7	2.03	133 K

Postseason

World Series	Chicago (NL) 4 vs. Detroit (AL) 1

Outstanding Performances

No-Hitters

Hooks Wiltse, NYG	vs. Phi on July 4
Nap Rucker, Bro	vs. Bos on September 5

1909 American League Standings

Team		Overall						Home Games						Road Games					Park Index			Record by Month				
	W	L	Pct	GB	DIF	W	L	R	OR	HR	OHR	W	L	R	OR	HR	OHR	Run	HR	M/A	May	June	July	Aug	S/O
Detroit	98	54	.645	—	161	57	19	377	246	12	12	41	35	289	247	7	4	116	218	10-3	15-9	18-9	17-13	17-9	21-11
Philadelphia	95	58	.621	3.5	18	49	27	293	200	9	4	46	31	312	208	12	5	96	77	5-5	16-9	15-11	20-13	18-9	21-11
Boston	88	63	.583	9.5	1	47	28	329	295	18	12	41	35	268	255	2	6	121	380	7-5	12-11	16-12	19-15	19-7	15-13
Chicago	78	74	.513	20.0	0	42	34	256	201	1	3	36	40	236	262	3	5	92	50	6-5	9-16	11-12	21-13	13-14	18-14
New York	74	77	.490	23.5	4	41	35	338	263	11	6	33	42	252	324	5	15	103	84	7-5	11-9	11-17	14-19	11-16	20-11
Cleveland	71	82	.464	27.5	2	39	37	262	259	2	0	32	45	231	273	8	9	105	12	4-8	12-13	16-8	17-15	13-17	9-21
St. Louis	61	89	.407	36.0	0	40	37	242	235	4	6	21	52	199	340	6	10	84	59	4-8	13-11	6-20	17-13	10-16	11-21
Washington	42	110	.276	56.0	2	27	48	197	271	5	3	15	62	183	385	4	9	85	63	3-7	7-17	11-15	5-29	7-20	9-22

Clinch Date—Detroit 9/30.

Team Batting

Team	G	AB	R	OR	H	2B	3B	HR	TB	RBI	TBB	IBB	SO	HBP	SH	SF	SB	CS	SB%	GDP	Avg	OBP	Slg
Detroit	158	5095	666	493	1360	209	58	19	1742	521	397	—	—	39	226	—	280	—	—	—	.267	.325	.342
Philadelphia	153	4906	605	408	1257	186	88	21	1682	498	403	—	—	64	248	—	205	—	—	—	.256	.321	.343
Boston	152	4979	597	550	1307	151	69	20	1656	474	348	—	—	77	174	—	215	—	—	—	.263	.321	.333
New York	153	4981	590	587	1234	143	61	16	1547	473	407	—	—	63	208	—	187	—	—	—	.248	.313	.311
Cleveland	155	5048	493	532	1216	173	81	10	1581	407	283	—	—	48	124	—	174	—	—	—	.241	.288	.313
Chicago	159	5018	492	463	1109	145	56	4	1378	393	441	—	—	57	232	—	211	—	—	—	.221	.291	.275
St. Louis	154	4964	441	575	1151	116	45	10	1387	352	331	—	—	51	130	—	136	—	—	—	.232	.287	.279
Washington	156	4983	380	656	1113	149	41	9	1371	306	321	—	—	42	193	—	136	—	—	—	.223	.276	.275
AL Total	1240	39974	4264	4264	9747	1272	499	109	12344	3424	2931	—	—	441	1535	—	1544	—	—	—	.244	.303	.309
AL Avg Team	155	4997	533	533	1218	159	62	14	1543	428	366	—	—	55	192	—	193	—	—	—	.244	.303	.309

Team Pitching

Team	G	CG	ShO	Rel	Sv	IP	H	R	ER	HR	SH	SF	HB	TBB	IBB	SO	WP	Bk	H/9	SO/9	BB/9	OAvg	OOBP	ERA
Philadelphia	153	110	27	62	3	1378.0	1069	408	296	9	—	—	62	386	—	728	31	4	7.0	4.8	2.5	.218	.283	1.93
Chicago	159	115	26	48	4	1430.1	1182	463	326	8	—	—	52	340	—	669	29	6	7.4	4.2	2.1	.235	.290	2.05
Detroit	158	117	17	50	12	1420.1	1254	493	357	16	—	—	56	359	—	528	38	1	7.9	3.3	2.3	.238	.293	2.26
Cleveland	155	110	15	51	3	1361.0	1212	532	363	9	—	—	47	348	—	568	40	4	8.0	3.8	2.3	.250	.307	2.40
Boston	152	75	11	94	15	1360.1	1214	550	392	18	—	—	47	384	—	555	31	3	8.0	3.7	2.5	.243	.303	2.59
New York	153	94	18	64	8	1350.1	1223	587	397	21	—	—	69	422	—	597	37	2	8.2	4.0	2.8	.246	.314	2.65
St. Louis	154	105	21	55	4	1354.2	1287	575	433	16	—	—	39	383	—	620	34	2	8.6	4.1	2.5	.258	.316	2.88
Washington	156	99	11	74	2	1374.2	1288	656	464	12	—	—	63	424	—	653	51	1	8.4	4.3	2.8	.248	.312	3.04
AL Total	1240	825	146	498	51	11029.2	9729	4264	3028	109	—	—	435	3046	—	4918	291	25	8.0	4.0	2.5	.244	.304	2.47
AL Avg Team	155	103	18	62	6	1378.2	1216	533	379	14	—	—	54	381	—	615	36	3	8.0	4.0	2.5	.244	.304	2.47

Team Fielding

Team	G	PO	A	E	TC	DP	PB	Pct
Chicago	159	4283	2280	246	6809	101	25	.964
Philadelphia	153	4105	1894	245	6244	92	14	.961
Detroit	158	4274	2208	276	6758	87	6	.959
St. Louis	154	4029	1970	267	6266	107	17	.957
Cleveland	155	4054	2059	278	6391	110	24	.957
Washington	156	4085	2069	280	6434	100	21	.956
Boston	152	4040	2068	292	6400	95	21	.954
New York	153	3979	1948	330	6257	94	15	.947
AL Total	1240	32849	16496	2214	51559	786	143	.957

Team vs. Team Records

	Bos	ChA	Cle	Det	NYA	Phi	StL	Was	Won
Bos	—	13	14	9	13	10	13	16	88
ChA	9	—	8	6	14	12	10	19	78
Cle	8	13	—	8	8	9	14	11	71
Det	13	15	14	—	14	8	18	16	98
NYA	9	8	14	8	—	8	13	14	74
Phi	11	10	13	14	14	—	14	19	95
StL	7	12	8	3	8	8	—	15	61
Was	6	3	11	6	6	3	7	—	42
Lost	63	74	82	54	77	58	89	110	

1909 American League Batting Leaders

Games			At-Bats			Runs			Hits			Doubles			Triples		
D. Bush, Det	157		R. Hartzell, StL	595		T. Cobb, Det	116		T. Cobb, Det	216		S. Crawford, Det	35		H. Baker, Phi	19	
T. Cobb, Det	156		S. Crawford, Det	589		D. Bush, Det	114		E. Collins, Phi	198		T. Cobb, Det	33		D. Murphy, Phi	14	
G. McBride, Was	156		T. Cobb, Det	573		E. Collins, Phi	104		S. Crawford, Det	185		N. Lajoie, Cle	33		S. Crawford, Det	14	
S. Crawford, Det	156		E. Collins, Phi	572		H. Lord, Bos	86		T. Speaker, Bos	168		E. Collins, Phi	30		3 tied with	13	
L. Tannehill, ChA	155		G. Stovall, Cle	565		S. Crawford, Det	83		H. Lord, Bos	166		D. Murphy, Phi	28				

Home Runs			Total Bases			Runs Batted In			Walks			Intentional Walks	Strikeouts
T. Cobb, Det	9		T. Cobb, Det	296		T. Cobb, Det	107		D. Bush, Det	88		Statistic unavailable	Statistic unavailable
T. Speaker, Bos	7		S. Crawford, Det	266		S. Crawford, Det	97		E. Collins, Phi	62			
J. Stahl, Bos	6		E. Collins, Phi	257		H. Baker, Phi	85		R. Demmitt, NYA	55			
S. Crawford, Det	6		H. Baker, Phi	242		T. Speaker, Bos	77		M. McIntyre, Det	54			
D. Murphy, Phi	5		T. Speaker, Bos	241		H. Davis, Phi	75		2 tied with	51			

Hit By Pitch			Sac Hits			Sac Flies	Stolen Bases			Caught Stealing	GDP
D. Altizer, ChA	16		D. Bush, Det	52		Statistic unavailable	T. Cobb, Det	76		Statistic unavailable	Statistic unavailable
J. Stahl, Bos	15		B. Ganley, 2tm	41			E. Collins, Phi	67			
J. Delahanty, 2tm	15		H. Baker, Phi	34			D. Bush, Det	53			
K. Elberfeld, NYA	14		D. Murphy, Phi	34			H. Lord, Bos	36			
H. Niles, Bos	13		W. Keeler, NYA	33			P. Dougherty, ChA	36			

Runs Created			Runs Created/27 Outs			Batting Average			On-Base Percentage			Slugging Percentage			OBP+Slugging		
T. Cobb, Det	138		T. Cobb, Det	9.27		T. Cobb, Det	.377		T. Cobb, Det	.431		T. Cobb, Det	.517		T. Cobb, Det	.947	
E. Collins, Phi	118		E. Collins, Phi	7.65		E. Collins, Phi	.346		E. Collins, Phi	.416		S. Crawford, Det	.452		E. Collins, Phi	.865	
S. Crawford, Det	105		S. Crawford, Det	6.27		N. Lajoie, Cle	.324		D. Bush, Det	.380		E. Collins, Phi	.449		S. Crawford, Det	.817	
T. Speaker, Bos	93		N. Lajoie, Cle	6.17		S. Crawford, Det	.314		N. Lajoie, Cle	.378		H. Baker, Phi	.447		J. Stahl, Bos	.812	
D. Bush, Det	85		J. Stahl, Bos	6.10		H. Lord, Bos	.311		J. Stahl, Bos	.377		T. Speaker, Bos	.443		N. Lajoie, Cle	.809	

1909 American League Pitching Leaders

Wins			Losses			Winning Percentage			Games			Games Started			Complete Games		
G. Mullin, Det	29		B. Groom, Was	26		G. Mullin, Det	.784		F. Smith, ChA	51		F. Smith, ChA	41		F. Smith, ChA	37	
F. Smith, ChA	25		W. Johnson, Was	25		E. Cicotte, Bos	.737		F. Arellanes, Bos	45		W. Johnson, Was	36		C. Young, Cle	30	
E. Willett, Det	21		D. Gray, Was	19		H. Krause, Phi	.692		B. Groom, Was	44		C. Morgan, 2tm	36		G. Mullin, Det	29	
3 tied with	19		F. Smith, ChA	17		C. Bender, Phi	.692		E. Willett, Det	41		G. Mullin, Det	35		W. Johnson, Was	27	
			C. Morgan, 2tm	17		E. Summers, Det	.679		3 tied with	40		2 tied with	34		C. Morgan, 2tm	26	

Shutouts			Saves			Games Finished			Batters Faced	Innings Pitched			Hits Allowed		
E. Walsh, ChA	8		F. Arellanes, Bos	8		F. Arellanes, Bos	15		Statistic unavailable	F. Smith, ChA	365.0		F. Smith, ChA	278	
H. Krause, Phi	7		J. Powell, StL	3		J. Dygert, Phi	13			G. Mullin, Det	303.2		C. Young, Cle	267	
F. Smith, ChA	7		5 tied with	2		4 tied with	12			W. Johnson, Was	296.1		G. Mullin, Det	258	
J. Coombs, Phi	6									C. Young, Cle	294.2		W. Johnson, Was	247	
4 tied with	5									C. Morgan, 2tm	293.1		E. Summers, Det	243	

Home Runs Allowed			Walks			Walks/9 Innings			Strikeouts			Strikeouts/9 Innings			Strikeout/Walk Ratio		
C. Smith, 2tm	6		B. Groom, Was	105		A. Joss, Cle	1.1		F. Smith, ChA	177		H. Berger, Cle	5.9		C. Bender, Phi	3.58	
E. Willett, Det	5		C. Morgan, 2tm	102		D. White, ChA	1.6		W. Johnson, Was	164		H. Krause, Phi	5.9		H. Krause, Phi	2.84	
E. Summers, Det	4		J. Scott, ChA	93		J. Powell, StL	1.6		H. Berger, Cle	162		C. Bender, Phi	5.8		H. Berger, Cle	2.79	
C. Young, Cle	4		W. Johnson, Was	84		C. Bender, Phi	1.6		C. Bender, Phi	161		R. Waddell, StL	5.8		E. Walsh, ChA	2.54	
10 tied with	3		J. Warhop, NYA	81		E. Summers, Det	1.7		R. Waddell, StL	141		B. Bailey, StL	5.2		F. Smith, ChA	2.53	

Earned Run Average			Component ERA			Hit Batsmen			Wild Pitches			Opponent Average			Opponent OBP		
H. Krause, Phi	1.39		E. Walsh, ChA	1.52		J. Warhop, NYA	26		H. Berger, Cle	13		C. Morgan, 2tm	.202		E. Walsh, ChA	.253	
E. Walsh, ChA	1.41		F. Smith, ChA	1.60		C. Morgan, 2tm	22		W. Johnson, Was	12		E. Walsh, ChA	.203		C. Bender, Phi	.254	
C. Bender, Phi	1.66		A. Joss, Cle	1.65		J. Scott, ChA	16		4 tied with	11		H. Krause, Phi	.204		A. Joss, Cle	.255	
A. Joss, Cle	1.71		H. Krause, Phi	1.65		W. Johnson, Was	15					J. Wood, Bos	.209		F. Smith, ChA	.257	
E. Killian, Det	1.71		C. Bender, Phi	1.68		E. Willett, Det	15					J. Coombs, Phi	.213		H. Krause, Phi	.266	

1909 American League Miscellaneous

Managers

Boston	Fred Lake	88-63
Chicago	Billy Sullivan	78-74
Cleveland	Nap Lajoie	57-57
	Deacon McGuire	14-25
Detroit	Hughie Jennings	98-54
New York	George Stallings	74-77
Philadelphia	Connie Mack	95-58
St. Louis	Jimmy McAleer	61-89
Washington	Joe Cantillon	42-110

Awards

STATS Most Valuable Player	Ty Cobb, of, Det
STATS Cy Young	George Mullin, Det
STATS Rookie of the Year	H. R. Baker, 3b, Phi
STATS Manager of the Year	Connie Mack, Phi

STATS All-Star Team

C	Bill Carrigan, Bos	.296	1	36
1B	Jake Stahl, Bos	.294	6	60
2B	Eddie Collins, Phi	.346	3	56
3B	Home Run Baker, Phi	.305	4	85
SS	Donie Bush, Det	.273	0	33
OF	Ty Cobb, Det	.377	9	107
OF	Sam Crawford, Det	.314	6	97
OF	Tris Speaker, Bos	.309	7	77
P	Chief Bender, Phi	18-8	1.66	161 K
P	Harry Krause, Phi	18-8	1.39	139 K
P	George Mullin, Det	29-8	2.22	124 K
P	Eddie Plank, Phi	19-10	1.76	132 K

Postseason

World Series	Detroit (AL) 3 vs. Pittsburgh (NL) 4

Outstanding Performances

Triple Crown
Ty Cobb, Det .377-9-107
Unassisted Triple Plays
Neal Ball, Cle on July 19

1909 National League Standings

Team	Overall					Home Games						Road Games						Park Index		Record by Month					
	W	L	Pct	GB	DIF	W	L	R	OR	HR	OHR	W	L	R	OR	HR	OHR	Run	HR	M/A	May	June	July	Aug	S/O
Pittsburgh	110	42	.724	—	155	56	21	354	237	10	6	54	21	345	210	15	6	104	74	6-6	20-6	18-3	20-10	22-7	24-10
Chicago	104	49	.680	6.5	6	47	29	281	199	8	0	57	20	354	191	12	6	89	45	8-5	16-11	14-6	19-8	22-8	25-11
New York	92	61	.601	18.5	0	44	33	298	294	19	23	48	28	325	252	7	5	101	345	4-6	13-11	16-6	18-12	18-11	18-20
Cincinnati	77	76	.503	33.5	6	39	38	282	299	5	2	38	38	324	300	17	3	92	35	8-7	11-14	13-8	13-15	14-12	18-20
Philadelphia	74	79	.484	36.5	3	40	37	266	279	6	10	34	42	250	239	6	13	110	83	6-4	12-12	10-14	13-17	16-13	16-18
Brooklyn	55	98	.359	55.5	1	34	45	238	311	12	9	21	53	206	316	4	22	99	76	4-6	12-12	5-20	11-18	9-20	14-22
St. Louis	54	98	.355	56.0	0	26	48	271	387	9	12	28	50	312	344	6	10	106	138	5-9	12-14	7-12	13-14	8-23	9-26
Boston	45	108	.294	65.5	10	27	47	219	326	10	9	18	61	216	357	4	14	102	113	6-4	6-20	4-18	9-22	7-22	13-22

Clinch Date—Pittsburgh 9/28.

Team Batting

Team	G	AB	R	OR	H	2B	3B	HR	TB	RBI	TBB	IBB	SO	HBP	SH	SF	SB	CS	SB%	GDP	Avg	OBP	Slg
Pittsburgh	154	5129	699	447	1332	218	92	25	1809	585	479	—	—	36	236	—	185	—	—	—	.260	.327	.353
Chicago	155	4999	635	390	1227	203	60	20	1610	496	420	—	—	31	246	—	187	—	—	—	.245	.308	.322
New York	158	5218	623	546	1327	173	68	26	1714	510	530	—	—	52	150	—	234	—	—	—	.254	.329	.328
Cincinnati	157	5088	606	599	1273	159	72	22	1642	507	478	—	—	38	229	—	280	—	—	—	.250	.319	.323
St. Louis	154	5108	583	731	1242	148	56	15	1547	479	568	—	—	62	136	—	161	—	—	—	.243	.326	.303
Philadelphia	154	5034	516	518	1228	185	53	12	1555	417	369	—	—	54	283	—	185	—	—	—	.244	.303	.309
Brooklyn	155	5056	444	627	1157	176	59	16	1499	370	330	—	—	20	175	—	141	—	—	—	.229	.279	.296
Boston	155	5017	435	683	1121	125	43	14	1374	338	400	—	—	30	207	—	135	—	—	—	.223	.285	.274
NL Total	1242	40649	4541	4541	9907	1387	503	150	12750	3702	3574	—	—	323	1662	—	1508	—	—	—	.244	.310	.314
NL Avg Team	155	5081	568	568	1238	173	63	19	1594	463	447	—	—	40	208	—	189	—	—	—	.244	.310	.314

Team Pitching

Team	G	CG	ShO	Rel	Sv	IP	H	R	ER	HR	SH	SF	HB	TBB	IBB	SO	WP	Bk	H/9	SO/9	BB/9	OAvg	OOBP	ERA
Chicago	155	111	32	57	11	1399.1	1094	390	272	6	—	—	45	364	—	680	30	2	7.0	4.4	2.3	.215	.273	1.75
Pittsburgh	154	93	21	82	11	1401.2	1174	447	322	12	—	—	48	320	—	490	14	0	7.5	3.1	2.1	.232	.284	2.07
New York	158	105	17	67	15	1440.2	1248	546	364	28	—	—	30	397	—	735	42	0	7.8	4.6	2.5	.238	.295	2.27
Philadelphia	154	89	17	84	6	1391.0	1190	518	377	23	—	—	40	472	—	612	34	0	7.7	4.0	3.1	.234	.304	2.44
Cincinnati	157	91	10	83	8	1407.0	1233	599	394	5	—	—	47	510	—	477	33	1	7.9	3.1	3.3	.240	.314	2.52
Brooklyn	155	126	18	30	3	1384.1	1277	627	477	31	—	—	49	528	—	594	26	2	8.3	3.9	3.4	.257	.334	3.10
Boston	155	98	13	69	6	1370.2	1329	683	487	23	—	—	40	543	—	414	46	8	8.7	2.7	3.6	.263	.339	3.20
St. Louis	154	84	5	92	4	1379.2	1368	731	523	22	—	—	44	483	—	435	52	1	8.9	2.8	3.2	.263	.331	3.41
NL Total	1242	797	133	564	64	11174.1	9913	4541	3216	150	—	—	343	3617	—	4437	277	14	8.0	3.6	2.9	.244	.311	2.59
NL Avg Team	155	100	17	71	8	1396.1	1239	568	402	19	—	—	43	452	—	555	35	2	8.0	3.6	2.9	.244	.311	2.59

Team Fielding

Team	G	PO	A	E	TC	DP	PB	Pct
Pittsburgh	154	4201	1929	228	6358	100	10	.964
Chicago	155	4252	1989	244	6485	95	7	.962
Philadelphia	154	4141	1977	241	6359	97	21	.962
Brooklyn	155	4131	1923	282	6336	86	7	.955
New York	158	4306	2066	307	6679	99	13	.954
Cincinnati	157	4201	1995	309	6505	120	21	.952
St. Louis	154	4099	1960	322	6381	90	9	.950
Boston	155	4097	2071	342	6510	101	22	.947
NL Total	1242	33428	15910	2275	51613	788	110	.956

Team vs. Team Records

	Bos	Bro	ChN	Cin	NYG	Phi	Pit	StL	Won
Bos	—	11	1	5	8	10	1	9	45
Bro	11	—	5	5	7	11	4	12	55
ChN	21	16	—	16	11	16	9	15	104
Cin	17	17	6	—	9	9	7	12	77
NYG	14	15	11	13	—	12	11	16	92
Phi	12	11	6	12	10	—	7	16	74
Pit	20	18	13	15	11	15	—	18	110
StL	13	10	7	10	5	6	3	—	54
Lost	108	98	49	76	61	79	42	98	

Seasons: Standings, Leaders

1909 National League Batting Leaders

Games		At-Bats		Runs		Hits		Doubles		Triples	
C. Wilson, Pit	154	E. Grant, Phi	631	T. Leach, Pit	126	L. Doyle, NYG	172	H. Wagner, Pit	39	M. Mitchell, Cin	17
E. Grant, Phi	154	A. Burch, Bro	601	F. Clarke, Pit	97	E. Grant, Phi	170	S. Magee, Phi	33	E. Konetchy, StL	14
S. Hofman, ChN	153	B. Byrne, 2tm	589	B. Byrne, 2tm	92	H. Wagner, Pit	168	D. Miller, Pit	31	S. Magee, Phi	14
4 tied with	152	T. Leach, Pit	587	H. Wagner, Pit	92	E. Konetchy, StL	165	T. Leach, Pit	29	D. Miller, Pit	13
		E. Konetchy, StL	576	2 tied with	88	A. Burch, Bro	163	J. Sheckard, ChN	29	3 tied with	12

Home Runs		Total Bases		Runs Batted In		Walks		Intentional Walks		Strikeouts	
R. Murray, NYG	7	H. Wagner, Pit	242	H. Wagner, Pit	100	F. Clarke, Pit	80	Statistic unavailable		Statistic unavailable	
B. Becker, Bos	6	L. Doyle, NYG	239	R. Murray, NYG	91	B. Byrne, 2tm	78				
L. Doyle, NYG	6	E. Konetchy, StL	228	D. Miller, Pit	87	J. Evers, ChN	73				
T. Leach, Pit	6	M. Mitchell, Cin	225	M. Mitchell, Cin	86	J. Sheckard, ChN	72				
H. Wagner, Pit	5	D. Miller, Pit	222	E. Konetchy, StL	80	A. Bridwell, NYG	67				

Hit By Pitch		Sac Hits		Sac Flies		Stolen Bases		Caught Stealing		GDP	
J. Titus, Phi	16	J. Bates, 2tm	48	Statistic unavailable		B. Bescher, Cin	54	Statistic unavailable		Statistic unavailable	
S. Evans, StL	14	J. Sheckard, ChN	46			R. Murray, NYG	48				
B. Byrne, 2tm	11	W. Clement, 2tm	38			D. Egan, Cin	39				
S. Magee, Phi	11	B. Becker, Bos	35			A. Burch, Bro	38				
A. Devlin, NYG	10	D. Shean, 2tm	34			S. Magee, Phi	38				

Runs Created		Runs Created/27 Outs		Batting Average		On-Base Percentage		Slugging Percentage		OBP+Slugging	
H. Wagner, Pit	115	H. Wagner, Pit	8.48	H. Wagner, Pit	.339	H. Wagner, Pit	.420	H. Wagner, Pit	.489	H. Wagner, Pit	.909
F. Clarke, Pit	97	M. Mitchell, Cin	6.39	M. Mitchell, Cin	.310	T. Jordan, Bro	.386	M. Mitchell, Cin	.430	M. Mitchell, Cin	.808
E. Konetchy, StL	92	F. Clarke, Pit	6.09	D. Hoblitzell, Cin	.308	A. Bridwell, NYG	.386	L. Doyle, NYG	.419	D. Hoblitzell, Cin	.782
M. Mitchell, Cin	92	J. Evers, ChN	5.84	L. Doyle, NYG	.302	F. Clarke, Pit	.384	D. Hoblitzell, Cin	.418	L. Doyle, NYG	.779
L. Doyle, NYG	89	E. Konetchy, StL	5.68	A. Bridwell, NYG	.294	M. Mitchell, Cin	.378	M. McCormick, NYG	.402	M. McCormick, NYG	.775

1909 National League Pitching Leaders

Wins		Losses		Winning Percentage		Games		Games Started		Complete Games	
T. F. Brown, ChN	27	G. Ferguson, Bos	23	H. Camnitz, Pit	.806	T. F. Brown, ChN	50	V. Willis, Pit	35	T. F. Brown, ChN	32
H. Camnitz, Pit	25	A. Mattern, Bos	21	C. Mathewson, NYG	.806	A. Mattern, Bos	47	A. Fromme, Cin	34	G. Bell, Bro	29
C. Mathewson, NYG	25	F. Beebe, StL	21	B. Adams, Pit	.800	H. Gaspar, Cin	44	F. Beebe, StL	34	N. Rucker, Bro	28
V. Willis, Pit	22	N. Rucker, Bro	19	T. F. Brown, ChN	.750	F. Beebe, StL	44	T. F. Brown, ChN	34	C. Mathewson, NYG	26
2 tied with	20	J. Lush, StL	18	J. Pfiester, ChN	.739	2 tied with	41	E. Moore, Phi	34	3 tied with	24

Shutouts		Saves		Games Finished		Batters Faced		Innings Pitched		Hits Allowed	
O. Overall, ChN	9	T. F. Brown, ChN	7	D. Crandall, NYG	20	Statistic unavailable		T. F. Brown, ChN	342.2	A. Mattern, Bos	322
T. F. Brown, ChN	8	D. Crandall, NYG	6	S. Melter, StL	18			A. Mattern, Bos	316.1	F. Beebe, StL	256
C. Mathewson, NYG	8	6 tied with	3	L. Richie, 2tm	17			N. Rucker, Bro	309.1	T. F. Brown, ChN	246
3 tied with	6			T. F. Brown, ChN	15			E. Moore, Phi	299.2	N. Rucker, Bro	245
				2 tied with	14			V. Willis, Pit	289.2	V. Willis, Pit	243

Home Runs Allowed		Walks		Walks/9 Innings		Strikeouts		Strikeouts/9 Innings		Strikeout/Walk Ratio	
H. Wiltse, NYG	9	A. Mattern, Bos	108	C. Mathewson, NYG	1.2	O. Overall, ChN	205	O. Overall, ChN	6.5	C. Mathewson, NYG	4.14
B. Raymond, NYG	7	E. Moore, Phi	108	T. F. Brown, ChN	1.4	N. Rucker, Bro	201	N. Rucker, Bro	5.8	T. F. Brown, ChN	3.25
E. Moore, Phi	7	J. Rowan, Cin	104	H. Wiltse, NYG	1.7	E. Moore, Phi	173	R. Ames, NYG	5.8	O. Overall, ChN	2.56
3 tied with	6	F. Beebe, StL	104	N. Maddox, Pit	1.7	T. F. Brown, ChN	172	R. Marquard, NYG	5.7	H. Wiltse, NYG	2.33
		2 tied with	101	G. McQuillan, Phi	2.0	R. Ames, NYG	156	E. Moore, Phi	5.2	N. Rucker, Bro	1.99

Earned Run Average		Component ERA		Hit Batsmen		Wild Pitches		Opponent Average		Opponent OBP	
C. Mathewson, NYG	1.14	C. Mathewson, NYG	1.29	H. McIntire, Bro	21	F. Beebe, StL	15	O. Overall, ChN	.198	C. Mathewson, NYG	.228
T. F. Brown, ChN	1.31	T. F. Brown, ChN	1.42	N. Maddox, Pit	15	A. Mattern, Bos	13	C. Mathewson, NYG	.200	T. F. Brown, ChN	.239
O. Overall, ChN	1.42	H. Camnitz, Pit	1.64	N. Rucker, Bro	14	R. Ames, NYG	13	A. Fromme, Cin	.201	O. Overall, ChN	.262
H. Camnitz, Pit	1.62	O. Overall, ChN	1.68	G. Ferguson, Bos	12	O. Overall, ChN	11	T. F. Brown, ChN	.202	H. Camnitz, Pit	.267
E. Reulbach, ChN	1.78	A. Fromme, Cin	1.81	2 tied with	11	B. Brown, 2tm	10	E. Moore, Phi	.210	G. McQuillan, Phi	.271

1909 National League Miscellaneous

Managers

Boston	Harry Smith	23-54
	Frank Bowerman	22-54
Brooklyn	Harry Lumley	55-98
Chicago	Frank Chance	104-49
Cincinnati	Clark Griffith	77-76
New York	John McGraw	92-61
Philadelphia	Billy Murray	74-79
Pittsburgh	Fred Clarke	110-42
St. Louis	Roger Bresnahan	54-98

Awards

STATS Most Valuable Player	Honus Wagner, ss, Pit
STATS Cy Young	C. Mathewson, NYG
STATS Rookie of the Year	Doc Hoblitzell, 1b, Cin
STATS Manager of the Year	Fred Clarke, Pit

STATS All-Star Team

C	George Gibson, Pit	.265	2	52
1B	Ed Konetchy, StL	.286	4	80
2B	Larry Doyle, NYG	.302	6	49
3B	Harry Steinfeldt, ChN	.252	2	59
SS	Honus Wagner, Pit	.339	5	100
OF	Fred Clarke, Pit	.287	3	68
OF	Moose McCormick, NYG	.291	3	27
OF	Mike Mitchell, Cin	.310	4	86
P	Three Finger Brown, ChN	27-9	1.31	172 K
P	Howie Camnitz, Pit	25-6	1.62	133 K
P	Christy Mathewson, NYG	25-6	1.14	149 K
P	Orval Overall, ChN	20-11	1.42	205 K

Postseason

World Series	Pittsburgh (NL) 4 vs. Detroit (AL) 3

Outstanding Performances

None

1910 American League Standings

Team	W	L	Pct	GB	DIF	W	L	R	OR	HR	OHR	W	L	R	OR	HR	OHR	Run	HR	M/A	May	June	July	Aug	S/O
		Overall						**Home Games**						**Road Games**				**Park Index**				**Record by Month**			
Philadelphia	102	48	.680	—	150	57	19	339	211	9	0	45	29	334	230	10	8	95	49	6-4	20-5	12-12	22-9	22-7	20-11
New York	88	63	.583	14.5	12	49	25	343	284	13	6	39	38	283	273	7	10	117	116	5-4	18-6	13-11	17-16	16-14	19-12
Detroit	86	68	.558	18.0	10	46	31	346	306	18	23	40	37	333	276	10	11	107	195	8-4	15-12	15-11	14-14	15-13	19-14
Boston	81	72	.529	22.5	3	51	28	338	262	32	21	30	44	300	302	11	9	93	248	7-6	12-10	13-11	16-16	10-23	20-13
Cleveland	71	81	.467	32.0	8	39	36	278	330	4	2	32	45	270	327	5	8	105	47	6-6	8-12	11-11	16-16	10-23	20-13
Chicago	68	85	.444	35.5	1	41	37	233	198	2	2	27	48	224	281	5	14	82	20	4-5	7-15	15-12	9-23	11-16	22-14
Washington	66	85	.437	36.5	4	38	35	265	252	2	7	28	50	236	298	7	12	103	51	5-9	11-13	8-16	14-15	18-14	10-18
St. Louis	47	107	.305	57.0	0	26	51	229	359	4	2	21	56	222	384	8	12	97	30	3-6	4-22	10-13	8-20	11-21	11-25

Clinch Date—Philadelphia 9/20.

Team Batting

Team	G	AB	R	OR	H	2B	3B	HR	TB	RBI	TBB	IBB	SO	HBP	SH	SF	SB	CS	SB%	GDP	Avg	OBP	Slg
Detroit	155	5039	**679**	582	1317	190	72	28	1735	548	459	—	—	51	198	—	249	—	—	—	.261	.329	.344
Philadelphia	155	5154	673	441	**1373**	191	105	19	1831	541	409	—	—	47	196	—	207	—	—	—	.266	.326	.355
Boston	158	5204	638	564	1350	175	87	**43**	1828	527	430	—	—	56	**227**	—	194	—	—	—	.259	.323	.351
New York	156	5051	626	557	1254	164	75	20	1628	492	**464**	—	—	71	176	—	**288**	—	—	—	.248	.320	.322
Cleveland	161	**5390**	548	657	1316	188	64	9	1659	460	366	—	—	37	190	—	189	—	—	—	.244	.297	.308
Washington	157	4989	501	550	1175	145	47	9	1441	393	449	—	—	82	172	—	192	—	—	—	.236	.309	.289
Chicago	156	5024	457	479	1058	115	58	7	1310	351	403	—	—	44	189	—	183	—	—	—	.211	.275	.261
St. Louis	158	5077	451	743	1105	131	60	12	1392	347	415	—	—	36	143	—	169	—	—	—	.218	.281	.274
AL Total	1256	40928	4573	4573	9948	1299	568	147	12824	3659	3395	—	—	424	1491	—	1671	—	—	—	.243	.308	.313
AL Avg Team	157	5116	572	572	1244	162	71	18	1603	457	424	—	—	53	186	—	209	—	—	—	.243	.308	.313

Team Pitching

Team	G	CG	ShO	Rel	Sv	IP	H	R	ER	HR	SH	SF	HB	TBB	IBB	SO	WP	Bk	H/9	SO/9	BB/9	OAvg	OOBP	ERA
Philadelphia	155	**123**	**24**	45	5	1421.2	1103	441	282	8	—	—	55	450	—	**789**	42	1	7.0	5.0	2.8	**.221**	.292	**1.79**
Chicago	156	103	23	66	7	1421.0	1130	479	320	16	—	—	38	381	—	785	31	**3**	7.2	5.0	2.4	.222	**.281**	2.03
Boston	158	100	12	70	6	1430.0	1236	564	390	30	—	—	45	414	—	670	32	1	7.8	4.2	2.6	.235	.297	2.45
Washington	157	119	19	43	3	1373.1	1215	550	376	19	—	—	51	375	—	674	**54**	**3**	8.0	4.4	2.5	.244	.304	2.46
New York	156	110	14	57	**8**	1399.0	1238	557	406	16	—	—	55	**364**	—	654	27	2	8.0	4.2	**2.3**	.243	.300	2.61
Detroit	155	108	17	64	5	1380.1	1257	582	433	34	—	—	67	460	—	532	31	0	8.2	3.5	3.0	.248	.319	2.82
Cleveland	161	92	13	**82**	5	**1467.0**	1392	657	470	10	—	—	64	488	—	617	43	0	8.5	3.8	3.0	.262	.331	2.88
St. Louis	158	101	9	73	3	1391.0	1356	743	477	14	—	—	53	532	—	557	34	2	8.8	3.6	3.4	.265	.341	3.09
AL Total	1256	856	131	500	42	11283.1	9927	4573	3154	147	—	—	428	3464	—	5278	294	12	7.9	4.2	2.8	.243	.308	2.52
AL Avg Team	157	107	16	63	5	1410.1	1241	572	394	18	—	—	54	433	—	660	37	2	7.9	4.2	2.8	.243	.308	2.52

Team Fielding

Team	G	PO	A	E	TC	DP	PB	Pct
Philadelphia	155	4255	2001	**230**	6486	**117**	10	**.965**
Cleveland	161	**4374**	2286	248	**6908**	112	19	.964
Washington	157	4129	2112	264	6505	99	**30**	.959
Detroit	155	4167	2162	288	6617	79	18	.956
New York	156	4150	2051	285	6486	95	19	.956
Boston	158	4275	2087	309	6671	80	20	.954
Chicago	156	4239	2209	314	6762	100	17	.954
St. Louis	158	4164	2206	385	6755	113	14	.943
AL Total	1256	33753	17114	2323	53190	795	147	.956

Team vs. Team Records

	Bos	ChA	Cle	Det	NYA	Phi	StL	Was	Won
Bos	—	10	14	12	9	4	16	16	81
ChA	12	—	10	9	8	8	12	9	68
Cle	8	12	—	9	8	7	18	9	71
Det	10	13	13	—	13	9	15	13	86
NYA	13	13	13	9	—	9	16	15	88
Phi	18	14	14	13	12	—	17	14	102
StL	6	10	4	7	6	5	—	9	47
Was	5	13	13	9	7	6	13	—	66
Lost	72	85	81	68	63	48	107	85	

Seasons: Standings, Leaders

1910 American League Batting Leaders

Games		At-Bats		Runs		Hits		Doubles		Triples	
N. Lajoie, Cle	159	N. Lajoie, Cle	591	T. Cobb, Det	106	N. Lajoie, Cle	227	N. Lajoie, Cle	51	S. Crawford, Det	19
H. Hooper, Bos	155	S. Crawford, Det	588	N. Lajoie, Cle	94	T. Cobb, Det	194	T. Cobb, Det	35	B. Lord, 2tm	18
G. McBride, Was	154	H. Hooper, Bos	584	T. Speaker, Bos	92	E. Collins, Phi	188	D. Lewis, Bos	29	D. Murphy, Phi	18
S. Crawford, Det	154	E. Collins, Phi	583	D. Bush, Det	90	T. Speaker, Bos	183	D. Murphy, Phi	28	B. Cree, NYA	16
E. Collins, Phi	153	T. Turner, Cle	574	C. Milan, Was	89	S. Crawford, Det	170	R. Oldring, Phi	27	J. Stahl, Bos	16

Home Runs		Total Bases		Runs Batted In		Walks		Intentional Walks		Strikeouts	
J. Stahl, Bos	10	N. Lajoie, Cle	304	S. Crawford, Det	120	D. Bush, Det	78	Statistic unavailable		Statistic unavailable	
D. Lewis, Bos	8	T. Cobb, Det	279	T. Cobb, Det	91	C. Milan, Was	71				
T. Cobb, Det	8	T. Speaker, Bos	252	E. Collins, Phi	81	H. Wolter, NYA	66				
T. Speaker, Bos	7	S. Crawford, Det	249	J. Stahl, Bos	77	T. Cobb, Det	64				
S. Crawford, Det	5	D. Murphy, Phi	244	N. Lajoie, Cle	76	3 tied with	62				

Hit By Pitch		Sac Hits		Sac Flies		Stolen Bases		Caught Stealing		GDP	
B. Daniels, NYA	16	H. Hooper, Bos	34	Statistic unavailable		E. Collins, Phi	81	Statistic unavailable		Statistic unavailable	
R. Killefer, Was	16	T. Jones, Det	33			T. Cobb, Det	65				
D. Gessler, Was	16	B. Purtell, 2tm	32			R. Zeider, ChA	49				
C. Milan, Was	15	D. Bush, Det	30			D. Bush, Det	49				
K. Elberfeld, Was	13	R. Killefer, Was	29			C. Milan, Was	44				

Runs Created		Runs Created/27 Outs		Batting Average		On-Base Percentage		Slugging Percentage		OBP+Slugging	
T. Cobb, Det	138	T. Cobb, Det	10.84	T. Cobb, Det	.383	T. Cobb, Det	.456	T. Cobb, Det	.551	T. Cobb, Det	1.008
N. Lajoie, Cle	135	N. Lajoie, Cle	9.07	N. Lajoie, Cle	.384	N. Lajoie, Cle	.445	N. Lajoie, Cle	.514	N. Lajoie, Cle	.960
E. Collins, Phi	109	T. Speaker, Bos	7.40	T. Speaker, Bos	.340	T. Speaker, Bos	.404	T. Speaker, Bos	.468	T. Speaker, Bos	.873
T. Speaker, Bos	105	E. Collins, Phi	6.76	E. Collins, Phi	.322	E. Collins, Phi	.381	D. Murphy, Phi	.436	E. Collins, Phi	.798
S. Crawford, Det	90	J. Knight, NYA	6.04	J. Knight, NYA	.312	C. Milan, Was	.379	R. Oldring, Phi	.430	J. Knight, NYA	.785

1910 American League Pitching Leaders

Wins		Losses		Winning Percentage		Games		Games Started		Complete Games	
J. Coombs, Phi	31	E. Walsh, ChA	20	C. Bender, Phi	.821	W. Johnson, Was	45	W. Johnson, Was	42	W. Johnson, Was	38
R. Ford, NYA	26	D. Gray, Was	19	R. Ford, NYA	.813	J. Coombs, Phi	45	J. Coombs, Phi	38	J. Coombs, Phi	35
W. Johnson, Was	25	J. Scott, ChA	18	J. Coombs, Phi	.775	E. Walsh, ChA	45	E. Walsh, ChA	36	E. Walsh, ChA	33
C. Bender, Phi	23	B. Bailey, StL	18	W. Donovan, Det	.708	J. Scott, ChA	41	C. Morgan, Phi	34	R. Ford, NYA	29
G. Mullin, Det	21	3 tied with	17	C. Smith, Bos	.647	2 tied with	38	R. Ford, NYA	33	G. Mullin, Det	27

Shutouts		Saves		Games Finished		Batters Faced		Innings Pitched		Hits Allowed	
J. Coombs, Phi	13	S. Hall, Bos	5	J. Scott, ChA	17	Statistic unavailable		W. Johnson, Was	370.0	W. Johnson, Was	262
R. Ford, NYA	8	E. Walsh, ChA	5	S. Hall, Bos	17			E. Walsh, ChA	369.2	G. Mullin, Det	260
W. Johnson, Was	8	F. Browning, Det	3	W. Mitchell, Cle	16			J. Coombs, Phi	353.0	B. Groom, Was	255
E. Walsh, ChA	7	6 tied with	2	E. Koestner, Cle	13			R. Ford, NYA	299.2	J. Coombs, Phi	248
2 tied with	5			J. Wood, Bos	13			C. Morgan, Phi	290.2	C. Falkenberg, Cle	246

Home Runs Allowed		Walks		Walks/9 Innings		Strikeouts		Strikeouts/9 Innings		Strikeout/Walk Ratio	
S. Stroud, Det	9	C. Morgan, Phi	117	E. Walsh, ChA	1.5	W. Johnson, Was	313	W. Johnson, Was	7.6	E. Walsh, ChA	4.23
B. Groom, Was	8	J. Coombs, Phi	115	C. Young, Cle	1.5	E. Walsh, ChA	258	J. Wood, Bos	6.6	W. Johnson, Was	4.12
E. Summers, Det	8	G. Mullin, Det	102	R. Collins, Bos	1.5	J. Coombs, Phi	224	E. Walsh, ChA	6.3	C. Bender, Phi	3.30
G. Mullin, Det	7	B. Bailey, StL	97	C. Bender, Phi	1.7	R. Ford, NYA	209	R. Ford, NYA	6.3	R. Ford, NYA	2.99
S. Hall, Bos	6	2 tied with	86	W. Johnson, Was	1.8	C. Bender, Phi	155	J. Coombs, Phi	5.7	R. Collins, Bos	2.66

Earned Run Average		Component ERA		Hit Batsmen		Wild Pitches		Opponent Average		Opponent OBP	
E. Walsh, ChA	1.27	E. Walsh, ChA	1.27	J. Warhop, NYA	18	W. Johnson, Was	21	E. Walsh, ChA	.187	E. Walsh, ChA	.226
J. Coombs, Phi	1.30	R. Ford, NYA	1.41	C. Morgan, Phi	18	C. Morgan, Phi	14	R. Ford, NYA	.188	R. Ford, NYA	.245
W. Johnson, Was	1.36	W. Johnson, Was	1.54	E. Willett, Det	17	E. Willett, Det	10	J. Coombs, Phi	.201	C. Bender, Phi	.255
C. Morgan, Phi	1.55	C. Bender, Phi	1.56	W. Mitchell, Cle	15	J. Coombs, Phi	10	W. Johnson, Was	.205	W. Johnson, Was	.257
C. Bender, Phi	1.58	J. Coombs, Phi	1.72	G. Mullin, Det	14	2 tied with	9	S. Hall, Bos	.207	R. Collins, Bos	.264

1910 American League Miscellaneous

Managers

Boston	Patsy Donovan	81-72
Chicago	Hugh Duffy	68-85
Cleveland	Deacon McGuire	71-81
Detroit	Hughie Jennings	86-68
New York	George Stallings	78-59
	Hal Chase	10-4
Philadelphia	Connie Mack	102-48
St. Louis	Jack O'Connor	47-107
Washington	Jimmy McAleer	66-85

Awards

STATS Most Valuable Player	Ty Cobb, of, Det
STATS Cy Young	Jack Coombs, Phi
STATS Rookie of the Year	Russ Ford, p, NYA
STATS Manager of the Year	Connie Mack, Phi

STATS All-Star Team

C	Ted Easterly, Cle	.306	0	55
1B	Jake Stahl, Bos	.271	10	77
2B	Nap Lajoie, Cle	.384	4	76
3B	Home Run Baker, Phi	.283	2	74
SS	John Knight, NYA	.312	3	45
OF	Ty Cobb, Det	.383	8	91
OF	Danny Murphy, Phi	.300	4	64
OF	Tris Speaker, Bos	.340	7	65
P	Chief Bender, Phi	23-5	1.58	155 K
P	Jack Coombs, Phi	31-9	1.30	224 K
P	Russ Ford, NYA	26-6	1.65	209 K
P	Walter Johnson, Was	25-17	1.36	313 K

Postseason

World Series	Philadelphia (AL) 4 vs. ChN (NL) 1

Outstanding Performances

No-Hitters
Addie Joss, Cle	@ ChA on April 20
Chief Bender, Phi	vs. Cle on May 12

Cycles
Danny Murphy, Phi	on August 25

1910 National League Standings

Team	W	L	Pct	GB	DIF	W	L	R	OR	HR	OHR	W	L	R	OR	HR	OHR	Run	HR	M/A	May	June	July	Aug	S/O
	Overall					**Home Games**						**Road Games**						**Park Index**		**Record by Month**					
Chicago	104	50	.675	—	144	58	19	354	231	18	9	46	31	358	268	16	9	93	108	6-4	16-8	16-9	21-9	21-7	24-13
New York	91	63	.591	13.0	10	52	26	352	255	20	17	39	37	363	312	11	13	88	150	9-3	14-11	13-8	15-14	16-12	24-15
Pittsburgh	86	67	.562	17.5	21	46	30	365	308	17	8	40	37	290	268	16	12	122	90	7-4	6-16	14-11	19-10	19-10	17-21
Philadelphia	78	75	.510	25.5	14	40	36	333	290	12	18	38	39	341	349	10	18	91	109	7-4	15-10	12-14	15-15	15-14	19-16
Cincinnati	75	79	.487	29.0	3	39	37	320	341	6	8	36	42	300	343	17	19	106	40	3-6	15-10	12-14	15-15	15-14	15-20
Brooklyn	64	90	.416	40.0	1	39	39	255	287	9	5	25	51	242	336	16	12	91	49	4-9	12-13	9-11	10-20	9-19	20-18
St. Louis	63	90	.412	40.5	0	35	41	312	316	3	14	28	49	327	402	12	16	87	62	4-8	14-12	11-14	10-18	9-19	15-19
Boston	53	100	.346	50.5	6	29	48	292	396	25	25	24	52	203	305	6	11	134	290	4-8	10-15	8-18	11-18	10-19	10-22

Clinch Date—Chicago 10/02.

Team Batting

Team	G	AB	R	OR	H	2B	3B	HR	TB	RBI	TBB	IBB	SO	HBP	SH	SF	SB	CS	SB%	GDP	Avg	OBP	Slg
New York	155	5061	**715**	567	**1391**	204	83	31	**1854**	623	562	—	489	57	193	—	282	—	—	—	.275	.354	.366
Chicago	154	4977	712	**499**	1333	219	**84**	**34**	1822	586	542	—	501	39	**234**	—	173	—	—	—	.268	.344	.366
Philadelphia	157	**5171**	674	639	1319	71	22	21	1750	565	506	—	559	43	205	—	199	—	—	—	.255	.327	.338
Pittsburgh	154	5125	655	576	1364	214	83	33	1843	543	437	—	524	34	198	—	148	—	—	—	.266	.328	.360
St. Louis	153	4912	639	718	1217	167	70	15	1569	527	**655**	—	581	**78**	153	—	179	—	—	—	.248	.345	.319
Cincinnati	156	5121	620	684	1326	150	79	23	1703	526	529	—	515	29	182	—	**310**	—	—	—	.259	.332	.333
Brooklyn	156	5125	497	623	1174	166	73	25	1561	408	434	—	**706**	40	183	—	151	—	—	—	.229	.294	.305
Boston	157	5123	495	701	1260	173	49	31	1624	421	359	—	540	47	181	—	152	—	—	—	.246	.301	.317
NL Total	1242	40615	5007	5007	10384	1516	592	214	13726	4199	4024	—	4415	367	1529	—	1594	—	—	—	.256	.328	.338
NL Avg Team	155	5077	626	626	1298	190	74	27	1716	525	503	—	552	46	191	—	199	—	—	—	.256	.328	.338

Team Pitching

Team	G	CG	ShO	Rel	Sv	IP	H	R	ER	HR	SH	SF	HB	TBB	IBB	SO	WP	Bk	H/9	SO/9	BB/9	OAvg	OOBP	ERA
Chicago	154	100	**25**	74	13	1378.2	**1171**	**499**	**384**	18	—	—	41	397	—	609	31	3	**7.6**	4.0	3.1	**.235**	**.307**	**2.51**
New York	155	96	9	80	10	1391.2	1290	567	414	30	—	—	38	397	—	**717**	30	1	8.3	**4.6**	2.6	.250	.308	2.68
Pittsburgh	154	73	13	100	12	1376.0	1254	576	433	20	—	—	57	**392**	—	479	15	**5**	8.2	3.1	**2.6**	.249	.310	2.83
Philadelphia	157	84	17	**107**	9	1411.1	1297	639	479	36	—	—	51	547	—	657	30	3	8.3	4.2	3.5	.253	.330	3.05
Brooklyn	156	**103**	15	65	5	**1420.1**	1331	623	484	17	—	—	38	545	—	555	35	0	8.4	3.5	3.5	.259	.335	3.07
Cincinnati	156	86	16	88	11	1386.2	1334	684	475	27	—	—	67	528	—	497	30	**5**	8.7	3.2	3.4	.261	.338	3.08
Boston	157	72	12	**107**	9	1390.1	1328	701	497	36	—	—	45	599	—	531	**40**	1	8.6	3.4	3.9	.265	.349	3.22
St. Louis	153	81	4	96	**14**	1337.1	1396	718	561	30	—	—	40	541	—	466	39	3	9.4	3.1	3.6	.275	.350	3.78
NL Total	1242	695	111	717	83	11092.1	10401	5007	3727	214	—	—	377	4023	—	4511	250	21	8.4	3.7	3.3	.256	.329	3.02
NL Avg Team	155	87	14	90	10	1386.1	1300	626	466	27	—	—	47	503	—	564	31	3	8.4	3.7	3.3	.256	.329	3.02

Team Fielding

Team	G	PO	A	E	TC	DP	PB	Pct
Brooklyn	156	**4238**	1979	235	6452	125	19	**.964**
Chicago	154	4118	1954	**230**	6302	110	15	.964
Pittsburgh	154	4115	1917	245	6277	102	8	.961
Philadelphia	157	4229	1971	258	6458	132	19	.960
St. Louis	153	4012	2021	261	6294	109	22	.959
New York	155	4183	1958	291	6432	117	22	.955
Cincinnati	156	4143	1995	291	6429	103	**23**	.955
Boston	157	4160	**2214**	305	**6679**	**137**	17	.954
NL Total	1242	33198	16009	2116	51323	935	145	.959

Team vs. Team Records

	Bos	Bro	ChN	Cin	NYG	Phi	Pit	StL	Won
Bos	—	10	5	8	6	4	8	12	53
Bro	12	—	6	7	8	9	10	12	**64**
ChN	17	16	—	16	14	14	12	15	**104**
Cin	14	15	6	—	8	10	10	12	75
NYG	16	14	8	14	—	15	12	12	91
Phi	17	13	8	12	7	—	11	10	78
Pit	14	12	10	12	10	11	—	17	86
StL	10	10	7	10	10	12	4	—	63
Lost	100	90	50	79	63	75	67	90	

Seasons: Standings, Leaders

1910 National League Batting Leaders

Games		At-Bats		Runs		Hits		Doubles		Triples	
Z. Wheat, Bro	156	D. Hoblitzell, Cin	611	S. Magee, Phi	110	B. Byrne, Pit	178	B. Byrne, Pit	43	M. Mitchell, Cin	18
M. Mitchell, Cin	156	Z. Wheat, Bro	606	B. Byrne, Pit	101	H. Wagner, Pit	178	S. Magee, Phi	39	S. Magee, Phi	17
D. Hoblitzell, Cin	155	B. Byrne, Pit	602	M. Huggins, StL	101	Z. Wheat, Bro	172	Z. Wheat, Bro	36	E. Konetchy, StL	16
F. Beck, Bos	154	B. Bescher, Cin	589	L. Doyle, NYG	97	S. Magee, Phi	172	F. Merkle, NYG	35	S. Hofman, ChN	16
S. Magee, Phi	154	B. Collins, Bos	584	B. Bescher, Cin	95	D. Hoblitzell, Cin	170	H. Wagner, Pit	34	3 tied with	15

Home Runs		Total Bases		Runs Batted In		Walks		Intentional Walks		Strikeouts	
F. Beck, Bos	10	S. Magee, Phi	263	S. Magee, Phi	123	M. Huggins, StL	116	Statistic unavailable		J. Hummel, Bro	81
W. Schulte, ChN	10	W. Schulte, ChN	257	M. Mitchell, Cin	88	J. Evers, ChN	108			Z. Wheat, Bro	80
J. Daubert, Bro	8	B. Byrne, Pit	251	R. Murray, NYG	87	S. Magee, Phi	94			B. Bescher, Cin	75
L. Doyle, NYG	8	Z. Wheat, Bro	244	S. Hofman, ChN	86	J. Titus, Phi	93			R. Ellis, StL	70
2 tied with	6	H. Wagner, Pit	240	H. Wagner, Pit	81	J. Sheckard, ChN	83			C. Wilson, Pit	68

Hit By Pitch		Sac Hits		Sac Flies		Stolen Bases		Caught Stealing		GDP	
S. Evans, StL	31	O. Knabe, Phi	37	Statistic unavailable		B. Bescher, Cin	70	Statistic unavailable		Statistic unavailable	
B. Herzog, Bos	15	E. Grant, Phi	34			R. Murray, NYG	57				
B. Collins, Bos	13	D. Egan, Cin	33			D. Paskert, Cin	51				
F. Snodgrass, NYG	13	3 tied with	31			S. Magee, Phi	49				
S. Magee, Phi	12					J. Devore, NYG	43				

Runs Created		Runs Created/27 Outs		Batting Average		On-Base Percentage		Slugging Percentage		OBP+Slugging	
S. Magee, Phi	132	S. Magee, Phi	9.15	S. Magee, Phi	.331	S. Magee, Phi	.445	S. Magee, Phi	.507	S. Magee, Phi	.952
H. Wagner, Pit	99	F. Snodgrass, NYG	7.44	S. Hofman, ChN	.325	F. Snodgrass, NYG	.440	S. Hofman, ChN	.461	F. Snodgrass, NYG	.871
B. Byrne, Pit	98	S. Hofman, ChN	7.05	F. Snodgrass, NYG	.321	J. Evers, ChN	.413	W. Schulte, ChN	.460	S. Hofman, ChN	.867
E. Konetchy, StL	97	E. Konetchy, StL	6.63	H. Wagner, Pit	.320	S. Hofman, ChN	.406	F. Merkle, NYG	.441	E. Konetchy, StL	.822
S. Hofman, ChN	97	J. Bates, Phi	6.45	J. Bates, Phi	.305	M. Huggins, StL	.399	F. Snodgrass, NYG	.432	H. Wagner, Pit	.822

1910 National League Pitching Leaders

Wins		Losses		Winning Percentage		Games		Games Started		Complete Games	
C. Mathewson, NYG	27	G. Bell, Bro	27	D. Phillippe, Pit	.875	A. Mattern, Bos	51	N. Rucker, Bro	39	N. Rucker, Bro	27
T. F. Brown, ChN	25	C. Curtis, Bos	24	K. Cole, ChN	.833	H. Gaspar, Cin	48	C. Curtis, Bos	37	T. F. Brown, ChN	27
E. Moore, Phi	22	B. Brown, Bos	23	D. Crandall, NYG	.810	4 tied with	46	A. Mattern, Bos	37	C. Mathewson, NYG	27
K. Cole, ChN	20	A. Mattern, Bos	19	C. Mathewson, NYG	.750			G. Bell, Bro	36	G. Bell, Bro	25
G. Suggs, Cin	20	S. Frock, 2tm	19	2 tied with	.667			2 tied with	35	C. Barger, Bro	25

Shutouts		Saves		Games Finished		Batters Faced		Innings Pitched		Hits Allowed	
T. F. Brown, ChN	7	H. Gaspar, Cin	7	D. Crandall, NYG	21	Statistic unavailable		N. Rucker, Bro	320.1	N. Rucker, Bro	293
A. Mattern, Bos	6	T. F. Brown, ChN	7	D. Phillippe, Pit	19			C. Mathewson, NYG	318.1	C. Mathewson, NYG	292
N. Rucker, Bro	6	D. Crandall, NYG	5	R. Dessau, Bro	18			G. Bell, Bro	310.0	A. Mattern, Bos	288
E. Moore, Phi	6	L. Richie, 2tm	4	B. Burke, Bos	16			A. Mattern, Bos	305.0	G. Bell, Bro	267
6 tied with	4	D. Phillippe, Pit	4	H. Gaspar, Cin	16			T. F. Brown, ChN	295.1	C. Barger, Bro	267

Home Runs Allowed		Walks		Walks/9 Innings		Strikeouts		Strikeouts/9 Innings		Strikeout/Walk Ratio	
D. Crandall, NYG	10	B. Harmon, StL	133	G. Suggs, Cin	1.6	E. Moore, Phi	185	L. Drucke, NYG	6.3	C. Mathewson, NYG	3.07
C. Curtis, Bos	9	K. Cole, ChN	130	C. Mathewson, NYG	1.7	C. Mathewson, NYG	184	S. Frock, 2tm	6.0	T. F. Brown, ChN	2.23
S. Frock, 2tm	8	C. Curtis, Bos	124	D. Crandall, NYG	1.9	S. Frock, 2tm	171	E. Moore, Phi	5.9	H. Camnitz, Pit	1.97
E. Stack, Phi	7	A. Mattern, Bos	121	T. F. Brown, ChN	2.0	L. Drucke, NYG	151	C. Mathewson, NYG	5.2	G. Suggs, Cin	1.90
6 tied with	6	E. Moore, Phi	121	H. Wiltse, NYG	2.0	N. Rucker, Bro	147	R. Ames, NYG	4.4	L. Drucke, NYG	1.84

Earned Run Average		Component ERA		Hit Batsmen		Wild Pitches		Opponent Average		Opponent OBP	
K. Cole, ChN	1.80	T. F. Brown, ChN	2.15	H. Gaspar, Cin	15	B. Harmon, StL	12	K. Cole, ChN	.211	T. F. Brown, ChN	.277
T. F. Brown, ChN	1.86	G. Bell, Bro	2.32	G. Suggs, Cin	14	K. Cole, ChN	9	L. Drucke, NYG	.228	C. Mathewson, NYG	.286
C. Mathewson, NYG	1.89	C. Mathewson, NYG	2.35	C. Curtis, Bos	12	C. Curtis, Bos	9	E. Moore, Phi	.228	D. Crandall, NYG	.289
R. Ames, NYG	2.22	B. Adams, Pit	2.41	B. Burns, Cin	12	B. Brown, Bos	9	T. F. Brown, ChN	.232	B. Adams, Pit	.291
B. Adams, Pit	2.24	R. Ames, NYG	2.50	H. Camnitz, Pit	12	R. Ames, NYG	9	D. Scanlan, Bro	.234	G. Bell, Bro	.296

1910 National League Miscellaneous

Managers

Boston	Fred Lake	53-100
Brooklyn	Bill Dahlen	64-90
Chicago	Frank Chance	104-50
Cincinnati	Clark Griffith	75-79
New York	John McGraw	91-63
Philadelphia	Red Dooin	78-75
Pittsburgh	Fred Clarke	86-67
St. Louis	Roger Bresnahan	63-90

Awards

STATS Most Valuable Player	Sherry Magee, of, Phi
STATS Cy Young	C. Mathewson, NYG
STATS Rookie of the Year	King Cole, p, ChN
STATS Manager of the Year	Frank Chance, ChN

Postseason

World Series	ChN (NL) 1 vs. Philadelphia (AL) 4

Outstanding Performances

Cycles
Chief Wilson, Pit	on July 3
Bill Collins, Bos	on October 6

STATS All-Star Team

C	Larry McLean, Cin	.298	2	71
1B	Ed Konetchy, StL	.302	3	78
2B	Larry Doyle, NYG	.285	8	69
3B	Bobby Byrne, Pit	.296	2	52
SS	Honus Wagner, Pit	.320	4	81
OF	Solly Hofman, ChN	.325	3	86
OF	Sherry Magee, Phi	.331	6	123
OF	Wildfire Schulte, ChN	.301	10	68
P	Three Finger Brown, ChN	25-13	1.86	143 K
P	King Cole, ChN	20-4	1.80	114 K
P	Christy Mathewson, NYG	27-9	1.89	184 K
P	Earl Moore, Phi	22-15	2.58	185 K

1911 American League Standings

	Overall					Home Games						Road Games						Park Index		Record by Month					
Team	W	L	Pct	GB	DIF	W	L	R	OR	HR	OHR	W	L	R	OR	HR	OHR	Run	HR	M/A	May	June	July	Aug	S/O
Philadelphia	101	50	.669	—	66	54	20	384	253	11	5	47	30	477	348	24	12	80	46	6-7	17-9	19-6	18-11	17-9	24-8
Detroit	89	65	.578	13.5	112	51	25	468	403	21	9	38	40	363	373	9	19	121	110	13-2	19-9	12-11	18-10	12-16	15-17
Cleveland	80	73	.523	22.0	0	46	30	368	344	7	13	34	43	323	368	13	4	104	119	6-10	12-14	12-14	18-12	12-10	20-13
Chicago	77	74	.510	24.0	0	39	37	341	299	8	15	38	37	378	325	12	7	90	119	7-7	12-10	13-11	16-15	13-17	16-14
Boston	78	75	.510	24.0	0	40	37	341	312	20	12	38	38	339	331	15	9	96	132	6-7	16-10	12-14	15-16	13-11	16-17
New York	76	76	.500	25.5	6	36	40	365	422	14	11	40	36	319	302	11	15	127	96	7-5	11-16	17-7	13-18	15-13	13-17
Washington	64	90	.416	38.5	3	39	38	323	356	11	6	25	52	302	410	5	33	95	45	6-6	8-20	10-17	10-17	17-11	13-19
St. Louis	45	107	.296	56.5	2	25	53	296	396	9	8	20	54	271	416	8	20	96	58	4-11	10-17	3-18	11-20	7-19	10-22

Clinch Date—Philadelphia 9/26.

Team Batting

Team	G	AB	R	OR	H	2B	3B	HR	TB	RBI	TBB	IBB	SO	HBP	SH	SF	SB	CS	SB%	GDP	Avg	OBP	Slg
Philadelphia	152	5199	861	601	1540	237	93	35	2068	692	424	—	—	65	232	—	226	—	—	—	.296	.357	.398
Detroit	154	5294	831	776	1544	230	96	30	2056	657	471	—	—	49	181	—	276	—	—	—	.292	.355	.388
Chicago	154	5213	719	624	1401	179	92	20	1824	593	385	—	—	48	208	—	201	—	—	—	.269	.325	.350
Cleveland	156	5321	691	712	1501	238	81	20	1961	579	354	—	—	50	160	—	209	—	—	—	.282	.333	.369
New York	153	5052	684	724	1374	190	96	25	1831	577	493	—	—	64	183	—	269	—	—	—	.272	.344	.362
Boston	153	5014	680	643	1379	203	66	35	1819	569	506	—	—	74	216	—	190	—	—	—	.275	.350	.363
Washington	154	5065	625	766	1308	159	54	16	1623	493	466	—	—	80	148	—	215	—	—	—	.258	.330	.320
St. Louis	152	4996	567	812	1192	187	63	17	1556	477	460	—	—	34	142	—	125	—	—	—	.239	.307	.311
AL Total	1228	41154	5658	5658	11239	1623	641	198	14738	4637	3559	—	—	464	1470	—	1711	—	—	—	.273	.338	.358
AL Avg Team	154	5144	707	707	1405	203	80	25	1842	580	445	—	—	58	184	—	214	—	—	—	.273	.338	.358

Team Pitching

Team	G	CG	ShO	Rel	Sv	IP	H	R	ER	HR	SH	SF	HB	TBB	IBB	SO	WP	Bk	H/9	SO/9	BB/9	OAvg	OOBP	ERA
Boston	153	87	10	85	8	1351.2	1309	643	412	21	—	—	48	473	—	711	33	2	8.7	4.7	3.1	.262	.332	2.74
Chicago	154	85	17	103	11	1386.1	1349	624	458	22	—	—	35	384	—	752	35	5	8.8	4.9	2.5	.255	.310	2.97
Philadelphia	152	97	13	77	13	1375.2	1343	601	460	17	—	—	81	487	—	739	34	4	8.8	4.8	3.2	.265	.339	3.01
Cleveland	156	93	6	73	6	1390.2	1382	712	519	17	—	—	66	552	—	675	55	8	8.9	4.4	3.6	.268	.347	3.36
Washington	154	106	14	62	3	1353.1	1471	766	529	39	—	—	48	410	—	628	57	1	9.8	4.2	2.7	.277	.334	3.52
New York	153	90	5	79	3	1360.2	1404	724	535	26	—	—	53	406	—	667	29	2	9.3	4.4	2.7	.270	.329	3.54
Detroit	154	108	8	67	3	1387.2	1514	776	575	28	—	—	69	460	—	538	40	1	9.8	3.5	3.0	.283	.348	3.73
St. Louis	152	92	8	80	1	1332.1	1465	812	571	28	—	—	53	463	—	383	30	4	9.9	2.6	3.1	.278	.342	3.86
AL Total	1228	758	80	626	48	10938.1	11237	5658	4059	198	—	—	453	3635	—	5093	313	27	9.2	4.2	3.0	.273	.339	3.34
AL Avg Team	154	95	10	78	6	1367.1	1405	707	507	25	—	—	57	454	—	637	39	3	9.2	4.2	3.0	.273	.339	3.34

Team Fielding

Team	G	PO	A	E	TC	DP	PB	Pct
Philadelphia	152	4121	1896	225	6242	100	14	.964
Chicago	154	4144	2091	252	6487	98	25	.961
Cleveland	156	4163	2081	302	6546	108	32	.954
Washington	154	4047	2162	305	6514	90	39	.953
Detroit	154	4143	2063	318	6524	78	15	.951
Boston	153	4037	1979	323	6339	93	28	.949
New York	153	4091	1971	328	6390	99	24	.949
St. Louis	152	3988	2125	358	6471	104	20	.945
AL Total	1228	32734	16368	2411	51513	770	197	.953

Team vs. Team Records

	Bos	ChA	Cle	Det	NYA	Phi	StL	Was	Won
Bos	—	11	11	10	12	9	12	13	78
ChA	11	—	6	8	13	9	17	13	77
Cle	11	15	—	6	14	5	15	14	80
Det	12	14	16	—	7	12	14	14	89
NYA	10	9	8	15	—	6	16	12	76
Phi	13	11	17	10	15	—	20	15	101
StL	9	5	7	8	5	2	—	9	45
Was	9	9	8	8	10	7	13	—	64
Lost	75	74	73	65	76	50	107	90	

1911 American League Batting Leaders

Games		At-Bats		Runs		Hits		Doubles		Triples	
C. Milan, Was	154	C. Milan, Was	616	T. Cobb, Det	147	T. Cobb, Det	248	T. Cobb, Det	47	T. Cobb, Det	24
G. McBride, Was	154	H. Baker, Phi	592	D. Bush, Det	126	J. Jackson, Cle	233	J. Jackson, Cle	45	B. Cree, NYA	22
D. Bush, Det	150	T. Cobb, Det	591	J. Jackson, Cle	126	S. Crawford, Det	217	H. Baker, Phi	42	J. Jackson, Cle	19
J. Austin, StL	148	B. Lord, Phi	574	C. Milan, Was	109	H. Baker, Phi	198	F. LaPorte, StL	37	H. Lord, ChA	18
H. Baker, Phi	148	S. Crawford, Det	574	S. Crawford, Det	109	C. Milan, Was	194	B. Lord, Phi	37	H. Wolter, NYA	15

Home Runs		Total Bases		Runs Batted In		Walks		Intentional Walks		Strikeouts	
H. Baker, Phi	11	T. Cobb, Det	367	T. Cobb, Det	127	D. Bush, Det	98	Statistic unavailable		Statistic unavailable	
T. Speaker, Bos	8	J. Jackson, Cle	337	H. Baker, Phi	115	C. Milan, Was	74				
T. Cobb, Det	8	S. Crawford, Det	302	S. Crawford, Det	115	D. Gessler, Was	74				
3 tied with	7	H. Baker, Phi	301	P. Bodie, ChA	97	H. Hooper, Bos	73				
		B. Cree, NYA	267	J. Delahanty, Det	94	J. Austin, StL	69				

Hit By Pitch		Sac Hits		Sac Flies		Stolen Bases		Caught Stealing		GDP	
K. Elberfeld, Was	25	J. Austin, StL	34	Statistic unavailable		T. Cobb, Det	83	Statistic unavailable		Statistic unavailable	
D. Gessler, Was	20	L. Gardner, Bos	32			C. Milan, Was	58				
B. Daniels, NYA	18	S. Yerkes, Bos	31			B. Cree, NYA	48				
E. Collins, Phi	15	H. Lord, ChA	31			N. Callahan, ChA	45				
T. Speaker, Bos	13	D. Bush, Det	30			H. Lord, ChA	43				

Runs Created		Runs Created/27 Outs		Batting Average		On-Base Percentage		Slugging Percentage		OBP+Slugging	
T. Cobb, Det	172	T. Cobb, Det	12.42	T. Cobb, Det	.420	J. Jackson, Cle	.468	T. Cobb, Det	.621	T. Cobb, Det	1.088
J. Jackson, Cle	147	J. Jackson, Cle	10.92	J. Jackson, Cle	.408	T. Cobb, Det	.467	J. Jackson, Cle	.590	J. Jackson, Cle	1.058
S. Crawford, Det	136	E. Collins, Phi	9.42	S. Crawford, Det	.378	E. Collins, Phi	.451	S. Crawford, Det	.526	S. Crawford, Det	.964
H. Baker, Phi	125	S. Crawford, Det	9.39	E. Collins, Phi	.365	S. Crawford, Det	.438	B. Cree, NYA	.513	E. Collins, Phi	.932
E. Collins, Phi	122	B. Cree, NYA	8.08	B. Cree, NYA	.348	T. Speaker, Bos	.418	H. Baker, Phi	.508	B. Cree, NYA	.928

1911 American League Pitching Leaders

Wins		Losses		Winning Percentage		Games		Games Started		Complete Games	
J. Coombs, Phi	28	J. Powell, StL	19	C. Bender, Phi	.773	E. Walsh, ChA	56	J. Coombs, Phi	40	W. Johnson, Was	36
E. Walsh, ChA	27	E. Walsh, ChA	18	V. Gregg, Cle	.767	J. Coombs, Phi	47	W. Johnson, Was	37	E. Walsh, ChA	33
W. Johnson, Was	25	B. Groom, Was	17	E. Plank, Phi	.742	J. Wood, Bos	44	E. Walsh, ChA	37	R. Ford, NYA	26
3 tied with	23	J. Wood, Bos	17	J. Coombs, Phi	.700	R. Caldwell, NYA	41	R. Ford, NYA	33	J. Coombs, Phi	26
		L. Hughes, Was	17	R. Works, Det	.688	3 tied with	40	J. Wood, Bos	33	2 tied with	25

Shutouts		Saves		Games Finished		Batters Faced		Innings Pitched		Hits Allowed	
W. Johnson, Was	6	S. Hall, Bos	5	J. Quinn, NYA	19	Statistic unavailable		E. Walsh, ChA	368.2	J. Coombs, Phi	360
E. Plank, Phi	6	E. Walsh, ChA	4	E. Walsh, ChA	19			J. Coombs, Phi	336.2	E. Walsh, ChA	327
V. Gregg, Cle	5	E. Plank, Phi	4	S. Hall, Bos	18			W. Johnson, Was	322.1	W. Johnson, Was	292
J. Wood, Bos	5	J. Wood, Bos	3	3 tied with	12			R. Ford, NYA	281.1	B. Groom, Was	280
E. Walsh, ChA	5	J. Coombs, Phi	3					J. Wood, Bos	276.2	E. Willett, Det	261

Home Runs Allowed		Walks		Walks/9 Innings		Strikeouts		Strikeouts/9 Innings		Strikeout/Walk Ratio	
B. Groom, Was	9	G. Krapp, Cle	136	D. White, ChA	1.5	E. Walsh, ChA	255	J. Wood, Bos	7.5	E. Walsh, ChA	3.54
W. Johnson, Was	8	J. Coombs, Phi	119	J. Lake, StL	1.7	J. Wood, Bos	231	J. Wood, Bos	6.2	J. Wood, Bos	3.04
J. Coombs, Phi	8	C. Morgan, Phi	113	E. Walsh, ChA	1.8	W. Johnson, Was	207	F. Lange, ChA	5.8	W. Johnson, Was	2.96
4 tied with	7	V. Gregg, Cle	86	J. Warhop, NYA	1.9	J. Coombs, Phi	185	W. Johnson, Was	5.8	R. Ford, NYA	2.08
		J. Scott, ChA	81	J. Powell, StL	1.9	R. Ford, NYA	158	G. Kahler, Cle	5.7	D. White, ChA	2.06

Earned Run Average		Component ERA		Hit Batsmen		Wild Pitches		Opponent Average		Opponent OBP	
V. Gregg, Cle	1.80	V. Gregg, Cle	1.89	C. Morgan, Phi	21	W. Johnson, Was	17	V. Gregg, Cle	.205	E. Walsh, ChA	.280
W. Johnson, Was	1.90	J. Wood, Bos	2.17	J. Coombs, Phi	16	G. Krapp, Cle	14	J. Wood, Bos	.223	W. Johnson, Was	.283
J. Wood, Bos	2.02	E. Walsh, ChA	2.20	J. Warhop, NYA	15	J. Coombs, Phi	12	G. Krapp, Cle	.232	J. Wood, Bos	.284
E. Plank, Phi	2.10	R. Ford, NYA	2.38	E. Willett, Det	14	D. Gray, Was	10	R. Ford, NYA	.237	V. Gregg, Cle	.286
C. Bender, Phi	2.16	W. Johnson, Was	2.40	E. Plank, Phi	14	J. Wood, Bos	10	W. Johnson, Was	.238	R. Ford, NYA	.291

1911 American League Miscellaneous

Managers		
Boston	Patsy Donovan	78-75
Chicago	Hugh Duffy	77-74
Cleveland	Deacon McGuire	6-11
	George Stovall	74-62
Detroit	Hughie Jennings	89-65
New York	Hal Chase	76-76
Philadelphia	Connie Mack	101-50
St. Louis	Bobby Wallace	45-107
Washington	Jimmy McAleer	64-90

Awards	
Most Valuable Player	Ty Cobb, of, Det
STATS Cy Young	Walter Johnson, Was
STATS Rookie of the Year	Joe Jackson, of, Cle
STATS Manager of the Year	George Stovall, Cle

STATS All-Star Team

C	Oscar Stanage, Det	.264	3	51
1B	Jim Delahanty, Det	.339	3	94
2B	Eddie Collins, Phi	.365	3	73
3B	Home Run Baker, Phi	.334	11	115
SS	Donie Bush, Det	.232	1	36
OF	Ty Cobb, Det	.420	8	127
OF	Sam Crawford, Det	.378	7	115
OF	Joe Jackson, Cle	.408	7	83
P	Vean Gregg, Cle	23-7	1.80	125 K
P	Walter Johnson, Was	25-13	1.90	207 K
P	Eddie Plank, Phi	23-8	2.10	149 K
P	Ed Walsh, ChA	27-18	2.22	255 K

Postseason	
World Series	Phi (AL) 4 vs. New York (NL) 2

Outstanding Performances

No-Hitters
Joe Wood, Bos — vs. StL on July 29
Ed Walsh, ChA — vs. Bos on August 27
Cycles
Home Run Baker, Phi on July 3

1911 National League Standings

Team	W	L	Pct	GB	DIF	W	L	R	OR	HR	OHR	W	L	R	OR	HR	OHR	Run	HR	M/A	May	June	July	Aug	S/O
	Overall					**Home Games**						**Road Games**						**Park Index**		**Record by Month**					
New York	99	54	.647	—	80	49	25	357	267	25	15	50	29	399	275	16	18	99	126	8-5	17-9	16-10	15-12	16-8	27-10
Chicago	92	62	.597	7.5	53	49	32	380	306	26	14	43	30	377	301	28	12	91	90	9-6	14-9	16-11	17-7	11-11	25-18
Pittsburgh	85	69	.552	14.5	4	48	29	393	246	29	6	37	40	351	311	20	17	97	70	8-5	15-12	14-10	18-10	15-12	15-20
Philadelphia	79	73	.520	19.5	51	42	34	352	357	48	26	37	39	306	312	12	17	115	255	3-7	15-12	17-11	16-12	8-15	15-21
St. Louis	75	74	.503	22.0	3	36	38	343	380	11	12	39	36	328	365	15	27	106	56	4-6	16-11	17-11	16-12	9-14	14-19
Cincinnati	70	83	.458	29.0	0	38	42	331	317	5	6	32	41	351	389	16	30	80	22	4-6	13-15	12-15	10-17	14-8	17-22
Brooklyn	64	86	.427	33.5	0	31	42	247	303	10	11	33	44	292	356	18	16	90	65	4-10	10-16	9-15	11-17	11-11	19-17
Boston	44	107	.291	54.0	1	19	54	391	536	28	47	25	53	308	485	9	29	125	211	5-10	5-21	5-19	5-23	10-15	14-19

Clinch Date—New York 10/04.

Team Batting

Team	G	AB	R	OR	H	2B	3B	HR	TB	RBI	TBB	IBB	SO	HBP	SH	SF	SB	CS	SB%	GDP	Avg	OBP	Slg
Chicago	157	5130	**757**	607	1335	218	101	54	1917	626	585	—	617	42	**202**	—	214	—	—	—	.260	.341	.374
New York	154	5006	756	**542**	1399	225	103	41	**1953**	651	530	—	506	85	160	—	**347**	—	—	—	**.279**	**.358**	**.390**
Pittsburgh	155	5137	744	557	1345	206	**106**	49	1910	633	525	—	583	52	193	—	160	—	—	—	.262	.336	.372
Boston	156	**5308**	699	1021	**1417**	249	54	37	1885	594	554	—	577	31	152	—	169	—	—	—	.267	.340	.355
Cincinnati	159	5291	682	706	1379	180	105	21	1832	595	578	—	594	35	185	—	289	—	—	—	.261	.337	.346
St. Louis	158	5132	671	745	1295	199	86	26	1744	567	**592**	—	650	65	181	—	175	—	—	—	.252	.337	.340
Philadelphia	153	5044	658	669	1307	214	56	**60**	1813	564	490	—	588	31	186	—	153	—	—	—	.259	.328	.359
Brooklyn	154	5059	539	659	1198	151	71	28	1575	465	425	—	**683**	39	157	—	184	—	—	—	.237	.301	.311
NL Total	1246	41107	5506	5506	10675	1642	682	316	14629	4695	4279	—	4798	380	1416	—	1691	—	—	—	.260	.335	.356
NL Avg Team	156	5138	688	688	1334	205	85	40	1829	587	535	—	600	48	177	—	211	—	—	—	.260	.335	.356

Team Pitching

Team	G	CG	ShO	Rel	Sv	IP	H	R	ER	HR	SH	SF	HB	TBB	IBB	SO	WP	Bk	H/9	SO/9	BB/9	OAvg	OOBP	ERA
New York	154	**95**	19	80	13	1368.0	1267	**542**	409	33	—	—	29	369	—	**771**	27	2	8.3	**5.1**	2.4	.246	**.300**	**2.69**
Pittsburgh	155	91	13	84	11	1380.1	**1249**	557	436	36	—	—	39	375	—	605	28	3	8.1	3.9	2.4	.248	.306	2.84
Chicago	157	85	12	97	**16**	1411.0	1270	607	454	**26**	—	—	47	525	—	582	35	2	**8.1**	3.7	3.3	**.245**	.320	2.90
Cincinnati	159	77	4	97	12	**1425.0**	1410	706	516	36	—	—	**65**	476	—	557	23	2	8.9	3.5	3.0	.265	.332	3.26
Philadelphia	153	90	**20**	78	10	1373.1	1285	669	503	43	—	—	54	598	—	697	30	**7**	8.4	4.6	3.9	.255	.340	3.30
Brooklyn	154	81	13	91	10	1371.2	1310	659	517	27	—	—	41	566	—	533	13	1	8.6	3.5	3.7	.263	.344	3.39
St. Louis	158	88	6	101	10	1402.1	1296	745	574	39	—	—	52	701	—	561	34	1	8.3	3.6	4.5	.254	.350	3.68
Boston	156	73	5	**115**	7	1374.0	1570	1021	776	76	—	—	56	672	—	486	**36**	4	10.3	3.2	4.4	.296	.381	5.08
NL Total	1246	680	92	743	89	11105.2	10657	5506	4185	316	—	—	383	4282	—	4792	226	22	8.7	3.9	3.5	.260	.335	3.39
NL Avg Team	156	85	12	93	11	1388.2	1332	688	523	40	—	—	48	535	—	599	28	3	8.7	3.9	3.5	.260	.335	3.39

Team Fielding

Team	G	PO	A	E	TC	DP	PB	Pct
Philadelphia	153	4108	1899	**231**	6238	113	23	**.963**
Pittsburgh	155	4122	1837	232	6191	**131**	15	.963
Brooklyn	154	4100	1970	241	6311	112	12	.962
Chicago	157	4217	2054	260	6531	114	11	.960
St. Louis	158	4188	2042	261	6491	106	17	.960
New York	154	4090	1925	256	6271	86	14	.959
Cincinnati	159	**4260**	2013	295	**6568**	108	15	.955
Boston	156	4105	**2065**	347	6517	110	19	.947
NL Total	1246	33190	15805	2123	51118	880	126	.958

Team vs. Team Records

	Bos	Bro	ChN	Cin	NYG	Phi	Pit	StL	Won
Bos	—	12	5	4	7	6	3	7	**44**
Bro	10	—	13	11	5	8	8	9	**64**
ChN	17	9	—	14	11	15	10	16	**92**
Cin	17	11	8	—	8	10	10	6	**70**
NYG	15	16	11	14	—	12	16	15	**99**
Phi	16	13	7	12	10	—	13	8	**79**
Pit	19	14	12	12	6	9	—	13	**85**
StL	13	11	6	16	7	13	9	—	**75**
Lost	107	86	62	83	54	73	69	74	

1911 National League Batting Leaders

Games			At-Bats			Runs			Hits			Doubles			Triples		
D. Hoblitzell, Cin	158		D. Hoblitzell, Cin	622		J. Sheckard, ChN	121		D. Miller, Bos	192		E. Konetchy, StL	38		L. Doyle, NYG	25	
E. Konetchy, StL	158		B. Bescher, Cin	599		B. Bescher, Cin	106		D. Miller, Bos	180		D. Miller, Bos	36		M. Mitchell, Cin	22	
J. Sheckard, ChN	156		B. Byrne, Pit	598		M. Huggins, StL	106		J. Daubert, Bro	176		C. Wilson, Pit	34		W. Schulte, ChN	21	
R. Ellis, StL	155		D. Miller, Bos	577		W. Schulte, ChN	105		W. Schulte, ChN	173		B. Herzog, 2tm	33		H. Zimmerman, ChN	17	
3 tied with	154		W. Schulte, ChN	577		L. Doyle, NYG	102		F. Luderus, Phi	166		B. Sweeney, Bos	33		B. Byrne, Pit	17	

Home Runs			Total Bases			Runs Batted In			Walks			Intentional Walks			Strikeouts		
W. Schulte, ChN	21		W. Schulte, ChN	308		C. Wilson, Pit	107		J. Sheckard, ChN	147		Statistic unavailable			B. Bescher, Cin	78	
F. Luderus, Phi	16		L. Doyle, NYG	277		W. Schulte, ChN	107		J. Bates, Cin	103					B. Coulson, Bro	78	
S. Magee, Phi	15		F. Luderus, Phi	260		F. Luderus, Phi	99		B. Bescher, Cin	102					F. Luderus, Phi	76	
L. Doyle, NYG	13		D. Hoblitzell, Cin	258		S. Magee, Phi	94		M. Huggins, StL	96					M. Carey, Pit	75	
2 tied with	12		C. Wilson, Pit	257		2 tied with	91		O. Knabe, Phi	94					D. Paskert, Phi	70	

Hit By Pitch			Sac Hits			Sac Flies			Stolen Bases			Caught Stealing			GDP		
S. Evans, StL	19		H. Lobert, Phi	38		Statistic unavailable			B. Bescher, Cin	80		Statistic unavailable			Statistic unavailable		
B. Herzog, 2tm	17		W. Schulte, ChN	31					J. Devore, NYG	61							
F. Snodgrass, NYG	15		B. Herzog, 2tm	30					F. Snodgrass, NYG	51							
A. Fletcher, NYG	14		D. Paskert, Phi	30					F. Merkle, NYG	49							
C. Meyers, NYG	13		2 tied with	28					2 tied with	48							

Runs Created			Runs Created/27 Outs			Batting Average			On-Base Percentage			Slugging Percentage			OBP+Slugging		
W. Schulte, ChN	127		H. Wagner, Pit	8.60		H. Wagner, Pit	.334		J. Sheckard, ChN	.434		W. Schulte, ChN	.534		H. Wagner, Pit	.930	
J. Sheckard, ChN	115		F. Clarke, Pit	7.91		D. Miller, Bos	.333		H. Wagner, Pit	.423		L. Doyle, NYG	.527		L. Doyle, NYG	.924	
L. Doyle, NYG	111		W. Schulte, ChN	7.46		C. Meyers, NYG	.332		J. Bates, Cin	.415		H. Wagner, Pit	.507		W. Schulte, ChN	.918	
H. Wagner, Pit	110		L. Doyle, NYG	7.41		F. Clarke, Pit	.324		F. Clarke, Pit	.407		F. Clarke, Pit	.492		F. Clarke, Pit	.900	
E. Konetchy, StL	104		J. Sheckard, ChN	7.26		A. Fletcher, NYG	.319		B. Sweeney, Bos	.404		S. Magee, Phi	.483		S. Magee, Phi	.849	

1911 National League Pitching Leaders

Wins			Losses			Winning Percentage			Games			Games Started			Complete Games		
P. Alexander, Phi	28		B. Steele, StL	19		R. Marquard, NYG	.774		T. F. Brown, ChN	53		B. Harmon, StL	41		P. Alexander, Phi	31	
C. Mathewson, NYG	26		E. Moore, Phi	19		D. Crandall, NYG	.750		B. Harmon, StL	51		P. Alexander, Phi	37		C. Mathewson, NYG	29	
R. Marquard, NYG	24		N. Rucker, Bro	18		K. Cole, ChN	.720		P. Alexander, Phi	48		B. Adams, Pit	37		B. Harmon, StL	28	
B. Harmon, StL	23		B. Brown, Bos	18		P. Alexander, Phi	.683		N. Rucker, Bro	48		L. Leifield, Pit	37		L. Leifield, Pit	26	
2 tied with	22		H. Gaspar, Cin	17		C. Mathewson, NYG	.667		2 tied with	45		C. Mathewson, NYG	37		B. Adams, Pit	24	

Shutouts			Saves			Games Finished			Batters Faced			Innings Pitched			Hits Allowed		
P. Alexander, Phi	7		T. F. Brown, ChN	13		D. Crandall, NYG	26		Statistic unavailable			P. Alexander, Phi	367.0		C. Mathewson, NYG	303	
B. Adams, Pit	6		D. Crandall, NYG	5		T. F. Brown, ChN	24					B. Harmon, StL	348.0		L. Leifield, Pit	301	
4 tied with	5		5 tied with	4		B. Pfeffer, Bos	16					L. Leifield, Pit	318.0		B. Harmon, StL	290	
						5 tied with	14					N. Rucker, Bro	315.2		B. Steele, StL	287	
												E. Moore, Phi	308.1		P. Alexander, Phi	285	

Home Runs Allowed			Walks			Walks/9 Innings			Strikeouts			Strikeouts/9 Innings			Strikeout/Walk Ratio		
A. Mattern, Bos	13		B. Harmon, StL	181		C. Mathewson, NYG	1.1		R. Marquard, NYG	237		R. Marquard, NYG	7.7		C. Mathewson, NYG	3.71	
N. Rucker, Bro	12		E. Moore, Phi	164		B. Adams, Pit	1.3		P. Alexander, Phi	227		P. Alexander, Phi	5.6		B. Adams, Pit	3.17	
L. Tyler, Bos	11		P. Alexander, Phi	129		E. Steele, 2tm	1.7		N. Rucker, Bro	190		N. Rucker, Bro	5.4		H. Wiltse, NYG	2.36	
E. Moore, Phi	11		R. Golden, StL	129		T. F. Brown, ChN	1.8		E. Moore, Phi	174		R. Ames, NYG	5.2		T. F. Brown, ChN	2.35	
3 tied with	10		B. Brown, Bos	116		H. Wiltse, NYG	1.9		B. Harmon, StL	144		E. Moore, Phi	5.1		R. Marquard, NYG	2.24	

Earned Run Average			Component ERA			Hit Batsmen			Wild Pitches			Opponent Average			Opponent OBP		
C. Mathewson, NYG	1.99		B. Adams, Pit	2.01		A. Fromme, Cin	16		K. Cole, ChN	11		P. Alexander, Phi	.219		B. Adams, Pit	.271	
L. Richie, ChN	2.31		R. Ames, NYG	2.08		L. Leifield, Pit	16		G. Chalmers, Phi	10		R. Marquard, NYG	.219		R. Ames, NYG	.277	
B. Adams, Pit	2.33		P. Alexander, Phi	2.22		H. Gaspar, Cin	14		R. Marquard, NYG	10		R. Ames, NYG	.223		C. Mathewson, NYG	.283	
R. Marquard, NYG	2.50		C. Mathewson, NYG	2.43		B. Humphries, 2tm	12		H. Camnitz, Pit	10		N. Rucker, Bro	.226		H. Wiltse, NYG	.292	
P. Alexander, Phi	2.57		B. Keefe, Cin	2.47		E. Moore, Phi	12		2 tied with	8		B. Keefe, Cin	.229		P. Alexander, Phi	.293	

1911 National League Miscellaneous

Managers

Boston	Fred Tenney	44-107
Brooklyn	Bill Dahlen	64-86
Chicago	Frank Chance	92-62
Cincinnati	Clark Griffith	70-83
New York	John McGraw	99-54
Philadelphia	Red Dooin	79-73
Pittsburgh	Fred Clarke	85-69
St. Louis	Roger Bresnahan	75-74

Awards

Most Valuable Player	Wildfire Schulte, of, ChN
STATS Cy Young	C. Mathewson, NYG
STATS Rookie of the Year	Pete Alexander, p, Phi
STATS Manager of the Year	John McGraw, NYG

STATS All-Star Team

C	Chief Meyers, NYG	.332	1	61
1B	Ed Konetchy, StL	.289	6	88
2B	Larry Doyle, NYG	.310	13	77
3B	Hans Lobert, Phi	.285	9	72
SS	Honus Wagner, Pit	.334	9	89
OF	Sherry Magee, Phi	.288	15	94
OF	Wildfire Schulte, ChN	.300	21	107
OF	Jimmy Sheckard, ChN	.276	4	50
P	Babe Adams, Pit	22-12	2.33	133 K
P	Pete Alexander, Phi	28-13	2.57	227 K
P	Rube Marquard, NYG	24-7	2.50	237 K
P	Christy Mathewson, NYG	26-13	1.99	141 K

Postseason

World Series	New York (NL) 2 vs. Phi (AL) 4

Outstanding Performances

Cycles

Mike Mitchell, Cin	on August 19

1912 American League Standings

Team	Overall					Home Games						Road Games						Park Index		Record by Month					
	W	L	Pct	GB	DIF	W	L	R	OR	HR	OHR	W	L	R	OR	HR	OHR	Run	HR	M/A	May	June	July	Aug	S/O
Boston	105	47	.691	—	130	57	20	417	286	10	10	48	27	382	258	19	8	107	72	9-4	15-9	21-8	22-9	20-7	18-10
Washington	91	61	.599	14.0	0	45	33	336	295	13	12	46	28	363	286	7	12	92	125	7-5	11-15	21-10	21-7	17-12	14-12
Philadelphia	90	62	.592	15.0	5	45	32	381	342	11	6	45	30	398	316	11	6	99	97	7-6	10-10	21-9	17-16	18-9	17-12
Chicago	78	76	.506	28.0	49	34	43	276	340	11	11	44	33	362	306	6	15	92	105	10-4	18-8	10-16	13-15	17-15	
Cleveland	75	78	.490	30.5	2	39	35	338	326	4	6	36	43	338	355	8	9	102	63	7-6	10-13	16-13	12-20	9-18	21-8
Detroit	69	84	.451	36.5	0	37	39	344	370	8	6	32	45	376	407	11	10	92	68	6-9	14-11	12-16	16-14	9-19	12-15
St. Louis	53	101	.344	53.0	0	27	50	287	379	6	11	26	51	265	385	13	6	102	89	5-9	7-17	6-20	11-20	13-16	11-19
New York	50	102	.329	55.0	0	31	44	352	423	14	16	19	58	278	419	4	12	114	193	2-10	10-12	6-21	13-18	14-17	5-24

Clinch Date—Boston 9/18.

Team Batting

Team	G	AB	R	OR	H	2B	3B	HR	TB	RBI	TBB	IBB	SO	HBP	SH	SF	SB	CS	SB%	GDP	Avg	OBP	Slg
Boston	154	5071	799	544	1404	269	84	29	1928	654	565	—	—	45	191	—	185	—	—	—	.277	.355	.380
Philadelphia	153	5111	779	658	1442	204	108	22	1928	620	485	—	—	38	201	—	258	—	—	—	.282	.349	.377
Detroit	154	5143	720	777	1376	189	86	19	1794	569	530	—	—	58	153	—	270	—	—	—	.268	.343	.349
Washington	154	5075	699	581	1298	202	86	20	1732	575	472	—	—	38	141	—	274	—	—	—	.256	.324	.341
Cleveland	155	5132	677	681	1403	219	77	12	1812	561	407	—	—	51	206	—	194	—	—	—	.273	.333	.353
Chicago	158	5182	639	648	1321	174	80	17	1706	537	423	—	—	51	221	—	205	—	—	—	.255	.317	.329
New York	153	5092	630	842	1320	168	79	18	1732	502	463	—	—	65	152	—	247	—	—	—	.259	.329	.334
St. Louis	157	5080	552	764	1262	166	71	19	1627	468	449	—	—	42	138	—	176	—	—	—	.248	.315	.320
AL Total	1238	40886	5495	5495	10826	1591	671	156	14227	4486	3794	—	—	388	1403	—	1809	—	—	—	.265	.333	.348
AL Avg Team	155	5111	687	687	1353	199	84	20	1778	561	474	—	—	49	175	—	226	—	—	—	.265	.333	.348

Team Pitching

Team	G	CG	ShO	Rel	Sv	IP	H	R	ER	HR	SH	SF	HB	TBB	IBB	SO	WP	Bk	H/9	SO/9	BB/9	OAvg	OOBP	ERA
Washington	154	98	11	72	7	1376.2	1219	581	412	24	—	—	54	525	—	828	48	5	8.0	5.4	3.4	.242	.320	2.69
Boston	154	108	18	56	6	1362.0	1243	544	417	18	—	—	35	385	—	712	20	3	8.2	4.7	2.5	.248	.306	2.76
Chicago	158	85	14	100	16	1413.0	1398	648	480	26	—	—	32	426	—	698	37	8	8.9	4.4	2.7	.263	.322	3.06
Cleveland	155	94	7	80	7	1352.2	1367	681	496	15	—	—	47	523	—	622	42	2	9.1	4.1	3.5	.272	.346	3.30
Philadelphia	153	95	11	81	9	1357.0	1273	658	501	12	—	—	57	518	—	601	30	2	8.4	4.0	3.4	.258	.336	3.32
St. Louis	157	85	8	91	5	1369.2	1433	764	565	17	—	—	58	442	—	547	39	1	9.4	3.6	2.9	.277	.341	3.71
Detroit	154	107	7	57	5	1367.1	1438	777	573	16	—	—	61	521	—	512	54	1	9.5	3.4	3.4	.279	.352	3.77
New York	153	105	5	60	3	1335.0	1448	842	612	28	—	—	45	436	—	637	37	4	9.8	4.3	2.9	.281	.343	4.13
AL Total	1238	777	81	600	58	10933.1	10819	5495	4056	156	—	—	389	3776	—	5157	307	26	8.9	4.2	3.1	.265	.333	3.34
AL Avg Team	155	97	10	75	7	1366.1	1352	687	507	20	—	—	49	472	—	645	38	3	8.9	4.2	3.1	.265	.333	3.34

Team Fielding

Team	G	PO	A	E	TC	DP	PB	Pct
Philadelphia	153	4100	2023	263	6386	115	17	.959
Boston	154	4109	1879	267	6255	88	20	.957
Chicago	158	4249	2111	291	6651	102	21	.956
Washington	154	4185	2032	297	6514	92	22	.954
Cleveland	155	4073	1917	287	6277	124	23	.954
Detroit	154	4137	2285	338	6760	91	28	.950
St. Louis	157	4117	1984	341	6442	127	15	.947
New York	153	4041	1915	382	6338	77	27	.940
AL Total	1238	33011	16146	2466	51623	816	173	.952

Team vs. Team Records

	Bos	ChA	Cle	Det	NYA	Phi	StL	Was	Won
Bos	—	16	11	15	19	15	17	12	105
ChA	6	—	11	14	13	12	13	9	78
Cle	11	11	—	13	13	8	15	4	75
Det	6	8	9	—	16	13	13	8	69
NYA	2	9	8	6	—	5	13	7	50
Phi	7	10	14	13	17	—	16	13	90
StL	5	9	7	9	9	6	—	8	53
Was	10	13	18	14	15	7	14	—	91
Lost	47	76	78	84	102	62	101	61	

1912 American League Batting Leaders

Games			At-Bats			Runs			Hits			Doubles			Triples		
M. Rath, ChA	157		E. Foster, Was	618		E. Collins, Phi	137		T. Cobb, Det	227		T. Speaker, Bos	53		J. Jackson, Cle	26	
D. Lewis, Bos	154		C. Milan, Was	601		T. Speaker, Bos	136		J. Jackson, Cle	226		J. Jackson, Cle	44		T. Cobb, Det	23	
E. Foster, Was	154		M. Rath, ChA	591		J. Jackson, Cle	121		T. Speaker, Bos	222		H. Baker, Phi	40		H. Baker, Phi	21	
B. Shotton, StL	154		H. Hooper, Bos	590		T. Cobb, Det	119		H. Baker, Phi	200		D. Lewis, Bos	36		S. Crawford, Det	21	
C. Milan, Was	154		2 tied with	581		H. Baker, Phi	116		2 tied with	189		3 tied with	34		L. Gardner, Bos	18	

Home Runs			Total Bases			Runs Batted In			Walks			Intentional Walks			Strikeouts		
H. Baker, Phi	10		J. Jackson, Cle	331		H. Baker, Phi	130		D. Bush, Det	117		Statistic unavailable			Statistic unavailable		
T. Speaker, Bos	10		T. Speaker, Bos	329		D. Lewis, Bos	109		E. Collins, Phi	101							
T. Cobb, Det	7		T. Cobb, Det	324		S. Crawford, Det	109		M. Rath, ChA	95							
3 tied with	6		H. Baker, Phi	312		S. McInnis, Phi	101		B. Shotton, StL	86							
			S. Crawford, Det	273		3 tied with	90		T. Speaker, Bos	82							

Hit By Pitch			Sac Hits			Sac Flies			Stolen Bases			Caught Stealing			GDP		
B. Daniels, NYA	18		D. Lewis, Bos	31		Statistic unavailable			C. Milan, Was	88		Statistic unavailable			Statistic unavailable		
J. Jackson, Cle	12		I. Olson, Cle	30					E. Collins, Phi	63							
B. Louden, Det	11		S. McInnis, Phi	29					T. Cobb, Det	61							
G. Moriarty, Det	11		H. Lord, ChA	29					T. Speaker, Bos	52							
B. Shotton, StL	9		E. Collins, Phi	29					R. Zeider, ChA	47							

Runs Created			Runs Created/27 Outs			Batting Average			On-Base Percentage			Slugging Percentage			OBP+Slugging		
T. Speaker, Bos	163		T. Speaker, Bos	11.36		T. Cobb, Det	.410		T. Speaker, Bos	.464		T. Cobb, Det	.586		T. Cobb, Det	1.043	
J. Jackson, Cle	148		T. Cobb, Det	11.27		J. Jackson, Cle	.395		J. Jackson, Cle	.458		J. Jackson, Cle	.579		J. Jackson, Cle	1.036	
T. Cobb, Det	148		J. Jackson, Cle	10.43		T. Speaker, Bos	.383		T. Cobb, Det	.458		T. Speaker, Bos	.567		T. Speaker, Bos	1.031	
H. Baker, Phi	132		H. Baker, Phi	8.66		N. Lajoie, Cle	.368		E. Collins, Phi	.450		H. Baker, Phi	.541		H. Baker, Phi	.945	
E. Collins, Phi	127		E. Collins, Phi	8.44		E. Collins, Phi	.348		N. Lajoie, Cle	.414		S. Crawford, Det	.470		E. Collins, Phi	.885	

1912 American League Pitching Leaders

Wins			Losses			Winning Percentage			Games			Games Started			Complete Games		
J. Wood, Bos	34		R. Ford, NYA	21		J. Wood, Bos	.872		E. Walsh, ChA	62		E. Walsh, ChA	41		J. Wood, Bos	35	
W. Johnson, Was	33		G. Kahler, Cle	19		E. Plank, Phi	.813		W. Johnson, Was	50		B. Groom, Was	40		W. Johnson, Was	34	
E. Walsh, ChA	27		J. Warhop, NYA	19		W. Johnson, Was	.733		B. Groom, Was	43		J. Wood, Bos	38		E. Walsh, ChA	32	
E. Plank, Phi	26		J. Lake, 2tm	18		H. Bedient, Bos	.690		J. Wood, Bos	43		W. Johnson, Was	37		R. Ford, NYA	30	
B. Groom, Was	24		5 tied with	17		J. Coombs, Phi	.677		4 tied with	41		R. Ford, NYA	35		B. Groom, Was	29	

Shutouts			Saves			Games Finished			Batters Faced			Innings Pitched			Hits Allowed		
J. Wood, Bos	10		E. Walsh, ChA	10		E. Walsh, ChA	18		Statistic unavailable			E. Walsh, ChA	393.0		E. Walsh, ChA	332	
W. Johnson, Was	7		5 tied with	3		J. Baskette, Cle	17					W. Johnson, Was	369.0		R. Ford, NYA	317	
E. Walsh, ChA	6					J. Warhop, NYA	15					J. Wood, Bos	344.0		B. Groom, Was	287	
E. Plank, Phi	5					J. Lake, 2tm	13					B. Groom, Was	316.0		E. Willett, Det	281	
R. Collins, Bos	4					W. Johnson, Was	13					R. Ford, NYA	291.2		J. Wood, Bos	267	

Home Runs Allowed			Walks			Walks/9 Innings			Strikeouts			Strikeouts/9 Innings			Strikeout/Walk Ratio		
R. Ford, NYA	10		G. Kahler, Cle	121		C. Bender, Phi	1.7		W. Johnson, Was	303		W. Johnson, Was	7.4		W. Johnson, Was	3.99	
L. Hughes, Bos	8		J. Dubuc, Det	109		W. Johnson, Was	1.9		J. Wood, Bos	258		J. Wood, Bos	6.8		J. Wood, Bos	3.15	
H. Bedient, Bos	6		C. Cashion, Was	103		R. Collins, Bos	1.9		E. Walsh, ChA	254		V. Gregg, Cle	6.1		C. Bender, Phi	2.73	
E. Walsh, ChA	6		3 tied with	94		J. Powell, StL	2.0		V. Gregg, Cle	184		E. Walsh, ChA	5.8		E. Walsh, ChA	2.70	
3 tied with	5					J. Warhop, NYA	2.1		B. Groom, Was	179		F. Lange, ChA	5.2		H. Bedient, Bos	2.22	

Earned Run Average			Component ERA			Hit Batsmen			Wild Pitches			Opponent Average			Opponent OBP		
W. Johnson, Was	1.39		W. Johnson, Was	1.52		E. Willett, Det	17		J. Dubuc, Det	16		W. Johnson, Was	.196		W. Johnson, Was	.248	
J. Wood, Bos	1.91		J. Wood, Bos	1.85		J. Warhop, NYA	16		C. Cashion, Was	11		J. Wood, Bos	.216		J. Wood, Bos	.272	
E. Walsh, ChA	2.15		E. Walsh, ChA	2.14		W. Johnson, Was	16		H. Vaughn, 2tm	11		E. Walsh, ChA	.231		E. Walsh, ChA	.279	
E. Plank, Phi	2.22		H. Bedient, Bos	2.44		3 tied with	12		W. Johnson, Was	11		B. Houck, Phi	.234		H. Bedient, Bos	.288	
R. Collins, Bos	2.53		B. O'Brien, Bos	2.54					2 tied with	10		J. Dubuc, Det	.235		R. Collins, Bos	.297	

1912 American League Miscellaneous

Managers

Boston	Jake Stahl	105-47
Chicago	Nixey Callahan	78-76
Cleveland	Harry Davis	54-71
	Joe Birmingham	21-7
Detroit	Hughie Jennings	69-84
New York	Harry Wolverton	50-102
Philadelphia	Connie Mack	90-62
St. Louis	Bobby Wallace	12-27
	George Stovall	41-74
Washington	Clark Griffith	91-61

Awards

Most Valuable Player	Tris Speaker, of, Bos
STATS Cy Young	Walter Johnson, Was
STATS Rookie of the Year	Del Pratt, 2b, StL
STATS Manager of the Year	Jake Stahl, Bos

STATS All-Star Team

C	Jack Lapp, Phi	.292	1	35
1B	Stuffy McInnis, Phi	.327	3	101
2B	Eddie Collins, Phi	.348	0	64
3B	Home Run Baker, Phi	.347	10	130
SS	Heinie Wagner, Bos	.274	2	68
OF	Ty Cobb, Det	.410	7	83
OF	Joe Jackson, Cle	.395	3	90
OF	Tris Speaker, Bos	.383	10	90
P	Walter Johnson, Was	33-12	1.39	303 K
P	Eddie Plank, Phi	26-6	2.22	110 K
P	Ed Walsh, ChA	27-17	2.15	254 K
P	Joe Wood, Bos	34-5	1.91	258 K

Postseason

World Series	Bos (AL) 4 vs. New York (NL) 3 (1 tie)

Outstanding Performances

No-Hitters

George Mullin, Det	vs. StL on July 4
Earl Hamilton, StL	@ Det on August 30

Cycles

Tris Speaker, Bos	on June 9
Bert Daniels, NYA	on July 25

1912 National League Standings

Team	W	L	Pct	GB	DIF	W	L	R	OR	HR	OHR	W	L	R	OR	HR	OHR	Run	HR	M/A	May	June	July	Aug	S/O
		Overall						**Home Games**						**Road Games**				**Park Index**				**Record by Month**			
New York	103	48	.682	—	151	**49**	**25**	387	302	**31**	21	54	23	436	269	16	**15**	102	175	8-3	20-4	22-4	17-13	15-12	21-12
Pittsburgh	93	58	.616	10.0	0	45	31	347	**275**	14	10	48	27	404	290	**25**	18	88	55	5-7	13-10	19-8	15-12	19-13	22-8
Chicago	91	59	.607	11.5	0	46	29	394	347	22	18	45	30	362	321	21	**15**	108	111	5-7	14-10	15-9	23-8	22-8	12-17
Cincinnati	75	78	.490	29.0	29	45	32	309	311	7	**2**	30	46	305	411	14	26	81	22	10-3	13-14	12-15	10-17	12-16	18-13
Philadelphia	73	79	.480	30.5	0	34	41	318	352	25	26	39	38	352	336	18	17	100	150	4-6	10-13	10-14	21-10	14-17	14-19
St. Louis	63	90	.412	41.0	6	37	40	354	414	14	9	26	50	305	416	13	22	105	65	5-8	15-14	7-20	14-13	12-14	10-21
Brooklyn	58	95	.379	46.0	0	33	43	303	368	17	20	25	52	348	386	15	25	93	94	4-7	8-15	12-14	11-23	9-17	14-19
Boston	52	101	.340	52.0	2	31	47	**407**	471	22	28	21	54	286	390	13	**15**	125	172	6-6	7-20	6-19	6-21	12-18	15-17

Clinch Date—New York 9/26.

Team Batting

Team	G	AB	R	OR	H	2B	3B	HR	TB	RBI	TBB	IBB	SO	HBP	SH	SF	SB	CS	SB%	GDP	Avg	OBP	Slg
New York	154	5067	**823**	571	1451	231	89	47	2001	702	514	—	497	69	152	—	319	—	—	—	.286	**.360**	.395
Chicago	152	5048	756	668	1398	**245**	90	43	1952	639	**560**	—	615	40	**182**	—	164	—	—	—	.277	.354	.387
Pittsburgh	152	5252	751	**565**	**1493**	222	**129**	39	**2090**	657	420	—	514	26	181	—	177	—	—	—	.284	.340	**.398**
Boston	155	**5361**	693	861	1465	227	68	35	1933	605	454	—	**690**	48	168	—	137	—	—	—	.273	.335	.361
Philadelphia	152	5077	670	688	1354	244	68	43	1863	570	464	—	615	34	179	—	159	—	—	—	.267	.332	.367
St. Louis	153	5092	659	830	1366	190	77	21	1791	545	508	—	620	47	166	—	193	—	—	—	.268	.340	.352
Cincinnati	155	5115	656	722	1310	183	89	21	1734	565	479	—	492	25	175	—	248	—	—	—	.256	.323	.339
Brooklyn	153	5141	651	754	1377	220	73	32	1839	561	490	—	584	40	159	—	179	—	—	—	.268	.336	.358
NL Total	1226	41153	5659	5659	11214	1762	683	287	15203	4860	3889	—	4627	329	1362	—	1576	—	—	—	.272	.340	.369
NL Avg Team	153	5144	707	707	1402	220	85	36	1900	608	486	—	578	41	170	—	197	—	—	—	.272	.340	.369

Team Pitching

Team	G	CG	ShO	Rel	Sv	IP	H	R	ER	HR	SH	SF	HB	TBB	IBB	SO	WP	Bk	H/9	SO/9	BB/9	OAvg	OOBP	ERA
New York	154	93	8	76	15	1369.2	1352	571	**393**	36	**136**	—	24	338	—	652	31	0	8.9	4.3	**2.2**	.259	**.307**	2.58
Pittsburgh	152	**94**	**18**	76	7	1385.0	**1268**	**565**	439	28	145	—	45	497	—	**664**	17	3	**8.2**	**4.3**	3.2	**.251**	.323	2.85
Philadelphia	152	81	10	99	9	1355.0	1381	688	489	43	146	—	39	515	—	616	36	2	9.2	4.1	3.4	.272	.344	3.25
Cincinnati	155	86	13	89	10	1377.2	1455	722	524	28	178	—	**61**	452	—	561	30	2	9.5	3.7	3.0	.279	.343	3.42
Chicago	152	80	15	105	9	1358.2	1307	668	517	33	176	—	47	493	—	554	34	2	8.7	3.7	3.3	.261	.332	3.42
Brooklyn	153	71	10	99	8	1357.0	1399	754	549	45	181	—	35	510	—	553	24	2	9.3	3.7	3.4	.273	.343	3.64
St. Louis	153	61	6	**134**	12	1353.0	1466	830	579	31	204	—	37	560	—	487	32	3	9.8	3.2	3.7	.287	.361	3.85
Boston	155	88	5	96	5	**1390.2**	1544	861	644	43	195	—	41	521	—	542	48	**5**	10.0	3.5	3.4	.291	.359	4.17
NL Total	1226	654	85	774	75	10946.2	11172	5659	4134	287	1361	—	329	3886	—	4629	252	19	9.2	3.8	3.2	.272	.339	3.40
NL Avg Team	153	82	11	97	9	1368.2	1397	707	517	36	170	—	41	486	—	579	32	2	9.2	3.8	3.2	.272	.339	3.40

Team Fielding

Team	G	PO	A	E	TC	DP	PB	Pct
Pittsburgh	152	**4144**	1832	**169**	6145	125	21	**.972**
Philadelphia	152	4059	1949	231	6239	98	25	.963
Chicago	152	4056	1990	249	6295	125	11	.960
Cincinnati	155	4112	1890	249	6251	102	6	.960
Brooklyn	153	4039	1941	255	6235	96	12	.959
St. Louis	153	4068	**2045**	274	6387	113	9	.957
New York	154	4098	1934	280	6312	123	18	.956
Boston	155	4134	1995	297	**6426**	**129**	21	.954
NL Total	1226	32710	15576	2004	50290	911	123	.960

Team vs. Team Records

	Bos	Bro	ChN	Cin	NYG	Phi	Pit	StL	Won
Bos	—	9	5	11	3	10	4	10	**52**
Bro	13	—	5	6	6	9	8	11	**58**
ChN	17	17	—	11	13	10	8	15	**91**
Cin	11	16	10	—	6	8	11	13	**75**
NYG	18	16	9	16	—	17	12	15	**103**
Phi	12	13	10	14	5	—	8	11	**73**
Pit	18	14	13	11	8	14	—	15	**93**
StL	12	10	7	9	7	11	7	—	**63**
Lost	101	95	59	78	48	79	58	90	

1912 National League Batting Leaders

Games		At-Bats		Runs		Hits		Doubles		Triples	
B. Sweeney, Bos	153	V. Campbell, Bos	624	B. Bescher, Cin	120	H. Zimmerman, ChN	207	H. Zimmerman, ChN	41	C. Wilson, Pit	36
C. Wilson, Pit	152	B. Sweeney, Bos	593	M. Carey, Pit	114	B. Sweeney, Bos	204	D. Paskert, Phi	37	R. Murray, NYG	20
M. Carey, Pit	150	M. Carey, Pit	587	V. Campbell, Bos	102	V. Campbell, Bos	185	H. Wagner, Pit	35	H. Wagner, Pit	20
D. Egan, Cin	149	C. Wilson, Pit	583	D. Paskert, Phi	102	L. Doyle, NYG	184	D. Miller, Pit	33	J. Daubert, Bro	16
3 tied with	148	F. Luderus, Phi	572	2 tied with	99	H. Wagner, Pit	181	L. Doyle, NYG	33	2 tied with	14

Home Runs		Total Bases		Runs Batted In		Walks		Intentional Walks		Strikeouts	
H. Zimmerman, ChN	14	H. Zimmerman, ChN	318	H. Wagner, Pit	102	J. Sheckard, ChN	122	Statistic unavailable		E. McDonald, Bos	91
W. Schulte, ChN	12	C. Wilson, Pit	299	B. Sweeney, Bos	100	D. Paskert, Phi	91			J. Sheckard, ChN	81
G. Cravath, Phi	11	H. Wagner, Pit	277	H. Zimmerman, ChN	99	M. Huggins, StL	87			M. Carey, Pit	79
C. Wilson, Pit	11	B. Sweeney, Bos	264	C. Wilson, Pit	95	B. Bescher, Cin	83			G. Cravath, Phi	77
F. Merkle, NYG	11	L. Doyle, NYG	263	R. Murray, NYG	92	J. Titus, 2tm	82			G. Jackson, Bos	72

Hit By Pitch		Sac Hits		Sac Flies		Stolen Bases		Caught Stealing		GDP	
S. Evans, StL	17	M. Carey, Pit	37	Statistic unavailable		B. Bescher, Cin	67	Statistic unavailable		Statistic unavailable	
A. Fletcher, NYG	14	J. Tinker, ChN	34			M. Carey, Pit	45				
G. Jackson, Bos	10	B. Sweeney, Bos	33			F. Snodgrass, NYG	43				
J. Titus, 2tm	10	D. Egan, Cin	29			R. Murray, NYG	38				
4 tied with	8	S. Magee, Phi	29			2 tied with	37				

Runs Created		Runs Created/27 Outs		Batting Average		On-Base Percentage		Slugging Percentage		OBP+Slugging	
H. Zimmerman, ChN	129	H. Zimmerman, ChN	8.96	H. Zimmerman, ChN	.372	C. Meyers, NYG	.441	H. Zimmerman, ChN	.571	H. Zimmerman, ChN	.989
B. Sweeney, Bos	114	C. Meyers, NYG	8.90	C. Meyers, NYG	.358	J. Evers, ChN	.431	C. Wilson, Pit	.513	C. Meyers, NYG	.918
L. Doyle, NYG	112	J. Evers, ChN	7.62	B. Sweeney, Bos	.344	M. Huggins, StL	.422	H. Wagner, Pit	.496	H. Wagner, Pit	.891
H. Wagner, Pit	111	L. Doyle, NYG	7.40	J. Evers, ChN	.341	D. Paskert, Phi	.420	C. Meyers, NYG	.477	J. Evers, ChN	.873
2 tied with	103	H. Wagner, Pit	7.32	L. Doyle, NYG	.330	H. Zimmerman, ChN	.418	L. Doyle, NYG	.471	L. Doyle, NYG	.864

1912 National League Pitching Leaders

Wins		Losses		Winning Percentage		Games		Games Started		Complete Games	
L. Cheney, ChN	26	L. Tyler, Bos	22	C. Hendrix, Pit	.727	R. Benton, Cin	50	R. Benton, Cin	39	L. Cheney, ChN	28
R. Marquard, NYG	26	R. Benton, Cin	21	L. Cheney, ChN	.722	S. Sallee, StL	48	R. Marquard, NYG	38	C. Mathewson, NYG	27
C. Hendrix, Pit	24	N. Rucker, Bro	21	J. Tesreau, NYG	.708	P. Alexander, Phi	46	L. Cheney, ChN	37	C. Hendrix, Pit	25
C. Mathewson, NYG	23	W. Dickson, Bos	19	R. Marquard, NYG	.703	N. Rucker, Bro	45	A. Fromme, Cin	37	P. Alexander, Phi	25
H. Camnitz, Pit	22	3 tied with	18	R. Ames, NYG	.688	T. Seaton, Phi	44	2 tied with	36	G. Suggs, Cin	25

Shutouts		Saves		Games Finished		Batters Faced		Innings Pitched		Hits Allowed	
N. Rucker, Bro	6	S. Sallee, StL	6	D. Crandall, NYG	25	R. Benton, Cin	1302	P. Alexander, Phi	310.1	G. Suggs, Cin	320
M. O'Toole, Pit	5	N. Rucker, Bro	4	R. Geyer, StL	18	P. Alexander, Phi	1290	C. Mathewson, NYG	310.0	R. Benton, Cin	316
G. Suggs, Cin	5	E. Reulbach, ChN	4	H. Robinson, Pit	15	L. Cheney, ChN	1267	L. Cheney, ChN	303.1	C. Mathewson, NYG	311
3 tied with	4	C. Mathewson, NYG	4	T. Seaton, Phi	14	C. Mathewson, NYG	1263	G. Suggs, Cin	303.0	H. Perdue, Bos	295
		5 tied with	3	E. Reulbach, ChN	14	G. Suggs, Cin	1256	R. Benton, Cin	302.0	2 tied with	289

Home Runs Allowed		Walks		Walks/9 Innings		Strikeouts		Strikeouts/9 Innings		Strikeout/Walk Ratio	
H. Perdue, Bos	11	M. O'Toole, Pit	159	C. Mathewson, NYG	1.0	P. Alexander, Phi	195	P. Alexander, Phi	5.7	C. Mathewson, NYG	3.94
P. Alexander, Phi	11	L. Tyler, Bos	126	H. Robinson, Pit	1.5	C. Hendrix, Pit	176	C. Hendrix, Pit	5.5	H. Robinson, Pit	2.63
E. Donnelly, Bos	10	R. Benton, Cin	118	G. Suggs, Cin	1.7	R. Marquard, NYG	175	R. Marquard, NYG	5.3	R. Marquard, NYG	2.19
E. Yingling, Bro	10	B. Harmon, StL	116	B. Adams, Pit	1.8	R. Benton, Cin	162	L. Tyler, Bos	5.1	N. Rucker, Bro	2.10
R. Marquard, NYG	9	L. Cheney, ChN	111	H. Perdue, Bos	2.0	N. Rucker, Bro	151	M. O'Toole, Pit	4.9	H. Perdue, Bos	1.87

Earned Run Average		Component ERA		Hit Batsmen		Wild Pitches		Opponent Average		Opponent OBP	
J. Tesreau, NYG	1.96	H. Robinson, Pit	2.12	R. Benton, Cin	18	L. Cheney, ChN	18	J. Tesreau, NYG	.204	C. Mathewson, NYG	.281
C. Mathewson, NYG	2.12	J. Tesreau, NYG	2.22	O. Hess, Bos	15	L. Tyler, Bos	13	L. Cheney, ChN	.234	H. Robinson, Pit	.284
N. Rucker, Bro	2.21	C. Mathewson, NYG	2.44	H. Camnitz, Pit	13	R. Benton, Cin	12	H. Robinson, Pit	.237	N. Rucker, Bro	.298
H. Robinson, Pit	2.26	N. Rucker, Bro	2.53	G. Suggs, Cin	11	E. Donnelly, Bos	10	B. Brown, Bos	.239	J. Tesreau, NYG	.298
E. Rixey, Phi	2.50	B. Brown, Bos	2.60	A. Fromme, Cin	11	2 tied with	9	M. O'Toole, Pit	.241	B. Adams, Pit	.303

1912 National League Miscellaneous

Managers

Boston	Johnny Kling	52-101
Brooklyn	Bill Dahlen	58-95
Chicago	Frank Chance	91-59
Cincinnati	Hank O'Day	75-78
New York	John McGraw	103-48
Philadelphia	Red Dooin	73-79
Pittsburgh	Fred Clarke	93-58
St. Louis	Roger Bresnahan	63-90

Awards

Most Valuable Player	Larry Doyle, 2b, NYG
STATS Cy Young	Rube Marquard, NYG
STATS Rookie of the Year	Larry Cheney, p, ChN
STATS Manager of the Year	John McGraw, NYG

STATS All-Star Team

C	Chief Meyers, NYG	.358	6	54
1B	Ed Konetchy, StL	.314	8	82
2B	Larry Doyle, NYG	.330	10	90
3B	Heinie Zimmerman, ChN	.372	14	99
SS	Honus Wagner, Pit	.324	7	102
OF	Dode Paskert, Phi	.315	2	43
OF	John Titus, 2tm	.309	5	70
OF	Chief Wilson, Pit	.300	11	95
P	Larry Cheney, ChN	26-10	2.85	140 K
P	Claude Hendrix, Pit	24-9	2.59	176 K
P	Rube Marquard, NYG	26-11	2.57	175 K
P	Christy Mathewson, NYG	23-12	2.12	134 K

Postseason

World Series	New York (NL) 3 vs. Bos (AL) 4 (1 tie)

Outstanding Performances

No-Hitters

Jeff Tesreau, NYG @ Phi on September 6

Cycles

Chief Meyers, NYG on June 10
Honus Wagner, Pit on August 22

1913 American League Standings

Team	Overall					Home Games						Road Games						Park Index		Record by Month					
	W	L	Pct	GB	DIF	W	L	R	OR	HR	OHR	W	L	R	OR	HR	OHR	Run	HR	M/A	May	June	July	Aug	S/O
Philadelphia	96	57	.627	—	173	50	26	388	271	19	14	46	31	406	321	14	10	92	139	9-3	19-7	20-7	19-12	14-12	15-16
Washington	90	64	.584	6.5	13	43	35	297	318	9	29	47	29	299	243	10	6	111	231	8-3	16-16	13-13	18-9	14-11	21-12
Cleveland	86	66	.566	9.5	1	45	35	336	284	4	9	41	35	297	252	12	10	113	59	10-5	19-7	12-17	19-9	15-11	11-17
Boston	79	71	.527	15.5	0	41	34	328	312	3	0	38	37	303	298	14	6	106	15	6-8	10-14	18-8	12-18	13-13	20-10
Chicago	78	74	.513	17.5	0	40	37	216	233	5	4	38	37	272	265	19	6	81	35	10-8	14-11	15-13	12-19	14-10	13-13
Detroit	66	87	.431	30.0	0	34	42	312	368	9	4	32	45	312	348	15	9	104	55	5-11	12-16	11-17	13-15	13-12	12-16
New York	57	94	.377	38.0	0	27	47	265	339	5	20	30	47	264	329	3	11	106	186	2-11	7-17	10-18	12-16	11-15	15-17
St. Louis	57	96	.373	39.0	3	31	46	247	309	13	11	26	50	281	333	5	10	89	158	8-9	10-19	11-17	11-18	8-18	9-15

Clinch Date—Philadelphia 9/22.

Team Batting

Team	G	AB	R	OR	H	2B	3B	HR	TB	RBI	TBB	IBB	SO	HBP	SH	SF	SB	CS	SB%	GDP	Avg	OBP	Slg
Philadelphia	153	5044	794	592	1412	223	80	33	1894	660	534	—	547	65	174	—	221	—	—	—	.280	.356	.375
Cleveland	155	5031	633	536	1349	206	74	16	1751	527	420	—	557	53	214	—	191	—	—	—	.268	.331	.348
Boston	151	4965	631	610	1334	220	101	17	1807	531	466	—	534	39	170	—	189	—	—	—	.269	.336	.364
Detroit	153	5064	624	716	1344	180	101	24	1798	519	496	—	501	46	161	—	218	—	—	—	.265	.336	.355
Washington	155	5074	596	561	1281	156	81	19	1656	484	440	—	595	42	106	—	287	—	—	—	.252	.326	.326
New York	153	4880	529	668	1157	155	45	8	1426	430	534	—	617	57	145	—	203	—	—	—	.237	.320	.292
St. Louis	155	5031	528	642	1193	179	73	18	1572	422	455	—	769	43	138	—	209	—	—	—	.237	.306	.312
Chicago	153	4822	488	498	1139	157	66	24	1500	410	398	—	550	36	192	—	156	—	—	—	.236	.299	.311
AL Total	1228	39911	4823	4823	10209	1476	621	159	13404	3983	3743	—	4670	381	1300	—	1674	—	—	—	.256	.325	.336
AL Avg Team	154	4989	603	603	1276	185	78	20	1676	498	468	—	584	48	163	—	209	—	—	—	.256	.325	.336

Team Pitching

Team	G	CG	ShO	Rel	Sv	IP	H	R	ER	HR	SH	SF	HB	TBB	IBB	SO	WP	Bk	H/9	SO/9	BB/9	OAvg	OOBP	ERA
Chicago	153	87	17	97	8	1360.1	1190	498	352	10	—	—	34	438	—	602	30	5	7.9	4.0	2.9	.239	.305	2.33
Cleveland	155	93	18	90	5	1386.2	1278	536	391	19	—	—	43	502	—	689	41	5	8.3	4.5	3.3	.248	.320	2.54
Washington	155	78	23	121	20	1396.1	1177	561	424	35	—	—	69	465	—	758	37	5	7.6	4.9	3.0	.226	.297	2.73
Boston	151	83	12	95	10	1358.1	1323	610	444	6	—	—	31	442	—	710	30	3	8.8	4.7	2.9	.262	.325	2.94
St. Louis	155	104	14	60	5	1382.1	1369	642	470	21	—	—	52	454	—	476	32	3	8.9	3.1	3.0	.266	.332	3.06
Philadelphia	153	69	17	124	22	1351.1	1200	592	479	24	—	—	39	532	—	630	48	3	8.0	4.2	3.5	.229	.304	3.19
New York	153	75	8	99	7	1344.0	1318	668	489	31	—	—	53	455	—	530	28	0	8.8	3.5	3.0	.255	.322	3.27
Detroit	153	90	4	87	7	1360.0	1359	716	511	13	—	—	49	504	—	468	46	0	9.0	3.1	3.3	.266	.338	3.38
AL Total	1228	679	113	773	84	10939.1	10214	4823	3560	159	—	—	370	3792	—	4863	292	24	8.4	4.0	3.1	.256	.326	2.93
AL Avg Team	154	85	14	97	11	1367.1	1277	603	445	20	—	—	46	474	—	608	37	3	8.4	4.0	3.1	.256	.326	2.93

Team Fielding

Team	G	PO	A	E	TC	DP	PB	Pct
Philadelphia	153	4048	1958	212	6218	108	13	.966
Cleveland	155	4143	1994	242	6379	124	13	.962
Boston	151	4051	1843	237	6131	84	23	.961
Chicago	153	4072	2078	255	6405	104	19	.960
Washington	155	4189	2085	261	6535	122	22	.960
Detroit	153	4076	2186	300	6562	105	18	.954
St. Louis	155	4131	2136	301	6568	125	22	.954
New York	153	4041	2052	293	6386	94	31	.954
AL Total	1228	32751	16332	2101	51184	866	161	.959

Team vs. Team Records

	Bos	ChA	Cle	Det	NYA	Phi	StL	Was	Won
Bos	—	10	8	13	14	11	17	6	79
ChA	11	—	9	13	11	11	12	11	78
Cle	13	13	—	14	14	9	16	7	86
Det	9	9	7	—	11	7	11	12	66
NYA	6	10	8	11	—	5	11	6	57
Phi	11	11	13	15	17	—	15	14	96
StL	5	10	6	11	11	6	—	8	57
Was	16	11	15	10	16	8	14	—	90
Lost	71	74	66	87	94	57	96	64	

1913 American League Batting Leaders

Games		At-Bats		Runs		Hits		Doubles		Triples	
D. Pratt, StL	155	S. Crawford, Det	610	E. Collins, Phi	125	J. Jackson, Cle	197	J. Jackson, Cle	39	S. Crawford, Det	23
C. Milan, Was	154	D. Bush, Det	597	H. Baker, Phi	116	S. Crawford, Det	193	T. Speaker, Bos	35	T. Speaker, Bos	22
D. Bush, Det	153	D. Pratt, StL	592	J. Jackson, Cle	109	H. Baker, Phi	190	H. Baker, Phi	34	J. Jackson, Cle	17
D. Moeller, Was	153	D. Moeller, Was	589	E. Murphy, Phi	105	T. Speaker, Bos	189	S. Crawford, Det	32	G. Williams, StL	16
S. Crawford, Det	153	H. Hooper, Bos	586	B. Shotton, StL	105	E. Collins, Phi	184	2 tied with	31	T. Cobb, Det	16

Home Runs		Total Bases		Runs Batted In		Walks		Intentional Walks		Strikeouts	
H. Baker, Phi	12	S. Crawford, Det	298	H. Baker, Phi	117	B. Shotton, StL	99	Statistic unavailable		D. Moeller, Was	103
S. Crawford, Det	9	J. Jackson, Cle	291	D. Lewis, Bos	90	E. Collins, Phi	85			G. Williams, StL	87
P. Bodie, ChA	8	H. Baker, Phi	278	S. McInnis, Phi	90	D. Bush, Det	80			D. Johnston, Cle	65
J. Jackson, Cle	7	T. Speaker, Bos	277	D. Pratt, StL	87	J. Jackson, Cle	80			R. Morgan, Was	63
3 tied with	5	E. Collins, Phi	242	J. Barry, Phi	85	H. Wolter, NYA	80			B. Shotton, StL	63

Hit By Pitch		Sac Hits		Sac Flies		Stolen Bases		Caught Stealing		GDP	
B. Daniels, NYA	18	R. Chapman, Cle	48	Statistic unavailable		C. Milan, Was	75	Statistic unavailable		Statistic unavailable	
N. Lajoie, Cle	15	T. Turner, Cle	33			D. Moeller, Was	62				
E. Murphy, Phi	10	S. Collins, ChA	28			E. Collins, Phi	55				
H. Baker, Phi	10	D. Lewis, Bos	28			T. Cobb, Det	52				
W. Schang, Phi	9	J. Barry, Phi	28			T. Speaker, Bos	46				

Runs Created		Runs Created/27 Outs		Batting Average		On-Base Percentage		Slugging Percentage		OBP+Slugging	
J. Jackson, Cle	132	J. Jackson, Cle	9.77	T. Cobb, Det	.390	T. Cobb, Det	.467	J. Jackson, Cle	.551	J. Jackson, Cle	1.011
H. Baker, Phi	125	T. Cobb, Det	9.19	J. Jackson, Cle	.373	J. Jackson, Cle	.460	T. Cobb, Det	.535	T. Cobb, Det	1.002
E. Collins, Phi	123	T. Speaker, Bos	8.44	T. Speaker, Bos	.363	E. Collins, Phi	.441	T. Speaker, Bos	.533	T. Speaker, Bos	.974
T. Speaker, Bos	116	H. Baker, Phi	8.26	E. Collins, Phi	.345	T. Speaker, Bos	.441	H. Baker, Phi	.492	H. Baker, Phi	.904
S. Crawford, Det	104	E. Collins, Phi	8.26	H. Baker, Phi	.336	H. Baker, Phi	.412	S. Crawford, Det	.489	E. Collins, Phi	.894

1913 American League Pitching Leaders

Wins		Losses		Winning Percentage		Games		Games Started		Complete Games	
W. Johnson, Was	36	C. Weilman, StL	20	W. Johnson, Was	.837	R. Russell, ChA	51	J. Scott, ChA	38	W. Johnson, Was	29
C. Falkenberg, Cle	23	J. Scott, ChA	20	J. Bush, Phi	.714	J. Scott, ChA	48	R. Russell, ChA	36	J. Scott, ChA	27
R. Russell, ChA	22	G. Baumgardner, StL	19	J. Boehling, Was	.708	W. Johnson, Was	48	B. Groom, Was	36	R. Russell, ChA	26
C. Bender, Phi	21	R. Ford, NYA	18	R. Collins, Bos	.704	C. Bender, Phi	48	W. Johnson, Was	36	V. Gregg, Cle	23
2 tied with	20	W. Leverenz, StL	17	B. Houck, Phi	.700	V. Gregg, Cle	44	C. Falkenberg, Cle	36	C. Falkenberg, Cle	23

Shutouts		Saves		Games Finished		Batters Faced		Innings Pitched		Hits Allowed	
W. Johnson, Was	11	C. Bender, Phi	13	S. Hall, Bos	22	Statistic unavailable		W. Johnson, Was	346.0	G. Baumgardner, StL	267
R. Russell, ChA	8	L. Hughes, Was	7	C. Bender, Phi	21			R. Russell, ChA	316.1	R. Mitchell, StL	265
E. Plank, Phi	7	H. Bedient, Bos	5	J. Bush, Phi	20			J. Scott, ChA	312.1	C. Weilman, StL	262
C. Falkenberg, Cle	6	3 tied with	4	L. Hughes, Was	18			V. Gregg, Cle	285.1	V. Gregg, Cle	258
4 tied with	4			2 tied with	16			C. Falkenberg, Cle	275.2	B. Groom, Was	258

Home Runs Allowed		Walks		Walks/9 Innings		Strikeouts		Strikeouts/9 Innings		Strikeout/Walk Ratio	
R. Ford, NYA	9	V. Gregg, Cle	124	W. Johnson, Was	1.0	W. Johnson, Was	243	J. Wood, Bos	7.6	W. Johnson, Was	6.39
W. Johnson, Was	9	B. Houck, Phi	122	R. Collins, Bos	1.4	V. Gregg, Cle	166	W. Johnson, Was	6.3	E. Plank, Phi	2.65
B. Groom, Was	8	D. Leonard, Bos	94	R. Mitchell, StL	1.7	C. Falkenberg, Cle	166	W. Mitchell, Cle	5.8	R. Collins, Bos	2.38
5 tied with	6	J. Dubuc, Det	91	E. Plank, Phi	2.1	J. Scott, ChA	158	E. Plank, Phi	5.6	C. Bender, Phi	2.29
		2 tied with	89	C. Weilman, StL	2.1	B. Groom, Was	156	C. Falkenberg, Cle	5.4	J. Wood, Bos	2.02

Earned Run Average		Component ERA		Hit Batsmen		Wild Pitches		Opponent Average		Opponent OBP	
W. Johnson, Was	1.14	W. Johnson, Was	1.27	V. Gregg, Cle	14	C. Falkenberg, Cle	13	W. Johnson, Was	.187	W. Johnson, Was	.217
E. Cicotte, ChA	1.58	R. Russell, ChA	1.92	L. Hughes, Was	14	C. Weilman, StL	11	W. Mitchell, Cle	.201	R. Russell, ChA	.274
W. Mitchell, Cle	1.87	W. Mitchell, Cle	2.02	H. Dauss, Det	13	B. Houck, Phi	11	R. Russell, ChA	.218	C. Bender, Phi	.277
J. Scott, ChA	1.90	J. Scott, ChA	2.09	J. Warhop, NYA	12	J. Dubuc, Det	11	B. Brown, Phi	.219	E. Cicotte, ChA	.283
R. Russell, ChA	1.91	E. Cicotte, ChA	2.17	E. Willett, Det	12	2 tied with	10	R. Caldwell, NYA	.222	E. Plank, Phi	.284

1913 American League Miscellaneous

Managers

Boston	Jake Stahl	39-41
	Bill Carrigan	40-30
Chicago	Nixey Callahan	78-74
Cleveland	Joe Birmingham	86-66
Detroit	Hughie Jennings	66-87
New York	Frank Chance	57-94
Philadelphia	Connie Mack	96-57
St. Louis	George Stovall	50-84
	Jimmy Austin	2-6
	Branch Rickey	5-6
Washington	Clark Griffith	90-64

Awards

Most Valuable Player	Walter Johnson, p, Was
STATS Cy Young	Walter Johnson, Was
STATS Rookie of the Year	Reb Russell, p, ChA
STATS Manager of the Year	Joe Birmingham, Cle

STATS All-Star Team

C	Jeff Sweeney, NYA	.265	2	40
1B	Stuffy McInnis, Phi	.326	4	90
2B	Eddie Collins, Phi	.345	3	73
3B	Home Run Baker, Phi	.336	12	117
SS	Jack Barry, Phi	.275	3	85
OF	Ty Cobb, Det	.390	4	67
OF	Joe Jackson, Cle	.373	7	71
OF	Tris Speaker, Bos	.363	3	71
P	Chief Bender, Phi	21-10	2.20	135 K
P	Cy Falkenberg, Cle	23-10	2.22	166 K
P	Walter Johnson, Was	36-7	1.14	243 K
P	Reb Russell, ChA	22-16	1.91	122 K

Postseason

World Series	Phil (AL) 4 vs. New York (NL) 1

Outstanding Performances

None

1913 National League Standings

Team	Overall					Home Games						Road Games						Park Index		Record by Month					
	W	L	Pct	GB	DIF	W	L	R	OR	HR	OHR	W	L	R	OR	HR	OHR	Run	HR	M/A	May	June	July	Aug	S/O
New York	101	51	.664	—	102	54	23	367	250	22	22	47	28	317	265	8	16	103	179	8-4	12-12	20-7	25-6	18-9	18-13
Philadelphia	88	63	.583	12.5	63	43	33	361	366	51	23	45	30	332	270	22	17	119	187	5-4	17-7	16-11	16-13	15-11	19-17
Chicago	88	65	.575	13.5	6	51	25	372	278	37	19	37	40	348	352	22	20	94	135	12-4	8-16	14-12	16-13	16-10	22-10
Pittsburgh	78	71	.523	21.5	1	41	35	324	277	13	6	37	36	349	308	22	20	88	43	8-7	11-13	11-15	17-11	18-11	13-14
Boston	69	82	.457	31.5	7	34	40	298	337	14	12	35	42	343	353	18	25	95	63	3-9	11-11	12-17	14-15	12-14	17-16
Brooklyn	65	84	.436	34.5	1	29	47	296	343	20	14	36	37	299	270	19	19	108	86	7-6	14-9	13-12	8-20	10-19	13-18
Cincinnati	64	89	.418	37.5	0	32	44	307	380	15	13	32	45	300	337	12	27	109	73	2-12	13-14	10-15	13-19	14-16	12-13
St. Louis	51	99	.340	49.0	5	25	48	239	346	8	20	26	51	289	409	7	37	88	67	8-7	11-15	9-16	9-21	8-21	6-19

Clinch Date—New York 9/27.

Team Batting

Team	G	AB	R	OR	H	2B	3B	HR	TB	RBI	TBB	IBB	SO	HBP	SH	SF	SB	CS	SB%	GDP	Avg	OBP	Slg
Chicago	155	5022	720	630	1289	195	96	59	1853	617	554	—	634	41	158	—	181	—	—	—	.257	.335	.369
Philadelphia	159	5400	693	636	1433	257	78	73	2065	597	383	—	578	35	183	—	156	—	—	—	.265	.318	.382
New York	156	5218	684	515	1427	226	71	30	1885	580	444	—	501	63	112	—	296	—	—	—	.273	.338	.361
Pittsburgh	155	5252	673	585	1383	210	86	35	1870	570	391	—	545	35	152	—	181	—	—	—	.263	.319	.356
Boston	154	5145	641	690	1318	191	60	32	1725	533	488	—	640	43	169	—	177	—	—	—	.256	.326	.335
Cincinnati	156	5132	607	717	1339	170	96	27	1782	541	458	—	579	29	162	—	226	—	—	—	.261	.325	.347
Brooklyn	152	5165	595	613	1394	193	86	39	1876	502	361	—	555	31	147	—	188	—	—	—	.270	.321	.363
St. Louis	153	4967	528	755	1229	152	72	15	1570	427	451	—	573	44	156	—	171	—	—	—	.247	.316	.316
NL Total	1240	41301	5141	5141	10812	1594	645	310	14626	4367	3530	—	4605	321	1239	—	1576	—	—	—	.262	.325	.354
NL Avg Team	155	5163	643	643	1352	199	81	39	1828	546	441	—	576	40	155	—	197	—	—	—	.262	.325	.354

Team Pitching

Team	G	CG	ShO	Rel	Sv	IP	H	R	ER	HR	SH	SF	HB	TBB	IBB	SO	WP	Bk	H/9	SO/9	BB/9	OAvg	OOBP	ERA
New York	156	82	12	94	17	1422.0	1276	515	383	38	119	—	21	315	—	651	21	2	8.1	4.1	2.0	.243	.289	2.42
Pittsburgh	155	74	9	109	7	1400.0	1344	585	451	26	157	—	29	434	—	590	28	1	8.6	3.8	2.8	.260	.320	2.90
Brooklyn	152	71	9	104	7	1373.0	1287	613	477	33	151	—	49	439	—	548	24	3	8.4	3.6	2.9	.255	.321	3.13
Chicago	155	89	12	90	15	1372.1	1330	630	478	39	141	—	40	478	—	556	43	1	8.7	3.6	3.1	.260	.328	3.13
Philadelphia	159	77	20	131	11	1455.1	1407	636	510	40	144	—	43	512	—	667	29	2	8.7	4.1	3.2	.261	.330	3.15
Boston	154	105	13	64	3	1373.1	1343	690	487	37	168	—	40	419	—	597	32	6	8.8	3.9	2.7	.263	.324	3.19
Cincinnati	156	71	10	113	10	1380.0	1398	717	530	40	185	—	47	456	—	522	36	7	9.1	3.4	3.0	.273	.338	3.46
St. Louis	153	74	6	114	11	1351.2	1426	755	636	57	172	—	51	477	—	465	24	5	9.5	3.1	3.2	.280	.347	4.23
NL Total	1240	643	91	819	81	11127.2	10811	5141	3952	310	1237	—	320	3530	—	4596	237	27	8.7	3.7	2.9	.262	.325	3.20
NL Avg Team	155	80	11	102	10	1390.2	1351	643	494	39	155	—	40	441	—	575	30	3	8.7	3.7	2.9	.262	.325	3.20

Team Fielding

Team	G	PO	A	E	TC	DP	PB	Pct
Philadelphia	159	4360	2081	214	6655	112	13	.968
St. Louis	153	4058	2057	219	6334	113	15	.965
Pittsburgh	155	4196	1851	226	6273	94	14	.964
Brooklyn	152	4105	1896	243	6244	125	13	.961
Cincinnati	156	4116	2055	251	6422	104	14	.961
New York	156	4252	1936	254	6442	107	14	.961
Chicago	155	4115	2003	260	6378	106	15	.959
Boston	154	4110	2002	273	6385	82	11	.957
NL Total	1240	33312	15881	1940	51133	843	109	.962

Team vs. Team Records

	Bos	Bro	ChN	Cin	NYG	Phi	Pit	StL	Won
Bos	—	10	9	8	8	7	11	16	69
Bro	10	—	9	9	8	8	8	13	65
ChN	13	13	—	13	7	13	13	16	88
Cin	14	13	9	—	5	5	8	10	64
NYG	14	14	14	17	—	14	14	14	101
Phi	15	13	9	17	8	—	9	17	88
Pit	10	14	9	13	8	11	—	13	78
StL	6	7	6	12	7	5	8	—	51
Lost	82	84	65	89	51	63	71	99	

1913 National League Batting Leaders

Games		At-Bats		Runs		Hits		Doubles		Triples	
F. Luderus, Phi	155	M. Carey, Pit	620	M. Carey, Pit	99	G. Cravath, Phi	179	R. Smith, Bro	40	V. Saier, ChN	21
C. Wilson, Pit	155	G. Burns, NYG	605	T. Leach, ChN	99	J. Daubert, Bro	178	G. Burns, NYG	37	D. Miller, Pit	20
M. Carey, Pit	154	G. Cutshaw, Bro	592	H. Lobert, Phi	98	G. Burns, NYG	173	S. Magee, Phi	36	E. Konetchy, StL	17
D. Miller, Pit	154	F. Luderus, Phi	588	V. Saier, ChN	94	M. Carey, Pit	172	G. Cravath, Phi	34	G. Cravath, Phi	14
F. Merkle, NYG	153	2 tied with	580	S. Magee, Phi	92	H. Lobert, Phi	172	2 tied with	32	C. Wilson, Pit	14

Home Runs		Total Bases		Runs Batted In		Walks		Intentional Walks		Strikeouts	
G. Cravath, Phi	19	G. Cravath, Phi	298	G. Cravath, Phi	128	B. Bescher, Cin	94	Statistic unavailable		G. Burns, NYG	74
F. Luderus, Phi	18	F. Luderus, Phi	254	H. Zimmerman, ChN	95	M. Huggins, StL	92			L. Mann, Bos	73
V. Saier, ChN	14	V. Saier, ChN	249	V. Saier, ChN	92	T. Leach, ChN	77			D. Paskert, Phi	69
S. Magee, Phi	11	D. Miller, Pit	243	D. Miller, Pit	90	A. Bridwell, ChN	74			3 tied with	68
C. Wilson, Pit	10	H. Lobert, Phi	243	F. Luderus, Phi	86	2 tied with	68				

Hit By Pitch		Sac Hits		Sac Flies		Stolen Bases		Caught Stealing		GDP	
A. Fletcher, NYG	15	O. Knabe, Phi	41	Statistic unavailable		M. Carey, Pit	61	Statistic unavailable		Statistic unavailable	
H. Myers, Bos	9	H. Myers, Bos	26			H. Myers, Bos	57				
C. Meyers, NYG	9	R. Oakes, StL	26			H. Lobert, Phi	41				
S. Magee, Phi	9	H. Lobert, Phi	26			G. Burns, NYG	40				
7 tied with	7	D. Miller, Pit	25			G. Cutshaw, Bro	39				

Runs Created		Runs Created/27 Outs		Batting Average		On-Base Percentage		Slugging Percentage		OBP+Slugging	
G. Cravath, Phi	117	G. Cravath, Phi	8.40	J. Daubert, Bro	.350	M. Huggins, StL	.432	G. Cravath, Phi	.568	G. Cravath, Phi	.974
V. Saier, ChN	101	H. Zimmerman, ChN	7.14	G. Cravath, Phi	.341	G. Cravath, Phi	.407	B. Becker, 2tm	.502	H. Zimmerman, ChN	.868
J. Viox, Pit	95	J. Viox, Pit	6.86	J. Viox, Pit	.317	J. Daubert, Bro	.405	H. Zimmerman, ChN	.490	B. Becker, 2tm	.862
H. Zimmerman, ChN	90	V. Saier, ChN	6.76	J. Tinker, Cin	.317	J. Viox, Pit	.399	V. Saier, ChN	.480	V. Saier, ChN	.850
H. Lobert, Phi	89	T. Leach, ChN	6.74	B. Becker, 2tm	.316	T. Leach, ChN	.391	S. Magee, Phi	.479	S. Magee, Phi	.848

1913 National League Pitching Leaders

Wins		Losses		Winning Percentage		Games		Games Started		Complete Games	
T. Seaton, Phi	27	D. Griner, StL	22	B. Humphries, ChN	.800	L. Cheney, ChN	54	J. Tesreau, NYG	38	L. Tyler, Bos	28
C. Mathewson, NYG	25	B. Harmon, StL	21	A. Demaree, NYG	.765	T. Seaton, Phi	52	B. Adams, Pit	37	L. Cheney, ChN	25
R. Marquard, NYG	23	H. Camnitz, 2tm	20	P. Alexander, Phi	.733	S. Sallee, StL	50	L. Cheney, ChN	36	C. Mathewson, NYG	25
J. Tesreau, NYG	22	F. Allen, Bro	18	G. Pearce, ChN	.722	P. Alexander, Phi	47	P. Alexander, Phi	36	B. Adams, Pit	24
P. Alexander, Phi	22	P. Ragan, Bro	18	R. Marquard, NYG	.697	H. Camnitz, 2tm	45	2 tied with	35	P. Alexander, Phi	23

Shutouts		Saves		Games Finished		Batters Faced		Innings Pitched		Hits Allowed	
P. Alexander, Phi	9	L. Cheney, ChN	11	D. Crandall, NYG	27	T. Seaton, Phi	1324	T. Seaton, Phi	322.1	B. Harmon, StL	291
T. Seaton, Phi	6	D. Crandall, NYG	6	T. F. Brown, Cin	21	L. Cheney, ChN	1255	B. Adams, Pit	313.2	C. Mathewson, NYG	291
5 tied with	4	T. F. Brown, Cin	6	R. Geyer, StL	20	P. Alexander, Phi	1234	P. Alexander, Phi	306.1	P. Alexander, Phi	288
		S. Sallee, StL	5	L. Cheney, ChN	18	B. Adams, Pit	1227	C. Mathewson, NYG	306.0	P. Ragan, Bro	284
		6 tied with	3	2 tied with	16	C. Mathewson, NYG	1195	L. Cheney, ChN	305.0	D. Griner, StL	279

Home Runs Allowed		Walks		Walks/9 Innings		Strikeouts		Strikeouts/9 Innings		Strikeout/Walk Ratio	
D. Griner, StL	12	T. Seaton, Phi	136	C. Mathewson, NYG	0.6	T. Seaton, Phi	168	J. Tesreau, NYG	5.3	C. Mathewson, NYG	4.43
O. Hess, Bos	12	J. Tesreau, NYG	119	B. Humphries, ChN	1.2	J. Tesreau, NYG	167	C. Hendrix, Pit	5.2	R. Marquard, NYG	3.08
S. Sallee, StL	11	L. Tyler, Bos	108	B. Adams, Pit	1.4	P. Alexander, Phi	159	B. James, Bos	4.8	B. Adams, Pit	2.94
3 tied with	10	H. Camnitz, 2tm	107	R. Marquard, NYG	1.5	R. Marquard, NYG	151	R. Marquard, NYG	4.7	B. Humphries, ChN	2.54
		B. Harmon, StL	99	H. Perdue, Bos	1.7	B. Adams, Pit	144	T. Seaton, Phi	4.7	H. Perdue, Bos	2.33

Earned Run Average		Component ERA		Hit Batsmen		Wild Pitches		Opponent Average		Opponent OBP	
C. Mathewson, NYG	2.06	B. Adams, Pit	2.03	J. Lavender, ChN	13	L. Cheney, ChN	19	J. Tesreau, NYG	.220	C. Mathewson, NYG	.266
B. Adams, Pit	2.15	C. Mathewson, NYG	2.16	L. Tyler, Bos	11	L. Tyler, Bos	12	T. Seaton, Phi	.226	B. Adams, Pit	.267
J. Tesreau, NYG	2.17	R. Marquard, NYG	2.17	4 tied with	10	R. Ames, 2tm	12	F. Allen, Bro	.231	R. Marquard, NYG	.273
A. Demaree, NYG	2.21	A. Demaree, NYG	2.29			T. Seaton, Phi	9	G. Pearce, ChN	.234	B. Humphries, ChN	.277
G. Pearce, ChN	2.31	B. Humphries, ChN	2.51			B. James, Bos	8	L. Tyler, Bos	.235	A. Demaree, NYG	.286

1913 National League Miscellaneous

Managers		
Boston	George Stallings	69-82
Brooklyn	Bill Dahlen	65-84
Chicago	Johnny Evers	88-65
Cincinnati	Joe Tinker	64-89
New York	John McGraw	101-51
Philadelphia	Red Dooin	88-63
Pittsburgh	Fred Clarke	78-71
St. Louis	Miller Huggins	51-99

Awards	
Most Valuable Player	Jake Daubert, 1b, Bro
STATS Cy Young	C. Mathewson, NYG
STATS Rookie of the Year	Jim Viox, 2b, Pit
STATS Manager of the Year	Red Dooin, Phi

STATS All-Star Team

C	Chief Meyers, NYG	.312	3	47
1B	Jake Daubert, Bro	.350	2	52
2B	Jim Viox, Pit	.317	2	65
3B	Heinie Zimmerman, ChN	.313	9	95
SS	Joe Tinker, Cin	.317	1	57
OF	Gavy Cravath, Phi	.341	19	128
OF	Tommy Leach, ChN	.287	6	32
OF	Sherry Magee, Phi	.306	11	70
P	Rube Marquard, NYG	23-10	2.50	151 K
P	Christy Mathewson, NYG	25-11	2.06	93 K
P	Tom Seaton, Phi	27-12	2.60	168 K
P	Jeff Tesreau, NYG	22-13	2.17	167 K

Postseason	
World Series	New York (NL) 1 vs. Phi (AL) 4

Outstanding Performances

None

1914 American League Standings

Team	Overall					Home Games						Road Games						Park Index		Record by Month					
	W	L	Pct	GB	DIF	W	L	R	OR	HR	OHR	W	L	R	OR	HR	OHR	Run	HR	M/A	May	June	July	Aug	S/O
Philadelphia	99	53	.651	—	130	51	24	354	247	17	13	48	29	395	282	12	5	91	181	5-5	16-8	18-13	20-7	23-5	17-15
Boston	91	62	.595	8.5	0	44	31	270	247	2	5	47	31	319	264	16	13	92	25	4-6	13-13	18-13	19-9	13-8	24-13
Washington	81	73	.526	19.0	6	40	33	282	246	9	7	41	40	290	273	9	13	104	81	6-5	17-10	12-15	16-12	10-14	20-17
Detroit	80	73	.523	19.5	33	42	35	315	318	11	9	38	38	300	300	14	8	104	90	10-4	13-13	16-14	10-16	12-14	19-12
St. Louis	71	82	.464	28.5	0	42	36	271	298	11	14	29	46	252	316	6	6	96	200	6-6	12-13	19-13	8-16	10-16	16-18
Chicago	70	84	.455	30.0	14	43	37	271	285	7	4	27	47	216	275	12	11	105	44	7-7	11-15	16-11	13-15	12-15	11-21
New York	70	84	.455	30.0	4	36	40	278	259	8	24	34	44	259	291	4	6	100	328	5-4	11-15	6-20	20-13	14-13	14-19
Cleveland	51	102	.333	48.5	0	32	47	289	380	4	3	19	55	249	329	6	7	108	50	3-9	10-16	11-17	6-24	9-18	12-18

Clinch Date—Philadelphia 9/27.

Team Batting

Team	G	AB	R	OR	H	2B	3B	HR	TB	RBI	TBB	IBB	SO	HBP	SH	SF	SB	CS	SB%	GDP	Avg	OBP	Slg
Philadelphia	158	5126	749	529	1392	165	80	29	1804	627	545	—	517	52	218	—	231	188	.55	—	.272	.348	.352
Detroit	157	5102	615	618	1318	195	84	25	1756	513	557	—	537	44	208	—	211	154	.58	—	.258	.336	.344
Boston	159	5117	589	510	1278	226	85	18	1728	513	490	—	549	39	173	—	177	176	.50	—	.250	.320	.338
Washington	158	5108	572	519	1245	176	81	18	1637	470	470	—	640	46	178	—	220	163	.57	—	.244	.313	.320
Cleveland	157	5157	538	709	1262	178	70	10	1610	438	450	—	685	39	155	—	167	157	.52	—	.245	.310	.312
New York	157	4992	537	550	1144	149	52	12	1433	416	577	—	711	47	145	—	251	191	.57	—	.229	.315	.287
St. Louis	159	5101	523	615	1241	185	75	17	1627	430	423	—	863	35	146	—	233	189	.55	—	.243	.306	.319
Chicago	157	5040	487	560	1205	161	71	19	1565	390	408	—	609	46	206	—	167	152	.52	—	.239	.302	.311
AL Total	1262	40743	4610	4610	10085	1435	598	148	13160	3797	3920	—	5111	348	1429	—	1657	1370	.55	—	.248	.319	.323
AL Avg Team	158	5093	576	576	1261	179	75	19	1645	475	490	—	639	44	179	—	207	171	.55	—	.248	.319	.323

Team Pitching

Team	G	CG	ShO	Rel	Sv	IP	H	R	ER	HR	SH	SF	HB	TBB	IBB	SO	WP	Bk	H/9	SO/9	BB/9	OAvg	OOBP	ERA
Boston	159	88	24	92	8	1427.1	1207	510	375	18	—	—	32	393	—	602	21	1	7.6	3.8	2.5	.236	.295	2.36
Chicago	157	74	17	125	11	1398.2	1207	560	385	15	—	—	29	401	—	660	31	0	7.8	4.2	2.6	.239	.298	2.48
Washington	158	75	25	120	20	1420.2	1170	519	401	20	—	—	51	520	—	784	46	6	7.4	5.0	3.3	.233	.311	2.54
Philadelphia	158	89	24	95	17	1404.0	1264	529	433	18	—	—	28	390	—	720	37	1	8.1	4.6	3.3	.249	.322	2.78
New York	157	98	9	83	5	1397.1	1277	550	437	30	—	—	32	390	—	563	37	1	8.2	3.6	2.5	.250	.308	2.81
St. Louis	159	81	15	113	11	1410.2	1309	615	446	20	—	—	49	540	—	553	42	2	8.4	3.5	3.4	.251	.327	2.85
Detroit	157	81	14	117	12	1412.0	1285	618	448	17	—	—	65	498	—	567	31	5	8.2	3.6	3.2	.249	.322	2.86
Cleveland	157	69	9	129	3	1391.2	1365	709	497	10	—	—	44	666	—	688	46	3	8.8	4.4	4.3	.268	.357	3.21
AL Total	1262	655	137	874	87	11262.1	10084	4610	3422	148	—	—	330	3929	—	5137	291	19	8.1	4.1	3.1	.248	.319	2.73
AL Avg Team	158	82	17	109	11	1407.1	1261	576	428	19	—	—	41	491	—	642	36	2	8.1	4.1	3.1	.248	.319	2.73

Team Fielding

Team	G	PO	A	E	TC	DP	PB	Pct
Philadelphia	158	4198	1938	213	6349	116	25	.966
New York	157	4184	2065	238	6487	93	15	.963
Boston	159	4273	1947	242	6462	99	19	.963
Washington	158	4251	1956	254	6461	116	22	.961
Detroit	157	4220	2274	286	6780	101	23	.958
Chicago	157	4185	2226	299	6710	90	16	.955
Cleveland	157	4136	2000	300	6436	119	30	.953
St. Louis	159	4242	2037	317	6596	114	30	.952
AL Total	1262	33689	16443	2149	52281	848	180	.959

Team vs. Team Records

	Bos	ChA	Cle	Det	NYA	Phi	StL	Was	Won
Bos	—	13	16	15	11	12	13	11	91
ChA	9	—	13	6	12	5	13	12	70
Cle	6	9	—	6	8	3	8	11	51
Det	7	16	16	—	13	9	9	10	80
NYA	11	10	14	9	—	8	11	7	70
Phi	9	17	19	12	14	—	15	13	99
StL	9	9	13	13	11	7	—	9	71
Was	11	10	11	12	15	9	13	—	81
Lost	62	84	102	73	84	53	82	73	

1914 American League Batting Leaders

Games		At-Bats		Runs		Hits		Doubles		Triples	
D. Pratt, StL	158	E. Foster, Was	616	E. Collins, Phi	122	T. Speaker, Bos	193	T. Speaker, Bos	46	S. Crawford, Det	26
T. Speaker, Bos	158	S. Collins, ChA	598	E. Murphy, Phi	101	S. Crawford, Det	183	D. Lewis, Bos	37	L. Gardner, Det	19
4 tied with	157	D. Bush, Det	596	T. Speaker, Bos	101	H. Baker, Phi	182	D. Pratt, StL	34	T. Speaker, Bos	18
		D. Pratt, StL	584	D. Bush, Det	97	S. McInnis, Phi	181	S. Collins, ChA	34	T. Walker, StL	16
		S. Crawford, Det	582	2 tied with	85	E. Collins, Phi	181	J. Leary, StL	28	H. Hooper, Bos	15

Home Runs		Total Bases		Runs Batted In		Walks		Intentional Walks	Strikeouts	
H. Baker, Phi	9	T. Speaker, Bos	287	S. Crawford, Det	104	D. Bush, Det	112	Statistic unavailable	G. Williams, StL	120
S. Crawford, Det	8	S. Crawford, Det	281	S. McInnis, Phi	95	E. Collins, Phi	97		D. Moeller, Was	89
J. Fournier, ChA	6	H. Baker, Phi	252	T. Speaker, Bos	90	E. Murphy, Phi	87		R. Peckinpaugh, NYA	73
T. Walker, StL	6	D. Pratt, StL	240	H. Baker, Phi	89	T. Speaker, Bos	77		T. Walker, StL	72
2 tied with	5	E. Collins, Phi	238	E. Collins, Phi	85	F. Maisel, NYA	76		J. Leary, StL	71

Hit By Pitch		Sac Hits		Sac Flies	Stolen Bases		Caught Stealing		GDP
G. Burns, Det	12	C. Gandil, Was	38	Statistic unavailable	F. Maisel, NYA	74	D. Cook, NYA	32	Statistic unavailable
E. Murphy, Phi	12	T. Turner, Cle	38		E. Collins, Phi	58	E. Murphy, Phi	32	
R. Morgan, Was	10	P. Bodie, ChA	34		T. Speaker, Bos	42	D. Lewis, Bos	31	
D. Cook, NYA	9	L. Blackburne, ChA	31		B. Shotton, StL	40	E. Collins, Phi	30	
W. Schang, Phi	9	J. Barry, Phi	31		2 tied with	38	2 tied with	29	

Runs Created		Runs Created/27 Outs		Batting Average		On-Base Percentage		Slugging Percentage		OBP+Slugging	
E. Collins, Phi	128	T. Cobb, Det	8.82	T. Cobb, Det	.368	T. Cobb, Det	.466	T. Cobb, Det	.513	T. Cobb, Det	.979
T. Speaker, Bos	123	E. Collins, Phi	8.43	E. Collins, Phi	.344	E. Collins, Phi	.452	T. Speaker, Bos	.503	T. Speaker, Bos	.926
H. Baker, Phi	107	T. Speaker, Bos	7.78	T. Speaker, Bos	.338	T. Speaker, Bos	.423	S. Crawford, Det	.483	E. Collins, Phi	.904
S. Crawford, Det	106	J. Jackson, Cle	6.96	J. Jackson, Cle	.338	J. Jackson, Cle	.399	J. Jackson, Cle	.464	S. Crawford, Det	.871
E. Murphy, Phi	90	H. Baker, Phi	6.83	H. Baker, Phi	.319	S. Crawford, Det	.388	E. Collins, Phi	.452	J. Jackson, Cle	.862

1914 American League Pitching Leaders

Wins		Losses		Winning Percentage		Games		Games Started		Complete Games	
W. Johnson, Was	28	J. Benz, ChA	19	C. Bender, Phi	.850	W. Johnson, Was	51	W. Johnson, Was	40	W. Johnson, Was	33
H. Coveleski, Det	22	E. Hamilton, StL	18	D. Leonard, Bos	.792	D. Ayers, Was	49	C. Weilman, StL	36	H. Coveleski, Det	23
R. Collins, Bos	20	J. Scott, ChA	18	H. Pennock, Phi	.733	J. Shaw, Was	48	H. Coveleski, Det	36	H. Dauss, Det	22
D. Leonard, Bos	19	W. Johnson, Was	18	E. Plank, Phi	.682	J. Benz, ChA	48	4 tied with	35	R. Caldwell, NYA	22
2 tied with	18	2 tied with	17	2 tied with	.667	3 tied with	45			3 tied with	20

Shutouts		Saves		Games Finished		Batters Faced	Innings Pitched		Hits Allowed	
W. Johnson, Was	9	R. Faber, ChA	4	G. Baumgardner, StL	23	Statistic unavailable	W. Johnson, Was	371.2	W. Johnson, Was	287
D. Leonard, Bos	7	J. Shaw, Was	4	H. Bedient, Bos	21		H. Coveleski, Det	303.1	H. Dauss, Det	286
C. Bender, Phi	7	J. Bentley, Was	4	R. Faber, ChA	17		E. Hamilton, StL	302.1	B. James, StL	269
R. Collins, Bos	6	H. Dauss, Det	4	F. Coumbe, 2tm	16		H. Dauss, Det	302.0	E. Hamilton, StL	265
6 tied with	5	R. Mitchell, StL	4	A. Collamore, Cle	16		C. Weilman, StL	299.0	C. Weilman, StL	260

Home Runs Allowed		Walks		Walks/9 Innings		Strikeouts		Strikeouts/9 Innings		Strikeout/Walk Ratio	
J. Warhop, NYA	8	J. Shaw, Was	137	M. McHale, NYA	1.6	W. Johnson, Was	225	D. Leonard, Bos	7.1	W. Johnson, Was	3.04
C. Pieh, NYA	6	W. Mitchell, Cle	124	W. Johnson, Was	1.8	W. Mitchell, Cle	179	W. Mitchell, Cle	6.3	D. Leonard, Bos	2.93
5 tied with	5	R. Hagerman, Cle	118	J. Warhop, NYA	1.8	D. Leonard, Bos	176	J. Shaw, Was	5.7	E. Plank, Phi	2.62
		B. James, StL	109	R. Collins, Bos	1.9	J. Shaw, Was	164	W. Johnson, Was	5.4	M. McHale, NYA	2.27
		J. Wyckoff, Phi	103	E. Plank, Phi	2.0	H. Dauss, Det	150	C. Bender, Phi	5.4	J. Benz, ChA	2.15

Earned Run Average		Component ERA		Hit Batsmen		Wild Pitches		Opponent Average		Opponent OBP	
D. Leonard, Bos	1.00	D. Leonard, Bos	1.41	H. Dauss, Det	18	J. Wyckoff, Phi	14	D. Leonard, Bos	.179	D. Leonard, Bos	.245
R. Foster, Bos	1.66	R. Caldwell, NYA	1.67	R. Faber, ChA	12	W. Johnson, Was	14	E. Shore, Bos	.195	E. Shore, Bos	.252
W. Johnson, Was	1.72	E. Shore, Bos	1.74	H. Coveleski, Det	12	R. Keating, NYA	11	R. Caldwell, NYA	.205	R. Caldwell, NYA	.260
R. Caldwell, NYA	1.94	W. Johnson, Was	1.75	3 tied with	11	B. James, StL	11	J. Shaw, Was	.216	W. Johnson, Was	.265
E. Shore, Bos	2.00	R. Foster, Bos	1.89			2 tied with	10	R. Foster, Bos	.217	R. Foster, Bos	.274

1914 American League Miscellaneous

Managers		
Boston	Bill Carrigan	91-62
Chicago	Nixey Callahan	70-84
Cleveland	Joe Birmingham	51-102
Detroit	Hughie Jennings	80-73
New York	Frank Chance	60-74
	Roger Peckinpaugh	10-10
Philadelphia	Connie Mack	99-53
St. Louis	Branch Rickey	71-82
Washington	Clark Griffith	81-73

Awards	
Most Valuable Player	Eddie Collins, 2b, Phi
STATS Cy Young	Walter Johnson, Was
STATS Rookie of the Year	George Burns, 1b, Det
STATS Manager of the Year	Bill Carrigan, Bos

STATS All-Star Team

C	Wally Schang, Phi	.287	3	45
1B	Stuffy McInnis, Phi	.314	1	95
2B	Eddie Collins, Phi	.344	2	85
3B	Home Run Baker, Phi	.319	9	89
SS	Donie Bush, Det	.252	0	32
OF	Ty Cobb, Det	.368	2	57
OF	Sam Crawford, Det	.314	8	104
OF	Tris Speaker, Bos	.338	4	90
P	Chief Bender, Phi	17-3	2.26	107 K
P	Harry Coveleski, Det	22-12	2.49	124 K
P	Walter Johnson, Was	28-18	1.72	225 K
P	Dutch Leonard, Bos	19-5	1.00	176 K

Postseason	
World Series	Philadelphia (AL) 0 vs. Boston (NL) 4

Outstanding Performances

No-Hitters
Joe Benz, ChA   vs. Cle on May 31

1914 National League Standings

Team	W	L	Pct	GB	DIF	W	L	R	OR	HR	OHR	W	L	R	OR	HR	OHR	Run	HR	M/A	May	June	July	Aug	S/O
			Overall					**Home Games**						**Road Games**				**Park Index**				**Record by Month**			
Boston	94	59	.614	—	34	51	25	339	279	19	16	43	34	318	269	16	22	107	93	2-7	8-15	16-13	18-10	19-6	31-8
New York	84	70	.545	10.5	100	43	36	316	288	15	24	41	34	356	288	15	23	89	97	4-4	17-7	16-12	15-12	11-15	21-20
St. Louis	81	72	.529	13.0	1	42	34	285	280	20	14	39	38	273	260	13	12	107	138	4-10	15-13	15-11	17-10	13-13	17-15
Chicago	78	76	.506	16.5	0	46	30	318	281	22	20	32	46	287	357	20	17	95	117	5-8	13-14	17-9	17-10	10-16	16-19
Brooklyn	75	79	.487	19.5	7	45	34	342	306	17	17	30	45	280	312	14	19	104	98	5-3	9-15	13-15	10-16	16-13	22-17
Philadelphia	74	80	.481	20.5	7	48	30	377	321	50	16	26	50	274	366	12	10	106	292	6-3	9-15	13-13	13-18	12-12	21-19
Pittsburgh	69	85	.448	25.5	39	39	36	234	214	3	6	30	49	269	326	15	21	79	26	10-2	11-12	9-17	9-18	13-14	17-22
Cincinnati	60	94	.390	34.5	3	34	42	290	328	4	5	26	52	240	323	12	25	113	25	7-6	18-9	8-17	11-16	10-15	6-31

Clinch Date—Boston 9/28.

Team Batting

Team	G	AB	R	OR	H	2B	3B	HR	TB	RBI	TBB	IBB	SO	HBP	SH	SF	SB	CS	SB%	GDP	Avg	OBP	Slg
New York	156	5146	**672**	576	1363	**222**	59	30	1793	566	447	—	479	57	139	—	**239**				.265	**.330**	.348
Boston	158	**5206**	657	548	1307	213	60	35	1745	**572**	**502**	—	617	50	**221**	—	139				.251	.323	.335
Philadelphia	154	5110	651	687	1345	211	52	**62**	**1846**	565	472	—	570	27	161	—	145				.263	.329	**.361**
Brooklyn	154	5152	622	618	**1386**	172	**90**	31	1831	529	376	—	559	33	190	—	173				**.269**	.323	.355
Chicago	156	5050	605	638	1229	199	74	42	1702	502	501	—	577	42	191	—	164				.243	.317	.337
St. Louis	157	5046	558	540	1249	203	65	33	1681	461	445	—	618	42	187	—	204				.248	.314	.333
Cincinnati	157	4991	530	651	1178	142	64	16	1496	432	441	—	**627**	54	149	—	224				.236	.305	.300
Pittsburgh	158	5145	503	540	1197	148	79	18	1557	487	416	—	608	36	156	—	147	101	.59		.233	.295	.303
NL Total	1250	40846	4798	4798	10254	1510	543	267	13651	4114	3600	—	4655	341	1394	—	1435	—	—	—	.251	.317	.334
NL Avg Team	156	5106	600	600	1282	189	68	33	1706	514	450	—	582	43	174	—	179	—	—	—	.251	.317	.334

Team Pitching

Team	G	CG	ShO	Rel	Sv	IP	H	R	ER	HR	SH	SF	HB	TBB	IBB	SO	WP	Bk	H/9	SO/9	BB/9	OAvg	OOBP	ERA
St. Louis	157	84	16	96	12	**1424.2**	1279	540	377	26	221	—	51	422	—	531	22	2	8.1	3.4	2.7	.249	.313	**2.38**
Pittsburgh	158	86	10	97	11	1405.0	1272	540	422	27	186	—	36	392	—	488	17	0	8.1	3.1	2.5	.249	.308	2.70
Chicago	156	70	14	**110**	11	1389.1	**1169**	638	418	37	181	—	39	528	—	**651**	60	2	**7.6**	4.2	3.4	**.233**	.311	2.71
Boston	158	**104**	19	69	6	1421.0	1272	548	433	38	**124**	—	49	477	—	606	37	2	8.1	3.8	3.0	.249	.319	2.74
Brooklyn	154	80	11	99	11	1368.1	1282	618	428	36	153	—	40	466	—	605	23	3	8.4	4.0	3.1	.253	.320	2.82
Cincinnati	157	74	15	106	15	1387.1	1259	651	453	30	194	—	48	489	—	607	40	6	8.2	3.9	3.2	.248	.320	2.94
New York	156	88	**20**	89	9	1390.2	1298	576	455	47	158	—	28	**367**	—	563	31	0	8.4	3.6	**2.4**	.253	**.306**	2.94
Philadelphia	154	85	14	98	7	1379.1	1403	687	469	**26**	169	—	**53**	452	—	650	27	5	9.2	**4.2**	2.9	.270	.335	3.06
NL Total	1250	671	119	764	82	11165.2	10234	4798	3455	267	1386	—	344	3593	—	4701	257	20	8.3	3.8	2.9	.251	.316	2.78
NL Avg Team	156	84	15	96	10	1395.2	1279	600	432	33	173	—	43	449	—	588	32	3	8.3	3.8	2.9	.251	.316	2.78

Team Fielding

Team	G	PO	A	E	TC	DP	PB	Pct
Pittsburgh	158	4211	2034	**223**	6468	96	22	**.966**
St. Louis	157	4256	2066	239	6561	109	14	.964
Boston	158	**4262**	2162	246	**6670**	**143**	17	.963
New York	156	4165	2032	254	6451	119	7	.961
Brooklyn	154	4109	1923	248	6280	112	19	.961
Cincinnati	157	4152	2090	314	6556	113	**39**	.952
Chicago	156	4135	1889	310	6334	87	29	.951
Philadelphia	154	4120	2016	324	6460	81	11	.950
NL Total	1250	33410	16212	2158	51780	860	158	.958

Team vs. Team Records

	Bos	Bro	ChN	Cin	NYG	Phi	Pit	StL	Won
Bos	—	9	16	14	11	12	17	15	**94**
Bro	13	—	10	11	9	11	16	5	75
ChN	6	12	—	17	9	12	12	10	78
Cin	8	11	5	—	9	8	8	10	60
NYG	11	13	13	13	—	12	13	9	84
Phi	10	11	10	13	10	—	12	8	74
Pit	5	6	10	14	9	10	—	15	69
StL	6	17	12	12	13	14	7	—	81
Lost	59	79	76	94	70	80	85	72	

Seasons: Standings, Leaders

1914 National League Batting Leaders

Games			At-Bats			Runs			Hits			Doubles			Triples		
R. Maranville, Bos	156		M. Carey, Pit	593		G. Burns, NYG	100		S. Magee, Phi	171		S. Magee, Phi	39		M. Carey, Pit	17	
M. Carey, Pit	156		R. Maranville, Bos	586		S. Magee, Phi	96		G. Burns, NYG	170		H. Zimmerman, ChN	36		G. Cutshaw, Bro	12	
D. Miller, StL	155		G. Cutshaw, Bro	583		J. Daubert, Bro	89		Z. Wheat, Bro	170		G. Burns, NYG	35		C. Wilson, StL	12	
4 tied with	154		C. Wilson, StL	580		V. Saier, ChN	87		B. Becker, Phi	167		J. Connolly, Bos	28		H. Zimmerman, ChN	12	
			W. Good, ChN	580		L. Doyle, NYG	87		H. Zimmerman, ChN	167		4 tied with	27		3 tied with	11	

Home Runs			Total Bases			Runs Batted In			Walks			Intentional Walks			Strikeouts		
G. Cravath, Phi	19		S. Magee, Phi	277		S. Magee, Phi	103		M. Huggins, StL	105		Statistic unavailable			F. Merkle, NYG	80	
V. Saier, ChN	18		G. Cravath, Phi	249		G. Cravath, Phi	100		V. Saier, ChN	94					B. Niehoff, Cin	77	
S. Magee, Phi	15		Z. Wheat, Bro	241		Z. Wheat, Bro	89		G. Burns, NYG	89					C. Dolan, StL	74	
F. Luderus, Phi	12		H. Zimmerman, ChN	239		D. Miller, StL	88		J. Evers, Bos	87					W. Good, ChN	74	
4 tied with	9		G. Burns, NYG	234		H. Zimmerman, ChN	87		G. Cravath, Phi	83					G. Cravath, Phi	72	

Hit By Pitch			Sac Hits			Sac Flies			Stolen Bases			Caught Stealing			GDP		
H. Groh, Cin	13		L. Magee, StL	35		Statistic unavailable			G. Burns, NYG	62		Statistic unavailable			Statistic unavailable		
A. Fletcher, NYG	13		J. Daubert, Bro	33					B. Herzog, Cin	46							
B. Schmidt, Bos	11		J. Evers, Bos	31					C. Dolan, StL	42							
L. Doyle, NYG	10		R. Maranville, Bos	27					M. Carey, Pit	38							
3 tied with	9		R. Smith, 2tm	27					2 tied with	36							

Runs Created			Runs Created/27 Outs			Batting Average			On-Base Percentage			Slugging Percentage			OBP+Slugging		
S. Magee, Phi	106		J. Connolly, Bos	7.50		J. Daubert, Bro	.329		C. Stengel, Bro	.404		S. Magee, Phi	.509		G. Cravath, Phi	.901	
G. Burns, NYG	105		G. Cravath, Phi	7.14		B. Becker, Phi	.325		G. Burns, NYG	.403		G. Cravath, Phi	.499		S. Magee, Phi	.890	
G. Cravath, Phi	103		S. Magee, Phi	7.01		J. Dalton, Bro	.319		G. Cravath, Phi	.402		J. Connolly, Bos	.494		J. Connolly, Bos	.886	
Z. Wheat, Bro	92		G. Burns, NYG	6.63		Z. Wheat, Bro	.319		R. Bresnahan, ChN	.401		Z. Wheat, Bro	.452		Z. Wheat, Bro	.830	
V. Saier, ChN	91		C. Stengel, Bro	6.48		C. Stengel, Bro	.316		M. Huggins, StL	.396		B. Becker, Phi	.446		C. Stengel, Bro	.829	

1914 National League Pitching Leaders

Wins			Losses			Winning Percentage			Games			Games Started			Complete Games		
P. Alexander, Phi	27		R. Ames, Cin	23		B. James, Bos	.788		L. Cheney, ChN	50		J. Tesreau, NYG	41		P. Alexander, Phi	32	
B. James, Bos	26		R. Marquard, NYG	22		B. Doak, StL	.760		E. Mayer, Phi	48		L. Cheney, ChN	40		D. Rudolph, Bos	31	
J. Tesreau, NYG	26		E. Mayer, Phi	19		J. Tesreau, NYG	.722		R. Ames, Cin	47		P. Alexander, Phi	39		B. James, Bos	30	
D. Rudolph, Bos	26		4 tied with	18		D. Rudolph, Bos	.722		3 tied with	46		E. Mayer, Phi	38		C. Mathewson, NYG	29	
C. Mathewson, NYG	24					J. Pfeffer, Bro	.657					2 tied with	37		J. Pfeffer, Bro	27	

Shutouts			Saves			Games Finished			Batters Faced			Innings Pitched			Hits Allowed		
J. Tesreau, NYG	8		S. Sallee, StL	6		Z. Zabel, ChN	18		P. Alexander, Phi	1459		P. Alexander, Phi	355.0		P. Alexander, Phi	327	
B. Doak, StL	7		R. Ames, Cin	6		J. Conzelman, Pit	17		E. Mayer, Phi	1343		D. Rudolph, Bos	336.1		C. Mathewson, NYG	314	
L. Cheney, ChN	6		L. Cheney, ChN	5		C. Hageman, 2tm	17		B. James, Bos	1316		B. James, Bos	332.1		E. Mayer, Phi	308	
P. Alexander, Phi	6		J. Pfeffer, Bro	4		A. Fromme, NYG	17		D. Rudolph, Bos	1302		J. Tesreau, NYG	322.1		D. Rudolph, Bos	288	
D. Rudolph, Bos	6		G. McQuillan, Pit	4		H. Wiltse, NYG	17		J. Tesreau, NYG	1299		E. Mayer, Phi	321.0		R. Ames, Cin	274	

Home Runs Allowed			Walks			Walks/9 Innings			Strikeouts			Strikeouts/9 Innings			Strikeout/Walk Ratio		
C. Mathewson, NYG	16		L. Cheney, ChN	140		C. Mathewson, NYG	0.7		P. Alexander, Phi	214		P. Alexander, Phi	5.4		C. Mathewson, NYG	3.48	
J. Lavender, ChN	11		J. Tesreau, NYG	128		B. Adams, Pit	1.2		J. Tesreau, NYG	189		J. Tesreau, NYG	5.3		P. Alexander, Phi	2.82	
4 tied with	9		B. James, Bos	118		R. Marquard, NYG	1.6		H. Vaughn, ChN	165		H. Vaughn, ChN	5.1		B. Adams, Pit	2.33	
			H. Vaughn, ChN	109		D. Rudolph, Bos	1.6		L. Cheney, ChN	157		L. Tyler, Bos	4.6		D. Rudolph, Bos	2.26	
			L. Tyler, Bos	101		P. Alexander, Phi	1.9		B. James, Bos	156		P. Ragan, Bro	4.6		R. Marquard, NYG	1.96	

Earned Run Average			Component ERA			Hit Batsmen			Wild Pitches			Opponent Average			Opponent OBP		
B. Doak, StL	1.72		B. Doak, StL	2.07		P. Perritt, StL	15		L. Cheney, ChN	26		J. Tesreau, NYG	.209		B. Adams, Pit	.276	
B. James, Bos	1.90		B. Adams, Pit	2.14		L. Tyler, Bos	14		H. Vaughn, ChN	13		L. Cheney, ChN	.215		D. Rudolph, Bos	.276	
J. Pfeffer, Bro	1.97		D. Rudolph, Bos	2.16		B. James, Bos	13		R. Marquard, NYG	12		B. Doak, StL	.216		C. Mathewson, NYG	.278	
H. Vaughn, ChN	2.05		J. Tesreau, NYG	2.24		E. Mayer, Phi	13		R. Ames, Cin	12		H. Vaughn, ChN	.222		P. Alexander, Phi	.290	
S. Sallee, StL	2.10		B. James, Bos	2.29		4 tied with	11		R. Benton, Cin	11		P. Douglas, Cin	.223		B. Doak, StL	.290	

1914 National League Miscellaneous

Managers		
Boston	George Stallings	94-59
Brooklyn	Wilbert Robinson	75-79
Chicago	Hank O'Day	78-76
Cincinnati	Buck Herzog	60-94
New York	John McGraw	84-70
Philadelphia	Red Dooin	74-80
Pittsburgh	Fred Clarke	69-85
St. Louis	Miller Huggins	81-72

Awards	
Most Valuable Player	Johnny Evers, 2b, Bos
STATS Cy Young	Bill James, Bos
STATS Rookie of the Year	Jeff Pfeffer, p, Bro
STATS Manager of the Year	George Stallings, Bos

STATS All-Star Team

C	Chief Meyers, NYG	.286	1	55
1B	Jake Daubert, Bro	.329	6	45
2B	Johnny Evers, Bos	.279	1	40
3B	Heinie Zimmerman, ChN	.296	4	87
SS	Rabbit Maranville, Bos	.246	4	78
OF	Joe Connolly, Bos	.306	9	65
OF	Gavy Cravath, Phi	.299	19	100
OF	Sherry Magee, Phi	.314	15	103
P	Pete Alexander, Phi	27-15	2.38	214 K
P	Bill James, Bos	26-7	1.90	156 K
P	Dick Rudolph, Bos	26-10	2.35	138 K
P	Jeff Tesreau, NYG	26-10	2.37	189 K

Postseason	
World Series	Boston (NL) 4 vs. Philadelphia (AL) 0

Outstanding Performances

No-Hitters

Iron Davis, Bos	vs. Phi on September 9

1914 Federal League Standings

Team	Overall					Home Games						Road Games						Park Index		Record by Month					
	W	L	Pct	GB	DIF	W	L	R	OR	HR	OHR	W	L	R	OR	HR	OHR	Run	HR	M/A	May	June	July	Aug	S/O
Indianapolis	88	65	.575	—	50	53	23	439	339	14	8	35	42	323	283	19	21	130	56	7-6	8-12	21-7	12-16	18-11	22-13
Chicago	87	67	.565	1.5	69	41	34	248	208	31	19	46	33	373	309	21	24	70	117	6-7	12-10	18-9	18-14	12-12	21-15
Baltimore	84	70	.545	4.5	51	53	26	350	298	25	15	31	44	295	330	7	19	98	146	6-4	16-7	11-16	16-13	12-13	23-17
Buffalo	80	71	.530	7.0	2	47	29	345	300	20	18	33	42	275	302	17	27	110	85	3-5	12-11	16-9	13-20	13-12	23-14
Brooklyn	77	77	.500	11.5	7	47	32	358	335	26	13	30	45	304	342	16	18	102	109	5-5	9-11	11-16	21-8	12-16	19-21
Kansas City	67	84	.444	20.0	0	38	37	322	306	28	21	29	47	322	377	11	16	91	184	5-8	13-12	13-15	12-17	14-10	10-22
Pittsburgh	64	86	.427	22.5	0	37	37	297	307	11	10	27	49	308	391	23	28	89	42	2-7	14-11	9-15	14-16	8-17	17-20
St. Louis	62	89	.411	25.0	13	31	44	304	368	12	23	31	45	261	329	14	15	115	122	10-2	8-18	8-20	13-15	14-12	9-22

Clinch Date—Indianapolis 10/07.

Team Batting

Team	G	AB	R	OR	H	2B	3B	HR	TB	RBI	TBB	IBB	SO	HBP	SH	SF	SB	CS	SB%	GDP	Avg	OBP	Slg
Indianapolis	157	5176	762	622	1474	230	90	33	1983	629	470	—	668	39	223	—	273	—	—	—	.285	.349	.383
Brooklyn	157	5221	662	677	1402	225	85	42	1923	573	404	—	665	45	135	—	220	—	—	—	.269	.326	.368
Baltimore	160	5120	645	628	1374	222	67	32	1826	551	487	—	589	46	181	—	152	—	—	—	.268	.337	.357
Kansas City	154	5127	644	683	1369	226	77	39	1866	557	399	—	621	36	149	—	171	—	—	—	.267	.324	.364
Chicago	157	5098	621	517	1314	227	50	52	1797	544	520	—	645	41	167	—	171	—	—	—	.258	.331	.352
Buffalo	155	5064	620	602	1264	177	74	37	1700	508	430	—	761	23	146	—	228	—	—	—	.250	.311	.336
Pittsburgh	154	5114	605	698	1339	180	90	34	1801	520	410	—	575	38	190	—	153	—	—	—	.262	.321	.352
St. Louis	154	5078	565	697	1254	193	65	26	1655	480	503	—	662	34	176	—	113	—	—	—	.247	.319	.326
FL Total	1248	40998	5124	5124	10790	1680	598	295	14551	4362	3623	—	5186	302	1367	—	1481	—	—	—	.263	.328	.355
FL Avg Team	156	5125	641	641	1349	210	75	37	1819	545	453	—	648	38	171	—	185	—	—	—	.263	.328	.355

Team Pitching

Team	G	CG	ShO	Rel	Sv	IP	H	R	ER	HR	SH	SF	HB	TBB	IBB	SO	WP	Bk	H/9	SO/9	BB/9	OAvg	OOBP	ERA
Chicago	157	93	17	87	8	1420.1	1204	517	385	43	—	—	32	393	—	650	24	0	7.6	4.1	2.5	.237	.296	2.44
Indianapolis	157	104	15	67	9	1397.2	1352	622	475	29	—	—	45	476	—	664	30	0	8.7	4.3	3.1	.262	.330	3.06
Baltimore	160	88	15	93	13	1392.0	1389	628	484	34	—	—	32	392	—	732	35	2	9.0	4.7	2.5	.268	.323	3.13
Buffalo	155	89	15	91	16	1387.0	1249	602	487	45	—	—	45	505	—	662	37	2	8.1	4.3	3.3	.248	.322	3.16
Brooklyn	157	91	11	92	9	1385.1	1375	677	513	31	—	52	559	—	636	31	0	8.9	4.1	3.6	.267	.345	3.33
Kansas City	154	82	10	92	12	1361.0	1387	683	515	37	—	48	445	—	600	38	4	9.2	4.0	2.9	.272	.336	3.41
Pittsburgh	154	97	9	71	6	1370.0	1416	698	542	38	—	23	444	—	510	21	1	9.3	3.4	2.9	.275	.335	3.56
St. Louis	154	97	9	73	6	1367.2	1418	697	545	38	—	52	409	—	661	35	2	9.3	4.3	2.7	.276	.335	3.59
FL Total	1248	741	101	666	79	11081.0	10790	5124	3946	295	—	329	3623	—	5115	251	11	8.8	4.2	2.9	.263	.328	3.20
FL Avg Team	156	93	13	83	10	1385.0	1349	641	493	37	—	41	453	—	639	31	1	8.8	4.2	2.9	.263	.328	3.20

Team Fielding

Team	G	PO	A	E	TC	DP	PB	Pct
Buffalo	155	4157	2002	242	6401	109	18	.962
Chicago	157	4259	2043	249	6551	114	14	.962
Pittsburgh	154	4103	1987	253	6343	92	24	.960
Baltimore	160	4172	2104	263	6539	105	20	.960
Kansas City	154	4081	2135	279	6495	135	23	.957
St. Louis	154	4097	1952	273	6322	94	18	.957
Indianapolis	157	4190	2049	289	6528	113	15	.956
Brooklyn	157	4155	1938	283	6376	120	17	.956
FL Total	1248	33214	16210	2131	51555	882	149	.959

Team vs. Team Records

	Bal	Bro	Buf	Chi	Ind	KC	Pit	STL	Won
Bal	—	9	14	12	10	12	10	17	84
Bro	13	—	11	9	3	11	17	13	77
Buf	8	11	—	10	11	12	13	15	80
Chi	10	13	12	—	13	14	12	13	87
Ind	12	19	10	9	—	13	12	13	88
KC	10	11	10	8	9	—	11	8	67
Pit	12	5	7	10	10	10	—	10	64
STL	5	9	7	9	9	12	11	—	62
Lost	70	77	71	67	65	84	86	89	

1914 Federal League Batting Leaders

Games		At-Bats		Runs		Hits		Doubles		Triples	
H. Swacina, Bal	158	H. Swacina, Bal	617	B. Kauff, Ind	120	B. Kauff, Ind	211	B. Kauff, Ind	44	J. Esmond, Ind	15
V. Duncan, Bal	157	C. Hanford, Buf	597	B. McKechnie, Ind	107	D. Zwilling, Chi	185	S. Evans, Bro	41	S. Evans, Bro	15
A. Wickland, Chi	157	D. Zwilling, Chi	592	V. Duncan, Bal	99	S. Evans, Bro	179	D. Kenworthy, KC	40	D. Kenworthy, KC	14
F. Beck, Chi	157	C. Chadbourne, KC	581	D. Kenworthy, KC	93	R. Oakes, Pit	178	D. Zwilling, Chi	38	3 tied with	13
J. Farrell, Chi	156	2 tied with	571	S. Evans, Bro	93	C. Hanford, Buf	174	2 tied with	31		

Home Runs		Total Bases		Runs Batted In		Walks		Intentional Walks		Strikeouts	
D. Zwilling, Chi	16	B. Kauff, Ind	305	F. LaPorte, Ind	107	A. Wickland, Chi	81	Statistic unavailable		Statistic unavailable	
D. Kenworthy, KC	15	D. Zwilling, Chi	287	S. Evans, Bro	96	J. Agler, Buf	77				
C. Hanford, Buf	13	D. Kenworthy, KC	286	B. Kauff, Ind	95	B. Kauff, Ind	72				
S. Evans, Bro	12	S. Evans, Bro	286	D. Zwilling, Chi	95	3 tied with	71				
2 tied with	11	C. Hanford, Buf	267	D. Kenworthy, KC	91						

Hit By Pitch		Sac Hits		Sac Flies		Stolen Bases		Caught Stealing		GDP	
T. Wisterzil, Bro	11	B. McKechnie, Ind	36	Statistic unavailable		B. Kauff, Ind	75	Statistic unavailable		Statistic unavailable	
V. Duncan, Bal	11	V. Duncan, Bal	28			B. McKechnie, Ind	47				
D. Kenworthy, KC	11	A. Wickland, Chi	27			H. Myers, Bro	43				
W. Miller, STL	10	O. Knabe, Bal	27			C. Chadbourne, KC	42				
S. Evans, Bro	10	M. Doolan, Bal	26			3 tied with	37				

Runs Created		Runs Created/27 Outs		Batting Average		On-Base Percentage		Slugging Percentage		OBP+Slugging	
B. Kauff, Ind	142	B. Kauff, Ind	9.56	B. Kauff, Ind	.370	B. Kauff, Ind	.447	S. Evans, Bro	.556	B. Kauff, Ind	.981
S. Evans, Bro	110	S. Evans, Bro	8.16	S. Evans, Bro	.348	D. Crandall, STL	.429	B. Kauff, Ind	.534	S. Evans, Bro	.973
D. Kenworthy, KC	107	E. Lennox, Pit	7.18	T. Easterly, KC	.335	S. Evans, Bro	.416	D. Kenworthy, KC	.525	E. Lennox, Pit	.907
C. Hanford, Buf	99	D. Kenworthy, KC	6.92	A. Shaw, Bro	.324	E. Lennox, Pit	.414	E. Lennox, Pit	.493	D. Kenworthy, KC	.896
D. Zwilling, Chi	99	D. Crandall, STL	6.81	V. Campbell, Ind	.318	W. Miller, STL	.397	D. Zwilling, Chi	.485	A. Shaw, Bro	.869

1914 Federal League Pitching Leaders

Wins		Losses		Winning Percentage		Games		Games Started		Complete Games	
C. Hendrix, Chi	29	W. Dickson, Pit	21	R. Ford, Buf	.778	C. Hendrix, Chi	49	C. Falkenberg, Ind	43	C. Hendrix, Chi	34
J. Quinn, Bal	26	H. Keupper, STL	20	C. Hendrix, Chi	.725	C. Falkenberg, Ind	49	J. Quinn, Bal	42	C. Falkenberg, Ind	33
T. Seaton, Bro	25	B. Groom, STL	20	J. Quinn, Bal	.650	K. Wilhelm, Bal	47	E. Moseley, Ind	38	E. Moseley, Ind	29
C. Falkenberg, Ind	25	E. Moseley, Ind	18	E. Knetzer, Pit	.645	J. Quinn, Bal	46	T. Seaton, Bro	38	J. Quinn, Bal	27
G. Suggs, Bal	24	H. Camnitz, Pit	18	T. Seaton, Bro	.641	G. Suggs, Bal	46	G. Suggs, Bal	38	2 tied with	26

Shutouts		Saves		Games Finished		Batters Faced		Innings Pitched		Hits Allowed	
C. Falkenberg, Ind	9	R. Ford, Buf	6	K. Wilhelm, Bal	18	Statistic unavailable		C. Falkenberg, Ind	377.1	J. Quinn, Bal	335
T. Seaton, Bro	7	C. Hendrix, Chi	5	D. Adams, KC	16			C. Hendrix, Chi	362.0	C. Falkenberg, Ind	332
C. Hendrix, Chi	6	D. Davenport, STL	4	S. Conley, Bal	15			J. Quinn, Bal	342.2	G. Suggs, Bal	322
G. Suggs, Bal	6	G. Packard, KC	4	E. Herbert, STL	15			G. Suggs, Bal	319.1	E. Moseley, Ind	303
2 tied with	5	K. Wilhelm, Bal	4	4 tied with	13			E. Moseley, Ind	316.2	T. Seaton, Bro	299

Home Runs Allowed		Walks		Walks/9 Innings		Strikeouts		Strikeouts/9 Innings		Strikeout/Walk Ratio	
R. Ford, Buf	11	E. Lafitte, Bro	127	R. Ford, Buf	1.5	C. Falkenberg, Ind	236	B. Bailey, Bal	9.2	R. Ford, Buf	3.00
K. Wilhelm, Bal	10	E. Moseley, Ind	123	G. Suggs, Bal	1.6	E. Moseley, Ind	205	D. Davenport, STL	5.9	C. Falkenberg, Ind	2.65
E. Knetzer, Pit	9	G. Krapp, Buf	115	J. Quinn, Bal	1.7	C. Hendrix, Chi	189	E. Moseley, Ind	5.8	J. Quinn, Bal	2.52
B. Groom, STL	9	T. Seaton, Bro	102	C. Hendrix, Chi	1.9	T. Seaton, Bro	172	C. Falkenberg, Ind	5.6	C. Hendrix, Chi	2.45
7 tied with	8	E. Moore, Buf	99	H. Keupper, STL	2.1	B. Groom, STL	167	B. Groom, STL	5.4	C. Johnson, KC	2.36

Earned Run Average		Component ERA		Hit Batsmen		Wild Pitches		Opponent Average		Opponent OBP	
R. Johnson, Chi	1.58	C. Hendrix, Chi	1.59	G. Kaiserling, Ind	17	M. Walker, Pit	12	C. Hendrix, Chi	.203	C. Hendrix, Chi	.251
C. Hendrix, Chi	1.69	R. Ford, Buf	1.83	E. Lafitte, Bro	16	G. Krapp, Buf	10	G. Krapp, Buf	.210	R. Ford, Buf	.254
R. Ford, Buf	1.82	R. Johnson, Chi	1.88	T. Seaton, Bro	13	8 tied with	9	R. Ford, Buf	.214	N. Cullop, KC	.275
D. Watson, 2tm	2.01	C. Falkenberg, Ind	2.30	3 tied with	12			N. Cullop, KC	.215	E. Lange, Chi	.282
C. Falkenberg, Ind	2.22	D. Watson, 2tm	2.31					E. Lange, Chi	.224	C. Falkenberg, Ind	.284

1914 Federal League Miscellaneous

Managers		
Baltimore	Otto Knabe	84-70
Brooklyn	Bill Bradley	77-77
Buffalo	Harry Schlafly	80-71
Chicago	Joe Tinker	87-67
Indianapolis	Bill Phillips	88-65
Kansas City	George Stovall	67-84
Pittsburgh	Doc Gessler	3-8
	Rebel Oakes	61-78
St. Louis	Three Finger Brown	50-63
	Fielder Jones	12-26

Awards

STATS Most Valuable Player	Benny Kauff, of, Ind
STATS Cy Young	Claude Hendrix, Chi
STATS Rookie of the Year	Benny Kauff, of, Ind
STATS Manager of the Year	Bill Phillips, Ind

STATS All-Star Team

C	Art Wilson, Chi	.291	10	64
1B	Fred Beck, Chi	.279	11	77
2B	Duke Kenworthy, KC	.317	15	91
3B	Ed Lennox, Pit	.312	11	84
SS	Baldy Louden, Buf	.313	6	63
OF	Steve Evans, Bro	.348	12	96
OF	Benny Kauff, Ind	.370	8	95
OF	Dutch Zwilling, Chi	.313	16	95
P	Cy Falkenberg, Ind	25-16	2.22	236 K
P	Russ Ford, Buf	21-6	1.82	123 K
P	Claude Hendrix, Chi	29-11	1.69	189 K
P	Jack Quinn, Bal	26-14	2.60	164 K

Postseason

None

Outstanding Performances

None

1915 American League Standings

Team	Overall					Home Games						Road Games						Park Index		Record by Month					
	W	L	Pct	GB	DIF	W	L	R	OR	HR	OHR	W	L	R	OR	HR	OHR	Run	HR	M/A	May	June	July	Aug	S/O
Boston	101	50	.669	—	84	55	20	323	221	5	4	46	30	346	278	9	14	88	40	5-6	12-9	19-8	22-10	21-6	22-11
Detroit	100	54	.649	2.5	23	50	26	410	314	11	7	50	28	368	283	12	7	114	97	12-5	13-11	14-10	18-10	23-7	20-11
Chicago	93	61	.604	9.5	59	54	24	353	236	9	4	39	37	364	273	16	10	90	49	10-7	16-7	19-7	13-14	15-13	20-13
Washington	85	68	.556	17.0	2	48	29	277	235	3	2	37	40	292	256	9	10	95	27	8-6	7-13	15-9	17-18	15-11	23-11
New York	69	83	.454	32.5	11	37	44	306	309	28	32	32	39	278	279	3	9	97	438	8-4	11-11	14-15	11-17	11-15	14-21
St. Louis	63	91	.409	39.5	0	35	38	237	315	6	7	28	53	284	364	13	14	95	53	4-12	11-11	7-17	16-15	9-19	16-17
Cleveland	57	95	.375	44.5	2	27	50	277	362	7	9	30	45	262	308	13	9	109	71	7-9	10-10	5-20	14-18	10-17	11-21
Philadelphia	43	109	.283	58.5	1	20	55	285	457	9	17	23	54	260	431	7	5	110	222	4-9	9-17	9-16	10-19	4-20	7-28

Clinch Date—Boston 9/30.

Team Batting

Team	G	AB	R	OR	H	2B	3B	HR	TB	RBI	TBB	IBB	SO	HBP	SH	SF	SB	CS	SB%	GDP	Avg	OBP	Slg
Detroit	156	5128	778	597	1372	207	94	23	1836	647	681	—	527	35	202	—	241	146	.62	—	.268	.357	.358
Chicago	155	4914	717	509	1269	163	102	25	1711	598	583	—	575	71	270	—	233	183	.56	—	.258	.345	.348
Boston	155	5024	669	499	1308	202	76	14	1704	575	527	—	476	49	265	—	118	117	.50	—	.260	.336	.339
New York	154	4982	584	588	1162	167	50	31	1522	459	570	—	669	44	168	—	198	133	.60	—	.233	.317	.305
Washington	155	5029	569	491	1225	152	79	12	1571	465	458	—	541	45	187	—	186	106	.64	—	.244	.312	.312
Philadelphia	154	5081	545	545	1204	183	72	16	1579	440	436	—	634	54	137	—	127	89	.59	—	.237	.304	.311
Cleveland	154	5034	539	670	1210	169	79	20	1597	456	490	—	681	37	179	—	138	117	.54	—	.240	.312	.317
St. Louis	159	5112	521	680	1255	166	65	19	1608	439	472	—	765	43	173	—	202	160	.56	—	.246	.315	.315
AL Total	1242	40304	4922	4922	10005	1409	617	160	13128	4079	4217	—	4868	378	1581	—	1443	1051	.58	—	.248	.325	.326
AL Avg Team	155	5038	615	615	1251	176	77	20	1641	510	527	—	609	47	198	—	180	131	.58	—	.248	.325	.326

Team Pitching

Team	G	CG	ShO	Rel	Sv	IP	H	R	ER	HR	SH	SF	HB	TBB	IBB	SO	WP	Bk	H/9	SO/9	BB/9	OAvg	OOBP	ERA
Washington	155	87	21	99	13	1393.2	1161	491	357	12	—	—	48	455	—	715	36	7	7.5	4.6	2.9	.232	.302	2.31
Boston	155	81	19	99	15	1397.0	1164	499	371	18	—	—	46	446	—	634	29	5	7.5	4.1	2.9	.231	.300	2.39
Chicago	155	91	16	91	9	1401.0	1242	509	378	14	—	—	33	350	—	635	19	6	8.0	4.1	2.2	.242	.295	2.43
Detroit	156	86	10	109	19	1413.1	1259	597	449	14	—	—	57	492	—	550	36	2	8.0	3.5	3.1	.243	.316	2.86
St. Louis	159	76	6	131	7	1403.0	1256	680	474	21	—	—	64	612	—	566	39	4	8.1	3.6	3.4	.249	.338	3.04
New York	154	101	12	66	2	1382.2	1272	588	470	41	—	—	48	517	—	559	20	0	8.3	3.6	3.4	.254	.329	3.06
Cleveland	154	62	11	138	10	1372.0	1287	670	477	18	—	—	27	518	—	610	35	6	8.4	4.0	3.4	.256	.329	3.13
Philadelphia	154	78	6	95	2	1348.1	1358	888	643	22	—	—	57	827	—	588	68	4	9.1	3.9	5.5	.278	.388	4.29
AL Total	1242	662	101	828	77	11111.0	9999	4922	3619	160	—	—	380	4217	—	4857	282	34	8.1	3.9	3.4	.248	.325	2.93
AL Avg Team	155	83	13	104	10	1388.0	1250	615	452	20	—	—	48	527	—	607	35	4	8.1	3.9	3.4	.248	.325	2.93

Team Fielding

Team	G	PO	A	E	TC	DP	PB	Pct
New York	154	4143	2008	217	6368	118	18	.966
Chicago	155	4198	1999	222	6419	95	19	.965
Boston	155	4186	1942	226	6354	95	22	.964
Washington	155	4184	1916	230	6330	101	14	.964
Detroit	156	4228	2170	258	6656	107	26	.961
Cleveland	154	4116	2051	280	6447	82	19	.957
St. Louis	159	4185	2068	336	6589	144	30	.949
Philadelphia	154	4044	2023	338	6405	118	17	.947
AL Total	1242	33284	16177	2107	51568	860	165	.959

Team vs. Team Records

	Bos	ChA	Cle	Det	NYA	Phi	StL	Was	Won
Bos	—	12	16	14	10	17	17	15	101
ChA	10	—	16	7	15	19	18	8	93
Cle	16	6	—	5	9	15	12	6	57
Det	8	15	17	—	17	17	13	13	100
NYA	12	7	13	5	—	11	12	9	69
Phi	5	3	7	5	9	—	6	8	43
StL	5	4	10	9	10	16	—	9	63
Was	6	14	16	9	13	14	13	—	85
Lost	50	61	95	54	83	109	91	68	

1915 American League Batting Leaders

Games		At-Bats		Runs		Hits		Doubles		Triples	
D. Pratt, StL	159	E. Foster, Was	618	T. Cobb, Det	144	T. Cobb, Det	208	B. Veach, Det	40	S. Crawford, Det	19
D. Lavan, StL	157	S. Crawford, Det	612	E. Collins, ChA	118	S. Crawford, Det	183	D. Pratt, StL	31	J. Fournier, ChA	18
B. Shotton, StL	156	D. Pratt, StL	602	O. Vitt, Det	116	B. Veach, Det	178	D. Lewis, Bos	31	B. Roth, 2tm	17
T. Cobb, Det	156	S. Collins, ChA	576	T. Speaker, Bos	108	T. Speaker, Bos	176	T. Cobb, Det	31	R. Chapman, Cle	17
S. Crawford, Det	156	C. Milan, Was	573	R. Chapman, Cle	101	D. Pratt, StL	175	S. Crawford, Det	31	S. Collins, ChA	17

Home Runs		Total Bases		Runs Batted In		Walks		Intentional Walks		Strikeouts	
B. Roth, 2tm	7	T. Cobb, Det	274	B. Veach, Det	112	E. Collins, ChA	119	Statistic unavailable		D. Lavan, StL	83
R. Oldring, Phi	6	S. Crawford, Det	264	S. Crawford, Det	112	B. Shotton, StL	118			R. Chapman, Cle	82
6 tied with	5	B. Veach, Det	247	T. Cobb, Det	99	D. Bush, StL	118			W. Pipp, NYA	81
		D. Pratt, StL	237	S. Collins, ChA	85	T. Cobb, Det	118			T. Walker, StL	77
		E. Collins, ChA	227	J. Jackson, 2tm	81	H. Hooper, Bos	89			E. Smith, Cle	75

Hit By Pitch		Sac Hits		Sac Flies		Stolen Bases		Caught Stealing		GDP	
J. Fournier, ChA	15	B. Weaver, ChA	42	Statistic unavailable		T. Cobb, Det	96	T. Cobb, Det	38	Statistic unavailable	
W. Schang, Phi	14	O. Vitt, Det	42			F. Maisel, NYA	51	B. Shotton, StL	32		
T. Cobb, Det	10	S. Collins, ChA	40			E. Collins, ChA	46	E. Collins, ChA	30		
L. Kopf, Phi	9	J. Austin, StL	35			B. Shotton, StL	43	D. Bush, Det	27		
6 tied with	8	E. Collins, ChA	35			C. Milan, Was	40	T. Speaker, Bos	25		

Runs Created		Runs Created/27 Outs		Batting Average		On-Base Percentage		Slugging Percentage		OBP+Slugging	
T. Cobb, Det	154	T. Cobb, Det	10.16	T. Cobb, Det	.369	T. Cobb, Det	.486	J. Fournier, ChA	.491	T. Cobb, Det	.973
E. Collins, ChA	128	J. Fournier, ChA	8.59	E. Collins, ChA	.332	E. Collins, ChA	.460	T. Cobb, Det	.487	J. Fournier, ChA	.920
S. Crawford, Det	108	E. Collins, ChA	8.22	J. Fournier, ChA	.322	J. Fournier, ChA	.429	M. Kavanagh, Det	.452	E. Collins, ChA	.896
T. Speaker, Bos	107	T. Speaker, Bos	6.87	T. Speaker, Bos	.322	T. Speaker, Bos	.416	J. Jackson, 2tm	.445	J. Jackson, 2tm	.830
B. Veach, Det	105	M. Kavanagh, Det	6.63	S. McInnis, Phi	.314	B. Shotton, StL	.409	B. Roth, 2tm	.438	M. Kavanagh, Det	.829

1915 American League Pitching Leaders

Wins		Losses		Winning Percentage		Games		Games Started		Complete Games	
W. Johnson, Was	27	J. Wyckoff, Phi	22	J. Wood, Bos	.750	R. Faber, ChA	50	W. Johnson, Was	39	W. Johnson, Was	35
R. Faber, ChA	24	C. Weilman, StL	19	R. Foster, Bos	.704	H. Coveleski, Det	50	H. Coveleski, Det	38	R. Caldwell, NYA	31
H. Dauss, Det	24	G. Lowdermilk, 2tm	18	E. Shore, Bos	.704	S. Jones, Cle	48	H. Dauss, Det	35	H. Dauss, Det	27
J. Scott, ChA	24	R. Bressler, Phi	17	B. Ruth, Bos	.692	J. Scott, ChA	48	R. Caldwell, NYA	35	J. Scott, ChA	23
H. Coveleski, Det	22	E. Hamilton, StL	17	J. Scott, ChA	.686	2 tied with	47	J. Scott, ChA	35	3 tied with	22

Shutouts		Saves		Games Finished		Batters Faced		Innings Pitched		Hits Allowed	
J. Scott, ChA	7	C. Mays, Bos	7	C. Mays, Bos	27	Statistic unavailable		W. Johnson, Was	336.2	H. Coveleski, Det	271
W. Johnson, Was	7	S. Jones, Cle	5	S. Jones, Cle	24			H. Coveleski, Det	312.2	R. Caldwell, NYA	266
G. Morton, Cle	6	5 tied with	4	D. Ayers, Was	17			H. Dauss, Det	309.2	R. Faber, ChA	264
R. Foster, Bos	5			B. Boland, Det	16			R. Caldwell, NYA	305.0	H. Dauss, Det	261
J. Dubuc, Det	5			3 tied with	15			R. Faber, ChA	299.2	W. Johnson, Was	258

Home Runs Allowed		Walks		Walks/9 Innings		Strikeouts		Strikeouts/9 Innings		Strikeout/Walk Ratio	
R. Fisher, NYA	7	J. Wyckoff, Phi	165	W. Johnson, Was	1.5	W. Johnson, Was	203	D. Leonard, Bos	5.7	W. Johnson, Was	3.63
J. Warhop, NYA	7	G. Lowdermilk, 2tm	157	J. Benz, ChA	1.6	R. Faber, ChA	182	W. Mitchell, Cle	5.7	G. Morton, Cle	2.23
C. Weilman, StL	6	B. James, 2tm	125	R. Russell, ChA	1.8	J. Wyckoff, Phi	157	R. Faber, ChA	5.5	E. Cicotte, ChA	2.21
R. Caldwell, NYA	6	J. Boehling, Was	119	E. Cicotte, ChA	1.9	H. Coveleski, Det	150	W. Johnson, Was	5.4	B. Gallia, Was	2.03
4 tied with	5	R. Bressler, Phi	118	B. Gallia, Was	2.2	W. Mitchell, Cle	149	G. Lowdermilk, 2tm	5.3	R. Russell, ChA	1.91

Earned Run Average		Component ERA		Hit Batsmen		Wild Pitches		Opponent Average		Opponent OBP	
J. Wood, Bos	1.49	W. Johnson, Was	1.67	H. Coveleski, Det	20	J. Wyckoff, Phi	14	D. Leonard, Bos	.208	W. Johnson, Was	.260
W. Johnson, Was	1.55	J. Wood, Bos	1.84	W. Johnson, Was	19	J. Dubuc, Det	11	B. Ruth, Bos	.212	G. Morton, Cle	.270
E. Shore, Bos	1.64	G. Morton, Cle	1.95	G. Lowdermilk, 2tm	17	J. Bush, Phi	10	W. Johnson, Was	.214	J. Wood, Bos	.275
J. Scott, ChA	2.03	D. Leonard, Bos	2.11	D. Leonard, Bos	14	B. Ruth, Bos	9	J. Wood, Bos	.216	J. Benz, ChA	.280
R. Fisher, NYA	2.11	J. Benz, ChA	2.14	2 tied with	12	2 tied with	8	G. Morton, Cle	.218	E. Shore, Bos	.283

1915 American League Miscellaneous

Managers

Boston	Bill Carrigan	101-50
Chicago	Pants Rowland	93-61
Cleveland	Joe Birmingham	12-16
	Lee Fohl	45-79
Detroit	Hughie Jennings	100-54
New York	Wild Bill Donovan	69-83
Philadelphia	Connie Mack	43-109
St. Louis	Branch Rickey	63-91
Washington	Clark Griffith	85-68

Awards

STATS Most Valuable Player	Ty Cobb, of, Det
STATS Cy Young	Walter Johnson, Was
STATS Rookie of the Year	Babe Ruth, p, Bos
STATS Manager of the Year	Hughie Jennings, Det

STATS All-Star Team

C	Ray Schalk, ChA	.266	1	54
1B	Jack Fournier, ChA	.322	5	77
2B	Eddie Collins, ChA	.332	4	77
3B	Ossie Vitt, Det	.250	1	48
SS	Ray Chapman, Cle	.270	3	67
OF	Ty Cobb, Det	.369	3	99
OF	Tris Speaker, Bos	.322	0	69
OF	Bobby Veach, Det	.313	3	112
P	Walter Johnson, Was	27-13	1.55	203 K
P	Jim Scott, ChA	24-11	2.03	120 K
P	Ernie Shore, Bos	19-8	1.64	102 K
P	Joe Wood, Bos	15-5	1.49	63 K

Postseason

World Series	Boston (AL) 4 vs. Philadelphia (NL) 1

Outstanding Performances

None

1915 National League Standings

Team	Overall W	L	Pct	GB	DIF	Home Games W	L	R	OR	HR	OHR	Road Games W	L	R	OR	HR	OHR	Park Index Run	HR	Record by Month M/A	May	June	July	Aug	S/O
Philadelphia	90	62	.592	—	135	49	27	313	235	46	18	41	35	276	228	12	8	109	320	11-3	9-12	12-12	19-12	15-12	24-11
Boston	83	69	.546	7.0	0	49	27	280	263	3	5	34	42	302	282	14	18	93	25	7-6	12-12	10-15	18-13	16-9	20-14
Brooklyn	80	72	.526	10.0	0	51	26	299	263	9	14	29	46	237	297	5	15	103	112	6-9	11-9	10-16	22-9	17-14	14-15
Chicago	73	80	.477	17.5	45	42	34	296	314	31	16	31	46	274	306	22	12	107	140	8-6	14-10	13-9	10-20	14-15	14-20
Pittsburgh	73	81	.474	18.0	1	40	37	290	241	8	6	33	44	267	279	16	15	97	45	5-9	13-10	13-9	16-17	11-20	15-16
St. Louis	72	81	.471	18.5	0	42	36	320	303	11	10	30	45	270	298	9	20	105	70	8-9	10-11	17-11	10-19	14-14	13-17
Cincinnati	71	83	.461	20.0	0	39	37	265	295	6	7	32	46	251	290	9	21	106	44	9-6	6-12	10-14	13-20	16-15	17-16
New York	69	83	.454	21.0	2	37	38	275	270	15	20	32	45	307	358	9	20	84	124	3-9	11-10	12-11	17-15	12-16	14-22

Clinch Date—Philadelphia 9/29.

Team Batting

Team	G	AB	R	OR	H	2B	3B	HR	TB	RBI	TBB	IBB	SO	HBP	SH	SF	SB	CS	SB%	GDP	Avg	OBP	Slg
St. Louis	157	5106	590	601	1297	159	92	20	1700	483	457	—	658	42	175	—	162	144	.53	—	.254	.320	.333
Philadelphia	153	4916	589	463	1216	202	39	58	1670	486	460	—	600	35	181	—	121	113	.52	—	.247	.316	.340
New York	155	5218	582	628	1312	195	68	24	1715	501	315	—	547	47	122	—	155	137	.53	—	.251	.300	.329
Boston	157	5070	582	545	1219	231	57	17	1615	496	549	—	620	56	194	—	121	98	.55	—	.240	.321	.319
Chicago	156	5114	570	620	1246	212	66	53	1749	485	393	—	639	41	182	—	166	124	.57	—	.244	.303	.342
Pittsburgh	156	5113	557	520	1259	197	91	24	1710	464	419	—	656	49	162	—	182	111	.62	—	.246	.309	.334
Brooklyn	154	5120	536	560	1268	165	73	14	1625	449	313	—	496	27	175	—	131	126	.51	—	.248	.295	.317
Cincinnati	160	5231	516	585	1323	194	84	15	1730	425	360	—	512	53	192	—	156	142	.52	—	.253	.308	.331
NL Total	1248	40888	4522	4522	10140	1555	572	225	13514	3789	3266	—	4728	350	1383	—	1194	995	.55	—	.248	.309	.331
NL Avg Team	156	5111	565	565	1268	194	72	28	1689	474	408	—	591	44	173	—	149	124	.55	—	.248	.309	.331

Team Pitching

Team	G	CG	ShO	Rel	Sv	IP	H	R	ER	HR	SH	SF	HB	TBB	IBB	SO	WP	Bk	H/9	SO/9	BB/9	OAvg	OOBP	ERA
Philadelphia	153	98	20	67	8	1374.1	1161	463	332	26	149	—	31	342	—	652	20	4	7.6	4.3	2.2	.234	.288	2.17
Boston	157	95	17	78	13	1405.2	1257	545	402	23	148	—	46	366	—	630	27	1	8.0	4.0	2.3	.247	.303	2.57
Pittsburgh	156	91	18	91	11	1380.0	1229	520	398	21	168	—	38	384	—	544	15	0	8.0	3.5	2.5	.246	.304	2.60
Brooklyn	154	87	16	91	8	1389.2	1252	560	410	29	174	—	67	473	—	499	31	3	8.1	3.2	3.1	.245	.318	2.66
Cincinnati	160	80	19	113	12	1432.1	1304	585	452	28	182	—	46	497	—	572	24	1	8.2	3.6	3.1	.250	.321	2.84
St. Louis	157	79	13	102	9	1400.2	1320	601	449	30	206	—	36	402	—	538	20	5	8.5	3.5	2.6	.256	.314	2.89
Chicago	156	71	18	119	8	1399.0	1272	620	483	28	184	—	44	480	—	657	40	0	8.2	4.2	3.1	.247	.316	3.11
New York	155	78	15	105	9	1385.0	1350	628	479	40	166	—	43	325	—	637	32	0	8.8	4.1	2.1	.260	.308	3.11
NL Total	1248	679	136	766	78	11166.2	10145	4522	3405	225	1377	—	351	3269	—	4729	209	14	8.2	3.8	2.6	.248	.309	2.74
NL Avg Team	156	85	17	96	10	1395.2	1268	565	426	28	172	—	44	409	—	591	26	2	8.2	3.8	2.6	.248	.309	2.74

Team Fielding

Team	G	PO	A	E	TC	DP	PB	Pct
Cincinnati	160	4294	2111	222	6627	148	12	.967
Boston	157	4204	1939	213	6356	115	7	.966
Pittsburgh	156	4129	1903	214	6246	100	16	.966
Philadelphia	153	4109	1950	216	6275	99	13	.966
St. Louis	157	4190	2041	235	6466	109	14	.964
Brooklyn	154	4160	1964	238	6362	96	13	.963
New York	155	4151	1969	256	6376	119	24	.960
Chicago	156	4157	1984	268	6409	94	18	.958
NL Total	1248	33394	15861	1862	51117	880	122	.964

Team vs. Team Records

	Bos	Bro	ChN	Cin	NYG	Phi	Pit	StL	Won
Bos	—	14	10	15	13	7	15	9	83
Bro	8	—	14	11	12	13	11	11	80
ChN	12	8	—	13	8	7	13	12	73
Cin	7	11	9	—	9	9	12	14	71
NYG	9	8	14	13	—	7	8	10	69
Phi	14	9	14	13	15	—	10	15	90
Pit	7	11	9	10	14	12	—	10	73
StL	12	11	10	8	12	7	12	—	72
Lost	69	72	80	83	83	62	81	81	

1915 National League Batting Leaders

Games		At-Bats		Runs		Hits		Doubles		Triples	
T. Griffith, Cin	160	G. Burns, NYG	622	G. Cravath, Phi	89	L. Doyle, NYG	189	L. Doyle, NYG	40	T. Long, StL	25
H. Groh, Cin	160	H. Myers, Bro	605	L. Doyle, NYG	86	T. Griffith, Cin	179	F. Luderus, Phi	36	H. Wagner, Pit	17
R. Smith, Bos	157	L. Doyle, NYG	591	D. Bancroft, Phi	85	B. Hinchman, Pit	177	V. Saier, ChN	35	T. Griffith, Cin	16
3 tied with	156	H. Groh, Cin	587	G. Burns, NYG	83	H. Groh, Cin	170	R. Smith, Bos	34	G. Burns, NYG	14
		T. Griffith, Cin	583	O. O'Mara, Bro	77	G. Burns, NYG	169	S. Magee, Bos	34	B. Hinchman, Pit	14

Home Runs		Total Bases		Runs Batted In		Walks		Intentional Walks		Strikeouts	
G. Cravath, Phi	24	G. Cravath, Phi	266	G. Cravath, Phi	115	G. Cravath, Phi	86	Statistic unavailable		D. Baird, Pit	88
C. Williams, ChN	13	L. Doyle, NYG	261	S. Magee, Bos	87	D. Bancroft, Phi	77			G. Cravath, Phi	77
W. Schulte, ChN	12	T. Griffith, Cin	254	T. Griffith, Cin	85	J. Viox, Pit	75			B. Hinchman, Pit	75
V. Saier, ChN	11	B. Hinchman, Pit	253	H. Wagner, Pit	78	M. Huggins, StL	74			W. Schulte, ChN	68
B. Becker, Phi	11	H. Wagner, Pit	239	B. Hinchman, Pit	77	R. Smith, Bos	67			M. Huggins, StL	68

Hit By Pitch		Sac Hits		Sac Flies		Stolen Bases		Caught Stealing		GDP	
R. Killefer, Cin	19	T. Fisher, ChN	42	Statistic unavailable		M. Carey, Pit	36	D. Bancroft, Phi	27	Statistic unavailable	
E. Fitzpatrick, Bos	14	J. Daubert, Bro	39			B. Herzog, Cin	35	T. Griffith, Cin	24		
A. Fletcher, NYG	14	D. Johnston, Pit	34			D. Baird, Pit	29	G. Cutshaw, Bro	23		
D. Johnston, Pit	13	H. Groh, Cin	31			V. Saier, ChN	29	H. Myers, Bro	22		
C. Williams, ChN	10	2 tied with	28			G. Cutshaw, Bro	28	2 tied with	20		

Runs Created		Runs Created/27 Outs		Batting Average		On-Base Percentage		Slugging Percentage		OBP+Slugging	
G. Cravath, Phi	114	G. Cravath, Phi	7.76	L. Doyle, NYG	.320	G. Cravath, Phi	.393	G. Cravath, Phi	.510	G. Cravath, Phi	.902
L. Doyle, NYG	103	F. Luderus, Phi	6.75	F. Luderus, Phi	.315	J. Connolly, Bos	.387	F. Luderus, Phi	.457	F. Luderus, Phi	.833
F. Luderus, Phi	92	L. Doyle, NYG	6.27	T. Griffith, Cin	.307	M. Huggins, StL	.377	T. Long, StL	.446	B. Hinchman, Pit	.807
B. Hinchman, Pit	92	V. Saier, ChN	5.99	B. Hinchman, Pit	.307	F. Luderus, Phi	.376	V. Saier, ChN	.445	L. Doyle, NYG	.799
2 tied with	89	J. Connolly, Bos	5.68	J. Daubert, Bro	.301	B. Hinchman, Pit	.368	L. Doyle, NYG	.442	V. Saier, ChN	.795

1915 National League Pitching Leaders

Wins		Losses		Winning Percentage		Games		Games Started		Complete Games	
P. Alexander, Phi	31	P. Schneider, Cin	19	P. Alexander, Phi	.756	T. Hughes, Bos	50	D. Rudolph, Bos	43	P. Alexander, Phi	36
D. Rudolph, Bos	22	D. Rudolph, Bos	19	A. Mamaux, Pit	.724	G. Dale, Cin	49	P. Alexander, Phi	42	D. Rudolph, Bos	30
A. Mamaux, Pit	21	P. Perritt, NYG	18	F. Toney, Cin	.714	P. Alexander, Phi	49	J. Tesreau, NYG	39	J. Pfeffer, Bro	26
E. Mayer, Phi	21	B. Doak, StL	18	S. Smith, Bro	.636	P. Schneider, Cin	48	B. Doak, StL	36	B. Harmon, Pit	25
H. Vaughn, ChN	20	R. Benton, 2tm	18	H. Vaughn, ChN	.625	S. Sallee, StL	46	2 tied with	35	J. Tesreau, NYG	24

Shutouts		Saves		Games Finished		Batters Faced		Innings Pitched		Hits Allowed	
P. Alexander, Phi	12	T. Hughes, Bos	9	T. Hughes, Bos	22	P. Alexander, Phi	1435	P. Alexander, Phi	376.1	D. Rudolph, Bos	304
A. Mamaux, Pit	8	R. Benton, 2tm	5	K. Lear, Cin	20	D. Rudolph, Bos	1362	D. Rudolph, Bos	341.1	B. Doak, StL	263
J. Tesreau, NYG	8	W. Cooper, Pit	4	P. Standridge, ChN	18	G. Dale, Cin	1207	J. Tesreau, NYG	306.0	G. Dale, Cin	256
J. Pfeffer, Bro	6	J. Lavender, ChN	4	R. Schauer, NYG	17	J. Tesreau, NYG	1198	G. Dale, Cin	296.2	P. Schneider, Cin	254
F. Toney, Cin	6	9 tied with	3	D. Griner, StL	16	J. Pfeffer, Bro	1177	J. Pfeffer, Bro	291.2	P. Alexander, Phi	253

Home Runs Allowed		Walks		Walks/9 Innings		Strikeouts		Strikeouts/9 Innings		Strikeout/Walk Ratio	
E. Mayer, Phi	9	G. Dale, Cin	107	C. Mathewson, NYG	1.0	P. Alexander, Phi	241	P. Alexander, Phi	5.8	P. Alexander, Phi	3.77
C. Mathewson, NYG	9	P. Schneider, Cin	104	B. Humphries, ChN	1.2	J. Tesreau, NYG	176	T. Hughes, Bos	5.5	T. Hughes, Bos	2.95
J. Pfeffer, Bro	8	W. Dell, Bro	100	B. Adams, Pit	1.2	T. Hughes, Bos	171	A. Mamaux, Pit	5.4	C. Mathewson, NYG	2.85
R. Marquard, 2tm	8	A. Mamaux, Pit	96	P. Alexander, Phi	1.5	A. Mamaux, Pit	152	J. Tesreau, NYG	5.2	R. Marquard, 2tm	2.42
2 tied with	7	J. Coombs, Bro	91	D. Rudolph, Bos	1.7	H. Vaughn, ChN	148	H. Vaughn, ChN	4.9	J. Tesreau, NYG	2.35

Earned Run Average		Component ERA		Hit Batsmen		Wild Pitches		Opponent Average		Opponent OBP	
P. Alexander, Phi	1.22	P. Alexander, Phi	1.33	R. Benton, 2tm	19	R. Schauer, NYG	10	P. Alexander, Phi	.191	P. Alexander, Phi	.234
F. Toney, Cin	1.58	T. Hughes, Bos	1.65	J. Pfeffer, Bro	17	G. Pearce, ChN	10	F. Toney, Cin	.207	T. Hughes, Bos	.265
A. Mamaux, Pit	2.04	F. Toney, Cin	1.80	J. Coombs, Bro	16	L. Cheney, 2tm	9	A. Mamaux, Pit	.208	J. Tesreau, NYG	.269
J. Pfeffer, Bro	2.10	J. Tesreau, NYG	1.84	E. Mayer, Phi	14	W. Cooper, Pit	8	T. Hughes, Bos	.213	F. Toney, Cin	.278
T. Hughes, Bos	2.12	A. Mamaux, Pit	2.11	P. Perritt, NYG	12	E. Rixey, Phi	8	J. Tesreau, NYG	.215	B. Adams, Pit	.280

1915 National League Miscellaneous

Managers

Boston	George Stallings	83-69
Brooklyn	Wilbert Robinson	80-72
Chicago	Roger Bresnahan	73-80
Cincinnati	Buck Herzog	71-83
New York	John McGraw	69-83
Philadelphia	Pat Moran	90-62
Pittsburgh	Fred Clarke	73-81
St. Louis	Miller Huggins	72-81

Awards

STATS Most Valuable Player	Pete Alexander, p, Phi
STATS Cy Young	Pete Alexander, Phi
STATS Rookie of the Year	Dave Bancroft, ss, StL
STATS Manager of the Year	Pat Moran, Phi

STATS All-Star Team

C	Frank Snyder, StL	.298	2	55
1B	Fred Luderus, Phi	.315	7	62
2B	Larry Doyle, NYG	.320	4	70
3B	Heine Groh, Cin	.290	3	50
SS	Buck Herzog, Cin	.264	1	42
OF	Gavy Cravath, Phi	.285	24	115
OF	Tommy Griffith, Cin	.307	4	85
OF	Bill Hinchman, Pit	.307	5	77
P	Pete Alexander, Phi	31-10	1.22	241 K
P	Al Mamaux, Pit	21-8	2.04	152 K
P	Erskine Mayer, Phi	21-15	2.36	114 K
P	Fred Toney, Cin	15-6	1.58	108 K

Postseason

World Series	Philadelphia (NL) 1 vs. Boston (AL) 4

Outstanding Performances

No-Hitters
Rube Marquard, NYG vs. Bro on April 15
J. Lavender, ChN @ NYG on August 31

Cycles
Heine Groh, Cin on July 5

1915 Federal League Standings

Team	Overall					Home Games						Road Games						Park Index		Record by Month					
	W	L	Pct	GB	DIF	W	L	R	OR	HR	OHR	W	L	R	OR	HR	OHR	Run	HR	M/A	May	June	July	Aug	S/O
Chicago	86	66	.566	—	38	44	32	310	252	21	10	42	34	330	286	29	23	91	60	8-5	15-11	14-14	18-10	11-19	20-7
St. Louis	87	67	.565	—	18	43	34	334	280	12	15	44	33	300	247	11	7	112	150	5-9	12-8	20-8	13-19	16-12	21-11
Pittsburgh	86	67	.562	0.5	69	45	31	292	269	4	10	41	36	300	255	16	27	102	33	9-7	14-9	12-12	16-13	18-11	17-15
Kansas City	81	72	.529	5.5	45	46	31	274	249	15	19	35	41	273	302	13	10	90	146	8-8	13-9	19-9	13-15	12-17	16-14
Newark	80	72	.526	6.0	17	40	39	267	271	4	2	40	33	318	291	13	13	82	21	10-6	10-11	13-16	16-11	16-7	15-21
Buffalo	74	78	.487	12.0	0	37	40	290	324	21	21	37	38	284	310	19	14	101	124	6-9	6-17	12-17	19-11	17-13	14-11
Brooklyn	70	82	.461	16.0	11	34	40	315	324	20	11	36	42	332	349	16	16	99	102	9-6	9-12	12-18	14-18	13-13	13-15
Baltimore	47	107	.305	40.0	0	24	51	299	419	29	36	23	56	251	341	7	16	128	298	6-11	9-11	9-17	10-22	6-17	7-29

Clinch Date—Chicago 10/03.

Team Batting

Team	G	AB	R	OR	H	2B	3B	HR	TB	RBI	TBB	IBB	SO	HBP	SH	SF	SB	CS	SB%	GDP	Avg	OBP	Slg
Brooklyn	153	5035	647	673	1348	205	75	36	1811	561	473	—	654	47	155	—	249	—	—	—	.268	.336	.360
Chicago	155	5133	640	538	1320	185	77	50	1809	558	444	—	590	30	181	—	161	—	—	—	.257	.320	.352
St. Louis	159	5145	634	527	1344	199	81	23	1774	546	576	—	502	36	235	—	195	—	—	—	.261	.340	.345
Pittsburgh	156	5040	592	524	1318	180	80	20	1718	507	448	—	561	38	206	—	224	—	—	—	.262	.326	.341
Newark	155	5097	585	562	1283	210	80	17	1704	486	438	—	550	34	202	—	184	—	—	—	.252	.315	.334
Buffalo	153	5065	574	634	1261	193	68	40	1710	506	420	—	587	19	120	—	184	—	—	—	.249	.309	.338
Baltimore	154	5060	550	760	1235	196	53	36	1645	465	470	—	641	37	177	—	128	—	—	—	.244	.313	.325
Kansas City	153	4937	547	551	1206	200	66	28	1622	483	368	—	503	46	202	—	144	—	—	—	.244	.303	.329
FL Total	1238	40512	4769	4769	10315	1568	580	250	13793	4112	3637	—	4588	287	1478	—	1469	—	—	—	.255	.320	.340
FL Avg Team	155	5064	596	596	1289	196	73	31	1724	514	455	—	574	36	185	—	184	—	—	—	.255	.320	.340

Team Pitching

Team	G	CG	ShO	Rel	Sv	IP	H	R	ER	HR	SH	SF	HB	TBB	IBB	SO	WP	Bk	H/9	SO/9	BB/9	OAvg	OOBP	ERA
Newark	155	100	16	76	7	1406.2	1308	562	407	15	—	—	53	453	—	581	33	3	8.4	3.7	2.9	.254	.321	2.60
Chicago	155	97	21	68	10	1397.2	1232	538	410	33	—	—	36	402	—	576	35	0	7.9	3.7	2.6	.244	.304	2.64
St. Louis	159	94	24	88	9	1426.0	1267	527	433	22	—	—	30	396	—	698	23	2	8.0	4.4	2.5	.245	.303	2.73
Pittsburgh	156	88	16	88	12	1382.1	1273	524	429	37	—	—	31	441	—	517	23	5	8.3	3.4	2.9	.252	.316	2.79
Kansas City	153	95	16	75	11	1359.0	1210	551	426	29	—	—	35	390	—	526	36	1	8.0	3.5	2.6	.246	.306	2.82
Brooklyn	153	78	10	99	16	1355.2	1299	673	507	27	—	—	23	536	—	467	37	3	8.6	3.1	3.6	.260	.334	3.37
Buffalo	153	79	14	97	11	1360.0	1271	634	511	35	—	—	29	553	—	594	28	3	8.4	3.9	3.7	.255	.333	3.38
Baltimore	154	85	5	92	7	1360.1	1455	760	598	52	—	—	41	466	—	570	24	4	9.6	3.8	3.1	.281	.345	3.96
FL Total	1238	716	122	683	83	11047.2	10315	4769	3721	250	—	—	278	3637	—	4529	239	21	8.4	3.7	3.0	.255	.320	3.03
FL Avg Team	155	90	15	85	10	1380.2	1289	596	465	31	—	—	35	455	—	566	30	3	8.4	3.7	3.0	.255	.320	3.03

Team Fielding

Team	G	PO	A	E	TC	DP	PB	Pct
Pittsburgh	156	4146	1951	182	6279	98	17	.971
St. Louis	159	4276	2021	212	6509	111	23	.967
Buffalo	153	4077	2057	232	6366	112	20	.964
Chicago	155	4189	1965	233	6387	102	15	.964
Newark	155	4218	2066	239	6523	124	6	.963
Kansas City	153	4073	2167	246	6486	96	17	.962
Baltimore	154	4080	2029	273	6382	140	7	.957
Brooklyn	153	4064	2078	290	6432	103	22	.955
FL Total	1238	33123	16334	1907	51364	886	127	.963

Team vs. Team Records

	Bal	Bro	Buf	Chi	KC	New	Pit	STL	Won
Bal	—	7	8	9	4	6	5	8	47
Bro	15	—	9	7	11	12	9	7	70
Buf	14	11	—	8	11	11	9	10	74
Chi	13	15	14	—	11	10	12	11	86
KC	18	11	11	11	—	11	8	11	81
New	16	10	11	10	11	—	12	10	80
Pit	17	13	13	10	13	10	—	10	86
STL	14	15	12	11	11	12	12	—	87
Lost	107	82	78	66	72	72	67	67	

1915 Federal League Batting Leaders

Games		At-Bats		Runs		Hits		Doubles		Triples	
B. Borton, STL	159	J. Tobin, STL	625	B. Borton, STL	97	J. Tobin, STL	184	S. Evans, 2tm	34	L. Mann, Chi	19
J. Tobin, STL	158	C. Chadbourne, KC	587	M. Berghammer, Pit	96	E. Konetchy, Pit	181	D. Zwilling, Chi	32	E. Konetchy, Pit	18
A. Scheer, New	155	R. Oakes, Pit	580	S. Evans, 2tm	94	S. Evans, 2tm	171	E. Konetchy, Pit	31	J. Kelly, Pit	17
J. Esmond, New	155	E. Konetchy, Pit	576	J. Tobin, STL	92	B. Kauff, Bro	165	H. Chase, Buf	31	G. Gilmore, KC	15
W. Miller, STL	154	J. Esmond, New	569	B. Kauff, Bro	92	H. Chase, Buf	165	2 tied with	30	3 tied with	14

Home Runs		Total Bases		Runs Batted In		Walks		Intentional Walks		Strikeouts	
H. Chase, Buf	17	E. Konetchy, Pit	278	D. Zwilling, Chi	94	B. Borton, STL	92	Statistic unavailable		Statistic unavailable	
D. Zwilling, Chi	13	H. Chase, Buf	267	E. Konetchy, Pit	93	B. Kauff, Bro	85				
B. Kauff, Bro	12	J. Tobin, STL	254	H. Chase, Buf	89	M. Berghammer, Pit	83				
E. Konetchy, Pit	10	B. Kauff, Bro	246	B. Borton, STL	83	W. Miller, STL	79				
J. Walsh, 2tm	9	D. Zwilling, Chi	242	B. Kauff, Bro	83	2 tied with	77				

Hit By Pitch		Sac Hits		Sac Flies		Stolen Bases		Caught Stealing		GDP	
S. Evans, 2tm	14	B. Vaughn, STL	42	Statistic unavailable		B. Kauff, Bro	55	Statistic unavailable		Statistic unavailable	
G. Gilmore, KC	13	J. Esmond, New	34			M. Mowrey, Pit	40				
M. Berghammer, Pit	12	V. Duncan, Bal	33			J. Kelly, Pit	38				
G. Anderson, Bro	8	A. Wickland, 2tm	31			M. Flack, Chi	37				
G. Hartley, STL	8	2 tied with	27			L. Magee, Bro	34				

Runs Created		Runs Created/27 Outs		Batting Average		On-Base Percentage		Slugging Percentage		OBP+Slugging	
B. Kauff, Bro	112	B. Kauff, Bro	8.82	B. Kauff, Bro	.342	B. Kauff, Bro	.446	B. Kauff, Bro	.509	B. Kauff, Bro	.955
E. Konetchy, Pit	97	W. Fischer, Chi	6.30	W. Fischer, Chi	.329	W. Miller, STL	.400	E. Konetchy, Pit	.483	E. Konetchy, Pit	.846
D. Zwilling, Chi	96	S. Evans, 2tm	6.23	L. Magee, Bro	.323	B. Borton, STL	.395	H. Chase, Buf	.471	W. Fischer, Chi	.832
J. Tobin, STL	95	E. Konetchy, Pit	6.04	E. Konetchy, Pit	.314	S. Evans, 2tm	.392	W. Fischer, Chi	.449	S. Evans, 2tm	.818
S. Evans, 2tm	95	D. Zwilling, Chi	6.01	M. Flack, Chi	.314	C. Cooper, Bro	.388	D. Zwilling, Chi	.442	D. Zwilling, Chi	.808

1915 Federal League Pitching Leaders

Wins		Losses		Winning Percentage		Games		Games Started		Complete Games	
G. McConnell, Chi	25	J. Quinn, Bal	22	G. McConnell, Chi	.714	D. Davenport, STL	55	D. Davenport, STL	46	D. Davenport, STL	30
F. Allen, Pit	23	B. Bailey, 2tm	20	T. F. Brown, Chi	.680	H. Bedient, Buf	53	A. Schulz, Buf	38	C. Hendrix, Chi	26
D. Davenport, STL	22	G. Krapp, Buf	19	E. Reulbach, New	.677	D. Crandall, STL	51	F. Allen, Pit	37	A. Schulz, Buf	25
N. Cullop, KC	22	D. Davenport, STL	18	N. Cullop, KC	.667	C. Johnson, KC	46	N. Cullop, KC	36	F. Allen, Pit	24
4 tied with	21	H. Bedient, Buf	18	F. Allen, Pit	.657	4 tied with	44	G. McConnell, Chi	35	3 tied with	23

Shutouts		Saves		Games Finished		Batters Faced		Innings Pitched		Hits Allowed	
D. Davenport, STL	10	H. Bedient, Buf	10	H. Bedient, Buf	19	Statistic unavailable		D. Davenport, STL	392.2	D. Crandall, STL	307
F. Allen, Pit	6	C. Barger, Pit	5	C. Barger, Pit	19			D. Crandall, STL	312.2	D. Davenport, STL	300
E. Plank, STL	6	H. Wiltse, Bro	5	G. LaClaire, 3tm	17			A. Schulz, Buf	309.2	J. Quinn, Bal	289
8 tied with	5	4 tied with	4	B. Upham, Bro	16			G. McConnell, Chi	303.0	G. Suggs, Bal	288
				P. Henning, KC	16			N. Cullop, KC	302.1	H. Bedient, Buf	284

Home Runs Allowed		Walks		Walks/9 Innings		Strikeouts		Strikeouts/9 Innings		Strikeout/Walk Ratio	
G. Suggs, Bal	12	A. Schulz, Buf	149	E. Plank, STL	1.8	D. Davenport, STL	229	F. Anderson, Buf	5.3	E. Plank, STL	2.72
F. Allen, Pit	9	B. Bailey, 2tm	125	C. Bender, Bal	1.9	A. Schulz, Buf	160	D. Davenport, STL	5.2	C. Bender, Bal	2.41
J. Quinn, Bal	9	G. Krapp, Buf	123	N. Cullop, KC	2.0	G. McConnell, Chi	151	E. Plank, STL	4.9	D. Davenport, STL	2.39
B. Bailey, 2tm	9	T. Seaton, 2tm	120	J. Quinn, Bal	2.1	E. Plank, STL	147	B. Bailey, 2tm	4.9	F. Anderson, Buf	1.97
3 tied with	8	F. Allen, Pit	100	D. Davenport, STL	2.2	2 tied with	142	B. Groom, STL	4.8	J. Quinn, Bal	1.87

Earned Run Average		Component ERA		Hit Batsmen		Wild Pitches		Opponent Average		Opponent OBP	
E. Moseley, New	1.91	E. Plank, STL	1.74	H. Moran, New	18	C. Johnson, KC	13	D. Davenport, STL	.215	E. Plank, STL	.262
E. Plank, STL	2.08	D. Davenport, STL	1.82	F. Allen, Pit	11	C. Hendrix, Chi	11	E. Plank, STL	.218	D. Davenport, STL	.268
T. F. Brown, Chi	2.09	T. F. Brown, Chi	2.04	D. Crandall, STL	10	G. McConnell, Chi	10	A. Main, KC	.219	T. F. Brown, Chi	.279
G. McConnell, Chi	2.20	F. Anderson, Buf	2.17	C. Falkenberg, 2tm	10	H. Finneran, Bro	9	T. F. Brown, Chi	.220	F. Anderson, Buf	.285
D. Davenport, STL	2.20	A. Main, KC	2.19	6 tied with	9	2 tied with	8	F. Anderson, Buf	.222	E. Reulbach, New	.287

1915 Federal League Miscellaneous

Managers		
Baltimore	Otto Knabe	47-107
Brooklyn	Lee Magee	53-64
	John Ganzel	17-18
Buffalo	Harry Schlafly	13-28
	Walter Blair	1-1
	Harry Lord	60-49
Chicago	Joe Tinker	86-66
Kansas City	George Stovall	81-72
Newark	Bill Phillips	26-27
	Bill McKechnie	54-45
Pittsburgh	Rebel Oakes	86-67
St. Louis	Fielder Jones	87-67

Awards

STATS Most Valuable Player	Benny Kauff, of, Bro	
STATS Cy Young	George McConnell, Chi	
STATS Rookie of the Year	Ernie Johnson, ss, STL	
STATS Manager of the Year	Joe Tinker, Chi	

STATS All-Star Team

C	Art Wilson, Chi	.305	7	31
1B	Ed Konetchy, Pit	.314	10	93
2B	Lee Magee, Bro	.323	4	49
3B	George Perring, KC	.259	7	67
SS	Jimmy Esmond, New	.258	5	62
OF	Steve Evans, 2tm	.308	4	67
OF	Benny Kauff, Bro	.342	12	83
OF	Dutch Zwilling, Chi	.286	13	94
P	Nick Cullop, KC	22-11	2.44	111 K
P	Dave Davenport, STL	22-18	2.20	229 K
P	George McConnell, Chi	25-10	2.20	151 K
P	Eddie Plank, STL	21-11	2.08	147 K

Postseason

None

Outstanding Performances

None

1916 American League Standings

Team	Overall					Home Games						Road Games						Park Index		Record by Month					
	W	L	Pct	GB	DIF	W	L	R	OR	HR	OHR	W	L	R	OR	HR	OHR	Run	HR	M/A	May	June	July	Aug	S/O
Boston	91	63	.591	—	73	49	28	252	205	1	1	42	35	298	275	13	9	80	9	9-6	12-12	13-12	20-10	17-12	20-11
Chicago	89	65	.578	2.0	6	49	28	326	254	9	5	40	37	275	243	8	9	112	82	9-9	8-12	16-8	22-13	14-15	20-8
Detroit	87	67	.565	4.0	6	49	28	350	313	7	8	38	39	320	282	10	4	110	107	9-6	9-16	16-10	18-15	18-10	17-10
New York	80	74	.519	11.0	35	46	31	306	277	22	22	34	43	271	284	13	15	105	105	7-5	15-10	15-11	16-17	13-16	14-15
St. Louis	79	75	.513	12.0	3	45	32	290	238	7	10	34	43	298	307	7	5	87	142	5-9	9-15	15-12	19-13	21-9	10-17
Cleveland	77	77	.500	14.0	47	44	33	323	293	4	9	33	44	307	309	12	7	100	68	8-7	16-8	12-13	15-16	16-16	10-17
Washington	76	77	.497	14.5	16	49	28	294	248	6	1	27	49	242	295	6	13	100	36	8-6	16-9	10-15	15-15	11-17	16-15
Philadelphia	36	117	.235	54.5	0	23	53	231	399	15	17	13	64	216	377	4	9	108	249	3-10	11-14	3-19	2-28	8-23	9-23

Clinch Date—Boston 10/01.

Team Batting

Team	G	AB	R	OR	H	2B	3B	HR	TB	RBI	TBB	IBB	SO	HBP	SH	SF	SB	CS	SB%	GDP	Avg	OBP	Slg
Detroit	155	5193	670	595	1371	202	96	17	1816	560	545	—	529	29	202	—	190	—	—	—	.264	.337	.350
Cleveland	157	5064	630	602	1264	233	66	16	1677	533	522	—	605	33	234	—	160	—	—	—	.250	.324	.331
Chicago	155	5081	601	497	1277	194	100	17	1722	484	447	—	591	60	221	—	197	—	—	—	.251	.319	.339
St. Louis	158	5159	588	545	1262	181	50	14	1585	499	627	—	640	42	164	—	234	—	—	—	.245	.331	.307
New York	156	5198	577	561	1277	194	59	35	1694	492	516	—	632	36	159	—	179	—	—	—	.246	.318	.326
Boston	156	5018	550	480	1246	197	56	14	1597	454	464	—	482	38	236	—	129	—	—	—	.248	.317	.318
Washington	159	5114	536	543	1238	170	60	12	1564	468	535	—	597	50	164	—	185	—	—	—	.242	.320	.306
Philadelphia	154	5010	447	776	1212	169	65	19	1568	380	406	—	631	30	157	—	151	—	—	—	.242	.303	.313
AL Total	1250	40837	4599	4599	10147	1540	552	144	13223	3870	4062	—	4707	318	1537	—	1425	—	—	—	.248	.321	.324
AL Avg Team	156	5105	575	575	1268	193	69	18	1653	484	508	—	588	40	192	—	178	—	—	—	.248	.321	.324

Team Pitching

Team	G	CG	ShO	Rel	Sv	IP	H	R	ER	HR	SH	SF	HB	TBB	IBB	SO	WP	Bk	H/9	SO/9	BB/9	OAvg	OOBP	ERA
Chicago	155	73	20	140	15	1412.1	1189	497	371	14	—	—	26	405	—	644	22	5	7.6	4.1	2.6	.236	.296	2.36
Boston	156	76	24	103	16	1410.2	1221	480	388	10	—	—	38	463	—	584	26	3	7.8	3.7	3.0	.239	.307	2.48
St. Louis	158	74	9	141	13	1443.2	1292	545	414	15	—	—	38	478	—	505	18	4	8.1	3.1	3.0	.248	.316	2.58
Washington	159	85	11	107	7	1430.2	1271	543	424	14	—	—	37	490	—	706	44	6	8.0	4.4	3.1	.244	.314	2.67
New York	156	84	12	102	17	1428.0	1249	561	440	37	—	—	47	476	—	616	22	1	7.9	3.9	3.0	.244	.314	2.77
Cleveland	157	65	9	140	16	1410.0	1383	602	455	16	—	—	33	467	—	537	33	5	8.8	3.4	3.0	.264	.328	2.90
Detroit	155	81	8	126	13	1410.0	1254	595	465	12	—	—	62	578	—	531	37	3	8.0	3.4	3.7	.248	.333	2.97
Philadelphia	154	94	11	80	3	1343.2	1311	776	585	26	—	—	31	715	—	575	53	5	8.8	3.9	4.8	.267	.364	3.92
AL Total	1250	632	104	939	100	11289.0	10170	4599	3542	144	—	—	312	4072	—	4698	255	32	8.1	3.7	3.2	.248	.322	2.82
AL Avg Team	156	79	13	117	13	1411.0	1271	575	443	18	—	—	39	509	—	587	32	4	8.1	3.7	3.2	.248	.322	2.82

Team Fielding

Team	G	PO	A	E	TC	DP	PB	Pct
Boston	156	4220	2046	183	6449	108	14	.972
Chicago	155	4235	1975	205	6415	134	6	.968
Detroit	155	4222	2073	211	6506	110	13	.968
New York	156	4280	2085	219	6584	119	10	.967
Cleveland	157	4233	2186	232	6651	130	23	.965
Washington	159	4274	1888	232	6394	119	32	.964
St. Louis	158	4333	2187	248	6768	120	20	.963
Philadelphia	154	4021	2126	314	6461	126	19	.951
AL Total	1250	33818	16566	1844	52228	966	137	.965

Team vs. Team Records

	Bos	ChA	Cle	Det	NYA	Phi	StL	Was	Won
Bos	—	14	15	14	11	16	10	11	91
ChA	8	—	13	13	10	18	15	12	89
Cle	7	9	—	11	12	18	11	9	77
Det	8	9	11	—	14	18	13	14	87
NYA	11	12	10	8	—	15	9	15	80
Phi	6	4	4	4	7	—	5	6	36
StL	12	7	11	9	13	17	—	10	79
Was	11	10	13	8	7	15	12	—	76
Lost	63	65	77	67	74	117	75	77	

Seasons: Standings, Leaders

1916 American League Batting Leaders

Games		At-Bats		Runs		Hits		Doubles		Triples	
D. Pratt, StL	158	B. Shotton, StL	614	T. Cobb, Det	113	T. Speaker, Cle	211	J. Graney, Cle	41	J. Jackson, ChA	21
E. Foster, Was	158	E. Foster, Was	606	J. Graney, Cle	106	J. Jackson, ChA	202	T. Speaker, Cle	41	E. Collins, ChA	17
B. Shotton, StL	156	O. Vitt, Det	597	T. Speaker, Cle	102	T. Cobb, Det	201	J. Jackson, ChA	40	W. Pipp, NYA	15
3 tied with	155	D. Pratt, StL	596	B. Shotton, StL	97	G. Sisler, StL	177	D. Pratt, StL	35	B. Veach, Det	15
		J. Jackson, ChA	592	B. Veach, Det	92	B. Shotton, StL	174	B. Veach, Det	33	2 tied with	14

Home Runs		Total Bases		Runs Batted In		Walks		Intentional Walks		Strikeouts	
W. Pipp, NYA	12	J. Jackson, ChA	293	D. Pratt, StL	103	B. Shotton, StL	110	Statistic unavailable		W. Pipp, NYA	82
H. Baker, NYA	10	T. Speaker, Cle	274	W. Pipp, NYA	93	J. Graney, Cle	102			W. Miller, StL	76
H. Felsch, ChA	7	T. Cobb, Det	267	B. Veach, Det	91	E. Collins, ChA	86			J. Graney, Cle	72
W. Schang, Phi	7	B. Veach, Det	245	T. Speaker, Cle	79	T. Speaker, Cle	82			W. Witt, Phi	71
4 tied with	5	2 tied with	233	J. Jackson, ChA	78	H. Hooper, Bos	80			H. Felsch, ChA	67

Hit By Pitch		Sac Hits		Sac Flies		Stolen Bases		Caught Stealing		GDP	
J. Barry, Bos	17	B. Weaver, ChA	44	Statistic unavailable		T. Cobb, Det	68	Statistic unavailable		Statistic unavailable	
B. Weaver, ChA	13	R. Chapman, Cle	40			A. Marsans, StL	46				
W. Schang, Phi	10	E. Collins, ChA	39			B. Shotton, StL	41				
R. Morgan, Was	10	O. Vitt, Det	32			E. Collins, ChA	40				
2 tied with	9	2 tied with	30			T. Speaker, Cle	35				

Runs Created		Runs Created/27 Outs		Batting Average		On-Base Percentage		Slugging Percentage		OBP+Slugging	
T. Speaker, Cle	136	T. Speaker, Cle	10.02	T. Speaker, Cle	.386	T. Speaker, Cle	.470	T. Speaker, Cle	.502	T. Speaker, Cle	.972
T. Cobb, Det	123	T. Cobb, Det	8.93	T. Cobb, Det	.371	T. Cobb, Det	.452	J. Jackson, ChA	.495	T. Cobb, Det	.944
J. Jackson, ChA	115	J. Jackson, ChA	7.30	J. Jackson, ChA	.341	E. Collins, ChA	.405	T. Cobb, Det	.493	J. Jackson, ChA	.888
E. Collins, ChA	97	E. Collins, ChA	6.01	A. Strunk, Phi	.316	J. Jackson, ChA	.393	B. Veach, Det	.433	A. Strunk, Phi	.814
B. Shotton, StL	96	B. Veach, Det	5.75	L. Gardner, Bos	.308	A. Strunk, Phi	.393	H. Baker, NYA	.428	E. Collins, ChA	.802

1916 American League Pitching Leaders

Wins		Losses		Winning Percentage		Games		Games Started		Complete Games	
W. Johnson, Was	25	J. Bush, Phi	24	N. Cullop, NYA	.684	D. Davenport, StL	59	B. Ruth, Bos	41	W. Johnson, Was	36
B. Shawkey, NYA	24	E. Myers, Phi	23	E. Cicotte, ChA	.682	R. Russell, ChA	56	H. Coveleski, Det	39	E. Myers, Phi	31
B. Ruth, Bos	23	J. Nabors, Phi	20	B. Ruth, Bos	.657	B. Shawkey, NYA	53	W. Johnson, Was	38	J. Bush, Phi	25
H. Coveleski, Det	21	W. Johnson, Was	20	H. Coveleski, Det	.656	B. Gallia, Was	49	E. Myers, Phi	35	B. Ruth, Bos	23
H. Dauss, Det	19	C. Weilman, StL	18	R. Faber, ChA	.654	3 tied with	48	2 tied with	34	H. Coveleski, Det	22

Shutouts		Saves		Games Finished		Batters Faced		Innings Pitched		Hits Allowed	
B. Ruth, Bos	9	B. Shawkey, NYA	8	B. Shawkey, NYA	23	Statistic unavailable		W. Johnson, Was	369.2	W. Johnson, Was	290
J. Bush, Phi	8	A. Russell, NYA	6	J. Bagby, Cle	19			H. Coveleski, Det	324.1	E. Myers, Phi	280
D. Leonard, Bos	6	D. Leonard, Bos	6	D. Davenport, StL	17			B. Ruth, Bos	323.2	B. Gallia, Was	278
R. Russell, ChA	5	J. Bagby, Cle	5	J. Dubuc, Det	16			E. Myers, Phi	315.0	H. Coveleski, Det	278
2 tied with	4	E. Cicotte, ChA	5	6 tied with	15			D. Davenport, StL	290.2	D. Davenport, StL	267

Home Runs Allowed		Walks		Walks/9 Innings		Strikeouts		Strikeouts/9 Innings		Strikeout/Walk Ratio	
A. Russell, NYA	8	E. Myers, Phi	168	R. Russell, ChA	1.4	W. Johnson, Was	228	W. Johnson, Was	5.6	W. Johnson, Was	2.78
E. Myers, Phi	7	J. Bush, Phi	130	H. Coveleski, Det	1.7	E. Myers, Phi	182	L. Williams, ChA	5.5	R. Russell, ChA	2.67
4 tied with	6	B. Ruth, Bos	118	E. Shore, Bos	2.0	B. Ruth, Bos	170	H. Harper, Was	5.4	D. Leonard, Bos	2.18
		H. Harper, Was	101	W. Johnson, Was	2.0	J. Bush, Phi	157	E. Myers, Phi	5.2	L. Williams, ChA	2.12
		D. Davenport, StL	100	D. Leonard, Bos	2.2	H. Harper, Was	149	J. Bush, Phi	4.9	H. Coveleski, Det	1.71

Earned Run Average		Component ERA		Hit Batsmen		Wild Pitches		Opponent Average		Opponent OBP	
B. Ruth, Bos	1.75	R. Russell, ChA	1.60	H. Dauss, Det	16	J. Bush, Phi	15	B. Ruth, Bos	.201	R. Russell, ChA	.254
E. Cicotte, ChA	1.78	W. Johnson, Was	1.79	E. Myers, Phi	14	E. Myers, Phi	13	B. Shawkey, NYA	.209	W. Johnson, Was	.270
W. Johnson, Was	1.90	B. Ruth, Bos	1.85	B. James, Det	11	H. Harper, Was	9	E. Cicotte, ChA	.218	B. Shawkey, NYA	.273
H. Coveleski, Det	1.97	B. Shawkey, NYA	1.86	H. Coveleski, Det	11	W. Johnson, Was	9	J. Bush, Phi	.219	B. Ruth, Bos	.280
R. Faber, ChA	2.02	E. Cicotte, ChA	1.99	2 tied with	9	3 tied with	8	W. Johnson, Was	.220	H. Coveleski, Det	.282

1916 American League Miscellaneous

Managers

Boston	Bill Carrigan	91-63
Chicago	Pants Rowland	89-65
Cleveland	Lee Fohl	77-77
Detroit	Hughie Jennings	87-67
New York	Wild Bill Donovan	80-74
Philadelphia	Connie Mack	36-117
St. Louis	Fielder Jones	79-75
Washington	Clark Griffith	76-77

Awards

STATS Most Valuable Player	Tris Speaker, of, Cle
STATS Cy Young	Babe Ruth, Bos
STATS Rookie of the Year	Jim Bagby, p, Cle
STATS Manager of the Year	Fielder Jones, StL

STATS All-Star Team

C	Les Nunamaker, NYA	.296	0	28
1B	Wally Pipp, NYA	.262	12	93
2B	Eddie Collins, ChA	.308	0	52
3B	Larry Gardner, Bos	.308	2	62
SS	Roger Peckinpaugh, NYA	.255	4	58
OF	Ty Cobb, Det	.371	5	68
OF	Joe Jackson, ChA	.341	3	78
OF	Tris Speaker, Cle	.386	2	79
P	Harry Coveleski, Det	21-11	1.97	108 K
P	Walter Johnson, Was	25-20	1.90	228 K
P	Babe Ruth, Bos	23-12	1.75	170 K
P	Bob Shawkey, NYA	24-14	2.21	122 K

Postseason

World Series	Boston (AL) 4 vs. Brooklyn (NL) 1

Outstanding Performances

No-Hitters

Rube Foster, Bos	vs. NYA on June 21
Joe Bush, Phi	vs. Cle on August 26
Dutch Leonard, Bos	vs. StL on August 30

1916 National League Standings

Team	Overall					Home Games						Road Games						Park Index		Record by Month					
	W	L	Pct	GB	DIF	W	L	R	OR	HR	OHR	W	L	R	OR	HR	OHR	Run	HR	M/A	May	June	July	Aug	S/O
Brooklyn	94	60	.610	—	152	50	27	300	233	19	9	44	33	285	238	9	15	102	117	5-3	17-9	14-11	18-11	18-10	22-16
Philadelphia	91	62	.595	2.5	18	50	29	281	233	29	17	41	33	300	256	13	11	87	180	7-3	13-14	13-11	16-10	18-11	24-13
Boston	89	63	.586	4.0	10	41	31	224	207	6	4	48	32	318	246	16	20	85	31	5-4	11-15	14-8	18-9	21-10	20-17
New York	86	66	.566	7.0	0	47	30	291	229	21	23	39	36	306	275	21	18	87	110	1-8	20-6	9-15	15-14	11-15	30-8
Chicago	67	86	.438	26.5	2	37	41	309	317	34	22	30	45	211	224	12	10	138	245	8-5	11-18	11-11	14-15	11-19	12-18
Pittsburgh	65	89	.422	29.0	0	37	40	268	298	9	5	28	49	216	288	11	19	112	47	6-8	11-14	11-9	11-18	16-15	10-25
Cincinnati	60	93	.392	33.5	0	32	44	242	312	4	10	28	49	263	305	10	25	99	41	7-8	13-14	8-13	10-22	8-21	14-15
St. Louis	60	93	.392	33.5	1	36	40	251	295	12	15	24	53	225	334	13	16	99	94	7-7	11-17	11-13	14-17	12-14	5-25

Clinch Date—Brooklyn 10/03.

Team Batting

Team	G	AB	R	OR	H	2B	3B	HR	TB	RBI	TBB	IBB	SO	HBP	SH	SF	SB	CS	SB%	GDP	Avg	OBP	Slg
New York	155	5152	597	504	1305	188	74	42	1767	500	356	—	558	44	134	—	206	—	—	—	.253	.307	.343
Brooklyn	156	5234	585	471	1366	195	80	28	1805	493	355	—	550	41	203	—	187	—	—	—	.261	.313	.345
Philadelphia	154	4985	581	489	1244	223	53	42	1699	486	399	—	571	34	179	—	149	—	—	—	.250	.310	.341
Boston	158	5075	542	453	1181	166	73	22	1559	472	437	—	646	46	202	—	141	—	—	—	.233	.299	.307
Chicago	156	5179	520	541	1237	194	56	46	1681	456	399	—	662	34	166	—	133	—	—	—	.239	.298	.325
Cincinnati	155	5254	505	617	1336	187	88	14	1741	422	362	—	573	40	127	—	157	—	—	—	.254	.307	.331
Pittsburgh	157	5181	484	586	1246	147	91	20	1635	406	372	—	618	50	166	—	173	—	—	—	.240	.298	.316
St. Louis	153	5030	476	629	1223	155	74	25	1601	413	335	—	651	33	116	—	182	—	—	—	.243	.295	.318
NL Total	1244	41090	4290	4290	10138	1455	589	239	13488	3648	3015	—	4829	322	1293	—	1328	—	—	—	.247	.303	.328
NL Avg Team	156	5136	536	536	1267	182	74	30	1686	456	377	—	604	40	162	—	166	—	—	—	.247	.303	.328

Team Pitching

Team	G	CG	ShO	Rel	Sv	IP	H	R	ER	HR	SH	SF	HB	TBB	IBB	SO	WP	Bk	H/9	SO/9	BB/9	OAvg	OOBP	ERA
Brooklyn	156	96	22	92	9	1427.1	1201	471	336	24	152	—	38	372	—	634	34	2	7.6	4.0	2.3	.233	.289	2.12
Boston	158	97	23	82	11	1415.2	1206	453	345	24	130	—	30	325	—	644	23	2	7.7	4.1	2.1	.235	.285	2.19
Philadelphia	154	97	25	78	9	1382.1	1238	489	362	28	158	—	45	295	—	601	34	2	8.1	3.9	1.9	.244	.292	2.36
New York	155	88	22	103	12	1397.1	1267	504	404	41	127	—	39	310	—	638	38	2	8.2	4.1	2.0	.245	.293	2.60
Chicago	156	72	17	119	13	1416.2	1265	541	417	32	194	—	43	365	—	616	37	0	8.0	3.9	2.3	.244	.299	2.65
Pittsburgh	157	88	11	102	7	1419.2	1277	586	436	24	193	—	36	443	—	596	21	7	8.1	3.8	2.8	.247	.311	2.76
Cincinnati	155	86	7	98	6	1408.0	1356	617	485	35	161	—	44	461	—	569	29	1	8.7	3.6	2.9	.261	.326	3.10
St. Louis	153	58	13	127	15	1355.0	1331	629	473	31	177	—	42	445	—	529	29	3	8.8	3.5	3.0	.265	.330	3.14
NL Total	1244	682	140	801	82	11222.0	10141	4290	3258	239	1292	—	317	3016	—	4827	245	19	8.1	3.9	2.4	.247	.303	2.61
NL Avg Team	156	85	18	100	10	1402.0	1268	536	407	30	162	—	40	377	—	603	31	2	8.1	3.9	2.4	.247	.303	2.61

Team Fielding

Team	G	PO	A	E	TC	DP	PB	Pct
Boston	158	4263	2052	212	6527	124	17	.968
New York	155	4184	2031	217	6432	108	17	.966
Cincinnati	155	4207	2091	228	6526	126	19	.965
Brooklyn	156	4259	1910	224	6393	90	19	.965
Philadelphia	154	4138	2004	234	6376	119	26	.963
Pittsburgh	157	4251	1902	260	6413	97	19	.959
Chicago	156	4233	2154	286	6673	104	20	.957
St. Louis	153	4049	2076	278	6403	124	22	.957
NL Total	1244	33584	16220	1939	51743	892	159	.963

Team vs. Team Records

	Bos	Bro	ChN	Cin	NYG	Phi	Pit	StL	Won
Bos	—	13	14	13	11	11	14	13	89
Bro	9	—	15	15	15	11	14	15	94
ChN	7	7	—	9	10	8	12	14	67
Cin	9	7	13	—	5	5	13	8	60
NYG	10	7	12	16	—	9	17	15	86
Phi	11	11	14	17	13	—	13	12	91
Pit	8	8	10	9	5	9	—	16	65
StL	9	7	8	14	7	9	6	—	60
Lost	63	60	86	93	66	62	89	93	

1916 National League Batting Leaders

Games		At-Bats		Runs		Hits		Doubles		Triples	
E. Konetchy, Bos	158	G. Burns, NYG	623	G. Burns, NYG	105	H. Chase, Cin	184	B. Niehoff, Phi	42	B. Hinchman, Pit	16
B. Herzog, 2tm	156	R. Maranville, Bos	604	M. Carey, Pit	90	D. Robertson, NYG	180	Z. Wheat, Bro	32	R. Hornsby, StL	15
T. Griffith, Cin	155	M. Carey, Pit	599	D. Robertson, NYG	88	Z. Wheat, Bro	177	D. Paskert, Phi	30	E. Roush, 2tm	15
R. Maranville, Bos	155	T. Griffith, Cin	595	H. Groh, Cin	85	B. Hinchman, Pit	175	4 tied with	29	B. Kauff, NYG	15
G. Burns, NYG	155	D. Robertson, NYG	587	D. Paskert, Phi	82	G. Burns, NYG	174			2 tied with	14

Home Runs		Total Bases		Runs Batted In		Walks		Intentional Walks		Strikeouts	
C. Williams, ChN	12	Z. Wheat, Bro	262	H. Zimmerman, 2tm	83	H. Groh, Cin	84	Statistic unavailable		G. Cravath, Phi	89
D. Robertson, NYG	12	D. Robertson, NYG	250	H. Chase, Cin	82	V. Saier, ChN	79			G. Neale, Cin	79
G. Cravath, Phi	11	H. Chase, Cin	249	B. Hinchman, Pit	76	D. Bancroft, Phi	74			B. Betzel, StL	77
B. Kauff, NYG	9	B. Hinchman, Pit	237	B. Kauff, NYG	74	B. Kauff, NYG	68			D. Paskert, Phi	76
Z. Wheat, Bro	9	G. Burns, NYG	229	Z. Wheat, Bro	73	G. Cravath, Phi	64			R. Maranville, Bos	69

Hit By Pitch		Sac Hits		Sac Flies		Stolen Bases		Caught Stealing		GDP	
A. Fletcher, NYG	14	M. Flack, ChN	39	Statistic unavailable		M. Carey, Pit	63	Statistic unavailable		Statistic unavailable	
B. Herzog, 2tm	10	J. Daubert, Bro	35			B. Kauff, NYG	40				
C. Williams, ChN	9	M. Mowrey, Bro	31			B. Bescher, StL	39				
F. Merkle, 2tm	9	P. Whitted, Phi	30			G. Burns, NYG	37				
2 tied with	8	G. Cutshaw, Bro	29			B. Herzog, 2tm	34				

Runs Created		Runs Created/27 Outs		Batting Average		On-Base Percentage		Slugging Percentage		OBP+Slugging	
Z. Wheat, Bro	94	G. Cravath, Phi	6.25	H. Chase, Cin	.339	G. Cravath, Phi	.379	Z. Wheat, Bro	.461	C. Williams, ChN	.831
G. Burns, NYG	88	Z. Wheat, Bro	6.09	J. Daubert, Bro	.316	H. Chase, Cin	.378	H. Chase, Cin	.459	Z. Wheat, Bro	.828
B. Kauff, NYG	86	C. Williams, ChN	5.83	B. Hinchman, Pit	.315	C. Williams, ChN	.372	C. Williams, ChN	.459	H. Chase, Cin	.822
B. Hinchman, Pit	86	R. Hornsby, StL	5.83	R. Hornsby, StL	.313	J. Daubert, Bro	.371	R. Hornsby, StL	.444	G. Cravath, Phi	.819
2 tied with	84	B. Hinchman, Pit	5.61	Z. Wheat, Bro	.312	H. Groh, Cin	.370	G. Cravath, Phi	.440	R. Hornsby, StL	.814

1916 National League Pitching Leaders

Wins		Losses		Winning Percentage		Games		Games Started		Complete Games	
P. Alexander, Phi	33	L. Meadows, StL	23	T. Hughes, Bos	.842	L. Meadows, StL	51	P. Alexander, Phi	45	P. Alexander, Phi	38
J. Pfeffer, Bro	25	P. Schneider, Cin	19	P. Alexander, Phi	.733	P. Alexander, Phi	48	F. Toney, Cin	38	J. Pfeffer, Bro	30
E. Rixey, Phi	22	A. Schulz, Cin	19	J. Pfeffer, Bro	.694	A. Mamaux, Pit	45	D. Rudolph, Bos	38	D. Rudolph, Bos	27
A. Mamaux, Pit	21	F. Toney, Cin	17	E. Rixey, Phi	.688	R. Ames, StL	45	A. Mamaux, Pit	37	A. Mamaux, Pit	26
2 tied with	19	2 tied with	16	R. Marquard, Bro	.684	3 tied with	44	2 tied with	36	A. Demaree, Phi	25

Shutouts		Saves		Games Finished		Batters Faced		Innings Pitched		Hits Allowed	
P. Alexander, Phi	16	R. Ames, StL	8	S. Williams, StL	21	P. Alexander, Phi	1500	P. Alexander, Phi	389.0	P. Alexander, Phi	323
J. Pfeffer, Bro	6	G. Packard, ChN	5	T. Hughes, Bos	19	J. Pfeffer, Bro	1298	J. Pfeffer, Bro	328.2	J. Pfeffer, Bro	274
L. Tyler, Bos	6	R. Marquard, Bro	5	F. Schupp, NYG	17	A. Mamaux, Pit	1291	D. Rudolph, Bos	312.0	H. Vaughn, ChN	269
4 tied with	5	T. Hughes, Bos	5	G. Packard, ChN	17	L. Meadows, StL	1217	A. Mamaux, Pit	310.0	D. Rudolph, Bos	266
		3 tied with	3	R. Ames, StL	17	D. Rudolph, Bos	1206	F. Toney, Cin	300.0	A. Mamaux, Pit	264

Home Runs Allowed		Walks		Walks/9 Innings		Strikeouts		Strikeouts/9 Innings		Strikeout/Walk Ratio	
P. Perritt, NYG	11	A. Mamaux, Pit	136	D. Rudolph, Bos	1.1	P. Alexander, Phi	167	L. Cheney, Bro	5.9	D. Rudolph, Bos	3.50
J. Tesreau, NYG	9	L. Meadows, StL	119	P. Alexander, Phi	1.2	L. Cheney, Bro	166	C. Hendrix, ChN	4.8	P. Alexander, Phi	3.34
G. McConnell, ChN	8	L. Cheney, Bro	105	A. Demaree, Phi	1.5	A. Mamaux, Pit	163	A. Mamaux, Pit	4.7	R. Marquard, Bro	2.82
4 tied with	7	A. Schulz, Cin	93	S. Sallee, 2tm	1.6	F. Toney, Cin	146	R. Marquard, Bro	4.7	A. Demaree, Phi	2.71
		P. Schneider, Cin	82	R. Marquard, Bro	1.7	H. Vaughn, ChN	144	F. Anderson, NYG	4.7	F. Anderson, NYG	2.58

Earned Run Average		Component ERA		Hit Batsmen		Wild Pitches		Opponent Average		Opponent OBP	
P. Alexander, Phi	1.55	P. Alexander, Phi	1.83	J. Pfeffer, Bro	17	L. Cheney, Bro	15	L. Cheney, Bro	.198	D. Rudolph, Bos	.261
R. Marquard, Bro	1.58	R. Marquard, Bro	1.87	L. Meadows, StL	14	E. Rixey, Phi	13	W. Cooper, Pit	.215	P. Alexander, Phi	.262
E. Rixey, Phi	1.85	D. Rudolph, Bos	1.89	P. Schneider, Cin	13	L. Meadows, StL	11	P. Ragan, Bos	.218	R. Marquard, Bro	.267
W. Cooper, Pit	1.87	P. Ragan, Bos	1.92	5 tied with	10	3 tied with	9	F. Miller, Pit	.226	P. Ragan, Bos	.270
J. Pfeffer, Bro	1.92	W. Cooper, Pit	2.00					L. Tyler, Bos	.226	L. Tyler, Bos	.276

1916 National League Miscellaneous

Managers

Boston	George Stallings	89-63
Brooklyn	Wilbert Robinson	94-60
Chicago	Joe Tinker	67-86
Cincinnati	Buck Herzog	34-49
	Ivy Wingo	1-1
	Christy Mathewson	25-43
New York	John McGraw	86-66
Philadelphia	Pat Moran	91-62
Pittsburgh	Nixey Callahan	65-89
St. Louis	Miller Huggins	60-93

Awards

STATS Most Valuable Player	Pete Alexander, p, Phi
STATS Cy Young	Pete Alexander, Phi
STATS Rookie of the Year	Rogers Hornsby, 3b, StL
STATS Manager of the Year	Wilbert Robinson, Bro

STATS All-Star Team

C	Ivy Wingo, Cin	.245	2	40
1B	Hal Chase, Cin	.339	4	82
2B	Larry Doyle, 2tm	.278	3	54
3B	Rogers Hornsby, StL	.313	6	65
SS	Art Fletcher, NYG	.286	3	66
OF	Gavy Cravath, Phi	.283	11	70
OF	Bill Hinchman, Pit	.315	4	76
OF	Zack Wheat, Bro	.312	9	73
P	Pete Alexander, Phi	33-12	1.55	167 K
P	Larry Cheney, Bro	18-12	1.92	166 K
P	Jeff Pfeffer, Bro	25-11	1.92	128 K
P	Eppa Rixey, Phi	22-10	1.85	134 K

Postseason

World Series	Brooklyn (NL) 1 vs. Boston (AL) 4

Outstanding Performances

No-Hitters

Tom Hughes, Bos   vs. Pit on June 16

1917 American League Standings

Team	Overall					Home Games						Road Games						Park Index		Record by Month					
	W	L	Pct	GB	DIF	W	L	R	OR	HR	OHR	W	L	R	OR	HR	OHR	Run	HR	M/A	May	June	July	Aug	S/O
Chicago	100	54	.649	—	126	56	21	327	204	7	3	44	33	329	260	11	7	90	56	10-6	17-7	16-10	18-14	22-9	17-8
Boston	90	62	.592	9.0	53	45	33	293	245	3	4	45	29	262	209	11	8	108	35	9-4	18-6	14-14	18-11	16-12	15-15
Cleveland	88	66	.571	12.0	5	43	34	317	314	5	8	45	32	267	229	8	9	127	76	8-9	14-12	12-13	19-13	16-13	19-6
Detroit	78	75	.510	21.5	0	34	41	285	303	5	5	44	34	354	274	20	7	97	39	5-9	10-12	17-10	20-14	14-15	12-15
Washington	74	79	.484	25.5	4	42	36	264	255	1	3	32	43	279	311	3	9	85	32	4-9	9-16	12-14	15-17	17-8	17-15
New York	71	82	.464	28.5	2	35	40	269	292	20	24	36	42	255	266	7	4	112	416	7-5	13-11	15-13	14-16	7-20	15-17
St. Louis	57	97	.370	43.0	0	31	46	252	337	7	11	26	51	259	350	8	8	97	113	8-7	7-16	10-17	11-22	13-18	8-17
Philadelphia	55	98	.359	44.5	0	29	47	264	319	11	17	26	51	265	372	6	6	93	236	6-8	7-15	10-15	11-19	10-20	11-21

Clinch Date—Chicago 9/21.

Team Batting

Team	G	AB	R	OR	H	2B	3B	HR	TB	RBI	TBB	IBB	SO	HBP	SH	SF	SB	CS	SB%	GDP	Avg	OBP	Slg
Chicago	156	5057	656	464	1281	152	81	18	1649	535	522	—	479	47	235	—	219	—	—	—	.253	.329	.326
Detroit	154	5093	639	577	1317	204	77	25	1750	535	483	—	476	45	193	—	163	—	—	—	.259	.328	.344
Cleveland	156	4994	584	543	1224	218	64	13	1609	475	549	—	596	34	255	—	105	—	—	—	.245	.324	.322
Boston	157	5048	555	454	1243	198	64	14	1611	476	466	—	473	34	310	—	105	—	—	—	.246	.314	.319
Washington	157	5142	543	566	1238	173	70	4	1563	462	500	—	574	43	179	—	166	—	—	—	.241	.313	.304
Philadelphia	154	5109	529	691	1296	177	62	17	1648	457	435	—	519	33	205	—	112	—	—	—	.254	.316	.323
New York	155	5136	524	558	1226	172	52	27	1583	445	496	—	535	38	188	—	136	—	—	—	.239	.310	.308
St. Louis	155	5091	511	687	1250	183	63	15	1604	425	405	—	540	31	166	—	157	—	—	—	.246	.305	.315
AL Total	1244	40670	4541	4540	10075	1477	533	133	13017	3810	3856	—	4192	306	1731	—	1268	—	—	—	.248	.318	.320
AL Avg Team	156	5084	568	568	1259	185	67	17	1627	476	482	—	524	38	216	—	159	—	—	—	.248	.318	.320

Team Pitching

Team	G	CG	ShO	Rel	Sv	IP	H	R	ER	HR	SH	SF	HB	TBB	IBB	SO	WP	Bk	H/9	SO/9	BB/9	OAvg	OOBP	ERA
Chicago	156	78	22	112	21	1424.1	1236	464	342	10	—	—	35	413	—	517	12	4	7.8	3.3	2.6	.237	.297	2.16
Boston	157	115	15	51	7	1421.1	1197	454	347	12	—	—	51	413	—	509	29	1	7.6	3.2	2.6	.231	.294	2.20
Cleveland	156	73	20	129	22	1412.2	1270	543	396	17	—	—	32	438	—	451	20	2	8.1	2.9	2.8	.246	.309	2.52
Detroit	154	78	20	113	15	1396.1	1209	577	397	12	—	—	55	504	—	516	18	1	7.8	3.3	3.2	.239	.314	2.56
New York	155	87	10	93	6	1411.1	1280	558	417	28	—	—	36	427	—	571	20	2	8.2	3.6	2.7	.251	.313	2.66
Washington	157	84	21	98	10	1413.0	1217	566	432	12	—	—	36	537	—	637	42	3	7.8	4.1	3.4	.238	.315	2.75
St. Louis	155	66	12	143	12	1385.1	1320	687	493	19	—	—	36	537	—	429	35	1	8.6	2.8	3.5	.255	.329	3.20
Philadelphia	154	80	8	95	8	1365.2	1310	691	496	23	—	—	23	562	—	516	37	2	8.6	3.4	3.7	.250	.326	3.27
AL Total	1244	661	128	834	101	11230.0	10039	4540	3320	133	—	—	304	3831	—	4146	213	16	8.1	3.3	3.1	.248	.316	2.66
AL Avg Team	156	83	16	104	13	1403.0	1255	568	415	17	—	—	38	479	—	518	27	2	8.1	3.3	3.1	.248	.316	2.66

Team Fielding

Team	G	PO	A	E	TC	DP	PB	Pct
Boston	157	4266	2110	183	6559	116	22	.972
Chicago	156	4253	1793	204	6250	117	10	.967
New York	155	4231	2054	225	6510	129	15	.965
Cleveland	156	4238	2176	242	6656	136	12	.964
Detroit	154	4186	1983	234	6403	95	21	.963
Philadelphia	154	4078	2064	251	6393	106	17	.961
Washington	157	4246	1889	251	6386	127	22	.961
St. Louis	155	4131	2099	281	6511	139	20	.957
AL Total	1244	33629	16168	1871	51668	965	139	.964

Team vs. Team Records

	Bos	ChA	Cle	Det	NYA	Phi	StL	Was	Won
Bos	—	10	10	9	13	18	17	13	90
ChA	12	—	14	16	12	15	16	15	100
Cle	12	8	—	12	15	15	14	11	88
Det	12	6	10	—	13	12	14	11	78
NYA	9	10	7	9	—	15	13	8	71
Phi	3	7	6	10	7	—	11	11	55
StL	5	6	8	8	9	11	—	10	57
Was	9	7	11	11	13	11	12	—	74
Lost	62	54	66	75	82	98	97	79	

1917 American League Batting Leaders

Games			At-Bats			Runs			Hits			Doubles			Triples		
E. Scott, Bos	157		T. Cobb, Det	588		D. Bush, Det	112		T. Cobb, Det	225		T. Cobb, Det	44		T. Cobb, Det	24	
R. Chapman, Cle	156		W. Pipp, NYA	587		T. Cobb, Det	107		G. Sisler, StL	190		T. Speaker, Cle	42		J. Jackson, ChA	17	
E. Collins, ChA	156		S. Rice, Was	586		R. Chapman, Cle	98		T. Speaker, Cle	184		B. Veach, Det	31		J. Judge, Was	15	
3 tied with	155		D. Bush, Det	581		J. Jackson, ChA	91		B. Veach, Det	182		G. Sisler, StL	30		R. Chapman, Cle	13	
			C. Milan, Was	579		E. Collins, ChA	91		2 tied with	177		B. Roth, Cle	30		3 tied with	12	

Home Runs			Total Bases			Runs Batted In			Walks			Intentional Walks			Strikeouts		
W. Pipp, NYA	9		T. Cobb, Det	335		B. Veach, Det	103		J. Graney, Cle	94		Statistic unavailable			B. Roth, Cle	73	
B. Veach, Det	8		B. Veach, Det	261		H. Felsch, ChA	102		E. Collins, ChA	89					B. D. Jacobson, StL	67	
P. Bodie, Phi	7		T. Speaker, Cle	254		T. Cobb, Det	102		H. Hooper, Bos	80					W. Pipp, NYA	66	
3 tied with	6		G. Sisler, StL	244		H. Heilmann, Det	86		D. Bush, Det	80					S. Risberg, ChA	65	
			P. Bodie, Phi	233		J. Jackson, ChA	75		N. Leibold, ChA	74					R. Chapman, Cle	65	

Hit By Pitch			Sac Hits			Sac Flies			Stolen Bases			Caught Stealing			GDP		
W. Schang, Phi	9		R. Chapman, Cle	67		Statistic unavailable			T. Cobb, Det	55		Statistic unavailable			Statistic unavailable		
B. Veach, Det	9		J. Barry, Bos	54					E. Collins, ChA	53							
E. Miller, NYA	9		R. Grover, Phi	43					R. Chapman, Cle	52							
T. Spencer, Det	9		E. Scott, Bos	41					B. Roth, Cle	51							
5 tied with	7		L. Gardner, Bos	40					G. Sisler, StL	37							

Runs Created			Runs Created/27 Outs			Batting Average			On-Base Percentage			Slugging Percentage			OBP+Slugging		
T. Cobb, Det	144		T. Cobb, Det	9.87		T. Cobb, Det	.383		T. Cobb, Det	.444		T. Cobb, Det	.570		T. Cobb, Det	1.014	
T. Speaker, Cle	111		T. Speaker, Cle	8.15		G. Sisler, StL	.352		T. Speaker, Cle	.432		T. Speaker, Cle	.486		T. Speaker, Cle	.918	
B. Veach, Det	108		B. Veach, Det	6.78		T. Speaker, Cle	.352		J. Harris, Cle	.398		B. Veach, Det	.457		B. Veach, Det	.850	
J. Jackson, ChA	99		G. Sisler, StL	6.57		B. Veach, Det	.319		B. Veach, Det	.393		G. Sisler, StL	.453		G. Sisler, StL	.843	
E. Collins, ChA	99		J. Jackson, ChA	6.51		H. Felsch, ChA	.308		G. Sisler, StL	.390		J. Jackson, ChA	.429		J. Jackson, ChA	.805	

1917 American League Pitching Leaders

Wins			Losses			Winning Percentage			Games			Games Started			Complete Games		
E. Cicotte, ChA	28		A. Sothoron, StL	19		E. Klepfer, Cle	.778		D. Danforth, ChA	50		D. Davenport, StL	39		B. Ruth, Bos	35	
B. Ruth, Bos	24		B. Groom, StL	19		R. Russell, ChA	.750		J. Bagby, Cle	49		B. Ruth, Bos	38		W. Johnson, Was	30	
J. Bagby, Cle	23		D. Davenport, StL	17		C. Mays, Bos	.710		E. Cicotte, ChA	49		J. Bagby, Cle	37		E. Cicotte, ChA	29	
W. Johnson, Was	23		D. Leonard, Bos	17		E. Cicotte, ChA	.700		A. Sothoron, StL	48		D. Leonard, Bos	36		C. Mays, Bos	27	
C. Mays, Bos	22		J. Bush, Phi	17		L. Williams, ChA	.680		3 tied with	47		S. Coveleski, Cle	36		2 tied with	26	

Shutouts			Saves			Games Finished			Batters Faced			Innings Pitched			Hits Allowed		
S. Coveleski, Cle	9		D. Danforth, ChA	9		D. Danforth, ChA	26		Statistic unavailable			E. Cicotte, ChA	346.2		J. Bagby, Cle	277	
J. Bagby, Cle	8		J. Bagby, Cle	7		G. Cunningham, Det	24					B. Ruth, Bos	326.1		D. Davenport, StL	273	
W. Johnson, Was	8		B. Boland, Det	6		D. Ayers, Was	21					W. Johnson, Was	326.0		A. Sothoron, StL	259	
E. Cicotte, ChA	7		F. Coumbe, Cle	5		S. Love, NYA	18					J. Bagby, Cle	320.2		D. Leonard, Bos	257	
2 tied with	6		4 tied with	4		6 tied with	14					S. Coveleski, Cle	298.2		W. Johnson, Was	248	

Home Runs Allowed			Walks			Walks/9 Innings			Strikeouts			Strikeouts/9 Innings			Strikeout/Walk Ratio		
R. Caldwell, NYA	8		J. Shaw, Was	123		R. Russell, ChA	1.5		W. Johnson, Was	188		W. Johnson, Was	5.2		W. Johnson, Was	2.76	
R. Schauer, Phi	6		J. Bush, Phi	111		G. Mogridge, NYA	1.8		E. Cicotte, ChA	150		H. Harper, Was	5.0		E. Cicotte, ChA	2.14	
J. Bagby, Cle	6		B. Ruth, Bos	108		E. Cicotte, ChA	1.8		D. Leonard, Bos	144		J. Bush, Phi	4.7		D. Leonard, Bos	2.00	
3 tied with	5		H. Harper, Was	106		W. Johnson, Was	1.9		S. Coveleski, Cle	133		D. Leonard, Bos	4.4		W. Mitchell, Det	1.74	
			D. Davenport, StL	105		J. Bagby, Cle	2.0		B. Ruth, Bos	128		S. Coveleski, Cle	4.0		R. Russell, ChA	1.69	

Earned Run Average			Component ERA			Hit Batsmen			Wild Pitches			Opponent Average			Opponent OBP		
E. Cicotte, ChA	1.53		E. Cicotte, ChA	1.48		C. Mays, Bos	14		D. Davenport, StL	11		S. Coveleski, Cle	.193		E. Cicotte, ChA	.248	
C. Mays, Bos	1.74		S. Coveleski, Cle	1.61		W. Mitchell, Det	13		E. Myers, Phi	10		E. Cicotte, ChA	.202		S. Coveleski, Cle	.260	
S. Coveleski, Cle	1.81		W. Johnson, Was	1.71		E. Shore, Bos	12		H. Harper, Was	10		B. Ruth, Bos	.210		W. Johnson, Was	.262	
R. Faber, ChA	1.92		B. Ruth, Bos	1.99		B. James, Det	12		B. Gallia, Was	9		W. Johnson, Was	.211		R. Russell, ChA	.278	
R. Russell, ChA	1.95		C. Mays, Bos	2.02		W. Johnson, Was	12		4 tied with	7		C. Mays, Bos	.221		J. Bagby, Cle	.281	

1917 American League Miscellaneous

Managers

Boston	Jack Barry	90-62
Chicago	Pants Rowland	100-54
Cleveland	Lee Fohl	88-66
Detroit	Hughie Jennings	78-75
New York	Wild Bill Donovan	71-82
Philadelphia	Connie Mack	55-98
St. Louis	Fielder Jones	57-97
Washington	Clark Griffith	74-79

Awards

STATS Most Valuable Player	Ty Cobb, of, Det
STATS Cy Young	Eddie Cicotte, ChA
STATS Rookie of the Year	Joe Harris, 1b, Cle
STATS Manager of the Year	Pants Rowland, ChA

STATS All-Star Team

C	Wally Schang, Phi	.285	3	36
1B	George Sisler, StL	.353	2	52
2B	Eddie Collins, ChA	.289	0	67
3B	Home Run Baker, NYA	.282	6	71
SS	Ray Chapman, Cle	.302	2	36
OF	Ty Cobb, Det	.383	6	102
OF	Tris Speaker, Cle	.352	2	60
OF	Bobby Veach, Det	.319	8	103
P	Jim Bagby, Cle	23-13	1.96	83 K
P	Eddie Cicotte, ChA	28-12	1.53	150 K
P	Carl Mays, Bos	22-9	1.74	91 K
P	Babe Ruth, Bos	24-13	2.01	128 K

Postseason

World Series	Chicago (AL) 4 vs. New York (NL) 2

Outstanding Performances

No-Hitters

Eddie Cicotte, ChA	@ StL on April 14
G. Mogridge, NYA	@ Bos on April 24
Ernie Koob, StL	vs. ChA on May 5
Bob Groom, StL	vs. ChA on May 6

1917 National League Standings

Team	Overall					Home Games						Road Games						Park Index		Record by Month					
	W	L	Pct	GB	DIF	W	L	R	OR	HR	OHR	W	L	R	OR	HR	OHR	Run	HR	M/A	May	June	July	Aug	S/O
New York	98	56	.636	—	151	50	28	294	220	21	17	48	28	341	237	18	12	87	123	8-4	12-7	18-11	19-8	19-12	22-14
Philadelphia	87	65	.572	10.0	23	46	29	297	270	26	20	41	36	281	230	12	5	114	278	6-7	15-6	16-11	9-16	21-11	20-14
St. Louis	82	70	.539	15.0	1	38	38	266	302	15	15	44	32	265	265	11	14	107	120	9-6	10-11	15-14	18-12	13-16	17-11
Cincinnati	78	76	.506	20.0	2	39	38	279	296	10	3	39	38	322	315	16	17	90	39	9-10	8-14	18-13	19-10	12-15	12-14
Chicago	74	80	.481	24.0	10	35	42	273	305	11	14	39	38	279	262	6	20	107	96	9-7	16-9	14-16	9-17	14-13	12-18
Boston	72	81	.471	25.5	1	35	42	240	269	13	3	37	39	296	283	9	16	87	63	6-5	6-12	12-18	14-17	12-14	22-15
Brooklyn	70	81	.464	26.5	0	36	38	270	288	14	14	34	43	241	271	11	18	113	100	3-7	10-10	14-16	17-13	15-14	11-21
Pittsburgh	51	103	.331	47.0	0	25	53	232	307	2	4	26	50	232	288	7	10	101	34	7-11	6-14	8-16	10-22	8-19	12-21

Clinch Date—New York 9/24.

Team Batting

Team	G	AB	R	OR	H	2B	3B	HR	TB	RBI	TBB	IBB	SO	HBP	SH	SF	SB	CS	SB%	GDP	Avg	OBP	Slg
New York	158	5211	635	457	1360	170	71	39	1789	544	373	—	533	52	151	—	162	—	—	—	.261	.317	.343
Cincinnati	157	5251	601	611	1385	196	100	26	1859	513	312	—	477	34	131	—	153	—	—	—	.264	.309	.354
Philadelphia	154	5084	578	500	1262	225	60	38	1721	526	435	—	533	20	186	—	109	—	—	—	.248	.310	.339
Chicago	157	5135	552	567	1229	194	67	17	1608	458	415	—	599	23	202	—	127	—	—	—	.239	.299	.313
Boston	157	5201	536	552	1280	169	75	22	1665	452	427	—	587	45	182	—	155	—	—	—	.246	.309	.320
St. Louis	154	5083	531	567	1271	159	93	26	1694	436	359	—	652	24	160	—	159	—	—	—	.250	.303	.333
Brooklyn	156	5251	511	559	1299	159	78	25	1689	429	334	—	527	29	162	—	130	—	—	—	.247	.296	.322
Pittsburgh	157	5169	464	595	1230	160	61	9	1539	396	399	—	580	46	174	—	150	—	—	—	.238	.298	.298
NL Total	1250	41385	4408	4408	10316	1432	605	202	13564	3754	3054	—	4488	273	1348	—	1145	—	—	—	.249	.305	.328
NL Avg Team	156	5173	551	551	1290	179	76	25	1696	469	382	—	561	34	169	—	143	—	—	—	.249	.305	.328

Team Pitching

Team	G	CG	ShO	Rel	Sv	IP	H	R	ER	HR	SH	SF	HB	TBB	IBB	SO	WP	Bk	H/9	SO/9	BB/9	OAvg	OOBP	ERA
New York	158	92	18	97	14	1426.2	1221	457	360	29	147	—	27	327	—	551	24	1	7.7	3.5	2.1	.234	.283	2.27
Philadelphia	154	102	22	65	5	1389.0	1258	500	379	25	129	—	36	325	—	616	21	4	8.2	4.0	2.1	.246	.295	2.46
Chicago	157	79	16	121	9	1404.0	1303	567	408	34	165	—	30	374	—	654	37	2	8.4	4.2	2.4	.253	.307	2.62
Cincinnati	157	94	12	85	6	1397.1	1358	611	416	20	178	—	33	402	—	488	16	2	8.7	3.1	2.6	.259	.315	2.68
Brooklyn	156	99	8	81	9	1421.2	1288	559	439	32	180	—	43	405	—	582	26	3	8.2	3.7	2.6	.247	.307	2.78
Boston	157	105	22	81	3	1424.2	1309	552	440	19	181	—	32	371	—	593	28	2	8.3	3.7	2.6	.250	.303	2.78
Pittsburgh	157	84	17	84	6	1417.2	1318	595	474	14	207	—	34	432	—	509	27	6	8.4	3.2	2.7	.253	.314	3.01
St. Louis	154	66	16	140	10	1392.2	1257	567	469	29	152	—	36	421	—	502	20	2	8.1	3.2	2.7	.248	.311	3.03
NL Total	1250	721	131	754	62	11273.2	10312	4408	3385	202	1339	—	271	3057	—	4495	199	22	8.2	3.6	2.4	.249	.305	2.70
NL Avg Team	156	90	16	94	8	1409.2	1289	551	423	25	167	—	34	382	—	562	25	3	8.2	3.6	2.4	.249	.305	2.70

Team Fielding

Team	G	PO	A	E	TC	DP	PB	Pct
New York	158	4274	2085	208	6567	122	7	.968
Philadelphia	154	4155	2106	212	6473	112	16	.967
St. Louis	154	4165	2291	221	6677	153	15	.967
Boston	157	4250	2070	224	6544	122	17	.966
Brooklyn	156	4248	2018	245	6511	102	14	.962
Cincinnati	157	4183	2051	247	6481	120	24	.962
Pittsburgh	157	4244	1965	251	6460	119	16	.961
Chicago	157	4193	2012	267	6472	121	26	.959
NL Total	1250	33712	16598	1875	52185	971	135	.964

Team vs. Team Records

	Bos	Bro	ChN	Cin	NYG	Phi	Pit	StL	Won
Bos	—	13	11	10	7	11	14	6	72
Bro	9	—	7	10	9	9	16	10	70
ChN	11	15	—	8	7	6	17	10	74
Cin	12	12	14	—	11	8	12	9	78
NYG	15	13	15	11	—	14	16	14	98
Phi	11	11	16	14	8	—	14	13	87
Pit	8	6	5	10	6	8	—	8	51
StL	15	11	12	13	8	9	14	—	82
Lost	81	81	80	76	56	65	103	70	

1917 National League Batting Leaders

Games		At-Bats		Runs		Hits		Doubles		Triples	
H. Groh, Cin	156	H. Chase, Cin	602	G. Burns, NYG	103	H. Groh, Cin	182	H. Groh, Cin	39	R. Hornsby, StL	17
M. Carey, Pit	155	H. Groh, Cin	599	H. Groh, Cin	91	G. Burns, NYG	180	R. Smith, Bos	31	G. Cravath, Phi	16
F. Luderus, Phi	154	G. Burns, NYG	597	B. Kauff, NYG	89	E. Roush, Cin	178	F. Merkle, 2tm	31	H. Chase, Cin	15
3 tied with	153	M. Carey, Pit	588	R. Hornsby, StL	86	M. Carey, Pit	174	G. Cravath, Phi	29	E. Roush, Cin	14
		H. Zimmerman, NYG	585	2 tied with	82	H. Zimmerman, NYG	174	H. Chase, Cin	28	T. Long, StL	14

Home Runs		Total Bases		Runs Batted In		Walks		Intentional Walks	Strikeouts	
D. Robertson, NYG	12	R. Hornsby, StL	253	H. Zimmerman, NYG	102	G. Burns, NYG	75	Statistic unavailable	C. Williams, ChN	78
G. Cravath, Phi	12	H. Groh, Cin	246	H. Chase, Cin	86	H. Groh, Cin	71		W. Cruise, StL	73
R. Hornsby, StL	8	G. Burns, NYG	246	G. Cravath, Phi	83	G. Cravath, Phi	70		D. Baird, 2tm	71
3 tied with	6	G. Cravath, Phi	238	C. Stengel, Bro	73	F. Luderus, Phi	65		J. Hickman, Bro	66
		2 tied with	237	F. Luderus, Phi	72	D. Paskert, Phi	62		J. Smith, StL	65

Hit By Pitch		Sac Hits		Sac Flies	Stolen Bases		Caught Stealing	GDP
A. Fletcher, NYG	19	C. Deal, ChN	29	Statistic unavailable	M. Carey, Pit	46	Statistic unavailable	Statistic unavailable
B. Herzog, NYG	13	M. Stock, Phi	28		G. Burns, NYG	40		
M. Carey, Pit	10	P. Whitted, Phi	28		B. Kauff, NYG	30		
C. Ward, Pit	8	C. Williams, ChN	26		R. Maranville, Bos	27		
H. Groh, Cin	8	L. Doyle, ChN	26		D. Baird, 2tm	26		

Runs Created		Runs Created/27 Outs		Batting Average		On-Base Percentage		Slugging Percentage		OBP+Slugging	
G. Burns, NYG	103	R. Hornsby, StL	6.68	E. Roush, Cin	.341	H. Groh, Cin	.385	R. Hornsby, StL	.484	R. Hornsby, StL	.868
H. Groh, Cin	100	E. Roush, Cin	6.54	R. Hornsby, StL	.327	R. Hornsby, StL	.385	G. Cravath, Phi	.473	G. Cravath, Phi	.842
R. Hornsby, StL	95	G. Burns, NYG	6.33	Z. Wheat, Bro	.312	G. Burns, NYG	.380	E. Roush, Cin	.454	E. Roush, Cin	.833
B. Kauff, NYG	92	G. Cravath, Phi	6.31	B. Kauff, NYG	.308	E. Roush, Cin	.379	Z. Wheat, Bro	.423	H. Groh, Cin	.796
G. Cravath, Phi	92	H. Groh, Cin	6.12	H. Groh, Cin	.304	B. Kauff, NYG	.379	G. Burns, NYG	.412	G. Burns, NYG	.792

1917 National League Pitching Leaders

Wins		Losses		Winning Percentage		Games		Games Started		Complete Games	
P. Alexander, Phi	30	J. Barnes, Bos	21	F. Schupp, NYG	.750	P. Douglas, ChN	51	P. Alexander, Phi	44	P. Alexander, Phi	35
F. Toney, Cin	24	E. Rixey, Phi	21	S. Sallee, NYG	.720	J. Barnes, Bos	50	P. Schneider, Cin	42	F. Toney, Cin	31
H. Vaughn, ChN	23	B. Doak, StL	20	P. Perritt, NYG	.708	P. Schneider, Cin	46	F. Toney, Cin	42	J. Barnes, Bos	27
F. Schupp, NYG	21	P. Douglas, ChN	20	P. Alexander, Phi	.698	P. Alexander, Phi	45	H. Vaughn, ChN	38	H. Vaughn, ChN	27
P. Schneider, Cin	20	3 tied with	19	A. Nehf, Bos	.680	B. Doak, StL	44	3 tied with	37	2 tied with	25

Shutouts		Saves		Games Finished		Batters Faced		Innings Pitched		Hits Allowed	
P. Alexander, Phi	8	S. Sallee, NYG	4	H. Eller, Cin	21	P. Alexander, Phi	1529	P. Alexander, Phi	388.0	P. Alexander, Phi	336
W. Cooper, Pit	7	5 tied with	3	B. Grimes, Pit	18	P. Schneider, Cin	1421	P. Schneider, Cin	341.2	P. Schneider, Cin	316
F. Toney, Cin	7			R. Ames, StL	17	F. Toney, Cin	1374	F. Toney, Cin	339.2	F. Toney, Cin	300
F. Schupp, NYG	6			M. Prendergast, ChN	16	H. Vaughn, ChN	1216	W. Cooper, Pit	297.2	W. Cooper, Pit	276
7 tied with	5			4 tied with	15	J. Barnes, Bos	1166	H. Vaughn, ChN	295.2	P. Douglas, ChN	269

Home Runs Allowed		Walks		Walks/9 Innings		Strikeouts		Strikeouts/9 Innings		Strikeout/Walk Ratio	
P. Douglas, ChN	13	P. Schneider, Cin	119	P. Alexander, Phi	1.3	P. Alexander, Phi	200	H. Vaughn, ChN	5.9	P. Alexander, Phi	3.57
J. Oeschger, Phi	7	H. Vaughn, ChN	91	S. Sallee, NYG	1.4	H. Vaughn, ChN	195	F. Schupp, NYG	4.9	P. Douglas, ChN	3.02
F. Schupp, NYG	7	L. Meadows, StL	90	A. Nehf, Bos	1.5	P. Douglas, ChN	151	P. Alexander, Phi	4.6	A. Nehf, Bos	2.59
J. Coombs, Bro	7	L. Tyler, Bos	86	J. Barnes, Bos	1.5	F. Schupp, NYG	147	P. Douglas, ChN	4.6	H. Vaughn, ChN	2.14
6 tied with	6	B. Doak, StL	85	P. Douglas, ChN	1.5	P. Schneider, Cin	142	R. Marquard, Bro	4.5	J. Barnes, Bos	2.14

Earned Run Average		Component ERA		Hit Batsmen		Wild Pitches		Opponent Average		Opponent OBP	
P. Alexander, Phi	1.83	F. Schupp, NYG	1.82	J. Pfeffer, Bro	16	P. Douglas, ChN	11	F. Schupp, NYG	.209	F. Schupp, NYG	.265
P. Perritt, NYG	1.88	P. Alexander, Phi	1.94	P. Schneider, Cin	11	L. Cheney, Bro	11	A. Nehf, Bos	.231	P. Alexander, Phi	.266
F. Schupp, NYG	1.95	A. Nehf, Bos	1.98	M. Watson, StL	9	B. Steele, 2tm	8	R. Marquard, Bro	.232	A. Nehf, Bos	.268
P. Schneider, Cin	1.98	J. Barnes, Bos	2.10	B. Doak, StL	9	J. Tesreau, NYG	8	J. Pfeffer, Bro	.234	J. Barnes, Bos	.277
H. Vaughn, ChN	2.01	P. Perritt, NYG	2.23	H. Vaughn, ChN	9	C. Hendrix, ChN	8	P. Alexander, Phi	.234	S. Sallee, NYG	.280

1917 National League Miscellaneous

Managers

Boston	George Stallings	72-81
Brooklyn	Wilbert Robinson	70-81
Chicago	Fred Mitchell	74-80
Cincinnati	Christy Mathewson	78-76
New York	John McGraw	98-56
Philadelphia	Pat Moran	87-65
Pittsburgh	Nixey Callahan	20-40
	Honus Wagner	1-4
	Hugo Bezdek	30-59
St. Louis	Miller Huggins	82-70

Awards

STATS Most Valuable Player	Rogers Hornsby, ss, StL
STATS Cy Young	Pete Alexander, Phi
STATS Rookie of the Year	Walter Holke, 1b, NYG
STATS Manager of the Year	Miller Huggins, StL

STATS All-Star Team

C	Ivy Wingo, Cin	.266	2	39
1B	Hal Chase, Cin	.277	4	86
2B	Larry Doyle, ChN	.254	6	61
3B	Heine Groh, Cin	.304	1	53
SS	Rogers Hornsby, StL	.327	8	66
OF	George Burns, NYG	.302	5	45
OF	Gavy Cravath, Phi	.280	12	83
OF	Edd Roush, Cin	.341	4	67
P	Pete Alexander, Phi	30-13	1.83	200 K
P	Ferdie Schupp, NYG	21-7	1.95	147 K
P	Fred Toney, Cin	24-16	2.20	123 K
P	Hippo Vaughn, ChN	23-13	2.01	195 K

Postseason

World Series	New York (NL) 2 vs. Chicago (AL) 4

Outstanding Performances

No-Hitters

Fred Toney, Cin	@ ChN on May 2

1918 American League Standings

Team	Overall					Home Games						Road Games						Park Index		Record by Month					
	W	L	Pct	GB	DIF	W	L	R	OR	HR	OHR	W	L	R	OR	HR	OHR	Run	HR	M/A	May	June	July	Aug	S/O
Boston	75	51	.595	—	129	49	21	272	165	2	3	26	30	202	215	13	6	84	21	11-2	14-12	14-14	20-9	15-13	1-1
Cleveland	73	54	.575	2.5	8	38	22	274	219	1	4	35	32	230	228	8	5	120	43	6-4	15-15	18-12	16-11	17-12	1-0
Washington	72	56	.563	4.0	0	41	32	268	238	1	6	31	24	193	174	3	4	104	75	4-7	11-15	21-11	16-10	18-12	2-1
New York	60	63	.488	13.5	8	37	29	251	237	10	22	23	34	242	238	10	3	88	213	6-7	16-8	14-11	11-19	12-16	1-2
St. Louis	58	64	.475	15.0	2	23	30	178	195	1	7	35	34	248	253	4	4	97	130	3-6	15-10	13-19	10-17	16-11	1-1
Chicago	57	67	.460	17.0	0	30	26	216	194	4	4	27	41	241	252	4	4	101	108	5-2	13-15	12-15	13-18	14-14	0-3
Detroit	55	71	.437	20.0	0	28	29	221	246	2	7	27	42	255	311	11	3	100	78	2-4	9-16	16-15	16-17	9-18	3-1
Philadelphia	52	76	.406	24.0	0	35	32	256	273	15	8	17	44	156	265	7	5	114	175	3-8	11-13	8-19	15-16	14-19	1-1

Clinch Date—Boston 8/31.

Team Batting

Team	G	AB	R	OR	H	2B	3B	HR	TB	RBI	TBB	IBB	SO	HBP	SH	SF	SB	CS	SB%	GDP	Avg	OBP	Slg
Cleveland	129	4166	504	447	1084	176	67	9	1421	423	491	—	386	42	168	—	165	—	—	—	.260	.344	.341
New York	126	4224	493	475	1085	160	45	20	1395	406	367	—	370	23	169	—	88	—	—	—	.257	.320	.330
Detroit	128	4262	476	557	1063	141	56	13	1355	389	452	—	380	22	140	—	123	—	—	—	.249	.325	.318
Boston	126	3982	474	380	990	159	54	15	1302	390	406	—	324	27	192	—	110	—	—	—	.249	.322	.327
Washington	130	4472	461	412	1144	156	49	4	1410	404	376	—	361	35	134	—	137	—	—	—	.256	.318	.315
Chicago	124	4132	457	446	1057	136	55	8	1327	375	375	—	358	27	161	—	116	—	—	—	.256	.322	.321
St. Louis	123	4019	426	448	1040	152	40	5	1287	360	397	—	340	35	176	—	138	—	—	—	.259	.331	.320
Philadelphia	130	4278	412	538	1039	124	44	22	1317	356	343	—	485	26	124	—	83	—	—	—	.243	.303	.308
AL Total	1016	33535	3703	3703	8502	1204	410	96	10814	3103	3207	—	3004	237	1266	—	960	—	—	—	.254	.323	.322
AL Avg Team	127	4192	463	463	1063	151	51	12	1352	388	401	—	376	30	158	—	120	—	—	—	.254	.323	.322

Team Pitching

Team	G	CG	ShO	Rel	Sv	IP	H	R	ER	HR	SH	SF	HB	TBB	IBB	SO	WP	Bk	H/9	SO/9	BB/9	OAvg	OOBP	ERA
Washington	130	75	19	74	8	1228.0	1021	412	292	10	111	—	29	395	—	505	35	3	7.5	3.7	2.9	.231	.299	2.14
Boston	126	105	26	28	2	1120.0	931	380	287	9	120	—	31	380	—	392	29	1	7.5	3.2	3.1	.231	.302	2.31
Cleveland	129	78	5	67	13	1161.0	1126	447	340	9	129	—	16	343	—	364	13	0	8.7	2.8	2.7	.262	.319	2.64
Chicago	124	76	9	68	8	1126.0	1092	446	342	9	115	—	18	300	—	349	11	1	8.7	2.8	2.4	.265	.318	2.73
St. Louis	123	67	8	79	8	1111.1	993	448	340	11	115	—	31	402	—	346	12	0	8.0	2.8	3.3	.246	.319	2.75
New York	126	59	8	88	13	1157.1	1103	475	386	25	99	—	39	463	—	370	14	2	8.6	2.9	3.6	.264	.343	3.00
Philadelphia	130	80	13	67	9	1156.0	1106	538	413	13	128	—	35	486	—	277	20	2	8.6	2.2	3.8	.264	.346	3.22
Detroit	128	74	8	76	7	1160.2	1130	557	439	10	137	—	33	437	—	374	18	1	8.8	2.9	3.4	.263	.335	3.40
AL Total	1016	614	96	547	68	9220.1	8502	3703	2839	96	954	—	232	3206	—	2977	152	10	8.3	2.9	3.1	.254	.323	2.77
AL Avg Team	127	77	12	68	9	1152.1	1063	463	355	12	119	—	29	401	—	372	19	1	8.3	2.9	3.1	.254	.323	2.77

Team Fielding

Team	G	PO	A	E	TC	DP	PB	Pct
Boston	126	3356	1721	152	5229	89	9	.971
New York	126	3468	1715	161	5344	137	11	.970
Chicago	124	3356	1560	169	5085	98	13	.967
St. Louis	123	3337	1663	190	5190	86	13	.963
Cleveland	129	3407	1695	207	5309	82	11	.961
Washington	130	3685	1689	226	5600	95	18	.960
Detroit	128	3452	1571	212	5235	77	15	.960
Philadelphia	130	3458	1850	228	5536	136	7	.959
AL Total	1016	27519	13464	1545	42528	800	97	.964

Team vs. Team Records

	Bos	ChA	Cle	Det	NYA	Phi	StL	Was	Won
Bos	—	12	10	13	6	13	14	7	75
ChA	7	—	10	6	12	11	5	6	57
Cle	10	11	—	10	11	13	10	8	73
Det	5	10	3	—	9	9	10	9	55
NYA	11	6	7	10	—	8	10	8	60
Phi	6	10	7	11	4	—	8	6	52
StL	5	5	6	10	10	10	—	12	58
Was	7	13	11	11	11	12	7	—	72
Lost	51	67	54	71	63	76	64	56	

1918 American League Batting Leaders

Games		At-Bats		Runs		Hits		Doubles		Triples	
J. Judge, Was	130	E. Foster, Was	519	R. Chapman, Cle	84	G. Burns, Phi	178	T. Speaker, Cle	33	T. Cobb, Det	14
G. Burns, Phi	130	G. Burns, Phi	505	T. Cobb, Det	83	T. Cobb, Det	161	B. Ruth, Bos	26	B. Veach, Det	13
E. Foster, Was	129	B. Shotton, Was	505	H. Hooper, Bos	81	G. Sisler, StL	154	H. Hooper, Bos	26	H. Hooper, Bos	13
3 tied with	128	H. Baker, NYA	504	D. Bush, Det	74	H. Baker, NYA	154	H. Baker, NYA	24	B. Roth, Cle	12
		C. Milan, Was	503	T. Speaker, Cle	73	T. Speaker, Cle	150	2 tied with	23	3 tied with	11

Home Runs		Total Bases		Runs Batted In		Walks		Intentional Walks		Strikeouts	
B. Ruth, Bos	11	G. Burns, Phi	236	B. Veach, Det	78	R. Chapman, Cle	84	Statistic unavailable		B. Ruth, Bos	58
T. Walker, Phi	11	T. Cobb, Det	217	G. Burns, Phi	70	D. Bush, Det	79			J. Dugan, Phi	55
G. Burns, Phi	6	H. Baker, NYA	206	B. Ruth, Bos	66	H. Hooper, Bos	75			M. Kopp, Phi	55
H. Baker, NYA	6	T. Speaker, Cle	205	J. Wood, Cle	66	E. Collins, ChA	73			R. Shannon, Phi	52
2 tied with	5	G. Sisler, StL	199	T. Cobb, Det	64	B. Shotton, Was	67			R. Chapman, Cle	46

Hit By Pitch		Sac Hits		Sac Flies		Stolen Bases		Caught Stealing		GDP	
B. Roth, Cle	8	D. Shean, Bos	36	Statistic unavailable		G. Sisler, StL	45	Statistic unavailable		Statistic unavailable	
G. Burns, Phi	8	R. Chapman, Cle	35			B. Roth, Cle	35				
J. Gedeon, StL	8	S. McInnis, Bos	32			T. Cobb, Det	34				
S. O'Neill, Cle	7	J. Judge, Was	28			R. Chapman, Cle	30				
3 tied with	6	E. Scott, Bos	26			T. Speaker, Cle	27				

Runs Created		Runs Created/27 Outs		Batting Average		On-Base Percentage		Slugging Percentage		OBP+Slugging	
T. Cobb, Det	90	T. Cobb, Det	8.66	T. Cobb, Det	.382	T. Cobb, Det	.440	T. Cobb, Det	.515	T. Cobb, Det	.955
G. Burns, Phi	88	G. Burns, Phi	6.80	G. Burns, Phi	.352	T. Speaker, Cle	.403	G. Burns, Phi	.467	G. Burns, Phi	.857
H. Hooper, Bos	84	T. Speaker, Cle	6.39	G. Sisler, StL	.341	G. Sisler, StL	.400	G. Sisler, StL	.440	G. Sisler, StL	.841
T. Speaker, Cle	82	G. Sisler, StL	6.24	T. Speaker, Cle	.318	H. Hooper, Bos	.391	T. Speaker, Cle	.435	T. Speaker, Cle	.839
H. Baker, NYA	77	H. Hooper, Bos	6.16	H. Baker, NYA	.306	2 tied with	.390	T. Walker, Phi	.423	H. Hooper, Bos	.796

1918 American League Pitching Leaders

Wins		Losses		Winning Percentage		Games		Games Started		Complete Games	
W. Johnson, Was	23	S. Perry, Phi	19	S. Jones, Bos	.762	J. Bagby, Cle	45	S. Perry, Phi	36	S. Perry, Phi	30
S. Coveleski, Cle	22	E. Cicotte, ChA	19	B. Ruth, Bos	.650	G. Mogridge, NYA	45	C. Mays, Bos	33	C. Mays, Bos	30
C. Mays, Bos	21	H. Dauss, Det	16	F. Coumbe, Cle	.650	S. Perry, Phi	44	S. Coveleski, Cle	33	W. Johnson, Was	29
S. Perry, Phi	20	J. Bagby, Cle	16	W. Johnson, Was	.639	J. Shaw, Was	41	H. Harper, Was	32	J. Bush, Bos	26
J. Bagby, Cle	17	2 tied with	15	G. Morton, Cle	.636	D. Ayers, Was	40	2 tied with	31	S. Coveleski, Cle	25

Shutouts		Saves		Games Finished		Batters Faced		Innings Pitched		Hits Allowed	
C. Mays, Bos	8	G. Mogridge, NYA	7	G. Mogridge, NYA	23	S. Perry, Phi	1342	S. Perry, Phi	332.1	S. Perry, Phi	295
W. Johnson, Was	8	J. Bagby, Cle	6	B. Houck, StL	22	W. Johnson, Was	1261	W. Johnson, Was	326.0	E. Cicotte, ChA	275
J. Bush, Bos	7	B. Geary, Phi	4	D. Danforth, ChA	19	S. Coveleski, Cle	1254	S. Coveleski, Cle	311.0	J. Bagby, Cle	274
S. Jones, Bos	5	A. Russell, NYA	4	D. Ayers, Was	14	C. Mays, Bos	1162	C. Mays, Bos	293.1	S. Coveleski, Cle	261
3 tied with	4	4 tied with	3	J. Bagby, Cle	14	J. Bagby, Cle	1147	J. Bush, Bos	272.2	H. Dauss, Det	243

Home Runs Allowed		Walks		Walks/9 Innings		Strikeouts		Strikeouts/9 Innings		Strikeout/Walk Ratio	
H. Finneran, 2tm	7	S. Love, NYA	116	E. Cicotte, ChA	1.4	W. Johnson, Was	162	G. Morton, Cle	5.2	E. Cicotte, ChA	2.60
A. Russell, NYA	6	S. Perry, Phi	111	G. Mogridge, NYA	1.6	J. Shaw, Was	129	J. Shaw, Was	4.8	W. Johnson, Was	2.31
G. Mogridge, NYA	6	H. Harper, Was	104	J. Benz, ChA	1.6	J. Bush, Bos	125	W. Johnson, Was	4.5	G. Morton, Cle	1.60
3 tied with	4	W. Adams, Phi	97	W. Johnson, Was	1.9	G. Morton, Cle	123	J. Bush, Bos	4.1	G. Mogridge, NYA	1.44
		J. Bush, Bos	91	H. Dauss, Det	2.1	C. Mays, Bos	114	S. Love, NYA	3.7	J. Shaw, Was	1.43

Earned Run Average		Component ERA		Hit Batsmen		Wild Pitches		Opponent Average		Opponent OBP	
W. Johnson, Was	1.27	W. Johnson, Was	1.63	W. Adams, Phi	12	H. Harper, Was	13	A. Sothoron, StL	.205	W. Johnson, Was	.260
S. Coveleski, Cle	1.82	B. Ruth, Bos	1.84	C. Mays, Bos	11	J. Shaw, Was	10	W. Johnson, Was	.210	A. Sothoron, StL	.274
A. Sothoron, StL	1.94	A. Sothoron, StL	1.86	S. Love, NYA	10	W. Johnson, Was	8	H. Harper, Was	.212	B. Ruth, Bos	.277
S. Perry, Phi	1.98	C. Mays, Bos	2.04	H. Dauss, Det	9	R. Kallio, Det	7	B. Ruth, Bos	.214	S. Coveleski, Cle	.279
J. Bush, Bos	2.11	S. Coveleski, Cle	2.07	4 tied with	8	D. Leonard, Bos	7	C. Mays, Bos	.221	C. Mays, Bos	.284

1918 American League Miscellaneous

Managers

Boston	Ed Barrow	75-51
Chicago	Pants Rowland	57-67
Cleveland	Lee Fohl	73-54
Detroit	Hughie Jennings	55-71
New York	Miller Huggins	60-63
Philadelphia	Connie Mack	52-76
St. Louis	Fielder Jones	22-24
	Jimmy Austin	7-9
	Jimmy Burke	29-31
Washington	Clark Griffith	72-56

Awards

STATS Most Valuable Player	Babe Ruth, of, Bos
STATS Cy Young	Walter Johnson, Was
STATS Rookie of the Year	Scott Perry, p, Phi
STATS Manager of the Year	Ed Barrow, Bos

STATS All-Star Team

C	Steve O'Neill, Cle	.242	1	35
1B	George Burns, Phi	.352	6	70
2B	Eddie Collins, ChA	.276	2	30
3B	Home Run Baker, NYA	.306	6	62
SS	Ray Chapman, Cle	.267	1	32
OF	Ty Cobb, Det	.382	3	64
OF	Babe Ruth, Bos	.300	11	66
OF	Tris Speaker, Cle	.318	0	61
P	Stan Coveleski, Cle	22-13	1.82	87 K
P	Walter Johnson, Was	23-13	1.27	162 K
P	Carl Mays, Bos	21-13	2.21	114 K
P	Scott Perry, Phi	20-19	1.98	81 K

Postseason

World Series	Boston (AL) 4 vs. Chicago (NL) 2

Outstanding Performances

No-Hitters

Dutch Leonard, Bos   @ Det on June 3

1918 National League Standings

Team	Overall					Home Games						Road Games						Park Index		Record by Month					
	W	L	Pct	GB	DIF	W	L	R	OR	HR	OHR	W	L	R	OR	HR	OHR	Run	HR	M/A	May	June	July	Aug	S/O
Chicago	84	45	.651	—	89	50	26	300	235	9	5	34	19	238	158	12	8	94	49	6-3	17-9	19-6	18-14	22-12	2-1
New York	71	53	.573	10.5	51	35	21	204	181	9	13	36	32	276	234	4	7	92	243	11-1	14-10	16-9	16-16	13-16	1-1
Cincinnati	68	60	.531	15.5	1	46	24	298	256	9	5	22	36	232	240	6	14	97	58	7-5	14-13	4-17	15-13	24-12	4-0
Pittsburgh	65	60	.520	17.0	0	41	27	270	232	9	4	24	33	196	180	6	9	112	73	4-4	13-13	11-17	20-9	16-15	1-2
Brooklyn	57	69	.452	25.5	0	33	21	173	185	4	12	24	48	187	278	6	10	103	133	2-9	11-15	12-10	15-16	16-18	1-1
Philadelphia	55	68	.447	26.0	0	27	29	220	261	19	13	28	39	210	246	6	9	126	255	8-4	7-16	13-12	14-15	12-20	1-1
Boston	53	71	.427	28.5	0	23	29	163	183	5	2	30	42	261	286	8	12	88	48	2-9	16-11	12-13	11-20	11-17	1-1
St. Louis	51	78	.395	33.0	2	32	40	241	280	14	7	19	38	213	247	13	9	90	76	3-8	10-15	11-14	14-20	13-17	0-4

Clinch Date—Chicago 8/24.

Team Batting

Team	G	AB	R	OR	H	2B	3B	HR	TB	RBI	TBB	IBB	SO	HBP	SH	SF	SB	CS	SB%	GDP	Avg	OBP	Slg
Chicago	131	4325	538	393	1147	164	53	21	1480	438	358	—	343	27	190	—	159	—	—	—	.265	.325	.342
Cincinnati	129	4265	530	496	1185	165	84	15	1563	447	304	—	303	31	162	—	128	—	—	—	.278	.330	.366
New York	124	4164	480	415	1081	150	53	13	1376	400	271	—	365	33	121	—	130	—	—	—	.260	.310	.330
Pittsburgh	126	4091	466	412	1016	170	72	15	1312	391	371	—	285	25	180	—	200	—	—	—	.248	.315	.321
St. Louis	131	4369	454	527	1066	147	64	27	1422	388	329	—	461	24	141	—	119	—	—	—	.244	.301	.325
Philadelphia	125	4192	430	507	1022	158	28	25	1311	376	346	—	400	20	119	—	97	—	—	—	.244	.305	.313
Boston	124	4162	424	469	1014	107	59	13	1278	353	350	—	438	28	151	—	83	—	—	—	.244	.307	.307
Brooklyn	126	4212	360	463	1052	121	62	10	1327	303	303	—	326	36	118	—	113	—	—	—	.250	.291	.315
NL Total	1016	33780	3682	3682	8583	1119	475	139	11069	3096	2541	—	2921	224	1182	—	1029	—	—	—	.254	.311	.328
NL Avg Team	127	4223	460	460	1073	140	59	17	1384	387	318	—	365	28	148	—	129	—	—	—	.254	.311	.328

Team Pitching

Team	G	CG	ShO	Rel	Sv	IP	H	R	ER	HR	SH	SF	HB	TBB	IBB	SO	WP	Bk	H/9	SO/9	BB/9	OAvg	OOBP	ERA
Chicago	131	92	23	52	8	1197.0	1050	393	290	13	139	—	22	296	—	472	19	2	7.9	3.5	2.2	.239	.291	2.18
Pittsburgh	126	85	10	52	7	1140.1	1005	412	314	13	148	—	32	299	—	367	12	1	7.9	2.9	2.4	.243	.300	2.48
New York	124	74	18	71	11	1111.2	1002	415	326	20	127	—	23	228	—	330	20	1	8.1	2.7	1.8	.243	.287	2.64
Brooklyn	126	85	17	51	2	1131.1	1024	463	353	22	138	—	28	320	—	395	34	2	8.1	3.1	2.5	.248	.307	2.81
Boston	124	96	13	31	0	1117.1	1111	469	360	14	137	—	25	277	—	340	11	1	8.9	2.7	2.2	.266	.316	2.90
St. Louis	131	72	3	79	5	1193.0	1148	527	393	16	155	—	43	352	—	361	11	2	8.7	2.7	2.7	.261	.321	2.96
Cincinnati	129	84	14	62	6	1142.1	1136	496	381	19	152	—	23	381	—	321	16	2	9.0	2.5	3.0	.268	.332	3.00
Philadelphia	125	78	10	61	6	1139.2	1086	507	399	22	175	—	30	369	—	312	24	2	8.6	2.5	2.9	.258	.323	3.15
NL Total	1016	666	108	459	45	9172.2	8562	3682	2816	139	1171	—	226	2522	—	2898	147	13	8.4	2.8	2.5	.254	.310	2.76
NL Avg Team	127	83	14	57	6	1146.2	1070	460	352	17	146	—	28	315	—	362	18	2	8.4	2.8	2.5	.254	.310	2.76

Team Fielding

Team	G	PO	A	E	TC	DP	PB	Pct
New York	124	3328	1664	152	5144	78	10	.970
Pittsburgh	126	3431	1722	179	5332	108	7	.966
Chicago	131	3581	1757	188	5526	91	12	.966
Boston	124	3321	1766	184	5271	89	10	.965
Cincinnati	129	3422	1684	192	5298	127	14	.964
Brooklyn	126	3381	1700	193	5274	74	16	.963
St. Louis	131	3578	1964	220	5762	116	10	.962
Philadelphia	125	3410	1758	211	5379	91	14	.961
NL Total	1016	27452	14015	1519	42986	774	93	.965

Team vs. Team Records

	Bos	Bro	ChN	Cin	NYG	Phi	Pit	StL	Won
Bos	—	8	5	10	1	7	10	12	53
Bro	6	—	10	6	8	9	10	8	57
ChN	14	9	—	10	14	12	10	15	84
Cin	8	12	7	—	12	12	4	13	68
NYG	15	12	6	7	—	10	8	13	71
Phi	12	8	6	7	3	—	11	8	55
Pit	9	9	8	12	11	7	—	9	65
StL	7	11	3	8	4	11	7	—	51
Lost	71	69	45	60	53	68	60	78	

Seasons: Standings, Leaders

1918 National League Batting Leaders

Games		At-Bats		Runs		Hits		Doubles		Triples	
C. Hollocher, ChN	131	C. Hollocher, ChN	509	H. Groh, Cin	88	C. Hollocher, ChN	161	H. Groh, Cin	28	J. Daubert, Bro	15
L. Mann, ChN	129	I. Olson, Bro	506	G. Burns, NYG	80	H. Groh, Cin	158	L. Mann, ChN	27	A. Wickland, Bos	13
F. Merkle, ChN	129	D. Bancroft, Phi	499	M. Flack, ChN	74	E. Roush, Cin	145	G. Cravath, Phi	27	L. Magee, Cin	13
D. Paskert, ChN	127	H. Groh, Cin	493	C. Hollocher, ChN	72	R. Youngs, NYG	143	I. Meusel, Phi	25	S. Magee, Cin	13
5 tied with	126	L. Mann, ChN	489	2 tied with	70	F. Merkle, ChN	143	F. Merkle, ChN	25	2 tied with	11

Home Runs		Total Bases		Runs Batted In		Walks		Intentional Walks		Strikeouts	
G. Cravath, Phi	8	C. Hollocher, ChN	202	S. Magee, Cin	76	M. Carey, Pit	62	Statistic unavailable		R. Youngs, NYG	49
W. Cruise, StL	6	E. Roush, Cin	198	G. Cutshaw, Pit	68	M. Flack, ChN	56			D. Paskert, ChN	49
C. Williams, Phi	6	H. Groh, Cin	195	F. Luderus, Phi	67	D. Bancroft, Phi	54			R. Smith, Bos	47
4 tied with	5	L. Mann, ChN	188	R. Smith, Bos	65	H. Groh, Cin	54			G. Cravath, Phi	46
		F. Merkle, ChN	187	F. Merkle, ChN	65	G. Cravath, Phi	54			L. Mann, ChN	45

Hit By Pitch		Sac Hits		Sac Flies		Stolen Bases		Caught Stealing		GDP	
A. Fletcher, NYG	15	E. Roush, Cin	33	Statistic unavailable		M. Carey, Pit	58	Statistic unavailable		Statistic unavailable	
O. O'Mara, Bro	10	F. Mollwitz, Pit	30			G. Burns, NYG	40				
S. Magee, Cin	9	G. Cutshaw, Pit	29			C. Hollocher, ChN	26				
H. Groh, Cin	7	L. Magee, Cin	27			D. Baird, StL	25				
6 tied with	6	2 tied with	26			G. Cutshaw, Pit	25				

Runs Created		Runs Created/27 Outs		Batting Average		On-Base Percentage		Slugging Percentage		OBP+Slugging	
C. Hollocher, ChN	84	H. Groh, Cin	5.97	Z. Wheat, Bro	.335	H. Groh, Cin	.395	E. Roush, Cin	.455	E. Roush, Cin	.823
H. Groh, Cin	80	E. Roush, Cin	5.87	E. Roush, Cin	.333	C. Hollocher, ChN	.379	J. Daubert, Bro	.429	H. Groh, Cin	.791
R. Youngs, NYG	73	C. Hollocher, ChN	5.83	H. Groh, Cin	.320	R. Smith, Bos	.373	R. Hornsby, StL	.416	J. Daubert, Bro	.789
E. Roush, Cin	73	S. Magee, Cin	5.62	C. Hollocher, ChN	.316	S. Magee, Cin	.370	S. Magee, Cin	.415	S. Magee, Cin	.785
G. Burns, NYG	72	R. Youngs, NYG	5.59	J. Daubert, Bro	.308	Z. Wheat, Bro	.369	C. Hollocher, ChN	.397	C. Hollocher, ChN	.775

1918 National League Pitching Leaders

Wins		Losses		Winning Percentage		Games		Games Started		Complete Games	
H. Vaughn, ChN	22	J. Oeschger, Phi	18	C. Hendrix, ChN	.741	B. Grimes, Bro	40	H. Vaughn, ChN	33	A. Nehf, Bos	28
C. Hendrix, ChN	20	R. Marquard, Bro	18	L. Tyler, ChN	.704	W. Cooper, Pit	38	A. Nehf, Bos	31	H. Vaughn, ChN	27
B. Grimes, Bro	19	P. Ragan, Bos	17	E. Mayer, 2tm	.696	H. Eller, Cin	37	P. Perritt, NYG	31	W. Cooper, Pit	26
W. Cooper, Pit	19	3 tied with	15	H. Vaughn, ChN	.688	3 tied with	35	3 tied with	30	L. Tyler, ChN	22
L. Tyler, ChN	19			B. Grimes, Bro	.679					C. Hendrix, ChN	21

Shutouts		Saves		Games Finished		Batters Faced		Innings Pitched		Hits Allowed	
L. Tyler, ChN	8	J. Oeschger, Phi	3	B. Sherdel, StL	14	A. Nehf, Bos	1167	H. Vaughn, ChN	290.1	A. Nehf, Bos	274
H. Vaughn, ChN	8	W. Cooper, Pit	3	B. Sanders, Pit	14	H. Vaughn, ChN	1146	A. Nehf, Bos	284.1	M. Prendergast, Phi	257
B. Grimes, Bro	7	F. Toney, 2tm	3	H. Eller, Cin	13	B. Grimes, Bro	1078	W. Cooper, Pit	273.1	R. Marquard, Bro	231
P. Perritt, NYG	6	F. Anderson, NYG	3	D. Davis, Phi	13	W. Cooper, Pit	1078	B. Grimes, Bro	269.2	E. Mayer, 2tm	230
4 tied with	4	7 tied with	2	3 tied with	10	L. Tyler, ChN	1066	L. Tyler, ChN	269.1	C. Hendrix, ChN	229

Home Runs Allowed		Walks		Walks/9 Innings		Strikeouts		Strikeouts/9 Innings		Strikeout/Walk Ratio	
J. Coombs, Bro	10	P. Schneider, Cin	117	S. Sallee, NYG	0.8	H. Vaughn, ChN	148	H. Vaughn, ChN	4.6	S. Sallee, NYG	2.75
R. Marquard, Bro	7	J. Oeschger, Phi	83	P. Perritt, NYG	1.5	W. Cooper, Pit	117	W. Cooper, Pit	3.9	H. Vaughn, ChN	1.95
M. Prendergast, Phi	6	B. Grimes, Bro	76	F. Toney, 2tm	1.5	B. Grimes, Bro	113	B. Grimes, Bro	3.8	W. Cooper, Pit	1.80
G. Packard, StL	6	A. Nehf, Bos	76	G. Packard, StL	1.6	L. Tyler, ChN	102	L. Cheney, Bro	3.7	P. Douglas, ChN	1.65
3 tied with	5	H. Vaughn, ChN	76	M. Prendergast, Phi	1.6	A. Nehf, Bos	96	H. Eller, Cin	3.5	D. Rudolph, Bos	1.60

Earned Run Average		Component ERA		Hit Batsmen		Wild Pitches		Opponent Average		Opponent OBP	
H. Vaughn, ChN	1.74	H. Vaughn, ChN	1.79	J. May, StL	13	L. Cheney, Bro	13	H. Vaughn, ChN	.208	S. Sallee, NYG	.259
L. Tyler, ChN	2.00	B. Grimes, Bro	1.95	P. Schneider, Cin	11	B. Grimes, Bro	11	B. Grimes, Bro	.216	H. Vaughn, ChN	.266
W. Cooper, Pit	2.11	L. Tyler, ChN	1.99	L. Meadows, StL	10	C. Hendrix, ChN	8	W. Cooper, Pit	.223	B. Grimes, Bro	.276
P. Douglas, ChN	2.13	W. Cooper, Pit	2.00	W. Cooper, Pit	10	G. Smith, 3tm	6	L. Tyler, ChN	.226	P. Perritt, NYG	.278
B. Grimes, Bro	2.14	S. Sallee, NYG	2.01	L. Cheney, Bro	10	4 tied with	5	E. Jacobs, 2tm	.233	W. Cooper, Pit	.279

1918 National League Miscellaneous

Managers

Boston	George Stallings	53-71
Brooklyn	Wilbert Robinson	57-69
Chicago	Fred Mitchell	84-45
Cincinnati	Christy Mathewson	61-57
	Heine Groh	7-3
New York	John McGraw	71-53
Philadelphia	Pat Moran	55-68
Pittsburgh	Hugo Bezdek	65-60
St. Louis	Jack Hendricks	51-78

Awards

STATS Most Valuable Player	Hippo Vaughn, p, ChN
STATS Cy Young	Hippo Vaughn, ChN
STATS Rookie of the Year	C. Hollocher, ss, ChN
STATS Manager of the Year	Fred Mitchell, ChN

STATS All-Star Team

C	Mike Gonzalez, StL	.252	3	20
1B	Sherry Magee, Cin	.298	2	76
2B	George Cutshaw, Pit	.285	5	68
3B	Heine Groh, Cin	.320	1	37
SS	Rogers Hornsby, StL	.281	5	60
OF	George Burns, NYG	.290	4	51
OF	Dode Paskert, ChN	.286	2	59
OF	Edd Roush, Cin	.333	5	62
P	Wilbur Cooper, Pit	19-14	2.11	117 K
P	Burleigh Grimes, Bro	19-9	2.14	113 K
P	Lefty Tyler, ChN	19-8	2.00	102 K
P	Hippo Vaughn, ChN	22-10	1.74	148 K

Postseason

World Series	Chicago (NL) 2 vs. Boston (AL) 4

Outstanding Performances

Cycles

Cliff Heathcote, StL   on June 13

1919 American League Standings

Team	Overall					Home Games						Road Games						Park Index		Record by Month					
	W	L	Pct	GB	DIF	W	L	R	OR	HR	OHR	W	L	R	OR	HR	OHR	Run	HR	M/A	May	June	July	Aug	S/O
Chicago	88	52	.629	—	134	48	22	344	279	5	11	40	30	323	255	20	13	108	48	6-1	18-6	11-16	22-10	18-9	13-10
Cleveland	84	55	.604	3.5	2	44	25	340	276	12	4	40	30	296	261	12	15	112	60	3-1	15-10	15-13	17-15	18-8	16-8
New York	80	59	.576	7.5	21	46	25	326	255	33	30	34	34	252	251	12	17	111	208	2-2	13-8	20-8	13-21	16-12	16-8
Detroit	80	60	.571	8.0	1	46	24	307	243	10	14	34	36	311	335	13	21	85	71	1-4	12-12	17-10	20-13	18-9	12-12
St. Louis	67	72	.482	20.5	0	40	30	280	249	19	23	27	42	253	318	12	12	91	173	1-5	14-8	12-15	20-12	13-16	7-16
Boston	66	71	.482	20.5	6	35	30	233	241	10	3	31	41	331	311	23	13	82	40	4-1	8-14	12-16	15-17	14-14	13-9
Washington	56	84	.400	32.0	1	32	40	265	282	2	5	24	44	268	288	22	15	93	18	2-4	6-15	16-14	14-19	6-20	12-12
Philadelphia	36	104	.257	52.0	0	21	49	266	400	29	31	15	55	191	342	6	13	125	316	2-3	4-17	8-19	10-24	6-21	6-20

Clinch Date—Chicago 9/24.

Team Batting

Team	G	AB	R	OR	H	2B	3B	HR	TB	RBI	TBB	IBB	SO	HBP	SH	SF	SB	CS	SB%	GDP	Avg	OBP	Slg
Chicago	140	4675	667	534	1343	218	70	25	1776	570	427	—	358	34	224	—	150	—	—	—	.287	.351	.380
Cleveland	139	4565	636	537	1268	254	72	24	1738	546	498	—	367	38	224	—	113	—	—	—	.278	.354	.381
Detroit	140	4665	618	578	1319	222	84	23	1778	544	429	—	427	25	211	—	121	—	—	—	.283	.346	.381
New York	141	4775	578	506	1275	193	49	45	1701	493	386	—	479	32	170	—	101	—	—	—	.267	.326	.356
Boston	138	4548	564	552	1188	181	49	33	1566	492	471	—	411	45	189	—	108	—	—	—	.261	.336	.344
St. Louis	140	4672	533	567	1234	187	73	31	1660	460	391	—	443	35	201	—	74	—	—	—	.264	.326	.355
Washington	142	4757	533	570	1238	177	63	24	1613	459	416	—	511	40	160	—	142	—	—	—	.260	.325	.339
Philadelphia	140	4730	457	742	1156	175	71	35	1578	395	349	—	565	30	125	—	103	—	—	—	.244	.300	.334
AL Total	1120	37387	4586	4586	10021	1607	531	240	13410	3959	3367	—	3561	279	1504	—	912	—	—	—	.268	.333	.359
AL Avg Team	140	4673	573	573	1253	201	66	30	1676	495	421	—	445	35	188	—	114	—	—	—	.268	.333	.359

Team Pitching

Team	G	CG	ShO	Rel	Sv	IP	H	R	ER	HR	SH	SF	HB	TBB	IBB	SO	WP	Bk	H/9	SO/9	BB/9	OAvg	OOBP	ERA
New York	141	85	14	90	7	1287.0	1143	506	403	47	—	—	37	433	—	500	19	0	8.0	3.5	3.0	.239	.307	2.82
Cleveland	139	80	10	93	10	1245.0	1242	537	407	19	—	—	33	362	—	432	16	1	9.0	3.1	2.6	.266	.323	2.94
Washington	142	68	13	97	10	1274.1	1237	570	426	20	—	—	38	451	—	536	35	5	8.7	3.8	3.2	.259	.328	3.01
Chicago	140	88	14	73	3	1265.2	1245	534	428	24	—	—	31	342	—	468	9	1	8.9	3.3	2.4	.262	.315	3.04
St. Louis	140	78	14	95	4	1256.0	1255	567	437	35	—	—	42	421	—	415	27	5	9.0	3.0	3.0	.263	.328	3.13
Detroit	140	85	10	74	4	1256.0	1254	578	461	35	—	—	38	436	—	428	24	1	9.0	3.1	3.1	.266	.333	3.30
Boston	138	89	15	66	8	1224.1	1251	552	450	16	—	—	28	421	—	381	36	2	9.2	2.8	3.1	.275	.341	3.31
Philadelphia	140	72	1	89	3	1239.1	1371	742	587	44	—	—	29	503	—	417	25	7	10.0	3.0	3.7	.290	.362	4.26
AL Total	1120	645	91	677	49	10047.2	9998	4586	3599	240	—	—	276	3369	—	3577	191	22	9.0	3.2	3.0	.268	.332	3.22
AL Avg Team	140	81	11	85	6	1255.2	1250	573	450	30	—	—	35	421	—	447	24	3	9.0	3.2	3.0	.268	.332	3.22

Team Fielding

Team	G	PO	A	E	TC	DP	PB	Pct
Boston	138	3630	1796	140	5566	118	20	.975
Chicago	140	3791	1749	176	5716	116	6	.969
New York	141	3867	1951	193	6011	108	13	.968
Cleveland	139	3724	1787	201	5712	102	6	.965
Detroit	140	3781	1758	205	5744	81	11	.964
St. Louis	140	3757	1811	215	5783	98	10	.963
Washington	142	3810	1653	227	5690	86	15	.960
Philadelphia	140	3702	1902	257	5861	96	9	.956
AL Total	1120	30062	14407	1614	46083	805	90	.965

Team vs. Team Records

	Bos	ChA	Cle	Det	NYA	Phi	StL	Was	Won
Bos	—	9	4	9	10	14	9	11	66
ChA	11	—	12	11	12	17	11	14	88
Cle	15	8	—	8	13	16	11	13	84
Det	11	9	12	—	8	14	14	12	80
NYA	9	8	7	12	—	18	12	14	80
Phi	6	3	4	6	2	—	7	8	36
StL	10	9	9	6	8	13	—	12	67
Was	9	6	7	8	6	12	8	—	56
Lost	71	52	55	60	59	104	72	84	

Seasons: Standings, Leaders

1919 American League Batting Leaders

Games			At-Bats			Runs			Hits			Doubles			Triples		
S. Rice, Was		141	B. Weaver, ChA		571	B. Ruth, Bos		103	B. Veach, Det		191	B. Veach, Det		45	B. Veach, Det		17
D. Lewis, NYA		141	H. Baker, NYA		567	G. Sisler, StL		96	T. Cobb, Det		191	T. Speaker, Cle		38	G. Sisler, StL		15
H. Baker, NYA		141	D. Lewis, NYA		559	T. Cobb, Det		92	J. Jackson, ChA		181	T. Cobb, Det		36	H. Heilmann, Det		15
5 tied with		140	S. Rice, Was		557	B. Weaver, ChA		89	G. Sisler, StL		180	S. O'Neill, Cle		35	J. Jackson, ChA		14
			B. Veach, Det		538	R. Peckinpaugh, NYA		89	S. Rice, Was		179	2 tied with		34	T. Cobb, Det		13

Home Runs			Total Bases			Runs Batted In			Walks			Intentional Walks		Strikeouts		
B. Ruth, Bos		29	B. Ruth, Bos		284	B. Ruth, Bos		114	J. Graney, Cle		105	Statistic unavailable		R. Shannon, 2tm		70
G. Sisler, StL		10	B. Veach, Det		279	B. Veach, Det		101	B. Ruth, Bos		101			B. Ruth, Bos		58
T. Walker, Phi		10	G. Sisler, StL		271	J. Jackson, ChA		96	J. Judge, Was		81			S. Vick, NYA		55
H. Baker, NYA		10	J. Jackson, ChA		261	H. Heilmann, Det		93	H. Hooper, Bos		79			B. Roth, 2tm		53
E. Smith, Cle		9	2 tied with		256	D. Lewis, NYA		89	D. Bush, Det		75			F. Thomas, Phi		52

Hit By Pitch			Sac Hits			Sac Flies		Stolen Bases			Caught Stealing		GDP	
G. Burns, Phi		12	R. Chapman, Cle		50	Statistic unavailable		E. Collins, ChA		33	Statistic unavailable		Statistic unavailable	
R. Shannon, 2tm		8	O. Vitt, Bos		47			G. Sisler, StL		28				
T. Speaker, Cle		8	R. Young, Det		46			T. Cobb, Det		28				
5 tied with		7	J. Gedeon, StL		40			S. Rice, Was		26				
			E. Collins, ChA		40			2 tied with		23				

Runs Created			Runs Created/27 Outs			Batting Average			On-Base Percentage			Slugging Percentage			OBP+Slugging		
B. Ruth, Bos		121	B. Ruth, Bos		10.53	T. Cobb, Det		.384	B. Ruth, Bos		.456	B. Ruth, Bos		.657	B. Ruth, Bos		1.114
J. Jackson, ChA		110	T. Cobb, Det		8.18	B. Veach, Det		.355	W. Schang, Bos		.436	G. Sisler, StL		.530	T. Cobb, Det		.944
B. Veach, Det		102	J. Jackson, ChA		8.05	G. Sisler, StL		.352	T. Cobb, Det		.429	B. Veach, Det		.519	J. Jackson, ChA		.928
T. Cobb, Det		100	B. Veach, Det		7.12	J. Jackson, ChA		.351	J. Jackson, ChA		.422	T. Cobb, Det		.515	G. Sisler, StL		.921
G. Sisler, StL		95	G. Sisler, StL		7.01	J. Tobin, StL		.327	N. Leibold, ChA		.404	J. Jackson, ChA		.506	B. Veach, Det		.916

1919 American League Pitching Leaders

Wins			Losses			Winning Percentage			Games			Games Started			Complete Games		
E. Cicotte, ChA		29	H. Harper, Was		21	E. Cicotte, ChA		.806	J. Shaw, Was		45	L. Williams, ChA		40	E. Cicotte, ChA		30
S. Coveleski, Cle		24	S. Jones, Bos		20	R. Caldwell, 2tm		.706	A. Russell, 2tm		44	J. Shaw, Was		38	L. Williams, ChA		27
L. Williams, ChA		23	R. Naylor, Phi		18	H. Dauss, Det		.700	W. Kinney, Phi		43	E. Cicotte, ChA		35	W. Johnson, Was		27
H. Dauss, Det		21	S. Perry, Phi		17	L. Williams, ChA		.676	S. Coveleski, Cle		43	S. Coveleski, Cle		34	C. Mays, 2tm		26
3 tied with		20	J. Shaw, Was		17	3 tied with		.667	2 tied with		41	2 tied with		32	S. Coveleski, Cle		24

Shutouts			Saves			Games Finished			Batters Faced		Innings Pitched			Hits Allowed		
W. Johnson, Was		7	A. Russell, 2tm		5	W. Kinney, Phi		21	Statistic unavailable		J. Shaw, Was		306.2	S. Coveleski, Cle		286
5 tied with		5	J. Shaw, Was		4	D. Kerr, ChA		20			E. Cicotte, ChA		306.2	J. Shaw, Was		274
			B. Shawkey, NYA		4	A. Russell, 2tm		19			L. Williams, ChA		297.0	L. Williams, ChA		265
			S. Coveleski, Cle		4	R. Wright, StL		16			S. Coveleski, Cle		296.0	H. Dauss, Det		262
			2 tied with		3	G. Cunningham, Det		15			W. Johnson, Was		290.1	2 tied with		258

Home Runs Allowed			Walks			Walks/9 Innings			Strikeouts			Strikeouts/9 Innings			Strikeout/Walk Ratio		
H. Thormahlen, NYA		10	H. Ehmke, Det		107	E. Cicotte, ChA		1.4	W. Johnson, Was		147	A. Russell, 2tm		4.8	W. Johnson, Was		2.88
B. Gallia, StL		10	J. Shaw, Was		101	W. Johnson, Was		1.6	J. Shaw, Was		128	W. Johnson, Was		4.6	E. Cicotte, ChA		2.24
T. Rogers, 2tm		9	H. Harper, Was		97	J. Bagby, Cle		1.6	L. Williams, ChA		125	W. Kinney, Phi		4.3	L. Williams, ChA		2.16
H. Dauss, Det		9	S. Jones, Bos		95	L. Williams, ChA		1.8	B. Shawkey, NYA		122	D. Leonard, Det		4.2	S. Coveleski, Cle		1.97
2 tied with		8	2 tied with		92	S. Coveleski, Cle		1.8	S. Coveleski, Cle		118	B. Shawkey, NYA		4.2	A. Russell, 2tm		1.59

Earned Run Average			Component ERA			Hit Batsmen			Wild Pitches			Opponent Average			Opponent OBP		
W. Johnson, Was		1.49	W. Johnson, Was		1.72	L. Williams, ChA		11	J. Shaw, Was		10	W. Johnson, Was		.219	W. Johnson, Was		.259
E. Cicotte, ChA		1.82	E. Cicotte, ChA		1.87	E. Myers, Cle		10	H. Harper, Was		9	E. Cicotte, ChA		.228	E. Cicotte, ChA		.261
C. Weilman, StL		2.07	L. Williams, ChA		2.37	C. Mays, 2tm		10	E. Erickson, 2tm		8	H. Thormahlen, NYA		.228	L. Williams, ChA		.289
C. Mays, 2tm		2.10	C. Mays, 2tm		2.45	A. Sothoron, StL		10	A. Sothoron, StL		8	B. Shawkey, NYA		.231	G. Mogridge, NYA		.294
A. Sothoron, StL		2.20	B. Shawkey, NYA		2.54	G. Lowdermilk, 2tm		9	H. Pennock, Bos		7	C. Mays, 2tm		.233	J. Quinn, NYA		.295

1919 American League Miscellaneous

Managers

Boston	Ed Barrow	66-71
Chicago	Kid Gleason	88-52
Cleveland	Lee Fohl	44-34
	Tris Speaker	40-21
Detroit	Hughie Jennings	80-60
New York	Miller Huggins	80-59
Philadelphia	Connie Mack	36-104
St. Louis	Jimmy Burke	67-72
Washington	Clark Griffith	56-84

Awards

STATS Most Valuable Player	Babe Ruth, of, Bos
STATS Cy Young	Eddie Cicotte, ChA
STATS Rookie of the Year	Ira Flagstead, of, Det
STATS Manager of the Year	Kid Gleason, ChA

STATS All-Star Team

C	Wally Schang, Bos	.306	0	55
1B	George Sisler, StL	.352	10	83
2B	Eddie Collins, ChA	.319	4	80
3B	Buck Weaver, ChA	.296	3	75
SS	Roger Peckinpaugh, NYA	.305	7	33
OF	Ty Cobb, Det	.384	1	70
OF	Joe Jackson, ChA	.351	7	96
OF	Babe Ruth, Bos	.322	29	114
P	Eddie Cicotte, ChA	29-7	1.82	110 K
P	Stan Coveleski, Cle	24-12	2.52	118 K
P	Walter Johnson, Was	20-14	1.49	147 K
P	Allen Sothoron, StL	20-13	2.20	106 K

Postseason

World Series	Chicago (AL) 3 vs. Cincinnati (NL) 5

Outstanding Performances

No-Hitters
Ray Caldwell, Cle   @ NYA on September 10

1919 National League Standings

Team	W	L	Pct	GB	DIF	W	L	R	OR	HR	OHR	W	L	R	OR	HR	OHR	Run	HR	M/A	May	June	July	Aug	S/O
		Overall						**Home Games**						**Road Games**				**Park Index**				**Record by Month**			
Cincinnati	96	44	.686	—	75	52	19	315	189	10	5	44	25	262	212	10	16	103	56	6-0	12-13	19-10	22-5	22-8	15-8
New York	87	53	.621	9.0	76	46	23	310	209	28	17	41	30	295	261	12	17	96	160	3-2	18-6	15-11	20-7	16-16	15-11
Chicago	75	65	.536	21.0	1	40	31	232	190	11	7	35	34	222	217	10	7	93	103	3-3	11-13	18-13	14-8	16-13	13-15
Pittsburgh	71	68	.511	24.5	0	40	30	273	218	8	7	31	38	199	248	9	16	108	59	2-3	13-13	17-11	10-19	14-11	15-11
Brooklyn	69	71	.493	27.0	21	36	33	243	227	12	10	33	38	282	286	13	11	85	94	4-1	13-11	12-17	12-13	16-17	12-12
Boston	57	82	.410	38.5	0	29	38	231	265	11	9	28	44	234	298	13	20	100	65	0-5	9-12	10-18	12-17	15-13	11-17
St. Louis	54	83	.394	40.5	0	34	35	240	244	9	10	20	48	223	308	9	15	90	78	1-6	9-14	17-13	3-19	10-20	14-11
Philadelphia	47	90	.343	47.5	0	26	44	307	378	29	24	21	46	203	321	13	16	125	175	3-2	9-12	6-21	11-16	11-22	7-17

Clinch Date—Cincinnati 9/16.

Team Batting

Team	G	AB	R	OR	H	2B	3B	HR	TB	RBI	TBB	IBB	SO	HBP	SH	SF	SB	CS	SB%	GDP	Avg	OBP	Slg
New York	140	4664	605	470	1254	204	64	40	1706	505	328	—	407	37	128	—	157	—	—	—	.269	.322	.366
Cincinnati	140	4577	577	401	1204	135	83	20	1565	489	368	—	405	33	199	—	143	—	—	—	.263	.304	.342
Brooklyn	141	4844	525	513	1272	167	66	25	1646	452	258	—	405	28	153	—	112	—	—	—	.263	.304	.340
Philadelphia	138	4746	510	699	1191	208	50	42	1625	434	323	—	469	28	123	—	114	—	—	—	.251	.303	.342
Pittsburgh	139	4538	472	466	1132	130	82	17	1477	394	344	—	381	24	143	—	196	—	—	—	.249	.306	.325
Boston	140	4746	465	563	1201	142	62	24	1539	401	355	—	481	42	156	—	145	—	—	—	.253	.311	.324
St. Louis	138	4588	463	552	1175	163	52	18	1496	398	298	—	418	18	142	—	148	—	—	—	.256	.305	.326
Chicago	140	4581	454	407	1174	166	58	21	1519	387	298	—	359	42	167	—	150	—	—	—	.256	.308	.332
NL Total	1116	37284	4071	4071	9603	1315	517	207	12573	3460	2615	—	3288	252	1211	—	1165	—	—	—	.258	.311	.337
NL Avg Team	140	4661	509	509	1200	164	65	26	1572	433	327	—	411	32	151	—	146	—	—	—	.258	.311	.337

Team Pitching

Team	G	CG	ShO	Rel	Sv	IP	H	R	ER	HR	SH	SF	HB	TBB	IBB	SO	WP	Bk	H/9	SO/9	BB/9	OAvg	OOBP	ERA
Chicago	140	80	21	79	5	1265.0	1127	407	311	14	131	—	28	294	—	495	20	1	8.0	3.5	2.1	.242	.291	2.21
Cincinnati	140	89	23	74	9	1274.0	1104	401	316	21	122	—	20	298	—	407	12	2	7.8	2.9	2.1	.239	.288	2.23
New York	140	72	11	96	13	1256.0	1153	470	377	34	142	—	25	305	—	340	11	1	8.3	2.4	2.2	.247	.296	2.70
Brooklyn	141	98	12	50	1	1281.0	1256	513	389	21	145	—	31	292	—	476	22	3	8.8	3.3	2.1	.262	.308	2.73
Pittsburgh	139	91	17	54	4	1249.0	1113	466	400	23	165	—	36	337	—	391	18	0	8.0	2.8	1.9	.244	.290	2.88
Boston	140	79	5	74	9	1270.1	1313	563	447	29	174	—	19	337	—	374	29	3	9.3	2.6	2.4	.275	.326	3.17
St. Louis	138	55	6	137	8	1217.1	1146	552	437	25	147	—	49	415	—	414	37	6	8.5	3.1	3.1	.256	.326	3.23
Philadelphia	138	93	6	57	2	1252.0	1391	699	576	40	185	—	45	408	—	397	34	5	10.0	2.9	2.9	.294	.356	4.14
NL Total	1116	657	101	621	51	10064.2	9603	4071	3253	207	1211	—	253	2612	—	3294	183	21	8.6	2.9	2.3	.258	.311	2.91
NL Avg Team	140	82	13	78	6	1258.2	1200	509	407	26	151	—	32	327	—	412	23	3	8.6	2.9	2.3	.258	.311	2.91

Team Fielding

Team	G	PO	A	E	TC	DP	PB	Pct
Cincinnati	140	3821	1846	151	5818	98	16	.974
Pittsburgh	139	3743	1668	165	5576	89	6	.970
Chicago	140	3789	1952	185	5926	87	6	.969
Boston	140	3810	1999	204	6013	111	12	.966
New York	140	3755	1997	216	5968	96	16	.964
Philadelphia	138	3762	1965	218	5945	112	19	.963
St. Louis	138	3648	1966	214	5828	112	13	.963
Brooklyn	141	3835	1876	219	5930	84	17	.963
NL Total	1116	30163	15269	1572	47004	789	105	.967

Team vs. Team Records

	Bos	Bro	ChN	Cin	NYG	Phi	Pit	StL	Won
Bos	—	7	7	4	6	15	8	10	57
Bro	13	—	9	7	8	12	9	11	69
ChN	13	11	—	8	6	13	11	13	75
Cin	16	13	12	—	12	15	14	14	96
NYG	14	12	14	8	—	14	11	14	87
Phi	5	8	7	5	6	—	6	10	47
Pit	11	11	9	6	9	14	—	11	71
StL	10	9	7	6	6	7	9	—	54
Lost	82	71	65	44	53	90	68	83	

Seasons: Standings, Leaders

1919 National League Batting Leaders

Games			At-Bats			Runs			Hits			Doubles			Triples		
T. Boeckel, 2tm	140		I. Olson, Bro	590		G. Burns, NYG	86		I. Olson, Bro	164		R. Youngs, NYG	31		B. Southworth, Pit	14
I. Olson, Bro	140		J. Daubert, Cin	537		H. Groh, Cin	79		R. Hornsby, StL	163		G. Burns, NYG	30		H. Myers, Bro	14
J. Daubert, Cin	140		M. Rath, Cin	537		J. Daubert, Cin	79		E. Roush, Cin	162		F. Luderus, Phi	30		5 tied with	12
3 tied with	139		Z. Wheat, Bro	536		M. Rath, Cin	77		G. Burns, NYG	162		B. Kauff, NYG	27			
			G. Burns, NYG	534		4 tied with	73		2 tied with	159		I. Meusel, Phi	26			

Home Runs			Total Bases			Runs Batted In			Walks			Intentional Walks		Strikeouts		
G. Cravath, Phi	12		H. Myers, Bro	223		H. Myers, Bro	73		G. Burns, NYG	82		Statistic unavailable		R. Powell, Bos	79
B. Kauff, NYG	10		R. Hornsby, StL	220		R. Hornsby, StL	71		M. Rath, Cin	64				A. McHenry, StL	57
C. Williams, Phi	9		Z. Wheat, Bro	219		E. Roush, Cin	71		H. Groh, Cin	56				G. Neale, Cin	51
R. Hornsby, StL	8		E. Roush, Cin	217		B. Kauff, NYG	67		F. Luderus, Phi	54				F. Luderus, Phi	48
L. Doyle, NYG	7		G. Burns, NYG	216		H. Groh, Cin	63		T. Boeckel, 2tm	53				R. Youngs, NYG	47

Hit By Pitch			Sac Hits			Sac Flies		Stolen Bases			Caught Stealing		GDP		
B. Herzog, 2tm	14		J. Daubert, Cin	39		Statistic unavailable		G. Burns, NYG	40		Statistic unavailable		Statistic unavailable	
C. Pick, 2tm	10		G. Neale, Cin	31				G. Cutshaw, Pit	36					
6 tied with	7		L. Blackburne, 2tm	28				C. Bigbee, Pit	31					
			W. Holke, Bos	26				J. Smith, StL	30					
			L. Magee, 2tm	26				2 tied with	28					

Runs Created			Runs Created/27 Outs			Batting Average			On-Base Percentage			Slugging Percentage			OBP+Slugging		
G. Burns, NYG	97		H. Groh, Cin	6.63		E. Roush, Cin	.321		G. Burns, NYG	.396		H. Myers, Bro	.436		H. Groh, Cin	.823
E. Roush, Cin	89		G. Burns, NYG	6.61		R. Hornsby, StL	.318		H. Groh, Cin	.392		L. Doyle, NYG	.433		R. Hornsby, StL	.814
R. Youngs, NYG	86		E. Roush, Cin	6.36		R. Youngs, NYG	.311		R. Hornsby, StL	.384		H. Groh, Cin	.431		E. Roush, Cin	.811
R. Hornsby, StL	84		R. Youngs, NYG	6.36		H. Groh, Cin	.310		R. Youngs, NYG	.384		E. Roush, Cin	.431		G. Burns, NYG	.801
H. Groh, Cin	83		R. Hornsby, StL	6.06		M. Stock, StL	.307		E. Roush, Cin	.380		R. Hornsby, StL	.430		R. Youngs, NYG	.799

1919 National League Pitching Leaders

Wins			Losses			Winning Percentage			Games			Games Started			Complete Games		
J. Barnes, NYG	25		L. Meadows, 2tm	20		D. Ruether, Cin	.760		O. Tuero, StL	45		H. Vaughn, ChN	37		W. Cooper, Pit	27
H. Vaughn, ChN	21		D. Rudolph, Bos	18		S. Sallee, Cin	.750		L. Meadows, 2tm	40		J. Barnes, NYG	34		J. Pfeffer, Bro	26
S. Sallee, Cin	21		E. Jacobs, 2tm	16		R. Fisher, Cin	.737		H. Eller, Cin	38		W. Cooper, Pit	32		H. Vaughn, ChN	25
H. Eller, Cin	20		4 tied with	14		J. Barnes, NYG	.735		J. Barnes, NYG	38		D. Rudolph, Bos	32		D. Rudolph, Bos	24
2 tied with	19					H. Eller, Cin	.690		H. Vaughn, ChN	38		A. Nehf, 2tm	31		2 tied with	23

Shutouts			Saves			Games Finished			Batters Faced			Innings Pitched			Hits Allowed		
P. Alexander, ChN	9		O. Tuero, StL	4		J. Dubuc, NYG	22		H. Vaughn, ChN	1224		H. Vaughn, ChN	306.2		D. Rudolph, Bos	282
H. Eller, Cin	7		5 tied with	3		O. Tuero, StL	20		J. Barnes, NYG	1178		J. Barnes, NYG	295.2		J. Pfeffer, Bro	270
B. Adams, Pit	6					P. Carter, ChN	20		W. Cooper, Pit	1147		W. Cooper, Pit	286.2		H. Vaughn, ChN	264
R. Fisher, Cin	5					B. Sherdel, StL	16		D. Rudolph, Bos	1125		D. Rudolph, Bos	273.2		J. Barnes, NYG	263
8 tied with	4					S. Martin, ChN	16		J. Pfeffer, Bro	1099		A. Nehf, 2tm	270.2		E. Jacobs, 2tm	231

Home Runs Allowed			Walks			Walks/9 Innings			Strikeouts			Strikeouts/9 Innings			Strikeout/Walk Ratio		
W. Cooper, Pit	10		J. May, StL	87		B. Adams, Pit	0.8		H. Vaughn, ChN	141		H. Eller, Cin	5.0		B. Adams, Pit	4.00
G. Smith, 2tm	8		D. Ruether, Cin	83		S. Sallee, Cin	0.8		H. Eller, Cin	137		P. Alexander, ChN	4.6		P. Alexander, ChN	3.18
A. Nehf, 2tm	8		L. Meadows, 2tm	79		J. Barnes, NYG	1.1		P. Alexander, ChN	121		L. Meadows, 2tm	4.3		H. Eller, Cin	2.74
J. Barnes, NYG	8		W. Cooper, Pit	74		L. Cadore, Bro	1.1		L. Meadows, 2tm	116		H. Vaughn, ChN	4.1		J. Barnes, NYG	2.63
A. Demaree, Bos	8		E. Jacobs, 2tm	69		P. Alexander, ChN	1.5		W. Cooper, Pit	106		B. Grimes, Bro	4.1		L. Cadore, Bro	2.41

Earned Run Average			Component ERA			Hit Batsmen			Wild Pitches			Opponent Average			Opponent OBP		
P. Alexander, ChN	1.72		B. Adams, Pit	1.52		W. Cooper, Pit	15		F. Woodward, 2tm	11		P. Alexander, ChN	.211		B. Adams, Pit	.241
H. Vaughn, ChN	1.79		P. Alexander, ChN	1.56		J. May, StL	14		D. Rudolph, Bos	11		B. Adams, Pit	.220		P. Alexander, ChN	.245
D. Ruether, Cin	1.82		R. Fisher, Cin	2.00		J. Pfeffer, Bro	12		L. Cheney, 3tm	8		D. Ruether, Cin	.223		J. Barnes, NYG	.260
F. Toney, NYG	1.84		J. Barnes, NYG	2.00		E. Jacobs, 2tm	11		B. Grimes, Bro	7		W. Cooper, Pit	.225		R. Fisher, Cin	.271
B. Adams, Pit	1.98		P. Douglas, 2tm	2.02		O. Tuero, StL	10		L. Meadows, 2tm	7		A. Nehf, 2tm	.225		F. Miller, Pit	.272

1919 National League Miscellaneous

Managers

Boston	George Stallings	57-82
Brooklyn	Wilbert Robinson	69-71
Chicago	Fred Mitchell	75-65
Cincinnati	Pat Moran	96-44
New York	John McGraw	87-53
Philadelphia	Jack Coombs	18-44
	Gavvy Cravath	29-46
Pittsburgh	Hugo Bezdek	71-68
St. Louis	Branch Rickey	54-83

Awards

STATS Most Valuable Player	Heine Groh, 3b, Cin
STATS Cy Young	Hippo Vaughn, ChN
STATS Rookie of the Year	Verne Clemons, c, StL
STATS Manager of the Year	Pat Moran, Cin

STATS All-Star Team

C	Ivy Wingo, Cin	.273	0	27
1B	Fred Luderus, Phi	.293	5	49
2B	Larry Doyle, NYG	.289	7	52
3B	Heine Groh, Cin	.310	5	63
SS	Rabbit Maranville, Bos	.267	5	43
OF	George Burns, NYG	.303	2	46
OF	Hi Myers, Bro	.307	5	73
OF	Edd Roush, Cin	.321	4	71
P	Jesse Barnes, NYG	25-9	2.40	92 K
P	Dutch Ruether, Cin	19-6	1.82	78 K
P	Slim Sallee, Cin	21-7	2.06	24 K
P	Hippo Vaughn, ChN	21-14	1.79	141 K

Postseason

World Series	Cincinnati (NL) 5 vs. Chicago (AL) 3

Outstanding Performances

No-Hitters

Hod Eller, Cin	vs. StL on May 11

1920 American League Standings

Team	Overall					Home Games						Road Games						Park Index		Record by Month					
	W	L	Pct	GB	DIF	W	L	R	OR	HR	OHR	W	L	R	OR	HR	OHR	Run	HR	M/A	May	June	July	Aug	S/O
Cleveland	98	56	.636	—	134	51	27	441	330	20	10	47	29	416	312	15	21	103	81	8-3	18-8	17-11	22-10	11-16	22-8
Chicago	96	58	.623	2.0	31	52	25	381	298	18	10	44	33	413	367	19	35	87	52	7-2	13-16	18-8	22-12	17-10	19-10
New York	95	59	.617	3.0	9	49	28	424	308	71	36	46	31	414	321	44	12	100	191	4-7	19-8	21-8	20-14	13-13	18-9
St. Louis	76	77	.497	21.5	0	40	38	473	415	31	33	36	39	324	351	19	20	126	158	5-4	9-18	17-12	14-15	17-9	14-19
Boston	72	81	.471	25.5	14	41	35	327	300	2	14	31	46	323	398	20	25	88	36	10-2	12-12	8-17	10-21	19-12	13-17
Washington	68	84	.447	29.0	0	37	38	343	386	5	7	31	46	380	416	31	44	94	16	5-6	14-12	13-10	12-19	8-19	16-18
Detroit	61	93	.396	37.0	0	32	46	336	452	12	24	29	47	316	381	18	22	110	88	0-11	11-14	10-18	14-15	13-15	13-20
Philadelphia	48	106	.312	50.0	1	25	50	254	401	35	40	23	56	304	433	9	16	94	316	3-7	10-18	4-24	12-20	10-14	9-23

Clinch Date—Cleveland 10/02.

Team Batting

Team	G	AB	R	OR	H	2B	3B	HR	TB	RBI	TBB	IBB	SO	HBP	SH	SF	SB	CS	SB%	GDP	Avg	OBP	Slg
Cleveland	154	5196	857	642	1574	300	95	35	2169	757	576	—	379	37	254	—	73	93	.44	—	.303	.376	.417
New York	154	5176	838	629	1448	268	71	115	2203	743	539	—	626	23	172	—	64	82	.44	—	.280	.350	.426
St. Louis	154	5358	797	766	1651	279	83	50	2246	707	427	—	339	38	208	—	121	79	.61	—	.308	.357	.419
Chicago	154	5328	794	665	1574	263	98	37	2144	692	433	—	543	56	198	—	160	114	.58	—	.295	.351	.402
Washington	153	5251	723	802	1526	233	81	36	2029	616	433	—	391	20	216	—	76	68	.53	—	.291	.351	.386
Detroit	155	5215	652	833	1408	228	72	30	1870	561	479	—	429	45	219	—	98	111	.47	—	.270	.334	.359
Boston	154	5199	650	698	1397	216	71	22	1821	569	533	—	355	38	188	—	50	67	.43	—	.269	.342	.350
Philadelphia	156	5256	558	834	1324	220	49	44	1774	465	471	—	593	43	169	—	109	96	.53	—	.252	.304	.338
AL Total	1234	41979	5869	5869	11902	2007	620	369	16256	5110	3811	—	3655	300	1624	—	751	710	.51	—	.284	.347	.387
AL Avg Team	154	5247	734	734	1488	251	78	46	2032	639	476	—	457	38	203	—	94	89	.51	—	.284	.347	.387

Team Pitching

Team	G	CG	ShO	Rel	Sv	IP	H	R	ER	HR	SH	SF	HB	TBB	IBB	SO	WP	Bk	H/9	SO/9	BB/9	OAvg	OOBP	ERA
New York	154	88	15	93	11	1368.0	1414	629	505	48	—	—	27	420	—	480	16	2	9.3	3.2	2.8	.264	.321	3.32
Cleveland	154	94	11	100	7	1377.0	1448	642	522	31	—	—	29	401	—	466	19	2	9.5	3.0	2.6	.275	.329	3.41
Chicago	154	109	9	66	10	1386.2	1467	665	553	45	—	—	25	405	—	438	22	1	9.5	2.8	2.6	.278	.332	3.59
Boston	154	92	11	76	6	1395.1	1481	698	592	39	—	—	27	461	—	481	33	4	9.6	3.1	3.0	.272	.332	3.82
Philadelphia	156	79	6	104	2	1380.1	1612	834	602	56	—	—	40	461	—	423	27	8	10.5	2.8	3.0	.300	.360	3.93
St. Louis	154	84	9	102	14	1378.2	1481	766	618	53	—	—	38	578	—	444	17	5	9.7	2.9	3.6	.277	.352	4.03
Detroit	155	74	9	122	10	1385.0	1487	833	622	46	—	—	56	561	—	483	25	4	9.7	3.1	3.6	.280	.355	4.04
Washington	153	81	10	102	7	1367.0	1521	802	633	51	—	—	43	520	—	418	51	4	10.0	2.8	3.4	.286	.355	4.17
AL Total	1234	701	80	765	67	11038.0	11911	5869	4647	369	—	—	285	3807	—	3633	210	30	9.7	3.0	3.1	.284	.347	3.79
AL Avg Team	154	88	10	96	8	1379.0	1489	734	581	46	—	—	36	476	—	454	26	4	9.7	3.0	3.1	.284	.347	3.79

Team Fielding

Team	G	PO	A	E	TC	DP	PB	Pct
Boston	154	4168	2100	183	6451	131	12	.972
Cleveland	154	4127	1985	184	6296	124	9	.971
New York	154	4107	2050	194	6351	129	7	.969
Chicago	154	4146	1920	198	6264	142	8	.968
Detroit	155	4136	2124	230	6490	95	16	.965
St. Louis	154	4117	1943	233	6293	119	6	.963
Washington	153	4077	1886	232	6195	95	12	.963
Philadelphia	156	4120	2173	266	6559	125	13	.959
AL Total	1234	32998	16181	1720	50899	960	83	.966

Team vs. Team Records

	Bos	ChA	Cle	Det	NYA	Phi	StL	Was	Won
Bos	—	12	6	13	9	13	9	10	72
ChA	10	—	10	19	10	16	14	17	96
Cle	16	12	—	15	9	16	15	15	98
Det	9	3	7	—	7	12	10	13	61
NYA	13	12	13	15	—	19	12	11	95
Phi	9	6	6	10	3	—	8	6	48
StL	13	8	7	12	10	14	—	12	76
Was	11	5	7	9	11	16	9	—	68
Lost	81	58	56	93	59	106	77	84	

Seasons: Standings, Leaders

1920 American League Batting Leaders

Games			At-Bats			Runs			Hits			Doubles			Triples		
7 tied with		154	G. Sisler, StL		631	B. Ruth, NYA		158	G. Sisler, StL		257	T. Speaker, Cle		50	J. Jackson, ChA		20
			B. Weaver, ChA		629	G. Sisler, StL		137	E. Collins, ChA		224	G. Sisler, StL		49	G. Sisler, StL		18
			S. Rice, Was		624	T. Speaker, Cle		137	J. Jackson, ChA		218	J. Jackson, ChA		42	H. Hooper, Bos		17
			B. Veach, Det		612	E. Collins, ChA		117	B. D. Jacobson, StL		216	3 tied with		40	3 tied with		15
			W. Pipp, NYA		610	2 tied with		109	T. Speaker, Cle		214						

Home Runs			Total Bases			Runs Batted In			Walks			Intentional Walks			Strikeouts		
B. Ruth, NYA		54	G. Sisler, StL		399	B. Ruth, NYA		137	B. Ruth, NYA		148	Statistic unavailable			A. Ward, NYA		84
G. Sisler, StL		19	B. Ruth, NYA		388	G. Sisler, StL		122	T. Speaker, Cle		97				B. Ruth, NYA		80
T. Walker, Phi		17	J. Jackson, ChA		336	B. D. Jacobson, StL		122	H. Hooper, Bos		88				J. Dykes, Phi		73
H. Felsch, ChA		14	T. Speaker, Cle		310	J. Jackson, ChA		121	R. Young, Det		85				B. Meusel, NYA		72
2 tied with		12	B. D. Jacobson, StL		305	L. Gardner, Cle		118	B. Roth, Was		75				T. Walker, Phi		59

Hit By Pitch			Sac Hits			Sac Flies			Stolen Bases			Caught Stealing			GDP		
B. Harris, Was		21	J. Gedeon, StL		48	Statistic unavailable			S. Rice, Was		63	S. Rice, Was		30	Statistic unavailable		
I. Griffin, Phi		11	D. Bush, Det		48				G. Sisler, StL		42	L. Gardner, Cle		20			
J. Dykes, Phi		9	S. McInnis, Bos		45				B. Roth, Was		24	M. Menosky, Bos		19			
R. Walters, Bos		9	R. Chapman, Cle		41				M. Menosky, Bos		23	B. Wambsganss, Cle		18			
M. Menosky, Bos		9	B. Wambsganss, Cle		40				J. Tobin, StL		21	H. Hooper, Bos		18			

Runs Created			Runs Created/27 Outs			Batting Average			On-Base Percentage			Slugging Percentage			OBP+Slugging		
B. Ruth, NYA		191	B. Ruth, NYA		16.44	G. Sisler, StL		.407	B. Ruth, NYA		.530	B. Ruth, NYA		.847	B. Ruth, NYA		1.378
G. Sisler, StL		154	T. Speaker, Cle		10.33	T. Speaker, Cle		.388	T. Speaker, Cle		.483	G. Sisler, StL		.632	G. Sisler, StL		1.082
T. Speaker, Cle		146	G. Sisler, StL		10.01	J. Jackson, ChA		.382	G. Sisler, StL		.449	J. Jackson, ChA		.589	T. Speaker, Cle		1.045
J. Jackson, ChA		138	J. Jackson, ChA		9.53	B. Ruth, NYA		.376	J. Jackson, ChA		.444	T. Speaker, Cle		.562	J. Jackson, ChA		1.033
E. Collins, ChA		131	E. Collins, ChA		8.19	E. Collins, ChA		.372	E. Collins, ChA		.438	H. Felsch, ChA		.540	E. Collins, ChA		.932

1920 American League Pitching Leaders

Wins			Losses			Winning Percentage			Games			Games Started			Complete Games		
J. Bagby, Cle		31	S. Perry, Phi		25	J. Bagby, Cle		.721	J. Bagby, Cle		48	R. Faber, ChA		39	J. Bagby, Cle		30
C. Mays, NYA		26	R. Naylor, Phi		23	C. Mays, NYA		.703	D. Ayers, Det		46	J. Bagby, Cle		39	R. Faber, ChA		28
S. Coveleski, Cle		24	H. Dauss, Det		21	D. Kerr, ChA		.700	D. Kerr, ChA		45	L. Williams, ChA		38	E. Cicotte, ChA		28
R. Faber, ChA		23	H. Ehmke, Det		18	E. Myers, 2tm		.688	C. Mays, NYA		45	C. Mays, NYA		37	3 tied with		26
L. Williams, ChA		22	J. Shaw, Was		18	E. Cicotte, ChA		.677	T. Zachary, Was		44	S. Coveleski, Cle		37			

Shutouts			Saves			Games Finished			Batters Faced			Innings Pitched			Hits Allowed		
C. Mays, NYA		6	D. Kerr, ChA		5	B. Karr, Bos		20	Statistic unavailable			J. Bagby, Cle		339.2	J. Bagby, Cle		338
U. Shocker, StL		5	U. Shocker, StL		5	B. Burwell, StL		18				R. Faber, ChA		319.0	R. Faber, ChA		332
B. Shawkey, NYA		5	B. Burwell, StL		4	R. Wilkinson, ChA		18				S. Coveleski, Cle		315.0	E. Cicotte, ChA		316
3 tied with		4	3 tied with		3	E. Rommel, Phi		16				C. Mays, NYA		312.0	S. Perry, Phi		310
						D. Ayers, Det		16				E. Cicotte, ChA		303.1	C. Mays, NYA		310

Home Runs Allowed			Walks			Walks/9 Innings			Strikeouts			Strikeouts/9 Innings			Strikeout/Walk Ratio		
L. Williams, ChA		15	D. Davis, StL		149	W. Johnson, Was		1.7	S. Coveleski, Cle		133	W. Johnson, Was		4.9	W. Johnson, Was		2.89
S. Perry, Phi		14	E. Erickson, Was		128	J. Quinn, NYA		1.7	L. Williams, ChA		128	B. Shawkey, NYA		4.2	J. Quinn, NYA		2.10
C. Mays, NYA		13	H. Ehmke, Det		124	S. Coveleski, Cle		1.9	B. Shawkey, NYA		126	H. Harper, Bos		3.9	S. Coveleski, Cle		2.05
E. Erickson, Was		13	J. Bush, Bos		94	J. Bagby, Cle		2.1	R. Faber, ChA		108	U. Shocker, StL		3.9	U. Shocker, StL		1.53
J. Shaw, Was		12	R. Oldham, Det		91	E. Cicotte, ChA		2.2	U. Shocker, StL		107	L. Williams, ChA		3.9	B. Shawkey, NYA		1.48

Earned Run Average			Component ERA			Hit Batsmen			Wild Pitches			Opponent Average			Opponent OBP		
B. Shawkey, NYA		2.45	S. Coveleski, Cle		2.34	H. Ehmke, Det		13	J. Shaw, Was		13	R. Collins, ChA		.239	S. Coveleski, Cle		.283
S. Coveleski, Cle		2.49	W. Johnson, Was		2.58	L. Williams, ChA		12	D. Leonard, Det		13	S. Coveleski, Cle		.241	W. Johnson, Was		.287
U. Shocker, StL		2.71	U. Shocker, StL		2.79	E. Erickson, Was		11	R. Naylor, Phi		11	B. Shawkey, NYA		.242	B. Shawkey, NYA		.301
J. Bagby, Cle		2.89	B. Shawkey, NYA		2.87	J. Bush, Bos		10	A. Sothoron, StL		10	W. Johnson, Was		.246	J. Quinn, NYA		.304
R. Faber, ChA		2.99	J. Bagby, Cle		2.94	2 tied with		9	2 tied with		9	U. Shocker, StL		.247	U. Shocker, StL		.304

1920 American League Miscellaneous

Managers

Boston	Ed Barrow	72-81
Chicago	Kid Gleason	96-58
Cleveland	Tris Speaker	98-56
Detroit	Hughie Jennings	61-93
New York	Miller Huggins	95-59
Philadelphia	Connie Mack	48-106
St. Louis	Jimmy Burke	76-77
Washington	Clark Griffith	68-84

Awards

STATS Most Valuable Player	Babe Ruth, of, NYA
STATS Cy Young	Jim Bagby, Cle
STATS Rookie of the Year	Bob Meusel, of, NYA
STATS Manager of the Year	Tris Speaker, Cle

STATS All-Star Team

C	Steve O'Neill, Cle	.321	3	55
1B	George Sisler, StL	.407	19	122
2B	Eddie Collins, ChA	.372	3	76
3B	Larry Gardner, Cle	.310	3	118
SS	Ray Chapman, Cle	.303	3	49
OF	Joe Jackson, ChA	.382	12	121
OF	Babe Ruth, NYA	.376	54	137
OF	Tris Speaker, Cle	.388	8	107
P	Jim Bagby, Cle	31-12	2.89	73 K
P	Stan Coveleski, Cle	24-14	2.49	133 K
P	Carl Mays, NYA	26-11	3.06	92 K
P	Bob Shawkey, NYA	20-13	2.45	126 K

Postseason

World Series Cleveland (AL) 5 vs. Brooklyn (NL) 2

Outstanding Performances

No-Hitters
Walter Johnson, Was @ Bos on July 1

Cycles
George Sisler, StL	on August 8
Bobby Veach, Det	on September 17

1920 National League Standings

Team		Overall				Home Games						Road Games						Park Index		Record by Month					
	W	L	Pct	GB	DIF	W	L	R	OR	HR	OHR	W	L	R	OR	HR	OHR	Run	HR	M/A	May	June	July	Aug	S/O
Brooklyn	93	61	.604	—	87	49	29	360	291	17	14	44	32	300	237	11	11	118	137	8-4	13-10	12-16	23-12	14-13	23-6
New York	86	68	.558	7.0	0	45	35	334	282	31	33	41	33	348	261	15	11	94	228	3-7	12-14	15-14	17-10	20-11	19-12
Cincinnati	82	71	.536	10.5	75	42	34	281	238	5	1	40	37	358	331	13	25	76	16	8-3	15-13	12-10	17-13	15-14	15-18
Pittsburgh	79	75	.513	14.0	15	42	35	276	263	6	4	37	40	254	289	10	21	99	92	4-8	13-12	10-13	18-15	16-13	16-17
Chicago	75	79	.487	18.0	4	43	34	322	302	19	15	32	45	297	333	15	22	98	49	5-7	12-15	17-9	10-20	17-13	14-15
St. Louis	75	79	.487	18.0	0	38	38	330	332	10	10	37	41	345	350	22	20	97	38	4-5	12-14	12-9	12-19	9-20	13-23
Boston	62	90	.408	30.0	4	36	37	271	292	5	11	26	53	252	378	18	28	127		6-5	8-19	11-13	13-17	12-19	12-15
Philadelphia	62	91	.405	30.5	1	32	45	339	380	50	30	30	46	226	334	14	5	127	416	6-5	8-19	11-13	13-17	12-19	12-18

Clinch Date—Brooklyn 9/27.

Team Batting

Team	G	AB	R	OR	H	2B	3B	HR	TB	RBI	TBB	IBB	SO	HBP	SH	SF	SB	CS	SB%	GDP	Avg	OBP	Slg
New York	155	5309	682	543	1427	210	76	46	1927	590	432	—	545	26	124	—	131	113	.54	—	.269	.327	.363
St. Louis	155	5495	675	682	1589	238	96	32	2115	600	373	—	484	26	192	—	126	114	.53	—	.289	.337	.385
Brooklyn	155	5399	660	528	1493	205	99	28	1980	566	359	—	391	19	189	—	70	80	.47	—	.277	.332	.367
Cincinnati	154	5176	639	569	1432	169	76	19	1807	546	382	—	367	47	194	—	158	128	.55	—	.277	.332	.349
Chicago	154	5117	619	635	1350	223	67	34	1809	535	428	—	421	46	220	—	115	129	.47	—	.264	.326	.354
Philadelphia	153	5264	565	714	1385	229	54	64	1914	483	283	—	531	36	159	—	100	83	.55	—	.263	.305	.364
Pittsburgh	155	5219	530	552	1342	162	90	16	1732	449	374	—	405	29	174	—	181	117	.61	—	.257	.324	.332
Boston	153	5218	523	670	1358	168	86	23	1767	456	385	—	488	33	166	—	88	98	.47	—	.260	.315	.339
NL Total	1234	42197	4893	4893	11376	1604	644	261	15051	4225	3016	—	3632	262	1418	—	969	862	.53	—	.270	.322	.357
NL Avg Team	154	5275	612	612	1422	201	81	33	1881	528	377	—	454	33	177	—	121	108	.53	—	.270	.322	.357

Team Pitching

Team	G	CG	ShO	Rel	Sv	IP	H	R	ER	HR	SH	SF	HB	TBB	IBB	SO	WP	Bk	H/9	SO/9	BB/9	OAvg	OOBP	ERA
Brooklyn	155	89	17	93	10	1427.1	1381	528	416	25	164	—	22	327	—	553	29	3	8.7	3.5	2.1	.259	.304	2.62
New York	155	86	18	103	9	1408.2	1379	543	439	25	164	—	19	297	—	380	23	3	8.8	2.4	1.9	.261	.303	2.80
Pittsburgh	155	92	17	85	10	1415.1	1389	552	454	25	165	—	27	280	—	444	27	2	8.8	2.8	1.8	.261	.301	2.89
Cincinnati	154	90	12	82	9	1391.2	1327	569	448	26	164	—	34	393	—	435	21	4	8.6	2.8	2.5	.258	.314	2.90
Chicago	154	95	13	93	9	1388.2	1459	635	504	37	166	—	25	382	—	508	22	1	9.5	3.3	2.5	.276	.328	3.27
St. Louis	155	72	9	135	12	1426.2	1488	682	544	30	188	—	58	479	—	529	23	6	9.4	3.3	3.0	.277	.343	3.43
Boston	153	93	14	73	6	1386.1	1464	670	545	35	190	—	35	415	—	368	27	1	9.5	2.7	2.7	.280	.337	3.54
Philadelphia	153	77	8	102	11	1380.2	1480	714	557	35	214	—	41	444	—	419	26	2	9.6	2.7	2.9	.284	.345	3.63
NL Total	1234	694	108	766	76	11225.1	11367	4893	3907	261	1415	—	261	3017	—	3636	198	22	9.1	2.9	2.4	.270	.322	3.13
NL Avg Team	154	87	14	96	10	1403.1	1421	612	488	33	177	—	33	377	—	455	25	3	9.1	2.9	2.4	.270	.322	3.13

Team Fielding

Team	G	PO	A	E	TC	DP	PB	Pct
Pittsburgh	155	4234	1946	186	6366	119	10	.971
New York	155	4232	2240	210	6682	137	15	.969
Cincinnati	154	4163	1924	200	6287	125	11	.968
Brooklyn	155	4277	2057	226	6560	118	19	.966
Chicago	154	4163	2125	225	6513	112	9	.965
Philadelphia	153	4126	2117	232	6475	135	21	.964
Boston	153	4164	2212	239	6615	125	5	.964
St. Louis	155	4277	2109	256	6642	136	18	.961
NL Total	1234	33636	16730	1774	52140	1007	108	.966

Team vs. Team Records

	Bos	Bro	ChN	Cin	NYG	Phi	Pit	StL	Won
Bos	—	8	7	9	10	10	7	11	62
Bro	14	—	13	10	15	14	12	15	93
ChN	15	9	—	9	7	14	11	10	75
Cin	12	12	13	—	6	14	12	13	82
NYG	12	7	15	16	—	12	13	11	86
Phi	11	8	8	8	10	—	9	8	62
Pit	15	10	11	10	9	13	—	11	79
StL	11	7	12	9	11	14	11	—	75
Lost	90	61	79	71	68	91	75	79	

Seasons: Standings, Leaders

1920 National League Batting Leaders

Games		At-Bats		Runs		Hits		Doubles		Triples	
G. Kelly, NYG	155	M. Stock, StL	639	G. Burns, NYG	115	R. Hornsby, StL	218	R. Hornsby, StL	44	H. Myers, Bro	22
M. Stock, StL	155	I. Olson, Bro	637	D. Bancroft, 2tm	102	R. Youngs, NYG	204	D. Bancroft, 2tm	36	R. Hornsby, StL	20
J. Johnston, Bro	155	J. Johnston, Bro	635	J. Daubert, Cin	97	M. Stock, StL	204	C. Williams, Phi	36	E. Roush, Cin	16
3 tied with	154	G. Burns, NYG	631	R. Hornsby, StL	96	E. Roush, Cin	196	H. Myers, Bro	36	C. Bigbee, Pit	15
		D. Bancroft, 2tm	613	R. Youngs, NYG	92	C. Williams, Phi	192	G. Burns, NYG	35	R. Maranville, Bos	15

Home Runs		Total Bases		Runs Batted In		Walks		Intentional Walks		Strikeouts	
C. Williams, Phi	15	R. Hornsby, StL	329	R. Hornsby, StL	94	G. Burns, NYG	76	Statistic unavailable		G. Kelly, NYG	92
I. Meusel, Phi	14	C. Williams, Phi	293	G. Kelly, NYG	94	R. Youngs, NYG	75			R. Powell, Bos	83
G. Kelly, NYG	11	R. Youngs, NYG	277	E. Roush, Cin	90	D. Paskert, ChN	64			A. McHenry, StL	73
A. McHenry, StL	10	Z. Wheat, Bro	270	P. Duncan, Cin	83	R. Hornsby, StL	60			D. Paskert, ChN	58
D. Robertson, ChN	10	H. Myers, Bro	269	H. Myers, Bro	80	H. Groh, Cin	60			R. Youngs, NYG	55

Hit By Pitch		Sac Hits		Sac Flies		Stolen Bases		Caught Stealing		GDP	
J. Fournier, StL	12	G. Cutshaw, Pit	37	Statistic unavailable		M. Carey, Pit	52	B. Southworth, Pit	25	Statistic unavailable	
A. Fletcher, 2tm	9	C. Deal, ChN	34			E. Roush, Cin	36	E. Roush, Cin	24		
5 tied with	8	Z. Terry, ChN	33			F. Frisch, NYG	34	D. Robertson, ChN	23		
		H. Myers, Bro	33			C. Bigbee, Pit	31	G. Burns, NYG	22		
		D. Lavan, StL	31			G. Neale, Cin	29	J. Fournier, StL	20		

Runs Created		Runs Created/27 Outs		Batting Average		On-Base Percentage		Slugging Percentage		OBP+Slugging	
R. Hornsby, StL	123	R. Hornsby, StL	8.37	R. Hornsby, StL	.370	R. Hornsby, StL	.431	R. Hornsby, StL	.559	R. Hornsby, StL	.990
R. Youngs, NYG	122	R. Youngs, NYG	8.02	R. Youngs, NYG	.351	R. Youngs, NYG	.427	C. Williams, Phi	.497	R. Youngs, NYG	.904
Z. Wheat, Bro	103	Z. Wheat, Bro	6.77	E. Roush, Cin	.339	E. Roush, Cin	.386	R. Youngs, NYG	.477	C. Williams, Phi	.861
E. Roush, Cin	101	E. Roush, Cin	6.26	Z. Wheat, Bro	.328	Z. Wheat, Bro	.385	I. Meusel, Phi	.473	Z. Wheat, Bro	.848
C. Williams, Phi	99	C. Williams, Phi	6.22	C. Williams, Phi	.325	H. Groh, Cin	.375	Z. Wheat, Bro	.463	E. Roush, Cin	.839

1920 National League Pitching Leaders

Wins		Losses		Winning Percentage		Games		Games Started		Complete Games	
P. Alexander, ChN	27	E. Rixey, Phi	22	B. Grimes, Bro	.676	J. Haines, StL	47	P. Alexander, ChN	40	P. Alexander, ChN	33
W. Cooper, Pit	24	J. Scott, Bos	21	P. Alexander, ChN	.659	P. Douglas, NYG	46	H. Vaughn, ChN	38	W. Cooper, Pit	28
B. Grimes, Bro	23	D. Fillingim, Bos	21	F. Toney, NYG	.656	P. Alexander, ChN	46	5 tied with	37	B. Grimes, Bro	25
A. Nehf, NYG	21	J. Haines, StL	20	J. Pfeffer, Bro	.640	J. Scott, Bos	44			E. Rixey, Phi	25
F. Toney, NYG	21	G. Smith, Phi	18	A. Nehf, NYG	.636	W. Cooper, Pit	44			H. Vaughn, ChN	24

Shutouts		Saves		Games Finished		Batters Faced		Innings Pitched		Hits Allowed	
B. Adams, Pit	8	B. Sherdel, StL	6	B. Sherdel, StL	28	P. Alexander, ChN	1447	P. Alexander, ChN	363.1	P. Alexander, ChN	335
P. Alexander, ChN	7	H. McQuillan, Bos	5	H. Betts, Phi	18	W. Cooper, Pit	1312	W. Cooper, Pit	327.0	J. Scott, Bos	308
5 tied with	5	P. Alexander, ChN	5	A. Mamaux, Bro	17	J. Haines, StL	1258	B. Grimes, Bro	303.2	W. Cooper, Pit	307
		B. Hubbell, 2tm	4	3 tied with	15	H. Vaughn, ChN	1255	J. Haines, StL	301.2	J. Haines, StL	303
		A. Mamaux, Bro	4			J. Oeschger, Bos	1250	H. Vaughn, ChN	301.0	H. Vaughn, ChN	301

Home Runs Allowed		Walks		Walks/9 Innings		Strikeouts		Strikeouts/9 Innings		Strikeout/Walk Ratio	
G. Smith, Phi	10	F. Schupp, StL	127	B. Adams, Pit	0.6	P. Alexander, ChN	173	P. Alexander, ChN	4.3	B. Adams, Pit	4.67
J. Oeschger, Bos	10	J. Oeschger, Bos	99	W. Cooper, Pit	1.4	B. Grimes, Bro	131	F. Schupp, StL	4.3	R. Marquard, Bro	2.54
J. Haines, StL	9	D. Ruether, Cin	96	A. Nehf, NYG	1.4	H. Vaughn, ChN	131	R. Marquard, Bro	4.2	P. Alexander, ChN	2.51
J. Barnes, NYG	9	J. Ring, Cin	92	R. Benton, NYG	1.4	J. Haines, StL	120	H. Vaughn, ChN	3.9	W. Cooper, Pit	2.19
6 tied with	8	L. Meadows, Phi	90	R. Marquard, Bro	1.7	F. Schupp, StL	119	B. Grimes, Bro	3.9	B. Grimes, Bro	1.96

Earned Run Average		Component ERA		Hit Batsmen		Wild Pitches		Opponent Average		Opponent OBP	
P. Alexander, ChN	1.91	B. Adams, Pit	1.94	J. Scott, Bos	13	E. Ponder, Pit	10	D. Luque, Cin	.225	B. Adams, Pit	.259
B. Adams, Pit	2.16	D. Luque, Cin	2.25	B. Sherdel, StL	11	B. Grimes, Bro	9	B. Grimes, Bro	.238	B. Grimes, Bro	.282
B. Grimes, Bro	2.22	B. Grimes, Bro	2.28	W. Cooper, Pit	11	J. Scott, Bos	9	B. Adams, Pit	.244	P. Alexander, ChN	.285
W. Cooper, Pit	2.39	E. Ponder, Pit	2.39	3 tied with	9	J. Ring, Cin	8	E. Ponder, Pit	.246	D. Luque, Cin	.286
D. Ruether, Cin	2.47	P. Alexander, ChN	2.40			E. Rixey, Phi	8	D. Ruether, Cin	.247	E. Ponder, Pit	.286

1920 National League Miscellaneous

Managers

Boston	George Stallings	62-90
Brooklyn	Wilbert Robinson	93-61
Chicago	Fred Mitchell	75-79
Cincinnati	Pat Moran	82-71
New York	John McGraw	86-68
Philadelphia	Gavvy Cravath	62-91
Pittsburgh	George Gibson	79-75
St. Louis	Branch Rickey	75-79

Awards

STATS Most Valuable Player	Rogers Hornsby, 2b, StL
STATS Cy Young	Pete Alexander, ChN
STATS Rookie of the Year	Pat Duncan, of, Cin
STATS Manager of the Year	Wilbert Robinson, Bro

STATS All-Star Team

C	Verne Clemons, StL	.281	1	36
1B	George Kelly, NYG	.266	11	94
2B	Rogers Hornsby, StL	.370	9	94
3B	Milt Stock, StL	.319	0	76
SS	Dave Bancroft, 2tm	.299	0	36
OF	Edd Roush, Cin	.339	4	90
OF	Zack Wheat, Bro	.328	9	73
OF	Ross Youngs, NYG	.351	6	78
P	Pete Alexander, ChN	27-14	1.91	173 K
P	Wilbur Cooper, Pit	24-15	2.39	114 K
P	Burleigh Grimes, Bro	23-11	2.22	131 K
P	Fred Toney, NYG	21-11	2.65	81 K

Postseason

World Series	Brooklyn (NL) 2 vs. Cleveland (AL) 5

Outstanding Performances

Cycles

George Burns, NYG   on September 17

1921 American League Standings

Team	Overall					Home Games						Road Games						Park Index		Record by Month					
	W	L	Pct	GB	DIF	W	L	R	OR	HR	OHR	W	L	R	OR	HR	OHR	Run	HR	M/A	May	June	July	Aug	S/O
New York	98	55	.641	—	54	53	25	500	355	83	34	45	30	448	353	51	17	103	165	6-6	18-10	17-12	17-7	17-11	23-9
Cleveland	94	60	.610	4.5	115	51	26	467	330	15	10	43	34	458	382	27	33	95	42	11-5	18-9	15-11	18-10	15-12	17-13
St. Louis	81	73	.526	17.5	1	43	34	423	434	42	43	38	39	412	411	25	28	104	160	5-8	14-15	12-15	13-12	21-11	16-12
Washington	80	73	.523	18.0	4	46	30	358	332	14	13	34	43	346	406	28	38	93	41	10-4	11-17	16-12	16-15	12-14	15-11
Boston	75	79	.487	23.5	1	41	36	332	333	3	16	34	43	336	363	14	37	95	37	5-5	11-14	16-14	10-19	16-10	17-17
Detroit	71	82	.464	27.0	1	37	40	433	412	19	28	34	42	450	440	39	43	94	57	6-7	18-15	10-14	14-15	12-17	11-14
Chicago	62	92	.403	36.5	0	37	40	378	399	12	20	25	52	305	459	23	32	102	58	4-6	13-17	9-15	16-16	11-18	9-20
Philadelphia	53	100	.346	45.0	0	28	47	353	464	65	59	25	53	304	430	17	26	116	300	3-9	11-17	12-14	10-20	7-18	10-22

Clinch Date—New York 10/01.

Team Batting

Team	G	AB	R	OR	H	2B	3B	HR	TB	RBI	TBB	IBB	SO	HBP	SH	SF	SB	CS	SB%	GDP	Avg	OBP	Slg
New York	153	5249	948	708	1576	285	87	134	2437	861	588	—	569	41	190	—	89	64	.58	—	.300	.375	.464
Cleveland	154	5383	925	712	1656	355	90	42	2317	829	376	—	376	37	232	—	51	42	.55	—	.308	.383	.430
Detroit	154	5461	883	852	1724	268	100	58	2366	793	582	—	376	29	227	—	95	89	.52	—	.316	.385	.433
St. Louis	154	5442	835	845	1655	246	106	67	2314	719	413	—	407	36	188	—	91	71	.56	—	.304	.357	.425
Washington	154	5294	704	738	1468	240	96	42	2026	610	462	—	472	58	185	—	112	66	.63	—	.277	.342	.383
Chicago	154	5329	683	858	1509	242	82	35	2020	609	445	—	474	43	183	—	93	93	.50	—	.283	.343	.379
Boston	154	5206	668	696	1440	284	69	17	1877	560	428	—	344	28	187	—	83	65	.56	—	.277	.335	.361
Philadelphia	155	5465	657	894	1497	256	64	82	2127	605	424	—	565	29	136	—	69	56	.55	—	.274	.330	.389
AL Total	1232	42829	6303	6303	12525	2140	694	477	17484	5586	3965	—	3583	301	1528	—	683	546	.56	—	.292	.357	.408
AL Avg Team	154	5354	788	788	1566	268	87	60	2186	698	496	—	448	38	191	—	85	68	.56	—	.292	.357	.408

Team Pitching

Team	G	CG	ShO	Rel	Sv	IP	H	R	ER	HR	SH	SF	HB	TBB	IBB	SO	WP	Bk	H/9	SO/9	BB/9	OAvg	OOBP	ERA
New York	153	92	8	96	15	1364.0	1461	708	579	51	143	—	51	470	—	481	23	3	9.6	3.2	3.1	.277	.342	3.82
Cleveland	154	81	11	114	14	1377.0	1534	712	597	43	201	—	27	431	—	475	20	3	10.0	3.1	2.8	.288	.344	3.90
Washington	154	80	10	108	10	1383.2	1568	738	611	51	171	—	35	442	—	452	28	2	10.2	2.9	2.9	.291	.349	3.97
Boston	154	88	9	82	5	1364.1	1521	696	604	53	198	—	41	452	—	446	15	1	10.0	2.9	3.0	.291	.352	3.98
Detroit	154	73	4	115	16	1386.1	1634	852	678	71	182	—	54	495	—	452	19	7	10.6	2.9	3.2	.297	.361	4.40
St. Louis	154	77	9	144	9	1379.0	1541	845	706	71	195	—	39	556	—	477	17	4	10.1	3.1	3.6	.288	.359	4.61
Philadelphia	155	75	2	119	7	1400.1	1645	894	717	85	217	—	32	548	—	431	34	7	10.6	2.8	3.5	.300	.367	4.61
Chicago	154	84	7	106	9	1365.1	1603	858	749	52	223	—	36	549	—	392	23	5	10.6	2.6	3.6	.303	.372	4.94
AL Total	1232	650	60	884	85	11020.0	12507	6303	5241	477	1530	—	315	3943	—	3606	179	32	10.2	2.9	3.2	.292	.356	4.28
AL Avg Team	154	81	8	111	11	1377.0	1563	788	655	60	191	—	39	493	—	451	22	4	10.2	2.9	3.2	.292	.356	4.28

Team Fielding

Team	G	PO	A	E	TC	DP	PB	Pct
Boston	154	4087	1964	157	6208	151	12	.975
Chicago	154	4099	2125	200	6424	155	12	.969
Cleveland	154	4123	1869	204	6196	124	12	.967
New York	153	4090	1965	222	6277	138	13	.965
St. Louis	154	4117	1881	224	6222	127	7	.964
Detroit	154	4158	1948	232	6338	107	15	.963
Washington	154	4131	1920	235	6286	153	8	.963
Philadelphia	155	4182	2005	274	6461	144	14	.958
AL Total	1232	32987	15677	1748	50412	1099	93	.965

Team vs. Team Records

	Bos	ChA	Cle	Det	NYA	Phi	StL	Was	Won
Bos	—	15	8	15	7	12	9	9	75
ChA	7	—	7	8	13	14	7	6	62
Cle	14	15	—	13	8	15	17	12	94
Det	7	14	9	—	5	14	12	10	71
NYA	15	9	14	17	—	17	13	13	98
Phi	10	8	7	7	5	—	5	11	53
StL	13	15	5	10	9	17	—	12	81
Was	13	16	10	12	8	11	10	—	80
Lost	79	92	60	82	55	100	73	73	

1921 American League Batting Leaders

Games		At-Bats		Runs		Hits		Doubles		Triples	
J. Dykes, Phi	155	J. Tobin, StL	671	B. Ruth, NYA	177	H. Heilmann, Det	237	T. Speaker, Cle	52	H. Shanks, Was	19
6 tied with	154	W. Witt, Phi	629	J. Tobin, StL	132	J. Tobin, StL	236	B. Ruth, NYA	44	G. Sisler, StL	18
		J. Judge, Was	622	R. Peckinpaugh, NYA	128	G. Sisler, StL	216	H. Heilmann, Det	43	J. Tobin, StL	18
		J. Dykes, Phi	613	G. Sisler, StL	125	B. D. Jacobson, StL	211	B. Veach, Det	43	3 tied with	16
		E. Johnson, ChA	613	T. Cobb, Det	124	B. Veach, Det	207	B. Meusel, NYA	40		

Home Runs		Total Bases		Runs Batted In		Walks		Intentional Walks		Strikeouts	
B. Ruth, NYA	59	B. Ruth, NYA	457	B. Ruth, NYA	171	B. Ruth, NYA	144	Statistic unavailable		B. Meusel, NYA	88
B. Meusel, NYA	24	H. Heilmann, Det	365	H. Heilmann, Det	139	L. Blue, Det	103			B. Ruth, NYA	81
K. Williams, StL	24	B. Meusel, NYA	334	B. Meusel, NYA	135	R. Peckinpaugh, NYA	84			J. Dykes, Phi	75
T. Walker, Phi	23	J. Tobin, StL	327	B. Veach, Det	128	J. Sewell, Cle	80			B. Falk, ChA	69
H. Heilmann, Det	19	G. Sisler, StL	326	K. Williams, StL	117	W. Schang, NYA	78			A. Ward, NYA	68

Hit By Pitch		Sac Hits		Sac Flies		Stolen Bases		Caught Stealing		GDP	
B. Harris, Was	18	B. Wambsganss, Cle	43	Statistic unavailable		G. Sisler, StL	35	J. Mulligan, ChA	18	Statistic unavailable	
J. Mostil, ChA	13	D. Bush, 2tm	41			B. Harris, Was	29	L. Blue, Det	17		
J. Sewell, Cle	11	S. McInnis, Bos	35			S. Rice, Was	25	K. Williams, StL	17		
3 tied with	9	J. Mulligan, ChA	34			E. Johnson, ChA	22	W. Witt, Phi	15		
		2 tied with	33			T. Cobb, Det	22	T. Cobb, Det	15		

Runs Created		Runs Created/27 Outs		Batting Average		On-Base Percentage		Slugging Percentage		OBP+Slugging	
B. Ruth, NYA	208	B. Ruth, NYA	15.47	H. Heilmann, Det	.394	B. Ruth, NYA	.512	B. Ruth, NYA	.846	B. Ruth, NYA	1.358
H. Heilmann, Det	141	H. Heilmann, Det	9.59	T. Cobb, Det	.389	T. Cobb, Det	.452	H. Heilmann, Det	.606	H. Heilmann, Det	1.051
G. Sisler, StL	127	T. Cobb, Det	9.27	B. Ruth, NYA	.378	H. Heilmann, Det	.444	T. Cobb, Det	.596	T. Cobb, Det	1.048
K. Williams, StL	124	T. Speaker, Cle	8.98	G. Sisler, StL	.371	T. Speaker, Cle	.439	K. Williams, StL	.561	K. Williams, StL	.990
T. Cobb, Det	120	G. Sisler, StL	8.53	T. Speaker, Cle	.362	K. Williams, StL	.429	G. Sisler, StL	.560	T. Speaker, Cle	.977

1921 American League Pitching Leaders

Wins		Losses		Winning Percentage		Games		Games Started		Complete Games	
U. Shocker, StL	27	E. Rommel, Phi	23	C. Mays, NYA	.750	C. Mays, NYA	49	S. Coveleski, Cle	40	R. Faber, ChA	32
C. Mays, NYA	27	R. Wilkinson, ChA	20	U. Shocker, StL	.692	B. Bayne, StL	47	U. Shocker, StL	39	U. Shocker, StL	31
R. Faber, ChA	25	D. Kerr, ChA	17	R. Collins, NYA	.688	U. Shocker, StL	47	R. Faber, ChA	39	C. Mays, NYA	30
S. Jones, Bos	23	5 tied with	16	B. Bayne, StL	.688	E. Rommel, Phi	46	C. Mays, NYA	38	S. Coveleski, Cle	29
S. Coveleski, Cle	23			J. Bush, Bos	.640	2 tied with	44	S. Jones, Bos	38	3 tied with	25

Shutouts		Saves		Games Finished		Batters Faced		Innings Pitched		Hits Allowed	
S. Jones, Bos	5	J. Middleton, Det	7	B. Burwell, StL	21	U. Shocker, StL	1401	C. Mays, NYA	336.2	D. Kerr, ChA	357
U. Shocker, StL	4	C. Mays, NYA	7	J. Middleton, Det	20	C. Mays, NYA	1400	R. Faber, ChA	330.2	U. Shocker, StL	345
R. Faber, ChA	4	4 tied with	4	A. Russell, Bos	19	D. Kerr, ChA	1360	U. Shocker, StL	326.2	S. Coveleski, Cle	341
G. Mogridge, Was	4			3 tied with	18	S. Coveleski, Cle	1360	S. Coveleski, Cle	316.0	C. Mays, NYA	332
4 tied with	3					R. Faber, ChA	1350	D. Kerr, ChA	308.2	S. Jones, Bos	318

Home Runs Allowed		Walks		Walks/9 Innings		Strikeouts		Strikeouts/9 Innings		Strikeout/Walk Ratio	
E. Rommel, Phi	21	D. Davis, StL	123	C. Mays, NYA	2.0	W. Johnson, Was	143	W. Johnson, Was	4.9	D. Leonard, Det	1.90
U. Shocker, StL	21	R. Moore, Phi	122	G. Mogridge, Was	2.1	U. Shocker, StL	132	B. Shawkey, NYA	4.6	W. Johnson, Was	1.55
D. Kerr, ChA	19	D. Kerr, ChA	96	J. Bagby, Cle	2.1	B. Shawkey, NYA	126	D. Leonard, Det	4.4	H. Pennock, Bos	1.54
S. Harriss, Phi	16	J. Bush, Bos	93	T. Zachary, Was	2.1	R. Faber, ChA	124	D. Mails, Cle	4.0	U. Shocker, StL	1.53
3 tied with	15	W. Johnson, Was	92	D. Leonard, Det	2.3	D. Leonard, Det	120	H. Pennock, Bos	3.7	G. Mogridge, Was	1.53

Earned Run Average		Component ERA		Hit Batsmen		Wild Pitches		Opponent Average		Opponent OBP	
R. Faber, ChA	2.48	R. Faber, ChA	2.53	H. Ehmke, Det	13	R. Moore, Phi	9	R. Faber, ChA	.242	R. Faber, ChA	.297
G. Mogridge, Was	3.00	C. Mays, NYA	2.93	H. Dauss, Det	13	5 tied with	7	C. Mays, NYA	.257	C. Mays, NYA	.303
C. Mays, NYA	3.05	S. Jones, Bos	3.27	D. Kerr, ChA	11			J. Bush, Bos	.260	G. Mogridge, Was	.313
W. Hoyt, NYA	3.09	G. Mogridge, Was	3.28	4 tied with	10			B. Shawkey, NYA	.263	U. Shocker, StL	.319
S. Jones, Bos	3.22	W. Johnson, Was	3.35					W. Johnson, Was	.263	W. Johnson, Was	.326

1921 American League Miscellaneous

Managers

Boston	Hugh Duffy	75-79
Chicago	Kid Gleason	62-92
Cleveland	Tris Speaker	94-60
Detroit	Ty Cobb	71-82
New York	Miller Huggins	98-55
Philadelphia	Connie Mack	53-100
St. Louis	Lee Fohl	81-73
Washington	George McBride	80-73

Awards

STATS Most Valuable Player	Babe Ruth, of, NYA
STATS Cy Young	Red Faber, ChA
STATS Rookie of the Year	Joe Sewell, ss, Cle
STATS Manager of the Year	George McBride, Was

STATS All-Star Team

C	Wally Schang, NYA	.316	6	55
1B	George Sisler, StL	.371	12	104
2B	Del Pratt, Bos	.324	5	100
3B	Larry Gardner, Cle	.319	3	115
SS	Joe Sewell, Cle	.318	4	91
OF	Ty Cobb, Det	.389	12	101
OF	Harry Heilmann, Det	.394	19	139
OF	Babe Ruth, NYA	.378	59	171
P	Red Faber, ChA	25-15	2.48	124 K
P	Sad Sam Jones, Bos	23-16	3.22	98 K
P	Carl Mays, NYA	27-9	3.05	70 K
P	Urban Shocker, StL	27-12	3.55	132 K

Postseason

World Series	NYA (AL) 3 vs. NYG (NL) 5

Outstanding Performances

Cycles

Bob Meusel, NYA	on May 7
George Sisler, StL	on August 13

1921 National League Standings

Team	Overall					Home Games						Road Games						Park Index		Record by Month					
	W	L	Pct	GB	DIF	W	L	R	OR	HR	OHR	W	L	R	OR	HR	OHR	Run	HR	M/A	May	June	July	Aug	S/O
New York	94	59	.614	—	32	**53**	**26**	**407**	321	49	46	41	33	**433**	316	26	33	91	151	7-6	20-8	13-12	20-11	18-13	16-9
Pittsburgh	90	63	.588	4.0	140	45	31	343	295	13	10	**45**	**32**	349	**300**	24	27	100	46	11-3	17-8	18-11	14-13	20-11	20-8
St. Louis	87	66	.569	7.0	0	48	29	397	307	43	25	39	37	412	374	40	36	88	88	2-9	14-11	18-12	13-15	14-19	12-17
Boston	79	74	.516	15.0	0	42	32	332	**292**	18	18	37	42	389	405	**43**	36	84	49	6-9	13-10	16-10	18-9	14-19	12-17
Brooklyn	77	75	.507	16.5	1	41	37	360	361	32	23	36	38	307	320	27	**23**	109	104	10-5	11-17	13-12	15-15	16-13	12-13
Cincinnati	70	83	.458	24.0	1	40	36	321	306	5	**2**	30	47	297	343	15	35	99	14	7-9	8-18	10-14	16-14	15-13	13-13
Chicago	64	89	.418	30.0	7	32	44	345	434	23	37	32	45	323	339	14	30	119	138	6-5	10-15	13-14	12-20	8-21	15-14
Philadelphia	51	103	.331	43.5	0	29	47	326	485	**67**	49	22	56	291	434	21	30	115	233	5-8	9-15	5-21	10-21	13-19	9-19

Clinch Date—New York 9/28.

Team Batting

Team	G	AB	R	OR	H	2B	3B	HR	TB	RBI	TBB	IBB	SO	HBP	SH	SF	SB	CS	SB%	GDP	Avg	OBP	Slg
New York	153	5278	**840**	637	1575	237	93	75	2223	**748**	469	—	390	33	166	—	**137**	114	.55	—	.298	**.359**	.421
St. Louis	154	5309	809	681	**1635**	**260**	88	83	**2320**	733	382	—	452	29	195	—	94	94	.50	—	**.308**	.358	**.437**
Boston	153	**5385**	721	697	1561	209	100	61	2153	630	377	—	470	22	198	—	94	100	.48	—	.290	.339	.400
Pittsburgh	154	5379	692	**595**	1533	231	**104**	37	2083	623	343	—	371	23	**208**	—	134	93	**.59**	—	.285	.330	.387
Chicago	153	5321	668	773	1553	234	56	37	2010	609	343	—	374	35	203	—	70	97	.42	—	.292	.339	.378
Brooklyn	152	5263	667	681	1476	209	85	59	2032	584	325	—	400	21	164	—	91	73	.55	—	.280	.325	.386
Cincinnati	153	5112	618	649	1421	221	94	20	1890	560	375	—	308	**45**	195	—	117	**120**	.49	—	.278	.333	.370
Philadelphia	154	5329	617	919	1512	238	50	**88**	2114	573	294	—	**615**	25	112	—	66	80	.45	—	.284	.324	.397
NL Total	1226	42376	5632	5632	12266	1839	670	460	16825	5060	2906	—	3380	233	1441	—	803	771	.51	—	.289	.338	.397
NL Avg Team	153	5297	704	704	1533	230	84	58	2103	633	363	—	423	29	180	—	100	96	.51	—	.289	.338	.397

Team Pitching

Team	G	CG	ShO	Rel	Sv	IP	H	R	ER	HR	SH	SF	HB	TBB	IBB	SO	WP	Bk	H/9	SO/9	BB/9	OAvg	OOBP	ERA
Pittsburgh	154	**88**	10	91	10	1415.2	**1448**	595	498	37	174	—	37	322	—	**500**	19	1	**9.2**	**3.2**	2.0	**.271**	**.316**	3.17
Cincinnati	153	83	7	95	9	1363.0	1500	649	524	37	183	—	15	305	—	408	18	3	9.9	2.7	2.0	.287	.328	3.46
New York	153	71	9	127	**18**	1372.1	1497	637	542	79	185	—	15	**295**	—	357	21	2	9.8	2.3	**1.9**	.286	.326	3.55
St. Louis	154	70	10	**155**	16	1371.2	1486	681	552	61	168	—	40	399	—	464	35	3	9.8	3.0	2.6	.282	.337	3.62
Brooklyn	152	82	8	106	12	1363.1	1556	681	560	46	175	—	32	361	—	471	23	0	10.3	3.1	2.4	.293	.342	3.70
Boston	153	74	**11**	124	12	1385.0	1488	697	600	54	**157**	—	38	420	—	382	8	3	9.7	2.5	2.7	.280	.337	3.90
Chicago	153	73	7	120	7	1363.0	1605	773	665	67	180	—	40	409	—	441	17	3	10.6	2.9	2.7	.303	.356	4.39
Philadelphia	154	82	5	107	8	1348.2	1665	919	671	79	209	—	32	371	—	333	**40**	3	11.1	2.2	2.5	.308	.356	4.48
NL Total	1226	623	67	925	92	10982.2	12245	5632	4612	460	1431	—	249	2882	—	3356	181	18	10.1	2.8	2.4	.289	.338	3.78
NL Avg Team	153	78	8	116	12	1372.2	1531	704	577	58	179	—	31	360	—	420	23	2	10.1	2.8	2.4	.289	.338	3.78

Team Fielding

Team	G	PO	A	E	TC	DP	PB	Pct
Chicago	153	4080	2052	**166**	6298	129	7	.974
Pittsburgh	154	**4239**	1867	172	6278	129	8	.973
New York	153	4111	2128	187	6426	**155**	8	.971
Cincinnati	153	4080	1951	193	6224	139	14	.969
Boston	153	4157	2040	199	6396	122	8	.969
St. Louis	154	4114	1958	219	6291	130	**17**	.965
Brooklyn	152	4087	2132	232	6451	142	14	.964
Philadelphia	154	4040	**2176**	295	**6511**	127	15	.955
NL Total	1226	32908	16304	1663	50875	1073	91	.967

Team vs. Team Records

	Bos	Bro	ChN	Cin	NYG	Phi	Pit	StL	Won
Bos	—	11	14	13	8	14	9	10	**79**
Bro	11	—	10	10	12	16	10	8	**77**
ChN	8	11	—	13	8	11	5	8	**64**
Cin	9	11	9	—	8	13	8	12	**70**
NYG	13	10	14	14	—	16	16	11	**94**
Phi	8	6	11	9	6	—	4	7	**51**
Pit	13	12	17	14	6	18	—	10	**90**
StL	12	14	14	10	11	15	11	—	**87**
Lost	74	75	89	83	59	103	63	66	

1921 National League Batting Leaders

Games		At-Bats		Runs		Hits		Doubles		Triples	
R. Hornsby, StL	154	I. Olson, Bro	652	R. Hornsby, StL	131	R. Hornsby, StL	235	R. Hornsby, StL	44	R. Hornsby, StL	18
5 tied with	153	C. Bigbee, Pit	632	F. Frisch, NYG	121	F. Frisch, NYG	211	G. Kelly, NYG	42	R. Powell, Bos	18
		R. Powell, Bos	624	D. Bancroft, NYG	121	C. Bigbee, Pit	204	J. Johnston, Bro	41	F. Frisch, NYG	17
		J. Johnston, Bro	624	R. Powell, Bos	114	J. Johnston, Bro	203	R. Grimes, ChN	38	C. Bigbee, Pit	17
		F. Frisch, NYG	618	G. Burns, NYG	111	2 tied with	201	A. McHenry, StL	37	C. Grimm, Pit	17

Home Runs		Total Bases		Runs Batted In		Walks		Intentional Walks		Strikeouts	
G. Kelly, NYG	23	R. Hornsby, StL	378	R. Hornsby, StL	126	G. Burns, NYG	80	Statistic unavailable		R. Powell, Bos	85
R. Hornsby, StL	21	G. Kelly, NYG	310	G. Kelly, NYG	122	R. Youngs, NYG	71			F. Parkinson, Phi	81
C. Williams, Phi	18	A. McHenry, StL	305	A. McHenry, StL	102	R. Grimes, ChN	70			G. Kelly, NYG	73
A. McHenry, StL	17	I. Meusel, 2tm	302	R. Youngs, NYG	102	M. Carey, Pit	70			R. Grimes, ChN	55
J. Fournier, StL	16	F. Frisch, NYG	300	F. Frisch, NYG	100	D. Bancroft, NYG	66			2 tied with	51

Hit By Pitch		Sac Hits		Sac Flies		Stolen Bases		Caught Stealing		GDP	
J. Fournier, StL	8	M. Stock, StL	36	Statistic unavailable		F. Frisch, NYG	49	S. Bohne, Cin	22	Statistic unavailable	
R. Hornsby, StL	7	B. Southworth, Bos	35			M. Carey, Pit	37	J. Fournier, StL	22		
5 tied with	6	Z. Terry, ChN	34			J. Johnston, Bro	28	4 tied with	20		
		J. Daubert, Cin	33			S. Bohne, Cin	26				
		M. Carey, Pit	30			R. Maranville, Pit	25				

Runs Created		Runs Created/27 Outs		Batting Average		On-Base Percentage		Slugging Percentage		OBP+Slugging	
R. Hornsby, StL	152	R. Hornsby, StL	10.41	R. Hornsby, StL	.397	R. Hornsby, StL	.458	R. Hornsby, StL	.639	R. Hornsby, StL	1.097
F. Frisch, NYG	120	W. Cruise, Bos	7.84	E. Roush, Cin	.352	W. Cruise, Bos	.429	A. McHenry, StL	.531	W. Cruise, Bos	.932
D. Bancroft, NYG	111	F. Frisch, NYG	7.09	A. McHenry, StL	.350	R. Youngs, NYG	.411	G. Kelly, NYG	.528	A. McHenry, StL	.924
J. Fournier, StL	110	A. McHenry, StL	6.93	W. Cruise, Bos	.346	J. Fournier, StL	.409	I. Meusel, 2tm	.515	J. Fournier, StL	.914
G. Kelly, NYG	109	R. Youngs, NYG	6.91	J. Fournier, StL	.343	R. Grimes, ChN	.406	J. Fournier, StL	.505	E. Roush, Cin	.905

1921 National League Pitching Leaders

Wins		Losses		Winning Percentage		Games		Games Started		Complete Games	
B. Grimes, Bro	22	G. Smith, Phi	20	W. Glazner, Pit	.737	J. Scott, Bos	47	W. Cooper, Pit	38	B. Grimes, Bro	30
W. Cooper, Pit	22	J. Ring, Phi	19	B. Adams, Pit	.737	J. Oeschger, Bos	46	D. Luque, Cin	36	W. Cooper, Pit	29
A. Nehf, NYG	20	D. Luque, Cin	19	B. Doak, StL	.714	H. McQuillan, Bos	45	J. Oeschger, Bos	36	D. Luque, Cin	25
J. Oeschger, Bos	20	E. Rixey, Cin	18	A. Nehf, NYG	.667	M. Watson, Bos	44	E. Rixey, Cin	36	3 tied with	21
E. Rixey, Cin	19	H. McQuillan, Bos	17	B. Grimes, Bro	.629	D. Fillingim, Bos	44	2 tied with	35		

Shutouts		Saves		Games Finished		Batters Faced		Innings Pitched		Hits Allowed	
8 tied with	3	L. North, StL	7	L. North, StL	26	W. Cooper, Pit	1377	W. Cooper, Pit	327.0	W. Cooper, Pit	341
		J. Barnes, NYG	6	H. Betts, Phi	22	E. Rixey, Cin	1260	D. Luque, Cin	304.0	E. Rixey, Cin	324
		H. McQuillan, Bos	5	H. Carlson, Pit	19	D. Luque, Cin	1259	B. Grimes, Bro	302.1	D. Luque, Cin	318
		4 tied with	4	S. Sallee, NYG	19	B. Grimes, Bro	1253	E. Rixey, Cin	301.0	B. Grimes, Bro	313
				2 tied with	17	J. Oeschger, Bos	1248	J. Oeschger, Bos	299.0	2 tied with	303

Home Runs Allowed		Walks		Walks/9 Innings		Strikeouts		Strikeouts/9 Innings		Strikeout/Walk Ratio	
B. Hubbell, Phi	18	J. Oeschger, Bos	97	B. Adams, Pit	1.0	B. Grimes, Bro	136	B. Grimes, Bro	4.0	B. Adams, Pit	3.06
A. Nehf, NYG	18	H. McQuillan, Bos	90	P. Alexander, ChN	1.2	W. Cooper, Pit	134	W. Cooper, Pit	3.7	P. Alexander, ChN	2.33
L. Cadore, Bro	17	J. Ring, Phi	88	J. Barnes, NYG	1.5	D. Luque, Cin	102	B. Doak, StL	3.6	B. Doak, StL	2.24
P. Douglas, NYG	17	W. Cooper, Pit	80	B. Hubbell, Phi	1.6	H. McQuillan, Bos	94	S. Martin, ChN	3.6	B. Grimes, Bro	1.79
J. Haines, StL	15	B. Grimes, Bro	76	B. Doak, StL	1.6	3 tied with	88	W. Glazner, Pit	3.4	R. Marquard, Cin	1.76

Earned Run Average		Component ERA		Hit Batsmen		Wild Pitches		Opponent Average		Opponent OBP	
B. Doak, StL	2.59	B. Adams, Pit	2.32	J. Oeschger, Bos	15	J. Ring, Phi	14	W. Glazner, Pit	.250	B. Adams, Pit	.272
B. Adams, Pit	2.64	J. Morrison, Pit	2.56	W. Glazner, Pit	12	L. Meadows, Phi	10	B. Adams, Pit	.251	J. Morrison, Pit	.305
W. Glazner, Pit	2.77	W. Glazner, Pit	2.71	B. Pertica, StL	10	D. Ruether, Bro	7	J. Morrison, Pit	.258	W. Glazner, Pit	.306
E. Rixey, Cin	2.78	B. Doak, StL	3.10	W. Cooper, Pit	10	B. Grimes, Bro	6	B. Pertica, StL	.267	A. Nehf, NYG	.311
B. Grimes, Bro	2.83	E. Rixey, Cin	3.17	V. Cheeves, ChN	9	E. Rixey, Cin	6	M. Watson, Bos	.270	D. Luque, Cin	.312

1921 National League Miscellaneous

Managers		
Boston	Fred Mitchell	79-74
Brooklyn	Wilbert Robinson	77-75
Chicago	Johnny Evers	41-55
	Bill Killefer	23-34
Cincinnati	Pat Moran	70-83
New York	John McGraw	94-59
Philadelphia	Wild Bill Donovan	25-62
	Kaiser Wilhelm	26-41
Pittsburgh	George Gibson	90-63
St. Louis	Branch Rickey	87-66

Awards

STATS Most Valuable Player	Rogers Hornsby, 2b, StL
STATS Cy Young	Burleigh Grimes, Bro
STATS Rookie of the Year	Ray Grimes, 1b, ChN
STATS Manager of the Year	Branch Rickey, StL

STATS All-Star Team

C	Frank Snyder, NYG	.320	8	45
1B	George Kelly, NYG	.308	23	122
2B	Rogers Hornsby, StL	.397	21	126
3B	Frankie Frisch, NYG	.341	8	100
SS	Dave Bancroft, NYG	.318	6	67
OF	Austin McHenry, StL	.350	17	102
OF	Irish Meusel, 2tm	.343	14	87
OF	Ross Youngs, NYG	.327	3	102
P	Wilbur Cooper, Pit	22-14	3.25	134 K
P	Burleigh Grimes, Bro	22-13	2.83	136 K
P	Art Nehf, NYG	20-10	3.63	67 K
P	Eppa Rixey, Cin	19-18	2.78	76 K

Postseason

World Series   NYG (NL) 5 vs. NYA (AL) 3

Outstanding Performances

Cycles
Dave Bancroft, NYG on June 1
Dave Robertson, Pit on August 30

1922 American League Standings

Team	Overall					Home Games						Road Games						Park Index		Record by Month					
	W	L	Pct	GB	DIF	W	L	R	OR	HR	OHR	W	L	R	OR	HR	OHR	Run	HR	M/A	May	June	July	Aug	S/O
New York	94	60	.610	—	95	50	27	387	291	53	48	44	33	371	327	42	25	97	151	11-5	17-12	11-15	18-12	20-6	17-10
St. Louis	93	61	.604	1.0	78	54	23	471	314	70	41	39	38	396	329	28	30	108	191	4-11	16-11	15-11	18-14	15-13	11-15
Detroit	79	75	.513	15.0	0	43	34	426	370	15	32	36	41	402	421	39	30	97	68	7-8	13-16	12-14	20-12	12-13	14-13
Cleveland	78	76	.506	16.0	10	44	35	423	424	12	20	34	41	345	393	20	38	109	52	8-6	11-17	15-7	19-16	12-13	14-13
Chicago	77	77	.500	17.0	0	43	34	351	335	10	21	34	43	340	356	35	36	99	44	8-9	11-15	15-7	19-16	10-17	14-14
Washington	69	85	.448	25.0	1	40	39	388	295	15	3	29	46	321	411	30	46	81	22	8-9	15-15	10-11	12-17	13-16	11-17
Philadelphia	65	89	.422	29.0	1	38	39	388	437	80	82	27	50	317	393	31	25	116	289	6-9	13-11	8-16	12-20	12-16	14-17
Boston	61	93	.396	33.0	0	31	42	280	344	6	17	30	51	318	425	39	31	93	36	6-8	11-15	13-16	9-20	9-16	13-18

Clinch Date—New York 9/30.

Team Batting

Team	G	AB	R	OR	H	2B	3B	HR	TB	RBI	TBB	IBB	SO	HBP	SH	SF	SB	CS	SB%	GDP	Avg	OBP	Slg
St. Louis	154	5416	867	643	1693	291	94	98	2466	785	473	—	381	35	205	—	136	76	.64	—	.313	.372	.455
Detroit	155	5360	828	791	1641	250	87	54	2227	735	530	—	378	36	244	—	78	62	.56	—	.306	.372	.415
Cleveland	155	5293	768	817	1544	320	73	32	2106	698	554	—	331	46	202	—	90	58	.61	—	.292	.364	.398
New York	154	5245	758	618	1504	220	75	95	2159	674	497	—	532	40	220	—	62	59	.51	—	.287	.353	.412
Philadelphia	155	5211	705	830	1409	229	63	111	2097	631	437	—	591	34	170	—	60	69	.47	—	.270	.331	.402
Chicago	155	5267	691	691	1463	243	62	45	1965	635	482	—	463	43	232	—	109	84	.56	—	.278	.343	.373
Washington	154	5201	650	706	1395	229	76	45	1911	575	458	—	442	56	153	—	97	63	.61	—	.268	.334	.367
Boston	154	5288	598	769	1392	250	55	45	1887	510	458	—	455	45	160	—	64	67	.49	—	.263	.316	.357
AL Total	1236	42281	5865	5865	12041	2032	585	525	16818	5243	3797	—	3573	335	1586	—	696	538	.56	—	.285	.348	.398
AL Avg Team	155	5285	733	733	1505	254	73	66	2102	655	475	—	447	42	198	—	87	67	.56	—	.285	.348	.398

Team Pitching

Team	G	CG	ShO	Rel	Sv	IP	H	R	ER	HR	SH	SF	HB	TBB	IBB	SO	WP	Bk	H/9	SO/9	BB/9	OAvg	OOBP	ERA
St. Louis	154	79	8	115	22	1392.0	1412	643	523	71	168	—	46	419	—	534	17	8	9.1	3.5	2.7	.268	.327	3.38
New York	154	100	7	69	14	1393.2	1402	618	525	73	148	—	21	423	—	458	20	1	9.1	3.0	2.7	.267	.325	3.39
Washington	154	84	13	97	10	1362.1	1485	706	577	49	196	—	45	500	—	422	31	7	9.8	2.8	3.3	.281	.349	3.81
Chicago	155	86	13	99	8	1403.2	1472	691	615	57	211	—	21	529	—	484	16	2	9.4	3.1	3.4	.277	.345	3.94
Detroit	155	67	7	133	15	1391.0	1554	791	660	62	186	—	84	473	—	461	19	2	10.1	3.0	3.1	.288	.354	4.27
Boston	154	71	10	130	6	1373.1	1508	769	656	48	233	—	43	503	—	359	28	3	9.9	2.4	3.3	.287	.354	4.30
Cleveland	155	76	14	135	7	1383.2	1605	817	705	58	189	—	42	464	—	489	28	3	10.4	3.2	3.0	.296	.356	4.59
Philadelphia	155	73	4	147	6	1362.1	1573	830	695	107	203	—	32	469	—	373	22	2	10.4	2.5	3.1	.297	.357	4.59
AL Total	1236	636	76	925	88	11062.0	12011	5865	4956	525	1534	—	334	3780	—	3580	181	28	9.8	2.9	3.1	.285	.348	4.03
AL Avg Team	155	80	10	116	11	1382.0	1501	733	620	66	192	—	42	473	—	448	23	4	9.8	2.9	3.1	.285	.348	4.03

Team Fielding

Team	G	PO	A	E	TC	DP	PB	Pct
Chicago	155	4197	1972	155	6324	143	3	.975
New York	154	4157	2029	157	6343	124	17	.975
Detroit	155	4163	2015	191	6369	133	10	.970
Washington	154	4051	2006	196	6253	168	11	.969
Cleveland	155	4139	1934	202	6275	147	20	.968
St. Louis	154	4156	1881	201	6238	158	7	.968
Philadelphia	155	4072	1978	215	6265	118	16	.966
Boston	154	4096	1999	224	6319	145	10	.965
AL Total	1236	33031	15814	1541	50386	1136	94	.969

Team vs. Team Records

	Bos	ChA	Cle	Det	NYA	Phi	StL	Was	Won
Bos	—	10	6	5	13	10	7	10	61
ChA	12	—	12	17	9	12	8	7	77
Cle	16	10	—	15	7	11	6	13	78
Det	17	5	7	—	11	16	9	14	79
NYA	9	13	15	11	—	17	14	15	94
Phi	12	10	11	6	5	—	9	12	65
StL	15	14	16	13	8	13	—	14	93
Was	12	15	9	8	7	10	8	—	69
Lost	93	77	76	75	60	89	61	85	

1922 American League Batting Leaders

Games		At-Bats		Runs		Hits		Doubles		Triples	
T. Rigney, Det	155	S. Rice, Was	633	G. Sisler, StL	134	G. Sisler, StL	246	T. Speaker, Cle	48	G. Sisler, StL	18
C. Galloway, Phi	155	J. Tobin, StL	625	L. Blue, Det	131	T. Cobb, Det	211	D. Pratt, Bos	44	B. D. Jacobson, StL	16
B. Veach, Det	155	B. Veach, Det	618	K. Williams, StL	128	J. Tobin, StL	207	G. Sisler, StL	42	T. Cobb, Det	16
7 tied with	154	D. Pratt, Bos	607	J. Tobin, StL	122	B. Veach, Det	202	T. Cobb, Det	42	J. Judge, Was	15
		M. McManus, StL	606	2 tied with	111	2 tied with	194	2 tied with	37	J. Mostil, ChA	14

Home Runs		Total Bases		Runs Batted In		Walks		Intentional Walks		Strikeouts	
K. Williams, StL	39	K. Williams, StL	367	K. Williams, StL	155	W. Witt, NYA	89	Statistic unavailable		J. Dykes, Phi	98
T. Walker, Phi	37	G. Sisler, StL	348	B. Veach, Det	126	B. Ruth, NYA	84			B. Ruth, NYA	80
B. Ruth, NYA	35	T. Walker, Phi	310	M. McManus, StL	109	L. Blue, Det	82			A. Ward, NYA	64
B. Miller, Phi	21	T. Cobb, Det	297	G. Sisler, StL	105	T. Speaker, Cle	77			T. Walker, Phi	64
H. Heilmann, Det	21	2 tied with	296	B. D. Jacobson, StL	102	K. Williams, StL	74			J. Wood, Cle	63

Hit By Pitch		Sac Hits		Sac Flies		Stolen Bases		Caught Stealing		GDP	
B. Harris, Was	14	B. Wambsganss, Cle	42	Statistic unavailable		G. Sisler, StL	51	K. Williams, StL	19	Statistic unavailable	
J. Mostil, ChA	14	T. Rigney, Det	39			K. Williams, StL	37	G. Sisler, StL	19		
F. Brower, Was	10	B. Veach, Det	36			B. Harris, Was	25	E. Johnson, ChA	18		
J. Dykes, Phi	10	G. Cutshaw, Det	33			E. Johnson, ChA	21	J. Judge, Was	15		
2 tied with	9	2 tied with	32			2 tied with	20	T. Cobb, Det	13		

Runs Created		Runs Created/27 Outs		Batting Average		On-Base Percentage		Slugging Percentage		OBP+Slugging	
G. Sisler, StL	140	T. Speaker, Cle	10.29	G. Sisler, StL	.420	T. Speaker, Cle	.474	B. Ruth, NYA	.672	B. Ruth, NYA	1.106
K. Williams, StL	134	G. Sisler, StL	9.78	T. Cobb, Det	.401	G. Sisler, StL	.467	K. Williams, StL	.627	T. Speaker, Cle	1.080
T. Cobb, Det	121	B. Ruth, NYA	9.73	T. Speaker, Cle	.378	T. Cobb, Det	.462	T. Speaker, Cle	.606	G. Sisler, StL	1.061
T. Speaker, Cle	110	H. Heilmann, Det	9.10	H. Heilmann, Det	.356	B. Ruth, NYA	.434	H. Heilmann, Det	.598	K. Williams, StL	1.040
3 tied with	107	T. Cobb, Det	8.93	B. Miller, Phi	.336	H. Heilmann, Det	.432	G. Sisler, StL	.594	H. Heilmann, Det	1.030

1922 American League Pitching Leaders

Wins		Losses		Winning Percentage		Games		Games Started		Complete Games	
E. Rommel, Phi	27	S. Harriss, Phi	20	J. Bush, NYA	.788	E. Rommel, Phi	51	G. Uhle, Cle	40	R. Faber, ChA	31
J. Bush, NYA	26	R. Francis, Was	18	R. Kolp, StL	.778	G. Uhle, Cle	50	U. Shocker, StL	38	U. Shocker, StL	29
U. Shocker, StL	24	4 tied with	17	E. Rommel, Phi	.675	U. Shocker, StL	48	R. Faber, ChA	38	G. Uhle, Cle	23
G. Uhle, Cle	22			D. Davis, StL	.647	S. Harriss, Phi	47	H. Pillette, Det	37	W. Johnson, Was	23
R. Faber, ChA	21			B. Shawkey, NYA	.625	2 tied with	45	C. Robertson, ChA	34	E. Rommel, Phi	22

Shutouts		Saves		Games Finished		Batters Faced		Innings Pitched		Hits Allowed	
G. Uhle, Cle	5	S. Jones, NYA	8	H. Pruett, StL	23	R. Faber, ChA	1464	R. Faber, ChA	353.0	U. Shocker, StL	365
5 tied with	4	H. Pruett, StL	7	S. Hodge, ChA	22	U. Shocker, StL	1441	U. Shocker, StL	348.0	R. Faber, ChA	334
		R. Wright, StL	5	B. Karr, Bos	20	G. Uhle, Cle	1263	B. Shawkey, NYA	299.2	G. Uhle, Cle	328
		3 tied with	4	C. Fullerton, Bos	17	B. Shawkey, NYA	1253	E. Rommel, Phi	294.0	G. Mogridge, Was	300
				2 tied with	16	H. Ehmke, Det	1232	G. Uhle, Cle	287.1	H. Ehmke, Det	299

Home Runs Allowed		Walks		Walks/9 Innings		Strikeouts		Strikeouts/9 Innings		Strikeout/Walk Ratio	
U. Shocker, StL	22	R. Collins, Bos	103	U. Shocker, StL	1.5	U. Shocker, StL	149	G. Morton, Cle	4.5	U. Shocker, StL	2.61
E. Rommel, Phi	21	H. Ehmke, Det	101	E. Vangilder, StL	1.8	R. Faber, ChA	148	S. Harriss, Phi	4.0	R. Faber, ChA	1.78
B. Hasty, Phi	20	W. Johnson, Was	99	C. Mays, NYA	1.9	B. Shawkey, NYA	130	B. Shawkey, NYA	3.9	S. Coveleski, Cle	1.53
S. Harriss, Phi	19	B. Shawkey, NYA	98	B. Hasty, Phi	1.9	H. Ehmke, Det	108	U. Shocker, StL	3.9	B. Shawkey, NYA	1.33
F. Heimach, Phi	18	H. Pillette, Det	95	E. Rommel, Phi	1.9	W. Johnson, Was	105	R. Faber, ChA	3.8	H. Dauss, Det	1.32

Earned Run Average		Component ERA		Hit Batsmen		Wild Pitches		Opponent Average		Opponent OBP	
R. Faber, ChA	2.80	R. Faber, ChA	2.68	H. Ehmke, Det	23	R. Francis, Was	7	J. Bush, NYA	.252	R. Faber, ChA	.299
H. Pillette, Det	2.85	J. Quinn, Bos	3.05	H. Pillette, Det	15	R. Collins, Bos	7	R. Faber, ChA	.252	U. Shocker, StL	.304
B. Shawkey, NYA	2.91	E. Vangilder, StL	3.16	O. Olsen, Det	14	H. Courtney, 2tm	7	B. Shawkey, NYA	.256	E. Rommel, Phi	.309
U. Shocker, StL	2.97	B. Shawkey, NYA	3.17	G. Uhle, Cle	13	H. Pennock, Bos	7	H. Pillette, Det	.258	E. Vangilder, StL	.310
W. Johnson, Was	2.99	U. Shocker, StL	3.19	2 tied with	11	2 tied with	6	D. Leverett, ChA	.264	J. Quinn, Bos	.311

1922 American League Miscellaneous

Managers

Boston	Hugh Duffy	61-93
Chicago	Kid Gleason	77-77
Cleveland	Tris Speaker	78-76
Detroit	Ty Cobb	79-75
New York	Miller Huggins	94-60
Philadelphia	Connie Mack	65-89
St. Louis	Lee Fohl	93-61
Washington	Clyde Milan	69-85

Awards

Most Valuable Player	George Sisler, 1b, StL
STATS Cy Young	Urban Shocker, StL
STATS Rookie of the Year	Herman Pillette, p, Det
STATS Manager of the Year	Lee Fohl, StL

STATS All-Star Team

C	Steve O'Neill, Cle	.311	2	65
1B	George Sisler, StL	.420	8	105
2B	Marty McManus, StL	.312	11	109
3B	Jimmy Dykes, Phi	.275	12	68
SS	Joe Sewell, Cle	.299	2	83
OF	Ty Cobb, Det	.401	4	99
OF	Babe Ruth, NYA	.315	35	96
OF	Ken Williams, StL	.332	39	155
P	Joe Bush, NYA	26-7	3.31	92 K
P	Red Faber, ChA	21-17	2.80	148 K
P	Eddie Rommel, Phi	27-13	3.28	54 K
P	Urban Shocker, StL	24-17	2.97	149 K

Postseason

World Series	NYA (AL) 0 vs. NYG (NL) 4 (1 tie)

Outstanding Performances

Perfect Games
C. Robertson, ChA @ Det on April 30
Three-Homer Games
Ken Williams, StL on April 22
Cycles
Ray Schalk, ChA on June 27
Bob Meusel, NYA on July 3

1922 National League Standings

Team	Overall W	L	Pct	GB	DIF	Home Games W	L	R	OR	HR	OHR	Road Games W	L	R	OR	HR	OHR	Park Index Run	HR	Record by Month M/A	May	June	July	Aug	S/O
New York	93	61	.604	—	162	51	27	439	333	47	38	42	34	413	325	33	33	102	125	12-3	14-12	17-9	15-14	16-10	19-13
Cincinnati	86	68	.558	7.0	0	48	29	378	297	8	13	38	39	388	380	37	36	88	29	5-11	17-13	12-9	19-14	15-10	18-11
Pittsburgh	85	69	.552	8.0	.0	45	33	439	390	22	16	40	36	426	346	30	36	105	56	7-8	17-8	8-17	16-14	20-9	17-13
St. Louis	85	69	.552	8.0	11	42	35	446	414	59	31	43	34	417	405	48	30	87	101	11-5	9-15	11-15	22-10	16-10	11-19
Chicago	80	74	.519	13.0	6	39	37	344	382	22	37	41	37	427	426	40	40	87	84	8-8	15-13	14-11	10-17	14-14	15-15
Brooklyn	76	78	.494	17.0	1	44	34	380	326	25	35	32	44	363	428	31	39			6-8	9-18	10-14	10-17	7-19	15-20
Philadelphia	57	96	.373	35.5	2	35	41	449	517	95	60	22	55	289	403	21	29	141	314	3-10	11-15	12-14	6-23	9-19	12-19
Boston	53	100	.346	39.5	0	32	43	287	373	6	15	21	57	309	449	26	42	91	32						

Clinch Date—New York 9/25.

Team Batting

Team	G	AB	R	OR	H	2B	3B	HR	TB	RBI	TBB	IBB	SO	HBP	SH	SF	SB	CS	SB%	GDP	Avg	OBP	Slg
Pittsburgh	155	5521	865	736	1698	239	110	52	2313	777	423	—	326	32	175	—	145	59	.71	—	.308	.360	.419
St. Louis	154	5425	863	819	1634	280	88	107	2411	787	447	—	425	28	161	—	73	63	.54	—	.301	.357	.444
New York	156	5454	852	658	1661	253	90	80	2334	756	448	—	421	48	159	—	116	83	.58	—	.305	.363	.428
Chicago	156	5335	771	808	1564	248	71	42	2080	667	525	—	447	27	205	—	97	108	.47	—	.293	.359	.390
Cincinnati	156	5282	766	677	1561	226	99	45	2120	686	436	—	381	36	189	—	130	136	.49	—	.296	.353	.401
Brooklyn	155	5413	743	754	1569	235	76	56	2124	674	339	—	318	25	178	—	79	60	.57	—	.290	.341	.392
Philadelphia	154	5459	738	920	1537	268	55	116	2263	685	450	—	611	39	140	—	48	60	.44	—	.282	.341	.415
Boston	154	5161	596	822	1355	162	73	32	1759	509	387	—	451	28	174	—	67	65	.51	—	.263	.317	.341
NL Total	1240	43050	6194	6194	12579	1911	662	530	17404	5541	3455	—	3380	263	1381	—	755	634	.54	—	.292	.348	.404
NL Avg Team	155	5381	774	774	1572	239	83	66	2176	693	432	—	423	33	173	—	94	79	.54	—	.292	.348	.404

Team Pitching

Team	G	CG	ShO	Rel	Sv	IP	H	R	ER	HR	SH	SF	HB	TBB	IBB	SO	WP	Bk	H/9	SO/9	BB/9	OAvg	OOBP	ERA
New York	156	76	7	135	15	1396.1	1454	658	536	71	146	—	21	393	—	388	24	1	9.4	2.5	2.5	.272	.324	3.45
Cincinnati	156	88	8	93	3	1385.2	1481	677	544	49	156	—	24	326	—	357	12	4	9.6	2.3	2.1	.278	.322	3.53
Pittsburgh	155	88	15	112	7	1387.1	1613	736	614	52	178	—	27	358	—	490	18	2	10.5	3.2	2.3	.296	.343	3.98
Brooklyn	155	82	12	115	8	1385.2	1574	754	624	74	196	—	35	490	—	499	24	2	10.2	3.2	3.2	.294	.357	4.05
Chicago	156	74	8	137	12	1397.2	1579	808	674	57	167	—	55	475	—	402	29	5	10.2	2.6	3.1	.292	.356	4.34
Boston	154	63	7	146	6	1348.0	1565	822	655	57	190	—	28	489	—	360	26	4	10.4	2.4	3.3	.298	.361	4.37
St. Louis	154	60	8	172	12	1362.2	1609	819	672	61	186	—	45	447	—	465	26	4	10.6	3.1	3.0	.300	.358	4.44
Philadelphia	154	73	6	118	5	1372.0	1692	920	707	89	174	—	40	460	—	394	42	5	11.1	2.6	3.0	.307	.365	4.64
NL Total	1240	604	71	1028	68	11035.1	12567	6194	5026	530	1393	—	275	3438	—	3355	201	27	10.3	2.7	2.8	.292	.348	4.10
NL Avg Team	155	76	9	129	9	1379.1	1571	774	628	66	174	—	34	430	—	419	25	3	10.3	2.7	2.8	.292	.348	4.10

Team Fielding

Team	G	PO	A	E	TC	DP	PB	Pct
New York	156	4181	2083	194	6458	145	16	.970
Pittsburgh	155	4159	1820	187	6166	126	13	.970
Cincinnati	156	4152	2084	205	6441	147	6	.968
Chicago	156	4183	2006	204	6393	154	6	.968
Brooklyn	155	4150	1933	208	6291	139	18	.967
Philadelphia	154	4132	2149	225	6506	152	10	.965
Boston	154	4038	1901	215	6154	121	8	.965
St. Louis	154	4088	1872	239	6199	122	9	.961
NL Total	1240	33083	15848	1677	50608	1106	86	.967

Team vs. Team Records

	Bos	Bro	ChN	Cin	NYG	Phi	Pit	StL	Won
Bos	—	7	4	5	8	8	10	11	53
Bro	15	—	11	8	8	15	11	8	76
ChN	18	11	—	11	8	9	10	13	80
Cin	17	14	11	—	10	15	11	8	86
NYG	14	14	14	12	—	15	11	13	93
Phi	13	7	13	7	7	—	3	7	57
Pit	12	11	12	11	11	19	—	9	85
StL	11	14	9	14	9	15	13	—	85
Lost	100	78	74	68	61	96	69	69	

Seasons: Standings, Leaders

1922 National League Batting Leaders

Games		At-Bats		Runs		Hits		Doubles		Triples	
B. Pinelli, Cin	156	R. Maranville, Pit	672	R. Hornsby, StL	141	R. Hornsby, StL	250	R. Hornsby, StL	46	J. Daubert, Cin	22
D. Bancroft, NYG	156	D. Bancroft, NYG	651	M. Carey, Pit	140	C. Bigbee, Pit	215	R. Grimes, ChN	45	I. Meusel, NYG	17
G. Burns, Cin	156	G. Burns, Cin	631	J. Smith, StL	117	D. Bancroft, NYG	209	P. Duncan, Cin	44	C. Bigbee, Pit	15
J. Daubert, Cin	156	M. Carey, Pit	629	D. Bancroft, NYG	117	M. Carey, Pit	207	D. Bancroft, NYG	41	R. Maranville, Pit	15
2 tied with	155	R. Hornsby, StL	623	R. Maranville, Pit	115	J. Daubert, Cin	205	C. Hollocher, ChN	37	2 tied with	14

Home Runs		Total Bases		Runs Batted In		Walks		Intentional Walks		Strikeouts	
R. Hornsby, StL	42	R. Hornsby, StL	450	R. Hornsby, StL	152	M. Carey, Pit	80	Statistic unavailable		F. Parkinson, Phi	93
C. Williams, Phi	26	I. Meusel, NYG	314	I. Meusel, NYG	132	B. O'Farrell, ChN	79			R. Powell, Bos	66
C. Lee, Phi	17	Z. Wheat, Bro	302	Z. Wheat, Bro	112	D. Bancroft, NYG	79			G. Kelly, NYG	65
G. Kelly, NYG	17	C. Williams, Phi	300	G. Kelly, NYG	107	G. Burns, Cin	78			R. Youngs, NYG	50
2 tied with	16	J. Daubert, Cin	300	2 tied with	99	R. Grimes, ChN	75			R. Hornsby, StL	50

Hit By Pitch		Sac Hits		Sac Flies		Stolen Bases		Caught Stealing		GDP	
C. Stengel, NYG	9	Z. Terry, ChN	39	Statistic unavailable		M. Carey, Pit	51	C. Hollocher, ChN	29	Statistic unavailable	
B. Henline, Phi	8	C. Hollocher, ChN	37			F. Frisch, NYG	31	P. Duncan, Cin	28		
4 tied with	7	J. Daubert, Cin	31			G. Burns, Cin	30	G. Burns, Cin	23		
		M. Krug, ChN	28			C. Bigbee, Pit	24	B. Pinelli, Cin	22		
		H. Myers, Bro	27			R. Maranville, Pit	24	2 tied with	17		

Runs Created		Runs Created/27 Outs		Batting Average		On-Base Percentage		Slugging Percentage		OBP+Slugging	
R. Hornsby, StL	179	R. Hornsby, StL	11.70	R. Hornsby, StL	.401	R. Hornsby, StL	.459	R. Hornsby, StL	.722	R. Hornsby, StL	1.181
M. Carey, Pit	129	R. Grimes, ChN	9.48	R. Grimes, ChN	.354	R. Grimes, ChN	.442	R. Grimes, ChN	.572	R. Grimes, ChN	1.014
R. Grimes, ChN	124	B. O'Farrell, ChN	7.65	H. Miller, ChN	.352	B. O'Farrell, ChN	.439	C. Lee, Phi	.540	C. Lee, Phi	.912
Z. Wheat, Bro	117	M. Carey, Pit	7.62	C. Bigbee, Pit	.350	M. Carey, Pit	.408	C. Tierney, Pit	.515	C. Williams, Phi	.905
2 tied with	115	Z. Wheat, Bro	7.41	C. Tierney, Pit	.345	C. Bigbee, Pit	.405	C. Williams, Phi	.514	H. Miller, ChN	.899

1922 National League Pitching Leaders

Wins		Losses		Winning Percentage		Games		Games Started		Complete Games	
E. Rixey, Cin	25	D. Luque, Cin	23	P. Douglas, NYG	.733	L. North, StL	53	E. Rixey, Cin	38	W. Cooper, Pit	27
W. Cooper, Pit	23	J. Oeschger, Bos	21	P. Donohue, Cin	.667	B. Sherdel, StL	47	W. Cooper, Pit	37	D. Ruether, Bro	26
D. Ruether, Bro	21	J. Ring, Phi	18	E. Rixey, Cin	.658	R. Ryan, NYG	46	D. Ruether, Bro	35	E. Rixey, Cin	26
A. Nehf, NYG	19	L. Meadows, Phi	18	J. Couch, Cin	.640	J. Oeschger, Bos	46	A. Nehf, NYG	35	4 tied with	20
J. Pfeffer, StL	19	5 tied with	15	D. Ruether, Bro	.636	J. Morrison, Pit	45	3 tied with	34		

Shutouts		Saves		Games Finished		Batters Faced		Innings Pitched		Hits Allowed	
J. Morrison, Pit	5	C. Jonnard, NYG	5	C. Barfoot, StL	25	E. Rixey, Cin	1303	E. Rixey, Cin	313.1	E. Rixey, Cin	337
D. Vance, Bro	5	L. North, StL	4	G. Stueland, ChN	21	W. Cooper, Pit	1251	W. Cooper, Pit	294.2	W. Cooper, Pit	330
W. Cooper, Pit	4	4 tied with	3	L. North, StL	20	J. Morrison, Pit	1231	J. Morrison, Pit	286.1	B. Grimes, Bro	324
B. Adams, Pit	4			J. Gillespie, Cin	19	D. Ruether, Bro	1157	A. Nehf, NYG	268.1	J. Morrison, Pit	315
2 tied with	3			C. Jonnard, NYG	19	B. Grimes, Bro	1153	D. Ruether, Bro	267.1	J. Couch, Cin	301

Home Runs Allowed		Walks		Walks/9 Innings		Strikeouts		Strikeouts/9 Innings		Strikeout/Walk Ratio	
J. Ring, Phi	19	J. Ring, Phi	103	B. Adams, Pit	0.8	D. Vance, Bro	134	D. Vance, Bro	4.9	B. Adams, Pit	2.60
B. Grimes, Bro	17	T. Osborne, ChN	95	P. Alexander, ChN	1.2	W. Cooper, Pit	129	J. Ring, Phi	4.2	W. Cooper, Pit	2.11
G. Smith, Phi	16	D. Vance, Bro	94	E. Rixey, Cin	1.3	J. Ring, Phi	116	W. Cooper, Pit	3.9	E. Rixey, Cin	1.78
T. Kaufmann, ChN	15	D. Ruether, Bro	92	P. Donohue, Cin	1.6	J. Morrison, Pit	104	W. Glazner, Pit	3.6	P. Donohue, Cin	1.53
A. Nehf, NYG	15	H. McQuillan, 2tm	90	J. Barnes, NYG	1.6	B. Grimes, Bro	99	R. Ryan, NYG	3.5	W. Glazner, Pit	1.48

Earned Run Average		Component ERA		Hit Batsmen		Wild Pitches		Opponent Average		Opponent OBP	
R. Ryan, NYG	3.01	B. Adams, Pit	2.95	T. Osborne, ChN	12	J. Ring, Phi	11	D. Luque, Cin	.268	E. Rixey, Cin	.303
P. Donohue, Cin	3.12	E. Rixey, Cin	3.11	V. Aldridge, ChN	12	J. Oeschger, Bos	11	R. Ryan, NYG	.269	R. Ryan, NYG	.307
W. Cooper, Pit	3.18	P. Donohue, Cin	3.14	L. Meadows, Phi	11	L. Weinert, Phi	7	E. Rixey, Cin	.275	J. Barnes, NYG	.311
A. Nehf, NYG	3.29	D. Luque, Cin	3.17	J. Pfeffer, StL	11	H. McQuillan, 2tm	7	D. Vance, Bro	.276	P. Donohue, Cin	.312
D. Luque, Cin	3.31	J. Barnes, NYG	3.42	2 tied with	10	G. Smith, Phi	7	P. Donohue, Cin	.276	D. Luque, Cin	.318

1922 National League Miscellaneous

Managers

Boston	Fred Mitchell	53-100
Brooklyn	Wilbert Robinson	76-78
Chicago	Bill Killefer	80-74
Cincinnati	Pat Moran	86-68
New York	John McGraw	93-61
Philadelphia	Kaiser Wilhelm	57-96
Pittsburgh	George Gibson	32-33
	Bill McKechnie	53-36
St. Louis	Branch Rickey	85-69

Awards

STATS Most Valuable Player	Rogers Hornsby, 2b, StL
STATS Cy Young	Wilbur Cooper, Pit
STATS Rookie of the Year	Hack Miller, of, ChN
STATS Manager of the Year	John McGraw, NYG

STATS All-Star Team

C	Bob O'Farrell, ChN	.324	4	60
1B	Ray Grimes, ChN	.354	14	99
2B	Rogers Hornsby, StL	.401	42	152
3B	Milt Stock, StL	.305	5	79
SS	Dave Bancroft, NYG	.321	4	60
OF	Carson Bigbee, Pit	.350	5	99
OF	Max Carey, Pit	.329	10	70
OF	Irish Meusel, NYG	.331	16	132
P	Wilbur Cooper, Pit	23-14	3.18	129 K
P	Pete Donohue, Cin	18-9	3.12	66 K
P	Eppa Rixey, Cin	25-13	3.53	80 K
P	Dutch Ruether, Bro	21-12	3.53	89 K

Postseason

World Series   NYG (NL) 4 vs. NYA (AL) 0 (1 tie)

Outstanding Performances

Triple Crown
Rogers Hornsby, StL .401-42-152
No-Hitters
Jesse Barnes, NYG   vs. Phi on May 7
Three-Homer Games
Butch Henline, Phi   on September 15
Cycles
Ross Youngs, NYG   on April 29
Jimmy Johnston, Bro on May 25

1923 American League Standings

Team	Overall					Home Games						Road Games						Park Index		Record by Month						
	W	L	Pct	GB	DIF	W	L	R	OR	HR	OHR	W	L	R	OR	HR	OHR	Run	HR	M/A	May	June	July	Aug	S/O
New York	98	54	.645	—	161	46	30	407	329	62	50	52	24	416	293	43	18	104	184	8-4	21-6	13-12	23-8	13-12	20-12
Detroit	83	71	.539	16.0	5	45	32	400	351	21	31	38	39	431	390	20	27	91	111	8-5	11-16	12-12	14-13	16-10	22-15
Cleveland	82	71	.536	16.5	15	42	36	455	393	22	16	40	35	433	353	37	20	104	64	10-3	12-14	11-15	20-13	13-10	16-16
Washington	75	78	.490	23.5	0	43	34	363	339	7	16	32	44	357	408	19	40	91	38	4-7	10-14	15-14	12-17	16-12	18-14
St. Louis	74	78	.487	24.0	0	40	36	377	364	50	43	34	42	311	356	32	16	111	194	4-7	13-13	13-13	19-11	12-13	13-21
Philadelphia	69	83	.454	29.0	3	34	41	345	360	28	32	35	42	316	401	25	36	101	101	6-4	14-12	14-14	8-21	10-16	17-16
Chicago	69	85	.448	30.0	0	30	45	327	348	13	24	39	40	365	393	29	25	94	72	2-9	12-13	15-9	16-17	10-16	14-21
Boston	61	91	.401	37.0	0	37	40	327	402	11	15	24	51	257	407	23	33	107	45	4-7	9-14	10-14	11-23	12-13	15-20

Clinch Date—New York 9/20.

Team Batting

Team	G	AB	R	OR	H	2B	3B	HR	TB	RBI	TBB	IBB	SO	HBP	SH	SF	SB	CS	SB%	GDP	Avg	OBP	Slg
Cleveland	153	5290	888	746	1594	301	75	59	2222	807	633	—	384	49	198	—	79	79	.50	—	.301	.381	.420
Detroit	155	5266	831	741	1579	270	69	41	2110	739	596	—	385	56	257	—	87	62	.58	—	.300	.377	.401
New York	152	5347	823	622	1554	231	79	105	2258	771	521	—	516	35	232	—	69	44	.48	—	.291	.357	.422
Washington	155	5244	720	747	1436	224	93	26	1924	628	532	—	448	50	232	—	102	68	.60	—	.274	.346	.367
Chicago	156	5246	692	741	1463	254	57	42	1957	604	532	—	458	40	248	—	191	118	.62	—	.279	.350	.373
St. Louis	154	5298	688	720	1489	248	62	82	2107	613	442	—	423	26	209	—	64	54	.54	—	.281	.339	.398
Philadelphia	153	5196	661	761	1407	229	64	53	1923	577	445	—	517	44	172	—	72	62	.54	—	.271	.318	.370
Boston	154	5181	584	809	1354	253	54	34	1817	480	441	—	480	41	157	—	79	91	.46	—	.261	.318	.351
AL Total	1232	42068	5887	5887	11876	2010	553	442	16318	5264	4092	—	3611	341	1617	—	743	608	.55	—	.282	.351	.388
AL Avg Team	154	5259	736	736	1485	251	69	55	2040	658	512	—	451	43	202	—	93	76	.55	—	.282	.351	.388

Team Pitching

Team	G	CG	ShO	Rel	Sv	IP	H	R	ER	HR	SH	SF	HB	TBB	IBB	SO	WP	Bk	H/9	SO/9	BB/9	OAvg	OOBP	ERA
New York	152	101	9	68	10	1380.2	1365	622	555	68	151	—	26	491	—	506	32	0	8.9	3.3	3.2	.263	.330	3.62
Cleveland	153	77	10	143	11	1376.0	1517	746	598	36	194	—	37	465	—	407	10	3	9.9	2.7	3.0	.284	.346	3.91
St. Louis	154	83	10	126	10	1373.1	1430	720	599	59	189	—	49	528	—	488	16	3	9.4	3.2	3.5	.275	.348	3.93
Washington	155	71	8	130	16	1374.1	1527	747	608	56	196	—	43	563	—	474	22	1	10.0	3.1	3.7	.291	.364	3.98
Chicago	156	74	5	126	11	1397.0	1512	741	629	49	232	—	37	534	—	467	26	7	9.7	3.0	3.4	.282	.351	4.05
Philadelphia	153	65	7	131	12	1364.2	1465	761	619	68	217	—	23	550	—	400	23	2	9.7	2.6	3.6	.280	.351	4.08
Detroit	155	61	9	163	12	1373.2	1502	741	624	58	188	—	54	449	—	447	19	2	9.8	2.9	2.9	.283	.345	4.09
Boston	154	77	3	115	11	1372.0	1534	809	640	48	211	—	68	520	—	412	28	3	10.1	2.7	3.4	.295	.367	4.20
AL Total	1232	609	61	1002	93	11011.2	11852	5887	4872	442	1578	—	337	4100	—	3601	176	21	9.7	2.9	3.4	.282	.350	3.98
AL Avg Team	154	76	8	125	12	1376.2	1482	736	609	55	197	—	42	513	—	450	22	3	9.7	2.9	3.4	.282	.350	3.98

Team Fielding

Team	G	PO	A	E	TC	DP	PB	Pct
New York	152	4145	1883	144	6172	131	21	.977
Chicago	156	4180	1933	184	6297	138	6	.971
St. Louis	154	4080	1770	177	6027	145	7	.971
Detroit	155	4129	2002	200	6331	103	11	.968
Washington	155	4144	2046	216	6406	182	10	.966
Cleveland	153	4100	2044	226	6370	143	18	.965
Philadelphia	153	4064	1935	221	6220	127	23	.964
Boston	154	4098	1966	232	6296	126	13	.963
AL Total	1232	32940	15579	1600	50119	1095	109	.968

Team vs. Team Records

	Bos	ChA	Cle	Det	NYA	Phi	StL	Was	Won
Bos	—	9	10	10	8	13	4	7	61
ChA	13	—	9	9	7	10	11	10	69
Cle	12	13	—	9	12	12	14	10	82
Det	12	13	13	—	10	12	12	11	83
NYA	14	15	10	12	—	16	15	16	98
Phi	7	12	10	10	6	—	9	15	69
StL	18	11	8	10	5	13	—	9	74
Was	15	12	11	11	6	7	13	—	75
Lost	91	85	71	71	54	83	78	78	

1923 American League Batting Leaders

Games			At-Bats			Runs			Hits			Doubles			Triples		
E. Sheely, ChA	156		J. Dugan, NYA	644		B. Ruth, NYA	151		C. Jamieson, Cle	222		T. Speaker, Cle	59		G. Goslin, Was	18	
M. McManus, StL	154		C. Jamieson, Cle	644		T. Speaker, Cle	133		T. Speaker, Cle	218		G. Burns, Bos	47		S. Rice, Was	18	
W. Gerber, StL	154		J. Tobin, StL	637		C. Jamieson, Cle	130		H. Heilmann, Det	211		B. Ruth, NYA	45		J. Mostil, ChA	15	
R. Peckinpaugh, Was	154		W. Gerber, StL	605		H. Heilmann, Det	121		B. Ruth, NYA	205		H. Heilmann, Det	44		J. Tobin, StL	15	
2 tied with	153		G. Goslin, Was	600		S. Rice, Was	117		J. Tobin, StL	202		J. Sewell, Cle	41		2 tied with	13	

Home Runs			Total Bases			Runs Batted In			Walks			Intentional Walks			Strikeouts		
B. Ruth, NYA	41		B. Ruth, NYA	399		B. Ruth, NYA	131		B. Ruth, NYA	170		Statistic unavailable			B. Ruth, NYA	93	
K. Williams, StL	29		T. Speaker, Cle	350		T. Speaker, Cle	130		J. Sewell, Cle	98					W. Kamm, ChA	82	
H. Heilmann, Det	18		K. Williams, StL	346		H. Heilmann, Det	115		L. Blue, Det	96					A. Ward, NYA	65	
J. Hauser, Phi	17		H. Heilmann, Det	331		J. Sewell, Cle	109		T. Speaker, Cle	93					D. Schliebner, StL	60	
T. Speaker, Cle	17		J. Tobin, StL	303		W. Pipp, NYA	108		E. Collins, ChA	84					R. Lutzke, Cle	57	

Hit By Pitch			Sac Hits			Sac Flies			Stolen Bases			Caught Stealing			GDP		
H. Manush, Det	17		R. Peckinpaugh, Was	40		Statistic unavailable			E. Collins, ChA	49		E. Collins, ChA	29		Statistic unavailable		
B. Harris, Was	13		E. Collins, ChA	39					J. Mostil, ChA	41		B. Ruth, NYA	21				
J. Hauser, Phi	12		H. McClellan, ChA	36					B. Harris, Was	23		H. Hooper, ChA	18				
J. Mostil, ChA	12		T. Rigney, Det	33					S. Rice, Was	20		J. Mostil, ChA	17				
W. Schang, NYA	9		B. Jones, Det	29					C. Jamieson, Cle	19		K. Williams, StL	17				

Runs Created			Runs Created/27 Outs			Batting Average			On-Base Percentage			Slugging Percentage			OBP+Slugging		
B. Ruth, NYA	193		B. Ruth, NYA	14.86		H. Heilmann, Det	.403		B. Ruth, NYA	.545		B. Ruth, NYA	.764		B. Ruth, NYA	1.309	
T. Speaker, Cle	154		H. Heilmann, Det	11.02		B. Ruth, NYA	.393		H. Heilmann, Det	.481		H. Heilmann, Det	.632		H. Heilmann, Det	1.113	
H. Heilmann, Det	144		T. Speaker, Cle	10.45		T. Speaker, Cle	.380		T. Speaker, Cle	.469		K. Williams, StL	.623		T. Speaker, Cle	1.079	
K. Williams, StL	129		K. Williams, StL	8.82		E. Collins, ChA	.360		J. Sewell, Cle	.456		T. Speaker, Cle	.610		K. Williams, StL	1.062	
J. Sewell, Cle	125		J. Sewell, Cle	8.46		K. Williams, StL	.357		E. Collins, ChA	.455		J. Harris, Bos	.520		J. Sewell, Cle	.935	

1923 American League Pitching Leaders

Wins			Losses			Winning Percentage			Games			Games Started			Complete Games		
G. Uhle, Cle	26		E. Rommel, Phi	19		H. Pennock, NYA	.760		E. Rommel, Phi	56		G. Uhle, Cle	44		G. Uhle, Cle	29	
S. Jones, NYA	21		H. Pillette, Det	19		S. Jones, NYA	.724		G. Uhle, Cle	54		H. Ehmke, Bos	39		H. Ehmke, Bos	28	
H. Dauss, Det	21		C. Robertson, ChA	18		B. Cole, Det	.722		B. Cole, Det	52		H. Dauss, Det	39		U. Shocker, StL	24	
U. Shocker, StL	20		4 tied with	17		W. Hoyt, NYA	.654		A. Russell, Was	52		H. Pillette, Det	37		J. Bush, NYA	23	
H. Ehmke, Bos	20					2 tied with	.632		H. Dauss, Det	50		B. Hasty, Phi	36		H. Dauss, Det	22	

Shutouts			Saves			Games Finished			Batters Faced			Innings Pitched			Hits Allowed		
S. Coveleski, Cle	5		A. Russell, Was	9		S. Thurston, 2tm	30		G. Uhle, Cle	1548		G. Uhle, Cle	357.2		G. Uhle, Cle	378	
E. Vangilder, StL	4		J. Quinn, Bos	7		A. Russell, Was	28		H. Dauss, Det	1340		H. Ehmke, Bos	316.2		H. Dauss, Det	331	
H. Dauss, Det	4		S. Harriss, Phi	6		B. Cole, Det	26		H. Ehmke, Bos	1331		H. Dauss, Det	316.0		H. Ehmke, Bos	318	
6 tied with	3		4 tied with	5		E. Rommel, Phi	20		E. Rommel, Phi	1292		E. Rommel, Phi	297.2		E. Rommel, Phi	306	
						L. O'Doul, Bos	17		E. Vangilder, StL	1210		E. Vangilder, StL	282.1		J. Quinn, Bos	302	

Home Runs Allowed			Walks			Walks/9 Innings			Strikeouts			Strikeouts/9 Innings			Strikeout/Walk Ratio		
B. Shawkey, NYA	17		E. Vangilder, StL	120		U. Shocker, StL	1.6		W. Johnson, Was	130		W. Johnson, Was	4.5		U. Shocker, StL	2.22	
F. Heimach, Phi	14		H. Ehmke, Bos	119		S. Coveleski, Cle	1.7		B. Shawkey, NYA	125		B. Shawkey, NYA	4.3		W. Johnson, Was	1.78	
E. Rommel, Phi	14		J. Bush, NYA	117		J. Quinn, Bos	2.0		J. Bush, NYA	125		J. Bush, NYA	4.1		R. Faber, ChA	1.47	
4 tied with	12		E. Rommel, Phi	108		H. Dauss, Det	2.2		H. Ehmke, Bos	121		D. Danforth, StL	3.8		H. Pennock, NYA	1.37	
			M. Cvengros, ChA	107		G. Mogridge, Was	2.4		2 tied with	109		H. Pennock, NYA	3.7		H. Dauss, Det	1.35	

Earned Run Average			Component ERA			Hit Batsmen			Wild Pitches			Opponent Average			Opponent OBP		
S. Coveleski, Cle	2.76		W. Hoyt, NYA	2.92		H. Ehmke, Bos	20		J. Bush, NYA	12		B. Shawkey, NYA	.246		U. Shocker, StL	.306	
W. Hoyt, NYA	3.02		R. Faber, ChA	3.02		W. Johnson, Was	20		B. Shawkey, NYA	8		W. Hoyt, NYA	.253		W. Hoyt, NYA	.307	
E. Vangilder, StL	3.06		U. Shocker, StL	3.12		B. Piercy, Bos	14		T. Blankenship, ChA	7		S. Jones, NYA	.257		R. Faber, ChA	.311	
G. Mogridge, Was	3.11		S. Jones, NYA	3.18		M. Cvengros, ChA	13		5 tied with	6		R. Faber, ChA	.259		S. Jones, NYA	.312	
E. Rommel, Phi	3.27		B. Shawkey, NYA	3.28		2 tied with	12					J. Bush, NYA	.260		H. Pennock, NYA	.314	

1923 American League Miscellaneous

Managers

Boston	Frank Chance	61-91
Chicago	Kid Gleason	69-85
Cleveland	Tris Speaker	82-71
Detroit	Ty Cobb	83-71
New York	Miller Huggins	98-54
Philadelphia	Connie Mack	69-83
St. Louis	Lee Fohl	52-49
	Jimmy Austin	22-29
Washington	Donie Bush	75-78

Awards

Most Valuable Player	Babe Ruth, of, NYA
STATS Cy Young	George Uhle, Cle
STATS Rookie of the Year	Willie Kamm, 3b, ChA
STATS Manager of the Year	Miller Huggins, NYA

STATS All-Star Team

C	Muddy Ruel, Was	.316	0	54
1B	Joe Hauser, Phi	.307	17	94
2B	Eddie Collins, ChA	.360	5	67
3B	Willie Kamm, ChA	.292	6	87
SS	Joe Sewell, Cle	.353	3	109
OF	Harry Heilmann, Det	.403	18	115
OF	Babe Ruth, NYA	.393	41	131
OF	Tris Speaker, Cle	.380	17	130
P	Waite Hoyt, NYA	17-9	3.02	60 K
P	Herb Pennock, NYA	19-6	3.33	93 K
P	Urban Shocker, StL	20-12	3.41	109 K
P	George Uhle, Cle	26-16	3.77	109 K

Postseason

World Series	NYA (AL) 4 vs. NYG (NL) 2

Outstanding Performances

No-Hitters
Sad Sam Jones, NYA @ Phi on September 4
Howard Ehmke, Bos @ Phi on September 7

Unassisted Triple Plays
George Burns, Bos   on September 14

1923 National League Standings

Team	Overall W	L	Pct	GB	DIF	Home Games W	L	R	OR	HR	OHR	Road Games W	L	R	OR	HR	OHR	Park Index Run	HR	Record by Month M/A	May	June	July	Aug	S/O
New York	95	58	.621	—	174	47	30	408	362	44	53	48	28	446	317	41	29	100	137	10-4	20-7	15-10	18-13	17-13	15-11
Cincinnati	91	63	.591	4.5	1	46	32	337	300	6	4	45	31	371	329	39	24	89	15	7-6	11-14	18-7	23-11	15-11	17-14
Pittsburgh	87	67	.565	8.5	1	47	30	381	322	16	9	40	37	405	374	33	44	90	32	7-6	11-15	18-11	14-15	19-9	14-15
Chicago	83	71	.539	12.5	0	46	31	402	354	63	57	37	40	354	350	27	29	107	214	6-7	14-15	12-13	14-15	13-13	17-11
St. Louis	79	74	.516	16.0	0	42	35	335	320	22	27	37	39	411	412	41	43	79	58	6-7	14-15	12-13	16-15	9-18	18-14
Brooklyn	76	78	.494	19.5	1	37	40	348	383	26	27	39	38	405	358	36	28	96	83	3-9	18-9	12-13	16-15	13-14	17-11
Boston	54	100	.351	41.5	0	22	55	291	429	7	27	32	45	345	369	25	37	101	55	6-6	10-17	5-22	6-24	13-14	14-17
Philadelphia	50	104	.325	45.5	0	20	55	418	597	76	77	30	49	330	411	36	23	144	273	5-5	7-23	7-18	12-19	9-17	10-22

Clinch Date—New York 9/28.

Team Batting

Team	G	AB	R	OR	H	2B	3B	HR	TB	RBI	TBB	IBB	SO	HBP	SH	SF	SB	CS	SB%	GDP	Avg	OBP	Slg
New York	153	5452	854	679	1610	248	76	85	2265	790	487	—	406	31	113	—	106	70	.60	—	.295	.356	.415
Pittsburgh	154	5405	786	696	1592	224	111	49	2185	701	407	—	362	28	103	—	154	75	.67	—	.295	.347	.404
Chicago	154	5259	756	704	1516	243	52	90	2133	675	455	—	485	31	148	—	181	143	.56	—	.288	.340	.387
Brooklyn	155	5476	753	741	1559	214	81	62	2121	677	425	—	382	33	148	—	71	50	.59	—	.285	.340	.387
Philadelphia	155	5491	748	1008	1528	259	39	112	2201	677	414	—	556	39	110	—	70	73	.49	—	.278	.333	.401
St. Louis	154	5526	746	732	1582	274	76	63	2197	676	438	—	446	38	135	—	89	61	.59	—	.286	.343	.398
Cincinnati	154	5278	708	629	1506	237	95	45	2068	645	439	—	367	33	185	—	96	105	.48	—	.285	.344	.392
Boston	155	5329	636	798	1455	213	58	32	1880	569	429	—	404	31	168	—	57	80	.42	—	.273	.331	.353
NL Total	1234	43216	5987	5987	12348	1912	588	538	17050	5407	3494	—	3408	264	1113	—	824	657	.56	—	.286	.343	.395
NL Avg Team	154	5402	748	748	1544	239	74	67	2131	676	437	—	426	33	139	—	103	82	.56	—	.286	.343	.395

Team Pitching

Team	G	CG	ShO	Rel	Sv	IP	H	R	ER	HR	SH	SF	HB	TBB	IBB	SO	WP	Bk	H/9	SO/9	BB/9	OAvg	OOBP	ERA
Cincinnati	154	88	11	97	9	1391.1	1465	629	497	28	135	—	33	359	—	450	18	3	9.5	2.9	2.3	.273	.322	3.21
Brooklyn	155	94	8	92	5	1396.2	1503	741	580	55	135	—	39	476	—	548	27	2	9.7	3.5	3.1	.274	.336	3.74
Chicago	154	80	8	107	11	1366.2	1419	704	580	86	128	—	31	435	—	408	18	3	9.3	2.7	2.9	.269	.328	3.82
St. Louis	154	77	9	126	7	1398.1	1539	732	601	70	161	—	44	456	—	398	22	1	9.9	2.6	2.9	.284	.344	3.87
Pittsburgh	154	92	5	99	9	1376.1	1513	696	592	53	137	—	24	402	—	414	20	1	9.9	2.7	2.6	.284	.337	3.87
New York	153	62	10	159	18	1378.0	1440	679	597	82	123	—	21	424	—	453	19	2	9.4	3.0	2.8	.271	.328	3.90
Boston	155	54	13	153	7	1392.2	1662	798	652	64	146	—	32	394	—	351	16	2	10.7	2.3	2.5	.302	.352	4.21
Philadelphia	155	68	3	150	5	1376.1	1801	1008	816	100	147	—	38	549	—	384	43	5	11.8	2.5	3.6	.321	.385	5.34
NL Total	1234	615	67	983	74	11076.1	12342	5987	4915	538	1112	—	262	3495	—	3406	183	19	10.0	2.8	2.8	.286	.343	3.99
NL Avg Team	154	77	8	123	9	1384.1	1543	748	614	67	139	—	33	437	—	426	23	2	10.0	2.8	2.8	.286	.343	3.99

Team Fielding

Team	G	PO	A	E	TC	DP	PB	Pct
New York	153	4131	1988	176	6295	141	7	.972
Pittsburgh	154	4122	1952	179	6253	157	5	.971
Cincinnati	154	4167	2058	202	6427	144	13	.969
Chicago	154	4092	1958	208	6258	144	7	.967
Philadelphia	155	4123	1960	217	6300	172	19	.966
Boston	155	4148	2011	230	6389	157	16	.964
St. Louis	154	4196	1905	232	6333	141	14	.963
Brooklyn	155	4188	2047	293	6528	137	20	.955
NL Total	1234	33167	15879	1737	50783	1193	101	.966

Team vs. Team Records

	Bos	Bro	ChN	Cin	NYG	Phi	Pit	StL	Won
Bos	—	8	6	7	6	13	5	9	54
Bro	14	—	10	8	11	12	11	10	76
ChN	16	12	—	9	10	13	11	12	83
Cin	15	14	13	—	12	19	8	10	91
NYG	16	11	12	10	—	19	13	14	95
Phi	9	10	9	3	3	—	9	7	50
Pit	17	11	11	14	9	13	—	12	87
StL	13	12	10	12	7	15	10	—	79
Lost	100	78	71	63	58	104	67	74	

Seasons: Standings, Leaders

1923 National League Batting Leaders

Games		At-Bats		Runs		Hits		Doubles		Triples	
J. Statz, ChN	154	J. Statz, ChN	655	R. Youngs, NYG	121	F. Frisch, NYG	223	E. Roush, Cin	41	P. Traynor, Pit	19
G. Burns, Cin	154	F. Frisch, NYG	641	M. Carey, Pit	120	J. Statz, ChN	209	G. Grantham, ChN	36	M. Carey, Pit	19
S. McInnis, Bos	154	J. Johnston, Bro	625	F. Frisch, NYG	116	P. Traynor, Pit	208	C. Tierney, 2tm	36	E. Roush, Cin	18
3 tied with	153	P. Traynor, Pit	616	J. Johnston, Bro	111	J. Johnston, Bro	203	J. Bottomley, StL	34	B. Southworth, Bos	16
		G. Burns, Cin	614	J. Statz, ChN	110	R. Youngs, NYG	200	4 tied with	33	2 tied with	14

Home Runs		Total Bases		Runs Batted In		Walks		Intentional Walks		Strikeouts	
C. Williams, Phi	41	F. Frisch, NYG	311	I. Meusel, NYG	125	G. Burns, Cin	101	Statistic unavailable		G. Grantham, ChN	92
J. Fournier, Bro	22	C. Williams, Phi	308	C. Williams, Phi	114	H. Sand, Phi	82			G. Felix, Bos	65
H. Miller, ChN	20	J. Fournier, Bro	303	F. Frisch, NYG	111	R. Youngs, NYG	73			G. Kelly, NYG	64
I. Meusel, NYG	19	P. Traynor, Pit	301	G. Kelly, NYG	103	M. Carey, Pit	73			C. Williams, Phi	57
R. Hornsby, StL	17	J. Statz, ChN	288	J. Fournier, Bro	102	G. Grantham, ChN	71			H. Sand, Phi	56

Hit By Pitch		Sac Hits		Sac Flies		Stolen Bases		Caught Stealing		GDP	
B. Hargrave, Cin	12	S. McInnis, Bos	37	Statistic unavailable		M. Carey, Pit	51	G. Grantham, ChN	28	Statistic unavailable	
R. Blades, StL	9	P. Duncan, Cin	28			G. Grantham, ChN	43	J. Statz, ChN	23		
B. Henline, Phi	9	G. Grantham, ChN	24			C. Heathcote, ChN	32	4 tied with	19		
J. Fournier, Bro	9	3 tied with	23			J. Smith, StL	32				
3 tied with	7					2 tied with	29				

Runs Created		Runs Created/27 Outs		Batting Average		On-Base Percentage		Slugging Percentage		OBP+Slugging	
F. Frisch, NYG	124	R. Hornsby, StL	10.27	R. Hornsby, StL	.384	R. Hornsby, StL	.459	R. Hornsby, StL	.627	R. Hornsby, StL	1.086
J. Fournier, Bro	119	J. Fournier, Bro	9.02	J. Bottomley, StL	.371	J. Bottomley, StL	.425	J. Fournier, Bro	.588	J. Fournier, Bro	.999
M. Carey, Pit	116	J. Bottomley, StL	8.09	J. Fournier, Bro	.351	B. Hargrave, Cin	.419	C. Williams, Phi	.576	C. Barnhart, Pit	.972
P. Traynor, Pit	111	C. Barnhart, Pit	8.04	E. Roush, Cin	.351	R. Youngs, NYG	.412	C. Barnhart, Pit	.563	J. Bottomley, StL	.960
R. Youngs, NYG	111	B. Hargrave, Cin	7.92	F. Frisch, NYG	.348	J. Fournier, Bro	.411	J. Bottomley, StL	.535	C. Williams, Phi	.947

1923 National League Pitching Leaders

Wins		Losses		Winning Percentage		Games		Games Started		Complete Games	
D. Luque, Cin	27	W. Cooper, Pit	19	D. Luque, Cin	.771	C. Jonnard, NYG	45	B. Grimes, Bro	38	B. Grimes, Bro	33
J. Morrison, Pit	25	B. Grimes, Bro	18	R. Ryan, NYG	.762	R. Ryan, NYG	45	W. Cooper, Pit	38	D. Luque, Cin	28
P. Alexander, ChN	22	L. Weinert, Phi	17	J. Scott, NYG	.696	J. Oeschger, Bos	44	J. Morrison, Pit	37	J. Morrison, Pit	27
P. Donohue, Cin	21	J. Ring, Phi	16	J. Morrison, Pit	.658	J. Genewich, Bos	43	D. Luque, Cin	37	W. Cooper, Pit	26
B. Grimes, Bro	21	7 tied with	15	B. Adams, Pit	.650	J. Barnes, 2tm	43	E. Rixey, Cin	37	P. Alexander, ChN	26

Shutouts		Saves		Games Finished		Batters Faced		Innings Pitched		Hits Allowed	
D. Luque, Cin	6	C. Jonnard, NYG	5	C. Jonnard, NYG	25	B. Grimes, Bro	1418	B. Grimes, Bro	327.0	B. Grimes, Bro	356
H. McQuillan, NYG	5	R. Ryan, NYG	4	F. Fussell, ChN	22	J. Ring, Phi	1333	D. Luque, Cin	322.0	J. Ring, Phi	336
J. Barnes, 2tm	5	8 tied with	3	C. Barfoot, StL	22	D. Luque, Cin	1301	E. Rixey, Cin	309.0	E. Rixey, Cin	334
7 tied with	3			3 tied with	18	E. Rixey, Cin	1294	P. Alexander, ChN	305.0	W. Cooper, Pit	331
						J. Morrison, Pit	1270	J. Ring, Phi	304.1	2 tied with	308

Home Runs Allowed		Walks		Walks/9 Innings		Strikeouts		Strikeouts/9 Innings		Strikeout/Walk Ratio	
V. Aldridge, ChN	17	J. Ring, Phi	115	P. Alexander, ChN	0.9	D. Vance, Bro	197	D. Vance, Bro	6.3	P. Alexander, ChN	2.40
P. Alexander, ChN	17	J. Morrison, Pit	110	B. Adams, Pit	1.4	D. Luque, Cin	151	D. Luque, Cin	4.2	D. Vance, Bro	1.97
W. Glazner, 2tm	16	B. Grimes, Bro	100	J. Genewich, Bos	1.8	B. Grimes, Bro	119	J. Bentley, NYG	3.9	D. Luque, Cin	1.72
3 tied with	15	D. Vance, Bro	100	E. Rixey, Cin	1.9	J. Morrison, Pit	114	J. Morrison, Pit	3.4	B. Adams, Pit	1.52
		T. Osborne, ChN	89	L. Meadows, 2tm	2.2	J. Ring, Phi	112	J. Ring, Phi	3.3	E. Rixey, Cin	1.49

Earned Run Average		Component ERA		Hit Batsmen		Wild Pitches		Opponent Average		Opponent OBP	
D. Luque, Cin	1.93	D. Luque, Cin	2.32	T. Kaufmann, ChN	11	J. Ring, Phi	14	D. Luque, Cin	.235	P. Alexander, ChN	.277
E. Rixey, Cin	2.80	P. Alexander, ChN	2.64	B. Grimes, Bro	11	J. Morrison, Pit	9	D. Vance, Bro	.250	D. Luque, Cin	.291
V. Keen, ChN	3.00	J. Morrison, Pit	3.12	D. Vance, Bro	11	L. Weinert, Phi	8	V. Aldridge, ChN	.251	V. Aldridge, ChN	.307
T. Kaufmann, ChN	3.10	E. Rixey, Cin	3.19	W. Cooper, Pit	11	L. Dickerman, Bro	7	J. Morrison, Pit	.253	H. McQuillan, NYG	.315
J. Haines, StL	3.11	D. Vance, Bro	3.19	P. Donohue, Cin	10	2 tied with	6	V. Keen, ChN	.255	V. Keen, ChN	.319

1923 National League Miscellaneous

Managers

Boston	Fred Mitchell	54-100
Brooklyn	Wilbert Robinson	76-78
Chicago	Bill Killefer	83-71
Cincinnati	Pat Moran	91-63
New York	John McGraw	95-58
Philadelphia	Art Fletcher	50-104
Pittsburgh	Bill McKechnie	87-67
St. Louis	Branch Rickey	79-74

Awards

STATS Most Valuable Player	Dolf Luque, p, Cin
STATS Cy Young	Dolf Luque, Cin
STATS Rookie of the Year	G. Grantham, 2b, ChN
STATS Manager of the Year	Pat Moran, Cin

STATS All-Star Team

C	Bubbles Hargrave, Cin	.333	10	78
1B	Jack Fournier, Bro	.351	22	102
2B	Rogers Hornsby, StL	.384	17	83
3B	Pie Traynor, Pit	.338	12	101
SS	Dave Bancroft, NYG	.304	1	31
OF	Edd Roush, Cin	.351	6	88
OF	Cy Williams, Phi	.293	41	114
OF	Ross Youngs, NYG	.336	3	87
P	Pete Alexander, ChN	22-12	3.19	72 K
P	Dolf Luque, Cin	27-8	1.93	151 K
P	Johnny Morrison, Pit	25-13	3.49	114 K
P	Eppa Rixey, Cin	20-15	2.80	97 K

Postseason

World Series	NYG (NL) 2 vs. NYA (AL) 4

Outstanding Performances

Three-Homer Games
Cy Williams, Phi — on May 11
George Kelly, NYG — on September 17

Cycles
Pie Traynor, Pit — on July 7

Unassisted Triple Plays
Ernie Padgett, Bos — on October 6

1924 American League Standings

Team	Overall					Home Games						Road Games						Park Index		Record by Month					
	W	L	Pct	GB	DIF	W	L	R	OR	HR	OHR	W	L	R	OR	HR	OHR	Run	HR	M/A	May	June	July	Aug	S/O
Washington	92	62	.597	—	52	47	30	371	280	1	7	45	32	384	333	21	27	91	17	5-8	12-11	21-9	18-15	18-12	18-7
New York	89	63	.586	2.0	97	45	32	397	324	57	46	44	31	401	343	41	13	94	186	9-4	13-10	12-15	23-14	14-12	18-8
Detroit	86	68	.558	6.0	27	45	33	427	393	17	28	41	35	422	403	18	27	97	97	9-4	14-13	14-15	18-11	13-16	18-9
St. Louis	74	78	.487	17.0	1	41	36	426	445	44	49	33	42	343	364	23	19	120	216	4-9	14-10	13-12	18-16	17-14	8-17
Philadelphia	71	81	.467	20.0	0	36	39	328	391	31	24	35	42	357	387	32	19	99	111	6-5	8-17	9-19	17-18	18-12	13-10
Cleveland	67	86	.438	24.5	0	37	38	374	375	13	18	30	48	381	439	28	25	95	61	5-6	9-15	17-12	15-20	14-16	7-17
Boston	67	87	.435	25.0	16	41	36	402	391	8	17	26	51	335	415	22	26	106	52	4-7	17-7	11-18	11-22	15-14	9-19
Chicago	66	87	.431	25.5	6	37	39	403	414	13	23	29	48	390	444	28	29	99	64	7-6	9-13	16-13	15-19	7-20	12-16

Clinch Date—Washington 9/29.

Team Batting

Team	G	AB	R	OR	H	2B	3B	HR	TB	RBI	TBB	IBB	SO	HBP	SH	SF	SB	CS	SB%	GDP	Avg	OBP	Slg
Detroit	156	5389	849	796	1604	315	76	35	2176	759	607	—	400	41	224	.56	—	100	77	.56	—	.298	.373	.404
New York	153	5240	798	667	1516	248	86	98	2230	734	478	—	420	27	186		—	69	67	.51	—	.289	.352	.426
Chicago	154	5255	793	858	1512	254	58	41	2005	710	604	—	421	35	232		—	137	92	.60	—	.288	.365	.382
St. Louis	153	5236	769	809	1543	266	62	67	2134	679	465	—	349	35	192		—	85	85	.50	—	.295	.356	.408
Cleveland	153	5332	755	814	1580	306	59	41	2127	677	492	—	371	48	160		—	85	57	.60	—	.296	.361	.399
Washington	156	5304	755	613	1558	255	88	22	2055	688	513	—	392	55	234		—	116	85	.58	—	.294	.362	.387
Boston	157	5340	737	806	1481	302	63	30	1999	666	603	—	417	46	195		—	78	61	.56	—	.277	.356	.374
Philadelphia	152	5184	685	778	1459	251	59	63	2017	608	374	—	484	38	157		—	77	68	.53	—	.281	.334	.389
AL Total	1234	42280	6141	6141	12253	2197	551	397	16743	5521	4136		3254	325	1580		—	747	592	.56	—	.290	.358	.396
AL Avg Team	154	5285	768	768	1532	275	69	50	2093	690	517		407	41	198			93	74	.56		.290	.358	.396

Team Pitching

Team	G	CG	ShO	Rel	Sv	IP	H	R	ER	HR	SH	SF	HB	TBB	IBB	SO	WP	Bk	H/9	SO/9	BB/9	OAvg	OOBP	ERA
Washington	156	74	13	128	25	1383.0	1329	613	513	34	204	—	44	505	—	469	13	4	8.6	3.1	3.3	.258	.329	3.34
New York	153	76	13	*111	13	1359.1	1483	667	583	59	162	—	26	522	—	487	35	5	9.8	3.2	3.5	.281	.349	3.86
Detroit	156	60	5	158	20	1394.2	1586	796	650	55	197	—	45	467	—	441	13	2	10.2	2.8	3.0	.291	.352	4.19
Boston	157	73	8	141	16	1391.1	1563	806	673	43	222	—	63	523	—	414	22	4	10.1	2.7	3.4	.285	.354	4.35
Philadelphia	152	68	8	144	10	1345.0	1527	778	656	43	185	—	28	597	—	371	19	3	10.2	2.5	4.0	.292	.367	4.39
Cleveland	153	87	7	119	7	1349.0	1603	814	659	43	180	—	38	503	—	315	29	1	10.7	2.1	3.4	.299	.363	4.40
St. Louis	153	65	11	174	7	1353.1	1511	809	687	68	199	—	45	517	—	386	15	2	10.0	2.6	3.4	.287	.356	4.57
Chicago	154	76	1	118	11	1370.2	1635	858	722	52	213	—	29	512	—	360	31	2	10.7	2.4	3.4	.300	.363	4.74
AL Total	1234	579	66	1093	109	10946.1	12237	6141	5143	397	1562	—	318	4146	—	3243	177	23	10.1	2.7	3.4	.290	.357	4.23
AL Avg Team	154	72	8	137	14	1368.1	1530	768	643	50	195	—	40	518	—	405	22	3	10.1	2.7	3.4	.290	.357	4.23

Team Fielding

Team	G	PO	A	E	TC	DP	PB	Pct
New York	153	4093	1823	156	6072	131	20	.974
Washington	156	4130	1732	171	6033	149	5	.972
Detroit	156	4192	2030	187	6409	142	4	.971
Philadelphia	152	4025	1943	180	6148	157	12	.971
St. Louis	153	4030	1805	184	6019	142	6	.969
Boston	157	4189	1987	210	6386	126	22	.967
Cleveland	153	4047	1944	205	6196	130	14	.967
Chicago	154	4071	1921	229	6221	136	17	.963
AL Total	1234	32777	15185	1522	49484	1113	100	.969

Team vs. Team Records

	Bos	ChA	Cle	Det	NYA	Phi	StL	Was	Won
Bos	—	10	14	6	5	12	11	9	67
ChA	12	—	11	8	6	11	13	5	66
Cle	8	11	—	7	8	11	11	11	67
Det	16	14	15	—	13	11	9	8	86
NYA	17	16	14	9	—	12	12	9	89
Phi	10	11	11	11	8	—	13	7	71
StL	11	8	10	13	10	9	—	13	74
Was	13	17	11	14	13	15	9	—	92
Lost	87	87	86	68	63	81	78	62	

1924 American League Batting Leaders

Games			At-Bats			Runs			Hits			Doubles			Triples		
B. Wambsganss, Bos	156		S. Rice, Was	646		B. Ruth, NYA	143		S. Rice, Was	216		J. Sewell, Cle	45		W. Pipp, NYA	19	
R. Peckinpaugh, Was	155		G. Sisler, StL	636		T. Cobb, Det	115		C. Jamieson, Cle	213		H. Heilmann, Det	45		G. Goslin, Was	17	
T. Cobb, Det	155		B. Wambsganss, Bos	636		E. Collins, ChA	108		T. Cobb, Det	211		B. D. Jacobson, StL	41		H. Heilmann, Det	16	
G. Goslin, Was	154		T. Cobb, Det	625		H. Heilmann, Det	107		B. Ruth, NYA	200		B. Wambsganss, Bos	41		S. Rice, Was	14	
S. Rice, Was	154		J. Dugan, NYA	610		H. Hooper, ChA	107		G. Goslin, Was	199		B. Meusel, NYA	40		B. D. Jacobson, StL	12	

Home Runs			Total Bases			Runs Batted In			Walks			Intentional Walks			Strikeouts		
B. Ruth, NYA	46		B. Ruth, NYA	391		G. Goslin, Was	129		B. Ruth, NYA	142		Statistic unavailable			B. Ruth, NYA	81	
J. Hauser, Phi	27		B. D. Jacobson, StL	306		B. Ruth, NYA	121		T. Rigney, Det	102					A. Simmons, Phi	60	
B. D. Jacobson, StL	19		H. Heilmann, Det	304		B. Meusel, NYA	120		E. Sheely, ChA	95					W. Kamm, ChA	59	
K. Williams, StL	18		G. Goslin, Was	299		J. Hauser, Phi	115		E. Collins, ChA	89					J. Dykes, Phi	59	
I. Boone, Bos	13		J. Hauser, Phi	290		H. Heilmann, Det	114		T. Cobb, Det	85					J. Hauser, Phi	52	

Hit By Pitch			Sac Hits			Sac Flies			Stolen Bases			Caught Stealing			GDP		
H. Manush, Det	16		B. Harris, Was	46		Statistic unavailable			E. Collins, ChA	42		G. Sisler, StL	17		Statistic unavailable		
G. Burns, Cle	15		B. Wambsganss, Bos	37					B. Meusel, NYA	26		E. Collins, ChA	17				
I. Flagstead, Bos	11		W. Kamm, ChA	32					S. Rice, Was	24		A. Simmons, Phi	15				
B. Miller, Phi	10		T. Rigney, Det	31					T. Cobb, Det	23		3 tied with	14				
3 tied with	9		H. Severeid, StL	31					C. Jamieson, Cle	21							

Runs Created			Runs Created/27 Outs			Batting Average			On-Base Percentage			Slugging Percentage			OBP+Slugging		
B. Ruth, NYA	179		B. Ruth, NYA	13.39		B. Ruth, NYA	.378		B. Ruth, NYA	.513		B. Ruth, NYA	.739		B. Ruth, NYA	1.252	
H. Heilmann, Det	127		H. Heilmann, Det	8.18		C. Jamieson, Cle	.359		J. Bassler, Det	.441		H. Heilmann, Det	.533		H. Heilmann, Det	.961	
G. Goslin, Was	118		K. Williams, StL	7.87		B. Falk, ChA	.352		E. Collins, ChA	.441		K. Williams, StL	.533		K. Williams, StL	.958	
E. Collins, ChA	118		T. Speaker, Cle	7.60		E. Collins, ChA	.349		T. Speaker, Cle	.432		B. D. Jacobson, StL	.529		T. Speaker, Cle	.943	
T. Cobb, Det	118		E. Collins, ChA	7.55		J. Bassler, Det	.346		H. Heilmann, Det	.428		G. Myatt, Cle	.518		G. Goslin, Was	.937	

1924 American League Pitching Leaders

Wins			Losses			Winning Percentage			Games			Games Started			Complete Games		
W. Johnson, Was	23		J. Shaute, Cle	17		W. Johnson, Was	.767		F. Marberry, Was	50		W. Johnson, Was	38		S. Thurston, ChA	28	
H. Pennock, NYA	21		A. Ferguson, Bos	17		H. Pennock, NYA	.700		K. Holloway, Det	49		S. Thurston, ChA	36		H. Ehmke, Bos	26	
S. Thurston, ChA	20		H. Ehmke, Bos	17		K. Holloway, Det	.700		J. Shaute, Cle	46		H. Ehmke, Bos	36		H. Pennock, NYA	25	
J. Shaute, Cle	20		J. Bush, NYA	16		S. Baumgartner, Phi	.684		W. Hoyt, NYA	46		3 tied with	34		J. Shaute, Cle	21	
H. Ehmke, Bos	19		S. Coveleski, Cle	16		R. Collins, Det	.667		H. Ehmke, Bos	45					E. Rommel, Phi	21	

Shutouts			Saves			Games Finished			Batters Faced			Innings Pitched			Hits Allowed		
W. Johnson, Was	6		F. Marberry, Was	15		F. Marberry, Was	30		H. Ehmke, Bos	1377		H. Ehmke, Bos	315.0		S. Thurston, ChA	330	
D. Davis, StL	5		A. Russell, Was	8		S. Connally, ChA	24		S. Thurston, ChA	1251		S. Thurston, ChA	291.0		H. Ehmke, Bos	324	
U. Shocker, StL	4		J. Quinn, Bos	7		K. Holloway, Det	21		J. Shaute, Cle	1228		H. Pennock, NYA	286.1		J. Shaute, Cle	317	
H. Ehmke, Bos	4		S. Connally, ChA	6		3 tied with	20		H. Pennock, NYA	1220		J. Shaute, Cle	283.0		E. Rommel, Phi	302	
H. Pennock, NYA	4		H. Dauss, Det	6					E. Rommel, Phi	1164		E. Rommel, Phi	278.0		H. Pennock, NYA	302	

Home Runs Allowed			Walks			Walks/9 Innings			Strikeouts			Strikeouts/9 Innings			Strikeout/Walk Ratio		
S. Thurston, ChA	17		J. Bush, NYA	109		S. Smith, Cle	1.5		W. Johnson, Was	158		W. Johnson, Was	5.1		W. Johnson, Was	2.05	
D. Danforth, StL	16		A. Ferguson, Bos	108		S. Thurston, ChA	1.9		H. Ehmke, Bos	119		B. Shawkey, NYA	4.9		U. Shocker, StL	1.69	
L. Stoner, Det	13		E. Rommel, Phi	94		U. Shocker, StL	1.9		B. Shawkey, NYA	114		H. Ehmke, Bos	3.4		H. Pennock, NYA	1.58	
H. Pennock, NYA	13		S. Gray, Phi	89		H. Pennock, NYA	2.0		H. Pennock, NYA	101		U. Shocker, StL	3.2		B. Shawkey, NYA	1.54	
2 tied with	11		E. Wingard, StL	85		J. Quinn, Bos	2.0		U. Shocker, StL	88		H. Pennock, NYA	3.2		H. Ehmke, Bos	1.47	

Earned Run Average			Component ERA			Hit Batsmen			Wild Pitches			Opponent Average			Opponent OBP		
W. Johnson, Was	2.72		W. Johnson, Was	2.39		E. Whitehill, Det	13		R. Meeker, Phi	7		W. Johnson, Was	.224		W. Johnson, Was	.284	
T. Zachary, Was	2.75		R. Collins, Det	2.78		G. Uhle, Cle	13		J. Bush, NYA	7		R. Collins, Det	.248		R. Collins, Det	.306	
H. Pennock, NYA	2.83		T. Zachary, Was	2.98		J. Quinn, Bos	12		6 tied with	5		D. Davis, StL	.259		H. Pennock, NYA	.309	
S. Baumgartner, Phi	2.88		S. Smith, Cle	3.09		H. Ehmke, Bos	11					H. Ehmke, Bos	.259		S. Smith, Cle	.310	
S. Smith, Cle	3.02		H. Ehmke, Bos	3.13		2 tied with	10					E. Wingard, StL	.260		H. Ehmke, Bos	.310	

1924 American League Miscellaneous

Managers

Boston	Lee Fohl	67-87
Chicago	Johnny Evers	10-11
	Ed Walsh	1-2
	Eddie Collins	14-13
	Johnny Evers	41-61
Cleveland	Tris Speaker	67-86
Detroit	Ty Cobb	86-68
New York	Miller Huggins	89-63
Philadelphia	Connie Mack	71-81
St. Louis	George Sisler	74-78
Washington	Bucky Harris	92-62

Awards

Most Valuable Player	Walter Johnson, p, Was
STATS Cy Young	Walter Johnson, Was
STATS Rookie of the Year	Firpo Marberry, p, Was
STATS Manager of the Year	Bucky Harris, Was

STATS All-Star Team

C	Glenn Myatt, Cle	.342	8	73
1B	Joe Hauser, Phi	.288	27	115
2B	Eddie Collins, ChA	.349	6	86
3B	Joe Dugan, NYA	.302	3	56
SS	Joe Sewell, Cle	.316	4	104
OF	Goose Goslin, Was	.344	12	129
OF	Harry Heilmann, Det	.346	10	114
OF	Babe Ruth, NYA	.378	46	121
P	Walter Johnson, Was	23-7	2.72	158 K
P	Herb Pennock, NYA	21-9	2.83	101 K
P	Sloppy Thurston, ChA	20-14	3.80	37 K
P	Tom Zachary, Was	15-9	2.75	45 K
RP	Firpo Marberry, Was	11-12	3.09	15 Sv

Postseason

World Series	Washington (AL) 4 vs. NYG (NL) 3

Outstanding Performances

Three-Homer Games

Joe Hauser, Phi	on August 2

Cycles

B. D. Jacobson, StL	on April 17
Goose Goslin, Was	on August 28

Seasons: Standings, Leaders

1924 National League Standings

Team	W	L	Pct	GB	DIF	W	L	R	OR	HR	OHR	W	L	R	OR	HR	OHR	Run	HR	M/A	May	June	July	Aug	S/O
		Overall					Home Games						Road Games					Park Index			Record by Month				
New York	93	60	.608	—	153	51	26	385	272	51	40	42	34	472	369	44	37	77	111	9-2	16-12	19-8	17-12	14-15	18-11
Brooklyn	92	62	.597	1.5	1	46	31	342	338	26	30	46	31	375	337	46	28	96	76	5-7	15-10	15-12	16-17	21-8	20-8
Pittsburgh	90	63	.588	3.0	0	49	28	393	293	20	17	41	35	331	295	24	25	108	75	6-8	13-12	14-10	19-11	21-10	17-12
Cincinnati	83	70	.542	10.0	9	43	33	311	283	3	3	40	37	338	296	33	27	95	10	8-5	13-14	13-16	16-15	17-12	16-8
Chicago	81	72	.529	12.0	5	46	31	373	341	33	68	35	41	325	358	33	21	103	185	9-6	15-12	13-8	17-14	13-17	13-15
St. Louis	65	89	.422	28.5	1	40	37	419	359	42	37	25	52	321	391	35	33	109	101	5-9	12-13	7-20	17-14	13-18	11-15
Philadelphia	55	96	.364	37.0	0	26	49	369	483	58	64	29	47	307	366	36	20	128	221	2-6	9-18	14-14	13-19	11-18	6-21
Boston	53	100	.346	40.0	3	28	48	254	366	9	8	25	52	266	434	16	41	90	30	4-5	12-14	11-18	9-23	9-21	8-19

Clinch Date—New York 9/27.

Team Batting

Team	G	AB	R	OR	H	2B	3B	HR	TB	RBI	TBB	IBB	SO	HBP	SH	SF	SB	CS	SB%	GDP	Avg	OBP	Slg
New York	154	5445	857	641	1634	269	81	95	2350	781	467	—	479	28	127	—	82	53	.61	—	.300	.358	.432
St. Louis	154	5349	740	750	1552	270	87	67	2197	672	382	—	418	33	145	—	86	86	.50	—	.290	.341	.411
Pittsburgh	153	5288	724	588	1517	222	122	44	2115	658	366	—	396	28	151	—	181	92	.66	—	.287	.345	.400
Brooklyn	154	5339	717	675	1534	227	54	72	2085	662	447	—	357	22	143	—	34	46	.43	—	.287	.345	.391
Chicago	154	5134	698	699	1419	207	59	66	1942	634	469	—	521	30	163	—	137	149	.48	—	.276	.340	.378
Philadelphia	152	5306	676	849	1459	256	56	94	2109	615	382	—	452	36	131	—	57	67	.46	—	.275	.328	.397
Cincinnati	153	5301	649	579	1539	236	111	36	2105	586	349	—	334	26	159	—	103	98	.51	—	.290	.337	.397
Boston	154	5283	520	800	1355	194	52	25	1728	520	459	—	451	26	104	—	74	68	.52	—	.256	.306	.327
NL Total	1228	42445	5581	5581	12009	1881	622	499	16631	5067	3216	—	3408	229	1123	—	754	659	.53	—	.283	.337	.392
NL Avg Team	154	5306	698	698	1501	235	78	62	2079	633	402	—	426	29	140	—	94	82	.53	—	.283	.337	.392

Team Pitching

Team	G	CG	ShO	Rel	Sv	IP	H	R	ER	HR	SH	SF	HB	TBB	IBB	SO	WP	Bk	H/9	SO/9	BB/9	OAvg	OOBP	ERA
Cincinnati	153	77	14	104	9	1378.0	1408	579	477	30	139	—	28	293	—	451	15	3	9.2	2.9	1.9	.267	.309	3.12
Pittsburgh	153	85	15	105	5	1382.0	1387	588	502	42	146	—	24	323	—	364	19	3	9.0	2.4	2.1	.267	.313	3.27
New York	154	71	4	148	21	1378.2	1464	641	554	77	111	—	19	392	—	406	19	7	9.6	2.7	2.6	.274	.326	3.62
Brooklyn	154	97	10	84	5	1376.1	1432	675	557	58	109	—	37	403	—	638	18	0	9.4	4.2	2.6	.270	.326	3.64
Chicago	154	85	4	107	6	1380.2	1459	699	587	89	130	—	23	438	—	416	17	4	9.5	2.7	2.9	.275	.333	3.83
St. Louis	154	79	7	119	6	1364.2	1528	750	629	70	148	—	40	486	—	393	20	5	10.1	2.6	3.2	.290	.354	4.15
Boston	154	66	10	123	4	1379.1	1607	800	684	49	188	—	29	402	—	364	21	5	10.5	2.4	2.6	.301	.353	4.46
Philadelphia	152	59	7	154	10	1354.1	1689	849	733	84	155	—	30	469	—	349	32	3	11.2	2.3	3.1	.313	.372	4.87
NL Total	1228	619	71	944	66	10994.0	11974	5581	4723	499	1126	—	230	3206	—	3381	161	30	9.8	2.8	2.6	.283	.336	3.87
NL Avg Team	154	77	9	118	8	1374.0	1497	698	590	62	141	—	29	401	—	423	20	4	9.8	2.8	2.6	.283	.336	3.87

Team Fielding

Team	G	PO	A	E	TC	DP	PB	Pct
Boston	154	4129	2029	168	6326	154	18	.973
Philadelphia	152	4065	2025	175	6265	168	11	.972
Pittsburgh	153	4148	2047	183	6378	161	12	.971
New York	154	4130	2031	186	6347	160	5	.971
St. Louis	154	4080	1876	188	6144	162	12	.969
Brooklyn	154	4126	1848	196	6170	121	9	.968
Cincinnati	153	4131	2089	217	6437	142	10	.966
Chicago	154	4135	1985	218	6338	153	13	.966
NL Total	1228	32944	15930	1531	50405	1221	90	.970

Team vs. Team Records

	Bos	Bro	ChN	Cin	NYG	Phi	Pit	StL	Won
Bos	—	7	6	12	5	10	7	6	53
Bro	15	—	12	12	8	17	13	15	92
ChN	15	10	—	9	9	16	7	15	81
Cin	10	10	13	—	9	16	12	13	83
NYG	17	14	13	13	—	14	9	13	93
Phi	12	5	6	5	7	—	8	12	55
Pit	15	9	15	10	13	13	—	15	90
StL	16	7	7	9	9	10	7	—	65
Lost	100	62	72	70	60	96	63	89	

1924 National League Batting Leaders

Games		At-Bats		Runs		Hits		Doubles		Triples	
J. Fournier, Bro	154	G. Wright, Pit	616	F. Frisch, NYG	121	R. Hornsby, StL	227	R. Hornsby, StL	43	E. Roush, Cin	21
G. Wright, Pit	153	F. Frisch, NYG	603	R. Hornsby, StL	121	Z. Wheat, Bro	212	Z. Wheat, Bro	41	R. Maranville, Pit	20
R. Maranville, Pit	152	M. Carey, Pit	599	M. Carey, Pit	113	F. Frisch, NYG	198	G. Kelly, NYG	37	G. Wright, Pit	18
T. Jackson, NYG	151	T. Jackson, NYG	596	R. Youngs, NYG	112	A. High, Bro	191	3 tied with	33	K. Cuyler, Pit	16
C. Grimm, Pit	151	R. Maranville, Pit	594	C. Williams, Phi	101	J. Fournier, Bro	188			F. Frisch, NYG	15

Home Runs		Total Bases		Runs Batted In		Walks		Intentional Walks		Strikeouts	
J. Fournier, Bro	27	R. Hornsby, StL	373	G. Kelly, NYG	136	R. Hornsby, StL	89	Statistic unavailable		G. Grantham, ChN	63
R. Hornsby, StL	25	Z. Wheat, Bro	311	J. Fournier, Bro	116	J. Fournier, Bro	83			K. Cuyler, Pit	62
C. Williams, Phi	24	C. Williams, Phi	308	G. Wright, Pit	111	R. Youngs, NYG	77			H. Sand, Phi	57
G. Kelly, NYG	21	G. Kelly, NYG	303	J. Bottomley, StL	111	C. Williams, Phi	67			E. Padgett, Bos	56
2 tied with	16	J. Fournier, Bro	302	I. Meusel, NYG	102	B. Friberg, ChN	66			T. Jackson, NYG	56

Hit By Pitch		Sac Hits		Sac Flies		Stolen Bases		Caught Stealing		GDP	
H. Groh, NYG	11	B. Pinelli, Cin	33	Statistic unavailable		M. Carey, Pit	49	B. Friberg, ChN	27	Statistic unavailable	
R. Blades, StL	10	B. Friberg, ChN	21			K. Cuyler, Pit	32	C. Heathcote, ChN	24		
J. Fournier, Bro	10	I. Meusel, NYG	19			C. Heathcote, ChN	26	G. Grantham, ChN	21		
B. Henline, Phi	8	M. Stock, Bro	19			P. Traynor, Pit	24	D. Grigsby, ChN	19		
4 tied with	7	M. Carey, Pit	19			J. Smith, StL	24	P. Traynor, Pit	18		

Runs Created		Runs Created/27 Outs		Batting Average		On-Base Percentage		Slugging Percentage		OBP+Slugging	
R. Hornsby, StL	162	R. Hornsby, StL	12.73	R. Hornsby, StL	.424	R. Hornsby, StL	.507	R. Hornsby, StL	.696	R. Hornsby, StL	1.203
J. Fournier, Bro	123	R. Youngs, NYG	8.75	Z. Wheat, Bro	.375	R. Youngs, NYG	.441	C. Williams, Phi	.552	Z. Wheat, Bro	.978
Z. Wheat, Bro	120	Z. Wheat, Bro	8.67	R. Youngs, NYG	.356	J. Fournier, Bro	.428	Z. Wheat, Bro	.549	J. Fournier, Bro	.965
R. Youngs, NYG	118	J. Fournier, Bro	8.21	K. Cuyler, Pit	.354	Z. Wheat, Bro	.428	K. Cuyler, Pit	.539	R. Youngs, NYG	.962
C. Williams, Phi	113	K. Cuyler, Pit	7.86	E. Roush, Cin	.348	C. Williams, Phi	.403	J. Fournier, Bro	.536	C. Williams, Phi	.955

1924 National League Pitching Leaders

Wins		Losses		Winning Percentage		Games		Games Started		Complete Games	
D. Vance, Bro	28	J. Barnes, Bos	20	E. Yde, Pit	.842	R. Kremer, Pit	41	B. Grimes, Bro	36	B. Grimes, Bro	30
B. Grimes, Bro	22	J. Genewich, Bos	19	D. Vance, Bro	.824	J. Morrison, Pit	41	W. Cooper, Pit	35	D. Vance, Bro	30
C. Mays, Cin	20	J. Haines, StL	19	A. Nehf, NYG	.778	V. Keen, ChN	40	D. Vance, Bro	34	W. Cooper, Pit	25
W. Cooper, Pit	20	H. Carlson, Phi	17	J. Bentley, NYG	.762	T. Sheehan, Cin	39	3 tied with	32	J. Barnes, Bos	21
R. Kremer, Pit	18	3 tied with	16	P. Alexander, ChN	.706	5 tied with	38			V. Aldridge, ChN	20

Shutouts		Saves		Games Finished		Batters Faced		Innings Pitched		Hits Allowed	
6 tied with	4	J. May, Cin	6	J. May, Cin	21	B. Grimes, Bro	1345	B. Grimes, Bro	310.2	B. Grimes, Bro	351
		C. Jonnard, NYG	5	B. Sherdel, StL	20	D. Vance, Bro	1221	D. Vance, Bro	308.1	W. Cooper, Pit	296
		R. Ryan, NYG	5	H. Betts, Phi	19	J. Barnes, Bos	1109	W. Cooper, Pit	268.2	J. Barnes, Bos	292
		6 tied with	3	T. Sheehan, Cin	19	W. Cooper, Pit	1109	J. Barnes, Bos	267.2	J. Haines, StL	275
				R. Lucas, Bos	18	R. Kremer, Pit	1066	R. Kremer, Pit	259.1	H. Carlson, Phi	267

Home Runs Allowed		Walks		Walks/9 Innings		Strikeouts		Strikeouts/9 Innings		Strikeout/Walk Ratio	
T. Kaufmann, ChN	21	J. Ring, Phi	108	P. Alexander, ChN	1.3	D. Vance, Bro	262	D. Vance, Bro	7.6	D. Vance, Bro	3.40
V. Keen, ChN	17	B. Grimes, Bro	91	W. Cooper, Pit	1.3	B. Grimes, Bro	135	B. Grimes, Bro	3.9	P. Donohue, Cin	2.00
B. Grimes, Bro	15	A. Sothoron, StL	84	C. Mays, Cin	1.4	D. Luque, Cin	86	A. Nehf, NYG	3.8	C. Mays, Cin	1.75
3 tied with	14	V. Keen, ChN	80	P. Donohue, Cin	1.5	J. Morrison, Pit	85	D. Luque, Cin	3.5	A. Nehf, NYG	1.71
		V. Aldridge, ChN	80	R. Kremer, Pit	1.8	T. Kaufmann, ChN	79	T. Kaufmann, ChN	3.4	D. Luque, Cin	1.62

Earned Run Average		Component ERA		Hit Batsmen		Wild Pitches		Opponent Average		Opponent OBP	
D. Vance, Bro	2.16	D. Vance, Bro	2.02	A. Sothoron, StL	10	C. Mitchell, Phi	9	D. Vance, Bro	.213	D. Vance, Bro	.269
H. McQuillan, NYG	2.69	E. Rixey, Cin	2.32	P. Donohue, Cin	9	J. Morrison, Pit	7	E. Yde, Pit	.244	E. Rixey, Cin	.285
E. Rixey, Cin	2.76	E. Yde, Pit	2.69	D. Vance, Bro	9	J. Haines, StL	6	J. Morrison, Pit	.245	P. Alexander, ChN	.299
E. Yde, Pit	2.83	J. Morrison, Pit	2.70	J. Genewich, Bos	8	3 tied with	5	E. Rixey, Cin	.246	A. Nehf, NYG	.301
P. Alexander, ChN	3.03	C. Mays, Cin	2.88	V. Aldridge, ChN	7			A. Nehf, NYG	.254	C. Mays, Cin	.302

1924 National League Miscellaneous

Managers

Boston	Dave Bancroft	27-38
	Dick Rudolph	11-27
	Dave Bancroft	15-35
Brooklyn	Wilbert Robinson	92-62
Chicago	Bill Killefer	81-72
Cincinnati	Jack Hendricks	83-70
New York	John McGraw	16-13
	Hughie Jennings	32-13
	John McGraw	45-35
Philadelphia	Art Fletcher	55-96
Pittsburgh	Bill McKechnie	90-63
St. Louis	Branch Rickey	65-89

Awards

Most Valuable Player	Dazzy Vance, p, Bro
STATS Cy Young	Dazzy Vance, Bro
STATS Rookie of the Year	Glenn Wright, ss, Pit
STATS Manager of the Year	Wilbert Robinson, Bro

STATS All-Star Team

C	Gabby Hartnett, ChN	.299	16	67
1B	Jack Fournier, Bro	.334	27	116
2B	Rogers Hornsby, StL	.424	25	94
3B	Pie Traynor, Pit	.294	5	82
SS	Glenn Wright, Pit	.287	7	111
OF	Kiki Cuyler, Pit	.354	9	85
OF	Zack Wheat, Bro	.375	14	97
OF	Ross Youngs, NYG	.356	10	74
P	Ray Kremer, Pit	18-10	3.19	64 K
P	Carl Mays, Cin	20-9	3.15	63 K
P	Dazzy Vance, Bro	28-6	2.16	262 K
P	Emil Yde, Pit	16-3	2.83	53 K
RP	Claude Jonnard, NYG	4-5	2.41	5 Sv

Postseason

World Series	NYG (NL) 3 vs. Washington (AL) 4

Outstanding Performances

No-Hitters
Jesse Haines, StL   vs. Bos on July 17
Three-Homer Games
George Kelly, NYG   on June 14

1925 American League Standings

Team	Overall					Home Games						Road Games						Park Index		Record by Month					
	W	L	Pct	GB	DIF	W	L	R	OR	HR	OHR	W	L	R	OR	HR	OHR	Run	HR	M/A	May	June	July	Aug	S/O
Washington	96	55	.636	—	76	53	22	408	298	13	13	43	33	421	372	43	36	90	33	9-3	17-12	19-8	15-12	19-10	17-10
Philadelphia	88	64	.579	8.5	98	51	26	435	351	35	37	37	38	396	362	41	23	101	110	8-3	20-8	16-12	18-9	12-15	14-17
St. Louis	82	71	.536	15.0	0	45	32	503	501	73	73	37	39	397	405	37	26	124	229	7-8	14-16	11-14	16-12	18-9	16-12
Detroit	81	73	.526	16.5	1	43	34	451	399	18	36	38	39	452	430	32	34	96	82	4-11	14-15	16-9	15-14	15-11	17-13
Chicago	79	75	.513	18.5	0	44	33	366	378	13	32	35	42	445	392	25	37	89	73	9-6	14-12	14-12	17-16	14-12	11-17
Cleveland	70	84	.455	27.5	17	37	39	421	430	23	19	33	45	361	387	29	22	117	85	9-4	11-15	8-21	18-13	14-15	10-16
New York	69	85	.448	28.5	1	42	36	354	356	54	56	27	49	352	418	56	22	90	137	4-7	11-18	14-13	12-17	9-17	19-13
Boston	47	105	.309	49.5	0	28	47	309	441	10	28	19	58	330	481	31	39	95	56	2-10	12-17	9-18	6-24	7-19	11-17

Clinch Date—Washington 9/24.

Team Batting

Team	G	AB	R	OR	H	2B	3B	HR	TB	RBI	TBB	IBB	SO	HBP	SH	SF	SB	CS	SB%	GDP	Avg	OBP	Slg
Detroit	156	5371	903	829	1621	277	84	50	2216	798	640	—	386	32	220	—	97	63	.61	—	.302	.379	.413
St. Louis	154	5440	900	906	1620	304	68	110	2390	800	498	—	375	31	143	—	85	78	.52	—	.298	.360	.439
Philadelphia	153	5399	831	713	1659	298	79	76	2343	768	453	—	432	31	187	—	67	60	.53	—	.307	.364	.434
Washington	152	5206	829	670	1577	251	71	56	2138	747	533	—	427	44	210	—	135	92	.59	—	.303	.372	.411
Chicago	154	5224	811	770	1482	299	59	38	2013	738	662	—	405	48	231	—	131	87	.60	—	.284	.369	.385
Cleveland	155	5436	782	817	1613	285	58	52	2170	697	520	—	379	28	180	—	90	77	.54	—	.297	.361	.399
New York	156	5353	706	774	1471	247	74	110	2196	652	470	—	482	24	171	—	69	73	.49	—	.275	.336	.410
Boston	152	5166	639	922	1375	257	64	41	1883	591	513	—	422	29	133	—	42	56	.43	—	.266	.336	.364
AL Total	1232	42595	6401	6401	12418	2218	557	533	17349	5791	4289	—	3308	267	1475	—	716	586	.55	—	.292	.360	.407
AL Avg Team	154	5324	800	800	1552	277	70	67	2169	724	536	—	414	33	184	—	90	73	.55	—	.292	.360	.407

Team Pitching

Team	G	CG	ShO	Rel	Sv	IP	H	R	ER	HR	SH	SF	HB	TBB	IBB	SO	WP	Bk	H/9	SO/9	BB/9	OAvg	OOBP	ERA
Washington	152	69	10	145	21	1358.1	1434	670	558	49	146	—	34	543	—	463	17	0	9.5	3.1	3.6	.278	.351	3.70
Philadelphia	153	61	8	161	18	1381.2	1468	713	594	60	161	—	36	544	—	495	30	3	9.6	3.2	3.5	.276	.347	3.87
Chicago	154	71	12	129	13	1385.2	1579	770	661	69	186	—	19	489	—	374	20	1	10.3	2.4	3.2	.294	.356	4.29
New York	156	80	8	123	13	1387.2	1560	774	668	78	142	—	31	505	—	492	20	3	10.1	3.2	3.3	.289	.353	4.33
Cleveland	155	93	6	103	9	1372.1	1604	817	685	41	183	—	40	493	—	345	17	1	10.5	2.3	3.2	.296	.359	4.49
Detroit	156	66	2	142	18	1383.2	1582	829	708	70	201	—	42	556	—	419	27	3	10.3	2.7	3.6	.296	.366	4.61
St. Louis	154	67	7	160	10	1379.2	1588	906	754	99	219	—	32	675	—	419	31	4	10.4	2.7	4.4	.299	.381	4.92
Boston	152	68	6	128	6	1326.2	1615	922	732	67	232	—	39	510	—	310	14	7	11.0	2.1	3.5	.308	.374	4.97
AL Total	1232	575	59	1091	108	10975.2	12430	6401	5360	533	1470	—	273	4315	—	3317	176	23	10.2	2.7	3.5	.292	.361	4.40
AL Avg Team	154	72	7	136	14	1371.2	1554	800	670	67	184	—	34	539	—	415	22	3	10.2	2.7	3.5	.292	.361	4.40

Team Fielding

Team	G	PO	A	E	TC	DP	PB	Pct
New York	156	4153	1844	160	6157	150	12	.974
Detroit	156	4119	1935	173	6227	143	7	.972
Washington	152	4062	1811	170	6043	166	7	.972
Chicago	154	4124	1967	200	6291	162	6	.968
Philadelphia	153	4117	1931	211	6259	148	13	.966
Cleveland	155	4109	1901	210	6220	146	8	.966
St. Louis	154	4171	1925	226	6322	164	15	.964
Boston	152	3976	1993	271	6240	150	16	.957
AL Total	1232	32831	15307	1621	49759	1229	84	.967

Team vs. Team Records

	Bos	ChA	Cle	Det	NYA	Phi	StL	Was	Won
Bos	—	9	7	5	9	5	5	7	47
ChA	13	—	14	13	13	8	9	9	79
Cle	15	8	—	11	10	11	11	4	70
Det	17	9	11	—	14	8	12	10	81
NYA	13	9	12	8	—	9	11	7	69
Phi	17	14	11	14	13	—	12	7	88
StL	16	13	11	10	11	10	—	11	82
Was	14	13	18	12	15	13	11	—	96
Lost	105	75	84	73	85	64	71	55	

1925 American League Batting Leaders

Games		At-Bats		Runs		Hits		Doubles		Triples	
B. Meusel, NYA	156	A. Simmons, Phi	658	J. Mostil, ChA	135	A. Simmons, Phi	253	M. McManus, StL	44	G. Goslin, Was	20
J. Sewell, Cle	155	S. Rice, Was	649	A. Simmons, Phi	122	S. Rice, Was	227	A. Simmons, Phi	43	J. Mostil, ChA	16
M. McManus, StL	154	G. Sisler, StL	649	E. Combs, NYA	117	H. Heilmann, Det	225	E. Sheely, ChA	43	G. Sisler, StL	15
B. Falk, ChA	154	B. Meusel, NYA	624	G. Goslin, Was	116	G. Sisler, StL	224	G. Burns, Cle	41	3 tied with	13
G. Robertson, StL	154	J. Sewell, Cle	608	S. Rice, Was	111	J. Sewell, Cle	204	2 tied with	40		

Home Runs		Total Bases		Runs Batted In		Walks		Intentional Walks		Strikeouts	
B. Meusel, NYA	33	A. Simmons, Phi	392	B. Meusel, NYA	138	W. Kamm, ChA	90	Statistic unavailable		M. McManus, StL	69
K. Williams, StL	25	B. Meusel, NYA	338	H. Heilmann, Det	134	J. Mostil, ChA	90			B. Ruth, NYA	68
B. Ruth, NYA	25	G. Goslin, Was	329	A. Simmons, Phi	129	M. Bishop, Phi	87			J. Tavener, Det	60
A. Simmons, Phi	24	H. Heilmann, Det	326	G. Goslin, Was	113	E. Collins, ChA	87			I. Davis, ChA	58
L. Gehrig, NYA	20	G. Sisler, StL	311	E. Sheely, ChA	111	L. Blue, Det	83			O. Bluege, Was	56

Hit By Pitch		Sac Hits		Sac Flies		Stolen Bases		Caught Stealing		GDP	
J. Mostil, ChA	12	B. Harris, Was	41	Statistic unavailable		J. Mostil, ChA	43	J. Mostil, ChA	21	Statistic unavailable	
F. O'Rourke, Det	11	I. Davis, ChA	40			G. Goslin, Was	26	C. Jamieson, Cle	18		
P. Todt, Bos	10	W. Kamm, ChA	37			S. Rice, Was	26	E. McNeely, Was	16		
E. McNeely, Was	9	L. Blue, Det	34			3 tied with	19	3 tied with	14		
B. Harris, Was	9	F. O'Rourke, Det	29								

Runs Created		Runs Created/27 Outs		Batting Average		On-Base Percentage		Slugging Percentage		OBP+Slugging	
H. Heilmann, Det	142	T. Cobb, Det	10.67	H. Heilmann, Det	.393	T. Cobb, Det	.479	K. Williams, StL	.613	T. Cobb, Det	1.066
A. Simmons, Phi	140	T. Speaker, Cle	10.31	T. Speaker, Cle	.389	T. Cobb, Det	.468	T. Cobb, Det	.598	T. Speaker, Cle	1.057
G. Goslin, Was	126	H. Heilmann, Det	9.85	A. Simmons, Phi	.384	E. Collins, ChA	.461	A. Simmons, Phi	.596	H. Heilmann, Det	1.026
G. Sisler, StL	113	H. Rice, StL	9.66	T. Cobb, Det	.378	H. Heilmann, Det	.457	T. Speaker, Cle	.578	H. Rice, StL	1.018
2 tied with	111	A. Wingo, Det	8.83	A. Wingo, Det	.370	A. Wingo, Det	.456	H. Heilmann, Det	.569	A. Simmons, Phi	1.012

1925 American League Pitching Leaders

Wins		Losses		Winning Percentage		Games		Games Started		Complete Games	
T. Lyons, ChA	21	S. Jones, NYA	21	S. Coveleski, Was	.800	F. Marberry, Was	55	E. Whitehill, Det	33	H. Ehmke, Bos	22
E. Rommel, Phi	21	H. Ehmke, Bos	20	K. Holloway, Det	.765	R. Walberg, Phi	53	S. Harriss, Phi	33	S. Smith, Cle	22
S. Coveleski, Was	20	T. Wingfield, Bos	19	W. Johnson, Was	.741	E. Rommel, Phi	52	T. Zachary, Was	33	H. Pennock, NYA	21
W. Johnson, Was	20	R. Ruffing, Bos	18	D. Leonard, Det	.733	E. Vangilder, StL	52	3 tied with	32	T. Lyons, ChA	19
S. Harriss, Phi	19	H. Pennock, NYA	17	D. Ruether, Was	.720	H. Pennock, NYA	47			T. Wingfield, Bos	18

Shutouts		Saves		Games Finished		Batters Faced		Innings Pitched		Hits Allowed	
T. Lyons, ChA	5	F. Marberry, Was	15	F. Marberry, Was	39	E. Rommel, Phi	1154	H. Pennock, NYA	277.0	S. Smith, Cle	296
J. Giard, StL	4	J. Doyle, Det	8	J. Doyle, Det	34	H. Pennock, NYA	1143	T. Lyons, ChA	262.2	E. Rommel, Phi	285
S. Gray, Phi	4	S. Connally, ChA	8	S. Connally, ChA	28	H. Ehmke, Bos	1134	E. Rommel, Phi	261.0	H. Ehmke, Bos	285
4 tied with	3	R. Walberg, Phi	7	3 tied with	23	T. Lyons, ChA	1110	H. Ehmke, Bos	260.2	M. Gaston, StL	284
		2 tied with	6			T. Wingfield, Bos	1105	T. Wingfield, Bos	254.1	W. Hoyt, NYA	283

Home Runs Allowed		Walks		Walks/9 Innings		Strikeouts		Strikeouts/9 Innings		Strikeout/Walk Ratio	
D. Danforth, StL	19	L. Grove, Phi	131	S. Smith, Cle	1.8	L. Grove, Phi	116	W. Johnson, Was	4.2	W. Johnson, Was	1.38
J. Bush, StL	18	D. Davis, StL	106	J. Quinn, 2tm	1.8	W. Johnson, Was	108	S. Gray, Phi	3.5	U. Shocker, NYA	1.28
U. Shocker, NYA	17	D. Ruether, Was	105	U. Shocker, NYA	2.1	S. Harriss, Phi	95	S. Harriss, Phi	3.4	S. Gray, Phi	1.27
3 tied with	14	S. Jones, NYA	104	R. Faber, ChA	2.2	H. Ehmke, Bos	95	S. Jones, NYA	3.4	H. Pennock, NYA	1.24
		M. Gaston, StL	101	H. Pennock, NYA	2.3	S. Jones, NYA	92	T. Blankenship, ChA	3.3	R. Faber, ChA	1.20

Earned Run Average		Component ERA		Hit Batsmen		Wild Pitches		Opponent Average		Opponent OBP	
S. Coveleski, Was	2.84	H. Pennock, NYA	2.92	H. Ehmke, Bos	11	L. Grove, Phi	9	W. Johnson, Was	.243	H. Pennock, NYA	.303
H. Pennock, NYA	2.96	W. Johnson, Was	2.97	E. Whitehill, Det	10	M. Gaston, StL	6	T. Blankenship, ChA	.253	T. Blankenship, ChA	.308
W. Johnson, Was	3.07	S. Coveleski, Was	2.99	L. Stoner, Det	9	D. Davis, StL	6	H. Pennock, NYA	.254	W. Johnson, Was	.311
H. Dauss, Det	3.16	T. Blankenship, ChA	3.14	4 tied with	8	7 tied with	5	S. Coveleski, Was	.255	S. Coveleski, Was	.312
T. Blankenship, ChA	3.16	S. Gray, Phi	3.30					S. Gray, Phi	.260	S. Gray, Phi	.319

1925 American League Miscellaneous

Managers

Boston	Lee Fohl	47-105
Chicago	Eddie Collins	79-75
Cleveland	Tris Speaker	70-84
Detroit	Ty Cobb	81-73
New York	Miller Huggins	69-85
Philadelphia	Connie Mack	88-64
St. Louis	George Sisler	82-71
Washington	Bucky Harris	96-55

Awards

Most Valuable Player	Peckinpaugh, ss, Was
STATS Cy Young	Stan Coveleski, Was
STATS Rookie of the Year	Earle Combs, of, NYA
STATS Manager of the Year	Connie Mack, Phi

STATS All-Star Team

C	Mickey Cochrane, Phi	.331	6	55
1B	George Sisler, StL	.345	12	105
2B	Eddie Collins, ChA	.346	3	80
3B	Sammy Hale, Phi	.345	8	63
SS	Joe Sewell, Cle	.336	1	98
OF	Ty Cobb, Det	.378	12	102
OF	Harry Heilmann, Det	.393	13	134
OF	Al Simmons, Phi	.384	24	129
P	Ted Blankenship, ChA	17-8	3.16	81 K
P	Stan Coveleski, Was	20-5	2.84	58 K
P	Walter Johnson, Was	20-7	3.07	108 K
P	Ted Lyons, ChA	21-11	3.26	45 K
RP	Firpo Marberry, Was	8-6	3.47	15 Sv

Postseason

World Series	Was (AL) 3 vs. Pittsburgh (NL) 4

Outstanding Performances

Three-Homer Games

Ty Cobb, Det	on May 5
M. Cochrane, Phi	on May 21
Goose Goslin, Was	on June 19

Cycles

Roy Carlyle, Bos	on July 21

1925 National League Standings

Team	Overall					Home Games						Road Games						Park Index		Record by Month					
	W	L	Pct	GB	DIF	W	L	R	OR	HR	OHR	W	L	R	OR	HR	OHR	Run	HR	M/A	May	June	July	Aug	S/O
Pittsburgh	95	58	.621	—	93	52	25	481	342	27	31	43	33	431	373	51	50	101	57	5-8	16-9	18-8	17-11	21-10	18-12
New York	86	66	.566	8.5	75	47	29	362	334	55	39	39	37	374	368	59	34	94	101	9-4	18-8	13-14	17-13	16-18	13-9
Cincinnati	80	73	.523	15.0	6	44	32	334	285	11	5	36	41	356	358	33	30	88	26	9-5	10-15	13-13	19-11	16-14	13-15
St. Louis	77	76	.503	18.0	0	48	28	449	359	66	41	29	48	379	405	43	45	104	123	5-8	9-17	19-9	12-18	15-16	17-8
Boston	70	83	.458	25.0	2	37	39	315	383	15	14	33	44	393	419	26	53	87	37	4-7	13-14	9-18	13-20	17-13	14-11
Philadelphia	68	85	.444	27.0	0	38	39	488	547	73	74	30	46	324	383	27	43	144	207	6-6	12-13	12-16	12-13	12-21	14-16
Brooklyn	68	85	.444	27.0	2	40	37	383	407	25	41	28	48	403	459	39	34	90	89	5-7	18-10	10-16	13-12	15-18	7-22
Chicago	68	86	.442	27.5	2	37	40	367	359	57	63	31	46	356	414	29	39	94	176	8-6	9-19	13-13	11-16	15-17	12-15

Clinch Date—Pittsburgh 9/23.

Team Batting

Team	G	AB	R	OR	H	2B	3B	HR	TB	RBI	TBB	IBB	SO	HBP	SH	SF	SB	CS	SB%	GDP	Avg	OBP	Slg
Pittsburgh	153	5372	912	715	1651	316	105	78	2411	820	499	—	363	30	135	—	159	63	.72	—	.307	.369	.449
St. Louis	153	5329	828	764	1592	292	80	109	2371	752	446	—	414	27	134	—	70	51	.58	—	.299	.356	.445
Philadelphia	153	5412	812	930	1598	288	58	100	2302	731	456	—	542	34	133	—	48	59	.45	—	.295	.354	.425
Brooklyn	153	5468	786	866	1617	250	80	64	2219	722	437	—	383	26	114	—	37	30	.55	—	.296	.351	.406
New York	152	5327	736	702	1507	239	61	114	2210	682	411	—	494	25	95	—	79	65	.55	—	.283	.337	.415
Chicago	154	5353	723	773	1473	254	70	86	2125	660	397	—	470	33	150	—	94	70	.57	—	.275	.329	.397
Boston	153	5365	708	802	1567	260	70	41	2090	645	405	—	380	30	145	—	77	72	.52	—	.292	.345	.390
Cincinnati	153	5233	690	643	1490	221	90	44	2023	624	409	—	327	23	173	—	108	107	.50	—	.285	.339	.387
NL Total	1224	42859	6195	6195	12495	2120	614	636	17751	5636	3460	—	3373	228	1079	—	672	517	.57	—	.292	.348	.414
NL Avg Team	153	5357	774	774	1562	265	77	80	2219	705	433	—	422	29	135	—	84	65	.57	—	.292	.348	.414

Team Pitching

Team	G	CG	ShO	Rel	Sv	IP	H	R	ER	HR	SH	SF	HB	TBB	IBB	SO	WP	Bk	H/9	SO/9	BB/9	OAvg	OOBP	ERA
Cincinnati	153	92	11	103	12	1375.1	1447	643	517	35	115	—	33	324	—	437	17	1	9.5	2.9	2.1	.272	.317	3.38
Pittsburgh	153	77	2	119	13	1354.2	1526	715	583	81	123	—	36	387	—	386	23	3	10.1	2.6	2.6	.287	.339	3.87
New York	152	80	6	112	8	1354.0	1532	702	593	73	139	—	16	408	—	446	10	0	10.2	3.0	2.7	.289	.342	3.94
St. Louis	153	82	8	105	7	1335.2	1480	764	647	86	113	—	40	470	—	428	21	3	10.0	2.9	3.2	.283	.347	4.36
Boston	153	77	5	129	4	1366.2	1567	802	667	67	168	—	17	458	—	351	23	0	10.3	2.3	3.0	.291	.348	4.39
Chicago	154	75	5	115	10	1370.0	1575	773	671	102	112	—	29	485	—	435	12	1	10.3	2.9	3.2	.292	.353	4.41
Brooklyn	153	82	4	128	4	1350.2	1608	866	716	75	167	—	35	477	—	518	33	2	10.7	3.5	3.2	.301	.362	4.77
Philadelphia	153	69	8	151	9	1350.2	1753	930	754	117	134	—	22	444	—	371	33	2	11.7	2.5	3.0	.315	.368	5.02
NL Total	1224	634	49	962	67	10857.2	12488	6195	5148	636	1071	—	228	3453	—	3372	172	12	10.4	2.8	2.9	.292	.347	4.27
NL Avg Team	153	79	6	120	8	1357.2	1561	774	644	80	134	—	29	432	—	422	22	2	10.4	2.8	2.9	.292	.347	4.27

Team Fielding

Team	G	PO	A	E	TC	DP	PB	Pct
Chicago	154	4106	2025	198	6329	161	9	.969
New York	152	4078	1999	199	6276	129	10	.968
Cincinnati	153	4122	2046	203	6371	161	15	.968
St. Louis	153	3999	1801	204	6004	156	4	.966
Brooklyn	153	4043	1908	210	6161	130	17	.966
Philadelphia	153	4049	1857	211	6117	147	12	.966
Boston	153	4101	1894	221	6216	145	6	.964
Pittsburgh	153	4064	1882	224	6170	171	13	.964
NL Total	1224	32562	15412	1670	49644	1200	86	.966

Team vs. Team Records

	Bos	Bro	ChN	Cin	NYG	Phi	Pit	StL	Won
Bos	—	13	12	9	11	6	7	12	70
Bro	8	—	11	12	10	11	5	11	68
ChN	10	11	—	10	7	10	12	8	68
Cin	13	10	12	—	9	16	8	12	80
NYG	11	12	15	13	—	13	10	12	86
Phi	16	11	12	6	8	—	8	7	68
Pit	15	17	10	13	12	14	—	14	95
StL	10	11	14	10	9	15	8	—	77
Lost	83	85	86	73	66	85	58	76	

1925 National League Batting Leaders

Games		At-Bats		Runs		Hits		Doubles		Triples	
G. Wright, Pit	153	S. Adams, ChN	627	K. Cuyler, Pit	144	J. Bottomley, StL	227	J. Bottomley, StL	44	K. Cuyler, Pit	26
L. Bell, StL	153	J. Bottomley, StL	619	R. Hornsby, StL	133	Z. Wheat, Bro	221	K. Cuyler, Pit	43	C. Walker, Cin	16
J. Bottomley, StL	153	E. Brown, Bro	618	Z. Wheat, Bro	125	K. Cuyler, Pit	220	Z. Wheat, Bro	42	E. Roush, Cin	16
K. Cuyler, Pit	153	K. Cuyler, Pit	617	P. Traynor, Pit	114	R. Hornsby, StL	203	D. Burrus, Bos	41	J. Fournier, Bro	16
E. Brown, Bro	153	Z. Wheat, Bro	616	R. Blades, StL	112	M. Stock, Bro	202	R. Hornsby, StL	41	2 tied with	14

Home Runs		Total Bases		Runs Batted In		Walks		Intentional Walks		Strikeouts	
R. Hornsby, StL	39	R. Hornsby, StL	381	R. Hornsby, StL	143	J. Fournier, Bro	86	Statistic unavailable		G. Hartnett, ChN	77
G. Hartnett, ChN	24	K. Cuyler, Pit	369	J. Fournier, Bro	130	R. Hornsby, StL	83			H. Sand, Phi	65
J. Fournier, Bro	22	J. Bottomley, StL	358	J. Bottomley, StL	128	E. Moore, Pit	73			B. Friberg, 2tm	57
J. Bottomley, StL	21	Z. Wheat, Bro	333	G. Wright, Pit	121	R. Youngs, NYG	66			K. Cuyler, Pit	56
I. Meusel, NYG	21	J. Fournier, Bro	310	C. Barnhart, Pit	114	M. Carey, Pit	66			G. Kelly, NYG	54

Hit By Pitch		Sac Hits		Sac Flies		Stolen Bases		Caught Stealing		GDP	
K. Cuyler, Pit	13	B. Pinelli, Cin	34	Statistic unavailable		M. Carey, Pit	46	E. Roush, Cin	20	Statistic unavailable	
J. Welsh, Bos	8	E. Brown, Bro	24			K. Cuyler, Pit	41	B. Pinelli, Cin	19		
B. Henline, Phi	8	H. Critz, Cin	21			S. Adams, ChN	26	H. Critz, Cin	13		
J. Fournier, Bro	8	E. Moore, Pit	19			E. Roush, Cin	22	K. Cuyler, Pit	13		
2 tied with	7	C. Barnhart, Pit	19			F. Frisch, NYG	21	B. Southworth, NYG	13		

Runs Created		Runs Created/27 Outs		Batting Average		On-Base Percentage		Slugging Percentage		OBP+Slugging	
R. Hornsby, StL	158	R. Hornsby, StL	12.88	R. Hornsby, StL	.403	R. Hornsby, StL	.489	R. Hornsby, StL	.756	R. Hornsby, StL	1.245
K. Cuyler, Pit	149	K. Cuyler, Pit	9.21	J. Bottomley, StL	.367	J. Fournier, Bro	.446	K. Cuyler, Pit	.598	K. Cuyler, Pit	1.021
J. Bottomley, StL	134	J. Fournier, Bro	9.17	Z. Wheat, Bro	.359	C. Williams, Phi	.435	J. Bottomley, StL	.578	J. Fournier, Bro	1.015
J. Fournier, Bro	130	J. Bottomley, StL	8.55	K. Cuyler, Pit	.357	R. Blades, StL	.423	J. Fournier, Bro	.569	J. Bottomley, StL	.992
Z. Wheat, Bro	125	Z. Wheat, Bro	8.07	J. Fournier, Bro	.350	K. Cuyler, Pit	.423	G. Harper, Phi	.558	R. Blades, StL	.958

1925 National League Pitching Leaders

Wins		Losses		Winning Percentage		Games		Games Started		Complete Games	
D. Vance, Bro	22	B. Grimes, Bro	19	B. Sherdel, StL	.714	J. Morrison, Pit	44	P. Donohue, Cin	38	P. Donohue, Cin	27
P. Donohue, Cin	21	S. Blake, ChN	18	D. Vance, Bro	.710	G. Bush, ChN	42	J. Ring, Phi	37	D. Vance, Bro	26
E. Rixey, Cin	21	D. Luque, Cin	18	A. Reinhart, StL	.688	P. Donohue, Cin	42	D. Luque, Cin	36	D. Luque, Cin	22
L. Meadows, Pit	19	C. Mitchell, Phi	17	V. Aldridge, Pit	.682	T. Osborne, Bro	41	E. Rixey, Cin	36	E. Rixey, Cin	22
3 tied with	17	2 tied with	16	R. Kremer, Pit	.680	R. Kremer, Pit	40	H. Carlson, Phi	32	J. Ring, Phi	21

Shutouts		Saves		Games Finished		Batters Faced		Innings Pitched		Hits Allowed	
H. Carlson, Phi	4	E. Yde, Pit	4	E. Dyer, StL	19	J. Ring, Phi	1239	P. Donohue, Cin	301.0	J. Ring, Phi	325
D. Vance, Bro	4	G. Bush, ChN	4	T. Sheehan, 2tm	18	P. Donohue, Cin	1232	D. Luque, Cin	291.0	P. Donohue, Cin	310
D. Luque, Cin	4	5 tied with	3	G. Bush, ChN	17	D. Luque, Cin	1196	E. Rixey, Cin	287.1	B. Grimes, Bro	305
P. Donohue, Cin	3			J. Wisner, NYG	16	E. Rixey, Cin	1186	J. Ring, Phi	270.0	E. Rixey, Cin	302
8 tied with	2			3 tied with	15	B. Grimes, Bro	1129	D. Vance, Bro	265.1	H. Carlson, Phi	281

Home Runs Allowed		Walks		Walks/9 Innings		Strikeouts		Strikeouts/9 Innings		Strikeout/Walk Ratio	
C. Mitchell, Phi	23	J. Ring, Phi	119	P. Alexander, ChN	1.1	D. Vance, Bro	221	D. Vance, Bro	7.5	D. Vance, Bro	3.35
R. Kremer, Pit	19	S. Blake, ChN	114	P. Donohue, Cin	1.5	D. Luque, Cin	140	D. Luque, Cin	4.3	P. Alexander, ChN	2.17
H. Carlson, Phi	19	B. Grimes, Bro	102	E. Rixey, Cin	1.5	S. Blake, ChN	93	V. Aldridge, Pit	3.7	D. Luque, Cin	1.79
J. Cooney, Bos	18	L. Dickerman, StL	79	J. Cooney, Bos	1.8	J. Ring, Phi	93	S. Blake, ChN	3.6	P. Donohue, Cin	1.59
W. Cooper, ChN	18	D. Luque, Cin	78	B. Sherdel, StL	1.9	V. Aldridge, Pit	88	K. Greenfield, NYG	3.5	J. Scott, NYG	1.58

Earned Run Average		Component ERA		Hit Batsmen		Wild Pitches		Opponent Average		Opponent OBP	
D. Luque, Cin	2.63	D. Luque, Cin	2.53	D. Vance, Bro	10	J. Ring, Phi	14	D. Luque, Cin	.239	D. Luque, Cin	.291
E. Rixey, Cin	2.88	P. Donohue, Cin	2.75	R. Kremer, Pit	9	R. Ehrhardt, Bro	8	L. Benton, Bos	.249	P. Donohue, Cin	.299
A. Reinhart, StL	3.05	D. Vance, Bro	2.78	L. Meadows, Pit	8	B. Grimes, Bro	8	D. Vance, Bro	.250	D. Vance, Bro	.304
P. Donohue, Cin	3.08	E. Rixey, Cin	3.04	8 tied with	7	D. Luque, Cin	8	P. Donohue, Cin	.268	E. Rixey, Cin	.307
L. Benton, Bos	3.09	L. Benton, Bos	3.07			L. Meadows, Pit	5	J. Scott, NYG	.269	J. Cooney, Bos	.312

1925 National League Miscellaneous

Managers		
Boston	Dave Bancroft	70-83
Brooklyn	Wilbert Robinson	68-85
Chicago	Bill Killefer	33-42
	Rabbit Maranville	23-30
	George Gibson	12-14
Cincinnati	Jack Hendricks	80-73
New York	John McGraw	10-4
	Hughie Jennings	21-11
	John McGraw	55-51
Philadelphia	Art Fletcher	68-85
Pittsburgh	Bill McKechnie	95-58
St. Louis	Branch Rickey	13-25
	Rogers Hornsby	64-51

Awards	
Most Valuable Player	Rogers Hornsby, 2b, StL
STATS Cy Young	Eppa Rixey, Cin
STATS Rookie of the Year	Jimmy Welsh, of, Bos
STATS Manager of the Year	Bill McKechnie, Pit

STATS All-Star Team

C	Gabby Hartnett, ChN	.289	24	67	
1B	Jack Fournier, Bro	.350	22	130	
2B	Rogers Hornsby, StL	.403	39	143	
3B	Pie Traynor, Pit	.320	6	106	
SS	Glenn Wright, Pit	.308	18	121	
OF	Ray Blades, StL	.342	12	57	
OF	Kiki Cuyler, Pit	.357	18	102	
OF	Zack Wheat, Bro	.359	14	103	
P	Pete Donohue, Cin	21-14	3.08	78 K	
P	Lee Meadows, Pit	19-10	3.67	87 K	
P	Eppa Rixey, Cin	21-11	2.88	69 K	
P	Dazzy Vance, Bro	22-9	3.53	221 K	
RP	Jakie May, Cin	8-9	3.87	2 Sv	

Postseason

World Series	Pit (NL) 4 vs. Was (AL) 3

Outstanding Performances

Triple Crown
Rogers Hornsby, StL   .403-39-143

No-Hitters
Dazzy Vance, Bro   vs. Phi on September 13

Cycles
Kiki Cuyler, Pit   on June 4
Max Carey, Pit   on June 20

Unassisted Triple Plays
Glenn Wright, Pit   on May 7

1926 American League Standings

Team	Overall					Home Games						Road Games						Park Index		Record by Month					
	W	L	Pct	GB	DIF	W	L	R	OR	HR	OHR	W	L	R	OR	HR	OHR	Run	HR	M/A	May	June	July	Aug	S/O
New York	91	63	.591	—	158	50	25	417	326	58	33	41	38	430	387	63	23	96	111	12-3	19-9	17-10	18-12	13-15	12-14
Cleveland	88	66	.571	3.0	13	49	31	376	301	11	19	39	35	362	311	16	30	93	60	10-5	12-17	16-12	20-10	16-11	14-11
Philadelphia	83	67	.553	6.0	0	44	27	365	314	34	27	39	40	312	256	27	11	133	179	6-10	21-10	10-14	15-14	19-9	12-10
Washington	81	69	.540	8.0	4	42	30	373	378	4	15	39	39	429	383	39	30	100	30	9-8	15-12	10-14	15-13	17-13	15-9
Chicago	81	72	.529	9.5	7	47	31	332	294	8	19	34	41	398	371	24	28	78	50	11-6	13-16	16-11	11-17	12-16	18-6
Detroit	79	75	.513	12.0	1	39	41	380	445	16	38	40	34	413	385	20	20	96	125	6-9	17-12	14-13	15-16	15-11	12-14
St. Louis	62	92	.403	29.0	0	40	39	375	429	53	64	22	53	307	416	19	22	106	271	5-12	9-18	14-13	13-16	11-18	10-15
Boston	46	107	.301	44.5	0	25	51	288	438	9	16	21	56	274	397	23	29	110	49	5-11	7-19	8-18	11-20	11-21	4-18

Clinch Date—New York 9/25.

Team Batting

Team	G	AB	R	OR	H	2B	3B	HR	TB	RBI	TBB	IBB	SO	HBP	SH	SF	SB	CS	SB%	GDP	Avg	OBP	Slg
New York	155	5221	847	713	1508	262	75	121	2283	787	642	—	580	23	217	—	79	62	.56	—	.289	.369	.437
Washington	152	5223	802	761	1525	244	43	43	2092	721	555	—	369	37	194	—	117	91	.56	—	.292	.364	.401
Detroit	157	5315	793	830	1547	281	90	36	2116	717	599	—	423	33	237	—	88	71	.55	—	.291	.366	.398
Cleveland	154	5293	738	612	1529	333	49	27	2041	643	455	—	332	35	224	—	88	42	.68	—	.289	.349	.386
Chicago	155	5220	730	665	1508	314	60	32	2038	666	556	—	381	34	229	—	123	78	.61	—	.289	.361	.390
St. Louis	155	5259	682	845	1449	253	78	72	2074	608	437	—	472	35	203	—	64	66	.49	—	.276	.335	.394
Philadelphia	150	5046	677	570	1359	259	65	61	1931	619	523	—	452	26	238	—	56	45	.55	—	.269	.341	.383
Boston	154	5185	562	835	1325	249	54	32	1778	521	465	—	454	32	168	—	52	48	.52	—	.256	.321	.343
AL Total	1232	41762	5831	5831	11750	2195	568	424	16353	5282	4232	—	3463	255	1710	—	667	503	.57	—	.281	.351	.392
AL Avg Team	154	5220	729	729	1469	274	71	53	2044	660	529	—	433	32	214	—	83	63	.57	—	.281	.351	.392

Team Pitching

Team	G	CG	ShO	Rel	Sv	IP	H	R	ER	HR	SH	SF	HB	TBB	IBB	SO	WP	Bk	H/9	SO/9	BB/9	OAvg	OOBP	ERA
Philadelphia	150	62	10	156	16	1346.0	1362	570	448	38	179	—	31	451	—	571	22	1	9.1	3.8	3.0	.268	.332	3.00
Cleveland	154	96	11	81	4	1374.0	1412	612	519	49	188	—	44	450	—	381	24	1	9.2	2.5	2.9	.271	.334	3.40
Chicago	155	85	11	100	12	1380.0	1426	665	573	47	175	—	11	506	—	458	12	2	9.3	3.0	3.3	.271	.336	3.74
New York	155	63	4	147	20	1372.1	1442	713	588	56	202	—	26	478	—	486	21	3	9.5	3.2	3.1	.274	.337	3.86
Washington	152	65	5	143	26	1348.1	1489	761	650	45	218	—	37	566	—	418	12	2	9.9	2.8	3.8	.292	.361	4.34
Detroit	157	57	10	163	18	1394.2	1570	830	683	58	197	—	46	555	—	469	16	6	10.1	3.0	3.6	.292	.363	4.41
St. Louis	155	64	5	139	9	1368.0	1549	845	709	86	258	—	32	654	—	337	27	4	10.2	2.2	4.3	.297	.379	4.66
Boston	154	53	6	162	5	1362.0	1520	835	715	45	288	—	31	546	—	336	23	4	10.0	2.2	3.6	.294	.365	4.72
AL Total	1232	545	62	1091	110	10945.1	11770	5831	4885	424	1705	—	258	4206	—	3456	157	23	9.7	2.8	3.5	.281	.351	4.02
AL Avg Team	154	68	8	136	14	1368.1	1471	729	611	53	213	—	32	526	—	432	20	3	9.7	2.8	3.5	.281	.351	4.02

Team Fielding

Team	G	PO	A	E	TC	DP	PB	Pct
Chicago	155	4152	1880	165	6197	122	9	.973
Cleveland	154	4115	1914	173	6202	153	5	.972
Philadelphia	150	4041	1869	171	6081	131	10	.972
Boston	154	4069	2105	193	6367	143	12	.970
Washington	152	4057	1771	184	6012	129	8	.969
Detroit	157	4180	1899	193	6272	151	9	.969
New York	155	4096	1792	210	6098	117	15	.966
St. Louis	155	4089	2006	235	6330	167	13	.963
AL Total	1232	32799	15236	1524	49559	1113	81	.969

Team vs. Team Records

	Bos	ChA	Cle	Det	NYA	Phi	StL	Was	Won
Bos	—	6	6	7	5	8	11	3	46
ChA	16	—	13	14	8	6	13	11	81
Cle	16	9	—	11	11	14	11	16	88
Det	15	8	11	—	10	11	12	12	79
NYA	17	14	11	12	—	9	16	12	91
Phi	14	15	8	11	13	—	15	7	83
StL	11	9	11	10	6	7	—	8	62
Was	18	11	6	10	10	12	14	—	81
Lost	107	72	66	75	63	67	92	69	

Seasons: Standings, Leaders

1926 American League Batting Leaders

Games		At-Bats		Runs		Hits		Doubles		Triples	
J. Tavener, Det	156	S. Rice, Was	641	B. Ruth, NYA	139	S. Rice, Was	216	G. Burns, Cle	64	L. Gehrig, NYA	20
T. Lazzeri, NYA	155	M. Koenig, NYA	617	L. Gehrig, NYA	135	G. Burns, Cle	216	A. Simmons, Phi	53	C. Gehringer, Det	17
L. Gehrig, NYA	155	F. Spurgeon, Cle	614	J. Mostil, ChA	120	G. Goslin, Was	201	T. Speaker, Cle	52	G. Goslin, Was	15
B. Falk, ChA	155	G. Sisler, StL	613	E. Combs, NYA	113	A. Simmons, Phi	199	B. D. Jacobson, 2tm	51	J. Mostil, ChA	15
3 tied with	154	E. Combs, NYA	606	G. Goslin, Was	105	J. Mostil, ChA	197	L. Gehrig, NYA	47	4 tied with	14

Home Runs		Total Bases		Runs Batted In		Walks		Intentional Walks		Strikeouts	
B. Ruth, NYA	47	B. Ruth, NYA	365	B. Ruth, NYA	146	B. Ruth, NYA	144	Statistic unavailable		T. Lazzeri, NYA	96
A. Simmons, Phi	19	A. Simmons, Phi	329	T. Lazzeri, NYA	114	M. Bishop, Phi	116			B. Ruth, NYA	76
T. Lazzeri, NYA	18	L. Gehrig, NYA	314	G. Burns, Cle	114	T. Rigney, Bos	108			L. Gehrig, NYA	73
G. Goslin, Was	17	G. Goslin, Was	308	L. Gehrig, NYA	112	L. Gehrig, NYA	105			M. McManus, StL	62
K. Williams, StL	17	G. Burns, Cle	298	A. Simmons, Phi	109	T. Speaker, Cle	94			P. Collins, NYA	56

Hit By Pitch		Sac Hits		Sac Flies		Stolen Bases		Caught Stealing		GDP	
J. Mostil, ChA	10	F. Spurgeon, Cle	35	Statistic unavailable		J. Mostil, ChA	35	S. Rice, Was	23	Statistic unavailable	
B. Harris, Was	9	B. Hunnefield, ChA	31			S. Rice, Was	25	B. Meusel, NYA	17		
4 tied with	8	4 tied with	28			B. Hunnefield, ChA	24	J. Mostil, ChA	14		
						E. McNeely, Was	18	B. Fothergill, Det	12		
						J. Sewell, Cle	17	B. Miller, 2tm	12		

Runs Created		Runs Created/27 Outs		Batting Average		On-Base Percentage		Slugging Percentage		OBP+Slugging	
B. Ruth, NYA	167	B. Ruth, NYA	13.23	H. Manush, Det	.378	B. Ruth, NYA	.516	B. Ruth, NYA	.737	B. Ruth, NYA	1.253
G. Goslin, Was	128	G. Goslin, Was	8.51	B. Ruth, NYA	.372	H. Heilmann, Det	.445	A. Simmons, Phi	.566	H. Manush, Det	.985
L. Gehrig, NYA	127	H. Heilmann, Det	8.44	B. Fothergill, Det	.367	E. Collins, ChA	.441	H. Manush, Det	.564	H. Heilmann, Det	.979
A. Simmons, Phi	122	H. Manush, Det	8.31	H. Heilmann, Det	.367	P. Collins, NYA	.433	L. Gehrig, NYA	.549	L. Gehrig, NYA	.969
3 tied with	113	A. Simmons, Phi	8.07	G. Burns, Cle	.358	M. Bishop, Phi	.431	G. Goslin, Was	.542	G. Goslin, Was	.967

1926 American League Pitching Leaders

Wins		Losses		Winning Percentage		Games		Games Started		Complete Games	
G. Uhle, Cle	27	M. Gaston, StL	18	G. Uhle, Cle	.711	F. Marberry, Was	64	G. Uhle, Cle	36	G. Uhle, Cle	32
H. Pennock, NYA	23	P. Zahniser, Bos	18	H. Pennock, NYA	.676	J. Pate, Phi	47	E. Whitehill, Det	34	T. Lyons, ChA	24
U. Shocker, NYA	19	T. Wingfield, Bos	16	H. Dauss, Det	.667	G. Rommel, Phi	45	S. Coveleski, Was	34	W. Johnson, Was	22
T. Lyons, ChA	18	T. Lyons, ChA	16	U. Shocker, NYA	.633	T. Thomas, ChA	44	4 tied with	33	L. Grove, Phi	20
3 tied with	16	W. Johnson, Was	16	F. Marberry, Was	.632	2 tied with	43			2 tied with	19

Shutouts		Saves		Games Finished		Batters Faced		Innings Pitched		Hits Allowed	
E. Wells, Det	4	F. Marberry, Was	22	F. Marberry, Was	47	G. Uhle, Cle	1367	G. Uhle, Cle	318.1	G. Uhle, Cle	300
9 tied with	3	H. Dauss, Det	9	J. Pate, Phi	34	T. Lyons, ChA	1208	T. Lyons, ChA	283.2	H. Pennock, NYA	294
		J. Pate, Phi	6	G. Braxton, NYA	23	H. Pennock, NYA	1124	H. Pennock, NYA	266.1	U. Shocker, NYA	272
		L. Grove, Phi	6	H. Dauss, Det	23	U. Shocker, NYA	1108	W. Johnson, Was	260.2	S. Coveleski, Was	272
		S. Jones, NYA	5	2 tied with	22	W. Johnson, Was	1101	U. Shocker, NYA	258.1	E. Whitehill, Det	271

Home Runs Allowed		Walks		Walks/9 Innings		Strikeouts		Strikeouts/9 Innings		Strikeout/Walk Ratio	
T. Zachary, StL	14	G. Uhle, Cle	118	H. Pennock, NYA	1.5	L. Grove, Phi	194	L. Grove, Phi	6.8	L. Grove, Phi	1.92
M. Gaston, StL	13	T. Thomas, ChA	110	S. Smith, Cle	1.5	G. Uhle, Cle	159	T. Thomas, ChA	4.6	H. Pennock, NYA	1.81
T. Blankenship, ChA	13	T. Lyons, ChA	106	E. Rommel, Phi	2.2	T. Thomas, ChA	127	G. Uhle, Cle	4.5	W. Johnson, Was	1.71
U. Shocker, NYA	13	L. Grove, Phi	101	U. Shocker, NYA	2.5	W. Johnson, Was	125	W. Johnson, Was	4.3	E. Whitehill, Det	1.38
W. Johnson, Was	13	M. Gaston, StL	101	W. Johnson, Was	2.5	E. Whitehill, Det	109	E. Whitehill, Det	3.9	G. Uhle, Cle	1.35

Earned Run Average		Component ERA		Hit Batsmen		Wild Pitches		Opponent Average		Opponent OBP	
L. Grove, Phi	2.51	L. Grove, Phi	2.91	G. Uhle, Cle	13	W. Ballou, StL	8	T. Thomas, ChA	.244	H. Pennock, NYA	.313
G. Uhle, Cle	2.83	T. Lyons, ChA	3.03	D. Levsen, Cle	8	G. Uhle, Cle	8	L. Grove, Phi	.244	E. Rommel, Phi	.314
T. Lyons, ChA	3.01	W. Hoyt, NYA	3.11	E. Whitehill, Det	8	W. Beall, NYA	7	T. Lyons, ChA	.252	W. Hoyt, NYA	.316
E. Rommel, Phi	3.08	T. Thomas, ChA	3.12	K. Holloway, Det	8	S. Harriss, 2tm	7	G. Uhle, Cle	.253	W. Johnson, Was	.317
S. Coveleski, Was	3.12	G. Uhle, Cle	3.13	H. Ehmke, 2tm	8	2 tied with	6	D. Levsen, Cle	.261	U. Shocker, NYA	.318

1926 American League Miscellaneous

Managers

Boston	Lee Fohl	46-107
Chicago	Eddie Collins	81-72
Cleveland	Tris Speaker	88-66
Detroit	Ty Cobb	79-75
New York	Miller Huggins	91-63
Philadelphia	Connie Mack	83-67
St. Louis	George Sisler	62-92
Washington	Bucky Harris	81-69

Awards

Most Valuable Player	George Burns, 1b, Cle
STATS Cy Young	George Uhle, Cle
STATS Rookie of the Year	Tony Lazzeri, 2b, NYA
STATS Manager of the Year	Miller Huggins, NYA

STATS All-Star Team

C	Wally Schang, StL	.330	8	50
1B	Lou Gehrig, NYA	.313	16	112
2B	Tony Lazzeri, NYA	.275	18	114
3B	Marty McManus, StL	.284	9	68
SS	Joe Sewell, Cle	.324	4	85
OF	Goose Goslin, Was	.354	17	108
OF	Harry Heilmann, Det	.367	9	103
OF	Babe Ruth, NYA	.372	47	146
P	Ted Lyons, ChA	18-16	3.01	51 K
P	Herb Pennock, NYA	23-11	3.62	78 K
P	Urban Shocker, NYA	19-11	3.38	59 K
P	George Uhle, Cle	27-11	2.83	159 K
RP	Firpo Marberry, Was	12-7	3.00	22 Sv

Postseason

World Series	New York (AL) 3 vs. St. Louis (NL) 4

Outstanding Performances

No-Hitters

Ted Lyons, ChA	@ Bos on August 21

Cycles

Bob Fothergill, Det	on September 26

1926 National League Standings

Team	Overall W	L	Pct	GB	DIF	Home Games W	L	R	OR	HR	OHR	Road Games W	L	R	OR	HR	OHR	Park Index Run	HR	Record by Month M/A	May	June	July	Aug	S/O
St. Louis	89	65	.578	—	30	47	30	411	359	**54**	42	**42**	**35**	**406**	319	**36**	34	106	137	8-8	15-16	16-6	14-16	22-8	14-11
Cincinnati	87	67	.565	2.0	75	**53**	**23**	372	**259**	8	8	34	44	375	392	27	32	84	28	8-6	21-10	14-11	13-18	18-9	13-13
Pittsburgh	84	69	.549	4.5	38	49	28	**446**	374	18	16	35	41	323	315	26	34	127	56	7-10	16-8	11-12	21-10	16-12	13-17
Chicago	82	72	.532	7.0	0	49	28	295	295	35	17	33	44	**307**	351	31	14	110	98	8-7	15-10	11-17	16-14	19-10	13-14
New York	74	77	.490	13.5	11	43	33	333	317	45	43	31	44	330	351	28	27	94	158	9-6	11-16	14-13	14-14	12-15	14-13
Brooklyn	71	82	.464	17.5	16	38	38	314	331	23	26	33	44	309	374	17	24	96	121	9-5	12-14	14-12	16-18	9-21	11-12
Boston	66	86	.434	22.0	0	43	34	296	266	4	**5**	23	52	328	453	12	41	70	17	5-10	7-17	13-15	15-15	8-20	18-9
Philadelphia	58	93	.384	29.5	5	33	42	392	470	46	42	25	51	295	430	29	26	120	162	7-9	9-15	10-17	12-16	9-18	11-18

Clinch Date—St. Louis 9/25.

Team Batting

Team	G	AB	R	OR	H	2B	3B	HR	TB	RBI	TBB	IBB	SO	HBP	SH	SF	SB	CS	SB%	GDP	Avg	OBP	Slg
St. Louis	156	**5381**	**817**	678	**1541**	259	82	**90**	**2234**	**756**	478	—	**518**	33	212	—	83	—	—	—	.286	.348	**.415**
Pittsburgh	157	5312	769	689	1514	243	106	44	2101	707	434	—	350	33	190	—	91	—	—	—	.285	.343	.396
Cincinnati	157	5320	747	651	**1541**	242	**120**	35	2128	692	454	—	333	**34**	**239**	—	51	—	—	—	**.290**	**.349**	.400
Philadelphia	152	5254	687	900	1479	244	50	75	2048	632	422	—	479	22	153	—	47	—	—	—	.281	.337	.390
Chicago	155	5229	682	**602**	1453	**291**	49	66	2040	630	445	—	447	29	199	—	85	—	—	—	.278	.338	.390
New York	151	5167	663	668	1435	214	58	73	1984	617	339	—	420	22	139	—	**94**	—	—	—	.278	.325	.384
Boston	153	5216	624	719	1444	209	62	16	1825	560	426	—	348	29	199	—	81	—	—	—	.277	.335	.350
Brooklyn	155	5130	623	705	1348	246	62	40	1838	568	475	—	464	27	158	—	76	—	—	—	.263	.328	.358
NL Total	1236	42009	5612	5612	11755	1948	589	439	16198	5162	3473	—	3359	229	1489	—	608	—	—	—	.280	.338	.386
NL Avg Team	155	5251	702	702	1469	244	74	55	2025	645	434	—	420	29	186	—	76	—	—	—	.280	.338	.386

Team Pitching

Team	G	CG	ShO	Rel	Sv	IP	H	R	ER	HR	SH	SF	HB	TBB	IBB	SO	WP	Bk	H/9	SO/9	BB/9	OAvg	OOBP	ERA
Chicago	155	77	13	114	14	1378.1	1407	**602**	499	39	183	—	**37**	486	—	508	20	2	9.2	3.3	3.2	.273	.340	3.26
Cincinnati	157	88	**14**	107	8	**1408.2**	1449	651	535	40	178	—	28	**324**	—	424	12	2	9.3	2.7	**2.1**	.271	**.316**	3.42
Pittsburgh	157	83	12	131	**18**	1379.1	1422	689	562	50	192	—	36	455	—	387	9	2	9.3	2.5	3.0	.272	.334	3.67
St. Louis	156	**90**	10	118	6	1398.2	1423	678	570	76	164	—	21	397	—	365	14	2	**9.2**	2.3	2.6	.269	.322	3.67
New York	151	61	4	135	15	1341.2	**1370**	668	562	70	**150**	—	18	427	—	419	21	0	9.2	2.8	2.9	**.269**	.328	3.77
Brooklyn	155	83	5	108	9	1361.2	1440	705	578	50	216	—	24	472	—	**517**	22	**6**	9.5	**3.4**	3.1	.276	.339	3.82
Boston	153	60	9	132	9	1365.1	1536	719	608	46	230	—	36	455	—	408	23	0	10.1	2.7	3.0	.294	.354	4.01
Philadelphia	152	68	5	**171**	5	1344.1	1699	900	751	68	173	—	21	454	—	331	**31**	2	11.4	2.2	3.0	.315	.371	5.03
NL Total	1236	610	72	1016	84	10978.0	11746	5612	4665	439	1486	—	221	3470	—	3359	152	16	9.6	2.8	2.8	.280	.338	3.82
NL Avg Team	155	76	9	127	11	1372.0	1468	702	583	55	186	—	28	434	—	420	19	2	9.6	2.8	2.8	.280	.338	3.82

Team Fielding

Team	G	PO	A	E	TC	DP	PB	Pct
Chicago	155	4133	2006	**162**	6301	**174**	17	.974
Cincinnati	157	**4196**	**2085**	183	**6464**	160	15	.972
New York	151	4029	1941	186	6156	150	15	.970
St. Louis	156	4191	1921	198	6310	141	5	.969
Boston	153	4089	1946	208	6243	150	**19**	.967
Pittsburgh	157	4144	1929	220	6293	161	9	.965
Philadelphia	152	3993	2019	224	6236	153	15	.964
Brooklyn	155	4114	1929	229	6272	95	12	.963
NL Total	1236	32889	15776	1610	50275	1184	107	.968

Team vs. Team Records

	Bos	Bro	ChN	Cin	NYG	Phi	Pit	StL	Won
Bos	—	6	12	12	12	7	10	7	66
Bro	15	—	14	4	9	13	9	7	71
ChN	10	8	—	13	14	16	10	11	82
Cin	10	18	9	—	7	16	13	14	87
NYG	10	13	8	15	—	12	6	10	74
Phi	15	9	6	6	7	—	8	7	58
Pit	11	13	12	9	16	14	—	9	84
StL	15	15	11	8	12	15	13	—	89
Lost	86	82	72	67	77	93	69	65	

1926 National League Batting Leaders

Games		At-Bats		Runs		Hits		Doubles		Triples	
K. Cuyler, Pit	157	S. Adams, ChN	624	K. Cuyler, Pit	113	E. Brown, Bos	201	J. Bottomley, StL	40	P. Waner, Pit	22
T. Thevenow, StL	156	K. Cuyler, Pit	614	P. Waner, Pit	101	K. Cuyler, Pit	197	E. Roush, Cin	37	C. Walker, Cin	20
4 tied with	155	E. Brown, Bos	612	H. Sand, Phi	99	S. Adams, ChN	193	H. Wilson, ChN	36	P. Traynor, Pit	17
		H. Critz, Cin	607	B. Southworth, 2tm	99	L. Bell, StL	189	3 tied with	35	3 tied with	15
		J. Bottomley, StL	603	2 tied with	98	2 tied with	182				

Home Runs		Total Bases		Runs Batted In		Walks		Intentional Walks		Strikeouts	
H. Wilson, ChN	21	J. Bottomley, StL	305	J. Bottomley, StL	120	H. Wilson, ChN	69	Statistic unavailable		B. Friberg, Phi	77
J. Bottomley, StL	19	L. Bell, StL	301	H. Wilson, ChN	109	P. Waner, Pit	66			K. Cuyler, Pit	66
C. Williams, Phi	18	H. Wilson, ChN	285	L. Bell, StL	100	H. Sand, Phi	66			L. Bell, StL	62
L. Bell, StL	17	P. Waner, Pit	283	B. Southworth, 2tm	99	D. Bancroft, Bos	64			H. Wilson, ChN	61
B. Southworth, 2tm	16	K. Cuyler, Pit	282	W. Pipp, Cin	99	R. Blades, StL	62			R. Blades, StL	57

Hit By Pitch		Sac Hits		Sac Flies		Stolen Bases		Caught Stealing		GDP	
R. Blades, StL	11	T. Douthit, StL	37	Statistic unavailable		K. Cuyler, Pit	35	Statistic unavailable		Statistic unavailable	
K. Cuyler, Pit	9	J. Welsh, Bos	32			S. Adams, ChN	27				
J. Welsh, Bos	8	L. Bell, StL	31			T. Douthit, StL	23				
H. Mueller, 2tm	8	C. Walker, Cin	30			F. Frisch, NYG	23				
2 tied with	6	E. Roush, Cin	30			R. Youngs, NYG	21				

Runs Created		Runs Created/27 Outs		Batting Average		On-Base Percentage		Slugging Percentage		OBP+Slugging	
P. Waner, Pit	118	C. Williams, Phi	8.30	B. Hargrave, Cin	.353	C. Christensen, Cin	.426	C. Williams, Phi	.568	C. Williams, Phi	.986
L. Bell, StL	114	P. Waner, Pit	8.23	C. Christensen, Cin	.350	C. Williams, Phi	.418	H. Wilson, ChN	.539	H. Wilson, ChN	.944
J. Bottomley, StL	112	B. Hargrave, Cin	7.55	E. Smith, Pit	.346	P. Waner, Pit	.413	P. Waner, Pit	.528	P. Waner, Pit	.941
K. Cuyler, Pit	111	H. Wilson, ChN	7.54	C. Williams, Phi	.345	R. Blades, StL	.409	B. Hargrave, Cin	.525	B. Hargrave, Cin	.930
H. Wilson, ChN	108	G. Grantham, Pit	7.35	P. Waner, Pit	.336	E. Smith, Pit	.407	L. Bell, StL	.518	L. Bell, StL	.901

1926 National League Pitching Leaders

Wins		Losses		Winning Percentage		Games		Games Started		Complete Games	
F. Rhem, StL	20	C. Root, ChN	17	R. Kremer, Pit	.769	J. Scott, NYG	50	P. Donohue, Cin	38	C. Mays, Cin	24
R. Kremer, Pit	20	J. Petty, Bro	17	J. Haines, StL	.765	C. Willoughby, Phi	47	F. Rhem, StL	34	J. Petty, Bro	23
P. Donohue, Cin	20	W. Dean, Phi	16	F. Rhem, StL	.741	P. Donohue, Cin	47	H. Carlson, Phi	34	C. Root, ChN	21
L. Meadows, Pit	20	J. Genewich, Bos	16	L. Meadows, Pit	.690	D. Ulrich, Phi	45	J. Petty, Bro	33	F. Rhem, StL	20
C. Mays, Cin	19	D. Luque, Cin	16	A. Reinhart, StL	.667	J. May, Cin	45	C. Mays, Cin	33	H. Carlson, Phi	20

Shutouts		Saves		Games Finished		Batters Faced		Innings Pitched		Hits Allowed	
P. Donohue, Cin	5	C. Davies, NYG	6	C. Davies, NYG	29	P. Donohue, Cin	1191	P. Donohue, Cin	285.2	P. Donohue, Cin	298
B. Smith, Bos	4	R. Kremer, Pit	5	R. Ehrhardt, Bro	28	C. Mays, Cin	1158	C. Mays, Cin	281.0	H. Carlson, Phi	293
S. Blake, ChN	4	J. Scott, NYG	5	J. Scott, NYG	24	J. Petty, Bro	1152	J. Petty, Bro	275.2	C. Mays, Cin	286
6 tied with	3	R. Ehrhardt, Bro	4	G. Mogridge, Bos	24	C. Root, ChN	1110	C. Root, ChN	271.1	C. Root, ChN	267
		4 tied with	3	J. May, Cin	22	H. Carlson, Phi	1110	H. Carlson, Phi	267.1	B. Sherdel, StL	255

Home Runs Allowed		Walks		Walks/9 Innings		Strikeouts		Strikeouts/9 Innings		Strikeout/Walk Ratio	
K. Greenfield, NYG	17	S. Blake, ChN	92	P. Donohue, Cin	1.2	D. Vance, Bro	140	D. Vance, Bro	7.5	D. Vance, Bro	2.41
V. Keen, StL	15	P. Jones, ChN	90	P. Alexander, 2tm	1.4	C. Root, ChN	127	P. Jones, ChN	4.5	C. Root, ChN	2.05
B. Sherdel, StL	15	W. Dean, Phi	89	H. Carlson, Phi	1.6	L. Benton, Bos	103	S. Blake, ChN	4.3	P. Donohue, Cin	1.87
J. Knight, Phi	14	B. Grimes, Bro	88	C. Mays, Cin	1.7	J. May, Cin	103	C. Root, ChN	4.2	J. Scott, NYG	1.55
J. Scott, NYG	13	D. McWeeny, Bro	84	B. Sherdel, StL	1.9	J. Petty, Bro	101	L. Benton, Bos	4.0	P. Alexander, 2tm	1.52

Earned Run Average		Component ERA		Hit Batsmen		Wild Pitches		Opponent Average		Opponent OBP	
R. Kremer, Pit	2.61	P. Alexander, 2tm	2.51	D. Songer, Pit	11	C. Willoughby, Phi	9	J. Petty, Bro	.240	P. Alexander, 2tm	.281
C. Root, ChN	2.82	J. Petty, Bro	2.56	J. Werts, Bos	10	J. Ring, NYG	9	P. Alexander, 2tm	.250	J. Petty, Bro	.296
J. Petty, Bro	2.84	R. Kremer, Pit	2.76	P. Donohue, Cin	9	G. Boehler, Bro	8	F. Rhem, StL	.250	R. Kremer, Pit	.296
F. Fitzsimmons, NYG	2.88	C. Mays, Cin	2.80	D. McWeeny, Bro	8	W. Dean, Phi	6	R. Kremer, Pit	.252	P. Donohue, Cin	.298
T. Kaufmann, ChN	3.02	P. Donohue, Cin	2.83	3 tied with	7	S. Blake, ChN	6	P. Jones, ChN	.256	F. Rhem, StL	.305

1926 National League Miscellaneous

Managers		
Boston	Dave Bancroft	66-86
Brooklyn	Wilbert Robinson	71-82
Chicago	Joe McCarthy	82-72
Cincinnati	Jack Hendricks	87-67
New York	John McGraw	74-77
Philadelphia	Art Fletcher	58-93
Pittsburgh	Bill McKechnie	84-69
St. Louis	Rogers Hornsby	89-65

Awards

Most Valuable Player	Bob O'Farrell, c, StL
STATS Cy Young	Ray Kremer, Pit
STATS Rookie of the Year	Paul Waner, of, Pit
STATS Manager of the Year	Rogers Hornsby, StL

STATS All-Star Team

C	Bob O'Farrell, StL	.293	7	68
1B	Jim Bottomley, StL	.299	19	120
2B	Rogers Hornsby, StL	.317	11	93
3B	Les Bell, StL	.325	17	100
SS	Travis Jackson, NYG	.327	8	51
OF	Kiki Cuyler, Pit	.321	8	92
OF	Paul Waner, Pit	.336	8	79
OF	Hack Wilson, ChN	.321	21	109
P	Pete Donohue, Cin	20-14	3.37	73 K
P	Ray Kremer, Pit	20-6	2.61	74 K
P	Carl Mays, Cin	19-12	3.14	58 K
P	Flint Rhem, StL	20-7	3.21	72 K
RP	Jakie May, Cin	13-9	3.22	3 Sv

Postseason

World Series	St. Louis (NL) 4 vs. New York (AL) 3

Outstanding Performances

Three-Homer Games
Jack Fournier, Bro   on July 13

1927 American League Standings

Team	Overall					Home Games						Road Games						Park Index		Record by Month					
	W	L	Pct	GB	DIF	W	L	R	OR	HR	OHR	W	L	R	OR	HR	OHR	Run	HR	M/A	May	June	July	Aug	S/O
New York	110	44	.714	—	173	57	19	479	267	83	30	53	25	496	332	75	12	92	133	9-5	19-9	21-6	24-7	16-10	21-7
Philadelphia	91	63	.591	19.0	1	50	27	412	327	26	36	41	36	429	399	30	29	89	105	9-5	13-15	15-12	14-15	21-7	19-9
Washington	85	69	.552	25.0	4	51	28	416	308	10	19	34	41	366	422	19	34	87	52	7-7	12-12	18-10	22-10	8-18	18-12
Detroit	82	71	.536	27.5	2	44	32	467	433	25	28	38	39	378	372	26	24	122	107	6-6	12-16	16-8	18-14	16-12	14-15
Chicago	70	83	.458	39.5	0	38	37	337	343	6	22	32	46	325	365	30	33	102	46	9-7	18-10	13-15	10-19	9-13	11-19
Cleveland	66	87	.431	43.5	1	35	42	333	367	10	11	31	45	335	399	16	26	94	49	7-9	13-14	11-15	10-21	14-11	11-17
St. Louis	59	94	.386	50.5	1	38	38	440	457	42	57	21	56	284	447	13	22	124	287	6-6	13-16	8-16	12-20	10-17	10-19
Boston	51	103	.331	59.0	0	29	49	299	409	5	29	22	54	298	447	23	27	93	66	3-11	8-16	4-24	14-18	10-16	12-18

Clinch Date—New York 9/13.

Team Batting

Team	G	AB	R	OR	H	2B	3B	HR	TB	RBI	TBB	IBB	SO	HBP	SH	SF	SB	CS	SB%	GDP	Avg	OBP	Slg
New York	155	5347	975	599	1644	291	103	158	2615	908	635	—	605	22	204	—	90	64	.58	—	.307	.383	.489
Detroit	156	5299	845	805	1533	282	100	51	2168	755	587	—	420	25	198	—	139	73	.66	—	.289	.363	.409
Philadelphia	155	5296	841	726	1606	281	70	56	2195	767	551	—	326	30	219	—	101	63	.62	—	.303	.372	.414
Washington	157	5389	782	730	1549	268	87	29	2078	696	498	—	359	32	198	—	133	52	.72	—	.287	.351	.386
St. Louis	155	5220	724	904	1440	262	59	55	1985	657	443	—	420	42	192	—	90	66	.58	—	.276	.337	.380
Cleveland	153	5202	668	766	1471	321	52	26	1974	616	381	—	366	48	214	—	65	72	.47	—	.283	.337	.379
Chicago	153	5157	662	708	1433	285	61	36	1948	610	493	—	389	26	235	—	89	75	.54	—	.278	.344	.378
Boston	154	5207	597	856	1348	271	78	28	1859	550	430	—	456	39	191	—	81	46	.64	—	.259	.320	.357
AL Total	1238	42117	6094	6094	12024	2261	610	439	16822	5559	4018	—	3341	264	1651	—	788	511	.61	—	.285	.351	.399
AL Avg Team	155	5265	762	762	1503	283	76	55	2103	695	502	—	418	33	206	—	99	64	.61	—	.285	.351	.399

Team Pitching

Team	G	CG	ShO	Rel	Sv	IP	H	R	ER	HR	SH	SF	HB	TBB	IBB	SO	WP	Bk	H/9	SO/9	BB/9	OAvg	OOBP	ERA
New York	155	82	11	109	20	1389.2	1403	599	494	42	177	—	18	409	—	431	16	2	9.1	2.8	2.6	.267	.323	3.20
Chicago	153	85	10	95	8	1367.0	1467	708	594	55	203	—	29	440	—	365	12	3	9.7	2.4	2.9	.283	.342	3.91
Washington	157	62	10	163	23	1402.0	1434	730	618	53	186	—	41	491	—	497	15	5	9.2	3.2	3.2	.269	.336	3.97
Philadelphia	155	66	8	160	25	1384.0	1467	726	611	65	183	—	36	442	—	553	18	2	9.5	3.6	2.9	.278	.338	3.97
Detroit	156	75	5	131	17	1387.2	1542	805	638	52	222	—	47	577	—	421	25	7	10.0	2.7	3.7	.290	.364	4.14
Cleveland	153	72	5	132	8	1353.1	1542	766	642	37	216	—	37	508	—	366	30	3	10.3	2.4	3.4	.295	.361	4.27
Boston	154	63	6	134	7	1366.1	1603	856	716	56	251	—	41	558	—	381	23	6	10.6	2.5	3.7	.305	.376	4.72
St. Louis	155	80	4	121	8	1353.1	1592	904	744	79	208	—	21	604	—	385	34	4	10.6	2.6	4.0	.297	.371	4.95
AL Total	1238	585	59	1045	116	11003.1	12050	6094	5057	439	1646	—	270	4029	—	3399	173	32	9.8	2.8	3.3	.285	.352	4.14
AL Avg Team	155	73	7	131	15	1375.1	1506	762	632	55	206	—	34	504	—	425	22	4	9.8	2.8	3.3	.285	.352	4.14

Team Fielding

Team	G	PO	A	E	TC	DP	PB	Pct
Chicago	153	4107	1905	178	6190	131	7	.971
Philadelphia	155	4161	1897	190	6248	124	10	.970
New York	155	4176	2009	195	6380	123	6	.969
Washington	157	4209	1876	195	6280	125	3	.969
Cleveland	153	4061	1981	201	6243	146	10	.968
Detroit	156	4167	1978	206	6351	173	8	.968
Boston	154	4088	2013	228	6329	167	13	.964
St. Louis	155	4037	1947	248	6232	166	13	.960
AL Total	1238	33006	15606	1641	50253	1155	70	.967

Team vs. Team Records

	Bos	ChA	Cle	Det	NYA	Phi	StL	Was	Won
Bos	—	11	15	5	4	6	6	4	51
ChA	11	—	8	13	5	8	15	10	70
Cle	7	14	—	7	10	10	10	8	66
Det	17	8	15	—	8	9	14	11	82
NYA	18	17	12	14	—	14	21	14	110
Phi	16	14	12	13	8	—	16	12	91
StL	16	7	11	8	1	6	—	10	59
Was	18	12	14	11	8	10	12	—	85
Lost	103	83	87	71	44	63	94	69	

1927 American League Batting Leaders

Games		At-Bats		Runs		Hits		Doubles		Triples	
L. Gehrig, NYA	155	E. Combs, NYA	648	B. Ruth, NYA	158	E. Combs, NYA	231	L. Gehrig, NYA	52	E. Combs, NYA	23
T. Lazzeri, NYA	153	G. Sisler, StL	614	L. Gehrig, NYA	149	L. Gehrig, NYA	218	G. Burns, Cle	51	L. Gehrig, NYA	18
J. Sewell, Cle	153	S. Rice, Was	603	E. Combs, NYA	137	G. Sisler, StL	201	H. Heilmann, Det	50	H. Manush, Det	18
E. Combs, NYA	152	H. Manush, Det	593	C. Gehringer, Det	110	H. Heilmann, Det	201	J. Sewell, Cle	48	G. Goslin, Was	15
H. Manush, Det	152	L. Gehrig, NYA	584	H. Heilmann, Det	106	G. Goslin, Was	194	B. Meusel, NYA	47	S. Rice, Was	14

Home Runs		Total Bases		Runs Batted In		Walks		Intentional Walks		Strikeouts	
B. Ruth, NYA	60	L. Gehrig, NYA	447	L. Gehrig, NYA	175	B. Ruth, NYA	138	Statistic unavailable		B. Ruth, NYA	89
L. Gehrig, NYA	47	B. Ruth, NYA	417	B. Ruth, NYA	164	L. Gehrig, NYA	109			L. Gehrig, NYA	84
T. Lazzeri, NYA	18	E. Combs, NYA	331	G. Goslin, Was	120	M. Bishop, Phi	105			T. Lazzeri, NYA	82
K. Williams, StL	17	H. Heilmann, Det	311	H. Heilmann, Det	120	H. Heilmann, Det	72			B. Meusel, NYA	58
A. Simmons, Phi	15	G. Goslin, Was	300	B. Fothergill, Det	114	L. Blue, Det	71			A. Ward, ChA	56

Hit By Pitch		Sac Hits		Sac Flies		Stolen Bases		Caught Stealing		GDP	
F. O'Rourke, StL	12	B. Harris, Was	30	Statistic unavailable		G. Sisler, StL	27	J. Sewell, Cle	16	Statistic unavailable	
A. Metzler, ChA	9	S. Hale, Phi	28			B. Meusel, NYA	24	T. Cobb, Phi	16		
B. Miller, StL	9	H. Summa, Cle	27			T. Lazzeri, NYA	22	B. Fothergill, Det	15		
J. Sewell, Cle	9	J. Barrett, ChA	26			J. Neun, Det	22	T. Lazzeri, NYA	14		
I. Flagstead, Bos	9	W. Kamm, ChA	25			T. Cobb, Phi	22	2 tied with	13		

Runs Created		Runs Created/27 Outs		Batting Average		On-Base Percentage		Slugging Percentage		OBP+Slugging	
L. Gehrig, NYA	182	B. Ruth, NYA	12.53	H. Heilmann, Det	.398	B. Ruth, NYA	.487	B. Ruth, NYA	.772	B. Ruth, NYA	1.259
B. Ruth, NYA	177	L. Gehrig, NYA	12.00	A. Simmons, Phi	.392	H. Heilmann, Det	.475	L. Gehrig, NYA	.765	L. Gehrig, NYA	1.240
H. Heilmann, Det	142	H. Heilmann, Det	11.35	L. Gehrig, NYA	.373	L. Gehrig, NYA	.474	A. Simmons, Phi	.645	H. Heilmann, Det	1.091
E. Combs, NYA	131	A. Simmons, Phi	10.07	B. Fothergill, Det	.359	M. Bishop, Phi	.442	H. Heilmann, Det	.616	A. Simmons, Phi	1.081
G. Goslin, Was	117	E. Combs, NYA	7.85	T. Cobb, Phi	.357	T. Cobb, Phi	.440	K. Williams, StL	.527	K. Williams, StL	.932

1927 American League Pitching Leaders

Wins		Losses		Winning Percentage		Games		Games Started		Complete Games	
T. Lyons, ChA	22	S. Harriss, Bos	21	W. Hoyt, NYA	.759	G. Braxton, Was	58	T. Thomas, ChA	36	T. Lyons, ChA	30
W. Hoyt, NYA	22	H. Wiltse, Bos	18	U. Shocker, NYA	.750	F. Marberry, Was	56	H. Lisenbee, Was	34	T. Thomas, ChA	24
L. Grove, Phi	20	M. Gaston, StL	17	W. Moore, NYA	.731	L. Grove, Phi	51	T. Lyons, ChA	34	W. Hoyt, NYA	23
3 tied with	19	T. Blankenship, ChA	17	H. Pennock, NYA	.704	W. Moore, NYA	50	R. Walberg, Phi	34	M. Gaston, StL	21
		G. Buckeye, Cle	17	B. Hadley, Was	.700	R. Walberg, Phi	46	T. Blankenship, ChA	34	2 tied with	18

Shutouts		Saves		Games Finished		Batters Faced		Innings Pitched		Hits Allowed	
H. Lisenbee, Was	4	W. Moore, NYA	13	G. Braxton, Was	32	T. Lyons, ChA	1262	T. Thomas, ChA	307.2	W. Hudlin, Cle	291
8 tied with	3	G. Braxton, Was	13	W. Moore, NYA	30	T. Thomas, ChA	1252	T. Lyons, ChA	307.2	T. Lyons, ChA	291
		L. Grove, Phi	9	F. Marberry, Was	30	W. Hudlin, Cle	1156	W. Hudlin, Cle	264.2	T. Blankenship, ChA	280
		F. Marberry, Was	9	J. Pate, Phi	19	M. Gaston, StL	1117	L. Grove, Phi	262.1	H. Wiltse, Bos	276
		2 tied with	6	S. Connally, ChA	19	L. Grove, Phi	1106	W. Hoyt, NYA	256.1	M. Gaston, StL	275

Home Runs Allowed		Walks		Walks/9 Innings		Strikeouts		Strikeouts/9 Innings		Strikeout/Walk Ratio	
M. Gaston, StL	18	E. Whitehill, Det	105	J. Quinn, Phi	1.6	L. Grove, Phi	174	L. Grove, Phi	6.0	L. Grove, Phi	2.20
R. Walberg, Phi	18	E. Vangilder, StL	102	U. Shocker, NYA	1.8	R. Walberg, Phi	136	R. Walberg, Phi	4.9	W. Hoyt, NYA	1.59
T. Thomas, ChA	16	S. Jones, StL	102	W. Hoyt, NYA	1.9	T. Thomas, ChA	107	R. Ruffing, Bos	4.4	R. Walberg, Phi	1.49
S. Thurston, Was	16	M. Gaston, StL	100	T. Lyons, ChA	2.0	H. Lisenbee, Was	105	G. Uhle, Cle	4.1	H. Lisenbee, Was	1.35
T. Blankenship, ChA	14	T. Thomas, ChA	94	H. Pennock, NYA	2.1	G. Braxton, Was	96	H. Lisenbee, Was	3.9	W. Moore, NYA	1.27

Earned Run Average		Component ERA		Hit Batsmen		Wild Pitches		Opponent Average		Opponent OBP	
W. Moore, NYA	2.28	W. Moore, NYA	2.33	H. Ehmke, Phi	14	G. Buckeye, Cle	10	W. Moore, NYA	.234	W. Moore, NYA	.289
W. Hoyt, NYA	2.63	T. Lyons, ChA	2.54	W. Hudlin, Cle	11	E. Wingard, StL	8	T. Thomas, ChA	.244	T. Lyons, ChA	.292
U. Shocker, NYA	2.84	W. Hoyt, NYA	2.69	5 tied with	9	M. Gaston, StL	8	B. Hadley, Was	.244	W. Hoyt, NYA	.294
T. Lyons, ChA	2.84	T. Thomas, ChA	2.75			D. Lundgren, Bos	7	H. Lisenbee, Was	.245	T. Thomas, ChA	.303
B. Hadley, Was	2.85	H. Lisenbee, Was	2.75			3 tied with	6	T. Lyons, ChA	.251	U. Shocker, NYA	.306

1927 American League Miscellaneous

Managers

Boston	Bill Carrigan	51-103
Chicago	Ray Schalk	70-83
Cleveland	Jack McCallister	66-87
Detroit	George Moriarty	82-71
New York	Miller Huggins	110-44
Philadelphia	Connie Mack	91-63
St. Louis	Dan Howley	59-94
Washington	Bucky Harris	85-69

Awards

Most Valuable Player	Lou Gehrig, 1b, NYA
STATS Cy Young	Waite Hoyt, NYA
STATS Rookie of the Year	Wilcy Moore, p, NYA
STATS Manager of the Year	Miller Huggins, NYA

STATS All-Star Team

C	Mickey Cochrane, Phi	.338	12	80
1B	Lou Gehrig, NYA	.373	47	175
2B	Tony Lazzeri, NYA	.309	18	102
3B	Sammy Hale, Phi	.313	5	81
SS	Joe Sewell, Cle	.316	1	92
OF	Harry Heilmann, Det	.398	14	120
OF	Babe Ruth, NYA	.356	60	164
OF	Al Simmons, Phi	.392	15	108
P	Lefty Grove, Phi	20-13	3.19	174 K
P	Waite Hoyt, NYA	22-7	2.63	86 K
P	Ted Lyons, ChA	22-14	2.84	71 K
P	Urban Shocker, NYA	18-6	2.84	35 K
RP	Wilcy Moore, NYA	19-7	2.28	13 Sv

Postseason

World Series	NYA (AL) 4 vs. Pittsburgh (NL) 0

Outstanding Performances

Three-Homer Games

Tony Lazzeri, NYA	on June 8
Lou Gehrig, NYA	on June 23

Unassisted Triple Plays

Johnny Neun, Det	on May 31

1927 National League Standings

Team	Overall					Home Games						Road Games						Park Index		Record by Month					
	W	L	Pct	GB	DIF	W	L	R	OR	HR	OHR	W	L	R	OR	HR	OHR	Run	HR	M/A	May	June	July	Aug	S/O
Pittsburgh	94	60	.610	—	104	48	31	406	345	25	23	46	29	411	314	29	35	98	71	8-6	18-6	13-12	18-14	14-12	23-10
St. Louis	92	61	.601	1.5	10	55	25	433	354	55	51	37	36	321	311	29	21	114	193	9-5	13-11	17-9	16-17	14-8	23-11
New York	92	62	.597	2.0	19	49	25	389	342	62	49	43	37	428	378	47	28	98	160	11-4	11-13	11-16	21-14	16-5	22-10
Chicago	85	68	.556	8.5	49	50	28	398	315	37	19	35	40	352	346	37	31	98	79	7-7	15-10	17-10	18-12	16-11	12-18
Cincinnati	75	78	.490	18.5	0	45	35	348	320	3	11	30	43	295	333	26	25	97	25	5-11	7-19	13-13	19-11	11-12	20-12
Brooklyn	65	88	.425	28.5	1	34	39	266	296	20	35	31	49	275	323	19	28	103	128	4-12	17-11	10-12	12-19	10-16	12-18
Boston	60	94	.390	34.0	0	32	41	296	339	5	10	28	53	355	432	32	33	90	26	8-9	5-11	11-13	12-22	15-14	9-25
Philadelphia	51	103	.331	43.0	0	34	43	375	429	32	46	17	60	303	474	25	38	103	124	8-6	9-14	9-16	12-19	7-25	6-23

Clinch Date—Pittsburgh 10/01.

Team Batting

Team	G	AB	R	OR	H	2B	3B	HR	TB	RBI	TBB	IBB	SO	HBP	SH	SF	SB	CS	SB%	GDP	Avg	OBP	Slg
New York	155	5372	817	720	1594	251	62	109	2296	765	461	—	462	32	180	—	73	—	—	—	.297	.356	.427
Pittsburgh	156	5397	817	659	1648	258	78	54	2224	759	437	—	355	29	214	—	65	—	—	—	.305	.361	.412
St. Louis	153	5207	754	665	1450	264	79	84	2124	700	484	—	511	26	171	—	110	—	—	—	.278	.343	.408
Chicago	153	5303	750	661	1505	266	63	74	2119	692	481	—	492	27	207	—	65	—	—	—	.284	.346	.400
Philadelphia	155	5317	678	903	1487	216	46	57	1966	617	434	—	482	28	177	—	68	—	—	—	.280	.337	.370
Boston	155	5370	651	771	1498	216	61	37	1947	582	346	—	363	28	197	—	100	—	—	—	.279	.326	.363
Cincinnati	153	5185	643	653	1439	222	77	29	1902	575	402	—	332	21	219	—	62	—	—	—	.278	.332	.367
Brooklyn	154	5193	541	619	1314	195	74	39	1774	499	368	—	494	25	166	—	106	—	—	—	.253	.306	.342
NL Total	1234	42344	5651	5651	11935	1888	540	483	16352	5189	3413	—	3491	216	1531	—	649	—	—	—	.282	.339	.386
NL Avg Team	154	5293	706	706	1492	236	68	60	2044	649	427	—	436	27	191	—	81	—	—	—	.282	.339	.386

Team Pitching

Team	G	CG	ShO	Rel	Sv	IP	H	R	ER	HR	SH	SF	HB	TBB	IBB	SO	WP	Bk	H/9	SO/9	BB/9	OAvg	OOBP	ERA
Brooklyn	154	74	7	131	10	1375.1	1382	619	513	63	198	—	26	418	—	574	16	2	9.0	3.8	2.7	.265	.323	3.36
Cincinnati	153	87	12	93	12	1368.0	1472	653	538	36	197	—	21	316	—	407	25	1	9.7	2.7	2.1	.281	.325	3.54
St. Louis	153	89	14	110	11	1367.1	1416	665	543	72	160	—	18	363	—	394	14	1	9.3	2.6	2.4	.271	.320	3.57
Chicago	153	75	11	114	5	1385.0	1439	661	562	50	168	—	38	514	—	465	16	3	9.4	3.0	3.3	.273	.342	3.65
Pittsburgh	156	90	10	107	10	1385.0	1400	659	563	58	206	—	23	418	—	435	19	0	9.1	2.8	2.7	.267	.323	3.66
New York	155	65	7	147	16	1381.2	1520	720	609	77	151	—	24	453	—	442	22	1	9.9	2.9	3.0	.283	.341	3.97
Boston	155	52	3	155	11	1390.0	1602	771	652	43	239	—	29	468	—	402	29	2	10.4	2.6	3.0	.296	.356	4.22
Philadelphia	155	81	5	112	6	1355.1	1710	903	807	84	211	—	35	462	—	377	23	1	11.4	2.5	3.1	.317	.374	5.36
NL Total	1234	613	69	969	81	11007.2	11941	5651	4787	483	1530	—	214	3412	—	3496	164	11	9.8	2.9	2.8	.282	.339	3.91
NL Avg Team	154	77	9	121	10	1375.2	1493	706	598	60	191	—	27	427	—	437	21	1	9.8	2.9	2.8	.282	.339	3.91

Team Fielding

Team	G	PO	A	E	TC	DP	PB	Pct
Cincinnati	153	4102	1946	165	6213	160	9	.973
Philadelphia	155	4054	1902	169	6125	152	12	.972
Chicago	153	4140	1969	181	6290	152	15	.971
New York	155	4138	2041	195	6374	160	12	.969
Pittsburgh	156	4139	1739	187	6065	130	13	.969
St. Louis	153	4103	1948	213	6264	170	7	.966
Boston	155	4161	1898	231	6290	130	11	.963
Brooklyn	154	4115	1798	229	6142	117	9	.963
NL Total	1234	32952	15241	1570	49763	1171	88	.968

Team vs. Team Records

	Bos	Bro	ChN	Cin	NYG	Phi	Pit	StL	Won
Bos	—	12	7	4	7	14	9	7	60
Bro	10	—	7	11	10	11	8	8	65
ChN	15	15	—	14	10	13	9	9	85
Cin	18	10	8	—	7	16	8	8	75
NYG	15	12	12	15	—	15	11	12	92
Phi	8	11	9	6	7	—	7	3	51
Pit	13	14	13	14	11	15	—	14	94
StL	15	14	12	14	10	19	8	—	92
Lost	94	88	68	78	62	103	60	61	

Seasons: Standings, Leaders

1927 National League Batting Leaders

Games		At-Bats		Runs		Hits		Doubles		Triples	
P. Waner, Pit	155	S. Adams, ChN	647	L. Waner, Pit	133	P. Waner, Pit	237	R. Stephenson, ChN	46	P. Waner, Pit	17
E. Brown, Bos	155	L. Waner, Pit	629	R. Hornsby, NYG	133	L. Waner, Pit	223	P. Waner, Pit	40	J. Bottomley, StL	15
R. Hornsby, NYG	155	P. Waner, Pit	623	H. Wilson, ChN	119	F. Frisch, StL	208	C. Dressen, Cin	36	F. Thompson, Phi	14
F. Thompson, Phi	153	F. Frisch, StL	617	P. Waner, Pit	113	R. Hornsby, NYG	205	F. Lindstrom, NYG	36	B. Terry, NYG	13
F. Frisch, StL	153	F. Thompson, Phi	597	F. Frisch, StL	112	R. Stephenson, ChN	199	E. Brown, Bos	35	H. Wilson, ChN	12

Home Runs		Total Bases		Runs Batted In		Walks		Intentional Walks		Strikeouts	
H. Wilson, ChN	30	P. Waner, Pit	338	P. Waner, Pit	131	R. Hornsby, NYG	86	Statistic unavailable		H. Wilson, ChN	70
C. Williams, Phi	30	R. Hornsby, NYG	333	H. Wilson, ChN	129	G. Harper, NYG	84			L. Bell, StL	63
R. Hornsby, NYG	26	H. Wilson, ChN	319	R. Hornsby, NYG	125	G. Grantham, Pit	74			H. Sand, Phi	59
B. Terry, NYG	20	B. Terry, NYG	307	J. Bottomley, StL	124	J. Bottomley, StL	74			C. Williams, Phi	57
J. Bottomley, StL	19	J. Bottomley, StL	292	B. Terry, NYG	121	2 tied with	71			B. Terry, NYG	53

Hit By Pitch		Sac Hits		Sac Flies		Stolen Bases		Caught Stealing		GDP	
C. Williams, Phi	9	P. Traynor, Pit	35	Statistic unavailable		F. Frisch, StL	48	Statistic unavailable		Statistic unavailable	
J. Welsh, Bos	8	J. Welsh, Bos	28			M. Carey, Bro	32				
F. Leach, Phi	8	H. Sand, Phi	28			H. Hendrick, Bro	29				
F. Frisch, StL	7	C. Walker, Cin	27			S. Adams, ChN	26				
6 tied with	6	4 tied with	26			L. Richbourg, Bos	24				

Runs Created		Runs Created/27 Outs		Batting Average		On-Base Percentage		Slugging Percentage		OBP+Slugging	
P. Waner, Pit	141	R. Hornsby, NYG	9.24	P. Waner, Pit	.380	R. Hornsby, NYG	.448	C. Hafey, StL	.590	R. Hornsby, NYG	1.035
R. Hornsby, NYG	139	P. Waner, Pit	8.92	R. Hornsby, NYG	.361	P. Waner, Pit	.437	R. Hornsby, NYG	.586	C. Hafey, StL	.990
H. Wilson, ChN	121	C. Hafey, StL	8.55	L. Waner, Pit	.355	G. Harper, NYG	.435	H. Wilson, ChN	.579	H. Wilson, ChN	.980
R. Stephenson, ChN	116	H. Wilson, ChN	7.94	R. Stephenson, ChN	.344	R. Stephenson, ChN	.415	P. Waner, Pit	.543	P. Waner, Pit	.980
J. Bottomley, StL	114	G. Harper, NYG	7.74	P. Traynor, Pit	.342	J. Harris, Pit	.402	B. Terry, NYG	.529	G. Harper, NYG	.930

1927 National League Pitching Leaders

Wins		Losses		Winning Percentage		Games		Games Started		Complete Games	
C. Root, ChN	26	J. Scott, Phi	21	L. Benton, 2tm	.708	C. Root, ChN	48	L. Meadows, Pit	38	J. Haines, StL	25
J. Haines, StL	24	B. Smith, Bos	18	J. Haines, StL	.706	J. Scott, Phi	48	C. Root, ChN	36	L. Meadows, Pit	25
C. Hill, Pit	22	J. Petty, Bro	18	R. Kremer, Pit	.704	R. Ehrhardt, Bro	46	J. Haines, StL	36	D. Vance, Bro	25
P. Alexander, StL	21	H. Pruett, Phi	17	B. Grimes, NYG	.704	D. Henry, NYG	45	V. Aldridge, Pit	34	C. Hill, Pit	22
3 tied with	19	C. Robertson, Bos	17	P. Alexander, StL	.677	J. May, Cin	44	B. Grimes, NYG	34	P. Alexander, StL	22

Shutouts		Saves		Games Finished		Batters Faced		Innings Pitched		Hits Allowed	
J. Haines, StL	6	B. Sherdel, StL	6	R. Ehrhardt, Bro	26	C. Root, ChN	1316	C. Root, ChN	309.0	L. Meadows, Pit	315
R. Lucas, Cin	4	A. Nehf, 2tm	5	A. Nehf, 2tm	19	L. Meadows, Pit	1263	J. Haines, StL	300.2	J. Scott, Phi	304
C. Root, ChN	4	G. Mogridge, Bos	5	J. Werts, Bos	18	J. Haines, StL	1228	L. Meadows, Pit	299.1	B. Smith, Bos	297
R. Kremer, Pit	3	D. Henry, NYG	4	C. Willoughby, Phi	18	C. Hill, Pit	1165	C. Hill, Pit	277.2	C. Root, ChN	296
15 tied with	2	7 tied with	3	3 tied with	17	J. Petty, Bro	1137	D. Vance, Bro	273.1	H. Carlson, 2tm	281

Home Runs Allowed		Walks		Walks/9 Innings		Strikeouts		Strikeouts/9 Innings		Strikeout/Walk Ratio	
B. Sherdel, StL	17	C. Root, ChN	117	P. Alexander, StL	1.3	D. Vance, Bro	184	D. Vance, Bro	6.1	D. Vance, Bro	2.67
C. Root, ChN	16	H. Pruett, Phi	89	R. Lucas, Cin	1.5	C. Root, ChN	145	J. Elliott, Bro	4.7	J. Petty, Bro	1.91
V. Aldridge, Pit	16	B. Grimes, NYG	87	P. Donohue, Cin	1.5	J. May, Cin	121	J. May, Cin	4.6	J. May, Cin	1.73
H. Carlson, 2tm	16	S. Blake, ChN	82	H. Carlson, 2tm	1.6	B. Grimes, NYG	102	H. Pruett, Phi	4.4	J. Elliott, Bro	1.65
3 tied with	15	L. Benton, 2tm	81	J. Petty, Bro	1.8	J. Petty, Bro	101	C. Root, ChN	4.2	P. Donohue, Cin	1.50

Earned Run Average		Component ERA		Hit Batsmen		Wild Pitches		Opponent Average		Opponent OBP	
R. Kremer, Pit	2.47	R. Lucas, Cin	2.47	J. May, Cin	14	J. May, Cin	8	D. Vance, Bro	.239	P. Alexander, StL	.286
P. Alexander, StL	2.52	R. Kremer, Pit	2.50	H. Pruett, Phi	12	J. Werts, Bos	6	R. Kremer, Pit	.244	R. Lucas, Cin	.287
D. Vance, Bro	2.70	D. Vance, Bro	2.56	C. Root, ChN	9	M. Cvengros, Pit	6	J. Haines, StL	.245	R. Kremer, Pit	.289
J. Haines, StL	2.72	P. Alexander, StL	2.58	D. McWeeny, Bro	8	D. Luque, Cin	6	C. Hill, Pit	.249	D. Vance, Bro	.291
J. Petty, Bro	2.98	J. Haines, StL	2.65	L. Meadows, Pit	8	E. Rixey, Cin	6	C. Root, ChN	.254	J. Petty, Bro	.293

1927 National League Miscellaneous

Managers

Boston	Dave Bancroft	60-94
Brooklyn	Wilbert Robinson	65-88
Chicago	Joe McCarthy	85-68
Cincinnati	Jack Hendricks	75-78
New York	John McGraw	70-52
	Rogers Hornsby	22-10
Philadelphia	Stuffy McInnis	51-103
Pittsburgh	Donie Bush	94-60
St. Louis	Bob O'Farrell	92-61

Awards

Most Valuable Player	Paul Waner, of, Pit
STATS Cy Young	Jesse Haines, StL
STATS Rookie of the Year	Lloyd Waner, of, Pit
STATS Manager of the Year	Donie Bush, Pit

STATS All-Star Team

C	Gabby Hartnett, ChN	.294	10	80
1B	Bill Terry, NYG	.326	20	121
2B	Rogers Hornsby, NYG	.361	26	125
3B	Pie Traynor, Pit	.342	5	106
SS	Travis Jackson, NYG	.318	14	98
OF	Chick Hafey, StL	.329	18	63
OF	Paul Waner, Pit	.380	9	131
OF	Hack Wilson, ChN	.318	30	129
P	Pete Alexander, StL	21-10	2.52	48 K
P	Jesse Haines, StL	24-10	2.72	89 K
P	Ray Kremer, Pit	19-8	2.47	63 K
P	Charlie Root, ChN	26-15	3.76	145 K
RP	George Mogridge, Bos	6-4	3.70	5 Sv

Postseason

World Series	Pittsburgh (NL) 0 vs. NYA (AL) 4

Outstanding Performances

Cycles
Jim Bottomley, StL   on July 15
Cy Williams, Phi   on August 5

Unassisted Triple Plays
Jimmy Cooney, ChN   on May 30

1928 American League Standings

Grouped columns: Overall (W, L, Pct, GB, DIF) · Home Games (W, L, R, OR, HR, OHR) · Road Games (W, L, R, OR, HR, OHR) · Park Index (Run, HR) · Record by Month (M/A, May, June, July, Aug, S/O)

Team	W	L	Pct	GB	DIF	H-W	H-L	H-R	H-OR	H-HR	H-OHR	R-W	R-L	R-R	R-OR	R-HR	R-OHR	PI-Run	PI-HR	M/A	May	June	July	Aug	S/O
New York	101	53	.656	—	165	52	25	400	301	69	36	49	28	494	384	64	23	80	121	10-3	24-5	16-8	20-15	14-11	17-11
Philadelphia	98	55	.641	2.5	2	52	25	430	295	54	33	46	30	399	320	35	33	100	126	6-4	19-10	14-14	25-8	19-9	15-10
St. Louis	82	72	.532	19.0	5	44	33	398	389	51	64	38	39	374	353	12	29	108	280	11-8	10-15	16-9	15-20	17-8	13-12
Washington	75	79	.487	26.0	0	37	43	363	378	16	12	38	36	355	327	24	28	101	50	5-8	9-18	17-11	15-20	12-12	17-10
Chicago	72	82	.468	29.0	0	37	40	316	369	11	28	35	42	340	356	13	38	98	76	7-10	9-17	12-13	17-16	11-14	16-12
Detroit	68	86	.442	33.0	0	36	41	382	400	33	26	32	45	362	404	29	32	102	97	7-13	11-13	8-17	16-14	16-14	10-15
Cleveland	62	92	.403	39.0	12	29	48	366	443	10	15	33	44	308	387	24	37	116	41	12-6	11-14	9-18	15-17	11-17	4-20
Boston	57	96	.373	43.5	1	26	47	283	363	10	15	31	49	306	407	28	34	99	44	4-10	11-12	12-14	11-24	8-23	11-13

Clinch Date—New York 9/28.

Team Batting

Team	G	AB	R	OR	H	2B	3B	HR	TB	RBI	TBB	IBB	SO	HBP	SH	SF	SB	CS	SB%	GDP	Avg	OBP	Slg
New York	154	5337	894	685	1578	269	79	133	2404	817	562	—	544	23	145	—	51	51	.50	—	.296	.365	.450
Philadelphia	153	5226	829	615	1540	323	75	89	2280	759	533	—	442	37	196	—	59	48	.55	—	.295	.364	.436
St. Louis	154	5217	772	742	1431	276	76	63	2048	707	548	—	479	29	211	—	76	43	.64	—	.274	.347	.393
Detroit	154	5292	744	804	1476	265	97	62	2121	686	469	—	438	23	163	—	110	59	.65	—	.279	.340	.401
Washington	155	5320	718	705	1510	277	93	40	2093	680	481	—	426	36	180	—	50	52	.49	—	.284	.347	.393
Cleveland	155	5386	674	830	1535	299	61	34	2058	619	377	—	488	31	201	—	139	82	.63	—	.285	.335	.382
Chicago	155	5207	656	725	1405	231	77	24	1862	592	469	—	512	20	205	—	99	64	.61	—	.264	.319	.361
Boston	154	5132	589	770	1356	260	62	38	1854	544	389	—	390	31	189	—	113	77	.59	—	.264	.320	.361
AL Total	1234	42117	5876	5876	11831	2200	620	483	16720	5404	3828	—	3719	230	1490	—	697	476	.59	—	.281	.344	.397
AL Avg Team	154	5265	735	735	1479	275	78	60	2090	676	479	—	465	29	186	—	87	60	.59	—	.281	.344	.397

Team Pitching

Team	G	CG	ShO	Rel	Sv	IP	H	R	ER	HR	SH	SF	HB	TBB	IBB	SO	WP	Bk	H/9	SO/9	BB/9	OAvg	OOBP	ERA
Philadelphia	153	81	15	103	16	1367.2	1349	615	511	66	140	—	22	424	—	607	19	0	8.9	4.0	2.8	.256	.314	3.36
New York	154	82	13	118	21	1375.1	1466	685	571	59	158	—	18	452	—	487	19	1	9.6	3.2	3.0	.264	.322	3.74
Washington	155	77	15	118	10	1384.0	1420	705	596	40	181	—	30	466	—	462	17	3	9.2	3.0	3.0	.268	.331	3.88
Chicago	155	88	6	93	11	1378.0	1518	725	610	66	181	—	32	501	—	418	17	2	9.9	2.7	3.3	.273	.331	3.98
St. Louis	154	80	6	128	15	1374.1	1487	742	637	93	192	—	16	454	—	456	11	1	9.7	3.0	3.0	.276	.350	4.17
Detroit	154	65	5	130	16	1372.0	1481	804	658	58	206	—	36	567	—	451	19	1	9.7	3.0	3.7	.281	.342	4.32
Boston	154	70	5	131	9	1352.0	1492	770	660	49	202	—	40	452	—	407	11	3	9.9	2.7	3.0	.296	.361	4.39
Cleveland	155	71	4	122	15	1378.0	1615	830	684	52	213	—	43	511	—	416	25	3	10.5	2.7	3.3	.281	.344	4.47
AL Total	1234	614	69	937	113	10981.1	11828	5876	4927	483	1473	—	237	3827	—	3704	138	15	9.7	3.0	3.1	.281	.344	4.04
AL Avg Team	154	77	9	117	14	1372.1	1479	735	616	60	184	—	30	478	—	463	17	2	9.7	3.0	3.1	.281	.344	4.04

Team Fielding

Team	G	PO	A	E	TC	DP	PB	Pct
Washington	155	4111	1937	178	6226	146	13	.971
Boston	154	4029	1943	178	6150	139	7	.971
Philadelphia	153	4107	1728	181	6016	124	10	.970
Chicago	155	4116	1850	186	6152	149	10	.970
St. Louis	154	4112	1768	189	6069	146	8	.969
New York	154	4121	1743	194	6058	136	9	.968
Cleveland	155	4126	2048	221	6395	187	16	.965
Detroit	154	4107	1847	218	6172	140	12	.965
AL Total	1234	32829	14864	1545	49238	1167	85	.969

Team vs. Team Records

	Bos	ChA	Cle	Det	NYA	Phi	StL	Was	Won
Bos	—	10	9	7	6	3	9	13	57
ChA	12	—	12	13	9	6	10	10	72
Cle	13	10	—	10	6	6	7	10	62
Det	15	9	12	—	7	8	9	8	68
NYA	16	13	16	15	—	16	12	13	101
Phi	18	16	16	14	6	—	16	12	98
StL	13	12	15	13	10	6	—	13	82
Was	9	12	12	14	9	10	9	—	75
Lost	96	82	92	86	53	55	72	79	

1928 American League Batting Leaders

Games		At-Bats		Runs		Hits		Doubles		Triples	
W. Kamm, ChA	155	C. Lind, Cle	650	B. Ruth, NYA	163	H. Manush, StL	241	L. Gehrig, NYA	47	E. Combs, NYA	21
J. Sewell, Cle	155	H. Manush, StL	638	L. Gehrig, NYA	139	L. Gehrig, NYA	210	H. Manush, StL	47	H. Manush, StL	20
6 tied with	154	E. Combs, NYA	626	E. Combs, NYA	118	S. Rice, Was	202	B. Meusel, NYA	45	C. Gehringer, Det	16
		S. Rice, Was	616	L. Blue, StL	116	E. Combs, NYA	194	F. Schulte, StL	44	3 tied with	15
		C. Gehringer, Det	603	C. Gehringer, Det	108	C. Gehringer, Det	193	C. Lind, Cle	42		

Home Runs		Total Bases		Runs Batted In		Walks		Intentional Walks		Strikeouts	
B. Ruth, NYA	54	B. Ruth, NYA	380	L. Gehrig, NYA	142	B. Ruth, NYA	135	Statistic unavailable		B. Ruth, NYA	87
L. Gehrig, NYA	27	H. Manush, StL	367	B. Ruth, NYA	142	L. Blue, StL	105			R. Kress, StL	70
G. Goslin, Was	17	L. Gehrig, NYA	364	B. Meusel, NYA	113	M. Bishop, Phi	97			L. Gehrig, NYA	69
J. Hauser, Phi	16	E. Combs, NYA	290	H. Manush, StL	108	L. Gehrig, NYA	95			F. Schulte, StL	60
A. Simmons, Phi	15	H. Heilmann, Det	283	2 tied with	107	J. Judge, Was	80			B. Meusel, NYA	56

Hit By Pitch		Sac Hits		Sac Flies		Stolen Bases		Caught Stealing		GDP	
E. McNeely, StL	8	P. Todt, Bos	31	Statistic unavailable		B. Myer, Bos	30	J. Mostil, ChA	21	Statistic unavailable	
O. Bluege, Was	8	B. Clancy, ChA	29			J. Mostil, ChA	23	B. Myer, Bos	16		
B. Miller, Phi	8	W. Kamm, ChA	28			H. Rice, Det	20	H. Rice, Det	13		
J. Sewell, Cle	7	C. Lind, Cle	27			B. Cissell, ChA	18	M. McManus, Det	13		
4 tied with	6	2 tied with	26			O. Bluege, Was	18	C. Jamieson, Cle	12		

Runs Created		Runs Created/27 Outs		Batting Average		On-Base Percentage		Slugging Percentage		OBP+Slugging	
B. Ruth, NYA	165	B. Ruth, NYA	11.48	G. Goslin, Was	.379	L. Gehrig, NYA	.467	B. Ruth, NYA	.709	B. Ruth, NYA	1.170
L. Gehrig, NYA	156	L. Gehrig, NYA	10.77	H. Manush, StL	.378	B. Ruth, NYA	.461	L. Gehrig, NYA	.648	L. Gehrig, NYA	1.115
H. Manush, StL	149	G. Goslin, Was	9.49	L. Gehrig, NYA	.374	G. Goslin, Was	.443	G. Goslin, Was	.614	G. Goslin, Was	1.057
E. Combs, NYA	114	H. Manush, StL	9.24	A. Simmons, Phi	.351	M. Bishop, Phi	.435	H. Manush, StL	.575	H. Manush, StL	.989
G. Goslin, Was	111	A. Simmons, Phi	7.86	T. Lazzeri, NYA	.332	J. Foxx, Phi	.416	A. Simmons, Phi	.558	J. Foxx, Phi	.964

1928 American League Pitching Leaders

Wins		Losses		Winning Percentage		Games		Games Started		Complete Games	
L. Grove, Phi	24	R. Ruffing, Bos	25	G. Crowder, StL	.808	F. Marberry, Was	48	G. Pipgras, NYA	38	R. Ruffing, Bos	25
G. Pipgras, NYA	24	J. Shaute, Cle	17	W. Hoyt, NYA	.767	E. Morris, Bos	47	R. Ruffing, Bos	34	T. Thomas, ChA	24
W. Hoyt, NYA	23	G. Uhle, Cle	17	L. Grove, Phi	.750	G. Pipgras, NYA	46	T. Thomas, ChA	32	L. Grove, Phi	24
G. Crowder, StL	21	4 tied with	16	H. Pennock, NYA	.739	E. Rommel, Phi	43	J. Shaute, Cle	32	G. Pipgras, NYA	22
S. Gray, StL	20			E. Rommel, Phi	.722	3 tied with	42	6 tied with	31	3 tied with	21

Shutouts		Saves		Games Finished		Batters Faced		Innings Pitched		Hits Allowed	
H. Pennock, NYA	5	W. Hoyt, NYA	8	F. Marberry, Was	26	G. Pipgras, NYA	1352	G. Pipgras, NYA	300.2	G. Pipgras, NYA	314
L. Grove, Phi	4	W. Hudlin, Cle	7	G. Smith, Det	21	R. Ruffing, Bos	1273	R. Ruffing, Bos	289.1	R. Ruffing, Bos	303
G. Pipgras, NYA	4	T. Lyons, ChA	6	B. Bayne, Cle	21	T. Thomas, ChA	1223	T. Thomas, ChA	283.0	J. Shaute, Cle	295
S. Jones, Was	4	G. Braxton, Was	6	E. Vangilder, Det	21	W. Hoyt, NYA	1153	W. Hoyt, NYA	273.0	W. Hoyt, NYA	279
J. Quinn, Phi	4	2 tied with	5	P. Simmons, Bos	19	S. Gray, StL	1133	S. Gray, StL	262.2	T. Thomas, ChA	277

Home Runs Allowed		Walks		Walks/9 Innings		Strikeouts		Strikeouts/9 Innings		Strikeout/Walk Ratio	
G. Blaeholder, StL	23	H. Johnson, NYA	104	J. Quinn, Phi	1.4	L. Grove, Phi	183	L. Grove, Phi	6.3	L. Grove, Phi	2.86
J. Ogden, StL	23	G. Pipgras, NYA	103	H. Pennock, NYA	1.7	G. Pipgras, NYA	139	H. Johnson, NYA	5.0	G. Braxton, Was	2.14
R. Walberg, Phi	19	G. Earnshaw, Phi	100	G. Braxton, Was	1.8	T. Thomas, ChA	129	R. Walberg, Phi	4.3	R. Walberg, Phi	1.75
3 tied with	16	B. Hadley, Was	100	J. Russell, Bos	1.8	R. Ruffing, Bos	118	E. Whitehill, Det	4.3	T. Thomas, ChA	1.70
		R. Ruffing, Bos	96	W. Hoyt, NYA	2.0	G. Earnshaw, Phi	117	G. Pipgras, NYA	4.2	G. Uhle, Cle	1.54

Earned Run Average		Component ERA		Hit Batsmen		Wild Pitches		Opponent Average		Opponent OBP	
G. Braxton, Was	2.51	G. Braxton, Was	1.92	H. Johnson, NYA	12	G. Earnshaw, Phi	7	G. Braxton, Was	.217	G. Braxton, Was	.261
H. Pennock, NYA	2.56	L. Grove, Phi	2.35	R. Ruffing, Bos	10	J. Shaute, Cle	7	L. Grove, Phi	.227	L. Grove, Phi	.274
L. Grove, Phi	2.58	H. Pennock, NYA	2.74	B. Bayne, Cle	10	4 tied with	5	H. Johnson, NYA	.232	H. Pennock, NYA	.299
S. Jones, Was	2.84	S. Jones, Was	2.94	B. Hadley, Was	8			G. Crowder, StL	.248	T. Thomas, ChA	.299
J. Quinn, Phi	2.90	T. Thomas, ChA	2.98	G. Uhle, Cle	8			T. Thomas, ChA	.249	W. Hoyt, NYA	.303

1928 American League Miscellaneous

Managers

Boston	Bill Carrigan	57-96
Chicago	Ray Schalk	32-42
	Lena Blackburne	40-40
Cleveland	Roger Peckinpaugh	62-92
Detroit	George Moriarty	68-86
New York	Miller Huggins	101-53
Philadelphia	Connie Mack	98-55
St. Louis	Dan Howley	82-72
Washington	Bucky Harris	75-79

Awards

Most Valuable Player	Mickey Cochrane, c, Phi
STATS Cy Young	Lefty Grove, Phi
STATS Rookie of the Year	Red Kress, ss, StL
STATS Manager of the Year	Dan Howley, StL

STATS All-Star Team

C	Mickey Cochrane, Phi	.293	10	57
1B	Lou Gehrig, NYA	.374	27	142
2B	Charlie Gehringer, Det	.320	6	74
3B	Jimmie Foxx, Phi	.328	13	79
SS	Joe Sewell, Cle	.323	4	70
OF	Goose Goslin, Was	.379	17	102
OF	Heinie Manush, StL	.378	13	108
OF	Babe Ruth, NYA	.323	54	142
P	Lefty Grove, Phi	24-8	2.58	183 K
P	Waite Hoyt, NYA	23-7	3.36	67 K
P	Herb Pennock, NYA	17-6	2.56	53 K
P	George Pipgras, NYA	24-13	3.38	139 K
RP	Eddie Rommel, Phi	13-5	3.06	4 Sv

Postseason

World Series	New York (AL) 4 vs. St. Louis (NL) 0

Outstanding Performances

Cycles

Bob Meusel, NYA	on July 26

1928 National League Standings

Team	W	L	Pct	GB	DIF	W	L	R	OR	HR	OHR	W	L	R	OR	HR	OHR	Run	HR	M/A	May	June	July	Aug	S/O
	Overall					**Home Games**						**Road Games**						**Park Index**		**Record by Month**					
St. Louis	95	59	.617	—	107	42	35	367	336	62	51	53	24	440	300	51	35	95	131	8-7	17-12	20-6	18-11	14-13	18-10
New York	93	61	.604	2.0	32	51	26	411	315	80	46	42	35	396	338	38	31	99	183	7-4	16-11	16-11	15-14	14-13	25-8
Chicago	91	63	.591	4.0	7	52	25	335	264	40	18	39	38	379	351	52	38	82	64	9-10	17-9	13-13	19-12	16-11	17-8
Pittsburgh	85	67	.559	9.0	0	47	30	479	356	16	14	38	37	358	348	36	52	115	33	6-8	12-16	13-11	20-9	11-14	14-11
Cincinnati	78	74	.513	16.0	30	44	33	324	318	3	17	34	41	324	368	29	41	90	28	9-7	21-10	9-16	20-9	11-14	8-18
Brooklyn	77	76	.503	17.5	4	41	35	330	296	30	25	36	41	335	344	36	34	93	80	9-5	13-14	15-11	14-18	10-16	16-12
Boston	50	103	.327	44.5	0	25	51	309	448	24	62	25	52	322	430	28	38	102	132	5-7	11-16	4-20	8-19	12-16	10-25
Philadelphia	43	109	.283	51.0	2	26	49	360	521	54	67	17	60	300	436	31	41	123	173	4-9	3-22	11-13	6-22	11-19	8-24

Clinch Date—St. Louis 9/29.

Team Batting

Team	G	AB	R	OR	H	2B	3B	HR	TB	RBI	TBB	IBB	SO	HBP	SH	SF	SB	CS	SB%	GDP	Avg	OBP	Slg
Pittsburgh	152	5371	**837**	704	**1659**	246	**100**	52	2261	**768**	435	—	352	29	202	—	64	—	—	—	**.309**	**.364**	.421
New York	155	**5459**	807	653	1600	276	59	118	**2348**	758	444	—	376	27	173	—	62	—	—	—	.293	.349	**.430**
St. Louis	154	5357	807	636	1505	**292**	70	113	2276	749	568	—	438	32	187	—	82	—	—	—	.281	.353	.425
Chicago	154	5260	714	615	1460	251	64	92	2115	665	665	—	**517**	31	210	—	83	—	—	—	.278	.345	.402
Brooklyn	155	5243	665	640	1393	229	70	66	1960	621	557	—	510	**32**	160	—	81	—	—	—	.266	.340	.374
Philadelphia	152	5234	660	957	1396	257	47	85	2002	606	503	—	510	21	159	—	53	—	—	—	.267	.333	.382
Cincinnati	153	5184	648	686	1449	229	67	32	1908	588	386	—	330	26	**212**	—	83	—	—	—	.280	.335	.368
Boston	153	5228	631	878	1439	241	41	52	1918	577	447	—	510	27	191	—	60	—	—	—	.275	.335	.367
NL Total	1228	42336	5769	5769	11901	2021	518	610	16788	5332	3848	—	3410	225	1494	—	568	—	—	—	.281	.344	.397
NL Avg Team	154	5292	721	721	1488	253	65	76	2099	667	481	—	426	28	187	—	71	—	—	—	.281	.344	.397

Team Pitching

Team	G	CG	ShO	Rel	Sv	IP	H	R	ER	HR	SH	SF	HB	TBB	IBB	SO	WP	Bk	H/9	SO/9	BB/9	OAvg	OOBP	ERA
Brooklyn	155	75	**16**	141	15	1396.0	**1378**	640	504	59	196	—	31	468	—	551	10	2	8.9	3.6	3.0	**.261**	.324	3.25
St. Louis	154	**83**	4	119	21	1415.1	1470	636	531	86	**153**	—	27	399	—	422	16	4	9.3	2.7	**2.5**	.270	**.323**	3.38
Chicago	154	75	12	122	14	1380.2	1383	**615**	521	**56**	163	—	32	508	—	531	18	1	9.0	3.5	3.3	.267	.336	3.40
New York	155	79	7	126	16	1394.0	1454	653	568	77	167	—	20	405	—	399	**25**	0	9.4	2.6	2.6	.273	.327	3.67
Cincinnati	153	68	11	120	11	1371.2	1516	686	600	58	205	—	16	410	—	355	11	2	9.9	2.3	2.7	.289	.342	3.94
Pittsburgh	152	82	8	112	11	1354.0	1422	704	594	66	206	—	26	524	—	343	23	1	9.5	2.3	3.5	.274	.335	3.95
Boston	153	54	1	168	6	1360.0	1596	878	730	100	191	—	30	524	—	404	23	2	10.6	2.3	3.5	.298	.363	4.83
Philadelphia	152	42	4	189	11	1352.2	1658	957	836	108	221	—	**41**	675	—	404	22	2	11.0	2.7	4.5	.315	.397	5.56
NL Total	1228	558	63	1097	105	11024.1	11877	5769	4884	610	1502	—	223	3835	—	3390	148	14	9.7	2.8	3.1	.281	.343	3.99
NL Avg Team	154	70	8	137	13	1378.1	1485	721	611	76	188	—	28	479	—	424	19	2	9.7	2.8	3.1	.281	.343	3.99

Team Fielding

Team	G	PO	A	E	TC	DP	PB	Pct
Chicago	154	4141	1971	**156**	6268	176	8	.975
St. Louis	154	**4248**	1819	160	6227	134	9	.974
Cincinnati	153	4112	1926	162	6200	**194**	10	.974
New York	155	4180	**2028**	178	**6386**	175	4	.972
Philadelphia	152	4034	1936	181	6151	171	7	.971
Boston	153	4084	1897	193	6174	141	**13**	.969
Pittsburgh	152	4059	1803	201	6063	123	10	.967
Brooklyn	155	4186	1870	217	6273	113	8	.965
NL Total	1228	33044	15250	1448	49742	1227	69	.971

Team vs. Team Records

	Bos	Bro	ChN	Cin	NYG	Phi	Pit	StL	Won
Bos	—	7	5	10	6	13	5	4	50
Bro	15	—	10	10	9	15	9	9	77
ChN	17	12	—	13	14	13	11	11	91
Cin	12	12	9	—	8	13	12	12	78
NYG	16	13	8	14	—	17	11	14	93
Phi	9	7	9	7	5	—	4	2	43
Pit	16	12	11	10	11	18	—	7	85
StL	18	13	11	10	8	20	15	—	95
Lost	103	76	63	74	61	109	67	59	

Seasons: Standings, Leaders

1928 National League Batting Leaders

Games		At-Bats		Runs		Hits		Doubles		Triples	
D. Bissonette, Bro	155	L. Waner, Pit	659	P. Waner, Pit	142	F. Lindstrom, NYG	231	P. Waner, Pit	50	J. Bottomley, StL	20
T. Douthit, StL	154	T. Douthit, StL	648	J. Bottomley, StL	123	P. Waner, Pit	223	C. Hafey, StL	46	P. Waner, Pit	19
H. Critz, Cin	153	F. Lindstrom, NYG	646	L. Waner, Pit	121	L. Waner, Pit	221	J. Bottomley, StL	42	L. Waner, Pit	14
F. Lindstrom, NYG	153	H. Critz, Cin	641	T. Douthit, StL	111	L. Richbourg, Bos	206	R. Hornsby, Bos	42	D. Bissonette, Bro	13
L. Bell, Bos	153	F. Thompson, Phi	634	F. Frisch, StL	107	P. Traynor, Pit	192	F. Lindstrom, NYG	39	R. Bressler, Bro	13

Home Runs		Total Bases		Runs Batted In		Walks		Intentional Walks		Strikeouts	
H. Wilson, ChN	31	J. Bottomley, StL	362	J. Bottomley, StL	136	R. Hornsby, Bos	107	Statistic unavailable		H. Wilson, ChN	94
J. Bottomley, StL	31	F. Lindstrom, NYG	330	P. Traynor, Pit	124	T. Douthit, StL	84			D. Bissonette, Bro	75
C. Hafey, StL	27	P. Waner, Pit	329	H. Wilson, ChN	120	R. Bressler, Bro	80			K. Cuyler, ChN	61
D. Bissonette, Bro	25	D. Bissonette, Bro	319	C. Hafey, StL	111	P. Waner, Pit	77			C. Beck, ChN	58
R. Hornsby, Bos	21	C. Hafey, StL	314	F. Lindstrom, NYG	107	H. Wilson, ChN	77			J. Bottomley, StL	54

Hit By Pitch		Sac Hits		Sac Flies		Stolen Bases		Caught Stealing		GDP	
T. Douthit, StL	10	P. Traynor, Pit	42	Statistic unavailable		K. Cuyler, ChN	37	Statistic unavailable		Statistic unavailable	
S. Hogan, NYG	8	F. Maguire, ChN	37			F. Frisch, StL	29				
J. Welsh, NYG	8	T. Jackson, NYG	33			F. Thompson, Phi	19				
K. Cuyler, ChN	7	C. Grimm, ChN	28			C. Walker, Cin	19				
2 tied with	6	3 tied with	25			2 tied with	18				

Runs Created		Runs Created/27 Outs		Batting Average		On-Base Percentage		Slugging Percentage		OBP+Slugging	
P. Waner, Pit	143	R. Hornsby, Bos	10.87	R. Hornsby, Bos	.387	R. Hornsby, Bos	.498	R. Hornsby, Bos	.632	R. Hornsby, Bos	1.130
R. Hornsby, Bos	135	P. Waner, Pit	9.48	P. Waner, Pit	.370	P. Waner, Pit	.446	J. Bottomley, StL	.628	J. Bottomley, StL	1.030
J. Bottomley, StL	133	J. Bottomley, StL	8.52	F. Lindstrom, NYG	.358	G. Grantham, Pit	.408	C. Hafey, StL	.604	H. Wilson, ChN	.992
D. Bissonette, Bro	116	C. Hafey, StL	7.79	G. Sisler, Bos	.340	G. Harper, 2tm	.407	H. Wilson, ChN	.588	P. Waner, Pit	.992
F. Lindstrom, NYG	116	H. Wilson, ChN	7.64	B. Herman, Bro	.340	R. Stephenson, ChN	.407	P. Waner, Pit	.547	C. Hafey, StL	.990

1928 National League Pitching Leaders

Wins		Losses		Winning Percentage		Games		Games Started		Complete Games	
L. Benton, NYG	25	E. Brandt, Bos	21	L. Benton, NYG	.735	B. Grimes, Pit	48	B. Grimes, Pit	37	L. Benton, NYG	28
B. Grimes, Pit	25	R. Benge, Phi	18	J. Haines, StL	.714	R. Kolp, Cin	44	E. Rixey, Cin	37	B. Grimes, Pit	28
D. Vance, Bro	22	C. Root, ChN	18	G. Bush, ChN	.714	E. Rixey, Cin	43	L. Benton, NYG	35	D. Vance, Bro	24
B. Sherdel, StL	21	E. Rixey, Cin	18	F. Fitzsimmons, NYG	.690	4 tied with	42	3 tied with	32	J. Haines, StL	20
2 tied with	20	3 tied with	17	D. Vance, Bro	.688					B. Sherdel, StL	20

Shutouts		Saves		Games Finished		Batters Faced		Innings Pitched		Hits Allowed	
R. Lucas, Cin	4	H. Haid, StL	5	B. McGraw, Phi	20	B. Grimes, Pit	1377	B. Grimes, Pit	330.2	E. Rixey, Cin	317
D. McWeeny, Bro	4.	B. Sherdel, StL	5	P. Appleton, Cin	18	L. Benton, NYG	1263	L. Benton, NYG	310.1	B. Grimes, Pit	311
S. Blake, ChN	4	L. Benton, NYG	4	A. Walsh, Phi	17	E. Rixey, Cin	1219	E. Rixey, Cin	291.1	L. Benton, NYG	299
B. Grimes, Pit	4	H. Carlson, ChN	4	J. Faulkner, NYG	17	D. Vance, Bro	1126	D. Vance, Bro	280.1	B. Smith, Bos	274
D. Vance, Bro	4	9 tied with	3	J. Dawson, Pit	17	F. Fitzsimmons, NYG	1084	F. Fitzsimmons, NYG	261.1	2 tied with	264

Home Runs Allowed		Walks		Walks/9 Innings		Strikeouts		Strikeouts/9 Innings		Strikeout/Walk Ratio	
J. Genewich, 2tm	24	D. McWeeny, Bro	114	P. Alexander, StL	1.4	D. Vance, Bro	200	D. Vance, Bro	6.4	D. Vance, Bro	2.78
E. Brandt, Bos	22	E. Brandt, Bos	109	B. Sherdel, StL	2.0	P. Malone, ChN	155	P. Malone, ChN	5.6	W. Clark, Bro	1.70
J. Petty, Bro	18	J. Ring, Phi	103	L. Benton, NYG	2.1	C. Root, ChN	122	C. Root, ChN	4.6	C. Root, ChN	1.67
B. Sherdel, StL	17	S. Blake, ChN	101	E. Rixey, Cin	2.1	B. Grimes, Pit	97	W. Clark, Bro	3.9	P. Alexander, StL	1.59
3 tied with	16	P. Malone, ChN	99	B. Grimes, Pit	2.1	L. Benton, NYG	90	E. Brandt, Bos	3.4	P. Malone, ChN	1.57

Earned Run Average		Component ERA		Hit Batsmen		Wild Pitches		Opponent Average		Opponent OBP	
D. Vance, Bro	2.09	D. Vance, Bro	2.20	L. Sweetland, Phi	15	P. Malone, ChN	10	D. Vance, Bro	.221	D. Vance, Bro	.277
S. Blake, ChN	2.47	B. Grimes, Pit	2.70	B. Grimes, Pit	9	F. Fitzsimmons, NYG	6	D. McWeeny, Bro	.235	B. Grimes, Pit	.297
A. Nehf, ChN	2.65	W. Clark, Bro	2.84	4 tied with	7	L. Benton, NYG	6	P. Malone, ChN	.236	L. Benton, NYG	.300
W. Clark, Bro	2.68	L. Benton, NYG	2.85			5 tied with	5	S. Blake, ChN	.240	B. Sherdel, StL	.303
L. Benton, NYG	2.73	S. Blake, ChN	2.88					C. Root, ChN	.242	R. Lucas, Cin	.304

1928 National League Miscellaneous

Managers		
Boston	Jack Slattery	11-20
	Rogers Hornsby	39-83
Brooklyn	Wilbert Robinson	77-76
Chicago	Joe McCarthy	91-63
Cincinnati	Jack Hendricks	78-74
New York	John McGraw	93-61
Philadelphia	Burt Shotton	43-109
Pittsburgh	Donie Bush	85-67
St. Louis	Bill McKechnie	95-59

Awards

Most Valuable Player	Jim Bottomley, 1b, StL
STATS Cy Young	Larry Benton, NYG
STATS Rookie of the Year	Del Bissonette, 1b, Bro
STATS Manager of the Year	Bill McKechnie, StL

Postseason

World Series	St. Louis (NL) 0 vs. New York (AL) 4

Outstanding Performances

Three-Homer Games

Les Bell, Bos	on June 2
George Harper, StL	on September 20

Cycles

Bill Terry, NYG	on May 29

STATS All-Star Team

C	Gabby Hartnett, ChN	.302	14	57
1B	Jim Bottomley, StL	.325	31	136
2B	Rogers Hornsby, Bos	.387	21	94
3B	Freddy Lindstrom, NYG	.358	14	107
SS	Travis Jackson, NYG	.270	14	77
OF	Chick Hafey, StL	.337	27	111
OF	Paul Waner, Pit	.370	6	86
OF	Hack Wilson, ChN	.313	31	120
P	Larry Benton, NYG	25-9	2.73	90 K
P	Burleigh Grimes, Pit	25-14	2.99	97 K
P	Bill Sherdel, StL	21-10	2.86	72 K
P	Dazzy Vance, Bro	22-10	2.09	200 K
RP	Joe Dawson, Pit	7-7	3.29	3 Sv

1929 American League Standings

Team	W	L	Pct	GB	DIF	W	L	R	OR	HR	OHR	W	L	R	OR	HR	OHR	Run	HR	M/A	May	June	July	Aug	S/O
			Overall					Home Games						Road Games				Park Index				Record by Month			
Philadelphia	104	46	.693	—	159	57	16	484	302	72	47	47	30	417	313	50	26	114	165	7-4	22-5	19-8	24-9	15-14	17-6
New York	88	66	.571	18.0	10	49	28	463	362	69	55	37	39	436	413	73	28	97	123	6-4	14-12	18-10	22-7	13-18	15-15
Cleveland	81	71	.533	24.0	3	44	32	359	363	27	21	37	39	358	373	35	35	99	69	5-8	14-12	12-14	20-13	13-12	17-12
St. Louis	79	73	.520	26.0	11	41	36	370	341	22	58	38	37	363	372	24	42	94	118	10-4	15-11	16-11	12-18	13-14	13-15
Washington	71	81	.467	34.0	0	37	40	376	390	10	17	34	41	354	386	38	31	101	38	3-7	10-16	13-14	10-20	20-11	15-13
Detroit	70	84	.455	36.0	0	38	39	476	453	57	33	32	45	450	475	53	40	100	97	6-9	18-12	14-12	9-17	11-16	12-18
Chicago	59	93	.388	46.0	0	35	41	306	366	19	41	24	52	321	426	18	43	90	98	6-6	10-20	7-20	15-15	12-13	9-19
Boston	58	96	.377	48.0	0	32	45	328	399	11	36	26	51	277	404	17	42	107	80	4-5	7-22	11-21	7-20	15-14	14-14

Clinch Date—Philadelphia 9/14.

Team Batting

Team	G	AB	R	OR	H	2B	3B	HR	TB	RBI	TBB	IBB	SO	HBP	SH	SF	SB	CS	SB%	GDP	Avg	OBP	Slg
Detroit	155	5592	926	928	1671	339	97	110	2534	851	521	—	496	20	124	—	95	72	.57	—	.299	.361	.453
Philadelphia	151	5204	901	615	1539	288	76	122	2345	844	543	—	440	29	214	—	61	38	.62	—	.296	.365	.451
New York	154	5379	899	775	1587	262	74	142	2423	828	554	—	518	23	146	—	51	44	.54	—	.295	.363	.450
St. Louis	154	5174	733	713	1426	277	64	46	1969	672	589	—	431	25	190	—	72	46	.61	—	.276	.352	.381
Washington	153	5237	730	776	1445	244	66	48	1965	656	556	—	400	17	186	—	86	61	.59	—	.276	.347	.375
Cleveland	152	5187	717	736	1525	294	79	62	2163	683	453	—	436	22	210	—	75	85	.47	—	.294	.353	.417
Chicago	152	5248	627	792	1406	240	74	37	1905	569	425	—	436	21	157	—	109	65	.63	—	.268	.325	.363
Boston	155	5160	605	803	1377	285	69	28	1884	561	413	—	494	29	178	—	85	80	.52	—	.267	.325	.365
AL Total	1226	42181	6138	6138	11976	2229	599	595	17188	5664	4054	—	3578	186	1405	—	634	491	.56	—	.284	.349	.407
AL Avg Team	153	5273	767	767	1497	279	75	74	2149	708	507	—	447	23	176	—	79	61	.56	—	.284	.349	.407

Team Pitching

Team	G	CG	ShO	Rel	Sv	IP	H	R	ER	HR	SH	SF	HB	TBB	IBB	SO	WP	Bk	H/9	SO/9	BB/9	OAvg	OOBP	ERA
Philadelphia	151	70	9	126	24	1357.0	1371	615	519	73	136	—	15	487	—	573	28	2	9.1	3.8	3.2	.264	.329	3.44
Cleveland	152	80	8	102	10	1352.0	1570	736	609	56	163	—	26	488	—	389	10	4	10.5	2.6	3.2	.295	.357	4.05
St. Louis	154	83	15	117	10	1371.0	1469	713	621	100	171	—	16	462	—	415	15	6	9.6	2.7	3.0	.280	.340	4.08
New York	154	64	12	144	18	1366.2	1475	775	637	83	150	—	24	485	—	484	20	6	9.7	3.2	3.2	.276	.342	4.34
Washington	153	62	3	138	17	1354.2	1429	776	653	48	168	—	31	496	—	494	29	2	9.5	3.3	3.3	.284	.351	4.41
Chicago	152	78	5	100	7	1357.2	1481	792	666	84	197	—	28	505	—	328	22	3	9.8	2.2	3.3	.291	.355	4.43
Boston	155	84	9	105	5	1366.2	1537	803	672	78	188	—	28	496	—	416	36	0	10.1	2.7	3.3	.301	.377	4.96
Detroit	155	82	5	139	9	1390.1	1641	928	766	73	212	—	28	646	—	467	31	3	10.6	3.0	4.2			4.96
AL Total	1226	603	66	971	100	10916.0	11973	6138	5143	595	1385	—	192	4065	—	3566	191	26	9.9	2.9	3.4	.284	.349	4.24
AL Avg Team	153	75	8	121	13	1364.0	1497	767	643	74	173	—	24	508	—	446	24	3	9.9	2.9	3.4	.284	.349	4.24

Team Fielding

Team	G	PO	A	E	TC	DP	PB	Pct
Philadelphia	151	4065	1587	146	5798	117	10	.975
St. Louis	154	4111	1863	156	6130	148	7	.975
New York	154	4079	1745	178	6002	153	7	.970
Chicago	152	4052	1905	188	6145	153	11	.969
Cleveland	152	4060	2015	198	6273	162	14	.968
Washington	153	4060	1839	195	6094	156	9	.968
Boston	155	4090	1877	218	6185	159	8	.965
Detroit	155	4162	1827	242	6231	149	13	.961
AL Total	1226	32679	14658	1521	48858	1197	79	.969

Team vs. Team Records

	Bos	ChA	Cle	Det	NYA	Phi	StL	Was	Won
Bos	—	11	9	8	5	4	11	10	58
ChA	11	—	9	10	6	9	4	10	59
Cle	13	12	—	11	14	7	10	14	81
Det	14	12	11	—	9	4	10	10	70
NYA	17	16	8	13	—	8	14	12	88
Phi	18	13	14	18	14	—	11	16	104
StL	11	17	12	12	8	10	—	9	79
Was	12	12	8	12	10	4	13	—	71
Lost	96	93	71	84	66	46	73	81	

1929 American League Batting Leaders

Games			At-Bats			Runs			Hits			Doubles			Triples		
D. Alexander, Det		155	R. Johnson, Det		640	C. Gehringer, Det		131	D. Alexander, Det		215	R. Johnson, Det		45	C. Gehringer, Det		19
C. Gehringer, Det		155	C. Gehringer, Det		634	R. Johnson, Det		128	C. Gehringer, Det		215	C. Gehringer, Det		45	R. Scarritt, Bos		17
L. Gehrig, NYA		154	D. Alexander, Det		626	L. Gehrig, NYA		127	A. Simmons, Phi		212	H. Manush, StL		45	B. Miller, Phi		16
M. McManus, Det		154	B. Cissell, ChA		618	J. Foxx, Phi		123	L. Fonseca, Cle		209	L. Fonseca, Cle		44	3 tied with		15
F. O'Rourke, StL		154	S. Rice, Was		616	B. Ruth, NYA		121	H. Manush, StL		204	2 tied with		43			

Home Runs			Total Bases			Runs Batted In			Walks			Intentional Walks			Strikeouts		
B. Ruth, NYA		46	A. Simmons, Phi		373	A. Simmons, Phi		157	M. Bishop, Phi		128	Statistic unavailable			J. Foxx, Phi		70
L. Gehrig, NYA		35	D. Alexander, Det		363	B. Ruth, NYA		154	L. Blue, StL		126				L. Gehrig, NYA		68
A. Simmons, Phi		34	B. Ruth, NYA		348	D. Alexander, Det		137	L. Gehrig, NYA		122				D. Alexander, Det		63
J. Foxx, Phi		33	C. Gehringer, Det		337	L. Gehrig, NYA		126	J. Foxx, Phi		103				R. Johnson, Det		60
D. Alexander, Det		25	J. Foxx, Phi		323	H. Heilmann, Det		120	J. Cronin, Was		85				B. Ruth, NYA		60

Hit By Pitch			Sac Hits			Sac Flies			Stolen Bases			Caught Stealing			GDP		
B. Reeves, Bos		7	J. Sewell, Cle		41	Statistic unavailable			C. Gehringer, Det		27	B. Cissell, ChA		17	Statistic unavailable		
J. Dykes, Phi		7	M. Haas, Phi		40				B. Cissell, ChA		26	R. Johnson, Det		15			
W. Schang, StL		7	F. O'Rourke, StL		28				B. Miller, Phi		24	4 tied with		13			
C. Gehringer, Det		6	J. Kerr, ChA		26				J. Rothrock, Bos		23						
L. Fonseca, Cle		6	P. Todt, Bos		25				R. Johnson, Det		20						

Runs Created			Runs Created/27 Outs			Batting Average			On-Base Percentage			Slugging Percentage			OBP+Slugging		
J. Foxx, Phi		145	J. Foxx, Phi		10.64	L. Fonseca, Cle		.369	J. Foxx, Phi		.463	B. Ruth, NYA		.697	B. Ruth, NYA		1.128
A. Simmons, Phi		141	B. Ruth, NYA		10.54	A. Simmons, Phi		.365	L. Gehrig, NYA		.431	A. Simmons, Phi		.642	J. Foxx, Phi		1.088
B. Ruth, NYA		138	A. Simmons, Phi		9.54	H. Manush, StL		.355	T. Lazzeri, NYA		.430	J. Foxx, Phi		.625	A. Simmons, Phi		1.040
L. Gehrig, NYA		137	L. Gehrig, NYA		8.90	T. Lazzeri, NYA		.354	B. Ruth, NYA		.430	L. Gehrig, NYA		.582	L. Gehrig, NYA		1.013
2 tied with		136	T. Lazzeri, NYA		8.61	J. Foxx, Phi		.354	L. Fonseca, Cle		.426	D. Alexander, Det		.580	T. Lazzeri, NYA		.992

1929 American League Pitching Leaders

Wins			Losses			Winning Percentage			Games			Games Started			Complete Games		
G. Earnshaw, Phi		24	R. Ruffing, Bos		22	L. Grove, Phi		.769	F. Marberry, Was		49	L. Grove, Phi		37	T. Thomas, ChA		24
W. Ferrell, Cle		21	T. Lyons, ChA		20	G. Earnshaw, Phi		.750	G. Earnshaw, Phi		44	S. Gray, StL		37	S. Gray, StL		23
L. Grove, Phi		20	M. Gaston, Bos		19	W. Ferrell, Cle		.677	W. Ferrell, Cle		43	G. Crowder, StL		34	G. Uhle, Det		23
F. Marberry, Was		19	3 tied with		18	3 tied with		.647	S. Gray, StL		43	4 tied with		33	W. Hudlin, Cle		22
3 tied with		18							2 tied with		42				2 tied with		21

Shutouts			Saves			Games Finished			Batters Faced			Innings Pitched			Hits Allowed		
D. MacFayden, Bos		4	F. Marberry, Was		11	W. Moore, NYA		27	S. Gray, StL		1310	S. Gray, StL		305.0	S. Gray, StL		336
G. Crowder, StL		4	W. Moore, NYA		8	F. Marberry, Was		21	W. Hudlin, Cle		1201	W. Hudlin, Cle		280.1	W. Hudlin, Cle		299
G. Blaeholder, StL		4	B. Shores, Phi		7	B. Shores, Phi		19	L. Grove, Phi		1168	L. Grove, Phi		275.0	G. Uhle, Det		283
S. Gray, StL		4	W. Ferrell, Cle		5	E. Yde, Det		16	R. Walberg, Phi		1139	R. Walberg, Phi		267.2	R. Ruffing, Bos		280
5 tied with		3	7 tied with		4	E. Rommel, Phi		16	G. Crowder, StL		1128	G. Crowder, StL		266.2	L. Grove, Phi		278

Home Runs Allowed			Walks			Walks/9 Innings			Strikeouts			Strikeouts/9 Innings			Strikeout/Walk Ratio		
G. Crowder, StL		22	G. Earnshaw, Phi		125	J. Russell, Bos		1.6	L. Grove, Phi		170	L. Grove, Phi		5.6	L. Grove, Phi		2.10
R. Walberg, Phi		22	R. Ruffing, Bos		118	T. Thomas, ChA		2.1	G. Earnshaw, Phi		149	G. Earnshaw, Phi		5.3	F. Marberry, Was		1.75
E. Wells, NYA		19	W. Ferrell, Cle		109	G. Uhle, Det		2.1	G. Pipgras, NYA		125	G. Pipgras, NYA		5.0	G. Uhle, Det		1.72
G. Blaeholder, StL		18	V. Sorrell, Det		106	W. Hudlin, Cle		2.3	F. Marberry, Was		121	F. Marberry, Was		4.4	G. Pipgras, NYA		1.32
S. Gray, StL		18	R. Walberg, Phi		99	R. Faber, ChA		2.3	2 tied with		109	R. Ruffing, Bos		4.0	G. Earnshaw, Phi		1.19

Earned Run Average			Component ERA			Hit Batsmen			Wild Pitches			Opponent Average			Opponent OBP		
L. Grove, Phi		2.81	F. Marberry, Was		2.78	H. McKain, ChA		10	M. Gaston, Bos		17	G. Earnshaw, Phi		.241	F. Marberry, Was		.308
F. Marberry, Was		3.06	L. Grove, Phi		3.19	R. Faber, ChA		9	L. Brown, Was		9	E. Wells, NYA		.248	T. Thomas, ChA		.310
T. Thomas, ChA		3.19	W. Hudlin, Cle		3.29	O. Carroll, Det		8	G. Earnshaw, Phi		8	F. Marberry, Was		.252	L. Grove, Phi		.316
G. Earnshaw, Phi		3.29	T. Thomas, ChA		3.33	B. Bayne, Bos		8	L. Grove, Phi		8	R. Walberg, Phi		.254	W. Hudlin, Cle		.318
W. Hudlin, Cle		3.34	G. Earnshaw, Phi		3.37	J. Miller, Cle		7	E. Morris, Bos		8	L. Grove, Phi		.262	R. Walberg, Phi		.320

1929 American League Miscellaneous

Managers

Boston	Bill Carrigan	58-96
Chicago	Lena Blackburne	59-93
Cleveland	Roger Peckinpaugh	81-71
Detroit	Bucky Harris	70-84
New York	Miller Huggins	82-61
	Art Fletcher	6-5
Philadelphia	Connie Mack	104-46
St. Louis	Dan Howley	79-73
Washington	Walter Johnson	71-81

Awards

STATS Most Valuable Player	Jimmie Foxx, 1b, Phi
STATS Cy Young	Lefty Grove, Phi
STATS Rookie of the Year	Dale Alexander, 1b, Det
STATS Manager of the Year	Roger Peckinpaugh, Cle

STATS All-Star Team

C	Mickey Cochrane, Phi	.331	7	95
1B	Jimmie Foxx, Phi	.354	33	117
2B	Charlie Gehringer, Det	.339	13	106
3B	Marty McManus, Det	.280	18	90
SS	Red Kress, StL	.305	9	107
OF	Harry Heilmann, Det	.344	15	120
OF	Babe Ruth, NYA	.345	46	154
OF	Al Simmons, Phi	.365	34	157
P	George Earnshaw, Phi	24-8	3.29	149 K
P	Wes Ferrell, Cle	21-10	3.60	100 K
P	Lefty Grove, Phi	20-6	2.81	170 K
P	Firpo Marberry, Was	19-12	3.06	121 K
RP	Bill Shores, Phi	11-6	3.60	7 Sv

Postseason

World Series	Philadelphia (AL) 4 vs. ChN (NL) 1

Outstanding Performances

Three-Homer Games

Lou Gehrig, NYA	on May 4

Cycles

Ski Melillo, StL	on May 23
Joe Cronin, Was	on September 2

1929 National League Standings

Team	Overall W	L	Pct	GB	DIF	Home Games W	L	R	OR	HR	OHR	Road Games W	L	R	OR	HR	OHR	Park Index Run	HR	Record by Month M/A	May	June	July	Aug	S/O
Chicago	98	54	.645	—	102	**52**	25	490	374	76	41	46	29	492	384	63	36	96	115	7-5	15-9	17-9	24-8	20-10	15-13
Pittsburgh	88	65	.575	10.5	40	45	31	471	382	27	37	43	34	433	398	33	59	104	70	4-6	19-8	17-11	18-11	13-16	17-13
New York	84	67	.556	13.5	7	39	37	418	374	79	59	45	30	479	**335**	57	43	96	136	4-4	13-13	21-12	17-16	12-12	17-10
St. Louis	78	74	.513	20.0	19	43	32	414	386	48	50	35	42	417	420	52	51	98	98	7-5	19-10	10-15	13-19	16-11	17-14
Philadelphia	71	82	.464	27.5	0	39	37	503	580	86	74	32	45	394	452	67	48	130	141	4-6	15-11	9-22	10-19	16-11	17-13
Brooklyn	70	83	.458	28.5	0	42	35	371	413	53	48	28	48	384	475	46	44	90	111	4-7	10-15	17-14	12-18	13-12	14-17
Cincinnati	66	88	.429	33.0	1	38	39	356	**356**	7	**18**	28	49	330	404	27	43	97	36	5-7	7-19	12-14	16-17	12-15	14-16
Boston	56	98	.364	43.0	18	34	43	318	403	11	39	22	55	339	473	22	64	89	58	7-2	8-21	12-18	15-17	6-17	8-23

Clinch Date—Chicago 9/18.

Team Batting

Team	G	AB	R	OR	H	2B	3B	HR	TB	RBI	TBB	IBB	SO	HBP	SH	SF	SB	CS	SB%	GDP	Avg	OBP	Slg
Chicago	156	5471	**982**	758	1655	310	46	139	2474	**933**	**589**	—	567	29	163	—	103	—	—	—	.303	.373	.452
Pittsburgh	154	**5490**	904	780	1663	285	**116**	60	2360	828	503	—	335	29	176	—	59	—	—	—	.303	.364	.430
Philadelphia	154	5484	897	1032	**1693**	305	51	**153**	2559	841	573	—	470	**36**	135	—	85	—	—	—	**.309**	**.377**	**.467**
New York	152	5388	897	**709**	1594	251	47	136	2347	829	482	—	405	24	154	—	85	—	—	—	.296	.358	.436
St. Louis	154	5364	831	806	1569	310	84	100	2347	779	490	—	455	22	154	—	72	—	—	—	.293	.355	.437
Brooklyn	153	5273	755	888	1535	282	69	99	2252	705	504	—	454	26	155	—	**134**	—	—	—	.291	.336	.427
Cincinnati	155	5269	686	760	1478	258	79	34	1996	618	412	—	347	26	175	—	65	—	—	—	.280	.335	.379
Boston	154	5291	657	876	1481	252	77	33	1986	598	408	—	432	27	**197**	—	65	—	—	—	.280	.335	.375
NL Total	1232	43030	6609	6609	12668	2253	569	754	18321	6131	3961	—	3465	215	1309	—	692	—	—	—	.294	.357	.426
NL Avg Team	154	5379	826	826	1584	282	71	94	2290	766	495	—	433	27	164	—	87	—	—	—	.294	.357	.426

Team Pitching

Team	G	CG	ShO	Rel	Sv	IP	H	R	ER	HR	SH	SF	HB	TBB	IBB	SO	WP	Bk	H/9	SO/9	BB/9	OAvg	OOBP	ERA
New York	152	68	9	131	13	1372.0	1536	**709**	605	102	170	—	17	**387**	—	431	16	1	10.1	2.8	**2.5**	.287	**.337**	3.97
Chicago	156	79	**14**	139	21	**1398.2**	1542	758	646	77	**128**	—	21	537	—	548	23	2	**9.9**	3.5	3.5	.285	.352	4.16
Pittsburgh	154	79	5	134	13	1379.0	**1530**	780	668	96	163	—	21	439	—	409	22	0	10.0	2.7	2.9	**.284**	.340	4.36
Cincinnati	155	75	5	121	8	1369.1	1558	760	671	**61**	177	—	23	413	—	347	12	2	10.2	2.3	2.7	.292	.346	4.41
St. Louis	154	**83**	6	115	8	1359.2	1604	806	704	101	132	—	29	474	—	**549**	32	**7**	10.6	3.0	3.1	.297	.357	4.66
Brooklyn	153	59	8	173	16	1358.0	1553	888	743	92	180	—	38	549	—	549	**32**	4	10.3	**3.6**	3.6	.302	.367	4.92
Boston	154	78	4	108	12	1352.2	1604	876	770	103	178	—	24	530	—	366	18	0	10.7	2.4	3.5	.324	.398	5.12
Philadelphia	154	45	5	**204**	24	1348.0	1743	1032	918	122	176	—	**39**	616	—	369	21	4	11.6	2.5	4.1	.324	.398	6.13
NL Total	1232	566	56	1125	115	10937.1	12670	6609	5725	754	1304	—	212	3945	—	3472	164	18	10.4	2.9	3.2	.294	.357	4.71
NL Avg Team	154	71	7	141	14	1367.1	1584	826	716	94	163	—	27	493	—	434	21	2	10.4	2.9	3.2	.294	.357	4.71

Team Fielding

Team	G	PO	A	E	TC	DP	PB	Pct
Chicago	156	**4190**	1920	154	6264	169	13	.975
New York	152	4117	**2008**	158	**6283**	163	8	.975
Cincinnati	155	4103	1978	162	6243	148	7	.974
St. Louis	154	4073	1754	174	6001	149	6	.971
Pittsburgh	154	4135	1810	181	6126	136	9	.970
Philadelphia	154	4040	1969	191	6200	153	9	.969
Brooklyn	153	4070	1782	192	6044	113	13	.968
Boston	154	4055	1917	204	6176	146	**14**	.967
NL Total	1232	32783	15138	1416	49337	1177	79	.971

Team vs. Team Records

	Bos	Bro	ChN	Cin	NYG	Phi	Pit	StL	Won
Bos	—	11	7	8	9	5	8	8	56
Bro	11	—	6	11	14	9	9	10	70
ChN	15	16	—	14	12	17	9	15	98
Cin	14	11	8	—	10	11	9	3	66
NYG	13	7	10	12	—	16	13	13	84
Phi	17	13	5	11	5	—	11	9	71
Pit	14	13	13	13	8	11	—	16	88
StL	14	12	5	19	9	13	6	—	78
Lost	98	83	54	88	67	82	65	74	

1929 National League Batting Leaders

Games			At-Bats			Runs			Hits			Doubles			Triples	
R. Hornsby, ChN	156		L. Waner, Pit	662		R. Hornsby, ChN	156		L. O'Doul, Phi	254		J. Frederick, Bro	52		L. Waner, Pit	20
D. Hurst, Phi	154		L. O'Doul, Phi	638		L. O'Doul, Phi	152		L. Waner, Pit	234		C. Hafey, StL	47		P. Waner, Pit	15
P. Whitney, Phi	154		G. Sisler, Bos	629		M. Ott, NYG	138		R. Hornsby, ChN	229		R. Hornsby, ChN	47		C. Walker, Cin	15
L. O'Doul, Phi	154		J. Frederick, Bro	628		H. Wilson, ChN	135		B. Terry, NYG	226		C. Klein, Phi	45		P. Whitney, Phi	14
G. Sisler, Bos	154		F. Thompson, Phi	623		L. Waner, Pit	134		C. Klein, Phi	219		G. Kelly, Cin	45		3 tied with	13

Home Runs			Total Bases			Runs Batted In			Walks			Intentional Walks			Strikeouts	
C. Klein, Phi	43		R. Hornsby, ChN	409		H. Wilson, ChN	159		M. Ott, NYG	113		Statistic unavailable			H. Wilson, ChN	83
M. Ott, NYG	42		C. Klein, Phi	405		M. Ott, NYG	151		G. Grantham, Pit	93					R. Hornsby, ChN	65
H. Wilson, ChN	39		L. O'Doul, Phi	397		R. Hornsby, ChN	149		P. Waner, Pit	89					C. Klein, Phi	61
R. Hornsby, ChN	39		H. Wilson, ChN	355		C. Klein, Phi	145		R. Hornsby, ChN	87					G. Kelly, Cin	61
L. O'Doul, Phi	32		B. Herman, Bro	348		J. Bottomley, StL	137		C. Walker, Cin	85					D. Bissonette, Bro	58

Hit By Pitch			Sac Hits			Sac Flies			Stolen Bases			Caught Stealing			GDP	
J. Welsh, 2tm	11		F. Maguire, Bos	26		Statistic unavailable			K. Cuyler, ChN	43		Statistic unavailable			Statistic unavailable	
L. Waner, Pit	9		P. Traynor, Pit	24					E. Swanson, Cin	33						
W. Gilbert, Bro	7		W. Gilbert, Bro	23					F. Frisch, StL	24						
R. Stephenson, ChN	7		R. Maranville, Bos	23					E. Allen, Cin	21						
3 tied with	6		5 tied with	22					B. Herman, Bro	21						

Runs Created			Runs Created/27 Outs			Batting Average			On-Base Percentage			Slugging Percentage			OBP+Slugging	
R. Hornsby, ChN	178		R. Hornsby, ChN	11.58		L. O'Doul, Phi	.398		L. O'Doul, Phi	.465		R. Hornsby, ChN	.679		R. Hornsby, ChN	1.139
L. O'Doul, Phi	157		M. Ott, NYG	10.60		B. Herman, Bro	.381		R. Hornsby, ChN	.459		C. Klein, Phi	.657		L. O'Doul, Phi	1.087
M. Ott, NYG	155		L. O'Doul, Phi	10.17		R. Hornsby, ChN	.380		G. Grantham, Pit	.454		M. Ott, NYG	.635		M. Ott, NYG	1.084
H. Wilson, ChN	148		R. Stephenson, ChN	9.77		B. Terry, NYG	.372		M. Ott, NYG	.449		C. Hafey, StL	.632		C. Klein, Phi	1.065
C. Klein, Phi	140		H. Wilson, ChN	9.71		R. Stephenson, ChN	.362		R. Stephenson, ChN	.445		L. O'Doul, Phi	.622		B. Herman, Bro	1.048

1929 National League Pitching Leaders

Wins			Losses			Winning Percentage			Games			Games Started			Complete Games	
P. Malone, ChN	22		W. Clark, Bro	19		C. Root, ChN	.760		G. Bush, ChN	50		W. Clark, Bro	36		R. Lucas, Cin	28
R. Lucas, Cin	19		L. Benton, NYG	17		G. Bush, ChN	.720		C. Willoughby, Phi	49		C. Hubbell, NYG	35		6 tied with	19
C. Root, ChN	19		B. Smith, Bos	17		B. Grimes, Pit	.708		L. Sweetland, Phi	43		C. Willoughby, Phi	34			
3 tied with	18		S. Seibold, Bos	17		P. Malone, ChN	.688		P. Collins, Phi	43		R. Lucas, Cin	32			
			D. Luque, Cin	16		H. Carlson, ChN	.688		C. Root, ChN	43		2 tied with	31			

Shutouts			Saves			Games Finished			Batters Faced			Innings Pitched			Hits Allowed	
P. Malone, ChN	5		G. Bush, ChN	8		B. McGraw, Phi	24		W. Clark, Bro	1189		W. Clark, Bro	279.0		W. Clark, Bro	295
F. Fitzsimmons, NYG	4		J. Morrison, Bro	8		J. Morrison, Bro	22		G. Bush, ChN	1176		C. Root, ChN	272.0		C. Willoughby, Phi	288
C. Root, ChN	4		L. Koupal, 2tm	6		P. Collins, Phi	20		C. Root, ChN	1158		G. Bush, ChN	270.2		C. Root, ChN	286
4 tied with	3		3 tied with	5		C. Mays, NYG	19		P. Malone, ChN	1152		R. Lucas, Cin	270.0		P. Malone, ChN	283
						3 tied with	17		C. Hubbell, NYG	1130		C. Hubbell, NYG	268.0		B. Sherdel, StL	278

Home Runs Allowed			Walks			Walks/9 Innings			Strikeouts			Strikeouts/9 Innings			Strikeout/Walk Ratio	
R. Benge, Phi	24		S. Blake, ChN	130		D. Vance, Bro	1.8		P. Malone, ChN	166		P. Malone, ChN	5.6		D. Vance, Bro	2.68
L. Sweetland, Phi	23		C. Willoughby, Phi	108		R. Lucas, Cin	1.9		W. Clark, Bro	140		D. Vance, Bro	4.9		W. Clark, Bro	1.97
R. Kremer, Pit	21		G. Bush, ChN	107		J. Petty, Pit	2.1		D. Vance, Bro	126		W. Clark, Bro	4.5		P. Malone, ChN	1.63
J. Haines, StL	21		P. Malone, ChN	102		C. Hubbell, NYG	2.3		C. Root, ChN	124		J. May, Cin	4.2		C. Hubbell, NYG	1.58
B. Smith, Bos	20		D. McWeeny, Bro	93		W. Clark, Bro	2.3		C. Hubbell, NYG	106		C. Root, ChN	4.1		C. Root, ChN	1.49

Earned Run Average			Component ERA			Hit Batsmen			Wild Pitches			Opponent Average			Opponent OBP	
B. Walker, NYG	3.09		R. Lucas, Cin	2.94		C. Dudley, Bro	10		D. McWeeny, Bro	11		R. Lucas, Cin	.258		R. Lucas, Cin	.298
B. Grimes, Pit	3.13		C. Hubbell, NYG	3.36		L. Sweetland, Phi	9		G. Bush, ChN	7		S. Johnson, StL	.265		C. Hubbell, NYG	.313
C. Root, ChN	3.47		W. Clark, Bro	3.43		D. Vance, Bro	9		4 tied with	6		C. Hubbell, NYG	.265		W. Clark, Bro	.316
P. Malone, ChN	3.57		D. Vance, Bro	3.45		3 tied with	7					G. Bush, ChN	.265		D. Vance, Bro	.316
R. Lucas, Cin	3.60		J. Petty, Pit	3.45								B. Grimes, Pit	.269		J. Petty, Pit	.317

1929 National League Miscellaneous

Managers

Boston	Judge Fuchs	56-98
Brooklyn	Wilbert Robinson	70-83
Chicago	Joe McCarthy	98-54
Cincinnati	Jack Hendricks	66-88
New York	John McGraw	84-67
Philadelphia	Burt Shotton	71-82
Pittsburgh	Donie Bush	67-51
	Jewel Ens	21-14
St. Louis	Billy Southworth	43-45
	Gabby Street	1-0
	Bill McKechnie	34-29

Awards

Most Valuable Player	R. Hornsby, 2b, ChN
STATS Cy Young	Pat Malone, ChN
STATS Rookie of the Year	J. Frederick, of, Bro
STATS Manager of the Year	Joe McCarthy, ChN

STATS All-Star Team

C	Jimmie Wilson, StL	.325	4	71
1B	Jim Bottomley, StL	.314	29	137
2B	Rogers Hornsby, ChN	.380	39	149
3B	Pie Traynor, Pit	.356	4	108
SS	Travis Jackson, NYG	.294	21	94
OF	Lefty O'Doul, Phi	.398	32	122
OF	Mel Ott, NYG	.328	42	151
OF	Hack Wilson, ChN	.345	39	159
P	Burleigh Grimes, Pit	17-7	3.13	62 K
P	Red Lucas, Cin	19-12	3.60	72 K
P	Pat Malone, ChN	22-10	3.57	166 K
P	Charlie Root, ChN	19-6	3.47	124 K
RP	Johnny Morrison, Bro	13-7	4.48	8 Sv

Postseason

World Series	ChN (NL) 1 vs. Philadelphia (AL) 4

Outstanding Performances

No-Hitters

Carl Hubbell, NYG	vs. Pit on May 8

Cycles

Mel Ott, NYG	on May 16

1930 American League Standings

Team	W	L	Pct	GB	DIF	W	L	R	OR	HR	OHR	W	L	R	OR	HR	OHR	Run	HR	M/A	May	June	July	Aug	S/O
	Overall					**Home Games**						**Road Games**						**Park Index**		**Record by Month**					
Philadelphia	102	52	.662	—	134	58	18	485	329	76	49	44	34	466	422	49	35	94	153	6-5	21-9	19-11	23-9	19-10	14-8
Washington	94	60	.610	8.0	31	56	21	474	300	17	15	38	39	418	389	40	37	96	42	10-3	17-11	15-11	17-15	21-9	14-11
New York	86	68	.558	16.0	0	47	29	471	390	69	54	39	39	591	508	83	39	80	103	8-4	15-14	12-16	18-16	16-13	12-10
Cleveland	81	73	.526	21.0	6	44	33	494	469	34	46	37	40	396	446	38	39	114	104	5-10	13-14	11-17	19-15	14-14	13-9
Detroit	75	79	.487	27.0	3	45	33	441	419	45	48	30	46	342	414	37	38	111	121	6-7	11-16	12-18	13-21	11-16	11-12
St. Louis	64	90	.416	38.0	0	38	40	432	475	35	72	26	50	319	411	40	52	121	113	6-4	9-19	9-17	19-18	8-19	11-15
Chicago	62	92	.403	40.0	2	34	44	393	457	25	42	28	48	336	427	38	32	109	93	5-8	7-20	14-14	9-23	8-18	9-19
Boston	52	102	.338	50.0	1	30	46	287	354	15	31	22	56	325	460	32	44	84	62						

Clinch Date—Philadelphia 9/18.

Team Batting

Team	G	AB	R	OR	H	2B	3B	HR	TB	RBI	TBB	IBB	SO	HBP	SH	SF	SB	CS	SB%	GDP	Avg	OBP	Slg
New York	154	5448	1062	898	1683	298	110	152	2657	986	644	—	569	18	162	—	91	60	.60	—	.309	.384	.488
Philadelphia	154	5345	951	751	1573	319	74	125	2415	895	599	—	531	31	188	—	48	33	.59	—	.294	.369	.452
Washington	154	5370	892	689	1620	300	98	57	2287	819	537	—	438	38	173	—	101	67	.60	—	.302	.369	.426
Cleveland	154	5439	890	915	1654	358	59	72	2346	830	490	—	461	25	145	—	51	47	.52	—	.304	.364	.431
Detroit	154	5297	783	833	1504	298	90	82	2228	728	461	—	508	25	145	—	98	70	.58	—	.284	.344	.421
St. Louis	154	5278	751	886	1415	289	67	75	2063	691	497	—	550	15	156	—	93	71	.57	—	.276	.333	.391
Chicago	154	5419	729	884	1496	256	90	63	2121	679	389	—	479	32	152	—	74	40	.65	—	.276	.328	.391
Boston	154	5286	612	814	1393	257	67	47	1925	533	358	—	552	19	144	—	42	35	.55	—	.264	.313	.364
AL Total	1232	42882	6670	6670	12338	2375	655	673	18042	6161	3975	—	4088	203	1294	—	598	423	.59	—	.288	.351	.421
AL Avg Team	154	5360	834	834	1542	297	82	84	2255	770	497	—	511	25	162	—	75	53	.59	—	.288	.351	.421

Team Pitching

Team	G	CG	ShO	Rel	Sv	IP	H	R	ER	HR	SH	SF	HB	TBB	IBB	SO	WP	Bk	H/9	SO/9	BB/9	OAvg	OOBP	ERA
Washington	154	78	6	111	14	1369.0	1367	689	603	52	138	—	25	504	—	524	15	2	9.0	3.4	3.3	.264	.332	3.96
Philadelphia	154	72	8	135	21	1371.0	1457	751	652	84	140	—	20	488	—	672	25	5	9.6	4.4	3.2	.274	.337	4.28
Boston	154	78	4	92	5	1360.1	1515	814	708	75	182	—	20	488	—	356	18	2	10.0	2.4	3.2	.286	.348	4.68
Detroit	154	68	4	137	17	1351.2	1507	833	706	86	152	—	33	570	—	574	27	0	10.0	3.8	3.8	.286	.359	4.70
Chicago	154	63	2	146	10	1361.0	1629	884	713	74	191	—	29	407	—	471	17	1	10.8	3.1	2.7	.300	.352	4.71
New York	154	65	7	150	15	1367.2	1566	898	741	93	148	—	29	524	—	572	38	1	10.3	3.8	3.5	.287	.352	4.88
Cleveland	154	68	5	139	14	1360.0	1663	915	738	85	174	—	21	528	—	442	23	9	11.0	2.9	3.5	.305	.368	4.88
St. Louis	154	68	5	122	10	1371.2	1639	886	773	124	159	—	25	449	—	470	10	1	10.8	3.1	2.9	.300	.356	5.07
AL Total	1232	560	41	1032	106	10912.1	12343	6670	5634	673	1284	—	202	3958	—	4081	173	23	10.2	3.4	3.3	.288	.351	4.65
AL Avg Team	154	70	5	129	13	1364.1	1543	834	704	84	161	—	25	495	—	510	22	3	10.2	3.4	3.3	.288	.351	4.65

Team Fielding

Team	G	PO	A	E	TC	DP	PB	Pct
Philadelphia	154	4127	1651	145	5923	121	11	.976
Washington	154	4105	1781	157	6043	150	4	.974
St. Louis	154	4114	1870	188	6172	152	4	.970
Boston	154	4084	1824	196	6104	161	12	.968
Detroit	154	4031	1650	192	5873	156	17	.967
New York	154	4081	1688	207	5976	132	12	.965
Cleveland	154	4076	1920	237	6233	156	8	.962
Chicago	154	4079	1865	235	6179	136	15	.962
AL Total	1232	32697	14249	1557	48503	1164	83	.968

Team vs. Team Records

	Bos	ChA	Cle	Det	NYA	Phi	StL	Was	Won
Bos	—	13	7	8	6	4	9	5	52
ChA	9	—	10	9	8	6	12	8	62
Cle	15	12	—	11	10	7	16	10	81
Det	14	13	11	—	9	7	11	10	75
NYA	16	14	12	13	—	10	16	5	86
Phi	18	16	15	15	12	—	16	10	102
StL	13	10	6	11	6	6	—	12	64
Was	17	14	12	12	17	12	10	—	94
Lost	102	92	73	79	68	52	90	60	

1930 American League Batting Leaders

Games		At-Bats		Runs		Hits		Doubles		Triples	
8 tied with	154	T. Oliver, Bos	646	A. Simmons, Phi	152	J. Hodapp, Cle	225	J. Hodapp, Cle	51	E. Combs, NYA	22
		J. Hodapp, Cle	635	B. Ruth, NYA	150	L. Gehrig, NYA	220	H. Manush, 2tm	49	C. Reynolds, ChA	18
		S. Jolley, ChA	616	C. Gehringer, Det	144	A. Simmons, Phi	211	E. Morgan, Cle	47	L. Gehrig, NYA	17
		R. Kress, StL	614	L. Gehrig, NYA	143	S. Rice, Was	207	C. Gehringer, Det	47	A. Simmons, Phi	16
		C. Gehringer, Det	610	E. Combs, NYA	129	E. Morgan, Cle	204	2 tied with	43	2 tied with	15

Home Runs		Total Bases		Runs Batted In		Walks		Intentional Walks		Strikeouts	
B. Ruth, NYA	49	L. Gehrig, NYA	419	L. Gehrig, NYA	174	B. Ruth, NYA	136	Statistic unavailable		E. Morgan, Cle	66
L. Gehrig, NYA	41	A. Simmons, Phi	392	A. Simmons, Phi	165	M. Bishop, Phi	128			J. Foxx, Phi	66
J. Foxx, Phi	37	B. Ruth, NYA	379	J. Foxx, Phi	156	L. Gehrig, NYA	101			L. Gehrig, NYA	63
G. Goslin, 2tm	37	J. Foxx, Phi	358	B. Ruth, NYA	153	J. Foxx, Phi	93			T. Lazzeri, NYA	62
A. Simmons, Phi	36	2 tied with	351	G. Goslin, 2tm	138	L. Blue, StL	81			2 tied with	61

Hit By Pitch		Sac Hits		Sac Flies		Stolen Bases		Caught Stealing		GDP	
J. Dykes, Phi	10	M. Haas, Phi	33	Statistic unavailable		M. McManus, Det	23	C. Gehringer, Det	15	Statistic unavailable	
O. Bluege, Was	8	O. Bluege, Was	27			C. Gehringer, Det	19	L. Gehrig, NYA	14		
C. Reynolds, ChA	7	L. Funk, Det	23			R. Johnson, Det	17	B. Miller, Phi	13		
C. Gehringer, Det	7	J. Cronin, Was	22			J. Cronin, Was	17	R. Kress, StL	12		
2 tied with	6	B. Ruth, NYA	21			G. Goslin, 2tm	17	2 tied with	11		

Runs Created		Runs Created/27 Outs		Batting Average		On-Base Percentage		Slugging Percentage		OBP+Slugging	
L. Gehrig, NYA	182	B. Ruth, NYA	12.69	A. Simmons, Phi	.381	B. Ruth, NYA	.493	B. Ruth, NYA	.732	B. Ruth, NYA	1.225
B. Ruth, NYA	176	L. Gehrig, NYA	12.12	L. Gehrig, NYA	.379	L. Gehrig, NYA	.473	L. Gehrig, NYA	.721	L. Gehrig, NYA	1.194
A. Simmons, Phi	156	A. Simmons, Phi	11.28	B. Ruth, NYA	.359	J. Foxx, Phi	.429	A. Simmons, Phi	.708	A. Simmons, Phi	1.130
J. Foxx, Phi	150	J. Foxx, Phi	9.84	C. Reynolds, ChA	.359	M. Bishop, Phi	.426	J. Foxx, Phi	.637	J. Foxx, Phi	1.066
E. Morgan, Cle	140	E. Morgan, Cle	9.09	M. Cochrane, Phi	.357	E. Combs, NYA	.424	2 tied with	.601	E. Morgan, Cle	1.014

1930 American League Pitching Leaders

Wins		Losses		Winning Percentage		Games		Games Started		Complete Games	
L. Grove, Phi	28	J. Russell, Bos	20	L. Grove, Phi	.848	L. Grove, Phi	50	G. Earnshaw, Phi	39	T. Lyons, ChA	29
W. Ferrell, Cle	25	M. Gaston, Bos	20	E. Wells, NYA	.800	G. Earnshaw, Phi	49	T. Lyons, ChA	36	W. Ferrell, Cle	25
G. Earnshaw, Phi	22	D. Coffman, StL	18	F. Marberry, Was	.750	H. Johnson, NYA	44	W. Ferrell, Cle	35	G. Crowder, 2tm	25
T. Lyons, ChA	22	H. Lisenbee, Bos	17	B. Shores, Phi	.750	G. Pipgras, NYA	44	G. Crowder, 2tm	35	L. Stewart, StL	23
L. Stewart, StL	20	D. Henry, ChA	17	S. Jones, Was	.682	W. Ferrell, Cle	43	2 tied with	34	L. Grove, Phi	22

Shutouts		Saves		Games Finished		Batters Faced		Innings Pitched		Hits Allowed	
C. Brown, Cle	3	L. Grove, Phi	9	C. Kimsey, StL	30	G. Earnshaw, Phi	1299	T. Lyons, ChA	297.2	T. Lyons, ChA	331
G. Earnshaw, Phi	3	G. Braxton, 2tm	6	E. Walsh, ChA	21	W. Ferrell, Cle	1274	W. Ferrell, Cle	296.2	J. Russell, Bos	302
G. Pipgras, NYA	3	J. Quinn, Phi	6	P. Appleton, Cle	21	T. Lyons, ChA	1258	G. Earnshaw, Phi	296.0	G. Earnshaw, Phi	299
6 tied with	2	C. Sullivan, Det	5	E. Rommel, Phi	20	L. Grove, Phi	1191	L. Grove, Phi	291.0	W. Ferrell, Cle	299
		H. McKain, ChA	5	3 tied with	19	G. Crowder, 2tm	1188	G. Crowder, 2tm	279.2	D. MacFayden, Bos	293

Home Runs Allowed		Walks		Walks/9 Innings		Strikeouts		Strikeouts/9 Innings		Strikeout/Walk Ratio	
L. Stewart, StL	21	G. Earnshaw, Phi	139	H. Pennock, NYA	1.2	L. Grove, Phi	209	L. Grove, Phi	6.5	L. Grove, Phi	3.48
G. Earnshaw, Phi	20	V. Sorrell, Det	106	T. Lyons, ChA	1.7	G. Earnshaw, Phi	193	G. Earnshaw, Phi	5.9	H. Pennock, NYA	2.30
H. Lisenbee, Bos	20	W. Ferrell, Cle	106	L. Grove, Phi	1.9	B. Hadley, Was	162	B. Hadley, Was	5.6	R. Ruffing, 2tm	1.93
G. Blaeholder, StL	20	B. Hadley, Was	105	J. Russell, Bos	2.1	W. Ferrell, Cle	143	R. Ruffing, 2tm	5.3	G. Pipgras, NYA	1.59
G. Uhle, Det	18	H. Johnson, NYA	104	C. Brown, Cle	2.1	R. Ruffing, 2tm	131	G. Pipgras, NYA	4.5	G. Uhle, Det	1.56

Earned Run Average		Component ERA		Hit Batsmen		Wild Pitches		Opponent Average		Opponent OBP	
L. Grove, Phi	2.54	L. Grove, Phi	2.56	C. Hogsett, Det	9	H. Johnson, NYA	11	L. Grove, Phi	.247	L. Grove, Phi	.288
W. Ferrell, Cle	3.31	B. Hadley, Was	3.14	E. Whitehill, Det	8	M. Gaston, Bos	11	B. Hadley, Was	.247	L. Stewart, StL	.315
L. Stewart, StL	3.45	T. Lyons, ChA	3.44	G. Pipgras, NYA	8	G. Earnshaw, Phi	10	G. Crowder, 2tm	.259	T. Lyons, ChA	.319
G. Uhle, Det	3.65	G. Crowder, 2tm	3.46	D. MacFayden, Bos	6	R. Sherid, NYA	7	M. Gaston, Bos	.259	G. Crowder, 2tm	.321
B. Hadley, Was	3.73	M. Gaston, Bos	3.46	B. Hadley, Was	6	C. Sullivan, Det	6	R. Walberg, Phi	.262	H. Pennock, NYA	.322

1930 American League Miscellaneous

Managers		
Boston	Heinie Wagner	52-102
Chicago	Donie Bush	62-92
Cleveland	Roger Peckinpaugh	81-73
Detroit	Bucky Harris	75-79
New York	Bob Shawkey	86-68
Philadelphia	Connie Mack	102-52
St. Louis	Bill Killefer	64-90
Washington	Walter Johnson	94-60

Awards	
STATS Most Valuable Player	Lefty Grove, p, Phi
STATS Cy Young	Lefty Grove, Phi
STATS Rookie of the Year	Ben Chapman, 3b, NYA
STATS Manager of the Year	Walter Johnson, Was

STATS All-Star Team

C	Mickey Cochrane, Phi	.357	10	85
1B	Lou Gehrig, NYA	.379	41	174
2B	Charlie Gehringer, Det	.330	16	98
3B	Marty McManus, Det	.320	9	89
SS	Joe Cronin, Was	.346	13	126
OF	Goose Goslin, 2tm	.308	37	138
OF	Babe Ruth, NYA	.359	49	153
OF	Al Simmons, Phi	.381	36	165
P	Wes Ferrell, Cle	25-13	3.31	143 K
P	Lefty Grove, Phi	28-5	2.54	209 K
P	Ted Lyons, ChA	22-15	3.78	69 K
P	Lefty Stewart, StL	20-12	3.45	79 K
RP	Jack Quinn, Phi	9-7	4.42	6 Sv

Postseason	
World Series	Philadelphia (AL) 4 vs. StL (NL) 2

Outstanding Performances

Three-Homer Games

Babe Ruth, NYA	on May 21
Lou Gehrig, NYA	on May 22
Carl Reynolds, ChA	on July 2
Goose Goslin, StL	on August 19
Earl Averill, Cle	on September 17

1930 National League Standings

Team	Overall					Home Games						Road Games						Park Index		Record by Month					
	W	L	Pct	GB	DIF	W	L	R	OR	HR	OHR	W	L	R	OR	HR	OHR	Run	HR	M/A	May	June	July	Aug	S/O
St. Louis	92	62	.597	—	22	53	24	541	383	52	50	39	38	463	401	52	37	107	115	6-8	17-9	10-15	15-17	23-9	21-4
Chicago	90	64	.584	2.0	40	51	26	538	454	96	62	39	38	460	416	75	49	113	127	8-8	15-11	20-7	15-15	19-10	13-13
New York	87	67	.565	5.0	28	47	31	468	395	91	63	40	36	491	419	52	54	92	142	7-3	10-19	17-10	21-12	16-11	16-12
Brooklyn	86	68	.558	6.0	76	49	27	438	336	73	66	37	41	433	402	49	49	95	146	5-7	20-8	14-10	21-14	12-19	14-10
Pittsburgh	80	74	.519	12.0	6	42	35	433	454	27	51	38	39	458	474	59	77	95	57	9-3	11-15	10-16	18-15	20-12	12-13
Boston	70	84	.455	22.0	0	39	38	329	401	29	51	31	46	364	434	37	26	91	78	5-5	13-13	12-15	15-20	13-17	12-14
Cincinnati	59	95	.383	33.0	0	37	40	300	368	20	21	22	55	365	489	54	54	78	38	4-8	12-15	11-17	17-12	9-21	6-22
Philadelphia	52	102	.338	40.0	4	35	42	543	644	72	72	17	60	401	555	54	70	124	116	5-7	7-15	12-16	8-25	10-23	10-16

Clinch Date—St. Louis 9/26.

Team Batting

Team	G	AB	R	OR	H	2B	3B	HR	TB	RBI	TBB	IBB	SO	HBP	SH	SF	SB	CS	SB%	GDP	Avg	OBP	Slg
St. Louis	154	5512	1004	784	1732	373	89	104	2595	942	479	—	496	28	185	—	72	—	—	—	.314	.372	.471
Chicago	156	5581	998	870	1722	305	72	171	2684	940	588	—	635	37	148	—	70	—	—	—	.309	.378	.481
New York	154	5553	959	814	1769	264	83	143	2628	880	422	—	382	21	165	—	34	—	—	—	.319	.369	.473
Philadelphia	156	5667	944	1199	1783	345	44	126	2594	884	450	—	449	23	196	—	59	—	—	—	.315	.367	.458
Pittsburgh	154	5346	891	928	1622	285	119	86	2403	844	494	—	541	22	147	—	76	—	—	—	.303	.365	.449
Brooklyn	154	5433	871	738	1654	303	73	122	2469	836	481	—	489	27	147	—	53	—	—	—	.304	.364	.454
Boston	154	5356	693	835	1503	246	78	66	2103	631	332	—	397	28	154	—	69	—	—	—	.281	.326	.393
Cincinnati	154	5245	665	857	1475	265	67	74	2096	625	445	—	459	16	174	—	48	—	—	—	.281	.339	.400
NL Total	1236	43693	7025	7025	13260	2386	625	892	19572	6582	3691	—	3848	202	1317	—	481	—	—	—	.303	.360	.448
NL Avg Team	155	5462	878	878	1658	298	78	112	2447	823	461	—	481	25	165	—	60	—	—	—	.303	.360	.448

Team Pitching

Team	G	CG	ShO	Rel	Sv	IP	H	R	ER	HR	SH	SF	HB	TBB	IBB	SO	WP	Bk	H/9	SO/9	BB/9	OAvg	OOBP	ERA
Brooklyn	154	74	13	138	15	1372.0	1480	738	614	115	140	—	19	394	—	526	18	3	9.7	3.5	2.6	.278	.330	4.03
St. Louis	154	63	5	150	21	1380.2	1596	784	669	117	153	—	24	476	—	639	42	0	10.4	4.2	3.1	.294	.354	4.36
New York	154	64	6	157	19	1363.1	1546	814	699	117	133	—	31	439	—	522	19	1	10.2	3.4	2.9	.288	.345	4.61
Chicago	156	67	6	174	12	1403.2	1642	870	749	111	138	—	26	528	—	601	28	1	10.5	3.9	3.4	.294	.357	4.80
Boston	154	71	6	124	11	1361.0	1624	835	743	117	190	—	23	475	—	424	12	2	10.7	2.8	3.1	.302	.360	4.91
Cincinnati	154	61	6	149	11	1335.0	1650	857	753	75	178	—	29	438	—	361	28	4	11.1	2.4	2.7	.310	.361	5.08
Pittsburgh	154	80	7	107	13	1361.1	1730	928	793	128	174	—	29	438	—	393	25	0	11.4	2.6	2.9	.313	.367	5.24
Philadelphia	156	54	3	201	7	1372.2	1993	1199	1024	142	210	—	33	543	—	384	23	2	13.1	2.5	3.6	.346	.405	6.71
NL Total	1236	534	52	1200	109	10949.2	13261	7025	6044	892	1316	—	199	3687	—	3850	195	13	10.9	3.2	3.0	.303	.360	4.97
NL Avg Team	155	67	7	150	14	1368.2	1658	878	756	112	165	—	25	461	—	481	24	2	10.9	3.2	3.0	.303	.360	4.97

Team Fielding

Team	G	PO	A	E	TC	DP	PB	Pct
New York	154	4079	1976	164	6219	144	7	.974
Cincinnati	154	4006	1870	161	6037	164	13	.973
Chicago	156	4166	1881	170	6217	167	13	.973
Brooklyn	154	4115	1865	174	6154	167	14	.972
Boston	154	4082	1778	178	6038	167	14	.971
St. Louis	154	4137	1786	183	6106	176	11	.970
Pittsburgh	154	4083	1865	216	6164	164	8	.965
Philadelphia	156	4124	2000	239	6363	169	11	.962
NL Total	1236	32792	15021	1485	49298	1318	91	.970

Team vs. Team Records

Team	Bos	Bro	ChN	Cin	NYG	Phi	Pit	StL	Won
Bos	—	9	5	13	11	14	10	8	70
Bro	13	—	8	13	13	15	13	11	86
ChN	17	14	—	11	10	16	11	11	90
Cin	9	9	11	—	7	12	8	3	59
NYG	11	9	12	15	—	16	14	10	87
Phi	8	7	6	10	6	—	9	6	52
Pit	12	9	11	14	8	13	—	13	80
StL	14	11	11	19	12	16	9	—	92
Lost	84	68	64	95	67	102	74	62	

1930 National League Batting Leaders

Games			At-Bats			Runs			Hits			Doubles			Triples		
C. Klein, Phi		156	T. Douthit, StL		664	C. Klein, Phi		158	B. Terry, NYG		254	C. Klein, Phi		59	A. Comorosky, Pit		23
W. English, ChN		156	H. Critz, 2tm		662	K. Cuyler, ChN		155	C. Klein, Phi		250	K. Cuyler, ChN		50	P. Waner, Pit		18
T. Thevenow, Phi		156	C. Klein, Phi		648	W. English, ChN		152	B. Herman, Bro		241	B. Herman, Bro		48	W. English, ChN		17
K. Cuyler, ChN		156	K. Cuyler, ChN		642	H. Wilson, ChN		146	F. Lindstrom, NYG		231	A. Comorosky, Pit		47	K. Cuyler, ChN		17
H. Wilson, ChN		155	W. English, ChN		638	B. Herman, Bro		143	K. Cuyler, ChN		228	F. Frisch, StL		46	B. Terry, NYG		15

Home Runs			Total Bases			Runs Batted In			Walks			Intentional Walks			Strikeouts		
H. Wilson, ChN		56	C. Klein, Phi		445	H. Wilson, ChN		190	H. Wilson, ChN		105	Statistic unavailable			H. Wilson, ChN		84
C. Klein, Phi		40	H. Wilson, ChN		423	C. Klein, Phi		170	M. Ott, NYG		103				W. English, ChN		72
W. Berger, Bos		38	B. Herman, Bro		416	K. Cuyler, ChN		134	W. English, ChN		100				G. Wright, Bro		70
G. Hartnett, ChN		37	B. Terry, NYG		392	B. Herman, Bro		130	G. Grantham, Pit		81				W. Berger, Bos		69
B. Herman, Bro		35	K. Cuyler, ChN		351	B. Terry, NYG		129	G. Suhr, Pit		80				2 tied with		66

Hit By Pitch			Sac Hits			Sac Flies			Stolen Bases			Caught Stealing			GDP		
K. Cuyler, ChN		10	A. Comorosky, Pit		33	Statistic unavailable			K. Cuyler, ChN		37	Statistic unavailable			Statistic unavailable		
F. Blair, ChN		7	T. Thevenow, Phi		26				B. Herman, Bro		18						
C. Hafey, StL		7	J. Bottomley, StL		24				P. Waner, Pit		18						
F. Leach, NYG		7	P. Traynor, Pit		23				3 tied with		15						
2 tied with		6	H. Ford, Cin		23												

Runs Created			Runs Created/27 Outs			Batting Average			On-Base Percentage			Slugging Percentage			OBP+Slugging		
C. Klein, Phi		171	H. Wilson, ChN		11.12	B. Terry, NYG		.401	M. Ott, NYG		.458	H. Wilson, ChN		.723	H. Wilson, ChN		1.177
H. Wilson, ChN		171	B. Herman, Bro		10.79	B. Herman, Bro		.393	B. Herman, Bro		.455	C. Klein, Phi		.687	B. Herman, Bro		1.132
B. Herman, Bro		163	C. Klein, Phi		10.69	C. Klein, Phi		.386	H. Wilson, ChN		.454	B. Herman, Bro		.678	C. Klein, Phi		1.123
B. Terry, NYG		160	B. Terry, NYG		10.33	L. O'Doul, Phi		.383	L. O'Doul, Phi		.453	C. Hafey, StL		.652	B. Terry, NYG		1.071
K. Cuyler, ChN		143	L. O'Doul, Phi		10.17	F. Lindstrom, NYG		.379	B. Terry, NYG		.452	G. Hartnett, ChN		.630	C. Hafey, StL		1.059

1930 National League Pitching Leaders

Wins			Losses			Winning Percentage			Games			Games Started			Complete Games		
P. Malone, ChN		20	B. Frey, Cin		18	B. Teachout, ChN		.733	H. Elliott, Phi		48	R. Kremer, Pit		38	E. Brame, Pit		22
R. Kremer, Pit		20	L. French, Pit		18	F. Fitzsimmons, NYG		.731	P. Collins, Phi		47	L. French, Pit		35	P. Malone, ChN		22
F. Fitzsimmons, NYG		19	C. Willoughby, Phi		17	P. Malone, ChN		.690	G. Bush, ChN		46	P. Malone, ChN		35	L. French, Pit		21
5 tied with		17	R. Lucas, Cin		16	T. Zachary, Bos		.688	P. Malone, ChN		45	B. Walker, NYG		34	S. Seibold, Bos		20
			S. Seibold, Bos		16	E. Brame, Pit		.680	H. Pruett, NYG		45	S. Seibold, Bos		33	D. Vance, Bro		20

Shutouts			Saves			Games Finished			Batters Faced			Innings Pitched			Hits Allowed		
C. Root, ChN		4	H. Bell, StL		8	J. Heving, NYG		22	L. French, Pit		1232	R. Kremer, Pit		276.0	R. Kremer, Pit		366
D. Vance, Bro		4	J. Heving, NYG		6	G. Spencer, Pit		22	R. Kremer, Pit		1232	L. French, Pit		274.2	L. French, Pit		325
L. French, Pit		3	W. Clark, Bro		6	H. Elliott, Phi		20	P. Malone, ChN		1197	P. Malone, ChN		271.2	R. Benge, Phi		305
C. Hubbell, NYG		3	3 tied with		5	J. Lindsey, StL		19	S. Seibold, Bos		1109	D. Vance, Bro		258.2	B. Frey, Cin		295
11 tied with		2				2 tied with		18	P. Collins, Phi		1089	S. Seibold, Bos		251.0	2 tied with		291

Home Runs Allowed			Walks			Walks/9 Innings			Strikeouts			Strikeouts/9 Innings			Strikeout/Walk Ratio		
R. Kremer, Pit		29	W. Hallahan, StL		126	R. Lucas, Cin		1.9	W. Hallahan, StL		177	W. Hallahan, StL		6.7	D. Vance, Bro		3.15
F. Fitzsimmons, NYG		26	S. Blake, ChN		99	D. Vance, Bro		1.9	D. Vance, Bro		173	D. Vance, Bro		6.0	C. Hubbell, NYG		2.02
B. Smith, Bos		25	P. Malone, ChN		96	R. Kremer, Pit		2.1	P. Malone, ChN		142	C. Root, ChN		5.1	C. Root, ChN		1.97
L. Sweetland, Phi		24	L. French, Pit		89	E. Brame, Pit		2.1	C. Root, ChN		124	P. Malone, ChN		4.7	P. Malone, ChN		1.48
2 tied with		22	B. Walker, NYG		88	C. Hubbell, NYG		2.2	C. Hubbell, NYG		117	C. Hubbell, NYG		4.4	W. Hallahan, StL		1.40

Earned Run Average			Component ERA			Hit Batsmen			Wild Pitches			Opponent Average			Opponent OBP		
D. Vance, Bro		2.61	D. Vance, Bro		2.74	C. Hubbell, NYG		11	G. Bush, ChN		12	D. Vance, Bro		.246	D. Vance, Bro		.289
C. Hubbell, NYG		3.87	C. Hubbell, NYG		3.65	P. Collins, Phi		10	W. Hallahan, StL		11	W. Hallahan, StL		.260	F. Fitzsimmons, NYG		.314
B. Walker, NYG		3.93	F. Fitzsimmons, NYG		3.73	C. Root, ChN		7	L. Benton, 2tm		9	F. Fitzsimmons, NYG		.266	C. Hubbell, NYG		.327
P. Malone, ChN		3.94	P. Malone, ChN		3.85	B. Grimes, 2tm		7	3 tied with		7	B. Walker, NYG		.268	R. Phelps, Bro		.332
B. Grimes, 2tm		4.07	B. Walker, NYG		3.98	E. Rixey, Cin		7				P. Malone, ChN		.271	B. Walker, NYG		.332

1930 National League Miscellaneous

Managers

Boston	Bill McKechnie	70-84
Brooklyn	Wilbert Robinson	86-68
Chicago	Joe McCarthy	86-64
	Rogers Hornsby	4-0
Cincinnati	Dan Howley	59-95
New York	John McGraw	87-67
Philadelphia	Burt Shotton	52-102
Pittsburgh	Jewel Ens	80-74
St. Louis	Gabby Street	92-62

Awards

STATS Most Valuable Player	Hack Wilson, of, ChN
STATS Cy Young	Pat Malone, ChN
STATS Rookie of the Year	Wally Berger, of, Bos
STATS Manager of the Year	Gabby Street, StL

STATS All-Star Team

C	Gabby Hartnett, ChN	.339	37	122
1B	Bill Terry, NYG	.401	23	129
2B	Frankie Frisch, StL	.346	10	114
3B	Freddy Lindstrom, NYG	.379	22	106
SS	Glenn Wright, Bro	.321	22	126
OF	Babe Herman, Bro	.393	35	130
OF	Chuck Klein, Phi	.386	40	170
OF	Hack Wilson, ChN	.356	56	190
P	Freddie Fitzsimmons, NYG	19-7	4.25	76 K
P	Carl Hubbell, NYG	17-12	3.87	117 K
P	Pat Malone, ChN	20-9	3.94	142 K
P	Dazzy Vance, Bro	17-15	2.61	173 K
RP	Hi Bell, StL	4-3	3.90	8 Sv

Postseason

World Series	StL (NL) 2 vs. Philadelphia (AL) 4

Outstanding Performances

Three-Homer Games

Hack Wilson, ChN	on July 26
Mel Ott, NYG	on August 31

Cycles

F. Lindstrom, NYG	on May 8
Hack Wilson, ChN	on June 23
Chick Hafey, StL	on August 21

Team	Overall					Home Games						Road Games						Park Index		Record by Month					
	W	L	Pct	GB	DIF	W	L	R	OR	HR	OHR	W	L	R	OR	HR	OHR	Run	HR	M/A	May	June	July	Aug	S/O
Philadelphia	107	45	.704	—	140	60	15	446	289	59	37	47	30	412	337	59	36	101	104	5-6	23-4	20-9	26-7	16-9	17-10
New York	94	59	.614	13.5	14	51	25	545	337	85	39	43	34	522	423	70	28	95	128	8-6	14-10	13-14	22-9	16-14	21-6
Washington	92	62	.597	16.0	4	55	22	453	308	13	24	37	40	390	383	36	49	98	44	8-5	16-11	22-8	15-13	14-14	17-11
Cleveland	78	76	.506	30.0	18	45	31	503	405	38	32	33	45	382	428	33	32	115	111	9-4	11-16	14-14	13-16	11-22	10-16
St. Louis	63	91	.409	45.0	3	39	38	407	425	42	48	24	53	315	445	34	36	109	129	3-8	10-14	16-15	13-16	11-22	10-16
Boston	62	90	.408	45.0	0	39	40	332	362	11	29	23	50	293	438	26	25	88	72	3-7	11-18	12-13	12-21	11-16	13-15
Detroit	61	93	.396	47.0	0	36	41	349	432	19	43	25	52	302	404	24	36	111	103	7-7	11-19	8-17	10-21	15-12	10-17
Chicago	56	97	.366	51.5	0	31	45	341	421	11	45	25	52	363	518	16	37	88	107	6-6	11-15	6-21	13-18	14-17	6-20

Clinch Date—Philadelphia 9/15.

Team Batting

Team	G	AB	R	OR	H	2B	3B	HR	TB	RBI	TBB	IBB	SO	HBP	SH	SF	SB	CS	SB%	GDP	Avg	OBP	Slg
New York	155	5608	1067	760	1667	277	78	155	2565	990	748	—	554	27	87	—	138	68	.67	—	.297	.383	.457
Cleveland	155	5445	885	833	1612	321	69	71	2284	812	555	—	433	21	90	—	63	60	.51	—	.296	.363	.419
Philadelphia	153	5377	858	626	1544	311	64	118	2337	798	528	—	543	35	78	—	25	23	.52	—	.287	.355	.435
Washington	156	5576	843	691	1588	308	93	49	2229	788	481	—	459	31	97	—	72	64	.53	—	.285	.345	.400
St. Louis	154	5374	722	870	1455	287	62	76	2094	666	488	—	580	12	61	—	73	80	.48	—	.271	.333	.390
Chicago	156	5481	704	939	1423	238	69	27	1880	649	483	—	445	30	104	—	94	39	.71	—	.260	.323	.343
Detroit	154	5430	651	836	1456	292	69	43	2015	600	480	—	468	20	63	—	117	75	.61	—	.268	.330	.371
Boston	153	5379	625	800	1409	289	34	37	1877	572	405	—	565	11	68	—	42	43	.49	—	.262	.315	.349
AL Total	1236	43670	6355	6355	12154	2323	538	576	17281	5875	4168	—	4047	187	648	—	624	452	.58	—	.278	.344	.396
AL Avg Team	155	5459	794	794	1519	290	67	72	2160	734	521	—	506	23	81	—	78	57	.58	—	.278	.344	.396

Team Pitching

Team	G	CG	ShO	Rel	Sv	IP	H	R	ER	HR	SH	SF	HB	TBB	IBB	SO	WP	Bk	H/9	SO/9	BB/9	OAvg	OOBP	ERA
Philadelphia	153	97	12	82	16	1365.1	1342	626	526	73	63	—	9	457	—	574	20	2	8.8	3.8	3.0	.258	.319	3.47
Washington	156	60	7	145	24	1394.1	1434	691	583	73	70	—	13	498	—	582	21	3	9.3	3.8	3.2	.264	.327	3.76
New York	155	78	4	132	17	1410.1	1461	760	658	67	84	—	25	543	—	686	24	3	9.3	4.4	3.5	.263	.332	4.20
Detroit	154	86	5	92	6	1392.0	1549	836	706	79	99	—	27	597	—	511	26	2	10.0	3.3	3.9	.282	.355	4.56
Boston	153	61	5	161	10	1366.2	1559	800	698	54	96	—	25	473	—	365	18	2	10.3	2.4	3.1	.285	.344	4.60
Cleveland	155	76	6	124	9	1354.2	1577	833	697	64	61	—	25	561	—	470	23	2	10.5	3.1	3.7	.286	.355	4.63
St. Louis	154	65	4	129	10	1362.0	1623	870	720	84	63	—	21	444	—	436	14	1	10.7	2.9	2.9	.293	.348	4.76
Chicago	156	54	6	169	10	1390.1	1613	939	778	82	98	—	33	588	—	421	20	5	10.4	2.7	3.8	.288	.359	5.04
AL Total	1236	577	49	1034	102	11035.2	12158	6355	5366	576	634	—	178	4161	—	4045	166	20	9.9	3.3	3.4	.278	.344	4.38
AL Avg Team	155	72	6	129	13	1379.2	1520	794	671	72	79	—	22	520	—	506	21	3	9.9	3.3	3.4	.278	.344	4.38

Team Fielding

Team	G	PO	A	E	TC	DP	PB	Pct
Washington	156	4188	1684	142	6014	148	7	.976
Philadelphia	153	4088	1614	141	5843	151	10	.976
New York	155	4221	1672	169	6062	131	0	.972
Boston	153	4102	2010	188	6300	127	10	.970
Detroit	154	4159	1802	220	6181	139	7	.964
St. Louis	154	4093	1886	232	6211	160	6	.963
Cleveland	155	4063	1900	232	6195	143	7	.963
Chicago	156	4160	1812	245	6217	131	9	.961
AL Total	1236	33074	14380	1569	49023	1130	56	.968

Team vs. Team Records

	Bos	ChA	Cle	Det	NYA	Phi	StL	Was	Won
Bos	—	12	13	12	6	4	8	7	62
ChA	10	—	7	11	6	3	12	7	56
Cle	9	15	—	13	13	4	16	8	78
Det	10	11	9	—	8	4	11	8	61
NYA	16	15	9	14	—	11	16	13	94
Phi	16	19	18	18	11	—	14	11	107
StL	14	10	6	11	6	8	—	8	63
Was	15	15	14	14	9	11	14	—	92
Lost	90	97	76	93	59	45	91	62	

1931 American League Batting Leaders

Games		At-Bats		Runs		Hits		Doubles		Triples	
J. Cronin, Was	156	E. Averill, Cle	627	L. Gehrig, NYA	163	L. Gehrig, NYA	211	E. Webb, Bos	67	R. Johnson, Det	19
L. Lary, NYA	155	R. Johnson, Det	621	B. Ruth, NYA	149	E. Averill, Cle	209	D. Alexander, Det	47	L. Gehrig, NYA	15
E. Averill, Cle	155	L. Gehrig, NYA	619	E. Averill, Cle	140	A. Simmons, Phi	200	R. Kress, StL	46	L. Blue, ChA	15
L. Gehrig, NYA	155	S. Melillo, StL	617	B. Chapman, NYA	120	B. Ruth, NYA	199	J. Cronin, Was	44	J. Vosmik, Cle	14
L. Blue, ChA	155	H. Manush, Was	616	E. Combs, NYA	120	E. Webb, Bos	196	2 tied with	43	C. Reynolds, ChA	14

Home Runs		Total Bases		Runs Batted In		Walks		Intentional Walks		Strikeouts	
L. Gehrig, NYA	46	L. Gehrig, NYA	410	L. Gehrig, NYA	184	B. Ruth, NYA	128	Statistic unavailable		J. Foxx, Phi	84
B. Ruth, NYA	46	B. Ruth, NYA	374	B. Ruth, NYA	163	L. Blue, ChA	127			J. Levey, StL	83
E. Averill, Cle	32	E. Averill, Cle	361	E. Averill, Cle	143	L. Gehrig, NYA	117			T. Lazzeri, NYA	80
J. Foxx, Phi	30	A. Simmons, Phi	329	A. Simmons, Phi	128	M. Bishop, Phi	112			B. Chapman, NYA	77
G. Goslin, StL	24	G. Goslin, StL	328	J. Cronin, Was	126	L. Lary, NYA	88			L. Blue, ChA	60

Hit By Pitch		Sac Hits		Sac Flies		Stolen Bases		Caught Stealing		GDP	
B. Miller, Phi	10	M. Haas, Phi	19	Statistic unavailable		B. Chapman, NYA	61	B. Chapman, NYA	23	Statistic unavailable	
J. Sewell, NYA	9	J. Sewell, NYA	17			R. Johnson, Det	33	R. Johnson, Det	21		
5 tied with	6	M. Owen, Det	12			J. Burns, StL	19	R. Kress, StL	16		
		W. Kamm, 2tm	12			B. Cissell, ChA	18	B. Myer, Was	14		
		2 tied with	11			T. Lazzeri, NYA	18	J. Stone, Det	13		

Runs Created		Runs Created/27 Outs		Batting Average		On-Base Percentage		Slugging Percentage		OBP+Slugging	
L. Gehrig, NYA	179	B. Ruth, NYA	13.93	A. Simmons, Phi	.390	B. Ruth, NYA	.494	B. Ruth, NYA	.700	B. Ruth, NYA	1.194
B. Ruth, NYA	179	L. Gehrig, NYA	11.19	B. Ruth, NYA	.373	E. Morgan, Cle	.451	L. Gehrig, NYA	.662	L. Gehrig, NYA	1.108
E. Averill, Cle	143	A. Simmons, Phi	11.19	E. Morgan, Cle	.351	L. Gehrig, NYA	.446	A. Simmons, Phi	.641	A. Simmons, Phi	1.085
A. Simmons, Phi	134	E. Morgan, Cle	9.25	M. Cochrane, Phi	.349	A. Simmons, Phi	.444	E. Averill, Cle	.576	E. Averill, Cle	.979
G. Goslin, StL	134	M. Cochrane, Phi	9.08	L. Gehrig, NYA	.341	L. Blue, ChA	.430	J. Foxx, Phi	.567	M. Cochrane, Phi	.976

1931 American League Pitching Leaders

Wins		Losses		Winning Percentage		Games		Games Started		Complete Games	
L. Grove, Phi	31	P. Caraway, ChA	24	L. Grove, Phi	.886	B. Hadley, Was	55	S. Gray, StL	37	W. Ferrell, Cle	27
W. Ferrell, Cle	22	S. Gray, StL	24	F. Marberry, Was	.800	W. Moore, Bos	53	T. Thomas, ChA	36	L. Grove, Phi	27
L. Gomez, NYA	21	J. Russell, Bos	18	R. Mahaffey, Phi	.789	P. Caraway, ChA	51	W. Ferrell, Cle	35	G. Earnshaw, Phi	23
G. Earnshaw, Phi	21	L. Stewart, StL	17	G. Earnshaw, Phi	.750	V. Frasier, ChA	46	R. Walberg, Phi	35	E. Whitehill, Det	22
R. Walberg, Phi	20	2 tied with	16	L. Gomez, NYA	.700	C. Fischer, Was	46	2 tied with	34	L. Stewart, StL	20

Shutouts		Saves		Games Finished		Batters Faced		Innings Pitched		Hits Allowed	
L. Grove, Phi	4	W. Moore, Bos	10	C. Kimsey, StL	35	R. Walberg, Phi	1248	R. Walberg, Phi	291.0	S. Gray, StL	323
G. Earnshaw, Phi	3	B. Hadley, Was	8	W. Moore, Bos	31	W. Ferrell, Cle	1227	L. Grove, Phi	288.2	W. Hudlin, Cle	313
11 tied with	2	C. Kimsey, StL	7	B. Hadley, Was	28	E. Whitehill, Det	1197	G. Earnshaw, Phi	281.2	J. Russell, Bos	298
		F. Marberry, Was	7	C. Sullivan, Det	19	G. Earnshaw, Phi	1174	W. Ferrell, Cle	276.1	R. Walberg, Phi	298
		G. Earnshaw, Phi	6	G. Braxton, 2tm	18	L. Grove, Phi	1160	E. Whitehill, Det	271.2	T. Thomas, ChA	296

Home Runs Allowed		Walks		Walks/9 Innings		Strikeouts		Strikeouts/9 Innings		Strikeout/Walk Ratio	
E. Whitehill, Det	22	W. Ferrell, Cle	130	H. Pennock, NYA	1.4	L. Grove, Phi	175	L. Gomez, NYA	5.6	L. Grove, Phi	2.82
S. Gray, StL	20	V. Frasier, ChA	127	S. Gray, StL	1.9	G. Earnshaw, Phi	152	L. Grove, Phi	5.5	H. Pennock, NYA	2.17
P. Caraway, ChA	17	E. Whitehill, Det	118	L. Grove, Phi	1.9	L. Gomez, NYA	150	R. Ruffing, NYA	5.0	G. Earnshaw, Phi	2.03
T. Thomas, ChA	17	V. Sorrell, Det	114	C. Brown, Cle	2.1	R. Ruffing, NYA	132	G. Earnshaw, Phi	4.9	L. Gomez, NYA	1.76
L. Stewart, StL	17	R. Walberg, Phi	109	G. Blaeholder, StL	2.2	B. Hadley, Was	124	W. Ferrell, Cle	4.0	S. Gray, StL	1.63

Earned Run Average		Component ERA		Hit Batsmen		Wild Pitches		Opponent Average		Opponent OBP	
L. Grove, Phi	2.06	L. Grove, Phi	2.23	A. Herring, Det	8	T. Bridges, Det	9	L. Gomez, NYA	.226	L. Grove, Phi	.271
L. Gomez, NYA	2.63	L. Gomez, NYA	2.56	P. Caraway, ChA	7	G. Uhle, Det	6	L. Grove, Phi	.229	G. Earnshaw, Phi	.288
L. Brown, Was	3.20	G. Earnshaw, Phi	2.71	D. MacFayden, Bos	7	G. Earnshaw, Phi	5	G. Earnshaw, Phi	.236	L. Gomez, NYA	.295
F. Marberry, Was	3.45	D. Coffman, StL	3.00	3 tied with	6	H. Johnson, NYA	5	D. Coffman, StL	.241	D. Coffman, StL	.298
G. Uhle, Det	3.50	G. Uhle, Det	3.11			10 tied with	4	F. Marberry, Was	.252	G. Uhle, Det	.304

1931 American League Miscellaneous

Managers		
Boston	Shano Collins	62-90
Chicago	Donie Bush	56-97
Cleveland	Roger Peckinpaugh	78-76
Detroit	Bucky Harris	61-93
New York	Joe McCarthy	94-59
Philadelphia	Connie Mack	107-45
St. Louis	Bill Killefer	63-91
Washington	Walter Johnson	92-62

Awards

Most Valuable Player	Lefty Grove, p, Phi
STATS Cy Young	Lefty Grove, Phi
STATS Rookie of the Year	Joe Vosmik, of, Cle
STATS Manager of the Year	Connie Mack, Phi

STATS All-Star Team

C	Mickey Cochrane, Phi	.349	17	89
1B	Lou Gehrig, NYA	.341	46	184
2B	Max Bishop, Phi	.294	5	37
3B	Red Kress, StL	.311	16	114
SS	Joe Cronin, Was	.306	12	126
OF	Earl Averill, Cle	.333	32	143
OF	Babe Ruth, NYA	.373	46	163
OF	Al Simmons, Phi	.390	22	128
P	George Earnshaw, Phi	21-7	3.67	152 K
P	Wes Ferrell, Cle	22-12	3.75	123 K
P	Lefty Gomez, NYA	21-9	2.63	150 K
P	Lefty Grove, Phi	31-4	2.06	175 K
RP	Bump Hadley, Was	11-10	3.06	8 Sv

Postseason

World Series	Philadelphia (AL) 3 vs. StL (NL) 4

Outstanding Performances

No-Hitters

Wes Ferrell, Cle	vs. StL on April 29
Bobby Burke, Was	vs. Bos on August 8

Seasons: Standings, Leaders

1931 National League Standings

Team	W	L	Pct	GB	DIF	W	L	R	OR	HR	OHR	W	L	R	OR	HR	OHR	Run	HR	M/A	May	June	July	Aug	S/O
		Overall					Home Games						Road Games					Park Index			Record by Month				
St. Louis	101	53	.656	—	164	54	24	439	320	30	29	47	29	376	294	30	36	110	87	8-3	15-8	19-13	21-13	21-8	17-8
New York	87	65	.572	13.0	5	50	27	379	274	80	47	37	38	389	325	21	24	89	275	9-4	14-9	15-14	13-16	22-11	14-11
Chicago	84	70	.545	17.0	5	50	27	414	311	40	22	34	43	414	399	44	32	89	82	8-3	13-12	15-14	17-15	18-16	13-10
Brooklyn	79	73	.520	21.0	0	46	29	363	317	44	22	33	44	318	356	27	34	104	111	3-10	16-10	17-12	17-15	15-14	11-12
Pittsburgh	75	79	.487	26.0	0	44	33	343	327	25	16	31	46	293	364	16	39	102	75	6-8	11-14	8-18	19-10	15-20	16-9
Philadelphia	66	88	.429	35.0	0	40	36	391	423	51	33	26	52	293	405	30	42	120	120	5-7	13-13	11-16	10-22	16-15	11-15
Boston	64	90	.416	37.0	7	36	41	278	318	16	24	28	49	255	362	18	42	97	67	9-5	10-13	16-15	12-14	12-21	5-22
Cincinnati	58	96	.377	43.0	0	38	39	312	328	6	3	20	57	280	414	15	48	92	14	1-9	8-21	16-15	12-16	8-22	13-13

Clinch Date—St. Louis 9/16.

Team Batting

Team	G	AB	R	OR	H	2B	3B	HR	TB	RBI	TBB	IBB	SO	HBP	SH	SF	SB	CS	SB%	GDP	Avg	OBP	Slg
Chicago	156	5451	828	710	1578	340	66	84	2302	765	577	—	641	25	125	—	49	—	—	—	.289	.360	.422
St. Louis	154	5435	815	614	1554	353	74	60	2235	751	383	—	475	32	90	—	114	—	—	—	.286	.342	.411
New York	153	5372	768	599	1554	251	64	60	2236	727	383	—	395	26	59	—	83	—	—	—	.289	.340	.416
Philadelphia	155	5375	684	828	1502	299	52	81	2148	649	437	—	492	23	100	—	42	—	—	—	.279	.336	.400
Brooklyn	153	5309	681	673	1464	240	77	71	2071	633	409	—	512	27	69	—	45	—	—	—	.276	.331	.390
Pittsburgh	155	5360	636	691	1425	243	70	41	1931	597	493	—	454	16	130	—	59	—	—	—	.266	.330	.360
Cincinnati	154	5343	592	742	1439	241	70	21	1883	562	403	—	463	22	93	—	24	—	—	—	.269	.323	.352
Boston	156	5296	533	680	1367	221	59	34	1808	490	368	—	430	22	123	—	46	—	—	—	.258	.309	.341
NL Total	1236	42941	5537	5537	11883	2188	532	493	16614	5174	3502	—	3862	193	789	—	462	—	—	—	.277	.334	.387
NL Avg Team	155	5368	692	692	1485	274	67	62	2077	647	438	—	483	24	99	—	58	—	—	—	.277	.334	.387

Team Pitching

Team	G	CG	ShO	Rel	Sv	IP	H	R	ER	HR	SH	SF	HB	TBB	IBB	SO	WP	Bk	H/9	SO/9	BB/9	OAvg	OOBP	ERA
New York	153	90	17	105	12	1360.2	1341	599	499	71	71	—	22	422	—	570	20	2	8.9	3.8	2.8	.255	.313	3.30
St. Louis	154	80	17	111	20	1384.2	1470	614	531	65	77	—	22	449	—	626	35	1	9.6	4.1	2.9	.273	.332	3.45
Pittsburgh	155	89	9	97	5	1390.0	1489	691	565	55	102	—	21	442	—	345	23	5	9.6	2.2	2.9	.274	.331	3.66
Brooklyn	153	64	9	142	18	1356.0	1520	673	578	56	94	—	17	351	—	546	17	1	10.1	3.6	2.3	.283	.329	3.84
Boston	156	78	12	122	9	1380.1	1465	680	598	66	113	—	17	406	—	419	20	2	9.6	2.7	2.6	.272	.325	3.90
Chicago	156	80	8	144	8	1385.2	1448	710	612	54	94	—	36	524	—	541	23	2	9.4	3.5	3.4	.268	.337	3.97
Cincinnati	154	70	7	133	6	1345.0	1545	742	630	51	142	—	21	399	—	317	14	3	10.3	2.1	2.7	.294	.346	4.22
Philadelphia	155	60	6	163	16	1360.1	1603	828	692	75	98	—	36	511	—	499	29	6	10.6	3.3	3.4	.293	.358	4.58
NL Total	1236	611	85	1017	94	10962.2	11881	5537	4705	493	791	—	192	3504	—	3863	181	22	9.8	3.2	2.9	.277	.334	3.86
NL Avg Team	155	76	11	127	12	1370.2	1485	692	588	62	99	—	24	438	—	483	23	3	9.8	3.2	2.9	.277	.334	3.86

Team Fielding

Team	G	PO	A	E	TC	DP	PB	Pct
St. Louis	154	4150	1787	160	6097	169	6	.974
New York	153	4076	1772	159	6007	126	8	.974
Cincinnati	154	4028	1826	165	6019	194	9	.973
Chicago	156	4151	1837	169	6157	141	15	.973
Boston	156	4133	1874	170	6177	141	9	.972
Brooklyn	153	4067	1814	187	6068	154	10	.969
Pittsburgh	155	4166	1801	194	6161	167	7	.969
Philadelphia	155	4077	1787	210	6074	149	9	.965
NL Total	1236	32848	14498	1414	48760	1241	73	.971

Team vs. Team Records

	Bos	Bro	ChN	Cin	NYG	Phi	Pit	StL	Won
Bos	—	11	8	8	6	11	11	9	64
Bro	11	—	14	10	10	13	11	10	79
ChN	14	8	—	14	12	14	14	8	84
Cin	14	12	8	—	7	9	6	2	58
NYG	16	10	10	15	—	14	12	10	87
Phi	11	9	8	13	8	—	13	4	66
Pit	11	11	8	16	10	9	—	10	75
StL	13	12	14	20	12	18	12	—	101
Lost	90	73	70	96	65	88	79	53	

Seasons: Standings, Leaders

1931 National League Batting Leaders

Games		At-Bats		Runs		Hits		Doubles		Triples	
W. Berger, Bos	156	L. Waner, Pit	681	C. Klein, Phi	121	L. Waner, Pit	214	S. Adams, StL	46	B. Terry, NYG	20
W. English, ChN	156	W. English, ChN	634	B. Terry, NYG	121	B. Terry, NYG	213	W. Berger, Bos	44	B. Herman, Bro	16
P. Traynor, Pit	155	W. Berger, Bos	617	W. English, ChN	117	W. English, ChN	202	D. Bartell, Phi	43	P. Traynor, Pit	15
3 tied with	154	P. Traynor, Pit	615	K. Cuyler, ChN	110	K. Cuyler, ChN	202	B. Herman, Bro	43	D. Bissonette, Bro	14
		K. Cuyler, ChN	613	M. Ott, NYG	104	C. Klein, Phi	200	B. Terry, NYG	43	2 tied with	13

Home Runs		Total Bases		Runs Batted In		Walks		Intentional Walks		Strikeouts	
C. Klein, Phi	31	C. Klein, Phi	347	C. Klein, Phi	121	M. Ott, NYG	80	Statistic unavailable		N. Cullop, Cin	86
M. Ott, NYG	29	B. Terry, NYG	323	M. Ott, NYG	115	P. Waner, Pit	73			W. English, ChN	80
W. Berger, Bos	19	B. Herman, Bro	320	B. Terry, NYG	112	K. Cuyler, ChN	72			W. Berger, Bos	70
B. Arlett, Phi	18	W. Berger, Bos	316	P. Traynor, Pit	103	G. Grantham, Pit	71			H. Wilson, ChN	69
B. Herman, Bro	18	K. Cuyler, ChN	290	B. Herman, Bro	97	W. English, ChN	68			G. Watkins, StL	66

Hit By Pitch		Sac Hits		Sac Flies		Stolen Bases		Caught Stealing		GDP	
V. Barton, ChN	9	F. Maguire, Bos	31	Statistic unavailable		F. Frisch, StL	28	Statistic unavailable		Statistic unavailable	
W. English, ChN	7	D. Bartell, Phi	30			B. Herman, Bro	17				
J. Vergez, NYG	6	K. Cuyler, ChN	20			P. Martin, StL	16				
J. Frederick, Bro	6	W. English, ChN	18			S. Adams, StL	16				
W. Gilbert, Bro	6	2 tied with	17			G. Watkins, StL	15				

Runs Created		Runs Created/27 Outs		Batting Average		On-Base Percentage		Slugging Percentage		OBP+Slugging	
B. Terry, NYG	122	C. Hafey, StL	8.82	C. Hafey, StL	.349	R. Hornsby, ChN	.421	C. Klein, Phi	.584	R. Hornsby, ChN	.996
C. Klein, Phi	119	R. Hornsby, ChN	8.55	B. Terry, NYG	.349	C. Hafey, StL	.404	R. Hornsby, ChN	.574	C. Klein, Phi	.982
K. Cuyler, ChN	115	J. Bottomley, StL	8.31	J. Bottomley, StL	.348	K. Cuyler, ChN	.404	C. Hafey, StL	.569	C. Hafey, StL	.973
B. Herman, Bro	110	B. Terry, NYG	7.86	C. Klein, Phi	.337	P. Waner, Pit	.404	M. Ott, NYG	.545	M. Ott, NYG	.937
W. Berger, Bos	107	C. Klein, Phi	7.74	L. O'Doul, Bro	.336	J. Bottomley, StL	.403	B. Arlett, Phi	.538	J. Bottomley, StL	.937

1931 National League Pitching Leaders

Wins		Losses		Winning Percentage		Games		Games Started		Complete Games	
W. Hallahan, StL	19	S. Johnson, Cin	19	J. Haines, StL	.800	J. Elliott, Phi	52	H. Meine, Pit	35	R. Lucas, Cin	24
J. Elliott, Phi	19	R. Benge, Phi	18	P. Derringer, StL	.692	S. Johnson, Cin	42	L. French, Pit	33	E. Brandt, Bos	23
H. Meine, Pit	19	S. Seibold, Bos	18	W. Hallahan, StL	.679	P. Collins, Phi	42	S. Johnson, Cin	33	H. Meine, Pit	22
3 tied with	18	P. Collins, Phi	16	G. Bush, ChN	.667	4 tied with	39	F. Fitzsimmons, NYG	33	C. Hubbell, NYG	21
		3 tied with	15	B. Grimes, StL	.654			2 tied with	31	L. French, Pit	20

Shutouts		Saves		Games Finished		Batters Faced		Innings Pitched		Hits Allowed	
B. Walker, NYG	6	J. Quinn, Bro	15	J. Quinn, Bro	29	H. Meine, Pit	1202	H. Meine, Pit	284.0	L. French, Pit	301
P. Derringer, StL	4	J. Lindsey, StL	7	J. Lindsey, StL	19	L. French, Pit	1170	L. French, Pit	275.2	J. Elliott, Phi	288
C. Hubbell, NYG	4	J. Elliott, Phi	5	H. Haid, Bos	17	S. Johnson, Cin	1113	S. Johnson, Cin	262.1	H. Meine, Pit	278
F. Fitzsimmons, NYG	4	W. Hallahan, StL	4	3 tied with	16	J. Elliott, Phi	1098	F. Fitzsimmons, NYG	253.2	S. Johnson, Cin	273
9 tied with	3	P. Collins, Phi	4			W. Hallahan, StL	1061	C. Root, ChN	251.0	P. Collins, Phi	268

Home Runs Allowed		Walks		Walks/9 Innings		Strikeouts		Strikeouts/9 Innings		Strikeout/Walk Ratio	
F. Rhem, StL	17	W. Hallahan, StL	112	S. Johnson, StL	1.4	W. Hallahan, StL	159	D. Vance, Bro	6.2	D. Vance, Bro	2.83
F. Fitzsimmons, NYG	16	P. Malone, ChN	88	R. Lucas, Cin	1.5	C. Hubbell, NYG	155	W. Hallahan, StL	5.8	S. Johnson, StL	2.83
J. Elliott, Phi	15	H. Meine, Pit	87	W. Clark, Bro	2.0	D. Vance, Bro	150	P. Derringer, StL	5.7	C. Hubbell, NYG	2.31
3 tied with	14	P. Collins, Phi	83	T. Zachary, Bos	2.1	P. Derringer, StL	134	C. Hubbell, NYG	5.6	P. Derringer, StL	2.06
		J. Elliott, Phi	83	D. Vance, Bro	2.2	C. Root, ChN	131	C. Root, ChN	4.7	R. Benge, Phi	1.92

Earned Run Average		Component ERA		Hit Batsmen		Wild Pitches		Opponent Average		Opponent OBP	
B. Walker, NYG	2.26	B. Walker, NYG	2.44	B. Grimes, StL	10	W. Hallahan, StL	11	C. Hubbell, NYG	.227	C. Hubbell, NYG	.282
C. Hubbell, NYG	2.65	C. Hubbell, NYG	2.52	E. Baecht, ChN	8	C. Dudley, Phi	7	B. Walker, NYG	.231	B. Walker, NYG	.283
E. Brandt, Bos	2.92	S. Johnson, StL	2.79	C. Root, ChN	7	S. Bolen, Phi	7	E. Brandt, Bos	.244	S. Johnson, StL	.286
H. Meine, Pit	2.98	E. Brandt, Bos	2.88	H. Meine, Pit	7	5 tied with	6	F. Fitzsimmons, NYG	.251	F. Fitzsimmons, NYG	.296
S. Johnson, StL	3.00	F. Fitzsimmons, NYG	2.94	2 tied with	6			C. Root, ChN	.252	B. Smith, ChN	.303

1931 National League Miscellaneous

Managers		
Boston	Bill McKechnie	64-90
Brooklyn	Wilbert Robinson	79-73
Chicago	Rogers Hornsby	84-70
Cincinnati	Dan Howley	58-96
New York	John McGraw	87-65
Philadelphia	Burt Shotton	66-88
Pittsburgh	Jewel Ens	75-79
St. Louis	Gabby Street	101-53

Awards

Most Valuable Player	Frankie Frisch, 2b, StL
STATS Cy Young	Ed Brandt, Bos
STATS Rookie of the Year	Paul Derringer, p, StL
STATS Manager of the Year	Gabby Street, StL

STATS All-Star Team

C	Gabby Hartnett, ChN	.282	8	70
1B	Bill Terry, NYG	.349	9	112
2B	Frankie Frisch, StL	.311	4	82
3B	Pie Traynor, Pit	.298	2	103
SS	Woody English, ChN	.319	2	53
OF	Chick Hafey, StL	.349	16	95
OF	Chuck Klein, Phi	.337	31	121
OF	Mel Ott, NYG	.292	29	115
P	Ed Brandt, Bos	18-11	2.92	112 K
P	Freddie Fitzsimmons, NYG	18-11	3.05	78 K
P	Wild Bill Hallahan, StL	19-9	3.29	159 K
P	Heinie Meine, Pit	19-13	2.98	58 K
RP	Jack Quinn, Bro	5-4	2.66	15 Sv

Postseason

World Series	StL (NL) 4 vs. Philadelphia (AL) 3

Outstanding Performances

Three-Homer Games

R. Hornsby, ChN	on April 24
George Watkins, StL	on June 24

Cycles

Babe Herman, Bro	on May 18
Chuck Klein, Phi	on July 1
Babe Herman, Bro	on July 24

1932 American League Standings

	Overall					Home Games						Road Games						Park Index		Record by Month					
Team	W	L	Pct	GB	DIF	W	L	R	OR	HR	OHR	W	L	R	OR	HR	OHR	Run	HR	M/A	May	June	July	Aug	S/O
New York	107	47	.695	—	141	62	15	482	300	81	44	45	32	520	424	79	49	83	98	10-3	18-8	20-8	20-14	23-5	16-9
Philadelphia	94	60	.610	13.0	1	51	26	572	406	109	80	43	34	409	346	63	32	130	199	4-10	19-8	17-12	21-12	19-9	14-9
Washington	93	61	.604	14.0	23	51	26	431	325	21	26	42	35	409	391	40	47	95	54	11-4	14-13	12-14	19-14	18-9	19-7
Cleveland	87	65	.572	19.0	1	43	33	460	401	36	33	44	32	385	346	42	37	118	87	11-6	13-14	13-12	21-10	14-16	15-7
Detroit	76	75	.503	29.5	9	42	34	423	399	29	50	34	41	376	388	51	39	106	87	10-5	14-11	14-12	13-18	14-16	11-13
St. Louis	63	91	.409	44.0	0	33	42	385	428	47	56	30	49	351	470	20	47	104	162	6-10	13-14	16-8	11-22	9-17	8-20
Chicago	49	102	.325	56.5	3	28	49	300	390	10	36	21	53	367	507	26	52	76	57	5-11	10-16	8-16	10-21	6-23	10-15
Boston	43	111	.279	64.0	0	27	50	295	439	18	31	16	61	271	476	35	48	98	59	3-11	4-21	5-23	14-18	11-19	6-19

Clinch Date—New York 9/13.

Team Batting

Team	G	AB	R	OR	H	2B	3B	HR	TB	RBI	TBB	IBB	SO	HBP	SH	SF	SB	CS	SB%	GDP	Avg	OBP	Slg
New York	156	5477	1002	724	1564	279	82	160	2487	954	766	—	527	27	76	—	77	66	.54	—	.286	.376	.454
Philadelphia	154	5537	981	752	1606	303	52	172	2529	923	647	—	630	21	94	—	38	23	.62	—	.290	.366	.457
Cleveland	153	5412	845	747	1544	310	74	78	2236	786	566	—	454	32	110	—	52	54	.49	—	.285	.356	.413
Washington	154	5515	840	716	1565	303	100	61	2251	776	505	—	442	24	95	—	70	47	.60	—	.284	.346	.408
Detroit	153	5409	799	787	1479	291	80	80	2170	742	486	—	523	13	84	—	103	49	.68	—	.273	.335	.401
St. Louis	154	5449	736	898	1502	274	69	67	2115	684	507	—	528	19	90	—	69	62	.53	—	.276	.339	.388
Chicago	152	5336	667	897	1426	274	56	36	1920	608	459	—	386	18	89	—	89	58	.61	—	.267	.327	.360
Boston	154	5295	566	915	1331	253	57	53	1857	529	469	—	539	12	80	—	46	46	.50	—	.251	.314	.351
AL Total	1230	43430	6436	6436	12017	2287	570	707	17565	6002	4405	—	4029	166	718	—	544	405	.57	—	.277	.346	.404
AL Avg Team	154	5429	805	805	1502	286	71	88	2196	750	551	—	504	21	90	—	68	51	.57	—	.277	.346	.404

Team Pitching

Team	G	CG	ShO	Rel	Sv	IP	H	R	ER	HR	SH	SF	HB	TBB	IBB	SO	WP	Bk	H/9	SO/9	BB/9	OAvg	OOBP	ERA
New York	156	96	11	93	15	1408.0	1425	724	623	93	90	—	20	561	—	780	27	1	9.1	5.0	3.6	.260	.331	3.98
Cleveland	153	94	6	92	8	1377.1	1506	747	630	70	66	—	12	446	—	439	18	1	9.8	2.9	2.9	.273	.329	4.12
Washington	154	66	11	139	22	1383.1	1463	716	639	73	76	—	9	526	—	437	17	3	9.5	2.8	3.4	.271	.337	4.16
Detroit	153	67	9	120	17	1362.2	1421	787	651	89	106	—	31	592	—	521	26	1	9.4	3.4	3.9	.269	.346	4.30
Philadelphia	154	95	10	92	10	1386.0	1477	752	686	112	75	—	18	511	—	595	21	1	9.6	3.9	3.3	.271	.336	4.45
Chicago	152	50	2	166	12	1348.2	1551	897	723	88	90	—	29	580	—	379	27	5	10.4	2.5	3.9	.287	.359	4.82
St. Louis	154	63	7	150	11	1376.2	1592	898	766	103	94	—	21	574	—	496	23	5	10.4	3.2	3.8	.290	.359	5.01
Boston	154	42	3	188	7	1362.0	1574	915	759	79	117	—	30	612	—	365	27	7	10.4	2.4	4.0	.289	.364	5.02
AL Total	1230	573	59	1040	102	11004.2	12009	6436	5477	707	714	—	170	4402	—	4012	186	24	9.8	3.3	3.6	.277	.345	4.48
AL Avg Team	154	72	7	130	13	1375.2	1501	805	685	88	89	—	21	550	—	502	23	3	9.8	3.3	3.6	.277	.345	4.48

Team Fielding

Team	G	PO	A	E	TC	DP	PB	Pct
Philadelphia	154	4160	1736	124	6020	142	15	.979
Washington	154	4145	1741	125	6011	157	6	.979
St. Louis	154	4128	1798	188	6114	156	6	.969
Detroit	153	4081	1774	187	6042	154	5	.969
Cleveland	153	4132	1823	191	6146	129	6	.969
New York	156	4227	1623	188	6038	124	10	.969
Boston	154	4086	1956	233	6275	165	5	.963
Chicago	152	4033	1914	264	6211	170	10	.957
AL Total	1230	32992	14365	1500	48857	1197	63	.969

Team vs. Team Records

	Bos	ChA	Cle	Det	NYA	Phi	StL	Was	Won
Bos	—	12	4	6	5	4	7	5	43
ChA	10	—	7	8	5	7	8	4	49
Cle	18	14	—	11	7	10	16	11	87
Det	16	12	10	—	5	7	15	11	76
NYA	17	17	15	17	—	14	16	11	107
Phi	18	15	12	15	8	—	16	10	94
StL	15	14	6	7	6	6	—	9	63
Was	17	18	11	11	11	12	13	—	93
Lost	111	102	65	75	47	60	91	61	

1932 American League Batting Leaders

Games		At-Bats		Runs		Hits		Doubles		Triples	
L. Gehrig, NYA	156	A. Simmons, Phi	670	J. Foxx, Phi	151	A. Simmons, Phi	216	E. McNair, Phi	47	J. Cronin, Was	18
S. Melillo, StL	154	E. Averill, Cle	631	H. Manush, Was	144	H. Manush, Was	214	C. Gehringer, Det	44	T. Lazzeri, NYA	16
J. Foxx, Phi	154	H. Manush, Was	625	E. Combs, NYA	143	J. Foxx, Phi	213	J. Cronin, Was	43	B. Myer, Was	16
A. Simmons, Phi	154	J. Vosmik, Cle	621	L. Gehrig, NYA	138	L. Gehrig, NYA	208	3 tied with	42	B. Chapman, NYA	15
3 tied with	153	D. Porter, Cle	621	H. Manush, Was	121	E. Averill, Cle	198			2 tied with	14

Home Runs		Total Bases		Runs Batted In		Walks		Intentional Walks		Strikeouts	
J. Foxx, Phi	58	J. Foxx, Phi	438	J. Foxx, Phi	169	B. Ruth, NYA	130	Statistic unavailable		B. Campbell, 2tm	104
B. Ruth, NYA	41	L. Gehrig, NYA	370	A. Simmons, Phi	151	J. Foxx, Phi	116			J. Foxx, Phi	96
A. Simmons, Phi	35	A. Simmons, Phi	367	L. Gehrig, NYA	151	M. Bishop, Phi	110			A. Simmons, Phi	76
L. Gehrig, NYA	34	E. Averill, Cle	359	B. Ruth, NYA	137	L. Gehrig, NYA	108			U. Pickering, Bos	71
E. Averill, Cle	32	H. Manush, Was	325	E. Averill, Cle	124	M. Cochrane, Phi	100			R. Johnson, 2tm	67

Hit By Pitch		Sac Hits		Sac Flies		Stolen Bases		Caught Stealing		GDP	
B. Campbell, 2tm	6	M. Haas, Phi	27	Statistic unavailable		B. Chapman, NYA	38	B. Chapman, NYA	18	Statistic unavailable	
E. Averill, Cle	6	J. Burns, StL	21			G. Walker, Det	30	L. Funk, ChA	15		
4 tied with	5	O. Bluege, Was	20			R. Johnson, 2tm	20	B. Cissell, 2tm	15		
		H. Davis, Det	17			B. Cissell, 2tm	18	3 tied with	11		
		2 tied with	14			3 tied with	17				

Runs Created		Runs Created/27 Outs		Batting Average		On-Base Percentage		Slugging Percentage		OBP+Slugging	
J. Foxx, Phi	189	J. Foxx, Phi	13.19	D. Alexander, 2tm	.367	B. Ruth, NYA	.489	J. Foxx, Phi	.749	J. Foxx, Phi	1.218
L. Gehrig, NYA	163	B. Ruth, NYA	12.83	J. Foxx, Phi	.364	J. Foxx, Phi	.469	B. Ruth, NYA	.661	B. Ruth, NYA	1.150
B. Ruth, NYA	147	L. Gehrig, NYA	10.78	L. Gehrig, NYA	.349	D. Alexander, 2tm	.454	L. Gehrig, NYA	.621	L. Gehrig, NYA	1.072
E. Averill, Cle	139	D. Alexander, 2tm	8.68	H. Manush, Was	.342	L. Gehrig, NYA	.451	E. Averill, Cle	.569	D. Alexander, 2tm	.966
A. Simmons, Phi	135	E. Averill, Cle	8.34	B. Ruth, NYA	.341	M. Bishop, Phi	.412	A. Simmons, Phi	.548	E. Averill, Cle	.961

1932 American League Pitching Leaders

Wins		Losses		Winning Percentage		Games		Games Started		Complete Games	
G. Crowder, Was	26	B. Hadley, 2tm	21	J. Allen, NYA	.810	F. Marberry, Was	54	G. Crowder, Was	39	L. Grove, Phi	27
L. Grove, Phi	25	L. Stewart, StL	19	L. Gomez, NYA	.774	S. Gray, StL	52	G. Blaeholder, StL	36	W. Ferrell, Cle	26
L. Gomez, NYA	24	M. Gaston, ChA	17	R. Ruffing, NYA	.720	G. Crowder, Was	50	B. Hadley, 2tm	35	R. Ruffing, NYA	22
W. Ferrell, Cle	23	B. Weiland, Bos	16	L. Grove, Phi	.714	3 tied with	47	W. Ferrell, Cle	34	4 tied with	21
M. Weaver, NYA	22	3 tied with	15	T. Freitas, Phi	.706			R. Walberg, Phi	34		

Shutouts		Saves		Games Finished		Batters Faced		Innings Pitched		Hits Allowed	
T. Bridges, Det	4	F. Marberry, Was	13	C. Kimsey, 2tm	29	G. Crowder, Was	1356	G. Crowder, Was	327.0	G. Crowder, Was	319
L. Grove, Phi	4	W. Moore, 2tm	8	W. Moore, 2tm	28	W. Ferrell, Cle	1244	L. Grove, Phi	291.2	R. Walberg, Phi	305
7 tied with	3	C. Hogsett, Det	7	R. Faber, ChA	28	L. Grove, Phi	1207	W. Ferrell, Cle	287.2	G. Blaeholder, StL	304
		L. Grove, Phi	7	C. Hogsett, Det	27	R. Walberg, Phi	1203	R. Walberg, Phi	272.0	W. Ferrell, Cle	299
		R. Faber, ChA	6	F. Marberry, Was	26	B. Hadley, 2tm	1155	L. Gomez, NYA	265.1	C. Brown, Cle	298

Home Runs Allowed		Walks		Walks/9 Innings		Strikeouts		Strikeouts/9 Innings		Strikeout/Walk Ratio	
G. Earnshaw, Phi	28	B. Hadley, 2tm	171	C. Brown, Cle	1.7	R. Ruffing, NYA	190	R. Ruffing, NYA	6.6	L. Grove, Phi	2.38
R. Mahaffey, Phi	27	T. Bridges, Det	119	G. Crowder, Was	2.1	L. Grove, Phi	188	L. Gomez, NYA	6.0	L. Gomez, NYA	1.68
L. Gomez, NYA	23	R. Ruffing, NYA	115	M. Harder, Cle	2.4	L. Gomez, NYA	176	L. Grove, Phi	5.8	R. Ruffing, NYA	1.65
B. Hadley, 2tm	23	M. Weaver, Was	112	L. Grove, Phi	2.4	B. Hadley, 2tm	145	B. Hadley, 2tm	5.3	J. Allen, NYA	1.43
L. Stewart, StL	22	L. Gomez, NYA	105	L. Brown, Was	2.4	G. Pipgras, NYA	111	J. Allen, NYA	5.1	G. Crowder, Was	1.34

Earned Run Average		Component ERA		Hit Batsmen		Wild Pitches		Opponent Average		Opponent OBP	
L. Grove, Phi	2.84	L. Grove, Phi	2.74	B. Hadley, 2tm	8	G. Earnshaw, Phi	9	R. Ruffing, NYA	.226	L. Grove, Phi	.292
R. Ruffing, NYA	3.09	J. Allen, NYA	2.89	B. Marrow, Det	6	I. Andrews, 2tm	7	J. Allen, NYA	.228	G. Crowder, Was	.295
T. Lyons, ChA	3.28	G. Crowder, Was	2.93	B. Weiland, Bos	6	L. Brown, Was	7	T. Bridges, Det	.233	J. Allen, NYA	.306
G. Crowder, Was	3.33	R. Ruffing, NYA	3.06	G. Pipgras, NYA	6	5 tied with	6	L. Grove, Phi	.241	R. Ruffing, NYA	.311
T. Bridges, Det	3.36	V. Sorrell, Det	3.38	4 tied with	5			G. Crowder, Was	.252	C. Brown, Cle	.314

1932 American League Miscellaneous

Managers		
Boston	Shano Collins	11-44
	Marty McManus	32-67
Chicago	Lew Fonseca	49-102
Cleveland	Roger Peckinpaugh	87-65
Detroit	Bucky Harris	76-75
New York	Joe McCarthy	107-47
Philadelphia	Connie Mack	94-60
St. Louis	Bill Killefer	63-91
Washington	Walter Johnson	93-61

Awards	
Most Valuable Player	Jimmie Foxx, 1b, Phi
STATS Cy Young	Lefty Grove, Phi
STATS Rookie of the Year	Johnny Allen, p, NYA
STATS Manager of the Year	Joe McCarthy, NYA

STATS All-Star Team

C	Mickey Cochrane, Phi	.293	23	112
1B	Jimmie Foxx, Phi	.364	58	169
2B	Tony Lazzeri, NYA	.300	15	113
3B	Willie Kamm, Cle	.286	3	83
SS	Joe Cronin, Was	.318	6	116
OF	Earl Averill, Cle	.314	32	124
OF	Babe Ruth, NYA	.341	41	137
OF	Al Simmons, Phi	.322	35	151
P	General Crowder, Was	26-13	3.33	103 K
P	Wes Ferrell, Cle	23-13	3.66	105 K
P	Lefty Grove, Phi	25-10	2.84	188 K
P	Red Ruffing, NYA	18-7	3.09	190 K
RP	Firpo Marberry, Was	8-4	4.01	13 Sv

Postseason	
World Series	New York (AL) 4 vs. Chicago (NL) 0

Outstanding Performances

Four-Homer Games
Lou Gehrig, NYA   on June 3

Three-Homer Games
Goose Goslin, StL   on June 23
Ben Chapman, NYA   on July 9
Jimmie Foxx, Phi   on July 10
Al Simmons, Phi   on July 15

Cycles
Tony Lazzeri, NYA   on June 3
M. Cochrane, Phi   on July 22

1932 National League Standings

Team	Overall					Home Games						Road Games						Park index		Record by Month					
	W	L	Pct	GB	DIF	W	L	R	OR	HR	OHR	W	L	R	OR	HR	OHR	Run	HR	M/A	May	June	July	Aug	S/O
Chicago	90	64	.584	—	102	53	24	390	303	31	33	37	40	330	330	38	35	105	88	11-3	16-13	9-14	17-15	22-6	15-13
Pittsburgh	86	68	.558	4.0	44	45	31	352	338	22	25	41	37	349	373	26	61	98	55	6-9	14-11	14-7	25-13	10-20	17-8
Brooklyn	81	73	.526	9.0	1	44	34	378	353	59	31	37	39	374	394	51	41	93	95	4-9	17-13	14-14	15-16	20-10	11-11
Philadelphia	78	76	.506	12.0	7	45	32	507	429	86	71	33	44	337	367	36	36	133	218	8-7	11-18	18-11	16-14	12-16	13-10
Boston	77	77	.500	13.0	22	44	33	285		27	20	33	44	350	370	36	41	81	61	10-3	14-15	12-14	15-17	12-19	14-9
St. Louis	72	82	.468	18.0	2	42	35	354	357	37	38	30	47	330	360	39	38	103	97	5-10	14-14	14-9	14-19	16-13	9-17
New York	72	82	.468	18.0	0	37	40	362	359	78	71	35	42	393	347	38	41	97	189	5-8	12-14	13-11	15-20	14-17	13-12
Cincinnati	60	94	.390	30.0	1	33	44	270	344	11	11	27	50	305	371	36	58	91	23	8-8	16-16	7-21	13-16	11-16	5-17

Clinch Date—Chicago 9/20.

Team Batting

Team	G	AB	R	OR	H	2B	3B	HR	TB	RBI	TBB	IBB	SO	HBP	SH	SF	SB	CS	SB%	GDP	Avg	OBP	Slg
Philadelphia	154	5510	844	796	1608	330	67	122	2438	780	446	—	547	27	125	—	71	—	—	—	.292	.348	.442
New York	154	5530	755	706	1527	263	54	116	2246	718	348	—	391	23	49	—	31	—	—	—	.276	.322	.406
Brooklyn	154	5433	752	747	1538	296	59	110	2282	703	388	—	574	24	99	—	61	—	—	—	.283	.334	.420
Chicago	154	5462	720	633	1519	296	60	69	2142	665	398	—	514	28	118	—	48	—	—	—	.278	.330	.392
Pittsburgh	154	5421	701	711	1543	274	90	48	2141	653	358	—	385	31	96	—	71	—	—	—	.285	.333	.395
St. Louis	156	5458	684	717	1467	307	51	76	2104	626	420	—	514	25	69	—	92	—	—	—	.269	.324	.385
Boston	155	5506	649	655	1460	262	53	63	2017	594	347	—	496	19	105	—	36	—	—	—	.265	.324	.366
Cincinnati	155	5443	715	715	1429	265	68	47	1971	546	436	—	436	20	100	—	35	—	—	—	.263	.320	.362
NL Total	1236	43763	5680	5680	12091	2293	502	651	17341	5285	3141	—	3857	197	761	—	445	—	—	—	.276	.328	.396
NL Avg Team	155	5470	710	710	1511	287	63	81	2168	661	393	—	482	25	95	—	56	—	—	—	.276	.328	.396

Team Pitching

Team	G	CG	ShO	Rel	Sv	IP	H	R	ER	HR	SH	SF	HB	TBB	IBB	SO	WP	Bk	H/9	SO/9	BB/9	OAvg	OOBP	ERA
Chicago	154	79	9	132	7	1401.0	1444	633	536	68	75	—	28	420	—	527	26	2	9.3	3.4	2.6	.264	.319	3.44
Boston	155	72	8	124	8	1414.0	1483	655	554	61	128	—	29	420	—	440	15	1	9.4	2.8	2.7	.272	.328	3.53
Pittsburgh	154	71	12	126	12	1377.0	1472	711	573	86	85	—	18	338	—	377	24	1	9.6	2.5	2.2	.270	.314	3.75
Cincinnati	155	83	6	112	6	1394.2	1505	715	587	69	94	—	20	276	—	359	15	3	9.7	2.3	1.8	.274	.311	3.79
New York	154	57	3	156	16	1375.1	1533	706	585	112	92	—	24	387	—	506	23	3	10.0	3.3	2.5	.280	.330	3.83
St. Louis	156	70	13	139	9	1396.0	1533	717	616	76	107	—	23	455	—	681	36	3	9.9	4.4	2.9	.282	.340	3.97
Brooklyn	154	61	7	153	16	1379.2	1538	747	655	72	92	—	25	403	—	497	24	1	10.0	3.2	2.6	.282	.334	4.27
Philadelphia	154	59	4	160	17	1384.0	1589	796	687	107	85	—	30	450	—	459	19	3	10.3	3.0	2.9	.287	.344	4.47
NL Total	1236	552	62	1102	91	11121.2	12097	5680	4793	651	758	—	197	3138	—	3846	182	17	9.8	3.1	2.5	.276	.328	3.88
NL Avg Team	155	69	8	138	11	1390.2	1512	710	599	81	95	—	25	392	—	481	23	2	9.8	3.1	2.5	.276	.328	3.88

Team Fielding

Team	G	PO	A	E	TC	DP	PB	Pct
Boston	155	4235	1900	152	6287	145	7	.976
Chicago	154	4199	1937	173	6309	146	17	.973
St. Louis	156	4191	1748	175	6114	155	7	.971
Cincinnati	155	4180	1836	178	6194	129	20	.971
Brooklyn	154	4151	1969	183	6303	169	7	.971
New York	154	4126	1898	191	6215	143	10	.969
Pittsburgh	154	4131	1640	185	5956	124	9	.969
Philadelphia	154	4149	1755	194	6098	133	4	.968
NL Total	1236	33362	14683	1431	49476	1144	81	.971

Team vs. Team Records

	Bos	Bro	ChN	Cin	NYG	Phi	Pit	StL	Won
Bos	—	15	8	9	11	11	10	13	77
Bro	7	—	10	15	15	8	12	14	81
ChN	14	12	—	12	15	16	9	12	90
Cin	13	7	10	—	7	9	8	6	60
NYG	11	7	7	15	—	11	7	14	72
Phi	11	14	6	13	11	—	14	9	78
Pit	12	10	13	14	15	8	—	14	86
StL	9	8	10	16	8	13	8	—	72
Lost	77	73	64	94	82	76	68	82	

1932 National League Batting Leaders

Games		At-Bats		Runs		Hits		Doubles		Triples	
10 tied with	154	H. Critz, NYG	659	C. Klein, Phi	152	C. Klein, Phi	226	P. Waner, Pit	62	B. Herman, Cin	19
		B. Herman, ChN	656	B. Terry, NYG	124	B. Terry, NYG	225	C. Klein, Phi	50	G. Suhr, Pit	16
		C. Klein, Phi	650	L. O'Doul, Bro	120	L. O'Doul, Bro	219	R. Stephenson, ChN	49	C. Klein, Phi	15
		B. Terry, NYG	643	M. Ott, NYG	119	P. Waner, Pit	215	D. Bartell, Phi	48	3 tied with	11
		P. Waner, Pit	630	D. Bartell, Phi	118	B. Herman, ChN	206	4 tied with	42		

Home Runs		Total Bases		Runs Batted In		Walks		Intentional Walks		Strikeouts	
C. Klein, Phi	38	C. Klein, Phi	420	D. Hurst, Phi	143	M. Ott, NYG	100	Statistic unavailable		H. Wilson, Bro	85
M. Ott, NYG	38	B. Terry, NYG	373	C. Klein, Phi	137	D. Hurst, Phi	65			W. English, ChN	73
B. Terry, NYG	28	M. Ott, NYG	340	P. Whitney, Phi	124	D. Bartell, Phi	64			R. Collins, StL	67
D. Hurst, Phi	24	L. O'Doul, Bro	330	M. Ott, NYG	123	G. Suhr, Pit	63			W. Berger, Bos	66
H. Wilson, Bro	23	P. Waner, Pit	321	H. Wilson, Bro	123	2 tied with	60			P. Whitney, Phi	66

Hit By Pitch		Sac Hits		Sac Flies		Stolen Bases		Caught Stealing		GDP	
G. Watkins, StL	8	D. Bartell, Phi	35	Statistic unavailable		C. Klein, Phi	20	Statistic unavailable		Statistic unavailable	
T. Piet, Pit	7	B. Herman, ChN	22			T. Piet, Pit	19				
D. Hurst, Phi	7	B. Urbanski, Bos	22			G. Watkins, StL	18				
L. O'Doul, Bro	7	J. Stripp, Bro	21			F. Frisch, StL	18				
2 tied with	6	P. Whitney, Phi	19			K. Davis, Phi	16				

Runs Created		Runs Created/27 Outs		Batting Average		On-Base Percentage		Slugging Percentage		OBP+Slugging	
C. Klein, Phi	153	M. Ott, NYG	9.65	L. O'Doul, Bro	.368	M. Ott, NYG	.424	C. Klein, Phi	.646	C. Klein, Phi	1.050
M. Ott, NYG	143	C. Klein, Phi	9.47	B. Terry, NYG	.350	L. O'Doul, Bro	.423	M. Ott, NYG	.601	M. Ott, NYG	1.025
B. Terry, NYG	137	L. O'Doul, Bro	8.88	C. Klein, Phi	.348	D. Hurst, Phi	.412	B. Terry, NYG	.580	L. O'Doul, Bro	.978
L. O'Doul, Bro	129	B. Terry, NYG	8.58	P. Waner, Pit	.341	C. Klein, Phi	.404	L. O'Doul, Bro	.555	B. Terry, NYG	.962
D. Hurst, Phi	124	D. Hurst, Phi	8.20	D. Hurst, Phi	.339	S. Davis, Phi	.399	D. Hurst, Phi	.548	D. Hurst, Phi	.959

1932 National League Pitching Leaders

Wins		Losses		Winning Percentage		Games		Games Started		Complete Games	
L. Warneke, ChN	22	O. Carroll, Cin	19	L. Warneke, ChN	.786	L. French, Pit	47	W. Clark, Bro	36	R. Lucas, Cin	28
W. Clark, Bro	20	P. Malone, ChN	17	B. Brown, Bos	.667	D. Dean, StL	46	V. Mungo, Bro	33	L. Warneke, ChN	25
G. Bush, ChN	19	R. Lucas, Cin	17	S. Swetonic, Pit	.647	T. Carleton, StL	44	D. Dean, StL	33	C. Hubbell, NYG	22
3 tied with	18	L. French, Pit	16	G. Bush, ChN	.633	P. Collins, Phi	43	L. French, Pit	33	3 tied with	19
		E. Brandt, Bos	16	W. Hallahan, StL	.632	2 tied with	42	P. Malone, ChN	33		

Shutouts		Saves		Games Finished		Batters Faced		Innings Pitched		Hits Allowed	
D. Dean, StL	4	J. Quinn, Bro	8	J. Quinn, Bro	31	D. Dean, StL	1203	D. Dean, StL	286.0	L. French, Pit	301
L. Warneke, ChN	4	R. Benge, Phi	6	B. Cantwell, Bos	27	L. French, Pit	1167	C. Hubbell, NYG	284.0	P. Derringer, StL	296
S. Swetonic, Pit	4	B. Cantwell, Bos	5	S. Gibson, NYG	23	C. Hubbell, NYG	1151	L. Warneke, ChN	277.0	F. Fitzsimmons, NYG	287
3 tied with	3	D. Luque, NYG	5	D. Luque, NYG	22	W. Clark, Bro	1136	L. French, Pit	274.1	W. Clark, Bro	282
		3 tied with	4	2 tied with	20	L. Warneke, ChN	1117	W. Clark, Bro	273.0	D. Dean, StL	280

Home Runs Allowed		Walks		Walks/9 Innings		Strikeouts		Strikeouts/9 Innings		Strikeout/Walk Ratio	
B. Walker, NYG	23	V. Mungo, Bro	115	B. Swift, Pit	1.1	D. Dean, StL	191	D. Dean, StL	6.0	C. Hubbell, NYG	3.42
P. Collins, Phi	21	B. Brown, Bos	104	R. Lucas, Cin	1.2	C. Hubbell, NYG	137	W. Hallahan, StL	5.5	B. Swift, Pit	2.46
C. Hubbell, NYG	20	D. Dean, StL	102	C. Hubbell, NYG	1.3	P. Malone, ChN	120	P. Malone, ChN	4.6	W. Clark, Bro	2.02
J. Mooney, NYG	18	F. Fitzsimmons, NYG	83	H. Betts, Bos	1.4	T. Carleton, StL	113	C. Hubbell, NYG	4.3	D. Dean, StL	1.87
F. Fitzsimmons, NYG	18	P. Malone, ChN	78	W. Clark, Bro	1.6	B. Brown, Bos	110	V. Mungo, Bro	4.3	R. Lucas, Cin	1.80

Earned Run Average		Component ERA		Hit Batsmen		Wild Pitches		Opponent Average		Opponent OBP	
L. Warneke, ChN	2.37	R. Lucas, Cin	2.44	O. Carroll, Cin	9	P. Derringer, StL	9	S. Swetonic, Pit	.221	C. Hubbell, NYG	.268
C. Hubbell, NYG	2.50	C. Hubbell, NYG	2.45	G. Bush, ChN	7	P. Malone, ChN	8	L. Warneke, ChN	.237	B. Swift, Pit	.272
H. Betts, Bos	2.80	L. Warneke, ChN	2.50	8 tied with	6	F. Fitzsimmons, NYG	7	C. Hubbell, NYG	.238	R. Lucas, Cin	.275
S. Swetonic, Pit	2.82	B. Swift, Pit	2.59			W. Hallahan, StL	7	P. Malone, ChN	.244	L. Warneke, ChN	.283
R. Lucas, Cin	2.84	S. Swetonic, Pit	2.61			J. Quinn, Bro	7	B. Swift, Pit	.248	S. Swetonic, Pit	.286

1932 National League Miscellaneous

Managers

Boston	Bill McKechnie	77-77
Brooklyn	Max Carey	81-73
Chicago	Rogers Hornsby	53-46
	Charlie Grimm	37-18
Cincinnati	Dan Howley	60-94
New York	John McGraw	17-23
	Bill Terry	55-59
Philadelphia	Burt Shotton	78-76
Pittsburgh	George Gibson	86-68
St. Louis	Gabby Street	72-82

Awards

Most Valuable Player	Chuck Klein, of, Phi
STATS Cy Young	Lon Warneke, ChN
STATS Rookie of the Year	Billy Herman, 2b, ChN
STATS Manager of the Year	George Gibson, Pit

STATS All-Star Team

C	Spud Davis, Phi	.336	14	70
1B	Bill Terry, NYG	.350	28	117
2B	Billy Herman, ChN	.314	1	51
3B	Pinky Whitney, Phi	.298	13	124
SS	Dick Bartell, Phi	.308	1	53
OF	Chuck Klein, Phi	.348	38	137
OF	Lefty O'Doul, Bro	.368	21	90
OF	Mel Ott, NYG	.318	38	123
P	Guy Bush, ChN	19-11	3.21	73 K
P	Dizzy Dean, StL	18-15	3.30	191 K
P	Carl Hubbell, NYG	18-11	2.50	137 K
P	Lon Warneke, ChN	22-6	2.37	106 K
RP	Ben Cantwell, Bos	13-11	2.96	5 Sv

Postseason

World Series	Chicago (NL) 0 vs. New York (AL) 4

Outstanding Performances

Three-Homer Games

Bill Terry, NYG	on August 13

1933 American League Standings

Team	Overall					Home Games						Road Games						Park Index		Record by Month					
	W	L	Pct	GB	DIF	W	L	R	OR	HR	OHR	W	L	R	OR	HR	OHR	Run	HR	M/A	May	June	July	Aug	S/O
Washington	99	53	.651	—	102	46	30	358	338	14	**16**	53	23	492	**327**	46	48	85	32	10-6	14-12	20-7	17-10	21-8	17-10
New York	91	59	.607	7.0	76	**51**	23	**421**	324	79	26	40	36	**506**	444	65	40	81	103	11-4	14-9	18-13	17-10	13-15	18-8
Philadelphia	79	72	.523	19.5	0	46	29	414	387	**82**	50	33	43	461	466	57	**27**	88	159	6-10	15-6	14-16	12-17	14-14	18-9
Cleveland	75	76	.497	23.5	9	45	32	353	341	22	24	30	44	301	328	28	36	106	69	9-7	13-12	13-17	14-16	19-11	7-13
Detroit	75	79	.487	25.0	0	43	35	394	382	27	36	32	44	328	351	30	48	111	79	8-8	8-15	17-14	14-14	16-15	12-13
Chicago	67	83	.447	31.0	3	35	41	355	426	20	42	32	42	328	388	23	43	106	91	10-6	10-12	14-17	11-17	15-16	7-15
Boston	63	86	.423	34.5	0	32	40	341	377	23	35	31	46	359	381	27	40	104	93	4-11	9-14	15-16	16-10	11-22	8-13
St. Louis	55	96	.364	43.5	0	30	46	389	480	43	68	25	50	280	340	21	28	138	224	6-12	10-13	10-21	12-19	9-17	8-14

Clinch Date—Washington 9/21.

Team Batting

Team	G	AB	R	OR	H	2B	3B	HR	TB	RBI	TBB	IBB	SO	HBP	SH	SF	SB	CS	SB%	GDP	Avg	OBP	Slg
New York	152	5274	**927**	768	1495	241	75	**144**	2318	**849**	**700**	—	506	17	78	—	**76**	59	.56	—	.283	**.369**	.440
Philadelphia	152	5330	875	853	1519	**297**	57	139	**2347**	831	625	—	**618**	15	80	—	34	34	.50	—	.285	.362	**.440**
Washington	153	**5524**	850	**665**	**1586**	281	**86**	60	2219	793	539	—	395	20	**130**	—	65	50	.57	—	**.287**	.353	.402
Detroit	155	5502	722	733	1479	283	78	57	2089	676	475	—	523	20	93	—	68	50	.58	—	.269	.329	.380
Boston	149	5201	700	758	1407	294	56	50	1963	642	525	—	464	15	115	—	58	37	**.61**	—	.271	.339	.377
Chicago	151	5318	683	814	1448	231	53	43	1914	642	538	—	416	27	108	—	43	46	.48	—	.272	.342	.360
St. Louis	153	5285	669	820	1337	244	64	64	1901	606	520	—	556	14	87	—	72	**60**	.55	—	.253	.322	.360
Cleveland	151	5240	654	669	1366	218	77	50	1888	611	448	—	426	17	101	—	36	40	.47	—	.261	.321	.360
AL Total	1216	42674	6080	6080	11637	2089	546	607	16639	5650	4370	—	3904	145	792	—	452	376	.55	—	.273	.342	.390
AL Avg Team	152	5334	760	760	1455	261	68	76	2080	706	546	—	488	18	99	—	57	47	.55	—	.273	.342	.390

Team Pitching

Team	G	CG	ShO	Rel	Sv	IP	H	R	ER	HR	SH	SF	HB	TBB	IBB	SO	WP	Bk	H/9	SO/9	BB/9	OAvg	OOBP	ERA
Cleveland	151	**74**	**12**	124	7	1350.0	**1382**	669	**556**	60	90	—	16	465	—	437	14	3	9.2	2.9	3.1	.264	.325	3.71
Washington	153	68	5	150	**26**	1389.2	1415	**665**	590	64	**76**	—	16	**452**	—	447	15	2	9.2	2.9	**2.9**	.263	**.322**	3.82
Detroit	155	69	6	129	17	**1398.0**	1415	733	613	84	116	—	23	561	—	575	15	**6**	**9.1**	3.7	3.6	**.263**	.335	3.95
Boston	149	60	4	146	14	1327.2	1396	758	642	66	115	—	21	591	—	467	19	1	9.5	3.2	4.0	.271	.348	4.35
New York	152	70	8	123	22	1354.2	1426	768	657	66	84	—	14	612	—	**711**	**33**	2	9.5	**4.7**	4.1	.267	.344	4.36
Chicago	151	53	8	**167**	13	1371.1	1505	814	678	85	104	—	**28**	519	—	423	31	1	9.9	2.8	3.4	.277	.343	4.45
Philadelphia	152	69	6	142	14	1343.2	1523	853	718	77	106	—	17	644	—	423	**33**	2	10.2	2.8	4.3	.283	.361	4.81
St. Louis	153	55	7	147	10	1360.2	1574	820	729	96	93	—	16	531	—	426	26	1	10.4	2.8	3.5	.289	.354	4.82
AL Total	1216	518	56	1128	123	10895.2	11636	6080	5183	607	784	—	151	4375	—	3909	186	18	9.6	3.2	3.6	.273	.342	4.28
AL Avg Team	152	65	7	141	15	1361.2	1455	760	648	76	98	—	19	547	—	489	23	2	9.6	3.2	3.6	.273	.342	4.28

Team Fielding

Team	G	PO	A	E	TC	DP	PB	Pct
Washington	153	4169	1826	**131**	6126	149	7	.979
St. Louis	153	4096	1858	149	6103	162	4	.976
Cleveland	151	4040	1882	156	6078	127	4	.974
New York	152	4062	1609	165	5836	122	**12**	.972
Detroit	155	**4193**	1830	178	6201	**167**	6	.971
Chicago	151	4116	**1930**	186	**6232**	143	11	.970
Philadelphia	152	4032	1750	203	5985	121	9	.966
Boston	149	3972	1767	204	5943	133	3	.966
AL Total	1216	32680	14452	1372	48504	1124	56	.972

Team vs. Team Records

	Bos	ChA	Cle	Det	NYA	Phi	StL	Was	Won
Bos	—	11	6	11	8	14	9	4	63
ChA	7	—	9	10	7	12	15	7	67
Cle	16	13	—	10	7	6	15	8	75
Det	11	12	12	—	7	11	14	8	75
NYA	14	15	13	15	—	12	14	8	91
Phi	8	10	16	11	9	—	14	11	79
StL	13	7	7	8	7	6	—	7	55
Was	17	15	13	14	14	11	15	—	99
Lost	86	83	76	79	59	72	96	53	

1933 American League Batting Leaders

Games		At-Bats		Runs		Hits		Doubles		Triples	
B. Rogell, Det	155	D. Cramer, Phi	661	L. Gehrig, NYA	138	H. Manush, Was	221	J. Cronin, Was	45	H. Manush, Was	17
C. Gehringer, Det	155	H. Manush, Was	658	J. Foxx, Phi	125	J. Foxx, Phi	204	B. Johnson, Phi	44	E. Averill, Cle	16
J. Kuhel, Was	153	C. Gehringer, Det	628	H. Manush, Was	115	C. Gehringer, Det	204	J. Burns, StL	43	E. Combs, NYA	16
H. Manush, Was	153	L. Appling, ChA	612	B. Chapman, NYA	112	A. Simmons, ChA	200	B. Rogell, Det	42	B. Myer, Was	15
4 tied with	152	A. Simmons, ChA	605	D. Cramer, Phi	109	L. Gehrig, NYA	198	C. Gehringer, Det	42	C. Reynolds, StL	14

Home Runs		Total Bases		Runs Batted In		Walks		Intentional Walks		Strikeouts	
J. Foxx, Phi	48	J. Foxx, Phi	403	J. Foxx, Phi	163	B. Ruth, NYA	114	Statistic unavailable		J. Foxx, Phi	93
B. Ruth, NYA	34	L. Gehrig, NYA	359	L. Gehrig, NYA	139	M. Cochrane, Phi	106			B. Ruth, NYA	90
L. Gehrig, NYA	32	H. Manush, Was	302	A. Simmons, ChA	119	M. Bishop, Phi	106			H. Greenberg, Det	78
B. Johnson, Phi	21	C. Gehringer, Det	294	J. Cronin, Was	118	J. Foxx, Phi	96			B. Campbell, StL	77
T. Lazzeri, NYA	18	A. Simmons, ChA	291	J. Kuhel, Was	107	E. Swanson, ChA	93			B. Johnson, Phi	74

Hit By Pitch		Sac Hits		Sac Flies		Stolen Bases		Caught Stealing		GDP	
J. Dykes, ChA	12	M. Haas, ChA	30	Statistic unavailable		B. Chapman, NYA	27	B. Chapman, NYA	18	Statistic unavailable	
E. Averill, Cle	5	D. Cramer, Phi	21			G. Walker, Det	26	L. Gehrig, NYA	13		
B. Chapman, NYA	4	O. Bluege, Was	21			E. Swanson, ChA	19	F. Schulte, Was	12		
R. Johnson, Bos	4	W. Kamm, Cle	16			J. Kuhel, Was	17	3 tied with	11		
12 tied with	3	3 tied with	15			2 tied with	15				

Runs Created		Runs Created/27 Outs		Batting Average		On-Base Percentage		Slugging Percentage		OBP+Slugging	
J. Foxx, Phi	166	J. Foxx, Phi	11.85	J. Foxx, Phi	.356	M. Cochrane, Phi	.459	J. Foxx, Phi	.703	J. Foxx, Phi	1.153
L. Gehrig, NYA	149	B. Ruth, NYA	9.91	H. Manush, Was	.336	J. Foxx, Phi	.449	L. Gehrig, NYA	.605	L. Gehrig, NYA	1.030
B. Ruth, NYA	122	L. Gehrig, NYA	9.65	L. Gehrig, NYA	.334	M. Bishop, Phi	.446	B. Ruth, NYA	.582	B. Ruth, NYA	1.023
C. Gehringer, Det	118	M. Cochrane, Phi	9.24	A. Simmons, ChA	.331	B. Ruth, NYA	.442	M. Cochrane, Phi	.515	M. Cochrane, Phi	.974
H. Manush, Was	117	B. Johnson, Phi	7.30	C. Gehringer, Det	.325	L. Gehrig, NYA	.424	B. Johnson, Phi	.505	B. Johnson, Phi	.892

1933 American League Pitching Leaders

Wins		Losses		Winning Percentage		Games		Games Started		Complete Games	
G. Crowder, Was	24	T. Lyons, ChA	21	L. Grove, Phi	.750	G. Crowder, Was	52	E. Whitehill, Was	37	L. Grove, Phi	21
L. Grove, Phi	24	B. Hadley, StL	20	R. Van Atta, NYA	.750	J. Russell, Was	50	B. Hadley, StL	36	B. Hadley, StL	19
E. Whitehill, Was	22	G. Blaeholder, StL	19	E. Whitehill, Was	.733	J. Welch, Bos	47	G. Blaeholder, StL	36	E. Whitehill, Was	19
3 tied with	16	M. Harder, Cle	17	L. Stewart, Was	.714	B. Kline, Bos	46	G. Crowder, Was	35	R. Ruffing, NYA	18
		L. Brown, 2tm	17	J. Allen, NYA	.682	3 tied with	45	2 tied with	32	2 tied with	17

Shutouts		Saves		Games Finished		Batters Faced		Innings Pitched		Hits Allowed	
O. Hildebrand, Cle	6	J. Russell, Was	13	C. Hogsett, Det	34	B. Hadley, StL	1365	B. Hadley, StL	316.2	G. Crowder, Was	311
L. Gomez, NYA	4	C. Hogsett, Det	9	J. Russell, Was	31	G. Crowder, Was	1268	G. Crowder, Was	299.1	B. Hadley, StL	309
G. Blaeholder, StL	3	W. Moore, NYA	8	J. Welch, Bos	30	L. Grove, Phi	1173	L. Grove, Phi	275.1	G. Blaeholder, StL	283
13 tied with	2	J. Heving, ChA	6	W. Moore, NYA	26	E. Whitehill, Was	1149	E. Whitehill, Was	270.0	L. Grove, Phi	280
		L. Grove, Phi	6	R. Faber, ChA	24	G. Blaeholder, StL	1091	G. Blaeholder, StL	255.2	E. Whitehill, Was	271

Home Runs Allowed		Walks		Walks/9 Innings		Strikeouts		Strikeouts/9 Innings		Strikeout/Walk Ratio	
G. Blaeholder, StL	24	B. Hadley, StL	141	C. Brown, Cle	1.7	L. Gomez, NYA	163	L. Gomez, NYA	6.3	L. Gomez, NYA	1.54
B. Weiland, Bos	19	S. Cain, Phi	137	F. Marberry, Det	2.3	B. Hadley, StL	149	J. Allen, NYA	5.8	C. Brown, Cle	1.38
L. Stewart, Was	19	T. Bridges, Det	110	L. Stewart, Was	2.3	R. Ruffing, NYA	122	R. Ruffing, NYA	4.7	F. Marberry, Det	1.38
S. Cain, Phi	18	L. Gomez, NYA	106	M. Harder, Cle	2.4	T. Bridges, Det	120	T. Bridges, Det	4.6	L. Grove, Phi	1.37
V. Sorrell, Det	18	2 tied with	100	G. Blaeholder, StL	2.4	J. Allen, NYA	119	R. Van Atta, NYA	4.4	J. Allen, NYA	1.37

Earned Run Average		Component ERA		Hit Batsmen		Wild Pitches		Opponent Average		Opponent OBP	
M. Pearson, Cle	2.33	M. Pearson, Cle	2.63	B. Kline, Bos	6	J. Allen, NYA	10	M. Pearson, Cle	.221	M. Pearson, Cle	.297
M. Harder, Cle	2.95	T. Bridges, Det	2.94	T. Bridges, Det	6	L. Brown, 2tm	10	T. Bridges, Det	.226	F. Marberry, Det	.302
T. Bridges, Det	3.09	F. Marberry, Det	3.03	J. Miller, ChA	6	T. Lyons, ChA	10	L. Gomez, NYA	.240	L. Stewart, Was	.304
L. Gomez, NYA	3.18	M. Harder, Cle	3.11	E. Durham, ChA	5	H. McDonald, 2tm	9	J. Allen, NYA	.242	M. Harder, Cle	.309
L. Grove, Phi	3.20	M. Weaver, Was	3.16	B. Weiland, Bos	5	B. Hadley, StL	8	B. Weiland, Bos	.244	C. Brown, Cle	.310

1933 American League Miscellaneous

Managers		
Boston	Marty McManus	63-86
Chicago	Lew Fonseca	67-83
Cleveland	Roger Peckinpaugh	26-25
	Bibb Falk	1-0
	Walter Johnson	48-51
Detroit	Bucky Harris	73-79
	Del Baker	2-0
New York	Joe McCarthy	91-59
Philadelphia	Connie Mack	79-72
St. Louis	Bill Killefer	34-57
	Allen Sothoron	2-6
	Rogers Hornsby	19-33
Washington	Joe Cronin	99-53

Awards

Most Valuable Player	Jimmie Foxx, 1b, Phi
STATS Cy Young	Lefty Grove, Phi
STATS Rookie of the Year	Mike Higgins, 3b, Phi
STATS Manager of the Year	Joe Cronin, Was

STATS All-Star Team

C	Mickey Cochrane, Phi	.322	15	60
1B	Jimmie Foxx, Phi	.356	48	163
2B	Charlie Gehringer, Det	.325	12	105
3B	Mike Higgins, Phi	.314	13	99
SS	Joe Cronin, Was	.309	5	118
OF	Bob Johnson, Phi	.290	21	93
OF	Babe Ruth, NYA	.301	34	103
OF	Al Simmons, ChA	.331	14	119
P	General Crowder, Was	24-15	3.97	110 K
P	Lefty Gomez, NYA	16-10	3.18	163 K
P	Lefty Grove, Phi	24-8	3.20	114 K
P	Earl Whitehill, Was	22-8	3.33	96 K
RP	Jack Russell, Was	12-6	2.69	13 Sv

Postseason

World Series	Washington (AL) 1 vs. NYG (NL) 4

Outstanding Performances

Triple Crown
Jimmie Foxx, Phi .356-48-163

Three-Homer Games
Jimmie Foxx, Phi on June 8

Cycles
M. Cochrane, Phi on August 2
Mike Higgins, Phi on August 6
Jimmie Foxx, Phi on August 14
Earl Averill, Cle on August 17

1933 National League Standings

Team	Overall					Home Games						Road Games						Park Index		Record by Month					
	W	L	Pct	GB	DIF	W	L	R	OR	HR	OHR	W	L	R	OR	HR	OHR	Run	HR	M/A	May	June	July	Aug	S/O
New York	91	61	.599	—	126	48	27	298	241	55	44	43	34	338	274	27	17	90	231	8-4	13-12	19-9	17-12	16-11	18-13
Pittsburgh	87	67	.565	5.0	44	50	27	332	272	12	13	37	40	335	347	27	41	89	37	10-3	14-12	12-18	20-10	12-13	19-11
Chicago	86	68	.558	6.0	1	55	24	334	239	40	32	31	44	312	297	32	19	89	134	6-8	16-12	14-15	17-11	16-12	17-10
Boston	83	71	.539	9.0	0	45	31	265	230	27	26	38	40	287	301	27	28	86	99	7-7	10-17	17-11	14-14	22-6	13-16
St. Louis	82	71	.536	9.5	4	46	31	347	315	18	25	36	40	340	294	39	30	103	62	6-9	19-7	14-13	13-16	17-14	13-12
Brooklyn	65	88	.425	26.5	2	36	41	306	352	33	29	29	47	311	343	29	22	99	120	7-6	9-14	15-15	8-19	13-18	13-16
Philadelphia	60	92	.395	31.0	0	32	40	355	437	45	46	28	52	252	323	15	41	153	181	5-10	9-17	14-15	13-12	9-19	10-19
Cincinnati	58	94	.382	33.0	0	37	42	264	321	5	10	21	52	232	322	29	37	98	21	5-7	15-14	10-19	11-19	7-19	10-16

Clinch Date—New York 9/19.

Team Batting

Team	G	AB	R	OR	H	2B	3B	HR	TB	RBI	TBB	IBB	SO	HBP	SH	SF	SB	CS	SB%	GDP	Avg	OBP	Slg
St. Louis	154	5387	687	609	1486	256	61	57	2035	629	391	—	528	32	101	—	99	—	—	131	.276	.329	.378
Pittsburgh	154	5429	667	619	1548	249	84	39	2082	618	366	—	334	20	147	—	34	—	—	106	.285	.333	.383
Chicago	154	5255	646	536	1422	256	51	72	1996	608	392	—	475	30	108	—	52	—	—	161	.271	.326	.380
New York	156	5461	636	515	1437	204	41	82	1969	598	377	—	477	15	86	—	31	—	—	137	.263	.312	.361
Brooklyn	157	5367	617	695	1413	224	51	62	1925	566	397	—	453	18	90	—	82	—	—	139	.263	.316	.359
Philadelphia	152	5261	607	760	1439	240	41	60	1941	570	381	—	479	29	125	—	55	—	—	128	.274	.326	.369
Boston	156	5243	552	531	1320	217	56	54	1811	511	349	—	428	25	134	—	25	—	—	142	.252	.299	.345
Cincinnati	153	5156	496	643	1267	208	37	34	1651	455	349	—	354	33	115	—	30	—	—	161	.246	.298	.320
NL Total	1236	42559	4908	4908	11332	1854	422	460	15410	4555	2979	—	3528	202	906	—	408	—	—	1105	.266	.317	.362
NL Avg Team	155	5320	614	614	1417	232	53	58	1926	569	372	—	441	25	113	—	51	—	—	138	.266	.317	.362

Team Pitching

Team	G	CG	ShO	Rel	Sv	IP	H	R	ER	HR	SH	SF	HB	TBB	IBB	SO	WP	Bk	H/9	SO/9	BB/9	OAvg	OOBP	ERA
New York	156	75	23	126	15	1408.2	1280	515	424	61	101	—	25	400	—	555	30	2	8.2	3.5	2.6	.250	.307	2.71
Chicago	154	95	16	97	9	1362.0	1316	536	443	51	107	—	30	413	—	488	32	1	8.7	3.2	2.7	.254	.312	2.93
Boston	156	85	15	102	16	1403.0	1391	531	462	54	134	—	11	355	—	383	13	3	8.9	2.5	2.3	.261	.309	2.96
Pittsburgh	154	70	16	144	12	1373.1	1417	619	499	54	97	—	24	313	—	401	17	2	9.3	2.6	2.1	.264	.308	3.27
St. Louis	154	73	11	128	16	1382.2	1391	609	518	55	98	—	17	452	—	635	26	1	9.1	4.1	2.9	.261	.321	3.37
Cincinnati	153	74	13	113	8	1352.0	1470	643	514	47	130	—	14	257	—	310	24	2	9.8	2.1	1.7	.279	.314	3.42
Brooklyn	157	71	9	133	10	1386.1	1502	695	567	51	127	—	40	374	—	415	34	2	9.8	2.7	2.4	.275	.326	3.68
Philadelphia	152	52	10	170	13	1336.2	1563	760	645	87	112	—	41	410	—	341	30	4	10.5	2.3	2.8	.293	.348	4.34
NL Total	1236	595	113	1013	99	11004.2	11330	4908	4072	460	906	—	202	2974	—	3528	206	17	9.3	2.9	2.4	.266	.317	3.33
NL Avg Team	155	74	14	127	12	1375.2	1416	614	509	58	113	—	25	372	—	441	26	2	9.3	2.9	2.4	.266	.317	3.33

Team Fielding

Team	G	PO	A	E	TC	DP	PB	Pct
Boston	156	4195	1893	138	6226	148	7	.978
St. Louis	154	4148	1667	162	5977	119	11	.973
Chicago	154	4089	1869	168	6126	163	5	.973
New York	156	4224	2087	178	6489	156	12	.973
Pittsburgh	154	4118	1721	166	6005	133	7	.972
Brooklyn	157	4159	1776	177	6112	120	4	.971
Cincinnati	153	4050	1862	177	6089	139	13	.971
Philadelphia	152	4010	1845	183	6038	156	11	.970
NL Total	1236	32993	14720	1349	49062	1134	70	.973

Team vs. Team Records

	Bos	Bro	ChN	Cin	NYG	Phi	Pit	StL	Won
Bos	—	13	7	12	12	11	13	15	83
Bro	9	—	9	10	8	13	7	9	65
ChN	15	13	—	11	9	15	12	11	86
Cin	10	12	11	—	4	7	7	7	58
NYG	10	14	13	17	—	15	13	9	91
Phi	11	9	7	14	6	—	7	6	60
Pit	9	15	10	15	9	15	—	14	87
StL	7	12	11	15	13	16	8	—	82
Lost	71	88	68	94	61	92	67	71	

1933 National League Batting Leaders

Games		At-Bats		Runs		Hits		Doubles		Triples	
G. Suhr, Pit	154	C. Fullis, Phi	647	P. Martin, StL	122	C. Klein, Phi	223	C. Klein, Phi	44	A. Vaughan, Pit	19
P. Waner, Pit	154	P. Traynor, Pit	624	C. Klein, Phi	101	C. Fullis, Phi	200	J. Medwick, StL	40	P. Waner, Pit	16
P. Traynor, Pit	154	P. Waner, Pit	618	P. Waner, Pit	101	P. Waner, Pit	191	F. Lindstrom, Pit	39	P. Martin, StL	12
B. Herman, ChN	153	P. Waner, Pit	618	M. Ott, NYG	98	P. Traynor, Pit	190	P. Waner, Pit	38	B. Herman, ChN	12
5 tied with	152	C. Klein, Phi	606	J. Medwick, StL	92	P. Martin, StL	189	W. Berger, Bos	37	2 tied with	11

Home Runs		Total Bases		Runs Batted In		Walks		Intentional Walks		Strikeouts	
C. Klein, Phi	28	C. Klein, Phi	365	C. Klein, Phi	120	M. Ott, NYG	75	Statistic unavailable		W. Berger, Bos	77
W. Berger, Bos	27	W. Berger, Bos	299	W. Berger, Bos	106	G. Suhr, Pit	72			J. Vergez, NYG	66
M. Ott, NYG	23	J. Medwick, StL	296	M. Ott, NYG	103	P. Martin, StL	67			B. Ryan, NYG	62
J. Medwick, StL	18	P. Waner, Pit	282	J. Medwick, StL	98	A. Vaughan, Pit	64			G. Watkins, StL	62
3 tied with	16	A. Vaughan, Pit	274	A. Vaughan, Pit	97	P. Waner, Pit	60			B. Herman, ChN	57

Hit By Pitch		Sac Hits		Sac Flies		Stolen Bases		Caught Stealing		GDP	
G. Watkins, StL	12	D. Bartell, Phi	37	Statistic unavailable		P. Martin, StL	26	Statistic unavailable		E. Lombardi, Cin	26
S. Leslie, 2tm	8	F. Lindstrom, Pit	25			C. Fullis, Phi	18			J. Morrissey, Cin	21
J. Bottomley, Cin	7	H. Critz, NYG	21			F. Frisch, StL	18			B. Herman, ChN	21
T. Piet, Pit	6	B. Jordan, Bos	19			C. Klein, Phi	15			S. Davis, Phi	21
H. Rice, Cin	6	3 tied with	17			E. Orsatti, StL	14			4 tied with	20

Runs Created		Runs Created/27 Outs		Batting Average		On-Base Percentage		Slugging Percentage		OBP+Slugging	
C. Klein, Phi	138	C. Klein, Phi	9.52	C. Klein, Phi	.368	C. Klein, Phi	.422	C. Klein, Phi	.602	C. Klein, Phi	1.025
W. Berger, Bos	111	W. Berger, Bos	8.05	S. Davis, Phi	.349	S. Davis, Phi	.395	W. Berger, Bos	.566	W. Berger, Bos	.932
P. Martin, StL	110	P. Martin, StL	7.06	T. Piet, Pit	.323	A. Vaughan, Pit	.388	B. Herman, ChN	.502	S. Davis, Phi	.867
M. Ott, NYG	105	A. Vaughan, Pit	6.61	B. Terry, NYG	.322	P. Martin, StL	.387	J. Medwick, StL	.497	A. Vaughan, Pit	.866
A. Vaughan, Pit	102	M. Ott, NYG	6.57	W. Schulmerich, 2tm	.318	B. Terry, NYG	.375	A. Vaughan, Pit	.478	B. Herman, ChN	.855

1933 National League Pitching Leaders

Wins		Losses		Winning Percentage		Games		Games Started		Complete Games	
C. Hubbell, NYG	23	P. Derringer, 2tm	27	B. Tinning, ChN	.684	D. Dean, StL	48	L. French, Pit	35	D. Dean, StL	26
D. Dean, StL	20	B. Beck, Bro	20	B. Cantwell, Bos	.667	L. French, Pit	47	F. Fitzsimmons, NYG	35	L. Warneke, ChN	26
B. Cantwell, Bos	20	D. Dean, StL	18	C. Hubbell, NYG	.657	A. Liska, Phi	45	B. Beck, Bro	35	E. Brandt, Bos	23
G. Bush, ChN	20	S. Johnson, Cin	18	H. Meine, Pit	.652	C. Hubbell, NYG	45	D. Dean, StL	34	C. Hubbell, NYG	22
H. Schumacher, NYG	19	R. Benge, Bro	17	G. Bush, ChN	.625	T. Carleton, StL	44	L. Warneke, ChN	34	3 tied with	21

Shutouts		Saves		Games Finished		Batters Faced		Innings Pitched		Hits Allowed	
C. Hubbell, NYG	10	P. Collins, Phi	6	A. Liska, Phi	25	L. French, Pit	1209	C. Hubbell, NYG	308.2	L. French, Pit	290
H. Schumacher, NYG	7	C. Hubbell, NYG	5	S. Johnson, StL	24	C. Hubbell, NYG	1206	D. Dean, StL	293.0	D. Dean, StL	279
L. French, Pit	5	H. Bell, NYG	5	D. Luque, NYG	22	D. Dean, StL	1202	L. French, Pit	291.1	B. Beck, Bro	270
4 tied with	4	B. Harris, Pit	5	3 tied with	21	L. Warneke, ChN	1175	E. Brandt, Bos	287.2	P. Derringer, 2tm	264
		6 tied with	4			T. Carleton, StL	1168	L. Warneke, ChN	287.1	T. Carleton, StL	263

Home Runs Allowed		Walks		Walks/9 Innings		Strikeouts		Strikeouts/9 Innings		Strikeout/Walk Ratio	
E. Holley, Phi	18	W. Hallahan, StL	98	R. Lucas, Cin	0.7	D. Dean, StL	199	D. Dean, StL	6.1	C. Hubbell, NYG	3.32
T. Carleton, StL	15	T. Carleton, StL	97	C. Hubbell, NYG	1.4	C. Hubbell, NYG	156	R. Parmelee, NYG	5.4	D. Dean, StL	3.11
F. Fitzsimmons, NYG	14	V. Mungo, Bro	84	B. Swift, Pit	1.5	T. Carleton, StL	147	T. Carleton, StL	4.8	R. Lucas, Cin	2.22
C. Root, ChN	14	H. Schumacher, NYG	84	L. French, Pit	1.7	L. Warneke, ChN	133	C. Hubbell, NYG	4.5	B. Swift, Pit	1.78
R. Lucas, Cin	13	3 tied with	77	B. Cantwell, Bos	1.9	R. Parmelee, NYG	132	L. Warneke, ChN	4.2	L. Warneke, ChN	1.77

Earned Run Average		Component ERA		Hit Batsmen		Wild Pitches		Opponent Average		Opponent OBP	
C. Hubbell, NYG	1.66	C. Hubbell, NYG	1.84	R. Parmelee, NYG	14	R. Parmelee, NYG	14	H. Schumacher, NYG	.214	C. Hubbell, NYG	.260
L. Warneke, ChN	2.00	H. Schumacher, NYG	2.18	E. Holley, Phi	13	O. Carroll, Bro	10	C. Hubbell, NYG	.227	H. Schumacher, NYG	.280
H. Schumacher, NYG	2.16	E. Brandt, Bos	2.59	B. Beck, Bro	11	W. Hallahan, StL	8	R. Parmelee, NYG	.232	B. Swift, Pit	.285
E. Brandt, Bos	2.60	H. Betts, Bos	2.60	C. Root, ChN	10	V. Mungo, Bro	7	V. Mungo, Bro	.236	H. Betts, Bos	.290
C. Root, ChN	2.60	L. Warneke, ChN	2.61	O. Carroll, Bro	7	P. Derringer, 2tm	7	L. Warneke, ChN	.244	B. Cantwell, Bos	.291

1933 National League Miscellaneous

Managers

Boston	Bill McKechnie	83-71
Brooklyn	Max Carey	65-88
Chicago	Charlie Grimm	86-68
Cincinnati	Donie Bush	58-94
New York	Bill Terry	91-61
Philadelphia	Burt Shotton	60-92
Pittsburgh	George Gibson	87-67
St. Louis	Gabby Street	46-45
	Frank Frisch	36-26

Awards

Most Valuable Player	Carl Hubbell, p, NYG
STATS Cy Young	Carl Hubbell, NYG
STATS Rookie of the Year	Joe Medwick, of, StL
STATS Manager of the Year	Bill Terry, NYG

STATS All-Star Team

C	Gabby Hartnett, ChN	.276	16	88
1B	Ripper Collins, StL	.310	10	68
2B	Frankie Frisch, StL	.303	4	66
3B	Pepper Martin, StL	.316	8	57
SS	Arky Vaughan, Pit	.314	9	97
OF	Wally Berger, Bos	.313	27	106
OF	Chuck Klein, Phi	.368	28	120
OF	Mel Ott, NYG	.283	23	103
P	Ben Cantwell, Bos	20-10	2.62	57 K
P	Carl Hubbell, NYG	23-12	1.66	156 K
P	Hal Schumacher, NYG	19-12	2.16	96 K
P	Lon Warneke, ChN	18-13	2.00	133 K
RP	Hi Bell, NYG	6-5	2.05	5 Sv

Postseason

World Series	NYG (NL) 4 vs. Washington (AL) 1

Outstanding Performances

Triple Crown
Chuck Klein, Phi   .368-28-120
Three-Homer Games
Babe Herman, ChN   on July 20
Cycles
Pepper Martin, StL   on May 5
Chuck Klein, Phi   on May 26
Arky Vaughan, Pit   on June 24
Babe Herman, ChN   on September 30

1934 American League Standings

Team	Overall W	L	Pct	GB	DIF	Home Games W	L	R	OR	HR	OHR	Road Games W	L	R	OR	HR	OHR	Park Index Run	HR	Record by Month M/A	May	June	July	Aug	S/O
Detroit	101	53	.656	—	100	54	26	479	345	28	32	47	27	479	363	46	54	91	56	6-4	15-14	19-8	20-11	23-6	18-10
New York	94	60	.610	7.0	61	53	24	416	275	75	34	41	36	426	394	60	37	84	112	7-4	15-12	18-8	19-12	20-12	15-12
Cleveland	85	69	.552	16.0	9	47	31	435	362	45	34	38	38	379	401	55	36	100	85	5-4	16-10	12-16	21-12	10-17	21-10
Boston	76	76	.500	24.0	0	42	35	447	405	23	24	34	41	373	370	28	46	112	62	5-6	12-15	18-11	17-15	13-15	11-14
Philadelphia	68	82	.453	31.0	1	34	40	371	410	81	48	34	42	393	428	63	36	98	134	5-7	11-15	11-16	11-17	12-15	18-12
St. Louis	67	85	.441	33.0	0	36	39	356	405	35	60	31	46	318	395	27	34	110	160	4-5	14-14	11-15	13-15	15-17	10-19
Washington	66	86	.434	34.0	2	34	40	368	397	14	26	32	46	361	409	37	48	105	50	6-6	15-13	15-13	8-21	11-16	11-17
Chicago	53	99	.349	47.0	0	29	46	370	464	47	82	24	53	334	482	24	57	105	164	4-6	11-16	7-24	12-18	11-17	8-18

Clinch Date—Detroit 9/24.

Team Batting

Team	G	AB	R	OR	H	2B	3B	HR	TB	RBI	TBB	IBB	SO	HBP	SH	SF	SB	CS	SB%	GDP	Avg	OBP	Slg
Detroit	154	5475	958	708	1644	349	53	74	2321	872	639	—	528	24	103	—	125	55	.69	—	.300	.376	.424
New York	154	5368	842	669	1494	226	61	135	2247	789	700	—	597	20	90	—	71	46	.61	—	.278	.364	.419
Boston	153	5339	820	775	1465	287	70	51	2045	756	610	—	535	11	85	—	116	47	.71	—	.274	.350	.383
Cleveland	154	5396	814	763	1550	340	46	100	2282	765	526	—	433	19	87	—	52	32	.62	—	.287	.353	.423
Philadelphia	153	5317	764	838	1491	236	50	144	2259	708	491	—	584	13	99	—	57	35	.62	—	.280	.343	.425
Washington	155	5448	729	806	1512	278	70	51	2083	680	570	—	447	21	128	—	47	42	.53	—	.278	.348	.382
Chicago	153	5301	704	946	1395	237	40	71	1925	668	565	—	524	17	111	—	36	27	.57	—	.263	.336	.363
St. Louis	154	5288	674	800	1417	252	59	62	1973	632	514	—	631	19	101	—	43	31	.58	—	.268	.335	.373
AL Total	1230	42932	6305	6305	11968	2205	449	688	17135	5870	4615	—	4279	144	804	—	547	315	.63	—	.279	.351	.399
AL Avg Team	154	5367	788	788	1496	276	56	86	2142	734	577	—	535	18	101	—	68	39	.63	—	.279	.351	.399

Team Pitching

Team	G	CG	ShO	Rel	Sv	IP	H	R	ER	HR	SH	SF	HB	TBB	IBB	SO	WP	Bk	H/9	SO/9	BB/9	OAvg	OOBP	ERA
New York	154	83	13	111	10	1382.2	1349	669	577	71	74	—	11	542	—	656	13	3	8.8	4.3	3.5	.254	.324	3.76
Detroit	154	74	13	128	14	1370.2	1467	708	618	86	71	—	13	488	—	640	19	3	9.6	4.2	3.2	.273	.335	4.06
Cleveland	154	72	8	143	19	1367.0	1476	763	650	70	99	—	27	582	—	554	40	4	9.7	3.6	3.8	.275	.349	4.28
Boston	153	68	9	138	9	1361.0	1527	775	653	70	115	—	23	543	—	538	29	1	10.1	3.6	3.6	.283	.351	4.32
St. Louis	154	50	6	172	20	1350.0	1499	800	674	94	95	—	12	632	—	499	27	3	10.0	3.3	4.2	.283	.361	4.49
Washington	155	61	4	163	12	1381.1	1622	806	718	74	124	—	14	503	—	412	28	4	10.6	2.7	3.3	.295	.355	4.68
Philadelphia	153	68	8	144	8	1337.0	1429	838	745	84	113	—	23	693	—	480	33	3	9.6	3.2	4.7	.275	.363	5.01
Chicago	153	72	5	118	8	1355.0	1599	946	814	139	95	—	21	628	—	506	44	3	10.6	3.4	4.2	.292	.367	5.41
AL Total	1230	548	66	1117	100	10904.2	11968	6305	5449	688	786	—	144	4611	—	4285	233	24	9.9	3.5	3.8	.279	.351	4.50
AL Avg Team	154	69	8	140	13	1363.2	1496	788	681	86	98	—	18	576	—	536	29	3	9.9	3.5	3.8	.279	.351	4.50

Team Fielding

Team	G	PO	A	E	TC	DP	PB	Pct
Washington	155	4145	1914	162	6221	167	8	.974
Detroit	154	4099	1776	159	6034	150	6	.974
New York	154	4149	1582	157	5888	151	9	.973
Cleveland	154	4100	1842	172	6114	164	9	.972
Boston	153	4083	1784	188	6055	141	7	.969
St. Louis	154	4050	1743	187	5980	160	10	.969
Philadelphia	153	4012	1809	196	6017	166	12	.967
Chicago	153	4066	1788	207	6061	126	16	.966
AL Total	1230	32704	14238	1428	48370	1225	77	.970

Team vs. Team Records

	Bos	ChA	Cle	Det	NYA	Phi	StL	Was	Won
Bos	—	11	7	8	10	12	14	14	76
ChA	10	—	8	5	5	9	7	9	53
Cle	15	14	—	6	11	13	15	11	85
Det	14	17	16	—	12	12	15	15	101
NYA	12	17	11	10	—	15	17	12	94
Phi	9	13	9	10	7	—	9	11	68
StL	8	14	7	7	5	12	—	14	67
Was	8	13	11	7	10	9	8	—	66
Lost	76	99	69	53	60	82	85	86	

Seasons: Standings, Leaders

1934 American League Batting Leaders

Games		At-Bats		Runs		Hits		Doubles		Triples	
7 tied with	154	D. Cramer, Phi	649	C. Gehringer, Det	134	C. Gehringer, Det	214	H. Greenberg, Det	63	B. Chapman, NYA	13
		H. Trosky, Cle	625	B. Werber, Bos	129	L. Gehrig, NYA	210	C. Gehringer, Det	50	H. Manush, Was	11
		B. Werber, Bos	623	E. Averill, Cle	128	H. Trosky, Cle	206	E. Averill, Cle	48	5 tied with	10
		G. Goslin, Det	614	L. Gehrig, NYA	128	D. Cramer, Phi	202	H. Trosky, Cle	45		
		J. Burns, StL	612	J. Foxx, Phi	120	H. Greenberg, Det	201	O. Hale, Cle	44		

Home Runs		Total Bases		Runs Batted In		Walks		Intentional Walks		Strikeouts	
L. Gehrig, NYA	49	L. Gehrig, NYA	409	L. Gehrig, NYA	165	J. Foxx, Phi	111	Statistic unavailable		H. Clift, StL	100
J. Foxx, Phi	44	H. Trosky, Cle	374	H. Trosky, Cle	142	L. Gehrig, NYA	109			H. Greenberg, Det	93
H. Trosky, Cle	35	H. Greenberg, Det	356	H. Greenberg, Det	139	B. Ruth, NYA	103			J. Foxx, Phi	75
B. Johnson, Phi	34	J. Foxx, Phi	352	J. Foxx, Phi	130	B. Myer, Was	102			M. Higgins, Phi	70
E. Averill, Cle	31	E. Averill, Cle	340	C. Gehringer, Det	127	2 tied with	99			B. Chapman, NYA	68

Hit By Pitch		Sac Hits		Sac Flies		Stolen Bases		Caught Stealing		GDP	
F. Pytlak, Cle	5	M. Haas, ChA	24	Statistic unavailable		B. Werber, Bos	40	B. Chapman, NYA	16	Statistic unavailable	
F. Crosetti, NYA	5	R. Warstler, Phi	15			J. White, Det	28	B. Werber, Bos	15		
6 tied with	4	B. Werber, Bos	15			B. Chapman, NYA	26	O. Hale, Cle	12		
		L. Lary, 2tm	15			P. Fox, Det	25	P. Fox, Det	10		
		3 tied with	13			G. Walker, Det	20	G. Walker, Det	9		

Runs Created		Runs Created/27 Outs		Batting Average		On-Base Percentage		Slugging Percentage		OBP+Slugging	
L. Gehrig, NYA	171	L. Gehrig, NYA	11.93	L. Gehrig, NYA	.363	L. Gehrig, NYA	.465	L. Gehrig, NYA	.706	L. Gehrig, NYA	1.172
C. Gehringer, Det	145	J. Foxx, Phi	10.38	C. Gehringer, Det	.356	C. Gehringer, Det	.449	J. Foxx, Phi	.653	J. Foxx, Phi	1.102
J. Foxx, Phi	144	C. Gehringer, Det	9.46	H. Manush, Was	.349	J. Foxx, Phi	.449	H. Greenberg, Det	.600	H. Greenberg, Det	1.005
H. Greenberg, Det	142	H. Greenberg, Det	9.12	A. Simmons, ChA	.344	B. Ruth, NYA	.447	H. Trosky, Cle	.598	H. Trosky, Cle	.987
2 tied with	136	B. Ruth, NYA	8.73	J. Vosmik, Cle	.341	M. Cochrane, Det	.428	E. Averill, Cle	.569	B. Ruth, NYA	.984

1934 American League Pitching Leaders

Wins		Losses		Winning Percentage		Games		Games Started		Complete Games	
L. Gomez, NYA	26	B. Newsom, StL	20	L. Gomez, NYA	.839	J. Russell, Was	54	T. Bridges, Det	35	L. Gomez, NYA	25
S. Rowe, Det	24	M. Gaston, ChA	19	S. Rowe, Det	.750	B. Newsom, StL	47	M. Pearson, Cle	33	T. Bridges, Det	23
T. Bridges, Det	22	G. Blaeholder, StL	18	F. Marberry, Det	.750	S. Rowe, Det	45	L. Gomez, NYA	33	T. Lyons, ChA	21
M. Harder, Cle	20	S. Cain, Phi	17	W. Ferrell, Bos	.737	J. Knott, StL	45	G. Blaeholder, StL	33	S. Rowe, Det	20
R. Ruffing, NYA	19	B. Hadley, StL	16	E. Auker, Det	.682	2 tied with	44	3 tied with	32	2 tied with	19

Shutouts		Saves		Games Finished		Batters Faced		Innings Pitched		Hits Allowed	
L. Gomez, NYA	6	J. Russell, Was	7	A. McColl, Was	26	B. Newsom, StL	1159	L. Gomez, NYA	281.2	G. Blaeholder, StL	276
M. Harder, Cle	6	L. Brown, Cle	6	J. Heving, ChA	21	T. Bridges, Det	1153	T. Bridges, Det	275.0	E. Whitehill, Was	269
R. Ruffing, NYA	5	B. Newsom, StL	5	P. Gallivan, ChA	20	L. Gomez, NYA	1142	S. Rowe, Det	266.0	S. Rowe, Det	259
B. Dietrich, Phi	4	5 tied with	4	J. Russell, Was	20	M. Pearson, Cle	1136	B. Newsom, StL	262.1	B. Newsom, StL	259
3 tied with	3			H. Pennock, Bos	20	S. Rowe, Det	1111	R. Ruffing, NYA	256.1	2 tied with	257

Home Runs Allowed		Walks		Walks/9 Innings		Strikeouts		Strikeouts/9 Innings		Strikeout/Walk Ratio	
G. Earnshaw, ChA	28	B. Newsom, StL	149	W. Ferrell, Bos	2.4	L. Gomez, NYA	158	R. Ruffing, NYA	5.2	S. Rowe, Det	1.84
L. Tietje, ChA	20	M. Pearson, Cle	130	E. Auker, Det	2.5	T. Bridges, Det	151	L. Gomez, NYA	5.0	L. Gomez, NYA	1.65
R. Ruffing, NYA	18	S. Cain, Phi	128	G. Blaeholder, StL	2.6	S. Rowe, Det	149	S. Rowe, Det	5.0	E. Auker, Det	1.54
J. Knott, StL	17	B. Hadley, StL	127	S. Rowe, Det	2.7	R. Ruffing, NYA	149	M. Pearson, Cle	4.9	T. Bridges, Det	1.45
6 tied with	16	B. Dietrich, Phi	114	M. Weaver, Was	2.8	M. Pearson, Cle	140	T. Bridges, Det	4.9	R. Ruffing, NYA	1.43

Earned Run Average		Component ERA		Hit Batsmen		Wild Pitches		Opponent Average		Opponent OBP	
L. Gomez, NYA	2.33	L. Gomez, NYA	2.33	J. Welch, Bos	8	M. Pearson, Cle	15	L. Gomez, NYA	.215	L. Gomez, NYA	.282
M. Harder, Cle	2.61	M. Harder, Cle	3.08	M. Harder, Cle	7	M. Gaston, ChA	13	R. Ruffing, NYA	.236	R. Ruffing, NYA	.310
J. Murphy, NYA	3.12	S. Rowe, Det	3.15	B. Hadley, StL	6	W. Hudlin, Cle	7	T. Bridges, Det	.241	S. Rowe, Det	.312
E. Auker, Det	3.42	T. Bridges, Det	3.16	W. Hudlin, Cle	5	5 tied with	6	J. Murphy, NYA	.250	T. Bridges, Det	.312
S. Rowe, Det	3.45	J. Murphy, NYA	3.22	H. Johnson, Bos	5			M. Harder, Cle	.254	M. Harder, Cle	.316

1934 American League Miscellaneous

Managers		
Boston	Bucky Harris	76-76
Chicago	Lew Fonseca	4-11
	Jimmy Dykes	49-88
Cleveland	Walter Johnson	85-69
Detroit	Mickey Cochrane	101-53
New York	Joe McCarthy	94-60
Philadelphia	Connie Mack	68-82
St. Louis	Rogers Hornsby	67-85
Washington	Joe Cronin	66-86

Awards

Most Valuable Player	Mickey Cochrane, c, Det
STATS Cy Young	Lefty Gomez, NYA
STATS Rookie of the Year	Hal Trosky, 1b, Cle
STATS Manager of the Year	Mickey Cochrane, Det

STATS All-Star Team

C	Mickey Cochrane, Det	.320	2	76
1B	Lou Gehrig, NYA	.363	49	165
2B	Charlie Gehringer, Det	.356	11	127
3B	Bill Werber, Bos	.321	11	67
SS	Billy Rogell, Det	.296	3	100
OF	Earl Averill, Cle	.313	31	113
OF	Bob Johnson, Phi	.307	34	92
OF	Al Simmons, ChA	.344	18	104
P	Tommy Bridges, Det	22-11	3.67	151 K
P	Lefty Gomez, NYA	26-5	2.33	158 K
P	Mel Harder, Cle	20-12	2.61	91 K
P	Schoolboy Rowe, Det	24-8	3.45	149 K
RP	Jack Russell, Was	5-10	4.17	7 Sv

Postseason

World Series	Detroit (AL) 3 vs. St. Louis (NL) 4

Outstanding Performances

Triple Crown
Lou Gehrig, NYA   .363-49-165
Three-Homer Games
Hal Trosky, Cle   on May 30
Ed Coleman, Phi   on August 17
Cycles
Doc Cramer, Phi   on June 10
Lou Gehrig, NYA   on June 25
Moose Solters, Bos   on August 19

1934 National League Standings

Team	Overall					Home Games						Road Games						Park Index		Record by Month					
	W	L	Pct	GB	DIF	W	L	R	OR	HR	OHR	W	L	R	OR	HR	OHR	Run	HR	M/A	May	June	July	Aug	S/O
St. Louis	95	58	.621	—	13	48	29	451	363	56	43	47	29	348	293	48	34	125	119	4-7	21-6	13-14	17-13	19-11	21-7
New York	93	60	.608	2.0	127	49	26	363	254	75	43	44	34	397	329	51	32	88	148	8-3	17-13	17-9	19-11	19-10	13-14
Chicago	86	65	.570	8.0	25	47	30	347	301	53	44	39	35	358	338	48	36	89	111	10-2	15-14	16-10	17-12	16-13	12-14
Boston	78	73	.517	16.0	0	40	35	280	280	36	27	38	38	403	434	47	51	68	65	6-5	15-11	14-13	11-19	14-16	14-13
Pittsburgh	74	76	.493	19.5	10	45	32	421	369	22	38	29	44	314	344	30	40	114	81	5-5	15-11	14-13	13-15	14-14	17-12
Brooklyn	71	81	.467	23.5	1	43	33	390	355	42	38	28	48	358	440	37	43	93	100	5-6	11-16	11-18	13-15	14-14	17-12
Philadelphia	56	93	.376	37.0	0	35	36	384	400	28	72	21	57	291	394	28	54	126	134	3-8	8-16	13-18	18-13	4-21	10-17
Cincinnati	52	99	.344	42.0	0	30	47	331	406	17	24	22	52	259	395	38	37	108	53	3-8	5-19	13-16	12-19	12-17	7-20

Clinch Date—St. Louis 9/30.

Team Batting

Team	G	AB	R	OR	H	2B	3B	HR	TB	RBI	TBB	IBB	SO	HBP	SH	SF	SB	CS	SB%	GDP	Avg	OBP	Slg
St. Louis	154	5502	799	656	1582	294	75	104	2338	748	392	—	535	18	76	—	69	—	—	117	.288	.337	.425
New York	153	5396	760	583	1485	240	41	126	2185	716	526	—	526	24	108	—	19	—	—	102	.275	.329	.405
Brooklyn	153	5427	748	795	1526	284	52	79	2151	699	548	—	555	22	77	—	55	—	—	112	.281	.350	.396
Pittsburgh	151	5361	735	713	1541	281	77	52	2132	679	440	—	398	18	59	—	44	—	—	130	.287	.344	.398
Chicago	152	5347	705	639	1494	263	44	101	2148	664	375	—	630	26	93	—	59	—	—	112	.279	.330	.402
Boston	152	5370	683	714	1460	233	44	83	2030	649	375	—	440	28	81	—	30	—	—	128	.272	.323	.378
Philadelphia	149	5218	675	794	1480	286	35	56	2004	634	398	—	534	29	79	—	52	—	—	131	.284	.338	.384
Cincinnati	152	5361	590	801	1428	227	65	55	1950	560	313	—	532	33	78	—	34	—	—	136	.266	.311	.364
NL Total	1216	42982	5695	5695	11996	2108	433	656	16938	5349	3247	—	4150	198	651	—	362	—	—	968	.279	.333	.394
NL Avg Team	152	5373	712	712	1500	264	54	82	2117	669	406	—	519	25	81	—	45	—	—	121	.279	.333	.394

Team Pitching

Team	G	CG	ShO	Rel	Sv	IP	H	R	ER	HR	SH	SF	HB	TBB	IBB	SO	WP	Bk	H/9	SO/9	BB/9	OAvg	OOBP	ERA
New York	153	68	13	129	30	1370.0	1384	583	486	75	70	—	16	351	—	499	34	1	9.1	3.3	2.3	.260	.308	3.19
St. Louis	154	78	15	146	16	1386.2	1463	656	568	77	71	—	32	411	—	689	23	2	9.5	4.5	2.7	.268	.323	3.69
Chicago	152	73	11	129	9	1361.1	1432	639	568	80	86	—	19	417	—	633	32	3	9.5	4.2	2.8	.269	.325	3.76
Boston	152	62	12	138	20	1359.2	1512	714	621	78	83	—	17	405	—	462	13	2	10.0	3.1	2.7	.279	.331	4.11
Pittsburgh	151	63	8	159	8	1329.2	1523	713	620	78	83	—	31	354	—	487	18	2	10.3	3.3	2.4	.284	.332	4.20
Cincinnati	152	51	3	182	19	1347.2	1645	801	654	61	97	—	26	389	—	438	20	2	11.0	2.9	2.6	.299	.348	4.37
Brooklyn	153	66	6	166	12	1354.1	1540	795	674	81	72	—	27	475	—	520	37	1	10.2	3.5	3.2	.285	.346	4.48
Philadelphia	149	52	8	175	15	1297.0	1501	794	686	126	86	—	29	437	—	416	17	4	10.4	2.9	3.0	.288	.347	4.76
NL Total	1216	513	76	1224	129	10806.1	12000	5695	4877	656	648	—	197	3239	—	4144	194	17	10.0	3.5	2.7	.279	.333	4.06
NL Avg Team	152	64	10	153	16	1350.1	1500	712	610	82	81	—	25	405	—	518	24	2	10.0	3.5	2.7	.279	.333	4.06

Team Fielding

Team	G	PO	A	E	TC	DP	PB	Pct
Chicago	152	4085	1794	137	6016	135	13	.977
Pittsburgh	151	3983	1584	145	5712	118	4	.975
St. Louis	154	4158	1674	166	5998	141	8	.972
Boston	152	4074	1824	169	6067	120	6	.972
New York	153	4107	2031	179	6317	141	12	.972
Brooklyn	153	4060	1860	180	6100	141	16	.970
Cincinnati	152	4042	1816	181	6039	136	15	.970
Philadelphia	149	3899	1693	197	5789	140	11	.966
NL Total	1216	32408	14276	1354	48038	1072	85	.972

Team vs. Team Records

	Bos	Bro	ChN	Cin	NYG	Phi	Pit	StL	Won
Bos	—	16	12	15	7	14	9	5	78
Bro	6	—	8	13	8	13	16	7	71
ChN	10	12	—	14	11	13	14	12	86
Cin	7	9	8	—	6	9	7	6	52
NYG	15	14	10	16	—	15	14	9	93
Phi	8	9	9	10	7	—	7	6	56
Pit	11	6	8	15	8	13	—	13	74
StL	16	15	10	16	13	16	9	—	95
Lost	73	81	65	99	60	93	76	58	

1934 National League Batting Leaders

Games		At-Bats		Runs		Hits		Doubles		Triples	
R. Collins, StL	154	J. Rothrock, StL	647	P. Waner, Pit	122	P. Waner, Pit	217	E. Allen, Phi	42	J. Medwick, StL	18
J. Rothrock, StL	154	M. Koenig, Cin	633	M. Ott, NYG	119	B. Terry, NYG	213	K. Cuyler, ChN	42	P. Waner, Pit	16
M. Ott, NYG	153	J. Medwick, StL	620	R. Collins, StL	116	R. Collins, StL	200	A. Vaughan, Pit	41	G. Suhr, Pit	13
B. Terry, NYG	153	W. Berger, Bos	615	A. Vaughan, Pit	115	J. Medwick, StL	198	J. Medwick, StL	40	R. Collins, StL	12
2 tied with	151	L. Waner, Pit	611	J. Medwick, StL	110	2 tied with	192	R. Collins, StL	40	3 tied with	11

Home Runs		Total Bases		Runs Batted In		Walks		Intentional Walks		Strikeouts	
R. Collins, StL	35	R. Collins, StL	369	M. Ott, NYG	135	A. Vaughan, Pit	94	Statistic unavailable		D. Camilli, 2tm	94
M. Ott, NYG	35	M. Ott, NYG	344	R. Collins, StL	128	M. Ott, NYG	85			J. Medwick, StL	83
W. Berger, Bos	34	W. Berger, Bos	336	W. Berger, Bos	121	L. Koenecke, Bro	70			B. Herman, ChN	71
G. Hartnett, ChN	22	J. Medwick, StL	328	J. Medwick, StL	106	S. Leslie, Bro	69			T. Jackson, NYG	71
C. Klein, ChN	20	P. Waner, Pit	323	G. Suhr, Pit	103	P. Waner, Pit	68			B. Ryan, NYG	68

Hit By Pitch		Sac Hits		Sac Flies		Stolen Bases		Caught Stealing		GDP	
D. Bartell, Phi	9	H. Critz, NYG	22	Statistic unavailable		P. Martin, StL	23	Statistic unavailable		E. Lombardi, Cin	24
H. Pool, Cin	7	B. Terry, NYG	19			K. Cuyler, ChN	15			P. Traynor, Pit	23
4 tied with	6	E. Allen, Phi	16			D. Bartell, Phi	13			M. Koenig, Cin	17
		G. Slade, Cin	15			D. Taylor, Bro	12			F. Frisch, StL	17
		2 tied with	14			3 tied with	11			3 tied with	16

Runs Created		Runs Created/27 Outs		Batting Average		On-Base Percentage		Slugging Percentage		OBP+Slugging	
M. Ott, NYG	143	M. Ott, NYG	9.51	P. Waner, Pit	.362	A. Vaughan, Pit	.431	R. Collins, StL	.615	R. Collins, StL	1.008
R. Collins, StL	138	R. Collins, StL	8.94	B. Terry, NYG	.354	P. Waner, Pit	.429	M. Ott, NYG	.591	M. Ott, NYG	1.006
P. Waner, Pit	131	A. Vaughan, Pit	8.87	K. Cuyler, ChN	.338	M. Ott, NYG	.415	W. Berger, Bos	.546	P. Waner, Pit	.968
A. Vaughan, Pit	126	P. Waner, Pit	8.67	R. Collins, StL	.333	B. Terry, NYG	.414	P. Waner, Pit	.539	A. Vaughan, Pit	.942
B. Terry, NYG	121	B. Terry, NYG	7.80	A. Vaughan, Pit	.333	L. Koenecke, Bro	.411	J. Medwick, StL	.529	L. Koenecke, Bro	.919

1934 National League Pitching Leaders

Wins		Losses		Winning Percentage		Games		Games Started		Complete Games	
D. Dean, StL	30	S. Johnson, Cin	22	D. Dean, StL	.811	C. Davis, Phi	51	V. Mungo, Bro	38	C. Hubbell, NYG	25
H. Schumacher, NYG	23	P. Derringer, Cin	21	B. Walker, StL	.750	D. Dean, StL	50	F. Fitzsimmons, NYG	37	D. Dean, StL	24
L. Warneke, ChN	22	L. French, Pit	18	W. Hoyt, Pit	.714	S. Hansen, Phi	50	H. Schumacher, NYG	36	L. Warneke, ChN	23
C. Hubbell, NYG	21	P. Collins, Phi	18	H. Schumacher, NYG	.697	L. French, Pit	49	L. Warneke, ChN	35	V. Mungo, Bro	22
2 tied with	19	C. Davis, Phi	17	L. Warneke, ChN	.688	C. Hubbell, NYG	49	L. French, Pit	35	E. Brandt, Bos	20

Shutouts		Saves		Games Finished		Batters Faced		Innings Pitched		Hits Allowed	
D. Dean, StL	7	C. Hubbell, NYG	8	B. Smith, Bos	25	V. Mungo, Bro	1329	V. Mungo, Bro	315.1	V. Mungo, Bro	300
P. Dean, StL	5	D. Dean, StL	7	S. Johnson, 2tm	21	D. Dean, StL	1291	C. Hubbell, NYG	313.0	H. Schumacher, NYG	299
C. Hubbell, NYG	5	D. Luque, NYG	7	W. Hoyt, Pit	20	C. Hubbell, NYG	1255	D. Dean, StL	311.2	L. French, Pit	299
B. Lee, ChN	4	H. Bell, NYG	6	D. Luque, NYG	19	H. Schumacher, NYG	1254	H. Schumacher, NYG	297.0	P. Derringer, Cin	297
8 tied with	3	7 tied with	5	2 tied with	18	L. Warneke, ChN	1198	L. Warneke, ChN	291.1	2 tied with	288

Home Runs Allowed		Walks		Walks/9 Innings		Strikeouts		Strikeouts/9 Innings		Strikeout/Walk Ratio	
P. Collins, Phi	30	V. Mungo, Bro	104	C. Hubbell, NYG	1.1	D. Dean, StL	195	P. Dean, StL	5.8	C. Hubbell, NYG	3.19
P. Dean, StL	19	H. Schumacher, NYG	89	B. Frey, Cin	1.5	V. Mungo, Bro	184	D. Dean, StL	5.6	P. Dean, StL	2.88
C. Hubbell, NYG	17	P. Collins, Phi	87	D. Leonard, Bro	1.6	P. Dean, StL	150	V. Mungo, Bro	5.3	D. Dean, StL	2.60
H. Betts, Bos	17	S. Johnson, Cin	84	F. Fitzsimmons, NYG	1.7	L. Warneke, ChN	143	B. Walker, StL	4.5	L. Warneke, ChN	2.17
3 tied with	16	E. Brandt, Bos	83	H. Betts, Bos	1.8	P. Derringer, Cin	122	L. Warneke, ChN	4.4	P. Derringer, Cin	2.07

Earned Run Average		Component ERA		Hit Batsmen		Wild Pitches		Opponent Average		Opponent OBP	
C. Hubbell, NYG	2.30	C. Hubbell, NYG	2.27	B. Swift, Pit	8	H. Schumacher, NYG	10	C. Hubbell, NYG	.239	C. Hubbell, NYG	.263
D. Dean, StL	2.66	D. Dean, StL	2.69	C. Davis, Phi	7	B. Lee, ChN	9	D. Dean, StL	.241	L. Warneke, ChN	.287
C. Davis, Phi	2.95	L. Warneke, ChN	2.75	T. Carleton, StL	7	F. Fitzsimmons, NYG	9	L. Warneke, ChN	.244	D. Dean, StL	.289
F. Fitzsimmons, NYG	3.04	F. Fitzsimmons, NYG	2.97	S. Johnson, Cin	7	O. Carroll, Bro	8	P. Dean, StL	.248	P. Dean, StL	.292
B. Walker, StL	3.12	P. Dean, StL	3.07	3 tied with	6	2 tied with	7	V. Mungo, Bro	.249	F. Fitzsimmons, NYG	.297

1934 National League Miscellaneous

Managers

Boston	Bill McKechnie	78-73
Brooklyn	Casey Stengel	71-81
Chicago	Charlie Grimm	86-65
Cincinnati	Bob O'Farrell	30-60
	Burt Shotton	1-0
	Chuck Dressen	21-39
New York	Bill Terry	93-60
Philadelphia	Jimmie Wilson	56-93
Pittsburgh	George Gibson	27-24
	Pie Traynor	47-52
St. Louis	Frank Frisch	95-58

Awards

Most Valuable Player	Dizzy Dean, p, StL
STATS Cy Young	Dizzy Dean, StL
STATS Rookie of the Year	Curt Davis, p, Phi
STATS Manager of the Year	Frank Frisch, StL

STATS All-Star Team

C	Gabby Hartnett, ChN	.299	22	90
1B	Ripper Collins, StL	.333	35	128
2B	Frankie Frisch, StL	.305	3	75
3B	Pepper Martin, StL	.289	5	49
SS	Arky Vaughan, Pit	.333	12	94
OF	Wally Berger, Bos	.298	34	121
OF	Mel Ott, NYG	.326	35	135
OF	Paul Waner, Pit	.362	14	90
P	Curt Davis, Phi	19-17	2.95	99 K
P	Dizzy Dean, StL	30-7	2.66	195 K
P	Carl Hubbell, NYG	21-12	2.30	118 K
P	Hal Schumacher, NYG	23-10	3.18	112 K
RP	Dolf Luque, NYG	4-3	3.83	7 Sv

Postseason

World Series	St. Louis (NL) 4 vs. Detroit (AL) 3

Outstanding Performances

No-Hitters
Paul Dean, StL @ Bro on September 21

Three-Homer Games
Hal Lee, Bos on July 6

1935 American League Standings

Team	Overall					Home Games						Road Games						Park Index		Record by Month					
	W	L	Pct	GB	DIF	W	L	R	OR	HR	OHR	W	L	R	OR	HR	OHR	Run	HR	M/A	May	June	July	Aug	S/O
Detroit	93	58	.616	—	66	53	25	467	304	45	38	40	33	452	361	61	40	89	77	5-9	15-8	18-12	20-8	23-7	12-14
New York	89	60	.597	3.0	57	41	33	341	294	60	51	48	27	477	338	44	40	79	134	9-4	15-10	16-10	12-13	20-15	17-8
Cleveland	82	71	.536	12.0	18	48	29	391	340	53	30	34	42	385	399	40	38	92	105	8-2	12-13	17-11	8-19	19-14	18-12
Boston	78	75	.510	16.0	6	41	37	393	404	26	29	37	38	325	328	43	38	117	65	7-5	12-12	13-16	17-11	14-18	15-13
Chicago	74	78	.487	19.5	23	42	34	418	396	50	61	32	44	320	354	24	44	121	163	9-3	12-11	11-14	19-9	11-23	12-18
Washington	67	86	.438	27.0	2	37	39	388	414	5	28	30	47	435	489	27	61	88	38	7-6	10-13	12-16	10-20	13-17	15-14
St. Louis	65	87	.428	28.5	0	31	44	374	513	36	49	34	43	344	417	37	43	120	109	2-10	7-14	10-19	11-18	19-14	16-12
Philadelphia	58	91	.389	34.0	0	30	42	369	414	63	39	28	49	341	455	49	34	105	131	2-10	10-12	14-13	13-12	12-23	7-21

Clinch Date—Detroit 9/21.

Team Batting

Team	G	AB	R	OR	H	2B	3B	HR	TB	RBI	TBB	IBB	SO	HBP	SH	SF	SB	CS	SB%	GDP	Avg	OBP	Slg
Detroit	152	5423	919	665	1573	301	83	106	2358	836	627	—	456	19	112	—	70	45	.61	—	.290	.366	.435
Washington	154	5592	823	903	1591	255	95	32	2132	762	596	—	406	37	75	—	54	37	.59	—	.285	.358	.381
New York	149	5214	818	632	1462	255	70	104	2169	737	755	—	469	28	71	—	68	46	.60	—	.280	.358	.416
Cleveland	156	5534	776	739	1573	324	77	93	2330	737	460	—	567	17	87	—	63	54	.54	—	.284	.341	.421
Chicago	153	5314	738	750	1460	262	42	74	2028	690	580	—	405	19	112	—	46	28	.62	—	.275	.348	.382
St. Louis	155	5365	718	930	1446	291	51	73	2058	674	593	—	561	14	116	—	45	25	.64	—	.270	.344	.384
Boston	154	5288	718	732	1458	281	63	69	2072	674	609	—	470	21	137	—	91	59	.61	—	.276	.353	.392
Philadelphia	149	5269	710	869	1470	243	44	112	2137	674	475	—	602	17	86	—	43	35	.55	—	.279	.341	.406
AL Total	1222	42999	6220	6220	12033	2212	525	663	17284	5788	4544	—	3936	172	796	—	480	329	.59	—	.280	.351	.402
AL Avg Team	153	5375	778	778	1504	277	66	83	2161	724	568	—	492	22	100	—	60	41	.59	—	.280	.351	.402

Team Pitching

Team	G	CG	ShO	Rel	Sv	IP	H	R	ER	HR	SH	SF	HB	TBB	IBB	SO	WP	Bk	H/9	SO/9	BB/9	OAvg	OOBP	ERA
New York	149	76	12	120	13	1331.0	1276	632	533	91	85	—	12	516	—	594	21	2	8.6	4.0	3.5	.251	.321	3.60
Detroit	152	87	16	95	11	1364.0	1440	665	579	78	69	—	30	522	—	584	20	4	9.5	3.9	3.4	.271	.339	3.82
Boston	154	82	6	138	11	1376.0	1520	732	619	67	103	—	20	520	—	470	23	1	9.9	3.1	3.4	.280	.346	4.05
Cleveland	156	67	12	138	21	1396.0	1527	739	644	68	115	—	17	457	—	498	15	3	9.8	3.2	2.9	.278	.335	4.15
Chicago	153	80	8	102	8	1360.2	1443	750	662	105	85	—	22	574	—	436	33	3	9.5	2.9	3.8	.272	.346	4.38
Philadelphia	149	58	7	148	10	1326.1	1486	869	754	73	121	—	25	704	—	469	35	4	10.1	3.2	4.8	.285	.372	5.12
Washington	154	67	5	143	12	1378.2	1672	903	804	89	112	—	27	613	—	456	29	4	10.9	3.0	4.0	.302	.374	5.25
St. Louis	155	42	4	219	15	1380.1	1667	930	807	92	99	—	18	641	—	435	32	1	10.9	2.8	4.2	.297	.371	5.26
AL Total	1222	559	70	1103	101	10913.0	12031	6220	5402	663	789	—	171	4547	—	3942	208	22	9.9	3.3	3.7	.280	.351	4.46
AL Avg Team	153	70	9	138	13	1364.0	1504	778	675	83	99	—	21	568	—	493	26	3	9.9	3.3	3.7	.280	.351	4.46

Team Fielding

Team	G	PO	A	E	TC	DP	PB	Pct
Detroit	152	4088	1713	128	5929	154	6	.978
Chicago	153	4080	1890	146	6116	133	11	.976
New York	149	3990	1562	151	5703	114	9	.974
Washington	154	4134	1840	171	6145	186	15	.972
Cleveland	156	4191	1912	177	6280	147	9	.972
St. Louis	155	4143	1810	187	6140	138	6	.970
Boston	154	4125	1847	194	6166	136	10	.969
Philadelphia	149	3964	1690	190	5844	150	11	.967
AL Total	1222	32715	14264	1344	48323	1158	77	.972

Team vs. Team Records

	Bos	ChA	Cle	Det	NYA	Phi	StL	Was	Won
Bos	—	13	9	9	9	16	10	12	78
ChA	9	—	10	11	9	12	11	12	74
Cle	13	12	—	7	8	12	15	15	82
Det	13	11	15	—	11	14	17	12	93
NYA	12	11	14	11	—	14	12	15	89
Phi	6	10	10	5	6	—	11	10	58
StL	12	11	6	5	10	11	—	10	65
Was	10	10	7	10	7	12	11	—	67
Lost	75	78	71	58	60	91	87	86	

1935 American League Batting Leaders

Games		At-Bats		Runs		Hits		Doubles		Triples	
H. Trosky, Cle	154	D. Cramer, Phi	644	L. Gehrig, NYA	125	J. Vosmik, Cle	216	J. Vosmik, Cle	47	J. Vosmik, Cle	20
L. Appling, ChA	153	R. Rolfe, NYA	639	C. Gehringer, Det	123	B. Myer, Was	215	H. Greenberg, Det	46	J. Stone, Was	18
H. Greenberg, Det	152	J. Kuhel, Was	633	H. Greenberg, Det	121	D. Cramer, Phi	214	M. Solters, 2tm	45	H. Greenberg, Det	16
J. Vosmik, Cle	152	H. Trosky, Cle	632	B. Chapman, NYA	118	H. Greenberg, Det	203	P. Fox, Det	38	J. Cronin, Bos	14
4 tied with	151	M. Solters, 2tm	631	J. Foxx, Phi	118	2 tied with	201	B. Chapman, NYA	38	E. Averill, Cle	13

Home Runs		Total Bases		Runs Batted In		Walks		Intentional Walks		Strikeouts	
H. Greenberg, Det	36	H. Greenberg, Det	389	H. Greenberg, Det	170	L. Gehrig, NYA	132	Statistic unavailable		J. Foxx, Phi	99
J. Foxx, Phi	36	J. Foxx, Phi	340	L. Gehrig, NYA	119	L. Appling, ChA	122			B. Berger, Cle	97
L. Gehrig, NYA	30	J. Vosmik, Cle	333	J. Foxx, Phi	115	J. Foxx, Phi	114			H. Greenberg, Det	91
B. Johnson, Phi	28	M. Solters, 2tm	314	H. Trosky, Cle	113	B. Myer, Was	96			B. Johnson, Phi	76
H. Trosky, Cle	26	L. Gehrig, NYA	312	M. Solters, 2tm	112	M. Cochrane, Det	96			T. Lazzeri, NYA	75

Hit By Pitch		Sac Hits		Sac Flies		Stolen Bases		Caught Stealing		GDP	
C. Travis, Was	9	J. Burns, StL	20	Statistic unavailable		B. Werber, Bos	29	O. Hale, Cle	13	Statistic unavailable	
H. Clift, StL	6	R. Warstler, Phi	17			L. Lary, 2tm	28	B. Knickerbocker, Cle	12		
P. Fox, Det	6	C. Gehringer, Det	17			M. Almada, Bos	20	R. Johnson, Bos	12		
B. Dickey, NYA	6	M. Owen, Det	16			J. White, Det	19	J. White, Det	10		
2 tied with	5	J. Hayes, ChA	16			B. Chapman, NYA	17	B. Chapman, NYA	10		

Runs Created		Runs Created/27 Outs		Batting Average		On-Base Percentage		Slugging Percentage		OBP+Slugging	
H. Greenberg, Det	156	L. Gehrig, NYA	10.40	B. Myer, Was	.349	L. Gehrig, NYA	.466	J. Foxx, Phi	.636	J. Foxx, Phi	1.096
L. Gehrig, NYA	145	J. Foxx, Phi	10.31	J. Vosmik, Cle	.348	J. Foxx, Phi	.461	H. Greenberg, Det	.628	L. Gehrig, NYA	1.049
J. Foxx, Phi	139	H. Greenberg, Det	9.68	J. Foxx, Phi	.346	M. Cochrane, Det	.452	L. Gehrig, NYA	.583	H. Greenberg, Det	1.039
B. Myer, Was	132	B. Myer, Was	8.43	D. Cramer, Phi	.332	B. Myer, Was	.440	J. Vosmik, Cle	.537	J. Vosmik, Cle	.946
C. Gehringer, Det	130	M. Cochrane, Det	8.25	C. Gehringer, Det	.330	L. Appling, ChA	.437	P. Fox, Det	.513	C. Gehringer, Det	.911

1935 American League Pitching Leaders

Wins		Losses		Winning Percentage		Games		Games Started		Complete Games	
W. Ferrell, Bos	25	B. Newsom, 2tm	18	E. Auker, Det	.720	R. Van Atta, 2tm	58	W. Ferrell, Bos	38	W. Ferrell, Bos	31
M. Harder, Cle	22	R. Van Atta, 2tm	16	J. Allen, NYA	.684	J. Walkup, StL	55	M. Harder, Cle	35	T. Bridges, Det	23
T. Bridges, Det	21	4 tied with	15	J. Broaca, NYA	.682	I. Andrews, StL	50	S. Rowe, Det	34	L. Grove, Bos	23
L. Grove, Bos	20			T. Bridges, Det	.677	F. Thomas, StL	49	T. Bridges, Det	34	S. Rowe, Det	21
S. Rowe, Det	19			3 tied with	.667	J. Knott, StL	48	E. Whitehill, Was	34	4 tied with	19

Shutouts		Saves		Games Finished		Batters Faced		Innings Pitched		Hits Allowed	
S. Rowe, Det	6	J. Knott, StL	7	C. Hogsett, Det	30	W. Ferrell, Bos	1391	W. Ferrell, Bos	322.1	W. Ferrell, Bos	336
T. Bridges, Det	4	5 tied with	5	R. Van Atta, 2tm	25	E. Whitehill, Was	1239	M. Harder, Cle	287.1	E. Whitehill, Was	318
M. Harder, Cle	4			W. Wyatt, ChA	25	M. Harder, Cle	1206	E. Whitehill, Was	279.1	M. Harder, Cle	313
5 tied with	3			J. Russell, Was	24	T. Bridges, Det	1195	S. Rowe, Det	275.2	T. Bridges, Det	277
				L. Pettit, Was	22	S. Rowe, Det	1146	T. Bridges, Det	274.1	B. Newsom, 2tm	276

Home Runs Allowed		Walks		Walks/9 Innings		Strikeouts		Strikeouts/9 Innings		Strikeout/Walk Ratio	
T. Bridges, Det	22	S. Cain, 2tm	123	M. Harder, Cle	1.7	T. Bridges, Det	163	J. Allen, NYA	6.1	S. Rowe, Det	2.06
L. Gomez, NYA	18	T. Bridges, Det	113	L. Grove, Bos	2.1	S. Rowe, Det	140	T. Bridges, Det	5.3	J. Allen, NYA	1.95
B. Hadley, Was	18	W. Ferrell, Bos	108	S. Rowe, Det	2.2	L. Gomez, NYA	138	L. Gomez, NYA	5.0	L. Grove, Bos	1.86
4 tied with	17	J. Walkup, StL	104	I. Andrews, StL	2.2	L. Grove, Bos	121	S. Rowe, Det	4.6	M. Harder, Cle	1.79
		E. Whitehill, Was	104	W. Hudlin, Cle	2.4	J. Allen, NYA	113	M. Pearson, Cle	4.5	L. Gomez, NYA	1.60

Earned Run Average		Component ERA		Hit Batsmen		Wild Pitches		Opponent Average		Opponent OBP	
L. Grove, Bos	2.70	L. Grove, Bos	2.83	W. Wilshere, Phi	10	F. Thomas, StL	9	J. Allen, NYA	.238	S. Rowe, Det	.301
T. Lyons, ChA	3.02	S. Rowe, Det	2.99	E. Auker, Det	9	L. Gomez, NYA	8	R. Ruffing, NYA	.239	L. Grove, Bos	.302
R. Ruffing, NYA	3.12	J. Allen, NYA	3.10	E. Whitehill, Was	7	5 tied with	7	L. Gomez, NYA	.242	R. Ruffing, NYA	.303
L. Gomez, NYA	3.18	R. Ruffing, NYA	3.13	C. Hogsett, Det	5			J. Whitehead, ChA	.250	J. Allen, NYA	.307
M. Harder, Cle	3.29	L. Gomez, NYA	3.14	R. Mahaffey, Phi	5			J. Broaca, NYA	.254	M. Harder, Cle	.307

1935 American League Miscellaneous

Managers

Boston	Joe Cronin	78-75
Chicago	Jimmy Dykes	74-78
Cleveland	Walter Johnson	46-48
	Steve O'Neill	36-23
Detroit	Mickey Cochrane	93-58
New York	Joe McCarthy	89-60
Philadelphia	Connie Mack	58-91
St. Louis	Rogers Hornsby	65-87
Washington	Bucky Harris	67-86

Awards

Most Valuable Player	H. Greenberg, 1b, Det
STATS Cy Young	Wes Ferrell, Bos
STATS Rookie of the Year	Jake Powell, of, Was
STATS Manager of the Year	Jimmy Dykes, ChA

STATS All-Star Team

C	Mickey Cochrane, Det	.319	5	47
1B	Hank Greenberg, Det	.328	36	170
2B	Buddy Myer, Was	.349	5	100
3B	Odell Hale, Cle	.304	16	101
SS	Luke Appling, ChA	.307	1	71
OF	Pete Fox, Det	.321	15	73
OF	Bob Johnson, Phi	.299	28	109
OF	Joe Vosmik, Cle	.348	10	110
P	Tommy Bridges, Det	21-10	3.51	163 K
P	Wes Ferrell, Bos	25-14	3.52	110 K
P	Lefty Grove, Bos	20-12	2.70	121 K
P	Mel Harder, Cle	22-11	3.29	95 K
RP	Johnny Murphy, NYA	10-5	4.08	5 Sv

Postseason

World Series	Detroit (AL) 4 vs. Chicago (NL) 2

Outstanding Performances

No-Hitters
Vern Kennedy, ChA   vs. Cle on August 31
Three-Homer Games
Mike Higgins, Phi   on June 27
Moose Solters, StL   on July 7

1935 National League Standings

Team	Overall					Home Games						Road Games						Park Index		Record by Month					
	W	L	Pct	GB	DIF	W	L	R	OR	HR	OHR	W	L	R	OR	HR	OHR	Run	HR	M/A	May	June	July	Aug	S/O
Chicago	100	54	.649	—	18	56	21	426	264	43	40	44	33	421	333	45	45	92	92	8-5	10-9	18-14	26-8	15-15	23-3
St. Louis	96	58	.623	4.0	20	53	24	441	298	39	27	43	34	388	327	47	41	103	75	6-7	15-8	15-14	19-10	22-7	19-12
New York	91	62	.595	8.5	130	50	27	386	302	84	66	41	35	384	373	39	40	90	187	7-3	19-6	18-9	16-15	16-14	15-15
Pittsburgh	86	67	.562	13.5	1	46	31	398	340	32	25	40	36	345	307	34	38	112	78	6-8	17-11	16-11	15-14	20-11	12-12
Brooklyn	70	83	.458	29.5	10	38	38	349	346	32	43	32	45	362	421	27	45	90	106	9-4	10-13	10-17	12-18	16-16	13-15
Cincinnati	68	85	.444	31.5	4	41	35	331	320	18	18	27	50	315	452	55	47	86	36	7-7	9-13	13-16	13-17	12-20	14-12
Philadelphia	64	89	.418	35.5	0	35	43	416	499	52	68	29	46	269	372	40	38	137	148	2-9	9-13	15-16	14-15	13-18	11-18
Boston	38	115	.248	61.5	3	25	50	309	381	34	41	13	65	266	471	41	40	97	96	5-7	4-20	11-19	5-23	8-21	5-25

Clinch Date—Chicago 9/27.

Team Batting

Team	G	AB	R	OR	H	2B	3B	HR	TB	RBI	TBB	IBB	SO	HBP	SH	SF	SB	CS	SB%	GDP	Avg	OBP	Slg
Chicago	154	5486	847	597	1581	303	62	88	2272	782	464	—	471	33	150	—	66	—	—	115	.288	.347	.414
St. Louis	154	5457	829	625	1548	286	59	86	2210	762	404	—	521	19	97	—	71	—	—	100	.284	.335	.405
New York	156	5623	770	675	1608	248	56	123	2337	703	392	—	479	32	116	—	32	—	—	117	.286	.336	.416
Pittsburgh	153	5415	743	647	1543	255	90	66	2176	682	457	—	437	24	77	—	30	—	—	135	.285	.343	.402
Brooklyn	154	5410	711	767	1496	235	62	59	2032	666	430	—	520	27	70	—	60	—	—	120	.277	.333	.376
Philadelphia	156	5442	685	871	1466	249	32	92	2055	624	392	—	661	26	84	—	52	—	—	91	.269	.322	.378
Cincinnati	154	5296	646	772	1403	244	68	73	2002	605	392	—	547	30	80	—	72	—	—	93	.265	.319	.378
Boston	153	5309	575	852	1396	233	33	75	1920	544	353	—	436	19	80	—	20	—	—	139	.263	.311	.362
NL Total	1234	43438	5806	5806	12041	2053	462	662	17004	5368	3284	—	4072	210	754	—	403	—	—	910	.277	.331	.391
NL Avg Team	154	5430	726	726	1505	257	58	83	2126	671	411	—	509	26	94	—	50	—	—	114	.277	.331	.391

Team Pitching

Team	G	CG	ShO	Rel	Sv	IP	H	R	ER	HR	SH	SF	HB	TBB	IBB	SO	WP	Bk	H/9	SO/9	BB/9	OAvg	OOBP	ERA
Chicago	154	81	12	118	14	1394.1	1417	597	505	85	78	—	20	400	—	589	32	2	9.1	3.8	2.6	.263	.317	3.26
Pittsburgh	153	76	15	118	11	1365.2	1428	647	519	63	93	—	20	312	—	549	25	3	9.4	3.6	2.1	.265	.307	3.42
St. Louis	154	73	10	139	18	1384.2	1445	625	542	68	78	—	26	377	—	602	24	2	9.4	3.9	2.5	.267	.318	3.52
New York	156	76	10	134	11	1403.2	1433	675	590	106	100	—	30	411	—	524	38	1	9.2	3.4	2.6	.263	.318	3.78
Brooklyn	154	62	11	145	20	1358.0	1519	767	637	88	83	—	18	436	—	480	38	2	10.1	3.2	2.9	.281	.337	4.22
Cincinnati	154	59	9	161	13	1356.0	1490	772	648	65	109	—	29	438	—	500	20	1	9.9	3.3	2.9	.278	.336	4.30
Philadelphia	156	53	8	202	15	1374.2	1652	871	727	106	92	—	47	505	—	475	20	2	10.8	3.1	3.3	.295	.358	4.76
Boston	153	54	6	136	5	1330.0	1645	852	729	81	118	—	20	404	—	355	14	2	11.1	2.4	2.7	.303	.354	4.93
NL Total	1234	534	81	1153	107	10967.0	12029	5806	4897	662	751	—	210	3283	—	4074	211	15	9.9	3.3	2.7	.277	.331	4.02
NL Avg Team	154	67	10	144	13	1370.0	1504	726	612	83	94	—	26	410	—	509	26	2	9.9	3.3	2.7	.277	.331	4.02

Team Fielding

Team	G	PO	A	E	TC	DP	PB	Pct
St. Louis	154	4157	1595	164	5916	133	10	.972
New York	156	4211	1874	174	6259	129	8	.972
Chicago	154	4180	1858	186	6224	163	13	.970
Brooklyn	154	4076	1824	188	6088	146	11	.969
Pittsburgh	153	4094	1672	190	5956	94	9	.968
Boston	153	3991	1759	197	5947	101	7	.967
Cincinnati	154	4065	1790	204	6059	139	20	.966
Philadelphia	156	4121	1795	228	6144	145	8	.963
NL Total	1234	32895	14167	1531	48593	1050	86	.968

Team vs. Team Records

	Bos	Bro	ChN	Cin	NYG	Phi	Pit	StL	Won
Bos	—	6	3	10	5	8	2	4	38
Bro	16	—	5	11	9	12	11	6	70
ChN	19	17	—	14	14	13	15	8	100
Cin	12	11	8	—	8	13	8	8	68
NYG	16	13	8	14	—	12	14	14	91
Phi	14	9	9	9	10	—	6	7	64
Pit	20	11	7	13	8	16	—	11	86
StL	18	16	14	14	8	15	11	—	96
Lost	115	83	54	85	62	89	67	58	

Seasons: Standings, Leaders

1935 National League Batting Leaders

Games		At-Bats		Runs		Hits		Doubles		Triples	
D. Camilli, Phi	156	J. Moore, NYG	681	A. Galan, ChN	133	B. Herman, ChN	227	B. Herman, ChN	57	I. Goodman, Cin	18
E. Allen, Phi	156	B. Herman, ChN	666	J. Medwick, StL	132	J. Medwick, StL	224	J. Medwick, StL	46	L. Waner, Pit	14
J. Moore, NYG	155	A. Galan, ChN	646	P. Martin, StL	121	4 tied with	203	E. Allen, Phi	46	J. Medwick, StL	13
4 tied with	154	E. Allen, Phi	645	B. Herman, ChN	113			A. Galan, ChN	41	4 tied with	12
		J. Medwick, StL	634	M. Ott, NYG	113			P. Martin, StL	41		

Home Runs		Total Bases		Runs Batted In		Walks		Intentional Walks		Strikeouts	
W. Berger, Bos	34	J. Medwick, StL	365	W. Berger, Bos	130	A. Vaughan, Pit	97	Statistic unavailable		D. Camilli, Phi	113
M. Ott, NYG	31	M. Ott, NYG	329	J. Medwick, StL	126	A. Galan, ChN	87			A. Kampouris, Cin	84
D. Camilli, Phi	25	W. Berger, Bos	323	R. Collins, StL	122	M. Ott, NYG	82			B. Myers, Cin	81
J. Medwick, StL	23	B. Herman, ChN	317	M. Ott, NYG	114	G. Suhr, Pit	70			W. Berger, Bos	80
R. Collins, StL	23	H. Leiber, NYG	314	H. Leiber, NYG	107	L. Frey, Bro	66			G. Watkins, Phi	78

Hit By Pitch		Sac Hits		Sac Flies		Stolen Bases		Caught Stealing		GDP	
H. Leiber, NYG	10	B. Herman, ChN	24	Statistic unavailable		A. Galan, ChN	22	Statistic unavailable		H. Leiber, NYG	20
J. Moore, NYG	8	D. Bartell, NYG	21			P. Martin, StL	20			B. Herman, ChN	17
A. Vaughan, Pit	7	J. Rothrock, StL	20			F. Bordagaray, Bro	18			4 tied with	16
K. Cuyler, 2tm	7	B. Jurges, ChN	18			I. Goodman, Cin	14				
2 tied with	6	B. Terry, NYG	16			S. Hack, ChN	14				

Runs Created		Runs Created/27 Outs		Batting Average		On-Base Percentage		Slugging Percentage		OBP+Slugging	
J. Medwick, StL	143	A. Vaughan, Pit	11.93	A. Vaughan, Pit	.385	A. Vaughan, Pit	.491	A. Vaughan, Pit	.607	A. Vaughan, Pit	1.098
A. Vaughan, Pit	142	J. Medwick, StL	8.97	J. Medwick, StL	.353	M. Ott, NYG	.407	J. Medwick, StL	.576	J. Medwick, StL	.962
A. Galan, ChN	135	R. Collins, StL	8.58	G. Hartnett, ChN	.344	S. Hack, ChN	.406	M. Ott, NYG	.555	M. Ott, NYG	.962
M. Ott, NYG	130	M. Ott, NYG	8.47	E. Lombardi, Cin	.343	G. Hartnett, ChN	.404	W. Berger, Bos	.548	G. Hartnett, ChN	.949
R. Collins, StL	129	G. Hartnett, ChN	8.31	B. Herman, ChN	.341	A. Galan, ChN	.399	G. Hartnett, ChN	.545	E. Lombardi, Cin	.918

1935 National League Pitching Leaders

Wins		Losses		Winning Percentage		Games		Games Started		Complete Games	
D. Dean, StL	28	B. Cantwell, Bos	25	B. Lee, ChN	.769	O. Jorgens, Phi	53	D. Dean, StL	36	D. Dean, StL	29
C. Hubbell, NYG	23	E. Brandt, Bos	19	R. Henshaw, ChN	.722	D. Dean, StL	50	C. Hubbell, NYG	35	C. Hubbell, NYG	24
P. Derringer, Cin	22	B. Smith, Bos	18	S. Castleman, NYG	.714	J. Bivin, Phi	47	P. Dean, StL	33	C. Blanton, Pit	23
B. Lee, ChN	20	3 tied with	15	D. Dean, StL	.700	P. Dean, StL	46	P. Derringer, Cin	33	P. Derringer, Cin	20
L. Warneke, ChN	20			H. Schumacher, NYG	.679	B. Smith, Bos	46	H. Schumacher, NYG	33	L. Warneke, ChN	20

Shutouts		Saves		Games Finished		Batters Faced		Innings Pitched		Hits Allowed	
C. Blanton, Pit	4	D. Leonard, Bro	8	A. Stout, NYG	22	D. Dean, StL	1362	D. Dean, StL	325.1	D. Dean, StL	324
V. Mungo, Bro	4	S. Johnson, Phi	6	B. Smith, Bos	22	C. Hubbell, NYG	1265	C. Hubbell, NYG	302.2	C. Hubbell, NYG	314
L. French, ChN	4	W. Hoyt, Pit	6	L. Benton, Bos	19	P. Derringer, Cin	1153	P. Derringer, Cin	276.2	P. Derringer, Cin	295
J. Weaver, Pit	4	6 tied with	5	H. Betts, Bos	19	P. Dean, StL	1125	P. Dean, StL	269.2	L. French, ChN	279
F. Fitzsimmons, NYG	4			W. Hoyt, Pit	19	H. Schumacher, NYG	1074	2 tied with	261.2	F. Frankhouse, Bos	278

Home Runs Allowed		Walks		Walks/9 Innings		Strikeouts		Strikeouts/9 Innings		Strikeout/Walk Ratio	
C. Hubbell, NYG	27	R. Parmelee, NYG	97	W. Clark, Bro	1.2	D. Dean, StL	190	V. Mungo, Bro	6.0	C. Hubbell, NYG	3.06
J. Bivin, Phi	20	O. Jorgens, Phi	96	C. Hubbell, NYG	1.5	C. Hubbell, NYG	150	D. Dean, StL	5.3	P. Dean, StL	2.60
R. Parmelee, NYG	20	V. Mungo, Bro	90	P. Derringer, Cin	1.6	P. Dean, StL	143	C. Blanton, Pit	5.0	C. Blanton, Pit	2.58
L. Warneke, ChN	19	B. Lee, ChN	84	L. French, ChN	1.6	V. Mungo, Bro	143	P. Dean, StL	4.8	D. Dean, StL	2.47
T. Carleton, ChN	17	F. Frankhouse, Bos	81	B. Swift, Pit	1.6	C. Blanton, Pit	142	C. Hubbell, NYG	4.5	P. Derringer, Cin	2.45

Earned Run Average		Component ERA		Hit Batsmen		Wild Pitches		Opponent Average		Opponent OBP	
C. Blanton, Pit	2.58	C. Blanton, Pit	2.08	P. Dean, StL	9	L. Warneke, ChN	10	C. Blanton, Pit	.229	C. Blanton, Pit	.272
B. Swift, Pit	2.70	B. Swift, Pit	2.49	R. Parmelee, NYG	9	W. Hallahan, StL	10	H. Schumacher, NYG	.238	B. Swift, Pit	.282
H. Schumacher, NYG	2.89	H. Schumacher, NYG	2.67	O. Jorgens, Phi	8	D. Leonard, Bro	9	B. Swift, Pit	.247	W. Clark, Bro	.289
L. French, ChN	2.96	P. Dean, StL	2.92	L. Herrmann, Cin	8	R. Parmelee, NYG	8	P. Dean, StL	.249	H. Schumacher, NYG	.292
B. Lee, ChN	2.96	W. Clark, Bro	2.93	4 tied with	7	6 tied with	7	R. Parmelee, NYG	.249	P. Dean, StL	.292

1935 National League Miscellaneous

Managers		
Boston	Bill McKechnie	38-115
Brooklyn	Casey Stengel	70-83
Chicago	Charlie Grimm	100-54
Cincinnati	Chuck Dressen	68-85
New York	Bill Terry	91-62
Philadelphia	Jimmie Wilson	64-89
Pittsburgh	Pie Traynor	86-67
St. Louis	Frank Frisch	96-58

Awards	
Most Valuable Player	Gabby Hartnett, c, ChN
STATS Cy Young	Dizzy Dean, StL
STATS Rookie of the Year	Cy Blanton, p, Pit
STATS Manager of the Year	Charlie Grimm, ChN

STATS All-Star Team

C	Gabby Hartnett, ChN	.344	13	91
1B	Ripper Collins, StL	.313	23	122
2B	Billy Herman, ChN	.341	7	83
3B	Stan Hack, ChN	.311	4	64
SS	Arky Vaughan, Pit	.385	19	99
OF	Wally Berger, Bos	.295	34	130
OF	Joe Medwick, StL	.353	23	126
OF	Mel Ott, NYG	.322	31	114
P	Cy Blanton, Pit	18-13	2.58	142 K
P	Dizzy Dean, StL	28-12	3.04	190 K
P	Carl Hubbell, NYG	23-12	3.27	150 K
P	Bill Lee, ChN	20-6	2.96	100 K
RP	Syl Johnson, Phi	10-8	3.56	6 Sv

Postseason	
World Series	Chicago (NL) 2 vs. Detroit (AL) 4

Outstanding Performances

Three-Homer Games

Babe Ruth, Bos	on May 25

Cycles

Joe Medwick, StL	on June 29

1936 American League Standings

Team	Overall					Home Games						Road Games						Park Index		Record by Month					
	W	L	Pct	GB	DIF	W	L	R	OR	HR	OHR	W	L	R	OR	HR	OHR	Run	HR	M/A	May	June	July	Aug	S/O
New York	102	51	.667	—	141	**56**	**21**	492	311	82	41	46	30	**573**	420	**100**	43	80	85	10-5	20-8	17-9	18-12	21-8	16-9
Detroit	83	71	.539	19.5	1	44	33	448	399	51	58	39	38	473	472	43	42	90	128	7-6	16-15	13-11	16-14	16-16	15-9
Chicago	81	70	.536	20.0	8	43	32	453	419	23	55	38	38	467	454	37	49	96	92	4-8	15-13	12-14	20-11	16-16	14-8
Washington	82	71	.536	20.0	2	42	35	433	380	16	**27**	40	36	456	419	46	46	92	46	9-8	13-14	14-11	13-17	17-12	16-9
Cleveland	80	74	.519	22.5	7	49	30	**535**	433	73	33	31	44	386	429	50	**40**	113	112	8-6	16-11	12-15	21-11	12-15	11-16
Boston	74	80	.481	28.5	17	47	29	437	360	38	31	27	51	338	**404**	48	47	110	75	11-5	15-13	12-14	16-14	10-19	10-15
St. Louis	57	95	.375	44.5	0	31	43	443	552	47	63	26	52	361	512	32	52	120	138	3-12	9-18	9-12	13-21	12-18	11-14
Philadelphia	53	100	.346	49.0	0	31	46	383	531	43	77	22	54	331	514	29	54	107	143	6-8	7-19	11-14	8-25	15-15	6-19

Clinch Date—New York 9/09.

Team Batting

Team	G	AB	R	OR	H	2B	3B	HR	TB	RBI	TBB	IBB	SO	HBP	SH	SF	SB	CS	SB%	GDP	Avg	OBP	Slg
New York	155	5591	**1065**	731	1676	315	83	**182**	2703	997	700	—	594	33	40	—	77	40	.66	—	.300	**.381**	**.483**
Cleveland	157	**5646**	921	862	**1715**	**357**	82	123	2605	853	514	—	470	16	77	—	66	**53**	.55	—	**.304**	.364	.461
Detroit	154	5464	921	871	1638	326	55	94	2356	848	640	—	462	**34**	88	—	73	49	.60	—	.300	.377	.431
Chicago	153	5466	920	873	1597	282	56	60	2171	862	684	—	417	25	107	—	66	29	.69	—	.292	.373	.397
Washington	153	5433	889	799	1601	293	**84**	62	2248	823	576	—	398	22	61	—	**104**	42	.71	—	.295	.356	.414
St. Louis	155	5391	804	1064	1502	299	66	79	2170	761	625	—	**627**	19	72	—	62	20	**.76**	—	.279	.349	.403
Boston	155	5383	775	764	1485	288	62	86	2155	718	584	—	465	23	**108**	—	55	44	.56	—	.276	.349	.400
Philadelphia	154	5373	714	1045	1443	240	60	72	2019	663	524	—	590	19	74	—	59	43	.58	—	.269	.336	.376
AL Total	1236	43747	7009	7009	12657	2400	548	758	18427	6525	4847	—	4023	191	654	—	562	320	.64	—	.289	.363	.421
AL Avg Team	155	5468	876	876	1582	300	69	95	2303	816	606	—	503	24	82	—	70	40	.64	—	.289	.363	.421

Team Pitching

Team	G	CG	ShO	Rel	Sv	IP	H	R	ER	HR	SH	SF	HB	TBB	IBB	SO	WP	Bk	H/9	SO/9	BB/9	OAvg	OOBP	ERA
New York	155	77	6	119	21	1400.1	1474	731	649	84	75	—	13	663	—	624	34	0	9.5	4.0	4.3	.271	.351	4.17
Boston	155	78	11	143	9	1372.1	1501	764	669	78	82	—	18	**552**	—	584	30	3	9.8	3.8	**3.6**	.277	**.346**	4.39
Washington	153	78	8	112	14	1345.2	1484	799	685	**73**	**70**	—	22	588	—	462	40	4	9.9	3.1	3.9	.279	.353	4.58
Cleveland	157	74	6	155	12	1389.1	1604	862	746	100	91	—	27	607	—	619	45	7	10.4	4.0	3.9	.289	.362	4.83
Detroit	154	76	**13**	127	13	1360.0	1568	871	755	100	83	—	20	562	—	526	33	2	10.4	3.5	3.7	.289	.358	5.00
Chicago	153	**80**	5	104	8	1365.0	1603	873	768	104	77	—	23	578	—	414	32	0	10.6	2.7	3.8	.293	.363	5.06
Philadelphia	154	68	3	130	12	1352.1	1645	1045	913	131	90	—	24	696	—	405	**67**	7	10.9	2.7	4.6	.300	.381	6.08
St. Louis	155	54	3	**193**	13	1348.1	1776	1064	935	115	73	—	47	609	—	399	44	5	11.9	2.7	4.1	.314	.385	6.24
AL Total	1236	585	55	1083	102	10933.1	12655	7009	6120	758	641	—	194	4855	—	4033	325	28	10.4	3.3	4.0	.289	.363	5.04
AL Avg Team	155	73	7	135	13	1366.1	1582	876	765	95	80	—	24	607	—	504	41	4	10.4	3.3	4.0	.289	.363	5.04

Team Fielding

Team	G	PO	A	E	TC	DP	PB	Pct
Detroit	154	4080	1779	**153**	6012	159	16	.975
New York	155	**4195**	1692	163	6050	148	7	.973
Chicago	153	4092	**1966**	168	**6226**	**174**	11	.973
Boston	155	4134	1664	165	5963	139	7	.972
Cleveland	157	4167	1812	178	6157	154	14	.971
Washington	153	4039	1780	182	6001	163	7	.970
St. Louis	155	4040	1745	188	5973	143	9	.969
Philadelphia	154	4061	1773	209	6043	152	21	.965
AL Total	1236	32808	14211	1406	48425	1232	92	.971

Team vs. Team Records

	Bos	ChA	Cle	Det	NYA	Phi	StL	Was	Won
Bos	—	12	9	13	7	13	12	8	**74**
ChA	10	—	12	8	7	15	13	16	**81**
Cle	13	10	—	9	6	13	15	14	**80**
Det	9	14	13	—	8	17	11	11	**83**
NYA	15	14	16	14	—	16	14	13	**102**
Phi	9	7	9	5	6	—	11	6	**53**
StL	10	8	7	11	8	10	—	3	**57**
Was	14	5	8	11	9	16	19	—	**82**
Lost	80	70	74	71	51	100	95	71	

Seasons: Standings, Leaders

1936 American League Batting Leaders

Games		At-Bats		Runs		Hits		Doubles		Triples	
B. Bell, StL	155	L. Finney, Phi	653	L. Gehrig, NYA	167	E. Averill, Cle	232	C. Gehringer, Det	60	J. DiMaggio, NYA	15
B. Knickerbocker, Cle	155	D. Cramer, Bos	643	H. Clift, StL	145	C. Gehringer, Det	227	G. Walker, Det	55	R. Rolfe, NYA	15
L. Lary, StL	155	C. Gehringer, Det	641	C. Gehringer, Det	144	H. Trosky, Cle	216	O. Hale, Cle	50	E. Averill, Cle	15
J. Foxx, Bos	155	R. Hughes, Cle	638	F. Crosetti, NYA	137	B. Bell, StL	212	B. Chapman, 2tm	50	B. Johnson, Phi	14
L. Gehrig, NYA	155	J. DiMaggio, NYA	637	E. Averill, Cle	136	R. Radcliff, ChA	207	2 tied with	45	2 tied with	13

Home Runs		Total Bases		Runs Batted In		Walks		Intentional Walks		Strikeouts	
L. Gehrig, NYA	49	H. Trosky, Cle	405	H. Trosky, Cle	162	L. Gehrig, NYA	130	Statistic unavailable		J. Foxx, Bos	119
H. Trosky, Cle	42	L. Gehrig, NYA	403	L. Gehrig, NYA	152	L. Lary, StL	117			F. Crosetti, NYA	83
J. Foxx, Bos	41	E. Averill, Cle	385	J. Foxx, Bos	143	H. Clift, StL	115			M. Solters, StL	76
J. DiMaggio, NYA	29	J. Foxx, Bos	369	Z. Bonura, ChA	138	J. Foxx, Bos	105			B. Johnson, Phi	71
E. Averill, Cle	28	J. DiMaggio, NYA	367	M. Solters, StL	134	T. Lazzeri, NYA	97			2 tied with	70

Hit By Pitch		Sac Hits		Sac Flies		Stolen Bases		Caught Stealing		GDP	
F. Crosetti, NYA	12	M. Haas, ChA	23	Statistic unavailable		L. Lary, StL	37	B. Knickerbocker, Cle	14	Statistic unavailable	
T. Piet, ChA	9	R. Warstler, Phi	17			J. Powell, 2tm	26	B. Werber, Bos	13		
G. Walker, Det	8	D. Cramer, Bos	16			B. Werber, Bos	23	J. Powell, 2tm	11		
3 tied with	7	M. Kreevich, ChA	15			R. Hughes, Cle	20	B. Rogell, Det	10		
		3 tied with	12			B. Chapman, 2tm	20	4 tied with	9		

Runs Created		Runs Created/27 Outs		Batting Average		On-Base Percentage		Slugging Percentage		OBP+Slugging	
L. Gehrig, NYA	181	L. Gehrig, NYA	12.32	L. Appling, ChA	.388	L. Gehrig, NYA	.478	L. Gehrig, NYA	.696	L. Gehrig, NYA	1.174
J. Foxx, Bos	152	L. Appling, ChA	10.41	E. Averill, Cle	.378	L. Appling, ChA	.473	H. Trosky, Cle	.644	J. Foxx, Bos	1.071
E. Averill, Cle	150	B. Dickey, NYA	10.11	B. Dickey, NYA	.362	J. Foxx, Bos	.440	J. Foxx, Bos	.631	E. Averill, Cle	1.065
C. Gehringer, Det	149	E. Averill, Cle	10.06	C. Gehringer, Det	.354	E. Averill, Cle	.438	E. Averill, Cle	.627	B. Dickey, NYA	1.045
H. Trosky, Cle	139	J. Foxx, Bos	10.03	L. Gehrig, NYA	.354	C. Gehringer, Det	.431	B. Dickey, NYA	.617	H. Trosky, Cle	1.026

1936 American League Pitching Leaders

Wins		Losses		Winning Percentage		Games		Games Started		Complete Games	
T. Bridges, Det	23	G. Rhodes, Phi	20	B. Hadley, NYA	.778	R. Van Atta, StL	52	T. Bridges, Det	38	W. Ferrell, Bos	28
V. Kennedy, ChA	21	J. Knott, StL	17	P. Malone, NYA	.750	J. Knott, StL	47	B. Newsom, Was	38	T. Bridges, Det	26
J. Allen, Cle	20	5 tied with	16	M. Pearson, NYA	.731	4 tied with	43	W. Ferrell, Bos	38	R. Ruffing, NYA	25
W. Ferrell, Bos	20			V. Kennedy, ChA	.700			S. Rowe, Det	35	B. Newsom, Was	24
R. Ruffing, NYA	20			T. Bridges, Det	.676			V. Kennedy, ChA	34	L. Grove, Bos	22

Shutouts		Saves		Games Finished		Batters Faced		Innings Pitched		Hits Allowed	
L. Grove, Bos	6	P. Malone, NYA	9	C. Brown, ChA	29	W. Ferrell, Bos	1341	W. Ferrell, Bos	301.0	W. Ferrell, Bos	330
T. Bridges, Det	5	J. Knott, StL	6	P. Malone, NYA	25	T. Bridges, Det	1272	T. Bridges, Det	294.2	B. Newsom, Was	294
S. Rowe, Det	4	J. Murphy, NYA	5	R. Van Atta, StL	20	B. Newsom, Was	1258	B. Newsom, Was	285.1	M. Harder, Cle	294
J. Allen, Cle	4	C. Brown, ChA	5	J. Wilson, Bos	19	V. Kennedy, ChA	1214	V. Kennedy, ChA	274.1	T. Bridges, Det	289
B. Newsom, Was	4	O. Hildebrand, Cle	4	3 tied with	17	R. Ruffing, NYA	1151	R. Ruffing, NYA	271.0	C. Hogsett, 2tm	286

Home Runs Allowed		Walks		Walks/9 Innings		Strikeouts		Strikeouts/9 Innings		Strikeout/Walk Ratio	
G. Rhodes, Phi	26	V. Kennedy, ChA	147	T. Lyons, ChA	2.2	T. Bridges, Det	175	J. Allen, Cle	6.1	L. Grove, Bos	2.00
T. Thomas, StL	25	B. Newsom, Was	146	L. Grove, Bos	2.3	J. Allen, Cle	165	T. Bridges, Det	5.3	S. Rowe, Det	1.80
R. Ruffing, NYA	22	M. Pearson, NYA	135	S. Rowe, Det	2.3	B. Newsom, Was	156	L. Gomez, NYA	5.0	J. Allen, Cle	1.70
4 tied with	21	L. Gomez, NYA	122	I. Andrews, StL	2.4	L. Grove, Bos	130	B. Newsom, Was	4.9	T. Bridges, Det	1.52
		W. Ferrell, Bos	119	M. Harder, Cle	2.8	M. Pearson, NYA	118	M. Pearson, NYA	4.8	J. Broaca, NYA	1.27

Earned Run Average		Component ERA		Hit Batsmen		Wild Pitches		Opponent Average		Opponent OBP	
L. Grove, Bos	2.81	L. Grove, Bos	2.88	C. Hogsett, 2tm	15	S. Flythe, Phi	16	M. Pearson, NYA	.233	L. Grove, Bos	.297
J. Allen, Cle	3.44	J. Allen, Cle	3.26	E. Caldwell, StL	15	J. Allen, Cle	13	L. Grove, Bos	.246	S. Rowe, Det	.321
P. Appleton, Was	3.53	P. Appleton, Was	3.42	4 tied with	6	J. Knott, StL	11	L. Gomez, NYA	.254	R. Ruffing, NYA	.323
T. Bridges, Det	3.60	T. Bridges, Det	3.67			B. Ross, Phi	10	P. Appleton, Was	.254	P. Appleton, Was	.324
M. Pearson, NYA	3.71	S. Rowe, Det	3.69			J. Whitehead, ChA	10	T. Bridges, Det	.255	T. Bridges, Det	.326

1936 American League Miscellaneous

Managers		
Boston	Joe Cronin	74-80
Chicago	Jimmy Dykes	81-70
Cleveland	Steve O'Neill	80-74
Detroit	Mickey Cochrane	29-24
	Del Baker	18-16
	Mickey Cochrane	36-31
New York	Joe McCarthy	102-51
Philadelphia	Connie Mack	53-100
St. Louis	Rogers Hornsby	57-95
Washington	Bucky Harris	82-71

Awards

Most Valuable Player	Lou Gehrig, 1b, NYA
STATS Cy Young	Tommy Bridges, Det
STATS Rookie of the Year	Joe DiMaggio, of, NYA
STATS Manager of the Year	Joe McCarthy, NYA

STATS All-Star Team

C	Bill Dickey, NYA	.362	22	107	
1B	Lou Gehrig, NYA	.354	49	152	
2B	Charlie Gehringer, Det	.354	15	116	
3B	Harlond Clift, StL	.302	20	73	
SS	Luke Appling, ChA	.388	6	128	
OF	Earl Averill, Cle	.378	28	126	
OF	Joe DiMaggio, NYA	.323	29	125	
OF	Goose Goslin, Det	.315	24	125	
P	Johnny Allen, Cle	20-10	3.44	165 K	
P	Tommy Bridges, Det	23-11	3.60	175 K	
P	Lefty Grove, Bos	17-12	2.81	130 K	
P	Red Ruffing, NYA	20-12	3.85	102 K	
RP	Pat Malone, NYA	12-4	3.81	9 Sv	

Postseason

World Series	NYA (AL) 4 vs. NYG (NL) 2

Outstanding Performances

Three-Homer Games
Tony Lazzeri, NYA   on May 24

1936 National League Standings

Team	W	L	Pct	GB	DIF	W	L	R	OR	HR	OHR	W	L	R	OR	HR	OHR	Run	HR	M/A	May	June	July	Aug	S/O
	Overall					**Home Games**						**Road Games**						**Park Index**		**Record by Month**					
New York	92	62	.597	—	55	**52**	**26**	378	296	68	54	40	36	364	325	29	**21**	95	238	8-5	17-12	12-14	16-14	24-3	15-14
Chicago	87	67	.565	5.0	31	50	27	404	**290**	34	41	37	40	351	**313**	42	36	105	96	8-6	12-14	21-5	17-11	16-17	13-14
St. Louis	87	67	.565	5.0	85	43	33	363	386	38	43	**44**	**34**	**432**	408	50	46	92	87	6-5	21-9	16-11	15-13	16-14	13-15
Pittsburgh	84	70	.545	8.0	2	46	30	375	342	23	25	38	40	429	376	37	49	91	57	6-6	15-14	17-11	13-15	15-15	18-9
Cincinnati	74	80	.481	18.0	0	42	34	358	350	20	**21**	32	46	364	410	**62**	30	94	46	7-7	12-16	17-7	11-18	13-17	14-15
Boston	71	83	.461	21.0	0	35	43	292	339	26	23	36	40	339	376	41	46	86	55	5-7	15-16	12-15	13-14	13-15	13-16
Brooklyn	67	87	.435	25.0	0	37	40	360	397	15	46	30	47	302	355	18	38	115	109	6-8	12-17	4-21	13-16	16-12	16-13
Philadelphia	54	100	.351	38.0	1	30	48	**408**	499	**69**	56	24	52	318	375	34	31	128	187	7-9	11-17	4-19	16-13	4-24	12-18

Clinch Date—New York 9/24.

Team Batting

Team	G	AB	R	OR	H	2B	3B	HR	TB	RBI	TBB	IBB	SO	HBP	SH	SF	SB	CS	SB%	GDP	Avg	OBP	Slg
Pittsburgh	156	**5586**	804	718	**1596**	283	**80**	60	2219	732	**517**	—	502	26	82	—	37	—	—	122	**.286**	**.349**	.397
St. Louis	155	5537	795	794	1554	**332**	60	76	**2270**	**733**	442	—	577	15	**137**	—	**69**	—	—	125	.281	.349	**.410**
Chicago	154	5409	755	**603**	1545	275	36	76	2120	707	491	—	462	32	137	—	68	—	—	138	.286	.349	.392
New York	154	5449	742	621	1529	237	48	97	2153	687	431	—	452	**35**	123	—	31	—	—	116	.281	.337	.395
Philadelphia	154	5465	726	874	1538	250	46	**103**	2189	682	451	—	**586**	21	103	—	50	—	—	121	.281	.339	.401
Cincinnati	154	5393	722	760	1476	224	73	82	2092	674	410	—	584	34	67	—	68	—	—	121	.274	.329	.388
Brooklyn	156	5574	662	752	1518	263	43	33	1966	596	390	—	458	25	79	—	55	—	—	114	.272	.323	.353
Boston	157	5478	631	715	1450	207	45	67	1948	594	433	—	582	31	99	—	23	—	—	**146**	.265	.322	.356
NL Total	1240	43891	5837	5837	12206	2071	431	606	16957	5405	3565	—	4203	219	761	—	401	—	—	1003	.278	.335	.386
NL Avg Team	155	5486	730	730	1526	259	54	76	2120	676	446	—	525	27	95	—	50	—	—	125	.278	.335	.386

Team Pitching

Team	G	CG	ShO	Rel	Sv	IP	H	R	ER	HR	SH	SF	HB	TBB	IBB	SO	WP	Bk	H/9	SO/9	BB/9	OAvg	OOBP	ERA
New York	154	60	12	148	22	1385.2	1458	621	532	75	86	—	22	401	—	500	29	0	9.5	3.2	2.6	.273	.327	3.46
Chicago	154	**77**	**18**	139	10	1382.1	**1413**	**603**	543	77	**76**	—	29	434	—	597	23	0	**9.2**	3.9	2.8	**.265**	.324	3.54
Pittsburgh	156	67	5	137	12	1395.1	1475	718	603	74	106	—	21	**379**	—	559	27	1	9.5	3.6	**2.4**	.269	**.318**	3.89
Boston	157	61	7	134	13	**1413.1**	1566	715	619	69	91	—	23	451	—	421	21	1	10.0	2.7	2.9	.281	.337	3.94
Brooklyn	156	59	7	**169**	18	1403.0	1466	752	621	84	101	—	25	528	—	**651**	30	**4**	9.4	**4.2**	3.4	.266	.333	3.98
Cincinnati	154	50	6	161	23	1367.1	1576	760	641	**51**	101	—	27	418	—	459	34	**4**	10.4	3.0	2.8	.287	.341	4.22
St. Louis	155	65	5	166	**24**	1398.0	1610	794	694	89	120	—	34	434	—	559	**41**	2	10.4	3.6	2.8	.289	.344	4.47
Philadelphia	154	51	7	**169**	14	1365.1	1630	874	704	87	83	—	**37**	515	—	454	27	1	10.7	3.0	3.4	.292	.356	4.64
NL Total	1240	490	67	1223	136	11110.1	12194	5837	4957	606	764	—	218	3560	—	4200	232	13	9.9	3.4	2.9	.278	.335	4.02
NL Avg Team	155	61	8	153	17	1388.1	1524	730	620	76	96	—	27	445	—	525	29	2	9.9	3.4	2.9	.278	.335	4.02

Team Fielding

Team	G	PO	A	E	TC	DP	PB	Pct
Chicago	154	4147	1763	**146**	6056	156	11	.976
St. Louis	155	4190	1669	156	6015	134	9	.974
New York	154	4154	**2068**	168	6390	164	5	.974
Boston	157	**4238**	2008	189	**6435**	175	5	.971
Cincinnati	154	4100	1858	191	6149	150	12	.969
Pittsburgh	156	4189	1672	199	6060	113	4	.967
Brooklyn	156	4202	1709	208	6119	107	**13**	.966
Philadelphia	154	4093	1803	252	6148	144	6	.959
NL Total	1240	33313	14550	1509	49372	1143	65	.969

Team vs. Team Records

	Bos	Bro	ChN	Cin	NYG	Phi	Pit	StL	Won
Bos	—	10	6	13	9	12	8	13	**71**
Bro	12	—	7	9	9	12	9	9	**67**
ChN	16	15	—	10	11	16	10	9	**87**
Cin	9	13	12	—	9	13	8	10	**74**
NYG	13	13	11	13	—	17	15	10	**92**
Phi	10	10	6	9	5	—	7	7	**54**
Pit	14	13	12	14	7	15	—	9	**84**
StL	9	13	13	12	12	15	13	—	**87**
Lost	83	87	67	80	62	100	70	67	

1936 National League Batting Leaders

Games		At-Bats		Runs		Hits		Doubles		Triples	
B. Hassett, Bro	156	W. Jensen, Pit	696	A. Vaughan, Pit	122	J. Medwick, StL	223	J. Medwick, StL	64	I. Goodman, Cin	14
A. Vaughan, Pit	156	J. Moore, NYG	649	P. Martin, StL	121	P. Waner, Pit	218	B. Herman, ChN	57	D. Camilli, Phi	13
G. Suhr, Pit	156	G. Moore, Bos	637	M. Ott, NYG	120	F. Demaree, ChN	212	P. Waner, Pit	53	J. Medwick, StL	13
J. Medwick, StL	155	J. Medwick, StL	636	J. Medwick, StL	115	B. Herman, ChN	211	T. Moore, StL	39	3 tied with	12
3 tied with	154	B. Hassett, Bro	635	G. Suhr, Pit	111	J. Moore, NYG	205	G. Moore, Bos	38		

Home Runs		Total Bases		Runs Batted In		Walks		Intentional Walks		Strikeouts	
M. Ott, NYG	33	J. Medwick, StL	367	J. Medwick, StL	138	A. Vaughan, Pit	118	Statistic unavailable		B. Brubaker, Pit	96
D. Camilli, Phi	28	M. Ott, NYG	314	M. Ott, NYG	135	D. Camilli, Phi	116			D. Camilli, Phi	84
W. Berger, Bos	25	C. Klein, 2tm	308	G. Suhr, Pit	118	M. Ott, NYG	111			W. Berger, Bos	84
C. Klein, 2tm	25	D. Camilli, Phi	306	C. Klein, 2tm	104	G. Suhr, Pit	95			G. Moore, Bos	80
J. Mize, StL	19	P. Waner, Pit	304	2 tied with	102	S. Hack, ChN	89			L. Norris, Phi	79

Hit By Pitch		Sac Hits		Sac Flies		Stolen Bases		Caught Stealing		GDP	
I. Goodman, Cin	9	L. Norris, Phi	21	Statistic unavailable		P. Martin, StL	23	Statistic unavailable		H. Lee, Bos	23
W. Berger, Bos	8	D. Bartell, NYG	18			S. Martin, StL	17			F. Demaree, ChN	20
L. Riggs, Cin	7	B. Whitehead, NYG	17			L. Chiozza, Phi	17			B. Jordan, Bos	20
B. Whitehead, NYG	7	F. Demaree, ChN	17			S. Hack, ChN	17			3 tied with	18
E. Lombardi, Cin	7	B. Herman, ChN	17			3 tied with	16				

Runs Created		Runs Created/27 Outs		Batting Average		On-Base Percentage		Slugging Percentage		OBP+Slugging	
M. Ott, NYG	140	M. Ott, NYG	10.02	P. Waner, Pit	.373	A. Vaughan, Pit	.453	M. Ott, NYG	.588	M. Ott, NYG	1.036
J. Medwick, StL	137	D. Camilli, Phi	9.43	B. Phelps, Bro	.367	M. Ott, NYG	.448	D. Camilli, Phi	.577	D. Camilli, Phi	1.018
P. Waner, Pit	133	P. Waner, Pit	9.29	J. Medwick, StL	.351	P. Waner, Pit	.446	J. Mize, StL	.577	J. Mize, StL	.979
A. Vaughan, Pit	132	J. Mize, StL	9.15	F. Demaree, ChN	.350	D. Camilli, Phi	.441	J. Medwick, StL	.577	P. Waner, Pit	.965
D. Camilli, Phi	130	A. Vaughan, Pit	9.01	A. Vaughan, Pit	.335	B. Phelps, Bro	.421	P. Waner, Pit	.520	J. Medwick, StL	.964

1936 National League Pitching Leaders

Wins		Losses		Winning Percentage		Games		Games Started		Complete Games	
C. Hubbell, NYG	26	B. Walters, Phi	21	C. Hubbell, NYG	.813	P. Derringer, Cin	51	V. Mungo, Bro	37	D. Dean, StL	28
D. Dean, StL	24	J. Bowman, Phi	20	R. Lucas, Pit	.789	D. Dean, StL	51	P. Derringer, Cin	37	C. Hubbell, NYG	25
P. Derringer, Cin	19	V. Mungo, Bro	19	L. French, ChN	.667	C. Passeau, Phi	49	D. Dean, StL	34	V. Mungo, Bro	22
3 tied with	18	P. Derringer, Cin	19	D. Dean, StL	.649	M. Brown, Pit	47	C. Hubbell, NYG	34	D. MacFayden, Bos	21
		B. Swift, Pit	16	J. Weaver, Pit	.636	2 tied with	45	2 tied with	33	B. Lee, ChN	20

Shutouts		Saves		Games Finished		Batters Faced		Innings Pitched		Hits Allowed	
7 tied with	4	D. Dean, StL	11	B. Reis, Bos	24	V. Mungo, Bro	1313	D. Dean, StL	315.0	P. Derringer, Cin	331
		D. Brennan, Cin	9	D. Coffman, NYG	24	D. Dean, StL	1303	V. Mungo, Bro	311.2	D. Dean, StL	310
		B. Smith, Bos	8	D. Brennan, Cin	23	P. Derringer, Cin	1207	C. Hubbell, NYG	304.0	B. Walters, Phi	284
		D. Coffman, NYG	7	C. Passeau, Phi	22	C. Hubbell, NYG	1202	P. Derringer, Cin	282.1	B. Swift, Pit	275
		S. Johnson, Phi	7	2 tied with	21	B. Walters, Phi	1159	D. MacFayden, Bos	266.2	V. Mungo, Bro	275

Home Runs Allowed		Walks		Walks/9 Innings		Strikeouts		Strikeouts/9 Innings		Strikeout/Walk Ratio	
D. Dean, StL	21	V. Mungo, Bro	118	R. Lucas, Pit	1.3	V. Mungo, Bro	238	V. Mungo, Bro	6.9	D. Dean, StL	3.68
T. Chaplin, Bos	21	B. Walters, Phi	115	P. Derringer, Cin	1.3	D. Dean, StL	195	D. Dean, StL	5.6	P. Derringer, Cin	2.88
B. Swift, Pit	18	R. Parmelee, StL	107	D. Dean, StL	1.5	C. Blanton, Pit	127	C. Blanton, Pit	4.9	C. Blanton, Pit	2.31
F. Frankhouse, Bro	18	B. Lee, ChN	93	C. Hubbell, NYG	1.7	C. Hubbell, NYG	123	J. Weaver, Pit	4.3	C. Hubbell, NYG	2.16
C. Davis, 2tm	17	F. Frankhouse, Bro	89	L. French, ChN	1.9	P. Derringer, Cin	121	L. Warneke, ChN	4.2	R. Lucas, Pit	2.04

Earned Run Average		Component ERA		Hit Batsmen		Wild Pitches		Opponent Average		Opponent OBP	
C. Hubbell, NYG	2.31	C. Hubbell, NYG	2.20	R. Parmelee, StL	10	W. Hallahan, 2tm	11	V. Mungo, Bro	.234	C. Hubbell, NYG	.276
D. MacFayden, Bos	2.87	R. Lucas, Pit	2.78	G. Jeffcoat, Bro	8	V. Mungo, Bro	10	C. Hubbell, NYG	.236	D. Dean, StL	.285
D. Dean, StL	3.17	V. Mungo, Bro	2.79	L. Stine, Cin	8	H. Schumacher, NYG	9	B. Lee, ChN	.246	R. Lucas, Pit	.287
R. Lucas, Pit	3.18	D. Dean, StL	2.84	O. Jorgens, Phi	7	3 tied with	8	D. Dean, StL	.253	C. Blanton, Pit	.301
B. Lee, ChN	3.31	C. Blanton, Pit	2.96	J. Bowman, Phi	7			C. Blanton, Pit	.257	V. Mungo, Bro	.305

1936 National League Miscellaneous

Managers		
Boston	Bill McKechnie	71-83
Brooklyn	Casey Stengel	67-87
Chicago	Charlie Grimm	87-67
Cincinnati	Chuck Dressen	74-80
New York	Bill Terry	92-62
Philadelphia	Jimmie Wilson	54-100
Pittsburgh	Pie Traynor	84-70
St. Louis	Frank Frisch	87-67

Awards	
Most Valuable Player	Carl Hubbell, p, NYG
STATS Cy Young	Carl Hubbell, NYG
STATS Rookie of the Year	Johnny Mize, 1b, StL
STATS Manager of the Year	Bill McKechnie, Bos

STATS All-Star Team

C	Ernie Lombardi, Cin	.333	12	68
1B	Dolph Camilli, Phi	.315	28	102
2B	Billy Herman, ChN	.334	5	93
3B	Stan Hack, ChN	.298	6	78
SS	Arky Vaughan, Pit	.335	9	78
OF	Joe Medwick, StL	.351	18	138
OF	Mel Ott, NYG	.328	33	135
OF	Paul Waner, Pit	.373	5	94
P	Dizzy Dean, StL	24-13	3.17	195 K
P	Larry French, ChN	18-9	3.39	104 K
P	Carl Hubbell, NYG	26-6	2.31	123 K
P	Danny MacFayden, Bos	17-13	2.87	86 K
RP	Bob Smith, Bos	6-7	3.77	8 Sv

Postseason	
World Series	NYG (NL) 2 vs. NYA (AL) 4

Outstanding Performances

Four-Homer Games
Chuck Klein, Phi   on July 10
Three-Homer Games
Johnny Moore, Phi   on July 22
Cycles
Sam Leslie, NYG   on May 24

1937 American League Standings

Team	Overall					Home Games						Road Games						Park Index		Record by Month					
	W	L	Pct	GB	DIF	W	L	R	OR	HR	OHR	W	L	R	OR	HR	OHR	Run	HR	M/A	May	June	July	Aug	S/O
New York	102	52	.662	—	143	57	20	520	298	94	41	45	32	459	373	80	51	98	103	5-2	18-10	16-9	20-8	21-8	22-15
Detroit	89	65	.578	13.0	10	49	28	521	448	91	58	40	37	414	393	59	44	120	145	4-2	16-15	15-10	16-10	19-12	19-16
Chicago	86	68	.558	16.0	2	47	30	397	365	39	62	39	38	383	365	28	53	102	125	3-3	15-14	18-9	19-10	14-17	17-15
Cleveland	83	71	.539	19.0	4	50	28	430	329	48	22	33	43	387	439	55	39	90	73	4-3	14-11	12-15	12-15	17-13	24-14
Boston	80	72	.526	21.0	6	44	29	420	368	53	43	36	43	401	407	47	49	106	108	3-2	13-13	15-10	18-12	15-15	16-20
Washington	73	80	.477	28.5	0	43	35	376	381	14	30	30	45	381	460	33	66	87	43	2-6	15-14	10-13	12-14	15-15	19-18
Philadelphia	54	97	.358	46.5	14	27	50	333	419	51	47	27	47	366	435	43	58	90	93	3-3	12-15	5-20	6-22	11-20	17-17
St. Louis	46	108	.299	56.0	1	25	51	385	513	39	74	21	57	330	510	32	69	110	115	2-5	8-19	10-15	9-21	9-21	8-27

Clinch Date—New York 9/23.

Team Batting

Team	G	AB	R	OR	H	2B	3B	HR	TB	RBI	TBB	IBB	SO	HBP	SH	SF	SB	CS	SB%	GDP	Avg	OBP	Slg
New York	157	5487	979	671	1554	282	73	174	2504	922	709	—	607	34	61	—	60	36	.63	—	.283	.369	.456
Detroit	155	5516	935	841	1611	309	62	150	2494	873	656	—	711	22	45	—	89	45	.66	—	.292	.370	.452
Boston	154	5354	821	775	1506	269	64	100	2203	769	601	—	557	26	104	—	79	61	.56	—	.281	.357	.411
Cleveland	156	5353	817	768	1499	304	76	103	2264	754	570	—	551	20	96	—	78	51	.60	—	.280	.352	.423
Chicago	154	5277	780	730	1478	280	76	67	2111	726	549	—	447	19	111	—	70	34	.67	—	.280	.350	.400
Washington	158	5578	757	841	1559	245	84	47	2113	691	591	—	503	23	67	—	61	35	.64	—	.279	.351	.379
St. Louis	156	5510	715	1023	1573	327	44	71	2201	682	514	—	510	14	85	—	30	27	.53	—	.285	.348	.399
Philadelphia	154	5228	699	854	1398	278	60	94	2078	649	583	—	557	5	70	—	95	48	.66	—	.267	.341	.397
AL Total	1244	43303	6503	6503	12178	2294	539	806	17968	6066	4773	—	4443	163	664	—	562	337	.63	—	.281	.355	.415
AL Avg Team	156	5413	813	813	1522	287	67	101	2246	758	597	—	555	20	83	—	70	42	.63	—	.281	.355	.415

Team Pitching

Team	G	CG	ShO	Rel	Sv	IP	H	R	ER	HR	SH	SF	HB	TBB	IBB	SO	WP	Bk	H/9	SO/9	BB/9	OAvg	OOBP	ERA
New York	157	82	15	100	21	1396.0	1417	671	566	92	70	—	12	506	—	652	16	2	9.1	4.2	3.3	.261	.325	3.65
Chicago	154	70	25	108	21	1351.1	1435	730	626	115	77	—	17	532	—	533	24	1	9.6	3.5	3.5	.273	.341	4.17
Cleveland	156	64	4	160	15	1364.2	1529	768	666	61	97	—	25	566	—	630	18	4	10.1	4.2	3.7	.285	.356	4.39
Boston	154	74	6	132	14	1366.0	1518	775	680	92	77	—	15	597	—	682	22	3	10.0	4.5	3.9	.279	.352	4.48
Washington	158	75	5	122	14	1398.2	1498	841	712	96	76	—	22	671	—	524	23	4	9.6	3.4	4.1	.275	.357	4.58
Philadelphia	154	65	6	143	9	1335.0	1490	854	720	105	83	—	17	613	—	469	40	3	10.0	3.2	4.1	.281	.357	4.85
Detroit	155	70	6	132	11	1378.0	1521	841	746	102	73	—	24	635	—	485	24	4	9.9	3.2	4.1	.279	.357	4.87
St. Louis	156	55	2	157	8	1363.0	1768	1023	909	143	96	—	30	653	—	468	34	0	11.7	3.1	4.3	.316	.391	6.00
AL Total	1244	555	69	1054	113	10952.2	12176	6503	5625	806	649	—	162	4773	—	4443	201	21	10.0	3.7	3.9	.281	.355	4.62
AL Avg Team	156	69	9	132	14	1369.2	1522	813	703	101	81	—	20	597	—	555	25	3	10.0	3.7	3.9	.281	.355	4.62

Team Fielding

Team	G	PO	A	E	TC	DP	PB	Pct
Detroit	155	4123	1823	147	6093	149	19	.976
Cleveland	156	4087	1865	159	6111	153	8	.974
Washington	158	4194	1774	170	6138	181	13	.972
New York	157	4191	1752	170	6113	134	7	.972
St. Louis	156	4088	1897	173	6158	166	8	.972
Chicago	154	4052	1867	174	6093	173	10	.971
Boston	154	4099	1656	177	5932	139	9	.970
Philadelphia	154	4002	1725	198	5925	150	15	.967
AL Total	1244	32836	14359	1368	48563	1245	89	.972

Team vs. Team Records

	Bos	ChA	Cle	Det	NYA	Phi	StL	Was	Won
Bos	—	10	11	12	7	17	15	8	80
ChA	12	—	10	8	9	15	18	14	86
Cle	11	12	—	11	7	13	18	11	83
Det	10	14	11	—	9	14	15	16	89
NYA	15	13	15	13	—	14	16	16	102
Phi	3	7	9	8	8	—	11	8	54
StL	7	4	4	7	6	11	—	7	46
Was	14	8	11	6	6	13	15	—	73
Lost	72	68	71	65	52	97	108	80	

1937 American League Batting Leaders

Games
L. Gehrig, NYA	157
B. Lewis, Was	156
B. Bell, StL	156
L. Lary, Cle	156
E. Averill, Cle	156

At-Bats
B. Lewis, Was	668
W. Moses, Phi	649
R. Rolfe, NYA	648
L. Lary, Cle	644
B. Bell, StL	642

Runs
J. DiMaggio, NYA	151
R. Rolfe, NYA	143
L. Gehrig, NYA	138
H. Greenberg, Det	137
C. Gehringer, Det	133

Hits
B. Bell, StL	218
J. DiMaggio, NYA	215
G. Walker, Det	213
B. Lewis, Was	210
C. Gehringer, Det	209

Doubles
B. Bell, StL	51
H. Greenberg, Det	49
W. Moses, Phi	48
J. Vosmik, StL	47
L. Lary, Cle	46

Triples
M. Kreevich, ChA	16
D. Walker, ChA	16
J. DiMaggio, NYA	15
J. Stone, Was	15
H. Greenberg, Det	14

Home Runs
J. DiMaggio, NYA	46
H. Greenberg, Det	40
L. Gehrig, NYA	37
J. Foxx, Bos	36
R. York, Det	35

Total Bases
J. DiMaggio, NYA	418
H. Greenberg, Det	397
L. Gehrig, NYA	366
W. Moses, Phi	357
H. Trosky, Cle	329

Runs Batted In
H. Greenberg, Det	183
J. DiMaggio, NYA	167
L. Gehrig, NYA	159
B. Dickey, NYA	133
H. Trosky, Cle	128

Walks
L. Gehrig, NYA	127
H. Greenberg, Det	102
J. Foxx, Bos	99
H. Clift, StL	98
B. Johnson, Phi	98

Intentional Walks
Statistic unavailable

Strikeouts
F. Crosetti, NYA	105
H. Greenberg, Det	101
J. Foxx, Bos	96
H. Clift, StL	80
T. Lazzeri, NYA	76

Hit By Pitch
F. Crosetti, NYA	12
F. Pytlak, Cle	7
4 tied with	6

Sac Hits
D. Walker, ChA	17
D. Cramer, Bos	17
M. Kreevich, ChA	16
J. Hayes, ChA	15
S. Newsome, Phi	14

Sac Flies
Statistic unavailable

Stolen Bases
B. Werber, Phi	35
B. Chapman, 2tm	35
G. Walker, Det	23
3 tied with	18

Caught Stealing
B. Werber, Phi	13
B. Chapman, 2tm	12
L. Appling, ChA	10
M. Solters, Cle	9
4 tied with	8

GDP
Statistic unavailable

Runs Created
L. Gehrig, NYA	167
J. DiMaggio, NYA	163
H. Greenberg, Det	160
C. Gehringer, Det	132
B. Dickey, NYA	125

Runs Created/27 Outs
L. Gehrig, NYA	11.59
H. Greenberg, Det	10.36
J. DiMaggio, NYA	10.32
C. Gehringer, Det	9.37
B. Dickey, NYA	9.04

Batting Average
C. Gehringer, Det	.371
L. Gehrig, NYA	.351
J. DiMaggio, NYA	.346
Z. Bonura, ChA	.345
C. Travis, Was	.344

On-Base Percentage
L. Gehrig, NYA	.473
C. Gehringer, Det	.458
H. Greenberg, Det	.436
B. Johnson, Phi	.425
B. Dickey, NYA	.417

Slugging Percentage
J. DiMaggio, NYA	.673
H. Greenberg, Det	.668
R. York, Det	.651
L. Gehrig, NYA	.643
Z. Bonura, ChA	.573

OBP+Slugging
L. Gehrig, NYA	1.116
H. Greenberg, Det	1.105
J. DiMaggio, NYA	1.085
R. York, Det	1.026
B. Dickey, NYA	.987

1937 American League Pitching Leaders

Wins
L. Gomez, NYA	21
R. Ruffing, NYA	20
R. Lawson, Det	18
E. Auker, Det	17
L. Grove, Bos	17

Losses
H. Kelley, Phi	21
G. Caster, Phi	19
C. Hogsett, StL	19
W. Ferrell, 2tm	19
J. Knott, StL	18

Winning Percentage
J. Allen, Cle	.938
J. Murphy, NYA	.765
M. Stratton, ChA	.750
R. Ruffing, NYA	.741
G. Gill, Det	.733

Games
C. Brown, ChA	53
J. Wilson, Bos	51
B. Newsom, 2tm	41
H. Kelley, Phi	41
J. Heving, Cle	40

Games Started
B. Newsom, 2tm	37
W. Ferrell, 2tm	35
J. DeShong, Was	34
L. Gomez, NYA	34
G. Caster, Phi	33

Complete Games
W. Ferrell, 2tm	26
L. Gomez, NYA	25
R. Ruffing, NYA	22
L. Grove, Bos	21
J. DeShong, Was	20

Shutouts
L. Gomez, NYA	6
M. Stratton, ChA	5
P. Appleton, Was	4
R. Ruffing, NYA	4
4 tied with	3

Saves
C. Brown, ChA	18
J. Murphy, NYA	10
J. Wilson, Bos	7
P. Malone, NYA	6
2 tied with	5

Games Finished
C. Brown, ChA	48
J. Murphy, NYA	30
J. Wilson, Bos	23
S. Cohen, Was	21
L. Nelson, Phi	21

Batters Faced
W. Ferrell, 2tm	1266
B. Newsom, 2tm	1247
J. DeShong, Was	1179
L. Gomez, NYA	1148
L. Grove, Bos	1127

Innings Pitched
W. Ferrell, 2tm	281.0
L. Gomez, NYA	278.1
B. Newsom, 2tm	275.1
J. DeShong, Was	264.1
L. Grove, Bos	262.0

Hits Allowed
W. Ferrell, 2tm	325
J. DeShong, Was	290
B. Newsom, 2tm	269
M. Harder, Cle	269
L. Grove, Bos	269

Home Runs Allowed
J. Knott, StL	25
W. Ferrell, 2tm	25
G. Caster, Phi	23
M. Weaver, Was	21
T. Lyons, ChA	21

Walks
B. Newsom, 2tm	167
V. Kennedy, ChA	124
J. DeShong, Was	124
W. Ferrell, 2tm	122
J. Wilson, Bos	119

Walks/9 Innings
M. Stratton, ChA	2.0
W. Hudlin, Cle	2.2
R. Ruffing, NYA	2.4
T. Lyons, ChA	2.4
T. Lee, ChA	2.6

Strikeouts
L. Gomez, NYA	194
B. Newsom, 2tm	166
L. Grove, Bos	153
B. Feller, Cle	150
T. Bridges, Det	138

Strikeouts/9 Innings
L. Gomez, NYA	6.3
J. Wilson, Bos	5.6
B. Newsom, 2tm	5.4
L. Grove, Bos	5.3
T. Bridges, Det	5.1

Strikeout/Walk Ratio
L. Gomez, NYA	2.09
R. Ruffing, NYA	1.93
M. Stratton, ChA	1.86
L. Grove, Bos	1.84
T. Bridges, Det	1.52

Earned Run Average
L. Gomez, NYA	2.33
M. Stratton, ChA	2.40
J. Allen, Cle	2.55
R. Ruffing, NYA	2.98
L. Grove, Bos	3.02

Component ERA
M. Stratton, ChA	2.36
L. Gomez, NYA	2.47
J. Allen, Cle	2.94
R. Ruffing, NYA	3.00
L. Grove, Bos	3.34

Hit Batsmen
B. Trotter, StL	7
E. Auker, Det	6
B. Newsom, 2tm	6
E. Whitehill, Cle	6
5 tied with	5

Wild Pitches
G. Turbeville, Phi	9
B. Ross, Phi	8
J. Walkup, StL	8
V. Kennedy, ChA	8
3 tied with	6

Opponent Average
L. Gomez, NYA	.223
M. Stratton, ChA	.234
E. Smith, Phi	.242
J. Allen, Cle	.244
R. Ruffing, NYA	.247

Opponent OBP
M. Stratton, ChA	.280
L. Gomez, NYA	.287
R. Ruffing, NYA	.296
T. Lee, ChA	.312
J. Allen, Cle	.313

1937 American League Miscellaneous

Managers
Boston	Joe Cronin	80-72
Chicago	Jimmy Dykes	86-68
Cleveland	Steve O'Neill	83-71
Detroit	Mickey Cochrane	16-13
	Del Baker	34-20
	Mickey Cochrane	39-32
New York	Joe McCarthy	102-52
Philadelphia	Connie Mack	39-80
	Earle Mack	15-17
St. Louis	Rogers Hornsby	25-52
	Jim Bottomley	21-56
Washington	Bucky Harris	73-80

Awards
Most Valuable Player	C. Gehringer, 2b, Det
STATS Cy Young	Lefty Gomez, NYA
STATS Rookie of the Year	Rudy York, c, Det
STATS Manager of the Year	Joe McCarthy, NYA

STATS All-Star Team
C	Bill Dickey, NYA	.332	29	133
1B	Lou Gehrig, NYA	.351	37	159
2B	Charlie Gehringer, Det	.371	14	96
3B	Harlond Clift, StL	.306	29	118
SS	Joe Cronin, Bos	.307	18	110
OF	Earl Averill, Cle	.299	21	92
OF	Joe DiMaggio, NYA	.346	46	167
OF	Bob Johnson, Phi	.306	25	108
P	Johnny Allen, Cle	15-1	2.55	87 K
P	Lefty Gomez, NYA	21-11	2.33	194 K
P	Lefty Grove, Bos	17-9	3.02	153 K
P	Red Ruffing, NYA	20-7	2.98	131 K
RP	Clint Brown, ChA	7-7	3.42	18 Sv

Postseason
World Series	NYA (AL) 4 vs. NYG (NL) 1

Outstanding Performances

No-Hitters
Bill Dietrich, ChA   vs. StL on June 1

Three-Homer Games
Joe DiMaggio, NYA   on June 13
Hal Trosky, Cle   on July 5

Cycles
Gee Walker, Det   on April 20
Joe DiMaggio, NYA   on July 9
Lou Gehrig, NYA   on August 1

1937 National League Standings

Team	Overall W	L	Pct	GB	DIF	Home Games W	L	R	OR	HR	OHR	Road Games W	L	R	OR	HR	OHR	Park Index Run	HR	Record by Month M/A	May	June	July	Aug	S/O
New York	95	57	.625	—	50	50	25	353	288	76	57	45	32	379	314	35	28	95	217	5-2	18-13	15-10	16-13	17-9	24-10
Chicago	93	61	.604	3.0	75	46	32	412	361	47	48	47	29	399	321	49	43	105	101	2-6	20-10	16-8	20-8	15-15	20-14
Pittsburgh	86	68	.558	10.0	42	46	32	360	332	13	28	40	36	344	314	34	43	102	52	5-2	18-10	12-15	12-15	15-16	24-10
St. Louis	81	73	.526	15.0	9	45	33	406	379	52	51	36	40	383	354	42	44	104	117	7-1	11-17	17-8	12-16	18-12	16-19
Boston	79	73	.520	16.0	0	43	33	252	224	26	15	36	40	327	332	37	45	72	50	4-5	11-14	11-17	19-11	13-15	21-11
Brooklyn	62	91	.405	33.5	0	36	39	336	389	20	30	26	52	280	383	17	38	114	95	3-5	13-13	11-15	9-18	12-18	14-22
Philadelphia	61	92	.399	34.5	4	29	45	379	481	65	69	32	47	345	388	38	47	125	168	4-4	12-17	8-17	13-18	14-12	10-24
Cincinnati	56	98	.364	40.0	0	28	51	268	347	13	14	28	47	344	360	60	24	83	31	1-6	10-19	13-13	12-14	10-17	10-29

Clinch Date—New York 9/30.

Team Batting

Team	G	AB	R	OR	H	2B	3B	HR	TB	RBI	TBB	IBB	SO	HBP	SH	SF	SB	CS	SB%	GDP	Avg	OBP	Slg
Chicago	154	5349	811	682	1537	253	74	96	2226	762	538	—	496	22	119	—	71	—	—	120	.287	.355	.416
St. Louis	157	5476	789	733	1543	264	67	94	2223	731	385	—	569	16	89	—	78	—	—	116	.282	.331	.406
New York	152	5329	732	602	1484	251	41	111	2150	677	412	—	492	31	90	—	45	—	—	108	.278	.334	.403
Philadelphia	155	5424	724	869	1482	258	37	103	2123	668	478	—	640	16	75	—	66	—	—	109	.273	.334	.391
Pittsburgh	154	5433	704	646	1550	223	86	47	2086	649	463	—	480	11	89	—	32	—	—	117	.285	.343	.384
Brooklyn	155	5295	616	772	1401	258	53	37	1876	554	469	—	583	20	109	—	69	—	—	130	.265	.327	.354
Cincinnati	155	5230	612	707	1329	215	59	73	1881	567	437	—	586	24	72	—	53	—	—	134	.254	.314	.360
Boston	152	5124	579	556	1265	200	41	63	1736	534	485	—	707	18	113	—	45	—	—	122	.247	.314	.339
NL Total	1234	42660	5567	5567	11591	1922	458	624	16301	5142	3667	—	4553	158	756	—	459	—	—	956	.272	.332	.382
NL Avg Team	154	5333	696	696	1449	240	57	78	2038	643	458	—	569	20	95	—	57	—	—	120	.272	.332	.382

Team Pitching

Team	G	CG	ShO	Rel	Sv	IP	H	R	ER	HR	SH	SF	HB	TBB	IBB	SO	WP	Bk	H/9	SO/9	BB/9	OAvg	OOBP	ERA
Boston	152	85	16	103	10	1359.1	1344	556	486	60	96	—	11	372	—	387	9	2	8.9	2.6	2.5	.259	.310	3.22
New York	152	67	11	142	17	1361.0	1341	602	519	85	98	—	20	404	—	653	25	2	8.9	4.3	2.7	.258	.314	3.43
Pittsburgh	154	67	12	149	17	1366.1	1398	646	541	71	79	—	19	428	—	643	24	0	9.2	4.2	2.8	.264	.321	3.56
Cincinnati	155	64	10	162	18	1358.1	1428	707	594	38	96	—	18	533	—	581	31	3	9.5	3.8	3.5	.270	.339	3.94
Chicago	154	73	11	148	13	1381.1	1434	682	610	91	78	—	22	502	—	596	32	1	9.3	3.9	3.3	.267	.332	3.97
St. Louis	157	81	10	141	4	1392.0	1546	733	615	95	103	—	14	448	—	571	29	5	10.0	3.7	2.9	.281	.337	3.98
Brooklyn	155	63	5	160	8	1362.2	1470	772	625	68	109	—	21	476	—	592	26	6	9.7	3.9	3.1	.274	.336	4.13
Philadelphia	155	59	6	177	15	1373.2	1629	869	771	116	88	—	31	501	—	529	16	1	10.7	3.5	3.3	.297	.359	5.05
NL Total	1234	559	81	1182	102	10954.2	11590	5567	4761	624	747	—	156	3664	—	4552	192	20	9.5	3.7	3.0	.272	.332	3.91
NL Avg Team	154	70	10	148	13	1369.2	1449	696	595	78	93	—	20	458	—	569	24	3	9.5	3.7	3.0	.272	.332	3.91

Team Fielding

Team	G	PO	A	E	TC	DP	PB	Pct
Chicago	154	4142	1792	151	6085	141	12	.975
Boston	152	4079	1922	157	6158	128	5	.975
New York	152	4083	1984	159	6226	143	6	.974
St. Louis	157	4170	1690	164	6024	127	14	.973
Pittsburgh	154	4099	1781	181	6061	135	5	.970
Philadelphia	155	4098	1872	184	6154	157	11	.970
Cincinnati	155	4074	1867	208	6149	139	16	.966
Brooklyn	155	4089	1752	217	6058	127	16	.964
NL Total	1234	32834	14660	1421	48915	1097	85	.971

Team vs. Team Records

	Bos	Bro	ChN	Cin	NYG	Phi	Pit	StL	Won
Bos	—	15	9	11	10	14	11	9	79
Bro	7	—	8	12	6	10	12	7	62
ChN	13	14	—	14	12	14	9	17	93
Cin	11	10	8	—	8	11	1	7	56
NYG	10	16	10	14	—	15	16	14	95
Phi	8	11	8	11	7	—	11	5	61
Pit	11	10	13	21	6	11	—	14	86
StL	13	15	5	15	8	17	8	—	81
Lost	73	91	61	98	57	92	68	73	

1937 National League Batting Leaders

Games		At-Bats		Runs		Hits		Doubles		Triples	
J. Medwick, StL	156	J. Medwick, StL	633	J. Medwick, StL	111	J. Medwick, StL	237	J. Medwick, StL	56	A. Vaughan, Pit	17
F. Demaree, ChN	154	P. Waner, Pit	619	S. Hack, ChN	106	P. Waner, Pit	219	J. Mize, StL	40	G. Suhr, Pit	14
S. Hack, ChN	154	F. Demaree, ChN	615	B. Herman, ChN	106	J. Mize, StL	204	D. Bartell, NYG	38	L. Handley, Pit	12
P. Waner, Pit	154	A. Galan, ChN	611	A. Galan, ChN	104	F. Demaree, ChN	199	B. Phelps, Bro	37	I. Goodman, Cin	12
2 tied with	152	S. Hack, ChN	582	F. Demaree, ChN	104	B. Herman, ChN	189	J. Moore, NYG	37	B. Herman, ChN	11

Home Runs		Total Bases		Runs Batted In		Walks		Intentional Walks		Strikeouts	
J. Medwick, StL	31	J. Medwick, StL	406	J. Medwick, StL	154	M. Ott, NYG	102	Statistic unavailable		V. DiMaggio, Bos	111
M. Ott, NYG	31	J. Mize, StL	333	F. Demaree, ChN	115	D. Camilli, Phi	90			G. Brack, Bro	93
D. Camilli, Phi	27	F. Demaree, ChN	298	J. Mize, StL	113	S. Hack, ChN	83			D. Camilli, Phi	82
J. Mize, StL	25	M. Ott, NYG	285	S. Hack, ChN	97	G. Suhr, Pit	83			G. Moore, Bos	73
A. Galan, ChN	18	D. Camilli, Phi	279	M. Ott, NYG	95	A. Galan, ChN	79			M. Ott, NYG	69

Hit By Pitch		Sac Hits		Sac Flies		Stolen Bases		Caught Stealing		GDP	
D. Bartell, NYG	10	J. Brown, StL	26	Statistic unavailable		A. Galan, ChN	23	Statistic unavailable		F. Demaree, ChN	23
I. Goodman, Cin	7	R. Warstler, Bos	22			S. Hack, ChN	16			P. Whitney, Phi	19
B. Jurges, ChN	6	B. Hassett, Bro	14			4 tied with	13			A. Kampouris, Cin	17
4 tied with	5	F. Demaree, ChN	14							C. Lavagetto, Bro	17
		D. Bartell, NYG	14							L. Durocher, StL	17

Runs Created		Runs Created/27 Outs		Batting Average		On-Base Percentage		Slugging Percentage		OBP+Slugging	
J. Medwick, StL	163	J. Medwick, StL	10.62	J. Medwick, StL	.374	D. Camilli, Phi	.446	J. Medwick, StL	.641	J. Medwick, StL	1.056
J. Mize, StL	143	J. Mize, StL	10.53	J. Mize, StL	.364	J. Mize, StL	.427	J. Mize, StL	.595	D. Camilli, Phi	1.034
D. Camilli, Phi	122	D. Camilli, Phi	10.14	G. Hartnett, ChN	.354	G. Hartnett, ChN	.424	D. Camilli, Phi	.587	J. Mize, StL	1.021
M. Ott, NYG	120	G. Hartnett, ChN	8.72	P. Waner, Pit	.354	J. Medwick, StL	.414	G. Hartnett, ChN	.548	G. Hartnett, ChN	.971
P. Waner, Pit	110	M. Ott, NYG	8.12	P. Whitney, Phi	.341	P. Waner, Pit	.413	M. Ott, NYG	.523	M. Ott, NYG	.931

1937 National League Pitching Leaders

Wins		Losses		Winning Percentage		Games		Games Started		Complete Games	
C. Hubbell, NYG	22	W. LaMaster, Phi	19	C. Hubbell, NYG	.733	H. Mulcahy, Phi	56	C. Passeau, Phi	34	J. Turner, Bos	24
J. Turner, Bos	20	C. Passeau, Phi	18	C. Root, ChN	.722	O. Jorgens, Phi	52	C. Blanton, Pit	34	L. Fette, Bos	23
L. Fette, Bos	20	H. Mulcahy, Phi	18	C. Melton, NYG	.690	4 tied with	50	B. Walters, Phi	34	B. Weiland, StL	21
C. Melton, NYG	20	L. Grissom, Cin	17	R. Bauers, Pit	.684			B. Weiland, StL	34	4 tied with	18
L. Warneke, StL	18	5 tied with	15	3 tied with	.667			3 tied with	33		

Shutouts		Saves		Games Finished		Batters Faced		Innings Pitched		Hits Allowed	
J. Turner, Bos	5	C. Melton, NYG	7	M. Brown, Pit	27	C. Passeau, Phi	1276	C. Passeau, Phi	292.1	C. Passeau, Phi	348
L. Fette, Bos	5	M. Brown, Pit	7	M. Ryba, StL	22	B. Lee, ChN	1146	B. Lee, ChN	272.1	B. Walters, Phi	292
L. Grissom, Cin	5	L. Grissom, Cin	6	D. Coffman, NYG	21	B. Weiland, StL	1146	B. Weiland, StL	264.1	B. Lee, ChN	289
5 tied with	4	A. Hollingsworth, Cin	5	C. Root, ChN	20	B. Walters, Phi	1094	C. Hubbell, NYG	261.2	B. Weiland, StL	283
		C. Root, ChN	5	O. Jorgens, Phi	19	C. Hubbell, NYG	1087	L. Fette, Bos	259.0	L. Warneke, StL	280

Home Runs Allowed		Walks		Walks/9 Innings		Strikeouts		Strikeouts/9 Innings		Strikeout/Walk Ratio	
L. Warneke, StL	32	H. Mulcahy, Phi	97	D. Dean, StL	1.5	C. Hubbell, NYG	159	V. Mungo, Bro	6.8	D. Dean, StL	3.64
W. LaMaster, Phi	24	T. Carleton, ChN	94	W. Hoyt, 2tm	1.7	L. Grissom, Cin	149	L. Grissom, Cin	6.0	C. Hubbell, NYG	2.89
S. Johnson, Phi	20	B. Weiland, StL	94	J. Turner, Bos	1.8	C. Blanton, Pit	143	R. Bauers, Pit	5.7	C. Melton, NYG	2.58
S. Castleman, NYG	19	L. Grissom, Cin	93	S. Castleman, NYG	1.9	C. Melton, NYG	142	W. LaMaster, Phi	5.5	S. Castleman, NYG	2.36
2 tied with	18	H. Schumacher, NYG	89	C. Hubbell, NYG	1.9	2 tied with	135	D. Dean, StL	5.5	V. Mungo, Bro	2.18

Earned Run Average		Component ERA		Hit Batsmen		Wild Pitches		Opponent Average		Opponent OBP	
J. Turner, Bos	2.38	C. Melton, NYG	2.37	H. Kelleher, Phi	7	R. Parmelee, ChN	11	V. Mungo, Bro	.229	J. Turner, Bos	.274
C. Melton, NYG	2.61	J. Turner, Bos	2.40	H. Mulcahy, Phi	7	A. Hollingsworth, Cin	8	L. Grissom, Cin	.232	C. Melton, NYG	.280
D. Dean, StL	2.69	V. Mungo, Bro	2.51	R. Parmelee, ChN	7	L. Grissom, Cin	8	C. Melton, NYG	.233	S. Castleman, NYG	.287
R. Bauers, Pit	2.88	L. Hamlin, Bro	2.81	C. Melton, NYG	6	H. Mulcahy, Phi	7	J. Turner, Bos	.235	D. Dean, StL	.291
L. Fette, Bos	2.88	D. Dean, StL	2.87	6 tied with	5	C. Hubbell, NYG	7	T. Carleton, ChN	.236	C. Hubbell, NYG	.298

1937 National League Miscellaneous

Managers		
Boston	Bill McKechnie	79-73
Brooklyn	Burleigh Grimes	62-91
Chicago	Charlie Grimm	93-61
Cincinnati	Chuck Dressen	51-78
	Bobby Wallace	5-20
New York	Bill Terry	95-57
Philadelphia	Jimmie Wilson	61-92
Pittsburgh	Pie Traynor	86-68
St. Louis	Frank Frisch	81-73

Awards

Most Valuable Player	Joe Medwick, of, StL
STATS Cy Young	Cliff Melton, NYG
STATS Rookie of the Year	Cliff Melton, p, NYG
STATS Manager of the Year	Bill Terry, NYG

STATS All-Star Team

C	Gabby Hartnett, ChN	.354	12	82
1B	Johnny Mize, StL	.364	25	113
2B	Billy Herman, ChN	.335	8	65
3B	Pinky Whitney, Phi	.341	8	79
SS	Dick Bartell, NYG	.306	14	62
OF	Frank Demaree, ChN	.324	17	115
OF	Joe Medwick, StL	.374	31	154
OF	Mel Ott, NYG	.294	31	95
P	Lou Fette, Bos	20-10	2.88	70 K
P	Carl Hubbell, NYG	22-8	3.20	159 K
P	Cliff Melton, NYG	20-9	2.61	142 K
P	Jim Turner, Bos	20-11	2.38	69 K
RP	Charlie Root, ChN	13-5	3.38	5 Sv

Postseason

World Series	NYG (NL) 1 vs. NYA (AL) 4

Outstanding Performances

Triple Crown
Joe Medwick, StL   .374-31-154

Three-Homer Games
Alex Kampouris, Cin on May 9

1938 American League Standings

Team	W	L	Pct	GB	DIF	W	L	R	OR	HR	OHR	W	L	R	OR	HR	OHR	Run	HR	M/A	May	June	July	Aug	S/O
	Overall					Home Games						Road Games						Park Index		Record by Month					
New York	99	53	.651	—	87	55	22	524	342	112	43	44	31	442	368	62	42	104	145	7-6	13-8	17-11	20-5	20-8	14-15
Boston	88	61	.591	9.5	8	52	23	481	356	67	52	36	38	421	395	31	50	101	145	6-5	13-12	16-10	16-8	18-15	19-11
Cleveland	86	66	.566	13.0	72	46	30	425	363	54	35	40	36	422	419	59	65	94	72	8-3	16-9	16-10	13-8	15-23	18-13
Detroit	84	70	.545	16.0	0	48	31	447	392	83	60	36	39	415	403	54	50	97	131	5-6	13-12	15-15	13-13	16-14	22-10
Washington	75	76	.497	23.5	10	44	33	412	413	33	27	31	43	402	460	52	65	92	49	7-5	15-13	12-15	12-14	15-15	14-14
Chicago	65	83	.439	32.0	3	33	39	326	364	24	41	32	44	383	388	43	60	94	67	5-5	7-13	12-15	11-12	16-22	14-16
St. Louis	55	97	.362	44.0	1	31	43	385	487	52	62	24	54	370	475	40	70	109	109	4-8	7-15	8-19	9-17	16-17	11-21
Philadelphia	53	99	.349	46.0	0	28	47	378	486	55	64	25	52	348	470	43	78	108	101	3-7	11-13	12-13	3-20	15-25	9-21

Clinch Date—New York 9/18.

Team Batting

Team	G	AB	R	OR	H	2B	3B	HR	TB	RBI	TBB	IBB	SO	HBP	SH	SF	SB	CS	SB%	GDP	Avg	OBP	Slg
New York	157	5410	966	710	1480	283	63	174	2411	917	749	—	616	39	61	—	91	28	.76	—	.274	.366	.446
Boston	150	5229	902	751	1566	298	56	98	2270	860	650	—	463	13	112	—	55	51	.52	—	.299	.378	.434
Detroit	155	5270	862	795	1434	219	52	137	2168	804	693	—	581	21	75	—	76	41	.65	—	.272	.359	.411
Cleveland	153	5356	847	782	1506	300	89	113	2323	799	550	—	605	16	78	—	83	36	.70	—	.281	.350	.434
Washington	152	5474	814	873	1602	278	72	85	2279	768	573	—	379	18	93	—	65	37	.64	—	.293	.362	.416
St. Louis	156	5333	755	962	1498	273	36	92	2119	713	590	—	528	20	106	—	51	40	.56	—	.281	.355	.397
Philadelphia	154	5229	726	956	1410	243	62	98	2071	686	605	—	590	22	78	—	65	53	.55	—	.270	.348	.396
Chicago	149	5199	709	752	1439	239	55	67	1989	657	514	—	489	14	78	—	56	39	.59	—	.277	.343	.383
AL Total	1226	42500	6581	6581	11935	2133	485	864	17630	6204	4924	—	4251	163	681	—	542	325	.63	—	.281	.358	.415
AL Avg Team	153	5313	823	823	1492	267	61	108	2204	776	616	—	531	20	85	—	68	41	.63	—	.281	.358	.415

Team Pitching

Team	G	CG	ShO	Rel	Sv	IP	H	R	ER	HR	SH	SF	HB	TBB	IBB	SO	WP	Bk	H/9	SO/9	BB/9	OAvg	OOBP	ERA
New York	157	91	11	91	13	1382.0	1436	710	601	85	74	—	8	566	—	567	28	4	9.4	3.7	3.7	.268	.339	3.91
Chicago	149	83	5	84	9	1316.1	1449	752	638	101	106	—	19	550	—	432	23	3	9.9	3.0	3.8	.279	.350	4.36
Boston	150	67	10	147	15	1316.1	1472	751	652	102	84	—	20	528	—	484	20	4	10.1	3.3	3.6	.281	.349	4.46
Cleveland	153	68	5	145	17	1353.0	1416	782	691	100	64	—	30	681	—	717	28	2	9.4	4.8	4.5	.268	.355	4.60
Detroit	155	75	3	134	11	1348.1	1532	795	717	110	93	—	14	608	—	435	22	3	10.2	2.9	4.1	.287	.361	4.79
Washington	152	59	6	156	11	1360.1	1472	873	746	92	94	—	29	655	—	515	47	3	9.7	3.4	4.3	.276	.358	4.94
Philadelphia	154	56	4	143	12	1324.0	1573	956	806	142	81	—	18	599	—	473	28	4	10.7	3.2	4.1	.292	.365	5.48
St. Louis	156	71	3	134	7	1344.2	1584	962	867	132	82	—	26	737	—	632	27	3	10.6	4.2	4.1	.295	.382	5.80
AL Total	1226	570	47	1034	95	10745.0	11934	6581	5718	864	678	—	164	4924	—	4255	223	26	10.0	3.6	4.1	.281	.358	4.79
AL Avg Team	153	71	6	129	12	1343.0	1492	823	715	108	85	—	21	616	—	532	28	3	10.0	3.6	4.1	.281	.358	4.79

Team Fielding

Team	G	PO	A	E	TC	DP	PB	Pct
Detroit	155	4062	1832	147	6041	172	15	.976
St. Louis	156	3998	1579	145	5722	163	10	.975
Cleveland	153	4042	1625	151	5818	145	11	.974
New York	157	4147	1898	169	6214	177	11	.973
Washington	152	4081	1703	180	5964	179	13	.970
Boston	150	3952	1721	190	5863	172	7	.968
Chicago	149	3950	1767	196	5913	155	10	.967
Philadelphia	154	3964	1637	206	5807	119	15	.965
AL Total	1226	32196	13762	1384	47342	1282	92	.971

Team vs. Team Records

	Bos	ChA	Cle	Det	NYA	Phi	StL	Was	Won
Bos	—	12	12	10	11	14	17	12	88
ChA	6	—	9	7	8	12	13	10	65
Cle	10	13	—	12	8	18	13	12	86
Det	12	15	10	—	8	14	12	13	84
NYA	11	14	13	14	—	16	15	16	99
Phi	8	10	4	8	5	—	12	6	53
StL	5	8	9	10	7	7	—	7	55
Was	9	11	9	9	6	16	15	—	75
Lost	61	83	66	70	53	99	97	76	

1938 American League Batting Leaders

Games			At-Bats			Runs			Hits			Doubles			Triples	
F. Crosetti, NYA	157		D. Cramer, Bos	658		H. Greenberg, Det	144		J. Vosmik, Bos	201		J. Cronin, Bos	51		J. Heath, Cle	18
L. Gehrig, NYA	157		B. Lewis, Was	656		J. Foxx, Bos	139		D. Cramer, Bos	198		G. McQuinn, StL	42		E. Averill, Cle	15
P. Fox, Det	155		P. Fox, Det	634		C. Gehringer, Det	133		M. Almada, 2tm	197		H. Trosky, Cle	40		J. DiMaggio, NYA	13
H. Greenberg, Det	155		M. Almada, 2tm	633		R. Rolfe, NYA	132		J. Foxx, Bos	197		B. Chapman, Bos	40		3 tied with	12
2 tied with	152		2 tied with	631		J. DiMaggio, NYA	129		R. Rolfe, NYA	196		J. Vosmik, Bos	37			

Home Runs			Total Bases			Runs Batted In			Walks			Intentional Walks		Strikeouts	
H. Greenberg, Det	58		J. Foxx, Bos	398		J. Foxx, Bos	175		H. Greenberg, Det	119		Statistic unavailable		F. Crosetti, NYA	97
J. Foxx, Bos	50		H. Greenberg, Det	380		H. Greenberg, Det	146		J. Foxx, Bos	119				S. Chapman, Phi	94
H. Clift, StL	34		J. DiMaggio, NYA	348		J. DiMaggio, NYA	140		H. Clift, StL	118				H. Greenberg, Det	92
R. York, Det	33		B. Johnson, Phi	311		R. York, Det	127		C. Gehringer, Det	112				B. Berger, ChA	80
J. DiMaggio, NYA	32		J. Heath, Cle	302		H. Clift, StL	118		L. Gehrig, NYA	107				J. Foxx, Bos	76

Hit By Pitch			Sac Hits			Sac Flies		Stolen Bases			Caught Stealing			GDP	
F. Crosetti, NYA	15		B. Doerr, Bos	22		Statistic unavailable		F. Crosetti, NYA	27		B. Werber, Phi	15		Statistic unavailable	
D. Lodigiani, Phi	7		O. Hale, Cle	18				L. Lary, Cle	23		F. Crosetti, NYA	12			
H. Clift, StL	5		B. Newsom, StL	14				B. Werber, Phi	19		B. Doerr, Bos	10			
J. Cronin, Bos	5		G. McQuinn, StL	13				B. Lewis, Was	17		3 tied with	9			
L. Gehrig, NYA	5		C. Travis, Was	13				P. Fox, Det	16						

Runs Created			Runs Created/27 Outs			Batting Average		On-Base Percentage		Slugging Percentage		OBP+Slugging	
J. Foxx, Bos	172		J. Foxx, Bos	11.87		J. Foxx, Bos	.349	J. Foxx, Bos	.462	J. Foxx, Bos	.704	J. Foxx, Bos	1.166
H. Greenberg, Det	163		H. Greenberg, Det	10.79		J. Heath, Cle	.343	B. Myer, Was	.454	H. Greenberg, Det	.683	H. Greenberg, Det	1.122
J. DiMaggio, NYA	136		B. Dickey, NYA	9.05		B. Chapman, Bos	.340	H. Greenberg, Det	.438	J. Heath, Cle	.602	R. York, Det	.995
L. Gehrig, NYA	131		R. York, Det	8.98		B. Myer, Was	.336	E. Averill, Cle	.429	J. DiMaggio, NYA	.581	J. Heath, Cle	.985
C. Gehringer, Det	130		E. Averill, Cle	8.77		C. Travis, Was	.335	J. Cronin, Bos	.428	R. York, Det	.579	B. Dickey, NYA	.981

1938 American League Pitching Leaders

Wins			Losses			Winning Percentage		Games			Games Started			Complete Games	
R. Ruffing, NYA	21		G. Caster, Phi	20		L. Grove, Bos	.778	J. Humphries, Cle	45		G. Caster, Phi	40		B. Newsom, StL	31
B. Newsom, StL	20		B. Ross, Phi	16		R. Ruffing, NYA	.750	B. Newsom, StL	44		B. Newsom, StL	40		R. Ruffing, NYA	22
L. Gomez, NYA	18		B. Newsom, StL	16		J. Bagby Jr., Bos	.737	J. Bagby Jr., Bos	43		B. Feller, Cle	36		B. Feller, Cle	20
B. Feller, Cle	17		J. Wilson, Bos	15		F. Ostermueller, Bos	.722	E. Smith, Phi	43		L. Gomez, NYA	32		G. Caster, Phi	20
M. Harder, Cle	17		D. Leonard, Was	15		M. Pearson, NYA	.696	P. Appleton, Was	43		2 tied with	31		L. Gomez, NYA	20

Shutouts			Saves			Games Finished		Batters Faced			Innings Pitched			Hits Allowed	
L. Gomez, NYA	4		J. Murphy, NYA	11		E. Smith, Phi	27	B. Newsom, StL	1475		B. Newsom, StL	329.2		B. Newsom, StL	334
J. Wilson, Bos	3		J. Humphries, Cle	6		J. Murphy, NYA	26	G. Caster, Phi	1250		G. Caster, Phi	281.1		G. Caster, Phi	310
D. Leonard, Was	3		A. McKain, Bos	6		J. Humphries, Cle	25	B. Feller, Cle	1248		B. Feller, Cle	277.2		B. Thomas, Phi	259
R. Ruffing, NYA	3		N. Potter, Phi	5		P. Appleton, Was	23	T. Lee, ChA	1074		R. Ruffing, NYA	247.1		M. Harder, Cle	257
5 tied with	2		P. Appleton, Was	5		E. Cole, StL	21	R. Ruffing, NYA	1043		T. Lee, ChA	245.1		T. Lee, ChA	252

Home Runs Allowed			Walks			Walks/9 Innings		Strikeouts			Strikeouts/9 Innings			Strikeout/Walk Ratio	
B. Newsom, StL	30		B. Feller, Cle	208		D. Leonard, Was	2.1	B. Feller, Cle	240		B. Feller, Cle	7.8		L. Grove, Bos	1.90
L. Nelson, Phi	29		B. Newsom, StL	192		M. Harder, Cle	2.3	B. Newsom, StL	226		B. Newsom, StL	6.2		T. Bridges, Det	1.74
G. Caster, Phi	25		G. Caster, Phi	117		T. Lyons, ChA	2.4	L. Mills, StL	134		T. Bridges, Det	6.0		M. Harder, Cle	1.65
B. Ross, Phi	23		L. Mills, StL	116		S. Chandler, NYA	2.5	L. Gomez, NYA	129		L. Mills, StL	5.7		R. Ruffing, NYA	1.55
B. Thomas, Phi	23		3 tied with	113		M. Stratton, ChA	2.7	R. Ruffing, NYA	127		L. Grove, Bos	5.4		M. Stratton, ChA	1.46

Earned Run Average			Component ERA			Hit Batsmen		Wild Pitches			Opponent Average			Opponent OBP	
L. Grove, Bos	3.08		D. Leonard, Was	3.08		E. Whitehill, Cle	9	D. Leonard, Was	11		B. Feller, Cle	.220		D. Leonard, Was	.305
R. Ruffing, NYA	3.31		S. Chandler, NYA	3.47		L. Mills, StL	8	M. Pearson, NYA	9		J. Allen, Cle	.246		M. Stratton, ChA	.315
L. Gomez, NYA	3.35		L. Grove, Bos	3.48		C. Hogsett, Was	8	P. Appleton, Was	8		M. Stratton, ChA	.255		R. Ruffing, NYA	.317
D. Leonard, Was	3.43		R. Ruffing, NYA	3.48		3 tied with	7	3 tied with	7		D. Leonard, Was	.256		M. Harder, Cle	.319
T. Lee, ChA	3.49		L. Gomez, NYA	3.53							R. Ruffing, NYA	.258		L. Grove, Bos	.319

1938 American League Miscellaneous

Managers		
Boston	Joe Cronin	88-61
Chicago	Jimmy Dykes	65-83
Cleveland	Ossie Vitt	86-66
Detroit	Mickey Cochrane	47-51
	Del Baker	37-19
New York	Joe McCarthy	99-53
Philadelphia	Connie Mack	53-99
St. Louis	Gabby Street	53-90
	Oscar Melillo	2-7
Washington	Bucky Harris	75-76

Awards

Most Valuable Player	Jimmie Foxx, 1b, Bos
STATS Cy Young	Red Ruffing, NYA
STATS Rookie of the Year	Jeff Heath, of, Cle
STATS Manager of the Year	Joe Cronin, Bos

STATS All-Star Team

C	Rudy York, Det	.298	33	127
1B	Jimmie Foxx, Bos	.349	50	175
2B	Charlie Gehringer, Det	.306	20	107
3B	Harlond Clift, StL	.290	34	118
SS	Joe Cronin, Bos	.325	17	94
OF	Earl Averill, Cle	.330	14	93
OF	Joe DiMaggio, NYA	.324	32	140
OF	Jeff Heath, Cle	.343	21	112
P	Bob Feller, Cle	17-11	4.08	240 K
P	Lefty Gomez, NYA	18-12	3.35	129 K
P	Mel Harder, Cle	17-10	3.83	102 K
P	Red Ruffing, NYA	21-7	3.31	127 K
RP	Johnny Murphy, NYA	8-2	4.24	11 Sv

Postseason

World Series	New York (AL) 4 vs. Chicago (NL) 0

Outstanding Performances

No-Hitters
Monte Pearson, NYA vs. Cle on August 27
Three-Homer Games
Merv Connors, ChA on September 17
Cycles
Odell Hale, Cle on July 12

1938 National League Standings

Team	W	L	Pct	GB	DIF	W	L	R	OR	HR	OHR	W	L	R	OR	HR	OHR	Run	HR	M/A	May	June	July	Aug	S/O
		Overall					Home Games						Road Games					Park Index		Record by Month					
Chicago	89	63	.586	—	10	44	33	349	326	24	41	45	30	364	272	41	30	103	89	8-4	16-11	11-14	16-12	16-15	22-7
Pittsburgh	86	64	.573	2.0	87	44	33	348	330	22	22	42	31	359	300	43	49	98	45	8-3	9-15	16-7	24-7	16-16	13-16
New York	83	67	.553	5.0	74	43	30	365	297	89	58	40	37	340	340	36	29	103	239	10-1	15-10	15-13	14-15	13-16	16-12
Cincinnati	82	68	.547	6.0	0	43	34	344	323	50	31	39	34	379	311	60	44	92	74	4-8	15-10	16-9	15-15	18-14	14-12
Boston	77	75	.507	12.0	0	45	30	233	241	12	19	32	45	328	377	42	47	69	36	5-4	13-10	10-14	13-19	20-12	16-16
St. Louis	71	80	.470	17.5	0	36	41	414	425	58	45	35	39	311	296	33	32	133	152	3-8	11-12	14-11	10-21	20-13	13-15
Brooklyn	69	80	.463	18.5	1	31	41	319	349	38	44	38	39	385	361	23	44	96	131	5-6	9-19	12-11	16-13	13-18	14-13
Philadelphia	45	105	.300	43.0	0	26	48	286	439	23	40	19	57	264	401	17	36	112	122	1-10	10-11	5-20	13-19	9-21	7-24

Clinch Date—Chicago 10/01.

Team Batting

Team	G	AB	R	OR	H	2B	3B	HR	TB	RBI	TBB	IBB	SO	HBP	SH	SF	SB	CS	SB%	GDP	Avg	OBP	Slg
St. Louis	156	5528	725	721	1542	288	74	91	2251	680	412	—	492	16	83	—	55	—		124	.279	.331	.407
Cincinnati	151	5391	723	634	1495	251	57	110	2190	679	366	—	518	32	89	—	19	—		125	.277	.327	.406
Chicago	154	5333	713	598	1435	242	70	65	2012	673	522	—	476	29	88	—	49	—		157	.269	.338	.377
Pittsburgh	152	5422	707	630	1511	265	66	65	2103	659	485	—	409	19	81	—	47	—		139	.279	.340	.388
New York	152	5255	705	637	1424	210	36	125	2081	672	465	—	528	33	88	—	31	—		112	.271	.334	.396
Brooklyn	151	5142	704	710	1322	225	79	61	1888	647	611	—	615	20	80	—	66	—		118	.257	.338	.367
Boston	153	5250	561	618	1311	199	39	54	1750	519	424	—	548	23	78	—	49	—		134	.250	.309	.333
Philadelphia	151	5192	550	840	1318	233	29	40	1729	503	423	—	507	12	86	—	38	—		129	.254	.312	.333
NL Total	1220	42513	5388	5388	11358	1913	450	611	16004	5032	3708	—	4093	184	673	—	354	—		1038	.267	.329	.376
NL Avg Team	153	5314	674	674	1420	239	56	76	2001	629	464	—	512	23	84	—	44	—		130	.267	.329	.376

Team Pitching

Team	G	CG	ShO	Rel	Sv	IP	H	R	ER	HR	SH	SF	HB	TBB	IBB	SO	WP	Bk	H/9	SO/9	BB/9	OAvg	OOBP	ERA
Chicago	154	67	16	148	18	1396.2	1414	598	523	71	81	—	17	454	—	583	31	5	9.1	3.8	2.9	.263	.322	3.37
Boston	153	83	15	109	12	1380.0	1375	618	522	66	90	—	30	465	—	413	17	2	9.0	2.7	3.0	.258	.322	3.40
Pittsburgh	152	57	8	144	15	1379.2	1406	630	531	71	97	—	27	432	—	557	17	3	9.2	3.6	2.8	.266	.324	3.46
Cincinnati	151	72	11	130	16	1362.0	1329	634	548	75	90	—	13	463	—	542	26	4	8.8	3.6	3.1	.254	.316	3.62
New York	152	59	8	142	18	1349.0	1370	637	543	87	71	—	21	389	—	497	10	0	9.1	3.3	2.6	.261	.314	3.62
St. Louis	156	58	10	179	16	1384.2	1482	721	591	77	85	—	20	474	—	534	21	1	9.6	3.5	3.1	.272	.333	3.84
Brooklyn	151	56	12	155	14	1332.0	1464	710	602	88	78	—	30	446	—	469	38	3	9.9	3.2	3.0	.278	.338	4.07
Philadelphia	151	68	3	140	6	1329.1	1516	840	728	76	82	—	26	582	—	492	27	2	10.3	3.3	3.9	.285	.358	4.93
NL Total	1220	520	83	1147	115	10913.1	11356	5388	4588	611	674	—	184	3705	—	4087	187	20	9.4	3.4	3.1	.267	.329	3.78
NL Avg Team	153	65	10	143	14	1364.1	1420	674	574	76	84	—	23	463	—	511	23	3	9.4	3.4	3.1	.267	.329	3.78

Team Fielding

Team	G	PO	A	E	TC	DP	PB	Pct
Chicago	154	4164	1837	135	6136	151	11	.978
Pittsburgh	152	4139	1917	163	6219	168	7	.974
Brooklyn	151	3992	1706	157	5845	148	14	.973
New York	152	4043	1920	168	6131	147	10	.973
Boston	153	4133	1861	173	6167	136	6	.972
Cincinnati	151	4085	1766	172	6023	133	13	.971
St. Louis	156	4115	1758	199	6112	145	15	.967
Philadelphia	151	3985	1700	201	5886	135	13	.966
NL Total	1220	32696	14455	1368	48519	1163	89	.972

Team vs. Team Records

	Bos	Bro	ChN	Cin	NYG	Phi	Pit	StL	Won
Bos	—	12	10	11	8	14	9	13	77
Bro	10	—	9	9	8	15	9	9	69
ChN	12	11	—	11	12	18	12	13	89
Cin	9	13	11	—	12	14	10	13	82
NYG	14	14	10	9	—	16	9	11	83
Phi	8	7	4	7	5	—	8	6	45
Pit	13	11	10	12	13	12	—	15	86
StL	9	12	9	9	9	16	7	—	71
Lost	75	80	63	68	67	105	64	80	

1938 National League Batting Leaders

Games		At-Bats		Runs		Hits		Doubles		Triples	
S. Hack, ChN	152	F. McCormick, Cin	640	M. Ott, NYG	116	F. McCormick, Cin	209	J. Medwick, StL	47	J. Mize, StL	16
B. Herman, ChN	152	P. Waner, Pit	625	S. Hack, ChN	109	S. Hack, ChN	195	F. McCormick, Cin	40	D. Gutteridge, StL	15
H. Craft, Cin	151	B. Herman, ChN	624	D. Camilli, Bro	106	L. Waner, Pit	194	H. Martin, Phi	36	G. Suhr, Pit	14
F. McCormick, Cin	151	L. Waner, Pit	619	I. Goodman, Cin	103	J. Medwick, StL	190	P. Young, Pit	36	E. Koy, Bro	13
2 tied with	150	H. Craft, Cin	612	J. Medwick, StL	100	J. Mize, StL	179	2 tied with	35	L. Riggs, Cin	13

Home Runs		Total Bases		Runs Batted In		Walks		Intentional Walks		Strikeouts	
M. Ott, NYG	36	J. Mize, StL	326	J. Medwick, StL	122	D. Camilli, Bro	119	Statistic unavailable		V. DiMaggio, Bos	134
I. Goodman, Cin	30	J. Medwick, StL	316	M. Ott, NYG	116	M. Ott, NYG	118			D. Camilli, Bro	101
J. Mize, StL	27	M. Ott, NYG	307	J. Rizzo, Pit	111	A. Vaughan, Pit	104			B. Myers, Cin	80
D. Camilli, Bro	24	I. Goodman, Cin	303	F. McCormick, Cin	106	S. Hack, ChN	94			E. Koy, Bro	76
J. Rizzo, Pit	23	J. Rizzo, Pit	285	J. Mize, StL	102	G. Suhr, Pit	87			J. Hudson, Bro	76

Hit By Pitch		Sac Hits		Sac Flies		Stolen Bases		Caught Stealing		GDP	
I. Goodman, Cin	15	D. Young, Phi	15	Statistic unavailable		S. Hack, ChN	16	Statistic unavailable		E. Lombardi, Cin	30
D. Bartell, NYG	8	J. Ripple, NYG	14			E. Koy, Bro	15			A. Todd, Pit	25
5 tied with	5	J. Stripp, 2tm	14			C. Lavagetto, Bro	15			B. Herman, ChN	24
		C. Melton, NYG	13			D. Gutteridge, StL	14			B. Jurges, ChN	22
		L. Riggs, Cin	13			A. Vaughan, Pit	14			J. Medwick, StL	21

Runs Created		Runs Created/27 Outs		Batting Average		On-Base Percentage		Slugging Percentage		OBP+Slugging	
M. Ott, NYG	134	M. Ott, NYG	9.68	E. Lombardi, Cin	.342	M. Ott, NYG	.442	J. Mize, StL	.614	J. Mize, StL	1.036
J. Mize, StL	125	J. Mize, StL	9.20	J. Mize, StL	.337	A. Vaughan, Pit	.433	M. Ott, NYG	.583	M. Ott, NYG	1.024
S. Hack, ChN	120	A. Vaughan, Pit	7.77	F. McCormick, Cin	.327	P. Weintraub, Phi	.422	J. Medwick, StL	.536	E. Lombardi, Cin	.915
I. Goodman, Cin	112	D. Camilli, Bro	7.66	J. Medwick, StL	.322	J. Mize, StL	.422	I. Goodman, Cin	.533	J. Medwick, StL	.905
D. Camilli, Bro	110	S. Hack, ChN	7.62	A. Vaughan, Pit	.322	S. Hack, ChN	.411	E. Lombardi, Cin	.524	I. Goodman, Cin	.901

1938 National League Pitching Leaders

Wins		Losses		Winning Percentage		Games		Games Started		Complete Games	
B. Lee, ChN	22	H. Mulcahy, Phi	20	B. Lee, ChN	.710	M. Brown, Pit	51	B. Lee, ChN	37	P. Derringer, Cin	26
P. Derringer, Cin	21	L. French, ChN	19	B. Klinger, Pit	.706	D. Coffman, NYG	51	P. Derringer, Cin	37	J. Turner, Bos	22
C. Bryant, ChN	19	J. Turner, Bos	18	V. Tamulis, Bro	.667	B. McGee, StL	47	4 tied with	34	B. Walters, 2tm	20
B. Weiland, StL	16	C. Passeau, Phi	18	C. Bryant, ChN	.633	H. Mulcahy, Phi	46			B. Lee, ChN	19
4 tied with	15	A. Hollingsworth, 2tm	18	M. Brown, Pit	.625	5 tied with	44			D. MacFayden, Bos	19

Shutouts		Saves		Games Finished		Batters Faced		Innings Pitched		Hits Allowed	
B. Lee, ChN	9	D. Coffman, NYG	12	D. Coffman, NYG	35	P. Derringer, Cin	1263	P. Derringer, Cin	307.0	P. Derringer, Cin	315
D. MacFayden, Bos	5	C. Root, ChN	8	M. Brown, Pit	32	H. Mulcahy, Phi	1201	B. Lee, ChN	291.0	H. Mulcahy, Phi	294
P. Derringer, Cin	4	D. Errickson, Bos	6	J. Brown, NYG	32	B. Lee, ChN	1194	C. Bryant, ChN	270.1	C. Passeau, Phi	281
H. Schumacher, NYG	4	L. Hamlin, Bro	6	J. Cascarella, Cin	23	C. Bryant, ChN	1146	J. Turner, Bos	268.0	B. Lee, ChN	281
L. Warneke, StL	4	3 tied with	5	P. Sivess, Phi	22	B. Walters, 2tm	1111	H. Mulcahy, Phi	267.1	J. Turner, Bos	267

Home Runs Allowed		Walks		Walks/9 Innings		Strikeouts		Strikeouts/9 Innings		Strikeout/Walk Ratio	
J. Turner, Bos	21	C. Bryant, ChN	125	P. Derringer, Cin	1.4	C. Bryant, ChN	135	C. Hubbell, NYG	5.2	C. Hubbell, NYG	3.15
P. Derringer, Cin	20	H. Mulcahy, Phi	120	C. Hubbell, NYG	1.7	P. Derringer, Cin	132	J. Vander Meer, Cin	5.0	P. Derringer, Cin	2.69
C. Melton, NYG	19	B. Walters, 2tm	108	J. Turner, Bos	1.8	J. Vander Meer, Cin	125	B. Weiland, StL	4.6	B. Weiland, StL	1.75
B. Lee, ChN	18	J. Vander Meer, Cin	103	F. Fitzsimmons, Bro	1.9	B. Lee, ChN	121	C. Bryant, ChN	4.5	C. Blanton, Pit	1.74
2 tied with	17	R. Bauers, Pit	99	P. Davis, Cin	2.1	2 tied with	117	2 tied with	4.3	C. Melton, NYG	1.66

Earned Run Average		Component ERA		Hit Batsmen		Wild Pitches		Opponent Average		Opponent OBP	
B. Lee, ChN	2.66	J. Vander Meer, Cin	2.75	T. Pressnell, Bro	8	T. Carleton, ChN	12	J. Vander Meer, Cin	.213	C. Hubbell, NYG	.285
P. Derringer, Cin	2.93	R. Bauers, Pit	2.86	C. Passeau, Phi	8	B. Walters, 2tm	11	R. Bauers, Pit	.233	P. Derringer, Cin	.291
D. MacFayden, Bos	2.95	D. MacFayden, Bos	2.88	T. Carleton, ChN	8	B. Posedel, Bro	9	C. Bryant, ChN	.235	H. Schumacher, NYG	.299
B. Klinger, Pit	2.99	C. Hubbell, NYG	2.93	H. Gumbert, NYG	7	A. Hollingsworth, 2tm	8	D. MacFayden, Bos	.247	J. Turner, Bos	.299
F. Fitzsimmons, Bro	3.02	C. Bryant, ChN	2.97	5 tied with	6	V. Mungo, Bro	8	H. Schumacher, NYG	.248	B. Lee, ChN	.302

1938 National League Miscellaneous

Managers		
Boston	Casey Stengel	77-75
Brooklyn	Burleigh Grimes	69-80
Chicago	Charlie Grimm	45-36
	Gabby Hartnett	44-27
Cincinnati	Bill McKechnie	82-68
New York	Bill Terry	83-67
Philadelphia	Jimmie Wilson	45-103
	Hans Lobert	0-2
Pittsburgh	Pie Traynor	86-64
St. Louis	Frank Frisch	63-72
	Mike Gonzalez	8-8

Awards	
Most Valuable Player	Ernie Lombardi, c, Cin
STATS Cy Young	Bill Lee, ChN
STATS Rookie of the Year	Johnny Rizzo, of, Pit
STATS Manager of the Year	Gabby Hartnett, ChN

STATS All-Star Team

C	Ernie Lombardi, Cin	.342	19	95
1B	Johnny Mize, StL	.337	27	102
2B	Billy Herman, ChN	.277	1	56
3B	Mel Ott, NYG	.311	36	116
SS	Arky Vaughan, Pit	.322	7	68
OF	Ival Goodman, Cin	.292	30	92
OF	Joe Medwick, StL	.322	21	122
OF	Johnny Rizzo, Pit	.301	23	111
P	Clay Bryant, ChN	19-11	3.10	135 K
P	Paul Derringer, Cin	21-14	2.93	132 K
P	Bill Lee, ChN	22-9	2.66	121 K
P	Johnny Vander Meer, Cin	15-10	3.12	125 K
RP	Dick Coffman, NYG	8-4	3.48	12 Sv

Postseason	
World Series	Chicago (NL) 0 vs. New York (AL) 4

Outstanding Performances

No-Hitters
J. Vander Meer, Cin   vs. Bos on June 11
J. Vander Meer, Cin   @ Bro on June 15

Three-Homer Games
Johnny Mize, StL   on July 13
Johnny Mize, StL   on July 20

1939 American League Standings

Team	Overall					Home Games						Road Games						Park Index		Record by Month					
	W	L	Pct	GB	DIF	W	L	R	OR	HR	OHR	W	L	R	OR	HR	OHR	Run	HR	M/A	May	June	July	Aug	S/O
New York	106	45	.702	—	159	52	25	382	261	84	48	54	20	585	295	82	37	70	107	5-3	24-4	21-7	16-12	21-10	19-9
Boston	89	62	.589	17.0	7	42	32	458	445	57	39	47	30	432	350	67	38	120	95	5-3	16-9	12-12	23-10	18-14	15-14
Cleveland	87	67	.565	20.5	2	44	33	363	347	30	33	43	34	434	353	55	42	90	65	4-6	15-9	14-14	15-13	18-14	21-11
Chicago	85	69	.552	22.5	0	50	27	414	366	38	51	35	42	341	371	26	48	110	120	6-4	13-12	12-14	21-12	16-14	17-13
Detroit	81	73	.526	26.5	3	42	35	461	434	66	65	39	38	388	328	58	39	125	135	6-5	10-17	18-8	14-16	17-12	16-15
Washington	65	87	.428	41.5	0	37	39	326	337	11	19	28	48	376	460	33	56	79	34	5-4	9-18	11-20	14-15	15-15	11-15
Philadelphia	55	97	.362	51.5	1	28	48	354	523	45	83	27	49	357	499	53	65	102	108	2-7	11-15	13-15	8-20	10-22	11-18
St. Louis	43	111	.279	64.5	1	18	59	372	561	47	80	25	52	361	474	44	53	112	131	4-5	7-21	7-18	8-21	8-22	9-24

Clinch Date—New York 9/16.

Team Batting

Team	G	AB	R	OR	H	2B	3B	HR	TB	RBI	TBB	IBB	SO	HBP	SH	SF	SB	CS	SB%	GDP	Avg	OBP	Slg
New York	152	5300	967	556	1521	259	55	166	2388	904	701	—	543	36	92	—	72	37	.66	99	.287	.374	.451
Boston	152	5308	890	795	1543	287	57	124	2316	832	505	—	505	15	140	—	42	44	.49	146	.291	.363	.436
Detroit	155	5326	849	762	1487	277	67	124	2270	802	620	—	592	16	145	—	88	38	.70	125	.279	.356	.426
Cleveland	154	5316	797	700	1490	291	79	85	2194	730	557	—	574	14	120	—	72	46	.61	108	.280	.350	.413
Chicago	155	5279	755	737	1451	220	56	64	1975	679	579	—	502	21	154	—	113	61	.65	108	.275	.349	.374
St. Louis	156	5422	733	1035	1453	242	50	91	2068	696	559	—	606	20	133	—	48	38	.56	121	.268	.336	.381
Philadelphia	153	5309	711	1022	1438	282	55	98	2124	667	503	—	532	15	138	—	60	34	.64	122	.271	.336	.400
Washington	153	5334	702	797	1483	249	79	44	2022	647	547	—	460	12	134	—	94	47	.67	103	.278	.347	.379
AL Total	1230	42594	6404	6404	11866	2107	498	796	17357	5957	4657	—	4314	149	1056	—	589	345	.63	932	.279	.352	.407
AL Avg Team	154	5324	801	801	1483	263	62	100	2170	745	582	—	539	19	132	—	74	43	.63	117	.279	.352	.407

Team Pitching

Team	G	CG	ShO	Rel	Sv	IP	H	R	ER	HR	SH	SF	HB	TBB	IBB	SO	WP	Bk	H/9	SO/9	BB/9	OAvg	OOBP	ERA
New York	152	87	15	93	26	1348.2	1208	556	496	85	100	—	11	567	—	565	21	1	8.1	3.8	3.8	.241	.319	3.31
Cleveland	154	69	10	142	13	1364.2	1394	700	619	75	138	—	16	602	—	614	32	6	9.2	4.0	4.0	.267	.344	4.08
Detroit	155	64	8	150	16	1367.1	1430	762	652	104	114	—	18	574	—	633	33	2	9.4	4.2	3.8	.268	.341	4.29
Chicago	155	62	5	125	24	1377.0	1470	737	659	99	143	—	16	454	—	535	23	3	9.6	3.5	3.0	.275	.333	4.31
Boston	152	52	4	187	20	1350.2	1533	795	684	77	130	—	19	543	—	539	25	2	10.2	3.6	3.6	.287	.355	4.56
Washington	153	72	4	122	10	1354.2	1420	797	693	75	139	—	20	602	—	521	44	4	9.4	3.5	4.0	.271	.348	4.60
Philadelphia	153	50	6	155	12	1342.2	1687	1022	864	148	153	—	19	579	—	397	35	4	11.3	2.7	3.9	.307	.375	5.79
St. Louis	156	56	3	181	3	1371.1	1724	1035	916	133	139	—	29	739	—	516	32	3	11.3	3.4	4.9	.310	.393	6.01
AL Total	1230	512	55	1155	124	10877.0	11866	6404	5583	796	1056	—	148	4660	—	4320	245	25	9.8	3.6	3.9	.279	.352	4.62
AL Avg Team	154	64	7	144	16	1359.0	1483	801	698	100	132	—	19	583	—	540	31	3	9.8	3.6	3.9	.279	.352	4.62

Team Fielding

Team	G	PO	A	E	TC	DP	PB	Pct
New York	152	4045	1631	126	5802	159	8	.978
Chicago	155	4130	1685	167	5982	140	12	.972
Boston	152	4052	1798	180	6030	147	6	.970
Cleveland	154	4089	1657	180	5926	148	5	.970
St. Louis	156	4114	1813	199	6126	144	17	.968
Detroit	155	4101	1654	198	5953	147	14	.967
Washington	153	4071	1737	205	6013	167	26	.966
Philadelphia	153	4028	1678	210	5916	131	14	.965
AL Total	1230	32630	13653	1465	47748	1183	102	.969

Team vs. Team Records

	Bos	ChA	Cle	Det	NYA	Phi	StL	Was	Won
Bos	—	8	11	10	11	18	16	15	89
ChA	14	—	12	12	4	11	18	14	85
Cle	11	10	—	11	7	18	16	14	87
Det	12	10	11	—	9	11	14	14	81
NYA	8	18	15	13	—	18	19	15	106
Phi	4	11	4	11	4	—	13	8	55
StL	6	4	6	8	3	9	—	7	43
Was	7	8	8	8	7	12	15	—	65
Lost	62	69	67	73	45	97	111	87	

Seasons: Standings, Leaders

1939 American League Batting Leaders

Games		At-Bats		Runs		Hits		Doubles		Triples	
K. Keltner, Cle	154	F. Crosetti, NYA	656	R. Rolfe, NYA	139	R. Rolfe, NYA	213	R. Rolfe, NYA	46	B. Lewis, Was	16
G. McQuinn, StL	154	R. Rolfe, NYA	648	T. Williams, Bos	131	G. McQuinn, StL	195	T. Williams, Bos	44	B. McCosky, Det	14
F. Crosetti, NYA	152	G. McQuinn, StL	617	J. Foxx, Bos	130	K. Keltner, Cle	191	H. Greenberg, Det	42	G. McQuinn, StL	13
R. Rolfe, NYA	152	B. McCosky, Det	611	B. McCosky, Det	120	B. McCosky, Det	190	G. McQuinn, StL	37	B. Campbell, Cle	13
2 tied with	151	G. Walker, ChA	598	B. Johnson, Phi	115	T. Williams, Bos	185	K. Keltner, Cle	35	4 tied with	11

Home Runs		Total Bases		Runs Batted In		Walks		Intentional Walks		Strikeouts	
J. Foxx, Bos	35	T. Williams, Bos	344	T. Williams, Bos	145	H. Clift, StL	111	Statistic unavailable		H. Greenberg, Det	95
H. Greenberg, Det	33	J. Foxx, Bos	324	J. DiMaggio, NYA	126	T. Williams, Bos	107			B. Nagel, Phi	86
T. Williams, Bos	31	R. Rolfe, NYA	321	B. Johnson, Phi	114	L. Appling, ChA	105			F. Crosetti, NYA	81
J. DiMaggio, NYA	30	G. McQuinn, StL	318	H. Greenberg, Det	112	G. Selkirk, NYA	103			J. Foxx, Bos	72
J. Gordon, NYA	28	H. Greenberg, Det	311	2 tied with	111	B. Johnson, Phi	99			2 tied with	64

Hit By Pitch		Sac Hits		Sac Flies		Stolen Bases		Caught Stealing		GDP	
F. Crosetti, NYA	13	M. Kreevich, ChA	22	Statistic unavailable		G. Case, Was	51	G. Case, Was	17	J. Vosmik, Bos	27
G. Selkirk, NYA	8	B. Chapman, Cle	20			P. Fox, Det	23	P. Fox, Det	12	B. Chapman, Cle	19
G. Walker, ChA	7	J. Cronin, Bos	20			M. Kreevich, ChA	23	4 tied with	10	J. Cronin, Bos	18
H. Clift, StL	5	B. Lewis, Was	19			B. McCosky, Det	20			B. Doerr, Bos	17
4 tied with	4	G. McQuinn, StL	18			2 tied with	18			J. Foxx, Bos	17

Runs Created		Runs Created/27 Outs		Batting Average		On-Base Percentage		Slugging Percentage		OBP+Slugging	
T. Williams, Bos	153	J. Foxx, Bos	11.78	J. DiMaggio, NYA	.381	J. Foxx, Bos	.464	J. Foxx, Bos	.694	J. Foxx, Bos	1.158
J. Foxx, Bos	142	J. DiMaggio, NYA	11.71	J. Foxx, Bos	.360	G. Selkirk, NYA	.452	J. DiMaggio, NYA	.671	J. DiMaggio, NYA	1.119
R. Rolfe, NYA	136	T. Williams, Bos	10.44	B. Johnson, Phi	.338	J. DiMaggio, NYA	.448	H. Greenberg, Det	.622	T. Williams, Bos	1.045
J. DiMaggio, NYA	132	G. Selkirk, NYA	9.57	H. Trosky, Cle	.335	C. Keller, NYA	.447	T. Williams, Bos	.609	H. Greenberg, Det	1.042
H. Greenberg, Det	130	H. Greenberg, Det	9.55	C. Keller, NYA	.334	B. Johnson, Phi	.440	H. Trosky, Cle	.589	H. Trosky, Cle	.994

1939 American League Pitching Leaders

Wins		Losses		Winning Percentage		Games		Games Started		Complete Games	
B. Feller, Cle	24	V. Kennedy, 2tm	20	A. Donald, NYA	.813	C. Brown, ChA	61	B. Newsom, 2tm	37	B. Feller, Cle	24
R. Ruffing, NYA	21	K. Chase, Was	19	L. Grove, Bos	.789	C. Dean, Phi	54	B. Feller, Cle	35	B. Newsom, 2tm	24
D. Leonard, Was	20	J. Krakauskas, Was	17	R. Ruffing, NYA	.750	E. Dickman, Bos	48	D. Leonard, Was	34	R. Ruffing, NYA	22
B. Newsom, 2tm	20	J. Kramer, StL	16	B. Feller, Cle	.727	J. Heving, Bos	46	3 tied with	31	D. Leonard, Was	21
T. Bridges, Det	17	B. Ross, Phi	14	D. Leonard, Was	.714	3 tied with	41			L. Grove, Bos	17

Shutouts		Saves		Games Finished		Batters Faced		Innings Pitched		Hits Allowed	
R. Ruffing, NYA	5	J. Murphy, NYA	19	C. Brown, ChA	56	B. Newsom, 2tm	1261	B. Feller, Cle	296.2	D. Leonard, Was	273
B. Feller, Cle	4	C. Brown, ChA	18	C. Dean, Phi	38	B. Feller, Cle	1243	B. Newsom, 2tm	291.2	B. Newsom, 2tm	272
12 tied with	2	C. Dean, Phi	7	J. Murphy, NYA	34	D. Leonard, Was	1133	D. Leonard, Was	269.1	J. Kramer, StL	269
		J. Heving, Bos	7	P. Appleton, Was	27	K. Chase, Was	1019	T. Lee, ChA	235.0	T. Lee, ChA	260
		P. Appleton, Was	6	J. Heving, Bos	26	T. Lee, ChA	1008	R. Ruffing, NYA	233.1	N. Potter, Phi	258

Home Runs Allowed		Walks		Walks/9 Innings		Strikeouts		Strikeouts/9 Innings		Strikeout/Walk Ratio	
J. Marcum, 2tm	27	B. Feller, Cle	142	T. Lyons, ChA	1.4	B. Feller, Cle	246	B. Feller, Cle	7.5	T. Lyons, ChA	2.50
L. Nelson, Phi	27	J. Kramer, StL	127	D. Leonard, Was	2.0	B. Newsom, 2tm	192	B. Newsom, 2tm	5.9	T. Bridges, Det	2.11
N. Potter, Phi	26	B. Newsom, 2tm	126	T. Lee, ChA	2.7	T. Bridges, Det	129	T. Bridges, Det	5.9	B. Feller, Cle	1.73
V. Kennedy, 2tm	22	V. Kennedy, 2tm	124	L. Grove, Bos	2.7	J. Rigney, ChA	119	J. Rigney, ChA	4.9	B. Newsom, 2tm	1.52
B. Newsom, 2tm	19	2 tied with	114	M. Harder, Cle	2.8	K. Chase, Was	118	L. Gomez, NYA	4.6	D. Leonard, Was	1.49

Earned Run Average		Component ERA		Hit Batsmen		Wild Pitches		Opponent Average		Opponent OBP	
L. Grove, Bos	2.54	T. Lyons, ChA	2.40	L. Mills, StL	8	B. Feller, Cle	14	B. Feller, Cle	.210	T. Lyons, ChA	.276
T. Lyons, ChA	2.76	B. Feller, Cle	2.66	T. Bridges, Det	6	N. Potter, Phi	12	L. Gomez, NYA	.235	R. Ruffing, NYA	.301
B. Feller, Cle	2.85	L. Grove, Bos	2.95	4 tied with	5	K. Chase, Was	11	R. Ruffing, NYA	.240	B. Feller, Cle	.303
R. Ruffing, NYA	2.93	R. Ruffing, NYA	2.98			B. Harris, 2tm	10	T. Bridges, Det	.243	T. Bridges, Det	.304
L. Gomez, NYA	3.41	T. Bridges, Det	3.09			J. Kramer, StL	9	B. Newsom, 2tm	.243	D. Leonard, Was	.305

1939 American League Miscellaneous

Managers

Boston	Joe Cronin	89-62
Chicago	Jimmy Dykes	85-69
Cleveland	Ossie Vitt	87-67
Detroit	Del Baker	81-73
New York	Joe McCarthy	106-45
Philadelphia	Connie Mack	25-37
	Earle Mack	30-60
St. Louis	Fred Haney	43-111
Washington	Bucky Harris	65-87

Awards

Most Valuable Player	Joe DiMaggio, of, NYA
STATS Cy Young	Bob Feller, Cle
STATS Rookie of the Year	Ted Williams, of, Bos
STATS Manager of the Year	Jimmy Dykes, ChA

STATS All-Star Team

C	Bill Dickey, NYA	.302	24	105
1B	Jimmie Foxx, Bos	.360	35	105
2B	Charlie Gehringer, Det	.325	16	86
3B	Red Rolfe, NYA	.329	14	80
SS	Joe Cronin, Bos	.308	19	107
OF	Joe DiMaggio, NYA	.381	30	126
OF	Bob Johnson, Phi	.338	23	114
OF	Ted Williams, Bos	.327	31	145
P	Bob Feller, Cle	24-9	2.85	246 K
P	Lefty Grove, Bos	15-4	2.54	81 K
P	Dutch Leonard, Was	20-8	3.54	88 K
P	Red Ruffing, NYA	21-7	2.93	95 K
RP	Clint Brown, ChA	11-10	3.88	18 Sv

Postseason

World Series	NYA (AL) 4 vs. Cincinnati (NL) 0

Outstanding Performances

Three-Homer Games

Ken Keltner, Cle	on May 25
Jim Tabor, Bos	on July 4
Bill Dickey, NYA	on July 26

Cycles

Sam Chapman, Phi	on May 5
C. Gehringer, Det	on May 27

1939 National League Standings

Team	Overall W	L	Pct	GB	DIF	Home Games W	L	R	OR	HR	OHR	Road Games W	L	R	OR	HR	OHR	Park Index Run	HR	Record by Month M/A	May	June	July	Aug	S/O
Cincinnati	97	57	.630	—	138	55	25	404	307	49	39	42	32	363	288	49	42	101	89	6-2	19-11	13-10	22-7	13-15	24-12
St. Louis	92	61	.601	4.5	19	51	27	431	317	63	42	41	34	348	316	35	34	108	146	5-4	17-10	11-13	15-15	20-9	24-10
Brooklyn	84	69	.549	12.5	0	51	27	385	329	41	49	33	42	323	316	37	44	107	107	4-4	13-14	12-11	15-16	16-11	24-13
Chicago	84	70	.545	13.0	6	44	34	379	343	44	35	40	36	345	335	47	39	103	90	6-4	14-14	15-12	14-15	19-10	16-15
New York	77	74	.510	18.5	2	41	33	360	315	84	58	36	41	343	370	32	28	99	246	3-6	14-15	18-7	9-18	15-12	18-16
Pittsburgh	68	85	.444	28.5	1	35	42	339	365	24	29	33	43	327	356	39	41	102	65	1-8	18-10	8-13	19-11	8-22	14-21
Boston	63	88	.417	32.5	9	37	35	254	272	13	14	26	53	318	387	43	49	82	32	7-3	8-18	10-14	17-13	10-18	11-22
Philadelphia	45	106	.298	50.5	0	29	44	288	384	18	49	16	62	265	472	31	57	97	81	4-5	8-19	7-14	7-23	13-17	6-28

Clinch Date—Cincinnati 9/28.

Team Batting

Team	G	AB	R	OR	H	2B	3B	HR	TB	RBI	TBB	IBB	SO	HBP	SH	SF	SB	CS	SB%	GDP	Avg	OBP	Slg
St. Louis	155	5447	779	633	1601	332	62	98	2351	732	475	—	566	27	167	—	44	—	—	116	.294	.354	.432
Cincinnati	156	5378	767	595	1493	269	60	98	2176	714	500	—	538	35	193	—	46	—	—	110	.278	.343	.405
Chicago	156	5293	724	678	1407	263	62	91	2067	671	523	—	553	34	140	—	61	—	—	124	.266	.336	.391
Brooklyn	157	5350	708	645	1420	265	57	78	2033	653	564	—	639	26	107	—	59	—	—	131	.265	.338	.380
New York	151	5129	703	685	1395	211	38	116	2030	651	498	—	499	32	108	—	26	—	—	153	.272	.340	.396
Pittsburgh	153	5269	666	721	1453	261	60	63	2023	617	477	—	420	21	156	—	44	—	—	128	.276	.338	.384
Boston	152	5286	572	659	1395	199	39	56	1840	534	366	—	494	21	122	—	41	—	—	119	.264	.314	.348
Philadelphia	152	5133	553	856	1341	232	40	49	1800	510	421	—	486	9	144	—	47	—	—	133	.261	.318	.351
NL Total	1232	42285	5472	5472	11505	2032	418	649	16320	5082	3824	—	4195	205	1137	—	368	—	—	1014	.272	.335	.386
NL Avg Team	154	5286	684	684	1438	254	52	81	2040	635	478	—	524	26	142	—	46	—	—	127	.272	.335	.386

Team Pitching

Team	G	CG	ShO	Rel	Sv	IP	H	R	ER	HR	SH	SF	HB	TBB	IBB	SO	WP	Bk	H/9	SO/9	BB/9	OAvg	OOBP	ERA
Cincinnati	156	86	13	143	9	1403.2	1340	595	510	81	140	—	28	499	—	637	26	6	8.6	4.1	3.2	.255	.322	3.27
St. Louis	155	45	18	210	32	1384.2	1377	633	552	76	120	—	19	498	—	603	27	4	9.0	3.9	3.2	.260	.326	3.59
Brooklyn	157	69	9	138	13	1410.1	1431	645	571	93	138	—	30	399	—	528	21	3	9.1	3.4	2.5	.263	.317	3.64
Boston	152	68	11	144	15	1358.1	1400	659	560	63	158	—	19	513	—	430	20	5	9.3	2.8	3.4	.271	.339	3.71
Chicago	156	72	8	136	13	1392.1	1504	678	588	74	126	—	19	430	—	584	20	3	9.7	3.8	2.8	.276	.331	3.80
New York	151	55	6	163	20	1319.0	1412	685	596	86	119	—	25	477	—	505	30	1	9.6	3.4	3.3	.275	.340	4.07
Pittsburgh	153	53	10	157	15	1354.0	1537	721	625	70	151	—	22	423	—	464	18	1	10.2	3.1	2.8	.287	.342	4.15
Philadelphia	152	67	3	133	12	1326.2	1502	856	762	106	177	—	44	579	—	447	38	1	10.2	3.0	3.9	.289	.365	5.17
NL Total	1232	515	78	1224	129	10949.0	11503	5472	4764	649	1129	—	206	3818	—	4198	200	24	9.5	3.5	3.1	.272	.335	3.92
NL Avg Team	154	64	10	153	16	1368.0	1438	684	596	81	141	—	26	477	—	525	25	3	9.5	3.5	3.1	.272	.335	3.92

Team Fielding

Team	G	PO	A	E	TC	DP	PB	Pct
New York	151	3964	1893	153	6010	151	10	.975
Cincinnati	156	4211	1837	162	6210	170	19	.974
Pittsburgh	153	4049	1852	168	6069	153	8	.972
Brooklyn	157	4231	1812	176	6219	157	9	.972
Boston	152	4074	1912	181	6167	178	10	.971
St. Louis	155	4150	1693	177	6020	140	16	.971
Philadelphia	152	3990	1629	171	5790	136	9	.970
Chicago	156	4172	1802	186	6160	126	13	.970
NL Total	1232	32841	14430	1374	48645	1211	94	.972

Team vs. Team Records

	Bos	Bro	ChN	Cin	NYG	Phi	Pit	StL	Won
Bos	—	10	6	6	10	13	9	9	63
Bro	12	—	11	10	12	17	13	9	84
ChN	16	11	—	10	11	12	14	10	84
Cin	16	12	12	—	11	19	16	11	97
NYG	11	10	11	11	—	14	11	9	77
Phi	8	4	10	3	7	—	8	5	45
Pit	12	9	8	6	11	14	—	8	68
StL	13	13	12	11	12	17	14	—	92
Lost	88	69	70	57	74	106	85	61	

1939 National League Batting Leaders

Games		At-Bats		Runs		Hits		Doubles		Triples	
D. Camilli, Bro	157	J. Brown, StL	645	B. Werber, Cin	115	F. McCormick, Cin	209	E. Slaughter, StL	52	B. Herman, ChN	18
F. McCormick, Cin	156	S. Hack, ChN	641	S. Hack, ChN	112	J. Medwick, StL	201	J. Medwick, StL	48	I. Goodman, Cin	16
S. Hack, ChN	156	F. McCormick, Cin	630	B. Herman, ChN	111	J. Mize, StL	197	J. Mize, StL	44	J. Mize, StL	14
B. Herman, ChN	156	B. Herman, ChN	623	D. Camilli, Bro	105	E. Slaughter, StL	193	F. McCormick, Cin	41	D. Camilli, Bro	12
2 tied with	153	J. Medwick, StL	606	2 tied with	104	J. Brown, StL	192	2 tied with	37	2 tied with	11

Home Runs		Total Bases		Runs Batted In		Walks		Intentional Walks	Strikeouts	
J. Mize, StL	28	J. Mize, StL	353	F. McCormick, Cin	128	D. Camilli, Bro	110	Statistic unavailable	D. Camilli, Bro	107
M. Ott, NYG	27	F. McCormick, Cin	312	J. Medwick, StL	117	M. Ott, NYG	100		B. Myers, Cin	90
D. Camilli, Bro	26	J. Medwick, StL	307	J. Mize, StL	108	J. Mize, StL	92		D. Gutteridge, StL	70
H. Leiber, ChN	24	D. Camilli, Bro	296	D. Camilli, Bro	104	B. Werber, Cin	91		E. Koy, Bro	64
E. Lombardi, Cin	20	E. Slaughter, StL	291	H. Leiber, ChN	88	C. Lavagetto, Bro	78		W. Berger, Cin	63

Hit By Pitch		Sac Hits		Sac Flies	Stolen Bases		Caught Stealing	GDP	
I. Goodman, Cin	7	P. May, Phi	25	Statistic unavailable	L. Handley, Pit	17	Statistic unavailable	B. Jurges, NYG	26
D. Bartell, ChN	7	L. Frey, Cin	25		S. Hack, ChN	17		B. Herman, ChN	24
A. Vaughan, Pit	6	B. Myers, Pit	22		B. Werber, Cin	15		E. Lombardi, Cin	24
B. Jurges, NYG	6	I. Goodman, Cin	22		C. Lavagetto, Bro	14		F. McCormick, Cin	23
B. Werber, Cin	6	A. Vaughan, Pit	22		B. Hassett, Bos	13		Z. Bonura, NYG	22

Runs Created		Runs Created/27 Outs		Batting Average		On-Base Percentage		Slugging Percentage		OBP+Slugging	
J. Mize, StL	138	M. Ott, NYG	9.86	J. Mize, StL	.349	M. Ott, NYG	.449	J. Mize, StL	.626	J. Mize, StL	1.070
D. Camilli, Bro	123	J. Mize, StL	9.56	F. McCormick, Cin	.332	J. Mize, StL	.444	M. Ott, NYG	.581	M. Ott, NYG	1.030
F. McCormick, Cin	109	H. Leiber, ChN	8.15	J. Medwick, StL	.332	H. Leiber, ChN	.411	H. Leiber, ChN	.556	H. Leiber, ChN	.967
M. Ott, NYG	107	D. Camilli, Bro	7.87	P. Waner, Pit	.328	D. Camilli, Bro	.409	D. Camilli, Bro	.524	D. Camilli, Bro	.933
B. Herman, ChN	105	I. Goodman, Cin	7.57	M. Arnovich, Phi	.324	I. Goodman, Cin	.401	I. Goodman, Cin	.515	I. Goodman, Cin	.916

1939 National League Pitching Leaders

Wins		Losses		Winning Percentage		Games		Games Started		Complete Games	
B. Walters, Cin	27	B. Klinger, Pit	17	P. Derringer, Cin	.781	C. Shoun, StL	53	B. Lee, ChN	36	B. Walters, Cin	31
P. Derringer, Cin	25	M. Butcher, 2tm	17	J. Thompson, Cin	.722	R. Sewell, Pit	52	L. Hamlin, Bro	36	P. Derringer, Cin	28
C. Davis, StL	22	H. Mulcahy, Phi	16	B. Bowman, StL	.722	B. Bowman, StL	51	B. Walters, Cin	36	B. Lee, ChN	20
L. Hamlin, Bro	20	C. Davis, StL	16	B. Walters, Cin	.711	C. Davis, StL	49	C. Passeau, 2tm	35	L. Hamlin, Bro	19
B. Lee, ChN	19	3 tied with	15	B. McGee, StL	.706	M. Brown, Pit	47	P. Derringer, Cin	35	B. Posedel, Bos	18

Shutouts		Saves		Games Finished		Batters Faced		Innings Pitched		Hits Allowed	
L. Fette, Bos	6	B. Bowman, StL	9	C. Shoun, StL	25	B. Walters, Cin	1283	B. Walters, Cin	319.0	P. Derringer, Cin	321
B. Posedel, Bos	5	C. Shoun, StL	9	J. Russell, ChN	24	P. Derringer, Cin	1245	P. Derringer, Cin	301.0	B. Lee, ChN	295
P. Derringer, Cin	5	M. Brown, Pit	7	I. Hutchinson, Bro	21	B. Lee, ChN	1202	B. Lee, ChN	282.1	C. Davis, StL	279
B. McGee, StL	4	C. Davis, StL	7	3 tied with	20	C. Passeau, 2tm	1150	C. Passeau, 2tm	274.1	C. Passeau, 2tm	269
4 tied with	3	J. Brown, NYG	7			L. Hamlin, Bro	1100	L. Hamlin, Bro	269.2	H. Gumbert, NYG	257

Home Runs Allowed		Walks		Walks/9 Innings		Strikeouts		Strikeouts/9 Innings		Strikeout/Walk Ratio	
L. Hamlin, Bro	27	K. Higbe, 2tm	123	P. Derringer, Cin	1.0	C. Passeau, 2tm	137	L. French, ChN	4.5	P. Derringer, Cin	3.66
H. Gumbert, NYG	21	B. Walters, Cin	109	C. Hubbell, NYG	1.4	B. Walters, Cin	137	C. Passeau, 2tm	4.5	C. Hubbell, NYG	2.58
H. Mulcahy, Phi	19	M. Cooper, StL	97	C. Davis, StL	1.7	M. Cooper, StL	130	K. Higbe, 2tm	4.1	L. French, ChN	1.96
B. Lee, ChN	18	J. Vander Meer, Cin	95	L. Hamlin, Bro	1.8	P. Derringer, Cin	128	B. Walters, Cin	3.9	C. Passeau, 2tm	1.88
C. Davis, StL	16	W. Moore, Cin	95	T. Pressnell, Bro	1.9	B. Lee, ChN	105	P. Derringer, Cin	3.8	L. Hamlin, Bro	1.63

Earned Run Average		Component ERA		Hit Batsmen		Wild Pitches		Opponent Average		Opponent OBP	
B. Walters, Cin	2.29	B. Walters, Cin	2.41	H. Mulcahy, Phi	11	H. Mulcahy, Phi	11	B. Walters, Cin	.220	C. Hubbell, NYG	.280
C. Hubbell, NYG	2.75	C. Hubbell, NYG	2.77	C. Casey, Bro	11	T. Sunkel, StL	9	L. Fette, Bos	.229	L. Hamlin, Bro	.285
H. Casey, Bro	2.93	L. Fette, Bos	2.89	K. Higbe, 2tm	10	B. Walters, Cin	8	L. Hamlin, Bro	.248	B. Walters, Cin	.291
P. Derringer, Cin	2.93	L. Hamlin, Bro	2.97	V. Tamulis, Bro	8	K. Higbe, 2tm	7	C. Hubbell, NYG	.249	P. Derringer, Cin	.295
L. Fette, Bos	2.96	C. Passeau, 2tm	3.00	J. Bowman, Pit	7	2 tied with	6	C. Passeau, 2tm	.256	C. Passeau, 2tm	.307

1939 National League Miscellaneous

Managers

Boston	Casey Stengel	63-88
Brooklyn	Leo Durocher	84-69
Chicago	Gabby Hartnett	84-70
Cincinnati	Bill McKechnie	97-57
New York	Bill Terry	77-74
Philadelphia	Doc Prothro	45-106
Pittsburgh	Pie Traynor	68-85
St. Louis	Ray Blades	92-61

Awards

Most Valuable Player	Bucky Walters, p, Cin
STATS Cy Young	Bucky Walters, Cin
STATS Rookie of the Year	Bob Bowman, p, StL
STATS Manager of the Year	Bill McKechnie, Cin

STATS All-Star Team

C	Harry Danning, NYG	.313	16	74
1B	Johnny Mize, StL	.349	28	108
2B	Billy Herman, ChN	.307	7	70
3B	Cookie Lavagetto, Bro	.300	10	87
SS	Arky Vaughan, Pit	.306	6	62
OF	Hank Leiber, ChN	.310	24	88
OF	Joe Medwick, StL	.332	14	117
OF	Mel Ott, NYG	.308	27	80
P	Hugh Casey, Bro	15-10	2.93	79 K
P	Curt Davis, StL	22-16	3.63	70 K
P	Paul Derringer, Cin	25-7	2.93	128 K
P	Bucky Walters, Cin	27-11	2.29	137 K
RP	Bob Bowman, StL	13-5	2.60	9 Sv

Postseason

World Series	Cincinnati (NL) 0 vs. NYA (AL) 4

Outstanding Performances

Three-Homer Games
Hank Leiber, ChN   on July 4
Cycles
Arky Vaughan, Pit   on July 19

1940 American League Standings

Team	W	L	Pct	GB	DIF	W	L	R	OR	HR	OHR	W	L	R	OR	HR	OHR	Run	HR	M/A	May	June	July	Aug	S/O
	Overall					**Home Games**						**Road Games**						**Park Index**		**Record by Month**					
Detroit	90	64	.584	—	49	50	29	512	389	82	64	40	35	376	328	52	38	122	154	6-5	14-10	18-10	19-13	15-15	18-11
Cleveland	89	65	.578	1.0	73	51	30	350	281	37	27	38	35	360	356	64	59	79	47	8-3	15-10	19-12	15-13	17-12	15-15
New York	88	66	.571	2.0	0	52	24	414	284	83	63	36	42	403	387	72	56	91	117	4-6	13-12	15-14	16-12	20-10	20-12
Boston	82	72	.532	8.0	57	45	34	468	421	73	64	37	38	404	404	72	60	104	99	7-4	15-6	14-16	14-18	19-14	13-14
Chicago	82	72	.532	8.0	0	41	36	357	363	36	65	41	36	378	309	37	46	105	122	3-7	13-14	12-13	18-10	17-16	19-12
St. Louis	67	87	.435	23.0	2	37	39	419	460	68	68	30	48	338	422	50	45	119	147	5-5	9-16	17-16	8-21	12-18	16-11
Washington	64	90	.416	26.0	0	36	41	316	368	19	28	28	49	349	443	33	65	86	48	6-5	10-17	11-19	15-14	10-16	12-19
Philadelphia	54	100	.351	36.0	1	29	42	336	409	44	62	25	58	367	523	61	73	98	92	4-8	9-13	11-17	14-18	8-17	8-27

Clinch Date—Detroit 9/27.

Team Batting

Team	G	AB	R	OR	H	2B	3B	HR	TB	RBI	TBB	IBB	SO	HBP	SH	SF	SB	CS	SB%	GDP	Avg	OBP	Slg
Detroit	155	5418	888	717	1549	312	65	134	2393	829	664	—	556	23	77	—	66	39	.63	115	.286	.366	.442
Boston	154	5481	872	825	1566	301	80	145	2462	808	590	—	597	10	91	—	55	49	.53	129	.286	.356	.449
New York	155	5286	817	671	1371	243	66	155	2211	757	648	—	606	36	76	—	59	36	.62	124	.259	.344	.418
St. Louis	156	5415	757	882	1423	278	58	118	2171	715	556	—	642	16	63	—	51	40	.56	106	.263	.333	.401
Chicago	155	5386	735	672	1499	238	63	73	2082	671	496	—	569	10	110	—	52	60	.46	122	.278	.340	.387
Cleveland	155	5361	710	637	1422	287	61	101	2134	661	519	—	597	16	61	—	53	36	.60	127	.265	.332	.398
Philadelphia	154	5304	703	932	1391	242	53	105	2054	648	556	—	656	19	69	—	48	33	.59	127	.262	.334	.387
Washington	154	5365	665	811	1453	266	67	52	2009	602	468	—	504	18	61	—	94	40	.70	99	.271	.331	.374
AL Total	1238	43016	6147	6147	11674	2167	513	883	17516	5691	4497	—	4727	148	608	—	478	333	.59	933	.271	.342	.407
AL Avg Team	155	5377	768	768	1459	271	64	110	2190	711	562	—	591	19	76	—	60	42	.59	117	.271	.342	.407

Team Pitching

Team	G	CG	ShO	Rel	Sv	IP	H	R	ER	HR	SH	SF	HB	TBB	IBB	SO	WP	Bk	H/9	SO/9	BB/9	OAvg	OOBP	ERA
Cleveland	155	72	13	151	22	1375.0	1328	637	555	86	66	—	25	512	—	686	28	2	8.7	4.5	3.4	.254	.324	3.63
Chicago	155	83	10	91	18	1386.2	1335	672	576	111	72	—	14	480	—	574	31	2	8.7	3.7	3.1	.250	.313	3.74
New York	155	76	10	125	14	1373.0	1389	671	593	119	68	—	16	511	—	559	22	3	9.1	3.7	3.3	.261	.328	3.89
Detroit	155	59	10	171	23	1375.1	1425	717	613	102	74	—	17	570	—	752	25	5	9.3	4.9	3.7	.266	.338	4.01
Washington	154	74	6	122	7	1350.0	1494	811	689	93	95	—	21	618	—	618	47	4	10.0	4.1	4.1	.281	.359	4.59
Boston	154	51	4	178	16	1379.2	1568	825	749	124	71	—	23	625	—	613	36	1	10.2	4.0	4.1	.284	.359	4.89
St. Louis	156	64	4	180	9	1373.1	1592	882	782	113	76	—	20	646	—	439	42	3	10.4	2.9	4.2	.290	.367	5.12
Philadelphia	154	72	4	117	12	1345.0	1543	932	780	135	83	—	15	534	—	488	40	5	10.3	3.3	3.6	.283	.348	5.22
AL Total	1238	551	61	1135	121	10958.0	11674	6147	5337	883	605	—	151	4496	—	4729	271	25	9.6	3.9	3.7	.271	.342	4.38
AL Avg Team	155	69	8	142	15	1369.0	1459	768	667	110	76	—	19	562	—	591	34	3	9.6	3.9	3.7	.271	.342	4.38

Team Fielding

Team	G	PO	A	E	TC	DP	PB	Pct
Cleveland	155	4118	1622	149	5889	164	5	.975
New York	155	4121	1718	152	5991	158	6	.975
St. Louis	156	4120	1891	158	6169	179	18	.974
Boston	154	4140	1808	173	6121	156	12	.972
Chicago	155	4159	1649	185	5993	125	15	.969
Detroit	155	4122	1722	194	6038	116	8	.968
Washington	154	4058	1747	194	5999	166	23	.968
Philadelphia	154	4035	1667	238	5940	131	15	.960
AL Total	1238	32873	13824	1443	48140	1195	102	.970

Team vs. Team Records

	Bos	ChA	Cle	Det	NYA	Phi	StL	Was	Won
Bos	—	11	8	11	9	18	12	13	82
ChA	11	—	6	13	11	16	13	12	82
Cle	14	16	—	11	10	14	11	13	89
Det	11	9	11	—	14	11	18	16	90
NYA	13	11	12	8	—	13	14	17	88
Phi	4	6	8	11	9	—	8	8	54
StL	10	9	11	4	8	14	—	11	67
Was	9	10	9	6	5	14	11	—	64
Lost	72	72	65	64	66	100	87	90	

1940 American League Batting Leaders

Games			At-Bats			Runs			Hits			Doubles			Triples		
L. Boudreau, Cle	155		D. Cramer, Bos	661		T. Williams, Bos	134		B. McCosky, Det	200		H. Greenberg, Det	50		B. McCosky, Det	19	
J. Gordon, NYA	155		G. Case, Was	656		H. Greenberg, Det	129		R. Radcliff, StL	200		L. Boudreau, Cle	46		C. Keller, NYA	15	
B. Dahlgren, NYA	155		L. Boudreau, Cle	627		B. McCosky, Det	123		D. Cramer, Bos	200		R. York, Det	46		L. Finney, Bos	15	
R. York, Det	155		J. Gordon, NYA	616		J. Gordon, NYA	112		L. Appling, ChA	197		T. Williams, Bos	43		T. Williams, Bos	14	
J. Kuhel, ChA	155		B. Kennedy, ChA	606		J. Kuhel, ChA	111		T. Wright, ChA	196		W. Moses, Phi	41		L. Appling, ChA	13	

Home Runs			Total Bases			Runs Batted In			Walks			Intentional Walks			Strikeouts		
H. Greenberg, Det	41		H. Greenberg, Det	384		H. Greenberg, Det	150		C. Keller, NYA	106		Statistic unavailable			S. Chapman, Phi	96	
J. Foxx, Bos	36		R. York, Det	343		R. York, Det	134		H. Clift, StL	104					R. York, Det	88	
R. York, Det	33		T. Williams, Bos	333		J. DiMaggio, NYA	133		J. Foxx, Bos	101					J. Foxx, Bos	87	
J. DiMaggio, NYA	31		J. DiMaggio, NYA	318		J. Foxx, Bos	119		C. Gehringer, Det	101					R. Mack, Cle	77	
B. Johnson, Phi	31		J. Gordon, NYA	315		T. Williams, Bos	113		T. Williams, Bos	96					F. Crosetti, NYA	77	

Hit By Pitch			Sac Hits			Sac Flies			Stolen Bases			Caught Stealing			GDP		
F. Crosetti, NYA	10		M. Kreevich, ChA	21		Statistic unavailable			G. Case, Was	35		M. Tresh, ChA	10		L. Boudreau, Cle	23	
G. Case, Was	5		D. Cramer, Bos	14					G. Walker, Was	21		J. Tabor, Bos	10		B. Dahlgren, NYA	20	
B. Dahlgren, NYA	5		J. Cronin, Bos	13					J. Gordon, NYA	18		G. Case, Was	10		B. Johnson, Phi	20	
D. Bartell, Det	5		J. Rigney, ChA	12					B. Lewis, Was	15		B. Lewis, Was	10		B. Chapman, Cle	19	
3 tied with	4		2 tied with	11					M. Kreevich, ChA	15		B. McCosky, Det	9		2 tied with	18	

Runs Created			Runs Created/27 Outs			Batting Average			On-Base Percentage			Slugging Percentage			OBP+Slugging		
H. Greenberg, Det	152		H. Greenberg, Det	10.22		J. DiMaggio, NYA	.352		T. Williams, Bos	.442		H. Greenberg, Det	.670		H. Greenberg, Det	1.103	
T. Williams, Bos	139		J. DiMaggio, NYA	9.90		L. Appling, ChA	.348		H. Greenberg, Det	.433		J. DiMaggio, NYA	.626		J. DiMaggio, NYA	1.051	
R. York, Det	134		T. Williams, Bos	9.66		T. Williams, Bos	.344		L. Rosenthal, ChA	.432		T. Williams, Bos	.594		T. Williams, Bos	1.036	
J. DiMaggio, NYA	128		R. York, Det	8.56		R. Radcliff, StL	.342		C. Gehringer, Det	.428		R. York, Det	.583		R. York, Det	.993	
J. Kuhel, ChA	116		C. Keller, NYA	8.06		H. Greenberg, Det	.340		J. DiMaggio, NYA	.425		J. Foxx, Bos	.581		J. Foxx, Bos	.993	

1940 American League Pitching Leaders

Wins			Losses			Winning Percentage			Games			Games Started			Complete Games		
B. Feller, Cle	27		G. Caster, Phi	19		S. Rowe, Det	.842		B. Feller, Cle	43		B. Feller, Cle	37		B. Feller, Cle	31	
B. Newsom, Det	21		D. Leonard, Was	19		B. Newsom, Det	.808		A. Benton, Det	42		D. Leonard, Was	35		T. Lee, ChA	24	
A. Milnar, Cle	18		J. Rigney, ChA	18		B. Feller, Cle	.711		E. Heusser, Phi	41		E. Auker, StL	35		D. Leonard, Was	23	
S. Hudson, Was	17		K. Chase, Was	17		A. Smith, Cle	.682		J. Wilson, Bos	41		K. Chase, Was	34		4 tied with	20	
2 tied with	16		V. Kennedy, StL	17		J. Wilson, Bos	.667		J. Dobson, Cle	40		B. Newsom, Det	34				

Shutouts			Saves			Games Finished			Batters Faced			Innings Pitched			Hits Allowed		
B. Feller, Cle	4		A. Benton, Det	17		C. Brown, ChA	36		B. Feller, Cle	1304		B. Feller, Cle	320.1		D. Leonard, Was	328	
A. Milnar, Cle	4		C. Brown, ChA	10		A. Benton, Det	35		D. Leonard, Was	1245		D. Leonard, Was	289.0		E. Auker, StL	299	
T. Lyons, ChA	4		J. Murphy, NYA	9		J. Murphy, NYA	28		E. Auker, StL	1176		J. Rigney, ChA	280.2		S. Hudson, Was	272	
5 tied with	3		4 tied with	5		E. Heusser, Phi	26		K. Chase, Was	1165		B. Newsom, Det	264.0		V. Kennedy, StL	263	
						J. Heving, Bos	21		J. Rigney, ChA	1152		E. Auker, StL	263.2		K. Chase, Was	260	

Home Runs Allowed			Walks			Walks/9 Innings			Strikeouts			Strikeouts/9 Innings			Strikeout/Walk Ratio		
B. Harris, StL	24		K. Chase, Was	143		T. Lyons, ChA	1.8		B. Feller, Cle	261		B. Feller, Cle	7.3		B. Feller, Cle	2.21	
R. Ruffing, NYA	24		V. Kennedy, StL	122		T. Lee, ChA	2.2		B. Newsom, Det	164		T. Bridges, Det	6.1		T. Lyons, ChA	1.95	
J. Rigney, ChA	22		B. Feller, Cle	118		S. Rowe, Det	2.3		J. Rigney, ChA	141		B. Newsom, Det	5.6		B. Newsom, Det	1.64	
C. Dean, Phi	21		B. Newsom, Det	100		D. Leonard, Was	2.4		T. Bridges, Det	133		E. Smith, ChA	5.2		D. Leonard, Was	1.59	
3 tied with	20		A. Milnar, Cle	99		M. Russo, NYA	2.6		K. Chase, Was	129		J. Niggeling, StL	4.8		M. Russo, NYA	1.58	

Earned Run Average			Component ERA			Hit Batsmen			Wild Pitches			Opponent Average			Opponent OBP		
B. Feller, Cle	2.61		B. Feller, Cle	2.32		S. Chandler, NYA	6		P. Vaughan, Phi	12		B. Feller, Cle	.210		B. Feller, Cle	.285	
B. Newsom, Det	2.83		J. Rigney, ChA	2.82		A. Smith, Cle	6		K. Chase, Was	12		E. Smith, ChA	.228		T. Lyons, ChA	.287	
J. Rigney, ChA	3.11		T. Lee, ChA	3.05		5 tied with	5		N. Potter, Phi	10		T. Bridges, Det	.229		J. Rigney, ChA	.292	
E. Smith, ChA	3.21		T. Bridges, Det	3.07					D. Leonard, Was	10		J. Rigney, ChA	.230		T. Lee, ChA	.300	
K. Chase, Was	3.23		T. Lyons, ChA	3.15					3 tied with	8		B. Newsom, Det	.238		M. Russo, NYA	.303	

1940 American League Miscellaneous

Managers

Boston	Joe Cronin	82-72
Chicago	Jimmy Dykes	82-72
Cleveland	Ossie Vitt	89-65
Detroit	Del Baker	90-64
New York	Joe McCarthy	88-66
Philadelphia	Connie Mack	54-100
St. Louis	Fred Haney	67-87
Washington	Bucky Harris	64-90

Awards

Most Valuable Player	Hank Greenberg, of, Det
STATS Cy Young	Bob Feller, Cle
STATS Rookie of the Year	Wally Judnich, of, StL
STATS Manager of the Year	Del Baker, Det

STATS All-Star Team

C	Frankie Hayes, Phi	.308	16	70
1B	Rudy York, Det	.316	33	134
2B	Joe Gordon, NYA	.281	30	103
3B	Harlond Clift, StL	.273	20	87
SS	Joe Cronin, Bos	.285	24	111
OF	Joe DiMaggio, NYA	.352	31	133
OF	Hank Greenberg, Det	.340	41	150
OF	Ted Williams, Bos	.344	23	113
P	Bob Feller, Cle	27-11	2.61	261 K
P	Al Milnar, Cle	18-10	3.27	99 K
P	Bobo Newsom, Det	21-5	2.83	164 K
P	Schoolboy Rowe, Det	16-3	3.46	61 K
RP	Johnny Murphy, NYA	8-4	3.69	9 Sv

Postseason

World Series	Detroit (AL) 3 vs. Cincinnati (NL) 4

Outstanding Performances

No-Hitters

Bob Feller, Cle	@ ChA on April 16

Three-Homer Games

Mike Higgins, Det	on May 20
Charlie Keller, NYA	on July 28

Cycles

Buddy Rosar, NYA	on July 19
Joe Cronin, Bos	on August 2
Joe Gordon, NYA	on September 8

1940 National League Standings

Team	W	L	Pct	GB	DIF	W	L	R	OR	HR	OHR	W	L	R	OR	HR	OHR	Run	HR	M/A	May	June	July	Aug	S/O
		Overall						Home Games						Road Games				Park Index				Record by Month			
Cincinnati	100	53	.654	—	139	55	21	352	240	47	36	45	32	355	288	42	37	93	106	6-3	19-7	16-11	20-8	16-16	23-8
Brooklyn	88	65	.575	12.0	50	41	37	369	358	40	55	47	28	328	263	53	46	118	92	9-0	12-10	17-11	16-16	15-15	19-13
St. Louis	84	69	.549	16.0	0	41	36	368	364	69	47	43	33	379	335	50	36	101	133	4-6	9-14	11-14	20-11	19-11	21-13
Pittsburgh	78	76	.506	22.5	8	40	34	390	354	26	22	38	42	419	429	50	50	95	52	4-6	5-15	15-13	18-12	20-12	16-18
Chicago	75	79	.487	25.5	0	40	37	333	316	40	32	35	42	348	320	46	42	97	82	7-7	11-12	16-14	12-17	13-19	13-15
New York	72	80	.474	27.5	0	39	37	340	320	61	75	33	43	323	339	30	35	100	209	4-4	15-8	18-10	12-17	13-19	10-22
Boston	65	87	.428	34.5	0	35	40	328	352	25	30	30	47	295	393	34	53	101	65	1-7	10-11	9-17	9-24	21-13	15-15
Philadelphia	50	103	.327	50.0	7	24	55	232	403	33	50	26	48	262	347	42	42	98	93	3-5	9-13	9-21	11-17	7-23	11-24

Clinch Date—Cincinnati 9/18.

Team Batting

Team	G	AB	R	OR	H	2B	3B	HR	TB	RBI	TBB	IBB	SO	HBP	SH	SF	SB	CS	SB%	GDP	Avg	OBP	Slg
Pittsburgh	156	5466	809	783	1511	276	68	76	2151	740	553	—	494	33	63	—	69	—	—	116	.276	.346	.394
St. Louis	156	5499	747	699	1514	266	61	119	2259	709	479	—	610	21	88	—	97	—	—	103	.275	.336	.411
Cincinnati	155	5372	707	528	1427	264	38	89	2034	649	453	—	503	36	125	—	72	—	—	108	.266	.327	.379
Brooklyn	156	5470	697	621	1421	256	70	93	2096	653	522	—	570	20	77	—	56	—	—	112	.260	.327	.383
Chicago	154	5389	681	636	1441	272	48	86	2067	627	482	—	566	29	70	—	63	—	—	108	.267	.331	.384
New York	152	5324	663	659	1423	201	46	91	1989	614	453	—	478	37	86	—	45	—	—	130	.267	.329	.374
Boston	152	5329	623	745	1366	219	50	59	1862	558	402	—	581	17	62	—	48	—	—	101	.256	.311	.349
Philadelphia	153	5137	494	750	1225	180	35	75	1700	459	435	—	527	14	87	—	25	—	—	115	.238	.300	.331
NL Total	1234	42986	5421	5421	11328	1934	416	688	16158	5009	3779	—	4329	207	658	—	475	—	—	893	.264	.326	.376
NL Avg Team	154	5373	678	678	1416	242	52	86	2020	626	472	—	541	26	82	—	59	—	—	112	.264	.326	.376

Team Pitching

Team	G	CG	ShO	Rel	Sv	IP	H	R	ER	HR	SH	SF	HB	TBB	IBB	SO	WP	Bk	H/9	SO/9	BB/9	OAvg	OOBP	ERA
Cincinnati	155	91	10	106	11	1407.2	1263	528	477	73	76	—	18	445	—	557	11	3	8.1	3.6	2.8	.240	.302	3.05
Brooklyn	156	65	17	169	14	1433.0	1366	621	557	101	78	—	31	393	—	639	15	1	8.6	4.0	2.5	.248	.302	3.50
Chicago	154	69	12	151	14	1392.0	1418	636	548	74	104	—	16	430	—	564	10	2	9.2	3.6	2.8	.262	.318	3.54
New York	152	57	11	166	18	1360.1	1383	659	573	110	70	—	18	473	—	606	27	2	9.1	4.0	3.1	.262	.325	3.79
St. Louis	156	71	10	168	14	1396.1	1457	699	594	83	83	—	27	488	—	550	35	5	9.4	3.5	3.1	.267	.330	3.83
Boston	152	76	9	148	12	1359.0	1444	745	658	83	75	—	35	573	—	435	24	5	9.6	2.9	3.8	.274	.349	4.36
Pittsburgh	156	49	8	215	24	1388.2	1569	783	673	72	75	—	32	492	—	491	28	4	10.2	3.2	3.2	.283	.345	4.36
Philadelphia	153	66	5	133	8	1357.0	1429	750	663	92	95	—	26	475	—	485	36	5	9.5	3.2	3.2	.270	.333	4.40
NL Total	1234	544	82	1256	115	11093.2	11329	5421	4743	688	656	—	203	3769	—	4327	186	27	9.2	3.5	3.1	.264	.326	3.85
NL Avg Team	154	68	10	157	14	1386.2	1416	678	593	86	82	—	25	471	—	541	23	3	9.2	3.5	3.1	.264	.326	3.85

Team Fielding

Team	G	PO	A	E	TC	DP	PB	Pct
Cincinnati	155	4223	1816	117	6156	158	11	.981
New York	152	4081	1896	139	6116	132	9	.977
St. Louis	156	4184	1654	174	6012	134	10	.971
Philadelphia	153	4074	1831	181	6086	136	12	.970
Brooklyn	156	4286	1627	183	6096	110	7	.970
Boston	152	4075	1865	184	6124	169	7	.970
Chicago	154	4176	1922	199	6297	143	11	.968
Pittsburgh	156	4165	1941	217	6323	161	4	.966
NL Total	1234	33264	14552	1394	49210	1143	71	.972

Team vs. Team Records

	Bos	Bro	ChN	Cin	NYG	Phi	Pit	StL	Won
Bos	—	9	8	9	7	15	9	8	65
Bro	13	—	10	8	16	17	15	9	88
ChN	14	12	—	6	12	12	11	8	75
Cin	12	14	16	—	15	16	12	100
NYG	15	5	10	7	—	12	12	11	72
Phi	6	5	10	7	10	—	6	6	50
Pit	13	7	11	6	10	16	—	15	78
StL	14	13	14	10	10	16	7	—	84
Lost	87	65	79	53	80	103	76	69	

1940 National League Batting Leaders

Games			At-Bats			Runs			Hits			Doubles			Triples		
A. Vaughan, Pit		156	F. McCormick, Cin		618	A. Vaughan, Pit		113	F. McCormick, Cin		191	F. McCormick, Cin		44	A. Vaughan, Pit		15
J. Hack, StL		155	S. Hack, ChN		603	J. Mize, StL		111	S. Hack, ChN		191	A. Vaughan, Pit		40	C. Ross, Bos		14
F. McCormick, Cin		155	A. Vaughan, Pit		594	B. Werber, Cin		105	J. Mize, StL		182	J. Gleeson, ChN		39	E. Slaughter, StL		13
E. Miller, Bos		151	B. Werber, Cin		584	L. Frey, Cin		102	A. Vaughan, Pit		178	S. Hack, ChN		38	J. Mize, StL		13
M. Ott, NYG		151	J. Medwick, 2tm		581	S. Hack, ChN		101	J. Medwick, 2tm		175	D. Walker, Bro		37	D. Camilli, Bro		13

Home Runs			Total Bases			Runs Batted In			Walks			Intentional Walks		Strikeouts		
J. Mize, StL		43	J. Mize, StL		368	J. Mize, StL		137	E. Fletcher, Pit		119	Statistic unavailable		C. Ross, Bos		127
B. Nicholson, ChN		25	F. McCormick, Cin		298	F. McCormick, Cin		127	M. Ott, NYG		100			J. Orengo, StL		90
J. Rizzo, 3tm		24	J. Medwick, 2tm		280	M. Van Robays, Pit		116	D. Camilli, Bro		89			V. DiMaggio, 2tm		83
D. Camilli, Bro		23	D. Camilli, Bro		271	E. Fletcher, Pit		104	A. Vaughan, Pit		88			D. Camilli, Bro		83
3 tied with		19	A. Vaughan, Pit		269	B. Young, NYG		101	J. Mize, StL		82			H. Leiber, ChN		68

Hit By Pitch			Sac Hits			Sac Flies		Stolen Bases			Caught Stealing		GDP		
E. Fletcher, Pit		9	H. Schulte, Phi		20	Statistic unavailable		L. Frey, Cin		22	Statistic unavailable		F. McCormick, Cin		23
B. Werber, Cin		8	M. McCormick, Cin		20			S. Hack, ChN		21			J. Medwick, 2tm		19
E. Lombardi, Cin		7	L. Frey, Cin		17			T. Moore, StL		18			H. Danning, NYG		18
J. Moore, NYG		7	J. Orengo, StL		16			B. Werber, Cin		16			E. Lombardi, Cin		18
3 tied with		6	F. Demaree, NYG		16			P. Reese, Bro		15			5 tied with		16

Runs Created			Runs Created/27 Outs			Batting Average			On-Base Percentage			Slugging Percentage			OBP+Slugging		
J. Mize, StL		138	J. Mize, StL		9.12	D. Garms, Pit		.355	E. Fletcher, Pit		.419	J. Mize, StL		.636	J. Mize, StL		1.039
A. Vaughan, Pit		117	D. Garms, Pit		8.29	E. Lombardi, Cin		.319	M. Ott, NYG		.407	B. Nicholson, ChN		.534	D. Camilli, Bro		.926
F. McCormick, Cin		108	D. Camilli, Bro		7.81	J. Cooney, Bos		.318	J. Mize, StL		.404	D. Camilli, Bro		.529	B. Nicholson, ChN		.899
D. Camilli, Bro		108	E. Fletcher, Pit		7.46	S. Hack, ChN		.317	D. Camilli, Bro		.397	V. DiMaggio, 2tm		.519	D. Garms, Pit		.895
S. Hack, ChN		108	A. Vaughan, Pit		7.41	J. Mize, StL		.314	D. Garms, Pit		.395	E. Slaughter, StL		.504	V. DiMaggio, 2tm		.884

1940 National League Pitching Leaders

Wins			Losses			Winning Percentage			Games			Games Started			Complete Games		
B. Walters, Cin		22	H. Mulcahy, Phi		22	F. Fitzsimmons, Bro		.889	C. Shoun, StL		54	P. Derringer, Cin		37	B. Walters, Cin		29
C. Passeau, ChN		20	K. Higbe, Phi		19	J. Beggs, Cin		.800	M. Brown, StL		48	K. Higbe, Phi		36	P. Derringer, Cin		26
P. Derringer, Cin		20	B. Posedel, Bos		17	R. Sewell, Pit		.762	C. Passeau, ChN		46	H. Mulcahy, Phi		36	H. Mulcahy, Phi		21
5 tied with		16	B. Lee, ChN		17	B. Walters, Cin		.688	H. Casey, Bro		44	B. Walters, Cin		36	K. Higbe, Phi		20
			B. Lohrman, NYG		15	J. Turner, Cin		.667	Raffensberger, ChN		43	W. Wyatt, Bro		34	C. Passeau, ChN		20

Shutouts			Saves			Games Finished			Batters Faced			Innings Pitched			Hits Allowed		
M. Salvo, Bos		5	J. Beggs, Cin		7	J. Beggs, Cin		27	B. Walters, Cin		1207	B. Walters, Cin		305.0	H. Mulcahy, Phi		283
B. Lohrman, NYG		5	M. Brown, Pit		7	J. Brown, NYG		23	P. Derringer, Cin		1205	P. Derringer, Cin		296.2	P. Derringer, Cin		280
W. Wyatt, Bro		5	J. Brown, NYG		7	C. Shoun, StL		22	K. Higbe, Phi		1194	K. Higbe, Phi		283.0	B. Posedel, Bos		263
3 tied with		4	C. Passeau, ChN		5	M. Brown, Pit		21	H. Mulcahy, Phi		1189	C. Passeau, ChN		280.2	C. Passeau, ChN		259
			C. Shoun, StL		5	H. Casey, Bro		19	C. Passeau, ChN		1172	H. Mulcahy, Phi		280.0	B. Lee, ChN		246

Home Runs Allowed			Walks			Walks/9 Innings			Strikeouts			Strikeouts/9 Innings			Strikeout/Walk Ratio		
C. Hubbell, NYG		22	K. Higbe, Phi		121	P. Derringer, Cin		1.5	K. Higbe, Phi		137	H. Schumacher, NYG		4.9	P. Derringer, Cin		2.40
B. Lohrman, NYG		19	J. Thompson, Cin		96	J. Turner, Cin		1.5	C. Passeau, ChN		124	W. Wyatt, Bro		4.7	C. Passeau, ChN		2.10
B. Walters, Cin		19	B. McGee, StL		96	F. Fitzsimmons, Bro		1.7	W. Wyatt, Bro		124	K. Higbe, Phi		4.4	W. Wyatt, Bro		2.00
W. Wyatt, Bro		19	H. Schumacher, NYG		96	L. Warneke, StL		1.8	H. Schumacher, NYG		123	J. Thompson, Cin		4.1	L. Warneke, StL		1.81
6 tied with		17	B. Walters, Cin		92	C. Passeau, ChN		1.9	2 tied with		115	C. Passeau, ChN		4.0	C. Shoun, StL		1.78

Earned Run Average			Component ERA			Hit Batsmen			Wild Pitches			Opponent Average			Opponent OBP		
B. Walters, Cin		2.48	F. Fitzsimmons, Bro		2.30	C. Doyle, 2tm		10	K. Higbe, Phi		9	B. Walters, Cin		.220	F. Fitzsimmons, Bro		.269
C. Passeau, ChN		2.50	C. Passeau, ChN		2.42	B. Beck, Phi		9	B. McGee, StL		9	K. Higbe, Phi		.232	P. Derringer, Cin		.276
R. Sewell, Pit		2.80	B. Walters, Cin		2.43	N. Strincevich, Bos		8	H. Gumbert, NYG		8	F. Fitzsimmons, Bro		.233	C. Passeau, ChN		.278
F. Fitzsimmons, Bro		2.81	P. Derringer, Cin		2.55	J. Sullivan, Bos		8	K. Heintzelman, Pit		7	J. Thompson, Cin		.233	B. Walters, Cin		.283
J. Turner, Cin		2.89	R. Sewell, Pit		2.84	2 tied with		7	H. Mulcahy, Phi		6	C. Passeau, ChN		.237	J. Turner, Cin		.296

1940 National League Miscellaneous

Managers		
Boston	Casey Stengel	65-87
Brooklyn	Leo Durocher	88-65
Chicago	Gabby Hartnett	75-79
Cincinnati	Bill McKechnie	100-53
New York	Bill Terry	72-80
Philadelphia	Doc Prothro	50-103
Pittsburgh	Frank Frisch	78-76
St. Louis	Ray Blades	14-24
	Mike Gonzalez	1-5
	Billy Southworth	69-40

Awards

Most Valuable Player	F. McCormick, 1b, Cin
STATS Cy Young	Bucky Walters, Cin
STATS Rookie of the Year	Babe Young, 1b, NYG
STATS Manager of the Year	Bill McKechnie, Cin

STATS All-Star Team

C	Ernie Lombardi, Cin	.319	14	74
1B	Johnny Mize, StL	.314	43	137
2B	Lonny Frey, Cin	.266	8	54
3B	Debs Garms, Pit	.355	5	57
SS	Arky Vaughan, Pit	.300	7	95
OF	Bill Nicholson, ChN	.297	25	98
OF	Mel Ott, NYG	.289	19	79
OF	Enos Slaughter, StL	.306	17	73
P	Paul Derringer, Cin	20-12	3.06	115 K
P	Freddie Fitzsimmons, Bro	16-2	2.81	35 K
P	Claude Passeau, ChN	20-13	2.50	124 K
P	Bucky Walters, Cin	22-10	2.48	115 K
RP	Joe Beggs, Cin	12-3	2.00	7 Sv

Postseason

World Series	Cincinnati (NL) 4 vs. Detroit (AL) 3

Outstanding Performances

No-Hitters
Tex Carleton, Bro @ Cin on April 30

Three-Homer Games
Johnny Mize, StL on May 13
Johnny Mize, StL on September 8

Cycles
Harry Craft, Cin on June 8
Harry Danning, NYG on June 15
Johnny Mize, StL on July 13

1941 American League Standings

Team	Overall					Home Games						Road Games						Park Index		Record by Month					
	W	L	Pct	GB	DIF	W	L	R	OR	HR	OHR	W	L	R	OR	HR	OHR	Run	HR	M/A	May	June	July	Aug	S/O
New York	101	53	.656	—	99	51	26	396	295	76	44	50	27	434	336	75	37	90	107	10-6	13-13	19-7	25-4	21-14	13-9
Boston	84	70	.545	17.0	9	47	30	461	371	70	51	37	40	404	379	54	51	106	133	7-6	12-13	17-11	14-16	18-17	16-7
Chicago	77	77	.500	24.0	2	38	39	288	297	17	40	39	38	350	352	30	49	83	72	9-4	16-12	11-16	11-19	21-13	9-13
Cleveland	75	79	.487	26.0	60	42	35	340	322	45	35	33	44	337	346	58	36	97	85	11-4	18-13	13-13	13-12	10-21	10-16
Detroit	75	79	.487	26.0	0	43	34	381	377	50	43	32	45	350	366	31	37	113	137	6-7	17-13	12-16	10-19	17-14	13-10
St. Louis	70	84	.455	31.0	2	40	37	407	408	49	63	30	47	358	415	42	57	105	113	3-8	10-19	11-14	14-16	20-14	12-13
Washington	70	84	.455	31.0	0	40	37	367	387	13	19	30	47	361	411	39	50	98	36	4-10	10-18	12-14	11-14	16-17	17-11
Philadelphia	64	90	.416	37.0	2	36	41	373	432	43	75	28	49	340	408	42	61	108	115	4-9	17-12	11-15	15-13	10-23	7-18

Clinch Date—New York 9/04.

Team Batting

Team	G	AB	R	OR	H	2B	3B	HR	TB	RBI	TBB	IBB	SO	HBP	SH	SF	SB	CS	SB%	GDP	Avg	OBP	Slg
Boston	155	5359	865	750	1517	304	55	124	2303	806	683	—	567	20	115	—	67	51	.57	127	.283	.366	.430
New York	156	5444	830	631	1464	243	60	151	2280	774	616	—	565	28	49	—	51	33	.61	119	.269	.360	.419
St. Louis	157	5408	765	823	1440	281	58	91	2110	729	775	—	552	13	89	—	50	39	.56	119	.266	.360	.390
Washington	156	5521	728	798	1502	257	80	52	2075	671	470	—	488	14	62	—	79	36	.69	115	.272	.331	.376
Philadelphia	154	5336	713	840	1431	240	69	85	2064	659	574	—	588	8	76	—	27	36	.43	139	.268	.340	.387
Detroit	155	5370	686	743	1412	247	55	81	2012	636	602	—	584	23	82	—	43	28	.61	118	.263	.340	.375
Cleveland	155	5283	677	668	1350	249	84	103	2076	618	512	—	605	18	101	—	63	47	.57	129	.256	.322	.393
Chicago	156	5404	649		1376	245	47	47	1856	567	510	—	476	24	74	—	91	53	.63	129	.255	.322	.343
AL Total	1244	43125	5902	5902	11492	2066	508	734	16776	5460	4742	—	4425	148	648	—	471	323	.59	943	.266	.341	.389
AL Avg Team	156	5391	738	738	1437	258	64	92	2097	683	593	—	553	19	81	—	59	40	.59	118	.266	.341	.389

Team Pitching

Team	G	CG	ShO	Rel	Sv	IP	H	R	ER	HR	SH	SF	HB	TBB	IBB	SO	WP	Bk	H/9	SO/9	BB/9	OAvg	OOBP	ERA
Chicago	156	106	14	63	4	1416.0	1362	649	554	89	95	—	26	521	—	564	30	0	8.7	3.6	3.3	.252	.320	3.52
New York	156	75	13	119	26	1396.1	1309	631	547	81	75	—	10	598	—	589	30	1	8.4	3.8	3.9	.248	.325	3.53
Cleveland	155	68	10	133	19	1377.0	1366	668	596	71	70	—	21	660	—	617	29	2	8.9	4.0	4.3	.259	.344	3.90
Detroit	155	52	8	157	16	1381.2	1399	743	641	80	84	—	13	645	—	697	29	4	9.1	4.5	4.2	.260	.341	4.18
Boston	155	70	8	137	11	1372.0	1453	750	638	88	89	—	20	611	—	574	34	7	9.5	3.8	4.0	.270	.347	4.19
Washington	156	69	8	140	7	1389.1	1524	798	672	69	90	—	18	603	—	544	44	3	9.9	3.5	3.9	.279	.353	4.35
St. Louis	157	65	7	158	10	1389.0	1563	823	728	120	70	—	22	549	—	454	28	1	10.1	2.9	3.6	.283	.351	4.72
Philadelphia	154	64	3	125	18	1365.1	1516	840	733	136	76	—	18	557	—	386	46	3	10.0	2.5	3.7	.279	.348	4.83
AL Total	1244	569	71	1032	111	11086.2	11492	5902	5109	734	649	—	148	4744	—	4425	270	18	9.3	3.6	3.9	.266	.341	4.15
AL Avg Team	156	71	9	129	14	1385.2	1437	738	639	92	81	—	19	593	—	553	34	2	9.3	3.6	3.9	.266	.341	4.15

Team Fielding

Team	G	PO	A	E	TC	DP	PB	Pct
Cleveland	155	4131	1737	142	6010	158	5	.976
St. Louis	157	4146	1749	151	6046	156	15	.975
New York	156	4190	1734	165	6089	196	6	.973
Boston	155	4115	1769	172	6056	139	9	.972
Chicago	156	4247	1774	180	6201	145	19	.971
Washington	156	4175	1767	187	6129	169	24	.969
Detroit	155	4145	1733	186	6064	129	10	.969
Philadelphia	154	4095	1733	200	6028	150	20	.967
AL Total	1244	33244	13996	1383	48623	1242	108	.972

Team vs. Team Records

	Bos	ChA	Cle	Det	NYA	Phi	StL	Was	Won
Bos	—	16	9	11	9	16	9	14	84
ChA	6	—	17	12	8	10	11	13	77
Cle	13	5	—	10	7	15	13	12	75
Det	11	10	12	—	11	13	11	7	75
NYA	13	14	15	11	—	14	18	16	101
Phi	6	12	7	9	8	—	11	11	64
StL	13	11	9	11	4	11	—	11	70
Was	8	9	10	15	6	11	11	—	70
Lost	70	77	79	79	53	90	84	84	

Seasons: Standings, Leaders

1941 American League Batting Leaders

Games		At-Bats		Runs		Hits		Doubles		Triples	
J. Gordon, NYA	156	D. Cramer, Was	660	T. Williams, Bos	135	C. Travis, Was	218	L. Boudreau, Cle	45	J. Heath, Cle	20
R. York, Det	155	G. Case, Was	649	J. DiMaggio, NYA	122	J. Heath, Cle	199	J. DiMaggio, NYA	43	C. Travis, Was	19
H. Clift, StL	154	C. Travis, Was	608	D. DiMaggio, Bos	117	J. DiMaggio, NYA	193	W. Judnich, StL	40	K. Keltner, Cle	13
L. Appling, ChA	154	J. Kuhel, ChA	600	H. Clift, StL	108	L. Appling, ChA	186	C. Travis, Was	39	4 tied with	11
D. Cramer, Was	154	L. Appling, ChA	592	3 tied with	106	T. Williams, Bos	185	J. Kuhel, ChA	39		

Home Runs		Total Bases		Runs Batted In		Walks		Intentional Walks		Strikeouts	
T. Williams, Bos	37	J. DiMaggio, NYA	348	J. DiMaggio, NYA	125	T. Williams, Bos	145	Statistic unavailable		J. Foxx, Bos	103
C. Keller, NYA	33	J. Heath, Cle	343	J. Heath, Cle	123	R. Cullenbine, StL	121			H. Clift, StL	93
T. Henrich, NYA	31	T. Williams, Bos	335	C. Keller, NYA	122	H. Clift, StL	113			R. York, Det	88
J. DiMaggio, NYA	30	C. Travis, Was	316	T. Williams, Bos	120	C. Keller, NYA	102			J. Gordon, NYA	80
R. York, Det	27	S. Chapman, Phi	300	R. York, Det	111	3 tied with	95			B. Johnson, Phi	75

Hit By Pitch		Sac Hits		Sac Flies		Stolen Bases		Caught Stealing		GDP	
D. DiMaggio, Bos	7	B. Harris, StL	14	Statistic unavailable		G. Case, Was	33	J. Heath, Cle	12	P. Suder, Phi	23
T. Wright, ChA	6	L. Boudreau, Cle	14			J. Kuhel, ChA	20	M. Hoag, 2tm	10	F. Hayes, Phi	23
D. Cramer, Was	6	J. Cronin, Bos	14			J. Heath, Cle	18	5 tied with	9	J. Foxx, Bos	21
3 tied with	5	S. Newsome, Bos	13			J. Tabor, Bos	17			M. Higgins, Det	20
		M. Kreevich, ChA	13			M. Kreevich, ChA	17			J. Cronin, Bos	20

Runs Created		Runs Created/27 Outs		Batting Average		On-Base Percentage		Slugging Percentage		OBP+Slugging	
T. Williams, Bos	170	T. Williams, Bos	16.09	T. Williams, Bos	.406	T. Williams, Bos	.551	T. Williams, Bos	.735	T. Williams, Bos	1.286
J. DiMaggio, NYA	146	J. DiMaggio, NYA	11.06	C. Travis, Was	.359	R. Cullenbine, StL	.452	J. DiMaggio, NYA	.643	J. DiMaggio, NYA	1.083
J. Heath, Cle	127	C. Keller, NYA	9.29	J. DiMaggio, NYA	.357	J. DiMaggio, NYA	.440	J. Heath, Cle	.586	C. Keller, NYA	.996
C. Travis, Was	127	J. Heath, Cle	8.42	J. Heath, Cle	.340	C. Keller, NYA	.416	C. Keller, NYA	.580	J. Heath, Cle	.982
C. Keller, NYA	125	C. Travis, Was	8.42	D. Siebert, Phi	.334	J. Foxx, Bos	.412	S. Chapman, Phi	.543	C. Travis, Was	.930

1941 American League Pitching Leaders

Wins		Losses		Winning Percentage		Games		Games Started		Complete Games	
B. Feller, Cle	25	B. Newsom, Det	20	L. Gomez, NYA	.750	B. Feller, Cle	44	B. Feller, Cle	40	T. Lee, ChA	30
T. Lee, ChA	22	A. Milnar, Cle	19	A. Benton, Det	.714	B. Newsom, Det	43	B. Newsom, Det	36	B. Feller, Cle	28
D. Newsome, Bos	19	K. Chase, Was	18	R. Ruffing, NYA	.714	C. Brown, Cle	41	T. Lee, ChA	34	E. Smith, ChA	21
D. Leonard, Was	18	E. Smith, ChA	17	J. Dobson, Bos	.706	M. Ryba, Bos	40	3 tied with	33	D. Leonard, Was	19
3 tied with	15	3 tied with	15	T. Lee, ChA	.667	A. Benton, Det	38			T. Lyons, ChA	19

Shutouts		Saves		Games Finished		Batters Faced		Innings Pitched		Hits Allowed	
B. Feller, Cle	6	J. Murphy, NYA	15	J. Murphy, NYA	31	B. Feller, Cle	1466	B. Feller, Cle	343.0	B. Feller, Cle	284
J. Humphries, ChA	4	T. Ferrick, Phi	7	C. Brown, Cle	28	T. Lee, ChA	1224	T. Lee, ChA	300.1	D. Leonard, Was	271
S. Chandler, NYA	4	A. Benton, Det	7	T. Ferrick, Phi	25	B. Newsom, Det	1130	E. Smith, ChA	263.1	E. Auker, StL	268
D. Leonard, Was	4	M. Ryba, Bos	6	M. Ryba, Bos	25	E. Smith, ChA	1125	D. Leonard, Was	256.0	B. Newsom, Det	265
5 tied with	3	2 tied with	5	N. Branch, NYA	22	D. Leonard, Was	1073	B. Newsom, Det	250.1	T. Lee, ChA	258

Home Runs Allowed		Walks		Walks/9 Innings		Strikeouts		Strikeouts/9 Innings		Strikeout/Walk Ratio	
J. Rigney, ChA	21	B. Feller, Cle	194	T. Lyons, ChA	1.8	B. Feller, Cle	260	B. Feller, Cle	6.8	T. Lyons, ChA	1.70
E. Auker, StL	20	H. Newhouser, Det	137	D. Leonard, Was	1.9	B. Newsom, Det	175	B. Newsom, Det	6.3	D. Leonard, Was	1.69
J. Knott, Phi	20	P. Marchildon, Phi	118	B. Muncrief, StL	2.2	T. Lee, ChA	130	T. Bridges, Det	5.5	B. Newsom, Det	1.48
3 tied with	18	B. Newsom, Det	118	R. Ruffing, NYA	2.6	J. Rigney, ChA	119	M. Harris, Bos	5.1	T. Lee, ChA	1.41
		A. Milnar, Cle	116	T. Lee, ChA	2.8	2 tied with	111	J. Rigney, ChA	4.5	B. Feller, Cle	1.34

Earned Run Average		Component ERA		Hit Batsmen		Wild Pitches		Opponent Average		Opponent OBP	
T. Lee, ChA	2.37	T. Lee, ChA	2.71	D. Newsome, Bos	7	P. Marchildon, Phi	12	B. Feller, Cle	.226	T. Lee, ChA	.293
C. Wagner, Bos	3.07	S. Chandler, NYA	2.82	J. Bagby Jr., Cle	6	K. Chase, Was	11	T. Lee, ChA	.232	R. Ruffing, NYA	.306
M. Russo, NYA	3.09	D. Leonard, Was	3.14	4 tied with	5	D. Leonard, Was	9	T. Bridges, Det	.233	S. Chandler, NYA	.307
B. Feller, Cle	3.15	R. Ruffing, NYA	3.17			4 tied with	8	A. Donald, NYA	.237	T. Lyons, ChA	.308
E. Smith, ChA	3.18	T. Lyons, ChA	3.27					S. Chandler, NYA	.239	D. Leonard, Was	.309

1941 American League Miscellaneous

Managers

Boston	Joe Cronin	84-70
Chicago	Jimmy Dykes	77-77
Cleveland	Roger Peckinpaugh	75-79
Detroit	Del Baker	75-79
New York	Joe McCarthy	101-53
Philadelphia	Connie Mack	64-90
St. Louis	Fred Haney	15-29
	Luke Sewell	55-55
Washington	Bucky Harris	70-84

Awards

Most Valuable Player	Joe DiMaggio, of, NYA
STATS Cy Young	Bob Feller, Cle
STATS Rookie of the Year	Phil Rizzuto, ss, NYA
STATS Manager of the Year	Joe McCarthy, NYA

STATS All-Star Team

C	Frankie Hayes, Phi	.280	12	63
1B	Jimmie Foxx, Bos	.300	19	105
2B	Joe Gordon, NYA	.276	24	87
3B	Ken Keltner, Cle	.269	23	84
SS	Cecil Travis, Was	.359	7	101
OF	Joe DiMaggio, NYA	.357	30	125
OF	Charlie Keller, NYA	.298	33	122
OF	Ted Williams, Bos	.406	37	120
P	Bob Feller, Cle	25-13	3.15	260 K
P	Thornton Lee, ChA	22-11	2.37	130 K
P	Dutch Leonard, Was	18-13	3.45	91 K
P	Marius Russo, NYA	14-10	3.09	105 K
RP	Johnny Murphy, NYA	8-3	1.98	15 Sv

Postseason

World Series	New York (AL) 4 vs. Brooklyn (NL) 1

Outstanding Performances

Three-Homer Games
Rudy York, Det   on September 1
Cycles
George McQuinn, StL on July 19

1941 National League Standings

Team	Overall					Home Games						Road Games						Park Index		Record by Month					
	W	L	Pct	GB	DIF	W	L	R	OR	HR	OHR	W	L	R	OR	HR	OHR	Run	HR	M/A	May	June	July	Aug	S/O
Brooklyn	100	54	.649	—	85	52	25	421	282	55	40	48	29	379	299	46	41	104	109	13-4	17-8	17-11	13-13	22-10	18-8
St. Louis	97	56	.634	2.5	81	53	24	405	324	37	53	44	32	329	265	33	32	121	137	10-3	21-8	16-12	15-11	19-11	16-11
Cincinnati	88	66	.571	12.0	0	45	34	308	273	27	27	43	32	308	291	37	34	92	72	7-8	12-15	17-10	16-9	17-12	19-12
Pittsburgh	81	73	.526	19.0	0	45	32	346	336	20	28	36	41	344	307	36	38	105	65	3-10	11-11	14-12	22-9	18-15	13-16
New York	74	79	.484	25.5	12	38	39	360	358	68	69	36	40	307	348	27	21	108	282	8-6	12-11	17-13	8-15	15-21	14-13
Chicago	70	84	.455	30.0	2	38	39	311	306	37	20	32	45	355	364	62	40	86	56	5-7	12-14	14-18	13-13	12-21	14-11
Boston	62	92	.403	38.0	0	32	44	276	321	17	28	30	48	316	399	31	47	86	59	6-9	7-15	11-15	14-17	14-18	10-18
Philadelphia	43	111	.279	57.0	1	23	52	255	384	34	37	20	59	246	409	30	42	103	104	5-10	7-17	7-22	6-20	11-20	7-22

Clinch Date—Brooklyn 9/25.

Team Batting

Team	G	AB	R	OR	H	2B	3B	HR	TB	RBI	TBB	IBB	SO	HBP	SH	SF	SB	CS	SB%	GDP	Avg	OBP	Slg
Brooklyn	157	5485	800	581	1494	286	69	101	2221	747	600	—	535	27	106	—	36	—	—	103	.272	.347	.405
St. Louis	155	5457	734	589	1482	254	56	70	2058	664	540	—	543	28	126	—	47	—	—	102	.272	.340	.377
Pittsburgh	156	5297	690	643	1417	233	65	56	1948	634	547	—	516	15	95	—	59	—	—	119	.268	.338	.368
New York	156	5395	667	706	1401	248	35	95	2004	625	504	—	518	23	96	—	36	—	—	116	.260	.326	.371
Chicago	155	5230	666	670	1323	239	25	99	1909	610	559	—	670	14	98	—	39	—	—	102	.253	.327	.365
Cincinnati	154	5218	616	564	1288	213	33	64	1759	567	477	—	428	22	102	—	68	—	—	122	.247	.313	.337
Boston	156	5414	592	720	1357	231	38	48	1808	552	471	—	608	13	70	—	61	—	—	120	.251	.312	.334
Philadelphia	155	5233	501	793	1277	188	38	64	1733	467	451	—	596	22	90	—	65	—	—	142	.244	.307	.331
NL Total	1244	42729	5266	5266	11039	1892	359	597	15440	4866	4149	—	4414	164	783	—	411	—	—	926	.258	.326	.361
NL Avg Team	156	5341	658	658	1380	237	45	75	1930	608	519	—	552	21	98	—	51	—	—	116	.258	.326	.361

Team Pitching

Team	G	CG	ShO	Rel	Sv	IP	H	R	ER	HR	SH	SF	HB	TBB	IBB	SO	WP	Bk	H/9	SO/9	BB/9	OAvg	OOBP	ERA
Brooklyn	157	66	17	157	22	1421.0	1236	581	496	81	80	—	17	495	—	603	23	5	7.8	3.8	3.1	.233	.300	3.14
Cincinnati	154	89	19	112	10	1386.2	1300	564	488	61	106	—	16	510	—	627	19	0	8.4	4.1	3.3	.248	.317	3.17
St. Louis	155	64	15	171	20	1416.1	1289	589	502	85	97	—	22	502	—	659	26	3	8.2	4.2	3.2	.242	.310	3.19
Pittsburgh	156	71	8	150	12	1374.1	1392	643	532	66	82	—	13	492	—	410	30	1	9.1	2.7	3.2	.260	.323	3.48
Chicago	155	74	8	145	9	1364.2	1431	670	564	60	96	—	21	449	—	548	21	2	9.4	3.6	3.0	.267	.327	3.72
New York	156	55	12	175	18	1391.2	1455	706	610	90	100	—	15	539	—	566	29	2	9.4	3.7	3.5	.269	.337	3.94
Boston	156	62	10	176	9	1385.2	1440	720	608	75	106	—	32	554	—	446	28	1	9.4	2.9	3.6	.269	.341	3.95
Philadelphia	155	35	4	201	9	1372.1	1499	793	686	79	109	—	26	606	—	552	35	1	9.8	3.6	4.0	.279	.355	4.50
NL Total	1244	516	93	1287	109	11112.2	11042	5266	4486	597	776	—	162	4147	—	4411	211	15	8.9	3.6	3.4	.258	.326	3.63
NL Avg Team	156	65	12	161	14	1389.2	1380	658	561	75	97	—	20	518	—	551	26	2	8.9	3.6	3.4	.258	.326	3.63

Team Fielding

Team	G	PO	A	E	TC	DP	PB	Pct
Cincinnati	154	4159	1775	152	6086	147	20	.975
New York	156	4177	1800	160	6137	144	8	.974
Brooklyn	157	4265	1769	162	6196	125	6	.974
St. Louis	155	4250	1839	172	6261	146	6	.973
Chicago	155	4089	1756	180	6025	139	9	.970
Boston	156	4161	1902	191	6254	174	8	.969
Philadelphia	155	4116	1782	187	6085	147	11	.969
Pittsburgh	156	4121	1853	196	6170	130	3	.968
NL Total	1244	33338	14476	1400	49214	1152	71	.972

Team vs. Team Records

	Bos	Bro	ChN	Cin	NYG	Phi	Pit	StL	Won
Bos	—	4	11	9	6	14	10	8	62
Bro	18	—	13	14	14	18	12	11	100
ChN	11	9	—	8	9	14	9	10	70
Cin	13	8	14	—	15	16	12	10	88
NYG	16	8	13	7	—	16	8	6	74
Phi	8	4	8	6	6	—	6	5	43
Pit	12	10	13	10	14	16	—	6	81
StL	14	11	12	12	15	17	16	—	97
Lost	92	54	84	66	79	111	73	56	

1941 National League Batting Leaders

Games		At-Bats		Runs		Hits		Doubles		Triples	
M. Marion, StL	155	J. Rucker, NYG	622	P. Reiser, Bro	117	S. Hack, ChN	186	P. Reiser, Bro	39	P. Reiser, Bro	17
B. Bragan, Phi	154	F. McCormick, Cin	603	S. Hack, ChN	111	P. Reiser, Bro	184	J. Mize, StL	39	E. Fletcher, Pit	13
E. Miller, Bos	154	P. Reese, Bro	595	J. Medwick, Bro	100	D. Litwhiler, Phi	180	J. Rucker, NYG	38	J. Hopp, StL	11
F. McCormick, Cin	154	D. Litwhiler, Phi	590	J. Rucker, NYG	95	J. Rucker, NYG	179	Dallessandro, ChN	36	B. Elliott, Pit	10
3 tied with	152	S. Hack, ChN	586	E. Fletcher, Pit	95	J. Medwick, Bro	171	2 tied with	33	J. Medwick, Bro	10

Home Runs		Total Bases		Runs Batted In		Walks		Intentional Walks		Strikeouts	
D. Camilli, Bro	34	P. Reiser, Bro	299	D. Camilli, Bro	120	E. Fletcher, Pit	118	Statistic unavailable		D. Camilli, Bro	115
M. Ott, NYG	27	D. Camilli, Bro	294	B. Young, NYG	104	D. Camilli, Bro	104			V. DiMaggio, Pit	100
B. Nicholson, ChN	26	J. Medwick, Bro	278	V. DiMaggio, Pit	100	M. Ott, NYG	100			B. Nicholson, ChN	91
B. Young, NYG	25	D. Litwhiler, Phi	275	J. Mize, StL	100	S. Hack, ChN	99			L. Stringer, ChN	86
B. Dahlgren, 2tm	23	B. Young, NYG	265	B. Nicholson, ChN	98	2 tied with	82			S. Benjamin, Phi	81

Hit By Pitch		Sac Hits		Sac Flies		Stolen Bases		Caught Stealing		GDP	
P. Reiser, Bro	11	M. Marion, StL	28	Statistic unavailable		D. Murtaugh, Phi	18	Statistic unavailable		F. McCormick, Cin	22
C. Crespi, StL	9	J. Marty, Phi	16			S. Benjamin, Phi	17			J. Medwick, Bro	20
B. Young, NYG	5	M. Owen, Bro	15			L. Handley, Pit	16			E. Lombardi, Cin	19
E. Miller, Bos	5	L. Handley, Pit	15			L. Frey, Cin	16			3 tied with	18
6 tied with	4	2 tied with	14			J. Hopp, StL	15				

Runs Created		Runs Created/27 Outs		Batting Average		On-Base Percentage		Slugging Percentage		OBP+Slugging	
D. Camilli, Bro	121	P. Reiser, Bro	8.58	P. Reiser, Bro	.343	E. Fletcher, Pit	.421	P. Reiser, Bro	.558	P. Reiser, Bro	.964
P. Reiser, Bro	117	D. Camilli, Bro	8.39	J. Cooney, Bos	.319	S. Hack, ChN	.417	D. Camilli, Bro	.556	D. Camilli, Bro	.962
S. Hack, ChN	116	J. Mize, StL	8.20	J. Medwick, Bro	.318	D. Camilli, Bro	.407	J. Mize, StL	.535	J. Mize, StL	.941
E. Fletcher, Pit	111	E. Fletcher, Pit	7.90	S. Hack, ChN	.317	P. Reiser, Bro	.406	J. Medwick, Bro	.517	M. Ott, NYG	.898
M. Ott, NYG	110	M. Ott, NYG	7.71	J. Mize, StL	.317	J. Mize, StL	.406	E. Slaughter, StL	.496	E. Slaughter, StL	.886

1941 National League Pitching Leaders

Wins		Losses		Winning Percentage		Games		Games Started		Complete Games	
K. Higbe, Bro	22	R. Sewell, Pit	17	E. Riddle, Cin	.826	K. Higbe, Bro	48	K. Higbe, Bro	39	B. Walters, Cin	27
W. Wyatt, Bro	22	M. Salvo, Bos	16	K. Higbe, Bro	.710	I. Pearson, Phi	46	B. Walters, Cin	35	W. Wyatt, Bro	23
E. Riddle, Cin	19	A. Johnson, Bos	15	E. White, StL	.708	H. Casey, Bro	45	W. Wyatt, Bro	35	J. Tobin, Bos	20
B. Walters, Cin	19	B. Walters, Cin	15	W. Wyatt, Bro	.688	J. Hutchings, 2tm	44	3 tied with	32	C. Passeau, ChN	20
3 tied with	17	6 tied with	14	H. Gumbert, 2tm	.667	A. Johnson, Bos	43			2 tied with	19

Shutouts		Saves		Games Finished		Batters Faced		Innings Pitched		Hits Allowed	
W. Wyatt, Bro	7	J. Brown, NYG	8	I. Pearson, Phi	30	K. Higbe, Bro	1266	B. Walters, Cin	302.0	B. Walters, Cin	292
J. Vander Meer, Cin	6	B. Crouch, 2tm	7	J. Beggs, Cin	27	B. Walters, Cin	1252	K. Higbe, Bro	298.0	C. Passeau, ChN	262
C. Davis, Bro	5	H. Casey, Bro	7	H. Casey, Bro	25	W. Wyatt, Bro	1147	W. Wyatt, Bro	288.1	M. Butcher, Pit	249
B. Walters, Cin	5	I. Pearson, Phi	6	J. Brown, NYG	25	R. Sewell, Pit	1055	R. Sewell, Pit	249.0	K. Higbe, Bro	244
2 tied with	4	2 tied with	5	2 tied with	22	M. Butcher, Pit	1017	L. Warneke, StL	246.0	P. Derringer, Cin	233

Home Runs Allowed		Walks		Walks/9 Innings		Strikeouts		Strikeouts/9 Innings		Strikeout/Walk Ratio	
L. Warneke, StL	19	K. Higbe, Bro	132	C. Davis, Bro	1.6	J. Vander Meer, Cin	202	J. Vander Meer, Cin	8.0	W. Wyatt, Bro	2.15
R. Sewell, Pit	18	J. Vander Meer, Cin	126	C. Passeau, ChN	2.0	W. Wyatt, Bro	176	M. Cooper, StL	5.7	C. Davis, Bro	1.85
P. Derringer, Cin	17	M. Salvo, Bos	93	P. Derringer, Cin	2.1	B. Walters, Cin	129	W. Wyatt, Bro	5.5	M. Cooper, StL	1.71
K. Higbe, Bro	16	B. Walters, Cin	88	J. Tobin, Bos	2.3	K. Higbe, Bro	121	E. White, StL	5.0	E. White, StL	1.67
2 tied with	15	R. Sewell, Pit	84	B. Lee, ChN	2.3	M. Cooper, StL	118	C. Hubbell, NYG	4.1	J. Vander Meer, Cin	1.60

Earned Run Average		Component ERA		Hit Batsmen		Wild Pitches		Opponent Average		Opponent OBP	
E. Riddle, Cin	2.24	W. Wyatt, Bro	2.06	I. Pearson, Phi	8	K. Higbe, Bro	9	W. Wyatt, Bro	.212	W. Wyatt, Bro	.270
W. Wyatt, Bro	2.34	E. Riddle, Cin	2.32	E. White, StL	6	L. Grissom, 2tm	8	J. Vander Meer, Cin	.214	C. Davis, Bro	.280
E. White, StL	2.40	C. Davis, Bro	2.47	A. Javery, Bos	6	R. Sewell, Pit	8	E. White, StL	.217	E. Riddle, Cin	.282
J. Vander Meer, Cin	2.82	E. White, StL	2.52	K. Higbe, Bro	6	M. Cooper, StL	7	K. Higbe, Bro	.220	E. White, StL	.287
B. Walters, Cin	2.83	J. Vander Meer, Cin	2.86	3 tied with	5	B. Walters, Cin	7	E. Riddle, Cin	.224	R. Sewell, Pit	.299

1941 National League Miscellaneous

Managers

Boston	Casey Stengel	62-92
Brooklyn	Leo Durocher	100-54
Chicago	Jimmie Wilson	70-84
Cincinnati	Bill McKechnie	88-66
New York	Bill Terry	74-79
Philadelphia	Doc Prothro	43-111
Pittsburgh	Frank Frisch	81-73
St. Louis	Billy Southworth	97-56

Awards

Most Valuable Player	Dolph Camilli, 1b, Bro
STATS Cy Young	Whit Wyatt, Bro
STATS Rookie of the Year	Elmer Riddle, p, Cin
STATS Manager of the Year	Leo Durocher, Bro

Postseason

World Series	Brooklyn (NL) 1 vs. New York (AL) 4

Outstanding Performances

No-Hitters
Lon Warneke, StL   @ Cin on August 30

STATS All-Star Team

C	Ernie Lombardi, Cin	.264	10	60
1B	Dolph Camilli, Bro	.285	34	120
2B	Billy Herman, 2tm	.285	3	41
3B	Stan Hack, ChN	.317	7	45
SS	Arky Vaughan, Pit	.316	6	38
OF	Joe Medwick, Bro	.318	18	88
OF	Mel Ott, NYG	.286	27	90
OF	Pete Reiser, Bro	.343	14	76
P	Kirby Higbe, Bro	22-9	3.14	121 K
P	Elmer Riddle, Cin	19-4	2.24	80 K
P	Bucky Walters, Cin	19-15	2.83	129 K
P	Whit Wyatt, Bro	22-10	2.34	176 K
RP	Hugh Casey, Bro	14-11	3.89	7 Sv

1942 American League Standings

Team	W	L	Pct	GB	DIF	W	L	R	OR	HR	OHR	W	L	R	OR	HR	OHR	Run	HR	M/A	May	June	July	Aug	S/O
		Overall				Home Games						Road Games						Park Index			Record by Month				
New York	103	51	.669	—	157	58	19	394	226	62	39	45	32	407	281	46	32	90	129	10-5	21-6	16-12	21-9	18-12	17-7
Boston	93	59	.612	9.0	8	53	24	403	299	54	33	40	35	358	295	49	32	105	105	9-6	14-14	19-7	14-17	23-9	14-6
St. Louis	82	69	.543	19.5	5	40	37	376	350	55	37	42	32	354	287	43	26	109	128	7-11	16-13	10-15	20-12	15-10	14-8
Cleveland	75	79	.487	28.0	12	39	39	266	308	20	24	36	40	324	351	30	37	83	64	12-3	12-18	17-12	16-14	10-16	8-16
Detroit	73	81	.474	30.0	0	43	34	344	302	50	40	30	47	245	285	26	20	122	196	11-7	15-15	15-13	8-19	15-14	9-13
Chicago	66	82	.446	34.0	0	35	35	256	275	6	31	31	47	282	334	19	43	96	66	3-12	15-14	12-13	13-16	14-13	9-14
Washington	62	89	.411	39.5	0	35	42	339	409	13	11	27	47	314	408	27	39	100	35	8-9	9-18	9-19	15-15	9-14	12-14
Philadelphia	55	99	.357	48.0	0	25	51	249	415	16	42	30	48	300	386	17	47	99	93	5-12	14-18	11-18	12-17	7-23	6-11

Clinch Date—New York 9/14.

Team Batting

Team	G	AB	R	OR	H	2B	3B	HR	TB	RBI	TBB	IBB	SO	HBP	SH	SF	SB	CS	SB%	GDP	Avg	OBP	Slg
New York	154	5305	801	507	1429	223	57	108	2090	744	591	—	556	29	84	—	69	33	.68	104	.269	.346	.394
Boston	152	5248	761	594	1451	244	55	103	2114	702	591	—	508	22	123	—	68	61	.53	94	.276	.352	.403
St. Louis	151	5229	730	637	1354	239	62	98	2011	669	609	—	607	13	96	—	37	38	.49	115	.259	.338	.385
Washington	151	5295	653	817	1364	224	49	40	1806	593	581	—	536	19	54	—	98	29	.77	106	.258	.333	.341
Cleveland	156	5317	590	659	1344	223	58	50	1833	539	500	—	544	24	90	—	69	74	.48	109	.253	.320	.345
Detroit	156	5327	589	587	1313	217	37	76	1832	547	509	—	476	19	73	—	39	40	.49	138	.246	.314	.344
Philadelphia	154	5285	549	801	1315	213	46	33	1719	517	440	—	490	23	74	—	44	45	.49	129	.249	.309	.325
Chicago	148	4949	538	609	1215	214	36	25	1576	486	497	—	427	16	90	—	114	70	.62	102	.246	.316	.318
AL Total	1222	41955	5211	5211	10785	1797	400	533	14981	4797	4318	—	4144	165	684	—	538	390	.58	897	.257	.329	.357
AL Avg Team	153	5244	651	651	1348	225	50	67	1873	600	540	—	518	21	86	—	67	49	.58	112	.257	.329	.357

Team Pitching

Team	G	CG	ShO	Rel	Sv	IP	H	R	ER	HR	SH	SF	HB	TBB	IBB	SO	WP	Bk	H/9	SO/9	BB/9	OAvg	OOBP	ERA
New York	154	88	18	89	17	1375.0	1259	507	444	71	61	—	17	431	—	558	17	3	8.2	3.7	2.8	.244	.304	2.91
Detroit	156	65	12	126	14	1399.1	1321	587	487	60	89	—	23	598	—	671	31	3	8.5	4.3	3.8	.248	.326	3.13
Boston	152	84	11	108	17	1358.2	1260	594	520	65	86	—	16	553	—	500	23	3	8.3	3.3	3.7	.247	.322	3.44
Chicago	148	86	8	75	8	1314.1	1304	609	523	74	84	—	26	473	—	432	32	3	8.9	3.0	3.2	.258	.325	3.58
St. Louis	151	68	12	140	13	1363.0	1387	637	544	63	86	—	25	505	—	488	29	4	9.2	3.2	3.3	.262	.330	3.59
Cleveland	156	61	12	162	11	1402.2	1353	659	560	61	87	—	21	560	—	448	15	3	8.7	2.9	3.6	.254	.327	3.59
Philadelphia	154	67	5	114	9	1374.2	1404	801	679	89	97	—	21	639	—	546	35	3	9.2	3.6	4.2	.263	.344	4.45
Washington	151	68	12	125	11	1346.2	1496	817	686	50	90	—	17	558	—	496	22	3	10.0	3.3	3.7	.279	.349	4.58
AL Total	1222	587	90	939	100	10934.1	10784	5211	4443	533	680	—	166	4317	—	4139	204	23	8.9	3.4	3.6	.257	.329	3.66
AL Avg Team	153	73	11	117	13	1366.1	1348	651	555	67	85	—	21	540	—	517	26	3	8.9	3.4	3.6	.257	.329	3.66

Team Fielding

Team	G	PO	A	E	TC	DP	PB	Pct
New York	154	4126	1757	142	6025	190	4	.976
Boston	152	4077	1772	157	6006	156	11	.974
Cleveland	156	4208	1817	163	6188	175	9	.974
St. Louis	151	4089	1757	167	6013	143	22	.972
Chicago	148	3936	1727	173	5836	144	11	.970
Detroit	156	4175	1801	194	6170	142	11	.969
Philadelphia	154	4062	1678	188	5928	124	23	.968
Washington	151	4046	1634	222	5902	133	19	.962
AL Total	1222	32719	13943	1406	48068	1207	110	.971

Team vs. Team Records

	Bos	ChA	Cle	Det	NYA	Phi	StL	Was	Won
Bos	—	13	14	15	12	14	11	14	93
ChA	8	—	11	9	7	12	6	13	66
Cle	8	11	—	9	7	16	9	15	75
Det	7	13	13	—	7	13	11	9	73
NYA	10	15	15	15	—	16	15	17	103
Phi	8	10	6	9	6	—	6	10	55
StL	11	13	13	11	7	16	—	11	82
Was	7	7	7	13	5	12	11	—	62
Lost	59	82	79	81	51	99	69	89	

1942 American League Batting Leaders

Games		At-Bats		Runs		Hits		Doubles		Triples	
L. Fleming, Cle	156	D. Cramer, Det	630	T. Williams, Bos	141	J. Pesky, Bos	205	D. Kolloway, ChA	40	S. Spence, Was	15
B. McCosky, Det	154	S. Spence, Was	629	J. DiMaggio, NYA	123	S. Spence, Was	203	H. Clift, StL	39	J. Heath, Cle	13
J. DiMaggio, NYA	154	K. Keltner, Cle	624	D. DiMaggio, Bos	110	T. Williams, Bos	186	J. Heath, Cle	37	J. DiMaggio, NYA	13
R. York, Det	153	D. DiMaggio, Bos	622	H. Clift, StL	108	J. DiMaggio, NYA	186	D. DiMaggio, Bos	36	G. McQuillen, StL	12
D. Siebert, Phi	153	M. Vernon, Was	621	C. Keller, NYA	106	K. Keltner, Cle	179	2 tied with	35	2 tied with	11

Home Runs		Total Bases		Runs Batted In		Walks		Intentional Walks		Strikeouts	
T. Williams, Bos	36	T. Williams, Bos	338	T. Williams, Bos	137	T. Williams, Bos	145	Statistic unavailable		J. Gordon, NYA	95
C. Laabs, StL	27	J. DiMaggio, NYA	304	J. DiMaggio, NYA	114	C. Keller, NYA	114			C. Laabs, StL	88
C. Keller, NYA	26	C. Keller, NYA	279	C. Keller, NYA	108	L. Fleming, Cle	106			G. McQuinn, StL	77
J. DiMaggio, NYA	21	S. Spence, Was	272	J. Gordon, NYA	103	H. Clift, StL	106			R. York, Det	71
R. York, Det	21	D. DiMaggio, Bos	272	B. Doerr, Bos	102	R. Cullenbine, 3tm	92			J. Heath, Cle	66

Hit By Pitch		Sac Hits		Sac Flies		Stolen Bases		Caught Stealing		GDP	
F. Crosetti, NYA	9	J. Pesky, Bos	22	Statistic unavailable		G. Case, Was	44	L. Boudreau, Cle	16	J. Gordon, NYA	22
P. Rizzuto, NYA	6	L. Boudreau, Cle	19			M. Vernon, Was	25	D. Kolloway, ChA	14	G. McQuillen, StL	21
D. DiMaggio, Bos	6	K. Keltner, Cle	16			P. Rizzuto, NYA	22	J. Tabor, Bos	13	M. Higgins, Det	21
L. Fleming, Cle	6	G. McQuinn, StL	16			J. Kuhel, ChA	22	D. Gutteridge, StL	13	P. Suder, Phi	20
2 tied with	5	D. Gutteridge, StL	14			2 tied with	17	R. Weatherly, Cle	13	B. Estalella, Was	19

Runs Created		Runs Created/27 Outs		Batting Average		On-Base Percentage		Slugging Percentage		OBP+Slugging	
T. Williams, Bos	160	T. Williams, Bos	12.40	T. Williams, Bos	.356	T. Williams, Bos	.499	T. Williams, Bos	.648	T. Williams, Bos	1.147
C. Keller, NYA	131	C. Keller, NYA	9.04	J. Pesky, Bos	.331	C. Keller, NYA	.417	C. Keller, NYA	.513	C. Keller, NYA	.930
J. DiMaggio, NYA	121	W. Judnich, StL	8.17	S. Spence, Was	.323	W. Judnich, StL	.413	W. Judnich, StL	.499	W. Judnich, StL	.912
J. Gordon, NYA	110	J. DiMaggio, NYA	7.54	J. Gordon, NYA	.322	L. Fleming, Cle	.412	J. DiMaggio, NYA	.498	J. Gordon, NYA	.900
S. Spence, Was	109	J. Gordon, NYA	7.46	G. Case, Was	.320	J. Gordon, NYA	.409	C. Laabs, StL	.498	C. Laabs, StL	.878

1942 American League Pitching Leaders

Wins		Losses		Winning Percentage		Games		Games Started		Complete Games	
T. Hughson, Bos	22	E. Smith, ChA	20	T. Bonham, NYA	.808	J. Haynes, ChA	40	J. Bagby Jr., Cle	35	T. Hughson, Bos	22
T. Bonham, NYA	21	D. Trout, Det	18	H. Borowy, NYA	.789	G. Caster, StL	39	E. Auker, StL	34	T. Bonham, NYA	22
P. Marchildon, Phi	17	S. Hudson, Was	17	T. Hughson, Bos	.786	4 tied with	38	P. Marchildon, Phi	31	T. Lyons, ChA	20
J. Bagby Jr., Cle	17	B. Newsom, Was	17	S. Chandler, NYA	.762			S. Hudson, Was	31	S. Hudson, Was	19
S. Chandler, NYA	16	E. Wynn, Was	16	T. Lyons, ChA	.700			2 tied with	30	2 tied with	18

Shutouts		Saves		Games Finished		Batters Faced		Innings Pitched		Hits Allowed	
T. Bonham, NYA	6	J. Murphy, NYA	11	J. Haynes, ChA	35	T. Hughson, Bos	1150	T. Hughson, Bos	281.0	E. Auker, StL	273
7 tied with	4	J. Haynes, ChA	6	J. Murphy, NYA	26	J. Bagby Jr., Cle	1111	J. Bagby Jr., Cle	270.2	J. Bagby Jr., Cle	267
		M. Brown, Bos	6	G. Caster, StL	24	E. Auker, StL	1093	E. Auker, StL	249.0	S. Hudson, Was	266
		H. Newhouser, Det	5	M. Brown, Bos	23	P. Marchildon, Phi	1081	P. Marchildon, Phi	244.0	T. Hughson, Bos	258
		G. Caster, StL	5	3 tied with	19	S. Hudson, Was	1048	S. Hudson, Was	239.1	E. Wynn, Was	246

Home Runs Allowed		Walks		Walks/9 Innings		Strikeouts		Strikeouts/9 Innings		Strikeout/Walk Ratio	
J. Bagby Jr., Cle	19	P. Marchildon, Phi	140	T. Bonham, NYA	1.0	T. Hughson, Bos	113	H. Newhouser, Det	5.0	T. Bonham, NYA	2.96
E. Smith, ChA	17	H. Newhouser, Det	114	T. Lyons, ChA	1.3	B. Newsom, Was	113	T. Bridges, Det	5.0	R. Ruffing, NYA	1.95
R. Wolff, Phi	16	R. Christopher, Phi	99	R. Ruffing, NYA	1.9	P. Marchildon, Phi	110	B. Newsom, Was	4.8	T. Lyons, ChA	1.92
E. Auker, StL	16	C. Wagner, Bos	95	J. Bagby Jr., Cle	2.1	A. Benton, Det	110	J. Niggeling, StL	4.7	T. Bridges, Det	1.59
B. Dietrich, ChA	16	J. Niggeling, StL	93	J. Humphries, ChA	2.3	J. Niggeling, StL	107	H. Borowy, NYA	4.3	T. Hughson, Bos	1.51

Earned Run Average		Component ERA		Hit Batsmen		Wild Pitches		Opponent Average		Opponent OBP	
T. Lyons, ChA	2.10	T. Bonham, NYA	2.11	J. Niggeling, StL	11	P. Marchildon, Phi	13	H. Newhouser, Det	.207	T. Bonham, NYA	.259
T. Bonham, NYA	2.27	T. Lyons, ChA	2.50	J. Humphries, ChA	7	D. Trout, Det	8	J. Niggeling, StL	.226	T. Lyons, ChA	.275
S. Chandler, NYA	2.38	T. Hughson, Bos	2.68	5 tied with	5	V. Trucks, Det	7	J. Dobson, Bos	.231	R. Ruffing, NYA	.292
H. Newhouser, Det	2.45	A. Donald, NYA	2.74			O. Judd, Bos	7	H. Borowy, NYA	.233	T. Hughson, Bos	.296
H. Borowy, NYA	2.52	H. Borowy, NYA	2.78			J. Niggeling, StL	7	L. Harris, Phi	.234	A. Donald, NYA	.296

1942 American League Miscellaneous

Managers

Boston	Joe Cronin	93-59
Chicago	Jimmy Dykes	66-82
Cleveland	Lou Boudreau	75-79
Detroit	Del Baker	73-81
New York	Joe McCarthy	103-51
Philadelphia	Connie Mack	55-99
St. Louis	Luke Sewell	82-69
Washington	Bucky Harris	62-89

Awards

Most Valuable Player	Joe Gordon, 2b, NYA
STATS Cy Young	Tex Hughson, Bos
STATS Rookie of the Year	Johnny Pesky, ss, Bos
STATS Manager of the Year	Luke Sewell, StL

STATS All-Star Team

C	Bill Dickey, NYA	.295	2	37
1B	Les Fleming, Cle	.292	14	82
2B	Joe Gordon, NYA	.322	18	103
3B	Harlond Clift, StL	.274	7	55
SS	Johnny Pesky, Bos	.331	2	51
OF	Joe DiMaggio, NYA	.305	21	114
OF	Charlie Keller, NYA	.292	26	108
OF	Ted Williams, Bos	.356	36	137
P	Tiny Bonham, NYA	21-5	2.27	71 K
P	Spud Chandler, NYA	16-5	2.38	74 K
P	Tex Hughson, Bos	22-6	2.59	113 K
P	Ted Lyons, ChA	14-6	2.10	50 K
RP	Joe Haynes, ChA	8-5	2.62	6 Sv

Postseason

World Series	New York (AL) 1 vs. St. Louis (NL) 4

Outstanding Performances

Triple Crown
Ted Williams, Bos .356-36-137

1942 National League Standings

Team	W	L	Pct	GB	DIF	W	L	R	OR	HR	OHR	W	L	R	OR	HR	OHR	Run	HR	M/A	May	June	July	Aug	S/O
			Overall					Home Games						Road Games				Park Index				Record by Month			
St. Louis	106	48	.688	—	16	60	17	419	229	31	24	46	31	336	253	29	25	110	102	7-7	18-11	13-9	22-9	25-8	21-4
Brooklyn	104	50	.675	2.0	148	57	22	381	250	30	35	47	28	361	260	32	38	96	88	14-3	18-10	16-7	22-9	18-11	16-10
New York	85	67	.559	20.0	0	47	31	376	296	80	67	38	36	299	304	29	27	106	249	8-8	15-15	14-12	15-12	19-11	14-9
Cincinnati	76	76	.500	29.0	0	38	39	264	276	30	23	38	37	263	269	36	24	99	86	5-10	17-12	17-10	14-13	11-19	12-12
Pittsburgh	66	81	.449	36.5	4	41	34	333	301	15	21	25	47	252	330	39	43	105	43	9-6	10-21	13-9	11-16	15-15	8-14
Chicago	68	86	.442	38.0	1	36	41	298	318	36	27	32	45	293	347	39	43	96	77	7-9	14-15	15-14	11-17	13-18	8-13
Boston	59	89	.399	44.0	6	33	36	250	271	36	34	26	53	265	374	32	48	93	100	9-8	16-14	8-21	8-19	10-17	8-10
Philadelphia	42	109	.278	62.5	0	23	51	182	340	18	31	19	58	212	366	26	30	94	91	4-12	10-20	5-19	9-17	8-20	6-21

Clinch Date—St. Louis 9/27.

Team Batting

Team	G	AB	R	OR	H	2B	3B	HR	TB	RBI	TBB	IBB	SO	HBP	SH	SF	SB	CS	SB%	GDP	Avg	OBP	Slg
St. Louis	156	5421	755	482	1454	282	69	60	2054	680	551	—	507	22	130	—	71	—	—	90	.268	.338	.379
Brooklyn	155	5285	742	510	1398	263	34	62	1915	678	572	—	484	14	119	—	81	—	—	95	.265	.338	.362
New York	154	5210	675	600	1323	162	35	109	1882	632	558	—	511	34	80	—	39	—	—	140	.254	.330	.361
Chicago	155	5352	591	665	1360	224	41	75	1891	533	509	—	607	19	104	—	63	—	—	110	.254	.321	.353
Pittsburgh	151	5104	585	631	1250	173	49	54	1683	544	537	—	536	26	86	—	41	—	—	105	.245	.320	.330
Cincinnati	154	5260	527	545	1216	198	39	66	1690	488	483	—	549	23	92	—	42	—	—	96	.231	.299	.321
Boston	150	5077	515	645	1216	210	19	68	1668	479	474	—	507	20	89	—	49	—	—	114	.240	.307	.329
Philadelphia	151	5060	394	706	1174	168	37	44	1548	356	392	—	488	16	89	—	37	—	—	109	.232	.289	.306
NL Total	1226	41769	4784	4784	10391	1680	323	538	14331	4390	4076	—	4189	174	789	—	423	—	—	859	.249	.318	.343
NL Avg Team	153	5221	598	598	1299	210	40	67	1791	549	510	—	524	22	99	—	53	—	—	107	.249	.318	.343

Team Pitching

Team	G	CG	ShO	Rel	Sv	IP	H	R	ER	HR	SH	SF	HB	TBB	IBB	SO	WP	Bk	H/9	SO/9	BB/9	OAvg	OOBP	ERA
St. Louis	156	70	18	149	15	1410.1	1192	482	399	49	75	—	19	473	—	651	31	1	7.6	4.2	3.0	.228	.294	2.55
Cincinnati	154	80	12	115	8	1411.2	1213	545	442	47	88	—	20	526	—	616	15	2	7.7	3.9	3.4	.230	.302	2.82
Brooklyn	155	67	16	165	24	1398.2	1205	510	442	73	84	—	33	493	—	612	14	1	7.8	3.9	3.2	.232	.302	2.84
New York	154	70	12	153	13	1370.0	1299	600	504	94	103	—	13	493	—	497	24	0	8.5	3.3	3.2	.250	.316	3.31
Pittsburgh	151	64	13	156	11	1351.1	1376	631	538	62	116	—	13	435	—	426	21	3	9.2	2.8	2.9	.262	.320	3.58
Chicago	155	71	10	150	14	1400.2	1447	665	560	70	97	—	18	525	—	507	27	4	9.3	3.3	3.4	.267	.334	3.60
Boston	150	68	9	162	8	1334.0	1326	645	557	82	98	—	29	518	—	414	26	4	8.9	2.8	3.5	.260	.331	3.76
Philadelphia	151	51	2	184	6	1341.0	1328	706	614	61	115	—	26	605	—	472	27	6	8.9	3.2	4.1	.260	.342	4.12
NL Total	1226	541	92	1234	99	11017.2	10386	4784	4056	538	776	—	171	4068	—	4195	185	21	8.5	3.4	3.3	.249	.318	3.31
NL Avg Team	153	68	12	154	12	1377.2	1298	598	507	67	97	—	21	509	—	524	23	3	8.5	3.4	3.3	.249	.318	3.31

Team Fielding

Team	G	PO	A	E	TC	DP	PB	Pct
New York	154	4108	1816	138	6062	128	5	.977
Brooklyn	155	4191	1677	138	6006	150	5	.977
Boston	150	4006	1795	142	5943	138	14	.976
Chicago	155	4203	1871	170	6244	136	10	.973
St. Louis	156	4230	1698	169	6097	137	12	.972
Cincinnati	154	4238	1793	177	6208	158	13	.971
Pittsburgh	151	4053	1713	184	5950	128	8	.969
Philadelphia	151	4015	1803	194	6012	147	9	.968
NL Total	1226	33044	14166	1312	48522	1122	76	.973

Team vs. Team Records

	Bos	Bro	ChN	Cin	NYG	Phi	Pit	StL	Won
Bos	—	6	13	5	8	14	7	6	59
Bro	16	—	16	15	14	18	16	9	104
ChN	9	6	—	13	9	14	11	6	68
Cin	16	7	9	—	9	16	12	7	76
NYG	12	8	13	13	—	17	15	7	85
Phi	8	4	8	6	5	—	6	5	42
Pit	12	6	11	9	7	13	—	8	66
StL	16	13	16	15	15	17	14	—	106
Lost	89	50	86	76	67	109	81	48	

Seasons: Standings, Leaders

1942 National League Batting Leaders

Games		At-Bats		Runs		Hits		Doubles		Triples	
B. Herman, Bro	155	J. Brown, StL	606	M. Ott, NYG	118	E. Slaughter, StL	188	M. Marion, StL	38	E. Slaughter, StL	17
B. Haas, Cin	154	D. Litwhiler, Phi	591	E. Slaughter, StL	100	B. Nicholson, ChN	173	J. Medwick, Bro	37	B. Nicholson, ChN	11
E. Slaughter, StL	152	E. Slaughter, StL	591	J. Mize, NYG	97	B. Elliott, Pit	166	S. Hack, ChN	36	S. Musial, StL	10
B. Nicholson, ChN	152	B. Nicholson, ChN	588	S. Hack, ChN	91	J. Medwick, Bro	166	B. Herman, Bro	34	D. Litwhiler, Phi	9
M. Ott, NYG	152	B. Haas, Cin	585	2 tied with	89	S. Hack, ChN	166	P. Reiser, Bro	33	6 tied with	7

Home Runs		Total Bases		Runs Batted In		Walks		Intentional Walks		Strikeouts	
M. Ott, NYG	30	E. Slaughter, StL	292	J. Mize, NYG	110	M. Ott, NYG	109	Statistic unavailable		V. DiMaggio, Pit	87
J. Mize, NYG	26	J. Mize, NYG	282	D. Camilli, Bro	109	E. Fletcher, Pit	105			D. Camilli, Bro	85
D. Camilli, Bro	26	B. Nicholson, ChN	280	E. Slaughter, StL	98	D. Camilli, Bro	97			B. Nicholson, ChN	80
B. Nicholson, ChN	21	M. Ott, NYG	273	J. Medwick, Bro	96	S. Hack, ChN	94			N. Fernandez, Bos	61
M. West, Bos	16	D. Camilli, Bro	247	M. Ott, NYG	93	E. Slaughter, StL	88			M. Ott, NYG	61

Hit By Pitch		Sac Hits		Sac Flies		Stolen Bases		Caught Stealing		GDP	
B. Nicholson, ChN	8	L. Merullo, ChN	22	Statistic unavailable		P. Reiser, Bro	20	Statistic unavailable		M. Witek, NYG	23
D. Bartell, NYG	8	D. Murtaugh, Phi	21			N. Fernandez, Bos	15			B. Jurges, NYG	20
D. Litwhiler, Phi	7	M. Marion, StL	20			P. Reese, Bro	15			W. Cooper, StL	18
3 tied with	6	M. Owen, Bro	18			L. Merullo, ChN	14			E. Lombardi, Bos	17
		2 tied with	14			J. Hopp, StL	14			4 tied with	16

Runs Created		Runs Created/27 Outs		Batting Average		On-Base Percentage		Slugging Percentage		OBP+Slugging	
E. Slaughter, StL	128	M. Ott, NYG	8.39	E. Lombardi, Bos	.330	E. Fletcher, Pit	.417	J. Mize, NYG	.521	M. Ott, NYG	.912
M. Ott, NYG	124	E. Slaughter, StL	8.39	E. Slaughter, StL	.318	M. Ott, NYG	.415	M. Ott, NYG	.497	E. Slaughter, StL	.906
J. Mize, NYG	113	S. Musial, StL	7.97	S. Musial, StL	.315	E. Slaughter, StL	.412	E. Slaughter, StL	.494	J. Mize, NYG	.901
D. Camilli, Bro	104	J. Mize, NYG	7.91	P. Reiser, Bro	.310	E. Lombardi, Bos	.403	S. Musial, StL	.490	S. Musial, StL	.888
B. Nicholson, ChN	103	P. Reiser, Bro	7.49	J. Mize, NYG	.305	S. Hack, ChN	.402	E. Lombardi, Bos	.482	E. Lombardi, Bos	.886

1942 National League Pitching Leaders

Wins		Losses		Winning Percentage		Games		Games Started		Complete Games	
M. Cooper, StL	22	J. Tobin, Bos	21	H. Krist, StL	.813	A. Adams, NYG	61	A. Javery, Bos	37	J. Tobin, Bos	28
J. Beazley, StL	21	R. Melton, Phi	20	L. French, Bro	.789	H. Casey, Bro	50	M. Cooper, StL	35	C. Passeau, ChN	24
C. Passeau, ChN	19	S. Johnson, Phi	19	J. Beazley, StL	.778	J. Beazley, StL	43	C. Passeau, ChN	34	M. Cooper, StL	22
W. Wyatt, Bro	19	T. Hughes, Phi	18	M. Cooper, StL	.759	J. Podgajny, Phi	43	4 tied with	33	J. Vander Meer, Cin	21
J. Vander Meer, Cin	18	2 tied with	16	B. Lohrman, 2tm	.737	2 tied with	42			B. Walters, Cin	21

Shutouts		Saves		Games Finished		Batters Faced		Innings Pitched		Hits Allowed	
M. Cooper, StL	10	H. Casey, Bro	13	A. Adams, NYG	49	J. Tobin, Bos	1224	J. Tobin, Bos	287.2	C. Passeau, ChN	284
A. Javery, Bos	5	A. Adams, NYG	11	J. Beggs, Cin	30	C. Passeau, ChN	1177	M. Cooper, StL	278.2	J. Tobin, Bos	283
C. Davis, Bro	5	J. Beggs, Cin	8	H. Casey, Bro	29	R. Starr, Cin	1136	C. Passeau, ChN	278.1	R. Sewell, Pit	259
R. Sewell, Pit	5	J. Sain, Bos	6	C. Shoun, 2tm	27	A. Javery, Bos	1108	R. Starr, Cin	276.2	A. Javery, Bos	251
3 tied with	4	H. Gumbert, StL	5	J. Sain, Bos	24	M. Cooper, StL	1100	A. Javery, Bos	261.0	R. Starr, Cin	228

Home Runs Allowed		Walks		Walks/9 Innings		Strikeouts		Strikeouts/9 Innings		Strikeout/Walk Ratio	
J. Tobin, Bos	20	R. Melton, Phi	114	L. Warneke, 2tm	1.8	J. Vander Meer, Cin	186	J. Vander Meer, Cin	6.9	M. Cooper, StL	2.24
K. Higbe, Bro	17	K. Higbe, Bro	106	B. Lohrman, 2tm	1.8	M. Cooper, StL	152	M. Cooper, StL	4.9	C. Melton, NYG	1.85
C. Hubbell, NYG	17	R. Starr, Cin	106	C. Hubbell, NYG	1.9	K. Higbe, Bro	115	K. Higbe, Bro	4.7	J. Vander Meer, Cin	1.82
B. Carpenter, NYG	13	J. Vander Meer, Cin	102	C. Melton, NYG	2.1	B. Walters, Cin	109	R. Melton, Phi	4.6	C. Hubbell, NYG	1.79
C. Passeau, ChN	13	T. Hughes, Phi	99	P. Derringer, Cin	2.1	R. Melton, Phi	107	W. Wyatt, Bro	4.3	W. Wyatt, Bro	1.65

Earned Run Average		Component ERA		Hit Batsmen		Wild Pitches		Opponent Average		Opponent OBP	
M. Cooper, StL	1.78	M. Cooper, StL	1.81	J. Podgajny, Phi	11	R. Melton, Phi	8	M. Cooper, StL	.204	M. Cooper, StL	.258
J. Beazley, StL	2.13	J. Vander Meer, Cin	2.33	C. Davis, Bro	7	J. Beazley, StL	7	J. Vander Meer, Cin	.208	C. Melton, NYG	.276
C. Davis, Bro	2.36	C. Melton, NYG	2.43	W. Wyatt, Bro	7	J. Tobin, Bos	7	K. Higbe, Bro	.223	B. Lohrman, 2tm	.281
J. Vander Meer, Cin	2.43	J. Beazley, StL	2.43	J. Tobin, Bos	6	5 tied with	5	W. Wyatt, Bro	.225	W. Wyatt, Bro	.286
B. Lohrman, 2tm	2.48	W. Wyatt, Bro	2.51	5 tied with	5			R. Starr, Cin	.226	L. Warneke, 2tm	.286

1942 National League Miscellaneous

Managers

Boston	Casey Stengel	59-89
Brooklyn	Leo Durocher	104-50
Chicago	Jimmie Wilson	68-86
Cincinnati	Bill McKechnie	76-76
New York	Mel Ott	85-67
Philadelphia	Hans Lobert	42-109
Pittsburgh	Frank Frisch	66-81
St. Louis	Billy Southworth	106-48

Awards

Most Valuable Player	Mort Cooper, p, StL
STATS Cy Young	Mort Cooper, StL
STATS Rookie of the Year	Johnny Beazley, p, StL
STATS Manager of the Year	Billy Southworth, StL

STATS All-Star Team

C	Ernie Lombardi, Bos	.330	11	46
1B	Johnny Mize, NYG	.305	26	110
2B	Lonny Frey, Cin	.266	2	39
3B	Stan Hack, ChN	.300	6	39
SS	Pee Wee Reese, Bro	.255	3	53
OF	Stan Musial, StL	.315	10	72
OF	Mel Ott, NYG	.295	30	93
OF	Enos Slaughter, StL	.318	13	98
P	Johnny Beazley, StL	21-6	2.13	91 K
P	Mort Cooper, StL	22-7	1.78	152 K
P	Johnny Vander Meer, Cin	18-12	2.43	186 K
P	Whit Wyatt, Bro	19-7	2.73	104 K
RP	Ace Adams, NYG	7-4	1.84	11 Sv

Postseason

World Series	St. Louis (NL) 4 vs. New York (AL) 1

Outstanding Performances

Three-Homer Games
Jim Tobin, Bos   on May 13
C. McCullough, ChN   on July 26

1943 American League Standings

Team	Overall W	L	Pct	GB	DIF	Home Games W	L	R	OR	HR	OHR	Road Games W	L	R	OR	HR	OHR	Park Index Run	HR	Record by Month M/A	May	June	July	Aug	S/O
New York	98	56	.636	—	158	54	23	321	241	60	33	44	33	348	301	40	27	87	139	5-2	14-11	15-11	21-11	22-11	21-10
Washington	84	69	.549	13.5	5	44	32	345	307	9	14	40	37	321	288	38	34	108	32	6-3	13-13	15-13	14-18	21-11	15-11
Cleveland	82	71	.536	15.5	7	44	33	269	247	16	21	38	38	331	330	39	31	77	52	5-2	13-15	12-15	14-14	21-11	17-14
Chicago	82	72	.532	16.0	0	40	36	264	311	20	25	42	36	309	283	13	29	100	110	1-4	12-12	15-14	19-14	17-16	18-12
Detroit	78	76	.506	20.0	0	45	32	345	284	45	26	33	44	287	276	32	25	112	125	4-3	12-13	11-14	19-14	17-14	15-18
St. Louis	72	80	.474	25.0	3	44	33	319	290	49	51	28	47	277	314	29	23	100	187	2-3	9-15	16-13	15-15	14-20	16-14
Boston	68	84	.447	29.0	1	39	36	293	312	29	25	29	48	270	295	28	36	110	87	2-5	15-14	15-12	13-16	14-20	9-17
Philadelphia	49	105	.318	49.0	0	27	51	261	387	14	36	22	54	236	330	12	37	112	99	3-6	16-11	11-18	8-21	3-26	8-23

Clinch Date—New York 9/25.

Team Batting

Team	G	AB	R	OR	H	2B	3B	HR	TB	RBI	TBB	IBB	SO	HBP	SH	SF	SB	CS	SB%	GDP	Avg	OBP	Slg
New York	155	5282	669	542	1350	218	59	100	1986	635	624	—	562	25	93	—	46	60	.43	132	.256	.337	.376
Washington	153	5233	666	595	1328	245	50	47	1814	619	605	—	579	39	88	—	142	55	.72	94	.254	.336	.347
Detroit	155	5364	632	560	1401	200	47	77	1926	572	483	—	553	13	123	—	40	43	.48	159	.261	.324	.359
Cleveland	153	5269	600	577	1344	246	45	55	1845	564	567	—	521	11	120	—	47	58	.45	110	.255	.329	.350
St. Louis	153	5175	596	604	1269	229	36	78	1804	552	569	—	646	14	105	—	37	43	.46	107	.245	.322	.349
Chicago	155	5254	573	594	1297	193	46	33	1681	508	561	—	581	22	72	—	173	87	.67	110	.247	.322	.320
Boston	155	5392	563	607	1314	223	42	57	1792	511	486	—	591	19	113	—	86	61	.59	103	.244	.308	.332
Philadelphia	155	5244	497	717	1219	174	44	26	1559	462	430	—	465	29	95	—	55	42	.57	132	.232	.294	.297
AL Total	1234	42213	4796	4796	10522	1728	369	473	14407	4423	4325	—	4498	172	809	—	626	449	.58	947	.249	.322	.341
AL Avg Team	154	5277	600	600	1315	216	46	59	1801	553	541	—	562	22	101	—	78	56	.58	118	.249	.322	.341

Team Pitching

Team	G	CG	ShO	Rel	Sv	IP	H	R	ER	HR	SH	SF	HB	TBB	IBB	SO	WP	Bk	H/9	SO/9	BB/9	OAvg	OOBP	ERA
New York	155	83	14	98	13	1415.1	1229	542	460	60	91	—	13	489	—	653	20	5	7.8	4.2	3.1	.234	.301	2.93
Detroit	155	67	18	130	20	1411.2	1226	560	471	51	89	—	14	549	—	706	20	3	7.8	4.5	3.5	.234	.308	3.00
Cleveland	153	64	14	158	20	1406.1	1234	577	492	52	96	—	22	606	—	585	10	1	7.9	3.7	3.9	.239	.322	3.15
Washington	153	61	16	134	21	1388.0	1293	595	491	48	93	—	15	540	—	495	32	4	8.4	3.2	3.5	.246	.318	3.18
Chicago	155	70	12	109	19	1400.1	1352	594	498	54	100	—	37	501	—	476	16	2	8.7	3.1	3.2	.255	.324	3.20
St. Louis	153	64	10	130	14	1385.0	1397	604	525	74	107	—	22	488	—	572	25	8	9.1	3.7	3.2	.263	.327	3.41
Boston	155	62	13	140	16	1426.1	1369	607	547	61	117	—	15	615	—	513	34	7	8.6	3.2	3.9	.257	.335	3.45
Philadelphia	155	73	5	107	13	1394.0	1421	717	627	73	113	—	35	536	—	503	24	4	9.2	3.2	3.5	.265	.336	4.05
AL Total	1234	544	102	1006	136	11227.0	10521	4796	4111	473	806	—	173	4324	—	4503	181	34	8.4	3.6	3.5	.249	.322	3.30
AL Avg Team	154	68	13	126	17	1403.0	1315	600	514	59	101	—	22	541	—	563	23	4	8.4	3.6	3.5	.249	.322	3.30

Team Fielding

Team	G	PO	A	E	TC	DP	PB	Pct
Boston	155	4274	1892	153	6319	179	11	.976
Cleveland	153	4239	1835	157	6231	183	3	.975
St. Louis	153	4147	1659	152	5958	127	7	.974
New York	155	4244	1756	160	6160	166	11	.974
Philadelphia	155	4180	1741	162	6083	148	19	.973
Chicago	155	4201	1833	166	6200	167	19	.973
Detroit	155	4235	1772	177	6184	130	12	.971
Washington	153	4172	1786	179	6137	145	17	.971
AL Total	1234	33692	14274	1306	49272	1245	99	.973

Team vs. Team Records

	Bos	ChA	Cle	Det	NYA	Phi	StL	Was	Won
Bos	—	8	12	11	5	11	11	10	68
ChA	14	—	7	9	10	18	10	14	82
Cle	10	15	—	15	9	16	9	8	82
Det	11	13	7	—	10	13	11	13	78
NYA	17	12	13	12	—	16	17	11	98
Phi	11	4	6	9	6	—	8	5	49
StL	9	12	13	11	5	14	—	8	72
Was	12	8	13	9	11	17	14	—	84
Lost	84	72	71	76	56	105	80	69	

1943 American League Batting Leaders

Games		At-Bats		Runs		Hits		Doubles		Triples	
B. Johnson, NYA	155	D. Wakefield, Det	633	G. Case, Was	102	D. Wakefield, Det	200	D. Wakefield, Det	38	J. Lindell, NYA	12
D. Wakefield, Det	155	G. Case, Was	613	C. Keller, NYA	97	L. Appling, ChA	192	G. Case, Was	36	W. Moses, ChA	12
B. Doerr, Bos	155	T. Lupien, Bos	608	D. Wakefield, Det	91	D. Cramer, Det	182	N. Etten, NYA	35	C. Keller, NYA	11
R. York, Det	155	D. Cramer, Det	606	R. York, Det	90	G. Case, Was	180	D. Gutteridge, StL	35	R. York, Det	11
L. Appling, ChA	155	B. Doerr, Bos	604	M. Vernon, Was	89	2 tied with	166	2 tied with	33	S. Spence, Was	10

Home Runs		Total Bases		Runs Batted In		Walks		Intentional Walks		Strikeouts	
R. York, Det	34	R. York, Det	301	R. York, Det	118	C. Keller, NYA	106	Statistic unavailable		C. Laabs, StL	105
C. Keller, NYA	31	D. Wakefield, Det	275	N. Etten, NYA	107	J. Gordon, NYA	98			J. Hoover, Det	101
V. Stephens, StL	22	C. Keller, NYA	269	B. Johnson, NYA	94	R. Cullenbine, Cle	96			R. York, Det	88
J. Heath, Cle	18	B. Doerr, Bos	249	V. Stephens, StL	91	L. Boudreau, Cle	90			J. Priddy, Was	76
2 tied with	17	V. Stephens, StL	247	S. Spence, Was	88	L. Appling, ChA	90			J. Gordon, NYA	75

Hit By Pitch		Sac Hits		Sac Flies		Stolen Bases		Caught Stealing		GDP	
M. Vernon, Was	10	J. Hoover, Det	28	Statistic unavailable		G. Case, Was	61	O. Hockett, Cle	18	J. Bloodworth, Det	29
F. Crosetti, NYA	7	E. Mayo, Phi	23			W. Moses, ChA	56	T. Tucker, ChA	17	B. Johnson, NYA	27
J. Kuhel, ChA	7	L. Boudreau, Cle	20			T. Tucker, ChA	29	G. Case, Was	14	D. Wakefield, Det	23
I. Hall, Phi	6	P. Fox, Bos	18			L. Appling, ChA	27	W. Moses, ChA	14	R. York, Det	22
R. Hodgin, ChA	6	R. Mack, Cle	14			M. Vernon, Was	24	G. Curtright, ChA	12	D. Siebert, Phi	19

Runs Created		Runs Created/27 Outs		Batting Average		On-Base Percentage		Slugging Percentage		OBP+Slugging	
C. Keller, NYA	108	C. Keller, NYA	7.67	L. Appling, ChA	.328	L. Appling, ChA	.419	R. York, Det	.527	C. Keller, NYA	.922
R. York, Det	108	L. Appling, ChA	7.15	D. Wakefield, Det	.316	R. Cullenbine, Cle	.407	C. Keller, NYA	.525	R. York, Det	.893
L. Appling, ChA	108	R. York, Det	6.62	R. Hodgin, ChA	.315	C. Keller, NYA	.396	V. Stephens, StL	.482	J. Heath, Cle	.850
D. Wakefield, Det	101	J. Heath, Cle	6.27	D. Cramer, Det	.300	L. Boudreau, Cle	.388	J. Heath, Cle	.481	V. Stephens, StL	.839
S. Spence, Was	93	V. Stephens, StL	6.26	G. Case, Was	.294	G. Curtright, ChA	.382	D. Wakefield, Det	.434	L. Appling, ChA	.825

1943 American League Pitching Leaders

Wins		Losses		Winning Percentage		Games		Games Started		Complete Games	
D. Trout, Det	20	L. Harris, Phi	21	S. Chandler, NYA	.833	M. Brown, Bos	49	E. Wynn, Was	33	T. Hughson, Bos	20
S. Chandler, NYA	20	H. Newhouser, Det	17	J. Murphy, NYA	.750	D. Trout, Det	44	J. Bagby Jr., Cle	33	S. Chandler, NYA	20
E. Wynn, Was	18	D. Black, Phi	16	A. Smith, Cle	.708	R. Wolff, Phi	41	T. Hughson, Bos	32	B. Wensloff, NYA	18
J. Bagby Jr., Cle	17	R. Wolff, Phi	15	M. Haefner, Was	.688	M. Ryba, Bos	40	3 tied with	30	O. Grove, ChA	18
A. Smith, Cle	17	T. Hughson, Bos	15	N. Potter, StL	.667	A. Carrasquel, Was	39			D. Trout, Det	18

Shutouts		Saves		Games Finished		Batters Faced		Innings Pitched		Hits Allowed	
D. Trout, Det	5	G. Maltzberger, ChA	14	M. Brown, Bos	41	J. Bagby Jr., Cle	1135	J. Bagby Jr., Cle	273.0	J. Bagby Jr., Cle	248
S. Chandler, NYA	5	M. Brown, Bos	9	G. Maltzberger, ChA	33	T. Hughson, Bos	1080	T. Hughson, Bos	266.0	T. Hughson, Bos	242
T. Hughson, Bos	4	J. Heving, Cle	9	G. Caster, StL	32	E. Wynn, Was	1067	E. Wynn, Was	256.2	L. Harris, Phi	241
T. Bonham, NYA	4	G. Caster, StL	8	J. Murphy, NYA	32	D. Trout, Det	1019	S. Chandler, NYA	253.0	R. Wolff, Phi	232
14 tied with	3	J. Murphy, NYA	8	J. Haynes, ChA	26	S. Chandler, NYA	989	D. Trout, Det	246.2	E. Wynn, Was	232

Home Runs Allowed		Walks		Walks/9 Innings		Strikeouts		Strikeouts/9 Innings		Strikeout/Walk Ratio	
T. Hughson, Bos	23	H. Newhouser, Det	111	D. Leonard, Was	1.9	A. Reynolds, Cle	151	A. Reynolds, Cle	6.8	S. Chandler, NYA	2.48
L. Harris, Phi	17	D. Black, Phi	110	S. Chandler, NYA	1.9	H. Newhouser, Det	144	H. Newhouser, Det	6.6	V. Trucks, Det	2.27
E. Wynn, Was	15	A. Reynolds, Cle	109	T. Bonham, NYA	2.1	S. Chandler, NYA	134	T. Bridges, Det	5.8	T. Bridges, Det	2.03
J. Bagby Jr., Cle	15	D. Trout, Det	101	B. Muncrief, StL	2.1	T. Bridges, Det	124	V. Trucks, Det	5.2	B. Muncrief, StL	1.67
3 tied with	13	E. Wynn, Was	83	V. Trucks, Det	2.3	V. Trucks, Det	118	S. Chandler, NYA	4.8	J. Flores, Phi	1.61

Earned Run Average		Component ERA		Hit Batsmen		Wild Pitches		Opponent Average		Opponent OBP	
S. Chandler, NYA	1.64	S. Chandler, NYA	1.82	A. Reynolds, Cle	7	L. Harris, Phi	8	A. Reynolds, Cle	.202	S. Chandler, NYA	.261
T. Bonham, NYA	2.27	J. Niggeling, 2tm	2.20	D. Black, Phi	6	O. Judd, Bos	7	J. Niggeling, 2tm	.204	V. Trucks, Det	.276
T. Bridges, Det	2.39	B. Wensloff, NYA	2.23	J. Humphries, ChA	6	D. Trout, Det	6	S. Chandler, NYA	.215	B. Wensloff, NYA	.282
D. Trout, Det	2.48	V. Trucks, Det	2.37	J. Niggeling, 2tm	6	D. Leonard, Was	6	B. Wensloff, NYA	.219	T. Bonham, NYA	.282
B. Wensloff, NYA	2.54	T. Bridges, Det	2.49	B. Swift, ChA	6	4 tied with	5	H. Newhouser, Det	.224	J. Niggeling, 2tm	.282

1943 American League Miscellaneous

Managers		
Boston	Joe Cronin	68-84
Chicago	Jimmy Dykes	82-72
Cleveland	Lou Boudreau	82-71
Detroit	Steve O'Neill	78-76
New York	Joe McCarthy	98-56
Philadelphia	Connie Mack	49-105
St. Louis	Luke Sewell	72-80
Washington	Ossie Bluege	84-69

Awards

Most Valuable Player	Spud Chandler, p, NYA
STATS Cy Young	Spud Chandler, NYA
STATS Rookie of the Year	Dick Wakefield, of, Det
STATS Manager of the Year	Ossie Bluege, Was

STATS All-Star Team

C	Jake Early, Was	.258	5	60
1B	Rudy York, Det	.271	34	118
2B	Joe Gordon, NYA	.249	17	69
3B	Bill Johnson, NYA	.280	5	94
SS	Luke Appling, ChA	.328	3	80
OF	Jeff Heath, Cle	.274	18	79
OF	Charlie Keller, NYA	.271	31	86
OF	Dick Wakefield, Det	.316	7	79
P	Tiny Bonham, NYA	15-8	2.27	71 K
P	Spud Chandler, NYA	20-4	1.64	134 K
P	Al Smith, Cle	17-7	2.55	72 K
P	Dizzy Trout, Det	20-12	2.48	111 K
RP	Gordon Maltzberger, ChA	7-4	2.46	14 Sv

Postseason

World Series	New York (AL) 4 vs. St. Louis (NL) 1

Outstanding Performances

Cycles
Leon Culberson, Bos on July 3

1943 National League Standings

Team	Overall					Home Games						Road Games						Park Index		Record by Month					
	W	L	Pct	GB	DIF	W	L	R	OR	HR	OHR	W	L	R	OR	HR	OHR	Run	HR	M/A	May	June	July	Aug	S/O
St. Louis	105	49	.682	—	121	58	21	355	243	33	17	47	28	324	232	37	16	102	90	4-3	18-10	16-10	22-8	20-12	25-6
Cincinnati	87	67	.565	18.0	3	48	29	282	280	17	15	39	38	326	263	26	23	95	65	4-3	13-15	13-13	18-14	21-8	18-14
Brooklyn	81	72	.529	23.5	44	46	31	389	323	21	30	35	41	327	351	18	29	104	107	5-1	20-12	17-13	10-18	13-14	16-14
Pittsburgh	80	74	.519	25.0	1	47	30	364	296	19	15	33	44	305	309	23	29	107	65	3-4	13-13	16-11	18-13	17-20	13-13
Chicago	74	79	.484	30.5	0	36	38	292	300	24	19	38	41	340	300	28	34	99	74	3-4	9-19	13-15	20-9	14-17	15-15
Boston	68	85	.444	36.5	0	38	39	247	327	25	34	30	46	218	285	14	32	113	127	3-2	13-13	12-17	10-18	16-15	14-20
Philadelphia	64	90	.416	41.0	0	33	43	269	314	29	18	31	47	302	362	37	41	90	62	1-4	15-15	14-12	12-23	12-16	10-20
New York	55	98	.359	49.5	0	34	43	291	326	63	52	21	55	267	387	18	28	93	247	2-4	13-17	9-19	11-18	9-20	11-20

Clinch Date—St. Louis 9/18.

Team Batting

Team	G	AB	R	OR	H	2B	3B	HR	TB	RBI	TBB	IBB	SO	HBP	SH	SF	SB	CS	SB%	GDP	Avg	OBP	Slg
Brooklyn	153	5309	716	674	1444	263	35	39	1894	658	580	—	422	21	100	—	58	33	.64	114	.272	.346	.357
St. Louis	157	5438	679	475	1515	259	72	70	2128	638	428	—	438	19	173	—	40	—	—	92	.279	.333	.391
Pittsburgh	157	5353	669	605	1401	240	73	42	1913	620	573	—	566	17	83	—	64	—	—	113	.262	.335	.357
Chicago	154	5279	632	600	1380	207	56	52	1855	579	574	—	522	21	97	—	53	—	—	117	.261	.336	.351
Cincinnati	155	5329	608	543	1362	229	47	43	1814	559	445	—	476	17	120	—	49	—	—	104	.256	.315	.340
Philadelphia	157	5297	571	676	1321	186	36	66	1777	528	499	—	556	21	99	—	29	—	—	143	.249	.316	.335
New York	156	5290	558	713	1309	153	33	81	1771	518	480	—	470	22	103	—	35	33	.51	147	.247	.313	.335
Boston	153	5196	465	612	1213	202	36	39	1604	433	469	—	609	14	99	—	56	—	—	104	.233	.299	.309
NL Total	1242	42491	4898	4898	10945	1739	388	432	14756	4533	4048	—	4059	152	874	—	384	—	—	934	.258	.324	.347
NL Avg Team	155	5311	612	612	1368	217	49	54	1845	567	506	—	507	19	109	—	48	—	—	117	.258	.324	.347

Team Pitching

Team	G	CG	ShO	Rel	Sv	IP	H	R	ER	HR	SH	SF	HB	TBB	IBB	SO	WP	Bk	H/9	SO/9	BB/9	OAvg	OOBP	ERA
St. Louis	157	94	21	104	15	1427.0	1246	475	407	33	89	—	18	477	—	639	20	4	7.9	4.0	3.0	.237	.303	2.57
Pittsburgh	157	74	11	157	12	1404.0	1424	605	481	44	105	—	15	422	—	396	17	3	9.1	2.5	2.7	.263	.319	3.08
Cincinnati	155	78	18	119	17	1404.0	1299	543	489	38	110	—	11	579	—	498	15	2	8.3	3.2	3.7	.251	.328	3.13
Boston	153	87	13	99	4	1397.2	1361	612	505	66	105	—	23	441	—	409	15	3	8.8	2.6	2.8	.255	.314	3.25
Chicago	154	67	13	160	14	1386.0	1379	600	510	53	102	—	18	394	—	513	20	1	9.0	3.3	2.6	.258	.311	3.31
Philadelphia	157	66	10	140	14	1392.2	1436	676	586	59	136	—	20	451	—	431	32	4	9.3	2.8	2.9	.267	.326	3.79
Brooklyn	153	50	13	182	22	1369.2	1326	674	591	59	94	—	29	637	—	588	22	4	8.7	3.9	4.2	.254	.338	3.88
New York	156	35	6	208	19	1394.2	1474	713	633	80	110	—	21	626	—	588	32	1	9.5	3.4	4.0	.272	.350	4.08
NL Total	1242	551	105	1169	117	11175.2	10945	4898	4202	432	851	—	155	4027	—	4062	173	22	8.8	3.3	3.2	.258	.324	3.38
NL Avg Team	155	69	13	146	15	1396.2	1368	612	525	54	106	—	19	503	—	508	22	3	8.8	3.3	3.2	.258	.324	3.38

Team Fielding

Team	G	PO	A	E	TC	DP	PB	Pct
Cincinnati	155	4210	1950	125	6285	193	6	.980
St. Louis	157	4280	1780	151	6211	183	13	.976
New York	156	4189	1892	166	6247	140	11	.973
Pittsburgh	157	4198	1881	170	6249	159	3	.973
Chicago	154	4148	1824	168	6140	138	14	.973
Boston	153	4191	2007	176	6374	139	2	.972
Brooklyn	153	4111	1679	168	5958	137	13	.972
Philadelphia	157	4182	1807	189	6178	143	11	.969
NL Total	1242	33509	14820	1313	49642	1232	73	.974

Team vs. Team Records

	Bos	Bro	ChN	Cin	NYG	Phi	Pit	StL	Won
Bos	—	12	8	11	11	11	12	3	68
Bro	9	—	10	13	14	17	11	7	81
ChN	14	12	—	9	12	10	8	9	74
Cin	11	9	13	—	16	19	9	10	87
NYG	11	8	9	6	—	8	9	4	55
Phi	11	5	12	3	14	—	10	9	64
Pit	10	11	14	13	13	12	—	7	80
StL	19	15	13	12	18	13	15	—	105
Lost	85	72	79	67	98	90	74	49	

1943 National League Batting Leaders

Games			At-Bats			Runs			Hits			Doubles			Triples		
S. Musial, StL		157	T. Holmes, Bos		629	A. Vaughan, Bro		112	S. Musial, StL		220	S. Musial, StL		48	S. Musial, StL		20
V. DiMaggio, Pit		157	L. Klein, StL		627	S. Musial, StL		108	M. Witek, NYG		195	V. DiMaggio, Pit		41	L. Klein, StL		14
B. Elliott, Pit		156	M. Witek, NYG		622	B. Nicholson, ChN		95	B. Herman, Bro		193	B. Herman, Bro		41	P. Lowrey, ChN		12
4 tied with		154	S. Musial, StL		617	P. Cavarretta, ChN		93	B. Nicholson, ChN		188	A. Vaughan, Bro		39	B. Elliott, Pit		12
			C. Workman, Bos		615	E. Stanky, ChN		92	A. Vaughan, Bro		186	T. Holmes, Bos		33	2 tied with		11

Home Runs			Total Bases			Runs Batted In			Walks			Intentional Walks			Strikeouts		
B. Nicholson, ChN		29	S. Musial, StL		347	B. Nicholson, ChN		128	A. Galan, Bro		103	Statistic unavailable			V. DiMaggio, Pit		126
M. Ott, NYG		18	B. Nicholson, ChN		323	B. Elliott, Pit		101	E. Fletcher, Pit		95				B. Nicholson, ChN		86
R. Northey, Phi		16	B. Elliott, Pit		258	B. Herman, Bro		100	M. Ott, NYG		95				E. Joost, Bos		80
C. Triplett, 2tm		15	L. Klein, StL		257	V. DiMaggio, Pit		88	E. Stanky, ChN		92				C. Workman, Bos		72
V. DiMaggio, Pit		15	2 tied with		252	2 tied with		81	E. Tipton, Cin		85				B. Adams, 2tm		71

Hit By Pitch			Sac Hits			Sac Flies			Stolen Bases			Caught Stealing			GDP		
D. Bartell, NYG		7	H. Walker, StL		36	Statistic unavailable			A. Vaughan, Bro		20	Statistic unavailable			S. Gordon, NYG		26
E. Fletcher, Pit		6	E. Miller, Cin		19				P. Lowrey, ChN		13				B. Dahlgren, Phi		22
B. Nicholson, ChN		5	S. Mesner, Cin		17				J. Russell, Pit		12				M. Witek, NYG		21
3 tied with		4	C. Ryan, Bos		16				F. Gustine, Pit		12				B. Herman, Bro		19
			3 tied with		15				C. Workman, Bos		12				2 tied with		18

Runs Created			Runs Created/27 Outs			Batting Average			On-Base Percentage			Slugging Percentage			OBP+Slugging		
S. Musial, StL		130	S. Musial, StL		8.23	S. Musial, StL		.357	S. Musial, StL		.425	S. Musial, StL		.562	S. Musial, StL		.988
B. Nicholson, ChN		119	B. Nicholson, ChN		7.48	B. Herman, Bro		.330	A. Galan, Bro		.412	B. Nicholson, ChN		.531	B. Nicholson, ChN		.917
A. Vaughan, Bro		100	A. Galan, Bro		7.24	W. Cooper, StL		.318	B. Herman, Bro		.398	W. Cooper, StL		.463	B. Elliott, Pit		.820
B. Herman, Bro		100	E. Tipton, Cin		6.69	B. Elliott, Pit		.315	E. Fletcher, Pit		.395	B. Elliott, Pit		.444	E. Tipton, Cin		.819
A. Galan, Bro		97	M. Ott, NYG		6.38	M. Witek, NYG		.313	E. Tipton, Cin		.395	C. Triplett, 2tm		.439	A. Galan, Bro		.818

1943 National League Pitching Leaders

Wins			Losses			Winning Percentage			Games			Games Started			Complete Games		
E. Riddle, Cin		21	N. Andrews, Bos		20	C. Shoun, Cin		.737	A. Adams, NYG		70	J. Vander Meer, Cin		36	R. Sewell, Pit		25
M. Cooper, StL		21	A. Gerheauser, Phi		19	W. Wyatt, Bro		.737	L. Webber, Bro		54	A. Javery, Bos		35	M. Cooper, StL		24
R. Sewell, Pit		21	R. Barrett, Bos		18	M. Cooper, StL		.724	E. Head, Bro		47	N. Andrews, Bos		34	J. Tobin, Bos		24
H. Bithorn, ChN		18	A. Javery, Bos		16	R. Sewell, Pit		.700	C. Shoun, Cin		45	B. Walters, Cin		34	N. Andrews, Bos		23
A. Javery, Bos		17	J. Vander Meer, Cin		16	H. Krist, StL		.688	V. Mungo, NYG		45	2 tied with		33	2 tied with		21

Shutouts			Saves			Games Finished			Batters Faced			Innings Pitched			Hits Allowed		
H. Bithorn, ChN		7	L. Webber, Bro		10	A. Adams, NYG		52	A. Javery, Bos		1286	A. Javery, Bos		303.0	A. Javery, Bos		288
M. Cooper, StL		6	A. Adams, NYG		9	C. Shoun, Cin		29	J. Vander Meer, Cin		1204	J. Vander Meer, Cin		289.0	R. Sewell, Pit		267
4 tied with		5	C. Shoun, Cin		7	L. Webber, Bro		27	N. Andrews, Bos		1167	N. Andrews, Bos		283.2	N. Andrews, Bos		253
			E. Head, Bro		6	J. Beggs, Cin		26	R. Sewell, Pit		1113	M. Cooper, StL		274.0	C. Passeau, ChN		245
			J. Beggs, Cin		6	N. Kimball, 2tm		21	M. Cooper, StL		1109	R. Sewell, Pit		265.1	B. Walters, Cin		244

Home Runs Allowed			Walks			Walks/9 Innings			Strikeouts			Strikeouts/9 Innings			Strikeout/Walk Ratio		
J. Wittig, NYG		14	J. Vander Meer, Cin		162	S. Rowe, Phi		1.3	J. Vander Meer, Cin		174	J. Vander Meer, Cin		5.4	P. Derringer, ChN		1.92
A. Javery, Bos		13	B. Walters, Cin		109	P. Derringer, ChN		2.0	M. Cooper, StL		141	M. Lanier, StL		5.2	H. Pollet, StL		1.91
J. Tobin, Bos		12	E. Riddle, Cin		107	W. Wyatt, Bro		2.1	A. Javery, Bos		134	H. Pollet, StL		4.6	W. Wyatt, Bro		1.86
R. Barrett, Bos		11	A. Javery, Bos		99	W. Hebert, Pit		2.2	M. Lanier, StL		123	M. Cooper, StL		4.6	S. Rowe, Phi		1.79
N. Andrews, Bos		11	K. Higbe, Bro		95	R. Barrett, Bos		2.2	K. Higbe, Bro		108	W. Wyatt, Bro		4.0	M. Cooper, StL		1.78

Earned Run Average			Component ERA			Hit Batsmen			Wild Pitches			Opponent Average			Opponent OBP		
H. Pollet, StL		1.75	H. Pollet, StL		1.66	N. Andrews, Bos		6	B. Walters, Cin		8	H. Pollet, StL		.200	W. Wyatt, Bro		.255
M. Lanier, StL		1.90	W. Wyatt, Bro		1.81	V. Mungo, NYG		6	5 tied with		6	W. Wyatt, Bro		.207	H. Pollet, StL		.261
M. Cooper, StL		2.30	M. Cooper, StL		2.27	6 tied with		5				J. Vander Meer, Cin		.224	S. Rowe, Phi		.276
W. Wyatt, Bro		2.49	S. Rowe, Phi		2.53							M. Cooper, StL		.226	M. Cooper, StL		.286
R. Sewell, Pit		2.54	H. Bithorn, ChN		2.59							D. Barrett, 2tm		.237	N. Andrews, Bos		.291

1943 National League Miscellaneous

Managers

Boston	Bob Coleman	21-25
	Casey Stengel	47-60
Brooklyn	Leo Durocher	81-72
Chicago	Jimmie Wilson	74-79
Cincinnati	Bill McKechnie	87-67
New York	Mel Ott	55-98
Philadelphia	Bucky Harris	38-52
	Freddie Fitzsimmons	26-38
Pittsburgh	Frank Frisch	80-74
St. Louis	Billy Southworth	105-49

Awards

Most Valuable Player	Stan Musial, of, StL
STATS Cy Young	Mort Cooper, StL
STATS Rookie of the Year	Lou Klein, 2b, StL
STATS Manager of the Year	Frank Frisch, Pit

STATS All-Star Team

C	Walker Cooper, StL	.318	9	81
1B	Phil Cavarretta, ChN	.291	8	73
2B	Billy Herman, Bro	.330	2	100
3B	Bob Elliott, Pit	.315	7	101
SS	Arky Vaughan, Bro	.305	5	66
OF	Augie Galan, Bro	.287	9	67
OF	Stan Musial, StL	.357	13	81
OF	Bill Nicholson, ChN	.309	29	128
P	Mort Cooper, StL	21-8	2.30	141 K
P	Max Lanier, StL	15-7	1.90	123 K
P	Elmer Riddle, Cin	21-11	2.66	69 K
P	Rip Sewell, Pit	21-9	2.54	65 K
RP	Ace Adams, NYG	11-7	2.82	9 Sv

Postseason

World Series	St. Louis (NL) 1 vs. New York (AL) 4

Outstanding Performances

None

1944 American League Standings

Team	Overall					Home Games						Road Games						Park Index		Record by Month					
	W	L	Pct	GB	DIF	W	L	R	OR	HR	OHR	W	L	R	OR	HR	OHR	Run	HR	M/A	May	June	July	Aug	S/O
St. Louis	89	65	.578	—	128	54	23	368	272	45	24	35	42	316	315	27	34	101	113	10-2	14-16	15-11	19-13	13-14	18-9
Detroit	88	66	.571	1.0	14	43	34	325	318	38	21	45	32	333	263	22	18	108	148	4-7	17-13	10-16	17-14	19-8	21-8
New York	83	71	.539	6.0	32	47	31	388	307	58	45	36	40	286	310	38	37	114	134	5-4	15-11	13-15	17-15	19-13	14-13
Boston	77	77	.500	12.0	0	47	30	389	311	48	34	30	47	350	365	21	32	98	155	5-5	13-16	18-10	16-14	16-15	9-17
Cleveland	72	82	.468	17.0	0	39	38	345	328	27	16	33	44	298	349	43	24	104	64	4-6	15-16	12-14	19-13	11-18	11-15
Philadelphia	72	82	.468	17.0	2	39	37	277	270	18	28	33	45	248	324	18	30	98	98	5-4	14-15	11-17	13-19	19-13	10-14
Chicago	71	83	.461	18.0	2	41	36	302	304	11	24	30	47	241	358	12	44	101	63	3-6	13-15	14-9	16-18	12-19	13-16
Washington	64	90	.416	25.0	0	40	37	286	268	9	13	24	53	306	396	24	35	79	37	3-5	16-15	13-14	10-21	11-20	11-15

Clinch Date—St. Louis 10/01.

Team Batting

Team	G	AB	R	OR	H	2B	3B	HR	TB	RBI	TBB	IBB	SO	HBP	SH	SF	SB	CS	SB%	GDP	Avg	OBP	Slg
Boston	156	5400	739	676	1456	277	56	69	2052	691	522	—	505	20	110	—	60	40	.60	111	.270	.336	.380
St. Louis	154	5269	684	587	1328	223	45	72	1857	629	531	—	604	21	107	—	44	33	.57	93	.252	.323	.352
New York	154	5331	674	617	1410	216	74	96	2062	631	523	—	627	22	102	—	91	31	.75	130	.264	.333	.387
Detroit	156	5344	658	581	1405	220	44	60	1893	591	532	—	500	24	111	—	61	55	.53	132	.263	.332	.354
Cleveland	155	5481	643	677	1458	270	50	70	2038	615	512	—	593	19	105	—	48	42	.53	134	.266	.331	.372
Washington	154	5319	592	664	1386	186	42	33	1755	530	470	—	477	29	108	—	127	59	.68	111	.261	.324	.330
Chicago	154	5292	543	662	1307	210	55	23	1696	494	439	—	448	21	67	—	66	47	.58	111	.247	.307	.320
Philadelphia	155	5312	525	594	1364	169	47	36	1735	475	422	—	490	17	121	—	42	32	.57	146	.257	.314	.327
AL Total	1238	42748	5058	5058	11114	1771	413	459	15088	4656	3951	—	4244	173	831	—	539	339	.61	968	.260	.325	.353
AL Avg Team	155	5344	632	632	1389	221	52	57	1886	582	494	—	531	22	104	—	67	42	.61	121	.260	.325	.353

Team Pitching

Team	G	CG	ShO	Rel	Sv	IP	H	R	ER	HR	SH	SF	HB	TBB	IBB	SO	WP	Bk	H/9	SO/9	BB/9	OAvg	OOBP	ERA
Detroit	156	87	20	119	8	1400.0	1373	581	480	39	88	—	22	452	—	568	20	5	8.8	3.7	2.9	.257	.318	3.09
St. Louis	154	71	16	127	17	1397.1	1392	587	492	58	98	—	12	469	—	581	18	3	9.0	3.7	3.0	.259	.320	3.17
Philadelphia	155	72	10	107	14	1397.1	1345	594	506	58	100	—	31	390	—	534	30	4	8.7	3.4	2.5	.252	.307	3.26
New York	154	78	9	111	13	1390.1	1351	617	523	82	111	—	13	532	—	529	30	3	8.7	3.4	3.4	.257	.326	3.39
Washington	154	83	13	110	11	1381.0	1410	664	536	48	109	—	24	475	—	503	29	3	9.2	3.3	3.1	.264	.327	3.49
Chicago	154	64	5	112	17	1390.2	1411	662	553	68	127	—	20	420	—	481	26	4	9.1	3.1	2.7	.264	.320	3.58
Cleveland	155	48	7	200	18	1419.1	1428	677	576	40	110	—	28	621	—	524	30	2	9.1	3.3	3.9	.265	.344	3.65
Boston	156	58	7	150	17	1394.1	1404	676	592	66	84	—	23	592	—	524	28	5	9.1	3.4	3.8	.263	.339	3.82
AL Total	1238	561	87	1036	115	11170.1	11114	5058	4258	459	827	—	173	3951	—	4244	211	29	9.0	3.4	3.2	.260	.325	3.43
AL Avg Team	155	70	11	130	14	1396.1	1389	632	532	57	103	—	22	494	—	531	26	4	9.0	3.4	3.2	.260	.325	3.43

Team Fielding

Team	G	PO	A	E	TC	DP	PB	Pct
New York	154	4173	1707	156	6036	170	8	.974
Cleveland	155	4257	1929	165	6351	192	10	.974
Boston	156	4183	1792	171	6146	154	12	.972
St. Louis	154	4185	1745	171	6101	142	12	.972
Philadelphia	155	4192	1745	176	6113	127	12	.971
Chicago	154	4169	1832	183	6184	154	18	.970
Detroit	156	4198	1952	190	6340	184	12	.970
Washington	154	4144	1752	218	6114	156	33	.964
AL Total	1238	33501	14454	1430	49385	1279	117	.971

Team vs. Team Records

	Bos	ChA	Cle	Det	NYA	Phi	StL	Was	Won
Bos	—	17	8	10	11	11	10	10	77
ChA	5	—	14	9	10	9	8	16	71
Cle	14	8	—	10	8	12	10	10	72
Det	12	13	12	—	14	11	9	17	88
NYA	11	12	14	8	—	13	10	15	83
Phi	11	13	10	11	9	—	9	9	72
StL	12	14	12	13	12	13	—	13	89
Was	12	6	12	5	7	13	9	—	64
Lost	77	83	82	66	71	82	65	90	

1944 American League Batting Leaders

Games			At-Bats			Runs			Hits			Doubles			Triples		
M. Rocco, Cle	155		M. Rocco, Cle	653		S. Stirnweiss, NYA	125		S. Stirnweiss, NYA	205		L. Boudreau, Cle	45		S. Stirnweiss, NYA	16
F. Hayes, Phi	155		S. Stirnweiss, NYA	643		B. Johnson, Bos	106		L. Boudreau, Cle	191		K. Keltner, Cle	41		J. Lindell, NYA	16
4 tied with	154		E. Mayo, Det	607		R. Cullenbine, Cle	98		S. Spence, Was	187		B. Johnson, Bos	40		D. Gutteridge, StL	11
			D. Gutteridge, StL	603		B. Doerr, Bos	95		J. Lindell, NYA	178		P. Fox, Bos	38		B. Doerr, Bos	10
			J. Lindell, NYA	594		C. Metkovich, Bos	94		M. Rocco, Cle	174		S. Stirnweiss, NYA	35		5 tied with	9

Home Runs			Total Bases			Runs Batted In			Walks			Intentional Walks			Strikeouts		
N. Etten, NYA	22		J. Lindell, NYA	297		V. Stephens, StL	109		N. Etten, NYA	97		Statistic unavailable			P. Seerey, Cle	99
V. Stephens, StL	20		S. Stirnweiss, NYA	296		B. Johnson, Bos	106		B. Johnson, Bos	95					S. Stirnweiss, NYA	87
J. Lindell, NYA	18		S. Spence, Was	288		J. Lindell, NYA	103		R. Cullenbine, Cle	87					G. McQuinn, StL	74
S. Spence, Was	18		B. Johnson, Bos	277		S. Spence, Was	100		G. McQuinn, StL	85					R. York, Det	73
R. York, Det	18		2 tied with	267		R. York, Det	98		M. Higgins, Det	81					B. Johnson, Bos	67

Hit By Pitch			Sac Hits			Sac Flies			Stolen Bases			Caught Stealing			GDP		
R. Ortiz, Was	8		E. Mayo, Det	28		Statistic unavailable			S. Stirnweiss, NYA	55		G. Case, Was	18		G. Kell, Phi	28
G. Myatt, Was	7		G. Myatt, Was	21					G. Case, Was	49		E. Mayo, Det	13		K. Keltner, Cle	23
4 tied with	6		G. McQuinn, StL	21					G. Myatt, Was	26		T. Tucker, ChA	12		E. Busch, Phi	20
			R. Schalk, ChA	21					W. Moses, ChA	21		S. Stirnweiss, NYA	11		G. Torres, Was	20
			4 tied with	19					D. Gutteridge, StL	20		2 tied with	10		2 tied with	18

Runs Created			Runs Created/27 Outs			Batting Average			On-Base Percentage			Slugging Percentage			OBP+Slugging		
B. Johnson, Bos	120		B. Johnson, Bos	8.66		L. Boudreau, Cle	.327		B. Johnson, Bos	.431		B. Doerr, Bos	.528		B. Johnson, Bos	.959
S. Stirnweiss, NYA	118		B. Doerr, Bos	8.49		B. Doerr, Bos	.325		L. Boudreau, Cle	.406		B. Johnson, Bos	.528		B. Doerr, Bos	.927
S. Spence, Was	113		S. Spence, Was	7.32		B. Johnson, Bos	.324		B. Doerr, Bos	.399		J. Lindell, NYA	.500		S. Spence, Was	.877
V. Stephens, StL	107		V. Stephens, StL	7.19		S. Stirnweiss, NYA	.319		N. Etten, NYA	.399		S. Spence, Was	.486		N. Etten, NYA	.865
N. Etten, NYA	104		A. Zarilla, StL	7.08		S. Spence, Was	.316		M. Byrnes, StL	.396		2 tied with	.466		J. Lindell, NYA	.851

1944 American League Pitching Leaders

Wins			Losses			Winning Percentage			Games			Games Started			Complete Games		
H. Newhouser, Det	29		E. Wynn, Was	17		T. Hughson, Bos	.783		J. Heving, Cle	63		D. Trout, Det	40		D. Trout, Det	33
D. Trout, Det	27		B. Dietrich, ChA	17		H. Newhouser, Det	.763		J. Berry, Phi	53		B. Dietrich, ChA	36		H. Newhouser, Det	25
N. Potter, StL	19		4 tied with	15		N. Potter, StL	.731		D. Trout, Det	49		H. Newhouser, Det	34		4 tied with	19
T. Hughson, Bos	18					G. Maltzberger, ChA	.667		E. Klieman, Cle	47		O. Grove, ChA	33			
2 tied with	17					D. Trout, Det	.659		H. Newhouser, Det	47		B. Newsom, Phi	33			

Shutouts			Saves			Games Finished			Batters Faced			Innings Pitched			Hits Allowed		
D. Trout, Det	7		G. Maltzberger, ChA	12		J. Berry, Phi	47		D. Trout, Det	1421		D. Trout, Det	352.1		D. Trout, Det	314
H. Newhouser, Det	6		J. Berry, Phi	12		G. Maltzberger, ChA	41		H. Newhouser, Det	1271		H. Newhouser, Det	312.1		B. Dietrich, ChA	269
S. Jakucki, StL	4		G. Caster, StL	12		J. Heving, Cle	38		B. Newsom, Phi	1095		B. Newsom, Phi	265.0		H. Newhouser, Det	264
8 tied with	3		J. Heving, Cle	10		G. Caster, StL	34		B. Dietrich, ChA	1061		J. Kramer, StL	257.0		B. Newsom, Phi	243
			F. Barrett, Bos	8		J. Turner, NYA	28		J. Kramer, StL	1058		H. Borowy, NYA	252.2		O. Grove, ChA	237

Home Runs Allowed			Walks			Walks/9 Innings			Strikeouts			Strikeouts/9 Innings			Strikeout/Walk Ratio		
S. Jakucki, StL	17		R. Gentry, Det	108		L. Harris, Phi	1.3		H. Newhouser, Det	187		H. Newhouser, Det	5.4		T. Hughson, Bos	2.73
H. Borowy, NYA	15		H. Newhouser, Det	102		D. Leonard, Was	1.5		D. Trout, Det	144		J. Niggeling, Was	5.3		H. Newhouser, Det	1.83
B. Dietrich, ChA	15		A. Reynolds, Cle	91		T. Bonham, NYA	1.7		B. Newsom, Phi	142		S. Gromek, Cle	5.1		B. Muncrief, StL	1.76
T. Bonham, NYA	14		E. O'Neill, Bos	89		T. Hughson, Bos	1.8		J. Kramer, StL	124		T. Hughson, Bos	5.0		D. Trout, Det	1.73
J. Bowman, Bos	14		3 tied with	88		S. Overmire, Det	1.8		J. Niggeling, Was	121		B. Newsom, Phi	4.8		B. Newsom, Phi	1.73

Earned Run Average			Component ERA			Hit Batsmen			Wild Pitches			Opponent Average			Opponent OBP		
D. Trout, Det	2.12		T. Hughson, Bos	2.04		R. Christopher, Phi	9		D. Leonard, Was	9		S. Gromek, Cle	.219		T. Hughson, Bos	.267
H. Newhouser, Det	2.22		S. Gromek, Cle	2.27		O. Grove, ChA	8		E. O'Neill, Bos	8		J. Niggeling, Was	.221		D. Leonard, Was	.284
T. Hughson, Bos	2.26		H. Newhouser, Det	2.42		E. Klieman, Cle	7		O. Grove, ChA	8		T. Hughson, Bos	.225		D. Trout, Det	.284
J. Niggeling, Was	2.32		D. Trout, Det	2.42		P. Woods, Bos	6		B. Newsom, Phi	8		H. Newhouser, Det	.230		S. Gromek, Cle	.290
J. Kramer, StL	2.49		J. Kramer, StL	2.55		R. Wolff, Was	6		3 tied with	6		H. Borowy, NYA	.236		H. Newhouser, Det	.293

1944 American League Miscellaneous

Managers

Boston	Joe Cronin	77-77
Chicago	Jimmy Dykes	71-83
Cleveland	Lou Boudreau	72-82
Detroit	Steve O'Neill	88-66
New York	Joe McCarthy	83-71
Philadelphia	Connie Mack	72-82
St. Louis	Luke Sewell	89-65
Washington	Ossie Bluege	64-90

Awards

Most Valuable Player	Hal Newhouser, p, Det
STATS Cy Young	Hal Newhouser, Det
STATS Rookie of the Year	Joe Berry, p, Phi
STATS Manager of the Year	Luke Sewell, StL

STATS All-Star Team

C	Frankie Hayes, Phi	.248	13	78
1B	Nick Etten, NYA	.293	22	91
2B	Bobby Doerr, Bos	.325	15	81
3B	Ken Keltner, Cle	.295	13	91
SS	Vern Stephens, StL	.293	20	109
OF	Bob Johnson, Bos	.324	17	106
OF	Stan Spence, Was	.316	18	100
OF	Dick Wakefield, Det	.355	12	53
P	Tex Hughson, Bos	18-5	2.26	112 K
P	Jack Kramer, StL	17-13	2.49	124 K
P	Hal Newhouser, Det	29-9	2.22	187 K
P	Dizzy Trout, Det	27-14	2.12	144 K
RP	Joe Berry, Phi	10-8	1.94	12 Sv

Postseason

World Series	St. Louis (AL) 2 vs. St. Louis (NL) 4

Outstanding Performances

Cycles

Bobby Doerr, Bos	on May 17
Bob Johnson, Bos	on July 6

1944 National League Standings

Team	W	L	Pct	GB	DIF	W	L	R	OR	HR	OHR	W	L	R	OR	HR	OHR	Run	HR	M/A	May	June	July	Aug	S/O
	Overall					Home Games						Road Games						Park Index		Record by Month					
St. Louis	105	49	.682	—	163	54	22	360	230	39	14	51	27	412	260	61	41	90	53	9-2	16-11	17-6	26-7	23-4	14-19
Pittsburgh	90	63	.588	14.5	0	49	28	399	357	23	31	41	35	345	305	47	34	115	66	3-5	16-10	14-11	17-14	21-10	19-13
Cincinnati	89	65	.578	16.0	2	45	33	253	252	14	23	44	32	320	285	37	37	81	49	7-4	15-11	12-15	19-12	14-9	22-14
Chicago	75	79	.487	30.0	1	35	42	346	342	32	40	40	37	356	327	39	35	101	97	1-9	10-14	11-12	20-12	12-18	21-14
New York	67	87	.435	38.0	11	39	36	372	382	75	86	28	51	310	391	18	30	113	353	7-3	11-17	13-19	11-17	10-20	
Boston	65	89	.422	40.0	0	38	40	293	307	51	44	27	49	300	367	29	36	88	145	3-8	16-14	8-17	12-17	11-18	15-15
Brooklyn	63	91	.409	42.0	0	37	39	372	413	27	34	26	52	318	419	29	41	109	89	5-6	13-14	15-13	5-24	10-20	15-14
Philadelphia	61	92	.399	43.5	1	29	49	271	346	20	21	32	43	268	312	35	28	102	63	6-4	9-15	10-17	12-19	11-17	13-20

Clinch Date—St. Louis 9/21.

Team Batting

Team	G	AB	R	OR	H	2B	3B	HR	TB	RBI	TBB	IBB	SO	HBP	SH	SF	SB	CS	SB%	GDP	Avg	OBP	Slg
St. Louis	157	5475	772	490	1507	274	59	100	2199	722	544	—	473	27	124	—	37	—	—	96	.275	.344	.402
Pittsburgh	158	5428	744	662	1441	248	80	70	2059	706	573	—	616	18	79	—	86	—	—	122	.265	.338	.379
Chicago	157	5462	702	669	1425	236	46	71	1966	639	520	—	521	21	105	—	53	—	—	105	.261	.328	.360
Brooklyn	155	5393	690	832	1450	255	51	56	1975	631	486	—	451	14	117	—	45	15	.75	109	.269	.331	.366
New York	155	5306	682	773	1398	191	47	93	1962	644	512	—	480	20	115	—	39	20	.66	121	.263	.331	.370
Boston	155	5282	593	674	1299	250	39	79	1864	558	456	—	509	18	112	—	37	—	—	92	.246	.308	.353
Cincinnati	155	5271	573	537	1340	229	31	51	1784	528	423	—	391	27	99	—	51	—	—	126	.254	.313	.338
Philadelphia	154	5301	539	658	1331	199	42	55	1779	495	470	—	500	31	109	—	32	—	—	114	.251	.316	.336
NL Total	1246	42918	5295	5295	11191	1882	395	575	15588	4923	3984	—	3941	176	860	—	380	—	—	885	.261	.326	.363
NL Avg Team	156	5365	662	662	1399	235	49	72	1949	615	498	—	493	22	108	—	48	—	—	111	.261	.326	.363

Team Pitching

Team	G	CG	ShO	Rel	Sv	IP	H	R	ER	HR	SH	SF	HB	TBB	IBB	SO	WP	Bk	H/9	SO/9	BB/9	OAvg	OOBP	ERA
St. Louis	157	89	26	113	12	1427.0	1228	490	424	55	68	—	22	468	—	637	13	4	7.7	4.0	3.0	.233	.298	2.67
Cincinnati	155	93	17	96	12	1398.1	1292	537	462	60	84	—	19	390	—	369	9	0	8.3	2.4	2.5	.245	.299	2.97
Pittsburgh	158	77	10	140	19	1414.1	1466	662	540	65	116	—	17	435	—	452	12	1	9.3	2.9	2.8	.265	.321	3.44
Chicago	157	70	11	156	13	1400.2	1484	669	558	75	72	—	7	458	—	545	25	0	9.5	3.5	2.9	.272	.330	3.59
Philadelphia	154	66	11	155	6	1395.1	1407	658	564	49	112	—	17	459	—	496	28	4	9.1	3.2	3.0	.260	.320	3.64
Boston	155	70	13	132	12	1388.1	1430	674	566	80	109	—	16	527	—	454	16	2	9.3	2.9	3.4	.267	.335	3.67
New York	155	47	4	200	21	1363.2	1413	773	650	116	107	—	33	587	—	499	38	2	9.3	3.3	3.9	.265	.341	4.29
Brooklyn	155	50	4	187	13	1367.2	1471	832	711	75	131	—	36	660	—	487	36	2	9.7	3.2	4.3	.275	.358	4.68
NL Total	1246	562	96	1179	108	11155.1	11191	5295	4475	575	829	—	167	3984	—	3939	177	15	9.0	3.2	3.2	.261	.326	3.61
NL Avg Team	156	70	12	147	14	1394.1	1399	662	559	72	104	—	21	498	—	492	22	2	9.0	3.2	3.2	.261	.326	3.61

Team Fielding

Team	G	PO	A	E	TC	DP	PB	Pct
St. Louis	157	4276	1678	112	6066	162	9	.982
Cincinnati	155	4194	1929	137	6260	153	5	.978
Philadelphia	154	4177	1875	177	6229	138	13	.972
Boston	155	4159	1896	182	6237	160	6	.971
New York	155	4095	1797	179	6071	128	11	.971
Chicago	157	4202	1878	186	6266	151	10	.970
Pittsburgh	158	4248	1857	191	6296	122	11	.970
Brooklyn	155	4095	1577	197	5869	112	12	.966
NL Total	1246	33446	14487	1361	49294	1126	77	.972

Team vs. Team Records

	Bos	Bro	ChN	Cin	NYG	Phi	Pit	StL	Won
Bos	—	9	11	8	9	11	9	8	65
Bro	13	—	8	8	10	16	4	4	63
ChN	11	14	—	9	10	13	12	6	75
Cin	14	14	13	—	15	13	12	8	89
NYG	13	12	12	7	—	10	7	6	67
Phi	11	6	9	9	12	—	9	5	61
Pit	13	18	10	10	15	12	—	12	90
StL	14	18	16	14	16	17	10	—	105
Lost	89	91	79	65	87	92	63	49	

Seasons: Standings, Leaders

1944 National League Batting Leaders

Games		At-Bats		Runs		Hits		Doubles		Triples	
B. Dahlgren, Pit	158	W. Williams, Cin	653	B. Nicholson, ChN	116	S. Musial, StL	197	S. Musial, StL	51	J. Barrett, Pit	19
B. Nicholson, ChN	156	T. Holmes, Bos	631	S. Musial, StL	112	P. Cavarretta, ChN	197	A. Galan, Bro	43	B. Elliott, Pit	16
4 tied with	155	P. Cavarretta, ChN	614	J. Russell, Pit	109	T. Holmes, Bos	195	T. Holmes, Bos	42	P. Cavarretta, ChN	15
		D. Johnson, ChN	608	J. Hopp, StL	106	D. Walker, Bro	191	3 tied with	37	J. Russell, Pit	14
		R. Sanders, StL	601	P. Cavarretta, ChN	106	J. Russell, Pit	181			S. Musial, StL	14

Home Runs		Total Bases		Runs Batted In		Walks		Intentional Walks		Strikeouts	
B. Nicholson, ChN	33	B. Nicholson, ChN	317	B. Nicholson, ChN	122	A. Galan, Bro	101	Statistic unavailable		V. DiMaggio, Pit	83
M. Ott, NYG	26	S. Musial, StL	312	B. Elliott, Pit	108	B. Nicholson, ChN	93			B. Adams, Phi	74
R. Northey, Phi	22	T. Holmes, Bos	288	R. Northey, Phi	104	S. Musial, StL	90			B. Nicholson, ChN	71
W. Kurowski, StL	20	R. Northey, Phi	283	R. Sanders, StL	102	M. Ott, NYG	90			H. Schultz, Bro	67
F. McCormick, Cin	20	D. Walker, Bro	283	F. McCormick, Cin	102	J. Barrett, Pit	86			J. Russell, Pit	63

Hit By Pitch		Sac Hits		Sac Flies		Stolen Bases		Caught Stealing		GDP	
D. Litwhiler, StL	10	G. Hausmann, NYG	27	Statistic unavailable		J. Barrett, Pit	28	Statistic unavailable		E. Lombardi, NYG	23
B. Adams, Phi	7	E. Verban, StL	19			T. Lupien, Phi	18			B. Dahlgren, Pit	20
B. Nicholson, ChN	6	B. Adams, Phi	17			R. Hughes, ChN	16			F. McCormick, Cin	19
B. Dahlgren, Pit	6	R. Hughes, ChN	17			J. Hopp, StL	15			E. Tipton, Cin	18
5 tied with	5	M. Marion, StL	16			B. Kerr, NYG	14			M. Owen, Bro	18

Runs Created		Runs Created/27 Outs		Batting Average		On-Base Percentage		Slugging Percentage		OBP+Slugging	
S. Musial, StL	134	D. Walker, Bro	9.44	D. Walker, Bro	.357	S. Musial, StL	.440	S. Musial, StL	.549	S. Musial, StL	.990
B. Nicholson, ChN	132	S. Musial, StL	9.42	S. Musial, StL	.347	D. Walker, Bro	.434	B. Nicholson, ChN	.545	M. Ott, NYG	.967
D. Walker, Bro	124	M. Ott, NYG	9.02	J. Medwick, NYG	.337	A. Galan, Bro	.426	M. Ott, NYG	.544	D. Walker, Bro	.963
A. Galan, Bro	121	A. Galan, Bro	8.44	J. Hopp, StL	.336	M. Ott, NYG	.423	D. Walker, Bro	.529	P. Weintraub, NYG	.935
P. Cavarretta, ChN	115	B. Nicholson, ChN	8.38	P. Cavarretta, ChN	.321	P. Weintraub, NYG	.412	P. Weintraub, NYG	.524	B. Nicholson, ChN	.935

1944 National League Pitching Leaders

Wins		Losses		Winning Percentage		Games		Games Started		Complete Games	
B. Walters, Cin	23	K. Raffensberger, Phi	20	T. Wilks, StL	.810	A. Adams, NYG	65	B. Voiselle, NYG	41	J. Tobin, Bos	28
M. Cooper, StL	22	A. Javery, Bos	19	H. Brecheen, StL	.762	X. Rescigno, Pit	48	J. Tobin, Bos	36	B. Walters, Cin	27
B. Voiselle, NYG	21	J. Tobin, Bos	19	M. Cooper, StL	.759	L. Webber, Bro	48	H. Wyse, ChN	34	B. Voiselle, NYG	25
R. Sewell, Pit	21	D. Barrett, Phi	18	B. Walters, Cin	.742	B. Voiselle, NYG	43	N. Andrews, Bos	34	R. Sewell, Pit	24
J. Tobin, Bos	18	5 tied with	16	N. Strincevich, Pit	.667	J. Tobin, Bos	43	3 tied with	33	M. Cooper, StL	22

Shutouts		Saves		Games Finished		Batters Faced		Innings Pitched		Hits Allowed	
M. Cooper, StL	7	A. Adams, NYG	13	A. Adams, NYG	44	B. Voiselle, NYG	1327	B. Voiselle, NYG	312.2	H. Wyse, ChN	277
B. Walters, Cin	6	F. Schmidt, StL	5	X. Rescigno, Pit	25	J. Tobin, Bos	1249	J. Tobin, Bos	299.1	B. Voiselle, NYG	276
M. Lanier, StL	5	X. Rescigno, Pit	5	L. Webber, Bro	23	R. Sewell, Pit	1218	R. Sewell, Pit	286.0	J. Tobin, Bos	271
J. Tobin, Bos	5	C. Cuccurullo, Pit	4	A. Karl, Phi	20	B. Walters, Cin	1162	B. Walters, Cin	285.0	N. Andrews, Bos	263
M. Butcher, Pit	5	C. Davis, Bro	4	2 tied with	17	N. Andrews, Bos	1095	K. Raffensberger, Phi	258.2	R. Sewell, Pit	263

Home Runs Allowed		Walks		Walks/9 Innings		Strikeouts		Strikeouts/9 Innings		Strikeout/Walk Ratio	
B. Voiselle, NYG	31	H. Gregg, Bro	137	K. Raffensberger, Phi	1.6	B. Voiselle, NYG	161	M. Lanier, StL	5.7	K. Raffensberger, Phi	3.02
H. Feldman, NYG	18	B. Voiselle, NYG	118	N. Strincevich, Pit	1.8	M. Lanier, StL	141	A. Javery, Bos	4.9	M. Lanier, StL	1.99
J. Tobin, Bos	18	A. Javery, Bos	118	C. Davis, Bro	1.8	A. Javery, Bos	137	K. Raffensberger, Phi	4.7	H. Brecheen, StL	1.91
R. Sewell, Pit	15	C. Schanz, Phi	103	C. Shoun, Cin	1.9	K. Raffensberger, Phi	136	B. Voiselle, NYG	4.6	C. Passeau, ChN	1.78
N. Andrews, Bos	14	R. Sewell, Pit	99	E. Heusser, Cin	2.0	2 tied with	97	H. Brecheen, StL	4.2	M. Cooper, StL	1.62

Earned Run Average		Component ERA		Hit Batsmen		Wild Pitches		Opponent Average		Opponent OBP	
E. Heusser, Cin	2.38	E. Heusser, Cin	2.30	H. Gregg, Bro	9	H. Gregg, Bro	10	B. Walters, Cin	.219	T. Wilks, StL	.275
B. Walters, Cin	2.40	B. Walters, Cin	2.33	C. Schanz, Phi	6	L. Webber, Bro	8	T. Wilks, StL	.227	E. Heusser, Cin	.275
M. Cooper, StL	2.46	T. Wilks, StL	2.34	R. Fischer, NYG	6	B. Voiselle, NYG	7	E. Heusser, Cin	.231	B. Walters, Cin	.281
T. Wilks, StL	2.64	M. Cooper, StL	2.48	E. Pyle, NYG	6	D. Barrett, Phi	7	B. Voiselle, NYG	.232	K. Raffensberger, Phi	.285
M. Lanier, StL	2.65	M. Lanier, StL	2.52	4 tied with	5	3 tied with	6	M. Lanier, StL	.234	M. Cooper, StL	.288

1944 National League Miscellaneous

Managers

Boston	Bob Coleman	65-89
Brooklyn	Leo Durocher	63-91
Chicago	Jimmie Wilson	1-9
	Roy Johnson	0-1
	Charlie Grimm	74-69
Cincinnati	Bill McKechnie	89-65
New York	Mel Ott	67-87
Philadelphia	Freddie Fitzsimmons	61-92
Pittsburgh	Frank Frisch	90-63
St. Louis	Billy Southworth	105-49

Awards

Most Valuable Player	Marty Marion, ss, StL
STATS Cy Young	Bucky Walters, Cin
STATS Rookie of the Year	Bill Voiselle, p, NYG
STATS Manager of the Year	Billy Southworth, StL

STATS All-Star Team

C	Walker Cooper, StL	.317	13	72
1B	Phil Cavarretta, ChN	.321	5	82
2B	Pete Coscarart, Pit	.264	4	42
3B	Bob Elliott, Pit	.297	10	108
SS	Marty Marion, StL	.267	6	63
OF	Stan Musial, StL	.347	12	94
OF	Bill Nicholson, ChN	.287	33	122
OF	Dixie Walker, Bro	.357	13	91
P	Mort Cooper, StL	22-7	2.46	97 K
P	Bill Voiselle, NYG	21-16	3.02	161 K
P	Bucky Walters, Cin	23-8	2.40	77 K
P	Ted Wilks, StL	17-4	2.64	70 K
RP	Ace Adams, NYG	8-11	4.25	13 Sv

Postseason

World Series	St. Louis (NL) 4 vs. St. Louis (AL) 2

Outstanding Performances

No-Hitters
Jim Tobin, Bos   vs. Bro on April 27
Clyde Shoun, Cin   vs. Bos on May 15

Three-Homer Games
Bill Nicholson, ChN   on July 23

Cycles
Dixie Walker, Bro   on September 2

1945 American League Standings

Team	Overall					Home Games						Road Games						Park Index		Record by Month					
	W	L	Pct	GB	DIF	W	L	R	OR	HR	OHR	W	L	R	OR	HR	OHR	Run	HR	M/A	May	June	July	Aug	S/O
Detroit	88	65	.575	—	113	50	26	333	285	43	28	38	39	300	280	34	20	108	133	6-3	13-9	18-12	14-12	18-17	19-12
Washington	87	67	.565	1.5	1	46	31	278	255	1	6	41	36	344	307	26	36	82	11	6-5	9-14	16-10	14-12	24-15	18-11
St. Louis	81	70	.536	6.0	1	47	27	353	291	32	33	34	43	244	257	31	26	134	119	4-5	12-11	10-15	16-13	23-12	16-14
New York	81	71	.533	6.5	25	48	28	395	297	65	51	33	43	281	309	28	15	117	270	7-4	15-9	13-12	12-15	17-16	17-15
Cleveland	73	72	.503	11.0	0	44	33	292	273	27	15	29	39	265	275	38	24	92	60	2-7	12-10	12-16	18-11	19-13	10-15
Chicago	71	78	.477	15.0	37	44	29	305	277	8	34	27	49	291	356	14	29	94	102	5-2	12-14	15-14	12-15	16-16	11-17
Boston	71	83	.461	17.5	0	42	35	306	299	22	28	29	48	293	375	28	30	91	86	3-8	13-11	16-8	14-16	13-23	12-17
Philadelphia	52	98	.347	34.5	0	39	35	265	270	16	21	13	63	229	368	17	34	92	75	6-5	8-16	6-19	10-16	8-26	14-16

Clinch Date—Detroit 9/30.

Team Batting

Team	G	AB	R	OR	H	2B	3B	HR	TB	RBI	TBB	IBB	SO	HBP	SH	SF	SB	CS	SB%	GDP	Avg	OBP	Slg
New York	152	5176	676	606	1343	189	61	93	1933	639	618	—	567	36	95	—	64	43	.60	102	.259	.343	.373
Detroit	155	5257	633	565	1345	227	47	77	1897	588	517	—	533	9	102	—	60	54	.53	112	.256	.324	.361
Washington	156	5326	622	562	1375	197	63	27	1779	569	545	—	489	23	114	—	110	65	.63	116	.258	.330	.334
Boston	157	5367	599	674	1393	225	44	50	1856	559	541	—	534	23	87	—	72	50	.59	117	.260	.330	.346
St. Louis	154	5227	597	548	1302	215	37	63	1780	557	500	—	555	15	124	—	25	31	.45	102	.249	.316	.341
Chicago	150	5077	596	633	1330	204	55	22	1710	544	470	—	467	14	100	—	78	54	.59	116	.262	.326	.337
Cleveland	147	4898	557	548	1249	216	48	65	1756	521	505	—	578	14	119	—	19	31	.38	116	.255	.326	.359
Philadelphia	153	5296	494	638	1297	201	37	33	1671	440	449	—	463	19	96	—	25	45	.36	105	.245	.306	.316
AL Total	1224	41624	4774	4774	10634	1674	392	430	14382	4417	4145	—	4186	153	837	—	453	373	.55	890	.255	.325	.346
AL Avg Team	153	5203	597	597	1329	209	49	54	1798	552	518	—	523	19	105	—	57	47	.55	111	.255	.325	.346

Team Pitching

Team	G	CG	ShO	Rel	Sv	IP	H	R	ER	HR	SH	SF	HB	TBB	IBB	SO	WP	Bk	H/9	SO/9	BB/9	OAvg	OOBP	ERA
Washington	156	82	19	110	11	1412.1	1307	562	459	42	87	—	15	440	—	550	18	4	8.3	3.5	2.8	.242	.301	2.92
Detroit	155	78	19	131	16	1393.2	1305	565	463	48	108	—	23	538	—	588	29	5	8.4	3.8	3.5	.250	.322	2.99
St. Louis	154	91	10	110	8	1382.2	1307	548	483	59	108	—	5	506	—	570	16	3	8.5	3.7	3.3	.249	.316	3.14
Cleveland	147	76	14	116	12	1302.1	1269	548	479	39	103	—	22	501	—	497	23	5	8.8	3.4	3.5	.257	.328	3.31
New York	152	78	9	102	14	1355.0	1277	606	520	66	97	—	11	485	—	474	27	4	8.5	3.1	3.2	.250	.316	3.45
Philadelphia	153	65	11	120	8	1381.0	1380	638	556	55	121	—	22	571	—	531	18	1	9.0	3.5	3.7	.262	.337	3.62
Chicago	150	84	13	86	13	1330.2	1400	633	546	63	91	—	30	448	—	486	17	2	9.5	3.3	3.0	.270	.332	3.69
Boston	157	71	15	135	13	1390.2	1389	674	587	58	119	—	26	656	—	490	30	4	9.0	3.2	4.2	.264	.348	3.80
AL Total	1224	625	110	910	95	10948.1	10634	4774	4093	430	834	—	154	4145	—	4186	178	28	8.7	3.4	3.4	.255	.325	3.36
AL Avg Team	153	78	14	114	12	1368.1	1329	597	512	54	104	—	19	518	—	523	22	4	8.7	3.4	3.4	.255	.325	3.36

Team Fielding

Team	G	PO	A	E	TC	DP	PB	Pct
Cleveland	147	3909	1561	126	5596	149	18	.977
St. Louis	154	4148	1674	143	5965	123	6	.976
Detroit	155	4182	1877	158	6217	173	11	.975
Boston	157	4168	1964	169	6301	198	18	.973
Philadelphia	153	4140	1903	168	6211	160	9	.973
New York	152	4065	1733	175	5973	170	8	.971
Washington	156	4245	1766	183	6194	124	40	.970
Chicago	150	3991	1814	180	5985	139	9	.970
AL Total	1224	32848	14292	1302	48442	1236	119	.973

Team vs. Team Records

	Bos	ChA	Cle	Det	NYA	Phi	StL	Was	Won
Bos	—	9	11	12	6	14	8	11	71
ChA	13	—	11	10	9	12	8	8	71
Cle	11	8	—	11	12	12	11	8	73
Det	10	12	11	—	15	15	15	10	88
NYA	16	12	9	7	—	16	7	14	81
Phi	8	10	6	7	6	—	10	5	52
StL	14	13	10	6	15	12	—	11	81
Was	11	14	14	12	8	17	11	—	87
Lost	83	78	72	65	71	98	70	67	

1945 American League Batting Leaders

Games		At-Bats		Runs		Hits		Doubles		Triples	
R. York, Det	155	S. Stirnweiss, NYA	632	S. Stirnweiss, NYA	107	S. Stirnweiss, NYA	195	W. Moses, ChA	35	S. Stirnweiss, NYA	22
R. Cullenbine, 2tm	154	I. Hall, Phi	616	V. Stephens, StL	90	W. Moses, ChA	168	G. Binks, Was	32	J. Kuhel, Was	15
S. Stirnweiss, NYA	152	R. York, Det	595	R. Cullenbine, 2tm	83	V. Stephens, StL	165	S. Stirnweiss, NYA	32	J. Dickshot, ChA	13
N. Etten, NYA	152	D. Siebert, Phi	573	3 tied with	81	I. Hall, Phi	161	G. McQuinn, StL	31	J. Dickshot, ChA	10
2 tied with	151	V. Stephens, StL	571			N. Etten, NYA	161	2 tied with	30	H. Peck, Phi	9

Home Runs		Total Bases		Runs Batted In		Walks		Intentional Walks		Strikeouts	
V. Stephens, StL	24	S. Stirnweiss, NYA	301	N. Etten, NYA	111	R. Cullenbine, 2tm	112	Statistic unavailable		P. Seerey, Cle	97
N. Etten, NYA	18	V. Stephens, StL	270	R. Cullenbine, 2tm	93	E. Lake, Bos	106			R. York, Det	85
R. Cullenbine, 2tm	18	N. Etten, NYA	247	V. Stephens, StL	89	O. Grimes, NYA	97			M. Byrnes, StL	84
R. York, Det	18	R. York, Det	246	R. York, Det	87	N. Etten, NYA	90			O. Grimes, NYA	73
J. Heath, Cle	15	W. Moses, ChA	239	G. Binks, Was	81	J. Kuhel, Was	79			2 tied with	70

Hit By Pitch		Sac Hits		Sac Flies		Stolen Bases		Caught Stealing		GDP	
F. Crosetti, NYA	10	R. Schalk, ChA	24	Statistic unavailable		S. Stirnweiss, NYA	33	S. Stirnweiss, NYA	17	R. York, Det	23
C. Metkovich, Bos	6	L. Boudreau, Cle	20			G. Myatt, Was	30	G. Case, Was	16	N. Etten, NYA	21
I. Hall, Phi	6	G. Myatt, Was	20			G. Case, Was	30	B. Maier, Det	11	J. Dickshot, ChA	16
O. Grimes, NYA	6	M. Byrnes, StL	19			C. Metkovich, Bos	19	G. Myatt, Was	11	B. Estalella, Phi	15
5 tied with	4	S. Newsome, Bos	17			J. Dickshot, ChA	18	I. Hall, Phi	10	3 tied with	14

Runs Created		Runs Created/27 Outs		Batting Average		On-Base Percentage		Slugging Percentage		OBP+Slugging	
S. Stirnweiss, NYA	114	R. Cullenbine, 2tm	6.86	S. Stirnweiss, NYA	.309	E. Lake, Bos	.412	S. Stirnweiss, NYA	.476	S. Stirnweiss, NYA	.862
R. Cullenbine, 2tm	103	S. Stirnweiss, NYA	6.57	T. Cuccinello, ChA	.308	R. Cullenbine, 2tm	.401	V. Stephens, StL	.473	R. Cullenbine, 2tm	.845
W. Moses, ChA	99	W. Moses, ChA	6.51	J. Dickshot, ChA	.302	B. Estalella, Phi	.399	R. Cullenbine, 2tm	.444	B. Estalella, Phi	.834
V. Stephens, StL	97	V. Stephens, StL	6.20	B. Estalella, Phi	.299	O. Grimes, NYA	.395	N. Etten, NYA	.437	V. Stephens, StL	.825
N. Etten, NYA	93	E. Lake, Bos	6.18	G. Myatt, Was	.296	N. Etten, NYA	.387	B. Estalella, Phi	.435	N. Etten, NYA	.824

1945 American League Pitching Leaders

Wins		Losses		Winning Percentage		Games		Games Started		Complete Games	
H. Newhouser, Det	25	B. Newsom, Phi	20	B. Muncrief, StL	.765	J. Berry, Phi	52	H. Newhouser, Det	36	H. Newhouser, Det	29
B. Ferriss, Bos	21	D. Trout, Det	15	H. Newhouser, Det	.735	M. Pieretti, Was	44	B. Newsom, Phi	34	B. Ferriss, Bos	26
R. Wolff, Was	20	J. Kramer, StL	15	D. Leonard, Was	.708	A. Reynolds, Cle	44	N. Potter, StL	32	R. Wolff, Was	21
S. Gromek, Cle	19	M. Haefner, Was	14	S. Gromek, Cle	.679	D. Trout, Det	41	B. Ferriss, Bos	31	S. Gromek, Cle	21
2 tied with	18	J. Humphries, ChA	14	B. Ferriss, Bos	.677	H. Newhouser, Det	40	D. Trout, Det	31	N. Potter, StL	21

Shutouts		Saves		Games Finished		Batters Faced		Innings Pitched		Hits Allowed	
H. Newhouser, Det	8	J. Turner, NYA	10	J. Berry, Phi	40	H. Newhouser, Det	1261	H. Newhouser, Det	313.1	B. Ferriss, Bos	263
B. Ferriss, Bos	5	J. Berry, Phi	5	F. Barrett, Bos	26	B. Newsom, Phi	1116	B. Ferriss, Bos	264.2	B. Newsom, Phi	255
A. Benton, Det	5	5 tied with	4	J. Turner, NYA	26	B. Ferriss, Bos	1103	B. Newsom, Phi	257.1	D. Trout, Det	252
5 tied with	4			J. Johnson, ChA	19	A. Reynolds, Cle	1074	N. Potter, StL	255.1	H. Newhouser, Det	239
				2 tied with	18	D. Trout, Det	1041	S. Gromek, Cle	251.0	M. Pieretti, Was	235

Home Runs Allowed		Walks		Walks/9 Innings		Strikeouts		Strikeouts/9 Innings		Strikeout/Walk Ratio	
J. Kramer, StL	13	A. Reynolds, Cle	130	T. Bonham, NYA	1.1	H. Newhouser, Det	212	H. Newhouser, Det	6.1	D. Leonard, Was	2.74
B. Bevens, NYA	12	E. O'Neill, Bos	117	D. Leonard, Was	1.5	N. Potter, StL	129	J. Kramer, StL	4.6	R. Wolff, Was	2.04
O. Grove, ChA	12	H. Newhouser, Det	110	R. Wolff, Was	1.9	B. Newsom, Phi	127	N. Potter, StL	4.5	H. Newhouser, Det	1.93
B. Newsom, Phi	12	B. Newsom, Phi	103	S. Gromek, Cle	2.4	A. Reynolds, Cle	112	B. Newsom, Phi	4.4	T. Bonham, NYA	1.91
3 tied with	11	T. Shirley, StL	93	N. Potter, StL	2.4	2 tied with	108	T. Lee, ChA	4.3	N. Potter, StL	1.90

Earned Run Average		Component ERA		Hit Batsmen		Wild Pitches		Opponent Average		Opponent OBP	
H. Newhouser, Det	1.81	R. Wolff, Was	1.87	T. Lee, ChA	10	H. Newhouser, Det	10	H. Newhouser, Det	.211	R. Wolff, Was	.258
A. Benton, Det	2.02	H. Newhouser, Det	2.07	R. Christopher, Phi	9	L. Knerr, Phi	7	R. Wolff, Was	.215	N. Potter, StL	.279
R. Wolff, Was	2.12	N. Potter, StL	2.27	B. Ferriss, Bos	7	E. O'Neill, Bos	6	N. Potter, StL	.226	D. Leonard, Was	.279
D. Leonard, Was	2.13	D. Leonard, Was	2.46	A. Gettel, NYA	7	H. Borowy, NYA	6	B. Muncrief, StL	.239	H. Newhouser, Det	.281
T. Lee, ChA	2.44	S. Gromek, Cle	2.61	M. Haefner, Was	7	O. Grove, ChA	6	A. Benton, Det	.241	T. Bonham, NYA	.288

1945 American League Miscellaneous

Managers

Boston	Joe Cronin	71-83
Chicago	Jimmy Dykes	71-78
Cleveland	Lou Boudreau	73-72
Detroit	Steve O'Neill	88-65
New York	Joe McCarthy	81-71
Philadelphia	Connie Mack	52-98
St. Louis	Luke Sewell	81-70
Washington	Ossie Bluege	87-67

Awards

Most Valuable Player	Hal Newhouser, p, Det
STATS Cy Young	Hal Newhouser, Det
STATS Rookie of the Year	Boo Ferriss, p, Bos
STATS Manager of the Year	Steve O'Neill, Det

STATS All-Star Team

C	Frankie Hayes, 2tm	.234	9	57
1B	Nick Etten, NYA	.285	18	111
2B	Snuffy Stirnweiss, NYA	.309	10	64
3B	Tony Cuccinello, ChA	.308	2	49
SS	Vern Stephens, StL	.289	24	89
OF	Roy Cullenbine, 2tm	.272	18	93
OF	Hank Greenberg, Det	.311	13	60
OF	Jeff Heath, Cle	.305	15	61
P	Boo Ferriss, Bos	21-10	2.96	94 K
P	Dutch Leonard, Was	17-7	2.13	96 K
P	Hal Newhouser, Det	25-9	1.81	212 K
P	Roger Wolff, Was	20-10	2.12	108 K
RP	Joe Berry, Phi	8-7	2.35	5 Sv

Postseason

World Series	Detroit (AL) 4 vs. Chicago (NL) 3

Outstanding Performances

No-Hitters
Dick Fowler, Phi   vs. StL on September 9
Three-Homer Games
Pat Seerey, Cle   on July 13

1945 National League Standings

Team	Overall W	L	Pct	GB	DIF	Home Games W	L	R	OR	HR	OHR	Road Games W	L	R	OR	HR	OHR	Park Index Run	HR	Record by Month M/A	May	June	July	Aug	S/O
Chicago	98	56	.636	—	88	49	26	330	253	24	17	49	30	405	279	33	40	90	59	7-4	11-12	14-11	26-5	18-13	22-11
St. Louis	95	59	.617	3.0	0	48	29	368	286	29	29	47	30	388	297	35	41	95	76	5-4	15-13	16-10	19-14	19-8	21-10
Brooklyn	87	67	.565	11.0	22	48	30	387	347	29	34	39	37	408	377	28	40	91	90	5-5	16-11	19-8	13-15	15-14	19-14
Pittsburgh	82	72	.532	16.0	3	45	34	407	352	31	25	37	38	346	334	41	36	106	69	4-7	15-9	14-14	16-16	18-16	15-10
New York	78	74	.513	19.0	58	47	30	366	325	83	47	31	44	302	375	31	38	99	184	8-4	18-7	10-19	14-17	17-10	11-17
Boston	67	85	.441	30.0	0	36	38	411	395	69	63	31	47	310	333	32	36	132	205	6-5	7-15	17-11	12-21	14-16	11-17
Cincinnati	61	93	.396	37.0	2	36	41	267	307	25	23	25	52	269	387	31	47	87	62	5-6	10-12	13-13	14-17	7-25	12-20
Philadelphia	46	108	.299	52.0	0	22	55	261	450	23	28	24	53	287	415	33	33	101	77	3-8	7-20	7-24	9-18	11-17	9-21

Clinch Date—Chicago 9/29.

Team Batting

Team	G	AB	R	OR	H	2B	3B	HR	TB	RBI	TBB	IBB	SO	HBP	SH	SF	SB	CS	SB%	GDP	Avg	OBP	Slg
Brooklyn	155	5418	795	724	1468	257	71	57	2038	722	629	—	434	25	111	—	75	—	—	87	.271	.349	.376
St. Louis	155	5487	756	583	1498	256	44	64	2034	698	515	—	488	26	138	—	55	—	—	75	.273	.338	.371
Pittsburgh	155	5343	753	686	1425	259	56	72	2012	695	590	—	480	17	88	—	81	—	—	122	.267	.342	.377
Chicago	155	5298	735	532	1465	229	52	57	1969	674	554	—	462	32	150	—	69	—	—	93	.277	.349	.372
Boston	154	5441	721	728	1453	229	25	101	2035	668	520	—	510	26	91	—	82	—	—	107	.267	.334	.374
New York	154	5350	668	700	1439	175	35	114	2026	626	501	—	457	40	100	—	38	—	—	111	.269	.336	.379
Philadelphia	154	5203	548	865	1278	197	27	56	1697	503	449	—	501	15	71	—	54	—	—	113	.246	.307	.326
Cincinnati	154	5283	536	694	1317	221	26	56	1758	498	392	—	532	26	95	—	71	—	—	112	.249	.304	.333
NL Total	1236	42823	5512	5512	11343	1823	336	577	15569	5084	4150	—	3864	207	844	—	525	—	—	820	.265	.333	.364
NL Avg Team	155	5353	689	689	1418	228	42	72	1946	636	519	—	483	26	106	—	66	—	—	103	.265	.333	.364

Team Pitching

Team	G	CG	ShO	Rel	Sv	IP	H	R	ER	HR	SH	SF	HB	TBB	IBB	SO	WP	Bk	H/9	SO/9	BB/9	OAvg	OOBP	ERA
Chicago	155	86	15	135	14	1366.1	1301	532	452	57	76	—	21	385	—	541	19	2	8.6	3.6	2.5	.249	.303	2.98
St. Louis	155	77	18	156	9	1408.2	1351	583	507	70	86	—	27	497	—	510	12	2	8.6	3.3	3.2	.253	.319	3.24
Brooklyn	155	61	7	163	18	1392.1	1357	724	573	74	95	—	34	586	—	557	32	2	8.8	3.6	3.8	.253	.330	3.70
Pittsburgh	155	73	8	142	16	1387.1	1477	686	580	61	85	—	19	455	—	518	17	2	9.6	3.4	3.0	.272	.330	3.76
Cincinnati	154	77	11	132	6	1365.2	1438	694	607	70	116	—	27	534	—	372	20	1	9.5	2.5	3.5	.271	.341	4.00
Boston	154	57	7	166	13	1391.2	1474	728	624	99	107	—	19	557	—	404	21	4	9.5	2.6	3.6	.272	.342	4.04
New York	154	53	13	179	21	1374.2	1401	700	620	85	117	—	25	528	—	530	21	5	9.2	3.5	3.5	.263	.332	4.06
Philadelphia	154	31	4	212	26	1352.2	1544	865	697	61	122	—	29	608	—	432	38	5	10.3	2.9	4.0	.285	.361	4.64
NL Total	1236	515	83	1285	123	11039.1	11343	5512	4660	577	804	—	201	4150	—	3864	180	23	9.2	3.2	3.4	.265	.333	3.80
NL Avg Team	155	64	10	161	15	1379.1	1418	689	583	72	101	—	25	519	—	483	23	3	9.2	3.2	3.4	.265	.333	3.80

Team Fielding

Team	G	PO	A	E	TC	DP	PB	Pct
Chicago	155	4098	1782	121	6001	124	5	.980
St. Louis	155	4226	1641	137	6004	150	12	.977
Cincinnati	154	4102	1828	146	6076	138	11	.976
New York	154	4124	1844	166	6134	112	12	.973
Pittsburgh	155	4158	1827	178	6163	141	7	.971
Boston	154	4172	1809	193	6174	160	4	.969
Brooklyn	155	4174	1678	230	6082	144	9	.962
Philadelphia	154	4047	1818	234	6099	150	12	.962
NL Total	1236	33101	14227	1405	48733	1119	72	.971

Team vs. Team Records

	Bos	Bro	ChN	Cin	NYG	Phi	Pit	StL	Won
Bos	—	9	7	10	10	14	7	10	67
Bro	13	—	8	11	15	19	12	9	87
ChN	15	14	—	21	11	17	14	6	98
Cin	12	11	1	—	6	12	10	9	61
NYG	10	7	11	16	—	17	11	6	78
Phi	8	3	5	10	5	—	6	9	46
Pit	15	10	8	12	11	16	—	10	82
StL	12	13	16	13	16	13	12	—	95
Lost	85	67	56	93	74	108	72	59	

1945 National League Batting Leaders

Games			At-Bats			Runs			Hits			Doubles			Triples		
E. Verban, StL	155		D. Clay, Cin	656		E. Stanky, Bro	128		T. Holmes, Bos	224		T. Holmes, Bos	47		L. Olmo, Bro	13	
G. Hausmann, NYG	154		T. Holmes, Bos	636		G. Rosen, Bro	126		G. Rosen, Bro	197		D. Walker, Bro	42		A. Pafko, ChN	12	
T. Holmes, Bos	154		B. Adams, 2tm	634		T. Holmes, Bos	125		S. Hack, ChN	193		B. Elliott, Pit	36		J. Rucker, NYG	11	
B. Adams, 2tm	154		G. Hausmann, NYG	623		A. Galan, Bro	114		D. Clay, Cin	184		A. Galan, Bro	36		G. Rosen, Bro	11	
D. Walker, Bro	154		D. Walker, Bro	607		S. Hack, ChN	110		2 tied with	182		P. Cavarretta, ChN	34		P. Cavarretta, ChN	10	

Home Runs			Total Bases			Runs Batted In			Walks			Intentional Walks			Strikeouts		
T. Holmes, Bos	28		T. Holmes, Bos	367		D. Walker, Bro	124		E. Stanky, Bro	148		Statistic unavailable			V. DiMaggio, Phi	91	
C. Workman, Bos	25		B. Adams, 2tm	279		T. Holmes, Bos	117		A. Galan, Bro	114					B. Adams, 2tm	80	
B. Adams, 2tm	22		G. Rosen, Bro	279		A. Pafko, ChN	110		S. Hack, ChN	99					B. Nicholson, ChN	73	
W. Kurowski, StL	21		D. Walker, Bro	266		L. Olmo, Bro	110		B. Nicholson, ChN	92					C. Gillenwater, Bos	70	
M. Ott, NYG	21		W. Kurowski, StL	261		B. Adams, 2tm	109		R. Sanders, StL	83					J. Barrett, Pit	68	

Hit By Pitch			Sac Hits			Sac Flies			Stolen Bases			Caught Stealing			GDP		
A. Pafko, ChN	8		D. Johnson, ChN	22		Statistic unavailable			R. Schoendienst, StL	26		Statistic unavailable			B. Dahlgren, Pit	23	
N. Reyes, NYG	8		A. Pafko, ChN	21					J. Barrett, Pit	25					F. McCormick, Cin	20	
M. Ott, NYG	8		P. Lowrey, ChN	21					D. Clay, Cin	19					C. Gillenwater, Bos	17	
C. Workman, Bos	6		E. Stanky, Bro	19					3 tied with	15					S. Mesner, Cin	17	
B. Nicholson, ChN	6		2 tied with	17											B. Elliott, Pit	16	

Runs Created			Runs Created/27 Outs			Batting Average			On-Base Percentage			Slugging Percentage			OBP+Slugging		
T. Holmes, Bos	151		T. Holmes, Bos	9.51		P. Cavarretta, ChN	.355		P. Cavarretta, ChN	.449		T. Holmes, Bos	.577		T. Holmes, Bos	.997	
A. Galan, Bro	121		P. Cavarretta, ChN	9.34		T. Holmes, Bos	.352		A. Galan, Bro	.423		W. Kurowski, StL	.511		P. Cavarretta, ChN	.949	
P. Cavarretta, ChN	115		A. Galan, Bro	7.86		G. Rosen, Bro	.325		S. Hack, ChN	.420		P. Cavarretta, ChN	.500		M. Ott, NYG	.910	
G. Rosen, Bro	113		M. Ott, NYG	7.54		S. Hack, ChN	.323		T. Holmes, Bos	.420		M. Ott, NYG	.499		W. Kurowski, StL	.894	
S. Hack, ChN	113		W. Kurowski, StL	7.36		W. Kurowski, StL	.323		E. Stanky, Bro	.417		L. Olmo, Bro	.462		A. Galan, Bro	.864	

1945 National League Pitching Leaders

Wins			Losses			Winning Percentage			Games			Games Started			Complete Games		
R. Barrett, 2tm	23		D. Barrett, Phi	20		H. Brecheen, StL	.789		A. Karl, Phi	67		B. Voiselle, NYG	35		R. Barrett, 2tm	24	
H. Wyse, ChN	22		E. Heusser, Cin	16		K. Burkhart, StL	.692		A. Adams, NYG	65		H. Gregg, Bro	34		H. Wyse, ChN	23	
K. Burkhart, StL	18		C. Schanz, Phi	15		H. Wyse, ChN	.688		J. Hutchings, Bos	57		H. Wyse, ChN	34		C. Passeau, ChN	19	
H. Gregg, Bro	18		V. Kennedy, 2tm	15		V. Mungo, NYG	.667		H. Fox, Cin	45		R. Barrett, 2tm	34		N. Strincevich, Pit	18	
C. Passeau, ChN	17		2 tied with	14		R. Barrett, 2tm	.657		R. Barrett, 2tm	45		P. Roe, Pit	31		E. Heusser, Cin	18	

Shutouts			Saves			Games Finished			Batters Faced			Innings Pitched			Hits Allowed		
C. Passeau, ChN	5		A. Karl, Phi	15		A. Adams, NYG	50		R. Barrett, 2tm	1175		R. Barrett, 2tm	284.2		R. Barrett, 2tm	287	
K. Burkhart, StL	4		A. Adams, NYG	15		A. Karl, Phi	41		H. Wyse, ChN	1139		H. Wyse, ChN	278.1		H. Wyse, ChN	272	
B. Donnelly, StL	4		X. Rescigno, Pit	9		D. Hendrickson, Bos	27		H. Gregg, Bro	1092		H. Gregg, Bro	254.1		B. Voiselle, NYG	249	
B. Voiselle, NYG	4		3 tied with	5		X. Rescigno, Pit	27		B. Voiselle, NYG	1034		P. Roe, Pit	235.0		E. Heusser, Cin	248	
E. Heusser, Cin	4					C. King, Bro	25		N. Strincevich, Pit	966		B. Voiselle, NYG	232.1		N. Strincevich, Pit	235	

Home Runs Allowed			Walks			Walks/9 Innings			Strikeouts			Strikeouts/9 Innings			Strikeout/Walk Ratio		
J. Hutchings, Bos	21		H. Gregg, Bro	120		C. Davis, Bro	1.3		P. Roe, Pit	148		P. Roe, Pit	5.7		P. Roe, Pit	3.22	
R. Barrett, 2tm	18		B. Voiselle, NYG	97		R. Barrett, 2tm	1.7		H. Gregg, Bro	139		H. Gregg, Bro	4.9		C. Davis, Bro	1.86	
H. Wyse, ChN	17		D. Barrett, Phi	92		P. Roe, Pit	1.8		B. Voiselle, NYG	115		B. Voiselle, NYG	4.5		P. Derringer, ChN	1.69	
B. Voiselle, NYG	15		R. Sewell, Pit	91		H. Wyse, ChN	1.8		V. Mungo, NYG	101		C. Passeau, ChN	3.9		C. Passeau, ChN	1.66	
2 tied with	14		2 tied with	87		N. Strincevich, Pit	1.9		J. Hutchings, Bos	99		P. Derringer, ChN	3.6		N. Strincevich, Pit	1.51	

Earned Run Average			Component ERA			Hit Batsmen			Wild Pitches			Opponent Average			Opponent OBP		
H. Borowy, ChN	2.13		C. Passeau, ChN	2.46		C. Schanz, Phi	9		D. Barrett, Phi	8		H. Borowy, ChN	.231		C. Passeau, ChN	.289	
C. Passeau, ChN	2.46		H. Brecheen, StL	2.59		H. Gregg, Bro	8		H. Gregg, Bro	7		H. Gregg, Bro	.232		R. Barrett, 2tm	.295	
H. Brecheen, StL	2.52		H. Borowy, ChN	2.63		P. Erickson, ChN	7		O. Judd, Phi	7		H. Brecheen, StL	.238		H. Wyse, ChN	.296	
B. Walters, Cin	2.68		P. Roe, Pit	2.86		D. Barrett, Phi	7		3 tied with	6		C. Passeau, ChN	.238		P. Roe, Pit	.296	
H. Wyse, ChN	2.68		H. Wyse, ChN	2.96		J. Bowman, Cin	7					H. Feldman, NYG	.251		H. Brecheen, StL	.298	

1945 National League Miscellaneous

Managers		
Boston	Bob Coleman	42-51
	Del Bissonette	25-34
Brooklyn	Leo Durocher	87-67
Chicago	Charlie Grimm	98-56
Cincinnati	Bill McKechnie	61-93
New York	Mel Ott	78-74
Philadelphia	Freddie Fitzsimmons	18-51
	Ben Chapman	28-57
Pittsburgh	Frank Frisch	82-72
St. Louis	Billy Southworth	95-59

Awards

Most Valuable Player	Phil Cavarretta, 1b, ChN
STATS Cy Young	Hank Wyse, ChN
STATS Rookie of the Year	Ken Burkhart, p, StL
STATS Manager of the Year	Charlie Grimm, ChN

STATS All-Star Team

C	Bill Salkeld, Pit	.311	15	52
1B	Phil Cavarretta, ChN	.355	6	97
2B	Eddie Stanky, Bro	.258	1	39
3B	Whitey Kurowski, StL	.323	21	102
SS	Marty Marion, StL	.277	1	59
OF	Tommy Holmes, Bos	.352	28	117
OF	Goody Rosen, Bro	.325	12	75
OF	Dixie Walker, Bro	.300	8	124
P	Red Barrett, 2tm	23-12	3.00	76 K
P	Hank Borowy, ChN	11-2	2.13	47 K
P	Claude Passeau, ChN	17-9	2.46	98 K
P	Hank Wyse, ChN	22-10	2.68	77 K
RP	Andy Karl, Phi	8-8	2.99	15 Sv

Postseason

World Series	Chicago (NL) 3 vs. Detroit (AL) 4

Outstanding Performances

Cycles

Bob Elliott, Pit	on July 15
Bill Salkeld, Pit	on August 4

Seasons: Standings, Leaders

269

1946 American League Standings

Team	Overall					Home Games						Road Games						Park Index		Record by Month					
	W	L	Pct	GB	DIF	W	L	R	OR	HR	OHR	W	L	R	OR	HR	OHR	Run	HR	M/A	May	June	July	Aug	S/O
Boston	104	50	.675	—	164	61	16	469	315	65	44	43	34	323	279	44	45	130	122	11-3	21-6	18-10	20-10	21-11	13-10
Detroit	92	62	.597	12.0	2	48	30	391	300	75	68	44	32	313	267	33	29	116	225	7-5	15-14	14-11	20-10	15-13	21-9
New York	87	67	.565	17.0	5	47	30	342	262	68	34	40	37	342	285	68	32	96	102	9-5	18-11	15-12	15-13	19-11	11-15
Washington	76	78	.494	28.0	0	38	38	253	343	16	25	38	40	355	363	44	56	85	42	5-8	15-9	13-16	17-14	12-18	14-13
Chicago	74	80	.481	30.0	0	40	38	272	290	17	20	34	42	290	305	20	34	92	114	5-8	10-13	11-17	13-20	18-13	17-9
Cleveland	68	86	.442	36.0	4	36	41	231	264	25	36	32	45	306	374	54	48	73	60	5-5	12-18	13-15	17-14	11-18	10-16
St. Louis	66	88	.429	38.0	0	35	41	313	344	46	29	31	47	308	366	38	44	100	94	6-7	11-16	14-13	11-18	11-18	13-16
Philadelphia	49	105	.318	55.0	0	31	46	297	351	21	38	18	59	232	329	19	45	116	92	3-10	6-21	11-15	8-22	14-19	7-18

Clinch Date—Boston 9/13.

Team Batting

Team	G	AB	R	OR	H	2B	3B	HR	TB	RBI	TBB	IBB	SO	HBP	SH	SF	SB	CS	SB%	GDP	Avg	OBP	Slg
Boston	156	5318	792	594	1441	268	50	109	2136	737	687	—	661	15	106	—	45	36	.56	133	.271	.356	.402
Detroit	155	5318	704	567	1373	212	41	108	1991	644	622	—	616	13	104	—	65	41	.61	125	.258	.337	.374
New York	154	5139	684	547	1275	208	50	136	1991	649	627	—	706	33	80	—	48	35	.58	106	.248	.334	.387
St. Louis	156	5373	621	710	1350	220	46	84	1914	576	465	—	713	16	67	—	23	35	.40	128	.251	.313	.356
Washington	155	5337	608	706	1388	260	63	60	1954	554	511	—	641	24	86	—	51	50	.50	115	.260	.327	.366
Chicago	155	5312	562	595	1364	206	44	37	1769	515	501	—	600	20	78	—	78	64	.55	134	.257	.323	.333
Cleveland	156	5242	537	638	1285	233	56	79	1867	497	506	—	697	13	96	—	57	49	.54	116	.245	.313	.356
Philadelphia	155	5200	529	680	1317	220	51	40	1759	483	482	—	594	9	105	—	39	30	.57	126	.253	.318	.338
AL Total	1242	42239	5037	5037	10793	1827	401	653	15381	4655	4401	—	5228	143	722	—	406	340	.54	977	.256	.328	.364
AL Avg Team	155	5280	630	630	1349	228	50	82	1923	582	550	—	654	18	90	—	51	43	.54	122	.256	.328	.364

Team Pitching

Team	G	CG	ShO	Rel	Sv	IP	H	R	ER	HR	SH	SF	HB	TBB	IBB	SO	WP	Bk	H/9	SO/9	BB/9	OAvg	OOBP	ERA
Chicago	155	62	9	142	16	1392.1	1348	595	479	80	91	—	23	508	—	550	33	1	8.7	3.6	3.3	.255	.323	3.10
New York	154	68	17	152	17	1361.0	1232	547	474	66	95	—	13	552	—	653	12	6	8.1	4.3	3.7	.243	.319	3.13
Detroit	155	94	18	101	15	1402.0	1277	567	501	97	66	—	11	497	—	896	21	2	8.2	5.8	3.2	.241	.307	3.22
Boston	156	79	15	151	20	1396.2	1359	594	525	89	86	—	14	501	—	667	15	3	8.8	4.3	3.2	.254	.319	3.38
Cleveland	156	63	16	170	13	1388.2	1282	638	558	84	100	—	17	649	—	789	20	0	8.3	5.1	4.2	.245	.331	3.62
Washington	155	71	8	157	10	1396.1	1459	706	580	81	82	—	30	547	—	537	27	2	9.4	3.5	3.5	.269	.339	3.74
Philadelphia	155	61	10	145	5	1342.2	1371	680	582	83	97	—	25	577	—	562	13	6	9.2	3.8	3.9	.264	.340	3.90
St. Louis	156	63	13	193	12	1382.1	1465	710	607	73	100	—	9	573	—	574	27	3	9.5	3.7	3.7	.272	.343	3.95
AL Total	1242	561	106	1211	108	11062.0	10793	5037	4306	653	717	—	142	4404	—	5228	168	23	8.8	4.3	3.6	.256	.328	3.50
AL Avg Team	155	70	13	151	14	1382.0	1349	630	538	82	90	—	18	551	—	654	21	3	8.8	4.3	3.6	.256	.328	3.50

Team Fielding

Team	G	PO	A	E	TC	DP	PB	Pct
Boston	156	4191	1754	139	6084	163	9	.977
Cleveland	156	4153	1591	147	5891	147	16	.975
New York	154	4083	1751	150	5984	174	11	.975
Detroit	155	4199	1684	155	6038	138	14	.974
St. Louis	156	4146	1721	159	6026	157	19	.974
Chicago	155	4176	1875	175	6226	170	16	.972
Philadelphia	155	4028	1594	167	5789	141	7	.971
Washington	155	4190	1737	211	6138	162	37	.966
AL Total	1242	33166	13707	1303	48176	1252	129	.973

Team vs. Team Records

	Bos	ChA	Cle	Det	NYA	Phi	StL	Was	Won
Bos	—	13	15	15	14	17	14	16	104
ChA	9	—	13	10	8	12	12	10	74
Cle	7	9	—	5	10	15	15	7	68
Det	7	12	17	—	13	17	14	12	92
NYA	8	14	12	9	—	16	14	14	87
Phi	5	10	7	5	6	—	10	6	49
StL	8	10	7	8	8	12	—	13	66
Was	6	12	15	10	8	16	9	—	76
Lost	50	80	86	62	67	105	88	78	

1946 American League Batting Leaders

Games		At-Bats		Runs		Hits		Doubles		Triples	
E. Lake, Det	155	J. Pesky, Bos	621	T. Williams, Bos	142	J. Pesky, Bos	208	M. Vernon, Was	51	H. Edwards, Cle	16
R. York, Bos	154	E. Lake, Det	587	J. Pesky, Bos	115	M. Vernon, Was	207	S. Spence, Was	50	B. Lewis, Was	13
J. Pesky, Bos	153	M. Vernon, Was	587	E. Lake, Det	105	L. Appling, ChA	180	J. Pesky, Bos	43	G. Kell, 2tm	10
S. Spence, Was	152	B. Doerr, Bos	583	C. Keller, NYA	98	T. Williams, Bos	176	T. Williams, Bos	37	S. Spence, Was	10
B. Doerr, Bos	151	3 tied with	582	B. Doerr, Bos	95	B. Lewis, Was	170	B. Doerr, Bos	34	C. Keller, NYA	10

Home Runs		Total Bases		Runs Batted In		Walks		Intentional Walks		Strikeouts	
H. Greenberg, Det	44	T. Williams, Bos	343	H. Greenberg, Det	127	T. Williams, Bos	156	Statistic unavailable		P. Seerey, Cle	101
T. Williams, Bos	38	H. Greenberg, Det	316	T. Williams, Bos	123	C. Keller, NYA	113			C. Keller, NYA	101
C. Keller, NYA	30	M. Vernon, Was	298	R. York, Bos	119	E. Lake, Det	103			R. York, Bos	93
P. Seerey, Cle	26	S. Spence, Was	287	B. Doerr, Bos	116	R. Cullenbine, Det	88			H. Greenberg, Det	88
J. DiMaggio, NYA	25	C. Keller, NYA	287	C. Keller, NYA	101	T. Henrich, NYA	87			2 tied with	73

Hit By Pitch		Sac Hits		Sac Flies		Stolen Bases		Caught Stealing		GDP	
T. Henrich, NYA	7	G. Kell, 2tm	15	Statistic unavailable		G. Case, Cle	28	G. Case, Cle	11	S. Chapman, Phi	22
P. Rizzuto, NYA	6	L. Boudreau, Cle	15			S. Stirnweiss, NYA	18	T. Tucker, ChA	10	B. Rosar, Phi	20
J. Grace, 2tm	6	J. Pesky, Bos	14			E. Lake, Det	15	M. Vernon, Was	10	B. Doerr, Bos	18
7 tied with	4	B. Lewis, Was	13			3 tied with	14	E. Lake, Det	9	3 tied with	17
		3 tied with	12					3 tied with	8		

Runs Created		Runs Created/27 Outs		Batting Average		On-Base Percentage		Slugging Percentage		OBP+Slugging	
T. Williams, Bos	163	T. Williams, Bos	12.56	M. Vernon, Was	.353	T. Williams, Bos	.497	T. Williams, Bos	.667	T. Williams, Bos	1.164
C. Keller, NYA	118	C. Keller, NYA	7.97	T. Williams, Bos	.342	C. Keller, NYA	.405	H. Greenberg, Det	.604	H. Greenberg, Det	.977
H. Greenberg, Det	115	H. Greenberg, Det	7.81	J. Pesky, Bos	.335	M. Vernon, Was	.403	C. Keller, NYA	.533	C. Keller, NYA	.938
J. Pesky, Bos	108	M. Vernon, Was	7.07	G. Kell, 2tm	.322	J. Pesky, Bos	.401	J. DiMaggio, NYA	.511	M. Vernon, Was	.910
M. Vernon, Was	106	J. Heath, 2tm	6.61	D. DiMaggio, Bos	.316	D. DiMaggio, Bos	.393	H. Edwards, Cle	.509	J. DiMaggio, NYA	.878

1946 American League Pitching Leaders

Wins		Losses		Winning Percentage		Games		Games Started		Complete Games	
H. Newhouser, Det	26	L. Knerr, Phi	16	B. Ferriss, Bos	.806	B. Feller, Cle	48	B. Feller, Cle	42	B. Feller, Cle	36
B. Feller, Cle	26	D. Fowler, Phi	16	E. Caldwell, ChA	.765	B. Ferriss, Bos	40	B. Ferriss, Bos	35	H. Newhouser, Det	29
B. Ferriss, Bos	25	P. Marchildon, Phi	16	H. Newhouser, Det	.743	B. Savage, Phi	40	T. Hughson, Bos	35	B. Ferriss, Bos	26
T. Hughson, Bos	20	4 tied with	15	S. Chandler, NYA	.714	T. Hughson, Bos	39	H. Newhouser, Det	34	D. Trout, Det	23
S. Chandler, NYA	20			M. Harris, Bos	.654	E. Caldwell, ChA	39	2 tied with	32	T. Hughson, Bos	21

Shutouts		Saves		Games Finished		Batters Faced		Innings Pitched		Hits Allowed	
B. Feller, Cle	10	B. Klinger, Bos	9	E. Caldwell, ChA	37	B. Feller, Cle	1512	B. Feller, Cle	371.1	B. Feller, Cle	277
B. Ferriss, Bos	6	E. Caldwell, ChA	8	J. Murphy, NYA	24	H. Newhouser, Det	1176	H. Newhouser, Det	292.2	B. Ferriss, Bos	274
T. Hughson, Bos	6	J. Murphy, NYA	7	T. Ferrick, 2tm	22	D. Trout, Det	1142	T. Hughson, Bos	278.0	T. Hughson, Bos	252
H. Newhouser, Det	6	T. Ferrick, 2tm	6	B. Klinger, Bos	20	B. Ferriss, Bos	1141	D. Trout, Det	276.1	D. Trout, Det	244
S. Chandler, NYA	6	3 tied with	4	G. Caster, Det	19	T. Hughson, Bos	1128	B. Ferriss, Bos	274.0	M. Harris, Bos	236

Home Runs Allowed		Walks		Walks/9 Innings		Strikeouts		Strikeouts/9 Innings		Strikeout/Walk Ratio	
V. Trucks, Det	23	B. Feller, Cle	153	T. Hughson, Bos	1.7	B. Feller, Cle	348	H. Newhouser, Det	8.5	T. Hughson, Bos	3.37
S. Gromek, Cle	20	P. Marchildon, Phi	114	E. Lopat, ChA	1.9	H. Newhouser, Det	275	B. Feller, Cle	8.4	H. Newhouser, Det	2.81
E. Lopat, ChA	18	A. Reynolds, Cle	108	B. Ferriss, Bos	2.3	T. Hughson, Bos	172	V. Trucks, Det	6.1	B. Feller, Cle	2.27
M. Harris, Bos	18	T. Shirley, StL	105	D. Galehouse, StL	2.6	V. Trucks, Det	161	F. Hutchinson, Det	6.0	V. Trucks, Det	2.15
D. Fowler, Phi	16	H. Newhouser, Det	98	B. Bevens, NYA	2.8	D. Trout, Det	151	T. Hughson, Bos	5.6	F. Hutchinson, Det	2.09

Earned Run Average		Component ERA		Hit Batsmen		Wild Pitches		Opponent Average		Opponent OBP	
H. Newhouser, Det	1.94	H. Newhouser, Det	2.00	B. Newsom, 2tm	7	O. Grove, ChA	10	H. Newhouser, Det	.201	H. Newhouser, Det	.269
S. Chandler, NYA	2.10	S. Chandler, NYA	2.25	R. Hamner, ChA	5	H. Newhouser, Det	8	B. Feller, Cle	.208	T. Hughson, Bos	.274
B. Feller, Cle	2.18	B. Feller, Cle	2.29	M. Haefner, Was	5	P. Marchildon, Phi	7	S. Chandler, NYA	.218	S. Chandler, NYA	.288
B. Bevens, NYA	2.23	T. Hughson, Bos	2.45	R. Wolff, Was	5	3 tied with	6	B. Bevens, NYA	.232	E. Lopat, ChA	.288
D. Trout, Det	2.34	B. Bevens, NYA	2.58	7 tied with	4			F. Hutchinson, Det	.236	B. Feller, Cle	.291

1946 American League Miscellaneous

Managers

Boston	Joe Cronin	104-50
Chicago	Jimmy Dykes	10-20
	Ted Lyons	64-60
Cleveland	Lou Boudreau	68-86
Detroit	Steve O'Neill	92-62
New York	Joe McCarthy	22-13
	Bill Dickey	57-48
	Johnny Neun	8-6
Philadelphia	Connie Mack	49-105
St. Louis	Luke Sewell	53-71
	Zack Taylor	13-17
Washington	Ossie Bluege	76-78

Awards

Most Valuable Player	Ted Williams, of, Bos
STATS Cy Young	Hal Newhouser, Det
STATS Rookie of the Year	Hoot Evers, of, Det
STATS Manager of the Year	Joe Cronin, Bos

STATS All-Star Team

C	Aaron Robinson, NYA	.297	16	64
1B	Hank Greenberg, Det	.277	44	127
2B	Bobby Doerr, Bos	.271	18	116
3B	George Kell, 2tm	.322	4	52
SS	Johnny Pesky, Bos	.335	2	55
OF	Roy Cullenbine, Det	.335	15	56
OF	Charlie Keller, NYA	.275	30	101
OF	Ted Williams, Bos	.342	38	123
P	Spud Chandler, NYA	20-8	2.10	138 K
P	Bob Feller, Cle	26-15	2.18	348 K
P	Tex Hughson, Bos	20-11	2.75	172 K
P	Hal Newhouser, Det	26-9	1.94	275 K
RP	Earl Caldwell, ChA	13-4	2.08	8 Sv

Postseason

World Series	Boston (AL) 3 vs. St. Louis (NL) 4

Outstanding Performances

No-Hitters

Bob Feller, Cle	@ NYA on April 30

Three-Homer Games

Ted Williams, Bos	on July 14
Sam Chapman, Phi	on August 15

Cycles

Mickey Vernon, Was	on May 19
Ted Williams, Bos	on July 21

1946 National League Standings

Team		Overall				Home Games						Road Games						Park Index		Record by Month					
	W	L	Pct	GB	DIF	W	L	R	OR	HR	OHR	W	L	R	OR	HR	OHR	Run	HR	M/A	May	June	July	Aug	S/O
St. Louis	98	58	.628	—	70	49	29	370	288	41	36	49	29	342	257	40	27	110	115	9-4	14-10	14-14	19-11	22-9	20-10
Brooklyn	96	60	.615	2.0	122	56	22	374	273	19	22	40	38	327	297	36	36	104	57	8-4	17-8	18-11	16-14	16-13	21-10
Chicago	82	71	.536	14.5	5	44	33	291	260	24	30	38	38	335	321	32	28	83	89	7-5	10-13	17-10	18-15	16-12	14-16
Boston	81	72	.529	15.5	1	45	31	300	268	14	31	36	41	330	324	30	45	88	61	7-4	10-15	14-17	14-13	18-11	18-12
Philadelphia	69	85	.448	28.0	0	41	36	280	335	38	34	28	49	280	370	42	39	95	89	2-9	9-15	17-9	12-20	14-17	15-15
Cincinnati	67	87	.435	30.0	0	35	42	267	289	37	39	32	45	256	281	28	31	104	129	5-7	12-9	12-16	18-16	9-21	11-18
Pittsburgh	63	91	.409	34.0	1	37	40	303	342	24	23	26	51	249	326	36	27	112	75	5-8	10-10	11-19	11-19	11-15	15-20
New York	61	93	.396	36.0	2	38	39	340	336	76	75	23	54	272	349	45	39	109	180	5-7	12-14	11-18	15-15	10-18	8-21

Clinch Date—St. Louis 10/03.

Team Batting

Team	G	AB	R	OR	H	2B	3B	HR	TB	RBI	TBB	IBB	SO	HBP	SH	SF	SB	CS	SB%	GDP	Avg	OBP	Slg
St. Louis	156	5372	712	545	1426	265	56	81	2046	665	530	—	537	21	97	—	58	—	—	95	.265	.334	.381
Brooklyn	157	5285	701	570	1376	233	66	55	1906	642	691	—	575	17	141	—	100	41	.71	103	.260	.348	.361
Boston	154	5225	630	592	1377	238	48	44	1843	596	558	—	468	22	135	—	60	—	—	111	.264	.337	.353
Chicago	155	5298	626	581	1344	223	50	56	1835	566	586	—	599	24	116	—	43	—	—	129	.254	.331	.346
New York	154	5191	612	685	1326	176	37	121	1939	576	532	—	546	27	86	—	46	26	.64	121	.255	.328	.374
Philadelphia	155	5233	560	705	1351	209	40	80	1880	517	417	—	590	19	102	—	41	—	—	102	.258	.315	.359
Pittsburgh	155	5199	552	668	1300	202	52	60	1786	508	592	—	555	15	101	—	48	—	—	125	.250	.328	.344
Cincinnati	156	5291	523	570	1262	206	33	65	1729	481	493	—	604	28	122	—	82	—	—	102	.239	.307	.327
NL Total	1242	42094	4916	4916	10762	1752	382	562	14964	4551	4399	—	4474	173	900	—	478	—	—	888	.256	.329	.355
NL Avg Team	155	5262	615	615	1345	219	48	70	1871	569	550	—	559	22	113	—	60	—	—	111	.256	.329	.355

Team Pitching

Team	G	CG	ShO	Rel	Sv	IP	H	R	ER	HR	SH	SF	HB	TBB	IBB	SO	WP	Bk	H/9	SO/9	BB/9	OAvg	OOBP	ERA
St. Louis	156	75	18	180	15	1397.0	1326	545	467	63	96	—	31	493	—	607	19	1	8.5	3.9	3.2	.253	.320	3.01
Brooklyn	157	52	14	223	28	1418.0	1280	570	480	58	135	—	20	671	—	647	27	4	8.1	4.1	4.3	.243	.331	3.05
Cincinnati	156	69	17	146	11	1413.1	1334	570	483	70	102	—	15	467	—	506	13	1	8.5	3.2	3.0	.252	.314	3.08
Chicago	155	59	15	187	11	1393.0	1370	581	502	58	104	—	19	527	—	619	15	2	8.9	4.0	3.4	.256	.325	3.24
Boston	154	73	10	167	12	1371.0	1291	592	510	76	99	—	15	478	—	566	26	4	8.5	3.7	3.1	.248	.313	3.35
Pittsburgh	155	61	10	181	6	1370.0	1406	668	566	50	121	—	20	561	—	458	18	0	9.2	3.0	3.7	.268	.341	3.72
New York	154	47	8	216	13	1353.1	1313	685	589	114	111	—	18	660	—	581	29	1	8.7	3.9	4.4	.256	.343	3.92
Philadelphia	155	55	11	185	23	1369.0	1442	705	607	73	107	—	34	542	—	490	32	0	9.5	3.2	3.6	.273	.344	3.99
NL Total	1242	491	103	1485	119	11084.2	10762	4916	4204	562	875	—	172	4399	—	4474	179	13	8.7	3.6	3.6	.256	.329	3.41
NL Avg Team	155	61	13	186	15	1385.2	1345	615	526	70	109	—	22	550	—	559	22	2	8.7	3.6	3.6	.256	.329	3.41

Team Fielding

Team	G	PO	A	E	TC	DP	PB	Pct
St. Louis	156	4194	1777	124	6095	167	10	.980
Chicago	155	4202	1778	146	6126	119	13	.976
Cincinnati	156	4231	1924	155	6310	192	4	.975
Philadelphia	155	4100	1702	148	5950	144	12	.975
New York	154	4056	1742	159	5957	121	9	.973
Brooklyn	157	4249	1728	174	6151	154	17	.972
Boston	154	4121	1668	169	5958	129	6	.972
Pittsburgh	155	4111	1786	184	6081	127	10	.970
NL Total	1242	33264	14105	1259	48628	1153	81	.974

Team vs. Team Records

	Bos	Bro	ChN	Cin	NYG	Phi	Pit	StL	Won
Bos	—	5	12	15	13	14	15	7	81
Bro	17	—	11	14	15	17	14	8	96
ChN	9	11	—	13	17	12	12	8	82
Cin	7	8	9	—	14	8	13	8	67
NYG	9	7	5	8	—	12	10	10	61
Phi	8	5	10	14	10	—	14	8	69
Pit	7	8	10	9	12	8	—	9	63
StL	15	16	14	14	12	14	13	—	98
Lost	72	60	71	87	93	85	91	58	

1946 National League Batting Leaders

Games			At-Bats			Runs			Hits		
S. Musial, StL	156		S. Musial, StL	624		S. Musial, StL	124		S. Musial, StL	228	
E. Slaughter, StL	156		E. Slaughter, StL	609		E. Slaughter, StL	100		D. Walker, Bro	184	
P. Reese, Bro	152		R. Schoendienst, StL	606		E. Stanky, Bro	98		E. Slaughter, StL	183	
D. Walker, Bro	150		D. Walker, Bro	576		R. Schoendienst, StL	94		T. Holmes, Bos	176	
T. Holmes, Bos	149		T. Holmes, Bos	568		P. Cavarretta, ChN	89		R. Schoendienst, StL	170	

Doubles			Triples		
S. Musial, StL	50		S. Musial, StL	20	
T. Holmes, Bos	35		P. Reese, Bro	10	
W. Kurowski, StL	32		P. Cavarretta, ChN	10	
B. Herman, 2tm	31		D. Walker, Bro	9	
3 tied with	30		5 tied with	8	

Home Runs			Total Bases			Runs Batted In			Walks		
R. Kiner, Pit	23		S. Musial, StL	366		E. Slaughter, StL	130		E. Stanky, Bro	137	
J. Mize, NYG	22		E. Slaughter, StL	283		D. Walker, Bro	116		E. Fletcher, Pit	111	
E. Slaughter, StL	18		D. Ennis, Phi	262		S. Musial, StL	103		P. Cavarretta, ChN	88	
D. Ennis, Phi	17		D. Walker, Bro	258		W. Kurowski, StL	89		P. Reese, Bro	87	
2 tied with	16		T. Holmes, Bos	241		R. Kiner, Pit	81		S. Hack, ChN	83	

Intentional Walks			Strikeouts		
Statistic unavailable			R. Kiner, Pit	109	
			A. Seminick, Phi	86	
			P. Reese, Bro	71	
			D. Ennis, Phi	65	
			2 tied with	63	

Hit By Pitch			Sac Hits			Sac Flies			Stolen Bases		
B. Blattner, NYG	6		E. Stanky, Bro	20		Statistic unavailable			P. Reiser, Bro	34	
D. Clay, Cin	5		B. Kerr, NYG	19					B. Haas, Cin	22	
W. Kurowski, StL	5		P. Lowrey, ChN	17					J. Hopp, Bos	21	
J. Hopp, Bos	5		S. Newsome, Phi	17					B. Adams, Cin	16	
J. Mize, NYG	5		M. Marion, StL	15					D. Walker, Bro	14	

Caught Stealing			GDP		
Statistic unavailable			A. Seminick, Phi	19	
			A. Libke, Cin	16	
			P. Cavarretta, ChN	16	
			6 tied with	15	

Runs Created			Runs Created/27 Outs			Batting Average			On-Base Percentage		
S. Musial, StL	152		S. Musial, StL	10.01		S. Musial, StL	.365		E. Stanky, Bro	.436	
E. Slaughter, StL	109		W. Kurowski, StL	6.77		J. Hopp, Bos	.333		S. Musial, StL	.434	
D. Walker, Bro	100		E. Slaughter, StL	6.64		D. Walker, Bro	.319		P. Cavarretta, ChN	.401	
W. Kurowski, StL	96		D. Walker, Bro	6.62		D. Ennis, Phi	.313		B. Herman, 2tm	.395	
2 tied with	91		E. Stanky, Bro	6.45		T. Holmes, Bos	.310		D. Walker, Bro	.391	

Slugging Percentage			OBP+Slugging		
S. Musial, StL	.587		S. Musial, StL	1.021	
D. Ennis, Phi	.485		W. Kurowski, StL	.853	
E. Slaughter, StL	.465		D. Ennis, Phi	.849	
W. Kurowski, StL	.462		D. Walker, Bro	.839	
D. Walker, Bro	.448		E. Slaughter, StL	.838	

1946 National League Pitching Leaders

Wins			Losses			Winning Percentage			Games		
H. Pollet, StL	21		D. Koslo, NYG	19		S. Rowe, Phi	.733		K. Trinkle, NYG	48	
J. Sain, Bos	20		B. Voiselle, NYG	15		M. Dickson, StL	.714		H. Behrman, Bro	47	
K. Higbe, Bro	17		N. Strincevich, Pit	15		H. Behrman, Bro	.688		M. Dickson, StL	47	
H. Brecheen, StL	15		H. Brecheen, StL	15		H. Casey, Bro	.688		H. Casey, Bro	46	
M. Dickson, StL	15		K. Raffensberger, Phi	15		K. Higbe, Bro	.680		2 tied with	42	

Games Started			Complete Games		
D. Koslo, NYG	35		J. Sain, Bos	24	
J. Sain, Bos	34		H. Pollet, StL	22	
H. Pollet, StL	32		D. Koslo, NYG	17	
J. Schmitz, ChN	31		F. Ostermueller, Pit	16	
2 tied with	30		M. Cooper, Bos	15	

Shutouts			Saves			Games Finished			Batters Faced		
E. Blackwell, Cin	6		K. Raffensberger, Phi	6		J. Thompson, NYG	27		D. Koslo, NYG	1136	
H. Brecheen, StL	5		A. Karl, Phi	5		H. Casey, Bro	27		J. Sain, Bos	1086	
J. Vander Meer, Cin	5		H. Pollet, StL	5		A. Karl, Phi	23		H. Pollet, StL	1083	
H. Pollet, StL	4		H. Casey, Bro	5		E. Kush, ChN	19		H. Brecheen, StL	954	
7 tied with	3		A. Herring, Bro	5		H. Gumbert, Cin	19		J. Hatten, Bro	949	

Innings Pitched			Hits Allowed		
H. Pollet, StL	266.0		D. Koslo, NYG	251	
D. Koslo, NYG	265.1		H. Pollet, StL	228	
J. Sain, Bos	265.0		J. Sain, Bos	225	
H. Brecheen, StL	231.1		H. Borowy, ChN	220	
J. Schmitz, ChN	224.1		H. Brecheen, StL	212	

Home Runs Allowed			Walks			Walks/9 Innings			Strikeouts		
M. Cooper, Bos	17		M. Kennedy, NYG	116		M. Cooper, Bos	1.8		J. Schmitz, ChN	135	
D. Koslo, NYG	16		J. Hatten, Bro	110		K. Raffensberger, Phi	1.8		K. Higbe, Bro	134	
J. Beggs, Cin	15		K. Higbe, Bro	107		J. Beggs, Cin	1.8		J. Sain, Bos	129	
M. Kennedy, NYG	14		D. Koslo, NYG	101		N. Strincevich, Pit	2.3		D. Koslo, NYG	121	
B. Voiselle, NYG	14		J. Schmitz, ChN	94		H. Wyse, ChN	2.3		H. Brecheen, StL	117	

Strikeouts/9 Innings			Strikeout/Walk Ratio		
K. Higbe, Bro	5.7		M. Cooper, Bos	2.13	
J. Schmitz, ChN	5.4		K. Raffensberger, Phi	1.87	
E. Blackwell, Cin	4.6		H. Brecheen, StL	1.75	
H. Brecheen, StL	4.6		J. Sain, Bos	1.48	
B. Voiselle, NYG	4.5		M. Dickson, StL	1.46	

Earned Run Average			Component ERA			Hit Batsmen			Wild Pitches		
H. Pollet, StL	2.10		J. Sain, Bos	2.51		J. Hatten, Bro	7		C. Schanz, Phi	6	
J. Sain, Bos	2.21		E. Blackwell, Cin	2.53		S. Rowe, Phi	6		K. Higbe, Bro	6	
J. Beggs, Cin	2.32		J. Schmitz, ChN	2.60		5 tied with	5		6 tied with	5	
E. Blackwell, Cin	2.45		M. Dickson, StL	2.66							
H. Brecheen, StL	2.49		M. Cooper, Bos	2.68							

Opponent Average			Opponent OBP		
J. Schmitz, ChN	.221		M. Cooper, Bos	.276	
M. Kennedy, NYG	.224		J. Beggs, Cin	.287	
E. Blackwell, Cin	.226		J. Sain, Bos	.294	
K. Higbe, Bro	.229		M. Dickson, StL	.295	
J. Sain, Bos	.230		C. Passeau, ChN	.298	

1946 National League Miscellaneous

Managers

Boston	Billy Southworth	81-72
Brooklyn	Leo Durocher	96-60
Chicago	Charlie Grimm	82-71
Cincinnati	Bill McKechnie	64-86
	Hank Gowdy	3-1
New York	Mel Ott	61-93
Philadelphia	Ben Chapman	69-85
Pittsburgh	Frank Frisch	62-89
	Spud Davis	1-2
St. Louis	Eddie Dyer	98-58

Awards

Most Valuable Player	Stan Musial, 1b, StL
STATS Cy Young	Howie Pollet, StL
STATS Rookie of the Year	Del Ennis, of, Phi
STATS Manager of the Year	Eddie Dyer, StL

STATS All-Star Team

C	Andy Seminick, Phi	.264	12	52
1B	Stan Musial, StL	.365	16	103
2B	Eddie Stanky, Bro	.273	0	36
3B	Whitey Kurowski, StL	.301	14	89
SS	Pee Wee Reese, Bro	.284	5	60
OF	Phil Cavarretta, ChN	.294	8	78
OF	Enos Slaughter, StL	.300	18	130
OF	Dixie Walker, Bro	.319	9	116
P	Joe Beggs, Cin	12-10	2.32	38 K
P	Kirby Higbe, Bro	17-8	3.03	134 K
P	Howie Pollet, StL	21-10	2.10	107 K
P	Johnny Sain, Bos	20-14	2.21	129 K
RP	Hugh Casey, Bro	11-5	1.99	5 Sv

Postseason

World Series	St. Louis (NL) 4 vs. Boston (AL) 3

Outstanding Performances

No-Hitters

Ed Head, Bro	vs. Bos on April 23

1947 American League Standings

Team	Overall					Home Games						Road Games						Park Index		Record by Month					
	W	L	Pct	GB	DIF	W	L	R	OR	HR	OHR	W	L	R	OR	HR	OHR	Run	HR	M/A	May	June	July	Aug	S/O
New York	97	57	.630	—	112	55	22	392	242	54	49	42	35	402	326	61	46	87	96	7-5	13-12	21-9	24-6	18-13	14-12
Detroit	85	69	.552	12.0	39	46	31	370	345	62	47	39	38	344	297	41	32	112	149	6-6	18-8	8-17	17-12	20-17	16-9
Boston	83	71	.539	14.0	6	49	30	421	355	61	39	34	41	299	314	42	45	120	109	6-6	13-13	15-11	18-13	17-13	14-15
Cleveland	80	74	.519	17.0	1	38	39	314	279	52	51	42	35	373	309	60	43	87	100	5-5	11-9	12-14	15-17	20-16	17-13
Philadelphia	78	76	.506	19.0	2	39	38	296	324	33	41	39	38	309	290	28	44	99	103	4-6	14-13	14-13	10-21	18-11	10-17
Chicago	70	84	.455	27.0	19	32	43	244	322	20	31	38	41	309	339	33	45	92	69	6-4	12-18	14-13	12-18	18-11	10-17
Washington	64	90	.416	33.0	0	36	41	244	326	10	20	28	49	252	349	32	43	95	40	4-5	12-14	14-13	12-18	10-24	12-16
St. Louis	59	95	.383	38.0	0	29	48	286	401	52	57	30	47	278	343	38	46	111	130	5-6	9-15	9-18	11-20	12-23	13-13

Clinch Date—New York 9/15.

Team Batting

Team	G	AB	R	OR	H	2B	3B	HR	TB	RBI	TBB	IBB	SO	HBP	SH	SF	SB	CS	SB%	GDP	Avg	OBP	Slg
New York	155	5308	794	568	1439	230	72	115	2158	748	610	—	581	26	86	—	27	23	.54	122	.271	.349	.407
Boston	157	5322	720	669	1412	206	54	103	2035	674	666	—	590	16	95	—	41	35	.54	130	.265	.349	.382
Detroit	158	5276	714	642	1363	234	42	103	1990	662	762	—	565	13	97	—	52	60	.46	130	.258	.353	.377
Cleveland	157	5367	687	588	1392	234	51	112	2064	649	502	—	609	14	93	—	29	25	.54	107	.259	.324	.385
Philadelphia	156	5198	633	614	1311	218	52	61	1816	581	605	—	563	24	144	—	37	33	.53	117	.252	.333	.349
St. Louis	154	5145	564	744	1238	189	52	90	1801	526	583	—	664	15	76	—	69	49	.58	118	.241	.320	.350
Chicago	155	5274	553	661	1350	211	41	53	1802	519	492	—	527	14	56	—	91	57	.61	142	.256	.321	.342
Washington	154	5112	496	675	1234	186	48	42	1642	459	525	—	534	7	72	—	53	51	.51	131	.241	.313	.321
AL Total	1246	42002	5161	5161	10739	1708	412	679	15308	4818	4745	—	4633	129	719	—	399	333	.55	1007	.256	.333	.364
AL Avg Team	156	5250	645	645	1342	214	52	85	1914	602	593	—	579	16	90	—	50	42	.55	126	.256	.333	.364

Team Pitching

Team	G	CG	ShO	Rel	Sv	IP	H	R	ER	HR	SH	SF	HB	TBB	IBB	SO	WP	Bk	H/9	SO/9	BB/9	OAvg	OOBP	ERA
New York	155	73	14	140	21	1374.1	1221	568	518	95	76	—	20	628	—	691	16	2	8.0	4.5	4.1	.238	.323	3.39
Cleveland	157	55	13	182	29	1402.1	1244	588	536	94	91	—	22	628	—	590	29	6	8.0	3.8	4.0	.240	.325	3.44
Philadelphia	156	70	12	125	15	1391.1	1291	614	543	85	55	—	14	597	—	493	14	2	8.4	3.2	3.9	.247	.326	3.51
Detroit	158	77	15	137	18	1398.2	1382	642	555	79	94	—	16	531	—	648	27	1	8.9	4.2	3.4	.258	.326	3.57
Chicago	155	47	11	184	27	1391.0	1384	661	562	76	121	—	20	603	—	522	35	1	9.0	3.4	3.9	.261	.339	3.64
Boston	157	64	13	184	19	1391.1	1383	669	589	84	88	—	16	575	—	586	36	6	8.9	3.8	3.7	.261	.335	3.81
Washington	154	67	15	143	12	1362.0	1408	675	601	63	89	—	17	579	—	551	16	6	9.3	3.6	3.8	.267	.342	3.97
St. Louis	154	50	7	141	13	1365.0	1426	744	656	103	105	—	7	604	—	552	17	2	9.4	3.6	4.0	.272	.348	4.33
AL Total	1246	503	100	1236	154	11076.0	10739	5161	4560	679	719	—	132	4745	—	4633	190	25	8.7	3.8	3.9	.256	.333	3.71
AL Avg Team	156	63	13	155	19	1384.0	1342	645	570	85	90	—	17	593	—	579	24	3	8.7	3.8	3.9	.256	.333	3.71

Team Fielding

Team	G	PO	A	E	TC	DP	PB	Pct
Cleveland	157	4207	1776	104	6087	178	7	.983
New York	155	4121	1521	109	5751	151	11	.981
St. Louis	154	4096	1694	134	5924	169	11	.977
Boston	157	4173	1736	137	6046	172	11	.977
Philadelphia	156	4174	1689	143	6006	161	5	.976
Washington	154	4081	1640	143	5864	151	7	.976
Chicago	155	4172	1827	155	6154	180	13	.975
Detroit	158	4162	1746	155	6063	142	8	.974
AL Total	1246	33186	13629	1080	47895	1304	73	.977

Team vs. Team Records

	Bos	ChA	Cle	Det	NYA	Phi	StL	Was	Won
Bos	—	16	9	12	9	10	15	12	83
ChA	6	—	11	7	10	11	11	14	70
Cle	13	11	—	8	7	11	17	13	80
Det	10	15	14	—	8	11	15	12	85
NYA	13	12	15	14	—	13	15	15	97
Phi	12	11	11	11	9	—	13	11	78
StL	7	11	5	7	7	9	—	13	59
Was	10	8	9	10	7	11	9	—	64
Lost	71	84	74	69	57	76	95	90	

1947 American League Batting Leaders

Games		At-Bats		Runs		Hits		Doubles		Triples	
E. Lake, Det	158	J. Pesky, Bos	638	T. Williams, Bos	125	J. Pesky, Bos	207	L. Boudreau, Cle	45	T. Henrich, NYA	13
T. Williams, Bos	156	E. Lake, Det	602	T. Henrich, NYA	109	G. Kell, Det	188	T. Williams, Bos	40	M. Vernon, Was	12
J. Pesky, Bos	155	M. Vernon, Was	600	J. Pesky, Bos	106	T. Williams, Bos	181	T. Henrich, NYA	35	D. Philley, ChA	11
J. Gordon, Cle	155	G. Kell, Det	588	S. Stirnweiss, NYA	102	B. McCosky, Phi	179	J. DiMaggio, NYA	31	3 tied with	10
2 tied with	154	R. York, 2tm	584	J. DiMaggio, NYA	97	2 tied with	168	4 tied with	29		

Home Runs		Total Bases		Runs Batted In		Walks		Intentional Walks		Strikeouts	
T. Williams, Bos	32	T. Williams, Bos	335	T. Williams, Bos	114	T. Williams, Bos	162	Statistic unavailable		E. Joost, Phi	110
J. Gordon, Cle	29	J. Gordon, Cle	279	T. Henrich, NYA	98	R. Cullenbine, Det	137			J. Heath, StL	87
J. Heath, StL	27	J. DiMaggio, NYA	279	J. DiMaggio, NYA	97	E. Lake, Det	120			R. York, 2tm	87
R. Cullenbine, Det	24	T. Henrich, NYA	267	J. Jones, 2tm	96	E. Joost, Phi	114			J. Jones, 2tm	85
R. York, 2tm	21	J. Pesky, Bos	250	2 tied with	95	F. Fain, Phi	95			J. Priddy, Was	79

Hit By Pitch		Sac Hits		Sac Flies		Stolen Bases		Caught Stealing		GDP	
P. Rizzuto, NYA	8	E. Joost, Phi	24	Statistic unavailable		B. Dillinger, StL	34	D. Philley, ChA	16	B. Doerr, Bos	25
B. Johnson, NYA	6	5 tied with	14			D. Philley, ChA	21	B. Dillinger, StL	13	D. Kolloway, ChA	22
H. Evers, Det	6					J. Pesky, Bos	12	M. Vernon, Was	12	R. York, 2tm	22
H. Majeski, Phi	5					M. Vernon, Was	12	G. Kell, Det	11	B. Johnson, NYA	21
5 tied with	4					4 tied with	11	E. Lake, Det	10	2 tied with	18

Runs Created		Runs Created/27 Outs		Batting Average		On-Base Percentage		Slugging Percentage		OBP+Slugging	
T. Williams, Bos	161	T. Williams, Bos	11.99	T. Williams, Bos	.343	T. Williams, Bos	.499	T. Williams, Bos	.634	T. Williams, Bos	1.133
J. DiMaggio, NYA	109	J. DiMaggio, NYA	7.67	B. McCosky, Phi	.328	F. Fain, Phi	.414	J. DiMaggio, NYA	.522	J. DiMaggio, NYA	.913
T. Henrich, NYA	103	T. Henrich, NYA	6.75	J. Pesky, Bos	.324	R. Cullenbine, Det	.401	J. Gordon, Cle	.496	T. Henrich, NYA	.857
J. Pesky, Bos	100	G. McQuinn, NYA	6.72	T. Wright, ChA	.324	T. Wright, ChA	.398	T. Henrich, NYA	.485	J. Heath, StL	.850
G. McQuinn, NYA	96	F. Fain, Phi	6.39	G. Kell, Det	.320	B. McCosky, Phi	.395	J. Heath, StL	.485	J. Gordon, Cle	.842

1947 American League Pitching Leaders

Wins		Losses		Winning Percentage		Games		Games Started		Complete Games	
B. Feller, Cle	20	H. Newhouser, Det	17	S. Shea, NYA	.737	E. Klieman, Cle	58	B. Feller, Cle	37	H. Newhouser, Det	24
A. Reynolds, NYA	19	F. Sanford, StL	16	A. Reynolds, NYA	.704	J. Page, NYA	56	H. Newhouser, Det	36	E. Lopat, ChA	22
P. Marchildon, Phi	19	W. Masterson, Was	16	J. Haynes, ChA	.700	E. Johnson, Bos	45	P. Marchildon, Phi	35	E. Wynn, Was	22
F. Hutchinson, Det	18	J. Kramer, StL	16	J. Dobson, Bos	.692	B. Savage, Phi	44	5 tied with	31	P. Marchildon, Phi	21
J. Dobson, Bos	18	2 tied with	15	2 tied with	.688	R. Christopher, Phi	44			B. Feller, Cle	20

Shutouts		Saves		Games Finished		Batters Faced		Innings Pitched		Hits Allowed	
B. Feller, Cle	5	J. Page, NYA	17	J. Page, NYA	44	B. Feller, Cle	1218	B. Feller, Cle	299.0	H. Newhouser, Det	268
M. Haefner, Was	4	E. Klieman, Cle	17	R. Christopher, Phi	38	H. Newhouser, Det	1216	H. Newhouser, Det	285.0	E. Wynn, Was	251
A. Reynolds, NYA	4	R. Christopher, Phi	12	E. Klieman, Cle	34	P. Marchildon, Phi	1172	P. Marchildon, Phi	276.2	B. Ferriss, Bos	241
W. Masterson, Was	4	T. Ferrick, Was	9	E. Caldwell, ChA	30	E. Wynn, Was	1058	W. Masterson, Was	253.0	E. Lopat, ChA	241
10 tied with	3	2 tied with	8	G. Moulder, StL	25	E. Lopat, ChA	1047	E. Lopat, ChA	252.2	B. Feller, Cle	230

Home Runs Allowed		Walks		Walks/9 Innings		Strikeouts		Strikeouts/9 Innings		Strikeout/Walk Ratio	
A. Reynolds, NYA	23	P. Marchildon, Phi	141	D. Galehouse, 2tm	2.5	B. Feller, Cle	196	B. Feller, Cle	5.9	F. Hutchinson, Det	1.85
6 tied with	17	B. Feller, Cle	127	F. Hutchinson, Det	2.5	H. Newhouser, Det	176	T. Hughson, Bos	5.7	T. Hughson, Bos	1.68
		A. Reynolds, NYA	123	E. Lopat, ChA	2.6	W. Masterson, Was	135	H. Newhouser, Det	5.6	S. Chandler, NYA	1.66
		H. Newhouser, Det	110	J. Dobson, Bos	2.9	A. Reynolds, NYA	129	E. Kinder, StL	5.1	H. Newhouser, Det	1.60
		F. Papish, ChA	98	S. Chandler, NYA	2.9	P. Marchildon, Phi	128	A. Reynolds, NYA	4.8	B. Feller, Cle	1.54

Earned Run Average		Component ERA		Hit Batsmen		Wild Pitches		Opponent Average		Opponent OBP	
S. Chandler, NYA	2.46	S. Chandler, NYA	2.13	B. Ferriss, Bos	7	H. Newhouser, Det	11	S. Shea, NYA	.200	S. Chandler, NYA	.277
B. Feller, Cle	2.68	S. Shea, NYA	2.62	P. Marchildon, Phi	7	J. Dobson, Bos	11	S. Chandler, NYA	.214	J. Dobson, Bos	.299
D. Fowler, Phi	2.81	B. Feller, Cle	2.66	K. Drews, NYA	5	A. Reynolds, NYA	8	B. Feller, Cle	.215	B. Feller, Cle	.300
E. Lopat, ChA	2.81	W. Masterson, Was	2.83	E. Wynn, Was	5	B. Feller, Cle	7	P. Marchildon, Phi	.224	S. Shea, NYA	.303
H. Newhouser, Det	2.87	J. Dobson, Bos	2.92	6 tied with	4	6 tied with	6	A. Reynolds, NYA	.227	F. Hutchinson, Det	.304

1947 American League Miscellaneous

Managers		
Boston	Joe Cronin	83-71
Chicago	Ted Lyons	70-84
Cleveland	Lou Boudreau	80-74
Detroit	Steve O'Neill	85-69
New York	Bucky Harris	97-57
Philadelphia	Connie Mack	78-76
St. Louis	Muddy Ruel	59-95
Washington	Ossie Bluege	64-90

Awards	
Most Valuable Player	Joe DiMaggio, of, NYA
STATS Cy Young	Bob Feller, Cle
STATS Rookie of the Year	Ferris Fain, 1b, Phi
STATS Manager of the Year	Connie Mack, Phi

STATS All-Star Team

C	Aaron Robinson, NYA	.270	5	36
1B	George McQuinn, NYA	.304	13	80
2B	Joe Gordon, Cle	.272	29	93
3B	George Kell, Det	.320	5	93
SS	Lou Boudreau, Cle	.307	4	67
OF	Joe DiMaggio, NYA	.315	20	97
OF	Tommy Henrich, NYA	.287	16	98
OF	Ted Williams, Bos	.343	32	114
P	Joe Dobson, Bos	18-8	2.95	110 K
P	Bob Feller, Cle	20-11	2.68	196 K
P	Phil Marchildon, Phi	19-9	3.22	128 K
P	Allie Reynolds, NYA	19-8	3.20	129 K
RP	Joe Page, NYA	14-8	2.48	17 Sv

Postseason	
World Series	New York (AL) 4 vs. Brooklyn (NL) 3

Outstanding Performances

Triple Crown
Ted Williams, Bos	.343-32-114

No-Hitters
Don Black, Cle	vs. Phi on July 10
Bill McCahan, Phi	vs. Was on September 3

Cycles
Bobby Doerr, Bos	on May 13
Vic Wertz, Det	on September 14

1947 National League Standings

Team	Overall					Home Games						Road Games						Park Index		Record by Month					
	W	L	Pct	GB	DIF	W	L	R	OR	HR	OHR	W	L	R	OR	HR	OHR	Run	HR	M/A	May	June	July	Aug	S/O
Brooklyn	94	60	.610	—	113	52	25	409	343	37	57	42	35	365	325	46	47	109	101	8-3	12-14	18-11	25-8	18-13	13-11
St. Louis	89	65	.578	5.0	0	46	31	400	331	45	49	43	34	380	303	70	57	107	74	2-9	13-13	18-10	18-12	21-11	17-10
Boston	86	68	.558	8.0	18	50	27	332	289	29	39	36	41	369	333	56	54	88	62	7-5	13-12	17-10	13-18	23-13	13-10
New York	81	73	.526	13.0	18	45	31	417	380	131	75	36	42	413	381	90	47	103	154	4-7	17-7	13-13	15-15	15-20	17-11
Cincinnati	73	81	.474	21.0	1	42	35	318	330	48	47	31	46	363	425	47	55	82	93	7-8	9-14	17-13	14-17	14-19	12-10
Chicago	69	85	.448	25.0	13	36	43	280	384	29	51	33	42	287	338	42	55	101	78	8-5	13-11	12-17	11-19	13-19	12-14
Philadelphia	62	92	.403	32.0	3	38	38	309	323	24	43	24	54	280	364	36	55	101	76	6-8	11-14	10-18	13-17	13-18	9-17
Pittsburgh	62	92	.403	32.0	11	32	45	384	437	95	87	30	47	360	380	61	68	111	141	8-5	9-12	8-21	15-18	14-18	8-18

Clinch Date—Brooklyn 9/22.

Team Batting

Team	G	AB	R	OR	H	2B	3B	HR	TB	RBI	TBB	IBB	SO	HBP	SH	SF	SB	CS	SB%	GDP	Avg	OBP	Slg
New York	155	5343	830	761	1446	220	48	221	2425	790	494	—	568	23	64	—	29	16	.64	114	.271	.335	.454
St. Louis	156	5422	780	634	1462	235	65	115	2172	718	612	—	511	29	68	—	28	—	—	136	.272	.364	.384
Brooklyn	155	5249	774	668	1428	241	50	83	2018	719	732	—	561	29	115	—	88	45	.66	87	.272	.364	.384
Pittsburgh	156	5307	744	817	1385	216	44	156	2157	699	607	—	687	24	70	—	30	—	—	136	.261	.340	.406
Boston	154	5253	701	622	1444	265	42	85	2048	645	558	—	500	14	129	—	58	—	—	130	.275	.346	.390
Cincinnati	154	5299	681	755	1372	242	43	95	1985	637	539	—	530	21	95	—	46	—	—	97	.259	.330	.375
Philadelphia	155	5256	589	687	1354	210	52	60	1849	544	464	—	594	26	82	—	60	—	—	119	.258	.321	.352
Chicago	155	5305	567	722	1373	231	48	71	1913	540	471	—	578	19	64	—	22	—	—	112	.259	.321	.361
NL Total	1240	42434	5666	5666	11264	1860	392	886	16566	5292	4477	—	4529	185	687	—	361	—	—	931	.265	.338	.390
NL Avg Team	155	5304	708	708	1408	233	49	111	2071	662	560	—	566	23	86	—	45	—	—	116	.265	.338	.390

Team Pitching

Team	G	CG	ShO	Rel	Sv	IP	H	R	ER	HR	SH	SF	HB	TBB	IBB	SO	WP	Bk	H/9	SO/9	BB/9	OAvg	OOBP	ERA
St. Louis	156	65	12	187	20	1397.2	1417	634	548	106	73	—	21	495	—	642	20	1	9.1	4.1	3.2	.266	.330	3.53
Boston	154	74	14	167	13	1362.2	1342	622	548	93	67	—	13	453	—	494	15	1	8.9	3.3	3.0	.255	.316	3.62
Brooklyn	155	47	14	223	34	1375.0	1299	668	583	104	81	—	31	626	—	592	36	6	8.5	3.9	4.1	.251	.336	3.82
Philadelphia	155	70	8	161	14	1362.0	1399	687	599	98	90	—	25	513	—	514	25	4	9.2	3.4	3.4	.276	.345	3.96
Chicago	155	46	8	216	15	1367.0	1449	722	613	106	102	—	20	618	—	571	30	3	9.5	3.8	4.1	.274	.353	4.04
Cincinnati	154	54	13	190	13	1365.1	1442	755	669	102	90	—	18	589	—	633	16	5	9.5	4.2	3.9	.274	.349	4.41
New York	155	58	6	212	14	1363.2	1428	761	673	122	85	—	19	590	—	553	34	4	9.4	3.6	3.9	.272	.347	4.44
Pittsburgh	156	44	9	211	13	1374.0	1488	817	715	155	67	—	27	592	—	530	24	2	9.7	3.5	3.9	.275	.350	4.68
NL Total	1240	458	84	1567	136	10967.1	11264	5666	4948	886	655	—	174	4476	—	4529	200	26	9.2	3.7	3.7	.265	.338	4.06
NL Avg Team	155	57	11	196	17	1370.1	1408	708	619	111	82	—	22	560	—	566	25	3	9.2	3.7	3.7	.265	.338	4.06

Team Fielding

Team	G	PO	A	E	TC	DP	PB	Pct
St. Louis	156	4192	1740	128	6060	169	13	.979
Brooklyn	155	4126	1691	129	5946	169	11	.978
Cincinnati	154	4090	1646	138	5874	134	6	.977
Chicago	155	4100	1859	150	6109	159	10	.975
Pittsburgh	156	4120	1625	149	5894	131	18	.975
Philadelphia	155	4090	1716	152	5958	140	27	.974
Boston	154	4086	1723	153	5962	124	7	.974
New York	155	4095	1775	155	6025	136	6	.974
NL Total	1240	32899	13775	1154	47828	1162	98	.976

Team vs. Team Records

	Bos	Bro	ChN	Cin	NYG	Phi	Pit	StL	Won
Bos	—	12	13	13	13	14	12	9	86
Bro	10	—	15	15	14	14	15	11	94
ChN	9	7	—	12	7	16	8	10	69
Cin	9	7	10	—	13	13	13	8	73
NYG	9	8	15	9	—	12	15	13	81
Phi	8	8	6	9	10	—	13	8	62
Pit	10	7	14	9	7	9	—	6	62
StL	13	11	12	14	9	14	16	—	89
Lost	68	60	85	81	73	92	92	65	

1947 National League Batting Leaders

Games		At-Bats		Runs		Hits		Doubles		Triples	
F. Gustine, Pit	156	R. Schoendienst, StL	659	J. Mize, NYG	137	T. Holmes, Bos	191	E. Miller, Cin	38	H. Walker, 2tm	16
E. Verban, Phi	155	F. Baumholtz, Cin	643	J. Robinson, Bro	125	H. Walker, 2tm	186	B. Elliott, Bos	35	S. Musial, StL	13
W. Marshall, NYG	155	T. Holmes, Bos	618	R. Kiner, Pit	118	S. Musial, StL	183	C. Ryan, Bos	33	E. Slaughter, StL	13
J. Mize, NYG	154	F. Gustine, Pit	616	S. Musial, StL	113	F. Gustine, Pit	183	T. Holmes, Bos	33	F. Baumholtz, Cin	9
R. Kiner, Pit	152	J. Robinson, Bro	590	W. Kurowski, StL	108	F. Baumholtz, Cin	182	F. Baumholtz, Cin	32	R. Schoendienst, StL	9

Home Runs		Total Bases		Runs Batted In		Walks		Intentional Walks		Strikeouts	
R. Kiner, Pit	51	R. Kiner, Pit	361	J. Mize, NYG	138	P. Reese, Bro	104	Statistic unavailable		B. Nicholson, ChN	83
J. Mize, NYG	51	J. Mize, NYG	360	R. Kiner, Pit	127	H. Greenberg, Pit	104			R. Kiner, Pit	81
W. Marshall, NYG	36	W. Marshall, NYG	310	W. Cooper, NYG	122	E. Stanky, Bro	103			B. Thomson, NYG	78
W. Cooper, NYG	35	W. Cooper, NYG	302	B. Elliott, Bos	113	R. Kiner, Pit	98			H. Greenberg, Pit	73
B. Thomson, NYG	29	S. Musial, StL	296	W. Marshall, NYG	107	D. Walker, Bro	97			H. Schultz, 2tm	70

Hit By Pitch		Sac Hits		Sac Flies		Stolen Bases		Caught Stealing		GDP	
W. Kurowski, StL	10	J. Robinson, Bro	28	Statistic unavailable		J. Robinson, Bro	29	Statistic unavailable		A. Pafko, ChN	19
J. Robinson, Bro	9	H. Walker, 2tm	18			P. Reiser, Bro	14			W. Kurowski, StL	19
5 tied with	5	B. Kerr, NYG	13			H. Walker, 2tm	13			S. Musial, StL	18
		3 tied with	12			J. Hopp, Bos	13			D. Ennis, Phi	17
						E. Torgeson, Bos	11			C. Furillo, Bro	17

Runs Created		Runs Created/27 Outs		Batting Average		On-Base Percentage		Slugging Percentage		OBP+Slugging	
R. Kiner, Pit	142	R. Kiner, Pit	9.36	H. Walker, 2tm	.363	H. Walker, 2tm	.436	R. Kiner, Pit	.639	R. Kiner, Pit	1.055
J. Mize, NYG	138	J. Mize, NYG	8.79	B. Elliott, Bos	.317	W. Kurowski, StL	.420	J. Mize, NYG	.614	J. Mize, NYG	.998
S. Musial, StL	117	W. Kurowski, StL	8.07	P. Cavarretta, ChN	.314	R. Kiner, Pit	.417	W. Cooper, NYG	.586	W. Kurowski, StL	.964
W. Kurowski, StL	115	H. Walker, 2tm	7.82	R. Kiner, Pit	.313	D. Walker, Bro	.415	W. Kurowski, StL	.544	B. Elliott, Bos	.927
W. Marshall, NYG	112	B. Elliott, Bos	7.33	S. Musial, StL	.312	P. Reese, Bro	.414	W. Marshall, NYG	.528	W. Cooper, NYG	.926

1947 National League Pitching Leaders

Wins		Losses		Winning Percentage		Games		Games Started		Complete Games	
E. Blackwell, Cin	22	J. Schmitz, ChN	18	L. Jansen, NYG	.808	K. Trinkle, NYG	62	R. Branca, Bro	36	E. Blackwell, Cin	23
L. Jansen, NYG	21	K. Higbe, 2tm	17	G. Munger, StL	.762	H. Behrman, 2tm	50	J. Sain, Bos	35	J. Sain, Bos	22
R. Branca, Bro	21	M. Dickson, StL	16	E. Blackwell, Cin	.733	K. Higbe, 2tm	50	W. Spahn, Bos	35	W. Spahn, Bos	22
J. Sain, Bos	21	O. Judd, Phi	15	J. Hatten, Bro	.680	E. Kush, ChN	47	E. Blackwell, Cin	33	L. Jansen, NYG	20
W. Spahn, Bos	21	P. Roe, Pit	15	W. Spahn, Bos	.677	M. Dickson, StL	47	K. Higbe, 2tm	33	D. Leonard, Phi	19

Shutouts		Saves		Games Finished		Batters Faced		Innings Pitched		Hits Allowed	
W. Spahn, Bos	7	H. Casey, Bro	18	K. Trinkle, NYG	38	W. Spahn, Bos	1174	W. Spahn, Bos	289.2	J. Sain, Bos	265
G. Munger, StL	6	K. Trinkle, NYG	10	H. Casey, Bro	37	R. Branca, Bro	1158	R. Branca, Bro	280.0	R. Branca, Bro	251
E. Blackwell, Cin	6	H. Gumbert, Cin	10	H. Gumbert, Cin	34	J. Sain, Bos	1131	E. Blackwell, Cin	273.0	W. Spahn, Bos	245
R. Branca, Bro	5	H. Behrman, 2tm	8	E. Kush, ChN	23	E. Blackwell, Cin	1086	J. Sain, Bos	266.0	L. Jansen, NYG	241
M. Dickson, StL	4	4 tied with	5	2 tied with	19	K. Higbe, 2tm	1051	L. Jansen, NYG	248.0	S. Rowe, Phi	232

Home Runs Allowed		Walks		Walks/9 Innings		Strikeouts		Strikeouts/9 Innings		Strikeout/Walk Ratio	
L. Jansen, NYG	23	K. Higbe, 2tm	122	L. Jansen, NYG	2.1	E. Blackwell, Cin	193	E. Blackwell, Cin	6.4	E. Blackwell, Cin	2.03
D. Koslo, NYG	23	J. Hatten, Bro	105	S. Rowe, Phi	2.1	R. Branca, Bro	148	G. Munger, StL	4.9	L. Jansen, NYG	1.82
R. Branca, Bro	22	R. Branca, Bro	98	D. Leonard, Phi	2.2	J. Sain, Bos	132	R. Branca, Bro	4.8	D. Leonard, Phi	1.81
K. Higbe, 2tm	22	E. Blackwell, Cin	95	Raffensberger, 2tm	2.3	G. Munger, StL	123	J. Sain, Bos	4.5	J. Sain, Bos	1.67
S. Rowe, Phi	22	P. Erickson, ChN	93	R. Barrett, Bos	2.3	W. Spahn, Bos	123	M. Dickson, StL	4.3	S. Rowe, Phi	1.64

Earned Run Average		Component ERA		Hit Batsmen		Wild Pitches		Opponent Average		Opponent OBP	
W. Spahn, Bos	2.33	W. Spahn, Bos	2.50	R. Branca, Bro	6	O. Judd, Phi	8	H. Taylor, Bro	.225	W. Spahn, Bos	.283
E. Blackwell, Cin	2.47	E. Blackwell, Cin	2.66	H. Taylor, Bro	5	E. Erautt, Cin	7	W. Spahn, Bos	.226	R. Barrett, Bos	.292
R. Branca, Bro	2.67	R. Barrett, Bos	3.01	J. Hatten, Bro	5	M. Kennedy, NYG	7	E. Blackwell, Cin	.234	E. Blackwell, Cin	.304
D. Leonard, Phi	2.68	D. Leonard, Phi	3.03	P. Erickson, ChN	5	R. Branca, Bro	7	R. Branca, Bro	.240	D. Leonard, Phi	.306
M. Dickson, StL	3.07	R. Branca, Bro	3.22	J. Bagby Jr., Pit	5	K. Higbe, 2tm	7	M. Dickson, StL	.243	L. Jansen, NYG	.306

1947 National League Miscellaneous

Managers

Boston	Billy Southworth	86-68
Brooklyn	Clyde Sukeforth	2-0
	Burt Shotton	92-60
Chicago	Charlie Grimm	69-85
Cincinnati	Johnny Neun	73-81
New York	Mel Ott	81-73
Philadelphia	Ben Chapman	62-92
Pittsburgh	Billy Herman	61-92
	Bill Burwell	1-0
St. Louis	Eddie Dyer	89-65

Awards

Most Valuable Player	Bob Elliott, 3b, Bos
STATS Cy Young	Ewell Blackwell, Cin
Rookie of the Year	J. Robinson, 1b, Bro
STATS Manager of the Year	Burt Shotton, Bro

STATS All-Star Team

C	Walker Cooper, NYG	.305	35	122
1B	Johnny Mize, NYG	.302	51	138
2B	Bill Rigney, NYG	.267	17	59
3B	Bob Elliott, Bos	.317	22	113
SS	Pee Wee Reese, Bro	.284	12	73
OF	Ralph Kiner, Pit	.313	51	127
OF	Willard Marshall, NYG	.291	36	107
OF	Harry Walker, 2tm	.363	1	41
P	Ewell Blackwell, Cin	22-8	2.47	193 K
P	Ralph Branca, Bro	21-12	2.67	148 K
P	Larry Jansen, NYG	21-5	3.16	104 K
P	Warren Spahn, Bos	21-10	2.33	123 K
RP	Hugh Casey, Bro	10-4	3.99	18 Sv

Postseason

World Series	Brooklyn (NL) 3 vs. New York (AL) 4

Outstanding Performances

No-Hitters

Ewell Blackwell, Cin vs. Bos on June 18

Three-Homer Games

Johnny Mize, NYG	on April 24
W. Marshall, NYG	on July 18
Ralph Kiner, Pit	on August 16
Ralph Kiner, Pit	on September 11

1948 American League Standings

Team	W	L	Pct	GB	DIF	W	L	R	OR	HR	OHR	W	L	R	OR	HR	OHR	Run	HR	M/A	May	June	July	Aug	S/O
		Overall						Home Games						Road Games				Park Index				Record by Month			
Cleveland	97	58	.626	—	115	48	30	398	272	77	41	49	28	442	296	78	41	90	98	6-0	17-11	16-12	14-15	22-12	22-8
Boston	96	59	.619	1.0	40	55	23	481	336	60	43	41	36	426	384	61	40	100	101	3-6	11-17	19-6	24-9	19-10	20-11
New York	94	60	.610	2.5	2	50	27	413	315	70	54	44	33	444	318	69	40	96	114	6-3	15-12	17-12	16-12	21-10	19-11
Philadelphia	84	70	.545	12.5	23	36	41	347	396	33	47	48	29	382	339	35	39	103	108	5-5	15-12	10-14	15-14	15-14	11-16
Detroit	78	76	.506	18.5	3	39	38	327	355	39	61	39	38	373	371	39	31	92	143	4-7	15-13	10-14	17-14	13-13	19-15
St. Louis	59	94	.386	37.0	0	34	42	363	451	29	64	25	52	308	398	34	39	117	129	4-4	12-13	8-21	10-17	13-19	12-20
Washington	56	97	.366	40.0	0	29	48	312	419	11	24	27	49	266	377	20	57	112	45	5-5	12-16	13-13	10-19	8-24	8-20
Chicago	51	101	.336	44.5	0	27	48	278	378	21	36	24	53	281	436	34	53	94	67	3-6	6-20	10-14	12-22	11-20	9-19

Clinch Date—Cleveland 10/04.

Team Batting

Team	G	AB	R	OR	H	2B	3B	HR	TB	RBI	TBB	IBB	SO	HBP	SH	SF	SB	CS	SB%	GDP	Avg	OBP	Slg
Boston	155	5363	907	720	1471	277	40	121	2191	854	823	—	552	32	66	—	38	17	.69	144	.274	.374	.409
New York	154	5324	857	633	1480	251	75	139	2298	806	623	—	478	23	78	—	24	24	.50	136	.278	.356	.432
Cleveland	156	5446	840	568	1534	242	54	155	2349	801	646	—	575	24	85	—	54	44	.55	132	.282	.360	.431
Philadelphia	154	5181	729	735	1345	231	47	68	1874	684	726	—	523	22	120	—	40	32	.56	137	.260	.353	.362
Detroit	154	5235	700	726	1396	219	58	78	1965	661	671	—	504	26	130	—	22	32	.41	134	.267	.353	.375
St. Louis	155	5303	671	849	1438	251	62	63	2002	625	578	—	572	19	113	—	63	44	.59	130	.271	.345	.378
Washington	154	5111	578	796	1245	203	75	31	1691	537	568	—	572	20	84	—	76	48	.61	124	.244	.322	.331
Chicago	154	5192	559	814	1303	172	39	55	1718	532	595	—	528	11	73	—	46	47	.49	119	.251	.329	.331
AL Total	1236	42155	5841	5841	11212	1846	450	710	16088	5500	5230	—	4304	177	749	—	363	288	.56	1056	.266	.349	.382
AL Avg Team	155	5269	730	730	1402	231	56	89	2011	688	654	—	538	22	94	—	45	36	.56	132	.266	.349	.382

Team Pitching

Team	G	CG	ShO	Rel	Sv	IP	H	R	ER	HR	SH	SF	HB	TBB	IBB	SO	WP	Bk	H/9	SO/9	BB/9	OAvg	OOBP	ERA
Cleveland	156	66	26	196	30	1409.1	1246	568	505	82	81	—	19	625	—	593	16	3	8.0	3.8	4.0	.239	.323	3.22
New York	154	62	16	162	24	1365.2	1289	633	569	94	90	—	24	641	—	654	27	7	8.5	4.3	4.2	.250	.336	3.75
Detroit	154	60	5	187	22	1377.0	1367	726	635	92	104	—	15	589	—	678	31	2	8.9	4.4	3.8	.259	.335	4.15
Boston	155	70	11	141	13	1379.1	1445	720	653	83	68	—	19	592	—	513	26	6	9.4	3.3	3.9	.270	.345	4.26
Philadelphia	154	74	7	137	18	1368.2	1456	735	673	86	102	—	15	638	—	486	35	4	9.6	3.2	4.2	.275	.355	4.43
Washington	154	42	4	201	22	1357.1	1439	796	702	81	99	—	27	734	—	446	19	0	9.5	3.0	4.9	.273	.364	4.65
Chicago	154	35	2	210	23	1345.2	1454	814	731	89	122	—	30	673	—	403	32	6	9.7	2.7	4.5	.280	.365	4.89
St. Louis	155	35	4	243	20	1373.1	1513	849	764	103	78	—	30	737	—	531	47	2	9.9	3.5	4.8	.283	.373	5.01
AL Total	1236	444	75	1477	172	10976.1	11209	5841	5232	710	744	—	179	5229	—	4304	233	30	9.2	3.5	4.3	.266	.349	4.29
AL Avg Team	155	56	9	185	22	1372.1	1401	730	654	89	93	—	22	654	—	538	29	4	9.2	3.5	4.3	.266	.349	4.29

Team Fielding

Team	G	PO	A	E	TC	DP	PB	Pct
Cleveland	156	4229	1849	114	6192	183	8	.982
Philadelphia	154	4108	1710	113	5931	180	7	.981
Boston	155	4143	1796	116	6055	174	5	.981
New York	154	4108	1494	120	5722	161	13	.979
Washington	154	4071	1662	154	5887	144	12	.974
Detroit	154	4123	1644	155	5922	143	13	.974
Chicago	154	4033	1763	160	5956	176	15	.973
St. Louis	155	4119	1736	168	6023	190	7	.972
AL Total	1236	32934	13654	1100	47688	1351	80	.977

Team vs. Team Records

	Bos	ChA	Cle	Det	NYA	Phi	StL	Was	Won
Bos	—	14	11	15	14	12	15	15	96
ChA	8	—	6	8	6	6	8	9	51
Cle	12	16	—	13	10	16	14	16	97
Det	7	14	9	—	9	12	11	16	78
NYA	8	16	12	13	—	12	16	17	94
Phi	10	16	6	10	10	—	18	14	84
StL	7	13	8	11	6	4	—	10	59
Was	7	12	6	6	5	8	12	—	56
Lost	59	101	58	76	60	70	94	97	

Seasons: Standings, Leaders

1948 American League Batting Leaders

Games		At-Bats		Runs		Hits		Doubles		Triples	
V. Stephens, Bos	155	D. DiMaggio, Bos	648	T. Henrich, NYA	138	B. Dillinger, StL	207	T. Williams, Bos	44	T. Henrich, NYA	14
D. DiMaggio, Bos	155	B. Dillinger, StL	644	D. DiMaggio, Bos	127	D. Mitchell, Cle	204	T. Henrich, NYA	42	B. Stewart, 2tm	13
T. Lupien, ChA	154	V. Stephens, Bos	635	J. Pesky, Bos	124	L. Boudreau, Cle	199	H. Majeski, Phi	41	E. Yost, Was	11
3 tied with	153	T. Lupien, ChA	617	T. Williams, Bos	124	J. DiMaggio, NYA	190	J. Priddy, StL	40	P. Mullin, Det	11
		D. Mitchell, Cle	608	L. Boudreau, Cle	116	T. Williams, Bos	188	D. DiMaggio, Bos	40	J. DiMaggio, NYA	11

Home Runs		Total Bases		Runs Batted In		Walks		Intentional Walks		Strikeouts	
J. DiMaggio, NYA	39	J. DiMaggio, NYA	355	J. DiMaggio, NYA	155	T. Williams, Bos	126	Statistic unavailable		P. Seerey, 2tm	102
J. Gordon, Cle	32	T. Henrich, NYA	326	V. Stephens, Bos	137	E. Joost, Phi	119			E. Joost, Phi	87
K. Keltner, Cle	31	T. Williams, Bos	313	T. Williams, Bos	127	F. Fain, Phi	113			G. Coan, Was	78
V. Stephens, Bos	29	V. Stephens, Bos	299	J. Gordon, Cle	124	D. DiMaggio, Bos	101			L. Doby, Cle	77
B. Doerr, Bos	27	L. Boudreau, Cle	299	H. Majeski, Phi	120	J. Pesky, Bos	99			J. Hegan, Cle	74

Hit By Pitch		Sac Hits		Sac Flies		Stolen Bases		Caught Stealing		GDP	
J. DiMaggio, NYA	8	B. McCosky, Phi	22	Statistic unavailable		B. Dillinger, StL	28	D. Mitchell, Cle	18	V. Stephens, Bos	25
S. Vico, Det	7	C. Stevens, StL	18			G. Coan, Was	23	B. Dillinger, StL	11	S. Vico, Det	23
G. Coan, Was	7	E. Mayo, Det	18			M. Vernon, Was	15	M. Vernon, Was	11	K. Keltner, Cle	23
J. Pesky, Bos	6	S. Vico, Det	17			D. Mitchell, Cle	13	F. Baker, ChA	10	B. Johnson, NYA	22
H. Majeski, Phi	6	L. Boudreau, Cle	16			3 tied with	11	D. Philley, ChA	10	B. Tebbetts, Bos	22

Runs Created		Runs Created/27 Outs		Batting Average		On-Base Percentage		Slugging Percentage		OBP+Slugging	
T. Williams, Bos	160	T. Williams, Bos	12.92	T. Williams, Bos	.369	T. Williams, Bos	.497	T. Williams, Bos	.615	T. Williams, Bos	1.112
J. DiMaggio, NYA	137	L. Boudreau, Cle	8.82	L. Boudreau, Cle	.355	L. Boudreau, Cle	.453	J. DiMaggio, NYA	.598	J. DiMaggio, NYA	.994
L. Boudreau, Cle	130	J. DiMaggio, NYA	8.62	D. Mitchell, Cle	.336	L. Appling, ChA	.423	T. Henrich, NYA	.554	L. Boudreau, Cle	.987
T. Henrich, NYA	128	T. Henrich, NYA	7.98	A. Zarilla, StL	.329	B. Goodman, Bos	.414	L. Boudreau, Cle	.534	T. Henrich, NYA	.945
D. DiMaggio, Bos	114	B. Doerr, Bos	7.36	B. McCosky, Phi	.326	F. Fain, Phi	.412	K. Keltner, Cle	.522	K. Keltner, Cle	.917

1948 American League Pitching Leaders

Wins		Losses		Winning Percentage		Games		Games Started		Complete Games	
H. Newhouser, Det	21	F. Sanford, StL	21	J. Kramer, Bos	.783	J. Page, NYA	55	B. Feller, Cle	38	B. Lemon, Cle	20
G. Bearden, Cle	20	B. Wight, ChA	20	G. Bearden, Cle	.741	A. Widmar, StL	49	B. Lemon, Cle	37	H. Newhouser, Det	19
B. Lemon, Cle	20	E. Wynn, Was	19	V. Raschi, NYA	.704	F. Biscan, StL	47	H. Newhouser, Det	35	V. Raschi, NYA	18
V. Raschi, NYA	19	A. Houtteman, Det	16	A. Reynolds, NYA	.696	D. Thompson, Was	46	F. Sanford, StL	33	B. Feller, Cle	18
B. Feller, Cle	19	S. Hudson, Was	16	3 tied with	.652	2 tied with	45	2 tied with	32	3 tied with	16

Shutouts		Saves		Games Finished		Batters Faced		Innings Pitched		Hits Allowed	
B. Lemon, Cle	10	R. Christopher, Cle	17	J. Page, NYA	38	B. Feller, Cle	1214	B. Lemon, Cle	293.2	B. Lemon, Cle	255
G. Bearden, Cle	6	J. Page, NYA	16	R. Christopher, Cle	28	B. Feller, Cle	1186	B. Feller, Cle	280.1	F. Sanford, StL	250
V. Raschi, NYA	6	A. Houtteman, Det	10	T. Ferrick, Was	26	H. Newhouser, Det	1146	H. Newhouser, Det	272.1	H. Newhouser, Det	249
J. Dobson, Bos	5	T. Ferrick, Was	10	D. Thompson, Was	24	J. Dobson, Bos	1044	J. Dobson, Bos	245.1	E. Lopat, NYA	246
4 tied with	3	H. Judson, ChA	8	F. Biscan, StL	22	A. Reynolds, NYA	1017	A. Reynolds, NYA	236.1	A. Reynolds, NYA	240

Home Runs Allowed		Walks		Walks/9 Innings		Strikeouts		Strikeouts/9 Innings		Strikeout/Walk Ratio	
F. Hutchinson, Det	32	B. Wight, ChA	135	F. Hutchinson, Det	2.0	B. Feller, Cle	164	L. Brissie, Phi	5.9	F. Hutchinson, Det	1.92
B. Feller, Cle	20	P. Marchildon, Phi	131	E. Lopat, NYA	2.6	B. Lemon, Cle	147	B. Feller, Cle	5.3	V. Raschi, NYA	1.68
F. Sanford, StL	19	B. Lemon, Cle	129	J. Kramer, Bos	2.8	H. Newhouser, Det	143	V. Raschi, NYA	5.0	H. Newhouser, Det	1.44
P. Marchildon, Phi	19	W. Masterson, Was	122	V. Raschi, NYA	3.0	L. Brissie, Phi	127	H. Newhouser, Det	4.7	B. Feller, Cle	1.41
E. Wynn, Was	18	B. Kennedy, 2tm	117	E. Kinder, Bos	3.2	V. Raschi, NYA	124	B. Lemon, Cle	4.5	L. Brissie, Phi	1.34

Earned Run Average		Component ERA		Hit Batsmen		Wild Pitches		Opponent Average		Opponent OBP	
G. Bearden, Cle	2.43	B. Lemon, Cle	2.65	T. Byrne, NYA	9	A. Reynolds, NYA	9	B. Lemon, Cle	.216	F. Hutchinson, Det	.297
B. Lemon, Cle	2.82	G. Bearden, Cle	2.95	F. Biscan, StL	9	L. Brissie, Phi	7	G. Bearden, Cle	.229	B. Lemon, Cle	.302
H. Newhouser, Det	3.01	H. Newhouser, Det	2.96	B. Ferriss, Bos	7	B. Stephens, StL	7	B. Feller, Cle	.241	H. Newhouser, Det	.309
M. Parnell, Bos	3.14	V. Raschi, NYA	3.23	4 tied with	6	V. Trucks, Det	7	H. Newhouser, Det	.242	V. Raschi, NYA	.310
D. Trout, Det	3.43	B. Feller, Cle	3.38			P. Marchildon, Phi	7	C. Fannin, StL	.245	B. Feller, Cle	.317

1948 American League Miscellaneous

Managers		
Boston	Joe McCarthy	96-59
Chicago	Ted Lyons	51-101
Cleveland	Lou Boudreau	97-58
Detroit	Steve O'Neill	78-76
New York	Bucky Harris	94-60
Philadelphia	Connie Mack	84-70
St. Louis	Zack Taylor	59-94
Washington	Joe Kuhel	56-97

Awards	
Most Valuable Player	Lou Boudreau, ss, Cle
STATS Cy Young	Gene Bearden, Cle
STATS Rookie of the Year	Gene Bearden, p, Cle
STATS Manager of the Year	Lou Boudreau, Cle

STATS All-Star Team

C	Birdie Tebbetts, Bos	.280	5	68
1B	Ferris Fain, Phi	.281	7	88
2B	Bobby Doerr, Bos	.285	27	111
3B	Ken Keltner, Cle	.297	31	119
SS	Lou Boudreau, Cle	.355	18	106
OF	Joe DiMaggio, NYA	.320	39	155
OF	Tommy Henrich, NYA	.308	25	100
OF	Ted Williams, Bos	.369	25	127
P	Gene Bearden, Cle	20-7	2.43	80 K
P	Bob Feller, Cle	19-15	3.56	164 K
P	Bob Lemon, Cle	20-14	2.82	147 K
P	Hal Newhouser, Det	21-12	3.01	143 K
RP	Russ Christopher, Cle	3-2	2.90	17 Sv

Postseason	
World Series	Cleveland (AL) 4 vs. Boston (NL) 2

Outstanding Performances

No-Hitters
Bob Lemon, Cle   @ Det on June 30
Four-Homer Games
Pat Seerey, ChA   on July 18
Three-Homer Games
Joe DiMaggio, NYA   on May 23
Cycles
Joe DiMaggio, NYA   on May 20

1948 National League Standings

Team	W	L	Pct	GB	DIF	W	L	R	OR	HR	OHR	W	L	R	OR	HR	OHR	Run	HR	M/A	May	June	July	Aug	S/O
		Overall						Home Games						Road Games				Park Index				Record by Month			
Boston	91	62	.595	—	109	45	31	349	297	32	40	46	31	390	287	63	53	97	63	5-7	12-10	20-10	19-11	14-17	21-7
St. Louis	85	69	.552	6.5	26	44	33	359	327	47	43	41	36	383	319	58	60	98	76	4-4	16-11	15-13	12-17	21-12	17-12
Brooklyn	84	70	.545	7.5	8	36	41	352	386	43	68	48	29	392	281	48	51	110	112	5-5	11-15	11-13	21-10	20-10	16-17
Pittsburgh	83	71	.539	8.5	8	47	31	384	370	69	64	36	40	322	329	39	56	113	136	6-4	14-12	13-13	13-16	19-9	18-17
New York	78	76	.506	13.5	23	37	40	366	374	89	82	41	36	414	330	75	40	99	149	7-4	13-10	12-16	18-13	10-17	18-16
Philadelphia	66	88	.429	25.5	5	32	44	276	332	32	44	34	44	315	397	59	51	88	71	5-6	14-13	14-14	15-16	7-19	11-20
Cincinnati	64	89	.418	27.0	1	32	45	312	398	68	52	32	44	276	354	36	52	111	135	6-6	12-15	11-15	12-19	11-16	12-18
Chicago	64	90	.416	27.5	0	35	42	282	323	38	34	29	48	315	383	49	55	87	69	4-6	10-16	13-15	12-20	13-15	12-18

Clinch Date—Boston 9/26.

Team Batting

Team	G	AB	R	OR	H	2B	3B	HR	TB	RBI	TBB	IBB	SO	HBP	SH	SF	SB	CS	SB%	GDP	Avg	OBP	Slg
New York	155	5277	780	704	1352	210	49	164	2152	733	599	—	648	19	65	—	51	—	—	113	.256	.334	.408
Brooklyn	155	5328	744	667	1393	256	54	91	2030	671	601	—	684	18	100	—	114	—	—	100	.261	.338	.381
St. Louis	155	5302	742	646	1396	238	58	105	2065	680	594	—	521	22	76	—	24	—	—	125	.263	.340	.389
Boston	154	5297	739	584	1458	272	49	95	2113	695	671	—	536	17	140	—	43	—	—	116	.275	.359	.399
Pittsburgh	156	5286	706	699	1388	191	54	108	2011	650	580	—	578	21	56	—	68	—	—	100	.263	.338	.380
Chicago	155	5352	597	706	1402	225	44	87	1976	564	443	—	578	29	70	—	39	—	—	104	.262	.322	.369
Philadelphia	155	5287	591	729	1367	227	39	91	1945	548	440	—	598	21	81	—	68	—	—	99	.259	.318	.368
Cincinnati	153	5127	588	752	1266	221	37	104	1873	548	478	—	586	16	79	—	42	—	—	121	.247	.313	.365
NL Total	1238	42256	5487	5487	11022	1840	384	845	16165	5089	4406	—	4729	163	667	—	449	—	—	878	.261	.333	.383
NL Avg Team	155	5282	686	686	1378	230	48	106	2021	636	551	—	591	20	83	—	56	—	—	110	.261	.333	.383

Team Pitching

Team	G	CG	ShO	Rel	Sv	IP	H	R	ER	HR	SH	SF	HB	TBB	IBB	SO	WP	Bk	H/9	SO/9	BB/9	OAvg	OOBP	ERA
Boston	154	70	10	167	17	1389.1	1354	584	521	93	74	—	14	430	—	579	11	0	8.8	3.8	2.8	.254	.311	3.38
Brooklyn	155	52	9	211	22	1392.2	1328	667	581	119	76	—	31	633	—	670	35	2	8.6	4.3	4.1	.253	.337	3.75
St. Louis	155	60	13	205	18	1368.0	1392	646	594	103	81	—	10	476	—	625	22	2	9.2	4.1	3.1	.264	.326	3.91
New York	155	54	15	230	21	1373.0	1425	704	599	122	84	—	27	556	—	527	23	1	9.3	3.5	3.6	.269	.341	3.93
Chicago	155	51	7	220	10	1355.1	1385	706	603	89	97	—	17	619	—	636	27	2	9.0	4.2	4.1	.261	.341	4.00
Philadelphia	155	61	6	162	15	1362.1	1385	729	617	95	74	—	17	556	—	550	26	3	9.1	3.6	3.7	.269	.342	4.08
Pittsburgh	156	65	5	166	19	1371.2	1373	699	632	120	71	—	24	564	—	543	36	5	9.0	3.6	3.7	.260	.334	4.15
Cincinnati	153	40	8	211	20	1343.1	1410	752	667	104	89	—	18	572	—	599	20	2	9.4	4.0	3.8	.270	.344	4.47
NL Total	1238	453	73	1572	142	10955.2	11022	5487	4814	845	646	—	158	4406	—	4729	200	17	9.1	3.9	3.6	.261	.333	3.95
NL Avg Team	155	57	9	197	18	1369.2	1378	686	602	106	81	—	20	551	—	591	25	2	9.1	3.9	3.6	.261	.333	3.95

Team Fielding

Team	G	PO	A	E	TC	DP	PB	Pct
St. Louis	155	4107	1716	119	5942	138	8	.980
Pittsburgh	156	4114	1757	137	6008	150	20	.977
Boston	154	4164	1677	143	5984	132	8	.976
New York	155	4106	1711	156	5973	134	7	.974
Brooklyn	155	4172	1646	161	5979	151	14	.973
Cincinnati	153	4018	1644	158	5820	135	10	.973
Chicago	155	4062	1811	172	6045	152	11	.972
Philadelphia	155	4092	1606	210	5908	126	19	.964
NL Total	1238	32835	13568	1256	47659	1118	97	.974

Team vs. Team Records

	Bos	Bro	ChN	Cin	NYG	Phi	Pit	StL	Won
Bos	—	14	16	13	11	14	12	11	91
Bro	8	—	11	18	11	15	9	12	84
ChN	6	11	—	10	11	7	8	11	64
Cin	8	4	12	—	10	11	9	10	64
NYG	11	11	11	12	—	14	12	7	78
Phi	8	7	15	11	8	—	12	5	66
Pit	10	13	14	13	10	10	—	13	83
StL	11	10	11	12	15	17	9	—	85
Lost	62	70	90	89	76	88	71	69	

1948 National League Batting Leaders

Games		At-Bats		Runs		Hits		Doubles		Triples	
R. Kiner, Pit	156	S. Rojek, Pit	641	S. Musial, StL	135	S. Musial, StL	230	S. Musial, StL	46	S. Musial, StL	18
S. Rojek, Pit	156	S. Musial, StL	611	W. Lockman, NYG	117	T. Holmes, Bos	190	D. Ennis, Phi	40	J. Hopp, Pit	12
S. Musial, StL	155	D. Ennis, Phi	589	J. Mize, NYG	110	S. Rojek, Pit	186	A. Dark, Bos	39	E. Slaughter, StL	11
D. Ennis, Phi	152	T. Holmes, Bos	585	J. Robinson, Bro	108	E. Slaughter, StL	176	J. Robinson, Bro	38	W. Lockman, NYG	10
J. Mize, NYG	152	W. Lockman, NYG	584	R. Kiner, Pit	104	A. Dark, Bos	175	T. Holmes, Bos	35	E. Waitkus, ChN	10

Home Runs		Total Bases		Runs Batted In		Walks		Intentional Walks		Strikeouts	
R. Kiner, Pit	40	S. Musial, StL	429	S. Musial, StL	131	B. Elliott, Bos	131	Statistic unavailable		H. Sauer, Cin	85
J. Mize, NYG	40	J. Mize, NYG	316	J. Mize, NYG	125	R. Kiner, Pit	112			J. Blatnik, Phi	77
S. Musial, StL	39	D. Ennis, Phi	309	R. Kiner, Pit	123	J. Mize, NYG	94			B. Thomson, NYG	77
H. Sauer, Cin	35	R. Kiner, Pit	296	S. Gordon, NYG	107	3 tied with	81			R. Smalley, ChN	76
2 tied with	30	A. Pafko, ChN	283	A. Pafko, ChN	101					2 tied with	68

Hit By Pitch		Sac Hits		Sac Flies		Stolen Bases		Caught Stealing		GDP	
J. Robinson, Bro	7	J. Sain, Bos	16	Statistic unavailable		R. Ashburn, Phi	32	Statistic unavailable		N. Jones, StL	25
5 tied with	5	H. Jeffcoat, ChN	14			P. Reese, Bro	25			T. Holmes, Bos	18
		C. Corbitt, Cin	11			S. Rojek, Pit	24			S. Musial, StL	18
		E. Verban, 2tm	11			J. Robinson, Bro	22			S. Gordon, NYG	18
		P. Masi, Bos	11			E. Torgeson, Bos	19			D. Litwhiler, 2tm	18

Runs Created		Runs Created/27 Outs		Batting Average		On-Base Percentage		Slugging Percentage		OBP+Slugging	
S. Musial, StL	177	S. Musial, StL	11.72	S. Musial, StL	.376	S. Musial, StL	.450	S. Musial, StL	.702	S. Musial, StL	1.152
J. Mize, NYG	133	J. Mize, NYG	8.70	R. Ashburn, Phi	.333	B. Elliott, Bos	.423	J. Mize, NYG	.564	J. Mize, NYG	.959
R. Kiner, Pit	115	S. Gordon, NYG	7.60	T. Holmes, Bos	.325	R. Ashburn, Phi	.410	S. Gordon, NYG	.537	S. Gordon, NYG	.927
S. Gordon, NYG	112	E. Slaughter, StL	7.40	A. Dark, Bos	.322	E. Slaughter, StL	.409	R. Kiner, Pit	.533	R. Kiner, Pit	.924
E. Slaughter, StL	109	G. Hermanski, Bro	7.36	E. Slaughter, StL	.321	J. Mize, NYG	.395	D. Ennis, Phi	.525	B. Elliott, Bos	.897

1948 National League Pitching Leaders

Wins		Losses		Winning Percentage		Games		Games Started		Complete Games	
J. Sain, Bos	24	D. Leonard, Phi	17	R. Sewell, Pit	.813	H. Gumbert, Cin	61	J. Sain, Bos	39	J. Sain, Bos	28
H. Brecheen, StL	20	M. Dickson, StL	16	H. Brecheen, StL	.741	T. Wilks, StL	57	L. Jansen, NYG	36	H. Brecheen, StL	21
L. Jansen, NYG	18	K. Peterson, Cin	15	B. Chesnes, Pit	.700	K. Higbe, Pit	56	W. Spahn, Bos	35	J. Schmitz, ChN	18
J. Schmitz, ChN	18	J. Sain, Bos	15	V. Bickford, Bos	.688	S. Jones, NYG	55	R. Barney, Bro	34	W. Spahn, Bos	16
J. Vander Meer, Cin	17	J. Vander Meer, Cin	14	S. Jones, NYG	.667	J. Dobernic, ChN	54	J. Vander Meer, Cin	33	D. Leonard, Phi	16

Shutouts		Saves		Games Finished		Batters Faced		Innings Pitched		Hits Allowed	
H. Brecheen, StL	7	H. Gumbert, Cin	17	H. Gumbert, Cin	46	J. Sain, Bos	1313	J. Sain, Bos	314.2	J. Sain, Bos	297
L. Jansen, NYG	4	T. Wilks, StL	13	K. Trinkle, NYG	31	L. Jansen, NYG	1137	L. Jansen, NYG	277.0	L. Jansen, NYG	283
R. Barney, Bro	4	K. Higbe, Pit	10	K. Higbe, Pit	31	W. Spahn, Bos	1064	W. Spahn, Bos	257.0	M. Dickson, StL	257
J. Sain, Bos	4	H. Behrman, Bro	7	T. Wilks, StL	28	M. Dickson, StL	1064	M. Dickson, StL	252.1	W. Spahn, Bos	237
K. Raffensberger, Cin	4	K. Trinkle, NYG	7	J. Dobernic, ChN	27	R. Barney, Bro	1028	R. Barney, Bro	246.2	J. Hatten, Bro	228

Home Runs Allowed		Walks		Walks/9 Innings		Strikeouts		Strikeouts/9 Innings		Strikeout/Walk Ratio	
M. Dickson, StL	39	J. Vander Meer, Cin	124	L. Jansen, NYG	1.8	H. Brecheen, StL	149	H. Brecheen, StL	5.7	H. Brecheen, StL	3.04
L. Jansen, NYG	25	R. Barney, Bro	122	H. Brecheen, StL	1.9	R. Barney, Bro	138	R. Branca, Bro	5.1	L. Jansen, NYG	2.33
R. Branca, Bro	24	C. Simmons, Phi	108	D. Leonard, Phi	2.2	J. Sain, Bos	137	R. Barney, Bro	5.0	D. Leonard, Phi	1.70
H. Wehmeier, Cin	21	J. Schmitz, ChN	97	J. Sain, Bos	2.4	L. Jansen, NYG	126	J. Vander Meer, Cin	4.7	J. Sain, Bos	1.65
R. Poat, NYG	21	J. Hatten, Bro	94	W. Spahn, Bos	2.7	R. Branca, Bro	122	L. Jansen, NYG	4.1	R. Branca, Bro	1.52

Earned Run Average		Component ERA		Hit Batsmen		Wild Pitches		Opponent Average		Opponent OBP	
H. Brecheen, StL	2.24	H. Brecheen, StL	2.01	S. Jones, NYG	6	S. Jones, NYG	10	J. Schmitz, ChN	.215	H. Brecheen, StL	.265
D. Leonard, Phi	2.51	J. Schmitz, ChN	2.47	K. Peterson, Cin	6	E. Singleton, Pit	9	R. Barney, Bro	.217	J. Schmitz, ChN	.295
J. Sain, Bos	2.60	J. Sain, Bos	2.96	R. Barney, Bro	6	R. Branca, Bro	9	H. Brecheen, StL	.222	J. Sain, Bos	.296
J. Schmitz, ChN	2.64	W. Spahn, Bos	3.05	3 tied with	5	E. Riddle, Pit	9	V. Bickford, Bos	.226	W. Spahn, Bos	.298
R. Barney, Bro	3.10	R. Barney, Bro	3.06			3 tied with	6	R. Branca, Bro	.232	L. Jansen, NYG	.303

1948 National League Miscellaneous

Managers

Boston	Billy Southworth	91-62
Brooklyn	Leo Durocher	35-37
	Ray Blades	1-0
	Burt Shotton	48-33
Chicago	Charlie Grimm	64-90
Cincinnati	Johnny Neun	44-56
	Bucky Walters	20-33
New York	Mel Ott	37-38
	Leo Durocher	41-38
Philadelphia	Ben Chapman	37-42
	Dusty Cooke	6-6
	Eddie Sawyer	23-40
Pittsburgh	Billy Meyer	83-71
St. Louis	Eddie Dyer	85-69

Awards

Most Valuable Player	Stan Musial, of, StL
STATS Cy Young	Johnny Sain, Bos
Rookie of the Year	Al Dark, ss, Bos
STATS Manager of the Year	Billy Southworth, Bos

STATS All-Star Team

C	Walker Cooper, NYG	.266	16	54
1B	Johnny Mize, NYG	.289	40	125
2B	Jackie Robinson, Bro	.296	12	85
3B	Sid Gordon, NYG	.299	30	107
SS	Pee Wee Reese, Bro	.274	9	75
OF	Ralph Kiner, Pit	.265	40	123
OF	Stan Musial, StL	.376	39	131
OF	Enos Slaughter, StL	.321	11	90
P	Harry Brecheen, StL	20-7	2.24	149 K
P	Johnny Sain, Bos	24-15	2.60	137 K
P	Johnny Schmitz, ChN	18-13	2.64	100 K
P	Johnny Vander Meer, Cin	17-14	3.41	120 K
RP	Ted Wilks, StL	6-6	2.62	13 Sv

Postseason

World Series	Boston (NL) 2 vs. Cleveland (AL) 4

Outstanding Performances

No-Hitters
Rex Barney, Bro   @ NYG on September 9

Three-Homer Games
Ralph Kiner, Pit   on July 5
Gene Hermanski, Bro on August 5

Cycles
Wally Westlake, Pit   on July 30
Jackie Robinson, Bro on August 29

1949 American League Standings

	Overall					Home Games						Road Games						Park Index		Record by Month					
Team	W	L	Pct	GB	DIF	W	L	R	OR	HR	OHR	W	L	R	OR	HR	OHR	Run	HR	M/A	May	June	July	Aug	S/O
New York	97	57	.630	—	164	54	23	419	304	72	53	43	34	410	333	43	45	97	142	10-2	15-10	19-12	16-11	17-12	20-10
Boston	96	58	.623	1.0	7	61	16	514	310	71	43	35	42	382	357	60	39	112	115	5-6	15-10	15-15	18-12	24-8	19-7
Cleveland	89	65	.578	8.0	0	49	28	319	263	61	42	40	37	356	311	51	40	87	113	6-3	11-15	18-12	21-9	18-14	15-12
Detroit	87	67	.565	10.0	2	50	27	402	350	57	60	37	40	349	305	31	42	115	160	6-5	14-14	18-12	16-15	18-12	15-9
Philadelphia	81	73	.526	16.0	0	52	25	389	326	42	42	29	48	337	399	40	63	97	82	6-5	15-12	18-11	14-16	14-13	14-14
Chicago	63	91	.409	34.0	0	32	45	327	353	15	52	31	46	321	384	28	56	96	80	6-5	13-15	8-22	14-15	11-18	11-16
St. Louis	53	101	.344	44.0	1	36	41	394	426	69	56	17	60	273	487	48	57	108	119	3-8	7-22	10-16	13-17	14-19	6-19
Washington	50	104	.325	47.0	0	26	51	254	426	20	14	24	53	330	442	61	65	88	27	3-9	18-10	10-16	5-22	6-26	8-21

Clinch Date—New York 10/02.

Team Batting

Team	G	AB	R	OR	H	2B	3B	HR	TB	RBI	TBB	IBB	SO	HBP	SH	SF	SB	CS	SB%	GDP	Avg	OBP	Slg
Boston	155	5320	896	667	1500	272	36	131	2237	835	835	—	510	17	78	—	43	25	.63	169	.282	.381	.420
New York	155	5196	829	637	1396	215	60	115	2076	760	731	—	539	32	84	—	58	30	.66	141	.269	.362	.400
Detroit	155	5259	751	655	1405	215	51	88	1986	707	751	—	502	23	107	—	39	52	.43	164	.267	.361	.378
Philadelphia	154	5123	726	725	1331	214	49	82	1889	680	783	—	493	25	117	—	36	25	.59	160	.260	.361	.369
Cleveland	154	5221	675	574	1358	194	58	112	2004	640	601	—	534	23	113	—	44	40	.52	137	.260	.339	.384
St. Louis	155	5112	667	913	1301	213	30	117	1925	628	631	—	700	21	83	—	38	39	.49	138	.254	.339	.377
Chicago	154	5204	648	737	1340	207	66	43	1808	591	702	—	596	13	84	—	62	55	.53	136	.254	.347	.347
Washington	154	5234	584	868	1330	207	41	81	1862	546	593	—	495	22	63	—	46	33	.58	132	.254	.333	.356
AL Total	1236	41669	5776	5776	10961	1737	391	769	15787	5387	5627	—	4369	176	729	—	366	299	.55	1177	.263	.353	.379
AL Avg Team	155	5209	722	722	1370	217	49	96	1973	673	703	—	546	22	91	—	46	37	.55	147	.263	.353	.379

Team Pitching

Team	G	CG	ShO	Rel	Sv	IP	H	R	ER	HR	SH	SF	HB	TBB	IBB	SO	WP	Bk	H/9	SO/9	BB/9	OAvg	OOBP	ERA
Cleveland	154	65	10	168	19	1383.2	1275	574	516	82	95	—	16	611	—	594	28	3	8.3	3.9	4.0	.247	.329	3.36
New York	155	59	12	159	36	1371.1	1231	637	563	98	76	—	36	812	—	671	35	4	8.1	4.4	5.3	.242	.351	3.69
Detroit	155	70	19	152	12	1393.2	1338	655	584	102	73	—	18	628	—	631	30	0	8.6	4.1	4.1	.254	.335	3.77
Boston	155	84	16	120	16	1377.0	1375	667	608	82	73	—	24	661	—	598	27	6	9.0	3.9	4.3	.262	.347	3.97
Philadelphia	154	85	9	107	11	1365.0	1359	725	642	105	67	—	19	758	—	490	33	5	9.0	3.2	5.0	.263	.360	4.23
Chicago	154	57	10	174	17	1363.1	1362	737	651	108	111	—	15	693	—	502	27	4	9.0	3.3	4.6	.264	.353	4.30
Washington	154	44	9	206	9	1345.2	1438	868	762	79	127	—	25	779	—	451	41	2	9.6	3.0	5.2	.276	.373	5.10
St. Louis	155	43	3	231	16	1341.1	1583	913	777	113	106	—	23	685	—	432	35	7	10.6	2.9	4.6	.294	.377	5.21
AL Total	1236	507	88	1317	136	10941.0	10961	5776	5103	769	728	—	176	5627	—	4369	256	31	9.0	3.6	4.6	.263	.353	4.20
AL Avg Team	155	63	11	165	17	1367.0	1370	722	638	96	91	—	22	703	—	546	32	4	9.0	3.6	4.6	.263	.353	4.20

Team Fielding

Team	G	PO	A	E	TC	DP	PB	Pct
Cleveland	154	4150	1816	103	6069	192	5	.983
Boston	155	4139	1737	120	5996	207	4	.980
Detroit	155	4170	1723	131	6024	174	10	.978
Chicago	154	4089	1844	141	6074	180	7	.977
New York	155	4109	1627	138	5874	195	5	.977
Philadelphia	154	4102	1710	140	5952	217	10	.976
Washington	154	4031	1748	161	5940	168	6	.973
St. Louis	155	4031	1625	166	5822	154	6	.971
AL Total	1236	32821	13830	1100	47751	1487	53	.977

Team vs. Team Records

	Bos	ChA	Cle	Det	NYA	Phi	StL	Was	Won
Bos	—	17	8	15	9	14	15	18	96
ChA	5	—	7	8	7	6	15	15	63
Cle	14	15	—	13	10	9	15	13	89
Det	7	14	9	—	11	14	14	18	87
NYA	13	15	12	11	—	14	17	15	97
Phi	8	16	13	8	8	—	12	16	81
StL	7	7	7	8	5	10	—	9	53
Was	4	7	9	4	7	6	13	—	50
Lost	58	91	65	67	57	73	101	104	

1949 American League Batting Leaders

Games		At-Bats		Runs		Hits		Doubles		Triples	
V. Wertz, Det	155	D. Mitchell, Cle	640	T. Williams, Bos	150	D. Mitchell, Cle	203	T. Williams, Bos	39	D. Mitchell, Cle	23
V. Stephens, Bos	155	P. Rizzuto, NYA	614	E. Joost, Phi	128	T. Williams, Bos	194	G. Kell, Det	38	B. Dillinger, StL	13
T. Williams, Bos	155	V. Stephens, Bos	610	D. DiMaggio, Bos	126	D. DiMaggio, Bos	186	D. DiMaggio, Bos	34	E. Valo, Phi	12
C. Michaels, ChA	154	V. Wertz, Det	608	V. Stephens, Bos	113	V. Wertz, Det	185	A. Zarilla, 2tm	33	3 tied with	9
S. Chapman, Phi	154	D. DiMaggio, Bos	605	J. Pesky, Bos	111	J. Pesky, Bos	185	V. Stephens, Bos	31		

Home Runs		Total Bases		Runs Batted In		Walks		Intentional Walks		Strikeouts	
T. Williams, Bos	43	T. Williams, Bos	368	V. Stephens, Bos	159	T. Williams, Bos	162	Statistic unavailable		D. Kokos, StL	91
V. Stephens, Bos	39	V. Stephens, Bos	329	T. Williams, Bos	159	E. Joost, Phi	149			L. Doby, Cle	90
4 tied with	24	V. Wertz, Det	283	V. Wertz, Det	133	F. Fain, Phi	136			J. Hegan, Cle	89
		D. Mitchell, Cle	274	B. Doerr, Bos	109	L. Appling, ChA	121			J. Priddy, StL	81
		B. Doerr, Bos	269	S. Chapman, Phi	108	E. Valo, Phi	119			E. Joost, Phi	80

Hit By Pitch		Sac Hits		Sac Flies		Stolen Bases		Caught Stealing		GDP	
L. Doby, Cle	7	P. Rizzuto, NYA	25	Statistic unavailable		B. Dillinger, StL	20	B. Dillinger, StL	14	B. Doerr, Bos	31
E. Robinson, Was	7	C. Kress, ChA	17			P. Rizzuto, NYA	18	L. Appling, ChA	12	S. Chapman, Phi	23
N. Fox, Phi	6	G. Kell, Det	16			E. Valo, Phi	14	E. Valo, Phi	11	L. Appling, ChA	23
Y. Berra, NYA	6	M. Vernon, Cle	15			D. Philley, ChA	13	L. Doby, Cle	9	T. Williams, Bos	22
2 tied with	5	H. Newhouser, Det	14			3 tied with	10	E. Lake, Det	8	3 tied with	20

Runs Created		Runs Created/27 Outs		Batting Average		On-Base Percentage		Slugging Percentage		OBP+Slugging	
T. Williams, Bos	174	T. Williams, Bos	11.73	G. Kell, Det	.343	T. Williams, Bos	.490	T. Williams, Bos	.650	T. Williams, Bos	1.141
V. Stephens, Bos	128	T. Henrich, NYA	8.64	T. Williams, Bos	.343	L. Appling, ChA	.439	V. Stephens, Bos	.539	T. Henrich, NYA	.942
E. Joost, Phi	117	E. Joost, Phi	7.83	B. Dillinger, StL	.324	E. Joost, Phi	.429	T. Henrich, NYA	.526	V. Stephens, Bos	.930
V. Wertz, Det	109	V. Stephens, Bos	7.51	D. Mitchell, Cle	.317	G. Kell, Det	.424	B. Doerr, Bos	.497	G. Kell, Det	.892
D. DiMaggio, Bos	109	G. Kell, Det	7.34	B. Doerr, Bos	.309	C. Michaels, ChA	.417	Y. Berra, NYA	.480	B. Doerr, Bos	.890

1949 American League Pitching Leaders

Wins		Losses		Winning Percentage		Games		Games Started		Complete Games	
M. Parnell, Bos	25	N. Garver, StL	17	E. Kinder, Bos	.793	J. Page, NYA	60	V. Raschi, NYA	37	M. Parnell, Bos	27
E. Kinder, Bos	23	P. Calvert, Was	17	M. Parnell, Bos	.781	D. Welteroth, Was	52	H. Newhouser, Det	35	B. Lemon, Cle	22
B. Lemon, Cle	22	S. Hudson, Was	17	A. Reynolds, NYA	.739	T. Ferrick, StL	50	M. Parnell, Bos	33	H. Newhouser, Det	22
V. Raschi, NYA	21	R. Gumpert, ChA	16	M. Garcia, Cle	.737	B. Kennedy, StL	48	B. Wight, ChA	33	V. Raschi, NYA	21
A. Kellner, Phi	20	2 tied with	15	B. Lemon, Cle	.688	M. Surkont, ChA	44	B. Lemon, Cle	33	2 tied with	19

Shutouts		Saves		Games Finished		Batters Faced		Innings Pitched		Hits Allowed	
E. Kinder, Bos	6	J. Page, NYA	27	J. Page, NYA	48	M. Parnell, Bos	1240	M. Parnell, Bos	295.1	H. Newhouser, Det	277
V. Trucks, Det	6	A. Benton, Cle	10	T. Ferrick, StL	29	H. Newhouser, Det	1228	H. Newhouser, Det	292.0	M. Parnell, Bos	258
M. Garcia, Cle	5	T. Ferrick, StL	6	D. Welteroth, Was	25	V. Raschi, NYA	1186	B. Lemon, Cle	279.2	B. Wight, ChA	254
4 tied with	4	S. Paige, Cle	5	D. Trout, Det	24	B. Lemon, Cle	1159	V. Trucks, Det	275.0	E. Kinder, Bos	251
		5 tied with	4	M. Surkont, ChA	23	V. Trucks, Det	1133	V. Raschi, NYA	274.2	J. Coleman, Phi	249

Home Runs Allowed		Walks		Walks/9 Innings		Strikeouts		Strikeouts/9 Innings		Strikeout/Walk Ratio	
R. Gumpert, ChA	22	T. Byrne, NYA	179	A. Houtteman, Det	2.6	V. Trucks, Det	153	T. Byrne, NYA	5.9	A. Houtteman, Det	1.44
E. Kinder, Bos	21	V. Raschi, NYA	138	E. Lopat, NYA	2.9	H. Newhouser, Det	144	V. Trucks, Det	5.0	E. Kinder, Bos	1.39
L. Brissie, Phi	20	B. Lemon, Cle	137	R. Gumpert, ChA	3.2	E. Kinder, Bos	138	E. Kinder, Bos	4.9	H. Newhouser, Det	1.30
4 tied with	19	M. Parnell, Bos	134	H. Newhouser, Det	3.4	B. Lemon, Cle	138	L. Brissie, Phi	4.6	B. Feller, Cle	1.29
		A. Kellner, Phi	129	B. Wight, ChA	3.5	T. Byrne, NYA	129	B. Feller, Cle	4.6	V. Trucks, Det	1.23

Earned Run Average		Component ERA		Hit Batsmen		Wild Pitches		Opponent Average		Opponent OBP	
M. Parnell, Bos	2.77	V. Trucks, Det	2.68	T. Byrne, NYA	13	G. Bearden, Cle	11	T. Byrne, NYA	.183	V. Trucks, Det	.301
V. Trucks, Det	2.81	B. Lemon, Cle	2.88	K. Drews, StL	9	D. Weik, Was	10	B. Lemon, Cle	.211	B. Lemon, Cle	.309
B. Lemon, Cle	2.99	M. Parnell, Bos	3.09	M. Haefner, 2tm	7	N. Garver, StL	10	V. Trucks, Det	.211	R. Gumpert, ChA	.318
E. Lopat, NYA	3.26	H. Newhouser, Det	3.42	R. Scarborough, Was	7	L. Brissie, Phi	10	M. Parnell, Bos	.237	H. Newhouser, Det	.319
B. Wight, ChA	3.31	B. Feller, Cle	3.57	2 tied with	6	V. Raschi, NYA	10	V. Raschi, NYA	.241	B. Feller, Cle	.320

1949 American League Miscellaneous

Managers		
Boston	Joe McCarthy	96-58
Chicago	Jack Onslow	63-91
Cleveland	Lou Boudreau	89-65
Detroit	Red Rolfe	87-67
New York	Casey Stengel	97-57
Philadelphia	Connie Mack	81-73
St. Louis	Zack Taylor	53-101
Washington	Joe Kuhel	50-104

Awards	
Most Valuable Player	Ted Williams, of, Bos
STATS Cy Young	Mel Parnell, Bos
Rookie of the Year	Roy Sievers, of, StL
STATS Manager of the Year	Casey Stengel, NYA

STATS All-Star Team

C	Yogi Berra, NYA	.277	20	91
1B	Eddie Robinson, Was	.294	18	78
2B	Bobby Doerr, Bos	.309	18	109
3B	George Kell, Det	.343	3	59
SS	Vern Stephens, Bos	.290	39	159
OF	Tommy Henrich, NYA	.287	24	85
OF	Vic Wertz, Det	.304	20	133
OF	Ted Williams, Bos	.343	43	159
P	Ellis Kinder, Bos	23-6	3.36	138 K
P	Bob Lemon, Cle	22-10	2.99	138 K
P	Mel Parnell, Bos	25-7	2.77	122 K
P	Virgil Trucks, Det	19-11	2.81	153 K
RP	Joe Page, NYA	13-8	2.59	27 Sv

Postseason	
World Series	New York (AL) 4 vs. Brooklyn (NL) 1

Outstanding Performances

Three-Homer Games

Pat Mullin, Det	on June 26

1949 National League Standings

	Overall					Home Games						Road Games						Park Index		Record by Month					
Team	W	L	Pct	GB	DIF	W	L	R	OR	HR	OHR	W	L	R	OR	HR	OHR	Run	HR	M/A	May	June	July	Aug	S/O
Brooklyn	97	57	.630	—	71	48	29	431	335	86	73	49	28	448	316	66	59	100	127	6-6	17-11	18-9	15-12	20-11	21-8
St. Louis	96	58	.623	1.0	64	51	26	427	325	48	33	45	32	339	291	54	33	119	75	5-5	14-13	21-9	18-10	20-11	18-10
Philadelphia	81	73	.526	16.0	1	40	37	336	326	61	35	41	36	326	342	61	69	99	74	7-5	16-12	15-15	13-14	15-14	9-19
Boston	75	79	.487	22.0	30	43	34	344	328	40	40	32	45	362	391	63	70	89	60	6-5	16-13	11-16	16-12	14-16	10-19
New York	73	81	.474	24.0	23	43	34	404	331	94	78	30	47	332	362	53	54	106	161	5-6	11-18	11-15	18-10	12-19	14-15
Pittsburgh	71	83	.461	26.0	2	36	41	341	397	77	75	35	42	340	363	49	67	105	131	5-6	14-15	7-19	11-20	12-16	12-15
Cincinnati	62	92	.403	35.0	4	35	42	326	349	50	54	27	50	301	421	36	70	93	98	6-4	14-15	11-20	11-20	12-16	12-13
Chicago	61	93	.396	36.0	0	33	44	285	365	53	38	28	49	308	408	44	66	91	83	5-6	10-16	11-20	10-20	13-18	12-13

Clinch Date—Brooklyn 10/02.

Team Batting

Team	G	AB	R	OR	H	2B	3B	HR	TB	RBI	TBB	IBB	SO	HBP	SH	SF	SB	CS	SB%	GDP	Avg	OBP	Slg
Brooklyn	156	5400	879	651	1477	236	47	152	2263	816	638	—	570	33	102	—	117	44	.73	127	.274	.354	.419
St. Louis	157	5463	766	616	1513	281	54	102	2208	720	569	—	482	25	94	—	17	—		124	.277	.348	.404
New York	156	5308	736	693	1383	203	52	147	2131	690	684	—	656	23	96	—	43	25	.63	130	.261	.345	.401
Boston	157	5336	706	719	1376	246	33	103	1997	654	613	—	523	22	86	—	48	—		96	.258	.337	.374
Pittsburgh	154	5214	681	760	1350	191	41	126	2001	626	548	—	554	24	64	—	27	—		116	.259	.332	.384
Philadelphia	154	5307	662	668	1349	232	55	122	2057	622	528	—	670	26	74	—	31	—		116	.254	.325	.388
Cincinnati	156	5469	627	770	1423	264	35	86	2015	588	429	—	559	20	76	—	53	—		121	.256	.316	.373
Chicago	154	5214	593	773	1336	212	53	97	1945	539	396	—	573	26	87	—	28	—		125	.256	.312	.373
NL Total	1244	42711	5650	5650	11207	1865	370	935	16617	5255	4405	—	4587	199	679	—	364	—		955	.262	.334	.389
NL Avg Team	156	5339	706	706	1401	233	46	117	2077	657	551	—	573	25	85	—	46	—		119	.262	.334	.389

Team Pitching

Team	G	CG	ShO	Rel	Sv	IP	H	R	ER	HR	SH	SF	HB	TBB	IBB	SO	WP	Bk	H/9	SO/9	BB/9	OAvg	OOBP	ERA
St. Louis	157	64	13	188	19	1407.2	1356	616	538	87	97	—	26	507	—	606	21	1	8.7	3.9	3.2	.254	.322	3.44
Brooklyn	156	62	15	193	17	1408.2	1306	651	595	132	64	—	25	582	—	743	20	3	8.3	4.7	3.7	.248	.326	3.80
New York	156	68	10	186	9	1374.1	1328	693	584	132	53	—	21	544	—	516	32	5	8.7	3.4	3.6	.251	.323	3.82
Philadelphia	154	58	12	190	15	1391.2	1389	668	602	104	97	—	17	502	—	495	17	6	9.0	3.2	3.2	.270	.337	3.89
Boston	157	68	12	159	11	1400.0	1466	719	620	110	101	—	22	520	—	589	22	1	9.4	3.8	3.3	.270	.336	3.99
Cincinnati	156	55	10	210	6	1401.2	1423	770	675	124	91	—	28	640	—	538	29	4	9.1	3.5	4.1	.266	.348	4.33
Chicago	154	44	8	200	17	1357.2	1487	773	679	104	84	—	22	575	—	544	36	4	9.9	3.6	3.8	.280	.352	4.50
Pittsburgh	154	53	9	179	15	1356.0	1452	760	688	142	80	—	33	535	—	556	21	1	9.6	3.7	3.6	.276	.346	4.57
NL Total	1244	472	89	1505	109	11097.2	11207	5650	4981	935	667	—	194	4405	—	4587	198	25	9.1	3.7	3.6	.262	.334	4.04
NL Avg Team	156	59	11	188	14	1387.2	1401	706	623	117	83	—	24	551	—	573	25	3	9.1	3.7	3.6	.262	.334	4.04

Team Fielding

Team	G	PO	A	E	TC	DP	PB	Pct
Brooklyn	156	4224	1618	122	5964	162	11	.980
Pittsburgh	154	4073	1723	132	5928	173	13	.978
Cincinnati	156	4206	1717	138	6061	150	19	.977
St. Louis	157	4220	1822	146	6188	149	8	.976
Boston	157	4201	1727	148	6076	144	8	.976
Philadelphia	154	4177	1653	156	5986	141	18	.974
New York	156	4121	1675	161	5957	134	11	.973
Chicago	154	4063	1887	186	6136	160	20	.970
NL Total	1244	33285	13822	1189	48296	1213	108	.975

Team vs. Team Records

	Bos	Bro	ChN	Cin	NYG	Phi	Pit	StL	Won
Bos	—	10	12	12	12	11	12	6	75
Bro	12	—	17	17	14	11	16	10	97
ChN	10	5	—	9	12	6	11	8	61
Cin	10	5	13	—	7	13	9	5	62
NYG	10	8	10	15	—	11	12	7	73
Phi	11	11	16	9	11	—	13	10	81
Pit	10	6	11	13	10	9	—	12	71
StL	16	12	14	17	15	12	10	—	96
Lost	79	57	93	92	81	73	83	58	

1949 National League Batting Leaders

Games			At-Bats			Runs			Hits			Doubles			Triples		
S. Musial, StL		157	R. Ashburn, Phi		662	P. Reese, Bro		132	S. Musial, StL		207	S. Musial, StL		41	S. Musial, StL		13
J. Robinson, Bro		156	G. Hamner, Phi		662	S. Musial, StL		128	J. Robinson, Bro		203	D. Ennis, Phi		39	E. Slaughter, StL		13
B. Thomson, NYG		156	B. Thomson, NYG		641	J. Robinson, Bro		122	B. Thomson, NYG		198	J. Robinson, Bro		38	J. Robinson, Bro		12
G. Hodges, Bro		156	R. Schoendienst, StL		640	R. Kiner, Pit		116	E. Slaughter, StL		191	G. Hatton, Cin		38	R. Ashburn, Phi		11
P. Reese, Bro		155	2 tied with		617	R. Schoendienst, StL		102	R. Schoendienst, StL		190	2 tied with		35	D. Ennis, Phi		11

Home Runs			Total Bases			Runs Batted In			Walks			Intentional Walks			Strikeouts		
R. Kiner, Pit		54	S. Musial, StL		382	R. Kiner, Pit		127	R. Kiner, Pit		117	Statistic unavailable			D. Snider, Bro		92
S. Musial, StL		36	R. Kiner, Pit		361	J. Robinson, Bro		124	P. Reese, Bro		116				R. Smalley, ChN		77
H. Sauer, 2tm		31	B. Thomson, NYG		332	S. Musial, StL		123	E. Stanky, Bos		113				A. Seminick, Phi		74
B. Thomson, NYG		27	D. Ennis, Phi		320	G. Hodges, Bro		115	S. Musial, StL		107				W. Westlake, Pit		69
S. Gordon, NYG		26	J. Robinson, Bro		313	D. Ennis, Phi		110	S. Gordon, NYG		95				J. Russell, Bos		68

Hit By Pitch			Sac Hits			Sac Flies			Stolen Bases			Caught Stealing			GDP		
A. Pafko, ChN		9	J. Robinson, Bro		17	Statistic unavailable			J. Robinson, Bro		37	Statistic unavailable			S. Gordon, NYG		24
J. Robinson, Bro		8	M. Marion, StL		17				P. Reese, Bro		26				J. Robinson, Bro		22
E. Fletcher, Bos		8	S. Rojek, Pit		16				4 tied with		12				P. H. Jones, Phi		20
T. Glaviano, StL		6	G. Hamner, Phi		13										G. Hamner, Phi		20
W. Westlake, Pit		6	E. Fletcher, Bos		13										W. Cooper, 2tm		19

Runs Created			Runs Created/27 Outs			Batting Average			On-Base Percentage			Slugging Percentage			OBP+Slugging		
S. Musial, StL		155	R. Kiner, Pit		10.07	J. Robinson, Bro		.342	S. Musial, StL		.438	R. Kiner, Pit		.658	R. Kiner, Pit		1.089
R. Kiner, Pit		147	S. Musial, StL		9.90	S. Musial, StL		.338	J. Robinson, Bro		.432	S. Musial, StL		.624	S. Musial, StL		1.062
J. Robinson, Bro		139	J. Robinson, Bro		8.63	E. Slaughter, StL		.336	R. Kiner, Pit		.432	J. Robinson, Bro		.528	J. Robinson, Bro		.960
P. Reese, Bro		119	E. Slaughter, StL		8.06	C. Furillo, Bro		.322	E. Slaughter, StL		.418	D. Ennis, Phi		.525	E. Slaughter, StL		.929
E. Slaughter, StL		118	R. Campanella, Bro		7.34	R. Kiner, Pit		.310	E. Stanky, Bos		.417	B. Thomson, NYG		.518	S. Gordon, NYG		.909

1949 National League Pitching Leaders

Wins			Losses			Winning Percentage			Games			Games Started			Complete Games		
W. Spahn, Bos		21	H. Fox, Cin		19	R. Branca, Bro		.722	T. Wilks, StL		59	W. Spahn, Bos		38	W. Spahn, Bos		25
H. Pollet, StL		20	B. Rush, ChN		18	P. Roe, Bro		.714	J. Konstanty, Phi		53	K. Raffensberger, Cin		38	K. Raffensberger, Cin		20
K. Raffensberger, Cin		18	J. Sain, Bos		17	H. Pollet, StL		.690	E. Palica, Bro		49	V. Bickford, Bos		36	D. Newcombe, Bro		19
3 tied with		17	K. Raffensberger, Cin		17	D. Newcombe, Bro		.680	J. Banta, Bro		48	J. Sain, Bos		36	L. Jansen, NYG		17
			2 tied with		16	R. Meyer, Phi		.680	B. Muncrief, 2tm		47	L. Jansen, NYG		35	H. Pollet, StL		17

Shutouts			Saves			Games Finished			Batters Faced			Innings Pitched			Hits Allowed		
D. Newcombe, Bro		5	T. Wilks, StL		9	H. Gumbert, 2tm		34	W. Spahn, Bos		1258	W. Spahn, Bos		302.1	K. Raffensberger, Cin		289
H. Pollet, StL		5	J. Konstanty, Phi		7	T. Wilks, StL		30	K. Raffensberger, Cin		1190	K. Raffensberger, Cin		284.0	J. Sain, Bos		285
K. Raffensberger, Cin		5	N. Potter, Bos		7	N. Potter, Bos		29	L. Jansen, NYG		1101	L. Jansen, NYG		259.2	W. Spahn, Bos		283
K. Heintzelman, Phi		5	G. Staley, StL		6	E. Palica, Bro		27	J. Sain, Bos		1072	K. Heintzelman, Phi		250.0	L. Jansen, NYG		271
3 tied with		4	E. Palica, Bro		6	J. Konstanty, Phi		27	K. Heintzelman, Phi		1041	D. Newcombe, Bro		244.1	V. Bickford, Bos		246

Home Runs Allowed			Walks			Walks/9 Innings			Strikeouts			Strikeouts/9 Innings			Strikeout/Walk Ratio		
L. Jansen, NYG		36	H. Wehmeier, Cin		117	D. Koslo, NYG		1.8	W. Spahn, Bos		151	D. Newcombe, Bro		5.5	P. Roe, Bro		2.48
W. Spahn, Bos		27	V. Bickford, Bos		106	P. Roe, Bro		1.9	D. Newcombe, Bro		149	C. Chambers, Pit		4.7	B. Werle, Pit		2.08
P. Roe, Bro		25	M. Kennedy, NYG		100	B. Werle, Pit		2.1	L. Jansen, NYG		113	P. Roe, Bro		4.6	D. Newcombe, Bro		2.04
K. Raffensberger, Cin		23	K. Heintzelman, Phi		93	L. Jansen, NYG		2.1	R. Branca, Bro		109	W. Spahn, Bos		4.5	D. Leonard, ChN		1.93
B. Werle, Pit		22	J. Schmitz, ChN		92	D. Leonard, ChN		2.2	P. Roe, Bro		109	B. Werle, Pit		4.3	H. Pollet, StL		1.83

Earned Run Average			Component ERA			Hit Batsmen			Wild Pitches			Opponent Average			Opponent OBP		
D. Koslo, NYG		2.50	D. Koslo, NYG		2.57	S. Jones, NYG		10	H. Wehmeier, Cin		7	D. Koslo, NYG		.239	D. Koslo, NYG		.278
H. Pollet, StL		2.77	H. Pollet, StL		3.01	B. Werle, Pit		8	D. Leonard, ChN		7	M. Kennedy, NYG		.242	P. Roe, Bro		.293
P. Roe, Bro		2.79	D. Newcombe, Bro		3.02	H. Wehmeier, Cin		7	B. Rush, ChN		6	D. Newcombe, Bro		.243	W. Spahn, Bos		.299
K. Heintzelman, Phi		3.02	W. Spahn, Bos		3.18	H. Brecheen, StL		7	A. Hansen, NYG		6	W. Spahn, Bos		.245	D. Newcombe, Bro		.301
W. Spahn, Bos		3.07	R. Meyer, Phi		3.22	D. Leonard, ChN		7	B. Voiselle, Bos		6	S. Jones, NYG		.248	H. Pollet, StL		.304

1949 National League Miscellaneous

Managers

Boston	Billy Southworth	55-54
	Johnny Cooney	20-25
Brooklyn	Burt Shotton	97-57
Chicago	Charlie Grimm	19-31
	Frank Frisch	42-62
Cincinnati	Bucky Walters	61-90
	Luke Sewell	1-2
New York	Leo Durocher	73-81
Philadelphia	Eddie Sawyer	81-73
Pittsburgh	Billy Meyer	71-83
St. Louis	Eddie Dyer	96-58

Awards

Most Valuable Player	J. Robinson, 2b, Bro
STATS Cy Young	Warren Spahn, Bos
Rookie of the Year	Don Newcombe, p, Bro
STATS Manager of the Year	Eddie Sawyer, Phi

STATS All-Star Team

C	Roy Campanella, Bro	.287	22	82
1B	Gil Hodges, Bro	.285	23	115
2B	Jackie Robinson, Bro	.342	16	124
3B	Sid Gordon, NYG	.284	26	90
SS	Pee Wee Reese, Bro	.279	16	73
OF	Ralph Kiner, Pit	.310	54	127
OF	Stan Musial, StL	.338	36	123
OF	Enos Slaughter, StL	.336	13	96
P	Russ Meyer, Phi	17-8	3.08	78 K
P	Don Newcombe, Bro	17-8	3.17	149 K
P	Howie Pollet, StL	20-9	2.77	108 K
P	Warren Spahn, Bos	21-14	3.07	151 K
RP	Jim Konstanty, Phi	9-5	3.25	7 Sv

Postseason

World Series	Brooklyn (NL) 1 vs. New York (AL) 4

Outstanding Performances

Three-Homer Games

Andy Seminick, Phi	on June 2
Walker Cooper, Cin	on July 6
Bob Elliott, Bos	on September 24

Cycles

Wally Westlake, Pit	on June 14
Gil Hodges, Bro	on June 25
Stan Musial, StL	on July 24

1950 American League Standings

Team	Overall					Home Games						Road Games						Park Index		Record by Month					
	W	L	Pct	GB	DIF	W	L	R	OR	HR	OHR	W	L	R	OR	HR	OHR	Run	HR	M/A	May	June	July	Aug	S/O
New York	98	56	.636	—	50	53	24	440	333	78	51	45	32	474	358	81	67	93	87	6-4	20-6	15-17	19-8	20-11	18-10
Detroit	95	59	.617	3.0	120	50	30	405	346	60	72	45	29	432	367	54	69	87	99	6-3	16-9	21-9	16-13	18-13	18-12
Boston	94	60	.610	4.0	2	55	22	625	427	100	67	39	38	402	377	61	54	135	145	7-6	17-12	16-13	14-12	24-6	16-11
Cleveland	92	62	.597	6.0	0	49	28	386	297	102	57	43	34	420	357	62	63	88	127	4-3	16-14	19-10	20-11	17-14	16-10
Washington	67	87	.435	31.0	1	35	42	347	407	18	28	32	45	343	406	58	71	101	36	5-4	14-13	11-20	14-12	12-19	11-19
Chicago	60	94	.390	38.0	0	35	42	316	352	52	55	25	52	309	397	41	52	95	115	2-4	11-19	16-14	9-23	12-17	10-17
St. Louis	58	96	.377	40.0	4	27	47	368	484	52	69	31	49	316	432	54	60	123	115	3-5	5-20	13-18	13-18	9-20	15-15
Philadelphia	52	102	.338	46.0	0	29	48	314	406	45	67	23	54	356	507	55	71	83	89	4-8	10-16	10-20	10-18	10-22	8-18

Clinch Date—New York 9/29.

Team Batting

Team	G	AB	R	OR	H	2B	3B	HR	TB	RBI	TBB	IBB	SO	HBP	SH	SF	SB	CS	SB%	GDP	Avg	OBP	Slg
Boston	154	5516	1027	804	1665	287	61	161	2557	974	719	—	582	25	62	—	32	17	.65	153	.302	.385	.464
New York	155	5361	914	691	1511	234	70	159	2362	860	687	—	463	28	85	—	41	28	.59	122	.282	.366	.441
Detroit	157	5381	837	713	1518	285	50	114	2245	788	722	—	480	19	110	—	23	40	.37	162	.282	.369	.417
Cleveland	155	5263	806	654	1417	222	46	164	2223	758	693	—	624	38	86	—	40	34	.54	146	.269	.358	.422
Washington	155	5251	690	813	1365	190	53	76	1889	659	671	—	606	32	70	—	42	25	.63	134	.260	.347	.360
St. Louis	154	5163	684	916	1269	235	43	106	1908	642	690	—	744	20	97	—	39	40	.49	138	.246	.337	.370
Philadelphia	154	5212	670	913	1361	204	53	100	1971	627	685	—	493	23	73	—	42	25	.63	170	.261	.349	.378
Chicago	156	5260	625	749	1368	172	47	93	1913	592	551	—	566	28	102	—	19	22	.46	156	.260	.333	.364
AL Total	1240	42407	6253	6253	11474	1829	423	973	17068	5900	5418	—	4558	213	685	—	278	231	.55	1181	.271	.356	.402
AL Avg Team	155	5301	782	782	1434	229	53	122	2134	738	677	—	570	27	86	—	35	29	.55	148	.271	.356	.402

Team Pitching

Team	G	CG	ShO	Rel	Sv	IP	H	R	ER	HR	SH	SF	HB	TBB	IBB	SO	WP	Bk	H/9	SO/9	BB/9	OAvg	OOBP	ERA
Cleveland	155	69	11	184	16	1378.1	1289	654	575	120	82	—	18	647	—	674	23	4	8.4	4.4	4.2	.248	.333	3.75
Detroit	157	72	9	153	20	1407.1	1444	713	645	141	93	—	31	553	—	576	22	4	9.2	3.7	3.5	.267	.339	4.12
New York	155	66	12	141	31	1372.2	1322	691	633	118	72	—	35	708	—	712	20	14	8.7	4.7	4.6	.255	.348	4.15
Chicago	156	62	7	182	9	1365.2	1370	749	669	107	88	—	21	734	—	566	27	2	9.0	3.7	4.8	.263	.356	4.41
Washington	155	59	7	156	18	1364.2	1479	813	706	99	109	—	26	648	—	486	27	7	9.8	3.2	4.3	.278	.359	4.66
Boston	154	66	6	183	28	1362.1	1413	804	739	121	90	—	23	748	—	630	27	5	9.3	4.2	4.9	.270	.364	4.88
St. Louis	154	56	7	188	14	1365.1	1629	916	789	129	74	—	32	651	—	448	28	6	10.7	3.0	4.3	.295	.372	5.20
Philadelphia	154	50	3	153	18	1346.1	1528	913	821	138	85	—	31	729	—	466	39	5	10.2	3.1	4.9	.287	.376	5.49
AL Total	1240	500	62	1340	154	10962.2	11474	6253	5577	973	693	—	217	5418	—	4558	213	47	9.4	3.7	4.4	.271	.356	4.58
AL Avg Team	155	63	8	168	19	1370.2	1434	782	697	122	87	—	27	677	—	570	27	6	9.4	3.7	4.4	.271	.356	4.58

Team Fielding

Team	G	PO	A	E	TC	DP	PB	Pct
Boston	154	4084	1735	111	5930	181	11	.981
Detroit	157	4214	1875	120	6209	194	11	.981
New York	155	4108	1573	119	5800	188	7	.979
Cleveland	155	4135	1618	129	5882	160	6	.978
Chicago	156	4099	1730	140	5969	181	9	.977
Philadelphia	154	4033	1732	155	5920	208	9	.974
Washington	155	4100	1763	167	6030	181	10	.972
St. Louis	154	4090	1657	196	5943	155	9	.967
AL Total	1240	32863	13683	1137	47683	1448	72	.976

Team vs. Team Records

	Bos	ChA	Cle	Det	NYA	Phi	StL	Was	Won
Bos	—	15	10	10	9	19	19	12	94
ChA	7	—	8	6	8	11	12	8	60
Cle	12	14	—	13	8	17	13	15	92
Det	12	16	9	—	11	17	17	13	95
NYA	13	14	14	11	—	15	17	14	98
Phi	3	11	5	5	7	—	8	13	52
StL	3	10	9	5	5	14	—	12	58
Was	10	14	7	9	8	9	10	—	67
Lost	60	94	62	59	56	102	96	87	

Seasons: Standings, Leaders

1950 American League Batting Leaders

Games		At-Bats		Runs		Hits		Doubles		Triples	
J. Groth, Det	157	G. Kell, Det	641	D. DiMaggio, Bos	131	G. Kell, Det	218	G. Kell, Det	56	H. Evers, Det	11
G. Kell, Det	157	V. Stephens, Bos	628	V. Stephens, Bos	125	P. Rizzuto, NYA	200	V. Wertz, Det	37	D. DiMaggio, Bos	11
J. Priddy, Det	157	D. Philley, ChA	619	P. Rizzuto, NYA	125	D. DiMaggio, Bos	193	P. Rizzuto, NYA	36	B. Doerr, Bos	11
D. Philley, ChA	156	J. Priddy, Det	618	Y. Berra, NYA	116	Y. Berra, NYA	192	H. Evers, Det	35	4 tied with	10
5 tied with	155	P. Rizzuto, NYA	617	3 tied with	114	V. Stephens, Bos	185	V. Stephens, Bos	34		

Home Runs		Total Bases		Runs Batted In		Walks		Intentional Walks		Strikeouts	
A. Rosen, Cle	37	W. Dropo, Bos	326	W. Dropo, Bos	144	E. Yost, Was	141	Statistic unavailable		G. Zernial, ChA	110
W. Dropo, Bos	34	V. Stephens, Bos	321	V. Stephens, Bos	144	F. Fain, Phi	133			L. Easter, Cle	95
J. DiMaggio, NYA	32	Y. Berra, NYA	318	Y. Berra, NYA	124	J. Pesky, Bos	104			J. Priddy, Det	95
V. Stephens, Bos	30	G. Kell, Det	310	V. Wertz, Det	123	E. Joost, Phi	103			D. Lenhardt, StL	94
G. Zernial, ChA	29	J. DiMaggio, NYA	307	J. DiMaggio, NYA	122	A. Rosen, Cle	100			S. Chapman, Phi	79

Hit By Pitch		Sac Hits		Sac Flies		Stolen Bases		Caught Stealing		GDP	
L. Easter, Cle	10	P. Rizzuto, NYA	19	Statistic unavailable		D. DiMaggio, Bos	15	H. Evers, Det	9	B. Hitchcock, Phi	30
A. Rosen, Cle	10	J. Lipon, Det	18			P. Rizzuto, NYA	12	D. Kokos, StL	8	A. Rosen, Cle	27
S. Lollar, StL	8	G. Kell, Det	16			E. Valo, Phi	12	P. Rizzuto, NYA	8	S. Dente, Was	25
E. Yost, Was	8	B. Kennedy, Cle	15			G. Coan, Was	10	4 tied with	7	G. Kell, Det	23
3 tied with	7	O. Friend, StL	14			J. Lipon, Det	9			J. Priddy, Det	22

Runs Created		Runs Created/27 Outs		Batting Average		On-Base Percentage		Slugging Percentage		OBP+Slugging	
P. Rizzuto, NYA	124	L. Doby, Cle	8.90	B. Goodman, Bos	.354	L. Doby, Cle	.442	J. DiMaggio, NYA	.585	L. Doby, Cle	.986
Y. Berra, NYA	122	J. DiMaggio, NYA	8.46	G. Kell, Det	.340	E. Yost, Was	.440	W. Dropo, Bos	.583	J. DiMaggio, NYA	.979
J. DiMaggio, NYA	121	A. Zarilla, Bos	8.45	D. DiMaggio, Bos	.328	J. Pesky, Bos	.437	H. Evers, Det	.551	W. Dropo, Bos	.961
W. Dropo, Bos	120	W. Dropo, Bos	8.09	L. Doby, Cle	.326	F. Fain, Phi	.430	L. Doby, Cle	.545	H. Evers, Det	.959
V. Wertz, Det	120	V. Wertz, Det	7.91	A. Zarilla, Bos	.325	B. Goodman, Bos	.427	A. Rosen, Cle	.543	A. Rosen, Cle	.948

1950 American League Pitching Leaders

Wins		Losses		Winning Percentage		Games		Games Started		Complete Games	
B. Lemon, Cle	23	A. Kellner, Phi	20	V. Raschi, NYA	.724	M. Harris, Was	53	B. Lemon, Cle	37	N. Garver, StL	22
V. Raschi, NYA	21	L. Brissie, Phi	19	D. Trout, Det	.722	E. Kinder, Bos	48	A. Houtteman, Det	34	B. Lemon, Cle	22
A. Houtteman, Det	19	N. Garver, StL	18	E. Lopat, NYA	.692	H. Judson, ChA	46	B. Feller, Cle	34	M. Parnell, Bos	21
3 tied with	18	R. Scarborough, 2tm	18	E. Wynn, Cle	.692	L. Brissie, Phi	46	V. Raschi, NYA	32	A. Houtteman, Det	21
		2 tied with	16	F. Hutchinson, Det	.680	T. Ferrick, 2tm	46	E. Lopat, NYA	32	2 tied with	17

Shutouts		Saves		Games Finished		Batters Faced		Innings Pitched		Hits Allowed	
A. Houtteman, Det	4	M. Harris, Was	15	M. Harris, Was	43	B. Lemon, Cle	1254	B. Lemon, Cle	288.0	B. Lemon, Cle	281
5 tied with	3	J. Page, NYA	13	J. Page, NYA	33	A. Houtteman, Det	1147	A. Houtteman, Det	274.2	F. Hutchinson, Det	269
		T. Ferrick, 2tm	11	T. Ferrick, 2tm	32	N. Garver, StL	1124	N. Garver, StL	260.0	N. Garver, StL	264
		E. Kinder, Bos	9	C. Scheib, Phi	23	V. Raschi, NYA	1085	V. Raschi, NYA	256.2	S. Hudson, Was	261
		L. Brissie, Phi	8	B. Hooper, Phi	22	L. Brissie, Phi	1083	M. Parnell, Bos	249.0	A. Houtteman, Det	257

Home Runs Allowed		Walks		Walks/9 Innings		Strikeouts		Strikeouts/9 Innings		Strikeout/Walk Ratio	
A. Houtteman, Det	29	T. Byrne, NYA	160	F. Hutchinson, Det	1.9	B. Lemon, Cle	170	E. Wynn, Cle	6.0	F. Hutchinson, Det	1.48
A. Kellner, Phi	28	B. Lemon, Cle	146	E. Lopat, NYA	2.5	A. Reynolds, NYA	160	A. Reynolds, NYA	6.0	E. Wynn, Cle	1.42
B. Lemon, Cle	28	A. Reynolds, NYA	138	D. Trout, Det	3.1	V. Raschi, NYA	155	V. Raschi, NYA	5.4	D. Trout, Det	1.38
3 tied with	23	B. Pierce, ChA	137	A. Houtteman, Det	3.2	E. Wynn, Cle	143	B. Lemon, Cle	5.3	V. Raschi, NYA	1.34
		M. McDermott, Bos	124	E. Kinder, Bos	3.4	B. Feller, Cle	119	T. Byrne, NYA	5.2	E. Kinder, Bos	1.22

Earned Run Average		Component ERA		Hit Batsmen		Wild Pitches		Opponent Average		Opponent OBP	
E. Wynn, Cle	3.20	E. Wynn, Cle	3.03	T. Byrne, NYA	17	C. Scheib, Phi	9	E. Wynn, Cle	.212	E. Wynn, Cle	.305
N. Garver, StL	3.39	V. Raschi, NYA	3.55	H. Dorish, StL	9	A. Kellner, Phi	8	B. Pierce, ChA	.228	E. Lopat, NYA	.317
B. Feller, Cle	3.43	B. Feller, Cle	3.61	A. Houtteman, Det	8	B. Kuzava, 2tm	8	A. Reynolds, NYA	.242	A. Houtteman, Det	.322
E. Lopat, NYA	3.47	B. Pierce, ChA	3.62	A. Reynolds, NYA	8	3 tied with	7	V. Raschi, NYA	.243	B. Feller, Cle	.325
A. Houtteman, Det	3.54	E. Lopat, NYA	3.64	H. Wyse, Phi	8			B. Cain, ChA	.244	V. Raschi, NYA	.327

1950 American League Miscellaneous

Managers

Boston	Joe McCarthy	31-28
	Steve O'Neill	63-32
Chicago	Jack Onslow	8-22
	Red Corriden	52-72
Cleveland	Lou Boudreau	92-62
Detroit	Red Rolfe	95-59
New York	Casey Stengel	98-56
Philadelphia	Connie Mack	52-102
St. Louis	Zack Taylor	58-96
Washington	Bucky Harris	67-87

Awards

Most Valuable Player	Phil Rizzuto, ss, NYA
STATS Cy Young	Bob Lemon, Cle
Rookie of the Year	Walt Dropo, 1b, Bos
STATS Manager of the Year	Casey Stengel, NYA

STATS All-Star Team

C	Yogi Berra, NYA	.322	28	124
1B	Walt Dropo, Bos	.322	34	144
2B	Bobby Doerr, Bos	.294	27	120
3B	Al Rosen, Cle	.287	37	116
SS	Phil Rizzuto, NYA	.324	7	66
OF	Joe DiMaggio, NYA	.301	32	122
OF	Larry Doby, Cle	.326	25	102
OF	Ted Williams, Bos	.317	28	97
P	Art Houtteman, Det	19-12	3.54	88 K
P	Bob Lemon, Cle	23-11	3.84	170 K
P	Ed Lopat, NYA	18-8	3.47	72 K
P	Early Wynn, Cle	18-8	3.20	143 K
RP	Tom Ferrick, 2tm	9-7	3.79	11 Sv

Postseason

World Series	NYA (AL) 4 vs. Philadelphia (NL) 0

Outstanding Performances

Three-Homer Games

Bobby Doerr, Bos	on June 8
Larry Doby, Cle	on August 2
Joe DiMaggio, NYA	on September 10
Johnny Mize, NYA	on September 15
Gus Zernial, ChA	on October 1

Cycles

George Kell, Det	on June 2
Elmer Valo, Phi	on August 2
Hoot Evers, Det	on September 7

Team	Overall W	L	Pct	GB	DIF	Home Games W	L	R	OR	HR	OHR	Road Games W	L	R	OR	HR	OHR	Park Index Run	HR	Record by Month M/A	May	June	July	Aug	S/O
Philadelphia	91	63	.591	—	104	47	30	348	279	58	53	44	33	374	345	67	69	87	82	6-6	16-9	14-11	22-13	20-8	13-16
Brooklyn	89	65	.578	2.0	41	48	30	458	386	110	96	41	35	389	338	84	67	113	133	7-2	16-11	12-13	15-14	19-10	20-15
New York	86	68	.558	5.0	0	44	32	362	290	84	67	42	36	373	353	49	73	92	127	1-6	11-14	19-11	14-16	20-10	21-11
Boston	83	71	.539	8.0	6	46	31	343	294	59	45	37	40	442	442	89	84	72	60	6-6	13-10	16-12	18-12	15-14	15-17
St. Louis	78	75	.510	12.5	30	47	29	389	303	50	43	31	46	304	367	52	76	104	74	5-5	17-9	15-13	16-14	12-16	13-18
Cincinnati	66	87	.431	24.5	0	38	38	355	373	52	81	28	49	299	361	47	64	112	121	4-6	6-19	11-16	17-14	11-18	17-14
Chicago	64	89	.418	26.5	10	35	42	352	411	79	63	29	47	291	361	57	67	116	94	3-2	15-14	13-14	10-21	13-19	10-19
Pittsburgh	57	96	.373	33.5	0	33	44	370	447	81	79	24	52	311	410	57	73	112	121	6-5	10-18	7-17	11-19	8-23	15-14

Clinch Date—Philadelphia 10/01.

Team Batting

Team	G	AB	R	OR	H	2B	3B	HR	TB	RBI	TBB	IBB	SO	HBP	SH	SF	SB	CS	SB%	GDP	Avg	OBP	Slg
Brooklyn	155	5364	847	724	1461	247	46	194	2382	774	607	—	632	27	88	—	77	—		139	.272	.349	.444
Boston	156	5363	785	736	1411	246	36	148	2173	726	615	—	616	27	74	—	71	—		136	.263	.342	.405
New York	154	5238	735	643	1352	204	50	133	2055	684	627	—	629	41	75	—	42	—		104	.258	.342	.392
Philadelphia	157	5426	722	624	1440	225	55	125	2150	673	535	—	569	24	66	—	33	—		144	.265	.334	.396
St. Louis	153	5215	693	670	1353	255	50	102	2014	646	606	—	604	23	73	—	23	—		123	.259	.339	.386
Pittsburgh	154	5327	681	857	1404	227	59	138	2163	634	564	—	693	31	54	—	43	—		142	.264	.338	.406
Cincinnati	153	5253	654	734	1366	257	27	99	1974	617	504	—	497	16	72	—	37	—		135	.260	.327	.376
Chicago	154	5230	643	772	1298	224	47	161	2099	615	479	—	767	31	54	—	46	—		122	.248	.315	.401
NL Total	1236	42416	5760	5760	11085	1885	370	1100	17010	5369	4537	—	5007	220	556	—	372	—		1045	.261	.336	.401
NL Avg Team	155	5302	720	720	1386	236	46	138	2126	671	567	—	626	28	70	—	47	—		131	.261	.336	.401

Team Pitching

Team	G	CG	ShO	Rel	Sv	IP	H	R	ER	HR	SH	SF	HB	TBB	IBB	SO	WP	Bk	H/9	SO/9	BB/9	OAvg	OOBP	ERA
Philadelphia	157	57	13	167	27	1406.0	1324	624	546	122	66	—	13	530	—	620	28	14	8.5	4.0	3.4	.250	.320	3.50
New York	154	70	19	179	15	1375.0	1268	643	567	140	74	—	31	536	—	596	25	3	8.3	3.9	3.5	.246	.320	3.71
St. Louis	153	57	10	185	14	1356.0	1398	670	598	119	81	—	25	535	—	603	20	8	9.3	4.0	3.6	.268	.339	3.97
Boston	156	88	7	135	10	1385.1	1411	736	637	129	75	—	30	554	—	615	26	13	9.2	4.0	3.6	.263	.336	4.14
Chicago	154	55	9	199	19	1371.1	1452	772	652	130	74	—	27	593	—	559	31	10	9.5	3.7	3.9	.271	.347	4.28
Brooklyn	155	62	10	195	21	1389.2	1397	724	661	163	46	—	21	591	—	772	27	12	9.0	5.0	3.8	.263	.339	4.28
Cincinnati	153	67	7	157	13	1357.2	1363	734	651	145	66	—	41	582	—	686	32	7	9.0	4.5	3.9	.259	.338	4.32
Pittsburgh	154	42	6	213	16	1368.2	1472	857	754	152	73	—	32	616	—	556	30	9	9.7	3.7	4.1	.275	.353	4.96
NL Total	1236	498	81	1430	135	11009.2	11085	5760	5066	1100	555	—	220	4537	—	5007	219	76	9.1	4.1	3.7	.261	.336	4.14
NL Avg Team	155	62	10	179	17	1376.2	1386	720	633	138	69	—	28	567	—	626	27	10	9.1	4.1	3.7	.261	.336	4.14

Team Fielding

Team	G	PO	A	E	TC	DP	PB	Pct
Brooklyn	155	4169	1693	127	5989	183	8	.979
St. Louis	153	4066	1797	130	5993	172	11	.978
New York	154	4124	1779	137	6040	181	12	.977
Pittsburgh	154	4103	1741	136	5980	165	9	.977
Cincinnati	153	4067	1588	140	5795	132	17	.976
Philadelphia	157	4216	1731	151	6098	155	6	.975
Boston	156	4155	1683	182	6020	146	9	.970
Chicago	154	4119	1945	201	6265	169	12	.968
NL Total	1236	33019	13957	1204	48180	1303	84	.975

Team vs. Team Records

	Bos	Bro	ChN	Cin	NYG	Phi	Pit	StL	Won
Bos	—	9	9	17	13	9	15	11	83
Bro	13	—	10	12	12	11	19	12	89
ChN	13	12	—	4	5	9	11	10	64
Cin	5	10	17	—	11	4	12	7	66
NYG	9	10	17	11	—	12	16	11	86
Phi	13	11	13	18	10	—	14	12	91
Pit	7	3	11	10	6	8	—	12	57
StL	11	10	12	15	11	10	9	—	78
Lost	71	65	89	87	68	63	96	75	

1950 National League Batting Leaders

Games		At-Bats		Runs		Hits		Doubles		Triples	
P. H. Jones, Phi	157	R. Schoendienst, StL	642	E. Torgeson, Bos	120	D. Snider, Bro	199	R. Schoendienst, StL	43	R. Ashburn, Phi	14
G. Hamner, Phi	157	E. Waitkus, Phi	641	E. Stanky, NYG	115	S. Musial, StL	192	S. Musial, StL	41	G. Bell, Pit	11
E. Torgeson, Bos	156	G. Hamner, Phi	637	R. Kiner, Pit	112	C. Furillo, Bro	189	J. Robinson, Bro	39	D. Snider, Bro	10
B. Kerr, Bos	155	D. Snider, Bro	620	D. Snider, Bro	109	D. Ennis, Phi	185	T. Kluszewski, Cin	37	R. Smalley, ChN	9
3 tied with	154	C. Furillo, Bro	620	S. Musial, StL	105	E. Waitkus, Phi	182	A. Dark, NYG	36	R. Schoendienst, StL	9

Home Runs		Total Bases		Runs Batted In		Walks		Intentional Walks		Strikeouts	
R. Kiner, Pit	47	D. Snider, Bro	343	D. Ennis, Phi	126	E. Stanky, NYG	144	Statistic unavailable		R. Smalley, ChN	114
A. Pafko, ChN	36	S. Musial, StL	331	R. Kiner, Pit	118	R. Kiner, Pit	122			S. Jethroe, Bos	93
G. Hodges, Bro	32	D. Ennis, Phi	328	G. Hodges, Bro	113	E. Torgeson, Bos	119			D. Snider, Bro	79
H. Sauer, ChN	32	R. Kiner, Pit	323	T. Kluszewski, Cin	111	W. Westrum, NYG	92			R. Kiner, Pit	79
3 tied with	31	A. Pafko, ChN	304	S. Musial, StL	109	P. Reese, Bro	91			W. Westlake, Pit	78

Hit By Pitch		Sac Hits		Sac Flies		Stolen Bases		Caught Stealing		GDP	
E. Stanky, NYG	12	R. Schoendienst, StL	16	Statistic unavailable		S. Jethroe, Bos	35	Statistic unavailable		D. Ennis, Phi	25
A. Pafko, ChN	11	B. Kerr, Bos	14			P. Reese, Bro	17			R. Kiner, Pit	22
W. Westlake, Pit	7	R. Ashburn, Phi	11			D. Snider, Bro	16			B. Kerr, Bos	21
3 tied with	6	A. Dark, NYG	11			E. Torgeson, Bos	15			M. Goliat, Phi	20
		G. Hodges, Bro	11			R. Ashburn, Phi	14			T. Kluszewski, Cin	20

Runs Created		Runs Created/27 Outs		Batting Average		On-Base Percentage		Slugging Percentage		OBP+Slugging	
S. Musial, StL	136	S. Musial, StL	9.69	S. Musial, StL	.346	E. Stanky, NYG	.460	S. Musial, StL	.596	S. Musial, StL	1.034
D. Snider, Bro	127	S. Gordon, Bos	8.22	J. Robinson, Bro	.328	S. Musial, StL	.437	A. Pafko, ChN	.591	R. Kiner, Pit	.998
E. Torgeson, Bos	123	A. Pafko, ChN	8.18	D. Snider, Bro	.321	J. Robinson, Bro	.423	R. Kiner, Pit	.590	A. Pafko, ChN	.989
R. Kiner, Pit	118	E. Stanky, NYG	8.03	D. Ennis, Phi	.311	T. Glaviano, StL	.421	S. Gordon, Bos	.557	S. Gordon, Bos	.960
E. Stanky, NYG	116	J. Robinson, Bro	8.01	T. Kluszewski, Cin	.307	E. Torgeson, Bos	.412	D. Snider, Bro	.553	D. Snider, Bro	.932

1950 National League Pitching Leaders

Wins		Losses		Winning Percentage		Games		Games Started		Complete Games	
W. Spahn, Bos	21	B. Rush, ChN	20	S. Maglie, NYG	.818	J. Konstanty, Phi	74	R. Roberts, Phi	39	V. Bickford, Bos	27
R. Roberts, Phi	20	K. Raffensberger, Cin	19	J. Hearn, 2tm	.733	M. Dickson, Pit	51	V. Bickford, Bos	39	J. Sain, Bos	25
J. Sain, Bos	20	H. Wehmeier, Cin	18	F. Hiller, ChN	.706	B. Werle, Pit	48	W. Spahn, Bos	39	W. Spahn, Bos	25
4 tied with	19	W. Spahn, Bos	17	J. Konstanty, Phi	.696	S. Maglie, NYG	47	J. Sain, Bos	37	R. Roberts, Phi	21
		3 tied with	16	C. Simmons, Phi	.680	A. Brazle, StL	46	3 tied with	35	L. Jansen, NYG	21

Shutouts		Saves		Games Finished		Batters Faced		Innings Pitched		Hits Allowed	
R. Roberts, Phi	5	J. Konstanty, Phi	22	J. Konstanty, Phi	62	V. Bickford, Bos	1325	V. Bickford, Bos	311.2	J. Sain, Bos	294
L. Jansen, NYG	5	B. Werle, Pit	8	V. Lombardi, Phi	23	R. Roberts, Phi	1228	R. Roberts, Phi	304.1	V. Bickford, Bos	293
J. Hearn, 2tm	5	B. Hogue, Bos	7	D. Leonard, ChN	21	W. Spahn, Bos	1217	W. Spahn, Bos	293.0	R. Roberts, Phi	282
S. Maglie, NYG	5	R. Branca, Bro	7	B. Hogue, Bos	20	J. Sain, Bos	1178	J. Sain, Bos	278.1	K. Raffensberger, Cin	271
2 tied with	4	2 tied with	6	A. Brazle, StL	20	E. Blackwell, Cin	1102	L. Jansen, NYG	275.0	C. Chambers, Pit	262

Home Runs Allowed		Walks		Walks/9 Innings		Strikeouts		Strikeouts/9 Innings		Strikeout/Walk Ratio	
J. Sain, Bos	34	H. Wehmeier, Cin	135	K. Raffensberger, Cin	1.5	W. Spahn, Bos	191	E. Blackwell, Cin	6.5	L. Jansen, NYG	2.93
K. Raffensberger, Cin	34	V. Bickford, Bos	122	L. Jansen, NYG	1.8	E. Blackwell, Cin	188	C. Simmons, Phi	6.1	K. Raffensberger, Cin	2.17
P. Roe, Bro	34	E. Blackwell, Cin	112	J. Sain, Bos	2.3	L. Jansen, NYG	161	W. Spahn, Bos	5.9	R. Roberts, Phi	1.90
L. Jansen, NYG	31	W. Spahn, Bos	111	R. Roberts, Phi	2.3	R. Roberts, Phi	146	E. Palica, Bro	5.9	P. Roe, Bro	1.89
R. Roberts, Phi	29	E. Palica, Bro	98	P. Roe, Bro	2.4	C. Simmons, Phi	146	L. Jansen, NYG	5.3	H. Brecheen, StL	1.78

Earned Run Average		Component ERA		Hit Batsmen		Wild Pitches		Opponent Average		Opponent OBP	
J. Hearn, 2tm	2.49	J. Hearn, 2tm	1.74	E. Blackwell, Cin	13	H. Wehmeier, Cin	11	J. Hearn, 2tm	.182	J. Hearn, 2tm	.253
S. Maglie, NYG	2.71	E. Blackwell, Cin	2.68	S. Maglie, NYG	10	E. Blackwell, Cin	11	E. Blackwell, Cin	.210	L. Jansen, NYG	.271
E. Blackwell, Cin	2.97	L. Jansen, NYG	2.68	F. Smith, Cin	8	W. Spahn, Bos	8	C. Simmons, Phi	.223	R. Roberts, Phi	.297
L. Jansen, NYG	3.01	W. Spahn, Bos	2.93	G. Staley, StL	7	R. Barney, Bro	7	S. Maglie, NYG	.226	H. Brecheen, StL	.298
R. Roberts, Phi	3.02	C. Simmons, Phi	3.05	S. Jones, NYG	7	3 tied with	6	W. Spahn, Bos	.227	W. Spahn, Bos	.299

1950 National League Miscellaneous

Managers		
Boston	Billy Southworth	83-71
Brooklyn	Burt Shotton	89-65
Chicago	Frank Frisch	64-89
Cincinnati	Luke Sewell	66-87
New York	Leo Durocher	86-68
Philadelphia	Eddie Sawyer	91-63
Pittsburgh	Billy Meyer	57-96
St. Louis	Eddie Dyer	78-75

Awards

Most Valuable Player	Jim Konstanty, p, Phi
STATS Cy Young	Jim Konstanty, Phi
Rookie of the Year	Sam Jethroe, of, Bos
STATS Manager of the Year	Eddie Sawyer, Phi

STATS All-Star Team

C	Roy Campanella, Bro	.281	31	89
1B	Earl Torgeson, Bos	.290	23	87
2B	Jackie Robinson, Bro	.328	14	81
3B	Bob Elliott, Bos	.305	24	107
SS	Al Dark, NYG	.279	16	67
OF	Ralph Kiner, Pit	.272	47	118
OF	Stan Musial, StL	.346	28	109
OF	Andy Pafko, ChN	.304	36	92
P	Ewell Blackwell, Cin	17-15	2.97	188 K
P	Sal Maglie, NYG	18-4	2.71	96 K
P	Robin Roberts, Phi	20-11	3.02	146 K
P	Warren Spahn, Bos	21-17	3.16	191 K
RP	Jim Konstanty, Phi	16-7	2.66	22 Sv

Postseason

World Series	Philadelphia (NL) 0 vs. NYA (AL) 4

Outstanding Performances

No-Hitters
Vern Bickford, Bos   vs. Bro on August 11
Four-Homer Games
Gil Hodges, Bro   on August 31
Three-Homer Games
Duke Snider, Bro   on May 30
Wes Westrum, NYG   on June 24
Andy Pafko, ChN   on August 2
Roy Campanella, Bro   on August 26
Hank Sauer, ChN   on August 28
Tommy Brown, Bro   on September 18
Cycles
Ralph Kiner, Pit   on June 25
Roy Smalley, ChN   on June 28

1951 American League Standings

Team	Overall					Home Games						Road Games						Park Index		Record by Month					
	W	L	Pct	GB	DIF	W	L	R	OR	HR	OHR	W	L	R	OR	HR	OHR	Run	HR	M/A	May	June	July	Aug	S/O
New York	98	56	.636	—	83	56	22	366	258	72	43	42	34	432	363	68	49	76	96	8-4	18-9	16-11	17-11	21-12	18-9
Cleveland	93	61	.604	5.0	45	53	24	324	249	76	42	40	37	372	345	64	44	80	109	7-3	12-16	17-11	22-8	22-11	13-12
Boston	87	67	.565	11.0	11	50	25	460	348	80	65	37	42	344	377	47	35	118	186	7-4	17-9	16-14	17-12	18-12	12-16
Chicago	81	73	.526	17.0	45	39	38	334	310	28	47	42	35	380	334	58	62	90	63	6-4	20-5	17-15	11-21	16-13	11-15
Detroit	73	81	.474	25.0	1	36	41	358	402	58	60	37	40	327	339	46	42	114	134	8-5	13-13	15-14	14-16	12-16	11-17
Philadelphia	70	84	.455	28.0	1	38	41	406	407	54	59	32	43	330	338	48	50	116	109	1-12	10-15	15-14	13-19	14-17	17-7
Washington	62	92	.403	36.0	13	32	44	319	362	13	35	30	48	353	402	41	75	93	42	7-3	9-17	9-19	18-14	10-19	9-20
St. Louis	52	102	.338	46.0	1	24	53	327	486	41	66	28	49	284	396	45	65	120	97	4-8	7-21	9-17	11-18	8-22	13-16

Clinch Date—New York 9/28.

Team Batting

Team	G	AB	R	OR	H	2B	3B	HR	TB	RBI	TBB	IBB	SO	HBP	SH	SF	SB	CS	SB%	GDP	Avg	OBP	Slg
Boston	154	5378	804	725	1428	233	32	127	2106	757	756	—	594	18	59	—	20	21	.49	169	.266	.358	.392
New York	154	5194	798	621	1395	208	48	140	2119	741	605	—	547	36	91	—	78	39	.67	138	.269	.349	.408
Philadelphia	154	5277	736	745	1381	229	43	102	2035	685	677	—	565	34	61	—	47	36	.57	118	.262	.349	.386
Chicago	155	5378	714	644	1453	229	64	86	2068	668	596	—	524	27	103	—	99	70	.59	121	.270	.349	.385
Cleveland	155	5250	696	594	1346	208	35	140	2044	658	606	—	632	27	63	—	52	35	.60	125	.256	.336	.389
Detroit	154	5336	685	741	1413	231	35	104	2026	636	568	—	525	18	86	—	37	34	.52	138	.265	.338	.380
Washington	154	5329	672	764	1399	242	45	54	1893	627	560	—	515	26	64	—	45	38	.54	151	.263	.336	.355
St. Louis	154	5219	641	882	1288	223	47	86	1863	555	521	—	693	16	92	—	35	38	.48	151	.247	.317	.357
AL Total	1234	42361	5716	5716	11103	1836	349	839	16154	5327	4889	—	4595	226	619	—	413	311	.57	1105	.262	.342	.381
AL Avg Team	154	5295	715	715	1388	230	44	105	2019	666	611	—	574	28	77	—	52	39	.57	138	.262	.342	.381

Team Pitching

Team	G	CG	ShO	Rel	Sv	IP	H	R	ER	HR	SH	SF	HB	TBB	IBB	SO	WP	Bk	H/9	SO/9	BB/9	OAvg	OOBP	ERA
Cleveland	155	76	10	135	19	1391.1	1287	594	523	86	86	—	24	577	—	642	20	2	8.3	4.2	3.7	.245	.323	3.38
Chicago	155	74	11	150	14	1418.1	1353	644	552	109	81	—	15	549	—	572	17	4	8.6	3.6	3.5	.252	.323	3.50
New York	154	66	24	158	22	1367.0	1290	621	541	92	72	—	28	562	—	664	24	4	8.5	4.4	3.7	.250	.328	3.56
Boston	154	46	7	210	24	1399.0	1413	725	643	100	87	—	34	599	—	658	27	2	9.1	4.2	3.9	.264	.342	4.14
Detroit	154	51	8	195	17	1384.0	1385	741	660	102	89	—	40	602	—	597	40	6	9.0	3.9	3.9	.262	.342	4.29
Philadelphia	154	52	7	157	22	1358.0	1421	745	674	109	67	—	32	569	—	437	30	3	9.4	2.9	3.7	.272	.347	4.47
Washington	154	58	6	160	13	1366.1	1429	764	681	110	64	—	16	630	—	475	12	10	9.4	3.1	4.1	.269	.348	4.49
St. Louis	154	56	5	180	9	1370.1	1525	882	788	131	73	—	38	801	—	550	26	2	10.0	3.6	5.3	.282	.379	5.18
AL Total	1234	479	78	1345	140	11054.1	11103	5716	5062	839	619	—	227	4889	—	4595	196	33	9.0	3.7	4.0	.262	.342	4.12
AL Avg Team	154	60	10	168	18	1381.1	1388	715	633	105	77	—	28	611	—	574	25	4	9.0	3.7	4.0	.262	.342	4.12

Team Fielding

Team	G	PO	A	E	TC	DP	PB	Pct
Cleveland	155	4170	1674	134	5978	151	9	.978
Philadelphia	154	4073	1849	136	6058	204	12	.978
Boston	154	4191	1814	141	6146	184	10	.977
Chicago	155	4253	1753	151	6157	176	8	.975
New York	154	4100	1625	144	5869	190	4	.975
Detroit	154	4171	1832	163	6166	166	13	.974
Washington	154	4097	1587	160	5844	148	11	.973
St. Louis	154	4108	1665	172	5945	179	15	.971
AL Total	1234	33163	13799	1201	48163	1398	82	.975

Team vs. Team Records

	Bos	ChA	Cle	Det	NYA	Phi	StL	Was	Won
Bos	—	11	8	12	11	15	15	15	87
ChA	11	—	12	12	8	9	15	14	81
Cle	14	10	—	17	7	16	16	13	93
Det	10	10	5	—	10	13	12	13	73
NYA	11	14	15	12	—	13	17	16	98
Phi	7	13	6	9	9	—	14	12	70
StL	7	7	6	10	5	8	—	9	52
Was	7	8	9	9	6	10	13	—	62
Lost	67	73	61	81	56	84	102	92	

1951 American League Batting Leaders

Games			At-Bats			Runs			Hits			Doubles			Triples		
A. Rosen, Cle	154		D. DiMaggio, Bos	639		D. DiMaggio, Bos	113		G. Kell, Det	191		S. Mele, Was	36		M. Minoso, 2tm	14	
E. Yost, Was	154		B. Young, StL	611		M. Minoso, 2tm	112		N. Fox, ChA	189		E. Yost, Was	36		N. Fox, ChA	12	
J. Priddy, Det	154		N. Fox, ChA	604		E. Yost, Was	109		D. DiMaggio, Bos	189		G. Kell, Det	36		R. Coleman, 2tm	12	
R. Boone, Cle	151		G. Kell, Det	598		T. Williams, Bos	109		M. Minoso, 2tm	173		3 tied with	34		B. Young, StL	9	
E. Robinson, ChA	151		J. Priddy, Det	584		E. Joost, Phi	107		T. Williams, Bos	169					2 tied with	8	

Home Runs			Total Bases			Runs Batted In			Walks			Intentional Walks			Strikeouts		
G. Zernial, 2tm	33		T. Williams, Bos	295		G. Zernial, 2tm	129		T. Williams, Bos	144		Statistic unavailable			G. Zernial, 2tm	101	
T. Williams, Bos	30		G. Zernial, 2tm	292		T. Williams, Bos	126		E. Yost, Was	126					L. Doby, Cle	81	
E. Robinson, ChA	29		E. Robinson, ChA	279		E. Robinson, ChA	117		E. Joost, Phi	106					M. Mantle, NYA	74	
3 tied with	27		Y. Berra, NYA	269		L. Easter, Cle	103		L. Doby, Cle	101					J. Priddy, Det	73	
			D. DiMaggio, Bos	267		A. Rosen, Cle	102		A. Rosen, Cle	85					J. Hegan, Cle	72	

Hit By Pitch			Sac Hits			Sac Flies			Stolen Bases			Caught Stealing			GDP		
M. Minoso, 2tm	16		P. Rizzuto, NYA	26		Statistic unavailable			M. Minoso, 2tm	31		N. Fox, ChA	12		S. Mele, Was	22	
N. Fox, ChA	14		N. Fox, ChA	20					J. Busby, ChA	26		J. Busby, ChA	11		V. Stephens, Bos	22	
E. Yost, Was	11		B. Young, StL	19					P. Rizzuto, NYA	18		M. Minoso, 2tm	10		S. Lollar, StL	20	
L. Easter, Cle	9		B. Avila, Cle	13					3 tied with	14		J. Delsing, StL	9		C. Vollmer, Bos	20	
E. Valo, Phi	8		V. Raschi, NYA	13								2 tied with	8		J. Priddy, Det	18	

Runs Created			Runs Created/27 Outs			Batting Average			On-Base Percentage			Slugging Percentage			OBP+Slugging		
T. Williams, Bos	144		T. Williams, Bos	10.42		F. Fain, Phi	.344		T. Williams, Bos	.464		T. Williams, Bos	.556		T. Williams, Bos	1.019	
E. Yost, Was	118		F. Fain, Phi	8.32		M. Minoso, 2tm	.326		F. Fain, Phi	.451		L. Doby, Cle	.512		L. Doby, Cle	.941	
M. Minoso, 2tm	110		L. Doby, Cle	8.28		G. Kell, Det	.319		L. Doby, Cle	.428		G. Zernial, 2tm	.511		M. Minoso, 2tm	.922	
E. Joost, Phi	110		M. Minoso, 2tm	7.75		T. Williams, Bos	.318		E. Yost, Was	.423		V. Wertz, Det	.511		F. Fain, Phi	.921	
D. DiMaggio, Bos	103		E. Yost, Was	7.42		N. Fox, ChA	.313		M. Minoso, 2tm	.422		M. Minoso, 2tm	.500		V. Wertz, Det	.894	

1951 American League Pitching Leaders

Wins			Losses			Winning Percentage			Games			Games Started			Complete Games		
B. Feller, Cle	22		6 tied with	14		B. Feller, Cle	.733		E. Kinder, Bos	63		V. Raschi, NYA	34		N. Garver, StL	24	
V. Raschi, NYA	21					M. Martin, Phi	.733		L. Brissie, 2tm	56		B. Lemon, Cle	34		E. Wynn, Cle	21	
E. Lopat, NYA	21					E. Lopat, NYA	.700		M. Garcia, Cle	47		E. Wynn, Cle	34		E. Lopat, NYA	20	
3 tied with	20					A. Reynolds, NYA	.680		C. Scheib, Phi	46		B. Feller, Cle	32		B. Pierce, ChA	18	
						V. Raschi, NYA	.677		2 tied with	42		E. Lopat, NYA	31		2 tied with	17	

Shutouts			Saves			Games Finished			Batters Faced			Innings Pitched			Hits Allowed		
A. Reynolds, NYA	7		E. Kinder, Bos	14		E. Kinder, Bos	41		B. Lemon, Cle	1139		E. Wynn, Cle	274.1		B. Lemon, Cle	244	
V. Raschi, NYA	4		C. Scheib, Phi	10		C. Scheib, Phi	34		E. Wynn, Cle	1138		B. Lemon, Cle	263.1		M. Garcia, Cle	239	
E. Lopat, NYA	4		L. Brissie, 2tm	9		M. Harris, Was	29		V. Raschi, NYA	1081		V. Raschi, NYA	258.1		B. Feller, Cle	239	
B. Feller, Cle	4		A. Reynolds, NYA	7		L. Brissie, 2tm	26		M. Garcia, Cle	1066		M. Garcia, Cle	254.0		N. Garver, StL	237	
5 tied with	3		M. Garcia, Cle	6		J. Kucab, Phi	21		B. Feller, Cle	1061		B. Feller, Cle	249.2		B. Pierce, ChA	237	

Home Runs Allowed			Walks			Walks/9 Innings			Strikeouts			Strikeouts/9 Innings			Strikeout/Walk Ratio		
D. Starr, 2tm	22		T. Byrne, 2tm	150		F. Hutchinson, Det	1.3		V. Raschi, NYA	164		M. McDermott, Bos	6.6		F. Hutchinson, Det	1.96	
B. Feller, Cle	22		B. Lemon, Cle	124		E. Lopat, NYA	2.7		E. Wynn, Cle	133		T. Gray, Det	6.0		V. Raschi, NYA	1.59	
R. Scarborough, Bos	21		D. Pillette, StL	115		B. Pierce, ChA	2.7		B. Lemon, Cle	132		V. Raschi, NYA	5.7		B. Pierce, ChA	1.55	
3 tied with	20		E. Wynn, Cle	107		B. Hooper, Phi	2.9		T. Gray, Det	131		A. Reynolds, NYA	5.1		M. Garcia, Cle	1.44	
			V. Raschi, NYA	103		M. Garcia, Cle	2.9		M. McDermott, Bos	127		B. Lemon, Cle	4.5		M. McDermott, Bos	1.38	

Earned Run Average			Component ERA			Hit Batsmen			Wild Pitches			Opponent Average			Opponent OBP		
S. Rogovin, 2tm	2.78		A. Reynolds, NYA	2.77		T. Byrne, 2tm	15		A. Kellner, Phi	9		A. Reynolds, NYA	.213		E. Lopat, NYA	.298	
E. Lopat, NYA	2.91		E. Lopat, NYA	2.79		B. Cain, 2tm	14		V. Raschi, NYA	8		E. Wynn, Cle	.225		S. Rogovin, 2tm	.301	
E. Wynn, Cle	3.02		E. Wynn, Cle	2.84		R. Scarborough, Bos	14		4 tied with	6		M. McDermott, Bos	.226		E. Wynn, Cle	.301	
B. Pierce, ChA	3.03		S. Rogovin, 2tm	2.94		C. Scheib, Phi	8					S. Rogovin, 2tm	.235		F. Hutchinson, Det	.302	
A. Reynolds, NYA	3.05		M. Garcia, Cle	3.01		3 tied with	7					E. Lopat, NYA	.239		A. Reynolds, NYA	.304	

1951 American League Miscellaneous

Managers

Boston	Steve O'Neill	87-67
Chicago	Paul Richards	81-73
Cleveland	Al Lopez	93-61
Detroit	Red Rolfe	73-81
New York	Casey Stengel	98-56
Philadelphia	Jimmy Dykes	70-84
St. Louis	Zack Taylor	52-102
Washington	Bucky Harris	62-92

Awards

Most Valuable Player	Yogi Berra, c, NYA
STATS Cy Young	Ed Lopat, NYA
Rookie of the Year	Gil McDougald, 3b, NYA
STATS Manager of the Year	Paul Richards, ChA

STATS All-Star Team

C	Yogi Berra, NYA	.294	27	88
1B	Ferris Fain, Phi	.344	6	57
2B	Nellie Fox, ChA	.313	4	55
3B	Eddie Yost, Was	.283	12	65
SS	Eddie Joost, Phi	.289	19	78
OF	Minnie Minoso, 2tm	.326	10	76
OF	Ted Williams, Bos	.318	30	126
OF	Gus Zernial, 2tm	.268	33	129
P	Mike Garcia, Cle	20-13	3.15	118 K
P	Ned Garver, StL	20-12	3.73	84 K
P	Ed Lopat, NYA	21-9	2.91	93 K
P	Early Wynn, Cle	20-13	3.02	133 K
RP	Ellis Kinder, Bos	11-2	2.55	14 Sv

Postseason

World Series NYA (AL) 4 vs. NYG (NL) 2

Outstanding Performances

No-Hitters

Bob Feller, Cle	vs. Det on July 1
Allie Reynolds, NYA	@ Cle on July 12
Allie Reynolds, NYA	vs. Bos on September 28

Three-Homer Games

Bobby Avila, Cle	on June 20
Clyde Vollmer, Bos	on July 26

Seasons: Standings, Leaders

1951 National League Standings

Team	W	L	Pct	GB	DIF	W	L	R	OR	HR	OHR	W	L	R	OR	HR	OHR	Run	HR	M/A	May	June	July	Aug	S/O
		Overall						Home Games						Road Games				Park Index				Record by Month			
New York	98	59	.624	—	7	50	28	399	308	115	89	48	31	382	333	64	59	100	168	3-12	18-9	17-11	18-12	20-9	22-6
Brooklyn	97	60	.618	1.0	147	49	29	412	316	100	81	48	31	443	356	84	69	92	120	8-5	16-10	18-10	21-7	19-13	15-15
St. Louis	81	73	.526	15.5	8	44	34	370	323	44	56	37	39	313	348	51	63	102	85	6-3	16-14	12-15	12-16	15-14	20-11
Boston	76	78	.494	20.5	10	42	35	367	310	59	37	34	43	356	352	71	59	96	74	10-5	11-14	10-15	14-15	19-12	12-17
Philadelphia	73	81	.474	23.5	2	38	39	312	305	43	50	35	42	336	339	65	60	91	74	7-6	10-18	16-10	16-15	14-17	10-15
Cincinnati	68	86	.442	28.5	0	35	42	289	320	44	46	33	44	270	347	44	73	99	77	4-7	14-14	14-12	12-18	10-23	14-12
Pittsburgh	64	90	.416	32.5	5	32	45	388	465	72	84	32	45	301	380	65	73	125	113	5-5	10-18	10-17	14-17	16-17	9-16
Chicago	62	92	.403	34.5	3	32	45	304	364	45	59	30	47	310	386	58	66	96	84	5-5	14-12	9-16	11-18	14-22	9-19

Clinch Date—New York 10/03.

Team Batting

Team	G	AB	R	OR	H	2B	3B	HR	TB	RBI	TBB	IBB	SO	HBP	SH	SF	SB	CS	SB%	GDP	Avg	OBP	Slg
Brooklyn	158	5492	855	672	1511	249	37	184	2386	794	603	—	649	44	75	—	89	70	.56	147	.275	.352	.434
New York	157	5360	781	641	1396	201	53	179	2240	734	671	—	624	40	82	—	55	34	.62	139	.260	.336	.418
Boston	155	5293	723	662	1385	234	37	130	2083	683	565	—	617	31	79	—	80	34	.70	139	.262	.336	.394
Pittsburgh	155	5318	689	845	1372	218	56	137	2113	648	557	—	615	22	76	—	29	27	.52	130	.258	.331	.397
St. Louis	155	5317	683	671	1404	230	57	95	2033	629	569	—	492	31	86	—	30	30	.50	134	.264	.339	.382
Philadelphia	154	5332	648	644	1384	199	47	108	2001	609	505	—	525	21	103	—	63	28	.69	111	.260	.326	.375
Chicago	155	5307	614	750	1327	200	47	103	1930	572	477	—	647	22	56	—	63	30	.68	139	.250	.304	.364
Cincinnati	155	5285	559	667	1309	215	33	88	1854	528	415	—	577	11	64	—	44	40	.52	125	.248	.304	.351
NL Total	1244	42704	5552	5552	11088	1746	367	1024	16640	5197	4362	—	4746	222	621	—	453	293	.61	1041	.260	.331	.390
NL Avg Team	156	5338	694	694	1386	218	46	128	2080	650	545	—	593	28	78	—	57	37	.61	130	.260	.331	.390

Team Pitching

Team	G	CG	ShO	Rel	Sv	IP	H	R	ER	HR	SH	SF	HB	TBB	IBB	SO	WP	Bk	H/9	SO/9	BB/9	OAvg	OOBP	ERA
New York	157	64	9	189	18	1412.2	1334	641	546	148	61	—	20	482	—	625	26	4	8.5	4.0	3.1	.248	.312	3.48
Cincinnati	155	55	14	204	23	1390.2	1357	667	572	119	82	—	42	490	—	584	34	4	8.8	3.8	3.2	.255	.323	3.70
Boston	155	73	16	164	12	1389.0	1378	662	578	96	78	—	32	595	—	604	31	3	8.9	3.9	3.9	.259	.337	3.75
Philadelphia	154	57	19	179	15	1384.2	1373	644	586	110	72	—	22	497	—	570	32	3	8.9	3.7	3.2	.258	.324	3.81
Brooklyn	158	64	10	179	13	1423.1	1360	672	613	150	66	—	25	549	—	693	35	0	8.6	4.4	3.5	.253	.326	3.88
St. Louis	155	58	9	183	23	1387.2	1391	671	609	119	71	—	21	568	—	546	18	4	9.0	3.5	3.7	.263	.337	3.95
Chicago	155	48	10	185	10	1385.2	1416	750	668	125	89	—	29	572	—	544	43	7	9.2	3.5	3.7	.265	.340	4.34
Pittsburgh	155	40	9	226	22	1380.1	1479	845	735	157	86	—	31	609	—	580	27	7	9.6	3.8	4.0	.274	.352	4.79
NL Total	1244	459	96	1509	136	11154.0	11088	5552	4907	1024	605	—	222	4362	—	4746	246	32	8.9	3.8	3.5	.260	.331	3.96
NL Avg Team	156	57	12	189	17	1394.0	1386	694	613	128	76	—	28	545	—	593	31	4	8.9	3.8	3.5	.260	.331	3.96

Team Fielding

Team	G	PO	A	E	TC	DP	PB	Pct
St. Louis	155	4162	1870	125	6157	187	8	.980
Brooklyn	158	4270	1760	129	6159	192	4	.979
Cincinnati	155	4172	1677	140	5989	141	14	.977
Philadelphia	154	4153	1607	146	5898	146	14	.977
Boston	155	4167	1672	145	5984	157	13	.976
New York	157	4238	1785	171	6194	175	9	.972
Pittsburgh	155	4138	1808	170	6116	178	9	.972
Chicago	155	4157	1828	181	6166	161	17	.971
NL Total	1244	33457	14007	1199	48663	1337	88	.975

Team vs. Team Records

	Bos	Bro	ChN	Cin	NYG	Phi	Pit	StL	Won
Bos	—	10	10	10	8	12	13	13	76
Bro	12	—	14	14	14	15	10	18	97
ChN	12	8	—	10	7	7	9	9	62
Cin	12	8	12	—	5	11	12	8	68
NYG	14	11	15	17	—	16	14	11	98
Phi	10	7	15	11	6	—	15	9	73
Pit	9	12	13	10	8	7	—	5	64
StL	9	4	13	14	11	13	17	—	81
Lost	78	60	92	86	59	81	90	73	

1951 National League Batting Leaders

Games		At-Bats		Runs		Hits		Doubles		Triples	
C. Furillo, Bro	158	C. Furillo, Bro	667	R. Kiner, Pit	124	R. Ashburn, Phi	221	A. Dark, NYG	41	G. Bell, Pit	12
G. Hodges, Bro	158	A. Dark, NYG	646	S. Musial, StL	124	S. Musial, StL	205	T. Kluszewski, Cin	35	S. Musial, StL	12
A. Dark, NYG	156	R. Ashburn, Phi	643	G. Hodges, Bro	118	C. Furillo, Bro	197	R. Campanella, Bro	33	M. Irvin, NYG	11
E. Torgeson, Bos	155	P. Reese, Bro	616	A. Dark, NYG	114	A. Dark, NYG	196	J. Robinson, Bro	33	S. Jethroe, Bos	10
3 tied with	154	W. Lockman, NYG	614	J. Robinson, Bro	106	J. Robinson, Bro	185	2 tied with	32	F. Baumholtz, ChN	10

Home Runs		Total Bases		Runs Batted In		Walks		Intentional Walks		Strikeouts	
R. Kiner, Pit	42	S. Musial, StL	355	M. Irvin, NYG	121	R. Kiner, Pit	137	Statistic unavailable		G. Hodges, Bro	99
G. Hodges, Bro	40	R. Kiner, Pit	333	R. Kiner, Pit	109	E. Stanky, NYG	127			D. Snider, Bro	97
R. Campanella, Bro	33	G. Hodges, Bro	307	S. Gordon, Bos	109	W. Westrum, NYG	104			W. Westrum, NYG	93
B. Thomson, NYG	32	R. Campanella, Bro	298	R. Campanella, Bro	108	E. Torgeson, Bos	102			S. Jethroe, Bos	88
S. Musial, StL	32	2 tied with	293	S. Musial, StL	108	S. Musial, StL	98			G. Strickland, Pit	83

Hit By Pitch		Sac Hits		Sac Flies		Stolen Bases		Caught Stealing		GDP	
A. Pafko, 2tm	12	P. H. Jones, Phi	19	Statistic unavailable		S. Jethroe, Bos	35	P. Reese, Bro	14	S. Gordon, Bos	28
S. Jethroe, Bos	11	R. Ashburn, Phi	17			R. Ashburn, Phi	29	E. Torgeson, Bos	11	J. Adcock, Cin	25
M. Irvin, NYG	9	P. Castiglione, Pit	16			J. Robinson, Bro	25	D. Snider, Bro	10	D. Snider, Bro	23
J. Robinson, Bro	9	R. Roberts, Phi	14			E. Torgeson, Bos	20	B. Adams, Cin	10	R. Jackson, ChN	21
C. Furillo, Bro	7	2 tied with	13			P. Reese, Bro	20	2 tied with	8	G. Hamner, Phi	20

Runs Created		Runs Created/27 Outs		Batting Average		On-Base Percentage		Slugging Percentage		OBP+Slugging	
S. Musial, StL	147	S. Musial, StL	10.30	S. Musial, StL	.355	R. Kiner, Pit	.452	R. Kiner, Pit	.627	R. Kiner, Pit	1.079
R. Kiner, Pit	144	R. Kiner, Pit	10.28	R. Ashburn, Phi	.344	S. Musial, StL	.449	S. Musial, StL	.614	S. Musial, StL	1.063
J. Robinson, Bro	127	J. Robinson, Bro	8.86	J. Robinson, Bro	.338	J. Robinson, Bro	.429	R. Campanella, Bro	.590	R. Campanella, Bro	.983
G. Hodges, Bro	117	R. Campanella, Bro	8.20	R. Campanella, Bro	.325	M. Irvin, NYG	.415	B. Thomson, NYG	.562	J. Robinson, Bro	.957
M. Irvin, NYG	116	M. Irvin, NYG	7.79	M. Irvin, NYG	.312	E. Stanky, NYG	.401	G. Hodges, Bro	.527	B. Thomson, NYG	.947

1951 National League Pitching Leaders

Wins		Losses		Winning Percentage		Games		Games Started		Complete Games	
L. Jansen, NYG	23	W. Ramsdell, Cin	17	P. Roe, Bro	.880	T. Wilks, 2tm	65	R. Roberts, Phi	39	W. Spahn, Bos	26
S. Maglie, NYG	23	P. Minner, ChN	17	S. Maglie, NYG	.793	B. Werle, Pit	59	S. Maglie, NYG	37	R. Roberts, Phi	22
W. Spahn, Bos	22	K. Raffensberger, Cin	17	D. Newcombe, Bro	.690	J. Konstanty, Phi	58	D. Newcombe, Bro	36	S. Maglie, NYG	22
P. Roe, Bro	22	M. Surkont, Bos	16	L. Jansen, NYG	.676	G. Spencer, NYG	57	W. Spahn, Bos	36	M. Dickson, Pit	19
R. Roberts, Phi	21	M. Dickson, Pit	16	C. King, Bro	.667	A. Brazle, StL	56	M. Dickson, Pit	35	P. Roe, Bro	19

Shutouts		Saves		Games Finished		Batters Faced		Innings Pitched		Hits Allowed	
W. Spahn, Bos	7	T. Wilks, 2tm	13	J. Konstanty, Phi	45	W. Spahn, Bos	1289	R. Roberts, Phi	315.0	M. Dickson, Pit	294
R. Roberts, Phi	6	F. Smith, Cin	11	T. Wilks, 2tm	40	R. Roberts, Phi	1274	W. Spahn, Bos	310.2	R. Roberts, Phi	284
K. Raffensberger, Cin	5	J. Konstanty, Phi	9	F. Smith, Cin	35	M. Dickson, Pit	1241	S. Maglie, NYG	298.0	W. Spahn, Bos	278
3 tied with	4	A. Brazle, StL	7	C. King, Bro	31	S. Maglie, NYG	1210	M. Dickson, Pit	288.2	L. Jansen, NYG	254
		3 tied with	6	2 tied with	28	L. Jansen, NYG	1133	L. Jansen, NYG	278.2	S. Maglie, NYG	254

Home Runs Allowed		Walks		Walks/9 Innings		Strikeouts		Strikeouts/9 Innings		Strikeout/Walk Ratio	
M. Dickson, Pit	32	W. Spahn, Bos	109	K. Raffensberger, Cin	1.4	D. Newcombe, Bro	164	M. Queen, Pit	6.6	L. Jansen, NYG	2.59
P. Roe, Bro	30	M. Dickson, Pit	101	L. Jansen, NYG	1.8	W. Spahn, Bos	164	B. Rush, ChN	5.5	K. Raffensberger, Cin	2.13
K. Raffensberger, Cin	29	M. Queen, Pit	99	R. Roberts, Phi	1.8	S. Maglie, NYG	146	D. Newcombe, Bro	5.4	R. Roberts, Phi	1.98
S. Maglie, NYG	27	E. Blackwell, Cin	97	P. Roe, Bro	2.2	L. Jansen, NYG	145	R. Branca, Bro	5.2	B. Rush, ChN	1.90
L. Jansen, NYG	26	D. Newcombe, Bro	91	J. Sain, Bos	2.5	B. Rush, ChN	129	W. Spahn, Bos	4.8	D. Newcombe, Bro	1.80

Earned Run Average		Component ERA		Hit Batsmen		Wild Pitches		Opponent Average		Opponent OBP	
C. Nichols, Bos	2.88	R. Roberts, Phi	2.57	F. Hiller, ChN	9	W. Ramsdell, Cin	9	S. Maglie, NYG	.230	R. Roberts, Phi	.278
S. Maglie, NYG	2.93	L. Jansen, NYG	2.79	E. Blackwell, Cin	9	R. Meyer, Phi	9	D. Newcombe, Bro	.230	L. Jansen, NYG	.279
W. Spahn, Bos	2.98	S. Maglie, NYG	2.84	W. Ramsdell, Cin	8	C. Nichols, Bos	8	E. Blackwell, Cin	.233	K. Raffensberger, Cin	.279
R. Roberts, Phi	3.03	D. Newcombe, Bro	2.91	G. Staley, StL	8	S. Jones, NYG	8	M. Queen, Pit	.233	S. Maglie, NYG	.289
L. Jansen, NYG	3.04	K. Raffensberger, Cin	2.92	M. Surkont, Bos	7	5 tied with	7	R. Branca, Bro	.237	D. Newcombe, Bro	.297

1951 National League Miscellaneous

Managers

Boston	Billy Southworth	28-31
	Tommy Holmes	48-47
Brooklyn	Chuck Dressen	97-60
Chicago	Frank Frisch	35-45
	Phil Cavarretta	27-47
Cincinnati	Luke Sewell	68-86
New York	Leo Durocher	98-59
Philadelphia	Eddie Sawyer	73-81
Pittsburgh	Billy Meyer	64-90
St. Louis	Marty Marion	81-73

Awards

Most Valuable Player	Roy Campanella, c, Bro
STATS Cy Young	Sal Maglie, NYG
Rookie of the Year	Willie Mays, of, NYG
STATS Manager of the Year	Leo Durocher, NYG

STATS All-Star Team

C	Roy Campanella, Bro	.325	33	108
1B	Gil Hodges, Bro	.268	40	103
2B	Jackie Robinson, Bro	.338	19	88
3B	Puddin' Head Jones, Phi	.285	22	81
SS	Al Dark, NYG	.303	14	69
OF	Monte Irvin, NYG	.312	24	121
OF	Ralph Kiner, Pit	.309	42	109
OF	Stan Musial, StL	.355	32	108
P	Larry Jansen, NYG	23-11	3.04	145 K
P	Sal Maglie, NYG	23-6	2.93	146 K
P	Preacher Roe, Bro	22-3	3.04	113 K
P	Warren Spahn, Bos	22-14	2.98	164 K
RP	Ted Wilks, 2tm	3-5	2.86	13 Sv

Postseason

World Series   NYA (NL) 2 vs. NYG (AL) 4

Outstanding Performances

No-Hitters
Cliff Chambers, Pit   @ Bos on May 6
Three-Homer Games
Ralph Kiner, Pit   on July 18
Del Wilber, Phi   on August 27
Don Mueller, NYG   on September 1
Cycles
Gus Bell, Pit   on June 4

1952 American League Standings

Team	Overall					Home Games						Road Games						Park Index		Record by Month					
	W	L	Pct	GB	DIF	W	L	R	OR	HR	OHR	W	L	R	OR	HR	OHR	Run	HR	M/A	May	June	July	Aug	S/O
New York	95	59	.617	—	111	49	28	345	264	64	48	46	31	382	293	65	46	90	101	5-6	13-11	21-9	20-15	17-13	19-5
Cleveland	93	61	.604	2.0	37	49	28	333	260	72	43	44	33	430	346	76	51	76	91	9-5	16-12	12-15	19-12	18-12	19-5
Chicago	81	73	.526	14.0	0	44	33	305	276	42	39	37	40	305	292	38	47	97	95	8-6	15-13	16-13	13-18	15-12	14-11
Philadelphia	79	75	.513	16.0	0	45	32	382	403	55	60	34	43	282	320	34	53	130	132	2-8	13-11	12-14	21-13	20-14	11-15
Washington	78	76	.506	17.0	0	42	35	299	292	13	18	36	41	299	316	37	60	96	32	4-6	17-11	14-13	18-16	13-17	12-13
Boston	76	78	.494	19.0	22	50	27	406	309	68	49	26	51	262	349	45	58	117	114	10-2	12-15	15-14	16-13	16-14	7-20
St. Louis	64	90	.416	31.0	4	42	35	321	346	47	52	22	55	283	387	35	59	100	105	8-6	12-19	12-13	9-23	13-16	10-13
Detroit	50	104	.325	45.0	0	32	45	284	366	65	59	18	59	273	372	38	52	101	138	2-9	10-16	10-21	13-19	8-22	7-17

Clinch Date—New York 9/26.

Team Batting

Team	G	AB	R	OR	H	2B	3B	HR	TB	RBI	TBB	IBB	SO	HBP	SH	SF	SB	CS	SB%	GDP	Avg	OBP	Slg
Cleveland	155	5330	763	606	1399	211	49	148	2152	721	626	—	749	20	84	—	46	39	.54	124	.262	.342	.404
New York	154	5294	727	557	1411	233	34	129	2131	670	566	—	652	36	94	—	52	42	.55	93	.267	.341	.403
Boston	154	5246	668	658	1338	233	34	113	1978	628	542	—	739	32	66	—	59	47	.56	133	.255	.329	.377
Philadelphia	155	5163	664	723	1305	212	35	89	1854	632	683	—	561	27	102	—	52	43	.55	152	.253	.343	.359
Chicago	156	5316	610	568	1337	199	38	80	1852	560	541	—	521	58	121	—	61	38	.62	121	.252	.327	.348
St. Louis	155	5353	604	733	1340	225	46	82	1903	574	540	—	720	21	86	—	30	34	.47	112	.250	.321	.356
Washington	157	5357	598	608	1282	225	44	50	1745	555	580	—	607	30	79	—	48	37	.56	137	.239	.317	.326
Detroit	156	5258	557	738	1278	190	37	103	1851	529	553	—	605	22	80	—	27	38	.42	146	.243	.318	.352
AL Total	1242	42317	5191	5191	10690	1716	339	794	15466	4869	4631	—	5154	246	712	—	375	318	.54	1018	.253	.330	.365
AL Avg Team	155	5290	649	649	1336	215	42	99	1933	609	579	—	644	31	89	—	47	40	.54	127	.253	.330	.365

Team Pitching

Team	G	CG	ShO	Rel	Sv	IP	H	R	ER	HR	SH	SF	HB	TBB	IBB	SO	WP	Bk	H/9	SO/9	BB/9	OAvg	OOBP	ERA
New York	154	72	21	143	27	1381.0	1240	557	482	94	74	—	34	581	—	666	16	2	8.1	4.3	3.8	.243	.324	3.14
Chicago	156	53	15	190	28	1416.2	1251	568	512	86	96	—	20	578	—	774	31	1	7.9	4.9	3.7	.238	.316	3.25
Cleveland	155	80	19	143	18	1407.0	1278	606	519	94	99	—	24	556	—	671	29	2	8.2	4.3	3.6	.241	.316	3.32
Washington	157	75	10	137	15	1429.2	1405	608	536	78	67	—	30	577	—	574	23	1	8.8	3.6	3.6	.258	.332	3.37
Boston	154	53	7	176	24	1372.1	1332	658	580	107	91	—	38	623	—	624	27	3	8.7	4.1	4.1	.256	.340	3.80
St. Louis	155	48	6	181	18	1399.0	1388	733	640	111	95	—	41	598	—	581	26	4	8.9	3.7	3.8	.260	.339	4.12
Philadelphia	155	73	11	137	16	1384.1	1402	723	639	113	84	—	35	526	—	562	21	2	9.1	3.7	3.4	.263	.333	4.15
Detroit	156	51	10	182	14	1388.1	1394	738	656	111	106	—	25	591	—	702	37	4	9.0	4.6	3.8	.262	.338	4.25
AL Total	1242	505	99	1289	160	11178.1	10690	5191	4564	794	712	—	247	4630	—	5154	210	19	8.6	4.1	3.7	.253	.330	3.67
AL Avg Team	155	63	12	161	20	1397.1	1336	649	571	99	89	—	31	579	—	644	26	2	8.6	4.1	3.7	.253	.330	3.67

Team Fielding

Team	G	PO	A	E	TC	DP	PB	Pct
Chicago	156	4248	1690	123	6061	158	6	.980
New York	154	4146	1790	127	6063	199	5	.979
Washington	157	4278	1638	132	6048	152	11	.978
Philadelphia	155	4150	1766	140	6056	148	11	.977
Boston	154	4116	1820	145	6081	181	10	.976
Detroit	156	4165	1778	152	6095	145	13	.975
Cleveland	155	4217	1734	155	6106	141	5	.975
St. Louis	155	4185	1672	155	6012	176	12	.974
AL Total	1242	33505	13888	1129	48522	1300	73	.977

Team vs. Team Records

	Bos	ChA	Cle	Det	NYA	Phi	StL	Was	Won
Bos	—	12	9	16	8	12	11	8	76
ChA	10	—	8	17	8	11	14	13	81
Cle	13	14	—	16	10	13	15	12	93
Det	6	5	6	—	9	5	8	11	50
NYA	14	14	12	13	—	13	14	15	95
Phi	10	11	9	17	9	—	14	9	79
StL	11	8	7	14	8	8	—	8	64
Was	14	9	10	11	7	13	14	—	78
Lost	78	73	61	104	59	75	90	76	

1952 American League Batting Leaders

Games		At-Bats		Runs		Hits		Doubles		Triples	
E. Yost, Was	157	N. Fox, ChA	648	L. Doby, Cle	104	N. Fox, ChA	192	F. Fain, Phi	43	B. Avila, Cle	11
E. Robinson, ChA	155	B. Avila, Cle	597	B. Avila, Cle	102	B. Avila, Cle	179	M. Mantle, NYA	37	H. Simpson, Cle	10
M. Vernon, Was	154	E. Robinson, ChA	594	A. Rosen, Cle	101	F. Fain, Phi	176	E. Robinson, ChA	33	N. Fox, ChA	10
5 tied with	152	W. Dropo, 2tm	591	Y. Berra, NYA	97	E. Robinson, ChA	176	M. Vernon, Was	33	P. Rizzuto, NYA	10
		J. Jensen, 2tm	589	M. Minoso, ChA	96	2 tied with	171	2 tied with	32	4 tied with	9

Home Runs		Total Bases		Runs Batted In		Walks		Intentional Walks		Strikeouts	
L. Doby, Cle	32	A. Rosen, Cle	297	A. Rosen, Cle	105	E. Yost, Was	129	Statistic unavailable		M. Mantle, NYA	111
L. Easter, Cle	31	M. Mantle, NYA	291	L. Doby, Cle	104	E. Joost, Phi	122			L. Doby, Cle	111
Y. Berra, NYA	30	W. Dropo, 2tm	282	E. Robinson, ChA	104	F. Fain, Phi	105			E. Joost, Phi	94
G. Zernial, Phi	29	L. Doby, Cle	281	G. Zernial, Phi	100	E. Valo, Phi	101			G. Zernial, Phi	87
W. Dropo, 2tm	29	E. Robinson, ChA	277	Y. Berra, NYA	98	L. Doby, Cle	90			J. Rivera, 2tm	86

Hit By Pitch		Sac Hits		Sac Flies		Stolen Bases		Caught Stealing		GDP	
M. Minoso, ChA	14	P. Rizzuto, NYA	23	Statistic unavailable		M. Minoso, ChA	22	M. Minoso, ChA	16	D. Philley, Phi	29
S. Lollar, ChA	12	B. Avila, Cle	19			J. Rivera, 2tm	21	E. Valo, Phi	11	W. Dropo, 2tm	26
E. Robinson, ChA	12	D. Philley, Phi	17			J. Jensen, 2tm	18	P. Runnels, Was	10	F. Fain, Phi	19
B. Martin, NYA	8	G. McDougald, NYA	16			P. Rizzuto, NYA	17	B. Avila, Cle	10	3 tied with	18
E. Yost, Was	8	N. Fox, ChA	15			F. Throneberry, Bos	16	J. Groth, Det	10		

Runs Created		Runs Created/27 Outs		Batting Average		On-Base Percentage		Slugging Percentage		OBP+Slugging	
M. Mantle, NYA	112	M. Mantle, NYA	7.87	F. Fain, Phi	.327	F. Fain, Phi	.438	L. Doby, Cle	.541	M. Mantle, NYA	.924
A. Rosen, Cle	112	L. Doby, Cle	7.80	D. Mitchell, Cle	.323	G. Woodling, NYA	.397	M. Mantle, NYA	.530	L. Doby, Cle	.924
L. Doby, Cle	111	F. Fain, Phi	7.30	M. Mantle, NYA	.311	M. Mantle, NYA	.394	A. Rosen, Cle	.524	A. Rosen, Cle	.911
F. Fain, Phi	105	A. Rosen, Cle	7.18	G. Kell, 2tm	.311	E. Joost, Phi	.388	L. Easter, Cle	.513	V. Wertz, 2tm	.887
E. Robinson, ChA	105	G. Woodling, NYA	6.92	G. Woodling, NYA	.309	A. Rosen, Cle	.387	V. Wertz, 2tm	.506	G. Woodling, NYA	.870

1952 American League Pitching Leaders

Wins		Losses		Winning Percentage		Games		Games Started		Complete Games	
B. Shantz, Phi	24	A. Houtteman, Det	20	B. Shantz, Phi	.774	B. Kennedy, ChA	47	M. Garcia, Cle	36	B. Lemon, Cle	28
E. Wynn, Cle	23	V. Trucks, Det	19	V. Raschi, NYA	.727	M. Garcia, Cle	46	B. Lemon, Cle	36	B. Shantz, Phi	27
M. Garcia, Cle	22	T. Gray, Det	17	A. Reynolds, NYA	.714	S. Paige, StL	46	B. Shantz, Phi	33	A. Reynolds, NYA	24
B. Lemon, Cle	22	H. Byrd, Phi	15	3 tied with	.667	B. Hooper, Phi	43	A. Kellner, Phi	33	M. Garcia, Cle	19
A. Reynolds, NYA	20	B. Hooper, Phi	15			4 tied with	42	E. Wynn, Cle	33	E. Wynn, Cle	19

Shutouts		Saves		Games Finished		Batters Faced		Innings Pitched		Hits Allowed	
M. Garcia, Cle	6	H. Dorish, ChA	11	S. Paige, StL	35	B. Lemon, Cle	1252	B. Lemon, Cle	309.2	M. Garcia, Cle	284
A. Reynolds, NYA	6	S. Paige, StL	10	H. White, Det	31	M. Garcia, Cle	1236	M. Garcia, Cle	292.1	H. Byrd, Phi	244
B. Shantz, Phi	5	J. Sain, NYA	7	H. Dorish, ChA	27	E. Wynn, Cle	1190	E. Wynn, Cle	285.2	E. Wynn, Cle	239
B. Lemon, Cle	5	4 tied with	6	B. Kennedy, ChA	24	B. Shantz, Phi	1103	B. Shantz, Phi	279.2	B. Lemon, Cle	236
3 tied with	4			B. Hooper, Phi	21	B. Pierce, ChA	1042	B. Pierce, ChA	255.1	B. Shantz, Phi	230

Home Runs Allowed		Walks		Walks/9 Innings		Strikeouts		Strikeouts/9 Innings		Strikeout/Walk Ratio	
E. Wynn, Cle	23	E. Wynn, Cle	132	B. Shantz, Phi	2.0	A. Reynolds, NYA	160	M. McDermott, Bos	6.5	B. Shantz, Phi	2.41
B. Shantz, Phi	21	T. Byrne, StL	112	D. Pillette, StL	2.4	E. Wynn, Cle	153	A. Reynolds, NYA	5.9	B. Pierce, ChA	1.82
A. Kellner, Phi	21	B. Lemon, Cle	105	C. Marrero, Was	2.6	B. Shantz, Phi	152	V. Trucks, Det	5.9	J. Dobson, ChA	1.68
T. Gray, Det	21	T. Gray, Det	101	A. Houtteman, Det	2.6	B. Pierce, ChA	144	T. Gray, Det	5.5	A. Houtteman, Det	1.68
C. Scheib, Phi	21	H. Byrd, Phi	98	M. Garcia, Cle	2.7	M. Garcia, Cle	143	M. Grissom, ChA	5.3	A. Reynolds, NYA	1.65

Earned Run Average		Component ERA		Hit Batsmen		Wild Pitches		Opponent Average		Opponent OBP	
A. Reynolds, NYA	2.06	B. Lemon, Cle	2.28	E. Harrist, StL	10	G. Bearden, StL	10	B. Lemon, Cle	.208	B. Shantz, Phi	.272
M. Garcia, Cle	2.37	B. Shantz, Phi	2.39	T. Byrne, StL	10	B. Wight, 2tm	8	V. Raschi, NYA	.216	B. Lemon, Cle	.279
B. Shantz, Phi	2.48	J. Dobson, ChA	2.42	6 tied with	7	B. Lemon, Cle	8	A. Reynolds, NYA	.218	J. Dobson, ChA	.280
B. Lemon, Cle	2.50	B. Pierce, ChA	2.52			8 tied with	5	J. Dobson, ChA	.222	B. Pierce, ChA	.289
J. Dobson, ChA	2.51	A. Reynolds, NYA	2.63					B. Shantz, Phi	.225	A. Reynolds, NYA	.300

1952 American League Miscellaneous

Managers

Boston	Lou Boudreau	76-78
Chicago	Paul Richards	81-73
Cleveland	Al Lopez	93-61
Detroit	Red Rolfe	23-49
	Fred Hutchinson	27-55
New York	Casey Stengel	95-59
Philadelphia	Jimmy Dykes	79-75
St. Louis	Rogers Hornsby	22-29
	Marty Marion	42-61
Washington	Bucky Harris	78-76

Awards

Most Valuable Player	Bobby Shantz, p, Phi
STATS Cy Young	Bobby Shantz, Phi
Rookie of the Year	Harry Byrd, p, Phi
STATS Manager of the Year	Bucky Harris, Was

STATS All-Star Team

C	Yogi Berra, NYA	.273	30	98
1B	Ferris Fain, Phi	.327	2	59
2B	Bobby Avila, Cle	.300	7	45
3B	Al Rosen, Cle	.302	28	105
SS	Eddie Joost, Phi	.244	20	75
OF	Larry Doby, Cle	.276	32	104
OF	Mickey Mantle, NYA	.311	23	87
OF	Vic Wertz, 2tm	.277	23	70
P	Mike Garcia, Cle	22-11	2.37	143 K
P	Bob Lemon, Cle	22-11	2.50	131 K
P	Allie Reynolds, NYA	20-8	2.06	160 K
P	Bobby Shantz, Phi	24-7	2.48	152 K
RP	Satchel Paige, StL	12-10	3.07	10 Sv

Postseason

World Series	New York (AL) 4 vs. Brooklyn (NL) 3

Outstanding Performances

No-Hitters
Virgil Trucks, Det   vs. Was on May 15
Virgil Trucks, Det   @ NYA on August 25

Three-Homer Games
Al Rosen, Cle   on April 29

Cycles
Larry Doby, Cle   on June 4

Team	\ W	Overall\ L	\ Pct	\ GB	\ DIF	\ W	Home Games\ L	\ R	\ OR	\ HR	\ OHR	\ W	Road Games\ L	\ R	\ OR	\ HR	\ OHR	Park Index\ Run	\ HR	M/A	Record by Month\ May	\ June	\ July	\ Aug	\ S/O
Brooklyn	96	57	.627	—	152	45	33	389	324	76	78	51	24	386	279	77	43	103	123	8-2	18-8	21-8	17-11	19-13	13-15
New York	92	62	.597	4.5	20	50	27	369	327	103	74	42	35	353	312	48	47	105	186	7-4	20-6	17-12	14-13	16-16	18-11
St. Louis	88	66	.571	8.5	2	48	29	343	291	46	59	40	37	334	339	51	60	94	95	6-7	12-15	20-12	19-8	16-14	15-10
Philadelphia	87	67	.565	9.5	0	47	29	318	269	42	43	40	38	339	283	51	52	97	85	4-7	13-13	13-16	22-10	18-12	17-9
Chicago	77	77	.500	19.5	2	42	35	329	316	51	40	35	42	299	315	56	61	105	78	9-4	14-12	15-14	12-18	15-19	12-10
Cincinnati	69	85	.448	27.5	0	38	39	318	319	43	43	31	46	297	340	61	68	100	67	8-5	11-15	12-18	8-22	17-14	13-11
Boston	64	89	.418	32.0	0	31	45	257	314	48	44	33	44	312	337	62	62	89	75	5-9	8-13	14-20	14-13	14-17	9-17
Pittsburgh	42	112	.273	54.5	0	23	54	261	414	45	72	19	58	254	379	47	61	107	108	3-12	7-21	8-20	10-21	10-20	4-18

Clinch Date—Brooklyn 9/23.

Team Batting

Team	G	AB	R	OR	H	2B	3B	HR	TB	RBI	TBB	IBB	SO	HBP	SH	SF	SB	CS	SB%	GDP	Avg	OBP	Slg
Brooklyn	155	5266	775	603	1380	199	32	153	2102	725	663	—	699	35	104	—	90	49	.65	151	.262	.348	.399
New York	154	5229	722	639	1337	186	56	151	2088	663	536	—	672	38	88	—	30	31	.49	96	.256	.329	.399
St. Louis	154	5200	677	630	1386	247	54	97	2032	643	537	—	479	43	107	—	60	41	.59	115	.267	.332	.391
Philadelphia	154	5205	657	552	1353	223	45	107	1959	606	422	—	712	21	63	—	50	40	.56	133	.264	.321	.383
Chicago	155	5330	628	631	1408	223	45	107	2042	595	480	—	709	18	53	—	32	42	.43	110	.249	.314	.366
Cincinnati	154	5234	615	659	1303	212	45	104	1917	562	540	—	711	22	65	—	58	34	.63	117	.233	.301	.343
Boston	155	5221	569	651	1214	187	31	110	1793	530	483	—	724	32	92	—	43	41	.51	104	.231	.300	.331
Pittsburgh	155	5193	515	793	1201	181	30	92	1718	478	486	—	534	26	70	—	33	32	.51	122	.231	.300	.331
NL Total	1236	41878	5158	5158	10582	1672	338	907	15651	4802	4147	—	5240	235	642	—	396	310	.56	948	.253	.323	.374
NL Avg Team	155	5235	645	645	1323	209	42	113	1956	600	518	—	655	29	80	—	50	39	.56	119	.253	.323	.374

Team Pitching

Team	G	CG	ShO	Rel	Sv	IP	H	R	ER	HR	SH	SF	HB	TBB	IBB	SO	WP	Bk	H/9	SO/9	BB/9	OAvg	OOBP	ERA
Philadelphia	154	80	17	142	16	1386.2	1306	552	473	95	72	—	17	373	—	609	14	1	8.5	4.0	2.4	.249	.301	3.07
Brooklyn	155	45	11	196	24	1399.1	1295	603	549	101	63	—	28	544	—	773	24	4	8.3	5.0	3.5	.240	.314	3.53
Chicago	155	59	15	168	15	1386.1	1265	631	552	101	80	—	32	534	—	661	47	2	8.2	4.3	3.5	.240	.314	3.58
New York	154	49	12	226	31	1371.0	1282	639	547	121	77	—	35	538	—	655	14	1	8.4	4.3	3.5	.248	.323	3.59
St. Louis	154	49	12	208	27	1361.1	1274	630	553	119	83	—	29	501	—	712	20	3	8.4	4.7	3.3	.247	.317	3.66
Boston	155	63	11	175	13	1396.0	1388	651	586	106	87	—	30	525	—	687	28	4	8.9	4.4	3.4	.259	.329	3.78
Cincinnati	154	56	11	173	12	1363.1	1377	659	608	111	90	—	38	517	—	579	18	1	9.1	3.8	3.4	.267	.338	4.01
Pittsburgh	155	43	5	204	8	1363.2	1395	793	704	133	90	—	27	615	—	564	30	5	9.2	3.7	4.1	.266	.346	4.65
NL Total	1236	444	94	1492	146	11027.2	10582	5158	4572	907	642	—	236	4147	—	5240	195	21	8.6	4.3	3.4	.253	.323	3.73
NL Avg Team	155	56	12	187	18	1378.2	1323	645	572	113	80	—	30	518	—	655	24	3	8.6	4.3	3.4	.253	.323	3.73

Team Fielding

Team	G	PO	A	E	TC	DP	PB	Pct
Brooklyn	155	4197	1622	106	5925	169	13	.982
Cincinnati	154	4090	1660	107	5857	145	6	.982
St. Louis	154	4084	1795	141	6020	159	11	.977
Chicago	155	4159	1684	146	5989	123	18	.976
Philadelphia	154	4160	1710	150	6020	145	3	.975
Boston	155	4189	1714	154	6057	143	17	.975
New York	154	4113	1750	158	6021	175	23	.974
Pittsburgh	155	4091	1769	182	6042	167	4	.970
NL Total	1236	33083	13704	1144	47931	1226	95	.976

Team vs. Team Records

	Bos	Bro	ChN	Cin	NYG	Phi	Pit	StL	Won
Bos	—	3	12	9	9	9	15	7	64
Bro	18	—	13	17	8	10	19	11	96
ChN	10	9	—	13	10	10	14	11	77
Cin	13	5	9	—	6	10	16	10	69
NYG	13	14	12	16	—	10	15	12	92
Phi	13	12	12	12	12	—	16	10	87
Pit	7	3	8	6	7	6	—	5	42
StL	15	11	11	12	10	12	17	—	88
Lost	89	57	77	85	62	67	112	66	

1952 National League Batting Leaders

Games		At-Bats		Runs		Hits		Doubles		Triples	
6 tied with	154	B. Adams, Cin	637	S. Hemus, StL	105	S. Musial, StL	194	S. Musial, StL	42	B. Thomson, NYG	14
		R. Schoendienst, StL	620	S. Musial, StL	105	R. Schoendienst, StL	188	R. Schoendienst, StL	40	E. Slaughter, StL	12
		R. Ashburn, Phi	613	J. Robinson, Bro	104	B. Adams, Cin	180	R. McMillan, Cin	32	T. Kluszewski, Cin	11
		S. Jethroe, Bos	608	W. Lockman, NYG	99	A. Dark, NYG	177	R. Ashburn, Phi	31	D. Ennis, Phi	10
		B. Thomson, NYG	608	P. Reese, Bro	94	W. Lockman, NYG	176	H. Sauer, ChN	31	2 tied with	9

Home Runs		Total Bases		Runs Batted In		Walks		Intentional Walks		Strikeouts	
R. Kiner, Pit	37	S. Musial, StL	311	H. Sauer, ChN	121	R. Kiner, Pit	110	Statistic unavailable		E. Mathews, Bos	115
H. Sauer, ChN	37	H. Sauer, ChN	301	B. Thomson, NYG	108	G. Hodges, Bro	107			S. Jethroe, Bos	112
G. Hodges, Bro	32	B. Thomson, NYG	293	D. Ennis, Phi	107	J. Robinson, Bro	106			H. Sauer, ChN	92
E. Mathews, Bos	25	D. Ennis, Phi	281	G. Hodges, Bro	102	S. Hemus, StL	96			G. Hodges, Bro	90
S. Gordon, Bos	25	D. Snider, Bro	264	E. Slaughter, StL	101	S. Musial, StL	96			B. Serena, ChN	83

Hit By Pitch		Sac Hits		Sac Flies		Stolen Bases		Caught Stealing		GDP	
S. Hemus, StL	20	G. Hamner, Phi	17	Statistic unavailable		P. Reese, Bro	30	B. Cox, Bro	12	R. Campanella, Bro	22
J. Robinson, Bro	14	P. Reese, Bro	15			S. Jethroe, Bos	28	D. Fondy, ChN	11	D. Groat, Pit	18
S. Jethroe, Bos	9	R. Roberts, Phi	13			J. Robinson, Bro	24	R. Ashburn, Phi	11	G. Hamner, Phi	18
D. Williams, NYG	8	S. Maglie, NYG	12			R. Ashburn, Phi	16	3 tied with	9	4 tied with	17
R. Kiner, Pit	7	6 tied with	11			2 tied with	13				

Runs Created		Runs Created/27 Outs		Batting Average		On-Base Percentage		Slugging Percentage		OBP+Slugging	
S. Musial, StL	125	S. Musial, StL	8.35	S. Musial, StL	.336	J. Robinson, Bro	.440	S. Musial, StL	.538	S. Musial, StL	.970
J. Robinson, Bro	115	J. Robinson, Bro	8.09	F. Baumholtz, ChN	.325	S. Musial, StL	.432	H. Sauer, ChN	.531	J. Robinson, Bro	.904
G. Hodges, Bro	104	T. Kluszewski, Cin	7.19	T. Kluszewski, Cin	.320	S. Hemus, StL	.392	T. Kluszewski, Cin	.509	T. Kluszewski, Cin	.892
R. Kiner, Pit	103	G. Hodges, Bro	7.09	J. Robinson, Bro	.308	G. Hodges, Bro	.386	R. Kiner, Pit	.500	H. Sauer, ChN	.892
H. Sauer, ChN	103	R. Kiner, Pit	6.99	D. Snider, Bro	.303	E. Slaughter, StL	.386	G. Hodges, Bro	.500	G. Hodges, Bro	.886

1952 National League Pitching Leaders

Wins		Losses		Winning Percentage		Games		Games Started		Complete Games	
R. Roberts, Pit	28	M. Dickson, Pit	21	H. Wilhelm, NYG	.833	H. Wilhelm, NYG	71	R. Roberts, Phi	37	R. Roberts, Phi	30
S. Maglie, NYG	18	W. Spahn, Bos	19	R. Roberts, Phi	.800	J. Black, Bro	56	W. Spahn, Bos	35	M. Dickson, Pit	21
B. Rush, ChN	17	B. Friend, Pit	17	J. Black, Bro	.789	E. Yuhas, StL	54	J. Hearn, NYG	34	W. Spahn, Bos	19
G. Staley, StL	17	H. Pollet, Pit	16	A. Brazle, StL	.706	F. Smith, Cin	53	M. Dickson, Pit	34	K. Raffensberger, Cin	18
K. Raffensberger, Cin	17	K. Drews, Phi	15	C. Erskine, Bro	.700	W. Main, Pit	48	3 tied with	33	B. Rush, ChN	17

Shutouts		Saves		Games Finished		Batters Faced		Innings Pitched		Hits Allowed	
C. Simmons, Phi	6	A. Brazle, StL	16	J. Black, Bro	41	R. Roberts, Phi	1310	R. Roberts, Phi	330.0	R. Roberts, Phi	292
K. Raffensberger, Cin	6	J. Black, Bro	15	F. Smith, Cin	37	W. Spahn, Bos	1190	W. Spahn, Bos	290.0	M. Dickson, Pit	278
4 tied with	5	H. Wilhelm, NYG	11	D. Leonard, ChN	36	M. Dickson, Pit	1157	M. Dickson, Pit	277.2	W. Spahn, Bos	263
		D. Leonard, ChN	11	T. Wilks, Pit	34	B. Rush, ChN	1044	B. Rush, ChN	250.1	K. Raffensberger, Cin	247
		2 tied with	7	2 tied with	32	K. Raffensberger, Cin	1006	K. Raffensberger, Cin	247.0	G. Staley, StL	238

Home Runs Allowed		Walks		Walks/9 Innings		Strikeouts		Strikeouts/9 Innings		Strikeout/Walk Ratio	
M. Dickson, Pit	26	V. B. Mizell, StL	103	R. Roberts, Phi	1.2	W. Spahn, Bos	183	V. B. Mizell, StL	6.9	R. Roberts, Phi	3.29
H. Wehmeier, Cin	23	H. Wehmeier, Cin	103	W. Hacker, ChN	1.5	B. Rush, ChN	157	C. Simmons, Phi	6.3	W. Hacker, ChN	2.71
R. Roberts, Phi	22	J. Hearn, NYG	97	K. Raffensberger, Cin	1.6	R. Roberts, Phi	148	H. Wilhelm, NYG	6.1	W. Spahn, Bos	2.51
H. Pollet, Pit	22	B. Wade, Bro	94	G. Staley, StL	2.0	V. B. Mizell, StL	146	B. Wade, Bro	5.9	P. Roe, Bro	2.13
2 tied with	21	T. Lown, ChN	93	K. Drews, Phi	2.0	C. Simmons, Phi	141	C. Erskine, Bro	5.7	K. Raffensberger, Cin	2.07

Earned Run Average		Component ERA		Hit Batsmen		Wild Pitches		Opponent Average		Opponent OBP	
H. Wilhelm, NYG	2.43	W. Hacker, ChN	2.02	F. Smith, Cin	7	J. Klippstein, ChN	12	W. Hacker, ChN	.212	W. Hacker, ChN	.247
W. Hacker, ChN	2.58	R. Roberts, Phi	2.31	G. Staley, StL	7	B. Kelly, ChN	7	B. Rush, ChN	.216	R. Roberts, Phi	.263
R. Roberts, Phi	2.59	B. Rush, ChN	2.50	H. Wehmeier, Cin	7	B. Friend, Pit	7	H. Wilhelm, NYG	.220	B. Rush, ChN	.282
B. Loes, Bro	2.69	C. Simmons, Phi	2.69	7 tied with	6	M. Surkont, Bos	7	C. Erskine, Bro	.220	C. Erskine, Bro	.289
B. Rush, ChN	2.70	C. Erskine, Bro	2.72			B. Rush, ChN	7	B. Loes, Bro	.224	W. Spahn, Bos	.291

1952 National League Miscellaneous

Managers

Boston	Tommy Holmes	13-22
	Charlie Grimm	51-67
Brooklyn	Chuck Dressen	96-57
Chicago	Phil Cavarretta	77-77
Cincinnati	Luke Sewell	39-59
	Earle Brucker	3-2
	Rogers Hornsby	27-24
New York	Leo Durocher	92-62
Philadelphia	Eddie Sawyer	28-35
	Steve O'Neill	59-32
Pittsburgh	Billy Meyer	42-112
St. Louis	Eddie Stanky	88-66

Awards

Most Valuable Player	Hank Sauer, of, ChN
STATS Cy Young	Robin Roberts, Phi
Rookie of the Year	Joe Black, p, Bro
STATS Manager of the Year	Phil Cavarretta, ChN

STATS All-Star Team

C	Roy Campanella, Bro	.269	22	97	
1B	Gil Hodges, Bro	.254	32	102	
2B	Jackie Robinson, Bro	.308	19	75	
3B	Bobby Thomson, NYG	.270	24	108	
SS	Solly Hemus, StL	.268	15	52	
OF	Ralph Kiner, Pit	.244	37	87	
OF	Stan Musial, StL	.336	21	91	
OF	Hank Sauer, ChN	.270	37	121	
P	Warren Hacker, ChN	15-9	2.58	84 K	
P	Sal Maglie, NYG	18-8	2.92	112 K	
P	Robin Roberts, Phi	28-7	2.59	148 K	
P	Bob Rush, ChN	17-13	2.70	157 K	
RP	Joe Black, Bro	15-4	2.15	15 Sv	

Postseason

World Series	Brooklyn (NL) 3 vs. New York (AL) 4

Outstanding Performances

No-Hitters

Carl Erskine, Bro   vs. ChN on June 19

Three-Homer Games

Hank Sauer, ChN   on June 11

Eddie Mathews, Bos on September 27

1953 American League Standings

Team		Overall					Home Games						Road Games						Park Index		Record by Month					
	W	L	Pct	GB	DIF	W	L	R	OR	HR	OHR	W	L	R	OR	HR	OHR	Run	HR	M/A	May	June	July	Aug	S/O
New York	99	52	.656	—	159	50	27	347	255	64	39	49	25	454	292	75	55	78	76	11-3	16-8	19-10	20-12	20-10	13-9
Cleveland	92	62	.597	8.5	9	53	24	379	272	88	46	39	38	391	355	72	46	87	114	8-3	14-12	19-11	16-16	19-12	16-8
Chicago	89	65	.578	11.5	1	41	36	349	328	30	56	48	29	367	264	44	57	107	85	8-6	17-12	16-11	20-10	17-13	11-13
Boston	84	69	.549	16.0	2	38	38	335	354	57	59	46	31	321	278	44	33	117	153	6-6	15-15	17-13	19-11	15-15	12-9
Washington	76	76	.500	23.5	1	39	36	305	283	10	31	37	40	382	331	59	81	85	30	4-10	19-10	12-16	13-17	18-14	10-9
Detroit	60	94	.390	40.5	1	30	47	369	462	55	97	30	47	326	461	53	57	106	138	2-13	8-18	10-18	15-15	13-19	12-11
Philadelphia	59	95	.383	41.5	2	27	50	299	447	49	74	32	45	333	352	67	47	109	108	7-6	11-18	14-15	11-17	9-23	7-16
St. Louis	54	100	.351	46.5	7	23	54	281	447	58	64	31	46	274	331	54	37	120	134	7-6	11-18	9-22	7-23	12-17	8-14

Clinch Date—New York 9/14.

Team Batting

Team	G	AB	R	OR	H	2B	3B	HR	TB	RBI	TBB	IBB	SO	HBP	SH	SF	SB	CS	SB%	GDP	Avg	OBP	Slg
New York	151	5194	801	547	1420	226	52	139	2167	762	656	—	644	34	77	—	34	44	.44	105	.273	.359	.417
Cleveland	155	5285	770	627	1426	201	29	160	2165	730	609	—	683	35	90	—	33	29	.53	125	.270	.349	.410
Chicago	156	5212	716	592	1345	226	53	74	1899	669	601	—	530	54	120	—	73	54	.57	146	.258	.341	.364
Detroit	158	5553	695	923	1479	259	44	108	2150	660	506	—	603	30	63	—	30	35	.46	139	.266	.331	.387
Washington	152	5149	687	614	1354	230	53	69	1897	644	596	—	604	31	82	—	65	36	.64	134	.263	.343	.368
Boston	153	5246	656	632	1385	255	37	101	2017	614	496	—	601	38	99	—	33	45	.42	109	.264	.332	.384
Philadelphia	157	5455	632	799	1398	205	38	116	2027	588	498	—	602	24	51	—	41	24	.63	141	.256	.321	.372
St. Louis	154	5264	555	778	1310	214	25	112	1910	522	507	—	644	17	89	—	17	34	.33	144	.249	.317	.363
AL Total	1236	42358	5512	5512	11117	1816	331	879	16232	5189	4469	—	4911	263	671	—	326	302	.52	1043	.262	.337	.383
AL Avg Team	155	5295	689	689	1390	227	41	110	2029	649	559	—	614	33	84	—	41	38	.52	130	.262	.337	.383

Team Pitching

Team	G	CG	ShO	Rel	Sv	IP	H	R	ER	HR	SH	SF	HB	TBB	IBB	SO	WP	Bk	H/9	SO/9	BB/9	OAvg	OOBP	ERA
New York	151	50	18	176	39	1358.1	1286	547	483	94	64	—	33	500	—	604	15	2	8.5	4.0	3.3	.251	.321	3.20
Chicago	156	57	17	184	33	1403.2	1299	592	532	113	76	—	23	583	—	714	37	5	8.3	4.6	3.7	.246	.324	3.41
Boston	153	41	15	214	37	1373.0	1333	632	546	92	77	—	23	584	—	642	28	3	8.7	4.2	3.8	.254	.331	3.58
Cleveland	155	81	11	135	15	1373.0	1311	627	556	92	72	—	35	519	—	586	24	2	8.6	3.8	3.4	.253	.325	3.64
Washington	152	76	16	132	10	1344.2	1313	614	547	112	86	—	26	478	—	515	16	2	8.8	3.4	3.2	.258	.324	3.66
St. Louis	154	28	10	250	24	1383.2	1467	778	688	101	81	—	25	626	—	639	33	3	9.5	4.2	4.1	.273	.351	4.48
Philadelphia	157	51	7	165	11	1409.0	1475	799	731	121	92	—	57	594	—	566	51	4	9.4	3.6	3.8	.271	.349	4.67
Detroit	158	50	2	218	16	1415.0	1633	923	826	154	122	—	41	585	—	645	43	2	10.4	4.1	3.7	.291	.363	5.25
AL Total	1236	434	96	1474	185	11060.1	11117	5512	4909	879	670	—	263	4469	—	4911	247	21	9.0	4.0	3.6	.262	.337	3.99
AL Avg Team	155	54	12	184	23	1382.1	1390	689	614	110	84	—	33	559	—	614	31	3	9.0	4.0	3.6	.262	.337	3.99

Team Fielding

Team	G	PO	A	E	TC	DP	PB	Pct
Chicago	156	4209	1776	125	6110	144	4	.980
Washington	152	4031	1638	120	5789	173	12	.979
Cleveland	155	4121	1800	127	6048	197	13	.979
New York	151	4076	1742	126	5944	182	10	.979
Detroit	158	4243	1783	135	6161	149	20	.978
Philadelphia	157	4218	1710	137	6065	161	15	.977
Boston	153	4127	1731	148	6006	173	8	.975
St. Louis	154	4150	1644	152	5946	165	8	.974
AL Total	1236	33175	13824	1070	48069	1344	90	.978

Team vs. Team Records

	Bos	ChA	Cle	Det	NYA	Phi	StL	Was	Won
Bos	—	6	13	13	10	15	17	10	84
ChA	16	—	11	14	9	10	17	12	89
Cle	9	11	—	14	11	19	17	11	92
Det	9	8	8	—	6	11	7	11	60
NYA	11	13	11	16	—	17	17	14	99
Phi	7	12	3	11	5	—	13	8	59
StL	5	5	5	15	5	9	—	10	54
Was	12	10	11	11	6	14	12	—	76
Lost	69	65	62	94	52	95	100	76	

1953 American League Batting Leaders

Games		At-Bats		Runs		Hits		Doubles		Triples	
D. Philley, Phi	157	H. Kuenn, Det	679	A. Rosen, Cle	115	H. Kuenn, Det	209	M. Vernon, Was	43	J. Rivera, ChA	16
J. Rivera, ChA	156	N. Fox, ChA	624	E. Yost, Was	107	M. Vernon, Was	205	G. Kell, Bos	41	M. Vernon, Was	11
E. Robinson, Phi	156	D. Philley, Phi	620	M. Mantle, NYA	105	A. Rosen, Cle	201	S. White, Bos	34	J. Piersall, Bos	9
H. Kuenn, Det	155	E. Robinson, Phi	615	M. Minoso, ChA	104	D. Philley, Phi	188	H. Kuenn, Det	33	D. Philley, Phi	9
A. Rosen, Cle	155	M. Vernon, Was	608	M. Vernon, Was	101	J. Busby, Was	183	B. Goodman, Bos	33	5 tied with	8

Home Runs		Total Bases		Runs Batted In		Walks		Intentional Walks		Strikeouts	
A. Rosen, Cle	43	A. Rosen, Cle	367	A. Rosen, Cle	145	E. Yost, Was	123	Statistic unavailable		L. Doby, Cle	121
G. Zernial, Phi	42	M. Vernon, Was	315	M. Vernon, Was	115	F. Fain, ChA	108			M. Mantle, NYA	90
L. Doby, Cle	29	G. Zernial, Phi	311	R. Boone, 2tm	114	L. Doby, Cle	96			D. Gernert, Bos	82
Y. Berra, NYA	27	Y. Berra, NYA	263	G. Zernial, Phi	108	D. Gernert, Bos	88			G. Zernial, Phi	79
R. Boone, 2tm	26	D. Philley, Phi	263	Y. Berra, NYA	108	A. Rosen, Cle	85			J. Rivera, ChA	70

Hit By Pitch		Sac Hits		Sac Flies		Stolen Bases		Caught Stealing		GDP	
M. Minoso, ChA	17	J. Piersall, Bos	19	Statistic unavailable		M. Minoso, ChA	25	M. Minoso, ChA	16	M. Minoso, ChA	23
J. Piersall, Bos	9	P. Rizzuto, NYA	18			J. Rivera, ChA	22	J. Rivera, ChA	15	W. Dropo, Det	22
S. Lollar, ChA	8	B. Glynn, Cle	14			J. Jensen, Was	18	J. Piersall, Bos	10	D. Philley, Phi	22
N. Fox, ChA	7	B. Avila, Cle	14			J. Busby, Was	13	J. Jensen, Was	8	3 tied with	19
5 tied with	6	B. Young, StL	14			D. Philley, Phi	13	B. Avila, Cle	8		

Runs Created		Runs Created/27 Outs		Batting Average		On-Base Percentage		Slugging Percentage		OBP+Slugging	
A. Rosen, Cle	143	A. Rosen, Cle	9.07	M. Vernon, Was	.337	A. Rosen, Cle	.422	A. Rosen, Cle	.613	A. Rosen, Cle	1.034
M. Vernon, Was	123	M. Vernon, Was	7.73	A. Rosen, Cle	.336	M. Minoso, ChA	.410	G. Zernial, Phi	.559	M. Vernon, Was	.921
M. Minoso, ChA	110	M. Mantle, NYA	7.72	B. Goodman, Bos	.313	F. Fain, ChA	.405	Y. Berra, NYA	.523	G. Zernial, Phi	.914
G. Zernial, Phi	104	R. Boone, 2tm	7.20	M. Minoso, ChA	.313	E. Yost, Was	.403	R. Boone, 2tm	.519	R. Boone, 2tm	.909
E. Yost, Was	104	Y. Berra, NYA	7.00	J. Busby, Was	.312	M. Vernon, Was	.403	M. Vernon, Was	.518	M. Mantle, NYA	.895

1953 American League Pitching Leaders

Wins		Losses		Winning Percentage		Games		Games Started		Complete Games	
B. Porterfield, Was	22	H. Byrd, Phi	20	E. Lopat, NYA	.800	E. Kinder, Bos	69	H. Byrd, Phi	37	B. Porterfield, Was	24
M. Parnell, Bos	21	T. Gray, Det	15	W. Ford, NYA	.750	M. Stuart, StL	60	B. Lemon, Cle	36	B. Lemon, Cle	23
B. Lemon, Cle	21	B. Lemon, Cle	15	M. Parnell, Bos	.724	M. Martin, Phi	58	M. Garcia, Cle	35	M. Garcia, Cle	21
V. Trucks, 2tm	20	C. Bishop, Phi	14	B. Porterfield, Was	.688	S. Paige, StL	57	M. Parnell, Bos	34	B. Pierce, ChA	19
4 tied with	18	B. Hoeft, Det	14	V. Raschi, NYA	.684	H. Dorish, ChA	55	E. Wynn, Cle	34	V. Trucks, 2tm	17

Shutouts		Saves		Games Finished		Batters Faced		Innings Pitched		Hits Allowed	
B. Porterfield, Was	9	E. Kinder, Bos	27	E. Kinder, Bos	51	B. Lemon, Cle	1216	B. Lemon, Cle	286.2	B. Lemon, Cle	283
B. Pierce, ChA	7	H. Dorish, ChA	18	M. Martin, Phi	41	M. Garcia, Cle	1133	M. Garcia, Cle	271.2	H. Byrd, Phi	279
M. Parnell, Bos	5	A. Reynolds, NYA	13	H. Dorish, ChA	37	B. Pierce, ChA	1113	B. Pierce, ChA	271.1	M. Garcia, Cle	260
V. Trucks, 2tm	5	S. Paige, StL	11	S. Paige, StL	34	V. Trucks, 2tm	1101	V. Trucks, 2tm	264.1	B. Porterfield, Was	243
B. Lemon, Cle	5	J. Sain, NYA	9	M. Stuart, StL	30	H. Byrd, Phi	1090	B. Porterfield, Was	255.0	2 tied with	234

Home Runs Allowed		Walks		Walks/9 Innings		Strikeouts		Strikeouts/9 Innings		Strikeout/Walk Ratio	
T. Gray, Det	25	M. Parnell, Bos	116	E. Lopat, NYA	1.6	B. Pierce, ChA	186	B. Pierce, ChA	6.2	J. Sain, NYA	1.87
B. Hoeft, Det	24	H. Byrd, Phi	115	J. Sain, NYA	2.1	V. Trucks, 2tm	149	T. Gray, Det	5.9	B. Pierce, ChA	1.82
H. Byrd, Phi	23	W. Ford, NYA	110	A. Kellner, Phi	2.3	E. Wynn, Cle	138	W. Masterson, Was	5.1	M. Garcia, Cle	1.65
M. Fricano, Phi	21	B. Lemon, Cle	110	B. Porterfield, Was	2.6	M. Parnell, Bos	136	M. Parnell, Bos	5.1	A. Kellner, Phi	1.59
B. Pierce, ChA	20	M. McDermott, Bos	109	B. Hoeft, Det	2.6	M. Garcia, Cle	134	V. Trucks, 2tm	5.1	E. Lopat, NYA	1.56

Earned Run Average		Component ERA		Hit Batsmen		Wild Pitches		Opponent Average		Opponent OBP	
E. Lopat, NYA	2.42	V. Raschi, NYA	2.51	H. Byrd, Phi	14	A. Kellner, Phi	10	B. Pierce, ChA	.218	V. Raschi, NYA	.283
B. Pierce, ChA	2.72	B. Pierce, ChA	2.69	B. Lemon, Cle	11	B. Lemon, Cle	9	M. McDermott, Bos	.224	E. Lopat, NYA	.288
V. Trucks, 2tm	2.93	E. Lopat, NYA	2.85	A. Houtteman, 2tm	9	6 tied with	7	V. Raschi, NYA	.224	B. Pierce, ChA	.292
W. Ford, NYA	3.00	M. McDermott, Bos	3.11	S. Gromek, 2tm	9			W. Masterson, Was	.232	W. Masterson, Was	.304
J. Sain, NYA	3.00	V. Trucks, 2tm	3.18	M. Martin, Phi	8			V. Trucks, 2tm	.238	M. Garcia, Cle	.307

1953 American League Miscellaneous

Managers

Boston	Lou Boudreau	84-69
Chicago	Paul Richards	89-65
Cleveland	Al Lopez	92-62
Detroit	Fred Hutchinson	60-94
New York	Casey Stengel	99-52
Philadelphia	Jimmy Dykes	59-95
St. Louis	Marty Marion	54-100
Washington	Bucky Harris	76-76

Awards

Most Valuable Player	Al Rosen, 3b, Cle
STATS Cy Young	Virgil Trucks, ChA
Rookie of the Year	Harvey Kuenn, ss, Det
STATS Manager of the Year	Casey Stengel, NYA

STATS All-Star Team

C	Yogi Berra, NYA	.296	27	108
1B	Mickey Vernon, Was	.337	15	115
2B	Billy Goodman, Bos	.313	2	41
3B	Al Rosen, Cle	.336	43	145
SS	Harvey Kuenn, Det	.308	2	48
OF	Mickey Mantle, NYA	.295	21	92
OF	Minnie Minoso, ChA	.313	15	104
OF	Gus Zernial, Phi	.284	42	108
P	Ed Lopat, NYA	16-4	2.42	50 K
P	Mel Parnell, Bos	21-8	3.06	136 K
P	Bob Porterfield, Was	22-10	3.35	77 K
P	Virgil Trucks, 2tm	20-10	2.93	149 K
RP	Ellis Kinder, Bos	10-6	1.85	27 Sv

Postseason

World Series	New York (AL) 4 vs. Brooklyn (NL) 2

Outstanding Performances

No-Hitters

Bobo Holloman, StL vs. Phi on May 6

Team	Overall W	L	Pct	GB	DIF	Home Games W	L	R	OR	HR	OHR	Road Games W	L	R	OR	HR	OHR	Park Index Run	HR	Record by Month M/A	May	June	July	Aug	S/O
Brooklyn	105	49	.682	—	112	60	17	517	333	110	82	45	32	438	356	98	87	107	104	9-5	18-9	15-12	23-8	25-6	15-9
Milwaukee	92	62	.597	13.0	40	45	31	332	260	51	44	47	31	406	329	105	63	83	58	6-5	19-8	17-14	15-15	23-9	12-11
Philadelphia	83	71	.539	22.0	27	48	29	363	304	63	65	35	42	353	362	52	73	93	102	9-4	11-10	17-13	17-15	19-17	10-12
St. Louis	83	71	.539	22.0	1	48	30	420	321	65	58	35	41	348	392	75	81	98	77	6-4	17-11	17-14	13-15	17-14	13-13
New York	70	84	.455	35.0	1	38	39	395	345	109	81	32	45	373	402	67	65	95	144	5-9	14-10	15-14	18-10	10-25	8-16
Cincinnati	68	86	.442	37.0	0	38	39	367	391	89	96	30	47	347	397	77	83	102	116	2-7	10-17	18-14	15-17	13-18	10-13
Chicago	65	89	.422	40.0	2	43	34	351	417	74	69	22	55	282	418	63	82	110	99	5-4	7-20	11-19	12-18	15-19	15-9
Pittsburgh	50	104	.325	55.0	0	26	51	338	460	53	88	24	53	284	427	46	80	112	112	5-9	8-19	12-22	8-23	8-22	9-9

Clinch Date—Brooklyn 9/12.

Team Batting

Team	G	AB	R	OR	H	2B	3B	HR	TB	RBI	TBB	IBB	SO	HBP	SH	SF	SB	CS	SB%	GDP	Avg	OBP	Slg
Brooklyn	155	5373	955	689	1529	274	59	208	2545	887	655	—	686	35	75	—	90	47	.66	115	.285	.366	.474
New York	155	5362	768	747	1452	195	45	176	2265	739	499	—	608	28	67	—	31	21	.60	129	.271	.336	.422
St. Louis	157	5397	768	713	1474	281	56	140	2287	722	574	—	617	39	55	—	18	22	.45	141	.273	.347	.424
Milwaukee	157	5349	738	589	1422	227	52	156	2221	691	439	—	637	27	80	—	46	27	.63	122	.266	.325	.415
Philadelphia	156	5290	716	666	1400	228	62	115	2097	657	530	—	597	29	67	—	42	21	.67	109	.265	.335	.396
Cincinnati	155	5343	714	788	1396	190	34	166	2152	669	485	—	701	16	68	—	25	20	.56	113	.261	.325	.403
Chicago	155	5272	633	835	1372	204	57	137	2101	588	514	—	746	14	73	—	49	21	.70	140	.260	.328	.399
Pittsburgh	154	5253	622	887	1297	178	49	99	1870	571	524	—	715	36	89	—	41	39	.51	117	.247	.319	.356
NL Total	1244	42639	5914	5914	11342	1777	414	1197	17538	5524	4220	—	5307	224	574	—	342	218	.61	986	.266	.335	.411
NL Avg Team	156	5330	739	739	1418	222	52	150	2192	691	528	—	663	28	72	—	43	27	.61	123	.266	.335	.411

Team Pitching

Team	G	CG	ShO	Rel	Sv	IP	H	R	ER	HR	SH	SF	HB	TBB	IBB	SO	WP	Bk	H/9	SO/9	BB/9	OAvg	OOBP	ERA
Milwaukee	157	72	14	159	15	1387.0	1282	589	508	107	65	—	21	539	—	738	21	7	8.3	4.8	3.5	.245	.318	3.30
Philadelphia	156	76	13	165	15	1369.2	1410	666	578	138	77	—	28	410	—	637	19	1	9.3	4.2	2.7	.265	.320	3.80
Brooklyn	155	51	11	212	29	1380.2	1337	689	629	169	46	—	17	509	—	817	24	4	8.7	5.3	3.3	.253	.320	4.10
St. Louis	157	51	11	234	36	1386.2	1406	713	651	139	79	—	42	533	—	732	30	5	9.1	4.8	3.5	.262	.333	4.23
New York	155	46	10	217	20	1365.2	1403	747	645	146	68	—	26	610	—	647	35	3	9.2	4.3	4.0	.264	.343	4.25
Cincinnati	155	47	7	202	15	1365.0	1484	788	703	179	73	—	31	488	—	506	17	1	9.8	3.3	3.2	.279	.343	4.64
Chicago	155	38	3	238	22	1359.0	1491	835	723	151	76	—	38	554	—	623	27	4	9.9	4.1	3.7	.276	.347	4.79
Pittsburgh	154	49	4	211	10	1358.0	1529	887	788	168	90	—	21	577	—	607	44	4	10.1	4.0	3.8	.285	.356	5.22
NL Total	1244	430	73	1638	162	10971.2	11342	5914	5225	1197	574	—	224	4220	—	5307	217	29	9.3	4.4	3.5	.266	.335	4.29
NL Avg Team	156	54	9	205	20	1371.2	1418	739	653	150	72	—	28	528	—	663	27	4	9.3	4.4	3.5	.266	.335	4.29

Team Fielding

Team	G	PO	A	E	TC	DP	PB	Pct
Brooklyn	155	4141	1608	118	5867	161	4	.980
Cincinnati	155	4094	1713	129	5936	176	7	.978
St. Louis	157	4160	1823	138	6121	161	10	.977
Milwaukee	157	4161	1714	143	6018	169	10	.976
Philadelphia	156	4107	1578	147	5832	161	14	.975
New York	155	4097	1721	151	5969	151	16	.975
Pittsburgh	154	4074	1770	163	6007	139	32	.973
Chicago	155	4079	1627	197	5903	141	8	.967
NL Total	1244	32913	13554	1186	47653	1259	101	.975

Team vs. Team Records

	Bro	ChN	Cin	Mil	NYG	Phi	Pit	StL	Won
Bro	—	13	15	13	15	14	20	15	105
ChN	9	—	12	8	9	5	11	11	65
Cin	7	10	—	8	9	12	15	7	68
Mil	9	14	14	—	14	13	15	13	92
NYG	7	13	13	8	—	9	11	9	70
Phi	8	17	10	9	13	—	15	11	83
Pit	2	11	7	7	11	7	—	5	50
StL	7	11	15	9	13	11	17	—	83
Lost	49	89	86	62	84	71	104	71	

1953 National League Batting Leaders

Games		At-Bats		Runs		Hits		Doubles		Triples	
R. Kiner, 2tm	158	A. Dark, NYG	647	D. Snider, Bro	132	R. Ashburn, Phi	205	S. Musial, StL	53	J. Gilliam, Bro	17
R. Jablonski, StL	157	R. Ashburn, Phi	622	S. Musial, StL	127	S. Musial, StL	200	A. Dark, NYG	41	B. Bruton, Mil	14
E. Mathews, Mil	157	B. Bruton, Mil	613	A. Dark, NYG	126	D. Snider, Bro	198	D. Snider, Bro	38	D. Fondy, ChN	11
J. Adcock, Mil	157	J. Logan, Mil	611	J. Gilliam, Bro	125	A. Dark, NYG	194	C. Furillo, Bro	38	S. Hemus, StL	11
S. Musial, StL	157	G. Bell, Cin	610	3 tied with	110	R. Schoendienst, StL	193	G. Bell, Cin	37	3 tied with	9

Home Runs		Total Bases		Runs Batted In		Walks		Intentional Walks		Strikeouts	
E. Mathews, Mil	47	D. Snider, Bro	370	R. Campanella, Bro	142	S. Musial, StL	105	Statistic unavailable		S. Bilko, StL	125
D. Snider, Bro	42	E. Mathews, Mil	363	E. Mathews, Mil	135	J. Gilliam, Bro	100			D. Fondy, ChN	106
R. Campanella, Bro	41	S. Musial, StL	361	D. Snider, Bro	126	R. Kiner, 2tm	100			B. Bruton, Mil	100
T. Kluszewski, Cin	40	T. Kluszewski, Cin	325	D. Ennis, Phi	125	E. Mathews, Mil	99			F. Thomas, Pit	93
R. Kiner, 2tm	35	G. Bell, Cin	320	G. Hodges, Bro	122	S. Hemus, StL	86			D. Snider, Bro	90

Hit By Pitch		Sac Hits		Sac Flies		Stolen Bases		Caught Stealing		GDP	
S. Hemus, StL	12	P. Reese, Bro	15	Statistic unavailable		B. Bruton, Mil	26	C. Bernier, Pit	14	J. Adcock, Mil	22
R. Repulski, StL	9	R. Ashburn, Phi	14			P. Reese, Bro	22	J. Gilliam, Bro	14	R. Jackson, ChN	20
J. Logan, Mil	7	E. Miksis, ChN	13			J. Gilliam, Bro	21	B. Bruton, Mil	11	M. Irvin, NYG	20
J. Robinson, Bro	7	3 tied with	12			J. Robinson, Bro	17	D. Fondy, ChN	7	A. Dark, NYG	19
3 tied with	6					D. Snider, Bro	16	D. Snider, Bro	7	R. Schoendienst, StL	19

Runs Created		Runs Created/27 Outs		Batting Average		On-Base Percentage		Slugging Percentage		OBP+Slugging	
D. Snider, Bro	148	D. Snider, Bro	9.50	C. Furillo, Bro	.344	S. Musial, StL	.437	D. Snider, Bro	.627	D. Snider, Bro	1.046
E. Mathews, Mil	145	S. Musial, StL	9.47	R. Schoendienst, StL	.342	J. Robinson, Bro	.425	E. Mathews, Mil	.627	S. Musial, StL	1.046
S. Musial, StL	145	E. Mathews, Mil	9.31	S. Musial, StL	.337	D. Snider, Bro	.419	R. Campanella, Bro	.611	E. Mathews, Mil	1.033
R. Campanella, Bro	120	R. Campanella, Bro	8.58	D. Snider, Bro	.336	M. Irvin, NYG	.406	S. Musial, StL	.609	R. Campanella, Bro	1.006
T. Kluszewski, Cin	120	C. Furillo, Bro	8.11	D. Mueller, NYG	.333	E. Mathews, Mil	.406	C. Furillo, Bro	.580	C. Furillo, Bro	.973

1953 National League Pitching Leaders

Wins		Losses		Winning Percentage		Games		Games Started		Complete Games	
R. Roberts, ChN	23	W. Hacker, ChN	19	C. Erskine, Bro	.769	H. Wilhelm, NYG	68	R. Roberts, Phi	41	R. Roberts, Phi	33
W. Spahn, Mil	23	M. Dickson, Pit	19	W. Spahn, Mil	.767	A. Brazle, StL	60	H. Haddix, StL	33	W. Spahn, Mil	24
H. Haddix, StL	20	J. Lindell, 2tm	17	L. Burdette, Mil	.750	J. Hetki, Pit	54	V. B. Mizell, StL	33	H. Haddix, StL	19
C. Erskine, Bro	20	4 tied with	16	R. Meyer, Bro	.750	F. Smith, Cin	50	C. Erskine, Bro	33	C. Simmons, Phi	19
G. Staley, StL	18			F. Baczewski, 2tm	.733	2 tied with	49	5 tied with	32	C. Erskine, Bro	16

Shutouts		Saves		Games Finished		Batters Faced		Innings Pitched		Hits Allowed	
H. Haddix, StL	6	A. Brazle, StL	18	H. Wilhelm, NYG	39	R. Roberts, Phi	1412	R. Roberts, Phi	346.2	R. Roberts, Phi	324
R. Roberts, Phi	5	H. Wilhelm, NYG	15	A. Brazle, StL	33	W. Spahn, Mil	1055	W. Spahn, Mil	265.2	G. Staley, StL	243
W. Spahn, Mil	5	J. Hughes, Bro	9	J. Hetki, Pit	31	H. Haddix, StL	1031	H. Haddix, StL	253.0	M. Dickson, Pit	240
C. Erskine, Bro	4	L. Burdette, Mil	8	F. Smith, Cin	27	C. Erskine, Bro	1030	C. Erskine, Bro	246.2	P. Minner, ChN	227
C. Simmons, Phi	4	D. Leonard, ChN	8	D. Leonard, ChN	27	C. Simmons, Phi	993	C. Simmons, Phi	238.0	W. Hacker, ChN	225

Home Runs Allowed		Walks		Walks/9 Innings		Strikeouts		Strikeouts/9 Innings		Strikeout/Walk Ratio	
W. Hacker, ChN	35	J. Lindell, 2tm	139	R. Roberts, Phi	1.6	R. Roberts, Phi	198	V. B. Mizell, StL	6.9	R. Roberts, Phi	3.25
G. Staley, StL	31	V. B. Mizell, StL	114	K. Raffensberger, Cin	1.7	C. Erskine, Bro	187	C. Erskine, Bro	6.8	H. Haddix, StL	2.36
R. Roberts, Phi	30	J. Klippstein, ChN	107	P. Minner, ChN	1.8	V. B. Mizell, StL	173	J. Antonelli, Mil	6.7	P. Roe, Bro	2.13
M. Dickson, Pit	27	R. Gomez, NYG	101	G. Staley, StL	2.1	H. Haddix, StL	163	J. Klippstein, ChN	6.1	W. Spahn, Mil	2.11
P. Roe, Bro	27	C. Erskine, Bro	95	W. Hacker, ChN	2.2	W. Spahn, Mil	148	H. Haddix, StL	5.8	C. Erskine, Bro	1.97

Earned Run Average		Component ERA		Hit Batsmen		Wild Pitches		Opponent Average		Opponent OBP	
W. Spahn, Mil	2.10	W. Spahn, Mil	2.19	G. Staley, StL	17	J. Lindell, 2tm	11	W. Spahn, Mil	.217	W. Spahn, Mil	.270
R. Roberts, Phi	2.75	R. Roberts, Phi	2.75	K. Drews, Phi	10	J. Klippstein, ChN	10	R. Gomez, NYG	.218	R. Roberts, Phi	.276
B. Buhl, Mil	2.97	H. Haddix, StL	2.87	J. Klippstein, ChN	8	J. Hearn, NYG	10	V. B. Mizell, StL	.227	H. Haddix, StL	.287
H. Haddix, StL	3.06	C. Simmons, Phi	3.02	B. Podbielan, Cin	8	3 tied with	9	C. Erskine, Bro	.230	W. Hacker, ChN	.299
J. Antonelli, Mil	3.18	C. Erskine, Bro	3.14	J. Nuxhall, Cin	8			H. Haddix, StL	.232	C. Simmons, Phi	.302

1953 National League Miscellaneous

Managers

Brooklyn	Chuck Dressen	105-49
Chicago	Phil Cavarretta	65-89
Cincinnati	Rogers Hornsby	64-82
	Buster Mills	4-4
Milwaukee	Charlie Grimm	92-62
New York	Leo Durocher	70-84
Philadelphia	Steve O'Neill	83-71
Pittsburgh	Fred Haney	50-104
St. Louis	Eddie Stanky	83-71

Awards

Most Valuable Player	Roy Campanella, c, Bro
STATS Cy Young	Warren Spahn, Mil
Rookie of the Year	Jim Gilliam, 2b, Bro
STATS Manager of the Year	Chuck Dressen, Bro

STATS All-Star Team

C	Roy Campanella, Bro	.312	41	142
1B	Gil Hodges, Bro	.302	31	122
2B	Red Schoendienst, StL	.342	15	79
3B	Eddie Mathews, Mil	.302	47	135
SS	Al Dark, NYG	.300	23	88
OF	Carl Furillo, Bro	.344	21	92
OF	Stan Musial, StL	.337	30	113
OF	Duke Snider, Bro	.336	42	126
P	Carl Erskine, Bro	20-6	3.54	187 K
P	Harvey Haddix, StL	20-9	3.06	163 K
P	Robin Roberts, Phi	23-16	2.75	198 K
P	Warren Spahn, Mil	23-7	2.10	148 K
RP	Hoyt Wilhelm, NYG	7-8	3.04	15 Sv

Postseason

World Series	Brooklyn (NL) 2 vs. New York (AL) 4

Outstanding Performances

Three-Homer Games
Dusty Rhodes, NYG on August 26
Jim Pendleton, Mil on August 30

1954 American League Standings

Team	Overall W	L	Pct	GB	DIF	Home Games W	L	R	OR	HR	OHR	Road Games W	L	R	OR	HR	OHR	Park Index Run	HR	Record by Month M/A	May	June	July	Aug	S/O
Cleveland	111	43	.721	—	134	59	18	376	252	78	57	52	25	370	252	78	32	101	123	6-6	22-7	20-9	21-8	26-6	16-7
New York	103	51	.669	8.0	4	54	23	388	274	68	42	49	28	384	289	65	44	94	101	6-7	19-10	20-10	23-7	21-7	14-10
Chicago	94	60	.610	17.0	22	45	32	327	294	39	51	49	28	384	227	55	43	102	92	9-5	19-10	18-11	18-13	21-8	9-13
Boston	69	85	.448	42.0	0	38	39	357	384	69	70	31	46	343	344	54	48	99	119	7-4	13-13	11-20	14-18	12-18	11-13
Detroit	68	86	.442	43.0	18	35	42	285	336	44	80	33	44	299	328	46	58	97	50	6-6	11-17	12-17	13-14	11-22	13-12
Washington	66	88	.429	45.0	4	37	41	320	335	27	27	29	47	312	345	54	52	91	48	5-8	9-18	13-18	9-21	7-25	11-10
Baltimore	54	100	.351	57.0	2	32	45	235	313	19	23	22	55	248	355	33	55	108	136	6-6	11-17	12-17	13-14	11-22	13-12
Philadelphia	51	103	.331	60.0	2	29	47	260	467	44	85	22	56	282	408	50	56	108	125	6-5	8-22	14-14	7-23	9-23	7-16

Clinch Date—Cleveland 9/18.

Team Batting

Team	G	AB	R	OR	H	2B	3B	HR	TB	RBI	TBB	IBB	SO	HBP	SH	SF	SB	CS	SB%	GDP	Avg	OBP	Slg
New York	155	5226	805	563	1400	215	59	133	2132	747	650	—	632	20	84	47	34	41	.45	94	.268	.356	.408
Cleveland	156	5222	746	504	1368	188	39	156	2102	714	637	—	668	23	107	59	30	33	.48	114	.262	.351	.403
Chicago	155	5168	711	521	1382	203	47	94	1961	655	604	—	536	51	96	53	98	58	.63	148	.267	.353	.379
Boston	156	5399	700	728	1436	244	41	123	2131	657	654	—	719	27	77	42	37	21	.64	111	.246	.332	.355
Washington	155	5249	632	680	1292	188	69	81	1861	592	610	—	603	19	80	41	48	44	.52	148	.258	.329	.367
Detroit	155	5233	584	664	1351	215	41	90	1918	552	492	—	603	23	78	53	51	30	.63	106	.258	.329	.367
Philadelphia	156	5206	542	875	1228	191	41	94	1783	503	504	—	677	28	54	31	30	29	.51	106	.236	.310	.342
Baltimore	154	5206	483	668	1309	195	49	52	1758	451	468	—	634	21	99	44	30	31	.49	131	.251	.321	.338
AL Total	1242	41909	5203	5203	10766	1639	386	823	15646	4871	4619	—	5129	212	675	370	358	287	.56	980	.257	.331	.373
AL Avg Team	155	5239	650	650	1346	205	48	103	1956	609	577	—	641	27	84	46	45	36	.56	123	.257	.331	.373

Team Pitching

Team	G	CG	ShO	Rel	Sv	IP	H	R	ER	HR	SH	SF	HB	TBB	IBB	SO	WP	Bk	H/9	SO/9	BB/9	OAvg	OOBP	ERA
Cleveland	156	77	12	160	36	1419.1	1220	504	439	89	70	40	16	486	—	678	13	2	7.7	4.3	3.1	.232	.297	2.78
Chicago	155	60	23	176	33	1383.0	1255	521	469	86	68	31	12	552	—	701	23	2	8.2	4.6	3.4	.244	.313	3.05
New York	155	51	16	182	37	1379.1	1284	563	500	86	78	48	29	552	—	655	20	3	8.4	4.3	3.6	.251	.325	3.26
Detroit	155	58	13	179	13	1383.0	1375	664	585	138	96	39	38	506	—	603	14	1	8.9	3.9	3.3	.261	.328	3.81
Washington	155	69	10	158	7	1383.1	1396	680	590	79	101	41	23	573	—	562	25	7	9.1	3.7	3.7	.265	.338	3.84
Baltimore	154	58	6	156	8	1373.1	1279	668	592	78	88	57	19	688	—	668	20	1	8.4	4.4	4.5	.250	.338	3.88
Boston	156	41	10	224	22	1412.1	1434	728	630	118	96	45	36	612	—	707	24	6	9.1	4.5	3.9	.265	.341	4.01
Philadelphia	156	49	3	182	13	1371.1	1523	875	789	141	78	69	39	685	—	555	40	6	10.0	3.6	4.5	.285	.366	5.18
AL Total	1242	463	93	1417	169	11105.0	10766	5203	4594	823	675	370	212	4619	—	5129	179	28	8.7	4.2	3.7	.257	.339	3.72
AL Avg Team	155	58	12	177	21	1388.0	1346	650	574	103	84	46	27	577	—	641	22	4	8.7	4.2	3.7	.257	.339	3.72

Team Fielding

Team	G	PO	A	E	TC	DP	PB	Pct
Chicago	155	4144	1647	108	5899	149	4	.982
New York	155	4135	1751	126	6012	198	7	.979
Cleveland	156	4258	1641	128	6027	148	6	.979
Detroit	155	4145	1719	129	5993	131	5	.978
Washington	155	4149	1740	137	6026	172	8	.977
Baltimore	154	4122	1622	147	5891	152	12	.975
Boston	156	4234	1832	176	6242	163	13	.972
Philadelphia	156	4104	1655	169	5928	163	12	.971
AL Total	1242	33291	13607	1120	48018	1276	67	.977

Team vs. Team Records

	Bal	Bos	ChA	Cle	Det	NYA	Phi	Was	Won
Bal	—	11	7	3	8	5	10	10	54
Bos	11	—	5	2	14	9	15	13	69
ChA	15	17	—	11	12	7	17	15	94
Cle	19	20	11	—	14	11	18	18	111
Det	14	8	10	8	—	6	13	9	68
NYA	17	13	15	11	16	—	18	13	103
Phi	12	7	5	4	9	4	—	10	51
Was	12	9	7	4	13	9	12	—	66
Lost	100	85	60	43	86	51	103	88	

Seasons: Standings, Leaders

1954 American League Batting Leaders

Games		At-Bats		Runs		Hits		Doubles		Triples	
H. Kuenn, Det	155	H. Kuenn, Det	656	M. Mantle, NYA	129	H. Kuenn, Det	201	M. Vernon, Was	33	M. Minoso, ChA	18
J. Busby, Was	155	N. Fox, ChA	631	M. Minoso, ChA	119	N. Fox, ChA	201	M. Minoso, ChA	29	P. Runnels, Was	15
C. Carrasquel, ChA	155	J. Busby, Was	628	B. Avila, Cle	112	B. Avila, Cle	189	A. Smith, Cle	29	M. Vernon, Was	14
N. Fox, ChA	155	C. Carrasquel, ChA	620	N. Fox, ChA	111	J. Busby, Was	187	3 tied with	28	M. Mantle, NYA	12
E. Yost, Was	155	M. Vernon, Was	597	C. Carrasquel, ChA	106	M. Minoso, ChA	182			B. Tuttle, Det	11

Home Runs		Total Bases		Runs Batted In		Walks		Intentional Walks		Strikeouts	
L. Doby, Cle	32	M. Minoso, ChA	304	L. Doby, Cle	126	T. Williams, Bos	136	Statistic unavailable		M. Mantle, NYA	107
T. Williams, Bos	29	M. Vernon, Was	294	Y. Berra, NYA	125	E. Yost, Was	131			L. Doby, Cle	94
M. Mantle, NYA	27	M. Mantle, NYA	285	J. Jensen, Bos	117	M. Mantle, NYA	102			R. Sievers, Was	77
J. Jensen, Bos	25	Y. Berra, NYA	285	M. Minoso, ChA	116	A. Smith, Cle	88			E. Yost, Was	71
2 tied with	24	L. Doby, Cle	279	3 tied with	102	3 tied with	85			B. Consolo, Bos	69

Hit By Pitch		Sac Hits		Sac Flies		Stolen Bases		Caught Stealing		GDP	
M. Minoso, ChA	16	B. Avila, Cle	19	J. Jensen, Bos	11	J. Jensen, Bos	22	M. Minoso, ChA	11	J. Jensen, Bos	32
B. Wilson, 2tm	8	P. Rizzuto, NYA	18	R. Sievers, Was	11	M. Minoso, ChA	18	J. Rivera, ChA	10	A. Kaline, Det	21
A. Smith, Cle	7	N. Fox, ChA	15	A. Rosen, Cle	11	J. Rivera, ChA	18	4 tied with	9	M. Minoso, ChA	20
A. Carey, NYA	7	B. Hunter, Bal	13	L. Doby, Cle	9	S. Jacobs, Phi	17			H. Kuenn, Det	19
S. Lollar, ChA	7	M. Bolling, Bos	13	G. Kell, 2tm	9	J. Busby, Was	17			J. Groth, ChA	19

Runs Created		Runs Created/27 Outs		Batting Average		On-Base Percentage		Slugging Percentage		OBP+Slugging	
M. Mantle, NYA	126	M. Mantle, NYA	8.68	B. Avila, Cle	.341	M. Minoso, ChA	.411	M. Minoso, ChA	.535	M. Minoso, ChA	.946
M. Minoso, ChA	121	M. Minoso, ChA	7.56	M. Minoso, ChA	.320	M. Mantle, NYA	.408	M. Mantle, NYA	.525	M. Mantle, NYA	.933
T. Williams, Bos	117	A. Rosen, Cle	7.46	I. Noren, NYA	.319	E. Yost, Was	.405	A. Rosen, Cle	.506	A. Rosen, Cle	.910
Y. Berra, NYA	109	B. Avila, Cle	7.05	N. Fox, ChA	.319	A. Rosen, Cle	.404	M. Vernon, Was	.492	B. Avila, Cle	.880
2 tied with	106	I. Noren, NYA	7.04	Y. Berra, NYA	.307	B. Avila, Cle	.402	Y. Berra, NYA	.488	I. Noren, NYA	.859

1954 American League Pitching Leaders

Wins		Losses		Winning Percentage		Games		Games Started		Complete Games	
B. Lemon, Cle	23	D. Larsen, Bal	21	S. Consuegra, ChA	.842	S. Dixon, 2tm	54	E. Wynn, Cle	36	B. Porterfield, Was	21
E. Wynn, Cle	23	A. Portocarrero, Phi	18	B. Feller, Cle	.813	C. Pascual, Was	48	B. Turley, Bal	35	B. Lemon, Cle	21
B. Grim, NYA	20	A. Kellner, Phi	17	B. Grim, NYA	.769	M. Martin, 2tm	48	M. Garcia, Cle	34	E. Wynn, Cle	20
M. Garcia, Cle	19	J. Coleman, Bal	17	B. Lemon, Cle	.767	E. Kinder, Bos	48	3 tied with	33	S. Gromek, Det	17
V. Trucks, ChA	19	S. Gromek, Det	16	A. Reynolds, NYA	.765	2 tied with	46			3 tied with	16

Shutouts		Saves		Games Finished		Batters Faced		Innings Pitched		Hits Allowed	
M. Garcia, Cle	5	J. Sain, NYA	22	J. Sain, NYA	39	E. Wynn, Cle	1102	E. Wynn, Cle	270.2	B. Porterfield, Was	249
V. Trucks, ChA	5	E. Kinder, Bos	15	E. Kinder, Bos	34	B. Turley, Bal	1092	V. Trucks, ChA	264.2	S. Gromek, Det	236
7 tied with	4	R. Narleski, Cle	13	M. Burtschy, Phi	30	V. Trucks, ChA	1090	M. Garcia, Cle	258.2	A. Portocarrero, Phi	233
		4 tied with	7	S. Dixon, 2tm	29	A. Portocarrero, Phi	1086	B. Lemon, Cle	258.1	B. Lemon, Cle	228
				B. Chakales, 2tm	28	B. Lemon, Cle	1077	S. Gromek, Det	252.2	E. Wynn, Cle	225

Home Runs Allowed		Walks		Walks/9 Innings		Strikeouts		Strikeouts/9 Innings		Strikeout/Walk Ratio	
S. Gromek, Det	26	B. Turley, Bal	181	E. Lopat, NYA	1.7	B. Turley, Bal	185	B. Pierce, ChA	7.1	B. Hoeft, Det	1.93
A. Portocarrero, Phi	25	A. Portocarrero, Phi	114	S. Gromek, Det	2.0	E. Wynn, Cle	155	J. Harshman, ChA	6.8	F. Sullivan, Bos	1.88
B. Hoeft, Det	22	M. McDermott, Was	110	S. Consuegra, ChA	2.0	V. Trucks, ChA	152	B. Turley, Bal	6.7	E. Wynn, Cle	1.87
G. Zuverink, Det	22	W. Ford, NYA	101	N. Garver, Det	2.3	B. Pierce, ChA	148	B. Hoeft, Det	5.9	M. Garcia, Cle	1.82
E. Wynn, Cle	21	2 tied with	96	M. Garcia, Cle	2.5	J. Harshman, ChA	134	A. Reynolds, NYA	5.7	S. Gromek, Det	1.79

Earned Run Average		Component ERA		Hit Batsmen		Wild Pitches		Opponent Average		Opponent OBP	
M. Garcia, Cle	2.64	M. Garcia, Cle	2.30	S. Gromek, Det	12	A. Portocarrero, Phi	9	B. Turley, Bal	.203	M. Garcia, Cle	.282
S. Consuegra, ChA	2.69	E. Wynn, Cle	2.62	W. Nixon, Bos	9	M. Burtschy, Phi	7	E. Wynn, Cle	.225	E. Wynn, Cle	.283
B. Lemon, Cle	2.72	V. Trucks, ChA	2.71	G. Zuverink, Det	8	4 tied with	6	W. Ford, NYA	.227	N. Garver, Det	.287
E. Wynn, Cle	2.73	S. Consuegra, ChA	2.73	M. Burtschy, Phi	8			V. Trucks, ChA	.228	S. Consuegra, ChA	.289
S. Gromek, Det	2.74	N. Garver, Det	2.74	3 tied with	7			M. Garcia, Cle	.229	S. Gromek, Det	.294

1954 American League Miscellaneous

Managers

Baltimore	Jimmy Dykes	54-100
Boston	Lou Boudreau	69-85
Chicago	Paul Richards	91-54
	Marty Marion	3-6
Cleveland	Al Lopez	111-43
Detroit	Fred Hutchinson	68-86
New York	Casey Stengel	103-51
Philadelphia	Eddie Joost	51-103
Washington	Bucky Harris	66-88

Awards

Most Valuable Player	Yogi Berra, c, NYA
STATS Cy Young	Bob Lemon, Cle
Rookie of the Year	Bob Grim, p, NYA
STATS Manager of the Year	Al Lopez, Cle

STATS All-Star Team

C	Yogi Berra, NYA	.307	22	125
1B	Mickey Vernon, Was	.290	20	97
2B	Bobby Avila, Cle	.341	15	67
3B	Al Rosen, Cle	.300	24	102
SS	Chico Carrasquel, ChA	.255	12	62
OF	Mickey Mantle, NYA	.300	27	102
OF	Minnie Minoso, ChA	.320	19	116
OF	Ted Williams, Bos	.345	29	89
P	Mike Garcia, Cle	19-8	2.64	129 K
P	Steve Gromek, Det	18-16	2.74	102 K
P	Bob Lemon, Cle	23-7	2.72	110 K
P	Early Wynn, Cle	23-11	2.73	155 K
RP	Johnny Sain, NYA	6-6	3.16	22 Sv

Postseason

World Series	Cleveland (AL) 0 vs. NYG (NL) 4

Outstanding Performances

Three-Homer Games

Bill Glynn, Cle	on July 5

1954 National League Standings

Team	Overall					Home Games						Road Games						Park Index		Record by Month					
	W	L	Pct	GB	DIF	W	L	R	OR	HR	OHR	W	L	R	OR	HR	OHR	Run	HR	M/A	May	June	July	Aug	S/O
New York	97	57	.630	—	110	53	23	387	254	120	67	44	34	345	296	66	46	103	171	8-6	15-13	24-4	18-14	17-10	15-10
Brooklyn	92	62	.597	5.0	26	45	32	380	393	101	92	47	30	398	347	85	72	104	123	9-6	14-12	21-8	17-15	18-10	13-11
Milwaukee	89	65	.578	8.0	11	43	34	285	251	43	29	46	31	385	305	96	77	78	42	5-8	18-8	11-18	21-11	19-9	15-11
Philadelphia	75	79	.487	22.0	19	39	39	315	305	47	60	36	40	344	309	55	73	93	81	7-6	15-13	15-11	11-21	12-18	15-10
Cincinnati	74	80	.481	23.0	15	41	36	380	407	94	105	33	44	349	356	53	64	112	170	9-7	12-14	13-15	16-17	14-14	10-13
St. Louis	72	82	.468	25.0	4	33	44	386	431	57	90	39	38	413	359	62	80	106	104	7-6	16-15	10-15	17-14	10-20	12-12
Chicago	64	90	.416	33.0	3	40	37	366	385	86	59	24	53	334	381	73	72	105	100	4-6	16-16	4-21	18-15	13-18	9-14
Pittsburgh	53	101	.344	44.0	1	31	46	277	422	22	42	22	55	280	423	54	86	99	46	6-10	8-23	9-15	10-21	13-17	7-15

Clinch Date—New York 9/20.

Team Batting

Team	G	AB	R	OR	H	2B	3B	HR	TB	RBI	TBB	IBB	SO	HBP	SH	SF	SB	CS	SB%	GDP	Avg	OBP	Slg
St. Louis	154	5405	799	790	1518	285	58	119	2276	748	582	—	586	30	44	66	63	46	.58	127	.281	.361	.421
Brooklyn	154	5251	778	740	1418	246	56	186	2334	741	634	—	625	35	79	59	46	39	.54	137	.270	.359	.444
New York	154	5245	732	550	1386	194	42	186	2222	701	522	—	561	33	84	52	30	23	.57	110	.264	.341	.424
Cincinnati	154	5234	729	763	1369	221	46	147	2123	685	557	—	645	29	101	51	47	30	.61	103	.262	.342	.406
Chicago	154	5359	700	766	1412	229	45	159	2208	640	478	—	693	32	56	40	46	31	.60	119	.263	.332	.412
Milwaukee	154	5261	670	556	1395	217	41	139	2111	636	471	—	619	35	110	44	54	31	.64	115	.265	.335	.401
Philadelphia	154	5184	659	614	1384	224	58	102	2049	620	604	—	620	10	84	55	30	27	.53	125	.267	.333	.395
Pittsburgh	154	5088	557	845	1260	181	57	76	1783	526	566	—	737	25	99	58	21	13	.62	125	.248	.333	.350
NL Total	1232	42027	5624	5624	11142	1816	403	1114	17106	5297	4414	—	5086	229	657	425	337	240	.58	979	.265	.335	.407
NL Avg Team	154	5253	703	703	1393	227	50	139	2138	662	552	—	636	29	82	53	42	30	.58	122	.265	.335	.407

Team Pitching

Team	G	CG	ShO	Rel	Sv	IP	H	R	ER	HR	SH	SF	HB	TBB	IBB	SO	WP	Bk	H/9	SO/9	BB/9	OAvg	OOBP	ERA
New York	154	45	19	235	33	1390.0	1258	550	478	113	84	38	36	613	—	692	21	4	8.1	4.5	4.0	.243	.326	3.09
Milwaukee	154	63	13	193	21	1394.2	1296	556	494	106	75	41	29	553	—	698	23	2	8.4	4.5	3.6	.250	.323	3.19
Philadelphia	154	78	14	139	12	1365.1	1329	614	545	133	77	45	17	450	—	570	20	1	8.8	3.8	3.0	.256	.315	3.59
Brooklyn	154	39	8	231	36	1393.2	1399	740	667	164	83	44	19	533	—	762	28	0	9.0	4.9	3.4	.261	.328	4.31
St. Louis	154	40	11	262	18	1390.1	1484	790	695	170	76	53	44	535	—	680	35	2	9.6	4.4	3.5	.275	.343	4.50
Cincinnati	154	34	8	235	27	1367.1	1491	763	684	169	76	51	35	547	—	537	24	1	9.8	3.5	3.5	.282	.351	4.50
Chicago	154	41	6	210	15	1374.1	1375	766	688	131	84	74	26	619	—	622	35	2	9.0	4.1	4.1	.264	.340	4.51
Pittsburgh	154	37	4	195	15	1346.0	1510	845	736	128	102	79	23	564	—	525	37	5	10.1	3.5	3.8	.287	.354	4.92
NL Total	1232	377	83	1700	181	11021.2	11142	5624	4987	1114	657	425	229	4414	—	5086	223	17	9.1	4.2	3.6	.265	.344	4.07
NL Avg Team	154	47	10	213	23	1377.2	1393	703	623	139	82	53	29	552	—	636	28	2	9.1	4.2	3.6	.265	.344	4.07

Team Fielding

Team	G	PO	A	E	TC	DP	PB	Pct
Milwaukee	154	4184	1763	116	6063	171	10	.981
Brooklyn	154	4181	1656	129	5966	138	4	.978
Cincinnati	154	4103	1657	137	5897	194	9	.977
St. Louis	154	4171	1850	146	6167	178	8	.976
Philadelphia	154	4096	1578	145	5819	133	9	.975
New York	154	4170	1734	154	6058	172	17	.975
Chicago	154	4123	1761	154	6038	164	14	.974
Pittsburgh	154	4038	1741	173	5952	136	9	.971
NL Total	1232	33066	13740	1154	47960	1286	80	.976

Team vs. Team Records

	Bro	ChN	Cin	Mil	NYG	Phi	Pit	StL	Won
Bro	—	15	16	10	9	13	15	14	92
ChN	7	—	8	6	7	7	15	14	64
Cin	6	14	—	10	7	14	15	8	74
Mil	12	16	12	—	10	13	14	12	89
NYG	13	15	15	12	—	16	14	12	97
Phi	9	15	8	9	6	—	16	12	75
Pit	7	7	7	8	8	6	—	10	53
StL	8	8	14	10	10	10	12	—	72
Lost	62	90	80	65	57	79	101	82	

1954 National League Batting Leaders

Games		At-Bats		Runs		Hits		Doubles		Triples	
E. Banks, ChN	154	A. Dark, NYG	644	D. Snider, Bro	120	D. Mueller, NYG	212	S. Musial, StL	41	W. Mays, NYG	13
R. McMillan, Cin	154	W. Moon, StL	635	S. Musial, StL	120	D. Snider, Bro	199	R. Repulski, StL	39	G. Hamner, Phi	11
J. Logan, Mil	154	R. Repulski, StL	619	W. Mays, NYG	119	W. Mays, NYG	195	D. Snider, Bro	39	D. Snider, Bro	10
A. Dark, NYG	154	G. Bell, Cin	619	R. Ashburn, Phi	111	S. Musial, StL	195	G. Hamner, Phi	39	3 tied with	9
G. Hodges, Bro	154	D. Mueller, NYG	619	J. Gilliam, Bro	107	W. Moon, StL	193	2 tied with	38		

Home Runs		Total Bases		Runs Batted In		Walks		Intentional Walks		Strikeouts	
T. Kluszewski, Cin	49	D. Snider, Bro	378	T. Kluszewski, Cin	141	R. Ashburn, Phi	125	Statistic unavailable		D. Snider, Bro	96
G. Hodges, Bro	42	W. Mays, NYG	377	D. Snider, Bro	130	E. Mathews, Mil	113			R. Kiner, ChN	90
W. Mays, NYG	41	T. Kluszewski, Cin	368	G. Hodges, Bro	130	S. Musial, StL	103			G. Allie, Pit	84
H. Sauer, ChN	41	S. Musial, StL	359	S. Musial, StL	126	H. Thompson, NYG	90			D. Fondy, ChN	84
2 tied with	40	G. Hodges, Bro	335	D. Ennis, Phi	119	P. Reese, Bro	90			G. Hodges, Bro	84

Hit By Pitch		Sac Hits		Sac Flies		Stolen Bases		Caught Stealing		GDP	
F. Thomas, Pit	10	R. McMillan, Cin	31	G. Hodges, Bro	19	B. Bruton, Mil	34	B. Bruton, Mil	13	D. Ennis, Phi	23
E. Banks, ChN	7	D. O'Connell, Mil	19	R. Jablonski, StL	11	J. Temple, Cin	21	W. Moon, StL	10	D. Cole, Pit	20
J. Robinson, Bro	7	J. Logan, Mil	15	F. Thomas, Pit	11	D. Fondy, ChN	20	E. Banks, ChN	10	S. Musial, StL	20
J. Logan, Mil	6	R. Ashburn, Phi	14	D. Ennis, Phi	11	W. Moon, StL	18	R. Repulski, StL	10	P. Reese, Bro	20
H. Sauer, ChN	6	R. Meyer, Bro	14	4 tied with	9	R. Ashburn, Phi	11	R. Ashburn, Phi	8	D. Mueller, NYG	19

Runs Created		Runs Created/27 Outs		Batting Average		On-Base Percentage		Slugging Percentage		OBP+Slugging	
T. Kluszewski, Cin	141	W. Mays, NYG	9.52	W. Mays, NYG	.345	R. Ashburn, Phi	.441	W. Mays, NYG	.667	W. Mays, NYG	1.078
S. Musial, StL	141	T. Kluszewski, Cin	9.39	D. Mueller, NYG	.342	S. Musial, StL	.428	D. Snider, Bro	.647	D. Snider, Bro	1.071
D. Snider, Bro	140	D. Snider, Bro	9.21	D. Snider, Bro	.341	D. Snider, Bro	.423	T. Kluszewski, Cin	.642	T. Kluszewski, Cin	1.049
W. Mays, NYG	139	S. Musial, StL	8.85	S. Musial, StL	.330	E. Mathews, Mil	.423	S. Musial, StL	.607	S. Musial, StL	1.036
E. Mathews, Mil	117	E. Mathews, Mil	8.77	T. Kluszewski, Cin	.326	W. Mays, NYG	.411	E. Mathews, Mil	.603	E. Mathews, Mil	1.026

1954 National League Pitching Leaders

Wins		Losses		Winning Percentage		Games		Games Started		Complete Games	
R. Roberts, Phi	23	M. Dickson, Phi	20	J. Antonelli, NYG	.750	J. Hughes, Bro	60	R. Roberts, Phi	38	R. Roberts, Phi	29
J. Antonelli, NYG	21	M. Surkont, Pit	18	H. Wilhelm, NYG	.750	J. Hetki, Pit	58	C. Erskine, Bro	37	W. Spahn, Mil	23
W. Spahn, Mil	21	4 tied with	15	B. Loes, Bro	.722	A. Brazle, StL	58	J. Antonelli, NYG	37	C. Simmons, Phi	21
H. Haddix, StL	18			B. Lawrence, StL	.714	H. Wilhelm, NYG	57	H. Haddix, StL	35	J. Antonelli, NYG	18
C. Erskine, Bro	18			J. Nuxhall, Cin	.706	M. Grissom, NYG	56	W. Spahn, Mil	34	2 tied with	13

Shutouts		Saves		Games Finished		Batters Faced		Innings Pitched		Hits Allowed	
J. Antonelli, NYG	6	J. Hughes, Bro	24	J. Hetki, Pit	46	R. Roberts, Phi	1331	R. Roberts, Phi	336.2	R. Roberts, Phi	289
5 tied with	4	F. Smith, Cin	20	F. Smith, Cin	43	W. Spahn, Mil	1175	W. Spahn, Mil	283.1	W. Spahn, Mil	262
		M. Grissom, NYG	19	J. Hughes, Bro	41	C. Erskine, Bro	1098	C. Erskine, Bro	260.1	A. Fowler, Cin	256
		D. Jolly, Mil	10	M. Grissom, NYG	36	H. Haddix, StL	1087	H. Haddix, StL	259.2	M. Dickson, Phi	256
		J. Hetki, Pit	9	D. Jolly, Mil	31	C. Simmons, Phi	1074	J. Antonelli, NYG	258.2	H. Haddix, StL	247

Home Runs Allowed		Walks		Walks/9 Innings		Strikeouts		Strikeouts/9 Innings		Strikeout/Walk Ratio	
R. Roberts, Phi	35	R. Gomez, NYG	109	R. Roberts, Phi	1.5	R. Roberts, Phi	185	H. Haddix, StL	6.4	R. Roberts, Phi	3.30
C. Erskine, Bro	31	B. Rush, ChN	103	P. Minner, ChN	2.1	H. Haddix, StL	184	C. Erskine, Bro	5.7	H. Haddix, StL	2.39
M. Dickson, Phi	31	C. Simmons, Phi	98	W. Hacker, ChN	2.1	C. Erskine, Bro	166	D. Littlefield, Pit	5.3	W. Hacker, ChN	2.16
W. Hacker, ChN	28	J. Klippstein, ChN	96	L. Burdette, Mil	2.3	J. Antonelli, NYG	152	J. Antonelli, NYG	5.3	C. Erskine, Bro	1.80
H. Haddix, StL	26	J. Antonelli, NYG	94	R. Meyer, Bro	2.4	W. Spahn, Mil	136	G. Conley, Mil	5.2	S. Maglie, NYG	1.67

Earned Run Average		Component ERA		Hit Batsmen		Wild Pitches		Opponent Average		Opponent OBP	
J. Antonelli, NYG	2.30	R. Roberts, Phi	2.51	B. Lawrence, StL	8	P. LaPalme, Pit	8	J. Antonelli, NYG	.219	R. Roberts, Phi	.266
L. Burdette, Mil	2.76	J. Antonelli, NYG	2.78	B. Purkey, Pit	7	B. Rush, ChN	8	R. Roberts, Phi	.231	J. Antonelli, NYG	.292
C. Simmons, Phi	2.81	L. Burdette, Mil	3.08	R. Gomez, NYG	7	H. Haddix, StL	7	C. Simmons, Phi	.239	W. Hacker, ChN	.299
R. Gomez, NYG	2.88	C. Simmons, Phi	3.10	G. Conley, Mil	7	3 tied with	6	D. Littlefield, Pit	.239	W. Spahn, Mil	.300
G. Conley, Mil	2.96	W. Spahn, Mil	3.14	M. Grissom, NYG	7			H. Wehmeier, 2tm	.239	L. Burdette, Mil	.300

1954 National League Miscellaneous

Managers

Brooklyn	Walter Alston	92-62
Chicago	Stan Hack	64-90
Cincinnati	Birdie Tebbetts	74-80
Milwaukee	Charlie Grimm	89-65
New York	Leo Durocher	97-57
Philadelphia	Steve O'Neill	40-37
	Terry Moore	35-42
Pittsburgh	Fred Haney	53-101
St. Louis	Eddie Stanky	72-82

Awards

Most Valuable Player	Willie Mays, of, NYG
STATS Cy Young	Johnny Antonelli, NYG
Rookie of the Year	Wally Moon, of, StL
STATS Manager of the Year	Leo Durocher, NYG

STATS All-Star Team

C	Smoky Burgess, Phi	.368	4	46
1B	Ted Kluszewski, Cin	.326	49	141
2B	Red Schoendienst, StL	.315	5	79
3B	Eddie Mathews, Mil	.290	40	103
SS	Pee Wee Reese, Bro	.309	10	69
OF	Willie Mays, NYG	.345	41	110
OF	Stan Musial, StL	.330	35	126
OF	Duke Snider, Bro	.341	40	130
P	Johnny Antonelli, NYG	21-7	2.30	152 K
P	Ruben Gomez, NYG	17-9	2.88	106 K
P	Robin Roberts, Phi	23-15	2.97	185 K
P	Warren Spahn, Mil	21-12	3.14	136 K
RP	Marv Grissom, NYG	10-7	2.35	19 Sv

Postseason

World Series	NYG (NL) 4 vs. Cleveland (AL) 0

Outstanding Performances

No-Hitters
Jim Wilson, Mil — vs. Phi on June 12

Four-Homer Games
Joe Adcock, Mil — on July 31

Three-Homer Games
Stan Musial, StL — on May 2
H. Thompson, NYG — on June 3
Dusty Rhodes, NYG — on July 28

Cycles
Don Mueller, NYG — on July 11

1955 American League Standings

	Overall					Home Games						Road Games						Park Index		Record by Month					
Team	W	L	Pct	GB	DIF	W	L	R	OR	HR	OHR	W	L	R	OR	HR	OHR	Run	HR	M/A	May	June	July	Aug	S/O
New York	96	58	.623	—	93	**52**	**25**	378	**248**	**89**	44	**44**	**33**	384	321	**86**	64	89	89	9-6	21-7	20-11	12-17	17-11	17-6
Cleveland	93	61	.604	3.0	43	49	28	343	318	84	58	44	33	355	283	64	53	104	121	9-6	18-9	15-15	20-11	17-11	14-9
Chicago	91	63	.591	5.0	27	49	28	357	262	54	47	42	35	368	295	62	64	93	80	9-5	16-11	17-11	20-12	14-13	12-12
Boston	84	70	.545	12.0	9	47	31	**470**	395	84	79	37	39	285	**257**	53	**49**	156	156	8-8	11-18	20-9	21-8	14-13	10-14
Detroit	79	75	.513	17.0	3	46	31	386	301	81	59	33	44	**389**	357	49	67	92	121	10-5	12-15	16-11	17-16	12-18	12-10
Kansas City	63	91	.409	33.0	1	33	43	333	447	70	110	30	48	305	464	51	65	104	159	6-8	10-17	12-16	15-19	11-16	9-15
Baltimore	57	97	.370	39.0	0	30	47	249	335	15	42	27	50	291	419	39	61	82	57	4-12	10-19	6-19	10-21	11-15	16-11
Washington	53	101	.344	43.0	2	28	49	282	357	20	**25**	25	52	316	432	60	74	85	34	5-10	12-14	8-22	10-21	11-14	7-20

Clinch Date—New York 9/23.

Team Batting

Team	G	AB	R	OR	H	2B	3B	HR	TB	RBI	TBB	IBB	SO	HBP	SH	SF	SB	CS	SB%	GDP	Avg	OBP	Slg
Detroit	154	5283	**775**	658	**1407**	211	38	130	2084	**724**	641	42	583	21	71	57	41	22	.65	130	.266	.354	.394
New York	154	5161	762	569	1342	179	**55**	**175**	**2156**	717	609	**48**	658	46	79	53	55	17	**.72**	125	.260	**.360**	**.418**
Boston	154	5273	755	652	1392	**241**	39	137	2122	709	707	44	733	28	69	53	43	17	.72	117	.264	.351	.402
Chicago	155	5220	725	**557**	1401	204	36	116	2025	677	567	40	595	35	**111**	59	**69**	45	.61	112	**.268**	.349	.388
Cleveland	154	5146	698	601	1325	195	31	148	2026	657	**723**	37	715	35	87	59	28	24	.54	**146**	.257	.359	.394
Kansas City	155	**5335**	638	911	1395	189	46	121	2039	592	463	32	725	26	57	34	22	36	.38	99	.261	.327	.382
Washington	154	5142	598	789	1277	178	54	80	1803	566	538	22	654	19	79	27	34	**46**	.43	127	.248	.328	.351
Baltimore	156	5257	540	754	1263	177	39	54	1680	503	560	28	**742**	59	70	18	25	40	.38	127	.240	.319	.320
AL Total	1236	41817	5491	5491	10802	1574	338	961	15935	5145	4808	293	5405	269	623	360	317	247	.56	983	.258	.336	.381
AL Avg Team	155	5227	686	686	1350	197	42	120	1992	643	601	37	676	34	78	45	40	31	.56	123	.258	.336	.381

Team Pitching

Team	G	CG	ShO	Rel	Sv	IP	H	R	ER	HR	SH	SF	HB	TBB	IBB	SO	WP	Bk	H/9	SO/9	BB/9	OAvg	OOBP	ERA
New York	154	52	19	190	33	1372.1	**1163**	569	493	108	66	32	22	688	31	731	26	3	7.6	4.8	4.5	**.232**	.326	3.23
Chicago	155	55	**20**	202	23	1378.0	1301	557	516	111	73	34	22	**497**	44	720	19	3	8.5	4.7	**3.2**	.251	**.317**	3.37
Cleveland	154	45	15	215	**36**	1386.1	1285	601	522	111	**53**	**31**	22	558	24	**877**	35	0	8.3	**5.7**	3.6	.245	.319	3.39
Boston	154	44	9	187	34	1384.1	1333	652	572	128	70	41	30	582	42	674	28	**4**	8.7	4.4	3.8	.253	.328	3.72
Detroit	154	**66**	16	185	12	1380.1	1381	658	582	126	60	40	32	517	40	629	27	2	9.0	4.1	3.4	.261	.328	3.79
Baltimore	156	35	10	235	20	**1388.2**	1403	754	650	103	100	63	49	625	33	595	**42**	1	9.1	3.9	4.1	.279	.359	4.21
Washington	154	37	10	229	16	1354.2	1450	789	696	**99**	108	60	49	634	39	607	28	3	9.6	4.0	4.2	.278	.363	4.62
Kansas City	155	29	9	**255**	22	1382.0	1486	911	822	175	94	63	42	707	**59**	572	36	3	9.7	3.7	4.6	.266	.344	5.35
AL Total	1236	363	108	1698	196	11026.2	10802	5491	4853	961	624	364	262	4808	312	5405	241	19	8.8	4.4	3.9	.258	.344	3.96
AL Avg Team	155	45	14	212	25	1378.2	1350	686	607	120	78	46	33	601	39	676	30	2	8.8	4.4	3.9	.258	.344	3.96

Team Fielding

Team	G	PO	A	E	TC	DP	PB	Pct
Cleveland	154	**4155**	1561	108	5824	152	13	.981
Chicago	155	4133	1717	111	5961	147	6	.981
New York	154	4122	1632	128	5882	**180**	5	.978
Boston	154	4141	1708	136	5985	140	5	.977
Detroit	154	4143	1604	139	5886	159	8	.976
Kansas City	155	4142	**1729**	146	**6017**	174	14	.976
Washington	154	4066	1695	154	5915	170	17	.974
Baltimore	156	4153	1697	167	**6017**	159	**22**	.972
AL Total	1236	33055	13343	1089	47487	1281	90	.977

Team vs. Team Records

	Bal	Bos	ChA	Cle	Det	KCA	NYA	Was	Won
Bal	—	8	10	3	9	10	3	14	**57**
Bos	14	—	9	11	13	14	8	15	**84**
ChA	12	13	—	10	14	14	11	17	**91**
Cle	19	11	12	—	12	17	13	9	**93**
Det	13	9	8	10	—	12	10	17	**79**
KCA	12	8	8	5	10	—	7	13	**63**
NYA	19	14	11	9	12	15	—	16	**96**
Was	8	7	5	13	5	9	6	—	**53**
Lost	97	70	63	61	75	91	58	101	

1955 American League Batting Leaders

Games		At-Bats		Runs		Hits		Doubles		Triples	
A. Smith, Cle	154	N. Fox, ChA	636	A. Smith, Cle	123	A. Kaline, Det	200	H. Kuenn, Det	38	A. Carey, NYA	11
B. Tuttle, Det	154	H. Kuenn, Det	620	A. Kaline, Det	121	N. Fox, ChA	198	V. Power, KCA	34	M. Mantle, NYA	11
N. Fox, ChA	154	A. Smith, Cle	607	M. Mantle, NYA	121	V. Power, KCA	190	B. Goodman, Bos	31	V. Power, KCA	10
W. Miranda, Bal	153	B. Tuttle, Det	603	B. Tuttle, Det	102	H. Kuenn, Det	190	J. Finigan, KCA	30	4 tied with	8
2 tied with	152	B. Goodman, Bos	599	H. Kuenn, Det	101	A. Smith, Cle	186	S. White, Bos	30		

Home Runs		Total Bases		Runs Batted In		Walks		Intentional Walks		Strikeouts	
M. Mantle, NYA	37	A. Kaline, Det	321	J. Jensen, Bos	116	M. Mantle, NYA	113	T. Williams, Bos	17	N. Zauchin, Bos	105
G. Zernial, KCA	30	M. Mantle, NYA	316	R. Boone, Det	116	B. Goodman, Bos	99	A. Kaline, Det	12	L. Doby, Cle	100
T. Williams, Bos	28	V. Power, KCA	301	Y. Berra, NYA	108	E. Yost, Was	95	S. Lollar, ChA	12	M. Mantle, NYA	97
3 tied with	27	A. Smith, Cle	287	R. Sievers, Was	106	F. Fain, 2tm	94	M. Vernon, Was	9	G. Zernial, KCA	90
		J. Jensen, Bos	275	A. Kaline, Det	102	A. Smith, Cle	93	3 tied with	8	2 tied with	77

Hit By Pitch		Sac Hits		Sac Flies		Stolen Bases		Caught Stealing		GDP	
N. Fox, ChA	17	B. Avila, Cle	18	J. Jensen, Bos	12	J. Rivera, ChA	25	J. Rivera, ChA	17	B. Tuttle, Det	25
A. Smith, Cle	15	G. Strickland, Cle	14	G. Zernial, KCA	8	M. Minoso, ChA	19	P. Runnels, Was	9	S. White, Bos	23
E. Yost, Was	11	N. Fox, ChA	14	A. Rosen, Cle	8	J. Jensen, Bos	16	N. Fox, ChA	9	J. Jensen, Bos	20
M. Minoso, ChA	10	3 tied with	13	M. Vernon, Was	8	J. Busby, 2tm	12	4 tied with	8	M. Minoso, ChA	18
S. Lollar, ChA	10			7 tied with	7	A. Smith, Cle	11			J. Finigan, KCA	18

Runs Created		Runs Created/27 Outs		Batting Average		On-Base Percentage		Slugging Percentage		OBP+Slugging	
M. Mantle, NYA	136	M. Mantle, NYA	9.91	A. Kaline, Det	.340	M. Mantle, NYA	.431	M. Mantle, NYA	.611	M. Mantle, NYA	1.042
A. Kaline, Det	134	A. Kaline, Det	8.68	V. Power, KCA	.319	A. Kaline, Det	.421	A. Kaline, Det	.546	A. Kaline, Det	.967
A. Smith, Cle	116	A. Smith, Cle	7.07	G. Kell, ChA	.312	A. Smith, Cle	.407	G. Zernial, KCA	.508	A. Smith, Cle	.880
T. Williams, Bos	101	L. Doby, Cle	6.42	N. Fox, ChA	.311	B. Goodman, Bos	.394	L. Doby, Cle	.505	L. Doby, Cle	.874
V. Power, KCA	100	V. Power, KCA	6.28	H. Kuenn, Det	.306	G. Kell, ChA	.389	V. Power, KCA	.505	V. Power, KCA	.859

1955 American League Pitching Leaders

Wins		Losses		Winning Percentage		Games		Games Started		Complete Games	
F. Sullivan, Bos	18	J. Wilson, Bal	18	T. Byrne, NYA	.762	R. Narleski, Cle	60	F. Sullivan, Bos	35	W. Ford, NYA	18
W. Ford, NYA	18	B. Porterfield, Was	17	W. Ford, NYA	.720	D. Mossi, Cle	57	B. Turley, NYA	34	B. Hoeft, Det	17
B. Lemon, Cle	18	N. Garver, Det	16	B. Hoeft, Det	.696	T. Gorman, KCA	57	W. Ford, NYA	33	5 tied with	16
B. Turley, NYA	17	F. Lary, Det	15	B. Lemon, Cle	.643	H. Dorish, 2tm	48	H. Score, Cle	32		
E. Wynn, Cle	17	C. Stobbs, Was	14	2 tied with	.625	R. Moore, Bal	46	N. Garver, Det	32		

Shutouts		Saves		Games Finished		Batters Faced		Innings Pitched		Hits Allowed	
B. Hoeft, Det	7	R. Narleski, Cle	19	E. Kinder, Bos	38	F. Sullivan, Bos	1100	F. Sullivan, Bos	260.0	N. Garver, Det	251
B. Turley, NYA	6	T. Gorman, KCA	18	R. Narleski, Cle	36	B. Turley, NYA	1075	W. Ford, NYA	253.2	F. Sullivan, Bos	235
B. Pierce, ChA	6	E. Kinder, Bos	18	T. Gorman, KCA	35	W. Ford, NYA	1027	B. Turley, NYA	246.2	F. Lary, Det	232
E. Wynn, Cle	6	J. Konstanty, NYA	11	J. Konstanty, NYA	30	F. Lary, Det	997	J. Wilson, Bal	235.1	M. Garcia, Cle	230
2 tied with	5	T. Morgan, NYA	10	D. Mossi, Cle	27	N. Garver, Det	992	F. Lary, Det	235.0	B. Lemon, Cle	218

Home Runs Allowed		Walks		Walks/9 Innings		Strikeouts		Strikeouts/9 Innings		Strikeout/Walk Ratio	
S. Gromek, Det	26	B. Turley, NYA	177	S. Gromek, Det	1.8	H. Score, Cle	245	H. Score, Cle	9.7	B. Pierce, ChA	2.45
A. Ditmar, KCA	23	H. Score, Cle	154	D. Donovan, ChA	2.3	B. Turley, NYA	210	B. Turley, NYA	7.7	M. Garcia, Cle	2.14
F. Sullivan, Bos	23	D. Stone, Was	114	M. Garcia, Cle	2.4	B. Pierce, ChA	157	B. Pierce, ChA	6.9	S. Gromek, Det	1.97
3 tied with	21	W. Ford, NYA	113	N. Garver, Det	2.6	W. Ford, NYA	137	J. Harshman, ChA	5.8	D. Donovan, ChA	1.83
		2 tied with	100	B. Porterfield, Was	2.7	B. Hoeft, Det	133	B. Hoeft, Det	5.4	B. Hoeft, Det	1.77

Earned Run Average		Component ERA		Hit Batsmen		Wild Pitches		Opponent Average		Opponent OBP	
B. Pierce, ChA	1.97	B. Pierce, ChA	2.49	P. Ramos, Was	11	H. Score, Cle	12	B. Turley, NYA	.193	B. Pierce, ChA	.277
W. Ford, NYA	2.63	W. Ford, NYA	2.77	H. Byrd, 2tm	9	D. Stone, Was	9	H. Score, Cle	.194	B. Hoeft, Det	.294
E. Wynn, Cle	2.82	B. Hoeft, Det	2.95	M. McDermott, Was	9	B. Lemon, Cle	8	W. Ford, NYA	.208	W. Ford, NYA	.296
H. Score, Cle	2.85	J. Wilson, Bal	2.96	S. Gromek, Det	9	6 tied with	7	B. Pierce, ChA	.213	J. Wilson, Bal	.297
F. Sullivan, Bos	2.91	E. Wynn, Cle	3.24	2 tied with	8			J. Harshman, ChA	.224	E. Wynn, Cle	.304

1955 American League Miscellaneous

Managers

Baltimore	Paul Richards	57-97
Boston	Pinky Higgins	84-70
Chicago	Marty Marion	91-63
Cleveland	Al Lopez	93-61
Detroit	Bucky Harris	79-75
Kansas City	Lou Boudreau	63-91
New York	Casey Stengel	96-58
Washington	Chuck Dressen	53-101

Awards

Most Valuable Player	Yogi Berra, c, NYA
STATS Cy Young	Whitey Ford, NYA
Rookie of the Year	Herb Score, p, Cle
STATS Manager of the Year	Pinky Higgins, Bos

STATS All-Star Team

C	Yogi Berra, NYA	.272	27	108
1B	Vic Power, KCA	.319	19	76
2B	Nellie Fox, ChA	.311	6	59
3B	Ray Boone, Det	.284	20	116
SS	Harvey Kuenn, Det	.306	8	62
OF	Al Kaline, Det	.340	27	102
OF	Mickey Mantle, NYA	.306	37	99
OF	Ted Williams, Bos	.356	28	83
P	Whitey Ford, NYA	18-7	2.63	137 K
P	Billy Pierce, ChA	15-10	1.97	157 K
P	Herb Score, Cle	16-10	2.85	245 K
P	Early Wynn, Cle	17-11	2.82	122 K
RP	Ellis Kinder, Bos	5-5	2.84	18 Sv

Postseason

World Series	New York (AL) 3 vs. Brooklyn (NL) 4

Outstanding Performances

Three-Homer Games

Al Kaline, Det	on April 17
Mickey Mantle, NYA	on May 13
Norm Zauchin, Bos	on May 27

1955 National League Standings

Team	W	L	Pct	GB	DIF	W	L	R	OR	HR	OHR	W	L	R	OR	HR	OHR	Run	HR	M/A	May	June	July	Aug	S/O
		Overall					Home Games						Road Games					Park Index			Record by Month				
Brooklyn	98	55	.641	—	166	56	21	461	318	119	85	42	34	396	332	82	83	106	122	14-2	18-9	20-8	19-13	13-14	14-9
Milwaukee	85	69	.552	13.5	2	46	31	342	297	75	51	39	38	401	371	107	87	83	65	9-6	12-16	18-10	18-13	16-14	12-10
New York	80	74	.519	18.5	0	44	35	362	327	95	91	36	39	340	346	74	64	95	128	6-8	18-13	10-17	20-12	14-13	12-11
Philadelphia	77	77	.500	21.5	3	46	31	371	309	76	78	31	46	304	357	56	83	103	111	9-7	10-19	13-14	21-14	17-10	7-13
Cincinnati	75	79	.487	23.5	0	46	31	425	341	102	91	29	48	336	343	79	70	113	130	4-12	14-11	14-12	14-21	19-15	10-8
Chicago	72	81	.471	26.0	5	43	33	348	322	80	62	29	48	278	391	84	91	101	82	7-8	20-9	13-17	10-22	14-16	8-9
St. Louis	68	86	.442	30.5	0	41	36	358	362	84	92	27	50	296	395	59	93	104	116	7-5	11-17	13-15	15-17	9-22	13-10
Pittsburgh	60	94	.390	38.5	0	36	39	298	337	34	48	24	55	262	430	57	94	97	57	3-11	11-20	10-18	14-19	14-12	8-14

Clinch Date—Brooklyn 9/08.

Team Batting

Team	G	AB	R	OR	H	2B	3B	HR	TB	RBI	TBB	IBB	SO	HBP	SH	SF	SB	CS	SB%	GDP	Avg	OBP	Slg
Brooklyn	154	5193	857	650	1406	230	44	201	2327	800	674	62	718	41	75	54	79	56	.59	132	.271	.365	.448
Cincinnati	154	5270	761	684	1424	216	28	181	2239	726	556	50	657	33	76	43	51	36	.59	104	.270	.348	.425
Milwaukee	154	5277	743	668	1377	219	55	182	2252	699	504	67	735	28	72	39	42	27	.61	113	.261	.333	.427
New York	154	5288	702	673	1377	173	34	169	2125	643	497	44	581	36	69	50	38	22	.63	108	.260	.334	.402
Philadelphia	154	5092	675	666	1300	214	50	132	2010	631	652	39	673	24	53	43	44	32	.58	139	.255	.347	.395
St. Louis	154	5266	654	757	1375	228	34	143	2104	608	458	53	597	31	56	44	64	59	.52	122	.261	.329	.400
Chicago	154	5214	626	713	1287	187	55	164	2076	597	428	45	806	22	69	33	37	35	.51	107	.247	.311	.398
Pittsburgh	154	5173	560	767	1262	210	60	91	1865	532	471	64	652	21	93	32	22	22	.50	132	.244	.313	.361
NL Total	1232	41773	5578	5578	10808	1677	362	1263	16998	5236	4240	424	5419	236	563	338	377	289	.57	957	.259	.328	.407
NL Avg Team	154	5222	697	697	1351	210	45	158	2125	655	530	53	677	30	70	42	47	36	.57	120	.259	.328	.407

Team Pitching

Team	G	CG	ShO	Rel	Sv	IP	H	R	ER	HR	SH	SF	HB	TBB	IBB	SO	WP	Bk	H/9	SO/9	BB/9	OAvg	OOBP	ERA
Brooklyn	154	46	11	209	37	1378.0	1296	650	564	168	56	24	19	483	34	773	35	2	8.5	5.0	3.2	.248	.313	3.68
New York	154	52	6	246	14	1386.2	1347	673	581	155	78	40	47	560	55	721	19	1	8.7	4.7	3.6	.257	.332	3.77
Milwaukee	154	61	5	203	12	1383.0	1339	668	591	138	80	38	19	591	64	654	30	3	8.7	4.3	3.8	.256	.331	3.85
Philadelphia	154	58	11	193	21	1356.2	1291	666	592	161	64	42	25	477	43	657	28	0	8.6	4.4	3.2	.251	.315	3.93
Cincinnati	154	38	12	245	22	1363.0	1373	684	598	161	62	46	24	443	42	576	28	3	9.1	3.8	2.9	.264	.322	3.95
Chicago	154	47	10	209	23	1378.1	1306	713	639	153	73	48	29	601	57	686	31	1	8.5	4.5	3.9	.251	.330	4.17
Pittsburgh	154	41	5	199	16	1362.0	1480	767	665	142	81	53	26	536	50	622	30	4	9.8	4.1	3.5	.281	.347	4.39
St. Louis	154	42	10	274	15	1376.2	1376	757	698	185	69	47	47	549	79	730	31	3	9.0	4.8	3.6	.262	.334	4.56
NL Total	1232	385	70	1778	160	10984.1	10808	5578	4928	1263	563	338	236	4240	424	5419	232	17	8.9	4.4	3.5	.259	.335	4.04
NL Avg Team	154	48	9	222	20	1373.1	1351	697	616	158	70	42	30	530	53	677	29	2	8.9	4.4	3.5	.259	.335	4.04

Team Fielding

Team	G	PO	A	E	TC	DP	PB	Pct
Philadelphia	154	4070	1475	110	5655	117	18	.981
Brooklyn	154	4134	1674	133	5941	156	5	.978
Cincinnati	154	4088	1689	139	5916	169	10	.977
New York	154	4160	1732	142	6034	165	23	.976
Chicago	154	4135	1706	147	5988	147	21	.975
St. Louis	154	4131	1650	146	5927	152	14	.975
Milwaukee	154	4149	1780	152	6081	155	10	.975
Pittsburgh	154	4087	1744	166	5997	175	19	.972
NL Total	1232	32954	13450	1135	47539	1236	120	.976

Team vs. Team Records

	Bro	ChN	Cin	Mil	NYG	Phi	Pit	StL	Won
Bro	—	14	12	15	13	16	14	14	98
ChN	7	—	11	7	12	10	11	14	72
Cin	10	11	—	9	9	11	14	11	75
Mil	7	15	13	—	14	14	11	11	85
NYG	9	10	13	8	—	10	17	13	80
Phi	6	12	11	8	12	—	15	13	77
Pit	8	11	8	11	5	7	—	10	60
StL	8	8	11	11	9	9	12	—	68
Lost	55	81	79	69	74	77	94	86	

Seasons: Standings, Leaders

1955 National League Batting Leaders

Games		At-Bats		Runs		Hits		Doubles		Triples	
6 tied with	154	B. Bruton, Mil	636	D. Snider, Bro	126	T. Kluszewski, Cin	192	H. Aaron, Mil	37	W. Mays, NYG	13
		T. Kluszewski, Cin	612	W. Mays, NYG	123	H. Aaron, Mil	189	J. Logan, Mil	37	D. Long, Pit	13
		G. Bell, Cin	610	W. Post, Cin	116	G. Bell, Cin	188	D. Snider, Bro	34	B. Bruton, Mil	12
		G. Baker, ChN	609	T. Kluszewski, Cin	116	W. Post, Cin	186	W. Post, Cin	33	R. Clemente, Pit	11
		D. Mueller, NYG	605	J. Gilliam, Bro	110	2 tied with	185	R. Ashburn, Phi	32	3 tied with	9

Home Runs		Total Bases		Runs Batted In		Walks		Intentional Walks		Strikeouts	
W. Mays, NYG	51	W. Mays, NYG	382	D. Snider, Bro	136	E. Mathews, Mil	109	T. Kluszewski, Cin	25	W. Post, Cin	102
T. Kluszewski, Cin	47	T. Kluszewski, Cin	358	W. Mays, NYG	127	R. Ashburn, Phi	105	E. Mathews, Mil	20	E. Mathews, Mil	98
E. Banks, ChN	44	E. Banks, ChN	355	D. Ennis, Phi	120	D. Snider, Bro	104	D. Snider, Bro	19	G. Hodges, Bro	91
D. Snider, Bro	42	W. Post, Cin	345	E. Banks, ChN	117	H. Thompson, NYG	84	S. Musial, StL	19	D. Fondy, ChN	87
E. Mathews, Mil	41	D. Snider, Bro	338	T. Kluszewski, Cin	113	3 tied with	80	W. Mays, NYG	13	D. Snider, Bro	87

Hit By Pitch		Sac Hits		Sac Flies		Stolen Bases		Caught Stealing		GDP	
S. Musial, StL	8	G. Baker, ChN	18	G. Hodges, Bro	10	B. Bruton, Mil	25	K. Boyer, StL	17	P. Reese, Bro	22
R. McMillan, Cin	7	G. Freese, Pit	16	B. Virdon, StL	9	W. Mays, NYG	24	J. Gilliam, Bro	15	H. Aaron, Mil	20
C. Furillo, Bro	7	J. Logan, Mil	16	R. Campanella, Bro	9	K. Boyer, StL	22	W. Moon, StL	11	D. Groat, Pit	20
4 tied with	6	P. Reese, Bro	13	P. H. Jones, Phi	9	J. Temple, Cin	19	B. Bruton, Mil	11	R. Repulski, StL	17
		2 tied with	11	D. Ennis, Phi	9	J. Gilliam, Bro	15	R. Ashburn, Phi	10	2 tied with	16

Runs Created		Runs Created/27 Outs		Batting Average		On-Base Percentage		Slugging Percentage		OBP+Slugging	
W. Mays, NYG	146	W. Mays, NYG	9.39	R. Ashburn, Phi	.338	R. Ashburn, Phi	.449	W. Mays, NYG	.659	W. Mays, NYG	1.059
D. Snider, Bro	137	D. Snider, Bro	9.25	W. Mays, NYG	.319	D. Snider, Bro	.418	D. Snider, Bro	.628	D. Snider, Bro	1.046
T. Kluszewski, Cin	127	E. Mathews, Mil	8.91	S. Musial, StL	.319	E. Mathews, Mil	.413	E. Mathews, Mil	.601	E. Mathews, Mil	1.014
E. Mathews, Mil	123	S. Musial, StL	7.96	R. Campanella, Bro	.318	S. Musial, StL	.408	E. Banks, ChN	.596	R. Campanella, Bro	.978
S. Musial, StL	120	R. Campanella, Bro	7.94	H. Aaron, Mil	.314	W. Mays, NYG	.400	T. Kluszewski, Cin	.585	S. Musial, StL	.974

1955 National League Pitching Leaders

Wins		Losses		Winning Percentage		Games		Games Started		Complete Games	
R. Roberts, Phi	23	S. Jones, ChN	20	D. Newcombe, Bro	.800	C. Labine, Bro	60	R. Roberts, Phi	38	R. Roberts, Phi	26
D. Newcombe, Bro	20	H. Haddix, StL	16	C. Labine, Bro	.722	H. Wilhelm, NYG	59	S. Jones, ChN	34	D. Newcombe, Bro	17
J. Nuxhall, Cin	17	J. Antonelli, NYG	16	R. Roberts, Phi	.622	P. LaPalme, StL	56	J. Antonelli, NYG	34	W. Spahn, Mil	16
W. Spahn, Mil	17	J. Hearn, NYG	16	L. Burdette, Mil	.619	M. Grissom, NYG	55	4 tied with	33	3 tied with	14
4 tied with	14	W. Hacker, ChN	15	G. Conley, Mil	.611	H. Freeman, Cin	52				

Shutouts		Saves		Games Finished		Batters Faced		Innings Pitched		Hits Allowed	
J. Nuxhall, Cin	5	J. Meyer, Phi	16	J. Meyer, Phi	36	R. Roberts, Phi	1256	R. Roberts, Phi	305.0	R. Roberts, Phi	292
S. Jones, ChN	4	E. Roebuck, Bro	12	C. Labine, Bro	32	S. Jones, ChN	1070	J. Nuxhall, Cin	257.0	L. Burdette, Mil	253
M. Dickson, Phi	4	H. Freeman, Cin	11	M. Grissom, NYG	32	J. Nuxhall, Cin	1061	W. Spahn, Mil	245.2	W. Spahn, Mil	249
3 tied with	3	C. Labine, Bro	11	E. Roebuck, Bro	27	W. Spahn, Mil	1025	S. Jones, ChN	241.2	J. Nuxhall, Cin	240
		M. Grissom, NYG	8	H. Freeman, Cin	27	L. Burdette, Mil	1001	J. Antonelli, NYG	235.1	J. Hearn, NYG	225

Home Runs Allowed		Walks		Walks/9 Innings		Strikeouts		Strikeouts/9 Innings		Strikeout/Walk Ratio	
R. Roberts, Phi	41	S. Jones, ChN	185	D. Newcombe, Bro	1.5	S. Jones, ChN	198	S. Jones, ChN	7.4	D. Newcombe, Bro	3.76
W. Hacker, ChN	38	B. Buhl, Mil	109	R. Roberts, Phi	1.6	R. Roberts, Phi	160	H. Haddix, StL	6.5	R. Roberts, Phi	3.02
D. Newcombe, Bro	35	J. Antonelli, NYG	82	W. Hacker, ChN	1.8	H. Haddix, StL	150	J. Podres, Bro	6.4	H. Haddix, StL	2.42
C. Erskine, Bro	29	M. Dickson, Phi	82	B. Friend, Pit	2.3	D. Newcombe, Bro	143	G. Conley, Mil	6.1	G. Conley, Mil	2.06
3 tied with	27	2 tied with	78	W. Spahn, Mil	2.4	J. Antonelli, NYG	143	D. Newcombe, Bro	5.5	J. Podres, Bro	2.00

Earned Run Average		Component ERA		Hit Batsmen		Wild Pitches		Opponent Average		Opponent OBP	
B. Friend, Pit	2.83	B. Friend, Pit	2.91	S. Jones, ChN	14	J. Davis, ChN	7	S. Jones, ChN	.206	D. Newcombe, Bro	.279
D. Newcombe, Bro	3.20	B. Rush, ChN	2.95	J. Antonelli, NYG	11	6 tied with	6	B. Buhl, Mil	.227	R. Roberts, Phi	.279
B. Buhl, Mil	3.21	R. Roberts, Phi	3.15	L. Jackson, StL	9			B. Rush, ChN	.234	W. Hacker, ChN	.282
W. Spahn, Mil	3.26	D. Newcombe, Bro	3.22	B. Lawrence, StL	7			J. Antonelli, NYG	.234	B. Friend, Pit	.291
R. Roberts, Phi	3.28	J. Antonelli, NYG	3.36	R. Gomez, NYG	7			M. Dickson, Phi	.238	B. Rush, ChN	.293

1955 National League Miscellaneous

Managers

Brooklyn	Walter Alston	98-55
Chicago	Stan Hack	72-81
Cincinnati	Birdie Tebbetts	75-79
Milwaukee	Charlie Grimm	85-69
New York	Leo Durocher	80-74
Philadelphia	Mayo Smith	77-77
Pittsburgh	Fred Haney	60-94
St. Louis	Eddie Stanky	17-19
	Harry Walker	51-67

Awards

Most Valuable Player	Roy Campanella, c, Bro
STATS Cy Young	Robin Roberts, Phi
Rookie of the Year	Bill Virdon, of, StL
STATS Manager of the Year	Walter Alston, Bro

STATS All-Star Team

C	Roy Campanella, Bro	.318	32	107
1B	Ted Kluszewski, Cin	.314	47	113
2B	Gene Baker, ChN	.268	11	52
3B	Eddie Mathews, Mil	.289	41	101
SS	Ernie Banks, ChN	.295	44	117
OF	Willie Mays, NYG	.319	51	127
OF	Wally Post, Cin	.309	40	109
OF	Duke Snider, Bro	.309	42	136
P	Bob Friend, Pit	14-9	2.83	98 K
P	Don Newcombe, Bro	20-5	3.20	143 K
P	Robin Roberts, Phi	23-14	3.28	160 K
P	Warren Spahn, Mil	17-14	3.26	110 K
RP	Clem Labine, Bro	13-5	3.24	11 Sv

Postseason

World Series	Brooklyn (NL) 4 vs. New York (AL) 3

Outstanding Performances

No-Hitters

Sam Jones, ChN	vs. Pit on May 12

Three-Homer Games

Duke Snider, Bro	on June 1
Gus Bell, Cin	on July 21
Del Ennis, Phi	on July 23
Smoky Burgess, Cin	on July 29
Ernie Banks, ChN	on August 4

1956 American League Standings

Team	W	L	Pct	GB	DIF	W	L	R	OR	HR	OHR	W	L	R	OR	HR	OHR	Run	HR	M/A	May	June	July	Aug	S/O
		Overall					Home Games						Road Games					Park Index			Record by Month				
New York	97	57	.630	—	157	49	28	412	303	88	48	48	29	445	328	102	66	92	81	8-3	21-10	15-12	23-6	16-15	14-11
Cleveland	88	66	.571	9.0	2	46	31	340	287	71	61	42	35	372	294	82	55	94	96	6-5	14-12	17-12	20-10	16-14	15-13
Chicago	85	69	.552	12.0	10	46	31	403	320	69	47	39	38	373	314	59	71	105	89	5-1	13-14	21-9	9-21	22-11	15-13
Boston	84	70	.545	13.0	3	43	34	408	388	68	64	41	36	372	363	71	66	108	96	4-5	16-14	15-12	18-13	15-14	16-12
Detroit	82	72	.532	15.0	0	37	40	359	357	75	77	45	32	430	342	75	63	93	110	4-6	14-15	12-15	15-17	17-12	20-7
Baltimore	69	85	.448	28.0	0	41	36	275	315	35	39	28	49	296	390	56	60	86	64	4-9	15-12	12-17	14-15	12-16	12-16
Washington	59	95	.383	38.0	0	32	45	354	481	63	95	27	50	298	443	49	76	113	126	7-6	9-19	13-18	10-17	13-14	7-21
Kansas City	52	102	.338	45.0	3	22	55	305	449	62	113	30	47	314	382	50	74	108	141	3-6	12-18	10-20	9-19	7-22	11-17

Clinch Date—New York 9/18.

Team Batting

Team	G	AB	R	OR	H	2B	3B	HR	TB	RBI	TBB	IBB	SO	HBP	SH	SF	SB	CS	SB%	GDP	Avg	OBP	Slg
New York	154	5312	857	631	1433	193	55	190	2306	788	615	40	755	30	82	36	51	37	.58	102	.270	.353	.434
Detroit	155	5364	789	699	1494	209	50	150	2253	745	644	30	618	28	58	50	43	26	.62	133	.279	.364	.420
Boston	155	5349	780	751	1473	261	45	139	2241	752	727	41	687	26	68	46	28	19	.60	153	.275	.370	.419
Chicago	154	5286	776	634	1412	218	43	128	2100	726	619	30	660	75	86	56	70	33	.68	130	.267	.358	.397
Cleveland	155	5148	712	581	1256	199	23	153	1960	677	681	35	764	40	81	38	40	32	.56	110	.244	.341	.381
Washington	155	5202	652	924	1302	198	62	112	1960	612	690	42	877	41	75	35	37	34	.52	142	.250	.347	.377
Kansas City	154	5256	619	831	1325	204	41	112	1947	584	480	31	727	20	67	37	40	30	.57	127	.252	.361	.370
Baltimore	154	5090	571	705	1242	198	34	91	1781	515	563	30	725	22	84	31	39	42	.48	133	.244	.326	.350
AL Total	1236	42007	5756	5756	10937	1680	353	1075	16548	5399	5019	279	5813	282	601	329	348	253	.58	1030	.260	.341	.394
AL Avg Team	155	5251	720	720	1367	210	44	134	2069	675	627	35	727	35	75	41	44	32	.58	129	.260	.341	.394

Team Pitching

Team	G	CG	ShO	Rel	Sv	IP	H	R	ER	HR	SH	SF	HB	TBB	IBB	SO	WP	Bk	H/9	SO/9	BB/9	OAvg	OOBP	ERA
Cleveland	155	67	17	182	24	1384.0	1233	581	511	116	75	40	30	564	34	845	31	3	8.0	5.5	3.7	.238	.314	3.32
New York	154	50	10	181	35	1382.0	1285	631	557	114	48	37	38	652	20	732	22	2	8.4	4.8	4.2	.249	.335	3.63
Chicago	154	65	11	196	13	1389.0	1351	634	575	118	72	30	26	524	43	722	33	5	8.8	4.7	3.4	.255	.324	3.73
Detroit	155	62	10	187	15	1379.0	1389	699	622	140	88	46	44	655	49	788	29	5	9.1	5.1	4.3	.264	.348	4.06
Boston	155	50	8	178	20	1398.0	1354	751	647	130	67	38	44	668	34	712	31	2	8.7	4.6	4.3	.254	.340	4.17
Baltimore	154	38	10	231	24	1360.2	1362	705	635	99	88	48	24	547	29	715	35	4	9.0	4.7	3.6	.264	.334	4.20
Kansas City	154	30	3	251	18	1370.1	1424	831	740	187	77	38	42	679	44	636	38	3	9.4	4.2	4.5	.271	.357	4.86
Washington	155	36	1	244	18	1368.2	1539	924	811	171	86	52	33	730	26	663	39	6	10.1	4.4	4.8	.287	.373	5.33
AL Total	1236	398	70	1650	167	11031.2	10937	5756	5098	1075	601	329	281	5019	279	5813	258	30	8.9	4.7	4.1	.260	.348	4.16
AL Avg Team	155	50	9	206	21	1378.2	1367	720	637	134	75	41	35	627	35	727	32	4	8.9	4.7	4.1	.260	.348	4.16

Team Fielding

Team	G	PO	A	E	TC	DP	PB	Pct
Chicago	154	4168	1630	122	5920	160	9	.979
Cleveland	155	4149	1527	129	5805	130	10	.978
New York	154	4145	1711	136	5992	214	9	.977
Baltimore	154	4083	1647	137	5867	142	5	.977
Detroit	155	4130	1547	140	5817	151	11	.976
Kansas City	154	4111	1785	166	6062	187	19	.973
Boston	155	4192	1764	169	6125	168	10	.972
Washington	155	4105	1770	171	6046	173	11	.972
AL Total	1236	33083	13381	1170	47634	1325	84	.975

Team vs. Team Records

	Bal	Bos	ChA	Cle	Det	KCA	NYA	Was	Won
Bal	—	6	9	5	13	15	9	12	69
Bos	16	—	14	13	12	12	8	9	84
ChA	13	8	—	15	13	14	9	13	85
Cle	17	9	7	—	11	17	10	17	88
Det	9	10	9	11	—	16	12	15	82
KCA	7	10	8	5	6	—	4	12	52
NYA	13	14	13	12	10	18	—	17	97
Was	10	13	9	5	7	10	5	—	59
Lost	85	70	69	66	72	102	57	95	

1956 American League Batting Leaders

Games		At-Bats		Runs		Hits		Doubles		Triples	
J. Piersall, Bos	155	N. Fox, ChA	649	M. Mantle, NYA	132	H. Kuenn, Det	196	J. Piersall, Bos	40	M. Minoso, ChA	11
N. Fox, ChA	154	A. Kaline, Det	617	N. Fox, ChA	109	A. Kaline, Det	194	A. Kaline, Det	32	H. Simpson, KCA	11
A. Kaline, Det	153	J. Piersall, Bos	601	M. Minoso, ChA	106	N. Fox, ChA	192	H. Kuenn, Det	32	J. Lemon, Was	11
3 tied with	152	H. Kuenn, Det	591	4 tied with	96	M. Mantle, NYA	188	4 tied with	29	J. Jensen, Bos	11
		2 tied with	578			J. Jensen, Bos	182			2 tied with	10

Home Runs		Total Bases		Runs Batted In		Walks		Intentional Walks		Strikeouts	
M. Mantle, NYA	52	M. Mantle, NYA	376	M. Mantle, NYA	130	E. Yost, Was	151	T. Williams, Bos	11	J. Lemon, Was	138
V. Wertz, Cle	32	A. Kaline, Det	327	A. Kaline, Det	128	M. Mantle, NYA	112	R. Sievers, Was	10	L. Doby, Cle	105
Y. Berra, NYA	30	J. Jensen, Bos	287	V. Wertz, Cle	106	L. Doby, ChA	102	V. Wertz, Cle	10	M. Mantle, NYA	99
R. Sievers, Was	29	M. Minoso, ChA	286	H. Simpson, KCA	105	T. Williams, Bos	102	L. Berberet, Was	9	R. Sievers, Was	88
C. Maxwell, Det	28	2 tied with	278	Y. Berra, NYA	105	R. Sievers, Was	100	E. Yost, Was	9	V. Wertz, Cle	87

Hit By Pitch		Sac Hits		Sac Flies		Stolen Bases		Caught Stealing		GDP	
M. Minoso, ChA	23	L. Aparicio, ChA	14	J. Piersall, Bos	12	L. Aparicio, ChA	21	J. Rivera, ChA	9	J. Jensen, Bos	23
S. Lollar, ChA	16	G. Kell, 2tm	14	H. Kuenn, Det	8	J. Rivera, ChA	20	G. McDougald, NYA	8	G. Triandos, Bal	21
N. Fox, ChA	10	N. Fox, ChA	13	C. Maxwell, Det	8	B. Avila, Cle	17	J. Piersall, Bos	7	4 tied with	19
C. Courtney, Was	9	3 tied with	9	4 tied with	7	M. Minoso, ChA	12	5 tied with	6		
F. Hatfield, 2tm	9					2 tied with	11				

Runs Created		Runs Created/27 Outs		Batting Average		On-Base Percentage		Slugging Percentage		OBP+Slugging	
M. Mantle, NYA	174	M. Mantle, NYA	13.20	M. Mantle, NYA	.353	T. Williams, Bos	.479	M. Mantle, NYA	.705	M. Mantle, NYA	1.169
M. Minoso, ChA	126	T. Williams, Bos	10.28	T. Williams, Bos	.345	M. Mantle, NYA	.464	T. Williams, Bos	.605	T. Williams, Bos	1.084
A. Kaline, Det	119	M. Minoso, ChA	8.48	H. Kuenn, Det	.332	B. Nieman, 2tm	.436	C. Maxwell, Det	.534	M. Minoso, ChA	.950
Y. Berra, NYA	109	C. Maxwell, Det	8.22	C. Maxwell, Det	.326	M. Minoso, ChA	.425	Y. Berra, NYA	.534	C. Maxwell, Det	.948
C. Maxwell, Det	108	B. Nieman, 2tm	7.69	B. Nieman, 2tm	.320	C. Maxwell, Det	.414	A. Kaline, Det	.530	B. Nieman, 2tm	.931

1956 American League Pitching Leaders

Wins		Losses		Winning Percentage		Games		Games Started		Complete Games	
F. Lary, Det	21	A. Ditmar, KCA	22	W. Ford, NYA	.760	G. Zuverink, Bal	62	F. Lary, Det	38	B. Pierce, ChA	21
5 tied with	20	C. Pascual, Was	18	H. Score, Cle	.690	J. Crimian, KCA	54	B. Lemon, Cle	35	B. Lemon, Cle	21
		C. Stobbs, Was	15	B. Pierce, ChA	.690	T. Gorman, KCA	52	E. Wynn, Cle	35	F. Lary, Det	20
		3 tied with	14	E. Wynn, Cle	.690	D. Mossi, Cle	48	A. Ditmar, KCA	34	3 tied with	18
				D. Larsen, NYA	.688	I. Delock, Bos	48	B. Hoeft, Det	34		

Shutouts		Saves		Games Finished		Batters Faced		Innings Pitched		Hits Allowed	
H. Score, Cle	5	G. Zuverink, Bal	16	G. Zuverink, Bal	40	F. Lary, Det	1269	F. Lary, Det	294.0	F. Lary, Det	289
5 tied with	4	D. Mossi, Cle	11	I. Delock, Bos	28	B. Pierce, ChA	1166	E. Wynn, Cle	277.2	B. Hoeft, Det	276
		T. Morgan, NYA	11	A. Aber, Det	28	E. Wynn, Cle	1144	B. Pierce, ChA	276.1	C. Stobbs, Was	264
		I. Delock, Bos	9	B. Shantz, KCA	26	A. Ditmar, KCA	1101	P. Foytack, Det	256.0	B. Pierce, ChA	261
		B. Shantz, KCA	9	D. Mossi, Cle	24	P. Foytack, Det	1098	B. Lemon, Cle	255.1	A. Ditmar, KCA	254

Home Runs Allowed		Walks		Walks/9 Innings		Strikeouts		Strikeouts/9 Innings		Strikeout/Walk Ratio	
C. Pascual, Was	33	P. Foytack, Det	142	C. Stobbs, Was	2.0	H. Score, Cle	263	H. Score, Cle	9.5	T. Sturdivant, NYA	2.12
A. Ditmar, KCA	30	H. Score, Cle	129	D. Donovan, ChA	2.3	B. Pierce, ChA	192	C. Pascual, Was	7.7	H. Score, Cle	2.04
C. Stobbs, Was	29	F. Lary, Det	116	J. Kucks, NYA	2.9	P. Foytack, Det	184	P. Foytack, Det	6.5	D. Donovan, ChA	2.03
S. Gromek, Det	25	T. Brewer, Bos	112	E. Wynn, Cle	2.9	B. Hoeft, Det	172	B. Pierce, ChA	6.3	C. Johnson, 2tm	1.97
2 tied with	24	B. Wiesler, Was	112	T. Sturdivant, NYA	3.0	F. Lary, Det	165	T. Sturdivant, NYA	6.3	B. Pierce, ChA	1.92

Earned Run Average		Component ERA		Hit Batsmen		Wild Pitches		Opponent Average		Opponent OBP	
W. Ford, NYA	2.47	H. Score, Cle	2.52	F. Lary, Det	12	H. Score, Cle	11	H. Score, Cle	.186	D. Donovan, ChA	.290
H. Score, Cle	2.53	E. Wynn, Cle	2.76	J. Kucks, NYA	10	P. Foytack, Det	8	D. Larsen, NYA	.204	H. Score, Cle	.290
E. Wynn, Cle	2.72	W. Ford, NYA	2.88	S. Gromek, Det	9	4 tied with	7	T. Brewer, Bos	.220	E. Wynn, Cle	.291
B. Lemon, Cle	3.03	T. Sturdivant, NYA	2.99	F. Sullivan, Bos	8			J. Harshman, ChA	.221	T. Sturdivant, NYA	.291
J. Harshman, ChA	3.10	J. Harshman, ChA	2.99	W. Nixon, Bos	8			T. Sturdivant, NYA	.224	W. Ford, NYA	.301

1956 American League Miscellaneous

Managers				Awards	
Baltimore	Paul Richards	69-85		Most Valuable Player	Mickey Mantle, of, NYA
Boston	Pinky Higgins	84-70		STATS Cy Young	Herb Score, Cle
Chicago	Marty Marion	85-69		Rookie of the Year	Luis Aparicio, ss, ChA
Cleveland	Al Lopez	88-66		STATS Manager of the Year	Casey Stengel, NYA
Detroit	Bucky Harris	82-72			
Kansas City	Lou Boudreau	52-102			
New York	Casey Stengel	97-57			
Washington	Chuck Dressen	59-95			

Postseason

World Series	New York (AL) 4 vs. Brooklyn (NL) 3

Outstanding Performances

Triple Crown
Mickey Mantle, NYA .353-52-130
No-Hitters
Mel Parnell, Bos   vs. ChA on July 14
Three-Homer Games
Jim Lemon, Was   on August 31

STATS All-Star Team

C	Yogi Berra, NYA	.298	30	105
1B	Bill Skowron, NYA	.308	23	90
2B	Nellie Fox, ChA	.296	4	52
3B	Ray Boone, Det	.308	25	81
SS	Harvey Kuenn, Det	.332	12	88
OF	Mickey Mantle, NYA	.353	52	130
OF	Minnie Minoso, ChA	.316	21	88
OF	Ted Williams, Bos	.345	24	82
P	Whitey Ford, NYA	19-6	2.47	141 K
P	Frank Lary, Det	21-13	3.15	165 K
P	Herb Score, Cle	20-9	2.53	263 K
P	Early Wynn, Cle	20-9	2.72	158 K
RP	George Zuverink, Bal	7-6	4.16	16 Sv

1956 National League Standings

Team	W	L	Pct	GB	DIF	W	L	R	OR	HR	OHR	W	L	R	OR	HR	OHR	Run	HR	M/A	May	June	July	Aug	S/O
	Overall					Home Games						Road Games						Park Index		Record by Month					
Brooklyn	93	61	.604	—	18	**52**	**25**	369	300	102	89	41	36	351	**301**	77	82	103	120	7-4	12-12	18-12	18-13	20-10	18-10
Milwaukee	92	62	.597	1.0	126	47	29	344	**265**	77	53	**45**	**33**	365	304	**100**	80	93	74	4-3	15-7	17-15	21-10	21-14	14-13
Cincinnati	91	63	.591	2.0	22	51	26	**426**	346	**128**	75	40	37	349	312	93	66	117	128	5-5	16-11	16-12	21-12	17-13	16-10
St. Louis	76	78	.494	17.0	4	43	34	358	328	58	73	33	44	320	370	66	82	99	89	6-3	17-13	13-15	11-16	16-18	13-13
Philadelphia	71	83	.461	22.0	2	40	37	337	335	61	74	31	46	331	403	60	98	92	85	5-6	8-16	15-16	17-14	14-13	12-18
New York	67	87	.435	26.0	2	37	40	269	306	94	86	30	47	271	344	51	**58**	93	165	5-6	10-15	11-17	8-20	16-16	17-13
Pittsburgh	66	88	.429	27.0	6	35	43	301	328	49	**45**	31	45	287	325	61	97	100	58	5-6	16-10	11-17	11-20	12-20	11-15
Chicago	60	94	.390	33.0	0	39	38	335	328	78	77	21	56	262	380	64	84	103	105	3-7	7-17	15-12	16-18	10-22	9-18

Clinch Date—Brooklyn 9/30.

Team Batting

Team	G	AB	R	OR	H	2B	3B	HR	TB	RBI	TBB	IBB	SO	HBP	SH	SF	SB	CS	SB%	GDP	Avg	OBP	Slg
Cincinnati	155	5291	**775**	658	1406	201	32	221	2334	734	528	69	760	**51**	90	43	45	22	.67	112	.266	.343	**.441**
Brooklyn	154	5098	720	601	1315	212	36	179	2136	680	**649**	**91**	738	17	86	34	65	37	.64	**146**	.258	.348	.419
Milwaukee	155	5207	709	**569**	1350	212	54	177	2201	667	486	76	714	20	**142**	31	29	20	.59	128	.259	.330	.423
St. Louis	156	**5378**	678	698	**1443**	234	49	124	2147	628	503	53	622	33	41	31	41	35	.54	128	**.268**	.338	.399
Philadelphia	154	5204	668	738	1313	207	49	121	1981	616	585	62	673	27	52	42	45	23	.66	132	.252	.336	.381
Chicago	157	5260	597	708	1281	202	50	142	2009	563	446	60	**776**	13	87	**46**	55	**38**	.59	99	.244	.310	.382
Pittsburgh	157	5221	588	653	1340	199	**57**	110	1983	546	383	43	752	18	95	40	24	33	.42	124	.257	.315	.380
New York	154	5190	540	650	1268	192	45	145	1985	497	402	50	659	21	59	37	**67**	34	.66	114	.244	.306	.382
NL Total	1242	41849	5275	5275	10716	1659	372	1219	16776	4931	3982	504	5694	200	652	315	371	242	.61	954	.256	.321	.401
NL Avg Team	155	5231	659	659	1340	207	47	152	2097	616	498	63	712	25	82	39	46	30	.61	119	.256	.321	.401

Team Pitching

Team	G	CG	ShO	Rel	Sv	IP	H	R	ER	HR	SH	SF	HB	TBB	IBB	SO	WP	Bk	H/9	SO/9	BB/9	OAvg	OOBP	ERA
Milwaukee	155	**64**	**12**	177	27	**1393.1**	1295	**569**	482	133	61	31	21	467	65	639	24	2	8.4	4.1	3.0	.247	.309	3.11
Brooklyn	154	46	**12**	201	30	1368.2	**1251**	**569**	543	131	68	31	21	441	41	**772**	42	**3**	**8.2**	**5.1**	3.0	**.244**	**.305**	3.57
Pittsburgh	157	37	8	**266**	24	1376.1	1406	653	572	142	90	41	20	469	72	662	37	1	9.2	4.3	3.1	.267	.327	3.74
New York	154	31	9	263	28	1378.0	1287	650	578	144	106	41	30	551	63	765	24	1	8.4	5.0	3.6	.250	.324	3.78
Cincinnati	155	47	4	231	29	1389.0	1406	658	594	141	77	47	28	458	48	653	18	2	9.1	4.2	3.0	.265	.325	3.85
Chicago	157	37	6	220	17	1392.0	1325	708	612	161	77	44	38	**613**	79	744	24	1	8.6	4.8	4.0	.252	.332	3.96
St. Louis	156	41	12	234	**30**	1388.2	1339	698	612	155	90	38	18	546	64	709	**45**	1	8.7	4.6	3.5	.257	.327	3.97
Philadelphia	154	57	4	212	15	1377.1	1407	738	643	172	83	42	29	**437**	72	750	20	2	9.2	4.9	**2.9**	.266	.323	4.20
NL Total	1242	360	67	1804	200	11063.1	10716	5275	4636	1219	652	315	200	3982	504	5694	234	13	8.7	4.6	3.2	.256	.328	3.77
NL Avg Team	155	45	8	226	25	1382.1	1340	659	580	152	82	39	25	498	63	712	29	2	8.7	4.6	3.2	.256	.328	3.77

Team Fielding

Team	G	PO	A	E	TC	DP	PB	Pct
Brooklyn	154	4106	1716	**111**	5933	149	9	.981
Cincinnati	155	4167	1722	113	6002	147	8	.981
Milwaukee	155	**4180**	1738	130	6048	159	5	.979
St. Louis	156	4166	**1758**	134	**6058**	**172**	8	.978
New York	154	4134	1660	144	5938	143	**24**	.976
Chicago	157	4175	1607	144	5926	141	17	.976
Philadelphia	154	4132	1481	144	5757	140	3	.975
Pittsburgh	157	4129	1663	162	5954	140	17	.973
NL Total	1242	33189	13345	1082	47616	1191	91	.977

Team vs. Team Records

	Bro	ChN	Cin	Mil	NYG	Phi	Pit	StL	Won
Bro	—	16	11	10	14	13	13	16	93
ChN	6	—	6	9	7	13	10	9	60
Cin	11	16	—	9	14	11	17	13	91
Mil	12	13	13	—	17	10	14	13	92
NYG	8	15	8	5	—	11	13	7	67
Phi	9	9	11	12	11	—	7	12	71
Pit	9	12	5	8	9	15	—	8	66
StL	6	13	9	9	15	10	14	—	76
Lost	61	94	63	62	87	83	88	78	

1956 National League Batting Leaders

Games		At-Bats		Runs		Hits		Doubles		Triples	
B. Virdon, 2tm	157	J. Temple, Cin	632	F. Robinson, Cin	122	H. Aaron, Mil	200	H. Aaron, Mil	34	B. Bruton, Mil	15
F. Thomas, Pit	157	D. Ennis, Phi	630	D. Snider, Bro	112	R. Ashburn, Phi	190	S. Lopata, Phi	33	H. Aaron, Mil	14
S. Musial, StL	156	R. Ashburn, Phi	628	H. Aaron, Mil	106	B. Virdon, 2tm	185	D. Snider, Bro	33	W. Moon, StL	11
J. Temple, Cin	154	A. Dark, 2tm	619	E. Mathews, Mil	103	S. Musial, StL	184	S. Musial, StL	33	L. Walls, Pit	11
R. Ashburn, Phi	154	H. Aaron, Mil	609	J. Gilliam, Bro	102	K. Boyer, StL	182	G. Bell, Cin	31	B. Virdon, 2tm	10

Home Runs		Total Bases		Runs Batted In		Walks		Intentional Walks		Strikeouts	
D. Snider, Bro	43	H. Aaron, Mil	340	S. Musial, StL	109	D. Snider, Bro	99	D. Snider, Bro	26	W. Post, Cin	124
F. Robinson, Cin	38	D. Snider, Bro	324	J. Adcock, Mil	103	J. Gilliam, Bro	95	T. Kluszewski, Cin	22	D. Snider, Bro	101
J. Adcock, Mil	38	W. Mays, NYG	322	T. Kluszewski, Cin	102	P. H. Jones, Phi	92	W. Mays, NYG	20	F. Robinson, Cin	95
E. Mathews, Mil	37	F. Robinson, Cin	319	D. Snider, Bro	101	E. Mathews, Mil	91	E. Banks, ChN	18	S. Lopata, Phi	93
2 tied with	36	S. Musial, StL	310	K. Boyer, StL	98	W. Moon, StL	80	E. Mathews, Mil	17	G. Hodges, Bro	91

Hit By Pitch		Sac Hits		Sac Flies		Stolen Bases		Caught Stealing		GDP	
F. Robinson, Cin	20	J. Logan, Mil	31	D. Long, Pit	11	W. Mays, NYG	40	W. Mays, NYG	10	C. Furillo, Bro	27
S. Hemus, 2tm	8	B. Bruton, Mil	18	D. Fondy, ChN	10	J. Gilliam, Bro	21	W. Moon, StL	9	F. Thomas, Pit	22
R. Repulski, StL	7	D. Groat, Pit	17	S. Lopata, Phi	9	B. White, NYG	15	E. Banks, ChN	9	H. Aaron, Mil	21
R. Jablonski, Cin	7	J. Temple, Cin	17	B. Bruton, Mil	8	J. Temple, Cin	14	J. Gilliam, Bro	9	R. Campanella, Bro	20
B. Del Greco, 2tm	6	D. O'Connell, Mil	16	A. Dark, 2tm	8	P. Reese, Bro	13	2 tied with	8	S. Musial, StL	19

Runs Created		Runs Created/27 Outs		Batting Average		On-Base Percentage		Slugging Percentage		OBP+Slugging	
D. Snider, Bro	119	D. Snider, Bro	7.72	H. Aaron, Mil	.328	D. Snider, Bro	.399	D. Snider, Bro	.598	D. Snider, Bro	.997
F. Robinson, Cin	114	E. Mathews, Mil	7.08	B. Virdon, 2tm	.319	J. Gilliam, Bro	.399	J. Adcock, Mil	.597	F. Robinson, Cin	.936
H. Aaron, Mil	112	F. Robinson, Cin	7.01	R. Clemente, Pit	.311	W. Moon, StL	.390	H. Aaron, Mil	.558	J. Adcock, Mil	.934
E. Mathews, Mil	109	H. Aaron, Mil	6.73	S. Musial, StL	.310	S. Musial, StL	.386	F. Robinson, Cin	.558	W. Mays, NYG	.926
S. Musial, StL	109	T. Kluszewski, Cin	6.68	K. Boyer, StL	.306	R. Ashburn, Phi	.384	W. Mays, NYG	.557	H. Aaron, Mil	.923

1956 National League Pitching Leaders

Wins		Losses		Winning Percentage		Games		Games Started		Complete Games	
D. Newcombe, Bro	27	R. Kline, Pit	18	D. Newcombe, Bro	.794	R. Face, Pit	68	B. Friend, Pit	42	R. Roberts, Phi	22
J. Antonelli, NYG	20	R. Roberts, Phi	18	H. Freeman, Cin	.737	H. Freeman, Cin	64	R. Kline, Pit	39	W. Spahn, Mil	20
W. Spahn, Mil	20	R. Gomez, NYG	17	S. Maglie, Bro	.722	H. Wilhelm, NYG	64	R. Roberts, Phi	37	B. Friend, Pit	19
3 tied with	19	B. Friend, Pit	17	B. Buhl, Mil	.692	C. Labine, Bro	62	D. Newcombe, Bro	36	D. Newcombe, Bro	18
		V. Law, Pit	16	2 tied with	.655	T. Lown, ChN	61	J. Antonelli, NYG	36	L. Burdette, Mil	16

Shutouts		Saves		Games Finished		Batters Faced		Innings Pitched		Hits Allowed	
L. Burdette, Mil	6	C. Labine, Bro	19	H. Freeman, Cin	47	B. Friend, Pit	1315	B. Friend, Pit	314.1	R. Roberts, Phi	328
D. Newcombe, Bro	5	H. Freeman, Cin	18	T. Lown, ChN	47	R. Roberts, Phi	1228	R. Roberts, Phi	297.1	B. Friend, Pit	310
J. Antonelli, NYG	5	T. Lown, ChN	13	C. Labine, Bro	47	W. Spahn, Mil	1113	W. Spahn, Mil	281.1	R. Kline, Pit	263
B. Friend, Pit	4	D. Bessent, Bro	9	H. Wilhelm, NYG	38	R. Kline, Pit	1102	D. Newcombe, Bro	268.0	W. Spahn, Mil	249
5 tied with	3	L. Jackson, StL	9	R. Face, Pit	34	J. Antonelli, NYG	1061	R. Kline, Pit	264.0	L. Burdette, Mil	234

Home Runs Allowed		Walks		Walks/9 Innings		Strikeouts		Strikeouts/9 Innings		Strikeout/Walk Ratio	
R. Roberts, Phi	46	S. Jones, ChN	115	R. Roberts, Phi	1.2	S. Jones, ChN	176	S. Jones, ChN	8.4	R. Roberts, Phi	3.92
D. Newcombe, Bro	33	B. Buhl, Mil	105	D. Newcombe, Bro	1.5	H. Haddix, 2tm	170	H. Haddix, 2tm	6.6	D. Newcombe, Bro	3.02
B. Rush, ChN	30	V. B. Mizell, StL	92	W. Spahn, Mil	1.7	B. Friend, Pit	166	V. B. Mizell, StL	6.6	H. Haddix, 2tm	2.62
W. Hacker, ChN	28	R. Craig, Bro	87	A. Fowler, Cin	1.8	R. Roberts, Phi	157	J. Nuxhall, Cin	5.4	W. Spahn, Mil	2.46
T. Poholsky, StL	27	J. Nuxhall, Cin	87	L. Burdette, Mil	1.8	V. B. Mizell, StL	153	A. Worthington, NYG	5.2	A. Fowler, Cin	2.46

Earned Run Average		Component ERA		Hit Batsmen		Wild Pitches		Opponent Average		Opponent OBP	
L. Burdette, Mil	2.70	D. Newcombe, Bro	2.42	J. Klippstein, Cin	10	E. Roebuck, Bro	10	D. Newcombe, Bro	.221	D. Newcombe, Bro	.257
W. Spahn, Mil	2.78	W. Spahn, Mil	2.61	R. Gomez, NYG	9	R. Kline, Pit	10	S. Jones, ChN	.221	W. Spahn, Mil	.275
J. Antonelli, NYG	2.86	S. Maglie, Bro	2.78	S. Jones, ChN	8	L. McDaniel, StL	8	V. B. Mizell, StL	.222	B. Rush, ChN	.280
S. Maglie, Bro	2.87	L. Burdette, Mil	2.79	T. Phillips, Mil	7	V. Law, Pit	8	S. Maglie, Bro	.222	S. Maglie, Bro	.281
D. Newcombe, Bro	3.06	J. Antonelli, NYG	2.81	V. B. Mizell, StL	7	4 tied with	7	R. Craig, Bro	.231	L. Burdette, Mil	.281

1956 National League Miscellaneous

Managers

Brooklyn	Walter Alston	93-61
Chicago	Stan Hack	60-94
Cincinnati	Birdie Tebbetts	91-63
Milwaukee	Charlie Grimm	24-22
	Fred Haney	68-40
New York	Bill Rigney	67-87
Philadelphia	Mayo Smith	71-83
Pittsburgh	Bobby Bragan	66-88
St. Louis	Fred Hutchinson	76-78

Awards

Most Valuable Player	Don Newcombe, p, Bro
Cy Young	Don Newcombe, Bro
Rookie of the Year	Frank Robinson, of, Cin
STATS Manager of the Year	Birdie Tebbetts, Cin

STATS All-Star Team

C	Stan Lopata, Phi	.267	32	95
1B	Stan Musial, StL	.310	27	109
2B	Jim Gilliam, Bro	.300	6	43
3B	Eddie Mathews, Mil	.272	37	95
SS	Ernie Banks, ChN	.297	28	85
OF	Hank Aaron, Mil	.328	26	92
OF	Frank Robinson, Cin	.290	38	83
OF	Duke Snider, Bro	.292	43	101
P	Johnny Antonelli, NYG	20-13	2.86	145 K
P	Lew Burdette, Mil	19-10	2.70	110 K
P	Don Newcombe, Bro	27-7	3.06	139 K
P	Warren Spahn, Mil	20-11	2.78	128 K
RP	Clem Labine, Bro	10-6	3.35	19 Sv

Postseason

World Series	Brooklyn (NL) 3 vs. New York (AL) 4

Outstanding Performances

No-Hitters

Carl Erskine, Bro	vs. NYG on May 12
Sal Maglie, Bro	vs. Phi on September 25

Three-Homer Games

Gus Bell, Cin	on May 29
Ed Bailey, Cin	on June 24
Ted Kluszewski, Cin	on July 1
Bob Thurman, Cin	on August 18

1957 American League Standings

Team	W	L	Pct	GB	DIF	W	L	R	OR	HR	OHR	W	L	R	OR	HR	OHR	Run	HR	M/A	May	June	July	Aug	S/O
		Overall						**Home Games**						**Road Games**				**Park Index**				**Record by Month**			
New York	98	56	.636	—	108	48	29	316	241	60	51	50	27	407	293	85	59	80	77	6-5	17-11	21-9	21-9	17-13	16-9
Chicago	90	64	.584	8.0	68	45	32	347	263	40	59	45	32	360	303	66	65	92	76	8-2	18-9	17-15	18-11	15-15	14-12
Boston	82	72	.532	16.0	2	44	33	408	360	72	67	38	39	313	308	81	49	124	107	8-4	13-17	17-12	16-12	14-15	14-12
Detroit	78	76	.506	20.0	0	45	44	351	304	71	86	33	44	263	310	45	61	114	148	5-8	16-12	14-15	14-14	15-16	14-11
Baltimore	76	76	.500	21.0	1	42	33	283	248	36	30	34	43	314	340	51	65	83	58	6-8	9-16	19-11	12-18	15-13	15-10
Cleveland	76	77	.497	21.5	0	40	37	348	384	71	74	36	40	334	338	69	56	108	114	6-6	16-11	15-15	13-17	13-18	13-10
Kansas City	59	94	.386	38.5	2	37	40	294	344	91	77	22	54	269	366	75	76	99	110	6-7	12-16	7-21	11-19	14-16	9-15
Washington	55	99	.357	43.0	0	28	49	304	415	60	79	27	50	299	393	51	70	104	115	5-10	10-19	9-21	11-16	15-12	5-21

Clinch Date—New York 9/23.

Team Batting

Team	G	AB	R	OR	H	2B	3B	HR	TB	RBI	TBB	IBB	SO	HBP	SH	SF	SB	CS	SB%	GDP	Avg	OBP	Slg
New York	154	5271	**723**	**534**	1412	200	54	145	2155	680	562	**66**	709	24	93	43	49	38	.56	128	.268	.346	**.409**
Boston	154	5267	721	668	1380	**231**	32	153	2134	**695**	624	55	739	25	21	38	29	21	.58	**154**	.262	.347	.405
Chicago	155	5265	707	566	1369	208	41	106	1977	670	**633**	33	745	**68**	75	42	**109**	51	**.68**	121	.260	**.352**	.375
Cleveland	153	5171	682	722	1304	199	26	140	1975	649	591	34	**786**	26	78	53	40	47	.46	109	.252	.338	.382
Detroit	154	**5348**	614	614	1376	224	37	116	2022	574	504	54	643	27	96	30	36	47	.43	127	.257	.328	.378
Washington	154	5231	603	808	1274	215	38	153	1898	572	527	41	733	46	50	41	13	38	.25	139	.244	.323	.363
Baltimore	154	5264	597	588	1326	191	39	87	1856	557	504	40	699	34	**110**	**54**	57	35	.62	126	.252	.328	.353
Kansas City	154	5170	563	710	1262	195	40	**166**	2035	536	364	30	760	24	62	36	35	27	.56	135	.244	.301	.394
AL Total	1232	41987	5210	5210	10703	1663	307	1024	16052	4933	4309	353	5814	274	605	337	368	304	.55	1039	.255	.326	.382
AL Avg Team	154	5248	651	651	1338	208	38	128	2007	617	539	44	727	34	76	42	46	38	.55	130	.255	.326	.382

Team Pitching

Team	G	CG	ShO	Rel	Sv	IP	H	R	ER	HR	SH	SF	HB	TBB	IBB	SO	WP	Bk	H/9	SO/9	BB/9	OAvg	OOBP	ERA
New York	154	41	13	179	**42**	1395.1	**1198**	534	465	110	**51**	35	39	580	19	**810**	26	4	7.7	5.2	3.7	**.234**	.315	3.00
Chicago	155	**59**	**16**	200	27	1401.2	1305	566	521	124	66	**31**	25	**470**	51	665	31	4	8.4	4.3	**3.0**	.248	.311	3.35
Baltimore	154	44	13	195	25	1408.0	1272	588	542	**95**	83	34	27	493	38	767	29	5	8.1	4.9	3.2	.243	**.310**	3.46
Detroit	154	52	9	209	21	**1417.2**	1330	614	560	147	108	46	**43**	505	56	756	19	3	8.4	4.8	3.2	.250	.318	3.56
Boston	154	55	9	171	23	1376.2	1391	668	593	116	66	40	36	498	39	692	25	2	9.1	4.5	3.3	.264	.329	3.88
Cleveland	153	46	7	204	23	1380.2	1381	722	623	130	74	41	**43**	618	**59**	807	39	3	9.0	**5.3**	4.0	.261	.340	4.06
Kansas City	154	26	6	**250**	19	1369.2	1344	710	637	153	69	56	25	565	47	626	**45**	**7**	8.8	4.1	3.7	.260	.333	4.19
Washington	154	31	5	234	16	1377.0	1482	808	742	149	88	54	36	580	44	691	29	3	9.7	4.5	3.8	.278	.349	4.85
AL Total	1232	354	78	1642	196	11126.2	10703	5210	4683	1024	605	337	274	4309	353	5814	243	31	8.7	4.7	3.5	.255	.333	3.79
AL Avg Team	154	44	10	205	25	1390.2	1338	651	585	128	76	42	34	539	44	727	30	4	8.7	4.7	3.5	.255	.333	3.79

Team Fielding

Team	G	PO	A	E	TC	DP	PB	Pct
Chicago	155	4205	1787	**107**	6099	169	11	.982
Baltimore	154	4221	1690	112	6023	159	14	.981
New York	154	4184	1748	123	6055	**183**	13	.980
Detroit	154	**4241**	1572	121	5934	151	12	.980
Kansas City	154	4108	1720	125	5953	162	**22**	.979
Washington	154	4123	1716	128	5967	159	15	.979
Boston	154	4129	**1865**	149	**6143**	179	9	.976
Cleveland	153	4139	1557	153	5849	154	21	.974
AL Total	1232	33350	13655	1018	48023	1316	117	.979

Team vs. Team Records

	Bal	Bos	ChA	Cle	Det	KCA	NYA	Was	Won
Bal	—	8	10	9	9	16	9	15	**76**
Bos	14	—	8	12	10	16	8	14	**82**
ChA	12	14	—	14	11	14	8	17	**90**
Cle	12	10	8	—	11	11	9	15	**76**
Det	13	12	11	11	—	8	10	13	**78**
KCA	5	6	8	11	14	—	3	12	**59**
NYA	13	14	14	13	12	19	—	13	**98**
Was	7	8	5	7	9	10	9	—	**55**
Lost	76	72	64	77	76	94	56	99	

1957 American League Batting Leaders

Games		At-Bats		Runs		Hits		Doubles		Triples	
N. Fox, ChA	155	B. Gardner, Bal	644	M. Mantle, NYA	121	N. Fox, ChA	196	M. Minoso, ChA	36	H. Simpson, 2tm	9
B. Gardner, Bal	154	F. Malzone, Bos	634	N. Fox, ChA	110	F. Malzone, Bos	185	B. Gardner, Bal	36	G. McDougald, NYA	9
M. Minoso, ChA	153	H. Kuenn, Det	624	J. Piersall, Bos	103	M. Minoso, ChA	176	F. Malzone, Bos	31	H. Bauer, NYA	9
F. Malzone, Bos	153	N. Fox, ChA	619	R. Sievers, Was	99	H. Kuenn, Det	173	H. Kuenn, Det	30	B. Boyd, Bal	8
R. Sievers, Was	152	J. Piersall, Bos	609	2 tied with	96	M. Mantle, NYA	173	2 tied with	29	N. Fox, ChA	8

Home Runs		Total Bases		Runs Batted In		Walks		Intentional Walks		Strikeouts	
R. Sievers, Was	42	R. Sievers, Was	331	R. Sievers, Was	114	M. Mantle, NYA	146	T. Williams, Bos	33	J. Lemon, Was	94
T. Williams, Bos	38	M. Mantle, NYA	315	V. Wertz, Cle	105	T. Williams, Bos	119	M. Mantle, NYA	23	V. Wertz, Cle	88
M. Mantle, NYA	34	T. Williams, Bos	307	M. Minoso, ChA	103	M. Minoso, ChA	79	F. House, Det	13	B. Nieman, Bal	86
V. Wertz, Cle	28	A. Kaline, Det	276	F. Malzone, Bos	103	A. Smith, Cle	79	R. Sievers, Was	11	C. Maxwell, Det	84
G. Zernial, KCA	27	F. Malzone, Bos	271	J. Jensen, Bos	103	V. Wertz, Cle	78	Y. Berra, NYA	10	G. Zernial, KCA	84

Hit By Pitch		Sac Hits		Sac Flies		Stolen Bases		Caught Stealing		GDP	
M. Minoso, ChA	21	G. McDougald, NYA	19	V. Wertz, Cle	11	L. Aparicio, ChA	28	M. Minoso, ChA	15	J. Jensen, Bos	22
N. Fox, ChA	16	B. Avila, Cle	16	M. Minoso, ChA	9	M. Minoso, ChA	18	E. Yost, Was	11	M. Minoso, ChA	19
S. Lollar, ChA	13	T. Kubek, NYA	13	A. Pilarcik, Bal	9	J. Rivera, ChA	18	F. Bolling, Det	9	E. Howard, NYA	18
C. Courtney, Was	12	P. Foytack, Det	12	B. Nieman, Bal	8	M. Mantle, NYA	16	A. Kaline, Det	9	4 tied with	17
2 tied with	8	2 tied with	11	4 tied with	7	3 tied with	14	2 tied with	8		

Runs Created		Runs Created/27 Outs		Batting Average		On-Base Percentage		Slugging Percentage		OBP+Slugging	
M. Mantle, NYA	155	T. Williams, Bos	14.38	T. Williams, Bos	.388	T. Williams, Bos	.526	T. Williams, Bos	.731	T. Williams, Bos	1.257
T. Williams, Bos	143	M. Mantle, NYA	13.54	M. Mantle, NYA	.365	M. Mantle, NYA	.512	M. Mantle, NYA	.665	M. Mantle, NYA	1.177
R. Sievers, Was	126	R. Sievers, Was	8.33	G. Woodling, Cle	.321	G. Woodling, Cle	.408	R. Sievers, Was	.579	R. Sievers, Was	.967
N. Fox, ChA	108	G. Woodling, Cle	8.03	B. Boyd, Bal	.318	M. Minoso, ChA	.408	G. Woodling, Cle	.521	G. Woodling, Cle	.929
M. Minoso, ChA	104	V. Wertz, Cle	6.79	N. Fox, ChA	.317	N. Fox, ChA	.403	V. Wertz, Cle	.485	M. Minoso, ChA	.862

1957 American League Pitching Leaders

Wins		Losses		Winning Percentage		Games		Games Started		Complete Games	
J. Bunning, Det	20	C. Stobbs, Was	20	T. Sturdivant, NYA	.727	G. Zuverink, Bal	56	E. Wynn, Cle	37	D. Donovan, ChA	16
B. Pierce, ChA	20	C. Pascual, Was	17	D. Donovan, ChA	.727	D. Hyde, Was	52	F. Lary, Det	35	B. Pierce, ChA	16
T. Sturdivant, NYA	16	E. Wynn, Cle	17	J. Bunning, Det	.714	T. Clevenger, Was	52	B. Pierce, ChA	34	T. Brewer, Bos	15
T. Brewer, Bos	16	P. Ramos, Was	16	3 tied with	.688	I. Delock, Bos	49	T. Brewer, Bos	32	3 tied with	14
D. Donovan, ChA	16	F. Lary, Det	16			V. Trucks, KCA	48	R. Moore, Bal	32		

Shutouts		Saves		Games Finished		Batters Faced		Innings Pitched		Hits Allowed	
J. Wilson, ChA	5	B. Grim, NYA	19	G. Zuverink, Bal	37	E. Wynn, Cle	1146	J. Bunning, Det	267.1	E. Wynn, Cle	270
B. Turley, NYA	4	R. Narleski, Cle	16	B. Grim, NYA	36	J. Bunning, Det	1081	E. Wynn, Cle	263.0	P. Ramos, Was	251
B. Pierce, ChA	4	I. Delock, Bos	11	I. Delock, Bos	33	B. Pierce, ChA	1062	B. Pierce, ChA	257.0	F. Lary, Det	250
3 tied with	3	G. Zuverink, Bal	9	B. Byerly, Was	33	T. Brewer, Bos	1013	C. Johnson, Bal	242.0	C. Stobbs, Was	235
		T. Clevenger, Was	8	4 tied with	24	F. Lary, Det	1012	F. Sullivan, Bos	240.2	B. Pierce, ChA	228

Home Runs Allowed		Walks		Walks/9 Innings		Strikeouts		Strikeouts/9 Innings		Strikeout/Walk Ratio	
P. Ramos, Was	43	R. Moore, Bal	112	F. Sullivan, Bos	1.8	E. Wynn, Cle	184	B. Turley, NYA	7.8	C. Johnson, Bal	2.68
J. Bunning, Det	33	P. Foytack, Det	104	D. Donovan, ChA	1.8	J. Bunning, Det	182	C. Johnson, Bal	6.6	F. Sullivan, Bos	2.65
E. Wynn, Cle	32	E. Wynn, Cle	104	B. Shantz, NYA	2.1	C. Johnson, Bal	177	E. Wynn, Cle	6.3	J. Bunning, Det	2.53
C. Stobbs, Was	28	T. Brewer, Bos	93	B. Loes, Bal	2.1	B. Pierce, ChA	171	J. Bunning, Det	6.1	B. Pierce, ChA	2.41
T. Brewer, Bos	24	D. Larsen, NYA	87	J. Bunning, Det	2.4	B. Turley, NYA	152	B. Pierce, ChA	6.0	B. Loes, Bal	2.32

Earned Run Average		Component ERA		Hit Batsmen		Wild Pitches		Opponent Average		Opponent OBP	
B. Shantz, NYA	2.45	F. Sullivan, Bos	2.46	F. Lary, Det	12	C. McLish, Cle	8	B. Turley, NYA	.194	F. Sullivan, Bos	.273
T. Sturdivant, NYA	2.54	B. Pierce, ChA	2.74	J. Bunning, Det	11	T. Brewer, Bos	7	J. Bunning, Det	.218	J. Bunning, Det	.277
J. Bunning, Det	2.69	C. Johnson, Bal	2.79	B. Daley, Cle	10	R. Moore, Bal	7	P. Foytack, Det	.226	B. Pierce, ChA	.287
B. Turley, NYA	2.71	B. Loes, Bal	2.79	B. Turley, NYA	9	V. Trucks, KCA	7	F. Sullivan, Bos	.230	C. Johnson, Bal	.287
F. Sullivan, Bos	2.73	J. Bunning, Det	2.80	2 tied with	8	3 tied with	6	T. Sturdivant, NYA	.232	D. Donovan, ChA	.291

1957 American League Miscellaneous

Managers

Baltimore	Paul Richards	76-76
Boston	Pinky Higgins	82-72
Chicago	Al Lopez	90-64
Cleveland	Kerby Farrell	76-77
Detroit	Jack Tighe	78-76
Kansas City	Lou Boudreau	36-67
	Harry Craft	23-27
New York	Casey Stengel	98-56
Washington	Chuck Dressen	4-16
	Cookie Lavagetto	51-83

Awards

Most Valuable Player	Mickey Mantle, of, NYA
STATS Cy Young	Jim Bunning, Det
Rookie of the Year	Tony Kubek, of, NYA
STATS Manager of the Year	Casey Stengel, NYA

STATS All-Star Team

C	Yogi Berra, NYA	.251	24	82
1B	Vic Wertz, Cle	.282	28	105
2B	Nellie Fox, ChA	.317	6	61
3B	Frank Malzone, Bos	.292	15	103
SS	Gil McDougald, NYA	.289	13	62
OF	Mickey Mantle, NYA	.365	34	94
OF	Roy Sievers, Was	.301	42	114
OF	Ted Williams, Bos	.388	38	87
P	Jim Bunning, Det	20-8	2.69	182 K
P	Dick Donovan, ChA	16-6	2.77	88 K
P	Billy Pierce, ChA	20-12	3.26	171 K
P	Tom Sturdivant, NYA	16-6	2.54	118 K
RP	Bob Grim, NYA	12-8	2.63	19 Sv

Postseason

World Series	NYA (AL) 3 vs. Milwaukee (NL) 4

Outstanding Performances

No-Hitters
Bob Keegan, ChA   vs. Was on August 20

Three-Homer Games
Ted Williams, Bos   on May 8
Ted Williams, Bos   on June 13

Cycles
Mickey Mantle, NYA   on July 23

1957 National League Standings

Team	Overall W	L	Pct	GB	DIF	Home Games W	L	R	OR	HR	OHR	Road Games W	L	R	OR	HR	OHR	Park Index Run	HR	Record by Month M/A	May	June	July	Aug	S/O
Milwaukee	95	59	.617	—	105	45	32	312	289	75	51	50	27	460	324	124	73	77	64	9-2	14-14	19-13	18-12	19-7	16-11
St. Louis	87	67	.565	8.0	36	42	35	356	348	64	70	45	32	381	318	68	70	101	97	5-5	14-14	19-11	21-10	13-16	15-11
Brooklyn	84	70	.545	11.0	10	43	34	383	348	84	88	41	36	307	243	63	56	133	145	8-3	15-12	14-17	20-10	16-14	11-14
Cincinnati	80	74	.519	15.0	35	45	32	417	410	118	101	35	42	330	371	69	78	118	149	5-7	21-7	16-16	13-14	9-20	16-10
Philadelphia	77	77	.500	18.0	1	38	39	299	322	60	60	39	38	324	334	57	79	94	88	5-7	18-10	13-17	20-11	9-18	12-14
New York	69	85	.448	26.0	1	37	40	353	341	99	86	32	45	290	360	58	64	107	152	7-6	11-17	18-13	8-21	18-13	7-15
Chicago	62	92	.403	33.0	1	31	46	301	353	81	68	31	46	327	369	66	76	94	105	3-8	9-16	10-18	11-23	16-11	13-16
Pittsburgh	62	92	.403	33.0	3	36	41	273	321	20	53	26	51	313	375	72	105	86	41	4-8	7-19	15-19	10-20	12-13	14-13

Clinch Date—Milwaukee 9/23.

Team Batting

Team	G	AB	R	OR	H	2B	3B	HR	TB	RBI	TBB	IBB	SO	HBP	SH	SF	SB	CS	SB%	GDP	Avg	OBP	Slg
Milwaukee	155	5458	772	613	1469	221	62	199	2411	722	461	66	729	30	64	37	35	16	.69	107	.269	.334	.442
Cincinnati	154	5389	747	781	1452	251	33	187	2330	713	546	49	752	37	84	48	51	36	.59	108	.269	.346	.432
St. Louis	154	5472	737	666	1497	235	43	132	2214	685	493	75	672	18	45	54	58	44	.57	118	.274	.342	.405
Brooklyn	154	5242	690	591	1325	188	38	147	2030	648	550	46	848	33	78	41	60	34	.64	131	.253	.332	.387
New York	154	5346	643	701	1349	171	54	157	2099	612	447	37	669	25	32	42	64	38	.63	112	.252	.318	.393
Chicago	156	5369	628	722	1312	223	31	147	2038	590	461	34	989	26	58	33	28	25	.53	105	.244	.311	.380
Philadelphia	156	5241	623	656	1311	213	44	117	1963	569	534	40	758	45	52	49	57	26	.69	143	.250	.330	.375
Pittsburgh	155	5402	586	696	1447	231	60	92	2074	551	374	41	733	23	97	46	46	35	.57	107	.268	.323	.384
NL Total	1238	42919	5426	5426	11162	1733	365	1178	17159	5090	3866	388	6150	237	510	350	399	254	.61	931	.260	.322	.400
NL Avg Team	155	5365	678	678	1395	217	46	147	2145	636	483	49	769	30	64	44	50	32	.61	116	.260	.322	.400

Team Pitching

Team	G	CG	ShO	Rel	Sv	IP	H	R	ER	HR	SH	SF	HB	TBB	IBB	SO	WP	Bk	H/9	SO/9	BB/9	OAvg	OOBP	ERA
Brooklyn	154	44	18	204	29	1399.0	1285	591	521	55	33	26	456	33	891	30	2	8.3	5.7	2.9	.244	.305	3.35	
Milwaukee	155	60	9	183	24	1411.0	1347	613	544	124	63	43	13	570	43	693	25	0	8.6	4.4	3.6	.253	.325	3.47
St. Louis	154	46	11	229	29	1413.1	1385	666	593	140	54	32	29	506	45	778	40	0	8.8	5.0	3.2	.257	.322	3.78
Philadelphia	156	54	9	209	23	1401.2	1363	656	591	139	61	45	20	412	62	858	28	3	8.8	5.5	2.6	.254	.307	3.79
Pittsburgh	155	47	9	264	15	1395.0	1463	696	601	158	63	40	29	421	66	663	26	1	9.4	4.3	2.7	.270	.323	3.88
New York	154	35	9	270	20	1398.2	1436	701	623	150	69	47	38	471	50	701	26	2	9.2	4.5	3.0	.267	.327	4.01
Chicago	156	30	5	263	26	1403.1	1397	722	644	144	67	55	31	601	42	859	34	5	9.0	5.5	3.9	.261	.336	4.13
Cincinnati	154	40	5	279	29	1395.2	1486	781	717	179	78	55	51	429	46	707	28	2	9.6	4.6	2.8	.275	.331	4.62
NL Total	1238	356	75	1901	195	11217.2	11162	5426	4834	1178	510	350	237	3866	387	6150	237	15	9.0	4.9	3.1	.260	.330	3.88
NL Avg Team	155	45	9	238	24	1402.2	1395	678	604	147	64	44	30	483	48	769	30	2	9.0	4.9	3.1	.260	.330	3.88

Team Fielding

Team	G	PO	A	E	TC	DP	PB	Pct
Cincinnati	154	4187	1554	107	5848	139	8	.982
Milwaukee	155	4233	1811	120	6164	173	6	.981
Brooklyn	154	4198	1684	127	6009	136	8	.979
St. Louis	154	4240	1776	131	6147	168	22	.979
Philadelphia	156	4203	1437	136	5776	117	9	.976
Chicago	156	4210	1613	149	5972	140	19	.975
New York	154	4196	1811	161	6168	180	14	.974
Pittsburgh	155	4185	1695	170	6050	143	14	.972
NL Total	1238	33652	13381	1101	48134	1196	100	.977

Team vs. Team Records

	Bro	ChN	Cin	Mil	NYG	Phi	Pit	StL	Won
Bro	—	17	12	10	12	9	12	12	84
ChN	5	—	7	9	9	8	12	12	62
Cin	10	15	—	4	12	16	14	9	80
Mil	12	13	18	—	13	12	16	11	95
NYG	10	13	10	9	—	10	9	8	69
Phi	13	14	6	10	12	—	13	9	77
Pit	10	10	8	6	13	9	—	6	62
StL	10	10	13	11	14	13	16	—	87
Lost	70	92	74	59	85	77	92	67	

1957 National League Batting Leaders

Games		At-Bats		Runs		Hits		Doubles		Triples	
E. Banks, ChN	156	D. Blasingame, StL	650	H. Aaron, Mil	118	R. Schoendienst, 2tm	200	D. Hoak, Cin	39	W. Mays, NYG	20
R. Ashburn, Phi	156	R. Schoendienst, 2tm	648	E. Banks, ChN	113	H. Aaron, Mil	198	S. Musial, StL	38	B. Virdon, Pit	11
E. Bouchee, Phi	154	R. Ashburn, Phi	626	W. Mays, NYG	112	F. Robinson, Cin	197	E. Bouchee, Phi	35	B. Bruton, Mil	9
D. Blasingame, StL	154	J. Gilliam, Bro	617	E. Mathews, Mil	109	W. Mays, NYG	195	E. Banks, ChN	34	E. Mathews, Mil	9
W. Mays, NYG	152	H. Aaron, Mil	615	D. Blasingame, StL	108	R. Ashburn, Phi	186	W. Moryn, ChN	33	5 tied with	8

Home Runs		Total Bases		Runs Batted In		Walks		Intentional Walks		Strikeouts	
H. Aaron, Mil	44	H. Aaron, Mil	369	H. Aaron, Mil	132	J. Temple, Cin	94	S. Musial, StL	19	D. Snider, Bro	104
E. Banks, ChN	43	W. Mays, NYG	366	D. Ennis, StL	105	R. Ashburn, Phi	94	H. Aaron, Mil	15	F. Robinson, Cin	92
D. Snider, Bro	40	E. Banks, ChN	344	E. Banks, ChN	102	E. Mathews, Mil	90	W. Mays, NYG	15	E. Bouchee, Phi	91
W. Mays, NYG	35	F. Robinson, Cin	323	S. Musial, StL	102	E. Bouchee, Phi	84	W. Moon, StL	12	G. Hodges, Bro	91
E. Mathews, Mil	32	E. Mathews, Mil	309	G. Hodges, Bro	98	D. Snider, Bro	77	D. Snider, Bro	12	W. Moryn, ChN	90

Hit By Pitch		Sac Hits		Sac Flies		Stolen Bases		Caught Stealing		GDP	
E. Bouchee, Phi	14	J. Temple, Cin	16	F. Thomas, Pit	12	W. Mays, NYG	38	W. Mays, NYG	19	G. Hamner, Phi	23
F. Robinson, Cin	12	D. Groat, Pit	14	R. Jablonski, NYG	8	J. Gilliam, Bro	26	D. Hoak, Cin	15	D. Ennis, StL	22
F. Torre, Mil	9	B. Mazeroski, Pit	11	D. Ennis, StL	8	D. Blasingame, StL	21	J. Gilliam, Bro	10	C. Fernandez, Phi	21
C. Neal, Bro	8	R. McMillan, Cin	11	S. Musial, StL	8	J. Temple, Cin	19	R. Ashburn, Phi	10	D. Snider, Bro	17
4 tied with	6	G. Cimoli, Bro	10	3 tied with	7	C. Fernandez, Phi	18	D. Blasingame, StL	9	2 tied with	16

Runs Created		Runs Created/27 Outs		Batting Average		On-Base Percentage		Slugging Percentage		OBP+Slugging	
W. Mays, NYG	135	S. Musial, StL	9.39	S. Musial, StL	.351	S. Musial, StL	.422	W. Mays, NYG	.626	S. Musial, StL	1.034
H. Aaron, Mil	126	W. Mays, NYG	8.59	W. Mays, NYG	.333	W. Mays, NYG	.407	S. Musial, StL	.612	W. Mays, NYG	1.033
E. Banks, ChN	120	H. Aaron, Mil	7.93	F. Robinson, Cin	.322	E. Bouchee, Phi	.394	H. Aaron, Mil	.600	H. Aaron, Mil	.978
S. Musial, StL	120	E. Mathews, Mil	7.68	H. Aaron, Mil	.322	R. Ashburn, Phi	.390	D. Snider, Bro	.587	D. Snider, Bro	.955
E. Mathews, Mil	117	E. Banks, ChN	7.31	D. Groat, Pit	.315	J. Temple, Cin	.387	E. Banks, ChN	.579	E. Banks, ChN	.939

1957 National League Pitching Leaders

Wins		Losses		Winning Percentage		Games		Games Started		Complete Games	
W. Spahn, Mil	21	R. Roberts, Phi	22	B. Buhl, Mil	.720	T. Lown, ChN	67	B. Friend, Pit	38	W. Spahn, Mil	18
J. Sanford, Phi	19	B. Friend, Pit	18	J. Sanford, Phi	.704	R. Face, Pit	59	R. Gomez, NYG	36	B. Friend, Pit	17
B. Buhl, Mil	18	J. Antonelli, NYG	18	T. Acker, Cin	.667	C. Labine, Bro	58	W. Spahn, Mil	35	R. Gomez, NYG	16
D. Drysdale, Bro	17	R. Kline, Pit	16	W. Spahn, Mil	.656	A. Worthington, NYG	55	3 tied with	33	J. Sanford, Phi	15
L. Burdette, Mil	17	B. Rush, ChN	16	2 tied with	.654	M. Grissom, NYG	55			3 tied with	14

Shutouts		Saves		Games Finished		Batters Faced		Innings Pitched		Hits Allowed	
J. Podres, Bro	6	C. Labine, Bro	17	T. Lown, ChN	47	B. Friend, Pit	1148	B. Friend, Pit	277.0	B. Friend, Pit	273
D. Drysdale, Bro	4	M. Grissom, NYG	14	M. Grissom, NYG	38	W. Spahn, Mil	1111	W. Spahn, Mil	271.0	L. Burdette, Mil	260
D. Newcombe, Bro	4	T. Lown, ChN	12	C. Labine, Bro	37	L. Burdette, Mil	1067	L. Burdette, Mil	256.2	R. Roberts, Phi	246
W. Spahn, Mil	4	H. Wilhelm, StL	11	T. Farrell, Phi	32	B. Lawrence, Cin	1045	B. Lawrence, Cin	250.1	W. Spahn, Mil	241
5 tied with	3	2 tied with	10	R. Face, Pit	32	R. Roberts, Phi	1033	R. Roberts, Phi	249.2	H. Jeffcoat, Cin	236

Home Runs Allowed		Walks		Walks/9 Innings		Strikeouts		Strikeouts/9 Innings		Strikeout/Walk Ratio	
R. Roberts, Phi	40	D. Drott, ChN	129	D. Newcombe, Bro	1.5	J. Sanford, Phi	188	S. Jones, StL	7.6	H. Haddix, Phi	3.49
H. Jeffcoat, Cin	29	B. Buhl, Mil	121	R. Roberts, Phi	1.6	D. Drott, ChN	170	H. Haddix, Phi	7.2	R. Roberts, Phi	2.98
4 tied with	28	J. Sanford, Phi	94	V. Law, Pit	1.7	M. Drabowsky, ChN	170	J. Sanford, Phi	7.1	D. Newcombe, Bro	2.73
		M. Drabowsky, ChN	94	B. Purkey, Pit	1.9	S. Jones, StL	154	D. Drott, ChN	6.7	J. Podres, Bro	2.48
		W. Spahn, Mil	78	H. Jeffcoat, Cin	2.0	D. Drysdale, Bro	148	M. Drabowsky, ChN	6.4	D. Drysdale, Bro	2.43

Earned Run Average		Component ERA		Hit Batsmen		Wild Pitches		Opponent Average		Opponent OBP	
J. Podres, Bro	2.66	J. Podres, Bro	2.55	M. Drabowsky, ChN	10	J. Sanford, Phi	12	J. Sanford, Phi	.221	J. Podres, Bro	.273
D. Drysdale, Bro	2.69	D. Drysdale, Bro	2.97	T. Acker, Cin	8	L. McDaniel, StL	9	J. Podres, Bro	.230	R. Roberts, Phi	.283
W. Spahn, Mil	2.69	W. Spahn, Mil	2.97	B. Lawrence, Cin	8	D. McDevitt, Bro	7	D. Drott, ChN	.234	D. Newcombe, Bro	.288
B. Buhl, Mil	2.74	J. Sanford, Phi	3.06	6 tied with	7	D. Drott, ChN	7	D. Drysdale, Bro	.236	V. Law, Pit	.290
V. Law, Pit	2.87	C. Simmons, Phi	3.13			W. Schmidt, StL	7	W. Spahn, Mil	.237	W. Spahn, Mil	.291

1957 National League Miscellaneous

Managers

Brooklyn	Walter Alston	84-70
Chicago	Bob Scheffing	62-92
Cincinnati	Birdie Tebbetts	80-74
Milwaukee	Fred Haney	95-59
New York	Bill Rigney	69-85
Philadelphia	Mayo Smith	77-77
Pittsburgh	Bobby Bragan	36-67
	Danny Murtaugh	26-25
St. Louis	Fred Hutchinson	87-67

Awards

Most Valuable Player	Hank Aaron, of, Mil
Cy Young	Warren Spahn, Mil
Rookie of the Year	Jack Sanford, p, Phi
STATS Manager of the Year	Fred Haney, Mil

STATS All-Star Team

C	Ed Bailey, Cin	.261	20	48
1B	Stan Musial, StL	.351	29	102
2B	Red Schoendienst, 2tm	.309	15	65
3B	Eddie Mathews, Mil	.292	32	94
SS	Ernie Banks, ChN	.285	43	102
OF	Hank Aaron, Mil	.322	44	132
OF	Willie Mays, NYG	.333	35	97
OF	Duke Snider, Bro	.274	40	92
P	Bob Buhl, Mil	18-7	2.74	117 K
P	Don Drysdale, Bro	17-9	2.69	148 K
P	Jack Sanford, Phi	19-8	3.08	188 K
P	Warren Spahn, Mil	21-11	2.69	111 K
RP	Turk Farrell, Phi	10-2	2.38	10 Sv

Postseason

World Series	Milwaukee (NL) 4 vs. NYA (AL) 3

Outstanding Performances

Three-Homer Games

Ernie Banks, ChN	on September 14

Cycles

Lee Walls, ChN	on July 2

1958 American League Standings

Team	Overall					Home Games						Road Games						Park Index		Record by Month					
	W	L	Pct	GB	DIF	W	L	R	OR	HR	OHR	W	L	R	OR	HR	OHR	Run	HR	M/A	May	June	July	Aug	S/O
New York	92	62	.597	—	165	44	33	362	318	78	62	48	29	397	259	86	54	104	100	9-4	17-6	17-13	22-11	15-16	12-12
Chicago	82	72	.532	10.0	0	47	30	318	282	47	68	35	42	316	333	54	84	92	83	3-9	16-11	14-16	16-14	20-10	13-12
Boston	79	75	.513	13.0	0	49	28	384	350	73	65	30	47	313	341	82	56	112	100	4-10	16-12	15-12	14-14	17-13	13-14
Cleveland	77	76	.503	14.5	0	42	34	324	293	72	59	35	42	370	342	89	64	88	87	7-7	14-15	13-16	14-14	14-16	15-8
Detroit	77	77	.500	15.0	2	43	34	348	306	59	79	34	43	311	300	50	54	107	133	8-7	11-16	15-11	12-18	15-14	16-11
Baltimore	74	79	.484	17.5	3	46	31	248	256	46	36	28	48	273	319	62	70	84	61	5-6	11-15	15-15	16-12	15-17	12-14
Kansas City	73	81	.474	19.0	2	43	34	365	363	88	96	30	47	277	350	50	54	116	177	8-4	12-13	15-16	11-17	13-19	14-12
Washington	61	93	.396	31.0	1	33	44	269	373	49	80	28	49	284	374	72	76	98	87	7-4	10-19	12-17	13-18	12-16	7-19

Clinch Date—New York 9/14.

Team Batting

Team	G	AB	R	OR	H	2B	3B	HR	TB	RBI	TBB	IBB	SO	HBP	SH	SF	SB	CS	SB%	GDP	Avg	OBP	Slg
New York	155	5294	759	577	1418	212	39	164	2200	717	537	39	822	26	72	42	48	32	.60	107	.268	.343	.416
Boston	155	5218	697	691	1335	229	30	155	2089	667	638	38	820	27	60	29	29	22	.57	149	.256	.343	.400
Cleveland	153	5201	694	635	1340	210	31	161	2095	653	494	29	819	40	69	36	50	49	.51	112	.258	.331	.403
Detroit	154	5194	659	606	1384	229	41	109	2022	612	463	37	678	22	75	51	48	32	.60	133	.266	.335	.389
Kansas City	156	5261	642	713	1297	196	50	138	2007	605	452	34	747	25	64	43	22	36	.38	133	.247	.314	.381
Chicago	155	5249	634	615	1348	191	42	101	1926	594	518	30	669	49	72	47	101	33	.75	120	.257	.335	.367
Washington	156	5156	553	747	1240	161	38	121	1840	526	477	21	751	35	57	38	22	41	.35	133	.240	.314	.357
Baltimore	154	5111	521	575	1233	195	19	108	1790	492	483	31	731	28	62	36	33	35	.49	134	.241	.315	.350
AL Total	1238	41684	5159	5159	10595	1623	290	1057	15969	4866	4062	259	6037	252	531	322	353	280	.56	1015	.254	.322	.383
AL Avg Team	155	5211	645	645	1324	203	36	132	1996	608	508	32	755	32	66	40	44	35	.56	127	.254	.322	.383

Team Pitching

Team	G	CG	ShO	Rel	Sv	IP	H	R	ER	HR	SH	SF	HB	TBB	IBB	SO	WP	Bk	H/9	SO/9	BB/9	OAvg	OOBP	ERA
New York	155	53	21	184	33	1379.0	1201	577	493	116	45	36	44	557	23	796	24	2	7.8	5.2	3.6	.235	.313	3.22
Baltimore	154	55	15	183	28	1369.2	1277	575	517	106	75	46	35	403	29	749	32	6	8.4	4.9	2.6	.249	.306	3.40
Detroit	154	59	8	220	19	1357.1	1294	606	542	133	68	38	42	437	25	797	27	4	8.6	5.3	2.9	.252	.314	3.59
Chicago	155	55	15	204	25	1389.2	1296	615	557	152	78	39	18	515	40	751	28	3	8.4	4.9	3.3	.250	.317	3.61
Cleveland	153	51	2	221	20	1373.1	1283	635	569	123	71	39	28	604	36	766	33	5	8.4	5.0	4.0	.249	.328	3.73
Boston	155	44	5	201	28	1380.0	1396	691	601	121	73	43	31	521	30	695	28	6	9.1	4.5	3.4	.264	.332	3.92
Kansas City	156	42	9	237	25	1398.1	1405	713	645	150	77	29	28	467	30	721	31	1	9.0	4.6	3.0	.262	.323	4.15
Washington	156	28	6	222	28	1376.2	1443	747	693	156	64	52	26	558	47	762	43	5	9.4	5.0	3.6	.272	.341	4.53
AL Total	1238	387	81	1672	206	11024.0	10595	5159	4617	1057	531	322	252	4062	260	6037	246	32	8.6	4.9	3.3	.254	.329	3.77
AL Avg Team	155	48	10	209	26	1378.0	1324	645	577	132	66	40	32	508	33	755	31	4	8.6	4.9	3.3	.254	.329	3.77

Team Fielding

Team	G	PO	A	E	TC	DP	PB	Pct
Detroit	154	4070	1557	106	5733	140	16	.982
Chicago	155	4156	1667	114	5937	160	11	.981
Baltimore	154	4103	1525	114	5742	159	14	.980
Washington	156	4125	1648	118	5891	163	15	.980
Kansas City	156	4196	1730	125	6051	166	34	.979
New York	155	4135	1679	128	5942	182	9	.978
Boston	155	4130	1799	145	6074	172	9	.976
Cleveland	153	4105	1571	152	5828	171	35	.974
AL Total	1238	33020	13176	1002	47198	1313	143	.979

Team vs. Team Records

	Bal	Bos	ChA	Cle	Det	KCA	NYA	Was	Won
Bal	—	10	9	10	10	12	8	15	74
Bos	12	—	10	12	10	12	9	14	79
ChA	13	12	—	12	10	12	7	16	82
Cle	11	10	10	—	14	10	7	15	77
Det	12	12	12	8	—	12	12	9	77
KCA	10	10	10	12	10	—	9	12	73
NYA	14	13	15	15	10	13	—	12	92
Was	7	8	6	7	13	10	10	—	61
Lost	79	75	72	76	77	81	62	93	

1958 American League Batting Leaders

Games		At-Bats		Runs		Hits		Doubles		Triples	
F. Malzone, Bos	155	F. Malzone, Bos	627	M. Mantle, NYA	127	N. Fox, ChA	187	H. Kuenn, Det	39	V. Power, 2tm	10
N. Fox, ChA	155	N. Fox, ChA	623	P. Runnels, Bos	103	F. Malzone, Bos	185	V. Power, 2tm	37	L. Aparicio, ChA	9
F. Bolling, Det	154	F. Bolling, Det	610	V. Power, 2tm	98	V. Power, 2tm	184	A. Kaline, Det	34	B. Tuttle, KCA	9
J. Jensen, Bos	154	V. Power, 2tm	590	M. Minoso, Cle	94	P. Runnels, Bos	183	P. Runnels, Bos	32	J. Lemon, Was	9
2 tied with	151	R. Maris, 2tm	583	B. Cerv, KCA	93	H. Kuenn, Det	179	J. Jensen, Bos	31	G. Harris, Det	8

Home Runs		Total Bases		Runs Batted In		Walks		Intentional Walks		Strikeouts	
M. Mantle, NYA	42	M. Mantle, NYA	307	J. Jensen, Bos	122	M. Mantle, NYA	129	M. Mantle, NYA	13	M. Mantle, NYA	120
R. Colavito, Cle	41	B. Cerv, KCA	305	R. Colavito, Cle	113	J. Jensen, Bos	99	T. Williams, Bos	12	J. Lemon, Was	120
R. Sievers, Was	39	R. Colavito, Cle	303	R. Sievers, Was	108	T. Williams, Bos	98	B. Cerv, KCA	10	D. Buddin, Bos	106
B. Cerv, KCA	38	R. Sievers, Was	299	B. Cerv, KCA	104	P. Runnels, Bos	87	H. Kuenn, Det	8	R. Colavito, Cle	89
J. Jensen, Bos	35	J. Jensen, Bos	293	M. Mantle, NYA	97	R. Colavito, Cle	84	J. Jensen, Bos	7	N. Siebern, NYA	87

Hit By Pitch		Sac Hits		Sac Flies		Stolen Bases		Caught Stealing		GDP	
M. Minoso, Cle	15	B. Martin, Det	13	H. Lopez, KCA	9	L. Aparicio, ChA	29	M. Minoso, Cle	14	H. Lopez, KCA	23
N. Fox, ChA	11	B. Avila, Cle	12	F. Bolling, Det	9	J. Rivera, ChA	21	H. Kuenn, Det	10	G. Triandos, Bal	22
C. Courtney, Was	9	N. Fox, ChA	12	H. Smith, KCA	8	J. Landis, ChA	19	B. Tuttle, KCA	9	F. Malzone, Bos	21
E. Yost, Was	9	A. Pearson, Was	11	4 tied with	7	M. Mantle, NYA	18	3 tied with	8	3 tied with	19
2 tied with	8	D. Sisler, Bos	11			M. Minoso, Cle	14				

Runs Created		Runs Created/27 Outs		Batting Average		On-Base Percentage		Slugging Percentage		OBP+Slugging	
M. Mantle, NYA	138	M. Mantle, NYA	9.78	T. Williams, Bos	.328	T. Williams, Bos	.458	R. Colavito, Cle	.620	T. Williams, Bos	1.042
R. Colavito, Cle	116	T. Williams, Bos	9.25	P. Runnels, Bos	.322	M. Mantle, NYA	.443	B. Cerv, KCA	.592	M. Mantle, NYA	1.035
J. Jensen, Bos	113	R. Colavito, Cle	8.60	H. Kuenn, Det	.319	P. Runnels, Bos	.416	M. Mantle, NYA	.592	R. Colavito, Cle	1.024
B. Cerv, KCA	109	B. Cerv, KCA	7.66	A. Kaline, Det	.313	R. Colavito, Cle	.405	T. Williams, Bos	.584	B. Cerv, KCA	.963
P. Runnels, Bos	104	J. Jensen, Bos	7.35	V. Power, 2tm	.312	J. Jensen, Bos	.396	R. Sievers, Was	.544	J. Jensen, Bos	.931

1958 American League Pitching Leaders

Wins		Losses		Winning Percentage		Games		Games Started		Complete Games	
B. Turley, NYA	21	P. Ramos, Was	18	B. Turley, NYA	.750	T. Clevenger, Was	55	P. Ramos, Was	37	F. Lary, Det	19
B. Pierce, ChA	17	E. Wynn, ChA	16	C. McLish, Cle	.667	D. Tomanek, 2tm	54	J. Bunning, Det	34	B. Turley, NYA	19
F. Lary, Det	16	F. Lary, Det	15	W. Ford, NYA	.667	D. Hyde, Was	53	F. Lary, Det	34	B. Pierce, ChA	19
C. McLish, Cle	16	R. Kemmerer, Was	15	I. Delock, Bos	.636	M. Wall, Bos	52	D. Donovan, ChA	34	J. Harshman, Bal	17
3 tied with	15	J. Harshman, Bal	15	B. Pierce, ChA	.607	2 tied with	50	E. Wynn, ChA	34	2 tied with	16

Shutouts		Saves		Games Finished		Batters Faced		Innings Pitched		Hits Allowed	
W. Ford, NYA	7	R. Duren, NYA	20	D. Hyde, Was	44	P. Ramos, Was	1112	F. Lary, Det	260.1	P. Ramos, Was	277
B. Turley, NYA	6	D. Hyde, Was	18	L. Kiely, Bos	35	F. Lary, Det	1085	P. Ramos, Was	259.1	F. Lary, Det	249
P. Ramos, Was	4	L. Kiely, Bos	12	R. Duren, NYA	33	D. Donovan, ChA	1030	D. Donovan, ChA	248.0	D. Donovan, ChA	240
D. Donovan, ChA	4	M. Wall, Bos	10	T. Clevenger, Was	29	E. Wynn, ChA	1016	B. Turley, NYA	245.1	R. Kemmerer, Was	234
E. Wynn, ChA	4	4 tied with	8	M. Wall, Bos	29	B. Turley, NYA	1013	B. Pierce, ChA	245.0	T. Brewer, Bos	227

Home Runs Allowed		Walks		Walks/9 Innings		Strikeouts		Strikeouts/9 Innings		Strikeout/Walk Ratio	
P. Ramos, Was	38	B. Turley, NYA	128	D. Donovan, ChA	1.9	E. Wynn, ChA	179	C. Pascual, Was	7.4	B. O'Dell, Bal	2.69
B. Pierce, ChA	33	M. Grant, Cle	104	B. O'Dell, Bal	2.1	J. Bunning, Det	177	J. Bunning, Det	7.3	C. Pascual, Was	2.43
R. Terry, KCA	29	E. Wynn, ChA	104	F. Sullivan, Bos	2.2	B. Turley, NYA	168	E. Wynn, ChA	6.7	D. Donovan, ChA	2.40
J. Bunning, Det	28	T. Brewer, Bos	93	F. Lary, Det	2.4	J. Harshman, Bal	161	B. Turley, NYA	6.2	W. Ford, NYA	2.34
E. Wynn, ChA	27	R. Narleski, Cle	91	B. Pierce, ChA	2.4	C. Pascual, Was	146	J. Harshman, Bal	6.1	J. Bunning, Det	2.24

Earned Run Average		Component ERA		Hit Batsmen		Wild Pitches		Opponent Average		Opponent OBP	
W. Ford, NYA	2.01	W. Ford, NYA	2.40	F. Lary, Det	12	D. Tomanek, 2tm	9	B. Turley, NYA	.206	W. Ford, NYA	.276
B. Pierce, ChA	2.68	B. O'Dell, Bal	2.67	J. Bunning, Det	10	H. Griggs, Was	8	G. Bell, Cle	.213	B. Pierce, ChA	.279
J. Harshman, Bal	2.89	A. Portocarrero, Bal	2.75	H. Moford, Det	9	J. Harshman, Bal	8	W. Ford, NYA	.217	B. O'Dell, Bal	.284
F. Lary, Det	2.90	B. Pierce, ChA	2.93	3 tied with	8	R. Kemmerer, Was	7	B. Pierce, ChA	.227	A. Portocarrero, Bal	.284
B. O'Dell, Bal	2.97	G. Bell, Cle	2.94			6 tied with	6	M. Grant, Cle	.228	J. Harshman, Bal	.292

1958 American League Miscellaneous

Managers

Baltimore	Paul Richards	74-79
Boston	Pinky Higgins	79-75
Chicago	Al Lopez	82-72
Cleveland	Bobby Bragan	31-36
	Joe Gordon	46-40
Detroit	Jack Tighe	21-28
	Bill Norman	56-49
Kansas City	Harry Craft	73-81
New York	Casey Stengel	92-62
Washington	Cookie Lavagetto	61-93

Awards

Most Valuable Player	Jackie Jensen, of, Bos
Cy Young	Bob Turley, NYA
Rookie of the Year	Albie Pearson, of, Was
STATS Manager of the Year	Casey Stengel, NYA

STATS All-Star Team

C	Sherm Lollar, ChA	.273	20	84
1B	Vic Power, 2tm	.312	16	80
2B	Pete Runnels, Bos	.322	8	59
3B	Frank Malzone, Bos	.295	15	87
SS	Luis Aparicio, ChA	.266	2	40
OF	Jackie Jensen, Bos	.286	35	122
OF	Mickey Mantle, NYA	.304	42	97
OF	Ted Williams, Bos	.328	26	85
P	Whitey Ford, NYA	14-7	2.01	145 K
P	Frank Lary, Det	16-15	2.90	131 K
P	Billy Pierce, ChA	17-11	2.68	144 K
P	Bob Turley, NYA	21-7	2.97	168 K
RP	Dick Hyde, Was	10-3	1.75	18 Sv

Postseason

World Series	NYA (AL) 4 vs. Milwaukee (NL) 3

Outstanding Performances

No-Hitters
Jim Bunning, Det @ Bos on July 20
Hoyt Wilhelm, Bal vs. NYA on September 20

Three-Homer Games
Hector Lopez, KCA on June 26
Preston Ward, KCA on September 9

1958 National League Standings

Team	Overall					Home Games						Road Games						Park Index		Record by Month					
	W	L	Pct	GB	DIF	W	L	R	OR	HR	OHR	W	L	R	OR	HR	OHR	Run	HR	M/A	May	June	July	Aug	S/O
Milwaukee	92	62	.597	—	126	48	29	291	**207**	72	48	44	33	**384**	334	**95**	77	69	70	8-5	17-10	13-13	16-14	23-11	15-9
Pittsburgh	84	70	.545	8.0	4	**49**	28	323	260	41	**40**	35	42	339	347	93	83	85	46	7-5	15-15	12-17	15-12	21-12	14-9
San Francisco	80	74	.519	12.0	29	44	33	363	354	85	88	36	41	364	344	85	78	101	106	9-5	18-12	10-17	17-11	14-17	12-12
Cincinnati	76	78	.494	16.0	1	40	37	**364**	337	71	86	36	41	331	284	52	**62**	114	138	6-5	10-15	17-13	16-16	11-20	12-11
Chicago	72	82	.468	20.0	18	35	40	350	381	101	72	37	40	359	344	81	70	104	115	8-5	14-19	12-13	15-14	11-20	12-11
St. Louis	72	82	.468	20.0	1	39	38	329	381	62	88	33	44	290	323	49	70	116	126	3-10	16-11	18-10	9-20	15-17	11-14
Los Angeles	71	83	.461	21.0	1	39	38	359	405	92	101	32	45	309	356	80	72	115	127	5-9	11-17	15-13	13-15	17-14	10-15
Philadelphia	69	85	.448	23.0	4	35	42	318	397	59	77	34	43	346	365	65	71	101	100	5-7	13-15	13-14	15-14	12-19	11-16

Clinch Date—Milwaukee 9/21.

Team Batting

Team	G	AB	R	OR	H	2B	3B	HR	TB	RBI	TBB	IBB	SO	HBP	SH	SF	SB	CS	SB%	GDP	Avg	OBP	Slg
San Francisco	154	5318	**727**	698	1399	**250**	42	170	2243	682	531	54	817	34	68	**45**	64	29	.69	119	.263	.339	.422
Chicago	154	5289	709	725	1402	207	49	182	**2253**	666	487	50	853	**45**	42	39	61	38	.62	109	.265	.337	**.426**
Cincinnati	154	5273	695	621	1359	242	40	123	2050	649	572	41	765	21	76	38	61	38	.62	109	.258	.337	.389
Milwaukee	154	5225	675	541	1388	221	21	167	2152	641	478	68	646	36	**79**	41	26	8	**.76**	132	**.266**	.336	.412
Los Angeles	154	5173	668	761	1297	166	50	172	2079	627	495	22	850	25	68	43	**73**	**47**	.61	132	.251	.324	.402
Philadelphia	154	**5363**	664	762	**1424**	238	56	124	2146	630	**573**	60	**871**	38	70	37	51	33	.61	133	.266	.324	.400
Pittsburgh	154	5247	662	607	1386	229	**68**	134	2153	625	396	56	753	28	68	40	30	15	.67	128	.264	.324	.410
St. Louis	154	5255	619	704	1371	216	39	111	1998	570	533	**69**	637	20	44	39	44	43	.51	**166**	.261	.336	.380
NL Total	1232	42143	5419	5419	11026	1769	365	1183	17074	5090	4065	420	6192	247	515	322	388	236	.62	1047	.262	.328	.405
NL Avg Team	154	5268	677	677	1378	221	46	148	2134	636	508	53	774	31	64	40	49	30	.62	131	.262	.328	.405

Team Pitching

Team	G	CG	ShO	Rel	Sv	IP	H	R	ER	HR	SH	SF	HB	TBB	IBB	SO	WP	Bk	H/9	SO/9	BB/9	OAvg	OOBP	ERA
Milwaukee	154	**72**	**16**	149	17	1376.0	**1261**	541	491	125	45	31	27	426	42	773	21	4	**8.2**	5.1	2.8	**.244**	**.303**	3.21
Pittsburgh	154	43	10	222	**41**	1367.0	1344	607	541	**123**	73	46	20	470	**66**	679	31	2	8.8	4.5	3.1	.261	.323	3.56
Cincinnati	154	50	7	219	20	1385.1	1422	621	574	148	67	38	27	**419**	53	705	17	1	9.2	4.6	**2.7**	.267	.322	3.73
San Francisco	154	38	7	255	25	1389.1	1400	698	614	166	67	44	39	512	46	775	33	5	9.1	5.0	3.3	.263	.330	3.98
St. Louis	154	45	6	240	25	1381.2	1398	704	632	158	70	35	**42**	567	53	822	35	6	9.1	5.4	3.7	.264	.338	4.12
Chicago	154	27	5	**293**	24	1361.0	1322	725	638	142	65	36	38	619	57	805	36	7	8.7	5.3	4.1	.254	.336	4.22
Philadelphia	154	51	6	221	15	**1397.0**	1480	762	671	148	66	53	21	446	46	778	37	3	9.5	5.0	2.9	.272	.326	4.32
Los Angeles	154	30	7	284	31	1368.1	1399	761	680	173	62	39	33	606	57	**855**	**70**	**10**	9.2	**5.6**	4.0	.267	.344	4.47
NL Total	1232	356	64	1883	198	11025.2	11026	5419	4841	1183	515	322	247	4065	420	6192	280	38	9.0	5.1	3.3	.262	.335	3.95
NL Avg Team	154	45	8	235	25	1378.2	1378	677	605	148	64	40	31	508	53	774	35	5	9.0	5.1	3.3	.262	.335	3.95

Team Fielding

Team	G	PO	A	E	TC	DP	PB	Pct
Cincinnati	154	4156	1645	**100**	5901	148	8	.983
Milwaukee	154	4128	**1800**	120	**6048**	152	6	.980
Philadelphia	154	**4191**	1499	129	5819	136	**21**	.978
Pittsburgh	154	4101	1726	133	5960	173	14	.978
Los Angeles	154	4105	1693	146	5944	**198**	6	.975
San Francisco	154	4168	1707	152	6027	156	8	.975
Chicago	154	4083	1678	150	5911	161	12	.975
St. Louis	154	4145	1691	153	5989	163	13	.974
NL Total	1232	33077	13439	1083	47599	1287	88	.977

Team vs. Team Records

	ChN	Cin	LA	Mil	Phi	Pit	SF	StL	Won
ChN	—	10	11	10	13	9	12	7	**72**
Cin	12	—	11	5	15	10	11	12	**76**
LA	11	11	—	14	10	8	6	11	**71**
Mil	12	17	8	—	13	11	16	15	**92**
Phi	9	7	12	9	—	12	8	12	**69**
Pit	13	12	14	11	10	—	12	12	**84**
SF	10	11	16	6	14	10	—	13	**80**
StL	15	10	11	7	10	10	9	—	**72**
Lost	82	78	83	62	85	70	74	82	

Seasons: Standings, Leaders

1958 National League Batting Leaders

Games			At-Bats			Runs			Hits			Doubles			Triples		
E. Banks, ChN		154	E. Banks, ChN		617	W. Mays, SF		121	R. Ashburn, Phi		215	O. Cepeda, SF		38	R. Ashburn, Phi		13
H. Aaron, Mil		153	R. Ashburn, Phi		615	E. Banks, ChN		119	W. Mays, SF		208	D. Groat, Pit		36	B. Virdon, Pit		11
4 tied with		152	B. Virdon, Pit		604	H. Aaron, Mil		109	H. Aaron, Mil		196	S. Musial, StL		35	E. Banks, ChN		11
			O. Cepeda, SF		603	K. Boyer, StL		101	E. Banks, ChN		193	H. Anderson, Phi		34	W. Mays, SF		11
			H. Aaron, Mil		601	R. Ashburn, Phi		98	O. Cepeda, SF		188	H. Aaron, Mil		34	2 tied with		10

Home Runs			Total Bases			Runs Batted In			Walks			Intentional Walks			Strikeouts		
E. Banks, ChN		47	E. Banks, ChN		379	E. Banks, ChN		129	R. Ashburn, Phi		97	S. Musial, StL		26	H. Anderson, Phi		95
F. Thomas, Pit		35	W. Mays, SF		350	F. Thomas, Pit		109	J. Temple, Cin		91	D. Crandall, Mil		18	T. Taylor, ChN		93
F. Robinson, Cin		31	H. Aaron, Mil		328	H. Anderson, Phi		97	E. Mathews, Mil		85	H. Aaron, Mil		16	D. Zimmer, LA		92
E. Mathews, Mil		31	O. Cepeda, SF		309	O. Cepeda, SF		96	J. Cunningham, StL		82	E. Banks, ChN		12	C. Neal, LA		91
H. Aaron, Mil		30	F. Thomas, Pit		297	W. Mays, SF		96	2 tied with		78	W. Mays, SF		12	2 tied with		87

Hit By Pitch			Sac Hits			Sac Flies			Stolen Bases			Caught Stealing			GDP		
W. Moryn, ChN		8	J. Davenport, SF		17	O. Cepeda, SF		9	W. Mays, SF		31	C. Flood, StL		12	G. Green, StL		24
L. Walls, ChN		8	J. Temple, Cin		17	5 tied with		8	R. Ashburn, Phi		30	R. Ashburn, Phi		12	H. Aaron, Mil		21
S. Hemus, Phi		8	J. Logan, Mil		13				T. Taylor, ChN		21	O. Cepeda, SF		11	D. Groat, Pit		21
5 tied with		7	C. Fernandez, Phi		10				D. Blasingame, StL		20	J. Gilliam, LA		11	3 tied with		19
			B. Friend, Pit		10				J. Gilliam, LA		18	3 tied with		8			

Runs Created			Runs Created/27 Outs			Batting Average			On-Base Percentage			Slugging Percentage			OBP+Slugging		
W. Mays, SF		138	W. Mays, SF		8.97	R. Ashburn, Phi		.350	R. Ashburn, Phi		.440	E. Banks, ChN		.614	W. Mays, SF		1.002
E. Banks, ChN		123	S. Musial, StL		7.55	W. Mays, SF		.347	S. Musial, StL		.423	W. Mays, SF		.583	E. Banks, ChN		.980
R. Ashburn, Phi		114	E. Banks, ChN		7.36	S. Musial, StL		.337	W. Mays, SF		.419	H. Aaron, Mil		.546	S. Musial, StL		.950
H. Aaron, Mil		111	R. Ashburn, Phi		7.17	H. Aaron, Mil		.326	J. Temple, Cin		.405	F. Thomas, Pit		.528	H. Aaron, Mil		.931
B. Skinner, Pit		98	H. Aaron, Mil		6.96	B. Skinner, Pit		.321	B. Skinner, Pit		.387	S. Musial, StL		.528	H. Anderson, Phi		.897

1958 National League Pitching Leaders

Wins			Losses			Winning Percentage			Games			Games Started			Complete Games		
B. Friend, Pit		22	R. Kline, Pit		16	W. Spahn, Mil		.667	D. Elston, ChN		69	B. Friend, Pit		38	W. Spahn, Mil		23
W. Spahn, Mil		22	J. Podres, LA		15	L. Burdette, Mil		.667	R. Face, Pit		57	L. Burdette, Mil		36	R. Roberts, Phi		21
L. Burdette, Mil		20	4 tied with		14	G. Hobbie, ChN		.625	J. Klippstein, 2tm		57	W. Spahn, Mil		36	L. Burdette, Mil		19
B. Purkey, Cin		17				B. Rush, Mil		.625	G. Hobbie, ChN		55	S. Jones, StL		35	B. Purkey, Cin		17
R. Roberts, Phi		17				2 tied with		.611	2 tied with		54	3 tied with		34	B. Friend, Pit		16

Shutouts			Saves			Games Finished			Batters Faced			Innings Pitched			Hits Allowed		
C. Willey, Mil		4	R. Face, Pit		20	R. Face, Pit		40	W. Spahn, Mil		1176	W. Spahn, Mil		290.0	B. Friend, Pit		299
G. Witt, Pit		3	C. Labine, LA		14	D. Elston, ChN		39	B. Friend, Pit		1146	L. Burdette, Mil		275.1	L. Burdette, Mil		279
B. Purkey, Cin		3	T. Farrell, Phi		11	T. Farrell, Phi		35	L. Burdette, Mil		1122	B. Friend, Pit		274.0	R. Roberts, Phi		270
J. Jay, Mil		3	3 tied with		10	C. Labine, LA		35	R. Roberts, Phi		1116	R. Roberts, Phi		269.2	B. Purkey, Cin		259
L. Burdette, Mil		3				M. Grissom, SF		35	S. Jones, StL		1041	2 tied with		250.0	W. Spahn, Mil		257

Home Runs Allowed			Walks			Walks/9 Innings			Strikeouts			Strikeouts/9 Innings			Strikeout/Walk Ratio		
D. Newcombe, 2tm		31	S. Jones, StL		107	L. Burdette, Mil		1.6	S. Jones, StL		225	S. Jones, StL		8.1	H. Haddix, Cin		2.56
J. Antonelli, SF		31	S. Koufax, LA		105	R. Roberts, Phi		1.7	W. Spahn, Mil		150	S. Koufax, LA		7.4	R. Roberts, Phi		2.55
R. Roberts, Phi		30	D. Drott, ChN		99	V. Law, Pit		1.7	J. Podres, LA		143	D. Drott, ChN		6.8	L. Jackson, StL		2.43
W. Spahn, Mil		29	G. Hobbie, ChN		93	B. Purkey, Cin		1.8	J. Antonelli, SF		143	J. Podres, LA		6.1	S. Miller, SF		2.43
H. Haddix, Cin		28	R. Kline, Pit		92	D. Newcombe, 2tm		1.9	B. Friend, Pit		135	S. Miller, SF		5.9	L. Burdette, Mil		2.26

Earned Run Average			Component ERA			Hit Batsmen			Wild Pitches			Opponent Average			Opponent OBP		
S. Miller, SF		2.47	S. Miller, SF		2.87	D. Drysdale, LA		14	S. Koufax, LA		17	S. Koufax, LA		.220	S. Miller, SF		.286
S. Jones, StL		2.88	W. Spahn, Mil		2.96	L. Jackson, StL		10	D. Drott, ChN		9	S. Jones, StL		.223	W. Spahn, Mil		.287
L. Burdette, Mil		2.91	L. Burdette, Mil		3.16	R. Gomez, SF		8	J. Klippstein, 2tm		9	S. Miller, SF		.233	R. Roberts, Phi		.292
W. Spahn, Mil		3.07	S. Jones, StL		3.22	3 tied with		7	T. Phillips, ChN		8	W. Spahn, Mil		.237	L. Burdette, Mil		.300
R. Roberts, Phi		3.24	R. Roberts, Phi		3.32				D. Drysdale, LA		8	J. Antonelli, SF		.239	B. Purkey, Cin		.304

1958 National League Miscellaneous

Managers

Chicago	Bob Scheffing	72-82
Cincinnati	Birdie Tebbetts	52-61
	Jimmy Dykes	24-17
Los Angeles	Walter Alston	71-83
Milwaukee	Fred Haney	92-62
Philadelphia	Mayo Smith	39-45
	Eddie Sawyer	30-40
Pittsburgh	Danny Murtaugh	84-70
St. Louis	Fred Hutchinson	69-75
	Stan Hack	3-7
San Francisco	Bill Rigney	80-74

Awards

Most Valuable Player	Ernie Banks, ss, ChN
STATS Cy Young	Warren Spahn, Mil
Rookie of the Year	Orlando Cepeda, 1b, SF
STATS Manager of the Year	Danny Murtaugh, Pit

STATS All-Star Team

C	Del Crandall, Mil	.272	18	63
1B	Orlando Cepeda, SF	.312	25	96
2B	Johnny Temple, Cin	.306	3	47
3B	Ken Boyer, StL	.307	23	90
SS	Ernie Banks, ChN	.313	47	129
OF	Hank Aaron, Mil	.326	30	95
OF	Richie Ashburn, Phi	.350	2	33
OF	Willie Mays, SF	.347	29	96
P	Lew Burdette, Mil	20-10	2.91	113 K
P	Bob Friend, Pit	22-14	3.68	135 K
P	Robin Roberts, Phi	17-14	3.24	130 K
P	Warren Spahn, Mil	22-11	3.07	150 K
RP	Roy Face, Pit	5-2	2.89	20 Sv

Postseason

World Series	Milwaukee (NL) 3 vs. NYA (AL) 4

Outstanding Performances

Three-Homer Games

Lee Walls, ChN	on April 24
Roman Mejias, Pit	on May 4
Walt Moryn, ChN	on May 30
Frank Thomas, Pit	on August 16

1959 American League Standings

Team	Overall					Home Games						Road Games						Park Index		Record by Month					
	W	L	Pct	GB	DIF	W	L	R	OR	HR	OHR	W	L	R	OR	HR	OHR	Run	HR	M/A	May	June	July	Aug	S/O
Chicago	94	60	.610	—	89	47	30	313	272	44	61	47	30	356	316	53	68	87	87	10-6	15-13	14-14	20-7	21-9	14-11
Cleveland	89	65	.578	5.0	90	43	34	346	316	84	74	46	31	399	330	83	74	91	101	10-4	15-13	15-13	19-12	16-13	14-10
New York	79	75	.513	15.0	4	40	37	293	305	63	45	39	38	394	342	90	75	81	65	7-8	12-15	18-12	12-16	15-15	15-9
Detroit	76	78	.494	18.0	0	41	36	401	411	95	105	35	42	312	321	65	72	128	146	2-13	18-10	18-13	12-18	15-11	11-13
Boston	75	79	.487	19.0	0	43	34	404	356	62	66	32	45	322	340	63	69	115	97	6-7	13-17	12-16	13-17	18-12	13-10
Baltimore	74	80	.481	20.0	1	38	39	260	299	53	50	36	41	291	322	56	61	91	88	9-7	16-14	13-14	13-17	10-14	13-14
Kansas City	66	88	.429	28.0	0	37	40	362	386	58	80	29	48	319	374	59	68	108	109	9-7	11-14	11-18	19-11	9-20	7-18
Washington	63	91	.409	31.0	5	34	43	307	360	83	68	29	48	312	341	80	55	102	112	8-9	13-17	12-13	10-20	9-19	11-13

Clinch Date—Chicago 9/22.

Team Batting

Team	G	AB	R	OR	H	2B	3B	HR	TB	RBI	TBB	IBB	SO	HBP	SH	SF	SB	CS	SB%	GDP	Avg	OBP	Slg
Cleveland	154	5288	745	646	1390	216	25	167	2157	682	433	25	721	39	60	40	33	36	.48	119	.263	.328	.408
Boston	154	5225	726	696	1335	248	28	125	2014	678	626	31	810	23	65	46	68	25	.73	120	.256	.343	.385
Detroit	154	5211	713	732	1346	196	30	160	2082	667	580	31	737	44	73	40	34	17	.67	101	.258	.342	.400
New York	155	5379	687	647	1397	224	40	153	2160	651	457	37	828	30	76	38	45	22	.67	101	.260	.326	.402
Kansas City	154	5264	681	760	1383	231	43	117	2051	637	481	32	780	33	69	38	34	24	.59	124	.263	.333	.390
Chicago	156	5297	669	588	1325	220	46	97	1928	620	580	46	634	49	84	44	113	53	.68	107	.250	.335	.364
Washington	154	5092	619	701	1205	173	32	163	1931	580	517	20	881	26	64	35	51	34	.60	127	.237	.314	.379
Baltimore	155	5208	551	621	1240	182	23	109	1795	514	536	36	690	20	88	31	36	24	.60	126	.238	.315	.345
AL Total	1236	41964	5391	5391	10621	1690	267	1091	16118	5029	4210	258	6081	264	579	312	414	235	.64	925	.253	.323	.384
AL Avg Team	155	5246	674	674	1328	211	33	136	2015	629	526	32	760	33	72	39	52	29	.64	116	.253	.323	.384

Team Pitching

Team	G	CG	ShO	Rel	Sv	IP	H	R	ER	HR	SH	SF	HB	TBB	IBB	SO	WP	Bk	H/9	SO/9	BB/9	OAvg	OOBP	ERA
Chicago	156	44	13	242	36	1425.1	1297	588	521	129	71	34	31	525	45	761	21	4	8.2	4.8	3.3	.242	.311	3.29
Baltimore	155	45	15	180	30	1400.1	1290	621	554	111	78	34	30	476	40	735	36	4	8.3	4.7	3.1	.246	.311	3.56
New York	155	38	15	222	28	1399.0	1281	647	560	120	66	44	28	594	29	836	30	5	8.2	5.4	3.8	.244	.322	3.60
Cleveland	154	58	7	190	23	1383.2	1230	646	576	148	84	41	24	635	33	799	45	3	8.0	5.2	4.1	.239	.323	3.75
Washington	154	46	10	214	21	1360.0	1358	701	606	123	78	48	34	467	35	694	37	9	9.0	4.6	3.1	.259	.321	4.01
Boston	154	38	9	222	25	1364.0	1386	696	632	135	72	39	26	589	33	724	38	3	9.1	4.8	3.9	.266	.341	4.17
Detroit	154	53	9	197	24	1360.0	1327	732	635	177	50	33	45	432	18	829	24	5	8.8	5.5	2.9	.254	.315	4.20
Kansas City	154	44	8	241	21	1360.2	1452	760	658	148	80	39	46	492	24	703	41	3	9.6	4.6	3.3	.274	.338	4.35
AL Total	1236	366	86	1708	208	11053.0	10621	5391	4742	1091	579	312	264	4210	257	6081	272	36	8.6	5.0	3.4	.253	.330	3.86
AL Avg Team	155	46	11	214	26	1381.0	1328	674	593	136	72	39	33	526	32	760	34	5	8.6	5.0	3.4	.253	.330	3.86

Team Fielding

Team	G	PO	A	E	TC	DP	PB	Pct
Chicago	156	4293	1752	130	6175	141	10	.979
New York	155	4195	1730	131	6056	160	11	.978
Cleveland	154	4147	1584	127	5858	138	6	.978
Detroit	154	4080	1515	124	5719	131	14	.978
Boston	154	4092	1699	131	5922	167	13	.978
Baltimore	155	4202	1760	146	6108	163	49	.976
Washington	154	4087	1787	162	6036	140	19	.973
Kansas City	154	4086	1669	160	5915	156	15	.973
AL Total	1236	33182	13496	1111	47789	1196	137	.977

Team vs. Team Records

	Bal	Bos	ChA	Cle	Det	KCA	NYA	Was	Won
Bal	—	8	11	10	13	8	12	12	74
Bos	14	—	8	8	11	11	13	10	75
ChA	11	14	—	15	13	12	13	16	94
Cle	12	14	7	—	14	15	11	16	89
Det	9	11	9	8	—	15	14	10	76
KCA	14	11	10	7	7	—	5	12	66
NYA	10	9	9	11	8	17	—	15	79
Was	10	12	6	6	12	10	7	—	63
Lost	80	79	60	65	78	88	75	91	

1959 American League Batting Leaders

Games		At-Bats		Runs		Hits		Doubles		Triples	
N. Fox, ChA	156	N. Fox, ChA	624	E. Yost, Det	115	H. Kuenn, Det	198	H. Kuenn, Det	42	B. Allison, Was	9
F. Malzone, Bos	154	L. Aparicio, ChA	612	M. Mantle, NYA	104	N. Fox, ChA	191	F. Malzone, Bos	34	G. McDougald, NYA	8
R. Colavito, Cle	154	F. Malzone, Bos	604	V. Power, Cle	102	P. Runnels, Bos	176	N. Fox, ChA	34	4 tied with	7
H. Killebrew, Was	153	V. Power, Cle	595	J. Jensen, Bos	101	M. Minoso, Cle	172	P. Runnels, Bos	33		
L. Aparicio, ChA	152	R. Colavito, Cle	588	H. Kuenn, Det	99	V. Power, Cle	172	D. Williams, KCA	33		

Home Runs		Total Bases		Runs Batted In		Walks		Intentional Walks		Strikeouts	
R. Colavito, Cle	42	R. Colavito, Cle	301	J. Jensen, Bos	112	E. Yost, Det	135	A. Kaline, Det	12	M. Mantle, NYA	126
H. Killebrew, Was	42	H. Killebrew, Was	282	R. Colavito, Cle	111	P. Runnels, Bos	95	B. Gardner, Bal	9	W. Held, Cle	118
J. Lemon, Was	33	H. Kuenn, Det	281	H. Killebrew, Was	105	M. Mantle, NYA	93	R. Colavito, Cle	8	H. Killebrew, Was	116
M. Mantle, NYA	31	M. Mantle, NYA	278	J. Lemon, Was	100	D. Buddin, Bos	92	J. DeMaestri, KCA	8	D. Buddin, Bos	99
C. Maxwell, Det	31	B. Allison, Was	275	C. Maxwell, Det	95	H. Killebrew, Was	90	N. Fox, ChA	8	J. Lemon, Was	99

Hit By Pitch		Sac Hits		Sac Flies		Stolen Bases		Caught Stealing		GDP	
M. Minoso, Cle	17	T. Kubek, NYA	13	J. Jensen, Bos	12	L. Aparicio, ChA	56	L. Aparicio, ChA	13	S. Lollar, ChA	27
E. Yost, Det	12	J. Landis, ChA	13	B. Cerv, KCA	11	M. Mantle, NYA	21	V. Power, Cle	13	B. Allison, Was	22
S. Lollar, ChA	9	A. Pilarcik, Bal	13	F. Malzone, Bos	10	J. Landis, ChA	20	M. Minoso, Cle	10	J. Jensen, Bos	20
J. Landis, ChA	8	B. Boyd, Bal	12	J. Landis, ChA	9	J. Jensen, Bos	20	J. Landis, ChA	9	V. Power, Cle	19
4 tied with	7	2 tied with	11	2 tied with	7	B. Allison, Was	13	B. Allison, Was	8	P. Runnels, Bos	17

Runs Created		Runs Created/27 Outs		Batting Average		On-Base Percentage		Slugging Percentage		OBP+Slugging	
E. Yost, Det	112	A. Kaline, Det	7.88	H. Kuenn, Det	.353	E. Yost, Det	.435	A. Kaline, Det	.530	A. Kaline, Det	.940
M. Mantle, NYA	110	H. Kuenn, Det	7.79	A. Kaline, Det	.327	P. Runnels, Bos	.415	H. Killebrew, Was	.516	M. Mantle, NYA	.904
H. Kuenn, Det	109	E. Yost, Det	7.74	P. Runnels, Bos	.314	A. Kaline, Det	.410	M. Mantle, NYA	.514	H. Kuenn, Det	.903
R. Colavito, Cle	108	M. Mantle, NYA	7.43	N. Fox, ChA	.306	H. Kuenn, Det	.402	R. Colavito, Cle	.512	E. Yost, Det	.871
2 tied with	107	G. Woodling, Bal	6.92	M. Minoso, Cle	.302	G. Woodling, Bal	.402	J. Lemon, Was	.510	H. Killebrew, Was	.870

1959 American League Pitching Leaders

Wins		Losses		Winning Percentage		Games		Games Started		Complete Games	
E. Wynn, ChA	22	P. Ramos, Was	19	B. Shaw, ChA	.750	G. Staley, ChA	67	P. Foytack, Det	37	C. Pascual, Was	17
C. McLish, Cle	19	R. Kemmerer, Was	17	C. McLish, Cle	.704	T. Lown, ChA	60	E. Wynn, ChA	37	M. Pappas, Bal	15
B. Shaw, ChA	18	B. Pierce, ChA	15	E. Wynn, ChA	.688	T. Clevenger, Was	50	J. Bunning, Det	35	D. Mossi, Det	15
4 tied with	17	P. Foytack, Det	14	D. Mossi, Det	.654	B. Shaw, ChA	47	P. Ramos, Was	35	J. Bunning, Det	14
		3 tied with	13	I. Delock, Bos	.647	2 tied with	46	B. Pierce, ChA	33	E. Wynn, ChA	14

Shutouts		Saves		Games Finished		Batters Faced		Innings Pitched		Hits Allowed	
C. Pascual, Was	6	T. Lown, ChA	15	T. Lown, ChA	37	E. Wynn, ChA	1076	E. Wynn, ChA	255.2	C. McLish, Cle	253
E. Wynn, ChA	5	R. Duren, NYA	14	G. Staley, ChA	37	J. Bunning, Det	1037	J. Bunning, Det	249.2	P. Foytack, Det	239
M. Pappas, Bal	4	B. Loes, Bal	14	B. Loes, Bal	31	C. McLish, Cle	1021	P. Foytack, Det	240.1	P. Ramos, Was	233
7 tied with	3	G. Staley, ChA	14	R. Duren, NYA	29	G. Bell, Cle	1005	C. Pascual, Was	238.2	F. Lary, Det	225
		M. Fornieles, Bos	11	M. Fornieles, Bos	26	P. Foytack, Det	1000	C. McLish, Cle	235.1	R. Kemmerer, Was	221

Home Runs Allowed		Walks		Walks/9 Innings		Strikeouts		Strikeouts/9 Innings		Strikeout/Walk Ratio	
J. Bunning, Det	37	E. Wynn, ChA	119	H. Brown, Bal	1.8	J. Bunning, Det	201	H. Score, Cle	8.2	F. Lary, Det	2.98
P. Foytack, Det	34	H. Score, Cle	115	F. Lary, Det	1.9	C. Pascual, Was	185	J. Bunning, Det	7.2	C. Pascual, Was	2.68
P. Ramos, Was	29	G. Bell, Cle	105	N. Garver, KCA	1.9	E. Wynn, ChA	179	C. Pascual, Was	7.0	J. Bunning, Det	2.68
G. Bell, Cle	28	J. Casale, Bos	89	D. Mossi, Det	1.9	H. Score, Cle	147	B. Turley, NYA	6.5	D. Mossi, Det	2.55
H. Score, Cle	28	W. Ford, NYA	89	P. Ramos, Was	2.0	H. Wilhelm, Bal	139	E. Wynn, ChA	6.3	H. Brown, Bal	2.53

Earned Run Average		Component ERA		Hit Batsmen		Wild Pitches		Opponent Average		Opponent OBP	
H. Wilhelm, Bal	2.19	A. Ditmar, NYA	2.39	J. Kucks, 2tm	12	M. Pappas, Bal	14	H. Score, Cle	.210	A. Ditmar, NYA	.268
C. Pascual, Was	2.64	C. Pascual, Was	2.45	B. Daley, KCA	11	H. Score, Cle	14	A. Ditmar, NYA	.211	C. Pascual, Was	.282
B. Shaw, ChA	2.69	H. Wilhelm, Bal	2.69	J. Bunning, Det	11	T. Brewer, Bos	11	E. Wynn, ChA	.216	B. O'Dell, Bal	.284
A. Ditmar, NYA	2.90	M. Pappas, Bal	2.73	F. Lary, Det	11	R. Kemmerer, Was	10	B. O'Dell, Bal	.220	D. Mossi, Det	.284
J. Walker, Bal	2.92	B. O'Dell, Bal	2.73	H. Wilhelm, Bal	10	G. Bell, Cle	8	H. Wilhelm, Bal	.224	H. Brown, Bal	.289

1959 American League Miscellaneous

Managers

Baltimore	Paul Richards	74-80
Boston	Pinky Higgins	31-42
	Rudy York	0-1
	Billy Jurges	44-36
Chicago	Al Lopez	94-60
Cleveland	Joe Gordon	89-65
Detroit	Bill Norman	2-15
	Jimmy Dykes	74-63
Kansas City	Harry Craft	66-88
New York	Casey Stengel	79-75
Washington	Cookie Lavagetto	63-91

Awards

Most Valuable Player	Nellie Fox, 2b, ChA
Cy Young	Early Wynn, ChA
Rookie of the Year	Bob Allison, of, Was
STATS Manager of the Year	Al Lopez, ChA

STATS All-Star Team

C	Sherm Lollar, ChA	.265	22	84
1B	Vic Power, Cle	.289	10	60
2B	Nellie Fox, ChA	.306	2	70
3B	Eddie Yost, Det	.278	21	61
SS	Luis Aparicio, ChA	.257	6	51
OF	Tito Francona, Cle	.363	20	79
OF	Al Kaline, Det	.327	27	94
OF	Mickey Mantle, NYA	.285	31	75
P	Camilo Pascual, Was	17-10	2.64	185 K
P	Bob Shaw, ChA	18-6	2.69	89 K
P	Hoyt Wilhelm, Bal	15-11	2.19	139 K
P	Early Wynn, ChA	22-10	3.17	179 K
RP	Gerry Staley, ChA	8-5	2.24	14 Sv

Postseason

World Series	Chicago (AL) 2 vs. LA (NL) 4

Outstanding Performances

Four-Homer Games
Rocky Colavito, Cle   on June 10

Three-Homer Games
Charlie Maxwell, Det on May 3
Bob Cerv, KCA   on August 20

1959 National League Standings

	Overall					Home Games						Road Games						Park Index		Record by Month					
Team	W	L	Pct	GB	DIF	W	L	R	OR	HR	OHR	W	L	R	OR	HR	OHR	Run	HR	M/A	May	June	July	Aug	S/O
Los Angeles	88	68	.564	—	15	46	32	363	333	82	90	42	36	342	337	66	67	103	129	11-6	14-17	18-12	15-12	14-12	16-9
Milwaukee	86	70	.551	2.0	89	49	29	350	274	83	64	37	41	374	349	94	64	86	93	9-4	19-12	14-15	13-13	15-16	16-10
San Francisco	83	71	.539	4.0	79	42	35	339	271	80	63	41	36	366	342	87	76	86	88	9-7	17-12	17-14	14-12	16-13	10-13
Pittsburgh	78	76	.506	9.0	0	47	30	348	334	47	53	31	46	303	346	65	81	105	68	6-8	18-14	15-15	11-16	20-9	8-14
Chicago	74	80	.481	13.0	1	38	39	336	329	87	76	36	41	337	359	76	76	96	107	8-8	15-16	13-13	14-14	12-16	12-13
Cincinnati	74	80	.481	13.0	2	43	34	423	367	101	84	31	46	341	371	60	78	111	134	8-7	13-18	12-16	14-14	16-13	11-12
St. Louis	71	83	.461	16.0	0	42	35	366	359	64	64	29	48	275	366	54	73	113	101	4-13	15-13	16-12	13-16	13-18	10-11
Philadelphia	64	90	.416	23.0	4	37	40	316	354	55	66	27	50	283	371	58	84	102	85	6-8	11-20	9-17	16-13	12-21	10-11

Clinch Date—Los Angeles 9/29.

Team Batting

Team	G	AB	R	OR	H	2B	3B	HR	TB	RBI	TBB	IBB	SO	HBP	SH	SF	SB	CS	SB%	GDP	Avg	OBP	Slg
Cincinnati	154	5288	764	738	1448	258	34	161	2257	721	499	43	763	32	53	50	65	28	.70	121	.274	.346	.427
Milwaukee	157	5388	724	623	1426	216	36	177	2245	683	488	64	765	27	64	43	41	14	.75	130	.265	.334	.417
San Francisco	154	5281	705	613	1377	239	35	167	2187	660	473	57	875	25	73	38	81	34	.70	96	.261	.329	.414
Los Angeles	156	5282	705	670	1360	196	46	148	2092	667	591	61	891	28	100	32	84	51	.62	115	.257	.339	.396
Chicago	155	5296	673	688	1321	209	44	163	2107	635	498	63	911	43	62	40	32	19	.63	106	.249	.324	.398
Pittsburgh	155	5369	651	680	1414	230	42	112	2064	617	442	59	715	24	77	40	32	26	.55	125	.263	.327	.384
St. Louis	154	5317	641	725	1432	244	49	118	2128	605	485	49	747	19	60	26	65	53	.55	108	.269	.336	.400
Philadelphia	155	5109	599	725	1360	196	38	118	1848	560	498	54	858	34	59	35	39	46	.46	111	.242	.318	.362
NL Total	1240	42330	5462	5462	11015	1788	324	1159	16928	5148	3974	450	6525	232	548	304	439	271	.62	912	.260	.325	.400
NL Avg Team	155	5291	683	683	1377	224	41	145	2116	644	497	56	816	29	69	38	55	34	.62	114	.260	.325	.400

Team Pitching

Team	G	CG	ShO	Rel	Sv	IP	H	R	ER	HR	SH	SF	HB	TBB	IBB	SO	WP	Bk	H/9	SO/9	BB/9	OAvg	OOBP	ERA
San Francisco	154	52	12	205	23	1376.1	1279	613	530	139	80	36	33	500	53	873	29	2	8.4	5.7	3.3	.246	.314	3.47
Milwaukee	157	69	18	167	18	1400.2	1406	623	546	128	55	31	21	429	37	775	25	2	9.0	5.0	2.8	.260	.315	3.51
Los Angeles	156	43	14	241	26	1411.2	1317	670	595	157	59	38	51	614	71	1077	40	4	8.4	6.9	3.9	.247	.329	3.79
Pittsburgh	155	48	7	225	17	1393.1	1432	680	604	134	82	39	20	418	84	730	43	2	9.2	4.7	2.7	.267	.320	3.90
Chicago	155	30	11	250	25	1391.0	1337	688	620	152	73	43	24	519	40	765	34	6	8.7	4.9	3.4	.254	.321	4.01
Philadelphia	155	54	8	190	15	1354.0	1357	725	643	150	74	40	28	474	46	769	39	4	9.0	5.1	3.2	.261	.324	4.27
Cincinnati	154	44	7	232	26	1357.1	1460	738	650	162	61	34	34	456	45	690	29	2	9.7	4.6	3.0	.275	.335	4.31
St. Louis	154	36	8	231	21	1363.0	1427	725	657	137	64	43	21	564	74	846	46	2	9.4	5.6	3.7	.271	.341	4.34
NL Total	1240	376	85	1741	171	11047.1	11015	5462	4845	1159	548	304	232	3974	450	6525	285	24	9.0	5.3	3.2	.260	.331	3.95
NL Avg Team	155	47	11	218	21	1380.1	1377	683	606	145	69	38	29	497	56	816	36	3	9.0	5.3	3.2	.260	.331	3.95

Team Fielding

Team	G	PO	A	E	TC	DP	PB	Pct
Los Angeles	156	4235	1680	114	6029	154	19	.981
Milwaukee	157	4202	1732	127	6061	138	5	.979
Cincinnati	154	4072	1597	126	5795	157	6	.978
Chicago	155	4173	1758	140	6071	142	12	.977
St. Louis	154	4089	1673	146	5908	158	15	.975
Pittsburgh	155	4180	1727	154	6061	165	10	.975
San Francisco	154	4129	1645	152	5926	118	7	.974
Philadelphia	155	4062	1578	154	5794	132	14	.973
NL Total	1240	33142	13390	1113	47645	1164	88	.977

Team vs. Team Records

	ChN	Cin	LA	Mil	Phi	Pit	SF	StL	Won
ChN	—	9	11	10	10	12	12	10	74
Cin	13	—	13	11	9	9	8	11	74
LA	11	9	—	14	17	11	14	12	88
Mil	12	11	10	—	13	15	12	13	86
Phi	12	13	5	9	—	9	9	7	64
Pit	10	13	11	7	13	—	10	14	78
SF	10	14	8	10	13	12	—	16	83
StL	12	11	10	9	15	8	6	—	71
Lost	80	80	68	70	90	76	71	83	

1959 National League Batting Leaders

Games		At-Bats		Runs		Hits		Doubles		Triples	
D. Hoak, Pit	155	V. Pinson, Cin	648	V. Pinson, Cin	131	H. Aaron, Mil	223	V. Pinson, Cin	47	C. Neal, LA	11
E. Banks, ChN	155	H. Aaron, Mil	629	W. Mays, SF	125	V. Pinson, Cin	205	H. Aaron, Mil	46	W. Moon, LA	11
V. Pinson, Cin	154	T. Taylor, ChN	624	E. Mathews, Mil	118	O. Cepeda, SF	192	W. Mays, SF	43	V. Pinson, Cin	9
H. Aaron, Mil	154	C. Neal, LA	616	H. Aaron, Mil	116	J. Temple, Cin	186	G. Cimoli, StL	40	B. White, StL	9
R. Ashburn, Phi	153	D. Blasingame, StL	615	F. Robinson, Cin	106	E. Mathews, Mil	182	2 tied with	35	A. Dark, ChN	9

Home Runs		Total Bases		Runs Batted In		Walks		Intentional Walks		Strikeouts	
E. Mathews, Mil	46	H. Aaron, Mil	400	E. Banks, ChN	143	J. Gilliam, LA	96	E. Banks, ChN	20	W. Post, Phi	101
E. Banks, ChN	45	E. Mathews, Mil	352	F. Robinson, Cin	125	J. Cunningham, StL	88	H. Aaron, Mil	17	O. Cepeda, SF	100
H. Aaron, Mil	39	E. Banks, ChN	351	H. Aaron, Mil	123	W. Moon, LA	81	H. Anderson, Phi	14	V. Pinson, Cin	98
F. Robinson, Cin	36	W. Mays, SF	335	G. Bell, Cin	115	E. Mathews, Mil	80	S. Taylor, ChN	13	H. Anderson, Phi	95
W. Mays, SF	34	V. Pinson, Cin	330	E. Mathews, Mil	114	R. Ashburn, Phi	79	D. Snider, LA	13	F. Robinson, Cin	93

Hit By Pitch		Sac Hits		Sac Flies		Stolen Bases		Caught Stealing		GDP	
F. Robinson, Cin	8	C. Neal, LA	21	J. Temple, Cin	13	W. Mays, SF	27	D. Blasingame, StL	15	D. Crandall, Mil	24
G. Altman, ChN	7	B. Friend, Pit	12	F. Robinson, Cin	9	T. Taylor, ChN	23	R. Ashburn, Phi	11	C. Neal, LA	22
E. Banks, ChN	7	M. McCormick, SF	11	H. Aaron, Mil	9	O. Cepeda, SF	23	B. White, StL	10	D. Groat, Pit	21
3 tied with	6	J. Temple, Cin	11	E. Banks, ChN	9	J. Gilliam, LA	23	J. Gilliam, LA	10	G. Cimoli, StL	19
		S. Jones, SF	11	G. Bell, Cin	8	V. Pinson, Cin	21	3 tied with	9	H. Aaron, Mil	19

Runs Created		Runs Created/27 Outs		Batting Average		On-Base Percentage		Slugging Percentage		OBP+Slugging	
H. Aaron, Mil	143	H. Aaron, Mil	8.86	H. Aaron, Mil	.355	J. Cunningham, StL	.453	H. Aaron, Mil	.636	H. Aaron, Mil	1.037
E. Mathews, Mil	131	E. Mathews, Mil	8.31	J. Cunningham, StL	.345	H. Aaron, Mil	.401	E. Banks, ChN	.596	E. Mathews, Mil	.983
W. Mays, SF	123	W. Mays, SF	7.95	O. Cepeda, SF	.317	W. Moon, LA	.394	E. Mathews, Mil	.593	F. Robinson, Cin	.975
E. Banks, ChN	121	F. Robinson, Cin	7.84	V. Pinson, Cin	.316	F. Robinson, Cin	.391	F. Robinson, Cin	.583	E. Banks, ChN	.970
V. Pinson, Cin	120	J. Cunningham, StL	7.56	W. Mays, SF	.313	E. Mathews, Mil	.390	W. Mays, SF	.583	W. Mays, SF	.964

1959 National League Pitching Leaders

Wins		Losses		Winning Percentage		Games		Games Started		Complete Games	
S. Jones, SF	21	B. Friend, Pit	19	R. Face, Pit	.947	D. Elston, ChN	65	L. Burdette, Mil	39	W. Spahn, Mil	21
L. Burdette, Mil	21	B. Purkey, Cin	18	R. Craig, LA	.688	B. Henry, ChN	65	J. Antonelli, SF	38	L. Burdette, Mil	20
W. Spahn, Mil	21	R. Roberts, Phi	17	V. Law, Pit	.667	L. McDaniel, StL	62	L. Jackson, StL	37	V. Law, Pit	20
J. Antonelli, SF	19	M. McCormick, SF	16	J. Antonelli, SF	.655	D. McMahon, Mil	60	3 tied with	36	R. Roberts, Phi	19
2 tied with	18	3 tied with	15	G. Conley, Phi	.632	S. Miller, SF	59			2 tied with	17

Shutouts		Saves		Games Finished		Batters Faced		Innings Pitched		Hits Allowed	
7 tied with	4	D. McMahon, Mil	15	D. McMahon, Mil	49	W. Spahn, Mil	1203	W. Spahn, Mil	292.0	L. Burdette, Mil	312
		L. McDaniel, StL	15	D. Elston, ChN	49	L. Burdette, Mil	1193	L. Burdette, Mil	289.2	W. Spahn, Mil	282
		D. Elston, ChN	13	L. McDaniel, StL	47	J. Antonelli, SF	1150	J. Antonelli, SF	282.0	L. Jackson, StL	271
		B. Henry, ChN	12	R. Face, Pit	47	S. Jones, SF	1148	D. Drysdale, LA	270.2	B. Friend, Pit	267
		2 tied with	10	B. Henry, ChN	35	D. Drysdale, LA	1142	S. Jones, SF	270.2	R. Roberts, Phi	267

Home Runs Allowed		Walks		Walks/9 Innings		Strikeouts		Strikeouts/9 Innings		Strikeout/Walk Ratio	
L. Burdette, Mil	38	S. Jones, SF	109	D. Newcombe, Cin	1.1	D. Drysdale, LA	242	D. Drysdale, LA	8.0	R. Roberts, Phi	3.91
R. Roberts, Phi	34	G. Hobbie, ChN	106	L. Burdette, Mil	1.2	S. Jones, SF	209	S. Jones, SF	6.9	D. Newcombe, Cin	3.70
J. Antonelli, SF	29	D. Drysdale, LA	93	R. Roberts, Phi	1.2	S. Koufax, LA	173	J. Podres, LA	6.7	H. Haddix, Pit	3.04
3 tied with	26	S. Koufax, LA	92	B. Purkey, Cin	1.8	J. Antonelli, SF	165	E. Broglio, StL	6.6	L. Burdette, Mil	2.76
		2 tied with	89	V. Law, Pit	1.8	M. McCormick, SF	151	M. McCormick, SF	6.0	D. Drysdale, LA	2.60

Earned Run Average		Component ERA		Hit Batsmen		Wild Pitches		Opponent Average		Opponent OBP	
S. Jones, SF	2.83	H. Haddix, Pit	2.62	D. Drysdale, LA	18	L. McDaniel, StL	10	S. Jones, SF	.228	H. Haddix, Pit	.271
S. Miller, SF	2.84	G. Conley, Phi	2.65	D. McDevitt, LA	14	G. Hobbie, ChN	9	H. Haddix, Pit	.228	D. Newcombe, Cin	.279
B. Buhl, Mil	2.86	V. Law, Pit	2.82	S. Williams, LA	9	M. McCormick, SF	9	J. Antonelli, SF	.233	G. Conley, Phi	.280
W. Spahn, Mil	2.96	J. Antonelli, SF	2.95	3 tied with	8	R. Kline, Pit	9	D. Drysdale, LA	.233	V. Law, Pit	.281
V. Law, Pit	2.98	D. Hillman, ChN	2.97			4 tied with	8	G. Conley, Phi	.235	J. Antonelli, SF	.285

1959 National League Miscellaneous

Managers		
Chicago	Bob Scheffing	74-80
Cincinnati	Mayo Smith	35-45
	Fred Hutchinson	39-35
Los Angeles	Walter Alston	88-68
Milwaukee	Fred Haney	86-70
Philadelphia	Eddie Sawyer	64-90
Pittsburgh	Danny Murtaugh	78-76
St. Louis	Solly Hemus	71-83
San Francisco	Bill Rigney	83-71

Awards

Most Valuable Player	Ernie Banks, ss, ChN
STATS Cy Young	Sam Jones, SF
Rookie of the Year	Willie McCovey, 1b, SF
STATS Manager of the Year	Walter Alston, LA

STATS All-Star Team

C	Del Crandall, Mil	.257	21	72
1B	Frank Robinson, Cin	.311	36	125
2B	Johnny Temple, Cin	.311	8	67
3B	Eddie Mathews, Mil	.306	46	114
SS	Ernie Banks, ChN	.304	45	143
OF	Hank Aaron, Mil	.355	39	123
OF	Willie Mays, SF	.313	34	104
OF	Vada Pinson, Cin	.316	20	84
P	Johnny Antonelli, SF	19-10	3.10	165 K
P	Sam Jones, SF	21-15	2.83	209 K
P	Vern Law, Pit	18-9	2.98	110 K
P	Warren Spahn, Mil	21-15	2.96	143 K
RP	Roy Face, Pit	18-1	2.70	10 Sv

Postseason

World Series	L A (NL) 4 vs. Chicago (AL) 2

Outstanding Performances

Three-Homer Games

Don Demeter, LA	on April 21
Hank Aaron, Mil	on June 21
Frank Robinson, Cin	on August 22

Cycles

Frank Robinson, Cin	on May 2

1960 American League Standings

Team	Overall W	L	Pct	GB	DIF	Home Games W	L	R	OR	HR	OHR	Road Games W	L	R	OR	HR	OHR	Park Index Run	HR	Record by Month M/A	May	June	July	Aug	S/O
New York	97	57	.630	—	105	55	22	350	273	92	52	42	35	396	354	101	71	83	84	6-4	13-13	21-8	13-14	22-11	22-7
Baltimore	89	65	.578	8.0	35	44	33	332	313	50	52	45	32	350	293	73	65	100	74	6-6	19-9	17-15	12-15	22-8	13-12
Chicago	87	67	.565	10.0	37	51	26	379	298	57	54	36	41	362	319	55	73	99	87	5-4	16-14	16-13	20-9	15-15	15-12
Cleveland	76	78	.494	21.0	17	39	38	315	351	62	84	37	40	352	342	65	77	96	103	4-5	17-10	16-13	11-17	12-20	16-13
Washington	73	81	.474	24.0	7	32	45	336	366	75	74	41	36	336	330	72	56	105	116	5-6	9-17	16-12	16-13	18-15	9-18
Detroit	71	83	.461	26.0	17	40	37	322	323	78	85	31	46	311	321	72	56	102	127	5-4	12-14	15-16	12-15	15-18	12-16
Boston	65	89	.422	32.0	6	36	41	347	413	65	69	29	48	311	362	59	58	113	115	5-6	9-15	10-22	15-12	16-16	10-18
Kansas City	58	96	.377	39.0	6	34	43	327	369	58	79	24	53	288	387	52	81	103	103	5-6	13-16	8-20	10-14	9-26	13-14

Clinch Date—New York 9/25.

Team Batting

Team	G	AB	R	OR	H	2B	3B	HR	TB	RBI	TBB	IBB	SO	HBP	SH	SF	SB	CS	SB%	GDP	Avg	OBP	Slg
New York	155	5290	746	627	1377	215	40	193	2251	699	537	41	818	28	81	45	37	23	.62	112	.260	.337	.426
Chicago	154	5191	741	617	1402	242	38	112	2056	684	567	36	648	54	95	59	122	48	.72	133	.270	.355	.396
Baltimore	154	5170	682	606	1307	206	33	123	1948	640	596	36	801	36	72	37	37	24	.61	127	.253	.338	.377
Washington	154	5248	672	696	1283	205	43	147	2015	626	584	42	883	48	86	38	52	43	.55	130	.244	.330	.384
Cleveland	154	5296	667	693	1415	218	20	127	2054	632	444	41	573	32	97	52	58	30	.70	113	.267	.334	.388
Boston	154	5215	658	775	1359	234	32	124	2029	623	570	33	798	25	70	51	34	28	.55	153	.261	.342	.389
Detroit	154	5202	633	644	1243	188	34	150	1949	601	636	31	728	33	85	34	66	32	.67	117	.239	.330	.375
Kansas City	155	5226	615	756	1303	212	34	110	1913	566	513	22	744	12	75	32	16	11	.59	154	.249	.322	.366
AL Total	1234	41838	5414	5414	10689	1720	274	1086	16215	5071	4447	282	5993	268	661	348	422	234	.64	1039	.255	.328	.388
AL Avg Team	154	5230	677	677	1336	215	34	136	2027	634	556	35	749	34	83	44	53	29	.64	130	.255	.328	.388

Team Pitching

Team	G	CG	ShO	Rel	Sv	IP	H	R	ER	HR	SH	SF	HB	TBB	IBB	SO	WP	Bk	H/9	SO/9	BB/9	OAvg	OOBP	ERA
New York	155	38	16	263	42	1398.0	1225	627	546	123	78	42	30	609	33	712	38	5	7.9	4.6	3.9	.238	.320	3.52
Baltimore	154	48	11	177	22	1375.2	1222	606	538	117	77	44	34	552	19	785	34	2	8.0	5.1	3.6	.241	.317	3.52
Chicago	154	42	11	254	26	1381.0	1338	617	553	127	86	46	16	533	36	695	22	0	8.7	4.5	3.5	.258	.326	3.60
Detroit	154	40	7	209	25	1405.2	1336	644	568	141	82	35	47	474	31	824	36	5	8.6	5.3	3.0	.251	.316	3.64
Washington	154	34	10	258	35	1405.1	1392	696	589	130	75	38	36	538	49	775	35	1	8.9	5.0	3.4	.260	.329	3.77
Cleveland	154	32	10	219	30	1382.1	1308	693	607	161	69	45	26	636	26	771	37	3	8.5	5.0	4.1	.252	.334	3.95
Kansas City	155	44	4	227	14	1374.0	1428	756	668	160	110	50	43	525	36	664	37	4	9.4	4.3	3.4	.271	.339	4.38
Boston	154	34	6	252	23	1361.0	1440	775	699	127	84	48	36	580	53	767	55	5	9.5	5.1	3.8	.273	.346	4.62
AL Total	1234	312	75	1859	217	11083.0	10689	5414	4768	1086	661	348	268	4447	283	5993	294	25	8.7	4.9	3.6	.255	.336	3.87
AL Avg Team	154	39	9	232	27	1385.0	1336	677	596	136	83	44	34	556	35	749	37	3	8.7	4.9	3.6	.255	.336	3.87

Team Fielding

Team	G	PO	A	E	TC	DP	PB	Pct
Chicago	154	4143	1785	109	6037	175	6	.982
Baltimore	154	4123	1680	108	5911	172	24	.982
New York	155	4194	1794	129	6117	162	14	.979
Kansas City	155	4122	1666	127	5915	149	17	.979
Cleveland	154	4148	1568	128	5844	165	15	.978
Detroit	154	4220	1606	138	5964	138	13	.977
Boston	154	4083	1644	141	5868	156	14	.976
Washington	154	4214	1718	165	6097	159	19	.973
AL Total	1234	33247	13461	1045	47753	1276	120	.978

Team vs. Team Records

	Bal	Bos	ChA	Cle	Det	KCA	NYA	Was	Won
Bal	—	16	13	14	13	13	9	11	89
Bos	6	—	5	9	14	13	7	11	65
ChA	9	17	—	11	11	15	10	14	87
Cle	8	13	11	—	7	15	6	16	76
Det	9	8	11	15	—	10	8	10	71
KCA	9	9	7	7	12	—	7	7	58
NYA	13	15	12	16	14	15	—	12	97
Was	11	11	8	6	12	15	10	—	73
Lost	65	89	67	78	83	96	57	81	

1960 American League Batting Leaders

Games			At-Bats			Runs			Hits			Doubles			Triples		
M. Minoso, ChA	154		N. Fox, ChA	605		M. Mantle, NYA	119		M. Minoso, ChA	184		T. Francona, Cle	36		N. Fox, ChA	10	
R. Hansen, Bal	153		L. Aparicio, ChA	600		R. Maris, NYA	98		B. Robinson, Bal	175		B. Skowron, NYA	34		B. Robinson, Bal	9	
L. Aparicio, ChA	153		B. Robinson, Bal	595		M. Minoso, ChA	89		N. Fox, ChA	175		M. Minoso, ChA	32		5 tied with	7	
M. Mantle, NYA	153		F. Malzone, Bos	595		J. Landis, ChA	89		A. Smith, ChA	169		G. Freese, ChA	32				
3 tied with	152		B. Gardner, Was	592		R. Sievers, ChA	87		P. Runnels, Bos	169		3 tied with	31				

Home Runs			Total Bases			Runs Batted In			Walks			Intentional Walks			Strikeouts		
M. Mantle, NYA	40		M. Mantle, NYA	294		R. Maris, NYA	112		E. Yost, Det	125		J. Lemon, Was	8		M. Mantle, NYA	125	
R. Maris, NYA	39		R. Maris, NYA	290		M. Minoso, ChA	105		M. Mantle, NYA	111		R. Sievers, ChA	8		J. Lemon, Was	114	
J. Lemon, Was	38		M. Minoso, ChA	284		V. Wertz, Bos	103		B. Allison, Was	92		5 tied with	7		H. Killebrew, Was	106	
R. Colavito, Det	35		B. Skowron, NYA	284		J. Lemon, Was	100		G. Woodling, Bal	84					B. Skowron, NYA	95	
H. Killebrew, Was	31		J. Lemon, Was	268		J. Gentile, Bal	98		J. Landis, ChA	80					2 tied with	94	

Hit By Pitch			Sac Hits			Sac Flies			Stolen Bases			Caught Stealing			GDP		
M. Minoso, ChA	13		L. Aparicio, ChA	20		M. Minoso, ChA	9		L. Aparicio, ChA	51		M. Minoso, ChA	13		B. Robinson, Bal	29	
N. Fox, ChA	10		C. Fernandez, Det	19		J. Lemon, Was	9		J. Landis, ChA	23		B. Allison, Was	9		S. Lollar, ChA	22	
J. Landis, ChA	9		V. Power, Cle	14		5 tied with	8		L. Green, Was	21		L. Green, Was	8		F. Malzone, Bos	20	
5 tied with	8		N. Fox, ChA	14					A. Kaline, Det	19		L. Aparicio, ChA	8		B. Tuttle, KCA	19	
			2 tied with	13					J. Piersall, Cle	18		4 tied with	6		3 tied with	18	

Runs Created			Runs Created/27 Outs			Batting Average			On-Base Percentage			Slugging Percentage			OBP+Slugging		
M. Mantle, NYA	118		M. Mantle, NYA	7.97		P. Runnels, Bos	.320		E. Yost, Det	.414		R. Maris, NYA	.581		M. Mantle, NYA	.957	
R. Maris, NYA	106		R. Maris, NYA	7.72		A. Smith, ChA	.315		G. Woodling, Bal	.401		M. Mantle, NYA	.558		R. Maris, NYA	.952	
M. Minoso, ChA	105		R. Sievers, ChA	7.53		M. Minoso, ChA	.311		P. Runnels, Bos	.401		H. Killebrew, Was	.534		R. Sievers, ChA	.930	
J. Lemon, Was	97		H. Killebrew, Was	7.24		B. Skowron, NYA	.309		M. Mantle, NYA	.399		R. Sievers, ChA	.534		H. Killebrew, Was	.909	
2 tied with	93		G. Woodling, Bal	6.88		H. Kuenn, Cle	.308		R. Sievers, ChA	.396		B. Skowron, NYA	.528		B. Skowron, NYA	.881	

1960 American League Pitching Leaders

Wins			Losses			Winning Percentage			Games			Games Started			Complete Games		
C. Estrada, Bal	18		P. Ramos, Was	18		J. Coates, NYA	.813		M. Fornieles, Bos	70		J. Perry, Cle	36		F. Lary, Det	15	
J. Perry, Cle	18		B. Daley, KCA	16		H. Brown, Bal	.706		G. Staley, ChA	64		P. Ramos, Was	36		P. Ramos, Was	14	
B. Daley, KCA	16		F. Sullivan, Bos	16		F. Baumann, ChA	.684		T. Clevenger, Was	53		F. Lary, Det	36		R. Herbert, KCA	14	
3 tied with	15		3 tied with	15		B. Pierce, ChA	.667		M. Kutyna, KCA	51		B. Daley, KCA	35		B. Daley, KCA	13	
						M. Fornieles, Bos	.667		R. Moore, 2tm	51		E. Wynn, ChA	35		E. Wynn, ChA	13	

Shutouts			Saves			Games Finished			Batters Faced			Innings Pitched			Hits Allowed		
J. Perry, Cle	4		M. Fornieles, Bos	14		M. Fornieles, Bos	48		P. Ramos, Was	1162		F. Lary, Det	274.1		F. Lary, Det	262	
W. Ford, NYA	4		J. Klippstein, Cle	14		G. Staley, ChA	45		F. Lary, Det	1148		P. Ramos, Was	274.0		J. Perry, Cle	257	
E. Wynn, ChA	4		R. Moore, 2tm	13		M. Kutyna, KCA	30		J. Perry, Cle	1103		J. Perry, Cle	261.1		R. Herbert, KCA	256	
6 tied with	3		B. Shantz, NYA	11		J. Klippstein, Cle	30		R. Herbert, KCA	1063		R. Herbert, KCA	252.2		P. Ramos, Was	254	
			2 tied with	10		2 tied with	24		2 tied with	1024		J. Bunning, Det	252.0		B. Daley, KCA	234	

Home Runs Allowed			Walks			Walks/9 Innings			Strikeouts			Strikeouts/9 Innings			Strikeout/Walk Ratio		
J. Perry, Cle	35		S. Barber, Bal	113		H. Brown, Bal	1.2		J. Bunning, Det	201		J. Bunning, Det	7.2		J. Bunning, Det	3.14	
D. Hall, KCA	28		E. Wynn, ChA	112		D. Mossi, Det	1.8		P. Ramos, Was	160		G. Bell, Cle	6.3		H. Brown, Bal	3.00	
B. Daley, KCA	27		C. Estrada, Bal	101		D. Hall, KCA	1.9		E. Wynn, ChA	158		C. Estrada, Bal	6.2		F. Lary, Det	2.40	
M. Grant, Cle	26		P. Ramos, Was	99		F. Lary, Det	2.0		F. Lary, Det	149		E. Wynn, ChA	6.0		B. Pierce, ChA	2.35	
2 tied with	25		B. Daley, KCA	96		B. Pierce, ChA	2.1		C. Estrada, Bal	144		B. Monbouquette, Bos	5.6		D. Mossi, Det	2.16	

Earned Run Average			Component ERA			Hit Batsmen			Wild Pitches			Opponent Average			Opponent OBP		
F. Baumann, ChA	2.67		J. Bunning, Det	2.79		F. Lary, Det	19		S. Barber, Bal	10		C. Estrada, Bal	.218		H. Brown, Bal	.283	
J. Bunning, Det	2.79		H. Brown, Bal	2.91		C. Estrada, Bal	15		M. Pappas, Bal	10		B. Turley, NYA	.222		J. Bunning, Det	.292	
H. Brown, Bal	3.06		F. Baumann, ChA	2.93		J. Bunning, Det	11		G. Bell, Cle	9		S. Barber, Bal	.226		D. Mossi, Det	.293	
A. Ditmar, NYA	3.06		W. Ford, NYA	2.98		B. Daley, KCA	10		D. Sisler, Det	9		W. Ford, NYA	.235		W. Ford, NYA	.297	
W. Ford, NYA	3.08		R. Terry, NYA	3.19		J. Tsitouris, KCA	8		T. Brewer, Bos	9		J. Bunning, Det	.236		D. Hall, KCA	.299	

1960 American League Miscellaneous

Managers		
Baltimore	Paul Richards	89-65
Boston	Billy Jurges	15-27
	Del Baker	2-5
	Pinky Higgins	48-57
Chicago	Al Lopez	87-67
Cleveland	Joe Gordon	49-46
	Jo-Jo White	1-0
	Jimmy Dykes	26-32
Detroit	Jimmy Dykes	44-52
	Billy Hitchcock	1-0
	Joe Gordon	26-31
Kansas City	Bob Elliott	58-96
New York	Casey Stengel	97-57
Washington	Cookie Lavagetto	73-81

Awards

Most Valuable Player	Roger Maris, of, NYA
STATS Cy Young	Chuck Estrada, Bal
Rookie of the Year	Ron Hansen, ss, Bal
STATS Manager of the Year	Casey Stengel, NYA

STATS All-Star Team

C	John Romano, Cle	.272	16	52
1B	Roy Sievers, ChA	.295	28	93
2B	Pete Runnels, Bos	.320	2	35
3B	Brooks Robinson, Bal	.294	14	88
SS	Ron Hansen, Bal	.255	22	86
OF	Mickey Mantle, NYA	.275	40	94
OF	Roger Maris, NYA	.283	39	112
OF	Ted Williams, Bos	.316	29	72
P	Art Ditmar, NYA	15-9	3.06	65 K
P	Chuck Estrada, Bal	18-11	3.58	144 K
P	Milt Pappas, Bal	15-11	3.37	126 K
P	Jim Perry, Cle	18-10	3.62	120 K
RP	Mike Fornieles, Bos	10-5	2.64	14 Sv

Postseason

World Series	NYA (AL) 3 vs. Pittsburgh (NL) 4

Outstanding Performances

Cycles

Brooks Robinson, Bal on July 15

1960 National League Standings

Team	Overall W	L	Pct	GB	DIF	Home Games W	L	R	OR	HR	OHR	Road Games W	L	R	OR	HR	OHR	Park Index Run	HR	Record by Month M/A	May	June	July	Aug	S/O
Pittsburgh	95	59	.617	—	146	52	25	362	287	51	36	43	34	372	306	69	69	96	63	11-3	16-11	15-11	15-14	21-10	17-10
Milwaukee	88	66	.571	7.0	3	51	26	342	270	90	56	37	40	382	388	80	74	79	95	7-5	9-11	22-11	16-13	16-15	18-11
St. Louis	86	68	.558	9.0	0	51	26	361	308	78	64	35	42	278	308	60	63	114	115	7-6	11-16	15-13	20-9	18-11	15-13
Los Angeles	82	72	.532	13.0	9	42	35	379	334	89	97	40	37	283	259	37	57	132	198	8-7	12-14	13-14	19-7	15-15	15-15
San Francisco	79	75	.513	16.0	30	45	32	296	256	46	34	34	43	375	375	84	73	74	51	10-5	16-11	11-16	13-11	12-19	17-13
Cincinnati	67	87	.435	28.0	2	37	40	314	347	75	68	30	47	326	345	65	66	99	109	4-10	18-10	10-15	10-19	14-18	11-15
Chicago	60	94	.390	35.0	2	33	44	331	390	52	78	27	50	303	386	67	74	105	92	3-10	11-11	13-18	8-21	16-14	9-20
Philadelphia	59	95	.383	36.0	0	31	46	300	373	54	74	28	49	246	318	45	59	119	123	5-9	9-18	14-15	10-17	10-20	11-16

Clinch Date—Pittsburgh 9/25.

Team Batting

Team	G	AB	R	OR	H	2B	3B	HR	TB	RBI	TBB	IBB	SO	HBP	SH	SF	SB	CS	SB%	GDP	Avg	OBP	Slg
Pittsburgh	155	5406	734	593	1493	236	56	120	2201	689	486	71	747	20	69	48	34	24	.59	119	.276	.343	.407
Milwaukee	154	5263	724	658	1393	198	48	170	2197	681	463	53	793	23	59	60	69	37	.65	101	.265	.334	.417
San Francisco	156	5324	671	631	1357	220	62	130	2091	622	467	61	846	33	60	66	95	53	.64	108	.255	.332	.393
Los Angeles	154	5227	662	593	1333	216	38	126	2003	606	529	46	837	27	102	50	73	37	.66	110	.255	.326	.383
Cincinnati	154	5289	640	692	1324	230	40	140	2054	604	512	44	858	34	60	45	86	45	.66	106	.250	.326	.388
St. Louis	155	5187	639	616	1317	213	48	138	2040	592	501	63	792	31	52	35	48	35	.58	118	.254	.327	.393
Chicago	156	5311	634	776	1293	213	48	119	1959	600	531	69	897	19	64	35	51	34	.60	109	.243	.319	.369
Philadelphia	154	5169	546	691	1235	186	44	99	1816	503	448	40	1054	33	66	32	45	48	.48	104	.239	.308	.351
NL Total	1238	42176	5250	5250	10745	1722	384	1042	16361	4897	3937	447	6824	220	532	344	501	313	.62	875	.255	.319	.388
NL Avg Team	155	5272	656	656	1343	215	48	130	2045	612	492	56	853	28	67	43	63	39	.62	109	.255	.319	.388

Team Pitching

Team	G	CG	ShO	Rel	Sv	IP	H	R	ER	HR	SH	SF	HB	TBB	IBB	SO	WP	Bk	H/9	SO/9	BB/9	OAvg	OOBP	ERA
Los Angeles	154	46	13	204	20	1398.0	1218	593	528	154	46	25	33	564	58	1122	45	5	7.8	7.2	3.6	.234	.311	3.44
San Francisco	156	55	16	214	26	1396.0	1288	631	534	107	85	39	23	512	58	897	48	8	8.3	5.8	3.3	.245	.313	3.44
Pittsburgh	155	47	11	205	33	1399.2	1363	593	543	105	71	39	11	386	61	811	25	1	8.8	5.2	2.5	.257	.307	3.49
St. Louis	155	37	11	217	30	1371.0	1316	616	555	127	57	47	12	511	44	906	41	3	8.6	5.9	3.4	.253	.319	3.64
Milwaukee	154	55	13	182	28	1387.1	1327	658	580	130	65	35	35	518	54	807	41	4	8.6	5.2	3.4	.251	.320	3.76
Cincinnati	154	33	8	253	35	1390.1	1417	692	618	134	70	44	42	442	54	740	33	2	9.2	4.8	2.9	.267	.326	4.00
Philadelphia	154	45	6	199	16	1375.1	1423	691	613	133	78	63	22	439	56	736	38	5	9.3	4.8	2.9	.270	.325	4.01
Chicago	156	36	6	260	25	1402.2	1393	776	678	152	60	52	42	565	56	805	39	4	8.9	5.2	3.6	.260	.333	4.35
NL Total	1238	354	84	1734	213	11120.1	10745	5250	4649	1042	532	344	220	3937	447	6824	310	30	8.7	5.5	3.2	.255	.327	3.76
NL Avg Team	155	44	11	217	27	1390.1	1343	656	581	130	67	43	28	492	56	853	39	4	8.7	5.5	3.2	.255	.327	3.76

Team Fielding

Team	G	PO	A	E	TC	DP	PB	Pct
Los Angeles	154	4194	1656	125	5975	142	18	.979
Pittsburgh	155	4199	1774	128	6101	163	10	.979
Cincinnati	154	4171	1658	125	5954	155	10	.979
Chicago	156	4208	1756	143	6107	133	15	.977
Milwaukee	154	4162	1665	141	5968	137	16	.976
St. Louis	155	4113	1629	141	5883	152	7	.976
Philadelphia	154	4126	1622	155	5903	129	15	.974
San Francisco	156	4188	1614	166	5968	117	7	.972
NL Total	1238	33361	13374	1124	47859	1128	98	.977

Team vs. Team Records

	ChN	Cin	LA	Mil	Phi	Pit	SF	StL	Won
ChN	—	10	9	7	10	7	9	8	60
Cin	12	—	12	9	9	6	11	8	67
LA	13	10	—	12	16	11	10	10	82
Mil	15	13	10	—	16	9	14	11	88
Phi	12	13	6	6	—	7	8	7	59
Pit	15	16	11	13	15	—	14	11	95
SF	13	11	12	8	14	8	—	13	79
StL	14	14	12	11	15	11	9	—	86
Lost	94	87	72	66	95	59	75	68	

1960 National League Batting Leaders

Games		At-Bats		Runs		Hits		Doubles		Triples	
E. Banks, ChN	156	V. Pinson, Cin	652	B. Bruton, Mil	112	W. Mays, SF	190	V. Pinson, Cin	37	B. Bruton, Mil	13
D. Hoak, Pit	155	B. Bruton, Mil	629	E. Mathews, Mil	108	V. Pinson, Cin	187	O. Cepeda, SF	36	V. Pinson, Cin	12
V. Pinson, Cin	154	E. Banks, ChN	597	V. Pinson, Cin	107	D. Groat, Pit	186	F. Robinson, Cin	33	W. Mays, SF	12
3 tied with	153	W. Mays, SF	595	W. Mays, SF	107	B. Bruton, Mil	180	B. Skinner, Pit	33	H. Aaron, Mil	11
		H. Aaron, Mil	590	H. Aaron, Mil	102	R. Clemente, Pit	179	E. Banks, ChN	32	3 tied with	10

Home Runs		Total Bases		Runs Batted In		Walks		Intentional Walks		Strikeouts	
E. Banks, ChN	41	H. Aaron, Mil	334	H. Aaron, Mil	126	R. Ashburn, ChN	116	E. Banks, ChN	28	P. Herrera, Phi	136
H. Aaron, Mil	40	E. Banks, ChN	331	E. Mathews, Mil	124	E. Mathews, Mil	111	B. Mazeroski, Pit	15	E. Mathews, Mil	113
E. Mathews, Mil	39	W. Mays, SF	330	E. Banks, ChN	117	J. Gilliam, LA	96	H. Smith, StL	13	F. Howard, LA	108
K. Boyer, StL	32	K. Boyer, StL	310	W. Mays, SF	103	F. Robinson, Cin	82	H. Aaron, Mil	13	D. Stuart, Pit	107
F. Robinson, Cin	31	V. Pinson, Cin	308	K. Boyer, StL	97	D. Spencer, StL	81	2 tied with	12	T. Taylor, 2tm	98

Hit By Pitch		Sac Hits		Sac Flies		Stolen Bases		Caught Stealing		GDP	
F. Robinson, Cin	9	J. Javier, StL	15	H. Aaron, Mil	12	M. Wills, LA	50	B. Bruton, Mil	13	R. Clemente, Pit	21
O. Cepeda, SF	8	C. Neal, LA	14	D. Crandall, Mil	12	V. Pinson, Cin	32	M. Wills, LA	12	W. Moon, LA	21
E. Kasko, Cin	6	D. Groat, Pit	12	N. Larker, LA	9	T. Taylor, 2tm	26	V. Pinson, Cin	12	F. Robinson, Cin	18
J. Cunningham, StL	6	B. Friend, Pit	11	W. Mays, SF	9	W. Mays, SF	25	T. Taylor, 2tm	11	C. Neal, LA	18
4 tied with	5	J. Podres, LA	10	B. Mazeroski, Pit	8	B. Bruton, Mil	22	2 tied with	10	2 tied with	17

Runs Created		Runs Created/27 Outs		Batting Average		On-Base Percentage		Slugging Percentage		OBP+Slugging	
E. Mathews, Mil	124	E. Mathews, Mil	8.05	D. Groat, Pit	.325	R. Ashburn, ChN	.415	F. Robinson, Cin	.595	F. Robinson, Cin	1.002
W. Mays, SF	122	F. Robinson, Cin	7.81	N. Larker, LA	.323	F. Robinson, Cin	.407	H. Aaron, Mil	.566	E. Mathews, Mil	.948
H. Aaron, Mil	117	W. Mays, SF	7.52	W. Mays, SF	.319	E. Mathews, Mil	.397	K. Boyer, StL	.562	W. Mays, SF	.936
E. Banks, ChN	113	H. Aaron, Mil	7.11	R. Clemente, Pit	.314	W. Moon, LA	.383	W. Mays, SF	.555	K. Boyer, StL	.932
K. Boyer, StL	105	K. Boyer, StL	6.96	K. Boyer, StL	.304	W. Mays, SF	.381	E. Banks, ChN	.554	H. Aaron, Mil	.919

1960 National League Pitching Leaders

Wins		Losses		Winning Percentage		Games		Games Started		Complete Games	
E. Broglio, StL	21	G. Hobbie, ChN	20	L. McDaniel, StL	.750	R. Face, Pit	68	L. Jackson, StL	38	L. Burdette, Mil	18
W. Spahn, Mil	21	J. Hook, Cin	18	E. Broglio, StL	.700	L. McDaniel, StL	65	B. Friend, Pit	37	V. Law, Pit	18
V. Law, Pit	20	J. Buzhardt, Phi	16	V. Law, Pit	.690	D. Elston, ChN	60	G. Hobbie, ChN	36	W. Spahn, Mil	18
L. Burdette, Mil	19	D. Cardwell, 2tm	16	W. Spahn, Mil	.677	T. Farrell, Phi	59	D. Drysdale, LA	36	G. Hobbie, ChN	16
3 tied with	18	R. Roberts, Phi	16	B. Buhl, Mil	.640	E. Roebuck, LA	58	2 tied with	35	B. Friend, Pit	16

Shutouts		Saves		Games Finished		Batters Faced		Innings Pitched		Hits Allowed	
J. Sanford, SF	6	L. McDaniel, StL	26	R. Face, Pit	61	L. Jackson, StL	1173	L. Jackson, StL	282.0	L. Jackson, StL	277
D. Drysdale, LA	5	R. Face, Pit	24	T. Farrell, Phi	50	G. Hobbie, ChN	1118	B. Friend, Pit	275.2	L. Burdette, Mil	277
5 tied with	4	B. Henry, Cin	17	L. McDaniel, StL	47	B. Friend, Pit	1118	L. Burdette, Mil	275.2	B. Friend, Pit	266
		J. Brosnan, Cin	12	L. Sherry, LA	38	L. Burdette, Mil	1117	V. Law, Pit	271.2	V. Law, Pit	266
		3 tied with	11	B. Henry, Cin	38	W. Spahn, Mil	1110	D. Drysdale, LA	269.0	B. Purkey, Cin	259

Home Runs Allowed		Walks		Walks/9 Innings		Strikeouts		Strikeouts/9 Innings		Strikeout/Walk Ratio	
J. Hook, Cin	31	B. Buhl, Mil	103	L. Burdette, Mil	1.1	D. Drysdale, LA	246	S. Koufax, LA	10.1	B. Friend, Pit	4.07
R. Roberts, Phi	31	G. Hobbie, ChN	101	R. Roberts, Phi	1.3	S. Koufax, LA	197	D. Drysdale, LA	8.2	R. Roberts, Phi	3.59
G. Hobbie, ChN	27	E. Broglio, StL	100	V. Law, Pit	1.3	S. Jones, SF	190	S. Williams, LA	7.6	D. Drysdale, LA	3.42
D. Drysdale, LA	27	S. Koufax, LA	100	B. Friend, Pit	1.5	E. Broglio, StL	188	E. Broglio, StL	7.5	V. Law, Pit	3.00
2 tied with	26	J. Sanford, SF	99	H. Haddix, Pit	2.0	B. Friend, Pit	183	S. Jones, SF	7.3	G. Conley, Phi	2.79

Earned Run Average		Component ERA		Hit Batsmen		Wild Pitches		Opponent Average		Opponent OBP	
M. McCormick, SF	2.70	D. Drysdale, LA	2.62	D. Drysdale, LA	10	J. Sanford, SF	15	S. Koufax, LA	.207	D. Drysdale, LA	.274
E. Broglio, StL	2.74	M. McCormick, SF	2.70	G. Hobbie, ChN	9	M. McCormick, SF	12	S. Williams, LA	.210	B. Friend, Pit	.280
D. Drysdale, LA	2.84	B. Friend, Pit	2.72	B. Purkey, Cin	9	B. Buhl, Mil	11	E. Broglio, StL	.213	S. Williams, LA	.280
S. Williams, LA	3.00	E. Broglio, StL	2.86	3 tied with	7	3 tied with	9	D. Drysdale, LA	.215	V. Law, Pit	.286
B. Friend, Pit	3.00	L. Burdette, Mil	2.91					B. Buhl, Mil	.229	L. Burdette, Mil	.287

1960 National League Miscellaneous

Managers

Chicago	Charlie Grimm	6-11
	Lou Boudreau	54-83
Cincinnati	Fred Hutchinson	67-87
Los Angeles	Walter Alston	82-72
Milwaukee	Chuck Dressen	88-66
Philadelphia	Eddie Sawyer	0-1
	Andy Cohen	1-0
	Gene Mauch	58-94
Pittsburgh	Danny Murtaugh	95-59
St. Louis	Solly Hemus	86-68
San Francisco	Bill Rigney	33-25
	Tom Sheehan	46-50

Awards

Most Valuable Player	Dick Groat, ss, Pit
Cy Young	Vern Law, Pit
Rookie of the Year	Frank Howard, of, LA
STATS Manager of the Year	Danny Murtaugh, Pit

STATS All-Star Team

C	Del Crandall, Mil	.294	19	77
1B	Frank Robinson, Cin	.297	31	83
2B	Bill Mazeroski, Pit	.273	11	64
3B	Eddie Mathews, Mil	.277	39	124
SS	Ernie Banks, ChN	.271	41	117
OF	Hank Aaron, Mil	.292	40	126
OF	Orlando Cepeda, SF	.297	24	96
OF	Willie Mays, SF	.319	29	103
P	Ernie Broglio, StL	21-9	2.74	188 K
P	Bob Friend, Pit	18-12	3.00	183 K
P	Vern Law, Pit	20-9	3.08	120 K
P	Warren Spahn, Mil	21-10	3.50	154 K
RP	Lindy McDaniel, StL	12-4	2.09	26 Sv

Postseason

World Series	Pittsburgh (NL) 4 vs. NYA (AL) 3

Outstanding Performances

No-Hitters

Don Cardwell, ChN	vs. StL on May 15
Lew Burdette, Mil	vs. Phi on August 18
Warren Spahn, Mil	vs. Phi on September 16

Three-Homer Games

Dick Stuart, Pit	on June 30

Cycles

Bill White, StL	on August 14

1961 American League Standings

Team	Overall					Home Games						Road Games						Park Index		Record by Month					
	W	L	Pct	GB	DIF	W	L	R	OR	HR	OHR	W	L	R	OR	HR	OHR	Run	HR	M/A	May	June	July	Aug	S/O
New York	109	53	.673	—	85	65	16	411	251	112	59	44	37	416	361	128	78	85	83	9-5	14-12	22-10	20-9	22-9	22-8
Detroit	101	61	.623	8.0	77	50	31	389	324	90	95	51	30	452	347	90	75	89	112	10-4	19-12	19-10	16-12	22-9	15-14
Baltimore	95	67	.586	14.0	0	48	33	320	283	61	46	47	34	371	305	88	63	89	71	8-8	17-12	15-15	18-11	20-11	17-10
Chicago	86	76	.531	23.0	4	53	28	411	320	80	55	33	48	354	406	58	103	96	84	7-6	9-21	22-10	13-16	19-10	16-13
Cleveland	78	83	.484	30.5	14	40	41	342	380	74	98	38	42	395	372	76	80	93	109	8-8	18-9	17-16	12-16	12-17	11-17
Boston	76	86	.469	33.0	0	50	31	401	386	63	91	26	55	328	406	49	76	107	123	7-7	10-16	21-13	9-22	17-14	12-14
Minnesota	70	90	.438	38.0	11	36	44	380	423	92	89	34	46	327	355	75	74	118	121	9-6	10-18	10-21	16-11	12-18	13-16
Los Angeles	70	91	.435	38.5	4	46	36	447	421	122	126	24	55	297	363	67	54	127	197	4-9	12-16	12-22	17-10	13-19	12-15
Washington	61	100	.379	47.5	0	33	46	288	366	34	53	28	54	330	410	85	78	92	55	5-11	17-12	11-19	12-14	5-24	11-20
Kansas City	61	100	.379	47.5	4	33	47	365	434	33	61	28	53	318	429	57	80	108	69	5-8	14-12	10-23	8-20	11-22	13-15

Clinch Date—New York 9/20.

Team Batting

Team	G	AB	R	OR	H	2B	3B	HR	TB	RBI	TBB	IBB	SO	HBP	SH	SF	SB	CS	SB%	GDP	Avg	OBP	Slg
Detroit	163	5561	841	671	1481	215	53	180	2342	779	673	39	867	38	64	42	98	36	.73	125	.266	.354	.421
New York	163	5559	827	612	1461	194	40	240	2455	782	543	45	785	35	57	45	28	18	.61	120	.263	.337	.442
Chicago	163	5556	765	726	1475	216	46	138	2197	704	550	30	612	57	71	51	100	40	.71	118	.265	.343	.395
Los Angeles	162	5424	744	784	1331	218	22	189	2160	700	681	25	1068	30	80	37	37	28	.57	116	.245	.337	.398
Cleveland	161	5609	737	752	1493	257	39	150	2278	682	492	33	720	28	73	50	34	11	.76	133	.266	.334	.406
Boston	163	5508	729	792	1401	251	37	112	2062	682	647	28	847	29	81	42	56	36	.61	129	.254	.340	.374
Minnesota	161	5417	707	778	1353	215	40	167	2149	665	597	25	840	33	67	42	47	43	.52	141	.250	.333	.397
Baltimore	163	5481	691	588	1393	227	36	149	2139	638	581	25	902	23	78	48	39	30	.57	140	.254	.333	.390
Kansas City	162	5423	683	863	1342	216	47	90	1922	631	580	10	772	25	89	47	58	22	.73	107	.247	.328	.354
Washington	161	5366	618	776	1307	217	44	119	1969	578	558	30	917	21	73	44	81	47	.63	127	.244	.322	.367
AL Total	1622	54904	7342	7342	14037	2226	404	1534	21673	6841	5902	290	8330	319	733	448	578	311	.65	1256	.256	.329	.395
AL Avg Team	162	5490	734	734	1404	223	40	153	2167	684	590	29	833	32	73	45	58	31	.65	126	.256	.329	.395

Team Pitching

Team	G	CG	ShO	Rel	Sv	IP	H	R	ER	HR	SH	SF	HB	TBB	IBB	SO	WP	Bk	H/9	SO/9	BB/9	OAvg	OOBP	ERA
Baltimore	163	54	21	201	33	1471.1	1226	588	526	109	71	35	32	617	30	926	45	3	7.5	5.7	3.8	.227	.308	3.22
New York	163	47	14	201	39	1451.0	1288	612	558	137	56	32	32	542	27	866	33	3	8.0	5.4	3.4	.239	.311	3.46
Detroit	163	62	12	220	30	1459.1	1404	671	575	170	61	42	29	469	27	836	29	2	8.7	5.2	2.9	.252	.311	3.55
Chicago	163	39	3	260	33	1448.2	1491	726	653	158	106	47	12	498	25	814	29	2	9.3	5.1	3.1	.268	.326	4.06
Cleveland	161	35	12	228	23	1443.1	1426	752	665	178	58	47	32	599	32	801	44	3	8.9	5.0	3.7	.258	.331	4.15
Washington	161	39	8	220	21	1425.0	1405	776	670	131	90	55	34	586	40	666	55	4	8.9	4.2	3.7	.260	.333	4.23
Minnesota	161	49	14	217	23	1432.1	1415	778	681	163	64	36	45	570	29	914	42	1	8.9	5.7	3.6	.256	.329	4.28
Boston	163	35	6	231	30	1442.2	1472	792	688	167	89	45	16	679	21	831	36	3	9.2	5.2	4.2	.266	.345	4.29
Los Angeles	162	25	5	311	34	1438.0	1391	784	689	180	63	45	34	713	38	973	53	2	8.7	6.1	4.5	.254	.341	4.31
Kansas City	162	32	5	268	23	1415.0	1519	863	746	141	75	64	53	629	21	703	58	7	9.7	4.5	4.0	.275	.351	4.74
AL Total	1622	417	100	2324	289	14426.2	14037	7342	6451	1534	733	448	319	5902	290	8330	424	30	8.8	5.2	3.7	.256	.336	4.02
AL Avg Team	162	42	10	232	29	1442.2	1404	734	645	153	73	45	32	590	29	833	42	3	8.8	5.2	3.7	.256	.336	4.02

Team Fielding

Team	G	PO	A	E	TC	DP	PB	Pct
New York	163	4358	1756	124	6238	180	13	.980
Baltimore	163	4413	1772	128	6313	173	30	.980
Chicago	163	4343	1790	128	6261	138	6	.980
Cleveland	161	4320	1645	139	6104	142	14	.977
Boston	163	4310	1747	144	6201	170	19	.977
Detroit	163	4362	1545	146	6053	147	13	.976
Washington	161	4253	1850	156	6259	171	23	.975
Kansas City	162	4260	1755	175	6190	160	17	.972
Minnesota	161	4296	1628	174	6098	150	16	.971
Los Angeles	162	4298	1749	192	6239	154	24	.969
AL Total	1622	43213	17237	1506	61956	1585	175	.976

Team vs. Team Records

	Bal	Bos	ChA	Cle	Det	KCA	LAA	Min	NYA	Was	Won
Bal	—	11	11	9	9	13	8	11	9	14	95
Bos	7	—	9	5	8	10	11	11	5	10	76
ChA	7	9	—	12	6	14	10	9	6	13	86
Cle	9	13	6	—	6	8	10	10	4	12	78
Det	9	10	12	12	—	12	14	11	8	13	101
KCA	5	8	4	9	6	—	9	7	4	9	61
LAA	10	7	8	8	4	9	—	8	6	10	70
Min	7	7	9	8	7	11	9	—	4	8	70
NYA	9	13	12	14	10	14	12	14	—	11	109
Was	4	8	5	6	5	9	8	9	7	—	61
Lost	67	86	76	83	61	100	91	90	53	100	

1961 American League Batting Leaders

Games		At-Bats		Runs		Hits		Doubles		Triples	
B. Robinson, Bal	163	B. Robinson, Bal	668	R. Maris, NYA	132	N. Cash, Det	193	A. Kaline, Det	41	J. Wood, Det	14
R. Colavito, Det	163	J. Wood, Det	663	M. Mantle, NYA	132	B. Robinson, Bal	192	T. Kubek, NYA	38	M. Keough, Was	9
J. Wood, Det	162	B. Richardson, NYA	662	R. Colavito, Det	129	A. Kaline, Det	190	B. Robinson, Bal	38	J. Lumpe, KCA	9
B. Richardson, NYA	162	C. Schilling, Bos	646	N. Cash, Det	119	T. Francona, Cle	178	N. Siebern, KCA	36	3 tied with	8
R. Maris, NYA	161	L. Aparicio, ChA	625	A. Kaline, Det	116	B. Richardson, NYA	173	V. Power, Cle	34		

Home Runs		Total Bases		Runs Batted In		Walks		Intentional Walks		Strikeouts	
R. Maris, NYA	61	R. Maris, NYA	366	R. Maris, NYA	142	M. Mantle, NYA	126	N. Cash, Det	19	J. Wood, Det	141
M. Mantle, NYA	54	N. Cash, Det	354	J. Gentile, Bal	141	N. Cash, Det	124	W. Held, Cle	11	K. Hunt, LAA	120
J. Gentile, Bal	46	M. Mantle, NYA	353	R. Colavito, Det	140	R. Colavito, Det	113	S. Lollar, ChA	10	M. Mantle, NYA	112
H. Killebrew, Min	46	R. Colavito, Det	338	N. Cash, Det	132	H. Killebrew, Min	107	3 tied with	9	W. Held, Cle	111
R. Colavito, Det	45	H. Killebrew, Min	328	M. Mantle, NYA	128	B. Allison, Min	103			H. Killebrew, Min	109

Hit By Pitch		Sac Hits		Sac Flies		Stolen Bases		Caught Stealing		GDP	
M. Minoso, ChA	16	D. O'Connell, Was	15	M. Minoso, ChA	12	L. Aparicio, ChA	53	L. Aparicio, ChA	13	G. Green, Was	26
J. Gentile, Bal	11	N. Fox, ChA	15	L. Posada, KCA	12	D. Howser, KCA	37	L. Green, Min	11	B. Robinson, Bal	21
N. Cash, Det	9	Monbouquette, Bos	14	V. Power, Cle	12	J. Wood, Det	30	W. Tasby, Was	10	B. Skowron, NYA	21
N. Fox, ChA	9	T. Francona, Cle	12	B. Robinson, Bal	9	C. Hinton, Was	22	3 tied with	9	4 tied with	19
2 tied with	8	2 tied with	11	F. Malzone, Bos	9	B. Bruton, Det	22				

Runs Created		Runs Created/27 Outs		Batting Average		On-Base Percentage		Slugging Percentage		OBP+Slugging	
N. Cash, Det	158	M. Mantle, NYA	11.73	N. Cash, Det	.361	N. Cash, Det	.487	M. Mantle, NYA	.687	N. Cash, Det	1.148
M. Mantle, NYA	157	N. Cash, Det	11.58	A. Kaline, Det	.324	M. Mantle, NYA	.448	N. Cash, Det	.662	M. Mantle, NYA	1.135
R. Maris, NYA	134	J. Gentile, Bal	9.34	J. Piersall, Cle	.322	J. Gentile, Bal	.423	J. Gentile, Bal	.646	J. Gentile, Bal	1.069
R. Colavito, Det	133	H. Killebrew, Min	8.67	M. Mantle, NYA	.317	A. Pearson, LAA	.420	R. Maris, NYA	.620	H. Killebrew, Min	1.012
H. Killebrew, Min	130	R. Colavito, Det	8.13	J. Gentile, Bal	.302	H. Killebrew, Min	.405	H. Killebrew, Min	.606	R. Maris, NYA	.993

1961 American League Pitching Leaders

Wins		Losses		Winning Percentage		Games		Games Started		Complete Games	
W. Ford, NYA	25	P. Ramos, Min	20	W. Ford, NYA	.862	L. Arroyo, NYA	65	W. Ford, NYA	39	F. Lary, Det	22
F. Lary, Det	23	J. McClain, Was	18	R. Terry, NYA	.842	T. Lown, ChA	59	J. Bunning, Det	37	C. Pascual, Min	15
S. Barber, Bal	18	J. Kaat, Min	17	L. Arroyo, NYA	.750	T. Morgan, LAA	59	K. McBride, LAA	36	S. Barber, Bal	14
J. Bunning, Det	17	J. Perry, Cle	17	B. Latman, Cle	.722	B. Kunkel, KCA	58	F. Lary, Det	36	5 tied with	12
R. Terry, NYA	16	B. Daley, 2tm	17	F. Lary, Det	.719	M. Fornieles, Bos	57	2 tied with	35		

Shutouts		Saves		Games Finished		Batters Faced		Innings Pitched		Hits Allowed	
S. Barber, Bal	8	L. Arroyo, NYA	29	L. Arroyo, NYA	54	W. Ford, NYA	1159	W. Ford, NYA	283.0	P. Ramos, Min	265
C. Pascual, Min	8	H. Wilhelm, Bal	18	F. Funk, Cle	43	F. Lary, Det	1127	F. Lary, Det	275.1	J. Kralick, Min	257
M. Pappas, Bal	4	M. Fornieles, Bos	15	H. Wilhelm, Bal	43	P. Ramos, Min	1123	J. Bunning, Det	268.0	F. Lary, Det	252
J. Bunning, Det	4	R. Moore, Min	14	M. Fornieles, Bos	42	J. Bunning, Det	1110	P. Ramos, Min	264.1	B. Shaw, 2tm	250
F. Lary, Det	4	T. Fox, Det	12	R. Moore, Min	38	C. Pascual, Min	1056	C. Pascual, Min	252.1	F. Baumann, ChA	249

Home Runs Allowed		Walks		Walks/9 Innings		Strikeouts		Strikeouts/9 Innings		Strikeout/Walk Ratio	
P. Ramos, Min	39	C. Estrada, Bal	132	D. Mossi, Det	1.8	C. Pascual, Min	221	J. Pizarro, ChA	8.7	D. Mossi, Det	2.91
G. Conley, Bos	33	S. Barber, Bal	130	H. Brown, Bal	1.8	W. Ford, NYA	209	C. Pascual, Min	7.9	J. Bunning, Det	2.73
G. Bell, Cle	32	E. Grba, LAA	114	D. Donovan, Was	1.9	J. Bunning, Det	194	C. Estrada, Bal	6.8	W. Ford, NYA	2.27
M. Grant, Cle	32	D. Schwall, Bos	110	R. Terry, NYA	2.0	J. Pizarro, ChA	188	K. McBride, LAA	6.7	F. Lary, Det	2.21
D. Mossi, Det	29	M. Grant, Cle	109	J. McClain, Was	2.0	K. McBride, LAA	180	W. Ford, NYA	6.6	C. Pascual, Min	2.21

Earned Run Average		Component ERA		Hit Batsmen		Wild Pitches		Opponent Average		Opponent OBP	
D. Donovan, Was	2.40	D. Donovan, Was	2.21	J. Kaat, Min	11	J. Kaat, Min	10	C. Estrada, Bal	.207	D. Donovan, Was	.267
B. Stafford, NYA	2.68	R. Terry, NYA	2.72	C. Estrada, Bal	10	J. Fisher, Bal	10	M. Pappas, Bal	.208	R. Terry, NYA	.275
D. Mossi, Det	2.96	H. Brown, Bal	2.83	J. Walker, KCA	10	J. Klippstein, Was	10	C. Pascual, Min	.217	J. Bunning, Det	.284
M. Pappas, Bal	3.04	B. Stafford, NYA	2.84	B. Daley, 2tm	9	S. Barber, Bal	9	S. Barber, Bal	.218	H. Brown, Bal	.284
J. Pizarro, ChA	3.05	J. Bunning, Det	2.87	J. Bunning, Det	9	J. Walker, KCA	9	D. Donovan, Was	.224	F. Lary, Det	.290

1961 American League Miscellaneous

Managers

Baltimore	Paul Richards	78-57
	Lum Harris	17-10
Boston	Pinky Higgins	76-86
Chicago	Al Lopez	86-76
Cleveland	Jimmy Dykes	77-83
	Mel Harder	1-0
Detroit	Bob Scheffing	101-61
Kansas City	Joe Gordon	26-33
	Hank Bauer	35-67
Los Angeles	Bill Rigney	70-91
Minnesota	Cookie Lavagetto	19-30
	Sam Mele	2-5
	Cookie Lavagetto	4-6
	Sam Mele	45-49
New York	Ralph Houk	109-53
Washington	Mickey Vernon	61-100

Awards

Most Valuable Player	Roger Maris, of, NYA
Cy Young	Whitey Ford, NYA
Rookie of the Year	Don Schwall, p, Bos
STATS Manager of the Year	Bob Scheffing, Det

STATS All-Star Team

C	Elston Howard, NYA	.348	21	77
1B	Norm Cash, Det	.361	41	132
2B	Jerry Lumpe, KCA	.293	3	54
3B	Al Smith, ChA	.278	28	93
SS	Woodie Held, Cle	.267	23	78
OF	Rocky Colavito, Det	.290	45	140
OF	Mickey Mantle, NYA	.317	54	128
OF	Roger Maris, NYA	.269	61	142
P	Jim Bunning, Det	17-11	3.19	194 K
P	Whitey Ford, NYA	25-4	3.21	209 K
P	Frank Lary, Det	23-9	3.24	146 K
P	Juan Pizarro, ChA	14-7	3.05	188 K
RP	Luis Arroyo, NYA	15-5	2.19	29 Sv

Postseason

World Series	NYA (AL) 4 vs. Cincinnati (NL) 1

Outstanding Performances

Three-Homer Games

Willie Kirkland, Cle	on July 9
Rocky Colavito, Det	on August 27
Lee Thomas, LAA	on September 5

Team	Overall					Home Games						Road Games						Park Index		Record by Month					
	W	L	Pct	GB	DIF	W	L	R	OR	HR	OHR	W	L	R	OR	HR	OHR	Run	HR	M/A	May	June	July	Aug	S/O
Cincinnati	93	61	.604	—	114	47	30	345	355	70	75	46	31	365	298	88	72	106	91	6-10	20-6	19-12	18-12	16-13	14-8
Los Angeles	89	65	.578	4.0	27	45	32	373	358	83	109	44	33	362	339	74	58	104	145	10-8	17-11	16-12	19-7	11-15	16-12
San Francisco	85	69	.552	8.0	38	45	32	371	316	97	77	40	37	402	339	86	75	93	108	10-6	16-10	15-15	13-15	15-11	16-12
Milwaukee	83	71	.539	10.0	2	45	32	324	280	84	72	38	39	388	376	104	81	79	84	6-6	13-14	14-13	17-15	20-9	13-14
St. Louis	80	74	.519	13.0	5	48	29	413	362	54	69	32	45	290	306	49	67	130	106	7-9	11-13	13-16	16-14	20-9	13-13
Pittsburgh	75	79	.487	18.0	5	38	39	338	338	49	54	37	40	356	337	79	67	98	71	9-6	12-12	15-13	9-17	16-16	14-15
Chicago	64	90	.416	29.0	1	40	37	372	391	102	81	24	53	317	409	74	84	105	116	8-8	7-18	13-16	15-14	11-17	10-17
Philadelphia	47	107	.305	46.0	1	22	55	256	408	43	77	25	52	328	388	60	78	93	87	6-9	6-18	10-18	8-21	7-26	10-15

Clinch Date—Cincinnati 9/26.

Team Batting

Team	G	AB	R	OR	H	2B	3B	HR	TB	RBI	TBB	IBB	SO	HBP	SH	SF	SB	CS	SB%	GDP	Avg	OBP	Slg
San Francisco	155	5233	773	655	1379	219	32	183	2211	709	506	58	764	30	70	48	79	54	.59	124	.264	.337	.423
Los Angeles	154	5189	735	697	1358	193	40	157	2102	673	596	53	796	23	96	36	86	45	.66	117	.262	.344	.405
Milwaukee	155	5288	712	656	1365	199	34	188	2196	662	534	50	880	34	62	40	70	43	.62	133	.258	.335	.415
Cincinnati	154	5243	710	653	1414	247	35	158	2205	675	423	59	761	29	50	51	70	33	.68	109	.270	.334	.421
St. Louis	155	5307	703	668	1436	236	51	103	2083	657	494	61	745	33	70	40	46	28	.62	108	.271	.341	.393
Pittsburgh	154	5311	694	675	1448	232	57	128	2178	646	428	51	721	27	64	37	26	30	.46	140	.273	.334	.410
Chicago	156	5344	689	800	1364	238	51	176	2232	650	539	64	1027	32	52	33	35	25	.58	115	.255	.331	.418
Philadelphia	155	5213	584	796	1265	185	50	103	1859	549	475	46	928	46	108	28	46	30	.65	130	.243	.315	.357
NL Total	1238	42128	5600	5600	11029	1749	350	1196	17066	5221	3995	442	6622	254	572	313	468	288	.62	976	.262	.327	.405
NL Avg Team	155	5266	700	700	1379	219	44	150	2133	653	499	55	828	32	72	39	59	36	.62	122	.262	.327	.405

Team Pitching

Team	G	CG	ShO	Rel	Sv	IP	H	R	ER	HR	SH	SF	HB	TBB	IBB	SO	WP	Bk	H/9	SO/9	BB/9	OAvg	OOBP	ERA
St. Louis	155	49	10	184	24	1368.2	1334	668	569	136	58	45	24	570	48	823	44	3	8.8	5.4	3.7	.256	.330	3.74
San Francisco	155	39	9	235	30	1388.0	1306	655	582	152	65	36	33	502	70	924	33	8	8.5	6.0	3.3	.249	.316	3.77
Cincinnati	154	46	12	210	40	1370.0	1300	653	576	147	65	42	32	500	37	829	40	5	8.5	5.4	3.3	.250	.318	3.78
Milwaukee	155	57	8	194	16	1391.1	1357	656	602	153	87	32	23	493	35	652	30	6	8.8	4.2	3.2	.258	.322	3.89
Pittsburgh	154	34	9	236	29	1362.0	1442	675	593	121	68	38	25	400	68	759	39	1	9.5	5.0	2.6	.274	.326	3.92
Los Angeles	154	40	10	239	35	1378.1	1346	697	619	167	65	34	48	544	71	1105	66	7	8.8	7.2	3.6	.256	.329	4.04
Chicago	156	34	6	248	25	1385.0	1492	800	690	165	87	44	35	465	47	755	50	3	9.7	4.9	3.0	.277	.336	4.48
Philadelphia	155	29	7	257	13	1383.1	1452	796	708	155	77	42	34	521	66	775	54	0	9.4	5.0	3.4	.273	.340	4.61
NL Total	1238	328	73	1803	212	11026.2	11029	5600	4939	1196	572	313	254	3995	442	6622	356	33	9.0	5.4	3.3	.262	.334	4.03
NL Avg Team	155	41	9	225	27	1378.2	1379	700	617	150	72	39	32	499	55	828	45	4	9.0	5.4	3.3	.262	.334	4.03

Team Fielding

Team	G	PO	A	E	TC	DP	PB	Pct
Milwaukee	155	4174	1848	111	6133	152	11	.982
San Francisco	155	4164	1513	133	5810	126	10	.977
Cincinnati	154	4110	1594	134	5838	124	23	.977
Philadelphia	155	4150	1803	146	6099	179	26	.976
Los Angeles	154	4135	1573	144	5852	162	14	.975
Pittsburgh	154	4086	1793	150	6029	189	19	.975
St. Louis	155	4106	1756	166	6028	165	17	.972
Chicago	156	4155	1848	183	6186	175	35	.970
NL Total	1238	33080	13728	1167	47975	1272	155	.976

Team vs. Team Records

	ChN	Cin	LA	Mil	Phi	Pit	SF	StL	Won
ChN	—	12	7	9	13	11	5	7	64
Cin	10	—	12	15	19	11	12	14	93
LA	15	10	—	12	17	13	10	12	89
Mil	13	7	10	—	16	12	11	14	83
Phi	9	3	5	6	—	7	8	9	47
Pit	11	11	9	10	15	—	10	9	75
SF	17	10	12	11	14	12	—	9	85
StL	15	8	10	8	13	13	13	—	80
Lost	90	61	65	71	107	79	69	74	

1961 National League Batting Leaders

Games		At-Bats		Runs		Hits		Doubles		Triples	
H. Aaron, Mil	155	M. Wills, LA	613	W. Mays, SF	129	V. Pinson, Cin	208	H. Aaron, Mil	39	G. Altman, ChN	12
R. Santo, ChN	154	V. Pinson, Cin	607	F. Robinson, Cin	117	R. Clemente, Pit	201	V. Pinson, Cin	34	J. Callison, Phi	11
V. Pinson, Cin	154	H. Aaron, Mil	603	H. Aaron, Mil	115	H. Aaron, Mil	197	R. Santo, ChN	32	B. White, StL	11
W. Mays, SF	154	B. Virdon, Pit	599	K. Boyer, StL	109	K. Boyer, StL	194	F. Robinson, Cin	32	K. Boyer, StL	11
R. McMillan, Mil	154	D. Groat, Pit	596	2 tied with	105	O. Cepeda, SF	182	W. Mays, SF	32	3 tied with	10

Home Runs		Total Bases		Runs Batted In		Walks		Intentional Walks		Strikeouts	
O. Cepeda, SF	46	H. Aaron, Mil	358	O. Cepeda, SF	142	E. Mathews, Mil	93	F. Robinson, Cin	23	D. Stuart, Pit	121
W. Mays, SF	40	O. Cepeda, SF	356	F. Robinson, Cin	124	W. Moon, LA	89	E. Banks, ChN	21	P. Herrera, Phi	120
F. Robinson, Cin	37	W. Mays, SF	334	W. Mays, SF	123	W. Mays, SF	81	H. Aaron, Mil	20	E. Mathews, Mil	95
D. Stuart, Pit	35	F. Robinson, Cin	333	H. Aaron, Mil	120	J. Gilliam, LA	79	S. Musial, StL	17	J. Adcock, Mil	94
J. Adcock, Mil	35	R. Clemente, Pit	320	D. Stuart, Pit	117	2 tied with	73	W. Mays, SF	15	G. Altman, ChN	92

Hit By Pitch		Sac Hits		Sac Flies		Stolen Bases		Caught Stealing		GDP	
J. Cunningham, StL	11	M. Wills, LA	13	F. Robinson, Cin	10	M. Wills, LA	35	M. Wills, LA	15	R. Santo, ChN	25
F. Robinson, Cin	10	A. Mahaffey, Phi	12	H. Aaron, Mil	9	V. Pinson, Cin	23	B. White, StL	11	F. Bolling, Mil	25
O. Cepeda, SF	9	J. Davenport, SF	12	G. Bell, Cin	9	F. Robinson, Cin	22	V. Pinson, Cin	10	D. Stuart, Pit	22
T. Gonzalez, Phi	6	J. Gilliam, LA	12	V. Pinson, Cin	8	H. Aaron, Mil	21	H. Aaron, Mil	9	D. Groat, Pit	22
F. Thomas, 2tm	6	2 tied with	11	J. Davenport, SF	8	W. Mays, SF	18	W. Mays, SF	9	J. Adcock, Mil	22

Runs Created		Runs Created/27 Outs		Batting Average		On-Base Percentage		Slugging Percentage		OBP+Slugging	
W. Mays, SF	133	F. Robinson, Cin	8.59	R. Clemente, Pit	.351	W. Moon, LA	.434	F. Robinson, Cin	.611	F. Robinson, Cin	1.015
F. Robinson, Cin	127	W. Mays, SF	8.44	V. Pinson, Cin	.343	F. Robinson, Cin	.404	O. Cepeda, SF	.609	W. Mays, SF	.977
H. Aaron, Mil	125	W. Moon, LA	8.31	K. Boyer, StL	.329	E. Mathews, Mil	.402	H. Aaron, Mil	.594	H. Aaron, Mil	.974
O. Cepeda, SF	124	K. Boyer, StL	7.72	W. Moon, LA	.328	K. Boyer, StL	.397	W. Mays, SF	.584	O. Cepeda, SF	.970
E. Mathews, Mil	120	R. Clemente, Pit	7.70	H. Aaron, Mil	.327	W. Mays, SF	.393	D. Stuart, Pit	.581	R. Clemente, Pit	.949

1961 National League Pitching Leaders

Wins		Losses		Winning Percentage		Games		Games Started		Complete Games	
J. Jay, Cin	21	A. Mahaffey, Phi	19	J. Podres, LA	.783	J. Baldschun, Phi	65	D. Cardwell, ChN	38	W. Spahn, Mil	21
W. Spahn, Mil	21	B. Friend, Pit	19	S. Miller, SF	.737	S. Miller, SF	63	D. Drysdale, LA	37	S. Koufax, LA	15
J. O'Toole, Cin	19	J. Buzhardt, Phi	18	J. O'Toole, Cin	.679	R. Face, Pit	62	L. Burdette, Mil	36	J. Jay, Cin	14
3 tied with	18	M. McCormick, SF	16	J. Jay, Cin	.677	D. Elston, ChN	58	5 tied with	35	L. Burdette, Mil	14
		F. Sullivan, Phi	16	2 tied with	.625	B. Anderson, ChN	57			4 tied with	13

Shutouts		Saves		Games Finished		Batters Faced		Innings Pitched		Hits Allowed	
J. Jay, Cin	4	R. Face, Pit	17	R. Face, Pit	47	L. Burdette, Mil	1126	L. Burdette, Mil	272.1	L. Burdette, Mil	295
W. Spahn, Mil	4	S. Miller, SF	17	S. Miller, SF	46	D. Cardwell, ChN	1106	W. Spahn, Mil	262.2	B. Friend, Pit	271
9 tied with	3	J. Brosnan, Cin	16	J. Baldschun, Phi	39	S. Koufax, LA	1068	D. Cardwell, ChN	259.1	B. Purkey, Cin	245
		B. Henry, Cin	16	L. McDaniel, StL	39	W. Spahn, Mil	1064	S. Koufax, LA	255.2	D. Cardwell, ChN	243
		L. Sherry, LA	15	2 tied with	34	J. O'Toole, Cin	1061	J. O'Toole, Cin	252.2	2 tied with	236

Home Runs Allowed		Walks		Walks/9 Innings		Strikeouts		Strikeouts/9 Innings		Strikeout/Walk Ratio	
M. McCormick, SF	33	B. Gibson, StL	119	L. Burdette, Mil	1.1	S. Koufax, LA	269	S. Koufax, LA	9.5	S. Koufax, LA	2.80
L. Burdette, Mil	31	S. Williams, LA	108	B. Friend, Pit	1.7	S. Williams, LA	205	S. Williams, LA	7.8	L. Burdette, Mil	2.79
D. Drysdale, LA	29	R. Sadecki, StL	102	B. Purkey, Cin	1.9	D. Drysdale, LA	182	B. Gibson, StL	7.1	J. Marichal, SF	2.58
R. Sadecki, StL	28	B. Buhl, Mil	98	W. Spahn, Mil	2.2	J. O'Toole, Cin	178	D. Drysdale, LA	6.7	J. Gibbon, Pit	2.54
J. Buzhardt, Phi	28	S. Koufax, LA	96	D. Ellsworth, ChN	2.3	B. Gibson, StL	166	J. Gibbon, Pit	6.7	J. Podres, LA	2.43

Earned Run Average		Component ERA		Hit Batsmen		Wild Pitches		Opponent Average		Opponent OBP	
W. Spahn, Mil	3.02	W. Spahn, Mil	2.96	D. Drysdale, LA	20	C. Short, Phi	14	S. Koufax, LA	.222	W. Spahn, Mil	.291
J. O'Toole, Cin	3.10	S. Koufax, LA	3.08	D. Cardwell, ChN	10	S. Koufax, LA	12	J. Jay, Cin	.236	S. Koufax, LA	.295
C. Simmons, StL	3.13	J. O'Toole, Cin	3.20	S. Jones, SF	8	J. Baldschun, Phi	11	R. Sadecki, StL	.238	L. Burdette, Mil	.295
M. McCormick, SF	3.20	J. Gibbon, Pit	3.30	A. Mahaffey, Phi	7	A. McBean, Pit	10	B. Gibson, StL	.239	B. Purkey, Cin	.296
B. Gibson, StL	3.24	L. Jackson, StL	3.35	7 tied with	6	T. Farrell, 2tm	10	J. O'Toole, Cin	.240	L. Jackson, StL	.301

1961 National League Miscellaneous

Managers

Chicago	Vedie Himsl	5-6
	Harry Craft	4-8
	Vedie Himsl	5-12
	El Tappe	2-0
	Harry Craft	3-1
	Vedie Himsl	0-3
	El Tappe	35-43
	Lou Klein	5-6
	El Tappe	5-11
Cincinnati	Fred Hutchinson	93-61
Los Angeles	Walter Alston	89-65
Milwaukee	Chuck Dressen	71-58
	Birdie Tebbetts	12-13
Philadelphia	Gene Mauch	47-107
Pittsburgh	Danny Murtaugh	75-79
St. Louis	Solly Hemus	33-41
	Johnny Keane	47-33
San Francisco	Alvin Dark	85-69

Awards

Most Valuable Player	Frank Robinson, of, Cin
STATS Cy Young	Warren Spahn, Mil
Rookie of the Year	Billy Williams, of, ChN
STATS Manager of the Year	Fred Hutchinson, Cin

STATS All-Star Team

C	John Roseboro, LA	.251	18	59	
1B	Orlando Cepeda, SF	.311	46	142	
2B	Bill Mazeroski, Pit	.265	13	59	
3B	Ken Boyer, StL	.329	24	95	
SS	Ernie Banks, ChN	.278	29	80	
OF	Hank Aaron, Mil	.327	34	120	
OF	Willie Mays, SF	.308	40	123	
OF	Frank Robinson, Cin	.323	37	124	
P	Joey Jay, Cin	21-10	3.53	157 K	
P	Sandy Koufax, LA	18-13	3.52	269 K	
P	Jim O'Toole, Cin	19-9	3.10	178 K	
P	Warren Spahn, Mil	21-13	3.02	115 K	
RP	Stu Miller, SF	14-5	2.66	17 Sv	

Postseason

World Series	Cincinnati (NL) 1 vs. NYA (AL) 4

Outstanding Performances

No-Hitters
Warren Spahn, Mil   vs. SF on April 28
Four-Homer Games
Willie Mays, SF   on April 30
Three-Homer Games
Willie Mays, SF   on June 29
Bill White, StL   on July 5
Don Demeter, Phi   on September 12
Cycles
Ken Boyer, StL   on September 14

1962 American League Standings

Team	Overall W	L	Pct	GB	DIF	Home Games W	L	R	OR	HR	OHR	Road Games W	L	R	OR	HR	OHR	Park Index Run	HR	Record by Month M/A	May	June	July	Aug	S/O
New York	96	66	.593	—	133	50	30	369	306	92	67	46	36	448	374	107	79	84	88	10-5	15-13	14-13	23-8	17-18	17-9
Minnesota	91	71	.562	5.0	1	45	36	417	378	97	97	46	35	381	335	88	69	111	124	9-9	18-12	15-15	15-11	19-13	15-11
Los Angeles	86	76	.531	10.0	5	40	41	357	368	50	50	46	35	361	338	87	68	104	65	7-9	17-11	17-13	16-13	18-14	11-16
Detroit	85	76	.528	10.5	0	49	33	448	368	117	91	36	43	310	324	92	78	124	118	8-6	16-13	13-17	12-15	18-15	18-10
Chicago	85	77	.525	11.0	5	43	38	315	319	36	58	42	39	392	339	56	65	87	78	11-7	12-17	15-15	14-14	17-13	16-11
Cleveland	80	82	.494	16.0	47	43	38	348	350	103	89	37	44	334	395	77	85	96	119	9-6	17-11	15-15	11-17	14-21	14-12
Baltimore	77	85	.475	19.0	0	44	38	328	299	66	65	33	47	324	381	90	82	87	74	9-7	13-16	17-14	13-17	13-17	10-17
Boston	76	84	.475	19.0	0	39	40	369	377	72	76	37	44	338	379	74	83	107	97	7-9	11-17	17-14	11-16	17-15	13-13
Kansas City	72	90	.444	24.0	1	39	42	387	423	64	118	33	48	358	414	52	81	105	137	9-10	14-16	12-16	10-17	16-15	11-16
Washington	60	101	.373	35.5	6	27	53	293	364	65	79	33	48	306	352	67	72	101	105	2-13	11-18	13-16	13-15	14-22	7-17

Clinch Date—New York 9/25.

Team Batting

Team	G	AB	R	OR	H	2B	3B	HR	TB	RBI	TBB	IBB	SO	HBP	SH	SF	SB	CS	SB%	GDP	Avg	OBP	Slg
New York	162	5644	817	680	1509	240	29	199	2404	791	584	46	842	32	79	54	42	29	.59	123	.267	.345	.426
Minnesota	163	5561	798	713	1445	215	39	185	2293	758	649	36	823	31	71	50	33	20	.62	129	.260	.346	.412
Detroit	161	5456	758	692	1352	191	36	209	2242	719	651	40	894	33	56	38	69	21	.77	122	.248	.336	.411
Kansas City	162	5576	745	837	1467	220	58	116	2151	691	556	35	803	42	78	50	76	21	.78	108	.263	.340	.386
Los Angeles	162	5499	718	706	1377	232	35	137	2090	667	602	40	917	29	82	43	46	27	.63	110	.250	.332	.380
Boston	160	5530	707	756	1429	257	53	146	2230	671	525	39	923	27	56	36	39	33	.54	129	.258	.330	.403
Chicago	162	5514	707	658	1415	250	56	92	2053	662	620	41	674	41	82	40	76	40	.66	132	.257	.340	.372
Cleveland	162	5484	682	745	1341	202	22	180	2127	644	502	27	939	54	52	45	35	16	.69	117	.245	.319	.388
Baltimore	162	5491	652	680	1363	225	34	156	2124	617	516	36	931	32	75	44	45	32	.58	131	.248	.321	.387
Washington	162	5484	599	716	1370	206	38	132	2048	566	466	26	789	15	71	36	99	53	.65	135	.250	.314	.373
AL Total	1618	55239	7183	7183	14068	2238	400	1552	21762	6786	5671	366	8535	336	705	436	560	292	.66	1236	.255	.325	.394
AL Avg Team	162	5524	718	718	1407	224	40	155	2176	679	567	37	854	34	71	44	56	29	.66	124	.255	.325	.394

Team Pitching

Team	G	CG	ShO	Rel	Sv	IP	H	R	ER	HR	SH	SF	HB	TBB	IBB	SO	WP	Bk	H/9	SO/9	BB/9	OAvg	OOBP	ERA
Baltimore	162	32	8	253	33	1462.1	1373	680	600	147	73	31	28	549	48	898	46	2	8.5	5.5	3.4	.249	.318	3.69
Los Angeles	162	23	15	345	47	1466.0	1412	706	602	118	84	40	49	616	44	858	39	3	8.7	5.3	3.8	.253	.330	3.70
New York	162	33	10	248	42	1470.1	1375	680	605	146	52	54	29	499	33	838	27	1	8.4	5.1	3.1	.247	.310	3.70
Chicago	162	50	13	265	28	1451.2	1380	658	602	123	65	42	19	537	38	821	33	1	8.6	5.1	3.3	.251	.317	3.73
Detroit	161	46	8	245	35	1443.2	1452	692	611	169	67	39	32	503	27	873	35	6	9.1	5.4	3.1	.259	.321	3.81
Minnesota	163	53	11	241	27	1463.1	1400	713	633	166	75	39	43	493	31	948	55	3	8.6	5.8	3.0	.253	.317	3.89
Washington	162	38	11	266	13	1445.0	1400	716	649	151	87	48	21	593	42	771	31	9	8.7	4.8	3.7	.256	.328	4.04
Cleveland	162	45	12	242	31	1441.0	1410	745	663	174	59	48	31	594	49	780	27	9	8.8	4.9	3.7	.258	.331	4.14
Boston	160	34	12	222	40	1437.2	1416	756	674	159	74	47	42	632	22	923	48	5	8.9	5.8	4.0	.258	.337	4.22
Kansas City	162	32	4	274	33	1434.0	1450	837	764	199	69	48	42	655	32	825	63	5	9.1	5.2	4.1	.263	.343	4.79
AL Total	1618	386	104	2601	329	14515.0	14068	7183	6403	1552	705	436	336	5671	366	8535	404	44	8.7	5.3	3.5	.255	.333	3.97
AL Avg Team	162	39	10	260	33	1451.0	1407	718	640	155	71	44	34	567	37	854	40	4	8.7	5.3	3.5	.255	.333	3.97

Team Fielding

Team	G	PO	A	E	TC	DP	PB	Pct
Chicago	162	4335	1760	110	6205	153	13	.982
Baltimore	162	4384	1711	122	6217	152	32	.980
Minnesota	163	4379	1778	129	6286	173	13	.979
New York	162	4390	1754	131	6275	151	7	.979
Boston	160	4307	1698	131	6136	152	12	.979
Kansas City	162	4294	1724	132	6150	131	25	.979
Washington	162	4320	1776	139	6235	160	15	.978
Cleveland	162	4325	1708	139	6172	168	16	.977
Detroit	161	4327	1444	156	5927	114	10	.974
Los Angeles	162	4388	1787	175	6350	153	16	.972
AL Total	1618	43449	17140	1364	61953	1507	159	.978

Team vs. Team Records

	Bal	Bos	ChA	Cle	Det	KCA	LAA	Min	NYA	Was	Won
Bal	—	8	9	11	2	10	8	6	11	12	77
Bos	10	—	8	7	11	10	6	10	6	8	76
ChA	9	10	—	12	9	9	10	8	8	10	77
Cle	7	11	6	—	10	11	9	6	11	9	80
Det	16	6	9	8	—	12	11	5	7	11	85
KCA	8	8	9	7	6	—	6	8	5	15	72
LAA	10	12	8	9	7	12	—	9	8	11	86
Min	12	8	10	12	13	10	9	—	7	10	91
NYA	7	12	10	7	11	13	10	11	—	15	96
Was	6	9	8	9	7	3	7	8	3	—	60
Lost	85	84	77	82	76	90	76	71	66	101	

1962 American League Batting Leaders

Games		At-Bats		Runs		Hits		Doubles		Triples	
N. Siebern, KCA	162	B. Richardson, NYA	692	A. Pearson, LAA	115	B. Richardson, NYA	209	F. Robinson, ChA	45	G. Cimoli, KCA	15
B. Robinson, Bal	162	B. Moran, LAA	659	N. Siebern, KCA	114	J. Lumpe, KCA	193	C. Yastrzemski, Bos	43	F. Robinson, ChA	10
R. Colavito, Det	161	C. Yastrzemski, Bos	646	B. Allison, Min	102	B. Robinson, Bal	192	E. Bressoud, Bos	40	L. Clinton, Bos	10
B. Richardson, NYA	161	J. Lumpe, KCA	641	C. Yastrzemski, Bos	99	C. Yastrzemski, Bos	191	B. Richardson, NYA	38	J. Lumpe, KCA	10
6 tied with	160	B. Robinson, Bal	634	B. Richardson, NYA	99	F. Robinson, ChA	187	3 tied with	34	2 tied with	9

Home Runs		Total Bases		Runs Batted In		Walks		Intentional Walks		Strikeouts	
H. Killebrew, Min	48	R. Colavito, Det	309	H. Killebrew, Min	126	M. Mantle, NYA	122	J. Gentile, Bal	16	H. Killebrew, Min	142
N. Cash, Det	39	B. Robinson, Bal	308	N. Siebern, KCA	117	N. Siebern, KCA	110	N. Cash, Det	12	E. Bressoud, Bos	118
L. Wagner, LAA	37	L. Wagner, LAA	306	R. Colavito, Det	112	H. Killebrew, Min	106	R. Maris, NYA	11	B. Allison, Min	115
R. Colavito, Det	37	C. Yastrzemski, Bos	303	F. Robinson, ChA	109	N. Cash, Det	104	P. Runnels, Bos	11	J. Kindall, Cle	107
2 tied with	33	H. Killebrew, Min	301	L. Wagner, LAA	107	J. Cunningham, ChA	101	B. Allen, Min	10	W. Held, Cle	107

Hit By Pitch		Sac Hits		Sac Flies		Stolen Bases		Caught Stealing		GDP	
N. Cash, Det	13	B. Richardson, NYA	20	J. Gentile, Bal	10	L. Aparicio, ChA	31	L. Aparicio, ChA	12	C. Yastrzemski, Bos	27
B. Del Greco, KCA	13	B. Moran, LAA	14	B. Robinson, Bal	10	C. Hinton, Was	28	G. Geiger, Bos	11	M. Hershberger, ChA	20
M. Jimenez, KCA	11	N. Fox, ChA	13	4 tied with	9	J. Wood, Det	24	C. Hinton, Was	10	E. Battey, Min	20
W. Held, Cle	11	C. Fernandez, Det	12			E. Charles, KCA	20	B. Richardson, NYA	9	E. Howard, NYA	20
J. Landis, ChA	9	2 tied with	11			3 tied with	19	3 tied with	8	2 tied with	19

Runs Created		Runs Created/27 Outs		Batting Average		On-Base Percentage		Slugging Percentage		OBP+Slugging	
N. Siebern, KCA	124	N. Siebern, KCA	7.69	P. Runnels, Bos	.326	N. Siebern, KCA	.412	H. Killebrew, Min	.545	H. Killebrew, Min	.912
M. Mantle, NYA	114	P. Runnels, Bos	7.15	F. Robinson, ChA	.312	J. Cunningham, ChA	.410	R. Colavito, Det	.514	N. Siebern, KCA	.907
R. Colavito, Det	113	H. Killebrew, Min	6.87	C. Hinton, Was	.310	P. Runnels, Bos	.408	N. Cash, Det	.513	N. Cash, Det	.894
H. Killebrew, Min	111	F. Robinson, ChA	6.85	N. Siebern, KCA	.308	F. Robinson, ChA	.384	B. Allison, Min	.511	R. Colavito, Det	.885
F. Robinson, ChA	110	J. Cunningham, ChA	6.84	B. Robinson, Bal	.303	N. Cash, Det	.382	L. Wagner, LAA	.500	B. Allison, Min	.881

1962 American League Pitching Leaders

Wins		Losses		Winning Percentage		Games		Games Started		Complete Games	
R. Terry, NYA	23	E. Rakow, KCA	17	D. Wickersham, KCA	.733	D. Radatz, Bos	62	R. Terry, NYA	39	C. Pascual, Min	18
C. Pascual, Min	20	C. Estrada, Bal	17	D. Stigman, Min	.706	J. Wyatt, KCA	59	J. Kralick, Min	37	J. Kaat, Min	16
R. Herbert, ChA	20	B. Daniels, Was	16	R. Herbert, ChA	.690	4 tied with	57	W. Ford, NYA	37	D. Donovan, Cle	16
D. Donovan, Cle	20	D. Schwall, Bos	15	K. McBride, LAA	.688			5 tied with	35	R. Terry, NYA	14
J. Bunning, Det	19	E. Wynn, ChA	15	W. Ford, NYA	.680					2 tied with	12

Shutouts		Saves		Games Finished		Batters Faced		Innings Pitched		Hits Allowed	
J. Kaat, Min	5	D. Radatz, Bos	24	D. Radatz, Bos	53	R. Terry, NYA	1191	R. Terry, NYA	298.2	J. Bunning, Det	262
C. Pascual, Min	5	M. Bridges, NYA	18	H. Wilhelm, Bal	44	J. Kaat, Min	1112	J. Kaat, Min	269.0	R. Terry, NYA	257
D. Donovan, Cle	5	T. Fox, Det	16	G. Bell, Cle	37	J. Bunning, Det	1103	J. Bunning, Det	258.0	D. Donovan, Cle	255
K. McBride, LAA	4	H. Wilhelm, Bal	15	R. Moore, Min	36	W. Ford, NYA	1070	C. Pascual, Min	257.2	J. Kaat, Min	243
Monbouquette, Bos	4	G. Bell, Cle	12	M. Bridges, NYA	35	C. Pascual, Min	1053	W. Ford, NYA	257.2	W. Ford, NYA	243

Home Runs Allowed		Walks		Walks/9 Innings		Strikeouts		Strikeouts/9 Innings		Strikeout/Walk Ratio	
R. Terry, NYA	40	B. Belinsky, LAA	122	D. Donovan, Cle	1.7	C. Pascual, Min	206	J. Pizarro, ChA	7.7	C. Pascual, Min	3.49
E. Rakow, KCA	31	D. Schwall, Bos	121	R. Terry, NYA	1.7	J. Bunning, Det	184	T. Cheney, Was	7.6	D. Mossi, Det	3.36
M. Pappas, Bal	31	C. Estrada, Bal	121	D. Mossi, Det	1.8	R. Terry, NYA	176	C. Pascual, Min	7.2	R. Terry, NYA	3.09
J. Kralick, Min	30	E. Wilson, Bos	111	R. Roberts, Bal	1.9	J. Kaat, Min	173	B. Belinsky, LAA	7.0	R. Roberts, Bal	2.49
3 tied with	28	D. Pfister, KCA	106	C. Pascual, Min	2.1	J. Pizarro, ChA	173	C. Estrada, Bal	6.6	J. Bunning, Det	2.49

Earned Run Average		Component ERA		Hit Batsmen		Wild Pitches		Opponent Average		Opponent OBP	
H. Aguirre, Det	2.21	H. Aguirre, Det	2.20	J. Kaat, Min	18	J. Kaat, Min	13	H. Aguirre, Det	.205	H. Aguirre, Det	.267
R. Roberts, Bal	2.78	R. Terry, NYA	2.79	B. Belinsky, LAA	13	E. Wilson, Bos	11	T. Cheney, Was	.213	R. Terry, NYA	.268
W. Ford, NYA	2.90	R. Roberts, Bal	2.92	J. Bunning, Det	13	D. McDevitt, KCA	11	B. Belinsky, LAA	.216	C. Pascual, Min	.285
D. Chance, LAA	2.96	C. Pascual, Min	2.95	3 tied with	10	H. Wilhelm, Bal	11	R. Terry, NYA	.231	R. Roberts, Bal	.288
E. Fisher, ChA	3.10	E. Fisher, ChA	3.07			2 tied with	10	E. Wilson, Bos	.231	E. Fisher, ChA	.291

1962 American League Miscellaneous

Managers

Baltimore	Billy Hitchcock	77-85
Boston	Pinky Higgins	76-84
Chicago	Al Lopez	85-77
Cleveland	Mel McGaha	78-82
	Mel Harder	2-0
Detroit	Bob Scheffing	85-76
Kansas City	Hank Bauer	72-90
Los Angeles	Bill Rigney	86-76
Minnesota	Sam Mele	91-71
New York	Ralph Houk	96-66
Washington	Mickey Vernon	60-101

Awards

Most Valuable Player	Mickey Mantle, of, NYA
STATS Cy Young	Ralph Terry, NYA
Rookie of the Year	Tom Tresh, ss, NYA
STATS Manager of the Year	Bill Rigney, LAA

STATS All-Star Team

C	John Romano, Cle	.261	25	81
1B	Norm Siebern, KCA	.308	25	117
2B	Billy Moran, LAA	.282	17	74
3B	Rich Rollins, Min	.298	16	96
SS	Tom Tresh, NYA	.286	20	93
OF	Rocky Colavito, Det	.273	37	112
OF	Harmon Killebrew, Min	.243	48	126
OF	Mickey Mantle, NYA	.321	30	89
P	Hank Aguirre, Det	16-8	2.21	156 K
P	Whitey Ford, NYA	17-8	2.90	160 K
P	Camilo Pascual, Min	20-11	3.32	206 K
P	Ralph Terry, NYA	23-12	3.19	176 K
RP	Dick Radatz, Bos	9-6	2.24	24 Sv

Postseason

World Series   NYA (AL) 4 vs. San Francisco (NL) 3

Outstanding Performances

No-Hitters
Bo Belinsky, LAA   vs. Bal on May 5
Earl Wilson, Bos   vs. LAA on June 26
Monbouquette, Bos   @ ChA on August 1
Jack Kralick, Min   vs. KCA on August 26

Three-Homer Games
Rocky Colavito, Det   on July 5
Steve Boros, Det   on August 6

Cycles
Lu Clinton, Bos   on July 13

Team	Overall					Home Games						Road Games						Park Index		Record by Month						
	W	L	Pct	GB	DIF	W	L	R	OR	HR	OHR	W	L	R	OR	HR	OHR	Run	HR	M/A	May	June	July	Aug	S/O
San Francisco	103	62	.624	—	54	61	21	479	299	109	74	42	41	399	391	95	74	100	110	15-5	20-10	16-13	16-11	18-10	18-13
Los Angeles	102	63	.618	1.0	111	54	29	409	289	47	39	48	34	433	408	93	76	82	50	13-8	21-7	17-14	20-6	17-12	14-16
Cincinnati	98	64	.605	3.5	0	58	23	456	294	95	68	40	41	346	391	72	81	102	107	8-11	19-6	12-17	22-8	21-12	16-10
Pittsburgh	93	68	.578	8.0	19	51	30	358	315	48	56	42	38	348	311	60	62	101	84	13-5	13-13	18-14	17-12	18-12	14-12
Milwaukee	86	76	.531	15.5	0	49	32	374	307	93	74	37	44	356	358	88	77	95	101	8-11	13-16	16-12	17-13	18-12	14-12
St. Louis	84	78	.519	17.5	12	44	37	407	362	64	83	40	41	367	302	73	66	115	106	11-4	13-17	19-12	16-14	13-15	12-16
Philadelphia	81	80	.503	20.0	1	46	34	341	346	70	66	35	46	364	413	72	89	90	86	8-9	9-19	17-13	15-17	17-15	15-7
Houston	64	96	.400	36.5	3	32	48	268	340	44	41	32	48	324	377	61	72	87	64	7-8	12-19	13-14	5-24	12-19	15-12
Chicago	59	103	.364	42.5	0	32	49	333	456	71	94	27	54	299	371	55	65	118	138	4-16	11-16	14-18	10-16	10-19	10-16
New York	40	120	.250	60.5	0	22	58	335	510	93	120	18	62	282	438	46	72	117	181	3-13	9-17	8-23	6-23	8-26	6-18

Clinch Date—San Francisco 10/03.

Team Batting

Team	G	AB	R	OR	H	2B	3B	HR	TB	RBI	TBB	IBB	SO	HBP	SH	SF	SB	CS	SB%	GDP	Avg	OBP	Slg
San Francisco	165	5588	878	690	1552	235	32	204	2463	807	523	41	822	42	76	48	73	50	.59	120	.278	.349	.441
Los Angeles	165	5628	842	697	1510	192	65	140	2252	781	572	65	886	32	83	47	198	43	.82	126	.268	.344	.400
Cincinnati	162	5645	802	685	1523	252	40	167	2356	745	498	62	903	41	57	32	66	39	.63	114	.270	.337	.417
St. Louis	163	5643	774	664	1528	221	31	137	2222	707	515	41	846	45	69	35	86	41	.68	129	.271	.340	.394
Milwaukee	162	5458	730	665	1376	204	38	181	2199	685	581	44	975	34	47	35	57	27	.68	133	.252	.332	.403
Pittsburgh	161	5483	706	626	1468	240	65	108	2162	655	432	52	836	17	54	49	50	39	.56	123	.268	.329	.394
Philadelphia	161	5420	705	759	1410	199	39	142	2113	658	531	38	923	53	83	44	79	42	.65	121	.260	.337	.390
Chicago	162	5534	632	827	1398	196	56	126	2084	600	504	43	1044	39	54	42	78	50	.61	131	.253	.324	.377
New York	161	5492	617	948	1318	166	40	139	1981	573	616	29	991	32	58	44	59	48	.55	122	.240	.325	.361
Houston	162	5558	592	717	1370	170	47	105	1949	549	493	37	806	38	75	34	42	30	.58	132	.246	.316	.351
NL Total	1624	55449	7278	7278	14453	2075	453	1449	21781	6760	5265	452	9032	373	656	410	788	409	.66	1251	.261	.327	.393
NL Avg Team	162	5545	728	728	1445	208	45	145	2178	676	527	45	903	37	66	41	79	41	.66	125	.261	.327	.393

Team Pitching

Team	G	CG	ShO	Rel	Sv	IP	H	R	ER	HR	SH	SF	HB	TBB	IBB	SO	WP	Bk	H/9	SO/9	BB/9	OAvg	OOBP	ERA
Pittsburgh	161	40	13	263	41	1432.1	1433	626	537	118	63	32	21	466	71	897	42	3	9.0	5.6	2.9	.262	.320	3.37
St. Louis	163	53	17	208	25	1463.1	1394	664	577	149	71	30	31	517	44	914	53	5	8.6	5.6	3.2	.252	.318	3.55
Los Angeles	165	44	8	249	46	1488.2	1386	697	598	115	56	39	32	588	66	1104	54	4	8.4	6.7	3.6	.245	.317	3.62
Milwaukee	162	59	10	206	24	1434.2	1443	665	586	151	64	39	33	407	41	802	37	2	9.1	5.0	2.6	.263	.315	3.68
Cincinnati	162	51	3	222	35	1460.2	1397	685	609	149	79	48	48	567	35	964	45	10	8.6	5.9	3.5	.254	.321	3.75
San Francisco	165	62	10	216	39	1461.2	1399	690	616	148	61	36	26	503	39	886	34	5	8.6	5.5	3.1	.251	.314	3.79
Houston	162	34	9	264	19	1453.2	1446	717	618	113	62	43	37	471	19	1047	74	5	9.0	6.5	2.9	.259	.319	3.83
Philadelphia	161	43	7	247	24	1426.2	1469	759	678	155	58	42	47	574	49	863	69	4	9.3	5.4	3.6	.268	.341	4.28
Chicago	162	29	4	309	26	1438.1	1509	827	725	159	74	46	46	601	60	783	66	5	9.4	4.9	3.8	.272	.346	4.54
New York	161	43	4	254	10	1430.0	1577	948	801	192	68	55	52	571	28	772	71	5	9.9	4.9	3.6	.281	.349	5.04
NL Total	1624	458	95	2438	289	14490.0	14453	7278	6345	1449	656	410	373	5265	452	9032	545	48	9.0	5.6	3.3	.261	.333	3.94
NL Avg Team	162	46	10	244	29	1449.0	1445	728	635	145	66	41	37	527	45	903	55	5	9.0	5.6	3.3	.261	.333	3.94

Team Fielding

Team	G	PO	A	E	TC	DP	PB	Pct
Milwaukee	162	4304	1802	124	6230	154	13	.980
St. Louis	163	4390	1828	132	6350	170	23	.979
Philadelphia	161	4280	1708	138	6126	167	20	.977
Chicago	162	4315	1911	146	6372	171	33	.977
San Francisco	165	4385	1649	142	6176	153	13	.977
Cincinnati	162	4382	1685	145	6212	144	22	.977
Pittsburgh	161	4297	1839	152	6288	177	24	.976
Houston	162	4361	1774	173	6308	149	25	.973
Los Angeles	165	4466	1734	193	6393	144	17	.970
New York	161	4290	1902	210	6402	167	26	.967
NL Total	1624	43470	17832	1555	62857	1596	216	.975

Team vs. Team Records

	ChN	Cin	Hou	LA	Mil	NYN	Phi	Pit	SF	StL	Won
ChN	—	4	7	4	8	9	10	4	6	7	59
Cin	14	—	13	9	13	13	8	13	7	8	98
Hou	11	5	—	6	7	13	1	5	7	9	64
LA	14	9	12	—	10	16	14	10	10	7	102
Mil	10	5	11	8	—	12	11	10	7	12	86
NYN	9	5	3	2	6	—	4	2	4	5	40
Phi	8	10	17	4	7	14	—	7	5	9	81
Pit	14	5	13	8	8	16	10	—	7	12	93
SF	12	11	11	11	11	14	13	11	—	9	103
StL	11	10	9	11	6	13	9	6	9	—	84
Lost	103	64	96	63	76	120	80	68	62	78	

1962 National League Batting Leaders

Games			At-Bats			Runs			Hits			Doubles			Triples	
M. Wills, LA		165	M. Wills, LA		695	F. Robinson, Cin		134	T. Davis, LA		230	F. Robinson, Cin		51	W. Davis, LA	10
J. Pagan, SF		164	D. Groat, Pit		678	M. Wills, LA		130	M. Wills, LA		208	W. Mays, SF		36	M. Wills, LA	10
T. Davis, LA		163	T. Davis, LA		665	W. Mays, SF		130	F. Robinson, Cin		208	D. Groat, Pit		34	J. Callison, Phi	10
4 tied with		162	B. Virdon, Pit		663	H. Aaron, Mil		127	B. White, StL		199	3 tied with		31	B. Virdon, Pit	10
			K. Hubbs, ChN		661	T. Davis, LA		120	D. Groat, Pit		199				6 tied with	9

Home Runs			Total Bases			Runs Batted In			Walks			Intentional Walks			Strikeouts	
W. Mays, SF		49	W. Mays, SF		382	T. Davis, LA		153	E. Mathews, Mil		101	B. Mazeroski, Pit		16	K. Hubbs, ChN	129
H. Aaron, Mil		45	F. Robinson, Cin		380	W. Mays, SF		141	J. Gilliam, LA		93	F. Robinson, Cin		16	F. Howard, LA	108
F. Robinson, Cin		39	H. Aaron, Mil		366	F. Robinson, Cin		136	R. Ashburn, NYN		81	G. Altman, ChN		14	K. Boyer, StL	104
E. Banks, ChN		37	T. Davis, LA		356	H. Aaron, Mil		128	W. Mays, SF		78	H. Aaron, Mil		14	M. Jones, Mil	100
O. Cepeda, SF		35	O. Cepeda, SF		324	F. Howard, LA		119	3 tied with		76	2 tied with		11	L. Cardenas, Cin	99

Hit By Pitch			Sac Hits			Sac Flies			Stolen Bases			Caught Stealing			GDP	
F. Robinson, Cin		11	J. Gilliam, LA		15	D. Demeter, Phi		11	M. Wills, LA		104	M. Wills, LA		13	K. Hubbs, ChN	20
D. Demeter, Phi		10	K. Hubbs, ChN		13	E. Banks, ChN		10	W. Davis, LA		32	B. Virdon, Pit		13	E. Banks, ChN	19
C. Flood, StL		10	J. Javier, StL		13	W. Davis, LA		8	J. Javier, StL		26	5 tied with		9	W. Mays, SF	19
T. Gonzalez, Phi		9	R. Fairly, LA		11	T. Davis, LA		8	V. Pinson, Cin		26				5 tied with	18
3 tied with		8	5 tied with		10	5 tied with		7	T. Taylor, Phi		20					

Runs Created			Runs Created/27 Outs			Batting Average			On-Base Percentage			Slugging Percentage			OBP+Slugging	
F. Robinson, Cin		152	F. Robinson, Cin		9.56	T. Davis, LA		.346	F. Robinson, Cin		.421	F. Robinson, Cin		.624	F. Robinson, Cin	1.045
W. Mays, SF		146	W. Mays, SF		8.62	F. Robinson, Cin		.342	S. Musial, StL		.416	H. Aaron, Mil		.618	H. Aaron, Mil	1.008
H. Aaron, Mil		134	H. Aaron, Mil		8.43	S. Musial, StL		.330	B. Skinner, Pit		.395	W. Mays, SF		.615	W. Mays, SF	.999
T. Davis, LA		132	S. Musial, StL		8.04	B. White, StL		.324	G. Altman, ChN		.393	F. Howard, LA		.560	S. Musial, StL	.924
M. Wills, LA		115	T. Davis, LA		7.58	H. Aaron, Mil		.323	H. Aaron, Mil		.390	T. Davis, LA		.535	T. Davis, LA	.910

1962 National League Pitching Leaders

Wins			Losses			Winning Percentage			Games			Games Started			Complete Games	
D. Drysdale, LA		25	R. Craig, NYN		24	B. Purkey, Cin		.821	R. Perranoski, LA		70	D. Drysdale, LA		41	W. Spahn, Mil	22
J. Sanford, SF		24	A. Jackson, NYN		20	J. Sanford, SF		.774	J. Baldschun, Phi		67	J. Podres, LA		40	A. Mahaffey, Phi	20
B. Purkey, Cin		23	D. Ellsworth, ChN		20	D. Drysdale, LA		.735	E. Roebuck, LA		64	A. Mahaffey, Phi		39	B. O'Dell, SF	20
J. Jay, Cin		21	T. Farrell, Hou		20	B. Pierce, SF		.727	R. Face, Pit		63	B. O'Dell, SF		39	D. Drysdale, LA	19
2 tied with		19	J. Hook, NYN		19	C. McLish, Phi		.688	D. Olivo, Pit		62	J. Sanford, SF		38	2 tied with	18

Shutouts			Saves			Games Finished			Batters Faced			Innings Pitched			Hits Allowed	
B. Gibson, StL		5	R. Face, Pit		28	R. Face, Pit		57	D. Drysdale, LA		1289	D. Drysdale, LA		314.1	B. O'Dell, SF	282
B. Friend, Pit		5	R. Perranoski, LA		20	J. Baldschun, Phi		49	B. Purkey, Cin		1181	B. Purkey, Cin		288.1	B. Friend, Pit	280
4 tied with		4	S. Miller, SF		19	D. McMahon, 2tm		42	B. O'Dell, SF		1178	B. O'Dell, SF		280.2	D. Drysdale, LA	272
			L. McDaniel, StL		14	S. Miller, SF		41	J. Jay, Cin		1165	A. Mahaffey, Phi		274.0	J. Podres, LA	270
			2 tied with		13	R. Perranoski, LA		39	A. Mahaffey, Phi		1138	J. Jay, Cin		273.0	J. Jay, Cin	269

Home Runs Allowed			Walks			Walks/9 Innings			Strikeouts			Strikeouts/9 Innings			Strikeout/Walk Ratio	
A. Mahaffey, Phi		36	J. Hamilton, Phi		107	B. Shaw, Mil		1.8	D. Drysdale, LA		232	S. Koufax, LA		10.5	K. Johnson, Hou	3.87
R. Craig, NYN		35	J. Jay, Cin		100	B. Friend, Pit		1.8	S. Koufax, LA		216	K. Johnson, Hou		8.1	S. Koufax, LA	3.79
J. Marichal, SF		34	S. Williams, LA		98	W. Spahn, Mil		1.8	B. Gibson, StL		208	B. Gibson, StL		8.0	T. Farrell, Hou	3.69
J. Hook, NYN		31	B. Buhl, 2tm		98	B. Pierce, SF		1.9	T. Farrell, Hou		203	D. Bennett, Phi		7.7	D. Drysdale, LA	2.97
B. Purkey, Cin		28	B. Gibson, StL		95	B. Purkey, Cin		2.0	B. O'Dell, SF		195	T. Farrell, Hou		7.6	B. O'Dell, SF	2.95

Earned Run Average			Component ERA			Hit Batsmen			Wild Pitches			Opponent Average			Opponent OBP	
S. Koufax, LA		2.54	S. Koufax, LA		2.13	B. Purkey, Cin		14	J. Hamilton, Phi		22	S. Koufax, LA		.197	S. Koufax, LA	.261
B. Shaw, Mil		2.80	B. Gibson, StL		2.60	A. Mahaffey, Phi		12	D. Ellsworth, ChN		15	B. Gibson, StL		.204	T. Farrell, Hou	.279
B. Purkey, Cin		2.81	D. Drysdale, LA		2.63	B. Bruce, Hou		12	D. Giusti, Hou		13	D. Bennett, Phi		.224	D. Drysdale, LA	.282
D. Drysdale, LA		2.83	T. Farrell, Hou		2.70	B. Shaw, Mil		12	H. Woodeshick, Hou		13	D. Drysdale, LA		.230	B. Pierce, SF	.283
B. Gibson, StL		2.85	W. Spahn, Mil		2.90	D. Drysdale, LA		11	B. Miller, NYN		12	T. Farrell, Hou		.233	W. Spahn, Mil	.284

1962 National League Miscellaneous

Managers			Awards		Postseason	
Chicago	El Tappe	4-16	Most Valuable Player	Maury Wills, ss, LA	World Series	San Francisco (NL) 3 vs. NYA (AL) 4
	Lou Klein	12-18	Cy Young	Don Drysdale, LA		
	Charlie Metro	43-69	Rookie of the Year	Ken Hubbs, 2b, ChN		
Cincinnati	Fred Hutchinson	98-64	STATS Manager of the Year	Alvin Dark, SF	**Outstanding Performances**	
Houston	Harry Craft	64-96			**No-Hitters**	
Los Angeles	Walter Alston	102-63			Sandy Koufax, LA	vs. NYN on June 30
Milwaukee	Birdie Tebbetts	86-76	**STATS All-Star Team**		**Three-Homer Games**	
New York	Casey Stengel	40-120	C Smoky Burgess, Pit	.328 13 61	Ernie Banks, ChN	on May 29
Philadelphia	Gene Mauch	81-80	1B Orlando Cepeda, SF	.306 35 114	Stan Musial, StL	on July 8
Pittsburgh	Danny Murtaugh	93-68	2B Bill Mazeroski, Pit	.271 14 81		
St. Louis	Johnny Keane	84-78	3B Eddie Mathews, Mil	.265 29 90		
San Francisco	Alvin Dark	103-62	SS Maury Wills, LA	.299 6 48		
			OF Hank Aaron, Mil	.323 45 128		
			OF Willie Mays, SF	.304 49 141		
			OF Frank Robinson, Cin	.342 39 136		
			P Don Drysdale, LA	25-9 2.83 232 K		
			P Sandy Koufax, LA	14-7 2.54 216 K		
			P Bob Purkey, Cin	23-5 2.81 141 K		
			P Jack Sanford, SF	24-7 3.43 147 K		
			RP Roy Face, Pit	8-7 1.88 28 Sv		

Team	Overall					Home Games						Road Games						Park Index		Record by Month					
	W	L	Pct	GB	DIF	W	L	R	OR	HR	OHR	W	L	R	OR	HR	OHR	Run	HR	M/A	May	June	July	Aug	S/O
New York	104	57	.646	—	120	58	22	367	246	88	55	46	35	347	301	100	60	96	90	8-6	17-9	19-13	22-9	22-10	16-10
Chicago	94	68	.580	10.5	19	49	33	362	272	63	46	45	35	321	272	51	54	104	101	7-7	20-12	18-14	14-13	17-13	18-9
Minnesota	91	70	.565	13.0	0	48	33	377	306	112	99	43	37	390	296	113	63	98	118	9-10	14-12	20-10	14-17	18-10	16-11
Baltimore	86	76	.531	18.5	28	48	33	311	268	72	56	38	43	333	353	74	81	84	83	10-8	20-10	11-20	19-11	13-14	13-13
Cleveland	79	83	.488	25.5	1	41	40	308	341	88	87	38	43	327	361	81	69	94	103	5-8	12-16	23-12	13-19	12-18	14-10
Detroit	79	83	.488	25.5	4	47	34	395	339	94	109	32	49	305	364	54	86	110	145	8-10	11-16	10-19	14-14	22-8	14-16
Boston	76	85	.472	28.0	5	44	36	383	346	95	73	32	49	283	358	76	79	115	110	9-6	13-14	18-13	13-18	11-20	12-14
Kansas City	73	89	.451	31.5	11	36	45	326	390	52	87	37	44	289	314	43	69	119	124	12-7	13-12	9-21	14-17	11-17	14-15
Los Angeles	70	91	.435	34.0	1	39	42	264	306	24	44	31	49	333	354	71	76	82	46	11-10	11-17	19-12	12-19	8-18	9-15
Washington	56	106	.346	48.5	0	31	49	286	406	63	82	25	57	292	406	75	94	102	88	6-13	9-22	8-21	14-12	12-18	7-20

Clinch Date—New York 9/13.

Team Batting

Team	G	AB	R	OR	H	2B	3B	HR	TB	RBI	TBB	IBB	SO	HBP	SH	SF	SB	CS	SB%	GDP	Avg	OBP	Slg
Minnesota	161	5531	767	602	1408	223	35	225	2376	722	547	41	912	41	84	30	32	14	.70	116	.255	.329	.430
New York	161	5506	714	547	1387	197	35	188	2218	666	434	46	808	31	66	30	42	26	.62	91	.252	.314	.403
Detroit	162	5500	700	703	1388	195	36	148	2099	649	592	49	908	38	64	48	73	32	.70	127	.252	.334	.382
Chicago	162	5508	683	544	1379	208	40	114	2009	648	571	29	896	40	79	44	64	28	.70	97	.250	.330	.365
Boston	161	5575	666	704	1403	247	34	171	2231	623	475	40	954	26	44	37	27	16	.63	118	.252	.316	.400
Baltimore	162	5448	644	621	1359	207	32	146	2068	609	469	43	940	28	73	37	97	34	.74	119	.249	.316	.380
Cleveland	162	5496	635	702	1314	214	29	169	2093	592	469	46	1102	40	88	43	59	36	.62	105	.239	.309	.381
Kansas City	162	5495	615	704	1356	225	38	95	1942	582	529	47	829	25	77	46	47	26	.64	125	.247	.321	.353
Los Angeles	161	5506	597	660	1378	208	38	95	1947	551	448	43	916	43	84	46	43	30	.59	110	.250	.317	.354
Washington	162	5446	578	812	1237	190	35	138	1911	551	448	35	963	30	57	39	68	28	.71	111	.227	.300	.351
AL Total	1616	55011	6599	6599	13609	2114	352	1489	20894	6180	5031	419	9228	342	716	388	552	270	.67	1139	.247	.312	.380
AL Avg Team	162	5501	660	660	1361	211	35	149	2089	618	503	42	923	34	72	39	55	27	.67	114	.247	.312	.380

Team Pitching

Team	G	CG	ShO	Rel	Sv	IP	H	R	ER	HR	SH	SF	HB	TBB	IBB	SO	WP	Bk	H/9	SO/9	BB/9	OAvg	OOBP	ERA
Chicago	162	49	21	211	39	1469.0	1311	544	485	100	68	32	31	440	39	932	37	0	8.0	5.7	2.7	.239	.297	2.97
New York	161	59	19	180	31	1449.0	1239	547	495	115	61	32	22	476	25	965	33	3	7.7	6.0	3.0	.232	.295	3.07
Minnesota	161	58	13	234	30	1446.1	1322	602	527	162	56	33	24	459	27	941	57	3	8.2	5.9	2.9	.242	.302	3.28
Baltimore	162	35	8	248	43	1452.0	1353	621	557	137	79	32	29	507	63	913	31	5	8.4	5.7	3.1	.248	.314	3.45
Los Angeles	161	30	13	315	31	1455.1	1317	660	570	120	71	43	52	578	55	889	48	5	8.1	5.5	3.6	.242	.318	3.52
Cleveland	162	40	14	240	25	1469.0	1390	702	619	176	72	40	27	478	55	1018	38	3	8.5	6.2	2.9	.249	.309	3.79
Detroit	162	42	7	240	28	1456.1	1407	703	631	195	71	44	48	477	28	930	42	10	8.7	5.7	2.9	.253	.315	3.90
Kansas City	162	35	11	247	29	1458.0	1417	704	635	156	77	44	44	540	35	887	43	8	8.7	5.5	3.3	.256	.324	3.92
Boston	161	29	7	241	32	1449.2	1367	704	640	152	84	32	27	539	48	1009	50	3	8.5	6.3	3.3	.248	.316	3.97
Washington	162	29	8	276	25	1447.0	1486	812	710	176	77	59	38	537	44	744	49	7	9.2	4.6	3.3	.266	.331	4.42
AL Total	1616	406	121	2449	313	14551.2	13609	6599	5869	1489	716	388	342	5031	419	9228	428	47	8.4	5.7	3.1	.247	.319	3.63
AL Avg Team	162	41	12	245	31	1455.2	1361	660	587	149	72	39	34	503	42	923	43	5	8.4	5.7	3.1	.247	.319	3.63

Team Fielding

Team	G	PO	A	E	TC	DP	PB	Pct
Baltimore	162	4347	1703	99	6149	157	11	.984
New York	161	4338	1720	110	6168	162	9	.982
Detroit	162	4357	1628	113	6098	124	21	.981
Kansas City	162	4373	1722	127	6222	131	11	.980
Chicago	162	4395	1779	131	6305	163	23	.979
Boston	161	4345	1591	135	6071	119	12	.978
Cleveland	162	4405	1604	143	6152	129	12	.977
Minnesota	161	4333	1597	144	6074	140	13	.976
Los Angeles	161	4361	1829	163	6353	155	18	.974
Washington	162	4334	1826	182	6342	165	17	.971
AL Total	1616	43588	16999	1347	61934	1445	147	.978

Team vs. Team Records

	Bal	Bos	ChA	Cle	Det	KCA	LAA	Min	NYA	Was	Won
Bal	—	7	7	10	13	9	9	9	7	15	86
Bos	11	—	8	10	9	7	9	7	6	9	76
ChA	11	10	—	11	11	12	10	8	8	13	94
Cle	8	8	7	—	10	11	10	5	7	13	79
Det	5	9	7	8	—	13	12	8	8	9	79
KCA	9	11	6	7	5	—	10	9	6	10	73
LAA	9	8	8	8	6	8	—	9	5	9	70
Min	9	11	10	13	10	9	9	—	6	14	91
NYA	11	12	10	11	10	12	13	11	—	14	104
Was	3	9	5	5	9	8	9	4	4	—	56
Lost	76	85	68	83	83	89	91	70	57	106	

1963 American League Batting Leaders

Games		At-Bats		Runs		Hits		Doubles		Triples	
B. Robinson, Bal	161	B. Richardson, NYA	630	B. Allison, Min	99	C. Yastrzemski, Bos	183	C. Yastrzemski, Bos	40	Z. Versalles, Min	13
R. Colavito, Det	160	Z. Versalles, Min	621	A. Pearson, LAA	92	P. Ward, ChA	177	P. Ward, ChA	34	J. Fregosi, LAA	12
Z. Versalles, Min	159	D. Stuart, Bos	612	C. Yastrzemski, Bos	91	A. Pearson, LAA	176	M. Alvis, Cle	32	C. Hinton, Was	12
M. Alvis, Cle	158	E. Charles, KCA	603	T. Tresh, NYA	91	A. Kaline, Det	172	F. Torres, LAA	32	G. Cimoli, KCA	11
E. Charles, KCA	158	M. Alvis, Cle	602	R. Colavito, Det	91	J. Fregosi, LAA	170	W. Causey, KCA	32	2 tied with	8

Home Runs		Total Bases		Runs Batted In		Walks		Intentional Walks		Strikeouts	
H. Killebrew, Min	45	D. Stuart, Bos	319	D. Stuart, Bos	118	C. Yastrzemski, Bos	95	A. Kaline, Det	12	D. Nicholson, ChA	175
D. Stuart, Bos	42	P. Ward, ChA	289	A. Kaline, Det	101	A. Pearson, LAA	92	C. Boyer, NYA	11	D. Lock, Was	151
B. Allison, Min	35	H. Killebrew, Min	286	H. Killebrew, Min	96	B. Allison, Min	90	W. Held, Cle	10	D. Stuart, Bos	144
J. Hall, Min	33	A. Kaline, Det	283	B. Allison, Min	91	N. Cash, Det	89	J. Gentile, Bal	9	L. Clinton, Bos	118
E. Howard, NYA	28	B. Allison, Min	281	R. Colavito, Det	91	R. Colavito, Det	84	R. Colavito, Det	9	2 tied with	109

Hit By Pitch		Sac Hits		Sac Flies		Stolen Bases		Caught Stealing		GDP	
M. Alvis, Cle	10	V. Power, Min	13	B. Phillips, Det	10	L. Aparicio, Bal	40	A. Pearson, LAA	10	D. Stuart, Bos	24
J. Orsino, Bal	9	J. Bouton, NYA	11	E. Charles, KCA	8	C. Hinton, Was	25	C. Hinton, Was	9	F. Malzone, Bos	24
L. Thomas, LAA	9	8 tied with	10	D. Nicholson, ChA	8	J. Wood, Det	18	E. Charles, KCA	8	E. Charles, KCA	21
5 tied with	8			N. Siebern, KCA	8	R. Snyder, Bal	18	3 tied with	7	F. Torres, LAA	20
				R. Colavito, Det	8	A. Pearson, LAA	17			R. Hansen, ChA	19

Runs Created		Runs Created/27 Outs		Batting Average		On-Base Percentage		Slugging Percentage		OBP+Slugging	
C. Yastrzemski, Bos	109	B. Allison, Min	7.31	C. Yastrzemski, Bos	.321	C. Yastrzemski, Bos	.418	H. Killebrew, Min	.555	B. Allison, Min	.911
B. Allison, Min	107	C. Yastrzemski, Bos	7.30	A. Kaline, Det	.312	A. Pearson, LAA	.402	B. Allison, Min	.533	H. Killebrew, Min	.904
P. Ward, ChA	103	T. Tresh, NYA	6.97	R. Rollins, Min	.307	N. Cash, Det	.386	E. Howard, NYA	.528	C. Yastrzemski, Bos	.894
A. Kaline, Det	102	A. Kaline, Det	6.90	A. Pearson, LAA	.305	B. Allison, Min	.378	D. Stuart, Bos	.521	A. Kaline, Det	.889
T. Tresh, NYA	101	N. Cash, Det	6.63	P. Ward, ChA	.295	A. Kaline, Det	.375	J. Hall, Min	.521	E. Howard, NYA	.869

1963 American League Pitching Leaders

Wins		Losses		Winning Percentage		Games		Games Started		Complete Games	
W. Ford, NYA	24	O. Pena, KCA	20	W. Ford, NYA	.774	S. Miller, Bal	71	R. Terry, NYA	37	R. Terry, NYA	18
J. Bouton, NYA	21	D. Rudolph, Was	19	J. Bouton, NYA	.750	D. Radatz, Bos	66	W. Ford, NYA	37	C. Pascual, Min	18
C. Pascual, Min	21	D. Chance, LAA	18	A. Downing, NYA	.722	B. Dailey, Min	66	S. Barber, Bal	36	D. Stigman, Min	15
S. Barber, Bal	20	E. Wilson, Bos	16	D. Radatz, Bos	.714	J. Lamabe, Bos	65	K. McBride, LAA	36	H. Aguirre, Det	14
Monbouquette, Bos	20	4 tied with	15	L. Stange, Min	.706	J. Wyatt, KCA	63	Monbouquette, Bos	36	R. Herbert, ChA	14

Shutouts		Saves		Games Finished		Batters Faced		Innings Pitched		Hits Allowed	
R. Herbert, ChA	7	S. Miller, Bal	27	S. Miller, Bal	59	S. Barber, Bal	1096	W. Ford, NYA	269.1	Monbouquette, Bos	258
J. Bouton, NYA	6	D. Radatz, Bos	25	D. Radatz, Bos	58	Monbouquette, Bos	1090	R. Terry, NYA	268.0	S. Barber, Bal	253
5 tied with	4	J. Wyatt, KCA	21	J. Wyatt, KCA	53	R. Terry, NYA	1074	Monbouquette, Bos	266.2	R. Terry, NYA	246
		B. Dailey, Min	21	R. Kline, Was	46	W. Ford, NYA	1068	S. Barber, Bal	258.2	J. Bunning, Det	245
		H. Wilhelm, ChA	21	B. Dailey, Min	43	D. Chance, LAA	1058	R. Roberts, Bal	251.1	D. Wickersham, KCA	244

Home Runs Allowed		Walks		Walks/9 Innings		Strikeouts		Strikeouts/9 Innings		Strikeout/Walk Ratio	
J. Bunning, Det	38	E. Wilson, Bos	105	D. Donovan, Cle	1.2	C. Pascual, Min	202	A. Downing, NYA	8.8	Monbouquette, Bos	4.14
R. Roberts, Bal	35	D. Morehead, Bos	99	R. Terry, NYA	1.3	J. Bunning, Det	196	P. Ramos, Cle	8.2	P. Ramos, Cle	4.12
P. Regan, Det	33	S. Barber, Bal	92	R. Herbert, ChA	1.4	D. Stigman, Min	193	C. Pascual, Min	7.3	W. Ford, NYA	3.38
D. Stigman, Min	32	D. Chance, LAA	90	Monbouquette, Bos	1.4	G. Peters, ChA	189	D. Stigman, Min	7.2	R. Roberts, Bal	3.10
Monbouquette, Bos	31	2 tied with	87	R. Roberts, Bal	1.4	W. Ford, NYA	189	J. Bunning, Det	7.1	2 tied with	3.00

Earned Run Average		Component ERA		Hit Batsmen		Wild Pitches		Opponent Average		Opponent OBP	
G. Peters, ChA	2.33	A. Downing, NYA	2.09	K. McBride, LAA	14	E. Wilson, Bos	21	A. Downing, NYA	.184	R. Terry, NYA	.271
J. Pizarro, ChA	2.39	G. Peters, ChA	2.26	J. Duckworth, Was	10	L. Stange, Min	10	D. Morehead, Bos	.211	P. Ramos, Cle	.272
C. Pascual, Min	2.46	J. Bouton, NYA	2.54	D. Chance, LAA	10	D. Stigman, Min	10	J. Bouton, NYA	.212	R. Roberts, Bal	.272
J. Bouton, NYA	2.53	J. Pizarro, ChA	2.57	3 tied with	9	M. Pappas, Bal	10	M. Drabowsky, KCA	.214	A. Downing, NYA	.277
A. Downing, NYA	2.56	R. Terry, NYA	2.78			C. Pascual, Min	10	G. Peters, ChA	.216	G. Peters, ChA	.277

1963 American League Miscellaneous

Managers

Baltimore	Billy Hitchcock	86-76
Boston	Johnny Pesky	76-85
Chicago	Al Lopez	94-68
Cleveland	Birdie Tebbetts	79-83
Detroit	Bob Scheffing	24-36
	Chuck Dressen	55-47
Kansas City	Ed Lopat	73-89
Los Angeles	Bill Rigney	70-91
Minnesota	Sam Mele	91-70
New York	Ralph Houk	104-57
Washington	Mickey Vernon	14-26
	Eddie Yost	0-1
	Gil Hodges	42-79

Awards

Most Valuable Player	Elston Howard, c, NYA
STATS Cy Young	Dick Radatz, Bos
Rookie of the Year	Gary Peters, p, ChA
STATS Manager of the Year	Ralph Houk, NYA

STATS All-Star Team

C	Elston Howard, NYA	.287	28	85
1B	Dick Stuart, Bos	.261	42	118
2B	Jerry Lumpe, KCA	.271	5	59
3B	Pete Ward, ChA	.295	22	84
SS	Jim Fregosi, LAA	.287	9	50
OF	Bob Allison, Min	.271	35	91
OF	Al Kaline, Det	.312	27	101
OF	Harmon Killebrew, Min	.258	45	96
P	Jim Bouton, NYA	21-7	2.53	148 K
P	Whitey Ford, NYA	24-7	2.74	189 K
P	Camilo Pascual, Min	21-9	2.46	202 K
P	Gary Peters, ChA	19-8	2.33	189 K
RP	Dick Radatz, Bos	15-6	1.97	25 Sv

Postseason

World Series	NYA (AL) 0 vs. Los Angeles (NL) 4

Outstanding Performances

Three-Homer Games

Don Leppert, Was	on April 11
Bob Allison, Min	on May 17
Boog Powell, Bal	on August 10
H. Killebrew, Min	on September 21

1963 National League Standings

Team	W	L	Pct	GB	DIF	W	L	R	OR	HR	OHR	W	L	R	OR	HR	OHR	Run	HR	M/A	May	June	July	Aug	S/O
		Overall						Home Games						Road Games				Park Index				Record by Month			
Los Angeles	99	63	.611	—	98	53	28	296	248	42	43	46	35	344	302	68	68	84	63	10-11	17-9	16-12	21-10	16-12	19-9
St. Louis	93	69	.574	6.0	29	53	28	429	311	79	70	40	41	318	317	49	54	117	145	14-6	15-15	16-10	14-16	15-13	19-9
San Francisco	88	74	.543	11.0	48	50	31	363	289	101	64	38	43	362	352	96	62	91	104	11-9	19-9	14-15	16-14	14-14	14-13
Philadelphia	87	75	.537	12.0	6	45	36	340	282	61	60	42	39	302	296	65	53	104	103	8-10	14-15	13-16	21-10	16-13	15-11
Cincinnati	86	76	.531	13.0	1	46	35	344	300	65	46	40	41	304	294	57	71	108	87	6-10	16-13	19-12	16-16	16-14	13-11
Milwaukee	84	78	.519	15.0	2	45	36	341	307	68	81	39	42	336	296	71	68	103	107	12-9	9-17	17-11	16-16	19-9	11-16
Chicago	82	80	.506	17.0	1	43	38	298	302	63	70	39	42	272	276	64	49	109	118	9-10	16-12	15-13	16-13	13-17	13-15
Pittsburgh	74	88	.457	25.0	9	42	39	275	295	47	42	32	49	292	300	61	57	96	75	11-5	12-17	13-17	16-14	15-13	7-22
Houston	66	96	.407	33.0	0	44	37	236	268	25	34	22	59	228	372	37	61	84	60	7-13	13-16	9-20	12-18	9-18	16-11
New York	51	111	.315	48.0	0	34	47	276	381	61	93	17	64	225	393	35	69	106	148	7-12	11-19	11-17	4-25	9-19	9-19

Clinch Date—Los Angeles 9/24.

Team Batting

Team	G	AB	R	OR	H	2B	3B	HR	TB	RBI	TBB	IBB	SO	HBP	SH	SF	SB	CS	SB%	GDP	Avg	OBP	Slg
St. Louis	162	5678	747	628	1540	231	66	128	2287	697	458	51	915	25	85	37	77	42	.65	95	.271	.332	.403
San Francisco	162	5579	725	641	1442	206	35	197	2309	680	441	53	889	45	72	39	55	49	.53	125	.258	.322	.414
Milwaukee	163	5518	677	603	1345	204	39	139	2044	624	525	63	954	43	82	43	75	52	.59	108	.244	.319	.370
Cincinnati	162	5416	648	594	1333	225	44	122	2012	608	474	52	960	47	62	41	92	58	.61	95	.246	.317	.371
Philadelphia	162	5524	642	578	1390	228	54	126	2104	599	403	64	955	44	87	34	56	39	.59	99	.252	.312	.381
Los Angeles	163	5428	640	550	1361	178	34	110	1937	584	453	47	867	26	85	53	124	70	.64	121	.251	.318	.357
Chicago	162	5404	570	578	1286	205	44	127	1960	530	439	57	1049	36	64	44	68	60	.53	112	.238	.305	.363
Pittsburgh	162	5536	567	595	1385	181	49	108	1988	523	454	47	940	29	63	28	57	41	.58	137	.250	.314	.359
New York	162	5336	501	774	1168	156	36	96	1682	459	457	41	1078	47	46	35	41	52	.44	106	.219	.291	.301
Houston	162	5384	464	640	1184	170	39	62	1618	420	456	39	938	30	86	27	39	30	.57	119	.220	.288	.301
NL Total	1622	54803	6181	6181	13434	1984	439	1215	19941	5724	4560	514	9545	372	732	381	684	493	.58	1117	.245	.306	.364
NL Avg Team	162	5480	618	618	1343	198	44	122	1994	572	456	51	955	37	73	38	68	49	.58	112	.245	.306	.364

Team Pitching

Team	G	CG	ShO	Rel	Sv	IP	H	R	ER	HR	SH	SF	HB	TBB	IBB	SO	WP	Bk	H/9	SO/9	BB/9	OAvg	OOBP	ERA
Los Angeles	163	51	24	217	29	1469.2	1329	550	466	111	68	25	33	402	74	1095	45	12	8.1	6.7	2.5	.239	.293	2.85
Chicago	162	45	15	217	28	1457.0	1357	578	498	119	86	34	24	400	32	851	43	11	8.4	5.3	2.5	.249	.301	3.08
Philadelphia	162	45	12	242	31	1457.1	1262	578	500	113	66	41	38	553	60	1052	49	13	7.8	6.5	3.4	.235	.309	3.09
Pittsburgh	162	34	16	292	33	1448.0	1350	595	498	99	91	45	49	457	94	900	42	16	8.4	5.6	2.8	.249	.311	3.10
Milwaukee	163	56	18	262	25	1471.2	1327	603	534	149	66	36	24	489	78	924	54	19	8.1	5.7	3.0	.241	.304	3.27
Cincinnati	162	55	22	102	36	1439.2	1307	594	527	117	67	42	39	425	28	1048	64	14	8.2	6.6	2.7	.242	.300	3.29
St. Louis	162	49	17	243	32	1463.0	1329	628	540	124	60	43	48	463	35	978	49	9	8.2	6.0	2.8	.241	.303	3.32
San Francisco	162	46	9	247	30	1469.0	1380	641	546	126	76	17	34	464	64	954	40	12	8.5	5.8	2.8	.246	.306	3.35
Houston	162	36	16	232	20	1450.1	1341	640	554	95	91	58	35	378	23	937	43	19	8.3	5.8	2.3	.245	.295	3.44
New York	162	42	5	233	12	1427.2	1452	774	654	162	61	40	48	529	26	806	57	20	9.2	5.1	3.3	.263	.330	4.12
NL Total	1622	459	154	2359	276	14553.1	13434	6181	5317	1215	732	381	372	4560	514	9545	486	147	8.3	5.9	2.8	.245	.312	3.29
NL Avg Team	162	46	15	236	28	1455.1	1343	618	532	122	73	38	37	456	51	955	49	15	8.3	5.9	2.8	.245	.312	3.29

Team Fielding

Team	G	PO	A	E	TC	DP	PB	Pct
Milwaukee	163	4416	1848	129	6393	161	15	.980
Philadelphia	162	4372	1839	142	6353	147	13	.978
Cincinnati	162	4319	1576	135	6030	127	17	.978
St. Louis	162	4390	1613	147	6150	136	20	.976
Chicago	162	4371	1956	155	6482	172	19	.976
Los Angeles	163	4409	1753	159	6321	129	15	.975
San Francisco	162	4407	1613	156	6176	113	13	.975
Houston	162	4351	1626	162	6139	100	22	.974
Pittsburgh	162	4344	1969	182	6495	195	15	.972
New York	162	4282	1888	210	6380	151	24	.967
NL Total	1622	43661	17681	1577	62919	1431	173	.975

Team vs. Team Records

	ChN	Cin	Hou	LA	Mil	NYN	Phi	Pit	SF	StL	Won
ChN	—	9	9	7	12	11	9	8	10	7	82
Cin	9	—	11	8	10	10	8	11	8	11	86
Hou	9	7	—	5	5	13	8	6	8	5	66
LA	11	10	13	—	8	16	7	13	9	12	99
Mil	6	8	13	10	—	12	10	7	10	8	84
NYN	7	8	5	2	6	—	8	4	6	5	51
Phi	9	10	10	11	8	10	—	13	8	8	87
Pit	10	7	12	5	11	14	5	—	5	5	74
SF	8	10	10	9	8	12	10	13	—	8	88
StL	11	7	13	6	10	13	10	13	10	—	93
Lost	80	76	96	63	78	111	75	88	74	69	

Seasons: Standings, Leaders

1963 National League Batting Leaders

Games		At-Bats		Runs		Hits		Doubles		Triples	
R. Santo, ChN	162	C. Flood, StL	662	H. Aaron, Mil	121	V. Pinson, Cin	204	D. Groat, StL	43	V. Pinson, Cin	14
V. Pinson, Cin	162	B. White, StL	658	W. Mays, SF	115	H. Aaron, Mil	201	V. Pinson, Cin	37	T. Gonzalez, Phi	12
B. White, StL	162	V. Pinson, Cin	652	C. Flood, StL	112	D. Groat, StL	201	T. Gonzalez, Phi	36	L. Brock, ChN	11
3 tied with	161	T. Taylor, Phi	640	B. White, StL	106	C. Flood, StL	200	B. Williams, ChN	36	J. Callison, Phi	11
		2 tied with	631	W. McCovey, SF	103	B. White, StL	200	J. Callison, Phi	36	D. Groat, StL	11

Home Runs		Total Bases		Runs Batted In		Walks		Intentional Walks		Strikeouts	
W. McCovey, SF	44	H. Aaron, Mil	370	H. Aaron, Mil	130	E. Mathews, Mil	124	F. Robinson, Cin	20	D. Clendenon, Pit	136
H. Aaron, Mil	44	W. Mays, SF	347	K. Boyer, StL	111	F. Robinson, Cin	81	H. Aaron, Mil	18	H. Goss, Hou	128
W. Mays, SF	38	V. Pinson, Cin	335	B. White, StL	109	H. Aaron, Mil	78	E. Banks, ChN	16	L. Brock, ChN	122
O. Cepeda, SF	34	O. Cepeda, SF	326	V. Pinson, Cin	106	K. Boyer, StL	70	C. Dalrymple, Phi	15	J. Hickman, NYN	120
F. Howard, LA	28	B. White, StL	323	W. Mays, SF	103	D. Schofield, Pit	69	E. Mathews, Mil	14	2 tied with	119

Hit By Pitch		Sac Hits		Sac Flies		Stolen Bases		Caught Stealing		GDP	
F. Robinson, Cin	14	F. Bolling, Mil	17	R. Santo, ChN	11	M. Wills, LA	40	M. Wills, LA	19	R. Clemente, Pit	24
R. Hunt, NYN	13	C. Hiller, SF	13	R. Sievers, Phi	9	H. Aaron, Mil	31	P. Rose, Cin	15	F. Thomas, NYN	23
W. McCovey, SF	11	J. Javier, StL	13	E. Banks, ChN	8	V. Pinson, Cin	27	D. Clendenon, Pit	13	K. Boyer, StL	20
O. Cepeda, SF	10	J. Callison, Phi	13	5 tied with	7	F. Robinson, Cin	26	L. Brock, ChN	12	P. Runnels, Hou	20
2 tied with	9	J. Temple, Hou	13			W. Davis, LA	25	C. Flood, StL	12	J. Torre, Mil	19

Runs Created		Runs Created/27 Outs		Batting Average		On-Base Percentage		Slugging Percentage		OBP+Slugging	
H. Aaron, Mil	146	H. Aaron, Mil	8.80	T. Davis, LA	.326	E. Mathews, Mil	.399	H. Aaron, Mil	.586	H. Aaron, Mil	.977
W. Mays, SF	127	W. Mays, SF	7.95	R. Clemente, Pit	.320	H. Aaron, Mil	.391	W. Mays, SF	.582	W. Mays, SF	.962
V. Pinson, Cin	114	O. Cepeda, SF	7.18	H. Aaron, Mil	.319	W. Mays, SF	.380	W. McCovey, SF	.566	O. Cepeda, SF	.929
B. White, StL	113	W. McCovey, SF	7.07	D. Groat, StL	.319	F. Robinson, Cin	.379	O. Cepeda, SF	.563	W. McCovey, SF	.915
O. Cepeda, SF	111	E. Mathews, Mil	7.01	O. Cepeda, SF	.316	D. Groat, StL	.377	V. Pinson, Cin	.514	V. Pinson, Cin	.861

1963 National League Pitching Leaders

Wins		Losses		Winning Percentage		Games		Games Started		Complete Games	
J. Marichal, SF	25	R. Craig, NYN	22	R. Perranoski, LA	.842	R. Perranoski, LA	69	J. Sanford, SF	42	W. Spahn, Mil	22
S. Koufax, LA	25	L. Jackson, ChN	18	S. Koufax, LA	.833	J. Baldschun, Phi	65	D. Drysdale, LA	42	S. Koufax, LA	20
J. Maloney, Cin	23	J. Jay, Cin	18	A. McBean, Pit	.813	L. Bearnarth, NYN	58	J. Marichal, SF	40	D. Ellsworth, ChN	19
W. Spahn, Mil	23	4 tied with	17	J. Maloney, Cin	.767	T. Sisk, Pit	57	S. Koufax, LA	40	J. Marichal, SF	18
D. Ellsworth, ChN	22			W. Spahn, Mil	.767	L. McDaniel, ChN	57	B. Friend, Pit	38	D. Drysdale, LA	17

Shutouts		Saves		Games Finished		Batters Faced		Innings Pitched		Hits Allowed	
S. Koufax, LA	11	L. McDaniel, ChN	22	L. McDaniel, ChN	48	J. Marichal, SF	1270	J. Marichal, SF	321.1	D. Drysdale, LA	287
W. Spahn, Mil	7	R. Perranoski, LA	21	R. Perranoski, LA	47	D. Drysdale, LA	1266	D. Drysdale, LA	315.1	J. Sanford, SF	273
J. Maloney, Cin	6	J. Baldschun, Phi	16	J. Baldschun, Phi	44	S. Koufax, LA	1210	S. Koufax, LA	311.0	J. Marichal, SF	259
C. Simmons, StL	6	R. Face, Pit	16	H. Woodeshick, Hou	39	J. Sanford, SF	1184	D. Ellsworth, ChN	290.2	L. Jackson, ChN	256
5 tied with	5	B. Henry, Cin	14	R. Face, Pit	38	D. Ellsworth, ChN	1160	J. Sanford, SF	284.1	R. Craig, NYN	249

Home Runs Allowed		Walks		Walks/9 Innings		Strikeouts		Strikeouts/9 Innings		Strikeout/Walk Ratio	
D. Lemaster, Mil	30	R. Culp, Phi	102	B. Friend, Pit	1.5	S. Koufax, LA	306	J. Maloney, Cin	9.5	S. Koufax, LA	5.28
R. Craig, NYN	28	B. Gibson, StL	96	T. Farrell, Hou	1.6	J. Maloney, Cin	265	S. Koufax, LA	8.9	D. Drysdale, LA	4.40
J. Marichal, SF	27	E. Broglio, StL	90	J. Nuxhall, Cin	1.6	D. Drysdale, LA	251	R. Culp, Phi	7.8	J. Nuxhall, Cin	4.33
3 tied with	25	J. Maloney, Cin	88	D. Drysdale, LA	1.6	J. Marichal, SF	248	C. Short, Phi	7.3	J. Marichal, SF	4.07
		D. Lemaster, Mil	85	S. Koufax, LA	1.7	B. Gibson, StL	204	D. Lemaster, Mil	7.2	T. Farrell, Hou	4.03

Earned Run Average		Component ERA		Hit Batsmen		Wild Pitches		Opponent Average		Opponent OBP	
S. Koufax, LA	1.88	S. Koufax, LA	1.55	D. Cardwell, Pit	16	J. Maloney, Cin	19	S. Koufax, LA	.189	S. Koufax, LA	.230
D. Ellsworth, ChN	2.11	T. Farrell, Hou	1.98	B. Gibson, StL	13	D. Lemaster, Mil	13	J. Maloney, Cin	.202	T. Farrell, Hou	.255
B. Friend, Pit	2.34	D. Ellsworth, ChN	2.02	A. Jackson, NYN	12	E. Broglio, StL	13	R. Culp, Phi	.206	J. Marichal, SF	.255
J. Marichal, SF	2.41	J. Marichal, SF	2.19	J. Tsitouris, Cin	11	R. Sadecki, StL	12	D. Ellsworth, ChN	.210	D. Ellsworth, ChN	.262
C. Simmons, StL	2.48	B. Friend, Pit	2.25	D. Drysdale, LA	10	B. Miller, LA	12	E. Broglio, StL	.216	B. Friend, Pit	.267

1963 National League Miscellaneous

Managers		
Chicago	Bob Kennedy	82-80
Cincinnati	Fred Hutchinson	86-76
Houston	Harry Craft	66-96
Los Angeles	Walter Alston	99-63
Milwaukee	Bobby Bragan	84-78
New York	Casey Stengel	51-111
Philadelphia	Gene Mauch	87-75
Pittsburgh	Danny Murtaugh	74-88
St. Louis	Johnny Keane	93-69
San Francisco	Alvin Dark	88-74

Awards	
Most Valuable Player	Sandy Koufax, p, LA
Cy Young	Sandy Koufax, LA
Rookie of the Year	Pete Rose, 2b, Cin
STATS Manager of the Year	Bob Kennedy, ChN

STATS All-Star Team

C	Ed Bailey, SF	.263	21	68
1B	Orlando Cepeda, SF	.316	34	97
2B	Tony Taylor, Phi	.281	5	49
3B	Eddie Mathews, Mil	.263	23	84
SS	Dick Groat, StL	.319	6	73
OF	Hank Aaron, Mil	.319	44	130
OF	Willie Mays, SF	.314	38	103
OF	Willie McCovey, SF	.280	44	102
P	Dick Ellsworth, ChN	22-10	2.11	185 K
P	Sandy Koufax, LA	25-5	1.88	306 K
P	Jim Maloney, Cin	23-7	2.77	265 K
P	Juan Marichal, SF	25-8	2.41	248 K
RP	Ron Perranoski, LA	16-3	1.67	21 Sv

Postseason	
World Series	Los Angeles (NL) 4 vs. NYA (AL) 0

Outstanding Performances

No-Hitters
Sandy Koufax, LA   vs. SF on May 11
Don Nottebart, Hou vs. Phi on May 17
Juan Marichal, SF   vs. Hou on June 15

Three-Homer Games
Willie Mays, SF   on June 2
Ernie Banks, ChN   on June 9
Willie McCovey, SF on September 22

Cycles
Johnny Callison, Phi on June 27
Jim Hickman, NYN   on August 7

1964 American League Standings

Team	Overall					Home Games						Road Games						Park Index		Record by Month					
	W	L	Pct	GB	DIF	W	L	R	OR	HR	OHR	W	L	R	OR	HR	OHR	Run	HR	M/A	May	June	July	Aug	S/O
New York	99	63	.611	—	37	50	31	363	290	69	56	49	32	367	287	93	73	100	75	4-4	17-12	21-12	19-10	14-16	24-9
Chicago	98	64	.605	1.0	40	52	29	306	213	43	42	46	35	336	288	63	82	83	59	5-4	19-7	15-18	22-11	19-14	18-10
Baltimore	97	65	.599	2.0	83	49	32	351	296	79	64	48	33	328	271	83	65	108	97	6-5	21-10	19-11	17-14	16-12	18-13
Detroit	85	77	.525	14.0	3	46	35	340	320	85	89	39	42	359	358	72	75	92	118	7-6	11-18	14-14	19-12	20-10	15-12
Los Angeles	82	80	.506	17.0	2	45	36	230	226	32	31	37	44	314	325	70	69	71	45	6-7	10-22	19-12	19-12	14-15	14-12
Cleveland	79	83	.488	20.0	16	41	40	365	351	84	82	38	43	324	342	80	72	108	109	6-3	15-13	12-21	12-20	20-10	14-16
Minnesota	79	83	.488	20.0	3	40	41	386	336	115	88	39	42	351	342	106	93	104	102	7-6	17-13	15-16	11-18	16-13	13-17
Boston	72	90	.444	27.0	17	45	36	393	382	100	87	27	54	295	411	86	91	110	106	5-7	16-14	15-17	16-14	7-22	13-16
Washington	62	100	.383	37.0	0	31	50	294	380	71	95	31	50	284	353	54	77	106	127	6-8	13-21	12-16	10-21	12-15	9-19
Kansas City	57	105	.352	42.0	0	26	55	330	455	107	132	31	50	291	381	59	88	117	163	4-6	11-20	14-19	11-18	9-20	8-22

Clinch Date—New York 10/03.

Team Batting

Team	G	AB	R	OR	H	2B	3B	HR	TB	RBI	TBB	IBB	SO	HBP	SH	SF	SB	CS	SB%	GDP	Avg	OBP	Slg
Minnesota	163	5610	737	678	1413	227	46	221	2395	707	553	43	1019	44	74	37	46	22	.68	120	.252	.328	.427
New York	164	5705	730	577	1442	208	35	162	2206	688	520	64	976	31	68	34	54	18	.75	117	.253	.322	.387
Detroit	163	5513	699	678	1394	199	57	157	2178	658	517	40	912	40	71	42	60	27	.69	105	.253	.326	.395
Cleveland	164	5603	689	693	1386	208	22	164	2130	640	500	63	1063	49	63	42	79	51	.61	112	.247	.319	.380
Boston	162	5513	688	793	1425	253	29	186	2294	648	504	43	917	28	35	26	18	16	.53	144	.258	.327	.416
Baltimore	163	5463	679	567	1357	229	20	162	2112	632	537	54	1019	27	69	47	78	38	.67	126	.248	.324	.387
Chicago	162	5491	642	501	1356	184	40	106	1938	586	562	58	902	52	96	45	75	39	.66	100	.247	.328	.353
Kansas City	163	5524	621	836	1321	216	29	166	2093	594	548	32	1104	42	53	25	34	20	.63	152	.239	.315	.379
Washington	162	5396	578	733	1246	199	28	125	1876	528	514	34	1124	28	66	33	47	30	.61	119	.231	.315	.348
Los Angeles	162	5362	544	551	1297	186	27	102	1843	508	472	40	920	26	78	37	49	39	.56	145	.242	.311	.344
AL Total	1628	55180	6607	6607	13637	2109	333	1551	21065	6189	5227	471	9956	367	673	368	540	300	.64	1240	.247	.315	.382
AL Avg Team	163	5518	661	661	1364	211	33	155	2107	619	523	47	996	37	67	37	54	30	.64	124	.247	.315	.382

Team Pitching

Team	G	CG	ShO	Rel	Sv	IP	H	R	ER	HR	SH	SF	HB	TBB	IBB	SO	WP	Bk	H/9	SO/9	BB/9	OAvg	OOBP	ERA
Chicago	162	44	20	219	45	1467.2	1216	501	444	124	59	36	31	401	42	955	49	2	7.5	5.9	2.5	.226	.282	2.72
Los Angeles	162	30	28	285	41	1450.2	1273	551	469	100	58	25	50	530	54	965	42	1	7.9	6.0	3.3	.236	.309	2.91
New York	164	46	18	215	45	1506.2	1312	577	528	129	74	33	22	504	39	989	43	3	7.8	5.9	3.0	.234	.299	3.15
Baltimore	163	44	17	238	41	1458.2	1292	567	512	129	54	33	36	456	63	939	31	1	8.0	5.8	2.8	.239	.300	3.16
Minnesota	163	47	4	277	29	1477.2	1361	678	587	181	76	34	31	545	55	1099	73	6	8.3	6.7	3.3	.243	.312	3.58
Cleveland	164	37	16	277	37	1487.2	1443	693	620	154	73	40	33	565	59	1162	56	6	8.7	7.0	3.4	.255	.324	3.75
Detroit	163	35	11	248	35	1453.0	1343	678	620	164	64	27	53	536	23	993	45	3	8.3	6.2	3.3	.244	.316	3.84
Washington	162	27	5	291	26	1435.1	1417	733	635	172	64	45	27	505	58	794	44	3	8.9	5.0	3.2	.259	.322	3.98
Boston	162	21	9	252	38	1422.0	1464	793	711	178	75	51	30	571	37	1094	52	1	9.3	6.9	3.6	.266	.336	4.50
Kansas City	163	18	6	344	27	1455.2	1516	836	761	220	76	44	54	614	42	966	55	4	9.4	6.0	3.8	.269	.344	4.71
AL Total	1628	349	134	2646	364	14615.0	13637	6607	5887	1551	673	368	367	5227	472	9956	490	29	8.4	6.1	3.2	.247	.321	3.63
AL Avg Team	163	35	13	265	36	1461.0	1364	661	589	155	67	37	37	523	47	996	49	3	8.4	6.1	3.2	.247	.321	3.63

Team Fielding

Team	G	PO	A	E	TC	DP	PB	Pct
Baltimore	163	4368	1726	95	6189	159	20	.985
New York	164	4515	1851	109	6475	158	12	.983
Detroit	163	4368	1633	111	6112	137	14	.982
Cleveland	164	4441	1674	118	6233	149	27	.981
Chicago	162	4395	1808	122	6325	164	35	.981
Washington	162	4299	1717	127	6143	145	19	.979
Los Angeles	162	4343	1847	138	6328	168	8	.978
Boston	162	4267	1558	138	5963	123	9	.977
Minnesota	163	4416	1645	145	6206	131	18	.977
Kansas City	163	4361	1669	158	6188	152	18	.974
AL Total	1628	43773	17128	1261	62162	1486	180	.980

Team vs. Team Records

	Bal	Bos	ChA	Cle	Det	KCA	LAA	Min	NYA	Was	Won
Bal	—	11	10	8	11	13	11	10	10	13	97
Bos	7	—	4	9	5	12	9	5	9	12	72
ChA	8	14	—	12	11	16	10	9	6	12	98
Cle	10	9	6	—	11	10	9	10	3	11	79
Det	7	13	7	7	—	11	10	11	8	11	85
KCA	5	6	2	8	7	—	6	9	6	8	57
LAA	7	9	8	9	8	12	—	12	7	10	82
Min	8	13	9	8	7	9	6	—	8	11	79
NYA	8	9	12	15	10	12	11	10	—	12	99
Was	5	6	6	7	7	10	8	7	6	—	62
Lost	65	90	64	83	77	105	80	83	63	100	

1964 American League Batting Leaders

Games		At-Bats		Runs		Hits		Doubles		Triples	
L. Wagner, Cle	163	B. Richardson, NYA	679	T. Oliva, Min	109	T. Oliva, Min	217	T. Oliva, Min	43	R. Rollins, Min	10
B. Robinson, Bal	163	T. Oliva, Min	672	D. Howser, Cle	101	B. Robinson, Bal	194	E. Bressoud, Bos	41	Z. Versalles, Min	10
B. Knoop, LAA	162	Z. Versalles, Min	659	H. Killebrew, Min	95	B. Richardson, NYA	181	B. Robinson, Bal	35	C. Yastrzemski, Bos	9
D. Howser, Cle	162	L. Wagner, Cle	641	Z. Versalles, Min	94	E. Howard, NYA	172	Z. Versalles, Min	33	T. Oliva, Min	9
D. McAuliffe, Det	162	D. Howser, Cle	637	L. Wagner, Cle	94	Z. Versalles, Min	171	3 tied with	31	J. Fregosi, LAA	9

Home Runs		Total Bases		Runs Batted In		Walks		Intentional Walks		Strikeouts	
H. Killebrew, Min	49	T. Oliva, Min	374	B. Robinson, Bal	118	N. Siebern, Bal	106	M. Mantle, NYA	18	N. Mathews, KCA	143
B. Powell, Bal	39	B. Robinson, Bal	319	D. Stuart, Bos	114	M. Mantle, NYA	99	L. Wagner, Cle	12	D. Lock, Was	137
M. Mantle, NYA	35	H. Killebrew, Min	316	H. Killebrew, Min	111	H. Killebrew, Min	93	E. Howard, NYA	12	H. Killebrew, Min	135
R. Colavito, KCA	34	R. Colavito, KCA	298	M. Mantle, NYA	111	B. Allison, Min	92	4 tied with	11	D. Stuart, Bos	130
D. Stuart, Bos	33	D. Stuart, Bos	296	R. Colavito, KCA	102	W. Causey, KCA	88			D. Nicholson, ChA	126

Hit By Pitch		Sac Hits		Sac Flies		Stolen Bases		Caught Stealing		GDP	
B. Freehan, Det	8	D. Howser, Cle	16	B. Robinson, Bal	10	L. Aparicio, Bal	57	L. Aparicio, Bal	17	C. Yastrzemski, Bos	30
Z. Versalles, Min	8	B. Richardson, NYA	16	E. Battey, Min	8	A. Weis, ChA	22	V. Davalillo, Cle	11	E. Battey, Min	23
H. Killebrew, Min	8	A. Weis, ChA	15	7 tied with	7	V. Davalillo, Cle	21	5 tied with	7	C. Hinton, Was	21
5 tied with	7	D. Wickersham, Det	12			D. Howser, Cle	20			E. Charles, KCA	20
		J. Snyder, Min	11			C. Hinton, Was	17			J. Adair, Bal	20

Runs Created		Runs Created/27 Outs		Batting Average		On-Base Percentage		Slugging Percentage		OBP+Slugging	
T. Oliva, Min	120	M. Mantle, NYA	9.27	T. Oliva, Min	.323	M. Mantle, NYA	.423	B. Powell, Bal	.606	M. Mantle, NYA	1.015
M. Mantle, NYA	116	B. Powell, Bal	8.55	B. Robinson, Bal	.317	B. Allison, Min	.404	M. Mantle, NYA	.591	B. Powell, Bal	1.005
B. Robinson, Bal	112	B. Allison, Min	7.86	E. Howard, NYA	.313	B. Powell, Bal	.399	T. Oliva, Min	.557	B. Allison, Min	.957
H. Killebrew, Min	110	T. Oliva, Min	6.83	M. Mantle, NYA	.303	F. Robinson, ChA	.388	B. Allison, Min	.553	H. Killebrew, Min	.924
B. Allison, Min	105	H. Killebrew, Min	6.78	F. Robinson, ChA	.301	A. Kaline, Det	.383	H. Killebrew, Min	.548	T. Oliva, Min	.916

1964 American League Pitching Leaders

Wins		Losses		Winning Percentage		Games		Games Started		Complete Games	
D. Chance, LAA	20	D. Segui, KCA	17	W. Bunker, Bal	.792	J. Wyatt, KCA	81	J. Bouton, NYA	37	D. Chance, LAA	15
G. Peters, ChA	20	B. Narum, Was	15	W. Ford, NYA	.739	D. Radatz, Bos	79	6 tied with	36	C. Pascual, Min	14
W. Bunker, Bal	19	D. Morehead, Bos	15	G. Peters, ChA	.714	H. Wilhelm, ChA	73			J. Kaat, Min	13
D. Wickersham, Det	19	D. Stigman, Min	15	M. Pappas, Bal	.696	D. McMahon, Cle	70			M. Pappas, Bal	13
J. Pizarro, ChA	19	4 tied with	14	D. Chance, LAA	.690	S. Miller, Bal	66			C. Osteen, Was	13

Shutouts		Saves		Games Finished		Batters Faced		Innings Pitched		Hits Allowed	
D. Chance, LAA	11	D. Radatz, Bos	29	D. Radatz, Bos	67	C. Pascual, Min	1136	D. Chance, LAA	278.1	Monbouquette, Bos	258
W. Ford, NYA	8	H. Wilhelm, ChA	27	J. Wyatt, KCA	57	G. Peters, ChA	1117	G. Peters, ChA	273.2	C. Osteen, Was	256
M. Pappas, Bal	7	S. Miller, Bal	23	H. Wilhelm, ChA	55	D. Chance, LAA	1093	J. Bouton, NYA	271.1	C. Pascual, Min	245
M. Lolich, Det	6	J. Wyatt, KCA	20	R. Kline, Was	52	J. Bouton, NYA	1086	C. Pascual, Min	267.1	M. Grant, 2tm	244
Monbouquette, Bos	5	B. Lee, LAA	19	S. Miller, Bal	46	C. Osteen, Was	1070	C. Osteen, Was	257.0	J. Lamabe, Bos	235

Home Runs Allowed		Walks		Walks/9 Innings		Strikeouts		Strikeouts/9 Innings		Strikeout/Walk Ratio	
O. Pena, KCA	40	A. Downing, NYA	120	Monbouquette, Bos	1.5	A. Downing, NYA	217	S. McDowell, Cle	9.2	M. Pappas, Bal	3.27
E. Wilson, Bos	37	D. Morehead, Bos	112	M. Pappas, Bal	1.7	C. Pascual, Min	213	A. Downing, NYA	8.0	W. Ford, NYA	3.02
Monbouquette, Bos	34	G. Peters, ChA	104	F. Newman, LAA	1.8	D. Chance, LAA	207	O. Pena, KCA	7.6	M. Lolich, Det	3.00
J. Bouton, NYA	32	S. McDowell, Cle	100	J. Bouton, NYA	2.0	G. Peters, ChA	205	D. Stigman, Min	7.5	Monbouquette, Bos	3.00
M. Grant, 2tm	32	C. Pascual, Min	98	J. Pizarro, ChA	2.1	M. Lolich, Det	192	D. Morehead, Bos	7.5	J. Pizarro, ChA	2.95

Earned Run Average		Component ERA		Hit Batsmen		Wild Pitches		Opponent Average		Opponent OBP	
D. Chance, LAA	1.65	J. Horlen, ChA	1.72	K. McBride, LAA	16	G. Peters, ChA	15	J. Horlen, ChA	.190	J. Horlen, ChA	.248
J. Horlen, ChA	1.88	D. Chance, LAA	1.76	D. Wickersham, Det	12	A. Downing, NYA	14	D. Chance, LAA	.195	D. Chance, LAA	.260
W. Ford, NYA	2.13	W. Bunker, Bal	2.29	J. Kaat, Min	9	J. Kaat, Min	13	W. Bunker, Bal	.207	J. Pizarro, ChA	.267
G. Peters, ChA	2.50	W. Ford, NYA	2.37	D. McNally, Bal	9	D. McMahon, Cle	12	G. Peters, ChA	.219	W. Bunker, Bal	.267
J. Pizarro, ChA	2.56	J. Pizarro, ChA	2.43	J. Kralick, Cle	9	2 tied with	11	J. Pizarro, ChA	.219	J. Bouton, NYA	.272

1964 American League Miscellaneous

Managers

Baltimore	Hank Bauer	97-65
Boston	Johnny Pesky	70-90
	Billy Herman	2-0
Chicago	Al Lopez	98-64
Cleveland	George Strickland	33-39
	Birdie Tebbetts	46-44
Detroit	Chuck Dressen	85-77
Kansas City	Ed Lopat	17-35
	Mel McGaha	40-70
Los Angeles	Bill Rigney	82-80
Minnesota	Sam Mele	79-83
New York	Yogi Berra	99-63
Washington	Gil Hodges	62-100

Awards

Most Valuable Player	B. Robinson, 3b, Bal
Cy Young	Dean Chance, LAA
Rookie of the Year	Tony Oliva, of, Min
STATS Manager of the Year	Hank Bauer, Bal

STATS All-Star Team

C	Elston Howard, NYA	.313	15	84
1B	Bob Allison, Min	.287	32	86
2B	Bobby Richardson, NYA	.267	4	50
3B	Brooks Robinson, Bal	.317	28	118
SS	Jim Fregosi, LAA	.277	18	72
OF	Mickey Mantle, NYA	.303	35	111
OF	Tony Oliva, Min	.323	32	94
OF	Boog Powell, Bal	.290	39	99
P	Dean Chance, LAA	20-9	1.65	207 K
P	Whitey Ford, NYA	17-6	2.13	172 K
P	Gary Peters, ChA	20-8	2.50	205 K
P	Juan Pizarro, ChA	19-9	2.56	162 K
RP	Dick Radatz, Bos	16-9	2.29	29 Sv

Postseason

World Series	New York (AL) 3 vs. St. Louis (NL) 4

Outstanding Performances

Three-Homer Games

Jim King, Was	on June 8
Boog Powell, Bal	on June 27
Manny Jimenez, KCA	on July 4

Cycles

Jim King, Was	on May 26
Jim Fregosi, LAA	on July 28

1964 National League Standings

Team	W	L	Pct	GB	DIF	W	L	R	OR	HR	OHR	W	L	R	OR	HR	OHR	Run	HR	M/A	May	June	July	Aug	S/O
	Overall					Home Games						Road Games						Park Index		Record by Month					
St. Louis	93	69	.574	—	18	48	33	386	378	59	81	45	36	329	274	50	52	127	137	8-6	17-14	11-18	17-11	18-10	22-10
Cincinnati	92	70	.568	1.0	17	47	34	331	294	62	59	45	36	329	272	68	53	104	100	6-7	15-14	17-13	18-13	17-10	19-13
Philadelphia	92	70	.568	1.0	140	46	35	352	298	59	61	46	35	341	334	71	68	96	86	9-2	16-13	18-12	16-14	19-10	14-19
San Francisco	90	72	.556	3.0	53	44	37	314	299	86	63	46	35	342	288	79	55	97	111	8-3	18-14	19-11	14-16	14-15	17-13
Milwaukee	88	74	.543	5.0	12	45	36	405	356	89	78	43	38	398	388	70	82	97	110	8-5	15-16	13-16	17-11	13-16	22-10
Los Angeles	80	82	.494	13.0	13	41	40	259	259	26	38	39	42	355	313	53	50	78	62	6-10	15-13	13-15	16-12	13-16	17-16
Pittsburgh	80	82	.494	13.0	13	42	39	340	315	55	31	38	43	323	321	66	61	102	68	7-6	16-15	15-11	15-13	13-19	14-18
Chicago	76	86	.469	17.0	13	40	41	337	397	84	87	36	45	312	327	61	57	115	145	4-7	15-15	16-12	13-18	12-18	16-16
Houston	66	96	.407	27.0	15	41	40	246	290	29	44	25	56	249	338	41	61	91	72	7-9	14-17	14-14	10-20	12-15	9-21
New York	53	109	.327	40.0	12	33	48	298	363	58	61	20	61	271	413	45	69	97	104	2-10	12-22	8-22	10-18	12-14	9-23

Clinch Date—St. Louis 10/04.

Team Batting

Team	G	AB	R	OR	H	2B	3B	HR	TB	RBI	TBB	IBB	SO	HBP	SH	SF	SB	CS	SB%	GDP	Avg	OBP	Slg
Milwaukee	162	5591	803	744	1522	274	32	159	2337	755	486	54	825	38	54	37	53	41	.56	134	.272	.339	.418
St. Louis	162	5625	715	652	1531	240	53	109	2204	654	427	51	925	18	94	32	73	51	.59	96	.272	.329	.392
Philadelphia	162	5493	693	632	1415	241	51	130	2148	649	440	61	924	40	97	46	30	35	.46	108	.258	.322	.391
Pittsburgh	162	5566	663	636	1469	225	54	121	2165	630	408	55	970	24	87	34	39	33	.54	127	.264	.321	.389
Cincinnati	163	5561	660	566	1383	220	38	130	2069	605	457	64	974	33	65	37	90	36	.71	105	.249	.314	.372
San Francisco	162	5535	656	587	1360	185	38	165	2116	608	505	74	900	33	78	43	64	35	.65	118	.246	.317	.382
Chicago	162	5545	649	724	1391	239	50	145	2165	609	499	51	1041	25	55	33	70	49	.59	101	.251	.319	.390
Los Angeles	164	5499	614	572	1375	180	39	79	1870	555	438	55	893	19	120	44	141	60	.70	105	.250	.313	.340
New York	163	5566	569	776	1372	195	31	103	1938	527	353	34	932	48	52	26	36	31	.54	147	.246	.300	.348
Houston	162	5303	495	628	1214	162	41	70	1668	452	381	44	872	49	87	39	40	48	.45	113	.229	.292	.315
NL Total	1624	55284	6517	6517	14032	2161	427	1211	20680	6044	4394	543	9256	327	789	371	636	419	.60	1154	.254	.311	.374
NL Avg Team	162	5528	652	652	1403	216	43	121	2068	604	439	54	926	33	79	37	64	42	.60	115	.254	.311	.374

Team Pitching

Team	G	CG	ShO	Rel	Sv	IP	H	R	ER	HR	SH	SF	HB	TBB	IBB	SO	WP	Bk	H/9	SO/9	BB/9	OAvg	OOBP	ERA
Los Angeles	164	47	19	213	27	1483.2	1289	572	487	88	73	34	27	458	79	1062	51	4	7.8	6.4	2.8	.232	.292	2.95
Cincinnati	163	54	14	203	35	1467.0	1306	566	501	112	74	33	31	436	44	1122	51	4	8.0	6.9	2.7	.238	.296	3.07
San Francisco	162	48	17	251	30	1476.1	1348	587	523	118	70	33	37	480	59	1023	34	6	8.2	6.2	2.9	.241	.304	3.19
Philadelphia	162	37	17	273	41	1461.0	1402	632	546	129	91	24	51	440	50	1009	51	1	8.6	6.2	2.7	.252	.312	3.36
Houston	162	30	9	248	31	1428.0	1421	628	541	105	99	50	28	353	53	852	39	1	9.0	5.4	2.2	.260	.306	3.41
St. Louis	162	47	10	232	38	1445.1	1405	652	551	133	85	37	30	410	44	877	30	4	8.7	5.5	2.6	.255	.308	3.43
Pittsburgh	162	42	14	274	29	1443.2	1429	636	565	92	75	38	31	476	75	951	59	7	8.9	5.9	2.6	.260	.320	3.52
Chicago	162	58	11	255	19	1445.0	1510	724	655	144	69	40	17	423	64	737	50	3	9.4	4.6	2.6	.270	.321	4.08
Milwaukee	162	45	14	268	39	1434.2	1411	744	656	160	69	40	25	452	51	906	71	1	8.9	5.7	2.8	.257	.314	4.12
New York	163	40	10	266	15	1438.2	1511	776	680	130	84	42	50	466	24	717	53	5	9.5	4.5	2.9	.272	.332	4.25
NL Total	1624	448	135	2483	304	14523.1	14032	6517	5705	1211	789	371	327	4394	543	9256	489	36	8.7	5.7	2.7	.254	.317	3.54
NL Avg Team	162	45	14	248	30	1452.1	1403	652	571	121	79	37	33	439	54	926	49	4	8.7	5.7	2.7	.254	.317	3.54

Team Fielding

Team	G	PO	A	E	TC	DP	PB	Pct
Cincinnati	163	4402	1600	130	6132	137	18	.979
Milwaukee	162	4304	1758	143	6205	139	16	.977
Houston	162	4284	1785	149	6218	124	23	.976
Chicago	162	4335	2068	162	6565	147	15	.975
San Francisco	162	4428	1718	159	6305	136	11	.975
Philadelphia	162	4381	1675	157	6213	150	21	.975
New York	163	4316	1914	167	6397	154	32	.974
Los Angeles	164	4451	1706	170	6327	126	14	.973
St. Louis	162	4335	1784	172	6291	147	19	.973
Pittsburgh	162	4331	1925	177	6433	179	15	.972
NL Total	1624	43567	17933	1586	63086	1439	184	.975

Team vs. Team Records

	ChN	Cin	Hou	LA	Mil	NYN	Phi	Pit	SF	StL	Won
ChN	—	6	11	10	8	11	6	9	9	6	76
Cin	12	—	12	14	9	11	9	8	7	10	92
Hou	7	6	—	7	12	9	5	5	7	8	66
LA	8	4	11	—	8	15	8	10	6	10	80
Mil	10	9	6	10	—	14	10	12	9	8	88
NYN	7	7	9	3	4	—	3	6	7	7	53
Phi	12	9	13	10	8	15	—	10	10	5	92
Pit	9	10	13	8	6	12	8	—	8	6	80
SF	9	11	11	12	9	11	8	10	—	9	90
StL	12	8	10	8	10	11	13	12	9	—	93
Lost	86	70	96	82	74	109	70	82	72	69	

1964 National League Batting Leaders

Games		At-Bats		Runs		Hits		Doubles		Triples	
L. Cardenas, Cin	163	C. Flood, StL	679	D. Allen, Phi	125	C. Flood, StL	211	L. Maye, Mil	44	D. Allen, Phi	13
6 tied with	162	J. Callison, Phi	654	W. Mays, SF	121	R. Clemente, Pit	211	R. Clemente, Pit	40	R. Santo, ChN	13
		B. Williams, ChN	645	L. Brock, 2tm	111	D. Allen, Phi	201	B. Williams, ChN	39	L. Brock, 2tm	11
		D. Groat, StL	636	F. Robinson, Cin	103	B. Williams, ChN	201	D. Allen, Phi	38	V. Pinson, Cin	11
		L. Brock, 2tm	634	H. Aaron, Mil	103	L. Brock, 2tm	200	F. Robinson, Cin	38	2 tied with	10

Home Runs		Total Bases		Runs Batted In		Walks		Intentional Walks		Strikeouts	
W. Mays, SF	47	D. Allen, Phi	352	K. Boyer, StL	119	R. Santo, ChN	86	F. Robinson, Cin	20	D. Allen, Phi	138
B. Williams, ChN	33	W. Mays, SF	351	R. Santo, ChN	114	E. Mathews, Mil	85	R. Clemente, Pit	16	B. Cowan, ChN	128
J. Hart, SF	31	B. Williams, ChN	343	W. Mays, SF	111	W. Mays, SF	82	T. McCarver, StL	15	L. Brock, 2tm	127
J. Callison, Phi	31	R. Santo, ChN	334	J. Torre, Mil	109	F. Robinson, Cin	79	S. Boros, Cin	14	F. Howard, LA	113
O. Cepeda, SF	31	J. Callison, Phi	322	J. Callison, Phi	104	K. Boyer, StL	70	3 tied with	13	L. Cardenas, Cin	110

Hit By Pitch		Sac Hits		Sac Flies		Stolen Bases		Caught Stealing		GDP	
T. Taylor, Phi	13	N. Fox, Hou	20	C. Dalrymple, Phi	8	M. Wills, LA	53	L. Brock, 2tm	18	J. Torre, Mil	26
R. Hunt, NYN	11	D. Drysdale, LA	14	5 tied with	7	L. Brock, 2tm	43	M. Wills, LA	17	K. Boyer, StL	22
N. Fox, Hou	10	L. Brock, 2tm	13			W. Davis, LA	42	W. Davis, LA	13	H. Aaron, Mil	22
F. Robinson, Cin	9	H. Lanier, SF	12			T. Harper, Cin	24	C. Flood, StL	11	B. Mazeroski, Pit	21
3 tied with	8	C. Ruiz, Cin	12			F. Robinson, Cin	23	2 tied with	10	2 tied with	18

Runs Created		Runs Created/27 Outs		Batting Average		On-Base Percentage		Slugging Percentage		OBP+Slugging	
D. Allen, Phi	130	W. Mays, SF	8.06	R. Clemente, Pit	.339	R. Santo, ChN	.398	W. Mays, SF	.607	W. Mays, SF	.990
W. Mays, SF	127	F. Robinson, Cin	8.03	R. Carty, Mil	.330	F. Robinson, Cin	.396	R. Santo, ChN	.564	R. Santo, ChN	.962
F. Robinson, Cin	124	D. Allen, Phi	7.79	H. Aaron, Mil	.328	H. Aaron, Mil	.393	D. Allen, Phi	.557	F. Robinson, Cin	.943
R. Santo, ChN	122	R. Carty, Mil	7.79	J. Torre, Mil	.321	R. Clemente, Pit	.388	R. Carty, Mil	.554	R. Carty, Mil	.942
2 tied with	114	R. Santo, ChN	7.72	D. Allen, Phi	.318	R. Carty, Mil	.388	F. Robinson, Cin	.548	D. Allen, Phi	.939

1964 National League Pitching Leaders

Wins		Losses		Winning Percentage		Games		Games Started		Complete Games	
L. Jackson, ChN	24	T. Stallard, NYN	20	S. Koufax, LA	.792	B. Miller, LA	74	D. Drysdale, LA	40	J. Marichal, SF	22
J. Marichal, SF	21	G. Cisco, NYN	19	J. Marichal, SF	.724	R. Perranoski, LA	72	J. Bunning, Phi	39	D. Drysdale, LA	21
R. Sadecki, StL	20	D. Ellsworth, ChN	18	J. O'Toole, Cin	.708	J. Baldschun, Phi	71	B. Veale, Pit	38	L. Jackson, ChN	19
4 tied with	19	B. Friend, Pit	18	J. Bunning, Phi	.704	R. Taylor, StL	63	L. Jackson, ChN	38	B. Gibson, StL	17
		J. Fisher, NYN	17	L. Jackson, ChN	.686	L. McDaniel, ChN	63	2 tied with	36	D. Ellsworth, ChN	16

Shutouts		Saves		Games Finished		Batters Faced		Innings Pitched		Hits Allowed	
S. Koufax, LA	7	H. Woodeshick, Hou	23	R. Perranoski, LA	52	D. Drysdale, LA	1264	D. Drysdale, LA	321.1	D. Ellsworth, ChN	267
H. Fischer, Mil	5	A. McBean, Pit	22	J. Baldschun, Phi	51	L. Jackson, ChN	1200	L. Jackson, ChN	297.2	L. Jackson, ChN	265
D. Drysdale, LA	5	J. Baldschun, Phi	21	A. McBean, Pit	49	B. Gibson, StL	1191	B. Gibson, StL	287.1	J. Fisher, NYN	256
J. Bunning, Phi	5	L. McDaniel, ChN	15	H. Woodeshick, Hou	48	B. Veale, Pit	1161	J. Bunning, Phi	284.1	B. Friend, Pit	253
V. Law, Pit	5	3 tied with	14	L. McDaniel, ChN	40	J. Bunning, Phi	1145	B. Veale, Pit	279.2	B. Gibson, StL	250

Home Runs Allowed		Walks		Walks/9 Innings		Strikeouts		Strikeouts/9 Innings		Strikeout/Walk Ratio	
D. Ellsworth, ChN	34	B. Veale, Pit	124	J. Bunning, Phi	1.5	B. Veale, Pit	250	S. Koufax, LA	9.0	J. Bunning, Phi	4.76
D. Lemaster, Mil	27	B. Gibson, StL	86	B. Bruce, Hou	1.5	B. Gibson, StL	245	J. Maloney, Cin	8.9	S. Koufax, LA	4.21
B. Gibson, StL	25	J. Maloney, Cin	83	V. Law, Pit	1.5	D. Drysdale, LA	237	B. Veale, Pit	8.0	B. Bruce, Hou	4.09
C. Simmons, StL	24	T. Cloninger, Mil	82	J. Marichal, SF	1.7	S. Koufax, LA	223	B. Gibson, StL	7.7	J. Marichal, SF	3.96
4 tied with	23	A. Mahaffey, Phi	82	L. Jackson, ChN	1.8	J. Bunning, Phi	219	D. Lemaster, Mil	7.5	J. Jay, Cin	3.72

Earned Run Average		Component ERA		Hit Batsmen		Wild Pitches		Opponent Average		Opponent OBP	
S. Koufax, LA	1.74	S. Koufax, LA	1.66	J. Bunning, Phi	14	D. Lemaster, Mil	20	S. Koufax, LA	.191	S. Koufax, LA	.240
D. Drysdale, LA	2.18	D. Drysdale, LA	1.89	B. Bolin, SF	10	B. Veale, Pit	18	D. Drysdale, LA	.207	D. Drysdale, LA	.255
C. Short, Phi	2.20	C. Short, Phi	2.10	J. Fisher, NYN	10	J. Maloney, Cin	16	B. Veale, Pit	.217	C. Short, Phi	.266
J. Marichal, SF	2.48	J. O'Toole, Cin	2.38	D. Drysdale, LA	10	T. Cloninger, Mil	13	C. Short, Phi	.217	L. Jackson, ChN	.272
J. Bunning, Phi	2.63	L. Jackson, ChN	2.43	2 tied with	9	T. Stallard, NYN	12	B. Bolin, SF	.220	J. Marichal, SF	.272

1964 National League Miscellaneous

Managers

Chicago	Bob Kennedy	76-86
Cincinnati	Fred Hutchinson	54-45
	Dick Sisler	3-3
	Fred Hutchinson	6-4
	Dick Sisler	29-18
Houston	Harry Craft	61-88
	Lum Harris	5-8
Los Angeles	Walter Alston	80-82
Milwaukee	Bobby Bragan	88-74
New York	Casey Stengel	53-109
Philadelphia	Gene Mauch	92-70
Pittsburgh	Danny Murtaugh	80-82
St. Louis	Johnny Keane	93-69
San Francisco	Alvin Dark	90-72

Awards

Most Valuable Player	Ken Boyer, 3b, StL
STATS Cy Young	Sandy Koufax, LA
Rookie of the Year	Dick Allen, 3b, Phi
STATS Manager of the Year	Johnny Keane, StL

STATS All-Star Team

C	Joe Torre, Mil	.321	20	109
1B	Orlando Cepeda, SF	.304	31	97
2B	Bill Mazeroski, Pit	.268	10	64
3B	Ron Santo, ChN	.313	30	114
SS	Denis Menke, Mil	.283	20	65
OF	Hank Aaron, Mil	.328	24	95
OF	Willie Mays, SF	.296	47	111
OF	Frank Robinson, Cin	.306	29	96
P	Jim Bunning, Phi	19-8	2.63	219 K
P	Larry Jackson, ChN	24-11	3.14	148 K
P	Sandy Koufax, LA	19-5	1.74	223 K
P	Juan Marichal, SF	21-8	2.48	206 K
RP	Al McBean, Pit	8-3	1.91	22 Sv

Postseason

World Series	St. Louis (NL) 4 vs. New York (AL) 3

Outstanding Performances

Perfect Games
Jim Bunning, Phi @ NYN on June 21

No-Hitters
Ken Johnson, Hou vs. Cin on April 23
Sandy Koufax, LA @ Phi on June 4

Three-Homer Games
Willie McCovey, SF on April 22
Johnny Callison, Phi on September 27

Cycles
Ken Boyer, StL on June 16
Willie Stargell, Pit on July 22

1965 American League Standings

Team	Overall					Home Games						Road Games						Park Index		Record by Month					
	W	L	Pct	GB	DIF	W	L	R	OR	HR	OHR	W	L	R	OR	HR	OHR	Run	HR	M/A	May	June	July	Aug	S/O
Minnesota	102	60	.630	—	138	51	30	379	308	67	89	51	30	395	292	83	77	100	98	8-3	19-12	16-13	22-9	19-13	18-10
Chicago	95	67	.586	7.0	29	48	33	288	241	45	51	47	34	359	314	80	71	79	64	8-4	19-12	15-13	12-16	22-12	19-10
Baltimore	94	68	.580	8.0	0	46	33	302	282	62	71	48	35	339	296	63	49	97	125	7-6	18-15	16-11	17-10	14-15	22-11
Detroit	89	73	.549	13.0	8	47	34	362	310	96	85	42	39	318	292	66	52	110	153	8-4	17-15	14-12	17-12	17-16	16-14
Cleveland	87	75	.537	15.0	9	52	30	342	287	90	58	35	45	321	326	66	71	95	105	6-4	15-16	22-7	15-15	15-16	14-17
New York	77	85	.475	25.0	0	40	43	320	306	77	63	37	42	291	298	72	63	101	99	6-7	13-19	17-12	15-16	15-13	11-18
California	75	87	.463	27.0	0	46	34	265	254	36	35	29	53	262	315	56	56	92	65	6-7	18-17	9-17	14-14	14-17	14-15
Washington	70	92	.432	32.0	0	36	45	302	366	62	86	34	47	289	355	74	74	104	100	4-11	16-17	10-17	14-14	14-16	12-17
Boston	62	100	.383	40.0	4	34	47	375	433	94	88	28	53	294	358	71	70	124	129	5-5	16-16	8-21	9-21	13-20	11-17
Kansas City	59	103	.364	43.0	0	33	48	301	365	47	68	26	55	284	390	63	93	99	74	2-9	8-20	12-16	11-19	14-19	12-20

Clinch Date—Minnesota 9/26.

Team Batting

Team	G	AB	R	OR	H	2B	3B	HR	TB	RBI	TBB	IBB	SO	HBP	SH	SF	SB	CS	SB%	GDP	Avg	OBP	Slg
Minnesota	162	5488	774	600	1396	257	42	150	2187	711	554	79	969	35	77	59	92	33	.74	93	.254	.333	.399
Detroit	162	5368	680	602	1278	190	27	162	2008	635	554	50	952	37	69	36	57	41	.58	122	.238	.318	.374
Boston	162	5487	669	791	1378	244	40	165	2197	629	607	44	964	30	57	39	47	24	.66	157	.251	.333	.400
Cleveland	162	5469	663	613	1367	198	21	156	2075	615	506	63	857	33	90	40	109	46	.70	97	.250	.322	.379
Chicago	162	5509	647	555	1354	200	38	125	2005	587	533	62	916	43	89	43	50	33	.60	127	.246	.322	.364
Baltimore	162	5450	641	578	1299	227	38	125	1977	596	529	61	907	28	95	36	67	31	.68	139	.238	.313	.363
New York	162	5470	611	604	1286	196	31	149	1991	576	489	62	951	19	72	31	35	20	.64	118	.235	.304	.364
Washington	162	5374	591	721	1227	179	33	136	1880	563	570	36	1125	34	63	37	30	19	.61	112	.228	.311	.350
Kansas City	162	5393	585	755	1294	186	59	110	1928	546	521	29	1020	35	74	35	110	51	.68	120	.240	.315	.358
California	162	5354	527	569	1279	200	36	92	1827	486	443	48	973	22	93	44	107	59	.64	99	.239	.305	.341
AL Total	1620	54362	6388	6388	13158	2077	365	1370	20075	5944	5306	534	9634	316	779	400	704	357	.66	1184	.242	.311	.369
AL Avg Team	162	5436	639	639	1316	208	37	137	2008	594	531	53	963	32	78	40	70	36	.66	118	.242	.311	.369

Team Pitching

Team	G	CG	ShO	Rel	Sv	IP	H	R	ER	HR	SH	SF	HB	TBB	IBB	SO	WP	Bk	H/9	SO/9	BB/9	OAvg	OOBP	ERA
Baltimore	162	32	15	228	41	1477.2	1268	578	490	120	82	44	26	510	48	939	36	1	7.7	5.7	3.1	.233	.300	2.98
Chicago	162	21	14	267	53	1481.2	1261	555	493	122	70	39	29	460	71	946	63	0	7.7	5.7	2.8	.231	.292	2.99
Minnesota	162	32	12	299	45	1457.1	1278	600	508	166	70	37	27	503	32	934	44	2	7.9	5.8	3.1	.235	.301	3.14
California	162	39	14	236	33	1441.2	1259	569	508	91	89	32	27	563	59	847	52	9	7.9	5.3	3.5	.237	.312	3.17
New York	162	41	11	252	31	1459.2	1337	604	532	126	73	35	28	511	46	1001	39	2	8.2	6.2	3.2	.245	.311	3.28
Cleveland	162	41	13	282	41	1458.1	1254	613	534	129	77	33	28	500	52	1156	50	1	7.7	7.1	3.1	.232	.298	3.30
Detroit	162	45	14	240	31	1455.0	1283	602	542	137	77	43	47	509	41	1069	49	6	7.9	6.6	3.1	.237	.306	3.35
Washington	162	21	8	327	40	1435.2	1376	721	627	160	91	43	34	633	73	867	52	7	8.6	5.4	4.0	.254	.334	3.93
Kansas City	162	18	7	378	32	1433.0	1399	755	675	161	76	50	39	574	60	882	67	7	8.8	5.5	3.6	.256	.329	4.24
Boston	162	33	9	268	25	1439.1	1443	791	678	158	74	44	31	543	53	993	44	12	9.0	6.2	3.4	.260	.327	4.24
AL Total	1620	323	117	2777	372	14539.1	13158	6388	5587	1370	779	400	316	5306	534	9634	496	47	8.1	6.0	3.3	.242	.318	3.46
AL Avg Team	162	32	12	278	37	1453.1	1316	639	559	137	78	40	32	531	53	963	50	5	8.1	6.0	3.3	.242	.318	3.46

Team Fielding

Team	G	PO	A	E	TC	DP	PB	Pct
Cleveland	162	4366	1574	114	6054	127	24	.981
Detroit	162	4358	1591	116	6065	126	22	.981
California	162	4330	1868	123	6321	149	20	.981
Chicago	162	4436	1938	127	6501	156	45	.980
Baltimore	162	4411	1770	126	6307	152	12	.980
New York	162	4370	1810	137	6317	166	20	.978
Kansas City	162	4300	1620	139	6059	142	20	.977
Washington	162	4292	1646	143	6081	148	18	.976
Boston	162	4317	1644	162	6123	129	14	.974
Minnesota	162	4366	1770	172	6308	158	16	.973
AL Total	1620	43546	17231	1359	62136	1453	211	.978

Team vs. Team Records

	Bal	Bos	Cal	ChA	Cle	Det	KCA	Min	NYA	Was	Won
Bal	—	11	13	9	10	11	11	8	13	8	94
Bos	7	—	5	4	8	6	11	1	9	11	62
Cal	5	13	—	6	9	8	13	9	6	6	75
ChA	9	14	12	—	10	9	13	7	8	13	95
Cle	8	10	9	8	—	9	9	11	12	11	87
Det	7	12	10	9	9	—	13	8	10	11	89
KCA	7	7	5	5	9	5	—	8	7	6	59
Min	10	18	9	11	7	10	10	—	13	15	102
NYA	5	9	12	10	6	8	11	5	—	11	77
Was	10	7	12	5	7	7	12	3	7	—	70
Lost	68	100	87	67	75	73	103	60	85	92	

1965 American League Batting Leaders

Games		At-Bats		Runs		Hits		Doubles		Triples	
D. Wert, Det	162	Z. Versalles, Min	666	Z. Versalles, Min	126	T. Oliva, Min	185	C. Yastrzemski, Bos	45	B. Campaneris, KCA	12
R. Hansen, ChA	162	B. Richardson, NYA	664	T. Oliva, Min	107	Z. Versalles, Min	182	Z. Versalles, Min	45	Z. Versalles, Min	12
R. Colavito, Cle	162	D. Wert, Det	609	T. Tresh, NYA	94	R. Colavito, Cle	170	T. Oliva, Min	40	L. Aparicio, Bal	10
J. Fregosi, Cal	161	M. Alvis, Cle	604	D. Buford, ChA	93	T. Tresh, NYA	168	T. Tresh, NYA	29	W. Smith, Cal	9
2 tied with	160	2 tied with	602	R. Colavito, Cle	92	J. Fregosi, Cal	167	B. Richardson, NYA	28	2 tied with	8

Home Runs		Total Bases		Runs Batted In		Walks		Intentional Walks		Strikeouts	
T. Conigliaro, Bos	32	Z. Versalles, Min	308	R. Colavito, Cle	108	R. Colavito, Cle	93	D. Mincher, Min	15	Z. Versalles, Min	122
N. Cash, Det	30	T. Tresh, NYA	287	W. Horton, Det	104	C. Blefary, Bal	88	B. Powell, Bal	13	M. Alvis, Cle	121
W. Horton, Det	29	T. Oliva, Min	283	T. Oliva, Min	98	F. Mantilla, Bos	79	T. Oliva, Min	12	T. Conigliaro, Bos	116
L. Wagner, Cle	28	R. Colavito, Cle	277	F. Mantilla, Bos	92	N. Cash, Det	77	H. Killebrew, Min	12	D. Lock, Was	115
3 tied with	26	T. Conigliaro, Bos	267	F. Whitfield, Cle	90	F. Robinson, ChA	76	4 tied with	11	B. Allison, Min	114

Hit By Pitch		Sac Hits		Sac Flies		Stolen Bases		Caught Stealing		GDP	
B. Campaneris, KCA	9	J. Fregosi, Cal	15	T. Oliva, Min	10	B. Campaneris, KCA	51	B. Campaneris, KCA	19	J. Adair, Bal	26
M. Alvis, Cle	9	L. Aparicio, Bal	14	J. Fregosi, Cal	8	J. Cardenal, Cal	37	J. Cardenal, Cal	17	F. Mantilla, Bos	24
F. Mantilla, Bos	8	7 tied with	10	B. Rodgers, Cal	8	Z. Versalles, Min	27	W. Horton, Det	9	B. Skowron, ChA	22
B. Freehan, Det	7			Z. Versalles, Min	8	V. Davalillo, Cle	26	T. Oliva, Min	9	R. Hansen, ChA	21
Z. Versalles, Min	7			R. Hansen, ChA	8	L. Aparicio, Bal	26	D. McAuliffe, Det	9	M. Hershberger, KCA	19

Runs Created		Runs Created/27 Outs		Batting Average		On-Base Percentage		Slugging Percentage		OBP+Slugging	
T. Oliva, Min	113	T. Oliva, Min	7.29	T. Oliva, Min	.321	C. Yastrzemski, Bos	.395	C. Yastrzemski, Bos	.536	C. Yastrzemski, Bos	.932
Z. Versalles, Min	107	N. Cash, Det	7.02	C. Yastrzemski, Bos	.312	R. Colavito, Cle	.383	T. Conigliaro, Bos	.512	N. Cash, Det	.883
R. Colavito, Cle	105	L. Wagner, Cle	6.85	V. Davalillo, Cle	.301	C. Blefary, Bal	.381	N. Cash, Det	.512	T. Oliva, Min	.870
T. Tresh, NYA	102	C. Yastrzemski, Bos	6.78	B. Robinson, Bal	.297	T. Oliva, Min	.378	L. Wagner, Cle	.495	L. Wagner, Cle	.864
L. Wagner, Cle	95	C. Blefary, Bal	6.74	L. Wagner, Cle	.294	F. Mantilla, Bos	.374	T. Oliva, Min	.491	R. Colavito, Cle	.851

1965 American League Pitching Leaders

Wins		Losses		Winning Percentage		Games		Games Started		Complete Games	
M. Grant, Min	21	J. O'Donoghue, KCA	18	M. Grant, Min	.750	E. Fisher, ChA	82	J. Kaat, Min	42	M. Stottlemyre, NYA	18
M. Stottlemyre, NYA	20	D. Morehead, Bos	18	D. McLain, Det	.727	R. Kline, Was	74	M. Grant, Min	39	S. McDowell, Cle	14
J. Kaat, Min	18	Monbouquette, Bos	18	M. Stottlemyre, NYA	.690	B. Lee, Cal	69	M. Lolich, Det	37	M. Grant, Min	14
S. McDowell, Cle	17	J. Lonborg, Bos	17	E. Fisher, ChA	.682	J. Dickson, KCA	68	M. Stottlemyre, NYA	37	D. McLain, Det	13
3 tied with	16	F. Newman, Cal	16	3 tied with	.667	S. Miller, Bal	67	3 tied with	36	5 tied with	10

Shutouts		Saves		Games Finished		Batters Faced		Innings Pitched		Hits Allowed	
M. Grant, Min	6	R. Kline, Was	29	E. Fisher, ChA	60	M. Stottlemyre, NYA	1188	M. Stottlemyre, NYA	291.0	J. Kaat, Min	267
M. Stottlemyre, NYA	4	E. Fisher, ChA	24	R. Kline, Was	58	S. McDowell, Cle	1116	S. McDowell, Cle	273.0	M. Grant, Min	252
D. McLain, Det	4	S. Miller, Bal	24	D. Radatz, Bos	56	J. Kaat, Min	1115	M. Grant, Min	270.1	M. Stottlemyre, NYA	250
D. Chance, Cal	4	B. Lee, Cal	23	S. Miller, Bal	55	M. Grant, Min	1095	J. Kaat, Min	264.1	W. Ford, NYA	241
J. Horlen, ChA	4	D. Radatz, Bos	22	B. Lee, Cal	50	F. Newman, Cal	1044	F. Newman, Cal	260.2	Monbouquette, Bos	239

Home Runs Allowed		Walks		Walks/9 Innings		Strikeouts		Strikeouts/9 Innings		Strikeout/Walk Ratio	
M. Grant, Min	34	S. McDowell, Cle	132	R. Terry, Cle	1.2	S. McDowell, Cle	325	S. McDowell, Cle	10.7	S. Siebert, Cle	4.15
P. Ortega, Was	33	D. Morehead, Bos	113	Monbouquette, Bos	1.6	M. Lolich, Det	226	S. Siebert, Cle	9.1	R. Terry, Cle	3.65
Monbouquette, Bos	32	A. Downing, NYA	105	J. Horlen, ChA	1.6	D. McLain, Det	192	M. Lolich, Det	8.3	W. Ford, NYA	3.24
E. Wilson, Bos	27	D. Chance, Cal	101	W. Ford, NYA	1.8	S. Siebert, Cle	191	D. McLain, Det	7.8	J. Horlen, ChA	3.21
3 tied with	25	P. Ortega, Was	97	M. Grant, Min	2.0	A. Downing, NYA	179	D. Morehead, Bos	7.6	M. Lolich, Det	3.14

Earned Run Average		Component ERA		Hit Batsmen		Wild Pitches		Opponent Average		Opponent OBP	
S. McDowell, Cle	2.18	E. Fisher, ChA	1.97	M. Lolich, Det	12	S. McDowell, Cle	17	S. McDowell, Cle	.185	S. Siebert, Cle	.259
E. Fisher, ChA	2.40	S. Siebert, Cle	2.09	D. Wickersham, Det	11	J. Wyatt, KCA	13	E. Fisher, ChA	.205	E. Fisher, ChA	.259
S. Siebert, Cle	2.43	S. McDowell, Cle	2.19	H. Aguirre, Det	10	D. Morehead, Bos	11	S. Siebert, Cle	.206	R. Terry, Cle	.268
G. Brunet, Cal	2.56	G. Brunet, Cal	2.28	D. Chance, Cal	9	3 tied with	10	G. Brunet, Cal	.209	D. McLain, Det	.273
P. Richert, Was	2.60	F. Newman, Cal	2.50	5 tied with	7			P. Richert, Was	.210	J. Horlen, ChA	.279

1965 American League Miscellaneous

Managers

Baltimore	Hank Bauer	94-68
Boston	Billy Herman	62-100
California	Bill Rigney	75-87
Chicago	Al Lopez	95-67
Cleveland	Birdie Tebbetts	87-75
Detroit	Bob Swift	24-18
	Chuck Dressen	65-55
Kansas City	Mel McGaha	5-21
	Haywood Sullivan	54-82
Minnesota	Sam Mele	102-60
New York	Johnny Keane	77-85
Washington	Gil Hodges	70-92

Awards

Most Valuable Player	Zoilo Versalles, ss, Min
STATS Cy Young	Sam McDowell, Cle
Rookie of the Year	Curt Blefary, of, Bal
STATS Manager of the Year	Sam Mele, Min

STATS All-Star Team

C	Earl Battey, ChA	.297	6	60
1B	Norm Cash, Det	.266	30	82
2B	Felix Mantilla, Bos	.275	18	92
3B	Brooks Robinson, Bal	.297	18	80
SS	Zoilo Versalles, Min	.273	19	77
OF	Rocky Colavito, Cle	.287	26	108
OF	Tony Oliva, Min	.321	16	98
OF	Carl Yastrzemski, Bos	.312	20	72
P	Mudcat Grant, Min	21-7	3.30	142 K
P	Sam McDowell, Cle	17-11	2.18	325 K
P	Sonny Siebert, Cle	16-8	2.43	191 K
P	Mel Stottlemyre, NYA	20-9	2.63	155 K
RP	Stu Miller, Bal	14-7	1.89	24 Sv

Postseason

World Series	Minnesota (AL) 3 vs. LA (NL) 4

Outstanding Performances

No-Hitters
Dave Morehead, Bos vs. Cle on September 16

Three-Homer Games
Tom Tresh, NYA   on June 6

Cycles
C. Yastrzemski, Bos on May 14

1965 National League Standings

1965 National League Standings

Team	W	L	Pct	GB	DIF	W	L	R	OR	HR	OHR	W	L	R	OR	HR	OHR	Run	HR	M/A	May	June	July	Aug	S/O
		Overall						**Home Games**						**Road Games**				**Park Index**				**Record by Month**			
Los Angeles	97	65	.599	—	136	50	31	268	218	26	41	47	34	340	303	52	86	76	49	10-5	19-12	17-14	15-13	14-13	22-8
San Francisco	95	67	.586	2.0	21	51	30	365	327	81	81	44	37	317	266	78	56	119	121	7-9	19-11	14-13	15-10	17-14	23-10
Pittsburgh	90	72	.556	7.0	4	49	32	334	284	37	38	41	40	341	296	74	51	97	60	6-9	14-15	19-11	13-18	19-9	19-10
Cincinnati	89	73	.549	8.0	16	49	32	450	352	108	69	40	41	375	352	75	67	110	125	9-5	15-15	19-12	16-12	13-14	17-15
Milwaukee	86	76	.531	11.0	3	44	37	366	331	98	75	42	39	342	302	98	48	108	118	6-6	15-13	16-14	17-12	13-14	14-18
Philadelphia	85	76	.528	11.5	2	45	35	312	300	77	55	40	41	342	367	67	61	87	104	8-4	14-16	18-10	15-15	15-14	17-13
St. Louis	80	81	.497	16.5	0	42	39	379	361	68	103	38	42	328	313	41	63	114	162	5-8	18-13	11-20	17-10	15-16	14-14
Chicago	72	90	.444	25.0	4	40	41	330	380	79	94	32	49	305	343	55	60	110	150	7-6	13-14	14-16	16-16	13-16	9-18
Houston	65	97	.401	32.0	0	36	45	250	313	25	32	29	52	319	398	72	91	79	35	10-6	13-19	11-17	9-15	14-18	8-22
New York	50	112	.309	47.0	0	29	52	380	380	50	81	21	60	237	372	57	66	105	107	6-10	11-19	9-21	8-20	9-20	7-22

Clinch Date—Los Angeles 10/02.

Team Batting

Team	G	AB	R	OR	H	2B	3B	HR	TB	RBI	TBB	IBB	SO	HBP	SH	SF	SB	CS	SB%	GDP	Avg	OBP	Slg
Cincinnati	162	5658	**825**	704	**1544**	**268**	**61**	183	**2483**	776	**538**	**89**	1003	50	73	36	82	40	.67	120	**.273**	**.345**	**.439**
Milwaukee	162	5542	708	633	1419	243	28	**196**	2306	664	408	50	976	37	58	32	64	37	.63	121	.256	.315	.416
St. Louis	162	5579	707	674	1415	234	46	109	2068	645	477	49	882	35	72	41	100	52	.66	98	.254	.321	.371
San Francisco	163	5495	682	593	1384	169	43	159	2116	623	476	68	844	31	80	37	47	27	.64	149	.252	.319	.385
Pittsburgh	163	**5686**	675	580	1506	217	57	111	2170	631	419	75	1008	35	67	**42**	51	38	.57	138	.265	.324	.382
Philadelphia	162	5528	654	667	1380	205	53	144	2123	608	494	60	1091	36	75	39	46	32	.59	115	.250	.320	.384
Chicago	164	5540	635	723	1316	202	33	134	1986	590	532	62	948	43	48	**42**	65	47	.58	115	.238	.314	.358
Los Angeles	162	5425	608	**521**	1329	193	32	78	1820	548	492	57	891	52	**103**	35	**172**	**77**	.69	79	.245	.318	.335
Houston	162	5483	569	711	1299	188	42	97	1862	523	502	46	877	46	57	34	90	37	**.71**	125	.237	.310	.340
New York	164	5441	495	752	1202	203	27	107	1780	460	392	40	**1129**	39	76	28	28	42	.40	121	.221	.282	.327
NL Total	1626	55377	6558	6558	13794	2122	422	1318	20714	6068	4730	596	9649	404	709	366	745	429	.63	1181	.249	.311	.374
NL Avg Team	163	5538	656	656	1379	212	42	132	2071	607	473	60	965	40	71	37	75	43	.63	118	.249	.311	.374

Team Pitching

Team	G	CG	ShO	Rel	Sv	IP	H	R	ER	HR	SH	SF	HB	TBB	IBB	SO	WP	Bk	H/9	SO/9	BB/9	OAvg	OOBP	ERA
Los Angeles	162	**58**	**23**	202	34	1476.0	**1223**	**521**	461	127	78	25	33	425	53	1079	51	1	**7.5**	6.6	2.6	**.224**	**.283**	2.81
Pittsburgh	163	49	17	246	27	**1479.0**	1324	580	495	**89**	70	38	44	469	56	882	53	0	8.1	5.4	2.9	.241	.304	3.01
San Francisco	163	42	17	262	**42**	1465.1	1325	593	521	137	**54**	29	37	408	65	1060	49	3	8.1	6.5	2.5	.238	.293	3.20
Milwaukee	162	43	4	266	38	1447.2	1336	633	566	123	63	39	28	541	66	966	68	1	8.3	6.0	3.4	.246	.316	3.52
Philadelphia	162	50	18	246	21	1468.2	1426	667	576	116	94	39	**60**	464	64	1071	42	1	8.7	6.6	2.9	.256	.318	3.53
St. Louis	162	40	11	261	35	1461.1	1414	674	612	166	65	43	40	467	72	916	47	2	8.7	5.6	2.9	.255	.315	3.77
Chicago	164	33	9	292	35	1472.0	1470	723	618	154	76	34	27	481	**78**	855	51	2	9.0	5.2	2.9	.260	.320	3.78
Houston	162	29	7	256	26	1461.0	1459	711	624	123	81	38	40	**388**	69	931	53	4	9.0	5.7	**2.4**	.260	.310	3.84
Cincinnati	162	43	9	244	34	1457.1	1355	704	629	136	58	46	46	587	44	**1113**	**83**	4	8.4	**6.9**	3.6	.247	.322	3.88
New York	164	29	11	**301**	14	1454.2	1462	752	656	147	70	35	49	498	29	776	53	7	9.0	4.8	3.1	.262	.326	4.06
NL Total	1626	416	126	2576	306	14643.0	13794	6558	5758	1318	709	366	404	4730	596	9649	550	25	8.5	5.9	2.9	.249	.317	3.54
NL Avg Team	163	42	13	258	31	1464.0	1379	656	576	132	71	37	40	473	60	965	55	3	8.5	5.9	2.9	.249	.317	3.54

Team Fielding

Team	G	PO	A	E	TC	DP	PB	Pct
Cincinnati	162	4372	1543	**117**	6032	142	15	.981
St. Louis	162	4384	1746	130	6260	152	23	.979
Los Angeles	162	4428	1814	134	6376	135	9	.979
Milwaukee	162	4345	1742	140	6227	145	**28**	.978
Pittsburgh	163	**4437**	1977	152	6566	**189**	12	.977
San Francisco	163	4396	1706	148	6250	124	26	.976
Philadelphia	162	4406	1769	157	6332	153	21	.975
Chicago	164	4416	**2004**	171	**6591**	166	14	.974
Houston	162	4384	1762	166	6312	130	25	.974
New York	164	4364	1945	171	6480	153	19	.974
NL Total	1626	43932	18008	1486	63426	1489	192	.977

Team vs. Team Records

	ChN	Cin	Hou	LA	Mil	NYN	Phi	Pit	SF	StL	Won
ChN	—	7	8	8	9	11	8	5	6	10	**72**
Cin	11	—	12	6	12	11	13	8	6	10	**89**
Hou	10	6	—	5	4	14	6	8	3	9	**65**
LA	10	12	13	—	10	12	9	9	10	12	**97**
Mil	9	6	14	8	—	13	6	9	10	11	**86**
NYN	7	7	4	6	5	—	7	4	5	5	**50**
Phi	10	5	12	9	12	11	—	8	8	10	**85**
Pit	13	10	10	9	9	14	10	—	11	4	**90**
SF	12	12	15	8	8	13	10	7	—	10	**95**
StL	8	8	9	6	7	13	7	14	8	—	**80**
Lost	90	73	97	65	76	112	76	72	67	81	

1965 National League Batting Leaders

Games		At-Bats		Runs		Hits		Doubles		Triples	
R. Santo, ChN	164	P. Rose, Cin	670	T. Harper, Cin	126	P. Rose, Cin	209	H. Aaron, Mil	40	J. Callison, Phi	16
B. Williams, ChN	164	V. Pinson, Cin	669	W. Mays, SF	118	V. Pinson, Cin	204	B. Williams, ChN	39	D. Allen, Phi	14
E. Banks, ChN	163	M. Wills, LA	650	P. Rose, Cin	117	B. Williams, ChN	203	P. Rose, Cin	35	D. Clendenon, Pit	14
P. Rose, Cin	162	T. Harper, Cin	646	B. Williams, ChN	115	R. Clemente, Pit	194	L. Brock, StL	35	R. Clemente, Pit	14
D. Clendenon, Pit	162	B. Williams, ChN	645	2 tied with	109	C. Flood, StL	191	V. Pinson, Cin	34	J. Morgan, Hou	12

Home Runs		Total Bases		Runs Batted In		Walks		Intentional Walks		Strikeouts	
W. Mays, SF	52	W. Mays, SF	360	D. Johnson, Cin	130	J. Morgan, Hou	97	L. Cardenas, Cin	25	D. Allen, Phi	150
W. McCovey, SF	39	B. Williams, ChN	356	F. Robinson, Cin	113	W. McCovey, SF	88	E. Banks, ChN	19	D. Stuart, Phi	136
B. Williams, ChN	34	V. Pinson, Cin	324	W. Mays, SF	112	R. Santo, ChN	88	F. Robinson, Cin	18	D. Clendenon, Pit	128
R. Santo, ChN	33	H. Aaron, Mil	319	B. Williams, ChN	108	J. Wynn, Hou	84	J. Edwards, Cin	16	W. Stargell, Pit	127
F. Robinson, Cin	33	D. Johnson, Cin	317	W. Stargell, Pit	107	T. Harper, Cin	78	W. Mays, SF	16	T. Harper, Cin	127

Hit By Pitch		Sac Hits		Sac Flies		Stolen Bases		Caught Stealing		GDP	
F. Robinson, Cin	18	W. Parker, LA	19	D. Clendenon, Pit	10	M. Wills, LA	94	M. Wills, LA	31	J. Torre, Mil	22
L. Johnson, LA	16	F. Bolling, Mil	17	D. Johnson, Cin	10	L. Brock, StL	63	L. Brock, StL	27	H. Lanier, SF	21
T. Taylor, Phi	12	R. McMillan, NYN	16	B. Mazeroski, Pit	9	J. Wynn, Hou	43	B. Bailey, Pit	14	J. Alou, SF	21
L. Brock, StL	10	M. Wills, LA	14	E. Kranepool, NYN	8	T. Harper, Cin	35	4 tied with	9	B. Williams, ChN	20
D. Landrum, ChN	10	R. Fairly, LA	14	H. Aaron, Mil	8	W. Davis, LA	25			4 tied with	17

Runs Created		Runs Created/27 Outs		Batting Average		On-Base Percentage		Slugging Percentage		OBP+Slugging	
W. Mays, SF	139	W. Mays, SF	9.46	R. Clemente, Pit	.329	W. Mays, SF	.398	W. Mays, SF	.645	W. Mays, SF	1.043
B. Williams, ChN	131	H. Aaron, Mil	7.66	H. Aaron, Mil	.318	F. Robinson, Cin	.386	H. Aaron, Mil	.560	H. Aaron, Mil	.938
R. Santo, ChN	120	W. McCovey, SF	7.61	W. Mays, SF	.317	P. Rose, Cin	.382	B. Williams, ChN	.552	B. Williams, ChN	.929
H. Aaron, Mil	117	B. Williams, ChN	7.60	B. Williams, ChN	.315	W. McCovey, SF	.381	F. Robinson, Cin	.540	F. Robinson, Cin	.925
W. McCovey, SF	114	R. Santo, ChN	7.24	P. Rose, Cin	.312	H. Aaron, Mil	.379	W. McCovey, SF	.539	W. McCovey, SF	.920

1965 National League Pitching Leaders

Wins		Losses		Winning Percentage		Games		Games Started		Complete Games	
S. Koufax, LA	26	J. Fisher, NYN	24	S. Koufax, LA	.765	T. Abernathy, ChN	84	D. Drysdale, LA	42	S. Koufax, LA	27
T. Cloninger, Mil	24	L. Jackson, ChN	21	J. Nuxhall, Cin	.733	H. Woodeshick, 2tm	78	S. Koufax, LA	41	J. Marichal, SF	24
D. Drysdale, LA	23	A. Jackson, NYN	20	B. Bolin, SF	.700	L. McDaniel, ChN	71	C. Short, Phi	40	B. Gibson, StL	20
S. Ellis, Cin	22	B. Bruce, Hou	18	J. Maloney, Cin	.690	J. Baldschun, Phi	65	C. Osteen, LA	40	D. Drysdale, LA	20
J. Marichal, SF	22	W. Spahn, 2tm	16	S. Ellis, Cin	.688	3 tied with	62	3 tied with	39	T. Cloninger, Mil	16

Shutouts		Saves		Games Finished		Batters Faced		Innings Pitched		Hits Allowed	
J. Marichal, SF	10	T. Abernathy, ChN	31	T. Abernathy, ChN	62	S. Koufax, LA	1297	S. Koufax, LA	335.2	D. Drysdale, LA	270
S. Koufax, LA	8	B. McCool, Cin	21	H. Woodeshick, 2tm	47	D. Drysdale, LA	1262	D. Drysdale, LA	308.1	L. Jackson, ChN	268
B. Veale, Pit	7	F. Linzy, SF	21	B. McCool, Cin	43	B. Gibson, StL	1233	B. Gibson, StL	299.0	C. Short, Phi	260
D. Drysdale, LA	7	3 tied with	18	B. O'Dell, Mil	42	C. Short, Phi	1216	C. Short, Phi	297.1	C. Osteen, LA	253
J. Bunning, Phi	7			2 tied with	40	J. Bunning, Phi	1191	J. Marichal, SF	295.1	J. Bunning, Phi	253

Home Runs Allowed		Walks		Walks/9 Innings		Strikeouts		Strikeouts/9 Innings		Strikeout/Walk Ratio	
B. Gibson, StL	34	B. Veale, Pit	119	J. Marichal, SF	1.4	S. Koufax, LA	382	S. Koufax, LA	10.2	S. Koufax, LA	5.38
D. Drysdale, LA	30	T. Cloninger, Mil	119	V. Law, Pit	1.4	B. Veale, Pit	276	B. Veale, Pit	9.3	J. Marichal, SF	5.22
L. Jackson, ChN	28	W. Blasingame, Mil	116	B. Bruce, Hou	1.5	B. Gibson, StL	270	J. Maloney, Cin	8.6	J. Bunning, Phi	4.32
J. Marichal, SF	27	J. Maloney, Cin	110	T. Farrell, Hou	1.5	J. Bunning, Phi	268	J. Bunning, Phi	8.3	B. Bruce, Hou	3.82
4 tied with	26	S. Ellis, Cin	104	K. Johnson, 2tm	1.9	J. Maloney, Cin	244	B. Gibson, StL	8.1	T. Farrell, Hou	3.49

Earned Run Average		Component ERA		Hit Batsmen		Wild Pitches		Opponent Average		Opponent OBP	
S. Koufax, LA	2.04	S. Koufax, LA	1.56	R. Culp, Phi	12	T. Cloninger, Mil	22	S. Koufax, LA	.179	S. Koufax, LA	.227
J. Marichal, SF	2.13	J. Marichal, SF	1.92	D. Cardwell, Pit	12	J. Maloney, Cin	19	J. Marichal, SF	.205	J. Marichal, SF	.239
V. Law, Pit	2.15	V. Law, Pit	2.29	D. Drysdale, LA	12	B. Veale, Pit	17	J. Maloney, Cin	.206	V. Law, Pit	.261
J. Maloney, Cin	2.54	J. Maloney, Cin	2.56	J. Bunning, Phi	12	D. Ellsworth, ChN	15	B. Bolin, SF	.214	D. Drysdale, LA	.279
J. Bunning, Phi	2.60	J. Bunning, Phi	2.62	B. Gibson, StL	11	J. Tsitouris, Cin	15	B. Gibson, StL	.222	J. Bunning, Phi	.279

1965 National League Miscellaneous

Managers

Chicago	Bob Kennedy	24-32
	Lou Klein	48-58
Cincinnati	Dick Sisler	89-73
Houston	Lum Harris	65-97
Los Angeles	Walter Alston	97-65
Milwaukee	Bobby Bragan	86-76
New York	Casey Stengel	31-64
	Wes Westrum	19-48
Philadelphia	Gene Mauch	85-76
Pittsburgh	Harry Walker	90-72
St. Louis	Red Schoendienst	80-81
San Francisco	Herman Franks	95-67

Awards

Most Valuable Player	Willie Mays, of, SF
Cy Young	Sandy Koufax, LA
Rookie of the Year	Jim Lefebvre, 2b, LA
STATS Manager of the Year	Walter Alston, LA

STATS All-Star Team

C	Joe Torre, Mil	.291	27	80
1B	Willie McCovey, SF	.276	39	92
2B	Pete Rose, Cin	.312	11	81
3B	Deron Johnson, Cin	.287	32	130
SS	Maury Wills, LA	.286	0	33
OF	Hank Aaron, Mil	.318	32	89
OF	Willie Mays, SF	.317	52	112
OF	Billy Williams, ChN	.315	34	108
P	Don Drysdale, LA	23-12	2.77	210 K
P	Sandy Koufax, LA	26-8	2.04	382 K
P	Jim Maloney, Cin	20-9	2.54	244 K
P	Juan Marichal, SF	22-13	2.13	240 K
RP	Ted Abernathy, ChN	4-6	2.57	31 Sv

Postseason

World Series	LA (NL) 4 vs. Minnesota (AL) 3

Outstanding Performances

Perfect Games
Sandy Koufax, LA   vs. ChN on September 9
No-Hitters
Jim Maloney, Cin   @ ChN on August 19
Three-Homer Games
Johnny Callison, Phi   on June 6
Willie Stargell, Pit   on June 24
Jim Hickman, NYN   on September 3

1966 American League Standings

Team	Overall W	L	Pct	GB	DIF	Home W	L	R	OR	HR	OHR	Road W	L	R	OR	HR	OHR	Park Run	HR	M/A	May	June	July	Aug	S/O
Baltimore	97	63	.606	—	125	48	31	375	296	85	65	49	32	380	305	90	62	100	101	11-1	14-16	25-8	19-10	14-14	14-14
Minnesota	89	73	.549	9.0	3	49	32	375	311	94	83	40	41	288	270	50	56	123	167	4-6	16-15	15-17	16-14	21-11	17-10
Detroit	88	74	.543	10.0	5	42	39	360	374	97	101	46	35	359	324	82	84	107	119	10-6	13-12	21-9	11-20	16-14	17-13
Chicago	83	79	.512	15.0	2	45	36	273	217	31	36	38	43	301	300	56	65	82	55	10-3	9-18	14-17	18-15	20-12	12-14
Cleveland	81	81	.500	17.0	56	41	40	283	300	82	65	40	41	291	286	73	64	101	107	10-1	18-13	15-15	11-19	15-17	12-16
California	80	82	.494	18.0	0	42	39	303	315	54	67	38	43	301	328	68	69	98	88	7-6	16-14	16-15	15-14	13-17	13-16
Kansas City	74	86	.463	23.0	0	42	39	284	292	18	27	32	47	280	356	52	79	88	34	2-10	13-15	16-17	14-15	14-20	15-9
Washington	71	88	.447	25.5	0	42	36	273	292	62	84	29	52	284	367	64	70	90	113	3-9	17-14	11-21	16-17	15-15	9-12
Boston	72	90	.444	26.0	0	40	41	374	397	80	97	32	49	281	334	65	67	125	134	3-10	14-16	10-21	18-14	15-17	12-12
New York	70	89	.440	26.5	0	35	46	302	280	74	63	35	43	309	332	88	61	87	89	3-11	15-12	13-16	16-16	13-19	10-15

Clinch Date—Baltimore 9/22.

Team Batting

Team	G	AB	R	OR	H	2B	3B	HR	TB	RBI	TBB	IBB	SO	HBP	SH	SF	SB	CS	SB%	GDP	Avg	OBP	Slg
Baltimore	160	5529	755	601	1426	243	35	175	2264	703	514	59	926	39	82	35	55	43	.56	119	.258	.329	.409
Detroit	162	5507	719	698	1383	224	45	179	2234	682	551	45	987	33	67	37	41	34	.55	128	.249	.324	.382
Minnesota	162	5390	663	581	1341	219	33	144	2058	611	513	69	844	39	49	44	67	42	.61	138	.249	.324	.382
Boston	162	5498	655	731	1318	228	44	145	2069	617	542	54	1020	32	65	38	35	24	.59	131	.240	.316	.376
New York	160	5330	611	612	1254	182	36	162	1994	569	485	41	817	21	58	42	49	29	.63	111	.235	.307	.374
California	162	5360	604	643	1244	179	54	122	1897	562	525	52	1062	27	56	33	53	41	.56	113	.237	.302	.360
Cleveland	162	5474	574	586	1300	156	25	155	1971	536	450	55	914	27	56	33	53	41	.56	113	.237	.302	.360
Chicago	163	5348	574	517	1235	193	40	87	1769	524	476	50	872	44	109	44	153	78	.66	94	.231	.304	.331
Kansas City	160	5328	564	648	1259	212	56	70	1793	509	421	34	982	26	71	27	132	50	.73	100	.236	.299	.337
Washington	159	5318	557	659	1245	185	40	126	1888	525	450	31	1069	20	84	33	53	37	.59	130	.234	.300	.355
AL Total	1612	54082	6276	6276	13005	2021	408	1365	19937	5838	4927	490	9493	319	710	379	718	432	.62	1168	.240	.306	.369
AL Avg Team	161	5408	628	628	1301	202	41	137	1994	584	493	49	949	32	71	38	72	43	.62	117	.240	.306	.369

Team Pitching

Team	G	CG	ShO	Rel	Sv	IP	H	R	ER	HR	SH	SF	HB	TBB	IBB	SO	WP	Bk	H/9	SO/9	BB/9	OAvg	OOBP	ERA
Chicago	163	38	22	239	34	1475.1	1229	517	440	101	70	23	36	403	55	896	68	6	7.5	5.5	2.5	.226	.282	2.68
Minnesota	162	52	11	202	28	1438.2	1246	581	501	139	68	35	27	392	25	1015	52	1	7.8	6.3	2.5	.232	.286	3.13
Cleveland	162	49	15	226	28	1467.1	1260	586	526	129	70	38	29	489	44	1111	51	2	7.7	6.8	3.0	.232	.297	3.23
Baltimore	160	23	13	253	51	1466.1	1267	601	541	127	56	34	29	514	27	1070	53	6	7.8	6.6	3.2	.233	.301	3.32
New York	160	29	7	227	32	1415.2	1318	612	537	124	82	39	21	443	51	842	36	2	8.4	5.4	2.8	.248	.306	3.41
Kansas City	160	19	11	306	47	1435.0	1281	648	567	106	71	42	39	630	77	854	52	5	8.0	5.4	4.0	.241	.323	3.56
California	162	31	12	296	40	1457.1	1364	643	577	136	74	47	38	511	43	836	49	11	8.4	5.2	3.2	.251	.317	3.56
Washington	159	25	6	295	35	1419.0	1282	659	584	154	72	35	24	448	68	866	43	6	8.1	5.5	2.8	.242	.302	3.70
Detroit	162	36	11	271	38	1454.1	1356	698	622	185	70	39	42	520	39	1026	56	6	8.4	6.3	3.2	.247	.315	3.85
Boston	162	32	10	311	31	1463.2	1402	731	637	164	77	47	34	577	61	977	53	6	8.6	6.0	3.5	.253	.325	3.92
AL Total	1612	334	118	2626	364	14492.2	13005	6276	5532	1365	710	379	319	4927	490	9493	513	51	8.1	5.9	3.1	.240	.312	3.44
AL Avg Team	161	33	12	263	36	1449.2	1301	628	553	137	71	38	32	493	49	949	51	5	8.1	5.9	3.1	.240	.312	3.44

Team Fielding

Team	G	PO	A	E	TC	DP	PB	Pct
Baltimore	160	4400	1654	115	6169	142	23	.981
Detroit	162	4362	1622	120	6104	142	7	.980
California	162	4378	1859	136	6373	186	16	.979
Cleveland	162	4390	1595	138	6123	132	16	.977
Kansas City	160	4320	1646	139	6105	154	20	.977
New York	160	4244	1835	142	6221	142	9	.977
Minnesota	162	4316	1589	139	6044	118	5	.977
Washington	159	4256	1687	142	6085	139	14	.977
Chicago	163	4423	1971	159	6553	149	24	.976
Boston	162	4389	1709	155	6253	153	13	.975
AL Total	1612	43478	17167	1385	62030	1457	147	.978

Team vs. Team Records

	Bal	Bos	Cal	ChA	Cle	Det	KCA	Min	NYA	Was	Won
Bal	—	12	12	9	8	9	11	10	15	11	97
Bos	6	—	9	11	7	8	9	6	8	8	72
Cal	6	9	—	8	10	9	9	11	11	7	80
ChA	9	7	10	—	11	8	13	4	9	12	83
Cle	10	11	8	7	—	9	6	9	12	9	81
Det	9	10	9	10	9	—	6	11	11	13	88
KCA	5	9	9	5	12	12	—	8	5	9	74
Min	8	12	7	14	9	7	10	—	8	14	89
NYA	3	10	7	9	6	7	13	10	—	5	70
Was	7	10	11	6	9	5	9	4	10	—	71
Lost	63	90	82	79	81	74	86	73	89	88	

Seasons: Standings, Leaders

1966 American League Batting Leaders

Games		At-Bats		Runs		Hits		Doubles		Triples	
D. Buford, ChA	163	L. Aparicio, Bal	659	F. Robinson, Bal	122	T. Oliva, Min	191	C. Yastrzemski, Bos	39	B. Knoop, Cal	11
G. Scott, Bos	162	T. Agee, ChA	629	T. Oliva, Min	99	F. Robinson, Bal	182	B. Robinson, Bal	35	B. Campaneris, KCA	10
J. Fregosi, Cal	162	T. Oliva, Min	622	T. Agee, ChA	98	L. Aparicio, Bal	182	F. Robinson, Bal	34	E. Brinkman, Was	9
H. Killebrew, Min	162	B. Robinson, Bal	620	N. Cash, Det	98	T. Agee, ChA	172	T. Oliva, Min	32	5 tied with	8
B. Knoop, Cal	161	J. Fregosi, Cal	611	2 tied with	97	N. Cash, Det	168	J. Fregosi, Cal	32		

Home Runs		Total Bases		Runs Batted In		Walks		Intentional Walks		Strikeouts	
F. Robinson, Bal	49	F. Robinson, Bal	367	F. Robinson, Bal	122	H. Killebrew, Min	103	H. Killebrew, Min	18	G. Scott, Bos	152
H. Killebrew, Min	39	T. Oliva, Min	312	H. Killebrew, Min	110	J. Foy, Bos	91	G. Scott, Bos	13	B. Knoop, Cal	144
B. Powell, Bal	34	H. Killebrew, Min	306	B. Powell, Bal	109	F. Robinson, Bal	87	A. Etchebarren, Bal	12	T. Agee, ChA	127
N. Cash, Det	32	N. Cash, Det	288	W. Horton, Det	100	T. Tresh, NYA	86	F. Robinson, Bal	11	D. Lock, Was	126
J. Pepitone, NYA	31	T. Agee, ChA	281	B. Robinson, Bal	100	C. Yastrzemski, Bos	84	B. Robinson, Bal	11	B. Powell, Bal	125

Hit By Pitch		Sac Hits		Sac Flies		Stolen Bases		Caught Stealing		GDP	
R. Reichardt, Cal	13	D. Buford, ChA	17	7 tied with	7	B. Campaneris, KCA	52	D. Buford, ChA	22	G. Scott, Bos	25
T. Agee, ChA	10	L. Aparicio, Bal	12			D. Buford, ChA	51	T. Agee, ChA	18	R. Colavito, Cle	25
F. Valentine, Was	10	D. Wert, Det	11			T. Agee, ChA	44	Z. Versalles, Min	12	F. Robinson, Bal	24
F. Robinson, Bal	10	K. Berry, ChA	11			L. Aparicio, Bal	25	3 tied with	11	D. Wert, Det	20
G. Scott, Bos	8	4 tied with	10			J. Cardenal, Cal	24			B. Robinson, Bal	18

Runs Created		Runs Created/27 Outs		Batting Average		On-Base Percentage		Slugging Percentage		OBP+Slugging	
F. Robinson, Bal	141	F. Robinson, Bal	8.90	F. Robinson, Bal	.316	F. Robinson, Bal	.410	F. Robinson, Bal	.637	F. Robinson, Bal	1.047
H. Killebrew, Min	120	H. Killebrew, Min	7.65	T. Oliva, Min	.307	A. Kaline, Det	.392	H. Killebrew, Min	.538	H. Killebrew, Min	.929
T. Oliva, Min	107	A. Kaline, Det	7.62	A. Kaline, Det	.288	H. Killebrew, Min	.391	A. Kaline, Det	.534	A. Kaline, Det	.927
A. Kaline, Det	101	B. Powell, Bal	7.08	B. Powell, Bal	.287	D. McAuliffe, Det	.373	B. Powell, Bal	.532	B. Powell, Bal	.903
N. Cash, Det	100	D. McAuliffe, Det	6.60	H. Killebrew, Min	.281	B. Powell, Bal	.372	D. McAuliffe, Det	.509	D. McAuliffe, Det	.882

1966 American League Pitching Leaders

Wins		Losses		Winning Percentage		Games		Games Started		Complete Games	
J. Kaat, Min	25	M. Stottlemyre, NYA	20	D. Boswell, Min	.706	E. Fisher, 2tm	67	J. Kaat, Min	41	J. Kaat, Min	19
D. McLain, Det	20	D. Chance, Cal	17	D. McNally, Bal	.684	C. Cox, Was	66	D. McLain, Det	38	D. McLain, Det	14
E. Wilson, 2tm	18	G. Bell, Cle	15	S. Siebert, Cle	.667	J. Aker, KCA	66	D. Chance, Cal	37	E. Wilson, 2tm	13
S. Siebert, Cle	16	6 tied with	14	S. Barber, Bal	.667	A. Worthington, Min	65	E. Wilson, 2tm	37	G. Bell, Cle	12
J. Palmer, Bal	15			J. Kaat, Min	.658	R. Kline, Was	63	G. Bell, Cle	37	4 tied with	11

Shutouts		Saves		Games Finished		Batters Faced		Innings Pitched		Hits Allowed	
T. John, ChA	5	J. Aker, KCA	32	J. Aker, KCA	57	J. Kaat, Min	1227	J. Kaat, Min	304.2	J. Kaat, Min	271
L. Tiant, Cle	5	R. Kline, Was	23	E. Fisher, 2tm	50	D. McLain, Det	1080	D. McLain, Det	264.1	M. Grant, Min	248
S. McDowell, Cle	5	L. Sherry, Det	20	A. Worthington, Min	46	D. Chance, Cal	1067	E. Wilson, 2tm	264.0	M. Stottlemyre, NYA	239
3 tied with	4	E. Fisher, 2tm	19	R. Kline, Was	46	E. Wilson, 2tm	1059	D. Chance, Cal	259.2	E. Wilson, 2tm	214
		S. Miller, Bal	18	3 tied with	39	M. Stottlemyre, NYA	1042	G. Bell, Cle	254.1	D. McNally, Bal	212

Home Runs Allowed		Walks		Walks/9 Innings		Strikeouts		Strikeouts/9 Innings		Strikeout/Walk Ratio	
D. McLain, Det	42	D. Chance, Cal	114	J. Kaat, Min	1.6	S. McDowell, Cle	225	S. McDowell, Cle	10.4	J. Kaat, Min	3.73
P. Richert, Was	36	G. Brunet, Cal	106	F. Peterson, NYA	1.7	J. Kaat, Min	205	D. Boswell, Min	9.2	S. Hargan, Cle	2.93
E. Wilson, 2tm	30	D. McLain, Det	104	M. Grant, Min	1.8	E. Wilson, 2tm	200	M. Lolich, Det	7.6	G. Peters, ChA	2.87
J. Kaat, Min	29	S. McDowell, Cle	102	G. Peters, ChA	2.0	P. Richert, Was	195	P. Richert, Was	7.1	P. Richert, Was	2.83
P. Ortega, Was	29	J. Palmer, Bal	91	S. Hargan, Cle	2.1	G. Bell, Cle	194	G. Bell, Cle	6.9	E. Wilson, 2tm	2.70

Earned Run Average		Component ERA		Hit Batsmen		Wild Pitches		Opponent Average		Opponent OBP	
G. Peters, ChA	1.98	G. Peters, ChA	1.96	M. Lopez, Cal	9	J. Horlen, ChA	14	S. McDowell, Cle	.188	G. Peters, ChA	.260
J. Horlen, ChA	2.43	S. Hargan, Cle	2.57	D. Wickersham, Det	8	J. Kaat, Min	12	D. Boswell, Min	.197	P. Richert, Was	.270
S. Hargan, Cle	2.48	F. Peterson, NYA	2.58	T. John, ChA	7	D. Boswell, Min	12	G. Peters, ChA	.212	J. Kaat, Min	.270
J. Perry, Min	2.54	L. Krausse, KCA	2.60	J. Lonborg, Bos	7	M. Lopez, Cal	12	D. McLain, Det	.214	P. Ortega, Was	.274
T. John, ChA	2.62	S. Siebert, Cle	2.63	D. Chance, Cal	7	2 tied with	11	P. Richert, Was	.215	S. Siebert, Cle	.276

1966 American League Miscellaneous

Managers

Baltimore	Hank Bauer	97-63
Boston	Billy Herman	64-82
	Pete Runnels	8-8
California	Bill Rigney	80-82
Chicago	Eddie Stanky	83-79
Cleveland	Birdie Tebbetts	66-57
	George Strickland	15-24
Detroit	Chuck Dressen	16-10
	Bob Swift	32-25
	Frank Skaff	40-39
Kansas City	Alvin Dark	74-86
Minnesota	Sam Mele	89-73
New York	Johnny Keane	4-16
	Ralph Houk	66-73
Washington	Gil Hodges	71-88

Awards

Most Valuable Player	Frank Robinson, of, Bal
STATS Cy Young	Jim Kaat, Min
Rookie of the Year	Tommie Agee, of, ChA
STATS Manager of the Year	Hank Bauer, Bal

STATS All-Star Team

C	Bill Freehan, Det	.234	12	46
1B	Boog Powell, Bal	.287	34	109
2B	Bobby Knoop, Cal	.232	17	72
3B	Harmon Killebrew, Min	.281	39	110
SS	Dick McAuliffe, Det	.274	23	56
OF	Al Kaline, Det	.288	29	88
OF	Tony Oliva, Min	.307	25	87
OF	Frank Robinson, Bal	.316	49	122
P	Jim Kaat, Min	25-13	2.75	205 K
P	Gary Peters, ChA	12-10	1.98	129 K
P	Sonny Siebert, Cle	16-8	2.80	163 K
P	Earl Wilson, 2tm	18-11	3.07	200 K
RP	Jack Aker, KCA	8-4	1.99	32 Sv

Postseason

World Series	Baltimore (AL) 4 vs. LA (NL) 0

Outstanding Performances

Triple Crown
Frank Robinson, Bal .316-49-122
No-Hitters
Sonny Siebert, Cle   vs. Was on June 10
Three-Homer Games
Boog Powell, Bal   on August 15

1966 National League Standings

Team	Overall W	L	Pct	GB	DIF	Home Games W	L	R	OR	HR	OHR	Road Games W	L	R	OR	HR	OHR	Park Index Run	HR	Record by Month M/A	May	June	July	Aug	S/O
Los Angeles	95	67	.586	—	30	53	28	286	220	43	36	42	39	320	270	65	48	86	70	11-7	16-11	14-14	18-10	15-15	21-10
San Francisco	93	68	.578	1.5	88	47	34	317	312	91	77	46	34	358	314	90	63	92	108	11-7	19-9	18-12	13-16	17-11	15-13
Pittsburgh	92	70	.568	3.0	70	46	35	384	317	48	48	46	35	375	324	110	77	100	51	10-5	14-15	19-9	17-14	18-12	14-15
Philadelphia	87	75	.537	8.0	4	48	33	354	319	52	65	39	42	342	321	65	72	102	85	8-5	14-15	18-14	15-15	16-15	16-11
Atlanta	85	77	.525	10.0	1	43	38	394	335	119	82	42	39	388	348	88	47	99	149	10-8	10-19	14-17	14-12	15-12	22-9
St. Louis	83	79	.512	12.0	1	43	38	274	288	48	64	40	41	297	289	60	66	96	89	7-9	13-12	14-17	20-10	13-18	16-13
Cincinnati	76	84	.475	18.0	1	46	33	417	372	91	93	30	51	275	330	58	60	134	160	4-10	15-11	17-15	14-17	18-12	8-19
Houston	72	90	.444	23.0	1	45	36	318	317	48	48	27	54	294	378	64	82	94	66	9-9	16-12	14-15	10-18	12-18	11-18
New York	66	95	.410	28.5	1	32	49	276	372	51	94	34	46	311	389	47	72	91	120	5-6	10-16	14-19	18-14	11-21	8-19
Chicago	59	103	.364	36.0	1	32	49	342	410	80	100	27	54	302	399	60	84	107	125	3-12	10-17	10-20	9-22	14-15	13-17

Clinch Date—Los Angeles 10/02.

Team Batting

Team	G	AB	R	OR	H	2B	3B	HR	TB	RBI	TBB	IBB	SO	HBP	SH	SF	SB	CS	SB%	GDP	Avg	OBP	Slg
Atlanta	163	5617	782	683	1476	220	32	207	2381	734	512	75	913	40	72	45	59	47	.56	106	.263	.334	.424
Pittsburgh	162	5676	759	641	1586	238	66	158	2430	715	405	75	1011	35	73	40	64	60	.52	111	.279	.336	.428
Philadelphia	162	5607	696	640	1448	224	49	117	2121	628	510	64	969	29	78	32	56	42	.57	113	.258	.327	.378
Cincinnati	160	5521	692	702	1434	232	33	149	2179	651	394	56	877	20	69	39	70	50	.58	117	.260	.316	.395
San Francisco	161	5539	675	626	1373	195	31	181	2173	627	414	65	860	32	70	28	29	30	.49	142	.248	.319	.392
Chicago	162	5592	644	809	1418	203	43	140	2127	603	457	53	998	47	80	37	76	47	.62	112	.254	.319	.380
Houston	163	5511	612	695	1405	203	35	112	2014	570	491	61	885	34	97	37	90	47	.66	128	.255	.324	.365
Los Angeles	162	5471	606	490	1399	201	27	108	1978	565	430	54	830	49	84	32	94	64	.59	117	.256	.319	.362
New York	161	5371	587	761	1286	187	35	98	1837	534	446	44	992	42	63	29	55	46	.54	127	.239	.306	.342
St. Louis	162	5480	571	577	1377	196	61	108	2019	533	345	51	977	35	59	44	144	61	.70	114	.251	.305	.368
NL Total	1618	55385	6624	6624	14202	2099	412	1378	21259	6160	4404	598	9312	363	745	363	737	494	.60	1187	.256	.313	.384
NL Avg Team	162	5539	662	662	1420	210	41	138	2126	616	440	60	931	36	75	36	74	49	.60	119	.256	.313	.384

Team Pitching

Team	G	CG	ShO	Rel	Sv	IP	H	R	ER	HR	SH	SF	HB	TBB	IBB	SO	WP	Bk	H/9	SO/9	BB/9	OAvg	OOBP	ERA
Los Angeles	162	52	20	214	35	1458.0	1287	490	425	84	96	42	27	356	67	1084	42	3	7.9	6.7	2.2	.237	.286	2.62
St. Louis	162	47	19	261	32	1459.2	1345	577	505	130	74	35	34	448	81	892	42	7	8.3	5.5	2.8	.246	.306	3.11
San Francisco	161	52	14	250	27	1476.2	1370	626	531	140	65	31	34	359	54	973	44	3	8.3	5.9	2.2	.244	.292	3.24
Pittsburgh	162	35	12	285	43	1463.1	1445	641	573	125	67	24	36	463	57	898	42	5	8.9	5.5	2.8	.261	.321	3.52
Philadelphia	162	52	15	245	23	1459.2	1439	640	579	137	53	37	61	412	55	928	43	4	8.9	5.7	2.5	.258	.315	3.57
Atlanta	163	37	10	290	36	1469.1	1430	683	601	129	79	44	29	485	64	884	83	5	8.8	5.4	3.0	.257	.317	3.68
Houston	163	34	13	261	26	1443.2	1468	695	603	130	72	33	34	391	44	929	60	6	9.2	5.8	2.4	.262	.313	3.76
Cincinnati	160	28	10	270	35	1436.0	1408	702	651	153	80	38	45	490	55	1043	54	5	8.8	6.5	3.1	.258	.322	4.08
New York	161	37	9	288	22	1427.0	1497	761	661	166	79	36	35	521	57	773	76	3	9.4	4.9	3.3	.272	.337	4.17
Chicago	162	28	6	285	24	1458.0	1513	809	702	184	80	43	28	479	64	908	40	4	9.3	5.6	3.0	.268	.326	4.33
NL Total	1618	402	128	2649	303	14551.1	14202	6624	5831	1378	745	363	363	4404	598	9312	526	45	8.8	5.8	2.7	.256	.319	3.61
NL Avg Team	162	40	13	265	30	1455.1	1420	662	583	138	75	36	36	440	60	931	53	5	8.8	5.8	2.7	.256	.319	3.61

Team Fielding

Team	G	PO	A	E	TC	DP	PB	Pct
Philadelphia	162	4379	1825	113	6317	147	17	.982
Cincinnati	160	4308	1534	122	5964	133	11	.980
Los Angeles	162	4374	1774	133	6281	128	11	.979
Pittsburgh	162	4390	1917	141	6448	215	16	.978
St. Louis	162	4379	1834	145	6358	166	11	.977
Atlanta	163	4408	1734	154	6296	139	27	.976
New York	161	4281	1995	159	6435	171	16	.975
Chicago	162	4374	1883	166	6423	132	18	.974
San Francisco	161	4429	1816	168	6413	131	23	.974
Houston	163	4331	1664	174	6169	126	25	.972
NL Total	1618	43653	17976	1475	63104	1488	175	.977

Team vs. Team Records

	Atl	ChN	Cin	Hou	LA	NYN	Phi	Pit	SF	StL	Won
Atl	—	7	10	14	7	14	11	7	8	7	85
ChN	11	—	6	5	8	8	5	6	6	4	59
Cin	8	12	—	4	6	10	10	8	7	11	76
Hou	4	13	14	—	7	7	7	4	6	10	72
LA	11	10	12	11	—	12	11	9	9	10	95
NYN	4	10	7	11	6	—	7	5	9	7	66
Phi	7	13	8	11	7	11	—	10	10	10	87
Pit	11	12	10	14	9	13	8	—	7	8	92
SF	10	12	10	12	9	9	8	11	—	12	93
StL	11	14	7	8	8	11	8	10	6	—	83
Lost	77	103	84	90	67	95	75	70	68	79	

1966 National League Batting Leaders

Games		At-Bats		Runs		Hits		Doubles		Triples	
B. Williams, ChN	162	F. Alou, Atl	666	F. Alou, Atl	122	F. Alou, Atl	218	J. Callison, Phi	40	T. McCarver, StL	13
B. Mazeroski, Pit	162	G. Beckert, ChN	656	H. Aaron, Atl	117	P. Rose, Cin	205	P. Rose, Cin	38	L. Brock, StL	12
L. Cardenas, Cin	160	P. Rose, Cin	654	D. Allen, Phi	112	R. Clemente, Pit	202	V. Pinson, Cin	35	R. Clemente, Pit	11
C. Flood, StL	160	B. Williams, ChN	648	R. Clemente, Pit	105	G. Beckert, ChN	188	F. Alou, Atl	32	3 tied with	10
B. White, Phi	159	L. Brock, StL	643	B. Williams, ChN	100	2 tied with	183	2 tied with	31		

Home Runs		Total Bases		Runs Batted In		Walks		Intentional Walks		Strikeouts	
H. Aaron, Atl	44	F. Alou, Atl	355	H. Aaron, Atl	127	R. Santo, ChN	95	L. Cardenas, Cin	18	B. Browne, ChN	143
D. Allen, Phi	40	R. Clemente, Pit	342	R. Clemente, Pit	119	J. Morgan, Hou	89	W. Stargell, Pit	16	D. Clendenon, Pit	142
W. Mays, SF	37	D. Allen, Phi	331	D. Allen, Phi	110	W. McCovey, SF	76	B. Williams, ChN	16	D. Allen, Phi	136
W. McCovey, SF	36	H. Aaron, Atl	325	B. White, Phi	103	H. Aaron, Atl	76	H. Aaron, Atl	15	A. Phillips, 2tm	135
J. Torre, Atl	36	W. Mays, SF	307	W. Mays, SF	103	D. Menke, Atl	71	4 tied with	13	L. Brock, StL	134

Hit By Pitch		Sac Hits		Sac Flies		Stolen Bases		Caught Stealing		GDP	
L. Johnson, LA	14	S. Jackson, Hou	27	O. Cepeda, 2tm	9	L. Brock, StL	74	M. Wills, LA	24	J. Hart, SF	23
O. Cepeda, 2tm	14	G. Alley, Pit	20	R. Staub, Hou	8	S. Jackson, Hou	49	L. Brock, StL	18	B. Aspromonte, Hou	22
A. Phillips, 2tm	12	W. Woodward, Atl	17	R. Santo, ChN	8	M. Wills, LA	38	A. Phillips, 2tm	15	H. Lanier, SF	20
F. Alou, Atl	12	D. Kessinger, ChN	15	H. Aaron, Atl	8	A. Phillips, 2tm	32	M. Alou, Pit	15	D. Groat, Phi	20
R. Hunt, NYN	11	M. Wills, LA	13	4 tied with	7	T. Harper, Cin	29	S. Jackson, Hou	14	L. Cardenas, Cin	19

Runs Created		Runs Created/27 Outs		Batting Average		On-Base Percentage		Slugging Percentage		OBP+Slugging	
D. Allen, Phi	124	D. Allen, Phi	8.94	M. Alou, Pit	.342	R. Santo, ChN	.412	D. Allen, Phi	.632	D. Allen, Phi	1.027
F. Alou, Atl	119	W. McCovey, SF	8.74	F. Alou, Atl	.327	J. Morgan, Hou	.410	W. McCovey, SF	.586	W. McCovey, SF	.977
W. McCovey, SF	118	W. Mays, SF	7.65	R. Carty, Atl	.326	D. Allen, Phi	.396	W. Stargell, Pit	.581	W. Stargell, Pit	.962
W. Mays, SF	116	W. Stargell, Pit	7.57	D. Allen, Phi	.317	W. McCovey, SF	.391	J. Torre, Atl	.560	R. Santo, ChN	.950
2 tied with	115	R. Santo, ChN	7.49	R. Clemente, Pit	.317	R. Carty, Atl	.391	W. Mays, SF	.556	J. Torre, Atl	.943

1966 National League Pitching Leaders

Wins		Losses		Winning Percentage		Games		Games Started		Complete Games	
S. Koufax, LA	27	D. Ellsworth, ChN	22	P. Regan, LA	.933	C. Carroll, Atl	73	J. Bunning, Phi	41	S. Koufax, LA	27
J. Marichal, SF	25	S. Ellis, Cin	19	J. Marichal, SF	.806	P. Mikkelsen, Pit	71	S. Koufax, LA	41	J. Marichal, SF	25
G. Perry, SF	21	K. Holtzman, ChN	16	S. Koufax, LA	.750	D. Knowles, Phi	69	D. Drysdale, LA	40	B. Gibson, StL	20
B. Gibson, StL	21	D. Drysdale, LA	16	G. Perry, SF	.724	P. Regan, LA	65	C. Short, Phi	39	C. Short, Phi	19
C. Short, Phi	20	3 tied with	15	L. Jaster, StL	.688	L. McDaniel, SF	64	2 tied with	38	J. Bunning, Phi	16

Shutouts		Saves		Games Finished		Batters Faced		Innings Pitched		Hits Allowed	
6 tied with	5	P. Regan, LA	21	P. Regan, LA	48	S. Koufax, LA	1274	S. Koufax, LA	323.0	D. Ellsworth, ChN	321
		B. McCool, Cin	18	B. McCool, Cin	45	J. Bunning, Phi	1254	J. Bunning, Phi	314.0	D. Drysdale, LA	279
		R. Face, Pit	18	C. Raymond, Hou	42	J. Marichal, SF	1180	J. Marichal, SF	307.1	J. Bunning, Phi	260
		F. Linzy, SF	16	R. Face, Pit	42	D. Ellsworth, ChN	1169	B. Gibson, StL	280.1	C. Short, Phi	257
		C. Raymond, Hou	16	2 tied with	39	D. Drysdale, LA	1135	D. Drysdale, LA	273.2	L. Jackson, 2tm	257

Home Runs Allowed		Walks		Walks/9 Innings		Strikeouts		Strikeouts/9 Innings		Strikeout/Walk Ratio	
S. Ellis, Cin	35	T. Cloninger, Atl	116	J. Marichal, SF	1.1	S. Koufax, LA	317	S. Koufax, LA	8.8	J. Marichal, SF	6.17
J. Marichal, SF	32	B. Veale, Pit	102	V. Law, SF	1.2	J. Bunning, Phi	252	J. Maloney, Cin	8.7	G. Perry, SF	5.03
T. Cloninger, Atl	29	J. Maloney, Cin	90	G. Perry, SF	1.4	B. Veale, Pit	229	D. Sutton, LA	8.3	J. Bunning, Phi	4.58
C. Short, Phi	28	J. Hamilton, NYN	88	D. Drysdale, LA	1.5	B. Gibson, StL	225	B. Veale, Pit	7.7	S. Koufax, LA	4.12
D. Ellsworth, ChN	28	2 tied with	78	J. Bunning, Phi	1.6	J. Marichal, SF	222	F. Jenkins, 2tm	7.3	D. Sutton, LA	4.02

Earned Run Average		Component ERA		Hit Batsmen		Wild Pitches		Opponent Average		Opponent OBP	
S. Koufax, LA	1.73	J. Marichal, SF	1.80	J. Bunning, Phi	19	T. Cloninger, Atl	27	J. Marichal, SF	.202	J. Marichal, SF	.230
M. Cuellar, Hou	2.22	S. Koufax, LA	1.92	D. Drysdale, LA	17	J. Hamilton, NYN	18	S. Koufax, LA	.205	S. Koufax, LA	.252
J. Marichal, SF	2.23	B. Gibson, StL	2.19	B. Bolin, SF	10	D. Giusti, Hou	14	B. Gibson, StL	.207	B. Gibson, StL	.265
J. Bunning, Phi	2.41	M. Cuellar, Hou	2.25	J. Maloney, Cin	10	B. Gibson, StL	12	B. Bolin, SF	.211	J. Bunning, Phi	.268
B. Gibson, StL	2.44	J. Bunning, Phi	2.42	2 tied with	9	J. Fisher, NYN	12	J. Maloney, Cin	.214	M. Cuellar, Hou	.273

1966 National League Miscellaneous

Managers

Atlanta	Bobby Bragan	52-59
	Billy Hitchcock	33-18
Chicago	Leo Durocher	59-103
Cincinnati	Don Heffner	37-46
	Dave Bristol	39-38
Houston	Grady Hatton	72-90
Los Angeles	Walter Alston	95-67
New York	Wes Westrum	66-95
Philadelphia	Gene Mauch	87-75
Pittsburgh	Harry Walker	92-70
St. Louis	Red Schoendienst	83-79
San Francisco	Herman Franks	93-68

Awards

Most Valuable Player	R. Clemente, of, Pit
Cy Young	Sandy Koufax, LA
Rookie of the Year	Tommy Helms, 3b, Cin
STATS Manager of the Year	Walter Alston, LA

STATS All-Star Team

C	Joe Torre, Atl	.315	36	101
1B	Willie McCovey, SF	.295	36	96
2B	Pete Rose, Cin	.313	16	70
3B	Dick Allen, Phi	.317	40	110
SS	Gene Alley, Pit	.299	7	43
OF	Hank Aaron, Atl	.279	44	127
OF	Roberto Clemente, Pit	.317	29	119
OF	Willie Mays, SF	.288	37	103
P	Jim Bunning, Phi	19-14	2.41	252 K
P	Bob Gibson, StL	21-12	2.44	225 K
P	Sandy Koufax, LA	27-9	1.73	317 K
P	Juan Marichal, SF	25-6	2.23	222 K
RP	Phil Regan, LA	14-1	1.62	21 Sv

Postseason

World Series	LA (NL) 0 vs. Baltimore (AL) 4

Outstanding Performances

Three-Homer Games

Gene Oliver, Atl	on July 30
Art Shamsky, Cin	on August 12
Willie McCovey, SF	on September 17

Cycles

Billy Williams, ChN	on July 17
Randy Hundley, ChN	on August 11

1967 American League Standings

Team	Overall					Home Games						Road Games						Park Index		Record by Month					
	W	L	Pct	GB	DIF	W	L	R	OR	HR	OHR	W	L	R	OR	HR	OHR	Run	HR	M/A	May	June	July	Aug	S/O
Boston	92	70	.568	—	5	49	32	408	355	90	88	43	38	314	259	68	54	133	146	8-6	14-14	15-14	19-10	20-15	16-11
Detroit	91	71	.562	1.0	34	52	29	360	272	83	79	39	42	323	315	69	72	99	115	10-6	16-9	12-18	15-12	21-14	17-12
Minnesota	91	71	.562	1.0	43	52	29	372	292	70	63	39	42	299	298	61	52	111	118	5-10	15-12	16-12	17-13	21-11	17-13
Chicago	89	73	.549	3.0	92	49	33	243	222	38	38	40	40	288	269	51	49	81	74	9-7	16-8	17-13	16-14	15-17	16-14
California	84	77	.522	7.5	3	53	24	288	276	56	59	31	47	279	311	58	59	90	92	8-9	10-18	20-11	17-11	11-16	18-12
Baltimore	76	85	.472	15.5	11	35	42	283	275	64	49	41	43	371	317	74	67	88	87	8-8	12-12	14-18	11-16	14-17	17-14
Washington	76	85	.472	15.5	0	40	40	277	332	57	54	36	45	273	305	58	59	107	96	7-8	12-15	13-18	19-12	13-17	12-15
Cleveland	75	87	.463	17.0	1	36	45	274	316	76	69	39	42	285	297	55	51	101	137	7-8	14-12	16-16	9-20	17-15	12-16
New York	72	90	.444	20.0	6	43	38	268	271	60	47	29	52	254	350	40	63	89	104	9-6	9-16	15-16	11-18	15-19	13-15
Kansas City	62	99	.385	29.5	3	37	44	288	320	19	38	25	55	245	340	50	87	103	41	6-9	13-15	15-17	10-18	11-17	7-23

Clinch Date—Boston 10/01.

Team Batting

Team	G	AB	R	OR	H	2B	3B	HR	TB	RBI	TBB	IBB	SO	HBP	SH	SF	SB	CS	SB%	GDP	Avg	OBP	Slg
Boston	162	5471	722	614	1394	216	39	158	2162	666	522	65	1020	31	85	40	68	59	.54	103	.255	.328	.395
Detroit	163	5410	683	587	1315	192	36	152	2035	619	626	54	994	51	78	35	37	21	.64	114	.243	.331	.376
Minnesota	164	5458	671	590	1309	216	48	131	2014	619	512	52	976	46	66	34	55	37	.60	114	.240	.314	.369
Baltimore	161	5456	654	592	1312	215	44	138	2029	624	531	67	1002	41	82	54	54	37	.59	103	.240	.319	.372
California	161	5307	567	587	1265	170	37	114	1851	524	453	49	1021	31	40	36	43	36	.53	114	.238	.305	.349
Cleveland	162	5461	559	613	1282	213	35	131	1958	514	413	38	984	50	85	28	53	65	.45	102	.235	.298	.359
Washington	161	5441	550	637	1211	168	25	115	1774	521	472	34	1037	37	63	31	53	37	.59	114	.223	.293	.326
Kansas City	161	5349	533	660	1244	212	50	69	1763	481	452	39	1019	42	59	36	132	59	.69	79	.233	.302	.330
Chicago	162	5383	531	491	1209	181	34	89	1725	491	480	56	1019	38	67	32	124	82	.60	102	.225	.296	.320
New York	163	5443	522	621	1225	166	17	100	1725	473	532	37	1043	30	78	35	63	37	.63	115	.225	.302	.317
AL Total	1620	54179	5992	5992	12766	1949	365	1197	19036	5532	4993	491	9945	397	751	348	679	470	.59	1060	.236	.303	.351
AL Avg Team	162	5418	599	599	1277	195	37	120	1904	553	499	49	995	40	75	35	68	47	.59	106	.236	.303	.351

Team Pitching

Team	G	CG	ShO	Rel	Sv	IP	H	R	ER	HR	SH	SF	HB	TBB	IBB	SO	WP	Bk	H/9	SO/9	BB/9	OAvg	OOBP	ERA
Chicago	162	36	24	292	39	1490.1	1197	491	406	87	71	26	58	465	46	927	54	6	7.2	5.6	2.8	.219	.287	2.45
Minnesota	164	58	18	219	24	1461.0	1336	590	509	115	74	34	40	396	48	1089	49	3	8.2	6.7	2.4	.243	.296	3.14
California	161	19	14	301	46	1430.1	1246	587	507	118	74	44	40	525	58	892	61	7	7.8	5.6	3.3	.237	.308	3.19
New York	163	37	16	251	27	1480.2	1375	621	533	110	93	50	38	480	68	898	32	2	8.4	5.5	2.9	.249	.310	3.24
Cleveland	162	49	14	236	27	1477.2	1258	613	533	120	84	35	33	559	48	1189	64	6	7.7	7.2	3.4	.231	.305	3.25
Detroit	163	46	17	254	40	1443.2	1230	587	532	151	66	35	37	472	24	1038	44	2	7.7	6.5	2.9	.230	.295	3.32
Baltimore	161	29	17	248	36	1457.1	1218	592	538	116	73	24	30	566	34	1034	59	5	7.5	6.4	3.5	.228	.304	3.32
Boston	162	41	9	254	44	1459.1	1307	614	545	142	76	29	47	477	44	1010	56	4	8.1	6.2	2.9	.239	.304	3.36
Washington	161	24	14	330	39	1473.1	1334	637	554	113	60	44	37	495	56	878	44	8	8.1	5.4	3.0	.242	.307	3.38
Kansas City	161	26	10	265	34	1428.0	1265	660	584	125	80	28	37	558	65	990	44	4	8.0	6.2	3.5	.238	.313	3.68
AL Total	1620	365	153	2650	356	14601.2	12766	5992	5241	1197	751	348	397	4993	491	9945	507	47	7.9	6.1	3.1	.236	.309	3.23
AL Avg Team	162	37	15	265	36	1460.2	1277	599	524	120	75	35	40	499	49	995	51	5	7.9	6.1	3.1	.236	.309	3.23

Team Fielding

Team	G	PO	A	E	TC	DP	PB	Pct
California	161	4286	1707	111	6104	135	13	.982
Cleveland	162	4431	1602	116	6149	138	29	.981
Baltimore	161	4360	1708	124	6192	144	17	.980
Chicago	162	4462	1949	138	6549	149	30	.979
Detroit	163	4328	1663	132	6123	126	19	.978
Minnesota	164	4383	1595	132	6110	123	14	.978
Kansas City	161	4279	1533	132	5944	120	17	.978
Washington	161	4431	1863	144	6438	167	16	.978
Boston	162	4374	1650	142	6166	142	8	.977
New York	163	4441	1936	154	6531	144	8	.976
AL Total	1620	43775	17206	1325	62306	1388	171	.979

Team vs. Team Records

	Bal	Bos	Cal	ChA	Cle	Det	KCA	Min	NYA	Was	Won
Bal	—	10	6	7	9	3	10	8	13	10	76
Bos	8	—	10	8	13	11	12	7	12	11	92
Cal	11	8	—	7	14	8	14	7	9	6	84
ChA	11	10	11	—	12	8	8	9	12	8	89
Cle	9	5	4	6	—	8	11	10	9	13	75
Det	15	7	10	10	10	—	12	8	10	9	91
KCA	8	6	4	10	7	6	—	8	7	6	62
Min	10	11	11	9	8	10	10	—	12	10	91
NYA	5	6	9	6	9	8	11	6	—	12	72
Was	8	7	12	10	5	9	11	8	6	—	76
Lost	85	70	77	73	87	71	99	71	90	85	

1967 American League Batting Leaders

Games		At-Bats		Runs		Hits		Doubles		Triples	
C. Tovar, Min	164	C. Tovar, Min	649	C. Yastrzemski, Bos	112	C. Yastrzemski, Bos	189	T. Oliva, Min	34	P. Blair, Bal	12
H. Killebrew, Min	163	M. Alvis, Cle	637	H. Killebrew, Min	105	C. Tovar, Min	173	C. Tovar, Min	32	D. Buford, ChA	9
C. Yastrzemski, Bos	161	B. Robinson, Bal	610	C. Tovar, Min	98	G. Scott, Bos	171	C. Yastrzemski, Bos	31	7 tied with	7
M. Alvis, Cle	161	B. Campaneris, KCA	601	A. Kaline, Det	94	J. Fregosi, Cal	171	D. Johnson, Bal	30		
Z. Versalles, Min	160	J. Fregosi, Cal	590	D. McAuliffe, Det	92	B. Robinson, Bal	164	B. Campaneris, KCA	29		

Home Runs		Total Bases		Runs Batted In		Walks		Intentional Walks		Strikeouts	
C. Yastrzemski, Bos	44	C. Yastrzemski, Bos	360	C. Yastrzemski, Bos	121	H. Killebrew, Min	131	B. Freehan, Det	15	F. Howard, Was	155
H. Killebrew, Min	44	H. Killebrew, Min	305	H. Killebrew, Min	113	M. Mantle, NYA	107	H. Killebrew, Min	15	B. Knoop, Cal	136
F. Howard, Was	36	F. Robinson, Bal	276	F. Robinson, Bal	94	D. McAuliffe, Det	105	F. Robinson, Bal	14	G. Scott, Bos	119
F. Robinson, Bal	30	F. Howard, Was	265	F. Howard, Was	89	C. Yastrzemski, Bos	91	B. Knoop, Cal	13	D. McAuliffe, Det	118
2 tied with	25	B. Robinson, Bal	265	T. Oliva, Min	83	A. Kaline, Det	83	T. Oliva, Min	12		

Hit By Pitch		Sac Hits		Sac Flies		Stolen Bases		Caught Stealing		GDP	
B. Freehan, Det	20	M. Andrews, Bos	18	D. Johnson, Bal	8	B. Campaneris, KCA	55	D. Buford, ChA	21	B. Robinson, Bal	21
C. Tovar, Min	13	M. Alvis, Cle	16	B. Robinson, Bal	8	D. Buford, ChA	34	B. Campaneris, KCA	16	P. Casanova, Was	19
L. Wagner, Cle	12	R. Oyler, Det	15	H. Killebrew, Min	8	T. Agee, ChA	28	C. Tovar, Min	11	5 tied with	16
P. Ward, ChA	11	L. Brown, Cle	14	P. Blair, Bal	7	T. McCraw, ChA	24	3 tied with	10		
F. Valentine, Was	10	2 tied with	13	M. Hershberger, KCA	7	H. Clarke, NYA	21				

Runs Created		Runs Created/27 Outs		Batting Average		On-Base Percentage		Slugging Percentage		OBP+Slugging	
C. Yastrzemski, Bos	148	C. Yastrzemski, Bos	9.84	C. Yastrzemski, Bos	.326	C. Yastrzemski, Bos	.418	C. Yastrzemski, Bos	.622	C. Yastrzemski, Bos	1.040
H. Killebrew, Min	133	H. Killebrew, Min	8.53	F. Robinson, Bal	.311	A. Kaline, Det	.411	F. Robinson, Bal	.576	F. Robinson, Bal	.979
F. Robinson, Bal	108	F. Robinson, Bal	8.41	A. Kaline, Det	.308	H. Killebrew, Min	.408	H. Killebrew, Min	.558	H. Killebrew, Min	.965
G. Scott, Bos	99	A. Kaline, Det	7.85	G. Scott, Bos	.303	F. Robinson, Bal	.403	A. Kaline, Det	.541	A. Kaline, Det	.952
A. Kaline, Det	99	B. Allison, Min	6.56	P. Blair, Bal	.293	M. Mantle, NYA	.391	F. Howard, Was	.511	D. Mincher, Cal	.854

1967 American League Pitching Leaders

Wins		Losses		Winning Percentage		Games		Games Started		Complete Games	
J. Lonborg, Bos	22	G. Brunet, Cal	19	J. Santiago, Bos	.750	B. Locker, ChA	77	J. Lonborg, Bos	39	D. Chance, Min	18
E. Wilson, Det	22	S. Barber, 2tm	18	J. Horlen, ChA	.731	M. Rojas, Cal	72	D. Chance, Min	39	J. Lonborg, Bos	15
D. Chance, Min	20	C. Hunter, KCA	17	J. Lonborg, Bos	.710	B. Kelso, Cal	69	J. Kaat, Min	38	S. Hargan, Cle	15
J. Horlen, ChA	19	J. Nash, KCA	17	E. Wilson, Det	.667	D. Womack, NYA	65	E. Wilson, Det	38	3 tied with	13
D. McLain, Det	17	L. Krausse, KCA	17	J. Merritt, Min	.650	D. McMahon, 2tm	63	4 tied with	37		

Shutouts		Saves		Games Finished		Batters Faced		Innings Pitched		Hits Allowed	
T. John, ChA	6	M. Rojas, Cal	27	M. Rojas, Cal	53	D. Chance, Min	1161	D. Chance, Min	283.2	J. Kaat, Min	269
M. Lolich, Det	6	B. Locker, ChA	20	D. Womack, NYA	48	J. Lonborg, Bos	1130	J. Lonborg, Bos	273.1	D. Chance, Min	244
J. McGlothlin, Cal	6	J. Wyatt, Bos	20	B. Locker, ChA	47	J. Kaat, Min	1100	E. Wilson, Det	264.0	M. Stottlemyre, NYA	235
S. Hargan, Cle	6	D. Womack, NYA	18	A. Worthington, Min	44	E. Wilson, Det	1083	J. Kaat, Min	263.1	J. Lonborg, Bos	228
J. Horlen, ChA	6	A. Worthington, Min	16	J. Wyatt, Bos	43	M. Stottlemyre, NYA	1063	G. Peters, ChA	260.0	E. Wilson, Det	216

Home Runs Allowed		Walks		Walks/9 Innings		Strikeouts		Strikeouts/9 Innings		Strikeout/Walk Ratio	
D. McLain, Det	35	S. McDowell, Cle	123	J. Merritt, Min	1.2	J. Lonborg, Bos	246	L. Tiant, Cle	9.2	J. Merritt, Min	5.37
E. Wilson, Det	34	S. Barber, 2tm	115	J. Kaat, Min	1.4	S. McDowell, Cle	236	S. McDowell, Cle	9.0	J. Kaat, Min	5.02
L. Tiant, Cle	24	T. Phoebus, Bal	114	L. Stange, Bos	1.6	D. Chance, Min	220	D. Boswell, Min	8.2	L. Tiant, Cle	3.27
J. Lonborg, Bos	23	D. Boswell, Min	107	J. Horlen, ChA	2.0	L. Tiant, Cle	219	J. Lonborg, Bos	8.1	D. Chance, Min	3.24
G. Bell, 2tm	23	E. Wilson, Det	92	F. Peterson, NYA	2.1	G. Peters, ChA	215	T. Phoebus, Bal	7.7	L. Stange, Bos	3.16

Earned Run Average		Component ERA		Hit Batsmen		Wild Pitches		Opponent Average		Opponent OBP	
J. Horlen, ChA	2.06	J. Horlen, ChA	1.84	J. Lonborg, Bos	19	S. McDowell, Cle	18	G. Peters, ChA	.199	J. Horlen, ChA	.253
G. Peters, ChA	2.28	G. Peters, ChA	2.25	G. Peters, ChA	11	S. Barber, 2tm	14	D. Boswell, Min	.202	J. Merritt, Min	.260
S. Siebert, Cle	2.38	S. Siebert, Cle	2.33	B. Locker, ChA	10	J. McGlothlin, Cal	13	S. Siebert, Cle	.202	S. Siebert, Cle	.266
T. John, ChA	2.47	J. Merritt, Min	2.35	J. Kaat, Min	9	3 tied with	12	J. Horlen, ChA	.203	T. John, ChA	.275
J. Merritt, Min	2.53	T. John, ChA	2.39	J. Coleman, Was	9			A. Downing, NYA	.217	G. Peters, ChA	.276

1967 American League Miscellaneous

Managers

Baltimore	Hank Bauer	76-85
Boston	Dick Williams	92-70
California	Bill Rigney	84-77
Chicago	Eddie Stanky	89-73
Cleveland	Joe Adcock	75-87
Detroit	Mayo Smith	91-71
Kansas City	Alvin Dark	52-69
	Luke Appling	10-30
Minnesota	Sam Mele	25-25
	Cal Ermer	66-46
New York	Ralph Houk	72-90
Washington	Gil Hodges	76-85

Awards

Most Valuable Player	C. Yastrzemski, of, Bos
Cy Young	Jim Lonborg, Bos
Rookie of the Year	Rod Carew, 2b, Min
STATS Manager of the Year	Dick Williams, Bos

STATS All-Star Team

C	Bill Freehan, Det	.282	20	74
1B	Harmon Killebrew, Min	.269	44	113
2B	Dick McAuliffe, Det	.239	22	65
3B	Brooks Robinson, Bal	.269	22	77
SS	Jim Fregosi, Cal	.290	9	56
OF	Al Kaline, Det	.308	25	78
OF	Frank Robinson, Bal	.311	30	94
OF	Carl Yastrzemski, Bos	.326	44	121
P	Dean Chance, Min	20-14	2.73	220 K
P	Joe Horlen, ChA	19-7	2.06	103 K
P	Jim Lonborg, Bos	22-9	3.16	246 K
P	Gary Peters, ChA	16-11	2.28	215 K
RP	Minnie Rojas, Cal	12-9	2.52	27 Sv

Postseason

World Series	Boston (AL) 3 vs. St. Louis (NL) 4

Outstanding Performances

Triple Crown
C. Yastrzemski, Bos .326-44-121
No-Hitters
Dean Chance, Min @ Cle on August 25
Joe Horlen, ChA vs. Det on September 10
Three-Homer Games
Tom McCraw, ChA on May 24
Curt Blefary, Bal on June 6

Team	Overall					Home Games						Road Games						Park Index		Record by Month					
	W	L	Pct	GB	DIF	W	L	R	OR	HR	OHR	W	L	R	OR	HR	OHR	Run	HR	M/A	May	June	July	Aug	S/O
St. Louis	101	60	.627	—	119	49	32	326	301	53	54	52	28	369	256	62	43	99	101	9-6	15-10	20-11	18-13	21-11	18-9
San Francisco	91	71	.562	10.5	0	51	31	333	271	65	59	40	40	319	280	75	54	98	94	7-9	17-10	16-16	14-15	16-14	21-7
Chicago	87	74	.540	14.0	5	49	34	366	332	70	90	38	40	336	292	58	52	104	137	8-6	14-13	21-10	15-16	14-17	15-12
Cincinnati	87	75	.537	14.5	57	49	32	343	287	57	66	38	43	261	276	52	35	117	141	15-5	15-13	13-15	12-17	18-11	14-14
Philadelphia	82	80	.506	19.5	0	45	35	320	292	48	44	37	45	292	289	55	42	108	97	8-8	10-15	17-14	13-14	20-11	14-18
Pittsburgh	81	81	.500	20.5	2	49	32	370	321	43	49	32	49	309	372	48	59	101	86	7-5	16-13	13-17	13-16	15-18	17-12
Atlanta	77	85	.475	24.5	0	48	33	352	316	91	74	29	52	279	324	67	44	111	149	9-7	13-14	15-15	15-11	15-17	10-21
Los Angeles	73	89	.451	28.5	0	42	39	241	230	36	35	31	50	278	365	46	58	73	68	6-10	13-14	14-16	13-15	14-16	13-18
Houston	69	93	.426	32.5	2	46	35	337	315	31	32	23	58	289	427	62	88	91	42	5-13	11-15	11-19	19-12	9-21	14-13
New York	61	101	.377	40.5	0	36	42	258	307	44	61	25	59	240	365	39	63	101	111	6-11	8-15	11-18	14-17	12-18	10-22

Clinch Date—St. Louis 9/18.

Team Batting

Team	G	AB	R	OR	H	2B	3B	HR	TB	RBI	TBB	IBB	SO	HBP	SH	SF	SB	CS	SB%	GDP	Avg	OBP	Slg
Chicago	162	5463	702	624	1373	211	49	128	2066	642	509	84	912	34	93	49	63	50	.56	112	.251	.325	.378
St. Louis	161	5566	695	557	1462	225	40	115	2112	656	443	77	919	45	54	44	102	54	.65	105	.263	.327	.379
Pittsburgh	163	5724	679	693	1585	193	62	140	2175	615	387	97	914	36	63	45	79	37	.68	131	.277	.332	.380
San Francisco	162	5524	652	551	1354	201	39	140	2053	604	520	75	978	42	92	27	22	30	.42	121	.245	.318	.372
Atlanta	162	5450	631	640	1307	191	29	158	2030	596	512	73	947	33	57	36	55	45	.55	128	.240	.313	.372
Houston	162	5506	626	742	1372	259	46	93	2002	581	537	88	934	26	65	43	88	38	.70	123	.249	.324	.364
Philadelphia	162	5401	612	581	1306	221	47	103	1930	553	545	101	1033	27	90	33	79	62	.56	108	.242	.318	.357
Cincinnati	162	5519	604	563	1366	251	54	109	2052	560	372	74	969	31	56	34	92	63	.59	111	.248	.303	.372
Los Angeles	162	5456	519	595	1285	203	38	82	1810	465	485	75	881	43	91	35	56	47	.54	133	.236	.307	.332
New York	162	5417	498	672	1288	178	23	83	1761	461	362	60	981	37	68	44	58	44	.57	113	.238	.295	.325
NL Total	1620	55026	6218	6218	13698	2133	427	1102	19991	5733	4672	804	9468	354	729	390	694	470	.60	1185	.249	.310	.363
NL Avg Team	162	5503	622	622	1370	213	43	110	1999	573	467	80	947	35	73	39	69	47	.60	119	.249	.310	.363

Team Pitching

Team	G	CG	ShO	Rel	Sv	IP	H	R	ER	HR	SH	SF	HB	TBB	IBB	SO	WP	Bk	H/9	SO/9	BB/9	OAvg	OOBP	ERA
San Francisco	162	64	17	215	25	1474.1	1283	551	478	113	77	31	27	453	93	990	48	5	7.8	6.0	2.8	.234	.294	2.92
Cincinnati	162	34	18	235	39	1468.0	1328	563	497	101	58	43	42	498	62	1065	59	4	8.1	6.5	3.1	.241	.306	3.05
St. Louis	161	44	17	272	45	1465.0	1313	557	496	97	68	40	35	431	76	956	38	7	8.1	5.9	2.6	.239	.297	3.05
Philadelphia	162	46	17	214	23	1453.2	1372	581	501	86	76	31	41	403	85	967	37	4	8.5	6.0	2.5	.250	.304	3.10
Los Angeles	162	41	17	229	24	1473.0	1421	595	526	93	77	38	38	393	101	967	39	8	8.7	5.9	2.4	.254	.306	3.21
Atlanta	162	35	5	276	32	1454.0	1377	640	561	118	79	41	40	449	85	862	59	5	8.5	5.3	2.8	.251	.310	3.47
Chicago	162	47	7	244	28	1457.0	1352	624	564	142	58	43	28	463	74	888	35	2	8.4	5.5	2.9	.246	.306	3.48
New York	162	36	10	277	19	1433.2	1369	672	594	124	78	43	28	536	88	893	54	6	8.6	5.6	3.4	.253	.321	3.73
Pittsburgh	163	35	5	283	35	1458.1	1439	693	606	108	73	41	32	561	93	820	40	5	8.9	5.1	3.5	.261	.330	3.74
Houston	162	35	8	294	21	1445.2	1444	742	647	120	85	39	43	485	47	1060	69	8	9.0	6.6	3.0	.260	.322	4.03
NL Total	1620	417	121	2539	291	14582.2	13698	6218	5470	1102	729	390	354	4672	804	9468	478	54	8.5	5.8	2.9	.249	.316	3.38
NL Avg Team	162	42	12	254	29	1458.2	1370	622	547	110	73	39	35	467	80	947	48	5	8.5	5.8	2.9	.249	.316	3.38

Team Fielding

Team	G	PO	A	E	TC	DP	PB	Pct
Chicago	162	4371	1850	121	6342	143	4	.981
Cincinnati	162	4404	1598	121	6123	124	12	.980
San Francisco	162	4424	1902	134	6460	149	18	.979
Philadelphia	162	4360	1795	137	6292	174	16	.978
Pittsburgh	163	4339	1981	141	6461	186	15	.978
Atlanta	162	4362	1801	138	6301	148	42	.978
St. Louis	161	4395	1719	140	6254	127	10	.978
Los Angeles	162	4419	1899	160	6478	144	13	.975
New York	162	4301	1824	157	6282	147	22	.975
Houston	162	4337	1657	159	6153	120	23	.974
NL Total	1620	43712	18026	1408	63146	1462	175	.978

Team vs. Team Records

	Atl	ChN	Cin	Hou	LA	NYN	Phi	Pit	SF	StL	Won
Atl	—	11	5	11	8	8	10	8	10	6	77
ChN	7	—	12	8	9	13	11	11	10	6	87
Cin	13	6	—	15	8	12	10	10	8	5	87
Hou	7	10	3	—	10	11	7	9	6	6	69
LA	9	9	10	8	—	12	6	7	5	6	73
NYN	10	5	6	7	6	—	4	11	5	7	61
Phi	8	7	8	11	12	14	—	8	8	6	82
Pit	10	7	8	9	11	7	10	—	8	11	81
SF	8	8	10	12	13	13	10	10	—	7	91
StL	12	11	13	12	12	11	12	7	11	—	101
Lost	85	74	75	93	89	101	80	81	71	60	

1967 National League Batting Leaders

Games		At-Bats		Runs		Hits		Doubles		Triples	
B. Mazeroski, Pit	163	L. Brock, StL	689	L. Brock, StL	113	R. Clemente, Pit	209	R. Staub, Hou	44	V. Pinson, Cin	13
B. Williams, ChN	162	V. Pinson, Cin	650	H. Aaron, Atl	113	L. Brock, StL	206	O. Cepeda, StL	37	L. Brock, StL	12
R. Santo, ChN	161	B. Mazeroski, Pit	639	R. Santo, ChN	107	V. Pinson, Cin	187	H. Aaron, Atl	37	B. Williams, ChN	12
L. Brock, StL	159	B. Williams, ChN	634	R. Clemente, Pit	103	M. Alou, Pit	186	4 tied with	32	J. Morgan, Hou	11
3 tied with	158	M. Wills, Pit	616	J. Wynn, Hou	102	M. Wills, Pit	186			2 tied with	10

Home Runs		Total Bases		Runs Batted In		Walks		Intentional Walks		Strikeouts	
H. Aaron, Atl	39	H. Aaron, Atl	344	O. Cepeda, StL	111	R. Santo, ChN	96	A. Phillips, ChN	29	J. Wynn, Hou	137
J. Wynn, Hou	37	L. Brock, StL	325	R. Clemente, Pit	110	J. Morgan, Hou	81	W. Stargell, Pit	25	D. Allen, Phi	117
W. McCovey, SF	31	R. Clemente, Pit	324	H. Aaron, Atl	109	A. Phillips, ChN	80	O. Cepeda, StL	23	W. McCovey, SF	110
R. Santo, ChN	31	B. Williams, ChN	305	J. Wynn, Hou	107	J. Hart, SF	77	R. Staub, Hou	21	L. Brock, StL	109
J. Hart, SF	29	R. Santo, ChN	300	T. Perez, Cin	102	D. Allen, Phi	75	3 tied with	19	M. Jones, Atl	108

Hit By Pitch		Sac Hits		Sac Flies		Stolen Bases		Caught Stealing		GDP	
O. Cepeda, StL	12	C. Rojas, Phi	16	R. Santo, ChN	12	L. Brock, StL	52	L. Brock, StL	18	J. Torre, Atl	22
L. May, Cin	10	G. Perry, SF	15	M. Mota, Pit	8	J. Morgan, Hou	29	B. Harrelson, NYN	13	E. Banks, ChN	20
R. Hunt, LA	10	H. Lanier, SF	13	R. Fairly, LA	8	M. Wills, Pit	29	D. Kessinger, ChN	13	4 tied with	17
M. Jones, Atl	9	M. Wills, Pit	12	3 tied with	7	V. Pinson, Cin	26	J. Callison, Phi	12		
6 tied with	7	2 tied with	11			A. Phillips, ChN	24	4 tied with	10		

Runs Created		Runs Created/27 Outs		Batting Average		On-Base Percentage		Slugging Percentage		OBP+Slugging	
H. Aaron, Atl	124	D. Allen, Phi	8.43	R. Clemente, Pit	.357	D. Allen, Phi	.404	H. Aaron, Atl	.573	D. Allen, Phi	.970
R. Santo, ChN	123	R. Clemente, Pit	7.99	T. Gonzalez, Phi	.339	R. Clemente, Pit	.400	D. Allen, Phi	.566	R. Clemente, Pit	.954
R. Clemente, Pit	116	O. Cepeda, StL	7.73	M. Alou, Pit	.338	O. Cepeda, StL	.399	R. Clemente, Pit	.554	H. Aaron, Atl	.943
O. Cepeda, StL	115	H. Aaron, Atl	7.69	C. Flood, StL	.335	R. Staub, Hou	.398	W. McCovey, SF	.535	O. Cepeda, StL	.923
B. Williams, ChN	111	R. Santo, ChN	7.54	R. Staub, Hou	.333	T. Gonzalez, Phi	.396	O. Cepeda, StL	.524	W. McCovey, SF	.913

1967 National League Pitching Leaders

Wins		Losses		Winning Percentage		Games		Games Started		Complete Games	
M. McCormick, SF	22	J. Fisher, NYN	18	N. Briles, StL	.737	R. Perranoski, LA	70	J. Bunning, Phi	40	F. Jenkins, ChN	20
F. Jenkins, ChN	20	G. Perry, SF	17	D. Hughes, StL	.727	T. Abernathy, Cin	70	C. Osteen, LA	39	G. Perry, SF	18
C. Osteen, LA	17	C. Osteen, LA	17	M. McCormick, SF	.688	R. Willis, StL	65	F. Jenkins, ChN	38	T. Seaver, NYN	18
J. Bunning, Phi	17	D. Drysdale, LA	16	B. Veale, Pit	.667	R. Face, Pit	61	D. Drysdale, LA	38	J. Marichal, SF	18
5 tied with	16	4 tied with	15	R. Sadecki, SF	.667	3 tied with	57	2 tied with	37	2 tied with	16

Shutouts		Saves		Games Finished		Batters Faced		Innings Pitched		Hits Allowed	
J. Bunning, Phi	6	T. Abernathy, Cin	28	T. Abernathy, Cin	61	J. Bunning, Phi	1216	J. Bunning, Phi	302.1	C. Osteen, LA	298
G. Nolan, Cin	5	F. Linzy, SF	17	R. Perranoski, LA	47	C. Osteen, LA	1187	G. Perry, SF	293.0	D. Drysdale, LA	269
C. Osteen, LA	5	R. Face, Pit	17	R. Face, Pit	45	G. Perry, SF	1178	F. Jenkins, ChN	289.1	J. Fisher, NYN	251
M. McCormick, SF	5	R. Perranoski, LA	16	F. Linzy, SF	44	F. Jenkins, ChN	1156	C. Osteen, LA	288.1	L. Jackson, Phi	242
L. Jackson, Phi	4	J. Hoerner, StL	15	D. Hall, Phi	37	D. Drysdale, LA	1151	D. Drysdale, LA	282.0	J. Bunning, Phi	241

Home Runs Allowed		Walks		Walks/9 Innings		Strikeouts		Strikeouts/9 Innings		Strikeout/Walk Ratio	
F. Jenkins, ChN	30	B. Veale, Pit	119	M. Pappas, Cin	1.6	J. Bunning, Phi	253	G. Nolan, Cin	8.2	J. Marichal, SF	3.95
M. McCormick, SF	25	G. Perry, SF	84	C. Osteen, LA	1.6	F. Jenkins, ChN	236	B. Veale, Pit	7.9	B. Gibson, StL	3.67
D. Hughes, StL	22	F. Jenkins, ChN	83	K. Johnson, Atl	1.6	G. Perry, SF	230	S. Carlton, StL	7.8	J. Bunning, Phi	3.47
R. Culp, ChN	22	M. McCormick, SF	81	J. Niekro, ChN	1.7	G. Nolan, Cin	206	D. Wilson, Hou	7.8	M. Pappas, Cin	3.39
J. Fisher, NYN	21	2 tied with	78	L. Jackson, Phi	1.9	M. Cuellar, Hou	203	B. Gibson, StL	7.5	D. Hughes, StL	3.35

Earned Run Average		Component ERA		Hit Batsmen		Wild Pitches		Opponent Average		Opponent OBP	
P. Niekro, Atl	1.87	D. Hughes, StL	2.09	J. Bunning, Phi	13	P. Niekro, Atl	19	D. Hughes, StL	.203	D. Hughes, StL	.251
J. Bunning, Phi	2.29	J. Bunning, Phi	2.24	B. Singer, LA	8	B. Belinsky, Hou	16	D. Wilson, Hou	.209	J. Bunning, Phi	.271
C. Short, Phi	2.39	P. Niekro, Atl	2.27	B. Belinsky, Hou	8	G. Perry, SF	13	G. Perry, SF	.214	M. Queen, Cin	.271
G. Nolan, Cin	2.58	G. Perry, SF	2.32	D. Drysdale, LA	8	J. Maloney, Cin	13	M. Queen, Cin	.215	G. Perry, SF	.273
G. Perry, SF	2.61	M. Queen, Cin	2.47	4 tied with	7	B. Veale, Pit	11	J. Bunning, Phi	.217	P. Niekro, Atl	.275

1967 National League Miscellaneous

Managers

Atlanta	Billy Hitchcock	77-82
	Ken Silvestri	0-3
Chicago	Leo Durocher	87-74
Cincinnati	Dave Bristol	87-75
Houston	Grady Hatton	69-93
Los Angeles	Walter Alston	73-89
New York	Wes Westrum	57-94
	Salty Parker	4-7
Philadelphia	Gene Mauch	82-80
Pittsburgh	Harry Walker	42-42
	Danny Murtaugh	39-39
St. Louis	Red Schoendienst	101-60
San Francisco	Herman Franks	91-71

Awards

Most Valuable Player	O. Cepeda, 1b, StL
Cy Young	Mike McCormick, SF
Rookie of the Year	Tom Seaver, p, NYN
STATS Manager of the Year	Red Schoendienst, StL

STATS All-Star Team

C	Tim McCarver, StL	.295	14	69
1B	Orlando Cepeda, StL	.325	25	111
2B	Joe Morgan, Hou	.275	6	42
3B	Ron Santo, ChN	.300	31	98
SS	Gene Alley, Pit	.287	6	55
OF	Hank Aaron, Atl	.307	39	109
OF	Roberto Clemente, Pit	.357	23	110
OF	Jimmy Wynn, Hou	.249	37	107
P	Jim Bunning, Phi	17-15	2.29	253 K
P	Fergie Jenkins, ChN	20-13	2.80	236 K
P	Mike McCormick, SF	22-10	2.85	150 K
P	Gary Nolan, Cin	14-8	2.58	206 K
RP	Ted Abernathy, Cin	6-3	1.27	28 Sv

Postseason

World Series	St. Louis (NL) 4 vs. Boston (AL) 3

Outstanding Performances

No-Hitters

Don Wilson, Hou	vs. Atl on June 18

Three-Homer Games

R. Clemente, Pit	on May 15
Adolfo Phillips, ChN	on June 11
Jimmy Wynn, Hou	on June 15

1968 American League Standings

Team	Overall W	L	Pct	GB	DIF	Home Games W	L	R	OR	HR	OHR	Road Games W	L	R	OR	HR	OHR	Park Index Run	HR	Record by Month M/A	May	June	July	Aug	S/O
Detroit	103	59	.636	—	158	56	25	348	254	107	75	47	34	323	238	78	54	107	138	12-5	16-11	20-11	17-12	20-12	18-8
Baltimore	91	71	.562	12.0	11	47	33	288	248	57	54	44	38	291	249	76	47	102	93	10-6	16-13	12-15	19-11	22-12	12-14
Cleveland	86	75	.534	16.5	1	43	37	246	262	36	56	43	38	270	242	39	42	100	115	6-11	20-9	16-16	16-12	15-19	13-8
Boston	86	76	.531	17.0	1	46	35	325	299	58	61	40	41	289	312	67	54	104	98	8-8	14-15	13-15	19-10	19-16	13-12
New York	83	79	.512	20.0	3	39	42	268	268	56	50	44	37	268	263	53	49	101	104	8-9	13-15	12-15	15-13	19-16	16-11
Oakland	82	80	.506	21.0	0	44	38	296	258	38	58	38	42	273	286	56	66	97	77	8-10	13-14	17-12	15-15	16-17	13-12
Minnesota	79	83	.488	24.0	10	41	40	299	290	50	51	38	43	263	256	55	41	113	105	11-6	13-15	14-14	10-19	18-17	13-12
California	67	95	.414	36.0	0	32	49	229	299	49	66	35	46	269	316	34	65	90	116	8-10	14-15	15-13	11-18	13-21	6-18
Chicago	67	95	.414	36.0	0	36	45	225	273	29	47	31	50	238	254	42	50	101	83	2-12	16-13	13-15	14-15	12-24	10-16
Washington	65	96	.404	37.5	0	34	47	257	300	53	53	31	49	267	365	71	65	87	77	11-7	6-21	10-16	9-20	17-17	12-15

Clinch Date—Detroit 9/17.

Team Batting

Team	G	AB	R	OR	H	2B	3B	HR	TB	RBI	TBB	IBB	SO	HBP	SH	SF	SB	CS	SB%	GDP	Avg	OBP	Slg
Detroit	164	5490	671	492	1292	190	39	185	2115	640	521	53	964	61	73	34	26	32	.45	124	.235	.312	.385
Boston	162	5303	614	611	1253	207	17	125	1869	558	582	58	974	33	77	41	76	62	.55	121	.236	.320	.352
Baltimore	162	5275	579	497	1187	215	28	133	1857	534	570	63	1019	48	80	49	78	32	.71	102	.225	.312	.352
Oakland	163	5406	569	544	1300	192	40	94	1854	522	472	53	1022	35	78	35	147	61	.71	87	.240	.310	.343
Minnesota	162	5373	562	546	1274	207	41	105	1878	522	445	61	966	49	69	38	98	54	.64	106	.237	.310	.350
New York	164	5310	536	531	1137	154	34	109	1686	501	566	52	958	30	56	30	90	50	.64	100	.214	.297	.318
Washington	161	5400	524	665	1208	160	37	124	1814	489	454	50	960	39	46	32	29	19	.60	125	.224	.292	.336
Cleveland	162	5416	516	504	1266	210	36	75	1773	476	427	51	858	39	69	37	115	61	.65	96	.234	.299	.327
California	162	5331	498	615	1209	170	33	83	1694	453	447	41	1080	52	75	37	62	50	.55	103	.227	.298	.318
Chicago	162	5405	463	527	1233	169	33	71	1681	431	397	47	840	40	90	33	90	50	.64	108	.228	.290	.311
AL Total	1624	53709	5532	5532	12359	1874	338	1104	18221	5126	4881	529	9641	426	713	366	811	471	.63	1072	.230	.297	.339
AL Avg Team	162	5371	553	553	1236	187	34	110	1822	513	488	53	964	43	71	37	81	47	.63	107	.230	.297	.339

Team Pitching

Team	G	CG	ShO	Rel	Sv	IP	H	R	ER	HR	SH	SF	HB	TBB	IBB	SO	WP	Bk	H/9	SO/9	BB/9	OAvg	OOBP	ERA
Cleveland	162	48	23	222	32	1464.1	1087	504	432	98	62	36	53	540	64	1157	42	2	6.7	7.1	3.3	.206	.285	2.66
Baltimore	162	53	16	234	31	1451.1	1111	497	429	101	51	28	46	502	42	1044	53	12	6.9	6.5	3.1	.212	.285	2.66
Detroit	164	59	19	238	29	1489.2	1180	492	449	129	71	17	32	486	40	1115	38	4	7.1	6.7	2.9	.217	.284	2.71
Chicago	162	20	11	322	40	1468.0	1290	527	448	97	73	35	66	451	69	834	40	3	7.9	5.1	2.8	.236	.301	2.75
New York	164	45	14	204	27	1467.1	1308	531	455	99	90	39	30	424	62	831	27	5	8.0	5.1	2.6	.240	.297	2.79
Minnesota	162	46	14	229	29	1433.1	1224	546	461	92	67	43	42	414	46	996	52	6	7.7	6.3	2.6	.229	.288	2.89
Oakland	163	45	18	252	29	1455.2	1220	544	476	124	63	35	31	505	78	997	55	2	7.5	6.2	3.1	.227	.295	2.94
Boston	162	55	17	225	31	1447.0	1303	611	536	115	62	36	50	523	45	972	73	4	8.1	6.0	3.3	.241	.312	3.33
California	162	29	11	320	31	1437.0	1234	615	548	131	77	46	33	519	43	869	68	2	7.7	5.4	3.3	.233	.303	3.43
Washington	161	26	11	296	28	1439.2	1402	665	583	118	97	51	43	517	40	826	61	6	8.8	5.2	3.2	.258	.325	3.64
AL Total	1624	426	154	2542	307	14553.1	12359	5532	4817	1104	713	366	426	4881	529	9641	509	46	7.6	6.0	3.0	.230	.304	2.98
AL Avg Team	162	43	15	254	31	1455.1	1236	553	482	110	71	37	43	488	53	964	51	5	7.6	6.0	3.0	.230	.304	2.98

Team Fielding

Team	G	PO	A	E	TC	DP	PB	Pct
Detroit	164	4463	1615	105	6183	133	10	.983
Baltimore	162	4347	1702	120	6169	131	24	.981
Boston	162	4351	1678	128	6157	147	19	.979
Cleveland	162	4385	1461	127	5973	130	22	.979
New York	164	4388	1972	139	6499	142	7	.979
California	162	4307	1711	140	6158	156	18	.977
Chicago	162	4391	1939	151	6481	152	16	.977
Oakland	163	4363	1657	145	6165	136	20	.976
Washington	161	4315	1785	148	6248	144	21	.976
Minnesota	162	4300	1712	170	6182	117	9	.973
AL Total	1624	43610	17232	1373	62215	1388	166	.978

Team vs. Team Records

	Bal	Bos	Cal	ChA	Cle	Det	Min	NYA	Oak	Was	Won
Bal	—	9	10	11	7	8	10	13	9	14	91
Bos	9	—	9	14	10	6	9	10	8	11	86
Cal	8	9	—	8	7	5	7	6	5	12	67
ChA	7	4	10	—	5	5	10	6	10	10	67
Cle	11	8	11	13	—	6	14	10	6	7	86
Det	10	12	13	13	12	—	10	10	13	10	103
Min	8	9	11	8	4	8	—	12	8	11	79
NYA	5	8	12	12	8	8	6	—	10	14	83
Oak	9	10	13	8	12	5	10	8	—	7	82
Was	4	7	6	8	10	8	7	4	11	—	65
Lost	71	76	95	95	75	59	83	79	80	96	

1968 American League Batting Leaders

Games		At-Bats		Runs		Hits		Doubles		Triples	
S. Bando, Oak	162	B. Campaneris, Oak	642	D. McAuliffe, Det	95	B. Campaneris, Oak	177	R. Smith, Bos	37	J. Fregosi, Cal	13
B. Robinson, Bal	162	D. Unser, Was	635	C. Yastrzemski, Bos	90	C. Tovar, Min	167	B. Robinson, Bal	36	T. McCraw, ChA	12
B. Campaneris, Oak	159	L. Aparicio, ChA	622	R. White, NYA	89	F. Howard, Was	164	C. Yastrzemski, Bos	32	E. Stroud, Was	10
R. White, NYA	159	J. Fregosi, Cal	614	C. Tovar, Min	89	L. Aparicio, ChA	164	C. Tovar, Min	31	D. McAuliffe, Det	10
J. Fregosi, Cal	159	C. Tovar, Min	613	M. Stanley, Det	88	C. Yastrzemski, Bos	162	2 tied with	29	B. Campaneris, Oak	9

Home Runs		Total Bases		Runs Batted In		Walks		Intentional Walks		Strikeouts	
F. Howard, Was	44	F. Howard, Was	330	K. Harrelson, Bos	109	C. Yastrzemski, Bos	119	T. Oliva, Min	16	R. Jackson, Oak	171
W. Horton, Det	36	W. Horton, Det	278	F. Howard, Was	106	M. Mantle, NYA	106	C. Yastrzemski, Bos	13	R. Monday, Oak	143
K. Harrelson, Bos	35	K. Harrelson, Bos	277	J. Northrup, Det	90	J. Foy, Bos	84	R. Smith, Bos	13	F. Howard, Was	141
R. Jackson, Oak	29	C. Yastrzemski, Bos	267	W. Horton, Det	85	D. McAuliffe, Det	82	B. Powell, Bal	12	B. Knoop, Cal	128
2 tied with	25	J. Northrup, Det	259	B. Powell, Bal	85	M. Andrews, Bos	81	F. Howard, Was	12	R. Reichardt, Cal	118

Hit By Pitch		Sac Hits		Sac Flies		Stolen Bases		Caught Stealing		GDP	
B. Freehan, Det	24	D. McLain, Det	16	C. Blefary, Bal	8	B. Campaneris, Oak	62	B. Campaneris, Oak	22	M. Stanley, Det	22
R. Reichardt, Cal	18	M. Andrews, Bos	12	R. Repoz, Cal	8	J. Cardenal, Cle	40	J. Cardenal, Cle	18	D. Cater, Oak	21
C. Tovar, Min	17	L. Tiant, Cle	11	B. Robinson, Bal	8	C. Tovar, Min	35	R. Smith, Bos	18	D. Johnson, Bal	18
M. Epstein, Was	13	J. Hardin, Bal	11	W. Horton, Det	7	D. Buford, Bal	27	V. Davalillo, 2tm	16	K. Harrelson, Bos	18
F. Robinson, Bal	12	D. Wert, Det	11	5 tied with	6	J. Foy, Bos	26	C. Tovar, Min	13	R. Hansen, 2tm	18

Runs Created		Runs Created/27 Outs		Batting Average		On-Base Percentage		Slugging Percentage		OBP+Slugging	
C. Yastrzemski, Bos	121	C. Yastrzemski, Bos	8.21	C. Yastrzemski, Bos	.301	C. Yastrzemski, Bos	.426	F. Howard, Was	.552	C. Yastrzemski, Bos	.922
F. Howard, Was	110	W. Horton, Det	6.63	D. Cater, Oak	.290	F. Robinson, Bal	.390	W. Horton, Det	.543	W. Horton, Det	.895
W. Horton, Det	96	F. Howard, Was	6.59	T. Oliva, Min	.289	M. Mantle, NYA	.385	K. Harrelson, Bos	.518	F. Howard, Was	.890
K. Harrelson, Bos	96	B. Freehan, Det	6.28	W. Horton, Det	.285	R. Monday, Oak	.371	C. Yastrzemski, Bos	.495	K. Harrelson, Bos	.874
B. Freehan, Det	96	M. Mantle, NYA	6.22	T. Uhlaender, Min	.283	M. Andrews, Bos	.368	T. Oliva, Min	.477	F. Robinson, Bal	.834

1968 American League Pitching Leaders

Wins		Losses		Winning Percentage		Games		Games Started		Complete Games	
D. McLain, Det	31	G. Brunet, Cal	17	D. McLain, Det	.838	W. Wood, ChA	88	D. McLain, Det	41	D. McLain, Det	28
D. McNally, Bal	22	J. Coleman, Was	16	R. Culp, Bos	.727	H. Wilhelm, ChA	72	D. Chance, Min	39	L. Tiant, Cle	19
L. Tiant, Cle	21	J. Merritt, Min	16	L. Tiant, Cle	.700	B. Locker, ChA	70	S. McDowell, Cle	37	M. Stottlemyre, NYA	19
M. Stottlemyre, NYA	21	D. Chance, Min	16	D. Ellsworth, Bos	.696	R. Perranoski, Min	66	3 tied with	36	D. McNally, Bal	18
J. Hardin, Bal	18	3 tied with	15	D. McNally, Bal	.688	2 tied with	59			J. Hardin, Bal	16

Shutouts		Saves		Games Finished		Batters Faced		Innings Pitched		Hits Allowed	
L. Tiant, Cle	9	A. Worthington, Min	18	W. Wood, ChA	46	D. McLain, Det	1288	D. McLain, Det	336.0	M. Stottlemyre, NYA	243
5 tied with	6	W. Wood, ChA	16	R. Perranoski, Min	41	D. Chance, Min	1161	D. Chance, Min	292.0	D. McLain, Det	241
		D. Higgins, Was	13	E. Watt, Bal	39	M. Stottlemyre, NYA	1123	M. Stottlemyre, NYA	278.2	D. Chance, Min	224
		3 tied with	12	H. Wilhelm, ChA	39	S. McDowell, Cle	1098	D. McNally, Bal	273.0	S. Bahnsen, NYA	216
				D. Womack, NYA	36	S. Bahnsen, NYA	1070	S. McDowell, Cle	269.0	J. Coleman, Was	212

Home Runs Allowed		Walks		Walks/9 Innings		Strikeouts		Strikeouts/9 Innings		Strikeout/Walk Ratio	
D. McLain, Det	31	S. McDowell, Cle	110	F. Peterson, NYA	1.2	S. McDowell, Cle	283	S. McDowell, Cle	9.5	D. McLain, Det	4.44
C. Hunter, Oak	29	T. Phoebus, Bal	105	D. McLain, Det	1.7	D. McLain, Det	280	L. Tiant, Cle	9.2	F. Peterson, NYA	3.97
D. McNally, Bal	24	B. Odom, Oak	98	D. Ellsworth, Bos	1.7	L. Tiant, Cle	264	M. Lolich, Det	8.1	D. Chance, Min	3.71
M. Lolich, Det	23	S. Siebert, Cle	88	J. Kaat, Min	1.7	D. Chance, Min	234	R. Culp, Bos	7.9	D. McNally, Bal	3.67
G. Brunet, Cal	23	D. Boswell, Min	87	D. McNally, Bal	1.8	D. McNally, Bal	202	D. McLain, Det	7.5	L. Tiant, Cle	3.62

Earned Run Average		Component ERA		Hit Batsmen		Wild Pitches		Opponent Average		Opponent OBP	
L. Tiant, Cle	1.60	L. Tiant, Cle	1.51	J. Horlen, ChA	14	B. Odom, Oak	17	L. Tiant, Cle	.168	D. McNally, Bal	.232
S. McDowell, Cle	1.81	D. McNally, Bal	1.66	T. John, ChA	12	F. Bertaina, Was	17	D. McNally, Bal	.182	L. Tiant, Cle	.233
D. McNally, Bal	1.95	D. McLain, Det	1.91	J. Coleman, Was	12	R. Clark, Cal	13	S. McDowell, Cle	.189	D. McLain, Det	.243
D. McLain, Det	1.96	D. Chance, Min	1.99	M. Lolich, Det	11	D. Chance, Min	12	S. Siebert, Cle	.198	D. Chance, Min	.260
T. John, ChA	1.98	S. McDowell, Cle	2.16	J. Lonborg, Bos	11	3 tied with	10	D. McLain, Det	.200	J. Nash, Oak	.269

1968 American League Miscellaneous

Managers

Baltimore	Hank Bauer	43-37
	Earl Weaver	48-34
Boston	Dick Williams	86-76
California	Bill Rigney	67-95
Chicago	Eddie Stanky	34-45
	Les Moss	0-2
	Al Lopez	6-5
	Les Moss	12-22
	Al Lopez	15-21
Cleveland	Alvin Dark	86-75
Detroit	Mayo Smith	103-59
Minnesota	Cal Ermer	79-83
New York	Ralph Houk	83-79
Oakland	Bob Kennedy	82-80
Washington	Jim Lemon	65-96

Awards

Most Valuable Player	Denny McLain, p, Det
Cy Young	Denny McLain, Det
Rookie of the Year	Stan Bahnsen, p, NYA
STATS Manager of the Year	Mayo Smith, Det

STATS All-Star Team

C	Bill Freehan, Det	.263	25	84
1B	Norm Cash, Det	.263	25	63
2B	Dick McAuliffe, Det	.249	16	56
3B	Brooks Robinson, Bal	.253	17	75
SS	Bert Campaneris, Oak	.276	4	38
OF	Ken Harrelson, Bos	.275	35	109
OF	Frank Howard, Was	.274	44	106
OF	Carl Yastrzemski, Bos	.301	23	74
P	Sam McDowell, Cle	15-14	1.81	283 K
P	Denny McLain, Det	31-6	1.96	280 K
P	Dave McNally, Bal	22-10	1.95	202 K
P	Luis Tiant, Cle	21-9	1.60	264 K
RP	Wilbur Wood, ChA	13-12	1.87	16 Sv

Postseason

World Series	Detroit (AL) 4 vs. St. Louis (NL) 3

Outstanding Performances

Perfect Games
Catfish Hunter, Oak   vs. Min on May 8
No-Hitters
Tom Phoebus, Bal   vs. Bos on April 27
Three-Homer Games
Ken Harrelson, Bos   on June 14
Cycles
Jim Fregosi, Cal   on May 20
Unassisted Triple Plays
Ron Hansen, Was   on July 29

1968 National League Standings

Team	Overall					Home Games						Road Games						Park Index		Record by Month					
	W	L	Pct	GB	DIF	W	L	R	OR	HR	OHR	W	L	R	OR	HR	OHR	Run	HR	M/A	May	June	July	Aug	S/O
St. Louis	97	65	.599	—	160	47	34	267	218	31	35	50	31	316	254	42	47	85	74	13-5	11-16	22-9	24-6	16-15	11-14
San Francisco	88	74	.543	9.0	11	42	39	299	242	60	32	46	35	300	287	48	54	92	90	10-7	16-14	14-16	12-15	21-10	15-12
Chicago	84	78	.519	13.0	0	47	34	363	332	83	83	37	44	249	279	47	55	132	163	8-10	15-13	10-18	21-11	17-15	13-11
Cincinnati	83	79	.512	14.0	1	40	41	377	400	55	66	43	38	313	273	51	48	133	122	8-9	14-13	15-15	16-11	18-14	12-17
Atlanta	81	81	.500	16.0	1	41	40	241	241	42	43	40	41	273	308	38	44	83	104	8-10	17-11	14-15	16-15	13-18	13-12
Pittsburgh	80	82	.494	17.0	0	40	41	289	268	33	30	40	41	294	264	47	43	100	70	8-8	10-15	18-13	15-18	14-17	15-11
Los Angeles	76	86	.469	21.0	0	41	40	212	215	25	24	35	46	258	294	42	41	77	59	9-9	15-16	16-13	7-20	11-19	18-9
Philadelphia	76	86	.469	21.0	1	38	43	274	297	52	46	38	43	269	318	48	45	97	105	8-9	13-11	12-16	15-19	14-18	14-13
New York	73	89	.451	24.0	0	32	49	224	270	49	50	41	40	249	229	32	37	103	143	7-9	13-15	16-14	13-20	14-18	10-13
Houston	72	90	.444	25.0	9	42	39	279	269	22	30	30	51	231	319	44	38	100	63	7-10	14-14	11-19	13-17	19-13	8-17

Clinch Date—St. Louis 9/15.

Team Batting

Team	G	AB	R	OR	H	2B	3B	HR	TB	RBI	TBB	IBB	SO	HBP	SH	SF	SB	CS	SB%	GDP	Avg	OBP	Slg
Cincinnati	163	5767	690	673	1573	281	36	106	2244	638	379	95	938	37	64	39	59	55	.52	142	.273	.326	.389
Chicago	163	5458	612	611	1319	203	43	130	1998	576	415	58	854	36	74	37	41	30	.58	103	.242	.304	.366
San Francisco	163	5441	599	529	1301	162	33	108	1853	566	508	55	904	47	92	44	50	37	.57	117	.239	.315	.341
Pittsburgh	163	5569	583	532	1404	180	44	80	1912	538	422	93	953	33	96	43	130	59	.69	133	.252	.313	.343
St. Louis	162	5561	583	472	1383	227	48	73	1925	539	378	56	897	32	67	42	110	45	.71	91	.249	.305	.346
Philadelphia	162	5372	543	615	1253	178	30	100	1791	505	462	60	1003	22	64	46	58	51	.53	106	.233	.302	.333
Atlanta	163	5552	514	549	1399	179	31	80	1880	480	414	85	782	36	86	30	83	44	.65	145	.252	.312	.339
Houston	162	5336	510	588	1233	205	28	66	1692	473	479	81	988	48	97	34	44	51	.46	115	.231	.304	.317
New York	163	5503	473	499	1252	178	30	81	1733	434	379	50	1203	43	75	27	72	45	.62	104	.228	.286	.315
Los Angeles	162	5354	470	509	1234	202	36	67	1709	434	439	61	980	18	79	45	57	43	.57	89	.230	.296	.319
NL Total	1626	54913	5577	5577	13351	1995	359	891	18737	5183	4275	694	9502	352	794	387	704	460	.60	1145	.243	.300	.341
NL Avg Team	163	5491	558	558	1335	200	36	89	1874	518	428	69	950	35	79	39	70	46	.60	115	.243	.300	.341

Team Pitching

Team	G	CG	ShO	Rel	Sv	IP	H	R	ER	HR	SH	SF	HB	TBB	IBB	SO	WP	Bk	H/9	SO/9	BB/9	OAvg	OOBP	ERA
St. Louis	162	63	30	196	32	1479.1	1282	472	409	82	92	31	28	375	62	971	30	0	7.8	5.9	2.3	.234	.285	2.49
Los Angeles	162	38	23	218	31	1448.2	1293	509	433	65	83	47	37	414	79	994	43	7	8.0	6.2	2.6	.241	.297	2.69
San Francisco	163	77	20	167	16	1469.0	1302	529	442	86	71	26	24	344	87	942	56	2	8.0	5.8	2.1	.236	.282	2.71
New York	163	45	25	212	32	1483.1	1250	499	449	87	76	38	45	430	67	1014	59	3	7.6	6.2	2.6	.230	.290	2.72
Pittsburgh	163	42	19	244	30	1487.0	1322	532	453	73	80	30	36	485	61	897	51	4	8.0	5.4	2.9	.240	.304	2.74
Atlanta	163	44	16	199	29	1474.2	1326	549	478	87	87	41	33	362	69	871	54	5	8.1	5.3	2.2	.241	.290	2.92
Houston	162	50	12	243	23	1446.2	1362	588	524	68	81	53	36	479	85	1021	74	7	8.5	6.4	3.0	.249	.311	3.26
Philadelphia	162	42	12	227	27	1448.1	1416	615	541	91	76	32	41	421	55	935	30	3	8.8	5.8	2.6	.257	.313	3.36
Chicago	163	46	12	221	32	1453.2	1399	611	551	138	78	35	27	392	47	894	41	3	8.7	5.5	2.4	.254	.304	3.41
Cincinnati	163	24	16	321	38	1490.1	1399	673	590	114	70	54	45	573	82	963	60	3	8.4	5.8	3.5	.250	.321	3.56
NL Total	1626	471	185	2248	290	14681.0	13351	5577	4870	891	794	387	352	4275	694	9502	498	37	8.2	5.8	2.6	.243	.306	2.99
NL Avg Team	163	47	19	225	29	1468.0	1335	558	487	89	79	39	35	428	69	950	50	4	8.2	5.8	2.6	.243	.306	2.99

Team Fielding

Team	G	PO	A	E	TC	DP	PB	Pct
Chicago	163	4360	1896	119	6375	149	9	.981
Atlanta	163	4423	1803	125	6351	139	14	.980
Philadelphia	162	4344	1842	127	6313	163	19	.980
New York	163	4450	1778	133	6361	142	11	.979
Pittsburgh	163	4462	2000	139	6601	162	11	.979
Cincinnati	163	4471	1843	144	6458	144	19	.978
St. Louis	162	4437	1689	140	6266	135	10	.978
Los Angeles	162	4348	1806	144	6298	144	17	.977
Houston	162	4341	1714	156	6211	129	15	.975
San Francisco	163	4406	1834	162	6402	125	23	.975
NL Total	1626	44042	18205	1389	63636	1432	148	.978

Team vs. Team Records

	Atl	ChN	Cin	Hou	LA	NYN	Phi	Pit	SF	StL	Won
Atl	—	8	10	11	9	12	11	6	9	5	81
ChN	10	—	7	10	12	8	9	10	9	9	84
Cin	8	11	—	9	9	10	11	10	8	7	83
Hou	7	8	9	—	11	10	9	5	8	5	72
LA	9	6	9	7	—	7	10	10	9	9	76
NYN	6	10	8	8	11	—	8	9	7	6	73
Phi	7	9	7	9	8	10	—	9	9	8	76
Pit	12	8	8	13	8	9	9	—	7	6	80
SF	9	9	10	10	9	11	9	11	—	10	88
StL	13	9	11	13	9	12	10	12	8	—	97
Lost	81	78	79	90	86	89	86	82	74	65	

1968 National League Batting Leaders

Games		At-Bats		Runs		Hits		Doubles		Triples	
B. Williams, ChN	163	F. Alou, Atl	662	G. Beckert, ChN	98	P. Rose, Cin	210	L. Brock, StL	46	L. Brock, StL	14
R. Santo, ChN	162	L. Brock, StL	660	P. Rose, Cin	94	F. Alou, Atl	210	P. Rose, Cin	42	R. Clemente, Pit	12
R. Staub, Hou	161	D. Kessinger, ChN	655	T. Perez, Cin	93	G. Beckert, ChN	189	J. Bench, Cin	40	W. Davis, LA	10
6 tied with	160	G. Beckert, ChN	643	L. Brock, StL	92	A. Johnson, Cin	188	R. Staub, Hou	37	D. Allen, Phi	9
		W. Davis, LA	643	B. Williams, ChN	91	C. Flood, StL	186	F. Alou, Atl	37	B. Williams, ChN	8

Home Runs		Total Bases		Runs Batted In		Walks		Intentional Walks		Strikeouts	
W. McCovey, SF	36	B. Williams, ChN	321	W. McCovey, SF	105	R. Santo, ChN	96	R. Clemente, Pit	27	D. Clendenon, Pit	163
D. Allen, Phi	33	H. Aaron, Atl	302	R. Santo, ChN	98	J. Wynn, Hou	90	R. Staub, Hou	24	D. Allen, Phi	161
E. Banks, ChN	32	P. Rose, Cin	294	B. Williams, ChN	98	R. Hunt, SF	78	H. Aaron, Atl	23	J. Wynn, Hou	131
B. Williams, ChN	30	F. Alou, Atl	290	T. Perez, Cin	92	D. Allen, Phi	74	W. McCovey, SF	20	L. Brock, StL	124
H. Aaron, Atl	29	W. McCovey, SF	285	D. Allen, Phi	90	R. Staub, Hou	73	A. Phillips, ChN	20	M. Shannon, StL	114

Hit By Pitch		Sac Hits		Sac Flies		Stolen Bases		Caught Stealing		GDP	
R. Hunt, SF	25	P. Niekro, Atl	18	T. Haller, LA	9	L. Brock, StL	62	M. Wills, Pit	21	H. Aaron, Atl	21
O. Cepeda, StL	9	R. Hunt, SF	16	W. McCovey, SF	8	M. Wills, Pit	52	J. Wynn, Hou	17	L. May, Cin	20
4 tied with	7	F. Millan, Atl	14	J. Bench, Cin	8	W. Davis, LA	36	C. Jones, NYN	12	J. Alou, SF	20
		H. Lanier, SF	14	D. Clendenon, Pit	8	H. Aaron, Atl	28	L. Brock, StL	12	G. Alley, Pit	20
		2 tied with	12	5 tied with	7	C. Jones, NYN	23	2 tied with	11	2 tied with	19

Runs Created		Runs Created/27 Outs		Batting Average		On-Base Percentage		Slugging Percentage		OBP+Slugging	
W. McCovey, SF	110	W. McCovey, SF	7.69	P. Rose, Cin	.335	P. Rose, Cin	.391	W. McCovey, SF	.545	W. McCovey, SF	.923
P. Rose, Cin	110	P. Rose, Cin	6.82	M. Alou, Pit	.332	W. McCovey, SF	.378	D. Allen, Phi	.520	D. Allen, Phi	.872
B. Williams, ChN	109	W. Mays, SF	6.62	F. Alou, Atl	.317	J. Wynn, Hou	.376	B. Williams, ChN	.500	P. Rose, Cin	.861
L. Brock, StL	99	D. Allen, Phi	6.57	A. Johnson, Cin	.312	R. Staub, Hou	.373	H. Aaron, Atl	.498	W. Mays, SF	.860
D. Allen, Phi	98	B. Williams, ChN	6.22	C. Flood, StL	.301	W. Mays, SF	.372	W. Mays, SF	.488	H. Aaron, Atl	.852

1968 National League Pitching Leaders

Wins		Losses		Winning Percentage		Games		Games Started		Complete Games	
J. Marichal, SF	26	R. Sadecki, SF	18	S. Blass, Pit	.750	T. Abernathy, Cin	78	F. Jenkins, ChN	40	J. Marichal, SF	30
B. Gibson, StL	22	C. Osteen, LA	18	J. Marichal, SF	.743	P. Regan, 2tm	73	G. Perry, SF	38	B. Gibson, StL	28
F. Jenkins, ChN	20	B. Singer, LA	17	B. Gibson, StL	.710	C. Carroll, 2tm	68	J. Marichal, SF	38	F. Jenkins, ChN	20
3 tied with	19	L. Jackson, Phi	17	P. Regan, 2tm	.706	R. Taylor, NYN	58	4 tied with	36	G. Perry, SF	19
		2 tied with	16	R. Kline, Pit	.706	F. Linzy, SF	57			J. Koosman, NYN	17

Shutouts		Saves		Games Finished		Batters Faced		Innings Pitched		Hits Allowed	
B. Gibson, StL	13	P. Regan, 2tm	25	P. Regan, 2tm	62	J. Marichal, SF	1307	J. Marichal, SF	326.0	J. Marichal, SF	295
D. Drysdale, LA	8	C. Carroll, 2tm	17	T. Abernathy, Cin	53	F. Jenkins, ChN	1231	F. Jenkins, ChN	308.0	C. Osteen, LA	267
J. Koosman, NYN	7	J. Hoerner, StL	17	F. Linzy, SF	45	B. Gibson, StL	1161	B. Gibson, StL	304.2	F. Jenkins, ChN	255
S. Blass, Pit	7	J. Brewer, LA	14	C. Carroll, 2tm	44	G. Perry, SF	1159	G. Perry, SF	291.0	N. Briles, StL	251
2 tied with	6	4 tied with	13	R. Taylor, NYN	44	C. Short, Phi	1103	T. Seaver, NYN	277.2	G. Perry, SF	240

Home Runs Allowed		Walks		Walks/9 Innings		Strikeouts		Strikeouts/9 Innings		Strikeout/Walk Ratio	
F. Jenkins, ChN	26	B. Veale, Pit	94	B. Hands, ChN	1.3	B. Gibson, StL	268	B. Singer, LA	8.0	J. Marichal, SF	4.74
B. Hands, ChN	26	L. Dierker, Hou	89	J. Marichal, SF	1.3	F. Jenkins, ChN	260	B. Gibson, StL	7.9	B. Gibson, StL	4.32
C. Short, Phi	25	G. Culver, Cin	84	T. Seaver, NYN	1.6	B. Singer, LA	227	J. Maloney, Cin	7.9	T. Seaver, NYN	4.27
J. Marichal, SF	21	C. Short, Phi	81	M. Pappas, 2tm	1.6	J. Marichal, SF	218	F. Jenkins, ChN	7.6	B. Hands, ChN	4.11
2 tied with	18	J. Maloney, Cin	80	P. Niekro, Atl	1.6	R. Sadecki, SF	206	D. Wilson, Hou	7.5	F. Jenkins, ChN	4.00

Earned Run Average		Component ERA		Hit Batsmen		Wild Pitches		Opponent Average		Opponent OBP	
B. Gibson, StL	1.12	B. Gibson, StL	1.44	G. Culver, Cin	14	L. Dierker, Hou	20	B. Gibson, StL	.184	B. Gibson, StL	.233
B. Bolin, SF	1.99	B. Bolin, SF	1.89	D. Drysdale, LA	12	P. Niekro, Atl	16	B. Bolin, SF	.200	P. Jarvis, Atl	.252
B. Veale, Pit	2.05	P. Jarvis, Atl	1.97	D. Cardwell, NYN	10	B. Singer, LA	12	B. Veale, Pit	.211	B. Bolin, SF	.258
J. Koosman, NYN	2.08	B. Moose, Pit	1.99	C. Short, Phi	9	J. Maloney, Cin	12	P. Jarvis, Atl	.214	T. Seaver, NYN	.261
S. Blass, Pit	2.12	G. Perry, SF	2.04	K. Johnson, Atl	9	D. Giusti, Hou	11	B. Moose, Pit	.218	B. Hands, ChN	.262

1968 National League Miscellaneous

Managers

Atlanta	Lum Harris	81-81
Chicago	Leo Durocher	84-78
Cincinnati	Dave Bristol	83-79
Houston	Grady Hatton	23-38
	Harry Walker	49-52
Los Angeles	Walter Alston	76-86
New York	Gil Hodges	73-89
Philadelphia	Gene Mauch	27-27
	George Myatt	1-0
	Bob Skinner	48-59
Pittsburgh	Larry Shepard	80-82
St. Louis	Red Schoendienst	97-65
San Francisco	Herman Franks	88-74

Awards

Most Valuable Player	Bob Gibson, p, StL
Cy Young	Bob Gibson, StL
Rookie of the Year	Johnny Bench, c, Cin
STATS Manager of the Year	Red Schoendienst, StL

STATS All-Star Team

C	Johnny Bench, Cin	.275	15	82
1B	Willie McCovey, SF	.293	36	105
2B	Glenn Beckert, ChN	.294	4	37
3B	Ron Santo, ChN	.246	26	98
SS	Don Kessinger, ChN	.240	1	32
OF	Hank Aaron, Atl	.287	29	86
OF	Dick Allen, Phi	.263	33	90
OF	Pete Rose, Cin	.335	10	49
P	Steve Blass, Pit	18-6	2.12	132 K
P	Bob Gibson, StL	22-9	1.12	268 K
P	Jerry Koosman, NYN	19-12	2.08	178 K
P	Juan Marichal, SF	26-9	2.43	218 K
RP	Phil Regan, 2tm	12-5	2.27	25 Sv

Postseason

World Series	St. Louis (NL) 3 vs. Detroit (AL) 4

Outstanding Performances

No-Hitters

George Culver, Cin	@ Phi on July 29
Gaylord Perry, SF	vs. StL on September 17
Ray Washburn, StL	@ SF on September 18

Three-Homer Games

Willie Stargell, Pit	on May 22
Billy Williams, ChN	on September 10
Dick Allen, Phi	on September 29

1969 American League Standings

EAST	Overall W	L	Pct	GB	DIF	Home Games W	L	R	OR	HR	OHR	Road Games W	L	R	OR	HR	OHR	Park Index Run	HR	Record by Month M/A	May	June	July	Aug	S/O
Baltimore	109	53	.673	—	170	60	21	402	251	82	51	49	32	377	266	93	66	102	84	16-7	18-8	21-6	17-10	19-12	18-10
Detroit	90	72	.556	19.0	3	46	35	361	305	104	72	44	37	340	296	78	56	105	131	10-10	15-8	14-14	17-13	21-9	13-18
Boston	87	75	.537	22.0	6	46	35	392	391	105	78	41	40	351	345	92	77	113	108	11-9	18-7	14-15	14-15	13-15	17-14
Washington	86	76	.531	23.0	1	47	34	353	290	77	62	39	42	341	354	71	73	93	97	12-11	12-16	14-12	16-15	14-11	18-11
New York	80	81	.497	28.5	2	48	32	284	245	44	51	32	49	278	342	50	67	86	82	11-10	12-15	13-17	13-14	16-10	15-15
Cleveland	62	99	.385	46.5	0	33	48	276	341	56	60	29	51	297	376	63	74	91	84	2-15	10-14	17-15	14-18	11-17	8-20
WEST																									
Minnesota	97	65	.599	—	138	57	24	414	298	79	61	40	41	376	320	84	58	102	99	13-7	12-12	16-14	23-7	15-12	18-13
Oakland	88	74	.543	9.0	31	49	32	410	363	75	70	39	42	330	315	73	93	83	85	11-8	12-13	17-9	18-11	16-15	14-18
California	71	91	.438	26.0	3	43	38	277	305	49	65	28	53	251	347	39	61	97	114	6-10	8-19	11-18	15-14	15-12	16-18
Kansas City	69	93	.426	28.0	12	36	45	301	362	39	63	33	48	285	326	59	73	109	77	9-10	12-15	10-18	11-18	10-17	17-15
Chicago	68	94	.420	29.0	5	41	40	352	387	61	80	27	54	273	336	51	66	121	121	8-8	11-13	12-20	10-22	11-15	16-16
Seattle	64	98	.395	33.0	4	34	47	329	399	74	93	30	51	310	400	51	79	103	128	7-11	13-13	14-15	9-20	6-22	15-17

Clinch Date—Baltimore 9/13, Minnesota 9/22.

Team Batting

Team	G	AB	R	OR	H	2B	3B	HR	TB	RBI	TBB	IBB	SO	HBP	SH	SF	SB	CS	SB%	GDP	Avg	OBP	Slg
Minnesota	162	5677	790	618	1520	246	32	163	2319	733	599	78	906	43	65	40	115	70	.62	114	.268	.346	.408
Baltimore	162	5518	779	517	1465	234	29	175	2282	722	634	62	806	43	74	59	82	45	.65	138	.265	.352	.414
Boston	162	5494	743	736	1381	234	37	197	2280	701	658	61	923	32	67	43	41	47	.47	125	.251	.339	.415
Oakland	162	5614	740	678	1400	210	28	148	2110	680	617	66	953	63	74	35	100	39	.72	124	.249	.334	.376
Detroit	162	5441	701	601	1316	188	29	182	2108	649	578	43	922	30	63	43	35	28	.56	113	.242	.323	.387
Washington	162	5447	694	644	1365	171	40	148	2060	640	630	65	900	32	51	36	52	40	.57	158	.251	.336	.378
Seattle	163	5444	639	799	1276	179	27	125	1884	583	626	43	1015	34	72	29	167	59	.74	111	.234	.320	.346
Chicago	162	5450	625	723	1346	210	27	112	1946	585	552	45	844	49	70	37	54	22	.71	119	.247	.326	.357
Kansas City	163	5462	586	688	1311	179	32	98	1848	538	522	40	901	43	57	38	129	70	.65	125	.240	.316	.338
Cleveland	161	5365	573	717	1272	173	24	119	1850	534	535	49	906	26	47	43	85	37	.70	147	.237	.314	.345
New York	162	5308	562	587	1247	210	44	94	1827	521	565	51	840	14	63	40	119	74	.62	105	.235	.315	.344
California	163	5316	528	652	1221	151	29	88	1694	480	516	65	929	32	75	41	54	39	.58	105	.230	.307	.319
AL Total	1946	65536	7960	7960	16120	2385	378	1649	24208	7366	7032	668	10845	441	778	484	1033	570	.64	1484	.246	.321	.369
AL Avg Team	162	5461	663	663	1343	199	32	137	2017	614	586	56	904	37	65	40	86	48	.64	124	.246	.321	.369

Team Pitching

Team	G	CG	ShO	Rel	Sv	IP	H	R	ER	HR	SH	SF	HB	TBB	IBB	SO	WP	Bk	H/9	SO/9	BB/9	OAvg	OOBP	ERA
Baltimore	162	50	20	235	36	1473.2	1194	517	464	117	52	35	22	498	55	897	34	4	7.3	5.5	3.0	.223	.290	2.83
New York	162	53	13	199	20	1440.2	1258	587	517	118	74	40	18	522	65	801	46	0	7.9	5.0	3.3	.236	.304	3.23
Minnesota	162	41	8	302	43	1497.2	1388	618	539	119	59	35	38	524	76	906	48	1	8.3	5.4	3.1	.246	.313	3.24
Detroit	162	55	20	251	28	1455.1	1250	601	536	128	68	40	34	586	39	1032	49	5	7.7	6.4	3.6	.232	.310	3.31
Washington	162	28	10	311	41	1447.1	1310	644	562	135	73	47	36	656	37	835	57	5	8.1	5.2	4.1	.244	.328	3.49
California	163	25	9	285	39	1438.1	1294	652	566	126	53	27	51	517	46	885	64	7	8.1	5.5	3.2	.242	.313	3.54
Oakland	162	42	14	276	36	1480.2	1356	678	611	163	50	36	39	586	48	887	55	3	8.2	5.4	3.6	.245	.320	3.71
Kansas City	163	42	10	249	25	1464.2	1357	688	605	136	82	45	25	560	36	894	52	3	8.3	5.5	3.4	.246	.316	3.72
Boston	162	30	7	298	41	1466.2	1423	736	639	155	62	40	48	685	42	935	61	5	8.7	5.7	4.2	.256	.341	3.92
Cleveland	161	35	7	294	22	1437.0	1330	717	629	134	75	61	48	681	79	1000	50	6	8.3	6.3	4.3	.248	.335	3.94
Chicago	162	29	10	265	25	1437.2	1470	723	672	146	70	38	33	564	70	810	59	4	9.2	5.1	3.5	.267	.337	4.21
Seattle	163	21	6	357	33	1463.2	1490	799	707	172	60	40	47	653	75	963	61	9	9.2	5.9	4.0	.264	.343	4.35
AL Total	1946	451	134	3322	389	17503.1	16120	7960	7047	1649	778	484	439	7032	668	10845	636	52	8.3	5.6	3.6	.246	.328	3.62
AL Avg Team	162	38	11	277	32	1458.1	1343	663	587	137	65	40	37	586	56	904	53	4	8.3	5.6	3.6	.246	.328	3.62

Team Fielding

Team	G	PO	A	E	TC	DP	PB	Pct
Baltimore	162	4410	1729	101	6240	145	14	.984
Chicago	162	4299	1997	122	6418	163	36	.981
New York	162	4357	1869	131	6357	158	19	.979
Detroit	162	4361	1599	130	6090	130	11	.979
Oakland	162	4434	1787	136	6357	162	26	.979
California	163	4281	1755	136	6172	164	30	.978
Washington	162	4332	1864	140	6336	159	18	.978
Minnesota	162	4503	1856	150	6509	177	18	.977
Cleveland	161	4301	1588	145	6034	153	21	.976
Boston	162	4382	1779	157	6318	178	21	.975
Kansas City	163	4389	1652	157	6198	114	17	.975
Seattle	163	4388	1760	167	6315	149	21	.974
AL Total	1946	52437	21235	1672	75344	1852	247	.978

Team vs. Team Records

	Bal	Bos	Cal	ChA	Cle	Det	KC	Min	NYA	Oak	Sea	Was	Won
Bal	—	10	6	9	13	11	11	8	11	8	9	13	109
Bos	8	—	8	5	12	10	10	7	11	4	6	6	87
Cal	6	4	—	9	8	5	9	7	3	6	9	5	71
ChA	3	7	9	—	8	3	8	5	3	8	10	4	68
Cle	5	6	4	4	—	7	7	5	9	5	7	3	62
Det	7	8	7	9	11	—	8	6	10	7	10	7	90
KC	1	2	9	10	5	4	—	8	5	8	10	7	69
Min	4	5	11	13	7	6	10	—	10	13	12	6	97
NYA	7	7	9	9	8	8	7	2	—	6	7	10	80
Oak	4	8	12	10	7	5	10	5	6	—	13	8	88
Sea	3	6	9	8	5	2	8	6	5	5	—	7	64
Was	5	12	7	8	15	11	5	6	8	4	5	—	86
Lost	53	75	91	94	99	72	93	65	81	74	98	76	

Seasons: Standings, Leaders

1969 American League Batting Leaders

Games		At-Bats		Runs		Hits		Doubles		Triples	
S. Bando, Oak	162	H. Clarke, NYA	641	R. Jackson, Oak	123	T. Oliva, Min	197	T. Oliva, Min	39	D. Unser, Was	8
C. Yastrzemski, Bos	162	T. Oliva, Min	637	F. Howard, Was	111	H. Clarke, NYA	183	R. Jackson, Oak	36	R. Smith, Bos	7
H. Killebrew, Min	162	P. Blair, Bal	625	F. Robinson, Bal	111	P. Blair, Bal	178	D. Johnson, Bal	34	H. Clarke, NYA	7
J. Fregosi, Cal	161	T. Horton, Cle	625	S. Bando, Oak	106	F. Howard, Was	175	P. Blair, Bal	32	5 tied with	6
F. Howard, Was	161	S. Alomar, 2tm	617	H. Killebrew, Min	106	T. Horton, Cle	174	R. Petrocelli, Bos	32		

Home Runs		Total Bases		Runs Batted In		Walks		Intentional Walks		Strikeouts	
H. Killebrew, Min	49	F. Howard, Was	340	H. Killebrew, Min	140	H. Killebrew, Min	145	R. Jackson, Oak	20	R. Jackson, Oak	142
F. Howard, Was	48	R. Jackson, Oak	334	B. Powell, Bal	121	R. Jackson, Oak	114	H. Killebrew, Min	20	J. Hernandez, KC	111
R. Jackson, Oak	47	H. Killebrew, Min	324	R. Jackson, Oak	118	S. Bando, Oak	111	F. Howard, Was	19	T. Conigliaro, Bos	111
C. Yastrzemski, Bos	40	T. Oliva, Min	316	S. Bando, Oak	113	F. Howard, Was	102	R. Petrocelli, Bos	13	B. Melton, ChA	106
R. Petrocelli, Bos	40	R. Petrocelli, Bos	315	2 tied with	111	C. Yastrzemski, Bos	101	D. Mincher, Sea	13	2 tied with	103

Hit By Pitch		Sac Hits		Sac Flies		Stolen Bases		Caught Stealing		GDP	
F. Robinson, Bal	13	P. Blair, Bal	13	R. White, NYA	11	T. Harper, Sea	73	D. Buford, Bal	18	F. Howard, Was	29
R. Jackson, Oak	12	D. McLain, Det	13	B. Robinson, Bal	10	B. Campaneris, Oak	62	T. Harper, Sea	18	D. Cater, Oak	25
S. Bando, Oak	11	M. Lolich, Det	12	L. Piniella, KC	9	C. Tovar, Min	45	J. Foy, KC	15	J. Adair, KC	24
M. Epstein, Was	10	S. McDowell, Cle	11	J. Foy, KC	9	P. Kelly, KC	40	J. Kenney, NYA	14	E. Brinkman, Was	23
C. Tovar, Min	9	3 tied with	10	L. Cardenas, Min	9	J. Foy, KC	37	4 tied with	13	T. Horton, Cle	21

Runs Created		Runs Created/27 Outs		Batting Average		On-Base Percentage		Slugging Percentage		OBP+Slugging	
R. Jackson, Oak	138	R. Jackson, Oak	9.05	R. Carew, Min	.332	H. Killebrew, Min	.427	R. Jackson, Oak	.608	R. Jackson, Oak	1.018
H. Killebrew, Min	136	H. Killebrew, Min	8.69	R. Smith, Bos	.309	F. Robinson, Bal	.415	R. Petrocelli, Bos	.589	H. Killebrew, Min	1.011
F. Howard, Was	128	F. Robinson, Bal	8.11	T. Oliva, Min	.309	R. Jackson, Oak	.410	H. Killebrew, Min	.584	R. Petrocelli, Bos	.992
S. Bando, Oak	123	R. Petrocelli, Bos	7.95	F. Robinson, Bal	.308	R. Petrocelli, Bos	.403	F. Howard, Was	.574	F. Howard, Was	.976
R. Petrocelli, Bos	118	F. Howard, Was	7.72	B. Powell, Bal	.304	F. Howard, Was	.402	B. Powell, Bal	.559	F. Robinson, Bal	.955

1969 American League Pitching Leaders

Wins		Losses		Winning Percentage		Games		Games Started		Complete Games	
D. McLain, Det	24	L. Tiant, Cle	20	J. Palmer, Bal	.800	W. Wood, ChA	76	D. McLain, Det	41	M. Stottlemyre, NYA	24
M. Cuellar, Bal	23	6 tied with	16	J. Perry, Min	.769	R. Perranoski, Min	75	D. McNally, Bal	40	D. McLain, Det	23
4 tied with	20			D. McNally, Bal	.741	S. Lyle, Bos	71	M. Stottlemyre, NYA	39	S. McDowell, Cle	18
				D. Bosman, Was	.737	B. Locker, 2tm	68	M. Cuellar, Bal	39	M. Cuellar, Bal	18
				D. McLain, Det	.727	D. Segui, Sea	66	2 tied with	38	F. Peterson, NYA	16

Shutouts		Saves		Games Finished		Batters Faced		Innings Pitched		Hits Allowed	
D. McLain, Det	9	R. Perranoski, Min	31	R. Perranoski, Min	52	D. McLain, Det	1304	D. McLain, Det	325.0	D. McLain, Det	288
J. Palmer, Bal	6	K. Tatum, Cal	22	W. Wood, ChA	50	M. Stottlemyre, NYA	1244	M. Stottlemyre, NYA	303.0	M. Stottlemyre, NYA	267
M. Cuellar, Bal	5	S. Lyle, Bos	17	S. Lyle, Bos	44	M. Lolich, Det	1172	M. Cuellar, Bal	290.2	J. Kaat, Min	252
6 tied with	4	E. Watt, Bal	16	E. Watt, Bal	41	S. McDowell, Cle	1166	S. McDowell, Cle	285.0	C. Dobson, Oak	244
		D. Higgins, Was	16	D. Knowles, Was	40	M. Cuellar, Bal	1137	M. Lolich, Det	280.2	J. Perry, Min	244

Home Runs Allowed		Walks		Walks/9 Innings		Strikeouts		Strikeouts/9 Innings		Strikeout/Walk Ratio	
L. Tiant, Cle	37	L. Tiant, Cle	129	F. Peterson, NYA	1.4	S. McDowell, Cle	279	S. McDowell, Cle	8.8	F. Peterson, NYA	3.49
C. Hunter, Oak	34	M. Lolich, Det	122	D. Bosman, Was	1.8	M. Lolich, Det	271	M. Lolich, Det	8.7	S. McDowell, Cle	2.74
M. Pattin, Sea	29	B. Odom, Oak	112	D. McLain, Det	1.9	A. Messersmith, Cal	211	A. Messersmith, Cal	7.6	D. McLain, Det	2.70
W. Bunker, KC	29	M. Nagy, Bos	106	J. Perry, Min	2.3	D. Boswell, Min	190	B. Butler, KC	7.2	D. Bosman, Was	2.54
S. Bahnsen, NYA	28	G. Brabender, Sea	103	M. Cuellar, Bal	2.4	2 tied with	182	S. Williams, Cle	7.0	J. Perry, Min	2.32

Earned Run Average		Component ERA		Hit Batsmen		Wild Pitches		Opponent Average		Opponent OBP	
D. Bosman, Was	2.19	M. Cuellar, Bal	2.02	T. Murphy, Cal	21	T. Murphy, Cal	16	A. Messersmith, Cal	.190	M. Cuellar, Bal	.260
J. Palmer, Bal	2.34	F. Peterson, NYA	2.08	M. Lolich, Det	14	A. Messersmith, Cal	16	J. Palmer, Bal	.200	D. Bosman, Was	.260
M. Cuellar, Bal	2.38	D. Bosman, Was	2.14	G. Brabender, Sea	13	T. John, ChA	15	M. Cuellar, Bal	.204	F. Peterson, NYA	.261
A. Messersmith, Cal	2.52	A. Messersmith, Cal	2.23	S. Williams, Cle	12	D. Higgins, Was	15	M. Lolich, Det	.210	J. Palmer, Bal	.272
F. Peterson, NYA	2.55	J. Palmer, Bal	2.26	M. Nagy, Bos	11	2 tied with	14	S. McDowell, Cle	.213	A. Messersmith, Cal	.274

1969 American League Miscellaneous

Managers

Baltimore	Earl Weaver	109-53
Boston	Dick Williams	82-71
	Eddie Popowski	5-4
California	Bill Rigney	11-28
	Lefty Phillips	60-63
Chicago	Al Lopez	8-9
	Don Gutteridge	60-85
Cleveland	Alvin Dark	62-99
Detroit	Mayo Smith	90-72
Kansas City	Joe Gordon	69-93
Minnesota	Billy Martin	97-65
New York	Ralph Houk	80-81
Oakland	Hank Bauer	80-69
	John McNamara	8-5
Seattle	Joe Schultz	64-98
Washington	Ted Williams	86-76

Awards

Most Valuable Player	H. Killebrew, 3b, Min
Cy Young	Mike Cuellar, Bal
	Denny McLain, Det
Rookie of the Year	Lou Piniella, of, KC
STATS Manager of the Year	Billy Martin, Min

STATS All-Star Team

C	Bill Freehan, Det	.262	16	49
1B	Boog Powell, Bal	.304	37	121
2B	Rod Carew, Min	.332	8	56
3B	Harmon Killebrew, Min	.276	49	140
SS	Rico Petrocelli, Bos	.297	40	97
OF	Frank Howard, Was	.296	48	111
OF	Reggie Jackson, Oak	.275	47	118
OF	Frank Robinson, Bal	.308	32	100
P	Mike Cuellar, Bal	23-11	2.38	182 K
P	Sam McDowell, Cle	18-14	2.94	279 K
P	Denny McLain, Det	24-9	2.80	181 K
P	Andy Messersmith, Cal	16-11	2.52	211 K
RP	Ron Perranoski, Min	9-10	2.11	31 Sv

Postseason

LCS	Baltimore 3 vs. Minnesota 0
World Series	Baltimore (AL) 1 vs. New York (NL) 4

Outstanding Performances

No-Hitters

Jim Palmer, Bal	vs. Oak on August 13

Three-Homer Games

Mike Epstein, Was	on May 16
Joe Lahoud, Bos	on June 11
Bill Melton, ChA	on June 24
Reggie Jackson, Oak	on July 2

1969 National League Standings

		Overall				Home Games								Road Games						Park Index		Record by Month						
EAST	W	L	Pct	GB	DIF	W	L	R	OR	HR	OHR	W	L	R	OR	HR	OHR	Run	HR	M/A	May	June	July	Aug	S/O
New York	100	62	.617	—	24	52	30	312	270	56	59	48	32	320	271	53	60	96	99	9-11	12-12	19-9	15-12	21-10	24-8
Chicago	92	70	.568	8.0	156	49	32	387	321	84	64	43	38	333	290	58	54	114	132	16-7	16-9	18-11	15-14	18-11	9-18
Pittsburgh	88	74	.543	12.0	7	47	34	324	322	41	33	41	40	401	330	78	63	88	52	13-8	11-15	14-15	15-12	17-10	18-14
St. Louis	87	75	.537	13.0	1	42	38	273	273	41	43	45	37	322	267	49	56	95	82	9-12	12-13	14-16	20-8	16-13	16-13
Philadelphia	63	99	.389	37.0	1	30	51	317	378	75	64	33	48	328	367	62	70	100	105	8-11	10-13	15-15	9-21	10-18	11-21
Montreal	52	110	.321	48.0	2	24	57	288	421	73	87	28	53	294	370	52	58	107	145	7-13	4-19	10-20	12-18	8-23	11-17
WEST																									
Atlanta	93	69	.574	—	108	50	31	360	321	77	84	43	38	331	310	64	60	106	130	14-7	14-9	16-14	16-16	13-16	20-7
San Francisco	90	72	.556	3.0	27	52	29	362	317	77	61	38	43	351	319	59	59	101	117	15-6	9-16	15-14	18-11	17-12	16-13
Cincinnati	89	73	.549	4.0	19	50	31	407	373	97	74	39	42	391	395	74	75	99	115	9-11	15-8	14-14	15-11	19-14	17-15
Los Angeles	85	77	.525	8.0	30	50	31	325	258	41	55	35	46	320	303	56	67	94	78	14-7	13-11	17-11	12-17	16-12	13-19
Houston	81	81	.500	12.0	0	52	29	371	313	47	43	29	52	305	355	57	68	104	72	4-20	20-6	15-13	15-10	15-14	12-18
San Diego	52	110	.321	41.0	3	28	53	239	358	47	47	24	57	229	388	52	66	97	80	9-14	11-16	7-22	7-19	5-22	13-17

Clinch Date—New York 9/24, Atlanta 9/30.

Team Batting

Team	G	AB	R	OR	H	2B	3B	HR	TB	RBI	TBB	IBB	SO	HBP	SH	SF	SB	CS	SB%	GDP	Avg	OBP	Slg
Cincinnati	163	5634	798	768	1558	224	42	171	2379	750	474	63	1042	46	100	47	79	56	.59	117	.277	.343	.422
Pittsburgh	162	5626	725	652	1557	220	52	119	2238	651	454	86	944	46	73	36	74	34	.69	128	.277	.340	.398
Chicago	163	5530	720	611	1400	215	40	142	2121	671	559	58	928	36	72	46	30	32	.48	111	.253	.331	.384
San Francisco	162	5474	713	636	1325	187	28	136	1976	657	711	82	1054	66	82	42	71	32	.69	121	.242	.341	.361
Atlanta	162	5460	691	631	1411	195	22	141	2073	640	485	67	665	32	87	34	59	48	.55	130	.258	.326	.380
Houston	162	5348	676	668	1284	208	40	104	1884	618	699	70	972	41	68	40	101	64	.64	109	.240	.337	.352
Philadelphia	162	5408	645	745	1304	227	35	137	2012	593	549	60	1130	26	61	36	73	49	.60	119	.241	.318	.372
Los Angeles	162	5532	645	561	1405	185	52	97	1985	584	484	63	823	21	96	33	80	51	.61	110	.254	.320	.359
New York	162	5427	632	541	1311	184	41	109	1904	598	527	58	1089	33	82	33	66	43	.61	105	.242	.316	.351
St. Louis	162	5536	595	540	1403	228	44	90	1989	561	503	70	876	23	57	33	87	49	.64	112	.253	.322	.359
Montreal	162	5419	582	791	1300	202	33	125	1943	542	529	51	962	38	57	30	52	52	.50	132	.240	.315	.359
San Diego	162	5357	468	746	1203	180	42	99	1764	431	423	40	1143	35	56	20	45	44	.51	122	.225	.288	.329
NL Total	1946	65751	7890	7890	16461	2455	471	1470	24268	7296	6397	768	11628	443	891	430	817	548	.60	1416	.250	.319	.369
NL Avg Team	162	5479	658	658	1372	205	39	123	2022	608	533	64	969	37	74	36	68	46	.60	118	.250	.319	.369

Team Pitching

Team	G	CG	ShO	Rel	Sv	IP	H	R	ER	HR	SH	SF	HB	TBB	IBB	SO	WP	Bk	H/9	SO/9	BB/9	OAvg	OOBP	ERA
St. Louis	162	63	12	183	26	1460.1	1289	540	477	99	63	40	31	511	61	1004	43	4	7.9	6.2	3.1	.237	.305	2.94
New York	162	51	28	203	35	1468.1	1217	541	487	119	79	33	29	517	70	1012	56	8	7.5	6.2	3.2	.227	.296	2.99
Los Angeles	162	47	20	190	31	1457.0	1324	561	499	122	68	32	38	420	41	975	51	4	8.2	6.0	2.6	.242	.299	3.08
San Francisco	162	71	15	174	17	1473.2	1381	636	534	120	77	37	35	461	65	906	54	5	8.4	5.5	2.8	.248	.307	3.26
Chicago	163	58	22	245	27	1454.1	1366	611	540	118	65	31	29	475	72	1017	39	4	8.5	6.3	2.9	.248	.310	3.34
Atlanta	162	38	7	221	42	1445.0	1334	631	567	144	90	31	27	438	49	893	40	4	8.3	5.6	2.7	.245	.302	3.53
Houston	162	52	11	256	34	1435.2	1347	668	574	111	55	30	35	547	65	1221	73	9	8.4	7.7	3.4	.247	.318	3.60
Pittsburgh	162	39	9	267	33	1445.2	1348	652	580	96	65	32	24	553	48	1124	33	13	8.4	7.0	3.4	.248	.320	3.61
Cincinnati	163	23	11	307	44	1465.0	1478	768	669	149	83	36	56	611	78	818	76	6	9.1	5.0	3.8	.262	.338	4.11
Philadelphia	162	47	14	236	21	1434.0	1494	745	660	134	73	45	38	570	57	921	54	8	9.4	5.8	3.6	.270	.340	4.14
San Diego	162	16	9	322	25	1422.1	1454	746	670	113	93	38	39	592	86	764	65	5	9.2	4.8	3.7	.267	.341	4.24
Montreal	162	26	8	299	21	1426.0	1429	791	686	145	80	45	49	702	76	973	64	9	9.0	6.1	4.4	.263	.350	4.33
NL Total	1946	531	166	2903	356	17387.1	16461	7890	6943	1470	891	430	443	6397	768	11628	648	79	8.5	6.0	3.3	.250	.325	3.59
NL Avg Team	162	44	14	242	30	1448.1	1372	658	579	123	74	36	37	533	64	969	54	7	8.5	6.0	3.3	.250	.325	3.59

Team Fielding

Team	G	PO	A	E	TC	DP	PB	Pct
Atlanta	162	4335	1635	115	6085	114	31	.981
New York	162	4405	1696	122	6223	146	7	.980
Los Angeles	162	4371	1836	126	6333	130	17	.980
Chicago	163	4363	1868	136	6367	149	11	.979
Philadelphia	162	4302	1753	137	6192	157	22	.978
St. Louis	162	4381	1690	138	6209	144	17	.978
Pittsburgh	162	4337	1782	155	6274	169	17	.975
San Diego	162	4267	1814	156	6237	140	21	.975
Houston	162	4307	1624	153	6084	136	15	.975
San Francisco	162	4421	1928	169	6518	155	19	.974
Cincinnati	163	4395	1758	167	6320	158	17	.974
Montreal	162	4278	1784	184	6246	179	23	.971
NL Total	1946	52162	21168	1758	75088	1777	217	.977

Team vs. Team Records

	Atl	ChN	Cin	Hou	LA	Mon	NYN	Phi	Pit	SD	SF	StL	Won
Atl	—	3	12	15	9	8	4	6	8	13	9	6	93
ChN	9	—	6	8	6	10	8	12	7	11	6	9	92
Cin	6	6	—	9	10	8	6	10	5	11	10	8	89
Hou	3	4	9	—	6	11	10	8	3	10	10	7	81
LA	9	6	8	12	—	10	4	8	8	12	5	3	85
Mon	4	8	4	1	2	—	5	11	5	4	1	7	52
NYN	8	10	6	2	8	13	—	12	10	11	8	12	100
Phi	6	6	2	4	4	7	6	—	10	8	3	7	63
Pit	4	11	7	9	4	13	8	8	—	10	5	9	88
SD	5	1	7	8	6	8	1	4	2	—	6	4	52
SF	9	6	8	8	13	11	4	9	7	12	—	3	90
StL	6	9	4	5	9	11	6	11	9	8	9	—	87
Lost	69	70	73	81	77	110	62	99	74	110	72	75	

1969 National League Batting Leaders

Games		At-Bats		Runs		Hits		Doubles		Triples	
B. Williams, ChN	163	M. Alou, Pit	698	B. Bonds, SF	120	M. Alou, Pit	231	M. Alou, Pit	41	R. Clemente, Pit	12
F. Millan, Atl	162	D. Kessinger, ChN	664	P. Rose, Cin	120	P. Rose, Cin	218	D. Kessinger, ChN	38	P. Rose, Cin	11
M. Alou, Pit	162	L. Brock, StL	655	J. Wynn, Hou	113	L. Brock, StL	195	P. Rose, Cin	33	B. Tolan, Cin	10
T. Perez, Cin	160	F. Millan, Atl	652	D. Kessinger, ChN	109	B. Tolan, Cin	194	L. Brock, StL	33	L. Brock, StL	10
R. Santo, ChN	160	B. Williams, ChN	642	M. Alou, Pit	105	B. Williams, ChN	188	B. Williams, ChN	33	B. Williams, ChN	10

Home Runs		Total Bases		Runs Batted In		Walks		Intentional Walks		Strikeouts	
W. McCovey, SF	45	H. Aaron, Atl	332	W. McCovey, SF	126	J. Wynn, Hou	148	W. McCovey, SF	45	B. Bonds, SF	187
H. Aaron, Atl	44	T. Perez, Cin	331	R. Santo, ChN	123	W. McCovey, SF	121	H. Aaron, Atl	19	L. Hisle, Phi	152
L. May, Cin	38	W. McCovey, SF	322	T. Perez, Cin	122	R. Staub, Mon	110	P. Rose, Cin	18	D. Allen, Phi	144
T. Perez, Cin	37	L. May, Cin	321	L. May, Cin	110	J. Morgan, Hou	110	R. Clemente, Pit	16	L. May, Cin	142
J. Wynn, Hou	33	P. Rose, Cin	321	E. Banks, ChN	106	R. Santo, ChN	96	3 tied with	15	J. Wynn, Hou	142

Hit By Pitch		Sac Hits		Sac Flies		Stolen Bases		Caught Stealing		GDP	
R. Hunt, SF	25	J. Merritt, Cin	15	R. Santo, ChN	14	L. Brock, StL	53	M. Wills, 2tm	21	R. Santo, ChN	21
B. Tolan, Cin	15	M. Mota, 2tm	14	A. Johnson, Cin	11	J. Morgan, Hou	49	J. Morgan, Hou	14	T. Perez, Cin	20
M. Jones, Mon	15	R. Reed, Atl	13	D. Johnson, Phi	9	B. Bonds, SF	45	L. Brock, StL	14	T. Helms, Cin	20
A. Oliver, Pit	13	H. Lanier, SF	13	V. Pinson, StL	9	M. Wills, 2tm	40	B. Tolan, Cin	12	R. Clemente, Pit	19
B. Bonds, SF	10	R. Hunt, SF	12	C. Laboy, Mon	8	B. Tolan, Cin	26	4 tied with	10	A. Oliver, Pit	18

Runs Created		Runs Created/27 Outs		Batting Average		On-Base Percentage		Slugging Percentage		OBP+Slugging	
W. McCovey, SF	140	W. McCovey, SF	10.75	P. Rose, Cin	.348	W. McCovey, SF	.453	W. McCovey, SF	.656	W. McCovey, SF	1.108
P. Rose, Cin	133	J. Wynn, Hou	8.79	R. Clemente, Pit	.345	J. Wynn, Hou	.436	H. Aaron, Atl	.607	H. Aaron, Atl	1.003
H. Aaron, Atl	128	H. Aaron, Atl	8.43	C. Jones, NYN	.340	P. Rose, Cin	.428	D. Allen, Phi	.573	R. Clemente, Pit	.955
J. Wynn, Hou	124	P. Rose, Cin	8.17	M. Alou, Pit	.331	R. Staub, Mon	.426	W. Stargell, Pit	.556	R. Staub, Mon	.952
R. Staub, Mon	118	C. Jones, NYN	7.98	W. McCovey, SF	.320	C. Jones, NYN	.422	R. Clemente, Pit	.544	D. Allen, Phi	.949

1969 National League Pitching Leaders

Wins		Losses		Winning Percentage		Games		Games Started		Complete Games	
T. Seaver, NYN	25	C. Kirby, SD	20	B. Moose, Pit	.824	W. Granger, Cin	90	F. Jenkins, ChN	42	B. Gibson, StL	28
P. Niekro, Atl	23	B. Stoneman, Mon	19	T. Seaver, NYN	.781	D. McGinn, Mon	74	D. Sutton, LA	41	J. Marichal, SF	27
F. Jenkins, ChN	21	G. Jackson, Phi	18	J. Maloney, Cin	.706	C. Carroll, Cin	71	B. Hands, ChN	41	G. Perry, SF	26
J. Marichal, SF	21	J. Niekro, 2tm	18	C. Carroll, Cin	.667	P. Regan, ChN	71	C. Osteen, LA	41	F. Jenkins, ChN	23
5 tied with	20	D. Sutton, LA	18	P. Regan, ChN	.667	F. Reberger, SD	67	B. Singer, LA	40	P. Niekro, Atl	21

Shutouts		Saves		Games Finished		Batters Faced		Innings Pitched		Hits Allowed	
J. Marichal, SF	8	F. Gladding, Hou	29	W. Granger, Cin	55	G. Perry, SF	1345	G. Perry, SF	325.1	C. Osteen, LA	293
F. Jenkins, ChN	7	W. Granger, Cin	27	P. Regan, ChN	49	C. Osteen, LA	1291	C. Osteen, LA	321.0	G. Perry, SF	290
C. Osteen, LA	7	C. Upshaw, Atl	27	C. Upshaw, Atl	47	F. Jenkins, ChN	1275	B. Singer, LA	315.2	F. Jenkins, ChN	284
J. Koosman, NYN	6	J. Brewer, LA	20	R. Taylor, NYN	44	B. Gibson, StL	1270	B. Gibson, StL	314.0	D. Sutton, LA	269
K. Holtzman, ChN	6	P. Regan, ChN	17	2 tied with	43	B. Singer, LA	1263	F. Jenkins, ChN	311.1	J. Merritt, Cin	269

Home Runs Allowed		Walks		Walks/9 Innings		Strikeouts		Strikeouts/9 Innings		Strikeout/Walk Ratio	
J. Merritt, Cin	33	B. Stoneman, Mon	123	J. Marichal, SF	1.6	F. Jenkins, ChN	273	T. Griffin, Hou	9.6	F. Jenkins, ChN	3.85
F. Jenkins, ChN	27	T. Cloninger, Cin	103	P. Niekro, Atl	1.8	B. Gibson, StL	269	D. Wilson, Hou	9.4	J. Marichal, SF	3.80
B. Stoneman, Mon	26	C. Kirby, SD	100	F. Jenkins, ChN	2.1	B. Singer, LA	247	B. Moose, Pit	8.7	P. Niekro, Atl	3.39
D. Sutton, LA	25	D. Wilson, Hou	97	J. Niekro, 2tm	2.1	D. Wilson, Hou	235	D. Selma, 2tm	8.5	B. Singer, LA	3.34
P. Jarvis, Atl	25	M. Wegener, Mon	96	C. Osteen, LA	2.1	G. Perry, SF	233	B. Veale, Pit	8.5	L. Dierker, Hou	3.22

Earned Run Average		Component ERA		Hit Batsmen		Wild Pitches		Opponent Average		Opponent OBP	
J. Marichal, SF	2.10	J. Marichal, SF	2.07	B. Stoneman, Mon	12	D. Wilson, Hou	16	T. Seaver, NYN	.207	L. Dierker, Hou	.261
S. Carlton, StL	2.17	L. Dierker, Hou	2.11	W. Fryman, Phi	11	J. Maloney, Cin	16	J. Maloney, Cin	.208	J. Marichal, SF	.261
B. Gibson, StL	2.18	B. Singer, LA	2.19	G. Perry, SF	11	P. Niekro, Atl	15	B. Singer, LA	.210	B. Singer, LA	.261
T. Seaver, NYN	2.21	J. Koosman, NYN	2.24	B. Singer, LA	10	T. Cloninger, Cin	14	L. Dierker, Hou	.214	P. Niekro, Atl	.264
J. Koosman, NYN	2.28	P. Niekro, Atl	2.27	B. Gibson, StL	10	M. Wegener, Mon	13	S. Carlton, StL	.216	T. Seaver, NYN	.272

1969 National League Miscellaneous

Managers

Atlanta	Lum Harris	93-69
Chicago	Leo Durocher	92-70
Cincinnati	Dave Bristol	89-73
Houston	Harry Walker	81-81
Los Angeles	Walter Alston	85-77
Montreal	Gene Mauch	52-110
New York	Gil Hodges	100-62
Philadelphia	Bob Skinner	44-64
	George Myatt	19-35
Pittsburgh	Larry Shepard	84-73
	Alex Grammas	4-1
St. Louis	Red Schoendienst	87-75
San Diego	Preston Gomez	52-110
San Francisco	Clyde King	90-72

Awards

Most Valuable Player	Willie McCovey, 1b, SF
Cy Young	Tom Seaver, NYN
Rookie of the Year	Ted Sizemore, 2b, LA
STATS Manager of the Year	Gil Hodges, NYN

STATS All-Star Team

C	Johnny Bench, Cin	.293	26	90	
1B	Willie McCovey, SF	.320	45	126	
2B	Joe Morgan, Hou	.236	15	43	
3B	Ron Santo, ChN	.289	29	123	
SS	Denis Menke, Hou	.269	10	90	
OF	Hank Aaron, Atl	.300	44	97	
OF	Pete Rose, Cin	.348	16	82	
OF	Jimmy Wynn, Hou	.269	33	87	
P	Bob Gibson, StL	20-13	2.18	269 K	
P	Juan Marichal, SF	21-11	2.10	205 K	
P	Phil Niekro, Atl	23-13	2.56	193 K	
P	Tom Seaver, NYN	25-7	2.21	208 K	
RP	Wayne Granger, Cin	9-6	2.80	27 Sv	

Postseason

LCS	New York 3 vs. Atlanta 0
World Series	New York (NL) 4 vs. Baltimore (AL) 1

Outstanding Performances

No-Hitters

Bill Stoneman, Mon	@ Phi on April 17
Jim Maloney, Cin	vs. Hou on April 30
Don Wilson, Hou	@ Cin on May 1
Ken Holtzman, ChN	vs. Atl on August 19
Bob Moose, Pit	@ NYN on September 20

Three-Homer Games

Bob Tillman, Atl	on July 30
R. Clemente, Pit	on August 13

1970 American League Standings

EAST	Overall W	L	Pct	GB	DIF	Home Games W	L	R	OR	HR	OHR	Road Games W	L	R	OR	HR	OHR	Park Index Run	HR	Record by Month M/A	May	June	July	Aug	S/O
Baltimore	108	54	.667	—	169	59	22	386	256	88	58	49	32	406	318	91	81	89	85	13-6	20-9	14-13	17-11	23-8	21-7
New York	93	69	.574	15.0	0	53	28	317	257	60	40	40	41	363	355	51	90	80	71	9-12	17-11	17-7	13-16	18-13	19-10
Boston	87	75	.537	21.0	2	52	29	455	382	117	75	35	46	331	340	86	81	125	115	11-8	9-17	14-11	18-13	16-14	19-12
Detroit	79	83	.488	29.0	10	42	39	348	379	86	86	37	44	318	352	62	67	109	133	12-6	9-17	17-10	19-12	12-18	10-20
Cleveland	76	86	.469	32.0	0	43	38	386	370	133	103	33	48	263	305	50	60	133	215	7-11	9-16	16-12	17-15	15-16	12-16
Washington	70	92	.432	38.0	0	40	41	303	330	72	61	30	51	323	359	66	78	93	92	11-8	11-16	12-16	12-16	17-13	7-23
WEST																									
Minnesota	98	64	.605	—	172	51	30	366	285	66	53	47	34	378	320	87	77	93	73	12-6	19-7	14-12	17-11	14-18	22-10
Oakland	89	73	.549	9.0	2	49	32	337	265	83	56	40	41	341	328	88	78	90	84	8-12	17-11	17-10	15-12	13-17	19-11
California	86	76	.531	12.0	17	43	38	287	274	41	59	43	38	344	356	73	95	80	60	13-7	17-10	13-14	15-14	16-13	12-18
Kansas City	65	97	.401	33.0	1	35	44	305	331	46	48	30	53	306	374	51	90	98	70	7-12	12-15	7-19	12-19	13-16	14-16
Milwaukee	65	97	.401	33.0	1	38	42	313	362	68	72	27	55	300	389	58	74	100	109	5-15	10-15	11-18	12-18	12-17	15-14
Chicago	56	106	.346	42.0	1	31	53	346	469	78	97	25	53	287	353	45	67	118	145	7-12	11-17	9-19	10-20	12-18	7-20

Clinch Date—Baltimore 9/24, Minnesota 9/22.

Team Batting

Team	G	AB	R	OR	H	2B	3B	HR	TB	RBI	TBB	IBB	SO	HBP	SH	SF	SB	CS	SB%	GDP	Avg	OBP	Slg
Baltimore	162	5545	792	574	1424	213	25	179	2224	748	717	64	952	44	64	46	84	39	.68	110	.257	.351	.401
Boston	162	5535	786	722	1450	252	28	203	2367	743	594	47	855	40	34	47	50	48	.51	137	.262	.343	.428
Minnesota	162	5483	744	605	1438	230	41	153	2209	694	501	65	905	42	79	38	57	52	.52	132	.262	.333	.403
New York	163	5492	680	612	1381	208	41	111	2004	627	588	48	808	25	60	46	105	61	.63	115	.251	.332	.365
Oakland	162	5376	678	593	1338	208	24	171	2107	630	584	55	977	36	73	36	131	68	.66	121	.249	.331	.392
Detroit	162	5377	666	731	1282	207	38	148	2009	619	656	56	825	34	83	49	29	30	.49	134	.238	.330	.374
Cleveland	162	5463	649	675	1358	197	23	183	2150	617	503	42	909	37	76	45	25	36	.41	119	.249	.321	.394
Chicago	162	5514	633	822	1394	192	20	123	1995	587	477	41	872	42	51	48	53	33	.62	132	.253	.322	.362
California	162	5532	631	630	1391	197	40	114	2010	598	447	56	922	29	69	37	69	27	.72	118	.251	.315	.363
Washington	162	5460	626	689	1302	184	28	138	1956	583	635	68	989	46	44	38	72	42	.63	133	.238	.327	.358
Milwaukee	163	5395	613	751	1305	202	24	126	1933	571	592	54	985	36	115	32	91	73	.55	132	.242	.325	.358
Kansas City	162	5503	611	705	1341	202	41	97	1916	572	514	42	958	21	63	27	97	53	.65	123	.244	.314	.348
AL Total	1946	65675	8109	8109	16404	2492	373	1746	24880	7589	6808	638	10957	432	811	489	863	562	.61	1506	.250	.322	.379
AL Avg Team	162	5473	676	676	1367	208	31	146	2073	632	567	53	913	36	68	41	72	47	.61	126	.250	.322	.379

Team Pitching

Team	G	CG	ShO	Rel	Sv	IP	H	R	ER	HR	SH	SF	HB	TBB	IBB	SO	WP	Bk	H/9	SO/9	BB/9	OAvg	OOBP	ERA
Baltimore	162	60	12	228	31	1478.2	1317	574	517	139	70	44	23	469	40	941	44	5	8.0	5.7	2.9	.240	.300	3.15
Minnesota	162	26	12	269	58	1448.1	1329	605	520	130	55	42	37	486	51	940	38	4	8.3	5.8	3.0	.244	.308	3.23
New York	163	36	6	239	49	1471.2	1386	612	530	130	62	38	26	451	54	777	32	2	8.5	4.8	2.8	.249	.306	3.24
Oakland	162	33	15	309	40	1442.2	1253	593	529	134	66	31	34	542	45	858	56	3	7.8	5.4	3.4	.234	.307	3.30
California	162	21	10	314	49	1462.1	1280	630	566	154	63	32	43	559	67	922	52	10	7.9	5.7	3.4	.237	.312	3.48
Kansas City	162	30	11	268	25	1463.2	1346	705	615	138	92	47	34	641	29	915	56	5	8.3	5.6	3.9	.247	.328	3.78
Washington	162	20	11	316	40	1457.2	1375	689	615	139	62	50	27	611	75	823	51	5	8.5	5.1	3.8	.252	.328	3.80
Boston	162	38	8	284	44	1446.1	1391	722	622	156	59	30	44	594	49	1003	70	5	8.7	6.2	3.7	.251	.327	3.87
Cleveland	162	34	8	312	35	1451.1	1333	675	630	163	74	36	40	689	62	1076	53	4	8.3	6.7	4.3	.247	.335	3.91
Detroit	162	33	9	288	39	1447.1	1443	731	658	153	57	49	35	623	31	1045	56	5	9.0	6.5	3.9	.260	.336	4.09
Milwaukee	163	31	2	283	27	1446.2	1397	751	676	146	80	46	45	587	68	895	46	3	8.7	5.6	3.7	.255	.330	4.21
Chicago	162	20	6	280	30	1430.1	1554	822	722	164	71	44	44	556	67	762	63	4	9.8	4.8	3.5	.280	.347	4.54
AL Total	1946	382	110	3390	467	17447.0	16404	8109	7200	1746	811	489	432	6808	638	10957	617	55	8.5	5.7	3.5	.250	.329	3.71
AL Avg Team	162	32	9	283	39	1453.0	1367	676	600	146	68	41	36	567	53	913	51	5	8.5	5.7	3.5	.250	.329	3.71

Team Fielding

Team	G	PO	A	E	TC	DP	PB	Pct
Washington	162	4367	1943	116	6426	173	12	.982
Baltimore	162	4434	1699	117	6250	148	12	.981
New York	163	4407	1929	130	6466	146	12	.980
Minnesota	162	4345	1636	123	6104	130	11	.980
California	162	4381	1782	127	6290	169	27	.980
Cleveland	162	4358	1740	133	6231	168	23	.979
Detroit	162	4343	1640	133	6116	142	15	.978
Milwaukee	163	4321	1731	136	6188	142	9	.978
Oakland	162	4322	1670	141	6133	152	12	.977
Kansas City	162	4386	1700	152	6238	162	16	.976
Chicago	162	4287	2058	165	6510	187	27	.975
Boston	162	4324	1596	156	6076	131	13	.974
AL Total	1946	52275	21124	1629	75028	1850	189	.978

Team vs. Team Records

	Bal	Bos	Cal	ChA	Cle	Det	KC	Mil	Min	NYA	Oak	Was	Won
Bal	—	13	7	9	14	11	12	7	5	11	7	12	108
Bos	5	—	5	8	12	9	7	5	7	10	7	12	87
Cal	5	7	—	12	6	6	10	12	8	5	8	7	86
ChA	3	4	6	—	6	6	7	7	6	5	2	4	56
Cle	4	6	6	6	—	7	8	7	6	8	7	11	76
Det	7	9	6	6	11	—	6	8	4	7	6	9	79
KC	0	5	8	11	4	6	—	12	5	1	7	6	65
Mil	5	7	6	11	5	4	6	—	5	3	8	5	65
Min	7	5	10	12	6	8	13	13	—	5	13	6	98
NYA	7	8	7	7	10	11	11	9	7	—	6	10	93
Oak	5	5	10	16	5	6	11	10	5	6	—	10	89
Was	6	6	5	8	7	9	6	7	6	8	2	—	70
Lost	54	75	76	106	86	83	97	97	64	69	73	92	

Seasons: Standings, Leaders

1970 American League Batting Leaders

Games		At-Bats		Runs		Hits		Doubles		Triples	
R. White, NYA	162	H. Clarke, NYA	686	C. Yastrzemski, Bos	125	T. Oliva, Min	204	A. Otis, KC	36	C. Tovar, Min	13
S. Alomar, Cal	162	S. Alomar, Cal	672	C. Tovar, Min	120	A. Johnson, Cal	202	C. Tovar, Min	36	M. Stanley, Det	11
C. Yastrzemski, Bos	161	C. Tovar, Min	650	R. Smith, Bos	109	C. Tovar, Min	195	T. Oliva, Min	36	A. Otis, KC	9
C. Tovar, Min	161	T. Oliva, Min	628	R. White, NYA	109	C. Yastrzemski, Bos	186	T. Harper, Mil	35	5 tied with	7
F. Howard, Was	161	E. Brinkman, Was	625	T. Harper, Mil	104	R. White, NYA	180	L. Cardenas, Min	34		

Home Runs		Total Bases		Runs Batted In		Walks		Intentional Walks		Strikeouts	
F. Howard, Was	44	C. Yastrzemski, Bos	335	F. Howard, Was	126	F. Howard, Was	132	F. Howard, Was	29	R. Jackson, Oak	135
H. Killebrew, Min	41	T. Oliva, Min	323	T. Conigliaro, Bos	116	C. Yastrzemski, Bos	128	H. Killebrew, Min	23	D. Walton, Mil	126
C. Yastrzemski, Bos	40	T. Harper, Mil	315	B. Powell, Bal	114	H. Killebrew, Min	128	B. Powell, Bal	18	B. Oliver, KC	126
T. Conigliaro, Bos	36	F. Howard, Was	309	H. Killebrew, Min	113	S. Bando, Oak	118	T. Kubiak, Mil	16	F. Howard, Was	125
B. Powell, Bal	35	B. Powell, Bal	289	T. Oliva, Min	107	D. Buford, Bal	109	2 tied with	12	M. Epstein, Was	117

Hit By Pitch		Sac Hits		Sac Flies		Stolen Bases		Caught Stealing		GDP	
R. Foster, Cle	12	E. Leon, Cle	23	J. Heidemann, Cle	10	B. Campaneris, Oak	42	R. Jackson, Oak	17	H. Killebrew, Min	28
B. Melton, ChA	9	J. Niekro, Det	15	R. Petrocelli, Bos	10	T. Harper, Mil	38	P. Kelly, KC	16	C. May, ChA	25
M. Epstein, Was	9	C. Gutierrez, Det	14	B. Melton, ChA	9	S. Alomar, Cal	35	T. Harper, Mil	16	A. Johnson, Cal	25
R. Reichardt, 2tm	9	T. Kubiak, Mil	13	3 tied with	8	P. Kelly, KC	34	C. Tovar, Min	15	F. Howard, Was	23
5 tied with	8	L. Cardenas, Min	13			A. Otis, KC	33	C. Yastrzemski, Bos	13	A. Kaline, Det	20

Runs Created		Runs Created/27 Outs		Batting Average		On-Base Percentage		Slugging Percentage		OBP+Slugging	
C. Yastrzemski, Bos	145	C. Yastrzemski, Bos	9.64	A. Johnson, Cal	.329	C. Yastrzemski, Bos	.452	C. Yastrzemski, Bos	.592	C. Yastrzemski, Bos	1.044
F. Howard, Was	120	B. Powell, Bal	7.98	C. Yastrzemski, Bos	.329	F. Howard, Was	.416	B. Powell, Bal	.549	F. Howard, Was	.962
T. Harper, Mil	118	H. Killebrew, Min	7.48	T. Oliva, Min	.325	B. Powell, Bal	.412	H. Killebrew, Min	.546	B. Powell, Bal	.962
H. Killebrew, Min	117	F. Howard, Was	7.43	L. Aparicio, ChA	.313	H. Killebrew, Min	.411	F. Howard, Was	.546	H. Killebrew, Min	.957
2 tied with	116	F. Robinson, Bal	7.41	F. Robinson, Bal	.306	S. Bando, Oak	.407	T. Harper, Mil	.522	F. Robinson, Bal	.918

1970 American League Pitching Leaders

Wins		Losses		Winning Percentage		Games		Games Started		Complete Games	
D. McNally, Bal	24	M. Lolich, Det	19	M. Cuellar, Bal	.750	W. Wood, ChA	77	C. Hunter, Oak	40	M. Cuellar, Bal	21
J. Perry, Min	24	L. Krausse, Mil	18	D. McNally, Bal	.727	M. Grant, Oak	72	C. Dobson, Oak	40	S. McDowell, Cle	19
M. Cuellar, Bal	24	T. John, ChA	17	J. Perry, Min	.667	D. Knowles, Was	71	D. McNally, Bal	40	J. Palmer, Bal	17
C. Wright, Cal	22	J. Janeski, ChA	17	J. Palmer, Bal	.667	S. Williams, Min	68	J. Perry, Min	40	D. McNally, Bal	16
3 tied with	20	J. Horlen, ChA	16	D. Hall, Bal	.667	2 tied with	67	M. Cuellar, Bal	40	R. Culp, Bos	15

Shutouts		Saves		Games Finished		Batters Faced		Innings Pitched		Hits Allowed	
J. Palmer, Bal	5	R. Perranoski, Min	34	W. Wood, ChA	62	J. Palmer, Bal	1257	J. Palmer, Bal	305.0	D. McNally, Bal	277
C. Dobson, Oak	5	L. McDaniel, NYA	29	R. Perranoski, Min	52	S. McDowell, Cle	1257	S. McDowell, Cle	305.0	M. Cuellar, Bal	273
G. Peters, Bos	4	D. Knowles, Was	27	L. McDaniel, NYA	51	D. McNally, Bal	1218	M. Cuellar, Bal	297.2	M. Lolich, Det	272
J. Perry, Min	4	T. Timmermann, Det	27	D. Knowles, Was	49	M. Cuellar, Bal	1214	D. McNally, Bal	296.0	J. Palmer, Bal	263
M. Cuellar, Bal	4	M. Grant, Oak	24	M. Grant, Oak	49	M. Lolich, Det	1181	J. Perry, Min	278.2	M. Stottlemyre, NYA	262

Home Runs Allowed		Walks		Walks/9 Innings		Strikeouts		Strikeouts/9 Innings		Strikeout/Walk Ratio	
M. Cuellar, Bal	34	S. McDowell, Cle	131	F. Peterson, NYA	1.4	S. McDowell, Cle	304	S. McDowell, Cle	9.0	F. Peterson, NYA	3.17
L. Krausse, Mil	33	M. Lolich, Det	109	J. Perry, Min	1.8	M. Lolich, Det	230	B. Johnson, KC	8.7	J. Perry, Min	2.95
C. Hunter, Oak	32	J. Rooker, KC	102	C. Cox, Was	2.1	B. Johnson, KC	206	L. Cain, Det	7.8	B. Blyleven, Min	2.87
T. Murphy, Cal	32	T. John, ChA	101	M. Cuellar, Bal	2.1	J. Palmer, Bal	199	M. Lolich, Det	7.6	M. Cuellar, Bal	2.75
C. Dobson, Oak	32	2 tied with	100	J. Horlen, ChA	2.1	R. Culp, Bos	197	A. Messersmith, Cal	7.5	B. Johnson, KC	2.51

Earned Run Average		Component ERA		Hit Batsmen		Wild Pitches		Opponent Average		Opponent OBP	
D. Segui, Oak	2.56	J. Perry, Min	2.82	B. Johnson, KC	11	T. John, ChA	17	A. Messersmith, Cal	.205	F. Peterson, NYA	.279
J. Palmer, Bal	2.71	F. Peterson, NYA	2.83	R. Culp, Bos	11	S. McDowell, Cle	17	S. McDowell, Cle	.213	M. Cuellar, Bal	.284
C. Wright, Cal	2.83	A. Messersmith, Cal	2.83	5 tied with	9	G. Peters, Bos	16	D. Segui, Oak	.222	J. Perry, Min	.286
F. Peterson, NYA	2.90	D. Segui, Oak	2.84			3 tied with	14	R. Culp, Bos	.224	B. Blyleven, Min	.288
S. McDowell, Cle	2.92	J. Palmer, Bal	2.85					B. Johnson, KC	.228	A. Messersmith, Cal	.289

1970 American League Miscellaneous

Managers

Baltimore	Earl Weaver	108-54
Boston	Eddie Kasko	87-75
California	Lefty Phillips	86-76
Chicago	Don Gutteridge	49-87
	Bill Adair	4-6
	Chuck Tanner	3-13
Cleveland	Alvin Dark	76-86
Detroit	Mayo Smith	79-83
Kansas City	Charlie Metro	19-33
	Bob Lemon	46-64
Milwaukee	Dave Bristol	65-97
Minnesota	Bill Rigney	98-64
New York	Ralph Houk	93-69
Oakland	John McNamara	89-73
Washington	Ted Williams	70-92

Awards

Most Valuable Player	Boog Powell, 1b, Bal
Cy Young	Jim Perry, Min
Rookie of the Year	T. Munson, c, NYA
STATS Manager of the Year	Earl Weaver, Bal

STATS All-Star Team

C	Ray Fosse, Cle	.307	18	61
1B	Carl Yastrzemski, Bos	.329	40	102
2B	Dave Johnson, Bal	.281	10	53
3B	Harmon Killebrew, Min	.271	41	113
SS	Jim Fregosi, Cal	.278	22	82
OF	Frank Howard, Was	.283	44	126
OF	Tony Oliva, Min	.325	23	107
OF	Roy White, NYA	.296	22	94
P	Sam McDowell, Cle	20-12	2.92	304 K
P	Jim Palmer, Bal	20-10	2.71	199 K
P	Jim Perry, Min	24-12	3.04	168 K
P	Clyde Wright, Cal	22-12	2.83	110 K
RP	Lindy McDaniel, NYA	9-5	2.01	29 Sv

Postseason

LCS	Baltimore 3 vs. Minnesota 0
World Series	Baltimore (AL) 4 vs. Cincinnati (NL) 1

Outstanding Performances

No-Hitters

Clyde Wright, Cal	vs. Oak on July 3
Vida Blue, Oak	vs. Min on September 21

Three-Homer Games

Paul Blair, Bal	on April 29
Tony Horton, Cle	on May 24
Willie Horton, Det	on June 9
Bobby Murcer, NYA	on June 24

Cycles

Rod Carew, Min	on May 20
Tony Horton, Cle	on July 2

1970 National League Standings

	Overall					Home Games						Road Games						Park Index		Record by Month					
EAST	W	L	Pct	GB	DIF	W	L	R	OR	HR	OHR	W	L	R	OR	HR	OHR	Run	HR	M/A	May	June	July	Aug	S/O
Pittsburgh	89	73	.549	—	89	50	32	356	315	43	41	39	41	373	349	87	65	91	54	11-8	12-18	17-11	16-11	14-15	19-10
Chicago	84	78	.519	5.0	56	46	34	471	394	109	92	38	44	335	285	70	51	143	170	13-5	12-14	10-18	19-12	15-15	15-14
New York	83	79	.512	6.0	24	44	38	374	314	63	75	39	41	321	316	57	60	105	115	10-9	15-14	15-10	15-13	13-18	15-15
St. Louis	76	86	.469	13.0	17	34	47	377	418	51	44	42	39	367	329	62	58	114	79	9-7	12-17	16-13	8-21	19-11	12-17
Philadelphia	73	88	.453	15.5	10	40	40	293	337	48	63	33	48	301	393	53	69	92	92	10-9	10-18	12-13	14-14	16-16	11-18
Montreal	73	89	.451	16.0	1	39	41	363	385	77	91	34	48	324	422	59	71	103	132	5-13	11-17	13-14	15-15	13-16	16-14
WEST																									
Cincinnati	102	60	.630	—	177	57	24	416	334	100	58	45	36	359	347	91	60	106	105	16-6	20-8	16-8	20-12	14-15	16-11
Los Angeles	87	74	.540	14.5	0	39	42	310	316	35	82	48	32	439	368	52	82	77	86	10-10	18-10	15-12	16-10	13-16	15-16
San Francisco	86	76	.531	16.0	2	48	33	413	386	84	77	38	43	418	440	81	79	93	101	10-12	14-14	12-12	13-14	20-11	17-13
Houston	79	83	.488	23.0	1	44	37	350	351	51	64	35	46	394	412	78	67	87	79	7-14	14-15	12-14	13-14	16-13	17-13
Atlanta	76	86	.469	26.0	0	42	39	395	398	92	119	34	47	341	374	68	66	111	157	10-11	17-8	10-16	13-18	15-14	11-19
San Diego	63	99	.389	39.0	1	31	50	312	393	68	56	32	49	369	395	104	93	92	63	7-14	15-17	9-16	9-17	10-18	13-17

Clinch Date—Pittsburgh 9/27, Cincinnati 9/17.

Team Batting

Team	G	AB	R	OR	H	2B	3B	HR	TB	RBI	TBB	IBB	SO	HBP	SH	SF	SB	CS	SB%	GDP	Avg	OBP	Slg
San Francisco	162	5578	831	826	1460	257	35	165	2282	773	729	95	1005	56	66	40	83	27	.75	143	.262	.357	.409
Chicago	162	5491	806	679	1424	228	44	179	2277	761	607	65	844	20	75	36	39	16	.71	110	.259	.339	.415
Cincinnati	162	5540	775	681	1498	253	45	191	2414	726	547	70	984	29	58	48	115	52	.69	119	.270	.344	.436
Los Angeles	161	5606	749	684	1515	233	67	87	2143	695	541	67	841	24	72	50	138	57	.71	114	.270	.342	.382
Houston	162	5574	744	763	1446	250	47	129	2177	694	598	81	911	27	63	43	114	41	.74	144	.259	.339	.391
St. Louis	162	5689	744	747	1497	218	51	113	2156	688	569	65	961	26	52	40	117	47	.71	138	.263	.337	.379
Atlanta	162	5546	736	772	1495	215	24	160	2238	692	522	72	736	38	54	42	58	34	.63	140	.270	.341	.404
Pittsburgh	162	5637	729	664	1522	235	70	130	2287	676	444	82	871	44	53	53	66	34	.66	117	.270	.334	.406
New York	162	5443	695	630	1358	211	42	120	2013	640	684	60	1062	26	74	48	118	54	.69	139	.249	.341	.370
Montreal	162	5411	687	807	1284	211	35	136	1973	646	659	64	972	39	107	49	65	45	.59	106	.237	.328	.365
San Diego	162	5494	681	788	1353	208	36	172	2149	629	500	46	1164	39	83	29	60	45	.57	111	.246	.317	.391
Philadelphia	161	5456	594	730	1299	224	58	101	1942	553	519	59	1066	25	62	37	72	64	.53	133	.238	.311	.356
NL Total	1942	66465	8771	8771	17151	2743	554	1683	26051	8173	6919	826	11417	393	819	501	1045	516	.67	1514	.258	.329	.392
NL Avg Team	162	5539	731	731	1429	229	46	140	2171	681	577	69	951	33	68	42	87	43	.67	126	.258	.329	.392

Team Pitching

Team	G	CG	ShO	Rel	Sv	IP	H	R	ER	HR	SH	SF	HB	TBB	IBB	SO	WP	Bk	H/9	SO/9	BB/9	OAvg	OOBP	ERA
New York	162	47	10	228	32	1459.2	1260	630	559	135	80	42	26	575	96	1064	48	7	7.8	6.6	3.5	.233	.307	3.45
Cincinnati	162	32	15	252	60	1444.2	1370	681	592	118	67	30	29	592	74	843	43	9	8.5	5.3	3.7	.251	.325	3.69
Pittsburgh	162	36	13	288	43	1453.2	1386	664	597	106	64	34	36	625	84	990	35	3	8.6	6.1	3.9	.255	.334	3.70
Chicago	162	59	9	205	25	1435.0	1402	679	600	143	66	43	25	475	58	1000	40	4	8.8	6.3	3.0	.256	.316	3.76
Los Angeles	161	37	17	227	42	1458.2	1394	684	619	164	63	34	34	496	49	880	49	6	8.6	5.4	3.1	.250	.314	3.82
St. Louis	162	51	11	278	20	1475.2	1483	747	665	102	82	51	22	632	102	960	66	7	9.0	5.9	3.9	.263	.337	4.06
Philadelphia	161	24	8	277	36	1461.0	1483	730	677	132	75	53	33	538	51	1047	52	7	9.1	6.4	3.3	.265	.330	4.17
Houston	162	36	6	302	35	1456.0	1491	763	685	131	64	37	41	577	46	942	91	5	9.2	5.8	3.6	.265	.336	4.23
Atlanta	162	45	9	204	24	1430.2	1451	772	688	185	66	37	30	478	42	960	44	7	9.1	6.0	3.0	.261	.320	4.33
San Diego	162	24	9	279	32	1440.1	1483	788	700	149	75	57	38	611	92	886	39	5	9.3	5.5	3.8	.267	.341	4.37
San Francisco	162	50	7	253	30	1457.2	1514	826	729	156	70	43	30	604	57	931	76	7	9.3	5.7	3.7	.267	.339	4.50
Montreal	162	29	10	285	32	1438.2	1434	807	720	162	47	40	49	716	76	914	49	6	9.0	5.7	4.5	.261	.349	4.50
NL Total	1942	470	124	3078	411	17411.2	17151	8771	7831	1683	819	501	393	6919	826	11417	632	73	8.9	5.9	3.6	.258	.336	4.05
NL Avg Team	162	39	10	257	34	1450.2	1429	731	653	140	68	42	33	577	69	951	53	6	8.9	5.9	3.6	.258	.336	4.05

Team Fielding

Team	G	PO	A	E	TC	DP	PB	Pct
Philadelphia	161	4383	1568	114	6065	134	19	.981
New York	162	4379	1514	124	6017	136	6	.979
Pittsburgh	162	4361	1930	137	6428	195	20	.979
Los Angeles	161	4376	1768	135	6279	135	17	.978
Chicago	162	4305	1791	137	6233	146	19	.978
Houston	162	4368	1791	140	6299	144	12	.978
Montreal	162	4316	1751	141	6208	193	12	.977
Atlanta	162	4292	1684	141	6117	118	30	.977
St. Louis	162	4427	1834	150	6411	159	20	.977
Cincinnati	162	4334	1835	151	6320	173	10	.976
San Diego	162	4321	1798	158	6277	159	3	.975
San Francisco	162	4373	1774	170	6317	153	30	.973
NL Total	1942	52235	21038	1698	74971	1845	198	.977

Team vs. Team Records

	Atl	ChN	Cin	Hou	LA	Mon	NYN	Phi	Pit	SD	SF	StL	Won
Atl	—	8	5	9	6	6	6	7	6	9	7	7	76
ChN	4	—	7	7	6	13	7	9	8	9	7	7	84
Cin	13	5	—	15	13	7	8	7	8	9	9	9	102
Hou	9	5	3	—	8	8	6	4	6	14	10	6	79
LA	12	6	5	10	—	8	7	6	6	11	9	7	87
Mon	6	5	5	4	4	—	10	11	9	6	6	7	73
NYN	6	5	4	6	5	8	—	13	6	6	6	12	83
Phi	5	9	5	8	5	7	5	—	4	9	8	8	73
Pit	6	10	4	6	6	9	12	14	—	6	4	12	89
SD	9	3	10	4	7	6	6	3	6	—	5	4	63
SF	11	5	9	8	9	6	6	4	8	13	—	7	86
StL	5	11	3	6	5	11	6	10	6	8	5	—	76
Lost	86	78	60	83	74	89	79	88	73	99	76	86	

1970 National League Batting Leaders

Games		At-Bats		Runs		Hits		Doubles		Triples	
W. Parker, LA	161	M. Alou, Pit	677	B. Williams, ChN	137	P. Rose, Cin	205	W. Parker, LA	47	W. Davis, LA	16
J. Torre, StL	161	L. Brock, StL	664	B. Bonds, SF	134	B. Williams, ChN	205	W. McCovey, SF	39	D. Kessinger, ChN	14
B. Williams, ChN	161	B. Bonds, SF	663	P. Rose, Cin	120	J. Torre, StL	203	P. Rose, Cin	37	B. Bonds, SF	10
R. Staub, Mon	160	P. Rose, Cin	649	L. Brock, StL	114	L. Brock, StL	202	B. Bonds, SF	36	R. Clemente, Pit	10
3 tied with	159	2 tied with	636	B. Tolan, Cin	112	M. Alou, Pit	201	D. Dietz, SF	36	7 tied with	9

Home Runs		Total Bases		Runs Batted In		Walks		Intentional Walks		Strikeouts	
J. Bench, Cin	45	B. Williams, ChN	373	J. Bench, Cin	148	W. McCovey, SF	137	W. McCovey, SF	40	B. Bonds, SF	189
B. Williams, ChN	42	J. Bench, Cin	355	T. Perez, Cin	129	R. Staub, Mon	112	W. Parker, LA	18	T. Agee, NYN	156
T. Perez, Cin	40	T. Perez, Cin	346	B. Williams, ChN	129	D. Dietz, SF	109	D. Allen, StL	16	N. Colbert, SD	150
W. McCovey, SF	39	B. Bonds, SF	334	W. McCovey, SF	126	J. Wynn, Hou	106	J. Edwards, Hou	16	B. Grabarkewitz, LA	149
2 tied with	38	C. Gaston, SD	317	H. Aaron, Atl	118	J. Morgan, Hou	102	H. Aaron, Atl	15	C. Gaston, SD	142

Hit By Pitch		Sac Hits		Sac Flies		Stolen Bases		Caught Stealing		GDP	
R. Hunt, SF	26	P. Dobson, SD	19	J. Bench, Cin	11	B. Tolan, Cin	57	B. Tolan, Cin	20	C. Jones, NYN	26
A. Oliver, Pit	14	B. Harrelson, NYN	12	D. Menke, Hou	9	L. Brock, StL	51	T. Agee, NYN	15	D. Rader, Hou	23
M. Jones, Mon	13	M. Mota, LA	12	B. Harrelson, NYN	8	B. Bonds, SF	48	L. Brock, StL	15	J. Torre, StL	23
A. Ferrara, SD	11	3 tied with	11	W. Parker, LA	8	J. Morgan, Hou	42	W. Davis, LA	14	H. Lanier, SF	20
O. Cepeda, Atl	9			9 tied with	7	W. Davis, LA	38	4 tied with	13	2 tied with	19

Runs Created		Runs Created/27 Outs		Batting Average		On-Base Percentage		Slugging Percentage		OBP+Slugging	
B. Williams, ChN	144	W. McCovey, SF	9.58	R. Carty, Atl	.366	R. Carty, Atl	.454	W. McCovey, SF	.612	W. McCovey, SF	1.056
B. Bonds, SF	130	R. Carty, Atl	9.45	J. Torre, StL	.325	W. McCovey, SF	.444	T. Perez, Cin	.589	R. Carty, Atl	1.037
W. McCovey, SF	130	J. Hickman, ChN	9.21	M. Sanguillen, Pit	.325	D. Dietz, SF	.426	J. Bench, Cin	.587	J. Hickman, ChN	1.001
J. Hickman, ChN	125	B. Williams, ChN	8.70	B. Williams, ChN	.322	J. Hickman, ChN	.419	B. Williams, ChN	.586	T. Perez, Cin	.990
T. Perez, Cin	124	D. Dietz, SF	7.94	W. Parker, LA	.319	T. Perez, Cin	.401	R. Carty, Atl	.584	B. Williams, ChN	.977

1970 National League Pitching Leaders

Wins		Losses		Winning Percentage		Games		Games Started		Complete Games	
G. Perry, SF	23	S. Carlton, StL	19	W. Simpson, Cin	.824	R. Herbel, 2tm	76	G. Perry, SF	41	F. Jenkins, ChN	24
B. Gibson, StL	23	P. Niekro, Atl	18	B. Gibson, StL	.767	D. Selma, Phi	73	F. Jenkins, ChN	39	G. Perry, SF	23
F. Jenkins, ChN	22	4 tied with	16	G. Nolan, Cin	.720	W. Granger, Cin	67	D. Sutton, LA	38	B. Gibson, StL	23
J. Merritt, Cin	20			L. Walker, Pit	.714	F. Linzy, 2tm	67	K. Holtzman, ChN	38	T. Seaver, NYN	19
4 tied with	18			D. Wilson, Hou	.647	D. Giusti, Pit	66	B. Hands, ChN	38	L. Dierker, Hou	17

Shutouts		Saves		Games Finished		Batters Faced		Innings Pitched		Hits Allowed	
G. Perry, SF	5	W. Granger, Cin	35	W. Granger, Cin	59	G. Perry, SF	1336	G. Perry, SF	328.2	G. Perry, SF	292
D. Ellis, Pit	4	D. Giusti, Pit	26	D. Selma, Phi	47	F. Jenkins, ChN	1265	F. Jenkins, ChN	313.0	C. Morton, Mon	281
D. Sutton, LA	4	J. Brewer, LA	24	D. Giusti, Pit	47	C. Morton, Mon	1218	B. Gibson, StL	294.0	C. Osteen, LA	280
C. Morton, Mon	4	C. Raymond, Mon	23	F. Gladding, Hou	44	B. Gibson, StL	1213	T. Seaver, NYN	290.2	B. Hands, ChN	278
C. Osteen, LA	4	D. Selma, Phi	22	D. McMahon, SF	44	K. Holtzman, ChN	1208	K. Holtzman, ChN	287.2	K. Holtzman, ChN	271

Home Runs Allowed		Walks		Walks/9 Innings		Strikeouts		Strikeouts/9 Innings		Strikeout/Walk Ratio	
P. Niekro, Atl	40	C. Morton, Mon	125	F. Jenkins, ChN	1.7	T. Seaver, NYN	283	T. Seaver, NYN	8.8	F. Jenkins, ChN	4.57
D. Sutton, LA	38	C. Kirby, SD	120	J. Marichal, SF	1.8	F. Jenkins, ChN	274	B. Gibson, StL	8.4	T. Seaver, NYN	3.41
L. Dierker, Hou	31	S. Carlton, StL	109	C. Osteen, LA	1.8	B. Gibson, StL	274	B. Veale, Pit	7.9	B. Gibson, StL	3.11
F. Jenkins, ChN	30	B. Stoneman, Mon	109	J. McAndrew, NYN	1.9	G. Perry, SF	214	F. Jenkins, ChN	7.9	J. McAndrew, NYN	2.92
K. Holtzman, ChN	30	S. Renko, Mon	104	J. Merritt, Cin	2.0	K. Holtzman, ChN	202	B. Stoneman, Mon	7.6	J. Bunning, Phi	2.63

Earned Run Average		Component ERA		Hit Batsmen		Wild Pitches		Opponent Average		Opponent OBP	
T. Seaver, NYN	2.82	T. Seaver, NYN	2.39	B. Stoneman, Mon	14	R. Robertson, SF	18	W. Simpson, Cin	.198	F. Jenkins, ChN	.264
W. Simpson, Cin	3.02	F. Jenkins, ChN	2.48	D. Ellis, Pit	10	F. Reberger, SF	15	T. Seaver, NYN	.214	T. Seaver, NYN	.272
L. Walker, Pit	3.04	B. Gibson, StL	2.75	D. Sutton, LA	10	D. Wilson, Hou	15	L. Walker, Pit	.219	J. McAndrew, NYN	.279
B. Gibson, StL	3.12	J. McAndrew, NYN	2.79	J. Billingham, Hou	10	S. Carlton, StL	14	F. Jenkins, ChN	.224	G. Perry, SF	.289
J. Koosman, NYN	3.14	W. Simpson, Cin	2.83	3 tied with	9	L. Palmer, Phi	14	G. Gentry, NYN	.224	B. Gibson, StL	.293

1970 National League Miscellaneous

Managers

Atlanta	Lum Harris	76-86
Chicago	Leo Durocher	84-78
Cincinnati	Sparky Anderson	102-60
Houston	Harry Walker	79-83
Los Angeles	Walter Alston	87-74
Montreal	Gene Mauch	73-89
New York	Gil Hodges	83-79
Philadelphia	Frank Lucchesi	73-88
Pittsburgh	Danny Murtaugh	89-73
St. Louis	Red Schoendienst	76-86
San Diego	Preston Gomez	63-99
San Francisco	Clyde King	19-23
	Charlie Fox	67-53

Awards

Most Valuable Player	Johnny Bench, c, Cin
Cy Young	Bob Gibson, StL
Rookie of the Year	Carl Morton, p, Mon
STATS Manager of the Year	Sparky Anderson, Cin

STATS All-Star Team

C	Johnny Bench, Cin	.293	45	148
1B	Willie McCovey, SF	.289	39	126
2B	Joe Morgan, Hou	.268	8	52
3B	Tony Perez, Cin	.317	40	129
SS	Denis Menke, Hou	.304	13	92
OF	Rico Carty, Atl	.366	25	101
OF	Jim Hickman, ChN	.315	32	115
OF	Billy Williams, ChN	.322	42	129
P	Bob Gibson, StL	23-7	3.12	274 K
P	Fergie Jenkins, ChN	22-16	3.39	274 K
P	Gaylord Perry, SF	23-13	3.20	214 K
P	Tom Seaver, NYN	18-12	2.82	283 K
RP	Wayne Granger, Cin	6-5	2.66	35 Sv

Postseason

LCS	Cincinnati 3 vs. Pittsburgh 0
World Series	Cincinnati (NL) 1 vs. Baltimore (AL) 4

Outstanding Performances

No-Hitters

Dock Ellis, Pit	@ SD on June 12
Bill Singer, LA	vs. Phi on July 20

Three-Homer Games

Rico Carty, Atl	on May 31
Mike Lum, Atl	on July 3
Johnny Bench, Cin	on July 26
Orlando Cepeda, Atl	on July 26

Cycles

Wes Parker, LA	on May 7
Tommie Agee, NYN	on July 6
Jim Ray Hart, SF	on July 8

1971 American League Standings

EAST	W	L	Pct	GB	DIF	W	L	R	OR	HR	OHR	W	L	R	OR	HR	OHR	Run	HR	M/A	May	June	July	Aug	S/O
			Overall					Home Games						Road Games				Park Index				Record by Month			
Baltimore	101	57	.639	—	142	53	24	374	254	78	67	48	33	368	276	80	58	103	111	12-8	15-11	20-9	18-10	16-10	20-9
Detroit	91	71	.562	12.0	3	54	27	352	289	90	70	37	44	349	356	89	56	91	110	10-10	16-12	16-13	17-12		19-9
Boston	85	77	.525	18.0	39	47	33	375	338	88	75	38	44	316	329	73	61	113	125	12-7	17-11	14-14	16-14	11-19	15-13
New York	82	80	.506	21.0	0	44	37	327	297	39	61	38	43	321	344	58	65	94	81	8-10	13-16	14-16	17-13	14-13	16-12
Washington	63	96	.396	38.5	2	35	46	268	296	34	59	28	50	269	364	52	73	86	72	12-10	6-19	9-18	16-12	13-18	7-19
Cleveland	60	102	.370	43.0	0	29	52	297	400	62	99	31	50	246	347	47	55	118	158	6-14	14-12	16-15	8-21	10-19	6-21
WEST																									
Oakland	101	60	.627	—	166	46	35	325	300	84	74	55	25	366	264	76	57	98	117	17-8	16-10	17-8	14-13	23-8	14-13
Kansas City	85	76	.528	16.0	2	44	37	296	277	23	36	41	39	307	289	57	48	95	55	11-11	12-11	15-12	14-16	18-12	15-14
Chicago	79	83	.488	22.5	5	39	42	278	310	60	53	40	41	339	287	78	41	94	90	8-13	10-13	12-16	19-13	14-15	16-13
California	76	86	.469	25.5	4	35	46	233	297	39	55	41	40	278	279	57	46	95	91	12-11	11-16	12-18	17-11	11-16	13-14
Minnesota	74	86	.463	26.5	3	37	42	332	356	57	71	37	44	322	314	59	68	111	103	9-12	16-12	13-15	9-17	13-15	14-15
Milwaukee	69	92	.429	32.0	5	34	48	282	319	46	64	35	44	252	290	58	66	107	85	8-11	11-14	12-17	12-18	13-16	13-16

Clinch Date—Baltimore 9/21, Oakland 9/15.

Team Batting

Team	G	AB	R	OR	H	2B	3B	HR	TB	RBI	TBB	IBB	SO	HBP	SH	SF	SB	CS	SB%	GDP	Avg	OBP	Slg
Baltimore	158	5303	742	530	1382	207	25	158	2113	702	672	69	844	46	85	37	66	38	.63	126	.261	.353	.398
Detroit	162	5502	701	645	1399	214	38	179	2226	652	540	70	854	55	62	37	35	43	.45	129	.254	.331	.405
Boston	162	5401	691	667	1360	246	28	161	2145	650	552	46	871	32	75	47	51	34	.60	146	.252	.330	.397
Oakland	161	5494	691	564	1383	195	25	160	2108	642	542	54	1018	37	80	38	80	53	.60	113	.252	.327	.384
Minnesota	160	5414	654	670	1406	197	31	116	2013	618	512	61	846	25	64	57	66	44	.60	159	.260	.333	.372
New York	162	5413	648	641	1377	195	43	97	1949	607	581	58	717	37	77	56	75	55	.58	140	.254	.337	.360
Chicago	162	5382	617	597	1346	185	30	138	2005	568	562	45	870	51	81	38	83	65	.56	107	.250	.331	.373
Kansas City	161	5295	603	566	1323	225	40	80	1868	573	490	54	819	25	45	59	130	46	.74	128	.250	.323	.353
Cleveland	162	5467	543	747	1303	200	20	109	1870	507	467	44	868	31	67	29	57	37	.61	127	.238	.305	.342
Washington	159	5290	537	660	1219	189	30	86	1726	501	575	58	956	28	58	35	68	45	.60	127	.230	.313	.326
Milwaukee	161	5185	534	609	1188	160	23	104	1706	496	543	40	924	30	107	31	89	53	.61	103	.229	.311	.329
California	162	5495	511	576	1271	213	18	96	1808	476	441	61	827	29	83	31	72	34	.68	141	.231	.296	.329
AL Total	1932	64641	7472	7472	15957	2426	351	1484	23537	6992	6477	660	10414	426	884	503	865	547	.61	1546	.247	.317	.364
AL Avg Team	161	5387	623	623	1330	202	29	124	1961	583	540	55	868	36	74	42	72	46	.61	129	.247	.317	.364

Team Pitching

Team	G	CG	ShO	Rel	Sv	IP	H	R	ER	HR	SH	SF	HB	TBB	IBB	SO	WP	Bk	H/9	SO/9	BB/9	OAvg	OOBP	ERA
Baltimore	158	71	15	177	22	1415.1	1257	530	470	125	65	32	18	416	37	793	2	8	5.0	5.0	2.6	.239	.295	2.99
Oakland	161	57	18	227	36	1469.1	1229	564	498	131	70	34	33	501	57	999	37	4	7.5	6.1	3.1	.228	.296	3.05
California	162	39	11	243	32	1481.0	1246	576	510	101	68	40	36	607	71	904	60	4	7.6	5.5	3.7	.230	.310	3.10
Chicago	162	46	19	259	32	1450.1	1348	597	503	100	81	46	29	468	38	976	43	5	8.4	6.1	2.9	.247	.307	3.12
Kansas City	161	34	15	264	44	1420.1	1301	566	513	84	80	40	36	496	21	775	41	1	8.2	4.9	3.1	.247	.314	3.25
Milwaukee	161	32	23	238	32	1416.1	1303	609	532	130	65	49	27	569	78	795	32	4	8.3	5.1	3.6	.247	.321	3.38
New York	162	67	15	189	12	1452.0	1382	641	554	126	66	48	23	423	73	707	48	3	8.6	4.4	2.6	.252	.306	3.43
Detroit	162	53	11	265	32	1468.1	1355	645	593	126	76	38	49	609	32	1000	40	5	8.3	6.1	3.7	.247	.325	3.63
Washington	159	30	10	315	26	1418.2	1376	660	583	132	83	46	45	554	74	762	43	6	8.7	4.8	3.5	.258	.331	3.70
Boston	162	44	11	274	35	1443.0	1424	667	610	136	71	35	42	535	52	871	37	0	8.8	5.4	3.3	.259	.327	3.81
Minnesota	160	43	9	252	25	1416.2	1384	670	600	139	73	43	40	529	58	895	42	3	8.8	5.7	3.4	.257	.326	3.81
Cleveland	162	21	7	325	32	1440.0	1352	747	684	154	86	52	48	770	69	937	66	8	8.5	5.9	4.8	.252	.348	4.28
AL Total	1932	537	164	3001	360	17291.1	15957	7472	6650	1484	884	503	426	6477	660	10414	526	45	8.3	5.4	3.4	.247	.324	3.46
AL Avg Team	161	45	14	250	30	1440.1	1330	623	554	124	74	42	36	540	55	868	44	4	8.3	5.4	3.4	.247	.324	3.46

Team Fielding

Team	G	PO	A	E	TC	DP	PB	Pct
Detroit	162	4395	1747	106	6248	156	12	.983
Baltimore	158	4234	1678	112	6024	148	16	.981
Cleveland	162	4318	1706	116	6140	159	18	.981
Boston	162	4324	1622	116	6062	149	18	.981
Oakland	161	4398	1569	117	6084	157	17	.981
New York	162	4351	1983	125	6459	159	10	.981
Minnesota	160	4248	1603	118	5969	134	12	.980
California	162	4442	1896	131	6469	159	25	.980
Kansas City	161	4244	1805	132	6181	178	11	.979
Milwaukee	161	4245	1690	138	6073	152	9	.977
Washington	159	4256	1772	141	6169	170	23	.977
Chicago	162	4347	1843	160	6350	128	32	.975
AL Total	1932	51802	20914	1512	74228	1849	203	.980

Team vs. Team Records

	Bal	Bos	Cal	ChA	Cle	Det	KC	Mil	Min	NYA	Oak	Was	Won
Bal	—	9	7	8	13	8	6	9	10	11	7	13	101
Bos	9	—	6	10	11	12	1	6	8	7	3	12	85
Cal	5	6	—	8	8	6	8	6	12	6	7	4	76
ChA	4	2	10	—	3	7	9	11	7	5	11	10	79
Cle	5	7	4	9	—	6	2	4	4	8	4	7	60
Det	10	6	6	5	12	—	8	10	6	10	4	14	91
KC	5	11	10	9	10	4	—	8	9	5	5	9	85
Mil	3	6	12	7	8	2	10	—	10	2	3	6	69
Min	2	4	6	11	8	6	9	7	—	8	8	5	74
NYA	7	11	6	7	10	8	7	10	4	—	5	7	82
Oak	4	9	11	7	8	8	13	15	10	7	—	9	101
Was	3	6	8	2	11	4	3	6	6	11	3	—	63
Lost	57	77	86	83	102	71	76	92	86	80	60	96	

Seasons: Standings, Leaders

1971 American League Batting Leaders

Games		At-Bats		Runs		Hits		Doubles		Triples	
S. Alomar, Cal	162	S. Alomar, Cal	689	D. Buford, Bal	99	C. Tovar, Min	204	R. Smith, Bos	33	F. Patek, KC	11
P. Schaal, KC	161	C. Tovar, Min	657	B. Murcer, NYA	94	S. Alomar, Cal	179	P. Schaal, KC	31	R. Carew, Min	10
K. McMullen, Cal	160	H. Clarke, NYA	625	C. Tovar, Min	94	R. Carew, Min	177	A. Rodriguez, Det	30	P. Blair, Bal	8
3 tied with	159	R. Smith, Bos	618	R. Carew, Min	88	B. Murcer, NYA	175	T. Oliva, Min	30	4 tied with	7
		A. Rodriguez, Det	604	R. Jackson, Oak	87	R. Smith, Bos	175	2 tied with	29		

Home Runs		Total Bases		Runs Batted In		Walks		Intentional Walks		Strikeouts	
B. Melton, ChA	33	R. Smith, Bos	302	H. Killebrew, Min	119	H. Killebrew, Min	114	F. Howard, Was	20	R. Jackson, Oak	161
R. Jackson, Oak	32	R. Jackson, Oak	288	F. Robinson, Bal	99	C. Yastrzemski, Bos	106	D. Buford, Bal	15	F. Howard, Was	121
N. Cash, Det	32	B. Murcer, NYA	287	R. Smith, Bos	96	P. Schaal, KC	103	D. Green, Oak	14	R. Petrocelli, Bos	108
R. Smith, Bos	30	B. Melton, ChA	267	S. Bando, Oak	94	B. Murcer, NYA	91	H. Killebrew, Min	14	G. Mitterwald, Min	104
4 tied with	28	T. Oliva, Min	266	B. Murcer, NYA	94	R. Petrocelli, Bos	91	B. Murcer, NYA	13	2 tied with	102

Hit By Pitch		Sac Hits		Sac Flies		Stolen Bases		Caught Stealing		GDP	
M. Epstein, 2tm	12	R. Theobald, Mil	19	R. White, NYA	17	A. Otis, KC	52	F. Patek, KC	14	F. Howard, Was	29
B. Melton, ChA	11	R. Culp, Bos	17	L. Cardenas, Min	11	F. Patek, KC	49	C. Tovar, Min	14	R. Carew, Min	23
B. Freehan, Det	9	W. Wood, ChA	17	H. Killebrew, Min	10	S. Alomar, Cal	39	P. Blair, Bal	11	G. Scott, Bos	23
F. Robinson, Bal	9	M. Lolich, Det	16	R. Petrocelli, Bos	9	B. Campaneris, Oak	34	3 tied with	10	3 tied with	21
2 tied with	8	2 tied with	14	2 tied with	8	2 tied with	25				

Runs Created		Runs Created/27 Outs		Batting Average		On-Base Percentage		Slugging Percentage		OBP+Slugging	
B. Murcer, NYA	120	B. Murcer, NYA	8.64	T. Oliva, Min	.337	T. Oliva, Min	.427	T. Oliva, Min	.546	B. Murcer, NYA	.970
R. Smith, Bos	105	D. Buford, Bal	7.56	B. Murcer, NYA	.331	M. Rettenmund, Bal	.422	B. Murcer, NYA	.543	T. Oliva, Min	.915
R. Jackson, Oak	102	M. Rettenmund, Bal	7.11	M. Rettenmund, Bal	.318	D. Buford, Bal	.413	N. Cash, Det	.531	N. Cash, Det	.903
R. White, NYA	101	N. Cash, Det	7.03	C. Tovar, Min	.310	R. White, NYA	.388	F. Robinson, Bal	.510	F. Robinson, Bal	.894
2 tied with	95	T. Oliva, Min	6.89	R. Carew, Min	.307	P. Schaal, KC	.387	R. Jackson, Oak	.508	D. Buford, Bal	.890

1971 American League Pitching Leaders

Wins		Losses		Winning Percentage		Games		Games Started		Complete Games	
M. Lolich, Det	25	D. McLain, Was	22	D. McNally, Bal	.808	K. Sanders, Mil	83	M. Lolich, Det	45	M. Lolich, Det	29
V. Blue, Oak	24	5 tied with	17	V. Blue, Oak	.750	F. Scherman, Det	69	W. Wood, ChA	42	V. Blue, Oak	24
W. Wood, ChA	22			C. Dobson, Oak	.750	T. Burgmeier, KC	67	V. Blue, Oak	39	W. Wood, ChA	22
C. Hunter, Oak	21			P. Dobson, Bal	.714	T. Abernathy, KC	63	T. Bradley, ChA	39	M. Cuellar, Bal	21
D. McNally, Bal	21			3 tied with	.690	3 tied with	57	J. Perry, Min	39	J. Palmer, Bal	20

Shutouts		Saves		Games Finished		Batters Faced		Innings Pitched		Hits Allowed	
V. Blue, Oak	8	K. Sanders, Mil	31	K. Sanders, Mil	77	M. Lolich, Det	1538	M. Lolich, Det	376.0	M. Lolich, Det	336
M. Stottlemyre, NYA	7	T. Abernathy, KC	23	T. Abernathy, KC	46	W. Wood, ChA	1316	W. Wood, ChA	334.0	J. Kaat, Min	275
W. Wood, ChA	7	F. Scherman, Det	20	F. Scherman, Det	40	V. Blue, Oak	1207	V. Blue, Oak	312.0	T. Bradley, ChA	273
T. Bradley, ChA	6	R. Fingers, Oak	17	P. Hennigan, Cle	38	T. Bradley, ChA	1198	M. Cuellar, Bal	292.1	W. Wood, ChA	272
2 tied with	5	T. Burgmeier, KC	17	S. Lyle, Bos	36	J. Coleman, Det	1174	J. Coleman, Det	286.0	F. Peterson, NYA	269

Home Runs Allowed		Walks		Walks/9 Innings		Strikeouts		Strikeouts/9 Innings		Strikeout/Walk Ratio	
J. Perry, Min	39	S. McDowell, Cle	153	F. Peterson, NYA	1.4	M. Lolich, Det	308	V. Blue, Oak	8.7	B. Blyleven, Min	3.80
M. Lolich, Det	36	A. Messersmith, Cal	121	S. Kline, NYA	1.5	V. Blue, Oak	301	S. McDowell, Cle	8.0	V. Blue, Oak	3.42
D. McLain, Was	31	B. Johnson, ChA	111	J. Kaat, Min	1.6	J. Coleman, Det	236	B. Johnson, ChA	7.7	W. Wood, ChA	3.39
M. Cuellar, Bal	30	S. Dunning, Cle	109	W. Wood, ChA	1.7	B. Blyleven, Min	224	J. Coleman, Det	7.4	M. Lolich, Det	3.35
2 tied with	29	J. Palmer, Bal	106	D. Drago, KC	1.7	W. Wood, ChA	210	M. Lolich, Det	7.4	F. Peterson, NYA	3.31

Earned Run Average		Component ERA		Hit Batsmen		Wild Pitches		Opponent Average		Opponent OBP	
V. Blue, Oak	1.82	V. Blue, Oak	1.81	J. Lonborg, Bos	14	T. Murphy, Cal	17	V. Blue, Oak	.189	V. Blue, Oak	.251
W. Wood, ChA	1.91	W. Wood, ChA	2.18	P. Broberg, Was	10	A. Fitzmorris, KC	15	S. McDowell, Cle	.207	W. Wood, ChA	.263
J. Palmer, Bal	2.68	C. Wright, Cal	2.49	D. Drago, KC	9	S. McDowell, Cle	13	R. May, Cal	.213	S. Kline, NYA	.275
M. Hedlund, KC	2.71	M. Stottlemyre, NYA	2.61	T. Murphy, Cal	9	B. Johnson, ChA	11	A. Messersmith, Cal	.218	P. Dobson, Bal	.278
B. Blyleven, Min	2.81	R. May, Cal	2.65	4 tied with	8	3 tied with	10	J. Palmer, Bal	.221	C. Hunter, Oak	.281

1971 American League Miscellaneous

Managers

Baltimore	Earl Weaver	101-57
Boston	Eddie Kasko	85-77
California	Lefty Phillips	76-86
Chicago	Chuck Tanner	79-83
Cleveland	Alvin Dark	42-61
	Johnny Lipon	18-41
Detroit	Billy Martin	91-71
Kansas City	Bob Lemon	85-76
Milwaukee	Dave Bristol	69-92
Minnesota	Bill Rigney	74-86
New York	Ralph Houk	82-80
Oakland	Dick Williams	101-60
Washington	Ted Williams	63-96

Awards

Most Valuable Player	Vida Blue, p, Oak
Cy Young	Vida Blue, Oak
Rookie of the Year	C. Chambliss, 1b, Cle
STATS Manager of the Year	Dick Williams, Oak

STATS All-Star Team

C	Bill Freehan, Det	.277	21	71
1B	Norm Cash, Det	.283	32	91
2B	Dave Johnson, Bal	.282	18	72
3B	Graig Nettles, Cle	.261	28	86
SS	Leo Cardenas, Min	.264	18	75
OF	Bobby Murcer, NYA	.331	25	94
OF	Tony Oliva, Min	.337	22	81
OF	Frank Robinson, Bal	.281	28	99
P	Vida Blue, Oak	24-8	1.82	301 K
P	Mickey Lolich, Det	25-14	2.92	308 K
P	Jim Palmer, Bal	20-9	2.68	184 K
P	Wilbur Wood, ChA	22-13	1.91	210 K
RP	Ken Sanders, Mil	7-12	1.91	31 Sv

Postseason

LCS	Baltimore 3 vs. Oakland 0
World Series	Bal (AL) 3 vs. Pit (NL) 4

Outstanding Performances

Three-Homer Games
Bill Freehan, Det   on August 9

Cycles
Freddie Patek, KC   on July 9

1971 National League Standings

	Overall					Home Games						Road Games						Park Index		Record by Month					
EAST	W	L	Pct	GB	DIF	W	L	R	OR	HR	OHR	W	L	R	OR	HR	OHR	Run	HR	M/A	May	June	July	Aug	S/O
Pittsburgh	97	65	.599	—	125	52	28	393	279	66	49	45	37	395	320	88	59	96	80	12-10	17-9	20-10	18-10	14-17	16-9
St. Louis	90	72	.556	7.0	17	45	36	376	358	38	49	45	36	363	341	57	55	104	78	13-11	19-6	18-21	18-11	18-11	14-12
Chicago	83	79	.512	14.0	2	44	37	363	342	74	70	39	42	274	306	54	62	122	124	8-13	14-14	18-9	16-13	15-14	12-16
New York	83	79	.512	14.0	32	44	37	281	256	48	50	39	42	307	294	50	50	89	98	12-7	15-11	18-11	9-20	12-17	17-13
Montreal	71	90	.441	25.5	11	36	44	304	366	50	68	35	46	318	363	38	65	100	116	9-6	9-18	11-21	14-19	14-11	14-15
Philadelphia	67	95	.414	30.0	1	34	47	296	353	73	80	33	48	262	335	50	52	109	150	7-12	10-18	14-15	15-16	11-16	10-18
WEST																									
San Francisco	90	72	.556	—	176	51	30	372	300	71	58	39	42	334	344	69	70	99	93	18-5	19-9	13-15	15-14	14-13	11-16
Los Angeles	89	73	.549	1.0	0	42	39	324	286	43	56	47	34	339	301	52	54	95	93	13-11	13-13	17-11	13-16	15-13	18-9
Atlanta	82	80	.506	8.0	7	43	39	366	384	96	90	39	41	277	315	57	62	124	152	10-11	12-17	16-17	19-8	13-15	12-12
Cincinnati	79	83	.488	11.0	0	46	35	303	251	69	51	33	48	283	330	69	61	90	92	8-12	12-17	16-15	13-16	19-10	11-13
Houston	79	83	.488	11.0	1	39	42	256	263	18	27	40	41	329	304	53	48	82	45	11-12	14-12	12-15	16-14	11-18	15-12
San Diego	61	100	.379	28.5	0	33	48	233	296	42	43	28	52	253	314	54	50	92	81	5-16	10-20	13-16	10-19	13-14	10-15

Clinch Date—Pittsburgh 9/22, San Francisco 9/30.

Team Batting

Team	G	AB	R	OR	H	2B	3B	HR	TB	RBI	TBB	IBB	SO	HBP	SH	SF	SB	CS	SB%	GDP	Avg	OBP	Slg
Pittsburgh	162	5674	788	599	1555	223	61	154	2362	744	469	73	919	29	62	49	65	31	.68	120	.274	.338	.416
St. Louis	163	5610	739	699	1542	225	54	95	2160	686	543	67	757	25	63	59	53		.70	144	.275	.332	.385
San Francisco	162	5461	706	644	1348	224	36	140	2064	653	654	86	1042	37	69	37	101	36	.74	126	.247	.335	.378
Los Angeles	162	5523	663	587	1469	213	38	95	2043	631	489	62	755	21	72	50	76	40	.66	140	.266	.334	.370
Atlanta	162	5575	643	699	1434	192	30	153	2145	597	434	72	747	28	91	44	57	46	.55	120	.257	.319	.385
Chicago	162	5438	637	648	1401	202	34	128	2055	603	527	65	772	34	92	40	44	32	.58	144	.258	.332	.378
Montreal	162	5335	622	729	1312	197	29	88	1831	567	543	58	800	78	102	40	51	43	.54	136	.246	.329	.343
New York	162	5477	588	550	1365	203	29	98	1920	546	547	59	958	28	91	35	89	43	.67	147	.249	.324	.351
Cincinnati	162	5414	586	581	1306	203	28	138	1979	542	438	52	907	27	69	25	59	33	.64	138	.241	.304	.366
Houston	162	5492	585	567	1319	230	52	71	1866	547	478	44	888	29	65	41	101	51	.66	105	.240	.309	.340
Philadelphia	162	5538	558	688	1289	209	35	123	1937	522	499	56	1031	34	55	45	63	39	.62	98	.233	.305	.350
San Diego	161	5366	486	610	1250	184	31	96	1784	447	438	42	966	25	87	19	70	45	.61	134	.233	.296	.332
NL Total	1944	65903	7601	7601	16590	2505	457	1379	24146	7085	6059	736	10542	395	918	484	900	492	.65	1547	.252	.316	.366
NL Avg Team	162	5492	633	633	1383	209	38	115	2012	590	505	61	879	33	77	40	75	41	.65	129	.252	.316	.366

Team Pitching

Team	G	CG	ShO	Rel	Sv	IP	H	R	ER	HR	SH	SF	HB	TBB	IBB	SO	WP	Bk	H/9	SO/9	BB/9	OAvg	OOBP	ERA
New York	162	42	13	211	22	1466.1	1227	550	488	100	65	35	40	529	63	1157	41	3	7.5	7.1	3.2	.227	.299	3.00
Houston	162	43	10	245	25	1471.1	1318	567	512	75	77	39	60	475	52	914	64	3	8.1	5.6	2.9	.241	.307	3.13
San Diego	161	47	10	237	17	1438.0	1351	610	515	93	82	40	28	559	80	923	65	7	8.5	5.8	3.5	.249	.321	3.22
Los Angeles	162	48	18	187	33	1449.2	1363	587	521	110	80	44	19	399	25	853	42	4	8.5	5.3	2.5	.250	.301	3.23
Pittsburgh	162	43	15	229	48	1461.0	1426	599	537	108	68	40	31	470	78	813	37	2	8.8	5.0	2.9	.257	.316	3.31
San Francisco	162	45	14	252	30	1454.2	1324	644	536	128	68	54	30	471	49	831	42	5	8.2	5.1	2.9	.242	.303	3.32
Cincinnati	162	27	11	255	38	1444.0	1298	581	538	112	98	27	27	501	68	750	33	4	8.1	4.7	3.1	.243	.310	3.35
Chicago	162	75	17	202	13	1444.0	1458	648	579	132	62	38	26	411	53	900	38	6	9.1	5.6	2.6	.262	.314	3.61
Philadelphia	162	31	10	253	25	1470.2	1396	688	607	132	93	49	37	525	39	838	53	2	8.5	5.1	3.2	.254	.320	3.71
Atlanta	162	40	11	224	31	1474.2	1529	699	614	152	92	32	28	485	65	823	56	7	9.3	5.0	3.0	.269	.328	3.75
St. Louis	163	56	14	274	22	1467.0	1482	699	628	104	72	47	38	576	91	911	56	6	9.1	5.6	3.5	.263	.333	3.85
Montreal	162	49	8	215	25	1434.1	1418	729	657	133	61	39	31	658	73	829	62	3	8.9	5.2	4.1	.260	.341	4.12
NL Total	1944	546	151	2784	329	17475.2	16590	7601	6732	1379	918	484	395	6059	736	10542	589	52	8.5	5.4	3.1	.252	.323	3.47
NL Avg Team	162	46	13	232	27	1456.2	1383	633	561	115	77	40	33	505	61	879	49	4	8.5	5.4	3.1	.252	.323	3.47

Team Fielding

Team	G	PO	A	E	TC	DP	PB	Pct
Cincinnati	162	4332	1870	103	6305	174	11	.984
Houston	162	4414	1750	106	6270	152	18	.983
New York	162	4399	1572	114	6085	135	13	.981
Philadelphia	162	4412	1945	122	6479	158	27	.981
Chicago	162	4332	1825	126	6283	150	18	.980
Los Angeles	162	4349	1852	131	6332	159	14	.979
Pittsburgh	162	4383	1834	133	6350	164	17	.979
St. Louis	163	4401	1773	142	6316	155	24	.978
Atlanta	162	4424	1814	146	6384	180	33	.977
Montreal	162	4303	1812	150	6265	164	12	.976
San Diego	161	4314	1772	161	6247	144	5	.974
San Francisco	162	4364	1750	179	6293	153	23	.972
NL Total	1944	52427	21569	1613	75609	1888	215	.979

Team vs. Team Records

	Atl	ChN	Cin	Hou	LA	Mon	NYN	Phi	Pit	SD	SF	StL	Won
Atl	—	5	9	9	9	7	7	8	4	11	7	6	82
ChN	7	—	6	5	8	8	11	11	6	9	3	9	83
Cin	9	6	—	5	7	7	8	5	5	10	9	8	79
Hou	9	7	13	—	8	4	5	8	4	10	9	2	79
LA	9	4	11	10	—	8	5	7	4	13	12	6	89
Mon	5	10	5	8	4	—	9	6	7	6	7	4	71
NYN	5	7	4	7	7	9	—	13	10	7	4	10	83
Phi	4	7	7	4	5	12	5	—	6	4	6	7	67
Pit	8	12	7	8	8	11	8	12	—	9	3	11	97
SD	7	3	8	8	5	5	5	8	3	—	5	4	61
SF	11	9	9	9	6	5	8	6	9	13	—	5	90
StL	6	9	4	10	6	14	8	11	7	8	7	—	90
Lost	80	79	83	83	73	90	79	95	65	100	72	72	

Seasons: Standings, Leaders

1971 National League Batting Leaders

Games			At-Bats			Runs			Hits			Doubles			Triples		
R. Staub, Mon		162	L. Bowa, Phi		650	L. Brock, StL		126	J. Torre, StL		230	C. Cedeno, Hou		40	R. Metzger, Hou		11
C. Cedeno, Hou		161	W. Davis, LA		641	B. Bonds, SF		110	R. Garr, Atl		219	L. Brock, StL		37	J. Morgan, Hou		11
J. Torre, StL		161	L. Brock, StL		640	W. Stargell, Pit		104	L. Brock, StL		200	R. Staub, Mon		34	W. Davis, LA		10
P. Rose, Cin		160	R. Garr, Atl		639	R. Garr, Atl		101	W. Davis, LA		198	J. Torre, StL		34	C. Gaston, SD		9
J. Morgan, Hou		160	J. Torre, StL		634	J. Torre, StL		97	2 tied with		192	W. Davis, LA		33	5 tied with		8

Home Runs			Total Bases			Runs Batted In			Walks			Intentional Walks			Strikeouts		
W. Stargell, Pit		48	J. Torre, StL		352	J. Torre, StL		137	W. Mays, SF		112	W. McCovey, SF		21	W. Stargell, Pit		154
H. Aaron, Atl		47	H. Aaron, Atl		331	W. Stargell, Pit		125	D. Dietz, SF		97	H. Aaron, Atl		21	L. May, Cin		146
L. May, Cin		39	W. Stargell, Pit		321	H. Aaron, Atl		118	B. Bailey, Mon		97	W. Stargell, Pit		20	B. Bonds, SF		137
D. Johnson, Phi		34	B. Bonds, SF		317	B. Bonds, SF		102	D. Allen, LA		93	J. Torre, StL		20	L. May, Cin		135
2 tied with		33	B. Williams, ChN		300	W. Montanez, Phi		99	J. Morgan, Hou		88	B. Williams, ChN		18	W. Mays, SF		123

Hit By Pitch			Sac Hits			Sac Flies			Stolen Bases			Caught Stealing			GDP		
R. Hunt, Mon		50	R. Garr, Atl		18	W. Montanez, Phi		13	L. Brock, StL		64	L. Brock, StL		19	J. Bateman, Mon		27
R. Staub, Mon		9	B. Day, Mon		16	T. Simmons, StL		10	J. Morgan, Hou		40	R. Garr, Atl		14	D. Allen, LA		23
4 tied with		7	T. Fuentes, SF		16	A. Oliver, Pit		10	R. Garr, Atl		30	L. Bowa, Phi		11	M. Sanguillen, Pit		21
			D. Kessinger, ChN		14	B. Bailey, Mon		9	3 tied with		28	M. Alou, StL		10	R. Staub, Mon		21
			B. Harrelson, NYN		13	W. Parker, LA		8				2 tied with		9	5 tied with		20

Runs Created			Runs Created/27 Outs			Batting Average			On-Base Percentage			Slugging Percentage			OBP+Slugging		
J. Torre, StL		136	H. Aaron, Atl		9.51	J. Torre, StL		.363	W. Mays, SF		.425	H. Aaron, Atl		.669	H. Aaron, Atl		1.079
W. Stargell, Pit		123	W. Stargell, Pit		8.95	R. Garr, Atl		.343	J. Torre, StL		.421	W. Stargell, Pit		.628	W. Stargell, Pit		1.026
H. Aaron, Atl		122	J. Torre, StL		8.60	G. Beckert, ChN		.342	H. Aaron, Atl		.410	J. Torre, StL		.555	J. Torre, StL		.976
L. Brock, StL		114	W. Mays, SF		7.97	R. Clemente, Pit		.341	R. Hunt, Mon		.402	L. May, Cin		.532	W. Mays, SF		.907
R. Staub, Mon		113	R. Staub, Mon		6.86	H. Aaron, Atl		.327	W. Stargell, Pit		.398	B. Bonds, SF		.512	B. Williams, ChN		.888

1971 National League Pitching Leaders

Wins			Losses			Winning Percentage			Games			Games Started			Complete Games		
F. Jenkins, ChN		24	S. Arlin, SD		19	T. McGraw, NYN		.733	W. Granger, Cin		70	F. Jenkins, ChN		39	F. Jenkins, ChN		30
S. Carlton, StL		20	C. Morton, Mon		18	D. Gullett, Cin		.727	J. Johnson, SF		67	B. Stoneman, Mon		39	T. Seaver, NYN		21
T. Seaver, NYN		20	B. Hands, ChN		18	S. Carlton, StL		.690	M. Marshall, Mon		66	C. Osteen, LA		38	B. Stoneman, Mon		20
A. Downing, LA		20	D. Roberts, SD		17	A. Downing, LA		.690	C. Carroll, Cin		61	5 tied with		37	B. Gibson, StL		20
D. Ellis, Pit		19	B. Singer, LA		17	D. Ellis, Pit		.679	D. McMahon, SF		61				4 tied with		18

Shutouts			Saves			Games Finished			Batters Faced			Innings Pitched			Hits Allowed		
S. Blass, Pit		5	D. Giusti, Pit		30	M. Marshall, Mon		52	F. Jenkins, ChN		1299	F. Jenkins, ChN		325.0	F. Jenkins, ChN		304
A. Downing, LA		5	M. Marshall, Mon		23	D. Giusti, Pit		49	B. Stoneman, Mon		1243	B. Stoneman, Mon		294.2	M. Pappas, ChN		279
B. Gibson, StL		5	J. Brewer, LA		22	J. Johnson, SF		47	S. Renko, Mon		1193	T. Seaver, NYN		286.1	S. Carlton, StL		275
M. Pappas, ChN		5	J. Johnson, SF		18	D. Frisella, NYN		42	S. Carlton, StL		1171	G. Perry, SF		280.0	C. Osteen, LA		262
8 tied with		4	C. Upshaw, Atl		17	3 tied with		41	G. Perry, SF		1149	J. Marichal, SF		279.0	R. Wise, Phi		261

Home Runs Allowed			Walks			Walks/9 Innings			Strikeouts			Strikeouts/9 Innings			Strikeout/Walk Ratio		
F. Jenkins, ChN		29	B. Stoneman, Mon		146	F. Jenkins, ChN		1.0	T. Seaver, NYN		289	T. Seaver, NYN		9.1	F. Jenkins, ChN		7.11
B. Lersch, Phi		28	S. Renko, Mon		135	J. Marichal, SF		1.8	F. Jenkins, ChN		263	C. Kirby, SD		7.8	T. Seaver, NYN		4.74
P. Niekro, Atl		27	N. Ryan, NYN		116	G. Stone, Atl		1.8	B. Stoneman, Mon		251	B. Stoneman, Mon		7.7	D. Sutton, LA		3.53
B. Hands, ChN		27	J. Reuss, StL		109	B. Hands, ChN		1.9	C. Kirby, SD		231	F. Jenkins, ChN		7.3	G. Stone, Atl		3.14
J. Marichal, SF		27	2 tied with		103	D. Sutton, LA		1.9	D. Sutton, LA		194	G. Gentry, NYN		6.8	J. Marichal, SF		2.84

Earned Run Average			Component ERA			Hit Batsmen			Wild Pitches			Opponent Average			Opponent OBP		
T. Seaver, NYN		1.76	T. Seaver, NYN		1.90	J. Billingham, Hou		16	E. McAnally, Mon		18	D. Wilson, Hou		.202	T. Seaver, NYN		.252
D. Roberts, SD		2.10	D. Wilson, Hou		2.10	N. Ryan, NYN		15	C. Kirby, SD		13	T. Seaver, NYN		.206	D. Wilson, Hou		.266
D. Wilson, Hou		2.45	G. Nolan, Cin		2.33	W. Blasingame, Hou		13	S. Carlton, StL		12	C. Kirby, SD		.216	F. Jenkins, ChN		.269
K. Forsch, Hou		2.53	D. Sutton, LA		2.36	E. McAnally, Mon		8	A. Downing, LA		12	J. Cumberland, SF		.223	J. Marichal, SF		.273
D. Sutton, LA		2.54	D. Roberts, SD		2.43	6 tied with		7	2 tied with		11	G. Gentry, NYN		.224	G. Nolan, Cin		.275

1971 National League Miscellaneous

Managers		
Atlanta	Lum Harris	82-80
Chicago	Leo Durocher	83-79
Cincinnati	Sparky Anderson	79-83
Houston	Harry Walker	79-83
Los Angeles	Walter Alston	89-73
Montreal	Gene Mauch	71-90
New York	Gil Hodges	83-79
Philadelphia	Frank Lucchesi	67-95
Pittsburgh	Danny Murtaugh	97-65
St. Louis	Red Schoendienst	90-72
San Diego	Preston Gomez	61-100
San Francisco	Charlie Fox	90-72

Awards	
Most Valuable Player	Joe Torre, 3b, StL
Cy Young	Fergie Jenkins, ChN
Rookie of the Year	Earl Williams, c, Atl
STATS Manager of the Year	Red Schoendienst, StL

STATS All-Star Team

C	Earl Williams, Atl	.260	33	87
1B	Hank Aaron, Atl	.327	47	118
2B	Joe Morgan, Hou	.256	13	56
3B	Joe Torre, StL	.363	24	137
SS	Maury Wills, LA	.281	3	44
OF	Bobby Bonds, SF	.288	33	102
OF	Lou Brock, StL	.313	7	61
OF	Willie Stargell, Pit	.295	48	125
P	Al Downing, LA	20-9	2.68	136 K
P	Fergie Jenkins, ChN	24-13	2.77	263 K
P	Tom Seaver, NYN	20-10	1.76	289 K
P	Don Wilson, Hou	16-10	2.45	180 K
RP	Dave Giusti, Pit	5-6	2.93	30 Sv

Postseason	
LCS	Pittsburgh 3 vs. San Francisco 1
World Series	Pit (NL) 4 vs. Bal (AL) 3

Outstanding Performances

No-Hitters

Ken Holtzman, ChN	@ Cin on June 3
Rick Wise, Phi	@ Cin on June 23
Bob Gibson, StL	@ Pit on August 14

Three-Homer Games

Willie Stargell, Pit	on April 10
Willie Stargell, Pit	on April 21
Deron Johnson, Phi	on July 11

1972 American League Standings

EAST	Overall W	L	Pct	GB	DIF	Home Games W	L	R	OR	HR	OHR	Road Games W	L	R	OR	HR	OHR	Park Index Run	HR	Record by Month M/A	May	June	July	Aug	S/O
Detroit	86	70	.551	—	108	44	34	312	288	68	67	42	36	246	226	54	34	127	153	7-4	14-12	15-12	19-12	12-18	19-12
Boston	85	70	.548	0.5	24	52	26	373	303	71	49	33	44	267	317	53	52	114	113	4-7	11-12	12-15	20-12	17-12	21-12
Baltimore	80	74	.519	5.0	42	38	39	240	211	44	40	42	35	279	219	56	45	91	83	7-6	13-10	15-13	17-13	15-15	13-17
New York	79	76	.510	6.5	0	46	31	270	219	53	37	33	45	287	308	50	50	83	91	4-8	13-12	11-14	19-11	19-14	13-17
Cleveland	72	84	.462	14.0	16	43	34	263	261	59	79	29	50	209	258	32	44	115	186	6-6	12-11	9-19	15-16	16-14	14-18
Milwaukee	65	91	.417	21.0	3	37	42	243	286	36	45	28	49	250	309	52	71	92	64	3-7	9-15	14-15	11-21	12-17	16-16
WEST																									
Oakland	93	62	.600	—	131	48	29	287	210	68	52	45	33	317	247	66	44	89	111	7-4	18-8	18-11	16-15	14-13	20-11
Chicago	87	67	.565	5.5	16	55	23	341	252	65	44	32	44	225	286	43	50	113	114	8-5	14-11	17-11	14-16	18-9	16-15
Minnesota	77	77	.500	15.5	24	42	32	299	255	52	54	35	45	238	280	41	51	116	125	8-3	15-9	12-17	12-16	14-15	16-17
Kansas City	76	78	.494	16.5	4	44	33	309	257	29	28	32	45	271	288	49	57	101	54	6-8	7-16	18-9	15-16	14-14	16-15
California	75	80	.484	18.0	1	44	36	221	218	30	31	31	44	233	315	48	59	75	53	5-8	13-15	13-14	13-16	13-14	18-13
Texas	54	100	.351	38.5	0	31	46	235	288	33	41	23	54	226	340	23	51	92	100	7-6	10-18	10-14	12-19	10-19	5-24

Clinch Date—Detroit 10/03, Oakland 9/28.

Team Batting

Team	G	AB	R	OR	H	2B	3B	HR	TB	RBI	TBB	IBB	SO	HBP	SH	SF	SB	CS	SB%	GDP	Avg	OBP	Slg
Boston	155	5208	640	620	1289	229	34	124	1958	594	522	49	858	37	56	48	66	30	.69	111	.248	.326	.376
Oakland	155	5200	604	457	1248	195	29	134	1903	565	463	55	886	47	100	36	87	48	.64	112	.240	.312	.366
Kansas City	154	5167	580	545	1317	220	26	78	1823	547	534	57	711	34	72	38	85	44	.66	134	.255	.333	.353
Chicago	154	5083	566	538	1208	170	28	108	1758	528	511	69	991	34	68	25	100	52	.66	113	.238	.315	.346
Detroit	156	5099	558	514	1206	179	32	122	1815	531	483	65	793	31	74	34	17	21	.45	112	.237	.311	.356
New York	155	5168	557	527	1288	201	24	103	1846	526	491	47	689	29	74	31	71	44	.63	112	.249	.322	.357
Minnesota	154	5234	537	535	1277	182	31	93	1800	506	478	53	905	35	73	28	53	41	.56	129	.244	.315	.344
Baltimore	154	5028	519	430	1153	193	29	100	1704	483	507	57	935	36	65	40	78	41	.66	113	.229	.309	.339
Milwaukee	156	5124	493	595	1204	167	22	88	1679	461	472	42	868	29	78	30	64	57	.53	144	.235	.307	.328
Cleveland	156	5207	472	519	1220	187	18	91	1716	440	420	62	762	26	83	33	49	53	.48	112	.234	.299	.330
Texas	154	5029	461	628	1092	166	17	56	1460	424	503	41	926	30	84	34	126	73	.63	100	.217	.296	.290
California	155	5165	454	533	1249	171	26	78	1706	420	358	52	850	25	66	25	57	37	.61	125	.242	.297	.330
AL Total	1858	61712	6441	6441	14751	2260	316	1175	21168	6025	5742	649	10174	393	893	402	853	539	.61	1430	.239	.306	.343
AL Avg Team	155	5143	537	537	1229	188	26	98	1764	502	479	54	848	33	74	34	71	45	.61	119	.239	.306	.343

Team Pitching

Team	G	CG	ShO	Rel	Sv	IP	H	R	ER	HR	SH	SF	HB	TBB	IBB	SO	WP	Bk	H/9	SO/9	BB/9	OAvg	OOBP	ERA
Baltimore	154	62	20	167	21	1371.2	1116	430	386	85	75	23	15	395	52	788	35	2	7.3	5.2	2.6	.224	.282	2.53
Oakland	155	42	23	236	43	1417.2	1170	457	406	96	62	34	19	418	41	862	29	2	7.4	5.5	2.7	.226	.284	2.58
Minnesota	154	37	17	203	34	1399.1	1188	535	441	105	71	34	37	444	42	838	26	5	7.6	5.4	2.9	.230	.294	2.84
Cleveland	156	47	13	255	24	1410.0	1232	519	457	123	73	34	40	534	92	846	43	4	7.9	5.4	3.4	.237	.311	2.92
Detroit	156	46	11	248	33	1388.1	1212	514	457	101	76	33	47	465	41	952	41	0	7.9	6.2	3.0	.236	.304	2.96
New York	155	35	19	188	39	1373.1	1306	527	465	87	73	29	30	419	61	625	47	1	8.6	4.1	2.7	.252	.310	3.05
California	155	57	18	192	16	1377.2	1109	533	469	90	80	34	28	620	53	1000	49	3	7.2	6.5	4.1	.222	.310	3.06
Chicago	154	36	14	248	42	1385.1	1269	538	480	94	81	30	27	431	29	936	47	2	8.2	6.1	2.8	.245	.305	3.12
Kansas City	154	44	16	242	28	1381.1	1293	545	497	85	69	37	30	405	33	801	37	3	8.4	5.2	2.6	.251	.307	3.24
Milwaukee	156	37	14	216	32	1391.2	1289	595	534	116	70	39	33	486	82	740	41	1	8.3	4.8	3.1	.247	.312	3.45
Boston	155	48	20	216	25	1382.2	1309	620	533	101	81	31	39	512	49	918	32	2	8.5	6.0	3.3	.251	.321	3.47
Texas	154	11	6	324	34	1374.2	1258	628	539	92	82	44	48	613	74	868	44	4	8.2	5.7	4.0	.246	.305	3.53
AL Total	1858	502	191	2735	371	16653.2	14751	6441	5664	1175	893	402	393	5742	649	10174	471	29	8.0	5.5	3.1	.239	.312	3.06
AL Avg Team	155	42	16	228	31	1387.2	1229	537	472	98	74	34	33	479	54	848	39	2	8.0	5.5	3.1	.239	.312	3.06

Team Fielding

Team	G	PO	A	E	TC	DP	PB	Pct
Detroit	156	4161	1617	96	5874	137	14	.984
Baltimore	154	4113	1653	100	5866	150	6	.983
Cleveland	156	4227	1756	116	6099	157	16	.981
Kansas City	154	4140	1759	116	6015	164	17	.981
California	155	4132	1607	114	5853	135	21	.981
Oakland	155	4250	1695	130	6075	146	13	.979
New York	155	4120	1860	134	6114	179	10	.978
Boston	155	4145	1610	130	5885	141	10	.978
Chicago	154	4146	1686	135	5967	136	23	.977
Milwaukee	156	4205	1602	139	5946	145	10	.977
Minnesota	154	4198	1730	133	6087	133	7	.974
Texas	154	4116	1618	166	5900	147	14	.972
AL Total	1858	49953	20193	1535	71681	1770	161	.979

Team vs. Team Records

	Bal	Bos	Cal	ChA	Cle	Det	KC	Mil	Min	NYA	Oak	Tex	Won
Bal	—	7	6	8	8	10	6	10	6	7	6	6	80
Bos	11	—	8	6	8	5	6	11	4	9	9	8	85
Cal	6	4	—	7	8	5	9	7	7	4	8	10	75
ChA	4	6	11	—	8	5	8	9	8	7	7	14	87
Cle	10	7	4	4	—	10	6	5	8	7	2	9	72
Det	8	9	7	7	8	—	7	10	9	7	4	10	86
KC	6	6	6	9	6	5	—	7	9	7	7	8	76
Mil	5	7	5	3	10	8	5	—	4	9	4	5	65
Min	6	8	8	6	4	3	9	8	—	6	8	11	77
NYA	6	9	8	5	11	9	5	9	6	—	3	8	79
Oak	6	3	10	8	10	8	11	8	9	9	—	11	93
Tex	6	4	7	4	3	2	6	7	4	7	4	—	54
Lost	74	70	80	67	84	70	78	91	77	76	62	100	

1972 American League Batting Leaders

Games		At-Bats		Runs		Hits		Doubles		Triples	
E. Brinkman, Det	156	B. Campaneris, Oak	625	B. Murcer, NYA	102	J. Rudi, Oak	181	L. Piniella, KC	33	C. Fisk, Bos	9
R. White, NYA	155	S. Alomar, Cal	610	J. Rudi, Oak	94	L. Piniella, KC	179	J. Rudi, Oak	32	J. Rudi, Oak	9
S. Alomar, Cal	155	A. Rodriguez, Det	601	T. Harper, Bos	92	B. Murcer, NYA	171	B. Murcer, NYA	30	P. Blair, Bal	8
4 tied with	153	J. Rudi, Oak	593	D. Allen, ChA	90	R. Carew, Min	170	R. White, NYA	29	P. Kelly, ChA	7
		B. Murcer, NYA	585	C. Tovar, Min	86	C. May, ChA	161	T. Harper, Bos	29	B. Murcer, NYA	7

Home Runs		Total Bases		Runs Batted In		Walks		Intentional Walks		Strikeouts	
D. Allen, ChA	37	B. Murcer, NYA	314	D. Allen, ChA	113	R. White, NYA	99	E. Herrmann, ChA	19	B. Darwin, Min	145
B. Murcer, NYA	33	D. Allen, ChA	305	J. Mayberry, KC	100	D. Allen, ChA	99	S. Bando, Oak	17	G. Scott, Mil	130
M. Epstein, Oak	26	J. Rudi, Oak	288	B. Murcer, NYA	96	H. Killebrew, Min	94	D. Allen, ChA	16	D. Allen, ChA	126
H. Killebrew, Min	26	J. Mayberry, KC	255	G. Scott, Mil	88	C. May, ChA	79	R. Fosse, Cle	15	R. Jackson, Oak	125
2 tied with	25	L. Piniella, KC	253	B. Powell, Bal	81	3 tied with	78	2 tied with	14	B. Oliver, 2tm	109

Hit By Pitch		Sac Hits		Sac Flies		Stolen Bases		Caught Stealing		GDP	
C. Tovar, Min	14	B. Campaneris, Oak	20	C. Yastrzemski, Bos	9	B. Campaneris, Oak	52	D. Nelson, Tex	17	L. Piniella, KC	25
M. Epstein, Oak	11	M. Andrews, ChA	18	M. Stanley, Det	8	D. Nelson, Tex	51	B. Campaneris, Oak	14	B. Darwin, Min	24
4 tied with	9	4 tied with	15	6 tied with	7	F. Patek, KC	33	C. May, ChA	14	G. Scott, Mil	19
						P. Kelly, ChA	32	D. May, Mil	13	R. Scheinblum, KC	19
						A. Otis, KC	28	2 tied with	12	2 tied with	18

Runs Created		Runs Created/27 Outs		Batting Average		On-Base Percentage		Slugging Percentage		OBP+Slugging	
D. Allen, ChA	123	D. Allen, ChA	8.89	R. Carew, Min	.318	D. Allen, ChA	.420	D. Allen, ChA	.603	D. Allen, ChA	1.023
B. Murcer, NYA	104	C. Fisk, Bos	6.98	L. Piniella, KC	.312	C. May, ChA	.405	C. Fisk, Bos	.538	C. Fisk, Bos	.909
J. Rudi, Oak	97	M. Epstein, Oak	6.86	D. Allen, ChA	.308	J. Mayberry, KC	.394	B. Murcer, NYA	.537	J. Mayberry, KC	.900
C. May, ChA	96	J. Mayberry, KC	6.78	C. May, ChA	.308	R. White, NYA	.384	J. Mayberry, KC	.507	B. Murcer, NYA	.898
J. Mayberry, KC	93	C. May, ChA	6.65	J. Rudi, Oak	.305	R. Scheinblum, KC	.383	M. Epstein, Oak	.490	M. Epstein, Oak	.866

1972 American League Pitching Leaders

Wins		Losses		Winning Percentage		Games		Games Started		Complete Games	
G. Perry, Cle	24	P. Dobson, Bal	18	C. Hunter, Oak	.750	P. Lindblad, Tex	66	W. Wood, ChA	49	G. Perry, Cle	29
W. Wood, ChA	24	M. Stottlemyre, NYA	18	L. Tiant, Bos	.714	R. Fingers, Oak	65	S. Bahnsen, ChA	41	M. Lolich, Det	23
M. Lolich, Det	22	4 tied with	17	B. Odom, Oak	.714	W. Granger, Min	63	M. Lolich, Det	41	N. Ryan, Cal	20
3 tied with	21			J. Palmer, Bal	.677	3 tied with	62	G. Perry, Cle	40	W. Wood, ChA	20
				R. Nelson, KC	.647			T. Bradley, ChA	40	J. Palmer, Bal	18

Shutouts		Saves		Games Finished		Batters Faced		Innings Pitched		Hits Allowed	
N. Ryan, Cal	9	S. Lyle, NYA	35	S. Lyle, NYA	56	W. Wood, ChA	1490	W. Wood, ChA	376.2	W. Wood, ChA	325
W. Wood, ChA	8	T. Forster, ChA	29	K. Sanders, Mil	51	G. Perry, Cle	1345	G. Perry, Cle	342.2	M. Lolich, Det	282
M. Stottlemyre, NYA	7	R. Fingers, Oak	21	T. Forster, ChA	45	M. Lolich, Det	1321	M. Lolich, Det	327.1	F. Peterson, NYA	270
3 tied with	6	W. Granger, Min	19	D. LaRoche, Min	43	B. Blyleven, Min	1158	C. Hunter, Oak	295.1	S. Bahnsen, ChA	263
		K. Sanders, Mil	17	R. Fingers, Oak	41	N. Ryan, Cal	1154	B. Blyleven, Min	287.1	G. Perry, Cle	253

Home Runs Allowed		Walks		Walks/9 Innings		Strikeouts		Strikeouts/9 Innings		Strikeout/Walk Ratio	
M. Lolich, Det	29	N. Ryan, Cal	157	F. Peterson, NYA	1.6	N. Ryan, Cal	329	N. Ryan, Cal	10.4	R. Nelson, KC	3.87
W. Wood, ChA	28	J. Coleman, Det	110	R. Nelson, KC	1.6	M. Lolich, Det	250	A. Messersmith, Cal	7.5	M. Lolich, Det	3.38
B. Parsons, Mil	27	R. Hand, Tex	103	S. Kline, NYA	1.7	G. Perry, Cle	234	R. May, Cal	7.4	B. Blyleven, Min	3.30
J. Coleman, Det	23	D. Woodson, Min	101	K. Holtzman, Oak	1.8	B. Blyleven, Min	228	T. Bradley, ChA	7.2	T. Bradley, ChA	3.22
K. Holtzman, Oak	23	B. Odom, Oak	87	W. Wood, ChA	1.8	J. Coleman, Det	222	B. Blyleven, Min	7.1	G. Perry, Cle	2.85

Earned Run Average		Component ERA		Hit Batsmen		Wild Pitches		Opponent Average		Opponent OBP	
L. Tiant, Bos	1.91	R. Nelson, KC	1.66	P. Broberg, Tex	13	N. Ryan, Cal	18	N. Ryan, Cal	.171	R. Nelson, KC	.234
G. Perry, Cle	1.92	C. Hunter, Oak	1.70	G. Perry, Cle	12	P. Broberg, Tex	14	C. Hunter, Oak	.189	C. Hunter, Oak	.241
C. Hunter, Oak	2.04	G. Perry, Cle	1.93	M. Lolich, Det	11	G. Perry, Cle	11	R. Nelson, KC	.196	G. Perry, Cle	.261
J. Palmer, Bal	2.07	L. Tiant, Bos	2.08	J. Lonborg, Mil	11	W. Wood, ChA	11	L. Tiant, Bos	.202	J. Palmer, Bal	.268
R. Nelson, KC	2.08	A. Messersmith, Cal	2.24	3 tied with	10	2 tied with	9	G. Perry, Cle	.205	L. Tiant, Bos	.275

1972 American League Miscellaneous

Managers

Baltimore	Earl Weaver	80-74
Boston	Eddie Kasko	85-70
California	Del Rice	75-80
Chicago	Chuck Tanner	87-67
Cleveland	Ken Aspromonte	72-84
Detroit	Billy Martin	86-70
Kansas City	Bob Lemon	76-78
Milwaukee	Dave Bristol	10-20
	Roy McMillan	1-1
	Del Crandall	54-70
Minnesota	Bill Rigney	36-34
	Frank Quilici	41-43
New York	Ralph Houk	79-76
Oakland	Dick Williams	93-62
Texas	Ted Williams	54-100

Awards

Most Valuable Player	Dick Allen, 1b, ChA
Cy Young	Gaylord Perry, Cle
Rookie of the Year	Carlton Fisk, c, Bos
STATS Manager of the Year	Chuck Tanner, ChA

STATS All-Star Team

C	Carlton Fisk, Bos	.293	22	61
1B	Dick Allen, ChA	.308	37	113
2B	Rod Carew, Min	.318	0	51
3B	Graig Nettles, Cle	.253	17	70
SS	Bert Campaneris, Oak	.240	8	32
OF	Carlos May, ChA	.308	12	68
OF	Bobby Murcer, NYA	.292	33	96
OF	Joe Rudi, Oak	.305	19	75
P	Catfish Hunter, Oak	21-7	2.04	191 K
P	Jim Palmer, Bal	21-10	2.07	184 K
P	Gaylord Perry, Cle	24-16	1.92	234 K
P	Nolan Ryan, Cal	19-16	2.28	329 K
RP	Sparky Lyle, NYA	9-5	1.92	35 Sv

Postseason

LCS	Oakland 3 vs. Detroit 2
World Series	Oakland (AL) 4 vs. Cincinnati (NL) 3

Outstanding Performances

Cycles

Bobby Murcer, NYA	on August 29
Cesar Tovar, Min	on September 19

1972 National League Standings

EAST	W	L	Pct	GB	DIF	W	L	R	OR	HR	OHR	W	L	R	OR	HR	OHR	Run	HR	M/A	May	June	July	Aug	S/O
		Ov	eral	l			Ho	me G	ames				Ro	ad G	ames			Park	Index		Re	cord	by M	onth	
Pittsburgh	96	59	.619	—	113	49	29	351	259	53	34	47	30	340	253	57	56	102	76	5-8	19-7	16-10	20-10	17-11	19-13
Chicago	85	70	.548	11.0	0	46	31	392	305	83	63	39	39	293	262	50	49	127	149	4-10	16-8	17-11	14-17	16-12	18-12
New York	83	73	.532	13.5	50	41	37	254	264	45	56	42	36	274	314	60	62	88	83	8-4	21-7	12-15	11-15	11-17	20-15
St. Louis	75	81	.481	21.5	0	40	37	298	308	31	38	35	44	270	292	39	49	111	80	5-8	11-17	18-8	12-15	14-15	15-18
Montreal	70	86	.449	26.5	14	35	43	252	324	50	56	35	43	261	285	41	47	105	120	9-4	9-18	11-16	13-12	15-15	13-21
Philadelphia	59	97	.378	37.5	1	28	51	246	316	49	57	31	46	257	319	49	60	95	95	9-5	7-19	8-18	10-19	10-18	15-18
WEST																									
Cincinnati	95	59	.617	—	115	42	34	300	266	58	59	53	25	407	291	66	70	83	88	5-8	18-10	18-9	16-10	21-9	17-13
Houston	84	69	.549	10.5	31	41	36	367	355	58	56	43	33	341	281	76	58	115	84	10-4	14-13	17-11	13-16	18-10	12-15
Los Angeles	85	70	.548	10.5	29	41	34	267	221	46	37	44	36	317	306	52	46	84	90	11-4	15-12	10-16	13-14	17-11	19-13
Atlanta	70	84	.455	25.0	0	36	41	339	392	86	88	34	43	289	338	58	67	117	139	7-8	11-14	13-14	15-14	11-19	13-15
San Francisco	69	86	.445	26.5	4	34	43	336	321	86	65	35	43	326	328	64	65	102	119	6-10	9-21	13-15	16-8	12-16	13-16
San Diego	58	95	.379	36.5	2	26	54	217	315	41	64	32	41	271	350	61	57	78	81	5-11	11-15	8-18	12-15	10-19	12-17

Clinch Date—Pittsburgh 9/21, Cincinnati 9/22.

Team Batting

Team	G	AB	R	OR	H	2B	3B	HR	TB	RBI	TBB	IBB	SO	HBP	SH	SF	SB	CS	SB%	GDP	Avg	OBP	Slg
Houston	153	5267	708	636	1359	233	38	134	2070	660	524	69	907	32	62	51	111	56	.66	98	.258	.335	.393
Cincinnati	154	5241	707	557	1317	214	44	124	1991	650	606	85	914	37	65	54	140	63	.69	109	.251	.339	.380
Pittsburgh	155	5490	691	512	1505	251	47	110	2180	654	404	69	871	25	52	50	49	30	.62	110	.274	.332	.397
Chicago	156	5247	685	567	1346	206	40	133	2031	634	565	78	815	28	67	43	69	47	.59	126	.257	.337	.387
San Francisco	155	5245	662	649	1281	211	36	150	2014	600	480	42	964	30	64	39	123	45	.73	107	.244	.316	.384
Atlanta	155	5278	628	730	1363	186	17	144	2015	593	532	44	770	35	55	38	47	35	.57	131	.258	.335	.382
Los Angeles	155	5270	584	527	1349	178	39	98	1899	543	480	53	786	24	89	40	82	38	.68	121	.256	.326	.360
St. Louis	156	5326	568	600	1383	214	42	70	1891	518	437	61	793	27	58	36	104	48	.68	141	.260	.323	.355
New York	156	5135	528	578	1154	175	31	105	1706	490	589	70	990	34	86	39	41	41	.50	127	.225	.313	.332
Montreal	156	5156	513	609	1205	156	22	91	1678	462	474	55	828	49	108	30	68	66	.51	96	.234	.308	.325
Philadelphia	156	5248	503	635	1240	200	36	98	1806	469	487	50	930	22	69	36	42	50	.46	104	.236	.308	.344
San Diego	153	5213	488	665	1181	168	38	102	1731	452	407	53	976	15	90	25	78	46	.63	97	.227	.288	.332
NL Total	1860	63116	7265	7265	15683	2392	430	1359	23012	6725	5985	729	10544	358	865	481	954	566	.63	1367	.248	.315	.365
NL Avg Team	155	5260	605	605	1307	199	36	113	1918	560	499	61	879	30	72	40	80	47	.63	114	.248	.315	.365

Team Pitching

Team	G	CG	ShO	Rel	Sv	IP	H	R	ER	HR	SH	SF	HB	TBB	IBB	SO	WP	Bk	H/9	SO/9	BB/9	OAvg	OOBP	ERA
Los Angeles	155	50	23	176	29	1403.0	1196	527	434	83	85	37	34	429	36	856	43	3	7.7	5.5	2.8	.230	.291	2.78
Pittsburgh	155	39	15	205	48	1414.1	1282	512	442	90	64	35	29	433	60	838	34	3	8.2	5.3	2.8	.243	.302	2.81
Cincinnati	154	25	15	239	60	1412.1	1313	557	504	129	61	35	20	435	62	806	42	1	8.4	5.1	2.8	.247	.305	3.21
Chicago	156	54	19	197	32	1398.2	1329	567	500	112	77	31	34	421	56	824	32	4	8.6	5.3	2.7	.251	.309	3.22
New York	156	32	12	207	41	1414.2	1263	578	513	118	77	44	30	486	63	1059	53	2	8.0	6.7	3.1	.240	.306	3.26
St. Louis	156	64	13	216	13	1399.2	1290	600	532	87	70	37	21	531	82	912	53	5	8.3	5.9	3.4	.247	.317	3.42
Montreal	156	39	11	217	23	1401.1	1281	609	559	103	44	40	26	579	60	888	47	8	8.2	5.7	3.7	.245	.321	3.59
Philadelphia	156	43	13	263	15	1400.0	1318	635	570	117	71	50	29	536	75	927	51	8	8.5	6.0	3.4	.251	.321	3.66
San Francisco	155	44	8	219	23	1386.1	1309	649	569	130	81	40	31	507	57	771	53	6	8.5	5.0	3.3	.250	.318	3.69
Houston	153	38	14	245	31	1385.1	1340	636	580	114	77	40	38	498	33	971	58	4	8.7	6.3	3.2	.256	.323	3.77
San Diego	153	39	17	270	19	1403.2	1350	665	589	121	84	48	40	618	90	960	63	11	8.7	6.2	4.0	.255	.334	3.78
Atlanta	155	40	4	220	27	1377.0	1412	730	654	155	74	44	26	512	55	732	69	8	9.2	4.8	3.3	.266	.331	4.27
NL Total	1860	507	164	2674	361	16796.1	15683	7265	6446	1359	865	481	358	5985	729	10544	598	63	8.4	5.6	3.2	.248	.322	3.45
NL Avg Team	155	42	14	223	30	1399.1	1307	605	537	113	72	40	30	499	61	879	50	5	8.4	5.6	3.2	.248	.322	3.45

Team Fielding

Team	G	PO	A	E	TC	DP	PB	Pct
Cincinnati	154	4238	1668	110	6016	143	5	.982
Philadelphia	156	4200	1709	116	6025	142	15	.981
Houston	153	4156	1671	116	5943	151	17	.980
New York	156	4244	1539	116	5899	122	7	.980
Chicago	156	4196	1889	132	6217	148	12	.979
Montreal	156	4204	1789	134	6127	141	11	.978
Pittsburgh	155	4243	1741	136	6120	171	6	.978
St. Louis	156	4199	1665	141	6005	146	18	.977
San Diego	153	4211	1621	144	5976	146	12	.976
San Francisco	155	4159	1659	156	5974	121	10	.974
Los Angeles	155	4209	1806	162	6177	145	12	.974
Atlanta	155	4131	1633	156	5920	130	36	.974
NL Total	1860	50390	20390	1619	72399	1706	161	.978

Team vs. Team Records

	Atl	ChN	Cin	Hou	LA	Mon	NYN	Phi	Pit	SD	SF	StL	Won
Atl	—	5	9	7	7	4	7	6	6	6	7	6	70
ChN	7	—	8	3	8	10	10	10	3	9	7	10	85
Cin	9	4	—	11	9	8	8	10	8	8	10	10	95
Hou	7	9	6	—	11	7	8	6	9	3	12	8	84
LA	8	4	5	11	—	6	7	7	7	13	9	8	85
Mon	8	5	4	4	6	—	6	10	6	6	6	9	70
NYN	5	8	4	6	5	12	—	13	8	7	8	7	83
Phi	6	7	2	3	5	6	5	—	5	6	6	8	59
Pit	6	12	4	9	5	12	6	13	—	10	9	10	96
SD	11	3	10	2	5	6	5	6	2	—	4	4	58
SF	11	5	5	5	9	6	4	6	3	10	—	5	69
StL	6	8	2	8	4	8	9	7	8	8	7	—	75
Lost	84	70	59	69	70	86	73	97	59	95	86	81	

1972 National League Batting Leaders

Games		At-Bats		Runs		Hits		Doubles		Triples	
P. Rose, Cin	154	P. Rose, Cin	645	J. Morgan, Cin	122	P. Rose, Cin	198	C. Cedeno, Hou	39	L. Bowa, Phi	13
B. Bonds, SF	153	R. Metzger, Hou	641	B. Bonds, SF	118	L. Brock, StL	193	W. Montanez, Phi	39	P. Rose, Cin	11
R. Metzger, Hou	153	B. Bonds, SF	626	J. Wynn, Hou	117	B. Williams, ChN	191	T. Simmons, StL	36	C. Cedeno, Hou	8
L. Brock, StL	153	L. Brock, StL	621	P. Rose, Cin	107	T. Simmons, StL	180	B. Williams, ChN	34	M. Sanguillen, Pit	8
5 tied with	152	W. Davis, LA	615	C. Cedeno, Hou	103	R. Garr, Atl	180	3 tied with	33	L. Brock, StL	8

Home Runs		Total Bases		Runs Batted In		Walks		Intentional Walks		Strikeouts	
J. Bench, Cin	40	B. Williams, ChN	348	J. Bench, Cin	125	J. Morgan, Cin	115	J. Bench, Cin	23	L. May, Hou	145
N. Colbert, SD	38	C. Cedeno, Hou	300	B. Williams, ChN	122	J. Wynn, Hou	103	B. Williams, ChN	20	D. Kingman, SF	140
B. Williams, ChN	37	J. Bench, Cin	291	J. Bench, Cin	112	J. Bench, Cin	100	T. Perez, Cin	15	T. Simmons, StL	137
H. Aaron, Atl	34	L. May, Hou	290	N. Colbert, SD	111	H. Aaron, Atl	92	W. Stargell, Pit	15	W. Stargell, Pit	129
W. Stargell, Pit	33	N. Colbert, SD	286	L. May, Hou	98	D. Evans, Atl	90	H. Aaron, Atl	15	N. Colbert, SD	127

Hit By Pitch		Sac Hits		Sac Flies		Stolen Bases		Caught Stealing		GDP	
R. Hunt, Mon	26	L. Bowa, Phi	18	J. Bench, Cin	12	L. Brock, StL	63	C. Cedeno, Hou	21	M. Perez, Atl	21
B. Watson, Hou	8	T. Foli, Mon	16	T. Helms, Hou	10	J. Morgan, Cin	58	L. Brock, StL	18	J. Torre, StL	19
J. Torre, StL	8	E. Hernandez, SD	15	D. Evans, Atl	9	C. Cedeno, Hou	55	J. Morgan, Cin	17	4 tied with	18
P. Rose, Cin	7	B. Stoneman, Mon	13	D. Rader, Hou	9	B. Bonds, SF	44	B. Tolan, Cin	15	
8 tied with	6	D. Kessinger, ChN	13	5 tied with	8	B. Tolan, Cin	42	J. Cardenal, ChN	14	

Runs Created		Runs Created/27 Outs		Batting Average		On-Base Percentage		Slugging Percentage		OBP+Slugging	
B. Williams, ChN	130	B. Williams, ChN	8.73	B. Williams, ChN	.333	J. Morgan, Cin	.417	B. Williams, ChN	.606	B. Williams, ChN	1.005
J. Morgan, Cin	119	J. Morgan, Cin	7.72	R. Garr, Atl	.325	B. Williams, ChN	.398	W. Stargell, Pit	.558	W. Stargell, Pit	.930
C. Cedeno, Hou	116	C. Cedeno, Hou	7.58	D. Baker, Atl	.321	R. Santo, ChN	.391	J. Bench, Cin	.541	C. Cedeno, Hou	.921
P. Rose, Cin	111	W. Stargell, Pit	7.32	C. Cedeno, Hou	.320	H. Aaron, Atl	.390	C. Cedeno, Hou	.537	J. Bench, Cin	.920
J. Bench, Cin	110	J. Wynn, Hou	7.05	B. Watson, Hou	.312	J. Wynn, Hou	.389	H. Aaron, Atl	.514	H. Aaron, Atl	.904

1972 National League Pitching Leaders

Wins		Losses		Winning Percentage		Games		Games Started		Complete Games	
S. Carlton, Phi	27	S. Arlin, SD	21	G. Nolan, Cin	.750	M. Marshall, Mon	65	S. Carlton, Phi	41	S. Carlton, Phi	30
T. Seaver, NYN	21	R. Wise, StL	16	S. Carlton, Phi	.730	C. Carroll, Cin	65	S. Arlin, SD	37	F. Jenkins, ChN	23
F. Jenkins, ChN	20	B. Greif, SD	16	M. Pappas, ChN	.708	P. Borbon, Cin	62	P. Niekro, Atl	36	B. Gibson, StL	23
C. Osteen, LA	20	B. Singer, LA	16	S. Blass, Pit	.704	G. Ross, SD	60	F. Jenkins, ChN	36	R. Wise, StL	20
3 tied with	19	J. Marichal, SF	16	T. John, LA	.688	3 tied with	54	3 tied with	35	D. Sutton, LA	18

Shutouts		Saves		Games Finished		Batters Faced		Innings Pitched		Hits Allowed	
D. Sutton, LA	9	C. Carroll, Cin	37	M. Marshall, Mon	56	S. Carlton, Phi	1351	S. Carlton, Phi	346.1	S. Carlton, Phi	257
S. Carlton, Phi	8	T. McGraw, NYN	27	C. Carroll, Cin	54	F. Jenkins, ChN	1176	F. Jenkins, ChN	289.1	P. Niekro, Atl	254
F. Norman, SD	6	D. Giusti, Pit	22	T. McGraw, NYN	47	P. Niekro, Atl	1150	P. Niekro, Atl	282.1	F. Jenkins, ChN	253
F. Jenkins, ChN	5	M. Marshall, Mon	18	D. Giusti, Pit	44	B. Gibson, StL	1119	B. Gibson, StL	278.0	R. Wise, StL	250
L. Dierker, Hou	5	2 tied with	17	J. Brewer, LA	41	R. Wise, StL	1089	D. Sutton, LA	272.2	C. Osteen, LA	232

Home Runs Allowed		Walks		Walks/9 Innings		Strikeouts		Strikeouts/9 Innings		Strikeout/Walk Ratio	
F. Jenkins, ChN	32	S. Arlin, SD	122	M. Pappas, ChN	1.3	S. Carlton, Phi	310	T. Seaver, NYN	8.6	S. Carlton, Phi	3.56
T. Seaver, NYN	23	C. Kirby, SD	116	G. Nolan, Cin	1.5	T. Seaver, NYN	249	J. Reuss, Hou	8.2	D. Sutton, LA	3.29
P. Niekro, Atl	22	M. Torrez, Mon	103	P. Niekro, Atl	1.7	B. Gibson, StL	208	J. Koosman, NYN	8.1	T. Seaver, NYN	3.23
R. Cleveland, StL	21	B. Stoneman, Mon	102	D. Ellis, Pit	1.8	D. Sutton, LA	207	S. Carlton, Phi	8.1	P. Niekro, Atl	3.09
C. Kirby, SD	21	2 tied with	88	B. Moose, Pit	1.9	F. Jenkins, ChN	184	F. Norman, SD	7.1	B. Moose, Pit	3.06

Earned Run Average		Component ERA		Hit Batsmen		Wild Pitches		Opponent Average		Opponent OBP	
S. Carlton, Phi	1.97	D. Sutton, LA	1.63	J. Reuss, Hou	10	S. Arlin, SD	15	D. Sutton, LA	.189	D. Sutton, LA	.240
G. Nolan, Cin	1.99	S. Carlton, Phi	1.92	B. Kison, Pit	9	F. Norman, SD	13	S. Carlton, Phi	.206	S. Carlton, Phi	.257
D. Sutton, LA	2.08	G. Nolan, Cin	2.22	S. Arlin, SD	9	R. Reed, Atl	11	B. Gibson, StL	.224	G. Nolan, Cin	.259
J. Matlack, NYN	2.32	B. Gibson, StL	2.48	B. Greif, SD	8	D. Wilson, Hou	11	T. Seaver, NYN	.224	P. Niekro, Atl	.274
B. Gibson, StL	2.46	P. Niekro, Atl	2.62	M. Pappas, ChN	8	S. McDowell, SF	11	R. Bryant, SF	.224	F. Jenkins, ChN	.278

1972 National League Miscellaneous

Managers

Atlanta	Lum Harris	47-57
	Eddie Mathews	23-27
Chicago	Leo Durocher	46-44
	Whitey Lockman	39-26
Cincinnati	Sparky Anderson	95-59
Houston	Harry Walker	67-54
	Salty Parker	1-0
	Leo Durocher	16-15
Los Angeles	Walter Alston	85-70
Montreal	Gene Mauch	70-86
New York	Yogi Berra	83-73
Philadelphia	Frank Lucchesi	26-50
	Paul Owens	33-47
Pittsburgh	Bill Virdon	96-59
St. Louis	Red Schoendienst	75-81
San Diego	Preston Gomez	4-7
	Don Zimmer	54-88
San Francisco	Charlie Fox	69-86

Awards

Most Valuable Player	Johnny Bench, c, Cin
Cy Young	Steve Carlton, Phi
Rookie of the Year	Jon Matlack, p, NYN
STATS Manager of the Year	Sparky Anderson, Cin

STATS All-Star Team

C	Johnny Bench, Cin	.270	40	125
1B	Willie Stargell, Pit	.293	33	112
2B	Joe Morgan, Cin	.292	16	73
3B	Ron Santo, ChN	.302	17	74
SS	Chris Speier, SF	.269	15	71
OF	Cesar Cedeno, Hou	.320	22	82
OF	Billy Williams, ChN	.333	37	122
OF	Jimmy Wynn, Hou	.273	24	90
P	Steve Carlton, Phi	27-10	1.97	310 K
P	Bob Gibson, StL	19-11	2.46	208 K
P	Tom Seaver, NYN	21-12	2.92	249 K
P	Don Sutton, LA	19-9	2.08	207 K
RP	Clay Carroll, Cin	6-4	2.25	37 Sv

Postseason

LCS	Cincinnati 3 vs. Pittsburgh 2
World Series	Cincinnati (NL) 3 vs. Oakland (AL) 4

Outstanding Performances

No-Hitters

Burt Hooton, ChN	vs. Phi on April 16
Milt Pappas, ChN	vs. SD on September 2
Bill Stoneman, Mon	vs. NYN on October 2

Three-Homer Games

Rick Monday, ChN	on May 16
Nate Colbert, SD	on August 1

Cycles

Dave Kingman, SF	on April 16
Cesar Cedeno, Hou	on August 2

1973 American League Standings

EAST	W	L	Pct	GB	DIF	W	L	R	OR	HR	OHR	W	L	R	OR	HR	OHR	Run	HR	M/A	May	June	July	Aug	S/O
		Overall						Home Games						Road Games				Park Index				Record by Month			
Baltimore	97	65	.599	—	79	50	31	408	284	63	60	47	34	346	277	56	64	111	103	10-9	10-12	17-10	18-14	21-9	21-11
Boston	89	73	.549	8.0	13	48	33	390	339	83	83	41	40	348	308	64	75	111	119	7-10	13-13	15-12	19-14	18-13	17-11
Detroit	85	77	.525	12.0	43	47	34	329	332	86	71	38	43	313	342	71	83	101	102	10-10	15-11	12-17	19-10	15-16	14-13
New York	80	82	.494	17.0	47	50	31	359	263	74	42	30	51	282	347	57	67	99	94	9-10	15-13	19-10	17-15	9-18	11-16
Milwaukee	74	88	.457	23.0	15	40	41	349	343	73	52	34	47	359	388	72	67	93	90	9-9	10-17	18-10	13-17	16-14	8-21
Cleveland	71	91	.438	26.0	2	34	47	320	427	92	100	37	44	360	399	66	72	98	139	9-12	11-15	7-21	11-20	19-10	14-13
WEST																									
Oakland	94	68	.580	—	83	50	31	313	253	70	70	44	37	445	362	77	73	70	93	9-11	15-13	18-11	17-12	20-7	15-14
Kansas City	88	74	.543	6.0	29	48	33	422	404	54	61	40	41	333	348	60	53	121	102	13-8	14-15	15-15	18-10	14-12	14-14
Minnesota	81	81	.500	13.0	12	37	44	357	386	56	60	44	37	381	306	64	55	108	97	9-8	16-11	14-14	14-17	11-19	17-12
California	79	83	.488	15.0	4	43	38	316	294	41	49	36	45	313	363	52	55	90	84	9-8	15-12	15-15	10-19	12-14	18-15
Chicago	77	85	.475	17.0	63	40	41	329	368	56	58	37	44	323	337	55	52	106	107	10-5	17-10	11-18	14-20	12-17	13-15
Texas	57	105	.352	37.0	1	35	46	321	408	47	51	22	59	298	436	63	79	99	69	6-10	9-18	10-18	15-17	6-24	11-18

Clinch Date—Baltimore 9/22, Oakland 9/27.

Team Batting

Team	G	AB	R	OR	H	2B	3B	HR	TB	RBI	TBB	IBB	SO	HBP	SH	SF	SB	CS	SB%	GDP	Avg	OBP	Slg
Oakland	162	5507	758	615	1431	216	28	147	2144	714	595	53	919	35	67	53	128	57	.69	118	.260	.342	.389
Kansas City	162	5508	755	752	1440	239	40	114	2101	703	644	44	696	26	49	47	105	69	.60	114	.261	.347	.381
Baltimore	162	5537	754	561	1474	229	48	119	2156	692	648	49	752	43	58	49	146	64	.70	126	.266	.353	.389
Boston	162	5513	738	647	1472	235	30	147	2208	692	581	49	799	31	54	44	114	45	.72	143	.267	.345	.401
Minnesota	162	5625	738	692	1521	240	44	120	2209	688	598	49	954	34	34	40	87	46	.65	150	.270	.348	.393
Milwaukee	162	5526	708	731	1399	229	40	145	2143	669	563	44	977	42	61	35	110	66	.63	114	.253	.331	.388
Cleveland	162	5592	680	826	1429	205	29	158	2166	636	471	26	793	32	40	43	60	68	.47	125	.256	.322	.387
Chicago	162	5475	652	705	1400	228	38	111	2037	598	537	31	952	32	49	42	83	73	.53	146	.256	.330	.372
Detroit	162	5508	642	674	1400	213	32	157	2148	592	509	47	722	39	48	31	28	30	.48	147	.254	.325	.390
New York	162	5492	641	610	1435	212	17	131	2074	616	489	34	680	22	27	34	47	43	.52	142	.261	.328	.378
California	162	5505	629	657	1395	183	29	93	1915	595	509	42	816	34	60	45	59	47	.56	131	.253	.325	.348
Texas	162	5488	619	844	1397	195	29	110	1980	574	503	27	791	27	45	50	91	53	.63	132	.255	.326	.361
AL Total	1944	66276	8314	8314	17193	2624	404	1552	25281	7769	6647	495	9851	397	592	513	1058	661	.62	1608	.259	.328	.381
AL Avg Team	162	5523	693	693	1433	219	34	129	2107	647	554	41	821	33	49	43	88	55	.62	134	.259	.328	.381

Team Pitching

Team	G	CG	ShO	Rel	Sv	IP	H	R	ER	HR	SH	SF	HB	TBB	IBB	SO	WP	Bk	H/9	SO/9	BB/9	OAvg	OOBP	ERA
Baltimore	162	67	14	140	26	1461.2	1297	561	498	124	50	33	20	475	35	715	37	1	8.0	4.4	2.9	.240	.302	3.07
Oakland	162	46	16	203	41	1457.1	1311	615	532	143	40	43	30	494	27	797	52	5	8.1	4.9	3.1	.241	.305	3.29
New York	162	47	16	143	39	1427.2	1379	610	530	109	46	49	26	457	50	708	42	1	8.7	4.5	2.9	.254	.313	3.34
California	162	72	13	164	19	1456.1	1351	657	571	104	64	42	41	614	30	1010	56	6	8.3	6.2	3.8	.246	.324	3.53
Boston	162	67	10	144	33	1440.1	1417	647	584	158	56	39	32	499	35	808	25	2	8.9	5.0	3.1	.259	.323	3.65
Minnesota	162	48	18	190	34	1451.2	1443	692	608	115	48	46	36	519	16	879	61	5	8.9	5.4	3.2	.259	.324	3.77
Chicago	162	48	15	176	35	1456.0	1484	705	625	110	52	43	38	574	19	848	38	2	9.2	5.2	3.5	.266	.336	3.86
Detroit	162	39	11	211	46	1447.2	1468	674	627	154	52	33	30	493	37	911	48	2	9.1	5.7	3.1	.265	.326	3.90
Milwaukee	162	50	11	217	28	1454.0	1476	731	643	119	42	42	28	623	53	671	57	7	9.1	4.2	3.9	.265	.340	3.98
Kansas City	162	40	7	213	41	1449.1	1521	752	675	114	49	46	33	617	75	790	43	6	9.4	4.9	3.8	.273	.346	4.19
Cleveland	162	55	9	206	21	1464.2	1532	826	746	172	49	31	39	602	67	883	87	3	9.4	5.4	3.7	.271	.343	4.58
Texas	162	35	10	241	27	1430.0	1514	844	737	130	44	66	44	680	50	831	62	3	9.5	5.2	4.3	.273	.353	4.64
AL Total	1944	614	150	2248	390	17396.2	17193	8314	7376	1552	592	513	397	6647	494	9851	608	43	8.9	5.1	3.4	.259	.335	3.82
AL Avg Team	162	51	13	187	33	1449.2	1433	693	615	129	49	43	33	554	41	821	51	4	8.9	5.1	3.4	.259	.335	3.82

Team Fielding

Team	G	PO	A	E	TC	DP	PB	Pct
Detroit	162	4343	1709	112	6164	144	10	.982
Baltimore	162	4385	1911	119	6415	184	6	.981
Boston	162	4321	1723	127	6171	162	5	.979
Cleveland	162	4394	1898	139	6431	174	27	.978
Oakland	162	4371	1710	137	6218	170	9	.978
Minnesota	162	4355	1761	139	6255	147	19	.978
Chicago	162	4368	1868	144	6380	165	33	.977
Milwaukee	162	4359	1763	145	6267	145	9	.977
New York	162	4283	1937	156	6376	172	12	.976
California	162	4368	1688	156	6212	153	16	.975
Kansas City	162	4353	1912	167	6432	192	8	.974
Texas	162	4290	1705	161	6156	164	8	.974
AL Total	1944	52190	21585	1702	75477	1994	162	.977

Team vs. Team Records

	Bal	Bos	Cal	ChA	Cle	Det	KC	Mil	Min	NYA	Oak	Tex	Won
Bal	—	7	6	8	12	9	8	15	8	9	5	10	97
Bos	11	—	7	6	9	3	8	12	6	14	4	9	89
Cal	6	5	—	8	5	7	10	5	10	6	6	11	79
ChA	4	6	10	—	7	5	6	3	9	8	6	13	77
Cle	6	9	7	5	—	9	2	9	7	7	3	7	71
Det	9	15	5	7	9	—	4	12	5	7	7	5	85
KC	4	4	8	12	10	8	—	8	9	6	8	11	88
Mil	3	6	7	9	9	6	4	—	8	10	4	8	74
Min	4	6	8	5	7	9	4	—	3	14	12	81	
NYA	9	4	6	4	11	11	6	8	9	—	4	8	80
Oak	7	8	12	12	9	5	10	8	4	8	—	11	94
Tex	2	3	7	5	5	7	7	4	6	4	7	—	57
Lost	65	73	83	85	91	77	74	88	81	82	68	105	

1973 American League Batting Leaders

Games		At-Bats		Runs		Hits		Doubles		Triples	
S. Bando, Oak	162	R. White, NYA	639	R. Jackson, Oak	99	R. Carew, Min	203	S. Bando, Oak	32	A. Bumbry, Bal	11
B. Grich, Bal	162	B. Bell, Cle	631	R. Carew, Min	98	D. May, Mil	189	P. Garcia, Mil	32	R. Carew, Min	11
R. White, NYA	162	D. May, Mil	624	B. North, Oak	98	B. Murcer, NYA	187	R. Carew, Min	30	J. Orta, ChA	10
E. Brinkman, Det	162	A. Johnson, Tex	624	G. Scott, Mil	98	G. Scott, Mil	185	C. Chambliss, Cle	30	R. Coggins, Bal	9
5 tied with	160	B. Murcer, NYA	616	S. Bando, Oak	97	A. Johnson, Tex	179	G. Scott, Mil	30	B. Coluccio, Mil	8

Home Runs		Total Bases		Runs Batted In		Walks		Intentional Walks		Strikeouts	
R. Jackson, Oak	32	S. Bando, Oak	295	R. Jackson, Oak	117	J. Mayberry, KC	122	J. Mayberry, KC	17	B. Darwin, Min	137
J. Burroughs, Tex	30	D. May, Mil	295	G. Scott, Mil	107	B. Grich, Bal	107	T. Oliva, Min	14	L. Hisle, Min	128
F. Robinson, Cal	30	G. Scott, Mil	295	J. Mayberry, KC	100	C. Yastrzemski, Bos	105	C. Yastrzemski, Bos	13	P. Garcia, Mil	119
S. Bando, Oak	29	R. Jackson, Oak	286	S. Bando, Oak	98	G. Tenace, Oak	101	O. Cepeda, Bos	13	D. Johnson, Oak	116
3 tied with	26	B. Murcer, NYA	286	F. Robinson, Cal	97	J. Briggs, Mil	87	F. Robinson, Cal	12	2 tied with	111

Hit By Pitch		Sac Hits		Sac Flies		Stolen Bases		Caught Stealing		GDP	
D. Baylor, Bal	13	M. Belanger, Bal	15	J. Burroughs, Tex	11	T. Harper, Bos	54	B. North, Oak	20	O. Cepeda, Bos	24
B. Freehan, Det	11	E. Brinkman, Det	14	8 tied with	7	B. North, Oak	53	R. Carew, Min	16	L. Piniella, KC	22
4 tied with	10	D. Griffin, Bos	13			D. Nelson, Tex	43	D. Nelson, Tex	16	B. Darwin, Min	22
		S. Alomar, Cal	12			R. Carew, Min	41	P. Kelly, ChA	15	E. Brinkman, Det	22
		L. Aparicio, Bos	12			F. Patek, KC	36	B. Bell, Cle	15	B. Melton, ChA	20

Runs Created		Runs Created/27 Outs		Batting Average		On-Base Percentage		Slugging Percentage		OBP+Slugging	
J. Mayberry, KC	115	J. Mayberry, KC	8.23	R. Carew, Min	.350	J. Mayberry, KC	.417	R. Jackson, Oak	.531	R. Jackson, Oak	.914
S. Bando, Oak	114	R. Jackson, Oak	7.39	G. Scott, Mil	.306	R. Carew, Min	.411	S. Bando, Oak	.498	J. Mayberry, KC	.895
R. Jackson, Oak	112	R. Carew, Min	6.91	T. Davis, Bal	.306	C. Yastrzemski, Bos	.407	F. Robinson, Cal	.489	R. Carew, Min	.881
R. Carew, Min	108	S. Bando, Oak	6.87	B. Murcer, NYA	.304	G. Tenace, Oak	.387	G. Scott, Mil	.488	S. Bando, Oak	.873
A. Otis, KC	106	A. Otis, KC	6.64	D. May, Mil	.303	R. Jackson, Oak	.383	T. Munson, NYA	.487	C. Yastrzemski, Bos	.870

1973 American League Pitching Leaders

Wins		Losses		Winning Percentage		Games		Games Started		Complete Games	
W. Wood, ChA	24	S. Bahnsen, ChA	21	R. Moret, Bos	.867	J. Hiller, Det	65	W. Wood, ChA	48	G. Perry, Cle	29
J. Coleman, Det	23	W. Wood, ChA	20	C. Hunter, Oak	.808	R. Fingers, Oak	62	S. Bahnsen, ChA	42	N. Ryan, Cal	26
J. Palmer, Bal	22	G. Perry, Cle	19	J. Palmer, Bal	.710	D. Bird, KC	54	M. Lolich, Det	42	B. Blyleven, Min	25
3 tied with	21	C. Wright, Cal	19	V. Blue, Oak	.690	D. Knowles, Oak	52	G. Perry, Cle	41	L. Tiant, Bos	23
		3 tied with	17	2 tied with	.667	4 tied with	51	5 tied with	40	J. Colborn, Mil	22

Shutouts		Saves		Games Finished		Batters Faced		Innings Pitched		Hits Allowed	
B. Blyleven, Min	9	J. Hiller, Det	38	J. Hiller, Det	60	W. Wood, ChA	1531	W. Wood, ChA	359.1	W. Wood, ChA	381
G. Perry, Cle	7	S. Lyle, NYA	27	R. Fingers, Oak	49	G. Perry, Cle	1410	G. Perry, Cle	344.0	G. Perry, Cle	315
J. Palmer, Bal	6	R. Fingers, Oak	22	S. Lyle, NYA	45	N. Ryan, Cal	1355	N. Ryan, Cal	326.0	M. Lolich, Det	315
10 tied with	4	D. Bird, KC	20	C. Acosta, ChA	42	B. Singer, Cal	1348	B. Blyleven, Min	325.0	J. Colborn, Mil	297
		C. Acosta, ChA	18	D. Bird, KC	41	B. Blyleven, Min	1321	B. Singer, Cal	315.2	B. Blyleven, Min	296

Home Runs Allowed		Walks		Walks/9 Innings		Strikeouts		Strikeouts/9 Innings		Strikeout/Walk Ratio	
C. Hunter, Oak	39	N. Ryan, Cal	162	J. Kaat, 2tm	1.7	N. Ryan, Cal	383	N. Ryan, Cal	10.6	B. Blyleven, Min	3.85
M. Lolich, Det	35	B. Singer, Cal	130	B. Blyleven, Min	1.9	B. Blyleven, Min	258	J. Bibby, Tex	7.7	M. Lolich, Det	2.71
G. Perry, Cle	34	S. Bahnsen, ChA	117	K. Holtzman, Oak	2.0	B. Singer, Cal	241	B. Blyleven, Min	7.1	L. Tiant, Bos	2.64
L. Tiant, Bos	32	G. Perry, Cle	115	W. Wood, ChA	2.3	G. Perry, Cle	238	S. Stone, ChA	7.0	J. Kaat, 2tm	2.53
J. Coleman, Det	32	J. Palmer, Bal	113	M. Lolich, Det	2.3	M. Lolich, Det	214	B. Singer, Cal	6.9	K. Holtzman, Oak	2.38

Earned Run Average		Component ERA		Hit Batsmen		Wild Pitches		Opponent Average		Opponent OBP	
J. Palmer, Bal	2.40	J. Palmer, Bal	2.51	J. Coleman, Det	10	G. Perry, Cle	17	J. Bibby, Tex	.192	L. Tiant, Bos	.278
B. Blyleven, Min	2.52	B. Blyleven, Min	2.64	B. Blyleven, Min	9	V. Blue, Oak	15	N. Ryan, Cal	.203	C. Hunter, Oak	.282
B. Lee, Bos	2.75	L. Tiant, Bos	2.78	B. Singer, Cal	9	N. Ryan, Cal	15	J. Palmer, Bal	.211	B. Blyleven, Min	.284
N. Ryan, Cal	2.87	N. Ryan, Cal	2.78	4 tied with	8	B. Strom, Cle	13	L. Tiant, Bos	.219	K. Holtzman, Oak	.286
D. Medich, NYA	2.95	K. Holtzman, Oak	2.87			2 tied with	12	V. Blue, Oak	.224	J. Palmer, Bal	.288

1973 American League Miscellaneous

Managers

Baltimore	Earl Weaver	97-65
Boston	Eddie Kasko	88-73
	Eddie Popowski	1-0
California	Bobby Winkles	79-83
Chicago	Chuck Tanner	77-85
Cleveland	Ken Aspromonte	71-91
Detroit	Billy Martin	71-63
	Joe Schultz	14-14
Kansas City	Jack McKeon	88-74
Milwaukee	Del Crandall	74-88
Minnesota	Frank Quilici	81-81
New York	Ralph Houk	80-82
Oakland	Dick Williams	94-68
Texas	Whitey Herzog	47-91
	Del Wilber	1-0
	Billy Martin	9-14

Awards

Most Valuable Player	Reggie Jackson, of, Oak
Cy Young	Jim Palmer, Bal
Rookie of the Year	Al Bumbry, of, Bal
STATS Manager of the Year	Earl Weaver, Bal

STATS All-Star Team

C	Thurman Munson, NYA	.301	20	74
1B	John Mayberry, KC	.278	26	100
2B	Rod Carew, Min	.350	6	62
3B	Sal Bando, Oak	.287	29	98
SS	Bert Campaneris, Oak	.250	4	46
OF	Reggie Jackson, Oak	.293	32	117
OF	Amos Otis, KC	.300	26	93
OF	Reggie Smith, Bos	.303	21	69
DH	Frank Robinson, Cal	.266	30	97
P	Bert Blyleven, Min	20-17	2.52	258 K
P	Ken Holtzman, Oak	21-13	2.97	157 K
P	Jim Palmer, Bal	22-9	2.40	158 K
P	Nolan Ryan, Cal	21-16	2.87	383 K
RP	John Hiller, Det	10-5	1.44	38 Sv

Postseason

LCS	Oakland 3 vs. Baltimore 2
World Series	Oakland (AL) 4 vs. New York (NL) 3

Outstanding Performances

No-Hitters
Steve Busby, KC @ Det on April 27
Nolan Ryan, Cal @ KC on May 15
Nolan Ryan, Cal @ Det on July 15
Jim Bibby, Tex @ Oak on July 30

Three-Homer Games
George Hendrick, Cle on June 19
Tony Oliva, Min on July 3
Lee Stanton, Cal on July 10
Bobby Murcer, NYA on July 13

1973 National League Standings

EAST	Overall					Home Games						Road Games						Park Index		Record by Month					
	W	L	Pct	GB	DIF	W	L	R	OR	HR	OHR	W	L	R	OR	HR	OHR	Run	HR	M/A	May	June	July	Aug	S/O
New York	82	79	.509	—	21	43	38	314	283	39	61	39	41	294	305	46	66	98	88	12-8	9-14	11-17	12-18	18-14	20-8
St. Louis	81	81	.500	1.5	52	43	38	290	255	27	30	38	43	353	348	48	75	78	46	3-15	16-10	18-12	19-11	12-18	13-15
Pittsburgh	80	82	.494	2.5	35	41	40	334	301	72	42	39	42	370	392	82	68	83	76	8-7	13-14	13-18	17-12	14-14	15-17
Montreal	79	83	.488	3.5	1	43	38	364	353	63	70	36	45	304	349	62	58	110	111	7-11	12-11	15-15	16-16	13-17	16-13
Chicago	77	84	.478	5.0	86	41	39	327	356	66	72	36	45	287	299	51	56	118	131	12-8	18-11	17-13	8-19	9-18	13-15
Philadelphia	71	91	.438	11.5	1	38	43	358	381	78	80	33	48	284	336	56	51	119	148	9-9	10-18	16-13	14-17	13-15	9-19
WEST																									
Cincinnati	99	63	.611	—	33	50	31	330	287	47	67	49	32	411	334	90	68	83	72	13-8	14-13	12-16	24-7	17-11	19-8
Los Angeles	95	66	.590	3.5	79	50	31	338	271	63	62	45	35	337	294	47	67	95	108	11-11	19-8	21-8	15-13	17-12	12-14
San Francisco	88	74	.543	11.0	65	47	34	395	363	85	79	41	40	344	339	76	66	111	115	18-6	14-14	13-14	15-12	13-13	15-15
Houston	82	80	.506	17.0	9	41	40	315	322	58	53	41	40	366	350	76	58	89	83	14-10	15-12	14-14	12-17	14-15	13-12
Atlanta	76	85	.472	22.5	0	40	40	460	437	118	87	36	45	339	337	88	57	134	143	7-13	10-17	16-15	15-17	17-8	11-15
San Diego	60	102	.370	39.0	3	31	50	273	355	51	80	29	52	275	415	61	77	91	95	7-15	10-18	8-19	10-18	13-15	12-17

Clinch Date—New York 10/01, Cincinnati 9/24.

Team Batting

Team	G	AB	R	OR	H	2B	3B	HR	TB	RBI	TBB	IBB	SO	HBP	SH	SF	SB	CS	SB%	GDP	Avg	OBP	Slg
Atlanta	162	5631	799	774	1497	219	34	206	2402	758	608	66	870	34	65	46	84	40	.68	112	.266	.346	.427
Cincinnati	162	5505	741	621	1398	232	34	137	2109	686	639	74	947	31	78	51	148	55	.73	118	.254	.340	.383
San Francisco	162	5537	739	702	1452	212	52	161	2251	684	590	82	913	35	75	37	112	52	.68	113	.262	.341	.407
Pittsburgh	162	5608	704	693	1465	257	44	154	2272	664	432	73	842	27	60	40	23	30	.43	130	.261	.322	.405
Houston	162	5532	681	672	1391	216	35	134	2079	634	469	72	962	33	83	36	92	48	.66	135	.251	.318	.376
Los Angeles	162	5604	675	565	1473	219	29	110	2080	623	497	92	795	28	81	57	109	50	.69	123	.263	.332	.371
Montreal	162	5369	668	702	1345	190	23	125	1956	613	695	76	777	44	115	28	77	68	.53	144	.251	.344	.364
St. Louis	162	5478	643	603	1418	240	35	75	1953	592	531	82	796	29	89	50	100	46	.68	149	.259	.333	.357
Philadelphia	162	5546	642	717	1381	218	29	134	2059	592	476	68	979	33	56	45	51	47	.52	91	.249	.317	.371
Chicago	161	5363	614	655	1322	201	21	117	1916	570	575	77	855	20	75	37	65	58	.53	144	.247	.326	.357
New York	161	5457	608	588	1345	198	24	85	1846	553	540	54	805	23	108	36	27	22	.55	147	.246	.321	.338
San Diego	162	5457	548	770	1330	198	26	112	1916	516	401	46	966	21	73	33	88	36	.71	115	.244	.302	.351
NL Total	1942	66087	8062	8062	16817	2600	386	1550	24839	7485	6453	862	10507	358	958	496	976	552	.64	1521	.254	.322	.376
NL Avg Team	162	5507	672	672	1401	217	32	129	2070	624	538	72	876	30	80	41	81	46	.64	127	.254	.322	.376

Team Pitching

Team	G	CG	ShO	Rel	Sv	IP	H	R	ER	HR	SH	SF	HB	TBB	IBB	SO	WP	Bk	H/9	SO/9	BB/9	OAvg	OOBP	ERA
Los Angeles	162	45	15	212	38	1491.0	1270	565	497	129	82	30	29	461	38	961	47	4	7.7	5.8	2.8	.231	.292	3.00
St. Louis	162	42	14	264	36	1460.2	1366	603	528	105	84	38	30	486	73	867	45	5	8.4	5.3	3.0	.248	.310	3.25
New York	161	47	15	194	40	1465.0	1345	588	531	127	83	39	23	490	67	1027	39	1	8.3	6.3	3.0	.245	.307	3.26
Cincinnati	162	39	17	267	43	1473.0	1389	621	557	135	98	34	29	518	90	801	36	8	8.5	4.9	3.2	.252	.318	3.40
Chicago	161	27	13	249	40	1437.2	1471	655	584	128	75	41	30	438	67	885	47	4	9.2	5.5	2.7	.267	.322	3.66
Montreal	162	26	6	272	34	1451.2	1356	702	599	128	85	47	31	681	74	866	59	6	8.4	5.4	4.2	.250	.334	3.71
Pittsburgh	162	26	11	284	44	1450.2	1426	693	602	110	78	38	40	564	85	839	42	4	8.8	5.2	3.5	.258	.329	3.73
Houston	162	45	14	268	26	1460.2	1389	672	608	111	73	38	29	575	64	907	52	5	8.6	5.6	3.5	.252	.323	3.75
San Francisco	162	33	8	252	44	1452.1	1442	702	612	145	57	41	30	485	59	787	58	5	8.9	4.9	3.0	.257	.318	3.79
Philadelphia	162	49	11	257	22	1447.1	1435	717	642	131	87	38	32	632	97	919	61	2	8.9	5.7	3.9	.263	.341	3.99
San Diego	162	34	10	269	23	1430.0	1461	770	661	157	88	52	27	548	82	845	53	3	9.2	5.3	3.4	.267	.334	4.16
Atlanta	162	34	9	287	35	1462.0	1467	774	690	144	68	60	28	575	66	803	52	5	9.0	4.9	3.5	.263	.332	4.25
NL Total	1942	447	143	3075	429	17482.0	16817	8062	7111	1550	958	496	358	6453	862	10507	591	52	8.7	5.4	3.3	.254	.329	3.66
NL Avg Team	162	37	12	256	36	1456.0	1401	672	593	129	80	41	30	538	72	876	49	4	8.7	5.4	3.3	.254	.329	3.66

Team Fielding

Team	G	PO	A	E	TC	DP	PB	Pct
Cincinnati	162	4419	1840	115	6374	162	13	.982
Houston	162	4391	1675	116	6182	140	15	.981
Los Angeles	162	4473	1886	125	6484	166	24	.981
New York	161	4395	1685	126	6206	140	7	.980
Philadelphia	162	4342	1762	134	6238	179	19	.979
Pittsburgh	162	4352	1831	151	6334	156	9	.976
Chicago	161	4313	1934	157	6404	155	7	.975
St. Louis	162	4382	1700	159	6241	149	27	.975
Montreal	162	4355	1846	163	6364	156	24	.974
San Francisco	162	4357	1753	163	6273	138	15	.974
Atlanta	162	4386	1809	166	6361	142	23	.974
San Diego	162	4281	1798	170	6249	152	14	.973
NL Total	1942	52446	21519	1745	75710	1835	197	.977

Team vs. Team Records

	Atl	ChN	Cin	Hou	LA	Mon	NYN	Phi	Pit	SD	SF	StL	Won
Atl	—	7	5	11	2	6	6	6	7	12	8	6	76
ChN	5	—	8	6	5	9	10	10	6	7	2	9	77
Cin	13	4	—	11	11	8	8	8	7	13	10	6	99
Hou	7	6	7	—	11	6	6	7	6	10	11	5	82
LA	15	7	7	7	—	7	7	9	10	9	9	8	95
Mon	6	9	4	6	6	—	9	13	6	7	6	8	79
NYN	6	7	4	6	5	9	—	9	13	8	5	10	82
Phi	6	8	4	5	3	5	9	—	8	9	5	9	71
Pit	5	12	5	6	2	12	5	10	—	8	5	10	80
SD	6	5	5	8	9	5	4	3	4	—	7	4	60
SF	10	10	8	7	7	6	7	7	7	11	—	6	88
StL	6	9	6	7	4	10	8	9	8	8	6	—	81
Lost	85	84	63	80	66	83	79	91	82	102	74	81	

1973 National League Batting Leaders

Games		At-Bats		Runs		Hits		Doubles		Triples	
K. Singleton, Mon	162	P. Rose, Cin	680	B. Bonds, SF	131	P. Rose, Cin	230	W. Stargell, Pit	43	R. Metzger, Hou	14
B. Russell, LA	162	R. Garr, Atl	668	J. Morgan, Cin	116	R. Garr, Atl	200	A. Oliver, Pit	38	G. Maddox, SF	10
D. Evans, Atl	161	T. Fuentes, SF	656	P. Rose, Cin	115	L. Brock, StL	193	T. Simmons, StL	36	G. Matthews, SF	10
G. Luzinski, Phi	161	A. Oliver, Pit	654	D. Evans, Atl	114	T. Simmons, StL	192	R. Staub, NYN	36	W. Davis, LA	9
T. Simmons, StL	161	L. Brock, StL	650	L. Brock, StL	110	A. Oliver, Pit	191	P. Rose, Cin	36	3 tied with	8

Home Runs		Total Bases		Runs Batted In		Walks		Intentional Walks		Strikeouts	
W. Stargell, Pit	44	B. Bonds, SF	341	W. Stargell, Pit	119	D. Evans, Atl	124	W. McCovey, SF	25	B. Bonds, SF	148
D. Johnson, Atl	43	W. Stargell, Pit	337	L. May, Hou	105	K. Singleton, Mon	123	D. Rader, SF	23	N. Colbert, SD	146
D. Evans, Atl	41	D. Evans, Atl	331	D. Evans, Atl	104	J. Morgan, Cin	111	W. Stargell, Pit	22	M. Schmidt, Phi	136
H. Aaron, Atl	40	D. Johnson, Atl	305	J. Bench, Cin	104	W. McCovey, SF	105	B. Russell, LA	20	G. Luzinski, Phi	135
B. Bonds, SF	39	A. Oliver, Pit	303	K. Singleton, Mon	103	R. Monday, ChN	92	D. Kessinger, ChN	18	W. Stargell, Pit	129

Hit By Pitch		Sac Hits		Sac Flies		Stolen Bases		Caught Stealing		GDP	
R. Hunt, Mon	24	T. Sizemore, StL	25	J. Ferguson, LA	10	L. Brock, StL	70	L. Brock, StL	20	T. Simmons, StL	29
J. Torre, StL	10	F. Millan, NYN	18	J. Bench, Cin	10	J. Morgan, Cin	67	B. Bonds, SF	17	K. Singleton, Mon	27
M. Schmidt, Phi	9	T. Fuentes, SF	17	D. Baker, Atl	9	C. Cedeno, Hou	56	D. Lopes, LA	16	R. Santo, ChN	27
D. Johnson, Atl	9	J. Koosman, NYN	15	L. May, Hou	9	B. Bonds, SF	43	C. Cedeno, Hou	15	B. Bailey, Mon	23
N. Colbert, SD	8	J. Billingham, Cin	13	A. Oliver, Pit	9	D. Lopes, LA	36	J. Morgan, Cin	15	J. Bench, Cin	22

Runs Created		Runs Created/27 Outs		Batting Average		On-Base Percentage		Slugging Percentage		OBP+Slugging	
D. Evans, Atl	131	W. Stargell, Pit	9.11	P. Rose, Cin	.338	K. Singleton, Mon	.425	W. Stargell, Pit	.646	W. Stargell, Pit	1.038
J. Morgan, Cin	127	D. Evans, Atl	7.90	C. Cedeno, Hou	.320	R. Fairly, Mon	.422	D. Evans, Atl	.556	D. Evans, Atl	.959
W. Stargell, Pit	126	J. Morgan, Cin	7.79	G. Maddox, SF	.319	J. Morgan, Cin	.406	D. Johnson, Atl	.546	T. Perez, Cin	.919
B. Bonds, SF	122	T. Perez, Cin	7.62	T. Perez, Cin	.314	B. Watson, Hou	.403	C. Cedeno, Hou	.537	D. Johnson, Atl	.916
P. Rose, Cin	118	C. Cedeno, Hou	7.38	B. Watson, Hou	.312	D. Evans, Atl	.403	B. Bonds, SF	.530	C. Cedeno, Hou	.913

1973 National League Pitching Leaders

Wins		Losses		Winning Percentage		Games		Games Started		Complete Games	
R. Bryant, SF	24	S. Carlton, Phi	20	G. Stone, NYN	.800	M. Marshall, Mon	92	S. Carlton, Phi	40	S. Carlton, Phi	18
T. Seaver, NYN	19	C. Kirby, SD	18	P. Borbon, Cin	.733	P. Borbon, Cin	80	J. Reuss, Hou	40	T. Seaver, NYN	18
J. Billingham, Cin	19	B. Hooton, ChN	17	T. John, LA	.696	E. Sosa, SF	71	J. Billingham, Cin	40	J. Billingham, Cin	16
D. Sutton, LA	18	J. Barr, SF	17	D. Gullett, Cin	.692	D. Giusti, Pit	67	R. Bryant, SF	39	3 tied with	14
D. Gullett, Cin	18	B. Greif, SD	17	2 tied with	.667	D. Segui, StL	65	F. Jenkins, ChN	38		

Shutouts		Saves		Games Finished		Batters Faced		Innings Pitched		Hits Allowed	
J. Billingham, Cin	7	M. Marshall, Mon	31	M. Marshall, Mon	73	S. Carlton, Phi	1262	S. Carlton, Phi	293.1	S. Carlton, Phi	293
D. Roberts, Hou	6	T. McGraw, NYN	25	D. Giusti, Pit	60	J. Billingham, Cin	1205	J. Billingham, Cin	293.1	J. Reuss, Hou	271
R. Wise, StL	5	D. Giusti, Pit	20	T. McGraw, NYN	46	J. Reuss, Hou	1198	T. Seaver, NYN	290.0	F. Jenkins, ChN	267
W. Twitchell, Phi	5	J. Brewer, LA	20	E. Sosa, SF	46	R. Bryant, SF	1165	J. Reuss, Hou	279.1	D. Roberts, Hou	264
2 tied with	4	2 tied with	18	2 tied with	43	T. Seaver, NYN	1147	F. Jenkins, ChN	271.0	R. Wise, StL	259

Home Runs Allowed		Walks		Walks/9 Innings		Strikeouts		Strikeouts/9 Innings		Strikeout/Walk Ratio	
F. Jenkins, ChN	35	J. Reuss, Hou	117	J. Marichal, SF	1.6	T. Seaver, NYN	251	T. Seaver, NYN	7.8	T. Seaver, NYN	3.92
C. Kirby, SD	30	M. Torrez, Mon	115	F. Jenkins, ChN	1.9	S. Carlton, Phi	223	B. Moore, Mon	7.7	D. Sutton, LA	3.57
S. Carlton, Phi	29	R. Bryant, SF	115	J. Barr, SF	1.9	J. Matlack, NYN	205	J. Matlack, NYN	7.6	F. Jenkins, ChN	2.98
F. Norman, 2tm	27	S. Carlton, Phi	113	D. Sutton, LA	2.0	D. Sutton, LA	200	D. Sutton, LA	7.0	R. Reuschel, ChN	2.71
3 tied with	26	B. Moore, Mon	109	T. Seaver, NYN	2.0	2 tied with	177	S. Carlton, Phi	6.8	B. Gibson, StL	2.49

Earned Run Average		Component ERA		Hit Batsmen		Wild Pitches		Opponent Average		Opponent OBP	
T. Seaver, NYN	2.08	T. Seaver, NYN	2.05	S. Blass, Pit	12	M. Torrez, Mon	14	T. Seaver, NYN	.206	T. Seaver, NYN	.252
D. Sutton, LA	2.42	D. Sutton, LA	2.08	M. Corkins, SD	11	W. Twitchell, Phi	13	D. Sutton, LA	.209	D. Sutton, LA	.257
W. Twitchell, Phi	2.50	B. Gibson, StL	2.47	J. Billingham, Cin	10	C. Kirby, SD	13	D. Wilson, Hou	.213	A. Messersmith, LA	.278
M. Marshall, Mon	2.66	A. Messersmith, LA	2.63	W. Twitchell, Phi	10	P. Niekro, Atl	11	A. Messersmith, LA	.214	B. Gibson, StL	.281
A. Messersmith, LA	2.70	J. Rooker, Pit	2.64	2 tied with	9	6 tied with	10	S. Renko, Mon	.218	N. Briles, Pit	.287

1973 National League Miscellaneous

Managers

Atlanta	Eddie Mathews	76-85
Chicago	Whitey Lockman	77-84
Cincinnati	Sparky Anderson	99-63
Houston	Leo Durocher	82-80
Los Angeles	Walter Alston	95-66
Montreal	Gene Mauch	79-83
New York	Yogi Berra	82-79
Philadelphia	Danny Ozark	71-91
Pittsburgh	Bill Virdon	67-69
	Danny Murtaugh	13-13
St. Louis	Red Schoendienst	81-81
San Diego	Don Zimmer	60-102
San Francisco	Charlie Fox	88-74

Awards

Most Valuable Player	Pete Rose, of, Cin
Cy Young	Tom Seaver, NYN
Rookie of the Year	Gary Matthews, of, SF
STATS Manager of the Year	Gene Mauch, Mon

STATS All-Star Team

C	Joe Ferguson, LA	.263	25	88
1B	Tony Perez, Cin	.314	27	101
2B	Joe Morgan, Cin	.290	26	82
3B	Darrell Evans, Atl	.281	41	104
SS	Dave Concepcion, Cin	.287	8	46
OF	Hank Aaron, Atl	.301	40	96
OF	Pete Rose, Cin	.338	5	64
OF	Willie Stargell, Pit	.299	44	119
P	Jack Billingham, Cin	19-10	3.04	155 K
P	Ron Bryant, SF	24-12	3.53	143 K
P	Tom Seaver, NYN	19-10	2.08	251 K
P	Don Sutton, LA	18-10	2.42	200 K
RP	Mike Marshall, Mon	14-11	2.66	31 Sv

Postseason

LCS	New York 3 vs. Cincinnati 2
World Series	New York (NL) 3 vs. Oakland (AL) 4

Outstanding Performances

No-Hitters

Phil Niekro, Atl	vs. SD	on August 5

Three-Homer Games

Johnny Bench, Cin	on May 9
Lee May, Hou	on June 21

Cycles

Joe Torre, StL	on June 27

EAST	W	L	Pct	GB	DIF	W	L	R	OR	HR	OHR	W	L	R	OR	HR	OHR	Run	HR	M/A	May	June	July	Aug	S/O
			Overall					Home Games						Road Games				Park Index				Record by Month			
Baltimore	91	71	.562	—	25	46	35	281	293	48	46	45	36	378	319	68	55	82	76	11-8	11-16	16-10	14-16	14-15	25-6
New York	89	73	.549	2.0	38	47	34	315	295	42	50	42	39	356	328	59	54	89	81	13-10	10-17	12-12	16-13	18-10	20-11
Boston	84	78	.519	7.0	98	46	35	375	348	58	66	38	43	321	313	51	60	114	112	10-12	15-10	16-10	14-15	17-12	12-19
Cleveland	77	85	.475	14.0	7	40	41	338	349	72	92	37	44	324	345	59	46	103	156	10-11	12-14	16-9	14-15	13-16	12-20
Milwaukee	76	86	.469	15.0	25	40	41	342	329	58	69	36	45	305	331	62	57	106	107	9-8	15-12	12-15	15-17	12-18	13-16
Detroit	72	90	.444	19.0	3	36	45	335	412	74	84	36	45	285	356	57	64	117	131	9-10	13-14	16-12	11-17	13-17	10-20
WEST																									
Oakland	90	72	.556	—	142	49	32	345	265	69	43	41	40	344	286	63	47	97	102	10-10	17-11	14-14	20-8	15-14	14-15
Texas	84	76	.525	5.0	17	42	38	321	340	43	57	42	38	369	358	56	69	91	80	13-8	11-16	15-14	14-14	16-13	15-11
Minnesota	82	80	.506	8.0	3	48	33	365	317	60	56	34	47	308	352	51	59	103	105	9-11	11-12	12-19	18-12	15-14	17-12
Chicago	80	80	.500	9.0	9	46	34	360	365	66	43	34	46	324	356	69	60	107	84	8-11	14-10	14-15	15-15	14-17	15-12
Kansas City	77	85	.475	13.0	0	40	41	355	353	38	42	37	44	312	309	51	49	114	80	8-11	17-11	12-14	14-14	18-13	8-22
California	68	94	.420	22.0	16	36	45	291	287	46	47	32	49	327	370	49	54	83	90	11-11	12-15	9-20	9-18	11-17	16-13

Clinch Date—Baltimore 10/01, Oakland 9/28.

Team Batting

Team	G	AB	R	OR	H	2B	3B	HR	TB	RBI	TBB	IBB	SO	HBP	SH	SF	SB	CS	SB%	GDP	Avg	OBP	Slg
Boston	162	5499	696	661	1449	236	31	109	2074	658	569	57	811	33	64	49	104	58	.64	128	.264	.341	.377
Texas	161	5449	690	698	1482	198	39	99	2055	643	508	38	710	38	81	47	113	80	.59	155	.272	.343	.377
Oakland	162	5331	689	551	1315	205	37	132	1990	637	568	48	876	38	60	51	164	93	.64	108	.247	.329	.373
Chicago	163	5577	684	721	1492	225	23	135	2168	633	519	40	858	26	70	43	64	53	.55	156	.268	.337	.389
Minnesota	163	5632	673	669	1530	190	37	111	2127	632	520	43	791	46	64	40	74	45	.62	159	.272	.342	.378
New York	162	5524	671	623	1451	220	30	101	2034	637	515	52	690	21	49	72	53	35	.60	122	.263	.336	.368
Kansas City	162	5582	667	662	1448	232	42	89	2031	623	550	42	768	32	56	44	146	76	.66	133	.259	.334	.364
Cleveland	162	5474	662	694	1395	201	19	131	2027	616	432	31	756	26	56	31	79	68	.54	135	.255	.316	.370
Baltimore	162	5535	659	612	1418	226	27	116	2046	608	509	61	770	58	72	56	145	58	.71	124	.256	.331	.370
Milwaukee	162	5472	647	660	1335	228	49	120	2021	612	500	37	909	27	56	35	106	75	.59	102	.244	.314	.369
Detroit	162	5568	620	768	1375	200	35	131	2038	579	436	33	784	24	41	37	67	38	.64	132	.247	.309	.366
California	163	5401	618	657	1372	203	31	95	1922	550	509	38	801	45	82	48	119	79	.60	135	.254	.329	.356
AL Total	1946	66044	7976	7976	17062	2564	400	1369	24533	7428	6135	520	9524	414	751	552	1234	758	.62	1589	.258	.323	.371
AL Avg Team	162	5504	665	665	1422	214	33	114	2044	619	511	43	794	35	63	46	103	63	.62	132	.258	.323	.371

Team Pitching

Team	G	CG	ShO	Rel	Sv	IP	H	R	ER	HR	SH	SF	HB	TBB	IBB	SO	WP	Bk	H/9	SO/9	BB/9	OAvg	OOBP	ERA
Oakland	162	49	12	216	28	1439.2	1322	551	472	90	56	56	25	430	41	755	27	1	8.3	4.7	2.7	.246	.302	2.95
Baltimore	162	57	16	185	25	1474.0	1393	612	536	101	73	43	25	480	43	701	34	5	8.5	4.3	2.9	.253	.314	3.27
New York	162	53	13	182	24	1455.1	1402	623	535	104	62	35	33	528	45	829	47	7	8.7	5.1	3.3	.256	.323	3.31
Kansas City	162	54	13	209	17	1471.2	1477	662	574	91	86	45	30	482	64	731	42	4	9.0	4.5	2.9	.263	.322	3.51
California	163	64	13	190	12	1439.0	1339	657	563	101	62	37	47	649	24	986	50	7	8.4	6.2	4.1	.248	.332	3.52
Minnesota	163	43	11	189	29	1455.1	1436	669	589	115	60	41	38	513	18	934	36	3	8.9	5.8	3.2	.260	.325	3.64
Boston	162	71	12	139	18	1455.1	1462	661	601	126	49	45	30	463	38	751	41	4	9.0	4.6	2.9	.262	.320	3.72
Milwaukee	162	43	11	189	24	1457.2	1476	660	609	126	57	47	25	493	46	621	46	0	9.1	3.8	3.0	.266	.326	3.76
Cleveland	162	45	9	214	27	1445.2	1419	694	611	138	70	56	34	479	67	650	20	6	8.8	4.0	3.0	.260	.320	3.80
Texas	161	62	16	189	12	1433.2	1423	698	609	126	46	52	40	449	25	871	51	4	8.9	5.5	2.8	.260	.318	3.82
Chicago	163	55	11	201	29	1465.2	1470	721	641	103	55	52	51	548	40	826	41	4	9.0	5.1	3.4	.263	.332	3.94
Detroit	162	54	7	154	15	1455.2	1443	768	673	148	75	43	36	621	69	869	58	1	8.9	5.4	3.8	.262	.338	4.16
AL Total	1946	650	144	2257	260	17448.2	17062	7976	7013	1369	751	552	414	6135	520	9524	493	46	8.8	4.9	3.2	.258	.330	3.62
AL Avg Team	162	54	12	188	22	1454.2	1422	665	584	114	63	46	35	511	43	794	41	4	8.8	4.9	3.2	.258	.330	3.62

Team Fielding

Team	G	PO	A	E	TC	DP	PB	Pct
Baltimore	162	4422	1922	128	6472	174	16	.980
Milwaukee	162	4373	1823	127	6323	168	16	.980
New York	162	4364	1797	142	6303	158	7	.977
Oakland	162	4319	1704	141	6164	154	10	.977
Cleveland	162	4338	1862	146	6346	157	10	.977
Chicago	163	4397	1765	147	6309	188	19	.977
Boston	162	4365	1709	145	6219	156	10	.977
Kansas City	162	4415	1875	152	6442	166	29	.976
California	163	4317	1721	147	6185	150	23	.976
Minnesota	163	4367	1771	151	6289	164	7	.976
Detroit	162	4367	1784	158	6309	155	17	.975
Texas	161	4301	1753	163	6217	164	8	.974
AL Total	1946	52345	21486	1747	75578	1954	172	.977

Team vs. Team Records

	Bal	Bos	Cal	ChA	Cle	Det	KC	Mil	Min	NYA	Oak	Tex	Won
Bal	—	10	7	5	12	14	8	8	6	11	6	4	91
Bos	8	—	4	8	9	11	4	10	6	11	8	5	84
Cal	5	8	—	10	3	5	8	3	8	3	6	9	68
ChA	7	4	8	—	8	7	11	8	7	4	7	9	80
Cle	6	9	9	4	—	9	8	10	6	7	5	4	77
Det	4	7	7	5	9	—	7	9	3	11	5	5	72
KC	4	8	10	7	4	5	—	11	8	4	8	8	77
Mil	10	8	9	4	8	9	1	—	6	9	5	7	76
Min	6	6	10	11	6	9	10	6	—	4	5	9	82
NYA	7	7	8	11	7	7	8	9	8	—	7	8	89
Oak	6	4	12	11	7	7	10	7	13	5	—	8	90
Tex	8	7	9	7	8	7	10	5	9	4	10	—	84
Lost	71	78	94	80	85	90	85	86	80	73	72	76	

Seasons: Standings, Leaders

1974 American League Batting Leaders

Games		At-Bats		Runs		Hits		Doubles		Triples	
K. Henderson, ChA	162	D. Money, Mil	629	C. Yastrzemski, Bos	93	R. Carew, Min	218	J. Rudi, Oak	39	M. Rivers, Cal	11
T. Harrah, Tex	161	T. Davis, Bal	626	B. Grich, Bal	92	T. Davis, Bal	181	H. McRae, KC	36	A. Otis, KC	9
B. Grich, Bal	160	G. Sutherland, Det	619	R. Jackson, Oak	90	D. Money, Mil	178	G. Scott, Mil	36	4 tied with	8
A. Rodriguez, Det	159	B. Murcer, NYA	606	A. Otis, KC	87	K. Henderson, ChA	176	K. Henderson, ChA	35		
D. Money, Mil	159	G. Scott, Mil	604	R. Carew, Min	86	J. Rudi, Oak	174	J. Burroughs, Tex	33		

Home Runs		Total Bases		Runs Batted In		Walks		Intentional Walks		Strikeouts	
D. Allen, ChA	32	J. Rudi, Oak	287	J. Burroughs, Tex	118	G. Tenace, Oak	110	R. Jackson, Oak	20	B. Darwin, Min	127
R. Jackson, Oak	29	K. Henderson, ChA	281	S. Bando, Oak	103	C. Yastrzemski, Bos	104	C. Yastrzemski, Bos	16	B. Grich, Bal	117
G. Tenace, Oak	26	J. Burroughs, Tex	279	J. Rudi, Oak	99	J. Burroughs, Tex	91	F. Robinson, 2tm	14	L. Hisle, Min	112
J. Burroughs, Tex	25	R. Carew, Min	267	K. Henderson, ChA	95	B. Grich, Bal	90	B. Robinson, Bal	13	K. Henderson, ChA	112
B. Darwin, Min	25	2 tied with	261	B. Darwin, Min	94	2 tied with	86	2 tied with	12	L. Stanton, Cal	107

Hit By Pitch		Sac Hits		Sac Flies		Stolen Bases		Caught Stealing		GDP	
B. Grich, Bal	20	B. Dent, ChA	23	S. Bando, Oak	13	B. North, Oak	54	B. North, Oak	26	G. Scott, Mil	25
B. Darwin, Min	14	M. Belanger, Bal	20	J. Burroughs, Tex	12	R. Carew, Min	38	J. Lowenstein, Cle	17	C. Rojas, KC	24
G. Tenace, Oak	12	J. Sundberg, Tex	17	A. Otis, KC	12	J. Lowenstein, Cle	36	L. Randle, Tex	17	B. Oliver, 2tm	21
D. Baylor, Bal	10	L. Randle, Tex	16	B. Murcer, NYA	12	B. Campaneris, Oak	34	R. Carew, Min	16	T. Davis, Bal	20
F. Robinson, 2tm	10	F. Duffy, Cle	16	2 tied with	11	F. Patek, KC	33	H. Washington, Oak	16	2 tied with	18

Runs Created		Runs Created/27 Outs		Batting Average		On-Base Percentage		Slugging Percentage		OBP+Slugging	
J. Burroughs, Tex	110	R. Jackson, Oak	7.81	R. Carew, Min	.364	R. Carew, Min	.433	D. Allen, ChA	.563	D. Allen, ChA	.938
R. Carew, Min	110	J. Burroughs, Tex	7.10	J. Orta, ChA	.316	C. Yastrzemski, Bos	.414	R. Jackson, Oak	.514	R. Jackson, Oak	.905
R. Jackson, Oak	110	D. Allen, ChA	6.98	H. McRae, KC	.310	J. Burroughs, Tex	.397	J. Burroughs, Tex	.504	J. Burroughs, Tex	.901
C. Yastrzemski, Bos	99	R. Carew, Min	6.92	L. Piniella, NYA	.305	E. Maddox, NYA	.395	J. Rudi, Oak	.484	R. Carew, Min	.879
J. Rudi, Oak	98	C. Yastrzemski, Bos	6.87	E. Maddox, NYA	.303	R. Jackson, Oak	.391	H. McRae, KC	.475	C. Yastrzemski, Bos	.859

1974 American League Pitching Leaders

Wins		Losses		Winning Percentage		Games		Games Started		Complete Games	
F. Jenkins, Tex	25	M. Lolich, Det	21	B. Champion, Mil	.733	R. Fingers, Oak	76	W. Wood, ChA	42	F. Jenkins, Tex	29
C. Hunter, Oak	25	C. Wright, Mil	20	M. Cuellar, Bal	.688	T. Murphy, Mil	70	6 tied with	41	G. Perry, Cle	28
4 tied with	22	5 tied with	19	A. Fitzmorris, KC	.684	S. Foucault, Tex	69			M. Lolich, Det	27
				F. Jenkins, Tex	.676	S. Lyle, NYA	66			N. Ryan, Cal	26
				C. Hunter, Oak	.676	B. Campbell, Min	63			L. Tiant, Bos	25

Shutouts		Saves		Games Finished		Batters Faced		Innings Pitched		Hits Allowed	
L. Tiant, Bos	7	T. Forster, ChA	24	T. Murphy, Mil	66	N. Ryan, Cal	1392	N. Ryan, Cal	332.2	B. Lee, Bos	320
F. Jenkins, Tex	6	T. Murphy, Mil	20	R. Fingers, Oak	60	W. Wood, ChA	1316	F. Jenkins, Tex	328.1	M. Lolich, Det	310
C. Hunter, Oak	6	B. Campbell, Min	19	S. Lyle, NYA	59	F. Jenkins, Tex	1305	G. Perry, Cle	322.1	W. Wood, ChA	305
J. Bibby, Tex	5	R. Fingers, Oak	18	B. Campbell, Min	55	L. Tiant, Bos	1266	W. Wood, ChA	320.1	F. Jenkins, Tex	286
M. Cuellar, Bal	5	T. Buskey, 2tm	18	S. Foucault, Tex	53	M. Lolich, Det	1263	C. Hunter, Oak	318.1	S. Busby, KC	284

Home Runs Allowed		Walks		Walks/9 Innings		Strikeouts		Strikeouts/9 Innings		Strikeout/Walk Ratio	
M. Lolich, Det	38	N. Ryan, Cal	202	F. Jenkins, Tex	1.2	N. Ryan, Cal	367	N. Ryan, Cal	9.9	F. Jenkins, Tex	5.00
J. Coleman, Det	30	J. Coleman, Det	158	C. Hunter, Oak	1.3	B. Blyleven, Min	249	B. Blyleven, Min	8.0	B. Blyleven, Min	3.23
4 tied with	27	J. Bibby, Tex	113	K. Holtzman, Oak	1.8	F. Jenkins, Tex	225	F. Jenkins, Tex	6.2	C. Hunter, Oak	3.11
		S. Bahnsen, ChA	110	J. Kaat, ChA	2.0	G. Perry, Cle	216	S. Busby, KC	6.1	M. Lolich, Det	2.59
		J. Slaton, Mil	102	C. Wright, Mil	2.1	M. Lolich, Det	202	G. Perry, Cle	6.0	F. Tanana, Cal	2.34

Earned Run Average		Component ERA		Hit Batsmen		Wild Pitches		Opponent Average		Opponent OBP	
C. Hunter, Oak	2.49	G. Perry, Cle	2.20	J. Coleman, Det	12	B. Dal Canton, KC	16	N. Ryan, Cal	.190	C. Hunter, Oak	.258
G. Perry, Cle	2.51	C. Hunter, Oak	2.25	7 tied with	9	J. Slaton, Mil	14	G. Perry, Cle	.204	F. Jenkins, Tex	.262
A. Hassler, Cal	2.61	F. Jenkins, Tex	2.38			J. Coleman, Det	13	B. Dal Canton, KC	.211	G. Perry, Cle	.270
B. Blyleven, Min	2.66	B. Blyleven, Min	2.69			L. LaGrow, Det	12	A. Hassler, Cal	.225	B. Blyleven, Min	.290
A. Fitzmorris, KC	2.79	B. Dal Canton, KC	2.69			D. Segui, Bos	12	C. Hunter, Oak	.229	L. Tiant, Bos	.291

1974 American League Miscellaneous

Managers		
Baltimore	Earl Weaver	91-71
Boston	Darrell Johnson	84-78
California	Bobby Winkles	30-44
	Whitey Herzog	2-2
	Dick Williams	36-48
Chicago	Chuck Tanner	80-80
Cleveland	Ken Aspromonte	77-85
Detroit	Ralph Houk	72-90
Kansas City	Jack McKeon	77-85
Milwaukee	Del Crandall	76-86
Minnesota	Frank Quilici	82-80
New York	Bill Virdon	89-73
Oakland	Alvin Dark	90-72
Texas	Billy Martin	84-76

Awards	
Most Valuable Player	Jeff Burroughs, of, Tex
Cy Young	Catfish Hunter, Oak
Rookie of the Year	Mike Hargrove, 1b, Tex
STATS Manager of the Year	Billy Martin, Tex

STATS All-Star Team

C	Thurman Munson, NYA	.261	13	60
1B	Dick Allen, ChA	.301	32	88
2B	Rod Carew, Min	.364	3	55
3B	Sal Bando, Oak	.243	22	103
SS	Toby Harrah, Tex	.260	21	74
OF	Jeff Burroughs, Tex	.301	25	118
OF	Reggie Jackson, Oak	.289	29	93
OF	Joe Rudi, Oak	.293	22	99
DH	Hal McRae, KC	.310	15	88
P	Catfish Hunter, Oak	25-12	2.49	143 K
P	Fergie Jenkins, Tex	25-12	2.82	225 K
P	Gaylord Perry, Cle	21-13	2.51	216 K
P	Nolan Ryan, Cal	22-16	2.89	367 K
RP	Tom Murphy, Mil	10-10	1.90	20 Sv

Postseason	
LCS	Oakland 3 vs. Baltimore 1
World Series	Oakland (AL) 4 vs. LA (NL) 1

Outstanding Performances

No-Hitters

Steve Busby, KC	@ Mil on June 19
Dick Bosman, Cle	vs. Oak on July 19
Nolan Ryan, Cal	vs. Min on September 28

Three-Homer Games

Bobby Grich, Bal	on June 18

EAST	W	L	Pct	GB	DIF	W	L	R	OR	HR	OHR	W	L	R	OR	HR	OHR	Run	HR	M/A	May	June	July	Aug	S/O
								Home Games						Road Games				Park Index		Record by Month					
Pittsburgh	88	74	.543	—	29	52	29	380	303	47	32	36	45	371	354	67	61	94	62	6-12	11-15	15-13	18-14	20-8	18-12
St. Louis	86	75	.534	1.5	84	44	37	356	329	45	46	42	38	321	314	38	51	107	101	13-9	11-13	16-12	13-16	15-15	18-10
Philadelphia	80	82	.494	8.0	63	46	35	378	337	55	56	34	47	298	364	40	55	108	117	10-11	15-12	13-14	15-13	12-17	15-15
Montreal	79	82	.491	8.5	23	42	38	356	329	50	49	37	44	306	328	36	50	109	117	9-7	11-13	15-14	14-19	11-17	19-12
New York	71	91	.438	17.0	1	36	45	279	325	43	49	35	46	293	321	53	50	98	89	8-13	12-15	10-16	15-12	14-15	12-20
Chicago	66	96	.407	22.0	3	32	49	344	424	67	72	34	47	325	402	43	50	106	149	7-11	11-14	13-16	11-18	12-16	12-21
WEST																									
Los Angeles	102	60	.630	—	177	52	29	355	250	68	51	50	31	443	311	71	61	80	90	17-6	19-8	16-10	16-13	15-12	19-11
Cincinnati	98	64	.605	4.0	3	50	31	389	295	74	62	48	33	387	336	61	64	95	109	10-9	17-10	17-12	19-12	18-9	17-12
Atlanta	88	74	.543	14.0	0	46	35	337	290	65	44	42	39	324	273	55	53	105	101	11-12	15-10	16-13	12-16	19-9	15-14
Houston	81	81	.500	21.0	0	46	35	330	293	58	35	35	46	323	339	52	49	94	92	14-10	13-14	11-15	17-11	13-14	13-17
San Francisco	72	90	.444	30.0	9	37	44	340	398	50	61	35	46	294	325	43	55	119	113	11-12	16-13	7-20	14-13	12-15	12-17
San Diego	60	102	.370	42.0	0	36	45	272	381	47	54	24	57	269	449	52	70	91	83	10-14	8-22	17-11	9-16	6-20	10-19

Clinch Date—Pittsburgh 10/02, Los Angeles 10/01.

Team Batting

Team	G	AB	R	OR	H	2B	3B	HR	TB	RBI	TBB	IBB	SO	HBP	SH	SF	SB	CS	SB%	GDP	Avg	OBP	Slg
Los Angeles	162	5557	798	561	1511	231	34	139	2227	744	597	95	820	28	86	64	149	75	.67	117	.272	.352	.401
Cincinnati	163	5535	776	631	1437	271	35	135	2183	714	693	87	940	30	68	46	146	49	.75	121	.260	.350	.394
Pittsburgh	162	5702	751	657	1560	238	46	114	2232	692	514	74	828	38	54	53	55	31	.64	140	.274	.343	.391
St. Louis	161	5620	677	643	1492	216	46	83	2049	610	531	79	752	44	68	55	172	62	.74	142	.265	.340	.365
Philadelphia	162	5494	676	701	1434	233	50	95	2052	636	469	75	822	29	84	44	115	58	.66	112	.261	.327	.373
Chicago	162	5574	669	826	1397	221	42	110	2032	610	621	66	857	29	80	40	78	73	.52	121	.251	.333	.365
Montreal	161	5343	662	657	1355	201	29	86	1872	610	652	65	812	33	106	56	124	49	.72	127	.254	.345	.350
Atlanta	163	5533	661	563	1375	202	37	120	2011	599	571	78	772	24	109	42	72	44	.62	124	.249	.326	.363
Houston	162	5489	653	632	1441	222	41	110	2075	603	471	49	864	30	83	48	108	65	.62	124	.263	.329	.378
San Francisco	162	5482	634	723	1380	228	38	93	1963	568	548	57	869	30	75	24	107	51	.68	113	.252	.326	.358
New York	162	5468	572	646	1286	183	22	96	1801	538	597	56	735	29	87	45	43	23	.65	148	.235	.319	.329
San Diego	162	5415	541	830	1239	196	27	99	1786	506	564	52	900	20	83	35	85	45	.65	106	.229	.308	.330
NL Total	1944	66212	8070	8070	16907	2642	447	1280	24283	7430	6828	833	9971	360	983	552	1254	625	.67	1495	.255	.326	.367
NL Avg Team	162	5518	673	673	1409	220	37	107	2024	619	569	69	831	30	82	46	105	52	.67	125	.255	.326	.367

Team Pitching

Team	G	CG	ShO	Rel	Sv	IP	H	R	ER	HR	SH	SF	HB	TBB	IBB	SO	WP	Bk	H/9	SO/9	BB/9	OAvg	OOBP	ERA
Los Angeles	162	33	19	209	23	1465.1	1272	561	484	112	77	31	24	464	9	943	36	9	7.8	5.8	2.8	.233	.294	2.97
Atlanta	163	46	21	215	22	1474.1	1343	563	500	97	74	39	26	488	55	772	33	9	8.2	4.7	3.0	.244	.307	3.05
Cincinnati	163	34	11	256	27	1466.1	1364	631	556	126	82	41	17	536	62	875	53	9	8.4	5.4	3.3	.247	.314	3.41
New York	162	46	15	212	14	1470.1	1433	646	558	99	85	45	27	504	78	908	40	11	8.8	5.6	3.1	.257	.320	3.42
Houston	162	36	18	272	18	1450.2	1396	632	558	84	74	47	37	601	56	738	52	15	8.7	4.6	3.7	.255	.331	3.46
St. Louis	161	37	13	293	20	1473.1	1399	643	570	97	84	43	24	616	99	794	40	6	8.5	4.9	3.8	.254	.329	3.48
Pittsburgh	162	51	9	229	17	1466.0	1428	657	568	93	76	53	33	543	81	721	48	12	8.8	4.4	3.3	.256	.323	3.49
Montreal	161	35	8	223	27	1429.0	1340	657	571	99	55	40	29	544	52	822	61	12	8.4	5.2	3.4	.249	.319	3.60
San Francisco	162	27	11	292	25	1439.0	1409	723	604	116	92	47	24	559	61	756	38	10	8.8	4.7	3.5	.257	.325	3.78
Philadelphia	162	46	4	283	19	1447.1	1394	701	629	111	79	49	31	682	92	892	63	15	8.7	5.5	4.2	.257	.341	3.91
Chicago	162	23	6	347	26	1466.1	1593	826	697	122	105	56	40	576	72	895	61	20	9.8	5.5	3.5	.277	.344	4.28
San Diego	162	25	7	352	19	1445.2	1536	830	736	124	100	61	48	715	116	855	68	12	9.6	5.3	4.5	.275	.359	4.58
NL Total	1944	439	142	3183	257	17493.2	16907	8070	7031	1280	983	552	360	6828	833	9971	593	140	8.7	5.1	3.5	.255	.333	3.62
NL Avg Team	162	37	12	265	21	1457.2	1409	673	586	107	82	46	30	569	69	831	49	12	8.7	5.1	3.5	.255	.333	3.62

Team Fielding

Team	G	PO	A	E	TC	DP	PB	Pct
Houston	162	4352	1875	113	6340	161	13	.982
Atlanta	163	4423	1822	132	6377	161	31	.979
Cincinnati	163	4399	1735	134	6268	151	6	.979
St. Louis	161	4420	1779	147	6346	192	17	.977
Philadelphia	162	4342	1798	148	6288	168	12	.976
Montreal	161	4287	1923	153	6363	157	13	.976
New York	162	4411	1796	158	6365	150	12	.975
Los Angeles	162	4396	1760	157	6313	122	19	.975
Pittsburgh	162	4398	1854	162	6414	154	10	.975
San Diego	162	4337	1760	170	6267	126	3	.973
San Francisco	162	4317	1826	175	6318	153	13	.972
Chicago	162	4399	1875	199	6473	141	20	.969
NL Total	1944	52481	21803	1848	76132	1836	169	.976

Team vs. Team Records

	Atl	ChN	Cin	Hou	LA	Mon	NYN	Phi	Pit	SD	SF	StL	Won
Atl	—	4	7	6	8	9	8	8	4	17	8	9	88
ChN	8	—	5	4	2	5	8	9	6	6	6	6	66
Cin	11	7	—	14	6	6	9	8	8	12	11	6	98
Hou	12	8	4	—	5	6	6	6	5	11	10	8	81
LA	10	10	12	13	—	8	5	6	4	16	12	6	102
Mon	3	13	6	6	4	—	9	11	9	6	4	8	79
NYN	4	10	3	6	7	9	—	7	7	6	6	6	71
Phi	4	10	4	6	6	7	11	—	10	5	8	9	80
Pit	8	9	4	7	8	9	11	8	—	9	8	7	88
SD	1	6	6	2	6	6	7	3		—	11	5	60
SF	10	6	7	8	6	8	6	4	4	7	—	6	72
StL	3	13	6	4	6	9	12	9	11	7	6	—	86
Lost	74	96	64	81	60	82	91	82	74	102	90	75	

1974 National League Batting Leaders

Games		At-Bats		Runs		Hits		Doubles		Triples	
P. Rose, Cin	163	D. Cash, Phi	687	P. Rose, Cin	110	R. Garr, Atl	214	P. Rose, Cin	45	R. Garr, Atl	17
L. Bowa, Phi	162	R. Stennett, Pit	673	M. Schmidt, Phi	108	D. Cash, Phi	206	A. Oliver, Pit	38	A. Oliver, Pit	12
D. Cash, Phi	162	L. Bowa, Phi	669	J. Bench, Cin	108	S. Garvey, LA	200	J. Bench, Cin	38	D. Cash, Phi	11
M. Schmidt, Phi	162	P. Rose, Cin	652	J. Morgan, Cin	107	A. Oliver, Pit	198	W. Stargell, Pit	37	L. Bowa, Phi	10
5 tied with	160	S. Garvey, LA	642	L. Brock, StL	105	R. Stennett, Pit	196	2 tied with	35	R. Metzger, Hou	10

Home Runs		Total Bases		Runs Batted In		Walks		Intentional Walks		Strikeouts	
M. Schmidt, Phi	36	J. Bench, Cin	315	J. Bench, Cin	129	D. Evans, Atl	126	B. Russell, LA	25	M. Schmidt, Phi	138
J. Bench, Cin	33	M. Schmidt, Phi	310	M. Schmidt, Phi	116	J. Morgan, Cin	120	W. Stargell, Pit	21	B. Bonds, SF	134
J. Wynn, LA	32	R. Garr, Atl	305	S. Garvey, LA	111	J. Wynn, LA	108	L. Brock, StL	16	D. Rader, Hou	131
T. Perez, Cin	28	S. Garvey, LA	301	J. Wynn, LA	108	M. Schmidt, Phi	106	J. Bench, Cin	15	D. Kingman, SF	125
C. Cedeno, Hou	26	A. Oliver, Pit	293	T. Simmons, StL	103	P. Rose, Cin	106	2 tied with	14	T. Perez, Cin	112

Hit By Pitch		Sac Hits		Sac Flies		Stolen Bases		Caught Stealing		GDP	
R. Hunt, 2tm	16	F. Millan, NYN	24	B. Foote, Mon	12	L. Brock, StL	118	L. Brock, StL	33	K. Reitz, StL	25
B. McBride, StL	13	L. Lintz, Mon	23	J. Wynn, LA	11	D. Lopes, LA	59	G. Gross, Hou	20	T. Simmons, StL	22
D. Cash, Phi	9	R. Metzger, Hou	21	W. Davis, Mon	11	J. Morgan, Cin	58	D. Lopes, LA	18	B. Bailey, Mon	22
B. Tolan, SD	9	L. Bowa, Phi	20	R. Cey, LA	10	C. Cedeno, Hou	57	C. Cedeno, Hou	17	R. Staub, NYN	21
2 tied with	8	T. Sizemore, StL	18	2 tied with	9	L. Lintz, Mon	50	R. Garr, Atl	16	2 tied with	20

Runs Created		Runs Created/27 Outs		Batting Average		On-Base Percentage		Slugging Percentage		OBP+Slugging	
M. Schmidt, Phi	127	J. Morgan, Cin	8.45	R. Garr, Atl	.353	J. Morgan, Cin	.427	M. Schmidt, Phi	.546	W. Stargell, Pit	.944
J. Morgan, Cin	120	W. Stargell, Pit	8.05	A. Oliver, Pit	.321	W. Stargell, Pit	.407	W. Stargell, Pit	.537	M. Schmidt, Phi	.941
R. Garr, Atl	111	M. Schmidt, Phi	8.01	G. Gross, Hou	.314	B. Bailey, Mon	.396	R. Smith, StL	.528	J. Morgan, Cin	.921
J. Bench, Cin	111	R. Garr, Atl	7.15	B. Buckner, LA	.314	M. Schmidt, Phi	.395	J. Bench, Cin	.507	R. Smith, StL	.917
2 tied with	109	R. Smith, StL	7.01	B. Madlock, ChN	.313	G. Gross, Hou	.393	R. Garr, Atl	.503	R. Garr, Atl	.886

1974 National League Pitching Leaders

Wins		Losses		Winning Percentage		Games		Games Started		Complete Games	
P. Niekro, Atl	20	B. Bonham, ChN	22	T. John, LA	.813	M. Marshall, LA	106	D. Sutton, LA	40	P. Niekro, Atl	18
A. Messersmith, LA	20	R. Jones, SD	22	A. Messersmith, LA	.769	L. Hardy, SD	76	S. Carlton, Phi	39	S. Carlton, Phi	17
D. Sutton, LA	19	S. Rogers, Mon	22	M. Caldwell, SF	.737	P. Borbon, Cin	73	P. Niekro, Atl	39	J. Lonborg, Phi	16
J. Billingham, Cin	19	B. Greif, SD	19	C. Carroll, Cin	.706	K. Forsch, Hou	70	J. Lonborg, Phi	39	J. Rooker, Pit	15
2 tied with	17	2 tied with	16	D. Sutton, LA	.679	E. Sosa, SF	68	A. Messersmith, LA	39	2 tied with	14

Shutouts		Saves		Games Finished		Batters Faced		Innings Pitched		Hits Allowed	
J. Matlack, NYN	7	M. Marshall, LA	21	M. Marshall, LA	83	S. Carlton, Phi	1227	P. Niekro, Atl	302.1	C. Morton, Atl	293
P. Niekro, Atl	6	R. Moffitt, SF	15	R. Moffitt, SF	47	P. Niekro, Atl	1219	A. Messersmith, LA	292.1	J. Lonborg, Phi	280
4 tied with	5	P. Borbon, Cin	14	P. Borbon, Cin	44	A. Messersmith, LA	1179	S. Carlton, Phi	291.0	R. Reuschel, ChN	262
		D. Giusti, Pit	12	D. Giusti, Pit	41	C. Morton, Atl	1176	J. Lonborg, Phi	283.0	J. Reuss, Pit	259
		2 tied with	11	K. Forsch, Hou	40	J. Lonborg, Phi	1168	D. Sutton, LA	276.0	J. Koosman, NYN	258

Home Runs Allowed		Walks		Walks/9 Innings		Strikeouts		Strikeouts/9 Innings		Strikeout/Walk Ratio	
A. Messersmith, LA	24	S. Carlton, Phi	136	J. Barr, SF	1.8	S. Carlton, Phi	240	T. Seaver, NYN	7.7	T. Seaver, NYN	2.68
B. Gibson, StL	24	J. D'Acquisto, SF	124	R. Reed, Atl	2.0	A. Messersmith, LA	221	S. Carlton, Phi	7.4	J. Matlack, NYN	2.57
D. Sutton, LA	23	D. Ruthven, Phi	116	D. Ellis, Pit	2.1	T. Seaver, NYN	201	B. Bonham, ChN	7.1	M. Marshall, LA	2.55
J. Lonborg, Phi	22	D. Freisleben, SD	112	J. Lonborg, Phi	2.2	P. Niekro, Atl	195	J. D'Acquisto, SF	7.0	A. Messersmith, LA	2.35
D. Gullett, Cin	22	B. Bonham, ChN	109	M. Marshall, LA	2.4	J. Matlack, NYN	195	F. Norman, Cin	6.8	D. Sutton, LA	2.24

Earned Run Average		Component ERA		Hit Batsmen		Wild Pitches		Opponent Average		Opponent OBP	
B. Capra, Atl	2.28	J. Matlack, NYN	2.35	B. Greif, SD	14	S. Renko, Mon	19	B. Capra, Atl	.208	A. Messersmith, LA	.277
P. Niekro, Atl	2.38	B. Capra, Atl	2.47	B. Kison, Pit	11	C. Kirby, Cin	15	A. Messersmith, LA	.212	J. Matlack, NYN	.283
J. Matlack, NYN	2.41	A. Messersmith, LA	2.54	6 tied with	7	B. Bonham, ChN	13	D. Gullett, Cin	.222	P. Niekro, Atl	.284
M. Marshall, LA	2.42	P. Niekro, Atl	2.59			D. Freisleben, SD	12	P. Niekro, Atl	.225	R. Reed, Atl	.285
A. Messersmith, LA	2.59	J. Rooker, Pit	2.74			3 tied with	11	J. Matlack, NYN	.226	B. Capra, Atl	.286

1974 National League Miscellaneous

Managers		
Atlanta	Eddie Mathews	50-49
	Clyde King	38-25
Chicago	Whitey Lockman	41-52
	Jim Marshall	25-44
Cincinnati	Sparky Anderson	98-64
Houston	Preston Gomez	81-81
Los Angeles	Walter Alston	102-60
Montreal	Gene Mauch	79-82
New York	Yogi Berra	71-91
Philadelphia	Danny Ozark	80-82
Pittsburgh	Danny Murtaugh	88-74
St. Louis	Red Schoendienst	86-75
San Diego	John McNamara	60-102
San Francisco	Charlie Fox	34-42
	Wes Westrum	38-48

Awards

Most Valuable Player	Steve Garvey, 1b, LA
Cy Young	Mike Marshall, LA
Rookie of the Year	Bake McBride, of, StL
STATS Manager of the Year	Walter Alston, LA

STATS All-Star Team

C	Johnny Bench, Cin	.280	33	129
1B	Steve Garvey, LA	.312	21	111
2B	Joe Morgan, Cin	.293	22	67
3B	Mike Schmidt, Phi	.282	36	116
SS	Dave Concepcion, Cin	.281	14	82
OF	Reggie Smith, StL	.309	23	100
OF	Willie Stargell, Pit	.301	25	96
OF	Jimmy Wynn, LA	.271	32	108
P	Buzz Capra, Atl	16-8	2.28	137 K
P	Jon Matlack, NYN	13-15	2.41	195 K
P	Andy Messersmith, LA	20-6	2.59	221 K
P	Phil Niekro, Atl	20-13	2.38	195 K
RP	Mike Marshall, LA	15-12	2.42	21 Sv

Postseason

LCS	Los Angeles 3 vs. Pittsburgh 1
World Series	LA (NL) 1 vs. Oakland (AL) 4

Outstanding Performances

Three-Homer Games

G. Mitterwald, ChN	on April 17
Jimmy Wynn, LA	on May 11
Davey Lopes, LA	on August 20

Cycles

Richie Zisk, Pit	on June 9

1975 American League Standings

	Overall					Home Games						Road Games						Park Index		Record by Month					
EAST	W	L	Pct	GB	DIF	W	L	R	OR	HR	OHR	W	L	R	OR	HR	OHR	Run	HR	M/A	May	June	July	Aug	S/O
Boston	95	65	.594	—	134	47	34	427	399	74	83	48	31	369	310	60	62	119	126	7-9	16-9	18-13	22-11	16-12	16-11
Baltimore	90	69	.566	4.5	3	44	33	282	231	46	45	46	36	400	322	78	65	76	68	7-9	11-17	16-13	18-10	21-11	17-9
New York	83	77	.519	12.0	5	43	35	323	276	50	56	40	42	358	312	60	48	94	103	9-10	12-14	20-9	11-18	15-16	16-10
Cleveland	79	80	.497	15.5	4	41	39	331	367	79	85	38	41	357	336	74	51	99	130	7-8	12-16	13-17	14-14	15-13	18-12
Milwaukee	68	94	.420	28.0	35	36	45	348	398	72	63	32	49	327	394	74	70	103	94	9-7	12-14	19-13	12-19	7-23	9-18
Detroit	57	102	.358	37.5	10	31	49	301	421	63	83	26	53	269	365	62	54	112	124	10-6	9-15	8-24	19-14	6-22	5-21
WEST																									
Oakland	98	64	.605	—	161	54	27	366	247	75	43	44	37	392	359	76	59	82	87	12-8	16-10	19-9	19-11	15-16	17-10
Kansas City	91	71	.562	7.0	13	51	30	377	309	46	45	40	41	333	340	72	63	102	67	11-9	16-11	14-13	15-15	16-12	19-11
Texas	79	83	.488	19.0	5	39	41	349	366	52	70	40	42	365	367	82	53	100	93	9-9	14-14	13-16	12-18	19-12	12-14
Minnesota	76	83	.478	20.5	3	39	43	401	410	75	88	37	40	323	326	46	49	117	161	6-10	17-9	10-20	12-21	18-10	13-13
Chicago	75	86	.466	22.5	0	42	39	350	359	42	54	33	47	305	344	52	53	108	90	7-13	13-11	15-14	15-14	15-17	10-17
California	72	89	.447	25.5	3	35	46	294	349	24	52	37	43	334	374	31	71	90	74	12-8	10-18	13-17	12-16	15-14	10-16

Clinch Date—Boston 9/28, Oakland 9/24.

Team Batting

Team	G	AB	R	OR	H	2B	3B	HR	TB	RBI	TBB	IBB	SO	HBP	SH	SF	SB	CS	SB%	GDP	Avg	OBP	Slg
Boston	160	5448	796	709	1500	284	44	134	2274	756	565	57	741	34	75	53	66	58	.53	137	.275	.353	.417
Oakland	162	5415	758	606	1376	220	33	151	2115	703	609	45	846	51	74	35	183	82	.69	107	.254	.339	.391
Minnesota	159	5514	724	736	1497	215	28	121	2131	669	563	67	746	40	62	46	81	48	.63	127	.271	.348	.386
Texas	162	5599	714	733	1431	208	17	134	2075	675	613	48	863	25	64	41	102	62	.62	125	.256	.336	.371
Kansas City	162	5491	710	649	1431	263	58	118	2164	667	591	47	675	29	68	51	155	75	.67	109	.261	.341	.394
Cleveland	159	5404	688	703	1409	201	25	153	2119	643	525	36	667	24	64	40	106	89	.54	145	.261	.333	.392
Baltimore	159	5474	682	553	1382	224	33	124	2044	635	580	55	834	38	73	46	104	55	.65	114	.252	.333	.373
New York	160	5415	681	588	1430	230	39	110	2068	642	486	41	710	30	54	53	102	59	.63	142	.264	.334	.382
Milwaukee	162	5378	675	792	1343	242	34	146	2091	632	553	33	922	28	73	49	65	64	.50	131	.250	.328	.389
Chicago	161	5490	655	703	1400	209	38	94	1967	604	611	53	800	40	50	52	101	54	.65	149	.255	.340	.358
California	161	5377	628	723	1324	195	41	55	1766	572	593	36	811	26	97	47	220	108	.67	98	.246	.329	.328
Detroit	159	5366	570	786	1338	171	39	125	1962	546	383	26	872	28	37	38	63	57	.53	120	.249	.307	.366
AL Total	1926	65371	8281	8281	16861	2662	429	1465	24776	7744	6672	544	9487	393	791	551	1348	811	.62	1504	.258	.328	.379
AL Avg Team	161	5448	690	690	1405	222	36	122	2065	645	556	45	791	33	66	46	112	68	.62	125	.258	.328	.379

Team Pitching

Team	G	CG	ShO	Rel	Sv	IP	H	R	ER	HR	SH	SF	HB	TBB	IBB	SO	WP	Bk	H/9	SO/9	BB/9	OAvg	OOBP	ERA
Baltimore	159	70	19	149	21	1451.0	1285	553	511	110	74	37	12	500	46	717	42	3	8.0	4.4	3.1	.242	.306	3.17
Oakland	162	36	10	245	44	1448.0	1267	606	526	102	64	51	37	523	41	784	47	3	7.9	4.9	3.3	.236	.306	3.27
New York	160	70	11	147	20	1424.0	1325	588	520	104	50	53	21	502	41	809	39	3	8.4	5.1	3.2	.249	.314	3.29
Kansas City	162	52	11	204	25	1456.2	1422	649	561	108	66	40	30	498	52	815	40	2	8.8	5.0	3.1	.258	.320	3.47
Cleveland	159	37	6	218	33	1435.1	1395	703	613	136	67	40	35	509	78	800	51	9	8.7	5.0	3.8	.258	.333	3.84
Texas	162	60	16	224	17	1465.2	1456	733	629	123	75	45	43	518	60	792	49	7	8.9	4.9	3.2	.261	.327	3.86
California	161	59	19	192	16	1453.1	1386	723	628	123	62	59	39	613	34	975	62	5	8.6	6.0	3.8	.253	.330	3.89
Chicago	161	34	7	209	39	1452.1	1489	703	634	107	73	35	33	655	38	799	26	6	9.2	5.0	4.1	.268	.347	3.93
Boston	160	62	11	167	31	1436.2	1463	709	636	145	57	45	20	490	24	720	34	1	9.2	4.5	3.1	.265	.325	3.98
Minnesota	159	57	7	163	22	1423.0	1381	736	663	137	75	43	36	617	22	846	49	6	8.7	5.4	3.9	.257	.335	4.05
Detroit	159	52	10	155	17	1396.0	1496	786	663	137	66	57	30	533	47	787	48	3	9.6	5.1	3.4	.275	.340	4.27
Milwaukee	162	36	10	223	34	1431.2	1496	792	690	133	62	46	58	624	60	643	65	3	9.4	4.0	3.9	.271	.348	4.34
AL Total	1926	625	137	2296	319	17273.2	16861	8281	7251	1465	791	551	394	6672	543	9487	552	51	8.8	4.9	3.5	.258	.335	3.78
AL Avg Team	161	52	11	191	27	1439.2	1405	690	604	122	66	46	33	556	45	791	46	4	8.8	4.9	3.5	.258	.335	3.78

Team Fielding

Team	G	PO	A	E	TC	DP	PB	Pct
Baltimore	159	4353	1974	107	6434	175	5	.983
Cleveland	159	4305	1751	134	6190	156	15	.978
Chicago	161	4357	1859	140	6356	155	12	.978
New York	160	4272	1698	135	6105	148	9	.978
Boston	160	4310	1724	139	6173	142	3	.977
Oakland	162	4345	1689	143	6177	140	13	.977
Kansas City	162	4370	1831	155	6356	151	13	.976
Minnesota	159	4269	1842	170	6281	147	9	.973
Detroit	159	4188	1756	173	6117	141	11	.972
Milwaukee	162	4295	1776	180	6251	162	20	.971
Texas	162	4397	1980	191	6568	173	11	.971
California	161	4360	1705	184	6249	164	12	.971
AL Total	1926	51821	21585	1851	75257	1854	133	.975

Team vs. Team Records

	Bal	Bos	Cal	ChA	Cle	Det	KC	Mil	Min	NYA	Oak	Tex	Won
Bal	—	9	6	7	10	12	7	14	6	8	4	7	90
Bos	9	—	6	8	7	13	7	10	10	11	6	8	95
Cal	6	6	—	9	3	6	4	7	8	7	7	9	72
ChA	4	4	9	—	7	5	9	8	9	6	9	5	75
Cle	8	11	9	5	—	12	6	9	3	9	2	5	79
Det	4	5	7	7	6	—	6	7	4	6	6	1	57
KC	5	5	14	9	6	6	—	7	11	7	7	14	91
Mil	4	8	5	4	9	11	5	—	2	9	5	6	68
Min	6	2	10	9	6	8	7	10	—	4	6	8	76
NYA	10	5	5	6	9	12	5	9	8	—	6	8	83
Oak	8	6	11	9	10	6	11	7	12	6	—	12	98
Tex	5	4	13	13	7	11	4	6	10	4	6	—	79
Lost	69	65	89	86	80	102	71	94	83	77	64	83	

1975 American League Batting Leaders

Games		At-Bats		Runs		Hits		Doubles		Triples	
S. Bando, Oak	160	G. Brett, KC	634	F. Lynn, Bos	103	G. Brett, KC	195	F. Lynn, Bos	47	G. Brett, KC	13
P. Garner, Oak	160	G. Scott, Mil	617	J. Mayberry, KC	95	R. Carew, Min	192	R. Jackson, Oak	39	M. Rivers, Cal	13
G. Brett, KC	159	M. Rivers, Cal	616	B. Bonds, NYA	93	T. Munson, NYA	190	C. Chambliss, NYA	38	J. Orta, ChA	10
W. Horton, Det	159	W. Horton, Det	615	J. Rice, Bos	92	C. Washington, Oak	182	J. Mayberry, KC	38	A. Cowens, KC	8
3 tied with	158	B. Dent, ChA	602	2 tied with	91	2 tied with	176	H. McRae, KC	38	4 tied with	7

Home Runs		Total Bases		Runs Batted In		Walks		Intentional Walks		Strikeouts	
R. Jackson, Oak	36	G. Scott, Mil	318	G. Scott, Mil	109	J. Mayberry, KC	119	R. Carew, Min	18	J. Burroughs, Tex	155
G. Scott, Mil	36	R. Jackson, Oak	303	J. Mayberry, KC	106	K. Singleton, Bal	118	J. Mayberry, KC	16	R. LeFlore, Det	139
J. Mayberry, KC	34	J. Mayberry, KC	303	F. Lynn, Bos	105	B. Grich, Bal	107	T. Oliva, Min	15	B. Bonds, NYA	137
B. Bonds, NYA	32	F. Lynn, Bos	299	R. Jackson, Oak	104	G. Tenace, Oak	106	K. Henderson, ChA	14	R. Jackson, Oak	133
2 tied with	29	G. Brett, KC	289	2 tied with	102	T. Harrah, Tex	98	C. May, ChA	13	G. Tenace, Oak	127

Hit By Pitch		Sac Hits		Sac Flies		Stolen Bases		Caught Stealing		GDP	
D. Baylor, Bal	13	M. Belanger, Bal	23	G. Nettles, NYA	11	M. Rivers, Cal	70	J. Remy, Cal	21	L. May, Bal	26
T. Oliva, Min	13	P. Garner, Oak	21	R. Carew, Min	10	C. Washington, Oak	40	R. LeFlore, Det	20	G. Scott, Mil	26
G. Tenace, Oak	12	B. Campaneris, Oak	19	H. McRae, KC	10	A. Otis, KC	39	L. Randle, Tex	19	G. Hendrick, Cle	25
C. May, ChA	9	P. Blair, Bal	17	T. Munson, NYA	10	R. Carew, Min	35	D. Kuiper, Cle	18	T. Munson, NYA	23
3 tied with	8	R. Burleson, Bos	17	3 tied with	9	J. Remy, Cal	34	2 tied with	17	3 tied with	19

Runs Created		Runs Created/27 Outs		Batting Average		On-Base Percentage		Slugging Percentage		OBP+Slugging	
J. Mayberry, KC	122	F. Lynn, Bos	8.32	R. Carew, Min	.359	R. Carew, Min	.421	F. Lynn, Bos	.566	F. Lynn, Bos	.967
F. Lynn, Bos	117	J. Mayberry, KC	8.06	F. Lynn, Bos	.331	J. Mayberry, KC	.416	J. Mayberry, KC	.547	J. Mayberry, KC	.963
K. Singleton, Bal	116	R. Carew, Min	8.00	T. Munson, NYA	.318	K. Singleton, Bal	.415	G. Scott, Mil	.515	R. Carew, Min	.919
R. Carew, Min	112	T. Harrah, Tex	7.27	J. Rice, Bos	.309	T. Harrah, Tex	.403	B. Bonds, NYA	.512	B. Bonds, NYA	.888
T. Harrah, Tex	106	K. Singleton, Bal	7.26	C. Washington, Oak	.308	F. Lynn, Bos	.401	R. Jackson, Oak	.511	K. Singleton, Bal	.869

1975 American League Pitching Leaders

Wins		Losses		Winning Percentage		Games		Games Started		Complete Games	
J. Palmer, Bal	23	W. Wood, ChA	20	R. Moret, Bos	.824	R. Fingers, Oak	75	W. Wood, ChA	43	C. Hunter, NYA	30
C. Hunter, NYA	23	F. Jenkins, Tex	18	M. Torrez, Bal	.690	P. Lindblad, Oak	68	J. Kaat, ChA	41	G. Perry, 2tm	25
V. Blue, Oak	22	J. Slaton, Mil	18	D. Leonard, KC	.682	G. Gossage, ChA	62	C. Hunter, NYA	39	J. Palmer, Bal	25
J. Kaat, ChA	20	J. Coleman, Det	18	J. Palmer, Bal	.676	D. LaRoche, Cle	61	3 tied with	38	F. Jenkins, Tex	22
M. Torrez, Bal	20	M. Lolich, Det	18	V. Blue, Oak	.667	S. Foucault, Tex	59			B. Blyleven, Min	20

Shutouts		Saves		Games Finished		Batters Faced		Innings Pitched		Hits Allowed	
J. Palmer, Bal	10	G. Gossage, ChA	26	R. Fingers, Oak	59	C. Hunter, NYA	1294	C. Hunter, NYA	328.0	J. Kaat, ChA	321
C. Hunter, NYA	7	R. Fingers, Oak	24	G. Gossage, ChA	49	J. Kaat, ChA	1279	J. Palmer, Bal	323.0	W. Wood, ChA	309
4 tied with	5	T. Murphy, Mil	20	T. Murphy, Mil	43	J. Palmer, Bal	1268	G. Perry, 2tm	305.2	G. Perry, 2tm	277
		D. LaRoche, Cle	17	D. LaRoche, Cle	41	G. Perry, 2tm	1248	J. Kaat, ChA	303.2	B. Lee, Bos	274
		D. Drago, Bos	15	S. Foucault, Tex	40	W. Wood, ChA	1245	W. Wood, ChA	291.1	D. Medich, NYA	271

Home Runs Allowed		Walks		Walks/9 Innings		Strikeouts		Strikeouts/9 Innings		Strikeout/Walk Ratio	
F. Jenkins, Tex	37	M. Torrez, Bal	133	F. Jenkins, Tex	1.9	F. Tanana, Cal	269	F. Tanana, Cal	9.4	F. Tanana, Cal	3.68
R. Wise, Bos	34	N. Ryan, Cal	132	G. Perry, 2tm	2.1	B. Blyleven, Min	233	N. Ryan, Cal	8.5	G. Perry, 2tm	3.33
R. Grimsley, Bal	29	J. Hughes, Min	127	R. Grimsley, Bal	2.1	G. Perry, 2tm	233	B. Blyleven, Min	7.6	F. Jenkins, Tex	2.80
G. Perry, 2tm	28	K. Holtzman, Oak	108	J. Palmer, Bal	2.2	J. Palmer, Bal	193	D. Eckersley, Cle	7.3	B. Blyleven, Min	2.77
J. Slaton, Mil	28	P. Broberg, Mil	106	C. Hunter, NYA	2.3	V. Blue, Oak	189	G. Perry, 2tm	6.9	J. Palmer, Bal	2.41

Earned Run Average		Component ERA		Hit Batsmen		Wild Pitches		Opponent Average		Opponent OBP	
J. Palmer, Bal	2.09	C. Hunter, NYA	2.18	P. Broberg, Mil	16	J. Coleman, Det	15	C. Hunter, NYA	.208	C. Hunter, NYA	.261
C. Hunter, NYA	2.58	J. Palmer, Bal	2.20	J. Hughes, Min	13	N. Ryan, Cal	12	N. Ryan, Cal	.213	J. Palmer, Bal	.266
D. Eckersley, Cle	2.60	B. Blyleven, Min	2.63	B. Travers, Mil	11	J. Slaton, Mil	12	D. Eckersley, Cle	.215	B. Blyleven, Min	.281
F. Tanana, Cal	2.62	F. Tanana, Cal	2.69	4 tied with	9	S. Hargan, Tex	12	J. Palmer, Bal	.216	G. Perry, 2tm	.284
E. Figueroa, Cal	2.91	G. Perry, 2tm	2.88			D. Goltz, Min	11	B. Blyleven, Min	.219	F. Tanana, Cal	.286

1975 American League Miscellaneous

Managers

Baltimore	Earl Weaver	90-69
Boston	Darrell Johnson	95-65
California	Dick Williams	72-89
Chicago	Chuck Tanner	75-86
Cleveland	Frank Robinson	79-80
Detroit	Ralph Houk	57-102
Kansas City	Jack McKeon	50-46
	Whitey Herzog	41-25
Milwaukee	Del Crandall	67-94
	Harvey Kuenn	1-0
Minnesota	Frank Quilici	76-83
New York	Bill Virdon	53-51
	Billy Martin	30-26
Oakland	Alvin Dark	98-64
Texas	Billy Martin	44-51
	Frank Lucchesi	35-32

Awards

Most Valuable Player	Fred Lynn, of, Bos
Cy Young	Jim Palmer, Bal
Rookie of the Year	Fred Lynn, of, Bos
STATS Manager of the Year	Darrell Johnson, Bos

STATS All-Star Team

C	Gene Tenace, Oak	.255	29	87
1B	John Mayberry, KC	.291	34	106
2B	Rod Carew, Min	.359	14	80
3B	George Brett, KC	.308	11	89
SS	Toby Harrah, Tex	.293	20	93
OF	Bobby Bonds, NYA	.270	32	85
OF	Reggie Jackson, Oak	.253	36	104
OF	Fred Lynn, Bos	.331	21	105
DH	Willie Horton, Det	.275	25	92
P	Vida Blue, Oak	22-11	3.01	189 K
P	Catfish Hunter, NYA	23-14	2.58	177 K
P	Jim Palmer, Bal	23-11	2.09	193 K
P	Frank Tanana, Cal	16-9	2.62	269 K
RP	Goose Gossage, ChA	9-8	1.84	26 Sv

Postseason

LCS	Boston 3 vs. Oakland 0
World Series	Boston (AL) 3 vs. Cincinnati (NL) 4

Outstanding Performances

No-Hitters

Nolan Ryan, Cal	vs. Bal on June 1

Three-Homer Games

Fred Lynn, Bos	on June 18
John Mayberry, KC	on July 1
Don Baylor, Bal	on July 2
Tony Solaita, KC	on September 7

1975 National League Standings

	Overall					Home Games						Road Games						Park Index		Record by Month					
EAST	W	L	Pct	GB	DIF	W	L	R	OR	HR	OHR	W	L	R	OR	HR	OHR	Run	HR	M/A	May	June	July	Aug	S/O
Pittsburgh	92	69	.571	—	121	52	28	348	270	67	41	40	41	364	295	71	38	95	100	9-7	15-11	21-11	18-12	12-17	17-11
Philadelphia	86	76	.531	6.5	1	51	30	401	326	72	47	35	46	334	368	53	64	104	102	8-10	14-13	20-11	17-12	13-17	14-13
New York	82	80	.506	10.5	2	42	39	294	301	52	48	40	41	352	324	49	51	88	100	9-7	12-12	16-15	17-14	17-16	11-16
St. Louis	82	80	.506	10.5	0	45	36	351	352	46	39	37	44	311	337	35	59	108	90	7-10	12-14	17-13	16-15	20-11	10-17
Chicago	75	87	.463	17.5	51	42	39	392	427	54	71	33	48	320	400	41	59	114	125	12-5	13-15	11-21	13-17	13-16	13-13
Montreal	75	87	.463	17.5	2	39	42	326	375	53	57	36	45	275	315	45	45	119	122	5-11	10-14	16-15	11-18	16-17	17-12
WEST																									
Cincinnati	108	54	.667	—	122	64	17	457	275	70	52	44	37	383	311	54	60	105	107	12-11	16-10	21-7	20-9	21-8	18-9
Los Angeles	88	74	.543	20.0	4	49	32	329	221	54	52	39	42	329	313	54	52	84	109	15-8	15-12	13-16	12-16	17-12	16-10
San Francisco	80	81	.497	27.5	1	46	35	346	335	36	37	34	46	313	336	48	55	104	70	10-11	13-11	14-17	15-14	15-15	13-13
San Diego	71	91	.438	37.0	13	38	43	279	338	33	38	33	48	273	345	45	61	100	67	11-10	13-14	12-17	14-15	11-19	10-16
Atlanta	67	94	.416	40.5	1	37	43	280	350	58	63	30	51	303	389	49	38	92	141	12-12	11-15	11-16	13-16	12-18	8-17
Houston	64	97	.398	43.5	1	37	44	313	338	40	43	27	53	351	373	44	63	89	77	8-16	12-15	8-21	10-18	14-15	12-12

Clinch Date—Pittsburgh 9/22, Cincinnati 9/07.

Team Batting

Team	G	AB	R	OR	H	2B	3B	HR	TB	RBI	TBB	IBB	SO	HBP	SH	SF	SB	CS	SB%	GDP	Avg	OBP	Slg
Cincinnati	162	5581	840	586	1515	278	37	124	2239	779	691	67	916	35	66	45	168	36	.82	122	.271	.360	.401
Philadelphia	162	5592	735	694	1506	283	42	125	2248	687	610	78	960	31	88	42	126	57	.69	114	.269	.349	.402
Pittsburgh	161	5489	712	565	1444	255	47	138	2207	669	468	55	832	38	76	40	49	28	.64	124	.263	.330	.402
Chicago	162	5470	712	827	1419	229	41	95	2015	645	650	78	802	30	107	66	67	55	.55	112	.259	.348	.368
Houston	162	5515	664	711	1401	218	54	84	1979	606	523	66	762	32	97	44	133	62	.68	118	.254	.327	.359
St. Louis	163	5597	662	689	1527	239	46	81	2101	619	444	66	649	29	92	45	116	49	.70	137	.273	.334	.375
San Francisco	161	5447	659	671	1412	235	45	84	1989	606	604	52	775	22	62	51	99	47	.68	139	.259	.341	.365
Los Angeles	162	5453	648	534	1355	217	31	118	1988	606	611	72	825	31	104	47	138	52	.73	123	.248	.333	.365
New York	162	5587	646	625	1430	217	34	101	2018	604	501	70	805	37	75	37	32	26	.55	143	.256	.325	.361
Montreal	162	5518	601	690	1346	216	31	98	1918	542	579	73	954	27	110	38	108	58	.65	110	.244	.323	.348
Atlanta	161	5424	583	739	1323	179	28	107	1879	541	543	58	759	18	72	55	55	38	.59	139	.244	.319	.346
San Diego	162	5429	552	683	1324	215	22	78	1817	505	506	60	754	37	133	46	85	50	.63	128	.244	.318	.335
NL Total	1942	66102	8014	8014	17002	2781	458	1233	24398	7409	6730	795	9793	367	1082	536	1176	558	.68	1509	.257	.327	.369
NL Avg Team	162	5509	668	668	1417	232	38	103	2033	617	561	66	816	31	90	45	98	47	.68	126	.257	.327	.369

Team Pitching

Team	G	CG	ShO	Rel	Sv	IP	H	R	ER	HR	SH	SF	HB	TBB	IBB	SO	WP	Bk	H/9	SO/9	BB/9	OAvg	OOBP	ERA
Los Angeles	162	51	18	169	21	1469.2	1215	534	477	104	89	39	28	448	20	894	34	10	7.4	5.5	2.7	.225	.285	2.92
Pittsburgh	161	43	14	226	31	1437.1	1302	565	480	79	92	40	20	551	102	768	37	11	8.2	4.8	3.5	.243	.313	3.01
Cincinnati	162	22	8	277	50	1459.0	1422	586	546	112	79	37	29	487	63	663	49	10	8.8	4.1	3.0	.257	.319	3.37
New York	162	40	14	229	31	1466.0	1344	625	552	99	87	32	24	580	64	989	48	20	8.3	6.1	3.6	.246	.319	3.39
San Diego	162	40	12	290	20	1463.1	1494	683	566	99	124	49	24	521	94	713	44	9	9.2	4.4	3.2	.266	.329	3.48
St. Louis	163	33	13	272	36	1454.2	1452	689	577	98	70	53	24	571	94	824	55	5	9.0	5.1	3.5	.260	.328	3.57
Montreal	162	30	12	271	25	1480.0	1448	690	612	102	87	43	37	665	63	831	65	12	8.8	5.1	4.0	.259	.339	3.72
San Francisco	161	37	9	259	24	1432.2	1406	671	595	92	99	40	38	612	93	856	51	15	8.8	5.4	3.8	.259	.336	3.74
Philadelphia	162	33	11	283	30	1455.0	1353	694	618	111	79	47	25	546	49	897	50	20	8.4	5.5	3.4	.249	.317	3.82
Atlanta	161	32	4	267	24	1430.0	1543	739	622	101	107	51	44	519	50	669	55	17	9.7	4.2	3.3	.278	.341	3.91
Houston	162	39	6	265	25	1458.1	1436	711	654	106	80	56	34	679	44	839	83	15	8.9	5.2	4.2	.262	.343	4.04
Chicago	162	27	8	298	33	1444.1	1587	827	721	130	101	49	40	551	59	850	35	9	9.9	5.3	3.4	.281	.347	4.49
NL Total	1942	427	129	3106	350	17450.1	17002	8014	7020	1233	1082	536	367	6730	795	9793	606	153	8.8	5.1	3.5	.257	.334	3.62
NL Avg Team	162	36	11	259	29	1454.1	1417	668	585	103	90	45	31	561	66	816	51	13	8.8	5.1	3.5	.257	.334	3.62

Team Fielding

Team	G	PO	A	E	TC	DP	PB	Pct
Cincinnati	162	4377	1782	102	6261	173	3	.984
Los Angeles	162	4409	1654	127	6190	106	17	.979
Houston	162	4375	1880	137	6392	166	30	.979
San Francisco	161	4298	1768	146	6212	164	13	.976
New York	162	4398	1736	151	6285	144	8	.976
Philadelphia	162	4365	1795	152	6312	156	10	.976
Pittsburgh	161	4312	1802	151	6265	147	19	.976
St. Louis	163	4364	1723	171	6258	140	31	.973
Montreal	162	4440	1953	180	6573	179	20	.973
Atlanta	161	4290	1877	175	6342	147	35	.972
Chicago	162	4333	1907	179	6419	152	15	.972
San Diego	162	4390	1930	188	6508	163	7	.971
NL Total	1942	52351	21807	1859	76017	1837	208	.976

Team vs. Team Records

	Atl	ChN	Cin	Hou	LA	Mon	NYN	Phi	Pit	SD	SF	StL	Won
Atl	—	5	3	12	8	8	4	5	4	7	8	3	67
ChN	7	—	1	7	5	9	7	12	6	5	5	11	75
Cin	15	11	—	13	8	8	8	7	6	11	13	8	108
Hou	6	5	5	—	8	6	4	6	6	9	5	4	64
LA	10	7	10	12	—	5	6	7	5	11	10	5	88
Mon	4	9	4	4	7	—	10	7	7	7	5	11	75
NYN	8	11	4	8	6	8	—	7	5	8	8	9	82
Phi	7	6	5	7	6	11	11	—	11	7	7	10	86
Pit	8	12	6	5	7	11	13	7	—	8	5	10	92
SD	11	7	7	9	7	5	4	5	4	—	8	4	71
SF	9	7	5	13	8	7	4	5	7	10	—	5	80
StL	9	7	4	8	7	7	9	8	8	8	7	—	82
Lost	94	87	54	97	74	87	80	76	69	91	81	80	

1975 National League Batting Leaders

Games		At-Bats		Runs		Hits		Doubles		Triples	
D. Cash, Phi	162	D. Cash, Phi	699	P. Rose, Cin	112	D. Cash, Phi	213	P. Rose, Cin	47	R. Garr, Atl	11
P. Rose, Cin	162	F. Millan, NYN	676	D. Cash, Phi	111	S. Garvey, LA	210	D. Cash, Phi	40	V. Joshua, SF	10
F. Millan, NYN	162	P. Rose, Cin	662	D. Lopes, LA	108	P. Rose, Cin	210	A. Oliver, Pit	39	G. Gross, Hou	10
G. Luzinski, Phi	161	S. Garvey, LA	659	J. Morgan, Cin	107	T. Simmons, StL	193	J. Bench, Cin	39	D. Parker, Pit	10
K. Reitz, StL	161	A. Oliver, Pit	628	D. Thomas, SF	99	F. Millan, NYN	191	S. Garvey, LA	38	D. Kessinger, ChN	10

Home Runs		Total Bases		Runs Batted In		Walks		Intentional Walks		Strikeouts	
M. Schmidt, Phi	38	G. Luzinski, Phi	322	G. Luzinski, Phi	120	J. Morgan, Cin	132	G. Luzinski, Phi	17	M. Schmidt, Phi	180
D. Kingman, NYN	36	S. Garvey, LA	314	J. Bench, Cin	110	J. Wynn, LA	110	R. Garr, Atl	17	D. Kingman, NYN	153
G. Luzinski, Phi	34	D. Parker, Pit	302	T. Perez, Cin	109	D. Evans, Atl	105	T. Simmons, StL	16	G. Luzinski, Phi	151
J. Bench, Cin	28	M. Schmidt, Phi	294	R. Staub, NYN	105	M. Schmidt, Phi	101	R. Cey, LA	15	P. Mangual, Mon	115
2 tied with	25	P. Rose, Cin	286	3 tied with	101	2 tied with	91	M. Sanguillen, Pit	15	3 tied with	109

Hit By Pitch		Sac Hits		Sac Flies		Stolen Bases		Caught Stealing		GDP	
F. Millan, NYN	12	E. Hernandez, SD	24	B. Murcer, SF	12	D. Lopes, LA	77	C. Cedeno, Hou	17	W. Montanez, 2tm	26
P. Rose, Cin	11	T. Sizemore, StL	21	J. Morales, ChN	11	J. Morgan, Cin	67	L. Brock, StL	16	J. Torre, NYN	22
R. Hebner, Pit	10	4 tied with	17	W. Montanez, 2tm	10	L. Brock, StL	56	D. Thomas, SF	13	T. Simmons, StL	20
B. Tolan, SD	10			R. Staub, NYN	9	C. Cedeno, Hou	50	B. Tolan, SD	13	3 tied with	19
R. Staub, NYN	9			D. Kessinger, ChN	9	J. Cardenal, ChN	34	3 tied with	12		

Runs Created		Runs Created/27 Outs		Batting Average		On-Base Percentage		Slugging Percentage		OBP+Slugging	
J. Morgan, Cin	137	J. Morgan, Cin	10.52	B. Madlock, ChN	.354	J. Morgan, Cin	.466	D. Parker, Pit	.541	J. Morgan, Cin	.974
P. Rose, Cin	119	B. Madlock, ChN	7.25	T. Simmons, StL	.332	P. Rose, Cin	.406	G. Luzinski, Phi	.540	G. Luzinski, Phi	.934
G. Luzinski, Phi	114	W. Stargell, Pit	7.08	M. Sanguillen, Pit	.328	J. Wynn, LA	.403	M. Schmidt, Phi	.523	D. Parker, Pit	.898
J. Cardenal, ChN	103	G. Luzinski, Phi	6.99	J. Morgan, Cin	.327	B. Madlock, ChN	.402	J. Bench, Cin	.519	W. Stargell, Pit	.891
M. Schmidt, Phi	103	P. Rose, Cin	6.91	B. Watson, Hou	.324	J. Cardenal, ChN	.397	G. Foster, Cin	.518	M. Schmidt, Phi	.890

1975 National League Pitching Leaders

Wins		Losses		Winning Percentage		Games		Games Started		Complete Games	
T. Seaver, NYN	22	R. Reuschel, ChN	17	A. Hrabosky, StL	.813	G. Garber, Phi	71	A. Messersmith, LA	40	A. Messersmith, LA	19
R. Jones, SD	20	C. Morton, Atl	16	D. Gullett, Cin	.789	W. McEnaney, Cin	70	C. Morton, Atl	39	R. Jones, SD	18
A. Messersmith, LA	19	L. Dierker, Hou	16	F. Norman, Cin	.750	D. Tomlin, SD	67	D. Rau, LA	38	J. Reuss, Pit	15
B. Hooton, 2tm	18	4 tied with	15	T. Seaver, NYN	.710	P. Borbon, Cin	67	3 tied with	37	T. Seaver, NYN	15
J. Reuss, Pit	18			P. Darcy, Cin	.688	M. Garman, StL	66			2 tied with	14

Shutouts		Saves		Games Finished		Batters Faced		Innings Pitched		Hits Allowed	
A. Messersmith, LA	7	R. Eastwick, Cin	22	G. Garber, Phi	47	A. Messersmith, LA	1276	A. Messersmith, LA	321.2	C. Morton, Atl	302
R. Jones, SD	6	A. Hrabosky, StL	22	M. Marshall, LA	46	C. Morton, Atl	1199	R. Jones, SD	285.0	P. Niekro, Atl	285
J. Reuss, Pit	6	D. Giusti, Pit	17	T. House, Atl	45	P. Niekro, Atl	1160	T. Seaver, NYN	280.1	R. Reed, 2tm	274
T. Seaver, NYN	5	D. Knowles, ChN	15	D. Giusti, Pit	43	R. Jones, SD	1124	C. Morton, Atl	277.2	R. Burris, ChN	259
5 tied with	4	W. McEnaney, Cin	15	A. Hrabosky, StL	41	T. Seaver, NYN	1115	P. Niekro, Atl	275.2	B. Bonham, ChN	254

Home Runs Allowed		Walks		Walks/9 Innings		Strikeouts		Strikeouts/9 Innings		Strikeout/Walk Ratio	
P. Niekro, Atl	29	J. Richard, Hou	138	G. Nolan, Cin	1.2	T. Seaver, NYN	243	J. Montefusco, SF	7.9	D. Sutton, LA	2.82
R. Burris, ChN	25	P. Falcone, SF	111	R. Jones, SD	1.8	J. Montefusco, SF	215	J. Richard, Hou	7.8	T. Seaver, NYN	2.76
S. Carlton, Phi	24	B. Bonham, ChN	109	R. Reed, 2tm	1.9	A. Messersmith, LA	213	T. Seaver, NYN	7.8	J. Matlack, NYN	2.66
S. Stone, ChN	24	D. Blair, Mon	106	D. Rau, LA	2.1	S. Carlton, Phi	192	D. Warthen, Mon	6.9	R. Reed, 2tm	2.62
L. Dierker, Hou	24	S. Carlton, Phi	104	J. Barr, SF	2.1	J. Richard, Hou	176	S. Carlton, Phi	6.8	G. Nolan, Cin	2.55

Earned Run Average		Component ERA		Hit Batsmen		Wild Pitches		Opponent Average		Opponent OBP	
R. Jones, SD	2.24	D. Sutton, LA	2.20	P. Niekro, Atl	11	J. Richard, Hou	20	A. Messersmith, LA	.213	D. Sutton, LA	.263
A. Messersmith, LA	2.29	T. Seaver, NYN	2.26	J. Billingham, Cin	9	P. Niekro, Atl	15	D. Sutton, LA	.213	R. Jones, SD	.269
T. Seaver, NYN	2.38	R. Jones, SD	2.27	T. Dettore, ChN	9	S. Rogers, Mon	13	T. Seaver, NYN	.214	B. Hooton, 2tm	.274
J. Reuss, Pit	2.54	A. Messersmith, LA	2.33	C. Hough, LA	8	L. Dierker, Hou	13	D. Warthen, Mon	.217	A. Messersmith, LA	.275
B. Forsch, StL	2.86	B. Hooton, 2tm	2.50	J. Montefusco, SF	8	3 tied with	12	B. Hooton, 2tm	.219	G. Nolan, Cin	.275

1975 National League Miscellaneous

Managers		
Atlanta	Clyde King	58-76
	Connie Ryan	9-18
Chicago	Jim Marshall	75-87
Cincinnati	Sparky Anderson	108-54
Houston	Preston Gomez	47-80
	Bill Virdon	17-17
Los Angeles	Walter Alston	88-74
Montreal	Gene Mauch	75-87
New York	Yogi Berra	56-53
	Roy McMillan	26-27
Philadelphia	Danny Ozark	86-76
Pittsburgh	Danny Murtaugh	92-69
St. Louis	Red Schoendienst	82-80
San Diego	John McNamara	71-91
San Francisco	Wes Westrum	80-81

Awards	
Most Valuable Player	Joe Morgan, 2b, Cin
Cy Young	Tom Seaver, NYN
Rookie of the Year	John Montefusco, p, SF
STATS Manager of the Year	Sparky Anderson, Cin

STATS All-Star Team

C	Johnny Bench, Cin	.283	28	110
1B	Willie Stargell, Pit	.295	22	90
2B	Joe Morgan, Cin	.327	17	94
3B	Mike Schmidt, Phi	.249	38	95
SS	Chris Speier, SF	.271	10	69
OF	George Foster, Cin	.300	23	78
OF	Greg Luzinski, Phi	.300	34	120
OF	Dave Parker, Pit	.308	25	101
P	Randy Jones, SD	20-12	2.24	103 K
P	Andy Messersmith, LA	19-14	2.29	213 K
P	Jerry Reuss, Pit	18-11	2.54	131 K
P	Tom Seaver, NYN	22-9	2.38	243 K
RP	Al Hrabosky, StL	13-3	1.66	22 Sv

Postseason	
LCS	Cincinnati 3 vs. Pittsburgh 0
World Series	Cincinnati (NL) 4 vs. Boston (AL) 3

Outstanding Performances

No-Hitters

Ed Halicki, SF	vs. NYN on August 24

Cycles

Lou Brock, StL	on May 27

1976 American League Standings

EAST	Overall					Home Games						Road Games						Park Index		Record by Month					
	W	L	Pct	GB	DIF	W	L	R	OR	HR	OHR	W	L	R	OR	HR	OHR	Run	HR	M/A	May	June	July	Aug	S/O
New York	97	62	.610	—	172	45	35	349	294	67	51	52	27	381	281	53	46	96	118	10-3	16-12	17-11	18-12	18-11	18-13
Baltimore	88	74	.543	10.5	2	42	39	280	306	58	38	46	35	339	292	61	42	93	93	6-9	16-12	12-16	17-12	17-12	20-13
Boston	83	79	.512	15.5	0	46	35	408	352	71	61	37	44	308	308	63	48	123	119	6-7	13-15	15-13	12-19	16-14	21-11
Cleveland	81	78	.509	16.0	0	44	35	311	295	40	43	37	43	304	320	45	39	98	103	7-6	14-15	15-12	13-17	17-13	15-15
Detroit	74	87	.460	24.0	3	36	44	305	381	51	62	38	43	304	328	50	39	110	129	7-6	10-17	17-12	14-16	13-18	13-18
Milwaukee	66	95	.410	32.0	5	36	45	292	321	45	43	30	50	278	334	43	56	99	88	9-3	7-17	9-21	18-13	15-15	8-26
WEST																									
Kansas City	90	72	.556	—	140	49	32	368	287	37	35	41	40	345	324	28	48	98	95	5-7	20-10	19-10	17-12	17-14	12-19
Oakland	87	74	.540	2.5	5	51	30	353	284	56	57	36	44	333	314	57	39	97	116	9-8	12-17	15-13	17-11	17-12	17-13
Minnesota	85	77	.525	5.0	1	44	37	368	348	34	52	41	40	375	356	47	37	98	102	5-9	16-12	12-18	18-11	13-19	21-8
California	76	86	.469	14.0	1	38	43	249	284	24	35	38	43	301	347	39	60	82	60	5-12	14-18	12-15	14-14	13-15	18-12
Texas	76	86	.469	14.0	37	39	42	319	330	40	57	37	44	297	322	40	49	105	109	9-6	15-12	16-12	8-22	12-19	16-15
Chicago	64	97	.398	25.5	9	35	45	300	369	31	34	29	52	286	376	42	53	102	69	5-7	16-12	12-18	12-19	12-18	7-23

Clinch Date—New York 9/25, Kansas City 10/01.

Team Batting

Team	G	AB	R	OR	H	2B	3B	HR	TB	RBI	TBB	IBB	SO	HBP	SH	SF	SB	CS	SB%	GDP	Avg	OBP	Slg
Minnesota	162	5574	743	704	1526	222	51	81	2093	691	550	39	714	41	93	49	146	75	.66	121	.274	.349	.375
New York	159	5555	730	575	1496	231	36	120	2159	682	470	36	616	35	50	46	163	65	.71	94	.269	.335	.389
Boston	162	5511	716	660	1448	257	53	134	2213	664	500	35	832	29	55	59	95	70	.58	127	.263	.334	.402
Kansas City	162	5540	713	611	1490	259	57	65	2058	656	484	36	650	31	71	71	218	106	.67	103	.269	.339	.371
Oakland	161	5353	686	598	1319	208	33	113	1932	625	592	45	818	45	58	58	341	123	.73	91	.246	.333	.361
Baltimore	162	5457	619	598	1326	213	28	119	1952	576	519	34	883	23	57	35	150	61	.71	119	.243	.315	.358
Texas	162	5555	616	652	1390	213	26	80	1895	574	568	46	809	29	72	45	87	45	.66	141	.250	.328	.341
Cleveland	159	5412	615	615	1423	189	38	85	1943	567	479	42	631	11	67	60	75	69	.52	143	.263	.331	.359
Detroit	161	5441	609	709	1401	207	38	101	1987	566	450	35	730	31	46	50	107	59	.64	157	.257	.324	.365
Chicago	161	5532	586	745	1410	209	46	73	1930	538	471	43	739	34	79	55	120	53	.69	104	.255	.323	.349
Milwaukee	161	5396	570	655	1326	170	38	88	1836	536	511	30	909	23	78	48	62	61	.50	112	.246	.319	.340
California	162	5385	550	631	1265	210	23	63	1710	511	534	50	812	42	92	48	126	80	.61	130	.235	.314	.318
AL Total	1934	65711	7753	7753	16820	2588	467	1122	23708	7186	6128	471	9143	374	818	624	1690	867	.66	1442	.256	.320	.361
AL Avg Team	161	5476	646	646	1402	216	39	94	1976	599	511	39	762	31	68	52	141	72	.66	120	.256	.320	.361

Team Pitching

Team	G	CG	ShO	Rel	Sv	IP	H	R	ER	HR	SH	SF	HB	TBB	IBB	SO	WP	Bk	H/9	SO/9	BB/9	OAvg	OOBP	ERA
New York	159	62	15	156	37	1455.0	1300	575	516	97	53	57	17	448	16	674	39	3	8.0	4.2	2.8	.241	.298	3.19
Kansas City	162	41	12	248	35	1472.1	1356	611	525	83	49	61	31	493	42	735	29	5	8.3	4.5	3.0	.247	.309	3.21
Oakland	161	39	15	233	29	1459.1	1412	598	528	96	83	42	30	415	34	711	40	2	8.7	4.4	2.6	.255	.308	3.26
Baltimore	162	59	16	171	23	1468.2	1396	598	541	80	80	63	23	489	40	678	37	3	8.6	4.2	3.0	.255	.315	3.32
California	162	64	15	177	17	1477.1	1323	631	551	95	74	40	38	553	50	992	27	2	8.1	6.0	3.4	.241	.313	3.36
Texas	162	63	15	196	15	1472.0	1464	652	565	106	90	45	31	461	31	773	46	9	9.0	4.7	2.8	.262	.320	3.45
Cleveland	159	30	17	237	46	1432.0	1361	615	552	80	77	47	32	533	48	928	41	7	8.6	5.8	3.3	.255	.324	3.47
Boston	162	49	13	195	27	1458.0	1424	660	571	109	58	46	32	409	45	673	33	1	9.2	4.2	2.5	.267	.318	3.52
Milwaukee	161	45	10	202	27	1435.1	1406	655	581	99	68	56	39	567	62	677	53	6	8.8	4.2	3.6	.260	.331	3.64
Minnesota	162	29	11	221	23	1459.0	1421	704	599	89	53	51	38	610	39	762	61	12	8.8	4.7	3.8	.259	.335	3.69
Detroit	161	55	12	164	20	1431.1	1426	709	616	101	72	55	30	550	37	738	45	4	9.0	4.6	3.5	.263	.331	3.87
Chicago	161	54	10	166	22	1448.0	1460	745	684	87	61	61	33	600	27	802	46	6	9.1	5.0	3.7	.266	.338	4.25
AL Total	1934	590	161	2366	321	17468.1	16820	7753	6829	1122	818	624	374	6128	471	9143	491	60	8.7	4.7	3.2	.256	.329	3.52
AL Avg Team	161	49	13	197	27	1455.1	1402	646	569	94	68	52	31	511	39	762	41	5	8.7	4.7	3.2	.256	.329	3.52

Team Fielding

Team	G	PO	A	E	TC	DP	PB	Pct
Baltimore	162	4406	1870	118	6394	157	7	.982
Cleveland	159	4296	1710	121	6127	159	10	.980
New York	159	4365	1824	126	6315	141	16	.980
Chicago	161	4344	1793	130	6267	155	5	.979
Kansas City	162	4416	1854	139	6409	147	9	.978
Boston	162	4374	1761	141	6276	148	8	.978
Oakland	161	4378	1821	144	6343	130	11	.977
California	162	4432	1840	150	6422	139	15	.977
Texas	162	4416	1807	156	6379	142	11	.976
Milwaukee	161	4306	1718	152	6176	160	17	.975
Detroit	161	4294	1961	168	6423	161	7	.974
Minnesota	162	4377	1823	172	6372	182	11	.973
AL Total	1934	52404	21782	1717	75903	1821	127	.977

Team vs. Team Records

	Bal	Bos	Cal	ChA	Cle	Det	KC	Mil	Min	NYA	Oak	Tex	Won
Bal	—	7	8	8	7	12	6	11	4	13	4	8	88
Bos	11	—	7	6	9	14	3	12	7	7	4	3	83
Cal	4	5	—	11	7	6	8	4	8	5	6	12	76
ChA	4	6	7	—	3	6	8	7	7	1	5	7	64
Cle	11	9	5	9	—	6	6	11	9	4	4	7	81
Det	6	4	6	6	12	—	4	12	4	9	6	5	74
KC	6	9	10	10	6	8	—	8	10	7	9	7	90
Mil	7	6	8	5	6	6	4	—	4	5	5	10	66
Min	8	5	10	11	3	8	8	8	—	2	11	11	85
NYA	5	11	7	11	12	8	5	13	10	—	6	9	97
Oak	8	8	12	9	8	9	6	7	7	6	—	7	87
Tex	4	9	6	11	5	7	11	2	7	3	11	—	76
Lost	74	79	86	97	78	87	72	95	77	62	74	86	

1976 American League Batting Leaders

Games		At-Bats		Runs		Hits		Doubles		Triples	
J. Mayberry, KC	161	G. Brett, KC	645	R. White, NYA	104	G. Brett, KC	215	A. Otis, KC	40	G. Brett, KC	14
R. Staub, Det	161	C. Chambliss, NYA	641	R. Carew, Min	97	R. Carew, Min	200	G. Brett, KC	34	R. Carew, Min	12
R. Yount, Mil	161	R. Yount, Mil	638	M. Rivers, NYA	95	C. Chambliss, NYA	188	H. McRae, KC	34	P. Garner, Oak	12
3 tied with	159	J. Orta, ChA	636	G. Brett, KC	94	T. Munson, NYA	186	D. Evans, Bos	34	T. Poquette, KC	10
		R. White, NYA	626	3 tied with	93	M. Rivers, NYA	184	R. Carty, Cle	34	L. Bostock, Min	9

Home Runs		Total Bases		Runs Batted In		Walks		Intentional Walks		Strikeouts	
G. Nettles, NYA	32	G. Brett, KC	298	L. May, Bal	109	M. Hargrove, Tex	97	J. Spencer, ChA	19	J. Rice, Bos	123
S. Bando, Oak	27	C. Chambliss, NYA	283	T. Munson, NYA	105	T. Harrah, Tex	91	B. Williams, Oak	15	T. Grieve, Tex	119
R. Jackson, Bal	27	R. Carew, Min	280	C. Yastrzemski, Bos	102	B. Grich, Bal	86	R. Carew, Min	14	D. Ford, Min	118
3 tied with	25	J. Rice, Bos	280	3 tied with	96	R. Staub, Det	83	M. Hargrove, Tex	13	G. Scott, Mil	118
		G. Nettles, NYA	277			R. White, NYA	83	2 tied with	11	S. Lezcano, Mil	112

Hit By Pitch		Sac Hits		Sac Flies		Stolen Bases		Caught Stealing		GDP	
D. Baylor, Oak	20	R. Smalley, 2tm	25	J. Mayberry, KC	12	B. North, Oak	75	B. North, Oak	29	R. Staub, Det	23
D. Chalk, Cal	10	B. Campaneris, Oak	18	D. Baylor, Oak	11	R. LeFlore, Det	58	R. Carew, Min	22	J. Burroughs, Tex	22
D. Ford, Min	10	F. White, KC	18	B. Campaneris, Oak	11	B. Campaneris, Oak	54	R. LeFlore, Det	20	A. Rodriguez, Det	19
T. Munson, NYA	9	B. Dent, ChA	17	R. Staub, Det	11	D. Baylor, Oak	52	C. Washington, Oak	20	G. Scott, Mil	19
2 tied with	8	B. Randall, Min	17	3 tied with	10	F. Patek, KC	51	D. Collins, Cal	19	3 tied with	18

Runs Created		Runs Created/27 Outs		Batting Average		On-Base Percentage		Slugging Percentage		OBP+Slugging	
G. Brett, KC	115	H. McRae, KC	7.10	G. Brett, KC	.333	H. McRae, KC	.407	R. Jackson, Bal	.502	H. McRae, KC	.868
R. Carew, Min	113	G. Brett, KC	6.82	H. McRae, KC	.332	M. Hargrove, Tex	.397	J. Rice, Bos	.482	R. Carew, Min	.858
H. McRae, KC	101	R. Carew, Min	6.79	R. Carew, Min	.331	R. Carew, Min	.395	G. Nettles, NYA	.475	R. Jackson, Bal	.853
R. White, NYA	99	G. Tenace, Oak	6.35	L. Bostock, Min	.323	R. Staub, Det	.386	F. Lynn, Bos	.467	G. Brett, KC	.839
R. Staub, Det	98	F. Lynn, Bos	6.30	R. LeFlore, Det	.316	R. Carty, Cle	.379	R. Carew, Min	.463	F. Lynn, Bos	.835

1976 American League Pitching Leaders

Wins		Losses		Winning Percentage		Games		Games Started		Complete Games	
J. Palmer, Bal	22	N. Ryan, Cal	18	B. Campbell, Min	.773	B. Campbell, Min	78	J. Palmer, Bal	40	M. Fidrych, Det	24
L. Tiant, Bos	21	D. Roberts, Det	17	W. Garland, Bal	.741	R. Fingers, Oak	70	N. Ryan, Cal	39	J. Palmer, Bal	23
W. Garland, Bal	20	G. Gossage, ChA	17	D. Ellis, NYA	.680	P. Lindblad, Oak	65	M. Torrez, Oak	39	F. Tanana, Cal	23
3 tied with	19	4 tied with	16	M. Fidrych, Det	.679	S. Lyle, NYA	64	J. Slaton, Mil	38	3 tied with	21
				2 tied with	.655	D. LaRoche, Cle	61	L. Tiant, Bos	38		

Shutouts		Saves		Games Finished		Batters Faced		Innings Pitched		Hits Allowed	
N. Ryan, Cal	7	S. Lyle, NYA	23	B. Campbell, Min	68	J. Palmer, Bal	1256	J. Palmer, Bal	315.0	J. Slaton, Mil	287
V. Blue, Oak	6	D. LaRoche, Cle	21	R. Fingers, Oak	62	J. Slaton, Mil	1235	C. Hunter, NYA	298.2	B. Blyleven, 2tm	283
B. Blyleven, 2tm	6	R. Fingers, Oak	20	S. Lyle, NYA	58	B. Blyleven, 2tm	1225	V. Blue, Oak	298.1	L. Tiant, Bos	274
J. Palmer, Bal	6	B. Campbell, Min	20	J. Hiller, Det	46	C. Hunter, NYA	1210	B. Blyleven, 2tm	297.2	V. Blue, Oak	268
8 tied with	4	M. Littell, KC	16	D. LaRoche, Cle	43	V. Blue, Oak	1205	J. Slaton, Mil	292.2	C. Hunter, NYA	268

Home Runs Allowed		Walks		Walks/9 Innings		Strikeouts		Strikeouts/9 Innings		Strikeout/Walk Ratio	
C. Hunter, NYA	28	N. Ryan, Cal	183	D. Bird, KC	1.4	N. Ryan, Cal	327	N. Ryan, Cal	10.4	F. Tanana, Cal	3.58
L. Tiant, Bos	25	B. Singer, 2tm	96	F. Jenkins, Bos	1.9	F. Tanana, Cal	261	D. Eckersley, Cle	9.0	D. Bird, KC	3.45
F. Tanana, Cal	24	B. Travers, Mil	95	G. Perry, Tex	1.9	B. Blyleven, 2tm	219	F. Tanana, Cal	8.1	F. Jenkins, Bos	3.30
B. Travers, Mil	21	E. Figueroa, NYA	94	V. Blue, Oak	1.9	D. Eckersley, Cle	200	B. Blyleven, 2tm	6.6	G. Perry, Tex	2.75
4 tied with	20	J. Slaton, Mil	94	M. Fidrych, Det	1.9	C. Hunter, NYA	173	B. Campbell, Min	6.2	B. Blyleven, 2tm	2.70

Earned Run Average		Component ERA		Hit Batsmen		Wild Pitches		Opponent Average		Opponent OBP	
M. Fidrych, Det	2.34	F. Tanana, Cal	2.16	B. Blyleven, 2tm	12	D. Goltz, Min	15	N. Ryan, Cal	.195	F. Tanana, Cal	.261
V. Blue, Oak	2.35	V. Blue, Oak	2.39	D. Leonard, KC	11	J. Slaton, Mil	11	F. Tanana, Cal	.203	M. Fidrych, Det	.277
F. Tanana, Cal	2.43	M. Fidrych, Det	2.41	B. Singer, 2tm	11	K. Holtzman, 2tm	10	D. Eckersley, Cle	.214	J. Palmer, Bal	.278
M. Torrez, Oak	2.50	J. Palmer, Bal	2.46	P. Hartzell, Cal	10	J. Hughes, Min	9	J. Palmer, Bal	.224	V. Blue, Oak	.279
J. Palmer, Bal	2.51	G. Perry, Tex	2.70	2 tied with	9	4 tied with	8	K. Brett, 2tm	.233	D. Bird, KC	.279

1976 American League Miscellaneous

Managers

Baltimore	Earl Weaver	88-74
Boston	Darrell Johnson	41-45
	Don Zimmer	42-34
California	Dick Williams	39-57
	Norm Sherry	37-29
Chicago	Paul Richards	64-97
Cleveland	Frank Robinson	81-78
Detroit	Ralph Houk	74-87
Kansas City	Whitey Herzog	90-72
Milwaukee	Alex Grammas	66-95
Minnesota	Gene Mauch	85-77
New York	Billy Martin	97-62
Oakland	Chuck Tanner	87-74
Texas	Frank Lucchesi	76-86

Awards

Most Valuable Player	T. Munson, c, NYA
Cy Young	Jim Palmer, Bal
Rookie of the Year	Mark Fidrych, p, Det
STATS Manager of the Year	Billy Martin, NYA

STATS All-Star Team

C	Thurman Munson, NYA	.302	17	105
1B	Rod Carew, Min	.331	9	90
2B	Bobby Grich, Bal	.266	13	54
3B	George Brett, KC	.333	7	67
SS	Toby Harrah, Tex	.260	15	67
OF	Reggie Jackson, Bal	.277	27	91
OF	Fred Lynn, Bos	.314	10	65
OF	Rusty Staub, Det	.299	15	96
DH	Hal McRae, KC	.332	8	73
P	Vida Blue, Oak	18-13	2.35	166 K
P	Mark Fidrych, Det	19-9	2.34	97 K
P	Jim Palmer, Bal	22-13	2.51	159 K
P	Frank Tanana, Cal	19-10	2.43	261 K
RP	Rollie Fingers, Oak	13-11	2.47	20 Sv

Postseason

LCS	New York 3 vs. Kansas City 2
World Series	NYA (AL) 0 vs. Cincinnati (NL) 4

Outstanding Performances

Three-Homer Games
C. Yastrzemski, Bos   on May 19

Cycles
Larry Hisle, Min	on June 4
Lyman Bostock, Min	on July 24
Mike Hegan, Mil	on September 3

1976 National League Standings

EAST	W	L	Pct	GB	DIF	W	L	R	OR	HR	OHR	W	L	R	OR	HR	OHR	Run	HR	M/A	May	June	July	Aug	S/O
						Home Games						**Road Games**						**Park Index**		**Record by Month**					
Philadelphia	101	61	.623	—	157	53	28	424	277	63	49	48	33	346	280	47	49	112	117	8-6	22-5	20-9	17-12	16-15	18-14
Pittsburgh	92	70	.568	9.0	16	47	34	366	302	54	44	45	36	342	328	56	51	100	92	8-8	17-11	16-10	15-15	16-13	20-13
New York	86	76	.531	15.0	10	45	37	269	245	43	43	41	39	346	293	59	54	78	74	13-7	11-17	15-13	13-15	14-12	20-12
Chicago	75	87	.463	26.0	1	42	39	355	385	71	84	33	48	256	343	34	39	124	212	9-10	11-14	10-19	13-16	17-13	15-15
St. Louis	72	90	.444	29.0	2	37	44	335	346	27	40	35	46	294	325	36	51	110	77	8-10	12-15	11-16	11-15	14-14	16-20
Montreal	55	107	.340	46.0	1	27	53	266	374	45	41	28	54	265	360	49	48	105	91	6-11	10-12	8-20	10-18	9-20	12-26
WEST																									
Cincinnati	102	60	.630	—	155	49	32	**426**	337	**73**	46	**53**	**28**	**431**	296	**68**	54	105	98	10-7	18-10	18-12	20-9	18-11	18-11
Los Angeles	92	70	.568	10.0	20	49	32	296	265	42	48	43	38	312	**278**	49	49	95	92	10-9	18-10	14-15	13-12	19-10	18-14
Houston	80	82	.494	22.0	3	46	36	277	264	30	**27**	34	46	348	393	36	55	71	61	11-10	10-17	13-14	20-11	13-16	13-14
San Francisco	74	88	.457	28.0	4	40	41	314	352	44	32	34	47	281	334	41	36	108	99	7-10	11-20	13-17	15-11	10-18	18-12
San Diego	73	89	.451	29.0	1	42	38	254	271	30	38	31	51	316	391	34	49	76	84	9-10	15-11	15-15	10-20	14-14	10-19
Atlanta	70	92	.432	32.0	7	34	47	338	401	43	56	36	45	282	299	39	**30**	127	143	8-9	8-21	18-11	12-15	13-17	11-19

Clinch Date—Philadelphia 9/25, Cincinnati 9/21.

Team Batting

Team	G	AB	R	OR	H	2B	3B	HR	TB	RBI	TBB	IBB	SO	HBP	SH	SF	SB	CS	SB%	GDP	Avg	OBP	Slg
Cincinnati	162	**5702**	**857**	633	**1599**	**271**	**63**	**141**	**2419**	**802**	**681**	63	**902**	28	67	60	**210**	57	**.79**	103	**.280**	**.366**	**.424**
Philadelphia	162	5528	770	557	1505	259	45	110	2184	708	542	55	793	**40**	59	**67**	127	70	.64	119	.272	.349	.395
Pittsburgh	162	5604	708	630	1499	249	56	110	2190	660	433	56	807	29	61	50	130	45	.74	**131**	.267	.329	.391
St. Louis	162	5516	629	671	1432	243	57	63	1978	584	512	69	860	22	86	45	123	55	.69	127	.260	.330	.359
Houston	162	5464	625	657	1401	195	50	66	1894	571	530	54	719	21	57	39	150	57	.72	127	.256	.329	.347
Atlanta	162	5345	620	700	1309	170	30	82	1785	586	589	46	811	19	107	47	74	61	.55	**131**	.245	.327	.334
New York	162	5415	615	**538**	1334	198	34	102	1906	560	561	53	797	28	92	33	66	58	.53	127	.246	.324	.352
Chicago	162	5519	611	728	1386	216	24	105	1965	559	490	66	834	30	75	41	74	**74**	.50	126	.251	.320	.356
Los Angeles	162	5472	608	543	1371	200	34	91	1912	561	486	**71**	744	29	91	47	144	55	.72	129	.251	.320	.349
San Francisco	162	5452	595	686	1340	211	37	85	1880	552	518	52	778	25	80	48	88	55	.62	122	.246	.320	.345
San Diego	162	5369	570	662	1327	216	37	64	1809	528	488	57	716	23	**125**	42	92	46	.67	119	.247	.317	.337
Montreal	162	5428	531	734	1275	224	32	94	1845	507	433	43	841	16	75	40	86	44	.66	107	.235	.298	.340
NL Total	1944	65814	7739	7739	16778	2652	499	1113	23767	7178	6263	685	9602	310	975	559	1364	677	.67	1468	.255	.320	.361
NL Avg Team	162	5485	645	645	1398	221	42	93	1981	598	522	57	800	26	81	47	114	56	.67	122	.255	.320	.361

Team Pitching

Team	G	CG	ShO	Rel	Sv	IP	H	R	ER	HR	SH	SF	HB	TBB	IBB	SO	WP	Bk	H/9	SO/9	BB/9	OAvg	OOBP	ERA
New York	162	**53**	**18**	183	25	1449.0	**1248**	**538**	474	97	76	36	23	419	56	**1025**	43	12	**7.8**	6.4	2.6	**.233**	**.290**	2.94
Los Angeles	162	47	17	182	28	1470.2	1330	543	493	97	84	**35**	23	479	31	747	32	3	8.1	4.6	2.9	.243	.305	3.02
Philadelphia	162	34	9	247	44	1459.0	1377	557	499	98	**59**	40	19	**397**	43	918	38	7	8.5	5.7	**2.4**	.250	.301	3.08
Pittsburgh	162	45	12	237	35	1466.1	1402	630	548	95	84	52	18	460	70	762	26	6	8.6	4.7	2.8	.253	.310	3.36
Cincinnati	162	33	12	274	**45**	1471.0	1436	633	573	100	71	44	21	491	56	790	43	7	8.8	4.8	3.0	.258	.318	3.51
San Francisco	162	27	**18**	304	31	1461.2	1464	686	573	**68**	99	48	23	518	55	746	47	9	9.0	4.6	3.2	.263	.325	3.53
Houston	162	42	17	235	29	1444.1	1349	657	571	82	80	47	25	662	43	780	57	12	8.4	4.9	4.1	.250	.332	3.56
St. Louis	162	35	15	298	26	1453.2	1416	671	582	91	69	55	27	581	56	731	61	8	8.8	4.5	3.6	.258	.329	3.60
San Diego	162	47	11	258	18	1432.1	1368	662	581	87	72	45	20	543	**83**	652	48	**17**	8.6	4.1	3.4	.253	.321	3.65
Atlanta	162	33	13	264	27	1438.0	1435	700	617	86	90	50	40	564	57	818	60	16	9.0	5.1	3.5	.261	.332	3.86
Chicago	162	27	12	**329**	33	1471.1	1511	728	643	123	85	55	28	490	60	850	38	11	9.2	5.2	3.0	.268	.327	3.93
Montreal	162	26	10	309	21	1440.0	1442	734	639	89	106	52	**43**	659	75	783	**63**	8	9.0	4.9	4.1	.266	.347	3.99
NL Total	1944	449	164	3120	362	17457.1	16778	7739	6793	1113	975	559	310	6263	685	9602	556	116	8.6	5.0	3.2	.255	.328	3.50
NL Avg Team	162	37	14	260	30	1454.1	1398	645	566	93	81	47	26	522	57	800	46	10	8.6	5.0	3.2	.255	.328	3.50

Team Fielding

Team	G	PO	A	E	TC	DP	PB	Pct
Cincinnati	162	4413	1678	**102**	6193	157	6	.984
Philadelphia	162	4377	1671	115	6163	148	6	.981
Los Angeles	162	**4432**	1833	128	6393	154	14	.980
New York	162	4347	1683	131	6161	116	8	.979
Chicago	162	4414	1854	140	6408	145	11	.978
San Diego	162	4297	1901	141	6339	148	9	.978
Houston	162	4333	1800	140	6273	155	32	.978
Montreal	162	4320	**1956**	155	6431	**179**	11	.976
Pittsburgh	162	4399	1878	163	6440	142	13	.975
Atlanta	162	4314	1820	167	6301	151	**38**	.973
St. Louis	162	4361	1840	174	6375	163	16	.973
San Francisco	162	4385	1940	186	**6511**	153	15	.971
NL Total	1944	52392	21854	1742	75988	1811	179	.977

Team vs. Team Records

	Atl	ChN	Cin	Hou	LA	Mon	NYN	Phi	Pit	SD	SF	StL	Won
Atl	—	6	6	7	8	8	4	5	3	10	9	4	**70**
ChN	6	—	3	5	3	11	5	8	6	8	8	12	**75**
Cin	12	9	—	12	13	9	6	5	8	13	9	6	**102**
Hou	11	7	6	—	5	10	6	4	2	10	10	9	**80**
LA	10	9	5	13	—	10	7	5	9	6	8	10	**92**
Mon	4	7	3	2	2	—	8	3	8	4	7	7	**55**
NYN	8	13	6	6	5	10	—	5	10	7	7	9	**86**
Phi	7	10	7	8	7	15	13	—	8	8	6	12	**101**
Pit	9	10	4	10	3	10	8	10	—	7	9	12	**92**
SD	8	6	5	8	12	8	5	4	5	—	8	4	**73**
SF	9	4	9	8	10	5	5	6	3	10	—	5	**74**
StL	8	6	6	3	2	11	9	6	6	8	7	—	**72**
Lost	92	87	60	82	70	107	76	61	70	89	88	90	

1976 National League Batting Leaders

Games		At-Bats		Runs		Hits		Doubles		Triples	
W. Montanez, 2tm	163	D. Cash, Phi	666	P. Rose, Cin	130	P. Rose, Cin	215	P. Rose, Cin	42	D. Cash, Phi	12
S. Garvey, LA	162	P. Rose, Cin	665	J. Morgan, Cin	113	W. Montanez, 2tm	206	J. Johnstone, Phi	38	C. Geronimo, Cin	11
P. Rose, Cin	162	R. Stennett, Pit	654	M. Schmidt, Phi	112	S. Garvey, LA	200	S. Garvey, LA	37	D. Parker, Pit	10
D. Cash, Phi	160	W. Montanez, 2tm	650	K. Griffey Sr., Cin	111	B. Buckner, LA	193	G. Maddox, Phi	37	W. Davis, SD	10
M. Schmidt, Phi	160	B. Buckner, LA	642	R. Monday, ChN	107	2 tied with	189	2 tied with	36	5 tied with	9

Home Runs		Total Bases		Runs Batted In		Walks		Intentional Walks		Strikeouts	
M. Schmidt, Phi	38	M. Schmidt, Phi	306	G. Foster, Cin	121	J. Wynn, Atl	127	T. Simmons, StL	19	M. Schmidt, Phi	149
D. Kingman, NYN	37	P. Rose, Cin	299	J. Morgan, Cin	111	J. Morgan, Cin	114	B. Madlock, ChN	15	D. Kingman, NYN	135
R. Monday, ChN	32	G. Foster, Cin	298	M. Schmidt, Phi	107	M. Schmidt, Phi	100	M. Sanguillen, Pit	14	R. Monday, ChN	125
G. Foster, Cin	29	S. Garvey, LA	284	B. Watson, Hou	102	R. Cey, LA	89	B. Boone, Phi	14	H. Cruz, StL	119
J. Morgan, Cin	27	2 tied with	272	G. Luzinski, Phi	95	P. Rose, Cin	86	2 tied with	13	J. Wynn, Atl	111

Hit By Pitch		Sac Hits		Sac Flies		Stolen Bases		Caught Stealing		GDP	
G. Luzinski, Phi	11	R. Gilbreath, Atl	20	J. Morgan, Cin	12	D. Lopes, LA	63	L. Brock, StL	19	W. Montanez, 2tm	26
B. Madlock, ChN	11	E. Hernandez, SD	16	G. Luzinski, Phi	11	J. Morgan, Cin	60	C. Cedeno, Hou	15	K. Reitz, SF	24
M. Schmidt, Phi	11	T. Fuentes, SD	16	5 tied with	9	C. Cedeno, Hou	58	J. Cardenal, ChN	14	B. Madlock, ChN	21
S. Yeager, LA	7	R. Jones, SD	15			F. Taveras, Pit	58	J. Royster, Atl	13	4 tied with	20
F. Millan, NYN	7	2 tied with	14			L. Brock, StL	56	2 tied with	12		

Runs Created		Runs Created/27 Outs		Batting Average		On-Base Percentage		Slugging Percentage		OBP+Slugging	
J. Morgan, Cin	125	J. Morgan, Cin	9.85	B. Madlock, ChN	.339	J. Morgan, Cin	.444	J. Morgan, Cin	.576	J. Morgan, Cin	1.020
M. Schmidt, Phi	121	M. Schmidt, Phi	7.18	K. Griffey Sr., Cin	.336	B. Madlock, ChN	.412	G. Foster, Cin	.530	B. Madlock, ChN	.912
P. Rose, Cin	113	B. Madlock, ChN	7.01	G. Maddox, Phi	.330	P. Rose, Cin	.404	M. Schmidt, Phi	.524	M. Schmidt, Phi	.900
G. Foster, Cin	101	K. Griffey Sr., Cin	6.95	P. Rose, Cin	.323	K. Griffey Sr., Cin	.401	R. Monday, ChN	.507	G. Foster, Cin	.894
2 tied with	100	G. Luzinski, Phi	6.66	J. Morgan, Cin	.320	R. Cey, LA	.386	D. Kingman, NYN	.506	P. Rose, Cin	.854

1976 National League Pitching Leaders

Wins		Losses		Winning Percentage		Games		Games Started		Complete Games	
R. Jones, SD	22	S. Rogers, Mon	17	R. Rhoden, LA	.800	D. Murray, Mon	81	R. Jones, SD	40	R. Jones, SD	25
D. Sutton, LA	21	D. Ruthven, Atl	17	S. Carlton, Phi	.741	C. Hough, LA	77	J. Richard, Hou	39	J. Koosman, NYN	17
J. Koosman, NYN	21	P. Falcone, StL	16	S. Alcala, Cin	.733	B. Metzger, SD	77	P. Niekro, Atl	37	J. Matlack, NYN	16
S. Carlton, Phi	20	B. Strom, SD	16	B. Metzger, SD	.733	R. Eastwick, Cin	71	R. Reuschel, ChN	37	D. Sutton, LA	15
J. Richard, Hou	20	3 tied with	15	J. Candelaria, Pit	.696	P. Borbon, Cin	69	J. Barr, SF	37	J. Richard, Hou	14

Shutouts		Saves		Games Finished		Batters Faced		Innings Pitched		Hits Allowed	
J. Montefusco, SF	6	R. Eastwick, Cin	26	B. Metzger, SD	62	R. Jones, SD	1251	R. Jones, SD	315.1	R. Jones, SD	274
J. Matlack, NYN	6	S. Lockwood, NYN	19	R. Eastwick, Cin	59	J. Richard, Hou	1218	J. Richard, Hou	291.0	R. Reuschel, ChN	260
R. Jones, SD	5	K. Forsch, Hou	19	C. Hough, LA	55	P. Niekro, Atl	1157	T. Seaver, NYN	271.0	J. Barr, SF	260
T. Seaver, NYN	5	C. Hough, LA	18	D. Murray, Mon	55	D. Sutton, LA	1093	P. Niekro, Atl	270.2	D. Ruthven, Atl	255
10 tied with	4	B. Metzger, SD	16	K. Forsch, Hou	46	T. Seaver, NYN	1079	D. Sutton, LA	267.2	R. Burris, ChN	251

Home Runs Allowed		Walks		Walks/9 Innings		Strikeouts		Strikeouts/9 Innings		Strikeout/Walk Ratio	
G. Nolan, Cin	28	J. Richard, Hou	151	G. Nolan, Cin	1.0	T. Seaver, NYN	235	T. Seaver, NYN	7.8	G. Nolan, Cin	4.19
J. Candelaria, Pit	22	J. D'Acquisto, SF	102	J. Kaat, Phi	1.3	J. Richard, Hou	214	J. Koosman, NYN	7.3	T. Seaver, NYN	3.05
D. Sutton, LA	22	P. Niekro, Atl	101	R. Jones, SD	1.4	J. Koosman, NYN	200	S. Carlton, Phi	6.9	J. Koosman, NYN	3.03
R. Burris, ChN	22	B. Bonham, ChN	96	J. Matlack, NYN	2.0	S. Carlton, Phi	195	J. Richard, Hou	6.6	S. Carlton, Phi	2.71
J. Kaat, Phi	21	P. Falcone, StL	93	J. Lonborg, Phi	2.0	P. Niekro, Atl	173	P. Zachry, Cin	6.3	J. Matlack, NYN	2.68

Earned Run Average		Component ERA		Hit Batsmen		Wild Pitches		Opponent Average		Opponent OBP	
J. Denny, StL	2.52	R. Jones, SD	2.19	W. Fryman, Mon	9	P. Niekro, Atl	14	J. Richard, Hou	.212	R. Jones, SD	.265
D. Rau, LA	2.57	T. Seaver, NYN	2.23	5 tied with	8	J. Richard, Hou	13	T. Seaver, NYN	.213	J. Candelaria, Pit	.271
T. Seaver, NYN	2.59	J. Candelaria, Pit	2.48			J. Matlack, NYN	13	J. Candelaria, Pit	.216	T. Seaver, NYN	.272
J. Koosman, NYN	2.69	J. Koosman, NYN	2.52			B. Strom, SD	13	A. Messersmith, Atl	.219	G. Nolan, Cin	.275
P. Zachry, Cin	2.74	A. Messersmith, Atl	2.68			2 tied with	12	P. Falcone, StL	.222	J. Koosman, NYN	.278

1976 National League Miscellaneous

Managers

Atlanta	Dave Bristol	70-92
Chicago	Jim Marshall	75-87
Cincinnati	Sparky Anderson	102-60
Houston	Bill Virdon	80-82
Los Angeles	Walter Alston	90-68
	Tom Lasorda	2-2
Montreal	Karl Kuehl	43-85
	Charlie Fox	12-22
New York	Joe Frazier	86-76
Philadelphia	Danny Ozark	101-61
Pittsburgh	Danny Murtaugh	92-70
St. Louis	Red Schoendienst	72-90
San Diego	John McNamara	73-89
San Francisco	Bill Rigney	74-88

Awards

Most Valuable Player	Joe Morgan, 2b, Cin
Cy Young	Randy Jones, SD
Rookie of the Year	Butch Metzger, p, SD
	Pat Zachry, p, Cin
STATS Manager of the Year	Danny Ozark, Phi

STATS All-Star Team

C	Ted Simmons, StL	.291	5	75
1B	Bob Watson, Hou	.313	16	102
2B	Joe Morgan, Cin	.320	27	111
3B	Mike Schmidt, Phi	.262	38	107
SS	Dave Concepcion, Cin	.281	9	69
OF	George Foster, Cin	.306	29	121
OF	Ken Griffey Sr., Cin	.336	6	74
OF	Rick Monday, ChN	.272	32	77
P	Steve Carlton, Phi	20-7	3.13	195 K
P	Randy Jones, SD	22-14	2.74	93 K
P	Jerry Koosman, NYN	21-10	2.69	200 K
P	J.R. Richard, Hou	20-15	2.75	214 K
RP	Rawly Eastwick, Cin	11-5	2.09	26 Sv

Postseason

LCS	Cincinnati 3 vs. Philadelphia 0
World Series	Cincinnati (NL) 4 vs. NYA (AL) 0

Outstanding Performances

No-Hitters
Larry Dierker, Hou   vs. Mon on July 9
John Candelaria, Pit vs. LA on August 9
John Montefusco, SF   @ Atl on September 29

Four-Homer Games
Mike Schmidt, Phi   on April 17

Three-Homer Games
Reggie Smith, StL   on May 22
Dave Kingman, NYN   on June 4
Bill Robinson, Pit   on June 5
Gary Matthews, SF   on September 25

Cycles
Tim Foli, Mon   on April 21
Mike Phillips, NYN   on June 25
Cesar Cedeno, Hou   on August 9

1977 American League Standings

EAST	W	L	Pct	GB	DIF	W	L	R	OR	HR	OHR	W	L	R	OR	HR	OHR	Run	HR	M/A	May	June	July	Aug	S/O
								Home Games						**Road Games**				**Park Index**				**Record by Month**			
New York	100	62	.617	—	71	55	26	412	305	84	63	45	36	419	346	100	76	94	84	11-9	15-12	16-12	16-12	22-7	20-10
Baltimore	97	64	.602	2.5	36	54	27	356	269	74	62	43	37	363	384	74	62	83	99	9-8	17-10	13-18	20-8	16-11	22-9
Boston	97	64	.602	2.5	48	51	29	495	407	124	95	46	35	364	305	89	63	137	146	9-9	15-12	17-10	17-12	17-12	22-9
Detroit	74	88	.457	26.0	1	39	42	369	401	81	100	35	46	345	350	85	62	111	123	8-12	10-14	16-12	12-17	17-12	11-21
Cleveland	71	90	.441	28.5	9	37	44	339	357	54	66	34	46	337	382	46	70	96	102	6-11	13-12	17-12	8-21	18-14	9-20
Milwaukee	67	95	.414	33.0	22	37	44	305	365	49	54	30	51	334	400	76	82	91	65	11-6	14-19	11-13	10-19	11-23	10-15
Toronto	54	107	.335	45.5	4	25	55	297	444	45	94	29	52	308	378	55	58	109	125	10-11	8-17	10-17	7-21	10-18	9-23
WEST																									
Kansas City	102	60	.630	—	52	55	26	408	320	56	50	47	34	414	331	90	60	98	71	11-8	10-15	17-12	18-8	20-11	26-6
Texas	94	68	.580	8.0	9	44	37	369	368	62	78	50	31	398	289	73	56	107	109	10-8	11-13	14-16	19-8	19-13	21-10
Chicago	90	72	.556	12.0	61	48	33	434	370	85	58	42	39	410	401	107	78	99	77	10-8	15-11	15-13	22-6	11-18	17-16
Minnesota	84	77	.522	17.5	59	48	32	469	376	61	79	36	45	398	400	62	72	107	106	13-9	16-8	13-15	17-14	16-13	9-18
California	74	88	.457	28.0	2	39	42	320	321	69	65	35	46	355	374	62	71	88	101	9-13	15-10	12-12	11-18	14-15	13-20
Seattle	64	98	.395	38.0	0	29	52	303	419	75	103	35	46	321	436	58	91	95	119	8-16	13-14	13-15	12-16	6-22	12-15
Oakland	63	98	.391	38.5	6	35	46	302	347	58	69	28	52	303	402	59	76	91	93	12-9	10-15	10-17	10-19	10-18	11-20

Clinch Date—New York 10/01, Kansas City 9/23.

Team Batting

Team	G	AB	R	OR	H	2B	3B	HR	TB	RBI	TBB	IBB	SO	HBP	SH	SF	SB	CS	SB%	GDP	Avg	OBP	Slg
Minnesota	161	5639	867	776	1588	273	60	123	2350	804	563	53	754	43	81	56	105	65	.62	115	.282	.357	.417
Boston	161	5510	859	712	1551	258	56	213	2560	828	528	38	905	42	45	59	66	47	.58	132	.281	.355	.465
Chicago	162	5633	844	771	1568	254	52	192	2502	809	559	46	666	34	33	63	42	44	.49	120	.278	.354	.444
New York	162	5605	831	651	1576	267	47	184	2489	784	533	49	681	28	46	48	93	57	.62	117	.281	.352	.444
Kansas City	162	5594	822	651	1549	299	77	146	2440	773	522	50	687	45	49	58	170	87	.66	104	.277	.350	.436
Texas	162	5541	767	657	1497	265	39	135	2245	704	596	47	904	39	116	50	154	85	.64	118	.270	.350	.405
Baltimore	161	5494	719	653	1433	231	25	148	2158	677	560	50	945	24	48	47	90	51	.64	132	.261	.337	.393
Detroit	162	5604	714	751	1480	228	45	166	2296	676	452	20	764	20	45	56	60	46	.57	132	.264	.327	.410
Cleveland	161	5491	676	739	1476	221	46	100	2089	631	531	31	688	34	94	54	87	87	.50	153	.269	.343	.380
California	162	5410	675	695	1380	233	40	131	2086	636	542	42	880	36	74	51	159	89	.64	116	.255	.333	.386
Milwaukee	162	5517	639	765	1425	255	46	125	2147	598	443	23	862	22	60	45	85	67	.56	120	.258	.321	.389
Seattle	162	5460	624	855	1398	218	33	133	2081	589	426	22	769	35	81	42	110	67	.62	114	.256	.319	.381
Oakland	161	5358	605	749	1284	176	37	117	1885	548	516	37	910	36	64	46	176	89	.66	111	.240	.316	.352
Toronto	161	5418	605	822	1367	230	41	100	1979	553	499	34	819	23	81	34	65	55	.54	156	.252	.322	.365
AL Total	2262	77274	10247	10247	20572	3408	644	2013	31307	9610	7270	542	11234	461	917	709	1462	936	.61	1740	.266	.330	.405
AL Avg Team	162	5520	732	732	1469	243	46	144	2236	686	519	39	802	33	66	51	104	67	.61	124	.266	.330	.405

Team Pitching

Team	G	CG	ShO	Rel	Sv	IP	H	R	ER	HR	SH	SF	HB	TBB	IBB	SO	WP	Bk	H/9	SO/9	BB/9	OAvg	OOBP	ERA
Kansas City	162	41	15	219	42	1460.2	1377	651	571	110	66	52	36	499	27	850	56	9	8.5	5.2	3.1	.251	.315	3.52
Texas	162	49	17	200	31	1472.1	1412	657	583	134	81	42	31	471	30	864	44	2	8.6	5.3	2.9	.255	.315	3.56
New York	162	52	16	154	34	1449.1	1395	651	581	139	49	44	22	486	31	758	39	2	8.7	4.7	3.0	.254	.315	3.61
California	162	53	13	185	26	1437.2	1383	695	594	136	72	58	47	572	52	965	56	8	8.7	6.0	3.6	.256	.330	3.72
Baltimore	161	65	11	169	23	1451.0	1414	653	603	124	59	55	30	494	27	737	30	3	8.8	4.6	3.1	.260	.322	3.74
Oakland	161	32	4	249	26	1436.2	1459	749	645	145	69	24	560	49	788	55	4	9.1	4.9	3.5	.265	.333	4.04
Cleveland	161	45	8	230	30	1452.1	1441	739	661	136	82	38	27	550	64	876	47	8	8.9	5.4	3.4	.261	.329	4.10
Boston	161	40	13	209	40	1428.0	1555	712	652	158	49	39	25	378	31	758	15	4	9.8	4.8	2.4	.278	.325	4.11
Detroit	162	44	3	198	23	1457.0	1526	751	669	162	65	42	23	470	38	784	37	8	9.4	4.8	2.9	.271	.327	4.13
Chicago	162	34	3	221	40	1444.2	1557	771	683	136	87	55	42	516	24	842	43	3	9.7	5.2	3.2	.277	.339	4.25
Milwaukee	162	38	6	215	25	1431.0	1461	765	687	136	66	67	36	566	61	719	43	8	9.2	4.5	3.6	.268	.337	4.32
Minnesota	161	35	4	242	25	1442.0	1546	776	698	151	66	49	37	507	27	737	48	5	9.6	4.6	3.2	.278	.340	4.36
Toronto	161	40	3	187	20	1428.1	1538	822	726	152	64	70	20	623	40	771	62	5	9.7	4.9	3.9	.278	.350	4.57
Seattle	162	18	1	280	31	1433.0	1508	855	769	194	42	49	61	567	41	785	51	9	9.5	4.9	3.6	.272	.344	4.83
AL Total	2262	586	117	2958	416	20224.0	20572	10247	9122	2013	917	709	461	7270	542	11234	626	78	9.2	5.0	3.2	.266	.338	4.06
AL Avg Team	162	42	8	211	30	1444.0	1469	732	652	144	66	51	33	519	39	802	45	6	9.2	5.0	3.2	.266	.338	4.06

Team Fielding

Team	G	PO	A	E	TC	DP	PB	Pct
Baltimore	161	4353	1879	106	6338	189	7	.983
Texas	162	4417	1870	117	6404	156	5	.982
Cleveland	161	4357	1706	130	6193	145	8	.979
New York	162	4348	1735	132	6215	151	13	.979
Boston	161	4284	1764	133	6181	162	4	.978
Kansas City	162	4379	1788	137	6304	145	13	.978
Milwaukee	162	4293	1886	139	6318	165	18	.978
Detroit	162	4371	1933	142	6446	153	6	.978
Minnesota	161	4326	1932	143	6401	184	10	.978
Seattle	162	4299	1807	147	6253	162	13	.976
California	162	4313	1693	147	6153	137	5	.976
Chicago	162	4334	1620	159	6113	125	7	.974
Toronto	161	4285	1798	164	6247	133	7	.974
Oakland	161	4310	1762	190	6262	136	12	.970
AL Total	2262	60669	25173	1986	87828	2143	128	.977

Team vs. Team Records

	Bal	Bos	Cal	ChA	Cle	Det	KC	Mil	Min	NYA	Oak	Sea	Tex	Tor	Won
Bal	—	6	5	5	11	12	4	11	6	8	8	7	4	10	97
Bos	8	—	7	3	8	9	5	9	4	8	10	6	2	12	97
Cal	6	3	—	8	6	4	6	5	7	4	5	9	5	6	74
ChA	5	7	7	—	6	4	8	6	10	3	10	10	6	8	90
Cle	4	7	4	4	—	8	3	11	2	3	7	7	2	9	71
Det	3	6	6	6	7	—	3	10	5	6	5	5	2	10	74
KC	7	5	9	7	7	8	—	8	10	5	9	11	8	8	102
Mil	4	6	5	5	4	5	2	—	3	8	5	7	5	8	67
Min	4	6	8	5	9	5	5	8	—	2	8	7	8	9	84
NYA	7	7	7	7	12	9	5	7	8	—	9	6	7	9	100
Oak	2	3	10	5	3	5	6	5	6	2	—	7	2	7	63
Sea	3	1	6	5	3	4	4	8	4	3	8	—	9	4	64
Tex	6	4	10	9	9	9	8	7	5	7	13	6	—	7	94
Tor	5	3	4	3	5	5	2	7	1	6	3	6	4	—	54
Lost	64	64	88	72	90	88	60	95	77	62	98	98	68	107	

1977 American League Batting Leaders

Games		At-Bats		Runs		Hits		Doubles		Triples	
A. Cowens, KC	162	R. Burleson, Bos	663	R. Carew, Min	128	R. Carew, Min	239	H. McRae, KC	54	R. Carew, Min	16
H. McRae, KC	162	R. LeFlore, Det	652	C. Fisk, Bos	106	R. LeFlore, Det	212	R. Jackson, NYA	39	J. Rice, Bos	15
4 tied with	160	J. Rice, Bos	644	G. Brett, KC	105	J. Rice, Bos	206	R. Carew, Min	38	A. Cowens, KC	14
		C. Cooper, Mil	643	3 tied with	104	L. Bostock, Min	199	C. Lemon, ChA	38	G. Brett, KC	13
		H. McRae, KC	641			R. Burleson, Bos	194	3 tied with	36	L. Bostock, Min	12

Home Runs		Total Bases		Runs Batted In		Walks		Intentional Walks		Strikeouts	
J. Rice, Bos	39	J. Rice, Bos	382	L. Hisle, Min	119	T. Harrah, Tex	109	R. Carew, Min	15	B. Hobson, Bos	162
B. Bonds, Cal	37	R. Carew, Min	351	B. Bonds, Cal	115	K. Singleton, Bal	107	K. Singleton, Bal	13	B. Bonds, Cal	141
G. Nettles, NYA	37	H. McRae, KC	330	J. Rice, Bos	114	M. Hargrove, Tex	103	J. Spencer, ChA	11	R. Jackson, NYA	129
G. Scott, Bos	33	A. Cowens, KC	318	A. Cowens, KC	112	W. Gross, Oak	86	R. Fairly, Tor	11	R. LeFlore, Det	121
R. Jackson, NYA	32	R. LeFlore, Det	310	B. Hobson, Bos	112	J. Mayberry, KC	83	J. Rice, Bos	10	2 tied with	120

Hit By Pitch		Sac Hits		Sac Flies		Stolen Bases		Caught Stealing		GDP	
H. McRae, KC	13	B. Campaneris, Tex	40	A. Bannister, ChA	11	F. Patek, KC	53	B. Campaneris, Tex	20	R. Staub, Det	27
D. Baylor, Cal	12	D. Kuiper, Cle	21	C. Yastrzemski, Bos	11	M. Page, Oak	42	R. LeFlore, Det	19	G. Scott, Bos	24
A. Thornton, Cle	11	J. Sundberg, Tex	20	B. Bonds, Cal	10	B. Bonds, Cal	41	J. Beniquez, Tex	18	C. Chambliss, NYA	22
C. Lemon, ChA	11	J. Remy, Cal	19	C. Fisk, Bos	10	J. Remy, Cal	41	B. Bonds, Cal	18	E. Murray, Bal	22
2 tied with	10	2 tied with	15	R. Staub, Det	10	R. LeFlore, Det	39	R. Scott, Oak	18	J. Rice, Bos	21

Runs Created		Runs Created/27 Outs		Batting Average		On-Base Percentage		Slugging Percentage		OBP+Slugging	
R. Carew, Min	154	R. Carew, Min	10.33	R. Carew, Min	.388	R. Carew, Min	.449	J. Rice, Bos	.593	R. Carew, Min	1.019
J. Rice, Bos	129	M. Page, Oak	8.47	L. Bostock, Min	.336	K. Singleton, Bal	.438	R. Carew, Min	.570	J. Rice, Bos	.969
K. Singleton, Bal	119	K. Singleton, Bal	8.40	K. Singleton, Bal	.328	M. Hargrove, Tex	.420	R. Jackson, NYA	.550	K. Singleton, Bal	.945
L. Bostock, Min	118	R. Jackson, NYA	7.64	M. Rivers, NYA	.326	M. Page, Oak	.405	L. Hisle, Min	.533	M. Page, Oak	.926
M. Page, Oak	115	C. Fisk, Bos	7.53	R. LeFlore, Det	.325	C. Fisk, Bos	.402	G. Brett, KC	.532	R. Jackson, NYA	.925

1977 American League Pitching Leaders

Wins		Losses		Winning Percentage		Games		Games Started		Complete Games	
D. Goltz, Min	20	V. Blue, Oak	19	D. Gullett, NYA	.778	S. Lyle, NYA	72	D. Goltz, Min	39	N. Ryan, Cal	22
D. Leonard, KC	20	W. Garland, Cle	19	D. Bird, KC	.733	T. Johnson, Min	71	J. Palmer, Bal	39	J. Palmer, Bal	22
J. Palmer, Bal	20	R. Langford, Oak	19	D. Tidrow, NYA	.733	B. Campbell, Bos	69	V. Blue, Oak	38	W. Garland, Cle	21
N. Ryan, Cal	19	3 tied with	18	P. Splittorff, KC	.727	B. McClure, Mil	68	W. Garland, Cle	38	D. Leonard, KC	21
2 tied with	18			S. Lyle, NYA	.722	L. LaGrow, ChA	66	5 tied with	37	F. Tanana, Cal	20

Shutouts		Saves		Games Finished		Batters Faced		Innings Pitched		Hits Allowed	
F. Tanana, Cal	7	B. Campbell, Bos	31	S. Lyle, NYA	60	N. Ryan, Cal	1272	J. Palmer, Bal	319.0	V. Blue, Oak	284
B. Blyleven, Tex	5	S. Lyle, NYA	26	B. Campbell, Bos	60	J. Palmer, Bal	1269	D. Goltz, Min	303.0	D. Goltz, Min	284
R. Guidry, NYA	5	L. LaGrow, ChA	25	T. Johnson, Min	54	D. Goltz, Min	1253	N. Ryan, Cal	299.0	W. Garland, Cle	281
D. Leonard, KC	5	J. Kern, Cle	18	D. LaRoche, 2tm	50	D. Leonard, KC	1186	D. Leonard, KC	292.2	D. Lemanczyk, Tor	278
3 tied with	4	D. LaRoche, 2tm	17	L. LaGrow, ChA	49	2 tied with	1184	W. Garland, Cle	282.2	J. Palmer, Bal	263

Home Runs Allowed		Walks		Walks/9 Innings		Strikeouts		Strikeouts/9 Innings		Strikeout/Walk Ratio	
J. Garvin, Tor	33	N. Ryan, Cal	204	D. Rozema, Det	1.4	N. Ryan, Cal	341	N. Ryan, Cal	10.3	D. Eckersley, Cle	3.54
G. Abbott, Sea	32	J. Palmer, Bal	99	F. Jenkins, Bos	1.7	D. Leonard, KC	244	F. Tanana, Cal	7.6	F. Tanana, Cal	3.36
D. Eckersley, Cle	31	D. Goltz, Min	91	P. Hartzell, Cal	1.8	F. Tanana, Cal	205	R. Guidry, NYA	7.5	G. Perry, Tex	3.16
F. Jenkins, Bos	30	W. Garland, Cle	88	D. Eckersley, Cle	2.0	J. Palmer, Bal	193	D. Leonard, KC	7.5	D. Leonard, KC	3.09
C. Hunter, NYA	29	D. Lemanczyk, Tor	87	R. Cleveland, Bos	2.0	D. Eckersley, Cle	191	B. Blyleven, Tex	7.0	F. Jenkins, Bos	2.92

Earned Run Average		Component ERA		Hit Batsmen		Wild Pitches		Opponent Average		Opponent OBP	
F. Tanana, Cal	2.54	B. Blyleven, Tex	2.53	J. Colborn, KC	13	N. Ryan, Cal	21	N. Ryan, Cal	.193	D. Eckersley, Cle	.276
B. Blyleven, Tex	2.72	R. Guidry, NYA	2.55	G. Abbott, Sea	12	D. Lemanczyk, Tor	20	B. Blyleven, Tex	.214	B. Blyleven, Tex	.278
N. Ryan, Cal	2.77	D. Leonard, KC	2.61	F. Tanana, Cal	12	D. Leonard, KC	14	R. Guidry, NYA	.224	D. Leonard, KC	.283
R. Guidry, NYA	2.82	F. Tanana, Cal	2.70	J. Slaton, Mil	11	3 tied with	12	F. Tanana, Cal	.227	R. Guidry, NYA	.283
J. Palmer, Bal	2.91	J. Palmer, Bal	2.76	W. Wood, ChA	10			D. Leonard, KC	.227	F. Tanana, Cal	.284

1977 American League Miscellaneous

Managers

Baltimore	Earl Weaver	97-64
Boston	Don Zimmer	97-64
California	Norm Sherry	39-42
	Dave Garcia	35-46
Chicago	Bob Lemon	90-72
Cleveland	Frank Robinson	26-31
	Jeff Torborg	45-59
Detroit	Ralph Houk	74-88
Kansas City	Whitey Herzog	102-60
Milwaukee	Alex Grammas	67-95
Minnesota	Gene Mauch	84-77
New York	Billy Martin	100-62
Oakland	Jack McKeon	26-27
	Bobby Winkles	37-71
Seattle	Darrell Johnson	64-98
Texas	Frank Lucchesi	31-31
	Eddie Stanky	1-0
	Connie Ryan	2-4
	Billy Hunter	60-33
Toronto	Roy Hartsfield	54-107

Awards

Most Valuable Player	Rod Carew, 1b, Min
Cy Young	Sparky Lyle, NYA
Rookie of the Year	Eddie Murray, dh, Bal
STATS Manager of the Year	Bob Lemon, ChA

STATS All-Star Team

C	Carlton Fisk, Bos	.315	26	102	
1B	Rod Carew, Min	.388	14	100	
2B	Don Money, Mil	.279	25	83	
3B	George Brett, KC	.312	22	88	
SS	Rick Burleson, Bos	.293	3	52	
OF	Larry Hisle, Min	.302	28	119	
OF	Reggie Jackson, NYA	.286	32	110	
OF	Ken Singleton, Bal	.328	24	99	
DH	Jim Rice, Bos	.320	39	114	
P	Dennis Leonard, KC	20-12	3.04	244 K	
P	Jim Palmer, Bal	20-11	2.91	193 K	
P	Nolan Ryan, Cal	19-16	2.77	341 K	
P	Frank Tanana, Cal	15-9	2.54	205 K	
RP	Sparky Lyle, NYA	13-5	2.17	26 Sv	

Postseason

LCS	New York 3 vs. Kansas City 2
World Series	NYA (AL) 4 vs. Los Angeles (NL) 2

Outstanding Performances

No-Hitters
Jim Colborn, KC	vs. Tex on May 14
D. Eckersley, Cle	vs. Cal on May 20
Bert Blyleven, Tex	@ Cal on September 22

Three-Homer Games
Willie Horton, Tex	on May 15
John Mayberry, KC	on June 1
Cliff Johnson, NYA	on June 30
Jim Rice, Bos	on August 29

Cycles
John Mayberry, KC	on August 5
Jack Brohamer, ChA	on September 24

1977 National League Standings

EAST	Overall					Home Games						Road Games						Park Index		Record by Month					
	W	L	Pct	GB	DIF	W	L	R	OR	HR	OHR	W	L	R	OR	HR	OHR	Run	HR	M/A	May	June	July	Aug	S/O
Philadelphia	101	61	.623	—	60	60	21	453	299	101	63	41	40	394	369	85	71	99	105	7-9	18-10	15-13	19-11	22-7	20-11
Pittsburgh	96	66	.593	5.0	30	58	23	396	315	64	76	38	43	338	350	69	73	103	99	10-7	16-10	13-17	20-10	18-12	19-10
St. Louis	83	79	.512	18.0	22	52	31	379	314	41	53	31	48	358	374	55	86	90	63	12-7	16-11	13-15	15-15	15-14	12-17
Chicago	81	81	.500	20.0	72	46	35	411	402	69	82	35	46	281	337	42	46	132	172	7-9	21-7	19-8	14-17	11-19	9-21
Montreal	75	87	.463	26.0	5	38	43	329	362	66	65	37	44	336	374	72	70	97	92	8-8	10-18	12-16	18-12	12-18	15-15
New York	64	98	.395	37.0	5	35	44	282	297	46	56	29	54	305	366	42	62	91	103	8-9	8-21	15-13	12-16	8-22	13-17
WEST																									
Los Angeles	98	64	.605	—	175	51	30	386	273	96	65	47	34	383	309	95	54	95	108	17-3	16-12	17-11	16-12	14-15	18-11
Cincinnati	88	74	.543	10.0	3	48	33	408	355	83	83	40	41	394	370	98	73	100	97	9-10	13-13	18-10	11-18	21-11	16-12
Houston	81	81	.500	17.0	8	46	35	309	291	40	33	35	46	371	359	74	77	82	48	9-11	11-16	13-16	15-14	16-12	17-12
San Francisco	75	87	.463	23.0	0	38	43	353	371	62	56	37	44	320	340	72	58	110	91	8-11	13-16	14-16	12-15	15-14	13-15
San Diego	69	93	.426	29.0	0	35	46	299	368	53	70	34	47	393	466	67	90	78	78	8-15	16-13	8-18	13-16	14-14	10-17
Atlanta	61	101	.377	37.0	0	40	41	416	488	97	111	21	60	262	407	42	58	135	208	8-12	9-20	11-15	9-18	11-19	13-17

Clinch Date—Philadelphia 9/27, Los Angeles 9/20.

Team Batting

Team	G	AB	R	OR	H	2B	3B	HR	TB	RBI	TBB	IBB	SO	HBP	SH	SF	SB	CS	SB%	GDP	Avg	OBP	Slg
Philadelphia	162	5546	847	668	1548	266	56	186	2484	795	573	75	806	38	59	74	135	68	.67	121	.279	.358	.448
Cincinnati	162	5524	802	725	1513	269	42	181	2409	750	600	63	911	25	62	50	170	64	.73	112	.274	.353	.436
Los Angeles	162	5589	769	582	1484	223	28	191	2336	729	588	67	896	23	83	44	114	62	.65	103	.266	.343	.418
St. Louis	162	5527	737	688	1490	252	56	96	2142	686	489	71	823	25	66	29	134	112	.54	111	.270	.335	.388
Pittsburgh	162	5662	734	665	1550	278	57	133	2341	678	474	74	878	34	49	43	260	120	.68	96	.274	.338	.413
San Diego	162	5602	692	834	1397	245	49	120	2100	652	602	64	1057	29	90	30	133	57	.70	102	.249	.329	.375
Chicago	162	5604	692	739	1489	271	37	111	2167	649	534	59	796	27	69	52	64	45	.59	142	.266	.338	.387
Houston	162	5530	680	650	1405	263	60	114	2130	638	515	60	839	40	76	39	187	72	.72	98	.254	.326	.385
Atlanta	162	5534	678	895	1404	218	20	139	2079	638	537	50	876	17	83	34	82	53	.61	135	.254	.325	.376
San Francisco	162	5497	673	711	1392	241	41	134	2103	624	568	61	842	21	78	51	90	59	.60	118	.253	.331	.383
Montreal	162	5675	665	736	1474	294	50	138	2282	622	478	66	877	21	69	39	88	50	.64	125	.260	.324	.402
New York	162	5410	587	663	1319	227	30	88	1870	525	529	45	887	30	63	37	98	81	.55	136	.244	.319	.346
NL Total	1944	66700	8556	8556	17465	3033	526	1631	26443	7986	6487	755	10488	330	847	522	1555	843	.65	1399	.262	.328	.396
NL Avg Team	162	5558	713	713	1455	253	44	136	2204	666	541	63	874	28	71	44	130	70	.65	117	.262	.328	.396

Team Pitching

Team	G	CG	ShO	Rel	Sv	IP	H	R	ER	HR	SH	SF	HB	TBB	IBB	SO	WP	Bk	H/9	SO/9	BB/9	OAvg	OOBP	ERA
Los Angeles	162	34	13	238	39	1475.1	1393	582	528	119	82	30	29	438	31	930	35	4	8.5	5.7	2.7	.251	.308	3.22
Houston	162	37	11	234	28	1465.2	1384	650	577	110	66	44	25	545	33	871	46	17	8.5	5.3	3.3	.251	.319	3.54
Pittsburgh	162	25	15	278	39	1481.2	1406	665	594	149	67	54	21	485	43	890	44	12	8.5	5.4	2.9	.252	.311	3.61
Philadelphia	162	31	7	246	47	1455.2	1451	660	600	134	66	35	24	482	46	856	44	17	9.0	5.3	3.0	.263	.323	3.71
San Francisco	162	27	10	312	33	1459.0	1501	711	608	114	56	47	27	529	90	854	34	6	9.3	5.3	3.3	.267	.331	3.75
New York	162	27	12	248	28	1433.2	1378	663	601	118	63	42	32	490	76	911	25	16	8.7	5.7	3.1	.254	.317	3.77
St. Louis	162	26	10	305	31	1446.0	1420	688	612	139	61	50	25	532	40	768	43	9	8.8	4.8	3.3	.260	.326	3.81
Chicago	162	16	10	319	44	1468.0	1500	739	654	128	72	30	22	489	101	942	55	17	9.2	5.8	3.0	.266	.325	4.01
Montreal	162	31	11	307	33	1481.0	1426	736	660	135	80	49	25	579	49	856	50	6	8.7	5.2	3.5	.255	.325	4.01
Cincinnati	162	33	12	261	32	1437.1	1469	725	673	156	68	45	31	544	54	868	54	9	9.2	5.4	3.4	.267	.334	4.21
San Diego	162	6	5	382	44	1466.1	1556	834	722	160	80	51	27	673	106	827	46	25	9.6	5.1	4.1	.276	.353	4.43
Atlanta	162	28	5	327	31	1445.1	1581	895	779	169	86	45	42	701	86	915	64	19	9.8	5.7	4.4	.279	.360	4.85
NL Total	1944	321	121	3457	429	17515.0	17465	8556	7608	1631	847	522	330	6487	755	10488	540	157	9.0	5.4	3.3	.262	.335	3.91
NL Avg Team	162	27	10	288	36	1459.0	1455	713	634	136	71	44	28	541	63	874	45	13	9.0	5.4	3.3	.262	.335	3.91

Team Fielding

Team	G	PO	A	E	TC	DP	PB	Pct
Cincinnati	162	4312	1660	95	6067	154	7	.984
Philadelphia	162	4367	1952	120	6439	168	4	.981
Los Angeles	162	4426	1879	124	6429	160	13	.981
Montreal	162	4443	1848	129	6420	128	12	.980
St. Louis	162	4338	1850	139	6327	174	10	.978
New York	162	4301	1612	134	6047	132	11	.978
Houston	162	4397	1851	142	6390	136	24	.978
Pittsburgh	162	4445	1779	145	6369	137	13	.977
Chicago	162	4404	2104	153	6661	147	8	.977
Atlanta	162	4336	1705	175	6216	127	34	.972
San Francisco	162	4377	1749	179	6305	136	9	.972
San Diego	162	4399	1846	189	6434	142	21	.971
NL Total	1944	52545	21835	1724	76104	1741	166	.977

Team vs. Team Records

	Atl	ChN	Cin	Hou	LA	Mon	NYN	Phi	Pit	SD	SF	StL	Won
Atl	—	5	4	9	5	6	7	2	3	11	8	1	**61**
ChN	7	—	7	6	6	10	9	6	7	7	9	7	**81**
Cin	14	5	—	5	10	7	10	8	3	11	10	5	**88**
Hou	9	6	13	—	9	8	6	4	4	8	9	5	**81**
LA	13	6	8	9	—	7	8	6	9	12	14	6	**98**
Mon	6	8	5	4	5	—	10	7	7	5	6	12	**75**
NYN	5	9	2	6	4	8	—	5	4	6	7	8	**64**
Phi	10	12	4	8	6	11	13	—	8	9	9	11	**101**
Pit	9	11	9	8	3	11	14	10	—	10	2	9	**96**
SD	7	5	7	10	6	7	6	3	2	—	8	8	**69**
SF	10	3	8	9	4	6	5	3	10	10	—	7	**75**
StL	11	11	7	7	6	10	7	9	4	5	—		**83**
Lost	101	81	74	81	64	87	98	61	66	93	87	79	

1977 National League Batting Leaders

Games		At-Bats		Runs		Hits		Doubles		Triples	
S. Garvey, LA	162	P. Rose, Cin	655	G. Foster, Cin	124	D. Parker, Pit	215	D. Parker, Pit	44	G. Templeton, StL	18
P. Rose, Cin	162	D. Cash, Mon	650	K. Griffey Sr., Cin	117	P. Rose, Cin	204	D. Cash, Mon	42	B. Almon, SD	11
K. Hernandez, StL	161	S. Garvey, LA	646	M. Schmidt, Phi	114	G. Templeton, StL	200	W. Cromartie, Mon	41	G. Richards, SD	11
L. Mazzilli, NYN	159	D. Parker, Pit	637	J. Morgan, Cin	113	G. Foster, Cin	197	K. Hernandez, StL	41	M. Schmidt, Phi	11
D. Parker, Pit	159	B. Russell, LA	634	D. Parker, Pit	107	S. Garvey, LA	192	2 tied with	38	6 tied with	10

Home Runs		Total Bases		Runs Batted In		Walks		Intentional Walks		Strikeouts	
G. Foster, Cin	52	G. Foster, Cin	388	G. Foster, Cin	149	G. Tenace, SD	125	T. Simmons, StL	25	G. Luzinski, Phi	140
J. Burroughs, Atl	41	D. Parker, Pit	338	G. Luzinski, Phi	130	J. Morgan, Cin	117	T. Sizemore, Phi	21	J. Burroughs, Atl	126
G. Luzinski, Phi	39	G. Luzinski, Phi	329	S. Garvey, LA	115	M. Schmidt, Phi	104	W. McCovey, SF	16	M. Schmidt, Phi	122
M. Schmidt, Phi	38	S. Garvey, LA	322	J. Burroughs, Atl	114	R. Smith, LA	104	T. Perez, Mon	15	G. Tenace, SD	119
S. Garvey, LA	33	M. Schmidt, Phi	312	2 tied with	110	R. Cey, LA	93	B. Pocoroba, Atl	15	2 tied with	114

Hit By Pitch		Sac Hits		Sac Flies		Stolen Bases		Caught Stealing		GDP	
G. Tenace, SD	13	B. Almon, SD	20	J. Cruz, Hou	10	F. Taveras, Pit	70	G. Templeton, StL	24	B. Madlock, SF	25
C. Cedeno, Hou	11	B. Hooton, LA	14	B. Murcer, ChN	10	C. Cedeno, Hou	61	L. Brock, StL	24	T. Sizemore, Phi	25
M. Schmidt, Phi	9	L. Bowa, Phi	13	T. Perez, Mon	9	G. Richards, SD	56	J. Cruz, Hou	23	B. Russell, LA	23
4 tied with	7	T. Seaver, 2tm	13	M. Schmidt, Phi	9	O. Moreno, Pit	53	E. Cabell, Hou	22	T. Simmons, StL	20
		J. Barr, SF	13	8 tied with	8	J. Morgan, Cin	49	L. Randle, NYN	21	3 tied with	18

Runs Created		Runs Created/27 Outs		Batting Average		On-Base Percentage		Slugging Percentage		OBP+Slugging	
G. Foster, Cin	129	R. Smith, LA	8.86	D. Parker, Pit	.338	R. Smith, LA	.427	G. Foster, Cin	.631	G. Foster, Cin	1.013
G. Luzinski, Phi	120	G. Luzinski, Phi	8.07	G. Templeton, StL	.322	J. Morgan, Cin	.417	G. Luzinski, Phi	.594	R. Smith, LA	1.003
M. Schmidt, Phi	120	G. Foster, Cin	7.85	G. Foster, Cin	.320	G. Tenace, SD	.415	R. Smith, LA	.576	G. Luzinski, Phi	.988
D. Parker, Pit	117	J. Morgan, Cin	7.72	K. Griffey Sr., Cin	.318	T. Simmons, StL	.408	M. Schmidt, Phi	.574	M. Schmidt, Phi	.967
R. Smith, LA	116	M. Schmidt, Phi	7.71	T. Simmons, StL	.318	D. Parker, Pit	.397	J. Bench, Cin	.540	D. Parker, Pit	.927

1977 National League Pitching Leaders

Wins		Losses		Winning Percentage		Games		Games Started		Complete Games	
S. Carlton, Phi	23	P. Niekro, Atl	20	J. Candelaria, Pit	.800	R. Fingers, SD	78	P. Niekro, Atl	43	P. Niekro, Atl	20
T. Seaver, 2tm	21	J. Koosman, NYN	20	T. Seaver, 2tm	.778	D. Tomlin, SD	76	S. Rogers, Mon	40	T. Seaver, 2tm	19
4 tied with	20	B. Shirley, SD	18	L. Christenson, Phi	.760	D. Spillner, SD	76	R. Burris, ChN	39	S. Carlton, Phi	17
		E. Rasmussen, StL	17	B. Forsch, StL	.741	B. Metzger, 2tm	75	J. Barr, SF	38	S. Rogers, Mon	17
		3 tied with	16	T. John, LA	.741	2 tied with	73	2 tied with	37	J. Richard, Hou	13

Shutouts		Saves		Games Finished		Batters Faced		Innings Pitched		Hits Allowed	
T. Seaver, 2tm	7	R. Fingers, SD	35	R. Fingers, SD	69	P. Niekro, Atl	1428	P. Niekro, Atl	330.1	P. Niekro, Atl	315
R. Reuschel, ChN	4	B. Sutter, ChN	31	G. Gossage, Pit	55	S. Rogers, Mon	1235	S. Rogers, Mon	301.2	J. Barr, SF	286
S. Rogers, Mon	4	G. Gossage, Pit	26	P. Borbon, Cin	54	S. Carlton, Phi	1135	S. Carlton, Phi	283.0	S. Rogers, Mon	272
5 tied with	3	C. Hough, LA	22	C. Hough, LA	53	J. Richard, Hou	1092	J. Richard, Hou	267.0	R. Burris, ChN	270
		2 tied with	20	S. Lockwood, NYN	50	E. Halicki, SF	1076	T. Seaver, 2tm	261.1	E. Halicki, SF	241

Home Runs Allowed		Walks		Walks/9 Innings		Strikeouts		Strikeouts/9 Innings		Strikeout/Walk Ratio	
J. Candelaria, Pit	29	P. Niekro, Atl	164	J. Candelaria, Pit	2.0	P. Niekro, Atl	262	J. Koosman, NYN	7.6	T. Seaver, 2tm	2.97
R. Burris, ChN	29	J. Richard, Hou	104	T. John, LA	2.0	J. Richard, Hou	214	J. Richard, Hou	7.2	J. Matlack, NYN	2.86
F. Norman, Cin	28	B. Shirley, SD	100	D. Rau, LA	2.1	S. Rogers, Mon	206	P. Niekro, Atl	7.1	J. Candelaria, Pit	2.66
B. Capra, Atl	28	F. Norman, Cin	98	J. Barr, SF	2.2	S. Carlton, Phi	198	T. Seaver, 2tm	6.8	D. Rau, LA	2.57
E. Halicki, SF	27	S. Carlton, Phi	89	M. Lemongello, Hou	2.2	T. Seaver, 2tm	196	J. Matlack, NYN	6.6	B. Hooton, LA	2.55

Earned Run Average		Component ERA		Hit Batsmen		Wild Pitches		Opponent Average		Opponent OBP	
J. Candelaria, Pit	2.34	T. Seaver, 2tm	2.12	J. Billingham, Cin	10	P. Niekro, Atl	17	T. Seaver, 2tm	.209	T. Seaver, 2tm	.258
T. Seaver, 2tm	2.58	B. Hooton, LA	2.46	M. Leon, Atl	9	S. Rogers, Mon	14	J. Richard, Hou	.218	J. Candelaria, Pit	.274
B. Hooton, LA	2.62	J. Richard, Hou	2.74	P. Niekro, Atl	8	F. Norman, Cin	11	S. Carlton, Phi	.223	B. Hooton, LA	.279
S. Carlton, Phi	2.64	S. Carlton, Phi	2.74	4 tied with	7	J. Reuss, Pit	11	B. Hooton, LA	.225	S. Carlton, Phi	.286
T. John, LA	2.78	S. Rogers, Mon	2.81			R. Sawyer, SD	10	J. Koosman, NYN	.232	D. Sutton, LA	.289

1977 National League Miscellaneous

Managers

Atlanta	Dave Bristol	8-21
	Ted Turner	0-1
	Vern Benson	1-0
	Dave Bristol	52-79
Chicago	Herman Franks	81-81
Cincinnati	Sparky Anderson	88-74
Houston	Bill Virdon	81-81
Los Angeles	Tom Lasorda	98-64
Montreal	Dick Williams	75-87
New York	Joe Frazier	15-30
	Joe Torre	49-68
Philadelphia	Danny Ozark	101-61
Pittsburgh	Chuck Tanner	96-66
St. Louis	Vern Rapp	83-79
San Diego	John McNamara	20-28
	Bob Skinner	1-0
	Alvin Dark	48-65
San Francisco	Joe Altobelli	75-87

Awards

Most Valuable Player	George Foster, of, Cin
Cy Young	Steve Carlton, Phi
Rookie of the Year	Andre Dawson, of, Mon
STATS Manager of the Year	Tom Lasorda, LA

STATS All-Star Team

C	Ted Simmons, StL	.318	21	95
1B	Steve Garvey, LA	.297	33	115
2B	Joe Morgan, Cin	.288	22	78
3B	Mike Schmidt, Phi	.274	38	101
SS	Garry Templeton, StL	.322	8	79
OF	George Foster, Cin	.320	52	149
OF	Greg Luzinski, Phi	.309	39	130
OF	Reggie Smith, LA	.307	32	87
P	John Candelaria, Pit	20-5	2.34	133 K
P	Steve Carlton, Phi	23-10	2.64	198 K
P	Rick Reuschel, ChN	20-10	2.79	166 K
P	Tom Seaver, 2tm	21-6	2.58	196 K
RP	Bruce Sutter, ChN	7-3	1.34	31 Sv

Postseason

LCS	Los Angeles 3 vs. Philadelphia 1
World Series	Los Angeles (NL) 2 vs. NYA (AL) 4

Outstanding Performances

Three-Homer Games

Gary Carter, Mon	on April 20
Larry Parrish, Mon	on May 29
George Foster, Cin	on July 14

Cycles

Bob Watson, Hou	on June 24

1978 American League Standings

	Overall					Home Games						Road Games						Park Index		Record by Month					
EAST	W	L	Pct	GB	DIF	W	L	R	OR	HR	OHR	W	L	R	OR	HR	OHR	Run	HR	M/A	May	June	July	Aug	S/O
New York	100	63	.613	—	23	55	26	358	275	68	59	45	37	377	307	57	52	94	118	10-9	19-8	14-15	15-14	19-8	23-9
Boston	99	64	.607	1.0	116	59	23	445	334	94	72	40	41	351	323	78	65	114	115	11-9	23-7	18-7	13-15	19-10	15-16
Milwaukee	93	69	.574	6.5	11	54	27	446	318	94	50	39	42	358	332	79	59	111	104	9-11	14-11	21-9	15-12	17-14	17-12
Baltimore	90	71	.559	9.0	2	51	30	316	258	74	42	39	41	343	375	80	65	79	79	8-11	15-14	18-10	17-11	14-14	18-11
Detroit	86	76	.531	13.5	42	47	34	395	338	74	78	39	42	319	315	55	57	116	136	13-5	13-15	10-18	19-11	18-10	13-17
Cleveland	69	90	.434	29.0	3	42	36	319	287	50	37	27	54	320	407	56	63	87	76	8-11	13-13	14-15	14-15	8-21	12-15
Toronto	59	102	.366	40.0	2	37	44	334	366	50	75	22	58	256	409	48	74	104	101	8-13	9-18	9-17	13-18	16-14	4-22
WEST																									
Kansas City	92	70	.568	—	101	56	25	434	264	43	44	36	45	309	370	55	64	103	73	14-5	11-14	13-17	20-8	13-16	21-10
California	87	75	.537	5.0	23	50	31	371	316	56	58	37	44	320	350	52	67	103	96	14-7	11-14	15-15	16-14	14-13	17-12
Texas	87	75	.537	5.0	9	52	30	348	289	62	49	35	45	344	343	70	59	90	84	9-10	14-12	16-13	10-20	16-10	22-10
Minnesota	73	89	.451	19.0	1	38	43	322	308	44	39	35	46	344	370	38	63	88	82	8-16	11-12	11-13	15-15	13-19	15-14
Chicago	71	90	.441	20.5	5	38	42	342	349	56	58	33	48	292	382	50	70	104	96	6-12	11-16	17-12	10-19	12-16	15-15
Oakland	69	93	.434	23.0	45	38	42	281	330	52	51	31	51	251	360	48	55	103	103	16-5	11-15	11-18	17-13	7-21	7-21
Seattle	56	104	.350	35.0	2	32	49	343	423	68	93	24	55	271	411	39	62	110	146	8-18	9-15	10-18	9-18	13-13	7-22

Clinch Date—New York 10/02, Kansas City 9/26.

Team Batting

Team	G	AB	R	OR	H	2B	3B	HR	TB	RBI	TBB	IBB	SO	HBP	SH	SF	SB	CS	SB%	GDP	Avg	OBP	Slg
Milwaukee	162	5536	804	650	1530	265	38	173	2390	762	520	38	805	32	89	50	95	53	.64	94	.276	.347	.432
Boston	163	5587	796	657	1493	270	46	172	2371	738	582	43	835	24	65	58	74	51	.59	135	.267	.345	.424
Kansas City	162	5474	743	634	1469	305	59	98	2186	695	498	44	644	30	55	72	216	84	.72	95	.268	.341	.399
New York	163	5583	735	582	1489	228	38	125	2168	693	695	45	695	42	57	52	98	42	.70	126	.267	.338	.388
Detroit	162	5601	714	653	1520	218	34	129	2193	666	563	32	695	31	57	47	90	38	.70	145	.271	.346	.392
Texas	162	5347	692	632	1353	216	36	132	2037	650	624	45	779	32	83	55	196	91	.68	115	.253	.341	.381
California	162	5472	691	666	1417	226	28	108	2023	646	539	38	682	67	72	56	86	69	.55	135	.259	.339	.370
Minnesota	162	5522	666	678	1472	259	47	82	2071	621	604	43	684	33	109	41	99	56	.64	139	.267	.348	.375
Baltimore	161	5422	659	633	1397	248	19	154	2145	612	552	34	698	22	41	42	75	61	.55	136	.258	.333	.396
Cleveland	159	5365	639	694	1400	223	45	106	2031	596	488	31	698	26	92	40	64	63	.55	124	.261	.330	.379
Chicago	161	5393	634	731	1423	221	41	106	2044	595	409	20	625	33	63	57	83	68	.55	122	.264	.326	.379
Seattle	160	5358	614	834	1327	229	37	97	1921	571	522	25	702	22	68	53	123	47	.72	112	.248	.323	.359
Toronto	161	5430	590	775	1358	217	39	98	1947	551	448	23	645	23	77	37	28	52	.35	124	.250	.314	.359
Oakland	162	5321	532	690	1304	200	31	100	1866	492	433	33	800	25	108	27	144	117	.55	106	.245	.308	.351
AL Total	2262	76411	9509	9509	19952	3325	538	1680	29393	8888	7287	494	10153	442	1016	701	1471	892	.62	1708	.261	.326	.385
AL Avg Team	162	5458	679	679	1425	238	38	120	2100	635	521	35	725	32	73	50	105	64	.62	122	.261	.326	.385

Team Pitching

Team	G	CG	ShO	Rel	Sv	IP	H	R	ER	HR	SH	SF	HB	TBB	IBB	SO	WP	Bk	H/9	SO/9	BB/9	OAvg	OOBP	ERA
New York	163	39	16	188	36	1460.2	1321	582	516	111	79	42	32	478	30	817	43	4	8.1	5.0	2.9	.243	.306	3.18
Texas	162	54	12	170	25	1456.1	1431	632	543	108	75	44	24	421	31	776	35	3	8.8	4.8	2.6	.259	.312	3.36
Kansas City	162	53	14	208	33	1439.0	1350	634	550	108	84	52	34	478	37	657	37	6	8.4	4.1	3.0	.251	.313	3.44
Boston	163	57	15	178	26	1472.2	1530	657	579	137	61	40	35	464	45	706	16	5	9.4	4.3	2.8	.270	.327	3.54
Baltimore	161	65	16	161	33	1429.0	1340	633	566	107	53	37	15	509	29	754	44	6	8.4	4.7	3.2	.251	.316	3.56
Oakland	162	26	11	271	29	1433.1	1401	690	577	106	92	52	26	582	59	750	37	9	8.8	4.7	3.7	.259	.330	3.62
Detroit	162	60	12	157	21	1455.2	1441	653	589	135	67	59	36	503	23	684	48	2	8.9	4.2	3.1	.263	.325	3.64
California	162	44	13	193	33	1455.2	1382	666	590	125	69	52	32	599	60	892	36	14	8.5	5.5	3.7	.253	.327	3.65
Milwaukee	162	62	19	173	24	1436.0	1442	650	583	109	58	52	41	398	26	577	34	7	9.0	3.6	2.5	.262	.313	3.65
Minnesota	162	48	9	176	22	1459.2	1468	678	599	102	76	56	39	520	19	703	51	14	9.1	4.3	3.2	.266	.330	3.69
Cleveland	159	36	6	214	28	1407.1	1397	694	621	100	73	49	28	568	38	739	56	7	8.9	4.7	3.6	.261	.332	3.97
Chicago	161	38	9	200	33	1409.1	1380	731	660	128	79	51	43	586	18	710	38	2	8.8	4.5	3.7	.259	.334	4.21
Toronto	161	35	5	213	23	1429.1	1529	775	721	149	79	51	22	614	40	758	47	5	9.6	4.8	3.9	.279	.351	4.54
Seattle	160	28	4	249	20	1419.1	1440	834	737	151	64	41		567	39	630	31	5	9.8	4.0	3.6	.280	.348	4.67
AL Total	2262	645	161	2751	390	20163.1	19952	9509	8431	1680	1016	701	442	7287	494	10153	553	89	8.9	4.5	3.3	.261	.335	3.76
AL Avg Team	162	46	12	197	28	1440.1	1425	679	602	120	73	50	32	521	35	725	40	6	8.9	4.5	3.3	.261	.335	3.76

Team Fielding

Team	G	PO	A	E	TC	DP	PB	Pct
Baltimore	161	4287	1887	110	6284	166	7	.982
New York	163	4382	1758	113	6253	134	11	.982
Detroit	162	4367	1858	118	6343	177	10	.981
Cleveland	159	4222	1769	123	6114	142	15	.980
Toronto	161	4288	1763	131	6182	163	16	.979
California	162	4367	1624	136	6127	136	5	.978
Seattle	160	4258	1882	141	6281	174	6	.978
Minnesota	162	4379	1943	146	6468	171	7	.977
Boston	163	4418	1842	146	6406	171	8	.977
Chicago	161	4228	1715	139	6082	130	13	.977
Milwaukee	162	4308	1976	144	6434	144	4	.977
Texas	162	4369	1972	153	6494	140	12	.976
Kansas City	162	4317	1676	150	6143	153	11	.976
Oakland	162	4300	1626	179	6105	145	10	.971
AL Total	2262	60490	25291	1935	87716	2146	135	.978

Team vs. Team Records

	Bal	Bos	Cal	ChA	Cle	Det	KC	Mil	Min	NYA	Oak	Sea	Tex	Tor	Won
Bal	—	7	4	8	9	7	2	7	5	6	11	9	7	8	90
Bos	8	—	9	7	7	12	4	10	9	7	5	7	3	11	99
Cal	6	2	—	8	6	4	9	5	12	5	9	9	5	7	87
ChA	1	3	7	—	8	2	8	4	8	1	7	7	11	4	71
Cle	6	8	4	2	—	5	5	5	5	6	4	8	1	10	69
Det	8	3	7	9	10	—	4	7	4	4	6	8	7	9	86
KC	8	6	6	7	6	6	—	6	7	6	10	12	7	5	92
Mil	8	5	5	7	10	8	4	—	4	10	9	5	6	12	93
Min	5	2	3	7	5	6	8	7	—	3	9	6	6	6	73
NYA	9	9	5	9	9	11	5	5	7	—	8	6	6	11	100
Oak	0	5	6	8	6	4	5	1	6	2	—	13	6	7	69
Sea	1	3	8	8	1	2	3	5	9	5	2	—	3	8	56
Tex	4	7	10	4	9	3	8	4	9	4	9	12	—	4	87
Tor	7	4	3	6	4	6	5	3	4	4	4	2	7	—	59
Lost	71	64	75	90	90	76	70	69	89	63	93	104	75	102	

Seasons: Standings, Leaders

1978 American League Batting Leaders

Games		At-Bats		Runs		Hits		Doubles		Triples	
J. Rice, Bos	163	J. Rice, Bos	677	R. LeFlore, Det	126	J. Rice, Bos	213	G. Brett, KC	45	J. Rice, Bos	15
C. Chambliss, NYA	162	R. LeFlore, Det	666	J. Rice, Bos	121	R. LeFlore, Det	198	C. Fisk, Bos	39	R. Carew, Min	10
R. Staub, Det	162	R. Staub, Det	642	D. Baylor, Cal	103	R. Carew, Min	188	H. McRae, KC	39	D. Ford, Min	10
E. Murray, Bal	161	R. Burleson, Bos	626	A. Thornton, Cle	97	T. Munson, NYA	183	D. DeCinces, Bal	37	R. Yount, Mil	9
2 tied with	159	C. Chambliss, NYA	625	L. Hisle, Mil	96	R. Staub, Det	175	D. Ford, Min	36	R. Garr, ChA	9

Home Runs		Total Bases		Runs Batted In		Walks		Intentional Walks		Strikeouts	
J. Rice, Bos	46	J. Rice, Bos	406	J. Rice, Bos	139	M. Hargrove, Tex	107	R. Carew, Min	19	G. Alexander, 2tm	166
D. Baylor, Cal	34	E. Murray, Bal	293	R. Staub, Det	121	K. Singleton, Bal	98	D. Porter, KC	14	R. Jackson, NYA	133
L. Hisle, Mil	34	D. Baylor, Cal	279	L. Hisle, Mil	115	S. Kemp, Det	97	F. Lynn, Bos	11	G. Thomas, Mil	133
A. Thornton, Cle	33	R. Staub, Det	279	A. Thornton, Cle	105	A. Thornton, Cle	93	B. Oglivie, Mil	10	J. Rice, Bos	126
G. Thomas, Mil	32	J. Thompson, Det	278	2 tied with	99	R. Smalley, Min	85	D. Baylor, Cal	9	B. Hobson, Bos	122

Hit By Pitch		Sac Hits		Sac Flies		Stolen Bases		Caught Stealing		GDP	
D. Baylor, Cal	18	B. Campaneris, Tex	25	D. Baylor, Cal	12	R. LeFlore, Det	68	M. Dilone, Oak	23	L. Bostock, Cal	26
R. Jackson, NYA	9	R. Smalley, Min	23	A. Cowens, KC	11	J. Cruz, Sea	59	B. Bonds, 2tm	22	R. Staub, Det	24
R. Jackson, Cal	9	L. Gomez, Tor	19	R. Staub, Det	11	B. Wills, Tex	52	M. Edwards, Oak	21	B. Bell, Cle	24
L. Roberts, Sea	8	B. Grich, Cal	19	H. McRae, KC	11	M. Dilone, Oak	50	M. Page, Oak	19	G. Nettles, NYA	20
C. Lemon, ChA	8	M. Guerrero, Oak	17	2 tied with	10	W. Wilson, KC	46	R. LeFlore, Det	16	T. Munson, NYA	20

Runs Created		Runs Created/27 Outs		Batting Average		On-Base Percentage		Slugging Percentage		OBP+Slugging	
J. Rice, Bos	141	J. Rice, Bos	7.73	R. Carew, Min	.333	R. Carew, Min	.411	J. Rice, Bos	.600	J. Rice, Bos	.970
C. Fisk, Bos	101	A. Otis, KC	7.19	A. Oliver, Tex	.324	K. Singleton, Bal	.409	L. Hisle, Mil	.533	L. Hisle, Mil	.906
R. LeFlore, Det	101	L. Roberts, Sea	6.74	J. Rice, Bos	.315	M. Hargrove, Tex	.388	D. DeCinces, Bal	.526	A. Otis, KC	.905
F. Lynn, Bos	100	F. Lynn, Bos	6.63	L. Piniella, NYA	.314	W. Randolph, NYA	.381	A. Otis, KC	.525	A. Thornton, Cle	.893
A. Otis, KC	99	L. Hisle, Mil	6.63	B. Oglivie, Mil	.303	F. Lynn, Bos	.380	A. Thornton, Cle	.516	L. Roberts, Sea	.879

1978 American League Pitching Leaders

Wins		Losses		Winning Percentage		Games		Games Started		Complete Games	
R. Guidry, NYA	25	R. Wise, Cle	19	R. Guidry, NYA	.893	B. Lacey, Oak	74	M. Flanagan, Bal	40	M. Caldwell, Mil	23
M. Caldwell, Mil	22	D. Leonard, KC	17	B. Stanley, Bos	.882	D. Heaverlo, Oak	69	D. Leonard, KC	40	D. Leonard, KC	20
D. Leonard, KC	21	J. Jefferson, Tor	16	L. Gura, KC	.800	E. Sosa, Oak	68	D. Martinez, Bal	38	J. Palmer, Bal	19
J. Palmer, Bal	21	K. Kravec, ChA	16	D. Eckersley, Bos	.714	G. Gossage, NYA	63	J. Palmer, Bal	38	J. Matlack, Tex	18
2 tied with	20	5 tied with	15	M. Caldwell, Mil	.710	3 tied with	59	P. Splittorff, KC	38	2 tied with	17

Shutouts		Saves		Games Finished		Batters Faced		Innings Pitched		Hits Allowed	
R. Guidry, NYA	9	G. Gossage, NYA	27	G. Gossage, NYA	55	D. Leonard, KC	1218	J. Palmer, Bal	296.0	D. Leonard, KC	283
M. Caldwell, Mil	6	D. LaRoche, Cal	25	M. Marshall, Min	51	J. Palmer, Bal	1197	D. Leonard, KC	294.2	L. Sorensen, Mil	277
J. Palmer, Bal	6	D. Stanhouse, Bal	24	A. Hrabosky, KC	47	M. Caldwell, Mil	1176	M. Caldwell, Mil	293.1	M. Torrez, Bos	272
L. Tiant, Bos	5	M. Marshall, Min	21	D. Stanhouse, Bal	47	M. Flanagan, Bal	1160	M. Flanagan, Bal	281.1	M. Flanagan, Bal	271
5 tied with	4	A. Hrabosky, KC	20	J. Willoughby, ChA	47	L. Sorensen, Mil	1150	L. Sorensen, Mil	280.2	R. Erickson, Min	268

Home Runs Allowed		Walks		Walks/9 Innings		Strikeouts		Strikeouts/9 Innings		Strikeout/Walk Ratio	
D. Eckersley, Bos	30	N. Ryan, Cal	148	F. Jenkins, Tex	1.5	N. Ryan, Cal	260	N. Ryan, Cal	10.0	F. Jenkins, Tex	3.83
J. Jefferson, Tor	28	R. Gale, KC	100	L. Sorensen, Mil	1.6	R. Guidry, NYA	248	R. Guidry, NYA	8.2	R. Guidry, NYA	3.44
D. Leonard, KC	27	M. Torrez, Bos	99	M. Caldwell, Mil	1.7	D. Leonard, KC	183	K. Kravec, ChA	6.8	J. Matlack, Tex	3.08
J. Slaton, Det	27	J. Palmer, Bal	97	J. Matlack, Tex	1.7	M. Flanagan, Bal	167	T. Underwood, Tor	6.3	M. Caldwell, Mil	2.43
2 tied with	26	K. Kravec, ChA	95	D. Rozema, Det	1.8	D. Eckersley, Bos	162	C. Knapp, Cal	6.0	D. Leonard, KC	2.35

Earned Run Average		Component ERA		Hit Batsmen		Wild Pitches		Opponent Average		Opponent OBP	
R. Guidry, NYA	1.74	R. Guidry, NYA	1.71	K. Kravec, ChA	10	N. Ryan, Cal	13	R. Guidry, NYA	.193	R. Guidry, NYA	.249
J. Matlack, Tex	2.27	M. Caldwell, Mil	2.39	D. Leonard, KC	9	M. Keough, Oak	12	N. Ryan, Cal	.220	M. Caldwell, Mil	.273
M. Caldwell, Mil	2.36	L. Gura, KC	2.49	F. Tanana, Cal	9	D. Leonard, KC	12	J. Palmer, Bal	.227	F. Jenkins, Tex	.278
J. Palmer, Bal	2.46	J. Matlack, Tex	2.65	7 tied with	8	D. Clyde, Cle	11	L. Gura, KC	.229	J. Matlack, Tex	.283
D. Goltz, Min	2.49	F. Jenkins, Tex	2.71			4 tied with	10	L. Tiant, Bos	.234	L. Gura, KC	.283

1978 American League Miscellaneous

Managers

Baltimore	Earl Weaver	90-71
Boston	Don Zimmer	99-64
California	Dave Garcia	25-20
	Jim Fregosi	62-55
Chicago	Bob Lemon	34-40
	Larry Doby	37-50
Cleveland	Jeff Torborg	69-90
Detroit	Ralph Houk	86-76
Kansas City	Whitey Herzog	92-70
Milwaukee	George Bamberger	93-69
Minnesota	Gene Mauch	73-89
New York	Billy Martin	52-42
	Dick Howser	0-1
	Bob Lemon	48-20
Oakland	Bobby Winkles	24-15
	Jack McKeon	45-78
Seattle	Darrell Johnson	56-104
Texas	Billy Hunter	86-75
	Pat Corrales	1-0
Toronto	Roy Hartsfield	59-102

Awards

Most Valuable Player	Jim Rice, of, Bos
Cy Young	Ron Guidry, NYA
Rookie of the Year	Lou Whitaker, 2b, Det
STATS Manager of the Year	Bob Lemon, NYA

STATS All-Star Team

C	Carlton Fisk, Bos	.284	20	88
1B	Andre Thornton, Cle	.262	33	105
2B	Willie Randolph, NYA	.279	3	42
3B	Doug DeCinces, Bal	.286	28	80
SS	Roy Smalley, Min	.273	19	77
OF	Larry Hisle, Mil	.290	34	115
OF	Amos Otis, KC	.298	22	96
OF	Jim Rice, Bos	.315	46	139
DH	Don Baylor, Cal	.255	34	99
P	Mike Caldwell, Mil	22-9	2.36	131 K
P	Dennis Eckersley, Bos	20-8	2.99	162 K
P	Ron Guidry, NYA	25-3	1.74	248 K
P	Jim Palmer, Bal	21-12	2.46	138 K
RP	Goose Gossage, NYA	10-11	2.01	27 Sv

Postseason

LCS	New York 3 vs. Kansas City 1
World Series	NYA (AL) 4 vs. Los Angeles (NL) 2

Outstanding Performances

Cycles

Andre Thornton, Cle   on April 22
Mike Cubbage, Min   on July 27

1978 National League Standings

	Overall					Home Games						Road Games						Park Index		Record by Month					
EAST	W	L	Pct	GB	DIF	W	L	R	OR	HR	OHR	W	L	R	OR	HR	OHR	Run	HR	M/A	May	June	July	Aug	S/O
Philadelphia	90	72	.556	—	135	54	28	405	279	80	70	36	44	303	307	53	48	109	145	10-7	12-14	18-10	15-14	16-14	19-13
Pittsburgh	88	73	.547	1.5	6	55	26	389	310	57	61	33	47	295	327	58	42	111	117	10-9	12-16	13-13	13-14	18-12	22-9
Chicago	79	83	.488	11.0	31	44	38	393	387	41	76	35	45	271	337	31	49	125	143	11-9	13-11	14-15	13-16	15-14	13-18
Montreal	76	86	.469	14.0	11	41	39	299	283	46	49	35	47	334	328	75	68	90	68	11-8	14-14	12-16	13-19	11-16	15-13
St. Louis	69	93	.426	21.0	5	37	44	289	307	29	32	32	49	311	350	50	62	90	54	9-12	9-20	12-15	10-17	18-11	11-18
New York	66	96	.407	24.0	9	33	47	295	340	37	60	33	49	312	350	49	54	98	97	10-12	13-15	10-18	12-17	8-17	13-17
WEST																									
Los Angeles	95	67	.586	—	77	54	27	361	272	78	59	41	40	366	301	71	48	95	115	13-7	14-13	17-12	17-12	18-10	16-13
Cincinnati	92	69	.571	2.5	21	49	31	379	338	74	61	43	38	331	350	62	61	107	111	13-8	17-11	14-14	18-10	10-18	20-8
San Francisco	89	73	.549	6.0	94	50	31	291	244	47	30	39	42	322	350	70	54	80	62	10-10	20-6	17-13	16-14	14-13	12-17
San Diego	84	78	.519	11.0	2	50	31	291	245	31	23	34	47	300	353	44	51	82	57	7-12	14-17	16-13	17-13	16-13	14-13
Houston	74	88	.457	21.0	1	50	31	327	254	30	29	24	57	278	380	40	57	88	61	10-12	10-13	13-14	15-17	14-14	12-18
Atlanta	69	93	.426	26.0	1	39	42	364	400	87	89	30	51	236	350	36	43	130	223	6-14	12-13	13-16	17-13	11-17	10-20

Clinch Date—Philadelphia 9/30, Los Angeles 9/24.

Team Batting

Team	G	AB	R	OR	H	2B	3B	HR	TB	RBI	TBB	IBB	SO	HBP	SH	SF	SB	CS	SB%	GDP	Avg	OBP	Slg
Los Angeles	162	5437	727	573	1435	251	27	149	2187	686	610	76	818	20	111	47	137	52	.72	101	.264	.345	.402
Cincinnati	161	5392	710	688	1378	270	32	136	2120	669	636	72	899	26	84	54	137	58	.70	112	.258	.343	.393
Philadelphia	162	5448	708	586	1404	248	32	133	2115	661	552	88	866	42	61	49	152	58	.72	93	.258	.336	.388
Pittsburgh	161	5406	684	637	1390	239	54	115	2082	631	480	89	874	42	64	46	213	90	.70	95	.257	.328	.385
Chicago	162	5532	664	724	1461	224	48	72	1997	612	562	61	746	21	84	59	110	58	.65	125	.264	.341	.361
Montreal	162	5530	633	611	1404	269	31	121	2098	589	396	62	881	35	62	40	80	42	.66	126	.254	.312	.379
San Francisco	162	5364	613	594	1331	240	41	117	2004	576	554	75	814	17	127	40	87	54	.62	104	.248	.325	.374
New York	162	5433	607	690	1332	227	47	86	1911	561	549	59	829	24	71	55	100	77	.56	126	.245	.323	.352
Houston	162	5458	605	634	1408	231	45	70	1939	557	434	67	743	22	76	44	178	59	.75	134	.258	.320	.355
Atlanta	162	5381	600	750	1313	191	39	123	1951	558	550	53	874	27	61	47	90	65	.58	140	.244	.323	.363
St. Louis	162	5415	600	657	1351	263	44	79	1939	568	420	55	713	22	55	50	97	42	.70	131	.249	.312	.348
San Diego	162	5360	591	598	1349	208	42	75	1866	542	536	87	848	32	114	39	152	70	.68	81	.252	.328	.348
NL Total	1942	65156	7742	7742	16556	2861	482	1276	24209	7210	6279	844	9905	330	970	573	1533	725	.68	1368	.254	.320	.372
NL Avg Team	162	5430	645	645	1380	238	40	106	2017	601	523	70	825	28	81	48	128	60	.68	114	.254	.320	.372

Team Pitching

Team	G	CG	ShO	Rel	Sv	IP	H	R	ER	HR	SH	SF	HB	TBB	IBB	SO	WP	Bk	H/9	SO/9	BB/9	OAvg	OOBP	ERA
Los Angeles	162	46	16	198	38	1440.1	1362	573	500	83	34	23		440	43	800	35	8	8.5	5.0	2.7	.250	.307	3.12
San Diego	162	21	10	265	55	1433.2	1385	598	523	74	80	50	12	483	92	744	28	20	8.7	4.7	3.0	.257	.317	3.28
San Francisco	162	42	17	239	29	1455.0	1377	594	534	84	87	55	22	453	76	840	32	9	8.5	5.2	2.8	.252	.309	3.30
Philadelphia	162	38	9	234	29	1436.1	1343	586	532	118	75	38	25	393	49	813	29	22	8.4	5.1	2.5	.251	.303	3.33
Pittsburgh	161	30	13	272	44	1444.2	1366	637	548	103	82	39	33	499	61	880	40	12	8.5	5.5	3.1	.249	.313	3.41
Montreal	162	42	13	267	32	1446.0	1332	611	550	117	82	41	29	572	51	740	40	13	8.3	4.6	3.6	.249	.323	3.42
St. Louis	162	32	13	258	22	1437.2	1300	657	572	94	70	58	31	600	66	859	61	17	8.1	5.4	3.8	.245	.323	3.58
Houston	162	48	17	218	23	1440.1	1328	634	581	86	91	61	31	578	54	930	47	21	8.3	5.8	3.6	.247	.320	3.63
Cincinnati	161	16	10	299	46	1448.1	1437	688	613	122	78	57	21	567	83	908	36	17	8.9	5.6	3.5	.261	.329	3.81
New York	162	21	7	280	26	1455.1	1447	690	626	114	92	59	28	531	94	775	33	15	8.9	4.8	3.3	.265	.330	3.87
Chicago	162	24	7	327	38	1455.1	1475	724	655	125	76	44	33	539	93	768	53	12	9.1	4.7	3.3	.265	.331	4.05
Atlanta	162	29	12	293	32	1440.1	1404	750	653	132	89	37	42	624	82	848	67	18	8.8	5.3	3.9	.257	.335	4.08
NL Total	1942	389	144	3140	414	17333.1	16556	7742	6887	1276	970	573	330	6279	844	9905	501	184	8.6	5.1	3.3	.254	.328	3.58
NL Avg Team	162	32	12	262	35	1444.1	1380	645	574	106	81	48	28	523	70	825	42	15	8.6	5.1	3.3	.254	.328	3.58

Team Fielding

Team	G	PO	A	E	TC	DP	PB	Pct
Philadelphia	162	4309	1825	104	6238	156	6	.983
New York	162	4366	1792	132	6290	160	16	.979
Montreal	162	4338	1786	134	6258	150	3	.979
St. Louis	162	4313	1846	136	6295	155	11	.978
Cincinnati	161	4345	1676	134	6155	120	17	.978
Houston	162	4321	1617	133	6071	109	22	.978
Chicago	162	4366	2059	144	6569	154	9	.978
Los Angeles	162	4321	1824	140	6285	138	10	.978
San Francisco	162	4365	1705	146	6216	118	6	.977
Atlanta	162	4321	1739	153	6213	126	32	.975
San Diego	162	4301	1915	160	6376	171	16	.975
Pittsburgh	161	4334	1691	167	6192	133	13	.973
NL Total	1942	52000	21475	1683	75158	1690	161	.978

Team vs. Team Records

	Atl	ChN	Cin	Hou	LA	Mon	NYN	Phi	Pit	SD	SF	StL	Won
Atl	—	5	6	8	5	5	6	8	2	8	11	5	69
ChN	7	—	7	6	4	7	11	4	7	7	4	15	79
Cin	12	5	—	11	9	8	7	7	4	9	12	8	92
Hou	10	6	7	—	7	6	7	6	4	8	6	7	74
LA	13	8	9	11	—	8	7	7	7	9	11	5	95
Mon	7	11	4	6	4	—	8	9	7	6	5	9	76
NYN	6	7	5	5	10		—	6	7	5	3	7	66
Phi	4	14	5	6	5	9	12	—	11	8	6	10	90
Pit	10	11	7	8	5	11	11	7	—	5	4	9	88
SD	10	5	9	10	9	6	7	4	7	—	8	9	84
SF	7	8	6	12	7	7	9	6	8	10	—	9	89
StL	7	3	4	5	7	9	11	8	9	3	3	—	69
Lost	93	83	69	88	67	86	96	72	73	78	73	93	

Seasons: Standings, Leaders

1978 National League Batting Leaders

Games		At-Bats		Runs		Hits		Doubles		Triples	
E. Cabell, Hou	162	E. Cabell, Hou	660	I. DeJesus, ChN	104	S. Garvey, LA	202	P. Rose, Cin	51	G. Templeton, StL	13
S. Garvey, LA	162	D. Cash, Mon	658	P. Rose, Cin	103	P. Rose, Cin	198	J. Clark, SF	46	G. Richards, SD	12
I. DeJesus, ChN	160	P. Rose, Cin	655	D. Parker, Pit	102	E. Cabell, Hou	195	T. Simmons, StL	40	D. Parker, Pit	12
8 tied with	159	L. Bowa, Phi	654	G. Foster, Cin	97	D. Parker, Pit	194	L. Parrish, Mon	39	6 tied with	9
		F. Taveras, Pit	654	O. Moreno, Pit	95	L. Bowa, Phi	192	T. Perez, Mon	38		

Home Runs		Total Bases		Runs Batted In		Walks		Intentional Walks		Strikeouts	
G. Foster, Cin	40	D. Parker, Pit	340	G. Foster, Cin	120	J. Burroughs, Atl	117	D. Parker, Pit	23	D. Murphy, Atl	145
G. Luzinski, Phi	35	G. Foster, Cin	330	D. Parker, Pit	117	D. Evans, SF	105	D. Winfield, SD	20	G. Foster, Cin	138
D. Parker, Pit	30	S. Garvey, LA	319	S. Garvey, LA	113	G. Tenace, SD	101	W. Montanez, NYN	19	G. Luzinski, Phi	135
R. Smith, LA	29	J. Clark, SF	318	G. Luzinski, Phi	101	G. Luzinski, Phi	100	T. Simmons, StL	17	A. Dawson, Mon	128
2 tied with	28	D. Winfield, SD	293	J. Clark, SF	98	R. Cey, LA	96	3 tied with	16	D. Kingman, ChN	111

Hit By Pitch		Sac Hits		Sac Flies		Stolen Bases		Caught Stealing		GDP	
A. Dawson, Mon	12	O. Smith, SD	28	R. Smith, LA	13	O. Moreno, Pit	71	F. Taveras, Pit	25	S. Henderson, NYN	24
G. Luzinski, Phi	11	B. Hooton, LA	18	B. Robinson, Pit	11	F. Taveras, Pit	46	O. Moreno, Pit	22	L. Parrish, Mon	19
G. Tenace, SD	11	T. Whitfield, SF	17	B. Watson, Hou	11	D. Lopes, LA	45	G. Richards, SD	17	T. Simmons, StL	19
R. Hebner, Phi	9	O. Moreno, Pit	17	J. Morgan, Cin	11	I. DeJesus, ChN	41	J. Royster, Atl	17	3 tied with	18
J. Stearns, NYN	8	I. DeJesus, ChN	15	D. Evans, SF	10	O. Smith, SD	40	E. Cabell, Hou	15		

Runs Created		Runs Created/27 Outs		Batting Average		On-Base Percentage		Slugging Percentage		OBP+Slugging	
D. Parker, Pit	126	D. Parker, Pit	8.39	D. Parker, Pit	.334	J. Burroughs, Atl	.432	D. Parker, Pit	.585	D. Parker, Pit	.979
J. Burroughs, Atl	108	J. Burroughs, Atl	7.96	S. Garvey, LA	.316	D. Parker, Pit	.394	R. Smith, LA	.559	J. Burroughs, Atl	.961
G. Foster, Cin	108	R. Smith, LA	7.32	J. Cruz, Hou	.315	G. Tenace, SD	.392	G. Foster, Cin	.546	R. Smith, LA	.942
G. Luzinski, Phi	108	G. Luzinski, Phi	6.95	B. Madlock, SF	.309	G. Luzinski, Phi	.388	J. Clark, SF	.537	G. Luzinski, Phi	.914
2 tied with	101	T. Simmons, StL	6.66	D. Winfield, SD	.308	R. Smith, LA	.382	J. Burroughs, Atl	.529	G. Foster, Cin	.906

1978 National League Pitching Leaders

Wins		Losses		Winning Percentage		Games		Games Started		Complete Games	
G. Perry, SD	21	P. Niekro, Atl	18	G. Perry, SD	.778	K. Tekulve, Pit	91	P. Niekro, Atl	42	P. Niekro, Atl	22
R. Grimsley, Mon	20	B. Forsch, StL	17	D. Robinson, Pit	.700	M. Littell, StL	72	G. Perry, SD	37	R. Grimsley, Mon	19
B. Hooton, LA	19	5 tied with	15	B. Bonham, Cin	.688	D. Moore, ChN	71	6 tied with	36	B. Knepper, SF	16
P. Niekro, Atl	19			B. Hooton, LA	.655	D. Bair, Cin	70			J. Richard, Hou	16
2 tied with	18			R. Grimsley, Mon	.645	R. Moffitt, SF	70			2 tied with	12

Shutouts		Saves		Games Finished		Batters Faced		Innings Pitched		Hits Allowed	
B. Knepper, SF	6	R. Fingers, SD	37	K. Tekulve, Pit	65	P. Niekro, Atl	1389	P. Niekro, Atl	334.1	P. Niekro, Atl	295
V. Blue, SF	4	K. Tekulve, Pit	31	R. Fingers, SD	62	J. Richard, Hou	1139	J. Richard, Hou	275.1	R. Jones, SD	263
B. Blyleven, Pit	4	D. Bair, Cin	28	D. Bair, Cin	56	T. Seaver, Cin	1075	R. Grimsley, Mon	263.0	G. Perry, SD	241
E. Halicki, SF	4	B. Sutter, ChN	27	M. Littell, StL	51	R. Grimsley, Mon	1068	G. Perry, SD	260.2	R. Grimsley, Mon	237
P. Niekro, Atl	4	G. Garber, 2tm	25	G. Garber, 2tm	50	B. Knepper, SF	1062	B. Knepper, SF	260.0	R. Reuschel, ChN	235

Home Runs Allowed		Walks		Walks/9 Innings		Strikeouts		Strikeouts/9 Innings		Strikeout/Walk Ratio	
S. Carlton, Phi	30	J. Richard, Hou	141	L. Christenson, Phi	1.9	J. Richard, Hou	303	J. Richard, Hou	9.9	D. Sutton, LA	2.85
D. Sutton, LA	29	P. Niekro, Atl	102	J. Barr, SF	1.9	P. Niekro, Atl	248	T. Seaver, Cin	7.8	L. Christenson, Phi	2.79
T. Seaver, Cin	26	B. Forsch, StL	97	R. Reuschel, ChN	2.0	T. Seaver, Cin	226	P. Vuckovich, StL	6.8	B. Blyleven, Pit	2.76
J. Montefusco, SF	25	P. Hanna, Atl	93	E. Halicki, SF	2.0	B. Blyleven, Pit	182	B. Blyleven, Pit	6.7	J. Montefusco, SF	2.60
N. Espinosa, NYN	24	T. Seaver, Cin	89	D. Sutton, LA	2.0	J. Montefusco, SF	177	P. Niekro, Atl	6.7	S. Carlton, Phi	2.56

Earned Run Average		Component ERA		Hit Batsmen		Wild Pitches		Opponent Average		Opponent OBP	
C. Swan, NYN	2.43	E. Halicki, SF	2.29	P. Niekro, Atl	13	J. Richard, Hou	16	J. Richard, Hou	.196	E. Halicki, SF	.270
S. Rogers, Mon	2.47	C. Swan, NYN	2.31	R. Burris, ChN	10	R. Reuschel, ChN	13	C. Swan, NYN	.219	C. Swan, NYN	.275
P. Vuckovich, StL	2.54	B. Hooton, LA	2.48	J. Niekro, Hou	9	M. Mahler, Atl	12	E. Halicki, SF	.221	B. Hooton, LA	.275
B. Knepper, SF	2.63	J. Richard, Hou	2.53	M. Lemongello, Hou	9	3 tied with	11	B. Hooton, LA	.226	L. Christenson, Phi	.282
B. Hooton, LA	2.71	B. Knepper, SF	2.56	J. Koosman, NYN	8			T. Seaver, Cin	.227	D. Robinson, Pit	.283

1978 National League Miscellaneous

Managers

Atlanta	Bobby Cox	69-93
Chicago	Herman Franks	79-83
Cincinnati	Sparky Anderson	92-69
Houston	Bill Virdon	74-88
Los Angeles	Tom Lasorda	95-67
Montreal	Dick Williams	76-86
New York	Joe Torre	66-96
Philadelphia	Danny Ozark	90-72
Pittsburgh	Chuck Tanner	88-73
St. Louis	Vern Rapp	6-11
	Jack Krol	1-1
	Ken Boyer	62-81
San Diego	Roger Craig	84-78
San Francisco	Joe Altobelli	89-73

Awards

Most Valuable Player	Dave Parker, of, Pit
Cy Young	Gaylord Perry, SD
Rookie of the Year	Bob Horner, 3b, Atl
STATS Manager of the Year	Roger Craig, SD

STATS All-Star Team

C	Ted Simmons, StL	.287	22	80
1B	Willie Stargell, Pit	.295	28	97
2B	Davey Lopes, LA	.278	17	58
3B	Ron Cey, LA	.270	23	84
SS	Dave Concepcion, Cin	.301	6	67
OF	George Foster, Cin	.281	40	120
OF	Dave Parker, Pit	.334	30	117
OF	Reggie Smith, LA	.295	29	93

P	Vida Blue, SF	18-10	2.79	171 K
P	Burt Hooton, LA	19-10	2.71	104 K
P	Gaylord Perry, SD	21-6	2.73	154 K
P	J.R. Richard, Hou	18-11	3.11	303 K
RP	Rollie Fingers, SD	6-13	2.52	37 Sv

Postseason

LCS	Los Angeles 3 vs. Philadelphia 1
World Series	Los Angeles (NL) 2 vs. NYA (AL) 4

Outstanding Performances

No-Hitters

Bob Forsch, StL	vs. Phi on April 16
Tom Seaver, Cin	vs. StL on June 16

Three-Homer Games

Pete Rose, Cin	on April 29
Dave Kingman, ChN	on May 14
Larry Parrish, Mon	on July 30

Cycles

Chris Speier, Mon	on July 20

1979 American League Standings

EAST	W	L	Pct	GB	DIF	W	L	R	OR	HR	OHR	W	L	R	OR	HR	OHR	Run	HR	M/A	May	June	July	Aug	S/O
				Overall				Home Games						Road Games				Park Index				Record by Month			
Baltimore	102	57	.642	—	151	55	24	369	259	74	57	47	33	388	323	107	76	89	72	14-9	16-9	23-6	18-10	16-11	15-12
Milwaukee	95	66	.590	8.0	16	52	29	401	362	91	81	43	37	406	360	94	81	98	97	13-9	15-14	16-10	19-10	18-12	14-11
Boston	91	69	.569	11.5	24	51	29	470	357	121	59	40	40	371	354	73	74	114	122	13-7	14-12	20-8	15-13	16-13	13-16
New York	89	71	.556	13.5	1	51	30	360	308	77	59	38	41	374	364	73	64	88	97	10-11	16-12	15-13	16-12	15-11	17-12
Detroit	85	76	.528	18.0	1	46	34	394	323	101	74	39	42	376	415	63	93	92	114	7-9	15-12	13-16	18-13	20-12	12-14
Cleveland	81	80	.503	22.0	1	47	34	428	409	87	72	34	46	332	396	73	66	114	134	6-14	15-12	13-15	19-11	16-14	12-14
Toronto	53	109	.327	50.5	1	32	49	345	432	50	74	21	60	268	430	45	91	111	91	7-15	5-23	12-18	8-18	11-17	10-18
WEST																									
California	88	74	.543	—	124	49	32	408	339	71	55	39	42	458	429	93	76	84	75	15-8	15-12	14-15	17-11	11-17	16-11
Kansas City	85	77	.525	3.0	7	46	35	462	421	53	81	39	42	389	395	63	84	113	91	11-10	17-11	14-14	10-17	19-11	14-14
Texas	83	79	.512	5.0	27	44	37	382	335	69	63	39	42	368	363	71	72	98	92	12-7	16-13	16-13	11-16	9-22	19-8
Minnesota	82	80	.506	6.0	31	39	42	415	390	67	61	43	38	349	335	45	67	118	114	13-7	14-12	12-15	16-14	14-16	13-16
Chicago	73	87	.456	14.0	0	33	46	349	401	56	60	40	41	381	347	71	54	106	95	9-11	15-13	9-19	13-16	12-16	15-12
Seattle	67	95	.414	21.0	3	36	45	371	404	88	94	31	50	340	416	44	71	103	158	8-15	10-18	16-12	11-18	12-16	10-16
Oakland	54	108	.333	34.0	0	31	50	262	371	46	65	23	58	311	489	62	82	79	77	8-14	9-19	5-24	8-20	14-15	10-16

Clinch Date—Baltimore 9/22, California 9/25.

Team Batting

Team	G	AB	R	OR	H	2B	3B	HR	TB	RBI	TBB	IBB	SO	HBP	SH	SF	SB	CS	SB%	GDP	Avg	OBP	Slg
California	162	5550	866	768	1563	242	43	164	2383	808	589	42	843	37	79	56	100	53	.65	136	.282	.360	.429
Kansas City	162	5653	851	816	1596	286	79	116	2388	791	528	56	675	35	57	76	207	76	.73	114	.282	.355	.422
Boston	160	5538	841	711	1567	310	34	194	2527	805	512	38	708	33	42	59	60	43	.58	158	.283	.353	.456
Milwaukee	161	5536	807	722	1552	291	41	185	2480	766	549	48	745	20	72	50	100	53	.65	130	.280	.353	.448
Detroit	161	5375	770	738	1446	221	35	164	2229	729	575	28	814	22	56	52	176	86	.67	140	.269	.348	.415
Minnesota	162	5544	764	725	1544	256	42	112	2228	714	526	37	693	31	142	53	66	45	.59	116	.278	.350	.402
Cleveland	161	5376	760	805	1388	206	29	138	2066	707	657	31	786	42	70	60	143	90	.61	122	.258	.350	.384
Baltimore	159	5371	757	582	1401	258	24	181	2250	717	608	52	847	31	42	54	99	49	.67	143	.261	.345	.419
Texas	162	5562	750	698	1549	252	26	140	2273	718	461	49	607	33	78	59	79	51	.61	135	.278	.344	.409
New York	160	5421	734	672	1443	226	40	150	2199	694	509	48	590	18	50	63	65	46	.59	148	.266	.338	.406
Chicago	160	5463	730	748	1505	290	33	127	2242	680	454	29	668	36	58	45	97	62	.61	151	.275	.340	.410
Seattle	162	5544	711	820	1490	250	52	132	2240	676	515	45	725	28	61	54	126	52	.71	158	.269	.340	.404
Toronto	162	5423	613	862	1362	253	34	95	1968	562	448	21	663	36	65	38	75	56	.57	131	.251	.317	.363
Oakland	162	5348	573	860	1276	188	32	108	1852	541	482	36	751	20	75	46	104	69	.60	131	.239	.309	.346
AL Total	2256	76704	10527	10527	20682	3529	548	2006	31325	9908	7413	560	10115	422	947	765	1497	831	.64	1913	.270	.334	.408
AL Avg Team	161	5479	752	752	1477	252	39	143	2238	708	530	40	723	30	68	55	107	59	.64	137	.270	.334	.408

Team Pitching

Team	G	CG	ShO	Rel	Sv	IP	H	R	ER	HR	SH	SF	HB	TBB	IBB	SO	WP	Bk	H/9	SO/9	BB/9	OAvg	OOBP	ERA
Baltimore	159	52	12	167	30	1434.1	1279	582	520	133	59	44	14	467	20	786	36	5	8.0	4.9	2.9	.241	.301	3.26
New York	160	43	10	217	37	1432.1	1446	672	610	123	80	47	14	455	22	731	45	1	9.1	4.6	2.9	.268	.323	3.83
Texas	162	26	10	217	42	1437.0	1371	698	617	135	73	48	28	532	40	773	37	2	8.6	4.8	3.3	.253	.321	3.86
Boston	160	47	11	198	29	1431.1	1487	711	641	133	59	47	37	463	45	731	31	3	9.4	4.6	2.9	.270	.328	4.03
Milwaukee	161	61	12	204	23	1439.2	1563	722	645	162	50	53	20	381	24	580	48	1	9.8	3.6	2.4	.279	.324	4.03
Chicago	160	28	9	236	37	1409.0	1365	748	642	114	65	60	40	618	43	675	50	7	8.7	4.3	3.9	.256	.334	4.10
Minnesota	162	31	6	214	33	1444.1	1590	725	663	128	68	44	15	452	21	721	39	7	9.9	4.5	2.8	.285	.338	4.13
Detroit	161	25	5	221	37	1423.1	1429	738	676	167	72	57	48	547	56	802	51	4	9.0	5.1	3.5	.265	.335	4.27
California	162	46	9	209	33	1436.0	1463	768	692	131	58	63	33	573	33	820	53	5	9.2	5.1	3.6	.267	.336	4.34
Kansas City	162	42	7	239	27	1448.1	1477	816	716	165	81	60	28	536	48	640	40	2	9.2	4.0	3.3	.267	.331	4.45
Cleveland	161	28	7	241	32	1431.1	1502	805	727	138	62	65	23	570	32	781	44	5	9.4	4.9	3.6	.272	.349	4.57
Seattle	162	37	7	217	26	1438.0	1567	820	731	165	75	54	33	571	74	736	43	2	9.8	4.6	3.6	.281	.348	4.58
Oakland	162	41	4	243	20	1429.1	1606	860	754	147	78	70	49	654	67	726	72	4	10.1	4.6	4.1	.288	.363	4.75
Toronto	162	44	7	195	11	1417.0	1537	862	759	165	67	50	40	594	35	613	64	7	9.8	3.9	3.8	.281	.353	4.82
AL Total	2256	551	116	3018	417	20051.2	20682	10527	9393	2006	947	765	422	7413	560	10115	653	55	9.3	4.5	3.3	.270	.343	4.22
AL Avg Team	161	39	8	216	30	1432.2	1477	752	671	143	68	55	30	530	40	723	47	4	9.3	4.5	3.3	.270	.343	4.22

Team Fielding

Team	G	PO	A	E	TC	DP	PB	Pct
New York	160	4297	1970	122	6389	183	15	.981
Detroit	161	4270	1767	120	6157	184	24	.981
Milwaukee	161	4319	1905	127	6351	153	10	.980
Baltimore	159	4303	1764	125	6192	161	10	.980
Texas	162	4311	1862	130	6303	151	8	.979
Minnesota	162	4333	2007	134	6474	203	5	.979
Cleveland	161	4295	1642	134	6071	149	16	.978
Seattle	162	4314	1879	141	6334	170	7	.978
California	162	4308	1608	135	6051	172	12	.978
Boston	160	4294	1853	142	6289	166	20	.977
Kansas City	162	4345	1778	146	6269	160	15	.977
Toronto	162	4251	1878	159	6288	187	8	.975
Chicago	160	4227	1831	173	6231	142	17	.972
Oakland	162	4288	1718	174	6180	137	15	.972
AL Total	2256	60155	25462	1962	87579	2318	182	.978

Team vs. Team Records

	Bal	Bos	Cal	ChA	Cle	Det	KC	Mil	Min	NYA	Oak	Sea	Tex	Tor	Won
Bal	—	8	9	8	8	7	6	8	8	5	8	10	6	11	102
Bos	5	—	5	5	6	8	8	8	9	5	9	9	6	9	91
Cal	3	7	—	9	6	4	7	7	9	7	10	7	5	7	88
ChA	3	6	4	—	6	3	5	5	5	4	9	5	11	7	73
Cle	5	7	6	6	—	6	6	4	8	5	8	7	5	8	81
Det	6	5	8	9	6	—	5	6	4	7	7	7	6	9	85
KC	6	4	6	8	6	7	—	5	7	5	9	7	6	9	85
Mil	5	4	5	7	9	7	7	—	8	9	6	9	9	10	95
Min	4	3	4	8	4	8	6	4	—	7	9	10	4	11	82
NYA	6	8	5	8	8	6	7	4	5	—	9	6	8	9	89
Oak	4	3	3	4	4	5	4	6	4	3	—	3	8	2	54
Sea	2	4	6	8	5	5	6	3	3	6	5	—	6	8	67
Tex	6	6	8	2	7	6	7	3	9	4	11	7	—	7	83
Tor	2	4	5	5	4	4	4	4	4	5	3	1	8	—	53
Lost	57	69	74	87	80	76	77	66	80	71	108	95	79	109	

1979 American League Batting Leaders

Games		At-Bats		Runs		Hits		Doubles		Triples	
6 tied with	162	B. Bell, Tex	670	D. Baylor, Cal	120	G. Brett, KC	212	C. Cooper, Mil	44	G. Brett, KC	20
		C. Lansford, Cal	654	G. Brett, KC	119	J. Rice, Bos	201	C. Lemon, ChA	44	P. Molitor, Mil	16
		W. Horton, Sea	646	J. Rice, Bos	117	B. Bell, Tex	200	G. Brett, KC	42	W. Randolph, NYA	13
		G. Brett, KC	645	F. Lynn, Bos	116	C. Lansford, Cal	188	F. Lynn, Bos	42	W. Wilson, KC	13
		D. Baylor, Cal	628	C. Lansford, Cal	114	P. Molitor, Mil	188	B. Bell, Tex	42	3 tied with	10

Home Runs		Total Bases		Runs Batted In		Walks		Intentional Walks		Strikeouts	
G. Thomas, Mil	45	J. Rice, Bos	369	D. Baylor, Cal	139	D. Porter, KC	121	K. Singleton, Bal	16	G. Thomas, Mil	175
F. Lynn, Bos	39	G. Brett, KC	363	J. Rice, Bos	130	K. Singleton, Bal	109	G. Brett, KC	14	B. Bonds, Cle	135
J. Rice, Bos	39	F. Lynn, Bos	338	G. Thomas, Mil	123	G. Thomas, Mil	98	O. Gamble, 2tm	12	K. Singleton, Bal	118
D. Baylor, Cal	36	D. Baylor, Cal	333	F. Lynn, Bos	122	W. Randolph, NYA	95	B. Oglivie, Mil	12	C. Lansford, Cal	115
K. Singleton, Bal	35	K. Singleton, Bal	304	D. Porter, KC	112	A. Thornton, Cle	90	J. Spencer, NYA	11	W. Horton, Sea	112

Hit By Pitch		Sac Hits		Sac Flies		Stolen Bases		Caught Stealing		GDP	
C. Lemon, ChA	13	R. Wilfong, Min	25	D. Ford, Cal	13	W. Wilson, KC	83	B. Bonds, Cle	23	B. Bochte, Sea	27
G. Roenicke, Bal	12	J. Castino, Min	22	D. Porter, KC	13	R. LeFlore, Det	78	A. Griffin, Tor	16	G. Scott, 3tm	24
D. Baylor, Cal	11	N. Norman, Tex	18	D. Baylor, Cal	12	J. Cruz, Sea	49	M. Page, Oak	16	B. Hobson, Bos	23
R. Jackson, Min	9	A. Griffin, Tor	16	3 tied with	10	A. Bumbry, Bal	37	R. LeFlore, Det	14	L. Johnson, ChA	23
3 tied with	8	R. Smalley, Min	15			B. Wills, Tex	35	A. Trammell, Det	14	W. Randolph, NYA	23

Runs Created		Runs Created/27 Outs		Batting Average		On-Base Percentage		Slugging Percentage		OBP+Slugging	
F. Lynn, Bos	134	F. Lynn, Bos	9.72	F. Lynn, Bos	.333	F. Lynn, Bos	.423	F. Lynn, Bos	.637	F. Lynn, Bos	1.059
G. Brett, KC	131	S. Lezcano, Mil	8.02	G. Brett, KC	.329	D. Porter, KC	.421	J. Rice, Bos	.596	S. Lezcano, Mil	.987
J. Rice, Bos	131	J. Rice, Bos	7.88	B. Downing, Cal	.326	B. Downing, Cal	.418	S. Lezcano, Mil	.573	J. Rice, Bos	.977
D. Baylor, Cal	128	G. Brett, KC	7.71	J. Rice, Bos	.325	S. Lezcano, Mil	.414	G. Brett, KC	.563	S. Kemp, Det	.941
K. Singleton, Bal	120	D. Porter, KC	7.66	A. Oliver, Tex	.323	K. Singleton, Bal	.405	R. Jackson, NYA	.544	G. Brett, KC	.938

1979 American League Pitching Leaders

Wins		Losses		Winning Percentage		Games		Games Started		Complete Games	
M. Flanagan, Bal	23	P. Huffman, Tor	18	R. Davis, NYA	.875	M. Marshall, Min	90	D. Martinez, Bal	39	D. Martinez, Bal	18
T. John, NYA	21	M. Keough, Oak	17	M. Caldwell, Mil	.727	S. Monge, Cle	76	M. Flanagan, Bal	38	N. Ryan, Cal	17
J. Koosman, Min	20	P. Splittorff, KC	17	J. Kern, Tex	.722	J. Kern, Tex	71	F. Jenkins, Tex	37	D. Eckersley, Bos	17
R. Guidry, NYA	18	3 tied with	16	M. Flanagan, Bal	.719	S. Lyle, Tex	67	4 tied with	36	T. John, NYA	17
3 tied with	17			J. Morris, Det	.708	D. Heaverlo, Oak	62			3 tied with	16

Shutouts		Saves		Games Finished		Batters Faced		Innings Pitched		Hits Allowed	
N. Ryan, Cal	5	M. Marshall, Min	32	M. Marshall, Min	84	D. Martinez, Bal	1206	D. Martinez, Bal	292.1	D. Goltz, Min	282
M. Flanagan, Bal	5	J. Kern, Tex	29	J. Kern, Tex	57	T. John, NYA	1116	T. John, NYA	276.1	D. Martinez, Bal	279
D. Leonard, KC	5	D. Stanhouse, Bal	21	S. Lyle, Tex	53	M. Torrez, Bos	1109	M. Flanagan, Bal	265.2	T. John, NYA	268
M. Caldwell, Mil	4	A. Lopez, Det	21	S. Monge, Cle	53	J. Koosman, Min	1101	J. Koosman, Min	263.2	J. Koosman, Min	268
B. Stanley, Bos	4	S. Monge, Cle	19	A. Lopez, Det	49	F. Jenkins, Tex	1089	F. Jenkins, Tex	259.0	M. Torrez, Bos	254

Home Runs Allowed		Walks		Walks/9 Innings		Strikeouts		Strikeouts/9 Innings		Strikeout/Walk Ratio	
F. Jenkins, Tex	40	M. Torrez, Bos	121	S. McGregor, Bal	1.2	N. Ryan, Cal	223	N. Ryan, Cal	9.0	S. McGregor, Bal	3.52
D. Leonard, KC	33	N. Ryan, Cal	114	M. Caldwell, Mil	1.5	R. Guidry, NYA	201	R. Guidry, NYA	7.7	R. Guidry, NYA	2.83
B. Travers, Mil	33	K. Kravec, ChA	111	L. Sorensen, Mil	1.6	M. Flanagan, Bal	190	M. Flanagan, Bal	6.4	M. Flanagan, Bal	2.71
S. Stone, Bal	31	R. Wortham, ChA	100	B. Stanley, Bos	1.8	F. Jenkins, Tex	164	F. Jenkins, Tex	5.7	D. Eckersley, Bos	2.54
L. Sorensen, Mil	30	R. Gale, KC	99	T. John, NYA	2.1	J. Koosman, Min	157	F. Bannister, Sea	5.7	M. Caldwell, Mil	2.28

Earned Run Average		Component ERA		Hit Batsmen		Wild Pitches		Opponent Average		Opponent OBP	
R. Guidry, NYA	2.78	S. McGregor, Bal	2.83	K. Kravec, ChA	14	R. Langford, Oak	16	N. Ryan, Cal	.212	S. McGregor, Bal	.273
T. John, NYA	2.96	R. Guidry, NYA	2.92	M. Wilcox, Det	11	R. Wortham, ChA	14	K. Kravec, ChA	.233	R. Guidry, NYA	.292
D. Eckersley, Bos	2.99	T. John, NYA	2.97	S. McCatty, Oak	10	M. Keough, Oak	13	R. Guidry, NYA	.236	M. Flanagan, Bal	.296
M. Flanagan, Bal	3.08	N. Ryan, Cal	3.07	M. Norris, Oak	9	3 tied with	11	R. Baumgarten, ChA	.243	D. Eckersley, Bos	.297
J. Morris, Det	3.28	M. Flanagan, Bal	3.12	T. Underwood, Tor	9			J. Morris, Det	.244	D. Leonard, KC	.297

1979 American League Miscellaneous

Managers

Baltimore	Earl Weaver	102-57
Boston	Don Zimmer	91-69
California	Jim Fregosi	88-74
Chicago	Don Kessinger	46-60
	Tony La Russa	27-27
Cleveland	Jeff Torborg	43-52
	Dave Garcia	38-28
Detroit	Les Moss	27-26
	Dick Tracewski	2-0
	Sparky Anderson	56-50
Kansas City	Whitey Herzog	85-77
Milwaukee	George Bamberger	95-66
Minnesota	Gene Mauch	82-80
New York	Bob Lemon	34-31
	Billy Martin	55-40
Oakland	Jim Marshall	54-108
Seattle	Darrell Johnson	67-95
Texas	Pat Corrales	83-79
Toronto	Roy Hartsfield	53-109

Awards

Most Valuable Player	Don Baylor, of, Cal
Cy Young	Mike Flanagan, Bal
Rookie of the Year	John Castino, 3b, Min
	Alfredo Griffin, ss, Tor
STATS Manager of the Year	Earl Weaver, Bal

STATS All-Star Team

C	Darrell Porter, KC	.291	20	112
1B	Cecil Cooper, Mil	.308	24	106
2B	Bobby Grich, Cal	.294	30	101
3B	George Brett, KC	.329	23	107
SS	Roy Smalley, Min	.271	24	95
OF	Don Baylor, Cal	.296	36	139
OF	Fred Lynn, Bos	.333	39	122
OF	Jim Rice, Bos	.325	39	130
DH	Willie Horton, Sea	.279	29	106
P	Dennis Eckersley, Bos	17-10	2.99	150 K
P	Mike Flanagan, Bal	23-9	3.08	190 K
P	Ron Guidry, NYA	18-8	2.78	201 K
P	Tommy John, NYA	21-9	2.96	111 K
RP	Jim Kern, Tex	13-5	1.57	29 Sv

Postseason

LCS	Baltimore 3 vs. California 1
World Series	Bal (AL) 3 vs. Pit (NL) 4

Outstanding Performances

Three-Homer Games

Al Oliver, Tex	on May 23
Ben Oglivie, Mil	on July 8
C. Washington, ChA	on July 14
George Brett, KC	on July 22
Cecil Cooper, Mil	on July 27
Eddie Murray, Bal	on August 29
Carney Lansford, Cal	on September 1

Cycles

George Brett, KC	on May 28
Dan Ford, Cal	on August 10
Bob Watson, Bos	on September 15
Frank White, KC	on September 26

1979 National League Standings

EAST	W	L	Pct	GB	DIF	W	L	R	OR	HR	OHR	W	L	R	OR	HR	OHR	Run	HR	M/A	May	June	July	Aug	S/O
											Home Games						**Road Games**		**Park Index**				**Record by Month**			
Pittsburgh	98	64	.605	—	50	48	33	399	339	74	77	**50**	**31**	**376**	**304**	74	48	109	124	7-11	16-10	14-13	20-11	21-9	20-10
Montreal	95	65	.594	2.0	101	**56**	**25**	378	275	68	51	39	40	323	306	75	65	101	83	14-5	15-10	14-12	14-16	15-11	23-11
St. Louis	86	76	.531	12.0	9	42	39	379	372	48	65	44	37	352	321	52	62	112	99	9-10	15-10	12-14	15-15	19-12	16-15
Philadelphia	84	78	.519	14.0	31	43	38	332	342	52	72	41	40	351	376	67	63	93	95	14-5	13-15	12-16	15-13	12-18	18-11
Chicago	80	82	.494	18.0	1	45	36	**423**	370	79	72	35	46	283	337	56	55	128	136	8-9	12-16	16-8	18-13	17-14	9-22
New York	63	99	.389	35.0	6	28	53	267	354	30	58	35	46	326	352	44	62	92	83	8-10	8-18	15-11	13-17	8-22	11-21
WEST																									
Cincinnati	90	71	.559	—	45	48	32	360	298	71	53	42	39	371	346	61	50	93	113	11-10	15-13	15-14	17-14	19-7	13-13
Houston	89	73	.549	1.5	130	52	29	269	**234**	15	**31**	37	44	314	348	34	59	76	49	15-6	14-17	20-8	12-16	15-11	13-15
Los Angeles	79	83	.488	11.5	1	46	35	389	341	**106**	55	33	48	350	376	**77**	**46**	101	131	10-14	16-12	7-20	12-15	17-11	17-11
San Francisco	71	91	.438	19.5	7	38	43	298	361	53	61	33	48	374	390	72	82	86	74	9-14	16-12	13-13	14-16	8-19	11-17
San Diego	68	93	.422	22.0	1	39	42	287	335	36	47	29	51	316	346	57	61	93	69	9-14	15-15	11-17	14-13	8-19	11-15
Atlanta	66	94	.413	23.5	0	34	45	359	425	73	80	32	49	310	338	53	52	124	149	7-13	11-18	13-16	12-17	10-16	13-14

Clinch Date—Pittsburgh 9/30, Cincinnati 9/28.

Team Batting

Team	G	AB	R	OR	H	2B	3B	HR	TB	RBI	TBB	IBB	SO	HBP	SH	SF	SB	CS	SB%	GDP	Avg	OBP	Slg
Pittsburgh	163	5661	**775**	643	1541	264	52	148	**2353**	710	483	**102**	855	32	98	56	180	66	**.73**	113	.272	.339	**.416**
Los Angeles	162	5490	739	717	1443	220	24	**183**	2260	**713**	556	62	834	23	83	36	106	46	.70	**145**	.263	.337	.412
Cincinnati	161	5477	731	644	1445	266	31	132	2169	686	**614**	73	902	19	62	46	99	47	.68	128	.264	.345	.396
St. Louis	163	**5734**	731	693	**1594**	279	**63**	100	2299	685	460	69	838	27	63	**63**	116	69	.63	116	**.278**	.341	.401
Chicago	162	5550	706	707	1494	250	43	135	2235	663	478	49	762	35	77	42	73	52	.58	126	.269	.336	.403
Montreal	160	5465	701	**581**	1445	273	42	143	2231	651	432	68	890	27	67	38	121	56	.68	123	.264	.326	.408
Philadelphia	163	5463	683	718	1453	250	53	119	2166	641	602	66	764	**37**	60	57	128	76	.63	124	.266	**.349**	.396
San Francisco	162	5395	672	751	1328	192	36	125	1967	616	580	61	**925**	20	89	47	140	73	.66	100	.246	.327	.365
Atlanta	160	5422	669	763	1389	220	28	126	2043	626	490	47	818	23	62	38	98	50	.66	112	.256	.325	.377
San Diego	161	5446	603	681	1316	193	53	93	1894	559	534	81	770	32	**113**	43	100	58	.63	104	.242	.318	.348
New York	163	5591	593	706	1399	255	41	74	1958	558	498	53	817	35	66	40	135	79	.63	117	.250	.320	.350
Houston	162	5394	583	582	1382	224	52	49	1857	542	461	75	745	22	109	43	**190**	**95**	.67	105	.256	.322	.344
NL Total	1942	66088	8186	8186	17229	2886	518	1427	25432	7650	6188	806	9920	332	949	549	1486	767	.66	1413	.261	.325	.385
NL Avg Team	162	5507	682	682	1436	241	43	119	2119	638	516	67	827	28	79	46	124	64	.66	118	.261	.325	.385

Team Pitching

Team	G	CG	ShO	Rel	Sv	IP	H	R	ER	HR	SH	SF	HB	TBB	IBB	SO	WP	Bk	H/9	SO/9	BB/9	OAvg	OOBP	ERA
Montreal	160	33	18	260	39	1447.1	1379	**581**	505	116	84	**34**	23	**450**	51	813	28	7	8.6	5.1	**2.8**	.253	.310	3.14
Houston	162	**55**	**19**	237	31	1447.2	**1278**	582	514	**90**	65	39	24	504	24	854	**55**	5	**7.9**	5.3	3.1	**.237**	**.304**	3.20
Pittsburgh	163	24	7	326	**52**	**1493.1**	1424	643	566	125	74	46	31	504	77	904	52	9	8.6	5.4	3.0	.254	.316	3.41
Cincinnati	161	27	10	281	40	1440.1	1415	644	573	103	78	50	18	485	63	773	30	7	8.8	4.8	3.0	.260	.319	3.58
San Diego	161	29	7	279	25	1453.0	1438	681	596	108	108	40	23	513	68	779	23	9	8.9	4.8	3.2	.263	.326	3.69
St. Louis	163	38	10	275	25	1486.2	1449	693	615	127	73	47	18	501	54	788	45	10	8.8	4.8	3.0	.258	.318	3.72
Los Angeles	162	30	6	240	34	1444.0	1425	717	614	101	92	50	27	555	53	811	44	11	8.9	5.1	3.5	.260	.329	3.83
New York	163	16	10	**328**	36	1482.2	1486	706	633	120	88	56	24	607	**107**	819	45	11	9.0	5.0	3.7	.266	.338	3.84
Chicago	162	20	11	287	44	1446.2	1500	707	624	127	74	45	43	521	87	**933**	40	5	9.3	**5.8**	3.2	.270	.335	3.88
Philadelphia	163	33	14	261	29	1441.1	1455	718	666	135	**61**	52	29	477	65	787	36	**18**	9.1	4.9	3.0	.266	.325	4.16
San Francisco	162	25	6	302	34	1436.0	1484	751	664	143	82	46	27	577	95	880	50	9	9.3	5.5	3.6	.269	.338	4.16
Atlanta	160	24	7	328	36	1407.2	1496	763	654	142	32	70	44	494	62	779	45	10	9.6	5.0	3.2	.272	.335	4.18
NL Total	1942	362	121	3359	423	17426.2	17229	8186	7224	1427	949	549	332	6188	806	9920	493	111	8.9	5.1	3.2	.261	.332	3.73
NL Avg Team	162	30	10	280	35	1452.2	1436	682	602	119	79	46	28	516	67	827	41	9	8.9	5.1	3.2	.261	.332	3.73

Team Fielding

Team	G	PO	A	E	TC	DP	PB	Pct
Philadelphia	163	4324	1800	**106**	6230	148	5	.983
Los Angeles	162	4332	1669	118	6119	123	21	.981
Cincinnati	161	4321	1738	124	6183	152	9	.980
St. Louis	163	4460	1932	132	**6524**	166	16	.980
Pittsburgh	163	**4480**	1752	134	6366	163	10	.979
Montreal	160	4342	1717	131	6190	123	4	.979
San Diego	161	4359	**1943**	141	6443	154	12	.978
New York	163	4448	1768	140	6356	**168**	15	.978
Houston	162	4343	1707	138	6188	146	18	.978
Chicago	162	4340	1902	159	6401	163	8	.975
San Francisco	162	4308	1806	163	6277	138	17	.974
Atlanta	160	4223	1781	183	6187	139	**25**	.970
NL Total	1942	52280	21515	1669	75464	1783	160	.978

Team vs. Team Records

	Atl	ChN	Cin	Hou	LA	Mon	NYN	Phi	Pit	SD	SF	StL	Won
Atl	—	4	6	7	12	1	4	7	4	6	11	4	**66**
ChN	8	—	7	6	5	6	8	9	6	9	8	8	**80**
Cin	12	5	—	8	11	6	8	8	8	10	6	8	**90**
Hou	11	6	10	—	10	7	9	5	4	14	7	6	**89**
LA	6	7	7	8	—	6	9	3	4	9	14	6	**79**
Mon	9	12	6	5	6	—	15	11	7	7	7	10	**95**
NYN	8	10	4	3	3	3	—	5	8	4	8	7	**63**
Phi	5	9	4	7	9	7	13	—	8	9	6	7	**84**
Pit	8	12	4	8	8	11	10	10	—	7	9	11	**98**
SD	12	3	7	4	9	5	8	3	5	—	8	4	**68**
SF	7	4	12	11	4	5	4	6	3	10	—	5	**71**
StL	8	10	4	6	6	8	11	11	7	8	7	—	**86**
Lost	94	82	71	73	83	65	99	78	64	93	91	76	

1979 National League Batting Leaders

Games		At-Bats		Runs		Hits		Doubles		Triples	
F. Taveras, 2tm	164	O. Moreno, Pit	695	K. Hernandez, StL	116	G. Templeton, StL	211	K. Hernandez, StL	48	G. Templeton, StL	19
P. Rose, Phi	163	F. Taveras, 2tm	680	O. Moreno, Pit	110	K. Hernandez, StL	210	W. Cromartie, Mon	46	A. Dawson, Mon	12
S. Garvey, LA	162	G. Templeton, StL	672	D. Lopes, LA	109	P. Rose, Phi	208	D. Parker, Pit	45	B. McBride, Phi	12
O. Moreno, Pit	162	W. Cromartie, Mon	659	M. Schmidt, Phi	109	S. Garvey, LA	204	K. Reitz, StL	41	O. Moreno, Pit	12
K. Hernandez, StL	161	S. Garvey, LA	648	D. Parker, Pit	109	O. Moreno, Pit	196	P. Rose, Phi	40	2 tied with	11

Home Runs		Total Bases		Runs Batted In		Walks		Intentional Walks		Strikeouts	
D. Kingman, ChN	48	D. Winfield, SD	333	D. Winfield, SD	118	M. Schmidt, Phi	120	D. Winfield, SD	24	D. Kingman, ChN	131
M. Schmidt, Phi	45	D. Parker, Pit	327	D. Kingman, ChN	115	G. Tenace, SD	105	T. Simmons, StL	22	A. Dawson, Mon	115
D. Winfield, SD	34	D. Kingman, ChN	326	M. Schmidt, Phi	114	D. Lopes, LA	97	W. Cromartie, Mon	19	M. Schmidt, Phi	115
B. Horner, Atl	33	S. Garvey, LA	322	S. Garvey, LA	110	B. North, SF	96	J. Cruz, Hou	16	G. Tenace, SD	106
W. Stargell, Pit	32	G. Matthews, Atl	317	K. Hernandez, StL	105	P. Rose, Phi	95	S. Garvey, LA	16	2 tied with	105

Hit By Pitch		Sac Hits		Sac Flies		Stolen Bases		Caught Stealing		GDP	
G. Luzinski, Phi	10	C. Reynolds, Hou	34	C. Cedeno, Hou	9	O. Moreno, Pit	77	B. North, SF	24	S. Garvey, LA	25
T. Foli, 2tm	9	O. Smith, SD	22	M. Schmidt, Phi	9	B. North, SF	58	T. Puhl, Hou	22	E. Valentine, Mon	23
D. Parker, Pit	9	T. Foli, 2tm	19	D. Parker, Pit	9	D. Lopes, LA	44	O. Moreno, Pit	21	J. Stearns, NYN	21
R. Hebner, NYN	8	I. DeJesus, ChN	17	5 tied with	8	F. Taveras, 2tm	44	I. DeJesus, ChN	20	R. Knight, Cin	20
G. Richards, SD	8	B. Blyleven, Pit	15			R. Scott, Mon	39	F. Taveras, 2tm	20	B. Russell, LA	20

Runs Created		Runs Created/27 Outs		Batting Average		On-Base Percentage		Slugging Percentage		OBP+Slugging	
D. Winfield, SD	125	K. Hernandez, StL	7.89	K. Hernandez, StL	.344	P. Rose, Phi	.418	D. Kingman, ChN	.613	D. Kingman, ChN	.956
K. Hernandez, StL	123	D. Winfield, SD	7.81	P. Rose, Phi	.331	K. Hernandez, StL	.417	M. Schmidt, Phi	.564	D. Winfield, SD	.953
D. Parker, Pit	123	D. Parker, Pit	7.41	R. Knight, Cin	.318	G. Tenace, SD	.403	G. Foster, Cin	.561	M. Schmidt, Phi	.950
G. Matthews, Atl	117	G. Foster, Cin	7.37	S. Garvey, LA	.315	L. Mazzilli, NYN	.395	D. Winfield, SD	.558	G. Foster, Cin	.947
D. Lopes, LA	111	D. Kingman, ChN	7.17	B. Horner, Atl	.314	D. Winfield, SD	.395	B. Horner, Atl	.552	K. Hernandez, StL	.930

1979 National League Pitching Leaders

Wins		Losses		Winning Percentage		Games		Games Started		Complete Games	
J. Niekro, Hou	21	P. Niekro, Atl	20	J. Bibby, Pit	.750	K. Tekulve, Pit	94	P. Niekro, Atl	44	P. Niekro, Atl	23
P. Niekro, Atl	21	G. Garber, Atl	16	T. Seaver, Cin	.727	E. Romo, Pit	84	R. Jones, SD	39	J. Richard, Hou	19
S. Carlton, Phi	18	B. Shirley, SD	16	B. Blyleven, Pit	.706	G. Jackson, Pit	72	J. Niekro, Hou	38	S. Carlton, Phi	13
R. Reuschel, ChN	18	D. Sutton, LA	15	D. Tidrow, ChN	.688	G. Lavelle, SF	70	J. Richard, Hou	38	S. Rogers, Mon	13
J. Richard, Hou	18	5 tied with	14	2 tied with	.667	G. Garber, Atl	68	2 tied with	37	B. Hooton, LA	12

Shutouts		Saves		Games Finished		Batters Faced		Innings Pitched		Hits Allowed	
J. Niekro, Hou	5	B. Sutter, ChN	37	K. Tekulve, Pit	67	P. Niekro, Atl	1436	P. Niekro, Atl	342.0	P. Niekro, Atl	311
S. Rogers, Mon	5	K. Tekulve, Pit	31	B. Sutter, ChN	56	J. Richard, Hou	1175	J. Richard, Hou	292.1	R. Jones, SD	257
T. Seaver, Cin	5	G. Garber, Atl	25	G. Garber, Atl	55	J. Niekro, Hou	1095	J. Niekro, Hou	263.2	R. Reuschel, ChN	251
S. Carlton, Phi	4	J. Sambito, Hou	22	G. Lavelle, SF	55	R. Jones, SD	1088	R. Jones, SD	263.0	V. Blue, SF	246
J. Richard, Hou	4	G. Lavelle, SF	20	J. Sambito, Hou	51	V. Blue, SF	1041	C. Swan, NYN	251.1	2 tied with	241

Home Runs Allowed		Walks		Walks/9 Innings		Strikeouts		Strikeouts/9 Innings		Strikeout/Walk Ratio	
P. Niekro, Atl	41	P. Niekro, Atl	113	K. Forsch, Hou	1.8	J. Richard, Hou	313	J. Richard, Hou	9.6	J. Richard, Hou	3.19
B. Knepper, SF	30	V. Blue, SF	111	J. Candelaria, Pit	1.8	S. Carlton, Phi	213	S. Carlton, Phi	7.6	L. McGlothen, ChN	2.67
L. McGlothen, ChN	27	J. Niekro, Hou	107	T. Hume, Cin	1.8	P. Niekro, Atl	208	S. Sanderson, Mon	7.4	S. Sanderson, Mon	2.56
J. Candelaria, Pit	25	J. Denny, StL	100	B. Lee, Mon	1.9	B. Blyleven, Pit	172	B. Blyleven, Pit	6.5	C. Swan, NYN	2.54
S. Carlton, Phi	25	J. Richard, Hou	98	C. Swan, NYN	2.0	L. McGlothen, ChN	147	M. Krukow, ChN	6.5	J. Candelaria, Pit	2.46

Earned Run Average		Component ERA		Hit Batsmen		Wild Pitches		Opponent Average		Opponent OBP	
J. Richard, Hou	2.71	J. Richard, Hou	2.23	P. Niekro, Atl	11	J. Niekro, Hou	19	J. Richard, Hou	.209	K. Forsch, Hou	.273
T. Hume, Cin	2.76	K. Forsch, Hou	2.54	R. Reuschel, ChN	10	J. Richard, Hou	19	S. Carlton, Phi	.219	J. Richard, Hou	.276
D. Schatzeder, Mon	2.83	T. Seaver, Cin	2.77	B. Bonham, Cin	8	P. Niekro, Atl	18	D. Schatzeder, Mon	.225	D. Sutton, LA	.288
B. Hooton, LA	2.97	B. Hooton, LA	2.85	C. Hough, LA	8	3 tied with	10	J. Niekro, Hou	.228	T. Seaver, Cin	.289
J. Niekro, Hou	3.00	S. Carlton, Phi	2.88	J. Niekro, Hou	7			J. Andujar, Hou	.233	J. Candelaria, Pit	.290

1979 National League Miscellaneous

Managers

Atlanta	Bobby Cox	66-94
Chicago	Herman Franks	78-77
	Joey Amalfitano	2-5
Cincinnati	John McNamara	90-71
Houston	Bill Virdon	89-73
Los Angeles	Tom Lasorda	79-83
Montreal	Dick Williams	95-65
New York	Joe Torre	63-99
Philadelphia	Danny Ozark	65-67
	Dallas Green	19-11
Pittsburgh	Chuck Tanner	98-64
St. Louis	Ken Boyer	86-76
San Diego	Roger Craig	68-93
San Francisco	Joe Altobelli	61-79
	Dave Bristol	10-12

Awards

Most Valuable Player	Willie Stargell, 1b, Pit
	K. Hernandez, 1b, StL
Cy Young	Bruce Sutter, ChN
Rookie of the Year	Rick Sutcliffe, p, LA
STATS Manager of the Year	Dick Williams, Mon

STATS All-Star Team

C	Ted Simmons, StL	.283	26	87
1B	Keith Hernandez, StL	.344	11	105
2B	Davey Lopes, LA	.265	28	73
3B	Mike Schmidt, Phi	.253	45	114
SS	Garry Templeton, StL	.314	9	62
OF	Dave Kingman, ChN	.288	48	115
OF	Dave Parker, Pit	.310	25	94
OF	Dave Winfield, SD	.308	34	118
P	Steve Carlton, Phi	18-11	3.62	213 K
P	Joe Niekro, Hou	21-11	3.00	119 K
P	Phil Niekro, Atl	21-20	3.39	208 K
P	J.R. Richard, Hou	18-13	2.71	313 K
RP	Bruce Sutter, ChN	6-6	2.22	37 Sv

Postseason

LCS	Pittsburgh 3 vs. Cincinnati 0
World Series	Pit (NL) 4 vs. Bal (AL) 3

Outstanding Performances

No-Hitters

Ken Forsch, Hou vs. Atl on April 7

Three-Homer Games

Dave Kingman, ChN on May 17
Dale Murphy, Atl on May 18
Mike Schmidt, Phi on July 7
Dave Kingman, ChN on July 28

1980 American League Standings

EAST	Overall W	L	Pct	GB	DIF	Home Games W	L	R	OR	HR	OHR	Road Games W	L	R	OR	HR	OHR	Park Index Run	HR	Record by Month M/A	May	June	July	Aug	S/O
New York	103	59	.636	—	158	53	28	409	315	91	47	50	31	411	347	98	55	96	90	9-9	19-7	19-9	16-12	15-14	25-8
Baltimore	100	62	.617	3.0	3	50	31	397	319	75	81	50	31	408	321	81	53	98	116	7-11	15-13	17-9	16-11	21-8	24-10
Milwaukee	86	76	.531	17.0	12	40	42	368	336	90	65	46	34	443	346	113	72	87	82	7-8	16-12	18-10	13-16	15-18	17-12
Boston	83	77	.519	19.0	8	36	45	370	420	79	74	47	32	387	347	83	55	105	108	8-9	14-14	16-10	12-16	20-7	13-21
Detroit	84	78	.519	19.0	2	43	38	440	404	77	95	41	40	390	353	66	57	114	140	7-11	12-14	16-13	15-11	15-17	17-17
Cleveland	79	81	.494	23.0	1	44	35	400	389	55	66	35	46	338	418	34	71	107	118	5-10	16-13	13-13	15-11	18-15	12-19
Toronto	67	95	.414	36.0	16	35	46	311	386	56	75	32	49	313	376	70	60	101	101	9-7	13-14	10-17	11-17	11-20	13-20
WEST																									
Kansas City	97	65	.599	—	138	49	32	397	335	47	51	48	33	412	359	68	78	95	67	10-8	17-10	17-12	18-9	23-7	12-19
Oakland	83	79	.512	14.0	21	46	35	337	277	58	57	37	44	349	365	79	85	86	70	12-8	13-13	7-21	19-10	14-14	18-13
Minnesota	77	84	.478	19.5	1	44	36	392	361	51	63	33	48	278	363	48	57	119	110	10-10	8-19	13-13	16-12	10-21	20-9
Texas	76	85	.472	20.5	7	39	41	380	365	58	57	37	44	376	387	66	62	99	91	10-8	12-15	13-15	14-13	15-15	12-19
Chicago	70	90	.438	26.0	15	37	42	281	350	41	37	33	48	306	372	50	71	95	66	12-6	12-17	11-14	10-18	10-17	13-18
California	65	95	.406	31.0	1	35	44	330	403	49	76	35	44	368	394	57	65	94	100	8-10	11-15	6-21	12-16	14-15	14-18
Seattle	59	103	.364	38.0	4	36	45	340	389	74	99	23	58	270	404	30	60	108	192	11-10	12-14	9-18	7-19	8-21	12-21

Clinch Date—New York 10/04, Kansas City 9/17.

Team Batting

Team	G	AB	R	OR	H	2B	3B	HR	TB	RBI	TBB	IBB	SO	HBP	SH	SF	SB	CS	SB%	GDP	Avg	OBP	Slg
Detroit	163	5648	830	757	1543	232	53	143	2310	767	645	35	844	33	63	55	75	68	.52	144	.273	.357	.409
New York	162	5553	820	662	1484	239	34	189	2358	772	643	58	739	28	51	54	86	36	.70	136	.267	.352	.425
Milwaukee	162	5653	811	682	1555	298	36	203	2534	774	455	59	745	25	58	51	131	56	.70	98	.275	.337	.448
Kansas City	162	5714	809	694	1633	266	59	115	2362	766	508	45	709	38	34	63	185	43	.81	147	.286	.355	.413
Baltimore	162	5585	805	640	1523	258	29	156	2307	751	587	38	766	21	42	46	111	38	.74	158	.273	.349	.413
Boston	160	5603	757	767	1588	297	36	162	2443	717	475	48	720	32	40	50	79	48	.62	151	.283	.348	.436
Texas	163	5690	756	752	1616	263	27	124	2305	720	480	51	589	23	70	56	91	49	.65	156	.284	.348	.405
Cleveland	160	5470	738	807	1517	221	40	89	2085	692	617	51	625	37	60	74	118	58	.67	165	.277	.362	.381
California	160	5443	698	797	1442	236	32	106	2060	655	539	38	889	32	71	49	91	63	.59	141	.265	.340	.378
Oakland	162	5495	686	642	1424	212	35	137	2117	635	506	49	824	19	99	41	175	82	.68	124	.259	.328	.385
Minnesota	161	5530	670	724	1468	252	46	99	2109	634	436	40	703	21	92	51	62	46	.57	151	.265	.327	.381
Toronto	162	5571	624	762	1398	249	53	126	2131	580	448	44	813	33	63	34	67	72	.48	120	.251	.314	.383
Seattle	163	5489	610	793	1359	211	35	104	1952	564	483	44	727	19	106	44	116	62	.65	136	.248	.316	.356
Chicago	162	5444	587	722	1408	255	38	91	2012	547	399	46	670	39	67	51	68	54	.56	142	.259	.320	.370
AL Total	2264	77888	10201	10201	20958	3489	553	1844	31085	9574	7221	646	10363	400	916	719	1455	775	.65	1969	.269	.331	.399
AL Avg Team	162	5563	729	729	1497	249	40	132	2220	684	516	46	740	29	65	51	104	55	.65	141	.269	.331	.399

Team Pitching

Team	G	CG	ShO	Rel	Sv	IP	H	R	ER	HR	SH	SF	HB	TBB	IBB	SO	WP	Bk	H/9	SO/9	BB/9	OAvg	OOBP	ERA
Oakland	162	94	9	146	13	1471.2	1347	642	566	142	46	47	31	521	29	769	51	8	8.2	4.7	3.2	.244	.310	3.46
New York	162	29	15	210	50	1464.1	1433	662	583	102	75	56	22	463	26	845	45	3	8.8	5.2	2.8	.259	.316	3.58
Baltimore	162	42	10	190	41	1460.0	1438	640	591	134	51	39	21	507	33	789	43	4	8.9	4.9	3.1	.261	.323	3.64
Milwaukee	162	48	14	231	30	1450.0	1530	682	597	137	41	58	24	420	37	575	33	6	9.5	3.6	2.6	.273	.323	3.71
Kansas City	162	37	10	201	42	1459.1	1496	694	621	129	63	50	19	465	47	614	35	1	9.2	3.8	2.9	.267	.323	3.83
Chicago	162	32	12	236	42	1435.1	1434	722	625	108	91	58	39	563	44	724	48	12	9.0	4.5	3.5	.263	.333	3.92
Minnesota	161	35	9	213	30	1451.0	1502	724	634	120	67	55	23	468	32	744	32	10	9.3	4.6	2.9	.272	.328	3.93
Texas	163	35	6	256	25	1452.1	1561	752	649	119	65	52	37	519	49	890	58	5	9.7	5.5	3.2	.277	.339	4.02
Toronto	162	39	9	286	23	1466.0	1523	762	683	135	92	47	28	635	57	705	41	5	9.3	4.3	3.9	.274	.348	4.19
Detroit	163	40	9	210	30	1467.1	1505	757	693	152	71	49	27	558	72	741	52	6	9.2	4.5	3.4	.267	.334	4.25
Boston	160	30	8	238	43	1441.1	1557	767	701	129	59	49	31	481	54	696	28	6	9.7	4.3	3.0	.279	.337	4.38
Seattle	163	31	7	236	26	1457.1	1565	793	710	159	75	49	27	540	94	703	31	7	9.7	4.3	3.3	.278	.341	4.38
California	160	22	6	268	30	1428.1	1548	797	717	141	69	56	39	549	35	725	32	9	9.8	4.6	3.3	.278	.342	4.52
Cleveland	160	35	8	225	32	1428.0	1519	807	743	137	51	54	32	552	37	843	59	4	9.6	5.3	3.5	.275	.341	4.68
AL Total	2264	549	132	3146	457	20332.1	20958	10201	9113	1844	916	719	400	7221	646	10363	588	85	9.3	4.6	3.2	.269	.340	4.03
AL Avg Team	162	39	9	225	33	1452.1	1497	729	651	132	65	51	29	516	46	740	42	6	9.3	4.6	3.2	.269	.340	4.03

Team Fielding

Team	G	PO	A	E	TC	DP	PB	Pct
Baltimore	162	4380	1818	95	6293	178	11	.985
Cleveland	160	4284	1713	105	6102	143	10	.983
Toronto	162	4398	1939	133	6470	206	8	.979
Detroit	163	4402	1787	133	6322	165	26	.979
Oakland	162	4415	1631	130	6176	115	9	.979
New York	162	4393	1852	138	6383	160	16	.978
Kansas City	162	4378	1820	141	6339	150	15	.978
California	160	4285	1576	134	5995	144	10	.978
Minnesota	161	4353	1996	148	6497	192	8	.977
Milwaukee	162	4350	1886	147	6383	189	6	.977
Seattle	163	4372	1930	149	6451	189	13	.977
Boston	160	4324	1937	149	6410	206	6	.977
Texas	163	4357	1818	147	6322	169	21	.977
Chicago	162	4306	1923	171	6400	162	13	.973
AL Total	2264	60997	25626	1920	88543	2368	172	.978

Team vs. Team Records

	Bal	Bos	Cal	ChA	Cle	Det	KC	Mil	Min	NYA	Oak	Sea	Tex	Tor	Won
Bal	—	8	10	6	6	10	6	7	10	7	7	6	6	11	100
Bos	5	—	9	6	7	8	5	6	6	3	9	7	5	7	83
Cal	2	3	—	3	4	5	5	6	7	2	3	11	11	3	65
ChA	6	4	10	—	5	2	5	5	5	6	6	6	6	5	70
Cle	7	6	6	7	—	3	5	3	9	5	6	8	6	8	79
Det	3	5	7	10	10	—	2	7	6	5	6	10	4	9	84
KC	6	7	8	8	7	10	—	6	5	8	6	7	10	9	97
Mil	6	7	6	7	10	6	6	—	7	5	7	9	5	5	86
Min	2	6	6	6	3	6	8	5	—	4	6	7	9	7	77
NYA	6	10	10	7	8	8	4	8	8	—	8	9	7	10	103
Oak	5	3	10	7	6	6	7	5	7	4	—	8	7	8	83
Sea	6	5	2	7	4	2	6	3	6	3	5	—	4	6	59
Tex	6	7	2	7	6	8	3	7	3	5	6	9	—	7	76
Tor	2	6	9	7	5	4	3	8	5	3	4	6	5	—	67
Lost	62	77	95	90	81	78	65	76	84	59	79	103	85	95	

Seasons: Standings, Leaders

1980 American League Batting Leaders

Games		At-Bats		Runs		Hits		Doubles		Triples	
A. Oliver, Tex	163	W. Wilson, KC	705	W. Wilson, KC	133	W. Wilson, KC	230	R. Yount, Mil	49	A. Griffin, Tor	15
G. Thomas, Mil	162	A. Oliver, Tex	656	R. Yount, Mil	121	C. Cooper, Mil	219	A. Oliver, Tex	43	W. Wilson, KC	15
J. Morrison, ChA	162	A. Griffin, Tor	653	A. Bumbry, Bal	118	M. Rivers, Tex	210	J. Morrison, ChA	40	K. Landreaux, Min	11
W. Wilson, KC	161	A. Bumbry, Bal	645	R. Henderson, Oak	111	A. Oliver, Tex	209	H. McRae, KC	39	U. Washington, KC	11
3 tied with	160	R. Burleson, Bos	644	A. Trammell, Det	107	A. Bumbry, Bal	205	D. Evans, Bos	37	R. Yount, Mil	10

Home Runs		Total Bases		Runs Batted In		Walks		Intentional Walks		Strikeouts	
R. Jackson, NYA	41	C. Cooper, Mil	335	C. Cooper, Mil	122	W. Randolph, NYA	119	B. Oglivie, Mil	19	G. Thomas, Mil	170
B. Oglivie, Mil	41	B. Oglivie, Mil	333	G. Brett, KC	118	R. Henderson, Oak	117	G. Brett, KC	16	T. Armas, Oak	128
G. Thomas, Mil	38	E. Murray, Bal	322	B. Oglivie, Mil	118	M. Hargrove, Cle	111	C. Cooper, Mil	15	R. Jackson, NYA	122
T. Armas, Oak	35	R. Yount, Mil	317	A. Oliver, Tex	117	D. Murphy, Oak	102	R. Jackson, NYA	15	L. Parrish, Det	109
E. Murray, Bal	32	A. Oliver, Tex	315	E. Murray, Bal	116	T. Harrah, Cle	98	B. Bochte, Sea	13	B. Grich, Cal	108

Hit By Pitch		Sac Hits		Sac Flies		Stolen Bases		Caught Stealing		GDP	
C. Fisk, Bos	13	D. Murphy, Oak	22	C. Lansford, Cal	11	R. Henderson, Oak	100	R. Henderson, Oak	26	T. Perez, Bos	25
C. Lemon, ChA	12	J. Castino, Min	21	R. Cerone, NYA	10	W. Wilson, KC	79	A. Griffin, Tor	23	R. Burleson, Bos	24
D. Baylor, Cal	11	B. Wills, Tex	15	M. Hargrove, Cle	10	M. Dilone, Cle	61	M. Dilone, Cle	18	L. Parrish, Det	24
4 tied with	8	L. Milbourne, Sea	15	A. Otis, KC	10	J. Cruz, Sea	45	R. Carew, Cal	15	S. Kemp, Det	24
		J. Dybzinski, Cle	14	6 tied with	9	A. Bumbry, Bal	44	D. Murphy, Oak	15	J. Charboneau, Cle	24

Runs Created		Runs Created/27 Outs		Batting Average		On-Base Percentage		Slugging Percentage		OBP+Slugging	
R. Henderson, Oak	121	G. Brett, KC	10.72	G. Brett, KC	.390	G. Brett, KC	.454	G. Brett, KC	.664	G. Brett, KC	1.118
A. Bumbry, Bal	119	R. Jackson, NYA	8.54	C. Cooper, Mil	.352	W. Randolph, NYA	.427	R. Jackson, NYA	.597	R. Jackson, NYA	.995
G. Brett, KC	118	W. Randolph, NYA	7.46	M. Dilone, Cle	.341	R. Henderson, Oak	.420	B. Oglivie, Mil	.563	C. Cooper, Mil	.926
C. Cooper, Mil	118	C. Cooper, Mil	7.26	M. Rivers, Tex	.333	M. Hargrove, Cle	.415	C. Cooper, Mil	.539	B. Oglivie, Mil	.925
R. Jackson, NYA	117	R. Henderson, Oak	7.23	R. Carew, Cal	.331	J. Thompson, 2tm	.398	R. Yount, Mil	.519	K. Singleton, Bal	.882

1980 American League Pitching Leaders

Wins		Losses		Winning Percentage		Games		Games Started		Complete Games	
S. Stone, Bal	25	B. Kingman, Oak	20	S. Stone, Bal	.781	D. Quisenberry, KC	75	D. Leonard, KC	38	R. Langford, Oak	28
T. John, NYA	22	G. Zahn, Min	18	D. Darwin, Tex	.765	D. Corbett, Min	73	M. Flanagan, Bal	37	M. Norris, Oak	24
M. Norris, Oak	22	R. Honeycutt, Sea	17	R. May, NYA	.750	A. Lopez, Det	67	S. Stone, Bal	37	M. Keough, Oak	20
D. Leonard, KC	20	4 tied with	16	S. McGregor, Bal	.714	S. Monge, Cle	67	5 tied with	36	L. Gura, KC	16
S. McGregor, Bal	20			2 tied with	.710	3 tied with	64			T. John, NYA	16

Shutouts		Saves		Games Finished		Batters Faced		Innings Pitched		Hits Allowed	
T. John, NYA	6	G. Gossage, NYA	33	D. Quisenberry, KC	68	L. Gura, KC	1175	R. Langford, Oak	290.0	M. Flanagan, Bal	278
G. Zahn, Min	5	D. Quisenberry, KC	33	D. Corbett, Min	63	D. Leonard, KC	1172	M. Norris, Oak	284.1	R. Langford, Oak	276
L. Gura, KC	4	E. Farmer, ChA	30	A. Lopez, Det	59	R. Langford, Oak	1166	L. Gura, KC	283.1	G. Zahn, Min	273
S. McGregor, Bal	4	T. Stoddard, Bal	26	G. Gossage, NYA	58	M. Norris, Oak	1135	D. Leonard, KC	280.1	L. Gura, KC	272
D. Stieb, Tor	4	T. Burgmeier, Bos	24	E. Farmer, ChA	55	T. John, NYA	1089	T. John, NYA	265.1	D. Leonard, KC	271

Home Runs Allowed		Walks		Walks/9 Innings		Strikeouts		Strikeouts/9 Innings		Strikeout/Walk Ratio	
D. Leonard, KC	30	J. Clancy, Tor	128	J. Matlack, Tex	1.8	L. Barker, Cle	187	L. Barker, Cle	6.8	R. May, NYA	3.41
M. Caldwell, Mil	29	S. Stone, Bal	101	P. Splittorff, KC	1.9	M. Norris, Oak	180	R. May, NYA	6.8	J. Matlack, Tex	2.96
R. Langford, Oak	29	S. McCatty, Oak	99	T. John, NYA	1.9	R. Guidry, NYA	166	R. Guidry, NYA	6.8	D. Eckersley, Bos	2.75
3 tied with	27	J. Beattie, Sea	98	F. Tanana, Cal	2.0	F. Bannister, Sea	155	F. Bannister, Sea	6.4	M. Haas, Mil	2.61
		M. Keough, Oak	94	R. Langford, Oak	2.0	D. Leonard, KC	155	G. Perry, 2tm	5.9	F. Tanana, Cal	2.51

Earned Run Average		Component ERA		Hit Batsmen		Wild Pitches		Opponent Average		Opponent OBP	
R. May, NYA	2.46	M. Norris, Oak	2.26	S. Trout, ChA	9	L. Barker, Cle	14	M. Norris, Oak	.209	R. May, NYA	.268
M. Norris, Oak	2.53	R. May, NYA	2.38	G. Perry, 2tm	8	M. Keough, Oak	13	R. May, NYA	.224	M. Norris, Oak	.270
B. Burns, ChA	2.84	B. Burns, ChA	2.89	S. McCatty, Oak	8	M. Flanagan, Bal	12	J. Clancy, Tor	.233	D. Eckersley, Bos	.289
M. Keough, Oak	2.92	T. Underwood, NYA	3.16	F. Tanana, Cal	8	D. Leonard, KC	12	M. Keough, Oak	.236	B. Burns, ChA	.293
L. Gura, KC	2.95	R. Langford, Oak	3.18	C. Knapp, Cal	8	2 tied with	10	T. Underwood, NYA	.237	R. Langford, Oak	.294

1980 American League Miscellaneous

Managers

Baltimore	Earl Weaver	100-62
Boston	Don Zimmer	82-73
	Johnny Pesky	1-4
California	Jim Fregosi	65-95
Chicago	Tony La Russa	70-90
Cleveland	Dave Garcia	79-81
Detroit	Sparky Anderson	84-78
Kansas City	Jim Frey	97-65
Milwaukee	Buck Rodgers	26-21
	George Bamberger	47-45
	Buck Rodgers	13-10
Minnesota	Gene Mauch	54-71
	John Goryl	23-13
New York	Dick Howser	103-59
Oakland	Billy Martin	83-79
Seattle	Darrell Johnson	39-65
	Maury Wills	20-38
Texas	Pat Corrales	76-85
Toronto	Bobby Mattick	67-95

Awards

Most Valuable Player	George Brett, 3b, KC
Cy Young	Steve Stone, Bal
Rookie of the Year	Joe Charboneau, of, Cle
STATS Manager of the Year	Dick Howser, NYA

STATS All-Star Team

C	Lance Parrish, Det	.286	24	82
1B	Cecil Cooper, Mil	.352	25	122
2B	Willie Randolph, NYA	.294	7	46
3B	George Brett, KC	.390	24	118
SS	Robin Yount, Mil	.293	23	87
OF	Rickey Henderson, Oak	.303	9	53
OF	Reggie Jackson, NYA	.300	41	111
OF	Ben Oglivie, Mil	.304	41	118
DH	Hal McRae, KC	.297	14	83
P	Larry Gura, KC	18-10	2.95	113 K
P	Tommy John, NYA	22-9	3.43	78 K
P	Mike Norris, Oak	22-9	2.53	180 K
P	Steve Stone, Bal	25-7	3.23	149 K
RP	Goose Gossage, NYA	6-2	2.27	33 Sv

Postseason

LCS	Kansas City 3 vs. New York 0
World Series	KC (AL) 2 vs. Philadelphia (NL) 4

Outstanding Performances

Three-Homer Games

Otto Velez, Tor	on May 4
Freddie Patek, Cal	on June 20
Al Oliver, Tex	on August 17
Eddie Murray, Bal	on September 14

Cycles

Fred Lynn, Bos	on May 13
Gary Ward, Min	on September 18
Charlie Moore, Mil	on October 1

1980 National League Standings

EAST		Overall				Home Games						Road Games						Park Index		Record by Month					
	W	L	Pct	GB	DIF	W	L	R	OR	HR	OHR	W	L	R	OR	HR	OHR	Run	HR	M/A	May	June	July	Aug	S/O
Philadelphia	91	71	.562	—	26	49	32	398	334	64	44	42	39	330	305	53	43	115	113	6-9	17-9	14-14	15-14	16-14	23-11
Montreal	90	72	.556	1.0	73	51	29	357	286	51	40	39	43	337	343	63	60	97	76	6-10	15-10	18-11	15-14	15-16	21-11
Pittsburgh	83	79	.512	8.0	88	47	34	355	322	63	53	36	45	311	324	53	57	107	105	11-5	14-13	13-16	18-10	14-17	13-18
St. Louis	74	88	.457	17.0	2	41	40	396	357	41	42	33	48	342	353	60	48	108	77	8-10	8-18	15-14	14-13	12-16	17-17
New York	67	95	.414	24.0	2	38	44	306	336	35	80	29	51	305	366	26	60	93	130	6-10	13-13	15-14	14-14	11-20	8-24
Chicago	64	98	.395	27.0	3	37	44	338	385	54	62	27	54	276	343	53	54	117	116	9-6	11-15	11-18	9-18	11-20	13-21
WEST																									
Houston	93	70	.571	—	112	55	26	329	255	26	22	38	44	308	334	49	47	92	51	13-5	12-14	18-9	13-16	18-12	19-14
Los Angeles	92	71	.564	1.0	57	55	27	327	272	82	58	37	44	336	319	66	47	90	122	13-7	15-11	14-14	13-14	18-11	19-14
Cincinnati	89	73	.549	3.5	27	44	37	356	349	66	70	45	36	351	321	47	43	105	151	13-6	11-15	11-15	16-14	18-10	18-14
Atlanta	81	80	.503	11.0	0	50	30	352	297	84	79	31	50	278	363	60	52	103	147	6-11	11-15	15-13	14-15	19-11	16-15
San Francisco	75	86	.466	17.0	0	44	37	283	293	24	41	31	49	290	341	56	51	90	60	6-14	13-13	15-13	16-11	16-13	9-22
San Diego	73	89	.451	19.5	3	45	36	295	274	29	33	28	53	296	380	38	64	84	61	7-11	16-13	10-18	11-15	11-19	18-13

Clinch Date—Philadelphia 10/04, Houston 10/06.

Team Batting

Team	G	AB	R	OR	H	2B	3B	HR	TB	RBI	TBB	IBB	SO	HBP	SH	SF	SB	CS	SB%	GDP	Avg	OBP	Slg
St. Louis	162	5608	738	710	1541	300	49	101	2242	688	451	74	781	21	73	49	117	54	.68	141	.275	.336	.400
Philadelphia	162	5625	728	639	1517	272	54	117	2248	674	472	65	708	33	77	54	140	62	.69	116	.262	.336	.386
Cincinnati	163	5516	707	670	1445	256	45	113	2130	668	537	68	852	23	78	54	156	43	.78	116	.262	.336	.386
Montreal	162	5465	694	629	1407	250	61	114	2121	647	547	75	865	20	76	56	237	82	.74	102	.257	.333	.388
Pittsburgh	162	5517	666	646	1469	249	38	116	2142	626	452	85	760	25	75	56	209	102	.67	107	.266	.331	.388
Los Angeles	163	5568	663	591	1462	209	24	148	2163	638	492	52	846	24	96	41	123	72	.63	108	.263	.330	.388
Houston	163	5566	637	589	1455	231	67	75	2045	599	540	73	755	13	89	45	194	74	.72	96	.261	.333	.367
Atlanta	161	5402	630	660	1352	226	22	144	2054	597	434	49	899	20	69	33	73	52	.58	124	.250	.312	.380
Chicago	162	5619	614	728	1411	251	35	107	2053	578	471	54	912	18	69	40	93	64	.59	119	.251	.316	.365
New York	162	5478	611	702	1407	218	41	61	1890	554	501	63	840	25	73	53	158	99	.61	126	.257	.328	.345
San Diego	163	5540	591	654	1410	195	43	67	1892	546	563	70	791	21	92	38	239	73	.77	113	.255	.330	.342
San Francisco	161	5368	573	634	1310	199	44	80	1837	539	509	61	840	14	100	54	100	58	.63	122	.244	.317	.342
NL Total	1946	66272	7852	7852	17186	2856	523	1243	24817	7354	5969	789	9849	257	967	577	1839	835	.69	1394	.259	.320	.374
NL Avg Team	162	5523	654	654	1432	238	44	104	2068	613	497	66	821	21	81	48	153	70	.69	116	.259	.320	.374

Team Pitching

Team	G	CG	ShO	Rel	Sv	IP	H	R	ER	HR	SH	SF	HB	TBB	IBB	SO	WP	Bk	H/9	SO/9	BB/9	OAvg	OOBP	ERA
Houston	163	31	18	246	41	1482.2	1367	589	511	69	64	42	25	466	26	929	38	8	8.3	5.6	2.8	.246	.305	3.10
Los Angeles	163	24	19	266	42	1472.2	1358	591	531	105	77	49	12	480	48	835	32	15	8.3	5.1	2.9	.247	.306	3.25
Philadelphia	162	25	8	277	40	1480.0	1419	639	564	87	75	53	20	530	83	889	51	23	8.6	5.4	3.2	.255	.319	3.43
San Francisco	161	27	10	288	35	1448.1	1446	634	556	92	78	44	30	492	78	811	31	21	9.0	5.0	3.1	.261	.323	3.46
Montreal	162	33	15	280	36	1456.2	1447	629	563	100	83	45	22	460	42	823	37	6	8.9	5.1	2.8	.261	.317	3.48
Pittsburgh	162	25	8	271	43	1458.1	1422	646	580	110	74	42	27	451	52	832	28	12	8.8	5.1	2.8	.259	.316	3.58
San Diego	163	19	9	296	39	1466.1	1474	654	595	97	99	46	12	536	113	728	39	14	9.0	4.5	3.3	.267	.331	3.65
Atlanta	161	29	9	289	37	1428.0	1397	660	598	131	81	44	26	454	49	696	36	7	8.8	4.4	2.9	.258	.316	3.77
Cincinnati	163	30	12	262	37	1459.1	1404	670	624	113	74	38	13	506	60	833	35	19	8.7	5.1	3.1	.255	.317	3.85
New York	162	17	9	324	33	1451.1	1473	702	621	140	96	51	21	510	77	886	38	13	9.1	5.5	3.2	.267	.328	3.85
Chicago	162	13	6	344	35	1479.0	1525	728	639	109	105	66	28	589	85	923	39	17	9.3	5.6	3.6	.272	.340	3.89
St. Louis	162	34	9	297	27	1447.0	1454	710	632	90	61	57	21	495	76	664	39	17	9.0	4.1	3.1	.265	.326	3.93
NL Total	1946	307	132	3440	445	17529.2	17186	7852	7014	1243	967	577	257	5969	789	9849	443	172	8.8	5.1	3.1	.259	.328	3.60
NL Avg Team	162	26	11	287	37	1460.2	1432	654	585	104	81	48	21	497	66	821	37	14	8.8	5.1	3.1	.259	.328	3.60

Team Fielding

Team	G	PO	A	E	TC	DP	PB	Pct
Cincinnati	163	4378	1730	106	6214	144	12	.983
St. Louis	162	4341	1959	122	6422	174	12	.981
Los Angeles	163	4418	1830	123	6371	149	12	.981
San Diego	163	4399	2012	132	6543	157	6	.980
Philadelphia	162	4440	1936	136	6512	136	8	.979
Pittsburgh	162	4375	1819	137	6331	154	6	.978
Houston	163	4448	1784	140	6372	145	24	.978
Montreal	162	4370	1784	144	6298	126	7	.977
New York	162	4354	1682	154	6190	132	2	.975
San Francisco	161	4345	1825	159	6329	124	7	.975
Atlanta	161	4284	1950	162	6396	156	14	.975
Chicago	162	4437	2030	174	6641	149	12	.974
NL Total	1946	52589	22341	1689	76619	1746	122	.978

Team vs. Team Records

	Atl	ChN	Cin	Hou	LA	Mon	NYN	Phi	Pit	SD	SF	StL	Won
Atl	—	8	2	7	11	5	3	5	11	12	11	6	81
ChN	4	—	7	1	5	6	10	5	8	4	5	9	64
Cin	16	5	—	8	9	3	8	7	6	15	7	5	89
Hou	11	11	10	—	9	5	8	3	7	11	11	7	93
LA	7	7	9	10	—	11	7	6	6	9	13	7	92
Mon	7	12	9	7	1	—	10	9	6	10	7	12	90
NYN	9	8	4	4	5	8	—	6	10	1	3	9	67
Phi	7	13	5	9	6	9	12	—	7	8	6	9	91
Pit	1	10	6	5	6	6	12	8	—	6	8	10	83
SD	6	8	3	7	9	2	11	4	6	—	10	7	73
SF	6	7	11	7	5	5	9	6	4	8	—	7	75
StL	6	9	7	5	5	6	9	9	8	5	5	—	74
Lost	80	98	73	70	71	72	95	71	79	89	86	88	

1980 National League Batting Leaders

Games		At-Bats		Runs		Hits		Doubles		Triples	
S. Garvey, LA	163	O. Moreno, Pit	676	K. Hernandez, StL	111	S. Garvey, LA	200	P. Rose, Phi	42	R. Scott, Mon	13
5 tied with	162	S. Garvey, LA	658	M. Schmidt, Phi	104	G. Richards, SD	193	A. Dawson, Mon	41	O. Moreno, Pit	13
		P. Rose, Phi	655	D. Murphy, Atl	98	K. Hernandez, StL	191	B. Buckner, ChN	41	L. Herndon, SF	11
		G. Richards, SD	642	A. Dawson, Mon	96	B. Buckner, ChN	187	R. Knight, Cin	39	R. LeFlore, Mon	11
		D. Concepcion, Cin	622	2 tied with	95	2 tied with	185	K. Hernandez, StL	39	2 tied with	10

Home Runs		Total Bases		Runs Batted In		Walks		Intentional Walks		Strikeouts	
M. Schmidt, Phi	48	M. Schmidt, Phi	342	M. Schmidt, Phi	121	D. Driessen, Cin	93	W. Cromartie, Mon	24	D. Murphy, Atl	133
B. Horner, Atl	35	S. Garvey, LA	307	G. Hendrick, StL	109	J. Morgan, Hou	93	C. Speier, Mon	18	M. Schmidt, Phi	119
D. Murphy, Atl	33	K. Hernandez, StL	294	S. Garvey, LA	106	G. Tenace, SD	92	D. Driessen, Cin	17	D. Concepcion, Cin	107
D. Baker, LA	29	D. Baker, LA	291	G. Carter, Mon	101	M. Schmidt, Phi	89	3 tied with	14	J. Martin, ChN	107
G. Carter, Mon	29	D. Murphy, Atl	290	K. Hernandez, StL	99	K. Hernandez, StL	86			O. Moreno, Pit	101

Hit By Pitch		Sac Hits		Sac Flies		Stolen Bases		Caught Stealing		GDP	
6 tied with	6	O. Smith, SD	23	M. Schmidt, Phi	13	R. LeFlore, Mon	97	O. Moreno, Pit	33	W. Cromartie, Mon	24
		J. Niekro, Hou	18	D. Baker, LA	12	O. Moreno, Pit	96	D. Collins, Cin	21	R. Knight, Cin	24
		S. Rogers, Mon	15	J. Clark, SF	10	D. Collins, Cin	79	R. LeFlore, Mon	19	D. Concepcion, Cin	20
		B. Hooton, LA	14	A. Dawson, Mon	10	R. Scott, Mon	63	B. North, SF	19	J. Mumphrey, SD	18
		3 tied with	13	5 tied with	9	G. Richards, SD	61	F. Taveras, NYN	18	3 tied with	17

Runs Created		Runs Created/27 Outs		Batting Average		On-Base Percentage		Slugging Percentage		OBP+Slugging	
M. Schmidt, Phi	126	M. Schmidt, Phi	8.25	B. Buckner, ChN	.324	K. Hernandez, StL	.408	M. Schmidt, Phi	.624	M. Schmidt, Phi	1.004
K. Hernandez, StL	119	K. Hernandez, StL	7.50	K. Hernandez, StL	.321	C. Cedeno, Hou	.389	J. Clark, SF	.517	K. Hernandez, StL	.902
D. Murphy, Atl	101	T. Simmons, StL	6.79	G. Templeton, StL	.319	J. Clark, SF	.382	D. Murphy, Atl	.510	J. Clark, SF	.900
A. Dawson, Mon	100	J. Clark, SF	6.77	B. McBride, Phi	.309	M. Schmidt, Phi	.380	T. Simmons, StL	.505	T. Simmons, StL	.881
L. Mazzilli, NYN	98	K. Griffey Sr., Cin	6.43	C. Cedeno, Hou	.309	D. Driessen, Cin	.377	D. Baker, LA	.503	D. Murphy, Atl	.858

1980 National League Pitching Leaders

Wins		Losses		Winning Percentage		Games		Games Started		Complete Games	
S. Carlton, Phi	24	P. Niekro, Atl	18	J. Bibby, Pit	.760	D. Tidrow, ChN	84	S. Carlton, Phi	38	S. Rogers, Mon	14
J. Niekro, Hou	20	B. Knepper, SF	16	J. Reuss, LA	.750	T. Hume, Cin	78	P. Niekro, Atl	38	S. Carlton, Phi	13
J. Bibby, Pit	19	M. Krukow, ChN	15	V. Ruhle, Hou	.750	K. Tekulve, Pit	78	R. Reuschel, ChN	38	J. Niekro, Hou	11
J. Reuss, LA	18	5 tied with	14	S. Carlton, Phi	.727	R. Camp, Atl	77	D. Lamp, ChN	37	P. Niekro, Atl	11
D. Ruthven, Phi	17			D. Sutton, LA	.722	E. Romo, SD	74	S. Rogers, Mon	37	2 tied with	10

Shutouts		Saves		Games Finished		Batters Faced		Innings Pitched		Hits Allowed	
J. Reuss, LA	6	B. Sutter, ChN	28	T. Hume, Cin	62	S. Carlton, Phi	1228	S. Carlton, Phi	304.0	R. Reuschel, ChN	281
J. Richard, Hou	4	T. Hume, Cin	25	K. Tekulve, Pit	57	S. Rogers, Mon	1151	S. Rogers, Mon	281.0	J. Niekro, Hou	268
S. Rogers, Mon	4	R. Fingers, SD	23	T. McGraw, Phi	48	P. Niekro, Atl	1137	P. Niekro, Atl	275.0	D. Lamp, ChN	259
10 tied with	3	N. Allen, NYN	22	N. Allen, NYN	47	J. Niekro, Hou	1096	R. Reuschel, ChN	257.0	P. Niekro, Atl	256
		R. Camp, Atl	22	R. Fingers, SD	46	R. Reuschel, ChN	1094	J. Niekro, Hou	256.0	S. Rogers, Mon	247

Home Runs Allowed		Walks		Walks/9 Innings		Strikeouts		Strikeouts/9 Innings		Strikeout/Walk Ratio	
P. Niekro, Atl	30	N. Ryan, Hou	98	B. Forsch, StL	1.4	S. Carlton, Phi	286	M. Soto, Cin	8.6	S. Carlton, Phi	3.18
L. McWilliams, Atl	27	S. Carlton, Phi	90	J. Reuss, LA	1.6	N. Ryan, Hou	200	S. Carlton, Phi	8.5	B. Blyleven, Pit	2.85
L. McGlothen, ChN	24	J. Bibby, Pit	88	K. Forsch, Hou	1.7	M. Soto, Cin	182	N. Ryan, Hou	7.7	J. Reuss, LA	2.78
T. Seaver, Cin	24	S. Mura, SD	86	J. Candelaria, Pit	1.9	P. Niekro, Atl	176	B. Blyleven, Pit	7.0	D. Sutton, LA	2.72
B. Hooton, LA	22	2 tied with	85	D. Sutton, LA	2.0	B. Blyleven, Pit	168	B. Welch, LA	5.9	B. Forsch, StL	2.64

Earned Run Average		Component ERA		Hit Batsmen		Wild Pitches		Opponent Average		Opponent OBP	
D. Sutton, LA	2.20	J. Reuss, LA	2.08	T. Griffin, SF	8	S. Carlton, Phi	17	M. Soto, Cin	.187	D. Sutton, LA	.257
S. Carlton, Phi	2.34	M. Soto, Cin	2.15	B. Knepper, SF	8	J. Niekro, Hou	12	D. Sutton, LA	.211	J. Reuss, LA	.260
J. Reuss, LA	2.51	D. Sutton, LA	2.20	M. Krukow, ChN	8	J. Curtis, SD	10	S. Carlton, Phi	.218	F. Pastore, Cin	.275
V. Blue, SF	2.97	S. Carlton, Phi	2.29	K. Forsch, Hou	7	D. Lamp, ChN	10	T. Seaver, Cin	.225	S. Carlton, Phi	.276
S. Rogers, Mon	2.98	F. Pastore, Cin	2.54	L. McWilliams, Atl	7	N. Ryan, Hou	10	J. Reuss, LA	.227	M. Soto, Cin	.276

1980 National League Miscellaneous

Managers

Atlanta	Bobby Cox	81-80
Chicago	Preston Gomez	39-51
	Joey Amalfitano	25-47
Cincinnati	John McNamara	89-73
Houston	Bill Virdon	93-70
Los Angeles	Tom Lasorda	92-71
Montreal	Dick Williams	90-72
New York	Joe Torre	67-95
Philadelphia	Dallas Green	91-71
Pittsburgh	Chuck Tanner	83-79
St. Louis	Ken Boyer	18-33
	Jack Krol	0-1
	Whitey Herzog	38-35
	Red Schoendienst	18-19
San Diego	Jerry Coleman	73-89
San Francisco	Dave Bristol	75-86

Awards

Most Valuable Player	Mike Schmidt, 3b, Phi
Cy Young	Steve Carlton, Phi
Rookie of the Year	Steve Howe, p, LA
STATS Manager of the Year	Bill Virdon, Hou

STATS All-Star Team

C	Ted Simmons, StL	.303	21	98
1B	Keith Hernandez, StL	.321	16	99
2B	Manny Trillo, Phi	.292	7	43
3B	Mike Schmidt, Phi	.286	48	121
SS	Garry Templeton, StL	.319	4	43
OF	Andre Dawson, Mon	.308	17	87
OF	Mike Easler, Pit	.338	21	74
OF	Dale Murphy, Atl	.281	33	89
P	Jim Bibby, Pit	19-6	3.32	144 K
P	Steve Carlton, Phi	24-9	2.34	286 K
P	Jerry Reuss, LA	18-6	2.51	111 K
P	Steve Rogers, Mon	16-11	2.98	147 K
RP	Tug McGraw, Phi	5-4	1.46	20 Sv

Postseason

LCS	Philadelphia 3 vs. Houston 2
World Series	Philadelphia (NL) 4 vs. KC (AL) 2

Outstanding Performances

No-Hitters
Jerry Reuss, LA @ SF on June 27

Three-Homer Games
Larry Parrish, Mon on April 25
Johnny Bench, Cin on May 29
C. Washington, NYN on June 22

Cycles
Ivan DeJesus, ChN on April 22
Mike Easler, Pit on June 12

EAST	Overall					Home Games						Road Games						Park Index		Record by Month					
	W	L	Pct	GB	DIF	W	L	R	OR	HR	OHR	W	L	R	OR	HR	OHR	Run	HR	M/A	May	June	July	Aug	S/O
Milwaukee	62	47	.569	—	—	28	21	203	203	33	29	34	26	290	256	63	43	91	72	9-7	18-12	4-6	—	13-9	18-13
Baltimore	59	46	.562	1.0	—	33	22	231	217	49	47	26	24	198	220	39	36	97	116	7-8	21-8	3-7	—	11-9	17-14
New York	59	48	.551	2.0	—	32	19	203	154	47	24	27	29	218	189	53	40	96	84	11-6	14-14	9-2	—	11-10	14-16
Detroit	60	49	.550	2.0	—	32	23	241	196	43	44	28	26	186	208	22	39	109	140	8-11	15-13	8-2	—	13-8	16-15
Boston	59	49	.546	2.5	—	30	23	278	247	52	47	29	26	241	234	38	43	115	127	7-9	18-12	5-5	—	11-9	18-14
Cleveland	52	51	.505	7.0	—	25	29	210	216	19	33	27	22	221	226	20	34	86	87	8-4	15-13	3-7	—	10-12	16-15
Toronto	37	69	.349	23.5	—	17	36	172	272	34	41	20	33	157	194	27	31	126	129	7-12	9-20	0-10	—	9-10	12-17
WEST																									
Oakland	64	45	.587	—		35	21	234	183	57	46	29	24	224	220	47	34	89	120	18-3	13-17	6-3	—	10-9	17-13
Texas	57	48	.543	5.0	—	32	24	232	168	21	24	25	24	220	221	28	43	79	55	10-7	16-12	7-3	—	9-10	15-16
Chicago	54	52	.509	8.5	—	25	24	215	198	31	33	29	28	261	225	45	40	99	88	11-6	15-11	5-5	—	10-10	13-20
Kansas City	50	53	.485	11.0	—	19	28	163	197	17	27	31	25	234	208	44	48	97	57	3-10	12-15	5-5	—	10-11	20-12
California	51	59	.464	13.5	—	26	28	244	233	48	39	25	31	232	220	49	42	109	99	10-11	13-16	8-2	—	11-9	11-20
Seattle	44	65	.404	20.0	—	20	37	226	271	52	53	24	28	200	250	37	23	101	160	5-14	12-16	4-6	—	8-13	15-16
Minnesota	41	68	.376	23.0	—	24	36	213	292	25	47	17	32	165	194	22	32	115	109	6-12	8-20	3-7	—	9-13	15-16

Team Batting

Team	G	AB	R	OR	H	2B	3B	HR	TB	RBI	TBB	IBB	SO	HBP	SH	SF	SB	CS	SB%	GDP	Avg	OBP	Slg
Boston	108	3820	519	481	1052	168	17	90	1524	492	378	18	520	13	37	33	32	31	.51	98	.275	.348	.399
Milwaukee	109	3743	493	459	961	173	20	96	1462	475	300	35	461	29	35	45	39	36	.52	83	.257	.324	.391
California	110	3688	476	453	944	134	16	97	1401	439	393	23	571	29	51	30	44	33	.57	97	.256	.337	.380
Chicago	106	3615	476	423	982	135	27	76	1399	438	322	16	518	43	48	36	86	44	.66	90	.272	.344	.387
Oakland	109	3677	458	403	910	119	26	104	1393	430	342	26	647	16	46	32	98	47	.68	75	.247	.320	.379
Texas	105	3581	452	389	968	178	15	49	1323	418	295	40	396	21	36	39	44	41	.53	84	.270	.336	.369
Cleveland	103	3507	431	442	922	150	21	39	1231	397	343	31	379	13	46	43	119	37	.76	91	.263	.338	.351
Baltimore	105	3516	429	437	883	165	11	88	1334	408	404	29	454	15	26	24	41	34	.55	110	.251	.335	.379
Detroit	109	3600	427	404	922	148	29	65	1323	403	404	33	500	18	50	37	61	37	.62	98	.256	.340	.368
Seattle	110	3780	426	521	950	148	13	89	1391	406	329	24	553	27	41	24	100	50	.67	70	.251	.320	.368
New York	107	3529	421	343	889	148	22	100	1381	403	391	30	434	7	40	27	47	30	.61	99	.252	.332	.391
Kansas City	103	3560	397	405	952	169	29	61	1362	381	301	34	419	17	28	35	100	53	.65	84	.267	.334	.383
Minnesota	110	3676	378	486	884	147	36	47	1244	359	275	28	497	11	36	27	34	27	.56	95	.240	.300	.338
Toronto	106	3521	329	466	797	137	23	61	1163	314	284	23	556	20	44	18	66	57	.54	72	.226	.291	.330
AL Total	1500	50813	6112	6112	13016	2119	305	1062	18931	5763	4761	390	6905	279	564	450	913	557	.62	1246	.256	.321	.373
AL Avg Team	107	3630	437	437	930	151	22	76	1352	412	340	28	493	20	40	32	65	40	.62	89	.256	.321	.373

Team Pitching

Team	G	CG	ShO	Rel	Sv	IP	H	R	ER	HR	SH	SF	HB	TBB	IBB	SO	WP	Bk	H/9	SO/9	BB/9	OAvg	OOBP	ERA
New York	107	16	13	161	30	948.0	827	343	305	64	32	30	10	287	17	606	25	5	7.9	5.8	2.7	.235	.293	2.90
Oakland	109	60	11	112	10	993.0	883	403	364	80	50	32	28	370	17	505	30	11	8.0	4.6	3.4	.240	.311	3.30
Texas	105	23	13	142	18	940.1	851	389	355	67	50	23	17	322	34	488	18	2	8.1	4.7	3.1	.243	.308	3.40
Chicago	106	20	8	173	23	940.2	891	423	363	73	39	23	24	336	17	529	24	6	8.5	5.1	3.2	.252	.319	3.47
Detroit	109	33	13	146	22	969.1	840	404	380	83	36	34	27	373	41	476	24	5	7.8	4.4	3.5	.236	.310	3.53
Kansas City	103	24	8	127	24	922.1	909	405	365	75	41	44	20	273	36	404	13	4	8.9	3.9	2.7	.260	.313	3.56
Baltimore	105	25	10	133	23	940.0	923	437	386	83	32	27	14	347	22	489	29	5	8.8	4.7	3.3	.260	.326	3.70
California	110	27	8	155	19	971.1	958	453	399	81	36	34	21	323	24	426	17	5	8.9	3.9	3.0	.261	.321	3.70
Boston	108	19	4	157	24	987.1	983	481	418	90	49	29	28	354	28	536	18	1	9.0	4.9	3.2	.262	.328	3.81
Toronto	106	20	4	189	18	953.1	908	466	404	72	38	36	36	377	27	451	41	4	8.6	4.3	3.6	.252	.326	3.81
Cleveland	103	33	10	111	13	931.0	989	442	401	67	33	37	10	311	15	569	30	2	9.6	5.5	3.0	.274	.330	3.88
Milwaukee	109	11	4	199	35	986.0	994	459	428	72	47	34	11	352	33	448	31	2	9.1	4.1	3.2	.266	.328	3.91
Minnesota	110	13	6	165	22	979.2	1021	486	433	79	45	35	17	376	53	500	19	14	9.4	4.6	3.5	.272	.338	3.98
Seattle	110	10	5	199	23	997.1	1039	521	469	76	36	32	16	360	26	478	40	7	9.4	4.3	3.2	.271	.334	4.23
AL Total	1500	334	117	2169	304	13459.2	13016	6112	5470	1062	564	450	279	4761	390	6905	359	73	8.7	4.6	3.2	.256	.329	3.66
AL Avg Team	107	24	8	155	22	961.2	930	437	391	76	40	32	20	340	28	493	26	5	8.7	4.6	3.2	.256	.329	3.66

Team Fielding

Team	G	PO	A	E	TC	DP	PB	Pct
Detroit	109	2908	1263	67	4238	109	8	.984
Texas	105	2821	1340	69	4230	102	10	.984
Baltimore	105	2820	1212	68	4100	114	11	.983
New York	107	2844	1157	72	4073	100	5	.982
Milwaukee	109	2958	1358	79	4395	135	9	.982
Kansas City	103	2767	1100	72	3939	94	7	.982
Oakland	109	2979	1080	81	4140	74	2	.980
Seattle	110	2992	1285	91	4368	122	9	.979
Chicago	106	2822	1218	87	4127	113	2	.979
Boston	108	2962	1245	91	4298	108	9	.979
Cleveland	103	2793	1156	87	4036	91	8	.978
Minnesota	110	2939	1268	96	4303	103	3	.978
California	110	2914	1286	101	4301	120	6	.977
Toronto	106	2860	1164	105	4129	102	4	.975
AL Total	1500	40379	17132	1166	58677	1487	93	.980

Team vs. Team Records

	Bal	Bos	Cal	ChA	Cle	Det	KC	Mil	Min	NYA	Oak	Sea	Tex	Tor	Won
Bal	—	2	6	3	4	6	5	2	6	7	7	4	2	5	59
Bos	2	—	2	5	7	6	3	6	2	3	7	9	3	4	59
Cal	6	4	—	6	7	3	0	4	3	2	2	6	2	6	51
ChA	6	4	7	—	2	3	2	4	2	5	7	3	2	7	54
Cle	6	2	6	5	—	1	4	3	2	7	3	8	2	4	52
Det	7	1	3	3	5	—	3	5	9	3	1	5	9	6	60
KC	3	3	6	0	4	2	—	4	9	2	3	6	3	5	50
Mil	4	7	3	1	6	8	5	—	9	3	4	2	4	6	62
Min	0	5	3	4	1	3	4	3	—	3	2	3	5	5	41
NYA	6	3	2	7	5	7	10	3	3	—	4	2	5	2	64
Oak	5	5	8	6	2	2	3	2	8	3	—	6	4	10	64
Sea	2	3	4	3	4	1	7	2	6	3	1	—	5	3	44
Tex	1	6	4	4	2	3	4	5	8	4	2	8	—	6	57
Tor	2	0	6	5	2	4	3	4	1	3	2	3	2	—	37
Lost	46	49	59	52	51	49	53	47	68	48	45	65	48	69	

1981 American League Batting Leaders

Games		At-Bats		Runs		Hits		Doubles		Triples	
T. Armas, Oak	109	J. Rice, Bos	451	R. Henderson, Oak	89	R. Henderson, Oak	135	C. Cooper, Mil	35	J. Castino, Min	9
R. Burleson, Cal	109	T. Armas, Oak	440	D. Evans, Bos	84	C. Lansford, Bos	134	A. Oliver, Tex	29	G. Brett, KC	7
L. Whitaker, Det	109	W. Wilson, KC	439	C. Cooper, Mil	70	C. Cooper, Mil	133	T. Paciorek, Sea	28	W. Wilson, KC	7
3 tied with	108	R. Burleson, Cal	430	T. Harrah, Cle	64	W. Wilson, KC	133	G. Brett, KC	27	R. Henderson, Oak	7
		R. Henderson, Oak	423	M. Rivers, Tex	62	T. Paciorek, Sea	132	R. Dauer, Bal	27	H. Baines, ChA	7

Home Runs		Total Bases		Runs Batted In		Walks		Intentional Walks		Strikeouts	
T. Armas, Oak	22	D. Evans, Bos	215	E. Murray, Bal	78	D. Evans, Bos	85	W. Aikens, KC	12	T. Armas, Oak	115
B. Grich, Cal	22	T. Armas, Oak	211	T. Armas, Oak	76	D. Murphy, Oak	73	B. Oglivie, Mil	10	D. Murphy, Oak	91
E. Murray, Bal	22	C. Cooper, Mil	206	B. Oglivie, Mil	72	S. Kemp, Det	70	A. Oliver, Tex	10	L. Moseby, Tor	86
D. Evans, Bos	22	T. Paciorek, Sea	206	D. Evans, Bos	71	R. Henderson, Oak	64	E. Murray, Bal	10	G. Thomas, Mil	85
2 tied with	21	E. Murray, Bal	202	D. Winfield, NYA	68	W. Aikens, KC	62	B. Bell, Tex	10	D. Evans, Bos	85

Hit By Pitch		Sac Hits		Sac Flies		Stolen Bases		Caught Stealing		GDP	
C. Lemon, ChA	13	A. Trammell, Det	16	B. Bell, Tex	10	R. Henderson, Oak	56	R. Henderson, Oak	22	K. Singleton, Bal	21
C. Fisk, ChA	12	M. Mendoza, Tex	14	A. Otis, KC	9	J. Cruz, Sea	43	A. Bumbry, Bal	15	A. Oliver, Tex	17
J. Mayberry, Tor	8	J. Remy, Bos	13	B. Oglivie, Mil	8	R. LeFlore, ChA	36	A. Griffin, Tor	12	C. Cooper, Mil	16
D. Baylor, Cal	7	M. Squires, ChA	13	T. Harrah, Cle	8	W. Wilson, KC	34	R. LeFlore, ChA	11	D. Ford, Cal	16
B. Sample, Tex	7	R. Burleson, Cal	11	4 tied with	7	M. Dilone, Cle	29	4 tied with	10	L. Parrish, Det	16

Runs Created		Runs Created/27 Outs		Batting Average		On-Base Percentage		Slugging Percentage		OBP+Slugging	
D. Evans, Bos	91	D. Evans, Bos	8.05	C. Lansford, Bos	.336	M. Hargrove, Cle	.424	B. Grich, Cal	.543	D. Evans, Bos	.937
R. Henderson, Oak	84	B. Grich, Cal	7.44	T. Paciorek, Sea	.326	D. Evans, Bos	.415	E. Murray, Bal	.534	B. Grich, Cal	.921
C. Cooper, Mil	75	R. Henderson, Oak	7.09	C. Cooper, Mil	.320	R. Henderson, Oak	.408	D. Evans, Bos	.522	E. Murray, Bal	.895
B. Grich, Cal	72	C. Cooper, Mil	6.57	R. Henderson, Oak	.319	S. Kemp, Det	.389	T. Paciorek, Sea	.509	T. Paciorek, Sea	.888
T. Paciorek, Sea	71	E. Murray, Bal	6.51	M. Hargrove, Cle	.317	C. Lansford, Bos	.389	C. Cooper, Mil	.495	C. Lemon, ChA	.874

1981 American League Pitching Leaders

Wins		Losses		Winning Percentage		Games		Games Started		Complete Games	
P. Vuckovich, Mil	14	J. Berenguer, 2tm	13	P. Vuckovich, Mil	.778	D. Corbett, Min	54	D. Leonard, KC	26	R. Langford, Oak	18
D. Martinez, Bal	14	L. Leal, Tor	13	D. Martinez, Bal	.737	R. Fingers, Mil	47	J. Morris, Det	25	S. McCatty, Oak	16
S. McCatty, Oak	14	J. Koosman, 2tm	13	S. McGregor, Bal	.722	S. Rawley, Sea	46	D. Stieb, Tor	25	J. Morris, Det	15
J. Morris, Det	14	J. Clancy, Tor	12	R. Guidry, NYA	.688	J. Easterly, Mil	44	G. Zahn, Cal	25	L. Gura, KC	12
2 tied with	13	3 tied with	11	2 tied with	.667	2 tied with	43	4 tied with	24	M. Norris, Oak	12

Shutouts		Saves		Games Finished		Batters Faced		Innings Pitched		Hits Allowed	
K. Forsch, Cal	4	R. Fingers, Mil	28	D. Corbett, Min	45	D. Leonard, KC	837	D. Leonard, KC	201.2	D. Leonard, KC	202
R. Dotson, ChA	4	G. Gossage, NYA	20	R. Fingers, Mil	41	R. Langford, Oak	823	J. Morris, Det	198.0	R. Langford, Oak	190
S. McCatty, Oak	4	D. Quisenberry, KC	18	D. Quisenberry, KC	35	J. Morris, Det	798	R. Langford, Oak	195.1	G. Zahn, Cal	181
D. Medich, Tex	4	D. Corbett, Min	17	D. Aase, Cal	31	D. Martinez, Bal	753	S. McCatty, Oak	185.2	D. Martinez, Bal	173
3 tied with	3	K. Saucier, Det	13	2 tied with	30	D. Stieb, Tor	748	D. Stieb, Tor	183.2	R. Waits, Cle	173

Home Runs Allowed		Walks		Walks/9 Innings		Strikeouts		Strikeouts/9 Innings		Strikeout/Walk Ratio	
M. Caldwell, Mil	18	J. Morris, Det	78	R. Honeycutt, Tex	1.2	L. Barker, Cle	127	L. Barker, Cle	7.4	R. Guidry, NYA	4.00
G. Zahn, Cal	18	J. Denny, Cle	66	K. Forsch, Cal	1.6	B. Burns, ChA	108	R. Guidry, NYA	7.4	L. Barker, Cle	2.76
M. Norris, Oak	17	J. Clancy, Tor	64	L. Gura, KC	1.8	B. Blyleven, Cle	107	F. Bannister, Sea	6.3	B. Blyleven, Cle	2.67
F. Tanana, Bos	17	M. Norris, Oak	63	D. Leonard, KC	1.8	D. Leonard, KC	107	B. Burns, ChA	6.2	D. Leonard, KC	2.61
D. Leonard, KC	15	D. Martinez, Bal	62	R. Guidry, NYA	1.8	R. Guidry, NYA	104	B. Blyleven, Cle	6.0	R. Honeycutt, Tex	2.35

Earned Run Average		Component ERA		Hit Batsmen		Wild Pitches		Opponent Average		Opponent OBP	
S. McCatty, Oak	2.33	L. Gura, KC	2.23	D. Stieb, Tor	11	M. Norris, Oak	14	S. McCatty, Oak	.211	R. Guidry, NYA	.256
S. Stewart, Bal	2.32	R. Guidry, NYA	2.27	M. Witt, Cal	11	J. Clancy, Tor	12	R. Guidry, NYA	.214	L. Gura, KC	.265
D. Lamp, ChA	2.41	S. McCatty, Oak	2.37	M. Norris, Oak	10	J. Denny, Cle	10	D. Darwin, Tex	.218	R. Honeycutt, Tex	.272
T. John, NYA	2.63	D. Lamp, ChA	2.46	4 tied with	6	L. Leal, Tor	8	J. Morris, Det	.218	S. McCatty, Oak	.277
B. Burns, ChA	2.64	K. Forsch, Cal	2.65			S. Rawley, Sea	8	D. Lamp, ChA	.222	K. Forsch, Cal	.286

1981 American League Miscellaneous

Managers

Baltimore	Earl Weaver	59-46
Boston	Ralph Houk	59-49
California	Jim Fregosi	22-25
	Gene Mauch	29-34
Chicago	Tony La Russa	54-52
Cleveland	Dave Garcia	52-51
Detroit	Sparky Anderson	60-49
Kansas City	Jim Frey	30-40
	Dick Howser	20-13
Milwaukee	Buck Rodgers	62-47
Minnesota	John Goryl	11-25
	Billy Gardner	30-43
New York	Gene Michael	48-34
	Bob Lemon	11-14
Oakland	Billy Martin	64-45
Seattle	Maury Wills	6-18
	Rene Lachemann	38-47
Texas	Don Zimmer	57-48
Toronto	Bobby Mattick	37-69

Awards

Most Valuable Player	Rollie Fingers, p, Mil
Cy Young	Rollie Fingers, Mil
Rookie of the Year	Dave Righetti, p, NYA
STATS Manager of the Year	Billy Martin, Oak

STATS All-Star Team

C	Lance Parrish, Det	.244	10	46
1B	Eddie Murray, Bal	.294	22	78
2B	Bobby Grich, Cal	.304	22	61
3B	Carney Lansford, Bos	.336	4	52
SS	Robin Yount, Mil	.273	10	49
OF	Dwight Evans, Bos	.296	22	71
OF	Rickey Henderson, Oak	.319	6	35
OF	Tom Paciorek, Sea	.326	14	66
DH	Greg Luzinski, ChA	.265	21	62
P	Britt Burns, ChA	10-6	2.64	108 K
P	Ron Guidry, NYA	11-5	2.76	104 K
P	Steve McCatty, Oak	14-7	2.33	91 K
P	Jack Morris, Det	14-7	3.05	97 K
RP	Rollie Fingers, Mil	6-3	1.04	28 Sv

Postseason

Division Series	New York 3 vs. Milwaukee 2
	Oakland 3 vs. Kansas City 0
LCS	New York 3 vs. Oakland 0
World Series	NYA (AL) 2 vs. Los Angeles (NL) 4

Outstanding Performances

Perfect Games
Len Barker, Cle   vs. Tor on May 15

Three-Homer Games
Jeff Burroughs, Sea   on August 14

1981 National League Standings

EAST	W	L	Pct	GB	DIF	W	L	R	OR	HR	OHR	W	L	R	OR	HR	OHR	Run	HR	M/A	May	June	July	Aug	S/O
		Overall						**Home Games**						**Road Games**				**Park Index**				**Record by Month**			
St. Louis	59	43	.578	—	—	32	21	244	218	22	26	27	22	220	199	28	26	102	82	9-3	14-14	7-3	—	12-6	17-17
Montreal	60	48	.556	2.0	—	**38**	**18**	255	170	39	23	22	30	188	224	42	35	96	75	12-4	14-15	4-6	—	11-8	19-15
Philadelphia	59	48	.551	2.5	—	36	19	**295**	261	41	39	23	29	196	211	28	33	129	124	12-6	15-13	7-2	—	7-13	18-14
Pittsburgh	46	56	.451	13.0	—	22	28	189	207	29	29	24	28	218	218	26	31	94	106	7-6	13-14	5-3	—	7-15	14-18
New York	41	62	.398	18.5	—	24	27	186	207	30	38	17	35	162	225	27	36	104	110	4-10	11-17	2-7	—	11-10	13-18
Chicago	38	65	.369	21.5	—	27	30	239	254	**41**	38	11	35	131	229	16	21	111	172	2-13	8-20	5-4	—	11-10	12-18
WEST																									
Cincinnati	66	42	.611	—	—	32	22	226	230	26	41	**34**	**20**	**238**	210	38	26	102	105	11-7	16-13	8-1	—	10-10	21-11
Los Angeles	63	47	.573	4.0	—	33	23	221	171	37	34	30	24	229	**185**	**45**	**20**	91	105	14-5	19-10	3-6	—	12-9	15-17
Houston	61	49	.555	6.0	—	31	20	166	**106**	16	**9**	30	29	228	225	29	31	69	48	7-12	17-12	4-5	—	13-8	20-12
San Francisco	56	55	.505	11.5	—	29	24	218	204	28	19	27	31	209	210	35	38	110	70	9-12	16-13	2-7	—	12-8	17-15
Atlanta	50	56	.472	15.0	—	22	27	182	195	37	41	28	29	213	221	27	21	101	189	9-10	13-13	3-6	—	12-9	13-18
San Diego	41	69	.373	26.0	—	20	35	168	223	9	27	21	34	214	232	23	37	88	60	6-14	13-15	4-4	—	5-17	13-19

Team Batting

Team	G	AB	R	OR	H	2B	3B	HR	TB	RBI	TBB	IBB	SO	HBP	SH	SF	SB	CS	SB%	GDP	Avg	OBP	Slg
Philadelphia	107	3665	**491**	472	**1002**	165	25	69	**1424**	453	372	42	432	**23**	44	37	103	46	.69	79	**.273**	**.350**	**.389**
Cincinnati	108	3637	464	440	972	**190**	24	64	1402	429	375	38	553	18	53	**40**	58	37	.61	**98**	.267	.345	.385
St. Louis	103	3537	464	417	936	158	**45**	50	1334	431	379	41	495	16	46	35	88	45	.66	82	.265	.344	.377
Los Angeles	110	3751	450	356	984	133	20	**82**	1403	427	331	38	550	17	62	27	73	46	.61	83	.262	.329	.374
Montreal	108	3591	443	394	883	146	28	81	1328	424	368	**55**	498	16	63	30	**138**	40	**.78**	74	.246	.324	.370
San Francisco	111	**3766**	427	414	941	161	26	63	1343	399	**386**	49	543	14	65	27	89	50	.64	91	.250	.326	.357
Pittsburgh	103	3576	407	425	920	176	30	55	1321	384	278	37	494	15	54	36	122	52	.70	60	.257	.320	.369
Atlanta	107	3642	395	416	886	148	22	64	1270	366	321	38	540	18	56	18	98	39	.72	83	.243	.311	.349
Houston	110	3693	394	**331**	948	160	35	45	1313	369	340	49	488	8	**79**	35	81	43	.65	69	.257	.321	.356
San Diego	110	3757	382	455	963	170	35	32	1299	350	311	39	525	14	72	30	83	**62**	.57	87	.256	.321	.346
Chicago	106	3546	370	483	838	138	29	57	1205	348	342	44	**611**	13	53	30	72	41	.64	78	.236	.311	.340
New York	105	3493	348	432	868	136	35	57	1245	325	304	35	603	13	41	34	103	42	.71	78	.248	.317	.356
NL Total	1288	43654	5035	5035	11141	1881	354	719	15887	4688	4107	505	6332	185	688	379	1108	543	.67	962	.255	.319	.364
NL Avg Team	107	3638	420	420	928	157	30	60	1324	391	342	42	528	15	57	32	92	45	.67	80	.255	.319	.364

Team Pitching

Team	G	CG	ShO	Rel	Sv	IP	H	R	ER	HR	SH	SF	HB	TBB	IBB	SO	WP	Bk	H/9	SO/9	BB/9	OAvg	OOBP	ERA
Houston	110	23	**19**	164	25	990.0	**842**	**331**	293	40	50	28	11	300	24	**610**	36	4	**7.7**	5.5	2.7	**.231**	**.289**	2.66
Los Angeles	110	**26**	**19**	187	24	997.0	904	356	333	54	55	31	14	302	38	603	19	1	8.2	5.4	2.7	.245	.302	3.01
San Francisco	111	8	9	211	**33**	1009.1	970	414	368	57	65	28	**24**	393	56	561	36	13	8.6	5.0	3.5	.256	.327	3.28
Montreal	108	20	12	183	23	975.0	902	394	357	58	**44**	26	18	**268**	21	520	28	2	8.3	4.8	**2.5**	.247	.300	3.30
Atlanta	107	11	4	215	24	968.0	936	416	371	62	64	34	11	330	31	471	25	6	8.7	4.4	3.1	.257	.318	3.45
New York	105	7	3	234	24	926.1	906	432	365	74	67	35	13	336	35	490	26	10	8.8	4.8	3.3	.259	.323	3.55
Pittsburgh	103	11	5	201	29	942.0	953	425	373	60	59	28	15	346	51	492	32	11	9.1	4.7	3.3	.266	.331	3.56
St. Louis	103	11	5	219	**33**	943.0	902	417	380	52	45	**22**	15	290	45	388	22	11	8.6	3.7	2.8	.255	.312	3.63
San Diego	110	9	6	239	23	1002.0	1013	455	414	64	66	26	17	414	59	492	30	**19**	9.1	4.4	3.7	.268	.341	3.72
Cincinnati	108	25	14	182	20	965.2	863	440	400	67	45	38	12	393	40	593	27	7	8.0	5.5	3.7	.241	.315	3.73
Chicago	106	6	2	**263**	20	956.2	983	483	426	59	75	38	21	388	**60**	532	**42**	8	9.2	5.0	3.7	.270	.340	4.01
Philadelphia	107	19	5	184	23	960.1	967	472	432	72	53	45	14	347	45	580	32	16	9.1	5.4	3.3	.267	.329	4.05
NL Total	1288	176	103	2482	301	11635.1	11141	5035	4512	719	688	379	185	4107	505	6332	355	108	8.6	4.9	3.2	.255	.327	3.49
NL Avg Team	107	15	9	207	25	969.1	928	420	376	60	57	32	15	342	42	528	30	9	8.6	4.9	3.2	.255	.327	3.49

Team Fielding

Team	G	PO	A	E	TC	DP	PB	Pct
St. Louis	103	2829	1347	82	4258	108	5	.981
Cincinnati	108	2897	1132	**80**	4109	99	3	.981
Montreal	108	2925	1123	81	4129	88	5	.980
Los Angeles	110	2991	1244	87	4322	101	**13**	.980
Philadelphia	107	2881	1285	86	4252	90	2	.980
Houston	110	2970	1206	87	4263	81	8	.980
Pittsburgh	103	2826	1171	86	4083	106	7	.979
San Diego	110	3006	**1375**	102	**4483**	117	5	.977
San Francisco	111	**3028**	1313	102	4443	102	7	.977
Atlanta	107	2904	1284	102	4290	93	10	.976
Chicago	106	2870	1284	113	4267	103	6	.974
New York	105	2779	1195	130	4104	89	5	.968
NL Total	1288	34906	14959	1138	51003	1177	76	.978

Team vs. Team Records

	Atl	ChN	Cin	Hou	LA	Mon	NYN	Phi	Pit	SD	SF	StL	Won
Atl	—	3	6	4	7	3	3	4	2	9	5	4	**50**
ChN	2	—	1	6	4	4	5	2	4	3	5	5	**38**
Cin	5	5	—	8	8	5	7	5	4	10	9	0	**66**
Hou	8	6	4	—	4	5	6	4	2	11	9	2	**61**
LA	7	4	8	8	—	5	5	3	5	6	7	5	**63**
Mon	7	7	4	2	5	—	9	7	10	4	2	6	**60**
NYN	3	8	3	3	1	3	—	7	3	2	2	6	**41**
Phi	5	10	2	6	3	4	7	—	7	4	4	7	**59**
Pit	3	10	2	4	1	3	6	5	—	6	3	3	**46**
SD	6	3	2	3	5	2	5	2	4	—	6	3	**41**
SF	7	5	5	6	3	5	5	4	3	7	—	2	**56**
StL	3	4	5	4	5	9	5	6	8	7	3	—	**59**
Lost	56	65	42	49	47	48	62	48	56	69	55	43	

Seasons: Standings, Leaders

1981 National League Batting Leaders

Games		At-Bats		Runs		Hits		Doubles		Triples	
S. Garvey, LA	110	O. Smith, SD	450	M. Schmidt, Phi	78	P. Rose, Phi	140	B. Buckner, ChN	35	C. Reynolds, Hou	12
O. Smith, SD	110	O. Moreno, Pit	434	P. Rose, Phi	73	B. Buckner, ChN	131	R. Jones, SD	34	G. Richards, SD	12
L. Salazar, SD	109	S. Garvey, LA	431	A. Dawson, Mon	71	D. Concepcion, Cin	129	D. Concepcion, Cin	28	T. Herr, StL	9
G. Foster, Cin	108	P. Rose, Phi	431	G. Hendrick, StL	67	D. Baker, LA	128	K. Hernandez, StL	27	4 tied with	8
3 tied with	107	2 tied with	421	2 tied with	65	K. Griffey Sr., Cin	123	C. Chambliss, Atl	25		

Home Runs		Total Bases		Runs Batted In		Walks		Intentional Walks		Strikeouts	
M. Schmidt, Phi	31	M. Schmidt, Phi	228	M. Schmidt, Phi	91	M. Schmidt, Phi	73	M. Schmidt, Phi	18	D. Kingman, NYN	105
A. Dawson, Mon	24	A. Dawson, Mon	218	G. Foster, Cin	90	J. Morgan, SF	66	A. Dawson, Mon	14	O. Moreno, Pit	76
G. Foster, Cin	22	G. Foster, Cin	215	B. Buckner, ChN	75	K. Hernandez, StL	61	W. Cromartie, Mon	12	G. Foster, Cin	75
D. Kingman, NYN	22	B. Buckner, ChN	202	G. Carter, Mon	68	G. Matthews, Phi	59	3 tied with	10	L. Parrish, Mon	73
G. Hendrick, StL	18	G. Hendrick, StL	191	2 tied with	67	J. Thompson, Pit	59			2 tied with	72

Hit By Pitch		Sac Hits		Sac Flies		Stolen Bases		Caught Stealing		GDP	
A. Dawson, Mon	7	C. Reynolds, Hou	18	G. Maddox, Phi	8	T. Raines, Mon	71	O. Moreno, Pit	14	R. Knight, Cin	18
D. Collins, Cin	6	T. Foli, Pit	14	D. Concepcion, Cin	7	O. Moreno, Pit	39	O. Smith, SD	12	B. Buckner, ChN	17
L. Smith, Phi	5	R. Scott, Mon	13	J. Cruz, Hou	7	R. Scott, Mon	30	G. Templeton, StL	12	D. Concepcion, Cin	13
O. Smith, SD	5	J. Niekro, Hou	11	R. Jones, SD	7	3 tied with	26	M. Wilson, NYN	12	B. Russell, LA	13
7 tied with	4	2 tied with	10	R. Oester, Cin	7			2 tied with	11	7 tied with	12

Runs Created		Runs Created/27 Outs		Batting Average		On-Base Percentage		Slugging Percentage		OBP+Slugging	
M. Schmidt, Phi	91	M. Schmidt, Phi	9.61	B. Madlock, Pit	.340	M. Schmidt, Phi	.435	M. Schmidt, Phi	.644	M. Schmidt, Phi	1.080
A. Dawson, Mon	81	B. Madlock, Pit	7.67	P. Rose, Phi	.325	B. Madlock, Pit	.412	A. Dawson, Mon	.553	A. Dawson, Mon	.918
G. Foster, Cin	76	A. Dawson, Mon	7.61	D. Baker, LA	.320	K. Hernandez, StL	.401	G. Foster, Cin	.519	B. Madlock, Pit	.907
K. Hernandez, StL	72	T. Raines, Mon	7.41	M. Schmidt, Phi	.316	G. Matthews, Phi	.398	B. Madlock, Pit	.495	G. Foster, Cin	.892
G. Matthews, Phi	68	K. Hernandez, StL	7.00	B. Buckner, ChN	.311	P. Rose, Phi	.391	G. Hendrick, StL	.485	K. Hernandez, StL	.864

1981 National League Pitching Leaders

Wins		Losses		Winning Percentage		Games		Games Started		Complete Games	
T. Seaver, Cin	14	S. Mura, SD	14	T. Seaver, Cin	.875	G. Lucas, SD	57	M. Krukow, ChN	25	F. Valenzuela, LA	11
S. Carlton, Phi	13	P. Zachry, NYN	14	S. Carlton, Phi	.765	G. Minton, SF	55	M. Soto, Cin	25	S. Carlton, Phi	10
F. Valenzuela, LA	13	T. Boggs, Atl	13	N. Ryan, Hou	.688	T. Hume, Cin	51	F. Valenzuela, LA	25	M. Soto, Cin	10
3 tied with	12	M. Scott, NYN	10	B. Forsch, StL	.667	D. Tidrow, ChN	51	6 tied with	24	J. Reuss, LA	8
		D. Tidrow, ChN	10	F. Valenzuela, LA	.650	J. Sambito, Hou	49			S. Rogers, Mon	7

Shutouts		Saves		Games Finished		Batters Faced		Innings Pitched		Hits Allowed	
F. Valenzuela, LA	8	B. Sutter, StL	25	G. Minton, SF	44	S. Carlton, Phi	763	F. Valenzuela, LA	192.1	G. Perry, Atl	182
B. Knepper, Hou	5	G. Minton, SF	21	T. Hume, Cin	40	F. Valenzuela, LA	758	S. Carlton, Phi	190.0	D. Ruthven, Phi	162
B. Hooton, LA	4	N. Allen, NYN	18	G. Lucas, SD	40	M. Soto, Cin	717	M. Soto, Cin	175.0	S. Mura, SD	156
6 tied with	3	R. Camp, Atl	17	B. Sutter, StL	36	J. Niekro, Hou	676	T. Seaver, Cin	166.1	D. Alexander, SF	156
		2 tied with	13	N. Allen, NYN	35	T. Seaver, Cin	671	J. Niekro, Hou	166.0	S. Carlton, Phi	152

Home Runs Allowed		Walks		Walks/9 Innings		Strikeouts		Strikeouts/9 Innings		Strikeout/Walk Ratio	
M. Soto, Cin	13	B. Berenyi, Cin	77	G. Perry, Atl	1.4	F. Valenzuela, LA	180	S. Carlton, Phi	8.5	D. Sutton, Hou	3.59
P. Zachry, NYN	13	J. Eichelberger, SD	74	J. Reuss, LA	1.6	S. Carlton, Phi	179	N. Ryan, Hou	8.5	B. Gullickson, Mon	3.38
9 tied with	11	N. Ryan, Hou	68	D. Sutton, Hou	1.6	M. Soto, Cin	151	F. Valenzuela, LA	8.4	F. Valenzuela, LA	2.95
		T. Seaver, Cin	66	L. Sorensen, StL	1.7	N. Ryan, Hou	140	M. Soto, Cin	7.8	S. Carlton, Phi	2.89
		S. Carlton, Phi	62	E. Solomon, Pit	1.9	B. Gullickson, Mon	115	B. Berenyi, Cin	7.6	G. Perry, Atl	2.50

Earned Run Average		Component ERA		Hit Batsmen		Wild Pitches		Opponent Average		Opponent OBP	
N. Ryan, Hou	1.69	N. Ryan, Hou	2.02	T. Griffin, SF	7	N. Ryan, Hou	16	N. Ryan, Hou	.188	D. Sutton, Hou	.265
B. Knepper, Hou	2.18	D. Sutton, Hou	2.05	8 tied with	4	S. Carlton, Phi	9	F. Valenzuela, LA	.205	F. Valenzuela, LA	.270
B. Hooton, LA	2.28	F. Valenzuela, LA	2.13			M. Krukow, ChN	8	T. Seaver, Cin	.205	B. Knepper, Hou	.278
J. Reuss, LA	2.30	B. Knepper, Hou	2.26			5 tied with	7	B. Berenyi, Cin	.211	S. Sanderson, Mon	.278
S. Carlton, Phi	2.42	B. Hooton, LA	2.33					V. Blue, SF	.217	N. Ryan, Hou	.280

1981 National League Miscellaneous

Managers

Atlanta	Bobby Cox	50-56
Chicago	Joey Amalfitano	38-65
Cincinnati	John McNamara	66-42
Houston	Bill Virdon	61-49
Los Angeles	Tom Lasorda	63-47
Montreal	Dick Williams	44-37
	Jim Fanning	16-11
New York	Joe Torre	41-62
Philadelphia	Dallas Green	59-48
Pittsburgh	Chuck Tanner	46-56
St. Louis	Whitey Herzog	59-43
San Diego	Frank Howard	41-69
San Francisco	Frank Robinson	56-55

Awards

Most Valuable Player	Mike Schmidt, 3b, Phi
Cy Young	F. Valenzuela, LA
Rookie of the Year	F. Valenzuela, p, LA
STATS Manager of the Year	Whitey Herzog, StL

STATS All-Star Team

C	Gary Carter, Mon	.251	16	68
1B	Keith Hernandez, StL	.306	8	48
2B	Ron Oester, Cin	.271	5	42
3B	Mike Schmidt, Phi	.316	31	91
SS	Dave Concepcion, Cin	.306	5	67
OF	Andre Dawson, Mon	.302	24	64
OF	George Foster, Cin	.295	22	90
OF	Tim Raines, Mon	.304	5	37
P	Steve Carlton, Phi	13-4	2.42	179 K
P	Nolan Ryan, Hou	11-5	1.69	140 K
P	Tom Seaver, Cin	14-2	2.54	87 K
P	Fernando Valenzuela, LA	13-7	2.48	180 K
RP	Rick Camp, Atl	9-3	1.78	17 Sv

Postseason

Division Series	Los Angeles 3 vs. Houston 2
	Montreal 3 vs. Philadelphia 2
LCS	Los Angeles 3 vs. Montreal 2
World Series	Los Angeles (NL) 4 vs. NYA (AL) 2

Outstanding Performances

No-Hitters

Charlie Lea, Mon vs. SF on May 10
Nolan Ryan, Hou vs. LA on September 26

1982 American League Standings

EAST	W	L	Pct	GB	DIF	W	L	R	OR	HR	OHR	W	L	R	OR	HR	OHR	Run	HR	M/A	May	June	July	Aug	S/O
						Home Games						Road Games						Park Index		Record by Month					
Milwaukee	95	67	.586	—	93	48	34	431	319	89	64	47	33	460	398	127	88	85	69	9-8	13-16	20-7	16-11	19-11	18-14
Baltimore	94	68	.580	1.0	7	53	28	397	330	87	87	41	40	377	357	92	60	99	114	6-12	17-12	15-9	16-11	18-14	22-10
Boston	89	73	.549	6.0	59	49	32	434	370	67	82	40	41	319	343	69	73	121	105	13-7	17-10	14-12	14-14	15-15	16-15
Detroit	83	79	.512	12.0	32	47	34	378	328	108	100	36	45	351	357	69	72	100	148	13-8	16-9	9-16	13-16	15-15	17-15
New York	79	83	.488	16.0	1	42	39	346	338	73	55	37	44	363	378	88	58	92	88	7-11	17-10	9-16	17-10	17-16	12-20
Cleveland	78	84	.481	17.0	3	41	40	342	377	49	64	37	44	341	371	60	58	101	96	8-10	15-13	13-13	13-14	12-17	17-17
Toronto	78	84	.481	17.0	2	44	37	353	379	62	70	34	47	298	322	44	77	118	109	8-12	13-14	12-14	15-12	13-20	17-12
WEST																									
California	93	69	.574	—	96	52	29	414	322	99	69	41	40	400	348	87	55	98	118	15-7	16-11	14-12	13-14	17-12	18-13
Kansas City	90	72	.556	3.0	53	56	25	431	318	61	64	34	47	353	399	71	99	100	74	11-8	14-10	16-11	15-12	21-11	13-17
Chicago	87	75	.537	6.0	43	49	31	383	332	51	43	38	44	403	378	85	56	94	68	11-8	14-13	12-15	11-16	19-13	19-13
Seattle	76	86	.469	17.0	3	42	39	356	388	78	104	34	47	295	324	52	69	120	150	11-12	14-14	15-10	12-14	10-19	14-17
Oakland	68	94	.420	25.0	3	36	45	328	398	71	83	32	49	363	421	78	94	93	90	11-11	12-16	10-18	11-15	14-15	10-19
Texas	64	98	.395	29.0	2	38	43	286	333	43	66	26	55	304	416	72	62	86	81	6-11	8-18	14-11	11-19	12-20	13-19
Minnesota	60	102	.370	33.0	4	37	44	351	401	81	110	23	58	306	418	67	98	104	116	9-13	3-26	8-17	14-13	13-15	13-18

Clinch Date—Milwaukee 10/03, California 10/02.

Team Batting

Team	G	AB	R	OR	H	2B	3B	HR	TB	RBI	TBB	IBB	SO	HBP	SH	SF	SB	CS	SB%	GDP	Avg	OBP	Slg
Milwaukee	163	5733	891	717	1599	277	41	216	2606	843	484	42	714	18	56	46	84	52	.62	106	.279	.342	.455
California	162	5532	814	670	1518	268	26	186	2396	760	613	46	760	35	114	56	55	53	.51	130	.274	.356	.433
Chicago	162	5575	786	710	1523	266	52	136	2301	747	533	45	866	30	54	50	136	58	.70	117	.273	.345	.413
Kansas City	162	5629	784	717	1603	295	58	132	2410	746	442	37	758	25	32	49	133	48	.73	140	.285	.345	.428
Baltimore	163	5557	774	687	1478	259	27	179	2328	735	634	52	796	25	57	52	49	38	.56	141	.266	.349	.419
Boston	162	5596	753	713	1536	271	31	136	2277	705	547	34	736	28	53	38	42	39	.52	171	.274	.346	.407
Detroit	162	5590	729	685	1489	237	40	177	2337	684	470	29	807	26	41	39	93	66	.58	99	.266	.330	.418
New York	162	5526	709	716	1417	225	37	161	2199	666	590	45	719	24	55	49	69	45	.61	152	.256	.336	.398
Oakland	162	5448	691	819	1286	211	27	149	1998	659	582	20	948	20	50	54	232	87	.73	95	.236	.318	.367
Cleveland	162	5559	683	748	1458	225	32	109	2074	639	651	48	625	35	74	40	151	68	.69	143	.262	.347	.373
Minnesota	162	5544	657	819	1427	234	44	148	2193	624	474	31	887	24	22	51	38	33	.54	149	.257	.324	.396
Seattle	162	5626	651	712	1431	259	33	130	2146	614	456	31	806	22	42	35	131	82	.62	113	.254	.317	.381
Toronto	162	5526	651	701	1447	262	45	106	2117	605	415	38	749	28	48	50	118	81	.59	107	.262	.322	.383
Texas	162	5445	590	749	1354	204	26	115	1955	558	447	22	750	32	64	32	63	45	.58	134	.249	.313	.359
AL Total	2270	77886	10163	10163	20566	3493	519	2080	31337	9585	7338	520	10921	372	762	641	1394	795	.64	1797	.264	.328	.402
AL Avg Team	162	5563	726	726	1469	250	37	149	2238	685	524	37	780	27	54	46	100	57	.64	128	.264	.328	.402

Team Pitching

Team	G	CG	ShO	Rel	Sv	IP	H	R	ER	HR	SH	SF	HB	TBB	IBB	SO	WP	Bk	H/9	SO/9	BB/9	OAvg	OOBP	ERA
Detroit	162	45	5	228	27	1451.0	1371	685	613	172	50	35	23	554	50	740	53	4	8.5	4.6	3.4	.251	.321	3.80
California	162	40	10	248	27	1464.0	1436	670	621	124	47	32	42	482	33	728	36	4	8.8	4.5	3.0	.259	.321	3.82
Chicago	162	30	10	258	41	1439.0	1502	710	618	99	56	41	26	460	30	753	28	13	9.4	4.7	2.9	.270	.326	3.87
Seattle	162	23	11	303	39	1476.1	1431	712	636	173	62	33	25	547	23	1002	47	9	8.7	6.1	3.3	.256	.324	3.88
Toronto	162	41	13	220	25	1443.2	1428	701	633	147	46	31	25	493	29	776	38	3	8.9	4.8	3.1	.257	.319	3.95
Milwaukee	163	34	6	213	47	1467.1	1514	717	649	152	52	51	21	511	27	717	44	8	9.3	4.4	3.0	.270	.330	3.98
Baltimore	163	38	8	231	34	1462.1	1436	687	648	147	52	46	22	488	41	719	35	6	8.8	4.4	3.0	.257	.317	3.99
New York	162	24	8	251	39	1459.0	1471	716	647	113	69	59	22	491	40	939	41	15	9.1	5.8	3.0	.264	.323	3.99
Boston	162	23	11	214	33	1453.0	1557	713	651	155	46	43	35	478	36	816	24	6	9.6	5.1	3.0	.276	.334	4.03
Kansas City	162	16	12	228	45	1431.0	1443	717	649	163	46	54	26	471	30	650	43	11	9.1	4.1	3.0	.262	.320	4.08
Cleveland	162	31	9	221	30	1468.1	1433	748	672	122	56	66	22	589	32	882	56	8	8.8	5.4	3.6	.257	.327	4.12
Texas	162	32	5	214	24	1431.0	1554	749	681	128	69	51	41	483	68	690	34	4	9.8	4.3	3.0	.280	.339	4.28
Oakland	162	42	6	239	22	1456.0	1506	819	735	177	71	54	30	648	21	697	58	8	9.3	4.3	4.0	.268	.343	4.54
Minnesota	162	26	7	245	30	1433.0	1484	819	752	208	40	45	12	643	60	812	45	12	9.3	5.1	4.0	.269	.344	4.72
AL Total	2270	445	121	3313	463	20335.0	20566	10163	9205	2080	762	641	372	7338	520	10921	582	111	9.1	4.8	3.2	.264	.335	4.07
AL Avg Team	162	32	9	237	33	1452.0	1469	726	658	149	54	46	27	524	37	780	42	8	9.1	4.8	3.2	.264	.335	4.07

Team Fielding

Team	G	PO	A	E	TC	DP	PB	Pct
Baltimore	163	4387	1707	101	6195	140	7	.984
California	162	4392	1984	108	6484	171	4	.983
Minnesota	162	4299	1560	108	5967	162	6	.982
Detroit	162	4353	1844	117	6314	165	15	.981
Texas	162	4293	1916	121	6330	169	19	.981
Boston	162	4359	1830	121	6310	172	16	.981
Cleveland	162	4405	1740	123	6268	129	6	.980
Milwaukee	163	4402	1834	125	6361	185	12	.980
Kansas City	162	4293	1743	127	6163	140	6	.979
New York	162	4377	1701	128	6206	158	15	.979
Toronto	162	4331	1768	136	6235	146	7	.978
Seattle	162	4429	1773	139	6341	158	10	.978
Chicago	162	4317	1901	154	6372	173	13	.976
Oakland	162	4368	1647	160	6175	140	8	.974
AL Total	2270	61005	24948	1768	87721	2208	144	.980

Team vs. Team Records

	Bal	Bos	Cal	ChA	Cle	Det	KC	Mil	Min	NYA	Oak	Sea	Tex	Tor	Won
Bal	—	4	7	5	6	7	4	9	8	11	7	7	9	10	94
Bos	9	—	7	4	6	8	6	4	6	7	8	7	10	7	89
Cal	5	5	—	8	8	5	7	6	7	9	10	8	8		93
ChA	7	8	5	—	6	9	3	3	7	8	9	6	8	8	87
Cle	7	7	4	6	—	6	2	7	8	4	4	9	7	7	78
Det	6	5	7	3	7	—	6	3	9	8	9	6	8	6	83
KC	8	6	6	10	10	6	—	7	7	5	7	7	4		90
Mil	4	9	6	9	6	10	5	—	7	8	7	8	7	9	95
Min	4	6	6	6	4	3	6	5	—	2	3	5	5	5	60
NYA	2	6	5	4	5	4	5	5	10	—	7	6	7	6	79
Oak	5	4	4	4	8	3	6	5	10	5	—	6	5	3	68
Sea	5	5	3	7	3	6	6	4	8	6	7	—	9	7	76
Tex	3	2	5	5	5	4	6	5	8	5	8	4	—	4	64
Tor	3	6	4	4	6	7	8	4	7	7	9	5	8	—	78
Lost	68	73	69	75	84	79	72	67	102	83	94	86	98	84	

Seasons: Standings, Leaders

1982 American League Batting Leaders

Games		At-Bats		Runs		Hits		Doubles		Triples	
A. Griffin, Tor	162	P. Molitor, Mil	666	P. Molitor, Mil	136	R. Yount, Mil	210	R. Yount, Mil	46	W. Wilson, KC	15
D. Evans, Bos	162	C. Cooper, Mil	654	R. Yount, Mil	129	C. Cooper, Mil	205	H. McRae, KC	46	L. Herndon, Det	13
T. Harrah, Cle	162	J. Remy, Bos	636	D. Evans, Bos	122	P. Molitor, Mil	201	F. White, KC	45	R. Yount, Mil	12
A. Thornton, Cle	161	R. Yount, Mil	635	R. Henderson, Oak	119	W. Wilson, KC	194	D. DeCinces, Cal	42	J. Mumphrey, NYA	10
H. Baines, ChA	161	B. Downing, Cal	623	B. Downing, Cal	109	H. McRae, KC	189	A. Cowens, Sea	39	3 tied with	9

Home Runs		Total Bases		Runs Batted In		Walks		Intentional Walks		Strikeouts	
R. Jackson, Cal	39	R. Yount, Mil	367	H. McRae, KC	133	R. Henderson, Oak	116	A. Thornton, Cle	18	R. Jackson, Cal	156
G. Thomas, Mil	39	C. Cooper, Mil	345	C. Cooper, Mil	121	D. Evans, Bos	112	E. Murray, Bal	18	G. Thomas, Mil	143
D. Winfield, NYA	37	H. McRae, KC	332	A. Thornton, Cle	116	A. Thornton, Cle	109	G. Brett, KC	14	J. Martin, KC	138
B. Oglivie, Mil	34	D. Evans, Bos	325	R. Yount, Mil	114	M. Hargrove, Cle	101	B. Oglivie, Mil	13	T. Armas, Oak	128
5 tied with	32	D. DeCinces, Cal	315	G. Thomas, Mil	112	D. Murphy, Oak	94	2 tied with	12	D. Evans, Bos	125

Hit By Pitch		Sac Hits		Sac Flies		Stolen Bases		Caught Stealing		GDP	
C. Lemon, Det	15	T. Foli, Cal	26	G. Gaetti, Min	13	R. Henderson, Oak	130	R. Henderson, Oak	42	J. Rice, Bos	29
T. Harrah, Cle	12	B. Boone, Cal	23	R. Yount, Mil	10	D. Garcia, Tor	54	D. Garcia, Tor	20	J. Wathan, KC	26
G. Roenicke, Bal	9	J. Remy, Bos	18	4 tied with	9	J. Cruz, Sea	46	R. Carew, Cal	17	K. Singleton, Bal	24
T. Paciorek, ChA	9	3 tied with	16			P. Molitor, Mil	41	R. LeFlore, ChA	14	D. Stapleton, Bos	24
3 tied with	8					W. Wilson, KC	37	J. Simpson, Sea	14	M. Hargrove, Cle	22

Runs Created		Runs Created/27 Outs		Batting Average		On-Base Percentage		Slugging Percentage		OBP+Slugging	
R. Yount, Mil	136	R. Yount, Mil	7.97	W. Wilson, KC	.332	D. Evans, Bos	.402	R. Yount, Mil	.578	R. Yount, Mil	.957
D. Evans, Bos	127	D. Evans, Bos	7.54	R. Yount, Mil	.331	T. Harrah, Cle	.398	D. Winfield, NYA	.560	E. Murray, Bal	.940
P. Molitor, Mil	119	E. Murray, Bal	7.34	R. Carew, Cal	.319	R. Henderson, Oak	.398	E. Murray, Bal	.549	D. Evans, Bos	.936
C. Cooper, Mil	118	H. McRae, KC	7.08	E. Murray, Bal	.316	R. Carew, Cal	.396	D. DeCinces, Cal	.548	D. DeCinces, Cal	.916
H. McRae, KC	115	C. Cooper, Mil	6.84	C. Cooper, Mil	.313	E. Murray, Bal	.391	H. McRae, KC	.542	H. McRae, KC	.910

1982 American League Pitching Leaders

Wins		Losses		Winning Percentage		Games		Games Started		Complete Games	
L. Hoyt, ChA	19	M. Keough, Oak	18	P. Vuckovich, Mil	.750	E. Vande Berg, Sea	78	J. Clancy, Tor	40	D. Stieb, Tor	19
P. Vuckovich, Mil	18	F. Tanana, Tex	18	J. Palmer, Bal	.750	T. Martinez, Bal	76	D. Martinez, Bal	39	J. Morris, Det	17
L. Gura, KC	18	R. Honeycutt, Tex	17	B. Burns, ChA	.722	D. Quisenberry, KC	72	L. Leal, Tor	38	R. Langford, Oak	15
G. Zahn, Cal	18	R. Langford, Oak	16	G. Zahn, Cal	.692	D. Caudill, Sea	70	D. Stieb, Tor	38	L. Hoyt, ChA	14
3 tied with	17	J. Morris, Det	16	B. Kison, Cal	.667	D. Spillner, Cle	65	3 tied with	37	4 tied with	12

Shutouts		Saves		Games Finished		Batters Faced		Innings Pitched		Hits Allowed	
D. Stieb, Tor	5	D. Quisenberry, KC	35	D. Quisenberry, KC	68	D. Stieb, Tor	1187	D. Stieb, Tor	288.1	D. Stieb, Tor	271
K. Forsch, Cal	4	G. Gossage, NYA	30	B. Caudill, Sea	64	J. Morris, Det	1107	J. Clancy, Tor	266.2	M. Caldwell, Mil	269
G. Zahn, Cal	4	R. Fingers, Mil	29	D. Spillner, Cle	54	J. Clancy, Tor	1100	J. Morris, Det	266.1	R. Langford, Oak	265
7 tied with	3	B. Caudill, Sea	26	R. Davis, Min	53	D. Martinez, Bal	1093	M. Caldwell, Mil	258.0	D. Martinez, Bal	262
		R. Davis, Min	22	R. Fingers, Mil	45	M. Caldwell, Mil	1064	D. Martinez, Bal	252.0	3 tied with	251

Home Runs Allowed		Walks		Walks/9 Innings		Strikeouts		Strikeouts/9 Innings		Strikeout/Walk Ratio	
M. Keough, Oak	38	D. Righetti, NYA	108	T. John, 2tm	1.6	F. Bannister, Sea	209	D. Righetti, NYA	8.0	D. Eckersley, Bos	2.95
J. Morris, Det	37	P. Vuckovich, Mil	102	D. Eckersley, Bos	1.7	L. Barker, Cle	187	F. Bannister, Sea	7.6	F. Bannister, Sea	2.71
R. Langford, Oak	33	M. Keough, Oak	101	L. Hoyt, ChA	1.8	D. Righetti, NYA	163	J. Beattie, Sea	7.3	M. Haas, Mil	2.67
F. Bannister, Sea	32	D. Petry, Det	100	M. Haas, Mil	1.8	R. Guidry, NYA	162	L. Barker, Cle	6.9	L. Hoyt, ChA	2.58
B. Havens, Min	32	R. Sutcliffe, Cle	98	R. Langford, Oak	1.9	J. Tudor, Bos	146	J. Tudor, Bos	6.7	J. Tudor, Bos	2.47

Earned Run Average		Component ERA		Hit Batsmen		Wild Pitches		Opponent Average		Opponent OBP	
R. Sutcliffe, Cle	2.96	J. Palmer, Bal	2.92	K. Forsch, Cal	11	G. Perry, Sea	13	R. Sutcliffe, Cle	.226	J. Palmer, Bal	.286
B. Stanley, Bos	3.10	L. Barker, Cle	3.00	J. Tudor, Bos	8	L. Barker, Cle	10	D. Righetti, NYA	.229	D. Eckersley, Bos	.296
J. Palmer, Bal	3.13	J. Beattie, Sea	3.13	8 tied with	7	M. Keough, Oak	10	D. Ujdur, Det	.230	D. Stieb, Tor	.298
D. Petry, Det	3.22	R. Sutcliffe, Cle	3.19			J. Morris, Det	10	J. Palmer, Bal	.231	L. Barker, Cle	.299
D. Stieb, Tor	3.25	D. Stieb, Tor	3.24			5 tied with	9	L. Barker, Cle	.232	L. Hoyt, ChA	.301

1982 American League Miscellaneous

Managers

Baltimore	Earl Weaver	94-68
Boston	Ralph Houk	89-73
California	Gene Mauch	93-69
Chicago	Tony La Russa	87-75
Cleveland	Dave Garcia	78-84
Detroit	Sparky Anderson	83-79
Kansas City	Dick Howser	90-72
Milwaukee	Buck Rodgers	23-24
	Harvey Kuenn	72-43
Minnesota	Billy Gardner	60-102
New York	Bob Lemon	6-8
	Gene Michael	44-42
	Clyde King	29-33
Oakland	Billy Martin	68-94
Seattle	Rene Lachemann	76-86
Texas	Don Zimmer	38-58
	Darrell Johnson	26-40
Toronto	Bobby Cox	78-84

Awards

Most Valuable Player	Robin Yount, ss, Mil
Cy Young	Pete Vuckovich, Mil
Rookie of the Year	Cal Ripken Jr., ss, Bal
STATS Manager of the Year	Harvey Kuenn, Mil

STATS All-Star Team

C	Lance Parrish, Det	.284	32	87
1B	Eddie Murray, Bal	.316	32	110
2B	Bobby Grich, Cal	.261	19	65
3B	Doug DeCinces, Cal	.301	30	97
SS	Robin Yount, Mil	.331	29	114
OF	Dwight Evans, Bos	.292	32	98
OF	Reggie Jackson, Cal	.275	39	101
OF	Dave Winfield, NYA	.280	37	106
DH	Hal McRae, KC	.308	27	133
P	Jim Palmer, Bal	15-5	3.13	103 K
P	Dave Stieb, Tor	17-14	3.25	141 K
P	Rick Sutcliffe, Cle	14-8	2.96	142 K
P	Pete Vuckovich, Mil	18-6	3.34	105 K
RP	Bill Caudill, Sea	12-9	2.35	26 Sv

Postseason

LCS	Milwaukee 3 vs. California 2
World Series	Milwaukee (AL) 3 vs. St. Louis (NL) 4

Outstanding Performances

Three-Homer Games

Paul Molitor, Mil	on May 12
Larry Herndon, Det	on May 18
Ben Oglivie, Mil	on June 20
Harold Baines, ChA	on July 7
Doug DeCinces, Cal	on August 3
Doug DeCinces, Cal	on August 8

Cycles

Frank White, KC	on August 3

1982 National League Standings

	Overall					Home Games						Road Games						Park Index		Record by Month					
EAST	W	L	Pct	GB	DIF	W	L	R	OR	HR	OHR	W	L	R	OR	HR	OHR	Run	HR	M/A	May	June	July	Aug	S/O
St. Louis	92	70	.568	—	131	46	35	338	325	27	48	46	35	347	284	40	46	105	87	14-7	17-11	12-16	15-10	17-12	17-14
Philadelphia	89	73	.549	3.0	41	51	30	301	307	57	46	38	43	363	347	55	40	86	108	6-13	19-8	17-12	16-9	15-17	16-14
Montreal	86	76	.531	6.0	7	40	41	335	352	59	65	46	35	362	264	74	45	110	104	10-7	15-13	15-12	13-15	17-15	16-14
Pittsburgh	84	78	.519	8.0	1	42	39	391	394	77	65	42	39	333	302	57	53	124	129	8-10	10-17	17-9	17-10	17-16	14-16
Chicago	73	89	.451	19.0	3	38	43	352	371	53	62	35	46	324	338	49	63	109	103	7-14	14-14	8-20	11-17	18-10	15-14
New York	65	97	.401	27.0	3	33	48	307	357	48	60	32	49	302	366	49	59	99	100	10-10	17-11	9-18	9-17	5-24	15-17
WEST																									
Atlanta	89	73	.549	—	149	42	39	388	387	95	86	47	34	351	315	51	40	116	199	16-5	11-15	18-9	16-11	13-18	15-15
Los Angeles	88	74	.543	1.0	37	43	38	321	283	57	35	45	36	370	329	81	46	86	72	10-11	15-13	16-13	14-12	19-10	14-15
San Francisco	87	75	.537	2.0	1	45	36	319	312	55	54	42	39	354	375	78	55	87	82	9-11	12-18	14-13	14-12	17-12	21-9
San Diego	81	81	.500	8.0	2	43	38	316	286	33	76	38	43	359	372	48	63	82	98	13-6	12-15	17-11	13-16	13-17	13-16
Houston	77	85	.475	12.0	1	43	38	290	294	31	26	34	47	279	326	43	61	97	55	9-14	12-14	10-16	15-11	17-14	14-16
Cincinnati	61	101	.377	28.0	1	33	48	296	325	37	47	28	53	249	336	45	58	106	82	8-12	11-16	12-16	7-21	13-16	10-20

Clinch Date—St. Louis 9/27, Atlanta 10/03.

Team Batting

Team	G	AB	R	OR	H	2B	3B	HR	TB	RBI	TBB	IBB	SO	HBP	SH	SF	SB	CS	SB%	GDP	Avg	OBP	Slg
Atlanta	162	5507	739	702	1411	215	22	146	2108	687	554	64	869	29	96	43	151	77	.66	102	.256	.332	.383
Pittsburgh	162	5614	724	696	1535	272	40	134	2289	688	447	72	862	28	78	67	161	75	.68	116	.273	.337	.408
Montreal	162	5557	697	616	1454	270	38	133	2199	656	503	72	816	35	85	41	156	56	.74	107	.262	.331	.396
Los Angeles	162	5642	691	612	1487	222	32	138	2187	661	528	83	804	30	106	55	151	56	.73	98	.264	.336	.388
St. Louis	162	5455	685	609	1439	239	52	67	1983	632	569	66	805	30	87	55	200	91	.69	110	.264	.332	.364
Chicago	162	5531	676	709	1436	239	46	102	2073	647	460	62	869	25	76	49	132	70	.65	97	.260	.325	.375
San Diego	162	5575	675	658	1435	217	52	81	1999	611	429	78	877	22	86	47	165	77	.68	96	.257	.318	.359
San Francisco	162	5499	673	687	1393	213	30	133	2065	631	607	70	915	17	59	45	130	56	.70	131	.253	.334	.376
Philadelphia	162	5454	664	654	1417	245	25	112	2048	624	506	66	831	24	85	38	128	76	.63	134	.260	.330	.376
New York	162	5510	609	723	1361	227	26	97	1931	568	456	49	1005	25	64	53	137	58	.70	112	.247	.314	.350
Houston	162	5440	569	620	1342	236	48	74	1896	533	435	67	830	19	68	46	140	61	.70	104	.247	.310	.349
Cincinnati	162	5479	545	661	1375	228	34	82	1917	496	470	50	817	21	88	41	131	69	.66	143	.251	.317	.350
NL Total	1944	66263	7947	7947	17085	2823	445	1299	24695	7434	5964	799	10300	305	978	580	1782	822	.68	1350	.258	.319	.373
NL Avg Team	162	5522	662	662	1424	235	37	108	2058	620	497	67	858	25	82	48	149	69	.68	113	.258	.319	.373

Team Pitching

Team	G	CG	ShO	Rel	Sv	IP	H	R	ER	HR	SH	SF	HB	TBB	IBB	SO	WP	Bk	H/9	SO/9	BB/9	OAvg	OOBP	ERA
Los Angeles	162	37	16	295	28	1488.1	1356	612	539	81	96	35	22	468	89	932	35	10	8.2	5.6	2.8	.244	.303	3.26
Montreal	162	34	10	250	43	1460.2	1371	616	538	110	72	48	22	448	49	936	47	8	8.4	5.8	2.8	.250	.306	3.31
St. Louis	162	25	10	318	47	1465.1	1420	609	549	94	63	45	22	502	90	689	46	12	8.7	4.2	3.1	.258	.320	3.37
Houston	162	37	16	244	51	1446.2	1338	620	549	87	68	40	33	447	40	899	61	14	8.3	5.6	3.0	.247	.310	3.42
San Diego	162	20	11	277	41	1476.0	1348	658	578	139	88	48	27	502	39	765	28	12	8.2	4.7	3.1	.244	.307	3.52
Philadelphia	162	38	13	287	33	1456.1	1395	654	584	86	70	54	28	472	70	1002	49	17	8.6	6.2	2.9	.255	.314	3.61
San Francisco	162	18	4	323	45	1465.1	1507	687	592	109	94	61	25	466	89	810	33	19	9.3	5.0	2.9	.270	.326	3.64
Cincinnati	162	22	7	293	31	1460.1	1414	661	594	105	88	44	27	570	85	998	50	11	8.7	6.2	3.5	.258	.328	3.66
Pittsburgh	162	19	7	280	39	1466.2	1434	696	621	118	68	48	29	521	70	933	59	10	8.8	5.7	3.2	.257	.321	3.81
Atlanta	162	15	11	314	51	1463.0	1484	702	621	126	86	45	24	502	62	813	37	7	9.1	5.0	3.1	.267	.328	3.82
New York	162	15	5	278	37	1447.1	1508	723	624	119	91	53	17	582	49	759	32	13	9.4	4.7	3.6	.273	.341	3.88
Chicago	162	9	7	354	43	1447.1	1510	709	630	125	94	59	29	452	67	764	32	15	9.4	4.8	2.8	.272	.327	3.92
NL Total	1944	289	117	3513	469	17543.1	17085	7947	7019	1299	978	580	305	5964	799	10300	509	145	8.8	5.3	3.1	.258	.327	3.60
NL Avg Team	162	24	10	293	39	1461.1	1424	662	585	108	82	48	25	497	67	858	42	12	8.8	5.3	3.1	.258	.327	3.60

Team Fielding

Team	G	PO	A	E	TC	DP	PB	Pct
St. Louis	162	4396	2038	124	6558	169	14	.981
Philadelphia	162	4369	1821	121	6311	138	11	.981
Montreal	162	4382	1630	122	6134	117	8	.980
Cincinnati	162	4381	1763	128	6272	158	12	.980
Chicago	162	4342	1909	132	6383	110	13	.979
Los Angeles	162	4465	1946	139	6550	131	16	.979
Atlanta	162	4389	1922	137	6448	186	13	.979
Houston	162	4340	1827	136	6303	154	32	.978
Pittsburgh	162	4400	1858	145	6403	133	12	.977
San Diego	162	4428	1826	152	6406	142	11	.976
San Francisco	162	4396	1909	173	6478	125	7	.973
New York	162	4342	1836	175	6353	134	6	.972
NL Total	1944	52630	22285	1684	76599	1697	155	.978

Team vs. Team Records

	Atl	ChN	Cin	Hou	LA	Mon	NYN	Phi	Pit	SD	SF	StL	Won
Atl	—	8	14	10	7	5	9	6	4	11	8	7	89
ChN	4	—	6	9	5	6	9	9	4	6	6	6	73
Cin	4	6	—	7	7	4	7	5	4	6	5	5	61
Hou	8	3	11	—	7	4	8	7	9	9	5	6	77
LA	11	7	11	11	—	8	6	4	5	9	9	7	88
Mon	7	12	8	8	4	—	11	8	7	7	4	10	86
NYN	3	9	5	4	6	7	—	7	8	6	4	6	65
Phi	6	9	7	5	8	10	11	—	9	7	10	7	89
Pit	8	9	8	3	7	11	10	9	—	6	6	7	84
SD	7	8	12	9	5	9	6	5	6	—	10	4	81
SF	10	6	12	13	9	9	8	2	6	8	—	5	87
StL	5	12	7	6	5	8	12	11	11	8	7	—	92
Lost	73	89	101	85	74	76	97	73	78	81	75	70	

1982 National League Batting Leaders

Games		At-Bats		Runs		Hits		Doubles		Triples	
S. Garvey, LA	162	B. Buckner, ChN	657	L. Smith, StL	120	A. Oliver, Mon	204	A. Oliver, Mon	43	D. Thon, Hou	10
G. Matthews, Phi	162	T. Raines, Mon	647	D. Murphy, Atl	113	B. Buckner, ChN	201	T. Kennedy, SD	42	T. Puhl, Hou	9
P. Rose, Phi	162	J. Ray, Pit	647	M. Schmidt, Phi	108	A. Dawson, Mon	183	A. Dawson, Mon	37	O. Moreno, Pit	9
D. Murphy, Atl	162	O. Moreno, Pit	645	A. Dawson, Mon	107	L. Smith, StL	182	R. Knight, Hou	36	M. Wilson, NYN	9
J. Ray, Pit	162	C. Davis, SF	641	R. Sandberg, ChN	103	J. Ray, Pit	182	3 tied with	35	6 tied with	8

Home Runs		Total Bases		Runs Batted In		Walks		Intentional Walks		Strikeouts	
D. Kingman, NYN	37	A. Oliver, Mon	317	A. Oliver, Mon	109	M. Schmidt, Phi	107	K. Hernandez, StL	19	D. Kingman, NYN	156
D. Murphy, Atl	36	P. Guerrero, LA	308	D. Murphy, Atl	109	J. Thompson, Pit	101	M. Schmidt, Phi	17	D. Murphy, Atl	134
M. Schmidt, Phi	35	A. Dawson, Mon	303	B. Buckner, ChN	105	K. Hernandez, StL	100	P. Guerrero, LA	16	M. Schmidt, Phi	131
P. Guerrero, LA	32	D. Murphy, Atl	303	G. Hendrick, StL	104	D. Murphy, Atl	93	B. Madlock, Pit	16	G. Foster, NYN	123
B. Horner, Atl	32	B. Buckner, ChN	290	J. Clark, SF	103	J. Clark, SF	90	3 tied with	15	O. Moreno, Pit	121

Hit By Pitch		Sac Hits		Sac Flies		Stolen Bases		Caught Stealing		GDP	
L. Smith, StL	9	G. Hubbard, Atl	20	G. Hendrick, StL	14	T. Raines, Mon	78	L. Smith, StL	26	G. Matthews, Phi	23
A. Dawson, Mon	8	J. Reuss, LA	16	R. Knight, Hou	13	L. Smith, StL	68	O. Moreno, Pit	26	J. Clark, SF	20
J. Youngblood, 2tm	8	S. Sanderson, Mon	16	B. Madlock, Pit	13	O. Moreno, Pit	60	G. Richards, SD	20	D. Concepcion, Cin	20
P. Rose, Phi	7	R. Ramirez, Atl	16	K. Hernandez, StL	12	M. Wilson, NYN	58	S. Sax, LA	19	B. Diaz, Phi	20
3 tied with	6	B. Forsch, StL	14	B. Buckner, ChN	10	S. Sax, LA	49	3 tied with	16	G. Templeton, SD	19

Runs Created		Runs Created/27 Outs		Batting Average		On-Base Percentage		Slugging Percentage		OBP+Slugging	
D. Murphy, Atl	121	M. Schmidt, Phi	7.85	A. Oliver, Mon	.331	M. Schmidt, Phi	.403	M. Schmidt, Phi	.547	M. Schmidt, Phi	.949
M. Schmidt, Phi	114	L. Durham, ChN	7.25	B. Madlock, Pit	.319	J. Morgan, SF	.400	P. Guerrero, LA	.536	P. Guerrero, LA	.914
A. Oliver, Mon	114	D. Murphy, Atl	7.24	L. Durham, ChN	.312	K. Hernandez, StL	.397	L. Durham, ChN	.521	L. Durham, ChN	.909
P. Guerrero, LA	107	A. Oliver, Mon	7.20	L. Smith, StL	.307	A. Oliver, Mon	.392	A. Oliver, Mon	.514	A. Oliver, Mon	.906
J. Thompson, Pit	107	S. Lezcano, SD	7.13	B. Buckner, ChN	.306	J. Thompson, Pit	.391	J. Thompson, Pit	.511	J. Thompson, Pit	.902

1982 National League Pitching Leaders

Wins		Losses		Winning Percentage		Games		Games Started		Complete Games	
S. Carlton, Phi	23	B. Berenyi, Cin	18	P. Niekro, Atl	.810	K. Tekulve, Pit	85	S. Carlton, Phi	38	S. Carlton, Phi	19
S. Rogers, Mon	19	B. Knepper, Hou	15	S. Rogers, Mon	.704	G. Minton, SF	78	J. Andujar, StL	37	F. Valenzuela, LA	18
F. Valenzuela, LA	19	F. Jenkins, ChN	15	S. Carlton, Phi	.676	R. Scurry, Pit	76	J. Reuss, LA	37	J. Niekro, Hou	16
J. Reuss, LA	18	6 tied with	14	F. Breining, SF	.647	W. Hernandez, ChN	75	F. Valenzuela, LA	37	S. Rogers, Mon	14
2 tied with	17			T. Lollar, SD	.640	J. Reardon, Mon	75	B. Welch, LA	36	M. Soto, Cin	13

Shutouts		Saves		Games Finished		Batters Faced		Innings Pitched		Hits Allowed	
S. Carlton, Phi	6	B. Sutter, StL	36	G. Minton, SF	66	S. Carlton, Phi	1193	S. Carlton, Phi	295.2	S. Carlton, Phi	253
J. Andujar, StL	5	G. Garber, Atl	30	K. Tekulve, Pit	64	F. Valenzuela, LA	1156	F. Valenzuela, LA	285.0	F. Valenzuela, LA	247
J. Niekro, Hou	5	G. Minton, SF	30	B. Sutter, StL	58	S. Rogers, Mon	1122	S. Rogers, Mon	277.0	S. Rogers, Mon	245
3 tied with	4	J. Reardon, Mon	26	G. Garber, Atl	56	J. Niekro, Hou	1067	J. Niekro, Hou	270.0	R. Rhoden, Pit	239
		K. Tekulve, Pit	20	J. Reardon, Mon	53	J. Andujar, StL	1056	J. Andujar, StL	265.2	B. Forsch, StL	238

Home Runs Allowed		Walks		Walks/9 Innings		Strikeouts		Strikeouts/9 Innings		Strikeout/Walk Ratio	
D. Bird, ChN	26	N. Ryan, Hou	109	D. Bird, ChN	1.4	S. Carlton, Phi	286	M. Soto, Cin	9.6	M. Soto, Cin	3.86
D. Robinson, Pit	26	D. Robinson, Pit	103	A. Hammaker, SF	1.4	M. Soto, Cin	274	N. Ryan, Hou	8.8	A. Hammaker, SF	3.64
B. Gullickson, Mon	25	B. Berenyi, Cin	96	J. Andujar, StL	1.7	N. Ryan, Hou	245	S. Carlton, Phi	8.7	J. Candelaria, Pit	3.59
P. Falcone, NYN	24	C. Puleo, NYN	90	J. Reuss, LA	1.8	F. Valenzuela, LA	199	J. Candelaria, Pit	6.9	S. Carlton, Phi	3.33
S. Sanderson, Mon	24	T. Lollar, SD	87	J. Candelaria, Pit	1.9	S. Rogers, Mon	179	B. Welch, LA	6.7	D. Sutton, Hou	3.02

Earned Run Average		Component ERA		Hit Batsmen		Wild Pitches		Opponent Average		Opponent OBP	
S. Rogers, Mon	2.40	J. Niekro, Hou	2.35	N. Ryan, Hou	8	J. Niekro, Hou	19	N. Ryan, Hou	.213	M. Soto, Cin	.271
J. Niekro, Hou	2.47	M. Soto, Cin	2.37	J. Andujar, StL	7	N. Ryan, Hou	18	M. Soto, Cin	.215	D. Sutton, Hou	.277
J. Andujar, StL	2.47	J. Reuss, LA	2.44	4 tied with	6	D. Robinson, Pit	17	C. Lea, Mon	.222	J. Reuss, LA	.277
M. Soto, Cin	2.79	J. Andujar, StL	2.45			B. Berenyi, Cin	16	T. Lollar, SD	.224	J. Niekro, Hou	.278
F. Valenzuela, LA	2.87	D. Sutton, Hou	2.47			M. Krukow, Phi	13	J. Niekro, Hou	.229	J. Andujar, StL	.281

1982 National League Miscellaneous

Managers

Atlanta	Joe Torre	89-73
Chicago	Lee Elia	73-89
Cincinnati	John McNamara	34-58
	Russ Nixon	27-43
Houston	Bill Virdon	49-62
	Bob Lillis	28-23
Los Angeles	Tom Lasorda	88-74
Montreal	Jim Fanning	86-76
New York	George Bamberger	65-97
Philadelphia	Pat Corrales	89-73
Pittsburgh	Chuck Tanner	84-78
St. Louis	Whitey Herzog	92-70
San Diego	Dick Williams	81-81
San Francisco	Frank Robinson	87-75

Awards

Most Valuable Player	Dale Murphy, of, Atl
Cy Young	Steve Carlton, Phi
Rookie of the Year	Steve Sax, 2b, LA
STATS Manager of the Year	Joe Torre, Atl

STATS All-Star Team

C	Gary Carter, Mon	.293	29	97
1B	Al Oliver, Mon	.331	22	109
2B	Joe Morgan, SF	.289	14	61
3B	Mike Schmidt, Phi	.280	35	87
SS	Ozzie Smith, StL	.248	2	43
OF	Leon Durham, ChN	.312	22	90
OF	Pedro Guerrero, LA	.304	32	100
OF	Dale Murphy, Atl	.281	36	109
P	Steve Carlton, Phi	23-11	3.10	286 K
P	Joe Niekro, Hou	17-12	2.47	130 K
P	Steve Rogers, Mon	19-8	2.40	179 K
P	Fernando Valenzuela, LA	19-13	2.87	199 K
RP	Bruce Sutter, StL	9-8	2.90	36 Sv

Postseason

LCS	St. Louis 3 vs. Atlanta 0
World Series	St. Louis (NL) 4 vs. Milwaukee (AL) 3

Outstanding Performances

None

1983 American League Standings

EAST	W	L	Pct	GB	DIF	W	L	R	OR	HR	OHR	W	L	R	OR	HR	OHR	Run	HR	M/A	May	June	July	Aug	S/O
						Home Games						Road Games						Park Index		Record by Month					
Baltimore	98	64	.605	—	115	50	31	389	328	79	66	48	33	410	324	89	64	98	95	11-9	15-13	14-11	19-7	18-12	21-12
Detroit	92	70	.568	6.0	9	48	33	377	314	83	87	44	37	412	365	73	83	89	109	8-9	14-14	18-10	19-9	15-15	18-13
New York	91	71	.562	7.0	0	51	30	398	323	67	55	40	41	372	380	86	61	96	83	9-11	16-10	14-12	17-10	17-14	18-14
Toronto	89	73	.549	9.0	44	48	33	437	385	101	84	41	40	358	341	66	61	118	146	8-10	18-9	16-12	15-12	15-19	17-11
Milwaukee	87	75	.537	11.0	12	52	29	356	305	64	57	35	46	408	403	68	76	82	84	10-9	13-12	12-15	20-8	20-13	12-18
Boston	78	84	.481	20.0	18	38	43	373	390	65	76	40	41	351	385	77	82	104	89	10-9	16-11	11-16	14-14	12-19	15-15
Cleveland	70	92	.432	28.0	10	36	45	367	424	48	71	34	47	337	361	38	49	113	137	9-11	12-14	12-16	8-19	17-16	12-16
WEST																									
Chicago	99	63	.611	—	78	55	26	432	306	84	64	44	37	368	344	73	64	104	108	8-10	12-15	18-10	15-13	22-9	24-6
Kansas City	79	83	.488	20.0	9	45	36	381	369	50	66	34	47	315	398	59	67	105	92	10-7	11-13	14-14	13-15	16-18	15-16
Texas	77	85	.475	22.0	45	44	37	326	294	45	33	33	48	313	315	61	64	99	62	12-9	10-15	19-9	8-20	12-19	16-13
Oakland	74	88	.457	25.0	8	42	39	348	367	60	54	32	49	360	415	61	81	92	80	11-9	11-16	14-15	12-17	17-13	9-18
California	70	92	.432	29.0	60	35	46	368	354	86	67	35	46	354	425	68	63	93	117	13-8	14-12	13-14	9-20	12-18	9-20
Minnesota	70	92	.432	29.0	0	37	44	389	427	56	91	33	48	320	395	85	72	114	94	11-11	11-17	9-18	12-15	14-15	13-16
Seattle	60	102	.370	39.0	2	30	51	281	369	64	80	30	51	277	371	47	65	100	129	8-16	12-14	8-20	12-14	11-18	9-20

Clinch Date—Baltimore 9/25, Chicago 9/17.

Team Batting

Team	G	AB	R	OR	H	2B	3B	HR	TB	RBI	TBB	IBB	SO	HBP	SH	SF	SB	CS	SB%	GDP	Avg	OBP	Slg
Chicago	162	5484	800	650	1439	270	42	157	2264	762	527	50	888	43	53	56	165	50	.77	111	.262	.338	.413
Baltimore	162	5546	799	652	1492	283	27	168	2333	761	601	48	800	23	46	56	61	33	.65	144	.269	.349	.421
Toronto	162	5581	795	726	1546	268	58	167	2431	748	510	44	810	32	36	54	131	72	.65	117	.277	.347	.436
Detroit	162	5592	789	679	1530	283	53	156	2387	749	508	37	831	39	48	59	93	53	.64	123	.274	.345	.427
New York	162	5631	770	703	1535	269	40	153	2343	728	533	36	686	37	37	41	84	42	.67	148	.273	.344	.416
Milwaukee	162	5620	764	708	1556	281	57	132	2347	732	475	51	665	27	61	57	101	49	.67	135	.277	.342	.418
Boston	162	5590	724	775	1512	287	32	142	2289	691	536	44	758	28	49	48	30	26	.54	171	.270	.342	.409
California	162	5640	722	779	1467	241	22	154	2214	682	509	39	835	31	68	45	41	39	.51	142	.260	.330	.393
Minnesota	162	5601	709	822	1463	280	41	144	2248	671	467	27	802	29	29	45	44	29	.60	150	.261	.326	.401
Oakland	162	5516	708	782	1447	237	28	121	2103	662	524	47	872	31	55	62	235	98	.71	128	.262	.337	.381
Cleveland	162	5476	704	785	1451	249	31	86	2020	659	605	38	691	29	48	64	109	71	.61	146	.265	.348	.369
Kansas City	163	5598	696	767	1515	273	54	109	2223	653	397	41	722	23	32	33	182	47	.79	123	.271	.325	.397
Texas	163	5610	639	609	1429	242	33	106	2055	587	442	33	767	29	38	42	119	60	.66	123	.255	.317	.366
Seattle	162	5336	558	740	1280	247	31	111	1922	536	460	31	840	24	40	45	144	80	.64	113	.240	.308	.360
AL Total	2270	77821	10177	10177	20662	3710	549	1903	31179	9621	7094	566	10967	425	640	708	1539	749	.67	1879	.266	.328	.401
AL Avg Team	162	5559	727	727	1476	265	39	136	2227	687	507	40	783	30	46	51	110	54	.67	134	.266	.328	.401

Team Pitching

Team	G	CG	ShO	Rel	Sv	IP	H	R	ER	HR	SH	SF	HB	TBB	IBB	SO	WP	Bk	H/9	SO/9	BB/9	OAvg	OOBP	ERA
Texas	163	43	11	190	32	1466.2	1392	609	540	97	48	43	38	471	25	826	36	6	8.5	5.1	2.9	.252	.313	3.31
Baltimore	162	36	15	225	38	1452.1	1451	652	585	130	46	46	10	452	25	774	36	4	9.0	4.8	2.8	.261	.316	3.63
Chicago	162	35	12	243	48	1445.1	1355	650	589	128	37	39	33	447	32	877	38	2	8.4	5.5	2.8	.248	.307	3.67
Detroit	162	42	9	205	28	1451.0	1318	679	613	170	32	39	29	522	48	875	59	7	8.2	5.4	3.2	.242	.309	3.80
New York	162	47	12	202	32	1456.2	1449	703	624	116	54	59	20	455	24	892	36	7	9.0	5.5	2.8	.260	.315	3.86
Milwaukee	162	35	10	241	43	1454.0	1513	708	650	133	48	57	28	491	32	689	29	9	9.4	4.3	3.0	.270	.329	4.02
Seattle	162	25	9	282	39	1418.1	1455	740	649	145	45	40	40	544	46	910	48	16	9.2	5.8	3.5	.268	.337	4.12
Toronto	162	43	8	257	32	1445.1	1434	726	662	145	34	50	42	517	38	835	25	5	8.9	5.2	3.2	.259	.325	4.12
Kansas City	163	19	7	229	49	1437.2	1535	767	679	133	46	62	27	471	23	593	40	3	9.6	3.7	2.9	.274	.330	4.25
California	162	39	7	237	23	1474.0	1636	779	706	130	57	50	30	496	71	668	51	1	10.0	4.1	3.0	.284	.341	4.31
Boston	162	29	7	201	42	1446.1	1572	775	698	158	40	57	31	493	43	767	28	9	9.8	4.8	3.1	.279	.337	4.34
Oakland	162	22	12	287	33	1454.1	1462	782	702	135	55	59	31	626	44	719	43	9	9.0	4.4	3.9	.263	.337	4.34
Cleveland	162	34	8	226	25	1441.2	1531	785	710	120	43	54	31	529	61	794	54	6	9.6	5.0	3.3	.275	.339	4.43
Minnesota	162	20	5	268	39	1437.1	1559	822	745	163	55	53	35	580	54	748	41	13	9.8	4.7	3.6	.280	.348	4.66
AL Total	2270	469	133	3263	503	20281.0	20662	10177	9152	1903	640	708	425	7094	566	10967	564	97	9.2	4.9	3.1	.266	.336	4.06
AL Avg Team	162	34	10	233	36	1448.0	1476	727	654	136	46	51	30	507	40	783	40	7	9.2	4.9	3.1	.266	.336	4.06

Team Fielding

Team	G	PO	A	E	TC	DP	PB	Pct
Texas	163	4400	1899	113	6412	151	14	.982
Milwaukee	162	4362	1771	113	6246	162	8	.982
Toronto	162	4336	1637	115	6088	148	7	.981
Chicago	162	4336	1853	120	6309	158	12	.981
Baltimore	162	4357	1784	121	6262	159	5	.981
Cleveland	162	4325	1786	121	6232	174	17	.981
Minnesota	162	4312	1700	121	6133	170	10	.980
Detroit	162	4353	1703	125	6181	142	12	.980
Boston	162	4339	1719	130	6188	168	8	.979
Seattle	162	4255	1858	136	6249	159	16	.978
New York	162	4370	1733	139	6242	157	6	.978
California	162	4422	2077	154	6653	190	6	.977
Oakland	162	4363	1602	157	6122	157	14	.974
Kansas City	163	4313	1816	165	6294	178	4	.974
AL Total	2270	60843	24938	1830	87611	2273	139	.979

Team vs. Team Records

	Bal	Bos	Cal	ChA	Cle	Det	KC	Mil	Min	NYA	Oak	Sea	Tex	Tor	Won
Bal	—	8	7	7	6	5	8	11	8	6	8	8	9	7	98
Bos	5	—	6	6	7	4	5	4	5	7	8	7	7	7	78
Cal	5	6	—	3	8	4	6	6	6	5	6	6	6	4	70
ChA	5	6	10	—	8	8	9	4	8	8	8	12	8	5	99
Cle	7	6	4	4	—	5	7	3	6	6	7	8	3	4	70
Det	8	9	8	4	8	—	7	6	9	5	6	8	6	6	92
KC	4	7	7	4	5	5	—	6	6	6	7	6	5	4	79
Mil	2	9	6	8	10	7	6	—	8	4	6	5	8	8	87
Min	4	7	7	5	6	3	7	4	—	4	4	9	5	5	70
NYA	7	6	7	4	7	8	6	9	8	—	8	7	7	7	91
Oak	4	4	8	5	5	6	6	6	9	4	—	9	2	6	74
Sea	4	5	7	1	4	5	5	7	4	5	4	—	6	4	60
Tex	3	5	7	5	9	3	4	4	8	5	11	7	—	4	77
Tor	6	6	8	7	9	7	6	5	7	6	6	8	8	—	89
Lost	64	84	92	63	92	70	83	75	92	71	88	102	85	73	

1983 American League Batting Leaders

Games		At-Bats		Runs		Hits		Doubles		Triples	
A. Griffin, Tor	162	C. Ripken Jr., Bal	663	C. Ripken Jr., Bal	121	C. Ripken Jr., Bal	211	C. Ripken Jr., Bal	47	R. Yount, Mil	10
C. Ripken Jr., Bal	162	C. Cooper, Mil	661	E. Murray, Bal	115	W. Boggs, Bos	210	W. Boggs, Bos	44	A. Griffin, Tor	9
G. Wright, Tex	162	L. Whitaker, Det	643	C. Cooper, Mil	106	L. Whitaker, Det	206	L. Parrish, Det	42	L. Herndon, Det	9
L. Whitaker, Det	161	G. Wright, Tex	634	R. Henderson, Oak	105	C. Cooper, Mil	203	R. Yount, Mil	42	K. Gibson, Det	9
J. Gantner, Mil	161	J. Rice, Bos	626	L. Moseby, Tor	104	J. Rice, Bos	191	2 tied with	41	4 tied with	8

Home Runs		Total Bases		Runs Batted In		Walks		Intentional Walks		Strikeouts	
J. Rice, Bos	39	J. Rice, Bos	344	C. Cooper, Mil	126	R. Henderson, Oak	103	K. Singleton, Bal	19	R. Kittle, ChA	150
T. Armas, Bos	36	C. Ripken Jr., Bal	343	J. Rice, Bos	126	K. Singleton, Bal	99	A. Thornton, Cle	14	G. Thomas, 2tm	148
R. Kittle, ChA	35	C. Cooper, Mil	336	D. Winfield, NYA	116	W. Boggs, Bos	92	G. Brett, KC	13	R. Jackson, Cal	140
E. Murray, Bal	33	E. Murray, Bal	313	L. Parrish, Det	114	A. Thornton, Cle	87	E. Murray, Bal	13	T. Armas, Bos	131
2 tied with	32	D. Winfield, NYA	307	E. Murray, Bal	111	E. Murray, Bal	86	H. Baines, ChA	13	G. Gaetti, Min	121

Hit By Pitch		Sac Hits		Sac Flies		Stolen Bases		Caught Stealing		GDP	
C. Lemon, Det	20	A. Trammell, Det	15	L. Parrish, Det	13	R. Henderson, Oak	108	R. Henderson, Oak	19	T. Armas, Bos	31
D. Baylor, NYA	13	C. Moore, Mil	14	B. Almon, Oak	11	R. Law, ChA	77	D. Garcia, Tor	17	J. Rice, Bos	31
G. Luzinski, ChA	11	S. Lubratich, Cal	13	D. Lopes, Oak	10	W. Wilson, KC	59	M. Davis, Oak	15	D. Winfield, NYA	30
H. McRae, KC	10	J. Remy, Bos	12	G. Luzinski, ChA	10	J. Cruz, 2tm	57	S. Henderson, Sea	14	3 tied with	24
R. Kittle, ChA	8	7 tied with	11	2 tied with	9	B. Sample, Tex	44	3 tied with	12		

Runs Created		Runs Created/27 Outs		Batting Average		On-Base Percentage		Slugging Percentage		OBP+Slugging	
E. Murray, Bal	121	W. Boggs, Bos	8.15	W. Boggs, Bos	.361	W. Boggs, Bos	.444	G. Brett, KC	.563	G. Brett, KC	.947
W. Boggs, Bos	121	E. Murray, Bal	7.63	R. Carew, Cal	.339	R. Henderson, Oak	.414	J. Rice, Bos	.550	W. Boggs, Bos	.931
C. Ripken Jr., Bal	117	G. Brett, KC	7.52	L. Whitaker, Det	.320	R. Carew, Cal	.409	E. Murray, Bal	.538	E. Murray, Bal	.930
L. Whitaker, Det	111	R. Henderson, Oak	7.50	A. Trammell, Det	.319	K. Singleton, Bal	.393	C. Fisk, ChA	.518	J. Rice, Bos	.911
R. Henderson, Oak	110	R. Yount, Mil	6.91	C. Ripken Jr., Bal	.318	E. Murray, Bal	.393	C. Ripken Jr., Bal	.517	C. Ripken Jr., Bal	.888

1983 American League Pitching Leaders

Wins		Losses		Winning Percentage		Games		Games Started		Complete Games	
L. Hoyt, ChA	24	L. Gura, KC	18	M. Haas, Mil	.813	D. Quisenberry, KC	69	D. Petry, Det	38	R. Guidry, NYA	21
R. Dotson, ChA	22	B. Stoddard, Sea	17	R. Dotson, ChA	.759	E. Vande Berg, Sea	68	J. Morris, Det	37	J. Morris, Det	20
R. Guidry, NYA	21	D. Martinez, Bal	16	M. Flanagan, Bal	.750	R. Davis, Min	66	L. Hoyt, ChA	36	D. Stieb, Tor	14
J. Morris, Det	20	3 tied with	15	G. Gossage, NYA	.722	T. Martinez, Bal	65	S. McGregor, Bal	36	S. Rawley, NYA	13
D. Petry, Det	19			S. McGregor, Bal	.720	B. Stanley, Bos	64	D. Stieb, Tor	36	S. McGregor, Bal	12

Shutouts		Saves		Games Finished		Batters Faced		Innings Pitched		Hits Allowed	
M. Boddicker, Bal	5	D. Quisenberry, KC	45	D. Quisenberry, KC	62	J. Morris, Det	1204	J. Morris, Det	293.2	T. John, Cal	287
B. Burns, ChA	4	B. Stanley, Bos	33	R. Davis, Min	61	D. Stieb, Tor	1141	D. Stieb, Tor	278.0	S. McGregor, Bal	271
D. Stieb, Tor	4	R. Davis, Min	30	B. Caudill, Sea	54	D. Petry, Det	1115	D. Petry, Det	266.1	M. Caldwell, Mil	269
5 tied with	3	B. Caudill, Sea	26	B. Stanley, Bos	53	S. McGregor, Bal	1072	L. Hoyt, ChA	260.2	J. Morris, Det	257
		P. Ladd, Mil	25	T. Martinez, Bal	51	R. Sutcliffe, Cle	1061	S. McGregor, Bal	260.0	D. Petry, Det	256

Home Runs Allowed		Walks		Walks/9 Innings		Strikeouts		Strikeouts/9 Innings		Strikeout/Walk Ratio	
D. Petry, Det	37	R. Dotson, ChA	106	L. Hoyt, ChA	1.1	J. Morris, Det	232	F. Bannister, ChA	8.0	L. Hoyt, ChA	4.77
M. Caldwell, Mil	35	R. Sutcliffe, Cle	102	S. McGregor, Bal	1.6	F. Bannister, ChA	193	J. Morris, Det	7.1	J. Morris, Det	2.80
F. Viola, Min	34	D. Petry, Det	99	T. John, Cal	1.9	D. Stieb, Tor	187	D. Righetti, NYA	7.0	F. Bannister, ChA	2.72
J. Tudor, Bos	32	T. Conroy, Oak	98	R. Honeycutt, Tex	1.9	D. Righetti, NYA	169	T. Conroy, Oak	6.2	R. Guidry, NYA	2.60
J. Morris, Det	30	C. Hough, Tex	95	D. Eckersley, Bos	2.0	R. Sutcliffe, Cle	160	J. Gott, Tor	6.2	D. Righetti, NYA	2.52

Earned Run Average		Component ERA		Hit Batsmen		Wild Pitches		Opponent Average		Opponent OBP	
R. Honeycutt, Tex	2.42	M. Boddicker, Bal	2.41	D. Stieb, Tor	14	J. Morris, Det	18	M. Boddicker, Bal	.216	L. Hoyt, ChA	.260
M. Boddicker, Bal	2.77	L. Hoyt, ChA	2.53	B. Blyleven, Cle	10	D. Petry, Det	12	D. Stieb, Tor	.219	M. Boddicker, Bal	.273
D. Stieb, Tor	3.04	D. Stieb, Tor	2.78	K. Schrom, Min	9	T. John, Cal	11	T. Conroy, Oak	.232	J. Morris, Det	.287
C. Hough, Tex	3.18	D. Righetti, NYA	2.88	5 tied with	8	3 tied with	10	F. Bannister, ChA	.233	R. Guidry, NYA	.288
S. McGregor, Bal	3.18	M. Haas, Mil	2.97					J. Morris, Det	.233	D. Stieb, Tor	.291

1983 American League Miscellaneous

Managers		
Baltimore	Joe Altobelli	98-64
Boston	Ralph Houk	78-84
California	John McNamara	70-92
Chicago	Tony La Russa	99-63
Cleveland	Mike Ferraro	40-60
	Pat Corrales	30-32
Detroit	Sparky Anderson	92-70
Kansas City	Dick Howser	79-83
Milwaukee	Harvey Kuenn	87-75
Minnesota	Billy Gardner	70-92
New York	Billy Martin	91-71
Oakland	Steve Boros	74-88
Seattle	Rene Lachemann	26-47
	Del Crandall	34-55
Texas	Doug Rader	77-85
Toronto	Bobby Cox	89-73

Awards

Most Valuable Player	Cal Ripken Jr., ss, Bal
Cy Young	LaMarr Hoyt, ChA
Rookie of the Year	Ron Kittle, of, ChA
Manager of the Year	Tony La Russa, ChA

STATS All-Star Team

C	Carlton Fisk, ChA	.289	26	86
1B	Eddie Murray, Bal	.306	33	111
2B	Bobby Grich, Cal	.292	16	62
3B	Wade Boggs, Bos	.361	5	74
SS	Cal Ripken Jr., Bal	.318	27	102
OF	Rickey Henderson, Oak	.292	9	48
OF	Jim Rice, Bos	.305	39	126
OF	Dave Winfield, NYA	.283	32	116
DH	Greg Luzinski, ChA	.255	32	95
P	Rich Dotson, ChA	22-7	3.23	137 K
P	LaMarr Hoyt, ChA	24-10	3.66	148 K
P	Jack Morris, Det	20-13	3.34	232 K
P	Dave Stieb, Tor	17-12	3.04	187 K
RP	Dan Quisenberry, KC	5-3	1.94	45 Sv

Postseason

LCS	Baltimore 3 vs. Chicago 1
World Series	Bal (AL) 4 vs. Phi (NL) 1

Outstanding Performances

No-Hitters

Dave Righetti, NYA	vs. Bos on July 4
Mike Warren, Oak	vs. ChA on September 29

Three-Homer Games

George Brett, KC	on April 20
Ben Oglivie, Mil	on May 14
Dan Ford, Bal	on July 20
Jim Rice, Bos	on August 29

Seasons: Standings, Leaders

1983 National League Standings

EAST	Overall					Home Games						Road Games						Park Index		Record by Month					
	W	L	Pct	GB	DIF	W	L	R	OR	HR	OHR	W	L	R	OR	HR	OHR	Run	HR	M/A	May	June	July	Aug	S/O
Philadelphia	90	72	.556	—	70	50	31	361	310	61	61	40	41	335	325	64	50	102	107	11-7	9-13	14-15	17-13	16-16	23-8
Pittsburgh	84	78	.519	6.0	39	41	40	335	336	60	63	43	38	324	312	61	46	106	115	8-9	10-15	14-15	22-10	14-14	16-15
Montreal	82	80	.506	8.0	38	46	35	341	325	40	56	36	45	336	321	62	64	101	76	10-7	12-14	17-12	13-17	14-14	16-16
St. Louis	79	83	.488	11.0	58	44	37	334	350	38	58	35	46	345	360	45	57	97	94	10-6	15-12	12-19	16-13	12-15	14-18
Chicago	71	91	.438	19.0	1	43	38	384	341	71	69	28	53	317	378	69	48	104	120	6-14	11-14	18-11	12-17	12-17	12-18
New York	68	94	.420	22.0	5	41	41	300	329	63	53	27	53	275	351	49	44	98	122	6-11	10-17	13-18	10-19	16-13	13-16
WEST																									
Los Angeles	91	71	.562	—	105	48	32	316	296	74	49	43	39	338	313	72	48	96	105	14-6	18-8	14-14	11-17	20-10	14-16
Atlanta	88	74	.543	3.0	79	46	34	394	327	66	71	42	40	352	313	64	61	111	112	14-5	16-12	16-13	18-11	12-16	12-17
Houston	85	77	.525	6.0	0	46	36	294	278	26	28	39	41	349	368	71	66	78	38	8-14	14-14	15-11	15-11	18-12	15-15
San Diego	81	81	.500	10.0	4	47	34	350	299	53	82	34	47	303	354	40	62	99	132	10-12	11-13	17-12	13-15	15-17	15-12
San Francisco	79	83	.488	12.0	0	43	38	346	356	73	67	36	45	341	341	69	60	103	109	7-14	19-7	12-16	13-16	12-17	16-13
Cincinnati	74	88	.457	17.0	6	36	45	331	360	52	64	38	43	292	350	55	71	108	92	11-10	11-17	11-17	13-14	15-15	13-15

Clinch Date—Philadelphia 9/28, Los Angeles 9/30.

Team Batting

Team	G	AB	R	OR	H	2B	3B	HR	TB	RBI	TBB	IBB	SO	HBP	SH	SF	SB	CS	SB%	GDP	Avg	OBP	Slg
Atlanta	162	5472	746	640	1489	218	45	130	2187	691	582	72	847	17	78	46	146	88	.62	129	.272	.349	.400
Chicago	162	5512	701	719	1436	272	42	140	2212	649	470	63	868	29	71	50	84	40	.68	113	.261	.328	.401
Philadelphia	163	5426	696	635	1352	209	45	125	2026	649	640	75	906	26	80	46	143	75	.66	132	.249	.336	.373
San Francisco	162	5369	687	697	1324	206	30	142	2016	638	619	63	990	28	64	46	140	78	.64	129	.247	.333	.375
St. Louis	162	5550	679	710	1496	262	63	83	2133	636	543	66	879	24	72	49	207	89	.70	117	.270	.343	.384
Montreal	163	5611	677	646	1482	297	41	102	2167	632	509	76	733	38	78	57	138	44	.76	133	.264	.336	.386
Pittsburgh	162	5531	659	648	1460	238	29	121	2119	612	497	63	873	19	84	38	124	77	.62	121	.264	.331	.383
Los Angeles	163	5440	654	609	1358	197	34	146	2061	613	541	61	925	22	86	40	166	76	.69	112	.250	.325	.379
San Diego	163	5527	653	653	1384	207	34	93	1938	592	482	80	822	20	89	45	179	67	.73	121	.250	.318	.351
Houston	162	5502	643	646	1412	239	60	97	2062	615	517	71	869	19	81	54	164	95	.63	76	.257	.329	.375
Cincinnati	162	5333	623	710	1274	236	35	107	1901	577	588	69	1006	19	72	45	154	77	.67	121	.239	.322	.356
New York	162	5444	575	680	1314	172	26	112	1874	542	436	54	1031	31	66	32	141	64	.69	113	.241	.305	.344
NL Total	1948	65717	7993	7993	16781	2753	484	1398	24696	7446	6424	813	10749	292	921	548	1786	870	.67	1417	.255	.322	.376
NL Avg Team	162	5476	666	666	1398	229	40	117	2058	621	535	68	896	24	77	46	149	73	.67	118	.255	.322	.376

Team Pitching

Team	G	CG	ShO	Rel	Sv	IP	H	R	ER	HR	SH	SF	HB	TBB	IBB	SO	WP	Bk	H/9	SO/9	BB/9	OAvg	OOBP	ERA
Los Angeles	163	27	12	278	40	1464.0	1336	609	505	97	99	45	20	495	78	1000	38	12	8.2	6.1	3.0	.244	.307	3.10
Philadelphia	163	20	10	300	41	1461.2	1429	635	542	111	65	39	23	464	77	1092	44	18	8.8	6.7	2.9	.256	.314	3.34
Houston	162	22	14	261	48	1466.1	1276	646	562	94	65	52	27	570	49	904	49	14	7.8	5.5	3.5	.236	.309	3.45
Pittsburgh	162	25	14	290	41	1462.1	1378	648	577	109	64	46	18	563	67	1061	52	21	8.5	6.5	3.5	.252	.321	3.55
Montreal	163	38	15	252	34	1471.0	1406	646	585	120	67	37	33	479	50	899	38	9	8.6	5.5	2.9	.254	.315	3.58
San Diego	163	23	5	294	44	1467.2	1389	653	590	96	46	42	28	528	52	850	33	10	8.5	5.2	3.2	.253	.320	3.62
Atlanta	162	18	4	305	48	1440.2	1412	640	588	132	75	43	23	540	47	895	34	10	8.8	5.6	3.4	.260	.327	3.67
New York	162	18	7	274	33	1451.0	1384	680	593	97	83	47	21	615	82	717	46	14	8.6	4.4	3.8	.256	.331	3.68
San Francisco	162	20	9	276	47	1445.2	1431	697	594	127	78	52	31	520	95	881	53	20	8.9	5.5	3.2	.259	.323	3.70
St. Louis	162	22	10	327	27	1460.2	1479	710	615	115	88	45	23	525	73	709	55	19	9.1	4.4	3.2	.266	.330	3.79
Cincinnati	162	34	5	271	29	1441.1	1365	710	638	135	61	58	20	627	60	934	27	9	8.5	5.8	3.9	.253	.330	3.98
Chicago	162	9	10	369	42	1428.2	1496	719	647	117	80	42	25	498	83	807	43	13	9.4	5.1	3.1	.274	.335	4.08
NL Total	1948	276	115	3497	474	17461.0	16781	7993	7036	1398	921	548	292	6424	813	10749	512	169	8.6	5.5	3.3	.255	.329	3.63
NL Avg Team	162	23	10	291	40	1455.0	1398	666	586	117	77	46	24	535	68	896	43	14	8.6	5.5	3.3	.255	.329	3.63

Team Fielding

Team	G	PO	A	E	TC	DP	PB	Pct
Chicago	162	4286	1982	115	6383	164	24	.982
Pittsburgh	162	4387	1717	115	6219	165	9	.982
Montreal	163	4413	1687	116	6216	130	8	.981
Cincinnati	162	4324	1624	114	6062	121	16	.981
San Diego	163	4403	1729	129	6261	135	9	.979
Atlanta	162	4322	1850	137	6309	176	6	.978
Houston	162	4399	1839	147	6385	165	35	.977
St. Louis	162	4382	1922	152	6456	173	19	.976
New York	162	4353	1889	151	6393	171	12	.976
Philadelphia	163	4385	1804	152	6341	117	13	.976
Los Angeles	163	4392	1805	168	6365	132	20	.974
San Francisco	162	4337	1775	171	6283	109	11	.973
NL Total	1948	52383	21623	1667	75673	1758	182	.978

Team vs. Team Records

	Atl	ChN	Cin	Hou	LA	Mon	NYN	Phi	Pit	SD	SF	StL	Won
Atl	—	5	12	11	7	7	8	7	6	9	9	7	88
ChN	7	—	4	5	6	7	9	5	9	5	4	10	71
Cin	6	8	—	5	7	4	7	6	6	9	10	6	74
Hou	7	7	13	—	6	8	9	4	6	11	12	2	85
LA	11	6	11	12	—	7	7	11	6	6	5	9	91
Mon	5	11	8	4	5	—	8	8	8	8	8	9	82
NYN	4	9	5	3	5	10	—	6	9	6	5	6	68
Phi	5	13	6	8	1	10	12	—	11	5	5	14	90
Pit	6	9	6	9	6	6	10	9	—	9	6	10	84
SD	9	7	9	7	12	4	6	7	3	—	11	6	81
SF	9	8	8	6	13	4	7	7	6	7	—	4	79
StL	5	8	6	10	3	9	12	4	8	6	8	—	79
Lost	74	91	88	77	71	80	94	72	78	81	83	83	

Seasons: Standings, Leaders

1983 National League Batting Leaders

Games		At-Bats		Runs		Hits		Doubles		Triples	
D. Murphy, Atl	162	M. Wilson, NYN	638	T. Raines, Mon	133	J. Cruz, Hou	189	B. Buckner, ChN	38	B. Butler, Atl	13
D. Berra, Pit	161	A. Dawson, Mon	633	D. Murphy, Atl	131	A. Dawson, Mon	189	A. Oliver, Mon	38	O. Moreno, Hou	11
J. Cruz, Hou	160	R. Sandberg, ChN	633	A. Dawson, Mon	104	R. Ramirez, Atl	185	J. Ray, Pit	38	A. Dawson, Mon	10
P. Guerrero, LA	160	B. Buckner, ChN	626	M. Schmidt, Phi	104	A. Oliver, Mon	184	G. Carter, Mon	37	D. Green, StL	10
3 tied with	159	S. Sax, LA	623	3 tied with	94	T. Raines, Mon	183	2 tied with	36	2 tied with	9

Home Runs		Total Bases		Runs Batted In		Walks		Intentional Walks		Strikeouts	
M. Schmidt, Phi	40	A. Dawson, Mon	341	D. Murphy, Atl	121	M. Schmidt, Phi	128	D. Berra, Pit	19	M. Schmidt, Phi	148
D. Murphy, Atl	36	A. Dawson, Mon	318	A. Dawson, Mon	113	J. Thompson, Pit	99	I. DeJesus, Phi	18	J. Thompson, Pit	128
A. Dawson, Mon	32	P. Guerrero, LA	310	M. Schmidt, Phi	109	T. Raines, Mon	97	M. Schmidt, Phi	17	D. Strawberry, NYN	128
P. Guerrero, LA	32	D. Thon, Hou	283	P. Guerrero, LA	103	D. Murphy, Atl	90	A. Oliver, Mon	17	M. Marshall, LA	127
D. Evans, SF	30	M. Schmidt, Phi	280	T. Kennedy, SD	98	J. Morgan, Phi	89	B. Benedict, Atl	16	J. Leonard, SF	116

Hit By Pitch		Sac Hits		Sac Flies		Stolen Bases		Caught Stealing		GDP	
A. Dawson, Mon	9	S. Rogers, Mon	20	A. Dawson, Mon	18	T. Raines, Mon	90	S. Sax, LA	30	D. Concepcion, Cin	21
L. Smith, StL	9	J. Denny, Phi	17	R. Knight, Hou	11	A. Wiggins, SD	66	B. Butler, Atl	23	A. Oliver, Mon	21
G. Carter, Mon	7	A. Wiggins, SD	16	G. Hendrick, StL	11	S. Sax, LA	56	J. LeMaster, SF	19	R. Cey, ChN	20
T. Wallach, Mon	6	6 tied with	12	K. Moreland, ChN	10	M. Wilson, NYN	54	L. Smith, StL	18	G. Foster, NYN	19
6 tied with	5			3 tied with	9	L. Smith, StL	43	4 tied with	16	J. Bonilla, SD	19

Runs Created		Runs Created/27 Outs		Batting Average		On-Base Percentage		Slugging Percentage		OBP+Slugging	
D. Murphy, Atl	124	D. Murphy, Atl	7.69	B. Madlock, Pit	.323	M. Schmidt, Phi	.399	D. Murphy, Atl	.540	D. Murphy, Atl	.933
M. Schmidt, Phi	115	M. Schmidt, Phi	7.41	L. Smith, StL	.321	K. Hernandez, 2tm	.396	A. Dawson, Mon	.539	M. Schmidt, Phi	.923
T. Raines, Mon	112	D. Evans, SF	7.14	J. Cruz, Hou	.318	D. Murphy, Atl	.393	P. Guerrero, LA	.531	P. Guerrero, LA	.904
P. Guerrero, LA	111	P. Guerrero, LA	6.92	G. Hendrick, StL	.318	T. Raines, Mon	.393	M. Schmidt, Phi	.524	D. Evans, SF	.894
A. Dawson, Mon	106	T. Raines, Mon	6.53	R. Knight, Hou	.304	B. Madlock, Pit	.386	D. Evans, SF	.516	A. Dawson, Mon	.877

1983 National League Pitching Leaders

Wins		Losses		Winning Percentage		Games		Games Started		Complete Games	
J. Denny, Phi	19	M. Torrez, NYN	17	J. Denny, Phi	.760	B. Campbell, ChN	82	J. Niekro, Hou	38	M. Soto, Cin	18
B. Gullickson, Mon	17	J. Andujar, StL	16	J. Candelaria, Pit	.652	K. Tekulve, Pit	76	S. Carlton, Phi	37	S. Rogers, Mon	13
S. Rogers, Mon	17	S. Carlton, Phi	16	L. McWilliams, Pit	.652	W. Hernandez, 2tm	74	J. Denny, Phi	36	B. Gullickson, Mon	10
M. Soto, Cin	17	4 tied with	14	P. Perez, Atl	.652	G. Minton, SF	73	S. Rogers, Mon	36	3 tied with	9
C. Lea, Mon	16			J. Orosco, NYN	.650	B. Scherrer, Cin	73	4 tied with	35		

Shutouts		Saves		Games Finished		Batters Faced		Innings Pitched		Hits Allowed	
S. Rogers, Mon	5	L. Smith, ChN	29	K. Tekulve, Pit	56	S. Carlton, Phi	1183	S. Carlton, Phi	283.2	S. Carlton, Phi	277
L. McWilliams, Pit	4	A. Holland, Phi	25	L. Smith, ChN	56	S. Rogers, Mon	1125	M. Soto, Cin	273.2	S. Rogers, Mon	258
C. Lea, Mon	4	G. Minton, SF	22	A. Holland, Phi	53	M. Soto, Cin	1114	S. Rogers, Mon	273.0	R. Rhoden, Pit	256
F. Valenzuela, LA	4	J. Reardon, Mon	21	J. Reardon, Mon	53	J. Niekro, Hou	1113	J. Niekro, Hou	263.2	F. Valenzuela, LA	245
10 tied with	3	B. Sutter, StL	21	2 tied with	52	F. Valenzuela, LA	1094	F. Valenzuela, LA	257.0	J. Niekro, Hou	238

Home Runs Allowed		Walks		Walks/9 Innings		Strikeouts		Strikeouts/9 Innings		Strikeout/Walk Ratio	
M. Soto, Cin	28	M. Torrez, NYN	113	A. Hammaker, SF	1.7	S. Carlton, Phi	275	S. Carlton, Phi	8.7	A. Hammaker, SF	3.97
E. Show, SD	25	P. Niekro, Atl	105	D. Ruthven, 2tm	1.9	M. Soto, Cin	242	N. Ryan, Hou	8.4	J. Candelaria, Pit	3.49
J. Andujar, StL	23	B. Berenyi, Cin	102	J. Denny, Phi	2.0	L. McWilliams, Pit	199	M. Soto, Cin	8.0	S. Carlton, Phi	3.27
B. Forsch, StL	23	J. Niekro, Hou	101	J. Reuss, LA	2.0	F. Valenzuela, LA	189	L. McWilliams, Pit	7.5	J. Reuss, LA	2.86
E. Whitson, SD	23	N. Ryan, Hou	101	J. Candelaria, Pit	2.0	N. Ryan, Hou	183	B. Berenyi, Cin	7.3	P. Perez, Atl	2.82

Earned Run Average		Component ERA		Hit Batsmen		Wild Pitches		Opponent Average		Opponent OBP	
A. Hammaker, SF	2.25	A. Hammaker, SF	2.16	M. Bystrom, Phi	7	J. Niekro, Hou	14	N. Ryan, Hou	.195	A. Hammaker, SF	.266
J. Denny, Phi	2.37	A. Pena, LA	2.45	E. Show, SD	6	S. Carlton, Phi	13	M. Soto, Cin	.208	M. Soto, Cin	.278
B. Welch, LA	2.65	N. Ryan, Hou	2.56	F. Jenkins, ChN	6	F. Valenzuela, LA	12	B. Welch, LA	.222	A. Pena, LA	.283
M. Soto, Cin	2.70	M. Soto, Cin	2.63	8 tied with	5	D. LaPoint, StL	11	A. Hammaker, SF	.228	B. Welch, LA	.291
A. Pena, LA	2.75	B. Welch, LA	2.68			L. Tunnell, Pit	11	A. Pena, LA	.229	J. Denny, Phi	.293

1983 National League Miscellaneous

Managers

Atlanta	Joe Torre	88-74
Chicago	Lee Elia	54-69
	Charlie Fox	17-22
Cincinnati	Russ Nixon	74-88
Houston	Bob Lillis	85-77
Los Angeles	Tom Lasorda	91-71
Montreal	Bill Virdon	82-80
New York	George Bamberger	16-30
	Frank Howard	52-64
Philadelphia	Pat Corrales	43-42
	Paul Owens	47-30
Pittsburgh	Chuck Tanner	84-78
St. Louis	Whitey Herzog	79-83
San Diego	Dick Williams	81-81
San Francisco	Frank Robinson	79-83

Awards

Most Valuable Player	Dale Murphy, of, Atl
Cy Young	John Denny, Phi
Rookie of the Year	D. Strawberry, of, NYN
Manager of the Year	Tom Lasorda, LA

STATS All-Star Team

C	Gary Carter, Mon	.270	17	79
1B	Darrell Evans, SF	.277	30	82
2B	Bill Doran, Hou	.271	8	39
3B	Mike Schmidt, Phi	.255	40	109
SS	Dickie Thon, Hou	.286	20	79
OF	Andre Dawson, Mon	.299	32	113
OF	Dale Murphy, Atl	.302	36	121
OF	Tim Raines, Mon	.298	11	71
P	John Denny, Phi	19-6	2.37	139 K
P	Larry McWilliams, Pit	15-8	3.25	199 K
P	Nolan Ryan, Hou	14-9	2.98	183 K
P	Mario Soto, Cin	17-13	2.70	242 K
RP	Lee Smith, ChN	4-10	1.65	29 Sv

Postseason

LCS	Philadelphia 3 vs. Los Angeles 1
World Series	Phi (NL) 1 vs. Bal (AL) 4

Outstanding Performances

No-Hitters
Bob Forsch, StL   vs. Mon on September 26

Three-Homer Games
Darrell Evans, SF   on June 15

1984 American League Standings

EAST	Overall					Home Games						Road Games						Park Index		Record by Month					
	W	L	Pct	GB	DIF	W	L	R	OR	HR	OHR	W	L	R	OR	HR	OHR	Run	HR	M/A	May	June	July	Aug	S/O
Detroit	104	58	.642	—	182	53	29	406	295	85	69	51	29	423	348	102	61	89	92	18-2	19-7	18-12	16-12	16-15	17-10
Toronto	89	73	.549	15.0	1	49	32	387	339	59	78	40	41	363	357	84	62	101	94	13-9	19-6	13-16	14-14	18-12	12-16
New York	87	75	.537	17.0	1	51	30	372	292	62	49	36	45	386	387	68	71	86	80	8-13	12-14	13-14	17-11	21-10	16-13
Boston	86	76	.531	18.0	1	41	40	456	413	100	76	45	36	354	351	81	65	123	121	9-13	12-13	15-14	18-9	17-14	15-13
Baltimore	85	77	.525	19.0	1	44	37	319	306	82	59	41	40	362	361	78	78	86	90	10-13	18-8	14-14	15-13	15-13	13-16
Cleveland	75	87	.463	29.0	6	41	39	411	399	65	73	34	48	350	367	58	68	116	112	10-9	7-19	14-14	13-16	16-18	15-11
Milwaukee	67	94	.416	36.5	1	38	43	286	344	42	68	29	51	355	390	54	69	84	88	9-11	13-13	12-18	13-17	9-20	11-15
WEST																									
Kansas City	84	78	.519	—	26	44	37	344	326	48	59	40	41	329	360	69	77	97	73	8-11	12-15	13-14	17-15	17-12	17-11
California	81	81	.500	3.0	80	37	44	341	364	79	83	44	37	355	333	71	60	102	124	15-11	11-14	15-12	12-14	13-16	15-14
Minnesota	81	81	.500	3.0	58	47	34	372	337	63	77	34	47	301	338	51	82	111	105	11-13	13-12	13-14	17-10	15-16	12-16
Oakland	77	85	.475	7.0	21	44	37	356	344	77	72	33	48	382	452	81	83	84	91	14-10	9-17	15-14	10-18	14-14	15-12
Chicago	74	88	.457	10.0	10	43	38	394	389	103	77	31	50	285	347	69	78	124	122	8-13	14-13	15-13	13-15	12-17	12-17
Seattle	74	88	.457	10.0	12	42	39	357	394	68	82	32	49	325	380	61	56	107	128	12-11	11-16	14-15	12-16	10-18	15-12
Texas	69	92	.429	14.5	0	34	46	327	357	55	70	35	46	329	357	65	78	101	89	8-14	12-15	15-15	10-17	15-13	9-18

Clinch Date—Detroit 9/18, Kansas City 9/28.

Team Batting

Team	G	AB	R	OR	H	2B	3B	HR	TB	RBI	TBB	IBB	SO	HBP	SH	SF	SB	CS	SB%	GDP	Avg	OBP	Slg
Detroit	162	5644	829	643	1529	254	46	187	2436	788	602	51	941	34	48	45	106	68	.61	102	.271	.349	.432
Boston	162	5648	810	764	1598	259	45	181	2490	767	500	48	842	20	36	46	38	25	.60	148	.283	.348	.441
Cleveland	163	5643	761	766	1498	222	39	123	2167	704	600	34	815	27	37	67	126	77	.62	137	.265	.346	.384
New York	162	5661	758	679	1560	275	32	130	2289	725	534	41	673	38	64	59	62	38	.62	147	.276	.348	.404
Toronto	163	5687	750	696	1555	275	68	143	2395	702	460	46	816	52	35	49	193	67	.74	91	.273	.339	.421
Oakland	162	5457	738	796	1415	257	29	158	2204	697	568	29	871	22	37	77	145	64	.69	116	.259	.340	.404
California	162	5470	696	697	1363	241	30	150	2084	649	556	33	928	29	65	46	80	51	.61	140	.249	.327	.381
Seattle	162	5546	682	774	1429	244	34	129	2128	635	519	35	871	42	66	38	116	62	.65	101	.258	.330	.384
Baltimore	162	5456	681	667	1374	234	23	160	2134	647	620	48	884	22	45	43	51	36	.59	133	.252	.335	.391
Chicago	162	5513	679	736	1360	225	38	172	2177	640	523	43	883	39	37	44	109	49	.69	111	.247	.321	.395
Kansas City	162	5543	673	686	1487	269	52	117	2211	639	400	39	832	24	41	55	106	64	.62	128	.268	.326	.399
Minnesota	162	5562	673	675	1473	259	33	114	2140	636	437	45	735	24	26	58	39	30	.57	138	.265	.328	.385
Texas	161	5569	656	714	1452	227	29	120	2097	618	420	36	807	20	47	43	81	50	.62	130	.261	.320	.377
Milwaukee	161	5511	641	734	1446	232	36	96	2038	598	432	35	673	26	42	46	52	57	.48	152	.262	.324	.370
AL Total	2268	77910	10027	10027	20539	3443	534	1980	30990	9445	7171	563	11571	419	626	716	1304	738	.64	1774	.264	.326	.398
AL Avg Team	162	5565	716	716	1467	246	38	141	2214	675	512	40	827	30	45	51	93	53	.64	127	.264	.326	.398

Team Pitching

Team	G	CG	ShO	Rel	Sv	IP	H	R	ER	HR	SH	SF	HB	TBB	IBB	SO	WP	Bk	H/9	SO/9	BB/9	OAvg	OOBP	ERA
Detroit	162	19	8	268	51	1464.0	1358	643	568	130	41	42	30	489	41	914	47	6	8.3	5.6	3.0	.246	.308	3.49
Baltimore	162	48	13	208	32	1439.1	1393	667	594	137	42	52	23	512	46	714	58	6	8.7	4.5	3.2	.256	.320	3.71
New York	162	15	12	287	43	1465.1	1485	679	615	120	46	56	20	518	28	992	33	8	9.1	6.1	3.2	.264	.325	3.78
Minnesota	162	32	9	249	38	1437.2	1429	675	615	159	31	44	35	463	50	713	38	7	8.9	4.5	2.9	.260	.319	3.85
Toronto	163	34	10	257	33	1464.0	1433	696	628	140	54	45	34	528	40	875	42	2	8.8	5.4	3.2	.257	.323	3.86
Texas	161	38	6	190	21	1438.2	1443	714	625	148	45	39	34	518	37	863	62	11	9.0	5.4	3.2	.260	.325	3.91
Kansas City	162	18	9	214	50	1444.0	1426	686	629	136	37	52	27	433	20	724	31	8	8.9	4.5	2.7	.258	.312	3.92
California	162	36	12	203	58	1458.0	1526	697	641	143	48	54	27	474	59	754	44	3	9.4	4.7	2.9	.271	.328	3.96
Milwaukee	161	13	7	283	41	1433.0	1532	734	647	137	56	58	22	480	44	785	45	10	9.6	4.9	3.0	.274	.331	4.06
Chicago	162	43	9	238	32	1454.1	1416	736	668	155	50	49	35	483	26	840	39	3	8.8	5.2	3.0	.256	.317	4.13
Boston	162	40	12	201	32	1442.0	1524	764	669	141	37	40	30	517	38	927	37	7	9.5	5.8	3.2	.270	.332	4.18
Cleveland	163	21	7	308	35	1467.2	1523	766	695	141	55	73	27	545	47	803	46	11	9.3	4.9	3.3	.269	.332	4.26
Seattle	162	26	4	292	35	1442.0	1497	774	690	138	44	56	40	619	53	972	47	11	9.3	6.1	3.9	.270	.345	4.31
Oakland	162	15	6	282	44	1430.0	1554	796	712	155	40	56	35	592	34	695	47	7	9.8	4.4	3.7	.278	.348	4.48
AL Total	2268	398	124	3480	513	20280.0	20539	10027	8996	1980	626	716	419	7171	563	11571	616	100	9.1	5.1	3.2	.264	.335	3.99
AL Avg Team	162	28	9	249	37	1448.0	1467	716	643	141	45	51	30	512	40	827	44	7	9.1	5.1	3.2	.264	.335	3.99

Team Fielding

Team	G	PO	A	E	TC	DP	PB	Pct
Baltimore	162	4318	1910	123	6351	166	9	.981
Chicago	162	4363	1796	122	6281	160	4	.981
Minnesota	162	4313	1678	120	6111	134	4	.980
Toronto	163	4392	1669	123	6184	166	9	.980
California	162	4374	1803	128	6305	170	4	.980
Detroit	162	4392	1667	127	6186	162	16	.979
Kansas City	162	4332	1861	131	6324	157	3	.979
Seattle	162	4326	1700	128	6154	143	17	.979
Milwaukee	161	4299	1812	136	6247	156	8	.978
Texas	161	4316	1671	138	6125	138	33	.977
New York	162	4396	1750	142	6288	177	8	.977
Boston	162	4326	1737	143	6206	128	10	.977
Cleveland	163	4403	1719	146	6268	163	14	.977
Oakland	162	4290	1508	146	5944	159	9	.975
AL Total	2268	60840	24281	1853	86974	2179	148	.979

Team vs. Team Records

	Bal	Bos	Cal	ChA	Cle	Det	KC	Mil	Min	NYA	Oak	Sea	Tex	Tor	Won
Bal	—	6	8	7	7	7	5	7	5	5	6	9	9	4	85
Bos	7	—	9	7	10	7	3	9	6	7	7	4	5	5	86
Cal	4	3	—	8	8	4	6	8	4	8	7	9	5	7	81
ChA	5	5	5	—	8	4	5	7	8	7	6	5	5	4	74
Cle	6	3	4	4	—	4	6	9	7	2	7	8	9	6	75
Det	6	6	8	8	9	—	7	11	9	7	9	6	10	8	104
KC	7	9	7	8	6	5	—	6	6	5	5	9	6	5	84
Mil	6	4	4	5	4	2	6	—	5	6	4	6	5	10	67
Min	7	6	9	5	5	3	7	7	—	8	8	7	8	1	81
NYA	8	6	4	5	11	4	6	7	4	—	8	7	6	8	87
Oak	6	5	6	7	5	3	8	8	5	4	—	8	8	4	77
Sea	3	8	4	8	4	6	4	6	6	5	5	—	10	5	74
Tex	3	7	8	8	3	2	7	6	5	5	3		—	6	69
Tor	9	8	5	8	7	5	7	3	11	5	8	7	6	—	89
Lost	77	76	81	88	87	58	78	94	81	75	85	88	92	73	

1984 American League Batting Leaders

Games		At-Bats		Runs		Hits		Doubles		Triples	
E. Murray, Bal	162	J. Franco, Cle	658	D. Evans, Bos	121	D. Mattingly, NYA	207	D. Mattingly, NYA	44	D. Collins, Tor	15
D. Evans, Bos	162	J. Rice, Bos	657	R. Henderson, Oak	113	W. Boggs, Bos	203	L. Parrish, Tex	42	L. Moseby, Tor	15
G. Gaetti, Min	162	C. Ripken Jr., Bal	641	W. Boggs, Bos	109	C. Ripken Jr., Bal	195	G. Bell, Tor	39	K. Gibson, Det	10
C. Ripken Jr., Bal	162	T. Armas, Bos	639	B. Butler, Cle	108	D. Winfield, NYA	193	D. Evans, Bos	37	H. Baines, ChA	10
2 tied with	160	D. Garcia, Tor	633	T. Armas, Bos	107	2 tied with	188	C. Ripken Jr., Bal	37	3 tied with	9

Home Runs		Total Bases		Runs Batted In		Walks		Intentional Walks		Strikeouts	
T. Armas, Bos	43	T. Armas, Bos	339	T. Armas, Bos	123	E. Murray, Bal	107	E. Murray, Bal	25	T. Armas, Bos	156
D. Kingman, Oak	35	D. Evans, Bos	335	J. Rice, Bos	122	A. Davis, Sea	97	A. Davis, Sea	16	R. Jackson, Cal	141
L. Parrish, Det	33	C. Ripken Jr., Bal	327	D. Kingman, Oak	118	D. Evans, Bos	96	K. Hrbek, Min	15	S. Balboni, KC	139
A. Thornton, Cle	33	D. Mattingly, NYA	324	A. Davis, Sea	116	A. Thornton, Cle	91	W. Upshaw, Tor	14	R. Kittle, ChA	137
D. Murphy, Oak	33	M. Easler, Bos	310	2 tied with	110	W. Boggs, Bos	89	A. Thornton, Cle	11	M. Easler, Bos	134

Hit By Pitch		Sac Hits		Sac Flies		Stolen Bases		Caught Stealing		GDP	
D. Baylor, NYA	23	B. Meacham, NYA	14	D. Kingman, Oak	14	R. Henderson, Oak	66	B. Butler, Cle	22	J. Rice, Bos	36
D. Collins, Tor	9	A. Griffin, Tor	13	D. DeCinces, Cal	12	D. Collins, Tor	60	R. Henderson, Oak	18	T. Simmons, Mil	23
D. Garcia, Tor	9	D. Schofield, Cal	13	J. Gantner, Mil	10	B. Butler, Cle	52	R. Law, ChA	17	D. Motley, KC	23
4 tied with	8	3 tied with	12	R. Bush, Min	10	G. Pettis, Cal	48	G. Pettis, Cal	17	J. Franco, Cle	23
				J. Franco, Cle	10	W. Wilson, KC	47	D. Collins, Tor	14	2 tied with	22

Runs Created		Runs Created/27 Outs		Batting Average		On-Base Percentage		Slugging Percentage		OBP+Slugging	
D. Evans, Bos	124	E. Murray, Bal	7.59	D. Mattingly, NYA	.343	E. Murray, Bal	.410	H. Baines, ChA	.541	D. Evans, Bos	.920
E. Murray, Bal	120	D. Winfield, NYA	7.19	D. Winfield, NYA	.340	W. Boggs, Bos	.407	D. Mattingly, NYA	.537	E. Murray, Bal	.918
C. Ripken Jr., Bal	114	R. Henderson, Oak	7.17	W. Boggs, Bos	.325	R. Henderson, Oak	.399	D. Evans, Bos	.532	D. Mattingly, NYA	.918
D. Mattingly, NYA	113	D. Mattingly, NYA	7.11	B. Bell, Tex	.315	D. Winfield, NYA	.393	T. Armas, Bos	.531	D. Winfield, NYA	.908
3 tied with	110	D. Evans, Bos	7.09	A. Trammell, Det	.314	A. Davis, Sea	.391	K. Hrbek, Min	.522	K. Hrbek, Min	.906

1984 American League Pitching Leaders

Wins		Losses		Winning Percentage		Games		Games Started		Complete Games	
M. Boddicker, Bal	20	L. Hoyt, ChA	18	D. Alexander, Tor	.739	W. Hernandez, Det	80	C. Hough, Tex	36	C. Hough, Tex	17
B. Blyleven, Cle	19	M. Moore, Sea	17	B. Blyleven, Cle	.731	D. Quisenberry, KC	72	J. Clancy, Tor	36	M. Boddicker, Bal	16
J. Morris, Det	19	J. Beattie, Sea	16	D. Petry, Det	.692	A. Lopez, Det	71	M. Smithson, Min	36	R. Dotson, ChA	14
D. Petry, Det	18	J. Cocanower, Mil	16	M. Wilcox, Det	.680	E. Camacho, Cle	69	8 tied with	35	B. Blyleven, Cle	12
F. Viola, Min	18	4 tied with	15	2 tied with	.667	B. Caudill, Oak	68			J. Beattie, Sea	12

Shutouts		Saves		Games Finished		Batters Faced		Innings Pitched		Hits Allowed	
B. Ojeda, Bos	5	D. Quisenberry, KC	44	W. Hernandez, Det	68	C. Hough, Tex	1133	D. Stieb, Tor	267.0	C. Hough, Tex	260
G. Zahn, Cal	5	B. Caudill, Oak	36	D. Quisenberry, KC	67	D. Stieb, Tor	1085	C. Hough, Tex	266.0	J. Clancy, Tor	249
4 tied with	4	W. Hernandez, Det	32	B. Caudill, Oak	62	D. Alexander, Tor	1061	D. Alexander, Tor	261.2	D. Darwin, Tex	249
		D. Righetti, NYA	31	R. Davis, Min	56	F. Tanana, Tex	1054	M. Boddicker, Bal	261.1	M. Smithson, Min	246
		R. Davis, Min	29	D. Righetti, NYA	53	M. Boddicker, Bal	1051	F. Viola, Min	257.2	L. Hoyt, ChA	244

Home Runs Allowed		Walks		Walks/9 Innings		Strikeouts		Strikeouts/9 Innings		Strikeout/Walk Ratio	
M. Smithson, Min	35	M. Langston, Sea	118	L. Hoyt, ChA	1.6	M. Langston, Sea	204	M. Langston, Sea	8.2	L. Hoyt, ChA	2.93
L. Hoyt, ChA	31	R. Dotson, ChA	103	M. Smithson, Min	1.9	D. Stieb, Tor	198	M. Witt, Cal	7.2	R. Guidry, NYA	2.89
F. Bannister, ChA	30	B. Ojeda, Bos	96	R. Guidry, NYA	2.0	M. Witt, Cal	196	M. Moore, Sea	6.7	D. Sutton, Mil	2.80
F. Tanana, Tex	30	C. Hough, Tex	94	D. Alexander, Tor	2.0	B. Blyleven, Cle	170	D. Stieb, Tor	6.7	M. Smithson, Min	2.67
F. Viola, Min	28	R. Burris, Oak	90	M. Haas, Mil	2.0	C. Hough, Tex	164	J. Berenguer, Det	6.3	O. Boyd, Bos	2.53

Earned Run Average		Component ERA		Hit Batsmen		Wild Pitches		Opponent Average		Opponent OBP	
M. Boddicker, Bal	2.79	B. Blyleven, Cle	2.73	D. Stieb, Tor	11	J. Morris, Det	14	D. Stieb, Tor	.221	B. Black, KC	.283
D. Stieb, Tor	2.83	D. Stieb, Tor	2.77	C. Hough, Tex	9	D. Martinez, Bal	13	B. Blyleven, Cle	.224	D. Alexander, Tor	.284
B. Blyleven, Cle	2.87	B. Black, KC	2.82	J. Cocanower, Mil	9	J. Cocanower, Mil	13	M. Boddicker, Bal	.228	B. Blyleven, Cle	.285
P. Niekro, NYA	3.09	D. Alexander, Tor	2.86	5 tied with	8	3 tied with	12	M. Langston, Sea	.230	M. Mason, Tex	.285
G. Zahn, Cal	3.12	M. Mason, Tex	2.88					J. Berenguer, Det	.232	T. Seaver, ChA	.288

1984 American League Miscellaneous

Managers

Baltimore	Joe Altobelli	85-77
Boston	Ralph Houk	86-76
California	John McNamara	81-81
Chicago	Tony La Russa	74-88
Cleveland	Pat Corrales	75-87
Detroit	Sparky Anderson	104-58
Kansas City	Dick Howser	84-78
Milwaukee	Rene Lachemann	67-94
Minnesota	Billy Gardner	81-81
New York	Yogi Berra	87-75
Oakland	Steve Boros	20-24
	Jackie Moore	57-61
Seattle	Del Crandall	59-76
	Chuck Cottier	15-12
Texas	Doug Rader	69-92
Toronto	Bobby Cox	89-73

Awards

Most Valuable Player	Willie Hernandez, p, Det
Cy Young	Willie Hernandez, Det
Rookie of the Year	Alvin Davis, 1b, Sea
Manager of the Year	Sparky Anderson, Det

STATS All-Star Team

C	Lance Parrish, Det	.237	33	98
1B	Eddie Murray, Bal	.306	29	110
2B	Lou Whitaker, Det	.289	13	56
3B	Buddy Bell, Tex	.315	11	83
SS	Cal Ripken Jr., Bal	.304	27	86
OF	Dwight Evans, Bos	.295	32	104
OF	Rickey Henderson, Oak	.293	16	58
OF	Dave Winfield, NYA	.340	19	100
DH	Mike Easler, Bos	.313	27	91
P	Bert Blyleven, Cle	19-7	2.87	170 K
P	Mike Boddicker, Bal	20-11	2.79	128 K
P	Mark Langston, Sea	17-10	3.40	204 K
P	Dave Stieb, Tor	16-8	2.83	198 K
RP	Willie Hernandez, Det	9-3	1.92	32 Sv

Postseason

LCS	Detroit 3 vs. Kansas City 0
World Series	Detroit (AL) 4 vs. San Diego (NL) 1

Outstanding Performances

Perfect Games
Mike Witt, Cal @ Tex on September 30
No-Hitters
Jack Morris, Det @ ChA on April 7
Three-Homer Games
Dave Kingman, Oak on April 16
Harold Baines, ChA on September 17
Cycles
Cal Ripken Jr., Bal on May 6
Carlton Fisk, ChA on May 16
Dwight Evans, Bos on June 28

1984 National League Standings

EAST	W	L	Pct	GB	DIF	W	L	R	OR	HR	OHR	W	L	R	OR	HR	OHR	Run	HR	M/A	May	June	July	Aug	S/O
		Overall					Home Games						Road Games					Park Index		Record by Month					
Chicago	96	65	.596	—	106	51	29	414	360	86	70	45	36	348	298	50	29	121	200	12-8	15-12	15-14	18-10	20-10	16-11
New York	90	72	.556	6.5	66	48	33	336	327	56	47	42	39	316	349	51	57	100	95	12-8	10-13	16-12	21-9	15-17	16-13
St. Louis	84	78	.519	12.5	4	44	37	327	310	29	42	40	41	325	335	46	52	97	72	11-12	13-15	14-13	14-13	15-12	17-13
Philadelphia	81	81	.500	15.5	27	39	42	353	369	79	45	42	39	367	321	68	56	105	100	11-9	16-10	15-15	14-13	16-14	9-20
Montreal	78	83	.484	18.0	4	39	42	266	260	45	56	39	41	327	325	51	58	80	92	12-10	12-14	13-14	14-14	15-15	12-16
Pittsburgh	75	87	.463	21.5	1	41	40	282	263	48	44	34	47	333	304	50	58	86	85	7-13	12-13	11-20	15-15	13-15	17-11
WEST																									
San Diego	92	70	.568	—	146	48	33	344	300	60	61	44	37	342	334	49	61	95	110	15-8	10-13	19-10	19-11	15-14	14-14
Atlanta	80	82	.494	12.0	8	38	43	328	376	53	72	42	39	304	279	58	50	121	116	9-12	17-11	17-12	12-16	11-17	14-14
Houston	80	82	.494	12.0	0	43	38	309	292	18	29	37	44	384	338	61	62	83	38	8-14	12-14	17-13	13-16	18-10	12-15
Los Angeles	79	83	.488	13.0	29	40	41	287	321	49	40	39	42	293	279	53	36	106	100	17-8	11-15	13-16	11-16	11-17	16-11
Cincinnati	70	92	.432	22.0	2	39	42	356	381	58	73	31	50	271	366	48	55	116	127	10-13	16-10	10-19	8-19	11-19	15-12
San Francisco	66	96	.407	26.0	0	35	46	340	393	55	63	31	50	342	414	57	62	97	99	7-16	9-13	14-16	10-17	16-16	10-18

Clinch Date—Chicago 9/24, San Diego 9/20.

Team Batting

Team	G	AB	R	OR	H	2B	3B	HR	TB	RBI	TBB	IBB	SO	HBP	SH	SF	SB	CS	SB%	GDP	Avg	OBP	Slg
Chicago	161	5437	762	658	1415	240	47	136	2157	703	567	69	967	29	59	51	154	66	.70	102	.260	.339	.397
Philadelphia	162	5614	720	690	1494	235	51	147	2285	673	555	60	1084	29	39	46	186	60	.76	140	.266	.340	.407
Houston	162	5548	693	630	1465	222	67	79	2058	640	494	57	837	17	87	55	105	61	.63	88	.264	.332	.371
San Diego	162	5504	686	634	1425	207	42	109	2043	629	472	70	810	24	64	55	152	68	.69	132	.259	.326	.371
San Francisco	162	5650	682	807	1499	229	26	112	2116	646	528	44	980	17	51	44	126	76	.62	141	.265	.335	.375
New York	162	5438	652	676	1400	235	25	107	2006	607	500	73	1001	20	59	49	149	54	.73	132	.257	.328	.369
St. Louis	162	5433	652	645	1369	225	44	75	1907	610	516	49	924	23	68	46	220	71	.76	120	.252	.325	.351
Atlanta	162	5422	632	655	1338	234	27	111	1959	578	555	70	896	20	64	45	140	85	.62	113	.247	.324	.361
Cincinnati	162	5498	627	747	1342	238	30	106	1958	578	566	62	978	12	71	53	160	63	.72	99	.244	.322	.356
Pittsburgh	162	5537	615	567	1412	237	33	98	2009	586	438	47	841	19	81	44	96	62	.61	131	.255	.317	.363
Montreal	161	5439	593	585	1367	242	36	96	1969	553	470	50	782	25	74	34	131	38	.78	101	.251	.318	.362
Los Angeles	162	5399	580	600	1316	213	23	102	1881	530	488	56	829	14	92	48	109	69	.61	120	.244	.314	.348
NL Total	1942	65919	7894	7894	16842	2770	451	1278	24348	7333	6149	707	10929	249	809	570	1728	773	.69	1419	.255	.319	.369
NL Avg Team	162	5493	658	658	1404	231	38	107	2029	611	512	59	911	21	67	48	144	64	.69	118	.255	.319	.369

Team Pitching

Team	G	CG	ShO	Rel	Sv	IP	H	R	ER	HR	SH	SF	HB	TBB	IBB	SO	WP	Bk	H/9	SO/9	BB/9	OAvg	OOBP	ERA
Pittsburgh	162	27	13	246	34	1470.0	1344	567	508	102	66	46	11	502	48	995	43	16	8.2	6.1	3.1	.246	.308	3.11
Los Angeles	162	39	16	259	27	1460.2	1381	600	515	76	62	35	18	499	81	1033	41	11	8.5	6.4	3.1	.250	.313	3.17
Montreal	161	19	10	272	48	1431.0	1333	585	526	114	56	46	21	474	54	861	40	13	8.4	5.4	3.0	.249	.310	3.31
Houston	162	24	13	312	29	1449.1	1350	630	534	91	55	50	17	502	58	950	45	11	8.4	5.9	3.1	.248	.311	3.32
San Diego	162	13	17	285	44	1460.1	1327	634	565	122	84	44	22	563	28	812	44	13	8.2	5.0	3.5	.244	.315	3.48
Atlanta	162	17	7	278	49	1447.0	1401	655	574	122	81	46	18	525	60	859	37	14	8.7	5.3	3.3	.257	.322	3.57
St. Louis	162	19	12	313	51	1449.0	1427	645	577	94	66	41	25	494	68	808	50	20	8.9	5.0	3.1	.262	.324	3.58
New York	162	12	15	278	50	1442.2	1371	676	577	104	55	48	27	573	43	1028	41	20	8.6	6.4	3.6	.252	.324	3.60
Philadelphia	162	11	6	287	35	1458.1	1416	690	586	101	69	45	17	448	65	904	41	27	8.7	5.6	2.8	.253	.308	3.62
Chicago	161	19	8	291	50	1434.0	1458	658	598	99	67	57	22	442	62	879	40	10	9.2	5.5	2.8	.267	.321	3.75
Cincinnati	162	25	6	327	29	1461.1	1445	747	676	128	75	48	17	578	57	946	33	7	8.9	5.8	3.6	.259	.328	4.16
San Francisco	162	9	7	359	38	1461.0	1589	807	713	125	73	64	34	549	83	854	58	21	9.8	5.3	3.4	.278	.342	4.39
NL Total	1942	234	130	3487	480	17424.2	16842	7894	6949	1278	809	570	249	6149	707	10929	513	183	8.7	5.6	3.2	.255	.327	3.59
NL Avg Team	162	20	11	291	40	1452.2	1404	658	579	107	67	48	21	512	59	911	43	15	8.7	5.6	3.2	.255	.327	3.59

Team Fielding

Team	G	PO	A	E	TC	DP	PB	Pct
St. Louis	162	4347	2001	118	6466	184	14	.982
Chicago	161	4302	1850	121	6273	137	10	.981
Pittsburgh	162	4410	1792	128	6330	142	6	.980
Houston	162	4348	1844	133	6325	160	38	.979
New York	162	4328	1632	129	6089	154	14	.979
Atlanta	162	4341	1963	139	6443	153	7	.978
Montreal	161	4293	1663	132	6088	147	8	.978
San Diego	162	4381	1633	138	6152	144	12	.978
Cincinnati	162	4384	1629	139	6152	116	18	.977
Los Angeles	162	4382	1918	163	6463	146	11	.975
Philadelphia	162	4375	1792	161	6328	112	10	.975
San Francisco	162	4383	1843	173	6399	134	18	.973
NL Total	1942	52274	21560	1674	75508	1729	166	.978

Team vs. Team Records

	Atl	ChN	Cin	Hou	LA	Mon	NYN	Phi	Pit	SD	SF	StL	Won
Atl	—	3	13	12	6	5	4	7	8	7	10	5	80
ChN	9	—	7	6	7	10	12	9	8	6	9	13	96
Cin	5	5	—	8	7	7	3	5	7	7	12	4	70
Hou	6	6	10	—	9	7	4	6	6	6	12	8	80
LA	12	5	11	9	—	6	3	3	4	10	10	6	79
Mon	7	7	5	5	6	—	7	11	7	7	7	9	78
NYN	8	6	9	8	9	11	—	10	12	6	4	7	90
Phi	5	9	7	6	9	7	8	—	7	7	8	8	81
Pit	4	10	5	6	8	11	6	11	—	4	6	4	75
SD	11	6	11	12	8	5	6	5	8	—	13	7	92
SF	8	3	6	6	8	5	8	4	6	5	—	7	66
StL	7	5	8	4	6	9	11	10	14	5	5	—	84
Lost	82	65	92	82	83	83	72	81	87	70	96	78	

1984 National League Batting Leaders

Games			At-Bats			Runs			Hits			Doubles			Triples		
D. Murphy, Atl	162		J. Samuel, Phi	701		R. Sandberg, ChN	114		T. Gwynn, SD	213		T. Raines, Mon	38		R. Sandberg, ChN	19	
S. Garvey, SD	161		M. Wynne, Pit	653		T. Raines, Mon	106		R. Sandberg, ChN	200		J. Ray, Pit	38		J. Samuel, Phi	19	
4 tied with	160		R. Sandberg, ChN	636		A. Wiggins, SD	106		T. Raines, Mon	192		R. Sandberg, ChN	36		J. Cruz, Hou	13	
			T. Raines, Mon	622		J. Samuel, Phi	105		J. Samuel, Phi	191		J. Samuel, Phi	36		4 tied with	11	
			S. Garvey, SD	617		G. Matthews, ChN	101		J. Cruz, Hou	187		2 tied with	32				

Home Runs			Total Bases			Runs Batted In			Walks			Intentional Walks			Strikeouts		
M. Schmidt, Phi	36		D. Murphy, Atl	332		G. Carter, Mon	106		G. Matthews, ChN	103		G. Templeton, SD	23		J. Samuel, Phi	168	
D. Murphy, Atl	36		R. Sandberg, ChN	331		M. Schmidt, Phi	106		K. Hernandez, NYN	97		D. Murphy, Atl	20		D. Murphy, Atl	134	
G. Carter, Mon	27		J. Samuel, Phi	310		D. Murphy, Atl	100		M. Schmidt, Phi	92		H. Brooks, NYN	15		D. Strawberry, NYN	131	
D. Strawberry, NYN	26		G. Carter, Mon	290		R. Cey, ChN	97		J. Thompson, Pit	87		J. Davis, ChN	15		J. Leonard, SF	123	
R. Cey, ChN	25		M. Schmidt, Phi	283		D. Strawberry, NYN	97		T. Raines, Mon	87		D. Strawberry, NYN	15		G. Foster, NYN	122	

Hit By Pitch			Sac Hits			Sac Flies			Stolen Bases			Caught Stealing			GDP		
L. Smith, StL	9		C. Reynolds, Hou	16		J. Cruz, Hou	10		T. Raines, Mon	75		A. Wiggins, SD	21		S. Garvey, SD	25	
T. Wallach, Mon	7		A. Wiggins, SD	14		S. Garvey, SD	10		J. Samuel, Phi	72		S. Sax, LA	19		A. Oliver, 2tm	23	
J. Samuel, Phi	7		J. Koosman, Phi	14		G. Matthews, ChN	10		A. Wiggins, SD	70		M. Wynne, Pit	19		J. Davis, ChN	20	
3 tied with	6		3 tied with	12		C. Martinez, SD	10		L. Smith, StL	50		T. Gwynn, SD	18		O. Virgil, Phi	19	
						4 tied with	9		2 tied with	48		2 tied with	17		2 tied with	17	

Runs Created			Runs Created/27 Outs			Batting Average			On-Base Percentage			Slugging Percentage			OBP+Slugging		
R. Sandberg, ChN	127		R. Sandberg, ChN	7.50		T. Gwynn, SD	.351		G. Matthews, ChN	.410		D. Murphy, Atl	.547		M. Schmidt, Phi	.919	
D. Murphy, Atl	119		K. Hernandez, NYN	7.12		L. Lacy, Pit	.321		T. Gwynn, SD	.410		M. Schmidt, Phi	.536		D. Murphy, Atl	.919	
T. Raines, Mon	113		D. Murphy, Atl	7.11		C. Davis, SF	.315		K. Hernandez, NYN	.409		R. Sandberg, ChN	.520		R. Sandberg, ChN	.887	
T. Gwynn, SD	113		T. Gwynn, SD	7.06		R. Sandberg, ChN	.314		T. Raines, Mon	.393		C. Davis, SF	.507		C. Davis, SF	.875	
J. Cruz, Hou	110		G. Matthews, ChN	7.05		J. Ray, Pit	.312		M. Schmidt, Phi	.383		L. Durham, ChN	.505		L. Durham, ChN	.874	

1984 National League Pitching Leaders

Wins			Losses			Winning Percentage			Games			Games Started			Complete Games		
J. Andujar, StL	20		J. Russell, Cin	18		R. Sutcliffe, ChN	.941		T. Power, Cin	78		J. Niekro, Hou	38		M. Soto, Cin	13	
M. Soto, Cin	18		M. Davis, SF	17		B. Dawley, Hou	.733		G. Lavelle, SF	77		J. Andujar, StL	36		J. Andujar, StL	12	
D. Gooden, NYN	17		F. Valenzuela, LA	17		M. Soto, Cin	.720		G. Minton, SF	74		4 tied with	34		F. Valenzuela, LA	12	
J. Niekro, Hou	16		C. McMurtry, Atl	17		A. Pena, LA	.667		K. Tekulve, Pit	72					B. Knepper, Hou	11	
R. Sutcliffe, ChN	16		3 tied with	15		D. Gooden, NYN	.654		B. Sutter, StL	71					R. Mahler, Atl	9	

Shutouts			Saves			Games Finished			Batters Faced			Innings Pitched			Hits Allowed		
J. Andujar, StL	4		B. Sutter, StL	45		B. Sutter, StL	63		F. Valenzuela, LA	1078		J. Andujar, StL	261.1		M. Krukow, SF	234	
A. Pena, LA	4		L. Smith, ChN	33		A. Holland, Phi	61		J. Andujar, StL	1052		F. Valenzuela, LA	261.0		J. Koosman, Phi	232	
O. Hershiser, LA	4		J. Orosco, NYN	31		L. Smith, ChN	59		J. Niekro, Hou	1027		J. Niekro, Hou	248.1		W. Terrell, NYN	232	
4 tied with	3		A. Holland, Phi	29		J. Reardon, Mon	58		M. Soto, Cin	971		R. Rhoden, Pit	238.1		B. Gullickson, Mon	230	
			G. Gossage, SD	25		J. Orosco, NYN	52		S. Carlton, Phi	964		M. Soto, Cin	237.1		L. McWilliams, Pit	226	

Home Runs Allowed			Walks			Walks/9 Innings			Strikeouts			Strikeouts/9 Innings			Strikeout/Walk Ratio		
B. Gullickson, Mon	27		F. Valenzuela, LA	106		B. Gullickson, Mon	1.5		D. Gooden, NYN	276		D. Gooden, NYN	11.4		J. Candelaria, Pit	3.91	
B. Knepper, Hou	26		T. Lollar, SD	105		J. Candelaria, Pit	1.7		F. Valenzuela, LA	240		N. Ryan, Hou	9.7		D. Gooden, NYN	3.78	
M. Soto, Cin	26		R. Darling, NYN	104		E. Whitson, SD	2.0		N. Ryan, Hou	197		F. Valenzuela, LA	8.3		O. Hershiser, LA	3.00	
P. Perez, Atl	26		C. McMurtry, Atl	102		A. Pena, LA	2.1		M. Soto, Cin	185		B. Berenyi, 2tm	7.3		A. Pena, LA	2.93	
M. Davis, SF	25		B. Berenyi, 2tm	95		B. Knepper, Hou	2.1		S. Carlton, Phi	163		J. DeLeon, Pit	7.2		N. Ryan, Hou	2.86	

Earned Run Average			Component ERA			Hit Batsmen			Wild Pitches			Opponent Average			Opponent OBP		
A. Pena, LA	2.48		D. Gooden, NYN	2.08		J. Andujar, StL	7		D. LaPoint, StL	15		D. Gooden, NYN	.202		D. Gooden, NYN	.269	
D. Gooden, NYN	2.60		O. Hershiser, LA	2.42		D. Cox, StL	7		J. Niekro, Hou	12		M. Soto, Cin	.209		O. Hershiser, LA	.278	
O. Hershiser, LA	2.66		J. Andujar, StL	2.61		J. Robinson, SF	7		S. Rogers, Mon	12		N. Ryan, Hou	.211		J. Andujar, StL	.284	
R. Rhoden, Pit	2.72		N. Ryan, Hou	2.63		B. Laskey, SF	6		3 tied with	11		J. DeLeon, Pit	.214		M. Soto, Cin	.284	
J. Candelaria, Pit	2.72		A. Pena, LA	2.68		5 tied with	5					O. Hershiser, LA	.225		N. Ryan, Hou	.286	

1984 National League Miscellaneous

Managers		
Atlanta	Joe Torre	80-82
Chicago	Jim Frey	96-65
Cincinnati	Vern Rapp	51-70
	Pete Rose	19-22
Houston	Bob Lillis	80-82
Los Angeles	Tom Lasorda	79-83
Montreal	Bill Virdon	64-67
	Jim Fanning	14-16
New York	Davey Johnson	90-72
Philadelphia	Paul Owens	81-81
Pittsburgh	Chuck Tanner	75-87
St. Louis	Whitey Herzog	84-78
San Diego	Dick Williams	92-70
San Francisco	Frank Robinson	42-64
	Danny Ozark	24-32

Awards

Most Valuable Player	R. Sandberg, 2b, ChN
Cy Young	Rick Sutcliffe, ChN
Rookie of the Year	Dwight Gooden, p, NYN
Manager of the Year	Jim Frey, ChN

STATS All-Star Team

C	Gary Carter, Mon	.294	27	106
1B	Keith Hernandez, NYN	.311	15	94
2B	Ryne Sandberg, ChN	.314	19	84
3B	Mike Schmidt, Phi	.277	36	106
SS	Ozzie Smith, StL	.257	1	44
OF	Jose Cruz, Hou	.312	12	95
OF	Tony Gwynn, SD	.351	5	71
OF	Dale Murphy, Atl	.290	36	100
P	Joaquin Andujar, StL	20-14	3.34	147 K
P	Dwight Gooden, NYN	17-9	2.60	276 K
P	Mario Soto, Cin	18-7	3.53	185 K
P	Rick Sutcliffe, ChN	16-1	2.69	155 K
RP	Bruce Sutter, StL	5-7	1.54	45 Sv

Postseason

LCS	San Diego 3 vs. Chicago 2
World Series	San Diego (NL) 1 vs. Detroit (AL) 4

Outstanding Performances

Cycles

Willie McGee, StL   on June 23

1985 American League Standings

EAST	W	L	Pct	GB	DIF	W	L	R	OR	HR	OHR	W	L	R	OR	HR	OHR	Run	HR	M/A	May	June	July	Aug	S/O
			Overall					Home Games						Road Games				Park Index				Record by Month			
Toronto	99	62	.615	—	149	54	26	396	264	75	78	45	36	363	324	83	69	97	102	13-7	17-8	16-13	18-10	17-10	18-14
New York	97	64	.602	2.0	0	58	22	411	288	92	67	39	42	428	372	84	90	88	93	6-12	18-8	13-14	18-10	20-8	22-12
Detroit	84	77	.522	15.0	20	44	37	386	368	108	93	40	40	343	320	94	48	112	140	11-7	14-12	16-11	12-16	16-13	15-18
Baltimore	83	78	.516	16.0	21	45	36	414	374	103	87	38	42	404	390	111	73	98	102	12-7	14-12	11-15	14-14	16-11	16-19
Boston	81	81	.500	18.5	6	43	37	415	357	73	64	38	44	385	363	89	66	106	91	9-11	12-14	10-14	14-12	8-21	21-13
Milwaukee	71	90	.441	28.0	0	40	40	368	416	50	86	31	50	322	386	51	89	112	98	8-11	13-11	12-15	11-17	15-13	12-23
Cleveland	60	102	.370	39.5	0	38	43	380	379	52	76	22	59	349	482	64	94	91	81	7-13	9-17	7-19	9-19	14-15	14-19
WEST																									
Kansas City	91	71	.562	—	30	50	32	357	317	67	43	41	39	330	322	87	60	101	73	11-8	14-13	12-14	17-10	15-12	22-14
California	90	72	.556	1.0	142	49	30	370	331	75	93	41	42	362	372	78	78	100	113	14-7	12-13	15-12	16-11	16-13	17-16
Chicago	85	77	.525	6.0	11	45	36	359	361	74	83	40	41	377	359	72	78	98	105	9-8	13-13	13-14	14-12	14-17	22-13
Minnesota	77	85	.475	14.0	2	49	35	407	393	71	83	28	50	298	389	70	81	108	95	11-9	10-16	12-13	13-15	12-16	19-16
Oakland	77	85	.475	14.0	6	43	36	348	347	66	71	34	49	409	440	89	101	86	76	9-12	13-12	17-10	13-14	15-14	10-23
Seattle	74	88	.457	17.0	13	42	41	360	389	92	78	32	47	359	429	79	76	90	104	9-12	11-14	16-11	12-16	11-17	15-18
Texas	62	99	.385	28.5	0	37	43	356	406	76	102	25	56	261	379	53	71	121	145	7-12	10-17	11-17	11-16	9-18	14-19

Clinch Date—Toronto 10/05, Kansas City 10/05.

Team Batting

Team	G	AB	R	OR	H	2B	3B	HR	TB	RBI	TBB	IBB	SO	HBP	SH	SF	SB	CS	SB%	GDP	Avg	OBP	Slg
New York	161	5458	839	660	1458	272	31	176	2320	793	620	50	771	50	48	60	155	53	.75	119	.267	.354	.425
Baltimore	161	5517	818	764	1451	234	22	214	2371	773	604	30	908	19	31	40	69	43	.62	132	.263	.342	.430
Boston	163	5720	800	720	1615	292	31	162	2455	760	562	39	816	30	50	57	66	27	.71	164	.282	.355	.429
Toronto	161	5508	759	588	1482	281	53	158	2343	714	503	44	807	30	21	44	144	77	.65	121	.269	.338	.425
Oakland	162	5581	757	787	1475	230	34	155	2238	690	508	29	861	16	63	47	117	58	.67	129	.264	.333	.401
Chicago	163	5470	736	720	1386	247	37	146	2145	695	471	40	843	43	59	45	108	56	.66	119	.253	.323	.392
California	162	5442	732	703	1364	215	31	153	2100	685	648	51	902	39	99	35	106	51	.68	139	.251	.338	.386
Detroit	161	5575	729	688	1413	254	45	202	2363	703	526	56	926	27	40	53	75	41	.65	81	.253	.327	.424
Cleveland	162	5527	729	861	1465	254	31	116	2129	689	492	26	817	15	38	48	132	72	.65	139	.265	.332	.385
Seattle	162	5521	719	818	1410	277	38	171	2276	686	564	36	942	31	28	41	94	35	.73	147	.255	.334	.412
Minnesota	162	5509	705	782	1453	282	41	141	2240	678	502	36	779	31	39	47	68	44	.61	117	.264	.334	.407
Milwaukee	161	5568	690	802	1467	250	44	101	2108	636	462	33	746	19	54	55	69	34	.67	145	.263	.328	.379
Kansas City	162	5500	687	639	1384	261	49	154	2205	657	473	57	840	36	44	41	128	48	.73	125	.252	.320	.401
Texas	161	5361	617	785	1359	213	41	129	2041	578	530	30	819	33	34	45	130	76	.63	136	.253	.330	.381
AL Total	2264	77257	10317	10317	20182	3562	528	2178	31334	9737	7465	557	11777	419	648	658	1461	715	.67	1813	.261	.327	.406
AL Avg Team	162	5518	737	737	1442	254	38	156	2238	696	533	40	841	30	46	47	104	51	.67	130	.261	.327	.406

Team Pitching

Team	G	CG	ShO	Rel	Sv	IP	H	R	ER	HR	SH	SF	HB	TBB	IBB	SO	WP	Bk	H/9	SO/9	BB/9	OAvg	OOBP	ERA
Toronto	161	18	9	316	47	1448.0	1312	588	532	147	47	41	26	484	26	823	36	5	8.2	5.1	3.0	.243	.306	3.31
Kansas City	162	27	11	216	41	1461.0	1433	639	566	103	48	42	28	463	37	846	43	9	8.8	5.2	2.9	.257	.315	3.49
New York	161	25	9	271	49	1440.1	1373	660	590	157	32	42	13	518	20	907	34	5	8.6	5.7	3.2	.251	.316	3.69
Detroit	161	31	11	250	40	1456.0	1313	688	612	141	43	49	23	556	92	943	62	6	8.1	5.8	3.4	.240	.311	3.78
California	162	22	8	250	41	1457.1	1453	703	633	171	48	44	27	514	30	767	45	4	9.0	4.7	3.2	.263	.326	3.91
Boston	163	35	8	202	29	1461.1	1487	720	659	130	49	38	35	540	54	913	34	13	9.2	5.6	3.3	.265	.331	4.06
Chicago	163	20	8	305	39	1451.2	1411	720	656	161	57	47	36	569	35	1023	54	5	8.7	6.3	3.5	.256	.327	4.07
Baltimore	161	32	6	238	33	1427.1	1480	764	694	160	59	41	23	568	57	793	32	7	9.3	5.0	3.6	.270	.338	4.38
Milwaukee	161	34	5	248	31	1437.0	1510	802	701	175	52	51	33	499	31	777	51	4	9.5	4.9	3.1	.271	.331	4.39
Oakland	162	10	6	299	41	1453.0	1451	787	712	172	39	46	25	607	32	785	48	6	9.0	4.9	3.8	.259	.331	4.41
Minnesota	162	41	7	237	34	1426.1	1468	782	710	164	47	55	30	462	31	767	51	11	9.3	4.8	2.9	.268	.326	4.48
Texas	161	18	5	264	33	1411.2	1479	785	715	173	28	44	36	501	38	863	43	7	9.4	5.5	3.2	.269	.331	4.56
Seattle	162	23	8	335	30	1432.0	1456	818	744	154	38	48	41	637	54	868	61	18	9.2	5.5	4.0	.265	.343	4.68
Cleveland	162	24	7	306	28	1421.0	1556	861	776	170	61	70	43	547	45	702	46	7	9.9	4.4	3.5	.281	.346	4.91
AL Total	2264	360	108	3737	522	20184.0	20182	10317	9300	2178	648	658	419	7465	557	11777	640	107	9.0	5.3	3.3	.261	.335	4.15
AL Avg Team	162	26	8	267	37	1441.0	1442	737	664	156	46	47	30	533	40	841	46	8	9.0	5.3	3.3	.261	.335	4.15

Team Fielding

Team	G	PO	A	E	TC	DP	PB	Pct
California	162	4372	1841	112	6325	202	8	.982
Chicago	163	4355	1677	111	6143	152	11	.982
Seattle	162	4296	1836	122	6254	156	22	.980
Minnesota	162	4279	1732	120	6131	139	13	.980
Kansas City	162	4383	1907	127	6417	160	10	.980
Texas	161	4235	1703	120	6058	145	23	.980
Toronto	161	4344	1729	125	6198	164	3	.980
New York	161	4321	1563	126	6010	172	18	.979
Baltimore	161	4282	1714	129	6125	168	4	.979
Boston	163	4384	1846	145	6375	161	14	.977
Oakland	162	4359	1566	140	6065	137	19	.977
Cleveland	162	4263	1703	141	6107	161	13	.977
Milwaukee	161	4311	1686	142	6139	153	12	.977
Detroit	161	4368	1671	143	6182	152	10	.977
AL Total	2264	60552	24174	1803	86529	2222	180	.979

Team vs. Team Records

	Bal	Bos	Cal	ChA	Cle	Det	KC	Mil	Min	NYA	Oak	Sea	Tex	Tor	Won
Bal	—	5	5	7	8	8	6	9	6	1	7	6	10	4	83
Bos	8	—	5	4	5	6	5	5	7	5	8	6	5	9	81
Cal	5	7	—	8	8	8	4	9	9	3	6	9	9	5	90
ChA	4	8	5	—	10	6	5	5	6	6	8	9	10	3	85
Cle	5	5	4	2	—	5	2	7	4	6	3	6	7	4	60
Det	7	7	4	6	8	—	5	9	3	9	8	5	7	6	84
KC	6	7	9	8	10	7	—	8	7	5	8	3	6	7	91
Mil	4	8	3	7	6	4	4	—	9	7	3	4	8	4	71
Min	6	5	4	7	8	9	6	3	—	3	8	6	8	4	77
NYA	12	8	9	6	7	3	7	6	9	—	7	9	8	6	97
Oak	5	4	7	5	9	4	5	9	5	5	—	8	6	5	77
Sea	6	6	4	4	6	7	10	8	7	3	5	—	6	2	74
Tex	2	7	4	3	5	5	7	3	5	4	7	7	—	3	62
Tor	8	4	7	9	9	7	5	9	8	7	7	10	9	—	99
Lost	78	81	72	77	102	77	71	90	85	64	85	88	99	62	

Seasons: Standings, Leaders

1985 American League Batting Leaders

Games
G. Walker, ChA	163
A. Griffin, Oak	162
B. Buckner, Bos	162
5 tied with	161

At-Bats
K. Puckett, Min	691
B. Buckner, Bos	673
W. Boggs, Bos	653
D. Mattingly, NYA	652
C. Ripken Jr., Bal	642

Runs
R. Henderson, NYA	146
C. Ripken Jr., Bal	116
E. Murray, Bal	111
D. Evans, Bos	110
G. Brett, KC	108

Hits
W. Boggs, Bos	240
D. Mattingly, NYA	211
B. Buckner, Bos	201
K. Puckett, Min	199
H. Baines, ChA	198

Doubles
D. Mattingly, NYA	48
B. Buckner, Bos	46
W. Boggs, Bos	42
C. Cooper, Mil	39
2 tied with	38

Triples
W. Wilson, KC	21
B. Butler, Cle	14
K. Puckett, Min	13
T. Fernandez, Tor	10
2 tied with	9

Home Runs
D. Evans, Det	40
C. Fisk, ChA	37
S. Balboni, KC	36
D. Mattingly, NYA	35
G. Thomas, Sea	32

Total Bases
D. Mattingly, NYA	370
G. Brett, KC	322
P. Bradley, Sea	319
W. Boggs, Bos	312
E. Murray, Bal	305

Runs Batted In
D. Mattingly, NYA	145
E. Murray, Bal	124
D. Winfield, NYA	114
H. Baines, ChA	113
G. Brett, KC	112

Walks
D. Evans, Bos	114
T. Harrah, Tex	113
G. Brett, KC	103
R. Henderson, NYA	99
W. Boggs, Bos	96

Intentional Walks
G. Brett, KC	31
K. Gibson, Det	16
D. Mattingly, NYA	13
5 tied with	12

Strikeouts
S. Balboni, KC	166
J. Barfield, Tor	143
R. Jackson, Cal	138
K. Gibson, Det	137
2 tied with	129

Hit By Pitch
D. Baylor, NYA	24
C. Fisk, ChA	17
B. Downing, Cal	13
P. Bradley, Sea	12
C. Lemon, Det	10

Sac Hits
B. Meacham, NYA	23
B. Boone, Cal	16
D. Hill, Oak	16
3 tied with	12

Sac Flies
D. Mattingly, NYA	15
T. Brunansky, Min	13
B. Buckner, Bos	11
5 tied with	10

Stolen Bases
R. Henderson, NYA	80
G. Pettis, Cal	56
B. Butler, Cle	47
W. Wilson, KC	43
L. Smith, KC	40

Caught Stealing
B. Butler, Cle	20
D. Garcia, Tor	15
L. Moseby, Tor	15
A. Wiggins, Bal	13
2 tied with	12

GDP
J. Rice, Bos	35
C. Ripken Jr., Bal	32
J. Presley, Sea	29
J. Franco, Cle	26
2 tied with	24

Runs Created
R. Henderson, NYA	135
G. Brett, KC	134
D. Mattingly, NYA	133
W. Boggs, Bos	131
E. Murray, Bal	120

Runs Created/27 Outs
G. Brett, KC	9.29
R. Henderson, NYA	9.13
W. Boggs, Bos	8.03
E. Murray, Bal	7.54
D. Mattingly, NYA	7.53

Batting Average
W. Boggs, Bos	.368
G. Brett, KC	.335
D. Mattingly, NYA	.324
R. Henderson, NYA	.314
B. Butler, Cle	.311

On-Base Percentage
W. Boggs, Bos	.450
G. Brett, KC	.436
T. Harrah, Tex	.432
R. Henderson, NYA	.419
E. Murray, Bal	.383

Slugging Percentage
G. Brett, KC	.585
D. Mattingly, NYA	.567
J. Barfield, Tor	.536
E. Murray, Bal	.523
D. Evans, Det	.519

OBP+Slugging
G. Brett, KC	1.022
D. Mattingly, NYA	.939
R. Henderson, NYA	.934
W. Boggs, Bos	.928
E. Murray, Bal	.906

1985 American League Pitching Leaders

Wins
R. Guidry, NYA	22
B. Saberhagen, KC	20
B. Burns, ChA	18
F. Viola, Min	18
4 tied with	17

Losses
M. Young, Sea	19
D. Darwin, Mil	18
M. Boddicker, Bal	17
N. Heaton, Cle	17
2 tied with	16

Winning Percentage
R. Guidry, NYA	.786
B. Saberhagen, KC	.769
J. Key, Tor	.700
J. Cowley, NYA	.667
C. Leibrandt, KC	.654

Games
D. Quisenberry, KC	84
E. Vande Berg, Sea	76
W. Hernandez, Det	74
D. Righetti, NYA	74
E. Nunez, Sea	70

Games Started
B. Blyleven, 2tm	37
C. Codiroli, Oak	37
M. Smithson, Min	37
3 tied with	36

Complete Games
B. Blyleven, 2tm	24
C. Hough, Tex	14
M. Moore, Sea	14
J. Morris, Det	13
O. Boyd, Bos	13

Shutouts
B. Blyleven, 2tm	5
B. Burns, ChA	4
J. Morris, Det	4
5 tied with	3

Saves
D. Quisenberry, KC	37
B. James, ChA	32
W. Hernandez, Det	31
D. Moore, Cal	31
2 tied with	29

Games Finished
D. Quisenberry, KC	76
W. Hernandez, Det	64
B. James, ChA	60
D. Righetti, NYA	60
J. Howell, Oak	58

Batters Faced
B. Blyleven, 2tm	1203
O. Boyd, Bos	1132
D. Alexander, Tor	1090
M. Smithson, Min	1088
D. Stieb, Tor	1087

Innings Pitched
B. Blyleven, 2tm	293.2
O. Boyd, Bos	272.1
D. Stieb, Tor	265.0
D. Alexander, Tor	260.2
R. Guidry, NYA	259.0

Hits Allowed
O. Boyd, Bos	273
D. Alexander, Tor	268
B. Blyleven, 2tm	264
M. Smithson, Min	264
F. Viola, Min	262

Home Runs Allowed
D. Darwin, Mil	34
S. McGregor, Bal	34
B. Hurst, Bos	31
F. Bannister, ChA	30
4 tied with	29

Walks
P. Niekro, NYA	120
J. Morris, Det	110
F. Bannister, ChA	100
T. Lollar, 2tm	98
M. Witt, Cal	98

Walks/9 Innings
B. Saberhagen, KC	1.5
R. Guidry, NYA	1.5
J. Butcher, Min	1.9
J. Key, Tor	2.1
O. Boyd, Bos	2.2

Strikeouts
B. Blyleven, 2tm	206
F. Bannister, ChA	198
J. Morris, Det	191
B. Hurst, Bos	189
M. Witt, Cal	180

Strikeouts/9 Innings
F. Bannister, ChA	8.5
B. Hurst, Bos	7.4
B. Burns, ChA	6.8
J. Morris, Det	6.7
F. Tanana, 2tm	6.7

Strikeout/Walk Ratio
B. Saberhagen, KC	4.16
R. Guidry, NYA	3.40
F. Tanana, 2tm	2.79
B. Blyleven, 2tm	2.75
B. Hurst, Bos	2.70

Earned Run Average
D. Stieb, Tor	2.48
C. Leibrandt, KC	2.69
B. Saberhagen, KC	2.87
J. Key, Tor	3.00
B. Blyleven, 2tm	3.16

Component ERA
B. Saberhagen, KC	2.56
D. Stieb, Tor	2.75
C. Hough, Tex	2.77
D. Petry, Det	2.80
R. Guidry, NYA	2.91

Hit Batsmen
M. Smithson, Min	15
B. Blyleven, 2tm	9
D. Martinez, Bal	9
D. Stieb, Tor	9
A. Nipper, Bos	9

Wild Pitches
J. Morris, Det	15
J. Cocanower, Mil	13
M. Gubicza, KC	12
4 tied with	11

Opponent Average
D. Stieb, Tor	.213
C. Hough, Tex	.215
D. Petry, Det	.217
J. Morris, Det	.225
T. Higuera, Mil	.235

Opponent OBP
B. Saberhagen, KC	.271
R. Guidry, NYA	.277
J. Key, Tor	.282
C. Hough, Tex	.283
D. Petry, Det	.285

1985 American League Miscellaneous

Managers
Baltimore	Joe Altobelli	29-26
	Cal Ripken	1-0
	Earl Weaver	53-52
Boston	John McNamara	81-81
California	Gene Mauch	90-72
Chicago	Tony La Russa	85-77
Cleveland	Pat Corrales	60-102
Detroit	Sparky Anderson	84-77
Kansas City	Dick Howser	91-71
Milwaukee	George Bamberger	71-90
Minnesota	Billy Gardner	27-35
	Ray Miller	50-50
New York	Yogi Berra	6-10
	Billy Martin	91-54
Oakland	Jackie Moore	77-85
Seattle	Chuck Cottier	74-88
Texas	Doug Rader	9-23
	Bobby Valentine	53-76
Toronto	Bobby Cox	99-62

Awards
Most Valuable Player	Don Mattingly, 1b, NYA
Cy Young	Bret Saberhagen, KC
Rookie of the Year	Ozzie Guillen, ss, ChA
Manager of the Year	Bobby Cox, Tor

STATS All-Star Team
C	Carlton Fisk, ChA	.238	37	107
1B	Don Mattingly, NYA	.324	35	145
2B	Lou Whitaker, Det	.279	21	73
3B	George Brett, KC	.335	30	112
SS	Cal Ripken Jr., Bal	.282	26	110
OF	Jesse Barfield, Tor	.289	27	84
OF	Kirk Gibson, Det	.287	29	97
OF	Rickey Henderson, NYA	.314	24	72
DH	Gorman Thomas, Sea	.215	32	87
P	Ron Guidry, NYA	22-6	3.27	143 K
P	Jack Morris, Det	16-11	3.33	191 K
P	Bret Saberhagen, KC	20-6	2.87	158 K
P	Dave Stieb, Tor	14-13	2.48	167 K
RP	Donnie Moore, Cal	8-8	1.92	31 Sv

Postseason
LCS	Kansas City 4 vs. Toronto 3
World Series	KC (AL) 4 vs. St. Louis (NL) 3

Outstanding Performances
Three-Homer Games
G. Thomas, Sea	on April 11
Larry Parrish, Tex	on April 29
Eddie Murray, Bal	on August 26

Cycles
O. McDowell, Tex	on July 23
Rich Gedman, Bos	on September 18

1985 National League Standings

	Overall					Home Games						Road Games						Park Index		Record by Month					
EAST	W	L	Pct	GB	DIF	W	L	R	OR	HR	OHR	W	L	R	OR	HR	OHR	Run	HR	M/A	May	June	July	Aug	S/O
St. Louis	101	61	.623	—	89	54	27	358	255	36	39	47	34	389	317	51	59	87	68	8-11	16-10	19-8	17-9	17-11	24-12
New York	98	64	.605	3.0	68	51	30	344	254	58	59	47	34	351	314	76	53	90	90	12-6	15-10	11-18	21-7	17-11	22-12
Montreal	84	77	.522	16.5	11	44	37	300	289	45	45	40	40	333	347	73	54	86	70	12-8	15-12	16-12	13-14	15-11	13-20
Chicago	77	84	.478	23.5	36	41	39	399	423	98	104	36	45	287	306	52	52	140	197	12-6	15-11	12-16	13-14	10-18	15-19
Philadelphia	75	87	.463	26.0	1	41	40	350	338	72	57	34	47	317	335	69	58	106	102	8-11	9-17	15-12	13-14	16-12	14-21
Pittsburgh	57	104	.354	43.5	1	35	45	314	347	39	53	22	59	254	361	41	54	109	98	6-12	9-17	9-18	8-19	8-20	17-18
WEST																									
Los Angeles	95	67	.586	—	91	48	33	310	258	47	54	47	34	372	321	82	48	82	78	11-10	12-14	15-10	20-7	16-11	21-15
Cincinnati	89	72	.553	5.5	8	47	34	347	359	49	65	42	38	330	307	65	66	109	86	10-10	14-12	15-11	13-13	15-14	22-12
Houston	83	79	.512	12.0	3	44	37	333	338	47	48	39	42	373	353	74	71	92	66	10-10	14-12	14-15	8-18	14-12	23-12
San Diego	83	79	.512	12.0	78	44	37	321	323	63	77	39	42	329	299	46	50	103	146	10-9	17-9	17-13	10-16	14-13	15-19
Atlanta	66	96	.407	29.0	8	32	49	336	431	65	80	34	47	296	350	61	54	119	126	9-10	10-16	14-14	11-15	11-17	11-24
San Francisco	62	100	.383	33.0	2	38	43	265	307	58	67	24	57	291	367	57	58	87	109	7-12	10-16	10-20	13-14	11-14	11-24

Clinch Date—St. Louis 10/05, Los Angeles 10/02.

Team Batting

Team	G	AB	R	OR	H	2B	3B	HR	TB	RBI	TBB	IBB	SO	HBP	SH	SF	SB	CS	SB%	GDP	Avg	OBP	Slg
St. Louis	162	5467	747	572	1446	245	59	87	2070	687	586	61	853	18	70	41	314	96	.77	91	.264	.342	.379
Houston	162	5582	706	691	1457	261	42	121	2165	666	477	63	873	23	66	44	96	56	.63	127	.261	.327	.388
New York	162	5549	695	568	1425	239	35	134	2136	651	546	88	872	20	89	44	117	53	.69	131	.257	.330	.385
Chicago	162	5492	686	729	1397	239	28	150	2142	640	562	62	937	18	66	39	182	49	.79	119	.254	.330	.390
Los Angeles	162	5502	682	579	1434	226	28	129	2103	632	539	69	846	31	104	46	136	58	.70	108	.261	.335	.382
Cincinnati	162	5431	677	666	1385	249	34	114	2044	634	576	72	856	23	70	41	159	70	.69	136	.255	.334	.376
Philadelphia	162	5477	667	673	1343	238	47	141	2098	628	527	51	1095	25	49	44	122	51	.71	124	.245	.319	.383
San Diego	162	5507	650	622	1405	241	28	109	2029	611	513	68	809	23	75	32	60	39	.61	128	.255	.325	.368
Montreal	161	5429	633	636	1342	242	49	118	2036	593	492	73	880	26	61	45	169	77	.69	112	.247	.318	.375
Atlanta	162	5526	632	781	1359	213	28	126	2006	598	553	56	849	22	65	41	72	52	.58	154	.246	.322	.363
Pittsburgh	161	5436	568	708	1340	251	28	80	1887	535	514	64	842	14	91	44	110	60	.65	131	.247	.318	.347
San Francisco	162	5420	556	674	1263	217	31	115	1887	517	488	53	962	37	93	25	99	55	.64	121	.233	.304	.348
NL Total	1942	65818	7899	7899	16596	2861	437	1424	24603	7392	6373	780	10674	280	901	486	1636	716	.70	1482	.252	.319	.374
NL Avg Team	162	5485	658	658	1383	238	36	119	2050	616	531	65	890	23	75	41	136	60	.70	124	.252	.319	.374

Team Pitching

Team	G	CG	ShO	Rel	Sv	IP	H	R	ER	HR	SH	SF	HB	TBB	IBB	SO	WP	Bk	H/9	SO/9	BB/9	OAvg	OOBP	ERA
Los Angeles	162	37	21	250	36	1465.0	1280	579	482	102	57	38	21	462	56	979	42	10	7.9	6.0	2.8	.234	.295	2.96
St. Louis	162	37	20	296	44	1464.0	1343	572	505	98	60	39	28	453	80	798	33	6	8.3	4.9	2.8	.246	.305	3.10
New York	162	32	19	243	37	1488.0	1306	568	514	111	66	27	18	515	36	1039	41	14	7.9	6.3	3.1	.237	.302	3.11
San Diego	162	26	19	283	44	1451.1	1399	622	549	127	91	43	25	443	50	727	23	14	8.7	4.5	2.7	.257	.313	3.40
Montreal	161	13	13	323	53	1457.0	1346	636	574	99	87	35	21	509	70	870	46	12	8.3	5.4	3.1	.247	.312	3.55
San Francisco	162	13	5	321	24	1448.0	1348	674	581	125	88	40	19	572	76	985	57	16	8.4	6.1	3.6	.247	.319	3.61
Houston	162	17	9	282	42	1458.0	1393	691	594	119	72	58	25	543	50	909	69	8	8.6	5.6	3.4	.254	.321	3.67
Philadelphia	162	24	9	315	30	1447.0	1424	673	592	115	66	47	26	596	63	899	34	9	8.9	5.6	3.7	.259	.331	3.68
Cincinnati	162	24	11	287	45	1451.1	1347	666	598	131	74	51	14	535	61	910	42	5	8.4	5.6	3.3	.248	.315	3.71
Pittsburgh	161	15	6	297	29	1445.1	1406	708	638	107	57	28	32	584	72	962	48	11	8.8	6.0	3.6	.255	.329	3.97
Chicago	162	20	8	313	42	1442.1	1492	729	666	156	95	45	23	519	83	820	31	11	9.3	5.1	3.2	.271	.333	4.16
Atlanta	162	9	9	351	29	1457.1	1512	781	679	134	88	35	28	642	83	776	35	4	9.3	4.8	4.0	.271	.347	4.19
NL Total	1942	267	149	3561	455	17474.2	16596	7899	6972	1424	901	486	280	6373	780	10674	501	120	8.5	5.5	3.3	.252	.325	3.59
NL Avg Team	162	22	12	297	38	1456.2	1383	658	581	119	75	41	23	531	65	890	42	10	8.5	5.5	3.3	.252	.325	3.59

Team Fielding

Team	G	PO	A	E	TC	DP	PB	Pct
St. Louis	162	4392	1859	108	6359	166	15	.983
New York	162	4464	1696	115	6275	138	9	.982
Montreal	161	4371	1856	121	6348	152	16	.981
Cincinnati	162	4354	1679	122	6155	142	10	.980
San Diego	162	4354	1730	124	6208	158	6	.980
Chicago	162	4327	1934	134	6395	150	17	.979
Pittsburgh	161	4336	1799	133	6268	127	6	.979
Philadelphia	162	4341	1777	139	6257	142	15	.978
San Francisco	162	4344	1773	148	6265	134	20	.976
Houston	162	4374	1789	152	6315	159	36	.976
Atlanta	162	4372	2028	159	6559	197	8	.976
Los Angeles	162	4395	1903	166	6464	131	7	.974
NL Total	1942	52424	21823	1621	75868	1796	165	.979

Team vs. Team Records

	Atl	ChN	Cin	Hou	LA	Mon	NYN	Phi	Pit	SD	SF	StL	Won
Atl	—	5	7	8	5	3	2	10	6	7	10	3	66
ChN	7	—	5	5	5	7	4	13	13	8	6	4	77
Cin	11	6	—	11	7	8	4	7	9	9	12	5	89
Hou	10	7	7	—	6	6	4	4	6	12	15	6	83
LA	13	7	11	12	—	7	7	4	8	8	11	7	95
Mon	9	11	4	6	5	—	9	8	9	5	7	11	84
NYN	10	14	8	8	5	9	—	11	10	7	8	8	98
Phi	2	5	5	5	8	10	7	—	11	5	6	8	75
Pit	6	5	3	6	4	8	8	7	—	4	3	3	57
SD	11	4	9	6	10	7	5	7	8	—	12	4	83
SF	8	6	6	3	7	5	4	6	9	6	—	2	62
StL	9	14	7	6	5	7	10	10	15	8	10	—	101
Lost	96	84	72	79	67	77	64	87	104	79	100	61	

Seasons: Standings, Leaders

1985 National League Batting Leaders

Games		At-Bats		Runs		Hits		Doubles		Triples	
S. Garvey, SD	162	J. Samuel, Phi	663	D. Murphy, Atl	118	W. McGee, StL	216	D. Parker, Cin	42	W. McGee, StL	18
D. Murphy, Atl	162	S. Garvey, SD	654	T. Raines, Mon	115	D. Parker, Cin	198	G. Wilson, Phi	39	T. Raines, Mon	13
K. Moreland, ChN	161	V. Coleman, StL	636	W. McGee, StL	114	T. Gwynn, SD	197	T. Herr, StL	38	J. Samuel, Phi	13
G. Wilson, Phi	161	D. Parker, Cin	635	R. Sandberg, ChN	113	R. Sandberg, ChN	186	T. Wallach, Mon	36	P. Garner, Hou	10
J. Samuel, Phi	161	T. Gwynn, SD	622	V. Coleman, StL	107	D. Murphy, Atl	185	4 tied with	34	V. Coleman, StL	10

Home Runs		Total Bases		Runs Batted In		Walks		Intentional Walks		Strikeouts	
D. Murphy, Atl	37	D. Parker, Cin	350	D. Parker, Cin	125	D. Murphy, Atl	90	G. Templeton, SD	24	D. Murphy, Atl	141
D. Parker, Cin	34	D. Murphy, Atl	332	D. Murphy, Atl	111	M. Schmidt, Phi	87	D. Parker, Cin	24	J. Samuel, Phi	141
P. Guerrero, LA	33	W. McGee, StL	308	T. Herr, StL	110	C. Martinez, SD	87	L. Durham, ChN	24	M. Marshall, LA	137
M. Schmidt, Phi	33	R. Sandberg, ChN	307	K. Moreland, ChN	106	P. Rose, Cin	86	R. Oester, Cin	17	M. Schmidt, Phi	117
G. Carter, NYN	32	M. Schmidt, Phi	292	G. Wilson, Phi	102	V. Law, Mon	86	G. Carter, NYN	16	G. Wilson, Phi	117

Hit By Pitch		Sac Hits		Sac Flies		Stolen Bases		Caught Stealing		GDP	
C. Brown, SF	11	W. Backman, NYN	14	T. Herr, StL	13	V. Coleman, StL	110	V. Coleman, StL	25	D. Parker, Cin	26
T. Flannery, SD	9	N. Ryan, Hou	14	K. Hernandez, NYN	10	T. Raines, Mon	70	J. Samuel, Phi	19	S. Garvey, SD	25
B. Madlock, 2tm	8	A. Hawkins, SD	13	K. Moreland, ChN	9	W. McGee, StL	56	W. McGee, StL	16	G. Wilson, Phi	24
D. Gladden, SF	7	R. Darling, NYN	13	K. Landreaux, LA	8	R. Sandberg, ChN	54	B. Doran, Hou	15	D. Concepcion, Cin	23
G. Davis, Hou	7	M. Duncan, LA	13	H. Brooks, Mon	8	J. Samuel, Phi	53	D. Gladden, SF	15	R. Ramirez, Atl	21

Runs Created		Runs Created/27 Outs		Batting Average		On-Base Percentage		Slugging Percentage		OBP+Slugging	
D. Murphy, Atl	125	P. Guerrero, LA	8.40	W. McGee, StL	.353	P. Guerrero, LA	.422	P. Guerrero, LA	.577	P. Guerrero, LA	.999
T. Raines, Mon	120	T. Raines, Mon	7.86	P. Guerrero, LA	.320	M. Scioscia, LA	.407	D. Parker, Cin	.551	D. Murphy, Atl	.927
W. McGee, StL	120	W. McGee, StL	7.75	T. Raines, Mon	.320	T. Raines, Mon	.405	D. Murphy, Atl	.539	D. Parker, Cin	.916
M. Schmidt, Phi	110	D. Murphy, Atl	7.50	T. Gwynn, SD	.317	J. Clark, StL	.393	M. Schmidt, Phi	.532	M. Schmidt, Phi	.907
D. Parker, Cin	110	M. Schmidt, Phi	7.19	D. Parker, Cin	.312	D. Murphy, Atl	.388	M. Marshall, LA	.515	J. Clark, StL	.895

1985 National League Pitching Leaders

Wins		Losses		Winning Percentage		Games		Games Started		Complete Games	
D. Gooden, NYN	24	J. DeLeon, Pit	19	O. Hershiser, LA	.864	T. Burke, Mon	78	R. Mahler, Atl	39	D. Gooden, NYN	16
J. Andujar, StL	21	D. LaPoint, SF	17	D. Gooden, NYN	.857	M. Davis, SF	77	J. Andujar, StL	38	F. Valenzuela, LA	14
J. Tudor, StL	21	B. Laskey, 2tm	16	J. Franco, Cin	.800	S. Garrelts, SF	74	T. Browning, Cin	38	J. Tudor, StL	14
T. Browning, Cin	20	J. Tibbs, Cin	16	B. Smith, Mon	.783	D. Carman, Phi	71	B. Knepper, Hou	37	J. Andujar, StL	10
O. Hershiser, LA	19	4 tied with	15	B. Welch, LA	.778	G. Minton, SF	68	S. Bedrosian, Atl	37	D. Cox, StL	10

Shutouts		Saves		Games Finished		Batters Faced		Innings Pitched		Hits Allowed	
J. Tudor, StL	10	J. Reardon, Mon	41	L. Smith, ChN	57	J. Andujar, StL	1127	D. Gooden, NYN	276.2	R. Mahler, Atl	272
D. Gooden, NYN	8	L. Smith, ChN	33	J. Reardon, Mon	50	R. Mahler, Atl	1110	J. Tudor, StL	275.0	J. Andujar, StL	265
F. Valenzuela, LA	5	D. Smith, Hou	27	B. Sutter, Atl	50	F. Valenzuela, LA	1109	F. Valenzuela, LA	272.1	R. Rhoden, Pit	254
O. Hershiser, LA	5	T. Power, Cin	27	T. Power, Cin	50	T. Browning, Cin	1083	J. Andujar, StL	269.2	B. Knepper, Hou	253
2 tied with	4	G. Gossage, SD	26	D. Smith, Hou	46	D. Gooden, NYN	1065	R. Mahler, Atl	266.2	J. Denny, Phi	252

Home Runs Allowed		Walks		Walks/9 Innings		Strikeouts		Strikeouts/9 Innings		Strikeout/Walk Ratio	
M. Soto, Cin	30	R. Darling, NYN	114	L. Hoyt, SD	0.9	D. Gooden, NYN	268	S. Fernandez, NYN	9.5	D. Eckersley, ChN	6.16
T. Browning, Cin	29	S. Bedrosian, Atl	111	D. Eckersley, ChN	1.0	M. Soto, Cin	214	D. Gooden, NYN	8.7	L. Hoyt, SD	4.15
E. Show, SD	27	M. Soto, Cin	104	E. Lynch, NYN	1.3	N. Ryan, Hou	209	J. DeLeon, Pit	8.2	D. Gooden, NYN	3.88
R. Mahler, Atl	24	F. Valenzuela, LA	101	J. Tudor, StL	1.6	F. Valenzuela, LA	208	N. Ryan, Hou	8.1	J. Tudor, StL	3.45
2 tied with	23	J. Niekro, Hou	99	B. Smith, Mon	1.7	S. Fernandez, NYN	180	M. Soto, Cin	7.5	B. Smith, Mon	3.10

Earned Run Average		Component ERA		Hit Batsmen		Wild Pitches		Opponent Average		Opponent OBP	
D. Gooden, NYN	1.53	D. Gooden, NYN	1.83	J. Andujar, StL	11	J. Niekro, Hou	21	S. Fernandez, NYN	.181	J. Tudor, StL	.249
J. Tudor, StL	1.93	J. Tudor, StL	1.84	N. Ryan, Hou	9	N. Ryan, Hou	14	D. Gooden, NYN	.201	D. Eckersley, ChN	.254
O. Hershiser, LA	2.03	O. Hershiser, LA	2.01	L. McWilliams, Pit	7	J. Tibbs, Cin	12	O. Hershiser, LA	.206	D. Gooden, NYN	.254
R. Reuschel, Pit	2.27	R. Reuschel, Pit	2.10	K. Gross, Phi	7	3 tied with	10	J. Tudor, StL	.209	O. Hershiser, LA	.267
B. Welch, LA	2.31	D. Eckersley, ChN	2.23	T. Burke, Mon	7			M. Soto, Cin	.211	B. Smith, Mon	.268

1985 National League Miscellaneous

Managers

Atlanta	Eddie Haas	50-71
	Bobby Wine	16-25
Chicago	Jim Frey	77-84
Cincinnati	Pete Rose	89-72
Houston	Bob Lillis	83-79
Los Angeles	Tom Lasorda	95-67
Montreal	Buck Rodgers	84-77
New York	Davey Johnson	98-64
Philadelphia	John Felske	75-87
Pittsburgh	Chuck Tanner	57-104
St. Louis	Whitey Herzog	101-61
San Diego	Dick Williams	83-79
San Francisco	Jim Davenport	56-88
	Roger Craig	6-12

Awards

Most Valuable Player	Willie McGee, of, StL
Cy Young	Dwight Gooden, NYN
Rookie of the Year	Vince Coleman, of, StL
Manager of the Year	Whitey Herzog, StL

STATS All-Star Team

Pos	Player	AVG	HR	RBI
C	Gary Carter, NYN	.281	32	100
1B	Mike Schmidt, Phi	.277	33	93
2B	Ryne Sandberg, ChN	.305	26	83
3B	Tim Wallach, Mon	.260	22	81
SS	Ozzie Smith, StL	.276	6	54
OF	Pedro Guerrero, LA	.320	33	87
OF	Willie McGee, StL	.353	10	82
OF	Dale Murphy, Atl	.300	37	111
P	Dwight Gooden, NYN	24-4	1.53	268 K
P	Orel Hershiser, LA	19-3	2.03	157 K
P	John Tudor, StL	21-8	1.93	169 K
P	Fernando Valenzuela, LA	17-10	2.45	208 K
RP	Jeff Reardon, Mon	2-8	3.18	41 Sv

Postseason

LCS	St. Louis 4 vs. Los Angeles 2
World Series	St. Louis (NL) 3 vs. KC (AL) 4

Outstanding Performances

Three-Homer Games
D. Strawberry, NYN on August 5
Gary Carter, NYN on September 3
Andre Dawson, Mon on September 24

Cycles
Jeffrey Leonard, SF on June 27
K. Hernandez, NYN on July 4

1986 American League Standings

EAST	W	L	Pct	GB	DIF	W	L	R	OR	HR	OHR	W	L	R	OR	HR	OHR	Run	HR	M/A	May	June	July	Aug	S/O
								Home Games						**Road Games**				**Park Index**				**Record by Month**			
Boston	95	66	.590	—	147	51	30	389	350	55	85	44	36	405	346	89	82	97	81	11-8	21-7	17-10	10-16	17-13	19-12
New York	90	72	.556	5.5	29	41	39	384	396	93	96	49	33	413	**342**	95	79	106	111	14-6	16-12	12-16	14-12	14-15	20-11
Detroit	87	75	.537	8.5	4	49	32	403	**310**	96	83	38	43	395	404	**102**	100	89	89	10-9	13-13	14-15	17-11	14-16	19-11
Toronto	86	76	.531	9.5	1	42	39	415	389	87	89	44	37	394	344	94	75	109	104	9-11	14-15	17-11	15-11	18-10	13-18
Cleveland	84	78	.519	11.5	7	45	35	403	415	80	80	39	43	**428**	426	77	87	98	100	11-8	12-16	15-11	15-12	12-19	19-12
Milwaukee	77	84	.478	18.0	5	41	39	338	375	63	79	36	45	329	359	64	79	105	101	9-9	15-13	13-15	12-13	15-15	13-19
Baltimore	73	89	.451	22.5	0	37	42	348	362	91	98	36	47	360	398	78	79	98	126	10-10	18-8	11-17	16-11	10-19	8-24
WEST																									
California	92	70	.568	—	132	50	32	371	335	88	84	42	38	415	349	79	69	90	113	13-8	10-17	17-10	15-11	19-10	18-14
Texas	87	75	.537	5.0	47	51	30	374	343	87	61	36	45	397	400	97	84	90	82	9-10	15-13	16-13	12-14	17-12	18-13
Kansas City	76	86	.469	16.0	4	45	36	342	317	60	**46**	31	50	312	356	77	75	99	70	9-10	14-14	14-15	9-17	14-14	16-16
Oakland	76	86	.469	16.0	5	47	36	363	349	75	81	29	50	368	411	88	85	87	86	11-10	12-16	7-22	14-12	17-11	15-15
Chicago	72	90	.444	20.0	1	41	40	341	335	51	63	31	50	303	364	70	80	101	76	7-12	11-16	15-13	11-15	12-17	16-17
Minnesota	71	91	.438	21.0	6	43	38	426	439	116	107	28	53	315	400	80	93	121	129	8-13	11-16	14-13	10-16	12-17	16-16
Seattle	67	95	.414	25.0	7	41	41	410	427	97	99	26	54	308	408	61	77	114	144	7-14	11-17	14-15	13-12	13-16	9-21

Clinch Date—Boston 9/28, California 9/26.

Team Batting

Team	G	AB	R	OR	H	2B	3B	HR	TB	RBI	TBB	IBB	SO	HBP	SH	SF	SB	CS	SB%	GDP	Avg	OBP	Slg
Cleveland	163	5702	**831**	841	**1620**	270	45	157	2451	**775**	456	26	944	24	56	49	**141**	54	.72	129	**.284**	.345	.430
Toronto	163	**5716**	809	733	1540	285	35	181	2438	767	496	23	848	33	24	49	110	59	.65	122	.269	.337	.427
Detroit	162	5512	798	714	1447	234	30	**198**	2335	751	613	35	885	43	52	49	138	58	.70	99	.263	.346	.424
New York	162	5570	797	738	1512	275	23	188	2397	745	645	52	911	28	36	46	139	48	**.74**	142	**.271**	**.355**	**.430**
Boston	161	5498	794	696	1488	**320**	21	144	2282	752	595	**56**	707	**66**	44	52	41	34	.55	142	.271	.354	.415
California	162	5433	786	684	1387	236	36	167	2196	743	**671**	45	860	40	**91**	**61**	109	42	.72	134	.255	.348	.404
Texas	162	5529	771	743	1479	248	43	184	2365	725	511	33	1088	35	31	42	103	**85**	.55	133	.267	.338	.428
Minnesota	162	5531	741	839	1446	257	39	196	2369	700	501	33	977	37	44	38	81	61	.57	123	.261	.331	.428
Oakland	162	5435	731	760	1370	213	25	163	2122	683	553	24	983	32	56	51	139	61	.70	105	.252	.330	.390
Seattle	162	5498	718	835	1392	243	41	158	2191	681	572	38	**1148**	34	52	29	93	76	.55	125	.253	.331	.399
Baltimore	162	5524	708	760	1425	223	13	169	2181	669	563	26	862	31	33	51	64	34	.65	**159**	.258	.336	.395
Milwaukee	161	5461	667	734	1393	255	38	127	2105	625	530	26	986	27	53	53	100	50	.67	122	.255	.330	.385
Kansas City	162	5561	654	**673**	1403	264	45	137	2168	618	474	40	919	36	24	33	97	46	.68	101	.252	.319	.390
Chicago	162	5406	644	699	1335	197	34	121	1963	605	487	29	940	34	50	53	115	54	.68	125	.247	.319	.363
AL Total	2268	77376	10449	10449	20237	3520	468	2290	31563	9839	7667	486	13058	500	646	656	1470	762	.66	1759	.262	.330	.408
AL Avg Team	162	5527	746	746	1446	251	33	164	2255	703	548	35	933	36	46	47	105	54	.66	126	.262	.330	.408

Team Pitching

Team	G	CG	ShO	Rel	Sv	IP	H	R	ER	HR	SH	SF	HB	TBB	IBB	SO	WP	Bk	H/9	SO/9	BB/9	OAvg	OOBP	ERA
Kansas City	162	24	**13**	230	31	1440.2	1413	**673**	612	121	51	48	38	479	46	888	43	6	8.8	5.5	3.0	.258	.319	3.82
California	162	29	12	246	40	1456.0	1356	684	622	153	41	44	27	478	19	955	44	6	8.4	5.9	**3.0**	.248	**.309**	3.84
Chicago	162	18	8	297	38	1442.1	1361	699	630	143	54	43	33	561	28	895	55	3	8.5	5.6	3.5	.251	.323	3.93
Boston	161	36	6	254	41	1429.2	1469	696	625	167	38	48	26	**474**	35	1033	55	8	9.2	6.5	3.0	.266	.325	3.93
Milwaukee	161	29	12	237	32	1431.2	1478	734	638	158	42	49	29	494	22	952	57	9	9.3	6.0	3.1	.267	.328	4.01
Detroit	162	33	12	239	38	1443.2	1374	714	645	183	47	**35**	30	571	**61**	880	50	6	8.6	5.5	3.6	.251	.323	4.02
Toronto	163	16	12	290	44	**1476.0**	1467	733	669	164	59	51	45	487	39	1002	38	6	8.9	6.1	3.0	.261	.322	4.08
New York	162	13	8	289	**58**	1443.1	1461	738	659	175	48	44	24	492	25	878	40	3	9.1	5.5	3.1	.263	.323	4.11
Texas	162	15	8	**328**	32	1450.1	1356	743	663	145	**37**	42	41	736	37	**1059**	94	13	8.4	**6.6**	4.6	.249	.340	4.11
Baltimore	162	17	6	262	39	1436.2	1451	760	687	177	46	41	21	535	41	954	52	4	9.1	6.0	3.4	.263	.328	4.30
Oakland	162	22	8	286	37	1433.0	**1334**	760	687	166	44	55	34	667	35	937	62	**19**	8.4	5.9	4.2	**.247**	.330	4.31
Cleveland	163	31	7	290	34	1447.2	1548	841	736	167	55	60	**57**	605	34	744	63	13	9.6	4.6	3.8	.273	.346	4.58
Seattle	162	33	5	281	27	1439.2	1590	835	744	171	41	44	49	585	27	944	46	10	9.9	5.9	3.7	.283	.353	4.65
Minnesota	162	**39**	4	239	24	1432.2	1579	839	759	290	40	50	46	533	37	937	58	5	9.9	5.9	3.2	.281	.342	4.77
AL Total	2268	355	123	3769	524	20203.1	20237	10449	9376	2290	646	656	500	7667	486	13058	757	113	9.0	5.8	3.4	.262	.337	4.18
AL Avg Team	162	25	9	269	37	1443.1	1446	746	670	164	46	47	36	548	35	933	54	8	9.0	5.8	3.4	.262	.337	4.18

Team Fielding

Team	G	PO	A	E	TC	DP	PB	Pct
Toronto	163	**4428**	1684	**100**	6212	150	9	.984
California	162	4368	1718	107	6193	156	12	.983
Detroit	162	4331	1707	108	6146	163	12	.982
Chicago	162	4327	1667	117	6111	142	14	.981
Minnesota	162	4298	1626	118	6042	168	12	.980
Kansas City	162	4322	1757	123	6202	153	16	.980
Texas	162	4351	1655	122	6128	160	**25**	.980
New York	162	4330	1672	127	6129	153	17	.979
Boston	161	4289	1602	129	6020	146	16	.979
Baltimore	162	4310	1651	135	6096	163	7	.978
Oakland	162	4299	1597	135	6031	120	16	.978
Milwaukee	161	4295	1521	146	5962	146	15	.976
Seattle	162	4319	**1838**	156	**6313**	191	17	.975
Cleveland	163	4343	1703	157	6203	148	20	.975
AL Total	2268	60610	23398	1780	85788	2159	208	.979

Team vs. Team Records

	Bal	Bos	Cal	ChA	Cle	Det	KC	Mil	Min	NYA	Oak	Sea	Tex	Tor	Won
Bal	—	4	6	9	4	1	6	6	8	5	5	6	5	8	73
Bos	9	—	5	7	10	7	6	6	10	5	7	8	8	7	95
Cal	6	7	—	7	6	7	8	5	7	7	10	8	8	6	92
ChA	3	5	6	—	5	6	7	5	6	6	7	8	2	6	72
Cle	9	3	6	7	—	4	8	6	8	5	10	9	6	3	84
Det	12	6	5	6	9	—	5	8	7	6	6	6	7	4	87
KC	6	6	5	6	4	7	—	6	4	8	5	8	5	4	76
Mil	7	6	7	7	5	5	6	—	4	8	5	6	4	7	77
Min	4	2	6	7	6	5	7	8	—	4	6	6	6	4	71
NYA	8	8	5	6	8	7	5	5	8	—	5	8	7	7	90
Oak	7	5	3	6	2	6	5	7	7	7	—	10	3	6	76
Sea	6	4	5	5	3	6	8	6	7	4	3	—	4	6	67
Tex	7	4	5	11	6	5	8	8	7	5	10	9	—	5	87
Tor	5	6	6	6	10	9	7	6	8	6	4	6	7	—	86
Lost	89	66	70	90	78	75	86	84	91	72	86	95	75	76	

1986 American League Batting Leaders

Games		At-Bats		Runs		Hits		Doubles		Triples	
T. Fernandez, Tor	163	T. Fernandez, Tor	687	R. Henderson, NYA	130	D. Mattingly, NYA	238	D. Mattingly, NYA	53	B. Butler, Cle	14
A. Griffin, Oak	162	K. Puckett, Min	680	K. Puckett, Min	119	K. Puckett, Min	223	W. Boggs, Bos	47	R. Sierra, Tex	10
C. Ripken Jr., Bal	162	D. Mattingly, NYA	677	D. Mattingly, NYA	117	T. Fernandez, Tor	213	J. Rice, Bos	39	T. Fernandez, Tor	9
D. Mattingly, NYA	162	J. Carter, Cle	663	J. Carter, Cle	108	W. Boggs, Bos	207	B. Buckner, Bos	39	J. Carter, Cle	9
J. Carter, Cle	162	G. Bell, Tor	641	3 tied with	107	2 tied with	200	M. Barrett, Bos	39	7 tied with	7

Home Runs		Total Bases		Runs Batted In		Walks		Intentional Walks		Strikeouts	
J. Barfield, Tor	40	D. Mattingly, NYA	388	J. Carter, Cle	121	W. Boggs, Bos	105	G. Brett, KC	18	P. Incaviglia, Tex	185
D. Kingman, Oak	35	K. Puckett, Min	365	J. Canseco, Oak	117	D. Evans, Det	97	W. Boggs, Bos	14	R. Deer, Mil	179
G. Gaetti, Min	34	G. Bell, Tor	341	D. Mattingly, NYA	113	W. Randolph, NYA	94	M. Easler, NYA	13	J. Canseco, Oak	175
R. Deer, Mil	33	J. Carter, Cle	341	J. Rice, Bos	110	R. Jackson, Cal	92	R. Gedman, Bos	13	J. Presley, Sea	172
J. Canseco, Oak	33	J. Barfield, Tor	329	3 tied with	108	D. Evans, Det	91	3 tied with	11	D. Tartabull, Sea	157

Hit By Pitch		Sac Hits		Sac Flies		Stolen Bases		Caught Stealing		GDP	
D. Baylor, Bos	35	M. Barrett, Bos	18	W. Joyner, Cal	12	R. Henderson, NYA	87	R. Henderson, NYA	18	J. Franco, Cle	28
B. Downing, Cal	17	B. Butler, Cle	17	D. Mattingly, NYA	10	G. Pettis, Cal	50	J. Moses, Sea	18	B. Buckner, Bos	25
L. Smith, KC	10	G. Pettis, Cal	15	J. Rice, Bos	9	J. Cangelosi, ChA	50	J. Cangelosi, ChA	17	F. Lynn, Bal	20
W. Wilson, KC	9	W. Tolleson, 2tm	13	D. Schofield, Cal	9	W. Wilson, KC	34	A. Griffin, Oak	16	L. Whitaker, Det	20
4 tied with	8	G. Gagne, Min	13	J. Canseco, Oak	9	K. Gibson, Det	34	3 tied with	15	D. Winfield, NYA	20

Runs Created		Runs Created/27 Outs		Batting Average		On-Base Percentage		Slugging Percentage		OBP+Slugging	
D. Mattingly, NYA	134	W. Boggs, Bos	8.69	W. Boggs, Bos	.357	W. Boggs, Bos	.453	D. Mattingly, NYA	.573	D. Mattingly, NYA	.967
W. Boggs, Bos	128	D. Mattingly, NYA	7.71	D. Mattingly, NYA	.352	P. Bradley, Sea	.405	J. Barfield, Tor	.559	W. Boggs, Bos	.939
K. Puckett, Min	121	J. Barfield, Tor	7.19	K. Puckett, Min	.328	G. Brett, KC	.401	K. Puckett, Min	.537	J. Barfield, Tor	.927
J. Barfield, Tor	118	P. Bradley, Sea	6.88	P. Tabler, Cle	.326	E. Murray, Bal	.396	G. Bell, Tor	.532	K. Puckett, Min	.903
J. Carter, Cle	116	G. Brett, KC	6.86	J. Rice, Bos	.324	D. Mattingly, NYA	.394	G. Gaetti, Min	.518	G. Brett, KC	.881

1986 American League Pitching Leaders

Wins		Losses		Winning Percentage		Games		Games Started		Complete Games	
R. Clemens, Bos	24	R. Dotson, ChA	17	R. Clemens, Bos	.857	M. Williams, Tex	80	F. Viola, Min	37	T. Candiotti, Cle	17
J. Morris, Det	21	M. Morgan, Sea	17	D. Rasmussen, NYA	.750	D. Righetti, NYA	74	M. Moore, Sea	37	B. Blyleven, Min	16
T. Higuera, Mil	20	S. McGregor, Bal	15	E. King, Det	.733	G. Harris, Tex	73	B. Blyleven, Min	36	J. Morris, Det	15
M. Witt, Cal	18	N. Heaton, 2tm	15	J. Morris, Det	.724	M. Eichhorn, Tor	69	M. Langston, Sea	36	T. Higuera, Mil	15
D. Rasmussen, NYA	18	J. Guzman, Tex	15	M. Eichhorn, Tor	.700	2 tied with	66	2 tied with	35	M. Witt, Cal	14

Shutouts		Saves		Games Finished		Batters Faced		Innings Pitched		Hits Allowed	
J. Morris, Det	6	D. Righetti, NYA	46	D. Righetti, NYA	68	M. Moore, Sea	1145	B. Blyleven, Min	271.2	M. Moore, Sea	279
B. Hurst, Bos	4	D. Aase, Bal	34	G. Harris, Tex	63	B. Blyleven, Min	1126	M. Witt, Cal	269.0	B. Blyleven, Min	262
T. Higuera, Mil	4	T. Henke, Tor	27	D. Aase, Bal	58	J. Morris, Det	1092	J. Morris, Det	267.0	F. Viola, Min	257
5 tied with	3	W. Hernandez, Det	24	D. Quisenberry, KC	54	T. Candiotti, Cle	1078	M. Moore, Sea	266.0	M. Morgan, Sea	243
		D. Moore, Cal	21	W. Hernandez, Det	53	M. Witt, Cal	1071	R. Clemens, Bos	254.0	P. Niekro, Cle	241

Home Runs Allowed		Walks		Walks/9 Innings		Strikeouts		Strikeouts/9 Innings		Strikeout/Walk Ratio	
B. Blyleven, Min	50	B. Witt, Tex	143	R. Guidry, NYA	1.8	M. Langston, Sea	245	M. Langston, Sea	9.2	B. Blyleven, Min	3.71
J. Morris, Det	40	E. Correa, Tex	126	C. Boyd, Bos	1.9	R. Clemens, Bos	238	B. Hurst, Bos	8.6	R. Guidry, NYA	3.68
F. Viola, Min	37	M. Langston, Sea	123	B. Blyleven, Min	1.9	J. Morris, Det	223	R. Clemens, Bos	8.4	R. Clemens, Bos	3.55
S. McGregor, Bal	35	J. Rijo, Oak	108	B. Wegman, Mil	2.0	B. Blyleven, Min	215	E. Correa, Tex	8.4	B. Hurst, Bos	3.34
K. Schrom, Cle	34	T. Candiotti, Cle	106	D. Sutton, Cal	2.1	M. Witt, Cal	208	J. Rijo, Oak	8.2	O. Boyd, Bos	2.87

Earned Run Average		Component ERA		Hit Batsmen		Wild Pitches		Opponent Average		Opponent OBP	
R. Clemens, Bos	2.48	R. Clemens, Bos	2.03	D. Stieb, Tor	15	B. Witt, Tex	22	R. Clemens, Bos	.195	R. Clemens, Bos	.252
T. Higuera, Mil	2.79	M. Witt, Cal	2.55	M. Smithson, Min	14	E. Correa, Tex	19	D. Rasmussen, NYA	.217	M. Witt, Cal	.275
M. Witt, Cal	2.84	K. McCaskill, Cal	3.07	B. Schrom, Cle	12	C. Hough, Tex	16	M. Witt, Cal	.221	J. Morris, Det	.287
B. Hurst, Bos	2.99	C. Young, Oak	3.12	M. Moore, Sea	12	M. Smithson, Min	15	C. Hough, Tex	.221	D. Sutton, Cal	.287
D. Jackson, KC	3.20	D. Rasmussen, NYA	3.16	2 tied with	11	M. Gubicza, KC	15	E. Correa, Tex	.223	D. Rasmussen, NYA	.289

1986 American League Miscellaneous

Managers		
Baltimore	Earl Weaver	73-89
Boston	John McNamara	95-66
California	Gene Mauch	92-70
Chicago	Tony La Russa	26-38
	Doug Rader	1-1
	Jim Fregosi	45-51
Cleveland	Pat Corrales	84-78
Detroit	Sparky Anderson	87-75
Kansas City	Dick Howser	40-48
	Mike Ferraro	36-38
Milwaukee	George Bamberger	71-81
	Tom Trebelhorn	6-3
Minnesota	Ray Miller	59-80
	Tom Kelly	12-11
New York	Lou Piniella	90-72
Oakland	Jackie Moore	29-44
	Jeff Newman	2-8
	Tony La Russa	45-34
Seattle	Chuck Cottier	9-19
	Marty Martinez	0-1
	Dick Williams	58-75
Texas	Bobby Valentine	87-75
Toronto	Jimy Williams	86-76

Awards	
Most Valuable Player	Roger Clemens, p, Bos
Cy Young	Roger Clemens, Bos
Rookie of the Year	Jose Canseco, of, Oak
Manager of the Year	John McNamara, Bos

STATS All-Star Team

C	Lance Parrish, Det	.257	22	62	
1B	Don Mattingly, NYA	.352	31	113	
2B	Tony Bernazard, Cle	.301	17	73	
3B	Wade Boggs, Bos	.357	8	71	
SS	Cal Ripken Jr., Bal	.282	25	81	
OF	Jesse Barfield, Tor	.289	40	108	
OF	Rickey Henderson, NYA	.263	28	74	
OF	Kirby Puckett, Min	.328	31	96	
DH	Larry Parrish, Tex	.276	28	94	
P	Roger Clemens, Bos	24-4	2.48	238 K	
P	Teddy Higuera, Mil	20-11	2.79	207 K	
P	Jack Morris, Det	21-8	3.27	223 K	
P	Mike Witt, Cal	18-10	2.84	208 K	
RP	Dave Righetti, NYA	8-8	2.45	46 Sv	

Postseason	
LCS	Boston 4 vs. California 3
World Series	Boston (AL) 3 vs. New York (NL) 4

Outstanding Performances

No-Hitters
Joe Cowley, ChA	@ Cal on September 19

Three-Homer Games
Lee Lacy, Bal	on June 8
Juan Beniquez, Bal	on June 12
Joe Carter, Cle	on August 29
Jim Presley, Sea	on September 1
Reggie Jackson, Cal	on September 18

Cycles
Tony Phillips, Oak	on May 16
Kirby Puckett, Min	on August 1

Seasons: Standings, Leaders

1986 National League Standings

	Overall					Home Games						Road Games						Park Index		Record by Month					
EAST	W	L	Pct	GB	DIF	W	L	R	OR	HR	OHR	W	L	R	OR	HR	OHR	Run	HR	M/A	May	June	July	Aug	S/O
New York	108	54	.667	—	172	55	26	379	251	77	47	53	28	404	327	71	56	86	98	13-3	18-9	19-9	16-11	21-11	21-11
Philadelphia	86	75	.534	21.5	1	49	31	413	344	86	49	37	44	326	369	68	81	110	92	8-9	12-15	15-13	14-13	19-12	18-13
St. Louis	79	82	.491	28.5	16	42	39	321	303	27	63	37	43	280	308	31	72	105	86	8-10	9-17	15-14	14-12	19-12	14-17
Montreal	78	83	.484	29.5	1	36	44	296	347	42	56	42	39	341	341	68	63	95	76	9-9	17-10	15-12	9-16	12-18	16-18
Chicago	70	90	.438	37.0	1	42	38	394	399	89	79	28	52	286	382	66	64	119	129	7-12	12-15	10-17	15-11	11-20	15-15
Pittsburgh	64	98	.395	44.0	1	31	50	331	357	49	75	33	48	332	343	62	63	102	99	7-10	11-15	12-18	11-14	12-19	11-22
WEST																									
Houston	96	66	.593	—	149	52	29	327	289	49	56	44	37	327	280	76	60	101	77	14-6	13-13	14-15	16-11	16-12	23-9
Cincinnati	86	76	.531	10.0	2	43	38	383	377	86	73	43	38	349	340	58	63	110	131	5-12	13-14	14-15	15-11	19-12	20-12
San Francisco	83	79	.512	13.0	37	46	35	345	275	50	61	37	44	353	343	64	60	89	90	13-8	12-15	16-12	12-14	12-16	18-14
San Diego	74	88	.457	22.0	3	43	38	339	319	80	78	31	50	317	404	56	72	91	123	12-9	12-14	14-14	12-14	11-19	13-18
Los Angeles	73	89	.451	23.0	1	46	35	326	290	57	46	27	54	312	389	73	69	88	73	10-13	13-13	11-16	15-10	13-16	11-21
Atlanta	72	89	.447	23.5	2	41	40	331	360	77	71	31	49	284	359	61	46	106	137	7-12	18-10	14-14	7-19	15-13	11-21

Clinch Date—New York 9/17, Houston 9/25.

Team Batting

Team	G	AB	R	OR	H	2B	3B	HR	TB	RBI	TBB	IBB	SO	HBP	SH	SF	SB	CS	SB%	GDP	Avg	OBP	Slg
New York	162	5558	783	578	1462	261	31	148	2229	730	631	68	968	31	75	53	118	48	.71	122	.263	.347	.401
Philadelphia	161	5483	739	713	1386	266	39	154	2192	696	589	70	1154	40	66	51	153	59	.72	98	.253	.335	.400
Cincinnati	162	5536	732	717	1404	237	35	144	2143	670	586	55	920	18	65	41	177	53	.77	127	.254	.331	.387
San Francisco	162	5501	698	618	1394	269	29	114	2063	637	536	86	1087	37	101	34	148	93	.61	83	.253	.328	.375
Chicago	160	5499	680	781	1409	258	27	155	2186	638	508	56	966	15	54	51	132	62	.68	113	.256	.327	.398
Pittsburgh	162	5456	663	700	1366	273	33	111	2038	618	569	55	929	20	68	44	152	84	.64	132	.250	.328	.374
San Diego	162	5515	656	723	1442	239	25	136	2139	629	484	74	917	18	66	35	96	68	.59	130	.261	.327	.388
Houston	162	5441	654	569	1388	244	32	125	2071	613	536	78	916	24	53	41	163	75	.68	126	.255	.329	.381
Los Angeles	162	5471	638	679	1373	242	14	130	2023	599	478	58	966	32	81	39	155	67	.70	109	.251	.319	.370
Montreal	161	5508	637	688	1401	255	50	110	2086	602	537	72	1016	33	53	42	193	95	.67	113	.254	.329	.379
Atlanta	161	5384	615	719	1348	241	24	138	2051	575	538	62	904	24	79	42	93	76	.55	124	.250	.326	.381
St. Louis	161	5378	601	611	1270	216	48	58	1756	550	568	69	905	20	108	46	262	78	.77	83	.236	.317	.327
NL Total	1938	65730	8096	8096	16643	2991	387	1523	24977	7557	6560	803	11648	312	869	519	1842	858	.68	1360	.253	.322	.380
NL Avg Team	162	5478	675	675	1387	249	32	127	2081	630	547	67	971	26	72	43	154	72	.68	113	.253	.322	.380

Team Pitching

Team	G	CG	ShO	Rel	Sv	IP	H	R	ER	HR	SH	SF	HB	TBB	IBB	SO	WP	Bk	H/9	SO/9	BB/9	OAvg	OOBP	ERA
New York	162	27	11	252	46	1484.0	1304	578	513	103	62	43	31	509	29	1083	40	16	7.9	6.6	3.1	.236	.302	3.11
Houston	162	18	19	299	51	1456.1	1203	569	510	116	82	42	23	523	60	1160	50	11	7.4	7.2	3.2	.225	.295	3.15
San Francisco	162	18	10	346	35	1460.1	1264	618	541	121	79	44	29	592	78	992	58	15	7.8	6.1	3.6	.236	.313	3.33
St. Louis	161	17	4	287	46	1466.1	1364	611	549	135	53	54	22	485	73	761	38	13	8.4	4.7	3.0	.250	.311	3.37
Los Angeles	162	35	14	280	25	1454.1	1428	679	608	115	75	30	26	499	79	1051	51	10	8.8	6.5	3.1	.256	.319	3.76
Montreal	161	15	9	326	50	1466.1	1350	688	616	119	80	38	33	566	61	1051	49	20	8.3	6.5	3.5	.246	.318	3.78
Philadelphia	161	22	11	321	39	1451.2	1473	713	621	130	58	47	22	553	71	874	45	17	9.1	5.4	3.4	.265	.331	3.85
Pittsburgh	162	17	9	356	30	1450.2	1397	700	629	138	66	46	37	570	55	924	59	20	8.7	5.7	3.5	.255	.327	3.90
Cincinnati	162	14	8	313	45	1468.0	1465	717	638	136	86	60	17	524	81	924	39	5	9.0	5.7	3.2	.264	.326	3.91
Atlanta	161	17	5	309	39	1424.2	1443	719	629	117	70	34	26	576	63	932	44	11	9.1	5.9	3.6	.266	.338	3.97
San Diego	162	13	7	350	32	1443.1	1406	723	640	150	82	36	27	607	75	934	38	18	8.8	5.8	3.8	.258	.333	3.99
Chicago	160	14	6	346	42	1445.0	1546	781	721	143	76	45	19	557	78	962	55	20	9.6	6.0	3.5	.279	.344	4.49
NL Total	1938	224	113	3785	480	17471.0	16643	8096	7215	1523	869	519	312	6560	803	11648	566	176	8.6	6.0	3.4	.253	.329	3.72
NL Avg Team	162	19	9	315	40	1455.0	1387	675	601	127	72	43	26	547	67	971	47	15	8.6	6.0	3.4	.253	.329	3.72

Team Fielding

Team	G	PO	A	E	TC	DP	PB	Pct
St. Louis	161	4399	1804	123	6326	178	9	.981
Chicago	160	4335	1784	124	6243	147	17	.980
Montreal	161	4399	1787	133	6319	132	21	.979
Houston	162	4369	1565	130	6064	108	9	.979
New York	162	4452	1781	138	6371	145	8	.978
Atlanta	161	4274	2026	141	6441	181	11	.978
Philadelphia	161	4355	1761	137	6253	157	23	.978
Cincinnati	162	4404	1809	140	6353	160	13	.978
Pittsburgh	162	4352	1918	143	6413	134	9	.978
San Diego	162	4330	1629	137	6096	135	14	.978
San Francisco	162	4381	1794	143	6318	149	12	.977
Los Angeles	162	4363	1801	181	6345	118	11	.971
NL Total	1938	52413	21459	1670	75542	1744	157	.978

Team vs. Team Records

	Atl	ChN	Cin	Hou	LA	Mon	NYN	Phi	Pit	SD	SF	StL	Won
Atl	—	9	6	5	10	4	4	4	5	12	7	6	72
ChN	3	—	5	4	8	6	8	6	9	7	6	10	70
Cin	12	7	—	4	10	7	4	7	10	9	9	7	86
Hou	13	8	14	—	10	8	5	6	6	10	9	7	96
LA	8	6	8	8	—	5	3	5	8	6	8	8	73
Mon	7	10	5	4	7	—	8	8	11	4	5	9	78
NYN	8	12	8	7	9	10	—	8	11	10	7	12	108
Phi	8	8	5	6	7	10	10	—	11	6	9	6	86
Pit	7	11	2	6	4	7	1	7	—	8	4	7	64
SD	6	6	9	6	12	8	2	6	4	—	8	5	74
SF	11	6	9	9	10	7	5	3	8	10	—	5	83
StL	6	7	5	5	4	9	6	12	11	7	7	—	79
Lost	89	90	76	66	89	83	54	75	98	88	79	82	

1986 National League Batting Leaders

Games		At-Bats		Runs		Hits		Doubles		Triples	
D. Parker, Cin	162	T. Gwynn, SD	642	V. Hayes, Phi	107	T. Gwynn, SD	211	V. Hayes, Phi	46	M. Webster, Mon	13
M. Schmidt, Phi	160	D. Parker, Cin	637	T. Gwynn, SD	107	S. Sax, LA	210	S. Sax, LA	43	J. Samuel, Phi	12
D. Murphy, Atl	160	S. Sax, LA	633	M. Schmidt, Phi	97	T. Raines, Mon	194	S. Bream, Pit	37	T. Raines, Mon	10
T. Gwynn, SD	160	R. Sandberg, ChN	627	E. Davis, Cin	97	V. Hayes, Phi	186	S. Dunston, ChN	37	V. Coleman, StL	8
T. Pendleton, StL	159	D. Murphy, Atl	614	2 tied with	94	K. Bass, Hou	184	J. Samuel, Phi	36	6 tied with	7

Home Runs		Total Bases		Runs Batted In		Walks		Intentional Walks		Strikeouts	
M. Schmidt, Phi	37	D. Parker, Cin	304	M. Schmidt, Phi	119	K. Hernandez, NYN	94	M. Schmidt, Phi	25	J. Samuel, Phi	142
D. Parker, Cin	31	M. Schmidt, Phi	302	D. Parker, Cin	116	M. Schmidt, Phi	89	C. Davis, SF	23	D. Murphy, Atl	141
G. Davis, Hou	31	T. Gwynn, SD	300	G. Carter, NYN	105	C. Davis, SF	84	G. Templeton, SD	21	D. Strawberry, NYN	141
D. Murphy, Atl	29	D. Murphy, Atl	293	G. Davis, Hou	101	K. Oberkfell, Atl	83	J. Uribe, SF	19	D. Parker, Cin	126
3 tied with	27	V. Hayes, Phi	293	V. Hayes, Phi	98	B. Doran, Hou	81	3 tied with	16	S. Dunston, ChN	114

Hit By Pitch		Sac Hits		Sac Flies		Stolen Bases		Caught Stealing		GDP	
T. Wallach, Mon	10	R. Thompson, SF	18	G. Carter, NYN	15	V. Coleman, StL	107	B. Doran, Hou	19	G. Carter, NYN	21
G. Davis, Hou	9	D. Cox, StL	16	K. Moreland, ChN	11	E. Davis, Cin	80	S. Sax, LA	17	T. Pena, Pit	21
C. Brown, SF	9	W. Backman, NYN	14	B. Horner, Atl	10	T. Raines, Mon	70	O. Moreno, Atl	16	J. Ray, Pit	21
J. Samuel, Phi	8	J. Tudor, StL	13	4 tied with	9	M. Duncan, LA	48	W. McGee, StL	16	T. Gwynn, SD	20
M. Schmidt, Phi	7	D. Gooden, NYN	13			2 tied with	42	2 tied with	15	R. Knight, NYN	19

Runs Created		Runs Created/27 Outs		Batting Average		On-Base Percentage		Slugging Percentage		OBP+Slugging	
T. Raines, Mon	117	T. Raines, Mon	7.85	T. Raines, Mon	.334	T. Raines, Mon	.413	M. Schmidt, Phi	.547	M. Schmidt, Phi	.937
M. Schmidt, Phi	116	M. Schmidt, Phi	7.67	S. Sax, LA	.332	K. Hernandez, NYN	.413	D. Strawberry, NYN	.507	T. Raines, Mon	.889
V. Hayes, Phi	108	K. Hernandez, NYN	7.10	T. Gwynn, SD	.329	S. Sax, LA	.390	K. McReynolds, SD	.504	D. Strawberry, NYN	.865
S. Sax, LA	108	D. Strawberry, NYN	6.49	K. Bass, Hou	.311	M. Schmidt, Phi	.390	G. Davis, Hou	.493	K. McReynolds, SD	.862
T. Gwynn, SD	108	V. Hayes, Phi	6.45	K. Hernandez, NYN	.310	T. Gwynn, SD	.381	K. Bass, Hou	.486	V. Hayes, Phi	.859

1986 National League Pitching Leaders

Wins		Losses		Winning Percentage		Games		Games Started		Complete Games	
F. Valenzuela, LA	21	R. Mahler, Atl	18	B. Ojeda, NYN	.783	C. Lefferts, SD	83	R. Mahler, Atl	39	F. Valenzuela, LA	20
M. Krukow, SF	20	R. Reuschel, Pit	16	D. Gooden, NYN	.739	R. McDowell, NYN	75	T. Browning, Cin	39	R. Rhoden, Pit	12
M. Scott, Hou	18	Z. Smith, Atl	16	S. Fernandez, NYN	.727	J. Franco, Cin	74	B. Knepper, Hou	38	D. Gooden, NYN	12
B. Ojeda, NYN	18	R. Sutcliffe, ChN	14	R. Darling, NYN	.714	T. Worrell, StL	74	B. Gullickson, Cin	37	M. Krukow, SF	10
2 tied with	17	O. Hershiser, LA	14	J. Deshaies, Hou	.706	K. Tekulve, Phi	73	M. Scott, Hou	37	3 tied with	8

Shutouts		Saves		Games Finished		Batters Faced		Innings Pitched		Hits Allowed	
B. Knepper, Hou	5	T. Worrell, StL	36	T. Worrell, StL	60	F. Valenzuela, LA	1102	M. Scott, Hou	275.1	R. Mahler, Atl	283
M. Scott, Hou	5	J. Reardon, Mon	35	L. Smith, ChN	59	M. Scott, Hou	1065	F. Valenzuela, LA	269.1	B. Gullickson, Cin	245
B. Welch, LA	3	D. Smith, Hou	33	S. Bedrosian, Phi	56	R. Mahler, Atl	1056	B. Knepper, Hou	258.0	K. Gross, Phi	240
F. Valenzuela, LA	3	L. Smith, ChN	31	J. Franco, Cin	52	B. Knepper, Hou	1053	R. Rhoden, Pit	253.2	B. Knepper, Hou	232
10 tied with	2	2 tied with	29	R. McDowell, NYN	52	K. Gross, Phi	1040	D. Gooden, NYN	250.0	R. Reuschel, Pit	232

Home Runs Allowed		Walks		Walks/9 Innings		Strikeouts		Strikeouts/9 Innings		Strikeout/Walk Ratio	
K. Gross, Phi	28	F. Youmans, Mon	118	D. Eckersley, ChN	1.9	M. Scott, Hou	306	M. Scott, Hou	10.0	M. Scott, Hou	4.25
L. Hoyt, SD	27	Z. Smith, Atl	105	S. Sanderson, ChN	2.0	F. Valenzuela, LA	242	N. Ryan, Hou	9.8	S. Sanderson, ChN	3.35
T. Browning, Cin	26	D. Palmer, Atl	102	F. Youmans, Mon	2.0	F. Youmans, Mon	202	S. Fernandez, NYN	8.8	B. Welch, LA	3.33
R. Mahler, Atl	25	R. Sutcliffe, ChN	96	B. Welch, LA	2.1	S. Fernandez, NYN	200	F. Youmans, Mon	8.3	M. Krukow, SF	3.24
3 tied with	24	R. Mahler, Atl	95	B. Ojeda, NYN	2.2	D. Gooden, NYN	200	F. Valenzuela, LA	8.1	D. Eckersley, ChN	3.19

Earned Run Average		Component ERA		Hit Batsmen		Wild Pitches		Opponent Average		Opponent OBP	
M. Scott, Hou	2.22	M. Scott, Hou	1.67	R. Reuschel, Pit	8	N. Ryan, Hou	15	M. Scott, Hou	.186	M. Scott, Hou	.242
B. Ojeda, NYN	2.57	N. Ryan, Hou	2.46	K. Gross, Phi	8	R. Sutcliffe, ChN	13	N. Ryan, Hou	.188	M. Krukow, SF	.269
R. Darling, NYN	2.81	D. Gooden, NYN	2.48	L. McWilliams, Pit	7	F. Valenzuela, LA	13	F. Youmans, Mon	.188	B. Ojeda, NYN	.278
R. Rhoden, Pit	2.84	B. Ojeda, NYN	2.53	B. Welch, LA	7	B. Walk, Pit	12	D. Gooden, NYN	.215	D. Gooden, NYN	.278
D. Gooden, NYN	2.84	M. Krukow, SF	2.55	R. Aguilera, NYN	7	O. Hershiser, LA	12	S. Fernandez, NYN	.216	N. Ryan, Hou	.283

1986 National League Miscellaneous

Managers

Atlanta	Chuck Tanner	72-89
Chicago	Jim Frey	23-33
	John Vukovich	1-1
	Gene Michael	46-56
Cincinnati	Pete Rose	86-76
Houston	Hal Lanier	96-66
Los Angeles	Tom Lasorda	73-89
Montreal	Buck Rodgers	78-83
New York	Davey Johnson	108-54
Philadelphia	John Felske	86-75
Pittsburgh	Jim Leyland	64-98
St. Louis	Whitey Herzog	79-82
San Diego	Steve Boros	74-88
San Francisco	Roger Craig	83-79

Awards

Most Valuable Player	Mike Schmidt, 3b, Phi
Cy Young	Mike Scott, Hou
Rookie of the Year	Todd Worrell, p, StL
Manager of the Year	Hal Lanier, Hou

STATS All-Star Team

C	Gary Carter, NYN	.255	24	105
1B	Keith Hernandez, NYN	.310	13	83
2B	Steve Sax, LA	.332	6	56
3B	Mike Schmidt, Phi	.290	37	119
SS	Shawon Dunston, ChN	.250	17	68
OF	Eric Davis, Cin	.277	27	71
OF	Kevin McReynolds, SD	.288	26	96
OF	Tim Raines, Mon	.334	9	62
P	Dwight Gooden, NYN	17-6	2.84	200 K
P	Bobby Ojeda, NYN	18-5	2.57	148 K
P	Mike Scott, Hou	18-10	2.22	306 K
P	Fernando Valenzuela, LA	21-11	3.14	242 K
RP	Todd Worrell, StL	9-10	2.08	36 Sv

Postseason

LCS	New York 4 vs. Houston 2
World Series	New York (NL) 4 vs. Boston (AL) 3

Outstanding Performances

No-Hitters
Mike Scott, Hou   vs. SF on September 25

Four-Homer Games
Bob Horner, Atl   on July 6

Three-Homer Games
Ken Griffey Sr., Atl   on July 22
Eric Davis, Cin   on September 10

1987 American League Standings

EAST	W	L	Pct	GB	DIF	W	L	R	OR	HR	OHR	W	L	R	OR	HR	OHR	Run	HR	M/A	May	June	July	Aug	S/O
			Overall					Home Games						Road Games				Park Index				Record by Month			
Detroit	98	64	.605	—	33	54	27	442	338	125	101	44	37	454	397	100	79	92	126	9-12	15-11	17-9	17-9	19-11	21-12
Toronto	96	66	.593	2.0	55	52	29	425	319	101	83	44	37	420	336	114	75	98	97	12-8	16-11	17-11	15-12	17-12	19-12
Milwaukee	91	71	.562	7.0	38	48	33	440	420	72	79	43	38	422	397	91	90	105	83	18-3	6-18	13-15	15-13	18-11	21-11
New York	89	73	.549	9.0	68	51	30	401	346	98	88	38	43	387	412	98	91	93	98	14-7	17-11	17-11	15-11	11-17	15-16
Boston	78	84	.481	20.0	0	50	30	436	383	86	75	28	54	406	442	88	115	99	81	9-13	13-14	15-12	11-15	14-13	16-17
Baltimore	67	95	.414	31.0	2	31	51	351	456	110	125	36	44	378	424	101	101	98	113	9-12	17-11	5-23	16-10	13-15	7-24
Cleveland	61	101	.377	37.0	0	35	46	373	519	94	118	26	55	369	438	93	101	111	109	8-14	8-20	10-15	10-17	15-15	10-20
WEST																									
Minnesota	85	77	.525	—	138	56	25	411	348	106	92	29	52	375	458	90	118	91	95	12-9	14-14	17-11	13-14	13-15	16-14
Kansas City	83	79	.512	2.0	38	46	35	375	349	73	57	37	44	340	342	95	71	106	78	9-10	18-9	12-16	10-18	16-13	18-13
Oakland	81	81	.500	4.0	3	42	39	363	351	88	75	39	42	443	438	111	101	81	77	9-14	15-10	16-11	12-15	15-14	14-17
Seattle	78	84	.481	7.0	2	40	41	403	400	103	115	38	43	357	401	58	84	106	154	12-11	14-12	13-14	10-16	12-17	17-14
Chicago	77	85	.475	8.0	2	38	43	394	414	72	90	39	42	354	332	101	99	118	81	6-12	14-13	7-21	14-13	14-16	22-10
California	75	87	.463	10.0	13	38	43	377	405	88	116	37	44	393	398	84	96	99	113	12-11	9-17	17-11	15-11	13-16	9-21
Texas	75	87	.463	10.0	0	43	38	426	447	93	111	32	49	397	402	101	88	109	108	8-11	11-16	16-12	14-13	12-17	14-18

Clinch Date—Detroit 10/04, Minnesota 9/28.

Team Batting

Team	G	AB	R	OR	H	2B	3B	HR	TB	RBI	TBB	IBB	SO	HBP	SH	SF	SB	CS	SB%	GDP	Avg	OBP	Slg
Detroit	162	5649	896	735	1535	274	32	225	2548	840	653	44	913	46	39	56	106	50	.68	108	.272	.358	.451
Milwaukee	162	5625	862	817	1552	272	46	163	2405	832	598	40	1040	32	63	50	176	74	.70	104	.276	.354	.428
Toronto	162	5635	845	655	1514	277	38	215	2512	790	555	45	970	38	30	35	126	50	.72	136	.269	.342	.446
Boston	162	5586	842	825	1554	273	26	174	2401	802	606	41	825	57	45	58	77	45	.63	129	.278	.361	.430
Texas	162	5564	823	849	1478	264	35	194	2394	772	567	34	1081	24	42	51	120	71	.63	116	.266	.342	.430
Oakland	162	5511	806	789	1432	263	33	199	2358	761	593	39	1056	36	50	48	140	63	.69	113	.260	.341	.428
New York	162	5511	788	758	1445	239	16	196	2304	749	604	37	949	28	38	38	105	43	.71	150	.262	.342	.418
Minnesota	162	5441	786	806	1422	258	35	196	2338	733	523	45	898	38	47	39	113	65	.63	128	.261	.335	.430
California	162	5570	770	803	1406	257	26	172	2231	709	590	35	926	35	70	36	125	44	.74	115	.252	.332	.401
Seattle	162	5508	760	801	1499	282	48	161	2360	717	500	19	863	43	38	50	174	73	.70	132	.272	.343	.428
Chicago	162	5538	748	746	1427	283	36	173	2301	706	487	35	971	33	54	52	138	52	.73	117	.258	.327	.415
Cleveland	162	5606	742	957	1476	267	30	187	2364	691	489	30	977	31	44	42	140	54	.72	103	.263	.330	.422
Baltimore	162	5576	729	880	1437	219	20	211	2329	701	524	29	939	22	31	32	69	45	.61	139	.258	.327	.418
Kansas City	162	5499	715	691	1443	239	40	168	2266	677	523	32	1034	30	34	42	125	43	.74	127	.262	.334	.412
AL Total	2268	77819	11112	11112	20620	3667	461	2634	33111	10480	7812	505	13442	493	632	629	1734	772	.69	1717	.265	.333	.425
AL Avg Team	162	5559	794	794	1473	262	33	188	2365	749	558	36	960	35	45	45	124	55	.69	123	.265	.333	.425

Team Pitching

Team	G	CG	ShO	Rel	Sv	IP	H	R	ER	HR	SH	SF	HB	TBB	IBB	SO	WP	Bk	H/9	SO/9	BB/9	OAvg	OOBP	ERA
Toronto	162	18	8	336	43	1454.0	1323	655	605	158	56	32	22	567	65	1064	56	14	8.2	6.6	3.5	.244	.316	3.74
Kansas City	162	44	11	225	26	1424.0	1424	691	610	128	33	44	36	548	27	923	54	6	9.0	5.8	3.5	.261	.330	3.86
Detroit	162	33	10	247	31	1456.0	1430	735	651	180	35	48	33	563	61	976	72	6	8.8	6.0	3.5	.256	.325	4.02
Chicago	162	29	12	270	37	1447.2	1436	746	691	189	50	29	35	537	28	792	35	3	8.9	4.9	3.3	.259	.327	4.30
Oakland	162	18	6	328	40	1445.2	1442	789	694	176	43	46	36	531	21	1042	52	10	9.0	6.5	3.3	.258	.324	4.32
New York	162	19	10	278	47	1446.1	1475	758	700	179	51	48	32	542	31	900	61	9	9.2	5.6	3.4	.266	.332	4.36
California	162	20	7	244	36	1457.1	1481	803	710	212	50	34	32	504	30	941	54	7	9.1	5.8	3.1	.264	.327	4.38
Seattle	162	39	10	251	33	1430.2	1503	801	713	199	50	59	28	497	19	919	47	9	9.5	5.8	3.1	.272	.332	4.49
Milwaukee	162	28	6	282	45	1464.0	1548	817	752	169	38	50	26	529	33	1039	45	8	9.5	6.4	3.3	.271	.333	4.62
Minnesota	162	16	4	289	39	1427.1	1465	806	734	210	27	49	50	564	40	990	42	9	9.2	6.2	3.6	.266	.337	4.63
Texas	162	20	3	329	27	1444.1	1388	849	743	199	42	45	55	760	34	1103	61	26	8.6	6.9	4.7	.253	.347	4.63
Boston	162	47	13	236	16	1436.0	1584	825	761	190	60	46	31	517	38	1034	37	9	9.9	6.5	3.2	.282	.344	4.77
Baltimore	162	17	6	294	30	1439.2	1555	880	802	226	41	39	27	547	50	870	52	8	9.7	5.4	3.4	.277	.341	5.01
Cleveland	162	24	8	308	25	1422.2	1566	957	835	219	56	60	50	606	28	849	74	12	9.9	5.4	3.8	.279	.351	5.28
AL Total	2268	372	114	3917	475	20195.2	20620	11112	10001	2634	632	629	493	7812	505	13442	762	137	9.2	6.0	3.5	.265	.341	4.46
AL Avg Team	162	27	8	280	34	1442.2	1473	794	714	188	45	45	36	558	36	960	54	10	9.2	6.0	3.5	.265	.341	4.46

Team Fielding

Team	G	PO	A	E	TC	DP	PB	Pct
Minnesota	162	4282	1609	98	5989	147	21	.984
New York	162	4339	1685	102	6126	155	22	.983
Baltimore	162	4319	1747	111	6177	174	5	.982
Toronto	162	4362	1700	111	6173	148	13	.982
Boston	162	4308	1684	110	6102	158	30	.982
Chicago	162	4343	1782	116	6241	174	11	.981
California	162	4372	1640	117	6129	162	11	.981
Detroit	162	4368	1703	122	6193	147	13	.980
Seattle	162	4292	1756	122	6170	150	4	.980
Kansas City	162	4272	1853	131	6256	151	17	.979
Oakland	162	4337	1649	142	6128	122	18	.977
Milwaukee	162	4392	1606	145	6143	155	13	.976
Texas	162	4333	1685	151	6169	148	73	.976
Cleveland	162	4268	1626	153	6047	128	16	.975
AL Total	2268	60587	23725	1731	86043	2119	267	.980

Team vs. Team Records

	Bal	Bos	Cal	ChA	Cle	Det	KC	Mil	Min	NYA	Oak	Sea	Tex	Tor	Won
Bal	—	1	9	8	7	4	9	2	5	3	7	4	7	1	67
Bos	12	—	4	3	7	2	6	6	7	7	4	7	5	6	78
Cal	3	8	—	8	7	3	5	7	8	3	6	7	5	5	75
ChA	4	9	5	—	7	3	6	6	6	5	9	6	7	4	77
Cle	6	6	5	5	—	4	6	4	3	6	4	5	2	5	61
Det	9	11	9	9	9	—	5	6	8	5	8	9	7	8	98
KC	3	6	8	7	6	7	—	4	8	5	5	9	7	8	83
Mil	11	7	5	6	9	7	8	—	3	7	6	4	9	9	91
Min	7	5	5	7	9	4	4	9	—	6	10	9	6	3	85
NYA	10	6	9	7	7	8	7	6	6	—	5	7	5	6	89
Oak	5	8	7	4	8	7	6	8	3	7	—	5	6	7	81
Sea	3	5	5	6	7	3	4	8	4	5	8	—	9	2	78
Tex	5	5	8	6	10	4	6	3	7	7	7	4	—	3	75
Tor	12	7	7	8	8	6	4	4	9	7	5	10	9	—	96
Lost	95	84	87	85	101	64	79	71	77	73	81	84	87	66	

1987 American League Batting Leaders

Games		At-Bats		Runs		Hits		Doubles		Triples	
C. Ripken Jr., Bal	162	R. Sierra, Tex	643	P. Molitor, Mil	114	K. Puckett, Min	207	P. Molitor, Mil	41	W. Wilson, KC	15
K. Seitzer, KC	161	K. Seitzer, KC	641	G. Bell, Tor	111	K. Seitzer, KC	207	W. Boggs, Bos	40	P. Bradley, Sea	10
E. Murray, Bal	160	D. White, Cal	639	B. Downing, Cal	110	A. Trammell, Det	205	4 tied with	38	L. Polonia, Oak	10
H. Reynolds, Sea	160	R. Yount, Mil	635	L. Whitaker, Det	110	W. Boggs, Bos	200			R. Yount, Mil	9
4 tied with	159	J. Canseco, Oak	630	2 tied with	109	R. Yount, Mil	198			4 tied with	8

Home Runs		Total Bases		Runs Batted In		Walks		Intentional Walks		Strikeouts	
M. McGwire, Oak	49	G. Bell, Tor	369	G. Bell, Tor	134	B. Downing, Cal	106	W. Boggs, Bos	19	R. Deer, Mil	186
G. Bell, Tor	47	M. McGwire, Oak	344	D. Evans, Bos	123	D. Evans, Bos	106	G. Brett, KC	14	P. Incaviglia, Tex	168
5 tied with	34	K. Puckett, Min	333	M. McGwire, Oak	118	W. Boggs, Bos	105	D. Mattingly, NYA	13	C. Snyder, Cle	166
		A. Trammell, Det	329	W. Joyner, Cal	117	D. Evans, Det	100	K. Hrbek, Min	12	B. Jackson, KC	158
		W. Boggs, Bos	324	D. Mattingly, NYA	115	B. Butler, Cle	91	W. Joyner, Cal	12	2 tied with	157

Hit By Pitch		Sac Hits		Sac Flies		Stolen Bases		Caught Stealing		GDP	
D. Baylor, 2tm	28	M. Barrett, Bos	22	R. Sierra, Tex	12	H. Reynolds, Sea	60	H. Reynolds, Sea	20	G. Gaetti, Min	25
B. Downing, Cal	17	M. McLemore, Cal	15	C. Ripken Jr., Bal	11	W. Wilson, KC	59	J. Browne, Tex	17	J. Franco, Cle	23
B. Madlock, Det	10	B. Boone, Cal	14	P. O'Brien, Tex	10	G. Redus, ChA	52	B. Butler, Cle	16	J. Rice, Bos	22
4 tied with	9	J. Castillo, Mil	14	W. Joyner, Cal	10	P. Molitor, Mil	45	J. Moses, Sea	15	3 tied with	20
		D. White, Cal	14	3 tied with	9	R. Henderson, NYA	41	2 tied with	13		

Runs Created		Runs Created/27 Outs		Batting Average		On-Base Percentage		Slugging Percentage		OBP+Slugging	
W. Boggs, Bos	140	W. Boggs, Bos	10.01	W. Boggs, Bos	.363	W. Boggs, Bos	.461	M. McGwire, Oak	.618	W. Boggs, Bos	1.049
A. Trammell, Det	129	P. Molitor, Mil	9.88	P. Molitor, Mil	.353	P. Molitor, Mil	.438	G. Bell, Tor	.605	P. Molitor, Mil	1.003
M. McGwire, Oak	125	A. Trammell, Det	8.39	A. Trammell, Det	.343	D. Evans, Bos	.417	W. Boggs, Bos	.588	M. McGwire, Oak	.987
D. Evans, Bos	124	D. Evans, Bos	8.35	K. Puckett, Min	.332	W. Randolph, NYA	.411	D. Evans, Bos	.569	D. Evans, Bos	.986
G. Bell, Tor	122	M. McGwire, Oak	8.17	D. Mattingly, NYA	.327	A. Trammell, Det	.402	P. Molitor, Mil	.566	G. Bell, Tor	.957

1987 American League Pitching Leaders

Wins		Losses		Winning Percentage		Games		Games Started		Complete Games	
D. Stewart, Oak	20	M. Moore, Sea	19	J. Cerutti, Tor	.733	M. Eichhorn, Tor	89	C. Hough, Tex	40	R. Clemens, Bos	18
R. Clemens, Bos	20	T. Candiotti, Cle	18	L. Guetterman, Sea	.733	M. Williams, Tex	85	B. Blyleven, Min	37	B. Hurst, Bos	15
M. Langston, Sea	19	M. Gubicza, KC	18	J. Musselman, Tor	.706	D. Mohorcic, Tex	74	D. Stewart, Oak	37	B. Saberhagen, KC	15
4 tied with	18	D. Jackson, KC	18	R. Clemens, Bos	.690	T. Henke, Tor	72	J. Clancy, Tor	37	M. Langston, Sea	14
		M. Morgan, Sea	17	T. John, NYA	.684	J. Musselman, Tor	68	4 tied with	36	T. Higuera, Mil	14

Shutouts		Saves		Games Finished		Batters Faced		Innings Pitched		Hits Allowed	
R. Clemens, Bos	7	T. Henke, Tor	34	T. Henke, Tor	62	C. Hough, Tex	1231	C. Hough, Tex	285.1	M. Moore, Sea	268
B. Saberhagen, KC	4	J. Reardon, Min	31	J. Reardon, Min	58	R. Clemens, Bos	1157	R. Clemens, Bos	281.2	W. Terrell, Det	254
6 tied with	3	D. Righetti, NYA	31	D. Righetti, NYA	54	M. Langston, Sea	1152	M. Langston, Sea	272.0	M. Witt, Cal	252
		D. Plesac, Mil	23	D. Mohorcic, Tex	54	B. Blyleven, Min	1122	B. Blyleven, Min	267.0	B. Blyleven, Min	249
		D. Buice, Cal	17	C. Schiraldi, Bos	52	D. Stewart, Oak	1103	J. Morris, Det	266.0	R. Clemens, Bos	248

Home Runs Allowed		Walks		Walks/9 Innings		Strikeouts		Strikeouts/9 Innings		Strikeout/Walk Ratio	
B. Blyleven, Min	46	B. Witt, Tex	140	B. Long, ChA	1.5	M. Langston, Sea	262	M. Langston, Sea	8.7	R. Clemens, Bos	3.08
J. Morris, Det	39	C. Hough, Tex	124	B. Saberhagen, KC	1.9	R. Clemens, Bos	256	T. Higuera, Mil	8.3	B. Saberhagen, KC	3.08
D. Sutton, Cal	38	M. Gubicza, KC	120	D. Sutton, Cal	1.9	T. Higuera, Mil	240	R. Clemens, Bos	8.2	C. Bosio, Mil	3.00
F. Bannister, ChA	38	M. Langston, Sea	114	F. Bannister, ChA	1.9	C. Hough, Tex	223	C. Bosio, Mil	7.9	F. Viola, Min	2.98
C. Young, Oak	38	D. Jackson, KC	109	C. Young, Oak	2.0	J. Morris, Det	208	J. Nieves, Mil	7.5	C. Young, Oak	2.82

Earned Run Average		Component ERA		Hit Batsmen		Wild Pitches		Opponent Average		Opponent OBP	
J. Key, Tor	2.76	J. Key, Tor	2.48	C. Hough, Tex	19	J. Morris, Det	24	J. Key, Tor	.221	J. Key, Tor	.272
F. Viola, Min	2.90	R. Clemens, Bos	2.94	J. Niekro, 2tm	10	M. Gubicza, KC	14	C. Hough, Tex	.223	F. Bannister, ChA	.285
R. Clemens, Bos	2.97	B. Saberhagen, KC	3.24	D. Petry, Det	10	C. Bosio, Mil	14	J. Morris, Det	.228	J. Morris, Det	.293
B. Saberhagen, KC	3.36	T. Higuera, Mil	3.27	J. DeLeon, ChA	10	3 tied with	13	D. Stewart, Oak	.229	C. Young, Oak	.293
J. Morris, Det	3.38	F. Viola, Min	3.27	3 tied with	9			J. DeLeon, ChA	.230	F. Viola, Min	.293

1987 American League Miscellaneous

Managers

Baltimore	Cal Ripken	67-95
Boston	John McNamara	78-84
California	Gene Mauch	75-87
Chicago	Jim Fregosi	77-85
Cleveland	Pat Corrales	31-56
	Doc Edwards	30-45
Detroit	Sparky Anderson	98-64
Kansas City	Billy Gardner	62-64
	John Wathan	21-15
Milwaukee	Tom Trebelhorn	91-71
Minnesota	Tom Kelly	85-77
New York	Lou Piniella	89-73
Oakland	Tony La Russa	81-81
Seattle	Dick Williams	78-84
Texas	Bobby Valentine	75-87
Toronto	Jimy Williams	96-66

Awards

Most Valuable Player	George Bell, of, Tor
Cy Young	Roger Clemens, Bos
Rookie of the Year	Mark McGwire, 1b, Oak
Manager of the Year	Sparky Anderson, Det

STATS All-Star Team

C	Matt Nokes, Det	.289	32	87	
1B	Mark McGwire, Oak	.289	49	118	
2B	Willie Randolph, NYA	.305	7	67	
3B	Wade Boggs, Bos	.363	24	89	
SS	Alan Trammell, Det	.343	28	105	
OF	George Bell, Tor	.308	47	134	
OF	Kirby Puckett, Min	.332	28	99	
OF	Danny Tartabull, KC	.309	34	101	
DH	Paul Molitor, Mil	.353	16	75	
P	Roger Clemens, Bos	20-9	2.97	256 K	
P	Jimmy Key, Tor	17-8	2.76	161 K	
P	Jack Morris, Det	18-11	3.38	208 K	
P	Frank Viola, Min	17-10	2.90	197 K	
RP	Tom Henke, Tor	0-6	2.49	34 Sv	

Postseason

LCS	Minnesota 4 vs. Detroit 1
World Series	Minnesota (AL) 4 vs. St. Louis (NL) 3

Outstanding Performances

No-Hitters

Juan Nieves, Mil @ Bal on April 15

Three-Homer Games

Cory Snyder, Cle	on May 21
Joe Carter, Cle	on May 28
Mark McGwire, Oak	on June 27
Bill Madlock, Det	on June 28
Brook Jacoby, Cle	on July 3
Dale Sveum, Mil	on July 17
Mickey Brantley, Sea	on September 14
Ernie Whitt, Tor	on September 14
Wally Joyner, Cal	on October 3

1987 National League Standings

EAST	W	L	Pct	GB	DIF	W	L	R	OR	HR	OHR	W	L	R	OR	HR	OHR	Run	HR	M/A	May	June	July	Aug	S/O
			Overall					Home	Games					Road	Games			Park	Index			Record	by Month		
St. Louis	95	67	.586	—	168	49	32	387	339	42	60	46	35	411	354	52	69	95	84	12-8	17-9	17-11	16-11	17-12	16-16
New York	92	70	.568	3.0	16	49	32	407	335	93	63	43	38	416	363	99	72	95	91	11-9	13-14	16-12	16-11	18-11	18-13
Montreal	91	71	.562	4.0	1	48	33	401	371	62	74	43	38	340	349	58	71	112	105	8-12	17-11	15-12	18-8	15-14	18-14
Philadelphia	80	82	.494	15.0	1	43	38	385	373	80	78	37	44	317	376	89	89	109	89	7-13	15-11	13-15	18-9	15-15	12-19
Pittsburgh	80	82	.494	15.0	1	47	34	404	363	71	84	33	48	319	381	60	80	110	111	8-11	13-14	13-17	11-15	15-14	20-11
Chicago	76	85	.472	18.5	8	40	40	381	389	114	90	36	45	339	412	95	69	104	126	10-10	18-10	12-17	12-13	14-14	10-21
WEST																									
San Francisco	90	72	.556	—	89	46	35	373	312	118	72	44	37	410	357	87	74	89	118	16-7	11-15	11-16	14-13	18-11	20-10
Cincinnati	84	78	.519	6.0	111	42	39	396	401	94	97	42	39	387	351	98	73	108	112	15-7	13-14	14-13	13-14	9-20	20-10
Houston	76	86	.469	14.0	9	47	34	334	268	51	46	29	52	314	410	71	95	83	58	12-9	12-15	16-11	10-17	15-14	11-20
Los Angeles	73	89	.451	17.0	0	40	41	280	306	52	56	33	48	355	369	73	74	81	73	12-11	11-15	13-14	10-16	10-19	17-14
Atlanta	69	92	.429	20.5	3	42	39	421	450	82	88	27	53	326	379	70	75	122	116	9-12	16-12	11-16	9-17	11-17	13-18
San Diego	65	97	.401	25.0	0	37	44	338	357	60	97	28	53	330	406	53	78	94	120	6-17	6-22	15-12	11-14	16-12	11-20

Clinch Date—St. Louis 10/01, San Francisco 9/28.

Team Batting

Team	G	AB	R	OR	H	2B	3B	HR	TB	RBI	TBB	IBB	SO	HBP	SH	SF	SB	CS	SB%	GDP	Avg	OBP	Slg
New York	162	5601	823	698	1499	287	34	192	2430	771	592	74	1012	31	70	39	159	49	.76	94	.268	.345	.434
St. Louis	162	5500	798	693	1449	252	49	94	2081	746	644	61	933	18	84	51	248	72	.78	126	.263	.348	.378
San Francisco	162	5608	783	669	1458	274	32	205	2411	731	511	73	1094	39	55	35	126	97	.57	99	.260	.330	.430
Cincinnati	162	5560	783	752	1478	262	29	192	2374	747	514	55	928	31	57	34	169	46	.79	129	.266	.335	.427
Atlanta	161	5428	747	829	1401	284	24	152	2189	696	641	82	834	38	86	34	135	68	.67	133	.258	.344	.403
Montreal	162	5527	741	720	1467	310	39	120	2215	695	501	77	918	35	57	42	166	74	.69	100	.265	.335	.401
Pittsburgh	162	5536	723	744	1464	282	45	131	2229	684	535	67	914	29	71	58	140	58	.71	124	.264	.338	.403
Chicago	161	5583	720	801	1475	244	33	209	2412	683	504	45	1064	21	59	30	109	48	.69	109	.264	.331	.432
Philadelphia	162	5475	702	749	1390	248	51	169	2247	662	587	51	1109	25	63	40	111	49	.69	133	.254	.333	.410
San Diego	162	5456	668	763	1419	209	48	113	2063	621	577	75	992	27	81	36	198	91	.69	122	.260	.338	.378
Houston	162	5485	648	678	1386	238	28	122	2046	603	526	52	936	24	58	50	162	46	.78	115	.253	.326	.373
Los Angeles	162	5517	635	675	1389	236	23	125	2046	594	445	70	923	31	82	39	128	59	.68	126	.252	.316	.371
NL Total	1942	66276	8771	8771	17275	3126	435	1824	26743	8233	6577	782	11657	349	823	481	1851	757	.71	1407	.261	.328	.404
NL Avg Team	162	5523	731	731	1440	261	36	152	2229	686	548	65	971	29	69	40	154	63	.71	117	.261	.328	.404

Team Pitching

Team	G	CG	ShO	Rel	Sv	IP	H	R	ER	HR	SH	SF	HB	TBB	IBB	SO	WP	Bk	H/9	SO/9	BB/9	OAvg	OOBP	ERA
San Francisco	162	19	10	348	38	1471.0	1407	669	601	146	74	36	27	547	86	1038	59	25	8.6	6.4	3.3	.255	.323	3.68
Los Angeles	162	29	8	281	32	1455.0	1415	675	601	130	65	27	28	565	62	1097	54	18	8.8	6.8	3.5	.255	.325	3.72
Houston	162	13	13	316	33	1441.1	1363	678	615	141	76	33	26	525	61	1137	39	14	8.5	7.1	3.3	.250	.317	3.84
New York	162	16	7	308	51	1454.0	1407	698	621	135	68	47	34	510	51	1032	42	13	8.7	6.4	3.2	.254	.319	3.84
St. Louis	162	10	7	362	48	1466.0	1484	693	637	129	71	33	27	533	79	873	46	22	9.1	5.4	3.3	.266	.331	3.91
Montreal	162	16	8	335	50	1450.1	1428	720	632	145	69	43	26	446	45	1012	47	14	8.9	6.3	2.8	.257	.313	3.92
Philadelphia	162	13	7	389	48	1448.1	1453	749	673	167	68	51	35	587	86	877	35	23	9.0	5.4	3.6	.263	.335	4.18
Pittsburgh	162	25	13	313	39	1445.0	1377	744	674	164	67	40	22	562	60	914	61	18	8.6	5.7	3.5	.253	.324	4.20
Cincinnati	162	7	6	392	44	1452.1	1486	752	685	170	72	49	22	485	68	919	33	13	9.2	5.7	3.0	.267	.326	4.24
San Diego	162	14	10	335	33	1433.1	1402	763	680	175	59	31	36	602	62	897	55	21	8.8	5.6	3.8	.256	.332	4.27
Chicago	161	11	5	327	48	1434.2	1524	801	726	159	71	24	27	628	67	1024	58	29	9.6	6.4	3.9	.275	.349	4.55
Atlanta	161	16	4	324	32	1427.2	1529	829	735	163	63	49	39	587	55	837	42	9	9.6	5.3	3.7	.276	.347	4.63
NL Total	1942	189	98	4030	496	17379.0	17275	8771	7880	1824	823	481	349	6577	782	11657	571	219	8.9	6.0	3.4	.261	.335	4.08
NL Avg Team	162	16	8	336	41	1448.0	1440	731	657	152	69	40	29	548	65	971	48	18	8.9	6.0	3.4	.261	.335	4.08

Team Fielding

Team	G	PO	A	E	TC	DP	PB	Pct
St. Louis	162	4398	1870	116	6384	172	16	.982
Atlanta	161	4283	1921	116	6320	170	11	.982
Houston	162	4324	1617	116	6057	113	11	.981
Pittsburgh	162	4335	1834	123	6292	147	9	.980
Philadelphia	162	4345	1711	121	6177	137	17	.980
San Francisco	162	4413	1861	129	6403	183	15	.980
Chicago	161	4304	1787	130	6221	154	13	.979
Cincinnati	162	4357	1643	130	6130	137	13	.979
New York	162	4362	1797	137	6296	137	9	.978
San Diego	162	4300	1799	147	6246	135	22	.976
Montreal	162	4351	1679	147	6177	122	8	.976
Los Angeles	162	4365	1790	155	6310	144	8	.975
NL Total	1942	52137	21309	1567	75013	1751	152	.979

Team vs. Team Records

	Atl	ChN	Cin	Hou	LA	Mon	NYN	Phi	Pit	SD	SF	StL	Won
Atl	—	6	8	6	8	6	3	7	7	6	8	3	69
ChN	5	—	6	8	6	10	9	8	4	9	5	6	76
Cin	10	6	—	13	10	6	7	5	4	12	7	4	84
Hou	10	4	5	—	12	7	6	6	6	5	10	5	76
LA	12	6	8	6	—	3	6	2	6	11	10	3	73
Mon	9	8	6	5	9	—	8	10	11	9	5	11	91
NYN	5	9	6	6	6	10	—	13	12	8	9	9	92
Phi	5	10	7	6	10	8	5	—	11	8	2	8	80
Pit	5	14	8	6	6	7	6	7	—	8	6	7	80
SD	12	3	6	13	7	3	4	4	4	—	5	4	65
SF	10	7	11	8	8	7	3	10	6	13	—	7	90
StL	9	12	8	7	9	7	9	10	11	8	5	—	95
Lost	92	85	78	86	89	71	70	82	82	97	72	67	

Seasons: Standings, Leaders

1987 National League Batting Leaders

Games		At-Bats		Runs		Hits		Doubles		Triples	
B. Doran, Hou	162	J. Samuel, Phi	655	T. Raines, Mon	123	T. Gwynn, SD	218	T. Wallach, Mon	42	J. Samuel, Phi	15
J. Samuel, Phi	160	B. Doran, Hou	625	V. Coleman, StL	121	P. Guerrero, LA	184	O. Smith, StL	40	T. Gwynn, SD	13
D. Murphy, Atl	159	V. Coleman, StL	623	E. Davis, Cin	120	O. Smith, StL	182	A. Galarraga, Mon	40	W. McGee, StL	11
T. Pendleton, StL	159	A. Dawson, ChN	621	T. Gwynn, SD	119	V. Coleman, StL	180	4 tied with	37	A. Van Slyke, Pit	11
2 tied with	158	W. McGee, StL	620	D. Murphy, Atl	115	2 tied with	178			V. Coleman, StL	10

Home Runs		Total Bases		Runs Batted In		Walks		Intentional Walks		Strikeouts	
A. Dawson, ChN	49	A. Dawson, ChN	353	A. Dawson, ChN	137	J. Clark, StL	136	D. Murphy, Atl	29	J. Samuel, Phi	162
D. Murphy, Atl	44	J. Samuel, Phi	329	T. Wallach, Mon	123	V. Hayes, Phi	121	T. Raines, Mon	26	J. Clark, StL	139
D. Strawberry, NYN	39	D. Murphy, Atl	328	M. Schmidt, Phi	113	D. Murphy, Atl	115	T. Gwynn, SD	26	D. Murphy, Atl	136
E. Davis, Cin	37	D. Strawberry, NYN	310	J. Clark, StL	106	D. Strawberry, NYN	97	P. Guerrero, LA	18	E. Davis, Cin	134
H. Johnson, NYN	36	W. Clark, SF	307	2 tied with	105	T. Raines, Mon	90	H. Johnson, NYN	18	A. Galarraga, Mon	127

Hit By Pitch		Sac Hits		Sac Flies		Stolen Bases		Caught Stealing		GDP	
A. Galarraga, Mon	10	Z. Smith, Atl	14	T. Herr, StL	12	V. Coleman, StL	109	V. Coleman, StL	22	W. McGee, StL	24
B. Hatcher, Hou	9	O. Smith, StL	12	K. Moreland, ChN	9	T. Gwynn, SD	56	W. Clark, SF	17	L. Parrish, Phi	23
D. Parker, Cin	8	S. Rawley, Phi	12	J. Shelby, LA	9	B. Hatcher, Hou	53	G. Perry, Atl	16	T. Pena, StL	19
R. Thompson, SF	8	B. Forsch, StL	11	T. Pendleton, StL	9	T. Raines, Mon	50	J. Samuel, Phi	15	S. Bream, Pit	19
5 tied with	7	R. Sutcliffe, ChN	11	3 tied with	8	E. Davis, Cin	50	4 tied with	12	5 tied with	18

Runs Created		Runs Created/27 Outs		Batting Average		On-Base Percentage		Slugging Percentage		OBP+Slugging	
D. Murphy, Atl	132	J. Clark, StL	10.84	T. Gwynn, SD	.370	J. Clark, StL	.459	J. Clark, StL	.597	J. Clark, StL	1.055
T. Gwynn, SD	128	T. Raines, Mon	9.01	P. Guerrero, LA	.338	T. Gwynn, SD	.447	E. Davis, Cin	.593	D. Murphy, Atl	.997
J. Clark, StL	124	E. Davis, Cin	8.88	T. Raines, Mon	.330	T. Raines, Mon	.429	D. Strawberry, NYN	.583	E. Davis, Cin	.991
T. Raines, Mon	124	T. Gwynn, SD	8.60	J. Kruk, SD	.313	D. Murphy, Atl	.417	W. Clark, SF	.580	D. Strawberry, NYN	.981
D. Strawberry, NYN	121	D. Murphy, Atl	8.47	D. James, Atl	.312	P. Guerrero, LA	.416	D. Murphy, Atl	.580	T. Gwynn, SD	.958

1987 National League Pitching Leaders

Wins		Losses		Winning Percentage		Games		Games Started		Complete Games	
R. Sutcliffe, ChN	18	B. Knepper, Hou	17	D. Martinez, Mon	.733	K. Tekulve, Phi	90	M. Scott, Hou	36	R. Reuschel, 2tm	12
S. Rawley, Phi	17	N. Ryan, Hou	16	M. Dunne, Pit	.684	R. Murphy, Cin	87	S. Rawley, Phi	36	F. Valenzuela, LA	12
M. Scott, Hou	16	E. Show, SD	16	D. Gooden, NYN	.682	F. Williams, Cin	85	Z. Smith, Atl	36	O. Hershiser, LA	10
O. Hershiser, LA	16	K. Gross, Phi	16	J. Deshaies, Hou	.647	J. Robinson, 2tm	81	4 tied with	35	Z. Smith, Atl	9
3 tied with	15	O. Hershiser, LA	16	R. Sutcliffe, ChN	.643	L. McCullers, SD	78			M. Scott, Hou	8

Shutouts		Saves		Games Finished		Batters Faced		Innings Pitched		Hits Allowed	
R. Reuschel, 2tm	4	S. Bedrosian, Phi	40	J. Franco, Cin	60	F. Valenzuela, LA	1116	O. Hershiser, LA	264.2	F. Valenzuela, LA	254
B. Welch, LA	4	L. Smith, ChN	36	S. Bedrosian, Phi	56	O. Hershiser, LA	1093	B. Welch, LA	251.2	S. Rawley, Phi	250
8 tied with	3	T. Worrell, StL	33	L. Smith, ChN	55	Z. Smith, Atl	1035	F. Valenzuela, LA	251.0	O. Hershiser, LA	247
		J. Franco, Cin	32	D. Robinson, 2tm	54	B. Welch, LA	1027	M. Scott, Hou	247.2	Z. Smith, Atl	245
		R. McDowell, NYN	25	T. Worrell, StL	54	R. Sutcliffe, ChN	1012	Z. Smith, Atl	242.0	B. Ruffin, Phi	236

Home Runs Allowed		Walks		Walks/9 Innings		Strikeouts		Strikeouts/9 Innings		Strikeout/Walk Ratio	
E. Whitson, SD	36	F. Valenzuela, LA	124	R. Reuschel, 2tm	1.7	N. Ryan, Hou	270	N. Ryan, Hou	11.5	N. Ryan, Hou	3.10
D. Carman, Phi	34	R. Sutcliffe, ChN	106	N. Heaton, Mon	1.7	M. Scott, Hou	233	M. Scott, Hou	8.5	M. Scott, Hou	2.95
B. Gullickson, Cin	33	J. Moyer, ChN	97	B. Gullickson, Cin	2.1	B. Welch, LA	196	B. Sebra, Mon	7.9	N. Heaton, Mon	2.84
T. Power, Cin	28	R. Darling, NYN	96	B. Forsch, StL	2.3	F. Valenzuela, LA	190	D. Gooden, NYN	7.4	D. Gooden, NYN	2.79
J. Moyer, ChN	28	Z. Smith, Atl	91	D. Drabek, Pit	2.3	O. Hershiser, LA	190	R. Darling, NYN	7.2	D. Drabek, Pit	2.61

Earned Run Average		Component ERA		Hit Batsmen		Wild Pitches		Opponent Average		Opponent OBP	
N. Ryan, Hou	2.76	N. Ryan, Hou	2.50	K. Gross, Phi	10	F. Valenzuela, LA	14	N. Ryan, Hou	.200	M. Scott, Hou	.281
M. Dunne, Pit	3.03	R. Reuschel, 2tm	2.64	J. Magrane, StL	10	K. Downs, SF	12	M. Scott, Hou	.217	R. Reuschel, 2tm	.282
O. Hershiser, LA	3.06	M. Scott, Hou	2.65	E. Show, SD	9	O. Hershiser, LA	11	B. Welch, LA	.221	N. Ryan, Hou	.284
R. Reuschel, 2tm	3.09	B. Welch, LA	2.78	O. Hershiser, LA	9	J. Moyer, ChN	11	R. Darling, NYN	.233	B. Welch, LA	.289
D. Gooden, NYN	3.21	D. Gooden, NYN	2.98	2 tied with	8	3 tied with	10	M. Dunne, Pit	.240	D. Drabek, Pit	.294

1987 National League Miscellaneous

Managers

Atlanta	Chuck Tanner	69-92
Chicago	Gene Michael	68-68
	Frank Lucchesi	8-17
Cincinnati	Pete Rose	84-78
Houston	Hal Lanier	76-86
Los Angeles	Tom Lasorda	73-89
Montreal	Buck Rodgers	91-71
New York	Davey Johnson	92-70
Philadelphia	John Felske	29-32
	Lee Elia	51-50
Pittsburgh	Jim Leyland	80-82
St. Louis	Whitey Herzog	95-67
San Diego	Larry Bowa	65-97
San Francisco	Roger Craig	90-72

Awards

Most Valuable Player	Andre Dawson, of, ChN
Cy Young	Steve Bedrosian, Phi
Rookie of the Year	Benito Santiago, c, SD
Manager of the Year	Buck Rodgers, Mon

STATS All-Star Team

C	Benito Santiago, SD	.300	18	79
1B	Jack Clark, StL	.286	35	106
2B	Juan Samuel, Phi	.272	28	100
3B	Mike Schmidt, Phi	.293	35	113
SS	Ozzie Smith, StL	.303	0	75
OF	Eric Davis, Cin	.293	37	100
OF	Dale Murphy, Atl	.295	44	105
OF	Tim Raines, Mon	.330	18	68
P	Orel Hershiser, LA	16-16	3.06	190 K
P	Nolan Ryan, Hou	8-16	2.76	270 K
P	Mike Scott, Hou	16-13	3.23	233 K
P	Rick Sutcliffe, ChN	18-10	3.68	174 K
RP	Steve Bedrosian, Phi	5-3	2.83	40 Sv

Postseason

LCS	St. Louis 4 vs. San Francisco 3
World Series	St. Louis (NL) 3 vs. Minnesota (AL) 4

Outstanding Performances

Three-Homer Games

Eric Davis, Cin	on May 3
Tim Wallach, Mon	on May 4
Mike Schmidt, Phi	on June 14
Andre Dawson, ChN	on August 1
Glenn Davis, Hou	on September 10
Darnell Coles, Pit	on September 30

Cycles

Andre Dawson, ChN	on April 29
C. Maldonado, SF	on May 4
Tim Raines, Mon	on August 16
Albert Hall, StL	on September 23

EAST	Overall					Home Games						Road Games						Park Index		Record by Month					
	W	L	Pct	GB	DIF	W	L	R	OR	HR	OHR	W	L	R	OR	HR	OHR	Run	HR	M/A	May	June	July	Aug	S/O
Boston	89	73	.549	—	30	53	28	456	360	68	73	36	45	357	329	56	70	119	112	14-6	11-16	14-12	21-9	13-16	16-14
Detroit	88	74	.543	1.0	76	50	31	328	303	83	76	38	43	375	355	60	74	86	119	13-8	15-12	18-9	15-12	14-16	13-17
Milwaukee	87	75	.537	2.0	4	47	34	354	310	60	65	40	41	328	306	53	60	105	111	9-11	17-13	12-15	14-15	17-13	18-8
Toronto	87	75	.537	2.0	3	45	36	371	344	78	73	42	39	392	336	80	70	98	101	9-13	13-16	17-11	12-14	14-14	22-7
New York	85	76	.528	3.5	65	46	34	378	345	77	75	39	42	394	403	71	82	92	101	16-7	17-9	12-15	15-11	9-20	16-14
Cleveland	78	84	.481	11.0	18	44	37	353	359	62	52	34	47	313	372	72	68	104	81	16-6	15-13	10-17	11-17	12-16	14-15
Baltimore	54	107	.335	34.5	0	34	46	286	354	70	77	20	61	264	435	67	76	93	104	1-22	10-17	11-16	10-16	14-15	8-21
WEST																									
Oakland	104	58	.642	—	177	54	27	362	294	67	47	50	31	438	326	89	69	86	72	16-7	19-8	13-14	16-12	20-9	20-8
Minnesota	91	71	.562	13.0	0	47	34	402	354	76	79	44	37	357	318	75	67	112	109	8-13	17-10	17-10	15-12	17-13	17-13
Kansas City	84	77	.522	19.5	6	44	36	359	330	55	37	40	41	345	318	66	65	105	71	12-10	11-17	17-10	12-15	18-10	14-15
California	75	87	.463	29.0	1	35	46	333	368	58	71	40	41	381	403	66	64	89	99	10-13	9-19	15-11	19-8	15-14	7-22
Chicago	71	90	.441	32.5	7	40	41	311	373	55	64	31	49	320	384	77	74	96	78	11-10	10-17	13-15	12-16	12-17	13-15
Texas	70	91	.435	33.5	2	38	43	336	368	58	67	32	48	301	367	54	62	104	106	8-13	17-11	12-15	9-18	14-14	10-20
Seattle	68	93	.422	35.5	1	37	44	362	405	97	81	31	49	302	339	51	63	118	154	10-14	12-15	8-19	10-16	14-16	14-13

Clinch Date—Boston 9/30, Oakland 9/18.

Team Batting

Team	G	AB	R	OR	H	2B	3B	HR	TB	RBI	TBB	IBB	SO	HBP	SH	SF	SB	CS	SB%	GDP	Avg	OBP	Slg
Boston	162	5545	813	689	1569	310	39	124	2329	760	623	53	728	45	66	55	65	36	.64	139	.283	.366	.420
Oakland	162	5602	800	620	1474	251	22	156	2237	752	580	29	926	65	54	55	129	54	.70	142	.263	.345	.399
New York	161	5592	772	748	1469	272	12	148	2209	713	588	56	935	30	36	51	146	39	.79	154	.263	.340	.395
Toronto	162	5557	763	680	1491	271	47	158	2330	706	521	35	935	31	34	50	107	36	.75	145	.268	.340	.419
Minnesota	162	5510	759	672	1508	294	31	151	2317	710	528	52	832	55	37	50	107	63	.63	130	.274	.349	.421
California	162	5582	714	771	1458	258	31	124	2150	660	469	48	819	49	63	52	86	52	.62	120	.261	.330	.385
Kansas City	161	5469	704	648	1419	275	40	121	2137	671	486	44	944	33	46	51	137	37	.72	105	.259	.329	.391
Detroit	162	5433	703	658	1358	213	28	143	2056	650	588	38	841	29	66	37	87	42	.67	136	.250	.331	.378
Milwaukee	162	5488	682	616	1409	258	26	113	2058	632	439	55	911	37	59	41	159	55	.74	123	.257	.321	.375
Cleveland	162	5505	666	731	1435	235	28	134	2128	629	416	43	866	37	36	51	97	50	.66	108	.261	.323	.387
Seattle	161	5436	664	744	1397	271	27	148	2166	617	461	24	787	38	40	42	95	61	.61	135	.257	.324	.398
Texas	161	5479	637	735	1378	227	39	112	2019	589	542	43	1022	35	48	53	130	57	.70	111	.252	.329	.368
Chicago	161	5449	631	757	1327	224	35	132	2017	573	446	50	908	34	67	43	98	46	.68	118	.244	.310	.370
Baltimore	161	5358	550	789	1275	199	20	137	1925	517	504	31	869	32	40	45	69	44	.61	140	.238	.313	.359
AL Total	2262	77005	9858	9858	19967	3558	425	1901	30078	9179	7191	601	12323	550	692	676	1512	689	.69	1782	.259	.324	.391
AL Avg Team	162	5500	704	704	1426	254	30	136	2148	656	514	43	880	39	49	48	108	49	.69	127	.259	.324	.391

Team Pitching

Team	G	CG	ShO	Rel	Sv	IP	H	R	ER	HR	SH	SF	HB	TBB	IBB	SO	WP	Bk	H/9	SO/9	BB/9	OAvg	OOBP	ERA
Oakland	162	22	9	290	64	1489.1	1376	620	569	116	51	54	29	553	27	983	62	76	8.3	5.9	3.3	.247	.316	3.44
Milwaukee	162	30	8	252	51	1449.1	1355	616	555	125	47	56	19	437	47	832	36	39	8.4	5.2	2.7	.248	.303	3.45
Kansas City	161	29	12	253	32	1428.1	1415	648	580	102	37	39	33	465	39	886	55	27	8.9	5.6	2.9	.258	.318	3.65
Detroit	162	34	8	220	36	1445.2	1361	658	596	150	56	39	32	497	68	890	57	27	8.5	5.5	3.1	.248	.312	3.71
Toronto	162	16	17	294	47	1449.0	1404	680	611	143	61	37	59	528	49	904	48	29	8.7	5.6	3.3	.256	.326	3.80
Minnesota	162	18	9	265	52	1431.2	1457	672	625	146	49	42	42	453	28	897	43	38	9.2	5.6	2.8	.266	.325	3.93
Boston	162	26	14	250	37	1426.1	1415	689	629	143	44	41	37	493	34	1085	45	39	8.9	6.8	3.1	.259	.322	3.97
Texas	161	41	11	251	31	1438.2	1310	735	647	129	42	53	56	654	33	912	72	57	8.2	5.7	4.1	.244	.329	4.05
Chicago	161	11	9	293	43	1439.0	1467	757	659	138	57	61	35	533	34	754	61	30	9.2	4.7	3.3	.266	.331	4.12
Seattle	161	28	11	292	28	1428.0	1385	744	659	144	38	51	36	558	57	981	50	55	8.7	6.2	3.5	.256	.327	4.15
Cleveland	162	35	10	230	46	1434.0	1501	731	663	120	70	40	40	442	28	812	36	38	9.4	5.1	2.8	.270	.326	4.16
New York	161	16	5	304	43	1456.0	1512	748	689	157	49	51	49	487	42	861	36	41	9.3	5.3	3.0	.267	.328	4.26
California	162	26	9	262	33	1455.2	1503	771	698	135	52	67	42	568	67	817	68	37	9.3	5.1	3.5	.270	.338	4.32
Baltimore	161	20	7	287	26	1416.0	1506	789	714	153	39	45	43	523	48	709	42	25	9.6	4.5	3.3	.274	.340	4.54
AL Total	2262	352	139	3743	569	20187.0	19967	9858	8894	1901	692	676	550	7191	601	12323	711	558	8.9	5.5	3.2	.259	.332	3.97
AL Avg Team	162	25	10	267	41	1441.0	1426	704	635	136	49	48	39	514	43	880	51	40	8.9	5.5	3.2	.259	.332	3.97

Team Fielding

Team	G	PO	A	E	TC	DP	PB	Pct
Minnesota	162	4295	1500	84	5879	155	13	.986
Boston	162	4279	1542	93	5914	123	14	.984
Oakland	162	4468	1629	105	6202	151	13	.983
Toronto	162	4347	1737	110	6194	170	12	.982
Detroit	162	4337	1614	109	6060	129	8	.982
Milwaukee	162	4348	1714	120	6182	146	10	.981
Baltimore	161	4248	1726	119	6093	172	18	.980
Kansas City	161	4285	1714	124	6123	147	12	.980
Cleveland	162	4302	1686	124	6112	131	10	.980
Seattle	161	4284	1612	123	6019	168	16	.980
Texas	161	4316	1756	131	6203	145	36	.979
California	162	4367	1825	135	6327	175	13	.979
New York	161	4368	1660	134	6162	161	5	.978
Chicago	161	4317	1843	154	6314	177	10	.976
AL Total	2262	60561	23558	1665	85784	2150	190	.981

Team vs. Team Records

	Bal	Bos	Cal	ChA	Cle	Det	KC	Mil	Min	NYA	Oak	Sea	Tex	Tor	Won
Bal	—	4	5	4	4	5	0	4	3	3	4	7	6	5	54
Bos	9	—	8	7	8	6	6	10	7	9	3	6	8	2	89
Cal	7	4	—	9	8	5	5	3	4	6	4	6	8	6	75
ChA	7	5	4	—	3	3	7	6	4	3	5	9	8	7	71
Cle	9	5	4	9	—	4	6	9	6	4	5	6	6	5	78
Det	8	7	7	9	9	—	8	5	1	8	4	9	8	5	88
KC	12	6	8	6	6	4	—	3	7	6	8	7	7	4	84
Mil	9	3	9	6	4	8	9	—	7	6	3	8	8	7	87
Min	9	5	9	9	7	11	6	5	—	3	5	8	7	7	91
NYA	10	4	6	9	7	5	6	7	9	—	6	5	5	6	85
Oak	8	9	8	8	8	5	8	9	8	6	—	9	8	9	104
Sea	5	6	7	4	7	3	5	4	5	7	4	—	6	5	68
Tex	6	4	5	5	6	4	6	4	6	5	5	7	—	6	70
Tor	8	11	6	5	7	8	8	6	5	5	7	3	7	—	87
Lost	107	73	87	90	84	74	77	75	71	76	58	93	91	75	

1988 American League Batting Leaders

Games		At-Bats		Runs		Hits		Doubles		Triples	
R. Yount, Mil	162	K. Puckett, Min	657	W. Boggs, Bos	128	K. Puckett, Min	234	W. Boggs, Bos	45	W. Wilson, KC	11
E. Murray, Bal	161	T. Fernandez, Tor	648	J. Canseco, Oak	120	W. Boggs, Bos	214	G. Brett, KC	42	R. Yount, Mil	11
C. Ripken Jr., Bal	161	R. Yount, Mil	621	R. Henderson, NYA	118	M. Greenwell, Bos	192	J. Ray, Cal	42	H. Reynolds, Sea	11
8 tied with	158	J. Carter, Cle	621	P. Molitor, Mil	115	R. Yount, Mil	190	K. Puckett, Min	42	M. Greenwell, Bos	8
		R. Sierra, Tex	615	K. Puckett, Min	109	P. Molitor, Mil	190	T. Fernandez, Tor	41	4 tied with	7

Home Runs		Total Bases		Runs Batted In		Walks		Intentional Walks		Strikeouts	
J. Canseco, Oak	42	K. Puckett, Min	358	J. Canseco, Oak	124	W. Boggs, Bos	125	W. Boggs, Bos	18	R. Deer, Mil	153
F. McGriff, Tor	34	J. Canseco, Oak	347	K. Puckett, Min	121	J. Clark, NYA	113	M. Greenwell, Bos	18	P. Incaviglia, Tex	153
M. McGwire, Oak	32	M. Greenwell, Bos	313	M. Greenwell, Bos	119	C. Ripken Jr., Bal	102	G. Brock, Mil	16	F. McGriff, Tor	149
E. Murray, Bal	28	G. Brett, KC	300	D. Evans, Bos	111	A. Davis, Sea	95	G. Brett, KC	15	B. Jackson, KC	146
G. Gaetti, Min	28	J. Carter, Cle	297	D. Winfield, NYA	107	M. Greenwell, Bos	87	5 tied with	14	J. Clark, NYA	141

Hit By Pitch		Sac Hits		Sac Flies		Stolen Bases		Caught Stealing		GDP	
G. Larkin, Min	15	M. Barrett, Bos	20	C. Ripken Jr., Bal	10	R. Henderson, NYA	93	H. Reynolds, Sea	29	W. Boggs, Bos	23
B. Downing, Cal	14	J. Gantner, Mil	18	C. Davis, Cal	10	G. Pettis, Det	44	J. Canseco, Oak	16	R. Yount, Mil	21
D. Baylor, Oak	12	F. Manrique, ChA	16	K. Puckett, Min	9	P. Molitor, Mil	41	R. Henderson, NYA	13	H. Baines, ChA	21
S. Fletcher, Tex	12	S. Fletcher, Tex	15	7 tied with	8	J. Canseco, Oak	40	O. Guillen, ChA	13	G. Bell, Tor	21
J. Canseco, Oak	10	S. Lyons, ChA	15			2 tied with	35	J. Franco, Cle	11	2 tied with	20

Runs Created		Runs Created/27 Outs		Batting Average		On-Base Percentage		Slugging Percentage		OBP+Slugging	
J. Canseco, Oak	137	W. Boggs, Bos	8.15	W. Boggs, Bos	.366	W. Boggs, Bos	.476	J. Canseco, Oak	.569	W. Boggs, Bos	.965
M. Greenwell, Bos	126	J. Canseco, Oak	8.00	K. Puckett, Min	.356	M. Greenwell, Bos	.416	F. McGriff, Tor	.552	J. Canseco, Oak	.959
W. Boggs, Bos	122	M. Greenwell, Bos	8.00	M. Greenwell, Bos	.325	A. Davis, Sea	.412	G. Gaetti, Min	.551	M. Greenwell, Bos	.946
K. Puckett, Min	120	D. Winfield, NYA	7.81	D. Winfield, NYA	.322	D. Winfield, NYA	.398	K. Puckett, Min	.545	F. McGriff, Tor	.928
2 tied with	117	G. Brett, KC	7.26	P. Molitor, Mil	.312	R. Henderson, NYA	.394	M. Greenwell, Bos	.531	D. Winfield, NYA	.927

1988 American League Pitching Leaders

Wins		Losses		Winning Percentage		Games		Games Started		Complete Games	
F. Viola, Min	24	B. Blyleven, Min	17	F. Viola, Min	.774	C. Crim, Mil	70	D. Stewart, Oak	37	D. Stewart, Oak	14
D. Stewart, Oak	21	C. Hough, Tex	16	B. Hurst, Bos	.750	B. Thigpen, ChA	68	B. Welch, Oak	36	R. Clemens, Bos	14
M. Gubicza, KC	20	M. Witt, Cal	16	M. Gubicza, KC	.714	M. Williams, Tex	67	7 tied with	35	B. Witt, Tex	13
3 tied with	18	W. Terrell, Det	16	J. Key, Tor	.706	M. Henneman, Det	65			M. Witt, Cal	12
		B. Saberhagen, KC	16	S. Davis, Oak	.696	2 tied with	64			G. Swindell, Cle	12

Shutouts		Saves		Games Finished		Batters Faced		Innings Pitched		Hits Allowed	
R. Clemens, Bos	8	D. Eckersley, Oak	45	B. Thigpen, ChA	59	D. Stewart, Oak	1156	D. Stewart, Oak	275.2	B. Saberhagen, KC	271
D. Stieb, Tor	4	J. Reardon, Min	42	J. Reardon, Min	58	M. Gubicza, KC	1111	M. Gubicza, KC	269.2	M. Witt, Cal	263
M. Gubicza, KC	4	D. Jones, Cle	37	L. Smith, Bos	57	B. Saberhagen, KC	1089	R. Clemens, Bos	264.0	D. Alexander, Det	260
G. Swindell, Cle	4	B. Thigpen, ChA	34	D. Eckersley, Oak	53	M. Witt, Cal	1080	M. Langston, Sea	261.1	C. Leibrandt, KC	244
3 tied with	3	D. Plesac, Mil	30	2 tied with	51	M. Langston, Sea	1078	B. Saberhagen, KC	260.2	2 tied with	240

Home Runs Allowed		Walks		Walks/9 Innings		Strikeouts		Strikeouts/9 Innings		Strikeout/Walk Ratio	
W. Fraser, Cal	33	C. Hough, Tex	126	A. Anderson, Min	1.6	R. Clemens, Bos	291	R. Clemens, Bos	9.9	R. Clemens, Bos	4.69
M. Langston, Sea	32	D. Stewart, Oak	110	G. Swindell, Cle	1.7	M. Langston, Sea	235	M. Langston, Sea	8.1	G. Swindell, Cle	4.00
D. Alexander, Det	30	M. Langston, Sea	110	D. Alexander, Det	1.8	F. Viola, Min	193	B. Witt, Tex	7.6	F. Viola, Min	3.57
R. Dotson, NYA	27	B. Witt, Tex	101	C. Bosio, Mil	1.9	D. Stewart, Oak	192	T. Higuera, Mil	7.6	T. Higuera, Mil	3.25
2 tied with	26	S. Davis, Oak	91	F. Viola, Min	1.9	T. Higuera, Mil	192	M. Moore, Sea	7.2	B. Saberhagen, KC	2.90

Earned Run Average		Component ERA		Hit Batsmen		Wild Pitches		Opponent Average		Opponent OBP	
A. Anderson, Min	2.45	T. Higuera, Mil	2.10	B. Blyleven, Min	16	S. Davis, Oak	16	J. Robinson, Det	.197	T. Higuera, Mil	.263
T. Higuera, Mil	2.45	R. Clemens, Bos	2.36	M. Boddicker, 2tm	14	B. Witt, Tex	16	T. Higuera, Mil	.207	R. Clemens, Bos	.270
F. Viola, Min	2.64	J. Robinson, Det	2.68	D. Stieb, Tor	13	D. Stewart, Oak	14	D. Stieb, Tor	.210	J. Robinson, Det	.282
M. Gubicza, KC	2.70	M. Gubicza, KC	2.77	C. Hough, Tex	12	K. McCaskill, Cal	13	B. Witt, Tex	.216	F. Viola, Min	.286
R. Clemens, Bos	2.93	D. Stieb, Tor	2.81	2 tied with	10	M. Perez, ChA	13	R. Clemens, Bos	.220	G. Swindell, Cle	.286

1988 American League Miscellaneous

Managers

Baltimore	Cal Ripken	0-6
	Frank Robinson	54-101
Boston	John McNamara	43-42
	Joe Morgan	46-31
California	Cookie Rojas	75-79
	Moose Stubing	0-8
Chicago	Jim Fregosi	71-90
Cleveland	Doc Edwards	78-84
Detroit	Sparky Anderson	88-74
Kansas City	John Wathan	84-77
Milwaukee	Tom Trebelhorn	87-75
Minnesota	Tom Kelly	91-71
New York	Billy Martin	40-28
	Lou Piniella	45-48
Oakland	Tony La Russa	104-58
Seattle	Dick Williams	23-33
	Jimmy Snyder	45-60
Texas	Bobby Valentine	70-91
Toronto	Jimy Williams	87-75

Awards

Most Valuable Player	Jose Canseco, of, Oak
Cy Young	Frank Viola, Min
Rookie of the Year	Walt Weiss, ss, Oak
Manager of the Year	Tony La Russa, Oak

STATS All-Star Team

C	Ernie Whitt, Tor	.251	16	70
1B	George Brett, KC	.306	24	103
2B	Julio Franco, Cle	.303	10	54
3B	Wade Boggs, Bos	.366	5	58
SS	Alan Trammell, Det	.311	15	69
OF	Jose Canseco, Oak	.307	42	124
OF	Mike Greenwell, Bos	.325	22	119
OF	Kirby Puckett, Min	.356	24	121
DH	Jack Clark, NYA	.242	27	93
P	Roger Clemens, Bos	18-12	2.93	291 K
P	Mark Gubicza, KC	20-8	2.70	183 K
P	Teddy Higuera, Mil	16-9	2.45	192 K
P	Frank Viola, Min	24-7	2.64	193 K
RP	Dennis Eckersley, Oak	4-2	2.35	45 Sv

Postseason

LCS	Oakland 4 vs. Boston 0
World Series	Oakland (AL) 1 vs. LA (NL) 4

Outstanding Performances

Three-Homer Games

George Bell, Tor	on April 4
Jose Canseco, Oak	on July 3

Cycles

Robin Yount, Mil	on June 12
Mike Greenwell, Bos	on September 14

1988 National League Standings

EAST	Overall					Home Games						Road Games						Park Index		Record by Month					
	W	L	Pct	GB	DIF	W	L	R	OR	HR	OHR	W	L	R	OR	HR	OHR	Run	HR	M/A	May	June	July	Aug	S/O
New York	100	60	.625	—	158	56	24	313	218	67	34	44	36	390	314	85	44	75	78	15-6	19-9	14-12	14-12	15-14	22-6
Pittsburgh	85	75	.531	15.0	21	43	38	326	298	56	50	42	37	325	318	54	58	95	92	16-6	14-14	13-14	15-11	13-17	14-13
Montreal	81	81	.500	20.0	0	43	38	333	304	47	62	38	43	295	288	60	60	109	91	9-11	14-14	14-15	18-8	12-17	14-16
Chicago	77	85	.475	24.0	9	39	42	346	373	58	71	38	43	314	321	55	44	113	130	10-12	15-12	16-11	9-18	16-12	11-20
St. Louis	76	86	.469	25.0	0	41	40	314	318	29	39	35	46	264	315	42	52	109	72	8-14	18-10	11-16	8-19	17-12	14-15
Philadelphia	65	96	.404	35.5	1	38	42	327	361	62	64	27	54	270	373	44	64	108	130	7-12	12-16	15-13	11-18	9-19	11-18
WEST																									
Los Angeles	94	67	.584	—	163	45	36	316	297	49	38	49	31	312	247	50	46	108	90	13-7	14-13	17-11	16-12	17-12	17-12
Cincinnati	87	74	.540	7.0	4	45	35	333	312	75	71	42	39	308	284	47	50	110	152	11-11	12-16	12-15	16-11	17-11	19-10
San Diego	83	78	.516	11.0	0	47	34	303	267	56	56	36	44	291	316	38	56	93	118	9-12	9-20	16-13	14-12	17-10	18-11
San Francisco	83	79	.512	11.5	2	45	36	318	284	58	42	38	43	352	342	55	57	87	89	11-12	14-14	14-11	17-11	15-14	13-16
Houston	82	80	.506	12.5	19	44	37	293	282	33	50	38	43	324	349	63	73	85	61	14-7	13-14	13-16	16-11	15-14	11-18
Atlanta	54	106	.338	39.5	0	28	51	295	391	48	64	26	55	260	350	48	44	115	125	3-16	13-15	10-18	9-20	10-19	9-18

Clinch Date—New York 9/22, Los Angeles 9/26.

Team Batting

Team	G	AB	R	OR	H	2B	3B	HR	TB	RBI	TBB	IBB	SO	HBP	SH	SF	SB	CS	SB%	GDP	Avg	OBP	Slg
New York	160	5408	703	532	1387	251	24	152	2142	659	544	79	842	32	65	56	140	51	.73	94	.256	.334	.396
San Francisco	162	5450	670	626	1353	227	44	113	2007	629	550	71	1023	33	94	51	121	78	.61	96	.248	.327	.368
Chicago	163	5675	660	694	1481	262	46	113	2174	612	403	58	910	21	57	46	120	46	.72	109	.261	.317	.383
Pittsburgh	160	5379	651	616	1327	240	45	110	1987	619	553	65	947	32	66	60	119	60	.66	97	.247	.327	.369
Cincinnati	161	5426	641	596	1334	246	25	122	1996	588	479	60	922	37	69	51	207	56	.79	99	.246	.317	.368
Montreal	163	5573	628	592	1400	260	48	107	2077	575	454	71	1053	32	66	44	189	89	.68	120	.251	.316	.373
Los Angeles	162	5431	628	544	1346	217	25	99	1910	587	437	65	947	32	95	50	131	46	.74	118	.248	.313	.352
Houston	162	5494	617	631	1338	239	31	96	1927	575	474	67	840	38	77	44	198	71	.74	103	.244	.313	.351
Philadelphia	162	5403	597	734	1294	246	31	106	1920	567	489	51	981	47	67	48	112	49	.70	106	.239	.314	.355
San Diego	161	5366	594	583	1325	205	35	94	1882	566	494	59	892	21	106	45	123	50	.71	117	.247	.318	.351
St. Louis	162	5518	578	633	1373	207	33	71	1859	536	484	61	827	22	105	48	234	64	.79	110	.249	.317	.337
Atlanta	160	5440	555	741	1319	228	28	96	1891	527	432	59	848	21	74	46	95	69	.58	136	.242	.306	.348
NL Total	1938	65563	7522	7522	16277	2828	415	1279	23772	7040	5793	766	11032	368	938	589	1789	729	.71	1305	.248	.310	.363
NL Avg Team	162	5464	627	627	1356	236	35	107	1981	587	483	64	919	31	78	49	149	61	.71	109	.248	.310	.363

Team Pitching

Team	G	CG	ShO	Rel	Sv	IP	H	R	ER	HR	SH	SF	HB	TBB	IBB	SO	WP	Bk	H/9	SO/9	BB/9	OAvg	OOBP	ERA
New York	160	31	22	241	46	1439.0	1253	532	465	78	56	44	35	404	33	1100	41	40	7.8	6.9	2.5	.235	.291	2.91
Los Angeles	162	32	24	295	49	1463.1	1291	544	482	84	73	41	22	473	61	1029	43	30	7.9	6.3	2.9	.237	.299	2.96
Montreal	163	18	12	307	43	1482.2	1310	592	508	122	66	45	36	476	61	923	39	41	8.0	5.6	2.9	.238	.301	3.08
San Diego	161	30	9	238	39	1449.0	1332	583	528	112	78	48	21	439	52	885	41	16	8.3	5.5	2.7	.247	.304	3.28
Cincinnati	161	24	13	343	43	1455.0	1271	596	541	121	73	48	27	504	62	934	33	37	7.9	5.8	3.1	.237	.303	3.35
San Francisco	162	25	13	290	43	1462.1	1323	626	550	99	82	53	30	422	68	875	44	22	8.1	5.4	2.6	.242	.298	3.39
Houston	162	21	15	284	40	1474.2	1339	631	558	123	87	60	37	478	73	1049	31	34	8.2	6.4	2.9	.243	.304	3.41
Pittsburgh	160	12	11	313	46	1440.2	1349	616	555	108	85	55	32	469	47	790	66	40	8.4	4.9	2.9	.250	.311	3.47
St. Louis	162	17	14	333	42	1470.2	1387	633	567	91	86	48	18	486	90	881	60	33	8.5	5.4	3.0	.252	.312	3.47
Chicago	163	30	10	290	29	1464.1	1494	694	625	115	67	46	31	490	75	897	56	26	9.2	5.5	3.0	.265	.325	3.84
Atlanta	160	14	4	318	25	1446.0	1481	741	657	108	106	45	43	524	65	810	45	28	9.2	5.0	3.3	.268	.334	4.09
Philadelphia	162	16	6	336	36	1433.0	1447	734	659	118	79	56	36	628	79	859	52	19	9.1	5.4	3.9	.265	.341	4.14
NL Total	1938	270	153	3588	480	17480.2	16277	7522	6695	1279	938	589	368	5793	766	11032	551	366	8.4	5.7	3.0	.248	.318	3.45
NL Avg Team	162	23	13	299	40	1456.2	1356	627	558	107	78	49	31	483	64	919	46	31	8.4	5.7	3.0	.248	.318	3.45

Team Fielding

Team	G	PO	A	E	TC	DP	PB	Pct
St. Louis	162	4412	1902	121	6435	131	9	.981
New York	160	4317	1630	115	6062	127	15	.981
San Diego	161	4347	1767	120	6234	147	11	.981
Chicago	163	4393	1823	125	6341	128	15	.980
Cincinnati	161	4365	1802	125	6292	131	13	.980
Pittsburgh	160	4322	1804	125	6251	128	8	.980
San Francisco	162	4387	1796	129	6312	145	19	.980
Houston	162	4424	1718	138	6280	124	8	.978
Montreal	163	4448	1816	142	6406	145	14	.978
Los Angeles	162	4390	1746	142	6278	126	7	.977
Philadelphia	162	4299	1653	145	6097	139	18	.976
Atlanta	160	4338	1789	151	6278	138	12	.976
NL Total	1938	52442	21246	1578	75266	1609	149	.979

Team vs. Team Records

	Atl	ChN	Cin	Hou	LA	Mon	NYN	Phi	Pit	SD	SF	StL	Won
Atl	—	5	5	5	4	4	4	6	5	8	5	3	54
ChN	7	—	6	7	4	9	9	8	7	8	5	7	77
Cin	13	6	—	9	7	5	4	9	7	10	11	6	87
Hou	13	5	9	—	9	6	5	8	8	6	7	6	82
LA	14	8	11	9	—	8	1	11	6	7	12	7	94
Mon	8	9	7	6	4	—	6	9	8	4	7	13	81
NYN	8	9	7	7	10	12	—	10	12	7	4	14	100
Phi	6	10	3	4	1	9	8	—	7	4	7	6	65
Pit	5	11	5	4	6	10	6	11	—	8	8	11	85
SD	10	4	8	12	11	8	5	7	4	—	8	6	83
SF	13	7	7	11	6	5	8	5	4	10	—	7	83
StL	9	11	6	6	5	5	4	12	7	6	5	—	76
Lost	106	85	74	80	67	81	60	96	75	78	79	86	

1988 National League Batting Leaders

Games		At-Bats		Runs		Hits		Doubles		Triples	
W. Clark, SF	162	S. Sax, LA	632	B. Butler, SF	109	A. Galarraga, Mon	184	A. Galarraga, Mon	42	A. Van Slyke, Pit	15
S. Sax, LA	160	J. Samuel, Phi	629	K. Gibson, LA	106	A. Dawson, ChN	179	R. Palmeiro, ChN	41	V. Coleman, StL	10
T. Wallach, Mon	159	R. Sandberg, ChN	618	W. Clark, SF	102	R. Palmeiro, ChN	178	C. Sabo, Cin	40	B. Butler, SF	9
B. Bonilla, Pit	159	V. Coleman, StL	616	D. Strawberry, NYN	101	S. Sax, LA	175	S. Bream, Pit	37	J. Samuel, Phi	9
5 tied with	157	J. Lind, Pit	611	A. Van Slyke, Pit	101	B. Larkin, Cin	174	2 tied with	35	G. Young, Hou	9

Home Runs		Total Bases		Runs Batted In		Walks		Intentional Walks		Strikeouts	
D. Strawberry, NYN	39	A. Galarraga, Mon	329	W. Clark, SF	109	W. Clark, SF	100	W. Clark, SF	27	A. Galarraga, Mon	153
G. Davis, Hou	30	A. Dawson, ChN	298	D. Strawberry, NYN	101	B. Butler, SF	97	H. Johnson, NYN	25	J. Samuel, Phi	151
A. Galarraga, Mon	29	A. Van Slyke, Pit	297	A. Van Slyke, Pit	100	K. Daniels, Cin	87	D. Strawberry, NYN	21	W. Clark, SF	129
W. Clark, SF	29	D. Strawberry, NYN	296	B. Bonilla, Pit	100	H. Johnson, NYN	86	G. Davis, Hou	20	J. Shelby, LA	128
K. McReynolds, NYN	27	W. Clark, SF	292	2 tied with	99	2 tied with	85	B. Bonilla, Pit	19	D. Strawberry, NYN	127

Hit By Pitch		Sac Hits		Sac Flies		Stolen Bases		Caught Stealing		GDP	
P. Bradley, Phi	16	R. Reuschel, SF	19	A. Van Slyke, Pit	13	V. Coleman, StL	81	V. Coleman, StL	27	D. Murphy, Atl	24
J. Samuel, Phi	12	O. Hershiser, LA	19	G. Perry, Atl	10	G. Young, Hou	65	G. Young, Hou	27	H. Brooks, Mon	21
G. Davis, Hou	11	R. Alomar, SD	16	W. Clark, SF	10	O. Smith, StL	57	B. Butler, SF	20	T. Wallach, Mon	19
A. Galarraga, Mon	10	B. Knepper, Hou	14	3 tied with	9	O. Nixon, Mon	46	4 tied with	14	G. Perry, Atl	18
3 tied with	8	R. Thompson, SF	14			C. Sabo, Cin	46			B. Santiago, SD	18

Runs Created		Runs Created/27 Outs		Batting Average		On-Base Percentage		Slugging Percentage		OBP+Slugging	
W. Clark, SF	126	W. Clark, SF	7.94	T. Gwynn, SD	.313	K. Daniels, Cin	.397	D. Strawberry, NYN	.545	D. Strawberry, NYN	.911
B. Bonilla, Pit	108	E. Davis, Cin	7.27	R. Palmeiro, ChN	.307	B. Butler, SF	.393	A. Galarraga, Mon	.540	W. Clark, SF	.894
A. Galarraga, Mon	107	K. Daniels, Cin	7.04	A. Dawson, ChN	.303	W. Clark, SF	.386	W. Clark, SF	.508	A. Galarraga, Mon	.893
K. Gibson, LA	102	K. Gibson, LA	6.83	A. Galarraga, Mon	.302	K. Gibson, LA	.377	A. Van Slyke, Pit	.506	K. Gibson, LA	.860
D. Strawberry, NYN	102	K. McReynolds, NYN	6.73	G. Perry, Atl	.300	T. Gwynn, SD	.373	A. Dawson, ChN	.504	K. Daniels, Cin	.860

1988 National League Pitching Leaders

Wins		Losses		Winning Percentage		Games		Games Started		Complete Games	
O. Hershiser, LA	23	T. Glavine, Atl	17	D. Cone, NYN	.870	R. Murphy, Cin	76	R. Reuschel, SF	36	O. Hershiser, LA	15
D. Jackson, Cin	23	R. Mahler, Atl	16	T. Browning, Cin	.783	J. Agosto, Hou	75	T. Browning, Cin	36	D. Jackson, Cin	15
D. Cone, NYN	20	S. Rawley, Phi	16	J. Parrett, Mon	.750	J. Robinson, Pit	75	D. Jackson, Cin	35	E. Show, SD	13
R. Reuschel, SF	19	J. Moyer, ChN	15	O. Hershiser, LA	.742	K. Tekulve, Phi	70	9 tied with	34	R. Sutcliffe, ChN	12
3 tied with	18	P. Smith, Atl	15	D. Jackson, Cin	.742	J. Franco, Cin	70			D. Gooden, NYN	10

Shutouts		Saves		Games Finished		Batters Faced		Innings Pitched		Hits Allowed	
O. Hershiser, LA	8	J. Franco, Cin	39	J. Franco, Cin	61	O. Hershiser, LA	1068	O. Hershiser, LA	267.0	R. Mahler, Atl	279
T. Leary, LA	6	J. Gott, Pit	34	J. Gott, Pit	59	R. Mahler, Atl	1063	D. Jackson, Cin	260.2	R. Reuschel, SF	242
D. Jackson, Cin	6	T. Worrell, StL	32	T. Worrell, StL	54	G. Maddux, ChN	1047	T. Browning, Cin	250.2	D. Gooden, NYN	242
M. Scott, Hou	5	M. Davis, SD	28	M. Davis, SD	52	D. Jackson, Cin	1034	R. Mahler, Atl	249.0	R. Sutcliffe, ChN	232
B. Ojeda, NYN	5	S. Bedrosian, Phi	28	S. Bedrosian, Phi	49	D. Gooden, NYN	1024	G. Maddux, ChN	249.0	G. Maddux, ChN	230

Home Runs Allowed		Walks		Walks/9 Innings		Strikeouts		Strikeouts/9 Innings		Strikeout/Walk Ratio	
T. Browning, Cin	36	K. Gross, Phi	89	B. Smith, Mon	1.5	N. Ryan, Hou	228	N. Ryan, Hou	9.3	B. Ojeda, NYN	4.03
S. Rawley, Phi	27	M. Dunne, Pit	88	R. Mahler, Atl	1.5	D. Cone, NYN	213	S. Fernandez, NYN	9.1	B. Smith, Mon	3.81
R. Darling, NYN	24	P. Smith, Atl	88	R. Reuschel, SF	1.5	J. DeLeon, StL	208	J. Rijo, Cin	8.9	M. Scott, Hou	3.58
E. Show, SD	22	N. Ryan, Hou	87	B. Ojeda, NYN	1.6	M. Scott, Hou	190	J. DeLeon, StL	8.3	T. Leary, LA	3.21
2 tied with	21	J. DeLeon, StL	86	J. Tudor, 2tm	1.9	S. Fernandez, NYN	189	D. Cone, NYN	8.3	R. Mahler, Atl	3.12

Earned Run Average		Component ERA		Hit Batsmen		Wild Pitches		Opponent Average		Opponent OBP	
J. Magrane, StL	2.18	P. Perez, Mon	1.94	K. Gross, Phi	11	B. Walk, Pit	13	S. Fernandez, NYN	.191	P. Perez, Mon	.252
D. Cone, NYN	2.22	B. Ojeda, NYN	2.02	B. Smith, Mon	10	B. Ruffin, Phi	12	P. Perez, Mon	.196	M. Scott, Hou	.260
O. Hershiser, LA	2.26	M. Scott, Hou	2.15	G. Maddux, ChN	9	M. Dunne, Pit	12	M. Scott, Hou	.204	B. Ojeda, NYN	.261
J. Tudor, 2tm	2.32	D. Jackson, Cin	2.23	3 tied with	8	3 tied with	11	J. Rijo, Cin	.209	O. Hershiser, LA	.269
J. Rijo, Cin	2.39	T. Belcher, LA	2.24					D. Cone, NYN	.213	S. Fernandez, NYN	.271

1988 National League Miscellaneous

Managers

Atlanta	Chuck Tanner	12-27
	Russ Nixon	42-79
Chicago	Don Zimmer	77-85
Cincinnati	Pete Rose	11-12
	Tommy Helms	12-15
	Pete Rose	64-47
Houston	Hal Lanier	82-80
Los Angeles	Tom Lasorda	94-67
Montreal	Buck Rodgers	81-81
New York	Davey Johnson	100-60
Philadelphia	Lee Elia	60-92
	John Vukovich	5-4
Pittsburgh	Jim Leyland	85-75
St. Louis	Whitey Herzog	76-86
San Diego	Larry Bowa	16-30
	Jack McKeon	67-48
San Francisco	Roger Craig	83-79

Awards

Most Valuable Player	Kirk Gibson, of, LA
Cy Young	Orel Hershiser, LA
Rookie of the Year	Chris Sabo, 3b, Cin
Manager of the Year	Tom Lasorda, LA

STATS All-Star Team

C	Tony Pena, StL	.263	10	51	
1B	Will Clark, SF	.282	29	109	
2B	Ron Gant, Atl	.259	19	60	
3B	Bobby Bonilla, Pit	.274	24	100	
SS	Barry Larkin, Cin	.296	12	56	
OF	Kirk Gibson, LA	.290	25	76	
OF	Darryl Strawberry, NYN	.269	39	101	
OF	Andy Van Slyke, Pit	.288	25	100	
P	David Cone, NYN	20-3	2.22	213 K	
P	Orel Hershiser, LA	23-8	2.26	178 K	
P	Danny Jackson, Cin	23-8	2.73	161 K	
P	Greg Maddux, ChN	18-8	3.18	140 K	
RP	John Franco, Cin	6-6	1.57	39 Sv	

Postseason

LCS	Los Angeles 4 vs. New York 3
World Series	LA (NL) 4 vs. Oakland (AL) 1

Outstanding Performances

Perfect Games
Tom Browning, Cin   vs. LA on September 16

Cycles
Chris Speier, SF   on July 9

1989 American League Standings

EAST	Overall					Home Games						Road Games						Park Index		Record by Month					
	W	L	Pct	GB	DIF	W	L	R	OR	HR	OHR	W	L	R	OR	HR	OHR	Run	HR	M/A	May	June	July	Aug	S/O
Toronto	89	73	.549	—	35	46	35	330	308	64	50	43	38	401	343	78	49	86	90	9-16	11-15	17-10	15-12	20-9	17-11
Baltimore	87	75	.537	2.0	118	47	34	347	338	61	65	40	41	361	348	68	69	97	92	12-12	14-10	17-11	11-16	18-13	15-13
Boston	83	79	.512	6.0	23	46	35	419	374	52	70	37	44	355	361	56	61	111	104	10-12	14-12	12-15	14-12	18-15	15-13
Milwaukee	81	81	.500	8.0	6	45	36	344	321	69	54	36	45	363	358	57	75	92	93	10-12	12-16	15-14	14-12	16-15	14-12
New York	74	87	.460	14.5	5	41	40	373	419	64	88	33	47	325	373	66	62	112	117	12-12	11-15	15-12	11-16	10-21	15-11
Cleveland	73	89	.451	16.0	18	41	40	319	332	56	51	32	49	285	322	71	56	107	84	9-13	16-13	11-15	15-12	12-17	10-19
Detroit	59	103	.364	30.0	0	38	43	321	389	74	77	21	60	296	427	42	73	98	131	8-14	14-14	8-18	6-21	11-22	12-14
WEST																									
Oakland	99	63	.611	—	109	54	27	370	284	65	51	45	36	342	292	62	52	103	102	18-8	16-10	13-14	16-10	18-11	18-10
Kansas City	92	70	.568	7.0	3	55	26	335	288	38	26	37	44	355	347	63	60	89	52	16-8	14-13	14-12	13-14	21-8	14-15
California	91	71	.562	8.0	49	52	29	317	285	73	75	39	42	352	293	72	38	93	135	15-10	18-7	12-14	15-10	15-14	13-16
Texas	83	79	.512	16.0	29	45	36	352	371	75	63	38	43	343	343	47	56	105	134	17-5	11-17	16-13	13-12	12-16	15-16
Minnesota	80	82	.494	19.0	2	45	36	387	404	59	69	35	46	353	334	58	70	115	100	10-12	13-15	17-12	11-14	17-12	12-17
Seattle	73	89	.451	26.0	0	40	41	353	386	68	67	33	48	341	342	66	47	108	119	11-15	14-13	12-14	13-12	9-20	14-15
Chicago	69	92	.429	29.5	3	35	45	301	365	36	58	34	47	392	385	58	86	87	66	8-16	10-17	12-17	14-11	12-16	13-15

Clinch Date—Toronto 9/30, Oakland 9/27.

Team Batting

Team	G	AB	R	OR	H	2B	3B	HR	TB	RBI	TBB	IBB	SO	HBP	SH	SF	SB	CS	SB%	GDP	Avg	OBP	Slg
Boston	162	5666	774	735	1571	326	30	108	2281	716	643	57	755	36	52	58	56	35	.62	169	.277	.360	.403
Minnesota	162	5581	740	738	1542	278	35	117	2241	691	478	40	743	39	51	58	111	53	.68	126	.276	.344	.402
Toronto	162	5581	731	651	1449	265	40	142	2220	685	521	32	923	31	30	53	144	58	.71	124	.260	.332	.398
Oakland	162	5416	712	576	1414	220	25	127	2065	659	562	37	855	34	36	62	157	55	.74	163	.261	.341	.381
Baltimore	162	5440	708	686	1369	238	33	129	2060	659	593	44	957	30	63	47	118	55	.68	140	.252	.334	.379
Milwaukee	162	5473	707	679	1415	235	32	126	2092	660	455	41	791	50	51	54	165	62	.73	108	.259	.327	.382
New York	161	5458	698	792	1470	229	23	130	2135	657	502	48	831	27	58	49	137	60	.70	130	.269	.339	.391
Texas	162	5458	695	714	1433	260	46	122	2151	654	503	28	989	34	63	40	101	49	.67	151	.263	.333	.394
Seattle	162	5512	694	728	1417	237	29	134	2114	653	489	40	838	45	35	52	81	55	.60	109	.257	.328	.384
Chicago	161	5504	693	750	1493	262	36	94	2109	661	464	51	873	28	85	51	97	52	.65	113	.271	.337	.383
Kansas City	162	5475	690	635	1428	227	41	101	2040	653	554	50	897	29	42	50	154	51	.75	141	.261	.337	.373
California	162	5545	669	578	1422	208	37	145	2139	624	429	48	1011	28	54	46	89	40	.69	114	.256	.318	.386
Detroit	162	5432	617	816	1315	198	24	116	1909	564	585	25	899	37	35	43	103	50	.67	108	.242	.325	.351
Cleveland	162	5463	604	654	1340	221	26	127	1994	567	499	52	934	35	72	41	74	51	.59	109	.245	.317	.365
AL Total	2266	77004	9732	9732	20078	3404	457	1718	29550	9103	7277	593	12296	483	727	704	1587	726	.69	1835	.261	.326	.384
AL Avg Team	162	5500	695	695	1434	243	33	123	2111	650	520	42	878	35	52	50	113	52	.69	131	.261	.326	.384

Team Pitching

Team	G	CG	ShO	Rel	Sv	IP	H	R	ER	HR	SH	SF	HB	TBB	IBB	SO	WP	Bk	H/9	SO/9	BB/9	OAvg	OOBP	ERA
Oakland	162	17	20	317	57	1448.1	1287	576	497	103	46	44	28	510	23	930	71	6	8.0	5.8	3.2	.239	.305	3.09
California	162	32	20	252	38	1454.1	1384	578	530	113	54	50	29	465	19	897	51	9	8.6	5.6	2.9	.253	.312	3.28
Kansas City	162	27	13	264	38	1451.2	1415	635	572	86	50	43	25	455	56	978	56	7	8.8	6.1	2.8	.257	.314	3.55
Toronto	162	12	12	277	38	1467.0	1408	651	584	99	61	62	45	478	44	849	58	8	8.6	5.2	2.9	.255	.317	3.58
Cleveland	162	23	13	287	38	1453.0	1423	654	590	107	58	48	24	452	36	844	43	17	8.8	5.2	2.8	.257	.313	3.65
Milwaukee	162	16	8	291	45	1432.1	1463	679	604	129	42	49	29	457	43	812	35	8	9.2	5.1	2.9	.265	.321	3.80
Texas	162	26	7	321	44	1434.1	1279	714	623	119	47	50	48	654	42	1112	65	16	8.0	7.0	4.1	.239	.324	3.91
Seattle	162	15	10	330	44	1438.0	1422	728	639	114	56	49	42	560	44	897	47	13	8.9	5.6	3.5	.259	.330	4.00
Baltimore	162	16	7	312	44	1448.1	1518	686	644	134	53	42	25	486	43	676	38	13	9.4	4.2	3.0	.272	.331	4.00
Boston	162	14	9	297	42	1460.1	1448	735	650	131	51	59	35	548	51	1054	40	18	8.9	6.5	3.4	.261	.328	4.01
Chicago	161	9	5	321	46	1422.0	1472	750	668	144	60	56	35	539	23	778	55	15	9.3	4.9	3.4	.269	.335	4.23
Minnesota	162	19	8	297	38	1429.1	1495	738	680	139	50	43	38	500	26	851	46	13	9.4	5.4	3.1	.269	.332	4.28
New York	161	15	9	278	44	1414.2	1550	792	708	150	47	46	37	521	52	787	42	18	9.9	5.0	3.3	.281	.344	4.50
Detroit	162	24	4	252	26	1427.1	1514	816	719	150	52	64	43	652	91	831	50	7	9.5	5.2	4.1	.274	.352	4.53
AL Total	2266	265	145	4096	582	20181.0	20078	9732	8708	1718	727	704	483	7277	593	12296	697	168	9.0	5.5	3.2	.261	.334	3.88
AL Avg Team	162	19	10	293	42	1441.0	1434	695	622	123	52	50	35	520	42	878	50	12	9.0	5.5	3.2	.261	.334	3.88

Team Fielding

Team	G	PO	A	E	TC	DP	PB	Pct
Baltimore	162	4345	1795	87	6227	163	8	.986
California	162	4363	1887	96	6346	173	14	.985
Minnesota	162	4288	1598	107	5993	141	8	.982
Kansas City	162	4355	1761	114	6230	139	12	.982
Cleveland	162	4359	1750	118	6227	126	17	.981
Toronto	162	4401	1864	127	6392	164	16	.980
New York	161	4244	1743	122	6109	183	7	.980
Boston	162	4381	1709	127	6217	162	11	.980
Detroit	162	4282	1762	130	6174	153	10	.979
Oakland	162	4345	1640	129	6114	159	13	.979
Texas	162	4303	1651	136	6090	137	42	.978
Seattle	162	4314	1777	143	6234	168	10	.977
Chicago	161	4266	1718	151	6135	176	16	.975
Milwaukee	162	4297	1803	155	6255	164	11	.975
AL Total	2266	60543	24458	1742	86743	2208	195	.980

Team vs. Team Records

	Bal	Bos	Cal	ChA	Cle	Det	KC	Mil	Min	NYA	Oak	Sea	Tex	Tor	Won
Bal	—	6	6	6	7	10	6	7	4	8	5	6	9	7	87
Bos	7	—	4	7	8	11	4	6	6	7	5	5	6	5	83
Cal	6	8	—	8	5	11	4	7	11	6	5	7	6	7	91
ChA	6	5	5	—	7	4	6	10	5	5	5	7	3	1	69
Cle	6	5	7	5	—	5	8	3	5	9	2	6	7	5	73
Det	3	2	1	8	8	—	6	6	5	6	4	4	4	2	59
KC	6	8	9	7	4	7	—	8	7	6	7	9	8	7	92
Mil	6	7	5	2	10	7	4	—	9	8	5	7	5	9	81
Min	8	6	2	8	7	7	6	3	—	6	6	7	5	9	80
NYA	5	6	6	4	4	7	6	5	6	—	3	8	5	7	74
Oak	7	5	8	8	10	8	6	7	7	9	—	9	8	7	99
Sea	6	7	6	6	6	8	4	5	6	4	4	—	6	5	73
Tex	3	6	7	10	5	8	5	7	8	7	5	7	—	5	83
Tor	6	8	5	11	8	11	5	7	3	6	5	7	7	—	89
Lost	75	79	71	92	89	103	70	81	82	87	63	89	79	73	

1989 American League Batting Leaders

Games		At-Bats		Runs		Hits		Doubles		Triples	
C. Ripken Jr., Bal	162	S. Sax, NYA	651	R. Henderson, 2tm	113	K. Puckett, Min	215	W. Boggs, Bos	51	R. Sierra, Tex	14
J. Carter, Cle	162	J. Carter, Cle	651	W. Boggs, Bos	113	S. Sax, NYA	205	K. Puckett, Min	45	D. White, Cal	13
R. Sierra, Tex	162	C. Ripken Jr., Bal	646	R. Yount, Mil	101	W. Boggs, Bos	205	J. Reed, Bos	42	P. Bradley, Bal	10
F. McGriff, Tor	161	D. White, Cal	636	R. Sierra, Tex	101	R. Yount, Mil	195	G. Bell, Tor	41	4 tied with	9
D. Gallagher, ChA	161	K. Puckett, Min	635	F. McGriff, Tor	98	2 tied with	194	R. Yount, Mil	38		

Home Runs		Total Bases		Runs Batted In		Walks		Intentional Walks		Strikeouts	
F. McGriff, Tor	36	R. Sierra, Tex	344	R. Sierra, Tex	119	R. Henderson, 2tm	126	W. Boggs, Bos	19	B. Jackson, KC	172
J. Carter, Cle	35	R. Yount, Mil	314	D. Mattingly, NYA	113	F. McGriff, Tor	119	D. Mattingly, NYA	18	R. Deer, Mil	158
M. McGwire, Oak	33	J. Carter, Cle	303	N. Esasky, Bos	108	W. Boggs, Bos	107	P. O'Brien, Cle	17	J. Barfield, 2tm	150
B. Jackson, KC	32	D. Mattingly, NYA	301	J. Carter, Cle	105	K. Seitzer, KC	102	A. Davis, Sea	15	P. Incaviglia, Tex	136
N. Esasky, Bos	30	K. Puckett, Min	295	B. Jackson, KC	105	A. Davis, Sea	101	M. Greenwell, Bos	15	C. Snyder, Cle	134

Hit By Pitch		Sac Hits		Sac Flies		Stolen Bases		Caught Stealing		GDP	
J. Gantner, Mil	10	F. Fermin, Cle	32	G. Bell, Tor	14	R. Henderson, 2tm	77	C. Espy, Tex	20	J. Franco, Tex	27
C. Lansford, Oak	9	A. Espinoza, NYA	23	J. Leonard, Sea	12	C. Espy, Tex	45	H. Reynolds, Sea	18	M. McGwire, Oak	23
C. O'Brien, Mil	9	B. Ripken, Bal	19	J. Ray, Cal	12	D. White, Cal	44	S. Sax, NYA	17	C. Ripken Jr., Bal	22
G. Larkin, Min	9	D. Gallagher, ChA	16	M. McGwire, Oak	11	S. Sax, NYA	43	O. Guillen, ChA	17	7 tied with	21
2 tied with	8	M. Barrett, Bos	15	4 tied with	10	G. Pettis, Det	43	D. White, Cal	16		

Runs Created		Runs Created/27 Outs		Batting Average		On-Base Percentage		Slugging Percentage		OBP+Slugging	
R. Sierra, Tex	125	A. Davis, Sea	8.47	K. Puckett, Min	.339	W. Boggs, Bos	.430	R. Sierra, Tex	.543	F. McGriff, Tor	.924
R. Yount, Mil	124	R. Yount, Mil	7.61	C. Lansford, Oak	.336	A. Davis, Sea	.424	F. McGriff, Tor	.525	A. Davis, Sea	.920
A. Davis, Sea	116	R. Sierra, Tex	7.32	W. Boggs, Bos	.330	R. Henderson, 2tm	.411	R. Yount, Mil	.511	R. Yount, Mil	.896
W. Boggs, Bos	114	F. McGriff, Tor	7.11	R. Yount, Mil	.318	F. McGriff, Tor	.399	N. Esasky, Bos	.500	R. Sierra, Tex	.889
F. McGriff, Tor	113	J. Franco, Tex	7.00	J. Franco, Tex	.316	C. Lansford, Oak	.398	A. Davis, Sea	.496	W. Boggs, Bos	.879

1989 American League Pitching Leaders

Wins		Losses		Winning Percentage		Games		Games Started		Complete Games	
B. Saberhagen, KC	23	D. Alexander, Det	18	B. Saberhagen, KC	.793	C. Crim, Mil	76	D. Stewart, Oak	36	B. Saberhagen, KC	12
D. Stewart, Oak	21	M. Witt, Cal	15	B. Blyleven, Cal	.773	R. Murphy, Bos	74	M. Gubicza, KC	36	J. Morris, Det	10
S. Davis, Oak	19	A. Hawkins, NYA	15	M. Henneman, Det	.733	K. Rogers, Tex	73	B. Milacki, Bal	36	C. Finley, Cal	9
M. Moore, Oak	19	6 tied with	14	S. Davis, Oak	.731	J. Russell, Tex	71	4 tied with	35	5 tied with	8
J. Ballard, Bal	18			2 tied with	.700	L. Guetterman, NYA	70				

Shutouts		Saves		Games Finished		Batters Faced		Innings Pitched		Hits Allowed	
B. Blyleven, Cal	5	J. Russell, Tex	38	J. Russell, Tex	66	D. Stewart, Oak	1081	B. Saberhagen, KC	262.1	D. Stewart, Oak	260
B. Saberhagen, KC	4	B. Thigpen, ChA	34	J. Reardon, Min	61	M. Gubicza, KC	1060	D. Stewart, Oak	257.2	M. Witt, Cal	252
K. McCaskill, Cal	4	D. Eckersley, Oak	33	M. Schooler, Sea	60	R. Clemens, Bos	1044	M. Gubicza, KC	255.0	M. Gubicza, KC	252
3 tied with	3	D. Plesac, Mil	33	T. Henke, Tor	56	B. Milacki, Bal	1022	R. Clemens, Bos	253.1	D. Alexander, Det	245
		M. Schooler, Sea	33	B. Thigpen, ChA	56	B. Saberhagen, KC	1021	B. Milacki, Bal	243.0	J. Ballard, Bal	240

Home Runs Allowed		Walks		Walks/9 Innings		Strikeouts		Strikeouts/9 Innings		Strikeout/Walk Ratio	
C. Hough, Tex	28	B. Witt, Tex	114	J. Key, Tor	1.1	N. Ryan, Tex	301	N. Ryan, Tex	11.3	B. Saberhagen, KC	4.49
D. Alexander, Det	28	N. Ryan, Tex	98	B. Saberhagen, KC	1.5	R. Clemens, Bos	230	T. Gordon, KC	8.4	J. Key, Tor	4.37
M. Witt, Cal	26	C. Hough, Tex	95	B. Blyleven, Cal	1.6	B. Saberhagen, KC	193	R. Clemens, Bos	8.2	C. Bosio, Mil	3.60
D. Schmidt, Bal	24	R. Clemens, Bos	93	C. Bosio, Mil	1.8	M. Gubicza, KC	173	B. Witt, Tex	7.7	N. Ryan, Tex	3.07
4 tied with	23	M. Perez, ChA	90	M. Witt, Cal	2.0	C. Bosio, Mil	173	F. Viola, Min	7.1	B. Blyleven, Cal	2.98

Earned Run Average		Component ERA		Hit Batsmen		Wild Pitches		Opponent Average		Opponent OBP	
B. Saberhagen, KC	2.16	B. Saberhagen, KC	1.89	D. Stieb, Tor	13	N. Ryan, Tex	19	N. Ryan, Tex	.187	B. Saberhagen, KC	.251
C. Finley, Cal	2.57	N. Ryan, Tex	2.31	M. Boddicker, Bos	10	M. Moore, Oak	17	T. Gordon, KC	.210	N. Ryan, Tex	.275
M. Moore, Oak	2.61	M. Moore, Oak	2.59	M. Smithson, Bos	10	D. Stewart, Oak	13	B. Saberhagen, KC	.217	M. Moore, Oak	.286
B. Blyleven, Cal	2.73	B. Blyleven, Cal	2.77	N. Ryan, Tex	9	B. Black, Cle	13	D. Stieb, Tor	.219	B. Blyleven, Cal	.287
K. McCaskill, Cal	2.93	T. Candiotti, Cle	2.81	4 tied with	8	D. Ward, Tor	13	M. Moore, Oak	.219	C. Bosio, Mil	.289

1989 American League Miscellaneous

Managers		
Baltimore	Frank Robinson	87-75
Boston	Joe Morgan	83-79
California	Doug Rader	91-71
Chicago	Jeff Torborg	69-92
Cleveland	Doc Edwards	65-78
	John Hart	8-11
Detroit	Sparky Anderson	59-103
Kansas City	John Wathan	92-70
Milwaukee	Tom Trebelhorn	81-81
Minnesota	Tom Kelly	80-82
New York	Dallas Green	56-65
	Bucky Dent	18-22
Oakland	Tony La Russa	99-63
Seattle	Jim Lefebvre	73-89
Texas	Bobby Valentine	83-79
Toronto	Jimy Williams	12-24
	Cito Gaston	77-49

Awards	
Most Valuable Player	Robin Yount, of, Mil
Cy Young	Bret Saberhagen, KC
Rookie of the Year	Gregg Olson, p, Bal
Manager of the Year	Frank Robinson, Bal

STATS All-Star Team

C	Mickey Tettleton, Bal	.258	26	65
1B	Fred McGriff, Tor	.269	36	92
2B	Julio Franco, Tex	.316	13	92
3B	Wade Boggs, Bos	.330	3	54
SS	Cal Ripken Jr., Bal	.257	21	93
OF	Rickey Henderson, 2tm	.274	12	57
OF	Ruben Sierra, Tex	.306	29	119
OF	Robin Yount, Mil	.318	21	103
DH	Harold Baines, 2tm	.309	16	72
P	Bert Blyleven, Cal	17-5	2.73	131 K
P	Roger Clemens, Bos	17-11	3.13	230 K
P	Mike Moore, Oak	19-11	2.61	172 K
P	Bret Saberhagen, KC	23-6	2.16	193 K
RP	Dennis Eckersley, Oak	4-0	1.56	33 Sv

Postseason	
LCS	Oakland 4 vs. Toronto 1
World Series	Oakland (AL) 4 vs. SF (NL) 0

Outstanding Performances

Three-Homer Games

Joe Carter, Cle	on June 24
Joe Carter, Cle	on July 19

Cycles

Kelly Gruber, Tor	on April 16

1989 National League Standings

EAST	W	L	Pct	GB	DIF	W	L	R	OR	HR	OHR	W	L	R	OR	HR	OHR	Run	HR	M/A	May	June	July	Aug	S/O
						Home Games						Road Games						Park Index		Record by Month					
Chicago	93	69	.574	—	108	48	33	381	334	61	64	45	36	321	289	63	42	117	119	12-11	16-11	13-15	18-9	16-12	18-11
New York	87	75	.537	6.0	25	51	30	333	275	78	56	36	45	350	320	69	59	91	105	12-10	13-14	15-11	13-15	19-10	15-15
St. Louis	86	76	.531	7.0	14	46	35	319	308	27	36	40	41	313	300	46	48	102	67	13-9	10-16	15-12	16-10	18-13	14-16
Montreal	81	81	.500	12.0	49	44	37	336	309	55	60	37	44	296	321	45	60	105	110	13-11	14-14	17-10	17-9	11-17	9-20
Pittsburgh	74	88	.457	19.0	1	39	42	296	313	45	62	35	46	341	367	50	59	86	98	10-14	11-14	12-13	12-18	13-15	16-14
Philadelphia	67	95	.414	26.0	12	38	42	321	376	61	67	29	53	308	359	62	60	107	108	11-12	7-19	9-17	15-14	12-17	13-16
WEST																									
San Francisco	92	70	.568	—	140	53	28	368	255	63	61	39	42	331	345	78	59	92	91	12-12	17-10	18-10	14-12	14-14	17-12
San Diego	89	73	.549	3.0	1	46	35	324	312	66	82	43	38	318	314	54	51	101	141	14-12	15-13	10-16	12-13	18-11	20-8
Houston	86	76	.531	6.0	5	47	35	340	344	42	50	39	41	307	325	55	55	106	82	11-14	16-10	15-11	15-11	11-17	15-14
Los Angeles	77	83	.481	14.0	0	44	37	253	244	37	46	33	46	301	292	52	49	82	80	11-13	14-11	12-17	12-16	13-14	15-12
Cincinnati	75	87	.463	17.0	45	38	43	312	377	59	71	37	44	320	314	69	54	109	106	13-9	14-13	14-15	7-19	16-13	11-18
Atlanta	63	97	.394	28.0	4	33	46	309	334	55	61	30	51	275	346	73	53	106	94	10-15	12-14	10-17	11-16	10-18	10-17

Clinch Date—Chicago 9/26, San Francisco 9/27.

Team Batting

Team	G	AB	R	OR	H	2B	3B	HR	TB	RBI	TBB	IBB	SO	HBP	SH	SF	SB	CS	SB%	GDP	Avg	OBP	Slg
Chicago	162	5513	702	623	1438	235	45	124	2135	653	472	75	921	26	80	50	136	57	.70	114	.261	.328	.387
San Francisco	162	5469	699	600	1365	241	52	141	2133	647	508	83	1071	40	82	39	87	54	.62	84	.250	.322	.390
New York	162	5489	683	595	1351	280	21	147	2114	633	504	69	934	33	56	48	158	53	.75	87	.246	.319	.385
Houston	162	5516	647	669	1316	239	28	97	1902	598	530	62	860	27	83	44	144	62	.70	80	.239	.313	.345
San Diego	162	5422	642	626	1360	215	32	120	1999	598	552	79	1013	9	95	41	136	67	.67	115	.251	.326	.369
Pittsburgh	164	5539	637	680	1334	263	53	95	1988	584	563	91	914	24	83	51	155	69	.69	115	.241	.319	.359
Cincinnati	162	5520	632	691	1362	243	28	128	2045	588	493	67	1028	30	66	49	128	71	.64	96	.247	.317	.370
Montreal	162	5482	632	630	1353	267	30	100	1980	587	572	83	958	35	71	46	160	70	.70	119	.247	.327	.361
St. Louis	164	5492	632	608	1418	263	47	73	1994	587	507	59	848	21	78	43	155	54	.74	120	.258	.328	.363
Philadelphia	163	5447	629	735	1324	215	36	123	1980	594	558	57	926	22	57	42	106	50	.68	107	.243	.321	.364
Atlanta	161	5463	584	680	1281	241	22	128	1910	544	485	51	996	24	65	42	83	54	.61	94	.234	.305	.350
Los Angeles	160	5465	554	536	1313	241	17	89	1855	513	507	77	885	27	83	41	81	54	.60	98	.240	.313	.339
NL Total	1946	65817	7673	7673	16215	2903	411	1365	24035	7126	6251	853	11354	318	899	536	1529	715	.68	1229	.246	.312	.365
NL Avg Team	162	5485	639	639	1351	242	34	114	2003	594	521	71	946	27	75	45	127	60	.68	102	.246	.312	.365

Team Pitching

Team	G	CG	ShO	Rel	Sv	IP	H	R	ER	HR	SH	SF	HB	TBB	IBB	SO	WP	Bk	H/9	SO/9	BB/9	OAvg	OOBP	ERA
Los Angeles	160	25	19	285	36	1463.1	1278	536	479	95	74	39	27	504	73	1052	53	14	7.9	6.5	3.1	.237	.304	2.95
New York	162	24	12	274	38	1454.1	1260	595	532	115	51	46	26	532	45	1108	50	24	7.8	6.9	3.3	.231	.301	3.29
San Francisco	162	12	16	318	47	1457.0	1320	600	535	120	69	52	24	471	54	802	37	26	8.2	5.0	2.9	.243	.304	3.30
St. Louis	164	18	18	358	43	1461.0	1330	608	546	84	64	46	30	482	89	844	40	16	8.2	5.2	3.0	.243	.306	3.36
San Diego	162	21	11	245	52	1457.1	1359	626	548	133	84	44	21	481	51	933	42	15	8.4	5.8	3.0	.249	.310	3.38
Chicago	162	18	10	338	55	1460.1	1369	623	556	106	76	45	25	532	70	918	44	24	8.4	5.7	3.3	.250	.317	3.43
Montreal	162	20	13	287	35	1468.1	1344	630	568	120	76	42	31	519	62	1059	40	20	8.2	6.5	3.2	.245	.312	3.48
Pittsburgh	164	20	9	325	40	1487.2	1394	680	602	121	69	44	29	539	78	827	55	20	8.4	5.0	3.3	.248	.314	3.64
Houston	162	19	12	346	38	1479.1	1370	669	599	105	90	44	25	551	94	965	50	23	8.4	5.9	3.4	.247	.315	3.64
Atlanta	161	15	8	340	33	1447.2	1370	680	595	114	89	44	16	468	57	966	48	17	8.5	6.0	2.9	.250	.309	3.70
Cincinnati	162	16	9	339	37	1464.1	1404	691	607	125	83	50	33	559	105	981	39	22	8.6	6.0	3.4	.253	.323	3.73
Philadelphia	163	10	10	348	33	1433.1	1408	735	644	127	74	40	31	613	75	899	91	18	8.8	5.6	3.8	.259	.335	4.04
NL Total	1946	218	147	3803	487	17534.0	16215	7673	6811	1365	899	536	318	6251	853	11354	589	239	8.3	5.8	3.2	.246	.320	3.50
NL Avg Team	162	18	12	317	41	1461.0	1351	639	568	114	75	45	27	521	71	946	49	20	8.3	5.8	3.2	.246	.320	3.50

Team Fielding

Team	G	PO	A	E	TC	DP	PB	Pct
St. Louis	164	4383	1856	112	6351	134	12	.982
San Francisco	162	4371	1725	114	6210	135	11	.982
Los Angeles	160	4390	1668	118	6176	153	10	.981
Cincinnati	162	4393	1671	121	6185	108	8	.980
Chicago	162	4381	1722	124	6227	130	12	.980
Montreal	162	4405	1822	136	6363	126	11	.979
Philadelphia	163	4300	1771	133	6204	136	6	.979
Houston	162	4438	1653	142	6233	121	14	.977
New York	162	4363	1462	144	5969	110	11	.976
San Diego	162	4372	1822	154	6348	147	14	.976
Atlanta	161	4343	1722	152	6217	124	14	.976
Pittsburgh	164	4463	1756	160	6379	130	19	.975
NL Total	1946	52602	20650	1610	74862	1554	142	.978

Team vs. Team Records

	Atl	ChN	Cin	Hou	LA	Mon	NYN	Phi	Pit	SD	SF	StL	Won
Atl	—	5	8	8	6	6	2	8	4	7	6	3	63
ChN	7	—	7	5	7	10	10	10	12	8	6	11	93
Cin	10	5	—	8	8	4	4	4	7	9	8	8	75
Hou	10	7	10	—	10	4	6	9	7	8	8	7	86
LA	10	5	10	8	—	7	5	6	7	6	10	3	77
Mon	6	8	8	8	5	—	9	9	11	5	7	5	81
NYN	10	8	8	6	7	9	—	12	9	5	3	10	87
Phi	4	8	8	3	6	9	6	—	10	2	4	7	67
Pit	8	6	5	5	5	7	9	8	—	3	5	13	74
SD	11	4	9	10	12	7	7	10	9	—	8	2	89
SF	12	6	10	10	8	5	9	8	7	10	—	7	92
StL	9	7	4	5	9	13	8	11	5	10	5	—	86
Lost	97	69	87	76	83	81	75	95	88	73	70	76	

1989 National League Batting Leaders

Games		At-Bats		Runs		Hits		Doubles		Triples	
J. Oquendo, StL	163	T. Benzinger, Cin	628	R. Sandberg, ChN	104	T. Gwynn, SD	203	P. Guerrero, StL	42	R. Thompson, SF	11
B. Bonilla, Pit	163	R. Alomar, SD	623	H. Johnson, NYN	104	W. Clark, SF	196	T. Wallach, Mon	42	B. Bonilla, Pit	10
P. Guerrero, StL	162	B. Bonilla, Pit	616	W. Clark, SF	104	R. Alomar, SD	184	H. Johnson, NYN	41	A. Van Slyke, Pit	9
T. Pendleton, StL	162	T. Pendleton, StL	613	B. Butler, SF	100	P. Guerrero, StL	177	W. Clark, SF	38	V. Coleman, StL	9
2 tied with	161	R. Sandberg, ChN	606	K. Mitchell, SF	100	R. Sandberg, ChN	176	B. Bonilla, Pit	37	W. Clark, SF	9

Home Runs		Total Bases		Runs Batted In		Walks		Intentional Walks		Strikeouts	
K. Mitchell, SF	47	K. Mitchell, SF	345	K. Mitchell, SF	125	J. Clark, SD	132	K. Mitchell, SF	32	A. Galarraga, Mon	158
H. Johnson, NYN	36	W. Clark, SF	321	P. Guerrero, StL	117	V. Hayes, Phi	101	S. Owen, Mon	25	J. Clark, SD	145
G. Davis, Hou	34	H. Johnson, NYN	319	W. Clark, SF	111	T. Raines, Mon	93	E. Murray, LA	24	D. Murphy, Atl	142
E. Davis, Cin	34	B. Bonilla, Pit	302	H. Johnson, NYN	101	B. Bonds, Pit	93	B. Bonds, Pit	22	R. Thompson, SF	133
R. Sandberg, ChN	30	R. Sandberg, ChN	301	E. Davis, Cin	101	2 tied with	87	B. Bonilla, Pit	20	H. Johnson, NYN	126

Hit By Pitch		Sac Hits		Sac Flies		Stolen Bases		Caught Stealing		GDP	
A. Galarraga, Mon	13	R. Alomar, SD	17	P. Guerrero, StL	12	V. Coleman, StL	65	G. Young, Hou	25	T. Wallach, Mon	21
R. Thompson, SF	13	R. Reuschel, SF	16	E. Davis, Cin	11	J. Samuel, 2tm	42	R. Alomar, SD	17	C. James, 2tm	20
L. Smith, Atl	11	T. Browning, Cin	14	9 tied with	8	R. Alomar, SD	42	B. Butler, SF	16	T. Pena, StL	19
J. Samuel, 2tm	11	B. Butler, SF	13			T. Raines, Mon	41	T. Gwynn, SD	16	R. Jordan, Phi	19
G. Davis, Hou	7	J. Lind, Pit	13			H. Johnson, NYN	41	4 tied with	12	2 tied with	17

Runs Created		Runs Created/27 Outs		Batting Average		On-Base Percentage		Slugging Percentage		OBP+Slugging	
W. Clark, SF	141	W. Clark, SF	9.39	T. Gwynn, SD	.336	L. Smith, Atl	.415	K. Mitchell, SF	.635	K. Mitchell, SF	1.023
H. Johnson, NYN	129	L. Smith, Atl	8.77	W. Clark, SF	.333	J. Clark, SD	.410	H. Johnson, NYN	.559	W. Clark, SF	.953
K. Mitchell, SF	125	K. Mitchell, SF	8.47	L. Smith, Atl	.315	W. Clark, SF	.407	W. Clark, SF	.546	L. Smith, Atl	.948
P. Guerrero, StL	117	H. Johnson, NYN	8.26	M. Grace, ChN	.314	M. Grace, ChN	.405	E. Davis, Cin	.541	H. Johnson, NYN	.928
L. Smith, Atl	115	J. Clark, SD	7.75	P. Guerrero, StL	.311	T. Raines, Mon	.395	L. Smith, Atl	.533	E. Davis, Cin	.908

1989 National League Pitching Leaders

Wins		Losses		Winning Percentage		Games		Games Started		Complete Games	
M. Scott, Hou	20	D. Carman, Phi	15	S. Garrelts, SF	.737	M. Williams, ChN	76	T. Browning, Cin	37	B. Hurst, SD	10
G. Maddux, ChN	19	O. Hershiser, LA	15	S. Fernandez, NYN	.737	R. Dibble, Cin	74	J. DeLeon, StL	36	T. Belcher, LA	10
M. Bielecki, ChN	18	K. Hill, StL	15	D. Darwin, Hou	.733	J. Parrett, Phi	72	G. Maddux, ChN	35	M. Scott, Hou	9
J. Magrane, StL	18	4 tied with	14	M. Bielecki, ChN	.720	J. Agosto, Hou	71	3 tied with	34	T. Browning, Cin	9
R. Reuschel, SF	17			D. Martinez, Mon	.696	K. Dayley, StL	71			J. Magrane, StL	9

Shutouts		Saves		Games Finished		Batters Faced		Innings Pitched		Hits Allowed	
T. Belcher, LA	8	M. Davis, SD	44	M. Davis, SD	65	O. Hershiser, LA	1047	O. Hershiser, LA	256.2	R. Mahler, Cin	242
D. Drabek, Pit	5	M. Williams, ChN	36	M. Williams, ChN	61	T. Browning, Cin	1031	T. Browning, Cin	249.2	T. Browning, Cin	241
O. Hershiser, LA	4	J. Franco, Cin	32	S. Bedrosian, 2tm	60	G. Maddux, ChN	1002	B. Hurst, SD	244.2	D. Martinez, Mon	227
M. Langston, Mon	4	J. Howell, LA	28	R. McDowell, 2tm	56	D. Drabek, Pit	994	J. DeLeon, StL	244.2	O. Hershiser, LA	226
T. Glavine, Atl	4	T. Burke, Mon	28	J. Boever, Atl	53	B. Hurst, SD	990	D. Drabek, Pit	244.1	G. Maddux, ChN	222

Home Runs Allowed		Walks		Walks/9 Innings		Strikeouts		Strikeouts/9 Innings		Strikeout/Walk Ratio	
T. Browning, Cin	31	K. Hill, StL	99	D. Robinson, SF	1.7	J. DeLeon, StL	201	M. Langston, Mon	8.9	P. Perez, Mon	3.38
M. Scott, Hou	23	F. Valenzuela, LA	98	D. Lilliquist, Atl	1.8	T. Belcher, LA	200	S. Fernandez, NYN	8.1	D. Martinez, Mon	2.90
E. Whitson, SD	22	M. Langston, Mon	93	D. Martinez, Mon	1.9	S. Fernandez, NYN	198	T. Belcher, LA	7.8	M. Scott, Hou	2.77
D. Robinson, SF	22	K. Gross, Mon	88	E. Whitson, SD	1.9	D. Cone, NYN	190	D. Cone, NYN	7.8	B. Hurst, SD	2.71
J. Smiley, Pit	22	2 tied with	86	T. Glavine, Atl	1.9	B. Hurst, SD	179	J. DeLeon, StL	7.4	S. Fernandez, NYN	2.64

Earned Run Average		Component ERA		Hit Batsmen		Wild Pitches		Opponent Average		Opponent OBP	
S. Garrelts, SF	2.28	S. Garrelts, SF	2.02	R. Mahler, Cin	10	K. Howell, Phi	21	J. DeLeon, StL	.197	S. Garrelts, SF	.258
O. Hershiser, LA	2.31	J. DeLeon, StL	2.16	M. Williams, ChN	8	J. Wetteland, LA	16	S. Fernandez, NYN	.198	M. Scott, Hou	.267
M. Langston, Mon	2.39	M. Scott, Hou	2.43	5 tied with	7	J. Robinson, Pit	14	J. Smoltz, Atl	.212	J. DeLeon, StL	.268
E. Whitson, SD	2.66	S. Fernandez, NYN	2.43			D. Cone, NYN	14	S. Garrelts, SF	.212	S. Fernandez, NYN	.271
B. Hurst, SD	2.69	B. Smith, Mon	2.47			J. Magrane, StL	14	M. Scott, Hou	.212	J. Smiley, Pit	.273

1989 National League Miscellaneous

Managers

Atlanta	Russ Nixon	63-97
Chicago	Don Zimmer	93-69
Cincinnati	Pete Rose	59-66
	Tommy Helms	16-21
Houston	Art Howe	86-76
Los Angeles	Tom Lasorda	77-83
Montreal	Buck Rodgers	81-81
New York	Davey Johnson	87-75
Philadelphia	Nick Leyva	67-95
Pittsburgh	Jim Leyland	74-88
St. Louis	Whitey Herzog	86-76
San Diego	Jack McKeon	89-73
San Francisco	Roger Craig	92-70

Awards

Most Valuable Player	Kevin Mitchell, of, SF
Cy Young	Mark Davis, SD
Rookie of the Year	Jerome Walton, of, ChN
Manager of the Year	Don Zimmer, ChN

STATS All-Star Team

C	Craig Biggio, Hou	.257	13	60
1B	Will Clark, SF	.333	23	111
2B	Ryne Sandberg, ChN	.290	30	76
3B	Howard Johnson, NYN	.287	36	101
SS	Dickie Thon, Phi	.271	15	60
OF	Eric Davis, Cin	.281	34	101
OF	Kevin Mitchell, SF	.291	47	125
OF	Lonnie Smith, Atl	.315	21	79
P	Sid Fernandez, NYN	14-5	2.83	198 K
P	Greg Maddux, ChN	19-12	2.95	135 K
P	Joe Magrane, StL	18-9	2.91	127 K
P	Mike Scott, Hou	20-10	3.10	172 K
RP	Mark Davis, SD	4-3	1.85	44 Sv

Postseason

LCS	San Francisco 4 vs. Chicago 1
World Series	SF (NL) 0 vs. Oakland (AL) 4

Outstanding Performances

Three-Homer Games

Von Hayes, Phi	on August 29

Cycles

Eric Davis, Cin	on June 2
K. McReynolds, NYN	on August 1
Gary Redus, Pit	on August 25

1990 American League Standings

EAST	W	L	Pct	GB	DIF	W	L	R	OR	HR	OHR	W	L	R	OR	HR	OHR	Run	HR	M/A	May	June	July	Aug	S/O
						Home Games						Road Games						Park Index		Record by Month					
Boston	88	74	.543	—	97	51	30	394	318	61	44	37	44	305	346	45	48	109	113	11-8	12-14	20-9	12-17	19-9	14-17
Toronto	86	76	.531	2.0	49	44	37	385	341	93	82	42	39	382	320	74	61	103	130	12-9	14-14	15-13	14-12	13-16	18-12
Detroit	79	83	.488	9.0	0	39	42	372	399	92	75	40	41	378	355	80	79	105	105	8-12	12-17	16-12	13-15	14-13	16-14
Cleveland	77	85	.475	11.0	0	41	40	363	373	52	86	36	45	369	364	58	77	100	102	9-9	13-14	14-14	11-19	12-16	18-13
Baltimore	76	85	.472	11.5	2	40	40	320	337	74	82	36	45	349	361	58	79	94	115	9-11	12-15	13-15	17-11	9-18	15-13
Milwaukee	74	88	.457	14.0	33	39	42	356	374	60	59	35	46	376	386	68	62	96	92	12-6	11-15	10-19	13-15	16-14	13-19
New York	67	95	.414	21.0	7	37	44	296	361	64	78	30	51	307	388	83	66	95	95	7-10	10-17	11-17	12-17	16-14	11-20
WEST																									
Oakland	103	59	.636	—	169	51	30	321	244	69	52	52	29	412	326	95	71	77	73	14-5	18-9	15-12	17-14	18-9	21-10
Chicago	94	68	.580	9.0	11	49	31	345	315	41	53	45	37	337	318	65	53	103	82	10-6	18-10	17-10	13-14	17-15	19-13
Texas	83	79	.512	20.0	1	47	35	354	348	64	59	36	44	322	348	46	54	102	120	11-9	8-19	16-13	17-9	14-15	17-14
California	80	82	.494	23.0	0	42	39	360	354	89	55	38	43	330	352	58	51	105	132	8-11	15-14	15-13	12-16	16-12	14-16
Seattle	77	85	.475	26.0	1	38	43	310	341	49	60	39	42	330	339	58	60	97	92	8-12	15-14	11-16	15-12	10-18	13-17
Kansas City	75	86	.466	27.5	0	45	36	370	342	42	46	30	50	337	367	58	70	100	68	6-12	14-14	11-16	17-12	17-12	10-20
Minnesota	74	88	.457	29.0	0	41	40	373	380	46	69	33	48	293	349	54	65	117	97	7-12	21-7	7-21	15-14	9-19	15-15

Clinch Date—Boston 10/03, Oakland 9/25.

Team Batting

Team	G	AB	R	OR	H	2B	3B	HR	TB	RBI	TBB	IBB	SO	HBP	SH	SF	SB	CS	SB%	GDP	Avg	OBP	Slg
Toronto	162	5589	767	661	1479	263	50	167	2343	729	526	35	970	28	18	62	111	52	.68	125	.265	.338	.419
Detroit	162	5479	750	754	1418	241	32	172	2239	714	634	44	952	34	36	41	82	57	.59	139	.259	.344	.409
Oakland	162	5433	733	570	1379	209	22	164	2124	693	651	38	992	46	60	48	141	54	.72	122	.254	.344	.391
Milwaukee	162	5503	732	760	1408	247	36	128	2111	680	519	46	821	33	59	71	164	72	.69	101	.256	.332	.384
Cleveland	162	5485	732	737	1465	266	41	110	2143	675	458	33	836	29	54	61	107	52	.67	122	.267	.334	.391
Kansas City	161	5488	707	709	1465	316	44	100	2169	660	498	32	879	27	31	54	107	62	.63	132	.267	.337	.395
Boston	162	5516	699	664	1502	298	31	106	2180	660	598	59	795	28	48	44	53	52	.50	174	.272	.351	.395
California	162	5570	690	706	1448	237	27	147	2180	646	566	41	1000	28	58	45	69	43	.62	142	.260	.336	.391
Chicago	162	5402	682	633	1393	251	44	106	2050	637	478	50	903	36	75	47	140	90	.61	112	.258	.328	.379
Texas	162	5469	676	696	1416	257	27	110	2057	641	575	45	1054	34	54	44	115	48	.71	142	.259	.338	.376
Baltimore	161	5410	669	698	1328	234	22	132	2002	623	660	50	962	40	72	41	94	52	.64	131	.245	.336	.370
Minnesota	162	5499	666	729	1458	281	39	100	2117	625	445	32	749	53	40	49	96	53	.64	148	.265	.338	.385
Seattle	162	5474	640	680	1419	251	26	107	2043	610	596	41	749	40	41	54	105	51	.67	140	.259	.342	.373
New York	162	5483	603	749	1322	208	19	147	2009	561	427	41	1027	53	37	36	119	45	.73	114	.241	.306	.366
AL Total	2266	76800	9746	9746	19900	3559	460	1796	29767	9154	7631	587	12689	509	683	697	1503	783	.66	1844	.259	.327	.388
AL Avg Team	162	5486	696	696	1421	254	33	128	2126	654	545	42	906	36	49	50	107	56	.66	132	.259	.327	.388

Team Pitching

Team	G	CG	ShO	Rel	Sv	IP	H	R	ER	HR	SH	SF	HB	TBB	IBB	SO	WP	Bk	H/9	SO/9	BB/9	OAvg	OOBP	ERA
Oakland	162	18	16	303	64	1456.0	1287	570	514	123	40	50	27	494	19	831	50	7	8.0	5.1	3.1	.238	.302	3.18
Chicago	162	17	10	367	68	1449.1	1313	633	582	106	52	46	39	548	27	914	35	11	8.2	5.7	3.4	.244	.316	3.61
Seattle	162	21	7	312	41	1443.1	1319	680	592	120	48	50	41	606	55	1064	69	12	8.2	6.6	3.8	.243	.321	3.69
Boston	162	15	13	323	44	1442.0	1439	664	596	92	47	46	45	519	47	997	63	6	9.0	6.2	3.2	.261	.327	3.72
California	162	21	13	269	42	1454.0	1482	706	613	106	47	46	38	544	25	944	50	6	9.2	5.8	3.4	.267	.334	3.79
Texas	162	25	9	302	36	1444.2	1343	696	615	113	37	57	44	623	39	997	61	6	8.4	6.2	3.9	.248	.327	3.83
Toronto	162	6	9	317	48	1454.0	1434	661	620	143	48	38	37	445	44	892	43	5	8.9	5.5	2.8	.260	.317	3.84
Kansas City	161	18	8	312	33	1420.2	1449	709	621	116	48	44	46	560	45	1006	59	5	9.2	6.4	3.5	.264	.335	3.93
Baltimore	161	10	5	357	43	1435.1	1445	698	644	161	52	56	16	537	43	776	34	10	9.1	4.9	3.4	.264	.328	4.04
Milwaukee	162	23	13	340	43	1445.0	1558	760	655	121	50	63	38	469	39	771	47	7	9.7	4.8	2.9	.275	.331	4.08
Minnesota	162	13	13	310	43	1435.2	1509	729	658	134	47	46	27	489	40	872	55	5	9.5	5.5	3.1	.273	.332	4.12
New York	162	15	6	342	41	1444.2	1430	749	676	144	60	48	26	618	40	909	83	6	8.9	5.7	3.9	.261	.336	4.21
Cleveland	162	12	10	301	47	1427.1	1491	737	676	163	50	50	40	518	38	860	50	8	9.4	5.4	3.3	.270	.334	4.26
Detroit	162	13	10	300	45	1430.1	1401	754	697	106	54	57	45	661	86	856	76	7	8.8	5.4	4.2	.259	.341	4.39
AL Total	2266	229	144	4455	637	20182.1	19900	9746	8759	1796	683	697	509	7631	587	12689	775	101	8.9	5.7	3.4	.259	.336	3.91
AL Avg Team	162	16	10	318	46	1441.1	1421	696	626	128	49	50	36	545	42	906	55	7	8.9	5.7	3.4	.259	.336	3.91

Team Fielding

Team	G	PO	A	E	TC	DP	PB	Pct
Toronto	162	4362	1720	86	6168	144	14	.986
Oakland	162	4368	1630	87	6085	152	14	.986
Baltimore	161	4306	1651	93	6050	151	5	.985
Minnesota	162	4307	1705	101	6113	161	11	.983
Cleveland	162	4282	1648	117	6047	146	14	.981
Boston	162	4326	1743	123	6192	154	7	.980
Chicago	162	4348	1706	124	6178	169	13	.980
New York	162	4334	1791	126	6251	164	27	.980
Kansas City	161	4262	1598	122	5982	161	13	.980
Seattle	162	4330	1730	130	6190	152	18	.979
Detroit	162	4291	1774	131	6196	178	15	.979
Texas	162	4334	1721	133	6188	161	35	.979
California	162	4362	1871	142	6375	186	15	.978
Milwaukee	162	4335	1737	149	6221	152	11	.976
AL Total	2266	60547	24025	1664	86236	2231	212	.981

Team vs. Team Records

	Bal	Bos	Cal	ChA	Cle	Det	KC	Mil	Min	NYA	Oak	Sea	Tex	Tor	Won
Bal	—	4	7	6	6	6	8	7	6	6	4	3	8	5	76
Bos	9	—	7	6	9	8	4	5	4	9	4	8	5	10	88
Cal	5	5	—	5	7	5	7	7	9	6	4	5	8	7	80
ChA	6	6	8	—	5	5	9	10	7	10	8	8	7	5	94
Cle	7	4	5	7	—	5	6	9	7	5	4	7	7	4	77
Det	7	5	7	7	8	—	5	3	6	7	6	7	6	5	79
KC	3	8	6	4	6	7	—	4	8	3	6	4	7	5	75
Mil	6	8	5	2	4	10	8	—	4	6	5	4	5	7	74
Min	6	8	4	6	5	6	5	8	—	6	6	6	5	3	74
NYA	7	4	6	2	6	6	4	7	6	—	0	9	3	5	67
Oak	8	8	9	5	8	6	6	6	7	12	—	9	8	7	103
Sea	9	4	8	5	5	5	6	8	7	3	4	—	7	6	77
Tex	4	7	5	6	5	6	8	7	8	9	5	6	—	7	83
Tor	8	3	5	7	9	8	7	6	9	8	5	6	5	—	86
Lost	85	74	82	68	85	83	86	88	88	95	59	85	79	76	

Seasons: Standings, Leaders

1990 American League Batting Leaders

Games		At-Bats		Runs		Hits		Doubles		Triples	
R. Kelly, NYA	162	H. Reynolds, Sea	642	R. Henderson, Oak	119	R. Palmeiro, Tex	191	G. Brett, KC	45	T. Fernandez, Tor	17
C. Ripken Jr., Bal	161	R. Kelly, NYA	641	C. Fielder, Det	104	W. Boggs, Bos	187	J. Reed, Bos	45	S. Sosa, ChA	10
T. Fernandez, Tor	161	T. Fernandez, Tor	635	H. Reynolds, Sea	100	R. Kelly, NYA	183	W. Boggs, Bos	44	L. Polonia, 2tm	9
H. Reynolds, Sea	160	K. Seitzer, KC	622	R. Yount, Mil	98	M. Greenwell, Bos	181	I. Calderon, ChA	44	L. Johnson, ChA	9
O. Guillen, ChA	160	W. Boggs, Bos	619	T. Phillips, Det	97	2 tied with	179	B. Harper, Min	42	N. Liriano, 2tm	9

Home Runs		Total Bases		Runs Batted In		Walks		Intentional Walks		Strikeouts	
C. Fielder, Det	51	C. Fielder, Det	339	C. Fielder, Det	132	M. McGwire, Oak	110	W. Boggs, Bos	19	C. Fielder, Det	182
M. McGwire, Oak	39	K. Gruber, Tor	303	K. Gruber, Tor	118	M. Tettleton, Bal	106	C. Ripken Jr., Bal	18	M. Tettleton, Bal	160
J. Canseco, Oak	37	F. McGriff, Tor	295	M. McGwire, Oak	108	T. Phillips, Det	99	G. Brett, KC	14	J. Canseco, Oak	158
F. McGriff, Tor	35	K. Griffey Jr., Sea	287	J. Canseco, Oak	101	R. Henderson, Oak	97	D. Mattingly, NYA	13	J. Barfield, NYA	150
K. Gruber, Tor	31	E. Burks, Bos	286	R. Sierra, Tex	96	F. McGriff, Tor	94	R. Sierra, Tex	13	S. Sosa, ChA	150

Hit By Pitch		Sac Hits		Sac Flies		Stolen Bases		Caught Stealing		GDP	
P. Bradley, 2tm	11	M. Gallego, Oak	17	D. Parker, Mil	14	R. Henderson, Oak	65	L. Johnson, ChA	22	I. Calderon, ChA	26
P. Incaviglia, Tex	9	B. Ripken, Bal	17	K. Gruber, Tor	13	S. Sax, NYA	43	O. Guillen, ChA	17	R. Palmeiro, Tex	24
K. Gruber, Tor	8	O. Guillen, ChA	15	G. Bell, Tor	11	R. Kelly, NYA	42	R. Kelly, NYA	17	T. Pena, Bos	23
8 tied with	7	3 tied with	13	J. Browne, Cle	11	A. Cole, Cle	40	3 tied with	16	G. Gaetti, Min	22
				3 tied with	9	G. Pettis, Tex	38			3 tied with	20

Runs Created		Runs Created/27 Outs		Batting Average		On-Base Percentage		Slugging Percentage		OBP+Slugging	
R. Henderson, Oak	122	R. Henderson, Oak	9.19	G. Brett, KC	.329	R. Henderson, Oak	.439	C. Fielder, Det	.592	R. Henderson, Oak	1.016
C. Fielder, Det	122	C. Fielder, Det	7.54	R. Henderson, Oak	.325	F. McGriff, Tor	.400	R. Henderson, Oak	.577	C. Fielder, Det	.969
K. Gruber, Tor	110	G. Brett, KC	7.41	R. Palmeiro, Tex	.319	E. Martinez, Sea	.397	J. Canseco, Oak	.543	F. McGriff, Tor	.930
F. McGriff, Tor	110	F. McGriff, Tor	7.30	A. Trammell, Det	.304	G. Brett, KC	.387	F. McGriff, Tor	.530	J. Canseco, Oak	.914
G. Brett, KC	108	A. Trammell, Det	6.86	W. Boggs, Bos	.302	A. Davis, Sea	.387	G. Brett, KC	.515	G. Brett, KC	.902

1990 American League Pitching Leaders

Wins		Losses		Winning Percentage		Games		Games Started		Complete Games	
B. Welch, Oak	27	T. Leary, NYA	19	B. Welch, Oak	.818	B. Thigpen, ChA	77	D. Stewart, Oak	36	D. Stewart, Oak	11
D. Stewart, Oak	22	J. Morris, Det	18	R. Clemens, Bos	.778	D. Ward, Tor	73	J. Morris, Det	36	J. Morris, Det	11
R. Clemens, Bos	21	M. Young, Sea	18	D. Stieb, Tor	.750	J. Montgomery, KC	73	B. Welch, Oak	35	5 tied with	7
3 tied with	18	A. Anderson, Min	18	E. King, ChA	.750	K. Rogers, Tex	69	M. Perez, ChA	35		
		2 tied with	17	B. Jones, ChA	.733	M. Henneman, Det	69	3 tied with	34		

Shutouts		Saves		Games Finished		Batters Faced		Innings Pitched		Hits Allowed	
D. Stewart, Oak	4	B. Thigpen, ChA	57	B. Thigpen, ChA	73	D. Stewart, Oak	1088	D. Stewart, Oak	267.0	J. Abbott, Cal	246
R. Clemens, Bos	4	D. Eckersley, Oak	48	D. Jones, Cle	64	J. Morris, Det	1073	J. Morris, Det	249.2	G. Swindell, Cle	245
J. Morris, Det	3	D. Jones, Cle	43	D. Eckersley, Oak	61	B. Welch, Oak	979	B. Welch, Oak	238.0	J. Morris, Det	231
M. Perez, ChA	3	G. Olson, Bal	37	J. Montgomery, KC	59	E. Hanson, Sea	964	C. Finley, Cal	236.0	D. Stewart, Oak	226
K. Appier, KC	3	D. Righetti, NYA	36	2 tied with	58	M. Young, Sea	963	E. Hanson, Sea	236.0	M. Boddicker, Bos	225

Home Runs Allowed		Walks		Walks/9 Innings		Strikeouts		Strikeouts/9 Innings		Strikeout/Walk Ratio	
D. Johnson, Bal	30	R. Johnson, Sea	120	A. Anderson, Min	1.9	N. Ryan, Tex	232	N. Ryan, Tex	10.2	R. Clemens, Bos	3.87
S. Sanderson, Oak	27	C. Hough, Tex	119	G. Swindell, Cle	2.0	B. Witt, Tex	221	B. Witt, Tex	9.0	N. Ryan, Tex	3.14
G. Swindell, Cle	27	B. Witt, Tex	110	R. Clemens, Bos	2.1	E. Hanson, Sea	211	R. Clemens, Bos	8.2	E. Hanson, Sea	3.10
3 tied with	26	M. Young, Sea	107	M. Knudson, Mil	2.1	R. Clemens, Bos	209	T. Gordon, KC	8.1	G. Swindell, Cle	2.87
		M. Langston, Cal	104	D. Wells, Tor	2.1	M. Langston, Cal	195	E. Hanson, Sea	8.0	T. Higuera, Mil	2.58

Earned Run Average		Component ERA		Hit Batsmen		Wild Pitches		Opponent Average		Opponent OBP	
R. Clemens, Bos	1.93	N. Ryan, Tex	2.28	C. Hough, Tex	11	T. Leary, NYA	23	N. Ryan, Tex	.188	N. Ryan, Tex	.267
C. Finley, Cal	2.40	R. Clemens, Bos	2.33	M. Boddicker, Bos	10	J. Morris, Det	16	R. Johnson, Sea	.216	R. Clemens, Bos	.278
D. Stewart, Oak	2.56	D. Wells, Tor	2.67	D. Stieb, Tor	10	M. Young, Sea	16	R. Clemens, Bos	.228	D. Wells, Tor	.283
K. Appier, KC	2.76	E. Hanson, Sea	2.72	F. Tanana, Det	9	J. Robinson, Det	16	D. Stieb, Tor	.230	E. Hanson, Sea	.287
D. Stieb, Tor	2.93	D. Stewart, Oak	2.75	D. Kiecker, Bos	9	G. Cadaret, NYA	14	D. Stewart, Oak	.231	B. Black, 2tm	.290

1990 American League Miscellaneous

Managers

Baltimore	Frank Robinson	76-85
Boston	Joe Morgan	88-74
California	Doug Rader	80-82
Chicago	Jeff Torborg	94-68
Cleveland	John McNamara	77-85
Detroit	Sparky Anderson	79-83
Kansas City	John Wathan	75-86
Milwaukee	Tom Trebelhorn	74-88
Minnesota	Tom Kelly	74-88
New York	Bucky Dent	18-31
	Stump Merrill	49-64
Oakland	Tony La Russa	103-59
Seattle	Jim Lefebvre	77-85
Texas	Bobby Valentine	83-79
Toronto	Cito Gaston	86-76

Awards

Most Valuable Player	R. Henderson, of, Oak
Cy Young	Bob Welch, Oak
Rookie of the Year	Sandy Alomar Jr., c, Cle
Manager of the Year	Jeff Torborg, ChA

STATS All-Star Team

C	Carlton Fisk, ChA	.285	18	65
1B	Cecil Fielder, Det	.277	51	132
2B	Julio Franco, Tex	.296	11	69
3B	Kelly Gruber, Tor	.274	31	118
SS	Alan Trammell, Det	.304	14	89
OF	Jose Canseco, Oak	.274	37	101
OF	Ken Griffey Jr., Sea	.300	22	80
OF	Rickey Henderson, Oak	.325	28	61
DH	Dave Parker, Mil	.289	21	92
P	Roger Clemens, Bos	21-6	1.93	209 K
P	Chuck Finley, Cal	18-9	2.40	177 K
P	Dave Stewart, Oak	22-11	2.56	166 K
P	Bob Welch, Oak	27-6	2.95	127 K
RP	Dennis Eckersley, Oak	4-2	0.61	48 Sv

Postseason

LCS	Oakland 4 vs. Boston 0
World Series	Oakland (AL) 0 vs. Cincinnati (NL) 4

Outstanding Performances

No-Hitters

Randy Johnson, Sea	vs. Det on June 2
Nolan Ryan, Tex	@ Oak on June 11
Dave Stewart, Oak	@ Tor on June 29
Dave Stieb, Tor	@ Cle on September 2

Three-Homer Games

Cecil Fielder, Det	on May 6
Cecil Fielder, Det	on June 6
Randy Milligan, Bal	on June 9
Bo Jackson, KC	on July 17
Tom Brunansky, Bos	on September 29

Cycles

George Brett, KC	on July 25

1990 National League Standings

EAST	W	L	Pct	GB	DIF	W	L	R	OR	HR	OHR	W	L	R	OR	HR	OHR	Run	HR	M/A	May	June	July	Aug	S/O
		Overall						Home Games						Road Games				Park Index				Record by Month			
Pittsburgh	95	67	.586	—	152	49	32	351	299	59	63	46	35	382	320	79	72	93	81	14-6	15-11	14-13	15-11	17-14	20-12
New York	91	71	.562	4.0	19	52	29	397	280	86	52	39	42	378	333	86	67	95	90	9-10	11-13	21-7	17-11	16-14	17-16
Montreal	85	77	.525	10.0	6	47	34	328	268	48	62	38	43	334	330	66	65	90	84	10-9	15-12	17-13	13-14	13-14	17-15
Chicago	77	85	.475	18.0	10	39	42	372	437	75	73	38	43	318	337	61	48	124	136	8-11	13-15	12-18	14-12	15-12	15-17
Philadelphia	77	85	.475	18.0	1	41	40	311	367	47	67	36	45	335	362	56	57	97	101	10-9	14-11	11-17	14-13	11-19	17-16
St. Louis	70	92	.432	25.0	5	34	47	319	366	43	47	36	45	280	332	30	51	112	111	9-11	11-16	11-17	15-13	14-14	10-21
WEST																									
Cincinnati	91	71	.562	—	178	46	35	334	312	70	73	45	36	359	285	55	51	100	135	13-3	17-9	16-14	14-15	15-14	16-16
Los Angeles	86	76	.531	5.0	2	47	34	351	323	54	73	39	42	377	362	75	64	91	91	11-10	14-13	11-15	16-11	16-13	16-15
San Francisco	85	77	.525	6.0	0	49	32	380	340	81	70	36	45	339	370	71	61	102	114	8-12	11-17	19-8	17-10	12-17	18-13
Houston	75	87	.463	16.0	0	49	32	298	271	35	47	26	55	275	385	59	83	86	58	9-10	11-17	12-16	11-18	16-11	16-15
San Diego	75	87	.463	16.0	0	37	44	342	348	63	78	38	43	331	325	60	69	105	109	9-10	15-12	11-15	10-19	15-13	15-18
Atlanta	65	97	.401	26.0	0	37	44	352	427	85	70	28	53	330	394	77	58	108	115	4-13	13-14	13-15	10-19	11-19	14-17

Clinch Date—Pittsburgh 9/30, Cincinnati 9/29.

Team Batting

Team	G	AB	R	OR	H	2B	3B	HR	TB	RBI	TBB	IBB	SO	HBP	SH	SF	SB	CS	SB%	GDP	Avg	OBP	Slg
New York	162	5504	775	613	1410	278	21	172	2246	734	536	65	851	32	54	56	110	33	.77	89	.256	.332	.408
Pittsburgh	162	5388	733	619	1395	288	42	138	2181	693	582	64	914	24	66	66	137	52	.72	115	.259	.336	.405
Los Angeles	162	5491	728	685	1436	222	27	129	2099	669	538	78	952	31	71	48	141	65	.68	110	.262	.336	.382
San Francisco	162	5573	719	710	1459	221	35	152	2206	681	488	61	973	33	76	45	109	56	.66	83	.262	.330	.396
Cincinnati	162	5525	693	597	1466	284	40	125	2205	644	466	73	913	42	88	42	166	66	.72	99	.265	.332	.399
Chicago	162	5600	690	774	1474	240	36	136	2194	649	406	68	869	30	61	51	151	50	.75	100	.263	.322	.392
Atlanta	162	5504	682	821	1376	263	26	162	2177	636	473	36	1010	27	49	31	92	55	.63	101	.250	.316	.396
San Diego	162	5554	673	673	1429	243	35	123	2111	628	509	75	902	28	79	48	138	59	.70	117	.257	.328	.380
Montreal	162	5453	662	598	1363	227	43	114	2018	607	576	67	1024	26	87	47	235	99	.70	96	.250	.330	.370
Philadelphia	162	5535	646	729	1410	237	27	103	2010	619	582	92	915	30	59	39	108	35	.76	115	.255	.333	.363
St. Louis	162	5462	599	698	1398	255	41	73	1954	554	517	54	844	21	77	50	221	74	.75	101	.256	.328	.358
Houston	162	5379	573	656	1301	209	32	94	1856	536	548	64	997	28	79	41	179	83	.68	107	.242	.320	.345
NL Total	1944	65968	8173	8173	16917	2967	405	1521	25257	7650	6221	797	11164	352	876	564	1787	727	.71	1233	.256	.321	.383
NL Avg Team	162	5497	681	681	1410	247	34	127	2105	638	518	66	930	29	73	47	149	61	.71	103	.256	.321	.383

Team Pitching

Team	G	CG	ShO	Rel	Sv	IP	H	R	ER	HR	SH	SF	HB	TBB	IBB	SO	WP	Bk	H/9	SO/9	BB/9	OAvg	OOBP	ERA
Montreal	162	18	11	341	50	1473.1	1349	598	551	127	69	48	38	510	76	991	27	13	8.2	6.1	3.1	.245	.311	3.37
Cincinnati	162	14	12	316	50	1456.1	1338	597	549	124	64	37	34	543	60	1029	48	26	8.3	6.4	3.4	.246	.316	3.39
Pittsburgh	162	18	8	364	43	1447.0	1367	619	546	135	68	38	30	413	48	848	42	22	8.5	5.3	2.6	.251	.305	3.40
New York	162	18	14	268	41	1440.0	1339	613	548	119	53	41	27	444	35	1217	51	14	8.4	7.6	2.8	.246	.304	3.43
Houston	162	12	6	348	37	1450.0	1396	656	581	130	67	61	38	496	74	854	36	15	8.7	5.3	3.1	.255	.318	3.61
San Diego	162	21	4	288	35	1461.2	1437	673	598	147	79	37	19	507	69	928	39	19	8.8	5.7	3.1	.258	.320	3.68
Los Angeles	162	29	12	339	29	1442.0	1364	685	596	137	56	42	28	478	49	1021	63	10	8.5	6.4	3.0	.249	.310	3.72
St. Louis	162	8	13	364	39	1443.1	1432	698	621	98	70	64	34	475	72	833	45	5	8.9	5.2	3.0	.261	.320	3.87
Philadelphia	162	18	7	374	35	1449.0	1381	729	655	124	79	48	29	651	81	840	69	15	8.6	5.2	4.0	.253	.334	4.07
San Francisco	162	14	6	335	45	1446.1	1477	710	655	131	70	50	21	553	84	788	37	19	9.2	4.9	3.4	.267	.333	4.08
Chicago	162	13	7	346	42	1442.2	1510	774	695	121	107	44	28	572	85	877	62	14	9.4	5.5	3.6	.271	.340	4.34
Atlanta	162	17	8	346	30	1429.2	1527	821	728	128	94	54	26	579	64	938	61	15	9.6	5.9	3.6	.275	.343	4.58
NL Total	1944	200	116	4029	476	17381.1	16917	8173	7323	1521	876	564	352	6221	797	11164	580	187	8.8	5.8	3.2	.256	.329	3.79
NL Avg Team	162	17	10	336	40	1448.1	1410	681	610	127	73	47	29	518	66	930	48	16	8.8	5.8	3.2	.256	.329	3.79

Team Fielding

Team	G	PO	A	E	TC	DP	PB	Pct
Cincinnati	162	4369	1690	102	6161	126	19	.983
San Francisco	162	4339	1825	107	6271	148	11	.983
Montreal	162	4420	1648	110	6178	134	21	.982
Philadelphia	162	4347	1739	117	6203	150	8	.981
Chicago	162	4328	1756	124	6208	136	24	.980
St. Louis	162	4330	1734	130	6194	114	11	.979
Los Angeles	162	4326	1612	130	6068	123	10	.979
Pittsburgh	162	4341	1777	134	6252	125	9	.979
Houston	162	4350	1602	131	6083	124	18	.978
New York	162	4320	1565	132	6017	107	20	.978
San Diego	162	4385	1668	141	6194	141	9	.977
Atlanta	162	4289	1735	158	6182	133	15	.974
NL Total	1944	52144	20351	1516	74011	1561	175	.980

Team vs. Team Records

	Atl	ChN	Cin	Hou	LA	Mon	NYN	Phi	Pit	SD	SF	StL	Won
Atl	—	6	8	5	6	6	4	5	5	8	5	7	65
ChN	6	—	4	6	3	11	9	11	4	8	7	8	77
Cin	10	8	—	11	9	9	6	7	6	9	7	9	91
Hou	13	6	7	—	9	5	5	5	5	4	10	6	75
LA	12	9	9	9	—	6	5	8	4	9	8	7	86
Mon	6	7	3	7	6	—	8	10	13	7	7	11	85
NYN	8	9	6	7	7	10	—	10	10	5	7	12	91
Phi	7	7	5	7	4	8	8	—	6	7	8	10	77
Pit	7	14	6	7	8	5	8	12	—	10	8	10	95
SD	10	4	9	14	9	5	7	5	2	—	7	3	75
SF	13	5	11	8	10	5	5	4	4	11	—	9	85
StL	5	10	3	6	5	7	6	8	8	9	3	—	70
Lost	97	85	71	87	76	77	71	85	67	87	77	92	

Seasons: Standings, Leaders

1990 National League Batting Leaders

Games		At-Bats		Runs		Hits		Doubles		Triples	
J. Carter, SD	162	J. Carter, SD	634	R. Sandberg, ChN	116	B. Butler, SF	192	G. Jefferies, NYN	40	M. Duncan, Cin	11
T. Wallach, Mon	161	T. Wallach, Mon	626	B. Bonilla, Pit	112	L. Dykstra, Phi	192	B. Bonilla, Pit	39	T. Gwynn, SD	10
B. Butler, SF	160	B. Bonilla, Pit	625	B. Butler, SF	108	R. Sandberg, ChN	188	C. Sabo, Cin	38	L. Smith, Atl	9
B. Bonilla, Pit	160	B. Butler, SF	622	R. Gant, Atl	107	T. Wallach, Mon	185	T. Wallach, Mon	37	B. Butler, SF	9
2 tied with	159	M. Williams, SF	617	L. Dykstra, Phi	106	B. Larkin, Cin	185	H. Johnson, NYN	37	V. Coleman, StL	9

Home Runs		Total Bases		Runs Batted In		Walks		Intentional Walks		Strikeouts	
R. Sandberg, ChN	40	R. Sandberg, ChN	344	M. Williams, SF	122	J. Clark, SD	104	A. Dawson, ChN	21	A. Galarraga, Mon	169
D. Strawberry, NYN	37	B. Bonilla, Pit	324	B. Bonilla, Pit	120	B. Bonds, Pit	93	E. Murray, LA	21	M. Williams, SF	138
K. Mitchell, SF	35	R. Gant, Atl	310	J. Carter, SD	115	B. Butler, SF	90	T. Gwynn, SD	20	D. Murphy, 2tm	130
B. Bonds, Pit	33	M. Williams, SF	301	B. Bonds, Pit	114	L. Dykstra, Phi	89	J. Lind, Pit	19	J. Presley, Atl	130
M. Williams, SF	33	T. Wallach, Mon	295	D. Strawberry, NYN	108	V. Hayes, Phi	87	J. Carter, SD	18	J. Samuel, LA	126

Hit By Pitch		Sac Hits		Sac Flies		Stolen Bases		Caught Stealing		GDP	
G. Davis, Hou	8	J. Bell, Pit	39	B. Bonilla, Pit	15	V. Coleman, StL	77	E. Yelding, Hou	25	D. Murphy, 2tm	22
J. Carter, SD	7	D. Gooden, NYN	14	W. Clark, SF	13	E. Yelding, Hou	64	D. DeShields, Mon	22	J. Lind, Pit	20
L. Dykstra, Phi	7	E. Whitson, SD	13	P. Guerrero, StL	11	B. Bonds, Pit	52	J. Samuel, LA	20	E. Murray, LA	19
B. Larkin, Cin	7	J. Armstrong, Cin	13	H. Brooks, LA	11	B. Butler, SF	51	B. Butler, SF	19	G. Templeton, SD	17
M. Williams, SF	7	2 tied with	12	3 tied with	10	O. Nixon, Mon	50	V. Coleman, StL	17	2 tied with	16

Runs Created		Runs Created/27 Outs		Batting Average		On-Base Percentage		Slugging Percentage		OBP+Slugging	
B. Bonds, Pit	126	B. Bonds, Pit	8.72	W. McGee, StL	.335	L. Dykstra, Phi	.418	B. Bonds, Pit	.565	B. Bonds, Pit	.970
R. Sandberg, ChN	122	D. Magadan, NYN	7.87	E. Murray, LA	.330	D. Magadan, NYN	.417	R. Sandberg, ChN	.559	E. Murray, LA	.934
L. Dykstra, Phi	118	E. Murray, LA	7.79	D. Magadan, NYN	.328	E. Murray, LA	.414	K. Mitchell, SF	.544	K. Daniels, LA	.920
E. Murray, LA	116	K. Daniels, LA	7.76	L. Dykstra, Phi	.325	B. Bonds, Pit	.406	R. Gant, Atl	.539	R. Sandberg, ChN	.913
D. Strawberry, NYN	107	L. Dykstra, Phi	7.71	A. Dawson, ChN	.310	B. Butler, SF	.397	D. Justice, Atl	.535	D. Justice, Atl	.908

1990 National League Pitching Leaders

Wins		Losses		Winning Percentage		Games		Games Started		Complete Games	
D. Drabek, Pit	22	J. DeLeon, StL	19	D. Drabek, Pit	.786	J. Agosto, Hou	82	F. Viola, NYN	35	R. Martinez, LA	12
F. Viola, NYN	20	J. Magrane, StL	17	R. Martinez, LA	.769	Assenmacher, ChN	74	T. Browning, Cin	35	B. Hurst, SD	9
R. Martinez, LA	20	M. Morgan, LA	15	J. Tudor, StL	.750	G. Harris, SD	73	G. Maddux, ChN	35	D. Drabek, Pit	9
D. Gooden, NYN	19	D. Rasmussen, SD	15	D. Darwin, Hou	.733	R. McDowell, Phi	72	3 tied with	34	G. Maddux, ChN	8
2 tied with	15	G. Maddux, ChN	15	D. Gooden, NYN	.731	D. Akerfelds, Phi	71			3 tied with	7

Shutouts		Saves		Games Finished		Batters Faced		Innings Pitched		Hits Allowed	
B. Hurst, SD	4	J. Franco, NYN	33	R. McDowell, Phi	60	F. Viola, NYN	1016	F. Viola, NYN	249.2	G. Maddux, ChN	242
M. Morgan, LA	4	R. Myers, Cin	31	R. Myers, Cin	59	G. Maddux, ChN	1011	G. Maddux, ChN	237.0	T. Browning, Cin	235
6 tied with	3	L. Smith, StL	27	S. Bedrosian, SF	53	D. Gooden, NYN	983	R. Martinez, LA	234.1	T. Glavine, Atl	232
		D. Smith, Hou	23	J. Franco, NYN	48	J. Smoltz, Atl	966	D. Gooden, NYN	232.2	D. Gooden, NYN	229
		C. Lefferts, SD	23	L. Smith, StL	45	T. Browning, Cin	957	2 tied with	231.1	F. Viola, NYN	227

Home Runs Allowed		Walks		Walks/9 Innings		Strikeouts		Strikeouts/9 Innings		Strikeout/Walk Ratio	
D. Rasmussen, SD	28	J. Smoltz, Atl	90	D. Darwin, Hou	1.7	D. Cone, NYN	233	D. Cone, NYN	9.9	D. Cone, NYN	3.58
M. Scott, Hou	27	J. DeLeon, StL	86	E. Whitson, SD	1.8	D. Gooden, NYN	223	S. Fernandez, NYN	9.1	D. Darwin, Hou	3.52
T. Browning, Cin	24	P. Combs, Phi	86	C. Leibrandt, Atl	1.9	R. Martinez, LA	223	D. Gooden, NYN	8.6	R. Martinez, LA	3.33
R. Martinez, LA	22	J. Deshaies, Hou	84	D. Martinez, Mon	2.0	F. Viola, NYN	182	R. Martinez, LA	8.6	D. Gooden, NYN	3.19
5 tied with	21	2 tied with	78	T. Browning, Cin	2.1	S. Fernandez, NYN	181	J. DeLeon, StL	8.1	D. Martinez, Mon	3.18

Earned Run Average		Component ERA		Hit Batsmen		Wild Pitches		Opponent Average		Opponent OBP	
D. Darwin, Hou	2.21	D. Darwin, Hou	2.31	M. Gardner, Mon	9	J. Smoltz, Atl	14	S. Fernandez, NYN	.200	D. Darwin, Hou	.266
Z. Smith, 2tm	2.55	D. Drabek, Pit	2.40	J. Deshaies, Hou	8	F. Valenzuela, LA	13	J. Rijo, Cin	.212	D. Drabek, Pit	.274
E. Whitson, SD	2.60	D. Martinez, Mon	2.44	J. Magrane, StL	8	F. Viola, NYN	11	R. Martinez, LA	.221	D. Martinez, Mon	.274
F. Viola, NYN	2.67	J. Rijo, Cin	2.57	3 tied with	7	M. Bielecki, ChN	11	D. Drabek, Pit	.225	S. Fernandez, NYN	.277
J. Rijo, Cin	2.70	S. Fernandez, NYN	2.57			J. Magrane, StL	11	D. Darwin, Hou	.225	R. Martinez, LA	.278

1990 National League Miscellaneous

Managers		
Atlanta	Russ Nixon	25-40
	Bobby Cox	40-57
Chicago	Don Zimmer	77-85
Cincinnati	Lou Piniella	91-71
Houston	Art Howe	75-87
Los Angeles	Tom Lasorda	86-76
Montreal	Buck Rodgers	85-77
New York	Davey Johnson	20-22
	Bud Harrelson	71-49
Philadelphia	Nick Leyva	77-85
Pittsburgh	Jim Leyland	95-67
St. Louis	Whitey Herzog	33-47
	Red Schoendienst	13-11
	Joe Torre	24-34
San Diego	Jack McKeon	37-43
	Greg Riddoch	38-44
San Francisco	Roger Craig	85-77

Awards

Most Valuable Player	Barry Bonds, of, Pit
Cy Young	Doug Drabek, Pit
Rookie of the Year	David Justice, 1b, Atl
Manager of the Year	Jim Leyland, Pit

STATS All-Star Team

C	Darren Daulton, Phi	.268	12	57
1B	Eddie Murray, LA	.330	26	95
2B	Ryne Sandberg, ChN	.306	40	100
3B	Matt Williams, SF	.277	33	122
SS	Barry Larkin, Cin	.301	7	67
OF	Barry Bonds, Pit	.301	33	114
OF	Ron Gant, Atl	.303	32	84
OF	Darryl Strawberry, NYN	.277	37	108
P	Doug Drabek, Pit	22-6	2.76	131 K
P	Ramon Martinez, LA	20-6	2.92	223 K
P	Frank Viola, NYN	20-12	2.67	182 K
P	Ed Whitson, SD	14-9	2.60	127 K
RP	Randy Myers, Cin	4-6	2.08	31 Sv

Postseason

LCS	Cincinnati 4 vs. Pittsburgh 2
World Series	Cincinnati (NL) 4 vs. Oakland (AL) 0

Outstanding Performances

No-Hitters
F. Valenzuela, LA   vs. StL on June 29
Terry Mulholland, Phi vs. SF on August 15
Three-Homer Games
Kevin Mitchell, SF   on May 25
Jeff Treadway, Atl   on May 26
Glenn Davis, Hou   on June 1

1991 American League Standings

EAST	Overall W	L	Pct	GB	DIF	Home Games W	L	R	OR	HR	OHR	Road Games W	L	R	OR	HR	OHR	Park Index Run	HR	Record by Month M/A	May	June	July	Aug	S/O
Toronto	91	71	.562	—	134	46	35	359	344	75	72	45	36	325	278	58	49	117	137	12-9	15-12	16-12	15-11	15-14	18-13
Boston	84	78	.519	7.0	46	43	38	378	374	69	76	41	40	353	338	57	71	109	113	11-7	15-13	11-16	11-16	18-11	18-15
Detroit	84	78	.519	7.0	6	49	32	437	402	109	89	35	46	380	392	100	59	109	125	10-9	13-14	14-14	14-12	18-12	15-17
Milwaukee	83	79	.512	8.0	3	43	37	398	398	62	73	40	42	401	346	54	74	109	108	10-9	12-15	12-15	9-18	19-10	21-12
New York	71	91	.438	20.0	0	39	42	356	380	82	84	32	49	318	397	65	68	103	125	6-11	14-13	13-14	13-13	12-19	13-21
Baltimore	67	95	.414	24.0	0	33	48	329	387	80	72	34	47	357	409	90	75	93	92	6-12	10-17	14-14	10-17	13-16	14-19
Cleveland	57	105	.352	34.0	0	30	52	271	377	22	41	27	53	305	382	57	69	92	49	7-10	10-17	7-21	9-18	10-20	14-19
WEST																									
Minnesota	95	67	.586	—	108	51	30	404	342	62	75	44	37	372	310	78	64	109	96	9-11	14-14	22-6	16-10	17-12	17-14
Chicago	87	75	.537	8.0	19	46	35	378	337	74	79	41	40	380	344	65	75	99	109	11-6	10-17	17-12	19-8	12-18	18-14
Texas	85	77	.525	10.0	12	46	35	404	400	79	77	39	42	425	414	98	74	96	91	8-8	18-9	13-14	13-14	15-16	18-16
Oakland	84	78	.519	11.0	39	47	34	357	351	76	67	37	44	403	425	83	88	86	84	13-7	15-12	13-15	15-12	15-14	13-18
Seattle	83	79	.512	12.0	4	45	36	374	319	69	69	38	43	328	355	57	67	101	111	10-11	15-12	14-13	15-12	13-15	16-16
Kansas City	82	80	.506	13.0	1	40	41	344	378	47	40	42	39	383	344	70	65	99	64	8-11	13-14	12-15	16-10	18-11	15-19
California	81	81	.500	14.0	5	40	41	291	303	59	74	41	40	362	346	56	67	84	108	10-10	16-11	15-12	11-15	11-18	18-15

Clinch Date—Toronto 10/02, Minnesota 9/29.

Team Batting

Team	G	AB	R	OR	H	2B	3B	HR	TB	RBI	TBB	IBB	SO	HBP	SH	SF	SB	CS	SB%	GDP	Avg	OBP	Slg
Texas	162	5703	829	814	1539	288	31	177	2420	774	596	51	1039	42	59	41	102	50	.67	128	.270	.348	.424
Detroit	162	5547	817	794	1372	259	26	209	2310	778	699	40	1185	31	38	44	109	47	.70	90	.247	.340	.416
Milwaukee	162	5611	799	744	1523	247	53	116	2224	750	556	48	802	23	52	66	106	68	.61	137	.271	.347	.396
Minnesota	162	5556	776	652	1557	270	42	140	2331	733	526	38	747	40	44	49	107	68	.61	157	.280	.352	.420
Oakland	162	5410	760	776	1342	246	19	159	2103	716	642	56	981	50	41	49	151	64	.70	131	.248	.339	.389
Chicago	162	5594	758	681	1464	226	39	139	2185	722	610	45	896	37	76	41	134	74	.64	132	.262	.343	.391
Boston	162	5530	731	712	1486	305	25	126	2219	691	593	49	820	32	50	51	59	39	.60	143	.269	.348	.401
Kansas City	162	5584	727	722	1475	290	41	117	2198	689	523	47	969	35	53	47	119	68	.64	126	.264	.336	.394
Seattle	162	5494	702	674	1400	268	29	126	2104	665	588	57	811	37	55	62	97	44	.69	139	.255	.338	.383
Baltimore	162	5604	686	796	1421	256	29	170	2245	660	528	33	974	33	47	45	50	33	.60	147	.254	.326	.401
Toronto	162	5489	684	622	1412	295	45	133	2196	649	499	49	1043	58	56	56	148	53	.74	108	.257	.333	.400
New York	162	5541	674	777	1418	249	19	147	2146	630	473	38	861	39	37	50	109	36	.75	125	.256	.324	.387
California	162	5470	653	649	1396	245	29	115	2044	607	448	28	928	38	63	31	94	56	.63	114	.255	.320	.374
Cleveland	162	5470	576	759	1390	236	26	79	1915	546	449	24	888	43	62	46	84	58	.59	146	.254	.321	.350
AL Total	2268	77603	10172	10172	20195	3680	453	1953	30640	9610	7730	603	12944	538	733	687	1469	758	.66	1823	.260	.329	.395
AL Avg Team	162	5543	727	727	1443	263	32	140	2189	686	552	43	925	38	52	49	105	54	.66	130	.260	.329	.395

Team Pitching

Team	G	CG	ShO	Rel	Sv	IP	H	R	ER	HR	SH	SF	HB	TBB	IBB	SO	WP	Bk	H/9	SO/9	BB/9	OAvg	OOBP	ERA
Toronto	162	10	16	347	60	1462.2	1301	622	569	121	53	45	43	523	41	971	55	8	8.0	6.0	3.2	.238	.307	3.50
California	162	18	10	310	50	1441.2	1351	649	591	141	43	35	38	543	29	990	49	11	8.4	6.2	3.4	.250	.321	3.69
Minnesota	162	21	12	291	53	1449.1	1402	652	595	139	46	49	27	488	39	876	57	5	8.7	5.4	3.0	.255	.317	3.69
Chicago	162	28	8	338	40	1478.0	1302	681	622	154	64	50	31	601	25	923	44	6	7.9	5.6	3.7	.239	.315	3.79
Seattle	162	10	13	383	48	1464.1	1387	674	617	136	51	49	47	628	50	1003	82	7	8.5	6.2	3.9	.253	.332	3.79
Kansas City	162	17	12	295	41	1466.0	1473	722	639	105	55	41	43	529	44	1004	47	5	9.0	6.2	3.2	.261	.327	3.92
Boston	162	15	13	328	45	1439.2	1405	712	642	147	42	46	31	530	59	999	42	4	8.8	6.2	3.3	.257	.323	4.01
Milwaukee	162	23	11	341	41	1463.2	1498	744	674	147	60	47	45	527	31	859	53	5	9.2	5.3	3.2	.266	.332	4.14
Cleveland	162	22	8	289	33	1441.1	1551	759	678	110	59	69	39	441	61	862	48	6	9.7	5.4	2.8	.276	.329	4.23
New York	162	3	11	377	37	1444.0	1510	777	709	152	49	38	42	506	29	936	53	14	9.4	5.8	3.2	.271	.334	4.42
Texas	162	9	10	386	41	1479.0	1486	814	735	151	52	56	45	662	37	1022	77	12	9.0	6.2	4.0	.262	.341	4.47
Detroit	162	18	8	326	38	1450.1	1570	794	726	148	65	63	24	593	88	739	50	5	9.7	4.6	3.7	.281	.348	4.51
Oakland	162	14	10	397	49	1444.1	1425	776	734	155	51	54	55	605	30	892	59	7	8.9	5.6	4.1	.260	.342	4.57
Baltimore	162	8	8	372	42	1457.2	1534	796	743	147	43	45	28	504	40	868	49	8	9.5	5.4	3.1	.273	.333	4.59
AL Total	2268	216	150	4780	618	20382.0	20195	10172	9274	1953	733	687	538	7730	603	12944	765	103	8.9	5.7	3.4	.260	.337	4.10
AL Avg Team	162	15	11	341	44	1455.0	1443	727	662	140	52	49	38	552	43	925	55	7	8.9	5.7	3.4	.260	.337	4.10

Team Fielding

Team	G	PO	A	E	TC	DP	PB	Pct
Baltimore	162	4373	1807	91	6271	172	8	.985
Minnesota	162	4348	1779	95	6222	161	12	.985
California	162	4325	1858	102	6285	156	23	.984
Detroit	162	4351	1796	104	6251	171	12	.983
Seattle	162	4393	1783	110	6286	187	24	.983
Oakland	162	4333	1608	107	6048	150	8	.982
Chicago	162	4434	1740	116	6290	151	20	.982
Boston	162	4319	1768	116	6203	165	11	.981
Milwaukee	162	4390	1770	118	6278	125	16	.981
Kansas City	162	4398	1694	125	6217	141	11	.980
Toronto	162	4388	1686	127	6201	115	21	.980
Texas	162	4437	1712	134	6283	138	15	.979
New York	162	4332	1752	133	6217	181	13	.979
Cleveland	162	4324	1712	149	6185	150	19	.976
AL Total	2268	61145	24465	1627	87237	2214	213	.981

Team vs. Team Records

	Bal	Bos	Cal	ChA	Cle	Det	KC	Mil	Min	NYA	Oak	Sea	Tex	Tor	Won
Bal	—	8	6	4	7	5	4	3	4	5	3	4	9	5	67
Bos	5	—	4	7	9	5	7	7	3	6	8	9	5	9	84
Cal	6	8	—	8	7	5	9	6	8	6	1	6	5	6	81
ChA	8	5	8	—	6	4	7	7	8	8	7	7	8	7	87
Cle	6	4	5	6	—	7	4	5	2	6	5	2	4	1	57
Det	8	8	7	8	6	—	8	4	4	8	4	8	6	5	84
KC	8	5	4	6	8	4	—	9	6	7	6	7	7	5	82
Mil	10	6	6	5	8	9	3	—	6	8	3	7	6	6	83
Min	8	9	5	5	10	8	7	6	—	10	8	9	6	4	95
NYA	8	7	6	4	7	5	5	7	2	—	6	3	6	6	71
Oak	9	4	12	6	7	8	7	4	5	6	—	6	4	6	84
Sea	8	3	7	6	10	4	6	6	4	9	7	—	5	5	83
Tex	3	7	8	5	8	6	6	7	7	7	9	8	—	6	85
Tor	8	4	6	5	12	8	7	7	8	7	6	7	6	—	91
Lost	95	78	81	75	105	78	80	79	67	91	78	79	77	71	

Seasons: Standings, Leaders

1991 American League Batting Leaders

Games		At-Bats		Runs		Hits		Doubles		Triples	
C. Ripken Jr., Bal	162	P. Molitor, Mil	665	P. Molitor, Mil	133	P. Molitor, Mil	216	R. Palmeiro, Tex	49	P. Molitor, Mil	13
J. Carter, Tor	162	R. Sierra, Tex	661	J. Canseco, Oak	115	C. Ripken Jr., Bal	210	C. Ripken Jr., Bal	46	L. Johnson, ChA	13
C. Fielder, Det	162	S. Sax, NYA	652	R. Palmeiro, Tex	115	R. Sierra, Tex	203	R. Sierra, Tex	44	R. Alomar, Tor	11
3 tied with	161	C. Ripken Jr., Bal	650	D. White, Tor	110	R. Palmeiro, Tex	203	4 tied with	42	D. White, Tor	10
		D. White, Tor	642	R. Sierra, Tex	110	J. Franco, Tex	201			M. Devereaux, Bal	10

Home Runs		Total Bases		Runs Batted In		Walks		Intentional Walks		Strikeouts	
C. Fielder, Det	44	C. Ripken Jr., Bal	368	C. Fielder, Det	133	F. Thomas, ChA	138	W. Boggs, Bos	25	R. Deer, Det	175
J. Canseco, Oak	44	R. Palmeiro, Tex	336	J. Canseco, Oak	122	M. Tettleton, Det	101	H. Baines, Oak	22	J. Canseco, Oak	152
C. Ripken Jr., Bal	34	R. Sierra, Tex	332	R. Sierra, Tex	116	R. Henderson, Oak	98	K. Griffey Jr., Sea	21	C. Fielder, Det	151
J. Carter, Tor	33	P. Molitor, Mil	325	C. Ripken Jr., Bal	114	J. Clark, Bos	96	P. Molitor, Mil	16	T. Fryman, Det	149
F. Thomas, ChA	32	J. Carter, Tor	321	F. Thomas, ChA	109	C. Davis, Min	95	C. Ripken Jr., Bal	15	D. White, Tor	135

Hit By Pitch		Sac Hits		Sac Flies		Stolen Bases		Caught Stealing		GDP	
J. Carter, Tor	10	L. Sojo, Cal	19	A. Davis, Sea	10	R. Henderson, Oak	58	L. Polonia, Cal	23	K. Puckett, Min	27
D. Valle, Sea	9	R. Alomar, Tor	16	J. Olerud, Tor	10	R. Alomar, Tor	53	R. Henderson, Oak	18	A. Belle, Cle	24
J. Canseco, Oak	9	H. Reynolds, Sea	14	9 tied with	9	T. Raines, ChA	51	A. Cole, Cle	17	T. Pena, Bos	23
3 tied with	8	3 tied with	13			L. Polonia, Cal	48	T. Raines, ChA	15	R. Milligan, Bal	23
						M. Cuyler, Det	41	O. Guillen, ChA	15	R. Ventura, ChA	22

Runs Created		Runs Created/27 Outs		Batting Average		On-Base Percentage		Slugging Percentage		OBP+Slugging	
F. Thomas, ChA	137	F. Thomas, ChA	9.16	J. Franco, Tex	.341	F. Thomas, ChA	.453	D. Tartabull, KC	.593	F. Thomas, ChA	1.006
P. Molitor, Mil	132	D. Tartabull, KC	8.64	W. Boggs, Bos	.331	W. Randolph, Mil	.424	C. Ripken Jr., Bal	.566	D. Tartabull, KC	.990
C. Ripken Jr., Bal	125	P. Molitor, Mil	7.62	W. Randolph, Mil	.327	W. Boggs, Bos	.421	J. Canseco, Oak	.556	C. Ripken Jr., Bal	.940
R. Sierra, Tex	121	K. Griffey Jr., Sea	7.55	K. Griffey Jr., Sea	.327	J. Franco, Tex	.408	F. Thomas, ChA	.553	K. Griffey Jr., Sea	.926
C. Fielder, Det	117	L. Whitaker, Det	7.50	P. Molitor, Mil	.325	E. Martinez, Sea	.405	R. Palmeiro, Tex	.532	R. Palmeiro, Tex	.922

1991 American League Pitching Leaders

Wins		Losses		Winning Percentage		Games		Games Started		Complete Games	
B. Gullickson, Det	20	K. McCaskill, Cal	19	J. Hesketh, Bos	.750	D. Ward, Tor	81	6 tied with	35	J. McDowell, ChA	15
S. Erickson, Min	20	G. Swindell, Cle	16	S. Erickson, Min	.714	M. Jackson, Sea	72			R. Clemens, Bos	13
M. Langston, Cal	19	C. Nagy, Cle	15	M. Langston, Cal	.704	G. Olson, Bal	72			J. Morris, Min	10
4 tied with	18	3 tied with	14	B. Gullickson, Det	.690	B. Swift, Sea	71			J. Navarro, Mil	10
				B. Wegman, Mil	.682	2 tied with	70			W. Terrell, Det	8

Shutouts		Saves		Games Finished		Batters Faced		Innings Pitched		Hits Allowed	
R. Clemens, Bos	4	B. Harvey, Cal	46	B. Harvey, Cal	63	R. Clemens, Bos	1077	R. Clemens, Bos	271.1	W. Terrell, Det	257
J. McDowell, ChA	3	D. Eckersley, Oak	43	G. Olson, Bal	62	J. Morris, Min	1032	J. McDowell, ChA	253.2	B. Gullickson, Det	256
B. Holman, Sea	3	R. Aguilera, Min	42	R. Aguilera, Min	60	J. McDowell, ChA	1028	J. Morris, Min	246.2	D. Stewart, Oak	245
K. Appier, KC	3	J. Reardon, Bos	40	D. Eckersley, Oak	59	D. Stewart, Oak	1014	M. Langston, Cal	246.1	G. Swindell, Cle	241
S. Erickson, Min	3	J. Montgomery, KC	33	B. Thigpen, ChA	58	2 tied with	1002	K. Tapani, Min	244.0	J. Navarro, Mil	237

Home Runs Allowed		Walks		Walks/9 Innings		Strikeouts		Strikeouts/9 Innings		Strikeout/Walk Ratio	
R. DeLucia, Sea	31	R. Johnson, Sea	152	G. Swindell, Cle	1.2	R. Clemens, Bos	241	N. Ryan, Tex	10.6	G. Swindell, Cle	5.45
M. Langston, Cal	30	D. Stewart, Oak	105	S. Sanderson, NYA	1.3	R. Johnson, Sea	228	R. Johnson, Sea	10.2	S. Sanderson, NYA	4.48
F. Tanana, Det	26	M. Moore, Oak	105	K. Tapani, Min	1.5	N. Ryan, Tex	203	R. Clemens, Bos	8.0	R. Clemens, Bos	3.71
B. Welch, Oak	25	C. Finley, Cal	101	B. Gullickson, Det	1.7	J. McDowell, ChA	191	E. Hanson, Sea	7.4	K. Tapani, Min	3.38
3 tied with	24	M. Langston, Cal	96	B. Wegman, Mil	1.9	M. Langston, Cal	183	K. Appier, KC	6.8	B. Saberhagen, KC	3.02

Earned Run Average		Component ERA		Hit Batsmen		Wild Pitches		Opponent Average		Opponent OBP	
R. Clemens, Bos	2.62	N. Ryan, Tex	1.98	M. Boddicker, KC	13	J. Morris, Min	15	N. Ryan, Tex	.172	N. Ryan, Tex	.263
T. Candiotti, 2tm	2.65	R. Clemens, Bos	2.23	K. Brown, Tex	13	M. Moore, Oak	14	R. Johnson, Sea	.213	R. Clemens, Bos	.270
B. Wegman, Mil	2.84	B. Saberhagen, KC	2.51	T. Stottlemyre, Tor	12	E. Hanson, Sea	14	M. Langston, Cal	.215	K. Tapani, Min	.277
J. Abbott, Cal	2.89	T. Candiotti, 2tm	2.67	R. Johnson, Sea	12	3 tied with	12	R. Clemens, Bos	.221	S. Sanderson, NYA	.279
N. Ryan, Tex	2.91	K. Tapani, Min	2.79	2 tied with	11			T. Candiotti, 2tm	.228	B. Saberhagen, KC	.280

1991 American League Miscellaneous

Managers

Baltimore	Frank Robinson	13-24
	Johnny Oates	54-71
Boston	Joe Morgan	84-78
California	Doug Rader	61-63
	Buck Rodgers	20-18
Chicago	Jeff Torborg	87-75
Cleveland	John McNamara	25-52
	Mike Hargrove	32-53
Detroit	Sparky Anderson	84-78
Kansas City	John Wathan	15-22
	Bob Schaefer	1-0
	Hal McRae	66-58
Milwaukee	Tom Trebelhorn	83-79
Minnesota	Tom Kelly	95-67
New York	Stump Merrill	71-91
Oakland	Tony La Russa	84-78
Seattle	Jim Lefebvre	83-79
Texas	Bobby Valentine	85-77
Toronto	Cito Gaston	66-54
	Gene Tenace	19-14
	Cito Gaston	6-3

Awards

Most Valuable Player	Cal Ripken Jr., ss, Bal
Cy Young	Roger Clemens, Bos
Rookie of the Year	C. Knoblauch, 2b, Min
Manager of the Year	Tom Kelly, Min

STATS All-Star Team

C	Mickey Tettleton, Det	.263	31	89
1B	Cecil Fielder, Det	.261	44	133
2B	Julio Franco, Tex	.341	15	78
3B	Wade Boggs, Bos	.332	8	51
SS	Cal Ripken Jr., Bal	.323	34	114
OF	Jose Canseco, Oak	.266	44	122
OF	Ken Griffey Jr., Sea	.327	22	100
OF	Danny Tartabull, KC	.316	31	100
DH	Frank Thomas, ChA	.318	32	109
P	Jim Abbott, Cal	18-11	2.89	158 K
P	Roger Clemens, Bos	18-10	2.62	241 K
P	Scott Erickson, Min	20-8	3.18	108 K
P	Mark Langston, Cal	19-8	3.00	183 K
RP	Bryan Harvey, Cal	2-4	1.60	46 Sv

Postseason

LCS	Minnesota 4 vs. Toronto 1
World Series	Minnesota (AL) 4 vs. Atlanta (NL) 3

Outstanding Performances

No-Hitters
Nolan Ryan, Tex vs. Tor on May 1
Wilson Alvarez, ChA @ Bal on August 11
Bret Saberhagen, KC vs. ChA on August 26

Three-Homer Games
Dave Winfield, Cal on April 13
Harold Baines, Oak on May 7
Danny Tartabull, KC on July 6
Jack Clark, Bos on July 31
D. Henderson, Oak on August 3

Cycles
Paul Molitor, Mil on May 15

1991 National League Standings

EAST	W	L	Pct	GB	DIF	W	L	R	OR	HR	OHR	W	L	R	OR	HR	OHR	Run	HR	M/A	May	June	July	Aug	S/O
																		Park Index		Record by Month					
Pittsburgh	98	64	.605	—	172	52	32	382	314	61	55	46	32	386	318	65	62	92	85	13-7	17-8	15-12	15-12	17-12	21-13
St. Louis	84	78	.519	14.0	1	52	32	345	293	32	41	32	46	306	355	36	73	90	62	13-8	11-14	16-12	13-13	16-12	15-19
Philadelphia	78	84	.481	20.0	0	47	36	341	334	61	53	31	48	288	346	50	58	101	100	9-12	13-13	10-18	10-15	20-9	16-17
Chicago	77	83	.481	20.0	4	46	37	386	396	93	75	31	46	309	338	66	42	112	144	10-11	14-12	10-18	14-11	17-12	12-19
New York	77	84	.478	20.5	14	40	42	332	348	57	55	37	42	308	298	60	53	108	95	12-8	14-11	13-15	16-11	8-21	14-18
Montreal	71	90	.441	26.5	1	33	35	216	233	35	33	38	55	363	422	60	78	78	67	7-13	13-14	13-15	10-15	9-19	19-14
WEST																									
Atlanta	94	68	.580	—	27	48	33	418	368	83	73	46	35	331	276	58	45	129	151	8-10	17-9	12-17	16-10	19-11	22-11
Los Angeles	93	69	.574	1.0	132	54	27	342	280	57	46	39	42	323	285	51	50	102	102	10-10	17-10	18-9	13-13	13-16	22-11
San Diego	84	78	.519	10.0	22	42	39	315	320	65	72	42	39	321	326	56	67	98	111	11-10	13-15	14-14	10-14	15-14	21-11
San Francisco	75	87	.463	19.0	0	43	38	306	305	69	62	32	49	343	392	72	81	83	86	8-12	8-20	17-10	15-9	14-16	13-20
Cincinnati	74	88	.457	20.0	10	39	42	373	376	104	77	35	46	316	315	60	50	119	165	11-8	12-15	18-10	8-16	15-16	10-23
Houston	65	97	.401	29.0	0	37	44	302	330	27	44	28	53	303	387	52	85	92	52	8-11	10-18	11-17	12-13	12-17	12-21

Clinch Date—Pittsburgh 9/22, Atlanta 10/05.

Team Batting

Team	G	AB	R	OR	H	2B	3B	HR	TB	RBI	TBB	IBB	SO	HBP	SH	SF	SB	CS	SB%	GDP	Avg	OBP	Slg
Pittsburgh	162	5449	768	632	1433	259	50	126	2170	725	620	62	901	35	99	66	124	46	.73	111	.263	.349	.398
Atlanta	162	5456	749	644	1407	255	30	141	2145	704	563	55	906	32	86	45	165	76	.68	104	.258	.336	.393
Chicago	160	5522	695	734	1395	232	26	159	2156	654	442	41	879	36	75	55	123	64	.66	87	.253	.318	.390
Cincinnati	162	5501	689	691	1419	250	27	164	2215	654	488	54	1006	32	72	41	124	56	.69	85	.258	.327	.403
Los Angeles	162	5408	665	565	1366	191	29	108	1939	605	583	50	957	28	94	46	126	68	.65	109	.253	.334	.359
St. Louis	162	5362	651	648	1366	239	53	68	1915	599	532	48	857	21	58	47	202	110	.65	94	.255	.330	.357
San Francisco	162	5463	649	697	1345	215	48	141	2079	605	471	59	973	40	90	33	95	57	.63	91	.246	.314	.381
New York	161	5359	640	646	1305	250	24	117	1954	605	578	53	789	27	60	52	153	70	.69	97	.244	.326	.365
San Diego	162	5408	636	646	1321	204	36	124	1960	591	501	60	1069	32	78	38	101	64	.61	122	.244	.316	.362
Philadelphia	162	5521	629	680	1332	248	33	111	1979	590	490	48	1026	21	52	49	92	30	.75	114	.241	.311	.358
Houston	162	5504	605	717	1345	240	43	79	1908	570	502	45	1027	35	63	43	125	68	.65	87	.244	.316	.347
Montreal	161	5412	579	655	1329	236	42	95	1934	536	484	51	1056	28	65	47	221	100	.69	97	.246	.316	.357
NL Total	1940	65365	7955	7955	16363	2819	441	1430	24354	7438	6254	626	11446	367	892	562	1651	809	.67	1198	.250	.317	.373
NL Avg Team	162	5447	663	663	1364	235	37	119	2030	620	521	52	954	31	74	47	138	67	.67	100	.250	.317	.373

Team Pitching

Team	G	CG	ShO	Rel	Sv	IP	H	R	ER	HR	SH	SF	HB	TBB	IBB	SO	WP	Bk	H/9	SO/9	BB/9	OAvg	OOBP	ERA
Los Angeles	162	15	14	367	40	1458.0	1312	565	496	96	74	39	28	500	77	1028	48	12	8.1	6.3	3.1	.241	.306	3.06
Pittsburgh	162	18	11	353	51	1456.2	1411	632	557	117	59	34	30	401	34	919	40	12	8.7	5.7	2.5	.256	.308	3.44
Atlanta	162	18	7	345	48	1452.2	1304	644	564	118	74	39	28	481	39	969	66	13	8.1	6.0	3.0	.240	.303	3.49
New York	161	12	11	314	39	1437.1	1403	646	569	108	83	46	25	410	41	1028	59	14	8.8	6.4	2.6	.257	.309	3.56
San Diego	162	14	11	334	47	1452.2	1385	646	578	139	72	50	13	457	56	921	49	13	8.6	5.7	2.8	.252	.308	3.58
Montreal	161	12	14	367	39	1440.1	1304	655	583	111	67	33	32	584	42	909	51	9	8.1	5.7	3.6	.244	.320	3.64
St. Louis	162	9	5	369	51	1435.1	1367	648	588	114	75	52	47	454	52	822	33	7	8.6	5.2	2.8	.255	.315	3.69
Cincinnati	162	7	11	354	43	1440.0	1372	691	613	127	73	52	28	560	41	997	60	9	8.6	6.2	3.5	.253	.323	3.83
Philadelphia	162	16	11	321	35	1463.0	1346	680	628	111	78	61	43	670	58	988	81	6	8.3	6.1	4.1	.246	.329	3.86
Houston	162	7	13	365	36	1453.0	1347	717	646	129	69	52	29	651	62	1033	46	17	8.3	6.4	4.0	.247	.328	4.00
San Francisco	162	10	10	334	45	1442.0	1397	697	646	143	71	46	36	544	60	905	44	14	8.7	5.6	3.4	.257	.326	4.03
Chicago	162	12	4	360	40	1456.2	1415	734	653	117	96	58	28	542	62	942	47	18	8.7	5.7	3.3	.257	.324	4.03
NL Total	1940	150	122	4183	514	17387.2	16363	7955	7121	1430	891	562	367	6254	626	11446	625	138	8.5	5.9	3.2	.250	.325	3.69
NL Avg Team	162	13	10	349	43	1448.2	1364	663	593	119	74	47	31	521	52	954	52	12	8.5	5.9	3.2	.250	.325	3.69

Team Fielding

Team	G	PO	A	E	TC	DP	PB	Pct
St. Louis	162	4306	1689	107	6102	133	8	.982
San Francisco	162	4326	1753	109	6188	151	9	.982
Chicago	160	4370	1830	113	6313	120	19	.982
San Diego	162	4358	1731	113	6202	130	9	.982
Pittsburgh	162	4370	1846	120	6336	134	9	.981
Philadelphia	162	4389	1623	119	6131	111	9	.981
Los Angeles	162	4374	1795	123	6292	126	8	.980
Cincinnati	162	4320	1615	125	6060	131	20	.979
Montreal	161	4321	1796	133	6250	128	22	.979
Atlanta	162	4358	1834	138	6330	122	14	.978
New York	161	4312	1766	143	6221	112	12	.977
Houston	162	4359	1617	161	6137	129	16	.974
NL Total	1940	52163	20895	1504	74562	1527	155	.980

Team vs. Team Records

	Atl	ChN	Cin	Hou	LA	Mon	NYN	Phi	Pit	SD	SF	StL	Won
Atl	—	6	11	13	7	5	9	5	9	11	9	9	94
ChN	6	—	4	9	2	10	11	8	7	4	6	10	77
Cin	7	8	—	9	6	6	5	9	2	8	10	4	74
Hou	5	3	9	—	8	2	7	7	4	6	9	5	65
LA	11	10	12	10	—	5	7	7	7	10	8	6	93
Mon	7	7	6	10	7	—	4	4	6	6	7	7	71
NYN	3	6	7	5	5	14	—	11	6	7	6	7	77
Phi	7	10	3	5	5	14	7	—	6	9	6	6	78
Pit	3	11	10	8	5	12	12	12	—	7	7	11	98
SD	7	8	10	12	8	6	5	3	5	—	11	9	84
SF	9	6	8	9	10	5	6	6	5	7	—	4	75
StL	3	8	8	7	6	11	11	12	7	3	8	—	84
Lost	68	83	88	97	69	90	84	84	64	78	87	78	

Seasons: Standings, Leaders

1991 National League Batting Leaders

Games		At-Bats		Runs		Hits		Doubles		Triples	
B. Butler, LA	161	M. Grace, ChN	619	B. Butler, LA	112	T. Pendleton, Atl	187	B. Bonilla, Pit	44	R. Lankford, StL	15
M. Grace, ChN	160	B. Butler, LA	615	H. Johnson, NYN	108	B. Butler, LA	182	F. Jose, StL	40	T. Gwynn, SD	11
S. Finley, Hou	159	J. Bell, Pit	608	R. Sandberg, ChN	104	C. Sabo, Cin	175	P. O'Neill, Cin	36	S. Finley, Hou	10
R. Sandberg, ChN	158	S. Finley, Hou	596	B. Bonilla, Pit	102	B. Bonilla, Pit	174	T. Zeile, StL	36	M. Grissom, Mon	9
3 tied with	157	J. Samuel, LA	594	R. Gant, Atl	101	F. Jose, StL	173	2 tied with	35	L. Gonzalez, Hou	9

Home Runs		Total Bases		Runs Batted In		Walks		Intentional Walks		Strikeouts	
H. Johnson, NYN	38	T. Pendleton, Atl	303	H. Johnson, NYN	117	B. Butler, LA	108	F. McGriff, SD	26	D. DeShields, Mon	151
M. Williams, SF	34	W. Clark, SF	303	B. Bonds, Pit	116	B. Bonds, Pit	107	B. Bonds, Pit	25	F. McGriff, SD	135
R. Gant, Atl	32	H. Johnson, NYN	302	W. Clark, SF	116	F. McGriff, SD	105	E. Murray, LA	17	J. Samuel, LA	133
A. Dawson, ChN	31	M. Williams, SF	294	F. McGriff, SD	106	D. DeShields, Mon	95	J. Kruk, Phi	16	M. Williams, SF	128
F. McGriff, SD	31	C. Sabo, Cin	294	R. Gant, Atl	105	B. Bonilla, Pit	90	P. O'Neill, Cin	14	D. Strawberry, LA	125

Hit By Pitch		Sac Hits		Sac Flies		Stolen Bases		Caught Stealing		GDP	
J. Bagwell, Hou	13	J. Bell, Pit	30	H. Johnson, NYN	15	M. Grissom, Mon	76	B. Butler, LA	28	B. Santiago, SD	21
L. Smith, Atl	9	T. Glavine, Atl	15	B. Bonds, Pit	13	O. Nixon, Atl	72	D. DeShields, Mon	23	D. Murphy, Phi	20
L. Gonzalez, Hou	8	Z. Smith, Pit	13	A. Van Slyke, Pit	11	D. DeShields, Mon	56	O. Nixon, Atl	21	J. Lind, Pit	20
G. Carter, LA	7	R. Tomlin, Pit	13	S. Dunston, ChN	11	R. Lankford, StL	44	R. Lankford, StL	20	K. Caminiti, Hou	18
B. Hatcher, Cin	7	3 tied with	12	B. Bonilla, Pit	11	B. Bonds, Pit	43	S. Finley, Hou	18	E. Murray, LA	17

Runs Created		Runs Created/27 Outs		Batting Average		On-Base Percentage		Slugging Percentage		OBP+Slugging	
B. Bonds, Pit	124	B. Bonds, Pit	8.49	T. Pendleton, Atl	.319	B. Bonds, Pit	.410	W. Clark, SF	.536	B. Bonds, Pit	.924
R. Sandberg, ChN	123	W. Clark, SF	7.79	H. Morris, Cin	.318	B. Butler, LA	.401	H. Johnson, NYN	.535	W. Clark, SF	.895
W. Clark, SF	117	R. Sandberg, ChN	7.53	T. Gwynn, SD	.317	F. McGriff, SD	.396	T. Pendleton, Atl	.517	F. McGriff, SD	.890
B. Bonilla, Pit	111	B. Bonilla, Pit	6.95	W. McGee, SF	.312	B. Bonilla, Pit	.391	B. Bonds, Pit	.514	B. Larkin, Cin	.884
H. Johnson, NYN	104	B. Larkin, Cin	6.72	F. Jose, StL	.305	J. Bagwell, Hou	.387	B. Larkin, Cin	.506	B. Bonilla, Pit	.883

1991 National League Pitching Leaders

Wins		Losses		Winning Percentage		Games		Games Started		Complete Games	
J. Smiley, Pit	20	B. Black, SF	16	J. Smiley, Pit	.714	B. Jones, Mon	77	G. Maddux, ChN	37	D. Martinez, Mon	9
T. Glavine, Atl	20	F. Viola, NYN	15	J. Rijo, Cin	.714	Assenmacher, ChN	75	C. Leibrandt, Atl	36	T. Glavine, Atl	9
S. Avery, Atl	18	T. Browning, Cin	14	M. Williams, Phi	.706	M. Stanton, Atl	74	T. Browning, Cin	36	T. Mulholland, Phi	8
R. Martinez, LA	17	D. Drabek, Pit	14	S. Avery, Atl	.692	J. Agosto, StL	72	J. Smoltz, Atl	36	G. Maddux, ChN	7
2 tied with	16	D. Cone, NYN	14	B. Hurst, SD	.652	T. Burke, 2tm	72	4 tied with	35	2 tied with	6

Shutouts		Saves		Games Finished		Batters Faced		Innings Pitched		Hits Allowed	
D. Martinez, Mon	5	L. Smith, StL	47	L. Smith, StL	61	G. Maddux, ChN	1070	G. Maddux, ChN	263.0	F. Viola, NYN	259
R. Martinez, LA	4	R. Dibble, Cin	31	M. Williams, Phi	60	T. Glavine, Atl	989	T. Glavine, Atl	246.2	D. Drabek, Pit	245
B. Black, SF	3	J. Franco, NYN	30	R. Dibble, Cin	57	T. Browning, Cin	983	M. Morgan, LA	236.1	T. Browning, Cin	241
Z. Smith, Pit	3	M. Williams, Phi	30	D. Righetti, SF	49	F. Viola, NYN	980	D. Drabek, Pit	234.2	Z. Smith, Pit	234
T. Mulholland, Phi	3	D. Righetti, SF	24	J. Franco, NYN	48	D. Drabek, Pit	977	D. Cone, NYN	232.2	G. Maddux, ChN	232

Home Runs Allowed		Walks		Walks/9 Innings		Strikeouts		Strikeouts/9 Innings		Strikeout/Walk Ratio	
T. Browning, Cin	32	J. DeJesus, Phi	128	Z. Smith, Pit	1.1	D. Cone, NYN	241	D. Cone, NYN	9.3	Z. Smith, Pit	4.14
B. Black, SF	25	B. Barnes, Mon	84	B. Tewksbury, StL	1.8	G. Maddux, ChN	198	J. Rijo, Cin	7.6	D. Cone, NYN	3.30
F. Viola, NYN	25	D. Kile, Hou	84	T. Mulholland, Phi	1.9	T. Glavine, Atl	192	P. Harnisch, Hou	7.1	J. Rijo, Cin	3.13
J. Armstrong, Cin	25	P. Harnisch, Hou	83	J. Smiley, Pit	1.9	J. Rijo, Cin	172	D. Gooden, NYN	7.1	G. Maddux, ChN	3.00
A. Benes, SD	23	R. Myers, Cin	80	B. Smith, StL	2.0	P. Harnisch, Hou	172	T. Glavine, Atl	7.0	J. Smiley, Pit	2.93

Earned Run Average		Component ERA		Hit Batsmen		Wild Pitches		Opponent Average		Opponent OBP	
D. Martinez, Mon	2.39	J. Rijo, Cin	2.23	J. Burkett, SF	10	J. Smoltz, Atl	20	P. Harnisch, Hou	.212	J. Rijo, Cin	.272
J. Rijo, Cin	2.51	M. Morgan, LA	2.37	J. Agosto, StL	8	D. Cone, NYN	17	J. Rijo, Cin	.219	T. Glavine, Atl	.277
T. Glavine, Atl	2.55	D. Martinez, Mon	2.46	M. Williams, Phi	8	J. Grimsley, Phi	14	T. Glavine, Atl	.222	M. Morgan, LA	.278
T. Belcher, LA	2.62	T. Glavine, Atl	2.47	3 tied with	7	R. Darling, 3tm	13	K. Hill, StL	.224	D. Martinez, Mon	.282
P. Harnisch, Hou	2.70	P. Harnisch, Hou	2.65			2 tied with	11	J. DeJesus, Phi	.224	A. Benes, SD	.285

1991 National League Miscellaneous

Managers

Atlanta	Bobby Cox	94-68
Chicago	Don Zimmer	18-19
	Joe Altobelli	0-1
	Jim Essian	59-63
Cincinnati	Lou Piniella	74-88
Houston	Art Howe	65-97
Los Angeles	Tom Lasorda	93-69
Montreal	Buck Rodgers	20-29
	Tom Runnells	51-61
New York	Bud Harrelson	74-80
	Mike Cubbage	3-4
Philadelphia	Nick Leyva	4-9
	Jim Fregosi	74-75
Pittsburgh	Jim Leyland	98-64
St. Louis	Joe Torre	84-78
San Diego	Greg Riddoch	84-78
San Francisco	Roger Craig	75-87

Awards

Most Valuable Player	Terry Pendleton, 3b, Atl
Cy Young	Tom Glavine, Atl
Rookie of the Year	Jeff Bagwell, 1b, Hou
Manager of the Year	Bobby Cox, Atl

STATS All-Star Team

C	Craig Biggio, Hou	.295	4	46
1B	Will Clark, SF	.301	29	116
2B	Ryne Sandberg, ChN	.291	26	100
3B	Terry Pendleton, Atl	.319	22	86
SS	Barry Larkin, Cin	.302	20	69
OF	Barry Bonds, Pit	.292	25	116
OF	Bobby Bonilla, Pit	.302	18	100
OF	Ron Gant, Atl	.251	32	105
P	Tom Glavine, Atl	20-11	2.55	192 K
P	Dennis Martinez, Mon	14-11	2.39	123 K
P	Jose Rijo, Cin	15-6	2.51	172 K
P	John Smiley, Pit	20-8	3.08	129 K
RP	Lee Smith, StL	6-3	2.34	47 Sv

Postseason

LCS	Atlanta 4 vs. Pittsburgh 3
World Series	Atlanta (NL) 3 vs. Minnesota (AL) 4

Outstanding Performances

Perfect Games
D. Martinez, Mon   @ LA on July 28

No-Hitters
Tommy Greene, Phi @ Mon on May 23

Three-Homer Games
Barry Larkin, Cin   on June 28

Cycles
R. Thompson, SF   on April 22
Ray Lankford, StL   on September 15

1992 American League Standings

1992 American League Standings

EAST	Overall					Home Games						Road Games						Park Index		Record by Month					
	W	L	Pct	GB	DIF	W	L	R	OR	HR	OHR	W	L	R	OR	HR	OHR	Run	HR	M/A	May	June	July	Aug	S/O
Toronto	96	66	.593	—	161	53	28	390	334	79	60	43	38	390	348	84	64	98	94	16-7	15-12	14-12	16-10	14-16	21-9
Milwaukee	92	70	.568	4.0	0	53	28	339	254	35	51	39	42	401	350	47	76	79	70	10-9	13-15	16-11	16-12	15-14	22-9
Baltimore	89	73	.549	7.0	22	43	38	339	333	75	69	46	35	366	323	73	55	98	113	13-8	16-11	15-13	13-14	16-12	16-15
Cleveland	76	86	.469	20.0	0	41	40	366	397	62	94	35	46	308	349	65	65	116	120	8-15	11-16	12-15	13-13	16-12	16-15
New York	76	86	.469	20.0	7	41	40	385	387	88	70	35	46	348	359	75	59	109	118	13-8	13-14	11-17	11-15	13-17	15-15
Detroit	75	87	.463	21.0	0	38	42	389	399	91	90	37	45	402	395	91	65	101	119	7-14	14-14	14-14	15-13	15-13	12-18
Boston	73	89	.451	23.0	0	44	37	328	341	45	46	29	52	271	328	39	61	112	91	9-9	15-12	11-17	13-15	12-18	13-18
WEST																									
Oakland	96	66	.593	—	139	51	30	365	326	76	73	45	36	380	346	66	56	95	122	14-8	13-14	18-9	15-11	19-10	17-14
Minnesota	90	72	.556	6.0	41	48	33	375	326	56	56	42	39	372	327	48	65	100	99	9-12	18-8	18-11	16-11	12-17	17-13
Chicago	86	76	.531	10.0	11	50	32	368	314	54	62	36	44	370	376	56	61	89	97	11-8	12-15	14-14	13-14	18-10	18-15
Texas	77	85	.475	19.0	8	36	45	317	376	71	63	41	40	365	377	88	50	93	97	13-11	16-12	14-13	11-15	11-18	12-16
California	72	90	.444	24.0	0	41	40	311	340	44	60	31	50	268	331	44	70	109	91	10-17	10-17	14-13	14-13	13-16	13-17
Kansas City	72	90	.444	24.0	0	44	37	314	336	24	41	28	53	296	331	51	65	104	56	3-17	14-14	15-12	13-14	14-14	13-19
Seattle	64	98	.395	32.0	0	38	43	355	398	78	63	26	55	324	401	71	66	104	103	10-11	11-17	10-18	11-17	13-14	9-21

Clinch Date—Toronto 10/03, Oakland 9/28.

Team Batting

Team	G	AB	R	OR	H	2B	3B	HR	TB	RBI	TBB	IBB	SO	HBP	SH	SF	SB	CS	SB%	GDP	Avg	OBP	Slg
Detroit	162	5515	791	794	1411	256	16	182	2245	746	675	42	1055	24	43	53	66	45	.59	124	.256	.345	.407
Toronto	162	5536	780	682	1458	265	40	163	2292	737	561	41	933	47	26	54	129	39	.77	123	.263	.342	.414
Minnesota	162	5582	747	653	1544	275	27	104	2185	701	527	53	834	53	46	59	123	74	.62	130	.277	.351	.391
Oakland	162	5387	745	672	1389	219	24	142	2082	693	707	46	831	49	72	59	143	59	.71	139	.258	.386	.386
Milwaukee	162	5504	740	604	1477	272	35	82	2065	683	511	45	779	33	61	72	256	115	.69	102	.268	.342	.375
Chicago	162	5498	738	690	1434	269	36	110	2105	686	622	48	784	31	47	69	160	57	.74	134	.261	.347	.383
New York	162	5593	733	746	1462	281	18	163	2268	703	536	51	903	42	26	55	78	37	.68	138	.261	.336	.406
Baltimore	162	5485	705	656	1423	243	36	148	2182	680	647	55	827	51	50	59	89	48	.65	139	.259	.349	.398
Texas	162	5537	682	753	1387	266	23	159	2176	646	550	36	1036	50	56	45	81	44	.65	115	.250	.329	.393
Seattle	162	5564	679	799	1466	278	24	149	2239	638	474	47	841	38	52	51	100	55	.65	148	.263	.331	.402
Cleveland	162	5620	674	746	1495	227	24	127	2151	637	448	46	885	45	42	44	144	67	.68	140	.266	.330	.383
Kansas City	162	5501	610	667	1411	284	42	75	2004	568	439	30	741	51	45	46	131	71	.65	121	.256	.325	.364
Boston	162	5461	599	669	1343	259	21	84	1896	567	591	46	865	31	60	43	44	48	.48	117	.246	.328	.347
California	162	5364	579	671	1306	202	20	88	1812	537	416	40	882	40	56	40	160	101	.61	137	.243	.308	.338
AL Total	2268	77147	9802	9802	20006	3596	386	1776	29702	9222	7704	626	12196	585	682	749	1704	860	.66	1807	.259	.328	.385
AL Avg Team	162	5511	700	700	1429	257	28	127	2122	659	550	45	871	42	49	54	122	61	.66	129	.259	.328	.385

Team Pitching

Team	G	CG	ShO	Rel	Sv	IP	H	R	ER	HR	SH	SF	HB	TBB	IBB	SO	WP	Bk	H/9	SO/9	BB/9	OAvg	OOBP	ERA
Milwaukee	162	19	14	338	39	1457.0	1344	604	556	127	47	42	47	435	33	793	37	8	8.3	4.9	2.7	.246	.305	3.43
Boston	162	22	13	328	39	1448.2	1403	669	585	107	51	49	41	535	56	943	50	6	8.7	5.9	3.3	.255	.323	3.63
Minnesota	162	16	13	323	50	1453.0	1391	653	600	121	50	49	36	479	30	923	52	5	8.6	5.7	3.0	.254	.316	3.72
Oakland	162	8	9	400	58	1447.0	1396	672	599	129	56	56	41	601	46	843	67	4	8.7	5.2	3.7	.256	.332	3.73
Baltimore	162	20	16	290	48	1464.0	1419	656	617	124	59	47	36	518	38	846	45	6	8.7	5.2	3.2	.257	.322	3.79
Kansas City	162	9	12	340	44	1447.1	1426	667	613	106	50	67	39	512	50	834	42	10	8.9	5.2	3.2	.259	.323	3.81
Chicago	162	21	5	292	52	1461.2	1400	690	623	123	43	45	55	550	48	810	35	6	8.6	5.0	3.4	.252	.323	3.84
California	162	26	13	297	42	1446.0	1449	671	617	130	47	50	39	532	40	888	42	6	9.0	5.5	3.3	.264	.331	3.84
Toronto	162	18	14	284	49	1440.2	1346	682	627	124	32	55	45	541	37	954	66	6	8.4	6.0	3.4	.248	.318	3.92
Texas	162	19	3	359	42	1460.1	1471	753	665	113	44	64	48	598	30	1034	72	6	9.1	6.4	3.7	.264	.337	4.10
Cleveland	162	13	7	379	46	1470.0	1507	746	672	159	56	56	34	566	31	890	53	12	9.2	5.4	3.5	.268	.336	4.11
New York	162	20	9	308	44	1452.2	1453	746	681	129	39	53	35	612	49	851	52	7	9.0	5.3	3.8	.263	.338	4.22
Seattle	162	21	9	372	30	1445.0	1467	799	730	129	56	56	60	661	50	894	61	6	9.1	5.6	4.1	.266	.348	4.55
Detroit	162	10	4	355	36	1435.2	1534	794	736	155	52	63	29	564	88	693	57	3	9.6	4.3	3.5	.277	.343	4.61
AL Total	2268	242	141	4665	619	20329.0	20006	9802	8921	1776	682	749	585	7704	626	12196	731	90	8.9	5.4	3.4	.259	.337	3.95
AL Avg Team	162	17	10	333	44	1452.0	1429	700	637	127	49	54	42	550	45	871	52	6	8.9	5.4	3.4	.259	.337	3.95

Team Fielding

Team	G	PO	A	E	TC	DP	PB	Pct
Milwaukee	162	4371	1741	89	6201	146	5	.986
Baltimore	162	4392	1708	93	6193	168	15	.985
Minnesota	162	4359	1776	95	6230	155	14	.985
Toronto	162	4322	1591	93	6006	109	15	.985
Seattle	162	4335	1763	112	6210	170	9	.982
New York	162	4358	1739	114	6211	165	16	.982
Detroit	162	4307	1766	116	6189	164	8	.981
Kansas City	162	4342	1748	122	6212	164	14	.980
Chicago	162	4385	1778	129	6292	134	13	.979
Oakland	162	4341	1576	125	6042	158	8	.979
California	162	4338	1811	134	6283	172	5	.979
Boston	162	4346	1871	139	6356	170	8	.978
Cleveland	162	4410	1727	141	6278	176	9	.978
Texas	162	4381	1692	154	6227	153	19	.975
AL Total	2268	60987	24287	1656	86930	2204	158	.981

Team vs. Team Records

	Bal	Bos	Cal	ChA	Cle	Det	KC	Mil	Min	NYA	Oak	Sea	Tex	Tor	Won
Bal	—	8	8	6	7	10	8	6	6	5	6	7	7	5	89
Bos	5	—	8	6	6	4	7	5	3	7	5	6	4	7	73
Cal	4	4	—	3	6	7	8	5	2	7	5	7	9	5	72
ChA	6	6	10	—	7	10	7	5	8	8	5	4	5	5	86
Cle	6	7	6	5	—	5	5	5	6	7	6	7	5	6	76
Det	3	9	5	2	8	—	7	5	3	5	6	9	8	5	75
KC	4	5	5	6	7	5	—	7	6	5	4	7	6	5	72
Mil	7	8	7	7	8	8	5	—	6	6	7	8	7	8	92
Min	6	9	11	5	6	9	7	6	—	7	5	8	6	5	90
NYA	8	6	5	4	6	8	7	7	5	—	6	6	6	2	76
Oak	6	7	8	8	6	6	9	5	8	6	—	12	9	6	96
Sea	5	6	6	9	5	3	6	4	5	6	1	—	4	4	64
Tex	5	8	4	8	7	4	7	5	7	6	4	9	—	3	77
Tor	8	6	7	7	7	8	7	5	7	11	6	8	9	—	96
Lost	73	89	90	76	86	87	90	70	72	86	66	98	85	66	

1992 American League Batting Leaders

Games		At-Bats		Runs		Hits		Doubles		Triples	
C. Ripken Jr., Bal	162	T. Fryman, Det	659	T. Phillips, Det	114	K. Puckett, Min	210	E. Martinez, Sea	46	L. Johnson, ChA	12
C. Baerga, Cle	161	C. Baerga, Cle	657	F. Thomas, ChA	108	C. Baerga, Cle	205	F. Thomas, ChA	46	M. Devereaux, Bal	11
T. Fryman, Det	161	M. Devereaux, Bal	653	R. Alomar, Tor	105	P. Molitor, Mil	195	R. Yount, Mil	40	B. Anderson, Bal	10
K. Puckett, Min	160	D. White, Tor	641	K. Puckett, Min	104	S. Mack, Min	189	D. Mattingly, NYA	40	T. Raines, ChA	9
F. Thomas, ChA	160	D. Mattingly, NYA	640	C. Knoblauch, Min	104	F. Thomas, ChA	185	K. Griffey Jr., Sea	39	2 tied with	8

Home Runs		Total Bases		Runs Batted In		Walks		Intentional Walks		Strikeouts	
J. Gonzalez, Tex	43	K. Puckett, Min	313	C. Fielder, Det	124	M. Tettleton, Det	122	W. Boggs, Bos	19	D. Palmer, Tex	154
M. McGwire, Oak	42	J. Carter, Tor	310	J. Carter, Tor	119	F. Thomas, ChA	122	M. Tettleton, Det	18	C. Fielder, Det	151
C. Fielder, Det	35	J. Gonzalez, Tex	309	F. Thomas, ChA	115	T. Phillips, Det	114	K. Griffey Jr., Sea	15	J. Buhner, Sea	146
J. Carter, Tor	34	F. Thomas, ChA	307	G. Bell, ChA	112	R. Milligan, Bal	106	3 tied with	14	T. Fryman, Det	144
A. Belle, Cle	34	M. Devereaux, Bal	303	A. Belle, Cle	112	D. Tartabull, NYA	103			J. Gonzalez, Tex	143

Hit By Pitch		Sac Hits		Sac Flies		Stolen Bases		Caught Stealing		GDP	
S. Mack, Min	15	J. Browne, Oak	16	J. Carter, Tor	13	K. Lofton, Cle	66	L. Polonia, Cal	21	G. Bell, ChA	29
M. Macfarlane, KC	15	M. Bordick, Oak	14	R. Yount, Mil	12	P. Listach, Mil	54	C. Curtis, Cal	18	G. Jefferies, KC	24
K. Miller, KC	14	T. Pena, Bos	13	C. Knoblauch, Min	12	B. Anderson, Bal	53	P. Listach, Mil	18	T. Martinez, Sea	24
C. Baerga, Cle	13	3 tied with	12	P. Molitor, Mil	11	L. Polonia, Cal	51	B. Anderson, Bal	16	T. Steinbach, Oak	20
J. Carter, Tor	11			F. Thomas, ChA	11	R. Alomar, Tor	49	G. Vaughn, Mil	15	L. Johnson, ChA	20

Runs Created		Runs Created/27 Outs		Batting Average		On-Base Percentage		Slugging Percentage		OBP+Slugging	
F. Thomas, ChA	127	F. Thomas, ChA	8.15	E. Martinez, Sea	.343	F. Thomas, ChA	.439	M. McGwire, Oak	.585	F. Thomas, ChA	.975
P. Molitor, Mil	117	D. Tartabull, NYA	7.93	K. Puckett, Min	.329	D. Tartabull, NYA	.409	E. Martinez, Sea	.544	M. McGwire, Oak	.970
R. Alomar, Tor	117	M. McGwire, Oak	7.61	C. Baerga, Cle	.323	R. Alomar, Tor	.405	F. Thomas, ChA	.536	E. Martinez, Sea	.948
K. Puckett, Min	115	R. Alomar, Tor	7.54	P. Molitor, Mil	.320	E. Martinez, Sea	.404	K. Griffey Jr., Sea	.535	D. Tartabull, NYA	.898
B. Anderson, Bal	113	E. Martinez, Sea	7.40	S. Mack, Min	.315	S. Mack, Min	.394	J. Gonzalez, Tex	.529	K. Griffey Jr., Sea	.896

1992 American League Pitching Leaders

Wins		Losses		Winning Percentage		Games		Games Started		Complete Games	
J. Morris, Tor	21	E. Hanson, Sea	17	M. Mussina, Bal	.783	K. Rogers, Tex	81	R. Sutcliffe, Bal	36	J. McDowell, ChA	13
K. Brown, Tex	21	M. Perez, NYA	16	J. Morris, Tor	.778	D. Ward, Tor	79	M. Moore, Oak	36	R. Clemens, Bos	11
J. McDowell, ChA	20	R. Sutcliffe, Bal	15	J. Guzman, Tor	.762	S. Olin, Cle	72	4 tied with	35	K. Brown, Tex	11
R. Clemens, Bos	18	J. Armstrong, Cle	15	C. Bosio, Mil	.727	D. Lilliquist, Cle	71			M. Perez, NYA	10
M. Mussina, Bal	18	J. Abbott, Cal	15	J. McDowell, ChA	.667	G. Harris, Bos	70			C. Nagy, Cle	10

Shutouts		Saves		Games Finished		Batters Faced		Innings Pitched		Hits Allowed	
R. Clemens, Bos	5	D. Eckersley, Oak	51	D. Eckersley, Oak	65	K. Brown, Tex	1108	K. Brown, Tex	265.2	K. Brown, Tex	262
M. Mussina, Bal	4	R. Aguilera, Min	41	J. Montgomery, KC	62	B. Wegman, Mil	1079	B. Wegman, Mil	261.2	R. Sutcliffe, Bal	251
D. Fleming, Sea	4	J. Montgomery, KC	39	S. Olin, Cle	62	J. McDowell, ChA	1079	J. McDowell, ChA	260.2	B. Wegman, Mil	251
4 tied with	3	G. Olson, Bal	36	R. Aguilera, Min	61	R. Sutcliffe, Bal	1018	C. Nagy, Cle	252.0	J. McDowell, ChA	247
		T. Henke, Tor	34	2 tied with	56	C. Nagy, Cle	1018	M. Perez, NYA	247.2	C. Nagy, Cle	245

Home Runs Allowed		Walks		Walks/9 Innings		Strikeouts		Strikeouts/9 Innings		Strikeout/Walk Ratio	
B. Gullickson, Det	35	R. Johnson, Sea	144	C. Bosio, Mil	1.7	R. Johnson, Sea	241	R. Johnson, Sea	10.3	R. Clemens, Bos	3.35
B. McDonald, Bal	32	B. Witt, 2tm	114	M. Mussina, Bal	1.8	M. Perez, NYA	218	J. Guzman, Tor	8.2	C. Nagy, Cle	2.96
D. Cook, Cle	29	M. Moore, Oak	103	B. Wegman, Mil	1.9	R. Clemens, Bos	208	M. Perez, NYA	7.9	K. Tapani, Min	2.88
S. Sanderson, NYA	28	C. Finley, Cal	98	K. Tapani, Min	2.0	J. Guzman, Tex	179	R. Clemens, Bos	7.6	C. Bosio, Mil	2.73
B. Wegman, Mil	28	K. McCaskill, ChA	95	B. Gullickson, Det	2.0	J. McDowell, ChA	178	J. Guzman, Tex	7.2	M. Mussina, Bal	2.71

Earned Run Average		Component ERA		Hit Batsmen		Wild Pitches		Opponent Average		Opponent OBP	
R. Clemens, Bos	2.41	J. Guzman, Tor	2.34	R. Johnson, Sea	18	M. Moore, Oak	22	R. Johnson, Sea	.206	M. Mussina, Bal	.278
K. Appier, KC	2.46	R. Clemens, Bos	2.38	N. Ryan, Tex	12	J. Guzman, Tor	14	J. Guzman, Tor	.207	R. Clemens, Bos	.279
M. Mussina, Bal	2.54	K. Appier, KC	2.41	J. Morris, Tor	10	4 tied with	13	K. Appier, KC	.217	K. Appier, KC	.281
J. Guzman, Tor	2.64	M. Mussina, Bal	2.54	K. Brown, Tex	10			R. Clemens, Bos	.224	J. Smiley, Min	.286
J. Abbott, Cal	2.77	J. Smiley, Min	2.74	T. Stottlemyre, Tor	10			J. Smiley, Min	.231	J. Guzman, Tor	.286

1992 American League Miscellaneous

Managers

Baltimore	Johnny Oates	89-73
Boston	Butch Hobson	73-89
California	Buck Rodgers	19-20
	John Wathan	39-50
	Buck Rodgers	14-20
Chicago	Gene Lamont	86-76
Cleveland	Mike Hargrove	76-86
Detroit	Sparky Anderson	75-87
Kansas City	Hal McRae	72-90
Milwaukee	Phil Garner	92-70
Minnesota	Tom Kelly	90-72
New York	Buck Showalter	76-86
Oakland	Tony La Russa	96-66
Seattle	Bill Plummer	64-98
Texas	Bobby Valentine	45-41
	Toby Harrah	32-44
Toronto	Cito Gaston	96-66

Awards

Most Valuable Player	D. Eckersley, p, Oak
Cy Young	Dennis Eckersley, Oak
Rookie of the Year	Pat Listach, ss, Mil
Manager of the Year	Tony La Russa, Oak

STATS All-Star Team

C	Mickey Tettleton, Det	.238	32	83
1B	Frank Thomas, ChA	.323	24	115
2B	Roberto Alomar, Tor	.310	8	76
3B	Edgar Martinez, Sea	.343	18	73
SS	Travis Fryman, Det	.266	20	96
OF	Brady Anderson, Bal	.271	21	80
OF	Ken Griffey Jr., Sea	.308	27	103
OF	Kirby Puckett, Min	.329	19	110
DH	Dave Winfield, Tor	.290	26	108
P	Kevin Appier, KC	15-8	2.46	150 K
P	Roger Clemens, Bos	18-11	2.41	208 K
P	Jack McDowell, ChA	20-10	3.18	178 K
P	Mike Mussina, Bal	18-5	2.54	130 K
RP	Dennis Eckersley, Oak	7-1	1.91	51 Sv

Postseason

LCS	Toronto 4 vs. Oakland 2
World Series	Toronto (AL) 4 vs. Atlanta (NL) 2

Outstanding Performances

Three-Homer Games

Juan Gonzalez, Tex	on June 7
Albert Belle, Cle	on September 6

1992 National League Standings

EAST	W	L	Pct	GB	DIF	W	L	R	OR	HR	OHR	W	L	R	OR	HR	OHR	Run	HR	M/A	May	June	July	Aug	S/O
		Overall						Home Games						Road Games				Park Index				Record by Month			
Pittsburgh	96	66	.593	—	172	53	28	363	277	51	37	43	38	330	318	55	64	99	74	15-5	11-17	12-15	12-15	19-8	22-10
Montreal	87	75	.537	9.0	6	43	38	331	334	50	48	44	37	317	247	52	44	118	102	9-14	12-11	14-13	19-11	17-10	16-16
St. Louis	83	79	.512	13.0	10	45	36	328	297	55	52	38	43	303	307	39	66	102	102	11-11	16-11	10-16	11-16	16-11	19-14
Chicago	78	84	.481	18.0	1	43	38	315	297	59	49	35	46	278	327	45	58	101	105	7-13	13-15	18-10	11-13	18-12	11-21
New York	72	90	.444	24.0	1	41	40	288	305	42	49	31	50	311	348	51	49	90	91	13-9	12-15	11-17	13-11	11-17	12-21
Philadelphia	70	92	.432	26.0	2	41	40	369	331	67	49	29	52	317	386	51	64	100	101	10-12	12-13	12-15	11-18	8-18	17-16
WEST																									
Atlanta	98	64	.605	—	77	51	30	343	290	72	45	47	34	339	279	66	44	102	106	11-11	12-16	19-6	16-9	19-10	21-12
Cincinnati	90	72	.556	8.0	63	53	28	355	289	60	60	37	44	305	320	39	49	103	136	11-10	15-11	18-9	15-12	12-17	19-13
San Diego	82	80	.506	16.0	10	45	36	339	334	87	64	37	44	278	302	48	47	116	159	12-11	16-11	13-14	15-12	13-13	13-19
Houston	81	81	.500	17.0	9	47	34	302	293	49	41	34	47	306	375	47	73	87	75	10-11	11-17	14-14	11-14	15-14	20-11
San Francisco	72	90	.444	26.0	31	42	39	307	294	57	60	30	51	267	353	48	68	97	101	12-10	15-11	7-19	16-12	9-19	13-19
Los Angeles	63	99	.389	35.0	1	37	44	277	281	26	33	26	55	271	355	46	49	89	62	9-13	13-10	9-18	12-19	10-18	10-21

Clinch Date—Pittsburgh 9/27, Atlanta 9/29.

Team Batting

Team	G	AB	R	OR	H	2B	3B	HR	TB	RBI	TBB	IBB	SO	HBP	SH	SF	SB	CS	SB%	GDP	Avg	OBP	Slg
Pittsburgh	162	5527	693	595	1409	272	54	106	2107	656	569	88	872	25	89	56	110	53	.67	102	.255	.333	.381
Philadelphia	162	5500	686	717	1392	255	36	118	2073	638	509	45	1059	52	64	46	127	31	.80	111	.253	.327	.377
Atlanta	162	5480	682	569	1391	223	48	138	2124	641	493	58	924	26	93	50	126	60	.68	82	.254	.324	.388
Cincinnati	162	5460	660	609	1418	281	44	99	2084	606	563	83	888	21	66	52	125	65	.66	123	.260	.337	.382
Montreal	162	5477	648	581	1381	263	37	102	2024	601	463	43	976	43	82	55	196	63	.76	104	.252	.322	.370
St. Louis	162	5594	631	604	1464	262	44	94	2096	599	495	49	996	32	68	41	208	118	.64	96	.262	.330	.375
San Diego	162	5476	617	636	1396	255	30	135	2116	576	453	67	864	26	78	41	69	52	.57	127	.255	.320	.386
Houston	162	5480	608	668	1350	255	38	96	1969	582	506	65	1025	48	88	40	139	54	.72	97	.246	.320	.359
New York	162	5340	599	653	1254	259	17	93	1826	564	572	53	956	28	74	45	129	52	.71	117	.235	.317	.342
Chicago	162	5590	593	624	1420	221	41	104	2035	566	417	49	901	31	78	40	77	51	.60	121	.254	.314	.364
San Francisco	162	5456	574	647	1330	220	36	105	1937	532	435	53	1067	39	101	39	112	64	.64	111	.244	.309	.355
Los Angeles	162	5368	548	636	1333	201	34	72	1818	499	503	36	899	24	102	40	142	78	.65	111	.248	.320	.339
NL Total	1944	65748	7539	7539	16538	2967	459	1262	24209	7060	5978	689	11342	395	983	545	1560	741	.68	1302	.252	.315	.368
NL Avg Team	162	5479	628	628	1378	247	38	105	2017	588	498	57	945	33	82	45	130	62	.68	109	.252	.315	.368

Team Pitching

Team	G	CG	ShO	Rel	Sv	IP	H	R	ER	HR	SH	SF	HB	TBB	IBB	SO	WP	Bk	H/9	SO/9	BB/9	OAvg	OOBP	ERA
Atlanta	162	26	24	338	41	1460.0	1321	569	510	89	53	37	26	489	55	948	58	10	8.1	5.8	3.0	.242	.305	3.14
Montreal	162	11	14	349	49	1468.0	1296	581	530	92	77	35	50	525	41	1014	48	11	7.9	6.2	3.2	.238	.309	3.25
Pittsburgh	162	20	20	354	43	1479.2	1410	595	551	101	80	48	30	455	61	844	52	9	8.6	5.1	2.8	.254	.312	3.35
St. Louis	162	10	9	424	47	1480.0	1405	604	556	118	77	46	32	400	46	842	41	3	8.5	5.1	2.4	.252	.303	3.38
Chicago	162	16	11	372	37	1469.0	1337	624	554	107	88	52	44	575	75	901	68	14	8.2	5.5	3.5	.246	.320	3.39
Los Angeles	162	18	13	353	29	1438.0	1401	636	545	82	109	44	28	553	95	981	64	10	8.8	6.1	3.5	.257	.326	3.41
Cincinnati	162	9	11	357	55	1449.2	1362	609	558	109	78	47	28	470	51	1060	54	6	8.5	6.6	2.9	.251	.312	3.46
San Diego	162	9	11	363	46	1461.1	1444	636	581	111	93	43	21	439	53	971	25	15	8.9	6.0	2.7	.261	.315	3.58
San Francisco	162	9	12	386	30	1461.0	1385	647	586	128	88	42	35	502	61	927	33	22	8.5	5.7	3.1	.253	.318	3.61
New York	162	17	13	333	34	1446.2	1404	653	591	98	72	52	36	482	54	1025	34	9	8.7	6.4	3.0	.256	.318	3.68
Houston	162	5	12	422	45	1459.1	1386	668	606	114	87	46	38	539	60	978	45	14	8.5	6.0	3.3	.252	.320	3.74
Philadelphia	162	27	7	323	34	1428.0	1387	717	655	113	81	53	27	549	37	851	43	9	8.7	5.4	3.5	.257	.326	4.13
NL Total	1944	177	157	4374	490	17500.2	16538	7539	6823	1262	983	545	395	5978	689	11342	565	129	8.5	5.8	3.1	.252	.323	3.51
NL Avg Team	162	15	13	365	41	1458.2	1378	628	569	105	82	45	33	498	57	945	47	11	8.5	5.8	3.1	.252	.323	3.51

Team Fielding

Team	G	PO	A	E	TC	DP	PB	Pct
St. Louis	162	4440	1777	94	6311	146	8	.985
Pittsburgh	162	4439	1931	101	6471	144	11	.984
Cincinnati	162	4349	1665	96	6110	128	8	.984
Atlanta	162	4380	1703	109	6192	121	13	.982
Chicago	162	4407	1934	114	6455	142	14	.982
San Francisco	162	4383	1782	113	6278	174	17	.982
San Diego	162	4384	1719	115	6218	127	2	.982
Houston	162	4378	1621	114	6113	125	13	.981
New York	162	4340	1717	116	6173	134	10	.981
Montreal	162	4404	1774	124	6302	113	9	.980
Philadelphia	162	4284	1614	131	6029	128	13	.978
Los Angeles	162	4314	1827	174	6315	136	20	.972
NL Total	1944	52502	21064	1401	74967	1618	138	.981

Team vs. Team Records

	Atl	ChN	Cin	Hou	LA	Mon	NYN	Phi	Pit	SD	SF	StL	Won
Atl	—	10	9	13	12	4	7	6	7	13	11	6	98
ChN	2	—	5	8	6	7	9	9	8	5	8	11	78
Cin	9	7	—	10	11	5	7	7	6	11	10	7	90
Hou	5	4	8	—	13	8	5	8	6	7	12	5	81
LA	6	6	7	5	—	4	5	5	5	9	7	4	63
Mon	8	11	7	4	8	—	12	9	9	8	5	6	87
NYN	5	9	5	7	7	6	—	6	4	4	10	9	72
Phi	6	9	5	4	7	9	12	—	5	3	3	7	70
Pit	5	10	6	6	7	9	14	13	—	5	6	15	96
SD	5	7	7	11	9	4	8	9	7	—	11	4	82
SF	7	4	8	6	11	7	2	9	6	7	—	5	72
StL	6	7	5	7	8	12	9	11	3	8	7	—	83
Lost	64	84	72	81	99	75	90	92	66	80	90	79	

1992 National League Batting Leaders

Games		At-Bats		Runs		Hits		Doubles		Triples	
C. Biggio, Hou	162	M. Grissom, Mon	653	B. Bonds, Pit	109	A. Van Slyke, Pit	199	A. Van Slyke, Pit	45	D. Sanders, Atl	14
S. Finley, Hou	162	T. Pendleton, Atl	640	D. Hollins, Phi	104	T. Pendleton, Atl	199	M. Duncan, Phi	40	S. Finley, Hou	13
J. Bagwell, Hou	162	J. Bell, Pit	632	A. Van Slyke, Pit	103	R. Sandberg, ChN	186	W. Clark, SF	40	A. Van Slyke, Pit	12
T. Pendleton, Atl	160	T. Fernandez, SD	622	R. Sandberg, ChN	100	M. Grace, ChN	185	R. Lankford, StL	40	B. Butler, LA	11
2 tied with	159	A. Van Slyke, Pit	614	M. Grissom, Mon	99	G. Sheffield, SD	184	2 tied with	39	L. Alicea, StL	11

Home Runs		Total Bases		Runs Batted In		Walks		Intentional Walks		Strikeouts	
F. McGriff, SD	35	G. Sheffield, SD	323	D. Daulton, Phi	109	B. Bonds, Pit	127	B. Bonds, Pit	32	R. Lankford, StL	147
B. Bonds, Pit	34	R. Sandberg, ChN	312	T. Pendleton, Atl	105	F. McGriff, SD	96	F. McGriff, SD	23	D. Hollins, Phi	110
G. Sheffield, SD	33	A. Van Slyke, Pit	310	F. McGriff, SD	104	B. Butler, LA	95	W. Clark, SF	23	M. Williams, SF	109
D. Daulton, Phi	27	T. Pendleton, Atl	303	B. Bonds, Pit	103	C. Biggio, Hou	94	J. Oliver, Cin	19	3 tied with	108
D. Hollins, Phi	27	2 tied with	295	G. Sheffield, SD	100	J. Kruk, Phi	92	P. O'Neill, Cin	15		

Hit By Pitch		Sac Hits		Sac Flies		Stolen Bases		Caught Stealing		GDP	
D. Hollins, Phi	19	B. Butler, LA	24	J. Bagwell, Hou	13	M. Grissom, Mon	78	R. Lankford, StL	24	D. Jackson, SD	21
J. Bagwell, Hou	12	J. Bell, Pit	19	W. Clark, SF	11	D. DeShields, Mon	46	B. Butler, LA	21	G. Sheffield, SD	19
R. Amaro, Phi	9	S. Finley, Hou	16	A. Van Slyke, Pit	9	B. Roberts, Cin	44	T. Fernandez, SD	20	J. Bagwell, Hou	17
4 tied with	8	R. Belliard, Atl	13	4 tied with	8	S. Finley, Hou	44	O. Nixon, Atl	18	T. Pendleton, Atl	16
		G. Maddux, ChN	13			O. Smith, StL	43	2 tied with	16	5 tied with	15

Runs Created		Runs Created/27 Outs		Batting Average		On-Base Percentage		Slugging Percentage		OBP+Slugging	
B. Bonds, Pit	130	B. Bonds, Pit	10.08	G. Sheffield, SD	.330	B. Bonds, Pit	.456	B. Bonds, Pit	.624	B. Bonds, Pit	1.080
A. Van Slyke, Pit	113	D. Daulton, Phi	7.96	A. Van Slyke, Pit	.324	J. Kruk, Phi	.423	G. Sheffield, SD	.580	G. Sheffield, SD	.965
T. Pendleton, Atl	113	G. Sheffield, SD	7.24	J. Kruk, Phi	.323	B. Butler, LA	.413	F. McGriff, SD	.556	F. McGriff, SD	.950
R. Sandberg, ChN	109	F. McGriff, SD	7.14	B. Roberts, Cin	.323	F. McGriff, SD	.394	D. Daulton, Phi	.524	D. Daulton, Phi	.908
R. Lankford, StL	109	W. Clark, SF	7.11	T. Gwynn, SD	.317	B. Roberts, Cin	.393	R. Sandberg, ChN	.510	A. Van Slyke, Pit	.886

1992 National League Pitching Leaders

Wins		Losses		Winning Percentage		Games		Games Started		Complete Games	
G. Maddux, ChN	20	T. Candiotti, LA	15	B. Tewksbury, StL	.762	J. Boever, Hou	81	G. Maddux, ChN	35	T. Mulholland, Phi	12
T. Glavine, Atl	20	O. Hershiser, LA	15	T. Glavine, Atl	.714	D. Jones, Hou	80	J. Smoltz, Atl	35	D. Drabek, Pit	10
4 tied with	16	5 tied with	14	C. Leibrandt, Atl	.682	X. Hernandez, Hou	77	S. Avery, Atl	35	C. Schilling, Phi	10
				M. Morgan, ChN	.667	M. Perez, StL	77	6 tied with	34	G. Maddux, ChN	9
				D. Cone, NYN	.650	J. Innis, NYN	76			J. Smoltz, Atl	9

Shutouts		Saves		Games Finished		Batters Faced		Innings Pitched		Hits Allowed	
D. Cone, NYN	5	L. Smith, StL	43	D. Jones, Hou	70	G. Maddux, ChN	1061	G. Maddux, ChN	268.0	A. Benes, SD	230
T. Glavine, Atl	5	R. Myers, SD	38	J. Wetteland, Mon	58	D. Drabek, Pit	1021	D. Drabek, Pit	256.2	T. Mulholland, Phi	227
5 tied with	4	J. Wetteland, Mon	37	R. Myers, SD	57	J. Smoltz, Atl	1021	J. Smoltz, Atl	246.2	R. Tomlin, Pit	226
		D. Jones, Hou	36	M. Williams, Phi	56	S. Avery, Atl	969	M. Morgan, ChN	240.0	B. Hurst, SD	223
		M. Williams, Phi	29	L. Smith, StL	55	M. Morgan, ChN	966	S. Avery, Atl	233.2	D. Drabek, Pit	218

Home Runs Allowed		Walks		Walks/9 Innings		Strikeouts		Strikeouts/9 Innings		Strikeout/Walk Ratio	
B. Black, SF	23	D. Cone, NYN	82	B. Tewksbury, StL	0.8	J. Smoltz, Atl	215	D. Cone, NYN	9.8	B. Tewksbury, StL	4.55
B. Hurst, SD	22	B. Ojeda, LA	81	R. Cormier, StL	1.6	D. Cone, NYN	214	S. Fernandez, NYN	8.1	J. Rijo, Cin	3.89
O. Olivares, StL	20	T. Belcher, Cin	80	G. Swindell, Cin	1.7	G. Maddux, ChN	199	J. Smoltz, Atl	7.8	R. Cormier, StL	3.55
K. Abbott, Phi	20	J. Smoltz, Atl	80	T. Mulholland, Phi	1.8	S. Fernandez, NYN	193	J. Rijo, Cin	7.3	G. Swindell, Cin	3.37
F. Castillo, ChN	19	M. Morgan, ChN	79	R. Tomlin, Pit	1.8	D. Drabek, Pit	177	P. Harnisch, Hou	7.1	D. Drabek, Pit	3.28

Earned Run Average		Component ERA		Hit Batsmen		Wild Pitches		Opponent Average		Opponent OBP	
B. Swift, SF	2.08	C. Schilling, Phi	1.86	G. Maddux, ChN	14	J. Smoltz, Atl	17	C. Schilling, Phi	.201	C. Schilling, Phi	.254
B. Tewksbury, StL	2.16	G. Maddux, ChN	2.01	D. Martinez, Mon	9	D. Henry, Cin	12	G. Maddux, ChN	.210	B. Tewksbury, StL	.265
G. Maddux, ChN	2.18	D. Martinez, Mon	2.19	D. Cone, NYN	9	4 tied with	11	S. Fernandez, NYN	.210	D. Martinez, Mon	.271
C. Schilling, Phi	2.35	S. Fernandez, NYN	2.24	M. Gardner, Mon	9			D. Martinez, Mon	.211	G. Maddux, ChN	.272
D. Martinez, Mon	2.47	B. Tewksbury, StL	2.40	O. Hershiser, LA	8			D. Cone, NYN	.223	S. Fernandez, NYN	.273

1992 National League Miscellaneous

Managers

Atlanta	Bobby Cox	98-64
Chicago	Jim Lefebvre	78-84
Cincinnati	Lou Piniella	90-72
Houston	Art Howe	81-81
Los Angeles	Tom Lasorda	63-99
Montreal	Tom Runnells	17-20
	Felipe Alou	70-55
New York	Jeff Torborg	72-90
Philadelphia	Jim Fregosi	70-92
Pittsburgh	Jim Leyland	96-66
St. Louis	Joe Torre	83-79
San Diego	Greg Riddoch	78-72
	Jim Riggleman	4-8
San Francisco	Roger Craig	72-90

Awards

Most Valuable Player	Barry Bonds, of, Pit
Cy Young	Greg Maddux, ChN
Rookie of the Year	Eric Karros, 1b, LA
Manager of the Year	Jim Leyland, Pit

STATS All-Star Team

C	Darren Daulton, Phi	.270	27	109
1B	Fred McGriff, SD	.286	35	104
2B	Ryne Sandberg, ChN	.304	26	87
3B	Gary Sheffield, SD	.330	33	100
SS	Barry Larkin, Cin	.304	12	78
OF	Barry Bonds, Pit	.311	34	103
OF	Ray Lankford, StL	.293	20	86
OF	Andy Van Slyke, Pit	.324	14	89
P	Tom Glavine, Atl	20-8	2.76	129 K
P	Greg Maddux, ChN	20-11	2.18	199 K
P	Dennis Martinez, Mon	16-11	2.47	147 K
P	Bob Tewksbury, StL	16-5	2.16	91 K
RP	Doug Jones, Hou	11-8	1.85	36 Sv

Postseason

LCS	Atlanta 4 vs. Pittsburgh 3
World Series	Atlanta (NL) 2 vs. Toronto (AL) 4

Outstanding Performances

No-Hitters
Kevin Gross, LA   vs. SF on August 17
Three-Homer Games
Jeff Blauser, Atl   on July 12
Cycles
Andujar Cedeno, Hou on August 25
Unassisted Triple Plays
M. Morandini, Phi   on September 23

1993 American League Standings

EAST	W	L	Pct	GB	DIF	W	L	R	OR	HR	OHR	W	L	R	OR	HR	OHR	Run	HR	M/A	May	June	July	Aug	S/O
			Overall					Home Games						Road Games				Park Index				Record by Month			
Toronto	95	67	.586	—	96	48	33	437	390	90	81	47	34	410	352	69	53	109	140	13-10	16-12	19-9	12-14	17-12	18-10
New York	88	74	.543	7.0	18	50	31	389	342	88	85	38	43	432	419	90	85	86	99	12-9	17-13	17-11	14-12	15-13	13-16
Baltimore	85	77	.525	10.0	1	48	33	434	371	87	81	37	44	352	374	70	72	111	118	8-13	13-16	20-7	14-12	15-14	15-15
Detroit	85	77	.525	10.0	64	44	37	457	408	103	99	41	40	442	429	75	89	99	123	15-7	15-11	13-16	10-18	18-11	14-14
Boston	80	82	.494	15.0	22	43	38	393	363	54	53	37	44	293	335	60	74	120	80	13-9	14-14	11-16	20-7	11-16	11-20
Cleveland	76	86	.469	19.0	0	46	35	387	351	69	83	30	51	403	462	72	99	85	89	7-15	12-17	17-10	12-14	14-14	14-16
Milwaukee	69	93	.426	26.0	0	38	43	371	381	53	65	31	50	362	411	72	88	97	74	9-11	13-14	10-19	9-17	16-16	12-16
WEST																									
Chicago	94	68	.580	—	126	45	36	384	333	82	70	49	32	392	331	80	55	99	113	13-9	11-14	15-13	18-9	17-12	20-11
Texas	86	76	.531	8.0	16	50	31	414	341	90	72	36	45	421	410	91	72	91	99	11-10	14-14	10-16	17-11	17-12	17-13
Kansas City	84	78	.519	10.0	25	43	38	370	354	50	49	41	40	305	340	75	56	112	76	9-14	16-9	13-15	16-12	15-14	15-14
Seattle	82	80	.506	12.0	1	46	35	380	350	74	66	36	45	354	381	87	69	99	90	11-11	14-15	13-14	13-13	14-13	17-14
California	71	91	.438	23.0	26	44	37	363	398	64	84	27	54	321	372	50	69	110	124	13-6	14-15	10-17	11-17	11-17	12-19
Minnesota	71	91	.438	23.0	0	36	45	360	433	56	70	35	46	333	397	65	78	109	88	8-14	12-13	12-15	11-16	13-17	15-16
Oakland	68	94	.420	26.0	3	38	43	333	387	78	78	30	51	382	459	80	79	86	98	7-11	12-16	12-15	11-16	9-21	16-15

Clinch Date—Toronto 9/27, Chicago 9/27.

Team Batting

Team	G	AB	R	OR	H	2B	3B	HR	TB	RBI	TBB	IBB	SO	HBP	SH	SF	SB	CS	SB%	GDP	Avg	OBP	Slg
Detroit	162	5620	899	837	1546	282	38	178	2438	853	765	50	1122	35	33	52	104	63	.62	101	.275	.371	.434
Toronto	162	5579	847	742	1556	317	42	159	2434	796	588	57	861	52	46	54	170	49	.78	138	.279	.359	.436
Texas	162	5510	835	751	1472	284	39	181	2377	780	483	56	984	48	69	56	113	67	.63	111	.267	.338	.431
New York	162	5615	821	761	1568	294	24	178	2444	793	629	47	910	43	22	50	39	35	.53	149	.279	.361	.435
Cleveland	162	5619	790	813	1547	264	31	141	2296	747	488	57	843	49	39	72	159	55	.74	131	.275	.346	.409
Baltimore	162	5508	786	745	1470	287	24	157	2276	744	655	52	930	41	49	56	73	54	.57	131	.267	.355	.413
Chicago	162	5483	776	664	1454	228	44	162	2256	731	604	52	834	33	72	61	106	57	.65	126	.265	.348	.411
Seattle	162	5494	734	731	1429	272	24	161	2232	681	624	73	901	56	63	51	91	68	.57	132	.260	.347	.406
Milwaukee	162	5525	733	792	1426	240	25	125	2091	688	555	52	932	40	57	45	138	93	.60	117	.258	.335	.378
Oakland	162	5543	715	846	1408	260	21	158	2184	679	622	45	1048	33	46	49	131	59	.69	125	.254	.338	.394
Minnesota	162	5601	693	830	1480	261	27	121	2158	642	493	35	850	51	27	37	83	59	.58	150	.264	.333	.385
Boston	162	5496	686	698	1451	319	29	114	2170	644	508	69	871	62	80	49	73	38	.66	146	.264	.353	.395
California	162	5391	684	770	1399	259	24	114	2048	644	564	39	930	38	50	46	169	100	.63	129	.260	.339	.380
Kansas City	162	5522	675	694	1455	294	35	125	2194	641	428	50	936	52	48	51	100	75	.57	107	.263	.328	.397
AL Total	2268	77506	10674	10674	20661	3861	427	2074	31598	10063	8006	734	12952	633	701	729	1549	872	.64	1793	.267	.337	.408
AL Avg Team	162	5536	762	762	1476	276	31	148	2257	719	572	52	925	45	50	52	111	62	.64	128	.267	.337	.408

Team Pitching

Team	G	CG	ShO	Rel	Sv	IP	H	R	ER	HR	SH	SF	HB	TBB	IBB	SO	WP	Bk	H/9	SO/9	BB/9	OAvg	OOBP	ERA
Chicago	162	16	11	322	48	1454.0	1398	664	598	125	54	41	40	566	36	974	51	7	8.7	6.0	3.5	.255	.328	3.70
Boston	162	9	11	389	44	1452.1	1379	698	609	127	58	60	48	552	87	997	42	11	8.5	6.2	3.4	.252	.322	3.77
Kansas City	162	16	6	303	48	1445.1	1379	694	649	105	41	52	44	571	36	985	76	7	8.6	6.1	3.6	.254	.327	4.04
Seattle	162	22	10	353	41	1453.2	1421	731	679	135	55	45	66	605	56	1083	57	6	8.8	6.7	3.7	.259	.337	4.20
Toronto	162	11	9	344	50	1441.1	1441	742	674	134	38	52	32	620	38	1023	83	5	9.0	6.4	3.9	.261	.336	4.21
Texas	162	20	6	359	45	1438.1	1476	751	684	144	48	42	44	562	42	957	52	14	9.2	6.0	3.5	.267	.337	4.28
Baltimore	162	21	10	329	42	1442.2	1427	745	691	153	51	42	38	579	50	900	41	2	8.9	5.6	3.6	.261	.333	4.31
California	162	26	6	320	41	1430.1	1482	770	690	153	53	61	51	550	35	843	55	7	9.3	5.3	3.5	.270	.339	4.34
New York	162	11	13	332	38	1438.1	1467	761	695	170	50	47	29	552	58	899	33	5	9.2	5.6	3.5	.266	.333	4.35
Milwaukee	162	26	6	353	29	1447.0	1511	792	716	153	50	76	60	522	58	810	45	7	9.4	5.0	3.2	.271	.336	4.45
Cleveland	162	7	8	410	45	1445.2	1591	813	735	182	48	41	39	591	53	888	41	5	9.9	5.5	3.7	.281	.351	4.58
Detroit	162	11	7	375	36	1436.2	1547	837	742	188	56	57	48	542	92	828	68	5	9.7	5.2	3.4	.276	.342	4.65
Minnesota	162	5	3	356	44	1444.1	1591	830	756	148	42	66	45	514	34	901	43	13	9.9	5.6	3.2	.283	.344	4.71
Oakland	162	8	2	424	42	1452.1	1551	846	791	157	57	47	49	680	59	864	39	6	9.6	5.4	4.2	.276	.356	4.90
AL Total	2268	209	110	4969	593	20222.1	20661	10674	9709	2074	701	729	633	8006	734	12952	726	103	9.2	5.8	3.6	.267	.346	4.32
AL Avg Team	162	15	8	355	42	1444.1	1476	762	694	148	50	52	45	572	52	925	52	7	9.2	5.8	3.6	.267	.346	4.32

Team Fielding

Team	G	PO	A	E	TC	DP	PB	Pct
Seattle	162	4361	1726	90	6177	173	13	.985
Kansas City	162	4336	1709	97	6142	150	15	.984
Baltimore	162	4328	1789	100	6217	171	6	.984
Minnesota	162	4333	1755	100	6188	160	21	.984
New York	162	4315	1889	105	6309	166	7	.983
Toronto	162	4324	1582	107	6013	144	6	.982
Oakland	162	4357	1625	111	6093	161	15	.982
Chicago	162	4362	1665	112	6139	153	15	.982
California	162	4291	1694	120	6105	161	10	.980
Boston	162	4357	1692	122	6171	155	11	.980
Texas	162	4315	1780	132	6227	145	18	.979
Detroit	162	4310	1777	132	6219	148	9	.979
Milwaukee	162	4341	1632	131	6104	148	12	.979
Cleveland	162	4337	1661	148	6146	174	9	.976
AL Total	2268	60667	23976	1607	86250	2209	166	.981

Team vs. Team Records

	Bal	Bos	Cal	ChA	Cle	Det	KC	Mil	Min	NYA	Oak	Sea	Tex	Tor	Won
Bal	—	6	7	4	8	5	7	8	8	6	10	7	4	5	85
Bos	7	—	7	7	5	6	5	5	7	6	9	7	6	3	80
Cal	5	5	—	7	5	4	6	7	4	6	6	6	6	4	71
ChA	8	5	6	—	9	7	6	9	10	4	7	9	8	6	94
Cle	5	8	7	3	—	6	7	8	4	6	8	3	7	4	76
Det	8	7	8	5	7	—	5	8	6	4	8	7	6	6	85
KC	5	7	7	7	5	7	—	6	5	7	6	6	7	8	84
Mil	5	8	5	3	5	5	7	—	7	4	7	4	4	5	69
Min	4	5	9	3	8	6	6	5	—	4	8	4	7	2	71
NYA	7	7	6	8	6	9	6	9	8	—	6	7	3	5	88
Oak	2	3	7	6	4	4	7	5	5	6	—	9	5	5	68
Sea	5	5	7	4	9	5	6	9	5	4	—	8	7	82
Tex	8	6	7	5	6	6	6	8	6	9	8	5	—	7	86
Tor	8	10	8	6	9	7	4	8	10	8	7	5	5	—	95
Lost	77	82	91	68	86	77	78	93	91	74	94	80	76	67	

1993 American League Batting Leaders

Games		At-Bats		Runs		Hits		Doubles		Triples	
C. Ripken Jr., Bal	162	C. Ripken Jr., Bal	641	R. Palmeiro, Tex	124	P. Molitor, Tor	211	J. Olerud, Tor	54	L. Johnson, ChA	14
P. Molitor, Tor	160	P. Molitor, Tor	636	P. Molitor, Tor	121	J. Olerud, Tor	200	D. White, Tor	42	J. Cora, ChA	13
R. Palmeiro, Tex	160	R. Sierra, Oak	630	D. White, Tor	116	C. Baerga, Cle	200	R. Palmeiro, Tex	40	D. Hulse, Tex	10
3 tied with	159	B. McRae, KC	627	K. Lofton, Cle	116	R. Alomar, Tor	192	J. Valentin, Bos	40	T. Fernandez, Tor	9
		C. Baerga, Cle	624	R. Henderson, 2tm	114	K. Lofton, Cle	185	K. Puckett, Min	39	B. McRae, KC	9

Home Runs		Total Bases		Runs Batted In		Walks		Intentional Walks		Strikeouts	
J. Gonzalez, Tex	46	K. Griffey Jr., Sea	359	A. Belle, Cle	129	T. Phillips, Det	132	J. Olerud, Tor	33	R. Deer, 2tm	169
K. Griffey Jr., Sea	45	J. Gonzalez, Tex	339	F. Thomas, ChA	128	R. Henderson, 2tm	120	K. Griffey Jr., Sea	25	D. Tartabull, NYA	156
F. Thomas, ChA	41	F. Thomas, ChA	333	J. Carter, Tor	121	J. Olerud, Tor	114	F. Thomas, ChA	23	D. Palmer, Tex	154
A. Belle, Cle	38	R. Palmeiro, Tex	331	J. Gonzalez, Tex	118	F. Thomas, ChA	112	M. Vaughn, Bos	23	J. Buhner, Sea	144
R. Palmeiro, Tex	37	J. Olerud, Tor	330	C. Fielder, Det	117	M. Tettleton, Det	109	R. Palmeiro, Tex	22	M. Tettleton, Det	139

Hit By Pitch		Sac Hits		Sac Flies		Stolen Bases		Caught Stealing		GDP	
D. Valle, Sea	17	J. Cora, ChA	19	A. Belle, Cle	14	K. Lofton, Cle	70	L. Polonia, Cal	24	E. Sprague, Tor	23
M. Macfarlane, KC	16	J. Valentin, Bos	16	C. Baerga, Cle	13	L. Polonia, Cal	55	C. Curtis, Cal	24	C. Fielder, Det	22
A. Dawson, Bos	13	B. McRae, KC	14	F. Thomas, ChA	13	R. Alomar, Tor	55	M. McLemore, Bal	15	M. McLemore, Bal	21
J. Gonzalez, Tex	13	4 tied with	13	3 tied with	10	R. Henderson, 2tm	53	R. Alomar, Tor	15	G. Brett, KC	20
2 tied with	11					C. Curtis, Cal	48	3 tied with	14	D. Mattingly, NYA	20

Runs Created		Runs Created/27 Outs		Batting Average		On-Base Percentage		Slugging Percentage		OBP+Slugging	
J. Olerud, Tor	144	J. Olerud, Tor	10.40	J. Olerud, Tor	.363	J. Olerud, Tor	.473	J. Gonzalez, Tex	.632	J. Olerud, Tor	1.072
F. Thomas, ChA	136	F. Thomas, ChA	9.14	P. Molitor, Tor	.332	T. Phillips, Det	.443	K. Griffey Jr., Sea	.617	F. Thomas, ChA	1.033
P. Molitor, Tor	134	J. Gonzalez, Tex	9.10	R. Alomar, Tor	.326	R. Henderson, 2tm	.432	F. Thomas, ChA	.607	K. Griffey Jr., Sea	1.025
J. Gonzalez, Tex	130	C. Hoiles, Bal	8.25	K. Lofton, Cle	.325	F. Thomas, ChA	.426	J. Olerud, Tor	.599	C. Hoiles, Bal	1.001
R. Palmeiro, Tex	127	P. Molitor, Tor	7.98	C. Baerga, Cle	.321	C. Hoiles, Bal	.416	C. Hoiles, Bal	.585	J. Gonzalez, Tex	1.000

1993 American League Pitching Leaders

Wins		Losses		Winning Percentage		Games		Games Started		Complete Games	
J. McDowell, ChA	22	S. Erickson, Min	19	J. Guzman, Tor	.824	G. Harris, Bos	80	M. Moore, Det	36	C. Finley, Cal	13
R. Johnson, Sea	19	C. Eldred, Mil	16	B. Wickman, NYA	.778	S. Radinsky, ChA	73	C. Eldred, Mil	36	K. Brown, Tex	12
P. Hentgen, Tor	19	K. Tapani, Min	15	J. Key, NYA	.750	D. Ward, Tor	71	M. Langston, Cal	35	J. McDowell, ChA	10
3 tied with	18	7 tied with	14	D. Fleming, Sea	.706	T. Fossas, Bos	71	C. Finley, Cal	35	R. Johnson, Sea	10
				J. Bere, ChA	.706	J. Nelson, Sea	71	K. Tapani, Min	35	C. Eldred, Mil	8

Shutouts		Saves		Games Finished		Batters Faced		Innings Pitched		Hits Allowed	
J. McDowell, ChA	4	D. Ward, Tor	45	D. Ward, Tor	70	C. Eldred, Mil	1087	C. Eldred, Mil	258.0	S. Erickson, Min	266
M. Moore, Det	3	J. Montgomery, KC	45	R. Hernandez, ChA	67	J. McDowell, ChA	1067	J. McDowell, ChA	256.2	J. McDowell, ChA	261
K. Brown, Tex	3	T. Henke, Tex	40	J. Montgomery, KC	63	C. Finley, Cal	1065	M. Langston, Cal	256.1	J. Navarro, Mil	254
R. Johnson, Sea	3	R. Hernandez, ChA	38	R. Aguilera, Min	61	D. Cone, KC	1060	R. Johnson, Sea	255.1	C. Finley, Cal	243
5 tied with	2	D. Eckersley, Oak	36	T. Henke, Tex	60	R. Johnson, Sea	1043	D. Cone, KC	254.0	K. Tapani, Min	243

Home Runs Allowed		Walks		Walks/9 Innings		Strikeouts		Strikeouts/9 Innings		Strikeout/Walk Ratio	
M. Moore, Det	35	W. Alvarez, ChA	122	J. Key, NYA	1.6	R. Johnson, Sea	308	R. Johnson, Sea	10.9	J. Key, NYA	4.02
C. Eldred, Mil	32	D. Cone, KC	114	D. Darwin, Bos	1.9	M. Langston, Cal	196	M. Perez, NYA	8.2	D. Wells, Det	3.31
D. Darwin, Bos	31	J. Guzman, Tor	110	D. Wells, Det	2.0	J. Guzman, Tor	194	J. Guzman, Tor	7.9	R. Johnson, Sea	3.11
B. Gullickson, Det	28	R. Johnson, Sea	99	K. Tapani, Min	2.3	D. Cone, KC	191	R. Clemens, Bos	7.5	E. Hanson, Sea	2.72
R. Bones, Mil	28	2 tied with	91	J. Doherty, Det	2.3	C. Finley, Cal	187	W. Banks, Min	7.2	M. Mussina, Bal	2.66

Earned Run Average		Component ERA		Hit Batsmen		Wild Pitches		Opponent Average		Opponent OBP	
K. Appier, KC	2.56	K. Appier, KC	2.25	R. Johnson, Sea	16	J. Guzman, Tor	26	R. Johnson, Sea	.203	D. Darwin, Bos	.272
W. Alvarez, ChA	2.95	R. Johnson, Sea	2.73	K. Brown, Tex	15	T. Gordon, KC	17	K. Appier, KC	.212	K. Appier, KC	.279
J. Key, NYA	3.00	D. Darwin, Bos	2.82	R. Clemens, Bos	11	J. Morris, Tor	14	D. Cone, KC	.223	J. Key, NYA	.279
A. Fernandez, ChA	3.13	J. Key, NYA	2.94	J. Navarro, Mil	11	D. Cone, KC	14	B. McDonald, Bal	.228	R. Johnson, Sea	.290
F. Viola, Bos	3.14	M. Langston, Cal	3.02	4 tied with	10	D. Wells, Det	13	C. Bosio, Sea	.229	M. Langston, Cal	.295

1993 American League Miscellaneous

Managers

Baltimore	Johnny Oates	85-77
Boston	Butch Hobson	80-82
California	Buck Rodgers	71-91
Chicago	Gene Lamont	94-68
Cleveland	Mike Hargrove	76-86
Detroit	Sparky Anderson	85-77
Kansas City	Hal McRae	84-78
Milwaukee	Phil Garner	69-93
Minnesota	Tom Kelly	71-91
New York	Buck Showalter	88-74
Oakland	Tony La Russa	68-94
Seattle	Lou Piniella	82-80
Texas	Kevin Kennedy	86-76
Toronto	Cito Gaston	95-67

Awards

Most Valuable Player	Frank Thomas, 1b, ChA
Cy Young	Jack McDowell, ChA
Rookie of the Year	Tim Salmon, of, Cal
Manager of the Year	Gene Lamont, ChA

STATS All-Star Team

C	Chris Hoiles, Bal	.310	29	82
1B	John Olerud, Tor	.363	24	107
2B	Roberto Alomar, Tor	.326	17	93
3B	Robin Ventura, ChA	.262	22	94
SS	Travis Fryman, Det	.300	22	97
OF	Albert Belle, Cle	.290	38	129
OF	Juan Gonzalez, Tex	.310	46	118
OF	Ken Griffey Jr., Sea	.309	45	109
DH	Paul Molitor, Tor	.332	22	111
P	Kevin Appier, KC	18-8	2.56	186 K
P	Randy Johnson, Sea	19-8	3.24	308 K
P	Jimmy Key, NYA	18-6	3.00	173 K
P	Jack McDowell, ChA	22-10	3.37	158 K
RP	Duane Ward, Tor	2-3	2.13	45 Sv

Postseason

LCS	Toronto 4 vs. Chicago 2
World Series	Tor (AL) 4 vs. Phi (NL) 2

Outstanding Performances

No-Hitters

Chris Bosio, Sea	vs. Bos on April 22
Jim Abbott, NYA	vs. Cle on September 4

Three-Homer Games

Carlos Baerga, Cle	on June 17
Joe Carter, Tor	on August 23
Juan Gonzalez, Tex	on August 28

Cycles

Jay Buhner, Sea	on June 23
Travis Fryman, Det	on July 28

1993 National League Standings

	Overall					Home Games						Road Games						Park Index		Record by Month					
EAST	W	L	Pct	GB	DIF	W	L	R	OR	HR	OHR	W	L	R	OR	HR	OHR	Run	HR	M/A	May	June	July	Aug	S/O
Philadelphia	97	65	.599	—	181	52	29	441	371	80	57	45	36	436	369	76	72	101	93	17-5	17-10	18-10	14-14	16-11	15-15
Montreal	94	68	.580	3.0	0	55	26	367	315	62	50	39	42	365	367	60	69	93	87	13-10	14-12	14-14	15-12	17-12	21-8
St. Louis	87	75	.537	10.0	1	49	32	376	321	59	59	38	43	382	423	59	93	87	78	13-10	12-14	20-7	14-13	13-16	15-15
Chicago	84	78	.519	13.0	0	43	38	381	382	76	94	41	40	357	357	85	59	107	118	11-11	13-12	13-15	15-12	12-18	20-10
Pittsburgh	75	87	.463	22.0	4	40	41	372	388	64	67	35	46	335	418	46	86	101	99	11-11	12-14	14-14	10-18	15-13	13-17
Florida	64	98	.395	33.0	1	35	46	299	369	44	72	29	52	282	355	50	63	105	103	10-14	11-15	12-14	11-17	11-17	9-21
New York	59	103	.364	38.0	4	28	53	317	376	75	72	31	50	355	368	83	67	96	98	8-13	9-18	6-21	12-16	11-18	13-17
WEST																									
Atlanta	104	58	.642	—	31	51	30	366	291	78	52	53	28	401	268	91	49	98	93	12-13	17-10	15-11	19-9	19-7	22-8
San Francisco	103	59	.636	1.0	144	50	31	366	293	82	81	53	28	446	343	86	87	83	94	15-9	18-9	19-9	18-8	15-11	18-13
Houston	85	77	.525	19.0	11	44	37	363	285	62	56	41	40	353	345	76	61	93	86	14-8	13-14	11-15	16-13	15-13	16-14
Los Angeles	81	81	.500	23.0	1	41	40	330	318	66	48	40	41	345	344	64	55	94	96	8-15	18-8	14-13	14-13	12-15	15-17
Cincinnati	73	89	.451	31.0	2	41	40	363	383	69	81	32	49	359	402	68	77	98	103	8-14	17-12	13-14	15-13	13-15	7-21
Colorado	67	95	.414	37.0	0	39	42	489	551	77	107	28	53	269	416	65	74	152	132	8-14	7-22	11-14	10-17	14-16	17-12
San Diego	61	101	.377	43.0	0	34	47	345	376	87	79	27	54	334	396	66	69	99	123	10-12	10-18	9-19	11-16	12-15	9-21

Clinch Date—Philadelphia 9/28, Atlanta 10/03.

Team Batting

Team	G	AB	R	OR	H	2B	3B	HR	TB	RBI	TBB	IBB	SO	HBP	SH	SF	SB	CS	SB%	GDP	Avg	OBP	Slg
Philadelphia	162	5685	877	740	1555	297	51	156	2422	811	665	70	1049	42	84	51	91	32	.74	107	.274	.359	.426
San Francisco	162	5557	808	636	1534	269	33	168	2373	759	516	88	930	46	102	50	120	65	.65	121	.276	.348	.427
Atlanta	162	5515	767	559	1444	239	29	169	2248	712	560	46	946	36	73	50	125	48	.72	127	.262	.339	.408
Colorado	162	5517	758	967	1507	278	59	142	2329	704	388	40	944	46	70	52	146	90	.62	125	.273	.332	.422
St. Louis	162	5551	758	744	1508	262	34	118	2192	724	588	50	882	27	59	54	153	72	.68	128	.272	.350	.395
Chicago	163	5627	738	739	1521	259	32	161	2327	706	446	61	923	34	67	42	100	43	.70	131	.270	.332	.414
Montreal	163	5493	732	682	1410	270	36	122	2118	682	542	65	860	48	100	50	228	56	.80	95	.257	.334	.386
Cincinnati	162	5517	722	785	1457	261	28	137	2185	669	485	42	1025	32	63	66	142	59	.71	104	.264	.334	.396
Houston	162	5464	716	630	1459	288	37	138	2235	656	497	58	911	40	82	47	103	60	.63	125	.267	.338	.409
Pittsburgh	162	5549	707	806	1482	267	50	110	2179	664	536	50	972	55	76	52	92	55	.63	129	.267	.343	.393
San Diego	162	5503	679	772	1386	239	28	153	2140	633	443	43	1046	59	80	50	92	41	.69	111	.252	.320	.389
Los Angeles	162	5588	675	662	1458	234	28	130	2138	639	492	48	937	27	107	47	126	61	.67	105	.261	.329	.383
New York	162	5448	672	744	1350	228	37	158	2126	632	448	43	879	24	89	47	79	50	.61	108	.248	.313	.390
Florida	162	5475	581	724	1356	197	31	94	1897	542	498	39	1054	51	58	43	117	56	.68	122	.248	.321	.346
NL Total	2270	77489	10190	10190	20427	3588	513	1956	30909	9533	7104	743	13358	567	1110	701	1714	788	.69	1638	.264	.327	.399
NL Avg Team	162	5535	728	728	1459	256	37	140	2208	681	507	53	954	41	79	50	122	56	.69	117	.264	.327	.399

Team Pitching

Team	G	CG	ShO	Rel	Sv	IP	H	R	ER	HR	SH	SF	HB	TBB	IBB	SO	WP	Bk	H/9	SO/9	BB/9	OAvg	OOBP	ERA
Atlanta	162	18	16	353	46	1455.0	1297	559	507	101	77	39	22	480	59	1036	46	9	8.0	6.4	3.0	.240	.303	3.14
Houston	162	18	14	324	42	1441.1	1363	630	559	117	79	43	41	476	52	1056	60	12	8.5	6.6	3.0	.251	.313	3.49
Los Angeles	162	17	9	346	36	1472.2	1406	662	573	103	76	48	37	567	68	1043	47	20	8.6	6.4	3.5	.254	.324	3.50
Montreal	163	8	7	385	61	1456.2	1369	682	574	119	82	40	47	521	38	934	46	12	8.5	5.8	3.2	.249	.317	3.55
San Francisco	162	4	9	414	50	1456.2	1385	636	585	168	74	38	50	442	46	982	33	18	8.6	6.1	2.7	.253	.313	3.61
Philadelphia	162	24	11	350	46	1472.2	1419	740	647	129	65	42	37	573	33	1117	74	7	8.7	6.8	3.5	.252	.322	3.95
New York	162	16	8	297	22	1438.0	1483	744	647	139	87	58	50	434	61	867	32	14	9.3	5.4	2.7	.269	.324	4.05
St. Louis	162	5	7	423	54	1453.0	1553	744	660	152	80	57	43	383	50	775	40	7	9.6	4.8	2.4	.276	.324	4.09
Florida	162	4	5	409	48	1440.1	1437	724	661	135	80	50	32	598	58	945	85	20	9.0	5.9	3.7	.261	.334	4.13
Chicago	163	8	5	422	56	1449.2	1514	739	673	135	69	51	43	470	61	905	43	21	9.4	5.6	2.9	.273	.332	4.18
San Diego	162	8	6	397	32	1437.2	1470	772	675	148	89	62	34	558	72	957	57	14	9.2	6.0	3.5	.266	.334	4.23
Cincinnati	162	11	8	375	37	1434.0	1510	785	719	158	77	40	44	508	36	996	47	8	9.5	6.3	3.2	.272	.336	4.51
Pittsburgh	162	12	5	384	34	1445.2	1557	806	766	153	93	55	46	485	43	832	55	11	9.7	5.2	3.0	.280	.339	4.77
Colorado	162	9	0	453	35	1431.1	1664	967	860	181	82	78	41	609	66	913	82	22	10.5	5.7	3.8	.294	.362	5.41
NL Total	2270	162	110	5332	599	20284.2	20427	10190	9106	1956	1110	701	567	7104	743	13358	747	195	9.1	5.9	3.2	.264	.335	4.04
NL Avg Team	162	12	8	381	43	1448.2	1459	728	650	140	79	50	41	507	53	954	53	14	9.1	5.9	3.2	.264	.335	4.04

Team Fielding

Team	G	PO	A	E	TC	DP	PB	Pct
San Francisco	162	4370	1733	101	6204	169	15	.984
Pittsburgh	162	4337	1816	105	6258	161	19	.983
Atlanta	162	4365	1769	108	6242	146	13	.983
Chicago	163	4349	1889	115	6353	162	14	.982
Cincinnati	162	4302	1633	121	6056	133	12	.980
Florida	162	4321	1703	125	6149	130	29	.980
Houston	162	4324	1651	126	6101	141	7	.979
Los Angeles	162	4418	1838	133	6389	141	15	.979
Philadelphia	162	4418	1536	141	6095	123	12	.977
St. Louis	162	4359	1890	159	6408	157	14	.975
New York	162	4314	1781	156	6251	143	4	.975
Montreal	163	4370	1827	159	6356	144	14	.975
San Diego	162	4313	1616	160	6089	129	20	.974
Colorado	162	4294	1760	167	6221	149	11	.973
NL Total	2270	60854	24442	1876	87172	2028	199	.978

Team vs. Team Records

	Atl	ChN	Cin	Col	Fla	Hou	LA	Mon	NYN	Phi	Pit	SD	SF	StL	Won
Atl	—	7	10	13	7	8	8	7	9	6	7	9	7	6	104
ChN	5	—	7	8	6	4	7	5	8	7	5	8	6	8	84
Cin	3	5	—	9	7	6	5	4	6	4	8	9	2	5	73
Col	0	4	4	—	7	11	7	3	6	3	8	6	3	5	67
Fla	5	7	5	5	—	3	5	5	4	4	6	7	4	4	64
Hou	5	8	7	2	9	—	9	5	11	5	7	8	3	6	85
LA	5	5	8	6	7	4	—	6	8	2	8	9	7	6	81
Mon	5	8	9	9	8	7	6	—	9	6	8	10	3	7	94
NYN	3	5	6	6	9	1	4	4	—	3	4	5	4	5	59
Phi	6	6	9	9	9	7	10	7	10	—	7	6	4	8	97
Pit	5	8	4	4	7	5	4	5	9	6	—	9	5	4	75
SD	4	4	7	7	5	5	2	7	6	3	1	—	3	7	61
SF	6	6	11	10	8	10	6	9	8	8	7	10	—	4	103
StL	6	5	7	7	9	6	6	8	5	9	5	8	6	—	87
Lost	58	78	89	95	98	77	81	68	103	65	87	101	59	75	

Seasons: Standings, Leaders

1993 National League Batting Leaders

Games		At-Bats		Runs		Hits		Doubles		Triples	
J. Conine, Fla	162	L. Dykstra, Phi	637	L. Dykstra, Phi	143	L. Dykstra, Phi	194	C. Hayes, Col	45	S. Finley, Hou	13
T. Pendleton, Atl	161	T. Pendleton, Atl	633	B. Bonds, SF	129	M. Grace, ChN	193	L. Dykstra, Phi	44	B. Butler, LA	10
L. Dykstra, Phi	161	M. Grissom, Mon	630	R. Gant, Atl	113	M. Grissom, Mon	188	D. Bichette, Col	43	J. Bell, Pit	9
J. Blauser, Atl	161	E. Karros, LA	619	F. McGriff, 2tm	111	J. Bell, Pit	187	T. Gwynn, SD	41	M. Morandini, Phi	9
2 tied with	159	J. King, Pit	611	J. Blauser, Atl	110	G. Jefferies, StL	186	C. Biggio, Hou	41	3 tied with	8

Home Runs		Total Bases		Runs Batted In		Walks		Intentional Walks		Strikeouts	
B. Bonds, SF	46	B. Bonds, SF	365	B. Bonds, SF	123	L. Dykstra, Phi	129	B. Bonds, SF	43	C. Snyder, LA	147
D. Justice, Atl	40	M. Williams, SF	325	D. Justice, Atl	120	B. Bonds, SF	126	L. Walker, Mon	20	S. Sosa, ChN	135
M. Williams, SF	38	R. Gant, Atl	309	R. Gant, Atl	117	D. Daulton, Phi	117	M. Grace, ChN	14	J. Conine, Fla	135
F. McGriff, 2tm	37	L. Dykstra, Phi	307	M. Piazza, LA	112	J. Kruk, Phi	111	4 tied with	13	O. Destrade, Fla	130
R. Gant, Atl	36	M. Piazza, LA	307	M. Williams, SF	110	B. Butler, LA	86			P. Plantier, SD	124

Hit By Pitch		Sac Hits		Sac Flies		Stolen Bases		Caught Stealing		GDP	
J. Blauser, Atl	16	J. Offerman, LA	25	L. Gonzalez, Hou	10	C. Carr, Fla	58	C. Carr, Fla	22	M. Grace, ChN	25
D. Bell, SD	12	J. Reed, LA	17	8 tied with	9	M. Grissom, Mon	53	B. Butler, LA	19	C. Hayes, Col	25
C. Biggio, Hou	10	B. Butler, LA	14			O. Nixon, Atl	47	E. Young, Col	19	E. Murray, NYN	24
J. Clark, Col	10	K. Hill, Mon	14			G. Jefferies, StL	46	C. Biggio, Hou	17	M. Lemke, Atl	21
L. Gonzalez, Hou	10	A. Benes, SD	14			D. Lewis, SF	46	D. Lewis, SF	15	J. Bagwell, Hou	20

Runs Created		Runs Created/27 Outs		Batting Average		On-Base Percentage		Slugging Percentage		OBP+Slugging	
B. Bonds, SF	162	B. Bonds, SF	11.27	A. Galarraga, Col	.370	B. Bonds, SF	.458	B. Bonds, SF	.677	B. Bonds, SF	1.136
L. Dykstra, Phi	129	A. Galarraga, Col	9.43	T. Gwynn, SD	.358	J. Kruk, Phi	.430	A. Galarraga, Col	.602	A. Galarraga, Col	1.005
D. Justice, Atl	113	G. Jefferies, StL	7.77	G. Jefferies, StL	.342	L. Dykstra, Phi	.420	M. Williams, SF	.561	M. Piazza, LA	.932
J. Blauser, Atl	112	J. Kruk, Phi	7.67	B. Bonds, SF	.336	O. Merced, Pit	.414	M. Piazza, LA	.561	F. McGriff, 2tm	.924
2 tied with	111	L. Dykstra, Phi	7.44	M. Grace, ChN	.325	G. Jefferies, StL	.408	F. McGriff, 2tm	.549	J. Kruk, Phi	.905

1993 National League Pitching Leaders

Wins		Losses		Winning Percentage		Games		Games Started		Complete Games	
J. Burkett, SF	22	D. Drabek, Hou	18	M. Portugal, Hou	.818	M. Jackson, SF	81	J. Rijo, Cin	36	G. Maddux, Atl	8
T. Glavine, Atl	22	J. Armstrong, Fla	17	T. Greene, Phi	.800	D. West, Phi	76	G. Maddux, Atl	36	5 tied with	7
B. Swift, SF	21	G. Harris, 2tm	17	T. Glavine, Atl	.786	R. Beck, SF	76	T. Glavine, Atl	36		
G. Maddux, Atl	20	C. Hough, Fla	16	J. Burkett, SF	.759	G. McMichael, Atl	74	3 tied with	35		
2 tied with	18	A. Young, NYN	16	S. Avery, Atl	.750	2 tied with	73				

Shutouts		Saves		Games Finished		Batters Faced		Innings Pitched		Hits Allowed	
P. Harnisch, Hou	4	R. Myers, ChN	53	R. Beck, SF	71	G. Maddux, Atl	1064	G. Maddux, Atl	267.0	B. Tewksbury, StL	258
R. Martinez, LA	3	R. Beck, SF	48	R. Myers, ChN	69	J. Rijo, Cin	1029	J. Rijo, Cin	257.1	D. Drabek, Hou	242
11 tied with	2	B. Harvey, Fla	45	D. Jones, Hou	60	J. Smoltz, Atl	1028	J. Smoltz, Atl	243.2	G. Harris, 2tm	239
		3 tied with	43	J. Wetteland, Mon	58	T. Glavine, Atl	1014	T. Glavine, Atl	239.1	T. Glavine, Atl	236
				M. Williams, Phi	57	D. Drabek, Hou	991	D. Drabek, Hou	237.2	C. Schilling, Phi	234

Home Runs Allowed		Walks		Walks/9 Innings		Strikeouts		Strikeouts/9 Innings		Strikeout/Walk Ratio	
G. Harris, 2tm	33	R. Martinez, LA	104	B. Tewksbury, StL	0.8	J. Rijo, Cin	227	J. Rijo, Cin	7.9	B. Tewksbury, StL	4.85
J. Armstrong, Fla	29	J. Smoltz, Atl	100	R. Arocha, StL	1.5	J. Smoltz, Atl	208	J. Smoltz, Atl	7.7	G. Maddux, Atl	3.79
D. Martinez, Mon	27	T. Glavine, Atl	90	J. Burkett, SF	1.6	G. Maddux, Atl	197	J. Guzman, ChN	7.7	J. Rijo, Cin	3.66
F. Tanana, NYN	26	R. Bowen, Fla	87	S. Avery, Atl	1.7	C. Schilling, Phi	186	P. Harnisch, Hou	7.6	J. Burkett, SF	3.63
J. Guzman, ChN	25	A. Benes, SD	86	G. Maddux, Atl	1.8	P. Harnisch, Hou	185	T. Greene, Phi	7.5	C. Schilling, Phi	3.26

Earned Run Average		Component ERA		Hit Batsmen		Wild Pitches		Opponent Average		Opponent OBP	
G. Maddux, Atl	2.36	G. Maddux, Atl	2.32	D. Kile, Hou	15	T. Greene, Phi	15	P. Harnisch, Hou	.214	G. Maddux, Atl	.273
J. Rijo, Cin	2.48	J. Rijo, Cin	2.55	D. Martinez, Mon	11	A. Benes, SD	14	B. Swift, SF	.226	B. Swift, SF	.277
M. Portugal, Hou	2.77	B. Swift, SF	2.57	J. Burkett, SF	11	J. Smoltz, Atl	13	J. Rijo, Cin	.230	J. Rijo, Cin	.278
B. Swift, SF	2.82	T. Greene, Phi	2.80	6 tied with	9	B. Rivera, Phi	13	J. Smoltz, Atl	.230	T. Mulholland, Phi	.282
S. Avery, Atl	2.94	P. Harnisch, Hou	2.80			2 tied with	12	G. Maddux, Atl	.232	P. Harnisch, Hou	.289

1993 National League Miscellaneous

Managers

Atlanta	Bobby Cox	104-58
Chicago	Jim Lefebvre	84-78
Cincinnati	Tony Perez	20-24
	Davey Johnson	53-65
Colorado	Don Baylor	67-95
Florida	Rene Lachemann	64-98
Houston	Art Howe	85-77
Los Angeles	Tom Lasorda	81-81
Montreal	Felipe Alou	94-68
New York	Jeff Torborg	13-25
	Dallas Green	46-78
Philadelphia	Jim Fregosi	97-65
Pittsburgh	Jim Leyland	75-87
St. Louis	Joe Torre	87-75
San Diego	Jim Riggleman	61-101
San Francisco	Dusty Baker	103-59

Awards

Most Valuable Player	Barry Bonds, of, SF
Cy Young	Greg Maddux, Atl
Rookie of the Year	Mike Piazza, c, LA
Manager of the Year	Dusty Baker, SF

STATS All-Star Team

C	Mike Piazza, LA	.318	35	112
1B	Andres Galarraga, Col	.370	22	98
2B	Robby Thompson, SF	.312	19	65
3B	Matt Williams, SF	.294	38	110
SS	Jeff Blauser, Atl	.305	15	73
OF	Barry Bonds, SF	.336	46	123
OF	Lenny Dykstra, Phi	.305	19	66
OF	Ron Gant, Atl	.274	36	117
P	Tom Glavine, Atl	22-6	3.20	120 K
P	Greg Maddux, Atl	20-10	2.36	197 K
P	Jose Rijo, Cin	14-9	2.48	227 K
P	Bill Swift, SF	21-8	2.82	157 K
RP	John Wetteland, Mon	9-3	1.37	43 Sv

Postseason

LCS	Philadelphia 4 vs. Atlanta 2
World Series	Phi (NL) 2 vs. Tor (AL) 4

Outstanding Performances

No-Hitters
Darryl Kile, Hou — vs. NYN on September 8

Four-Homer Games
Mark Whiten, StL — on September 7

Cycles
Mark Grace, ChN — on May 9

1994 American League Standings

EAST	W	L	Pct	GB	DIF	W	L	R	OR	HR	OHR	W	L	R	OR	HR	OHR	Run	HR	M/A	May	June	July	Aug	S/O
						Home Games						Road Games						Park Index		Record by Month					
New York	70	43	.619	—	101	33	24	291	260	63	62	37	19	379	274	76	58	83	92	15-8	18-7	14-13	17-10	6-5	—
Baltimore	63	49	.563	6.5	8	28	27	294	272	75	70	35	22	295	225	64	61	113	120	15-8	12-13	16-12	13-13	7-3	—
Toronto	55	60	.478	16.0	13	33	26	293	275	63	64	22	34	273	304	52	63	93	105	14-10	10-16	8-18	17-10	6-6	—
Boston	54	61	.470	17.0	31	31	33	320	353	68	67	23	28	232	268	52	53	107	102	17-7	13-12	8-19	12-15	4-8	—
Detroit	53	62	.461	18.0	1	34	24	350	324	85	76	19	38	302	347	76	72	102	107	7-14	16-11	13-14	12-17	5-6	—
CENTRAL																									
Chicago	67	46	.593	—	69	34	19	296	206	62	43	33	27	337	292	59	72	90	91	13-10	16-9	14-13	19-10	5-4	—
Cleveland	66	47	.584	1.0	64	35	16	335	248	87	44	31	31	344	314	80	50	108	123	13-9	13-12	18-9	15-13	7-4	—
Kansas City	64	51	.557	4.0	1	35	24	325	287	41	48	29	27	249	245	59	47	118	80	9-11	16-13	15-13	18-10	6-4	—
Minnesota	53	60	.469	14.0	1	32	27	319	339	48	88	21	33	275	349	55	65	97	104	9-16	16-8	15-12	7-20	6-4	—
Milwaukee	53	62	.461	15.0	11	24	32	275	311	48	63	29	30	272	275	51	64	113	102	13-9	7-21	17-10	13-14	3-8	—
WEST																									
Texas	52	62	.456	—	91	31	32	334	353	63	67	21	30	279	344	61	90	89	70	9-12	14-14	12-15	15-14	2-7	—
Oakland	51	63	.447	1.0	10	24	32	241	262	51	54	27	31	308	327	62	74	82	80	7-17	8-19	17-9	15-11	4-7	—
Seattle	49	63	.438	2.0	8	22	22	248	244	63	44	27	41	321	372	90	65	110	107	10-13	11-16	12-15	7-18	9-1	—
California	47	68	.409	5.5	28	23	40	286	389	74	93	24	28	257	271	46	57	106	134	9-16	14-13	10-17	11-16	3-6	—

Team Batting

Team	G	AB	R	OR	H	2B	3B	HR	TB	RBI	TBB	IBB	SO	HBP	SH	SF	SB	CS	SB%	GDP	Avg	OBP	Slg
Cleveland	113	4022	679	562	1165	240	20	167	1946	647	382	40	629	18	33	38	131	48	.73	80	.290	.359	.484
New York	113	3986	670	534	1155	238	16	139	1842	632	530	34	660	31	27	37	55	40	.58	112	.290	.382	.462
Detroit	115	3955	652	671	1048	216	25	161	1797	622	520	28	897	34	17	48	46	33	.58	86	.265	.362	.454
Chicago	113	3942	633	498	1133	175	39	121	1749	602	497	47	568	20	51	46	77	27	.74	91	.287	.376	.444
Texas	114	3983	613	697	1114	198	27	124	1738	582	437	37	730	36	41	34	82	35	.70	95	.280	.361	.436
Minnesota	113	3952	594	688	1092	239	23	103	1686	556	359	26	635	41	22	34	94	30	.76	93	.276	.348	.427
Baltimore	112	3856	589	497	1047	185	20	139	1689	557	438	23	655	39	16	35	69	13	.84	89	.272	.357	.438
Kansas City	115	3911	574	532	1051	211	38	100	1638	538	376	23	698	33	32	38	140	62	.69	72	.269	.344	.419
Seattle	112	3883	569	616	1045	211	18	153	1751	549	372	42	652	26	48	32	48	21	.70	87	.269	.342	.451
Toronto	115	3962	566	579	1064	210	30	115	1679	534	387	34	691	38	30	44	79	26	.75	96	.269	.346	.424
Boston	115	3940	552	621	1038	222	19	120	1658	523	404	40	723	31	38	33	81	38	.68	87	.263	.342	.421
Oakland	114	3885	549	589	1009	178	13	113	1552	515	417	21	686	18	24	51	91	39	.70	79	.260	.342	.399
Milwaukee	115	3978	547	586	1045	238	21	99	1622	510	417	30	680	33	28	38	59	37	.61	85	.263	.343	.408
California	115	3943	543	660	1042	178	16	120	1612	518	402	24	715	27	42	29	65	54	.55	84	.264	.341	.409
AL Total	1594	55198	8330	8330	15048	2939	325	1774	23959	7885	5938	449	9619	425	449	537	1117	503	.69	1236	.273	.345	.434
AL Avg Team	114	3943	595	595	1075	210	23	127	1711	563	424	32	687	30	32	38	80	36	.69	88	.273	.345	.434

Team Pitching

Team	G	CG	ShO	Rel	Sv	IP	H	R	ER	HR	SH	SF	HB	TBB	IBB	SO	WP	Bk	H/9	SO/9	BB/9	OAvg	OOBP	ERA
Chicago	113	13	9	239	20	1011.1	964	498	445	115	32	32	17	377	24	754	19	3	8.6	6.7	3.4	.250	.317	3.96
Kansas City	115	5	6	247	38	1031.2	1018	532	485	95	34	49	33	392	31	717	60	5	8.9	6.3	3.4	.260	.328	4.23
Baltimore	112	13	4	234	37	997.2	1005	497	478	131	35	36	26	351	25	666	18	1	9.1	6.0	3.2	.263	.327	4.31
New York	113	8	2	241	31	1019.2	1045	534	492	120	31	36	21	398	24	656	46	4	9.2	5.8	3.5	.267	.335	4.34
Cleveland	113	17	5	222	21	1018.2	1097	562	494	94	25	36	41	404	28	666	58	6	9.7	5.9	3.6	.275	.346	4.36
Milwaukee	115	11	3	252	23	1036.0	1071	586	532	127	24	37	29	421	28	577	30	6	9.3	5.0	3.7	.269	.340	4.62
Toronto	115	13	4	221	26	1025.0	1053	579	535	127	29	38	32	482	23	832	54	7	9.2	7.3	4.0	.266	.348	4.70
Oakland	114	12	9	308	23	1003.1	979	589	535	128	37	36	34	510	30	732	42	12	8.8	6.6	4.6	.257	.347	4.80
Boston	115	6	3	308	30	1029.1	1104	621	564	120	34	42	31	450	46	729	46	4	9.7	6.4	3.9	.276	.351	4.93
Seattle	112	13	7	252	21	984.0	1051	616	546	109	28	33	28	486	39	763	41	1	9.6	7.0	4.4	.274	.357	4.99
Detroit	115	15	1	246	20	1018.0	1139	671	609	148	35	31	25	449	74	560	59	2	10.1	5.0	4.0	.282	.356	5.38
California	115	11	4	257	21	1027.0	1149	660	618	150	35	41	45	436	28	682	48	8	10.1	6.0	3.8	.287	.360	5.42
Texas	114	10	4	301	26	1023.0	1176	697	620	157	36	46	32	394	29	683	50	5	10.3	6.0	3.5	.288	.351	5.45
Minnesota	113	6	4	272	29	1005.0	1197	688	634	153	34	44	31	388	20	602	43	4	10.7	5.4	3.5	.299	.361	5.68
AL Total	1594	153	65	3600	366	14229.2	15048	8330	7587	1774	449	537	425	5938	449	9619	614	68	9.5	6.1	3.8	.273	.353	4.80
AL Avg Team	114	11	5	257	26	1016.2	1075	595	542	127	32	38	30	424	32	687	44	5	9.5	6.1	3.8	.273	.353	4.80

Team Fielding

Team	G	PO	A	E	TC	DP	PB	Pct
Baltimore	112	2993	1127	57	4177	103	5	.986
California	115	3081	1196	76	4353	110	11	.983
Minnesota	113	3015	1186	75	4276	99	5	.982
New York	113	3059	1326	80	4465	122	10	.982
Kansas City	115	3095	1253	80	4428	102	5	.982
Boston	115	3088	1193	81	4362	124	16	.981
Detroit	115	3054	1261	82	4397	90	8	.981
Milwaukee	115	3108	1302	85	4495	130	11	.981
Toronto	115	3075	1059	81	4215	105	14	.981
Chicago	113	3034	991	79	4104	91	12	.981
Cleveland	113	3056	1289	90	4435	119	7	.980
Oakland	114	3010	1122	88	4220	105	5	.979
Seattle	112	2952	1167	95	4214	102	8	.977
Texas	114	3069	1262	106	4437	106	9	.976
AL Total	1594	42689	16734	1155	60578	1508	126	.981

Team vs. Team Records

	Bal	Bos	Cal	ChA	Cle	Det	KC	Mil	Min	NYA	Oak	Sea	Tex	Tor	Won
Bal	—	4	8	2	4	3	4	7	4	4	6	4	3	7	63
Bos	2	—	7	2	3	4	4	5	1	3	9	6	1	7	54
Cal	4	5	—	5	0	3	6	3	3	4	3	2	6	3	47
ChA	4	4	5	—	7	8	3	9	2	4	6	9	4	2	67
Cle	6	7	5	5	—	8	1	5	9	0	6	3	5	6	66
Det	4	2	4	4	2	—	4	6	3	3	5	5	5	5	53
KC	1	2	4	7	4	8	—	5	6	4	7	6	4	6	64
Mil	3	5	3	3	2	4	7	—	6	2	4	4	3	7	53
Min	5	8	3	4	3	3	4	6	—	4	2	3	4	4	53
NYA	6	7	8	2	9	3	2	7	5	—	7	8	3	3	70
Oak	5	3	6	3	0	4	3	1	5	5	—	4	7	5	51
Sea	4	6	7	1	2	3	4	2	3	4	9	—	9	1	49
Tex	3	5	4	5	7	3	7	3	5	2	3	1	—	4	52
Tor	2	3	4	3	4	6	3	8	4	1	5	8	5	—	55
Lost	49	61	68	46	47	62	51	62	62	60	43	63	63	62	60

Seasons: Standings, Leaders

1994 American League Batting Leaders

Games		At-Bats		Runs		Hits		Doubles		Triples	
P. Molitor, Tor	115	T. Fryman, Det	464	F. Thomas, ChA	106	K. Lofton, Cle	160	C. Knoblauch, Min	45	L. Johnson, ChA	14
5 tied with	114	K. Lofton, Cle	459	K. Lofton, Cle	105	P. Molitor, Tor	155	A. Belle, Cle	35	V. Coleman, KC	12
		P. Molitor, Tor	454	K. Griffey Jr., Sea	94	A. Belle, Cle	147	T. Fryman, Det	34	K. Lofton, Cle	9
		B. Anderson, Bal	453	T. Phillips, Det	91	F. Thomas, ChA	141	F. Thomas, ChA	34	A. Diaz, Mil	7
		C. Curtis, Cal	453	A. Belle, Cle	90	2 tied with	140	4 tied with	32	3 tied with	6

Home Runs		Total Bases		Runs Batted In		Walks		Intentional Walks		Strikeouts	
K. Griffey Jr., Sea	40	A. Belle, Cle	294	K. Puckett, Min	112	F. Thomas, ChA	109	M. Vaughn, Bos	20	T. Fryman, Det	128
F. Thomas, ChA	38	K. Griffey Jr., Sea	292	J. Carter, Tor	103	M. Tettleton, Det	97	K. Griffey Jr., Sea	19	J. Canseco, Tex	114
A. Belle, Cle	36	F. Thomas, ChA	291	A. Belle, Cle	101	T. Phillips, Det	95	R. Ventura, ChA	15	M. Vaughn, Bos	112
J. Canseco, Tex	31	K. Lofton, Cle	246	F. Thomas, ChA	101	R. Henderson, Oak	72	P. O'Neill, NYA	13	D. Tartabull, NYA	111
C. Fielder, Det	28	R. Palmeiro, Bal	240	J. Franco, ChA	98	P. O'Neill, NYA	72	2 tied with	12	C. Fielder, Det	110

Hit By Pitch		Sac Hits		Sac Flies		Stolen Bases		Caught Stealing		GDP	
M. Macfarlane, KC	18	P. Kelly, NYA	14	J. Carter, Tor	13	K. Lofton, Cle	60	G. Gagne, KC	17	J. Canseco, Tex	20
E. Sprague, Tor	11	F. Fermin, Sea	12	T. Fryman, Det	13	V. Coleman, KC	50	F. Jose, KC	12	J. Gonzalez, Tex	18
4 tied with	10	J. Cora, ChA	11	R. Sierra, Oak	11	O. Nixon, Bos	42	L. Polonia, NYA	12	C. Ripken Jr., Bal	17
		O. Vizquel, Cle	11	3 tied with	8	C. Knoblauch, Min	35	K. Lofton, Cle	12	C. Fielder, Det	17
		G. DiSarcina, Cal	10			B. Anderson, Bal	31	C. Curtis, Cal	11	P. O'Neill, NYA	16

Runs Created		Runs Created/27 Outs		Batting Average		On-Base Percentage		Slugging Percentage		OBP+Slugging	
F. Thomas, ChA	116	F. Thomas, ChA	11.03	P. O'Neill, NYA	.359	F. Thomas, ChA	.487	F. Thomas, ChA	.729	F. Thomas, ChA	1.217
A. Belle, Cle	112	A. Belle, Cle	10.72	A. Belle, Cle	.357	P. O'Neill, NYA	.461	A. Belle, Cle	.714	A. Belle, Cle	1.152
P. Molitor, Tor	101	P. O'Neill, NYA	9.97	F. Thomas, ChA	.353	A. Belle, Cle	.438	K. Griffey Jr., Sea	.674	K. Griffey Jr., Sea	1.076
K. Griffey Jr., Sea	100	W. Clark, Tex	8.77	K. Lofton, Cle	.349	W. Boggs, NYA	.433	P. O'Neill, NYA	.603	P. O'Neill, NYA	1.064
K. Lofton, Cle	99	K. Griffey Jr., Sea	8.76	W. Boggs, NYA	.342	W. Clark, Tex	.431	B. Hamelin, KC	.599	B. Hamelin, KC	.987

1994 American League Pitching Leaders

Wins		Losses		Winning Percentage		Games		Games Started		Complete Games	
J. Key, NYA	17	T. Belcher, Det	15	J. Key, NYA	.810	B. Wickman, NYA	53	10 tied with	25	R. Johnson, Sea	9
D. Cone, KC	16	J. Deshaies, Min	12	D. Cone, KC	.762	J. Mesa, Cle	51			D. Martinez, Cle	7
M. Mussina, Bal	16	5 tied with	11	M. Mussina, Bal	.762	M. Guthrie, Min	50			C. Finley, Cal	7
B. McDonald, Bal	14			R. Johnson, Sea	.684	B. Brewer, KC	50			4 tied with	6
2 tied with	13			B. McDonald, Bal	.667	C. Willis, Min	49				

Shutouts		Saves		Games Finished		Batters Faced		Innings Pitched		Hits Allowed	
R. Johnson, Sea	4	L. Smith, Bal	33	R. Hernandez, ChA	43	C. Finley, Cal	774	C. Finley, Cal	183.1	K. Brown, Tex	218
5 tied with	3	J. Montgomery, KC	27	R. Aguilera, Min	40	C. Eldred, Mil	769	J. McDowell, ChA	181.0	T. Belcher, Det	192
		R. Aguilera, Min	23	B. Ayala, Sea	40	K. Brown, Tex	760	C. Eldred, Mil	179.0	J. McDowell, ChA	186
		D. Eckersley, Oak	19	L. Smith, Bal	39	J. McDowell, ChA	755	D. Martinez, Cle	176.2	K. Tapani, Min	181
		B. Ayala, Sea	18	D. Eckersley, Oak	39	T. Belcher, Det	750	M. Mussina, Bal	176.1	C. Finley, Cal	178

Home Runs Allowed		Walks		Walks/9 Innings		Strikeouts		Strikeouts/9 Innings		Strikeout/Walk Ratio	
J. Deshaies, Min	30	M. Moore, Det	89	M. Gubicza, KC	1.8	R. Johnson, Sea	204	R. Johnson, Sea	10.7	J. McDowell, ChA	3.02
M. Moore, Det	27	T. Van Poppel, Oak	89	B. Gullickson, Det	2.0	R. Clemens, Bos	168	R. Clemens, Bos	8.9	R. Johnson, Sea	2.83
S. Fernandez, Bal	27	T. Gordon, KC	87	B. Wegman, Mil	2.0	C. Finley, Cal	148	K. Appier, KC	8.4	B. Gullickson, Det	2.60
D. Stewart, Tor	26	C. Eldred, Mil	84	S. Ontiveros, Oak	2.0	P. Hentgen, Tor	147	M. Langston, Cal	8.2	P. Hentgen, Tor	2.49
A. Fernandez, ChA	25	J. Bere, ChA	80	J. McDowell, ChA	2.1	K. Appier, KC	145	J. Bere, ChA	8.1	K. Brown, Tex	2.46

Earned Run Average		Component ERA		Hit Batsmen		Wild Pitches		Opponent Average		Opponent OBP	
S. Ontiveros, Oak	2.65	S. Ontiveros, Oak	2.35	S. Erickson, Min	9	J. Morris, Cle	13	R. Clemens, Bos	.204	S. Ontiveros, Oak	.271
R. Clemens, Bos	2.85	D. Cone, KC	2.57	M. Leiter, Cal	9	J. Guzman, Tor	13	D. Cone, KC	.209	D. Cone, KC	.277
D. Cone, KC	2.94	R. Clemens, Bos	2.72	A. Sele, Bos	9	T. Gordon, KC	12	R. Johnson, Sea	.216	R. Clemens, Bos	.289
M. Mussina, Bal	3.06	R. Johnson, Sea	2.99	J. Nelson, Sea	8	K. Appier, KC	11	S. Ontiveros, Oak	.217	M. Mussina, Bal	.291
R. Johnson, Sea	3.19	M. Mussina, Bal	3.16	5 tied with	7	4 tied with	10	J. Bere, ChA	.229	D. Martinez, Cle	.298

1994 American League Miscellaneous

Managers

Baltimore	Johnny Oates	63-49
Boston	Butch Hobson	54-61
California	Buck Rodgers	16-23
	Bobby Knoop	1-1
	Marcel Lachemann	30-44
Chicago	Gene Lamont	67-46
Cleveland	Mike Hargrove	66-47
Detroit	Sparky Anderson	53-62
Kansas City	Hal McRae	64-51
Milwaukee	Phil Garner	53-62
Minnesota	Tom Kelly	53-60
New York	Buck Showalter	70-43
Oakland	Tony La Russa	51-63
Seattle	Lou Piniella	49-63
Texas	Kevin Kennedy	52-62
Toronto	Cito Gaston	55-60

Awards

Most Valuable Player	Frank Thomas, 1b, ChA
Cy Young	David Cone, KC
Rookie of the Year	Bob Hamelin, dh, KC
Manager of the Year	Buck Showalter, NYA

STATS All-Star Team

C	Mike Stanley, NYA	.300	17	57
1B	Frank Thomas, ChA	.353	38	101
2B	Carlos Baerga, Cle	.314	19	80
3B	Wade Boggs, NYA	.342	11	55
SS	Cal Ripken Jr., Bal	.315	13	75
OF	Albert Belle, Cle	.357	36	101
OF	Ken Griffey Jr., Sea	.323	40	90
OF	Paul O'Neill, NYA	.359	21	83
DH	Chili Davis, Cal	.311	26	84
P	Roger Clemens, Bos	9-7	2.85	168 K
P	David Cone, KC	16-5	2.94	132 K
P	Randy Johnson, Sea	13-6	3.19	204 K
P	Mike Mussina, Bal	16-5	3.06	99 K
RP	Lee Smith, Bal	1-4	3.29	33 Sv

Postseason

None

Outstanding Performances

Perfect Games
Kenny Rogers, Tex   vs. Cal on July 28
No-Hitters
Scott Erickson, Min   vs. Mil on April 27
Three-Homer Games
Tim Raines, ChA   on April 18
Jose Canseco, Tex   on June 13
Darnell Coles, Tor   on July 5
Jim Thome, Cle   on July 22
Cycles
Scott Cooper, Bos   on April 12
Unassisted Triple Plays
John Valentin, Bos   on July 15

1994 National League Standings

EAST	Overall					Home Games						Road Games						Park Index		Record by Month					S/O
	W	L	Pct	GB	DIF	W	L	R	OR	HR	OHR	W	L	R	OR	HR	OHR	Run	HR	M/A	May	June	July	Aug	
Montreal	74	40	.649	—	28	32	20	266	227	42	47	42	20	319	227	66	53	108	89	13-10	15-12	19-8	18-8	9-2	—
Atlanta	68	46	.596	6.0	105	31	24	230	231	61	37	37	22	312	217	76	39	93	91	15-8	16-10	17-10	14-14	6-4	—
New York	55	58	.487	18.5	5	23	30	235	271	53	60	32	28	271	255	64	57	109	106	11-11	14-14	9-18	16-10	5-5	—
Philadelphia	54	61	.470	20.5	5	34	26	268	243	45	40	20	35	253	254	35	58	92	84	9-14	15-13	15-12	12-15	3-7	—
Florida	51	64	.443	23.5	1	25	34	245	341	46	70	26	30	223	235	48	50	121	112	12-12	12-15	12-15	9-17	6-5	—
CENTRAL																									
Cincinnati	66	48	.579	—	120	37	22	306	263	59	65	29	26	303	227	65	52	100	99	15-7	14-15	15-11	17-10	5-5	—
Houston	66	49	.574	0.5	20	37	22	307	241	57	56	29	27	295	262	63	46	93	98	13-10	16-12	14-13	16-11	7-3	—
Pittsburgh	53	61	.465	13.0	1	32	29	271	291	45	61	21	32	195	289	35	56	101	101	12-10	9-18	17-10	11-17	4-6	—
St. Louis	53	61	.465	13.0	7	23	33	248	315	50	66	30	28	287	306	58	68	98	95	12-9	14-14	13-13	8-20	6-5	—
Chicago	49	64	.434	16.5	0	20	39	216	287	47	71	29	25	284	262	62	49	84	97	6-15	16-12	10-16	15-13	2-8	—
WEST																									
Los Angeles	58	56	.509	—	92	33	22	230	209	47	49	25	34	302	300	68	41	78	94	11-12	17-12	13-13	11-15	6-4	—
San Francisco	55	60	.478	3.5	44	29	31	259	258	56	74	26	29	245	242	67	48	97	104	12-11	13-16	8-19	19-8	3-6	—
Colorado	53	64	.453	6.5	1	25	32	317	356	59	61	28	32	256	282	66	59	132	101	10-12	13-15	13-16	14-14	3-7	—
San Diego	47	70	.402	12.5	1	26	31	240	251	51	57	21	39	239	280	41	42	100	137	7-17	11-17	13-14	10-18	6-4	—

Team Batting

Team	G	AB	R	OR	H	2B	3B	HR	TB	RBI	TBB	IBB	SO	HBP	SH	SF	SB	CS	SB%	GDP	Avg	OBP	Slg
Cincinnati	115	3999	609	490	1142	211	36	124	1797	569	388	51	738	29	53	42	119	51	.70	82	.286	.359	.449
Houston	115	3955	602	503	1099	252	25	120	1761	573	394	58	718	43	73	35	124	44	.74	73	.278	.355	.445
Montreal	114	4000	585	454	1111	246	30	108	1741	542	379	39	669	40	53	42	137	36	.79	77	.278	.352	.435
Colorado	117	4006	573	638	1098	206	39	125	1757	540	378	33	761	23	50	36	91	53	.63	96	.274	.345	.439
Atlanta	114	3861	542	448	1031	198	18	137	1676	510	377	39	668	22	60	29	48	31	.61	104	.267	.340	.434
St. Louis	115	3902	535	621	1026	213	27	108	1617	506	434	48	686	33	44	37	76	46	.62	80	.263	.347	.414
Los Angeles	114	3904	532	509	1055	160	29	115	1618	505	366	33	687	19	51	31	74	37	.67	89	.270	.341	.414
Philadelphia	115	3927	521	497	1028	208	28	80	1532	484	396	44	711	31	51	31	67	24	.74	95	.262	.339	.390
New York	113	3869	506	526	966	164	21	117	1523	477	336	40	807	52	59	31	25	26	.49	70	.250	.323	.394
San Francisco	115	3869	504	500	963	159	32	123	1555	472	364	47	719	39	65	27	114	40	.74	72	.249	.324	.402
Chicago	113	3918	500	549	1015	189	26	109	1583	464	364	26	750	27	54	23	69	53	.57	84	.259	.330	.404
San Diego	117	4068	479	531	1117	200	19	92	1631	445	319	47	762	31	67	33	79	37	.68	112	.275	.337	.401
Florida	115	3926	468	576	1043	180	24	94	1553	451	349	25	746	40	42	30	65	26	.71	81	.266	.336	.396
Pittsburgh	114	3864	466	580	1001	198	23	80	1485	435	349	29	725	22	36	28	53	25	.68	90	.259	.328	.384
NL Total	1606	55068	7422	7422	14695	2784	377	1532	22829	6973	5193	559	10147	451	758	455	1141	529	.68	1205	.267	.333	.415
NL Avg Team	115	3933	530	530	1050	199	27	109	1631	498	371	40	725	32	54	33	82	38	.68	86	.267	.333	.415

Team Pitching

Team	G	CG	ShO	Rel	Sv	IP	H	R	ER	HR	SH	SF	HB	TBB	IBB	SO	WP	Bk	H/9	SO/9	BB/9	OAvg	OOBP	ERA
Montreal	114	4	8	259	46	1036.2	970	454	410	100	44	36	38	288	28	805	32	2	8.4	7.0	2.5	.247	.302	3.56
Atlanta	114	16	8	244	26	1026.1	929	448	407	76	48	37	22	378	52	865	35	10	8.1	7.6	3.3	.242	.311	3.57
Cincinnati	115	6	6	261	27	1038.1	1037	490	436	117	56	24	27	339	23	799	41	10	9.0	6.9	2.9	.262	.322	3.78
Philadelphia	115	7	6	243	30	1024.1	1028	497	438	98	63	34	28	377	28	699	45	6	9.0	6.1	3.3	.261	.328	3.85
Houston	115	9	6	268	29	1029.2	1043	503	454	102	50	31	34	367	34	739	35	6	9.1	6.5	3.2	.265	.331	3.97
San Francisco	115	2	4	288	33	1025.1	1014	500	455	122	53	38	37	372	40	655	32	8	8.9	5.7	3.3	.262	.330	3.99
San Diego	117	8	6	273	27	1045.2	1008	531	474	99	66	24	25	393	62	862	48	6	8.7	7.4	3.4	.252	.321	4.08
New York	113	7	3	238	35	1023.0	1069	526	470	117	51	33	21	332	48	640	26	6	9.4	5.6	2.9	.271	.328	4.13
Los Angeles	114	14	5	239	20	1014.0	1041	509	470	90	52	31	33	354	36	732	42	7	9.2	6.5	3.1	.267	.331	4.17
Chicago	113	5	5	286	27	1023.2	1054	549	508	120	46	27	18	392	35	717	41	6	9.3	6.3	3.4	.268	.336	4.47
Florida	115	5	7	300	30	1015.0	1069	576	508	120	68	38	39	428	50	649	57	13	9.5	5.8	3.8	.274	.349	4.50
Pittsburgh	114	8	2	285	24	1005.2	1094	580	518	117	51	37	41	370	52	650	24	11	9.8	5.8	3.3	.281	.347	4.64
St. Louis	115	7	7	330	29	1018.0	1154	621	581	134	57	31	38	355	28	632	40	5	10.2	5.6	3.1	.289	.351	5.14
Colorado	117	4	5	329	28	1031.0	1185	638	590	134	49	34	49	448	43	703	50	11	10.3	6.1	3.9	.292	.366	5.15
NL Total	1606	102	78	3843	411	14356.2	14695	7422	6719	1532	758	455	451	5193	559	10147	548	106	9.2	6.4	3.3	.267	.340	4.21
NL Avg Team	115	7	6	275	29	1025.2	1050	530	480	109	54	33	32	371	40	725	39	8	9.2	6.4	3.3	.267	.340	4.21

Team Fielding

Team	G	PO	A	E	TC	DP	PB	Pct
San Francisco	115	3076	1275	68	4419	113	6	.985
Cincinnati	115	3115	1180	73	4368	91	17	.983
Houston	115	3089	1263	76	4428	110	16	.983
St. Louis	115	3054	1260	80	4394	119	6	.982
Chicago	113	3071	1257	81	4409	110	10	.982
Atlanta	114	3079	1232	81	4392	85	11	.982
Colorado	117	3093	1259	84	4436	117	5	.981
New York	113	3069	1285	89	4443	112	10	.980
Los Angeles	114	3042	1244	88	4374	104	12	.980
Pittsburgh	114	3017	1338	91	4446	131	11	.980
Montreal	114	3110	1178	94	4382	90	3	.979
Philadelphia	115	3073	1144	94	4311	96	11	.978
Florida	115	3045	1208	95	4348	111	18	.978
San Diego	117	3137	1201	111	4449	82	11	.975
NL Total	1606	43070	17324	1205	61599	1471	147	.980

Team vs. Team Records

	Atl	ChN	Cin	Col	Fla	Hou	LA	Mon	NYN	Phi	Pit	SD	SF	StL	Won
Atl	—	4	5	8	8	3	6	4	5	6	3	6	5	5	68
ChN	2	—	5	6	4	4	3	2	1	1	5	6	5	5	49
Cin	5	7	—	4	7	4	3	4	2	4	9	8	7	2	66
Col	2	6	4	—	3	5	4	4	5	2	2	5	3	8	53
Fla	4	5	5	9	—	2	3	2	6	4	1	5	2	3	51
Hou	3	8	6	5	4	—	1	2	3	5	8	5	8	8	66
LA	0	3	6	6	3	8	—	3	6	7	3	6	5	2	58
Mon	5	4	2	2	7	4	9	—	4	5	8	12	5	7	74
NYN	4	4	4	1	4	3	6	3	—	4	4	6	6	6	55
Phi	3	6	2	4	6	1	5	4	6	—	5	4	4	4	54
Pit	9	5	3	3	6	4	3	2	5	4	—	3	1	5	53
SD	1	3	2	5	1	5	4	0	6	8	3	—	5	4	47
SF	1	4	2	7	4	2	5	7	6	8	5	2	—	2	55
StL	7	5	2	4	7	4	4	3	3	5	5	2	4	—	53
Lost	46	64	48	64	64	49	56	40	58	61	61	70	60	61	

Seasons: Standings, Leaders

1994 National League Batting Leaders

Games		At-Bats		Runs		Hits		Doubles		Triples	
D. Bichette, Col	116	D. Bichette, Col	484	J. Bagwell, Hou	104	T. Gwynn, SD	165	L. Walker, Mon	44	B. Butler, LA	9
J. Conine, Fla	115	M. Grissom, Mon	475	M. Grissom, Mon	96	D. Bichette, Col	147	C. Biggio, Hou	44	D. Lewis, SF	9
C. Biggio, Hou	114	D. Lewis, SF	451	B. Bonds, SF	89	J. Bagwell, Hou	147	T. Gwynn, SD	35	M. Kingery, Col	8
D. Lewis, SF	114	J. Conine, Fla	451	R. Lankford, StL	89	H. Morris, Cin	146	J. Bell, Pit	35	R. Sanders, Cin	8
4 tied with	113	M. Williams, SF	445	C. Biggio, Hou	88	J. Conine, Fla	144	D. Bichette, Col	33	R. Mondesi, LA	8

Home Runs		Total Bases		Runs Batted In		Walks		Intentional Walks		Strikeouts	
M. Williams, SF	43	J. Bagwell, Hou	300	J. Bagwell, Hou	116	B. Bonds, SF	74	B. Bonds, SF	18	R. Sanders, Cin	114
J. Bagwell, Hou	39	M. Williams, SF	270	M. Williams, SF	96	D. Justice, Atl	69	T. Gwynn, SD	16	R. Lankford, StL	113
B. Bonds, SF	37	D. Bichette, Col	265	D. Bichette, Col	95	B. Butler, LA	68	K. Mitchell, Cin	15	B. Bonilla, NYN	101
F. McGriff, Atl	34	F. McGriff, Atl	264	F. McGriff, Atl	94	L. Dykstra, Phi	68	A. Cedeno, Hou	15	K. Abbott, Fla	98
A. Galarraga, Col	31	B. Bonds, SF	253	M. Piazza, LA	92	J. Bagwell, Hou	65	J. Bagwell, Hou	14	R. Thompson, NYN	94

Hit By Pitch		Sac Hits		Sac Flies		Stolen Bases		Caught Stealing		GDP	
F. Vina, NYN	12	K. Hill, Mon	16	D. Fletcher, Mon	12	C. Biggio, Hou	39	D. Sanders, 2tm	16	T. Gwynn, SD	20
J. Patterson, SF	11	S. Finley, Hou	13	E. Karros, LA	11	D. Sanders, 2tm	38	S. Sosa, ChN	13	D. Bichette, Col	17
B. Gilkey, StL	10	A. Benes, SD	13	J. Bagwell, Hou	10	M. Grissom, Mon	36	D. Lewis, SF	13	O. Merced, Pit	17
J. Kent, NYN	10	G. Swindell, Hou	12	K. Mitchell, Cin	8	C. Carr, Fla	32	L. Gonzalez, Hou	13	H. Morris, Cin	16
R. Thompson, NYN	10	2 tied with	10	M. Kingery, Col	8	D. Lewis, SF	30	2 tied with	11	J. Bell, Pit	15

Runs Created		Runs Created/27 Outs		Batting Average		On-Base Percentage		Slugging Percentage		OBP+Slugging	
J. Bagwell, Hou	114	J. Bagwell, Hou	11.02	T. Gwynn, SD	.394	T. Gwynn, SD	.454	J. Bagwell, Hou	.750	J. Bagwell, Hou	1.201
B. Bonds, SF	104	B. Bonds, SF	9.88	J. Bagwell, Hou	.368	J. Bagwell, Hou	.451	K. Mitchell, Cin	.681	K. Mitchell, Cin	1.110
F. McGriff, Atl	95	K. Mitchell, Cin	8.83	M. Alou, Mon	.339	K. Mitchell, Cin	.429	B. Bonds, SF	.647	B. Bonds, SF	1.073
C. Biggio, Hou	93	F. McGriff, Atl	8.46	H. Morris, Cin	.335	D. Justice, Atl	.427	F. McGriff, Atl	.623	T. Gwynn, SD	1.022
M. Alou, Mon	87	D. Justice, Atl	8.36	K. Mitchell, Cin	.326	B. Bonds, SF	.426	M. Williams, SF	.607	F. McGriff, Atl	1.012

1994 National League Pitching Leaders

Wins		Losses		Winning Percentage		Games		Games Started		Complete Games	
G. Maddux, Atl	16	A. Benes, SD	14	B. Saberhagen, NYN	.778	S. Reed, Col	61	J. Rijo, Cin	26	G. Maddux, Atl	10
K. Hill, Mon	16	G. Harris, Col	12	K. Hill, Mon	.762	J. Bautista, ChN	58	5 tied with	25	D. Drabek, Hou	6
B. Saberhagen, NYN	14	W. Banks, ChN	12	G. Maddux, Atl	.727	M. Rojas, Mon	58			T. Candiotti, LA	5
D. Jackson, Phi	14	D. Weathers, Fla	12	D. Jackson, Phi	.700	M. Munoz, Col	57			5 tied with	4
T. Glavine, Atl	13	2 tied with	11	P. Martinez, Mon	.688	D. Burba, SF	57				

Shutouts		Saves		Games Finished		Batters Faced		Innings Pitched		Hits Allowed	
G. Maddux, Atl	3	J. Franco, NYN	30	R. Beck, SF	47	G. Maddux, Atl	774	G. Maddux, Atl	202.0	B. Tewksbury, StL	190
R. Martinez, LA	3	R. Beck, SF	28	J. Franco, NYN	43	D. Jackson, Phi	755	D. Jackson, Phi	179.1	D. Jackson, Phi	183
D. Drabek, Hou	2	D. Jones, Phi	27	J. Wetteland, Mon	43	J. Rijo, Cin	733	B. Saberhagen, NYN	177.1	J. Rijo, Cin	177
A. Benes, SD	2	J. Wetteland, Mon	25	D. Jones, Phi	42	T. Glavine, Atl	731	J. Rijo, Cin	172.1	J. Burkett, SF	176
20 tied with	1	2 tied with	21	2 tied with	41	R. Martinez, LA	718	A. Benes, SD	172.1	G. Swindell, Hou	175

Home Runs Allowed		Walks		Walks/9 Innings		Strikeouts		Strikeouts/9 Innings		Strikeout/Walk Ratio	
P. Smith, NYN	25	D. Kile, Hou	82	B. Saberhagen, NYN	0.7	A. Benes, SD	189	A. Benes, SD	9.9	B. Saberhagen, NYN	11.00
G. Harris, Col	22	T. Glavine, Atl	70	B. Tewksbury, StL	1.3	J. Rijo, Cin	171	J. Rijo, Cin	8.9	S. Reynolds, Hou	5.24
S. Cooke, Pit	21	P. Rapp, Fla	69	G. Maddux, Atl	1.4	G. Maddux, Atl	156	P. Martinez, Mon	8.8	G. Maddux, Atl	5.03
3 tied with	20	D. West, Phi	61	S. Reynolds, Hou	1.5	B. Saberhagen, NYN	143	D. Neagle, Pit	8.0	E. Hanson, Cin	4.39
		D. Weathers, Fla	59	G. Swindell, Hou	1.6	P. Martinez, Mon	142	S. Reynolds, Hou	8.0	A. Benes, SD	3.71

Earned Run Average		Component ERA		Hit Batsmen		Wild Pitches		Opponent Average		Opponent OBP	
G. Maddux, Atl	1.56	G. Maddux, Atl	1.59	P. Martinez, Mon	11	D. Kile, Hou	10	G. Maddux, Atl	.207	G. Maddux, Atl	.243
B. Saberhagen, NYN	2.74	D. Drabek, Hou	2.52	C. Hough, Fla	10	R. Lewis, Fla	10	P. Martinez, Mon	.220	B. Saberhagen, NYN	.271
D. Drabek, Hou	2.84	B. Saberhagen, NYN	2.56	D. Kile, Hou	9	S. Sanders, SD	10	D. Drabek, Hou	.220	D. Drabek, Hou	.275
J. Fassero, Mon	2.99	P. Martinez, Mon	2.81	P. Wagner, Pit	8	4 tied with	9	S. Avery, Atl	.227	A. Ashby, SD	.285
S. Reynolds, Hou	3.05	A. Ashby, SD	2.82	A. Watson, StL	8			J. Fassero, Mon	.229	J. Fassero, Mon	.285

1994 National League Miscellaneous

Managers

Atlanta	Bobby Cox	68-46
Chicago	Tom Trebelhorn	49-64
Cincinnati	Davey Johnson	66-48
Colorado	Don Baylor	53-64
Florida	Rene Lachemann	51-64
Houston	Terry Collins	66-49
Los Angeles	Tom Lasorda	58-56
Montreal	Felipe Alou	74-40
New York	Dallas Green	55-58
Philadelphia	Jim Fregosi	54-61
Pittsburgh	Jim Leyland	53-61
St. Louis	Joe Torre	53-61
San Diego	Jim Riggleman	47-70
San Francisco	Dusty Baker	55-60

Awards

Most Valuable Player	Jeff Bagwell, 1b, Hou
Cy Young	Greg Maddux, Atl
Rookie of the Year	Raul Mondesi, of, LA
Manager of the Year	Felipe Alou, Mon

STATS All-Star Team

C	Mike Piazza, LA	.319	24	92	
1B	Jeff Bagwell, Hou	.368	39	116	
2B	Craig Biggio, Hou	.318	6	56	
3B	Matt Williams, SF	.267	43	96	
SS	Wil Cordero, Mon	.294	15	63	
OF	Moises Alou, Mon	.339	22	78	
OF	Barry Bonds, SF	.312	37	81	
OF	Tony Gwynn, SD	.394	12	64	
P	Doug Drabek, Hou	12-6	2.84	121 K	
P	Ken Hill, Mon	16-5	3.32	85 K	
P	Greg Maddux, Atl	16-6	1.56	156 K	
P	Bret Saberhagen, NYN	14-4	2.74	143 K	
RP	Doug Jones, Phi	2-4	2.17	27 Sv	

Postseason

None

Outstanding Performances

No-Hitters
Kent Mercker, Atl vs. LA on April 8

Three-Homer Games
Karl Rhodes, ChN on April 4
Cory Snyder, LA on April 17
Jeff Bagwell, Hou on June 24
Barry Bonds, SF on August 2

1995 American League Standings

EAST	Overall					Home Games						Road Games						Park Index		Record by Month					
	W	L	Pct	GB	DIF	W	L	R	OR	HR	OHR	W	L	R	OR	HR	OHR	Run	HR	M/A	May	June	July	Aug	S/O
Boston	86	58	.597	—	155	42	30	387	360	70	63	44	28	404	338	105	64	101	79	3-1	17-10	14-14	14-13	23-7	15-13
New York	79	65	.549	7.0	15	46	26	411	323	69	76	33	39	338	365	53	83	104	107	3-1	10-16	13-14	17-11	14-17	22-6
Baltimore	71	73	.493	15.0	1	36	36	357	325	90	84	35	37	347	315	83	65	103	118	2-3	11-15	13-15	17-10	11-19	17-11
Detroit	60	84	.417	26.0	2	35	37	354	426	92	93	25	47	300	418	67	77	109	128	2-3	13-15	15-13	10-16	7-21	13-16
Toronto	56	88	.389	30.0	3	29	43	322	388	73	79	27	45	320	389	67	66	100	114	3-2	11-16	9-16	15-14	11-18	7-22
CENTRAL																									
Cleveland	100	44	.694	—	149	54	18	400	272	99	60	46	26	440	335	108	75	87	87	2-2	19-7	20-8	18-9	21-9	20-9
Kansas City	70	74	.486	30.0	3	35	37	285	346	49	68	35	37	344	345	70	74	92	81	2-2	14-13	15-10	10-18	17-13	12-18
Chicago	68	76	.472	32.0	1	38	34	361	361	59	73	30	42	394	397	87	91	91	74	1-4	10-15	14-13	12-16	13-16	18-12
Milwaukee	65	79	.451	35.0	16	33	39	390	426	56	71	32	40	350	321	72	75	122	86	4-1	11-16	11-15	16-12	16-14	7-21
Minnesota	56	88	.389	44.0	1	29	43	368	448	59	120	27	45	335	441	61	90	105	119	2-3	8-20	7-19	13-14	12-16	14-16
WEST																									
Seattle	79	66	.545	—	31	46	27	424	344	101	73	33	39	372	364	81	76	103	109	3-1	16-12	11-17	13-14	16-13	20-9
California	78	67	.538	1.0	128	39	33	405	322	90	88	39	34	396	375	96	75	96	106	2-2	18-11	14-13	20-7	13-17	11-17
Texas	74	70	.514	4.5	22	41	31	379	368	81	73	33	39	312	352	57	79	113	113	2-3	16-12	17-10	9-18	15-14	15-13
Oakland	67	77	.465	11.5	2	38	34	330	343	80	75	29	43	400	418	89	78	82	93	1-4	16-12	16-12	8-20	17-12	9-17

Clinch Date—Boston 9/20, Cleveland 9/08, Seattle 10/02. **Wild Card**—New York.

Team Batting

Team	G	AB	R	OR	H	2B	3B	HR	TB	RBI	TBB	IBB	SO	HBP	SH	SF	SB	CS	SB%	GDP	Avg	OBP	Slg
Cleveland	144	5028	840	607	1461	279	23	207	2407	803	542	40	766	35	31	48	132	53	.71	128	.291	.369	.479
California	145	5019	801	697	1390	252	25	186	2250	761	564	40	889	36	33	38	58	39	.60	115	.277	.358	.448
Seattle	145	4996	796	708	1377	276	20	182	2239	767	549	53	871	39	52	34	110	41	.73	109	.276	.356	.448
Boston	144	4997	791	698	1399	286	31	175	2272	754	560	38	923	65	45	49	99	44	.69	129	.280	.366	.455
Chicago	145	5060	755	758	1417	252	37	146	2181	712	576	54	767	32	46	56	110	39	.74	106	.280	.364	.431
New York	145	4947	749	688	1365	280	34	122	2079	709	625	36	851	39	20	68	50	30	.63	139	.276	.369	.420
Milwaukee	144	5000	740	747	1329	249	42	128	2046	700	502	20	800	46	41	42	105	40	.72	105	.266	.343	.409
Oakland	144	4916	730	761	1296	228	18	169	2067	694	565	25	911	45	32	58	112	46	.71	108	.264	.352	.420
Baltimore	144	4837	704	640	1267	229	27	173	2069	668	574	36	803	39	40	41	92	45	.67	119	.262	.350	.428
Minnesota	144	5005	703	889	1398	270	34	120	2096	662	471	32	916	58	18	36	105	57	.65	152	.279	.352	.419
Texas	144	4913	691	720	1304	247	24	138	2013	651	526	28	877	33	49	45	90	47	.66	112	.265	.346	.410
Detroit	144	4865	654	844	1204	228	29	159	1967	619	551	30	987	41	35	43	73	36	.67	121	.247	.334	.404
Toronto	144	5036	642	777	1309	275	27	140	2058	613	492	27	906	44	33	45	75	16	.82	119	.260	.336	.409
Kansas City	144	4903	629	691	1275	240	35	119	1942	578	475	33	849	43	66	39	120	53	.69	105	.260	.336	.396
AL Total	2020	69522	10225	10225	18791	3591	406	2164	29686	9691	7572	492	12116	595	541	642	1331	586	.69	1667	.270	.344	.427
AL Avg Team	144	4966	730	730	1342	257	29	155	2120	692	541	35	865	43	39	46	95	42	.69	119	.270	.344	.427

Team Pitching

Team	G	CG	ShO	Rel	Sv	IP	H	R	ER	HR	SH	SF	HB	TBB	IBB	SO	WP	Bk	H/9	SO/9	BB/9	OAvg	OOBP	ERA
Cleveland	144	10	10	335	50	1301.0	1261	607	554	135	32	44	45	445	16	926	48	5	8.7	6.4	3.1	.255	.320	3.83
Baltimore	144	19	10	336	29	1267.0	1165	640	607	149	33	34	37	523	40	930	30	9	8.3	6.6	3.7	.245	.322	4.31
Boston	144	7	9	370	39	1292.2	1338	698	631	127	32	44	46	476	28	888	57	1	9.3	6.2	3.3	.268	.334	4.39
Kansas City	144	11	10	308	37	1288.0	1323	691	642	142	39	42	38	503	38	763	45	5	9.2	5.3	3.5	.268	.338	4.49
Seattle	145	9	8	324	39	1289.1	1343	708	644	149	39	52	47	591	37	1068	50	7	9.4	7.5	4.1	.268	.347	4.50
California	145	8	9	368	42	1284.1	1310	697	645	163	48	45	43	486	23	901	42	10	9.2	6.3	3.4	.265	.333	4.52
New York	145	18	5	302	35	1284.2	1286	688	651	159	35	37	32	535	21	908	50	5	9.0	6.4	3.7	.261	.334	4.56
Texas	144	14	4	310	34	1285.0	1385	720	666	152	41	48	36	514	38	838	60	6	9.7	5.9	3.6	.278	.346	4.66
Milwaukee	144	7	4	321	31	1286.0	1391	747	689	146	34	62	47	603	39	699	45	7	9.7	4.9	4.2	.280	.360	4.82
Chicago	145	12	4	373	36	1284.2	1374	758	693	164	37	50	39	617	47	892	45	8	9.6	6.2	4.3	.275	.356	4.85
Toronto	144	16	8	265	22	1292.2	1336	777	701	145	36	37	51	654	42	894	73	4	9.3	6.2	4.6	.268	.356	4.88
Oakland	144	8	4	358	34	1273.0	1320	761	698	153	52	44	53	566	26	890	56	4	9.3	6.3	4.0	.269	.347	4.93
Detroit	144	5	3	366	38	1275.0	1509	844	778	170	42	50	45	536	79	729	67	7	10.7	5.1	3.8	.296	.365	5.49
Minnesota	144	7	2	336	27	1272.2	1450	889	815	210	41	50	36	533	18	790	52	4	10.3	5.6	3.8	.287	.356	5.76
AL Total	2020	151	90	4672	493	17976.0	18791	10225	9414	2164	541	642	595	7572	492	12116	720	82	9.4	6.1	3.8	.270	.352	4.71
AL Avg Team	144	11	6	334	35	1284.0	1342	730	672	155	39	46	43	541	35	865	51	6	9.4	6.1	3.8	.270	.352	4.71

Team Fielding

Team	G	PO	A	E	TC	DP	PB	Pct
Baltimore	144	3801	1441	72	5314	141	8	.986
New York	145	3854	1417	74	5345	121	20	.986
Kansas City	144	3864	1660	90	5614	168	11	.984
Texas	144	3855	1589	98	5542	156	10	.982
California	145	3853	1416	95	5364	120	4	.982
Cleveland	144	3903	1597	101	5601	142	11	.982
Toronto	144	3878	1399	97	5374	131	31	.982
Minnesota	144	3818	1487	100	5405	141	11	.981
Milwaukee	144	3858	1669	105	5632	186	34	.981
Oakland	144	3819	1486	102	5407	151	4	.981
Detroit	144	3825	1594	106	5525	143	3	.981
Seattle	145	3868	1357	104	5329	108	13	.980
Chicago	145	3854	1415	108	5377	131	12	.980
Boston	144	3878	1581	120	5579	151	29	.978
AL Total	2020	53928	21108	1372	76408	1990	210	.982

Team vs. Team Records

	Bal	Bos	Cal	ChA	Cle	Det	KC	Mil	Min	NYA	Oak	Sea	Tex	Tor	Won
Bal	—	4	9	6	2	8	4	7	3	6	5	6	4	7	71
Bos	9	—	11	5	6	8	3	8	5	5	8	7	3	8	86
Cal	4	3	—	10	3	6	5	5	8	7	6	7	6	8	78
ChA	1	3	2	—	5	8	8	6	10	3	7	4	5	6	68
Cle	10	7	2	8	—	10	11	9	6	7	5	6	10	100	
Det	5	5	2	4	3	—	3	8	7	5	2	5	4	7	60
KC	5	2	7	5	1	4	—	10	6	3	5	7	8	7	70
Mil	5	4	2	7	4	5	2	—	9	5	7	3	5	7	65
Min	6	4	5	3	4	5	7	4	—	3	5	4	5	1	56
NYA	7	8	4	5	2	6	8	7	6	—	4	4	6	12	79
Oak	7	4	7	5	0	3	8	2	7	9	—	7	5	3	67
Sea	7	5	6	9	4	5	5	2	8	9	6	—	10	3	79
Tex	1	4	7	7	3	8	6	7	8	3	8	3	—	9	74
Tor	6	5	2	5	3	6	5	5	4	1	7	4	3	—	56
Lost	73	58	67	76	44	84	74	79	88	65	77	66	70	88	

1995 American League Batting Leaders

Games		At-Bats		Runs		Hits		Doubles		Triples	
E. Martinez, Sea	145	L. Johnson, ChA	607	E. Martinez, Sea	121	L. Johnson, ChA	186	E. Martinez, Sea	52	K. Lofton, Cle	13
F. Thomas, ChA	145	O. Nixon, Tex	589	A. Belle, Cle	121	E. Martinez, Sea	182	A. Belle, Cle	52	L. Johnson, ChA	12
5 tied with	144	C. Curtis, Det	586	J. Edmonds, Cal	120	C. Knoblauch, Min	179	K. Puckett, Min	39	B. Anderson, Bal	10
		T. Fryman, Det	567	T. Phillips, Cal	119	T. Salmon, Cal	177	J. Valentin, Bos	37	B. Williams, NYA	9
		B. Williams, NYA	563	T. Salmon, Cal	111	C. Baerga, Cle	175	T. Martinez, Sea	35	C. Knoblauch, Min	8

Home Runs		Total Bases		Runs Batted In		Walks		Intentional Walks		Strikeouts	
A. Belle, Cle	50	A. Belle, Cle	377	A. Belle, Cle	126	F. Thomas, ChA	136	F. Thomas, ChA	29	M. Vaughn, Bos	150
J. Buhner, Sea	40	R. Palmeiro, Bal	323	M. Vaughn, Bos	126	E. Martinez, Sea	116	E. Martinez, Sea	19	B. Gil, Tex	147
F. Thomas, ChA	40	E. Martinez, Sea	321	J. Buhner, Sea	121	T. Phillips, Cal	113	K. Puckett, Min	18	T. Phillips, Cal	135
3 tied with	39	T. Salmon, Cal	319	E. Martinez, Sea	113	M. Tettleton, Tex	107	M. Vaughn, Bos	17	J. Edmonds, Cal	130
		M. Vaughn, Bos	316	2 tied with	111	J. Thome, Cle	97	T. Martinez, Sea	15	M. Blowers, Sea	128

Hit By Pitch		Sac Hits		Sac Flies		Stolen Bases		Caught Stealing		GDP	
E. Sprague, Tor	15	T. Goodwin, KC	14	F. Thomas, ChA	12	K. Lofton, Cle	54	O. Nixon, Tex	21	P. O'Neill, NYA	25
M. Macfarlane, Bos	14	J. Cora, Sea	13	P. O'Neill, NYA	11	O. Nixon, Tex	50	C. Knoblauch, Min	18	A. Belle, Cle	24
M. Vaughn, Bos	14	L. Alicea, Bos	13	W. Clark, Tex	11	T. Goodwin, KC	50	T. Goodwin, KC	18	E. Sprague, Tor	19
M. McGwire, Oak	11	B. Mayne, KC	11	B. Gates, Oak	11	C. Knoblauch, Min	46	V. Coleman, 2tm	16	3 tied with	18
P. Meares, Min	11	4 tied with	10	O. Vizquel, Cle	10	V. Coleman, 2tm	42	2 tied with	15		

Runs Created		Runs Created/27 Outs		Batting Average		On-Base Percentage		Slugging Percentage		OBP+Slugging	
E. Martinez, Sea	151	E. Martinez, Sea	11.67	E. Martinez, Sea	.356	E. Martinez, Sea	.479	A. Belle, Cle	.690	E. Martinez, Sea	1.107
T. Salmon, Cal	132	F. Thomas, ChA	9.37	C. Knoblauch, Min	.333	F. Thomas, ChA	.454	E. Martinez, Sea	.628	A. Belle, Cle	1.091
F. Thomas, ChA	129	T. Salmon, Cal	9.36	T. Salmon, Cal	.330	J. Thome, Cle	.438	F. Thomas, ChA	.606	F. Thomas, ChA	1.061
A. Belle, Cle	121	C. Davis, Cal	8.40	W. Boggs, NYA	.324	T. Salmon, Cal	.429	T. Salmon, Cal	.594	T. Salmon, Cal	1.024
3 tied with	117	J. Thome, Cle	8.11	C. Davis, Cal	.318	C. Davis, Cal	.429	R. Palmeiro, Bal	.583	J. Thome, Cle	.996

1995 American League Pitching Leaders

Wins		Losses		Winning Percentage		Games		Games Started		Complete Games	
M. Mussina, Bal	19	M. Moore, Det	15	R. Johnson, Sea	.900	J. Orosco, Bal	65	M. Gubicza, KC	33	J. McDowell, NYA	8
D. Cone, 2tm	18	K. Gross, Tex	15	E. Hanson, Bos	.750	R. McDowell, Tex	64	C. Finley, Cal	32	S. Erickson, 2tm	7
R. Johnson, Sea	18	J. Bere, ChA	15	O. Hershiser, Cle	.727	S. Belinda, Bos	63	M. Mussina, Bal	32	M. Mussina, Bal	7
K. Rogers, Tex	17	4 tied with	14	C. Nagy, Cle	.727	B. Wickman, NYA	63	9 tied with	31	3 tied with	6
3 tied with	16			K. Rogers, Tex	.708	B. Ayala, Sea	63				

Shutouts		Saves		Games Finished		Batters Faced		Innings Pitched		Hits Allowed	
M. Mussina, Bal	4	J. Mesa, Cle	46	J. Mesa, Cle	57	D. Cone, 2tm	954	D. Cone, 2tm	229.1	P. Hentgen, Tor	236
R. Johnson, Sea	3	L. Smith, Cal	37	R. Hernandez, ChA	57	J. McDowell, NYA	927	M. Mussina, Bal	221.2	T. Stottlemyre, Oak	228
6 tied with	2	R. Aguilera, 2tm	32	J. Wetteland, NYA	56	T. Stottlemyre, Oak	920	J. McDowell, NYA	217.2	M. Gubicza, KC	222
		R. Hernandez, ChA	32	L. Smith, Cal	51	P. Hentgen, Tor	913	R. Johnson, Sea	214.1	R. Bones, Mil	218
		2 tied with	31	R. Aguilera, 2tm	51	M. Gubicza, KC	898	M. Gubicza, KC	213.1	S. Erickson, 2tm	213

Home Runs Allowed		Walks		Walks/9 Innings		Strikeouts		Strikeouts/9 Innings		Strikeout/Walk Ratio	
B. Radke, Min	32	A. Leiter, Tor	108	M. Mussina, Bal	2.0	R. Johnson, Sea	294	R. Johnson, Sea	12.3	R. Johnson, Sea	4.52
K. Gross, Tex	27	J. Bere, ChA	106	D. Martinez, Cle	2.2	T. Stottlemyre, Oak	205	T. Stottlemyre, Oak	8.8	M. Mussina, Bal	3.16
K. Rogers, Tex	26	C. Finley, Cal	93	B. Radke, Min	2.3	C. Finley, Cal	195	C. Finley, Cal	8.6	T. Stottlemyre, Oak	2.56
T. Stottlemyre, Oak	26	W. Alvarez, ChA	93	K. Brown, Bal	2.5	D. Cone, 2tm	191	K. Appier, KC	8.3	A. Fernandez, ChA	2.45
R. Bones, Mil	26	2 tied with	90	M. Gubicza, KC	2.6	K. Appier, KC	185	A. Leiter, Tor	7.5	K. Brown, Bal	2.44

Earned Run Average		Component ERA		Hit Batsmen		Wild Pitches		Opponent Average		Opponent OBP	
R. Johnson, Sea	2.48	R. Johnson, Sea	2.18	R. Clemens, Bos	14	A. Leiter, Tor	14	R. Johnson, Sea	.201	R. Johnson, Sea	.266
T. Wakefield, Bos	2.95	M. Mussina, Bal	2.66	D. Martinez, Cle	12	C. Finley, Cal	13	K. Appier, KC	.221	M. Mussina, Bal	.270
D. Martinez, Cle	3.08	K. Appier, KC	3.01	K. Brown, Bal	9	S. Bergman, Det	13	M. Mussina, Bal	.226	T. Wakefield, Bos	.300
M. Mussina, Bal	3.29	K. Brown, Bal	3.03	T. Wakefield, Bos	9	4 tied with	11	T. Wakefield, Bos	.227	K. Brown, Bal	.302
K. Rogers, Tex	3.38	T. Wakefield, Bos	3.28	4 tied with	8			D. Cone, 2tm	.228	D. Martinez, Cle	.302

1995 American League Miscellaneous

Managers		
Baltimore	Phil Regan	71-73
Boston	Kevin Kennedy	86-58
California	Marcel Lachemann	78-67
Chicago	Gene Lamont	11-20
	Terry Bevington	57-56
Cleveland	Mike Hargrove	100-44
Detroit	Sparky Anderson	60-84
Kansas City	Bob Boone	70-74
Milwaukee	Phil Garner	65-79
Minnesota	Tom Kelly	56-88
New York	Buck Showalter	79-65
Oakland	Tony La Russa	67-77
Seattle	Lou Piniella	79-66
Texas	Johnny Oates	74-70
Toronto	Cito Gaston	56-88

Awards	
Most Valuable Player	Mo Vaughn, 1b, Bos
Cy Young	Randy Johnson, Sea
Rookie of the Year	Marty Cordova, of, Min
Manager of the Year	Lou Piniella, Sea

STATS All-Star Team

C	Mike Stanley, NYA	.268	18	83
1B	Frank Thomas, ChA	.308	40	111
2B	Chuck Knoblauch, Min	.333	11	63
3B	Jim Thome, Cle	.314	25	73
SS	John Valentin, Bos	.298	27	102
OF	Albert Belle, Cle	.317	50	126
OF	Manny Ramirez, Cle	.308	31	107
OF	Tim Salmon, Cal	.330	34	105
DH	Edgar Martinez, Sea	.356	29	113
P	David Cone, 2tm	18-8	3.57	191 K
P	Randy Johnson, Sea	18-2	2.48	294 K
P	Mike Mussina, Bal	19-9	3.29	158 K
P	Tim Wakefield, Bos	16-8	2.95	119 K
RP	Jose Mesa, Cle	3-0	1.13	46 Sv

Postseason	
Division Series	Cleveland 3 vs. Boston 0
	Seattle 3 vs. New York 2
LCS	Cleveland 4 vs. Seattle 2
World Series	Cleveland (AL) 2 vs. Atlanta (NL) 4

Outstanding Performances

Three-Homer Games

John Valentin, Bos	on June 2
Mark McGwire, Oak	on June 11
Mike Stanley, NYA	on August 10
Paul O'Neill, NYA	on August 31
Albert Belle, Cle	on September 19

Cycles

T. Fernandez, NYA	on September 3

1995 National League Standings

	Overall					Home Games						Road Games						Park Index		Record by Month					
EAST	W	L	Pct	GB	DIF	W	L	R	OR	HR	OHR	W	L	R	OR	HR	OHR	Run	HR	M/A	May	June	July	Aug	S/O
Atlanta	90	54	.625	—	103	44	28	322	295	94	66	46	26	323	245	74	41	109	139	4-1	16-12	15-12	20-7	19-10	16-12
New York	69	75	.479	21.0	1	40	32	308	294	63	68	29	43	349	324	62	65	89	103	2-3	11-17	10-17	12-15	16-12	18-11
Philadelphia	69	75	.479	21.0	60	35	37	336	359	51	78	34	38	279	299	43	56	120	130	2-2	21-7	15-12	9-20	13-16	9-18
Florida	67	76	.469	22.5	1	37	34	331	321	68	60	30	42	342	352	76	79	95	84	1-4	7-20	13-13	14-13	17-13	15-13
Montreal	66	78	.458	24.0	4	31	41	303	318	43	55	35	37	318	320	75	73	97	66	3-2	16-13	10-16	14-14	13-15	10-18
CENTRAL																									
Cincinnati	85	59	.590	—	126	44	28	358	308	76	58	41	31	389	315	85	73	95	85	0-5	20-6	17-11	16-10	19-11	13-16
Houston	76	68	.528	9.0	7	36	36	321	296	41	48	40	32	426	378	68	70	77	64	2-3	13-13	16-11	19-10	9-20	17-11
Chicago	73	71	.507	12.0	38	34	38	339	350	83	83	39	33	354	321	75	79	102	108	4-1	16-10	9-20	14-13	15-14	15-13
St. Louis	62	81	.434	22.5	2	39	33	311	316	54	60	23	48	252	342	53	75	104	88	2-3	12-17	11-16	12-15	12-16	13-14
Pittsburgh	58	86	.403	27.0	1	31	41	329	396	69	67	27	45	300	340	56	63	113	114	1-3	11-15	12-15	12-16	13-18	9-19
WEST																									
Los Angeles	78	66	.542	—	40	39	33	281	276	62	48	39	33	353	333	78	77	81	71	3-2	11-17	18-10	13-13	16-14	17-10
Colorado	77	67	.535	1.0	118	44	28	485	490	134	107	33	39	300	293	66	53	164	203	4-1	13-15	15-12	17-11	11-17	17-11
San Diego	70	74	.486	8.0	1	40	32	304	313	55	72	30	42	364	359	61	70	85	97	4-1	10-18	16-10	11-17	15-13	14-15
San Francisco	67	77	.465	11.0	12	37	35	305	364	76	78	30	42	347	412	76	95	88	90	2-3	16-13	12-14	9-18	15-14	13-15

Clinch Date—Atlanta 9/13, Cincinnati 9/22, Los Angeles 10/01. **Wild Card**—Colorado.

Team Batting

Team	G	AB	R	OR	H	2B	3B	HR	TB	RBI	TBB	IBB	SO	HBP	SH	SF	SB	CS	SB%	GDP	Avg	OBP	Slg
Colorado	144	4994	785	783	1406	259	43	200	2351	749	484	47	943	56	82	31	125	59	.68	118	.282	.355	.471
Cincinnati	144	4903	747	623	1326	277	35	161	2156	694	519	42	946	40	62	50	190	68	.74	92	.270	.351	.440
Houston	144	5097	747	674	1403	260	22	109	2034	694	566	58	992	69	78	47	176	60	.75	114	.275	.361	.399
Chicago	144	4963	693	671	1315	267	39	158	2134	648	440	46	953	34	71	35	105	37	.74	110	.265	.333	.430
Florida	143	4886	673	673	1278	214	29	144	1982	636	517	36	916	49	69	48	131	53	.71	105	.262	.344	.406
San Diego	144	4950	668	672	1345	231	20	116	1964	618	447	45	872	35	56	38	124	46	.73	125	.272	.341	.397
New York	144	4958	657	618	1323	218	34	125	1984	617	446	44	994	42	92	43	58	39	.60	105	.267	.338	.400
San Francisco	144	4971	652	776	1256	229	33	152	2007	610	472	55	1060	57	79	24	138	46	.75	92	.253	.327	.404
Atlanta	144	4814	645	540	1202	210	27	168	1970	618	520	37	933	40	56	34	73	43	.63	106	.250	.332	.409
Los Angeles	144	4942	634	609	1303	191	31	140	1976	593	468	46	1023	30	68	35	127	45	.74	99	.264	.335	.400
Pittsburgh	144	4937	629	736	1281	245	27	125	1955	587	456	45	972	24	51	33	84	55	.60	88	.259	.329	.396
Montreal	144	4905	621	638	1268	265	24	118	1935	572	400	43	901	56	58	32	120	49	.71	107	.259	.326	.394
Philadelphia	144	4950	615	658	1296	263	30	94	1901	576	497	38	884	46	77	41	72	25	.74	107	.262	.340	.384
St. Louis	143	4779	563	658	1182	238	24	107	1789	533	436	31	920	46	48	40	79	46	.63	110	.247	.321	.374
NL Total	2014	69049	9329	9329	18184	3367	418	1917	28138	8745	6668	613	13309	624	947	531	1602	671	.70	1478	.263	.331	.408
NL Avg Team	144	4932	666	666	1299	241	30	137	2010	625	476	44	951	45	68	38	114	48	.70	106	.263	.331	.408

Team Pitching

Team	G	CG	ShO	Rel	Sv	IP	H	R	ER	HR	SH	SF	HB	TBB	IBB	SO	WP	Bk	H/9	SO/9	BB/9	OAvg	OOBP	ERA
Atlanta	144	18	11	339	34	1291.2	1184	540	494	107	63	34	32	436	46	1087	38	4	8.2	7.6	3.0	.244	.309	3.44
Los Angeles	144	16	11	355	37	1295.0	1188	609	526	125	59	33	37	462	45	1060	49	12	8.3	7.4	3.2	.243	.311	3.66
New York	144	9	9	298	36	1291.0	1296	618	556	133	62	40	35	401	48	901	39	12	9.0	6.3	2.8	.262	.320	3.88
Cincinnati	144	8	10	330	38	1289.1	1270	623	578	131	56	43	31	424	32	903	58	10	8.9	6.3	3.0	.260	.320	4.03
Houston	144	6	8	394	32	1320.1	1357	674	596	118	56	44	50	460	52	1056	53	6	9.2	7.2	3.1	.266	.331	4.06
St. Louis	143	4	6	377	38	1265.2	1290	658	575	135	83	35	40	445	37	842	51	6	9.2	6.0	3.2	.268	.333	4.09
Montreal	144	7	9	391	42	1283.2	1286	638	586	128	77	29	59	416	26	950	45	9	9.0	6.7	2.9	.262	.325	4.11
Chicago	144	8	12	414	45	1301.0	1313	671	597	162	63	40	34	518	68	926	38	6	9.1	6.4	3.6	.262	.333	4.13
San Diego	144	6	10	337	35	1284.2	1242	672	590	142	72	28	51	512	37	1047	60	5	8.7	7.3	3.6	.255	.331	4.13
Philadelphia	144	8	8	341	41	1290.1	1241	658	603	134	60	44	55	538	36	980	57	10	8.7	6.8	3.8	.254	.333	4.21
Florida	143	12	7	400	29	1286.0	1299	673	610	139	73	27	46	562	54	994	36	5	9.1	7.0	3.9	.264	.343	4.27
Pittsburgh	144	11	7	391	29	1275.1	1407	736	666	130	70	46	57	477	50	871	65	4	9.9	6.1	3.4	.283	.350	4.70
San Francisco	144	12	5	381	34	1293.2	1368	776	699	173	77	53	56	505	51	801	43	15	9.5	5.6	3.5	.275	.345	4.86
Colorado	144	1	1	456	43	1288.1	1443	783	711	160	76	35	41	512	31	891	62	13	10.1	6.2	3.6	.286	.355	4.97
NL Total	2014	124	114	5209	513	18056.0	18184	9329	8387	1917	947	531	624	6668	613	13309	694	117	9.1	6.6	3.3	.263	.338	4.18
NL Avg Team	144	9	8	372	37	1289.0	1299	666	599	137	68	38	45	476	44	951	50	8	9.1	6.6	3.3	.263	.338	4.18

Team Fielding

Team	G	PO	A	E	TC	DP	PB	Pct
Cincinnati	144	3868	1507	79	5454	140	11	.986
Philadelphia	144	3871	1520	97	5488	139	19	.982
Atlanta	144	3875	1569	100	5544	113	8	.982
Colorado	144	3865	1665	107	5637	146	10	.981
San Francisco	144	3881	1548	108	5537	142	7	.980
San Diego	144	3854	1538	108	5500	430	8	.980
Montreal	144	3851	1558	109	5518	119	6	.980
St. Louis	143	3797	1622	113	5532	156	9	.980
New York	144	3873	1603	115	5591	125	14	.979
Chicago	144	3903	1563	115	5581	115	19	.979
Florida	143	3858	1466	115	5439	143	8	.979
Houston	144	3961	1639	121	5721	120	14	.979
Pittsburgh	144	3826	1588	122	5536	138	12	.978
Los Angeles	144	3885	1490	130	5505	120	19	.976
NL Total	2014	54168	21876	1539	77583	2146	164	.980

Team vs. Team Records

	Atl	ChN	Cin	Col	Fla	Hou	LA	Mon	NYN	Phi	Pit	SD	SF	StL	Won
Atl	—	8	8	9	10	6	5	9	5	7	4	5	7	7	90
ChN	4	—	3	6	8	5	7	3	4	6	8	5	5	9	73
Cin	5	7	—	5	6	12	4	8	7	9	8	3	3	8	85
Col	4	7	7	—	5	4	4	7	5	4	8	9	8	5	77
Fla	3	4	6	7	—	8	3	6	7	6	5	3	5	4	67
Hou	6	8	1	4	4	—	3	9	6	5	9	7	5	9	76
LA	4	5	3	9	7	2	—	7	6	4	9	7	8	7	78
Mon	4	5	4	1	7	3	5	—	7	8	4	7	7	4	66
NYN	8	3	5	6	6	6	6	6	—	7	4	6	3	3	69
Phi	6	1	3	2	7	7	9	5	6	—	6	6	6	6	69
Pit	2	5	5	8	4	4	4	3	3		—	4	6	6	58
SD	2	7	6	4	2	6	6	5	7	6	8	—	6	7	70
SF	1	7	3	5	3	3	5	6	8	6	6	7	—	7	67
StL	5	4	5	7	3	4	5	3	4	4	7	5	6	—	62
Lost	54	71	59	67	76	68	66	78	75	75	86	74	77	81	

Seasons: Standings, Leaders

1995 National League Batting Leaders

Games		At-Bats		Runs		Hits		Doubles		Triples	
F. McGriff, Atl	144	B. McRae, ChN	580	C. Biggio, Hou	123	T. Gwynn, SD	197	M. Grace, ChN	51	B. Butler, 2tm	9
B. Bonds, SF	144	D. Bichette, Col	579	B. Bonds, SF	109	D. Bichette, Col	197	D. Bichette, Col	38	E. Young, Col	9
S. Sosa, ChN	144	S. Sosa, ChN	564	S. Finley, SD	104	M. Grace, ChN	180	B. McRae, ChN	38	S. Finley, SD	8
4 tied with	143	S. Finley, SD	562	D. Bichette, Col	102	3 tied with	167	R. Sanders, Cin	36	D. Sanders, 2tm	8
		A. Galarraga, Col	554	B. Larkin, Cin	98			2 tied with	35	L. Gonzalez, 2tm	8

Home Runs		Total Bases		Runs Batted In		Walks		Intentional Walks		Strikeouts	
D. Bichette, Col	40	D. Bichette, Col	359	D. Bichette, Col	128	B. Bonds, SF	120	B. Bonds, SF	22	A. Galarraga, Col	146
L. Walker, Col	36	L. Walker, Col	300	S. Sosa, ChN	119	W. Weiss, Col	98	J. Branson, Cin	14	S. Sosa, ChN	134
S. Sosa, ChN	36	V. Castilla, Col	297	A. Galarraga, Col	106	C. Biggio, Hou	80	L. Walker, Col	13	R. Sanders, Cin	122
B. Bonds, SF	33	E. Karros, LA	295	J. Conine, Fla	105	Q. Veras, Fla	80	J. Bagwell, Hou	12	E. Karros, LA	115
3 tied with	32	B. Bonds, SF	292	E. Karros, LA	105	J. Bagwell, Hou	79	T. Tarasco, Mon	12	R. Brogna, NYN	111

Hit By Pitch		Sac Hits		Sac Flies		Stolen Bases		Caught Stealing		GDP	
C. Biggio, Hou	22	B. Jones, NYN	18	J. Conine, Fla	12	Q. Veras, Fla	56	Q. Veras, Fla	21	C. Hayes, Phi	22
L. Walker, Col	14	A. Ashby, SD	17	J. King, Pit	8	B. Larkin, Cin	51	D. Lewis, 2tm	18	E. Williams, SD	21
A. Galarraga, Col	13	R. Martinez, LA	13	5 tied with	7	D. DeShields, LA	39	D. DeShields, LA	14	T. Gwynn, SD	20
J. Blauser, Atl	12	J. Vizcaino, NYN	13			S. Finley, SD	36	4 tied with	12	F. McGriff, Atl	19
J. Patterson, SF	12	4 tied with	12			R. Sanders, Cin	36			2 tied with	17

Runs Created		Runs Created/27 Outs		Batting Average		On-Base Percentage		Slugging Percentage		OBP+Slugging	
B. Bonds, SF	127	B. Bonds, SF	8.97	T. Gwynn, SD	.368	B. Bonds, SF	.431	D. Bichette, Col	.620	B. Bonds, SF	1.009
D. Bichette, Col	123	B. Larkin, Cin	8.28	D. Bichette, Col	.340	C. Biggio, Hou	.406	L. Walker, Col	.607	L. Walker, Col	.988
C. Biggio, Hou	112	R. Sanders, Cin	8.12	M. Grace, ChN	.326	T. Gwynn, SD	.404	R. Sanders, Cin	.579	D. Bichette, Col	.984
S. Sosa, ChN	112	D. Bichette, Col	8.04	B. Larkin, Cin	.319	W. Weiss, Col	.403	B. Bonds, SF	.577	R. Sanders, Cin	.975
2 tied with	109	T. Gwynn, SD	7.41	V. Castilla, Col	.309	J. Bagwell, Hou	.399	V. Castilla, Col	.564	V. Castilla, Col	.911

1995 National League Pitching Leaders

Wins		Losses		Winning Percentage		Games		Games Started		Complete Games	
G. Maddux, Atl	19	P. Wagner, Pit	16	G. Maddux, Atl	.905	C. Leskanic, Col	76	M. Portugal, 2tm	31	G. Maddux, Atl	10
P. Schourek, Cin	18	T. Candiotti, LA	14	P. Schourek, Cin	.720	D. Veres, Hou	72	D. Drabek, Hou	31	M. Leiter, SF	7
R. Martinez, LA	17	J. Burkett, Fla	14	R. Martinez, LA	.708	S. Reed, Col	71	A. Ashby, SD	31	I. Valdes, LA	6
T. Glavine, Atl	16	J. Fassero, Mon	14	J. Smiley, Cin	.706	Y. Perez, Fla	69	D. Neagle, Pit	31	D. Neagle, Pit	5
4 tied with	14	3 tied with	13	J. Navarro, ChN	.700	3 tied with	68	E. Loaiza, Pit	31	4 tied with	4

Shutouts		Saves		Games Finished		Batters Faced		Innings Pitched		Hits Allowed	
G. Maddux, ChN	3	R. Myers, ChN	38	H. Slocumb, Phi	54	D. Neagle, Pit	876	G. Maddux, Atl	209.2	D. Neagle, Pit	221
H. Nomo, LA	3	T. Henke, StL	36	R. Nen, Fla	54	R. Martinez, LA	859	D. Neagle, Pit	209.2	P. Quantrill, Phi	212
10 tied with	2	R. Beck, SF	33	T. Worrell, LA	53	J. Hamilton, SD	850	R. Martinez, LA	206.1	B. Jones, NYN	209
		T. Worrell, LA	32	R. Beck, SF	52	B. Jones, NYN	839	J. Hamilton, SD	204.1	J. Burkett, Fla	208
		H. Slocumb, Phi	32	2 tied with	51	J. Navarro, ChN	837	J. Navarro, ChN	200.1	J. Fassero, Mon	207

Home Runs Allowed		Walks		Walks/9 Innings		Strikeouts		Strikeouts/9 Innings		Strikeout/Walk Ratio	
K. Foster, ChN	32	R. Martinez, LA	81	G. Maddux, Atl	1.0	H. Nomo, LA	236	H. Nomo, LA	11.1	G. Maddux, Atl	7.87
T. Mulholland, SF	25	H. Nomo, LA	78	S. Reynolds, Hou	1.8	J. Smoltz, Atl	193	J. Smoltz, Atl	9.0	S. Reynolds, Hou	4.73
S. Trachsel, ChN	25	P. Rapp, Fla	76	D. Neagle, Pit	1.9	G. Maddux, Atl	181	S. Reynolds, Hou	8.3	P. Schourek, Cin	3.56
J. Bautista, SF	24	S. Trachsel, ChN	76	J. Smiley, Cin	2.0	S. Reynolds, Hou	175	P. Martinez, Mon	8.0	D. Neagle, Pit	3.33
D. Mlicki, NYN	23	M. Mimbs, Phi	75	P. Schourek, Cin	2.1	P. Martinez, Mon	174	K. Foster, ChN	7.8	J. Smiley, Cin	3.18

Earned Run Average		Component ERA		Hit Batsmen		Wild Pitches		Opponent Average		Opponent OBP	
G. Maddux, Atl	1.63	G. Maddux, Atl	1.41	M. Leiter, SF	17	H. Nomo, LA	19	H. Nomo, LA	.182	G. Maddux, Atl	.224
H. Nomo, LA	2.54	H. Nomo, LA	2.16	D. Kile, Hou	12	H. Carrasco, Cin	15	G. Maddux, Atl	.197	H. Nomo, LA	.270
A. Ashby, SD	2.94	I. Valdes, LA	2.62	A. Ashby, SD	11	J. Smoltz, Atl	13	P. Martinez, Mon	.227	I. Valdes, LA	.277
I. Valdes, LA	3.05	P. Schourek, Cin	2.70	P. Martinez, Mon	11	T. Borland, Phi	12	I. Valdes, LA	.228	P. Schourek, Cin	.281
T. Glavine, Atl	3.08	J. Smoltz, Atl	3.08	J. Hamilton, SD	11	2 tied with	11	P. Schourek, Cin	.228	S. Reynolds, Hou	.300

1995 National League Miscellaneous

Managers

Atlanta	Bobby Cox	90-54
Chicago	Jim Riggleman	73-71
Cincinnati	Davey Johnson	85-59
Colorado	Don Baylor	77-67
Florida	Rene Lachemann	67-76
Houston	Terry Collins	76-68
Los Angeles	Tom Lasorda	78-66
Montreal	Felipe Alou	66-78
New York	Dallas Green	69-75
Philadelphia	Jim Fregosi	69-75
Pittsburgh	Jim Leyland	58-86
St. Louis	Joe Torre	20-27
	Mike Jorgensen	42-54
San Diego	Bruce Bochy	70-74
San Francisco	Dusty Baker	67-77

Awards

Most Valuable Player	Barry Larkin, ss, Cin
Cy Young	Greg Maddux, Atl
Rookie of the Year	Hideo Nomo, p, LA
Manager of the Year	Don Baylor, Col

STATS All-Star Team

C	Mike Piazza, LA	.346	32	93
1B	Mark Grace, ChN	.326	16	92
2B	Craig Biggio, Hou	.302	22	77
3B	Ken Caminiti, SD	.302	26	94
SS	Barry Larkin, Cin	.319	15	66
OF	Dante Bichette, Col	.340	40	128
OF	Barry Bonds, SF	.294	33	104
OF	Reggie Sanders, Cin	.306	28	99
P	Tom Glavine, Atl	16-7	3.08	127 K
P	Greg Maddux, Atl	19-2	1.63	181 K
P	Hideo Nomo, LA	13-6	2.54	236 K
P	Pete Schourek, Cin	18-7	3.22	160 K
RP	Tom Henke, StL	1-1	1.82	36 Sv

Postseason

Division Series	Atlanta 3 vs. Colorado 1
	Cincinnati 3 vs. Los Angeles 0
LCS	Atlanta 4 vs. Cincinnati 0
World Series	Atlanta (NL) 4 vs. Cleveland (AL) 2

Outstanding Performances

No-Hitters
Ramon Martinez, LA vs. Fla on July 14
Three-Homer Games
A. Galarraga, Col on June 25
Reggie Sanders, Cin on August 15
Cycles
Rondell White, Mon on June 11
Gregg Jefferies, Phi on August 25

1996 American League Standings

EAST	Overall					Home Games						Road Games						Park Index		Record by Month					
	W	L	Pct	GB	DIF	W	L	R	OR	HR	OHR	W	L	R	OR	HR	OHR	Run	HR	M/A	May	June	July	Aug	S/O
New York	92	70	.568	—	159	49	31	448	374	76	76	43	39	423	413	86	67	101	102	13-10	16-11	18-11	16-10	13-17	16-11
Baltimore	88	74	.543	4.0	31	43	38	438	441	121	108	45	36	511	462	136	101	90	97	14-12	14-10	14-14	11-16	19-11	16-11
Boston	85	77	.525	7.0	1	47	34	517	464	121	93	38	43	411	457	88	92	113	119	7-19	14-12	13-14	13-13	22-9	16-10
Toronto	74	88	.457	18.0	6	35	46	364	433	87	102	39	42	402	376	90	85	102	108	11-14	13-15	12-15	13-14	14-15	11-15
Detroit	53	109	.327	39.0	1	27	54	391	539	100	130	26	55	392	564	104	111	97	107	9-18	4-23	10-17	12-14	14-15	4-22
CENTRAL																									
Cleveland	99	62	.615	—	171	51	29	488	389	102	75	48	33	464	380	116	98	105	84	16-8	19-9	14-14	16-11	15-13	19-7
Chicago	85	77	.525	14.5	3	44	37	398	370	76	90	41	40	500	424	119	84	83	82	15-10	17-10	14-14	12-15	15-15	12-13
Milwaukee	80	82	.494	19.5	9	38	43	451	460	82	104	42	39	443	439	96	109	103	91	13-12	11-16	17-11	12-16	14-16	14-11
Minnesota	78	84	.481	21.5	9	39	43	452	483	61	121	39	41	425	417	57	112	108	105	13-12	10-16	15-13	13-14	16-14	11-15
Kansas City	75	86	.466	24.0	1	37	43	372	369	50	90	38	43	374	417	73	86	95	89	9-18	15-12	10-17	14-13	14-15	13-11
WEST																									
Texas	90	72	.556	—	178	50	31	508	407	112	86	40	41	420	392	109	82	113	104	16-10	18-9	14-13	13-14	16-12	13-14
Seattle	85	76	.528	4.5	8	43	38	473	449	121	116	42	38	520	446	124	100	94	104	16-10	12-14	14-12	16-12	12-17	15-11
Oakland	78	84	.481	12.0	0	40	41	440	452	113	102	38	43	421	448	130	103	103	92	13-12	11-16	14-15	17-10	11-19	12-12
California	70	91	.435	19.5	0	43	38	387	451	104	123	27	53	375	492	88	96	95	122	13-12	13-14	15-14	10-16	11-18	8-17

Clinch Date—New York 9/25, Cleveland 9/17, Texas 9/27. **Wild Card**—Baltimore.

Team Batting

Team	G	AB	R	OR	H	2B	3B	HR	TB	RBI	TBB	IBB	SO	HBP	SH	SF	SB	CS	SB%	GDP	Avg	OBP	Slg
Seattle	161	5668	993	895	1625	343	19	245	2741	954	670	57	1052	75	46	58	90	39	.70	121	.287	.375	.484
Cleveland	161	5681	952	769	1665	335	23	218	2700	904	671	44	844	43	34	57	160	50	.76	164	.293	.378	.475
Baltimore	163	5689	949	903	1557	299	29	257	2685	914	645	49	915	61	31	67	76	40	.66	134	.274	.361	.472
Texas	163	5702	928	799	1622	323	32	221	2672	890	660	51	1041	31	32	69	83	26	.76	128	.284	.369	.469
Boston	162	5756	928	921	1631	308	31	209	2628	882	642	50	1020	67	33	47	91	44	.67	148	.283	.367	.457
Chicago	162	5644	898	794	1586	284	33	195	2521	860	701	68	927	34	56	52	105	41	.72	139	.281	.370	.447
Milwaukee	162	5662	894	899	1578	304	40	178	2496	845	624	35	986	53	45	50	101	48	.68	115	.279	.361	.441
Minnesota	162	5673	877	900	1633	332	47	118	2413	812	576	42	958	65	20	63	143	53	.73	172	.288	.366	.425
New York	162	5628	871	787	1621	293	28	162	2456	830	632	56	909	41	41	72	96	46	.68	153	.288	.371	.436
Oakland	162	5630	861	900	1492	283	21	243	2546	823	640	36	1114	58	35	39	58	35	.62	134	.265	.350	.452
Detroit	162	5530	783	1103	1413	257	21	204	2324	741	546	26	1268	29	48	49	50	64	.64	132	.256	.331	.420
Toronto	162	5599	766	809	1451	302	35	177	2354	712	529	19	1105	92	38	37	116	38	.75	120	.259	.337	.420
California	161	5686	762	943	1571	256	24	192	2451	727	527	40	974	29	45	33	53	39	.58	148	.276	.344	.431
Kansas City	161	5542	746	786	1477	286	38	123	2208	689	529	36	943	43	66	49	195	85	.70	102	.267	.340	.398
AL Total	2266	79090	12208	12208	21922	4205	421	2742	35195	11583	8592	609	14056	721	570	752	1454	634	.70	1910	.277	.350	.445
AL Avg Team	162	5649	872	872	1566	300	30	196	2514	827	614	44	1004	52	41	54	104	45	.70	136	.277	.350	.445

Team Pitching

Team	G	CG	ShO	Rel	Sv	IP	H	R	ER	HR	SH	SF	HB	TBB	IBB	SO	WP	Bk	H/9	SO/9	BB/9	OAvg	OOBP	ERA
Cleveland	161	13	9	382	46	1452.1	1530	769	701	173	39	46	39	484	42	1033	49	3	9.5	6.4	3.0	.271	.331	4.34
Chicago	162	7	4	391	43	1461.0	1529	794	733	174	41	42	36	616	60	1039	59	1	9.4	6.4	3.8	.270	.343	4.52
Kansas City	161	17	8	322	35	1450.0	1563	786	733	176	42	51	56	460	32	926	56	4	9.7	5.7	2.9	.277	.335	4.55
Toronto	162	19	7	303	35	1445.2	1476	809	734	187	31	48	36	610	37	1033	61		9.2	6.4	3.8	.266	.340	4.57
New York	162	6	9	411	52	1440.0	1469	787	744	143	44	45	49	610	35	1139	55	5	9.2	7.1	3.8	.265	.341	4.65
Texas	163	19	6	347	43	1449.1	1569	799	749	168	33	55	43	582	44	976	38	9	9.7	6.1	3.6	.278	.347	4.65
Boston	162	17	5	409	37	1458.0	1606	921	807	185	32	67	50	722	41	1165	51	6	9.9	7.2	4.5	.279	.360	4.98
Milwaukee	162	6	4	384	42	1447.1	1570	899	826	213	43	64	57	635	33	846	56	6	9.8	5.3	3.9	.278	.354	5.14
Baltimore	163	13	1	378	44	1468.2	1604	903	839	209	44	57	38	597	35	1047	38	5	9.8	6.4	3.7	.280	.349	5.14
Oakland	162	7	5	418	34	1456.1	1638	900	842	205	52	55	52	644	61	884	60	6	10.1	5.5	4.0	.287	.362	5.20
Seattle	161	4	4	403	34	1431.2	1562	895	829	216	42	47	60	605	52	1000	37	3	9.8	6.3	3.8	.279	.353	5.21
Minnesota	162	13	5	387	31	1439.2	1561	900	844	233	41	47	41	581	27	959	49	3	9.8	6.0	3.6	.277	.346	5.28
California	161	12	8	383	38	1439.0	1546	943	847	219	41	56	84	662	47	1052	80	8	9.7	6.6	4.1	.275	.357	5.30
Detroit	162	10	4	426	22	1432.2	1699	1103	1015	241	45	72	80	784	63	957	82	4	10.7	6.0	4.9	.296	.384	6.38
AL Total	2266	163	79	5344	536	20271.2	21922	12208	11243	2742	570	752	721	8592	609	14056	771	66	9.7	6.2	3.8	.277	.359	4.99
AL Avg Team	162	12	6	382	38	1447.2	1566	872	803	196	41	54	52	614	44	1004	55	5	9.7	6.2	3.8	.277	.359	4.99

Team Fielding

Team	G	PO	A	E	TC	DP	PB	Pct
Texas	163	4348	1647	87	6082	150	10	.986
New York	162	4320	1613	91	6024	146	17	.985
Baltimore	163	4406	1730	97	6233	173	14	.984
Minnesota	162	4319	1616	94	5932	142	11	.984
Oakland	162	4369	1778	103	6250	195	11	.984
Chicago	162	4383	1574	109	6066	145	8	.982
Kansas City	161	4350	1704	111	6165	184	11	.982
Toronto	162	4337	1608	110	6055	187	16	.982
Seattle	161	4295	1542	110	5947	155	8	.982
Cleveland	161	4357	1765	124	6246	156	11	.980
California	161	4317	1702	128	6147	156	12	.979
Milwaukee	162	4342	1693	134	6169	180	9	.978
Boston	162	4374	1638	135	6147	152	23	.978
Detroit	162	4298	1727	137	6162	157	7	.978
AL Total	2266	60815	23240	1570	85625	2278	168	.982

Team vs. Team Records

	Bal	Bos	Cal	ChA	Cle	Det	KC	Mil	Min	NYA	Oak	Sea	Tex	Tor	Won
Bal	—	7	6	4	5	11	9	9	7	3	9	7	3	8	88
Bos	6	—	8	6	1	12	3	7	6	7	8	7	6	8	85
Cal	6	4	—	6	4	6	4	7	4	7	6	5	4	7	70
ChA	8	6	6	—	5	10	7	6	6	5	5	8	7	8	85
Cle	7	11	9	8	—	12	7	7	10	3	6	8	4	7	99
Det	2	1	6	3	0	—	6	4	6	5	4	6	4	6	53
KC	3	9	8	6	6	6	—	4	6	4	5	7	6	5	75
Mil	3	5	5	7	6	8	9	—	9	6	7	4	6	5	80
Min	5	6	8	7	3	6	7	4	—	5	6	6	7	8	78
NYA	10	6	6	7	9	8	8	6	7	—	9	3	5	8	92
Oak	4	5	7	7	6	8	7	5	7	3	—	8	7	4	78
Sea	5	6	6	7	4	6	5	9	6	9	5	—	10	5	85
Tex	10	6	9	4	8	9	6	7	5	7	6	3	—	10	90
Tor	5	5	5	7	7	9	8	7	5	8	7	2		—	74
Lost	74	77	91	77	62	109	86	82	84	70	84	76	72	88	

Seasons: Standings, Leaders

1996 American League Batting Leaders

Games		At-Bats		Runs		Hits		Doubles		Triples	
C. Ripken Jr., Bal	163	K. Lofton, Cle	662	A. Rodriguez, Sea	141	P. Molitor, Min	225	A. Rodriguez, Sea	54	C. Knoblauch, Min	14
R. Palmeiro, Bal	162	P. Molitor, Min	660	C. Knoblauch, Min	140	A. Rodriguez, Sea	215	E. Martinez, Sea	52	F. Vina, Mil	10
P. Molitor, Min	161	C. Ripken Jr., Bal	640	R. Alomar, Bal	132	K. Lofton, Cle	210	I. Rodriguez, Tex	47	4 tied with	8
M. Vaughn, Bos	161	I. Rodriguez, Tex	639	K. Lofton, Cle	132	M. Vaughn, Bos	207	J. Cirillo, Mil	46		
C. Fielder, 2tm	160	M. Vaughn, Bos	635	K. Griffey Jr., Sea	125	C. Knoblauch, Min	197	M. Cordova, Min	46		

Home Runs		Total Bases		Runs Batted In		Walks		Intentional Walks		Strikeouts	
M. McGwire, Oak	52	A. Rodriguez, Sea	379	A. Belle, Cle	148	T. Phillips, ChA	125	F. Thomas, ChA	26	J. Buhner, Sea	159
B. Anderson, Bal	50	A. Belle, Cle	375	J. Gonzalez, Tex	144	E. Martinez, Sea	123	M. Vaughn, Bos	19	M. Nieves, Det	158
K. Griffey Jr., Sea	49	M. Vaughn, Bos	370	M. Vaughn, Bos	143	J. Thome, Cle	123	M. McGwire, Oak	16	M. Vaughn, Bos	154
A. Belle, Cle	48	B. Anderson, Bal	369	R. Palmeiro, Bal	142	M. McGwire, Oak	116	A. Belle, Cle	15	E. Sprague, Tor	146
J. Gonzalez, Tex	47	J. Gonzalez, Tex	348	K. Griffey Jr., Sea	140	F. Thomas, ChA	109	K. Griffey Jr., Sea	13	2 tied with	145

Hit By Pitch		Sac Hits		Sac Flies		Stolen Bases		Caught Stealing		GDP	
B. Anderson, Bal	22	T. Goodwin, KC	21	B. Bonilla, Bal	17	K. Lofton, Cle	75	T. Goodwin, KC	22	C. Ripken Jr., Bal	28
C. Knoblauch, Min	19	D. Howard, KC	17	R. Alomar, Bal	12	T. Goodwin, KC	66	K. Lofton, Cle	17	F. Thomas, ChA	25
C. O'Brien, Tor	17	K. Elster, Tex	16	K. Elster, Tex	11	O. Nixon, Tor	54	C. Knoblauch, Min	14	G. Anderson, Cal	22
M. Vaughn, Bos	14	G. DiSarcina, Cal	16	4 tied with	10	C. Knoblauch, Min	45	O. Nixon, Tor	13	P. Molitor, Min	21
2 tied with	13	D. Lewis, ChA	15			O. Vizquel, Cle	35	5 tied with	10	P. O'Neill, NYA	21

Runs Created		Runs Created/27 Outs		Batting Average		On-Base Percentage		Slugging Percentage		OBP+Slugging	
M. Vaughn, Bos	149	M. McGwire, Oak	11.79	A. Rodriguez, Sea	.358	M. McGwire, Oak	.467	M. McGwire, Oak	.730	M. McGwire, Oak	1.198
A. Rodriguez, Sea	147	F. Thomas, ChA	9.72	F. Thomas, ChA	.349	E. Martinez, Sea	.464	J. Gonzalez, Tex	.643	F. Thomas, ChA	1.085
A. Belle, Cle	146	C. Knoblauch, Min	9.53	P. Molitor, Min	.341	F. Thomas, ChA	.459	B. Anderson, Bal	.637	J. Thome, Cle	1.062
C. Knoblauch, Min	145	A. Rodriguez, Sea	9.47	C. Knoblauch, Min	.341	J. Thome, Cle	.450	A. Rodriguez, Sea	.631	E. Martinez, Sea	1.059
R. Palmeiro, Bal	141	E. Martinez, Sea	9.33	R. Greer, Tex	.332	C. Knoblauch, Min	.448	K. Griffey Jr., Sea	.628	A. Rodriguez, Sea	1.045

1996 American League Pitching Leaders

Wins		Losses		Winning Percentage		Games		Games Started		Complete Games	
A. Pettitte, NYA	21	J. Abbott, Cal	18	J. Moyer, 2tm	.813	E. Guardado, Min	83	M. Mussina, Bal	36	P. Hentgen, Tor	10
P. Hentgen, Tor	20	E. Hanson, Tor	17	C. Nagy, Cle	.773	M. Myers, Det	83	11 tied with	35	K. Hill, Tex	7
M. Mussina, Bal	19	R. Robertson, Min	17	A. Pettitte, NYA	.724	M. Stanton, 2tm	81			R. Pavlik, Tex	7
C. Nagy, Cle	17	C. Finley, Cal	16	D. Oliver, Tex	.700	H. Slocumb, Bos	75			4 tied with	6
3 tied with	16	B. Radke, Min	16	P. Hentgen, Tor	.667	2 tied with	73				

Shutouts		Saves		Games Finished		Batters Faced		Innings Pitched		Hits Allowed	
K. Hill, Tex	3	J. Wetteland, NYA	43	R. Hernandez, ChA	61	P. Hentgen, Tor	1100	P. Hentgen, Tor	265.2	C. Haney, KC	267
P. Hentgen, Tor	3	J. Mesa, Cle	39	J. Mesa, Cle	60	A. Fernandez, ChA	1071	A. Fernandez, ChA	258.0	M. Mussina, Bal	264
R. Robertson, Min	3	R. Hernandez, ChA	38	H. Slocumb, Bos	60	K. Hill, Tex	1061	K. Hill, Tex	250.2	T. Belcher, KC	262
R. Clemens, Bos	2	T. Percival, Cal	36	J. Wetteland, NYA	58	M. Mussina, Bal	1039	M. Mussina, Bal	243.1	S. Erickson, Bal	262
F. Lira, Det	2	M. Fetters, Mil	32	M. Timlin, Tor	56	C. Finley, Cal	1037	R. Clemens, Bos	242.2	K. Hill, Tex	250

Home Runs Allowed		Walks		Walks/9 Innings		Strikeouts		Strikeouts/9 Innings		Strikeout/Walk Ratio	
S. Boskie, Cal	40	R. Robertson, Min	116	C. Haney, KC	2.0	R. Clemens, Bos	257	R. Clemens, Bos	9.5	J. Guzman, Tor	3.11
B. Radke, Min	40	R. Clemens, Bos	106	D. Wells, Bal	2.0	C. Finley, Cal	215	K. Appier, KC	8.8	M. Mussina, Bal	2.96
T. Wakefield, Bos	38	T. Gordon, Bos	105	B. Radke, Min	2.2	K. Appier, KC	207	C. Finley, Cal	8.1	A. Fernandez, ChA	2.78
K. Tapani, ChA	34	E. Hanson, Tor	102	C. Nagy, Cle	2.5	M. Mussina, Bal	204	J. Guzman, Tor	7.9	K. Appier, KC	2.76
A. Fernandez, ChA	34	W. Alvarez, ChA	97	A. Fernandez, ChA	2.5	A. Fernandez, ChA	200	M. Mussina, Bal	7.5	C. Nagy, Cle	2.74

Earned Run Average		Component ERA		Hit Batsmen		Wild Pitches		Opponent Average		Opponent OBP	
J. Guzman, Tor	2.93	J. Guzman, Tor	3.00	J. Grimsley, Cal	13	C. Finley, Cal	17	J. Guzman, Tor	.228	J. Guzman, Tor	.289
P. Hentgen, Tor	3.22	P. Hentgen, Tor	3.26	S. Boskie, Cal	13	R. Lewis, Det	14	R. Clemens, Bos	.237	B. Radke, Min	.302
C. Nagy, Cle	3.41	K. Appier, KC	3.41	O. Hershiser, Cle	12	E. Hanson, Tor	13	P. Hentgen, Tor	.241	C. Nagy, Cle	.306
A. Fernandez, ChA	3.45	C. Nagy, Cle	3.50	T. Wakefield, Bos	12	J. Abbott, Cal	13	K. Appier, KC	.245	A. Fernandez, ChA	.307
K. Appier, KC	3.62	R. Clemens, Bos	3.52	3 tied with	11	K. Tapani, ChA	13	A. Fernandez, ChA	.253	P. Hentgen, Tor	.308

1996 American League Miscellaneous

Managers

Baltimore	Davey Johnson	88-74
Boston	Kevin Kennedy	85-77
California	Marcel Lachemann	53-64
	John McNamara	17-27
Chicago	Terry Bevington	85-77
Cleveland	Mike Hargrove	99-62
Detroit	Buddy Bell	53-109
Kansas City	Bob Boone	75-86
Milwaukee	Phil Garner	80-82
Minnesota	Tom Kelly	78-84
New York	Joe Torre	92-70
Oakland	Art Howe	78-84
Seattle	Lou Piniella	85-76
Texas	Johnny Oates	90-72
Toronto	Cito Gaston	74-88

Awards

Most Valuable Player	Juan Gonzalez, of, Tex
Cy Young	Pat Hentgen, Tor
Rookie of the Year	Derek Jeter, ss, NYA
Manager of the Year	Johnny Oates, Tex
	Joe Torre, NYA

STATS All-Star Team

C	Ivan Rodriguez, Tex	.300	19	86
1B	Mark McGwire, Oak	.312	52	113
2B	Chuck Knoblauch, Min	.341	13	72
3B	Jim Thome, Cle	.311	38	116
SS	Alex Rodriguez, Sea	.358	36	123
OF	Albert Belle, Cle	.311	48	148
OF	Juan Gonzalez, Tex	.314	47	144
OF	Ken Griffey Jr., Sea	.303	49	140
DH	Edgar Martinez, Sea	.327	26	103
P	Kevin Appier, KC	14-11	3.62	207 K
P	Alex Fernandez, ChA	16-10	3.45	200 K
P	Pat Hentgen, Tor	20-10	3.22	177 K
P	Charles Nagy, Cle	17-5	3.41	167 K
RP	Roberto Hernandez, ChA	6-5	1.91	38 Sv

Postseason

Division Series	Baltimore 3 vs. Cleveland 1
	New York 3 vs. Texas 1
LCS	New York 4 vs. Baltimore 1
World Series	New York (AL) 4 vs. Atlanta (NL) 2

Outstanding Performances

No-Hitters

Dwight Gooden, NYA vs. Sea on May 14

Three-Homer Games

Dan Wilson, Sea	on April 11
Cecil Fielder, Det	on April 16
Ernie Young, Oak	on May 10
G. Berroa, Oak	on May 22
Ken Griffey Jr., Sea	on May 24
Cal Ripken Jr., Bal	on May 28
Edgar Martinez, Sea	on July 6
D. Strawberry, NYA	on August 6
G. Berroa, Oak	on August 12
Frank Thomas, ChA	on September 15
Mo Vaughn, Bos	on September 24

Cycles

John Valentin, Bos on June 6

1996 National League Standings

	Overall					Home Games						Road Games						Park Index		Record by Month					
EAST	W	L	Pct	GB	DIF	W	L	R	OR	HR	OHR	W	L	R	OR	HR	OHR	Run	HR	M/A	May	June	July	Aug	S/O
Atlanta	96	66	.593	—	139	56	25	434	300	106	66	40	41	339	348	91	54	107	119	16-11	19-6	15-13	15-11	19-10	12-15
Montreal	88	74	.543	8.0	46	50	31	410	330	81	76	38	43	331	338	67	76	111	110	17-9	14-14	16-10	11-15	14-14	16-12
Florida	80	82	.494	16.0	1	52	29	369	277	73	44	28	53	319	426	77	69	87	80	11-16	16-11	12-14	10-17	16-13	15-11
New York	71	91	.438	25.0	4	42	39	335	350	64	72	29	52	411	429	83	87	82	80	11-13	11-17	15-13	15-13	8-20	11-15
Philadelphia	67	95	.414	29.0	2	35	46	313	379	55	82	32	49	337	411	77	78	93	88	13-11	13-15	6-21	11-16	11-19	13-13
CENTRAL																									
St. Louis	88	74	.543	—	88	48	33	391	326	70	81	40	41	368	380	72	92	96	92	12-15	12-14	17-10	15-11	15-15	17-9
Houston	82	80	.506	6.0	95	48	33	364	347	60	63	34	47	389	445	69	91	85	77	13-14	14-14	15-12	15-12	17-11	8-17
Cincinnati	81	81	.500	7.0	6	46	35	413	363	89	86	35	46	365	410	102	81	100	96	9-16	10-12	17-11	16-12	15-17	14-13
Chicago	76	86	.469	12.0	19	43	38	413	372	97	91	33	48	359	399	78	93	104	110	13-14	9-17	16-11	14-12	15-13	9-19
Pittsburgh	73	89	.451	15.0	8	36	44	384	429	74	81	37	45	392	404	64	102	105	96	12-14	9-18	15-12	12-15	8-20	17-10
WEST																									
San Diego	91	71	.562	—	134	45	36	356	337	75	72	46	35	415	345	72	66	91	107	17-10	17-10	9-19	15-12	18-10	15-10
Los Angeles	90	72	.556	1.0	57	47	34	314	283	62	49	43	38	389	369	88	76	79	68	14-14	15-12	13-14	15-11	17-10	16-11
Colorado	83	79	.512	8.0	6	55	26	658	559	149	122	28	53	303	405	72	76	172	183	11-14	14-11	15-14	14-14	16-14	13-12
San Francisco	68	94	.420	23.0	1	38	44	386	431	82	98	30	50	366	431	71	96	100	105	14-12	12-14	10-17	10-17	12-15	10-19

Clinch Date—Atlanta 9/22, St. Louis 9/24, San Diego 9/29. **Wild Card**—Los Angeles.

Team Batting

Team	G	AB	R	OR	H	2B	3B	HR	TB	RBI	TBB	IBB	SO	HBP	SH	SF	SB	CS	SB%	GDP	Avg	OBP	Slg
Colorado	162	5590	961	964	1607	297	37	221	2641	909	527	40	1108	82	81	52	201	66	.75	118	.287	.363	.472
Cincinnati	162	5455	778	773	1398	259	36	191	2302	733	604	47	1134	34	71	49	171	63	.73	115	.256	.339	.422
Pittsburgh	162	5665	776	833	1509	319	33	138	2308	738	510	46	989	40	72	49	126	49	.72	107	.266	.337	.407
Atlanta	162	5614	773	648	1514	264	28	197	2425	735	530	41	1032	27	69	50	83	43	.66	144	.270	.341	.432
Chicago	162	5531	772	771	1388	267	19	175	2218	725	523	48	1090	61	66	48	108	50	.68	126	.251	.328	.401
San Diego	162	5655	771	682	1499	285	24	147	2273	718	601	62	1014	50	59	52	109	55	.66	146	.265	.346	.402
St. Louis	162	5502	759	706	1468	281	31	142	2237	711	495	59	1089	44	88	49	149	58	.72	121	.267	.337	.407
Houston	162	5508	753	792	1445	297	29	129	2187	703	554	64	1057	84	68	55	180	63	.74	115	.262	.345	.397
San Francisco	162	5533	752	862	1400	245	21	153	2146	707	615	62	1189	48	77	43	113	53	.68	108	.253	.338	.388
New York	162	5618	746	779	1515	267	47	147	2317	697	445	54	1069	33	75	49	97	48	.67	114	.270	.332	.412
Montreal	162	5505	741	668	1441	297	27	148	2236	696	492	49	1077	58	79	36	108	34	.76	119	.262	.333	.406
Los Angeles	162	5538	703	652	1396	215	33	150	2127	661	516	59	1190	22	74	45	124	40	.76	112	.252	.322	.384
Florida	162	5498	688	703	1413	240	30	150	2163	650	553	51	1122	55	41	45	99	46	.68	138	.257	.336	.393
Philadelphia	162	5499	650	790	1405	249	39	132	2128	604	536	52	1092	45	54	37	117	41	.74	116	.256	.331	.387
NL Total	2268	77711	10623	10623	20398	3782	434	2220	31708	9987	7501	734	15252	683	974	648	1785	709	.72	1699	.262	.330	.408
NL Avg Team	162	5551	759	759	1457	270	31	159	2265	713	536	52	1089	49	70	46	128	51	.72	121	.262	.330	.408

Team Pitching

Team	G	CG	ShO	Rel	Sv	IP	H	R	ER	HR	SH	SF	HB	TBB	IBB	SO	WP	Bk	H/9	SO/9	BB/9	OAvg	OOBP	ERA
Los Angeles	162	6	9	383	50	1466.1	1378	652	564	125	77	47	39	534	66	1212	39	22	8.5	7.4	3.3	.249	.317	3.46
Atlanta	162	14	9	408	46	1469.0	1372	648	575	120	71	38	19	451	64	1245	49	5	8.4	7.6	2.8	.247	.304	3.52
San Diego	162	5	11	411	47	1489.0	1395	682	616	138	65	47	45	506	47	1194	59	10	8.4	7.2	3.1	.248	.313	3.72
Montreal	162	11	7	433	43	1441.1	1353	668	605	167	65	45	56	482	33	1206	46	9	8.4	7.5	3.0	.247	.313	3.78
Florida	162	8	13	417	41	1443.0	1386	703	634	113	69	37	57	598	49	1050	49	5	8.6	6.5	3.7	.256	.334	3.95
St. Louis	162	13	11	413	43	1452.1	1380	706	641	173	64	49	35	539	43	1050	44	6	8.6	6.5	3.3	.251	.319	3.97
New York	162	10	10	335	41	1440.0	1517	779	675	159	78	48	44	532	73	999	60	12	9.5	6.2	3.3	.272	.337	4.22
Cincinnati	162	6	8	425	52	1443.0	1447	773	692	167	80	58	42	591	66	1089	66	8	9.0	6.8	3.7	.263	.336	4.32
Chicago	162	10	10	439	34	1456.1	1447	771	705	184	61	42	55	546	55	1027	48	8	8.9	6.3	3.4	.260	.330	4.36
Houston	162	13	4	371	35	1447.0	1541	792	702	154	80	51	70	539	60	1163	65	12	9.6	7.2	3.4	.274	.342	4.37
Philadelphia	162	12	6	387	42	1423.1	1463	790	709	160	68	45	35	510	49	1044	71	7	9.3	6.6	3.2	.267	.331	4.48
Pittsburgh	162	5	7	422	37	1453.1	1602	833	744	183	59	48	50	479	50	1044	62	8	9.9	6.5	3.0	.281	.339	4.61
San Francisco	162	9	8	425	35	1442.1	1520	862	755	194	79	48	67	570	60	997	58	10	9.5	6.2	3.6	.273	.345	4.71
Colorado	162	5	4	447	34	1422.2	1597	964	884	198	56	45	69	624	19	932	66	11	10.1	5.9	3.9	.285	.362	5.59
NL Total	2268	127	117	5716	580	20289.0	20398	10623	9501	2220	974	648	683	7501	734	15252	782	131	9.0	6.8	3.3	.262	.338	4.21
NL Avg Team	162	9	8	408	41	1449.0	1457	759	679	159	70	46	49	536	52	1089	56	9	9.0	6.8	3.3	.262	.338	4.21

Team Fielding

Team	G	PO	A	E	TC	DP	PB	Pct
Chicago	162	4369	1767	104	6240	147	13	.983
Florida	162	4329	1796	111	6236	187	12	.982
San Diego	162	4467	1768	118	6353	136	14	.981
Philadelphia	162	4270	1582	116	5968	145	10	.981
Cincinnati	162	4329	1694	121	6144	145	7	.980
Pittsburgh	162	4360	1868	128	6356	144	10	.980
Los Angeles	162	4399	1636	125	6160	143	15	.980
St. Louis	162	4357	1666	125	6148	139	7	.980
Montreal	162	4324	1713	126	6163	121	10	.980
Atlanta	162	4407	1809	130	6346	143	11	.980
San Francisco	162	4327	1637	136	6100	165	13	.978
Houston	162	4341	1692	138	6171	130	14	.978
Colorado	162	4268	1901	149	6318	167	19	.976
New York	162	4320	1717	159	6196	163	10	.974
NL Total	2268	60867	24246	1786	86899	2075	165	.979

Team vs. Team Records

	Atl	ChN	Cin	Col	Fla	Hou	LA	Mon	NYN	Phi	Pit	SD	SF	StL	Won
Atl	—	7	7	5	6	6	5	10	7	9	9	9	7	9	96
ChN	5	—	5	5	6	8	6	7	7	4	6	7	5	6	76
Cin	5	8	—	7	3	7	4	3	6	10	5	9	9	5	81
Col	7	7	6	—	5	8	6	3	7	6	7	8	5	8	83
Fla	7	6	9	8	—	7	6	5	7	6	5	3	6	6	80
Hou	6	8	5	5	5	—	6	4	8	10	8	6	8	2	82
LA	7	5	8	7	7	6	—	9	8	7	6	5	7	8	90
Mon	3	6	9	9	9	9	3	—	7	6	7	4	9	8	88
NYN	6	5	6	5	6	4	4	6	—	7	8	3	6	5	71
Phi	4	6	6	7	2	6	7	6	7	—	7	6	7	7	67
Pit	3	9	8	5	7	6	6	5	5	5	—	4	8	3	73
SD	4	6	3	5	9	6	8	10	9	8	9	—	11	4	91
SF	5	5	8	4	8	7	4	6	4	6	4	2	—	7	68
StL	4	8	4	4	6	11	4	4	7	8	10	8	6	—	88
Lost	66	86	81	79	82	80	72	74	91	95	89	71	94	74	

1996 National League Batting Leaders

Games		At-Bats		Runs		Hits		Doubles		Triples	
C. Biggio, Hou	162	L. Johnson, NYN	682	E. Burks, Col	142	L. Johnson, NYN	227	J. Bagwell, Hou	48	L. Johnson, NYN	21
J. Bagwell, Hou	162	M. Grissom, Atl	671	S. Finley, SD	126	E. Burks, Col	211	E. Burks, Col	45	M. Grissom, Atl	10
G. Sheffield, Fla	161	Grudzielanek, Mon	657	B. Bonds, SF	122	M. Grissom, Atl	207	S. Finley, SD	45	T. Howard, Cin	10
S. Finley, SD	161	S. Finley, SD	655	A. Galarraga, Col	119	Grudzielanek, Mon	201	B. Gilkey, NYN	44	S. Finley, SD	9
2 tied with	160	M. Lansing, Mon	641	G. Sheffield, Fla	118	D. Bichette, Col	198	H. Rodriguez, Mon	42	3 tied with	8

Home Runs		Total Bases		Runs Batted In		Walks		Intentional Walks		Strikeouts	
A. Galarraga, Col	47	E. Burks, Col	392	A. Galarraga, Col	150	B. Bonds, SF	151	B. Bonds, SF	30	H. Rodriguez, Mon	160
B. Bonds, SF	42	A. Galarraga, Col	376	D. Bichette, Col	141	G. Sheffield, Fla	142	M. Piazza, LA	21	A. Galarraga, Col	157
G. Sheffield, Fla	42	S. Finley, SD	348	K. Caminiti, SD	130	J. Bagwell, Hou	135	J. Bagwell, Hou	20	T. Hundley, NYN	146
T. Hundley, NYN	41	V. Castilla, Col	345	B. Bonds, SF	129	R. Henderson, SD	125	G. Sheffield, Fla	19	S. Sosa, ChN	134
4 tied with	40	K. Caminiti, SD	339	E. Burks, Col	128	B. Larkin, Cin	96	K. Caminiti, SD	16	R. Lankford, StL	133

Hit By Pitch		Sac Hits		Sac Flies		Stolen Bases		Caught Stealing		GDP	
C. Biggio, Hou	27	D. Neagle, 2tm	16	K. Caminiti, SD	10	E. Young, Col	53	E. Young, Col	19	E. Karros, LA	27
E. Young, Col	21	P. Martinez, Mon	16	D. Bichette, Col	10	L. Johnson, NYN	50	R. Henderson, SD	15	G. Colbrunn, Fla	22
A. Galarraga, Col	17	T. Glavine, Atl	15	R. Wilkins, 2tm	10	D. DeShields, LA	48	R. Clayton, StL	15	M. Piazza, LA	21
J. Kendall, Pit	15	J. Smoltz, Atl	15	4 tied with	9	B. Bonds, SF	40	3 tied with	12	J. Mabry, StL	21
2 tied with	14	3 tied with	14			A. Martin, Pit	38			5 tied with	20

Runs Created		Runs Created/27 Outs		Batting Average		On-Base Percentage		Slugging Percentage		OBP+Slugging	
B. Bonds, SF	160	B. Bonds, SF	11.33	T. Gwynn, SD	.353	G. Sheffield, Fla	.465	E. Burks, Col	.639	G. Sheffield, Fla	1.090
A. Galarraga, Col	150	G. Sheffield, Fla	10.13	E. Burks, Col	.344	B. Bonds, SF	.461	G. Sheffield, Fla	.624	B. Bonds, SF	1.076
J. Bagwell, Hou	149	J. Bagwell, Hou	9.66	M. Piazza, LA	.336	J. Bagwell, Hou	.451	K. Caminiti, SD	.621	E. Burks, Col	1.047
E. Burks, Col	146	K. Caminiti, SD	9.24	L. Johnson, NYN	.333	M. Piazza, LA	.422	B. Bonds, SF	.615	K. Caminiti, SD	1.028
G. Sheffield, Fla	145	E. Burks, Col	9.14	M. Grace, ChN	.331	R. Henderson, SD	.410	A. Galarraga, Col	.601	J. Bagwell, Hou	1.021

1996 National League Pitching Leaders

Wins		Losses		Winning Percentage		Games		Games Started		Complete Games	
J. Smoltz, Atl	24	F. Castillo, ChN	16	J. Smoltz, Atl	.750	B. Clontz, Atl	81	T. Glavine, Atl	36	C. Schilling, Phi	8
A. Benes, StL	18	P. Rapp, Fla	16	R. Martinez, LA	.714	B. Patterson, ChN	79	5 tied with	35	J. Smoltz, Atl	6
K. Brown, Fla	17	4 tied with	14	I. Valdes, LA	.682	J. Shaw, Cin	78			4 tied with	5
K. Ritz, Col	17			U. Urbina, Mon	.667	M. Dewey, SF	78				
4 tied with	16			A. Benes, StL	.643	M. Wohlers, Atl	77				

Shutouts		Saves		Games Finished		Batters Faced		Innings Pitched		Hits Allowed	
K. Brown, Fla	3	T. Worrell, LA	44	T. Worrell, LA	67	J. Navarro, ChN	1007	J. Smoltz, Atl	253.2	J. Navarro, ChN	244
7 tied with	2	J. Brantley, Cin	44	R. Nen, Fla	66	J. Smoltz, Atl	995	G. Maddux, Atl	245.0	K. Ritz, Col	236
		T. Hoffman, SD	42	M. Rojas, Mon	64	T. Glavine, Atl	994	S. Reynolds, Hou	239.0	D. Kile, Hou	233
		M. Wohlers, Atl	39	M. Wohlers, Atl	64	S. Reynolds, Hou	981	J. Navarro, ChN	236.2	S. Reynolds, Hou	227
		M. Rojas, Mon	36	T. Hoffman, SD	62	G. Maddux, Atl	978	T. Glavine, Atl	235.1	D. Neagle, 2tm	226

Home Runs Allowed		Walks		Walks/9 Innings		Strikeouts		Strikeouts/9 Innings		Strikeout/Walk Ratio	
M. Leiter, 2tm	37	A. Leiter, Fla	119	G. Maddux, Atl	1.0	J. Smoltz, Atl	276	J. Smoltz, Atl	9.8	G. Maddux, Atl	6.14
T. Stottlemyre, StL	30	K. Ritz, Col	105	K. Brown, Fla	1.3	H. Nomo, LA	234	H. Nomo, LA	9.2	J. Smoltz, Atl	5.02
P. Harnisch, NYN	30	D. Burba, Cin	97	D. Darwin, 2tm	1.5	J. Fassero, Mon	222	P. Martinez, Mon	9.2	K. Brown, Fla	4.82
S. Trachsel, ChN	30	D. Kile, Hou	97	S. Reynolds, Hou	1.7	P. Martinez, Mon	222	D. Kile, Hou	9.0	S. Reynolds, Hou	4.64
4 tied with	28	T. Stottlemyre, StL	93	B. Tewksbury, SD	1.9	D. Kile, Hou	219	C. Schilling, Phi	8.9	J. Fassero, Mon	4.04

Earned Run Average		Component ERA		Hit Batsmen		Wild Pitches		Opponent Average		Opponent OBP	
K. Brown, Fla	1.89	K. Brown, Fla	2.00	K. Brown, Fla	16	M. Williams, Phi	16	A. Leiter, Fla	.202	J. Smoltz, Atl	.260
G. Maddux, Atl	2.72	J. Smoltz, Atl	2.17	M. Leiter, 2tm	16	J. Hamilton, SD	14	J. Smoltz, Atl	.216	K. Brown, Fla	.262
A. Leiter, Fla	2.93	G. Maddux, Atl	2.22	D. Kile, Hou	16	J. Isringhausen, NYN	14	H. Nomo, LA	.218	G. Maddux, Atl	.264
J. Smoltz, Atl	2.94	C. Schilling, Phi	2.59	M. Thompson, Col	13	3 tied with	13	K. Brown, Fla	.220	C. Schilling, Phi	.278
T. Glavine, Atl	2.98	H. Nomo, LA	2.86	2 tied with	12			C. Schilling, Phi	.223	S. Reynolds, Hou	.288

1996 National League Miscellaneous

Managers		
Atlanta	Bobby Cox	96-66
Chicago	Jim Riggleman	76-86
Cincinnati	Ray Knight	81-81
Colorado	Don Baylor	83-79
Florida	Rene Lachemann	39-47
	Cookie Rojas	1-0
	John Boles	40-35
Houston	Terry Collins	82-80
Los Angeles	Tom Lasorda	41-35
	Bill Russell	49-37
Montreal	Felipe Alou	88-74
New York	Dallas Green	59-72
	Bobby Valentine	12-19
Philadelphia	Jim Fregosi	67-95
Pittsburgh	Jim Leyland	73-89
St. Louis	Tony La Russa	88-74
San Diego	Bruce Bochy	91-71
San Francisco	Dusty Baker	68-94

Awards

Most Valuable Player	Ken Caminiti, 3b, SD
Cy Young	John Smoltz, Atl
Rookie of the Year	T. Hollandsworth, of, LA
Manager of the Year	Bruce Bochy, SD

STATS All-Star Team

C	Mike Piazza, LA	.336	36	105
1B	Jeff Bagwell, Hou	.315	31	120
2B	Craig Biggio, Hou	.288	15	75
3B	Ken Caminiti, SD	.326	40	130
SS	Barry Larkin, Cin	.298	33	89
OF	Barry Bonds, SF	.308	42	129
OF	Ellis Burks, Col	.344	40	128
OF	Gary Sheffield, Fla	.314	42	120
P	Kevin Brown, Fla	17-11	1.89	159 K
P	Al Leiter, Fla	16-12	2.93	200 K
P	Greg Maddux, Atl	15-11	2.72	172 K
P	John Smoltz, Atl	24-8	2.94	276 K
RP	Trevor Hoffman, SD	9-5	2.25	42 Sv

Postseason

Division Series	Atlanta 3 vs. Los Angeles 0
	St. Louis 3 vs. San Diego 0
LCS	Atlanta 4 vs. St. Louis 3
World Series	Atlanta (NL) 2 vs. New York (AL) 4

Outstanding Performances

No-Hitters

Al Leiter, Fla	vs. Col on May 11
Hideo Nomo, LA	@ Col on September 17

Three-Homer Games

Sammy Sosa, ChN	on June 5
Mike Piazza, LA	on June 29
Benito Santiago, Phi	on September 15
Willie Greene, Cin	on September 24

Cycles

John Mabry, StL	on May 18
Alex Ochoa, NYN	on July 3

1997 American League Standings

EAST	W	L	Pct	GB	DIF	W	L	R	OR	HR	OHR	W	L	R	OR	HR	OHR	Run	HR	M/A	May	June	July	Aug	S/O
						Home Games						Road Games						Park Index		Record by Month					
Baltimore	98	64	.605	—	181	46	35	389	351	107	89	52	29	423	330	89	75	98	120	16-7	20-8	15-12	16-11	18-10	13-16
New York	96	66	.593	2.0	1	47	33	399	333	75	71	49	33	492	355	86	73	89	94	14-13	15-12	17-8	15-11	18-11	17-11
Detroit	79	83	.488	19.0	1	42	39	413	380	98	91	37	44	371	410	78	87	102	115	11-16	14-11	11-15	13-14	14-16	16-11
Boston	78	84	.481	20.0	2	39	42	428	421	90	62	39	42	423	436	95	87	99	84	13-12	9-17	14-15	15-13	16-13	11-14
Toronto	76	86	.469	22.0	1	42	39	326	325	68	72	34	47	328	369	79	95	93	80	11-12	15-13	11-15	13-15	15-15	11-16
CENTRAL																									
Cleveland	86	75	.534	—	142	44	37	425	407	96	89	42	38	443	408	124	92	97	85	12-13	15-11	13-11	14-13	16-14	16-13
Chicago	80	81	.497	6.0	1	45	36	389	393	73	78	35	45	390	440	85	97	93	82	8-17	15-11	17-11	13-14	15-15	12-13
Milwaukee	78	83	.484	8.0	28	47	33	354	351	56	92	31	50	327	391	79	85	99	91	12-11	13-14	12-15	16-12	15-15	10-16
Minnesota	68	94	.420	18.5	12	35	46	394	438	59	92	33	48	378	423	73	95	104	90	11-15	12-16	12-13	13-14	8-20	12-16
Kansas City	67	94	.416	19.0	6	33	47	387	434	88	94	34	47	360	386	70	92	111	114	11-12	12-16	13-13	8-19	11-18	12-16
WEST																									
Seattle	90	72	.556	—	136	45	36	465	422	131	102	45	36	460	411	133	90	102	104	16-11	11-16	20-7	13-13	15-15	15-10
Anaheim	84	78	.519	6.0	14	46	36	444	419	87	123	38	42	385	375	74	79	111	134	12-12	16-12	13-15	19-9	14-15	10-15
Texas	77	85	.475	13.0	27	39	42	410	424	95	91	38	43	397	399	92	78	105	109	14-10	15-13	10-17	11-16	14-17	13-12
Oakland	65	97	.401	25.0	11	35	46	390	497	107	96	30	51	374	449	90	101	108	106	13-13	9-21	12-15	8-19	11-16	12-13

Clinch Date—Baltimore 9/24, Cleveland 9/23, Seattle 9/23. **Wild Card**—New York.

Team Batting

Team	G	AB	R	OR	H	2B	3B	HR	TB	RBI	TBB	IBB	SO	HBP	SH	SF	SB	CS	SB%	GDP	Avg	OBP	Slg
Seattle	162	5614	925	833	1574	312	21	264	2720	890	626	53	1110	49	46	49	89	40	.69	146	.280	.363	.485
New York	162	5710	891	688	1636	325	23	161	2490	846	676	51	954	37	34	70	99	58	.63	138	.287	.373	.436
Cleveland	161	5556	868	815	1589	301	22	220	2594	810	617	39	955	37	45	49	118	59	.67	152	.286	.366	.467
Boston	162	5781	851	857	1684	373	32	185	2676	810	514	54	1044	59	21	55	68	48	.59	155	.291	.361	.463
Anaheim	162	5628	829	794	1531	279	25	161	2343	775	617	37	953	45	40	57	126	72	.64	129	.272	.354	.416
Baltimore	162	5584	812	681	1498	264	22	196	2394	780	586	44	952	65	46	59	63	26	.71	121	.268	.351	.429
Texas	162	5651	807	823	1547	311	27	187	2473	773	500	39	1116	34	28	52	72	37	.66	118	.274	.342	.438
Detroit	162	5481	784	790	1415	268	32	176	2275	743	578	37	1164	49	34	47	161	72	.69	120	.258	.339	.415
Chicago	161	5491	779	833	1498	260	28	158	2288	740	569	40	901	33	47	60	106	52	.67	133	.273	.351	.417
Minnesota	162	5634	772	861	1522	305	40	132	2303	730	495	32	1121	60	20	56	151	52	.74	117	.270	.342	.409
Oakland	162	5589	764	946	1451	274	23	197	2362	714	642	23	1181	49	49	40	71	36	.66	133	.260	.345	.423
Kansas City	161	5599	747	820	1478	256	35	158	2278	711	561	34	1061	42	51	42	130	66	.66	108	.264	.340	.407
Milwaukee	161	5444	681	742	1415	294	27	135	2168	643	494	31	967	58	48	52	103	55	.65	123	.260	.334	.398
Toronto	162	5473	654	694	1333	275	41	147	2131	627	487	26	1138	59	38	52	134	50	.73	102	.244	.318	.389
AL Total	2264	78235	11164	11177	21171	4097	398	2477	33495	10592	7962	540	14617	676	547	740	1491	723	.67	1795	.271	.340	.428
AL Avg Team	162	5588	797	798	1512	293	28	177	2393	757	569	39	1044	48	39	53	107	52	.67	128	.271	.340	.428

Team Pitching

Team	G	CG	ShO	Rel	Sv	IP	H	R	ER	HR	SH	SF	HB	TBB	IBB	SO	WP	Bk	H/9	SO/9	BB/9	OAvg	OOBP	ERA
New York	162	11	10	368	51	1467.2	1463	688	627	144	42	34	45	532	41	1165	62	10	9.0	7.1	3.3	.260	.327	3.84
Baltimore	162	8	10	400	59	1461.0	1404	681	635	164	34	51	30	563	31	1139	43	4	8.6	7.0	3.5	.253	.323	3.91
Toronto	162	19	16	336	34	1442.2	1453	694	630	167	49	37	39	497	29	1150	54	5	9.1	7.2	3.1	.263	.326	3.93
Milwaukee	161	6	8	367	44	1427.1	1419	742	671	177	43	36	61	542	25	1016	46	5	8.9	6.4	3.4	.261	.333	4.23
Anaheim	162	9	5	400	39	1454.2	1506	794	730	202	46	56	54	605	34	1050	57	9	9.3	6.5	3.7	.269	.343	4.52
Detroit	162	13	8	417	42	1445.2	1476	790	733	178	37	61	43	552	33	982	51	3	9.2	6.1	3.4	.266	.334	4.56
Texas	162	8	9	382	33	1429.2	1598	823	747	169	30	58	38	541	40	925	55	6	10.1	5.8	3.4	.283	.347	4.70
Kansas City	161	11	5	393	29	1443.0	1530	820	755	186	51	57	54	531	42	961	62	6	9.5	6.0	3.3	.274	.340	4.71
Cleveland	161	4	3	428	39	1425.2	1528	815	749	181	45	52	51	575	53	1036	59	3	9.6	6.5	3.6	.276	.347	4.73
Chicago	161	6	7	389	52	1422.1	1505	833	749	175	43	52	32	575	45	961	71	9	9.5	6.1	3.6	.271	.340	4.74
Seattle	162	9	8	392	38	1447.2	1500	833	771	192	43	40	66	598	36	1207	57	5	9.3	7.5	3.7	.267	.342	4.79
Boston	162	7	4	417	40	1451.2	1569	857	783	149	32	57	70	611	52	987	51	1	9.7	6.1	3.8	.277	.351	4.85
Minnesota	162	10	4	390	30	1434.0	1596	861	800	187	34	47	33	495	31	908	66	6	10.0	5.7	3.1	.283	.342	5.02
Oakland	162	2	1	480	38	1445.1	1734	946	881	197	44	80	64	642	54	953	51	4	10.8	5.9	4.0	.301	.372	5.49
AL Total	2264	123	98	5559	568	20198.1	21281	11177	10261	2468	573	718	680	7859	546	14440	785	76	9.4	6.4	3.5	.271	.349	4.57
AL Avg Team	162	9	7	397	41	1442.1	1520	798	733	176	41	51	49	561	39	1031	56	5	9.4	6.4	3.5	.271	.349	4.57

Team Fielding

Team	G	PO	A	E	TC	DP	PB	Pct
Detroit	162	4337	1720	92	6149	146	11	.985
Kansas City	161	4329	1630	91	6050	168	14	.985
Toronto	162	4328	1536	94	5958	150	11	.984
Baltimore	162	4383	1666	97	6146	148	7	.984
Minnesota	162	4302	1694	101	6097	170	14	.983
New York	162	4403	1704	104	6211	156	19	.983
Cleveland	161	4277	1728	106	6111	159	8	.983
Oakland	162	4336	1765	122	6223	170	5	.980
Texas	162	4289	1666	121	6076	155	6	.980
Milwaukee	161	4282	1655	121	6058	171	11	.980
Anaheim	162	4364	1592	123	6079	140	19	.980
Seattle	162	4343	1572	126	6041	143	3	.979
Chicago	161	4267	1439	127	5833	131	16	.978
Boston	162	4355	1696	135	6186	179	36	.978
AL Total	2264	60595	23063	1560	85218	2186	180	.982

Team vs. Team Records

Team	Ana	Bal	Bos	ChA	Cle	Det	KC	Mil	Min	NYA	Oak	Sea	Tex	Tor	NL	Won
Ana	—	4	6	6	7	5	6	7	4	4	11	6	8	6	4	84
Bal	7	—	5	5	6	6	7	5	10	8	8	7	10	6	8	98
Bos	5	7	—	3	6	5	3	8	8	4	7	7	3	6	6	78
ChA	5	6	8	—	5	4	11	4	6	2	8	5	8	5	8	80
Cle	4	5	5	7	—	6	8	8	8	5	7	3	5	6	9	86
Det	6	6	7	7	5	—	6	4	4	2	7	4	7	6	8	79
KC	5	4	8	1	3	5	—	6	7	3	3	5	6	5	6	67
Mil	4	6	3	7	4	7	6	—	5	4	5	5	7	7	8	78
Min	7	1	3	6	4	4	7	5	—	3	7	5	3	7	6	68
NYA	7	8	4	9	6	10	8	7	8	—	6	4	7	7	5	96
Oak	1	3	4	3	4	4	8	6	4	5	—	5	5	6	7	65
Sea	6	4	4	8	7	6	6	6	7	7		—	8	8	7	90
Tex	4	1	8	8	6	4	5	4	8	4	7	4	—	4	10	77
Tor	5	6	6	6	5	6	6	4	8	5	5	3	7	—	4	76
Lost	78	64	84	81	75	83	94	83	94	66	97	72	85	86		

Seasons: Standings, Leaders

1997 American League Batting Leaders

Games		At-Bats		Runs		Hits		Doubles		Triples	
C. Ripken Jr., Bal	162	N. Garciaparra, Bos	684	K. Griffey Jr., Sea	125	N. Garciaparra, Bos	209	J. Valentin, Bos	47	N. Garciaparra, Bos	11
B. Hunter, Det	162	B. Hunter, Det	658	N. Garciaparra, Bos	122	R. Greer, Tex	193	J. Cirillo, Mil	46	C. Knoblauch, Min	10
A. Belle, ChA	161	D. Jeter, NYA	654	C. Knoblauch, Min	117	D. Jeter, NYA	190	A. Belle, ChA	45	J. Burnitz, Mil	8
D. Jeter, NYA	159	A. Belle, ChA	634	D. Jeter, NYA	116	G. Anderson, Ana	189	N. Garciaparra, Bos	44	J. Damon, KC	8
T. Clark, Det	159	R. Durham, ChA	634	2 tied with	112	I. Rodriguez, Tex	187	3 tied with	42	5 tied with	7

Home Runs		Total Bases		Runs Batted In		Walks		Intentional Walks		Strikeouts	
K. Griffey Jr., Sea	56	K. Griffey Jr., Sea	393	K. Griffey Jr., Sea	147	J. Thome, Cle	120	K. Griffey Jr., Sea	23	J. Buhner, Sea	175
T. Martinez, NYA	44	N. Garciaparra, Bos	365	T. Martinez, NYA	141	J. Buhner, Sea	119	M. Vaughn, Bos	17	M. Nieves, Det	157
J. Gonzalez, Tex	42	T. Martinez, NYA	343	J. Gonzalez, Tex	131	E. Martinez, Sea	119	C. Davis, KC	16	M. Vaughn, Bos	154
J. Buhner, Sea	40	F. Thomas, ChA	324	T. Salmon, Ana	129	F. Thomas, ChA	109	B. Surhoff, Bal	14	J. Thome, Cle	146
J. Thome, Cle	40	R. Greer, Tex	319	F. Thomas, ChA	125	T. Phillips, 2tm	102	T. Martinez, NYA	14	T. Clark, Det	144

Hit By Pitch		Sac Hits		Sac Flies		Stolen Bases		Caught Stealing		GDP	
B. Anderson, Bal	19	O. Vizquel, Cle	16	T. Martinez, NYA	13	B. Hunter, Det	74	B. Hunter, Det	18	A. Belle, ChA	26
C. Knoblauch, Min	17	D. Cruz, Sea	14	P. Molitor, Min	12	C. Knoblauch, Min	62	T. Goodwin, 2tm	16	J. Buhner, Sea	23
D. Easley, Det	16	M. Bordick, Bal	12	K. Griffey Jr., Sea	12	T. Goodwin, 2tm	50	R. Durham, ChA	16	M. Bordick, Bal	23
P. Meares, Min	16	4 tied with	11	J. King, KC	12	O. Nixon, Tor	47	3 tied with	13	E. Martinez, Sea	21
J. Cirillo, Mil	14			2 tied with	11	O. Vizquel, Cle	43			J. Valentin, Bos	21

Runs Created		Runs Created/27 Outs		Batting Average		On-Base Percentage		Slugging Percentage		OBP+Slugging	
F. Thomas, ChA	150	F. Thomas, ChA	10.93	F. Thomas, ChA	.347	F. Thomas, ChA	.456	K. Griffey Jr., Sea	.646	F. Thomas, ChA	1.067
K. Griffey Jr., Sea	148	D. Justice, Cle	8.91	E. Martinez, Sea	.330	E. Martinez, Sea	.456	F. Thomas, ChA	.611	K. Griffey Jr., Sea	1.028
T. Salmon, Ana	130	K. Griffey Jr., Sea	8.82	D. Justice, Cle	.329	J. Thome, Cle	.423	D. Justice, Cle	.596	D. Justice, Cle	1.013
E. Martinez, Sea	127	E. Martinez, Sea	8.67	B. Williams, NYA	.328	M. Vaughn, Bos	.420	J. Gonzalez, Tex	.589	E. Martinez, Sea	1.009
P. O'Neill, NYA	123	J. Thome, Cle	8.17	M. Ramirez, Cle	.328	D. Justice, Cle	.418	J. Thome, Cle	.579	J. Thome, Cle	1.001

1997 American League Pitching Leaders

Wins		Losses		Winning Percentage		Games		Games Started		Complete Games	
R. Clemens, Tor	21	C. Eldred, Mil	15	R. Johnson, Sea	.833	M. Myers, Det	88	J. Fassero, Sea	35	R. Clemens, Tor	9
R. Johnson, Sea	20	T. Wakefield, Bos	15	J. Moyer, Sea	.773	B. Groom, Oak	78	P. Hentgen, Tor	35	P. Hentgen, Tor	9
B. Radke, Min	20	J. Baldwin, ChA	15	R. Clemens, Tor	.750	J. Nelson, NYA	77	A. Pettitte, NYA	35	B. Tewksbury, Min	5
A. Pettitte, NYA	18	3 tied with	14	A. Pettitte, NYA	.720	P. Quantrill, Tor	77	B. Radke, Min	35	D. Wells, NYA	5
J. Moyer, Sea	17			O. Hershiser, Cle	.700	H. Slocumb, 2tm	76	6 tied with	34	R. Johnson, Sea	5

Shutouts		Saves		Games Finished		Batters Faced		Innings Pitched		Hits Allowed	
R. Clemens, Tor	3	R. Myers, Bal	45	D. Jones, Mil	73	P. Hentgen, Tor	1085	R. Clemens, Tor	264.0	J. Navarro, ChA	267
P. Hentgen, Tor	3	M. Rivera, NYA	43	H. Slocumb, 2tm	61	R. Clemens, Tor	1044	P. Hentgen, Tor	264.0	C. Nagy, Cle	253
6 tied with	2	D. Jones, Mil	36	J. Wetteland, Tex	58	J. Fassero, Sea	1010	A. Pettitte, NYA	240.1	P. Hentgen, Tor	253
		J. Wetteland, Tex	31	R. Aguilera, Min	57	C. Nagy, Cle	991	B. Radke, Min	239.2	B. Witt, Tex	245
		T. Jones, Det	31	R. Myers, Bal	57	B. Radke, Min	989	K. Appier, KC	235.2	T. Belcher, KC	242

Home Runs Allowed		Walks		Walks/9 Innings		Strikeouts		Strikeouts/9 Innings		Strikeout/Walk Ratio	
A. Watson, Ana	37	K. Hill, 2tm	95	J. Burkett, Tex	1.4	R. Clemens, Tor	292	R. Johnson, Sea	12.3	J. Burkett, Tex	4.63
B. Witt, Tex	33	C. Eldred, Mil	89	B. Tewksbury, Min	1.7	R. Johnson, Sea	291	D. Cone, NYA	10.2	R. Clemens, Tor	4.29
D. Springer, Ana	32	T. Wakefield, Bos	87	B. Radke, Min	1.8	D. Cone, NYA	222	R. Clemens, Tor	10.0	M. Mussina, Bal	4.04
J. Dickson, Ana	32	D. Cone, NYA	86	D. Wells, NYA	1.9	M. Mussina, Bal	218	M. Mussina, Bal	8.7	R. Johnson, Sea	3.78
4 tied with	31	J. Fassero, Sea	84	J. Moyer, Sea	2.1	K. Appier, KC	196	C. Finley, Ana	8.5	B. Radke, Min	3.63

Earned Run Average		Component ERA		Hit Batsmen		Wild Pitches		Opponent Average		Opponent OBP	
R. Clemens, Tor	2.05	R. Clemens, Tor	2.17	T. Wakefield, Bos	16	D. Cone, NYA	14	R. Johnson, Sea	.194	R. Clemens, Tor	.273
R. Johnson, Sea	2.28	R. Johnson, Sea	2.47	A. Sele, Bos	15	K. Appier, KC	14	R. Clemens, Tor	.213	R. Johnson, Sea	.277
D. Cone, NYA	2.82	J. Thompson, Det	2.87	O. Olivares, 2tm	13	J. Navarro, ChA	14	D. Cone, NYA	.218	M. Mussina, Bal	.282
A. Pettitte, NYA	2.88	M. Mussina, Bal	3.00	R. Clemens, Tor	12	J. Baldwin, ChA	14	T. Gordon, Bos	.226	J. Thompson, Det	.289
J. Thompson, Det	3.02	A. Pettitte, NYA	3.05	2 tied with	11	J. Fassero, Sea	13	J. Thompson, Det	.233	B. Radke, Min	.293

1997 American League Miscellaneous

Managers

Anaheim	Terry Collins	84-78
Baltimore	Davey Johnson	98-64
Boston	Jimy Williams	78-84
Chicago	Terry Bevington	80-81
Cleveland	Mike Hargrove	86-75
Detroit	Buddy Bell	79-83
Kansas City	Bob Boone	36-46
	Tony Muser	31-48
Milwaukee	Phil Garner	78-83
Minnesota	Tom Kelly	68-94
New York	Joe Torre	96-66
Oakland	Art Howe	65-97
Seattle	Lou Piniella	90-72
Texas	Johnny Oates	77-85
Toronto	Cito Gaston	72-85
	Mel Queen	4-1

Awards

Most Valuable Player	Ken Griffey Jr., of, Sea
Cy Young	Roger Clemens, Tor
Rookie of the Year	N. Garciaparra, ss, Bos
Manager of the Year	Davey Johnson, Bal

STATS All-Star Team

C	Ivan Rodriguez, Tex	.313	20	77
1B	Frank Thomas, ChA	.347	35	125
2B	Chuck Knoblauch, Min	.291	9	58
3B	Matt Williams, Cle	.263	32	105
SS	Nomar Garciaparra, Bos	.306	30	98
OF	Ken Griffey Jr., Sea	.304	56	147
OF	David Justice, Cle	.329	33	101
OF	Bernie Williams, NYA	.328	21	100
DH	Edgar Martinez, Sea	.330	28	108
P	Roger Clemens, Tor	21-7	2.05	292 K
P	Randy Johnson, Sea	20-4	2.28	291 K
P	Mike Mussina, Bal	15-8	3.20	218 K
P	Andy Pettitte, NYA	18-7	2.88	166 K
RP	Randy Myers, Bal	2-3	1.51	45 Sv

Postseason

Division Series	Baltimore 3 vs. Seattle 1
	Cleveland 3 vs. New York 2
LCS	Cleveland 4 vs. Baltimore 2
World Series	Cleveland (AL) 3 vs. Florida (NL) 4

Outstanding Performances

Three-Homer Games

Tino Martinez, NYA	on April 2
Ken Griffey Jr., Sea	on April 25
Matt Williams, Cle	on April 25
Roberto Alomar, Bal	on April 26
Mo Vaughn, Bos	on May 30
Bob Higginson, Det	on June 30
Ivan Rodriguez, Tex	on September 11

Cycles

Alex Rodriguez, Sea	on June 5

1997 National League Standings

	Overall					Home Games						Road Games						Park Index		Record by Month					
EAST	W	L	Pct	GB	DIF	W	L	R	OR	HR	OHR	W	L	R	OR	HR	OHR	Run	HR	M/A	May	June	July	Aug	S/O
Atlanta	101	61	.623	—	169	50	31	378	302	76	55	51	30	413	279	98	56	98	85	19-6	17-11	16-12	17-11	16-11	16-10
Florida	92	70	.568	9.0	13	52	29	358	324	63	66	40	41	382	345	73	66	94	92	15-10	16-11	13-13	19-10		12-15
New York	88	74	.543	13.0	0	50	31	398	339	74	71	38	43	379	370	79	89	98	86	12-14	18-9	15-12	15-11	13-16	15-12
Montreal	78	84	.481	23.0	4	45	36	358	374	81	69	33	48	333	366	91	80	105	88	12-12	16-12	17-11	10-16	12-17	11-16
Philadelphia	68	94	.420	33.0	1	38	43	353	394	61	81	30	51	315	446	55	90	98	98	8-16	11-18	4-22	10-16	17-10	18-12
CENTRAL																									
Houston	84	78	.519	—	153	46	35	373	297	59	56	38	43	404	363	74	78	87	76	15-11	11-17	14-14	19-7	11-17	14-12
Pittsburgh	79	83	.488	5.0	37	43	38	365	395	68	77	36	45	360	365	61	66	105	114	12-13	14-14	11-16	16-12	15-14	11-14
Cincinnati	76	86	.469	8.0	4	40	41	343	388	73	91	36	45	308	376	69	82	107	109	7-18	13-16	14-12	11-14	14-15	17-11
St. Louis	73	89	.451	11.0	4	41	40	345	325	68	59	32	49	344	383	76	65	92	90	11-14	13-14	15-13	12-15	12-17	10-16
Chicago	68	94	.420	16.0	0	42	39	403	363	79	106	26	55	284	396	48	79	113	146	6-19	15-13	11-17	11-17	12-16	13-12
WEST																									
San Francisco	90	72	.556	—	137	48	33	377	387	83	76	42	39	407	406	89	84	94	92	17-7	14-14	16-13	12-15	16-13	15-10
Los Angeles	88	74	.543	2.0	34	47	34	396	365	89	87	41	40	346	280	85	76	92	91	13-11	16-11	13-15	16-13	17-11	13-13
Colorado	83	79	.512	7.0	26	47	34	545	501	124	121	36	45	378	407	115	75	133	129	17-7	12-17	14-15	8-19	17-12	15-9
San Diego	76	86	.469	14.0	7	39	42	367	418	75	96	37	44	428	473	77	76	87	112	9-15	13-15	14-15	16-11	13-17	11-13

Clinch Date—Atlanta 9/22, Houston 9/25, San Francisco 9/27. **Wild Card**—Florida.

Team Batting

Team	G	AB	R	OR	H	2B	3B	HR	TB	RBI	TBB	IBB	SO	HBP	SH	SF	SB	CS	SB%	GDP	Avg	OBP	Slg
Colorado	162	5603	923	908	1611	269	40	239	2677	869	562	35	1060	63	73	35	137	65	.68	138	.288	.363	.478
San Diego	162	5609	795	891	1519	275	16	152	2282	761	604	40	1129	35	63	58	140	60	.70	130	.271	.351	.407
Atlanta	162	5528	791	581	1490	268	37	174	2354	755	597	45	1160	52	83	52	108	58	.65	143	.270	.352	.426
San Francisco	162	5485	784	793	1415	266	37	172	2271	746	642	72	1120	46	64	59	121	49	.71	111	.258	.347	.414
New York	162	5524	777	709	1448	274	28	153	2237	741	550	45	1029	57	58	59	97	74	.57	122	.262	.342	.405
Houston	162	5502	777	660	1427	314	40	133	2220	720	633	63	1085	100	74	53	171	74	.70	104	.259	.352	.403
Los Angeles	162	5544	742	645	1488	242	33	174	2318	706	498	46	1079	33	105	36	131	64	.67	109	.268	.336	.418
Florida	162	5439	740	669	1410	272	28	136	2146	703	686	55	1074	61	71	42	115	58	.66	132	.259	.353	.395
Pittsburgh	162	5503	725	760	1440	291	52	129	2222	686	481	27	1161	92	77	47	160	50	.76	105	.262	.336	.404
Montreal	162	5526	691	740	1423	339	34	172	2346	659	420	40	1084	73	72	40	75	46	.62	95	.258	.323	.425
St. Louis	162	5524	689	708	1409	269	39	144	2188	654	543	54	1191	42	58	44	164	60	.73	128	.255	.331	.396
Chicago	162	5489	687	759	1444	269	39	127	2172	642	451	40	1003	34	83	38	116	60	.66	119	.263	.327	.396
Philadelphia	162	5443	668	840	1390	290	35	116	2098	622	519	32	1002	45	74	50	92	56	.62	105	.255	.330	.385
Cincinnati	162	5484	651	764	1386	269	27	142	2135	612	518	35	1113	45	75	30	190	67	.74	104	.253	.326	.389
NL Total	2268	77203	10440	10427	20300	3907	485	2163	31666	9876	7704	629	15320	773	1030	643	1817	841	.68	1645	.263	.333	.410
NL Avg Team	162	5515	746	745	1450	279	35	155	2262	705	550	45	1094	55	74	46	130	60	.68	118	.263	.333	.410

Team Pitching

Team	G	CG	ShO	Rel	Sv	IP	H	R	ER	HR	SH	SF	HB	TBB	IBB	SO	WP	Bk	H/9	SO/9	BB/9	OAvg	OOBP	ERA
Atlanta	162	21	17	374	37	1465.2	1319	581	518	111	68	46	31	450	56	1196	38	4	8.1	7.3	2.8	.242	.301	3.18
Los Angeles	162	6	6	412	45	1459.1	1325	645	588	163	74	32	45	546	36	1232	36	14	8.2	7.6	3.4	.241	.313	3.63
Houston	162	16	12	354	37	1459.0	1379	660	595	134	76	42	52	511	25	1138	46	9	8.5	7.0	3.2	.252	.319	3.67
Florida	162	12	10	404	39	1446.2	1353	669	615	131	69	45	63	639	41	1188	41	4	8.4	7.4	4.0	.250	.334	3.83
St. Louis	162	5	3	399	39	1455.2	1422	708	628	124	81	52	59	536	34	1130	48	8	8.8	7.0	3.3	.259	.329	3.88
New York	162	7	8	376	49	1459.1	1452	709	641	160	63	44	47	504	43	982	47	7	9.0	6.1	3.1	.262	.326	3.95
Montreal	162	27	14	390	37	1447.0	1365	740	665	149	72	45	63	557	45	1138	52	4	8.5	7.1	3.5	.251	.325	4.14
Pittsburgh	162	6	8	451	41	1436.0	1503	760	683	143	78	47	64	560	71	1080	61	12	9.4	6.8	3.5	.271	.343	4.28
Cincinnati	162	5	8	423	49	1449.0	1408	764	711	173	75	43	77	558	62	1159	64	7	8.7	7.2	3.5	.256	.330	4.42
San Francisco	162	5	9	481	45	1446.0	1494	793	712	160	76	51	39	578	57	1044	48	10	9.3	6.5	3.6	.270	.340	4.43
Chicago	162	6	4	441	37	1429.0	1451	759	705	185	80	57	43	590	51	1072	35	8	9.1	6.8	3.7	.266	.339	4.44
Philadelphia	162	13	7	409	35	1420.1	1441	840	768	171	48	63	58	616	42	1209	73	12	9.1	7.7	3.9	.265	.342	4.87
San Diego	162	5	2	426	43	1450.0	1581	891	804	172	71	46	61	596	37	1059	58	7	9.8	6.6	3.7	.280	.352	4.99
Colorado	162	5		426	38	1432.2	1697	908	836	172	52	46	52	566	23	870	50	6	10.7	5.5	3.6	.300	.367	5.25
NL Total	2268	143	113	5766	571	20255.2	20190	10427	9469	2172	1004	665	769	7807	623	15497	697	112	9.0	6.9	3.5	.263	.340	4.21
NL Avg Team	162	10	8	412	41	1446.2	1442	745	676	155	72	48	55	558	45	1107	50	8	9.0	6.9	3.5	.263	.340	4.21

Team Fielding

Team	G	PO	A	E	TC	DP	PB	Pct
Colorado	162	4298	1946	111	6355	202	5	.983
Cincinnati	162	4347	1576	106	6029	129	13	.982
Philadelphia	162	4261	1547	108	5916	134	16	.982
Atlanta	162	4397	1669	114	6180	136	11	.982
Chicago	162	4287	1605	112	6004	117	16	.981
New York	162	4378	1881	120	6379	165	10	.981
Florida	162	4340	1650	116	6106	167	7	.981
Los Angeles	162	4378	1563	116	6057	104	11	.981
St. Louis	162	4367	1739	123	6229	156	18	.980
San Francisco	162	4338	1799	125	6262	157	9	.980
Houston	162	4377	1874	131	6382	169	8	.979
Pittsburgh	162	4308	1833	131	6272	149	11	.979
San Diego	162	4350	1819	132	6301	132	8	.979
Montreal	162	4341	1697	132	6170	150	13	.979
NL Total	2268	60767	24198	1677	86642	2067	154	.981

Team vs. Team Records

	Atl	ChN	Cin	Col	Fla	Hou	LA	Mon	NYN	Phi	Pit	SD	SF	StL	AL	Won
Atl	—	9	9	5	4	7	6	10	5	10	5	8	7	8	8	101
ChN	2	—	7	2	2	3	5	4	6	7	6	5	4	6	9	68
Cin	2	5	—	5	5	5	6	6	2	8	8	5	4	6	9	76
Col	6	9	6	—	7	5	5	7	4	4	4	4	7	9	6	83
Fla	8	9	6	4	—	7	7	7	4	6	7	5	5	5	12	92
Hou	4	9	7	6	4	—	7	8	7	4	6	3	9	4	6	84
LA	5	6	5	7	4	4	—	7	6	10	9	5	6	5	9	88
Mon	2	7	5	4	5	3	4	—	5	6	5	8	6	6	12	78
NYN	7	5	9	5	8	4	5	7	—	7	7	5	3	9	7	88
Phi	2	5	3	7	3	6	7	1	6	—	5	7	3	6	5	68
Pit	6	5	4	7	4	6	2	6	4	6	—	5	8	9	7	79
SD	3	5	4	8	6	5	7	3	6	4	6	—	4	5	8	76
SF	4	6	7	6	6	8	5	8	8	3	6	8	—	3	10	90
StL	3	8	6	4	3	6	5	5	2	5	3	6	8	—	8	73
Lost	61	94	86	79	70	78	74	84	74	94	83	86	72	89		

1997 National League Batting Leaders

Games			At-Bats			Runs			Hits			Doubles			Triples		
C. Biggio, Hou		162	Grudzielanek, Mon		649	C. Biggio, Hou		146	T. Gwynn, SD		220	Grudzielanek, Mon		54	D. DeShields, StL		14
S. Sosa, ChN		162	S. Sosa, ChN		642	L. Walker, Col		143	L. Walker, Col		208	T. Gwynn, SD		49	N. Perez, Col		10
J. Bagwell, Hou		162	T. Womack, Pit		641	B. Bonds, SF		123	M. Piazza, LA		201	L. Walker, Col		46	T. Womack, Pit		9
E. Karros, LA		162	E. Karros, LA		628	A. Galarraga, Col		120	3 tied with		191	M. Lansing, Mon		45	J. Randa, Pit		9
T. Zeile, LA		160	E. Young, 2tm		622	J. Bagwell, Hou		109				R. Mondesi, LA		42	W. Guerrero, LA		9

Home Runs			Total Bases			Runs Batted In			Walks			Intentional Walks			Strikeouts		
L. Walker, Col		49	L. Walker, Col		409	A. Galarraga, Col		140	B. Bonds, SF		145	B. Bonds, SF		34	S. Sosa, ChN		174
J. Bagwell, Hou		43	M. Piazza, LA		355	J. Bagwell, Hou		135	J. Bagwell, Hou		127	J. Bagwell, Hou		27	R. Gant, StL		162
A. Galarraga, Col		41	A. Galarraga, Col		351	L. Walker, Col		130	G. Sheffield, Fla		121	T. Hundley, NYN		16	H. Rodriguez, Mon		149
3 tied with		40	J. Bagwell, Hou		335	M. Piazza, LA		124	J. Snow, SF		96	L. Walker, Col		14	A. Galarraga, Col		141
			V. Castilla, Col		335	J. Kent, SF		121	R. Lankford, StL		95	J. Snow, SF		13	S. Rolen, Phi		138

Hit By Pitch			Sac Hits			Sac Flies			Stolen Bases			Caught Stealing			GDP		
C. Biggio, Hou		34	E. Renteria, Fla		19	T. Gwynn, SD		12	T. Womack, Pit		60	K. Lofton, Atl		20	F. McGriff, Atl		22
J. Kendall, Pit		31	T. Glavine, Atl		17	B. Gilkey, NYN		12	D. Sanders, Cin		56	R. Mondesi, LA		15	B. Huskey, NYN		21
F. Santangelo, Mon		25	B. Butler, LA		15	W. Joyner, SD		10	D. DeShields, StL		55	E. Renteria, Fla		15	G. Gaetti, StL		20
J. Blauser, Atl		20	R. Ordonez, NYN		14	J. Kent, SF		10	C. Biggio, Hou		47	D. DeShields, StL		14	4 tied with		19
A. Galarraga, Col		17	2 tied with		13	3 tied with		9	E. Young, 2tm		45	E. Young, 2tm		14			

Runs Created			Runs Created/27 Outs			Batting Average			On-Base Percentage			Slugging Percentage			OBP+Slugging		
L. Walker, Col		158	L. Walker, Col		10.99	T. Gwynn, SD		.372	L. Walker, Col		.452	L. Walker, Col		.720	L. Walker, Col		1.172
C. Biggio, Hou		147	M. Piazza, LA		9.71	L. Walker, Col		.366	B. Bonds, SF		.446	M. Piazza, LA		.638	M. Piazza, LA		1.070
J. Bagwell, Hou		142	T. Gwynn, SD		9.24	M. Piazza, LA		.362	M. Piazza, LA		.431	J. Bagwell, Hou		.592	B. Bonds, SF		1.031
T. Gwynn, SD		138	C. Biggio, Hou		8.89	K. Lofton, Atl		.333	J. Bagwell, Hou		.425	A. Galarraga, Col		.585	J. Bagwell, Hou		1.017
M. Piazza, LA		137	J. Bagwell, Hou		8.85	W. Joyner, SD		.327	G. Sheffield, Fla		.424	R. Lankford, StL		.585	R. Lankford, StL		.996

1997 National League Pitching Leaders

Wins			Losses			Winning Percentage			Games			Games Started			Complete Games		
D. Neagle, Atl		20	M. Leiter, Phi		17	G. Maddux, Atl		.826	J. Tavarez, SF		89	J. Smoltz, Atl		35	P. Martinez, Mon		13
G. Maddux, Atl		19	S. Cooke, Pit		15	D. Neagle, Atl		.800	S. Belinda, Cin		84	C. Schilling, Phi		35	C. Perez, Mon		8
D. Kile, Hou		19	J. Lieber, Pit		14	S. Estes, SF		.792	J. Shaw, Cin		78	4 tied with		34	J. Smoltz, Atl		7
S. Estes, SF		19	T. Mulholland, 2tm		13	D. Kile, Hou		.731	M. Rojas, 2tm		77				C. Schilling, Phi		7
3 tied with		17	C. Perez, Mon		13	J. Juden, Mon		.688	2 tied with		76				M. Hampton, Hou		7

Shutouts			Saves			Games Finished			Batters Faced			Innings Pitched			Hits Allowed		
C. Perez, Mon		5	J. Shaw, Cin		42	R. Beck, SF		66	D. Kile, Hou		1056	J. Smoltz, Atl		256.0	J. Smoltz, Atl		234
D. Kile, Hou		4	R. Beck, SF		37	R. Nen, Fla		65	J. Smoltz, Atl		1043	D. Kile, Hou		255.2	S. Trachsel, ChN		225
D. Neagle, Atl		4	T. Hoffman, SD		37	J. Shaw, Cin		62	C. Schilling, Phi		1009	C. Schilling, Phi		254.1	F. Castillo, 2tm		220
P. Martinez, Mon		4	D. Eckersley, StL		36	R. Bottalico, Phi		61	K. Brown, Fla		976	P. Martinez, Mon		241.1	M. Hampton, Hou		217
10 tied with		2	J. Franco, NYN		36	T. Hoffman, SD		59	T. Glavine, Atl		970	T. Glavine, Atl		240.0	M. Leiter, Phi		216

Home Runs Allowed			Walks			Walks/9 Innings			Strikeouts			Strikeouts/9 Innings			Strikeout/Walk Ratio		
S. Trachsel, ChN		32	S. Estes, SF		100	G. Maddux, Atl		0.8	C. Schilling, Phi		319	P. Martinez, Mon		11.4	G. Maddux, Atl		8.85
M. Gardner, SF		28	D. Kile, Hou		94	R. Reed, NYN		1.3	P. Martinez, Mon		305	C. Schilling, Phi		11.3	C. Schilling, Phi		5.50
K. Foster, ChN		27	H. Nomo, LA		92	D. Neagle, Atl		1.9	J. Smoltz, Atl		241	H. Nomo, LA		10.1	P. Martinez, Mon		4.55
R. Bailey, Col		27	A. Leiter, Fla		91	C. Schilling, Phi		2.1	H. Nomo, LA		233	A. Benes, StL		8.9	J. Smoltz, Atl		3.83
5 tied with		25	T. Glavine, Atl		79	C. Perez, Mon		2.1	2 tied with		205	J. Smoltz, Atl		8.5	R. Reed, NYN		3.65

Earned Run Average			Component ERA			Hit Batsmen			Wild Pitches			Opponent Average			Opponent OBP		
P. Martinez, Mon		1.90	P. Martinez, Mon		1.79	K. Brown, Fla		14	M. Remlinger, Cin		12	P. Martinez, Mon		.184	P. Martinez, Mon		.250
G. Maddux, Atl		2.20	G. Maddux, Atl		1.95	R. Bailey, Col		13	M. Leiter, Phi		11	C. Park, LA		.213	G. Maddux, Atl		.256
D. Kile, Hou		2.57	C. Schilling, Phi		2.55	5 tied with		12	J. Smoltz, Atl		10	S. Estes, SF		.223	C. Schilling, Phi		.271
I. Valdes, LA		2.65	D. Neagle, Atl		2.60				H. Nomo, LA		10	C. Schilling, Phi		.224	R. Reed, NYN		.272
K. Brown, Fla		2.69	R. Reed, NYN		2.61				S. Estes, SF		10	D. Kile, Hou		.225	D. Neagle, Atl		.277

1997 National League Miscellaneous

Managers

Atlanta	Bobby Cox	101-61
Chicago	Jim Riggleman	68-94
Cincinnati	Ray Knight	42-54
	Jack McKeon	34-32
Colorado	Don Baylor	83-79
Florida	Jim Leyland	92-70
Houston	Larry Dierker	84-78
Los Angeles	Bill Russell	88-74
Montreal	Felipe Alou	78-84
New York	Bobby Valentine	88-74
Philadelphia	Terry Francona	68-94
Pittsburgh	Gene Lamont	79-83
St. Louis	Tony La Russa	73-89
San Diego	Bruce Bochy	76-86
San Francisco	Dusty Baker	90-72

Awards

Most Valuable Player	Larry Walker, of, Col
Cy Young	Pedro Martinez, Mon
Rookie of the Year	Scott Rolen, 3b, Phi
Manager of the Year	Dusty Baker, SF

STATS All-Star Team

C	Mike Piazza, LA	.362	40	124
1B	Jeff Bagwell, Hou	.286	43	135
2B	Craig Biggio, Hou	.309	22	81
3B	Ken Caminiti, SD	.290	26	90
SS	Jeff Blauser, Atl	.308	17	70
OF	Barry Bonds, SF	.291	40	101
OF	Tony Gwynn, SD	.372	17	119
OF	Larry Walker, Col	.366	49	130
P	Darryl Kile, Hou	19-7	2.57	205 K
P	Greg Maddux, Atl	19-4	2.20	177 K
P	Pedro Martinez, Mon	17-8	1.90	305 K
P	Curt Schilling, Phi	17-11	2.97	319 K
RP	Jeff Shaw, Cin	4-2	2.38	42 Sv

Postseason

Division Series	Atlanta 3 vs. Houston 0
	Florida 3 vs. San Francisco 0
LCS	Florida 4 vs. Atlanta 2
World Series	Florida (NL) 4 vs. Cleveland (AL) 3

Outstanding Performances

No-Hitters
Kevin Brown, Fla @ SF on June 10

Three-Homer Games
Larry Walker, Col on April 5
Steve Finley, SD on May 19
Steve Finley, SD on June 23
Bobby Estalella, Phi on September 4

Cycles
John Olerud, NYN on September 11

Team Rosters

»1876 Chicago White Stockings 1st NL 52-14 .788 —

Al Spalding

Player	Gm by Position	B	Age	G	AB	R	H	2B	3B	HR	RBI	BB	SO	SB	Avg	OBP	Slg
Deacon White	C63,1B3,OF3*	L	28	66	303	66	104	18	1	1	60	7	3	—	.343	.358	.419
Cal McVey	1B55,P11,C6*	R	25	63	308	62	107	15	0	1	53	2	4	—	.347	.352	.406
Ross Barnes	2B66,P1	R	26	66	322	126	138	21	14	1	59	20	8	—	.429	.462	.590
Cap Anson	3B66,C2	R	24	66	309	63	110	9	7	2	59	12	8	—	.356	.380	.450
John Peters	SS66,P1	R	26	66	316	70	111	14	2	1	47	3	2	—	.351	.357	.418
Paul Hines	OF64,2B1	R	24	64	305	62	101	21	3	2	59	1	3	—	.331	.333	.439
John Glenn	OF56,1B15	R	27	66	276	55	84	9	2	0	32	12	6	—	.304	.333	.351
Bob Addy	OF32	L	31	32	142	36	40	4	1	0	16	5	0	—	.282	.306	.324
Al Spalding	P61,OF10,1B3*	R	25	66	292	54	91	14	2	0	44	6	3	—	.312	.326	.373
Oscar Bielaski	OF32	R	29	32	139	24	29	3	0	0	10	2	3	—	.209	.220	.230
Fred Andrus	OF8	R	25	8	36	6	11	3	0	0	2	0	5	—	.306	.306	.389

D. White, 1 G at P, 1 G at 3B; C. McVey, 1 G at 3B, 1 G at OF; A. Spalding, 1 G at SS

Pitcher	T	Age	G	GS	CG	ShO	IP	H	HR	BB	SO	W-L	Sv	ERA
Al Spalding	R	25	61	60	53	8	528.2	542	6	26	39	47-12	0	1.75
Cal McVey	R	25	11	6	5	0	59.1	57	0	2	9	5-2	2	1.52
Deacon White	R	28	1	0	0	0	2.0	1	0	0	3	0-0	1	0.00
Ross Barnes	R	26	1	0	0	0	1.1	7	0	0	0	0-0	0	20.25
John Peters	R	26	1	0	0	0	1.0	1	0	1	0	0-0	1	0.00

1876 St. Louis Brown Stockings 2nd NL 45-19 .703 6.0 GB

Mase Graffen (39-17)/George McManus (6-2)

Player	Gm by Position	B	Age	G	AB	R	H	2B	3B	HR	RBI	BB	SO	SB	Avg	OBP	Slg
John Clapp	C61,OF4,2B1	R	24	64	298	60	91	4	2	0	29	8	2	—	.305	.324	.332
Herman Dehlman	1B64	—	24	64	245	40	45	6	0	0	9	9	10	—	.184	.213	.208
Mike McGeary	2B56,C5,3B1*	R	25	61	276	48	72	3	0	0	30	2	1	—	.261	.266	.272
Joe Battin	3B63,2B1	R	24	64	283	34	85	11	4	0	46	6	6	—	.300	.315	.367
Denny Mack	SS41,2B5,OF2	R	25	48	180	32	39	5	0	1	7	11	5	—	.217	.262	.261
Ned Cuthbert	OF63	R	31	63	283	46	70	10	1	0	25	7	4	—	.247	.266	.290
Lip Pike	OF62,2B2	L	31	63	282	55	91	19	10	1	50	8	9	—	.323	.341	.472
Joe Blong	OF62,P1	R	22	62	264	30	62	7	4	0	30	2	9	—	.235	.241	.292
Dickey Pearce	SS23,2B1,OF1	R	40	25	102	12	21	1	0	0	10	3	5	—	.206	.229	.216

M. McGeary, 1 G at OF

Pitcher	T	Age	G	GS	CG	ShO	IP	H	HR	BB	SO	W-L	Sv	ERA
George Bradley	R	23	64	64	63	16	573.0	470	3	38	103	45-19	0	1.23
Joe Blong	R	22	1	0	0	0	4.0	2	0	1	0	0-0	0	0.00

1876 Hartford Dark Blues 3rd NL 47-21 .691 6.0 GB

Bob Ferguson

Player	Gm by Position	B	Age	G	AB	R	H	2B	3B	HR	RBI	BB	SO	SB	Avg	OBP	Slg
Doug Allison	C40,OF6	R	30	44	163	19	43	4	0	0	15	3	9	—	.264	.277	.288
Everett Mills	1B63	—	31	63	254	28	66	8	1	0	23	1	3	—	.260	.263	.299
Jack Burdock	2B69,3B1	R	24	69	309	66	80	9	1	0	23	13	16	—	.259	.289	.294
Bob Ferguson	3B69	S	31	69	310	48	82	8	5	0	32	2	11	—	.265	.269	.323
Tom Carey	SS68	R	27	68	289	51	78	7	0	0	26	3	4	—	.270	.277	.294
Jack Remsen	OF69	R	26	69	324	62	89	12	5	1	30	1	15	—	.275	.277	.352
Tom York	OF67	L	24	67	263	47	68	12	7	1	39	10	4	—	.259	.286	.369
Dick Higham	OF59,C13,2B1*	L	24	67	312	59	102	21	2	0	35	2	7	—	.327	.331	.407
Bill Harbidge	C24,OF6,1B2	L	21	30	106	11	23	2	1	0	6	3	2	—	.217	.239	.255
John Cassidy	OF8,1B4	R	19	12	47	6	13	2	0	0	8	1	0	—	.277	.292	.319

D. Higham, 1 G at SS

Pitcher	T	Age	G	GS	CG	ShO	IP	H	HR	BB	SO	W-L	Sv	ERA
Tommy Bond	R	20	45	45	45	6	408.0	355	2	13	88	31-13	0	1.68
Candy Cummings	R	27	24	24	24	5	216.0	215	0	14	26	16-8	0	1.67

1876 Boston Red Stockings 4th NL 39-31 .557 15.0 GB

Harry Wright

Player	Gm by Position	B	Age	G	AB	R	H	2B	3B	HR	RBI	BB	SO	SB	Avg	OBP	Slg
Lew Brown	C45,OF1	R	18	45	195	23	41	6	6	2	21	3	22	—	.210	.222	.333
Tim Murnane	1B65,OF3,2B1	L	24	69	308	60	87	4	3	2	34	8	12	—	.282	.301	.334
John Morrill	2B37,C23,OF5*	R	21	66	278	38	73	5	2	0	26	3	5	—	.263	.270	.295
Harry Schafer	3B70	R	29	70	286	47	72	11	0	0	35	4	11	—	.252	.262	.290
George Wright	SS68,2B2,P1	R	29	70	335	72	100	18	6	1	34	8	9	—	.299	.315	.397
Jim O'Rourke	OF68,1B2,C1	R	25	70	312	61	102	17	3	2	43	15	17	—	.327	.358	.420
Jack Manning	OF56,P34,2B1*	R	22	70	288	52	76	13	0	2	25	7	5	—	.264	.281	.330
Andy Leonard	OF35,2B30	R	30	64	303	53	85	10	2	0	27	4	6	—	.281	.290	.327
Frank Whitney	OF34,2B1	R	20	34	139	27	33	7	1	0	15	1	3	—	.237	.243	.302
Joe Borden	P29,OF16	R	22	32	121	19	25	3	0	0	7	3	3	—	.207	.226	.231
Foghorn Bradley	P22,OF4	R	20	22	82	12	19	2	1	0	8	2	3	—	.232	.250	.280
Tim McGinley	OF6,C3	—	—	9	40	5	6	0	0	0	2	0	1	—	.150	.150	.150
Dick McBride	P4,OF1	—	31	4	16	2	3	0	0	0	4	0	0	—	.188	.188	.188
Sam Wright	SS2	R	27	2	8	0	1	0	0	0	0	0	0	—	.125	.125	.125
Bill Parks	OF1	R	27	1	4	0	0	0	0	0	0	0	0	—	.000	.000	.000
Harry Wright	OF1	R	41	1	3	0	0	0	0	0	0	0	1	—	.000	.000	.000

J. Morrill, 3 G at 1B; J. Manning, 1 G at SS

Pitcher	T	Age	G	GS	CG	ShO	IP	H	HR	BB	SO	W-L	Sv	ERA
Joe Borden	R	22	29	24	16	2	218.1	257	4	51	34	11-12	1	2.89
Foghorn Bradley	R	20	22	21	16	1	173.1	201	1	16	16	9-10	1	2.49
Jack Manning	R	22	34	20	13	0	197.1	213	1	32	24	18-5	5	2.14
Dick McBride	R	31	4	4	3	0	33.0	53	1	5	2	0-4	0	2.73
Tricky Nichols	R	25	1	1	1	0	9.0	7	0	0	0	1-0	0	1.00
George Wright	R	29	1	0	0	0	1.0	1	0	0	1	0-0	0	0.00

1876 Louisville Grays 5th NL 30-36 .455 22.0 GB

Jack Chapman

Player	Gm by Position	B	Age	G	AB	R	H	2B	3B	HR	RBI	BB	SO	SB	Avg	OBP	Slg
Pop Snyder	C55,OF4	R	21	56	224	21	44	4	1	1	9	2	7	—	.196	.204	.237
Joe Gerhardt	1B54,2B5,SS3*	R	21	65	292	33	76	10	3	2	18	3	5	—	.260	.268	.336
Ed Somerville	2B64	R	23	64	256	29	48	5	1	0	14	1	6	—	.188	.191	.215
Bill Hague	3B67,SS1	R	24	67	294	31	78	8	0	1	22	2	10	—	.265	.270	.303
Chuck Fulmer	SS66	R	25	66	267	28	73	9	5	1	29	1	10	—	.273	.276	.356
Scott Hastings	OF65,C5	R	28	67	283	36	73	6	1	0	21	5	11	—	.258	.271	.286
Johnny Ryan	OF64,P1	—	22	64	241	32	61	5	1	1	18	6	23	—	.253	.271	.295
Art Allison	OF23,1B8	—	27	31	130	9	27	2	1	0	10	2	6	—	.208	.220	.238
Jim Devlin	P68,1B1	R	27	68	298	38	94	14	1	0	28	1	11	—	.315	.318	.369
Jack Chapman	OF17,3B1	—	33	17	67	4	16	1	0	0	5	1	3	—	.239	.250	.254
Jim Clinton	OF14,P1,1B1	R	25	16	65	8	22	2	0	0	0	0	0	—	.338	.338	.369
George Bechtel†	OF14	—	27	14	55	2	10	1	0	0	2	0	1	—	.182	.182	.200
Bill Holbert	C12	R	21	12	43	3	11	0	0	0	5	0	3	—	.256	.256	.256
Dan Collins	OF7	—	21	7	28	3	4	1	0	0	9	0	2	—	.143	.143	.179
John Carbine	1B6,OF1	—	20	7	25	3	4	0	0	0	1	0	0	—	.160	.160	.160

J. Gerhardt, 2 G at 3B, 2 G at OF

Pitcher	T	Age	G	GS	CG	ShO	IP	H	HR	BB	SO	W-L	Sv	ERA
Jim Devlin	R	27	68	68	66	5	622.0	566	3	37	122	30-35	0	1.56
Jim Clinton	R	25	1	1	1	0	9.0	12	0	0	1	0-1	0	6.00
Johnny Ryan	—	22	1	0	0	0	8.0	22	0	0	1	0-0	0	5.63
Frank Pearce	—	16	1	0	0	0	4.0	5	0	1	1	0-0	0	4.50

1876 New York Mutuals 6th NL 21-35 .375 26.0 GB

Bill Craver

Player	Gm by Position	B	Age	G	AB	R	H	2B	3B	HR	RBI	BB	SO	SB	Avg	OBP	Slg
Nat Hicks	C45	R	31	45	188	20	44	4	1	0	15	3	4	—	.234	.246	.266
Joe Start	1B56	L	33	56	264	40	73	6	0	0	21	1	2	—	.277	.279	.299
Bill Craver	2B42,C11,SS6	R	32	56	246	24	55	4	0	0	22	2	7	—	.224	.230	.240
Al Nichols	3B57	—	—	57	212	20	38	4	0	0	9	2	3	—	.179	.187	.198
Jimmy Hallinan	SS50,2B4,OF2	L	27	54	240	45	67	7	6	2	36	2	4	—	.279	.285	.383
Fred Treacey	OF57	—	29	57	256	47	54	5	1	0	18	1	5	—	.211	.214	.238
Eddie Booth	OF53,2B5,P1	—	—	57	228	17	49	2	1	0	7	2	4	—	.215	.222	.232
Jim Holdsworth	OF49,2B3	R	25	52	241	23	64	3	2	0	19	1	2	—	.266	.269	.295
Bobby Mathews	P56,OF1	R	24	56	218	19	40	4	1	0	9	3	2	—	.183	.195	.211
Mike Hayes	OF5	—	23	5	21	1	3	0	2	0	2	0	0	—	.143	.143	.333
George Bechtel†	OF2	—	27	2	10	2	3	0	0	0	0	0	0	—	.300	.300	.300
Jim Shanley	OF2	—	22	2	8	0	1	0	0	0	0	0	0	—	.125	.125	.125
John Maloney	OF2	—	—	2	7	1	2	0	1	0	2	0	1	—	.286	.286	.571
Pete Treacey	SS2	—	24	2	5	1	0	0	0	0	0	1	0	—	.000	.167	.000
George Fair	2B1	—	20	1	4	0	0	0	0	0	0	0	0	—	.000	.000	.000
John McGuinness	C1,2B1	—	19	1	4	0	0	0	0	0	0	0	0	—	.000	.000	.000
Billy West	2B1	—	35	1	4	0	0	0	0	0	0	0	0	—	.000	.000	.000
George Heubel	1B1	—	27	1	4	0	0	0	0	0	0	0	0	—	.000	.000	.000
John Hatfield	2B1	—	28	1	4	0	1	0	0	0	1	0	0	—	.250	.250	.250
Bob Valentine	C1	—	—	1	3	0	0	0	0	0	0	0	0	—	.000	.000	.000
George Seward	2B1	—	—	1	3	0	0	0	0	0	0	0	0	—	.000	.000	.000
Nealy Phelps†	OF1	—	35	1	3	0	0	0	0	0	0	0	1	—	.000	.000	.000
Davy Force†	SS1	R	26	1	3	0	0	0	0	0	0	0	0	—	.000	.000	.000

Pitcher	T	Age	G	GS	CG	ShO	IP	H	HR	BB	SO	W-L	Sv	ERA
Bobby Mathews	R	24	56	56	55	2	516.0	693	8	24	37	21-34	0	2.86
Terry Larkin	R	—	1	1	1	0	9.0	9	0	0	0	0-1	0	3.00
Eddie Booth	—	—	1	0	0	0	5.0	16	0	0	0	0-0	0	10.80

1876 Philadelphia Athletics 7th NL 14-45 .237 34.5 GB

Al Wright

Player	Gm by Position	B	Age	G	AB	R	H	2B	3B	HR	RBI	BB	SO	SB	Avg	OBP	Slg
Fergy Malone	C20,OF3,SS1	R	34	22	96	14	22	2	0	0	6	0	1	—	.229	.229	.250
Ezra Sutton	1B29,2B15,3B8*	R	25	54	236	45	70	12	7	1	31	3	2	—	.297	.305	.419
Wes Fisler	OF24,2B21,1B14*	R	34	59	278	42	80	15	1	1	30	2	4	—	.288	.293	.360
Levi Meyerle	3B49,2B3,OF3*	R	30	55	256	46	87	12	8	0	34	3	2	—	.340	.347	.449
Davy Force†	SS60,3B2	R	26	60	284	48	66	6	0	0	17	5	3	—	.232	.246	.254
George Hall	OF60	L	27	60	268	51	98	7	13	5	45	8	4	—	.366	.384	.545
Dave Eggler	OF39	R	25	39	174	28	52	4	0	0	19	2	4	—	.299	.307	.322
William Coon	OF29,C18,2B4*	—	21	54	220	30	50	5	1	0	22	2	4	—	.227	.234	.259
Lon Knight	P34,1B13,OF9*	R	23	55	240	32	60	9	3	0	24	2	2	—	.250	.256	.313
George Zettlein	P28,1B7,2B1*	R	31	32	128	11	27	2	1	0	11	0	5	—	.211	.211	.242
Bill Fouser	2B14,OF7,1B1	—	20	21	89	11	12	0	1	0	2	0	0	—	.135	.135	.157
Whitey Ritterson	C14,OF4,3B1	R	21	16	52	8	13	3	0	0	4	0	2	—	.250	.250	.308
Doc Bushong	C5	R	19	5	21	4	1	0	0	0	1	0	0	—	.048	.048	.048
Pete Curren	C2,OF1	—	—	3	12	5	4	1	0	0	2	0	0	—	.333	.333	.417
Lou Paul	C3	R	—	3	12	2	2	1	0	0	0	0	0	—	.167	.167	.250
John Bergh	C1,OF1	—	18	1	4	0	0	0	0	0	0	0	2	—	.000	.000	.000
Jim Ward	C1	—	21	1	4	1	2	0	0	0	1	0	1	—	.500	.500	.500
Nealy Phelps†	C1	—	35	1	4	0	0	0	0	0	0	0	0	—	.000	.000	.000
John Mullen	C1	L	—	1	3	0	0	0	0	0	0	0	0	—	.000	.000	.000
Fred Warner	OF1	—	21	1	3	0	0	0	0	0	0	0	0	—	.000	.000	.000

E. Sutton, 4 G at OF; W. Fisler, 1 G at SS; L. Meyerle, 2 G at P; W. Coon, 4 G at 3B, 2 G at P; L. Knight, 6 G at 2B; G. Zettlein, 1 G at OF

Pitcher	T	Age	G	GS	CG	ShO	IP	H	HR	BB	SO	W-L	Sv	ERA
Lon Knight	R	23	34	32	27	0	282.0	383	0	34	12	10-22	0	2.62
George Zettlein	R	31	28	25	23	1	234.0	358	2	6	10	4-20	2	3.88
Levi Meyerle	R	30	2	2	2	0	18.0	28	0	1	0	0-2	0	5.00
Flip Lafferty	R	22	1	1	1	0	9.0	5	0	0	0	0-1	0	0.00
William Coon	—	21	2	0	0	0	7.0	9	0	0	0	0-0	0	5.14

1876 Cincinnati Red Stockings 8th NL 9-56 .138 42.5 GB

Charlie Gould

Player	Gm by Position	B	Age	G	AB	R	H	2B	3B	HR	RBI	BB	SO	SB	Avg	OBP	Slg
Dave Pierson	C31,OF30,P1*	R	20	57	233	33	55	4	1	0	13	1	9	—	.236	.239	.262
Charlie Gould	1B61,P2	R	28	61	258	27	65	7	0	0	11	6	11	—	.252	.269	.279
Charlie Sweasy	2B55,OF1	R	28	56	225	18	46	5	2	0	10	2	5	—	.204	.211	.244
Will Foley	3B46,C20	R	20	58	221	19	50	3	2	0	9	0	14	—	.226	.226	.258
Henry Kessler	SS46,OF16	R	29	59	248	26	64	5	0	0	11	7	10	—	.258	.278	.278
Charley Jones	OF64	R	26	64	276	40	79	17	4	4	38	7	17	—	.286	.304	.420
Redleg Snyder	OF55	R	21	55	205	10	31	3	1	0	12	1	19	—	.151	.155	.176
Bobby Clack	OF17,2B8,1B5*	R	26	32	118	10	19	0	1	0	5	5	12	—	.161	.195	.178
Amos Booth	C24,3B24,SS22*	R	23	63	272	31	71	3	0	0	14	9	11	—	.261	.285	.272
Dory Dean	P30,OF5,SS2	R	23	34	138	9	36	3	1	0	4	2	13	—	.261	.271	.297
Cherokee Fisher	P28,OF11,1B1*	R	30	35	129	12	32	1	0	0	4	0	8	—	.248	.248	.256
Sam Field	C3,2B2	R	27	4	14	2	0	0	0	0	0	1	3	—	.000	.067	.000

D. Pierson, 1 G at 2B, 1 G at 3B, 1 G at SS; B. Clack, 3 G at 3B, 1 G at P; A. Booth, 3 G at P, 3 G at OF; C. Fisher, 1 G at SS

Pitcher	T	Age	G	GS	CG	ShO	IP	H	HR	BB	SO	W-L	Sv	ERA
Dory Dean	R	23	30	30	26	0	262.2	397	1	24	22	4-26	0	3.73
Cherokee Fisher	R	30	28	24	22	0	229.1	294	6	6	29	4-20	0	3.02
Dale Williams	R	20	9	9	9	0	83.0	123	1	4	9	1-8	0	4.23
Dave Pierson	R	20	1	1	0	0	0.0	2	1	0	0	0-1	0	—
Amos Booth	R	23	3	1	0	0	9.2	22	0	0	0	0-1	0	9.31
Charlie Gould	R	28	2	0	0	0	4.1	10	0	0	0	0-0	0	0.00
Bobby Clack	R	26	1	0	0	0	2.0	2	0	0	0	0-0	0	4.50

»1877 Boston Red Stockings 1st NL 42-18 .700 —

Harry Wright

Player	Gm by Position	B	Age	G	AB	R	H	2B	3B	HR	RBI	BB	SO	SB	Avg	OBP	Slg
Lew Brown	C55,1B4	R	19	58	221	27	56	12	8	1	31	6	33	—	.253	.273	.394
Deacon White	1B35,OF19,C7	L	29	59	266	51	103	14	11	2	49	8	3	—	.387	.405	.545
George Wright	2B58,SS3	R	30	61	290	58	80	15	1	0	35	9	15	—	.276	.298	.334
John Morrill	3B30,1B18,OF11*	R	22	61	242	47	73	5	1	0	28	6	15	—	.302	.319	.331
Ezra Sutton	SS36,3B22	R	26	58	253	43	74	10	6	0	39	4	10	—	.292	.304	.379
Jim O'Rourke	OF60,1B1	R	26	61	265	68	96	14	4	0	23	20	9	—	.362	.407	.445
Andy Leonard	OF37,SS21	R	31	58	272	46	78	5	0	0	27	5	5	—	.287	.300	.305
Tim Murnane	OF30,1B5	L	25	35	140	23	39	7	1	1	15	6	7	—	.279	.308	.364
Tommy Bond	P58,OF3	R	21	61	259	32	59	4	3	0	30	1	15	—	.228	.231	.266
Harry Schafer	OF23,3B9,SS1	R	30	33	141	20	39	5	2	0	13	0	7	—	.277	.277	.340
Harry Wright	OF1	R	42	1	4	0	0	0	0	0	0	0	1	—	.000	.000	.000

J. Morrill, 3 G at 2B

Pitcher	T	Age	G	GS	CG	ShO	IP	H	HR	BB	SO	W-L	Sv	ERA
Tommy Bond	R	21	58	58	58	6	521.0	530	5	36	170	40-17	0	2.11
Will White	R	22	3	3	3	1	27.0	27	0	2	7	2-1	0	3.00

1877 Louisville Grays 2nd NL 35-25 .583 7.0 GB

Jack Chapman

Player	Gm by Position	B	Age	G	AB	R	H	2B	3B	HR	RBI	BB	SO	SB	Avg	OBP	Slg
Pop Snyder	C61,SS1,OF1	R	22	61	248	23	64	7	2	2	28	3	14	—	.258	.267	.327
Jumbo Latham	1B59	R	24	59	278	42	81	10	6	0	22	5	6	—	.291	.304	.371
Joe Gerhardt	2B57,1B1,SS1*	R	22	59	250	41	76	6	5	1	35	5	8	—	.304	.318	.380
Bill Hague	3B59	R	25	59	263	38	70	7	1	1	24	7	18	—	.266	.285	.312
Bill Craver	SS57	R	33	57	238	33	63	5	2	0	29	5	11	—	.265	.280	.303
George Hall	OF61	L	28	61	269	53	87	15	8	0	26	12	19	—	.323	.352	.439
Orator Shaffer	OF60,1B1	L	25	61	260	38	74	9	5	3	34	9	17	—	.285	.309	.392
Bill Crowley	OF58,C2,SS2*	R	20	61	238	30	67	9	3	1	23	4	13	—	.282	.293	.357
Al Nichols	2B3,1B1,3B1*	—	—	6	19	1	4	0	1	0	0	0	2	—	.211	.211	.316
Flip Lafferty	OF4	—	23	4	17	2	1	1	0	0	0	0	4	—	.059	.059	.118
John Haldeman	2B1	L	21	1	4	0	0	0	0	0	0	0	0	—	.000	.000	.000
Harry Little†	2B1	—	—	1	3	0	0	0	0	0	0	1	1	—	.000	.250	.000

J. Gerhardt, 1 G at OF; B. Crowley, 1 G at 2B, 1 G at 3B; A. Nichols, 1 G at SS

Pitcher	T	Age	G	GS	CG	ShO	IP	H	HR	BB	SO	W-L	Sv	ERA
Jim Devlin	R	28	61	61	61	4	559.0	617	4	41	141	35-25	0	2.25

1877 Hartford Dark Blues 3rd NL 31-27 .534 10.0 GB

Bob Ferguson

Player	Gm by Position	B	Age	G	AB	R	H	2B	3B	HR	RBI	BB	SO	SB	Avg	OBP	Slg
Bill Harbidge	C32,OF5,2B4*	L	22	41	167	18	37	5	2	0	8	3	6	—	.222	.235	.275
Joe Start	1B60	L	34	60	271	55	90	3	6	1	21	6	2	—	.332	.347	.399
Jack Burdock	2B55,3B3	R	25	58	277	35	72	6	0	0	9	2	16	—	.260	.265	.282
Bob Ferguson	3B56,P3	S	32	58	254	40	65	7	2	0	35	3	10	—	.256	.265	.299
Tom Carey	SS60	R	28	60	274	38	70	3	2	1	20	0	9	—	.255	.255	.292
John Cassidy	OF58,P2	R	20	60	251	43	95	10	5	0	27	3	3	—	.378	.386	.458
Tom York	OF56	L	25	56	237	43	67	16	7	1	37	3	11	—	.283	.292	.422
Jim Holdsworth	OF55	R	26	55	260	26	66	5	2	0	20	2	8	—	.254	.260	.288
Terry Larkin	P56,3B2,2B1	R	—	58	228	28	52	6	5	1	18	5	23	—	.228	.245	.311
Doug Allison	C29	R	31	29	115	14	17	2	0	0	6	3	7	—	.148	.169	.165
Live Oak Taylor	OF2	—	—	2	8	0	3	0	0	0	0	0	2	—	.375	.375	.375
Jay Pike	OF1	L	—	1	4	0	1	0	0	0	0	0	0	—	.250	.250	.250
Josh Bunce	OF1	—	30	1	4	0	0	0	0	0	0	0	0	—	.000	.000	.000
John Maloney	OF1	—	—	1	4	0	1	0	0	0	0	0	0	—	.250	.250	.250
John Bass	OF1	—	27	1	4	1	1	0	0	0	0	0	0	—	.250	.250	.250

B. Harbidge, 1 G at 3B

Pitcher	T	Age	G	GS	CG	ShO	IP	H	HR	BB	SO	W-L	Sv	ERA
Terry Larkin	R	—	56	56	55	4	501.0	510	2	53	96	29-25	0	2.14
Bob Ferguson	R	32	3	2	2	0	25.0	38	0	2	1	1-1	0	3.96
John Cassidy	L	20	2	2	2	0	18.0	24	0	1	2	1-1	0	5.00

1877 St. Louis Brown Stockings 4th NL 28-32 .467 14.0 GB

George McManus

Player	Gm by Position	B	Age	G	AB	R	H	2B	3B	HR	RBI	BB	SO	SB	Avg	OBP	Slg
John Clapp	C53,OF10,1B1	R	25	60	255	47	81	6	6	0	34	8	6	—	.318	.338	.388
Herman Dehlman	1B31,OF1	—	25	32	119	24	22	4	0	0	11	7	21	—	.185	.230	.218
Mike McGeary	2B39,3B19	R	26	57	258	35	65	3	2	0	20	2	6	—	.252	.258	.279
Joe Battin	3B32,2B21,OF5*	R	25	57	226	28	45	3	7	1	22	6	17	—	.199	.220	.288
Davy Force	SS50,3B8	R	27	58	225	24	59	5	3	0	22	11	15	—	.262	.297	.311
Mike Dorgan	OF50,C12,3B2*	R	23	60	266	45	82	9	7	0	23	9	13	—	.308	.331	.395
Joe Blong	OF40,P25	R	23	58	218	17	47	8	3	0	13	4	22	—	.216	.230	.280
Jack Remsen	OF33	R	27	33	123	14	32	3	4	0	13	4	3	—	.260	.283	.350
Art Croft	1B28,OF25,2B1	—	22	54	220	23	51	5	2	0	27	1	15	—	.232	.235	.273
Tricky Nichols	P42,OF16	R	26	51	186	22	31	4	2	0	9	3	15	—	.167	.180	.210
Dickey Pearce	SS8	R	41	8	29	1	5	0	0	0	4	1	4	—	.172	.200	.172
Leonidas Lee	OF4,SS1	—	16	4	18	0	5	1	0	0	0	0	1	—	.278	.278	.333
Harry Little†	OF3	—	—	3	12	2	2	0	0	0	0	1	6	—	.167	.231	.167
Tom Loftus	OF3	R	20	3	11	2	2	0	0	0	0	0	1	—	.182	.182	.182
Ed McKenna	OF1	—	—	1	5	0	1	0	0	0	0	0	1	—	.200	.200	.200
Jack Gleason	OF1	R	22	1	4	0	1	0	0	0	0	0	1	—	.250	.250	.250
T.E. Newell	SS1	—	—	1	3	0	0	0	0	0	0	0	0	—	.000	.000	.000

J. Battin, 1 G at P; M. Dorgan, 1 G at 2B, 1 G at SS

Pitcher	T	Age	G	GS	CG	ShO	IP	H	HR	BB	SO	W-L	Sv	ERA
Tricky Nichols	R	26	42	39	35	1	350.0	376	2	53	80	18-23	0	2.60
Joe Blong	R	23	25	21	17	0	187.1	203	0	38	51	10-9	0	2.74
Joe Battin	R	25	1	0	0	0	3.2	3	0	1	1	0-0	0	4.91

1877 Chicago White Stockings 5th NL 26-33 .441 15.5 GB

Al Spalding

Player	Gm by Position	B	Age	G	AB	R	H	2B	3B	HR	RBI	BB	SO	SB	Avg	OBP	Slg
Cal McVey	C40,P17,3B17*	R	26	60	266	58	98	9	7	0	36	8	11	—	.368	.387	.455
Al Spalding	1B45,2B13,P4*	R	26	60	254	29	65	7	6	0	35	3	16	—	.256	.265	.331
Ross Barnes	2B22	R	27	22	92	16	25	1	0	0	5	7	4	—	.272	.323	.283
Cap Anson	3B40,C31	R	25	59	255	52	86	19	1	0	32	9	3	—	.337	.360	.420
John Peters	SS60	R	27	60	265	45	84	10	3	0	41	1	7	—	.317	.320	.377
Paul Hines	OF49,2B11	R	25	60	261	44	73	11	7	0	23	1	8	—	.280	.282	.375
John Glenn	OF36,1B14	R	28	50	202	31	46	6	1	0	20	8	16	—	.228	.257	.267
Dave Eggler	OF33	R	26	33	136	20	36	3	0	0	20	1	5	—	.265	.270	.287
George Bradley	P50,3B16,1B3*	R	24	55	214	31	52	7	3	0	12	6	19	—	.243	.264	.304
Harry Smith†	2B14,OF10	R	21	24	94	7	19	1	0	0	3	4	6	—	.202	.235	.213
Jimmy Hallinan†	OF19	L	28	19	89	17	25	4	1	0	11	4	2	—	.281	.312	.348
Charlie Eden	OF15	L	22	15	55	9	12	0	1	0	5	3	6	—	.218	.259	.255
Charlie Waitt	OF10	—	23	10	41	2	4	0	0	0	2	0	3	—	.098	.098	.098
Joe Quinn	OF4	—	27	4	14	1	1	0	0	0	0	1	0	—	.071	.133	.071
Charley Jones†	OF2	R	27	2	8	1	3	1	0	0	2	1	0	—	.375	.444	.500
Dave Rowe	OF2,P1	R	22	2	7	0	2	0	0	0	0	0	3	—	.286	.286	.286
Cherokee Fisher	3B1	R	31	1	4	0	0	0	0	0	0	0	2	—	.000	.000	.000

C. McVey, 1 G at 1B, 1 G at 2B; A. Spalding, 2 G at 3B; G. Bradley, 1 G at OF

Pitcher	T	Age	G	GS	CG	ShO	IP	H	HR	BB	SO	W-L	Sv	ERA
George Bradley	R	24	50	44	35	2	394.0	452	4	39	59	18-23	0	3.31
Cal McVey	R	26	17	10	6	0	92.0	129	2	11	20	4-8	2	4.50
Laurie Reis	R	18	4	4	4	1	36.0	29	1	6	11	3-1	0	0.75
Dave Rowe	R	22	1	1	0	0	1.0	3	0	2	0	0-1	0	18.00
Al Spalding	R	26	4	1	0	0	11.0	17	0	0	2	1-0	1	3.27

1877 Cincinnati Red Stockings 6th NL 15-42 .263 25.5 GB

Lip Pike (3-11)/Bob Addy (5-19)/Jack Manning (7-12)

Player	Gm by Position	B	Age	G	AB	R	H	2B	3B	HR	RBI	BB	SO	SB	Avg	OBP	Slg
Scott Hastings	C20,OF1	R	29	20	71	7	10	1	0	0	3	3	6	—	.141	.176	.155
Charlie Gould	1B24,OF1	R	29	24	91	5	25	2	1	0	13	5	5	—	.275	.313	.319
Lip Pike	OF38,2B22,SS2	L	32	58	262	45	78	12	4	4	23	9	7	—	.298	.321	.420
Will Foley	3B56	R	21	56	216	23	41	5	1	0	18	4	13	—	.190	.205	.222
Jack Manning	SS26,1B17,OF12*	R	23	57	252	47	80	16	7	0	36	5	6	—	.317	.331	.437
Bob Addy	OF57	L	32	57	245	27	68	2	3	0	31	6	5	—	.278	.295	.310
Charley Jones†	OF46,1B10	R	27	55	232	52	72	11	10	2	36	14	25	—	.310	.350	.470
Ned Cuthbert	OF12	R	32	12	56	6	10	5	0	0	2	1	2	—	.179	.193	.268
Amos Booth	SS13,P12,C12*	R	24	44	157	16	27	2	1	0	13	12	10	—	.172	.231	.197
Levi Meyerle	SS18,2B12,OF1	R	31	27	107	11	35	7	2	0	15	0	4	—	.327	.327	.430
Jimmy Hallinan†	2B16	L	28	16	73	18	27	1	1	0	7	1	1	—	.370	.378	.411
Candy Cummings	P19,OF3	R	28	19	70	6	14	1	2	0	4	4	6	—	.200	.243	.271
Bobby Mathews	P15,SS1,OF1	R	25	15	59	5	10	0	0	0	0	1	2	—	.169	.183	.169
Bobby Mitchell	P12,OF2	L	21	13	49	5	10	3	0	0	5	1	2	—	.204	.220	.265
George Miller	C11	R	24	11	37	4	6	1	0	0	3	5	2	—	.162	.262	.189
Harry Smith†	C8,2B3,OF3	R	21	10	36	4	9	2	1	0	3	1	5	—	.250	.270	.361
Chub Sullivan	1B8	R	21	8	32	4	8	0	0	0	4	1	0	—	.250	.273	.250
Nat Hicks	C8	R	32	8	32	3	6	0	0	0	3	1	2	—	.188	.212	.188
Johnny Ryan	OF6	—	23	6	26	2	4	0	1	0	2	1	5	—	.154	.185	.231
Henry Kessler	C5,1B1	R	30	6	20	0	2	0	0	0	0	2	1	—	.100	.182	.100
Billy Redmond	SS3	L	—	3	12	1	3	1	0	0	3	1	1	—	.250	.308	.333

J. Manning, 10 G at P, 2 G at 2B; A. Booth, 10 G at 2B, 3 G at 3B, 1 G at OF

Pitcher	T	Age	G	GS	CG	ShO	IP	H	HR	BB	SO	W-L	Sv	ERA
Candy Cummings	R	28	19	19	16	0	155.2	219	2	13	11	5-14	0	4.34
Bobby Mathews	R	25	15	15	13	0	129.1	208	0	17	9	3-12	0	4.04
Bobby Mitchell	L	21	12	12	11	1	100.0	123	0	11	41	6-5	0	3.51
Amos Booth	R	24	12	8	6	0	86.0	114	1	13	18	1-7	0	3.56
Jack Manning	R	23	10	4	2	0	44.0	83	1	7	6	0-4	1	6.95

»1878 Boston Red Stockings 1st NL 41-19 .683 —

Harry Wright

Player	Gm by Position	B	Age	G	AB	R	H	2B	3B	HR	RBI	BB	SO	SB	Avg	OBP	Slg
Pop Snyder	C58,OF2	R	23	60	226	21	48	5	0	0	14	1	19	—	.212	.216	.235
John Morrill	1B59,3B1,OF1	R	23	60	233	26	56	5	1	0	23	5	16	—	.240	.256	.270
Jack Burdock	2B60	R	26	60	246	37	64	12	6	0	25	3	17	—	.260	.269	.358
Ezra Sutton	3B59,SS1	R	27	60	239	31	54	9	3	1	29	2	14	—	.226	.232	.301
George Wright	SS59	R	31	59	267	35	60	5	1	0	12	6	22	—	.225	.242	.251
Andy Leonard	OF60	R	32	60	262	41	68	8	5	0	16	3	19	—	.260	.268	.328
Jack Manning	OF59,P3	R	24	60	248	41	63	10	1	0	23	10	16	—	.254	.283	.302
Jim O'Rourke	OF57,C2,1B2	R	27	60	255	44	71	17	7	1	29	5	21	—	.278	.292	.412
Tommy Bond	P59,OF2	R	22	59	236	22	50	4	1	0	23	0	9	—	.212	.212	.237
Harry Schafer	OF2	R	31	2	8	0	1	0	0	0	0	0	1	—	.125	.125	.125

Pitcher	T	Age	G	GS	CG	ShO	IP	H	HR	BB	SO	W-L	Sv	ERA
Tommy Bond	R	22	59	59	57	9	532.2	571	5	33	182	40-19	0	2.06
Jack Manning	R	24	3	1	1	0	11.1	24	1	5	2	1-0	0	14.29

1878 Cincinnati Red Stockings 2nd NL 37-23 .617 4.0 GB

Cal McVey

Player	Gm by Position	B	Age	G	AB	R	H	2B	3B	HR	RBI	BB	SO	SB	Avg	OBP	Slg
Deacon White	C48,OF16,3B1	L	30	61	258	41	81	4	1	0	29	10	5	—	.314	.340	.337
Chub Sullivan	1B61	R	22	61	244	29	63	4	2	0	20	2	9	—	.258	.264	.291
Joe Gerhardt	2B60	R	23	60	259	46	77	7	2	0	28	7	14	—	.297	.316	.340
Cal McVey	3B61,C3	R	27	61	271	43	83	10	4	2	25	5	10	—	.306	.319	.395
Billy Geer	SS60,2B2	—	28	61	237	31	52	13	2	0	20	10	18	—	.219	.251	.291
Charley Jones	OF61	R	28	61	261	50	81	11	7	3	39	4	17	—	.310	.321	.441
King Kelly	OF47,C17,3B2	R	20	60	237	29	67	7	1	0	27	7	7	—	.283	.303	.321
Lip Pike†	OF31	L	33	31	145	28	47	5	1	0	11	4	9	—	.324	.342	.372
Buttercup Dickerson	OF29	L	19	29	123	17	38	5	1	0	9	0	7	—	.309	.309	.366
Bobby Mitchell	P9,SS2,OF1	L	22	13	49	4	12	0	0	0	8	1	4	—	.245	.260	.245

Pitcher	T	Age	G	GS	CG	ShO	IP	H	HR	BB	SO	W-L	Sv	ERA
Will White	R	23	52	52	52	5	468.0	477	1	45	169	30-21	0	1.79
Bobby Mitchell	L	22	9	9	9	1	80.0	69	1	18	51	7-2	0	2.14

1878 Providence Grays 3rd NL 33-27 .550 8.0 GB

Tom York

Player	Gm by Position	B	Age	G	AB	R	H	2B	3B	HR	RBI	BB	SO	SB	Avg	OBP	Slg
Lew Brown	C45,1B15,P1*	R	20	58	243	44	74	21	6	1	43	7	37	—	.305	.324	.453
Tim Murnane	1B48,OF1	L	26	49	188	35	45	6	1	0	14	8	12	—	.239	.270	.282
Charlie Sweasy	2B55	R	30	55	212	23	37	3	0	0	8	7	23	—	.175	.201	.189
Bill Hague	3B62	R	26	62	250	21	51	3	0	0	25	5	34	—	.204	.220	.216
Tom Carey	SS61	R	29	61	253	33	60	10	3	0	24	0	14	—	.237	.237	.300
Dick Higham	OF62,C1	L	26	62	281	60	90	22	1	1	29	5	16	—	.320	.332	.416
Tom York	OF62	L	26	62	269	56	83	19	10	1	26	8	19	—	.309	.329	.465
Paul Hines	OF61,SS1	R	26	62	257	42	92	13	4	4	50	2	10	—	.358	.363	.486
Doug Allison	C19,P1	R	32	19	76	9	22	2	0	0	7	1	8	—	.289	.299	.316
Lip Pike†	2B5	L	33	5	22	4	5	0	1	0	4	1	1	—	.227	.261	.318
Fred Corey	P5,2B2,1B1	R	21	7	21	3	3	0	0	0	1	0	2	—	.143	.143	.143

L. Brown, 1 G at OF

Pitcher	T	Age	G	GS	CG	ShO	IP	H	HR	BB	SO	W-L	Sv	ERA
Monte Ward	R	18	37	37	37	6	334.0	308	3	34	116	22-13	0	1.51
Tricky Nichols	R	27	11	10	10	0	98.0	157	0	8	21	4-7	0	4.22
Harry Wheeler	R	20	7	6	6	0	62.0	70	1	25	25	6-1	0	3.48
Fred Corey	R	21	5	5	2	0	23.0	22	0	7	7	1-2	0	2.35
Tom Healey†	R	25	3	3	3	0	24.0	27	1	7	2	0-3	0	3.00
Cherokee Fisher	R	32	1	1	1	0	9.0	14	0	0	2	0-1	0	4.00
Doug Allison	R	32	1	0	0	0	5.0	11	0	1	0	0-0	0	1.80
Lew Brown	R	20	1	0	0	0	1.0	0	0	4	0	0-0	0	18.00

1878 Chicago White Stockings 4th NL 30-30 .500 11.0 GB

Bob Ferguson

Player	Gm by Position	B	Age	G	AB	R	H	2B	3B	HR	RBI	BB	SO	SB	Avg	OBP	Slg
Bill Harbidge	C53,OF8	L	23	54	240	32	71	12	0	0	37	6	13	—	.296	.313	.346
Joe Start	1B61	L	35	61	285	58	100	12	5	1	27	2	3	—	.351	.355	.439
Bill McClellan	2B42,SS5,OF1	L	22	48	205	26	46	6	1	0	29	2	13	—	.224	.232	.263
Frank Hankinson	3B57,P1	R	22	58	240	38	64	8	3	1	27	5	36	—	.267	.282	.338
Bob Ferguson	SS57,2B4,C1	S	33	61	259	44	91	10	2	0	39	10	12	—	.351	.375	.405
John Cassidy	OF60,C1	R	21	60	256	33	68	7	1	0	29	9	11	—	.266	.291	.301
Jack Remsen	OF56	R	28	56	224	32	52	11	1	1	19	17	33	—	.232	.286	.304
Cap Anson	OF48,2B9,C3*	R	26	60	261	55	89	12	2	0	40	13	1	—	.341	.372	.402
Terry Larkin	P56,3B1,OF1	R	—	58	226	33	65	9	4	0	32	17	17	—	.288	.337	.363
Jimmy Hallinan†	OF11,2B5	L	29	16	67	14	19	3	0	0	2	5	6	—	.284	.333	.328
Phil Powers	C8	R	23	8	31	2	5	1	1	0	2	1	5	—	.161	.188	.258
Laurie Reis	P4,OF1	R	19	5	20	2	3	0	0	0	0	1	6	—	.150	.190	.150
Bill Traffley	C2	R	18	2	9	1	1	0	0	0	1	0	1	—	.111	.111	.111
Bill Sullivan	OF2	—	24	2	6	1	1	0	0	0	0	0	0	—	.167	.167	.167
Al Spalding	2B1	R	27	1	4	0	2	0	0	0	0	0	0	—	.500	.500	.500

C. Anson, 3 G at 3B

Pitcher	T	Age	G	GS	CG	ShO	IP	H	HR	BB	SO	W-L	Sv	ERA
Terry Larkin	R	—	56	56	56	1	506.0	511	4	31	163	29-26	0	2.24
Laurie Reis	R	19	4	4	4	0	36.0	55	0	4	8	1-3	0	3.25
Frank Hankinson	R	22	1	1	1	0	9.0	11	0	0	4	0-1	0	6.00

1878 Indianapolis Browns 5th NL 24-36 .400 17.0 GB

John Clapp

Player	Gm by Position	B	Age	G	AB	R	H	2B	3B	HR	RBI	BB	SO	SB	Avg	OBP	Slg
Silver Flint	C59,OF9	R	22	63	254	23	57	7	0	0	18	2	15	—	.224	.230	.252
Art Croft	1B51,OF9	—	23	60	222	22	35	6	0	0	16	5	23	—	.158	.176	.185
Joe Quest	2B62	R	25	62	278	45	57	3	2	0	13	12	24	—	.205	.238	.230
Ned Williamson	3B63	R	20	63	250	31	58	10	2	1	19	5	15	—	.232	.247	.300
Fred Warner	SS41,OF2	—	23	43	165	19	41	4	0	0	10	2	15	—	.248	.257	.273
Orator Shaffer	OF63	L	26	63	266	48	90	19	6	0	30	13	20	—	.338	.369	.455
Russ McKelvy	OF62,P4	R	23	63	253	33	57	4	3	2	36	5	38	—	.225	.240	.289
John Clapp	OF44,1B12,C9*	R	26	63	263	42	80	10	2	0	29	13	8	—	.304	.337	.357
The Only Nolan	P38,OF1	L	20	38	152	11	37	8	0	0	16	2	10	—	.243	.253	.296
Candy Nelson	SS19	L	29	19	84	12	11	1	0	0	5	5	11	—	.131	.180	.143
Jim McCormick	P14,OF3	R	21	15	56	5	8	1	0	0	0	0	2	—	.143	.143	.161
Tom Healey†	P11,OF3	—	25	12	45	2	8	1	0	0	5	0	14	—	.178	.178	.200
Jimmy Hallinan†	OF3	L	29	3	12	0	3	2	0	0	1	0	2	—	.250	.250	.417

J. Clapp, 3 G at SS, 1 G at 2B

Pitcher	T	Age	G	GS	CG	ShO	IP	H	HR	BB	SO	W-L	Sv	ERA
The Only Nolan	R	20	38	38	37	1	347.0	357	1	56	125	13-22	0	2.57
Jim McCormick	R	21	14	14	12	1	117.0	128	0	15	36	5-8	0	1.69
Tom Healey†	R	25	11	10	9	0	89.0	98	1	13	18	6-4	1	2.22
Russ McKelvy	R	23	4	1	1	0	25.0	38	1	3	3	0-2	0	2.16

1878 Milwaukee Cream Citys 6th NL 15-45 .250 26.0 GB

Jack Chapman

Player	Gm by Position	B	Age	G	AB	R	H	2B	3B	HR	RBI	BB	SO	SB	Avg	OBP	Slg
Charlie Bennett	C35,OF20	R	23	49	184	16	45	9	0	1	12	10	26	—	.245	.284	.310
Jake Goodman	1B60	—	24	60	252	28	62	4	3	1	27	7	33	—	.246	.266	.298
John Peters	2B34,SS22	R	28	55	246	33	76	6	1	0	22	5	8	—	.309	.323	.341
Will Foley	3B53,C7	R	22	56	229	33	62	8	5	0	22	7	14	—	.271	.292	.349
Billy Redmond	SS39,OF7,3B3*	L	—	48	187	16	43	8	0	0	21	8	13	—	.230	.262	.273
Abner Dalrymple	OF61	L	20	61	271	52	96	10	4	0	15	6	29	—	.354	.368	.421
Mike Golden	OF39,P22,1B1	R	26	55	214	16	44	6	3	0	20	3	35	—	.206	.217	.262
Bill Holbert	OF30,C21	R	23	45	173	10	32	2	0	0	12	3	14	—	.185	.199	.197
George Creamer	2B28,OF17,3B6	R	23	50	193	30	41	7	3	0	15	5	15	—	.212	.232	.280
Sam Weaver	P45,OF9	R	22	48	170	15	34	4	1	0	3	11	14	—	.200	.249	.235
Bill Morgan	OF13,3B3,2B1	—	—	14	56	2	11	0	0	0	5	3	9	—	.196	.237	.196
Jake Knowdell	C2,SS1,OF1	—	37	4	14	2	3	1	0	0	2	0	3	—	.214	.214	.286
Joe Ellick	C2,P1,3B1	—	24	3	13	2	2	0	0	0	1	0	1	—	.154	.154	.154
Frank Bliss	C1,3B1	—	25	2	8	1	1	0	0	0	0	0	0	—	.125	.125	.125
Alamazoo Jennings	C1	—	27	1	2	0	0	0	0	0	0	1	0	—	.000	.333	.000

B. Redmond, 1 G at C

Pitcher	T	Age	G	GS	CG	ShO	IP	H	HR	BB	SO	W-L	Sv	ERA
Sam Weaver	R	22	45	43	39	1	383.0	371	2	21	95	12-31	0	1.95
Mike Golden	R	26	22	18	15	0	161.0	217	1	33	52	3-13	0	4.14
Joe Ellick	—	24	1	0	0	0	3.0	1	0	1	0	0-1	0	3.00

»1879 Providence Grays 1st NL 59-25 .702 —

George Wright

Player	Gm by Position	B	Age	G	AB	R	H	2B	3B	HR	RBI	BB	SO	SB	Avg	OBP	Slg
Lew Brown†	C48,OF6	R	21	53	229	23	59	13	4	2	38	4	24	—	.258	.270	.376
Joe Start	1B65,OF1	L	36	66	317	70	101	11	5	2	37	7	4	—	.319	.333	.404
Mike McGeary	2B73,3B12	R	28	85	374	62	103	7	2	0	35	5	13	—	.275	.285	.305
Bill Hague	3B51	R	27	51	209	20	47	3	1	0	21	3	19	—	.225	.236	.249
George Wright	SS85	R	32	85	388	79	107	15	10	1	42	13	20	—	.276	.299	.374
Paul Hines	OF85	R	27	85	409	81	146	25	10	2	52	8	16	—	.357	.369	.482
Tom York	OF81	L	27	81	342	69	106	25	5	1	50	19	28	—	.310	.346	.421
Jim O'Rourke	OF56,1B20,C5*	R	28	81	362	69	126	19	9	1	46	13	10	—	.348	.371	.459
Monte Ward	P70,3B16,OF8	L	19	83	364	71	104	9	4	2	41	7	14	—	.286	.299	.349
Bobby Mathews	P27,OF21,3B5	R	27	43	173	25	35	2	0	1	10	7	12	—	.202	.233	.231
Emil Gross	C30	R	21	30	132	31	46	9	5	0	24	4	8	—	.348	.368	.492
Jack Farrell†	2B12	R	21	12	51	5	13	2	0	0	5	0	0	—	.255	.255	.294
Denny Sullivan	3B4,OF1	—	21	5	19	5	5	2	0	0	2	1	1	—	.263	.300	.368
Dan O'Leary	OF2	L	22	2	7	1	3	0	0	0	2	0	0	—	.429	.429	.429
Rudy Kemmler	C2	R	19	2	7	0	1	0	0	0	0	0	1	—	.143	.143	.143
Doug Allison	C1	R	33	1	5	0	0	0	0	0	0	0	1	—	.000	.000	.000
Bill White	1B1	—	—	1	4	1	1	0	0	0	0	0	1	—	.250	.250	.250

J. O'Rourke, 3 G at 3B

Pitcher	T	Age	G	GS	CG	ShO	IP	H	HR	BB	SO	W-L	Sv	ERA
Monte Ward	R	19	70	60	58	2	587.0	571	5	36	239	47-19	1	2.15
Bobby Mathews	R	27	27	25	15	1	189.0	194	4	26	90	12-6	1	2.29

1879 Boston Red Stockings 2nd NL 54-30 .643 5.0 GB

Harry Wright

Player	Gm by Position	B	Age	G	AB	R	H	2B	3B	HR	RBI	BB	SO	SB	Avg	OBP	Slg
Pop Snyder	C80,OF2	R	24	81	329	42	78	16	3	2	35	5	31	—	.237	.249	.322
Ed Cogswell	1B49	R	25	49	236	51	76	8	1	1	18	8	5	—	.322	.344	.377
Jack Burdock	2B84	R	27	84	359	64	86	10	3	0	36	9	28	—	.240	.258	.284
John Morrill	3B51,1B33	R	24	84	348	56	98	18	5	0	49	14	32	—	.282	.309	.362
Ezra Sutton	SS51,3B33	R	28	84	339	54	84	13	4	0	34	2	18	—	.248	.252	.310
Charley Jones	OF83	R	29	83	355	85	112	22	10	9	62	29	38	—	.315	.367	.510
John O'Rourke	OF71	L	29	72	317	69	108	17	11	6	62	8	32	—	.341	.357	.521
Sadie Houck	OF47,SS33	R	23	80	356	69	95	24	9	2	49	4	11	—	.267	.275	.402
Tommy Bond	P64,OF5,1B1	R	23	65	257	35	62	3	1	0	21	6	8	—	.241	.259	.261
Bill Hawes	OF34,C5	R	25	38	155	19	31	3	3	0	9	2	13	—	.200	.210	.258
Curry Foley	P21,OF17,1B2	—	23	35	146	16	46	3	1	0	17	3	4	—	.315	.329	.349

Pitcher	T	Age	G	GS	CG	ShO	IP	H	HR	BB	SO	W-L	Sv	ERA
Tommy Bond	R	23	64	64	59	11	555.1	543	8	24	155	43-19	0	1.96
Curry Foley	L	23	21	16	16	1	161.2	175	1	15	57	9-9	0	2.51
Jim Tyng	—	23	3	3	3	0	27.0	35	0	6	7	1-2	0	5.00
Lee Richmond	L	22	1	1	1	0	9.0	4	0	1	11	1-0	0	2.00

1879 Buffalo Bisons 3rd NL 46-32 .590 10.0 GB

John Clapp

Player	Gm by Position	B	Age	G	AB	R	H	2B	3B	HR	RBI	BB	SO	SB	Avg	OBP	Slg
John Clapp	C63,OF7	R	27	70	292	47	77	12	5	1	36	11	11	—	.264	.290	.349
Oscar Walker	1B72	L	25	72	287	35	79	15	6	1	35	8	38	—	.275	.295	.380
Chuck Fulmer	2B76	R	28	76	306	30	82	11	5	0	28	5	34	—	.268	.280	.337
Hardy Richardson	3B78,C1	R	24	79	336	54	95	18	10	0	37	16	30	—	.283	.315	.396
Davy Force	SS78,3B1	R	29	79	316	36	66	5	2	0	8	13	37	—	.209	.240	.237
Dave Eggler	OF78	R	28	78	317	41	66	5	7	0	27	11	41	—	.208	.235	.268
Joe Hornung	OF77,1B1	R	22	78	319	46	85	18	7	0	38	2	27	—	.266	.271	.367
Bill Crowley	OF43,C10,1B7*	R	22	60	261	41	75	9	5	0	30	6	14	—	.287	.303	.360
Pud Galvin	P66,SS1	R	22	67	265	34	66	11	6	0	27	1	56	—	.249	.252	.336
Bill McGunnigle	OF34,P14	R	24	47	171	22	30	0	1	0	5	5	24	—	.175	.199	.187
Jack Rowe	C6,OF2	L	22	8	34	8	12	1	0	0	8	0	1	—	.353	.353	.382
Steve Libby	1B1	—	25	1	2	0	0	0	0	0	0	0	1	—	.000	.000	.000

B. Crowley, 3 G at 2B

Pitcher	T	Age	G	GS	CG	ShO	IP	H	HR	BB	SO	W-L	Sv	ERA
Pud Galvin	R	22	66	66	65	6	593.0	585	3	31	136	37-27	0	2.28
Bill McGunnigle	R	24	14	13	13	2	120.0	113	0	16	62	9-5	0	2.63

1879 Chicago White Stockings 4th NL 46-33 .582 10.5 GB

Cap Anson (41-21)/Silver Flint (5-12)

Player	Gm by Position	B	Age	G	AB	R	H	2B	3B	HR	RBI	BB	SO	SB	Avg	OBP	Slg
Silver Flint	C78,OF1	R	23	79	324	46	92	22	6	1	41	6	44	—	.284	.297	.398
Cap Anson	1B51	R	27	51	227	40	72	20	1	0	34	2	2	—	.317	.323	.414
Joe Quest	2B83	R	26	83	334	38	69	16	1	0	22	9	33	—	.207	.227	.260
Ned Williamson	3B70,1B6,C4	R	21	80	320	66	94	20	13	1	36	24	31	—	.294	.343	.447
John Peters	SS83	R	29	83	379	45	93	13	2	1	31	1	19	—	.245	.247	.298
Orator Shaffer	OF72,3B1	L	27	73	316	53	96	13	0	0	35	6	28	—	.304	.317	.345
Abner Dalrymple	OF71	L	21	71	333	47	97	25	1	0	23	4	29	—	.291	.300	.372
George Gore	OF54,1B9	L	22	63	266	43	70	17	4	0	32	8	30	—	.263	.285	.357
Terry Larkin	P58,OF3	R	—	60	228	26	50	12	2	0	18	8	24	—	.219	.246	.289
Frank Hankinson	P26,OF14,3B5	R	23	44	171	14	31	4	0	0	8	2	14	—	.181	.191	.205
Jack Remsen	OF31,1B11	R	29	42	152	14	33	4	2	0	8	2	23	—	.217	.227	.270
Lew Brown†	1B6	R	21	6	21	2	6	1	0	0	3	1	4	—	.286	.318	.333
Bill Harbidge	OF4	L	24	4	18	2	2	0	0	0	1	0	5	—	.111	.111	.111
John Stedronsky	3B4	—	—	4	12	0	1	0	0	0	0	0	3	—	.083	.083	.083
Herm Doscher†	3B3	R	26	3	11	1	2	0	0	0	1	0	3	—	.182	.182	.182
Tom Dolan	C1	R	20	1	4	0	0	0	0	0	0	0	2	—	.000	.000	.000

Pitcher	T	Age	G	GS	CG	ShO	IP	H	HR	BB	SO	W-L	Sv	ERA
Terry Larkin	R	—	58	58	57	4	513.1	514	5	30	142	31-23	0	2.44
Frank Hankinson	R	23	26	25	25	2	230.2	248	0	27	69	15-10	0	2.50

1879 Cincinnati Red Stockings 5th NL 43-37 .538 14.0 GB

Deacon White (9-9)/Cal McVey (34-28)

Player	Gm by Position	B	Age	G	AB	R	H	2B	3B	HR	RBI	BB	SO	SB	Avg	OBP	Slg
Deacon White	C59,OF21,1B2	L	31	78	333	55	110	16	6	1	52	6	9	—	.330	.342	.423
Cal McVey	1B72,OF7,P3*	R	28	81	354	64	105	18	6	0	55	8	13	—	.297	.312	.381
Joe Gerhardt	2B55,3B16,1B8*	R	24	79	313	22	62	12	3	1	39	3	19	—	.198	.206	.265
King Kelly	3B33,OF29,C21*	R	21	77	345	78	120	20	12	2	47	8	14	—	.348	.363	.493
Ross Barnes	SS61,2B16	R	29	77	323	55	86	9	2	1	30	16	25	—	.266	.301	.316
Buttercup Dickerson	OF81	L	20	81	350	73	102	18	14	2	57	3	27	—	.291	.297	.440
Pete Hotaling	OF69,C8,2B6*	R	22	81	369	64	103	20	9	1	27	12	17	—	.279	.302	.390
Will Foley	3B29,OF25,2B3	R	23	56	218	22	46	5	1	0	25	2	16	—	.211	.218	.243
Mike Burke	SS19,3B5,OF5	R	—	28	117	13	26	3	0	0	8	2	5	—	.222	.235	.248
Blondie Purcell†	OF10,P2	R	25	12	50	10	11	0	0	0	4	0	3	—	.220	.220	.220
Jack Neagle	P2,OF2	R	21	3	12	1	2	0	0	0	2	0	0	—	.167	.167	.167
John Magner	OF1	—	24	1	4	0	0	0	0	0	1	0	1	—	.000	.000	.000
Harry Wheeler	P1,OF1	R	21	1	3	0	0	0	0	0	0	0	2	—	.000	.000	.000

C. McVey, 1 G at C, 1 G at 3B; J. Gerhardt, 1 G at SS; K. Kelly, 1 G at 2B; P. Hotaling, 3 G at 3B

Pitcher	T	Age	G	GS	CG	ShO	IP	H	HR	BB	SO	W-L	Sv	ERA
Will White	R	24	76	75	75	4	680.0	676	10	68	232	43-31	0	1.99
Blondie Purcell†	R	25	2	2	2	0	18.0	27	0	2	3	0-2	0	4.00
Jack Neagle	R	21	2	2	1	0	13.0	13	0	5	4	0-1	0	3.46
Harry Wheeler	R	21	1	1	0	0	1.0	6	0	4	0	0-1	0	81.00
Cal McVey	R	28	3	1	1	0	14.0	34	1	2	7	0-2	0	8.36

1879 Cleveland Blues 6th NL 27-55 .329 31.0 GB

Jim McCormick

Player	Gm by Position	B	Age	G	AB	R	H	2B	3B	HR	RBI	BB	SO	SB	Avg	OBP	Slg
Doc Kennedy	C46,1B4	R	25	49	193	19	56	8	2	1	18	2	10	—	.290	.297	.368
Bill Phillips	1B75,C11,OF2	R	22	81	365	58	99	15	4	0	29	2	20	—	.271	.275	.334
Jack Glasscock	2B66,3B14	R	19	80	325	31	68	9	3	0	29	6	24	—	.209	.224	.255
Fred Warner	3B54,OF21,1B1	—	24	76	316	32	77	11	4	0	22	2	20	—	.244	.248	.304
Tom Carey	SS80	R	30	80	335	30	80	14	1	0	32	5	20	—	.239	.250	.287
Charlie Eden	OF80,1B3,C1	L	24	81	353	40	96	31	7	3	34	6	20	—	.272	.284	.425
George Strief	OF55,2B16	R	22	71	264	24	46	7	1	0	15	10	23	—	.174	.204	.208
Billy Riley	OF43,C1,1B1	R	24	44	165	14	24	2	0	0	9	2	26	—	.145	.156	.158
Jim McCormick	P62,OF13,1B4	R	22	75	282	35	62	10	2	0	20	1	9	—	.220	.223	.270
Barney Gilligan	C27,OF23,SS2	R	23	52	205	20	35	6	2	0	11	0	13	—	.171	.171	.220
Bobby Mitchell	P23,OF9	L	23	30	109	11	16	2	2	0	6	0	14	—	.147	.147	.202
Jack Allen†	3B14,OF2	R	23	16	60	7	7	1	1	0	4	1	9	—	.117	.131	.167
Len Stockwell	OF2	R	19	2	6	0	0	0	0	0	0	0	2	—	.000	.000	.000
Hickey Hoffman	C2,OF1	—	22	2	6	0	0	0	0	0	0	0	3	—	.000	.000	.000
Fred Gunkle	C1,OF1	—	—	1	3	1	0	0	0	0	0	0	1	—	.000	.000	.000

Pitcher	T	Age	G	GS	CG	ShO	IP	H	HR	BB	SO	W-L	Sv	ERA
Jim McCormick	R	22	62	60	59	3	546.1	582	3	74	197	20-40	0	2.42
Bobby Mitchell	L	23	23	22	20	0	194.2	236	1	42	90	7-15	0	3.28

1879 Syracuse Stars 7th NL 22-48 .314 30.0 GB

Mike Dorgan (17-26)/Jimmy Macullar (5-21)/Bill Holbert (0-1)

Player	Gm by Position	B	Age	G	AB	R	H	2B	3B	HR	RBI	BB	SO	SB	Avg	OBP	Slg
Bill Holbert†	C56,OF4	R	24	59	229	11	46	0	0	0	21	1	20	—	.201	.204	.201
Hick Carpenter	1B34,3B18,OF11*	R	23	65	261	30	53	6	0	0	20	2	15	—	.203	.209	.226
Jack Farrell†	2B54	R	21	54	241	40	73	6	2	1	21	3	13	—	.303	.311	.357
Red Woodhead	3B34	—	27	34	131	4	21	1	0	0	2	0	23	—	.160	.160	.168
Jimmy Macullar	SS37,OF26,2B4*	R	24	64	246	24	52	9	0	0	13	3	27	—	.211	.221	.248
Mike Mansell	OF67	L	21	67	242	24	52	4	2	1	13	5	45	—	.215	.231	.260
Blondie Purcell†	OF47,P22,C1	R	25	63	277	32	72	6	3	0	25	3	13	—	.260	.268	.303
John Richmond	OF35,SS28,C2	—	25	62	254	31	54	8	4	1	23	4	24	—	.213	.225	.287
Mike Dorgan	1B21,OF16,3B11*	R	25	59	270	38	72	11	5	1	17	4	13	—	.267	.277	.356
Harry McCormick	P54,OF7	R	23	57	230	21	51	4	1	1	21	0	22	—	.222	.222	.261
George Creamer	2B10,SS3,OF2	R	24	15	60	3	13	2	0	0	3	1	2	—	.217	.230	.250
John McGuinness	1B12	—	22	12	51	7	15	1	1	0	4	0	6	—	.294	.294	.353
Jack Allen†	3B8,OF3	R	23	11	48	7	9	2	1	0	3	1	5	—	.188	.204	.271
Kick Kelly†	C8,1B2	—	22	10	36	4	4	1	0	0	2	0	6	—	.111	.111	.139
George Adams	1B2,OF2	R	—	4	13	0	3	0	0	0	0	1	1	—	.231	.286	.231
Frank Decker	C2,1B1,OF1	R	23	3	10	0	1	0	0	0	0	0	3	—	.100	.100	.100
Charlie Osterhout	C1,OF1	—	23	2	8	0	0	0	0	0	0	0	0	—	.000	.000	.000
Tom Mansell†	OF1	L	24	1	4	0	1	0	0	0	0	0	0	—	.250	.250	.250

H. Carpenter, 3 G at 2B; J. Macullar, 1 G at 3B; M. Dorgan, 6 G at SS, 4 G at C, 2 G at P, 1 G at 2B

Pitcher	T	Age	G	GS	CG	ShO	IP	H	HR	BB	SO	W-L	Sv	ERA
Harry McCormick	R	23	54	54	49	5	457.1	517	3	31	96	18-33	0	2.99
Blondie Purcell†	R	25	22	17	15	0	179.2	245	1	19	28	4-15	0	3.76
Mike Dorgan	R	25	2	0	0	0	12.0	13	0	2	8	0-0	0	2.25

1879 Troy Trojans 8th NL 19-56 .253 35.5 GB

Horace Phillips (12-34)/Bob Ferguson (7-22)

Player	Gm by Position	B	Age	G	AB	R	H	2B	3B	HR	RBI	BB	SO	SB	Avg	OBP	Slg
Charlie Reilley	C49,1B11,OF2	R	23	62	236	17	54	5	1	0	19	1	20	—	.229	.232	.258
Dan Brouthers	1B37,P3	L	21	39	168	17	46	12	1	4	17	1	18	—	.274	.278	.429
Thorny Hawkes	2B64	R	26	64	250	24	52	6	1	0	20	4	14	—	.208	.220	.240
Herm Doscher†	3B47	R	26	47	191	16	42	8	0	0	18	2	10	—	.220	.228	.262
Ed Caskin	SS42,C22,2B6	R	27	70	304	32	78	13	2	0	21	2	14	—	.257	.261	.313
Jake Evans	OF72	—	22	72	280	30	65	9	5	0	17	5	18	—	.232	.246	.300
Al Hall	OF67	—	—	67	306	30	79	7	3	0	14	3	13	—	.258	.265	.301
Tom Mansell†	OF40	L	24	40	177	29	43	6	0	0	11	3	9	—	.243	.256	.277
George Bradley	P54,3B5,1B3*	R	26	63	251	36	62	9	5	0	23	1	20	—	.247	.250	.323
Aaron Clapp	1B25,OF11	—	22	36	146	24	39	9	3	0	18	6	10	—	.267	.296	.370
Bob Ferguson	3B24,2B6	S	34	30	123	18	31	5	2	0	4	4	3	—	.252	.276	.325
Candy Nelson	SS24,OF4	L	30	28	106	17	28	7	1	0	10	8	4	—	.264	.316	.349
Sandy Taylor	OF24	—	—	24	97	10	21	4	0	0	8	1	8	—	.216	.224	.258
John Shoupe	SS10,2B1	L	27	11	44	5	4	0	0	0	1	0	3	—	.091	.091	.091
Fred Goldsmith	P8,OF2,1B1	R	23	9	38	6	9	1	0	0	2	1	3	—	.237	.256	.263
John Cassidy	OF8,1B2	R	22	9	37	4	7	1	0	0	1	2	4	—	.189	.231	.216
Harry Salisbury	P10,OF1	L	24	10	36	3	2	0	0	0	0	1	7	—	.056	.081	.056
Kick Kelly†	C3,OF2,3B1	—	22	6	22	1	5	0	0	0	0	0	1	—	.227	.227	.227
Bill Holbert†	C4	R	24	4	15	1	4	0	0	0	2	0	1	—	.267	.267	.267

G. Bradley, 1 G at SS, 1 G at OF

Pitcher	T	Age	G	GS	CG	ShO	IP	H	HR	BB	SO	W-L	Sv	ERA
George Bradley	R	26	54	54	53	3	487.0	590	12	26	133	13-40	0	2.85
Harry Salisbury	—	24	10	10	9	0	89.0	103	0	11	31	4-6	0	2.22
Fred Goldsmith	R	23	8	7	7	0	63.0	61	0	1	31	2-4	0	1.57
Dan Brouthers	L	21	3	2	2	0	21.0	35	0	8	6	0-2	0	5.57
Pat McManus	—	—	2	2	2	0	21.0	24	1	1	6	0-2	0	3.00
Gid Gardner	—	20	2	2	2	0	14.0	27	0	0	3	0-2	0	5.79

»1880 Chicago White Stockings 1st NL 67-17 .798 —

Cap Anson

Player	Gm by Position	B	Age	G	AB	R	H	2B	3B	HR	RBI	BB	SO	SB	Avg	OBP	Slg
Silver Flint	C67,OF13	R	24	74	284	30	46	10	4	0	17	5	32	—	.162	.176	.225
Cap Anson	1B81,3B9,2B1*	R	28	86	356	54	120	24	1	1	74	14	12	—	.337	.362	.419
Joe Quest	2B80,SS2,3B1	R	27	82	300	37	71	12	1	0	27	8	16	—	.237	.256	.283
Ned Williamson	3B63,C11,2B3	R	22	75	311	65	78	20	2	0	31	15	26	—	.251	.285	.328
Tom Burns	SS79,3B9,C2*	R	23	85	333	47	103	17	3	0	43	12	23	—	.309	.333	.378
Abner Dalrymple	OF86	L	22	86	382	91	126	25	12	0	36	3	18	—	.330	.335	.458
George Gore	OF74,1B7	L	23	77	322	70	116	23	2	2	47	21	10	—	.360	.399	.463
King Kelly	OF64,C17,3B14*	R	22	84	344	72	100	17	9	1	60	12	22	—	.291	.315	.401
Larry Corcoran	P63,SS8,OF8	L	20	72	286	41	66	11	1	0	25	10	33	—	.231	.257	.276
Fred Goldsmith	P26,OF10,1B4	R	24	35	142	24	37	4	2	0	15	2	15	—	.261	.271	.317
Tommy Beals	OF10,2B3	R	—	13	46	4	7	0	0	0	3	1	6	—	.152	.170	.152
Tom Poorman†	OF7,P2	L	22	7	25	3	5	1	2	0	0	0	2	—	.200	.200	.400

C. Anson, 1 G at SS; T. Burns, 1 G at P; K. Kelly, 1 G at P, 1 G at 2B, 1 G at SS

Pitcher	T	Age	G	GS	CG	ShO	IP	H	HR	BB	SO	W-L	Sv	ERA
Larry Corcoran	R	20	63	60	57	4	536.1	404	6	99	268	43-14	2	1.95
Fred Goldsmith	R	24	26	24	22	4	210.1	189	2	18	90	21-3	1	1.75
Tom Poorman†	R	22	2	1	0	0	15.0	12	0	8	0	2-0	0	2.40
Charlie Guth	—	24	1	1	1	0	9.0	12	0	1	7	1-0	0	5.00
King Kelly	R	22	1	0	0	0	3.0	3	0	1	1	0-0	0	0.00
Tom Burns	R	23	1	0	0	0	1.1	2	0	2	1	0-0	0	0.00

1880 Providence Grays 2nd NL 52-32 .619 15.0 GB

Mike McGeary (8-7)/Monte Ward (18-13)/Mike Dorgan (26-12)

Player	Gm by Position	B	Age	G	AB	R	H	2B	3B	HR	RBI	BB	SO	SB	Avg	OBP	Slg
Emil Gross	C87	R	22	87	347	43	90	18	3	1	34	16	15	—	.259	.292	.337
Joe Start	1B82	L	37	82	345	53	96	14	6	0	27	13	20	—	.278	.304	.354
Jack Farrell	2B80	R	22	80	339	46	92	12	5	3	36	10	6	—	.271	.292	.363
George Bradley	3B57,P28,OF7*	R	27	82	309	32	70	7	6	0	23	5	38	—	.227	.239	.288
John Peters	SS86	R	30	86	359	30	82	5	0	0	24	5	15	—	.228	.239	.242
Mike Dorgan	OF77,3B2,P1	R	26	79	321	45	79	10	1	0	31	10	18	—	.246	.269	.283
Paul Hines	OF75,2B6,1B4	R	28	85	374	64	115	20	2	3	35	13	17	—	.307	.331	.396
Tom York	OF53	L	28	53	203	21	43	9	2	0	18	8	29	—	.212	.242	.276
Monte Ward	P70,3B25,OF2	L	20	86	356	53	81	12	2	0	27	6	16	—	.228	.240	.272
Sadie Houck†	OF49	R	24	49	184	27	37	7	7	1	22	3	6	—	.201	.214	.332
Mike McGeary†	3B17,2B2,SS1	R	29	18	59	5	8	0	0	0	1	0	6	—	.136	.136	.136

G. Bradley, 2 G at 1B

Pitcher	T	Age	G	GS	CG	ShO	IP	H	HR	BB	SO	W-L	Sv	ERA
Monte Ward	R	20	70	67	59	8	595.0	501	5	45	230	39-24	1	1.74
George Bradley	R	27	28	20	16	4	196.0	158	2	6	54	14-8	1	1.38
Mike Dorgan	R	26	1	0	0	0	8.0	4	0	0	2	0-0	0	1.13

1880 Cleveland Blues 3rd NL 47-37 .560 20.0 GB — Jim McCormick

Player	Gm by Position	B	Age	G	AB	R	H	2B	3B	HR	RBI	BB	SO	SB	Avg	OBP	Slg
Doc Kennedy	C65,OF2	R	26	66	250	26	50	10	1	0	18	5	12	—	.200	.216	.248
Bill Phillips	1B85	R	23	85	334	41	85	14	10	1	36	6	29	—	.254	.268	.365
Fred Dunlap	2B85	R	21	85	373	61	103	27	9	4	30	7	32	—	.276	.289	.429
Frank Hankinson	3B56,OF12,P4	R	24	69	263	32	55	7	4	1	19	1	23	—	.209	.212	.278
Jack Glasscock	SS77	R	20	77	296	37	72	13	3	0	27	2	21	—	.243	.248	.307
Orator Shaffer	OF83	L	28	83	338	62	90	14	9	0	21	17	36	—	.266	.301	.361
Pete Hotaling	OF78,C2	R	23	78	325	40	78	17	8	0	41	10	30	—	.240	.263	.342
Ned Hanlon	OF69,SS4	L	22	73	280	30	69	10	3	0	32	11	30	—	.246	.275	.304
Jim McCormick	P74,OF5	R	23	78	289	34	71	11	0	0	26	5	5	—	.246	.259	.284
Mike McGeary†	3B29,OF2	R	29	31	111	14	28	2	1	0	6	4	3	—	.252	.278	.288
Barney Gilligan	C23,SS4,OF4	R	24	30	99	9	17	4	3	1	13	6	12	—	.172	.219	.303
Gid Gardner	P9,OF1	—	21	10	32	0	6	1	1	0	4	2	4	—	.188	.235	.281
Al Hall	OF3	—	—	3	8	1	1	0	0	0	0	0	0	—	.125	.125	.125
Harry Wheeler†	OF1	R	22	1	4	0	1	0	0	0	0	0	0	—	.250	.250	.250

Pitcher	T	Age	G	GS	CG	ShO	IP	H	HR	BB	SO	W-L	Sv	ERA
Jim McCormick	R	23	74	74	72	7	657.2	585	2	75	260	45-28	0	1.85
Gid Gardner	—	21	9	9	9	0	77.0	80	2	20	21	1-8	0	2.57
Frank Hankinson	R	24	4	2	2	0	25.0	20	0	3	8	1-1	1	1.08

1880 Troy Trojans 4th NL 41-42 .494 25.5 GB — Bob Ferguson

Player	Gm by Position	B	Age	G	AB	R	H	2B	3B	HR	RBI	BB	SO	SB	Avg	OBP	Slg
Bill Holbert	C58,OF3	R	25	60	212	18	40	5	1	0	8	9	18	—	.189	.222	.222
Ed Cogswell	1B47	R	26	47	209	41	63	7	3	0	13	11	10	—	.301	.336	.364
Bob Ferguson	2B82	S	35	82	332	55	87	9	0	0	22	24	24	—	.262	.312	.289
Roger Connor	3B83	L	22	83	340	53	113	18	8	3	47	13	21	—	.332	.357	.459
Ed Caskin	SS82,C2	R	28	82	333	36	75	5	4	0	28	7	24	—	.225	.241	.264
John Cassidy	OF82,2B1	R	23	83	352	40	89	14	8	0	29	12	34	—	.253	.277	.338
Pete Gillespie	OF82	L	28	82	346	50	84	20	5	2	24	17	35	—	.243	.278	.347
Jake Evans	OF47,P1	—	23	47	180	31	46	8	1	0	22	7	15	—	.256	.283	.311
Mickey Welch	P65,OF2	R	20	66	251	25	72	20	3	0	27	5	24	—	.287	.301	.390
Bill Tobin†	1B33	L	25	33	136	14	22	1	1	0	8	4	20	—	.162	.186	.184
B. Dickerson†	OF30,SS1	L	21	30	119	15	23	2	2	0	10	2	3	—	.193	.207	.244
Buck Ewing	C10,OF4	R	20	13	45	1	8	1	0	0	5	1	3	—	.178	.196	.200
Bill Harbidge	C9,OF1	L	25	9	27	3	10	0	1	0	2	0	3	—	.370	.370	.444
Terry Larkin	P5,OF2,SS1	R	—	6	20	1	3	1	0	0	1	3	4	—	.150	.261	.200
Joe Straub	C3	R	22	3	12	1	3	0	0	0	3	1	3	—	.250	.308	.250
Dan Brouthers	1B3	L	22	3	12	0	2	0	0	0	1	1	0	—	.167	.231	.167
Mike Lawlor	C4	—	26	4	9	1	1	0	0	0	0	1	1	—	.111	.200	.111
Fred Haley	C2	—	27	2	7	0	0	0	0	0	0	1	2	—	.000	.125	.000
Dick Higham	C1,OF1	L	28	1	5	1	1	0	0	0	0	0	0	—	.200	.200	.200
Charlie Ahearn	C1	—	—	1	4	1	1	0	0	0	0	0	0	—	.250	.250	.250
Fatty Briody	C1	—	21	1	4	0	0	0	0	0	0	0	0	—	.000	.000	.000

Pitcher	T	Age	G	GS	CG	ShO	IP	H	HR	BB	SO	W-L	Sv	ERA
Mickey Welch	R	20	65	64	64	4	574.0	575	7	80	123	34-30	0	2.54
Tim Keefe	R	23	12	12	12	0	105.0	71	0	17	43	6-6	0	0.86
Terry Larkin	R	—	5	5	3	0	38.0	83	1	10	5	0-5	0	8.76
Frank Mountain	R	20	2	2	2	0	17.0	23	0	6	2	1-1	0	5.29
Jake Evans	R	23	1	0	0	0	4.0	11	0	0	0	0-0	0	13.50

1880 Worcester Brown Stockings 5th NL 40-43 .482 26.5 GB — Frank Bancroft

Player	Gm by Position	B	Age	G	AB	R	H	2B	3B	HR	RBI	BB	SO	SB	Avg	OBP	Slg
Charlie Bennett	C46,OF6	R	25	51	193	20	44	9	3	0	18	10	30	—	.228	.266	.306
Chub Sullivan	1B43	R	24	43	166	22	43	6	3	0	0	4	6	—	.259	.276	.331
George Creamer	2B85	R	25	85	306	40	61	6	3	0	27	4	21	—	.199	.210	.239
Art Whitney	3B76	R	22	76	302	38	67	13	5	1	36	9	15	—	.222	.244	.308
Arthur Irwin	SS82,3B3,C1	L	22	85	352	53	91	19	4	1	35	11	27	—	.259	.281	.344
George Wood	OF80,3B2,1B1	L	21	81	327	37	80	16	5	0	28	10	37	—	.245	.267	.324
Lon Knight	OF49	R	27	49	201	31	48	11	3	0	21	5	8	—	.239	.257	.323
Harry Stovey	OF46,1B37,P2	R	23	83	355	76	94	21	14	6	28	12	46	—	.265	.289	.454
Lee Richmond	P74,OF20	—	23	77	309	44	70	8	4	0	34	9	32	—	.227	.248	.278
Doc Bushong	C40,3B1,OF1	R	23	41	146	13	25	3	0	0	19	1	16	—	.171	.177	.192
Fred Corey	OF29,P25,SS3*	R	23	41	138	11	24	8	1	0	6	4	27	—	.174	.197	.246
B. Dickerson†	OF31	L	21	31	133	22	39	8	6	0	20	1	2	—	.293	.299	.444
Jerry Dorgan	OF9,C1	L	24	10	35	2	7	1	0	0	1	0	1	—	.200	.200	.229
Joe Ellick	3B5	—	26	5	18	1	1	0	0	0	0	1	2	—	.056	.105	.056
Bill Tobin†	1B5	L	25	5	16	1	2	0	0	0	3	0	5	—	.125	.125	.125
Steve Dignan†	OF3	—	21	3	10	1	3	0	1	0	2	0	1	—	.300	.300	.500
Billy Geer	SS1,OF1	—	30	2	6	0	0	0	0	0	0	0	0	—	.000	.000	.000
Bill McGunnigle†	OF1	R	25	1	4	0	0	0	0	0	0	0	2	—	.000	.000	.000

F. Corey, 1 G at 1B, 1 G at 3B

Pitcher	T	Age	G	GS	CG	ShO	IP	H	HR	BB	SO	W-L	Sv	ERA
Lee Richmond	L	23	74	66	57	5	590.2	541	7	74	243	32-32	3	2.15
Fred Corey	R	23	25	17	9	2	148.1	131	6	16	47	8-9	2	2.43
Tricky Nichols	R	29	2	2	2	0	17.2	29	0	4	4	0-2	0	4.08
Harry Stovey	R	23	2	0	0	0	6.0	8	0	3	3	0-0	0	4.50

1880 Boston Red Stockings 6th NL 40-44 .476 27.0 GB — Harry Wright

Player	Gm by Position	B	Age	G	AB	R	H	2B	3B	HR	RBI	BB	SO	SB	Avg	OBP	Slg
Phil Powers	C37,OF2	R	25	37	126	11	18	5	0	0	10	5	15	—	.143	.176	.183
John Morrill	1B46,3B40,P3	R	25	86	342	51	81	16	8	2	44	11	37	—	.237	.261	.348
Jack Burdock	2B86	R	28	86	356	58	90	17	4	2	35	8	26	—	.253	.269	.340
Ezra Sutton	SS39,3B37	R	29	76	288	41	72	9	2	0	25	7	7	—	.250	.268	.295
John Richmond	SS31,OF1	—	26	32	129	12	32	3	1	0	9	2	18	—	.248	.260	.287
John O'Rourke	OF81	L	30	81	313	30	86	22	8	3	36	18	32	—	.275	.314	.425
Charley Jones	OF66	R	30	66	280	44	84	15	3	5	37	11	27	—	.300	.326	.429
Jim O'Rourke	OF37,1B19,SS17*	R	29	86	363	71	100	20	11	6	45	21	8	—	.275	.315	.441
Curry Foley	P36,OF35,1B25	—	24	80	332	44	97	13	2	2	31	8	14	—	.292	.309	.361
Tommy Bond	P63,OF26,1B1*	R	24	76	282	27	62	4	1	0	24	8	14	—	.220	.241	.241
Sam Trott	C36,OF4	L	21	39	125	14	26	4	1	0	9	3	5	—	.208	.227	.256
Sadie Houck†	OF12	R	24	12	47	2	7	0	0	0	2	0	6	—	.149	.149	.149
John Bergh	C11	—	22	11	40	2	8	3	0	0	0	2	5	—	.200	.238	.275
Steve Dignan†	OF8	—	21	8	34	4	11	1	0	0	4	0	3	—	.324	.324	.353
Dan O'Leary	OF3	L	23	3	12	1	3	2	0	0	1	0	3	—	.250	.250	.417
Denny Sullivan	C1	—	22	1	4	1	1	0	0	0	1	0	1	—	.250	.250	.250
George Wright	SS1	R	33	1	4	2	1	0	0	0	0	0	0	—	.250	.250	.250
Jack Leary	P1,OF1	—	22	1	3	1	0	0	0	0	0	1	0	—	.000	.250	.000

J. O'Rourke, 10 G at 3B, 9 G at C; T. Bond, 1 G at 3B

Pitcher	T	Age	G	GS	CG	ShO	IP	H	HR	BB	SO	W-L	Sv	ERA
Tommy Bond	R	24	63	57	49	3	493.0	559	1	45	118	26-29	0	2.67
Curry Foley	L	24	36	28	21	1	238.0	264	1	40	68	14-14	0	3.89
Jack Leary	L	22	1	1	0	0	3.0	8	0	0	1	0-1	0	15.00
John Morrill	R	25	3	0	0	0	10.2	9	0	1	0	0-0	0	0.84

1880 Buffalo Bisons 7th NL 24-58 .293 42.0 GB — Sam Crane

Player	Gm by Position	B	Age	G	AB	R	H	2B	3B	HR	RBI	BB	SO	SB	Avg	OBP	Slg
Jack Rowe	C60,OF25,3B3	L	23	79	326	43	82	10	6	1	36	6	17	—	.252	.265	.328
Dude Esterbrook	1B47,OF15,2B6*	R	23	64	253	20	61	12	1	0	35	0	15	—	.241	.241	.296
Davy Force	2B53,SS30	R	30	81	290	22	49	10	0	0	17	10	35	—	.169	.197	.203
Hardy Richardson	3B81,C5	R	25	83	343	48	89	18	8	0	17	14	37	—	.259	.289	.359
Mike Moynahan	SS27	L	24	27	100	12	33	5	1	0	14	6	9	—	.330	.368	.400
Bill Crowley	OF74,C22	R	23	85	354	57	95	16	4	0	20	19	23	—	.268	.306	.336
Joe Hornung	OF67,1B18,2B5*	R	23	85	342	47	91	8	11	1	42	8	29	—	.266	.283	.363
Ecky Stearns	OF20,C8,3B5*	L	18	28	104	8	19	6	1	0	13	3	23	—	.183	.206	.260
Pud Galvin	P58,OF19	R	23	66	241	25	51	9	2	0	12	5	57	—	.212	.228	.266
Oscar Walker	1B24,OF11	L	26	34	126	12	29	4	2	1	15	6	18	—	.230	.265	.317
Arlie Latham	SS12,OF10,C1	R	20	22	79	9	10	3	1	0	3	1	8	—	.127	.138	.190
Stump Wiedman	P17,OF13	R	19	23	78	8	8	1	0	0	3	2	11	—	.103	.125	.115
Tom Poorman†	P11,OF10	L	22	19	70	5	11	1	0	0	1	0	13	—	.157	.157	.171
Denny Driscoll	OF14,P6	L	24	18	65	1	10	1	0	0	4	1	7	—	.154	.167	.169
Denny Mack	SS16,2B1	R	29	17	59	5	12	0	0	0	3	5	7	—	.203	.266	.203
Chuck Fulmer	2B11	R	29	11	44	3	7	0	0	0	1	2	4	—	.159	.196	.159
Sam Crane	2B10,OF1	R	26	10	31	4	4	0	0	0	2	1	8	—	.129	.156	.129
Bill McGunnigle†	P5,OF3	R	25	7	22	0	4	0	0	0	1	0	4	—	.182	.182	.182
Old Hoss Radbourn	2B3,OF3	R	25	6	21	1	3	0	0	0	1	0	1	—	.143	.143	.143
Tom Kearns	C2	R	19	2	7	0	0	0	0	0	0	0	0	—	.000	.000	.000
Jim Keenan	C2	R	22	2	7	1	1	0	0	0	0	1	1	—	.143	.250	.143

D. Esterbrook, 1 G at C, 1 G at SS; J. Hornung, 1 G at P; E. Stearns, 1 G at SS

Pitcher	T	Age	G	GS	CG	ShO	IP	H	HR	BB	SO	W-L	Sv	ERA
Pud Galvin	R	23	58	54	46	5	458.2	528	5	32	128	20-35	0	2.71
Stump Wiedman	R	19	17	13	9	0	113.2	141	1	9	25	0-9	0	3.40
Tom Poorman†	R	22	11	9	9	0	85.0	117	3	19	13	1-8	1	4.13
Bill McGunnigle	R	25	5	5	4	1	37.0	43	0	8	3	2-3	0	3.41
Denny Driscoll	L	24	6	4	4	0	41.2	48	1	9	17	1-3	0	3.89
Joe Hornung	R	23	1	0	0	0	3.0	2	0	1	0	0-0	0	6.00

1880 Cincinnati Red Stockings 8th NL 21-59 .263 44.0 GB

John Clapp

Player	Gm by Position	B	Age	G	AB	R	H	2B	3B	HR	RBI	BB	SO	SB	Avg	OBP	Slg
John Clapp	C73,OF10	R	28	80	323	33	91	16	4	1	20	21	10	—	.282	.326	.365
John Reilly	1B72,OF3	R	21	73	272	21	56	8	4	0	16	3	36	—	.206	.215	.265
Pop Smith	2B83	R	23	83	334	35	69	10	9	0	27	6	36	—	.207	.221	.290
Hick Carpenter	3B67,1B9,SS1	R	24	77	300	32	72	6	4	0	23	2	15	—	.240	.245	.287
Lou Say	SS48	R	26	48	191	14	38	8	1	0	15	4	31	—	.199	.215	.251
Blondie Purcell	OF55,P25,SS1	R	26	77	325	48	95	13	6	1	24	5	13	—	.292	.303	.378
Mike Mansell	OF53	L	22	53	187	22	36	6	2	2	12	4	37	—	.193	.209	.278
Jack Manning	OF47,1B1	R	26	48	190	20	41	6	3	2	17	7	15	—	.216	.244	.311
Will White	P62,OF3	S	25	62	207	16	35	7	1	0	14	6	29	—	.169	.192	.213
Deacon White	OF33,1B3,2B1	L	32	35	141	21	42	4	2	0	7	9	7	—	.298	.340	.355
Andy Leonard	SS23,3B10	R	34	33	133	15	28	3	0	1	17	8	11	—	.211	.255	.256
Charlie Reilley	OF16,C13,3B4	R	24	30	103	8	21	1	0	0	9	0	5	—	.204	.204	.214
Joe Sommer	OF22,C1,3B1*	R	21	24	88	10	16	1	0	0	6	0	2	—	.182	.182	.193
Harry Wheeler†	OF17	R	22	17	65	1	6	2	0	0	2	0	15	—	.092	.092	.123
Sam Wright	SS9	R	31	9	34	0	3	0	0	0	0	0	5	—	.088	.088	.088
Amos Booth	3B1	R	27	1	2	0	0	0	0	0	0	0	0	—	.000	.000	.000

J. Sommer, 1 G at SS

Pitcher	T	Age	G	GS	CG	ShO	IP	H	HR	BB	SO	W-L	Sv	ERA
Will White	R	25	62	62	58	3	517.1	550	9	56	161	18-42	0	2.14
Blondie Purcell	R	26	25	21	21	0	196.0	235	1	32	47	3-17	0	3.21

»1881 Chicago White Stockings 1st NL 56-28 .667 —

Cap Anson

Player	Gm by Position	B	Age	G	AB	R	H	2B	3B	HR	RBI	BB	SO	SB	Avg	OBP	Slg
Silver Flint	C80,OF8,1B1	R	25	80	306	46	95	18	0	1	34	6	39	—	.310	.324	.379
Cap Anson	1B84,C2,SS1	R	29	84	343	67	137	21	7	1	82	26	4	—	.399	.442	.510
Joe Quest	2B77,SS1	R	28	78	293	35	72	6	0	1	26	2	29	—	.246	.251	.276
Ned Williamson	3B76,2B4,P3*	R	23	82	343	56	92	12	6	1	48	19	19	—	.268	.307	.347
Tom Burns	SS80,2B3,3B3	R	24	84	342	41	95	20	3	4	42	14	22	—	.278	.306	.389
Abner Dalrymple	OF82	L	23	82	362	72	117	22	4	1	37	15	22	—	.323	.350	.414
King Kelly	OF72,C11,3B8	R	23	82	353	84	114	27	3	2	55	16	14	—	.323	.352	.433
George Gore	OF72,1B1,3B1	L	24	73	309	86	92	18	9	1	44	27	23	—	.298	.354	.424
Larry Corcoran	P45,SS2,OF1	L	21	47	189	25	42	8	0	0	9	5	22	—	.222	.242	.265
Fred Goldsmith	P39,OF3	R	25	42	158	24	38	3	4	0	16	6	17	—	.241	.268	.310
Hugh Nicol	OF26,SS1	R	23	26	108	13	22	2	0	0	7	4	12	—	.204	.232	.222
Andy Piercy	2B1,3B1	—	24	2	8	1	2	0	0	0	0	0	1	—	.250	.250	.250

N. Williamson, 2 G at SS, 1 G at C

Pitcher	T	Age	G	GS	CG	ShO	IP	H	HR	BB	SO	W-L	Sv	ERA
Larry Corcoran	R	21	45	44	43	4	396.2	380	10	78	150	31-14	0	2.31
Fred Goldsmith	R	25	39	39	37	5	330.0	328	4	44	76	24-13	0	2.59
Ned Williamson	R	23	3	1	1	0	18.0	14	0	0	2	1-1	0	2.00

1881 Providence Grays 2nd NL 47-37 .560 9.0 GB

Jack Farrell (24-27)/Tom York (23-10)

Player	Gm by Position	B	Age	G	AB	R	H	2B	3B	HR	RBI	BB	SO	SB	Avg	OBP	Slg
Emil Gross	C50,OF1	R	23	51	182	15	50	9	4	1	24	13	11	—	.275	.323	.385
Joe Start	1B79	L	38	79	348	56	114	12	6	0	29	9	7	—	.328	.345	.397
Jack Farrell	2B82,OF3	R	23	84	345	69	82	16	5	5	36	29	23	—	.238	.297	.357
Jerry Denny	3B85	R	22	85	320	38	77	16	2	1	24	5	44	—	.241	.252	.313
Bill McClellan	SS50,OF17,2B1	L	25	68	259	30	43	3	1	0	16	15	21	—	.166	.212	.185
Tom York	OF85	L	29	85	316	57	96	23	5	2	47	29	26	—	.304	.362	.427
Paul Hines	OF78,2B4,1B1	R	29	80	361	65	103	27	5	2	31	13	12	—	.285	.310	.404
Monte Ward	OF40,P39,SS13	L	21	85	357	56	87	18	6	0	53	5	10	—	.244	.254	.328
Old Hoss Radbourn	P41,OF25,SS13	R	26	72	270	27	59	9	0	0	28	10	15	—	.219	.246	.252
Barney Gilligan	C36,SS10,OF1	R	25	46	183	19	40	7	2	0	20	9	24	—	.219	.255	.279
Lew Brown†	OF13,1B5	R	23	18	75	9	18	3	1	0	10	4	13	—	.240	.278	.307
Bobby Mathews†	P14,OF5	R	29	16	57	6	11	1	0	0	4	5	6	—	.193	.258	.211
Henry Myers	SS1	R	23	1	4	0	0	0	0	0	0	0	2	—	.000	.000	.000

Pitcher	T	Age	G	GS	CG	ShO	IP	H	HR	BB	SO	W-L	Sv	ERA
Old Hoss Radbourn	R	26	41	36	34	3	325.1	309	1	64	117	25-11	0	2.43
Monte Ward	R	21	39	35	32	3	330.0	326	2	53	119	18-18	0	2.13
Bobby Mathews†	R	29	14	14	10	1	102.1	121	2	21	28	4-8	0	3.17

1881 Buffalo Bisons 3rd NL 45-38 .542 10.5 GB

Jim O'Rourke

Player	Gm by Position	B	Age	G	AB	R	H	2B	3B	HR	RBI	BB	SO	SB	Avg	OBP	Slg
Jack Rowe	C46,3B7,SS7*	L	24	64	246	30	82	11	11	1	43	1	12	—	.333	.336	.480
Dan Brouthers	OF35,1B30	L	23	65	270	60	86	18	9	8	45	18	22	—	.319	.361	.541
Davy Force	2B51,SS21,OF3*	R	31	75	278	21	50	9	1	0	15	11	29	—	.180	.211	.219
Jim O'Rourke	3B56,OF18,C8*	R	30	83	348	71	105	21	7	0	30	27	18	—	.302	.352	.402
John Peters	SS53,OF1	R	31	54	229	21	49	8	1	0	25	3	12	—	.214	.224	.258
Hardy Richardson	OF79,2B5,3B1*	R	26	83	344	62	100	18	9	2	53	12	27	—	.291	.315	.413
Curry Foley	OF55,1B27,P10	—	25	83	375	58	96	20	2	1	25	7	27	—	.256	.270	.328
Blondie Purcell†	OF25,P9	R	27	30	113	15	33	7	2	0	17	8	8	—	.292	.339	.389
Deacon White	1B26,2B25,OF17*	L	33	78	319	58	99	24	4	0	53	9	8	—	.310	.329	.411
Pud Galvin	P56,OF14,SS1	R	24	62	236	19	50	12	4	0	21	3	70	—	.212	.222	.297
Sleeper Sullivan	C31,OF5	R	—	35	121	13	23	4	0	0	15	1	21	—	.190	.197	.223
Jack Lynch	P20,OF6	R	24	23	78	6	13	3	0	0	3	4	8	—	.167	.207	.205
John Morrissey	3B12	—	24	12	47	3	10	2	0	0	3	0	3	—	.213	.213	.255
Pop Smith†	2B3	R	24	3	11	3	0	0	0	0	1	3	5	—	.000	.214	.000
Ed Swartwood	OF1	L	22	1	3	0	1	0	0	0	0	1	0	—	.333	.500	.333
Jack Manning	OF1	R	27	1	1	0	0	0	0	0	0	1	0	—	.000	.000	.000

J. Rowe, 5 G at OF; D. Force, 1 G at 3B; J. O'Rourke, 3 G at SS, 1 G at 1B; H. Richardson, 1 G at SS; D. White, 7 G at 3B, 4 G at C

Pitcher	T	Age	G	GS	CG	ShO	IP	H	HR	BB	SO	W-L	Sv	ERA
Pud Galvin	R	24	56	53	48	5	474.0	546	4	46	136	28-24	0	2.37
Jack Lynch	R	24	20	19	17	0	165.2	203	2	29	32	10-9	0	3.59
Curry Foley	L	25	10	6	2	0	41.0	70	1	5	2	3-4	0	5.27
Blondie Purcell	R	27	9	5	5	0	61.2	62	2	9	15	4-1	0	2.77

1881 Detroit Wolverines 4th NL 41-43 .488 15.0 GB

Frank Bancroft

Player	Gm by Position	B	Age	G	AB	R	H	2B	3B	HR	RBI	BB	SO	SB	Avg	OBP	Slg
Charlie Bennett	C70,3B5,OF3	R	26	76	299	44	90	18	7	7	64	18	37	—	.301	.341	.478
Martin Powell	1B55,C1	L	25	55	219	47	74	9	4	1	38	15	9	—	.338	.380	.429
Joe Gerhardt	2B79,3B1	R	26	80	297	35	72	13	6	0	36	7	31	—	.242	.260	.327
Art Whitney	3B58	R	23	58	214	23	39	7	5	0	9	7	15	—	.182	.208	.262
Sadie Houck	SS75	R	25	75	308	43	86	16	6	1	36	6	6	—	.279	.293	.380
Lon Knight	OF82,1B1,2B1	R	28	83	340	67	92	16	3	1	52	23	21	—	.271	.317	.344
George Wood	OF80	L	22	80	337	54	100	18	9	2	32	19	32	—	.297	.334	.421
Ned Hanlon	OF74,SS2	L	23	76	305	63	85	14	8	2	28	22	11	—	.279	.327	.397
George Derby	P56,OF4	L	23	59	236	17	44	3	1	0	12	4	29	—	.186	.200	.208
Lew Brown†	1B27	R	23	27	108	16	26	3	1	3	14	3	16	—	.241	.261	.370
Charlie Reilley†	C10,OF4,3B3*	R	25	19	70	8	12	2	0	0	3	0	10	—	.171	.171	.200
Dasher Troy	3B7,2B4	R	25	11	44	2	15	3	0	0	4	3	8	—	.341	.383	.409
Mike Dorgan†	OF5,3B2,1B1	R	27	8	34	5	8	1	0	0	5	1	0	—	.235	.257	.265
Sam Trott	C6	L	22	6	25	3	5	2	1	0	2	1	3	—	.200	.231	.360
Will Foley	3B5	R	25	5	15	0	2	0	0	0	1	2	3	—	.133	.235	.133
Jack Leary	P2,OF2	—	23	3	11	2	3	1	1	0	4	1	1	—	.273	.333	.545
Ecky Stearns	SS3	L	19	3	11	1	1	1	0	0	0	0	2	—	.091	.091	.182
Dan O'Leary	OF2	L	24	2	8	0	0	0	0	0	0	0	2	—	.000	.000	.000
Sam Wise	3B1	L	23	1	4	0	2	0	0	0	0	0	2	—	.500	.500	.500
Billy Taylor†	3B1	R	26	1	4	0	2	2	0	0	1	0	0	—	.500	.500	1.000
Mike Moynahan†	3B1	L	25	1	4	1	1	0	0	0	0	0	1	—	.250	.250	.250
George Bradley†	SS1	R	28	1	4	0	0	0	0	0	0	0	0	—	.000	.000	.000

C. Reilley, 3 G at SS, 1 G at 1B

Pitcher	T	Age	G	GS	CG	ShO	IP	H	HR	BB	SO	W-L	Sv	ERA
George Derby	R	23	56	55	55	9	494.2	505	3	86	212	29-26	0	2.20
Stump Wiedman	R	20	13	13	13	1	115.0	108	1	12	26	8-5	0	1.80
Frank Mountain	R	21	7	7	7	0	60.0	80	2	18	13	3-4	0	5.25
Tony Mullane	R	22	5	5	5	0	44.0	55	2	17	7	1-4	0	4.91
Will White	R	26	2	2	2	0	18.0	24	0	2	5	0-2	0	5.00
Jack Leary	L	23	2	2	1	0	13.0	13	0	2	2	0-2	0	4.15

1881 Troy Trojans 5th NL 39-45 .464 17.0 GB

Bob Ferguson

Player	Gm by Position	B	Age	G	AB	R	H	2B	3B	HR	RBI	BB	SO	SB	Avg	OBP	Slg
Buck Ewing	C44,SS22,OF2*	R	21	67	272	40	68	14	7	0	25	7	8	—	.250	.269	.353
Roger Connor	1B85	L	23	85	367	55	107	17	6	2	31	15	20	—	.292	.319	.387
Bob Ferguson	2B85	S	36	85	339	56	96	13	5	1	35	29	12	—	.283	.340	.360
Frank Hankinson	3B84,SS1	R	25	85	321	34	62	15	0	1	19	10	41	—	.193	.218	.249
Ed Caskin	SS63	R	29	63	234	33	53	7	1	0	21	13	29	—	.226	.267	.265
John Cassidy	OF84,SS1	R	24	85	370	57	82	13	3	1	11	18	21	—	.222	.258	.281
Pete Gillespie	OF84	L	29	84	348	43	96	14	3	0	41	9	24	—	.276	.294	.333
Jake Evans	OF83	—	24	83	315	35	76	11	5	0	28	14	30	—	.241	.274	.308
Bill Holbert	C43,OF3	R	26	46	180	16	49	3	0	0	14	3	13	—	.272	.284	.289
Tim Keefe	P45,OF1	R	24	46	152	18	35	7	1	0	19	21	26	—	.230	.324	.289

B. Ewing, 1 G at 3B

Pitcher	T	Age	G	GS	CG	ShO	IP	H	HR	BB	SO	W-L	Sv	ERA
Tim Keefe	R	24	45	45	45	4	402.0	442	4	81	103	18-27	0	3.25
Mickey Welch	R	21	40	40	40	4	368.0	371	7	78	104	21-18	0	2.67

1881 Boston Red Stockings 6th NL 38-45 .458 17.5 GB

Harry Wright

Player	Gm by Position	B	Age	G	AB	R	H	2B	3B	HR	RBI	BB	SO	SB	Avg	OBP	Slg
Pop Snyder	C60,2B1,SS1*	R	26	62	219	14	50	8	0	0	16	3	23	—	.228	.239	.265
John Morrill	1B74,2B4,P3*	R	26	81	311	47	90	19	3	1	39	12	30	—	.289	.316	.379
Jack Burdock	2B72,SS1	R	29	73	282	36	67	12	4	1	24	7	18	—	.238	.256	.319
Ezra Sutton	3B81,SS2	R	30	83	333	43	97	12	4	0	31	13	9	—	.291	.318	.351
Ross Barnes	SS63,2B7	R	31	69	295	42	80	14	1	0	17	16	16	—	.271	.309	.325
Joe Hornung	OF83	R	24	83	324	40	78	12	8	2	25	5	25	—	.241	.252	.346
Bill Crowley	OF72	R	24	72	279	33	71	12	0	0	31	14	15	—	.254	.290	.297
Fred Lewis	OF27	S	22	27	114	17	25	6	0	0	9	7	5	—	.219	.264	.272
Jim Whitney	P66,OF15,1B2	L	23	75	282	37	72	17	3	0	32	19	18	—	.255	.302	.337
Pat Deasley	C28,SS7,OF7*	R	23	43	147	13	35	5	2	0	8	5	10	—	.238	.263	.299
John Fox	P17,OF12,1B6	—	22	30	118	8	21	0	0	0	4	0	11	—	.178	.178	.178
John Richmond	OF25,SS2	—	27	27	98	13	27	2	2	1	12	6	7	—	.276	.317	.367
Bobby Mathews†	OF18,P5	R	29	19	71	2	12	2	0	0	4	0	5	—	.169	.169	.197
George Wright	SS7	R	34	7	25	4	5	0	0	0	0	3	1	—	.200	.286	.200
Patrick Quinn†	1B1	—	—	1	4	0	0	0	0	0	0	0	0	—	.000	.000	.000
Sam Wright	SS1	R	32	1	4	0	1	0	0	0	0	0	0	—	.250	.250	.250

P. Snyder, 1 G at OF; J. Morrill, 2 G at 3B; P. Deasley, 2 G at 1B

Pitcher	T	Age	G	GS	CG	ShO	IP	H	HR	BB	SO	W-L	Sv	ERA
Jim Whitney	R	23	66	63	57	6	552.1	548	6	90	162	31-33	0	2.48
John Fox	—	22	17	16	12	0	124.1	144	0	39	30	6-8	0	3.33
Tommy Bond	R	25	3	3	2	0	25.1	40	3	2	2	0-3	0	4.26
Bobby Mathews†	R	29	5	1	1	0	23.0	22	0	11	5	1-0	2	2.35
John Morrill	R	26	3	0	0	0	5.2	9	0	1	0	0-1	1	6.35

1881 Cleveland Blues 7th NL 36-48 .429 20.0 GB

Mike McGeary (4-7)/John Clapp (32-41)

Player	Gm by Position	B	Age	G	AB	R	H	2B	3B	HR	RBI	BB	SO	SB	Avg	OBP	Slg
John Clapp	C48,OF21	R	29	68	261	47	66	12	2	0	25	35	6	—	.253	.341	.314
Bill Phillips	1B85	R	24	85	357	51	97	18	10	1	44	5	19	—	.272	.282	.387
Fred Dunlap	2B79,3B1	R	22	80	351	60	114	25	4	3	24	18	24	—	.325	.358	.444
George Bradley†	3B48,P6,SS6*	R	28	60	241	21	60	10	1	2	18	4	25	—	.249	.261	.324
Jack Glasscock	SS79,2B6	R	21	85	335	49	86	9	5	0	33	15	8	—	.257	.289	.313
Orator Shaffer	OF85	L	29	85	343	48	88	13	6	1	34	23	20	—	.257	.303	.338
Jack Remsen	OF48	R	31	48	172	14	30	4	3	0	13	9	31	—	.174	.215	.233
Mike Moynahan†	OF32,3B1	L	25	33	135	12	31	5	1	0	8	3	14	—	.230	.246	.281
Jim McCormick	P59,OF10,2B1*	R	24	70	309	45	79	9	4	0	26	5	16	—	.256	.268	.311
The Only Nolan	P22,OF14,3B6	L	23	41	168	12	41	5	1	0	18	4	13	—	.244	.262	.286
Doc Kennedy	C35,OF3,3B1	R	27	39	150	19	47	7	1	0	15	5	13	—	.313	.335	.373
Billy Taylor†	OF23,P1,3B1	R	26	24	103	6	25	1	0	0	12	0	8	—	.243	.243	.252
Blondie Purcell†	OF20	R	27	20	80	3	14	2	1	0	4	5	8	—	.175	.224	.225
Mike McGeary	3B11	R	30	11	41	1	9	0	0	0	5	0	6	—	.220	.220	.220
Pop Smith†	3B10	R	24	10	34	1	4	0	0	0	3	0	8	—	.118	.118	.118
Herm Doscher	3B5	R	28	5	19	2	4	0	0	0	0	0	2	—	.211	.211	.211
Phil Powers	C4,3B1	R	26	5	15	1	1	0	0	0	0	1	2	—	.067	.125	.067
Rudy Kemmler	C1	R	21	1	3	0	0	0	0	0	0	0	1	—	.000	.000	.000

G. Bradley, 1 G at OF; J. McCormick, 1 G at 3B

Pitcher	T	Age	G	GS	CG	ShO	IP	H	HR	BB	SO	W-L	Sv	ERA
Jim McCormick	R	24	59	58	57	2	526.0	484	4	84	178	26-30	0	2.45
The Only Nolan	R	23	22	21	20	0	180.0	183	3	38	54	8-14	0	3.05
George Bradley	R	28	6	6	5	0	51.0	70	2	3	6	2-4	0	3.88
Billy Taylor†	R	26	1	0	0	0	3.0	0	0	1	2	0-0	0	0.00

1881 Worcester Brown Stockings 8th NL 32-50 .390 23.0 GB

Mike Dorgan (24-32)/Harry Stovey (8-18)

Player	Gm by Position	B	Age	G	AB	R	H	2B	3B	HR	RBI	BB	SO	SB	Avg	OBP	Slg
Doc Bushong	C76	R	24	76	275	35	64	7	4	0	21	21	23	—	.233	.287	.287
Harry Stovey	1B57,OF18	R	24	75	341	57	92	25	7	2	30	12	23	—	.270	.295	.402
George Creamer	2B80	R	26	80	309	42	64	9	2	0	25	11	27	—	.207	.234	.249
Hick Carpenter	3B83	R	25	83	347	40	75	12	2	2	31	3	19	—	.216	.223	.280
Arthur Irwin	SS50	L	23	50	206	27	55	8	2	0	24	7	4	—	.267	.291	.325
Buttercup Dickerson	OF80	L	22	80	367	48	116	18	6	1	31	8	8	—	.316	.331	.406
Pete Hotaling	OF74,C3	R	24	77	317	51	98	15	3	1	35	18	12	—	.309	.346	.385
Fred Corey	OF25,P23,SS7	R	24	51	203	22	45	8	4	0	10	5	10	—	.222	.240	.300
Lee Richmond	P53,OF11	—	24	61	252	31	63	5	1	0	28	10	10	—	.250	.279	.278
Mike Dorgan†	1B26,OF23,SS2	R	27	51	220	36	61	5	0	0	18	8	4	—	.277	.303	.300
Candy Nelson	SS24	L	32	24	103	13	29	1	0	1	15	5	6	—	.282	.315	.320
Harry McCormick	P9,OF3	R	25	12	45	1	6	0	0	0	3	5	6	—	.133	.220	.133
Pop Smith†	OF8,2B3	R	24	11	41	1	3	0	0	0	2	3	5	—	.073	.136	.073
Billy Taylor†	OF5,P1	R	26	6	28	3	3	1	0	0	2	0	2	—	.107	.107	.143
Lip Pike	OF5	L	36	5	18	1	2	0	0	0	0	4	3	—	.111	.273	.111
Charlie Reilley†	C2	R	25	2	8	2	3	0	0	0	1	0	1	—	.375	.375	.375
Patrick Quinn†	C2	—	—	2	7	0	1	0	0	0	1	1	2	—	.143	.250	.143
Asa Stratton	SS1	—	28	1	4	0	1	0	0	0	0	0	2	—	.250	.250	.250
Martin Flaherty	OF1	L	27	1	2	0	0	0	0	0	0	0	2	—	.000	.000	.000

Pitcher	T	Age	G	GS	CG	ShO	IP	H	HR	BB	SO	W-L	Sv	ERA
Lee Richmond	L	24	53	52	50	3	462.1	547	7	68	156	25-26	0	3.39
Fred Corey	R	24	23	21	20	1	188.2	231	3	31	33	6-15	0	3.72
Harry McCormick	R	25	9	9	9	1	78.1	89	1	15	7	1-8	0	3.56
Billy Taylor†	R	26	1	1	1	0	8.0	15	0	6	0	0-1	0	7.88

»1882 Chicago White Stockings 1st NL 55-29 .655 —

Cap Anson

Player	Gm by Position	B	Age	G	AB	R	H	2B	3B	HR	RBI	BB	SO	SB	Avg	OBP	Slg
Silver Flint	C81,OF10	R	26	81	331	48	83	18	8	4	44	2	50	—	.251	.255	.390
Cap Anson	1B82,C1	R	30	82	348	69	126	29	8	1	83	20	7	—	.362	.397	.500
Tom Burns	2B43,SS41	R	25	84	355	55	88	23	6	0	48	15	28	—	.248	.278	.346
Ned Williamson	3B83,P1	R	24	83	348	66	98	27	4	3	60	27	21	—	.282	.333	.408
King Kelly	SS42,OF38,C12*	R	24	84	377	81	115	37	4	1	55	10	27	—	.305	.323	.432
Abner Dalrymple	OF84	L	24	84	397	96	117	25	11	1	36	14	18	—	.295	.319	.421
George Gore	OF84	L	25	84	367	99	117	15	7	3	51	29	19	—	.319	.369	.422
Hugh Nicol	OF47,SS8	R	24	47	186	19	37	9	1	1	16	7	29	—	.199	.228	.274
Fred Goldsmith	P45,1B1	R	26	45	183	23	42	11	1	0	19	4	29	—	.230	.246	.301
Larry Corcoran	P39,3B1	L	22	40	169	23	35	10	2	1	24	6	18	—	.207	.234	.308
Joe Quest	2B41,SS1	R	29	42	159	24	32	5	2	0	15	8	16	—	.201	.240	.258
Milt Scott	1B1	R	16	1	5	1	2	0	0	0	0	0	0	—	.400	.400	.400

K. Kelly, 3 G at 3B, 1 G at 1B

Pitcher	T	Age	G	GS	CG	ShO	IP	H	HR	BB	SO	W-L	Sv	ERA
Fred Goldsmith	R	26	45	45	45	4	405.0	377	7	38	109	28-17	0	2.42
Larry Corcoran	R	22	39	39	38	3	355.2	281	5	63	170	27-12	0	1.95
Ned Williamson	R	24	1	0	0	0	3.0	9	1	1	0	0-0	0	6.00

1882 Providence Grays 2nd NL 52-32 .619 3.0 GB

Harry Wright

Player	Gm by Position	B	Age	G	AB	R	H	2B	3B	HR	RBI	BB	SO	SB	Avg	OBP	Slg
Barney Gilligan	C54,SS2	R	26	56	201	32	45	7	6	0	26	4	26	—	.224	.239	.318
Joe Start	1B82	L	39	82	356	58	117	8	10	0	48	11	7	—	.329	.349	.407
Jack Farrell	2B84	R	24	84	366	67	93	21	6	2	31	16	23	—	.254	.285	.361
Jerry Denny	3B84	R	23	84	329	54	81	10	9	2	42	4	46	—	.246	.255	.350
George Wright	SS46	R	35	46	185	14	30	1	2	0	9	4	36	—	.162	.180	.189
Paul Hines	OF82,1B2	R	30	84	379	73	117	28	10	4	34	10	14	—	.309	.326	.467
Tom York	OF81	L	30	81	321	48	86	23	7	1	40	19	14	—	.268	.309	.393
Monte Ward	OF50,P33,SS4	L	22	83	355	58	87	10	3	1	39	13	22	—	.245	.272	.299
Old Hoss Radbourn	P55,OF31,SS1	R	27	83	326	30	78	11	0	1	32	12	22	—	.239	.266	.282
Sandy Nava	C27,OF1	—	32	28	97	15	20	2	0	0	7	1	13	—	.206	.214	.227
Tim Manning	SS17,C4	R	28	21	76	7	8	0	0	0	8	5	13	—	.105	.160	.105
Cliff Carroll	OF10	S	22	10	41	4	5	0	0	0	2	0	4	—	.122	.122	.122
Art Whitney†	SS11	R	24	11	40	2	3	0	0	0	1	2	11	—	.075	.119	.075
Dasher Troy†	SS4	R	26	4	17	1	4	0	0	0	1	0	1	—	.235	.235	.235
Charlie Reilley	C3	R	26	3	11	0	2	0	0	0	2	1	2	—	.182	.250	.182
Charlie Sweeney	OF1	R	19	1	4	0	0	0	0	0	0	0	1	—	.000	.000	.000

Pitcher	T	Age	G	GS	CG	ShO	IP	H	HR	BB	SO	W-L	Sv	ERA
Old Hoss Radbourn	R	27	55	52	51	6	474.0	429	6	51	201	33-20	0	2.09
Monte Ward	R	22	33	32	29	4	278.0	261	6	36	72	19-12	1	2.59

1882 Boston Red Stockings 3rd NL 45-39 .536 10.0 GB

John Morrill

Player	Gm by Position	B	Age	G	AB	R	H	2B	3B	HR	RBI	BB	SO	SB	Avg	OBP	Slg
Pat Deasley	C56,OF14,SS1	R	24	67	264	36	70	8	0	0	29	7	22	—	.265	.284	.295
John Morrill	1B76,SS3,2B2*	R	27	83	349	73	101	19	11	2	54	18	29	—	.289	.324	.424
Jack Burdock	2B83	R	30	83	319	36	76	6	7	0	27	9	24	—	.238	.259	.301
Ezra Sutton	3B77,SS4	R	31	81	319	44	80	8	1	2	38	24	25	—	.251	.303	.301
Sam Wise	SS72,3B6	L	24	78	298	44	66	11	4	4	34	5	45	—	.221	.234	.326
Joe Hornung	OF84,1B1	R	25	85	388	67	117	14	11	1	50	2	25	—	.302	.305	.402
Pete Hotaling	OF84	R	25	84	378	64	98	16	5	0	28	16	21	—	.259	.289	.328
Ed Rowen	OF48,C34,SS6*	—	24	83	327	36	81	7	4	1	43	19	18	—	.248	.289	.303
Jim Whitney	P49,OF9,1B6	L	24	61	251	49	81	18	7	5	48	24	13	—	.323	.382	.510
Bobby Mathews	P34,OF13,SS1	R	30	45	169	17	38	6	0	0	13	8	18	—	.225	.260	.260
Charlie Buffinton	OF7,P5,1B4	R	21	15	50	5	13	1	0	0	4	2	3	—	.260	.288	.280
Hall McClure	OF2	R	22	2	6	1	2	0	0	0	0	0	1	—	.333	.333	.333

J. Morrill, 1 G at P, 1 G at 3B, 1 G at OF; E. Rowen, 1 G at 3B

Pitcher	T	Age	G	GS	CG	ShO	IP	H	HR	BB	SO	W-L	Sv	ERA
Jim Whitney	R	24	49	48	46	3	420.0	404	3	41	180	24-21	0	2.64
Bobby Mathews	R	30	34	32	31	0	285.0	278	5	22	153	19-15	0	2.87
Charlie Buffinton	R	21	5	5	4	1	42.0	53	2	14	17	2-3	0	4.07
John Morrill	R	27	1	0	0	0	2.0	3	0	0	2	0-0	0	0.00

1882 Buffalo Bisons 3rd NL 45-39 .536 10.0 GB — Jim O'Rourke

Player	Gm by Position	B	Age	G	AB	R	H	2B	3B	HR	RBI	BB	SO	SB	Avg	OBP	Slg
Jack Rowe	C46,SS22,3B7*	L	25	75	308	43	82	14	5	1	42	12	0	—	.266	.294	.354
Dan Brouthers	1B84	L	24	84	351	71	129	23	11	6	63	21	7	—	.368	.403	.547
Hardy Richardson	2B83	R	27	83	354	61	96	20	8	2	57	11	33	—	.271	.293	.390
Deacon White	3B63,C20	L	34	83	337	51	95	17	0	1	33	15	16	—	.282	.313	.341
Davy Force	SS61,3B11,2B1	R	32	73	278	39	67	10	1	1	28	12	17	—	.241	.272	.295
Curry Foley	OF84,P1	—	26	84	341	51	104	16	4	3	49	12	26	—	.305	.329	.402
Blondie Purcell	OF82,P6	R	28	84	380	79	105	18	6	2	40	14	27	—	.276	.302	.371
Jim O'Rourke	OF81,C2,SS2*	R	31	84	370	62	104	15	6	2	37	13	13	—	.281	.305	.370
Pud Galvin	P52,OF6	R	25	54	206	21	44	7	4	0	17	2	49	—	.214	.221	.286
Tom Dolan	C18,OF4,3B2	R	23	22	89	12	14	0	1	0	8	2	11	—	.157	.176	.180
Walter Burke	P1,OF1	—	—	1	4	0	0	0	0	0	0	0	1	—	.000	.000	.000

J. Rowe, 1 G at OF; J. O'Rourke, 1 G at 3B

Pitcher	T	Age	G	GS	CG	ShO	IP	H	HR	BB	SO	W-L	Sv	ERA
Pud Galvin	R	25	52	51	48	3	445.1	476	8	40	162	28-23	0	3.17
One Arm Daily	R	25	29	29	29	0	255.2	246	7	70	116	15-14	0	2.99
Blondie Purcell	R	28	6	3	2	0	31.0	44	1	4	9	2-1	0	4.94
Walter Burke	—	—	1	1	0	0	4.0	10	0	0	0	0-1	0	11.25
Curry Foley	L	26	1	0	0	0	1.0	2	0	0	0	0-0	0	18.00

1882 Cleveland Blues 5th NL 42-40 .512 12.0 GB — Jim McCormick (0-4)/Fred Dunlap (42-36)

Player	Gm by Position	B	Age	G	AB	R	H	2B	3B	HR	RBI	BB	SO	SB	Avg	OBP	Slg
Fatty Briody	C53	—	23	53	194	30	50	13	0	0	13	9	13	—	.258	.291	.325
Bill Phillips	1B78,C1	R	25	78	335	40	87	17	7	4	47	7	18	—	.260	.275	.388
Fred Dunlap	2B84	R	23	84	364	68	102	19	4	0	28	23	26	—	.280	.323	.354
Mike Muldoon	3B61,OF23	—	24	84	341	50	84	17	5	6	45	10	28	—	.246	.268	.378
Jack Glasscock	SS83,3B1	R	22	84	358	66	104	27	9	4	46	13	9	—	.291	.315	.450
Orator Shaffer	OF84	L	30	84	313	37	67	14	2	3	28	27	27	—	.214	.276	.300
Dude Esterbrook	OF45,1B1	R	25	45	179	13	44	4	3	0	19	5	12	—	.246	.266	.302
John Richmond†	OF41	—	28	41	140	12	24	6	2	0	11	11	27	—	.171	.232	.243
Jim McCormick	P68,OF4	R	25	70	262	35	57	7	3	2	15	2	22	—	.218	.223	.290
George Bradley	P18,OF9,1B6	R	29	30	115	16	21	5	0	0	6	4	16	—	.183	.210	.226
John Kelly	C30	R	23	30	104	6	14	2	0	0	5	1	24	—	.135	.143	.154
Herm Doscher	3B22,OF2,SS1	R	29	25	104	7	25	2	0	0	10	0	11	—	.240	.240	.260
Dave Rowe	OF23,P1	R	27	24	97	13	25	4	3	1	17	4	9	—	.258	.287	.392
John Tilley	OF15	—	26	15	56	2	5	1	1	0	4	2	11	—	.089	.121	.143
Julius Willigrod†	OF9	L	—	9	36	5	5	1	1	0	2	3	7	—	.139	.205	.222
Bill McGunnigle	OF1	R	27	1	5	2	1	0	0	0	0	0	1	—	.200	.200	.200
John Dwyer	C1,OF1	—	—	1	3	0	0	0	0	0	1	0	0	—	.000	.000	.000
Doc Kennedy	C1	R	28	1	3	0	1	0	0	0	0	1	0	—	.333	.500	.333

Pitcher	T	Age	G	GS	CG	ShO	IP	H	HR	BB	SO	W-L	Sv	ERA
Jim McCormick	R	25	68	67	65	4	595.2	550	14	103	200	36-30	0	2.37
George Bradley	R	29	18	16	15	0	147.0	164	5	22	32	6-9	0	3.73
Dave Rowe	R	27	1	1	1	0	9.0	29	3	7	0	0-1	0	12.00

1882 Detroit Wolverines 6th NL 42-41 .506 12.5 GB — Frank Bancroft

Player	Gm by Position	B	Age	G	AB	R	H	2B	3B	HR	RBI	BB	SO	SB	Avg	OBP	Slg
Charlie Bennett	C65,3B11,2B7*	R	27	84	342	43	103	16	10	5	51	20	33	—	.301	.340	.450
Martin Powell	1B80	L	26	80	338	44	81	13	0	0	29	19	27	—	.240	.280	.278
Dasher Troy†	2B31,SS11	R	26	40	152	22	37	7	2	0	14	5	10	—	.243	.268	.316
Joe Farrell	3B42,2B18,SS9	R	25	69	283	34	70	12	2	1	24	4	20	—	.247	.258	.314
Mike McGeary	SS33,2B3	R	31	34	133	14	19	4	1	0	2	2	20	—	.143	.156	.188
George Wood	OF84	L	23	84	375	69	101	12	12	7	29	14	30	—	.269	.296	.421
Lon Knight	OF84,1B2	R	29	86	347	39	72	12	6	0	24	16	21	—	.207	.242	.277
Ned Hanlon	OF82,2B1	L	24	82	347	68	80	18	6	5	38	26	25	—	.231	.284	.360
Stump Wiedman	P46,OF6,SS1	R	21	50	193	20	42	7	1	0	20	2	19	—	.218	.226	.264
George Derby	P40,OF2	L	24	40	149	13	29	2	1	0	8	7	23	—	.195	.231	.221
Sam Trott	C23,1B3,2B3*	L	23	32	129	11	31	7	1	0	12	0	13	—	.240	.240	.310
Art Whitney†	3B22,SS8,P3	R	24	31	115	10	21	0	0	0	4	1	12	—	.183	.190	.183
Tom Forster	2B21	R	23	21	76	5	7	0	0	0	2	5	12	—	.092	.148	.092
Walt Kinzie	SS13	R	25	13	53	5	5	0	1	0	2	0	8	—	.094	.094	.132
Yank Robinson	SS10,P1,OF1	R	22	11	39	1	7	1	0	0	2	1	13	—	.179	.200	.205
Bob Casey	3B8,2B1	—	23	9	39	5	9	2	1	1	7	0	15	—	.231	.231	.410
Tom Kearns	2B4	R	21	4	13	2	4	2	0	0	1	0	4	—	.308	.308	.462
Henry Luff†	2B3,OF1	—	25	3	11	1	3	2	0	0	1	0	0	—	.273	.273	.455
John Morrissey	3B2	—	25	2	7	1	2	0	0	0	0	0	2	—	.286	.286	.286
Julius Willigrod†	SS1	L	—	1	3	0	1	0	0	0	1	0	1	—	.333	.333	.333

C. Bennett, 1 G at 1B, 1 G at SS; S. Trott, 3 G at SS, 2 G at OF, 1 G at 3B

Pitcher	T	Age	G	GS	CG	ShO	IP	H	HR	BB	SO	W-L	Sv	ERA
Stump Wiedman	R	21	46	45	43	4	411.0	391	10	39	161	25-20	0	2.63
George Derby	R	24	40	39	38	3	362.0	386	8	81	182	17-20	0	3.26
Art Whitney	R	24	3	2	1	0	18.0	31	1	8	11	0-1	0	6.00
Yank Robinson	R	22	1	0	0	0	2.0	0	0	1	0	0-0	0	0.00

1882 Troy Trojans 7th NL 35-48 .422 19.5 GB — Bob Ferguson

Player	Gm by Position	B	Age	G	AB	R	H	2B	3B	HR	RBI	BB	SO	SB	Avg	OBP	Slg
Bill Holbert	C58,3B12,OF3	R	27	71	251	24	46	5	0	0	23	11	22	—	.183	.218	.203
Roger Connor	1B43,OF24,3B14	L	24	81	349	65	115	22	18	4	42	13	20	—	.330	.354	.530
Bob Ferguson	2B79,SS2	S	37	81	319	44	82	15	2	0	32	23	21	—	.257	.307	.317
Buck Ewing	3B44,C25,2B4*	R	22	74	328	67	89	16	11	2	29	10	15	—	.271	.293	.405
Fred Pfeffer	SS83,2B2	R	22	85	330	26	72	7	4	1	43	1	24	—	.218	.221	.273
Chief Roseman	OF82	R	25	82	331	41	78	21	6	1	29	3	41	—	.236	.243	.344
Pete Gillespie	OF74	L	30	74	298	46	82	5	4	2	33	9	14	—	.275	.296	.339
Bill Harbidge	OF23,1B6,C3	L	27	32	123	11	23	1	1	0	13	10	17	—	.187	.248	.211
Tim Keefe	P43,OF8,3B3	R	25	53	189	24	43	8	7	1	19	17	46	—	.228	.291	.360
Mickey Welch	P33,OF8	R	22	38	151	26	37	6	0	1	17	5	16	—	.245	.269	.305
John Smith†	1B35	—	24	35	149	27	36	4	3	0	14	3	24	—	.242	.257	.309
John Cassidy	OF16,3B13	R	25	29	121	14	21	3	1	0	9	3	16	—	.174	.194	.215
Jim Egan	OF18,P12,C2	R	24	30	115	15	23	3	2	0	10	1	21	—	.200	.207	.261
Jim Holdsworth	OF1	R	31	1	3	0	0	0	0	0	0	0	1	—	.000	.000	.000

B. Ewing, 1 G at P, 1 G at 1B, 1 G at OF

Pitcher	T	Age	G	GS	CG	ShO	IP	H	HR	BB	SO	W-L	Sv	ERA
Tim Keefe	R	25	43	42	41	1	375.0	368	4	81	116	17-26	0	2.50
Mickey Welch	R	22	33	33	30	5	281.0	334	7	62	53	14-16	0	3.46
Jim Egan	L	24	12	10	10	0	100.0	133	2	24	20	4-6	0	4.14
Buck Ewing	R	22	1	0	0	0	1.0	2	0	1	0	0-0	0	9.00

1882 Worcester Brown Stockings 8th NL 18-66 .214 37.0 GB — Freeman Brown (9-32)/Tommy Bond (2-4)/Jack Chapman (7-30)

Player	Gm by Position	B	Age	G	AB	R	H	2B	3B	HR	RBI	BB	SO	SB	Avg	OBP	Slg
Doc Bushong	C69	R	25	69	253	20	40	4	1	1	15	5	17	—	.158	.174	.194
Harry Stovey	1B43,OF41	R	25	84	360	90	104	13	10	5	26	22	34	—	.289	.330	.422
George Creamer	2B81	R	27	81	286	27	65	16	6	1	29	14	24	—	.227	.263	.336
Arthur Irwin	3B51,SS33	L	24	84	333	30	73	12	4	0	30	14	34	—	.219	.251	.279
Fred Corey	SS26,P21,OF15*	R	25	64	255	33	63	7	12	0	29	5	31	—	.247	.262	.369
Jake Evans	OF68,SS11,P1*	R	25	80	334	30	71	10	4	0	25	7	22	—	.213	.229	.266
Jackie Hayes	OF58,C15,3B5*	—	21	78	326	27	88	22	4	4	54	6	26	—	.270	.283	.399
Jim Clinton	OF26	R	31	26	98	9	16	2	0	0	3	7	13	—	.163	.219	.184
Lee Richmond	P48,OF11	—	25	55	228	30	64	8	9	2	28	9	11	—	.281	.308	.421
Tom O'Brien	OF20,2B2,3B1	R	22	22	89	9	18	1	1	0	7	1	10	—	.202	.211	.236
Frank Mountain†	P18,OF6,1B2*	R	22	25	86	9	20	2	2	2	6	3	23	—	.233	.258	.372
Fred Mann†	3B18,1B1	L	24	19	77	12	18	5	0	0	7	2	15	—	.234	.253	.299
John Smith†	1B19	—	24	19	70	10	17	3	2	0	5	5	10	—	.243	.293	.343
Frank McLaughlin	SS14,OF1	R	26	15	55	7	12	0	2	1	4	0	11	—	.218	.218	.345
Ed Cogswell	1B13	R	28	13	51	10	7	1	0	0	1	6	6	—	.137	.228	.157
Tommy Bond	OF8,P2	R	26	8	30	1	4	0	0	0	2	2	3	—	.133	.188	.133
Dan O'Leary	OF6	L	25	6	22	2	4	1	0	0	2	5	5	—	.182	.333	.227
John Clarkson	P3,1B1	R	20	3	11	0	4	2	0	0	2	0	3	—	.364	.364	.545
Ed Merrill	3B2	—	22	2	8	0	1	0	0	0	4	0	1	—	.125	.125	.125
Jim Halpin	3B2	—	18	2	8	0	0	0	0	0	0	0	2	—	.000	.000	.000
John Irwin	1B1	L	20	1	4	0	0	0	0	0	0	0	2	—	.000	.000	.000

F. Corey, 6 G at 3B, 5 G at 1B; J. Evans, 1 G at 2B, 1 G at 3B; J. Hayes, 1 G at SS; F. Mountain, 1 G at SS

Pitcher	T	Age	G	GS	CG	ShO	IP	H	HR	BB	SO	W-L	Sv	ERA
Lee Richmond	L	25	48	46	44	0	411.0	525	11	88	123	14-33	0	3.74
Frank Mountain†	R	22	18	18	16	0	144.0	185	4	35	29	2-16	0	3.69
Fred Corey	R	25	21	14	12	0	139.0	180	5	19	36	1-13	0	3.56
John Clarkson	R	20	3	3	2	0	24.0	49	0	2	3	1-2	0	4.50
Tommy Bond	R	26	2	2	0	0	12.1	12	0	7	2	0-1	0	4.38
Jake Evans	R	25	1	1	1	0	8.0	13	1	0	2	0-1	0	5.63

»1882 Cincinnati Reds 1st AA 55-25 .688 — — Pop Snyder

Player	Gm by Position	B	Age	G	AB	R	H	2B	3B	HR	RBI	BB	SO	SB	Avg	OBP	Slg
Pop Snyder	C70,1B2,OF1	R	27	72	309	49	90	12	2	1	50	9	—	—	.291	.311	.353
Ecky Stearns	1B35,OF12,2B2*	L	20	49	214	28	55	10	2	0	35	6	—	—	.257	.277	.322
Bid McPhee	2B78	R	22	78	311	43	71	8	7	1	31	11	—	—	.228	.255	.309
Hick Carpenter	3B80	R	26	80	351	78	120	15	5	1	62	10	—	—	.342	.360	.422
Chuck Fulmer	SS79	R	31	79	324	54	91	13	5	0	27	10	—	—	.281	.302	.346
Joe Sommer	OF80	R	23	80	354	82	102	12	6	1	29	24	—	—	.288	.333	.364
Jimmy Macullar	OF76	R	27	79	299	44	70	6	6	0	22	14	—	—	.234	.268	.294
Harry Wheeler	OF64,1B12,P4	R	24	76	344	59	86	11	11	1	—	7	—	—	.250	.265	.355
Will White	P54,OF2	S	27	54	207	28	55	4	0	0	—	5	—	—	.266	.283	.285
Henry Luff†	1B27,OF1	—	25	28	120	16	28	2	2	0	6	2	—	—	.233	.246	.283
Harry McCormick	P25,OF2	R	26	26	93	3	12	0	1	0	—	1	—	—	.129	.138	.151
Phil Powers	C10,1B5,OF1	R	27	16	60	4	13	1	1	0	5	3	—	—	.217	.254	.267
Rudy Kemmler†	C3,OF1	R	22	3	11	0	1	1	0	0	—	0	—	—	.091	.091	.182
Tug Thompson	OF1	L	—	1	5	0	1	0	0	0	—	0	—	—	.200	.200	.200
Bill Tierney	1B1	—	24	1	5	1	0	0	0	0	—	0	—	—	.000	.000	.000

E. Stearns, 1 G at SS

Pitcher	T	Age	G	GS	CG	ShO	IP	H	HR	BB	SO	W-L	Sv	ERA
Will White	R	27	54	54	52	8	480.0	411	3	71	122	40-12	0	1.54
Harry McCormick	R	26	25	25	24	3	219.2	177	4	42	33	14-11	0	1.52
Harry Wheeler	R	24	4	1	1	0	21.2	21	0	12	10	1-2	0	5.40

486 Seasons: Team Rosters

1882 Philadelphia Athletics 2nd AA 41-34 .547 11.5 GB

Juice Latham

Player	Gm by Position	B	Age	G	AB	R	H	2B	3B	HR	RBI	BB	SO	SB	Avg	OBP	Slg
Jack O'Brien	C45,OF18,1B1*	R	22	62	241	44	73	13	3	3	37	13	—	—	.303	.339	.419
Jumbo Latham	1B74	R	29	74	323	47	92	10	2	0	38	10	—	—	.285	.306	.328
Cub Stricker	2B72,P2,OF1	R	23	72	272	34	59	6	1	0	18	15	—	—	.217	.258	.246
Bob Blakiston	OF38,3B34,2B1	—	26	72	281	40	64	4	1	0	20	9	—	—	.228	.252	.249
Lou Say	SS49	R	28	49	199	35	45	4	3	1	28	8	—	—	.226	.256	.291
Jud Birchall	OF74,2B1	—	24	75	338	65	89	12	1	0	27	8	—	—	.263	.280	.305
John Mansell	OF31	L	21	31	126	17	30	3	1	0	17	4	—	—	.238	.262	.278
Jerry Dorgan	C25,OF22,3B1	L	26	44	181	25	51	9	1	0	24	4	—	—	.282	.297	.343
Sam Weaver	P42,OF2	R	26	43	155	19	36	3	0	0	—	12	—	—	.232	.287	.252
Fred Mann†	3B29	L	24	29	121	13	28	7	4	0	—	4	—	—	.231	.256	.355
Bill Sweeney	P20,OF5	—	—	23	88	8	14	4	0	0	—	4	—	—	.159	.196	.205
Jimmy Say†	SS22	—	20	22	82	12	17	2	0	1	—	1	—	—	.207	.217	.268
John Richmond†	OF18	—	28	18	65	8	12	2	2	0	4	11	—	—	.185	.303	.277
Pop Smith†	3B11,SS4,OF3*	R	25	20	65	10	6	0	0	0	2	12	—	—	.092	.234	.092
Frank Mountain†	P8,OF1	R	22	9	36	5	12	3	0	0	—	2	—	—	.333	.368	.417
Bill Kienzle	OF9	L	—	9	33	8	11	3	2	0	9	5	—	—	.333	.421	.545
Joe Straub	C7,OF1	R	24	8	32	2	6	2	0	0	1	1	—	—	.188	.212	.250
Bill Greenwood	OF7,2B2	S	25	7	30	8	9	1	0	0	1	1	—	—	.300	.323	.333
Doc Landis†	P2,OF1	R	27	3	12	1	2	0	0	0	—	0	—	—	.167	.167	.167
Charlie Reynolds	P2,OF1	—	24	2	8	1	1	0	0	0	—	0	—	—	.125	.125	.125
Bill Farrell	OF2,C1	—	—	2	7	2	2	1	0	0	1	1	—	—	.286	.375	.429
Tug Arundel	C1	—	20	1	5	0	0	0	0	0	—	0	—	—	.000	.000	.000

J. O'Brien, 1 G at 3B; P. Smith, 2 G at 2B

Pitcher	T	Age	G	GS	CG	ShO	IP	H	HR	BB	SO	W-L	Sv	ERA
Sam Weaver	R	26	42	41	41	2	371.0	374	6	35	104	26-15	0	2.74
Bill Sweeney	R	—	20	20	18	0	170.0	178	4	42	48	9-10	0	2.91
Frank Mountain†	R	22	8	8	8	0	69.0	72	1	11	15	2-6	0	3.91
Doc Landis†	—	27	2	2	2	0	17.0	16	1	1	13	1-1	0	3.18
Charlie Reynolds	—	24	2	2	1	0	12.0	18	0	3	4	1-1	0	5.25
George Snyder	—	33	1	1	1	0	9.0	4	0	2	0	1-0	0	0.00
Ed Halbriter	—	22	1	1	1	0	8.0	17	1	4	4	0-1	0	7.88
Cub Stricker	R	23	2	0	0	0	7.0	3	0	1	2	1-0	0	1.29

1882 Louisville Eclipse 3rd AA 42-38 .525 13.0 GB

Denny Mack

Player	Gm by Position	B	Age	G	AB	R	H	2B	3B	HR	RBI	BB	SO	SB	Avg	OBP	Slg
Dan Sullivan	C54,3B10,OF4*	—	25	67	286	44	78	8	2	0	—	9	—	—	.273	.295	.315
Guy Hecker	1B66,P13,OF2	R	26	78	340	62	94	14	4	3	—	5	—	—	.276	.287	.368
Pete Browning	2B42,SS18,3B13	R	21	69	288	67	109	17	3	5	—	26	—	—	.378	.430	.510
Bill Schenck	3B58,P2,SS2	—	—	60	231	37	60	11	3	0	—	8	—	—	.260	.285	.333
Denny Mack	SS49,2B24,OF5	R	31	72	264	41	48	3	1	0	—	16	—	—	.182	.229	.201
Leech Maskrey	OF76,2B1	R	28	76	288	30	65	14	2	0	—	9	—	—	.226	.249	.288
Chicken Wolf	OF70,SS9,P1*	R	20	78	318	46	95	11	8	0	—	9	—	—	.299	.318	.384
John Reccius	OF65,P13	—	22	74	266	46	63	12	3	1	—	23	—	—	.237	.298	.316
Tony Mullane	P55,1B13,OF12*	S	23	77	303	46	78	13	1	0	—	13	—	—	.257	.288	.307
John Strick	C21,2B6,OF6*	—	—	32	110	17	18	6	1	0	—	9	—	—	.164	.227	.236
Gracie Pierce†	2B9	L	—	9	33	3	10	1	0	0	—	1	—	—	.303	.324	.333
Joe Crotty†	C5	R	21	5	20	1	2	0	0	0	—	0	—	—	.100	.100	.100
Phil Reccius	OF4	—	20	4	15	0	2	0	0	0	—	0	—	—	.133	.133	.133
Charlie Bohn	P2,OF2	R	25	4	13	0	2	0	0	0	—	0	—	—	.154	.154	.154
L. Smith	SS3	—	31	3	11	1	2	0	0	0	—	0	—	—	.182	.182	.182
Harry Maskrey	OF1	—	20	1	4	0	0	0	0	0	—	0	—	—	.000	.000	.000
Jimmy Say†	3B1	—	20	1	4	1	1	0	0	0	—	0	—	—	.250	.250	.250
John Dyler	OF1	—	30	1	4	0	0	0	0	0	—	0	—	—	.000	.000	.000
Harry McCaffery†	2B1	R	23	1	4	1	1	0	0	0	—	0	—	—	.250	.250	.250
Amos Booth†	2B1	R	29	1	4	0	0	0	0	0	—	0	—	—	.000	.000	.000

D. Sullivan, 1 G at SS; C. Wolf, 1 G at 1B; T. Mullane, 2 G at 2B; J. Strick, 1 G at 1B, 1 G at SS

Pitcher	T	Age	G	GS	CG	ShO	IP	H	HR	BB	SO	W-L	Sv	ERA
Tony Mullane	S	23	55	55	51	5	460.1	418	4	78	170	30-24	0	1.88
Guy Hecker	R	26	13	11	10	0	104.0	75	0	5	33	6-6	0	1.30
John Reccius	—	22	13	10	9	1	95.0	106	3	22	31	4-6	0	3.03
Charlie Bohn	R	25	2	2	2	0	18.0	21	0	3	1	1-1	0	3.00
Bill Schenck	—	—	2	1	1	0	10.0	6	0	1	4	1-0	0	0.90
Chicken Wolf	R	20	1	0	0	0	6.0	11	0	3	1	0-0	0	9.00

1882 Pittsburgh Alleghenys 4th AA 39-39 .500 15.0 GB

Al Pratt

Player	Gm by Position	B	Age	G	AB	R	H	2B	3B	HR	RBI	BB	SO	SB	Avg	OBP	Slg
Billy Taylor	C27,1B23,3B14*	R	27	70	299	40	84	16	13	3	—	7	—	—	.281	.297	.452
Chappy Lane	1B43,OF13,C2	R	—	57	214	26	38	8	2	3	—	5	—	—	.178	.196	.276
George Strief	2B78,SS1	R	25	79	297	45	58	9	6	2	—	13	—	—	.195	.229	.286
Joe Battin	3B34	R	30	34	133	13	28	5	1	1	—	3	—	—	.211	.228	.286
John Peters	SS77,2B1	R	32	78	333	46	96	10	1	0	—	4	—	—	.288	.297	.324
Mike Mansell	OF79	L	24	79	347	59	96	18	16	2	—	7	—	—	.277	.291	.438
Ed Swartwood	OF73,1B4	L	23	76	325	86	107	18	11	4	—	21	—	—	.329	.370	.489
Jack Leary†	3B33,OF27,P3*	—	24	60	257	32	75	7	3	1	—	5	—	—	.292	.305	.354
Harry Salisbury	P38,OF1	L	27	39	145	17	22	2	0	0	—	4	—	—	.152	.174	.166
Charlie Morton†	OF25,3B3,SS1	R	27	25	103	12	29	0	3	0	—	5	—	—	.282	.315	.340
Rudy Kemmler†	C23,OF1	R	22	24	99	7	25	4	0	0	—	1	—	—	.253	.260	.293
Jim Keenan	C22,OF3,SS1	R	24	25	96	10	21	7	0	1	—	1	—	—	.219	.227	.323
Bill Morgan	OF11,C7	—	—	17	66	10	17	2	1	0	—	4	—	—	.258	.300	.318
Harry Arundel	P14,SS1	—	28	14	53	8	10	0	0	0	—	5	—	—	.189	.259	.189
Jake Goodman	1B10	—	28	10	41	5	13	2	2	0	—	2	—	—	.317	.349	.463
Russ McKelvy	OF1	R	27	1	4	0	0	0	0	0	—	0	—	—	.000	.000	.000
Ren Wylie	OF1	R	20	1	3	0	0	0	0	0	—	0	—	—	.000	.000	.000

B. Taylor, 8 G at OF, 1 G at P; J. Leary, 1 G at 1B, 1 G at 2B

Pitcher	T	Age	G	GS	CG	ShO	IP	H	HR	BB	SO	W-L	Sv	ERA
Harry Salisbury	—	27	38	38	38	1	335.0	315	1	37	135	20-18	0	2.63
Denny Driscoll	L	26	23	23	23	0	201.0	162	0	12	59	13-9	0	1.21
Harry Arundel	R	28	14	14	13	0	120.0	155	3	23	47	4-10	0	4.65
Jack Leary†	L	24	3	2	1	0	18.2	28	0	3	5	1-0	0	6.27
Morrie Critchley†	—	32	1	1	1	1	9.0	7	0	1	3	1-0	0	0.00
Jake Seymour	—	28	1	1	1	0	8.0	16	0	2	2	0-1	0	7.88
Billy Taylor	R	27	1	0	0	0	5.0	11	0	4	1	0-1	0	16.20

1882 St. Louis Browns 5th AA 37-43 .463 18.0 GB

Ned Cuthbert

Player	Gm by Position	B	Age	G	AB	R	H	2B	3B	HR	RBI	BB	SO	SB	Avg	OBP	Slg
Sleeper Sullivan	C51	R	—	51	188	24	34	3	3	0	—	3	—	—	.181	.194	.229
Charlie Comiskey	1B77,P2	R	22	78	329	58	80	9	5	1	45	4	—	—	.243	.252	.310
Bill Smiley†	2B57,OF2	—	26	59	240	30	51	4	2	0	—	6	—	—	.213	.232	.246
Jack Gleason	3B73,OF6,2B1	R	27	78	331	53	84	10	1	2	—	27	—	—	.254	.310	.308
Bill Gleason	SS79	R	23	79	347	63	100	11	6	1	—	6	—	—	.288	.300	.363
Oscar Walker	OF75,1B1,2B1	L	28	76	318	48	76	15	7	7	—	10	—	—	.239	.262	.396
Ned Cuthbert	OF60	R	37	60	233	28	52	16	5	0	—	17	—	—	.223	.276	.335
George Seward	OF35,C5	—	—	38	144	23	31	1	1	0	—	12	—	—	.215	.276	.236
Jumbo McGinnis	P45,OF6,2B1	—	18	51	203	17	44	6	4	0	—	3	—	—	.217	.228	.286
Harry McCaffery†	OF23,2B8,3B7*	R	23	38	153	23	42	8	6	0	—	3	—	—	.275	.288	.405
Eddie Fusselback	C19,OF15,P4	R	23	35	136	13	31	2	0	0	—	5	—	—	.228	.255	.243
Ed Brown	OF15,2B2,P1	—	—	17	60	4	11	0	0	0	—	4	—	—	.183	.234	.183
Jack Schappert	P15,1B1,OF1	R	—	15	50	7	9	1	0	0	—	7	—	—	.180	.281	.200
Charlie Morton†	2B7,OF3	R	27	9	32	2	2	0	1	0	—	2	—	—	.063	.118	.125
Joe Crotty†	C7,OF1	R	21	8	28	2	4	1	0	0	—	3	—	—	.143	.226	.179
Frank Decker	2B2	R	26	2	8	0	2	0	0	0	1	0	—	—	.250	.250	.250
John Shoupe	2B2	L	30	2	7	1	0	0	0	0	—	0	—	—	.000	.000	.000
Bobby Mitchell	P1,OF1	L	26	1	4	0	0	0	0	0	0	0	—	—	.000	.000	.000

H. McCaffery, 1 G at 1B

Pitcher	T	Age	G	GS	CG	ShO	IP	H	HR	BB	SO	W-L	Sv	ERA
Jumbo McGinnis	—	18	45	45	43	3	388.1	391	2	53	134	25-18	0	2.60
Jack Schappert	R	—	15	14	13	0	128.0	131	2	32	38	8-7	0	3.52
Bert Dorr	—	20	8	8	8	0	66.0	53	0	1	34	2-6	0	2.59
Morrie Critchley†	—	32	4	4	4	0	34.0	43	3	7	2	0-4	0	4.24
John Doyle	—	24	3	3	3	0	24.0	41	0	3	5	0-3	0	2.63
Eddie Fusselback	—	23	4	2	2	0	23.0	34	0	2	3	1-2	1	4.70
Eddie Hogan	—	22	1	1	1	0	8.0	10	0	0	4	0-1	0	1.13
Charlie Comiskey	R	22	2	1	1	0	8.0	12	0	3	2	0-1	0	0.00
Bobby Mitchell	L	26	1	1	0	0	7.0	12	0	2	2	0-1	0	7.71
Ed Brown	R	—	1	0	0	0	2.0	2	0	0	1	0-0	0	0.00

1882 Baltimore Orioles 6th AA 19-54 .260 32.5 GB

Henry Myers

Player	Gm by Position	B	Age	G	AB	R	H	2B	3B	HR	RBI	BB	SO	SB	Avg	OBP	Slg
Ed Whiting	C72,1B3,OF2	L	22	74	308	43	80	14	5	0	—	7	—	—	.260	.276	.338
Charlie Householder	1B74,C3	L	26	74	307	42	78	10	7	1	—	4	—	—	.254	.264	.342
Gracie Pierce†	2B38,OF3,SS1	L	—	41	151	8	30	2	1	0	—	3	—	—	.199	.214	.225
John Shetzline	3B52,2B20,SS1*	—	32	73	282	23	62	8	3	0	—	5	—	—	.220	.233	.270
Henry Myers	SS68,P6	R	24	69	294	43	53	3	0	0	—	12	—	—	.180	.212	.190
Charlie Waitt	OF72	—	28	72	250	19	39	4	0	0	—	13	—	—	.156	.198	.172
Tom Brown	OF45,P2	L	21	45	181	30	55	5	2	1	23	6	—	—	.304	.326	.370
Monk Cline	OF39,SS8,2B2*	L	24	44	172	18	38	6	2	0	—	3	—	—	.221	.234	.279
Doc Landis†	P42,OF15	R	27	50	175	9	29	1	0	0	—	3	—	—	.166	.180	.171
Harry Jacoby	3B19,OF13	—	—	31	121	17	21	1	1	1	—	7	—	—	.174	.219	.223
Tricky Nichols	P16,OF14	R	31	26	95	4	15	1	0	0	—	7	—	—	.158	.216	.168
Bill Smiley†	2B16,SS2	—	26	16	61	3	9	0	0	0	—	0	—	—	.148	.148	.148
Emil Geis	P13,OF4	R	—	13	41	2	6	0	1	0	—	1	—	—	.146	.167	.195
Nick Scharf	OF9,3B1	—	23	10	39	4	8	1	1	1	—	0	—	—	.205	.205	.359
Frank Burt	OF10	—	—	10	36	2	4	2	1	0	—	1	—	—	.111	.135	.222
Bill Wise	P3,OF2	—	21	5	20	2	2	1	0	0	—	0	—	—	.100	.100	.150
Jack Leary†	P3,OF1	—	24	4	18	3	4	1	0	0	—	0	—	—	.222	.222	.278
Bill Jones	C2,OF2	—	—	4	15	1	1	0	0	0	—	0	—	—	.067	.067	.067
Harry East	3B1	—	19	1	4	0	0	0	0	0	—	0	—	—	.000	.000	.000
Tom Evers	2B1	—	30	1	4	0	0	0	0	0	—	0	—	—	.000	.000	.000
John Russ	P1,OF1	—	22	1	3	0	1	0	0	0	—	0	—	—	.333	.333	.333
Pop Smith†	OF1	R	25	1	3	0	0	0	0	0	—	0	—	—	.000	.000	.000
Amos Booth†	3B1	R	29	1	3	0	0	0	0	0	—	0	—	—	.000	.000	.000

J. Shetzline, 1 G at OF; M. Cline, 1 G at 3B

Pitcher	T	Age	G	GS	CG	ShO	IP	H	HR	BB	SO	W-L	Sv	ERA
Doc Landis†	—	27	42	39	35	0	341.0	409	7	46	62	11-27	0	3.33
Tricky Nichols	R	31	16	13	12	0	118.1	155	2	17	21	1-12	0	5.02
Emil Geis	R	—	13	13	10	1	95.2	84	2	22	10	4-9	0	4.80
Bill Wise	—	21	3	3	3	0	26.0	30	1	4	9	1-2	0	2.77
Jack Leary†	L	24	3	3	3	0	26.0	29	1	8	2	2-1	0	1.38
John Russ	—	22	1	1	0	0	5.0	10	0	1	0	0-1	0	7.20
Henry Myers	R	24	6	2	1	0	26.0	30	2	4	7	0-2	0	6.58
Tom Brown	R	21	2	0	0	0	8.1	13	0	6	2	0-0	0	1.08

»1883 Boston Red Stockings 1st NL 63-35 .643 —

Jack Burdock (30-24)/John Morrill (33-11)

Player	Gm by Position	B	Age	G	AB	R	H	2B	3B	HR	RBI	BB	SO	SB	Avg	OBP	Slg
Mike Hines	C59,OF7	R	20	63	231	38	52	13	1	0	16	7	36	—	.225	.248	.290
John Morrill	1B81,OF7,3B6*	R	28	97	404	83	129	33	16	6	68	15	68	—	.319	.344	.525
Jack Burdock	2B96	R	31	96	400	80	132	27	8	5	88	14	35	—	.330	.353	.475
Ezra Sutton	3B93,SS1,OF1	R	32	94	414	101	134	28	15	3	73	17	12	—	.324	.350	.486
Sam Wise	SS96	L	25	96	406	73	110	25	7	4	58	13	74	—	.271	.294	.397
Joe Hornung	OF98,3B1	R	26	98	446	107	124	25	13	8	66	8	54	—	.278	.291	.446
Paul Radford	OF72	R	21	72	258	46	53	6	3	0	14	9	26	—	.205	.232	.252
Charlie Buffinton	OF51,P43,1B2	R	22	86	341	28	81	8	3	1	26	6	24	—	.238	.251	.287
Jim Whitney	P62,OF40,1B2	L	25	96	409	78	115	27	10	5	57	25	29	—	.281	.323	.433
Mert Hackett	C44,OF4	R	23	46	179	20	42	8	6	2	24	1	48	—	.235	.239	.380
Edgar Smith	OF30,C1	—	22	30	115	10	25	5	3	0	16	5	11	—	.217	.250	.313
Lew Brown†	1B14	R	25	14	54	5	13	4	1	0	9	3	6	—	.241	.281	.352

J. Morrill, 2 G at P, 2 G at 2B, 2 G at SS

Pitcher	T	Age	G	GS	CG	ShO	IP	H	HR	BB	SO	W-L	Sv	ERA
Jim Whitney	R	25	62	56	54	1	514.0	492	7	35	345	37-21	2	2.24
Charlie Buffinton	R	22	43	41	34	4	333.0	346	4	51	188	25-14	1	3.03
John Morrill	R	28	2	1	1	0	13.0	15	0	4	5	1-0	0	2.77

1883 Chicago White Stockings 2nd NL 59-39 .602 4.0 GB

Cap Anson

Player	Gm by Position	B	Age	G	AB	R	H	2B	3B	HR	RBI	BB	SO	SB	Avg	OBP	Slg
Silver Flint	C83,OF23	R	27	85	332	57	88	23	4	0	32	3	69	—	.265	.272	.358
Cap Anson	1B98,P2,C1*	R	31	98	413	70	127	36	5	0	68	18	9	—	.308	.336	.419
Fred Pfeffer	2B79,SS18,1B1*	R	23	96	371	41	87	22	7	1	45	8	50	—	.235	.251	.340
Ned Williamson	3B97,C3,P1	R	25	98	402	83	111	49	5	2	59	22	48	—	.276	.314	.438
Tom Burns	SS79,2B19,OF1	R	26	97	405	69	119	37	7	2	67	13	31	—	.294	.316	.435
George Gore	OF92	L	26	92	392	105	131	30	9	2	52	27	13	—	.334	.377	.472
King Kelly	OF82,C38,2B3*	R	25	98	428	92	109	28	10	3	61	16	35	—	.255	.282	.388
Abner Dalrymple	OF80	L	25	80	363	78	108	24	4	2	37	11	29	—	.298	.318	.402
Larry Corcoran	P56,OF13,SS3*	L	23	68	263	40	55	12	7	0	25	6	62	—	.209	.227	.308
Fred Goldsmith	P46,OF16,1B2	R	27	60	235	38	52	12	3	1	16	4	35	—	.221	.234	.311
Billy Sunday	OF14	L	20	14	54	6	13	4	0	0	5	1	18	—	.241	.255	.315

C. Anson, 1 G at OF; F. Pfeffer, 1 G at 3B; K. Kelly, 2 G at 3B, 1 G at P; L. Corcoran, 1 G at 2B

Pitcher	T	Age	G	GS	CG	ShO	IP	H	HR	BB	SO	W-L	Sv	ERA
Larry Corcoran	R	23	56	53	51	3	473.2	483	7	82	216	34-20	0	2.49
Fred Goldsmith	R	27	46	45	40	2	383.1	456	14	39	82	25-19	0	3.15
Cap Anson	R	31	2	0	0	0	3.0	1	0	1	0	0-0	1	0.00
Ned Williamson	R	25	1	0	0	0	1.0	1	0	1	1	0-0	0	9.00
King Kelly	R	25	1	0	0	0	1.0	1	0	0	0	0-0	0	0.00

1883 Providence Grays 3rd NL 58-40 .592 5.0 GB

Harry Wright

Player	Gm by Position	B	Age	G	AB	R	H	2B	3B	HR	RBI	BB	SO	SB	Avg	OBP	Slg
Barney Gilligan	C74	R	27	74	263	34	52	13	3	0	24	26	32	—	.198	.270	.270
Joe Start	1B87	L	40	87	370	63	105	16	7	1	57	22	16	—	.284	.324	.373
Jack Farrell	2B95	R	25	95	420	92	128	24	11	3	61	15	21	—	.305	.329	.436
Jerry Denny	3B98	R	24	98	393	73	108	26	8	8	55	9	48	—	.275	.291	.443
Arthur Irwin	SS94,2B4	L	25	98	406	67	116	22	7	0	44	12	38	—	.286	.306	.374
Paul Hines	OF89,1B9	R	31	97	442	94	132	32	4	4	45	18	23	—	.299	.326	.416
John Cassidy	OF88,1B1,2B1	R	26	89	366	46	87	16	5	0	42	9	38	—	.238	.256	.309
Cliff Carroll	OF58	S	23	58	238	37	63	12	3	1	20	4	28	—	.265	.277	.353
Old Hoss Radbourn	P76,OF20,1B2	R	28	89	381	59	108	11	3	3	48	14	16	—	.283	.309	.352
Lee Richmond	OF41,P12	—	26	49	194	41	55	8	6	1	19	15	19	—	.284	.335	.402
Sandy Nava	C27,OF2	—	33	29	100	18	24	4	2	0	16	3	17	—	.240	.262	.320
Charlie Sweeney	P20,OF7	R	20	22	87	9	19	3	0	0	15	2	10	—	.218	.236	.253
Joe Mulvey†	SS4	R	24	4	16	1	2	1	0	0	2	0	1	—	.125	.125	.188
Edgar Smith†	1B2,OF2	R	21	2	9	2	2	1	0	0	1	0	2	—	.222	.222	.333

Pitcher	T	Age	G	GS	CG	ShO	IP	H	HR	BB	SO	W-L	Sv	ERA
Old Hoss Radbourn	R	28	76	68	66	4	632.1	563	7	56	315	48-25	1	2.05
Charlie Sweeney	R	20	20	18	14	0	146.2	142	3	28	48	7-7	0	3.13
Lee Richmond	L	26	12	12	8	0	92.0	122	2	27	13	3-7	0	3.33

1883 Cleveland Blues 4th NL 55-42 .567 7.5 GB

Frank Bancroft

Player	Gm by Position	B	Age	G	AB	R	H	2B	3B	HR	RBI	BB	SO	SB	Avg	OBP	Slg
Doc Bushong	C63	R	26	63	215	15	37	5	0	0	9	7	19	—	.172	.198	.195
Bill Phillips	1B97	R	26	97	382	42	94	29	8	2	40	8	49	—	.246	.262	.380
Fred Dunlap	2B93,OF1	R	24	93	396	81	129	34	2	4	37	22	21	—	.326	.361	.452
Mike Muldoon	3B98,OF2	—	25	98	378	54	86	22	3	0	29	10	29	—	.228	.247	.302
Jack Glasscock	SS93,2B3	R	23	96	383	67	110	19	6	0	46	13	23	—	.287	.311	.368
Pete Hotaling	OF100	R	26	100	417	54	108	20	8	0	30	12	33	—	.259	.280	.345
Tom York	OF100	L	31	100	381	56	99	29	5	2	46	37	55	—	.260	.325	.378
Jake Evans	OF86,3B3,SS3*	—	26	90	332	36	79	13	2	0	31	8	38	—	.238	.256	.289
Jim McCormick	P43,1B1,OF1	R	26	43	157	21	37	2	2	0	13	2	14	—	.236	.245	.274
Fatty Briody	C33,2B4,1B2*	—	24	40	145	23	34	5	1	0	10	3	13	—	.234	.250	.283
One Arm Daily	P45,OF1	R	26	45	142	18	18	1	0	0	5	10	36	—	.127	.184	.134
Bill Crowley†	OF11	R	26	11	41	3	12	5	0	0	5	1	7	—	.293	.310	.415
George Bradley†	SS4	R	30	4	16	0	5	0	1	0	1	0	1	—	.313	.313	.438
Charlie Cady	OF2,P1	—	17	3	11	0	0	0	0	0	0	1	5	—	.000	.083	.000
Cal Broughton†	C4	R	22	4	10	2	2	0	0	0	1	2	2	—	.200	.333	.200
Lem Hunter	P1,OF1	—	20	1	4	1	1	0	0	0	0	0	2	—	.250	.250	.250

J. Evans, 1 G at P, 1 G at 2B; F. Briody, 1 G at 3B

Pitcher	T	Age	G	GS	CG	ShO	IP	H	HR	BB	SO	W-L	Sv	ERA
One Arm Daily	R	26	45	43	40	4	378.2	360	5	99	171	23-19	1	2.42
Jim McCormick	R	26	43	41	36	1	342.0	316	1	65	145	28-12	1	1.84
Will Sawyer	L	18	17	15	15	0	141.0	119	1	47	76	4-10	0	2.36
Charlie Cady	—	17	1	1	1	0	8.0	13	0	4	5	0-1	0	7.88
Lem Hunter	—	20	1	0	0	0	6.1	10	0	2	4	0-0	0	1.42
Jake Evans	R	26	1	0	0	0	3.0	0	0	0	1	0-0	0	0.00

1883 Buffalo Bisons 5th NL 52-45 .536 10.5 GB

Jim O'Rourke

Player	Gm by Position	B	Age	G	AB	R	H	2B	3B	HR	RBI	BB	SO	SB	Avg	OBP	Slg
Jack Rowe	C49,OF28,SS18*	L	26	87	374	65	104	18	7	1	38	15	14	—	.278	.306	.372
Dan Brouthers	1B97,P1,3B1	L	25	98	425	85	159	41	17	3	97	16	17	—	.374	.397	.572
Hardy Richardson	2B92	R	28	92	399	73	124	34	7	1	56	22	20	—	.311	.347	.439
Deacon White	3B77,C22	L	35	94	391	62	114	14	5	0	47	23	18	—	.292	.331	.353
Davy Force	SS78,3B13,2B7	R	33	96	378	40	82	11	3	0	35	12	39	—	.217	.241	.262
Orator Shaffer	OF95	L	31	95	401	67	117	11	3	0	41	27	39	—	.292	.336	.334
Jim O'Rourke	OF61,C33,3B8*	R	32	94	436	102	143	29	8	1	38	15	13	—	.328	.350	.438
Jim Lillie	OF47,P3,C2*	—	21	50	201	25	47	7	3	1	29	1	31	—	.234	.238	.313
Pud Galvin	P76,OF8	R	26	80	322	41	71	11	2	1	19	3	79	—	.220	.228	.276
Dave Eggler†	OF38	R	32	38	153	13	38	2	1	0	13	2	29	—	.248	.258	.275
Curry Foley	OF23,P1	—	27	23	111	23	30	5	3	0	6	4	12	—	.270	.296	.369
George Derby	P14,OF3	L	25	16	59	10	14	1	0	0	3	0	7	—	.237	.237	.254
Ed Cushman	P7,OF1	R	31	7	23	3	5	0	0	0	1	2	7	—	.217	.280	.217
Doc Kennedy	OF4,1B1	R	29	5	19	3	6	0	0	0	2	2	2	—	.316	.381	.316
Dell Darling	C6	R	21	6	18	1	3	0	0	0	1	2	5	—	.167	.250	.167
Tony Suck	C1,OF1	—	25	2	7	1	0	0	0	0	0	1	4	—	.000	.125	.000
Art Hagan†	P2,OF1	—	20	2	7	0	0	0	0	0	0	0	3	—	.000	.000	.000
Walter Burke	P1,OF1	—	—	1	5	0	1	0	0	0	0	0	3	—	.200	.200	.200

J. Rowe, 3 G at 3B; J. O'Rourke, 3 G at SS, 2 G at P; J. Lillie, 1 G at 2B, 1 G at 3B, 1 G at SS

Pitcher	T	Age	G	GS	CG	ShO	IP	H	HR	BB	SO	W-L	Sv	ERA
Pud Galvin	R	26	76	75	72	5	656.1	676	9	50	279	46-29	0	2.72
George Derby	R	25	14	13	12	0	107.2	173	3	15	34	2-10	1	5.85
Ed Cushman	L	31	7	7	5	0	50.1	61	0	17	34	3-3	0	3.93
Art Hagan†	R	20	2	2	1	0	15.0	17	0	6	7	0-2	0	3.60
Walter Burke	—	—	1	1	0	0	8.0	9	0	3	1	0-0	0	5.63
Jim Lillie	—	21	3	0	0	0	12.0	16	0	2	4	0-1	0	3.00
Jim O'Rourke	R	32	2	0	0	0	7.0	10	0	1	1	0-0	1	6.43
Dan Brouthers	L	25	1	0	0	0	2.0	9	0	3	2	0-0	0	31.50
Curry Foley	L	27	1	0	0	0	1.0	0	0	4	0	1-0	0	0.00

1883 New York Gothams 6th NL 46-50 .479 16.0 GB

John Clapp

Player	Gm by Position	B	Age	G	AB	R	H	2B	3B	HR	RBI	BB	SO	SB	Avg	OBP	Slg
Buck Ewing	C63,OF14,2B11*	R	23	88	376	90	114	11	13	10	41	20	14	—	.303	.338	.481
Roger Connor	1B98	L	25	98	409	80	146	28	15	1	50	25	16	—	.357	.394	.506
Dasher Troy	2B73,SS12	R	27	85	316	37	68	7	5	0	20	9	33	—	.215	.237	.269
Frank Hankinson	3B93,OF1	R	27	94	337	40	74	13	6	2	30	19	38	—	.220	.261	.312
Ed Caskin	SS81,2B13,C1	R	31	95	383	47	91	11	2	1	40	14	25	—	.238	.264	.285
Pete Gillespie	OF98	L	31	98	411	64	129	23	12	1	62	9	27	—	.314	.329	.436
Mike Dorgan	OF59,C6,P1	R	29	64	261	32	61	11	3	0	27	2	23	—	.234	.240	.299
Monte Ward	OF56,P34,3B5*	L	23	88	380	76	97	18	7	7	54	8	25	—	.255	.271	.395
Mickey Welch	P54,OF38	R	23	84	320	42	75	13	5	2	30	10	38	—	.234	.258	.325
John Humphries	C20,OF12	L	21	29	107	5	12	1	0	0	4	1	22	—	.112	.120	.121
Tip O'Neill	P19,OF7	R	25	23	76	8	15	3	0	0	5	3	15	—	.197	.228	.237
John Clapp	C16,OF5	R	31	20	73	6	13	0	0	0	5	5	4	—	.178	.231	.178
Gracie Pierce†	OF18,2B1	L	—	18	62	3	5	0	1	0	2	1	9	—	.081	.095	.113
Dick Cramer	OF2	—	—	2	6	0	0	0	0	0	0	1	5	—	.000	.143	.000
Dave Orr†	OF1	R	23	1	3	0	0	0	0	0	0	0	1	—	.000	.000	.000

B. Ewing, 4 G at SS, 1 G at 3B; M. Ward, 2 G at SS, 1 G at 2B

Pitcher	T	Age	G	GS	CG	ShO	IP	H	HR	BB	SO	W-L	Sv	ERA
Mickey Welch	R	23	54	52	46	4	426.0	431	11	66	144	25-23	0	2.73
Monte Ward	R	23	34	25	24	1	277.0	278	3	31	121	16-13	0	2.70
Tip O'Neill	R	25	19	19	15	0	148.0	182	5	64	55	5-12	0	4.07
Myron Allen	R	29	1	1	1	0	8.0	8	0	3	0	0-1	0	1.13
Mike Dorgan	R	29	1	1	1	0	7.0	8	0	6	3	0-1	0	3.86

1883 Detroit Wolverines 7th NL 40-58 .408 23.0 GB

Jack Chapman

Player	Gm by Position	B	Age	G	AB	R	H	2B	3B	HR	RBI	BB	SO	SB	Avg	OBP	Slg
Charlie Bennett	C72,2B15,OF12	R	28	92	371	56	113	34	7	5	55	26	59	—	.305	.350	.474
Martin Powell	1B101	L	27	101	421	76	115	17	5	1	48	28	23	—	.273	.318	.344
Sam Trott	2B42,C34,OF6*	L	24	75	295	27	72	14	1	0	29	10	23	—	.244	.269	.298
Joe Farrell	3B101	R	26	101	444	58	108	13	5	0	36	5	29	—	.243	.252	.295
Sadie Houck	SS101	R	27	101	416	52	105	18	12	0	40	9	18	—	.252	.268	.353
George Wood	OF99,P1	L	24	99	441	81	133	26	11	5	47	25	37	—	.302	.339	.444
Ned Hanlon	OF90,2B11	L	25	100	413	65	100	13	2	1	40	34	44	—	.242	.300	.291
Stump Wiedman	P52,OF35,2B4	R	22	79	313	34	58	6	1	1	24	4	38	—	.185	.196	.220
Dupee Shaw	P26,OF15	L	24	38	141	13	29	3	0	0	5	3	36	—	.206	.222	.227
Dick Burns	OF24,P17	L	19	37	140	11	26	7	1	0	5	2	22	—	.186	.197	.250
Joe Quest†	2B37	R	30	37	137	22	32	8	2	0	25	10	18	—	.234	.286	.321
Tom Mansell†	OF34,P1	L	28	34	131	22	29	4	1	0	10	8	13	—	.221	.266	.267
Jack Jones†	P12,OF3	—	22	12	42	3	8	1	0	0	3	1	11	—	.190	.209	.214
George Radbourn	P3,OF1	—	27	3	12	2	2	0	0	0	0	0	5	—	.167	.167	.167
Ben Guiney	OF1	S	24	1	5	1	1	0	0	0	0	0	1	—	.200	.200	.200

S. Trott, 1 G at 1B

Pitcher	T	Age	G	GS	CG	ShO	IP	H	HR	BB	SO	W-L	Sv	ERA
Stump Wiedman	R	22	52	47	41	3	402.1	435	8	72	183	20-24	2	3.53
Dupee Shaw	L	24	26	25	23	1	227.0	238	3	44	73	10-15	0	2.50
Dick Burns	L	19	17	13	13	0	127.2	172	8	33	30	2-12	0	4.51
Jack Jones†	R	22	12	12	9	1	92.2	103	0	19	33	6-5	0	3.50
George Radbourn	—	27	3	3	2	0	22.0	38	1	7	2	1-2	0	6.55
Frank McIntyre†	—	23	1	1	1	0	11.0	11	0	1	0	1-0	0	0.82
Tom Mansell	R	28	1	0	0	0	6.2	21	2	5	3	0-0	0	18.90
George Wood	R	24	1	0	0	0	5.0	8	0	3	0	0-0	0	7.20

1883 Philadelphia Phillies 8th NL 17-81 .173 46.0 GB

Bob Ferguson (4-13)/Blondie Purcell (13-68)

Player	Gm by Position	B	Age	G	AB	R	H	2B	3B	HR	RBI	BB	SO	SB	Avg	OBP	Slg
Emil Gross	C55,OF2	R	25	57	231	39	71	25	7	1	25	12	18	—	.307	.342	.489
Sid Farrar	1B99	—	23	99	377	41	88	19	8	0	29	4	37	—	.233	.241	.326
Bob Ferguson	2B86,P1	S	38	86	329	39	85	9	2	0	27	18	21	—	.258	.297	.298
Blondie Purcell	3B46,OF44,P11	R	29	97	425	70	114	20	5	1	32	13	26	—	.268	.290	.346
Bill McClellan	SS78,OF2,3B1	L	27	80	326	42	75	21	4	1	33	19	18	—	.230	.272	.328
Jack Manning	OF98	R	29	98	420	60	112	31	5	0	37	20	37	—	.267	.300	.364
Bill Harbidge	OF44,SS11,2B9*	L	28	73	280	32	62	12	3	0	21	24	20	—	.221	.283	.286
Fred Lewis†	OF38	S	24	38	160	21	40	7	0	0	18	4	13	—	.250	.268	.294
John Coleman	P65,OF31,2B1	L	20	90	354	33	83	12	8	0	32	15	39	—	.234	.266	.314
Frank Ringo	C39,OF11,SS6*	R	22	60	221	24	42	10	1	0	12	6	34	—	.190	.211	.244
Fred Warner	3B38,OF1	—	28	39	141	13	32	6	1	0	13	5	21	—	.227	.253	.284
Jack Neagle†	OF12,P8	R	25	18	73	6	12	1	0	0	4	1	9	—	.164	.176	.178
Conny Doyle	OF16	—	21	16	68	3	15	3	2	0	3	0	15	—	.221	.221	.324
Dick Pirie	SS5	—	30	5	19	1	3	0	0	0	0	0	2	—	.158	.158	.158
Art Benedict	2B3	R	21	3	15	3	4	1	0	0	4	0	4	—	.267	.267	.333
Joe Mulvey†	3B3	R	24	3	12	2	6	1	0	0	3	0	1	—	.500	.500	.583
Abe Wolstenholme	C2,OF1	—	22	3	11	0	1	1	0	0	0	0	0	—	.091	.091	.182
Hardie Henderson†	P1,OF1	R	20	2	8	1	2	1	0	0	0	0	1	—	.250	.250	.375
Bill Gallagher†	OF2	—	—	2	8	1	0	0	0	0	0	0	4	—	.000	.000	.000
Charlie Kelly	3B2	—	—	2	7	1	1	0	1	0	0	0	3	—	.143	.143	.429
Piggy Ward	3B1	S	16	1	5	0	0	0	0	0	0	0	2	—	.000	.000	.000
Buck Gladman	3B1	—	19	1	4	1	0	0	0	0	0	0	2	—	.000	.000	.000
Edgar Smith†	P1,OF1	R	21	1	4	1	3	0	0	0	1	0	0	—	.750	.750	.750
John Kelly†	OF1	R	24	1	3	0	0	0	0	0	0	0	2	—	.000	.000	.000
Charlie Waitt	OF1	—	29	1	3	0	1	0	0	0	0	0	1	—	.333	.333	.333
C.B. White	3B1,SS1	—	—	1	1	0	0	0	0	0	0	0	0	—	.000	.000	.000

B. Harbidge, 7 G at C, 5 G at 3B; F. Ringo, 5 G at 3B, 2 G at 2B

Pitcher	T	Age	G	GS	CG	ShO	IP	H	HR	BB	SO	W-L	Sv	ERA
John Coleman	R	20	65	61	59	3	538.1	772	17	48	159	12-48	0	4.87
Art Hagan†	R	20	17	16	15	0	137.0	207	2	33	39	1-14	0	5.45
Blondie Purcell	R	29	11	9	7	0	80.0	110	0	12	30	2-6	0	4.39
Jack Neagle†	R	25	8	7	6	0	61.1	88	0	21	13	1-7	0	6.90
Charlie Hilsey	—	19	3	3	3	0	26.0	36	1	4	8	0-3	0	5.54
Hardie Henderson†	R	20	1	1	1	0	9.0	26	0	2	2	0-1	0	19.00
Edgar Smith	R	21	1	1	0	0	7.0	18	0	3	2	0-1	0	15.43
Alonzo Breitenstein	—	25	1	1	0	0	5.0	8	0	2	0	0-1	0	9.00
Bob Ferguson	R	38	1	0	0	0	1.0	2	0	0	0	0-0	0	9.00

»1883 Philadelphia Athletics 1st AA 66-32 .673 —

Lon Knight

Player	Gm by Position	B	Age	G	AB	R	H	2B	3B	HR	RBI	BB	SO	SB	Avg	OBP	Slg
Jack O'Brien	C58,OF25,3B19*	R	23	94	390	74	113	14	10	0	—	25	—	—	.290	.333	.377
Harry Stovey	1B93,OF3,P1	R	26	94	421	110	127	31	6	14	—	26	—	—	.302	.342	.504
Cub Stricker	2B88,C2	R	24	89	330	67	90	8	0	1	—	19	—	—	.273	.312	.306
George Bradley†	3B44,P26,OF11*	R	30	76	312	47	73	8	5	1	—	8	—	—	.234	.253	.301
Mike Moynahan	SS95	L	27	95	400	90	123	18	10	1	—	30	—	—	.308	.356	.410
Jud Birchall	OF96	—	25	96	449	95	108	10	1	1	—	19	—	—	.241	.271	.274
Lon Knight	OF93,3B3,2B2	R	30	97	429	98	108	23	9	1	—	21	—	—	.252	.287	.354
Bob Blakiston	OF37,1B6,3B5	—	27	44	167	26	41	3	3	0	—	9	—	—	.246	.284	.299
Fred Corey	3B34,P18,OF14*	R	26	71	298	45	77	16	2	1	—	12	—	—	.258	.287	.336
Ed Rowen	C44,OF8,2B1*	—	25	49	196	28	43	10	1	0	—	10	—	—	.219	.257	.281
Bobby Mathews	P44,OF3	R	31	45	167	15	31	2	0	0	—	4	—	—	.186	.205	.198
Bill Crowley†	OF22,1B1	R	26	23	96	16	24	4	3	0	—	3	—	—	.250	.273	.354
Jersey Bakely	P8,OF1	R	19	8	26	4	5	1	0	0	—	6	—	—	.192	.344	.231
Al Hubbard	C1,SS1	—	22	2	6	2	2	0	0	0	—	1	—	—	.333	.429	.333
Charlie Mason	OF1	R	30	1	2	0	1	0	0	0	—	0	—	—	.500	.500	.500

J. O'Brien, 1 G at SS; G. Bradley, 2 G at 1B; F. Corey, 9 G at 2B, 1 G at C, 1 G at SS; E. Rowen, 1 G at 3B

Pitcher	T	Age	G	GS	CG	ShO	IP	H	HR	BB	SO	W-L	Sv	ERA
Bobby Mathews	R	31	44	44	41	1	381.0	396	11	31	203	30-13	0	2.46
George Bradley	R	30	26	23	22	0	214.1	215	7	22	56	16-7	0	3.15
Fred Corey	R	26	18	16	15	0	148.1	182	3	24	42	10-7	0	3.40
Jersey Bakely	R	19	8	8	7	0	61.1	65	0	12	14	5-3	0	3.23
Jack Jones†	R	22	7	7	7	0	65.0	58	1	6	28	5-2	0	2.63
Harry Stovey	R	26	1	0	0	0	3.0	5	0	0	4	0-0	0	9.00

1883 St. Louis Browns 2nd AA 65-33 .663 1.0 GB

Ted Sullivan (53-26)/Charlie Comiskey (12-7)

Player	Gm by Position	B	Age	G	AB	R	H	2B	3B	HR	RBI	BB	SO	SB	Avg	OBP	Slg
Pat Deasley	C56,OF2	R	25	58	206	27	53	2	1	0	—	6	—	—	.257	.278	.277
Charlie Comiskey	1B96,OF1	R	23	96	401	87	118	17	9	2	—	11	—	—	.294	.313	.397
George Strief	2B67,OF15	R	26	82	302	22	68	9	0	1	—	12	—	—	.225	.255	.265
Arlie Latham	3B98,C1	R	23	98	406	86	96	12	7	0	—	18	—	—	.236	.269	.300
Bill Gleason	SS98	R	24	98	425	81	122	21	9	2	—	16	—	—	.287	.313	.393
ugh Nicol	OF84,2B11	R	25	94	368	73	106	13	3	0	—	18	—	—	.288	.321	.340
Fred Lewis†	OF49	S	24	49	209	37	63	8	4	1	—	1	—	—	.301	.305	.392
Tom Dolan	C42,OF40,P1	R	24	81	295	32	63	9	2	1	—	9	—	—	.214	.237	.268
Tony Mullane	P53,OF30,2B3*	S	24	83	307	38	69	11	6	0	—	13	—	—	.225	.256	.300
Jumbo McGinnis	P45,OF4	—	19	45	180	20	36	4	2	0	—	0	—	—	.200	.200	.244
Tom Mansell†	OF28	L	28	28	112	23	45	8	1	0	—	7	—	—	.402	.437	.491
Joe Quest†	2B19	R	30	19	78	12	20	3	1	0	—	1	—	—	.256	.266	.321
Ned Cuthbert	OF20,1B1	R	38	21	71	3	12	1	0	0	—	4	—	—	.169	.213	.183
Jack Gleason†	OF9,3B1	R	28	9	34	2	8	0	0	0	—	4	—	—	.235	.316	.235
Sleeper Sullivan	C6,OF2	R	—	8	27	2	6	0	1	0	—	0	—	—	.222	.222	.296
Tom Loftus	OF6	R	26	6	22	1	4	0	0	0	—	2	—	—	.182	.250	.182
Harry McCaffery	OF5	R	24	5	18	0	1	0	0	0	—	1	—	—	.056	.105	.056
Henry Oberbeck†	OF4	—	25	4	14	0	0	0	0	0	—	0	—	—	.000	.000	.000
Charlie Hodnett	P4,OF1	—	22	4	11	3	2	0	0	0	—	2	—	—	.182	.308	.182
John Ewing	OF1	—	20	1	5	0	0	0	0	0	—	0	—	—	.000	.000	.000
Jack Gorman	OF1	—	24	1	4	0	0	0	0	0	—	0	—	—	.000	.000	.000

T. Mullane, 2 G at 1B

Pitcher	T	Age	G	GS	CG	ShO	IP	H	HR	BB	SO	W-L	Sv	ERA
Tony Mullane	R	24	53	49	49	3	460.2	372	3	74	191	35-15	1	2.19
Jumbo McGinnis	—	19	45	45	41	6	382.2	325	3	69	128	28-16	0	2.33
Charlie Hodnett	—	22	4	4	3	0	32.0	28	1	7	6	2-2	0	1.41
Tom Dolan	R	24	1	0	0	0	4.0	4	0	0	0	0-0	0	4.50

1883 Cincinnati Reds 3rd AA 61-37 .622 5.0 GB

Pop Snyder

Player	Gm by Position	B	Age	G	AB	R	H	2B	3B	HR	RBI	BB	SO	SB	Avg	OBP	Slg
Pop Snyder	C57,SS2	R	28	58	250	38	64	14	6	0	—	8	—	—	.256	.279	.360
John Reilly	1B98,OF1	R	24	98	437	103	136	21	14	9	—	9	—	—	.311	.325	.485
Bid McPhee	2B96	R	23	96	367	61	90	10	10	2	—	18	—	—	.245	.281	.343
Hick Carpenter	3B95	R	27	95	436	99	129	18	4	3	—	18	—	—	.296	.324	.376
Chuck Fulmer	SS92	R	32	92	361	52	93	13	5	5	—	13	—	—	.258	.283	.363
Joe Sommer	OF94,3B3,P1	R	24	97	413	79	115	5	7	3	—	20	—	—	.278	.312	.346
Charley Jones	OF90	R	33	90	391	84	115	15	12	10	—	20	—	—	.294	.328	.471
Pop Corkhill	OF85,1B2,2B2*	L	25	88	375	53	81	10	8	2	—	3	—	—	.216	.222	.301
Phil Powers	C17,OF13	R	28	30	114	16	28	1	4	0	—	3	—	—	.246	.265	.325
Bill Traffley	C29,SS2	R	23	30	105	17	21	5	0	0	—	4	—	—	.200	.229	.248
Ren Deagle	P18,OF1	R	25	19	70	9	9	2	0	0	—	1	—	—	.129	.141	.157
Jimmy Macullar	OF14,SS1	R	28	14	48	4	8	2	0	0	—	4	—	—	.167	.231	.208
Podge Weihe	OF1	R	20	1	4	1	1	0	0	0	—	0	—	—	.250	.250	.250

P. Corkhill, 2 G at SS

Pitcher	T	Age	G	GS	CG	ShO	IP	H	HR	BB	SO	W-L	Sv	ERA
Will White	R	28	65	64	64	6	577.0	473	16	104	141	43-22	0	2.09
Ren Deagle	R	25	18	18	17	1	148.0	136	0	34	48	10-8	0	2.31
Harry McCormick	R	27	15	15	14	1	128.2	139	1	27	21	8-6	0	2.87
Billy Mountjoy	R	24	1	1	1	0	8.0	9	0	2	3	0-1	0	2.25
Joe Sommer	R	24	1	0	0	0	5.0	9	0	1	2	0-0	0	5.40

1883 New York Metropolitans 4th AA 54-42 .563 11.0 GB

Jim Mutrie

Player	Gm by Position	B	Age	G	AB	R	H	2B	3B	HR	RBI	BB	SO	SB	Avg	OBP	Slg
Bill Holbert	C68,OF5,2B1	R	28	73	299	26	71	9	1	0	—	1	—	—	.237	.240	.274
Steve Brady	1B81,OF16	—	31	97	432	69	117	12	6	0	—	11	—	—	.271	.289	.326
Sam Crane	2B96,OF1	R	29	96	349	57	82	8	5	0	—	13	—	—	.235	.262	.287
Dude Esterbrook	3B97	R	26	97	407	55	103	9	7	0	—	15	—	—	.253	.280	.310
Candy Nelson	SS97	L	34	97	417	75	127	19	6	0	—	31	—	—	.305	.353	.379
Ed Kennedy	OF94	—	27	94	356	57	78	6	7	2	—	17	—	—	.219	.255	.292
Chief Roseman	OF91,1B2	R	26	93	398	48	100	13	6	0	—	11	—	—	.251	.271	.314
John O'Rourke	OF76,1B1	L	33	77	315	49	85	19	5	2	—	21	—	—	.270	.315	.381
Tim Keefe	P68,2B1,OF1	R	26	70	259	39	57	6	9	0	—	14	—	—	.220	.260	.313
C. Reipschlager	C29,OF8	R	—	37	145	8	27	4	2	0	—	4	—	—	.186	.208	.241
Dave Orr†	1B13	R	23	13	50	6	16	4	3	2	—	0	—	—	.320	.320	.640

Pitcher	T	Age	G	GS	CG	ShO	IP	H	HR	BB	SO	W-L	Sv	ERA
Tim Keefe	R	26	68	68	68	5	619.0	486	6	98	361	41-27	0	2.41
Jack Lynch	R	26	29	29	29	1	255.0	263	6	25	119	13-15	0	4.09

Seasons: Team Rosters 489

1883 Louisville Eclipse 5th AA 52-45 .536 13.5 GB

Joe Gerhardt

Player	Gm by Position	B	Age	G	AB	R	H	2B	3B	HR	RBI	BB	SO	SB	Avg	OBP	Slg
Ed Whiting	C50,OF6,2B2*	L	23	58	240	35	70	16	4	2	—	9	—	—	.292	.317	.417
Jumbo Latham	1B67,2B14,SS9	R	30	88	368	60	92	7	6	0	—	12	—	—	.250	.274	.302
Joe Gerhardt	2B78	R	28	78	319	56	84	11	9	0	—	14	—	—	.263	.294	.354
Jack Gleason†	3B83,SS1	R	28	84	355	69	105	11	4	2	—	25	—	—	.296	.342	.366
Jack Leary†	SS40	—	25	40	165	16	31	1	3	3	—	2	—	—	.188	.198	.285
Leech Maskrey	OF96,SS1	R	29	96	361	50	73	13	8	1	—	10	—	—	.202	.224	.291
Chicken Wolf	OF78,C20,SS5*	R	21	98	389	59	102	17	9	1	—	5	—	—	.262	.272	.360
Pete Browning	OF48,SS26,3B10*	R	22	84	358	95	121	15	9	4	—	23	—	—	.338	.378	.464
Guy Hecker	P51,OF23,1B10	R	27	79	322	56	88	6	6	1	—	10	—	—	.273	.295	.339
Sam Weaver	P48,OF6,1B1	R	27	55	203	22	39	6	1	0	—	13	—	—	.192	.241	.232
Dan Sullivan	C32,3B2,OF2*	—	26	37	147	8	31	5	2	0	—	3	—	—	.211	.227	.272
Tom McLaughlin	SS19,OF17,1B5*	—	23	42	146	16	28	1	2	0	—	5	—	—	.192	.219	.226
John Reccius	OF18,P1	—	23	18	63	10	9	2	0	0	—	7	—	—	.143	.229	.175
Lew Brown†	1B14,C1	R	25	14	60	6	11	2	1	0	—	1	—	—	.183	.197	.250
Henry Luff	1B4,OF2	—	26	6	23	1	4	0	0	0	—	0	—	—	.174	.174	.174
George Winkelman	OF4	L	22	4	13	2	0	0	0	0	—	1	—	—	.000	.071	.000
Walter Prince	1B2,OF2,SS1	L	22	4	11	1	2	0	0	0	—	0	—	—	.182	.182	.182
Jack Jones	OF2,SS1	—	—	2	7	1	0	0	0	0	—	0	—	—	.000	.000	.000
Phil Reccius	OF1	—	21	1	3	1	1	1	0	0	—	0	—	—	.333	.333	.667

E. Whiting, 1 G at 1B, 1 G at 3B; C. Wolf, 1 G at 2B; P. Browning, 3 G at 2B, 1 G at 1B; D. Sullivan, 1 G at SS; T. McLaughlin, 2 G at 2B, 2 G at 3B

Pitcher	T	Age	G	GS	CG	ShO	IP	H	HR	BB	SO	W-L	Sv	ERA
Guy Hecker	R	27	51	50	49	3	451.0	509	4	72	153	26-23	0	3.33
Sam Weaver	R	27	48	48	47	4	418.2	468	3	38	116	26-22	0	3.70
John Reccius	—	23	1	0	0	0	4.0	10	0	0	0	0-0	0	2.25

1883 Columbus Colts 6th AA 32-65 .330 33.5 GB

Horace Phillips

Player	Gm by Position	B	Age	G	AB	R	H	2B	3B	HR	RBI	BB	SO	SB	Avg	OBP	Slg
Rudy Kemmler	C82,OF2	R	23	84	318	27	66	6	2	0	—	13	—	—	.208	.239	.239
Jim Field	1B76	—	20	76	295	31	75	10	6	1	—	7	—	—	.254	.272	.339
Pop Smith	2B73,3B24,P3	R	26	97	405	82	106	14	17	4	—	22	—	—	.262	.300	.410
Bill Kuehne	3B69,2B18,SS7*	R	24	95	374	38	85	8	14	1	—	2	—	—	.227	.231	.332
John Richmond	SS91,OF2	—	29	92	385	63	109	7	8	0	—	25	—	—	.283	.327	.343
Tom Brown	OF96,P3	L	22	97	420	69	115	12	7	5	—	20	—	—	.274	.307	.371
Fred Mann	OF82,1B9,3B6*	L	25	96	394	61	98	18	13	1	—	18	—	—	.249	.282	.368
Harry Wheeler	OF82,P1,2B1	R	25	82	371	42	84	6	7	0	—	6	—	—	.226	.239	.280
Frank Mountain	P59,OF12	R	23	70	276	36	60	14	5	3	—	9	—	—	.217	.242	.337
Joe Straub	C14,1B12,OF1	R	25	27	100	4	13	0	0	0	—	4	—	—	.130	.163	.130
Ed Dundon	P20,OF9,2B1	—	23	26	93	8	15	1	0	0	—	3	—	—	.161	.188	.172
John Valentine	P13,OF4	—	27	16	60	9	17	4	0	0	—	2	—	—	.283	.306	.350
Gracie Pierce†	2B6,OF5	L	—	11	41	5	7	0	0	0	—	0	—	—	.171	.171	.171
Bill Schwartz	C1,1B1	R	19	2	4	0	1	0	0	0	—	0	—	—	.250	.250	.250

B. Kuehne, 3 G at OF; F. Mann, 1 G at SS

Pitcher	T	Age	G	GS	CG	ShO	IP	H	HR	BB	SO	W-L	Sv	ERA
Frank Mountain	R	23	59	59	57	4	503.0	546	8	123	159	26-33	0	3.60
Ed Dundon	R	23	20	19	16	0	166.2	213	7	38	31	3-16	0	4.48
John Valentine	—	27	13	12	11	0	102.0	130	0	17	13	2-10	0	3.53
Pete Fries	L	25	3	3	3	0	25.0	34	1	14	7	0-3	0	6.48
Frank McIntyre†	—	23	2	2	2	0	19.0	20	0	7	6	1-1	0	5.21
Harry Wheeler	R	25	1	1	0	0	5.0	13	0	2	0	0-1	0	7.20
Tom Brown	R	22	3	1	1	0	14.0	14	0	10	6	0-1	0	5.79
Pop Smith	R	26	3	0	0	0	5.2	10	0	0	0	0-0	0	6.35

1883 Pittsburgh Alleghenys 7th AA 31-67 .316 35.0 GB

Al Pratt (12-20)/Ormond Butler (17-36)/Joe Battin (2-11)

Player	Gm by Position	B	Age	G	AB	R	H	2B	3B	HR	RBI	BB	SO	SB	Avg	OBP	Slg
Jackie Hayes	C62,OF18,1B5*	—	22	85	351	41	92	23	5	3	—	15	—	—	.262	.292	.382
Ed Swartwood	1B60,OF37,C3	L	24	94	413	86	147	24	8	3	—	24	—	—	.356	.391	.475
George Creamer	2B91	R	28	91	369	54	94	7	9	0	—	20	—	—	.255	.293	.322
Joe Battin	3B98,P2	R	31	98	388	42	83	9	6	1	—	11	—	—	.214	.236	.276
Denny Mack	SS38,1B25,2B1	R	32	60	224	26	44	5	3	0	—	13	—	—	.196	.241	.246
Mike Mansell	OF96	L	25	96	412	90	106	12	13	3	—	25	—	—	.257	.300	.371
Buttercup Dickerson	OF78,SS8,2B2	L	24	85	355	62	88	15	1	0	—	17	—	—	.248	.282	.296
Billy Taylor	OF37,C33,P19*	R	28	83	369	43	96	13	7	2	—	9	—	—	.260	.278	.350
Denny Driscoll	P41,OF4,3B1	L	27	41	148	19	27	2	1	0	—	4	—	—	.182	.204	.209
Bob Barr	P26,OF14,1B4*	R	26	37	142	12	35	4	3	0	—	5	—	—	.246	.272	.317
Bill Morgan	SS21,OF6,C5*	—	—	32	114	12	18	2	1	0	—	7	—	—	.158	.207	.193
Frank McLaughlin	SS25,OF4,P2*	R	27	29	114	15	25	2	0	1	—	6	—	—	.219	.258	.263
Jack Neagle†	P16,OF15	R	25	27	101	14	19	0	1	0	—	5	—	—	.188	.226	.208
Wes Blogg	C6,OF3	—	28	9	34	0	5	0	0	0	—	0	—	—	.147	.147	.147
John Peters	SS8	R	33	8	28	3	3	0	0	0	—	0	—	—	.107	.107	.107
The Only Nolan	P7,OF1	L	25	7	26	4	8	1	0	0	—	1	—	—	.308	.333	.346
Norm Baker	P3,OF2	—	20	4	12	1	0	0	0	0	—	0	—	—	.000	.000	.000
Henry Oberbeck†	1B2	—	25	2	9	1	2	1	0	0	—	0	—	—	.222	.222	.333

J. Hayes, 5 G at SS, 1 G at 2B; B. Taylor, 9 G at 1B; B. Barr, 1 G at 3B; B. Morgan, 2 G at 2B; F. McLaughlin, 2 G at 2B

Pitcher	T	Age	G	GS	CG	ShO	IP	H	HR	BB	SO	W-L	Sv	ERA
Denny Driscoll	L	27	41	40	35	1	336.1	427	3	39	79	18-21	0	3.99
Bob Barr	R	26	26	23	19	0	203.1	263	5	28	81	6-18	1	4.38
Jack Neagle†	R	25	16	16	12	0	114.0	156	9	25	41	3-12	0	5.84
The Only Nolan	R	25	7	7	6	0	55.0	81	0	10	23	0-7	0	4.25
Norm Baker	—	20	3	3	2	0	19.0	24	0	11	5	0-2	0	3.32
Billy Taylor	R	28	19	9	8	0	127.0	166	4	34	41	4-7	0	5.39
Frank McLaughlin	R	27	2	0	0	0	9.0	14	0	3	1	0-0	0	13.00
Joe Battin	R	31	2	0	0	0	4.0	9	0	1	0	0-0	0	2.25

1883 Baltimore Orioles 8th AA 28-68 .292 37.0 GB

Billy Barnie

Player	Gm by Position	B	Age	G	AB	R	H	2B	3B	HR	RBI	BB	SO	SB	Avg	OBP	Slg
John Kelly†	C38,OF13	R	24	48	202	18	46	9	2	0	—	3	—	—	.228	.239	.292
Ecky Stearns	1B92,OF1	L	21	93	382	54	94	10	9	1	—	34	—	—	.246	.308	.327
Tim Manning	2B35	R	29	35	121	23	26	5	0	0	—	14	—	—	.215	.296	.256
Jerry McCormick	3B93	—	—	93	389	40	102	16	6	0	—	2	—	—	.262	.266	.334
Lou Say	SS74	R	29	74	324	52	83	13	2	1	—	10	—	—	.256	.278	.318
Jim Clinton	OF92,2B2	R	32	94	399	69	125	16	8	0	—	27	—	—	.313	.357	.393
Dave Eggler†	OF53	R	32	53	202	15	38	2	0	0	—	1	—	—	.188	.192	.198
Dave Rowe	OF50,SS7,1B3*	R	28	59	256	40	80	11	6	0	—	2	—	—	.313	.318	.402
Hardie Henderson†	P45,OF10,SS2*	R	20	51	191	13	31	5	1	1	—	10	—	—	.162	.204	.215
Gid Gardner	OF35,2B4,3B3*	—	24	42	161	28	44	10	3	1	—	18	—	—	.273	.346	.391
Tom O'Brien	2B29,OF4	R	23	33	138	16	37	6	4	0	—	5	—	—	.268	.294	.370
Phil Baker	C19,OF14,SS1	L	26	28	121	22	33	2	1	1	—	8	—	—	.273	.318	.331
Rooney Sweeney	C23,OF3	—	23	25	101	13	21	5	2	0	—	4	—	—	.208	.238	.297
Bob Emslie	P24,OF5	R	24	27	97	14	16	1	2	0	—	6	—	—	.165	.214	.216
Billy Reid	2B23,SS1	L	26	24	97	14	27	3	0	0	—	4	—	—	.278	.307	.309
John Fox	P20,OF4,1B1	—	24	23	92	12	14	3	0	0	—	4	—	—	.152	.188	.185
Bill Gallagher†	OF9,P7,SS4	—	—	16	61	9	10	3	1	0	—	3	—	—	.164	.203	.246
Billy Barnie	C13,OF6,SS1	—	30	17	55	7	11	0	0	0	—	2	—	—	.200	.228	.200
Jack Neagle†	P6,OF5	R	25	9	35	3	10	4	0	0	—	2	—	—	.286	.324	.400
Cal Broughton†	C8,OF1	R	22	9	32	1	6	0	0	0	—	1	—	—	.188	.212	.188
George Baker	SS4,C3,OF1	—	24	7	22	0	5	0	0	0	—	0	—	—	.227	.227	.227
Nick Scharf	SS3	—	24	3	13	1	2	1	0	0	—	1	—	—	.154	.214	.231
Jack Leary†	2B3	—	25	3	11	1	2	0	2	0	—	0	—	—	.182	.182	.545
Jim Devine	P2,OF1	—	24	2	9	4	2	0	0	0	—	0	—	—	.222	.222	.222
Bill Farrell	SS2	—	—	2	7	0	0	0	0	0	—	1	—	—	.000	.125	.000
Bill Loughlin	OF1	—	—	1	5	0	2	0	0	0	—	0	—	—	.400	.400	.400
Charlie Ingraham	C1	—	23	1	4	0	1	0	0	0	—	0	—	—	.250	.250	.250
Dave Oldfield	C1	S	18	1	4	0	0	0	0	0	—	0	—	—	.000	.000	.000
Doug Allison	C1,OF1	R	37	1	3	2	2	0	0	0	—	0	—	—	.667	.667	.667

D. Rowe, 1 G at P; H. Henderson, 1 G at 3B; G. Gardner, 2 G at P

Pitcher	T	Age	G	GS	CG	ShO	IP	H	HR	BB	SO	W-L	Sv	ERA
Hardie Henderson†	R	20	45	42	38	0	358.1	383	4	87	145	10-32	0	4.02
Bob Emslie	R	24	24	23	21	1	201.1	188	3	41	62	9-13	0	3.17
John Fox	—	24	20	19	18	0	165.1	209	2	32	49	6-13	0	4.03
Bill Gallagher	L	—	7	5	4	0	51.2	79	0	6	19	0-5	0	5.40
Jack Neagle†	R	25	6	5	4	0	46.0	48	1	20	9	1-4	0	4.89
Jim Devine	L	24	2	2	1	0	11.0	15	0	1	3	1-1	0	7.36
Gid Gardner	—	24	2	0	0	0	7.0	9	1	1	2	1-0	0	5.14
Dave Rowe	R	28	1	0	0	0	4.0	12	1	2	1	0-0	0	20.25

»1884 Providence Grays 1st NL 84-28 .750 —

Frank Bancroft

Player	Gm by Position	B	Age	G	AB	R	H	2B	3B	HR	RBI	BB	SO	SB	Avg	OBP	Slg
Barney Gilligan	C81,1B1,3B1	R	28	82	294	47	72	13	2	1	38	35	41	—	.245	.325	.313
Joe Start	1B93	L	41	93	381	80	105	10	5	2	32	35	25	—	.276	.337	.344
Jack Farrell	2B109,3B3	R	26	111	469	70	102	13	6	1	37	35	44	—	.217	.272	.277
Jerry Denny	3B99,1B9,2B3*	R	25	110	439	57	109	22	9	6	59	14	58	—	.248	.272	.380
Arthur Irwin	SS102,P1	L	26	102	404	73	97	14	3	2	44	28	52	—	.240	.289	.304
Cliff Carroll	OF113	S	24	113	452	90	118	16	4	3	54	29	39	—	.261	.306	.334
Paul Hines	OF108,1B7,P1	R	32	114	490	94	148	36	10	3	41	44	28	—	.302	.360	.435
Paul Radford	OF96,P2	R	22	97	355	56	70	11	2	1	29	25	43	—	.197	.250	.248
Old Hoss Radbourn	P75,OF7,1B5*	R	29	87	361	48	83	7	1	1	37	26	42	—	.230	.282	.263
Charlie Sweeney†	P27,OF17,1B1	R	21	41	168	24	50	9	0	1	19	11	17	—	.298	.341	.369
Sandy Nava	C27,SS6,2B1	—	34	34	116	10	11	0	0	0	6	11	35	—	.095	.173	.095
Charley Bassett	3B13,SS7,OF2*	R	21	27	79	10	11	2	1	0	6	4	15	—	.139	.181	.190
Miah Murray	C7,1B1,OF1	R	19	8	27	1	5	0	0	0	1	1	8	—	.185	.214	.185
Cyclone Miller†	P6,OF4	—	24	6	23	3	1	0	0	0	0	1	10	—	.043	.083	.043
John Cattanach†	P1,OF1	—	21	1	4	0	0	0	0	0	0	0	2	—	.000	.000	.000

J. Denny, 1 G at C; O. Radbourn, 2 G at SS, 1 G at 2B; C. Bassett, 1 G at 2B

Pitcher	T	Age	G	GS	CG	ShO	IP	H	HR	BB	SO	W-L	Sv	ERA
Old Hoss Radbourn	R	29	75	73	73	11	678.2	528	18	98	441	59-12	1	1.38
Charlie Sweeney†	R	21	27	24	22	4	221.0	153	4	29	145	17-8	1	1.55
Ed Conley	—	19	8	8	8	1	71.0	63	4	22	33	4-4	0	2.15
Cyclone Miller†	L	24	6	5	2	0	34.2	36	0	11	12	3-2	0	2.08
Paul Radford	R	22	2	2	1	0	13.0	27	0	3	2	0-2	0	7.62
Harry Arundel	R	30	1	1	1	0	9.0	8	0	4	4	1-0	0	1.00
John Cattanach†	—	21	1	1	0	0	5.0	2	0	4	2	0-0	0	9.00
Arthur Irwin	R	26	1	0	0	0	3.0	5	0	1	0	0-0	0	3.00
Paul Hines	R	32	1	0	0	0	1.0	3	0	0	0	0-0	0	0.00

1884 Boston Red Stockings 2nd NL 73-38 .658 10.5 GB

John Morrill

Player	Gm by Position	B	Age	G	AB	R	H	2B	3B	HR	RBI	BB	SO	SB	Avg	OBP	Slg
Mert Hackett	C71,3B1	R	24	72	268	28	55	13	2	1	20	2	66	—	.205	.211	.280
John Morrill	1B91,2B17,P7*	R	29	111	438	80	114	19	7	3	61	30	87	—	.260	.308	.356
Jack Burdock	2B87,3B1	R	32	87	361	65	97	14	4	6	49	15	52	—	.269	.298	.380
Ezra Sutton	3B110	R	33	110	468	102	162	28	7	3	61	29	22	—	.346	.384	.455
Sam Wise	SS107,2B7	L	26	114	426	60	91	15	9	4	41	25	104	—	.214	.257	.319
Joe Hornung	OF110,1B6	R	27	115	518	119	139	27	10	7	51	17	80	—	.268	.292	.400
Bill Crowley	OF108	R	27	108	407	50	110	14	6	6	61	33	74	—	.270	.325	.378
Jim Manning	OF73,2B9,SS9*	S	22	89	345	52	83	8	6	2	35	19	47	—	.241	.280	.316
Charlie Buffinton	P67,OF13,1B11	R	23	87	352	48	94	18	3	1	39	16	12	—	.267	.299	.344
Jim Whitney	P38,1B15,OF15*	L	26	66	270	41	70	17	5	3	40	16	38	—	.259	.301	.393
Mike Hines	C35	R	21	35	132	16	23	3	0	0	3	3	24	—	.174	.193	.197
Bill Annis	OF27	R	27	27	96	17	17	2	0	0	3	0	8	—	.177	.177	.198
Tom Gunning	C12	R	22	12	45	4	5	1	1	0	2	1	12	—	.111	.130	.178
Gene Moriarity†	OF4	L	19	4	16	1	1	0	0	0	0	0	8	—	.063	.063	.063
Daisy Davis†	P4,OF1	—	25	4	16	0	0	0	0	0	0	0	9	—	.000	.000	.000
Marty Barrett†	C3	R	23	3	6	0	0	0	0	0	0	0	4	—	.000	.000	.000

J. Morrill, 2 G at 3B, 1 G at OF; J. Manning, 3 G at 3B; J. Whitney, 1 G at 3B

Pitcher	T	Age	G	GS	CG	ShO	IP	H	HR	BB	SO	W-L	Sv	ERA
Charlie Buffinton	R	23	67	67	63	8	587.0	506	15	76	417	48-16	0	2.15
Jim Whitney	R	26	38	37	35	6	336.0	272	12	27	270	23-14	0	2.09
John Connor	—	29	7	7	7	0	60.0	70	1	18	29	1-4	0	3.15
Daisy Davis†	R	25	4	4	3	0	31.0	50	2	8	13	1-3	0	7.84
John Morrill	R	29	7	1	1	0	23.0	34	0	6	13	0-1	2	7.43

1884 Buffalo Bisons 3rd NL 64-47 .577 19.5 GB

Jim O'Rourke

Player	Gm by Position	B	Age	G	AB	R	H	2B	3B	HR	RBI	BB	SO	SB	Avg	OBP	Slg
Jack Rowe	C65,OF30,SS6	L	27	93	400	85	126	14	14	4	61	23	14	—	.315	.352	.450
Dan Brouthers	1B93,3B1	L	26	94	398	82	130	22	15	14	79	33	20	—	.327	.378	.563
Hardy Richardson	2B71,OF24,3B5*	R	29	102	439	85	132	27	9	6	60	22	41	—	.301	.334	.444
Deacon White	3B108,C3	L	36	110	452	82	147	16	11	5	74	32	13	—	.325	.370	.442
Davy Force	SS105,2B1	R	34	106	403	47	83	13	3	0	36	27	41	—	.206	.256	.253
Jim Lillie	OF114,P2	—	22	114	471	68	105	12	5	3	53	5	71	—	.223	.231	.289
Jim O'Rourke	OF86,1B18,C10*	R	33	108	467	119	162	33	7	5	63	35	17	—	.347	.392	.480
Dave Eggler	OF63	R	33	63	241	25	47	3	1	0	20	6	54	—	.195	.215	.216
George Myers	C49,OF34	R	23	78	325	34	59	9	2	2	32	13	33	—	.182	.213	.240
Pud Galvin	P72,OF1	R	27	72	274	34	49	6	1	0	24	2	80	—	.179	.185	.208
Chub Collins†	2B42,SS3	S	26	45	169	24	30	6	0	0	20	14	36	—	.178	.240	.213
Billy Serad	P37,OF3	R	21	37	137	12	24	2	1	0	9	3	33	—	.175	.193	.204
Bones Ely	P1,OF1	R	21	1	4	0	0	0	0	0	0	0	2	—	.000	.000	.000
Ed Coughlin	P1,OF1	—	22	1	4	0	1	0	0	0	1	0	2	—	.250	.250	.250

H. Richardson, 3 G at 1B; J. O'Rourke, 4 G at P, 1 G at 3B

Pitcher	T	Age	G	GS	CG	ShO	IP	H	HR	BB	SO	W-L	Sv	ERA
Pud Galvin	R	27	72	72	71	12	636.1	566	23	63	369	46-22	0	1.99
Billy Serad	R	21	37	37	34	2	308.0	373	21	111	150	16-20	0	4.27
Art Hagan	R	21	3	3	3	0	26.0	53	1	4	4	1-2	0	5.88
Jim Lillie	—	22	2	1	0	0	13.0	22	0	5	4	0-1	0	6.23
Bones Ely	R	21	1	1	0	0	5.0	17	1	5	4	0-1	0	14.40
Jim O'Rourke	R	33	4	0	0	0	12.2	7	0	1	3	0-1	1	2.84
Ed Coughlin	—	22	1	0	0	0	0.0	3	0	0	0	0-0	0	—

1884 Chicago White Stockings 4th NL 62-50 .554 22.0 GB

Cap Anson

Player	Gm by Position	B	Age	G	AB	R	H	2B	3B	HR	RBI	BB	SO	SB	Avg	OBP	Slg
Silver Flint	C73	R	28	73	279	35	57	5	2	9	45	7	57	—	.204	.224	.333
Cap Anson	1B112,C3,P1*	R	32	112	475	108	159	30	3	21	102	29	13	—	.335	.373	.543
Fred Pfeffer	2B112,P1	R	24	112	467	105	135	10	10	25	101	25	47	—	.289	.325	.514
Ned Williamson	3B99,C10,P2	R	26	107	417	84	116	18	8	27	84	42	56	—	.278	.344	.554
Tom Burns	SS80,3B3	R	27	83	343	54	84	14	2	7	44	13	50	—	.245	.272	.359
Abner Dalrymple	OF111	L	26	111	521	111	161	18	9	22	69	14	39	—	.309	.327	.505
George Gore	OF103	L	27	103	422	104	134	18	4	5	34	61	26	—	.318	.404	.415
King Kelly	OF63,C28,SS12*	R	26	108	452	120	160	28	5	13	95	46	24	—	.354	.414	.524
Larry Corcoran	P60,OF4,SS2	L	24	64	251	43	61	3	4	1	19	10	33	—	.243	.272	.299
Billy Sunday	OF43	L	21	43	176	25	39	4	1	4	28	4	36	—	.222	.239	.324
John Clarkson	P14,OF8,3B2*	R	22	21	84	16	22	6	2	3	17	2	16	—	.262	.279	.488
Walt Kinzie†	SS17,3B2	R	27	19	82	4	13	3	0	2	8	0	13	—	.159	.159	.268
Fred Goldsmith†	P21,OF2	R	28	22	81	11	11	2	0	2	6	7	26	—	.136	.205	.235
Joe Brown	OF9,P7,C1*	—	25	15	61	6	13	1	0	0	3	0	15	—	.213	.213	.230
Tom Lee†	P5,SS1	—	22	6	24	0	3	1	0	0	0	0	6	—	.125	.125	.167
Sy Sutcliffe	C4	L	22	4	15	4	3	1	0	0	2	2	4	—	.200	.294	.267
Dummy Lynch	P1,1B1	L	21	1	4	0	0	0	0	0	0	0	2	—	.000	.000	.000

C. Anson, 1 G at SS; K. Kelly, 10 G at 3B, 2 G at P, 2 G at 1B; J. Clarkson, 1 G at 1B; J. Brown, 1 G at 1B

Pitcher	T	Age	G	GS	CG	ShO	IP	H	HR	BB	SO	W-L	Sv	ERA
Larry Corcoran	S	24	60	59	57	7	516.2	473	35	116	272	35-23	0	2.40
Fred Goldsmith†	R	28	21	21	20	1	188.0	245	11	29	34	9-11	0	4.26
John Clarkson	R	22	14	13	12	0	118.0	94	10	25	102	10-3	0	2.14
Joe Brown	—	25	7	6	5	0	50.0	56	4	7	27	4-2	0	4.68
Tom Lee†	—	22	5	5	5	0	45.1	55	12	15	14	1-4	0	3.77
George Crosby	—	24	3	3	3	0	28.0	27	3	12	11	1-2	0	3.54
John Hibbard	L	19	2	2	2	1	17.0	18	1	9	4	1-1	0	2.65
Mike Corcoran	—	—	1	1	1	0	9.0	16	1	7	2	0-1	0	4.00
Fred Andrus	R	33	1	1	1	0	9.0	11	1	2	2	1-0	0	2.00
Dummy Lynch	—	21	1	1	0	0	7.0	7	1	3	2	0-0	0	2.57
King Kelly	R	26	2	0	0	0	5.1	12	2	2	1	0-1	0	8.44
Ned Williamson	R	26	2	0	0	0	2.0	8	0	2	0	0-0	0	18.00
Fred Pfeffer	R	24	1	0	0	0	1.0	3	0	1	0	0-0	0	9.00
Cap Anson	R	32	1	0	0	0	1.0	3	2	1	1	0-1	0	18.00

1884 New York Gothams 4th NL 62-50 .554 22.0 GB

Jim Price (56-42)/Monte Ward (6-8)

Player	Gm by Position	B	Age	G	AB	R	H	2B	3B	HR	RBI	BB	SO	SB	Avg	OBP	Slg
Buck Ewing	C80,OF12,SS3*	R	24	94	382	90	106	15	20	3	41	28	22	—	.277	.327	.445
Alex McKinnon	1B116	R	27	116	470	66	128	21	12	4	73	8	62	—	.272	.285	.394
Roger Connor	2B67,OF37,3B12	L	26	116	477	98	151	28	4	4	82	38	32	—	.317	.367	.417
Frank Hankinson	3B105,OF1	R	28	105	389	44	90	16	7	2	43	23	59	—	.231	.274	.324
Ed Caskin	SS96,C6	R	32	100	351	49	81	11	1	1	40	34	55	—	.231	.299	.276
Pete Gillespie	OF101	L	32	101	413	75	109	7	4	2	44	19	35	—	.264	.296	.315
Mike Dorgan	OF64,P14,C6*	R	30	83	341	61	94	11	6	1	48	13	27	—	.276	.302	.352
Monte Ward	OF59,2B47,P9	L	24	113	482	98	122	11	8	2	51	28	47	—	.253	.294	.322
Danny Richardson	OF55,SS19	R	21	74	277	36	70	8	1	1	27	16	17	—	.253	.294	.300
Mickey Welch	P65,OF7	R	24	71	249	47	60	14	3	3	29	16	49	—	.241	.287	.357
Ed Begley	P31,OF2	—	21	33	121	12	22	4	0	0	8	8	31	—	.182	.233	.215
John Humphries†	C20	L	22	20	64	6	6	0	0	0	2	9	19	—	.094	.205	.094
Sandy Griffin	OF16	R	25	16	62	7	11	2	0	0	6	1	19	—	.177	.190	.210
— Loughran	C9,OF1	—	—	9	29	4	3	1	1	0	3	7	11	—	.103	.278	.207
Charlie Manlove†	C3,OF1	R	21	3	10	0	0	0	0	0	0	0	4	—	.000	.000	.000
Henry Oxley†	C2	—	26	2	4	0	0	0	0	0	0	1	2	—	.000	.200	.000

B. Ewing, 1 G at P, 1 G at 3B; M. Dorgan, 3 G at 2B

Pitcher	T	Age	G	GS	CG	ShO	IP	H	HR	BB	SO	W-L	Sv	ERA
Mickey Welch	R	24	65	65	62	4	557.1	528	12	146	345	39-21	0	2.50
Ed Begley	—	21	31	30	30	0	266.0	296	9	99	104	12-18	0	4.16
Mike Dorgan	R	30	14	14	12	0	113.0	98	5	51	90	8-6	0	3.50
Monte Ward	R	24	9	5	5	0	60.2	72	2	18	23	3-3	0	3.41
Jim Brown†	—	23	1	1	1	0	9.0	10	0	8	2	0-1	0	5.00
Buck Ewing	R	24	1	1	1	0	8.0	7	0	4	3	0-1	0	1.13

1884 Philadelphia Phillies 6th NL 39-73 .348 45.0 GB

Harry Wright

Player	Gm by Position	B	Age	G	AB	R	H	2B	3B	HR	RBI	BB	SO	SB	Avg	OBP	Slg
John Crowley	C48	—	22	48	168	26	41	7	3	0	19	15	21	—	.244	.306	.321
Sid Farrar	1B111	—	24	111	428	62	105	16	6	1	45	9	25	—	.245	.261	.318
Ed Andrews	2B109	R	25	109	420	74	93	21	2	0	23	9	42	—	.221	.238	.281
Joe Mulvey	3B100	R	25	100	401	47	92	11	2	2	32	4	49	—	.229	.237	.282
Bill McClellan	SS111,OF1	L	28	111	450	71	116	13	2	3	33	28	43	—	.258	.301	.316
Jack Manning	OF104	R	30	104	424	71	115	29	4	5	52	40	67	—	.271	.334	.394
Blondie Purcell	OF103,P1	R	30	103	428	67	108	11	7	1	31	29	30	—	.252	.300	.318
Jim Fogarty	OF78,3B14,2B4*	R	20	97	378	42	80	12	6	1	37	20	54	—	.212	.251	.283
Charlie Ferguson	P50,OF5	S	21	52	203	26	50	6	3	0	20	19	54	—	.246	.311	.305
John Coleman†	OF27,P21,1B2	L	21	43	171	16	42	7	2	0	22	8	20	—	.246	.279	.310
Frank Ringo†	C26	R	23	26	91	4	12	2	0	0	6	3	19	—	.132	.160	.154
Bill Vinton	P21,OF1	R	19	21	78	9	9	1	0	0	4	3	21	—	.115	.148	.128
Tom Lynch†	C7,OF7	L	24	13	48	7	15	4	2	0	3	4	5	—	.313	.365	.479
Jim McElroy†	P13,OF2	—	21	14	48	3	7	0	0	0	3	1	12	—	.146	.163	.146
Jack Remsen†	OF12	R	34	12	43	9	9	2	0	0	3	6	9	—	.209	.306	.256
Buster Hoover†	OF10	R	21	10	42	6	8	1	0	1	4	4	9	—	.190	.261	.286
Jack Clements†	C9	L	19	9	30	3	7	0	0	0	0	4	8	—	.233	.324	.233
Tony Cusick†	C9	R	24	9	29	2	4	0	0	0	1	0	3	—	.138	.138	.138
Joe Kappel	C4	R	27	4	15	1	1	0	0	0	0	0	2	—	.067	.067	.067
G. Vadeboncoeur	C4	—	25	4	14	1	3	0	0	0	3	1	2	—	.214	.267	.214
Paul Cook	C3	R	21	3	12	0	1	0	0	0	0	0	2	—	.083	.083	.083
Mike DePangher	C4	L	25	4	10	0	2	0	0	0	0	1	3	—	.200	.273	.200
Lou Hardie	C3	—	19	3	8	0	3	2	0	0	0	0	2	—	.375	.375	.625
Bill Conway	C1	R	22	1	4	0	0	0	0	0	0	0	1	—	.000	.000	.000
Hezekiah Allen	C1	—	21	1	3	0	2	0	0	0	0	0	0	—	.667	.667	.667
Ed Sixsmith	C1	R	21	1	2	0	0	0	0	0	0	0	0	—	.000	.000	.000

J. Fogarty, 3 G at SS, 1 G at P

Pitcher	T	Age	G	GS	CG	ShO	IP	H	HR	BB	SO	W-L	Sv	ERA
Charlie Ferguson	R	21	50	47	46	2	416.2	443	13	93	194	21-25	1	3.54
Bill Vinton	R	19	21	21	20	0	182.0	166	6	35	105	10-10	0	2.23
John Coleman†	R	21	21	19	14	1	154.1	216	9	22	37	5-15	0	4.90
Jim McElroy†	—	21	13	13	13	0	111.0	115	1	54	45	1-12	0	4.86
Joe Knight	L	24	6	6	6	0	51.0	66	2	21	8	2-4	0	5.47
Con Murphy	R	20	3	3	3	0	26.0	37	1	6	10	0-3	0	6.58
Sparrow Morton	L	—	2	2	2	0	17.0	16	0	11	5	0-2	0	5.29
Shadow Pyle	L	22	1	1	1	0	9.0	9	0	6	4	0-1	0	4.00
Cyclone Miller†	L	24	1	1	1	0	9.0	17	5	6	1	0-1	0	10.00
Blondie Purcell	R	30	1	0	0	0	4.0	3	1	0	1	0-0	0	2.25
Jim Fogarty	R	20	1	0	0	0	1.0	2	0	0	1	0-0	0	0.00

1884 Cleveland Blues 7th NL 35-77 .313 49.0 GB

Charlie Hackett

Player	Gm by Position	B	Age	G	AB	R	H	2B	3B	HR	RBI	BB	SO	SB	Avg	OBP	Slg
Doc Bushong	C62,OF1	R	27	62	203	24	48	6	1	0	10	17	11	—	.236	.295	.276
Bill Phillips	1B111	R	27	111	464	58	128	25	12	3	46	18	80	—	.276	.303	.401
Germany Smith†	2B42,SS30	R	21	72	291	31	74	14	4	4	26	2	45	—	.254	.259	.371
Mike Muldoon	3B109,2B1,OF1	—	26	110	422	46	101	16	6	2	38	18	67	—	.239	.270	.320
Jack Glasscock†	SS69,2B3,P2	R	24	72	281	45	70	4	4	1	22	25	16	—	.249	.310	.302
Pete Hotaling	OF102,2B1	R	27	102	408	69	99	16	6	3	27	28	50	—	.243	.291	.333
Jake Evans	OF76,2B4,SS2	—	27	80	313	32	81	18	3	1	38	15	49	—	.259	.293	.345
Sam Moffett	OF42,P24,1B2*	R	27	67	256	26	47	12	2	0	15	8	56	—	.184	.208	.246
John Harkins	P46,OF17,3B1*	R	25	61	229	24	47	4	2	0	20	7	45	—	.205	.229	.240
Jim McCormick†	P42,OF8	R	27	49	190	15	50	5	4	0	23	1	11	—	.263	.267	.332
Willie Murphy†	OF42	L	20	42	168	18	38	3	3	1	9	1	23	—	.226	.231	.298
Fatty Briody†	C42,OF1	—	25	43	148	17	25	6	0	1	12	6	19	—	.169	.201	.230
George Pinckney	2B25,SS11	R	22	36	144	18	45	9	0	0	16	10	7	—	.313	.357	.375
Ernie Burch	OF32	L	28	32	124	9	26	4	0	0	7	5	24	—	.210	.240	.242
Joe Ardner	2B25,3B1	R	26	26	92	6	16	1	1	0	4	1	24	—	.174	.183	.207
Mike Moynahan†	2B6,SS3,OF3	L	28	12	45	9	13	2	1	0	6	7	11	—	.289	.385	.378
Gurdon Whiteley	OF8	—	24	8	34	4	5	0	0	0	0	1	8	—	.147	.171	.147
Jerrie Moore†	C9	L	—	9	30	1	6	0	0	0	10	0	5	—	.200	.200	.200
George Strief†	OF6,3B2	R	27	8	29	2	7	2	0	0	0	0	5	—	.241	.241	.310
John Henry	P5,OF4	—	20	9	26	2	4	0	0	0	0	0	12	—	.154	.154	.154
George Fisher†	2B6,C1	L	—	6	24	2	3	0	0	0	0	0	3	—	.125	.125	.125
Pit Gilman	OF2	L	20	2	10	0	1	0	0	0	0	0	3	—	.100	.100	.100
Bill Smith	OF1	—	—	1	3	0	0	0	0	0	0	0	2	—	.000	.000	.000

S. Moffett, 1 G at 2B, 1 G at 3B; J. Harkins, 1 G at SS

Pitcher	T	Age	G	GS	CG	ShO	IP	H	HR	BB	SO	W-L	Sv	ERA
John Harkins	R	25	46	45	42	3	391.0	399	7	108	192	12-32	0	3.68
Jim McCormick†	R	27	42	41	39	3	359.0	357	16	75	182	19-22	0	2.86
Sam Moffett	R	27	24	22	21	0	197.2	236	9	58	84	3-19	0	3.87
John Henry	L	20	5	5	5	1	42.0	46	2	26	23	1-4	0	3.64
Jack Glasscock	R	24	2	0	0	0	5.0	8	0	2	1	0-0	0	5.40

1884 Detroit Wolverines 8th NL 28-84 .250 56.0 GB

Jack Chapman

Player	Gm by Position	B	Age	G	AB	R	H	2B	3B	HR	RBI	BB	SO	SB	Avg	OBP	Slg
Charlie Bennett	C80,OF5,SS4*	R	29	90	341	37	90	18	6	3	40	36	40	—	.264	.334	.378
Milt Scott	1B110	R	18	110	438	29	108	17	5	3	50	9	62	—	.247	.262	.329
Bill Geiss	2B73,P1,1B1*	—	25	75	283	23	50	11	4	2	16	6	60	—	.177	.194	.265
Joe Farrell	3B110,OF1	R	27	110	461	59	104	10	5	3	41	14	66	—	.226	.248	.289
Frank Meinke	SS51,P35,OF4*	R	20	92	341	28	56	5	7	6	24	6	89	—	.164	.179	.273
George Wood	OF114,3B1	L	25	114	473	79	119	16	10	8	29	39	75	—	.252	.309	.378
Ned Hanlon	OF114	L	26	114	450	86	119	18	6	5	39	40	52	—	.264	.324	.364
Stump Wiedman	OF53,P26,2B1*	R	23	81	300	24	49	6	0	0	26	13	41	—	.163	.198	.183
Dupee Shaw†	P28,OF10	L	25	36	136	16	26	4	1	1	8	4	21	—	.191	.214	.257
Henry Jones	2B16,OF11,SS7	S	27	34	127	24	28	3	1	0	3	16	18	—	.220	.308	.260
Harry Buker	SS19,OF11	—	25	30	111	5	15	1	0	0	3	4	15	—	.135	.165	.144
Frank Cox	SS27	—	26	27	102	6	13	3	1	0	4	2	36	—	.127	.144	.176
Ed Gastfield	C19,1B2,OF2	R	18	23	82	6	6	1	0	0	2	2	34	—	.073	.095	.085
Tom Kearns	2B21	R	23	21	79	9	16	0	1	0	7	2	10	—	.203	.222	.228
Frank Brill	P12,OF1	R	20	13	44	5	6	0	0	0	2	1	13	—	.136	.156	.136
Fred Wood	C7,OF6,SS1	—	21	12	42	4	2	0	0	0	1	3	18	—	.048	.111	.048
Chief Zimmer	C6,OF2	R	23	8	29	0	2	1	0	0	0	1	14	—	.069	.100	.103
Edward Santry	SS5,2B1	—	—	6	22	1	4	0	0	0	0	1	2	—	.182	.217	.182
Walter Prince†	OF7	L	23	7	21	0	3	0	0	0	1	3	4	—	.143	.250	.143
Frank Jones	SS1,OF1	L	25	2	8	0	1	0	0	0	0	0	1	—	.125	.125	.125
Joe Weber	OF2	—	—	2	8	0	0	0	0	0	0	0	2	—	.000	.000	.000
Ben Guiney	C2	S	25	2	7	0	0	0	0	0	0	0	3	—	.000	.000	.000
Walt Walker	C1	—	24	1	4	1	1	0	0	0	0	0	0	—	.250	.250	.250
Dick Lowe	C1	—	30	1	3	0	1	0	0	0	0	0	1	—	.333	.333	.333
Dave Beatle	C1,OF1	—	23	1	3	0	0	0	0	0	0	0	2	—	.000	.000	.000

C. Bennett, 1 G at 1B, 1 G at 2B, 1 G at 3B; B. Geiss, 1 G at OF; F. Meinke, 3 G at 2B, 3 G at 3B; S. Wiedman, 1 G at SS

Pitcher	T	Age	G	GS	CG	ShO	IP	H	HR	BB	SO	W-L	Sv	ERA
Frank Meinke	R	20	35	31	31	1	289.0	341	10	63	124	8-23	0	3.18
Dupee Shaw†	L	25	28	28	25	0	227.2	219	8	72	142	9-18	0	3.04
Stump Wiedman	R	23	26	26	24	0	212.2	257	9	57	96	4-21	0	3.72
Charlie Getzien	R	20	17	17	17	1	147.1	118	2	25	107	5-12	0	1.95
Frank Brill	R	20	12	12	12	1	103.0	148	7	26	18	2-10	0	5.50
Bill Geiss	—	25	1	0	0	0	5.0	14	0	2	1	0-0	0	14.40

»1884 New York Metropolitans 1st AA 75-32 .701 —

Jim Mutrie

Player	Gm by Position	B	Age	G	AB	R	H	2B	3B	HR	RBI	BB	SO	SB	Avg	OBP	Slg
Bill Holbert	C59,OF5,SS1	R	29	65	255	28	53	5	0	0	—	7	—	—	.208	.235	.227
Dave Orr	1B110,OF3	R	24	110	458	82	162	32	13	9	—	5	—	—	.354	.362	.539
Dasher Troy	2B107	R	28	107	421	80	111	22	10	2	—	19	—	—	.264	.300	.378
Dude Esterbrook	3B112	R	27	112	477	110	150	29	11	1	—	12	—	—	.314	.345	.428
Candy Nelson	SS110,2B1	L	35	111	432	114	110	15	3	1	—	74	—	—	.255	.375	.310
Steve Brady	OF110,1B5,2B1	—	32	112	485	102	122	11	3	1	—	21	—	—	.252	.283	.293
Chief Roseman	OF107	R	27	107	436	97	130	16	11	4	—	21	—	—	.298	.339	.413
Ed Kennedy	OF100,C1,2B1*	—	28	103	378	49	72	6	2	1	—	16	—	—	.190	.225	.225
C. Reipschlager	C51,OF8	R	—	59	233	21	56	13	2	0	—	1	—	—	.240	.250	.313
Tim Keefe	P58,OF5	R	27	62	210	27	50	3	6	3	—	18	—	—	.238	.301	.352
Gracie Pierce	2B3,OF3	L	—	5	20	2	5	1	0	0	—	0	—	—	.250	.250	.300
Tony Murphy	C1	—	21	1	3	1	1	0	0	0	—	0	—	—	.333	.333	.333
Henry Oxley†	C1	—	26	1	3	0	0	0	0	0	—	0	—	—	.000	.000	.000

E. Kennedy, 1 G at SS

Pitcher	T	Age	G	GS	CG	ShO	IP	H	HR	BB	SO	W-L	Sv	ERA
Tim Keefe	R	27	57	57	56	4	482.2	378	5	75	317	37-17	0	2.26
Jack Lynch	R	27	55	54	54	5	496.0	420	10	42	292	37-15	0	2.67
Buck Becannon	—	24	1	1	1	0	6.0	2	0	2	2	1-0	0	1.50

1884 Columbus Colts 2nd AA 69-39 .639 6.5 GB

Gus Schmelz

Player	Gm by Position	B	Age	G	AB	R	H	2B	3B	HR	RBI	BB	SO	SB	Avg	OBP	Slg
Rudy Kemmler	C58,1B2,OF1	R	24	61	211	28	42	3	3	0	—	15	—	—	.199	.252	.242
Jim Field	1B105	—	21	105	417	74	97	9	7	4	—	23	—	—	.233	.292	.317
Pop Smith	2B108	R	27	108	445	78	106	18	10	6	—	20	—	—	.238	.289	.364
Bill Kuehne	3B110	R	25	110	415	48	98	13	16	5	—	9	—	—	.236	.254	.381
John Richmond	SS105	—	30	105	398	57	100	13	7	3	—	35	—	—	.251	.317	.342
Tom Brown	OF107,P4	L	23	107	451	93	123	9	11	5	—	24	—	—	.273	.315	.375
Fred Mann	OF97,2B2	L	26	99	366	70	101	12	18	7	—	25	—	—	.276	.341	.464
John Cahill	OF56,SS5,P2	R	19	59	210	28	46	3	3	0	—	6	—	—	.219	.248	.262
Fred Carroll	C54,OF15	R	19	69	252	46	70	13	5	6	—	13	—	—	.278	.326	.440
Frank Mountain	P42,OF17	R	24	58	210	26	50	7	3	4	—	9	—	—	.238	.283	.357
Ed Morris	P52,OF10	S	21	57	199	19	37	4	8	0	—	5	—	—	.186	.217	.286
Ed Dundon	OF16,P11,1B3	—	24	26	86	6	12	2	2	0	—	5	—	—	.140	.196	.209
Tom Mansell†	OF23	L	29	23	77	9	15	1	3	0	—	6	—	—	.195	.262	.286

Pitcher	T	Age	G	GS	CG	ShO	IP	H	HR	BB	SO	W-L	Sv	ERA
Ed Morris	L	21	52	52	47	3	429.2	335	3	51	302	34-13	0	2.18
Frank Mountain	R	24	42	41	40	5	360.2	289	7	78	156	23-17	1	2.45
Ed Dundon	R	24	11	9	7	0	81.0	85	9	15	37	6-4	0	3.78
Tom Sullivan	—	24	4	4	4	0	31.0	42	2	3	12	2-2	0	4.06
Al Bauers	L	34	3	3	3	0	25.0	22	1	14	13	1-2	0	4.68
John Cahill	R	19	2	1	1	0	16.0	15	0	4	1	1-0	0	5.06
Tom Brown	R	23	4	0	0	0	19.0	27	0	7	5	2-1	0	7.11

1884 Louisville Colonels 3rd AA 68-40 .630 7.5 GB

Mike Walsh

Player	Gm by Position	B	Age	G	AB	R	H	2B	3B	HR	RBI	BB	SO	SB	Avg	OBP	Slg
Dan Sullivan	C63,OF1	—	27	63	247	27	59	8	6	0	—	9	—	—	.239	.268	.320
Jumbo Latham	1B76,3B1	R	31	77	308	31	52	3	3	0	—	8	—	—	.169	.197	.198
Joe Gerhardt	2B106	R	29	106	404	39	89	7	8	0	—	13	—	—	.220	.254	.277
Pete Browning	3B52,OF24,1B23*	R	23	103	447	101	150	33	8	4	—	13	—	—	.336	.357	.472
Tom McLaughlin	SS94,3B4,2B1	—	24	98	335	41	67	11	6	0	—	22	—	—	.200	.262	.269
Leech Maskrey	OF103,3B3,SS1	R	30	105	412	48	103	13	4	0	—	17	—	—	.250	.281	.301
Chicken Wolf	OF101,C11,1B1*	R	22	110	486	79	146	24	11	3	—	4	—	—	.300	.310	.414
Monk Cline	OF90,SS6	L	26	94	396	91	115	16	7	2	—	27	—	—	.290	.342	.381
Guy Hecker	P75,OF5	R	28	78	316	53	94	14	8	4	—	10	—	—	.297	.323	.430
Phil Reccius	3B51,P18,SS10	—	22	73	263	23	63	9	2	3	—	5	—	—	.240	.267	.323
Ed Whiting	C40,1B2,OF2	L	24	42	157	16	35	7	3	0	—	9	—	—	.223	.274	.306
Wally Andrews	1B9,3B3,SS1*	R	24	14	49	10	10	5	1	0	—	4	—	—	.204	.264	.347
Denny Driscoll	P13,OF2	L	28	13	48	5	9	1	0	0	—	2	—	—	.188	.220	.208
Ren Deagle†	P12,OF3	R	26	12	45	2	6	1	0	0	—	0	—	—	.133	.133	.156
B. Dickerson†	OF8	L	25	8	28	6	4	0	2	1	—	3	—	—	.143	.226	.393
Len Stockwell	OF2,C1	R	24	2	9	0	1	0	0	0	—	0	—	—	.111	.111	.111
Bill Hunter	C2	—	29	2	7	1	1	0	0	0	—	0	—	—	.143	.143	.143

P. Browning, 4 G at 2B, 1 G at P; C. Wolf, 1 G at 3B, 1 G at SS; W. Andrews, 1 G at OF

Pitcher	T	Age	G	GS	CG	ShO	IP	H	HR	BB	SO	W-L	Sv	ERA
Guy Hecker	R	28	75	73	72	6	670.2	526	4	56	385	52-20	0	1.80
Denny Driscoll	L	28	13	13	10	0	102.0	110	3	7	16	6-6	0	3.44
Ren Deagle†	R	26	12	12	8	0	87.1	80	0	13	23	4-6	0	2.58
Phil Reccius	—	22	18	11	11	0	129.1	118	2	19	46	6-7	0	2.71
Pete Browning	R	23	1	1	0	0	0.1	2	0	2	0	0-1	0	54.00

1884 St. Louis Browns 4th AA 67-40 .626 8.0 GB

Player	Gm by Position	B	Age	G	AB	R	H	2B	3B	HR	RBI	BB	SO	SB	Avg	OBP	Slg
Pat Deasley	C75,OF2,1B1	R	26	75	254	27	52	5	4	0	—	7	—	—	.205	.235	.256
Charlie Comiskey	1B108,P1,2B1	R	24	108	460	76	110	17	6	2	—	5	—	—	.239	.255	.315
Joe Quest†	2B81	R	31	81	310	46	64	9	5	0	—	19	—	—	.206	.257	.268
Arlie Latham	3B110,C1	R	24	110	474	115	130	17	12	1	—	19	—	—	.274	.311	.367
Bill Gleason	SS110,3B1	R	25	110	472	97	127	21	7	1	—	28	—	—	.269	.326	.350
Hugh Nicol	OF87,2B23,3B1*	R	26	110	442	79	115	14	5	0	—	22	—	—	.260	.300	.314
Fred Lewis†	OF73	S	25	73	300	59	97	25	3	0	—	16	—	—	.323	.366	.427
Tip O'Neill	OF64,P17,1B1	R	26	78	297	49	82	13	11	3	—	12	—	—	.276	.309	.424
George Strief†	OF44,2B3,1B1	R	27	48	184	22	37	5	2	2	—	13	—	—	.201	.254	.283
Tom Dolan†	C34,OF2	R	25	35	137	19	36	6	2	0	—	6	—	—	.263	.299	.336
Dave Foutz	P25,OF14	R	27	33	119	17	27	4	0	0	—	8	—	—	.227	.276	.261
Daisy Davis†	P25,OF4	—	25	25	87	5	15	0	1	0	—	5	—	—	.172	.217	.195
Bob Caruthers	OF16,P13	L	20	23	82	15	21	2	0	2	—	4	—	—	.256	.291	.354
Charlie Krehmeyer	OF15,C7,1B1	L	20	21	70	3	16	0	1	0	—	2	—	—	.229	.250	.257
Johnny Lavin	OF16	—	—	16	52	9	11	2	0	0	—	3	—	—	.212	.268	.250
Walt Goldsby†	OF5	L	22	5	20	2	4	0	0	0	—	0	—	—	.200	.200	.200
Harry Wheeler†	OF5	R	26	5	19	0	5	2	0	0	—	1	—	—	.263	.300	.368
Walt Kinzie†	2B2	R	27	2	9	0	1	0	0	0	—	0	—	—	.111	.111	.111
Al Struve	C1,OF1	—	—	2	7	2	2	0	0	0	—	0	—	—	.286	.286	.286
Chuck Fulmer†	2B1	R	33	1	5	0	0	0	0	0	—	0	—	—	.000	.000	.000
Nin Alexander†	C1,OF1	R	25	1	4	0	0	0	0	0	—	0	—	—	.000	.000	.000
Jim McCauley	C1	L	21	1	2	0	0	0	0	0	—	0	—	—	.000	.000	.000

H. Nicol, 1 G at SS

Jimmy Williams (51-33)/Charlie Comiskey (16-7)

Pitcher	T	Age	G	GS	CG	ShO	IP	H	HR	BB	SO	W-L	Sv	ERA
Jumbo McGinnis	—	20	40	40	39	5	354.1	331	4	35	141	24-16	0	2.84
Dave Foutz	R	27	25	25	19	2	206.2	167	7	36	95	15-6	0	2.18
Daisy Davis†	R	25	25	24	20	1	198.1	196	1	35	143	10-12	0	2.90
Tip O'Neill	R	26	17	14	14	0	141.0	125	3	51	36	11-4	0	2.68
Bob Caruthers	R	20	13	7	7	0	82.2	61	1	15	58	7-2	0	2.61
Charlie Comiskey	R	24	1	0	0	0	4.0	1	0	0	4	0-0	0	2.25

1884 Cincinnati Reds 5th AA 68-41 .624 8.0 GB

Player	Gm by Position	B	Age	G	AB	R	H	2B	3B	HR	RBI	BB	SO	SB	Avg	OBP	Slg
Pop Snyder	C65,1B2,OF1	R	29	67	268	32	69	9	9	0	—	7	—	—	.257	.276	.358
John Reilly	1B103,OF3,SS1	R	25	105	448	114	152	24	19	11	—	5	—	—	.339	.366	.551
Bid McPhee	2B112	R	24	112	450	107	125	8	7	5	—	27	—	—	.278	.327	.360
Hick Carpenter	3B108,OF1	R	28	108	474	80	121	16	2	4	—	6	—	—	.255	.271	.323
Jimmy Peoples	SS47,C14,OF10*	—	20	69	267	28	45	2	2	1	—	6	—	—	.169	.187	.202
Charley Jones	OF112	R	34	112	472	117	148	19	17	7	—	37	—	—	.314	.376	.470
Pop Corkhill	OF92,SS11,1B6*	L	26	110	452	85	124	13	11	4	—	6	—	—	.274	.290	.378
Tom Mansell†	OF65	L	29	65	266	49	66	4	6	0	—	15	—	—	.248	.301	.308
Buck West	OF33	L	23	33	131	20	32	2	8	1	—	2	—	—	.244	.256	.405
Phil Powers	C31,1B2,OF2	R	29	34	130	10	18	1	0	0	—	5	—	—	.138	.170	.146
Frank Fennelly†	SS28	R	24	28	122	42	43	5	8	2	—	11	—	—	.352	.415	.574
Billy Mountjoy	P33,OF2	L	25	34	119	13	18	2	1	0	—	9	—	—	.151	.229	.185
Chuck Fulmer†	SS29,OF2,3B1	R	33	31	114	13	20	2	1	0	—	1	—	—	.175	.183	.211
Jimmy Woulfe†	OF7,3B1	—	24	8	34	3	5	0	1	0	—	1	—	—	.147	.171	.206
Frank Berkelbach	OF6	—	—	6	25	3	6	0	1	0	—	0	—	—	.240	.296	.320
George Miller	C6	R	31	6	20	6	5	1	1	0	—	1	—	—	.250	.318	.400
Icicle Reeder†	OF3	R	19	3	14	0	2	0	0	0	—	0	—	—	.143	.143	.143
John Parsons	OF1	—	—	1	3	0	0	0	0	0	—	0	—	—	.000	.000	.000

J. Peoples, 1 G at 1B, 1 G at 3B; P. Corkhill, 3 G at 3B, 1 G at P

Will White (44-27)/Pop Snyder (24-14)

Pitcher	T	Age	G	GS	CG	ShO	IP	H	HR	BB	SO	W-L	Sv	ERA
Will White	R	29	52	52	52	7	456.0	479	16	74	118	34-18	0	3.32
Billy Mountjoy	R	25	33	33	32	3	289.0	274	5	43	96	19-12	0	2.93
Gus Shallix	R	26	23	23	23	0	199.2	163	6	53	78	11-10	0	3.70
Ren Deagle†	R	26	4	4	4	1	34.0	39	0	9	12	3-1	0	5.03
Pop Corkhill	R	26	1	0	0	0	5.0	1	0	2	4	1-0	0	1.80

1884 Baltimore Orioles 6th AA 63-43 .594 11.5 GB

Player	Gm by Position	B	Age	G	AB	R	H	2B	3B	HR	RBI	BB	SO	SB	Avg	OBP	Slg
Sam Trott	C60,2B6,OF5	L	25	71	284	36	73	17	9	3	—	4	—	—	.257	.272	.412
Ecky Stearns	1B100,2B1	L	22	100	396	61	94	12	3	3	—	28	—	—	.237	.298	.306
Tim Manning	2B91	R	30	91	341	49	70	14	5	2	—	26	—	—	.205	.275	.293
Joe Sommer	3B97,OF9,2B1	R	25	107	479	96	129	11	10	4	—	8	—	—	.269	.293	.359
Jimmy Macullar	SS107	R	29	107	360	73	73	16	6	4	—	36	—	—	.203	.290	.314
Jim Clinton	OF104,2B1	R	33	104	437	82	118	12	6	4	—	29	—	—	.270	.334	.352
Tom York	OF83	L	32	83	314	64	70	14	7	1	—	34	—	—	.223	.318	.322
Gid Gardner†	OF40,1B2	—	25	41	173	32	37	6	8	2	—	14	—	—	.214	.280	.376
Bill Traffley	C47,OF6,1B1	R	24	53	210	25	37	4	6	0	—	3	—	—	.176	.192	.252
Hardie Henderson	P52,OF3	R	21	53	203	24	46	7	7	0	—	5	—	—	.227	.245	.330
Bob Emslie	P50,OF1	R	25	51	195	21	37	6	3	0	—	2	—	—	.190	.198	.251
Dennis Casey†	OF37	L	26	37	149	20	37	7	4	3	—	5	—	—	.248	.273	.409
Oyster Burns†	OF24,2B10,P2*	R	19	35	131	34	39	2	6	6	—	7	—	—	.298	.348	.542
B. Dickerson†	OF12,3B1	L	25	13	56	9	12	2	1	0	—	4	—	—	.214	.290	.286
John Ake	3B9,OF3,SS1	R	22	13	52	1	10	0	1	0	—	0	—	—	.192	.208	.231
Pat Burns†	1B6	—	—	6	25	3	5	2	1	0	—	3	—	—	.200	.286	.360
Jim McLaughlin	P3,OF3	L	23	5	22	3	5	1	1	0	—	0	—	—	.227	.227	.364
Fred Goldsmith†	P4,1B1	R	28	4	14	2	2	0	0	0	—	2	—	—	.143	.250	.143
Jim Roxburgh	C2	R	26	2	4	1	2	0	0	0	—	1	—	—	.500	.667	.500

O. Burns, 1 G at 3B

Billy Barnie

Pitcher	T	Age	G	GS	CG	ShO	IP	H	HR	BB	SO	W-L	Sv	ERA
Hardie Henderson	R	21	52	52	50	4	439.1	382	9	116	346	27-23	0	2.62
Bob Emslie	R	25	50	50	50	4	455.1	419	5	88	264	32-17	0	2.75
Fred Goldsmith†	R	28	4	4	3	0	30.0	29	0	2	11	3-1	0	2.70
Jim McLaughlin	L	23	3	2	2	0	22.0	27	2	11	8	1-2	0	3.68
Oyster Burns	R	19	2	0	0	0	9.0	12	0	2	6	0-0	1	3.00

1884 Philadelphia Athletics 7th AA 61-46 .570 14.0 GB

Player	Gm by Position	B	Age	G	AB	R	H	2B	3B	HR	RBI	BB	SO	SB	Avg	OBP	Slg
Jocko Milligan	C65,OF1	R	22	66	268	39	77	20	3	3	—	8	—	—	.287	.308	.418
Harry Stovey	1B104	R	27	104	448	124	146	22	23	10	—	26	—	—	.326	.368	.545
Cub Stricker	2B107,P1,C1*	R	25	107	399	59	92	16	11	1	—	19	—	—	.231	.267	.333
Fred Corey	3B104	R	27	104	439	64	121	17	16	5	—	17	—	—	.276	.306	.421
Sadie Houck	SS108,2B1	R	28	108	472	93	140	19	14	0	—	7	—	—	.297	.318	.396
Lon Knight	OF108,P2,1B1	R	31	108	484	94	131	18	12	1	—	10	—	—	.271	.287	.364
Henry Larkin	OF85,2B2	R	24	85	326	59	90	21	9	3	—	15	—	—	.276	.324	.423
Jud Birchall	OF52,3B2	—	26	54	221	36	57	2	2	0	—	4	—	—	.258	.287	.285
Bobby Mathews	P49,OF1	R	32	40	104	20	34	5	1	0	—	7	—	—	.185	.215	.223
Jack O'Brien	C30,OF5,1B1	R	24	36	138	25	39	6	1	1	—	9	—	—	.283	.340	.362
Bob Blakiston†	OF28,3B2,1B1*	—	28	32	128	21	33	6	0	0	—	11	—	—	.258	.336	.305
John Coleman†	OF24,P3,1B2	L	21	28	107	16	22	2	3	2	—	5	—	—	.206	.241	.336
Al Atkinson†	P22,OF2	R	23	22	83	13	16	3	1	0	—	4	—	—	.193	.239	.253
Mike Mansell†	OF20	L	26	20	70	6	14	1	1	0	—	5	—	—	.200	.253	.243
Charlie Hilsey	P3,OF3	—	20	6	24	5	5	1	1	0	—	0	—	—	.208	.208	.333
Frank Siffell	C7	—	24	7	17	3	3	1	0	0	—	0	—	—	.176	.222	.235
Ed Rowen	C4	—	26	4	15	4	6	1	0	0	—	1	—	—	.400	.471	.467
Elmer Foster†	C4,OF1	R	22	4	11	4	2	0	0	0	—	3	—	—	.182	.357	.182
Frank Ringo†	C2	R	23	2	6	0	0	0	0	0	—	0	—	—	.000	.000	.000
Mike Moynahan†	OF1	L	28	1	4	0	0	0	0	0	—	0	—	—	.000	.000	.000

C. Stricker, 1 G at OF; B. Blakiston, 1 G at 2B, 1 G at SS

Lon Knight

Pitcher	T	Age	G	GS	CG	ShO	IP	H	HR	BB	SO	W-L	Sv	ERA
Bobby Mathews	R	32	49	49	48	3	430.2	401	10	49	286	30-18	0	3.32
Billy Taylor†	R	29	30	30	30	1	260.0	232	3	44	130	18-12	0	2.53
Al Atkinson†	R	23	22	22	20	1	184.0	186	3	21	93	11-11	0	4.21
Charlie Hilsey	—	20	3	3	3	0	27.0	29	0	5	10	2-1	0	4.67
John Coleman†	R	21	3	2	2	0	21.0	28	0	2	5	0-2	0	3.43
Lon Knight	R	31	2	1	1	0	14.0	24	0	4	2	0-1	0	9.00
Phenomenal Smith†	L	19	1	1	1	0	9.0	14	0	1	3	0-1	0	4.00
Cub Stricker	R	25	1	0	0	0	3.0	6	0	1	1	0-0	0	6.00

1884 Toledo Blue Stockings 8th AA 46-58 .442 27.5 GB

Player	Gm by Position	B	Age	G	AB	R	H	2B	3B	HR	RBI	BB	SO	SB	Avg	OBP	Slg
Fleet Walker	C41,OF1	R	27	42	152	23	40	2	3	0	—	8	—	—	.263	.300	.316
Chappy Lane	1B46,OF9,3B2*	R	—	57	215	26	49	9	5	1	—	2	—	—	.228	.242	.330
Sam Barkley	2B103,C2	R	26	104	435	71	133	39	9	1	—	22	—	—	.306	.342	.444
Ed Brown	3B40,OF2,P1*	—	—	42	153	13	27	3	0	0	—	2	—	—	.176	.187	.196
Joe Miller	SS105	R	23	105	423	46	101	12	8	1	—	26	—	—	.239	.284	.312
Curt Welch	OF107,C2,2B2*	R	22	109	425	61	95	24	5	0	—	10	—	—	.224	.248	.304
Tom Poorman	OF93,P1	L	26	94	382	56	89	8	7	0	—	10	—	—	.233	.254	.291
Frank Olin†	OF26	L	24	26	86	16	22	0	1	1	—	5	—	—	.256	.304	.314
Tony Mullane	P68,OF18,1B7*	S	25	95	352	49	97	19	3	3	—	33	—	—	.276	.339	.372
Hank O'Day	P39,OF24,1B3*	—	21	64	242	23	51	9	1	0	—	10	—	—	.211	.245	.256
Joe Moffett	1B38,3B11,2B4*	—	25	56	204	17	41	5	3	0	—	2	—	—	.201	.209	.255
Deacon McGuire	C41,OF4,SS3	R	20	45	151	12	28	7	0	1	—	5	—	—	.185	.217	.252
John Meister	3B34	—	20	34	119	9	23	6	0	0	—	3	—	—	.193	.244	.244
Charlie Morton	3B16,OF15,P3*	R	29	32	111	11	18	6	2	0	—	7	—	—	.162	.212	.252
Trick McSorley	1B16,OF5,P1*	R	31	21	68	12	17	1	0	0	—	3	—	—	.250	.282	.265
John Tilley†	OF17	—	28	17	56	5	10	2	0	0	—	4	—	—	.179	.246	.214
Tug Arundel	C15	—	22	15	47	6	4	0	0	0	—	3	—	—	.085	.140	.085
Sim Bullas	C12,OF2	R	23	13	45	4	4	0	1	0	—	1	—	—	.089	.109	.133
Ed Miller	OF8	—	—	8	24	2	6	0	0	0	—	1	—	—	.250	.280	.250
Welday Walker	OF5	—	23	5	18	1	4	1	0	0	—	0	—	—	.222	.417	.278

C. Lane, 1 G at C; E. Brown, 1 G at C; C. Welch, 1 G at 1B; T. Mullane, 6 G at 3B, 1 G at 2B, 1 G at SS; H. O'Day, 3 G at 3B; J. Moffett, 3 G at OF; C. Morton, 1 G at 2B; T. McSorley, 1 G at 3B

Charlie Morton

Pitcher	T	Age	G	GS	CG	ShO	IP	H	HR	BB	SO	W-L	Sv	ERA
Tony Mullane	R	25	67	65	64	7	567.0	481	5	89	325	36-26	0	2.52
Hank O'Day	R	21	41	40	35	2	326.2	335	6	66	163	9-28	1	3.75
Ed Kent	R	25	1	1	1	0	9.0	14	0	3	4	0-1	0	6.00
Ed Brown	R	—	1	1	1	0	9.0	19	0	4	1	0-1	0	9.00
Tom Poorman	R	26	1	1	1	0	9.0	13	1	2	0	0-1	0	3.00
Charlie Morton	R	29	3	1	1	0	23.1	18	0	5	7	0-1	0	3.09
Trick McSorley	R	31	1	0	0	0	2.0	5	0	0	1	0-0	0	4.50

1884 Brooklyn Bridegrooms 9th AA 40-64 .385 33.5 GB

George Taylor

Player	Gm by Position	B	Age	G	AB	R	H	2B	3B	HR	RBI	BB	SO	SB	Avg	OBP	Slg
Jack Corcoran	C38,OF9,2B4*	—	24	52	185	17	39	4	3	0	—	8	—	—	.211	.251	.265
Charlie Householder	1B40,C31,OF6*	L	28	76	273	28	66	15	3	3	—	12	—	—	.242	.279	.352
Bill Greenwood	2B92,SS1	S	27	92	385	52	83	8	3	3	—	10	—	—	.216	.237	.275
Fred Warner	3B84	—	29	84	352	40	78	4	0	1	—	17	—	—	.222	.259	.241
Billy Geer†	SS107,P2,2B2	—	34	107	391	68	82	15	7	0	—	38	—	—	.210	.281	.284
John Cassidy	OF101,3B4,SS1	R	27	106	433	57	109	11	6	2	—	19	—	—	.252	.286	.319
Jack Remsen†	OF81	R	34	81	301	45	67	6	6	3	—	23	—	—	.223	.278	.312
Oscar Walker	OF59,1B36	L	30	95	382	59	103	12	8	2	—	9	—	—	.270	.292	.359
Adonis Terry	P57,OF13	R	19	68	240	16	56	10	3	0	—	8	—	—	.233	.258	.300
Ike Benners†	OF49	L	28	49	189	25	38	11	5	1	—	7	—	—	.201	.237	.328
Jimmy Knowles†	1B30,3B11	—	25	41	153	19	36	5	1	1	—	3	—	—	.235	.255	.301
Charlie Jones	2B13,3B11,OF2	—	—	25	90	10	16	1	0	0	—	5	—	—	.178	.221	.189
Tug Wilson	OF12,C10,1B3*	—	24	24	82	13	19	4	0	0	—	5	—	—	.232	.276	.280
John Farrow	C16	L	30	16	58	7	11	2	0	0	—	3	—	—	.190	.230	.224
Jackie Hayes†	C14,OF2	—	23	16	51	4	12	3	0	0	—	3	—	—	.235	.278	.294
Jim Conway	P13,SS2,OF2	—	25	14	47	1	6	0	0	0	—	0	—	—	.128	.128	.128
Jerry Dorgan†	C4	L	28	4	13	2	4	0	0	0	—	0	—	—	.308	.308	.308

J. Corcoran, 2 G at SS, 1 G at P; C. Householder, 1 G at 2B; T. Wilson, 1 G at 2B

Pitcher	T	Age	G	GS	CG	ShO	IP	H	HR	BB	SO	W-L	Sv	ERA
Adonis Terry	R	19	57	56	55	3	485.0	487	10	75	233	20-35	0	3.49
Sam Kimber	R	31	40	40	40	3	352.1	363	6	69	119	17-20	0	3.91
Jim Conway	R	25	13	13	10	0	105.1	132	4	15	25	3-9	0	4.44
Billy Geer	R	34	2	0	0	0	5.0	14	0	3	1	0-0	0	12.60
Jack Corcoran	—	24	1	0	0	0	1.0	0	0	1	0	0-0	0	0.00

1884 Richmond Virginians 10th AA 12-30 .286 32.5 GB

Felix Moses

Player	Gm by Position	B	Age	G	AB	R	H	2B	3B	HR	RBI	BB	SO	SB	Avg	OBP	Slg
John Hanna†	C21,SS1	—	20	22	67	6	13	2	1	0	—	0	—	—	.194	.206	.254
Jim Powell	1B41	—	24	41	151	23	37	8	4	0	—	7	—	—	.245	.296	.351
Terry Larkin†	2B40	R	—	40	139	17	28	1	4	0	—	9	—	—	.201	.265	.266
Billy Nash	3B45	R	19	45	166	31	33	8	8	1	—	12	—	—	.199	.281	.361
Bill Schenck	SS40,2B2	—	—	42	151	14	31	4	0	3	—	1	—	—	.205	.216	.291
Ed Glenn	OF43	R	23	43	175	26	43	2	4	1	—	5	—	—	.246	.271	.320
Dick Johnston	OF37,SS2	R	21	39	146	23	41	5	5	2	—	2	—	—	.281	.291	.425
Mike Mansell†	OF29	L	26	29	113	21	34	2	5	0	—	8	—	—	.301	.363	.407
Marshall Quinton	C14,OF10,SS2	—	—	26	94	12	22	5	0	0	—	0	—	—	.234	.242	.287
Pete Meegan	P22,OF1	—	20	23	75	6	12	1	2	0	—	2	—	—	.160	.182	.227
Ed Dugan	P20,2B2	—	20	22	70	4	8	0	0	0	—	5	—	—	.114	.184	.114
Walt Goldsby†	OF11	L	22	11	40	4	9	1	0	0	—	1	—	—	.225	.262	.250
Bill Dugan†	C9	—	20	9	28	4	2	1	0	0	—	0	—	—	.071	.103	.107
Bill Morgan†	C3,OF2,2B1	—	—	6	20	0	2	0	0	0	—	1	—	—	.100	.143	.100
Andy Swan†	1B3	—	39	3	10	2	5	0	0	0	—	0	—	—	.500	.500	.500
Wash Williams	OF2	—	—	2	8	0	2	0	0	0	—	0	—	—	.250	.250	.250
Ed Ford	1B1,SS1	—	22	2	5	0	0	0	0	0	—	0	—	—	.000	.000	.000

Pitcher	T	Age	G	GS	CG	ShO	IP	H	HR	BB	SO	W-L	Sv	ERA
Pete Meegan	—	20	22	22	22	1	179.0	177	7	29	106	7-12	0	4.32
Ed Dugan	—	20	20	20	20	0	166.1	196	5	15	60	5-14	0	4.49
Wes Curry	—	24	2	2	2	0	16.0	15	2	3	1	0-2	0	5.06
Ted Firth	—	29	1	1	1	0	9.0	14	0	5	0	0-1	0	8.00

1884 Pittsburgh Alleghenys 11th AA 30-78 .278 45.5 GB

D. McKnight (4-8)/B. Ferguson (11-31)/J. Battin (6-7)/G. Creamer (0-8)/H. Phillips (9-24)

Player	Gm by Position	B	Age	G	AB	R	H	2B	3B	HR	RBI	BB	SO	SB	Avg	OBP	Slg
Ed Colgan	C44,OF4	—	—	48	161	10	25	4	1	0	—	3	—	—	.155	.171	.193
Jimmy Knowles†	1B46	—	25	46	182	19	42	5	7	0	—	5	—	—	.231	.259	.335
George Creamer	2B98	R	29	98	339	38	62	8	5	0	—	16	—	—	.183	.224	.236
Joe Battin†	3B43	R	32	43	158	10	28	1	2	0	—	3	—	—	.177	.198	.209
Bill White	SS60,3B10,OF4	—	24	74	291	25	66	7	10	0	—	13	—	—	.227	.262	.320
Ed Swartwood	OF79,1B22,P1*	L	25	102	399	74	115	19	6	0	—	33	—	—	.288	.365	.366
Doggie Miller	OF49,C36,3B3*	R	19	89	347	46	78	10	2	0	—	13	—	—	.225	.257	.265
Live Oak Taylor	OF41	—	—	41	152	22	32	4	1	0	—	6	—	—	.211	.255	.250
Fleury Sullivan	P51,OF3	—	22	54	189	14	29	2	1	0	—	5	—	—	.153	.175	.175
Jack Neagle	P38,OF6	R	26	43	148	13	22	6	0	0	—	6	—	—	.149	.187	.189
Jim McDonald†	3B22,OF15,2B1	—	23	38	145	11	23	3	0	0	—	2	—	—	.159	.170	.179
Tom Forster	SS28,3B6,2B1	R	25	35	126	10	28	5	0	0	—	7	—	—	.222	.263	.262
Jackie Hayes†	C24,1B5,OF3*	—	23	33	124	11	28	6	1	0	—	4	—	—	.226	.256	.290
Charlie Eden	OF31,P2	L	29	32	122	12	33	7	4	1	—	7	—	—	.270	.341	.418
Jay Faatz	1B29	R	23	29	112	18	27	2	3	0	—	1	—	—	.241	.274	.313
Mike Mansell†	OF27	L	26	27	100	15	14	0	3	1	—	7	—	—	.140	.204	.230
Art Whitney	3B21,SS1,OF1	R	26	23	94	10	28	4	0	0	—	1	—	—	.298	.305	.340
Billy Reid	OF17,2B1,3B1	L	27	19	70	11	17	2	0	0	—	4	—	—	.243	.293	.271
Conny Doyle	OF14,SS1	—	22	15	58	8	17	3	2	0	—	2	—	—	.293	.317	.414
Jimmy Woulfe†	OF15	—	24	15	53	7	6	1	0	0	—	0	—	—	.113	.113	.132
Chuck Lauer	OF10,P3,1B1	—	19	13	44	5	5	0	0	0	—	0	—	—	.114	.114	.114
Joe Quest†	2B7,SS5	R	31	12	43	2	9	3	0	0	—	0	—	—	.209	.227	.279
Bob Ferguson	OF6,1B3,3B1	S	39	10	41	2	6	0	0	0	—	0	—	—	.146	.146	.146
Jim Dee	SS12	—	—	12	40	0	5	0	0	0	—	1	—	—	.125	.146	.125
Frank Smith	C7,OF3	—	26	10	36	3	9	0	1	0	—	0	—	—	.250	.250	.306
Jack Gorman†	P3,OF3,3B2	—	25	8	27	3	4	0	1	0	—	1	—	—	.148	.179	.222
John Fox	P7,SS1	—	25	8	25	4	6	2	0	0	—	0	—	—	.240	.240	.320
Charlie Hautz	1B5,OF2	R	32	7	24	0	5	0	0	0	—	3	—	—	.208	.296	.208
Gus Alberts†	SS2	R	16	2	5	1	1	0	0	0	—	0	—	—	.200	.200	.200
John Peters	SS1	R	34	1	4	0	0	0	0	0	—	0	—	—	.000	.000	.000
Jim Gray	3B1	—	21	1	2	0	1	0	0	0	—	0	—	—	.500	.500	.500

E. Swartwood, 1 G at 3B; D. Miller, 1 G at 2B; J. Hayes, 1 G at 2B

Pitcher	T	Age	G	GS	CG	ShO	IP	H	HR	BB	SO	W-L	Sv	ERA
Fleury Sullivan	—	22	51	51	51	2	441.0	496	15	96	189	16-35	0	4.20
Jack Neagle	R	26	38	38	37	2	326.0	354	6	70	85	11-26	0	3.73
John Fox	—	25	7	7	7	0	59.0	76	2	16	22	1-6	0	5.64
Bill Nelson	R	20	3	3	3	0	26.0	26	1	8	6	1-2	0	4.50
Frank Beck†	R	23	3	3	3	0	25.0	33	0	6	11	0-3	0	6.12
Jack Gorman	—	25	3	3	3	0	25.0	22	0	5	10	1-2	0	4.68
Chuck Lauer	R	19	3	3	2	0	19.0	23	0	9	8	0-2	0	7.58
Charlie Eden	L	29	2	1	1	0	12.0	12	1	3	3	0-1	0	6.00
Phenomenal Smith†	L	19	1	1	1	0	8.0	11	0	2	4	0-1	0	9.00
Ed Swartwood	R	25	1	0	0	0	2.1	6	0	1	0	0-0	0	11.57

1884 Indianapolis Blues 12th AA 29-78 .271 46.0 GB

Jim Gifford (25-60)/Bill Watkins (4-18)

Player	Gm by Position	B	Age	G	AB	R	H	2B	3B	HR	RBI	BB	SO	SB	Avg	OBP	Slg
Jim Keenan	C59,1B6,OF2*	R	26	68	249	36	73	14	4	3	—	16	—	—	.293	.343	.418
John Kerins	1B87,C5,OF5*	R	25	94	364	58	78	10	3	6	—	6	—	—	.214	.229	.308
Ed Merrill	2B55	—	24	55	196	14	35	3	1	0	—	6	—	—	.179	.207	.204
Pat Callahan	3B61	—	17	61	258	38	67	8	5	2	—	8	—	—	.260	.282	.353
Marr Phillips	SS97	R	27	97	413	41	111	18	8	0	—	5	—	—	.269	.279	.351
John Peltz	OF106	R	23	106	393	40	86	13	17	3	—	7	—	—	.219	.236	.361
Podge Weihe	OF58,2B4,1B3	R	21	63	256	29	65	13	2	4	—	9	—	—	.254	.279	.367
Jon Morrison	OF44	L	25	44	182	26	48	6	8	1	—	7	—	—	.264	.306	.401
Larry McKeon	P61,1B5,2B3*	—	18	70	250	29	53	8	1	0	—	1	—	—	.212	.215	.252
Jerry Dorgan†	OF29,C5	L	28	34	141	22	42	6	1	0	—	2	—	—	.298	.317	.355
Chub Collins†	2B38	S	26	38	138	18	31	3	1	0	—	9	—	—	.225	.272	.261
Jim Donnelly†	3B24,SS8,OF6*	R	18	40	134	22	34	2	2	0	—	5	—	—	.254	.301	.299
Bill Watkins	3B23,2B9,SS2	—	26	34	127	16	26	4	0	0	—	5	—	—	.205	.241	.236
Jon Sneed	OF27	—	—	27	102	14	22	4	0	1	—	6	—	—	.216	.259	.284
Tug Thompson	C12,OF12	L	—	24	97	10	20	3	0	0	—	2	—	—	.206	.222	.237
Charlie Robinson	C17,SS3,OF1	L	27	20	80	11	23	2	0	0	—	3	—	—	.288	.313	.313
Bob Barr†	P16,OF2	R	27	18	65	6	12	3	2	0	—	3	—	—	.185	.221	.292
Al McCauley	P10,1B5,OF3	L	21	17	53	7	10	0	1	0	—	12	—	—	.189	.358	.226
Jake Aydelott	P12,OF1	—	22	12	44	1	5	1	0	0	—	2	—	—	.114	.152	.136
Gene Moriarity†	OF7,P2,3B1	L	19	10	37	4	8	0	2	0	—	0	—	—	.216	.216	.324
Bill Butler	OF9	—	23	9	31	7	7	3	2	0	—	1	—	—	.226	.250	.452
Marshall Locke	OF7	—	27	7	29	5	7	0	1	0	—	0	—	—	.241	.241	.310
Tommy Bond†	P5,OF2	R	28	7	23	0	3	1	1	0	—	0	—	—	.130	.130	.261
Jim Tray	C4,1B2	—	24	6	21	2	6	0	0	0	—	2	—	—	.286	.348	.286
Bob Blakiston†	1B5,OF1	—	28	6	18	0	4	1	0	0	—	1	—	—	.222	.263	.278
Jim Holdsworth	OF5	R	33	5	18	1	2	0	0	0	—	2	—	—	.111	.200	.111
Harry Decker†	C4	R	29	4	15	1	4	1	0	0	—	1	—	—	.267	.313	.333
Marty Barrett†	C4,OF1	R	23	5	13	1	1	1	0	0	—	1	—	—	.077	.143	.154
Charlie Levis†	1B3	R	24	3	10	0	2	0	0	0	—	0	—	—	.200	.200	.200
Joe Webber	C3	—	22	3	8	0	0	0	0	0	—	0	—	—	.000	.111	.000
Charlie Reising	OF2	—	22	2	8	0	0	0	0	0	—	1	—	—	.000	.111	.000
Frank Monroe	C1,OF1	—	—	2	8	1	0	0	0	0	—	0	—	—	.000	.000	.000
George Mundinger	C3	R	29	3	8	1	2	0	0	0	—	0	—	—	.250	.250	.250
Pete Fries	OF1	L	26	1	3	0	1	1	0	0	—	1	—	—	.333	.500	.667

J. Keenan, 1 G at P, 1 G at SS; J. Kerins, 1 G at 3B; L. McKeon, 1 G at OF; J. Donnelly, 2 G at 2B

Pitcher	T	Age	G	GS	CG	ShO	IP	H	HR	BB	SO	W-L	Sv	ERA
Larry McKeon	—	18	61	60	59	2	512.0	488	20	94	308	18-41	0	3.50
Bob Barr†	R	27	16	16	15	0	132.0	160	2	19	69	3-11	0	4.98
Jake Aydelott	—	22	12	12	11	0	106.0	129	0	29	30	5-7	0	4.92
Al McCauley	L	21	10	9	9	0	76.0	87	2	25	34	2-7	0	5.09
Mac MacArthur	R	22	6	6	6	0	52.0	57	1	21	19	1-5	0	5.02
Tommy Bond†	R	28	5	5	5	0	43.0	62	5	4	15	0-5	0	5.65
Gene Moriarity	L	19	2	2	2	0	13.2	16	0	7	4	0-2	0	5.27
Jim Keenan	R	26	1	0	0	0	3.0	2	0	0	0	0-0	0	3.00

1884 Washington DC 13th AA 12-51 .190 41.0 GB

Holly Hollingshead (12-50)/Bickerson (0-1)

Player	Gm by Position	B	Age	G	AB	R	H	2B	3B	HR	RBI	BB	SO	SB	Avg	OBP	Slg
John Humphries†	C35,OF12,1B4	L	22	49	193	23	34	2	0	0	—	9	—	—	.176	.217	.187
Walter Prince†	1B43	L	23	43	166	22	36	3	2	1	—	13	—	—	.217	.286	.277
Thorny Hawkes	2B38,OF2	R	31	38	151	16	42	4	2	0	—	4	—	—	.278	.297	.331
Buck Gladman	3B53,OF2,SS1	—	20	56	224	17	35	5	3	1	—	3	—	—	.156	.178	.219
Frank Fennelly†	SS60,2B4	R	24	62	257	52	75	17	7	2	—	20	—	—	.292	.343	.436
Henry Mullin†	OF34,3B1	R	21	34	120	13	17	3	1	0	—	8	—	—	.142	.195	.183
Bill Morgan	OF31,C12,2B2*	—	—	45	162	8	28	1	1	0	—	8	—	—	.173	.216	.191
Ed Trumbull	OF15,P10	—	23	25	86	5	10	2	0	0	—	2	—	—	.116	.136	.140
Bob Barr†	P32,OF5,1B2	R	27	39	135	15	20	3	1	2	—	5	—	—	.148	.190	.230
Ed Yewell†	2B11,OF8,3B7*	—	21	27	93	14	23	3	1	0	—	1	—	—	.247	.263	.301
Frank Olin†	2B12,OF11	L	24	21	83	12	32	4	1	0	—	8	—	—	.386	.440	.458
John Hanna†	C18,OF6	—	20	23	76	8	5	0	0	0	—	6	—	—	.066	.134	.066
John Hamill	P19,OF3	R	23	21	71	5	7	0	2	0	—	6	—	—	.099	.169	.155
Edgar Smith	OF12,P3	R	22	14	57	5	5	0	1	0	—	1	—	—	.088	.103	.123
John Kiley	OF14	L	24	14	56	9	12	2	2	0	—	3	—	—	.214	.267	.321
Tom Farley	OF14	—	—	14	52	5	11	4	0	0	—	1	—	—	.212	.241	.288
Sam King	1B12	—	32	12	45	3	8	2	0	0	—	1	—	—	.178	.213	.222
Jack Beach	OF8	—	22	8	31	3	3	2	0	0	—	0	—	—	.097	.097	.161
Walt Goldsby†	OF6	L	22	6	24	4	9	0	0	0	—	1	—	—	.375	.400	.375
Andy Swan†	1B3,3B2	—	39	5	21	3	3	1	0	0	—	0	—	—	.143	.143	.190
Willie Murphy†	OF4,2B1	L	20	5	21	3	10	0	0	0	—	1	—	—	.476	.542	.476
— Jones	OF4	—	—	4	17	2	5	0	0	0	—	1	—	—	.294	.333	.294
— Wills†	OF4	—	—	4	15	1	2	2	0	0	—	0	—	—	.133	.133	.267
Lyman Drake	OF2	—	32	2	7	0	2	1	0	0	—	0	—	—	.286	.286	.429
Alex Gardner	C1	—	23	1	3	0	0	0	0	0	—	0	—	—	.000	.000	.000

B. Morgan, 2 G at SS; E. Yewell, 2 G at SS

Pitcher	T	Age	G	GS	CG	ShO	IP	H	HR	BB	SO	W-L	Sv	ERA
Bob Barr†	R	27	32	32	32	2	281.0	311	9	31	138	9-23	0	3.46
John Hamill	R	23	19	19	18	1	156.2	197	8	43	50	2-17	0	4.48
Ed Trumbull	—	23	10	10	10	0	84.0	108	4	31	43	1-9	0	4.71
Edgar Smith	R	22	3	2	2	0	22.0	27	0	5	4	0-2	0	4.91

»1884 St. Louis Maroons 1st UA 94-19 .832 —

Ted Sullivan (28-3)/Fred Dunlap (66-16)

Player	Gm by Position	B	Age	G	AB	R	H	2B	3B	HR	RBI	BB	SO	SB	Avg	OBP	Slg
George Baker	C68,2B4,OF4*	—	25	80	317	39	52	6	0	0	—	5	—	—	.164	.177	.183
Joe Quinn	1B100,OF3,SS1	R	19	103	429	74	116	21	1	0	—	9	—	—	.270	.285	.324
Fred Dunlap	2B100,P1,OF1	R	25	101	449	160	185	39	8	13	—	29	—	—	.412	.448	.621
Jack Gleason	3B92	R	29	92	395	90	128	30	2	4	—	23	—	—	.324	.361	.441
Milt Whitehead†	SS94,OF2,P1*	S	22	99	393	61	83	15	1	1	—	8	—	—	.211	.227	.262
Orator Shaffer	OF100,2B7,1B1	L	32	106	467	130	168	40	10	2	—	30	—	—	.360	.398	.501
Dave Rowe	OF92,SS14,1B2*	R	29	109	485	95	142	32	11	4	—	10	—	—	.293	.307	.429
Henry Boyle	OF43,P19,3B4*	—	23	65	262	41	68	10	3	4	—	9	—	—	.260	.284	.366
Jack Brennan	C33,OF16,3B7*	—	22	56	231	38	50	6	1	0	—	12	—	—	.216	.255	.251
B. Dickerson†	OF42,3B4	L	25	46	211	49	77	15	1	0	—	8	—	—	.365	.388	.445
Billy Taylor†	P33,1B10,OF4	R	29	43	186	44	68	23	1	3	—	7	—	—	.366	.389	.548
Charlie Sweeney†	P33,OF13,1B1	R	21	45	171	31	54	14	2	1	—	10	—	—	.316	.354	.439
Perry Werden	P16,OF6	R	18	18	76	7	18	2	0	0	—	2	—	—	.237	.256	.263
Tom Dolan†	C14,3B3,OF2	R	25	19	69	9	13	3	0	0	—	4	—	—	.188	.233	.232
Charlie Hodnett	P14,OF6	—	23	18	58	9	12	1	0	0	—	10	—	—	.207	.324	.224
Fred Lewis†	OF8	S	25	8	30	6	9	1	0	0	—	3	—	—	.300	.364	.333
Tom Ryder	OF8	L	—	8	28	4	7	1	0	0	—	2	—	—	.250	.300	.286
Sleeper Sullivan	P1,C1,OF1	R	—	2	9	0	1	0	0	0	—	0	—	—	.111	.111	.111
Dan Cronin†	OF1	—	27	1	5	0	0	0	0	0	—	0	—	—	.000	.000	.000
C.V. Matterson	P1,OF1	—	—	1	4	0	0	0	0	0	—	0	—	—	.000	.000	.000
Ed Callahan†	OF1	—	26	1	3	0	0	0	0	0	—	0	—	—	.000	.000	.000

G. Baker, 3 G at 3B, 2 G at SS; M. Whitehead, 1 G at 2B, 1 G at 3B; D. Rowe, 2 G at 2B, 1 G at P; H. Boyle, 1 G at 1B, 1 G at 2B, 1 G at SS; J. Brennan, 1 G at SS

Pitcher	T	Age	G	GS	CG	ShO	IP	H	HR	BB	SO	W-L	Sv	ERA
Charlie Sweeney†	R	21	33	32	31	2	271.0	207	2	13	192	24-7	0	1.83
Billy Taylor†	R	29	33	29	29	2	263.0	222	2	40	154	25-4	4	1.68
Henry Boyle	R	23	19	16	16	2	150.0	118	3	10	88	15-3	1	1.74
Perry Werden	R	18	16	16	12	1	141.1	113	1	22	51	12-1	0	1.97
Charlie Hodnett	—	23	14	14	12	1	121.0	121	0	16	41	12-2	0	2.01
John Cattanach†	—	21	2	2	2	0	17.0	12	0	4	13	1-1	0	2.12
Dave Rowe	R	29	1	1	1	0	9.0	10	0	0	2	1-0	0	2.00
Milt Whitehead	—	22	1	1	1	0	8.0	14	0	2	2	0-1	0	9.00
C.V. Matterson	—	—	1	1	0	0	6.0	9	1	3	3	1-0	0	9.00
Sleeper Sullivan	R	—	1	1	0	0	6.0	10	0	0	3	1-0	0	4.50
Fred Dunlap	R	25	1	0	0	0	0.2	2	0	0	1	0-0	1	13.50

1884 Milwaukee Grays 2nd UA 8-4 .667 50.5 GB

Tom Loftus

Player	Gm by Position	B	Age	G	AB	R	H	2B	3B	HR	RBI	BB	SO	SB	Avg	OBP	Slg
Cal Broughton	C7,OF5	R	23	11	39	5	12	5	0	0	—	0	—	—	.308	.308	.436
Thomas Griffin	1B11	—	27	11	41	5	9	2	0	0	—	3	—	—	.220	.273	.268
Bert Myers	2B12	R	20	12	46	6	15	6	0	0	—	0	—	—	.326	.326	.457
Tom Morrissey	3B12	—	23	12	47	3	8	2	0	0	—	0	—	—	.170	.170	.213
Tom Sexton	SS12	—	19	12	47	9	11	2	0	0	—	4	—	—	.234	.294	.277
Eddie Hogan	OF11	R	24	11	37	6	3	1	0	0	—	7	—	—	.081	.227	.108
Steve Behel	OF9	—	23	9	33	5	8	1	0	0	—	3	—	—	.242	.306	.273
Lady Baldwin	OF5,P2	L	25	7	27	6	6	3	0	0	—	0	—	—	.222	.222	.333
Henry Porter	P6,OF4,1B1	R	25	11	40	3	11	3	0	0	—	0	—	—	.275	.275	.350
Anton Falch	OF3,C2	—	23	5	18	0	2	0	0	0	—	0	—	—	.111	.111	.111
George Bignell	C4	—	25	4	9	4	2	0	0	0	—	1	—	—	.222	.300	.222

Pitcher	T	Age	G	GS	CG	ShO	IP	H	HR	BB	SO	W-L	Sv	ERA
Henry Porter	R	25	6	6	6	1	51.0	32	1	9	71	3-3	0	3.00
Ed Cushman	L	32	4	4	4	2	36.0	10	0	3	47	4-0	0	1.00
Lady Baldwin	L	25	2	2	2	0	17.0	7	0	1	21	1-1	0	2.65

1884 Cincinnati Outlaw Reds 3rd UA 69-36 .657 21.0 GB

Dan O'Leary (20-15)/Sam Crane (49-21)

Player	Gm by Position	B	Age	G	AB	R	H	2B	3B	HR	RBI	BB	SO	SB	Avg	OBP	Slg
John Kelly†	C37,OF2	R	25	38	142	23	40	5	1	1	—	6	—	—	.282	.311	.352
Martin Powell	1B43	L	28	43	185	46	59	4	2	1	—	13	—	—	.319	.364	.378
Sam Crane	2B80	R	30	80	309	56	72	9	3	1	—	11	—	—	.233	.259	.291
Charlie Barber	3B55	R	30	55	204	38	41	1	4	0	—	11	—	—	.201	.242	.245
Jack Jones	SS41,2B19,3B10	—	—	69	272	36	71	5	1	2	—	12	—	—	.261	.292	.309
Lou Sylvester	OF81,P6,SS2	R	29	82	333	67	89	13	8	2	—	18	—	—	.267	.305	.372
Bill Harbidge	OF80,SS3,1B2	L	29	82	341	59	95	12	5	2	—	25	—	—	.279	.328	.361
Bill Hawes	OF50,1B21	R	30	79	349	80	97	7	4	4	—	5	—	—	.278	.288	.355
Dick Burns	OF44,P40,SS2	L	20	79	350	84	107	17	12	4	—	5	—	—	.306	.315	.457
George Bradley	P41,OF16,SS5*	R	31	58	226	31	43	4	7	0	—	7	—	—	.190	.215	.270
Jack Glasscock†	SS36,2B2	R	24	38	172	48	72	9	5	2	—	8	—	—	.419	.444	.564
Mox McQuery	1B35	—	23	35	132	31	37	5	0	2	—	8	—	—	.280	.321	.364
Dan O'Leary	OF32	L	27	32	132	14	34	0	2	1	—	5	—	—	.258	.285	.311
Elmer Cleveland	3B29	R	21	29	115	24	37	9	2	0	—	4	—	—	.322	.345	.435
Jim McCormick†	P24,OF3	R	27	27	110	12	27	3	1	0	—	0	—	—	.245	.245	.291
Bill Schwartz	C25,OF3,3B1	R	20	29	106	14	25	4	0	1	—	3	—	—	.236	.257	.302
Fatty Briody†	C22	—	25	22	89	11	30	2	2	0	—	1	—	—	.337	.344	.404
Joe Crotty	C21	R	23	21	84	11	22	4	2	1	—	1	—	—	.262	.271	.393
Frank McLaughlin†	SS16	R	28	16	67	10	16	4	1	2	—	2	—	—	.239	.261	.418
Ed Kennedy	3B8,SS4,OF1	R	23	13	48	6	10	1	1	0	—	1	—	—	.208	.224	.271
Fred Robinson	2B3	R	27	3	13	1	3	0	0	0	—	0	—	—	.231	.231	.231
John Ewing†	OF1	—	21	1	4	0	0	0	0	0	—	0	—	—	.000	.000	.000
Lou Meyers	C2,OF1	R	24	2	3	1	0	0	0	0	—	1	—	—	.000	.250	.000

G. Bradley, 2 G at 1B

Pitcher	T	Age	G	GS	CG	ShO	IP	H	HR	BB	SO	W-L	Sv	ERA
Dick Burns	L	20	40	40	34	1	329.2	298	7	47	167	23-15	0	2.46
George Bradley	R	31	41	38	36	3	342.0	350	7	23	168	25-15	0	2.71
Jim McCormick†	R	27	24	24	24	7	210.0	151	3	14	161	21-3	0	1.54
Lou Sylvester	R	29	6	1	1	0	32.2	32	0	6	7	0-1	1	3.58

1884 Baltimore Monumentals 4th UA 58-47 .552 32.0 GB

Bill Henderson

Player	Gm by Position	B	Age	G	AB	R	H	2B	3B	HR	RBI	BB	SO	SB	Avg	OBP	Slg
Eddie Fusselback	C54,3B6,SS5*	R	25	68	303	60	86	16	3	1	—	3	—	—	.284	.291	.366
Charlie Levis†	1B87	R	24	87	373	59	85	11	4	6	—	3	—	—	.228	.234	.327
Dick Phelan	2B100,3B3	R	29	101	402	63	99	13	3	3	—	12	—	—	.246	.268	.316
Yank Robinson	3B71,SS14,P11*	R	24	102	415	101	111	24	4	2	—	37	—	—	.267	.327	.359
Lou Say†	SS78	R	30	78	339	65	81	14	2	2	—	11	—	—	.239	.263	.310
Emmett Seery†	OF103,C3,3B2	L	23	105	463	113	144	25	7	2	—	20	—	—	.311	.340	.408
Ned Cuthbert	OF44	R	39	44	168	29	34	5	0	0	—	10	—	—	.202	.247	.232
Bernie Graham†	OF40,1B1	—	24	41	167	21	45	11	0	0	—	2	—	—	.269	.278	.335
Bill Sweeney	P62,OF11,2B6*	—	—	74	296	35	71	7	0	0	—	9	—	—	.240	.262	.264
Rooney Sweeney	C33,OF16,3B1	—	24	48	186	37	42	7	1	0	—	15	—	—	.226	.284	.274
Henry Oberbeck†	OF28,3B8,P2	—	26	33	125	19	23	4	0	0	—	3	—	—	.184	.203	.216
Tom Lee†	P15,OF6,3B3*	—	22	21	82	11	23	1	0	0	—	5	—	—	.280	.322	.293
John O'Brien	OF18	—	32	18	77	7	19	1	1	0	—	2	—	—	.247	.266	.286
Harry Wheeler†	OF17	R	26	17	69	3	18	2	0	0	—	0	—	—	.261	.261	.290
Jumbo Schoeneck†	1B15,SS1	R	22	16	60	5	15	2	0	0	—	0	—	—	.250	.250	.283
Joe Battin†	3B17	R	32	17	59	3	6	1	0	0	—	0	—	—	.102	.102	.119
— Scott	OF13,3B1	—	—	13	53	10	12	1	1	1	—	2	—	—	.226	.255	.340
Phenomenal Smith†	P9,OF5	L	19	9	34	2	5	0	0	0	—	2	—	—	.147	.194	.147
Joe Ellick†	SS6,OF1	—	30	7	27	2	4	0	0	0	—	2	—	—	.148	.207	.148
John Ryan	P6,OF2	L	—	7	25	2	2	0	0	0	—	2	—	—	.080	.148	.080
Joe Stanley	OF6	—	—	6	21	3	5	1	0	0	—	0	—	—	.238	.238	.286
Frank Beck†	OF4,P2	—	23	5	20	1	2	1	0	0	—	0	—	—	.100	.100	.150
Chris McFarland	OF3,P1	—	22	3	14	2	3	1	0	0	—	0	—	—	.214	.214	.286
Frank Shaffer†	OF3	—	—	3	13	1	1	0	0	0	—	0	—	—	.077	.077	.077
John Cuff	C3	—	20	3	11	1	1	1	0	0	—	1	—	—	.091	.167	.182
Tony Suck†	C3	—	26	3	10	2	3	0	0	0	—	0	—	—	.300	.300	.300
Bill Morgan†	C1,2B1,OF1	—	—	2	9	1	2	0	0	0	—	1	—	—	.222	.300	.222
Frank Bahret	OF2	—	—	2	8	0	0	0	0	0	—	0	—	—	.000	.000	.000
Pat Burns†	1B1	—	—	1	4	0	2	0	0	0	—	0	—	—	.500	.500	.500
Gid Gardner†	SS1	—	25	1	4	0	1	0	0	0	—	0	—	—	.250	.250	.250
E. Morris	P1,OF1	—	—	1	3	0	0	0	0	0	—	0	—	—	.000	.000	.000
Charles Skinner†	OF1	—	—	1	3	0	1	0	0	0	—	0	—	—	.333	.333	.333
Jerry Dorsey	P1,OF1	—	30	1	3	0	0	0	0	0	—	0	—	—	.000	.000	.000
Bill Tierney	OF1	—	26	1	3	0	1	0	0	0	—	1	—	—	.333	.500	.333

E. Fusselback, 4 G at OF; Y. Robinson, 11 G at C, 3 G at 2B; B. Sweeney, 1 G at 1B, 1 G at SS; T. Lee, 1 G at SS

Pitcher	T	Age	G	GS	CG	ShO	IP	H	HR	BB	SO	W-L	Sv	ERA
Bill Sweeney	R	—	62	60	58	4	538.0	522	13	74	374	40-21	0	2.59
Tom Lee†	—	22	15	14	12	0	122.0	121	1	29	81	5-8	0	3.39
Al Atkinson†	R	23	8	8	8	0	69.2	60	4	12	50	3-5	0	2.33
Phenomenal Smith†	L	19	9	8	5	0	62.0	86	2	17	13	3-4	0	3.48
John Ryan	R	—	6	6	5	0	51.0	61	1	16	33	3-2	0	3.35
Frank Beck†	R	23	2	2	1	0	9.0	17	0	4	7	0-2	0	8.00
— Smith	—	—	1	1	0	0	6.0	12	0	2	2	0-0	0	9.00
Henry Oberbeck†	—	26	2	1	0	0	6.0	9	0	2	1	0-0	0	3.00
Jerry Dorsey	—	30	1	1	0	0	4.0	7	1	0	3	0-1	0	9.00
Chris McFarland	—	22	1	1	0	0	3.0	9	1	1	3	0-1	0	15.00
Yank Robinson	R	24	11	3	3	0	75.0	96	1	18	61	3-3	0	3.48
E. Morris	—	—	1	0	0	0	1.0	2	0	2	0	0-0	0	9.00

1884 Boston Unions 5th UA 58-51 .532 34.0 GB

Tim Murnane

Player	Gm by Position	B	Age	G	AB	R	H	2B	3B	HR	RBI	BB	SO	SB	Avg	OBP	Slg
Lew Brown	C54,1B33,OF2*	R	26	85	325	50	75	18	3	1	—	13	—	—	.231	.260	.314
Tim Murnane	1B63,OF16	L	32	76	311	55	73	5	2	0	—	22	—	—	.235	.285	.264
Tom O'Brien	2B99,OF3,1B2*	R	24	103	449	80	118	31	8	4	—	12	—	—	.263	.282	.394
John Irwin	3B105	L	22	105	432	81	101	22	6	1	—	15	—	—	.234	.260	.319
Walter Hackett	SS103	—	26	103	415	71	101	19	0	1	—	7	—	—	.243	.256	.296
Mike Slattery	OF96,1B11	L	17	106	413	60	86	6	2	0	—	4	—	—	.208	.216	.232
Ed Crane	OF57,C42,1B5*	R	22	101	428	83	122	23	6	12	—	14	—	—	.285	.308	.451
Kid Butler	OF53,2B12,SS6*	—	23	71	255	36	43	15	0	0	—	12	—	—	.169	.206	.227
Tommy McCarthy	OF48,P7	R	20	53	209	37	45	2	2	0	—	6	—	—	.215	.237	.244
Walter Burke	P38,OF13	—	—	47	184	21	41	8	3	0	—	6	—	—	.223	.247	.299
Tommy Bond†	P23,OF17,3B1	R	28	37	162	21	48	8	0	0	—	4	—	—	.296	.313	.346
Dupee Shaw†	P39,OF9	L	25	44	153	13	37	8	0	0	—	5	—	—	.242	.266	.294
Jim McKeever	C12,OF4	—	23	16	66	13	9	0	0	0	—	0	—	—	.136	.136	.136
Joe Flynn†	C7,OF4,1B1	—	—	9	31	4	7	2	0	0	—	2	—	—	.226	.273	.290
Patrick Scannell	OF6	—	23	6	24	2	7	1	0	0	—	0	—	—	.292	.292	.333
Ed Callahan†	OF4	—	26	4	13	2	5	0	0	0	—	1	—	—	.385	.429	.385
Joe Reilly	OF2,3B1	—	23	3	11	1	0	0	0	0	—	1	—	—	.000	.083	.000
Charlie Daniels	P2,OF1	—	22	3	11	1	3	0	0	0	—	2	—	—	.273	.385	.273
Henry Mullin†	OF2	R	21	2	8	1	0	0	0	0	—	0	—	—	.000	.000	.000
Art Sladen	OF2	—	23	2	7	0	0	0	0	0	—	0	—	—	.000	.000	.000
Clarence Dow	OF1	—	29	1	6	1	2	0	0	0	—	0	—	—	.333	.333	.333
John Rudderham	OF1	R	20	1	4	0	1	0	0	0	—	0	—	—	.250	.250	.250
— Murphy	C1,OF1	—	—	1	3	0	0	0	0	0	—	1	—	—	.000	.250	.000
Elias Peak†	OF1	—	25	1	3	2	2	0	0	0	—	1	—	—	.667	.750	.667

L. Brown, 1 G at P; T. O'Brien, 1 G at C; E. Crane, 4 G at P; K. Butler, 2 G at 3B

Pitcher	T	Age	G	GS	CG	ShO	IP	H	HR	BB	SO	W-L	Sv	ERA
Dupee Shaw†	L	25	39	38	35	5	315.2	227	1	37	309	21-15	0	1.77
Walter Burke	—	—	38	36	34	0	322.0	326	10	31	255	19-15	0	2.85
Tommy Bond†	R	28	23	21	19	0	189.0	185	3	14	128	13-9	0	3.00
Tommy McCarthy	R	20	7	6	5	0	56.0	73	2	14	18	0-7	0	4.82
Fred Tenney†	—	24	4	4	4	0	35.0	31	0	5	18	3-1	0	2.31
Ed Crane	R	22	4	2	1	0	18.0	17	1	6	13	0-2	0	4.00
Charlie Daniels	—	22	2	2	2	0	16.2	20	0	2	12	0-2	0	4.32
Lew Brown	R	26	1	0	0	0	1.0	6	0	1	0	0-0	1	36.00

1884 Chicago Browns 6th UA 34-39 .466 40.0 GB

Ed Hengle

Player	Gm by Position	B	Age	G	AB	R	H	2B	3B	HR	RBI	BB	SO	SB	Avg	OBP	Slg
Bill Krieg†	C43,OF19,1B1*	R	25	61	240	27	55	10	3	0	—	10	—	—	.229	.260	.296
Jumbo Schoeneck†	1B72	R	22	72	289	47	94	19	2	2	—	7	—	—	.325	.341	.426
Moxie Hengle†	2B19	R	26	19	74	9	15	2	1	0	—	3	—	—	.203	.234	.257
C. Householder†	3B41,OF23,SS3*	R	28	66	244	28	57	8	3	1	—	11	—	—	.234	.267	.303
Steve Matthias	SS36,OF2	—	24	37	142	24	39	7	1	0	—	5	—	—	.275	.299	.338
Joe Ellick†	OF57,SS15,2B4	—	30	74	314	58	80	8	0	0	—	13	—	—	.255	.284	.280
Charlie Briggs	OF37,2B12,SS2	—	23	49	182	29	31	8	2	1	—	11	—	—	.170	.218	.253
Harry Wheeler†	OF20	R	26	20	85	14	19	4	2	1	—	0	—	—	.224	.224	.353
One Arm Daily†	P46,2B2,OF2*	R	27	48	160	19	39	5	0	0	—	8	—	—	.244	.280	.275
Tony Suck†	C18,SS15,OF12*	—	26	43	153	15	22	2	0	0	—	12	—	—	.144	.206	.157
Emil Gross	C15,OF9	R	26	23	95	13	34	6	2	4	—	6	—	—	.358	.396	.589
Gid Gardner†	OF14,3B8,P1	—	25	22	85	14	21	7	0	0	—	5	—	—	.247	.289	.329
Will Foley	3B19	R	28	19	71	15	20	1	1	0	—	5	—	—	.282	.329	.324
Chippy McGarr	2B13,OF6	R	21	19	70	10	11	2	0	0	—	0	—	—	.157	.157	.186
P.J. Horan	P13,OF10	—	21	20	68	3	6	0	0	0	—	1	—	—	.088	.101	.088
Frank McLaughlin†	2B14,SS1,OF1	R	28	15	67	11	16	4	1	0	—	1	—	—	.239	.250	.328
Charlie Baker†	OF8,SS3,2B1	R	28	12	45	5	7	1	0	1	—	0	—	—	.156	.156	.244
Jack Leary†	2B4,3B3,OF3*	—	26	10	40	0	7	1	0	0	—	0	—	—	.175	.175	.200
Al Atkinson†	P8,OF2	R	23	10	35	3	10	0	0	0	—	0	—	—	.286	.286	.286
Charlie Cady†	P4,OF2	—	18	6	20	4	2	1	1	0	—	1	—	—	.100	.143	.250
Charlie Berry†	2B5	R	23	5	17	3	2	2	0	0	—	0	—	—	.118	.118	.235
Frank Bishop	3B3,SS1	—	23	4	16	1	3	1	0	0	—	0	—	—	.188	.188	.250
Frank Foreman†	P3,OF2	L	21	3	11	0	1	0	0	0	—	0	—	—	.091	.091	.091
Frank Wyman†	1B2	—	22	2	8	1	3	0	0	0	—	0	—	—	.375	.375	.375
Phil Corridan	2B2,OF1	—	—	2	7	1	1	0	0	0	—	0	—	—	.143	.143	.143
Bernie Graham†	OF1	—	24	1	5	2	1	0	0	0	—	0	—	—	.200	.200	.200
Art Richardson	2B1	—	22	1	4	0	0	0	0	0	—	0	—	—	.000	.000	.000
Dan Cronin†	2B1	—	27	1	4	1	1	0	0	0	—	0	—	—	.250	.250	.250
Charles Skinner†	OF1	—	—	1	3	1	1	0	0	0	—	0	—	—	.333	.333	.333
Charlie Fisher†	3B1	L	32	1	3	1	2	0	0	0	—	1	—	—	.667	.750	.667
Harry Koons†	3B1	R	21	1	3	0	0	0	0	0	—	0	—	—	.000	.000	.000

B. Krieg, 1 G at SS; C. Householder, 2 G at P; O. Daily, 1 G at SS; T. Suck, 1 G at 3B; J. Leary, 2 G at P

Pitcher	T	Age	G	GS	CG	ShO	IP	H	HR	BB	SO	W-L	Sv	ERA
One Arm Daily†	R	27	46	46	44	4	396.2	353	10	58	403	22-23	0	2.43
P.J. Horan	—	21	13	10	9	0	98.0	94	0	24	55	3-6	0	3.49
Al Atkinson†	R	23	8	8	8	1	71.0	65	1	8	51	4-4	0	2.66
Charlie Cady	—	18	4	4	4	0	35.0	37	0	13	15	3-1	0	2.83
Frank Foreman†	L	21	3	3	1	0	18.0	23	0	2	10	1-2	0	4.00
Jack Leary†	L	26	2	1	1	0	10.0	14	0	5	6	0-2	0	5.40
Cyclone Miller†	L	24	1	1	1	0	9.0	4	0	0	13	1-0	0	1.00
Gid Gardner	—	25	1	1	0	0	6.0	10	0	1	4	0-1	0	6.00
Charlie Householder	R	28	2	0	0	0	3.0	4	0	0	3	0-0	0	3.00

1884 Washington Nationals 7th UA 47-65 .420 46.5 GB

Mike Scanlon

Player	Gm by Position	B	Age	G	AB	R	H	2B	3B	HR	RBI	BB	SO	SB	Avg	OBP	Slg
Chris Fulmer	C34,OF16,1B5	R	25	48	181	39	50	9	0	0	—	11	—	—	.276	.318	.326
Phil Baker	1B39,OF32,C27	L	27	86	371	75	107	12	5	1	—	11	—	—	.288	.309	.356
Tom Evers	2B109	—	32	109	427	54	99	6	1	0	—	7	—	—	.232	.244	.251
Jerry McCormick†	3B38,SS4	—	—	42	157	23	34	8	2	0	—	1	—	—	.217	.222	.293
Jim Halpin	SS39,3B7	—	20	46	168	24	31	3	0	0	—	2	—	—	.185	.194	.202
Harry Moore	OF105,SS8	—	—	111	461	77	155	23	5	1	—	19	—	—	.336	.363	.414
Bill Wise	P50,OF43,3B8*	—	23	85	339	51	79	17	1	2	—	12	—	—	.233	.259	.307
Abner Powell	OF30,P18,3B2*	L	23	48	191	36	54	10	5	0	—	3	—	—	.283	.294	.387
Alex Voss†	P27,3B16,1B15*	R	26	63	245	33	47	9	0	0	—	5	—	—	.192	.208	.229
Joe Gunson	C33,OF18	R	21	45	166	15	23	2	0	0	—	3	—	—	.139	.154	.151
Charlie Geggus	P23,OF21,SS3*	—	22	44	154	14	38	7	1	0	—	4	—	—	.247	.266	.305
John Deasley†	SS31	—	23	31	134	20	29	1	1	0	—	3	—	—	.216	.234	.239
Pop Joy	1B36	—	24	36	130	12	28	0	0	0	—	2	—	—	.215	.227	.215
Fred Tenney†	OF27,1B6	—	24	32	119	17	28	3	1	0	—	6	—	—	.235	.272	.277
Ed McKenna	C23,OF10,3B7	—	—	32	117	19	22	1	0	0	—	4	—	—	.188	.215	.197
Terry Larkin†	3B17	R	—	17	70	11	17	0	0	0	—	4	—	—	.243	.284	.243
Milo Lockwood	P11,OF11,3B3	—	26	20	67	9	14	1	0	0	—	8	—	—	.209	.293	.224
Dave Drew†	SS8,1B5,OF1	—	—	13	53	8	16	1	2	0	—	1	—	—	.302	.315	.396
Bill Hughes	1B9,OF6	L	17	14	49	5	6	0	0	0	—	2	—	—	.122	.157	.122
Jim McLaughlin	SS9,3B1	—	—	10	37	3	7	3	0	0	—	0	—	—	.189	.189	.270
Jim Green	3B9,OF1	—	—	10	36	4	5	1	0	0	—	0	—	—	.139	.139	.167
Marty Creegan	OF6,C3,3B2*	—	—	9	33	4	5	0	0	0	—	1	—	—	.152	.176	.152
John Ryan†	OF7,3B1	—	—	7	28	2	4	0	1	0	—	1	—	—	.143	.172	.214
Warren White	3B2,2B1,SS1	—	—	4	18	2	1	0	0	0	—	0	—	—	.056	.056	.056
Frank McKee	OF3,3B2,C1	—	—	4	17	2	3	0	0	0	—	1	—	—	.176	.222	.176
Gus Alberts†	SS4	R	16	4	16	4	4	0	0	0	—	4	—	—	.250	.400	.250
Chick Carroll	OF4	—	16	4	16	1	4	0	0	0	—	0	—	—	.250	.250	.250
John Kelly†	C3,OF1	R	25	4	14	1	5	1	0	0	—	0	—	—	.357	.357	.429
Icicle Reeder†	OF3	R	19	3	12	0	2	0	0	0	—	0	—	—	.167	.167	.167
Mike Lehane	SS3,3B1,OF1	R	19	3	12	1	4	2	0	0	—	0	—	—	.333	.333	.500
Maury Pierce	3B2	—	—	2	7	0	1	0	0	0	—	0	—	—	.143	.143	.143
Mike Lawlor	C2	—	30	2	7	0	0	0	0	0	—	0	—	—	.000	.000	.000
Jim McDonald†	C1,OF1	—	23	2	6	0	1	0	0	0	—	0	—	—	.167	.167	.167
Charlie Kalbfus	OF1	R	19	1	5	1	1	0	0	0	—	0	—	—	.200	.200	.200
John Ewing†	OF1	—	21	1	5	1	1	0	1	0	—	0	—	—	.200	.200	.600
Frank Olin†	OF1	L	24	1	4	0	0	0	0	0	—	0	—	—	.000	.000	.000
— Wiley	3B1	—	—	1	4	0	0	0	0	0	—	0	—	—	.000	.000	.000
John Mulligan	3B1	—	—	1	4	2	1	0	0	0	—	0	—	—	.250	.250	.250
John Ward	OF1	—	—	1	4	0	1	0	0	0	—	0	—	—	.250	.250	.250
Ed Yewell†	3B1	—	21	1	4	0	0	0	0	0	—	0	—	—	.000	.000	.000
Emory Nusz	OF1	—	18	1	4	1	0	0	0	0	—	0	—	—	.000	.000	.000
Walter Prince†	1B1	L	23	1	4	0	1	0	0	0	—	0	—	—	.250	.250	.250
John Shoupe	OF1	L	32	1	4	1	3	0	0	0	—	0	—	—	.750	.750	.750
— Franklin	OF1	—	—	1	3	0	0	0	0	0	—	0	—	—	.000	.000	.000
— McRemer	OF1	—	—	1	3	0	0	0	0	0	—	0	—	—	.000	.000	.000
William Rollinson	C1	—	28	1	3	0	0	0	0	0	—	0	—	—	.000	.000	.000
Al Bradley	OF1	—	—	1	3	0	0	0	0	0	—	2	—	—	.000	.400	.000
P. Morris	SS1	—	—	1	3	0	0	0	0	0	—	0	—	—	.000	.000	.000
Charlie Levis†	1B1	R	24	1	3	0	0	0	0	0	—	0	—	—	.000	.000	.000

B. Wise, 2 G at SS, 1 G at 1B; A. Powell, 1 G at 2B, 1 G at SS; A. Voss, 13 G at OF, 1 G at SS; C. Geggus, 1 G at 2B; M. Creegan, 1 G at 1B

Pitcher	T	Age	G	GS	CG	ShO	IP	H	HR	BB	SO	W-L	Sv	ERA
Bill Wise	—	23	50	41	34	4	364.1	383	5	60	268	23-18	0	3.04
Charlie Geggus	—	22	23	21	19	0	177.1	143	2	38	156	10-9	0	2.54
Alex Voss†	R	26	27	20	18	0	186.1	206	2	32	112	5-14	0	3.57
Abner Powell	R	23	18	17	14	1	134.0	135	3	19	78	6-12	0	3.43
Milo Lockwood	—	26	11	10	6	0	67.2	99	4	15	48	1-9	0	7.45
One Arm Daily†	R	27	2	2	2	0	16.0	16	0	1	14	1-1	0	2.25
Art Thompson	—	—	1	1	1	0	8.0	10	0	3	8	0-1	0	6.75

1884 Pittsburgh Stogies 8th UA 7-11 .389 47.5 GB

Joe Ellick (6-6)/Joe Battin (1-5)

Player	Gm by Position	B	Age	G	AB	R	H	2B	3B	HR	RBI	BB	SO	SB	Avg	OBP	Slg
Tony Suck†	C10	—	26	10	35	3	6	0	0	0	—	1	—	—	.171	.194	.171
Jumbo Schoeneck†	1B18	R	22	18	77	9	22	3	0	0	—	1	—	—	.286	.295	.325
George Strief†	2B15	R	27	15	53	6	11	5	0	0	—	3	—	—	.208	.250	.302
Joe Battin†	3B18	R	32	18	69	8	13	2	0	0	—	0	—	—	.188	.188	.217
Joe Ellick†	SS18	—	30	18	80	13	13	3	0	0	—	3	—	—	.163	.193	.200
Harry Wheeler†	OF17	R	26	17	73	15	17	1	1	0	—	4	—	—	.233	.273	.274
C. Householder†	OF17	R	28	17	66	4	17	4	2	0	—	1	—	—	.258	.269	.379
Gid Gardner†	OF15,2B1	—	25	16	64	8	17	3	2	0	—	5	—	—	.266	.319	.375
Bill Krieg†	C9,OF1	R	25	10	39	8	14	5	1	0	—	1	—	—	.359	.375	.538
Al Atkinson†	P8,OF1	R	23	9	33	1	4	0	0	0	—	0	—	—	.121	.121	.121
Charlie Baker†	OF3	R	28	3	12	0	1	1	0	0	—	0	—	—	.083	.083	.167
Charlie Berry†	2B2	R	23	2	10	1	1	0	0	0	—	0	—	—	.100	.100	.100
Kid Baldwin†	C1	R	19	1	1	0	1	0	0	0	—	0	—	—	1.000	1.000	1.000

Pitcher	T	Age	G	GS	CG	ShO	IP	H	HR	BB	SO	W-L	Sv	ERA
One Arm Daily†	R	27	10	10	10	1	88.0	77	1	13	66	5-4	0	2.45
Al Atkinson†	R	23	8	8	8	0	69.0	62	0	13	53	2-6	0	2.87

1884 Philadelphia Keystones 9th UA 21-46 .313 50.0 GB

Fergy Malone

Player	Gm by Position	B	Age	G	AB	R	H	2B	3B	HR	RBI	BB	SO	SB	Avg	OBP	Slg
Tom Gillen	C27,OF3	—	22	29	116	5	18	2	0	0	—	1	—	—	.155	.162	.172
John McGuinness	1B48,2B5,SS1	—	27	53	220	25	52	8	1	0	—	5	—	—	.236	.253	.282
Elias Peak†	2B47,OF5,SS2	—	25	54	215	35	42	6	4	0	—	7	—	—	.195	.221	.260
Jerry McCormick†	3B54,2B5,OF5*	—	—	67	295	41	84	12	2	0	—	4	—	—	.285	.294	.339
Henry Easterday	SS28	R	19	28	115	12	28	5	0	0	—	5	—	—	.243	.275	.287
Bill Kienzle	OF67	L	—	67	299	76	76	13	8	0	—	21	—	—	.254	.303	.351
Joe Flynn†	OF43,C10,1B1*	—	—	52	209	38	52	9	4	4	—	11	—	—	.249	.286	.388
Buster Hoover†	OF37,SS15,1B6*	R	21	63	275	76	100	20	8	0	—	12	—	—	.364	.390	.495
Jack Clements†	OF22,C20,SS1	L	19	41	177	37	50	13	2	3	—	9	—	—	.282	.317	.429
Jersey Bakely†	P39,1B3,OF3*	R	20	45	167	21	22	4	2	0	—	11	—	—	.132	.185	.180
Henry Luff†	OF12,1B6,3B5*	—	27	26	111	9	30	4	2	0	—	4	—	—	.270	.296	.342
Sam Weaver	P17,OF6	R	28	20	84	11	18	2	0	0	—	2	—	—	.214	.233	.238
George Fisher†	P8,1B2	L	—	10	36	7	8	2	0	0	—	3	—	—	.222	.282	.278
Billy Geer†	SS9	—	34	9	36	7	9	2	1	0	—	4	—	—	.250	.325	.361
John Siegel	3B8	—	—	8	31	4	7	2	0	0	—	1	—	—	.226	.250	.290
Chris Rickley	SS6	—	24	6	25	5	5	2	0	0	—	2	—	—	.200	.259	.280
Pat Carroll†	C5	—	31	5	19	1	3	1	0	0	—	0	—	—	.158	.158	.211
Bill Jones	C4,OF1	—	—	4	14	2	2	0	0	0	—	1	—	—	.143	.200	.143
Levi Meyerle	1B2,OF1	R	38	3	11	0	1	1	0	0	—	0	—	—	.091	.091	.182
Dave Drew†	P1,2B1,SS1	—	—	2	9	1	4	0	0	0	—	0	—	—	.444	.444	.444
Clarence Cross†	SS2	—	28	2	9	0	2	0	0	0	—	0	—	—	.222	.222	.222
Con Daily	C2	L	19	2	8	0	0	0	0	0	—	0	—	—	.000	.000	.000
George Pattison	OF2	—	—	2	7	0	1	0	0	0	—	0	—	—	.143	.143	.143
John O'Donnell	C1	—	—	1	4	0	1	0	0	0	—	0	—	—	.250	.250	.250
Bill Johnson	OF1	L	21	1	4	0	0	0	0	0	—	0	—	—	.000	.000	.000
Fergy Malone	C1	R	42	1	4	0	1	0	0	0	—	0	—	—	.250	.250	.250
Elmer Foster†	C1	R	22	1	3	0	1	0	1	0	—	0	—	—	.333	.333	1.000

J. McCormick, 3 G at SS, 1 G at P; J. Flynn, 1 G at SS; B. Hoover, 6 G at 2B, 1 G at 3B; J. Bakely, 1 G at SS; H. Luff, 3 G at 2B

Pitcher	T	Age	G	GS	CG	ShO	IP	H	HR	BB	SO	W-L	Sv	ERA
Jersey Bakely†	R	20	39	38	38	1	344.2	390	0	76	204	14-25	0	4.47
Sam Weaver	R	28	17	17	14	0	136.0	206	3	11	40	5-10	0	5.76
George Fisher	—	—	8	8	8	0	70.2	76	0	13	42	1-7	0	3.57
Bill Gallagher	L	—	3	3	3	0	25.0	32	3	4	12	1-2	0	3.24
Al Maul	R	18	1	1	1	0	8.0	10	0	1	7	0-1	0	4.50
Dave Drew	—	—	1	0	0	0	7.0	7	0	0	2	0-1	0	3.86
Jerry McCormick	—	—	1	0	0	0	2.0	5	1	0	3	0-0	0	9.00

1884 St. Paul White Caps 10th UA 2-6 .250 52.5 GB

Andrew Thompson

Player	Gm by Position	B	Age	G	AB	R	H	2B	3B	HR	RBI	BB	SO	SB	Avg	OBP	Slg
Charlie Ganzel	C6,OF1	R	22	7	23	2	5	0	0	0	—	0	—	—	.217	.217	.217
Steve Dunn	1B9,3B1	—	25	9	32	2	8	2	0	0	—	0	—	—	.250	.250	.313
Moxie Hengel†	2B9	R	26	9	33	2	5	1	1	0	—	0	—	—	.152	.152	.242
Billy O'Brien†	3B8,P2	R	24	8	30	1	7	3	0	0	—	0	—	—	.233	.233	.333
Joe Werrick	SS9	R	22	9	27	3	2	0	0	0	—	1	—	—	.074	.107	.074
John Tilley†	OF9	—	28	9	26	2	4	1	0	0	—	3	—	—	.154	.241	.192
Scrappy Carroll	OF8,3B2	—	23	9	31	3	3	1	0	0	—	2	—	—	.097	.152	.129
Bill Barnes	OF8	—	—	8	30	2	6	1	0	0	—	0	—	—	.200	.200	.233
Jim Brown†	P6,1B1,OF1	—	23	6	16	5	5	4	0	0	—	1	—	—	.313	.353	.563
Pat Dealy	C4,OF1	R	—	5	15	2	2	0	0	0	—	0	—	—	.133	.133	.133

Pitcher	T	Age	G	GS	CG	ShO	IP	H	HR	BB	SO	W-L	Sv	ERA
Jim Brown†	—	23	6	6	4	1	36.0	43	1	14	20	1-4	0	3.75
Lou Galvin	—	22	3	3	3	0	25.0	21	0	10	17	0-2	0	2.88
Billy O'Brien	—	24	2	0	0	0	10.0	8	0	3	7	1-0	0	1.80

1884 Altoona Unions 11th UA 6-19 .240 44.0 GB

Ed Curtis

Player	Gm by Position	B	Age	G	AB	R	H	2B	3B	HR	RBI	BB	SO	SB	Avg	OBP	Slg
Jerrie Moore†	C12,OF9	L	—	20	80	10	25	3	1	1	—	0	—	—	.313	.313	.413
Frank Harris	1B17,OF7	R	25	24	95	10	25	2	1	0	—	3	—	—	.263	.286	.305
Charlie Dougherty	2B16,OF8,SS1	—	22	23	85	6	22	5	0	0	—	2	—	—	.259	.276	.318
Harry Koons†	3B21,C1	R	21	21	78	8	18	2	1	0	—	2	—	—	.231	.250	.282
Germany Smith†	SS25,P1	R	21	25	108	9	34	8	1	0	—	1	—	—	.315	.321	.407
Frank Shaffer†	OF17,C2,3B1	—	—	19	74	11	21	2	0	0	—	3	—	—	.284	.312	.311
Jim Brown†	OF14,P11	—	23	21	88	12	22	2	2	1	—	1	—	—	.250	.258	.352
John Murphy†	P14,OF10,2B4	—	—	23	94	10	14	1	0	0	—	4	—	—	.149	.184	.160
Pat Carroll†	C8,OF3	—	31	11	49	4	13	1	0	0	—	1	—	—	.265	.280	.286
John Grady	1B8,OF1	—	24	9	36	5	11	3	0	0	—	2	—	—	.306	.342	.389
Jack Leary†	OF6,P3,3B1	—	26	8	33	1	3	0	0	0	—	1	—	—	.091	.118	.091
Charlie Berry†	2B7	R	23	7	25	2	6	0	0	0	—	0	—	—	.240	.240	.240
George Noftsker	OF5,C3	R	24	7	25	0	1	0	0	0	—	0	—	—	.040	.040	.040
Joe Connors†	P1,3B1,OF1	—	—	3	11	0	1	0	0	0	—	0	—	—	.091	.091	.091
Charlie Manlove†	C1,OF1	R	21	2	7	1	3	0	0	0	—	0	—	—	.429	.429	.429
Clarence Cross†	3B2	—	28	2	7	1	4	1	0	0	—	2	—	—	.571	.667	.714
George Daisey	OF1	—	—	1	4	0	0	0	0	0	—	0	—	—	.000	.000	.000

Pitcher	T	Age	G	GS	CG	ShO	IP	H	HR	BB	SO	W-L	Sv	ERA
Jim Brown†	—	23	11	11	7	0	74.0	99	0	36	39	1-9	0	5.35
John Murphy†	—	—	14	10	10	0	111.2	141	3	9	46	5-6	0	3.87
Jack Leary†	L	26	3	3	2	0	24.0	31	0	2	7	0-3	0	5.25
Joe Connors†	—	—	1	1	1	0	9.0	18	0	5	0	0-1	0	7.00
Germany Smith	R	21	1	0	0	0	1.0	3	0	0	1	0-0	0	9.00

1884 Kansas City Unions 12th UA 16-63 .203 61.0 GB

Harry Wheeler (0-4)/Matt Porter (3-13)/Ted Sullivan (13-46)

Player	Gm by Position	B	Age	G	AB	R	H	2B	3B	HR	RBI	BB	SO	SB	Avg	OBP	Slg
Kid Baldwin†	C44,OF10,2B1*	R	19	50	191	19	37	6	3	0	—	4	—	—	.194	.210	.257
Jerry Sweeney	1B31	—	24	31	129	16	34	3	0	0	—	4	—	—	.264	.286	.287
Charlie Berry†	2B22,OF8,3B1	R	23	29	118	15	29	6	1	1	—	1	—	—	.246	.252	.339
Pat Sullivan	3B21,OF9,P1*	—	21	31	114	15	22	3	1	0	—	4	—	—	.193	.220	.237
Clarence Cross†	SS24,3B1	—	28	25	93	13	20	1	0	0	—	6	—	—	.215	.263	.226
Frank Shaffer†	OF41,C2,2B1*	—	—	44	164	18	28	3	2	0	—	15	—	—	.171	.240	.213
Frank Wyman†	OF25,P3,1B3*	—	22	30	124	16	27	4	0	0	—	3	—	—	.218	.236	.250
Barney McLaughlin	OF24,2B12,P7*	R	27	42	162	15	37	7	3	0	—	9	—	—	.228	.269	.309
Bob Black	OF19,P16,2B6*	—	21	38	146	25	36	14	2	1	—	10	—	—	.247	.295	.390
Jack Gorman†	1B24,OF5,3B4	—	25	33	137	25	38	5	2	0	—	4	—	—	.277	.298	.343
Frank McLaughlin†	2B10,OF10,3B9*	R	28	32	123	17	28	11	0	1	—	9	—	—	.228	.280	.341
Jim Cudworth	1B19,OF12,P2	R	25	32	116	7	17	3	1	0	—	2	—	—	.147	.161	.190
Henry Oberbeck†	3B15,OF7,P6*	—	26	27	90	7	17	3	0	0	—	7	—	—	.189	.247	.222
Peek-A-Boo Veach	OF14,P12,1B1*	—	22	27	82	9	11	1	0	1	—	9	—	—	.134	.220	.183
Harry Decker†	OF16,C11	R	29	23	75	8	10	2	0	0	—	5	—	—	.133	.188	.160
Ernie Hickman	P17,OF3,3B1	—	28	19	72	4	12	1	0	0	—	1	—	—	.167	.178	.181
Lou Say†	SS16,2B1	R	30	17	70	6	14	2	0	1	—	2	—	—	.200	.222	.271
Nin Alexander†	C17,SS2,OF2	R	25	19	65	2	9	0	0	0	—	1	—	—	.138	.152	.138
Harry Wheeler†	OF13,P1	R	26	14	62	11	16	1	0	0	—	3	—	—	.258	.292	.274
Joe Strauss	OF10,C3,2B2*	R	25	16	60	4	12	3	0	0	—	1	—	—	.200	.213	.250
George Strief†	2B15	R	27	15	56	5	6	5	0	0	—	4	—	—	.107	.167	.196
Jerry Turbidy	SS13	R	31	13	49	5	11	4	0	0	—	3	—	—	.224	.269	.306
Charlie Bastian†	2B11	R	23	11	46	6	9	3	0	1	—	4	—	—	.196	.260	.326
Alex Voss†	OF8,P7	R	26	14	45	1	4	0	0	0	—	0	—	—	.089	.089	.089
Al Dwight	C10,2B1,OF1	—	28	12	43	8	10	2	0	0	—	2	—	—	.233	.267	.279
John Deasley†	SS13	—	23	13	40	3	7	2	0	0	—	2	—	—	.175	.214	.225
Charlie Fisher†	3B9,SS1	L	32	10	40	3	8	2	0	0	—	0	—	—	.200	.200	.250
Jumbo Davis	3B7	L	22	7	29	3	6	0	0	0	—	0	—	—	.207	.207	.207
Jim Donnelly†	3B5,C1	R	18	6	23	2	3	1	0	0	—	1	—	—	.130	.167	.174
Milt Whitehead†	2B3,C1,3B1*	S	22	5	22	2	3	0	0	0	—	0	—	—	.136	.136	.136
— Wills†	OF5	—	—	5	21	2	3	1	0	0	—	0	—	—	.143	.143	.190
Jersey Bakely†	P5,OF3	R	20	6	20	3	3	1	0	0	—	1	—	—	.150	.190	.200
Henry Luff†	3B4,OF4	—	27	5	19	0	1	0	0	0	—	1	—	—	.053	.100	.053
Billy O'Brien†	3B3,1B1	R	24	4	17	2	4	0	0	0	—	0	—	—	.235	.235	.235
Dick Blaisdell	P3,OF1	—	22	4	16	1	5	1	0	0	—	0	—	—	.313	.313	.375
Doug Crothers	P3,OF1	R	24	4	15	2	2	0	0	0	—	0	—	—	.133	.133	.133
Jim Chatterton	1B2,OF2,P1	—	19	4	15	4	2	1	0	0	—	2	—	—	.133	.235	.200
Matthew Porter	OF3	—	—	3	12	1	1	1	0	0	—	0	—	—	.083	.083	.167
Ed Callahan†	SS3	—	26	3	11	0	4	0	0	0	—	0	—	—	.364	.364	.364
Joe Connors†	P2,OF2	—	—	3	11	2	1	0	0	0	—	1	—	—	.091	.167	.091
Ted Sullivan	OF2,SS1	—	33	3	9	0	3	0	0	0	—	1	—	—	.333	.400	.333
Jimmy Say†	3B2	—	22	2	8	0	2	0	0	0	—	0	—	—	.250	.250	.250
Joe Ellick†	2B1,OF1	—	30	2	8	0	0	0	0	0	—	0	—	—	.000	.000	.000
John Kirby	P2,OF1	—	19	2	7	1	1	0	0	0	—	0	—	—	.143	.143	.143
Bill Dugan†	OF3	—	20	3	6	0	0	0	0	0	—	0	—	—	.000	.000	.000
Emmett Seery†	OF1	L	23	1	4	2	2	1	0	0	—	1	—	—	.500	.600	.750
Frank Krueger	P1,OF1	—	—	1	3	0	0	0	0	0	—	0	—	—	.000	.000	.000
Charlie Cady†	C1,2B1	—	18	2	3	0	0	0	0	0	—	0	—	—	.000	.000	.000

K. Baldwin, 1 G at 3B; P. Sullivan, 1 G at C; F. Shaffer, 1 G at 3B, 1 G at SS; F. Wyman, 3 G at 3B; B. McLaughlin, 2 G at SS; B. Black, 1 G at SS; F. McLaughlin, 5 G at SS, 2 G at P; H. Oberbeck, 3 G at 1B; P. Veach, 1 G at 2B; J. Strauss, 1 G at 3B; M. Whitehead, 1 G at SS

Pitcher	T	Age	G	GS	CG	ShO	IP	H	HR	BB	SO	W-L	Sv	ERA
Ernie Hickman	—	28	17	17	15	0	137.1	172	5	36	68	4-13	0	4.52
Bob Black	—	21	16	15	13	0	123.0	127	1	17	93	4-9	0	3.22
Peek-A-Boo Veach	—	22	12	12	12	0	104.0	95	1	10	62	3-9	0	2.42
Alex Voss†	R	26	7	6	6	0	53.0	74	2	7	17	0-6	0	4.25
Jersey Bakely†	R	20	5	5	3	0	33.0	29	0	4	13	2-3	0	2.45
Barney McLaughlin	R	27	7	4	4	0	48.2	62	2	15	14	1-3	0	5.36
Henry Oberbeck†	—	26	6	4	3	0	29.2	47	0	3	6	0-5	0	5.76
Dick Blaisdell	—	22	3	3	3	0	26.0	49	0	4	8	0-3	0	8.65
Doug Crothers	R	24	3	3	3	0	25.0	26	0	6	11	1-2	0	1.80
Bill Hutchison	R	24	2	2	2	0	17.0	14	0	1	5	1-1	0	2.65
John Kirby	R	19	2	2	1	0	11.0	13	0	2	1	0-1	0	4.09
Jim Cudworth	R	25	2	1	1	0	17.0	19	1	3	6	0-0	0	4.24
Joe Connors†	—	—	2	1	1	0	12.0	24	1	0	1	0-1	0	4.50
Frank McLaughlin	R	28	2	1	0	0	10.0	15	0	2	3	0-0	0	5.40
Frank Foreman†	L	21	1	1	1	0	8.0	17	0	2	5	0-1	0	5.63
Harry Wheeler	R	26	1	1	1	0	8.0	7	0	0	6	0-1	0	1.13
Pat Sullivan	R	21	1	1	0	0	7.0	15	1	5	1	0-1	0	11.57
Frank Krueger	—	—	1	1	0	0	7.0	9	0	5	3	0-1	0	0.00
Jim Chatterton	—	19	1	1	0	0	5.0	11	0	2	2	0-1	0	3.60
Frank Wyman	—	22	3	1	1	0	21.0	37	0	3	9	0-1	0	6.86

1884 Wilmington Quicksteps 13th UA 2-16 .111 47.5 GB

Joe Simmons

Player	Gm by Position	B	Age	G	AB	R	H	2B	3B	HR	RBI	BB	SO	SB	Avg	OBP	Slg
Tom Lynch†	C8,OF8,1B1	L	24	16	58	6	16	3	1	0	—	5	—	—	.276	.333	.362
Redleg Snyder	1B16,OF1	R	29	17	52	4	10	0	0	0	—	1	—	—	.192	.208	.192
Charlie Bastian†	2B16,P1,SS1	R	23	17	60	6	12	1	3	2	—	3	—	—	.200	.238	.417
Jimmy Say†	3B16	—	22	16	59	3	13	1	2	0	—	1	—	—	.220	.233	.305
Henry Myers	SS5,2B1	R	26	6	24	3	3	0	0	0	—	0	—	—	.125	.125	.125
Big John Munce	OF7	—	26	7	21	1	4	0	0	0	—	1	—	—	.190	.227	.190
John Cullen	OF6,SS3	—	—	9	31	2	6	0	0	0	—	1	—	—	.194	.219	.194
George Fisher†	OF6,SS2	L	—	8	29	0	2	0	0	0	—	0	—	—	.069	.069	.069
Tony Cusick†	C6,SS3,OF3*	R	24	11	34	0	5	0	0	0	—	1	—	—	.147	.171	.147
The Only Nolan	P5,OF4	L	26	9	33	5	9	2	1	0	—	2	—	—	.273	.314	.394
John Murphy†	P7,SS2,OF2*	—	—	10	31	4	2	0	0	0	—	3	—	—	.065	.147	.065
Bill McCloskey	C5,OF5	—	30	9	30	0	3	0	0	0	—	0	—	—	.100	.100	.100
Ike Benners†	OF6	L	28	6	22	0	1	0	0	0	—	1	—	—	.045	.087	.045
Dennis Casey†	OF2	L	26	2	8	1	2	1	0	0	—	0	—	—	.250	.250	.375
Oyster Burns†	SS2	R	19	2	7	0	1	0	1	0	—	1	—	—	.143	.250	.429
John Ryan†	OF2	—	—	2	6	0	1	0	0	0	—	1	—	—	.167	.286	.167
Jim McElroy†	P1,OF1	—	21	1	2	0	0	0	0	0	—	0	—	—	.000	.000	.000

T. Cusick, 1 G at 2B, 1 G at 3B; J. Murphy, 1 G at 3B

Pitcher	T	Age	G	GS	CG	ShO	IP	H	HR	BB	SO	W-L	Sv	ERA
John Murphy†	—	—	7	6	5	0	48.0	52	3	2	27	0-6	0	3.00
The Only Nolan	R	26	5	5	5	0	40.0	44	1	7	52	1-4	0	2.93
Dan Casey	L	21	2	2	2	0	18.0	23	0	4	10	1-1	0	1.00
Jersey Bakely†	R	20	2	2	2	0	17.0	24	0	1	9	0-2	0	4.24
Fred Tenney†	—	24	1	1	1	0	8.0	6	0	4	10	0-1	0	1.13
Jim McElroy†	—	21	1	1	0	0	5.0	10	0	0	3	0-1	0	10.80
Charlie Bastian	R	23	1	0	0	0	6.0	6	0	0	2	0-0	0	3.00

»1885 Chicago White Stockings 1st NL 87-25 .777 —

Cap Anson

Player	Gm by Position	B	Age	G	AB	R	H	2B	3B	HR	RBI	BB	SO	SB	Avg	OBP	Slg
Silver Flint	C68,OF1	R	29	68	249	27	52	8	2	1	17	2	52	—	.209	.215	.269
Cap Anson	1B112,C1	R	33	112	464	100	144	35	7	7	108	34	13	—	.310	.357	.461
Fred Pfeffer	2B109,P5,OF1	R	25	112	469	90	113	12	7	5	73	26	47	—	.241	.281	.328
Ned Williamson	3B113,P2,C1	R	27	113	407	87	97	16	5	3	65	75	60	—	.238	.357	.324
Tom Burns	SS111,2B1	R	28	111	445	82	121	23	9	7	71	16	48	—	.272	.297	.411
Abner Dalrymple	OF113	L	27	113	492	109	135	27	12	11	61	46	42	—	.274	.336	.445
George Gore	OF109	L	28	109	441	115	138	21	13	5	57	68	25	—	.313	.405	.454
King Kelly	OF69,C37,2B6*	R	27	107	438	124	126	24	7	9	75	46	24	—	.288	.355	.436
John Clarkson	P70,OF3,3B1	R	23	72	283	34	61	11	5	4	31	3	44	—	.216	.224	.332
Billy Sunday	OF46	L	22	46	172	36	44	3	3	2	20	12	33	—	.256	.304	.343
Jim McCormick†	P24,OF1	R	28	25	103	13	23	1	4	0	16	1	18	—	.223	.231	.311
Sy Sutcliffe†	C11,OF1	L	23	11	43	5	8	1	1	0	4	2	5	—	.186	.222	.256
Ted Kennedy	P9,3B1	L	20	9	36	3	3	0	0	0	0	0	10	—	.083	.083	.083
Larry Corcoran†	P7,SS1	L	25	7	22	6	6	1	0	0	4	6	1	—	.273	.429	.318
Jimmy Ryan	SS2,OF1	R	22	3	13	2	6	1	0	0	2	1	1	—	.462	.500	.538
Jim McCauley†	C2,OF2	L	22	3	6	1	1	0	0	0	0	2	3	—	.167	.375	.167
Wash Williams	P1,OF1	—	—	1	4	0	1	0	0	0	0	0	0	—	.250	.250	.250
Ed Gastfield†	C1	R	19	1	3	0	0	0	0	0	0	0	1	—	.000	.000	.000
Bill Krieg†	OF1	R	26	1	3	0	0	0	0	0	0	0	2	—	.000	.000	.000

K. Kelly, 2 G at 1B, 2 G at 3B

Pitcher	T	Age	G	GS	CG	ShO	IP	H	HR	BB	SO	W-L	Sv	ERA
John Clarkson	R	23	70	70	68	10	623.0	497	21	97	308	53-16	0	1.85
Jim McCormick†	R	28	24	24	24	3	215.0	187	8	40	88	20-4	0	2.43
Ted Kennedy	—	20	9	9	8	0	78.2	91	5	28	36	7-2	0	3.43
Larry Corcoran†	R	25	7	7	6	1	59.1	63	2	24	10	5-2	0	3.64
Wash Williams	—	—	1	1	0	0	2.0	2	0	5	0	0-0	0	13.50
Fred Pfeffer	R	25	5	2	2	0	31.2	26	1	8	13	2-1	2	2.56
Ned Williamson	R	27	2	0	0	0	6.0	2	0	0	3	0-0	2	0.00

498 Seasons: Team Rosters

1885 New York Giants 2nd NL 85-27 .759 2.0 GB

Jim Mutrie

Player	Gm by Position	B	Age	G	AB	R	H	2B	3B	HR	RBI	BB	SO	SB	Avg	OBP	Slg
Buck Ewing	C63,OF14,3B8*	R	25	81	342	81	104	15	12	6	63	13	17	—	.304	.330	.471
Roger Connor	1B110	L	27	110	455	102	169	23	15	1	65	51	8	—	.371	.435	.495
Joe Gerhardt	2B112	R	30	112	399	43	62	12	2	0	33	24	47	—	.155	.203	.195
Dude Esterbrook	3B84,OF4	R	28	88	359	48	92	14	5	2	44	4	28	—	.256	.264	.340
Monte Ward	SS111	L	25	111	446	72	101	8	9	0	37	17	39	—	.226	.255	.285
Jim O'Rourke	OF112,C8	R	34	112	477	119	143	21	16	5	42	40	21	—	.300	.354	.442
Pete Gillespie	OF102	L	33	102	420	67	123	17	6	0	52	15	32	—	.293	.317	.362
Mike Dorgan	OF88,1B1	R	31	89	347	60	113	17	8	0	46	11	24	—	.326	.346	.421
Pat Deasley	C54,OF2,SS1	R	27	54	207	22	53	5	1	0	24	9	20	—	.256	.287	.290
Danny Richardson	OF22,3B21,P9	R	22	49	198	26	52	9	3	0	25	10	14	—	.263	.298	.338
Tim Keefe	P46,OF2	R	28	47	166	20	27	1	5	0	12	13	22	—	.163	.223	.229

B. Ewing, 1 G at P, 1 G at 1B, 1 G at SS

Pitcher	T	Age	G	GS	CG	ShO	IP	H	HR	BB	SO	W-L	Sv	ERA
Mickey Welch	R	25	56	55	55	7	492.0	372	4	131	258	44-11	1	1.66
Tim Keefe	R	28	46	46	45	7	398.0	297	6	103	230	32-13	0	1.58
Danny Richardson	R	22	9	8	7	1	75.0	58	0	18	21	7-1	0	2.40
Larry Corcoran†	R	25	3	3	2	0	25.0	24	1	11	10	2-1	0	2.88
Buck Ewing	R	25	1	0	0	0	2.0	4	0	3	0	0-1	0	4.50

1885 Philadelphia Phillies 3rd NL 56-54 .509 30.0 GB

Harry Wright

Player	Gm by Position	B	Age	G	AB	R	H	2B	3B	HR	RBI	BB	SO	SB	Avg	OBP	Slg
Jack Clements	C41,OF11	L	20	52	188	14	36	11	3	1	14	2	30	—	.191	.200	.298
Sid Farrar	1B111	—	25	111	420	49	103	20	3	3	36	28	34	—	.245	.292	.329
Bert Myers	2B93	R	21	93	357	25	73	13	2	1	28	11	41	—	.204	.228	.261
Joe Mulvey	3B107	R	26	107	443	74	119	25	6	6	64	3	18	—	.269	.274	.393
Charlie Bastian	SS103	R	24	103	389	63	65	11	5	4	29	35	82	—	.167	.236	.252
Jack Manning	OF107	R	31	107	445	61	114	24	4	3	40	37	27	—	.256	.313	.348
Ed Andrews	OF99,2B5	R	26	103	421	77	112	15	3	0	23	32	25	—	.266	.318	.316
Jim Fogarty	OF88,2B10,SS8*	R	21	111	427	49	99	13	3	0	39	30	37	—	.232	.282	.276
Charlie Ferguson	P48,OF15	S	22	61	235	42	72	8	3	1	27	23	18	—	.306	.368	.379
Tony Cusick	C38,OF1	R	25	39	141	12	25	1	0	0	5	1	24	—	.177	.183	.184
Charlie Ganzel	C33,OF1	R	23	34	125	15	21	3	1	0	6	4	13	—	.168	.194	.208
Tom Lynch	OF13	L	25	13	53	7	10	3	0	0	1	10	3	—	.189	.317	.245
Bill Vinton†	P9,OF1	R	20	9	30	2	2	0	0	0	1	1	12	—	.067	.097	.067
The Only Nolan	P7,OF1	L	27	7	26	1	2	1	0	0	0	3	8	—	.077	.172	.115
John Hiland	2B3	L	24	3	9	0	0	0	0	0	0	0	4	—	.000	.000	.000

J. Fogarty, 5 G at 3B

Pitcher	T	Age	G	GS	CG	ShO	IP	H	HR	BB	SO	W-L	Sv	ERA
Ed Daily	R	22	50	50	49	4	440.0	370	12	90	140	26-23	0	2.21
Charlie Ferguson	R	22	48	45	45	5	405.0	345	5	81	197	26-20	0	2.22
Bill Vinton†	R	20	9	9	8	0	77.0	90	0	23	21	3-6	0	3.04
The Only Nolan	R	27	7	7	6	0	54.0	55	1	24	20	1-5	0	4.17

1885 Providence Grays 4th NL 53-57 .482 33.0 GB

Frank Bancroft

Player	Gm by Position	B	Age	G	AB	R	H	2B	3B	HR	RBI	BB	SO	SB	Avg	OBP	Slg
Barney Gilligan	C65,SS5,2B1*	R	29	71	252	23	54	7	3	0	12	23	33	—	.214	.280	.266
Joe Start	1B101	L	42	101	374	47	103	11	4	0	41	39	10	—	.275	.344	.326
Jack Farrell	2B68	R	27	68	257	27	53	7	1	1	19	10	25	—	.206	.236	.253
Jerry Denny	3B83	R	26	83	318	40	71	14	4	3	24	12	53	—	.223	.252	.321
Arthur Irwin	SS58,2B1,3B1	L	27	59	218	16	39	2	1	0	14	14	29	—	.179	.228	.197
Cliff Carroll	OF104	S	25	104	426	62	99	12	3	1	40	29	29	—	.232	.281	.282
Paul Hines	OF92,1B4,2B1*	R	33	98	411	63	111	20	4	1	35	19	18	—	.270	.302	.345
Paul Radford	OF88,SS16,P3*	R	23	105	371	55	90	12	5	0	32	33	43	—	.243	.304	.302
Charley Bassett	2B39,SS23,3B20*	R	22	82	285	21	41	8	2	0	16	19	60	—	.144	.197	.186
Old Hoss Radbourn	P49,OF16,2B2	R	30	66	249	34	58	9	2	0	22	36	27	—	.233	.330	.285
Con Daily	C48,1B7,OF6	L	20	60	223	20	58	6	1	0	19	12	20	—	.260	.298	.296
Dupee Shaw	P49,OF2	L	26	49	165	17	22	2	0	0	9	4	38	—	.133	.154	.145
Lon Knight†	OF25,P1	R	32	25	81	8	13	1	0	0	8	11	17	—	.160	.261	.173
Tim Manning†	SS10	R	31	10	35	3	2	1	0	0	0	1	11	—	.057	.083	.086
Denny Lyons	3B4	R	19	4	16	3	2	1	0	0	1	0	3	—	.125	.125	.188
Wiman Andrus	3B1	—	26	1	4	0	0	0	0	0	0	0	1	—	.000	.000	.000
Mike Hines†	C1	R	22	1	3	0	0	0	0	0	0	0	2	—	.000	.000	.000
Ed Crane†	OF1	R	23	1	2	0	0	0	0	0	0	1	1	—	.000	.333	.000

B. Gilligan, 1 G at OF; P. Hines, 1 G at 3B, 1 G at SS; P. Radford, 1 G at 2B; C. Bassett, 1 G at C

Pitcher	T	Age	G	GS	CG	ShO	IP	H	HR	BB	SO	W-L	Sv	ERA
Old Hoss Radbourn	R	30	49	49	49	2	445.2	423	4	83	154	28-21	0	2.20
Dupee Shaw	L	26	49	49	47	6	399.2	343	7	99	194	23-26	0	2.57
Jim McCormick†	R	28	4	4	4	0	37.0	34	1	20	8	1-3	0	2.43
Paul Radford	R	23	3	2	2	0	18.1	34	1	8	3	0-2	0	7.85
Charlie Hallstrom	—	21	1	1	1	0	9.0	18	3	6	0	0-1	0	11.00
Edgar Smith	R	23	1	1	1	0	9.0	9	0	0	1	1-0	0	1.00
Bill Stellberger	L	20	1	1	1	0	8.0	14	0	4	0	0-1	0	7.88
John Foley	L	—	1	1	1	0	8.0	6	0	5	2	0-1	0	4.50
Sam Kimber	R	32	1	1	1	0	8.0	15	1	5	4	0-1	0	11.25
John Ward	—	—	1	1	1	0	8.0	10	0	1	3	0-1	0	4.50
Ed Seward	R	18	1	0	0	0	6.0	2	0	0	1	0-0	0	0.00
Lon Knight†	R	32	1	0	0	0	4.0	4	1	4	1	0-0	0	6.75

1885 Boston Red Stockings 5th NL 46-66 .411 41.0 GB

John Morrill

Player	Gm by Position	B	Age	G	AB	R	H	2B	3B	HR	RBI	BB	SO	SB	Avg	OBP	Slg
Tom Gunning	C48	R	23	48	174	17	32	3	0	0	15	5	29	—	.184	.207	.201
John Morrill	1B92,2B17,3B2	R	30	111	394	74	89	20	7	4	44	64	78	—	.226	.334	.343
Jack Burdock	2B45	R	33	45	169	18	24	5	0	0	7	8	18	—	.142	.181	.172
Ezra Sutton	3B91,SS16,2B2*	R	34	110	457	78	143	23	8	4	47	17	25	—	.313	.338	.425
Sam Wise	SS79,2B22,OF6	L	27	107	424	71	120	20	10	4	46	25	61	—	.283	.323	.406
Jim Manning†	OF83,SS1	S	23	84	306	34	63	8	9	2	27	19	36	—	.206	.252	.310
Tom Poorman	OF56	L	27	56	227	44	54	5	3	3	25	7	32	—	.238	.261	.326
Tommy McCarthy	OF40	R	21	40	148	16	27	2	0	0	11	5	25	—	.182	.209	.196
Charlie Buffinton	P51,OF18,1B15	R	24	82	338	26	81	12	3	1	33	3	26	—	.240	.246	.302
Jim Whitney	P51,OF17,1B5	L	27	72	290	35	68	8	4	0	36	17	24	—	.234	.277	.290
Gurdon Whiteley	OF32,C1	—	25	33	135	14	25	2	2	1	7	1	25	—	.185	.191	.252
Pat Dealy	C29,3B3,SS2*	R	—	35	130	18	29	4	1	1	9	2	14	—	.223	.235	.292
Walter Hackett	2B20,SS15	—	27	35	125	8	23	3	0	0	9	3	22	—	.184	.203	.208
Mert Hackett	C34	R	25	34	115	9	21	7	1	0	4	2	28	—	.183	.197	.261
Dick Johnston	OF26	R	22	26	111	17	26	6	3	1	23	0	15	—	.234	.234	.369
Joe Hornung	OF25	R	28	25	109	14	22	4	1	1	7	1	20	—	.202	.209	.284
Billy Nash	3B19,2B8	R	20	26	94	9	24	4	0	0	11	2	9	—	.255	.271	.298
Blondie Purcell†	OF21	R	31	21	87	9	19	1	1	0	3	3	15	—	.218	.244	.253
Mike Hines†	OF14	R	22	14	56	11	13	4	0	0	4	4	5	—	.232	.283	.304
Pop Tate	C4	R	24	4	13	1	2	0	0	0	2	1	3	—	.154	.214	.154
Bill Collver	OF1	—	18	1	4	0	0	0	0	0	0	0	1	—	.000	.000	.000

E. Sutton, 1 G at 1B; P. Dealy, 2 G at OF, 1 G at 1B

Pitcher	T	Age	G	GS	CG	ShO	IP	H	HR	BB	SO	W-L	Sv	ERA
Jim Whitney	R	27	51	50	50	2	441.1	503	14	37	200	18-32	0	2.98
Charlie Buffinton	R	24	51	50	49	6	434.1	425	10	112	242	22-27	0	2.88
Daisy Davis	R	26	11	11	10	1	94.1	110	2	28	30	5-6	0	4.29
Bill Stemmeyer	R	20	2	2	2	1	11.0	7	0	11	8	1-1	0	0.00

1885 Detroit Wolverines 6th NL 41-67 .380 44.0 GB

Charlie Morton (7-31)/Bill Watkins (34-36)

Player	Gm by Position	B	Age	G	AB	R	H	2B	3B	HR	RBI	BB	SO	SB	Avg	OBP	Slg
Charlie Bennett	C62,OF19,3B10	R	30	91	349	49	94	24	13	5	60	47	37	—	.269	.356	.456
Mox McQuery	1B69,OF1	—	24	70	278	34	76	15	4	3	30	8	29	—	.273	.294	.388
Sam Crane	2B68	R	31	68	245	23	47	4	6	1	20	13	45	—	.192	.233	.269
Jim Donnelly	3B55,1B1	R	19	56	211	24	49	4	3	1	22	10	29	—	.232	.267	.294
Marr Phillips†	SS33	R	28	33	139	13	29	5	0	0	17	0	13	—	.209	.209	.245
Ned Hanlon	OF105	L	27	105	424	93	128	18	8	1	29	47	18	—	.302	.372	.389
George Wood	OF70,3B12,P1*	L	26	82	362	62	105	19	8	5	28	13	19	—	.290	.315	.428
Sam Thompson	OF62,3B1	L	25	63	254	58	77	11	9	7	44	16	22	—	.303	.344	.500
Joe Quest	2B39,SS15,OF1	R	32	55	200	24	39	8	2	0	21	14	25	—	.195	.248	.255
Jerry Dorgan	OF39	L	29	39	161	23	46	6	2	0	24	8	10	—	.286	.320	.348
Stump Wiedman	P38,OF7,2B1	R	24	44	153	7	24	2	1	1	14	8	32	—	.157	.199	.203
Milt Scott†	1B38	R	19	38	148	14	39	7	0	0	12	4	16	—	.264	.283	.311
Charlie Getzien	P37,OF2	R	21	40	137	9	29	3	0	0	16	4	27	—	.212	.234	.234
Lady Baldwin	P21,OF12	L	26	31	124	12	30	6	3	0	18	6	22	—	.242	.277	.339
Deacon McGuire	C31,OF3	R	21	34	121	11	23	4	2	0	9	5	23	—	.190	.222	.256
Charlie Morton	3B18,SS4	R	30	22	79	9	14	1	2	0	3	5	10	—	.177	.226	.241
Jim Manning†	SS20	S	23	20	78	15	21	4	0	1	9	4	10	—	.269	.305	.359
Frank Ringo†	C8,3B8,OF1	R	24	17	65	12	16	3	0	0	2	0	7	—	.246	.246	.292
Chub Collins	SS14	S	27	14	55	8	10	0	2	0	6	0	11	—	.182	.182	.255
Jim Halpin	SS15	—	21	15	54	3	7	2	0	0	1	1	12	—	.130	.145	.167
Gene Moriarity	OF6,3B4,P1*	L	20	11	39	1	1	1	0	0	0	0	10	—	.026	.026	.051
Jerrie Moore	C6	L	—	6	23	2	4	1	0	0	0	1	3	—	.174	.208	.217
Nate Kellogg	SS5	—	26	5	17	4	2	1	0	0	0	1	5	—	.118	.167	.176
George Bryant	2B1	—	28	1	4	0	0	0	0	0	1	0	2	—	.000	.000	.000
Frank Olin	3B1	L	25	1	4	1	2	0	0	0	0	0	0	—	.500	.500	.500
Ed Gastfield†	C1	R	19	1	3	0	0	0	0	0	0	0	2	—	.000	.000	.000
Frank Meinke	P1,OF1	R	21	1	3	0	0	0	0	0	0	0	1	—	.000	.000	.000

G. Wood, 1 G at SS; G. Moriarity, 1 G at SS

Pitcher	T	Age	G	GS	CG	ShO	IP	H	HR	BB	SO	W-L	Sv	ERA
Stump Wiedman	R	24	38	38	37	3	330.0	343	7	63	149	14-24	0	3.14
Charlie Getzien	R	21	37	37	37	1	330.0	360	8	92	110	12-25	0	3.03
Lady Baldwin	L	26	21	20	19	1	179.1	137	2	28	135	11-9	1	1.86
Dan Casey	L	22	12	12	12	1	104.0	105	1	35	79	4-8	0	3.29
Frank Meinke	R	21	1	1	0	0	5.0	13	0	4	0	0-1	0	3.60
George Wood	R	26	1	0	0	0	4.0	5	0	1	1	0-0	0	0.00
Gene Moriarity	L	20	1	0	0	0	2.0	3	0	1	1	0-0	0	9.00

1885 Buffalo Bisons 7th NL 38-74 .339 49.0 GB

Pud Galvin (7-17)/Jack Chapman (31-57)

Player	Gm by Position	B	Age	G	AB	R	H	2B	3B	HR	RBI	BB	SO	SB	Avg	OBP	Slg
George Myers	C69,OF23	R	24	89	326	40	67	7	2	0	19	23	40	—	.206	.258	.239
Dan Brouthers	1B98	L	27	98	407	87	146	32	11	7	59	34	10	—	.359	.408	.543
Hardy Richardson	2B50,OF48,P1*	R	30	96	426	90	136	19	11	6	44	20	22	—	.319	.350	.458
Deacon White	3B98	L	37	98	404	54	118	6	6	0	57	12	11	—	.292	.313	.337
Jack Rowe	SS65,C23,OF12	L	28	98	421	62	122	28	8	2	51	13	19	—	.290	.311	.409
Jim Lillie	OF112,SS3,1B1	—	23	112	430	49	107	13	3	2	30	6	39	—	.249	.259	.307
Bill Crowley	OF92	R	28	92	344	29	83	14	1	1	36	21	32	—	.241	.285	.297
Ed Crane†	OF13	R	23	13	51	5	14	0	1	2	9	3	8	—	.275	.315	.431
Davy Force	2B42,SS24,3B6	R	35	71	253	20	57	6	1	0	15	13	19	—	.225	.263	.257
Ecky Stearns†	SS19,1B12,C2	L	23	30	105	7	21	6	1	0	9	8	23	—	.200	.257	.276
Pete Wood	P24,OF4,1B2	—	28	28	104	10	23	3	1	0	5	0	18	—	.221	.221	.269
Pete Conway	P27,OF2,1B1*	R	18	29	90	7	10	5	0	1	7	5	28	—	.111	.158	.200
Jim McCauley†	C21,OF4	L	22	24	84	4	15	2	1	0	7	11	12	—	.179	.274	.226
Scrappy Carroll	OF13	—	24	13	40	1	3	0	0	0	1	2	8	—	.075	.119	.075
Gil Hatfield	3B8,2B3	—	30	11	30	1	4	0	1	0	0	0	11	—	.133	.133	.200
Moxie Hengle	2B5,OF3	R	27	7	26	2	4	0	0	0	0	1	2	—	.154	.185	.154
Dave Eggler	OF6	R	34	6	24	0	2	0	0	0	0	2	4	—	.083	.154	.083
Joe Staples	OF6,2B1	—	—	7	22	0	1	0	0	0	0	0	9	—	.045	.045	.045
Buttercup Dickerson	OF5	L	26	5	21	1	1	1	0	0	0	1	4	—	.048	.091	.095
Denny Driscoll	2B7	L	29	7	19	2	3	0	0	0	0	2	5	—	.158	.238	.158
Dick Phelan†	2B4	R	30	4	16	2	2	0	0	1	3	0	3	—	.125	.125	.313
Jim McDonald	SS4,OF1	—	24	5	14	0	0	0	0	0	0	0	4	—	.000	.000	.000
Charlie Ritter	2B2	—	—	2	6	0	1	0	0	0	0	0	2	—	.167	.167	.167
Fred Wood	C1	—	22	1	4	0	1	0	0	0	0	0	0	—	.250	.250	.250

H. Richardson, 1 G at SS; P. Conway, 1 G at SS

Pitcher	T	Age	G	GS	CG	ShO	IP	H	HR	BB	SO	W-L	Sv	ERA
Pud Galvin†	R	28	33	32	31	3	284.0	356	8	37	93	13-19	1	4.09
Billy Serad	R	22	30	29	27	0	241.1	299	5	80	90	7-21	0	4.10
Pete Conway	R	18	27	27	26	1	210.0	256	10	44	94	10-17	0	4.67
Pete Wood	R	28	24	22	21	0	198.2	235	8	66	38	8-15	0	4.44
John Connor†	—	30	1	1	1	0	9.0	14	0	2	0	0-1	0	4.00
George Fisher	—	—	1	1	1	0	9.0	10	0	2	4	0-1	0	5.00
Hardy Richardson	R	30	1	0	0	0	4.0	5	0	3	1	0-0	0	2.25

1885 St. Louis Maroons 8th NL 36-72 .333 49.0 GB

Fred Dunlap (21-29)/Alex McKinnon (6-32)/Fred Dunlap (9-11)

Player	Gm by Position	B	Age	G	AB	R	H	2B	3B	HR	RBI	BB	SO	SB	Avg	OBP	Slg
Fatty Briody	C60,2B1,3B1*	—	26	62	215	14	42	9	0	1	17	12	23	—	.195	.238	.251
Alex McKinnon	1B100	R	28	100	411	42	121	21	6	1	44	8	31	—	.294	.308	.382
Fred Dunlap	2B106	R	26	106	423	70	114	11	5	2	25	41	24	—	.270	.334	.333
Ed Caskin	3B69,C23,SS1	R	33	71	262	31	47	3	0	0	12	12	22	—	.179	.215	.191
Jack Glasscock	SS110,2B1	R	25	111	446	66	125	18	3	1	40	29	10	—	.280	.324	.341
Orator Shaffer†	OF69	L	33	69	257	30	50	11	2	0	18	19	31	—	.195	.250	.253
Emmett Seery	OF59,3B1	L	24	59	216	20	35	7	0	1	14	16	37	—	.162	.220	.208
Joe Quinn	OF57,3B31,1B11	R	20	97	343	27	73	8	2	0	15	9	38	—	.213	.233	.248
Charlie Sweeney	OF39,P35	R	22	71	267	27	55	7	1	0	24	12	33	—	.206	.240	.240
Henry Boyle	P42,OF31,2B2	—	24	72	258	24	52	9	1	1	21	13	38	—	.202	.240	.256
Fred Lewis	OF45	S	26	45	181	12	53	9	0	1	27	9	10	—	.293	.326	.359
George Baker	C32,3B3,OF2*	—	26	38	131	5	16	0	0	0	5	9	28	—	.122	.179	.122
Dave Rowe	OF16	R	30	16	62	8	10	3	0	0	3	5	8	—	.161	.224	.210
Dick Burns	OF14,P1	L	21	14	54	2	12	2	1	0	4	3	8	—	.222	.263	.296
Sy Sutcliffe†	C14,OF2	L	23	16	49	2	6	1	0	0	4	5	10	—	.122	.204	.143
Rooney Sweeney	OF2,C1	—	25	3	11	1	1	0	0	0	0	0	4	—	.091	.091	.091
Jack Brennan	OF2,3B1	—	23	3	10	0	1	0	0	0	1	1	1	—	.100	.182	.100
Tom Dolan	C3	R	26	3	9	1	2	0	0	0	0	2	1	—	.222	.364	.222
Joe Fogarty	OF2	—	16	2	8	1	1	0	0	0	0	0	1	—	.125	.125	.125
Jack Gleason	3B2	R	30	2	7	0	1	0	0	0	0	0	1	—	.143	.143	.143
Trick McSorley	3B2	R	32	2	6	2	3	1	0	0	1	2	1	—	.500	.625	.667
Billy Alvord	3B2	—	21	2	5	0	0	0	0	0	0	1	2	—	.000	.167	.000
Dick Phelan†	3B2	R	30	2	4	1	1	1	0	0	1	0	2	—	.250	.250	.500
Charlie Krehmeyer†	C1	L	21	1	3	0	0	0	0	0	0	0	2	—	.000	.000	.000

F. Briody, 1 G at OF; G. Baker, 1 G at 2B

Pitcher	T	Age	G	GS	CG	ShO	IP	H	HR	BB	SO	W-L	Sv	ERA
Henry Boyle	R	24	42	39	39	1	366.2	346	2	100	133	16-24	0	2.75
Charlie Sweeney	R	22	35	35	32	2	275.0	276	6	50	84	11-21	0	3.93
John Kirby	R	20	14	14	14	0	129.1	118	0	44	46	5-8	0	3.55
One Arm Daily	R	28	11	11	10	1	91.1	92	5	44	31	3-8	0	3.94
Egyptian Healy	R	18	8	8	8	0	66.0	54	0	20	32	1-7	0	3.00
— Palmer	—	—	4	4	4	0	34.0	46	2	20	9	0-4	0	3.44
Dick Burns	L	21	1	0	0	0	3.0	3	0	0	2	0-0	0	9.00

»1885 St. Louis Browns 1st AA 79-33 .705 —

Charlie Comiskey

Player	Gm by Position	B	Age	G	AB	R	H	2B	3B	HR	RBI	BB	SO	SB	Avg	OBP	Slg
Doc Bushong	C85,3B1	R	28	85	300	42	80	13	5	0	21	11	—	—	.267	.297	.343
Charlie Comiskey	1B83	R	25	83	340	68	87	15	7	2	44	14	—	—	.256	.293	.359
Sam Barkley	2B96,1B11	R	27	106	418	67	112	18	10	3	53	25	—	—	.268	.312	.380
Arlie Latham	3B109,C2	R	25	110	485	84	100	15	3	1	34	18	—	—	.206	.242	.256
Bill Gleason	SS112	R	26	112	472	79	119	9	5	3	53	29	—	—	.252	.316	.311
Curt Welch	OF112	R	23	112	432	84	117	18	8	3	69	23	—	—	.271	.318	.370
Hugh Nicol	OF111,3B1	R	27	112	425	59	88	11	1	0	45	34	—	—	.207	.271	.238
Yank Robinson	OF52,2B19,C5*	R	25	78	287	63	75	8	8	0	35	29	—	—	.261	.344	.345
Dave Foutz	P47,1B15,OF4	R	28	65	238	42	59	6	4	0	34	11	—	—	.248	.281	.307
Bob Caruthers	P53,OF7	L	21	60	222	37	50	10	2	1	12	20	—	—	.225	.289	.302
Tip O'Neill	OF52	R	27	52	206	44	72	7	4	3	38	13	—	—	.350	.399	.466
Dan Sullivan†	C13,1B4	—	28	17	60	4	7	2	0	0	3	6	—	—	.117	.197	.150
Jumbo McGinnis	P13,OF1	—	21	13	50	3	11	0	0	1	7	1	—	—	.220	.235	.280
Mike Drissel	C6	R	20	6	20	0	1	0	0	0	0	0	—	—	.050	.050	.050
Cal Broughton†	C4	R	24	4	17	1	1	0	0	0	1	0	—	—	.059	.059	.059

Y. Robinson, 2 G at 3B, 1 G at 1B

Pitcher	T	Age	G	GS	CG	ShO	IP	H	HR	BB	SO	W-L	Sv	ERA
Bob Caruthers	R	21	53	53	53	6	482.1	430	3	57	190	40-13	0	2.07
Dave Foutz	R	28	47	46	46	2	407.2	351	8	92	147	33-14	0	2.63
Jumbo McGinnis	—	21	13	13	12	3	112.0	98	1	19	41	6-6	0	3.38

1885 Cincinnati Reds 2nd AA 63-49 .563 16.0 GB

Ollie Caylor

Player	Gm by Position	B	Age	G	AB	R	H	2B	3B	HR	RBI	BB	SO	SB	Avg	OBP	Slg
Pop Snyder	C38,1B1	R	30	39	152	13	36	4	3	1	19	6	—	—	.237	.270	.322
John Reilly	1B107,OF7	R	26	111	482	92	143	18	11	5	60	11	—	—	.297	.322	.411
Bid McPhee	2B110	R	25	110	431	78	114	12	4	0	46	19	—	—	.265	.306	.311
Hick Carpenter	3B112	R	29	112	473	89	131	12	8	2	61	9	—	—	.277	.295	.349
Frank Fennelly	SS112	R	25	112	454	82	124	14	17	10	89	38	—	—	.273	.333	.445
Charley Jones	OF112	R	35	112	487	108	157	19	17	5	35	21	—	—	.322	.362	.462
Pop Corkhill	OF110,P8,1B3	L	27	112	440	64	111	16	8	1	53	7	—	—	.252	.275	.318
Jim Clinton	OF105	R	34	105	408	48	97	5	5	0	34	15	—	—	.238	.277	.275
Jim Keenan	C33,1B4,P1	R	27	36	132	16	35	2	2	1	15	8	—	—	.265	.307	.333
Kid Baldwin	C25,OF6,P2*	R	20	34	126	9	17	1	0	1	8	3	—	—	.135	.155	.167
Larry McKeon	P33,OF1	—	19	33	121	14	20	3	1	0	8	0	—	—	.165	.165	.207
Phil Powers†	C15	R	30	15	60	6	16	2	0	0	7	0	—	—	.267	.267	.300
Gus Shallix	P13,OF3	R	27	13	39	3	5	0	0	0	2	3	—	—	.128	.227	.128
Jimmy Peoples†	C5,P2,OF1	—	21	7	22	1	4	0	0	0	1	1	—	—	.182	.217	.182

K. Baldwin, 2 G at 2B, 1 G at 3B

Pitcher	T	Age	G	GS	CG	ShO	IP	H	HR	BB	SO	W-L	Sv	ERA
Will White	R	30	34	34	33	2	293.1	295	9	64	80	18-15	0	3.53
Larry McKeon	—	19	33	33	32	2	290.0	273	5	50	117	20-13	0	2.86
Billy Mountjoy†	R	26	17	17	17	1	153.2	149	5	52	50	10-7	0	3.16
Gus Shallix	R	27	13	12	7	0	91.1	95	1	33	15	6-4	0	3.25
George Pechiney	R	23	11	11	11	1	98.0	95	1	30	49	7-4	0	2.02
Jimmy Peoples	R	21	2	2	1	0	15.0	30	0	2	4	0-2	0	12.00
Harry McCaffery	R	26	1	1	1	0	9.0	13	1	2	2	1-0	0	6.00
Kid Baldwin	R	20	2	1	0	0	4.0	5	0	6	1	0-0	0	9.00
Pop Corkhill	R	27	8	1	0	0	37.0	36	2	10	12	1-4	1	3.65
Jim Keenan	R	27	1	0	0	0	8.0	7	0	1	0	0-0	0	1.13

1885 Pittsburgh Alleghenys 3rd AA 56-55 .505 22.5 GB

Horace Phillips

Player	Gm by Position	B	Age	G	AB	R	H	2B	3B	HR	RBI	BB	SO	SB	Avg	OBP	Slg
Fred Carroll	C60,OF12	R	20	71	280	45	75	13	8	0	30	7	—	—	.268	.298	.371
Jim Field†	1B56	—	22	56	209	28	50	9	1	1	15	13	—	—	.239	.306	.306
Pop Smith	2B106	R	28	106	453	85	113	11	13	0	35	25	—	—	.249	.293	.331
Bill Kuehne	3B97,SS7	R	26	104	411	54	93	9	19	0	43	15	—	—	.226	.257	.341
Art Whitney	SS75,3B8,2B4*	R	27	90	373	53	87	10	4	0	28	16	—	—	.233	.267	.282
Tom Brown	OF108,P2	L	24	108	437	81	134	16	12	4	68	34	—	—	.307	.366	.426
Fred Mann	OF97,3B3	L	27	99	391	60	99	17	6	0	41	31	—	—	.253	.318	.327
Charlie Eden	OF96,P4,3B2	L	30	98	405	57	103	18	6	0	38	17	—	—	.254	.298	.328
Ed Morris	P63,OF1	S	22	64	237	19	44	3	6	0	14	5	—	—	.186	.202	.224
Milt Scott†	1B55	R	19	55	210	15	52	7	1	0	18	5	—	—	.248	.272	.290
Doggie Miller	C33,OF6,3B2*	R	20	42	166	19	27	3	1	0	13	4	—	—	.163	.182	.193
John Richmond	SS23,OF11	—	31	34	131	14	27	2	2	0	12	8	—	—	.206	.262	.252
Pete Meegan	P18,OF3,2B1	—	21	19	67	3	13	1	0	0	3	3	—	—	.194	.229	.209
Rudy Kemmler	C18	R	25	18	64	2	13	2	1	0	5	2	—	—	.203	.239	.266
Hank O'Day	P12,OF3	—	22	13	49	7	12	2	1	0	3	1	—	—	.245	.260	.327
Pud Galvin†	P11,OF1	R	28	11	38	2	4	0	0	0	2	0	—	—	.105	.105	.105
Marr Phillips†	SS4	R	28	4	15	1	4	0	0	0	2	2	—	—	.267	.353	.267
Frank Ringo†	C3	R	24	3	11	0	2	0	0	0	0	0	—	—	.182	.182	.182

A. Whitney, 3 G at OF; D. Miller, 2 G at SS

Pitcher	T	Age	G	GS	CG	ShO	IP	H	HR	BB	SO	W-L	Sv	ERA
Ed Morris	L	22	63	63	63	7	581.0	459	5	101	298	39-24	0	2.35
Pete Meegan	—	21	18	16	14	1	146.0	146	1	38	58	7-8	0	3.39
Hank O'Day	R	22	12	12	10	0	103.0	110	4	16	36	5-7	0	3.67
Pud Galvin†	R	28	11	11	9	0	88.1	97	2	7	27	3-7	0	3.67
Frank Mountain	R	25	5	5	5	0	46.0	56	1	24	7	1-4	0	4.30
John Hofford	—	22	3	3	3	0	25.0	28	1	9	21	0-3	0	3.60
Charlie Eden	L	30	4	1	0	0	15.2	22	0	3	5	1-2	0	5.17
Tom Brown	R	24	2	0	0	0	6.0	0	0	3	2	0-0	0	3.00

1885 Philadelphia Athletics 4th AA 55-57 .491 24.0 GB

Player	Gm by Position	B	Age	G	AB	R	H	2B	3B	HR	RBI	BB	SO	SB	Avg	OBP	Slg
Jocko Milligan	C61,1B6,OF2	R	23	67	265	35	71	15	4	2	39	7	—	—	.268	.289	.377
Harry Stovey	1B82,OF30	R	28	112	486	130	153	27	9	13	75	39	—	—	.315	.371	.488
Cub Stricker	2B106	R	26	106	398	71	93	9	3	1	41	21	—	—	.234	.284	.279
Fred Corey	3B92,P1,SS1	R	28	94	384	61	94	14	8	1	38	17	—	—	.245	.282	.331
Sadie Houck	SS93	R	29	93	388	74	99	10	9	0	54	10	—	—	.255	.286	.327
Henry Larkin	OF108	R	25	108	453	114	149	37	14	8	88	26	—	—	.329	.372	.525
John Coleman	OF93,P8	L	22	96	398	71	119	15	11	3	70	25	—	—	.299	.345	.415
Blondie Purcell†	OF66,P1	R	31	66	304	71	90	15	5	0	22	16	—	—	.296	.337	.378
Jack O'Brien	C43,SS9,1B7*	R	25	62	225	35	60	9	1	2	30	20	—	—	.267	.340	.342
Bobby Mathews	P48,OF1	R	33	48	179	22	30	3	0	0	12	10	—	—	.168	.212	.184
George Strief	3B19,SS10,OF8*	R	28	44	175	19	48	8	5	0	27	9	—	—	.274	.310	.377
Lon Knight†	OF29,P1	R	32	29	119	17	25	1	1	0	14	9	—	—	.210	.271	.235
Martin Powell	1B19	L	29	19	75	5	12	0	3	0	5	1	—	—	.160	.192	.240
Tom Lovett	P16,OF1	R	21	16	58	9	13	0	1	0	3	3	—	—	.224	.274	.259
Ed Knouff	P14,OF1	R	17	14	48	5	9	0	0	0	2	2	—	—	.188	.220	.188
Marshall Quinton	C7	—	—	7	29	6	6	1	0	0	4	1	—	—	.207	.258	.241
Bill Vinton†	P7,OF1	R	20	7	26	5	4	2	0	0	4	3	—	—	.154	.241	.231
Eddie Fusselback	C5	R	26	5	19	2	6	1	0	0	2	0	—	—	.316	.316	.368
Bill Hughes	P2,OF2	L	18	4	16	3	3	1	1	0	1	1	—	—	.188	.278	.375
Bob Emslie†	P4,OF1	R	26	4	12	1	1	0	0	0	0	0	—	—	.083	.083	.083
Frank Siffell	C2,OF1	—	25	3	10	0	1	0	0	0	0	0	—	—	.100	.100	.100
Orator Shaffer†	OF2	L	33	2	9	1	2	0	1	0	1	1	—	—	.222	.300	.444
Jim Conway	P2,OF1	—	26	2	6	2	0	0	0	0	0	1	—	—	.000	.250	.000

J. O'Brien, 3 G at OF, 2 G at 3B; G. Strief, 7 G at 2B

Harry Stovey

Pitcher	T	Age	G	GS	CG	ShO	IP	H	HR	BB	SO	W-L	Sv	ERA
Bobby Mathews	R	33	48	48	46	2	422.1	394	3	57	286	30-17	0	2.43
Tom Lovett	—	21	16	16	15	1	138.2	130	3	38	56	7-8	0	3.70
Ed Knouff	R	17	14	13	12	0	106.0	103	0	44	43	7-6	0	3.65
Ed Cushman†	L	33	10	10	10	0	87.0	101	1	17	37	3-7	0	3.52
Bill Vinton†	R	20	7	7	6	2	55.0	46	1	15	34	4-3	0	2.45
Billy Taylor	R	30	6	6	6	0	52.1	68	0	9	11	1-5	0	3.27
Bob Emslie†	R	26	4	4	3	0	28.2	37	1	6	9	0-4	0	6.28
Bill Hughes	L	18	2	2	2	0	16.2	18	0	10	4	0-2	0	4.86
Jim Conway	R	26	2	2	1	0	12.1	19	0	2	0	0-1	0	7.30
Fred Corey	R	28	1	1	1	0	9.0	18	2	1	3	1-0	0	7.00
Phenomenal Smith†	L	20	1	1	0	0	4.0	7	0	4	7	0-1	0	9.00
John Coleman	R	22	8	3	3	0	60.1	82	0	5	12	2-2	0	3.43
Blondie Purcell	R	31	1	0	0	0	6.0	11	0	2	3	0-1	0	6.00
Lon Knight†	R	32	1	0	0	0	5.0	4	0	2	1	0-0	0	1.80

1885 Louisville Colonels 5th AA 53-59 .473 26.0 GB

Player	Gm by Position	B	Age	G	AB	R	H	2B	3B	HR	RBI	BB	SO	SB	Avg	OBP	Slg
Joe Crotty	C38,1B1	R	24	39	129	14	20	2	0	0	7	3	—	—	.155	.193	.171
John Kerins	1B96,C19,OF3*	R	26	112	456	65	111	9	16	3	51	20	—	—	.243	.281	.353
Tom McLaughlin	2B93,SS19	—	25	112	411	49	87	13	9	2	41	15	—	—	.212	.245	.302
Phil Reccius	3B97,P7	—	23	102	402	57	97	8	10	1	38	13	—	—	.241	.267	.318
Joe Miller	SS79,3B11,2B8	R	24	98	339	44	62	9	5	0	24	28	—	—	.183	.249	.239
Pete Browning	OF112	R	24	112	481	98	174	34	10	9	73	25	—	—	.362	.393	.530
Chicken Wolf	OF111,C2,P1*	R	23	112	483	79	141	23	17	1	52	11	—	—	.292	.309	.416
Leech Maskrey	OF108,3B3	R	31	109	423	54	97	8	11	1	46	19	—	—	.229	.269	.307
Guy Hecker	P53,1B17,OF3	R	29	70	297	48	81	9	2	2	35	5	—	—	.273	.287	.337
Amos Cross	C35	—	24	35	130	11	37	2	1	0	14	0	—	—	.285	.290	.315
Billy Geer	SS14	—	35	14	51	2	6	2	0	0	3	2	—	—	.118	.167	.157
Dan Sullivan†	C13	—	28	13	44	3	8	1	0	0	4	2	—	—	.182	.234	.205
Miah Murray	C12,1B2	R	20	12	43	4	8	0	0	0	3	2	—	—	.186	.239	.186
Reddy Mack	2B11	—	19	11	41	7	10	1	0	0	5	2	—	—	.244	.295	.268
Charlie Krehmeyer†	C4,OF2,1B1	L	21	7	31	4	7	1	1	0	5	1	—	—	.226	.250	.323
Monk Cline	3B1,OF1	L	27	2	9	0	2	1	0	0	2	0	—	—	.222	.222	.333
Joe Strauss	C1,OF1	R	26	2	6	0	1	0	0	0	0	0	—	—	.167	.167	.167

J. Kerins, 1 G at 3B; C. Wolf, 1 G at 3B

Jim Hart

Pitcher	T	Age	G	GS	CG	ShO	IP	H	HR	BB	SO	W-L	Sv	ERA
Guy Hecker	R	29	53	53	51	2	480.0	454	6	54	209	30-23	0	2.18
Norm Baker	—	22	25	24	24	1	217.0	210	3	69	79	13-12	0	3.40
Al Mays	—	20	17	17	17	0	150.0	129	3	43	61	6-11	0	2.76
Toad Ramsey	L	20	9	9	9	0	79.0	44	1	28	83	3-6	0	1.94
Phil Reccius	—	23	7	5	4	0	40.0	46	0	11	10	0-4	1	3.83
John Connor†	—	30	4	4	4	0	35.0	43	0	12	19	1-3	0	4.89
Chicken Wolf	R	23	1	0	0	0	1.0	1	0	0	1	0-0	0	9.00

1885 Brooklyn Bridegrooms 5th AA 53-59 .473 26.0 GB

Player	Gm by Position	B	Age	G	AB	R	H	2B	3B	HR	RBI	BB	SO	SB	Avg	OBP	Slg
Jackie Hayes	C42	—	24	42	137	10	18	3	0	0	10	5	—	—	.131	.179	.153
Bill Phillips	1B99	R	28	99	391	65	118	16	11	3	63	27	—	—	.302	.364	.422
George Pinckney	2B57,3B51,SS3	R	23	110	447	77	124	16	5	0	42	27	—	—	.277	.328	.336
Bill McClellan	3B57,2B55	L	29	112	464	85	124	22	7	0	49	28	—	—	.267	.317	.345
Germany Smith	SS108	R	22	108	419	63	108	17	11	4	62	10	—	—	.258	.275	.379
Ed Swartwood	OF95,1B4,C1*	L	26	99	399	80	106	8	9	0	49	36	—	—	.266	.334	.331
Pete Hotaling	OF94	R	28	94	370	73	95	9	5	1	34	49	—	—	.257	.350	.316
John Cassidy	OF54	R	28	54	221	36	47	6	2	1	28	8	—	—	.213	.250	.271
Adonis Terry	OF47,P25,3B1	R	20	71	264	23	45	1	3	1	20	10	—	—	.170	.201	.208
John Harkins	P34,OF9,3B1	R	26	43	159	20	42	4	2	1	15	9	—	—	.264	.304	.333
Jimmy Peoples†	C37,SS2,1B1*	—	21	41	151	21	30	4	1	1	15	5	—	—	.199	.229	.258
Jim McTamany	OF35	R	21	35	131	21	36	7	2	1	13	9	—	—	.275	.321	.382
Bill Krieg†	C12,1B5	R	26	17	60	7	9	4	0	1	5	2	—	—	.150	.177	.267
Charlie Robinson	C11	L	28	11	40	5	6	2	1	0	4	3	—	—	.150	.209	.250
Frank Bell	C5,OF4,3B2	—	22	10	29	5	5	0	1	0	2	0	—	—	.172	.200	.241
Dave Oldfield	C9,OF2	S	20	10	25	2	8	1	0	0	2	3	—	—	.320	.414	.360
George McVey	C3,1B3	R	19	6	21	2	3	0	0	0	1	2	—	—	.143	.217	.143
Mike Hines†	C3	R	22	3	13	1	1	0	1	0	1	0	—	—	.077	.077	.231
Bill Schenck	3B1	—	—	1	4	0	0	0	0	0	0	0	—	—	.000	.000	.000

E. Swartwood, 1 G at SS; J. Peoples, 1 G at 3B, 1 G at OF

Charlie Hackett (15-22)/Charlie Byrne (38-37)

Pitcher	T	Age	G	GS	CG	ShO	IP	H	HR	BB	SO	W-L	Sv	ERA
Henry Porter	R	26	54	54	53	2	481.2	427	11	107	197	33-21	0	2.78
John Harkins	R	26	34	34	33	1	293.0	303	7	56	141	14-20	0	3.75
Adonis Terry	R	20	25	23	23	0	209.0	213	9	42	96	6-17	1	4.26
Phenomenal Smith†	L	20	1	1	1	0	8.0	12	0	6	2	0-1	0	12.38

1885 New York Metropolitans 7th AA 44-64 .407 33.0 GB

Player	Gm by Position	B	Age	G	AB	R	H	2B	3B	HR	RBI	BB	SO	SB	Avg	OBP	Slg
C. Reipschlager	C59,3B6,OF6*	R	—	72	268	29	65	11	1	0	21	9	—	—	.243	.270	.291
Dave Orr	1B107,P3	R	25	107	444	76	152	29	21	6	77	8	—	—	.342	.358	.543
Tom Forster	2B52,OF5	R	26	57	213	28	47	7	2	0	18	17	—	—	.221	.281	.272
Frank Hankinson	3B94,P1	R	29	94	362	43	81	12	2	2	44	12	—	—	.224	.251	.285
Candy Nelson	SS107,3B1	L	36	107	420	98	107	12	4	1	30	61	—	—	.255	.353	.310
Steve Brady	OF105,1B4,2B2*	—	33	108	434	60	128	14	5	3	58	25	—	—	.295	.342	.371
Chief Roseman	OF101,P1	R	28	101	410	72	114	13	14	4	47	26			.270	.335	.407
Ed Kennedy	OF96	—	29	96	349	35	71	8	4	2	21	12	—	—	.203	.238	.266
Bill Holbert	C39,OF13,3B5	R	30	56	202	13	35	3	0	0	13	8	—	—	.173	.205	.188
Dasher Troy	2B42,OF2,SS1	R	29	45	177	24	39	3	3	2	12	5	—	—	.220	.258	.305
Ed Begley	P15,OF4	—	22	15	52	5	9	1	0	1	3	1	—	—	.173	.189	.250
Cal Broughton†	C11	R	24	11	41	1	6	1	0	0	1	1	—	—	.146	.167	.171
Joe Reilly	2B8,3B2	—	24	10	40	6	7	3	0	0	3	2	—	—	.175	.214	.250
Dick Pierson	2B3	—	27	3	9	1	1	0	0	0	0	2	—	—	.111	.273	.111
— Jones	3B1	—	—	1	4	0	1	0	0	0	0	0	—	—	.250	.250	.250

C. Reipschlager, 1 G at 2B, 1 G at SS; S. Brady, 1 G at 3B

Jim Gifford

Pitcher	T	Age	G	GS	CG	ShO	IP	H	HR	BB	SO	W-L	Sv	ERA
Jack Lynch	R	28	44	43	43	1	379.0	410	17	42	177	23-21	0	3.61
Ed Cushman†	L	33	22	22	22	0	191.0	158	2	33	133	8-14	0	2.78
Doug Crothers	R	25	18	18	18	1	154.0	192	4	49	40	7-11	0	5.08
Ed Begley	—	22	15	14	10	0	115.0	131	5	48	44	4-9	0	4.93
Buck Becannon	—	25	10	10	10	0	85.0	108	5	24	13	2-8	0	6.25
Chief Roseman	R	28	1	1	0	0	1.0	3	0	2	0	0-1	0	27.00
Dave Orr	R	25	3	0	0	0	10.0	11	2	5	1	0-0	0	7.20
Frank Hankinson	R	29	1	0	0	0	2.0	2	1	1	0	0-0	0	4.50

1885 Baltimore Orioles 8th AA 41-68 .376 36.5 GB

Billy Barnie

Player	Gm by Position	B	Age	G	AB	R	H	2B	3B	HR	RBI	BB	SO	SB	Avg	OBP	Slg
Bill Traffley	C61,OF10,2B3	R	25	69	254	27	39	4	5	1	20	17	—	—	.154	.215	.220
Ecky Stearns†	1B63,OF3,C2	L	23	67	253	40	47	3	8	1	29	38	—	—	.186	.306	.273
Tim Manning†	2B41,3B3	R	31	43	157	17	32	8	1	0	16	10	—	—	.204	.265	.268
Mike Muldoon	3B101,2B1	—	27	102	410	47	103	20	6	2	52	20	—	—	.251	.293	.344
Jimmy Macullar	SS98,OF2,P1	R	30	100	320	52	61	7	6	3	26	49	—	—	.191	.306	.278
Joe Sommer	OF107,P2,3B2*	R	26	110	471	84	118	23	6	1	44	24	—	—	.251	.291	.331
Dennis Casey	OF63	L	27	63	264	50	76	10	5	3	29	21	—	—	.288	.347	.398
Ed Greer	OF47,C12	R	20	56	211	32	42	7	0	0	21	8	—	—	.199	.235	.232
Oyster Burns	OF45,P15,SS10*	R	20	78	321	47	74	11	6	5	37	16	—	—	.231	.280	.349
Hardie Henderson	P61,2B1,OF1	R	22	61	229	23	51	5	2	1	21	12	—	—	.223	.264	.275
Gid Gardner	2B39,OF5,P1*	—	26	44	170	22	37	5	4	0	17	12	—	—	.218	.269	.294
Jim Field†	1B38	—	22	38	144	16	30	3	2	0	10	13	—	—	.208	.278	.257
Sam Trott	C17,OF4,2B2*	L	26	21	88	12	24	2	2	0	12	5	—	—	.273	.312	.341
Tom York	OF22	L	33	22	87	6	23	4	2	0	12	8	—	—	.264	.326	.356
Jake Evans	OF20	—	28	20	77	18	17	1	1	0	7	7	—	—	.221	.318	.260
Bob Emslie†	P13,OF2	R	26	13	51	6	12	1	1	0	4	0	—	—	.235	.235	.294
Harry Jacoby	2B11	—	—	11	43	4	6	2	0	0	1	2	—	—	.140	.178	.186
John Henry	P9,OF1	—	21	10	34	4	9	3	0	0	3	1	—	—	.265	.286	.353
Phil Powers†	C8,OF1	R	30	9	34	6	4	1	0	0	2	1	—	—	.118	.143	.147
Tom O'Brien	1B6,2B2	R	25	8	33	4	7	3	0	0	5	2	—	—	.212	.257	.303
Gene Derby	C9,OF1	—	25	10	31	4	4	0	0	0	2	1	—	—	.129	.182	.129
Sandy Nava	C8	—	35	8	27	2	5	1	0	0	4	1	—	—	.185	.214	.222
George Mappes	2B6	—	19	6	19	2	4	0	1	0	0	1	—	—	.211	.250	.316
Joe Brown	P4,2B1	—	26	5	19	2	3	0	0	0	0	0	—	—	.158	.158	.158
Billy Mountjoy†	P6,OF1	L	26	7	18	5	1	0	0	0	0	7	—	—	.056	.320	.056
Frank Foreman	P3,OF1	L	22	3	14	4	4	0	1	0	2	0	—	—	.286	.286	.429
Oscar Walker	OF4	L	31	4	13	1	0	0	0	0	1	0	—	—	.000	.000	.000
Joe Visner	OF4	L	25	4	13	2	3	0	0	0	2	2	—	—	.231	.333	.231
John Tener	OF1	R	21	1	4	0	0	0	0	0	0	0	—	—	.000	.000	.000
Charlie Levis	1B1	R	25	1	4	2	1	0	0	0	0	0	—	—	.250	.400	.250
Sandy McDermott	2B1	—	29	1	0	0	0	0	0	0	0	0	—	—	—	—	—

J. Sommer, 2 G at SS, 1 G at 1B; O. Burns, 6 G at 2B, 6 G at 3B, 1 G at 1B; G. Gardner, 1 G at 1B; S. Trott, 1 G at SS

Pitcher	T	Age	G	GS	CG	ShO	IP	H	HR	BB	SO	W-L	Sv	ERA
Hardie Henderson	R	22	61	61	59	0	539.1	539	7	117	263	25-35	0	3.19
Bob Emslie†	R	26	13	13	11	0	107.0	131	0	30	27	3-10	0	4.29
Oyster Burns	R	20	15	11	10	1	105.2	112	2	21	30	7-4	3	3.58
John Henry	L	21	9	9	9	0	71.0	71	0	13	31	2-7	0	4.31
Billy Mountjoy†	R	26	6	6	6	1	53.0	72	1	13	15	2-4	0	5.43
Joe Brown	—	26	4	4	4	0	38.0	52	0	4	9	0-4	0	5.68
Frank Foreman	L	22	3	3	2	0	27.0	33	0	9	11	2-1	0	6.00
Shorty Wetzel	—	17	2	2	1	0	17.0	27	0	9	6	0-2	0	8.47
Gid Gardner	—	26	1	1	1	0	9.0	16	2	6	3	0-1	0	10.00
Joe Sommer	R	26	2	0	0	0	3.0	6	0	0	0	0-0	1	9.00
Jimmy Macullar	L	30	1	0	0	0	1.0	0	0	0	0	0-0	0	0.00

»1886 Chicago White Stockings 1st NL 90-34 .726 —

Cap Anson

Player	Gm by Position	B	Age	G	AB	R	H	2B	3B	HR	RBI	BB	SO	SB	Avg	OBP	Slg
Silver Flint	C54,1B3	R	30	54	173	30	35	6	2	1	13	12	36	1	.202	.254	.277
Cap Anson	1B125,C12	R	34	125	504	117	187	35	11	10	147	55	19	29	.371	.433	.544
Fred Pfeffer	2B118,1B1	R	26	118	474	88	125	17	8	7	95	36	46	30	.264	.316	.378
Tom Burns	3B112	R	29	112	445	64	123	18	10	3	65	14	40	15	.276	.298	.382
Ned Williamson	SS121,C4,P2	R	28	121	430	69	93	17	8	6	58	80	71	13	.216	.339	.335
George Gore	OF118	L	29	118	444	150	135	20	12	6	63	102	30	23	.304	.434	.444
Abner Dalrymple	OF82	L	28	82	331	62	77	7	12	3	26	33	44	16	.233	.302	.353
Jimmy Ryan	OF70,3B6,SS6*	R	23	84	327	58	100	17	6	4	53	12	28	10	.306	.330	.431
King Kelly	OF56,C53,1B9*	R	28	118	451	155	175	32	11	4	79	83	33	53	.388	.483	.534
John Clarkson	P55,OF5	R	24	55	210	21	49	9	1	3	23	0	38	2	.233	.233	.329
Jocko Flynn	P32,OF28	—	22	57	205	40	41	6	2	4	19	18	45	9	.200	.265	.307
Jim McCormick	P42,OF4	R	29	42	174	17	41	9	2	2	21	2	30	1	.236	.244	.345
Billy Sunday	OF28	L	23	28	103	16	25	2	2	0	6	7	26	10	.243	.291	.301
George Moolic	C15,OF2	R	19	16	56	9	8	3	0	0	2	2	17	0	.143	.172	.196
Lou Hardie	C13,OF2,3B1	—	21	16	51	4	9	0	0	0	3	4	10	1	.176	.236	.176

J. Ryan, 5 G at P, 5 G at 2B; K. Kelly, 8 G at 3B, 6 G at 2B, 5 G at SS

Pitcher	T	Age	G	GS	CG	ShO	IP	H	HR	BB	SO	W-L	Sv	ERA
John Clarkson	R	24	55	55	50	3	466.2	419	19	86	313	36-17	0	2.41
Jim McCormick	R	29	42	42	38	2	347.2	341	18	100	172	31-11	0	2.82
Jocko Flynn	R	22	32	29	28	2	257.0	207	9	63	146	23-6	1	2.24
Jimmy Ryan	L	23	5	0	0	0	23.1	19	3	13	15	0-0	1	4.63
Ned Williamson	R	28	2	0	0	0	3.0	2	0	0	1	0-0	1	0.00

1886 Detroit Wolverines 2nd NL 87-36 .707 2.5 GB

Bill Watkins

Player	Gm by Position	B	Age	G	AB	R	H	2B	3B	HR	RBI	BB	SO	SB	Avg	OBP	Slg
Charlie Bennett	C69,OF4,SS1	R	31	72	235	37	57	13	5	4	34	48	29	4	.243	.371	.391
Dan Brouthers	1B121	L	28	121	489	139	181	40	15	11	72	66	16	21	.370	.445	.581
Fred Dunlap†	2B51	R	27	51	196	32	56	8	3	4	37	16	21	13	.286	.340	.418
Deacon White	3B124	L	38	124	491	65	142	19	5	1	76	31	35	9	.289	.331	.354
Jack Rowe	SS110,C3	L	29	111	468	97	142	21	9	6	87	26	27	12	.303	.340	.425
Ned Hanlon	OF126,2B1	L	28	126	494	105	116	6	6	4	60	57	39	50	.235	.314	.296
Sam Thompson	OF122	L	26	122	503	101	156	18	13	8	89	35	31	13	.310	.355	.445
Hardy Richardson	OF80,2B42,P4*	R	31	125	538	125	189	27	11	11	61	46	27	42	.351	.402	.504
Charlie Ganzel†	C45,OF7,1B5	R	24	57	213	28	58	7	2	1	31	7	22	5	.272	.295	.338
Lady Baldwin	P56,OF2	L	27	57	204	25	41	6	3	0	25	18	44	3	.201	.266	.260
Sam Crane†	2B38,SS8,OF4	R	32	47	185	24	26	2	2	1	12	8	34	8	.141	.176	.189
Charlie Getzien	P43,OF1	R	22	43	165	14	29	3	3	0	19	6	46	3	.176	.205	.230
Jim Manning	OF26,SS1	S	24	26	97	14	18	2	3	0	7	6	10	7	.186	.233	.268
Harry Decker†	C14,OF1	R	31	14	54	2	12	1	0	0	5	2	9	0	.222	.250	.241
Pete Conway†	P11,OF1	R	19	12	43	10	8	1	0	2	3	1	8	0	.186	.205	.349
Bill Smith	P9,OF1	—	—	10	38	2	7	2	0	0	4	1	14	0	.184	.205	.237
Jack McGeachey†	OF6	R	22	6	27	3	9	0	1	0	4	0	3	2	.333	.333	.407
Billy Shindle	SS7	R	22	7	26	4	7	0	0	0	4	0	5	2	.269	.269	.269
Larry Twitchell	P4,OF2	R	22	4	16	0	1	0	0	0	0	0	2	0	.063	.063	.063
Tom Gillen	C2	—	24	2	10	2	4	0	0	0	4	0	1	0	.400	.400	.400

H. Richardson, 3 G at SS, 2 G at 3B

Pitcher	T	Age	G	GS	CG	ShO	IP	H	HR	BB	SO	W-L	Sv	ERA
Lady Baldwin	L	27	56	56	55	7	487.0	371	11	100	323	42-13	0	2.24
Charlie Getzien	R	22	43	43	42	1	386.2	388	6	85	172	30-11	0	3.03
Pete Conway†	R	19	11	11	11	0	91.0	93	1	25	35	6-5	0	3.36
Bill Smith	R	—	9	9	9	0	77.0	81	0	30	36	5-4	0	4.09
Larry Twitchell	R	22	4	4	2	0	25.0	35	1	12	6	0-2	0	6.48
Phenomenal Smith	L	21	3	3	3	0	25.0	16	0	8	15	1-1	0	2.16
Hardy Richardson	R	31	4	0	0	0	12.0	11	1	10	5	3-0	0	4.50

1886 New York Giants 3rd NL 75-44 .630 12.5 GB

Jim Mutrie

Player	Gm by Position	B	Age	G	AB	R	H	2B	3B	HR	RBI	BB	SO	SB	Avg	OBP	Slg
Buck Ewing	C50,OF23,1B2	R	26	73	275	59	85	11	7	4	31	16	17	18	.309	.347	.444
Roger Connor	1B118	L	28	118	485	105	172	29	20	7	71	41	15	17	.355	.405	.540
Joe Gerhardt	2B123	R	31	123	426	44	81	11	7	0	40	22	63	8	.190	.230	.249
Dude Esterbrook	3B123	R	29	123	473	62	125	20	6	3	43	8	43	13	.264	.277	.351
Monte Ward	SS122	L	26	122	491	82	134	17	5	2	81	19	46	36	.273	.300	.340
Mike Dorgan	OF116,1B3	R	32	118	442	61	129	19	4	2	79	29	37	9	.292	.335	.367
Pete Gillespie	OF97	L	34	97	396	65	108	13	8	0	58	16	30	17	.273	.301	.346
Danny Richardson	OF64,P5,2B1*	R	23	68	237	43	55	9	1	1	27	17	21	12	.232	.283	.291
Jim O'Rourke	OF63,C47,1B2	R	35	105	440	106	136	26	6	1	34	39	21	14	.309	.365	.402
Mickey Welch	P59,OF3	R	26	59	213	17	46	4	2	0	18	7	47	3	.216	.241	.254
Tim Keefe	P64,OF1	R	29	64	205	26	35	10	1	1	20	17	42	3	.171	.234	.244
Pat Deasley	C30,OF15	R	28	41	143	18	38	6	1	0	17	4	12	2	.266	.286	.322
Bill Finley	C8,OF8	—	22	13	44	2	8	0	0	0	5	1	8	2	.182	.200	.182
Gene Begley	C3,OF2	—	25	5	16	1	2	0	0	0	1	1	3	1	.125	.176	.125
Larry Corcoran†	OF1	L	26	1	4	0	0	0	0	0	0	0	2	0	.000	.000	.000
Ed Caskin	SS1	R	34	1	4	1	2	0	0	0	1	0	1	0	.500	.500	.500
Jim Devine	OF1	—	27	1	3	0	0	0	0	0	0	0	1	0	.000	.000	.000

D. Richardson, 1 G at 3B, 1 G at SS

Pitcher	T	Age	G	GS	CG	ShO	IP	H	HR	BB	SO	W-L	Sv	ERA
Tim Keefe	R	29	64	64	62	2	540.0	478	9	100	291	42-20	0	2.53
Mickey Welch	R	26	59	59	56	1	500.0	514	13	163	272	33-22	0	2.99
Danny Richardson	R	23	5	1	1	0	25.0	33	1	11	17	0-2	0	5.76
Jim Devlin	L	20	1	0	0	0	2.0	3	0	4	2	0-0	1	18.00

1886 Philadelphia Phillies 4th NL 71-43 .623 14.0 GB

Harry Wright

Player	Gm by Position	B	Age	G	AB	R	H	2B	3B	HR	RBI	BB	SO	SB	Avg	OBP	Slg
Deacon McGuire	C49,OF1	R	22	50	167	25	33	7	1	2	18	19	25	2	.198	.280	.287
Sid Farrar	1B118	—	26	118	439	55	109	19	7	5	50	16	47	10	.248	.275	.358
Charlie Bastian	2B87,SS10,3B8	R	25	105	373	46	81	9	11	2	38	33	73	29	.217	.281	.316
Joe Mulvey	3B107,OF1	R	27	107	430	71	115	16	10	2	53	15	31	27	.267	.292	.365
Arthur Irwin	SS100,3B1	L	28	101	373	51	87	6	6	0	34	35	39	24	.233	.299	.282
Ed Andrews	OF104,2B3	R	27	107	437	93	109	15	4	2	28	31	35	56	.249	.299	.316
George Wood	OF97,SS6,3B3	L	27	106	450	81	123	18	15	4	50	23	75	9	.273	.309	.407
Jim Fogarty	OF60,2B13,3B3*	R	22	77	280	54	82	13	5	3	47	42	16	30	.293	.385	.407
Ed Daily	OF56,P27	R	23	79	309	40	70	17	1	4	50	7	34	23	.227	.244	.327
Charlie Ferguson	P48,OF27	S	23	72	261	56	66	9	1	2	25	37	28	9	.253	.346	.318
Jack Clements	C47,OF7	L	21	54	185	15	38	5	1	0	11	7	34	4	.205	.234	.243
Dan Casey	P44,OF5	R	23	44	151	11	23	4	1	0	9	9	41	0	.152	.200	.192
Tony Cusick	C25,OF3,1B1	R	26	29	104	10	23	5	1	0	4	3	14	1	.221	.243	.288
Jack Farrell†	2B17	R	28	17	60	7	11	0	1	0	3	3	11	1	.183	.222	.217
Tommy McCarthy	OF8,P1	R	22	8	27	6	5	2	1	0	3	2	3	1	.185	.241	.333
John Strike	P2,OF1	—	21	2	7	0	0	0	0	0	0	0	4	0	.000	.000	.000
Charlie Ganzel†	C1	R	24	1	3	0	0	0	0	0	0	0	1	0	.000	.000	.000

J. Fogarty, 3 G at SS, 1 G at P

Pitcher	T	Age	G	GS	CG	ShO	IP	H	HR	BB	SO	W-L	Sv	ERA
Charlie Ferguson	R	23	48	45	43	4	395.2	317	11	69	212	30-9	2	1.98
Dan Casey	L	23	44	44	39	4	369.0	326	8	104	193	24-18	0	2.41
Ed Daily	R	23	27	23	22	1	218.0	211	7	59	95	16-9	0	3.06
Cannonball Titcomb	L	19	5	5	5	0	41.0	43	1	24	24	0-5	0	3.73
John Strike	—	21	2	2	1	0	15.0	19	1	7	11	1-1	0	4.80
Jim Fogarty	R	22	1	0	0	0	6.0	7	1	0	4	0-1	0	0.00
Tommy McCarthy	R	22	1	0	0	0	1.0	0	0	1	1	0-0	0	0.00

1886 Boston Red Stockings 5th NL 56-61 .479 30.5 GB

John Morrill

Player	Gm by Position	B	Age	G	AB	R	H	2B	3B	HR	RBI	BB	SO	SB	Avg	OBP	Slg
Con Daily	C49,OF1	L	21	50	180	25	43	4	2	0	21	19	29	2	.239	.312	.283
Sam Wise	1B57,2B20,SS18*	L	28	96	387	71	112	19	12	4	72	33	61	31	.289	.345	.432
Jack Burdock	2B59	R	34	59	221	26	48	6	1	0	25	11	27	3	.217	.254	.253
Billy Nash	3B90,SS17,OF2	R	21	109	417	61	117	11	8	1	45	24	28	16	.281	.320	.353
John Morrill	SS55,1B42,2B20*	R	31	117	430	86	106	25	6	7	69	56	81	9	.247	.333	.381
Dick Johnston	OF109	R	23	109	413	48	99	18	9	1	57	3	70	11	.240	.245	.334
Joe Hornung	OF94	R	29	94	424	67	109	12	2	2	40	10	62	16	.257	.274	.309
Tom Poorman	OF88	L	28	88	371	72	97	16	6	3	41	19	52	31	.261	.297	.361
Ezra Sutton	OF43,3B28,SS28*	R	35	116	499	83	138	21	6	3	48	26	21	18	.277	.312	.361
Old Hoss Radbourn	P58,OF6	R	31	66	253	30	60	5	1	2	22	17	36	5	.237	.285	.289
Charlie Buffinton	1B19,P18,OF9	R	25	44	176	27	51	4	1	1	30	6	12	3	.290	.313	.341
Pop Tate	C31	R	25	31	106	13	24	3	1	0	3	7	17	0	.226	.274	.274
Tom Gunning	C27	R	24	27	98	15	22	2	1	0	7	3	19	3	.224	.248	.265
Pat Dealy	C14,OF1	R	—	15	46	9	15	1	1	0	3	4	4	5	.326	.380	.391
Myron Allen	2B1	R	32	1	3	0	0	0	0	0	0	0	1	0	.000	.000	.000

S. Wise, 1 G at OF; J. Morrill, 1 G at P; E. Sutton, 18 G at 2B

Pitcher	T	Age	G	GS	CG	ShO	IP	H	HR	BB	SO	W-L	Sv	ERA
Old Hoss Radbourn	R	31	58	58	57	3	509.1	521	18	111	218	27-31	0	3.00
Bill Stemmeyer	R	21	41	41	41	0	348.2	300	11	144	239	22-18	0	3.02
Charlie Buffinton	R	25	18	17	16	0	151.0	203	4	39	47	7-10	0	4.59
Charlie Parsons	L	22	2	2	2	0	16.0	20	0	4	5	0-2	0	3.94
John Morrill	R	31	1	0	0	0	4.0	5	0	0	2	0-0	0	0.00

1886 St. Louis Maroons 6th NL 43-79 .352 46.0 GB

Gus Schmelz

Player	Gm by Position	B	Age	G	AB	R	H	2B	3B	HR	RBI	BB	SO	SB	Avg	OBP	Slg
George Myers	C72,OF6,3B1	R	25	79	295	26	56	7	3	0	27	18	42	6	.190	.236	.234
Alex McKinnon	1B119,OF3	R	29	122	491	75	148	24	7	8	72	21	23	10	.301	.330	.428
Fred Dunlap†	2B71,OF1	R	27	71	285	53	76	15	2	3	32	28	30	7	.267	.332	.365
Jerry Denny	3B117,SS3	R	27	119	475	58	122	24	6	9	62	14	68	16	.257	.278	.389
Jack Glasscock	SS120,OF1	R	26	121	486	96	158	29	7	3	40	38	13	38	.325	.374	.432
Emmett Seery	OF126,P2	L	25	126	453	73	108	22	6	2	48	57	82	24	.238	.324	.327
John Cahill	OF124,P2,3B1*	R	21	125	463	43	92	17	6	1	32	9	79	16	.199	.214	.268
Jack McGeachey†	OF55,2B2,3B2	R	22	59	226	31	46	12	3	2	24	1	37	8	.204	.207	.310
Joe Quinn	OF48,2B15,1B7*	R	21	75	271	33	63	11	3	1	21	8	31	12	.232	.254	.306
Egyptian Healy	P43,OF1	R	19	43	145	10	14	5	0	0	5	2	67	0	.097	.109	.131
Frank Graves	C41,OF3,P1	—	25	43	138	7	21	2	0	0	9	7	48	11	.152	.193	.167
John Kirby	P41,OF3	—	21	42	136	10	15	4	0	0	5	3	47	0	.110	.129	.140
Sam Crane†	2B39	R	32	39	116	10	20	3	1	0	7	13	27	6	.172	.256	.216
Henry Boyle	P25,OF6	—	25	30	108	8	27	2	2	1	13	5	19	0	.250	.283	.333
Charlie Sweeney	P11,OF4,SS2	R	23	17	64	4	16	2	0	0	7	3	10	0	.250	.284	.281
Tom Dolan†	C15	R	27	15	44	8	11	3	0	0	1	7	9	2	.250	.353	.318
Joe Murphy†	P4,OF1	—	19	4	14	0	3	1	0	0	1	0	8	0	.214	.214	.286
George Mappes	C3,3B2,2B1	—	20	6	14	1	2	0	0	0	0	1	5	0	.143	.200	.143
Red Connally	OF2	—	23	2	7	0	0	0	0	0	0	0	3	0	.000	.000	.000
Louis Pelouze	OF1	L	22	1	3	0	0	0	0	0	0	0	2	0	.000	.000	.000

J. Cahill, 1 G at SS; J. Quinn, 4 G at 3B, 2 G at SS

Pitcher	T	Age	G	GS	CG	ShO	IP	H	HR	BB	SO	W-L	Sv	ERA
Egyptian Healy	R	19	43	41	39	3	353.2	315	5	118	213	17-23	0	2.88
John Kirby	R	21	41	41	38	1	325.0	329	9	134	129	11-26	0	3.30
Henry Boyle	R	25	25	24	23	2	210.0	183	5	46	101	9-15	0	1.76
Charlie Sweeney	R	23	11	11	11	0	93.0	108	9	39	28	5-6	0	4.16
Joe Murphy†	—	19	4	4	3	0	33.0	45	3	16	11	0-4	0	8.18
Al Bauers	L	36	4	4	3	0	28.2	31	1	27	13	0-4	0	5.97
Jeremiah Reardon†	—	—	1	1	1	0	8.0	10	1	5	0	0-1	0	6.75
John Cahill	R	21	2	0	0	0	12.0	11	0	3	2	1-0	0	3.00
Emmett Seery	R	25	2	0	0	0	7.0	8	1	3	2	0-0	0	7.71
Frank Graves	—	25	1	0	0	0	7.0	10	0	1	2	0-0	0	9.00

1886 Kansas City Cowboys 7th NL 30-91 .248 58.5 GB

Dave Rowe

Player	Gm by Position	B	Age	G	AB	R	H	2B	3B	HR	RBI	BB	SO	SB	Avg	OBP	Slg
Fatty Briody	C54,OF2,1B1	—	27	56	215	14	51	10	3	0	29	3	35	0	.237	.248	.312
Mox McQuery	1B122	—	25	122	449	62	111	27	4	4	38	36	44	4	.247	.303	.352
Bert Myers	2B118	R	22	118	473	69	131	22	9	4	51	22	42	3	.277	.309	.387
Jim Donnelly	3B113	R	20	113	438	51	88	11	3	0	38	36	57	16	.201	.262	.240
Charley Bassett	SS82,3B8	R	23	90	342	41	89	19	8	2	32	36	43	6	.260	.331	.380
Jim Lillie	OF114,P1	—	24	114	416	37	73	9	0	0	22	11	80	13	.175	.197	.197
Paul Radford	OF92,SS30,2B1	R	24	122	493	78	113	17	5	0	20	58	48	39	.229	.310	.284
Dave Rowe	OF90,SS11,2B4	R	31	105	429	53	103	24	8	3	57	15	43	2	.240	.266	.354
Jim Whitney	P46,OF22,3B1	L	28	67	247	25	59	13	3	2	23	29	39	5	.239	.319	.340
Mert Hackett	C53,OF13	R	26	62	230	18	50	8	3	3	25	4	59	1	.217	.231	.317
Pete Conway†	OF31,P23	R	19	51	194	22	47	8	2	1	18	5	34	3	.242	.261	.320
Stump Wiedman	P51,OF3	R	25	51	179	13	30	2	0	0	7	5	46	3	.168	.190	.179
Frank Ringo†	C13,OF2,3B1	R	25	16	56	6	13	7	0	0	7	5	10	0	.232	.295	.357
Dan Dugdale	C7,OF6	—	21	12	40	4	7	0	0	0	2	2	13	1	.175	.214	.175
Silver King	P5,OF2	R	18	7	22	0	1	0	0	0	1	2	12	0	.045	.125	.045
George Baker	C1	—	27	1	4	1	1	0	0	0	0	0	1	0	.250	.250	.250

Pitcher	T	Age	G	GS	CG	ShO	IP	H	HR	BB	SO	W-L	Sv	ERA
Stump Wiedman	R	25	51	51	48	1	427.2	549	11	112	168	12-36	0	4.50
Jim Whitney	R	28	46	44	42	3	393.0	465	9	55	167	12-32	0	4.49
Pete Conway†	R	19	23	20	19	0	180.0	236	6	61	81	5-15	0	5.75
Silver King	R	18	5	5	5	0	39.0	43	1	9	23	1-3	0	4.85
Larry McKeon†	—	20	3	3	3	0	21.0	44	0	8	3	0-2	0	10.71
Jim Lillie	—	24	1	0	0	0	6.0	8	0	1	0	0-0	0	4.50

1886 Washington Senators 8th NL 28-92 .233 60.0 GB

Mike Scanlon (13-67)/John Gaffney (15-25)

Player	Gm by Position	B	Age	G	AB	R	H	2B	3B	HR	RBI	BB	SO	SB	Avg	OBP	Slg
Barney Gilligan	C71,OF14,3B1*	R	30	81	273	23	52	9	2	0	17	39	35	6	.190	.292	.238
Phil Baker	1B56,OF21,C4	L	29	81	325	37	72	6	5	1	34	20	32	16	.222	.267	.280
Jimmy Knowles	2B62,3B53	—	27	115	443	43	94	16	11	3	35	15	73	20	.212	.238	.318
Buck Gladman	3B44	—	22	44	152	17	21	5	3	1	15	12	30	5	.138	.201	.230
Davy Force	SS56,2B8,3B4	R	36	68	242	26	44	5	1	0	16	17	26	9	.182	.236	.211
Cliff Carroll	OF111	S	26	111	433	73	99	11	6	2	22	44	26	31	.229	.300	.296
Paul Hines	OF92,3B15,1B10*	R	34	121	487	80	152	30	8	9	56	35	21	21	.312	.358	.462
Ed Crane	OF68,P10,C4	R	24	80	292	20	50	11	3	0	20	13	54	8	.171	.207	.229
Sadie Houck†	SS51,2B1	R	30	52	195	14	42	3	0	0	14	2	28	4	.215	.223	.231
Jack Farrell†	2B47	R	28	47	171	24	41	11	4	2	18	15	12	12	.240	.301	.386
Dupee Shaw	P45,OF1	L	27	45	148	13	13	2	0	0	6	14	44	0	.088	.167	.101
Joe Start	1B31	L	43	31	122	10	27	4	1	0	17	5	13	4	.221	.252	.270
Bill Krieg	1B27	R	27	27	98	11	25	6	3	1	15	3	12	2	.255	.277	.408
George Shoch	OF25,SS1	R	27	26	95	11	28	2	1	1	18	2	13	2	.295	.309	.368
Jackie Hayes	C14,OF12,2B1	—	25	26	89	8	17	3	0	3	9	4	23	0	.191	.226	.326
Larry Corcoran†	OF11,SS9,P2	L	26	21	81	9	15	2	1	0	3	7	14	3	.105	.250	.235
Dave Oldfield†	C12,OF9	S	21	21	71	2	10	2	0	0	2	5	15	0	.141	.197	.169
Tony Madigan	P14,OF1	—	17	14	48	2	4	1	0	0	2	1	20	0	.083	.102	.104
Connie Mack	C10	R	23	10	36	4	13	2	1	0	5	0	2	0	.361	.361	.472
Harry Decker†	C4,3B2,SS1	R	31	7	23	0	5	1	1	0	2	1	5	0	.217	.250	.348
Ed Whiting	C6	L	26	6	21	0	0	0	0	0	0	1	12	0	.000	.045	.000
Walt Goldsby	OF6	L	24	6	18	0	4	1	0	0	1	2	3	0	.222	.300	.278
John McGlone	3B4	—	22	4	15	2	1	0	0	0	1	0	3	0	.067	.067	.067
Tom Kinslow	C3	R	20	3	8	1	2	0	0	0	1	0	1	0	.250	.250	.250
Ed Fuller	P2,OF1	R	17	2	7	0	1	0	0	0	0	0	3	0	.143	.143	.143
Jim Gallagher	SS1	—	—	1	5	1	1	0	0	0	0	0	2	0	.200	.200	.200
George Winkelman	P1,OF1	L	25	1	5	0	1	0	0	0	0	0	1	0	.200	.200	.200
Bill Wise	P1,OF1	—	25	1	3	0	0	0	0	0	0	0	1	0	.000	.000	.000
— Joyce	OF1	—	—	1	0	0	0	0	0	0	0	0	0	0	—	—	—

B. Gilligan, 1 G at SS; P. Hines, 5 G at SS, 3 G at 2B

Pitcher	T	Age	G	GS	CG	ShO	IP	H	HR	BB	SO	W-L	Sv	ERA
Dupee Shaw	L	27	45	44	43	1	385.2	384	12	91	177	13-31	0	3.34
Bob Barr	R	29	22	22	21	1	190.2	216	7	54	80	3-18	0	4.30
Tony Madigan	R	17	14	14	13	0	115.2	159	3	44	29	1-13	0	5.06
Frank Gilmore	—	22	9	9	9	1	75.0	57	3	22	75	4-4	0	2.52
Ed Crane	R	24	10	8	7	1	70.0	91	4	53	39	1-7	0	7.20
Hank O'Day	R	23	6	6	6	0	49.0	41	1	17	47	2-2	0	1.65
One Arm Daily	R	29	6	6	6	0	49.0	69	2	40	15	0-6	0	7.35
Sadie Keefe	L	19	4	4	4	0	31.1	28	0	15	5	0-3	0	5.17
John Henry	L	22	4	4	4	0	27.2	35	1	15	19	1-3	0	4.23
Larry Corcoran	R	26	2	1	1	0	14.0	16	0	4	3	0-1	0	5.79
Ed Fuller	R	17	2	1	1	0	13.0	15	0	5	3	0-1	0	6.92
John Fox	—	27	1	1	1	0	8.0	11	0	11	3	0-1	0	9.00
George Winkelman	L	25	1	1	0	0	6.0	12	0	5	4	0-1	0	10.50
Bill Wise	—	25	1	1	0	0	3.0	6	0	2	0	0-1	0	9.00
Joe Yingling	L	19	1	0	0	0	3.0	7	1	1	1	0-0	0	12.00

»1886 St. Louis Browns 1st AA 93-46 .669 —

Charlie Comiskey

Player	Gm by Position	B	Age	G	AB	R	H	2B	3B	HR	RBI	BB	SO	SB	Avg	OBP	Slg
Doc Bushong	C106,1B1	R	29	107	386	56	86	8	0	1	31	31	—	12	.223	.281	.251
Charlie Comiskey	1B121,2B9,OF3	R	26	131	578	95	147	15	9	3	76	10	—	41	.254	.267	.327
Yank Robinson	2B125,3B6,P1*	R	26	133	481	89	132	26	9	3	71	64	—	51	.274	.377	.385
Arlie Latham	3B133,2B1	R	26	134	578	152	174	23	8	1	47	55	—	60	.301	.368	.374
Bill Gleason	SS125	R	27	125	524	97	141	18	5	0	61	43	—	19	.269	.333	.323
Tip O'Neill	OF138	R	28	138	579	106	190	28	14	3	107	47	—	9	.328	.385	.440
Curt Welch	OF138,2B2	R	24	138	563	114	158	31	13	2	95	29	—	59	.281	.332	.393
Hugh Nicol	OF57,SS8,2B4	R	28	67	253	44	52	6	3	0	19	26	—	38	.206	.280	.253
Dave Foutz	P59,OF34,1B11	R	29	102	414	66	116	18	9	3	59	9	—	17	.280	.297	.389
Bob Caruthers	P44,OF43,2B2	L	22	87	317	91	106	21	14	4	61	64	—	26	.334	.448	.527
Nat Hudson	P29,OF12,1B3	R	17	43	150	16	35	4	1	0	17	11	—	2	.233	.286	.273
Rudy Kemmler	C32,1B3	R	26	35	123	13	17	2	0	0	6	8	—	0	.138	.197	.154
Trick McSorley	SS5	R	33	5	20	1	3	3	0	0	0	0	—	0	.150	.150	.300
Lou Harding	C1	—	—	1	3	0	1	1	0	0	1	0	—	0	.333	.333	.667

Y. Robinson, 1 G at SS, 1 G at OF

Pitcher	T	Age	G	GS	CG	ShO	IP	H	HR	BB	SO	W-L	Sv	ERA
Dave Foutz	R	29	59	57	55	11	504.0	418	5	144	283	41-16	1	2.11
Bob Caruthers	R	22	44	43	42	2	387.1	323	3	86	166	30-14	0	2.32
Nat Hudson	R	17	29	27	25	0	234.1	224	3	62	100	16-10	1	3.03
Jumbo McGinnis†	—	22	10	10	10	1	87.2	107	2	27	30	5-5	0	3.80
Yank Robinson	R	26	1	1	1	0	9.0	10	0	7	1	0-1	0	3.00
Joe Murphy†	—	19	1	1	1	0	7.0	5	0	3	3	1-0	0	3.86

1886 Pittsburgh Alleghenys 2nd AA 80-57 .584 12.0 GB

Horace Phillips

Player	Gm by Position	B	Age	G	AB	R	H	2B	3B	HR	RBI	BB	SO	SB	Avg	OBP	Slg
Fred Carroll	C70,OF27,1B25*	R	21	122	486	92	140	28	11	5	64	52	—	20	.288	.362	.422
Otto Schomberg	1B72	L	21	72	246	53	67	6	6	1	29	57	—	7	.272	.417	.358
Sam Barkley	2B112,OF8,1B2	R	28	122	478	77	127	31	8	1	69	58	—	22	.266	.345	.370
Art Whitney	3B95,SS42,P1	R	28	136	511	70	122	13	4	0	55	51	—	15	.239	.315	.280
Pop Smith	SS98,2B28,C1	R	29	126	483	75	105	20	9	2	57	42	—	38	.217	.288	.308
Fred Mann	OF116	L	28	116	440	85	110	16	14	2	60	45	—	26	.250	.335	.364
Tom Brown	OF115,P1	L	25	115	460	106	131	11	11	1	51	56	—	30	.285	.365	.363
Ed Glenn	OF71	R	25	71	277	32	53	6	5	0	26	17	—	19	.191	.241	.249
Bill Kuehne	OF54,3B47,1B18	R	27	117	481	73	98	16	17	1	49	19	—	26	.204	.237	.314
Doggie Miller	C61,OF22,2B1	R	21	83	317	70	80	15	1	2	36	43	—	35	.252	.343	.325
Frank Ringo†	1B9,C6	R	25	15	56	3	12	2	2	0	5	1	—	0	.214	.228	.321
Frank Mountain	1B16,P2	R	26	18	55	6	8	1	1	0	2	13	—	3	.145	.319	.200
Jim Handiboe	P14,OF2	R	19	14	44	10	5	1	0	0	2	6	—	1	.114	.220	.136
John Coleman†	OF11	L	23	11	43	3	15	2	1	0	9	2	—	1	.349	.378	.442
Tom Quinn	C3	R	22	3	11	1	0	0	0	0	0	0	—	1	.000	.000	.000
Dan Sullivan	C1	—	29	1	4	0	0	0	0	0	0	0	—	0	.000	.000	.000

F. Carroll, 1 G at SS

Pitcher	T	Age	G	GS	CG	ShO	IP	H	HR	BB	SO	W-L	Sv	ERA
Ed Morris	L	23	64	63	63	12	555.1	455	5	118	326	41-20	1	2.45
Pud Galvin	R	29	50	50	49	2	434.2	457	3	75	72	29-21	0	2.67
Jim Handiboe	R	19	14	14	12	1	114.0	82	1	33	83	7-7	0	3.32
John Hofford	—	23	9	9	9	0	81.0	88	1	40	25	3-6	0	4.33
Bill Bishop	—	16	2	2	2	0	17.0	17	0	11	4	0-1	0	3.18
Frank Mountain	R	26	2	2	2	0	16.0	22	0	14	2	0-2	0	7.88
Art Whitney	R	28	1	0	0	0	6.0	7	0	3	2	0-0	0	3.00
Tom Brown	R	25	1	0	0	0	2.0	2	0	5	1	0-0	0	9.00

1886 Brooklyn Bridegrooms 3rd AA 76-61 .555 16.0 GB

Charlie Byrne

Player	Gm by Position	B	Age	G	AB	R	H	2B	3B	HR	RBI	BB	SO	SB	Avg	OBP	Slg
Jimmy Peoples	C76,SS14,OF8*	—	22	93	340	43	74	7	3	3	38	20	—	20	.218	.261	.282
Bill Phillips	1B141	R	29	141	585	68	160	26	15	0	72	33	—	13	.274	.313	.369
Bill McClellan	2B141	L	30	141	595	131	152	33	9	1	71	56	—	43	.255	.322	.346
George Pinckney	3B141,P1	R	24	141	597	119	156	22	7	0	37	70	—	32	.261	.339	.322
Germany Smith	SS105,C1,OF1	R	23	105	426	66	105	17	6	2	45	19	—	22	.246	.279	.329
Ed Swartwood	OF122,C1	L	27	122	471	95	132	13	10	3	58	70	—	37	.280	.377	.369
Ernie Burch	OF113	L	30	113	456	78	119	22	6	2	72	39	—	16	.261	.321	.349
Jim McTamany	OF111	R	22	111	418	86	106	23	10	2	56	54	—	18	.254	.353	.371
Adonis Terry	P34,OF32,SS13	R	21	75	299	34	71	8	9	2	39	10	—	17	.237	.265	.344
Bob Clark	C44,OF17,SS12	R	23	71	269	37	58	8	2	0	26	17	—	14	.216	.262	.260
John Harkins	P34,OF8	R	27	41	142	18	32	4	2	1	15	17	—	2	.225	.308	.303
Steve Toole	P13,OF3	R	27	14	57	7	20	4	0	0	9	1	—	3	.351	.362	.421
Dave Oldfield†	C13,SS1,OF1	S	21	14	55	7	13	1	0	0	5	2	—	1	.236	.263	.255
Joe Strauss†	OF7,C2	R	27	9	36	6	9	1	1	0	5	1	—	4	.250	.270	.333
Jim McCauley	C11	L	23	11	30	5	7	1	0	0	3	11	—	2	.233	.439	.267
Ed Kennedy	OF6	—	30	6	22	1	4	0	0	0	2	2	—	1	.182	.250	.182
Pop Schriver	OF5,C3	R	20	8	21	2	1	0	0	0	0	2	—	0	.048	.130	.048

J. Peoples, 1 G at 3B

Pitcher	T	Age	G	GS	CG	ShO	IP	H	HR	BB	SO	W-L	Sv	ERA
Henry Porter	R	27	48	48	48	1	424.0	439	8	120	163	27-19	0	3.42
Adonis Terry	R	21	34	34	32	5	288.1	263	1	115	162	18-16	0	3.09
John Harkins	R	27	34	33	33	0	292.1	286	6	114	118	15-16	0	3.60
Hardie Henderson†	R	23	14	14	14	0	124.0	112	2	51	49	10-4	0	2.90
Steve Toole	L	27	13	12	11	0	104.0	100	0	64	48	6-6	0	4.41
George Pinckney	R	24	1	0	0	0	2.0	2	0	0	0	0-0	0	4.50

1886 Louisville Colonels 4th AA 66-70 .485 25.5 GB

Jim Hart

Player	Gm by Position	B	Age	G	AB	R	H	2B	3B	HR	RBI	BB	SO	SB	Avg	OBP	Slg
John Kerins	C65,1B47,OF7*	R	27	120	487	113	131	19	9	4	50	66	—	26	.269	.360	.370
Paul Cook	1B43,C21,OF2	R	23	66	262	28	54	5	2	0	14	10	—	6	.206	.235	.240
Reddy Mack	2B137	—	20	137	483	82	118	23	11	1	56	68	—	13	.244	.342	.344
Joe Werrick	3B136	R	24	136	561	75	140	20	14	3	62	33	—	19	.250	.294	.351
Bill White	SS135,P1	—	26	135	557	96	143	17	10	1	66	37	—	14	.257	.304	.329
Chicken Wolf	OF123,1B8,C3*	R	24	130	545	93	148	17	12	3	61	27	—	23	.272	.310	.363
Pete Browning	OF112	R	25	112	467	86	159	29	6	2	68	30	—	26	.340	.389	.441
Joe Strauss†	OF74,P2,C1	R	27	74	297	36	64	5	6	1	31	8	—	25	.215	.239	.283
Guy Hecker	P49,1B22,OF17	R	30	84	343	76	117	14	5	4	48	32	—	25	.341	.402	.446
Amos Cross	C51,1B20,SS2*	—	25	74	283	51	78	14	6	1	42	44	—	13	.276	.375	.378
Lou Sylvester†	OF45	R	31	45	154	41	35	5	3	0	17	29	—	3	.227	.350	.299
Hub Collins	OF24,3B2,1B1*	R	22	27	101	12	29	3	2	0	10	5	—	7	.287	.321	.356
Bones Ely	P6,OF5	R	23	10	32	5	5	0	0	0	6	2	—	1	.156	.206	.156
Tom Sullivan	P9,OF1	—	26	9	27	1	3	0	0	0	0	4	—	0	.111	.226	.111
Elton Chamberlin	P4,OF2	R	18	6	19	2	3	0	0	0	1	4	—	0	.158	.304	.158
Leech Maskrey†	OF5	R	32	5	19	1	3	1	0	0	2	1	—	0	.158	.200	.211
Phil Reccius	OF5,P1	—	24	5	13	4	4	1	1	0	2	3	—	0	.308	.471	.538
Jack Heinzman	1B1	R	22	1	5	1	0	0	0	0	0	0	—	0	.000	.000	.000
Joe Neale	OF2,P1	R	20	2	5	0	0	0	0	0	0	0	—	0	.000	.000	.000
Tom Terrell	C1,OF1	—	19	1	4	0	1	0	0	0	0	0	—	0	.250	.250	.250
Clarence Murphy	OF1	—	—	1	3	0	0	0	0	0	0	0	—	0	.000	.000	.000

J. Kerins, 1 G at SS; C. Wolf, 1 G at P, 1 G at 2B; A. Cross, 1 G at OF; H. Collins, 1 G at 2B, 1 G at SS

Pitcher	T	Age	G	GS	CG	ShO	IP	H	HR	BB	SO	W-L	Sv	ERA
Toad Ramsey	L	21	67	67	66	3	588.2	447	3	207	499	38-27	0	2.45
Guy Hecker	R	30	49	48	45	2	420.2	390	6	118	133	26-23	0	2.87
Tom Sullivan	—	26	9	9	8	0	75.0	94	6	33	27	2-7	0	3.96
Bones Ely	R	23	6	4	4	0	44.0	53	0	26	28	0-4	1	5.32
Ted Kennedy†	—	21	4	4	4	0	32.0	53	1	16	14	0-4	0	5.34
Elton Chamberlin	R	18	4	4	4	0	31.1	39	0	17	18	0-3	0	6.61
Joe Neale	R	20	1	1	0	0	7.0	11	0	7	0	0-1	0	7.71
Phil Reccius	—	24	1	1	0	0	3.0	7	0	3	0	0-1	0	9.00
Joe Strauss	R	27	2	0	0	0	4.0	6	0	3	0	0-0	1	4.50
Chicken Wolf	R	24	1	0	0	0	3.0	7	0	0	0	0-0	0	15.00
Bill White	—	26	1	0	0	0	1.0	2	0	2	1	0-0	0	9.00

1886 Cincinnati Reds 5th AA 65-73 .471 27.5 GB

Ollie Caylor

Player	Gm by Position	B	Age	G	AB	R	H	2B	3B	HR	RBI	BB	SO	SB	Avg	OBP	Slg
Kid Baldwin	C71,3B13,OF6	R	21	87	315	41	72	8	7	3	32	8	—	12	.229	.252	.327
John Reilly	1B110,OF6	R	27	115	441	92	117	12	11	6	79	31	—	19	.265	.321	.383
Bid McPhee	2B140	R	26	140	560	139	150	23	12	8	70	59	—	40	.268	.343	.395
Hick Carpenter	3B111	R	30	111	458	67	101	8	5	2	61	18	—	8	.221	.262	.273
Frank Fennelly	SS132	R	26	132	497	113	124	13	17	6	72	60	—	32	.249	.351	.380
Charley Jones	OF127	R	36	127	500	87	135	22	10	6	68	61	—	3	.270	.356	.390
Pop Corkhill	OF112,3B12,1B7*	L	28	129	540	81	143	9	7	5	97	23	—	24	.265	.302	.335
Fred Lewis	OF76,3B1	S	27	77	324	72	103	14	6	2	32	20	—	8	.318	.365	.417
Tony Mullane	P63,OF27,1B4*	S	27	91	324	59	73	12	5	0	39	25	—	20	.225	.283	.293
Pop Snyder	C41,1B19,OF1	R	31	60	220	33	41	8	3	0	28	13	—	11	.186	.242	.250
Jim Keenan	C30,OF7,3B5*	R	28	44	148	31	40	4	3	3	24	18	—	0	.270	.357	.399
George Pechiney	P40,OF4	R	24	41	144	14	30	4	2	1	21	6	—	1	.208	.240	.285
Leech Maskrey†	OF26,3B2	R	32	27	98	7	19	3	1	0	10	5	—	4	.194	.240	.245
Larry McKeon†	P19,1B2,2B1	—	20	19	75	9	19	2	3	0	9	0	—	0	.253	.253	.360
Abner Powell†	OF13,SS6,P4	L	25	19	74	13	17	1	1	0	8	4	—	0	.230	.269	.270
Lou Sylvester†	OF17	R	31	17	55	10	10	0	0	3	8	7	—	2	.182	.286	.345
Elmer Smith	P10,OF1	L	18	10	32	7	9	1	0	0	2	9	—	0	.281	.439	.375
Lefty Marr	OF8	L	23	8	29	2	8	1	1	0	2	1	—	1	.276	.323	.379
Lee Richmond	OF7,P3	—	29	8	29	3	8	0	0	0	3	3	—	0	.276	.344	.276
Jack Boyle	C1	R	20	1	5	0	1	0	0	0	0	0	—	0	.200	.200	.200
Farmer Vaughn	C1	R	22	1	3	0	0	0	0	0	0	1	—	0	.000	.250	.000
Jeremiah Reardon†	P1,OF1	—	—	1	3	0	0	0	0	0	0	0	—	0	.000	.000	.000

P. Corkhill, 3 G at SS, 1 G at P; T. Mullane, 2 G at 3B, 1 G at 2B, 1 G at SS; J. Keenan, 4 G at 1B, 2 G at P

Pitcher	T	Age	G	GS	CG	ShO	IP	H	HR	BB	SO	W-L	Sv	ERA
Tony Mullane	R	27	63	56	55	1	529.2	501	11	166	250	33-27	0	3.70
George Pechiney	R	24	40	40	35	2	330.1	355	4	133	110	15-21	0	4.14
Larry McKeon†	—	20	19	19	16	0	156.0	174	6	54	46	8-8	0	5.08
Elmer Smith	L	18	10	10	9	0	81.2	65	1	54	41	4-5	0	3.75
Joe Murphy†	—	19	5	5	5	0	46.0	50	0	21	11	2-3	0	4.89
Will White	R	31	3	3	3	0	26.0	28	1	10	6	1-2	0	4.15
Lee Richmond	L	29	3	2	1	0	18.0	24	0	11	6	0-2	0	8.00
Bill Irwin	R	26	2	2	2	0	17.0	18	2	8	6	0-2	0	5.82
Dan Bickham	R	21	1	1	1	0	9.0	13	0	3	6	1-0	0	3.00
Clarence Stephens	R	22	1	1	1	0	8.0	9	0	5	6	1-0	0	5.63
Jeremiah Reardon†	—	—	1	1	0	0	2.0	5	0	4	0	0-1	0	18.00
Abner Powell†	R	25	4	1	1	0	15.1	16	0	9	4	0-1	0	4.70
Jim Keenan	R	28	2	0	0	0	8.0	8	0	3	2	0-1	0	3.38
Pop Corkhill	R	28	1	0	0	0	0.2	1	0	0	1	0-0	0	13.50

1886 Philadelphia Athletics 6th AA 63-72 .467 28.0 GB

Lew Simmons (41-55)/Bill Sharsig (22-17)

Player	Gm by Position	B	Age	G	AB	R	H	2B	3B	HR	RBI	BB	SO	SB	Avg	OBP	Slg
Wilbert Robinson	C61,1B22,OF5	R	23	87	342	57	69	11	3	1	30	21	—	33	.202	.254	.260
Harry Stovey	OF63,1B62,P1	R	29	123	489	115	144	28	11	7	59	64	—	68	.294	.377	.440
Lou Bierbauer	2B133,C4,P2*	L	20	137	522	56	118	17	5	2	47	21	—	19	.226	.256	.289
Jack Gleason	3B77	R	31	77	299	39	56	8	7	1	31	16	—	8	.187	.255	.271
Chippy McGarr	SS71	R	23	71	267	41	71	9	3	2	31	9	—	17	.266	.295	.345
Henry Larkin	OF139	R	26	139	565	133	180	36	16	2	74	59	—	32	.319	.390	.450
John Coleman†	OF115,1B6,P3*	L	23	121	492	67	121	18	16	0	65	33	—	28	.246	.296	.348
Ed Greer†	OF70,C1	R	21	71	264	33	51	5	3	1	20	8	—	12	.193	.223	.246
Jack O'Brien	C36,3B27,1B24*	R	26	105	423	65	107	25	7	0	56	38	—	23	.253	.325	.345
Jocko Milligan	C40,1B29,OF5*	R	24	75	301	52	76	17	3	5	45	21	—	18	.252	.301	.379
Joe Quest	SS41,2B2	R	33	42	150	14	31	4	1	0	10	20	—	5	.207	.300	.247
Denny Lyons	3B32	R	20	32	123	22	26	3	1	0	11	8	—	7	.211	.281	.252
Bobby Mathews	P24,OF1	R	34	24	88	16	21	3	0	0	10	3	—	1	.239	.264	.273
Orator Shaffer	OF21	L	34	21	82	15	22	3	3	0	8	8	—	3	.268	.333	.378
Cyclone Miller	P19,3B1,OF1	—	26	21	66	8	9	2	0	0	1	14	—	3	.136	.296	.167
George Bradley	SS13	R	33	13	48	1	4	0	0	0	1	1	—	2	.083	.102	.125
John Irwin	SS2,3B1	L	24	3	13	4	3	1	0	0	1	0	—	0	.231	.231	.308
Sam Weaver	P2,1B1	R	30	2	7	0	1	0	0	0	0	0	—	0	.143	.143	.143
Jim Hyndman	P1,OF1	—	20	1	4	0	0	0	0	0	0	0	—	0	.000	.000	.000
Charlie Kelly	SS1	—	—	1	3	0	0	0	0	0	0	0	—	0	.000	.000	.000

L. Bierbauer, 2 G at SS; J. Coleman, 1 G at 2B; J. O'Brien, 10 G at SS, 7 G at 2B, 3 G at OF; J. Milligan, 2 G at 3B

Pitcher	T	Age	G	GS	CG	ShO	IP	H	HR	BB	SO	W-L	Sv	ERA
Al Atkinson	R	25	45	45	44	1	396.2	414	11	101	154	25-17	0	3.95
Bobby Mathews	R	34	24	24	22	0	197.2	226	3	53	93	13-9	0	3.96
Bill Hart	R	20	22	22	22	2	186.0	183	7	66	78	9-13	0	3.19
Ted Kennedy†	—	21	20	19	19	0	172.2	196	4	65	68	5-15	0	4.53
Cyclone Miller	L	26	19	19	19	1	169.2	158	6	59	99	10-8	0	2.97
Jake Aydelott	—	24	2	2	2	0	18.0	21	0	12	5	0-2	0	4.00
Sam Weaver	R	30	2	2	1	0	11.0	30	0	2	2	0-2	0	14.73
Rex Smith	—	22	1	1	1	0	9.0	15	0	5	4	0-1	0	7.00
Jim Brown	—	25	1	1	1	0	8.1	9	0	3	4	0-1	0	3.24
Charlie Gessner	—	—	1	1	1	0	8.0	13	0	5	0	0-1	0	9.00
Ed Clark	—	—	1	1	1	0	8.0	10	2	2	2	0-1	0	6.75
Jim Hyndman	—	20	1	1	0	0	2.0	5	1	5	1	0-1	0	27.00
John Coleman	R	23	3	1	1	0	20.2	18	1	5	2	1-1	0	2.61
Lou Bierbauer	R	20	2	0	0	0	10.2	8	0	5	1	0-0	0	4.22
Harry Stovey	R	29	1	0	0	0	0.1	2	0	0	0	0-0	0	27.00

1886 New York Metropolitans 7th AA 53-82 .393 38.0 GB

Jim Gifford (5-12)/Bob Ferguson (48-70)

Player	Gm by Position	B	Age	G	AB	R	H	2B	3B	HR	RBI	BB	SO	SB	Avg	OBP	Slg
C. Reipschlager	C57,OF9	R	—	65	232	21	49	4	6	0	25	9	—	2	.211	.244	.280
Dave Orr	1B136	R	26	136	571	93	193	25	31	7	91	17	—	16	.338	.363	.527
Tom Forster	2B62,OF4,SS1	R	27	67	251	33	49	3	2	1	20	20	—	9	.195	.263	.235
Frank Hankinson	3B136	R	30	136	522	66	126	14	5	2	63	49	—	10	.241	.306	.299
Candy Nelson	SS73,OF36	L	37	109	413	89	93	7	2	0	24	64	—	14	.225	.332	.252
Chief Roseman	OF134,P1	R	29	134	559	90	127	19	10	5	53	24	—	6	.227	.269	.324
Steve Brady	OF123,1B1	—	34	124	466	56	112	8	5	0	39	35	—	16	.240	.298	.279
Steve Behel	OF59	—	25	59	224	32	46	5	2	0	17	22	—	16	.205	.279	.246
Tom McLaughlin	SS63,2B10,OF1	—	26	74	250	27	34	3	1	0	16	26	—	13	.136	.220	.156
John Meister	2B45	—	23	45	186	35	44	7	3	2	21	4	—	1	.237	.253	.339
Jim Donahue	OF34,C19	R	24	49	186	14	37	0	0	0	9	10	—	1	.199	.251	.199
Bill Holbert	C45,OF3,SS1	R	31	48	171	8	35	4	2	0	13	6	—	4	.205	.232	.251
Elmer Foster	2B21,OF14	R	24	35	125	16	23	0	1	0	7	7	—	3	.184	.239	.200
Joe Crotty	C14	R	25	14	47	6	8	0	1	0	2	4	—	3	.170	.250	.213
Chief Zimmer	C6	R	25	6	19	1	3	0	0	0	1	1	—	0	.158	.238	.158
Pete Connell	3B1	—	—	1	5	0	0	0	0	0	0	0	—	0	.000	.000	.000
Harry Brooks	P1,OF1	—	20	1	1	0	0	0	0	0	0	0	—	0	.000	.000	.000

Pitcher	T	Age	G	GS	CG	ShO	IP	H	HR	BB	SO	W-L	Sv	ERA
Jack Lynch	R	29	51	50	50	1	432.2	485	10	116	193	20-30	0	3.95
Al Mays	—	21	41	41	39	1	350.0	330	7	140	163	11-28	0	3.39
Ed Cushman	L	34	38	37	37	2	325.2	278	6	99	167	17-20	0	3.12
John Shaffer	—	22	8	8	8	1	69.0	40	0	29	36	5-3	0	1.96
Harry Brooks	—	20	1	1	0	0	2.0	9	0	2	0	0-1	0	36.00
Chief Roseman	R	29	1	0	0	0	7.0	6	0	0	0	0-0	0	5.14

1886 Baltimore Orioles 8th AA 48-83 .366 41.0 GB

Billy Barnie

Player	Gm by Position	B	Age	G	AB	R	H	2B	3B	HR	RBI	BB	SO	SB	Avg	OBP	Slg
Chris Fulmer	C68,OF12,P1	R	27	80	270	54	66	9	3	1	30	48	—	29	.244	.363	.311
Milt Scott	1B137,P1	R	20	137	484	48	92	11	4	2	52	22	—	11	.190	.239	.242
Mike Muldoon	2B57,3B44	—	28	101	381	57	76	13	8	0	23	34	—	12	.199	.269	.276
Jumbo Davis	3B60	L	24	60	216	23	42	5	2	1	20	11	—	12	.194	.240	.250
Jimmy Macullar	SS82,OF2,P1*	R	31	85	268	49	55	7	1	0	26	49	—	23	.205	.332	.239
Jack Manning	OF137	R	32	137	556	78	124	18	7	1	45	50	—	24	.223	.291	.286
Joe Sommer	OF95,2B32,3B11*	R	27	139	560	79	117	18	4	1	52	24	—	31	.209	.245	.261
Pat O'Connell	OF41,P1,1B1	L	25	42	166	20	30	3	2	0	8	11	—	10	.181	.236	.223
Joe Farrell	2B45,3B27,OF1	R	29	73	301	36	63	8	3	1	31	12	—	5	.209	.240	.266
Sadie Houck†	SS55,2B5,OF1	R	30	61	260	29	50	8	1	0	17	4	—	25	.192	.216	.231
Matt Kilroy	P68,OF2	L	20	68	218	33	38	3	1	0	11	21	—	20	.174	.253	.197
Buster Hoover	OF40	R	23	40	157	25	34	2	6	0	10	16	—	15	.217	.297	.306
Tom Dolan†	C35,OF3	R	27	38	125	13	19	3	2	0	12	8	—	8	.152	.203	.208
Jumbo McGinnis†	P26,OF2	—	22	26	85	7	16	5	0	1	6	4	—	3	.188	.225	.282
Blondie Purcell	OF26,P1,SS1	R	32	26	85	17	19	0	1	0	8	17	—	13	.224	.365	.247
Bill Traffley	C25	R	26	25	85	15	18	0	1	0	7	10	—	8	.212	.295	.235
Jim Clinton	OF23	R	35	23	83	8	15	1	0	0	6	4	—	3	.181	.227	.193
Len Sowders	OF23,1B1	—	25	23	76	10	20	3	1	0	14	12	—	6	.263	.364	.329
Abner Powell†	P7,OF4	L	25	11	39	4	7	2	1	0	7	1	—	4	.179	.200	.282
Billy Taylor	P8,C1,1B1	R	31	10	39	4	12	0	1	0	8	1	—	1	.308	.325	.359
Ed Greer†	OF9,C2	R	21	11	38	2	5	1	0	0	4	2	—	4	.132	.175	.158
Dick Conway	P9,OF1	L	20	9	34	5	7	2	0	0	3	3	—	1	.206	.270	.265
Bill Conway	C7	R	24	7	14	4	2	0	0	0	3	7	—	0	.143	.429	.143
Ned Bligh	C3	R	22	3	9	0	0	0	0	0	0	1	—	0	.000	.100	.000
Billy Barnie	C1,OF1	—	33	2	6	0	0	0	0	0	0	1	—	0	.000	.143	.000
Sandy Nava	C1,SS1	—	36	2	5	0	1	0	0	0	0	0	—	1	.200	.200	.200
Tony Hellman	C1	—	25	1	3	0	0	0	0	0	0	0	—	0	.000	.000	.000
— Zay	P1,OF1	—	—	1	1	0	0	0	0	0	0	0	—	0	.000	.000	.000

J. Macullar, 1 G at 2B; J. Sommer, 3 G at SS, 1 G at P

Pitcher	T	Age	G	GS	CG	ShO	IP	H	HR	BB	SO	W-L	Sv	ERA
Matt Kilroy	L	20	68	68	66	5	583.0	476	10	182	513	29-34	0	3.37
Jumbo McGinnis†	—	22	26	25	24	0	209.1	235	6	48	70	11-13	0	3.48
Hardie Henderson†	R	23	19	19	19	0	171.1	188	0	66	88	3-15	0	4.62
Dick Conway	R	20	9	9	8	0	76.2	106	6	43	64	2-7	0	6.81
Billy Taylor	R	31	8	8	8	0	72.1	87	1	20	37	1-6	0	5.72
Abner Powell†	R	25	7	7	7	0	60.0	66	2	26	15	2-5	0	5.10
Ed Knouff	R	18	1	1	1	0	9.0	2	0	5	8	0-1	0	2.00
Frank Houseman	—	—	1	1	1	0	8.0	6	0	1	5	0-1	0	3.38
— Zay	—	—	1	1	0	0	2.0	4	0	4	2	0-1	0	9.00
Joe Sommer	R	27	1	0	0	0	4.0	14	0	3	1	0-0	0	18.00
Pat O'Connell	R	25	1	0	0	0	3.0	4	0	2	1	0-0	0	6.00
Milt Scott	—	20	1	0	0	0	3.0	2	0	2	0	0-0	0	3.00
Chris Fulmer	R	27	1	0	0	0	2.0	2	0	1	0	0-0	0	4.50
Jimmy Macullar	L	31	1	0	0	0	2.0	4	0	0	1	0-0	0	9.00
Blondie Purcell	R	32	1	0	0	0	1.0	1	0	0	0	0-0	0	9.00

»1887 Detroit Wolverines 1st NL 79-45 .637 —

Bill Watkins

Player	Gm by Position	B	Age	G	AB	R	H	2B	3B	HR	RBI	BB	SO	SB	Avg	OBP	Slg
Charlie Ganzel	C51,OF4,1B2*	R	25	57	227	40	59	6	5	0	20	8	2	3	.260	.288	.330
Dan Brouthers	1B123	L	29	123	500	153	169	36	20	12	101	71	9	34	.338	.426	.562
Fred Dunlap	2B65,P1	R	28	65	272	60	72	13	10	5	45	25	12	15	.265	.327	.441
Deacon White	3B106,OF3,1B2	L	39	111	449	71	136	20	11	3	75	26	15	20	.303	.353	.416
Jack Rowe	SS124	L	30	124	537	135	171	30	10	6	96	39	11	22	.318	.368	.445
Sam Thompson	OF127	L	27	127	545	118	203	29	23	11	166	32	19	22	.372	.416	.571
Ned Hanlon	OF118	L	29	118	471	79	129	13	7	4	69	30	24	69	.274	.320	.357
Hardy Richardson	2B64,OF59	R	32	120	543	131	178	25	18	8	94	31	40	29	.328	.366	.484
Larry Twitchell	OF53,P15	R	23	65	264	44	88	14	6	0	51	8	19	12	.333	.358	.432
Charlie Bennett	C45,1B1,OF1	R	32	46	160	26	39	6	5	3	20	30	22	7	.244	.363	.400
Charlie Getzien	P43,OF1	R	23	43	156	19	29	4	5	1	14	10	32	2	.186	.240	.295
Fatty Briody	C33	—	28	33	128	24	29	6	1	1	26	9	10	6	.227	.283	.313
Pete Conway	P17,OF8	R	20	24	95	16	22	5	1	1	7	2	9	0	.232	.247	.337
Billy Shindle	3B21,OF1	R	23	22	84	17	24	3	2	0	12	7	10	13	.286	.341	.369
Stump Wiedman†	P21,OF2	R	26	21	82	12	17	2	0	1	11	3	3	6	.207	.235	.268
Jim Manning	OF10,SS3	S	25	13	52	5	10	1	0	0	3	5	4	3	.192	.276	.212
Walter Burke	P2,OF1	—	—	2	8	1	2	0	0	0	1	0	1	0	.250	.250	.250

C. Ganzel, 1 G at 3B

Pitcher	T	Age	G	GS	CG	ShO	IP	H	HR	BB	SO	W-L	Sv	ERA
Charlie Getzien	R	23	43	42	41	2	366.2	373	24	106	135	29-13	0	3.73
Lady Baldwin	L	28	24	24	24	1	211.0	225	8	61	60	13-10	0	3.84
Stump Wiedman†	R	26	21	21	20	0	183.0	221	9	60	56	13-7	0	5.36
Pete Conway	R	20	17	17	16	0	146.0	132	3	47	40	8-9	0	2.90
Larry Twitchell	R	23	15	12	11	0	112.1	120	3	36	24	11-1	1	4.33
Henry Gruber	R	23	7	7	7	0	62.1	63	3	21	12	4-3	0	2.74
Ed Beatin	L	20	2	2	2	0	18.0	13	2	8	6	1-1	0	4.00
Walter Burke	—	—	2	2	1	0	15.0	21	0	5	3	0-1	0	6.00
Fred Dunlap	R	28	1	0	0	0	2.0	4	0	0	1	0-0	0	4.50

1887 Philadelphia Phillies 2nd NL 75-48 .610 3.5 GB

Harry Wright

Player	Gm by Position	B	Age	G	AB	R	H	2B	3B	HR	RBI	BB	SO	SB	Avg	OBP	Slg
Jack Clements	C59,3B4,SS3	L	22	66	246	48	69	13	7	1	47	9	24	7	.280	.317	.402
Sid Farrar	1B116	—	27	116	443	83	125	20	9	4	72	42	29	24	.282	.358	.395
Barney McLaughlin	2B50	R	30	50	205	26	45	8	3	1	26	11	27	2	.220	.263	.302
Joe Mulvey	3B111	R	28	111	474	93	136	21	6	2	78	21	14	43	.287	.321	.369
Arthur Irwin	SS100	L	29	100	374	65	95	14	8	2	56	48	26	19	.254	.344	.350
Jim Fogarty	OF123,3B2,SS2*	R	23	126	495	113	129	26	12	8	50	82	44	102	.261	.370	.410
George Wood	OF104,2B3,3B3*	L	28	113	491	118	142	22	19	14	66	40	51	19	.289	.350	.497
Ed Andrews	OF99,2B7,1B1	R	28	104	464	110	151	19	7	4	67	21	21	57	.325	.359	.422
Charlie Buffinton	P40,OF22,1B10	R	26	66	269	34	72	12	1	1	46	11	3	8	.268	.299	.331
Charlie Ferguson	P37,2B27,OF6*	S	24	72	264	67	89	14	6	3	85	34	19	13	.337	.417	.470
Charlie Bastian	2B39,SS18,3B4	R	26	60	221	33	47	11	1	1	21	19	29	11	.213	.284	.285
Dan Casey	P45,OF1	R	24	45	164	22	27	3	0	1	17	6	20	1	.165	.194	.201
Deacon McGuire	C41	R	23	41	150	22	46	6	6	2	23	11	8	3	.307	.362	.467
Ed Daily†	OF22,P6	R	24	26	106	18	30	11	1	1	17	3	9	8	.283	.303	.434
Tom Gunning	C28	R	25	28	104	22	27	6	1	1	16	5	6	18	.260	.306	.365
Tommy McCarthy	OF8,2B5,SS3*	R	23	18	70	7	13	4	0	0	6	2	5	15	.186	.219	.243
Al Maul	OF8,P7,1B2	R	21	16	56	15	17	2	2	1	4	15	10	5	.304	.451	.464
Tony Cusick	C4,1B3,2B1	R	27	7	24	3	7	1	0	0	5	3	1	0	.292	.393	.333
Harry Lyons†	OF1	R	21	1	4	0	0	0	0	0	0	1	0	0	.000	.200	.000

J. Fogarty, 1 G at P, 1 G at 2B; G. Wood, 3 G at SS; C. Ferguson, 5 G at 3B; T. McCarthy, 2 G at 3B

Pitcher	T	Age	G	GS	CG	ShO	IP	H	HR	BB	SO	W-L	Sv	ERA
Dan Casey	L	24	45	45	43	4	390.1	377	15	115	119	28-13	0	2.86
Charlie Buffinton	R	26	40	38	35	1	332.1	352	16	92	160	21-17	0	3.66
Charlie Ferguson	R	24	37	33	31	2	297.1	297	13	47	125	22-10	1	3.00
Al Maul	R	21	7	5	4	0	50.1	72	2	15	18	4-2	0	5.54
Ed Daily†	R	24	6	5	4	0	41.1	52	2	25	7	0-4	0	7.19
Jim Devlin	L	21	2	2	2	0	18.0	20	0	10	6	0-2	0	6.00
Jim Fogarty	R	23	1	0	0	0	3.0	3	0	1	0	0-0	0	9.00

1887 Chicago White Stockings 3rd NL 71-50 .587 6.5 GB

Cap Anson

Player	Gm by Position	B	Age	G	AB	R	H	2B	3B	HR	RBI	BB	SO	SB	Avg	OBP	Slg
Tom Daly	C64,OF8,1B2*	S	21	74	256	45	53	10	4	2	17	22	25	29	.207	.270	.301
Cap Anson	1B122,C1	R	35	122	472	107	164	33	13	7	102	60	18	27	.347	.422	.517
Fred Pfeffer	2B123,OF2	R	27	123	479	95	133	21	6	16	89	34	20	57	.278	.327	.447
Tom Burns	3B107,OF8	R	30	115	424	57	112	20	10	3	60	34	32	32	.264	.320	.380
Ned Williamson	SS127,P1	R	29	127	439	77	117	20	14	9	78	73	57	45	.267	.377	.437
Jimmy Ryan	OF122,P8,2B3	R	24	126	508	117	145	23	10	11	74	53	19	50	.285	.360	.435
Marty Sullivan	OF115,P1	R	24	115	472	98	134	13	16	7	77	36	53	35	.284	.340	.424
Billy Sunday	OF50	L	24	50	199	41	58	6	6	3	32	21	20	34	.291	.362	.427
John Clarkson	P60,OF5	R	25	63	215	40	52	5	5	6	25	11	25	6	.242	.279	.395
Silver Flint	C47,1B2	R	31	49	187	22	50	8	6	3	21	4	28	7	.267	.283	.422
George Van Haltren	OF27,P20	L	21	45	172	30	35	4	0	3	17	15	15	12	.203	.271	.279
Dell Darling	C20,OF20	R	25	38	141	28	45	7	4	3	20	22	18	19	.319	.411	.489
Mark Baldwin	P40,OF5,1B1	R	23	41	139	18	26	1	1	4	17	10	42	4	.187	.242	.295
Bob Pettit	OF32,P1,C1	L	25	32	138	29	36	3	3	2	12	8	15	16	.261	.301	.370
Patsy Tebeau	3B20	R	22	20	68	8	11	3	0	0	10	4	4	8	.162	.208	.206
Shadow Pyle	P4,OF1	—	25	4	16	1	3	1	0	1	4	0	0	1	.188	.188	.438
Charlie Sprague	P3,OF1	L	22	3	13	0	2	0	0	0	0	0	2	0	.154	.154	.154
Emil Geiss	P1,1B1,2B1	R	20	3	12	0	1	0	0	0	0	0	7	0	.083	.083	.083
Jocko Flynn	OF1	—	23	1	0	0	0	0	0	0	0	0	0	0	—	—	—

T. Daly, 2 G at 2B, 2 G at SS

Pitcher	T	Age	G	GS	CG	ShO	IP	H	HR	BB	SO	W-L	Sv	ERA
John Clarkson	R	25	60	59	56	2	523.0	513	20	92	237	38-21	0	3.08
Mark Baldwin	R	23	40	39	35	1	334.0	329	23	122	164	18-17	1	3.40
George Van Haltren	L	21	20	18	18	1	161.0	177	7	66	76	11-7	1	3.86
Shadow Pyle	L	25	4	4	3	0	26.2	32	1	21	5	1-3	0	4.73
Charlie Sprague	L	22	3	3	2	0	22.0	24	1	13	9	1-0	0	4.91
Emil Geiss	R	20	1	1	1	0	9.0	17	0	3	4	0-1	0	8.00
Jimmy Ryan	L	24	8	3	2	0	45.0	53	3	17	14	2-1	0	4.20
Marty Sullivan	R	24	1	0	0	0	2.1	6	0	1	1	0-0	0	7.71
Ned Williamson	R	29	1	0	0	0	2.0	2	0	1	0	0-0	0	9.00
Bob Pettit	R	25	1	0	0	0	1.0	3	0	2	0	0-0	1	0.00

1887 New York Giants 4th NL 68-55 .553 10.5 GB

Player	Gm by Position	B	Age	G	AB	R	H	2B	3B	HR	RBI	BB	SO	SB	Avg	OBP	Slg
Willard Brown	C46,3B3,OF2	R	21	49	170	17	37	3	2	0	25	10	15	10	.218	.273	.259
Roger Connor	1B127	L	29	127	471	113	134	26	22	17	104	75	50	43	.285	.392	.541
Danny Richardson	2B108,3B14,P1	R	24	122	450	79	125	19	10	3	62	36	25	41	.278	.337	.384
Buck Ewing	3B51,2B19,C8	R	27	77	318	83	97	17	13	6	44	30	33	26	.305	.370	.497
Monte Ward	SS129	L	27	129	545	114	184	16	5	1	53	29	12	111	.338	.375	.391
George Gore	OF111	L	30	111	459	95	133	16	5	1	49	42	18	39	.290	.358	.353
Mike Tiernan	OF103,P5	L	20	103	407	82	117	13	12	10	62	32	31	28	.287	.344	.452
Pete Gillespie	OF76,3B1	L	35	76	295	40	78	9	3	3	37	12	21	37	.264	.304	.346
Jim O'Rourke	C40,3B38,OF28*	R	36	103	397	73	113	15	13	3	88	36	11	46	.285	.352	.411
Mike Dorgan	OF69,1B2	R	33	71	283	41	73	10	0	0	34	15	20	22	.258	.302	.293
Tim Keefe	P56,OF2	R	30	56	191	27	42	7	6	2	23	20	41	2	.220	.294	.351
Mickey Welch	P40,OF1	R	27	40	148	16	36	4	2	2	15	6	1	2	.243	.277	.338
Pat Deasley	C24,3B7,SS1	R	29	30	118	12	37	5	0	0	23	9	7	3	.314	.367	.356
John Rainey	3B17	L	22	17	58	6	17	3	0	0	12	5	6	0	.293	.349	.345
Pat Murphy	C17	—	30	17	56	4	12	2	0	0	4	2	4	1	.214	.241	.250
Bill George	P13,OF1	R	22	13	53	6	9	0	0	0	5	1	6	2	.170	.185	.170
Mike Mattimore	P7,OF2	L	28	8	32	5	8	1	0	0	4	0	6	1	.250	.250	.281
Gil Hatfield	3B2	—	32	2	7	2	3	1	0	0	3	0	1	0	.429	.429	.571
Buck Becannon	3B1	—	27	1	5	0	0	0	0	0	0	0	2	0	.000	.000	.000
Roger Carey	2B1	—	—	1	4	0	0	0	0	0	2	0	1	0	.000	.000	.000
Joe Gerhardt†	3B1	R	32	1	4	0	0	0	0	0	0	0	0	0	.000	.000	.000
Candy Nelson†	3B1	L	38	1	2	0	0	0	0	0	0	0	1	0	.000	.000	.000

J. O'Rourke, 2 G at 2B

Jim Mutrie

Pitcher	T	Age	G	GS	CG	ShO	IP	H	HR	BB	SO	W-L	Sv	ERA
Tim Keefe	R	30	56	56	54	2	478.2	447	11	108	186	35-19	0	3.10
Mickey Welch	R	27	40	40	39	2	346.0	339	7	91	115	22-15	0	3.36
Bill George	L	22	13	13	11	0	108.0	126	1	89	49	3-9	0	5.25
C. Titcomb†	L	20	9	9	9	0	72.0	68	3	37	34	4-3	0	3.88
Mike Mattimore	L	28	7	7	6	1	57.1	47	2	28	12	3-3	0	2.35
Bill Swabach	—	—	2	2	2	0	16.0	27	1	6	6	0-2	0	5.06
John Roach	L	—	1	1	1	0	8.0	18	0	4	3	0-1	0	11.25
Stump Wiedman†	R	26	1	1	1	0	8.0	10	0	2	4	0-1	0	1.13
Mike Tiernan	L	20	5	0	0	0	19.2	33	2	7	3	1-2	1	8.69
Danny Richardson	R	24	1	0	0	0	0.0	0	0	1	0	0-0	0	—

1887 Boston Red Stockings 5th NL 61-60 .504 16.5 GB

Player	Gm by Position	B	Age	G	AB	R	H	2B	3B	HR	RBI	BB	SO	SB	Avg	OBP	Slg
Pop Tate	C53,OF8	R	26	60	231	34	60	5	3	0	27	8	9	7	.260	.296	.307
John Morrill	1B127	R	32	127	504	79	141	32	6	12	81	37	86	19	.280	.330	.438
Jack Burdock	2B65	R	35	65	237	36	61	6	0	0	29	18	22	19	.257	.320	.283
Billy Nash	3B117,OF5	R	22	121	475	100	140	24	12	6	94	60	30	43	.295	.376	.434
Sam Wise	SS72,OF27,2B16	L	29	113	467	103	156	27	17	9	92	36	44	43	.334	.390	.522
Dick Johnston	OF127	R	24	127	507	87	131	13	20	5	77	16	35	52	.258	.281	.393
Joe Hornung	OF98	R	30	98	437	85	118	10	6	5	49	17	28	41	.270	.302	.355
King Kelly	OF61,2B30,C24*	R	29	116	484	120	156	34	11	8	63	55	40	84	.322	.393	.488
Ezra Sutton	SS37,OF18,2B13*	R	36	77	326	58	99	14	9	3	46	13	6	17	.304	.342	.429
Old Hoss Radbourn	P50,OF2	R	32	51	175	25	40	2	2	1	24	18	21	6	.229	.308	.280
Bobby Wheelock	OF28,SS20,2B4	R	22	48	166	32	42	4	2	2	15	15	15	20	.253	.315	.337
Dick Conway	P26,OF16	L	21	42	145	20	36	4	1	0	10	16	16	5	.248	.327	.290
Kid Madden	P37,OF1	—	19	37	132	23	32	2	3	1	10	12	17	6	.242	.315	.326
Con Daily	C36	L	22	36	120	12	19	5	0	0	13	9	8	7	.158	.229	.200
Tom O'Rourke	C21,3B1,OF1	—	21	22	78	12	12	3	0	0	10	7	6	4	.154	.233	.192

K. Kelly, 3 G at P, 2 G at 3B, 2 G at SS; E. Sutton, 11 G at 3B

King Kelly (49-43)/John Morrill (12-17)

Pitcher	T	Age	G	GS	CG	ShO	IP	H	HR	BB	SO	W-L	Sv	ERA
Old Hoss Radbourn	R	32	50	50	48	1	425.0	505	20	133	87	24-23	0	4.55
Kid Madden	L	19	37	37	36	3	321.0	317	20	122	81	21-14	0	3.79
Dick Conway	R	21	26	26	25	0	222.1	249	10	86	45	9-15	0	4.66
Bill Stemmeyer	R	22	15	14	14	0	119.1	138	4	41	41	6-8	1	5.20
King Kelly	R	29	3	0	0	0	13.0	17	1	14	0	1-0	0	3.46

1887 Pittsburgh Alleghenys 6th NL 55-69 .444 24.0 GB

Player	Gm by Position	B	Age	G	AB	R	H	2B	3B	HR	RBI	BB	SO	SB	Avg	OBP	Slg
Doggie Miller	C73,OF14,3B1	R	22	87	342	58	83	17	4	1	34	35	13	33	.243	.317	.325
Sam Barkley	1B53,2B36	R	29	89	340	44	76	10	4	1	35	30	24	6	.224	.294	.285
Pop Smith	2B89,SS33	R	30	122	456	69	98	12	7	2	54	30	48	30	.215	.283	.285
Art Whitney	3B119	R	29	119	431	57	112	11	4	0	51	55	18	10	.260	.346	.304
Bill Kuehne	SS91,1B4,3B4*	R	28	102	402	68	120	18	15	1	41	14	39	17	.299	.324	.425
John Coleman	OF115,1B2	L	24	115	475	75	139	21	11	2	54	31	40	25	.293	.337	.396
Abner Dalrymple	OF92	L	29	92	358	45	76	18	5	2	31	45	43	29	.212	.311	.307
Tom Brown†	OF47	L	26	47	192	30	47	3	4	0	6	11	40	12	.245	.289	.302
Fred Carroll	OF46,C40,1B17*	R	22	102	421	71	138	24	15	6	54	36	21	23	.328	.383	.499
Alex McKinnon	1B48	R	30	48	200	26	68	16	4	1	30	8	9	6	.340	.365	.475
Pud Galvin	P49,OF1	R	30	49	193	10	41	7	3	2	22	2	47	5	.212	.221	.311
Ed Beecher	OF41	L	26	41	169	15	41	8	0	2	22	7	8	8	.243	.281	.325
Jocko Fields	OF27,C14,1B3*	R	22	43	164	26	44	9	2	0	17	7	13	7	.268	.306	.348

B. Kuehne, 3 G at OF; F. Carroll, 1 G at SS; J. Fields, 1 G at P, 1 G at 3B

Horace Phillips

Pitcher	T	Age	G	GS	CG	ShO	IP	H	HR	BB	SO	W-L	Sv	ERA
Pud Galvin	R	30	49	48	47	2	440.2	490	12	67	76	28-21	0	3.29
Ed Morris	L	24	38	38	37	1	317.2	375	13	71	91	14-22	0	4.31
Jim McCormick	R	30	36	36	36	0	322.1	377	12	84	77	13-23	0	4.30
Bill Bishop	—	17	3	3	3	0	27.0	45	2	22	4	0-3	0	13.33
Jocko Fields	R	22	1	0	0	0	1.0	0	0	2	0	0-0	0	0.00

1887 Washington Senators 7th NL 46-76 .377 32.0 GB

Player	Gm by Position	B	Age	G	AB	R	H	2B	3B	HR	RBI	BB	SO	SB	Avg	OBP	Slg
Connie Mack	C76,OF5,2B2	R	24	82	314	35	63	6	1	0	20	8	17	26	.201	.228	.226
Billy O'Brien	1B104,3B4,OF4*	R	27	113	453	71	126	16	12	19	73	21	17	11	.278	.317	.492
Bert Myers	2B78,SS27	R	23	105	362	45	84	9	5	2	36	40	26	18	.232	.312	.301
Jim Donnelly	3B115,SS2	R	21	117	425	51	85	9	6	1	46	16	26	42	.200	.234	.256
Jack Farrell	SS48,2B40	R	29	87	339	40	75	14	9	0	41	20	12	31	.221	.267	.316
Paul Hines	OF109,1B7,2B5*	R	35	123	478	83	147	32	5	10	72	48	24	46	.308	.380	.458
Cliff Carroll	OF103	S	27	103	420	79	104	17	4	4	37	17	30	40	.248	.291	.336
Ed Daily†	OF77,P1	R	24	78	311	39	78	6	10	2	36	14	27	26	.251	.285	.354
George Shoch	OF63,SS6,2B1	R	28	70	264	47	63	9	1	1	18	21	16	29	.239	.304	.292
Pat Dealy	C28,SS23,3B5*	R	—	58	212	33	55	8	2	1	18	8	8	36	.259	.293	.330
Jim Whitney	P47,OF7	L	29	54	201	29	53	9	6	2	22	18	24	10	.264	.324	.398
Hank O'Day	P30,SS6,OF2	—	24	36	116	10	23	3	0	0	7	7	15	1	.198	.244	.224
Bill Krieg	1B16,OF9	R	28	25	95	9	24	4	1	2	17	7	5	2	.253	.311	.379
Barney Gilligan	C26,SS3,OF1	R	31	28	90	7	18	2	0	1	6	5	18	2	.200	.242	.256
John Irwin	SS5,3B4	L	25	8	31	6	11	2	0	2	3	3	6	6	.355	.429	.613
Sam Crane	SS7	R	33	7	30	6	9	1	1	0	1	1	6	5	.300	.323	.400
Jerry O'Brien	2B1	—	23	1	4	0	0	0	0	0	0	0	2	0	.000	.000	.000
Bill Wright	C1	—	—	1	3	0	2	0	0	0	0	0	0	0	.667	.667	.667

B. O'Brien, 2 G at 2B; P. Hines, 4 G at SS; P. Dealy, 5 G at OF

John Gaffney

Pitcher	T	Age	G	GS	CG	ShO	IP	H	HR	BB	SO	W-L	Sv	ERA
Jim Whitney	R	29	47	47	46	3	404.2	430	16	42	146	24-21	0	3.22
Hank O'Day	R	24	30	30	29	0	254.2	255	15	109	86	8-20	0	4.17
Frank Gilmore	—	23	28	27	27	1	234.2	247	7	92	114	7-20	0	3.87
Dupee Shaw	L	28	21	20	20	0	181.1	263	8	46	47	7-13	0	6.45
George Keefe	L	20	1	1	1	0	8.0	16	1	4	0	0-1	0	9.00
Ed Daily†	R	24	1	1	1	0	7.0	5	0	6	3	0-1	0	7.71

1887 Indianapolis Hoosiers 8th NL 37-89 .294 43.0 GB

Player	Gm by Position	B	Age	G	AB	R	H	2B	3B	HR	RBI	BB	SO	SB	Avg	OBP	Slg
George Myers	C50,OF15,1B6*	R	26	69	235	25	51	8	1	1	20	22	7	26	.217	.298	.272
Otto Schomberg	1B112,OF1	L	22	112	419	91	129	18	16	5	83	56	32	21	.308	.397	.463
Charley Bassett	2B119	R	24	119	452	41	104	14	6	1	47	25	31	25	.230	.278	.294
Jerry Denny	3B116,SS4,2B1*	R	28	122	510	86	165	34	12	11	97	13	22	29	.324	.344	.502
Jack Glasscock	SS122,P1	R	27	122	483	91	142	18	7	0	40	41	8	62	.294	.361	.360
Emmett Seery	OF122,SS1	L	26	122	465	104	104	18	15	4	28	71	68	48	.224	.331	.353
Jack McGeachey	OF98,P1,3B1	R	23	99	405	49	109	17	3	1	56	5	16	27	.269	.280	.333
John Cahill	OF56,3B9,P6*	R	22	68	263	22	54	4	3	0	26	9	5	34	.205	.234	.243
Tug Arundel	C42,OF2,1B1	—	25	43	157	13	31	4	0	0	13	8	12	8	.197	.241	.223
Mert Hackett	C40,OF2,1B1	R	27	42	147	12	35	6	3	2	10	7	24	4	.238	.282	.361
Henry Boyle	P38,OF4	—	26	41	141	17	27	9	1	2	13	9	18	2	.191	.250	.312
Tom Brown†	OF36	L	26	36	140	20	25	3	0	2	9	8	25	13	.179	.228	.243
Mark Polhemus	OF20	—	24	20	75	6	18	1	0	0	8	2	9	4	.240	.260	.253
Gid Gardner	OF11,2B7	—	28	18	63	8	11	1	0	1	8	12	11	7	.175	.307	.238
Bill Johnson	OF11	L	24	11	42	3	8	0	0	0	3	0	6	5	.190	.209	.190
Sam Moffett	P6,OF5	R	30	11	41	6	5	1	0	0	1	1	6	2	.122	.143	.146
Henry Jackson	1B10	R	26	10	38	1	10	1	0	0	3	0	12	2	.263	.263	.289
John Kirby†	P8,OF3	—	22	8	29	3	4	0	1	0	2	0	7	0	.138	.138	.207
Hank Morrison	P7,OF1	R	21	7	26	4	3	0	0	0	3	2	4	2	.115	.179	.115
— Fast	P4,OF1	—	—	4	11	1	2	0	0	0	0	0	3	1	.182	.182	.182
Larry Corcoran	P2,OF2	L	27	3	10	2	2	0	0	0	0	2	1	2	.200	.333	.200
John Sowders	P1,OF1	R	20	1	2	0	0	0	0	0	0	0	1	0	.000	.000	.000

G. Myers, 1 G at 3B; J. Denny, 1 G at OF; J. Cahill, 1 G at SS

Watch Burnham (6-22)/Fred Thomas (11-18)/Horace Fogel (20-49)

Pitcher	T	Age	G	GS	CG	ShO	IP	H	HR	BB	SO	W-L	Sv	ERA
Egyptian Healy	R	20	41	41	40	3	341.0	415	24	108	75	12-29	0	5.17
Henry Boyle	R	26	38	38	37	0	328.0	356	11	69	85	13-24	0	3.65
Lev Shreve†	R	18	14	14	14	1	122.0	141	5	65	22	5-9	0	4.72
Doc Leitner	R	21	8	8	8	0	65.0	69	6	41	27	2-6	0	5.68
John Kirby†	R	22	8	8	5	0	62.0	70	3	43	7	1-6	0	6.10
Hank Morrison	R	21	7	7	5	0	57.0	79	2	27	13	3-4	0	7.58
Sam Moffett	R	30	6	6	6	0	50.0	47	1	23	3	1-5	0	3.78
— Fast	—	—	4	2	1	0	15.2	25	1	8	0	0-1	1	10.34
Larry Corcoran	R	27	2	2	1	0	15.0	23	3	19	4	0-2	0	12.60
John Cahill	R	22	6	1	1	0	22.0	40	2	19	5	0-2	0	14.32
Jack McGeachey	R	23	1	0	0	0	6.1	13	2	4	3	0-1	0	11.37
John Sowders	L	20	1	0	0	0	3.0	11	0	5	0	0-0	0	21.00
Jack Glasscock	R	27	1	0	0	0	1.0	0	0	0	1	0-0	0	0.00

»1887 St. Louis Browns 1st AA 95-40 .704 — Charlie Comiskey

Player	Gm by Position	B	Age	G	AB	R	H	2B	3B	HR	RBI	BB	SO	SB	Avg	OBP	Slg
Jack Boyle	C86,1B2,OF2*	R	21	88	350	48	66	3	1	2	41	20	—	7	.189	.237	.220
Charlie Comiskey	1B116,2B9,OF3	R	27	125	538	139	180	22	5	4	103	27	—	117	.335	.374	.416
Yank Robinson	2B117,3B6,SS2*	R	27	125	430	102	131	32	4	1	74	92	—	75	.305	.445	.405
Arlie Latham	3B132,2B5,C2	R	27	136	627	163	198	35	10	2	83	45	—	129	.316	.366	.413
Bill Gleason	SS135	R	28	135	598	135	172	19	1	0	76	41	—	23	.288	.342	.323
Tip O'Neill	OF124	R	29	124	517	167	225	52	19	14	123	50	—	30	.435	.490	.691
Curt Welch	OF123,2B8,1B1	R	25	131	544	98	151	32	7	3	108	25	—	89	.278	.322	.379
Bob Caruthers	OF54,P39,1B7	L	23	98	364	102	130	23	11	8	73	66	—	49	.357	.463	.547
Dave Foutz	OF50,P40,1B15	R	30	102	423	79	151	26	13	4	108	23	—	22	.357	.393	.508
Silver King	P46,OF18	R	19	62	222	28	46	6	1	0	19	24	—	10	.207	.285	.243
Doc Bushong	C52,3B2,OF2	R	30	53	201	35	51	4	0	0	26	11	—	14	.254	.299	.274
Lou Sylvester	OF29,2B1	R	32	29	112	20	25	4	3	1	18	13	—	13	.223	.310	.339
Ed Knouff†	OF9,P6	R	19	15	56	4	10	1	2	0	6	1	—	1	.179	.207	.268
Nat Hudson	P9,OF6	R	18	13	48	7	12	2	1	0	3	4	—	0	.250	.308	.333
Harry Lyons†	2B1,OF1	R	21	2	8	2	1	0	0	0	1	0	—	2	.125	.125	.125
Mike Goodfellow	C1	R	20	1	4	0	0	0	0	0	0	0	—	0	.000	.000	.000

J. Boyle, 1 G at 3B; Y. Robinson, 2 G at OF, 1 G at P, 1 G at C

Pitcher	T	Age	G	GS	CG	ShO	IP	H	HR	BB	SO	W-L	Sv	ERA
Silver King	R	19	46	44	43	2	390.0	401	4	109	128	32-12	1	3.78
Bob Caruthers	R	23	39	39	39	2	341.0	337	6	61	74	29-9	0	3.30
Dave Foutz	R	30	40	38	36	1	339.1	369	7	90	94	25-12	0	3.87
Nat Hudson	R	18	9	9	7	0	67.0	91	2	20	15	4-4	0	4.97
Ed Knouff†	R	19	6	6	6	1	50.0	40	0	36	18	4-2	0	4.50
Joe Murphy	—	20	1	1	1	0	9.0	13	0	4	5	1-0	0	5.00
Yank Robinson	R	27	1	0	0	0	3.0	3	0	3	0	0-0	1	3.00

1887 Cincinnati Reds 2nd AA 81-54 .600 14.0 GB Gus Schmelz

Player	Gm by Position	B	Age	G	AB	R	H	2B	3B	HR	RBI	BB	SO	SB	Avg	OBP	Slg
Kid Baldwin	C96,OF2	R	22	96	388	46	98	15	10	1	57	6	—	13	.253	.271	.351
John Reilly	1B127,OF9	R	28	134	551	106	170	35	14	10	96	22	—	50	.309	.352	.477
Bid McPhee	2B129	R	27	129	540	137	156	20	19	2	87	55	—	95	.289	.360	.407
Hick Carpenter	3B127	R	31	127	498	70	124	12	6	1	50	19	—	44	.249	.282	.303
Frank Fennelly	SS134	R	27	134	526	133	140	15	16	8	97	82	—	74	.266	.369	.401
Pop Corkhill	OF128,P5	L	29	128	541	79	168	19	11	5	97	14	—	30	.311	.333	.414
Hugh Nicol	OF125	R	29	125	475	122	102	18	2	1	34	86	—	138	.215	.341	.267
W. Wings Tebeau	OF84,P1	R	25	85	318	57	94	12	5	4	33	31	—	37	.296	.364	.403
Tony Mullane	P48,OF9	S	28	56	199	35	44	6	3	3	23	16	—	20	.221	.292	.327
Elmer Smith	P52,OF2	L	19	52	186	26	47	10	6	0	23	11	—	5	.253	.298	.371
Jim Keenan	C38,1B11	R	29	47	174	19	44	4	1	0	17	11	—	7	.253	.301	.287
Charley Jones†	OF41	R	37	41	153	28	48	7	4	2	40	19	—	7	.314	.400	.451
Billy Serad	P22,OF1	R	24	22	79	9	14	1	2	0	5	3	—	0	.177	.207	.241
Heinie Kappel	3B9,OF7,2B6*	R	23	23	78	11	22	3	2	0	15	2	—	3	.282	.309	.372
Jack O'Connor	OF7,C5	R	18	12	40	4	4	0	0	0	1	2	—	3	.100	.143	.100
Mother Watson	P2,OF1	—	22	2	8	1	1	0	0	0	0	1	—	0	.125	.300	.125

H. Kappel, 1 G at SS

Pitcher	T	Age	G	GS	CG	ShO	IP	H	HR	BB	SO	W-L	Sv	ERA
Elmer Smith	L	19	52	52	49	3	447.1	400	5	126	176	34-17	0	2.94
Tony Mullane	R	28	48	48	47	6	416.1	414	11	121	97	31-17	0	3.24
Billy Serad	R	24	22	21	20	2	187.1	201	7	80	34	10-11	1	4.08
Jumbo McGinnis	—	23	8	8	8	0	69.1	85	3	43	18	3-5	0	5.45
Mike Shea	R	20	2	2	2	0	16.2	26	0	10	0	1-1	0	7.02
Mother Watson	—	22	2	2	1	0	14.0	22	0	6	1	0-1	0	5.79
Wild Bill Widner	R	20	1	1	1	0	9.0	11	2	2	0	1-0	0	5.00
W. Wings Tebeau	R	25	1	1	1	0	8.0	21	0	3	1	0-1	0	13.50
Pop Corkhill	R	29	5	0	0	0	14.2	22	0	5	3	1-0	0	5.52

1887 Baltimore Orioles 3rd AA 77-58 .570 18.0 GB Billy Barnie

Player	Gm by Position	B	Age	G	AB	R	H	2B	3B	HR	RBI	BB	SO	SB	Avg	OBP	Slg
Sam Trott	C69,2B11,OF3*	L	28	85	300	44	77	16	3	0	37	27	—	8	.257	.322	.330
Tommy Tucker	1B136	S	23	136	524	114	144	15	9	6	84	29	—	85	.275	.347	.372
Bill Greenwood	2B117,OF1	S	30	118	495	114	130	16	6	0	65	54	—	71	.263	.336	.319
Jumbo Davis	3B87,SS43	L	25	130	485	81	150	23	19	8	109	28	—	49	.309	.353	.485
Oyster Burns	SS98,3B42,P3*	R	22	140	551	122	188	33	19	9	99	63	—	58	.341	.414	.519
Blondie Purcell	OF140,P1	R	33	140	567	101	142	25	8	4	96	46	—	88	.250	.318	.344
Mike Griffin	OF136	L	22	136	532	142	160	32	13	3	94	55	—	94	.301	.375	.427
Joe Sommer	OF110,2B13,3B10*	R	28	131	463	88	123	11	5	0	65	63	—	29	.266	.358	.311
Matt Kilroy	P69,OF4,SS1	L	21	72	239	46	59	5	6	0	25	31	—	12	.247	.336	.318
Phenomenal Smith	P58,OF7	L	22	64	205	37	48	7	6	1	18	26	—	7	.234	.323	.341
Chris Fulmer	C48,OF8	R	28	56	201	52	54	11	4	0	32	36	—	35	.269	.382	.363
Law Daniels	C26,OF15,1B4*	R	24	48	165	23	41	5	1	0	32	8	—	7	.248	.287	.291
Ed Knouff†	P9,OF3	R	19	9	31	4	9	0	0	0	3	1	—	1	.290	.313	.290
Jackie Hayes	OF4,3B3,C1	—	26	8	28	2	4	3	0	0	3	0	—	0	.143	.143	.250
Lev Shreve†	P5,OF2	R	18	6	24	3	4	0	1	0	2	1	—	1	.167	.200	.250
Fred Gardner	P3,3B1,SS1	—	—	4	11	2	3	0	0	0	1	1	—	0	.273	.333	.273

S. Trott, 2 G at 1B, 1 G at SS; O. Burns, 1 G at 2B; J. Sommer, 2 G at SS, 1 G at P; L. Daniels, 2 G at 2B, 1 G at 3B, 1 G at SS

Pitcher	T	Age	G	GS	CG	ShO	IP	H	HR	BB	SO	W-L	Sv	ERA
Matt Kilroy	L	21	69	69	66	6	589.1	585	9	157	217	46-19	0	3.07
Phenomenal Smith	L	22	58	55	54	1	491.1	526	7	176	206	25-30	0	3.79
Ed Knouff†	R	19	9	9	6	0	63.0	79	0	41	27	2-6	0	7.57
Lev Shreve†	R	18	5	5	4	1	38.0	33	0	19	13	3-1	0	3.79
Fred Gardner	—	—	3	2	1	0	13.0	23	0	10	3	0-1	0	11.08
Ed Keating	L	24	1	1	1	0	9.0	16	0	6	0	0-1	0	11.00
Oyster Burns	R	22	3	0	0	0	11.1	16	0	4	2	1-0	0	9.53
Blondie Purcell	R	33	1	0	0	0	4.0	8	0	4	2	0-0	0	15.75
Joe Sommer	R	28	1	0	0	0	1.0	2	0	1	0	0-0	0	9.00

1887 Louisville Colonels 4th AA 76-60 .559 19.5 GB Honest John Kelly

Player	Gm by Position	B	Age	G	AB	R	H	2B	3B	HR	RBI	BB	SO	SB	Avg	OBP	Slg
Paul Cook	C55,1B6	R	24	61	223	34	55	4	2	0	17	11	—	15	.247	.294	.283
John Kerins	1B74,C35,OF5	R	28	112	476	101	140	18	5	5	57	38	—	49	.294	.349	.443
Reddy Mack	2B128	—	21	128	478	117	147	23	8	1	69	83	—	22	.308	.415	.395
Joe Werrick	3B136	R	25	136	533	90	152	21	13	7	99	38	—	49	.285	.336	.413
Bill White	SS132	—	27	132	512	85	129	7	9	2	79	47	—	41	.252	.315	.313
Pete Browning	OF134	R	26	134	547	137	220	35	16	4	118	55	—	103	.402	.464	.547
Chicken Wolf	OF128,1B11	R	25	137	569	103	160	27	13	2	102	34	—	45	.281	.331	.385
Hub Collins	OF109,2B10,1B8*	R	23	130	559	122	162	22	8	1	66	39	—	71	.290	.338	.363
Guy Hecker	1B43,P34,OF16	R	31	91	370	89	118	21	6	4	50	31	—	48	.319	.381	.441
Lave Cross	C44,OF10	R	21	54	203	32	54	8	3	0	26	15	—	15	.266	.320	.335
Elton Chamberlin	P36,OF2	R	19	37	131	14	26	1	1	1	16	12	—	2	.198	.266	.244
Phil Reccius†	OF10,SS1	—	25	11	37	9	9	2	0	0	4	8	—	3	.243	.391	.297
Amos Cross	C5,1B2,OF1	—	26	8	28	0	3	0	0	0	0	1	—	0	.107	.138	.107
Ducky Hemp	OF1	—	19	1	3	1	1	1	0	0	0	1	—	0	.333	.500	.667

H. Collins, 4 G at SS, 1 G at 3B

Pitcher	T	Age	G	GS	CG	ShO	IP	H	HR	BB	SO	W-L	Sv	ERA
Toad Ramsey	L	22	65	64	61	0	561.0	544	9	167	355	37-27	0	3.43
Elton Chamberlin	R	19	36	36	35	1	309.0	340	8	117	118	18-16	0	3.79
Guy Hecker	R	31	34	32	32	2	285.1	325	9	50	58	18-12	1	4.16
Joe Neale	R	21	5	4	4	0	41.1	60	4	15	11	1-4	0	6.97
Peek-A-Boo Veach	—	25	1	1	1	0	9.0	5	1	8	2	0-1	0	4.00

1887 Philadelphia Athletics 5th AA 64-69 .481 30.0 GB Frank Bancroft (26-29)/Charlie Mason (38-40)

Player	Gm by Position	B	Age	G	AB	R	H	2B	3B	HR	RBI	BB	SO	SB	Avg	OBP	Slg
Wilbert Robinson	C67,1B3,OF1	R	24	68	264	28	60	6	2	1	24	14	—	15	.227	.269	.277
Jocko Milligan	1B50,C47,OF1	R	25	95	377	54	114	27	4	2	50	21	—	8	.302	.344	.411
Lou Bierbauer	2B126,P1	L	21	126	530	74	144	19	7	1	82	13	—	40	.272	.289	.340
Denny Lyons	3B137	R	21	137	570	128	209	43	14	6	102	47	—	73	.367	.421	.523
Chippy McGarr	SS137	R	24	137	536	93	158	23	6	1	63	23	—	84	.295	.326	.366
Tom Poorman	OF135,2B2,P1	L	29	135	585	140	155	18	19	4	61	35	—	88	.265	.317	.381
Henry Larkin	OF93,1B23,2B10	R	27	126	497	105	154	22	12	3	88	48	—	37	.310	.380	.421
Harry Stovey	OF80,1B46	R	30	124	497	125	142	31	12	4	77	56	—	74	.286	.366	.421
Ed Seward	P55,OF21	—	20	74	266	31	50	10	0	5	28	16	—	14	.188	.239	.282
Fred Mann†	OF55	L	29	55	229	42	63	14	6	0	32	15	—	16	.275	.336	.389
Gus Weyhing	P55,OF3	R	20	57	209	19	42	6	1	0	16	6	—	8	.201	.223	.239
George Townsend	C28,OF3	R	20	31	109	12	21	3	0	0	14	3	—	8	.193	.214	.220
Ed Flanagan	1B19	—	25	19	80	12	20	5	0	1	10	3	—	3	.250	.286	.350
Chief Roseman†	OF21	R	30	21	73	16	16	2	1	0	8	10	—	3	.219	.352	.274
Al Atkinson	P15,OF4	R	26	16	59	8	12	2	0	1	5	5	—	3	.203	.266	.288
Ed Greer†	OF3	R	22	3	11	1	2	0	0	0	0	0	—	2	.182	.182	.182
Jim Roxburgh	C2,2B1	R	29	2	8	0	1	0	0	0	0	0	—	0	.125	.125	.125

Pitcher	T	Age	G	GS	CG	ShO	IP	H	HR	BB	SO	W-L	Sv	ERA
Gus Weyhing	R	20	55	55	53	2	466.1	465	12	167	193	26-28	0	4.27
Ed Seward	R	20	55	52	52	3	470.2	445	7	140	155	25-25	0	4.13
Al Atkinson	R	26	15	15	11	0	124.2	156	2	54	34	6-8	0	5.92
Bobby Mathews	R	35	7	7	7	0	58.0	75	4	25	9	3-4	0	6.67
Bill Hart	R	21	3	3	3	0	26.0	28	1	17	4	1-2	0	4.50
C. Titcomb†	L	20	3	3	3	0	24.0	31	1	19	16	1-2	0	6.75
Billy Taylor	R	32	1	1	1	0	9.0	10	1	7	0	1-0	0	3.00
Fred Chapman	R	14	1	1	1	0	5.0	8	0	2	4	0-0	0	7.20
Bill Casey	—	—	1	0	0	0	1.0	4	0	1	0	0-0	0	18.00
Lou Bierbauer	R	21	1	0	0	0	1.0	0	0	0	1	0-0	1	0.00
Tom Poorman	R	29	1	0	0	0	0.2	5	1	1	1	0-0	0	40.50

1887 Brooklyn Bridegrooms 6th AA 60-74 .448 34.5 GB Charlie Byrne

Player	Gm by Position	B	Age	G	AB	R	H	2B	3B	HR	RBI	BB	SO	SB	Avg	OBP	Slg
Jimmy Peoples	C57,OF8,1B4*	—	23	73	268	36	68	14	2	1	38	16	—	22	.254	.306	.332
Bill Phillips	1B132	R	30	132	533	82	142	34	11	2	101	45	—	16	.266	.330	.383
Bill McClellan	2B136	L	31	136	548	109	144	24	6	1	53	80	—	70	.263	.363	.334
George Pinckney	3B136,SS2	R	25	138	580	133	155	26	6	3	69	61	—	59	.267	.343	.348
Germany Smith	SS101,3B2	R	24	103	435	79	128	19	16	4	72	13	—	26	.294	.316	.439
Jim McTamany	OF134	R	23	134	520	123	134	22	10	1	68	76	—	66	.258	.365	.344
Ed Swartwood	OF91	L	28	91	363	72	92	14	8	1	54	46	—	29	.253	.342	.344
Ed Greer†	OF76,C16	R	22	91	327	49	83	13	2	2	48	25	—	33	.254	.318	.324
Adonis Terry	OF49,P40,SS2	R	22	86	352	56	103	6	10	3	65	16	—	27	.293	.323	.392
Ernie Burch	OF49	L	31	49	188	47	55	4	4	2	26	29	—	15	.293	.395	.388
Bob Clark	C45,OF3	R	24	48	177	24	47	3	1	0	18	7	—	15	.266	.297	.294
Henry Porter	P40,OF1	R	28	40	146	16	29	2	4	1	12	10	—	6	.199	.250	.288
Jack O'Brien	C25,OF4,2B1	R	27	30	123	18	28	4	1	1	17	6	—	8	.228	.264	.301
Steve Toole	P24,1B3	R	28	26	103	19	24	6	0	1	13	3	—	4	.233	.255	.320
Billy Otterson	SS30	R	25	30	100	16	20	4	1	2	15	8	—	8	.200	.259	.320
John Harkins	P24,OF4,2B1	R	28	27	98	10	23	5	0	0	16	7	—	4	.235	.292	.286
Chief Roseman†	OF1	R	30	1	3	2	1	0	0	0	1	0	—	0	.333	.500	.333

J. Peoples, 4 G at SS, 1 G at 2B

Pitcher	T	Age	G	GS	CG	ShO	IP	H	HR	BB	SO	W-L	Sv	ERA
Henry Porter	R	28	40	40	38	1	339.2	416	7	96	74	15-24	0	4.21
Adonis Terry	R	22	40	35	35	1	318.0	331	10	99	138	16-16	3	4.02
John Harkins	R	28	24	24	22	0	199.0	262	6	77	36	10-14	0	6.02
Steve Toole	L	28	24	24	22	1	194.0	186	1	106	48	14-10	0	4.31
Hardie Henderson	R	24	13	12	12	0	111.2	127	3	63	28	5-8	0	3.95
Bert Cunningham	R	21	3	3	3	0	23.0	26	0	13	8	0-2	0	5.09

1887 New York Metropolitans 7th AA 44-89 .331 50.0 GB

Bob Ferguson (6-24)/Dave Orr (3-5)/Ollie Caylor (35-60)

Player	Gm by Position	B	Age	G	AB	R	H	2B	3B	HR	RBI	BB	SO	SB	Avg	OBP	Slg
Bill Holbert	C60,1B8,SS2*	R	32	69	255	20	58	4	3	0	32	7	—	12	.227	.248	.267
Dave Orr	1B81,OF3	R	27	84	345	63	127	25	10	2	66	22	—	17	.368	.408	.516
Joe Gerhardt†	2B84,3B1	R	32	85	307	40	68	13	2	0	27	24	—	15	.221	.280	.277
Frank Hankinson	3B127,2B1	R	31	127	512	79	137	29	11	1	71	38	—	19	.268	.318	.373
Paul Radford	SS76,OF37,2B18*	R	25	128	486	127	129	15	5	4	45	106	—	73	.265	.403	.342
Darby O'Brien	OF121,1B10,SS2*	R	23	127	522	97	157	30	13	5	73	40	—	49	.301	.355	.437
Charley Jones†	OF62,P2,1B1	R	37	62	247	30	63	11	3	3	29	12	—	8	.255	.306	.360
Chief Roseman†	OF59,1B3,P2	R	30	60	241	30	55	10	1	1	27	9	—	3	.228	.265	.290
Candy Nelson†	OF37,SS32,2B1	L	38	68	257	61	63	5	1	0	24	48	—	29	.245	.380	.272
Al Mays	P52,OF11,1B1	R	22	62	221	23	45	15	4	2	23	10	—	7	.204	.241	.335
Jim Donahue	C51,OF5,1B4*	R	25	60	220	33	62	4	1	1	29	21	—	6	.282	.350	.323
John Meister	OF22,2B14,3B3*	—	24	39	157	24	35	6	2	1	21	16	—	9	.223	.303	.306
Tom O'Brien	1B20,OF8,2B2*	R	27	31	129	13	25	3	2	0	18	2	—	10	.194	.212	.248
Eddie Hogan	OF29,SS4,3B1	R	27	32	120	22	24	6	1	0	5	30	—	12	.200	.373	.267
Pete Sommers	C31,1B1,OF1	R	20	33	116	9	21	3	0	1	12	7	—	6	.181	.234	.233
Dude Esterbrook	1B9,OF7,2B5*	R	30	26	101	11	17	1	0	0	7	6	—	8	.168	.222	.178
Ed Cushman	P26,OF1	R	35	26	93	14	23	4	2	0	9	10	—	2	.247	.333	.333
Jack Lynch	P21,1B2	R	30	23	83	4	14	1	0	0	6	7	—	3	.169	.250	.181
Jimmy Knowles	2B16,3B1	—	28	16	60	12	15	1	1	0	6	1	—	6	.250	.262	.300
Clarence Cross	SS13,3B4	—	31	16	55	9	11	2	1	0	5	2	—	0	.200	.267	.273
Stump Wiedman†	P12,OF3	R	26	14	46	5	7	1	1	0	1	4	—	2	.152	.220	.217
Jon Morrison	OF9	L	28	9	34	7	4	0	0	0	3	6	—	0	.118	.268	.118
Sadie Houck	SS10,2B1	R	31	10	33	3	5	1	0	0	0	3	—	2	.152	.243	.182
Cyclone Ryan	1B8,P2	—	21	8	32	4	7	1	0	0	3	3	—	1	.219	.286	.250
Fred O'Neill	OF6	—	22	6	26	4	8	1	1	0	3	1	—	3	.308	.357	.423
George McMullen	P3,OF1	—	—	3	12	2	1	0	0	0	1	0	—	0	.083	.083	.083
Charlie Hall	OF3	—	23	3	12	1	1	0	0	0	0	2	—	1	.083	.214	.083
Tom Kinslow	C2	R	21	2	6	0	0	0	0	0	0	0	—	0	.000	.000	.000
Hugh Collins	C1	—	—	1	4	0	1	0	0	0	0	0	—	0	.250	.250	.250
Lip Pike	OF1	L	42	1	4	0	0	0	0	0	0	0	—	0	.000	.000	.000

B. Holbert, 1 G at 2B; P. Radford, 2 G at P; D. O'Brien, 1 G at P, 1 G at 3B; J. Donahue, 1 G at 2B, 1 G at 3B; J. Meister, 1 G at SS; T. O'Brien, 2 G at 3B, 1 G at P; D. Esterbrook, 5 G at SS

Pitcher	T	Age	G	GS	CG	ShO	IP	H	HR	BB	SO	W-L	Sv	ERA
Al Mays	—	22	52	52	50	0	441.1	551	11	136	124	17-34	0	4.73
Ed Cushman	L	35	26	26	25	0	220.0	310	9	83	64	10-15	0	5.97
Jack Lynch	R	30	21	21	21	0	187.0	245	8	36	45	7-14	0	5.10
John Shaffer	—	23	13	13	13	0	112.0	148	3	53	22	2-11	0	6.19
Stump Wiedman†	R	26	12	12	11	1	97.0	122	3	25	37	4-8	0	4.64
Bill Fagan	L	18	6	6	6	0	45.0	55	1	24	12	1-4	0	4.00
Charlie Parsons	L	23	4	4	4	0	34.0	51	0	6	5	1-1	0	4.50
George McMullen	—	—	3	3	2	0	21.0	25	2	19	2	2-1	0	7.71
Cyclone Ryan	R	21	2	1	0	0	2.1	5	1	6	0	0-1	0	23.14
Chief Roseman	R	30	2	0	0	0	8.0	11	0	5	1	0-0	0	7.88
Paul Radford	R	25	2	0	0	0	5.0	15	1	3	4	0-0	0	18.00
Charley Jones	R	37	2	0	0	0	3.0	2	0	4	0	0-0	0	3.00
Tom O'Brien	R	27	1	0	0	0	3.2	4	0	5	0	0-0	0	7.36
Darby O'Brien	R	23	1	0	0	0	1.0	1	0	1	0	0-0	0	0.00

1887 Cleveland Spiders 8th AA 39-92 .298 54.0 GB

Jimmy Williams

Player	Gm by Position	B	Age	G	AB	R	H	2B	3B	HR	RBI	BB	SO	SB	Avg	OBP	Slg
Pop Snyder	C63,1B13	R	32	74	282	33	72	12	6	0	27	9	—	5	.255	.281	.340
Jim Toy	1B82,OF11,C10*	R	29	109	423	56	94	20	5	1	56	17	—	8	.222	.256	.300
Cub Stricker	2B126,SS6,P3	R	28	131	534	122	141	19	4	2	53	53	—	86	.264	.334	.326
Phil Reccius†	3B62,P1	—	25	62	229	23	47	6	3	0	29	24	—	9	.205	.295	.258
Ed McKean	SS123,2B8,OF4	R	23	132	539	97	154	16	13	2	54	60	—	76	.286	.358	.375
Pete Hotaling	OF126	R	30	126	505	108	151	28	13	3	94	53	—	43	.299	.373	.424
Myron Allen	OF115,3B3,P2*	R	33	117	463	66	128	22	10	4	77	36	—	26	.276	.335	.393
Fred Mann†	OF64	L	29	64	259	45	80	15	7	2	41	23	—	25	.309	.385	.444
C. Reipschlager	C48,1B16	R	—	63	231	20	49	8	3	0	17	11	—	7	.212	.251	.273
Scrappy Carroll	OF54,3B3,2B1	—	26	57	216	30	43	5	1	0	19	15	—	19	.199	.264	.231
Mike Morrison	P40,OF4,2B1*	R	20	41	141	23	27	3	2	0	12	11	—	5	.191	.255	.241
Charlie Sweeney	1B20,OF10,P3*	R	24	36	133	22	30	4	4	0	19	21	—	11	.226	.331	.316
Bob Gilks	P13,1B6,OF3*	R	22	22	83	12	26	2	0	0	13	3	—	5	.313	.352	.337
John McGlone	3B21	—	23	21	79	14	20	2	1	0	10	7	—	15	.253	.337	.304
Jimmy Say	3B16	—	25	16	64	9	24	5	3	0	12	1	—	0	.375	.385	.547
John Munyan	OF12,C3,3B2	—	26	16	58	9	14	1	1	0	6	3	—	4	.241	.279	.293
Chief Zimmer	C12,1B2	R	26	14	52	9	12	5	0	0	4	4	—	1	.231	.298	.327
Ed Herr	3B11	R	25	11	44	6	12	2	0	0	6	6	—	2	.273	.360	.318
Ed Flynn	3B6,OF1	L	23	7	27	0	5	1	0	0	4	1	—	3	.185	.214	.222
Hank Simon	OF3	R	24	3	10	1	1	0	0	0	0	0	—	0	.100	.100	.100
Frank Scheibeck	P1,3B1,SS1	R	22	3	9	2	2	0	0	0	0	2	—	0	.222	.364	.222

J. Toy, 8 G at 3B, 3 G at SS; M. Allen, 2 G at SS; M. Morrison, 1 G at 3B; C. Sweeney, 2 G at 3B, 2 G at SS; B. Gilks, 1 G at 2B

Pitcher	T	Age	G	GS	CG	ShO	IP	H	HR	BB	SO	W-L	Sv	ERA
Billy Crowell	R	21	45	45	45	1	389.1	541	9	138	72	14-31	0	4.88
Mike Morrison	R	20	40	40	35	0	316.2	385	13	205	158	12-25	0	4.92
One Arm Daily	R	30	16	16	16	0	139.2	181	1	44	30	4-12	0	3.67
Bob Gilks	R	22	13	13	12	1	108.0	104	1	42	28	7-5	0	3.08
George Pechiney	R	25	10	10	10	0	86.0	118	8	44	24	1-9	0	7.12
John Kirby†	R	22	5	5	5	0	41.0	62	1	28	6	0-5	0	9.00
Charlie Sweeney	R	24	3	3	3	0	24.0	42	0	13	8	0-3	0	8.25
Frank Scheibeck	R	22	1	1	1	0	9.0	17	1	4	3	0-1	0	12.00
Cub Stricker	R	28	3	0	0	0	5.2	5	0	7	2	0-0	1	3.18
Myron Allen	R	33	2	0	0	0	9.2	9	0	3	1	1-0	0	0.93
Phil Reccius	—	25	1	0	0	0	7.0	8	0	5	0	0-0	0	7.71

»1888 New York Giants 1st NL 84-47 .641 —

Jim Mutrie

Player	Gm by Position	B	Age	G	AB	R	H	2B	3B	HR	RBI	BB	SO	SB	Avg	OBP	Slg
Buck Ewing	C78,3B21,SS4*	R	28	103	415	83	127	18	15	6	58	24	28	53	.306	.348	.465
Roger Connor	1B133,2B1	L	30	134	481	98	140	15	17	14	71	73	44	27	.291	.389	.480
Danny Richardson	2B135	R	25	135	561	82	127	16	7	8	61	15	35	35	.226	.248	.323
Art Whitney	3B90	R	30	90	328	28	72	1	4	1	28	8	22	7	.220	.240	.256
Monte Ward	SS122	L	28	122	510	70	128	14	5	2	49	9	13	38	.251	.265	.310
Mike Tiernan	OF113	L	21	113	443	75	130	16	8	9	52	42	42	52	.293	.364	.427
Mike Slattery	OF103	L	21	103	391	50	96	12	6	1	35	13	28	26	.246	.272	.315
Jim O'Rourke	OF87,C15,1B4*	R	37	107	409	50	112	16	6	4	50	24	30	25	.274	.319	.372
George Gore	OF64	L	31	64	254	37	56	4	4	2	17	30	31	11	.220	.308	.291
Tim Keefe	P51,OF1	R	31	51	181	10	23	3	0	2	8	4	56	3	.127	.146	.177
Elmer Foster	OF37,3B1	R	26	37	136	15	20	3	2	0	10	9	20	13	.147	.216	.199
Pat Murphy	C28	—	31	28	106	11	18	1	0	0	4	6	11	3	.170	.214	.179
Gil Hatfield	3B14,SS13,2B1*	—	33	28	105	7	19	1	0	0	9	2	18	8	.181	.211	.190
Cannonball Titcomb	P23,3B1	L	21	23	82	6	10	1	0	0	5	1	22	5	.122	.133	.134
Willard Brown	C20	R	22	20	59	4	16	1	0	0	6	1	8	1	.271	.283	.288
Bill George	OF6,P4	R	23	9	39	7	9	1	0	1	6	0	2	1	.231	.231	.333
Elmer Cleveland†	3B9	R	25	9	34	6	8	0	2	2	5	3	1	1	.235	.297	.529

B. Ewing, 2 G at P; J. O'Rourke, 2 G at 3B; G. Hatfield, 1 G at OF

Pitcher	T	Age	G	GS	CG	ShO	IP	H	HR	BB	SO	W-L	Sv	ERA
Tim Keefe	R	31	51	51	48	8	434.1	316	5	91	333	35-12	0	1.74
Mickey Welch	R	28	47	47	47	5	425.1	328	12	108	167	26-19	0	1.93
Cannonball Titcomb	L	21	23	23	22	4	197.0	149	4	46	129	14-8	0	2.24
Ed Crane	R	26	12	11	11	2	92.2	70	3	40	58	5-6	1	2.43
Bill George	L	23	4	3	3	1	33.2	18	0	11	26	2-1	0	1.34
Stump Wiedman	R	27	2	2	2	0	18.0	17	2	8	5	1-1	0	3.50
Buck Ewing	R	28	2	0	0	0	7.0	8	1	4	6	0-0	0	2.57

1888 Chicago White Stockings 2nd NL 77-58 .570 9.0 GB

Cap Anson

Player	Gm by Position	B	Age	G	AB	R	H	2B	3B	HR	RBI	BB	SO	SB	Avg	OBP	Slg
Tom Daly	C62,OF4	S	22	65	219	34	42	2	6	0	29	10	26	10	.192	.230	.256
Cap Anson	1B134	R	36	134	515	101	177	20	12	12	84	47	24	28	.344	.400	.499
Fred Pfeffer	2B135	R	28	135	517	90	129	22	10	8	57	32	38	64	.250	.297	.377
Tom Burns	3B134	R	31	134	483	60	115	12	6	3	70	26	49	34	.238	.281	.306
Ned Williamson	SS132	R	30	132	452	75	113	9	14	8	73	65	71	25	.250	.352	.385
Jimmy Ryan	OF128,P8	R	25	129	549	115	182	33	10	16	64	35	50	60	.332	.377	.515
Marty Sullivan	OF75	R	25	75	314	40	74	12	6	7	39	15	32	9	.236	.273	.379
Hugh Duffy	OF67,SS3,3B1	R	21	71	298	60	84	10	4	7	41	9	32	13	.282	.305	.413
George Van Haltren	OF57,P30	L	22	81	318	46	90	9	14	4	34	22	34	21	.283	.329	.437
Duke Farrell	C33,OF31,1B1	S	21	64	241	34	56	6	3	3	19	4	41	8	.232	.245	.320
Bob Pettit	OF43	L	26	43	169	23	43	1	4	4	23	7	9	7	.254	.288	.379
Mark Baldwin	P30,OF3	R	24	30	106	11	16	1	2	1	5	5	47	4	.151	.196	.226
Silver Flint	C22	R	32	22	77	6	14	3	0	0	3	1	21	1	.182	.203	.221
Dell Darling	C20	R	26	20	75	12	16	3	1	2	7	3	12	0	.213	.253	.360
John Tener	P12,OF1	R	24	12	46	4	9	1	0	0	1	1	15	1	.196	.229	.217
George Borchers	P10,OF3	S	19	10	33	3	2	2	0	0	2	1	13	1	.061	.088	.121
Ad Gumbert	P6,OF2	R	19	7	24	3	8	0	1	0	2	0	2	0	.333	.360	.417
Tod Brynan	P3,OF1	R	24	3	11	1	2	0	1	0	1	0	3	0	.182	.182	.364
Willard Mains	P2,OF1	—	19	2	7	1	1	0	0	0	0	1	3	0	.143	.250	.143
Dad Clarke	P2,OF1	S	23	2	7	4	2	0	1	1	2	1	2	0	.286	.375	1.000

Pitcher	T	Age	G	GS	CG	ShO	IP	H	HR	BB	SO	W-L	Sv	ERA
Gus Krock	L	22	39	39	39	4	339.2	295	20	45	161	25-14	0	2.44
Mark Baldwin	R	24	30	30	27	2	251.0	241	13	99	157	13-15	0	2.76
George Van Haltren	L	22	30	24	24	4	245.2	263	15	60	139	13-13	1	3.52
John Tener	R	24	12	12	11	1	102.0	90	6	25	39	7-5	0	2.74
George Borchers	R	19	10	10	7	1	67.0	67	2	29	26	4-4	0	3.49
Ad Gumbert	R	19	6	6	5	0	48.2	44	0	10	16	3-3	0	3.14
Frank Dwyer	R	20	5	5	5	1	42.0	32	1	9	17	4-1	0	1.07
Tod Brynan	R	24	3	3	2	0	25.0	29	2	7	11	2-1	0	6.48
Dad Clarke	R	23	2	2	1	0	16.0	23	2	6	6	1-0	0	5.06
Willard Mains	R	19	2	2	1	0	11.0	8	0	6	5	1-1	0	4.91
Jimmy Ryan	L	25	8	2	1	0	38.1	47	2	12	11	4-0	0	3.05

1888 Philadelphia Phillies 3rd NL 69-61 .531 14.5 GB

Harry Wright

Player	Gm by Position	B	Age	G	AB	R	H	2B	3B	HR	RBI	BB	SO	SB	Avg	OBP	Slg
Jack Clements	C85,OF1	L	23	86	326	26	80	8	4	1	32	10	36	3	.245	.276	.304
Sid Farrar	1B131	—	28	131	508	53	124	24	7	1	53	31	38	21	.244	.304	.325
Charlie Bastian	2B65,3B14,SS1	R	27	80	275	30	53	4	1	1	17	27	41	12	.193	.282	.225
Joe Mulvey	3B100	R	29	100	398	37	86	12	3	0	39	9	33	18	.216	.235	.261
Arthur Irwin	SS122,2B3	L	30	125	448	51	98	12	4	0	28	33	56	19	.219	.277	.263
Ed Andrews	OF124	R	29	124	528	75	126	14	4	3	44	21	41	35	.239	.272	.297
Jim Fogarty	OF117,3B5,SS1	R	24	121	454	72	107	14	6	1	35	53	66	58	.236	.325	.300
George Wood	OF104,P2,3B2	L	29	106	433	67	99	19	6	6	51	39	44	20	.229	.303	.342
Ed Delahanty	2B56,OF17	R	20	74	290	40	66	12	2	1	31	12	26	38	.228	.261	.293
Ben Sanders	P31,OF25,3B1	R	23	57	236	26	58	11	2	1	25	8	12	13	.246	.276	.322
Charlie Buffinton	P46,OF1	R	27	46	160	14	29	4	1	0	12	7	5	1	.181	.216	.219
Pop Schriver	C27,3B6,SS6*	R	22	40	134	15	26	5	2	1	23	7	21	2	.194	.250	.284
Dan Casey	P33,OF1	R	25	33	118	11	18	2	1	0	5	3	28	2	.153	.174	.186
Kid Gleason	P24,OF1	S	21	24	83	4	17	2	0	0	5	3	16	3	.205	.233	.229
Bill Hallman	C10,2B4,OF3*	R	21	18	63	5	13	4	1	0	6	1	12	1	.206	.219	.302
Deacon McGuire†	C10,3B2	R	24	12	51	7	17	4	2	0	11	4	9	0	.333	.382	.490
Woodie Wagenhorst	3B2	—	25	2	8	2	1	0	0	0	0	0	1	0	.125	.125	.125
John Grim	2B1,OF1	R	20	2	7	0	1	0	0	0	0	0	0	0	.143	.143	.143
Cupid Childs	2B2	L	20	2	4	0	0	0	0	0	0	0	0	0	.000	.000	.000
Gid Gardner†	2B1	—	29	1	3	0	2	0	0	0	1	0	0	0	.667	.667	.667

P. Schriver, 1 G at OF; B. Hallman, 1 G at 3B, 1 G at SS

Pitcher	T	Age	G	GS	CG	ShO	IP	H	HR	BB	SO	W-L	Sv	ERA
Charlie Buffinton	R	27	46	46	43	6	400.1	324	6	59	199	28-17	0	1.91
Dan Casey	L	25	33	33	31	2	285.2	298	6	48	108	14-18	0	3.15
Ben Sanders	R	23	31	29	28	8	275.1	240	3	33	121	19-10	0	1.90
Kid Gleason	R	21	24	23	23	0	199.2	199	11	53	89	7-16	0	2.84
George Wood	R	29	2	0	0	0	2.0	3	0	1	0	0-0	2	4.50
Jim Tyng	—	32	1	0	0	0	4.0	8	0	2	2	0-0	1	4.50

1888 Boston Red Stockings 4th NL 70-64 .522 15.5 GB

John Morrill

Player	Gm by Position	B	Age	G	AB	R	H	2B	3B	HR	RBI	BB	SO	SB	Avg	OBP	Slg
King Kelly	C76,OF34	R	30	107	440	85	140	22	11	9	71	31	39	56	.318	.368	.480
John Morrill	1B133,2B2	R	33	135	486	60	96	18	7	4	39	55	68	21	.198	.282	.288
Joe Quinn	2B38	R	23	38	156	19	47	8	3	4	29	2	5	12	.301	.310	.468
Billy Nash	3B105,2B31	R	23	135	526	71	149	18	15	4	75	50	46	20	.283	.350	.397
Sam Wise	SS89,3B6,1B5*	L	30	105	417	66	100	19	12	4	40	34	66	33	.240	.306	.372
Dick Johnston	OF135	R	25	135	585	102	173	31	18	12	68	15	33	35	.296	.314	.472
Joe Hornung	OF107	R	31	107	431	61	103	11	7	3	53	16	39	29	.239	.269	.318
Tom Brown	OF107	L	27	107	420	62	104	10	7	9	49	30	68	46	.248	.299	.369
Irv Ray	SS48,2B3	L	24	50	206	26	51	2	3	2	26	6	11	7	.248	.272	.316
John Clarkson	P54,OF1	R	26	55	205	20	40	9	1	1	17	7	48	5	.195	.222	.263
Pop Tate	C41,OF1	R	27	41	148	18	34	7	1	1	6	8	7	3	.230	.278	.311
Ezra Sutton	3B27,SS1	R	37	28	110	16	24	3	1	1	16	7	3	10	.218	.277	.291
Billy Klusman	2B28	R	23	28	107	9	18	4	0	2	11	5	13	3	.168	.205	.262
Jack Burdock†	2B22	R	36	22	79	5	16	0	0	0	4	2	5	1	.203	.232	.203
Tom O'Rourke	C20,OF1	—	22	20	74	3	13	0	0	0	4	1	9	2	.176	.187	.176
Ed Glenn†	OF19,3B1	R	27	20	65	8	10	0	2	0	3	2	8	0	.154	.203	.215
Bill Higgins	2B14	—	26	14	54	5	10	1	0	0	4	1	3	1	.185	.200	.204
Dick Conway	P6,OF1	L	22	7	25	2	4	0	0	0	1	1	6	0	.160	.192	.160
Mike Hines	OF3,C1	R	25	4	16	3	2	0	1	0	2	2	0	0	.125	.222	.250
Pete Sommers	C4	R	21	4	13	1	3	1	0	0	0	0	3	0	.231	.231	.308
Nick Wise	C1,OF1	R	22	1	3	0	0	0	0	0	0	0	0	0	.000	.000	.000

S. Wise, 4 G at OF, 2 G at 2B

Pitcher	T	Age	G	GS	CG	ShO	IP	H	HR	BB	SO	W-L	Sv	ERA
John Clarkson	R	26	54	54	53	3	483.1	448	17	119	223	33-20	0	2.76
Bill Sowders	R	23	36	35	34	2	317.0	278	3	73	132	19-15	0	2.07
Old Hoss Radbourn	R	33	24	24	24	1	207.0	187	8	45	64	7-16	0	2.87
Kid Madden	L	20	20	18	17	1	165.0	142	6	24	53	7-11	0	2.95
Dick Conway	R	22	6	6	6	0	53.0	49	2	8	12	4-2	0	2.38

1888 Detroit Wolverines 5th NL 68-63 .519 16.0 GB

Bill Watkins (49-44)/Bob Leadley (19-19)

Player	Gm by Position	B	Age	G	AB	R	H	2B	3B	HR	RBI	BB	SO	SB	Avg	OBP	Slg
Charlie Bennett	C73,1B1	R	33	74	258	32	68	12	4	5	29	31	40	4	.264	.347	.399
Dan Brouthers	1B129	L	30	129	522	118	160	33	11	9	66	68	13	34	.307	.399	.464
Hardy Richardson	2B58	R	33	58	266	60	77	18	2	6	32	17	23	13	.289	.335	.440
Deacon White	3B125	L	40	125	527	75	157	22	5	4	71	21	24	12	.298	.336	.381
Jack Rowe	SS105	L	31	105	451	62	125	19	8	2	74	19	28	10	.277	.311	.368
Larry Twitchell	OF131,P2	R	24	131	524	71	128	19	4	5	67	28	45	14	.244	.286	.324
Ned Hanlon	OF109	L	30	109	459	64	122	6	8	5	39	15	32	38	.266	.295	.346
Count Campau	OF70	L	24	70	251	28	51	5	3	1	18	19	36	27	.203	.259	.259
Charlie Ganzel	2B49,C28,3B9*	R	26	95	386	45	96	13	5	1	46	14	15	12	.249	.277	.316
Sam Thompson	OF56	L	28	56	238	51	67	10	8	6	40	23	10	5	.282	.352	.466
Sy Sutcliffe	SS24,C14,1B5*	L	26	49	191	17	49	5	3	0	23	5	14	6	.257	.276	.314
Pete Conway	P45,OF1	R	21	45	167	28	46	4	2	3	23	8	25	1	.275	.320	.377
Ted Scheffler	OF27	R	24	27	94	17	19	3	1	0	4	9	9	4	.202	.286	.255
Parson Nicholson	2B24	—	25	24	85	11	22	2	3	1	9	2	7	6	.259	.284	.388
Jake Wells	C16	R	24	16	57	5	9	1	0	0	2	0	5	0	.158	.158	.175
Ed Beatin	P12,SS2,OF2	R	21	16	56	8	14	1	2	2	9	6	8	1	.250	.323	.446
Lady Baldwin	P6,OF1	L	29	6	23	5	6	0	0	0	3	3	3	0	.261	.346	.261
Deacon McGuire†	C3	R	24	3	13	0	0	0	0	0	0	0	4	0	.000	.000	.000
Sam LaRoque	2B2	—	24	2	9	1	4	0	0	0	2	1	1	0	.444	.500	.444
Barney Gilligan	C1	R	32	1	5	1	1	0	0	0	0	0	1	0	.200	.200	.200
Frank Scheibeck	SS1	R	23	1	4	0	0	0	0	0	0	0	0	0	.000	.000	.000
Cal Broughton	C1	R	27	1	4	0	0	0	0	0	0	0	0	0	.000	.000	.000

C. Ganzel, 5 G at OF, 3 G at SS, 1 G at 1B; S. Sutcliffe, 4 G at OF, 2 G at 2B

Pitcher	T	Age	G	GS	CG	ShO	IP	H	HR	BB	SO	W-L	Sv	ERA
Charlie Getzien	R	24	46	46	45	2	404.0	411	13	54	202	19-25	0	3.05
Pete Conway	R	21	45	45	43	4	391.0	315	11	57	176	30-14	0	2.26
Henry Gruber	R	24	27	25	25	3	240.0	196	8	41	71	11-14	0	2.29
Ed Beatin	L	21	12	12	12	1	107.0	111	6	16	44	5-7	0	2.86
Lady Baldwin	L	29	6	6	5	0	53.0	76	5	15	26	3-3	0	5.43
Larry Twitchell	R	24	2	0	0	0	4.0	6	1	0	3	0-0	1	6.75

1888 Pittsburgh Alleghenys 6th NL 66-68 .493 19.5 GB

Horace Phillips

Player	Gm by Position	B	Age	G	AB	R	H	2B	3B	HR	RBI	BB	SO	SB	Avg	OBP	Slg
Doggie Miller	C68,OF32,3B4	R	23	103	404	50	112	17	5	0	36	18	16	27	.277	.319	.344
Jake Beckley	1B71	L	20	71	283	35	97	15	3	0	27	7	22	20	.343	.363	.417
Fred Dunlap	2B82	R	29	82	321	41	84	12	4	1	36	16	30	24	.262	.303	.333
Bill Kuehne	3B75,SS63	R	29	138	524	60	123	22	11	3	62	9	68	34	.235	.250	.336
Pop Smith	SS75,2B56	R	31	131	481	61	99	15	2	4	52	22	78	37	.206	.248	.270
Billy Sunday	OF120	L	25	120	505	69	119	14	3	0	15	12	36	71	.236	.256	.275
John Coleman	OF91,1B25	L	25	116	438	49	101	11	4	0	26	29	52	15	.231	.285	.274
Abner Dalrymple	OF57	L	30	57	227	19	50	9	2	0	14	6	28	7	.220	.247	.278
Fred Carroll	C54,OF38,1B5*	R	23	97	366	62	91	14	5	2	48	32	31	18	.249	.326	.331
Al Maul	1B38,OF34,P3	R	22	74	259	21	54	9	4	0	31	21	45	9	.208	.276	.274
Pud Galvin	P50,OF1	R	31	50	175	6	25	1	1	1	3	1	51	4	.143	.148	.177
Jocko Fields	OF29,C14,3B3	R	23	45	169	22	33	7	2	1	15	8	19	9	.195	.232	.278
Elmer Cleveland†	3B30	R	25	30	108	10	24	2	1	2	11	5	23	3	.222	.270	.315
Pete McShannic	3B26	S	24	26	98	5	19	1	0	0	5	1	9	3	.194	.218	.204
Sam Nichol	OF8	R	19	8	22	3	1	0	0	0	0	2	2	0	.045	.125	.045
Cliff Carroll	OF5	S	28	5	20	1	0	0	0	0	0	0	8	2	.000	.000	.000
Hardie Henderson	P5,OF1	R	25	5	18	2	5	0	0	0	3	0	2	0	.278	.278	.278
Henry Yaik	C1,OF1	L	24	2	6	0	2	0	0	0	1	1	0	0	.333	.429	.333
Bill Farmer†	C1,OF1	R	17	2	4	0	0	0	0	0	0	0	1	0	.000	.000	.000

F. Carroll, 1 G at 3B

Pitcher	T	Age	G	GS	CG	ShO	IP	H	HR	BB	SO	W-L	Sv	ERA
Ed Morris	L	25	55	55	54	5	480.0	470	7	74	135	29-23	0	2.31
Pud Galvin	R	31	50	50	49	6	437.1	446	9	53	107	23-25	0	2.63
Harry Staley	R	21	25	24	24	2	207.1	185	6	53	89	12-12	0	2.69
Hardie Henderson	R	25	5	5	4	0	35.1	43	0	20	9	1-3	0	5.35
Phil Knell	L	23	3	3	3	0	26.1	20	1	18	15	1-2	0	3.76
Al Maul	R	22	3	1	1	0	17.0	26	0	5	12	0-2	0	6.35

1888 Indianapolis Hoosiers 7th NL 50-85 .370 36.0 GB

Harry Spence

Player	Gm by Position	B	Age	G	AB	R	H	2B	3B	HR	RBI	BB	SO	SB	Avg	OBP	Slg
Dick Buckley	C51,3B22,1B1*	—	29	71	260	28	71	9	3	5	22	6	24	4	.273	.289	.388
Dude Esterbrook†	1B61,3B3	R	31	64	246	21	54	8	0	0	17	2	20	11	.220	.232	.252
Charley Bassett	2B128	R	25	128	481	58	116	20	3	2	60	32	41	24	.241	.297	.308
Jerry Denny	3B96,SS25,2B5*	R	29	126	524	92	137	27	7	12	63	9	79	32	.261	.277	.408
Jack Glasscock	SS110,2B3,P1	R	28	113	442	63	119	17	3	1	45	14	17	48	.269	.302	.328
Emmett Seery	OF133,SS1	L	27	133	500	87	110	20	10	5	50	64	73	80	.220	.316	.330
Paul Hines	OF125,1B6,SS2	R	36	133	513	84	144	26	3	4	58	41	45	31	.281	.343	.366
Jack McGeachey	OF117,P1,SS1	R	24	118	452	45	99	15	2	0	30	5	21	49	.219	.231	.261
George Myers	C47,3B14,OF10*	R	27	66	248	36	59	9	0	2	16	16	14	28	.238	.292	.298
Con Daily	C42,1B5,3B5*	L	23	57	202	14	44	6	1	0	14	10	28	15	.218	.255	.257
Jumbo Schoeneck	1B48,P2	R	26	48	169	15	40	4	0	0	20	9	24	11	.237	.283	.260
Egyptian Healy	P37,OF1	R	21	37	131	14	30	9	0	1	13	1	39	5	.229	.235	.321
Henry Boyle	P37,1B1	—	27	37	125	13	18	2	0	1	6	6	31	1	.144	.189	.184
Lev Shreve	P35,OF1	R	19	36	115	10	21	3	0	0	2	4	9	5	.183	.210	.209
Otto Schomberg	1B15,OF15	L	23	30	112	11	24	5	1	1	10	10	12	6	.214	.290	.304
Bill Burdick	P20,OF1	R	28	21	68	6	10	0	0	0	1	2	11	0	.147	.194	.147
Sam Moffett	P7,OF3	R	31	10	35	6	4	0	0	0	0	5	4	0	.114	.225	.114

D. Buckley, 1 G at OF; J. Denny, 1 G at P, 1 G at OF; G. Myers, 1 G at 1B; C. Daily, 5 G at OF, 1 G at 2B

Pitcher	T	Age	G	GS	CG	ShO	IP	H	HR	BB	SO	W-L	Sv	ERA
Henry Boyle	R	27	37	37	36	3	323.0	315	11	58	98	15-22	0	3.26
Egyptian Healy	R	21	37	37	36	1	321.1	347	13	87	124	12-24	0	3.89
Lev Shreve	R	19	35	35	34	1	297.2	352	23	93	101	11-24	0	4.63
Bill Burdick	R	28	20	20	20	0	176.0	168	12	43	55	10-10	0	2.81
Sam Moffett	R	31	7	7	6	1	56.0	62	3	17	7	2-5	0	4.66
Jumbo Schoeneck	R	26	2	0	0	0	4.1	5	0	1	1	0-0	0	0.00
Jack McGeachey	R	24	1	0	0	0	5.0	5	1	3	0	0-0	0	7.20
Jerry Denny	R	29	1	0	0	0	4.0	5	1	4	1	0-0	0	9.00
Jack Glasscock	R	28	1	0	0	0	0.1	1	0	2	1	0-0	0	54.00

1888 Washington Senators 8th NL 48-86 .358 37.5 GB

Walter Hewett (10-29)/Ted Sullivan (38-57)

Player	Gm by Position	B	Age	G	AB	R	H	2B	3B	HR	RBI	BB	SO	SB	Avg	OBP	Slg
Connie Mack	C79,OF4,1B1*	R	25	85	300	49	56	5	6	3	29	17	18	31	.187	.249	.273
Billy O'Brien	1B132,3B1	R	28	133	528	42	119	15	2	9	66	9	70	10	.225	.238	.313
Bert Myers	2B132	R	24	132	502	46	104	12	7	2	46	37	46	20	.207	.270	.271
Jim Donnelly	3B117,SS5	R	22	122	428	43	86	9	4	0	23	20	16	44	.201	.242	.241
George Shoch	SS52,OF35,P1*	R	29	90	317	46	58	6	3	2	24	25	22	23	.183	.262	.240
Dummy Hoy	OF136	L	26	136	503	77	138	10	8	2	29	69	48	82	.274	.374	.338
Walt Wilmot	OF119	S	24	119	473	61	106	16	9	4	43	23	55	46	.224	.263	.321
Ed Daily	OF100,P9,1B1	R	25	110	453	56	102	8	4	7	39	7	42	44	.225	.239	.307
Shorty Fuller	SS47,2B2	R	20	49	170	11	31	5	2	0	12	10	14	6	.182	.232	.235
Hank O'Day	P46,SS2	—	25	47	166	6	23	2	0	0	6	4	41	3	.139	.159	.151
Jim Whitney	P39,OF3,1B1	L	30	42	141	13	24	0	0	1	17	7	20	3	.170	.209	.191
Pat Deasley	C31,2B1,SS1*	R	30	34	127	6	20	1	0	0	4	2	18	2	.157	.171	.165
John Irwin	SS27,3B10	L	26	37	126	14	28	5	2	0	8	5	18	15	.222	.263	.294
Wild Bill Widner	P13,OF2	R	21	15	60	4	12	0	0	0	6	0	8	1	.200	.200	.200
Tug Arundel	C17	—	26	17	51	2	10	0	1	0	3	5	10	1	.196	.268	.235
Pete Sweeney	3B8,OF3	R	24	11	44	3	8	0	1	0	5	0	4	0	.182	.182	.227
Miah Murray	C10,1B2	R	23	12	42	1	4	1	0	0	3	1	7	0	.095	.116	.119
Frank Gilmore	P12,C1,OF1	R	24	13	41	0	1	0	0	0	2	0	20	0	.024	.024	.024
Perry Werden	OF3	R	22	3	10	0	3	0	0	0	2	1	4	0	.300	.364	.300
Gid Gardner†	2B1,SS1	—	29	2	4	0	1	0	0	0	0	1	1	0	.250	.400	.250
Jim Banning	C1	L	22	1	0	0	0	0	0	0	0	0	0	0	—	—	—

C. Mack, 1 G at SS; G. Shoch, 1 G at 2B; P. Deasley, 1 G at OF

Pitcher	T	Age	G	GS	CG	ShO	IP	H	HR	BB	SO	W-L	Sv	ERA
Hank O'Day	R	25	46	46	46	3	403.0	359	19	117	186	16-29	0	3.10
Jim Whitney	R	30	39	39	37	2	325.0	317	7	54	79	18-21	0	3.05
Wild Bill Widner	R	21	13	13	13	0	115.0	111	7	22	33	5-7	0	2.82
George Keefe	L	21	13	13	13	1	114.0	87	2	43	52	6-7	0	2.84
Frank Gilmore	—	24	12	11	10	0	95.2	131	4	29	23	1-9	0	6.59
Ed Daily	R	25	9	8	8	0	73.2	88	7	19	20	2-7	0	4.89
Dupee Shaw	L	29	3	3	3	0	25.0	36	2	7	8	0-3	0	6.48
George Haddock	R	21	2	2	2	0	16.0	9	0	2	3	0-2	0	2.25
John Greening	—	—	1	1	1	0	9.0	17	2	4	2	0-1	0	11.00
George Shoch	R	29	1	0	0	0	3.0	2	0	1	0	0-0	0	0.00

»1888 St. Louis Browns 1st AA 92-43 .681 —

Charlie Comiskey

Player	Gm by Position	B	Age	G	AB	R	H	2B	3B	HR	RBI	BB	SO	SB	Avg	OBP	Slg
Jack Boyle	C70,OF1	R	22	71	257	33	62	8	1	1	23	13	—	11	.241	.286	.292
Charlie Comiskey	1B133,OF5,2B3	R	28	137	576	102	157	22	5	6	83	12	—	72	.273	.292	.359
Yank Robinson	2B102,SS34	R	28	134	455	111	105	17	6	3	53	116	—	56	.231	.400	.314
Arlie Latham	3B133,SS1	R	28	133	570	119	151	19	5	2	31	43	—	109	.265	.325	.326
Bill White†	SS74,2B2	—	28	76	275	31	48	2	3	2	30	21	—	6	.175	.238	.225
Tommy McCarthy	OF131,P2	R	24	131	511	107	140	20	3	1	68	38	—	93	.274	.328	.331
Tip O'Neill	OF130	R	30	130	529	96	177	24	10	5	98	44	—	26	.335	.390	.446
Harry Lyons	OF122,3B2,2B1*	R	22	123	499	66	97	10	5	4	63	20	—	36	.194	.230	.259
Jocko Milligan	C58,1B5	R	26	63	219	19	55	6	2	5	37	17	—	3	.251	.311	.365
Silver King	P66,OF2	R	20	66	207	25	43	4	6	1	14	40	—	6	.208	.339	.300
Nat Hudson	P39,OF16,1B3*	R	19	56	196	27	50	7	0	2	28	18	—	9	.255	.324	.321
Ed Herr	SS28,OF11,3B4	R	26	43	172	21	46	7	1	3	43	11	—	9	.267	.323	.372
Chippy McGarr	2B33,SS1	R	25	34	132	17	31	1	0	0	13	6	—	25	.235	.268	.242
Elton Chamberlin†	P14,OF1	R	20	14	50	6	5	0	0	1	2	3	—	3	.100	.182	.160
Tom Dolan	C11	R	29	11	36	1	7	1	0	0	1	1	—	1	.194	.216	.222

H. Lyons, 1 G at SS; N. Hudson, 1 G at SS

Pitcher	T	Age	G	GS	CG	ShO	IP	H	HR	BB	SO	W-L	Sv	ERA
Silver King	R	20	66	65	64	6	585.2	437	6	76	258	45-21	0	1.64
Nat Hudson	R	19	39	37	36	5	333.0	283	8	59	130	25-10	0	2.54
Elton Chamberlin†	R	20	14	14	13	1	112.0	61	1	27	57	11-2	0	1.61
Jim Devlin	L	22	11	11	10	0	90.1	82	3	20	45	6-5	0	3.19
Ed Knouff†	R	20	9	9	9	0	81.0	66	0	37	25	5-4	0	2.67
Julie Freeman	—	19	1	1	0	0	6.1	7	0	4	1	0-1	0	4.26
Tommy McCarthy	R	24	2	0	0	0	4.1	3	1	2	1	0-0	0	4.15

1888 Brooklyn Bridegrooms 2nd AA 88-52 .629 6.5 GB

Bill McGunnigle

Player	Gm by Position	B	Age	G	AB	R	H	2B	3B	HR	RBI	BB	SO	SB	Avg	OBP	Slg
Doc Bushong	C69	R	31	69	253	23	53	5	1	0	16	5	—	9	.209	.231	.237
Dave Orr	1B99	R	28	99	394	57	120	20	5	1	59	7	—	11	.305	.330	.388
Jack Burdock†	2B70	R	36	70	246	15	30	1	2	1	8	8	—	9	.122	.166	.154
George Pinckney	3B143	R	26	143	575	134	156	18	8	4	52	66	—	51	.271	.358	.351
Germany Smith	SS103,2B1	R	25	103	402	47	86	10	7	3	61	22	—	27	.214	.255	.296
Darby O'Brien	OF136	R	24	136	532	105	149	27	6	2	65	30	—	55	.280	.327	.365
Paul Radford	OF88,2B2	R	26	90	308	48	67	9	3	2	29	35	—	33	.218	.305	.286
Dave Foutz	OF78,1B42,P23	R	31	140	563	91	156	20	13	3	99	28	—	35	.277	.314	.375
Bob Caruthers	OF51,P44	L	24	94	335	58	77	10	5	5	53	45	—	23	.230	.328	.334
Bill McClellan†	2B56,OF18	L	32	74	278	33	57	7	3	0	21	40	—	13	.205	.307	.252
Oyster Burns†	SS36,OF14,2B3	R	23	52	204	40	58	9	6	2	25	14	—	21	.284	.339	.417
Bob Clark	C36,OF8,1B1	R	25	45	150	23	36	5	3	1	20	9	—	11	.240	.292	.333
Adonis Terry	P23,OF7,1B2	R	23	30	115	13	29	6	0	0	8	5	—	7	.252	.283	.304
Jimmy Peoples	C25,SS5,OF2	—	24	32	103	15	20	5	3	0	17	8	—	10	.194	.259	.301
Pop Corkhill†	OF19	L	30	19	71	17	27	4	3	1	19	4	—	3	.380	.429	.563
Al Mays	P18,OF1	R	23	18	63	4	5	1	1	0	5	5	—	2	.079	.159	.127
Bill Holbert	C15	R	33	15	50	4	6	1	0	0	1	2	—	0	.120	.170	.140
Ed Silch	OF14	—	23	14	48	5	13	4	0	0	3	4	—	4	.271	.327	.354
Hub Collins†	2B12	R	24	12	42	16	13	5	1	0	3	9	—	9	.310	.442	.476

Pitcher	T	Age	G	GS	CG	ShO	IP	H	HR	BB	SO	W-L	Sv	ERA
Bob Caruthers	R	24	44	43	42	4	391.2	337	4	53	140	29-15	0	2.39
Mickey Hughes	R	21	40	40	40	2	363.0	281	5	98	159	25-13	0	2.13
Adonis Terry	R	23	23	23	20	2	195.0	145	2	67	138	13-8	0	2.03
Dave Foutz	R	31	23	19	19	0	176.0	146	3	35	73	12-7	0	2.51
Al Mays	—	23	18	18	17	1	160.2	150	1	32	67	9-9	0	2.80

1888 Philadelphia Athletics 3rd AA 81-52 .609 10.0 GB

Bill Sharsig

Player	Gm by Position	B	Age	G	AB	R	H	2B	3B	HR	RBI	BB	SO	SB	Avg	OBP	Slg
Wilbert Robinson	C65,1B1	R	25	66	254	32	62	7	2	1	31	9	—	11	.244	.270	.299
Henry Larkin	1B122,2B14	R	28	135	546	92	147	28	12	7	101	33	—	20	.269	.326	.403
Lou Bierbauer	2B121,3B13,P1	L	22	134	535	83	143	20	9	0	80	25	—	34	.267	.301	.338
Denny Lyons	3B111	R	22	111	456	93	135	22	5	6	83	41	—	39	.296	.363	.406
Bill Gleason	SS121,1B1,3B1	R	29	123	499	55	112	10	2	0	61	12	—	27	.224	.256	.253
Curt Welch	OF135,2B3	R	26	136	549	125	155	22	8	1	61	33	—	95	.282	.355	.357
Harry Stovey	OF118,1B13	R	31	130	530	127	152	25	20	9	65	62	—	87	.287	.365	.460
Tom Poorman	OF97	L	30	97	383	76	87	16	6	2	44	31	—	46	.227	.294	.316
Ed Seward	P57,OF7	—	21	64	225	27	32	3	3	2	14	18	—	12	.142	.215	.209
Gus Weyhing	P47,OF2	R	21	48	184	19	40	6	8	1	14	1	—	5	.217	.222	.353
George Townsend	C42	R	21	42	161	13	25	6	0	0	12	4	—	2	.155	.181	.193
Mike Mattimore	P26,OF16	L	29	41	142	22	38	6	5	0	12	12	—	16	.268	.333	.380
Mike Sullivan	OF18,3B10	R	28	28	112	20	31	5	6	1	19	3	—	10	.277	.296	.455
Tom Gunning	C23	R	26	23	92	18	18	0	0	0	5	2	—	14	.196	.237	.196
Blondie Purcell†	OF17,3B1	R	34	18	66	10	11	3	1	0	6	5	—	10	.167	.236	.242
Frank Fennelly†	SS15	R	28	15	47	13	11	2	2	1	12	9	—	5	.234	.357	.426
Bill Blair	P4,OF1	L	24	4	13	1	4	1	0	0	1	1	—	0	.308	.357	.385
Bill Farmer†	C3	R	17	3	12	0	2	0	0	0	1	0	—	0	.167	.167	.167
Frank Zinn	C2	—	22	2	7	0	0	0	0	0	0	1	—	0	.000	.125	.000
Whitey Gibson	C1	—	19	1	3	0	0	0	0	0	0	0	—	0	.000	.000	.000

Pitcher	T	Age	G	GS	CG	ShO	IP	H	HR	BB	SO	W-L	Sv	ERA
Ed Seward	R	21	57	57	57	6	518.2	388	4	127	272	35-19	0	2.01
Gus Weyhing	R	21	47	47	45	3	404.0	314	4	111	204	28-18	0	2.25
Mike Mattimore	L	29	26	24	24	4	221.0	221	6	65	80	15-10	0	3.38
Bill Blair	L	24	4	4	3	0	31.0	29	0	8	16	1-3	0	2.61
Phenomenal Smith†	L	23	3	3	3	0	22.0	21	0	10	19	2-1	0	2.86
Bob Gamble	R	21	1	1	1	0	9.0	10	0	3	2	0-1	0	8.00
Lou Bierbauer	R	22	1	0	0	0	3.0	5	0	0	3	0-0	0	0.00

1888 Cincinnati Reds 4th AA 80-54 .597 11.5 GB

Gus Schmelz

Player	Gm by Position	B	Age	G	AB	R	H	2B	3B	HR	RBI	BB	SO	SB	Avg	OBP	Slg
Jim Keenan	C69,1B16	R	30	85	313	38	73	9	8	1	40	22	—	9	.233	.294	.323
John Reilly	1B117,OF10	R	29	127	527	112	169	28	14	13	103	17	—	82	.321	.363	.501
Bid McPhee	2B111	R	28	111	458	88	110	12	10	4	51	43	—	54	.240	.312	.336
Hick Carpenter	3B136	R	32	136	551	68	147	14	5	3	67	5	—	59	.267	.280	.327
Frank Fennelly†	SS112,2B4,OF4	R	28	120	448	64	88	8	7	2	56	63	—	43	.196	.297	.259
Hugh Nicol	OF125,2B12,SS1	R	30	135	548	112	131	10	2	1	35	67	—	103	.239	.330	.270
W. Wings Tebeau	OF121	R	26	121	411	72	94	12	12	3	51	61	—	37	.229	.338	.338
Pop Corkhill†	OF116,P2,1B1*	L	30	118	490	68	133	11	9	1	74	15	—	27	.271	.299	.337
Kid Baldwin	C65,OF2,1B1	R	23	67	271	27	59	11	3	1	25	3	—	4	.218	.235	.292
Tony Mullane	P44,1B4,OF3*	S	29	51	175	27	44	4	4	1	16	8	—	12	.251	.296	.337
Lee Viau	P42,OF1	R	21	43	149	16	13	1	2	0	8	11	—	5	.087	.150	.121
Heinie Kappel	SS25,2B10,3B1	R	24	36	143	18	37	4	4	1	15	2	—	20	.259	.274	.364
Jack O'Connor	OF34,C2	R	19	36	137	14	28	3	1	1	17	6	—	12	.204	.243	.263
Elmer Smith	P40,OF2	L	20	40	129	15	29	4	1	0	9	20	—	2	.225	.329	.271
Ned Bligh	C2,OF1	R	24	3	5	0	0	0	0	0	0	0	—	0	.000	.000	.000

P. Corkhill, 1 G at 2B; T. Mullane, 2 G at 2B

Pitcher	T	Age	G	GS	CG	ShO	IP	H	HR	BB	SO	W-L	Sv	ERA
Lee Viau	R	21	42	42	42	1	387.2	331	7	110	164	27-14	0	2.65
Tony Mullane	R	29	44	42	41	4	380.1	341	9	75	186	26-16	1	2.84
Elmer Smith	L	20	40	40	37	5	348.1	309	1	89	154	22-17	0	2.74
John Weyhing	L	19	8	8	7	0	65.2	52	0	17	30	3-4	0	1.23
Billy Serad	R	25	6	5	5	0	50.2	62	1	19	4	2-3	0	3.55
Pop Corkhill	R	30	2	0	0	0	5.0	8	1	0	1	0-0	1	10.80

1888 Baltimore Orioles 5th AA 57-80 .416 36.0 GB

Billy Barnie

Player	Gm by Position	B	Age	G	AB	R	H	2B	3B	HR	RBI	BB	SO	SB	Avg	OBP	Slg
Chris Fulmer	C45,OF7	R	29	52	166	20	31	5	1	0	10	21	—	10	.187	.286	.229
Tommy Tucker	1B129,OF7,P1	S	24	136	520	74	149	17	12	6	61	16	—	43	.287	.330	.400
Bill Greenwood	2B86,SS28,OF1	S	31	115	409	69	78	13	1	0	29	30	—	46	.191	.256	.227
Billy Shindle	3B135	R	24	135	514	61	107	14	8	1	53	20	—	52	.208	.249	.272
Jack Farrell	SS54,2B52	R	30	103	398	72	81	19	5	4	36	26	—	29	.204	.256	.307
Mike Griffin	OF137	L	23	137	542	103	139	21	11	0	46	55	—	46	.256	.331	.336
Blondie Purcell†	OF100,SS2,1B1	R	34	101	406	53	96	9	4	2	39	27	—	16	.236	.289	.293
Oyster Burns†	OF56,SS23,P5*	R	23	79	325	54	97	18	9	4	42	24	—	23	.298	.349	.446
Joe Sommer	OF44,SS34,2B2*	R	29	79	297	31	65	10	0	0	35	18	—	13	.219	.266	.253
Jack O'Brien	C37,OF13,1B7	R	28	57	196	25	44	11	5	0	18	17	—	14	.224	.300	.332
Bert Cunningham	P51,OF1	R	22	51	177	17	33	3	2	1	9	5	—	2	.186	.217	.243
Walt Goldsby	OF45	L	26	45	165	13	39	1	1	0	14	8	—	17	.236	.288	.255
Matt Kilroy	P40,OF7	L	22	43	145	13	26	5	2	0	19	11	—	10	.179	.242	.241
Bart Cantz	C33,OF4	—	28	37	126	7	21	2	1	0	9	2	—	0	.167	.180	.198
Phenomenal Smith†	P35,OF1	L	23	35	109	16	27	3	4	1	12	11	—	2	.248	.322	.376
Sam Trott	C27,OF3,1B1*	L	29	31	108	19	30	11	4	0	22	4	—	1	.278	.304	.454
John Peltz	OF1	R	27	1	4	1	1	0	0	0	0	0	—	1	.250	.250	.250
George Bradley	SS1	R	35	1	3	0	0	0	0	0	0	0	—	0	.000	.000	.000

O. Burns, 2 G at 3B, 1 G at 2B; J. Sommer, 1 G at 1B; S. Trott, 1 G at 2B

Pitcher	T	Age	G	GS	CG	ShO	IP	H	HR	BB	SO	W-L	Sv	ERA
Bert Cunningham	R	22	51	51	50	0	453.1	412	8	157	186	22-29	0	3.39
Matt Kilroy	L	22	40	40	35	2	321.0	347	5	79	135	17-21	0	4.04
Phenomenal Smith†	L	23	35	32	31	0	292.0	249	5	137	152	14-19	0	3.61
Sam Shaw	R	24	6	6	6	0	53.0	65	2	15	22	2-4	0	3.40
George Walker	—	25	4	4	4	1	35.0	36	2	14	18	1-3	0	5.91
Pat Whitaker	R	23	2	2	2	0	14.0	13	0	6	5	1-1	0	5.14
Mike Kilroy	R	15	1	1	1	0	9.0	12	1	5	1	0-1	0	8.00
John Harkins	R	29	1	1	1	0	8.0	12	0	3	2	0-1	0	6.75
Oyster Burns	R	23	5	0	0	0	12.2	12	0	3	2	0-1	0	4.26
Tommy Tucker	R	24	1	0	0	0	2.1	4	0	0	2	0-0	0	3.86

1888 Cleveland Spiders 6th AA 50-82 .379 40.5 GB

Jimmy Williams (20-44)/Tom Loftus (30-38)

Player	Gm by Position	B	Age	G	AB	R	H	2B	3B	HR	RBI	BB	SO	SB	Avg	OBP	Slg
Chief Zimmer	C59,1B3,OF3*	R	27	65	212	27	51	11	4	0	22	18	—	15	.241	.312	.330
Jay Faatz	1B120	R	27	120	470	73	124	10	2	0	51	12	—	64	.264	.312	.294
Cub Stricker	2B122,OF6,P2	R	29	127	493	80	115	13	6	1	33	50	—	60	.233	.311	.290
Gus Alberts	SS53,3B49	R	20	102	364	51	75	10	6	1	48	41	—	26	.206	.299	.275
Ed McKean	SS78,OF48,2B9*	R	24	131	548	94	164	21	15	6	68	28	—	52	.299	.340	.425
Pete Hotaling	OF98	R	31	98	403	67	101	7	6	0	55	26	—	35	.251	.307	.298
Bob Gilks	OF87,3B28,P4*	R	23	119	484	59	111	14	4	1	63	7	—	16	.229	.245	.281
Eddie Hogan	OF78	R	28	78	269	60	61	16	6	0	24	50	—	30	.227	.368	.331
Mike Goodfellow	OF62,C4,1B3*	R	21	68	269	24	66	7	0	0	29	11	—	7	.245	.283	.271
Pop Snyder	C58,1B4,OF3	R	33	64	237	22	51	7	3	0	14	6	—	9	.215	.238	.270
John McGlone	3B48,OF7	—	24	55	203	22	37	1	3	1	22	16	—	26	.182	.249	.232
Jersey Bakely	P61,SS1	R	24	61	194	19	26	0	1	1	9	26	—	1	.134	.236	.160
Darby O'Brien	P30,OF2	R	21	32	109	13	20	1	0	0	9	4	—	2	.183	.212	.193
Deacon McGuire†	C17,1B6,OF3	R	24	26	94	15	24	1	3	1	13	7	—	2	.255	.333	.362
Bill McClellan†	OF15,2B5,SS2	L	32	22	72	6	16	0	0	0	5	6	—	6	.222	.282	.222
Billy Crowell†	P18,OF1	R	22	18	58	5	5	2	0	0	3	3	—	1	.086	.131	.121
Dick Van Zant	3B10	—	23	10	31	1	8	1	0	0	1	1	—	1	.258	.303	.290
Bill Stemmeyer	P2,1B1	R	23	3	10	2	4	1	0	0	1	1	—	0	.400	.455	.500
Ed Knouff†	P2,2B1	R	20	2	6	0	1	1	0	0	0	1	—	0	.167	.286	.333

C. Zimmer, 1 G at SS; E. McKean, 1 G at 3B; B. Gilks, 4 G at SS, 1 G at 2B; M. Goodfellow, 1 G at SS

Pitcher	T	Age	G	GS	CG	ShO	IP	H	HR	BB	SO	W-L	Sv	ERA
Jersey Bakely	R	24	61	61	60	4	532.2	518	14	128	212	25-33	0	2.97
Darby O'Brien	R	21	30	30	30	1	259.0	245	5	99	135	11-19	0	3.30
Billy Crowell†	R	22	18	18	16	0	150.2	212	8	61	61	5-13	0	5.79
George Proeser	L	24	7	7	7	1	59.0	53	4	30	20	3-4	0	3.81
Ed Keas	—	25	6	6	6	0	51.0	53	1	12	18	3-3	0	2.29
Mike Morrison	R	21	4	4	4	0	35.0	40	3	19	14	1-3	0	5.40
Doc Oberlander	L	24	3	3	3	0	25.2	27	2	18	23	1-2	0	5.26
Bob Gilks	R	23	4	2	2	0	21.0	26	1	8	3	0-2	1	8.14
Bill Stemmeyer	R	23	2	2	2	0	16.0	37	0	9	7	0-2	0	9.00
Ed Knouff†	R	20	2	2	1	0	9.0	8	0	3	2	0-1	0	1.00
Cub Stricker	R	29	2	0	0	0	12.0	16	0	2	5	1-0	0	4.50

1888 Louisville Colonels 7th AA 48-87 .356 44.0 GB

H. John Kelly (10-29)/M. Davidson (1-2)/J. Kerins (3-4)/M. Davidson (34-52)

Player	Gm by Position	B	Age	G	AB	R	H	2B	3B	HR	RBI	BB	SO	SB	Avg	OBP	Slg
Paul Cook	C53,OF4,SS1	R	25	57	185	20	34	2	0	0	13	5	—	9	.184	.222	.195
Skyrocket Smith	1B58	R	20	58	206	27	49	9	4	1	31	24	—	5	.238	.349	.335
Reddy Mack	2B112	—	22	112	446	77	97	13	5	3	34	52	—	18	.217	.320	.289
Joe Werrick	3B89,SS11,2B8*	R	26	111	413	49	89	12	7	0	51	30	—	15	.215	.274	.278
Chicken Wolf	OF85,SS39,3B4*	R	26	128	538	80	154	28	11	0	67	25	—	41	.286	.320	.379
Pete Browning	OF99	R	27	99	383	58	120	22	8	3	72	37	—	36	.313	.380	.436
Hub Collins†	OF82,2B19,SS15	R	24	116	485	117	149	26	11	2	50	41	—	62	.307	.366	.419
John Kerins	OF47,C33,1B4*	R	29	83	319	38	75	11	4	2	41	25	—	16	.235	.297	.313
Scott Stratton	OF38,P33	L	18	67	249	35	64	8	1	1	29	12	—	10	.257	.310	.309
Guy Hecker	1B30,P26,OF1	R	32	56	211	32	48	9	2	0	29	11	—	20	.227	.285	.289
Bill White†	SS38,3B11	—	28	49	198	35	55	6	5	1	30	7	—	15	.278	.313	.374
Farmer Vaughn	OF28,C25	R	24	51	189	15	37	4	2	1	21	4	—	4	.196	.216	.254
Lave Cross	C37,OF12,SS2	R	22	47	181	20	41	3	0	0	15	2	—	10	.227	.239	.243
Toad Ramsey	P40,OF5	R	23	42	142	12	17	6	0	0	9	9	—	0	.120	.183	.162
Harry Raymond	3B31,OF1	—	26	32	123	8	26	2	0	0	13	1	—	7	.211	.218	.228
Phil Tomney	SS34	R	25	34	120	15	18	3	0	0	4	7	—	11	.150	.197	.175
Farmer Weaver	OF26	L	23	26	112	12	28	1	1	0	8	3	—	12	.250	.276	.277
Elton Chamberlin†	P24,OF4	R	20	26	94	11	18	4	2	0	3	6	—	8	.191	.240	.277
Wally Andrews	1B26	R	28	26	93	12	18	6	3	0	6	13	—	5	.194	.292	.323
Dude Esterbrook†	1B23	R	31	23	93	9	21	6	0	0	7	3	—	5	.226	.265	.290
Phil Reccius	3B2	—	26	2	9	0	2	1	0	0	4	1	—	0	.222	.300	.333
Hercules Burnett	OF1	R	18	1	4	1	0	0	0	0	0	1	—	1	.000	.200	.000
Eddie Fusselback	OF1	R	29	1	4	0	1	0	0	0	1	0	—	0	.250	.250	.250
Dan Long	OF1	—	20	1	2	0	0	0	0	0	0	1	—	0	.000	.333	.000

J. Werrick, 3 G at OF; C. Wolf, 3 G at C, 1 G at 1B; J. Kerins, 2 G at 3B, 1 G at 2B

Pitcher	T	Age	G	GS	CG	ShO	IP	H	HR	BB	SO	W-L	Sv	ERA
Toad Ramsey	L	23	40	40	37	1	342.1	362	10	86	228	8-30	0	3.42
Scott Stratton	R	18	33	28	28	2	269.2	287	7	53	97	10-17	0	3.64
Guy Hecker	R	32	26	25	25	0	223.1	251	5	43	63	8-17	0	3.39
Elton Chamberlin†	S	20	24	24	21	1	196.0	177	2	59	119	14-9	0	2.53
John Ewing	R	25	21	21	21	2	191.0	175	3	34	87	8-13	0	2.83
Billy Crowell†	R	22	1	1	1	0	9.0	12	1	6	5	0-1	0	6.00

1888 Kansas City Blues 8th AA 43-89 .326 47.5 GB

Dave Rowe (14-36)/Sam Barkley (21-36)/Bill Watkins (8-17)

Player	Gm by Position	B	Age	G	AB	R	H	2B	3B	HR	RBI	BB	SO	SB	Avg	OBP	Slg
Jim Donahue	C67,OF18,3B5*	R	26	88	337	29	79	11	3	1	28	21	—	12	.234	.281	.294
Bill Phillips	1B129	R	31	129	509	57	120	20	10	1	56	27	—	10	.236	.284	.320
Sam Barkley	2B116	R	30	116	482	67	104	21	6	4	51	26	—	15	.216	.262	.309
Jumbo Davis	3B113,SS8	L	26	121	491	70	131	22	8	3	61	20	—	42	.267	.304	.363
Henry Easterday	SS115	R	23	115	401	42	76	7	6	3	37	31	—	23	.190	.256	.259
Jim McTamany	OF130	R	24	130	516	94	127	12	10	4	41	67	—	55	.246	.345	.331
Monk Cline	OF70,2B3,3B1	L	30	73	293	45	69	13	2	0	19	20	—	29	.235	.289	.294
Myron Allen	OF35,P2	R	34	37	136	23	29	6	4	0	10	9	—	4	.213	.267	.316
Law Daniels	OF30,C29,3B2*	R	25	61	218	32	45	2	0	2	28	14	—	20	.206	.264	.243
Henry Porter	P55,OF2	R	29	55	195	12	28	3	0	0	10	8	—	1	.144	.177	.159
Frank Hankinson	2B13,SS9,3B7*	R	32	37	155	20	27	4	1	1	20	11	—	2	.174	.229	.232
Billy Hamilton	OF35	L	22	35	129	21	34	4	4	0	11	4	—	19	.264	.307	.357
Dave Rowe	OF32	R	33	32	122	14	21	3	4	0	13	6	—	2	.172	.217	.262
Jack Brennan	C25,3B5,OF5	—	26	34	118	5	20	2	0	0	6	3	—	3	.169	.203	.186
Tom Sullivan	P24,OF4	—	28	28	92	10	10	1	0	0	5	9	—	7	.109	.188	.120
Jim Burns	OF15	—	—	15	66	13	20	0	0	0	4	1	—	6	.303	.343	.303
Bill Fagan	P17,OF2	—	19	18	65	5	14	3	0	0	4	2	—	0	.215	.261	.262
Red Ehret	OF10,P7,1B1*	R	19	17	63	4	12	4	0	0	4	1	—	1	.190	.203	.254
Steve Toole	P12,OF2	R	29	13	48	6	10	2	2	0	7	1	—	2	.208	.224	.333
Fatty Briody	C13	—	29	13	48	1	10	1	0	0	8	1	—	0	.208	.224	.229
Charley Jones	OF6	R	38	6	25	2	4	0	1	0	5	1	—	1	.160	.192	.240
Charlie Hoover	C3	L	22	3	10	0	3	0	0	0	1	0	—	0	.300	.300	.300
Ed Glenn†	OF3	R	27	3	8	0	0	0	0	0	0	0	—	1	.000	.200	.000

J. Donahue, 1 G at 2B; L. Daniels, 1 G at SS; F. Hankinson, 7 G at OF, 2 G at 1B; R. Ehret, 1 G at 2B

Pitcher	T	Age	G	GS	CG	ShO	IP	H	HR	BB	SO	W-L	Sv	ERA
Henry Porter	R	29	55	54	53	4	474.0	527	16	120	145	18-37	0	4.16
Tom Sullivan	—	28	24	24	24	0	214.2	227	2	68	84	8-16	0	3.40
Bill Fagan	L	19	17	17	15	0	142.1	179	4	75	49	5-11	0	5.69
Frank Hoffman	R	—	12	12	12	0	104.0	102	3	42	38	3-9	0	2.77
Steve Toole	L	29	12	10	10	0	91.2	124	4	50	35	5-6	0	6.68
Red Ehret	R	19	7	6	5	0	52.0	58	1	22	12	3-2	0	3.98
John Kirby	R	23	5	5	5	0	43.0	48	0	7	11	1-4	0	4.19
Frank Hafner	R	20	2	2	2	0	18.0	24	2	16	5	0-2	0	7.00
Myron Allen	R	34	2	2	2	0	18.0	17	0	1	2	0-2	0	2.50

»1889 New York Giants 1st NL 83-43 .659 —

Jim Mutrie

Player	Gm by Position	B	Age	G	AB	R	H	2B	3B	HR	RBI	BB	SO	SB	Avg	OBP	Slg
Buck Ewing	C97,P3,OF1	R	29	99	407	91	133	23	13	4	87	37	32	34	.327	.383	.477
Roger Connor	1B131,3B1	L	31	131	496	117	157	32	17	13	130	93	46	21	.317	.426	.528
Danny Richardson	2B125	R	26	125	497	88	139	22	8	7	100	46	37	32	.280	.342	.398
Art Whitney	3B129,P1	R	31	129	473	71	103	12	2	1	59	56	39	19	.218	.303	.258
Monte Ward	SS108,2B7	L	29	114	479	87	143	13	4	1	67	27	7	62	.299	.339	.349
Jim O'Rourke	OF128,C1	R	38	128	502	89	161	36	7	3	81	40	34	33	.321	.372	.438
Mike Tiernan	OF122	L	22	122	499	147	167	23	14	10	73	96	62	33	.335	.447	.497
George Gore	OF120	L	32	120	488	132	149	21	7	7	54	84	28	28	.305	.416	.420
Willard Brown	C37,OF3	R	23	40	139	16	36	10	0	1	29	9	9	6	.259	.318	.353
Gil Hatfield	SS24,P6,3B2	—	34	32	125	21	23	2	0	1	12	9	15	9	.184	.250	.224
Ed Crane	P29,1B1	R	27	29	103	16	21	1	0	2	11	13	21	6	.204	.293	.272
Mike Slattery	OF12	L	22	12	48	7	14	2	0	1	12	4	3	2	.292	.346	.396
Pat Murphy	C9	—	32	9	28	5	10	1	1	1	4	2	0	0	.357	.400	.571
Harry Lyons	OF5	R	23	5	20	1	2	0	1	0	2	2	0	0	.100	.182	.200
Bill George†	OF3	R	24	3	15	1	4	0	0	0	0	0	3	1	.267	.267	.267
Elmer Foster	OF2	R	27	2	4	2	0	0	0	0	0	3	1	2	.000	.429	.000

Pitcher	T	Age	G	GS	CG	ShO	IP	H	HR	BB	SO	W-L	Sv	ERA
Tim Keefe	R	32	47	45	38	3	364.0	310	9	151	209	28-13	1	3.31
Mickey Welch	R	29	45	41	39	3	375.0	340	14	149	125	27-12	2	3.02
Ed Crane	R	27	29	25	23	0	230.0	221	10	136	130	14-10	0	3.68
Hank O'Day†	R	26	10	10	8	0	78.0	83	2	35	28	9-1	0	4.27
Gil Hatfield	R	34	6	5	5	0	52.0	53	2	25	28	2-4	0	3.98
Cannonball Titcomb	L	22	3	3	3	0	26.0	27	1	16	7	1-2	0	6.58
Buck Ewing	R	29	3	2	2	0	20.0	23	0	8	12	2-0	0	4.05
Art Whitney	R	31	1	0	0	0	6.0	7	0	3	3	0-1	0	3.00

1889 Boston Beaneaters 2nd NL 83-45 .648 1.0 GB

Jim Hart

Player	Gm by Position	B	Age	G	AB	R	H	2B	3B	HR	RBI	BB	SO	SB	Avg	OBP	Slg
Charlie Bennett	C82	R	34	82	247	42	57	8	2	4	28	21	43	7	.231	.296	.336
Dan Brouthers	1B126	L	31	126	485	105	181	26	9	7	118	66	6	22	.373	.462	.507
Hardy Richardson	2B86,OF46	R	34	132	536	122	163	33	10	6	79	48	44	47	.304	.367	.437
Billy Nash	3B128,P1	R	24	128	481	84	132	20	2	3	76	79	44	26	.274	.379	.343
Joe Quinn	SS63,2B47,3B2	R	24	112	444	57	116	13	5	2	69	25	21	24	.261	.308	.327
Dick Johnston	OF132	R	26	132	539	80	123	16	4	5	67	41	60	34	.228	.285	.301
King Kelly	OF113,C23	R	31	125	507	120	149	41	5	9	78	65	40	68	.294	.376	.448
Tom Brown	OF90	L	28	90	362	93	84	10	5	2	24	59	56	63	.232	.341	.304
Charlie Ganzel	C39,OF26,1B7*	R	27	73	275	30	73	3	5	1	43	15	11	13	.265	.308	.324
John Clarkson	P73,OF2,3B1	R	27	73	262	36	54	9	3	2	23	11	59	8	.206	.238	.286
Pop Smith†	SS59	R	32	59	208	21	54	13	4	0	32	23	30	11	.260	.345	.361
Old Hoss Radbourn	P33,OF2,3B1	R	34	35	122	17	23	1	0	1	13	9	19	3	.189	.256	.221
Kid Madden	P22,OF2	—	21	24	86	7	25	1	0	0	14	3	7	4	.291	.315	.302
Irv Ray†	SS5,3B4	L	25	9	33	8	10	1	0	0	2	4	0	1	.303	.378	.333
Jerry Hurley	C1,OF1	R	26	1	4	0	0	0	0	0	0	0	0	0	.000	.000	.000

C. Ganzel, 6 G at SS, 1 G at 3B

Pitcher	T	Age	G	GS	CG	ShO	IP	H	HR	BB	SO	W-L	Sv	ERA
John Clarkson	R	27	73	72	68	8	620.0	589	16	203	284	49-19	1	2.73
Old Hoss Radbourn	R	34	33	31	28	1	277.0	282	14	72	99	20-11	0	3.67
Kid Madden	L	21	22	19	18	1	178.0	194	7	71	64	10-10	1	4.40
Bill Daley	L	21	9	7	4	0	48.0	34	1	43	40	3-3	0	4.31
Bill Sowders†	R	24	7	4	3	0	42.0	53	3	23	10	1-2	2	5.14
Billy Nash	R	24	1	0	0	0	1.0	0	0	1	0	0-0	0	0.00

1889 Chicago White Stockings 3rd NL 67-65 .508 19.0 GB

Cap Anson

Player	Gm by Position	B	Age	G	AB	R	H	2B	3B	HR	RBI	BB	SO	SB	Avg	OBP	Slg
Duke Farrell	C76,OF25	S	22	101	407	66	101	19	7	11	75	41	21	13	.248	.318	.410
Cap Anson	1B134	R	37	134	518	100	161	32	7	7	117	86	19	27	.311	.414	.440
Fred Pfeffer	2B134	R	29	134	531	85	121	15	7	7	77	53	51	45	.228	.302	.322
Tom Burns	3B136	R	32	136	525	64	127	27	6	4	66	32	57	18	.242	.288	.339
Ned Williamson	SS47	R	31	47	173	16	41	3	1	1	30	23	22	2	.237	.340	.283
George Van Haltren	OF130,SS3,2B1	L	23	134	543	126	168	20	10	9	81	82	41	28	.309	.405	.433
Hugh Duffy	OF126,SS10	R	22	136	584	144	172	21	7	12	89	46	30	52	.295	.348	.416
Jimmy Ryan	OF106,SS29	R	26	135	576	140	177	31	14	17	72	70	62	45	.307	.388	.498
Charlie Bastian	SS45,2B1	R	28	46	155	19	21	0	0	0	10	25	46	1	.135	.256	.135
Ad Gumbert	P31,OF13	R	20	41	153	30	44	3	2	7	29	11	36	2	.288	.339	.471
John Tener	P35,OF6,1B2	R	25	42	150	18	41	4	2	1	19	7	22	2	.273	.306	.347
Frank Dwyer	P32,OF3,SS2	R	21	36	135	14	27	1	1	1	6	4	8	0	.200	.223	.244
Bill Hutchison	P37,OF1	R	29	37	133	14	21	1	1	1	7	7	40	2	.158	.200	.203
Dell Darling	C36	R	27	36	120	14	23	1	1	0	7	25	22	5	.192	.331	.217
Silver Flint	C15	R	33	15	56	6	13	1	0	1	9	3	18	1	.232	.271	.304
Pete Sommers†	C11,OF1	R	22	12	45	5	10	5	0	0	8	2	8	0	.222	.271	.333

Pitcher	T	Age	G	GS	CG	ShO	IP	H	HR	BB	SO	W-L	Sv	ERA
Bill Hutchison	R	29	37	36	33	3	318.0	306	11	117	136	16-17	0	3.54
John Tener	R	25	35	30	28	1	287.0	302	16	105	105	15-15	0	3.64
Frank Dwyer	R	21	32	30	27	0	276.0	307	14	72	63	16-13	0	3.59
Ad Gumbert	R	20	31	28	25	2	246.1	258	16	76	91	16-13	0	3.62
Gus Krock†	L	23	7	7	5	0	60.2	86	10	14	16	3-3	0	4.90
Egyptian Healy†	R	22	5	5	5	0	46.0	48	4	18	22	1-4	0	4.50
Bill Bishop	—	19	2	0	0	0	3.0	6	0	6	1	0-0	2	18.00

1889 Philadelphia Phillies 4th NL 63-64 .496 20.5 GB

Harry Wright

Player	Gm by Position	B	Age	G	AB	R	H	2B	3B	HR	RBI	BB	SO	SB	Avg	OBP	Slg
Jack Clements	C78	L	24	78	310	51	88	17	1	4	35	29	21	3	.284	.347	.384
Sid Farrar	1B130	—	29	130	477	70	128	22	2	3	58	52	36	28	.268	.348	.342
Bert Myers†	2B75	R	25	75	305	52	82	14	2	0	28	36	9	8	.269	.354	.328
Joe Mulvey	3B129	R	30	129	544	77	157	21	9	6	77	23	25	23	.289	.319	.393
Bill Hallman	SS106,2B13,C1	R	22	119	462	67	117	21	8	2	60	36	54	20	.253	.313	.346
Sam Thompson	OF128	L	29	128	533	103	158	36	4	20	111	36	22	24	.296	.348	.492
Jim Fogarty	OF128,P4	R	25	128	499	107	129	15	17	3	54	65	60	99	.259	.352	.375
George Wood†	OF92,SS6,P1	L	30	97	422	77	106	21	4	5	53	53	33	17	.251	.336	.355
Ed Delahanty	OF31,2B24,SS1	R	21	56	246	37	72	13	3	0	27	14	17	19	.293	.333	.370
Pop Schriver	C48,2B6,3B1	R	23	55	211	24	56	10	0	1	19	16	8	5	.265	.323	.327
Ben Sanders	P44,OF3	R	24	44	169	21	47	8	2	0	21	6	11	4	.278	.303	.349
Charlie Buffinton	P47,OF1	R	28	47	154	16	32	2	0	0	21	9	5	0	.208	.256	.221
Kid Gleason	P29,OF3,2B2	S	22	30	99	11	25	5	0	0	8	8	12	4	.253	.308	.303
Arthur Irwin†	SS18	L	31	18	73	9	16	5	0	0	10	6	6	6	.219	.278	.288
Ed Andrews†	OF9,2B1	R	30	10	39	10	11	1	0	0	7	2	4	7	.282	.317	.308
Harry Decker	2B7,C3,OF1	R	34	11	30	4	3	0	0	0	2	2	5	1	.100	.156	.100
Piggy Ward	2B6,OF1	S	22	7	25	0	4	1	0	0	4	0	7	1	.160	.160	.200

Pitcher	T	Age	G	GS	CG	ShO	IP	H	HR	BB	SO	W-L	Sv	ERA
Charlie Buffinton	R	28	47	43	37	2	380.0	390	10	121	153	28-16	0	3.24
Ben Sanders	R	24	44	39	34	1	349.2	406	9	96	123	19-18	1	3.55
Kid Gleason	R	22	29	21	15	0	205.0	242	8	97	64	9-15	1	5.58
Dan Casey	L	26	20	20	15	1	152.2	170	4	72	65	6-10	0	3.77
Bill Day	R	21	4	3	2	0	19.0	16	0	23	20	0-3	0	5.21
Pete Wood	R	32	3	2	2	0	19.0	28	0	3	8	1-1	0	5.21
Dave Anderson	L	20	5	2	1	0	23.0	30	2	14	8	0-1	0	7.43
Jim Fogarty	R	25	4	0	0	0	4.0	4	0	2	0	0-0	0	9.00
George Wood	R	30	1	0	0	0	1.0	2	0	0	2	0-0	0	18.00

1889 Pittsburgh Alleghenys 5th NL 61-71 .462 25.0 GB

Horace Phillips (28-43)/Fred Dunlap (7-10)/Ned Hanlon (26-18)

Player	Gm by Position	B	Age	G	AB	R	H	2B	3B	HR	RBI	BB	SO	SB	Avg	OBP	Slg
Doggie Miller	C76,OF27,3B3	R	24	104	422	77	113	25	3	6	56	31	11	16	.268	.321	.384
Jake Beckley	1B122,OF1	L	21	123	522	91	157	24	10	9	97	29	29	11	.301	.345	.437
Fred Dunlap	2B121	R	30	121	451	59	106	19	0	2	65	46	33	21	.235	.309	.290
Bill Kuehne	3B75,OF13,2B5*	R	30	97	390	43	96	20	5	5	57	9	36	15	.246	.263	.362
Jack Rowe	SS75	L	32	75	317	57	82	14	3	2	32	22	16	5	.259	.313	.341
Ned Hanlon	OF116	L	31	116	461	81	110	14	10	2	37	58	25	53	.239	.326	.325
Billy Sunday	OF81	L	26	81	321	62	77	10	6	2	25	27	33	47	.240	.307	.327
Al Maul	OF64,P6	R	23	68	257	37	71	6	6	4	44	29	41	18	.276	.356	.393
Fred Carroll	C43,OF41,1B7*	R	24	91	318	80	105	21	11	2	51	85	26	19	.330	.486	.484
Jocko Fields	OF60,C16	R	24	75	289	41	90	22	5	2	43	29	30	7	.311	.376	.443
Pop Smith†	SS58,2B9,3B3*	R	32	72	258	26	54	10	2	5	27	24	38	12	.209	.292	.322
Deacon White	3B52,1B3	L	41	55	225	35	57	10	1	0	26	16	18	2	.253	.314	.307
Harry Staley	P49,OF2	R	22	51	186	11	30	3	1	0	8	4	40	1	.161	.179	.188
Bill Sowders†	P13,OF2	R	24	15	48	4	13	1	0	0	4	3	10	0	.271	.314	.292
Chuck Lauer	C3,OF1	—	24	4	16	2	3	0	0	0	1	0	5	0	.188	.188	.188
Pete Conway	P3,OF1	R	22	3	10	2	1	0	0	1	2	1	3	1	.100	.182	.400

B. Kuehne, 2 G at 1B, 2 G at SS; F. Carroll, 1 G at 3B; P. Smith, 3 G at OF

Pitcher	T	Age	G	GS	CG	ShO	IP	H	HR	BB	SO	W-L	Sv	ERA
Harry Staley	R	22	49	47	46	1	420.0	433	11	116	159	21-26	1	3.51
Pud Galvin	R	32	41	40	38	4	341.0	392	19	78	77	23-16	0	4.17
Ed Morris	L	26	21	21	18	0	170.0	196	4	48	40	6-13	0	4.13
Bill Sowders†	R	24	13	11	9	0	52.2	94	1	29	33	6-5	0	7.35
Al Maul	R	23	6	4	4	0	42.0	64	3	28	11	1-4	0	9.86
Pete Conway	R	22	3	3	2	0	22.0	26	1	16	2	2-1	0	4.91
Bill Garfield	R	21	4	2	2	0	29.0	45	2	17	4	0-2	0	7.76
Alex Beam	—	18	2	2	2	0	18.0	11	0	15	1	1-1	0	6.50
Andy Dunning	R	17	2	2	2	0	18.0	20	1	16	4	0-2	0	7.00
Alex Jones	L	19	1	1	1	0	9.0	7	0	1	10	1-0	0	3.00
Al Krumm	R	—	1	1	1	0	9.0	8	0	10	4	0-1	0	10.00

1889 Cleveland Spiders 6th NL 61-72 .459 25.5 GB

Tom Loftus

Player	Gm by Position	B	Age	G	AB	R	H	2B	3B	HR	RBI	BB	SO	SB	Avg	OBP	Slg
Chief Zimmer	C81,1B3	R	28	84	259	47	67	9	9	1	21	44	35	14	.259	.368	.375
Jay Faatz	1B117	R	28	117	442	50	102	12	5	2	38	17	28	27	.231	.275	.294
Cub Stricker	2B135,SS1	R	30	136	566	83	142	10	4	1	47	58	18	32	.251	.323	.288
Patsy Tebeau	3B136	R	24	136	521	72	147	20	6	8	76	37	41	26	.282	.332	.390
Ed McKean	SS122,2B1	R	25	123	500	88	159	22	8	4	75	42	25	35	.318	.375	.418
Paul Radford	OF136,3B1	R	27	136	487	94	116	21	5	1	46	91	37	30	.238	.365	.308
Larry Twitchell	OF134,P1	R	25	134	549	73	151	16	11	4	95	29	37	17	.275	.315	.366
Jimmy McAleer	OF110	R	24	110	447	66	105	6	6	1	35	30	49	37	.235	.289	.282
Bob Gilks	OF29,SS13,1B10*	R	24	53	210	17	50	5	2	0	18	7	20	6	.238	.273	.281
Sy Sutcliffe	C37,1B8,OF1	L	27	46	161	17	40	3	2	1	21	14	6	5	.248	.309	.311
Ed Beatin	P36,OF1	R	22	37	121	13	14	0	0	1	8	14	33	0	.116	.207	.140
Jersey Bakely	P36,OF1	R	25	36	111	9	15	1	1	1	8	17	40	1	.135	.250	.189
Pop Snyder	C22	R	34	22	83	5	16	3	0	0	12	2	12	4	.193	.221	.229

B. Gilks, 1 G at 2B

Pitcher	T	Age	G	GS	CG	ShO	IP	H	HR	BB	SO	W-L	Sv	ERA
Darby O'Brien	R	22	41	41	39	1	346.2	345	9	167	122	22-17	0	4.15
Ed Beatin	L	22	36	36	35	3	317.2	316	12	141	126	20-15	0	3.57
Jersey Bakely	R	25	36	34	33	2	304.1	296	9	106	105	12-22	0	2.96
Henry Gruber	R	25	25	23	23	0	205.0	198	6	94	74	7-16	1	3.64
Charlie Sprague	L	24	2	2	2	0	17.0	27	0	10	8	0-2	0	8.47
Larry Twitchell	R	25	1	0	0	0	1.0	0	0	1	0	0-0	0	0.00

1889 Indianapolis Hoosiers 7th NL 59-75 .440 28.0 GB

Frank Bancroft (25-43)/Jack Glasscock (34-32)

Player	Gm by Position	B	Age	G	AB	R	H	2B	3B	HR	RBI	BB	SO	SB	Avg	OBP	Slg
Dick Buckley	C55,3B12,1B1*	—	30	68	260	35	67	11	0	8	41	15	32	5	.258	.301	.392
Paul Hines	1B109	R	37	121	486	77	148	27	1	6	72	49	22	34	.305	.374	.401
Charley Bassett	2B127	R	26	127	477	64	117	12	5	4	68	37	38	15	.245	.304	.317
Jerry Denny	3B123,2B7,SS5	R	30	133	578	96	163	24	0	18	112	27	63	22	.282	.314	.417
Jack Glasscock	SS132,2B2,P1	R	29	134	582	128	205	40	3	7	85	31	10	57	.352	.390	.467
Jack McGeachey	OF131,P3	R	25	131	532	83	142	32	1	2	63	9	39	37	.267	.282	.342
Emmett Seery	OF127	L	28	127	526	123	165	26	12	8	59	67	59	19	.314	.401	.454
Marty Sullivan	OF64,1B5	R	26	69	256	45	73	11	3	4	35	50	31	15	.285	.404	.398
Con Daily	C51,1B6,OF6*	L	24	62	219	35	55	6	2	0	26	28	21	14	.251	.347	.297
Ed Andrews†	OF40,2B1	R	30	40	173	32	53	11	0	0	22	5	10	7	.306	.330	.370
Henry Boyle	P46,3B1	—	28	46	155	17	38	10	0	1	17	9	23	4	.245	.291	.329
George Myers	OF23,C18,1B1	R	28	43	149	22	29	3	0	0	12	17	13	12	.195	.294	.215
Pete Sommers†	C21,OF2	R	22	23	84	12	21	2	2	2	14	1	16	2	.250	.267	.393
Jumbo Schoeneck	1B16	R	27	16	62	3	15	2	2	0	8	3	3	1	.242	.299	.339
Jim Whitney	P9,OF1	L	31	10	32	6	12	4	1	0	4	5	6	2	.375	.474	.563
Pete Weckbecker	C1	—	24	1	1	0	0	0	0	0	0	0	0	0	.000	.000	.000

D. Buckley, 1 G at OF; C. Daily, 1 G at 3B

Pitcher	T	Age	G	GS	CG	ShO	IP	H	HR	BB	SO	W-L	Sv	ERA
Henry Boyle	R	28	46	45	38	2	378.2	422	14	95	97	21-23	0	3.92
Charlie Getzien	R	25	45	44	36	0	349.0	395	27	100	139	18-22	1	4.54
Amos Rusie	R	18	33	22	19	1	225.0	246	12	116	109	12-10	0	5.32
Jim Whitney	R	31	9	8	7	0	70.0	106	4	19	16	2-7	0	6.81
Gus Krock†	L	23	4	4	3	0	32.0	48	2	14	10	2-2	0	7.31
Lev Shreve	R	20	3	3	1	0	15.2	25	3	12	5	0-3	0	13.79
Varney Anderson	R	23	2	1	1	0	12.0	13	0	9	3	0-1	0	4.50
Jack Fanning	R	26	1	1	0	0	1.0	3	0	2	0	0-1	0	18.00
Bill Burdick	R	29	10	4	2	0	45.2	58	7	13	16	2-4	1	4.53
Jack Fee	—	21	7	3	2	0	40.0	39	2	31	10	2-2	0	4.28
Jack McGeachey	R	25	3	0	0	0	4.2	7	2	6	3	0-0	0	11.57
Jack Glasscock	R	29	1	0	0	0	0.2	3	0	3	0	0-0	0	0.00

1889 Washington Senators 8th NL 41-83 .331 41.0 GB

John Morrill (13-38)/Arthur Irwin (28-45)

Player	Gm by Position	B	Age	G	AB	R	H	2B	3B	HR	RBI	BB	SO	SB	Avg	OBP	Slg
Tom Daly	C57,1B8,2B4*	S	23	71	250	39	75	13	5	1	40	38	28	18	.300	.394	.404
John Carney	1B53,OF16	R	22	69	273	25	63	7	0	1	29	14	14	12	.231	.271	.267
Sam Wise	2B72,SS26,3B13*	L	31	121	472	79	118	15	8	4	62	61	62	24	.250	.341	.341
John Irwin	3B58	L	27	58	228	42	66	11	4	0	25	25	14	10	.289	.370	.373
Arthur Irwin†	SS85,P1,2B1	L	31	85	313	49	73	10	5	0	32	42	37	9	.233	.326	.297
Dummy Hoy	OF127	L	27	127	507	98	139	11	6	0	39	75	30	35	.274	.374	.320
Walt Wilmot	OF108	S	25	108	432	88	125	19	19	9	57	51	32	40	.289	.367	.484
Ed Beecher	OF39,1B3	L	28	42	179	20	53	9	0	0	30	5	4	3	.296	.319	.346
Connie Mack	C45,OF34,1B22	R	26	98	386	51	113	16	1	0	42	15	12	26	.293	.333	.339
Pete Sweeney†	3B47,2B1,OF1	R	25	49	193	13	44	7	3	1	23	11	26	8	.228	.284	.311
Bert Myers†	2B46	R	25	46	176	24	46	3	0	0	20	22	7	10	.261	.347	.278
John Morrill	1B40,3B3,P1*	R	34	44	146	20	27	5	0	2	16	30	23	12	.185	.328	.260
Spider Clark	C14,SS13,OF9*	—	21	38	145	19	37	7	2	3	22	6	18	8	.255	.285	.393
George Haddock	P33,OF3	R	22	34	112	13	25	3	0	2	14	19	27	3	.223	.336	.304
George Shoch	OF29,SS1	R	30	30	109	12	26	2	0	0	11	20	5	9	.239	.385	.257
George Keefe	P30,OF1	L	22	30	98	7	16	2	1	0	1	8	29	2	.163	.226	.204
Hi Ebright	C9,OF4,SS3	R	30	16	59	7	15	2	2	1	6	3	8	1	.254	.302	.407
John Riddle	C9,OF2	R	25	11	37	3	8	3	0	0	3	2	8	0	.216	.256	.297
Jim Donnelly	3B4	R	23	4	13	3	2	0	0	0	0	2	0	1	.154	.267	.154
Billy O'Brien	1B2	R	29	2	8	1	0	0	0	0	0	1	1	0	.000	.111	.000
Art McCoy	2B2	—	24	2	6	0	0	0	0	0	0	2	1	0	.000	.250	.000
Harry Clarke	OF1	—	28	1	3	0	0	0	0	0	0	0	1	0	.000	.000	.000
Jim Banning	C2	L	23	2	1	0	0	0	0	0	0	0	0	0	.000	.000	.000

T. Daly, 3 G at OF, 1 G at SS; S. Wise, 10 G at OF; J. Morrill, 1 G at 2B; S. Clark, 2 G at 2B, 2 G at 3B

Pitcher	T	Age	G	GS	CG	ShO	IP	H	HR	BB	SO	W-L	Sv	ERA
Alex Ferson	R	22	36	34	28	1	288.1	319	9	105	85	17-17	0	3.90
George Haddock	R	22	33	31	30	0	276.1	299	10	123	106	11-19	0	4.20
George Keefe	L	22	30	27	24	0	230.0	266	6	143	90	8-18	0	5.13
Hank O'Day†	R	26	13	13	11	0	108.0	117	7	57	23	2-10	0	4.33
Egyptian Healy†	R	22	13	12	10	0	101.0	139	2	38	49	1-11	0	6.24
Gus Krock†	L	23	6	6	6	0	48.0	65	1	22	17	2-4	0	5.25
John Thornton	—	—	1	1	1	0	9.0	8	0	7	3	0-1	0	5.00
Mike Sullivan	—	22	9	3	3	0	41.0	47	2	32	15	0-3	0	7.24
Arthur Irwin	R	31	1	0	0	0	1.0	1	0	0	0	0-0	0	0.00
John Morrill	R	34	1	0	0	0	0.1	0	0	0	0	0-0	0	0.00

>>1889 Brooklyn Bridegrooms 1st AA 93-44 .679 —

Bill McGunnigle

Player	Gm by Position	B	Age	G	AB	R	H	2B	3B	HR	RBI	BB	SO	SB	Avg	OBP	Slg
Joe Visner	C53,OF29	L	29	80	295	56	76	12	10	8	68	36	36	13	.258	.346	.447
Dave Foutz	1B134,P12	R	32	138	553	118	152	19	8	6	113	64	23	43	.275	.353	.371
Hub Collins	2B138	R	25	138	560	139	149	18	3	2	73	80	41	65	.266	.365	.320
George Pinckney	3B138	R	27	138	545	103	134	25	7	4	82	59	43	47	.246	.327	.339
Germany Smith	SS120,OF1	R	26	121	446	89	103	22	3	3	53	40	42	35	.231	.296	.314
Pop Corkhill	OF138,1B1,SS1	L	31	138	537	91	134	21	9	8	78	42	24	22	.250	.308	.367
Darby O'Brien	OF136	R	25	136	567	146	170	30	11	5	80	61	76	91	.300	.384	.418
Oyster Burns	OF113,SS19	R	24	131	504	105	153	19	13	5	100	68	26	32	.304	.391	.423
Bob Clark	C53	R	26	53	182	32	50	5	2	0	22	26	7	18	.275	.368	.324
Bob Caruthers	P56,OF3,1B2	L	25	59	172	45	43	8	3	2	31	44	17	9	.250	.408	.366
Adonis Terry	P41,1B10	R	24	49	160	29	48	6	6	2	26	14	14	8	.300	.356	.450
Doc Bushong	C25	R	32	25	84	15	13	1	0	0	8	9	7	2	.155	.237	.167
Mickey Hughes	P20,OF1	—	22	20	68	4	12	0	0	0	5	4	15	0	.176	.222	.176
Charlie Reynolds†	C12	—	24	12	42	5	9	1	1	0	3	1	6	2	.214	.233	.286

Pitcher	T	Age	G	GS	CG	ShO	IP	H	HR	BB	SO	W-L	Sv	ERA
Bob Caruthers	R	25	56	50	46	7	445.0	444	16	104	118	40-11	1	3.13
Adonis Terry	R	24	41	39	35	2	326.0	285	6	126	186	22-15	0	3.29
Tom Lovett	—	25	29	28	23	1	229.0	234	3	65	92	17-10	0	4.32
Mickey Hughes	R	22	20	17	13	0	153.0	172	6	86	54	9-8	0	4.35
Dave Foutz	R	32	12	4	3	0	59.2	70	2	19	21	3-0	0	4.37

1889 St. Louis Browns 2nd AA 90-45 .667 2.0 GB

Charlie Comiskey

Player	Gm by Position	B	Age	G	AB	R	H	2B	3B	HR	RBI	BB	SO	SB	Avg	OBP	Slg
Jack Boyle	C80,3B12,OF5*	R	23	99	347	54	85	11	5	3	42	21	42	5	.245	.301	.331
Charlie Comiskey	1B134,2B3,OF3*	R	29	137	587	105	168	28	10	3	102	19	19	65	.286	.312	.383
Yank Robinson	2B132	R	29	132	452	97	94	17	3	5	70	118	55	39	.208	.378	.292
Arlie Latham	3B116,2B3	R	29	118	512	110	126	13	3	4	49	42	30	69	.246	.317	.307
Shorty Fuller	SS140	R	21	140	517	91	117	18	6	0	51	52	56	38	.226	.303	.284
Tommy McCarthy	OF140,2B2,P1	R	25	140	604	136	176	24	7	2	63	46	26	57	.291	.348	.364
Tip O'Neill	OF134	R	31	134	534	123	179	33	8	9	110	72	37	28	.335	.419	.478
Charlie Duffee	OF132,3B5,2B2	R	23	137	509	93	124	15	11	16	86	60	81	21	.244	.327	.411
Jocko Milligan	C66,1B9	R	27	72	273	53	100	30	2	12	76	16	19	2	.366	.408	.623
Silver King	P56,1B2,OF1	R	21	56	189	37	43	7	3	0	30	22	40	3	.228	.311	.296
Elton Chamberlin	P53,2B1	R	21	53	171	18	34	8	3	2	31	12	32	3	.199	.259	.316
Jack Stivetts	P26,OF1	R	21	27	79	12	18	2	2	0	7	3	13	0	.228	.265	.304
Nat Hudson	P9,OF6,1B3	R	20	13	52	6	13	1	1	1	10	2	11	1	.250	.278	.365
Pete Sweeney†	3B8,OF1	R	25	9	38	8	14	2	0	0	8	1	5	2	.368	.415	.421
Tom Gettinger	OF4	L	20	4	16	2	7	0	0	1	2	2	1	0	.438	.500	.625
Jim Gill	2B1,OF1	—	—	2	8	2	2	1	0	0	1	1	2	1	.250	.333	.375
Jumbo Davis†	SS1,OF1	L	27	2	4	1	0	0	0	0	0	1	1	0	.000	.200	.000
Dad Meek	C2	—	22	2	2	2	1	0	0	0	1	0	0	1	.500	.500	.500
John Bellman	C1	—	25	1	2	1	1	0	0	0	0	1	0	0	.500	.667	.500

J. Boyle, 4 G at 1B, 1 G at 2B; C. Comiskey, 1 G at P

Pitcher	T	Age	G	GS	CG	ShO	IP	H	HR	BB	SO	W-L	Sv	ERA
Silver King	R	21	56	53	47	3	458.0	462	15	125	188	34-16	1	3.14
Elton Chamberlin	R	21	53	51	44	2	421.2	376	18	165	202	32-15	1	2.97
Jack Stivetts	R	21	26	20	18	2	191.2	153	4	68	143	13-7	1	2.25
Jim Devlin	L	23	9	8	5	0	60.0	56	0	24	37	5-3	0	2.40
Nat Hudson	R	20	9	5	4	0	60.0	71	2	15	13	3-2	0	4.20
Toad Ramsey†	L	24	5	3	3	0	41.0	44	0	10	33	3-1	0	3.95
Tommy McCarthy	R	25	1	0	0	0	5.0	4	0	6	1	0-0	0	7.20
Charlie Comiskey	R	29	1	0	0	0	0.1	0	0	0	0	0-0	0	0.00

1889 Philadelphia Athletics 3rd AA 75-58 .564 16.0 GB

Bill Sharsig

Player	Gm by Position	B	Age	G	AB	R	H	2B	3B	HR	RBI	BB	SO	SB	Avg	OBP	Slg
Wilbert Robinson	C69	R	26	69	264	31	61	13	2	0	28	6	34	9	.231	.251	.295
Henry Larkin	1B131,2B1,3B1	R	29	133	516	105	164	23	12	3	74	83	41	11	.318	.428	.426
Lou Bierbauer	2B130,C1	L	23	130	549	80	167	27	7	7	105	29	30	17	.304	.344	.417
Denny Lyons	3B130,1B1	R	23	131	510	135	168	36	4	9	82	79	44	10	.329	.426	.469
Frank Fennelly	SS138	R	29	138	513	70	132	20	5	1	64	65	78	15	.257	.344	.322
Harry Stovey	OF137,1B1	R	32	137	556	152	171	38	13	19	119	77	68	63	.308	.393	.525
Blondie Purcell	OF129	R	35	129	507	72	160	19	7	0	85	50	27	22	.316	.383	.381
Curt Welch	OF125	R	27	125	516	134	140	39	6	0	39	67	30	66	.271	.375	.370
Lave Cross	C55	R	23	55	199	22	44	8	2	0	23	14	9	11	.221	.272	.281
Gus Weyhing	P54,OF1	R	22	54	191	16	25	2	0	0	12	9	59	4	.131	.174	.141
Ed Seward	P39,OF8,2B1	—	22	46	143	22	31	5	3	2	17	22	19	6	.217	.333	.336
Jack Brennan	C13,2B7,OF7*	—	27	31	113	12	25	4	0	0	15	10	15	1	.221	.285	.257
Sadie McMahon	P28,OF2	R	21	30	104	9	16	2	1	0	4	4	16	3	.154	.185	.192
Mike Mattimore†	OF12,1B7,P5	L	30	23	73	10	17	1	2	1	8	9	7	6	.233	.333	.342
Tom Gunning	C8	R	27	8	24	3	6	0	1	1	1	0	4	3	.250	.250	.458
John Coleman	P5,OF1	L	26	6	19	1	1	0	0	0	1	1	3	1	.053	.100	.053
Barney Graham	3B4	L	—	4	18	0	3	0	0	0	0	0	0	0	.167	.167	.167
Bill Collins	C1	R	26	1	4	0	1	0	0	0	1	1	0	1	.250	.400	.250

J. Brennan, 4 G at 3B

Pitcher	T	Age	G	GS	CG	ShO	IP	H	HR	BB	SO	W-L	Sv	ERA
Gus Weyhing	R	22	54	53	50	4	449.0	382	15	212	213	30-21	0	2.95
Ed Seward	R	22	39	38	35	3	320.0	353	8	101	102	21-15	0	3.97
Sadie McMahon	R	21	28	27	27	2	242.0	230	5	102	117	14-12	0	3.53
George Bausewine	—	20	7	6	6	0	55.1	64	1	33	18	1-4	0	3.90
Phenomenal Smith	L	24	5	5	5	0	43.0	53	2	25	12	2-3	0	4.40
John Coleman	R	26	5	5	4	0	34.0	38	2	14	6	3-2	0	2.91
Ed Knouff	R	21	3	3	2	0	25.0	37	2	9	5	2-0	0	3.96
Mike Mattimore†	L	30	5	1	1	0	31.0	43	0	13	6	2-1	1	5.81

1889 Cincinnati Reds 4th AA 76-63 .547 18.0 GB

Gus Schmelz

Player	Gm by Position	B	Age	G	AB	R	H	2B	3B	HR	RBI	BB	SO	SB	Avg	OBP	Slg
Jim Keenan	C66,1B21,3B1	R	31	87	300	52	86	10	11	6	60	48	35	18	.287	.395	.453
John Reilly	1B109,OF2	R	30	111	427	84	111	24	13	5	66	34	37	43	.260	.340	.412
Bid McPhee	2B135,3B1	R	29	135	540	109	145	25	7	5	57	60	29	63	.269	.346	.369
Hick Carpenter	3B121,1B2	R	33	123	486	67	127	23	6	0	63	18	41	47	.261	.293	.333
Ollie Beard	SS141	R	27	141	558	96	159	13	14	1	77	35	39	36	.285	.328	.364
Bug Holliday	OF135	R	22	135	563	107	181	28	7	19	104	43	59	46	.321	.372	.497
W. Wings Tebeau	OF134,1B1	R	27	135	496	110	125	21	11	7	70	69	62	61	.252	.350	.381
Hugh Nicol	OF115,2B7,3B3	R	31	122	474	82	121	7	8	2	58	54	35	80	.255	.338	.316
Kid Baldwin	C55,OF4,1B1*	R	24	60	223	34	55	14	2	1	34	5	32	7	.247	.273	.341
Tony Mullane	P33,3B18,OF12*	S	30	63	196	53	58	16	4	0	29	27	21	24	.296	.387	.418
Billy Earle	OF26,C23,1B5	R	21	53	169	37	45	4	7	4	31	30	24	26	.266	.386	.444
Jesse Duryea	P53,OF3	R	29	54	162	37	44	6	3	0	17	11	30	5	.272	.330	.346
Lee Viau	P47,OF1	R	22	47	147	14	21	2	1	0	9	11	47	4	.143	.208	.170

K. Baldwin, 1 G at 3B; T. Mullane, 4 G at 1B

Pitcher	T	Age	G	GS	CG	ShO	IP	H	HR	BB	SO	W-L	Sv	ERA
Jesse Duryea	R	29	53	48	38	2	401.0	372	9	127	183	32-19	1	2.56
Lee Viau	R	22	47	42	38	1	373.0	379	8	136	152	22-20	1	3.79
Tony Mullane	R	30	33	24	17	0	220.0	218	4	89	112	11-9	5	2.99
Elmer Smith	L	21	29	22	16	0	203.0	253	11	101	104	9-12	0	4.88
Charlie Petty	R	23	5	5	5	0	44.0	44	3	20	10	2-3	0	5.52
Ted Conover	R	21	1	0	0	0	2.0	4	0	2	1	0-0	1	13.50

1889 Baltimore Orioles 5th AA 70-65 .519 22.0 GB

Billy Barnie

Player	Gm by Position	B	Age	G	AB	R	H	2B	3B	HR	RBI	BB	SO	SB	Avg	OBP	Slg
Pop Tate	C62,1B10	R	28	72	253	28	46	6	3	1	27	13	37	4	.182	.236	.241
Tommy Tucker	1B123,OF12	S	25	134	527	103	196	22	11	5	99	42	26	63	.372	.450	.484
Reddy Mack	2B135,OF1	—	23	136	519	84	125	24	7	1	87	60	69	23	.241	.329	.320
Billy Shindle	3B138	R	25	138	567	122	178	24	7	3	64	42	37	56	.314	.369	.397
Jack Farrell	SS42	R	31	42	157	25	33	3	0	1	26	15	15	14	.210	.287	.248
Joe Hornung	OF134,3B1	R	32	135	533	73	122	13	9	1	78	22	72	34	.229	.269	.293
Mike Griffin	OF109,SS25,2B5	L	24	137	531	152	148	21	14	4	48	91	29	39	.279	.387	.394
Joe Sommer	OF105,SS1	R	30	106	386	51	85	13	2	1	36	42	49	18	.220	.298	.272
Matt Kilroy	P59,OF8	L	23	65	208	32	57	3	6	1	26	23	26	13	.274	.352	.361
Tom Quinn	C55	R	25	55	194	18	34	2	1	1	15	19	22	6	.175	.252	.211
Frank Foreman	P51,OF3	L	26	54	181	18	26	2	1	1	11	12	35	7	.144	.201	.182
Will Holland	SS39,OF1	—	—	40	143	13	27	1	2	0	16	9	28	4	.189	.247	.224
Bert Cunningham	P39,OF2,SS1	R	23	41	131	10	27	4	2	0	18	4	25	3	.206	.241	.267
Irv Ray†	SS20,OF6	L	25	26	106	20	36	4	1	0	17	7	6	12	.340	.397	.396
Joe Dowie	OF20	—	23	20	75	12	17	5	0	0	8	2	10	5	.227	.266	.293
Bart Cantz	C18,OF2	—	29	20	69	6	12	2	0	0	8	4	14	2	.174	.219	.203
Chris Fulmer	OF14,C2	R	30	16	58	11	15	3	1	0	13	6	12	2	.259	.338	.345
John Kerins†	1B9,C4,OF2*	R	30	16	53	7	15	2	0	0	12	2	4	2	.283	.321	.321
Dusty Miller	SS8,OF3	L	20	11	40	4	6	1	1	0	6	2	11	3	.150	.209	.225
George Wood†	OF3	L	30	3	10	1	2	0	0	0	1	0	2	1	.200	.200	.200
Chippy McGarr†	SS3	R	26	3	7	1	1	0	0	0	0	1	1	0	.143	.250	.143

J. Kerins, 1 G at SS

Pitcher	T	Age	G	GS	CG	ShO	IP	H	HR	BB	SO	W-L	Sv	ERA
Matt Kilroy	L	23	59	56	55	5	480.2	476	8	142	217	29-25	0	2.85
Frank Foreman	L	26	51	48	43	5	414.0	364	8	137	180	23-21	0	3.52
Bert Cunningham	R	23	39	33	29	0	279.1	306	11	141	140	16-19	1	4.87
George Goetz	—	—	1	1	0	0	9.0	12	0	0	2	1-0	0	4.00
Pat Whitaker	R	24	1	1	1	0	9.0	10	0	4	1	1-0	0	2.00

1889 Columbus Colts 6th AA 60-78 .435 33.5 GB

Al Buckenberger

Player	Gm by Position	B	Age	G	AB	R	H	2B	3B	HR	RBI	BB	SO	SB	Avg	OBP	Slg
Jack O'Connor	C84,OF19,2B4*	R	20	107	398	69	107	17	7	4	60	33	37	26	.269	.331	.377
Dave Orr	1B134	R	29	134	560	70	183	31	12	4	87	9	38	12	.327	.340	.446
Bill Greenwood	2B118	S	32	118	414	62	93	7	10	3	49	58	71	37	.225	.327	.312
Lefty Marr	3B66,OF47,SS26*	L	26	139	546	110	167	26	15	1	75	87	32	29	.306	.407	.414
Henry Easterday	SS89,2B5,3B1	R	24	95	324	43	56	5	8	4	34	41	57	10	.173	.270	.275
Jim McTamany	OF139	R	25	139	529	113	146	21	7	4	52	116	66	40	.276	.407	.365
Ed Daily	OF136,P2	R	26	136	578	105	148	22	8	3	70	38	65	60	.256	.303	.337
Spud Johnson	OF69,3B44,1B2*	L	29	116	459	91	130	14	10	2	79	39	47	34	.283	.355	.370
Mark Baldwin	P63,OF1	R	25	64	208	19	39	6	5	2	25	16	63	2	.188	.246	.293
Heinie Kappel	3B23,SS23	R	25	46	173	25	47	7	5	3	21	21	28	10	.272	.354	.422
Wild Bill Widner	P41,1B1,OF1	R	22	41	133	16	28	3	0	2	10	2	31	5	.211	.228	.278
Jimmy Peoples	C22,OF5,2B2*	—	25	29	100	13	23	6	2	1	16	6	8	3	.230	.274	.360
Ned Bligh	C28	R	25	28	93	6	13	1	1	0	5	4	14	2	.140	.200	.172
Al Mays	P21,OF2	R	24	21	54	4	7	1	0	0	4	11	10	1	.130	.277	.148
Jack Crooks	2B12	R	23	12	43	13	14	2	3	0	7	10	4	10	.326	.463	.512
Jack Doyle	C7,OF3,2B2	R	19	11	36	6	10	1	1	0	3	6	6	9	.278	.381	.361
Rudy Kemmler	C8	R	29	8	26	2	3	0	0	0	0	3	3	0	.115	.207	.115
Charlie Reilly	3B6	S	22	6	23	5	11	1	0	3	6	2	2	9	.478	.538	.913
Bill George†	OF4,P2	R	24	5	17	1	4	0	0	0	3	1	1	1	.235	.278	.235
Sparrow McCaffrey	C2	—	21	2	1	1	1	0	0	0	0	1	0	0	1.000	1.000	1.000

J. O'Connor, 3 G at 1B; L. Marr, 2 G at 1B, 1 G at C; S. Johnson, 1 G at SS; J. Peoples, 1 G at SS

Pitcher	T	Age	G	GS	CG	ShO	IP	H	HR	BB	SO	W-L	Sv	ERA
Mark Baldwin	R	25	63	59	54	6	513.2	458	9	274	368	27-34	1	3.61
Wild Bill Widner	R	22	41	34	25	2	294.0	368	11	85	63	12-20	1	5.20
Hank Gastright	R	24	32	26	21	0	222.2	255	8	104	115	10-16	0	4.57
Al Mays	—	24	21	19	13	1	140.0	167	4	56	52	10-7	0	4.82
Jack Easton	—	22	4	1	1	0	18.0	13	0	21	7	1-0	1	3.50
Bill George	L	24	2	0	0	0	8.0	11	1	3	3	0-0	0	7.88
Ed Daily	R	26	2	0	0	0	1.2	1	0	4	2	0-0	1	21.60
John Weyhing	L	20	1	0	0	0	1.0	1	0	4	0	0-0	0	27.00

1889 Kansas City Blues 7th AA 55-82 .401 38.0 GB

Bill Watkins

Player	Gm by Position	B	Age	G	AB	R	H	2B	3B	HR	RBI	BB	SO	SB	Avg	OBP	Slg
Charlie Hoover	C66,3B4,OF3	L	23	71	258	44	64	2	5	1	25	29	38	9	.248	.329	.306
Ecky Stearns	1B135,3B4	L	27	139	560	96	160	24	12	3	87	56	69	67	.286	.351	.388
Jim Manning	OF69,2B63,3B1*	S	27	132	506	68	103	16	7	3	68	54	61	58	.204	.297	.281
Jumbo Davis†	3B62	L	27	62	241	40	64	4	3	0	30	17	35	25	.266	.319	.307
Herman Long	SS128,2B8,OF1	L	23	136	574	137	158	32	6	3	60	64	63	89	.275	.358	.368
Billy Hamilton	OF137	L	23	137	534	144	161	17	12	3	77	87	41	111	.301	.413	.395
Jim Burns	OF134,3B1	—	—	134	579	103	176	23	11	5	97	20	68	56	.304	.335	.408
John Pickett	OF28,3B14,2B11	R	23	53	201	20	45	7	0	0	12	11	21	7	.224	.271	.259
Jim Donahue	C46,OF14,3B10	R	27	67	252	30	59	5	4	0	32	21	20	12	.234	.293	.286
Billy Alvord	3B34,2B8,SS8	—	25	50	186	23	43	8	9	0	18	10	35	3	.231	.270	.371
Sam Barkley	2B41,1B4	R	31	45	176	36	50	6	2	0	23	15	20	8	.284	.340	.341
Park Swartzel	P48,OF4	R	23	51	174	19	25	4	0	0	20	18	33	7	.144	.247	.167
Joe Gunson	C32,3B1,OF1	R	26	34	122	15	24	3	1	0	12	3	17	2	.197	.228	.238
Chippy McGarr†	3B11,OF6,2B5*	R	26	25	108	22	31	3	0	0	16	6	11	12	.287	.330	.315
John Sowders	P25,OF3	R	22	28	87	11	19	3	0	0	6	4	20	1	.218	.269	.253
John McCarty	P15,OF6	—	—	20	79	12	18	0	1	0	12	1	9	3	.228	.247	.253
Mike Mattimore†	OF19,P1	L	30	19	75	6	12	1	1	0	5	3	16	0	.160	.192	.200
Red Bittmann	2B4	—	26	4	14	2	4	0	0	0	2	1	1	1	.286	.333	.286
Frank Pears	P3,OF1	—	22	3	11	0	1	0	0	0	1	0	3	0	.091	.091	.091
Charlie Bell	P1,OF1	—	20	2	6	1	1	1	0	0	3	2	2	0	.167	.375	.333
Steve Ladew	P1,OF1	—	—	2	4	0	0	0	0	0	0	0	3	0	.000	.000	.000
Charlie Reynolds†	C1	—	24	1	4	1	1	0	0	0	1	0	1	0	.250	.250	.250

J. Manning, 1 G at SS; C. McGarr, 3 G at SS

Pitcher	T	Age	G	GS	CG	ShO	IP	H	HR	BB	SO	W-L	Sv	ERA
Park Swartzel	R	23	48	47	45	0	410.1	481	21	117	147	19-27	1	4.32
Jim Conway	R	30	41	37	33	0	335.0	334	12	90	115	19-19	0	3.25
John Sowders	L	22	25	23	20	0	185.0	204	9	105	104	6-16	1	4.82
John McCarty	R	—	15	14	13	0	119.2	147	4	61	36	8-6	0	3.91
Tom Sullivan	—	29	10	10	10	0	87.1	111	2	48	24	2-8	0	5.67
Henry Porter	R	30	4	4	3	0	23.0	52	0	14	9	0-3	0	12.52
Frank Pears	R	22	3	2	2	0	22.0	21	2	9	5	0-2	0	4.91
Charlie Bell	R	20	1	1	1	0	9.0	4	0	3	3	1-0	0	1.00
John Bates	—	21	1	1	1	0	8.0	15	0	5	3	0-1	0	13.50
Mike Mattimore†	L	30	1	0	0	0	3.0	3	1	2	1	0-0	0	3.00
Steve Ladew	—	—	1	0	0	0	2.0	1	0	3	0	0-0	0	4.50

1889 Louisville Colonels 8th AA 27-111 .196 66.5 GB

Dude Esterbrook (2-8)/Chicken Wolf (14-51)/Dan Shannon (10-46)/Jack Chapman (1-6)

Player	Gm by Position	B	Age	G	AB	R	H	2B	3B	HR	RBI	BB	SO	SB	Avg	OBP	Slg
Paul Cook	C74,OF7,1B1*	R	26	81	286	34	65	10	1	0	15	15	48	11	.227	.287	.269
Guy Hecker	1B65,P19,OF1	R	33	81	327	42	93	17	5	1	36	18	27	17	.284	.333	.376
Dan Shannon	2B121	—	24	121	498	90	128	22	12	4	48	42	52	26	.257	.315	.373
Harry Raymond	3B129,P1,OF1	—	27	130	515	58	123	12	9	0	47	19	45	19	.239	.270	.297
Phil Tomney	SS112	R	26	112	376	61	80	8	5	4	38	46	47	26	.213	.304	.293
Farmer Weaver	OF123,C2,2B1*	L	24	124	499	62	145	17	6	0	60	40	22	21	.291	.352	.349
Chicken Wolf	OF88,1B16,2B13*	R	27	130	546	72	159	20	9	3	57	29	34	18	.291	.333	.377
Pete Browning	OF83	R	28	83	324	39	83	19	5	2	32	34	30	21	.256	.327	.364
Farmer Vaughn	C54,OF20,1B18*	R	25	90	360	39	86	11	5	3	45	7	41	13	.239	.253	.322
Red Ehret	P45,OF22,2B1*	R	20	67	258	27	65	6	6	1	31	4	23	4	.252	.263	.333
Scott Stratton	OF29,P19,1B17	L	19	62	229	30	66	7	5	4	34	13	36	10	.288	.332	.415
John Ewing	P40,1B1	—	26	41	134	12	23	2	0	0	6	9	30	5	.172	.234	.187
Jim Galligan	OF31	—	27	31	120	6	20	0	2	0	7	6	17	1	.167	.213	.200
Fred Carl	OF18,2B6,3B1	L	30	25	99	13	20	2	2	0	13	16	22	0	.202	.313	.263
Ed Flanagan	1B23	—	27	23	88	11	22	7	3	0	8	7	11	1	.250	.305	.398
Jack Ryan	C15,OF4,3B2	R	20	21	79	8	14	1	0	0	2	3	17	2	.177	.207	.190
Bill Gleason	SS16	R	30	16	58	6	14	2	0	0	5	4	1	1	.241	.302	.276
Dude Esterbrook	1B8,OF2,SS1	R	32	11	44	8	14	3	0	0	9	5	2	6	.318	.400	.386
John Kerins†	OF2,C1	R	30	2	9	2	3	1	0	0	3	0	1	0	.333	.333	.444
Harry Scherer	OF1	—	—	1	3	0	1	0	0	0	0	0	0	0	.333	.333	.333
John Traffley	OF1	—	27	1	2	0	1	0	0	0	0	0	0	0	.500	.500	.500
Mike Gaule	OF1	L	19	1	2	0	0	0	0	0	0	0	1	0	.000	.000	.000
Charles Fisher	OF1	—	—	1	2	0	1	0	0	0	0	0	0	0	.500	.500	.500
Harry Smith	C1,OF1	R	33	1	2	0	1	0	0	0	1	0	1	0	.500	.500	.500

P. Cook, 1 G at SS; F. Weaver, 1 G at 3B; C. Wolf, 10 G at SS, 7 G at 3B; F. Vaughn, 3 G at 3B; R. Ehret, 1 G at 3B, 1 G at SS

Pitcher	T	Age	G	GS	CG	ShO	IP	H	HR	BB	SO	W-L	Sv	ERA
John Ewing	R	26	40	39	37	1	331.0	407	6	147	155	6-30	0	4.87
Red Ehret	R	20	45	38	35	1	364.0	441	11	115	135	10-29	0	4.80
Toad Ramsey†	L	24	18	18	15	0	140.0	175	7	71	60	1-16	0	5.59
Scott Stratton	R	19	19	17	13	0	133.2	157	6	42	42	3-13	1	3.23
Guy Hecker	R	33	19	16	15	0	151.1	215	7	47	33	5-13	0	5.59
Mike McDermott	R	26	9	9	9	0	84.1	108	4	34	22	1-8	0	4.16
Harry Raymond	—	27	1	1	1	0	9.0	8	0	11	1	1-0	0	1.00
Bill Robinson	—	—	1	1	1	0	8.0	10	2	6	2	0-1	0	10.13
Ed Springer	—	28	1	1	1	0	5.0	8	0	2	1	0-1	0	9.00

»1890 Brooklyn Bridegrooms 1st NL 86-43 .667 —

Bill McGunnigle

Player	Gm by Position	B	Age	G	AB	R	H	2B	3B	HR	RBI	BB	SO	SB	Avg	OBP	Slg
Tom Daly	C69,1B12,OF1	S	24	82	292	55	71	9	4	5	43	32	43	20	.243	.326	.353
Dave Foutz	1B113,OF13,P5	R	33	129	509	106	154	25	13	5	98	52	25	42	.303	.368	.432
Hub Collins	2B129	R	26	129	510	148	142	32	7	3	69	85	47	85	.278	.385	.386
George Pinckney	3B126	R	28	126	485	115	150	20	9	7	83	80	19	47	.309	.411	.431
Germany Smith	SS129	R	27	129	481	76	92	6	5	1	47	42	23	24	.191	.260	.231
Oyster Burns	OF116,3B3	R	25	119	472	102	134	22	12	13	128	51	42	21	.284	.359	.464
Darby O'Brien	OF85	R	26	85	350	78	110	28	6	2	63	32	43	38	.314	.378	.446
Adonis Terry	OF54,P46,1B1	R	25	99	363	63	101	17	9	4	59	40	34	32	.278	.356	.408
Bob Caruthers	OF39,P37	L	26	71	238	46	63	7	4	1	29	47	18	13	.265	.397	.340
Pop Corkhill	OF48,1B6	L	32	51	204	23	46	4	2	1	21	15	11	6	.225	.279	.279
Tom Lovett	P44,OF1	R	26	44	164	22	33	4	0	1	20	12	29	6	.201	.264	.244
Bob Clark	C42,OF1	R	27	43	151	24	33	3	3	0	15	15	8	10	.219	.306	.278
Patsy Donovan†	OF28	L	25	28	105	17	23	5	1	0	8	5	5	3	.219	.268	.286
Doc Bushong	C15,OF2	R	33	16	55	5	13	2	0	0	7	6	4	2	.236	.311	.273
George Stallings	C4	R	22	4	11	1	0	0	0	0	0	1	3	0	.000	.154	.000

Pitcher	T	Age	G	GS	CG	ShO	IP	H	HR	BB	SO	W-L	Sv	ERA
Adonis Terry	R	25	46	44	38	1	370.0	362	3	133	185	26-16	0	2.94
Tom Lovett	—	26	44	41	39	4	372.0	327	14	141	124	30-11	0	2.78
Bob Caruthers	R	26	37	33	30	1	300.0	292	9	87	64	23-11	0	3.09
Mickey Hughes†	R	23	9	8	6	0	66.1	77	1	30	22	4-4	0	5.16
Lady Baldwin†	L	31	2	1	0	0	7.2	15	0	4	4	1-0	0	7.04
Dave Foutz	R	33	5	2	2	0	29.0	29	0	6	4	2-1	2	1.86

1890 Chicago White Stockings 2nd NL 84-53 .613 6.0 GB

Cap Anson

Player	Gm by Position	B	Age	G	AB	R	H	2B	3B	HR	RBI	BB	SO	SB	Avg	OBP	Slg
Malachi Kittridge	C96	R	20	96	333	46	67	8	3	3	35	39	53	7	.201	.287	.270
Cap Anson	1B135,C3,2B2	R	38	139	504	95	157	14	5	7	107	113	23	29	.312	.443	.401
Bob Glenalvin	2B66	—	23	66	250	43	67	10	3	4	26	19	31	30	.268	.337	.380
Tom Burns	3B139	R	33	139	538	86	149	17	6	5	86	57	45	44	.277	.348	.359
Jimmy Cooney	SS135,C1	S	24	135	574	114	156	19	10	4	52	73	23	45	.272	.360	.361
Walt Wilmot	OF139	S	26	139	571	114	159	15	12	13	99	64	44	76	.278	.353	.415
Cliff Carroll	OF136	S	30	136	582	134	166	16	6	7	65	53	34	34	.285	.352	.369
Jim Andrews	OF53	—	25	53	202	32	38	4	2	3	17	23	41	11	.188	.278	.272
Howard Earl	OF49,2B39,SS4*	—	23	92	384	57	95	10	3	7	51	18	47	17	.247	.285	.344
Tom Nagle	C33,OF6	R	24	38	144	21	39	5	1	1	11	7	24	4	.271	.318	.340
Pat Luby	P34,1B2	—	21	36	116	27	31	5	3	3	17	9	6	3	.267	.331	.440
Pete O'Brien	2B27	R	23	27	106	15	30	7	0	3	16	5	10	4	.283	.315	.434
Elmer Foster	OF27	R	28	27	105	20	26	4	2	5	23	9	21	18	.248	.325	.467
Jake Stenzel	C6,OF6	R	23	11	41	3	11	1	0	0	3	1	0	0	.268	.286	.293
Ed Hutchinson	2B4	L	23	4	17	0	1	1	0	0	0	0	0	0	.059	.059	.118
Chuck Lauer	C2	—	25	2	8	1	2	1	0	0	2	0	0	0	.250	.250	.375
Dad Lytle†	OF1	R	28	1	4	1	0	0	0	0	0	0	1	0	.000	.000	.000
Marty Honan	C1	—	20	1	3	0	0	0	0	0	1	0	2	0	.000	.000	.000
Pat Wright	2B1	S	21	1	2	0	0	0	0	0	0	1	0	0	.000	.333	.000

H. Earl, 3 G at 1B

Pitcher	T	Age	G	GS	CG	ShO	IP	H	HR	BB	SO	W-L	Sv	ERA
Bill Hutchison	R	30	71	66	65	5	603.0	505	20	199	289	42-25	2	2.70
Pat Luby	R	21	34	31	26	0	267.2	226	6	95	85	20-9	1	3.19
Ed Stein	R	20	20	18	14	1	160.2	147	9	83	65	12-6	0	3.81
Mike Sullivan	—	23	12	12	10	0	96.0	108	3	58	33	5-6	0	4.59
Roscoe Coughlin	R	22	11	10	10	0	95.0	102	3	40	29	4-6	0	4.26
Robert Gibson†	R	20	1	1	1	0	9.0	6	0	2	1	1-0	0	0.00
Ed Eiteljorge	R	18	1	1	0	0	2.0	5	0	1	1	0-1	0	22.50
Fred Demarais	R	23	1	0	0	0	2.0	1	0	1	1	0-0	0	0.00
Ossie France	L	31	1	0	0	0	2.0	3	0	2	0	0-0	0	13.50

1890 Philadelphia Phillies 3rd NL 78-54 .591 9.5 GB

H. Wright (14-8)/J. Clements (13-6)/A. Reach (4-7)/B. Allen (25-10)/H. Wright (22-23)

Player	Gm by Position	B	Age	G	AB	R	H	2B	3B	HR	RBI	BB	SO	SB	Avg	OBP	Slg
Jack Clements	C91,1B5	L	25	97	381	64	120	23	8	7	74	45	30	10	.315	.392	.472
Al McCauley	1B112	L	27	112	418	63	102	25	7	1	42	57	38	8	.244	.346	.344
Bert Myers	2B117	R	26	117	487	95	135	29	7	2	81	57	46	44	.277	.365	.378
Ed Mayer	3B117,OF4	—	23	117	484	49	117	25	5	1	70	22	36	20	.242	.286	.320
Bob Allen	SS133	R	22	133	456	69	103	15	11	2	57	87	54	13	.226	.356	.320
Sam Thompson	OF132	L	30	132	549	116	172	41	9	4	102	42	29	25	.313	.371	.443
Billy Hamilton	OF123	L	24	123	496	133	161	13	9	2	49	83	37	102	.325	.430	.399
Eddie Burke†	OF96,2B4	L	23	100	430	85	113	16	11	4	50	49	40	38	.263	.349	.379
Kid Gleason	P60,2B2	S	23	63	224	22	47	3	0	0	17	12	21	10	.210	.250	.223
Pop Schriver	C34,1B10,3B8*	R	24	57	223	37	61	9	6	0	35	22	15	9	.274	.339	.368
Bill Grey	OF10,2B8,3B8*	—	19	34	128	20	31	8	4	0	21	6	3	5	.242	.287	.367
Billy Sunday†	OF31	L	27	31	119	26	31	3	1	0	6	18	7	28	.261	.367	.303
Phenomenal Smith†	P24,OF3	L	25	26	86	19	24	4	0	0	10	10	5	6	.279	.361	.326
Harry Decker†	1B2,OF2,C1	R	35	5	19	5	7	1	0	0	2	4	1	4	.368	.478	.421
Frank Motz	1B1	—	20	1	2	1	0	0	0	0	0	1	1	1	.000	.333	.000

P. Schriver, 3 G at 2B, 2 G at OF; B. Grey, 7 G at C, 1 G at 1B

Pitcher	T	Age	G	GS	CG	ShO	IP	H	HR	BB	SO	W-L	Sv	ERA
Kid Gleason	R	23	60	55	54	6	506.0	479	8	167	222	38-17	2	2.63
Tom Vickery	R	23	46	46	41	2	382.0	405	8	184	162	24-22	0	3.44
Phenomenal Smith†	L	25	24	20	19	1	204.0	209	5	89	81	8-12	0	4.28
Duke Esper†	L	21	5	5	4	0	41.0	40	1	16	18	5-0	0	3.07
Bill Day†	R	22	4	2	2	0	23.2	26	0	12	9	1-1	0	3.04
Dave Anderson†	L	21	3	2	1	0	19.1	31	0	11	7	1-1	0	7.45
Jack McFetridge	—	20	1	1	1	0	9.0	5	0	2	4	1-0	0	1.00
Sumner Bowman†	L	23	1	1	0	0	8.0	11	0	2	2	0-0	0	7.88
John Coleman	R	—	1	1	0	0	1.2	4	0	3	2	0-1	0	21.60

1890 Cincinnati Reds 4th NL 77-55 .583 10.5 GB

Tom Loftus

Player	Gm by Position	B	Age	G	AB	R	H	2B	3B	HR	RBI	BB	SO	SB	Avg	OBP	Slg
Jerry Harrington	C65	R	20	65	236	25	58	7	1	1	23	15	29	4	.246	.299	.297
John Reilly	1B132,OF1	R	31	133	553	114	166	25	26	6	86	16	41	29	.300	.328	.472
Bid McPhee	2B132	R	30	132	528	125	135	16	22	3	39	82	26	55	.256	.362	.386
Lefty Marr	OF64,3B63,SS3	L	27	130	527	91	158	17	12	1	73	46	29	44	.300	.363	.383
Ollie Beard	SS113,3B9	R	28	122	492	64	132	17	15	3	72	44	13	40	.268	.331	.382
Bug Holliday	OF131	R	23	131	518	93	140	18	14	4	75	49	36	50	.270	.341	.382
Joe Knight	OF127	L	30	127	481	67	150	26	8	4	67	38	31	17	.312	.367	.424
Hugh Nicol	OF46,SS3,2B1	R	32	50	186	28	39	1	4	0	19	19	12	24	.210	.283	.258
Tony Mullane	OF28,P25,3B21*	S	31	81	286	41	79	9	8	0	34	39	30	19	.276	.375	.364
Jim Keenan	C50,1B2,3B1*	R	32	54	202	21	28	4	2	3	19	19	36	5	.139	.216	.223
Arlie Latham†	3B41,OF1	R	30	41	164	35	41	6	2	0	15	23	18	20	.250	.346	.311
Jesse Duryea	P33,OF1	R	30	33	99	13	15	1	1	1	6	19	21	9	.152	.317	.212
Frank Foreman	P25,OF1	L	27	25	75	13	10	1	3	1	7	10	13	0	.133	.253	.267
Kid Baldwin†	C20,OF2	R	25	22	72	5	11	0	0	0	10	3	6	2	.153	.187	.153
Billy Clingman	SS6,2B1	S	20	7	27	2	7	1	0	0	5	1	0	0	.259	.286	.296

T. Mullane, 10 G at SS, 1 G at 1B; J. Keenan, 1 G at OF

Pitcher	T	Age	G	GS	CG	ShO	IP	H	HR	BB	SO	W-L	Sv	ERA
Billy Rhines	R	21	46	45	45	6	401.1	337	6	113	182	28-17	0	1.95
Jesse Duryea	R	30	33	32	29	2	274.0	270	11	60	108	16-12	0	2.92
Frank Foreman	L	27	25	24	20	0	198.1	201	6	89	57	13-10	0	3.95
Tony Mullane	R	31	25	21	21	0	209.0	175	7	96	91	12-10	1	2.24
Lee Viau†	R	23	13	10	7	1	90.0	97	8	39	41	7-5	0	4.50
John Dolan	R	22	2	2	2	0	18.0	17	3	10	9	1-1	0	4.50

1890 Boston Beaneaters 5th NL 76-57 .571 12.0 GB

Frank Selee

Player	Gm by Position	B	Age	G	AB	R	H	2B	3B	HR	RBI	BB	SO	SB	Avg	OBP	Slg
Charlie Bennett	C85	R	35	85	281	59	60	17	2	3	40	72	56	6	.214	.377	.320
Tommy Tucker	1B132	S	26	132	539	104	159	17	8	1	62	56	22	43	.295	.387	.362
Pop Smith	2B134,SS1	R	33	134	463	82	106	16	12	1	53	80	81	39	.229	.353	.322
Chippy McGarr	3B115,SS5,OF1	R	27	121	487	68	115	12	7	1	51	34	38	39	.236	.291	.296
Herman Long	SS101	L	24	101	431	95	108	15	3	8	52	40	34	49	.251	.320	.355
Steve Brodie	OF132	L	21	132	514	77	152	19	9	0	67	66	20	29	.296	.387	.368
Marty Sullivan	OF120,3B1	R	27	121	505	82	144	19	7	6	61	56	48	33	.285	.357	.386
Paul Hines†	OF69,1B1	R	38	69	273	41	72	12	3	2	48	32	20	9	.264	.350	.352
Bobby Lowe	SS24,OF15,3B12	R	21	52	207	35	58	13	2	2	21	26	32	15	.280	.366	.391
Lou Hardie	C25,OF15,3B7*	—	25	47	185	17	42	8	0	3	17	18	36	4	.227	.296	.319
Kid Nichols	P48,OF2	S	20	49	174	18	43	5	1	0	23	11	36	2	.247	.296	.287
John Clarkson	P44,OF1	R	28	45	173	18	43	6	3	2	26	8	31	2	.249	.286	.353
Charlie Ganzel	C22,OF15,SS3*	R	28	38	163	21	44	7	3	0	24	5	6	1	.270	.300	.350
Charlie Getzien	P40,OF1	R	26	41	147	27	34	9	2	2	25	16	25	4	.231	.315	.361
Patsy Donovan†	OF32	L	25	32	140	17	36	0	0	0	9	8	17	10	.257	.307	.257
Al Schellhase	OF5,C2,3B1*	R	25	9	29	1	4	0	0	0	1	1	10	0	.138	.167	.138

L. Hardie, 1 G at 1B, 1 G at SS; C. Ganzel, 1 G at 2B; A. Schellhase, 1 G at SS

Pitcher	T	Age	G	GS	CG	ShO	IP	H	HR	BB	SO	W-L	Sv	ERA
Kid Nichols	R	20	48	47	47	7	424.0	374	8	112	222	27-19	0	2.23
John Clarkson	R	28	44	44	43	2	383.0	370	14	140	138	26-18	0	3.27
Charlie Getzien	R	26	40	40	39	4	350.0	342	5	82	140	23-17	0	3.19
John Taber	R	22	2	1	1	0	13.0	11	0	8	3	0-1	1	4.15
Al Lawson†	R	21	1	1	1	0	9.0	12	0	4	1	0-1	0	4.00
Hon Von Fricken	R	20	1	1	1	0	8.0	23	0	8	2	0-1	0	10.13

1890 New York Giants 6th NL 63-68 .481 24.0 GB

Jim Mutrie

Player	Gm by Position	B	Age	G	AB	R	H	2B	3B	HR	RBI	BB	SO	SB	Avg	OBP	Slg
Dick Buckley	C62,3B8	—	31	70	266	39	68	11	0	2	26	23	35	3	.256	.324	.320
Dude Esterbrook	1B45	R	33	45	197	29	57	14	1	0	29	10	8	12	.289	.333	.371
Charley Bassett	2B100	R	27	100	410	52	98	13	8	0	54	29	25	14	.239	.300	.310
Jerry Denny	3B106,SS7,2B1	R	31	114	437	50	93	18	7	3	42	28	62	11	.213	.270	.307
Jack Glasscock	SS124	R	30	124	512	91	172	32	9	1	66	41	8	54	.336	.395	.439
Mike Tiernan	OF133	L	23	133	553	132	168	25	21	13	59	68	53	56	.304	.385	.495
Jesse Burkett	OF90,P21	L	21	101	401	67	124	23	13	4	60	33	52	14	.309	.366	.461
Joe Hornung	OF77,1B36,3B5*	R	33	120	513	62	122	18	5	0	65	12	37	39	.238	.258	.292
Artie Clarke	C36,OF33,3B16*	R	25	101	395	55	89	12	8	0	49	32	38	44	.225	.290	.296
Amos Rusie	P67,OF14	R	19	73	284	31	79	13	6	0	28	7	26	6	.278	.298	.366
Lew Whistler	1B45	—	22	45	170	27	49	9	7	2	29	20	37	8	.288	.366	.459
John Henry	OF37	—	26	37	144	19	35	6	0	0	16	7	12	12	.243	.283	.285
Pat Murphy	C29,OF3,SS1	—	33	32	119	14	28	5	1	0	9	14	13	3	.235	.321	.294
John Sharrott	P25,OF9	R	20	32	109	16	22	3	2	0	14	0	14	6	.202	.202	.266
Shorty Howe	2B18,3B1	—	—	19	64	4	11	0	0	0	4	3	2	3	.172	.221	.172
Pete Sommers†	C11,1B5,OF2	R	23	17	47	4	5	1	1	0	1	4	13	0	.106	.192	.170
George McMillan	OF10	—	—	10	35	4	5	1	0	0	1	7	4	1	.143	.286	.143
Ed Daily†	OF3,P2	R	27	4	15	1	2	1	0	0	1	0	4	0	.133	.133	.200
Sam Crane†	2B2,1B1,OF1	R	36	4	12	0	0	0	0	0	0	0	2	1	.000	.000	.000
Mort Scanlan	1B3	—	29	3	10	0	0	0	0	0	0	2	5	1	.000	.167	.000
Tom O'Rourke†	C2	—	24	2	7	1	0	0	0	0	0	1	0	0	.000	.125	.000

J. Hornung, 2 G at SS; A. Clarke, 15 G at 2B, 1 G at SS

Pitcher	T	Age	G	GS	CG	ShO	IP	H	HR	BB	SO	W-L	Sv	ERA
Amos Rusie	R	19	67	63	56	4	548.2	436	3	289	341	29-34	1	2.56
Mickey Welch	R	30	37	37	33	2	292.1	268	5	122	97	17-14	0	2.99
John Sharrott	R	20	25	20	18	0	184.0	162	3	88	84	11-10	0	2.89
Jesse Burkett	L	21	21	12	6	0	118.0	134	3	92	82	3-10	0	5.57
Bob Murphy	—	23	3	2	1	0	18.0	23	0	10	8	1-0	0	5.50
Ed Daily†	R	27	2	1	1	0	16.0	6	0	6	0	2-0	0	2.25

1890 Cleveland Spiders 7th NL 44-88 .333 43.5 GB

Gus Schmelz (21-55)/Bob Leadley (23-33)

Player	Gm by Position	B	Age	G	AB	R	H	2B	3B	HR	RBI	BB	SO	SB	Avg	OBP	Slg
Chief Zimmer	C125	R	29	125	444	54	95	16	6	2	57	46	54	15	.214	.303	.291
Peek-A-Boo Veach†	1B64	—	28	64	238	24	56	10	5	0	32	33	28	9	.235	.336	.319
Joe Ardner	2B84	R	32	84	323	28	72	13	1	0	35	17	40	9	.223	.266	.269
Will Smalley	3B136	R	19	136	502	62	107	11	1	0	42	60	44	10	.213	.303	.239
Ed McKean	SS134,2B3	R	26	136	530	95	157	15	14	7	61	87	25	23	.296	.401	.417
George Davis	OF133,2B2,SS1	S	19	136	526	98	139	22	9	6	73	53	34	22	.264	.336	.375
Bob Gilks	OF123,P4,SS3*	R	25	130	544	65	116	10	3	0	41	32	38	17	.213	.265	.243
Vince Dailey	OF64,P2	—	25	64	246	41	71	5	7	0	32	33	23	17	.289	.373	.366
Jake Virtue	1B62	S	25	62	223	39	68	6	5	2	25	49	15	9	.305	.432	.404
Tom Dowse	OF26,1B10,C3*	R	23	40	159	20	33	2	1	0	9	12	22	3	.208	.267	.233
Buck West	OF37	L	29	37	151	20	37	6	1	2	29	7	11	4	.245	.283	.338
Bill Delaney	2B36	R	27	36	116	16	22	1	1	1	7	21	19	5	.190	.314	.241
Rasty Wright†	OF13	L	27	13	45	7	5	1	0	0	2	12	4	3	.111	.298	.133
Pat Lyons	2B11	—	30	11	38	2	2	1	0	0	1	4	4	0	.053	.143	.079
Joe Sommer†	OF9,P1	R	31	9	35	4	8	1	0	0	0	2	2	0	.229	.270	.257
Pete Sommers†	C8,OF1	R	23	9	34	4	7	1	1	0	1	2	3	0	.206	.250	.294
Edgar Smith	P6,OF2	R	28	8	24	2	7	0	1	0	4	4	1	0	.292	.393	.375
Len Stockwell	1B1,OF1	R	30	2	7	2	2	1	0	0	0	0	3	0	.286	.286	.429

B. Gilks, 2 G at 2B; T. Dowse, 1 G at P

Pitcher	T	Age	G	GS	CG	ShO	IP	H	HR	BB	SO	W-L	Sv	ERA
Ed Beatin	L	23	54	54	53	1	474.1	518	11	186	155	22-30	0	3.83
Jack Wadsworth	R	22	20	19	19	0	169.2	202	6	81	26	2-16	0	5.20
Cy Young	R	23	17	16	16	0	147.2	145	6	30	38	9-7	0	3.47
Ezra Lincoln†	L	21	15	15	13	0	118.0	157	1	53	22	3-11	0	4.42
Lee Viau†	R	23	13	13	13	1	107.0	101	4	42	30	4-9	0	3.36
Bill Garfield	R	22	9	8	7	0	70.0	91	3	35	16	1-7	0	4.89
Edgar Smith	R	28	6	6	5	0	44.0	42	1	10	11	1-4	0	4.30
Bob Gilks	R	25	4	3	3	0	31.2	34	0	9	5	2-2	0	4.26
Charlie Parsons	L	26	2	1	0	0	9.0	12	0	6	2	0-1	0	6.00
Vince Dailey	—	25	2	1	0	0	7.0	12	0	7	0	0-1	0	7.71
Tom Dowse	R	23	1	0	0	0	5.0	6	0	1	0	0-0	0	5.40
Joe Sommer	R	31	1	0	0	0	1.0	2	1	2	0	0-0	0	0.00

1890 Pittsburgh Innocents 8th NL 23-113 .169 66.5 GB

Guy Hecker

Player	Gm by Position	B	Age	G	AB	R	H	2B	3B	HR	RBI	BB	SO	SB	Avg	OBP	Slg
Harry Decker†	C70,1B16,OF4*	R	35	92	354	52	97	14	3	5	38	26	36	8	.274	.324	.373
Guy Hecker	1B69,P14,OF7	R	34	86	340	43	77	13	9	0	38	19	17	13	.226	.285	.318
Sam LaRoque	2B78,SS31,1B2*	—	26	111	434	59	105	20	4	1	40	35	29	27	.242	.316	.313
Doggie Miller	3B88,OF25,SS13*	R	25	138	549	85	150	24	3	4	66	68	11	32	.273	.357	.350
Ed Sales	SS51	L	29	51	189	19	43	7	3	1	23	16	15	3	.228	.298	.312
Billy Sunday†	OF86,P1	L	27	86	358	58	92	9	2	1	33	32	20	56	.257	.327	.302
John Kelty	OF59	—	23	59	207	24	49	10	2	1	27	22	42	10	.237	.322	.319
Tun Berger	OF41,SS33,C21*	—	22	104	391	64	104	18	4	0	40	35	23	11	.266	.337	.332
Bill Wilson	C38,OF25,1B18*	—	22	83	304	30	65	11	3	0	21	22	50	5	.214	.271	.270
Fred Roat	3B44,1B9,OF4	—	22	57	215	18	48	2	0	2	17	16	22	7	.223	.286	.260
Fred Osborne	OF35,P8	—	—	41	168	24	40	8	3	1	14	6	18	0	.238	.269	.339
Mike Jordan	OF37	—	27	37	125	8	12	1	0	0	6	15	19	5	.096	.210	.104
Eddie Burke†	OF31	L	23	31	124	17	26	5	2	1	7	14	9	6	.210	.295	.306
Paul Hines†	1B17,OF14	R	38	31	121	11	22	1	0	0	9	11	7	6	.182	.256	.190
Sam Crane†	2B15,SS7,OF1	R	36	22	82	3	16	3	0	0	3	0	5	5	.195	.205	.232
Ducky Hemp†	OF21	—	22	21	81	9	19	0	2	0	4	8	12	3	.235	.311	.284
Fred Dunlap†	2B17	R	31	17	64	9	11	1	1	0	3	7	6	2	.172	.264	.219
Dad Lytle†	2B8,OF7	R	28	15	55	2	8	1	0	0	0	8	9	0	.145	.254	.164
Bill Sowders	P15,OF2	R	25	17	50	3	9	0	0	0	4	2	7	1	.180	.212	.180
Henry Youngman	3B7,2B6	—	25	13	47	6	6	1	1	0	4	6	9	1	.128	.226	.191
Bill Phillips	P10,OF4	R	21	14	46	6	11	2	0	0	2	3	13	0	.239	.286	.283
Charlie Heard	P6,OF6	R	18	12	43	2	8	2	0	0	0	1	15	0	.186	.205	.233
Billy Gumbert	P10,1B1	R	24	10	37	8	9	3	0	1	7	2	5	1	.243	.300	.405
Sumner Bowman†	P9,OF2	L	23	10	36	7	10	1	0	0	3	4	5	0	.278	.350	.306
Peek-A-Boo Veach†	1B8	—	28	8	30	6	9	1	1	2	5	8	3	0	.300	.447	.600
Robert Gibson†	P3,OF2	R	20	3	13	1	3	0	0	0	1	0	3	0	.231	.231	.231
John Coleman	P2,OF2	L	27	3	11	1	2	0	0	0	0	3	0	1	.182	.357	.182
John Gilbert	SS2	—	26	2	8	0	0	0	0	0	0	0	2	0	.000	.000	.000
Harry Gilbert	2B2	—	21	2	8	1	2	0	0	0	0	0	3	0	.250	.250	.250
Frank McGinn	OF1	—	21	1	4	0	0	0	0	0	0	0	2	0	.000	.000	.000
Phil Routcliffe	OF1	R	19	1	4	1	1	0	0	0	1	0	0	1	.250	.400	.250
Fred Truax	OF1	—	22	1	3	0	1	0	0	0	1	1	1	0	.333	.500	.333
Reddy Gray†	SS1	—	—	1	3	0	0	0	0	0	0	0	1	0	.000	.000	.000
Ed Clements	SS1	—	—	1	1	0	0	0	0	0	0	0	0	0	.000	.000	.000

H. Decker, 1 G at 2B, 1 G at SS; S. LaRoque, 1 G at OF; D. Miller, 10 G at C, 6 G at 2B; T. Berger, 6 G at 2B, 1 G at 3B; B. Wilson, 1 G at SS

Pitcher	T	Age	G	GS	CG	ShO	IP	H	HR	BB	SO	W-L	Sv	ERA
Kirtley Baker	R	21	25	21	19	2	178.1	209	11	86	76	3-19	0	5.60
Dave Anderson†	L	21	13	13	13	0	108.0	116	2	49	41	2-11	0	4.67
Guy Hecker	R	34	14	12	11	0	119.2	160	9	44	32	2-9	0	5.11
Bill Sowders	R	25	15	11	9	0	106.0	117	1	24	30	3-8	0	4.42
Crazy Schmit	L	24	11	10	9	1	83.1	108	3	42	35	1-9	0	5.83
Bill Phillips	R	21	10	10	9	0	82.0	123	8	29	25	1-9	0	7.57
Billy Gumbert	R	24	10	10	8	0	79.1	96	0	31	18	4-6	0	5.22
Sumner Bowman†	L	23	9	7	6	0	70.2	100	1	50	22	2-5	0	6.62
Bill Day†	R	22	6	6	6	0	50.0	66	1	24	10	0-6	0	5.22
Charlie Heard	R	18	6	6	5	0	44.0	75	5	32	13	0-6	0	8.39
Fred Osborne	L	—	8	5	5	0	58.0	82	6	45	14	0-5	0	8.38
Phenomenal Smith†	L	25	5	5	5	0	44.0	39	0	13	15	1-3	0	3.07
Charlie Gray	—	23	5	4	3	0	31.0	48	0	24	10	1-4	0	7.55
Henry Jones	—	33	5	4	2	0	31.0	35	1	14	13	2-1	0	3.48
Pete Daniels	L	26	4	4	3	0	28.0	40	1	12	8	1-2	0	7.07
Robert Gibson†	R	20	3	3	2	0	12.0	24	0	23	3	0-3	0	17.25
Duke Esper†	L	21	2	2	2	0	17.0	18	0	10	9	0-2	0	5.29
John Coleman	R	27	2	2	1	0	14.0	28	1	6	3	0-2	0	9.64
Al Lawson†	R	21	2	2	1	0	10.0	15	0	10	2	0-2	0	9.00
George Ziegler	—	18	1	1	0	0	6.0	12	0	0	1	0-1	0	10.50
John Heyner	—	—	1	0	0	0	4.0	7	2	5	1	0-0	0	13.50
Billy Sunday	R	27	1	0	0	0	0.0	2	0	0	0	0-0	0	—

»1890 Louisville Colonels 1st AA 88-44 .667 —

Jack Chapman

Player	Gm by Position	B	Age	G	AB	R	H	2B	3B	HR	RBI	BB	SO	SB	Avg	OBP	Slg
Jack Ryan	C89,OF3,1B1*	R	21	93	337	43	73	16	4	0	35	12	—	6	.217	.244	.288
Harry Taylor	1B118,SS12,2B4*	L	24	134	553	115	169	7	7	0	53	68	—	45	.306	.383	.344
Tim Shinnick	2B130,3B3	S	22	133	493	87	126	16	11	1	82	62	—	62	.256	.348	.339
Harry Raymond	3B119,SS4	—	28	123	521	91	135	7	4	2	51	22	—	18	.259	.293	.299
Phil Tomney	SS108	R	27	108	386	72	107	21	7	1	58	43	—	27	.277	.357	.376
Charlie Hamburg	OF133	—	26	133	485	93	132	22	2	3	77	69	—	46	.272	.370	.344
Farmer Weaver	OF127,SS2,3B1	L	25	130	557	101	161	27	9	3	67	29	—	45	.289	.333	.386
Chicken Wolf	OF123,3B12	R	28	134	543	100	197	29	11	4	98	43	—	46	.363	.421	.479
Scott Stratton	P50,OF5	L	20	55	189	29	61	3	5	0	24	16	—	8	.323	.385	.392
Pete Weckbecker	C32	—	25	32	101	17	24	1	0	0	11	8	—	7	.238	.300	.248
Ed Daily†	P12,OF11	R	27	23	80	24	20	0	2	0	9	13	—	13	.250	.355	.300
Ned Bligh†	C24	R	26	24	73	9	15	0	0	1	9	9	—	1	.205	.293	.247
George Meakim	P28,OF1	R	24	29	72	6	11	0	0	0	6	8	—	8	.153	.265	.153
Herb Goodall	P18,OF1	R	20	19	45	10	19	2	0	0	5	1	—	0	.422	.435	.467
Dan Phelan	1B8	—	25	8	32	4	8	1	1	0	4	0	—	1	.250	.250	.344
Dan O'Connor	1B6	L	21	6	26	3	12	1	1	0	5	1	—	5	.462	.481	.577
Henry Easterday†	SS6,3B1	R	25	7	24	2	2	0	0	0	1	2	—	1	.083	.185	.083
Chief Roseman†	1B2	R	33	2	8	0	2	0	0	0	0	0	—	0	.250	.250	.250
Pete Sweeney†	SS2	R	26	2	7	1	1	1	0	0	1	1	—	1	.143	.250	.286

J. Ryan, 1 G at SS; H. Taylor, 1 G at C

Pitcher	T	Age	G	GS	CG	ShO	IP	H	HR	BB	SO	W-L	Sv	ERA
Scott Stratton	R	20	50	49	44	4	431.0	398	3	61	207	34-14	0	2.36
Red Ehret	R	21	43	38	35	4	359.0	351	5	79	174	25-14	2	2.53
George Meakim	R	24	28	21	16	3	192.0	173	4	63	123	12-7	1	2.91
Herb Goodall	R	20	18	13	8	1	109.0	94	2	51	46	8-5	4	3.39
Ed Daily†	R	27	12	10	9	1	93.0	83	2	30	31	6-3	0	1.94
Mike Jones	L	24	3	3	2	0	22.0	21	2	9	6	2-0	0	3.27

1890 Columbus Colts 2nd AA 79-55 .590 10.0 GB

Al Buckenberger (39-41)/Gus Schmelz (38-13)/Pat Sullivan (2-1)

Player	Gm by Position	B	Age	G	AB	R	H	2B	3B	HR	RBI	BB	SO	SB	Avg	OBP	Slg
Jack O'Connor	C106,OF9,SS8*	R	21	121	457	89	148	14	10	2	66	38	—	29	.324	.377	.411
Mike Lehane	1B140	R	25	140	512	54	108	19	5	0	56	43	—	13	.211	.276	.268
Jack Crooks	2B134,3B1,OF1	R	24	135	485	86	107	5	4	1	62	96	—	57	.221	.357	.254
Charlie Reilly	3B137	S	23	137	530	75	141	23	3	4	77	35	—	43	.266	.319	.343
Henry Easterday†	SS58	R	25	58	197	25	31	5	1	1	17	23	—	5	.157	.249	.208
Spud Johnson	OF135	L	30	135	538	106	186	23	18	1	113	48	—	43	.346	.409	.461
Jon Sneed†	OF126,SS2	—	—	128	484	114	141	13	15	2	65	63	—	39	.291	.383	.393
Jim McTamany	OF125	R	26	125	466	140	120	27	7	1	48	112	—	43	.258	.405	.352
Jack Doyle	C38,SS25,OF9*	R	20	77	298	47	80	17	7	2	44	13	—	27	.268	.299	.393
Bobby Wheelock	SS52	R	25	52	190	24	45	6	1	1	16	25	—	34	.237	.326	.295
Jack Easton	P37,SS2,OF2*	—	23	41	107	14	19	0	2	0	6	10	—	6	.178	.261	.215
Sam Nichol	OF14	R	21	14	56	7	9	0	0	0	4	2	—	3	.161	.190	.161
Ned Bligh†	C8	R	26	8	29	2	6	2	0	0	5	2	—	0	.207	.258	.276
John Munyan†	OF2	—	29	2	7	1	1	0	0	0	0	0	—	0	.143	.250	.143

J. O'Connor, 2 G at 2B, 1 G at 3B; J. Doyle, 6 G at 2B, 3 G at 3B; J. Easton, 1 G at 2B

Pitcher	T	Age	G	GS	CG	ShO	IP	H	HR	BB	SO	W-L	Sv	ERA
Hank Gastright	R	25	48	45	41	4	401.1	312	8	135	199	30-14	0	2.94
Frank Knauss	L	22	37	34	28	3	275.2	206	3	106	148	17-12	2	2.81
Jack Easton	—	23	37	29	23	0	255.2	213	4	125	147	15-14	1	3.52
Elton Chamberlin†	R	22	25	21	19	6	175.0	128	2	70	114	12-6	0	2.21
Wild Bill Widner	R	23	13	10	8	1	96.0	103	3	24	14	4-8	0	3.28
Al Mays	—	25	1	1	1	0	9.0	14	0	8	2	0-1	0	8.00
Tom Ford†	—	24	1	0	0	0	2.0	0	0	3	0	0-0	0	0.00

516 Seasons: Team Rosters

1890 St. Louis Browns 3rd AA 77-58 .570 12.5 GB

T. McCarthy (11-11)/J. Kerins (9-8)/C. Roseman (7-8)/C. Campau (26-14)/T. McCarthy (4-1)/J. Gerhardt (20-16)

Player	Gm by Position	B	Age	G	AB	R	H	2B	3B	HR	RBI	BB	SO	SB	Avg	OBP	Slg
John Munyan†	C83,OF7,2B5*	—	29	96	342	61	91	15	7	4	42	32	—	11	.266	.341	.386
Ed Cartwright	1B75	R	30	75	300	70	90	12	4	8	60	29	—	26	.300	.367	.447
Bill Higgins†	2B67	—	28	67	258	39	65	6	2	0	35	24	—	7	.252	.316	.291
Charlie Duffee	OF66,3B33,SS1	R	24	98	378	68	104	11	7	3	54	37	—	20	.275	.344	.365
Shorty Fuller	SS130	R	22	130	526	118	146	9	9	1	40	73	—	60	.278	.377	.335
Tommy McCarthy	OF102,3B32,2B1	R	26	133	548	137	192	28	9	6	69	66	—	83	.350	.430	.467
Count Campau	OF74,1B1,3B1	L	26	75	314	68	101	9	12	9	75	26	—	36	.322	.374	.513
Chief Roseman†	OF58,1B22	R	33	80	302	47	103	26	0	2	58	30	—	7	.341	.449	.447
Tom Gettinger	OF58	L	21	58	227	31	54	7	5	3	30	20	—	8	.238	.302	.352
Jack Stivetts	P54,OF10,1B3	R	22	67	226	36	65	15	6	7	43	16	—	2	.288	.337	.500
Pete Sweeney†	2B23,3B21,1B3*	R	26	49	190	23	34	3	2	0	10	17	—	8	.179	.271	.216
Joe Gerhardt†	2B20,3B17	R	35	37	125	15	32	0	0	1	11	9	—	5	.256	.321	.280
Jake Wells	C28,OF3	R	26	30	105	17	25	3	0	0	12	10	—	1	.238	.333	.267
Dusty Miller	OF24,SS3	L	21	26	96	17	21	5	3	1	10	8	—	4	.219	.279	.365
Billy Hart	P26,OF1	—	24	27	78	7	15	1	0	1	8	9	—	1	.192	.292	.244
Billy Earle	C18,OF3,2B1*	R	22	22	73	16	17	3	1	0	12	7	—	6	.233	.317	.301
Jumbo Davis†	3B21	L	28	21	71	8	18	3	1	0	13	9	—	5	.254	.338	.324
Billy Klusman	2B15	R	25	15	65	9	18	4	1	1	11	1	—	1	.277	.288	.415
John Kerins	1B17,C1	R	31	18	63	8	8	2	0	0	3	8	—	2	.127	.225	.159
Pat Hartnett	1B14	—	26	14	53	6	10	2	1	0	4	6	—	1	.189	.283	.264
Mike Trost	C13,OF4	—	24	17	51	10	13	2	0	1	7	6	—	4	.255	.345	.353
Bill Whitrock	P16,OF1	—	20	16	48	7	7	3	0	0	3	2	—	0	.146	.180	.208
Jim Donnelly	3B11	R	24	11	42	11	14	0	0	0	3	8	—	5	.333	.451	.333
Ed Herr	2B7,OF4,3B1	R	28	12	41	5	9	2	1	0	1	5	—	2	.220	.347	.317
Joe Neale	P10,OF1	R	24	11	30	4	2	0	0	0	1	3	—	0	.067	.152	.067
Jerry Kane	1B5,C4	R	21	8	25	3	5	0	0	0	2	2	—	0	.200	.259	.200
Dad Meek	C4	—	23	4	16	3	5	0	0	0	1	0	—	1	.313	.313	.313
Gus Creely	SS4	—	20	4	15	0	0	0	0	0	0	0	—	1	.000	.000	.000
Ed Pabst†	OF4	—	22	4	14	1	2	0	1	0	0	0	—	0	.143	.143	.286
Joe Burke	3B2	—	—	2	6	3	4	0	0	0	2	1	—	0	.667	.750	.667
John Adams	C1	—	—	1	4	0	1	0	0	0	0	0	—	0	.250	.250	.250
Frank Millard	2B1	—	24	1	1	0	0	0	0	0	0	1	—	0	.000	.500	.000

J. Munyan, 3 G at 3B, 1 G at SS; P. Sweeney, 2 G at OF; B. Earle, 1 G at 3B, 1 G at SS

Pitcher	T	Age	G	GS	CG	ShO	IP	H	HR	BB	SO	W-L	Sv	ERA
Jack Stivetts	R	22	54	46	41	3	419.1	399	14	179	289	27-21	0	3.52
Toad Ramsey	L	25	44	40	34	1	348.2	325	10	102	257	24-17	0	3.69
Billy Hart	—	24	26	24	20	0	201.1	188	6	66	95	12-8	0	3.67
Bill Whitrock	R	20	16	11	10	0	105.0	104	2	40	39	5-6	1	3.51
Joe Neale	R	24	10	9	8	0	69.0	53	4	15	23	5-3	0	3.39
Elton Chamberlin†	R	22	5	5	3	0	35.0	47	1	26	14	3-1	0	5.91
George Nicol	L	19	3	3	2	0	17.0	11	1	19	16	2-1	0	4.76

1890 Toledo Maumees 4th AA 68-64 .515 20.0 GB

Charlie Morton

Player	Gm by Position	B	Age	G	AB	R	H	2B	3B	HR	RBI	BB	SO	SB	Avg	OBP	Slg
Harry Sage	C80,OF1	R	26	81	275	40	41	8	4	2	25	29	—	10	.149	.235	.229
Perry Werden	1B124,OF5	R	24	128	498	113	147	22	20	6	72	78	—	59	.295	.404	.456
Parson Nicholson	2B134,C1	—	27	134	523	78	140	16	11	4	72	42	—	46	.268	.333	.363
Billy Alvord	3B116	—	26	116	495	69	135	13	16	2	52	22	—	21	.273	.304	.376
Frank Scheibeck	SS134	R	25	134	485	72	117	13	5	1	49	76	—	57	.241	.350	.295
Ed Swartwood	OF126,P1	L	31	126	462	106	151	23	11	3	64	80	—	53	.327	.444	.444
Bill Van Dyke	OF110,3B18,2B2*	R	26	129	502	74	129	14	11	2	54	25	—	73	.257	.296	.341
W. Wings Tebeau	OF94,P1	R	28	94	381	71	102	16	10	1	36	51	—	55	.268	.359	.370
Charlie Sprague	OF40,P19	L	25	55	199	25	47	5	6	1	19	16	—	10	.236	.303	.337
Egyptian Healy	P46,1B2	R	23	48	156	27	34	7	4	1	10	15	—	7	.218	.307	.333
Fred Smith	P35,OF3	L	27	38	126	11	21	7	1	0	10	8	—	4	.167	.222	.238
Emmett Rogers	C34,OF1	S	25	35	110	18	19	3	3	0	7	14	—	2	.173	.266	.255
Tub Welsh	C25,1B10	—	23	35	108	15	31	3	1	1	14	8	—	7	.287	.358	.361
John Peltz†	OF20	R	29	20	73	8	18	2	2	0	13	3	—	7	.247	.286	.329
Jon Sneed†	OF9	—	—	9	30	3	6	0	0	0	4	8	—	5	.200	.368	.200
Floyd Ritter	C1	R	20	1	3	0	0	0	0	0	0	0	—	0	.000	.000	.000

B. Van Dyke, 1 G at C

Pitcher	T	Age	G	GS	CG	ShO	IP	H	HR	BB	SO	W-L	Sv	ERA
Egyptian Healy	R	23	46	46	44	2	389.0	326	5	127	225	22-21	0	2.89
Ed Cushman	L	38	40	38	34	0	315.2	346	5	107	125	17-21	1	4.19
Fred Smith	R	27	35	34	31	2	286.0	273	13	90	116	19-13	0	3.27
Charlie Sprague	L	25	19	12	9	0	122.2	111	0	78	59	9-5	0	3.89
Ed O'Neil†	R	31	2	2	2	0	16.0	27	0	13	2	0-2	0	7.88
Babe Doty	R	22	1	1	1	0	9.0	9	0	1	4	1-0	0	1.00
Dan Abbott	R	28	3	1	1	0	13.0	19	0	8	1	0-2	1	6.23
W. Wings Tebeau	R	28	1	0	0	0	5.0	9	0	5	0	0-0	0	9.00
Ed Swartwood	R	31	1	0	0	0	3.0	2	0	0	1	0-0	0	3.00

1890 Rochester Hop Bitters 5th AA 63-63 .500 22.0 GB

Pat Powers

Player	Gm by Position	B	Age	G	AB	R	H	2B	3B	HR	RBI	BB	SO	SB	Avg	OBP	Slg
Deacon McGuire	C71,1B15,OF3*	R	26	87	331	46	99	16	4	4	53	21	—	8	.299	.356	.408
Tom O'Brien	1B68,2B8	R	30	73	273	36	52	6	5	0	31	30	—	6	.190	.273	.249
Bill Greenwood	2B123,SS1	S	33	124	437	76	97	11	6	2	41	48	—	40	.222	.310	.288
Jimmy Knowles	3B123	—	31	123	491	83	138	12	8	5	84	59	—	55	.281	.359	.369
Marr Phillips	SS64	R	33	64	257	18	53	8	0	0	34	16	—	10	.206	.261	.237
Harry Lyons	OF132,3B2,P1*	R	24	133	584	83	152	11	11	3	58	27	—	47	.260	.294	.332
Ted Scheffler	OF119,C1	R	26	119	445	111	109	12	6	3	34	78	—	77	.245	.374	.319
Sandy Griffin	OF107,2B1	R	31	107	407	85	125	28	4	5	53	50	—	21	.307	.388	.432
Dave McKeough	C47,SS13,2B2*	—	26	62	218	38	49	5	0	0	20	29	—	14	.225	.316	.248
John Grim	SS21,C15,3B8*	R	22	50	192	30	51	6	9	2	34	7	—	14	.266	.299	.422
Jim Field	1B51,P2	—	27	52	188	30	38	7	5	4	25	21	—	8	.202	.309	.356
Will Callahan	P37,OF12	—	21	48	159	16	23	4	2	1	14	8	—	2	.145	.186	.214
Leo Smith	SS35	—	31	35	112	11	21	1	3	0	11	14	—	1	.188	.283	.250
Dan Burke†	OF29,C4,1B2	R	21	32	102	14	22	1	0	0	9	17	—	2	.216	.333	.225
Cannonball Titcomb	P20,2B1,3B1	L	23	21	75	3	8	0	1	0	6	3	—	0	.107	.141	.133
Bob Miller	P13,OF3	—	28	15	40	3	6	1	0	0	2	3	—	0	.150	.209	.175
Phil Reccius	OF1	—	28	1	4	0	0	0	0	0	1	0	—	0	.000	.000	.000

D. McGuire, 1 G at P; H. Lyons, 1 G at C; D. McKeough, 1 G at 3B; J. Grim, 4 G at 2B, 3 G at OF, 2 G at 1B, 1 G at P

Pitcher	T	Age	G	GS	CG	ShO	IP	H	HR	BB	SO	W-L	Sv	ERA
Bob Barr	R	33	57	54	52	3	493.1	458	7	219	209	28-24	0	3.25
Will Callahan	—	21	37	36	31	0	296.1	276	4	125	127	18-15	0	3.28
Cannonball Titcomb	L	23	20	19	19	1	168.2	168	6	97	73	10-9	0	3.74
Bob Miller	—	28	13	12	11	0	92.1	89	2	26	20	3-7	1	4.29
John Fitzgerald	—	—	11	11	8	1	78.0	77	0	45	35	3-8	0	4.04
Jim Field	—	27	2	1	1	0	9.2	7	0	4	2	1-0	1	2.79
Henry Blauvelt	—	17	2	0	0	0	12.1	19	0	8	5	0-0	0	10.22
Deacon McGuire	R	26	1	0	0	0	4.0	10	0	1	1	0-0	0	6.75
Harry Lyons	R	24	1	0	0	0	3.2	8	0	1	2	0-0	0	12.27
John Grim	R	22	1	0	0	0	3.1	3	0	4	3	0-0	0	0.00

1890 Baltimore Orioles 6th AA 15-19 .441 49.0 GB

Billy Barnie

Player	Gm by Position	B	Age	G	AB	R	H	2B	3B	HR	RBI	BB	SO	SB	Avg	OBP	Slg
George Townsend	C18	R	23	18	67	6	16	4	1	0	9	4	—	3	.239	.282	.328
Tom Power	1B26,2B12	—	—	38	125	11	26	3	1	0	6	13	—	6	.208	.293	.248
Reddy Mack	2B26	—	24	26	95	14	27	3	5	0	11	10	—	7	.284	.370	.421
Pete Gilbert	3B29	—	22	29	100	25	28	2	1	1	18	10	—	12	.280	.363	.350
Irv Ray	SS38	L	26	38	139	28	50	6	2	1	20	15	—	11	.360	.433	.453
Joe Sommer†	OF38	R	31	38	129	13	33	4	2	0	23	13	—	10	.256	.324	.318
Bill Johnson	OF24	L	27	24	95	15	28	2	3	0	6	7	—	8	.295	.350	.379
Dan Long	OF21	—	22	21	77	19	12	0	0	0	2	14	—	16	.156	.301	.156
Pop Tate	C11,1B8	R	29	19	71	7	13	1	1	0	6	4	—	3	.183	.284	.225
Curt Welch†	OF17,1B2	R	28	19	68	16	9	4	0	0	5	9	—	8	.132	.253	.191
Wilbert Robinson†	C11,1B3	R	27	14	48	7	13	1	0	0	4	3	—	1	.271	.314	.292
Joe McGuckin	OF11	—	28	11	37	2	4	0	0	0	2	6	—	3	.108	.250	.108
Belden Hill	3B9	R	25	9	30	3	5	2	0	0	2	3	—	6	.167	.306	.233
Mike O'Rourke	P5,OF3	—	—	8	26	5	3	1	0	0	1	5	—	0	.115	.258	.154

Pitcher	T	Age	G	GS	CG	ShO	IP	H	HR	BB	SO	W-L	Sv	ERA
Les German	R	21	17	16	15	0	132.1	147	2	54	37	5-11	0	4.83
Sadie McMahon†	R	22	12	11	11	1	99.0	84	1	33	66	7-3	0	3.00
Mike O'Rourke	—	—	5	5	5	0	41.0	45	0	10	8	1-2	0	3.95
Mike Morrison†	R	23	4	4	3	0	26.0	15	0	20	13	1-2	0	3.81
Norm Baker	—	27	2	2	2	0	17.0	16	0	6	10	1-1	0	3.71

1890 Syracuse Stars 7th AA 55-72 .433 30.5 GB

George Frazer (31-40)/Wally Fessenden (4-7)/George Frazer (20-25)

Player	Gm by Position	B	Age	G	AB	R	H	2B	3B	HR	RBI	BB	SO	SB	Avg	OBP	Slg
Grant Briggs	C46,OF33,3B5*	—	25	86	316	44	57	6	5	0	21	16	—	7	.180	.222	.231
Mox McQuery	1B122	—	29	122	461	64	142	17	6	2	55	53	—	26	.308	.383	.384
Cupid Childs	2B125,SS1	L	22	126	493	109	170	33	14	2	89	72	—	56	.345	.434	.481
Tim O'Rourke	3B87	L	26	87	332	48	94	13	6	1	46	36	—	22	.283	.360	.367
Barney McLaughlin	SS86	R	33	86	329	43	87	8	1	2	40	47	—	13	.264	.360	.313
Rasty Wright†	OF88	L	27	88	348	82	106	10	6	0	27	69	—	30	.305	.428	.368
Bones Ely	OF78,SS36,1B4*	R	27	119	496	72	130	16	6	0	64	31	—	44	.262	.308	.319
Pat Friel	OF62	S	30	62	261	51	65	8	2	3	21	17	—	34	.249	.302	.330
Dan Casey	P45,OF1	R	27	46	160	11	26	5	2	0	11	6	—	3	.163	.198	.219
Hank Simon†	OF38	R	27	38	156	33	47	5	3	2	23	17	—	12	.301	.370	.410
Tom O'Rourke†	C40,1B1	—	24	41	153	16	33	8	0	0	12	12	—	2	.216	.277	.268
Mike Dorgan	OF33	R	36	33	139	19	30	8	0	0	18	16	—	8	.216	.301	.273
Mike Morrison†	P17,OF16,SS1	R	23	34	120	17	29	3	4	1	12	6	—	3	.242	.278	.358
Joe Battin	3B29	R	38	29	119	15	25	2	1	0	13	8	—	8	.210	.260	.244
Herman Pitz†	C27,SS1,OF1	—	24	29	95	17	21	0	0	0	3	13	—	14	.221	.321	.221
Pat Dealy	C10,3B6,OF2	R	—	18	66	9	12	1	0	0	4	5	—	4	.182	.250	.197
George Proeser	OF13	L	26	13	53	11	13	1	1	1	6	10	—	1	.245	.365	.358
Ducky Hemp†	OF9	—	22	9	33	1	5	1	0	0	1	0	—	1	.152	.176	.182
John Leighton	OF7	—	28	7	27	6	8	2	0	0	0	3	—	2	.296	.367	.370
Bill Sullivan	P6,OF1	R	21	6	22	2	2	0	0	0	1	1	—	0	.091	.130	.091
Dan Burke†	C9	R	21	9	20	1	0	0	0	0	0	5	—	0	.000	.231	.000
John Peltz†	OF5	R	29	5	17	2	3	1	1	0	2	3	—	0	.176	.300	.353
Louis Graff	C1	—	23	1	5	0	2	1	0	0	3	0	—	0	.400	.400	.600
Bill Higgins†	2B1	—	28	1	4	1	1	1	0	0	1	0	—	0	.250	.250	.500

G. Briggs, 4 G at SS; B. Ely, 2 G at 2B, 1 G at P, 1 G at 3B

Pitcher	T	Age	G	GS	CG	ShO	IP	H	HR	BB	SO	W-L	Sv	ERA
Dan Casey	L	27	45	42	40	2	360.2	365	8	165	169	19-22	0	4.14
John Keefe	L	22	43	41	36	2	352.1	355	9	148	120	17-24	0	4.32
Mike Morrison†	R	23	17	14	13	1	127.0	131	4	81	69	6-9	0	5.88
Ed Mars	—	23	16	14	14	0	121.1	132	2	49	59	9-5	0	4.67
Bill Sullivan	R	21	6	6	4	0	42.0	51	2	27	13	1-4	0	7.93
C. McCullough†	R	23	3	3	3	0	26.0	29	1	14	8	1-2	0	7.27
Toby Lyons	—	21	3	3	2	0	22.1	40	1	21	6	0-2	0	10.48
Ezra Lincoln†	L	21	3	3	2	0	20.0	33	1	4	6	0-3	0	10.35
Frank Keffer	—	—	2	1	1	0	16.0	15	0	9	4	1-1	0	5.63
Bones Ely	R	27	1	0	0	0	2.0	7	0	0	0	0-0	0	22.50

1890 Philadelphia Athletics 8th AA 54-78 .409 34.0 GB

Bill Sharsig

Player	Gm by Position	B	Age	G	AB	R	H	2B	3B	HR	RBI	BB	SO	SB	Avg	OBP	Slg
Wilbert Robinson†	C82	R	27	82	329	32	78	13	4	4	42	16	—	20	.237	.279	.337
Jack O'Brien	1B109,C1,OF1	R	30	109	433	80	113	24	14	4	80	52	—	31	.261	.356	.409
Taylor Shaffer	2B69	—	19	69	261	28	45	3	4	0	21	28	—	19	.172	.258	.215
Denny Lyons	3B88	R	24	88	339	79	120	29	5	7	73	57	—	21	.354	.461	.531
Ben Conroy	SS74,2B42,OF1	—	19	117	404	45	69	13	1	0	21	45	—	17	.171	.262	.208
Blondie Purcell	OF110	R	36	110	463	110	128	28	3	2	59	43	—	48	.276	.343	.363
Curt Welch†	OF103,P1	R	28	103	396	100	106	21	4	2	40	49	—	64	.268	.392	.356
Orator Shaffer	OF98,1B3	L	38	100	390	55	110	15	5	1	58	47	—	29	.282	.367	.354
Joe Kappel	OF23,SS18,3B11*	R	33	56	208	29	50	8	1	1	22	20	—	12	.240	.310	.303
Sadie McMahon†	P48,1B1	R	22	49	175	27	40	5	1	2	19	7	—	2	.229	.266	.303
Ed Green	P25,3B10,SS3*	—	40	39	126	15	15	1	1	0	5	13	—	7	.119	.218	.143
George Carman	SS15,OF10,2B2*	—	24	28	97	9	17	2	0	0	7	8	—	5	.175	.245	.196
Kid Baldwin†	C19,3B5	R	25	24	90	5	21	1	2	0	12	4	—	2	.233	.274	.289
John Riddle	C13,OF12,2B2*	R	26	27	85	7	7	0	1	0	2	17	—	4	.082	.243	.106
Andy Knox	1B21	R	26	21	75	6	19	3	0	0	8	9	—	5	.253	.333	.293
Joe Daly	OF14,C9	—	21	21	75	8	21	4	1	0	7	3	—	1	.280	.308	.360
Ed Seward	P21,OF6	—	23	26	72	7	10	4	0	0	2	8	—	3	.139	.244	.194
Henry Easterday†	SS19	R	25	19	68	17	10	1	0	1	3	10	—	4	.147	.256	.206
Pete Sweeney†	2B9,OF4,3B2	R	26	14	49	5	8	1	1	0	0	7	—	0	.163	.281	.224
Al Sauters	3B11,2B2,OF2	—	—	14	41	1	4	0	0	0	0	11	—	0	.098	.288	.098
Charles Snyder	C5,OF5	R	—	9	33	5	9	1	0	0	4	2	—	0	.273	.314	.303
Ed O'Neil†	P6,OF3,3B1	—	31	10	31	0	5	0	0	0	2	3	—	0	.161	.235	.161
Charlie Stecher	P10,3B1	—	—	10	29	3	7	0	1	0	0	1	—	0	.241	.290	.310
Ed Pabst†	OF8	—	22	8	25	7	10	2	0	0	3	5	—	3	.400	.500	.480
Bart Cantz	C5	—	30	5	22	1	1	0	0	0	1	0	—	0	.045	.045	.045
Jim Whitney	P6,OF1	L	32	7	21	3	5	0	0	0	1	1	—	0	.238	.273	.238
Henry Meyers	3B5	—	30	5	19	2	3	0	0	0	1	1	—	2	.158	.238	.158
George Crawford	OF4,SS1	—	—	5	17	1	2	0	0	0	3	0	—	1	.118	.118	.118
Mickey Hughes†	P6,OF1	—	23	6	16	2	2	0	0	0	1	2	—	2	.125	.222	.125
Dennis Fitzgerald	SS2	—	25	2	8	0	2	0	0	0	0	0	—	0	.250	.250	.250
Pete Hasney	OF2	—	25	2	7	1	1	0	0	0	0	1	—	0	.143	.250	.143
Sam Campbell	2B2	—	—	2	5	0	0	0	0	0	0	1	—	0	.000	.167	.000
Bob Stafford	OF1	—	18	1	2	0	0	0	0	0	0	0	—	0	.000	.000	.000
John McBride	OF1	—	—	1	2	0	0	0	0	0	0	0	—	0	.000	.000	.000
Ham Sweigert	OF1	—	—	1	1	0	0	0	0	0	0	1	—	1	.000	.500	.000
— Macey	C1	—	—	1	1	0	0	0	0	0	0	0	—	0	.000	.000	.000
Bill Collins	SS1	R	27	1	1	0	0	0	0	0	0	0	—	0	.000	.000	.000

J. Kappel, 3 G at C, 2 G at 2B; E. Green, 2 G at 2B; G. Carman, 1 G at 3B; J. Riddle, 1 G at 3B

Pitcher	T	Age	G	GS	CG	ShO	IP	H	HR	BB	SO	W-L	Sv	ERA
Sadie McMahon†	R	22	48	46	44	0	410.0	414	5	133	225	29-18	1	3.34
Ed Green	—	40	25	22	20	1	191.0	267	4	94	56	7-15	1	5.80
Ed Seward	R	23	21	19	15	1	154.0	165	4	72	55	6-12	0	4.73
Duke Esper†	L	21	18	16	14	1	143.2	176	1	67	61	8-9	0	4.89
Charlie Stecher	—	—	10	10	9	0	68.0	111	1	60	18	0-10	0	10.32
Ed O'Neil†	R	31	6	6	6	0	52.0	84	0	32	17	0-6	0	9.69
Mickey Hughes†	R	23	6	5	4	0	41.1	64	0	21	15	1-3	0	5.44
Jim Whitney	R	32	6	4	3	0	40.0	61	1	11	6	2-2	0	5.18
Bill Price	—	—	1	1	1	0	9.0	6	0	7	1	1-0	0	2.00
Harry Stine	L	26	1	1	1	0	8.0	17	0	4	1	0-1	0	9.00
Horace Helmbold	—	22	1	1	1	0	7.0	17	0	6	3	0-1	0	14.14
John Sterling	—	—	1	1	1	0	5.0	16	1	4	1	0-1	0	21.60
— Lackey	—	—	1	0	0	0	2.0	1	0	3	1	0-0	0	9.00
Curt Welch	R	28	1	0	0	0	1.0	6	0	0	1	0-0	0	54.00

1890 Brooklyn Gladiators 9th AA 26-72 .265 45.0 GB

Jim Kennedy

Player	Gm by Position	B	Age	G	AB	R	H	2B	3B	HR	RBI	BB	SO	SB	Avg	OBP	Slg
Jim Toy	C44	R	32	44	160	11	29	3	0	0	7	11	—	2	.181	.238	.200
Billy O'Brien	1B96	R	30	96	388	47	108	25	8	4	67	28	—	5	.278	.332	.415
Joe Gerhardt†	2B99	R	35	99	369	34	75	10	4	2	40	30	—	9	.203	.270	.268
Jumbo Davis†	3B38	L	28	38	142	33	43	6	1	2	28	15	—	10	.303	.385	.437
Candy Nelson	SS57,OF4	L	41	60	223	44	56	3	2	0	12	35	—	12	.251	.365	.283
John Peltz†	OF98	R	29	98	384	55	87	9	6	1	33	32	—	10	.227	.289	.289
Hank Simon†	OF89	R	27	89	373	66	96	17	11	0	38	34	—	23	.257	.323	.362
Ed Daily†	OF64,P27	R	27	91	394	68	94	15	7	1	39	24	—	49	.239	.284	.320
Frank Bowes	C25,OF19,3B13*	—	25	61	232	28	53	5	2	0	24	7	—	11	.220	.246	.259
Herman Pitz†	C34,3B16,OF9*	—	24	61	189	26	26	0	0	0	6	45	—	25	.138	.312	.138
Frank Fennelly	SS38,3B7	R	30	45	178	40	44	8	3	2	18	30	—	6	.247	.356	.360
Mike Mattimore	P19,OF14	L	31	33	129	14	17	1	1	0	7	16	—	11	.132	.238	.155
Fred Siefke	3B16	—	20	16	58	1	8	2	0	0	3	5	—	2	.138	.206	.172
Con Murphy†	P12,OF5	—	26	16	50	4	9	2	0	1	0	3	—	0	.180	.241	.280
Pat O'Connell		L	29	11	40	7	9	2	1	0	3	7	—	3	.225	.340	.325
Tom Ford†	P7,SS4	—	24	10	30	1	1	0	0	0	0	1	—	1	.033	.065	.033
Hi Church	OF3	—	26	3	9	1	1	0	0	0	0	0	—	0	.111	.111	.111

F. Bowes, 3 G at 1B, 2 G at SS; H. Pitz, 2 G at SS, 1 G at 2B

Pitcher	T	Age	G	GS	CG	ShO	IP	H	HR	BB	SO	W-L	Sv	ERA
Ed Daily†	R	27	27	27	27	0	235.2	252	3	93	82	10-15	0	4.05
C. McCullough†	R	23	26	25	24	0	215.2	247	5	102	61	4-21	0	4.59
Mike Mattimore	L	31	19	19	19	0	178.1	201	3	76	33	6-13	0	4.54
Con Murphy†	R	26	12	12	10	0	96.0	121	6	46	26	3-9	0	5.72
Steve Toole	L	31	6	6	6	0	53.1	47	0	39	10	2-4	0	4.05
Tom Ford†	—	24	7	6	6	0	49.0	70	2	32	12	0-6	0	5.14
Jim Powers	—	22	4	2	2	0	30.0	38	1	16	3	1-2	0	5.70
Gus Williams	—	20	2	2	1	0	12.0	13	0	12	2	0-1	0	7.50
Jack Lynch	R	33	1	1	1	0	9.0	22	1	5	1	0-1	0	12.00

»1890 Boston Red Stockings 1st PL 81-48 .628 —

King Kelly

Player	Gm by Position	B	Age	G	AB	R	H	2B	3B	HR	RBI	BB	SO	SB	Avg	OBP	Slg
Morgan Murphy	C67,SS2,3B1*	R	23	68	246	38	56	10	2	2	32	24	31	16	.228	.301	.309
Dan Brouthers	1B123	L	32	123	460	117	152	36	9	1	97	99	17	28	.330	.466	.454
Joe Quinn	2B130	R	25	130	509	87	153	19	8	7	82	44	24	29	.301	.359	.411
Billy Nash	3B129,P1	R	25	129	488	103	130	28	6	5	90	88	43	26	.266	.383	.379
Arthur Irwin	SS96	L	32	96	354	60	92	17	1	0	45	57	29	16	.260	.364	.314
Tom Brown	OF128	L	29	128	543	146	150	23	14	4	61	86	84	79	.276	.378	.392
Hardy Richardson	OF124,SS6,1B1	R	35	130	555	126	181	26	14	13	146	52	46	42	.326	.384	.494
Harry Stovey	OF117,1B1	R	33	118	481	142	143	25	11	12	85	81	38	97	.297	.404	.470
King Kelly	C56,SS27,OF6*	R	32	89	340	83	111	18	6	4	66	52	22	51	.326	.419	.450
Old Hoss Radbourn	P41,OF4,1B1	R	35	45	154	20	39	6	0	0	16	9	20	7	.253	.299	.292
Ad Gumbert	P39,OF7	R	21	44	145	23	35	7	1	3	20	18	26	5	.241	.333	.366
Bill Daley	P34,OF3	—	22	37	110	14	17	1	0	2	7	9	15	1	.155	.225	.218
Pop Swett	C34,OF3	—	20	37	94	16	18	4	3	1	12	16	26	4	.191	.321	.330
Matt Kilroy	P30,OF2,3B1*	L	24	31	93	11	20	1	1	0	8	12	9	11	.215	.305	.247
Kid Madden	P10,OF2,SS1	—	22	13	38	5	7	2	0	0	4	3	3	0	.184	.244	.237
Dick Johnston†	OF2	R	27	2	9	0	1	0	0	0	0	0	1	0	.111	.111	.111
John Morrill	1B1,SS1	R	35	2	7	1	1	0	0	0	2	2	1	0	.143	.333	.143

M. Murphy, 1 G at OF; K. Kelly, 4 G at 1B, 2 G at 3B, 1 G at P; M. Kilroy, 1 G at SS

Pitcher	T	Age	G	GS	CG	ShO	IP	H	HR	BB	SO	W-L	Sv	ERA
Old Hoss Radbourn	R	35	41	38	36	1	343.0	352	8	100	80	27-12	0	3.31
Ad Gumbert	R	21	39	33	27	1	277.1	338	18	86	81	23-12	0	3.96
Matt Kilroy	L	24	30	27	18	0	217.2	268	14	87	48	9-15	0	4.26
Bill Daley	L	22	34	25	19	2	235.0	246	7	167	110	18-7	2	3.60
Kid Madden	L	22	10	7	5	1	62.0	85	2	25	24	3-2	0	4.79
King Kelly	R	32	1	0	0	0	2.0	1	0	2	2	1-0	0	4.50
Billy Nash	R	25	1	0	0	0	0.1	1	0	0	0	0-0	0	0.00

1890 Brooklyn Wonders 2nd PL 76-56 .576 6.5 GB

Monte Ward

Player	Gm by Position	B	Age	G	AB	R	H	2B	3B	HR	RBI	BB	SO	SB	Avg	OBP	Slg
Tom Kinslow	C64	R	24	64	242	30	64	11	6	4	46	10	22	2	.264	.299	.409
Dave Orr	1B107	R	30	107	464	89	173	32	13	6	124	30	11	10	.373	.416	.537
Lou Bierbauer	2B133	L	24	133	589	128	180	31	11	7	99	40	15	16	.306	.350	.431
Bill Joyce	3B133	L	24	133	489	121	123	18	18	1	78	123	77	43	.252	.413	.368
Monte Ward	SS128	L	30	128	561	134	189	15	12	4	60	51	22	63	.337	.394	.428
Jack McGeachey	OF104	R	26	104	443	84	108	24	4	1	65	19	12	21	.244	.278	.323
Emmett Seery	OF104	L	29	104	394	78	88	12	7	1	50	70	36	44	.223	.348	.297
Ed Andrews	OF94	R	31	94	395	84	100	12	2	3	38	40	32	21	.253	.323	.322
George Van Haltren	OF67,P28,SS3	L	24	92	376	84	126	8	9	5	54	41	23	35	.335	.405	.444
Paul Cook	C36,1B21,OF1	R	27	58	218	32	55	3	3	0	31	14	18	7	.252	.303	.294
Con Daily	C40,1B6,OF1	L	25	46	168	20	42	6	3	0	35	15	14	6	.250	.315	.321
John Sowders	P39,OF3	R	23	40	132	14	25	3	0	1	20	10	12	0	.189	.246	.235
Art Sunday	OF24	L	28	24	83	26	22	5	1	0	13	15	9	0	.265	.419	.349
Con Murphy†	P20,OF3	—	26	24	69	11	15	2	0	0	7	5	7	1	.217	.280	.246
George Hemming†	P19,OF1	R	21	19	57	5	9	0	1	0	8	1	11	1	.158	.172	.193
Jackie Hayes	OF6,SS3,C2*	—	29	12	42	3	8	0	0	0	5	2	4	0	.190	.227	.190

J. Hayes, 1 G at 3B

Pitcher	T	Age	G	GS	CG	ShO	IP	H	HR	BB	SO	W-L	Sv	ERA
Gus Weyhing	R	23	49	46	38	3	390.0	419	10	179	177	30-16	0	3.60
John Sowders	L	23	39	37	28	1	309.0	358	3	161	91	19-16	0	3.82
George Van Haltren	L	24	28	25	23	0	223.0	272	8	89	48	15-10	2	4.28
Con Murphy†	R	26	20	14	11	0	139.0	168	2	82	29	4-10	2	4.79
George Hemming†	R	21	19	11	11	0	123.0	117	3	59	32	8-4	3	3.80

1890 New York Giants 3rd PL 74-57 .565 8.0 GB

Buck Ewing

Player	Gm by Position	B	Age	G	AB	R	H	2B	3B	HR	RBI	BB	SO	SB	Avg	OBP	Slg
Buck Ewing	C81,P1,2B1	R	30	83	352	98	119	19	15	8	72	39	12	36	.338	.406	.545
Roger Connor	1B123	L	32	123	484	133	169	24	15	14	103	88	32	22	.349	.450	.548
Dan Shannon†	2B77,SS6	—	25	83	324	59	70	7	8	3	44	25	34	21	.216	.274	.315
Art Whitney	3B88,SS31	R	32	119	442	71	97	12	3	0	45	64	19	8	.219	.322	.260
Danny Richardson	SS68,2B56	R	27	123	528	102	135	12	9	4	80	37	19	37	.256	.307	.335
Jim O'Rourke	OF111	R	39	111	478	112	172	37	5	9	115	33	20	23	.360	.410	.515
Mike Slattery	OF97	L	23	97	411	80	126	20	11	5	67	27	25	18	.307	.352	.445
George Gore	OF93	L	33	93	399	132	127	26	8	10	55	77	23	28	.318	.432	.499
Dick Johnston†	OF76,SS2	R	27	77	306	37	74	9	7	1	43	18	25	7	.242	.288	.327
Gil Hatfield	3B42,SS27,P3*	—	35	71	287	32	80	13	6	2	37	17	19	12	.279	.328	.387
Willard Brown	C34,OF13,1B9*	R	24	60	230	47	64	8	4	4	43	13	13	5	.278	.320	.400
Farmer Vaughn	C30,OF12,2B1*	R	26	44	166	27	44	7	0	1	22	10	9	6	.265	.307	.325
Fred Dunlap†	2B1	R	31	1	4	1	2	0	0	0	0	0	0	0	.500	.500	.500

G. Hatfield, 1 G at OF; W. Brown, 3 G at 3B, 2 G at 2B; F. Vaughn, 1 G at 3B

Pitcher	T	Age	G	GS	CG	ShO	IP	H	HR	BB	SO	W-L	Sv	ERA
Ed Crane	R	28	43	35	28	0	330.1	323	12	210	117	16-19	0	4.63
Hank O'Day	R	27	43	35	32	1	329.0	356	11	163	94	22-13	3	4.21
John Ewing	R	27	35	31	27	1	267.1	293	6	104	145	18-12	2	4.24
Tim Keefe	R	33	30	30	23	1	229.0	228	6	85	88	17-11	0	3.38
Buck Ewing	R	30	1	1	1	0	9.0	11	1	3	2	0-1	0	4.00
Gil Hatfield	R	35	3	0	0	0	7.2	8	1	4	3	1-1	1	3.52

1890 Chicago Pirates 4th PL 75-62 .547 10.0 GB

Charlie Comiskey

Player	Gm by Position	B	Age	G	AB	R	H	2B	3B	HR	RBI	BB	SO	SB	Avg	OBP	Slg
Duke Farrell	C90,1B22,OF10	S	23	117	451	79	131	21	12	2	84	42	28	8	.290	.352	.404
Charlie Comiskey	1B88	R	30	88	377	53	92	11	3	0	59	14	17	34	.244	.277	.289
Fred Pfeffer	2B124	R	30	124	499	86	128	21	8	5	80	44	23	27	.257	.319	.361
Ned Williamson	3B52,SS21	R	32	73	261	34	51	7	3	2	26	36	35	3	.195	.311	.268
Charlie Bastian	SS64,2B12,3B4	R	29	80	283	38	54	10	5	0	29	33	37	4	.191	.287	.261
Hugh Duffy	OF137	R	23	138	596	161	191	36	16	7	82	59	20	78	.320	.384	.470
Tip O'Neill	OF137	R	32	137	577	112	174	20	16	3	75	65	36	29	.302	.377	.407
Jimmy Ryan	OF118	R	27	118	486	99	165	32	5	6	89	60	36	30	.340	.416	.463
Jack Boyle	C50,3B30,SS16*	R	24	100	369	56	96	9	5	1	49	44	29	11	.260	.347	.320
Dell Darling	1B29,SS15,C9*	R	28	58	221	45	57	12	4	2	39	29	28	5	.258	.352	.376
Arlie Latham†	3B52	R	30	52	214	47	49	7	2	1	20	22	22	32	.229	.310	.294
Silver King	P56,1B1,OF1	R	22	58	185	24	31	2	5	1	16	13	22	3	.168	.222	.249
Frank Shugart	SS25,OF5	S	23	29	106	8	20	5	5	0	15	5	13	5	.189	.232	.330
Frank Dwyer	P12,OF4	R	22	16	53	10	14	2	0	0	11	0	2	1	.264	.264	.302

J. Boyle, 7 G at 1B, 2 G at OF; D. Darling, 7 G at OF, 3 G at 2B, 1 G at 3B

Pitcher	T	Age	G	GS	CG	ShO	IP	H	HR	BB	SO	W-L	Sv	ERA
Mark Baldwin	R	26	59	57	54	1	501.0	498	10	249	211	34-24	0	3.31
Silver King	R	22	56	56	48	4	461.0	420	5	163	185	30-22	0	2.69
Charlie Bartson	—	25	25	19	16	0	188.0	222	8	66	47	8-10	1	4.26
Frank Dwyer	R	22	12	6	6	0	69.1	98	4	25	17	3-6	1	6.23

1890 Philadelphia Quakers 5th PL 68-63 .519 14.0 GB

Jim Fogarty (7-9)/Charlie Buffinton (61-54)

Player	Gm by Position	B	Age	G	AB	R	H	2B	3B	HR	RBI	BB	SO	SB	Avg	OBP	Slg
Jocko Milligan	C59,1B3	R	28	62	234	38	69	9	3	3	57	19	19	2	.295	.363	.397
Sid Farrar	1B127	—	30	127	481	84	122	17	11	1	69	51	23	9	.254	.331	.341
John Pickett	2B100	R	24	100	407	82	114	7	9	4	64	40	17	12	.280	.347	.371
Joe Mulvey	3B120	R	31	120	519	96	149	26	15	6	87	27	36	20	.287	.326	.430
Billy Shindle	SS130,3B2	R	26	132	584	127	188	21	21	10	90	40	30	51	.322	.369	.481
George Wood	OF132,3B1	L	31	132	539	115	156	20	14	9	102	51	35	20	.289	.360	.429
Mike Griffin	OF115	L	25	115	489	127	140	29	6	6	54	64	19	30	.286	.377	.407
Jim Fogarty	OF91,3B1	R	26	91	347	71	83	17	6	4	58	59	50	36	.239	.364	.357
Bill Hallman	OF34,C26,2B14*	R	23	84	356	59	95	16	7	1	37	33	24	6	.267	.338	.360
Lave Cross	C49,OF15	R	24	63	245	42	73	7	8	3	47	12	6	5	.298	.331	.429
Ben Sanders	P43,OF10	R	25	52	189	31	59	6	6	0	30	10	10	2	.312	.347	.407
Charlie Buffinton	P36,OF5,1B3	R	29	42	150	24	41	3	2	1	24	9	3	1	.273	.319	.340
Phil Knell	P35,OF2	R	25	36	132	19	29	3	3	1	18	7	17	3	.220	.264	.311
Dan Shannon†	2B19	—	25	19	75	15	18	5	1	1	16	4	12	4	.240	.278	.373
Bert Cunningham†	P14,OF1	R	24	15	52	6	6	1	1	0	3	2	11	1	.115	.148	.173

B. Hallman, 10 G at 3B, 2 G at SS

Pitcher	T	Age	G	GS	CG	ShO	IP	H	HR	BB	SO	W-L	Sv	ERA
Ben Sanders	R	25	43	40	37	2	346.2	412	13	69	107	19-18	1	3.76
Charlie Buffinton	R	29	36	33	28	0	283.1	312	8	126	89	19-15	1	3.81
Phil Knell	L	25	35	31	30	2	286.2	287	10	166	99	22-11	0	3.83
Bill Husted	—	23	18	17	12	0	129.0	148	2	67	33	5-10	0	4.88
Bert Cunningham†	R	24	14	11	11	0	108.2	133	0	67	33	3-9	0	5.22

1890 Pittsburgh Burghers 6th PL 60-68 .469 20.5 GB

Ned Hanlon

Player	Gm by Position	B	Age	G	AB	R	H	2B	3B	HR	RBI	BB	SO	SB	Avg	OBP	Slg
Fred Carroll	C56,OF49,1B7	R	25	111	416	95	124	20	7	2	71	75	22	35	.298	.418	.394
Jake Beckley	1B121	L	22	121	516	109	167	38	22	9	120	42	32	18	.324	.381	.535
Yank Robinson	2B98	R	30	98	306	59	70	10	3	0	38	101	33	17	.229	.434	.281
Bill Kuehne	3B126	R	31	126	528	66	126	21	12	5	73	28	37	21	.239	.277	.352
Tommy Corcoran	SS123	R	21	123	503	80	117	14	13	1	61	38	45	43	.233	.289	.318
Joe Visner	OF127	L	30	127	521	110	138	15	22	3	71	76	44	18	.265	.367	.395
Ned Hanlon	OF118	L	32	118	472	106	131	16	6	1	44	80	24	65	.278	.389	.343
Jocko Fields	OF80,2B30,C15*	R	25	126	526	101	149	18	20	9	86	57	52	24	.283	.357	.445
Tom Quinn	C55	R	26	55	207	23	44	4	3	1	15	17	8	1	.213	.282	.275
Harry Staley	P46,OF1	R	23	47	164	25	34	3	2	1	25	13	16	0	.207	.270	.268
Al Maul	P30,OF15,SS1	R	24	45	162	31	42	6	2	0	21	22	12	5	.259	.348	.321
John Tener	P14,3B2,OF2	R	26	18	63	7	12	0	0	2	5	7	10	1	.190	.301	.286
Jerry Hurley	C7,OF1	R	27	8	22	5	6	1	0	0	2	2	5	0	.273	.333	.318
Reddy Gray†	2B2	—	—	2	9	3	2	0	0	1	3	0	2	0	.222	.222	.556

J. Fields, 4 G at SS

Pitcher	T	Age	G	GS	CG	ShO	IP	H	HR	BB	SO	W-L	Sv	ERA
Harry Staley	R	23	46	46	44	3	387.2	392	5	74	145	21-25	0	3.23
Al Maul	R	24	30	28	26	2	246.2	258	13	104	81	16-12	0	3.79
Pud Galvin	R	33	26	25	23	1	217.0	275	3	49	35	12-13	0	4.35
Ed Morris	L	27	18	15	15	1	144.1	178	5	35	25	8-7	0	4.86
John Tener	R	26	14	14	13	0	117.0	160	6	70	30	3-11	0	7.31
Al Doe†	R	26	1	0	0	0	4.0	4	0	2	2	0-0	0	4.50

1890 Cleveland Infants 7th PL 55-75 .423 26.5 GB

Henry Larkin (34-45)/Patsy Tebeau (21-30)

Player	Gm by Position	B	Age	G	AB	R	H	2B	3B	HR	RBI	BB	SO	SB	Avg	OBP	Slg
Sy Sutcliffe	C84,OF15,SS4*	L	28	99	386	62	127	14	8	2	60	33	16	10	.329	.382	.422
Henry Larkin	1B125,OF1	R	30	125	506	93	168	32	15	5	112	65	18	5	.332	.420	.484
Cub Stricker	2B109,SS20	R	31	127	544	93	133	19	8	2	65	54	16	24	.244	.318	.320
Patsy Tebeau	3B110	R	25	110	450	86	135	26	6	5	74	34	20	14	.300	.353	.418
Ed Delahanty	SS76,2B20,OF18*	R	22	115	517	107	154	26	13	3	64	24	30	25	.298	.339	.416
Pete Browning	OF118	R	29	118	493	112	184	40	8	5	93	75	36	35	.373	.459	.517
Jimmy McAleer	OF86	R	25	86	341	58	91	8	7	1	42	37	33	21	.267	.340	.340
Paul Radford	OF80,SS36,3B7*	R	28	122	466	98	136	24	12	2	62	82	28	25	.292	.406	.408
Larry Twitchell†	OF57	R	26	57	233	33	52	6	3	2	36	17	17	4	.223	.279	.300
Jack Brennan	C42,3B14,OF6	—	28	59	233	32	59	3	7	0	26	13	29	8	.253	.304	.326
Henry Gruber	P48,OF3,3B1	R	26	50	163	21	36	3	3	0	9	26	29	0	.221	.328	.276
Jersey Bakely	P43,OF1	R	26	43	138	10	28	3	0	0	9	11	28	0	.203	.267	.225
Darby O'Brien	P25,OF1	R	23	26	96	12	15	1	1	0	6	2	6	0	.156	.173	.188
John Carney†	OF19,1B6	R	23	25	89	15	31	5	3	0	21	14	5	6	.348	.442	.472
Willie McGill	P24,OF1	—	16	24	68	10	10	2	0	0	6	21	16	0	.147	.356	.176
Pop Snyder	C13	R	35	13	48	5	9	1	0	0	12	1	9	1	.188	.220	.208
Neil Stynes	C2	R	21	2	8	0	0	0	0	0	0	0	0	0	.000	.000	.000
— Budd	OF1	—	—	1	4	0	0	0	0	0	0	0	3	0	.000	.000	.000

S. Sutcliffe, 2 G at 3B; E. Delahanty, 3 G at 3B, 1 G at 1B; P. Radford, 4 G at 2B, 1 G at P

Pitcher	T	Age	G	GS	CG	ShO	IP	H	HR	BB	SO	W-L	Sv	ERA
Henry Gruber	R	26	48	44	39	1	383.1	464	15	204	110	22-23	1	4.27
Jersey Bakely	R	26	43	38	32	0	326.1	412	13	147	67	12-25	0	4.47
Darby O'Brien	R	23	25	25	22	0	206.1	229	9	93	54	8-16	0	3.40
Willie McGill	L	16	24	20	19	0	183.2	222	5	96	82	11-9	0	4.12
Charlie Dewald	L	22	2	2	2	0	14.0	13	0	5	6	2-0	0	0.64
Bill Gleason	—	22	1	1	0	0	4.0	14	1	6	0	0-1	0	27.00
George Hemming†	R	21	3	1	1	0	21.0	25	1	19	3	0-1	0	6.86
Paul Radford	R	28	1	0	0	0	5.0	7	1	1	3	0-0	0	3.60

1890 Buffalo Bisons 8th PL 36-96 .273 46.5 GB

Jack Rowe (22-58)/Jay Faatz (9-24)/Jack Rowe (5-14)

Player	Gm by Position	B	Age	G	AB	R	H	2B	3B	HR	RBI	BB	SO	SB	Avg	OBP	Slg
Connie Mack	C112,OF9,1B5	R	27	123	503	95	134	15	12	0	53	47	13	16	.266	.353	.344
Deacon White	3B64,1B57,P1*	L	42	122	439	62	114	13	4	0	47	67	30	3	.260	.381	.308
Sam Wise	2B119	L	32	119	505	95	148	29	11	6	102	46	45	19	.293	.359	.430
John Irwin	3B64,1B12,2B1	L	28	77	308	62	72	11	4	0	34	43	19	18	.234	.335	.295
Jack Rowe	SS125	L	33	125	504	77	126	22	7	2	76	48	18	10	.250	.324	.333
Ed Beecher	OF126,P1	L	29	126	536	69	159	22	10	3	90	29	23	14	.297	.341	.392
Dummy Hoy	OF122,2B1	L	28	122	493	107	147	17	8	1	53	94	36	39	.298	.418	.371
Jocko Halligan	OF43,C16	L	21	57	211	28	53	9	2	3	33	20	19	7	.251	.319	.355
Spider Clark	OF34,C14,2B13*	—	22	69	260	45	69	11	1	1	25	20	16	8	.265	.325	.327
Larry Twitchell†	OF32,P13,1B3	R	26	44	172	24	38	3	1	2	17	23	12	4	.221	.316	.285
John Rainey	OF28,SS7,3B6*	L	25	42	166	29	39	5	1	1	20	24	15	12	.235	.349	.295
George Haddock	P35,OF7	R	23	42	146	21	36	11	0	0	24	24	32	3	.247	.360	.322
Jay Faatz	1B32	R	29	32	111	18	21	0	2	1	16	9	5	2	.189	.252	.252
John Carney†	1B24,OF4	R	23	28	107	11	29	3	0	0	13	7	14	2	.271	.333	.299
Bert Cunningham†	P25,OF4	R	24	28	101	11	23	5	1	0	11	6	23	0	.228	.271	.297
General Stafford	P12,OF4	R	21	15	49	11	7	1	0	0	3	7	8	2	.143	.250	.163
Alex Ferson	P10,OF1	R	23	11	32	4	7	0	0	0	2	6	7	1	.219	.359	.219
— Lewis	P1,OF1	—	—	1	5	1	1	0	0	0	0	0	0	0	.200	.200	.200
Jim Gillespie	OF1	L	31	1	3	0	0	0	0	0	0	0	2	0	.000	.000	.000

D. White, 1 G at SS; S. Clark, 6 G at 1B, 3 G at 3B, 1 G at P, 1 G at SS; J. Rainey, 2 G at 2B

Pitcher	T	Age	G	GS	CG	ShO	IP	H	HR	BB	SO	W-L	Sv	ERA
George Haddock	R	23	35	34	31	0	290.2	366	15	149	123	9-26	0	5.76
Bert Cunningham†	R	24	25	25	24	2	211.0	251	8	134	78	9-15	0	5.84
George Keefe	L	23	25	22	22	0	196.0	280	11	138	55	6-16	0	6.52
Larry Twitchell	R	26	13	12	12	0	104.1	112	3	72	29	5-7	0	4.57
General Stafford	R	21	12	12	11	0	98.0	123	8	43	21	3-9	0	5.14
Alex Ferson	R	23	10	10	7	0	71.0	88	5	40	13	1-7	0	5.45
Lady Baldwin†	L	31	7	7	7	0	62.0	90	5	24	13	2-5	0	4.50
John Buckley	R	20	4	4	4	0	34.0	49	5	16	4	1-3	0	7.68
Gus Krock	L	24	4	3	3	0	25.0	43	1	15	5	0-3	0	6.12
Bill Duzen	R	20	2	2	2	0	13.0	20	2	14	5	0-2	0	13.85
Dan Cotter	R	23	1	1	1	0	9.0	18	1	7	0	0-1	0	14.00
Al Doe†	R	26	1	1	1	0	6.0	10	0	7	2	0-1	0	12.00
— Lewis	—	—	1	1	0	0	3.0	13	3	7	1	0-1	0	60.00
Deacon White	R	42	1	0	0	0	8.0	18	0	2	0	0-0	0	9.00
Ed Beecher	L	29	1	0	0	0	6.0	10	0	3	0	0-0	0	12.00
Spider Clark	R	22	1	0	0	0	4.0	8	0	2	2	0-0	0	6.75

»1891 Boston Beaneaters 1st NL 87-51 .630 —

Frank Selee

Player	Gm by Position	B	Age	G	AB	R	H	2B	3B	HR	RBI	BB	SO	SB	Avg	OBP	Slg
Charlie Bennett	C75	R	36	75	256	35	55	9	3	5	39	42	61	3	.215	.332	.332
Tommy Tucker	1B140,P1	S	27	140	548	103	148	16	5	2	69	37	30	26	.270	.349	.328
Joe Quinn	2B124	R	26	124	508	70	122	8	10	3	63	28	28	24	.240	.288	.313
Billy Nash	3B140	R	26	140	537	92	148	24	9	5	95	74	50	28	.276	.369	.382
Herman Long	SS139	L	25	139	577	129	163	21	12	9	75	80	51	60	.282	.377	.407
Harry Stovey	OF134,1B1	R	34	134	544	118	152	31	20	16	95	78	69	57	.279	.372	.498
Steve Brodie	OF133	L	22	133	523	84	136	13	6	2	78	63	39	25	.260	.351	.319
Bobby Lowe	OF107,2B17,SS2*	R	22	125	497	92	129	19	5	6	74	53	54	43	.260	.342	.354
Charlie Ganzel	C59,OF13	R	29	70	263	33	68	18	5	1	29	12	13	7	.259	.304	.376
John Clarkson	P55,OF1	R	29	55	187	28	42	7	4	0	26	18	51	2	.225	.293	.305
Marty Sullivan†	OF17	R	28	17	67	15	15	1	0	2	7	5	3	7	.224	.288	.328
King Kelly†	C11,OF6	R	33	16	52	7	12	1	0	0	5	6	10	6	.231	.322	.250
Joe Kelley	OF12	R	19	12	45	7	11	1	1	0	3	2	7	0	.244	.277	.311
Charlie Getzien†	P11,OF3	R	27	14	41	4	7	2	1	1	6	7	18	0	.171	.292	.341
George Rooks	OF5	R	27	5	16	1	2	0	0	0	0	4	1	0	.125	.300	.125
Fred Lake	C4,OF1	R	24	5	7	1	1	0	0	0	0	2	4	0	.143	.333	.143

B. Lowe, 1 G at P, 1 G at 3B

Pitcher	T	Age	G	GS	CG	ShO	IP	H	HR	BB	SO	W-L	Sv	ERA
John Clarkson	R	29	55	51	47	3	460.2	435	18	154	141	33-19	3	2.79
Kid Nichols	R	21	52	48	45	5	425.1	413	15	103	240	30-17	3	2.39
Harry Staley†	R	24	31	30	26	1	252.1	236	11	69	114	20-8	0	2.50
Charlie Getzien†	R	27	11	9	7	0	89.0	112	4	23	29	4-5	0	3.84
John Kiley	L	31	1	1	1	0	8.0	13	2	5	1	0-1	0	6.75
Tod Brynan	R	27	1	1	0	0	1.0	4	0	3	0	0-1	0	54.00
Cyclone Ryan	R	25	1	0	0	0	3.0	2	0	1	0	0-0	0	0.00
Bobby Lowe	R	22	1	0	0	0	1.0	3	0	1	0	0-0	0	9.00
Tommy Tucker	R	27	1	0	0	0	1.0	3	0	0	0	0-0	0	9.00
Jim Sullivan†	R	22	1	0	0	0	0.1	2	0	5	0	0-0	0	81.00

1891 Chicago Colts 2nd NL 82-53 .607 3.5 GB

Cap Anson

Player	Gm by Position	B	Age	G	AB	R	H	2B	3B	HR	RBI	BB	SO	SB	Avg	OBP	Slg
Malachi Kittridge	C79	R	21	79	296	26	62	8	5	2	27	17	28	4	.209	.252	.291
Cap Anson	1B136,C2	R	39	136	540	81	157	24	8	8	120	75	29	17	.291	.378	.409
Fred Pfeffer	2B137	R	31	137	498	93	123	12	9	7	77	79	60	40	.247	.353	.349
Bill Dahlen	3B84,OF37,SS15	R	21	135	549	114	143	18	13	9	76	67	60	21	.260	.348	.390
Jimmy Cooney	SS118	S	25	118	465	84	114	15	3	0	42	48	17	21	.245	.318	.290
Cliff Carroll	OF130	S	31	130	515	87	132	20	8	7	80	50	42	31	.256	.340	.367
Walt Wilmot	OF121	S	27	121	498	102	139	14	10	11	71	55	21	42	.279	.357	.414
Jimmy Ryan	OF117,P2,SS2	R	28	118	505	110	140	22	15	9	66	53	38	27	.277	.355	.434
Bill Hutchison	P66,OF1	R	31	67	243	27	45	4	2	2	25	17	62	5	.185	.238	.243
Tom Burns	3B53,SS4,OF2	R	34	59	243	36	55	8	1	1	17	21	21	18	.226	.288	.280
Ad Gumbert	P32,1B1,OF1	R	22	34	105	18	32	7	4	0	16	13	14	4	.305	.397	.448
Pat Luby	P30,OF2,1B1	—	22	32	98	19	24	2	4	2	24	8	16	3	.245	.321	.408
Pop Schriver	C27,1B2	R	25	27	90	15	30	1	4	1	21	10	9	1	.333	.412	.467
Bill Bowman	C15	—	22	15	45	2	4	1	0	0	5	5	9	0	.089	.196	.111
Bill Merritt	C11,1B1	R	20	11	42	4	9	1	0	0	4	2	2	0	.214	.250	.238
Tom Vickery	P14,SS1	—	24	14	39	3	7	1	0	0	1	0	10	3	.179	.179	.205
Tom Nagle	C7,OF1	R	25	8	25	3	3	0	0	0	1	1	3	0	.120	.154	.120
Elmer Foster	OF4	R	29	4	16	3	3	0	0	1	1	1	2	1	.188	.235	.375
Marty Honan	C5	—	21	5	12	1	2	0	1	0	3	1	3	0	.167	.231	.333

Pitcher	T	Age	G	GS	CG	ShO	IP	H	HR	BB	SO	W-L	Sv	ERA
Bill Hutchison	R	31	66	58	56	4	561.0	508	26	178	261	44-19	1	2.81
Ad Gumbert	R	22	32	31	24	1	256.1	282	5	90	73	17-11	0	3.58
Pat Luby	R	22	30	24	18	0	206.0	221	11	94	52	8-11	1	4.76
Tom Vickery	R	24	14	12	7	0	79.2	72	4	44	39	6-5	0	4.07
Ed Stein	R	21	14	10	9	1	101.0	99	7	57	38	7-6	0	3.74
George Nicol	L	20	3	2	0	0	11.0	14	0	10	12	0-1	0	4.91
Jimmy Ryan	L	28	2	0	0	0	5.2	11	0	2	2	0-0	1	1.59

1891 New York Giants 3rd NL 71-61 .538 13.0 GB

Jim Mutrie

Player	Gm by Position	B	Age	G	AB	R	H	2B	3B	HR	RBI	BB	SO	SB	Avg	OBP	Slg
Dick Buckley	C74,3B1	—	32	75	253	23	55	9	1	4	31	11	30	3	.217	.258	.308
Roger Connor	1B129	L	33	129	479	112	139	29	13	7	94	83	39	27	.290	.399	.449
Danny Richardson	2B114,SS9	R	28	123	516	85	139	18	5	4	51	33	27	28	.269	.313	.347
Charley Bassett	3B121,2B9	R	28	130	524	60	136	19	8	4	68	36	29	16	.260	.312	.349
Jack Glasscock	SS97	R	31	97	369	46	89	12	6	0	55	36	11	29	.241	.317	.306
Mike Tiernan	OF134	L	24	134	542	111	166	30	12	16	73	69	32	53	.306	.388	.494
George Gore	OF130	L	34	130	528	103	150	22	7	2	48	74	34	19	.284	.379	.364
Jim O'Rourke	OF126,C14	R	40	136	555	92	164	28	7	5	95	26	29	19	.295	.334	.398
Lew Whistler	SS33,OF22,1B7*	—	23	72	265	39	65	8	7	3	38	24	45	4	.245	.315	.362
Amos Rusie	P61,OF1	R	20	62	220	30	54	5	2	0	15	3	25	2	.245	.256	.286
Artie Clarke	C42,3B5,OF2	R	26	48	174	17	33	2	2	0	21	15	16	5	.190	.254	.224
Buster Burrell	C15,OF1	R	24	15	53	1	5	0	0	0	1	3	12	2	.094	.158	.094
Buck Ewing	2B8,C6	R	31	14	49	8	17	2	1	0	18	5	5	5	.347	.407	.429
Jerry Denny†	3B4	R	32	4	16	0	4	1	0	0	1	0	3	2	.250	.250	.313

L. Whistler, 6 G at 2B, 5 G at 3B

Pitcher	T	Age	G	GS	CG	ShO	IP	H	HR	BB	SO	W-L	Sv	ERA
Amos Rusie	R	20	61	57	52	6	500.1	391	7	262	337	33-20	1	2.55
John Ewing	R	28	33	30	28	5	269.1	237	2	105	138	21-8	0	2.27
Mickey Welch	R	31	22	15	14	0	160.0	176	7	97	46	7-10	1	4.28
John Sharrott	R	21	10	9	6	0	69.1	47	2	35	41	4-5	1	2.60
Roscoe Coughlin	R	23	8	7	6	0	61.0	74	5	23	22	3-3	0	3.84
Tim Keefe†	R	34	8	7	4	0	55.0	71	1	27	29	1-5	0	5.24
Bob Barr	R	34	5	4	2	0	27.0	47	1	12	11	0-4	0	5.33
Mike Sullivan†	—	24	3	3	3	0	24.0	24	0	8	11	1-2	0	3.38
Jack Taylor	R	18	1	1	1	0	8.0	4	1	3	3	0-1	0	1.13
Andy Dunning	R	19	1	1	0	0	2.0	3	1	3	2	0-1	0	4.50
Dad Clarkson	R	24	5	2	1	0	28.0	24	0	18	11	1-2	0	2.89

1891 Philadelphia Phillies 4th NL 68-69 .496 18.5 GB

Harry Wright

Player	Gm by Position	B	Age	G	AB	R	H	2B	3B	HR	RBI	BB	SO	SB	Avg	OBP	Slg
Jack Clements	C107,1B2	L	26	107	423	58	131	29	4	4	75	43	19	3	.310	.380	.426
Willard Brown	1B97,C19,OF2	R	25	115	441	62	107	20	4	0	50	34	35	7	.243	.303	.306
Bert Myers	2B135	R	27	135	514	67	118	27	2	2	69	69	46	8	.230	.331	.302
Billy Shindle	3B100,SS3	R	27	103	415	68	87	13	1	0	38	33	39	17	.210	.278	.246
Bob Allen	SS118	R	23	118	438	46	97	7	4	1	51	43	44	12	.221	.291	.263
Sam Thompson	OF133	L	31	133	554	108	163	23	10	7	90	52	20	29	.294	.363	.410
Billy Hamilton	OF133	L	25	133	527	141	179	23	7	2	60	102	28	111	.340	.453	.421
Ed Delahanty	OF99,1B27,2B3	R	23	128	543	92	132	19	9	5	86	33	50	25	.243	.296	.339
Ed Mayer	3B31,OF29,SS7*	—	24	68	268	24	50	2	4	0	31	14	29	7	.187	.238	.224
Kid Gleason	P53,OF9,SS4	S	24	65	214	31	53	5	2	0	17	20	17	6	.248	.318	.290
John Thornton	P37,OF3	—	—	39	123	7	17	3	0	0	6	2	10	1	.138	.152	.163
Bill Grey	C11,OF10,SS3*	—	20	23	75	11	18	0	0	0	7	3	10	3	.240	.296	.240
Jerry Denny†	1B12,3B7	R	32	19	73	5	21	1	1	0	11	4	6	1	.288	.325	.329
Bill Kling	P12,OF1	L	24	13	31	3	6	0	0	0	2	7	3	0	.194	.342	.194
Jocko Fields†	C8	R	26	8	30	4	7	2	1	0	5	4	2	0	.233	.324	.367
Lew Graulich	C4,1B3	—	—	7	26	2	8	0	0	0	3	1	2	0	.308	.333	.308
Joe Donohue	OF4,SS2	—	22	6	22	2	7	1	0	0	2	1	3	0	.318	.375	.364
Harry Morelock	SS4	—	—	4	14	1	1	0	0	0	0	3	3	0	.071	.235	.071
Walter Plock	OF2	—	21	2	5	2	2	0	0	0	0	0	1	0	.400	.500	.400
Charlie Bastian†	SS1	R	30	1	0	0	0	0	0	0	0	0	0	0	—	—	—

E. Mayer, 1 G at 2B; B. Grey, 1 G at 3B

Pitcher	T	Age	G	GS	CG	ShO	IP	H	HR	BB	SO	W-L	Sv	ERA
Kid Gleason	R	24	53	44	40	1	418.0	431	10	165	100	24-22	1	3.51
Duke Esper	L	22	39	36	25	1	296.0	302	8	121	108	20-15	1	3.56
John Thornton	—	—	37	32	23	1	269.0	268	3	115	52	15-16	2	3.68
Tim Keefe†	R	34	11	10	9	0	78.1	84	2	28	35	3-6	1	3.91
Bill Kling	R	24	12	7	4	0	75.0	90	2	32	26	4-2	0	4.32
Ed Cassian†	R	23	6	4	3	0	38.0	40	0	16	10	1-3	0	2.84
Phenomenal Smith	L	26	3	2	0	0	19.0	20	1	8	3	1-1	0	4.26
Joe Gormley	L	24	1	1	1	0	8.0	10	0	5	2	0-1	0	5.63
John Schultze	—	—	6	1	0	0	15.0	18	1	11	4	0-1	0	6.60
Mike Kilroy	R	18	3	1	0	0	10.0	15	1	4	3	0-2	0	9.90
Phil Saylor	L	20	1	0	0	0	3.0	2	1	0	0	0-0	0	6.00

1891 Cleveland Spiders 5th NL 65-74 .468 22.5 GB

Bob Leadley (34-34)/Patsy Tebeau (31-40)

Player	Gm by Position	B	Age	G	AB	R	H	2B	3B	HR	RBI	BB	SO	SB	Avg	OBP	Slg
Chief Zimmer	C116,3B1	R	30	116	440	55	112	21	4	3	69	33	49	15	.255	.312	.341
Jake Virtue	1B139	S	26	139	517	82	135	19	14	2	72	75	40	15	.261	.363	.364
Cupid Childs	2B141	L	23	141	551	120	155	21	12	2	83	97	32	39	.281	.395	.374
Patsy Tebeau	3B61,OF1	R	26	61	249	38	65	8	3	1	41	16	13	12	.261	.313	.329
Ed McKean	SS141	R	27	141	603	115	170	13	12	6	69	64	19	14	.282	.352	.373
Jimmy McAleer	OF136	R	26	136	565	97	134	16	11	1	61	49	47	51	.237	.304	.310
George Davis	OF116,3B22,P3	S	20	136	570	115	165	35	12	3	89	53	29	42	.289	.354	.409
Spud Johnson	OF79,1B1	L	31	80	327	49	84	8	3	1	46	22	23	16	.257	.319	.309
Jack Doyle	C29,OF21,3B20*	R	21	69	250	43	69	14	4	0	43	26	44	24	.276	.351	.364
Jesse Burkett	OF40	L	22	40	167	29	45	7	4	0	13	23	19	1	.269	.358	.359
Lee Viau	P45,OF1	R	24	45	144	15	23	3	2	0	6	12	28	2	.160	.224	.208
Henry Gruber	P44,OF2	R	27	46	141	17	23	3	2	1	20	21	35	0	.163	.276	.234
Jerry Denny†	3B29,OF7	R	32	36	138	17	31	5	0	0	21	12	23	3	.225	.291	.261
John Shearon	OF25,P6	—	21	30	124	10	30	1	1	0	13	1	15	6	.242	.248	.266
Billy Alvord†	3B13	—	27	13	59	7	17	2	2	1	7	0	7	0	.288	.300	.441
Ed Seward	P3,OF3,1B1	—	24	7	19	2	4	2	0	0	1	3	4	0	.211	.318	.316
Marty Sullivan†	OF1	R	28	1	4	0	1	0	0	0	1	0	1	0	.250	.250	.250
Joe Daly	OF1	—	22	1	3	0	0	0	0	0	0	0	2	0	.000	.000	.000
Bill Collins	C1,OF1	R	28	2	3	0	0	0	0	0	0	0	0	0	.000	.000	.000

J. Doyle, 1 G at SS

Pitcher	T	Age	G	GS	CG	ShO	IP	H	HR	BB	SO	W-L	Sv	ERA
Cy Young	R	24	55	46	43	0	423.2	431	4	140	147	27-22	2	2.85
Henry Gruber	R	27	44	40	35	1	348.2	407	10	119	79	17-22	0	4.13
Lee Viau	R	24	45	38	31	0	343.2	367	3	138	130	18-17	0	3.01
John Shearon	—	21	6	5	4	0	46.0	57	2	24	19	1-3	0	3.52
Ed Beatin	L	24	4	4	2	0	29.0	39	1	21	4	0-3	0	5.28
Ed Seward	R	24	3	3	0	0	16.1	16	0	11	4	2-1	0	3.86
Frank Knauss	L	23	3	3	1	0	15.0	23	2	8	6	0-3	0	7.20
Charlie Getzien†	R	27	1	1	1	0	9.0	12	1	4	4	0-1	0	8.00
Henry Killeen	—	20	1	1	1	0	8.2	11	1	8	3	0-1	0	6.23
George Davis	R	20	3	0	0	0	4.0	8	0	3	4	0-1	1	15.75

1891 Brooklyn Bridegrooms 6th NL 61-76 .445 25.5 GB

Monte Ward

Player	Gm by Position	B	Age	G	AB	R	H	2B	3B	HR	RBI	BB	SO	SB	Avg	OBP	Slg
Tom Kinslow	C61	R	25	61	228	22	54	6	0	0	33	9	22	3	.237	.266	.263
Dave Foutz	1B124,P6,SS1	R	34	130	521	87	134	26	8	2	73	40	25	48	.257	.313	.349
Hub Collins	2B72,OF35	R	27	107	435	82	120	16	5	3	31	59	63	32	.276	.365	.356
George Pinckney	3B130,SS5	R	29	135	501	80	137	19	6	2	71	66	32	44	.273	.366	.347
Monte Ward	SS87,2B18	L	31	105	441	85	122	13	5	0	39	36	10	57	.277	.335	.329
Mike Griffin	OF134	L	26	134	521	106	139	36	9	3	65	57	31	65	.267	.340	.388
Oyster Burns	OF113,SS6,3B5	R	26	123	470	75	134	24	13	4	83	53	30	21	.285	.358	.417
Darby O'Brien	OF103	R	27	103	395	79	100	18	6	5	57	39	53	31	.253	.331	.367
Con Daily	C55,OF3,SS2*	L	26	60	206	25	66	10	1	0	30	15	13	7	.320	.378	.379
Tom Daly	C26,1B15,SS11*	S	25	58	200	29	50	11	5	2	27	21	34	7	.250	.327	.385
Bob Caruthers	P38,OF17,2B1	L	27	56	171	24	48	5	3	2	23	25	13	4	.281	.372	.380
John O'Brien	2B43	L	20	43	167	22	41	4	2	0	26	12	17	4	.246	.308	.293
Bones Ely	SS28,3B2,2B1	R	28	31	111	9	17	0	1	0	11	7	9	4	.153	.203	.171
Adonis Terry	P25,OF5	R	26	30	91	10	19	7	1	0	6	9	26	4	.209	.301	.308
Jack Burdock	2B3	R	39	3	12	1	1	0	0	0	1	1	1	0	.083	.154	.083
Dude Esterbrook	OF2,2B1	R	34	3	8	1	3	0	0	0	0	0	1	0	.375	.444	.375

C. Daily, 1 G at 1B; T. Daly, 7 G at OF

Pitcher	T	Age	G	GS	CG	ShO	IP	H	HR	BB	SO	W-L	Sv	ERA
Tom Lovett	—	27	44	43	39	3	365.2	361	14	129	129	23-19	0	3.69
Bob Caruthers	R	27	38	32	29	2	297.0	323	7	107	69	18-14	1	3.12
George Hemming	R	22	27	22	19	1	199.2	231	11	84	83	8-15	1	4.96
Adonis Terry	R	26	25	22	18	1	194.0	207	5	80	65	6-16	1	4.22
Bert Inks	L	20	13	13	11	1	96.1	99	2	43	47	3-10	0	4.02
Dave Foutz	R	34	6	5	5	0	52.0	51	1	16	14	3-2	0	3.29

1891 Cincinnati Reds 7th NL 56-81 .409 30.5 GB

Tom Loftus

Player	Gm by Position	B	Age	G	AB	R	H	2B	3B	HR	RBI	BB	SO	SB	Avg	OBP	Slg
Jerry Harrington	C92,3B1	R	21	92	333	25	76	10	5	2	41	19	34	4	.228	.272	.306
John Reilly	1B100,OF36	R	32	135	546	60	132	20	13	4	64	9	42	22	.242	.267	.348
Bid McPhee	2B138	R	31	138	562	107	144	14	16	6	38	74	35	33	.256	.345	.370
Arlie Latham	3B135,C1	R	31	135	533	119	145	20	10	7	53	74	35	87	.272	.372	.386
Germany Smith	SS138	R	28	138	512	50	103	11	5	3	53	38	32	16	.201	.258	.260
Bug Holliday	OF111	R	24	111	442	74	141	21	10	9	84	37	28	30	.319	.376	.473
Lefty Marr†	OF72	L	28	72	286	32	74	9	7	0	32	25	15	16	.259	.323	.339
Jocko Halligan	OF61	L	22	61	247	43	77	13	6	3	44	24	25	5	.312	.375	.449
Jim Keenan	1B41,C34,3B1	R	33	75	252	30	51	7	5	4	33	33	39	2	.202	.302	.317
Pete Browning†	OF55	R	30	55	216	29	74	10	3	0	33	24	23	12	.343	.413	.417
Tony Mullane	P51,OF12,3B3	S	32	64	209	16	31	1	2	0	10	18	33	4	.148	.229	.172
Mike Slattery†	OF41	L	24	41	158	24	33	3	2	1	16	10	10	1	.209	.256	.272
Jim Curtis†	OF27	L	29	27	108	11	29	3	3	1	13	9	19	3	.269	.331	.380
Old Hoss Radbourn	P26,OF2,3B1	R	36	29	96	11	17	2	2	0	10	4	11	1	.177	.225	.240
Bob Clark	C16	R	28	16	54	2	6	0	0	0	3	6	9	3	.111	.213	.111
Frank Foreman†	OF1	L	28	1	4	0	1	1	0	0	0	0	0	0	.250	.250	.500
Pop Corkhill†	OF1	L	33	1	4	0	0	0	0	0	0	0	1	0	.000	.000	.000

Pitcher	T	Age	G	GS	CG	ShO	IP	H	HR	BB	SO	W-L	Sv	ERA
Tony Mullane	R	32	51	47	42	1	426.1	390	15	187	124	23-26	0	3.23
Billy Rhines	R	22	48	43	40	1	372.2	364	4	124	138	17-24	1	2.87
Old Hoss Radbourn	R	36	26	24	23	2	218.0	236	13	62	54	11-13	0	4.25
Ed Crane†	R	29	15	13	11	1	116.2	134	3	64	51	4-8	0	4.09
Jesse Duryea†	R	31	10	10	8	0	77.0	101	4	25	23	1-9	0	5.38
Clarence Stephens	R	27	1	1	1	0	8.0	9	1	3	3	0-1	0	7.88

1891 Pittsburgh Pirates 8th NL 55-80 .407 30.5 GB

Ned Hanlon (31-47)/Bill McGunnigle (24-33)

Player	Gm by Position	B	Age	G	AB	R	H	2B	3B	HR	RBI	BB	SO	SB	Avg	OBP	Slg
Connie Mack	C72,1B3	R	28	75	280	43	60	10	0	0	29	19	11	4	.214	.286	.250
Jake Beckley	1B133	L	23	133	554	94	162	20	19	4	73	44	46	13	.292	.353	.419
Lou Bierbauer	2B121	L	25	121	500	60	103	13	6	1	47	28	19	12	.206	.252	.262
Charlie Reilly	3B99,SS11,OF4	S	24	114	415	43	91	8	5	3	44	29	58	20	.219	.277	.284
Frank Shugart	SS75	S	24	75	320	57	88	19	8	3	33	20	26	21	.275	.324	.413
Ned Hanlon	OF119,SS1	L	33	119	455	87	121	12	8	0	60	48	30	54	.266	.341	.327
Fred Carroll	OF91	R	26	91	353	55	77	13	4	4	48	48	36	22	.218	.315	.312
Pete Browning†	OF50	R	30	50	203	35	59	14	1	4	28	27	31	4	.291	.377	.429
Doggie Miller	C41,SS37,3B34*	R	26	135	548	80	156	19	6	4	57	59	26	35	.285	.357	.363
Al Maul	OF40,P8	R	25	47	149	15	28	2	4	0	14	20	28	4	.188	.284	.255
Silver King	P48,3B1	R	23	49	148	12	25	2	3	0	9	14	31	0	.169	.241	.223
Pop Corkhill†	OF41	L	33	41	145	16	33	1	1	3	20	7	10	7	.228	.268	.310
Dan Lally	OF41	L	23	41	143	24	32	6	2	1	17	16	20	0	.224	.319	.315
Tun Berger	C18,2B17,SS6*	—	23	43	134	15	32	2	1	1	14	12	10	4	.239	.315	.291
Jocko Fields†	C15,SS8	R	26	23	75	10	18	3	0	0	5	10	13	1	.240	.337	.280
John Newell	3B5	R	23	5	18	1	2	0	0	0	2	0	0	0	.111	.158	.111
Piggy Ward	OF5	S	24	6	18	3	6	0	0	0	2	3	3	3	.333	.455	.333
Ed Spurney	SS3	—	19	3	7	2	2	1	0	0	0	2	1	0	.286	.444	.429
Sam LaRoque†	3B1	—	27	1	4	0	0	0	0	0	0	0	1	0	.000	.000	.000

D. Miller, 24 G at OF, 1 G at 1B; T. Berger, 2 G at OF

Pitcher	T	Age	G	GS	CG	ShO	IP	H	HR	BB	SO	W-L	Sv	ERA
Mark Baldwin	R	27	53	50	48	2	437.2	385	10	227	197	22-28	0	2.76
Silver King	R	23	48	44	40	3	384.1	382	7	144	160	14-29	1	3.11
Pud Galvin	R	34	33	31	23	2	246.2	256	10	62	46	14-14	0	2.88
Harry Staley†	R	24	9	7	6	0	71.2	77	4	11	25	4-5	0	2.89
Scott Stratton†	R	21	2	2	2	0	18.1	16	0	5	5	0-2	0	2.45
Al Maul	R	25	8	3	3	0	39.0	44	0	16	13	1-2	1	2.31

»1891 Boston Red Stockings 1st AA 93-42 .689 —

Arthur Irwin

Player	Gm by Position	B	Age	G	AB	R	H	2B	3B	HR	RBI	BB	SO	SB	Avg	OBP	Slg
Morgan Murphy	C104,OF4	R	24	106	402	60	87	11	4	4	54	36	58	17	.216	.289	.294
Dan Brouthers	1B130	L	33	130	486	117	170	26	19	5	109	87	20	31	.350	.471	.512
Cub Stricker	2B139	R	32	139	514	96	111	15	4	0	46	63	34	54	.216	.309	.261
Duke Farrell	3B66,C37,OF23*	S	24	122	473	108	143	19	13	12	110	59	48	21	.302	.384	.474
Paul Radford	SS131,OF4,P1	R	29	133	456	102	118	11	5	0	65	96	36	55	.259	.393	.305
Tom Brown	OF137	L	30	137	589	177	189	30	21	5	71	70	96	106	.321	.397	.469
Hugh Duffy	OF124,3B3,SS1	R	24	127	536	134	180	20	8	9	110	61	29	85	.336	.408	.453
Hardy Richardson	OF60,3B9,SS4*	R	36	74	278	45	71	9	4	7	52	40	26	16	.255	.351	.392
Bill Joyce	3B64,1B1	L	25	65	243	76	75	9	15	3	51	63	27	36	.309	.460	.506
George Haddock	P51,OF8	R	24	58	185	30	45	4	1	3	23	21	46	3	.243	.324	.324
Charlie Buffinton	P48,OF10,1B4	R	30	58	181	16	34	2	1	1	16	19	15	0	.188	.269	.227
Jack McGeachey†	OF41	R	27	41	178	26	45	2	1	1	21	12	8	11	.253	.304	.292
John Irwin†	OF17,3B2,SS1	L	29	19	72	6	16	2	2	0	15	6	9	6	.222	.282	.306
Bill Daley	P19,OF2	—	23	20	59	5	10	0	1	0	9	1	6	1	.169	.183	.203
Clark Griffith†	P7,OF3	R	21	10	23	6	4	1	1	1	3	6	5	1	.174	.367	.435
Arthur Irwin	SS6	L	33	6	17	1	2	0	0	0	0	2	1	0	.118	.286	.118
King Kelly†	C4	R	33	4	15	2	4	0	0	1	4	0	2	1	.267	.267	.467
Tom Cotter	C5,OF1	R	24	6	12	1	3	0	0	0	4	1	2	0	.250	.308	.250
Tommy Dowd†	OF4	R	22	4	11	1	1	0	0	0	0	0	1	0	.091	.091	.091
Tim Donahue	C4	L	21	4	7	0	0	0	0	0	0	0	5	0	.000	.000	.000
Frank Quinlan	C1,OF1	—	22	2	5	0	0	0	0	0	0	0	2	0	.000	.000	.000
Mike Flynn	C1	—	19	1	2	0	0	0	0	0	0	0	1	0	.000	.000	.000

D. Farrell, 4 G at 1B; H. Richardson, 3 G at 1B

Pitcher	T	Age	G	GS	CG	ShO	IP	H	HR	BB	SO	W-L	Sv	ERA
George Haddock	R	24	51	47	37	5	379.2	330	8	137	169	34-11	1	2.49
Charlie Buffinton	R	30	48	43	33	2	363.2	303	8	120	158	29-9	1	2.55
Darby O'Brien	R	24	40	30	22	0	268.2	300	13	127	87	18-13	2	3.65
Bill Daley	L	23	19	11	10	0	126.2	119	6	81	68	8-6	2	2.98
Clark Griffith†	R	21	7	4	3	0	40.0	47	3	15	20	3-1	0	5.63
John Fitzgerald	—	21	6	3	2	0	32.0	49	2	11	16	1-1	1	5.63
Kid Madden†	L	23	1	1	1	0	8.0	10	2	6	6	0-1	0	6.75
Paul Radford	R	29	1	0	0	0	1.0	0	0	0	0	0-0	0	0.00

1891 St. Louis Browns 2nd AA 85-51 .625 8.5 GB

Charlie Comiskey

Player	Gm by Position	B	Age	G	AB	R	H	2B	3B	HR	RBI	BB	SO	SB	Avg	OBP	Slg
Jack Boyle	C91,SS26,3B8*	R	25	123	439	78	123	18	8	5	79	47	36	19	.280	.365	.392
Charlie Comiskey	1B141,OF2	R	31	141	580	86	152	16	2	3	93	33	25	41	.262	.310	.312
Bill Eagan	2B83	—	22	83	302	49	65	11	4	4	43	44	54	21	.215	.321	.318
Denny Lyons	3B120	R	25	120	451	124	142	24	3	11	84	88	58	9	.315	.445	.455
Shorty Fuller	SS103,2B39	R	23	137	586	107	127	15	7	2	63	67	28	42	.217	.301	.276
Dummy Hoy	OF141	L	29	141	567	136	165	14	5	5	66	119	25	59	.291	.424	.360
Tip O'Neill	OF129	R	33	129	521	112	167	28	4	10	95	62	33	25	.321	.402	.447
Tommy McCarthy	OF113,2B14,SS12*	R	27	136	578	127	179	21	6	8	95	50	19	37	.310	.375	.408
Jack Stivetts	P64,OF24	R	23	85	302	45	92	10	2	7	54	10	32	4	.305	.331	.421
John Munyan	C45,OF12,SS5*	—	30	62	182	44	42	4	3	0	20	43	39	13	.231	.389	.286
Dell Darling	C17,2B2,SS1	R	29	17	53	9	7	1	3	0	9	10	11	0	.132	.270	.264
George Rettger	P14,OF1	R	22	15	42	5	3	0	0	1	2	5	10	1	.071	.188	.143
Jack Easton†	P7,OF2	—	24	9	28	5	5	0	0	0	2	3	3	2	.179	.258	.179
Joe Visner†	OF6	L	31	6	27	2	4	0	1	0	1	0	3	0	.148	.148	.222
Paul Cook†	C7	R	28	7	25	3	5	0	0	0	1	1	2	0	.200	.259	.200
Harry Burrell	P7,OF2	—	22	9	22	2	5	2	0	0	6	1	5	0	.227	.261	.318
John Ricks	3B5	—	—	5	18	3	3	0	0	0	0	0	2	0	.167	.167	.167
Paul McSweeney	2B3,3B1	—	24	3	12	2	3	1	0	0	2	0	0	1	.250	.308	.333
Ted Breitenstein	P6,OF1	L	22	6	12	2	0	0	0	0	0	2	0	1	.000	.143	.000
Mart McQuaid	2B3,OF1	—	30	4	11	1	4	2	0	0	1	0	1	1	.364	.364	.545
Art Whitney†	3B3	R	33	3	11	0	0	0	0	0	0	1	2	0	.000	.083	.000
Bill Zies	C2	L	—	2	3	0	1	0	0	0	0	0	0	0	.333	.333	.333
Yank Robinson†	2B1	R	31	1	3	0	0	0	0	0	0	0	0	0	.000	.000	.000
John Schultz	C1	—	—	1	2	0	0	0	0	0	0	0	0	0	.000	.000	.000
Harry Fuller	3B1	—	28	1	2	0	0	0	0	0	0	0	1	0	.000	.000	.000

J. Boyle, 3 G at 1B, 3 G at 2B, 3 G at OF; T. McCarthy, 3 G at 3B, 1 G at P; J. Munyan, 3 G at 3B

Pitcher	T	Age	G	GS	CG	ShO	IP	H	HR	BB	SO	W-L	Sv	ERA
Jack Stivetts	R	23	64	56	40	3	440.0	357	15	232	259	33-22	1	2.86
Willie McGill†	L	17	35	31	22	1	249.0	225	10	131	154	18-10	1	2.93
Clark Griffith†	R	21	27	17	12	0	186.1	195	8	58	68	11-8	0	3.33
George Rettger	R	22	14	12	10	1	92.2	85	4	51	49	7-3	1	3.40
Joe Neale	R	25	15	11	9	1	110.1	109	4	36	24	6-4	1	4.24
Jack Easton†	—	24	7	6	4	0	47.2	48	3	23	22	3-2	0	5.10
Harry Burrell	L	22	7	4	3	0	43.0	51	4	21	19	5-2	0	4.81
Jesse Duryea†	R	31	3	3	2	0	24.0	19	0	10	13	1-1	0	3.38
Ted Breitenstein	L	22	6	1	1	1	28.2	15	2	14	13	2-0	1	2.20
Tommy McCarthy	R	27	1	0	0	0	1.0	2	0	0	0	0-0	0	9.00

1891 Milwaukee Brewers 3rd AA 21-15 .583 49.5 GB

Charlie Cushman

Player	Gm by Position	B	Age	G	AB	R	H	2B	3B	HR	RBI	BB	SO	SB	Avg	OBP	Slg
Farmer Vaughn†	C20,1B4,OF1	R	27	25	99	13	33	7	0	0	9	4	5	1	.333	.359	.404
John Carney†	1B31	R	24	31	110	22	33	5	2	3	23	13	8	5	.300	.389	.464
Jim Canavan†	2B24,SS11	R	24	35	142	33	38	2	4	3	21	16	10	7	.268	.342	.401
Gus Alberts	3B12	R	23	12	41	6	4	0	0	0	2	7	5	1	.098	.260	.098
George Shoch	SS25,3B9	R	32	34	127	29	40	7	1	1	16	18	5	12	.315	.435	.409
Eddie Burke	OF35	L	24	35	144	31	34	9	0	2	21	12	19	7	.236	.337	.340
Abner Dalrymple	OF32	L	33	32	135	31	42	7	5	1	22	7	18	6	.311	.345	.459
Howard Earl	OF30,1B2	—	24	31	129	21	32	5	2	1	17	5	13	3	.248	.281	.341
John Grim	C16,3B10,2B3	R	23	29	119	14	28	5	1	1	14	2	5	1	.235	.248	.319
Bob Pettit	2B9,OF7,3B6	L	29	21	80	10	14	4	0	1	5	7	7	2	.175	.267	.263
Frank Dwyer†	P10,OF1	R	23	11	40	1	9	1	0	0	2	1	2	1	.225	.262	.250
Tom Letcher	OF6	L	23	6	21	3	4	1	0	0	2	0	1	1	.190	.190	.238

Pitcher	T	Age	G	GS	CG	ShO	IP	H	HR	BB	SO	W-L	Sv	ERA
George Davies	—	23	12	12	12	1	102.0	94	2	35	61	7-5	0	2.65
Frank Killen	L	20	11	11	11	2	96.2	73	1	51	38	7-4	0	1.68
Frank Dwyer†	R	23	10	10	10	0	86.0	92	2	21	27	6-4	0	2.20
Willard Mains†	R	22	2	2	1	0	10.0	14	1	10	2	0-2	0	10.80
Jim Hughey	R	22	2	1	1	0	15.0	18	0	3	9	1-0	0	3.00

1891 Baltimore Orioles 4th AA 71-64 .526 22.0 GB

Billy Barnie

Player	Gm by Position	B	Age	G	AB	R	H	2B	3B	HR	RBI	BB	SO	SB	Avg	OBP	Slg
Wilbert Robinson	C92,OF1	R	28	93	334	25	72	8	5	2	46	16	37	18	.216	.251	.287
Perry Werden	1B139	R	25	139	552	102	160	20	18	6	104	52	59	46	.290	.363	.424
Sam Wise	2B99,SS4	L	33	103	388	70	96	14	5	1	48	62	52	33	.247	.364	.317
Pete Gilbert	3B139	—	23	139	513	81	118	15	7	3	72	37	77	31	.230	.317	.304
George Van Haltren	OF81,SS59,P6*	L	25	139	566	136	180	14	15	9	83	71	46	75	.318	.398	.443
Bill Johnson	OF129	L	28	129	480	101	130	13	14	2	79	89	55	32	.271	.389	.369
Curt Welch	OF113,2B21,SS2	R	29	132	514	122	138	22	10	3	55	77	42	50	.268	.400	.368
Irv Ray	OF64,SS40	L	27	103	418	72	116	17	5	0	58	54	18	28	.278	.366	.342
Sadie McMahon	P61,OF2	R	23	61	210	31	43	2	4	1	15	7	36	6	.205	.234	.267
George Townsend	C58,OF3	R	24	61	204	29	39	5	4	0	18	20	21	3	.191	.279	.255
John McGraw	SS21,OF9,2B3	L	18	33	115	17	31	3	5	0	14	12	17	4	.270	.359	.383
Kid Madden†	P32,OF7	—	23	38	107	18	29	2	2	1	15	9	10	2	.271	.339	.355
Joe Walsh	2B13,SS13	L	26	26	100	14	21	0	1	1	10	6	18	4	.210	.255	.260
Bert Cunningham	P30,OF2,SS1	R	25	31	100	17	15	3	1	1	11	13	20	4	.150	.248	.230
Lou Hardie	OF15	—	26	15	56	7	13	0	3	0	1	8	8	3	.232	.328	.339
John O'Connell	2B3,SS3,OF2	—	19	8	29	2	5	1	0	0	7	3	6	2	.172	.250	.207

G. Van Haltren, 2 G at 2B

Pitcher	T	Age	G	GS	CG	ShO	IP	H	HR	BB	SO	W-L	Sv	ERA
Sadie McMahon	R	23	61	58	53	5	503.0	493	13	149	219	35-24	1	2.81
Kid Madden†	L	23	32	27	20	1	224.0	239	4	88	56	13-12	1	4.10
Bert Cunningham	R	25	30	25	21	0	237.2	241	8	138	59	11-14	0	4.01
Egyptian Healy	R	24	23	22	19	0	170.1	179	6	57	54	8-10	0	3.75
Jersey Bakely†	R	27	8	6	5	0	59.0	48	1	30	13	4-2	0	2.29
George Van Haltren	L	25	6	1	0	0	23.0	38	1	10	7	0-1	0	5.09

1891 Philadelphia Athletic 5th AA 73-66 .525 22.0 GB

Bill Sharsig (6-11)/George Wood (67-55)

Player	Gm by Position	B	Age	G	AB	R	H	2B	3B	HR	RBI	BB	SO	SB	Avg	OBP	Slg
Jocko Milligan	C87,1B32	R	29	118	455	75	138	35	12	11	106	56	51	2	.303	.397	.505
Henry Larkin	1B111,OF23	R	31	133	526	94	147	27	14	10	93	66	56	2	.279	.376	.441
Bill Hallman	2B141	R	24	141	587	112	166	21	13	6	69	38	56	18	.283	.332	.394
Joe Mulvey	3B113	R	32	113	453	62	115	9	13	5	66	17	32	11	.254	.287	.364
Tommy Corcoran	SS133	R	22	133	511	84	130	11	15	7	71	29	56	30	.254	.307	.376
George Wood	OF122,3B6,SS5	L	32	132	528	105	163	18	14	3	61	72	52	22	.309	.399	.413
Pop Corkhill†	OF83	L	33	83	349	50	73	7	7	0	31	26	15	12	.209	.268	.269
Jim McTamany†	OF58	R	27	58	218	57	49	6	3	3	21	43	44	13	.225	.365	.321
Lave Cross	C43,OF43,3B24*	R	25	110	402	66	121	20	14	5	52	38	23	14	.301	.366	.458
Jack McGeachey†	OF50	R	27	50	201	24	46	4	3	2	13	6	12	9	.229	.255	.308
Gus Weyhing	P52,OF2	R	24	54	198	11	22	5	1	0	11	7	65	2	.111	.146	.146
Elton Chamberlin	P49,OF6	R	23	54	176	21	33	3	5	2	19	21	33	3	.188	.278	.295
Ben Sanders	OF22,P19	R	26	40	156	24	39	6	4	1	19	7	12	2	.250	.291	.359
Ed Beecher†	OF16	L	30	16	71	9	15	2	4	0	7	3	4	7	.211	.243	.352
Will Callahan	P13,3B1,SS1	—	22	15	56	6	11	1	0	0	4	5	8	0	.196	.262	.214
Sumner Bowman	P8,OF6	L	24	14	54	8	13	4	0	0	2	2	12	1	.241	.268	.315
Dave McKeough	C14,SS1	—	27	15	54	4	14	1	1	0	3	8	6	0	.259	.355	.315
Bill Clymer	SS3	—	17	3	11	0	0	0	0	0	0	1	2	1	.000	.154	.000
Pat Friel	OF2	S	31	2	8	2	2	1	0	0	0	0	0	0	.250	.250	.375
Bob Matthews	OF1	—	—	1	3	1	1	0	0	0	0	0	1	0	.333	.600	.333

L. Cross, 1 G at 2B, 1 G at SS

Pitcher	T	Age	G	GS	CG	ShO	IP	H	HR	BB	SO	W-L	Sv	ERA
Gus Weyhing	R	24	52	51	51	3	450.0	428	12	161	219	31-20	0	3.18
Elton Chamberlin	R	23	49	46	44	0	405.2	397	10	206	204	22-23	0	4.22
Ben Sanders	R	26	19	18	15	0	145.0	157	3	37	40	11-5	0	3.79
Will Callahan	—	22	13	11	11	0	112.0	151	7	47	28	6-6	0	6.43
Sumner Bowman	L	24	8	8	8	0	68.0	73	0	37	22	2-5	0	3.44
George Meakim	R	25	6	6	4	0	35.0	51	1	22	13	1-4	0	6.94
Mike Sullivan†	—	24	2	2	2	0	18.0	17	2	10	7	0-2	0	3.50

1891 Columbus Colts 6th AA 61-76 .445 33.0 GB

Gus Schmelz

Player	Gm by Position	B	Age	G	AB	R	H	2B	3B	HR	RBI	BB	SO	SB	Avg	OBP	Slg
Jim Donahue	C75,1B1,OF1	R	29	77	280	27	61	4	3	0	35	31	18	2	.218	.298	.254
Mike Lehane	1B137	R	26	137	511	59	110	12	7	1	52	34	77	16	.215	.268	.272
Jack Crooks	2B138	R	25	138	519	110	127	19	13	0	46	103	47	50	.245	.379	.331
Bill Kuehne†	3B68	R	32	68	261	32	56	9	0	2	22	10	22	21	.215	.244	.272
Bobby Wheelock	SS136	R	26	136	498	82	114	15	1	0	39	78	55	52	.229	.336	.263
Charlie Duffee	OF128,3B7,SS2	R	25	137	552	86	166	28	4	10	90	42	36	41	.301	.353	.420
Jon Sneed	OF99	—	—	99	366	66	94	9	6	1	61	55	29	24	.257	.366	.322
Jim McTamany†	OF81	R	27	81	304	59	76	17	9	3	35	58	48	20	.250	.374	.395
Jack O'Connor	OF40,C21	R	22	56	229	28	61	12	3	0	37	11	14	10	.266	.300	.345
Larry Twitchell	OF56,P6	R	27	57	224	32	62	9	4	2	35	20	28	10	.277	.341	.379
Phil Knell	P58,OF9,2B1	R	26	66	215	25	34	2	3	0	19	8	34	4	.158	.188	.195
Tom Dowse	C51,OF5	R	24	55	201	24	45	7	0	0	22	13	22	2	.224	.278	.259
Tim O'Rourke	3B34	L	27	34	136	22	38	1	3	0	12	15	7	9	.279	.359	.331
John Dolan	P27,OF1	—	23	28	78	6	7	3	0	1	8	8	33	1	.090	.184	.167
Jack Easton†	P20,OF5	—	24	24	74	11	15	4	1	0	8	3	12	4	.203	.244	.284
Jim Donnelly	3B17	R	25	17	54	6	13	0	0	0	9	13	5	7	.241	.388	.241
Elmer Cleveland	3B12	R	28	12	41	12	7	0	0	0	4	12	9	4	.171	.370	.171
Jack Leiper	P6,OF1	L	23	6	21	2	3	0	0	0	3	0	6	0	.143	.143	.143

Pitcher	T	Age	G	GS	CG	ShO	IP	H	HR	BB	SO	W-L	Sv	ERA
Phil Knell	L	26	58	52	47	5	462.0	363	4	226	228	28-27	0	2.92
Hank Gastright	R	26	35	33	28	1	283.2	280	7	136	109	12-19	0	3.78
John Dolan	R	23	27	24	19	0	203.1	216	8	84	68	12-11	0	4.16
Jack Easton†	—	24	20	18	15	0	150.1	160	5	63	65	5-12	0	4.43
Jack Leiper	L	23	6	5	4	0	45.0	41	3	39	19	2-2	0	5.40
Dad Clarke	R	26	4	3	2	0	21.0	30	0	16	2	1-2	0	6.86
Jim Sullivan†	R	22	1	1	1	0	9.0	10	1	5	1	0-1	0	4.00
Bill Lyston	R	28	1	1	1	0	6.0	10	0	6	1	0-1	0	10.50
Larry Twitchell	R	27	6	1	1	0	31.0	29	1	13	8	1-1	0	4.06
Ed Clark	—	—	1	0	0	0	2.0	2	0	0	1	0-0	0	0.00

1891 Cincinnati Porkers 7th AA 43-57 .430 32.5 GB

King Kelly

Player	Gm by Position	B	Age	G	AB	R	H	2B	3B	HR	RBI	BB	SO	SB	Avg	OBP	Slg
King Kelly†	C66,3B8,OF7*	R	33	82	283	56	84	15	7	1	53	51	28	22	.297	.408	.410
John Carney†	1B99	R	24	99	367	47	102	10	8	3	43	35	18	15	.278	.346	.373
Yank Robinson†	2B97	R	31	97	342	48	61	9	4	1	37	68	51	23	.178	.328	.237
Art Whitney†	3B93	R	33	93	347	42	69	6	1	3	33	31	20	8	.199	.270	.248
Jim Canavan†	SS101	R	24	101	426	74	97	13	14	7	66	27	44	21	.228	.282	.373
Dick Johnston	OF99	R	28	99	376	59	83	11	2	6	51	38	44	12	.221	.301	.309
Emmett Seery	OF97	L	30	97	372	77	106	15	10	4	36	81	52	19	.285	.423	.411
Ed Andrews	OF83	R	32	83	356	47	75	7	4	0	26	33	35	22	.211	.279	.253
Farmer Vaughn†	C44,OF6,1B2*	R	27	51	175	21	45	7	1	1	14	14	15	7	.257	.316	.326
Frank Dwyer†	P35,OF3,2B2	R	23	37	141	24	40	4	3	0	18	5	14	4	.284	.308	.355
Ed Crane†	P32,OF3	R	29	34	110	13	17	0	0	1	7	8	28	4	.155	.212	.182
Willard Mains†	P30,OF1	—	22	31	90	14	22	3	2	1	10	5	8	2	.244	.284	.356
Jerry Hurley	C24,1B1,OF1	R	28	24	66	10	14	3	2	0	6	12	13	2	.212	.333	.318
Lefty Marr†	OF14	L	28	14	57	9	11	1	0	0	4	7	4	2	.193	.281	.211
Matt Kilroy	P7,OF1	L	25	8	20	2	3	0	0	0	0	4	2	0	.150	.292	.150
Billy Clingman	2B1	S	21	1	5	0	1	1	0	0	0	0	0	0	.200	.200	.400
Joe Burke	2B1	—	—	1	4	0	1	0	0	0	1	0	2	0	.250	.250	.250
Charlie Bastian†	2B1	R	30	1	4	0	0	0	0	0	0	0	0	0	.000	.000	.000

K. Kelly, 6 G at 2B, 5 G at 1B, 3 G at P, 1 G at SS; F. Vaughn, 2 G at 3B, 1 G at P

Pitcher	T	Age	G	GS	CG	ShO	IP	H	HR	BB	SO	W-L	Sv	ERA
Frank Dwyer†	R	23	35	31	29	1	289.0	332	10	124	101	13-19	0	4.52
Ed Crane†	R	29	32	31	25	1	250.0	216	3	139	122	14-14	0	2.45
Willard Mains†	R	22	30	23	19	0	204.0	196	3	107	76	12-12	0	2.69
Willie McGill†	L	17	8	8	6	0	65.0	69	1	37	19	2-5	0	4.98
Matt Kilroy	L	25	7	6	4	0	45.1	51	1	19	6	1-4	0	2.98
Charlie Bell†	R	22	1	1	1	0	9.0	2	0	3	1	1-0	0	0.00
Kid Keenan	R	16	1	1	1	0	8.0	6	0	4	5	0-1	0	0.00
Wild Bill Widner	R	24	1	1	1	0	8.0	13	0	4	0	0-1	0	7.88
King Kelly	R	33	3	0	0	0	15.1	21	2	7	0	0-1	0	5.28
Farmer Vaughn	R	27	1	0	0	0	7.0	12	0	1	0	0-0	0	3.86
John Slagle	R	—	1	0	0	0	1.1	3	0	1	1	0-0	1	0.00

1891 Louisville Colonels 8th AA 54-83 .394 40.0 GB

Jack Chapman

Player	Gm by Position	B	Age	G	AB	R	H	2B	3B	HR	RBI	BB	SO	SB	Avg	OBP	Slg
Tom Cahill	C56,SS49,OF12*	—	22	120	433	70	111	18	7	3	47	41	51	39	.256	.329	.351
Harry Taylor	1B92,C1,2B1*	L	25	93	356	81	105	7	4	2	37	55	33	15	.295	.397	.354
Tim Shinnick	2B120,3B7,SS1	S	23	128	443	79	98	10	11	1	54	54	47	36	.221	.314	.300
Ollie Beard	3B61,SS7	R	29	68	257	35	62	4	5	0	24	33	9	7	.241	.330	.296
Hughie Jennings	SS70,1B17,3B3	R	22	90	360	53	105	10	8	1	58	17	36	12	.292	.339	.372
Chicken Wolf	OF133,1B5,3B1	R	29	138	537	67	136	17	8	1	82	42	36	13	.253	.317	.320
Farmer Weaver	OF132,C4	L	26	135	565	76	160	25	7	1	55	33	23	30	.283	.335	.358
Patsy Donovan†	OF105	L	26	105	439	73	141	10	3	2	53	30	18	27	.321	.375	.371
Jack Ryan	C56,1B11,3B6*	R	22	75	253	24	57	5	4	2	25	15	40	3	.225	.271	.300
Bill Kuehne†	3B41	R	32	41	159	28	44	3	1	1	18	8	13	10	.277	.315	.327
Paul Cook†	C35,1B10	R	28	45	153	21	35	3	1	0	23	11	17	4	.229	.285	.261
Scott Stratton†	P20,1B8,OF6	L	21	34	115	9	27	2	0	0	8	11	13	8	.235	.307	.252
John Fitzgerald	P33,OF1	—	—	34	112	15	19	2	2	1	10	14	38	3	.170	.273	.250
Jouett Meekin	P29,OF3,1B1	R	24	33	97	14	21	0	3	1	10	15	19	4	.216	.321	.309
Monk Cline	OF21	L	33	21	76	13	23	3	1	0	12	19	3	2	.303	.442	.368
Ed Daily†	P15,OF7	R	28	22	64	10	16	2	0	0	8	8	6	4	.250	.342	.281
Harry Raymond	SS14	—	29	14	59	4	12	2	0	0	2	5	6	3	.203	.288	.237
John Irwin†	3B14	L	29	14	55	7	15	1	1	0	7	5	6	1	.273	.344	.327
Sam LaRoque†	2B10,1B1	—	27	10	35	6	11	2	1	1	8	5	8	1	.314	.429	.514
Jim Long	OF6	—	28	6	25	5	6	0	0	0	4	3	6	1	.240	.367	.240
Al Schellhase	C7	R	26	7	20	4	3	0	0	0	1	1	2	3	.150	.190	.150
Paddy Fox	3B6	—	22	6	19	1	2	0	1	0	2	2	3	0	.105	.261	.211
Joe Gerhardt	2B2	R	36	2	6	0	0	0	0	0	0	1	0	0	.000	.143	.000
Pat Pettee	2B2	R	28	2	5	1	0	0	0	0	0	3	1	1	.000	.375	.000
Jack Wentz	2B1	R	28	1	4	0	1	0	0	0	0	0	0	0	.250	.250	.250
Grant Briggs	C1	—	26	1	4	0	1	0	0	0	0	0	0	0	.250	.250	.250
Jack Darragh	1B1	—	24	1	2	0	1	0	0	0	0	0	0	0	.500	.500	.500
Nick Reeder	3B1	R	24	1	2	0	0	0	0	0	0	0	1	0	.000	.000	.000

T. Cahill, 6 G at 2B, 2 G at 3B; H. Taylor, 1 G at 3B; J. Ryan, 4 G at OF, 3 G at 2B

Pitcher	T	Age	G	GS	CG	ShO	IP	H	HR	BB	SO	W-L	Sv	ERA
John Fitzgerald	L	—	33	32	29	3	276.0	280	6	95	111	14-18	0	3.59
Jouett Meekin	R	24	29	26	25	2	228.0	227	2	113	144	10-16	0	4.30
Red Ehret	R	22	26	24	23	2	220.2	225	2	70	76	13-13	0	3.47
Scott Stratton†	R	21	20	20	20	1	172.0	204	10	34	52	6-13	0	4.08
John Doran	L	24	15	14	12	1	126.0	160	3	75	55	5-10	0	5.43
Ed Daily	R	28	15	14	11	0	111.1	149	6	48	27	4-8	0	5.74
Charlie Bell†	R	22	10	9	8	0	77.0	93	4	20	16	2-6	0	4.68
George Boone	—	20	4	1	0	0	15.0	15	0	9	4	0-0	1	7.80

1891 Washington Senators 9th AA 44-91 .326 49.0 GB

Sam Trott (4-7)/Pop Snyder (23-46)/Dan Shannon (15-34)/Sandy Griffin (2-4)

Player	Gm by Position	B	Age	G	AB	R	H	2B	3B	HR	RBI	BB	SO	SB	Avg	OBP	Slg
Deacon McGuire	C98,OF18,3B3*	R	27	114	413	55	125	22	10	3	66	43	34	10	.303	.382	.426
Mox McQuery	1B68	—	30	68	261	40	63	9	4	2	37	18	19	3	.241	.305	.330
Tommy Dowd†	2B107,OF5	R	22	112	464	66	120	9	10	1	44	19	44	39	.259	.291	.328
Billy Alvord†	3B81	—	27	81	312	28	73	8	3	0	30	11	38	3	.234	.260	.279
Gil Hatfield	SS105,3B27,P4*	—	36	134	500	83	128	11	8	1	48	50	39	43	.256	.335	.316
Larry Murphy	OF101	L	—	101	400	73	106	15	3	1	35	63	27	29	.265	.372	.325
Ed Beecher†	OF58	L	30	58	235	35	57	11	3	2	28	27	9	17	.243	.333	.340
Paul Hines	OF47,1B8	R	39	54	206	25	58	7	5	0	31	21	16	6	.282	.376	.364
Al McCauley	1B59	L	28	59	206	36	58	5	8	1	31	30	13	9	.282	.378	.398
Sy Sutcliffe	OF35,C22,SS3*	L	29	53	201	29	71	8	3	2	33	17	17	8	.353	.409	.453
Kid Carsey	P54,OF7,SS2	L	20	61	187	25	28	5	2	0	15	19	38	2	.150	.236	.198
Frank Foreman†	P43,OF8	L	28	50	153	26	34	4	5	4	19	23	35	6	.222	.339	.392
Pete Lohman	C21,OF8,3B4*	—	26	32	109	18	21	1	4	1	11	16	17	1	.193	.302	.303
Jim Curtis†	OF29	L	29	29	103	17	26	3	2	0	12	13	16	2	.252	.347	.320
Pop Smith	2B19,SS5,3B4	R	34	27	90	13	16	2	2	0	13	13	16	2	.178	.295	.244
Jim Burns	OF20,SS1	—	—	20	82	15	26	6	0	0	10	6	10	2	.317	.378	.390
Ed Daily†	OF21	R	28	21	79	13	18	2	0	0	6	11	10	8	.228	.322	.253
Patsy Donovan†	OF17	L	26	17	70	9	14	1	0	0	3	4	5	1	.200	.243	.214
Sandy Griffin	OF20	R	32	20	69	15	19	4	2	0	10	10	3	2	.275	.398	.391
Joe Visner†	OF17,C1,3B1	L	31	18	68	13	19	2	3	1	7	8	7	2	.279	.355	.441
Dan Shannon	SS14,2B5	—	26	19	67	7	9	2	0	0	3	6	9	3	.134	.205	.164
Mike Slattery†	OF15	L	24	15	60	8	17	1	0	0	5	4	5	6	.283	.358	.300
Jumbo Davis	3B12	L	29	12	44	7	14	3	2	0	9	7	5	8	.318	.412	.477
Tom McLaughlin	SS14	—	31	14	41	9	11	0	1	0	3	7	6	3	.268	.400	.317
Will Smalley	3B9,2B2	R	20	11	38	5	6	0	1	0	3	5	2	0	.158	.256	.211
Pop Snyder	1B4,C3,OF1	R	36	8	27	4	5	0	1	0	2	0	3	0	.185	.241	.259
Fred Dunlap	2B8	R	32	8	25	4	5	1	1	0	4	5	4	3	.200	.355	.320
Tom Hart	C5,OF3	—	22	8	24	1	3	0	0	0	2	2	1	1	.125	.192	.125
Miah Murray	C2	R	26	2	8	0	0	0	0	0	0	0	1	0	.000	.000	.000

D. McGuire, 1 G at 1B; G. Hatfield, 3 G at OF; S. Sutcliffe, 1 G at 3B; P. Lohman, 1 G at 2B, 1 G at SS

Pitcher	T	Age	G	GS	CG	ShO	IP	H	HR	BB	SO	W-L	Sv	ERA
Kid Carsey	R	20	54	53	46	1	415.0	513	17	161	174	14-37	0	4.99
Frank Foreman	L	28	43	41	39	1	345.1	381	9	142	170	18-20	1	3.73
Jersey Bakely†	R	27	13	12	11	0	104.1	127	6	60	32	2-10	0	5.35
Ed Eiteljorge	R	19	8	7	6	0	61.1	79	3	41	23	1-5	0	6.16
Bob Miller	—	29	7	7	3	0	42.0	53	3	24	13	2-5	0	4.29
Ed Cassian†	R	23	7	5	5	0	53.0	73	4	35	14	2-4	0	5.60
Buck Freeman	L	19	5	4	4	0	44.0	35	0	33	28	3-2	0	3.89
George Keefe	L	24	5	4	4	0	37.0	44	0	17	11	0-3	1	2.68
Martin Duke	L	24	4	3	2	0	23.0	36	0	19	5	0-3	0	7.43
Bill Quarles	—	22	3	2	2	0	22.0	32	1	12	10	1-1	0	8.18
Gil Hatfield	R	36	4	0	0	0	18.0	29	1	14	3	0-0	0	11.00
Jimmy Mace	—	—	3	1	1	0	16.0	18	0	8	3	0-1	0	7.31

»1892 Boston Beaneaters NL 1st 52-22 .703 — (1) 2nd 50-26 .658 3.0 GB (2)

Frank Selee

Player	Gm by Position	B	Age	G	AB	R	H	2B	3B	HR	RBI	BB	SO	SB	Avg	OBP	Slg
King Kelly	C72,1B2,3B2*	R	34	78	281	40	53	7	0	2	41	39	31	24	.189	.288	.235
Tommy Tucker	1B149	S	28	149	542	85	153	15	7	1	62	45	35	22	.282	.365	.341
Joe Quinn	2B143	R	27	143	532	63	116	14	1	1	59	35	40	17	.218	.275	.254
Billy Nash	3B135,OF1	R	27	135	526	94	137	25	5	4	95	59	41	31	.260	.338	.350
Herman Long	SS141,OF12,3B1	L	26	151	646	115	181	33	6	6	78	44	36	57	.280	.334	.378
Tommy McCarthy	OF152	R	28	152	603	119	146	19	5	4	63	93	29	53	.242	.347	.310
Hugh Duffy	OF146,3B2	R	25	147	612	125	184	28	12	5	81	60	37	51	.301	.364	.410
Bobby Lowe	OF90,3B14,SS13*	R	23	124	475	79	115	16	7	3	57	37	46	36	.242	.308	.324
Jack Stivetts	P54,OF18,1B1	R	24	71	240	40	71	14	2	3	36	27	28	8	.296	.369	.408
Charlie Ganzel	C51,OF2,1B1	R	30	54	198	25	53	9	3	0	25	18	12	7	.268	.332	.343
Kid Nichols	P53,OF5	S	22	57	197	21	39	6	2	2	21	16	51	3	.198	.258	.279
Harry Stovey†	OF38	R	35	38	146	21	24	8	1	0	12	14	19	20	.164	.252	.233
Harry Staley	P37,OF1	R	25	38	122	9	16	2	0	1	9	9	38	2	.131	.191	.172
Charlie Bennett	C35	R	37	35	114	19	23	4	0	1	16	27	23	6	.202	.355	.263
Dan Burke	C1	R	23	1	4	0	0	0	0	0	0	0	2	0	.000	.000	.000
Joe Daly	C1	—	23	1	0	0	0	0	0	0	0	0	0	0	—	—	—

K. Kelly, 2 G at OF, 1 G at P; B. Lowe, 10 G at 2B

Pitcher	T	Age	G	GS	CG	ShO	IP	H	HR	BB	SO	W-L	Sv	ERA
Kid Nichols	R	22	53	51	49	5	453.0	404	15	121	187	35-16	0	2.84
Jack Stivetts	R	24	54	48	45	3	415.2	346	12	171	180	35-16	1	3.03
Harry Staley	R	25	37	35	31	3	299.2	273	10	97	93	22-10	0	3.03
John Clarkson†	R	30	16	16	15	4	145.2	115	4	60	48	8-6	0	2.35
Lee Viau†	R	25	1	1	1	0	9.0	5	0	4	1	1-0	0	0.00
Dad Clarkson	R	25	1	1	1	0	7.0	5	0	3	0	1-0	0	1.29
King Kelly	R	34	1	0	0	0	6.0	8	0	4	0	0-0	0	1.50

1892 Cleveland Spiders NL 5th 40-33 .548 11.5 GB (1) 1st 53-23 .697 — (2)

Patsy Tebeau

Player	Gm by Position	B	Age	G	AB	R	H	2B	3B	HR	RBI	BB	SO	SB	Avg	OBP	Slg
Chief Zimmer	C111	R	31	111	413	63	108	29	13	1	64	32	47	18	.262	.325	.402
Jake Virtue	1B147	S	27	147	557	98	157	15	20	2	89	84	68	14	.282	.380	.391
Cupid Childs	2B145	L	24	145	558	136	177	14	11	3	53	117	20	26	.317	.443	.398
George Davis	3B79,OF44,SS20*	S	21	144	597	95	144	27	12	5	82	58	51	36	.241	.312	.352
Ed McKean	SS129	R	28	129	531	76	139	14	10	0	93	49	28	19	.262	.325	.326
Jimmy McAleer	OF149	R	27	149	571	92	136	26	7	4	70	63	54	40	.238	.318	.329
Jesse Burkett	OF145	L	23	145	608	119	167	15	14	6	66	67	59	36	.275	.348	.375
Jack O'Connor	OF106,C34	R	23	140	572	71	142	22	5	1	58	25	48	17	.248	.282	.309
Patsy Tebeau	3B74,2B5,1B4*	R	27	86	340	47	83	13	3	2	49	23	34	6	.244	.307	.318
Nig Cuppy	P47,OF3	R	22	50	168	15	36	11	0	0	24	7	40	2	.214	.246	.280
Jack Doyle†	OF12,C9,1B1*	R	22	24	88	17	26	4	1	1	14	6	10	5	.295	.340	.398
Tom Williams	P2,OF1	—	21	3	10	1	1	0	0	0	0	0	2	0	.100	.100	.100

G. Davis, 3 G at 2B; P. Tebeau, 3 G at SS; J. Doyle, 1 G at SS

Pitcher	T	Age	G	GS	CG	ShO	IP	H	HR	BB	SO	W-L	Sv	ERA
Cy Young	R	25	53	49	48	9	453.0	363	8	118	168	36-12	0	1.93
Nig Cuppy	R	22	47	42	38	1	376.0	333	9	121	103	28-13	1	2.51
John Clarkson†	R	30	29	28	27	1	243.1	235	4	72	91	17-10	1	2.55
George Davies	—	24	26	26	23	0	215.2	201	4	69	95	10-16	0	2.59
George Rettger†	R	23	6	5	3	0	38.0	32	2	31	12	1-3	0	4.26
Tom Williams	—	21	2	1	1	0	9.0	9	1	1	3	1-0	0	3.00
Lee Viau†	R	25	1	1	0	0	1.0	5	0	1	0	0-1	0	36.00

1892 Brooklyn Bridegrooms NL 2nd 51-26 .662 2.5 GB (1) 3rd 44-33 .571 9.5 GB (2)

Monte Ward

Player	Gm by Position	B	Age	G	AB	R	H	2B	3B	HR	RBI	BB	SO	SB	Avg	OBP	Slg
Con Daily	C68,OF13	L	27	80	278	38	65	10	1	0	28	38	21	18	.234	.328	.277
Dan Brouthers	1B152	L	34	152	588	121	197	30	20	5	124	84	30	31	.335	.432	.480
Monte Ward	2B148	L	32	148	614	109	163	13	3	1	47	82	19	88	.265	.355	.301
Bill Joyce	3B94,OF3	L	26	97	372	89	91	15	12	6	45	82	55	23	.245	.392	.398
Tommy Corcoran	SS151	R	23	151	613	77	145	11	6	1	74	34	51	39	.237	.281	.279
Oyster Burns	OF129,3B7,SS5	R	27	141	542	88	171	27	18	4	96	65	42	33	.315	.395	.454
Mike Griffin	OF127,SS2	L	27	129	452	103	125	17	11	3	66	68	36	49	.277	.376	.383
Darby O'Brien	OF122	R	28	122	490	72	119	14	5	1	56	29	52	57	.243	.289	.298
Tom Daly	3B57,OF30,C27*	S	26	124	446	76	114	15	6	4	51	64	61	34	.256	.355	.343
Tom Kinslow	C66	R	26	66	246	37	75	6	11	2	40	13	16	4	.305	.342	.443
Dave Foutz	OF29,P27,1B6	R	35	61	220	33	41	5	3	1	26	14	14	19	.186	.235	.250
George Haddock	P46,OF1	R	25	47	158	23	28	6	1	0	11	12	31	2	.177	.240	.228
Bill Hart	P28,OF12	—	26	37	125	14	24	3	4	2	17	7	22	4	.192	.241	.328
Hub Collins	OF21	R	28	21	87	17	26	5	1	0	17	14	13	4	.299	.396	.379
Brickyard Kennedy	P26,OF1	R	24	26	85	12	14	3	2	0	11	4	8	3	.165	.211	.247

T. Daly, 10 G at 2B

Pitcher	T	Age	G	GS	CG	ShO	IP	H	HR	BB	SO	W-L	Sv	ERA
George Haddock	R	25	46	44	39	3	381.1	340	11	163	153	29-13	1	3.14
Ed Stein	R	22	48	42	38	6	377.1	310	6	150	190	27-16	1	2.84
Bill Hart	R	26	28	23	16	2	195.0	188	3	96	65	9-12	1	3.28
Brickyard Kennedy	R	24	26	21	18	0	191.0	189	3	95	108	13-8	1	3.86
Dave Foutz	R	35	27	20	17	0	203.0	210	3	63	56	13-8	1	3.41
Bert Inks†	L	21	9	8	4	1	58.0	48	0	33	25	4-2	0	3.88

1892 Philadelphia Phillies NL 3rd 46-30 .605 7.0 GB (1) 5th 41-36 .532 12.5 GB (2)

Harry Wright

Player	Gm by Position	B	Age	G	AB	R	H	2B	3B	HR	RBI	BB	SO	SB	Avg	OBP	Slg
Jack Clements	C109	L	27	109	402	50	106	25	6	8	76	43	40	7	.264	.339	.415
Roger Connor	1B155	L	34	155	564	123	166	37	11	12	73	116	39	22	.294	.420	.463
Bill Hallman	2B138	R	25	138	586	106	171	27	10	2	84	32	52	19	.292	.335	.382
Charlie Reilly	3B70,OF15,2B4	S	25	91	331	42	65	7	3	1	24	18	43	15	.196	.242	.245
Bob Allen	SS152	R	24	152	563	77	128	20	14	2	64	61	60	15	.227	.304	.323
Sam Thompson	OF153	L	32	153	609	109	186	28	11	9	104	59	19	28	.305	.377	.432
Billy Hamilton	OF139	L	26	139	554	132	183	21	7	3	53	81	29	57	.330	.423	.410
Ed Delahanty	OF121,3B4	R	24	123	477	79	146	30	21	6	91	31	32	29	.306	.360	.495
Lave Cross	3B65,C39,OF25*	R	26	140	541	84	149	15	10	4	69	39	16	18	.275	.328	.362
Gus Weyhing	P59,OF7	R	25	66	214	14	29	5	0	0	13	11	67	2	.136	.178	.159
Kid Carsey	P43,OF2	L	21	44	131	8	20	2	1	1	10	9	24	1	.153	.207	.206
Joe Mulvey	3B25	R	33	25	98	9	14	1	1	0	4	6	9	2	.143	.200	.173
Duke Esper†	P21,OF1	—	23	23	70	8	17	2	0	1	11	2	18	1	.243	.274	.314
Tom Dowse†	C15	R	25	16	54	3	10	0	0	0	6	2	4	1	.185	.228	.185
Dummy Stephenson	OF8	R	22	8	37	4	10	3	0	0	5	0	2	0	.270	.289	.351
John Thornton†	P3,OF2	—	—	5	13	1	5	0	0	0	2	0	0	0	.385	.385	.385
Jerry Connors	OF1	—	—	1	3	0	0	0	0	0	0	0	1	0	.000	.000	.000
Harry Morelock	3B1	—	—	1	3	0	0	0	0	0	0	1	0	0	.000	.250	.000

L. Cross, 14 G at 2B, 5 G at SS

Pitcher	T	Age	G	GS	CG	ShO	IP	H	HR	BB	SO	W-L	Sv	ERA
Gus Weyhing	R	25	59	49	46	6	469.2	411	9	168	202	32-21	3	2.66
Tim Keefe	R	35	39	38	31	2	313.1	264	4	100	127	19-16	0	2.36
Kid Carsey	R	21	43	36	30	1	317.2	320	6	104	76	19-16	1	3.12
Duke Esper†	L	23	21	18	14	0	160.1	171	2	58	45	11-6	1	3.42
Phil Knell†	L	27	11	9	7	0	80.0	87	0	35	43	5-5	0	4.05
Jack Taylor	R	19	3	3	2	0	26.0	28	2	10	7	1-0	0	1.38
John Thornton	—	—	3	2	1	0	12.0	16	1	17	2	0-2	0	12.75

1892 Cincinnati Reds NL 4th 44-31 .587 8.5 GB (1) 8th 38-37 .507 14.5 GB (2)

Charlie Comiskey

Player	Gm by Position	B	Age	G	AB	R	H	2B	3B	HR	RBI	BB	SO	SB	Avg	OBP	Slg
Morgan Murphy	C74	R	25	74	234	29	46	8	2	2	24	25	57	4	.197	.277	.274
Charlie Comiskey	1B141	R	32	141	551	61	125	14	6	3	71	32	16	30	.227	.274	.290
Bid McPhee	2B144	R	32	144	573	111	157	19	12	4	60	84	48	44	.274	.373	.370
Arlie Latham	3B142,2B9,OF1	R	32	152	622	111	148	20	4	0	44	60	54	66	.238	.310	.283
Germany Smith	SS139	R	29	139	506	58	121	13	6	8	63	42	52	19	.239	.297	.336
Bug Holliday	OF152,P1	R	25	152	602	114	176	23	16	13	91	57	39	43	.292	.355	.449
Tip O'Neill	OF109	R	34	109	419	63	105	14	6	2	52	53	25	14	.251	.339	.327
Pete Browning†	OF82,1B2	R	31	83	307	47	93	12	5	3	52	40	25	8	.303	.383	.404
Farmer Vaughn	C67,1B14,OF11*	R	28	91	346	45	88	10	5	2	50	16	13	10	.254	.295	.329
Elton Chamberlin	P52,OF1	R	24	53	160	13	36	3	1	2	15	7	17	1	.225	.257	.294
Frank Dwyer†	P33,OF6	R	24	40	132	15	21	0	2	0	6	4	9	2	.159	.184	.189
Tony Mullane	P37,1B2	S	33	39	118	14	20	3	1	0	9	9	8	4	.169	.246	.212
Frank Genins†	SS17,OF14,3B4	—	25	35	110	12	20	4	0	0	7	12	12	7	.182	.262	.218
George Wood†	OF30	L	33	30	107	10	21	2	4	0	14	10	17	4	.196	.271	.290
Jocko Halligan†	OF26	L	23	26	101	14	29	4	0	2	12	12	9	3	.287	.363	.386
Curt Welch†	OF25	R	30	25	94	14	19	0	2	1	7	7	8	7	.202	.299	.277
Jerry Harrington	C22,1B1	R	22	22	61	6	13	1	0	0	3	6	1	0	.213	.284	.230
Buster Hoover	OF14	R	29	14	51	7	9	0	0	0	2	5	4	1	.176	.250	.176
Eddie Burke†	OF14,3B1	L	25	15	41	6	6	1	0	0	4	9	4	2	.146	.300	.171
Billy Rhines	P12,OF1	R	23	13	27	2	5	0	1	1	4	3	8	0	.185	.267	.370
Bill Kuehne†	3B4,2B2	R	33	6	24	3	5	1	0	1	4	1	5	0	.208	.240	.375
Dan Mahoney	C5	R	28	5	21	1	4	0	1	0	1	1	4	0	.190	.227	.286
George Rettger†	P1,OF1	R	23	2	8	1	1	1	0	0	3	1	1	0	.125	.222	.250
Tom Dowse†	C1	R	25	1	4	0	0	0	0	0	0	0	0	0	.000	.000	.000

F. Vaughn, 6 G at 3B

Pitcher	T	Age	G	GS	CG	ShO	IP	H	HR	BB	SO	W-L	Sv	ERA
Elton Chamberlin	R	24	52	49	43	2	406.1	391	8	170	169	19-23	0	3.39
Tony Mullane	R	33	37	34	30	3	295.0	222	12	127	109	21-13	1	2.59
Frank Dwyer†	R	24	34	28	25	3	268.1	262	6	49	47	19-10	1	2.31
Mike Sullivan	—	25	21	16	15	0	166.1	179	8	74	56	12-4	0	3.08
Billy Rhines	R	23	11	9	6	0	74.2	102	0	36	10	4-7	0	5.42
Jesse Duryea†	R	32	9	7	5	0	68.0	55	3	26	21	2-5	0	3.57
Dan Daub	R	24	4	3	2	0	25.0	23	0	13	7	1-2	0	2.88
Willie McGill	L	18	3	3	1	0	17.0	18	0	5	7	1-1	0	5.29
George Meakim†	R	26	3	3	1	0	13.2	19	1	9	4	1-1	0	8.56
Bumpus Jones	R	22	1	1	1	0	9.0	0	0	4	3	1-0	0	0.00
George Rettger†	R	23	1	1	1	0	9.0	8	0	10	1	1-0	0	4.00
Clarence Stephens	R	28	1	1	0	0	7.0	12	0	4	1	0-1	0	1.29
Frank Knauss	L	24	1	0	0	0	8.0	13	0	5	2	0-0	0	3.38
George Hemming†	R	23	1	0	0	0	6.0	10	1	2	0	0-1	0	7.50
Bug Holliday	R	25	1	0	0	0	4.0	13	0	1	0	0-0	0	11.25

1892 Pittsburgh Pirates NL 6th 37-39 .487 16.0 GB (1) 4th 43-34 .558 10.5 GB (2)

A. Buckenberger (15-14)/T. Burns (27-32)/A. Buckenberger (38-27)

Player	Gm by Position	B	Age	G	AB	R	H	2B	3B	HR	RBI	BB	SO	SB	Avg	OBP	Slg
Connie Mack	C92,OF3,1B1	R	29	97	346	39	84	9	4	1	31	21	22	11	.243	.298	.301
Jake Beckley	1B151	L	24	151	614	102	145	21	19	10	96	31	44	30	.236	.288	.381
Lou Bierbauer	2B152	L	26	152	649	81	153	20	9	8	65	25	29	11	.236	.264	.331
Duke Farrell	3B133,OF20	S	25	152	605	96	130	10	13	8	77	46	53	20	.215	.276	.314
Frank Shugart	SS134,C2,OF1	S	25	137	554	94	148	19	14	0	62	47	48	28	.267	.329	.352
Elmer Smith	OF124,P17	L	24	138	511	86	140	16	14	4	63	82	43	22	.274	.375	.384
Patsy Donovan†	OF90	L	27	90	388	77	114	15	3	2	26	20	16	40	.294	.333	.363
Doggie Miller	OF76,C63,SS19*	R	27	149	623	103	158	15	12	2	59	69	14	28	.254	.335	.326
Pop Corkhill	OF68	L	34	68	256	23	47	1	4	0	25	12	19	6	.184	.229	.219
Joe Kelley†	OF56	R	20	56	205	26	49	7	7	0	28	17	21	8	.239	.297	.341
Adonis Terry†	P30,OF1	R	27	31	100	10	16	0	4	2	11	10	11	2	.160	.236	.300
G. Van Haltren†	OF13	L	26	13	55	10	11	2	2	0	5	6	0	6	.200	.279	.309
Harry Raymond†	3B12	—	30	12	49	4	4	0	1	0	2	4	8	1	.082	.151	.122
Ed Swartwood	OF13	L	33	13	42	8	10	1	0	0	4	13	11	1	.238	.418	.262
Tom Burns	3B8,OF3	R	35	12	39	7	8	0	0	0	4	3	8	1	.205	.262	.205
Billy Gumbert	P6,OF1	R	26	7	18	2	2	0	1	0	1	0	4	2	.111	.158	.222
Billy Earle	C5	R	24	5	13	5	7	2	0	0	3	4	1	2	.538	.647	.692
Jake Stenzel	OF2,C1	R	25	3	9	0	0	0	0	0	0	1	3	1	.000	.100	.000
Bobby Cargo	SS2	R	23	2	4	0	1	0	0	0	0	0	0	0	.250	.250	.250
Jock Menefee	P1,OF1	R	24	2	3	0	0	0	0	0	0	0	0	0	.000	.000	.000

D. Miller, 2 G at 3B

Pitcher	T	Age	G	GS	CG	ShO	IP	H	HR	BB	SO	W-L	Sv	ERA
Mark Baldwin	R	28	56	53	45	0	440.1	447	11	194	157	26-27	0	3.47
Red Ehret	R	23	39	36	32	0	316.0	290	7	83	101	16-20	0	2.65
Adonis Terry†	R	27	30	26	24	2	240.0	185	3	106	95	18-7	1	2.51
Elmer Smith	L	24	17	13	12	1	134.0	140	2	58	51	6-7	0	3.63
Pud Galvin†	R	35	12	12	10	0	96.0	104	0	28	29	5-6	0	2.63
Fred Woodcock	L	24	5	4	3	0	33.0	42	1	17	8	1-2	0	3.55
Billy Gumbert	R	26	6	3	2	0	39.2	30	0	23	3	3-2	0	1.36
Duke Esper†	L	23	3	3	1	0	18.1	18	0	12	5	2-0	0	5.40
Bill Thompson	R	21	1	1	0	0	3.0	3	0	5	0	0-1	0	3.00
Kid Camp	R	22	4	1	1	0	23.0	31	4	9	6	0-1	0	6.26
Jock Menefee	R	24	1	0	0	0	4.0	10	0	2	0	0-0	0	11.25

1892 Chicago Colts NL 8th 31-39 .443 19.0 GB (1) 7th 39-37 .513 14.0 GB (2)

Cap Anson

Player	Gm by Position	B	Age	G	AB	R	H	2B	3B	HR	RBI	BB	SO	SB	Avg	OBP	Slg
Pop Schriver	C82,OF10	R	26	92	326	40	73	10	6	1	34	27	25	4	.224	.297	.301
Cap Anson	1B146	R	40	146	559	62	152	25	9	1	74	67	30	13	.272	.354	.354
Jim Canavan	2B112,OF4,SS2	R	25	118	439	48	73	10	11	0	32	48	48	33	.166	.248	.239
Jiggs Parrott	3B78	—	20	78	333	38	67	8	5	2	22	8	30	7	.201	.222	.273
Bill Dahlen	SS72,3B68,OF2*	R	22	143	581	114	169	23	19	5	58	45	56	60	.291	.347	.422
Jimmy Ryan	OF120,SS9	R	29	128	505	105	148	21	11	10	65	61	41	27	.293	.375	.438
Sam Dungan	OF113	R	25	113	433	46	123	19	7	0	53	35	19	15	.284	.346	.360
Walt Wilmot	OF92	S	28	92	380	47	82	7	7	2	35	40	20	31	.216	.297	.287
George Decker	OF62,2B16	L	23	78	291	32	66	6	7	1	28	20	49	9	.227	.277	.306
Bill Hutchison	P75,OF2	R	32	77	263	23	57	10	5	1	22	10	60	8	.217	.245	.304
Jimmy Cooney†	SS65	S	26	65	238	18	41	1	0	0	20	23	5	10	.172	.248	.176
Malachi Kittridge	C69	R	22	69	229	19	41	5	0	0	10	11	27	2	.179	.217	.201
Ad Gumbert	P46,OF7	R	23	52	178	18	42	1	2	1	8	14	24	5	.236	.295	.281
Pat Luby	P31,OF16	—	23	45	163	14	31	3	2	2	20	12	27	3	.190	.250	.270
Charlie Newman†	OF16	R	23	16	61	4	10	0	0	0	2	1	6	2	.164	.177	.164
Jim Connor	2B9	R	29	9	34	0	2	0	0	0	0	1	7	0	.059	.111	.059
Fred Roat	2B8	—	24	8	31	4	6	0	1	0	2	2	3	2	.194	.242	.258

B. Dahlen, 1 G at 2B

Pitcher	T	Age	G	GS	CG	ShO	IP	H	HR	BB	SO	W-L	Sv	ERA
Bill Hutchison	R	32	75	70	67	5	622.0	571	11	190	312	37-36	1	2.76
Ad Gumbert	R	23	46	45	39	0	382.2	399	11	107	118	22-19	0	3.41
Pat Luby	R	23	31	27	24	1	252.1	248	10	103	68	10-16	0	3.07
Harry DeMiller	L	24	4	2	2	0	24.0	29	1	16	15	1-1	0	6.38
George Meakim†	R	26	1	1	1	0	9.0	18	0	2	0	0-1	0	11.00
Frank Griffith	L	19	1	1	0	0	4.0	3	1	6	3	0-1	0	11.25
John Hollison	L	22	1	0	0	0	4.0	1	1	0	2	0-0	0	2.25

1892 New York Giants NL 10th 31-43 .419 21.0 GB (1) 6th 40-37 .519 13.5 GB (2)

Pat Powers

Player	Gm by Position	B	Age	G	AB	R	H	2B	3B	HR	RBI	BB	SO	SB	Avg	OBP	Slg
Jack Boyle	C79,1B40,SS2*	R	26	120	436	52	80	8	8	0	32	36	40	10	.183	.252	.239
Buck Ewing	1B73,C30,2B2	R	32	105	393	58	122	10	15	8	76	38	26	42	.310	.371	.473
Eddie Burke†	2B59,OF30	L	25	89	363	81	94	10	5	6	41	46	37	42	.259	.350	.364
Denny Lyons	3B108	R	26	108	389	71	100	16	7	8	51	59	36	11	.257	.359	.396
Shorty Fuller	SS141	R	24	141	508	74	115	11	4	1	48	52	22	37	.226	.298	.270
Mike Tiernan	OF116	L	25	116	450	79	129	16	10	5	66	57	46	20	.287	.369	.400
Jim O'Rourke	OF111,C4,1B1	R	41	115	448	62	136	28	5	0	56	30	30	16	.304	.354	.388
Harry Lyons	OF96	R	26	96	411	67	98	5	2	0	53	33	29	25	.238	.297	.260
Jack Doyle†	2B31,C26,OF17*	R	22	90	366	61	109	22	1	5	55	18	30	42	.298	.336	.404
Amos Rusie	P64,OF4	R	21	69	252	18	53	6	4	1	26	3	29	4	.210	.220	.278
Hardy Richardson†	2B33,OF17,1B9*	R	37	64	248	36	53	11	5	2	34	21	26	14	.214	.278	.323
George Gore†	OF53	L	35	53	193	47	49	11	2	0	11	49	16	20	.254	.412	.332
Ed Crane	P47,OF1	R	30	48	163	20	40	1	1	0	14	11	30	2	.245	.297	.264
Jack McMahon	1B36,C5	R	22	40	147	21	33	5	7	1	24	10	9	3	.224	.278	.374
Charley Bassett†	2B30,3B5	R	29	35	130	9	27	2	3	0	16	6	10	0	.208	.254	.269
Jocko Fields	OF11,C10	R	27	21	66	8	18	4	2	0	5	9	10	2	.273	.368	.394
Jimmy Knowles	3B15,SS1	—	33	16	59	9	9	1	0	0	7	6	8	2	.153	.231	.169
Willie Keeler	3B14	L	20	14	53	7	17	3	0	0	6	3	3	5	.321	.368	.377
Danny Murphy	C8	—	27	8	26	2	3	0	0	0	0	5	4	0	.115	.258	.115
Charlie Newman†	OF3	R	23	3	12	1	4	0	0	0	1	2	0	3	.333	.429	.333
John Sharrott	OF3,P1	R	22	4	8	1	1	0	0	0	0	0	1	0	.125	.125	.125

J. Boyle, 2 G at OF; J. Doyle, 13 G at 3B, 7 G at SS; H. Richardson, 6 G at SS

Pitcher	T	Age	G	GS	CG	ShO	IP	H	HR	BB	SO	W-L	Sv	ERA
Amos Rusie	R	21	64	61	58	2	532.0	405	7	267	288	31-31	0	2.88
Silver King	R	24	52	47	46	1	419.1	397	15	174	177	23-24	0	3.24
Ed Crane	R	30	47	43	35	2	364.1	350	10	189	174	16-24	1	3.80
Mickey Welch	R	32	1	1	0	0	5.0	11	0	4	1	0-0	0	14.40
John Sharrott	R	22	1	0	0	0	2.0	2	0	1	1	0-0	0	4.50

1892 Louisville Colonels NL 11th 30-47 .390 23.5 GB (1) 9th 33-42 .440 19.5 GB (2)

Jack Chapman (21-33)/Fred Pfeffer (42-56)

Player	Gm by Position	B	Age	G	AB	R	H	2B	3B	HR	RBI	BB	SO	SB	Avg	OBP	Slg
John Grim	C69,1B11,2B10*	R	24	97	370	40	90	16	4	1	36	13	24	18	.243	.280	.316
Lew Whistler†	1B72,2B10	—	24	80	285	42	67	4	7	5	34	30	45	14	.235	.312	.351
Fred Pfeffer	2B116,1B10,P1	R	32	124	470	78	121	14	9	2	76	67	36	27	.257	.353	.338
Bill Kuehne†	3B76	R	33	76	287	22	48	4	5	0	36	13	36	6	.167	.203	.216
Hughie Jennings	SS152	R	23	152	594	65	132	16	4	2	61	30	30	28	.222	.270	.273
Tom Brown	OF153	L	31	153	660	105	150	16	8	2	45	47	94	78	.227	.284	.285
Farmer Weaver	OF122,C15,1B1	L	27	138	551	58	140	15	4	0	57	40	17	30	.254	.315	.296
Harry Taylor	OF73,1B34,2B14*	L	26	125	493	66	128	7	1	0	34	58	23	24	.260	.342	.278
Charley Bassett†	3B73,2B6	R	29	79	313	36	67	5	5	2	35	15	19	16	.214	.250	.281
Scott Stratton	P42,OF17,1B6	L	22	63	219	22	56	2	9	0	23	17	21	9	.256	.318	.347
Ben Sanders	P31,1B15,OF9	R	27	54	198	30	54	12	2	3	18	16	17	6	.273	.330	.399
Bill Merritt	C46	R	21	46	168	22	33	4	2	1	13	11	15	3	.196	.246	.262
Emmett Seery	OF42	L	31	42	154	18	31	6	1	0	15	24	19	6	.201	.309	.253
Tom Dowse†	C29,1B11,OF3*	R	25	41	145	10	21	2	0	0	7	2	15	1	.145	.173	.159
Pete Browning†	OF21	R	31	21	77	10	19	4	0	0	4	12	7	5	.247	.348	.299
Lee Viau†	P16,OF5	R	25	21	66	5	13	2	0	0	5	7	16	2	.197	.284	.227
Jouett Meekin†	P19,OF1	R	25	20	64	7	5	1	0	0	3	6	9	1	.078	.157	.094
Alex McFarlan	OF12,2B2	—	22	14	42	2	7	0	0	0	1	8	11	1	.167	.300	.167
Harry Dooms	OF1	—	25	1	4	0	0	0	0	0	0	1	3	0	.000	.200	.000

J. Grim, 8 G at OF, 1 G at 3B, 1 G at SS; H. Taylor, 5 G at 3B, 2 G at SS; T. Dowse, 1 G at 2B

Pitcher	T	Age	G	GS	CG	ShO	IP	H	HR	BB	SO	W-L	Sv	ERA
Scott Stratton	R	22	42	40	39	2	351.2	342	1	70	93	21-19	0	2.92
Ben Sanders	R	27	31	31	30	3	268.1	281	6	62	77	12-19	0	3.22
Fritz Clausen	L	23	24	24	24	2	200.0	181	3	87	94	9-13	0	3.06
Jouett Meekin†	R	25	19	18	17	0	156.1	168	3	78	67	7-10	0	4.03
Alex Jones†	L	22	18	16	13	1	146.2	130	3	56	44	5-11	0	3.31
Lee Viau†	R	25	16	15	14	1	130.2	156	7	56	36	4-11	0	3.99
George Hemming†	R	23	4	4	4	0	35.0	36	1	17	12	2-2	0	4.63
John Fitzgerald	L	—	4	4	4	0	34.0	45	2	11	3	1-3	0	4.24
Egyptian Healy†	R	25	2	2	2	0	18.1	15	0	5	4	1-1	0	1.96
Fred Pfeffer	R	32	1	0	0	0	5.0	4	0	5	0	0-0	0	1.80

1892 Washington Senators NL 7th 35-41 .460 18.0 GB (1) 12th 23-52 .307 29.5 GB (2)

B. Barnie (0-2)/A. Irwin (46-60)/D. Richardson (12-31)

Player	Gm by Position	B	Age	G	AB	R	H	2B	3B	HR	RBI	BB	SO	SB	Avg	OBP	Slg
Deacon McGuire	C89,1B8,OF1	R	28	97	315	46	73	14	4	4	43	61	48	7	.232	.360	.340
Henry Larkin	1B117,OF2	R	32	119	464	76	130	13	7	8	96	39	21	21	.280	.346	.390
Tommy Dowd	2B98,OF23,3B18*	R	23	144	584	94	142	9	10	1	50	34	49	49	.243	.286	.298
Yank Robinson	3B58,SS5,2B4	R	32	67	218	26	39	4	3	0	19	38	28	11	.179	.301	.225
Danny Richardson	SS93,2B49,3B1	R	29	142	551	48	132	13	4	3	58	25	45	25	.240	.274	.294
Dummy Hoy	OF152	L	30	152	593	108	166	19	8	3	75	86	23	60	.280	.375	.354
Charlie Duffee	OF125,3B6,1B4	R	26	132	492	64	122	12	11	6	51	36	33	28	.248	.302	.354
Paul Radford	OF62,3B54,SS20*	R	30	137	510	93	130	19	4	1	37	86	47	35	.255	.366	.314
Jocko Milligan	C59,1B28	R	30	88	323	40	89	20	9	4	43	26	24	2	.276	.335	.430
Larry Twitchell	OF48,SS3,3B1	R	28	51	192	20	42	9	5	0	20	11	31	8	.219	.275	.318
Frank Killen	P60,OF2	L	21	65	186	27	37	4	4	4	23	26	61	2	.199	.310	.328
Patsy Donovan†	OF40	L	27	40	163	29	39	3	3	0	12	11	13	16	.239	.295	.294
Tun Berger	SS18,C9	—	24	26	97	9	14	2	1	0	3	7	9	3	.144	.210	.186
Hardy Richardson†	OF7,3B2,2B1	R	37	10	37	2	4	0	0	0	0	5	3	2	.108	.214	.108
Jake Drauby	3B10	—	27	10	34	3	7	0	1	0	3	2	12	0	.206	.250	.265
Tom Dowse†	OF4,C3	R	25	7	27	5	7	1	0	0	2	0	3	0	.259	.259	.296
Jimmy Cooney†	SS6	S	26	6	25	5	4	0	1	0	4	4	3	1	.160	.276	.240
George Ulrich	3B3,C2,SS2	—	23	6	24	1	7	1	0	0	0	0	4	2	.292	.292	.333
Harry Raymond†	3B4	—	30	4	15	2	1	0	0	0	0	3	2	1	.067	.222	.067
Dan Potts	C1	—	—	1	4	0	1	0	0	0	0	0	1	0	.250	.250	.250
Frank Shannon	SS1	—	18	1	4	0	1	0	0	0	2	0	2	0	.250	.250	.250
Hal O'Hagen	C1	—	18	1	4	1	1	0	0	0	0	0	2	0	.250	.250	.250
Kohly Miller†	SS1	—	—	1	3	0	0	0	0	0	0	0	1	0	.000	.000	.000

T. Dowd, 6 G at SS; P. Radford, 2 G at 2B

Pitcher	T	Age	G	GS	CG	ShO	IP	H	HR	BB	SO	W-L	Sv	ERA
Frank Killen	L	21	60	52	46	2	459.2	448	15	182	147	29-26	0	3.31
Bert Abbey	R	22	27	23	19	0	195.2	207	7	76	77	5-18	1	3.45
Phil Knell†	L	27	22	21	17	1	170.0	156	4	76	74	9-13	0	3.65
Jesse Duryea†	R	32	18	15	13	1	127.0	102	6	45	48	3-11	2	2.41
Jouett Meekin†	R	25	14	14	13	1	112.0	112	2	48	58	3-10	0	3.46
Hank Gastright	R	27	11	7	6	0	79.2	94	3	38	32	3-3	0	5.08
Frank Foreman†	L	29	11	7	4	0	60.0	53	3	37	16	2-4	0	3.30
Cozy Dolan	L	19	5	4	3	0	37.0	39	0	15	8	2-2	0	4.38
Alex Jones†	L	22	4	4	3	0	27.0	33	0	14	7	0-3	0	4.00
Matt Kilroy	L	26	4	3	2	0	26.1	20	0	15	1	1-1	0	2.39
Bert Inks†	L	21	3	3	3	0	21.0	29	0	10	11	1-2	0	5.14

1892 St. Louis Browns NL 9th 31-42 .425 20.5 GB (1) 11th 25-52 .325 28.5 GB (2)

Glasscock (1-3)/Crooks (3-11)/Stricker (6-17)/Gore (6-9)/Crooks (24-22)/Caruthers (16-32)

Player	Gm by Position	B	Age	G	AB	R	H	2B	3B	HR	RBI	BB	SO	SB	Avg	OBP	Slg
Dick Buckley	C119,1B2	—	33	121	410	43	93	17	4	5	52	22	34	7	.227	.275	.324
Perry Werden	1B149	R	26	149	598	73	154	22	6	8	84	59	52	20	.258	.328	.355
Jack Crooks	2B102,3B24,OF2	R	26	128	445	82	95	7	4	7	38	136	52	23	.213	.400	.294
George Pinckney	3B78	R	30	78	290	31	50	3	2	0	25	36	26	4	.172	.268	.197
Jack Glasscock	SS139	R	32	139	566	83	151	27	5	3	72	44	19	26	.267	.327	.348
Steve Brodie	OF137,2B16,3B2	L	23	154	602	85	152	10	9	4	60	52	31	28	.252	.316	.319
Bob Caruthers	OF122,P16,2B6*	L	28	143	513	76	142	16	8	3	69	86	29	24	.277	.386	.357
Cliff Carroll	OF101	S	32	101	407	82	111	14	8	4	49	47	22	30	.273	.363	.376
Kid Gleason	P47,OF10,2B9*	S	25	66	233	35	50	4	2	3	25	34	23	7	.215	.315	.288
Gene Moriarty	OF47	L	27	47	177	20	31	4	1	3	19	4	37	7	.175	.207	.260
Lew Camp	3B39,OF3	L	24	42	145	19	30	3	1	2	13	17	27	12	.207	.294	.283
Ted Breitenstein	P39,OF10	L	23	47	131	16	16	1	1	0	6	16	20	4	.122	.228	.145
Cub Stricker†	2B27,SS1	R	33	28	98	12	20	1	0	0	11	10	7	5	.204	.297	.214
Bill Moran	C21,OF2	—	22	24	81	2	11	1	0	0	5	2	12	0	.136	.157	.148
George Gore†	OF20	L	35	20	73	9	15	0	1	0	4	18	6	2	.205	.363	.233
Grant Briggs	C15,OF8	—	27	22	55	2	4	1	0	0	1	5	14	2	.073	.164	.091
Frank Genins†	SS14,OF1	—	25	15	51	5	10	1	0	0	4	1	11	3	.196	.212	.216
Frank Bird	C17	R	23	17	50	9	10	3	1	1	1	6	11	2	.200	.286	.360
Bill Hawke	P14,OF1	R	22	15	45	2	4	0	0	0	1	0	6	0	.089	.109	.089
Bill Kuehne†	3B6,SS1	R	33	7	28	1	4	1	0	0	0	0	4	1	.143	.172	.179
Jack Easton	P5,OF1	—	25	5	17	1	3	1	0	0	2	0	3	1	.176	.176	.235
Bill Van Dyke	OF4	R	28	4	16	2	2	0	0	0	1	0	1	0	.125	.125	.125
Chicken Wolf	OF3	R	30	3	14	1	2	0	0	0	1	0	1	0	.143	.143	.143
Jim McCormick	2B2,3B1	R	23	3	11	0	0	0	0	0	0	1	5	0	.000	.083	.000
Kohly Miller†	3B1	—	—	1	4	0	0	0	0	0	0	0	0	0	.000	.000	.000
Ed Haigh	OF1	—	25	1	4	0	1	0	0	0	0	0	2	0	.250	.250	.250
Heinie Peitz	C1	R	21	1	3	0	0	0	0	0	0	0	0	0	.000	.000	.000
Mark McGrillis	3B1	—	19	1	3	0	0	0	0	0	0	0	1	0	.000	.000	.000
John Thornton†	OF1	—	—	1	3	0	0	0	0	0	0	0	2	0	.000	.000	.000
Hick Carpenter	3B1	R	36	1	3	0	1	0	0	0	0	1	1	0	.333	.500	.333
— Collins	OF1	—	—	1	2	0	0	0	0	0	0	0	2	0	.000	.000	.000
— Leonard	OF1	—	—	1	0	0	0	0	0	0	0	1	0	1	—	1.000	—

B. Caruthers, 4 G at 1B; K. Gleason, 1 G at 1B

Pitcher	T	Age	G	GS	CG	ShO	IP	H	HR	BB	SO	W-L	Sv	ERA
Kid Gleason	R	25	47	45	43	2	400.0	389	11	151	133	20-24	0	3.33
Ted Breitenstein	L	23	39	32	28	1	282.1	280	8	148	126	9-19	0	4.69
Pink Hawley	R	19	20	20	18	0	166.1	160	4	63	63	6-14	0	3.19
Charlie Getzien	R	28	13	13	12	0	108.0	159	5	31	32	5-8	0	5.67
Pud Galvin†	R	35	12	12	10	0	92.0	102	4	26	27	5-6	0	3.23
Bill Hawke	R	22	14	11	10	1	97.1	108	2	45	55	5-5	0	3.70
Bob Caruthers	R	28	16	10	10	0	101.2	131	10	27	21	2-10	1	5.84
Frank Dwyer†	R	24	10	10	6	0	64.0	90	1	24	16	2-8	0	5.63
Jack Easton	—	25	5	2	2	0	31.0	38	2	26	4	2-0	0	6.39
Joe Young	—	—	1	0	0	0	2.0	9	0	2	1	0-0	0	22.50

1892 Baltimore Orioles NL 12th 20-55 .267 32.5 GB (1) 10th 26-46 .361 25.0 GB (2)

G. Van Haltren (1-10)/J. Waltz (2-6)/N. Hanlon (43-85)

Player	Gm by Position	B	Age	G	AB	R	H	2B	3B	HR	RBI	BB	SO	SB	Avg	OBP	Slg
Wilbert Robinson	C87,1B2,OF1	R	29	90	330	36	88	14	4	2	57	15	35	5	.267	.303	.352
Sy Sutcliffe	1B66	L	30	66	276	41	77	10	7	1	27	14	15	12	.279	.316	.377
Cub Stricker†	2B75	R	33	75	269	45	71	5	5	3	37	32	18	13	.264	.344	.353
Billy Shindle	3B134,SS9	R	28	143	619	100	156	20	18	3	50	35	34	24	.252	.301	.357
Tim O'Rourke	SS58,OF4,3B1	L	28	63	239	40	74	8	4	0	35	24	19	12	.310	.373	.377
G. Van Haltren†	OF129,P4,3B3*	L	26	135	556	105	168	20	12	7	57	70	34	49	.302	.382	.419
Harry Stovey†	OF64,1B10	R	35	74	283	58	77	14	11	4	55	40	32	20	.272	.364	.442
Curt Welch†	OF63	R	30	63	237	42	56	1	3	1	22	36	9	14	.236	.363	.278
Joe Gunson	C67,OF20,1B2*	R	29	89	314	35	67	10	5	0	32	16	17	2	.213	.267	.277
George Shoch	SS57,OF12,3B7	R	33	76	308	42	85	15	3	1	50	24	19	14	.276	.340	.354
John McGraw	2B34,OF34,SS8*	L	19	79	286	41	77	13	2	1	26	32	21	15	.269	.355	.339
Lew Whistler†	1B51,OF1	—	24	52	209	32	47	6	6	2	21	18	22	12	.225	.296	.340
Piggy Ward	OF43,2B7,SS5*	S	25	56	186	28	54	6	5	1	33	31	18	10	.290	.403	.392
Jocko Halligan†	OF22,1B19,C5	L	23	46	178	38	47	4	7	2	43	30	24	8	.264	.376	.399
Sadie McMahon	P48,1B1	R	24	49	177	12	25	1	2	0	18	7	31	0	.141	.183	.169
George Cobb	P53,OF6	—	—	57	172	20	36	4	4	5	13	22	37	2	.209	.299	.308
John Pickett	2B36	R	26	36	141	13	30	2	3	1	12	7	10	2	.213	.260	.291
George Wood†	OF21	L	33	21	76	9	17	1	1	0	10	10	8	1	.224	.330	.263
Monte Cross	SS15	R	22	15	50	5	8	0	0	0	2	4	10	2	.160	.222	.160
Sun Daly	OF13	—	27	13	48	5	12	0	2	0	7	1	4	0	.250	.265	.333
Ned Hanlon	OF11	L	34	11	43	3	7	1	1	0	2	3	3	0	.163	.217	.233
Joe Kelley†	OF10	R	20	10	33	3	7	0	0	0	4	4	7	2	.212	.316	.212
Frank Foreman†	OF5,P4	L	29	7	23	2	4	1	0	0	1	3	3	1	.174	.269	.304
Crazy Schmit	P6,OF1	L	26	7	19	1	2	0	0	0	0	3	5	1	.105	.227	.105
Pete Gilbert	3B4	—	24	4	15	0	3	0	0	0	0	1	3	0	.200	.250	.200
Bill Johnson	OF4	L	29	4	15	2	2	0	0	0	2	2	0	0	.133	.235	.133
John Godar	OF5	R	27	5	14	2	3	0	0	0	1	2	1	1	.214	.353	.214
Tom Hess	C1	—	16	1	2	0	0	0	0	0	0	0	1	0	.000	.000	.000

G. Van Haltren, 2 G at 1B, 2 G at SS; J. Gunson, 1 G at 2B; J. McGraw, 3 G at 3B; P. Ward, 1 G at C

Pitcher	T	Age	G	GS	CG	ShO	IP	H	HR	BB	SO	W-L	Sv	ERA
George Cobb	—	—	53	47	42	0	394.1	495	21	140	159	10-37	0	4.86
Sadie McMahon	R	24	48	46	44	2	397.0	430	9	145	118	19-25	1	3.24
Tom Vickery	R	25	24	21	17	0	176.0	189	3	87	49	8-10	0	3.53
Charlie Buffinton	R	31	13	13	9	0	97.0	130	4	46	30	4-8	0	4.92
Egyptian Healy†	R	25	9	8	5	0	68.1	82	4	21	24	3-6	0	4.74
Crazy Schmit	L	26	6	6	6	0	47.1	37	0	26	17	1-4	0	3.23
Frank Foreman†	L	29	4	3	2	0	25.0	40	4	11	5	0-3	0	6.84
Bill Kling	R	25	2	2	0	0	11.0	17	1	7	7	0-2	0	11.45
Bill Gilbert	—	24	2	1	1	0	14.0	14	1	17	5	0-1	0	5.79
Alex Ferson	R	25	2	1	1	0	9.0	17	1	6	8	0-1	0	11.00
Adonis Terry†	R	27	1	1	1	0	9.0	7	0	7	3	0-1	0	4.00
Harry Ely	—	—	1	1	1	0	7.0	14	0	7	0	0-1	0	7.71
George Stephens	—	24	5	2	2	0	29.0	37	2	9	7	1-1	1	2.79
George Van Haltren	L	26	4	0	0	0	14.2	28	1	7	5	0-0	0	9.20

»1893 Boston Beaneaters 1st NL 86-43 .667 — Frank Selee

Player	Gm by Position	B	Age	G	AB	R	H	2B	3B	HR	RBI	BB	SO	SB	Avg	OBP	Slg
Charlie Bennett	C60	R	38	60	191	34	40	6	0	4	27	40	36	5	.209	.352	.304
Tommy Tucker	1B121	S	29	121	486	83	138	13	2	7	91	27	31	8	.284	.347	.362
Bobby Lowe	2B121,SS5	R	24	126	526	130	157	19	5	14	89	55	29	22	.298	.369	.433
Billy Nash	3B128	R	28	128	485	115	141	27	6	10	123	85	29	30	.291	.399	.433
Herman Long	SS123,2B5	L	27	128	552	149	159	22	6	6	58	73	32	38	.288	.376	.382
Hugh Duffy	OF131	R	26	131	560	147	203	23	7	6	118	50	13	44	.363	.416	.461
Cliff Carroll	OF120	S	33	120	438	80	98	7	5	2	54	88	28	29	.224	.360	.276
Tommy McCarthy	OF108,2B7,SS3	R	29	116	462	107	160	28	6	5	111	64	10	46	.346	.429	.465
Charlie Ganzel	C40,OF23,1B10	R	31	73	281	50	75	10	2	1	48	22	9	6	.267	.325	.327
Kid Nichols	P52,OF1	S	23	53	177	25	39	3	2	2	26	15	22	4	.220	.285	.294
Jack Stivetts	P37,OF8,3B3	R	25	50	172	32	51	5	6	3	25	12	14	6	.297	.342	.448
Bill Merritt	C37,OF2	R	22	39	141	30	49	6	3	3	26	13	13	3	.348	.403	.496
Hank Gastright†	P19,OF1	R	28	20	68	11	13	3	0	0	10	6	5	0	.191	.257	.235
Bill Van Dyke	OF3	R	29	3	12	2	3	1	0	0	1	0	1	1	.250	.250	.333

Pitcher	T	Age	G	GS	CG	ShO	IP	H	HR	BB	SO	W-L	Sv	ERA
Kid Nichols	R	23	52	44	43	1	425.0	426	15	118	94	34-14	1	3.52
Jack Stivetts	R	25	38	34	29	1	283.2	315	17	115	61	20-12	1	4.41
Harry Staley	R	26	36	31	23	0	263.0	344	22	81	61	18-10	0	5.13
Hank Gastright†	R	28	19	18	16	0	156.0	179	9	76	27	12-4	0	5.13
Bill Quarles	—	24	3	3	3	0	27.0	31	2	5	6	2-1	0	4.67
Bill Coyle	R	—	2	1	0	0	8.0	14	1	3	2	0-1	0	9.00
Jim Garry	L	23	1	0	0	0	1.0	5	0	4	2	0-1	0	63.00

1893 Pittsburgh Pirates 2nd NL 81-48 .628 5.0 GB Al Buckenberger

Player	Gm by Position	B	Age	G	AB	R	H	2B	3B	HR	RBI	BB	SO	SB	Avg	OBP	Slg
Doggie Miller	C40	R	28	41	154	23	28	6	1	0	17	17	8	3	.182	.284	.234
Jake Beckley	1B131	L	25	131	542	108	164	32	19	5	106	54	26	15	.303	.386	.459
Lou Bierbauer	2B128	L	27	128	528	84	150	19	11	4	94	36	12	11	.284	.335	.384
Denny Lyons	3B131	R	27	131	490	103	150	19	16	3	105	97	29	19	.306	.430	.429
Jack Glasscock†	SS66	R	33	66	293	49	100	7	11	1	74	17	4	16	.341	.385	.451
Elmer Smith	OF128	L	25	128	518	121	179	26	23	7	103	77	23	26	.346	.435	.525
Patsy Donovan	OF112	L	28	113	499	114	158	5	8	2	56	42	8	46	.317	.373	.371
George Van Haltren	OF111,SS12,2B2	L	27	124	529	129	179	14	11	3	79	75	25	37	.338	.422	.423
Jake Stenzel	OF45,C12,2B1*	R	26	60	224	57	81	13	4	4	37	24	17	16	.362	.423	.509
Frank Shugart†	SS51,OF1	S	26	52	210	37	55	7	3	1	32	19	15	12	.262	.332	.338
Connie Mack	C37	R	30	37	133	22	38	3	1	0	15	10	9	4	.286	.358	.323
Billy Earle	C27	R	25	27	95	21	24	4	4	2	15	7	6	1	.253	.304	.442
Ad Gumbert	P22,OF7	R	24	29	95	17	21	3	3	0	10	10	16	0	.221	.295	.316
Joe Sugden	C27	S	22	27	92	20	24	4	3	0	12	10	11	1	.261	.340	.370
Reddy Gray	SS2	—	—	2	9	0	4	1	0	0	2	0	1	0	.444	.444	.556
Sam Gillen	SS3	—	22	3	6	0	0	0	0	0	0	0	1	0	.000	.000	.000

J. Stenzel, 1 G at SS

Pitcher	T	Age	G	GS	CG	ShO	IP	H	HR	BB	SO	W-L	Sv	ERA
Frank Killen	L	22	55	48	38	2	415.0	401	12	140	99	36-14	0	3.64
Red Ehret	R	24	39	35	32	4	314.1	322	3	115	70	18-18	0	3.44
Ad Gumbert	R	24	22	20	16	2	162.2	207	5	78	40	11-7	0	5.15
Adonis Terry	R	28	26	19	14	0	170.0	177	5	99	52	12-8	0	4.45
Hank Gastright†	R	28	9	5	3	0	59.0	74	3	39	12	3-1	0	6.25
Mark Baldwin†	R	29	1	1	0	0	2.1	6	0	1	0	0-0	0	11.57
Tom Colcolough	R	22	8	3	1	0	43.2	45	1	32	7	1-0	1	4.12

1893 Cleveland Spiders 3rd NL 73-55 .570 12.5 GB Patsy Tebeau

Player	Gm by Position	B	Age	G	AB	R	H	2B	3B	HR	RBI	BB	SO	SB	Avg	OBP	Slg
Jack O'Connor	C56,OF44	R	24	96	384	72	110	23	1	4	75	29	12	29	.286	.341	.383
Jake Virtue	1B73,OF13,3B5*	S	28	97	378	87	100	16	10	1	60	54	14	11	.265	.358	.368
Cupid Childs	2B123	L	25	124	485	145	158	19	10	3	65	120	12	23	.326	.463	.425
Chippy McGarr	3B63	R	30	63	249	38	77	12	0	0	28	20	15	24	.309	.363	.357
Ed McKean	SS125	R	29	125	545	103	169	29	24	4	133	50	14	16	.310	.372	.473
Jesse Burkett	OF125	L	24	125	511	145	178	25	15	6	82	98	23	39	.348	.459	.491
Buck Ewing	OF112,2B5,C1*	R	33	116	500	117	172	28	15	6	122	41	18	47	.344	.394	.496
Jimmy McAleer	OF91	R	28	91	350	63	83	5	1	2	41	35	21	32	.237	.314	.274
Patsy Tebeau	1B57,3B56,2B3	R	28	116	486	90	160	32	8	2	102	32	11	19	.329	.375	.440
Chief Zimmer	C56,3B1	R	32	57	227	27	70	13	7	2	41	16	15	4	.308	.357	.454
John Clarkson	P36,OF1	R	31	37	131	18	27	6	2	1	17	4	20	2	.206	.230	.305
Nig Cuppy	P31,OF2	R	23	32	109	14	27	6	2	0	14	8	15	1	.248	.299	.339
Joe Gunson†	C20	R	30	21	73	11	19	1	0	0	9	6	0	0	.260	.316	.274
Charlie Hastings	P15,OF1	—	22	16	39	6	7	0	2	0	1	8	12	1	.179	.319	.282
Ed McFarland	OF5,3B2,C1	R	18	8	22	5	9	2	1	0	6	1	2	0	.409	.458	.591
Tom Williams	P5,OF3	—	22	8	18	5	5	0	0	0	2	4	4	2	.278	.409	.278
Billy Alvord	3B3	—	29	3	12	2	2	0	0	0	2	0	1	0	.167	.167	.167
Jim Gilman	3B2	—	—	2	7	1	2	0	0	0	1	0	2	0	.286	.286	.286
Frank Boyd	C2	R	25	2	5	3	1	1	0	0	3	1	0	0	.200	.333	.400
Pete Allen	C1	R	25	1	4	0	0	0	0	0	0	0	0	0	.000	.000	.000
John Stafford	P2,OF1	R	23	2	4	0	0	0	0	0	0	0	0	0	.000	.000	.000

J. Virtue, 5 G at SS, 1 G at P; B. Ewing, 1 G at 1B

Pitcher	T	Age	G	GS	CG	ShO	IP	H	HR	BB	SO	W-L	Sv	ERA
Cy Young	R	26	53	46	42	1	422.2	442	10	103	102	34-16	1	3.36
John Clarkson	R	31	36	35	31	0	295.0	358	11	95	62	16-17	0	4.45
Nig Cuppy	R	23	31	30	24	0	243.2	316	6	75	39	17-10	0	4.47
Charlie Hastings	—	22	15	9	6	0	92.0	128	5	33	14	4-5	1	4.70
George Davies†	—	25	3	3	1	0	15.0	28	1	10	3	0-2	0	11.40
Chauncey Fisher	R	21	2	2	2	0	18.0	26	0	9	9	0-2	0	5.50
John Scheible	L	27	2	2	2	1	18.0	15	0	11	1	1-1	0	2.00
Tom Williams	—	22	5	2	2	0	24.0	33	1	10	6	1-1	0	4.88
John Stafford	R	23	2	0	0	0	7.0	12	1	7	4	0-1	0	14.14
Jake Virtue	L	28	1	0	0	0	5.0	3	0	3	2	0-0	0	1.80

1893 Philadelphia Phillies 4th NL 72-57 .558 14.0 GB Harry Wright

Player	Gm by Position	B	Age	G	AB	R	H	2B	3B	HR	RBI	BB	SO	SB	Avg	OBP	Slg
Jack Clements	C92,1B1	L	28	94	376	64	107	20	3	17	80	39	29	3	.285	.360	.489
Jack Boyle	1B112,C6,2B2	R	27	116	504	105	144	29	9	4	81	41	30	22	.286	.351	.403
Bill Hallman	2B120,1B12	R	26	132	596	119	183	28	7	5	76	51	27	22	.307	.367	.403
Charlie Reilly	3B104	S	26	104	416	64	102	16	7	4	56	33	36	13	.245	.314	.346
Bob Allen	SS124	R	25	124	471	86	126	19	12	8	90	71	40	8	.268	.369	.410
Sam Thompson	OF131,1B1	L	33	131	600	130	222	37	13	11	126	50	17	18	.370	.424	.530
Ed Delahanty	OF117,2B15,1B6	R	25	132	595	145	219	35	18	19	146	47	20	37	.368	.423	.583
Billy Hamilton	OF82	L	27	82	355	110	135	22	7	5	44	63	7	43	.380	.490	.524
Lave Cross	C40,3B30,SS10*	R	27	96	415	81	124	17	6	4	78	26	7	18	.299	.342	.398
Tuck Turner	OF36	S	20	36	155	32	50	4	3	1	13	9	19	7	.323	.364	.406
John Sharrott	OF39,P12	R	23	50	152	25	38	4	3	1	22	8	14	6	.250	.288	.336
Gus Weyhing	P42,OF1	R	26	43	147	14	22	3	0	0	11	14	39	1	.150	.224	.170
Jack Taylor	P25,OF3	R	20	31	93	11	20	5	1	0	18	1	8	1	.215	.232	.290
Tom Vickery	P13,2B1	—	26	15	35	1	11	1	0	0	4	1	2	0	.314	.368	.343

L. Cross, 10 G at OF, 6 G at 1B

Pitcher	T	Age	G	GS	CG	ShO	IP	H	HR	BB	SO	W-L	Sv	ERA
Gus Weyhing	R	26	42	40	33	2	345.1	399	10	145	101	23-16	0	4.74
Kid Carsey	R	22	39	35	30	1	318.1	375	7	124	50	20-15	0	4.81
Tim Keefe	R	36	22	22	17	0	178.0	202	3	79	53	10-7	0	4.40
Jack Taylor	R	20	25	16	14	0	170.0	189	8	77	41	10-9	1	4.24
Tom Vickery	R	26	13	11	7	0	80.0	100	1	37	15	4-5	0	5.40
Albert McGinnis†	L	—	5	4	4	1	37.1	39	0	17	12	1-3	0	4.34
John Sharrott	R	23	12	4	2	0	56.0	53	1	33	11	4-2	0	4.50
Frank O'Connor	L	22	3	1	0	0	4.0	2	0	9	0	0-0	1	11.25

1893 New York Giants 5th NL 68-64 .515 19.5 GB Monte Ward

Player	Gm by Position	B	Age	G	AB	R	H	2B	3B	HR	RBI	BB	SO	SB	Avg	OBP	Slg
Jack Doyle	C48,OF29,SS4*	R	23	82	318	56	102	17	5	1	51	27	12	40	.321	.383	.415
Roger Connor	1B135,3B1	L	35	135	511	111	156	25	8	11	105	91	26	24	.305	.413	.450
Monte Ward	2B134	L	33	135	588	129	193	27	9	2	77	47	5	46	.328	.379	.415
George Davis	3B133,SS1	S	22	133	549	112	195	22	27	11	119	42	20	37	.355	.410	.554
Shorty Fuller	SS130	R	25	130	474	78	112	14	8	0	51	60	21	26	.236	.325	.300
Eddie Burke	OF135	L	26	135	537	122	150	23	10	9	80	51	32	54	.279	.369	.410
Mike Tiernan	OF125	L	26	125	511	114	158	19	12	15	102	72	24	26	.309	.399	.481
General Stafford	OF67	R	24	67	281	58	79	7	4	5	27	25	31	19	.281	.344	.388
Harry Lyons	OF47	R	27	47	187	27	51	5	2	0	21	14	6	10	.273	.323	.321
Jocko Milligan†	C42	R	31	42	147	16	34	5	6	1	25	14	13	2	.231	.302	.367
Parke Wilson	C31	R	25	31	114	16	28	4	1	2	21	7	9	5	.246	.289	.351
Les German	P20,3B1,OF1	R	24	22	74	10	23	0	1	0	15	5	1	1	.311	.354	.338
King Kelly	C17,OF1	R	35	20	67	9	18	1	0	0	15	6	5	3	.269	.329	.284
Jack McMahon	C11	R	23	11	30	5	10	2	1	0	4	2	0	0	.333	.375	.467
Ed Crane†	P10,1B1,OF1	R	31	12	26	8	12	1	0	0	3	7	0	0	.462	.576	.500
Willie Keeler†	OF3,2B2,SS2	L	21	7	24	5	8	2	1	1	7	5	1	3	.333	.448	.625
Shorty Howe	3B1	—	—	1	5	1	3	0	0	0	2	0	0	1	.600	.600	.600
— Kinsler	OF1	—	—	1	3	1	0	0	0	0	0	1	1	0	.000	.250	.000

J. Doyle, 3 G at 3B, 1 G at 1B

Pitcher	T	Age	G	GS	CG	ShO	IP	H	HR	BB	SO	W-L	Sv	ERA
Amos Rusie	R	22	56	52	50	4	482.0	451	15	218	208	33-21	1	3.23
Mark Baldwin†	R	29	45	39	33	2	331.1	335	6	141	100	16-20	2	4.10
Les German	R	24	20	18	14	0	152.0	162	6	70	35	8-8	0	4.14
Ed Crane†	R	31	10	7	4	0	68.1	84	2	41	11	2-4	0	5.93
Silver King†	R	25	7	7	4	0	49.0	69	4	26	13	3-4	0	8.63
Charlie Petty	R	27	9	6	4	0	54.0	66	0	28	12	5-2	0	3.33
Crazy Schmit†	L	27	4	4	1	0	20.2	30	0	17	5	0-2	0	7.40
Frank Foreman	L	30	2	1	0	0	5.2	19	1	10	0	0-1	0	27.00
Bumpus Jones†	R	23	1	1	0	0	4.0	5	0	10	1	0-1	0	11.25
George Davies†	—	25	5	1	1	0	36.1	41	1	13	7	1-1	0	6.19
Red Donahue	R	20	2	0	0	0	5.0	8	1	3	1	0-0	1	9.00
Seth Sigsby	—	19	1	0	0	0	3.0	1	0	4	2	0-0	0	9.00

526 Seasons: Team Rosters

1893 Cincinnati Reds 6th NL 65-63 .508 20.5 GB

Charlie Comiskey

Player	Gm by Position	B	Age	G	AB	R	H	2B	3B	HR	RBI	BB	SO	SB	Avg	OBP	Slg
Farmer Vaughn	C80,OF23,1B21	R	29	121	483	68	135	17	12	1	108	35	17	16	.280	.332	.371
Charlie Comiskey	1B64	R	33	64	259	38	57	12	1	0	26	11	2	9	.220	.257	.274
Bid McPhee	2B127	R	33	127	491	101	138	17	11	3	68	94	20	25	.281	.401	.379
Arlie Latham	3B127	R	33	127	531	101	150	18	6	2	49	62	20	57	.282	.368	.350
Germany Smith	SS130	R	30	130	500	63	118	18	6	4	56	38	20	14	.236	.293	.320
Bug Holliday	OF125,1B1	R	26	126	500	108	155	24	10	5	89	73	22	32	.310	.401	.428
Jim Canavan	OF116,2B5,3B1	R	26	121	461	65	104	13	7	5	64	51	20	31	.226	.305	.317
Jack McCarthy	OF47,1B2	L	24	49	195	28	55	8	3	0	22	22	7	6	.282	.355	.354
Morgan Murphy	C56,1B1	R	26	57	200	25	47	5	1	1	19	14	35	1	.235	.295	.285
Frank Motz	1B43	—	23	43	156	16	40	7	1	2	25	19	10	3	.256	.352	.353
Piggy Ward†	OF40,1B1	S	26	42	150	44	42	4	1	0	10	37	10	27	.280	.440	.320
Frank Dwyer	P37,1B1,OF1	R	25	38	120	22	24	1	2	1	17	9	5	2	.200	.256	.267
George Henry	OF21	R	29	21	83	11	23	3	0	0	13	11	12	2	.277	.375	.313
Tom Parrott†	P22,OF1	R	25	24	68	5	13	1	1	1	9	1	9	0	.191	.203	.279
Tony Mullane†	P15,3B1	S	34	16	52	11	15	0	0	1	6	5	3	1	.288	.383	.346
Bob Caruthers†	OF13	L	29	13	48	14	14	2	0	1	8	16	1	4	.292	.477	.396
Jud Smith†	OF9,3B6,SS1	R	24	17	43	7	10	1	0	1	5	9	5	1	.233	.365	.326
Connie Murphy	C4	L	22	6	17	3	3	1	0	0	2	1	2	0	.176	.222	.235
Charlie Duffee	OF4	R	27	4	12	3	2	1	0	0	0	5	0	0	.167	.412	.250
George Ulrich	OF1	—	24	1	3	0	0	0	0	0	0	0	0	1	.000	.250	.000

Pitcher	T	Age	G	GS	CG	ShO	IP	H	HR	BB	SO	W-L	Sv	ERA
Frank Dwyer	R	25	37	30	28	1	287.1	332	17	93	53	18-15	2	4.13
Elton Chamberlin	R	25	34	27	19	1	241.0	248	3	112	59	16-12	0	3.73
Mike Sullivan	—	26	27	18	14	0	183.2	200	5	103	40	8-11	1	5.05
Tom Parrott†	R	25	22	17	11	1	154.0	174	1	70	33	10-7	0	4.09
Silver King†	R	25	17	15	8	1	105.0	119	2	56	30	5-6	1	4.89
Tony Mullane†	R	34	15	13	11	0	122.1	130	4	65	24	6-6	1	4.41
Bumpus Jones†	R	23	6	5	2	0	28.2	37	1	23	6	1-3	0	10.05
George Darby	R	24	4	3	2	0	29.0	41	2	18	6	1-1	0	7.76
Lem Cross	R	21	3	3	2	0	21.0	24	3	9	7	0-2	0	5.57

1893 Brooklyn Bridegrooms 6th NL 65-63 .508 20.5 GB

Dave Foutz

Player	Gm by Position	B	Age	G	AB	R	H	2B	3B	HR	RBI	BB	SO	SB	Avg	OBP	Slg
Tom Kinslow	C76,OF2	R	27	78	312	38	76	8	4	4	45	11	13	4	.244	.272	.333
Dan Brouthers	1B77	L	35	77	282	57	95	21	11	2	59	52	10	9	.337	.450	.511
Tom Daly	2B82,3B45	S	27	126	470	94	136	21	14	8	70	76	65	32	.289	.388	.445
George Shoch	OF46,3B37,SS11*	R	34	94	327	53	86	17	1	2	54	48	13	9	.263	.366	.339
Tommy Corcoran	SS115	R	24	115	459	61	126	11	10	2	58	27	12	14	.275	.318	.355
Oyster Burns	OF108,SS1	R	28	109	415	68	112	22	8	7	60	36	16	14	.270	.334	.412
Mike Griffin	OF93,2B2	L	28	95	362	85	103	21	7	6	59	59	23	30	.285	.396	.431
Dave Foutz	OF77,1B54,P6	R	36	130	557	91	137	20	10	7	67	32	34	39	.246	.287	.355
Con Daily	C51,OF9	L	28	61	215	33	57	4	2	1	32	20	12	13	.265	.342	.316
Danny Richardson	2B46,3B5,SS3	R	30	54	206	36	46	6	2	0	27	13	18	7	.223	.279	.272
Harry Stovey†	OF48	R	36	48	175	43	44	6	6	1	29	44	11	22	.251	.402	.371
Gil Hatfield	3B34	—	38	34	120	24	35	3	3	2	19	17	5	9	.292	.388	.417
George Haddock	P23,OF7	R	26	29	85	21	24	1	2	1	7	8	15	2	.282	.344	.376
Willie Keeler†	3B12,OF8	L	21	20	80	14	25	1	1	1	9	4	4	2	.313	.353	.388
Tom Lovett	P14,OF4,1B1	R	29	18	50	8	9	1	0	0	5	3	3	0	.180	.226	.200
Candy LaChance	C6,OF5	S	23	11	35	1	6	1	0	0	6	2	12	0	.171	.237	.200
Ed Crane†	P2,OF1	R	31	3	5	1	2	1	0	0	0	0	0	0	.400	.400	.600

G. Shoch, 3 G at 2B

Pitcher	T	Age	G	GS	CG	ShO	IP	H	HR	BB	SO	W-L	Sv	ERA
Brickyard Kennedy	R	25	46	44	40	2	382.2	376	15	168	107	25-20	1	3.72
Ed Stein	R	23	37	34	28	1	298.1	294	4	119	81	19-15	0	3.77
George Haddock	R	26	23	20	12	0	151.0	193	10	89	37	8-9	0	5.60
Dan Daub	R	25	12	12	12	0	103.0	104	3	61	25	6-6	0	3.84
George Sharrott	L	23	13	10	10	0	95.0	114	3	58	24	4-6	1	5.87
Tom Lovett	—	29	14	8	6	0	96.0	134	2	35	15	3-5	1	6.56
Ed Crane†	R	31	2	2	1	0	10.0	19	2	9	5	0-2	0	13.50
Dave Foutz	R	36	6	0	0	0	18.0	28	2	8	3	0-0	0	7.50

1893 Baltimore Orioles 8th NL 60-70 .462 26.5 GB

Ned Hanlon

Player	Gm by Position	B	Age	G	AB	R	H	2B	3B	HR	RBI	BB	SO	SB	Avg	OBP	Slg
Wilbert Robinson	C93,1B1	R	30	95	359	49	120	21	3	3	57	26	22	17	.334	.382	.435
Harry Taylor	1B88	L	27	88	360	50	102	9	1	1	54	32	11	24	.283	.347	.322
Heinie Reitz	2B130	L	26	130	490	90	140	17	13	1	76	65	32	24	.286	.377	.380
Billy Shindle	3B125	R	29	125	521	100	136	22	11	1	75	66	17	17	.261	.353	.351
John McGraw	SS117,OF11	L	20	127	480	123	154	9	10	5	64	101	11	38	.321	.454	.413
Joe Kelley	OF125	R	21	125	502	120	153	27	16	9	76	77	44	33	.305	.401	.476
George Treadway	OF115	L	—	115	458	78	119	16	17	1	67	57	50	24	.260	.347	.376
Jim Long	OF55	—	30	55	226	31	48	8	1	2	25	16	27	23	.212	.276	.283
Boileryard Clarke	C38,1B11	R	24	49	183	23	32	1	3	1	24	19	14	2	.175	.274	.230
Tim O'Rourke†	OF25,3B5,SS1	L	29	31	135	22	49	4	1	0	19	12	4	5	.363	.423	.407
Tony Mullane†	P34,OF2,1B1	S	34	38	114	15	26	2	1	0	14	5	14	5	.228	.261	.263
Jocko Milligan†	1B22,C1	R	31	24	102	19	25	5	2	1	19	5	7	2	.245	.294	.363
Steve Brodie†	OF25	L	24	25	97	18	35	7	2	0	19	12	2	8	.361	.446	.474
Bob Gilks	OF15	R	28	15	64	10	17	2	0	0	7	0	3	3	.266	.277	.297
Kirtley Baker	P15,OF3	R	24	19	57	9	17	1	1	0	6	8	6	1	.298	.385	.351
Hughie Jennings†	SS15,OF1	R	24	16	55	6	14	0	0	1	6	4	3	0	.255	.339	.309
Piggy Ward†	OF9,1B2	S	26	11	49	11	12	1	3	0	5	5	2	4	.245	.327	.388
Willard Brown†	1B7	R	27	7	32	5	4	3	0	0	5	1	3	0	.125	.152	.219
Harry Stovey†	OF7	R	36	8	26	4	4	2	0	0	5	8	3	1	.154	.353	.231

Pitcher	T	Age	G	GS	CG	ShO	IP	H	HR	BB	SO	W-L	Sv	ERA
Sadie McMahon	R	25	43	40	35	0	346.1	378	6	156	79	23-18	1	4.37
Bill Hawke†	R	23	29	29	22	1	225.0	248	8	108	69	11-16	0	4.76
Tony Mullane†	R	34	34	26	23	0	244.2	277	4	124	71	12-16	1	4.45
Edgar McNabb	R	27	21	14	12	0	142.0	167	5	53	18	8-7	0	4.12
Kirtley Baker	R	24	15	12	8	0	91.2	138	5	58	26	3-8	0	8.44
Crazy Schmit†	L	27	9	6	4	0	49.0	67	1	22	10	3-2	0	6.61
Jack Wadsworth	R	25	3	3	0	0	16.0	37	0	8	2	0-3	0	11.25
Stub Brown	L	22	2	0	0	0	9.0	13	0	5	0	0-0	0	6.00

1893 Chicago Colts 9th NL 56-71 .441 29.0 GB

Cap Anson

Player	Gm by Position	B	Age	G	AB	R	H	2B	3B	HR	RBI	BB	SO	SB	Avg	OBP	Slg
Malachi Kittridge	C70	R	23	70	255	32	59	9	5	2	30	17	15	3	.231	.279	.329
Cap Anson	1B101	R	41	103	398	70	125	24	2	0	91	68	12	13	.314	.415	.384
Bill Lange	2B57,OF40,3B8*	R	22	117	469	92	132	8	7	8	88	52	20	47	.281	.358	.380
Jiggs Parrott	3B99,2B7,OF4	—	21	110	455	54	111	10	9	1	65	13	25	25	.244	.267	.312
Bill Dahlen	SS88,OF17,2B10*	R	23	116	485	113	146	28	15	5	64	58	30	31	.301	.381	.452
Sam Dungan	OF107	R	26	107	465	86	138	23	7	2	64	29	8	11	.297	.350	.389
Walt Wilmot	OF93	S	29	94	392	69	118	14	14	3	61	40	8	39	.301	.367	.431
Jimmy Ryan	OF73,SS10,P1	R	30	83	341	82	102	21	7	3	30	59	25	8	.299	.407	.428
George Decker	OF33,1B27,2B20*	L	24	81	328	57	89	9	8	2	48	24	22	22	.271	.325	.366
Pop Schriver	C56,OF5	R	27	64	229	49	65	8	3	4	34	14	9	4	.284	.336	.397
Bill Hutchison	P44,OF2	R	33	46	162	14	41	7	3	0	25	7	20	2	.253	.284	.333
Lew Camp	3B16,OF11,2B9*	L	25	38	156	37	41	7	7	2	17	19	19	30	.263	.347	.436
Charlie Irwin	SS21	L	24	21	82	14	25	6	2	0	13	10	1	4	.305	.394	.427
Bob Glenalvin	2B16	—	26	16	61	11	21	3	1	0	12	7	3	7	.344	.412	.426
Tom Parrott†	P4,3B2,2B1	R	25	7	27	4	7	1	0	0	3	1	2	0	.259	.286	.296
Albert McGinnis†	P13,OF1	—	—	13	25	8	6	0	0	0	7	9	2	0	.240	.441	.240
Bill Eagan	2B6	—	24	6	19	3	5	0	0	0	2	5	5	4	.263	.417	.263
Henry Lynch	OF4	S	27	4	14	0	3	2	0	0	2	1	1	0	.214	.267	.357
John O'Brien	2B4	L	22	4	14	3	5	0	1	0	1	2	2	0	.357	.471	.500
Bob Caruthers†	OF1	L	29	1	3	0	0	0	0	0	0	0	1	0	.000	.000	.000

B. Lange, 7 G at C, 7 G at SS; B. Dahlen, 3 G at 3B; G. Decker, 2 G at SS; L. Camp, 3 G at SS

Pitcher	T	Age	G	GS	CG	ShO	IP	H	HR	BB	SO	W-L	Sv	ERA
Bill Hutchison	R	33	44	40	38	2	348.1	420	9	156	80	16-24	0	4.75
Willie McGill	L	19	39	34	26	1	302.2	311	6	181	91	17-18	0	4.61
Hal Mauck	R	24	23	18	12	1	143.0	168	2	60	23	8-10	0	4.41
Fritz Clausen†	L	24	10	9	8	0	76.0	71	1	39	31	6-2	1	3.08
Bert Abbey	R	23	7	7	5	0	56.0	74	1	20	6	2-4	0	5.46
Frank Donnelly	—	23	7	5	3	0	42.0	51	1	17	6	3-1	2	5.36
Tom Parrott†	R	25	4	3	2	0	27.0	35	1	17	7	0-3	0	6.67
Clark Griffith	R	23	4	2	2	0	19.2	24	1	5	9	1-2	0	5.03
Sam Shaw	R	29	2	2	1	0	16.0	12	2	13	1	1-0	0	5.63
Jim Hughey	R	24	2	2	1	0	9.0	14	0	3	4	0-1	0	11.00
Gus Yost	—	—	1	1	0	0	2.2	3	0	8	1	0-1	0	13.50
Albert McGinnis†	L	—	13	5	3	0	67.1	85	2	31	13	2-5	0	5.35
Jimmy Ryan	L	30	1	0	0	0	4.2	3	0	0	1	0-0	0	0.00
Doc Parker	R	21	1	0	0	0	2.0	5	0	1	0	0-0	1	13.50
Abe Johnson	—	—	1	0	0	0	1.0	2	0	2	0	0-0	1	36.00

1893 St. Louis Browns 10th NL 57-75 .432 30.5 GB

Bill Watkins

Player	Gm by Position	B	Age	G	AB	R	H	2B	3B	HR	RBI	BB	SO	SB	Avg	OBP	Slg
Heinie Peitz	C74,SS11,OF10*	R	22	96	362	53	92	12	9	1	45	54	20	12	.254	.353	.345
Perry Werden	1B124,OF1	R	27	125	500	73	138	22	29	1	94	49	25	11	.276	.349	.442
Joe Quinn	2B135	R	28	135	547	68	126	18	6	0	71	33	7	24	.230	.279	.285
Jack Crooks	3B123,SS4,C1	R	27	128	448	93	106	10	9	1	48	121	37	31	.237	.408	.306
Jack Glasscock†	SS48	R	33	48	195	32	56	8	1	1	26	25	3	20	.287	.382	.354
Tommy Dowd	OF132,2B1	R	24	132	581	114	164	18	7	1	54	49	23	59	.282	.340	.343
Steve Brodie†	OF107	L	24	107	469	71	149	16	8	2	79	33	16	41	.318	.376	.399
Charlie Frank	OF40	—	23	40	164	29	55	6	3	1	17	18	8	8	.335	.408	.427
Frank Shugart†	OF28,SS23,3B9	S	26	59	246	41	69	10	4	0	28	22	10	13	.280	.354	.354
Kid Gleason	P48,OF11,SS1	S	26	59	199	25	51	6	4	0	20	19	8	2	.256	.327	.327
Bones Ely	SS44	R	30	44	178	25	45	1	6	0	16	17	13	2	.253	.318	.326
Ted Breitenstein	P48,OF2	L	24	49	160	20	29	1	1	1	14	18	15	3	.181	.268	.219
Joe Gunson†	C35,OF5	R	30	40	151	20	41	5	0	0	15	6	6	0	.272	.321	.305
Duff Cooley	OF15,C10,SS5	L	20	29	107	20	37	2	3	0	21	8	9	8	.346	.391	.421
Jimmy Bannon	OF24,SS2,P1	R	22	26	107	9	36	3	4	0	15	4	5	8	.336	.366	.439
Sandy Griffin	OF23	R	34	23	92	9	18	1	1	0	9	16	2	2	.196	.315	.228
Dad Clarkson	P24,OF1	R	26	25	75	8	10	1	0	0	5	9	16	0	.133	.226	.147
Art Twineham	C14	L	26	14	48	8	15	2	0	0	11	1	2	0	.313	.340	.354
Lew Whistler†	OF9,1B1	—	25	10	38	5	9	1	0	0	2	3	2	0	.237	.293	.263
Bill Goodenough	OF10	—	30	10	31	4	5	1	0	0	2	3	4	2	.161	.297	.194
Denny O'Neill	1B7	L	26	7	25	3	3	0	0	0	2	4	0	3	.120	.241	.120
Dick Buckley	C9	—	34	9	23	2	4	1	0	0	1	0	0	0	.174	.174	.217
Pat McCauley	C5	—	23	5	16	0	1	0	0	0	0	0	1	0	.063	.063	.063
Jud Smith†	3B4	R	24	4	13	1	1	0	0	0	0	1	2	0	.077	.200	.077
Kid Summers	C1,OF1	—	—	2	1	1	0	0	0	0	0	0	0	0	.000	.500	.000

H. Peitz, 5 G at 1B

Pitcher	T	Age	G	GS	CG	ShO	IP	H	HR	BB	SO	W-L	Sv	ERA
Kid Gleason	R	26	48	45	37	1	380.1	436	18	187	86	21-22	1	4.61
Ted Breitenstein	L	24	48	42	38	1	382.2	359	8	156	102	19-24	1	3.18
Pink Hawley	R	20	31	24	21	0	227.0	249	6	103	73	5-17	1	4.60
Dad Clarkson	R	26	24	21	17	1	186.1	194	4	79	37	12-9	0	3.48
Bill Hawke†	R	23	1	1	0	0	5.1	9	0	3	1	0-1	0	5.06
Jimmy Bannon	R	22	1	1	0	0	4.0	10	1	5	1	0-1	0	22.50
John Dolan	R	25	3	1	1	0	17.1	26	1	7	1	0-1	1	4.15
Frank Pears	R	26	1	0	0	0	4.0	9	0	2	0	0-0	0	13.50

1893 Louisville Colonels 11th NL 50-75 .400 34.0 GB

Billy Barnie

Player	Gm by Position	B	Age	G	AB	R	H	2B	3B	HR	RBI	BB	SO	SB	Avg	OBP	Slg
John Grim	C92,1B3,2B2*	R	25	99	415	68	111	19	8	3	54	12	10	15	.267	.303	.373
Willard Brown†	1B111,C1	R	27	111	461	80	140	23	7	1	85	50	32	9	.304	.373	.390
Fred Pfeffer	2B125	R	33	125	508	85	129	29	12	3	75	51	18	32	.254	.322	.376
George Pinckney	3B118	R	31	118	446	64	105	12	6	1	62	50	8	12	.235	.323	.296
Tim O'Rourke†	SS60,OF26,3B6	L	29	92	352	80	99	8	4	0	53	77	15	22	.281	.421	.327
Tom Brown	OF122	L	32	122	529	104	127	15	7	5	54	56	63	66	.240	.319	.323
Farmer Weaver	OF85,C21	L	28	106	439	79	128	17	7	2	49	27	12	17	.292	.348	.376
Pete Browning	OF57	R	32	57	220	38	78	11	3	1	37	44	15	8	.355	.466	.445
Scott Stratton	P38,OF23,1B1	L	23	61	221	34	50	8	5	0	16	25	15	6	.226	.308	.308
Larry Twitchell	OF45	R	29	45	187	37	58	11	3	2	31	17	20	7	.310	.377	.433
Jerry Denny	SS42,3B2	R	34	44	175	22	43	5	4	1	22	9	15	4	.246	.283	.337
George Hemming	P41,OF4	R	24	45	158	17	32	5	2	0	19	12	20	0	.203	.259	.259
Hughie Jennings†	SS23	R	24	23	88	6	12	3	0	0	9	3	3	0	.136	.174	.170
Jock Menefee	P15,OF7	R	25	22	73	10	20	2	1	0	12	13	5	2	.274	.391	.329
Lew Whistler†	1B13	—	25	13	47	5	10	1	1	0	9	5	5	1	.213	.302	.277
Curt Welch	OF14	R	31	14	47	5	8	1	0	0	2	16	4	1	.170	.400	.191
Jerry Harrington	C10	R	23	10	36	4	4	1	0	0	6	3	9	0	.111	.179	.139
Bob Clark	C10,SS1,OF1	R	30	12	28	3	3	1	0	0	3	5	5	0	.107	.242	.143
Bill Whitrock	P6,OF1	—	23	7	21	5	6	0	1	0	4	1	1	1	.286	.348	.381

J. Grim, 1 G at SS, 1 G at OF

Pitcher	T	Age	G	GS	CG	ShO	IP	H	HR	BB	SO	W-L	Sv	ERA
Scott Stratton	R	23	38	36	35	1	323.2	451	8	104	44	12-24	0	5.45
George Hemming	R	24	41	33	33	1	332.0	373	7	176	79	18-17	1	5.18
Bill Rhodes	—	—	20	19	17	0	151.2	244	10	66	22	5-12	0	7.60
Jock Menefee	R	25	15	15	14	1	129.1	150	3	40	30	8-7	0	4.24
Bill Whitrock	R	23	6	6	4	0	37.2	54	3	14	7	2-4	0	7.88
Matt Kilroy	L	27	5	5	5	1	35.0	57	2	23	4	3-2	0	9.00
Fritz Clausen†	L	24	5	5	3	0	33.0	41	2	22	4	1-4	0	6.00
Billy Rhines	R	24	5	5	3	0	31.0	49	3	19	0	1-4	0	8.71
Con Lucid	—	19	2	1	0	0	6.0	10	0	10	0	0-1	0	15.00
Billy Gumbert	R	27	1	1	0	0	0.2	2	0	5	0	0-0	0	27.00

1893 Washington Senators 12th NL 40-89 .310 46.0 GB

Jim O'Rourke

Player	Gm by Position	B	Age	G	AB	R	H	2B	3B	HR	RBI	BB	SO	SB	Avg	OBP	Slg
Duke Farrell	C81,3B41,1B3	S	26	124	511	84	143	13	13	4	75	47	12	11	.280	.346	.380
Henry Larkin	1B81	R	33	81	319	54	101	20	3	4	73	50	5	1	.317	.422	.436
Sam Wise	2B91,3B31	L	35	122	521	102	162	27	17	5	77	49	27	20	.311	.375	.457
Joe Mulvey	3B55	R	34	55	226	21	53	9	4	0	19	7	8	2	.235	.264	.310
Joe Sullivan	SS128	—	23	128	508	72	135	16	13	2	64	36	24	7	.266	.324	.360
Dummy Hoy	OF130	L	31	130	564	106	138	12	6	0	45	66	9	48	.245	.337	.287
Paul Radford	OF123,P1,2B1	R	31	124	464	87	106	18	3	2	34	105	42	32	.228	.380	.293
Jim O'Rourke	OF87,1B33,C9	R	42	129	547	75	157	22	5	3	95	49	26	15	.287	.354	.362
Deacon McGuire	C50,1B12	R	29	63	237	29	62	14	3	1	26	26	12	3	.262	.342	.359
Cub Stricker	2B39,OF12,3B4*	R	34	59	218	28	40	7	1	0	20	20	12	4	.183	.252	.225
Al Maul	P37,OF7	R	27	44	134	10	34	8	4	0	12	33	14	1	.254	.405	.373
Charlie Abbey	OF31	L	26	31	116	11	30	1	4	0	12	12	6	9	.259	.333	.336
Jouett Meekin	P31,OF3	R	26	33	113	15	29	3	2	3	20	4	11	0	.257	.282	.398
Otis Stocksdale	P11,1B1,OF1	L	21	12	40	7	12	0	2	0	6	2	2	1	.300	.333	.400

C. Stricker, 4 G at SS

Pitcher	T	Age	G	GS	CG	ShO	IP	H	HR	BB	SO	W-L	Sv	ERA
Duke Esper	L	24	42	36	34	0	334.1	442	14	156	78	12-28	0	4.71
Al Maul	R	27	37	33	29	1	297.0	355	17	144	72	12-21	0	5.30
Jouett Meekin	R	26	31	28	24	1	245.0	289	6	140	91	10-15	0	4.96
Jesse Duryea	R	33	17	15	9	0	117.0	182	8	56	20	4-10	0	7.54
Otis Stocksdale	R	21	11	11	7	0	69.0	111	4	32	12	2-8	0	8.22
George Stephens	—	25	9	6	6	0	63.2	83	1	31	14	0-6	0	5.80
John Graff	—	—	2	1	1	0	12.0	21	2	13	4	0-1	0	11.25
Paul Radford	R	31	1	0	0	0	1.0	2	2	2	1	0-0	0	18.00

»1894 Baltimore Orioles 1st NL 89-39 .695 —

Ned Hanlon

Player	Gm by Position	B	Age	G	AB	R	H	2B	3B	HR	RBI	BB	SO	SB	Avg	OBP	Slg
Wilbert Robinson	C109	R	31	109	414	69	146	21	4	1	98	46	18	12	.353	.421	.430
Dan Brouthers	1B123	L	36	123	525	137	182	39	23	9	128	67	9	38	.347	.425	.560
Heinie Reitz	2B97,3B12	L	27	108	446	86	135	22	31	2	105	42	24	18	.303	.372	.504
John McGraw	3B118,2B6	L	21	124	512	156	174	18	14	1	92	91	12	78	.340	.451	.436
Hughie Jennings	SS128	R	25	128	501	134	168	28	16	4	109	37	17	37	.335	.411	.479
Steve Brodie	OF129	L	25	129	573	134	210	25	11	3	113	18	8	42	.366	.399	.464
Joe Kelley	OF129	R	22	129	507	165	199	48	20	6	111	107	36	46	.393	.502	.602
Willie Keeler	OF128,2B1	L	22	129	590	165	219	27	22	5	94	40	6	32	.371	.427	.517
Frank Bonner	2B27,OF4,3B2*	R	24	33	118	27	38	10	2	0	24	17	5	12	.322	.412	.441
Boileryard Clarke	C23,1B5	R	25	28	100	18	24	8	0	1	19	16	14	2	.240	.361	.350
Kid Gleason†	P21,1B1	S	27	26	86	22	30	5	1	0	17	7	2	1	.349	.398	.430
Kirtley Baker	P1,OF1	R	25	2	4	0	0	0	0	0	0	0	1	0	.000	.000	.000

F. Bonner, 1 G at SS

Pitcher	T	Age	G	GS	CG	ShO	IP	H	HR	BB	SO	W-L	Sv	ERA
Sadie McMahon	R	26	35	33	26	0	275.2	317	7	111	60	25-8	0	4.21
Bill Hawke	R	24	32	25	17	0	205.0	264	9	78	68	16-9	3	5.84
Kid Gleason†	R	27	21	20	19	0	172.0	224	3	44	35	15-5	0	4.45
Tony Mullane†	R	35	21	15	9	0	122.2	155	4	90	43	6-9	4	6.31
Bert Inks†	L	23	22	14	10	0	133.0	181	4	54	30	9-4	1	5.55
Duke Esper†	L	25	16	9	8	0	102.0	107	1	36	25	10-2	2	3.88
Stub Brown	L	23	9	6	3	0	49.2	59	3	24	8	4-0	0	4.89
George Hemming†	R	25	6	6	4	0	45.1	48	0	26	4	4-0	0	3.57
Jack Horner	—	30	2	1	1	0	11.0	15	0	7	2	0-1	1	9.00
Kirtley Baker	R	25	1	0	0	0	0.0	1	0	2	0	0-1	0	—

1894 New York Giants 2nd NL 88-44 .667 3.0 GB

Monte Ward

Player	Gm by Position	B	Age	G	AB	R	H	2B	3B	HR	RBI	BB	SO	SB	Avg	OBP	Slg
Duke Farrell	C104,3B5,1B4	S	27	114	401	47	114	20	12	4	66	35	15	9	.284	.346	.424
Jack Doyle	1B99,C6	R	24	105	422	90	155	30	8	3	100	35	3	42	.367	.420	.498
Monte Ward	2B136	L	34	136	540	100	143	12	5	0	77	34	6	39	.265	.310	.306
George Davis	3B122	S	23	122	477	120	168	26	19	8	91	66	10	40	.352	.435	.537
Shorty Fuller	SS89,3B2,OF2*	R	26	93	368	81	104	14	4	2	46	52	16	32	.283	.374	.359
George Van Haltren	OF137	L	28	137	519	109	172	22	4	7	104	55	22	43	.331	.400	.430
Eddie Burke	OF136	L	27	136	566	121	172	23	11	4	77	37	35	34	.304	.357	.405
Mike Tiernan	OF111	L	27	112	424	84	117	19	13	5	77	54	21	28	.276	.359	.417
Yale Murphy	SS49,OF20,3B3*	L	24	74	280	64	76	6	2	0	28	51	23	28	.271	.384	.307
Parke Wilson	C34,1B15	R	26	49	175	35	58	5	5	1	32	14	5	8	.331	.387	.434
Roger Connor†	1B21,OF1	L	36	22	82	10	24	7	0	1	14	8	0	2	.293	.356	.415
General Stafford	3B6,OF5,1B1*	R	25	14	46	10	10	1	1	0	4	10	7	2	.217	.368	.283

S. Fuller, 1 G at 2B; Y. Murphy, 1 G at 1B, 1 G at 2B; G. Stafford, 1 G at 2B

Pitcher	T	Age	G	GS	CG	ShO	IP	H	HR	BB	SO	W-L	Sv	ERA
Amos Rusie	R	23	54	50	45	3	444.0	426	10	200	195	36-13	1	2.78
Jouett Meekin	R	27	52	48	40	1	409.0	404	13	171	133	33-9	2	3.70
Huyler Westervelt	—	23	23	18	11	1	141.0	170	4	76	35	7-10	0	5.04
Les German	R	25	23	15	10	0	134.0	178	7	66	17	9-8	1	5.78
Dad Clarke	R	29	15	6	5	0	84.0	114	3	26	15	3-4	1	4.93

1894 Boston Beaneaters 3rd NL 83-49 .629 8.0 GB

Frank Selee

Player	Gm by Position	B	Age	G	AB	R	H	2B	3B	HR	RBI	BB	SO	SB	Avg	OBP	Slg
Charlie Ganzel	C59,1B7,OF3*	R	32	70	266	51	74	7	6	3	56	19	6	1	.278	.326	.383
Tommy Tucker	1B123,OF1	S	30	123	500	112	165	24	6	3	100	53	21	18	.330	.412	.420
Bobby Lowe	2B130,SS2,3B1	R	25	133	613	158	212	34	11	17	115	50	25	23	.346	.401	.520
Billy Nash	3B132	R	29	132	512	132	148	23	6	8	87	91	23	20	.289	.399	.404
Herman Long	SS98,OF5,2B3	L	28	104	475	136	154	28	11	12	79	35	17	24	.324	.375	.505
Jimmy Bannon	OF128,P1	R	23	128	494	130	166	29	10	13	114	62	42	47	.336	.414	.514
Tommy McCarthy	OF127,SS2,P1*	R	30	127	539	118	188	21	8	13	126	59	17	43	.349	.419	.490
Hugh Duffy	OF124,SS2	R	27	125	539	160	237	51	16	18	145	66	15	48	.440	.502	.694
Jack Stivetts	P45,OF16,1B4	R	26	68	244	55	80	12	7	8	64	16	21	3	.328	.369	.533
Jack Ryan	C51,1B2	R	25	53	201	39	54	12	7	1	29	13	16	3	.269	.316	.413
Frank Connaughton	SS33,C7,OF4	R	25	46	171	42	59	9	2	2	33	16	8	3	.345	.407	.456
Kid Nichols	P50,OF1	S	24	51	170	39	50	11	2	0	34	16	24	1	.294	.358	.382
Fred Tenney	C20,OF6,1B1	L	22	27	86	23	34	7	1	2	21	12	9	6	.395	.469	.570
Harry Staley	P27,OF1	R	27	28	85	12	20	2	1	2	25	13	9	0	.235	.343	.353
Bill Merritt†	C8,OF1	R	23	10	26	3	6	1	0	0	6	8	0	0	.231	.412	.269

C. Ganzel, 2 G at SS, 1 G at 2B; T. McCarthy, 1 G at 2B

Pitcher	T	Age	G	GS	CG	ShO	IP	H	HR	BB	SO	W-L	Sv	ERA
Kid Nichols	R	24	50	46	40	3	407.0	488	23	121	113	32-13	0	4.75
Jack Stivetts	R	26	45	39	30	0	338.0	429	27	127	76	26-14	0	4.90
Harry Staley	R	27	27	21	18	0	208.2	305	15	61	32	12-10	0	6.81
Tom Lovett	—	30	15	13	10	0	104.0	155	12	36	23	8-6	0	5.97
George Hodson	R	24	12	11	8	0	74.0	103	4	35	12	4-4	0	5.84
George Stultz	—	21	1	1	1	0	9.0	4	0	5	1	1-0	0	0.00
Scott Hawley	—	—	1	1	1	0	7.0	10	0	7	1	0-1	0	7.71
Henry Lampe	L	21	2	1	0	0	5.1	17	5	7	1	0-1	0	11.81
Tom Smith	R	22	2	0	0	0	6.0	8	2	6	2	0-0	1	15.00
Frank West	—	20	1	0	0	0	3.0	5	0	2	1	0-0	0	9.00
Jimmy Bannon	R	23	1	0	0	0	2.0	4	1	1	0	0-0	0	0.00
Tommy McCarthy	R	30	1	0	0	0	2.0	1	0	3	0	0-0	0	4.50

1894 Philadelphia Phillies 4th NL 71-57 .555 18.0 GB

Arthur Irwin

Player	Gm by Position	B	Age	G	AB	R	H	2B	3B	HR	RBI	BB	SO	SB	Avg	OBP	Slg
Jack Clements	C45	L	29	45	159	26	55	6	5	3	36	24	7	6	.346	.455	.503
Jack Boyle	1B114,2B1,3B1	R	28	114	495	98	149	21	10	4	88	45	26	21	.301	.363	.408
Bill Hallman	2B119	R	27	119	505	107	156	19	7	0	66	36	15	36	.309	.360	.374
Lave Cross	3B100,C16,SS7*	R	28	119	529	123	204	34	9	7	125	29	7	21	.386	.421	.524
Joe Sullivan†	SS75	—	24	75	304	63	107	10	8	3	63	23	10	10	.352	.407	.467
Billy Hamilton	OF129	L	28	129	544	192	220	25	15	4	87	126	17	98	.404	.523	.528
Sam Thompson	OF99	L	34	99	437	108	178	29	27	13	141	40	13	24	.407	.458	.686
Ed Delahanty	OF88,1B12,3B9*	R	26	114	489	147	199	39	18	4	131	60	16	21	.407	.478	.585
Tuck Turner	OF78,P1	S	21	80	339	91	141	21	9	1	82	23	13	11	.416	.456	.540
Mike Grady	C44,1B11,OF2	R	24	60	190	45	69	13	8	0	40	14	13	3	.363	.427	.516
Dick Buckley†	C42,1B1	—	35	43	160	18	47	7	3	1	26	6	13	0	.294	.327	.394
Bob Allen	SS40	R	26	40	149	26	38	10	3	0	19	17	11	4	.255	.335	.362
Charlie Reilly	3B28,OF5,2B4*	S	27	39	135	21	40	1	2	0	19	16	10	9	.296	.383	.333
Tom Delahanty	2B1	L	22	1	4	0	1	0	0	0	0	0	1	0	.250	.250	.250
Joe Yingling	SS1	R	27	1	4	0	1	0	0	0	0	0	1	0	.250	.250	.250
Tom Murray	SS1	—	28	1	2	0	0	0	0	0	0	0	2	0	.000	.000	.000
Arthur Irwin	SS1	L	36	1	0	0	0	0	0	0	0	0	0	0	—	—	—

L. Cross, 1 G at 2B; E. Delahanty, 8 G at SS, 6 G at 2B; C. Reilly, 1 G at 1B, 1 G at SS

Pitcher	T	Age	G	GS	CG	ShO	IP	H	HR	BB	SO	W-L	Sv	ERA
Jack Taylor	R	21	41	34	31	1	298.0	347	13	96	76	23-13	1	4.08
Gus Weyhing	R	27	38	34	25	2	266.1	365	12	116	81	16-14	1	5.81
Kid Carsey	R	23	35	31	26	0	277.0	349	22	102	41	18-12	0	5.56
George Harper	R	27	12	9	7	0	86.1	128	3	49	24	6-6	0	5.32
George Haddock†	R	27	10	7	5	0	56.0	63	0	34	7	4-3	0	5.79
Jack Fanning	R	31	5	4	2	0	32.1	45	4	20	7	1-3	0	8.07
John Johnson	L	24	4	3	2	0	32.2	44	3	15	10	1-1	0	6.06
Al Lukens	—	25	3	2	1	0	15.0	26	0	10	0	0-1	0	10.20
Alex Jones	L	24	1	1	1	0	9.0	10	0	0	2	1-0	0	2.00
Frank Figgemeier	—	21	1	1	1	0	8.0	12	1	4	2	0-1	0	11.25
John Scheible	L	28	1	1	0	0	0.1	6	0	2	0	0-1	0	189.00
Nixey Callahan	R	20	9	2	1	0	33.2	64	3	17	9	1-2	2	9.89
Tuck Turner	L	21	1	0	0	0	6.0	9	1	2	3	0-0	0	7.50
Al Burris	R	20	1	0	0	0	5.0	14	0	2	0	0-0	0	18.00

1894 Brooklyn Bridegrooms 5th NL 70-61 .534 20.5 GB

Dave Foutz

Player	Gm by Position	B	Age	G	AB	R	H	2B	3B	HR	RBI	BB	SO	SB	Avg	OBP	Slg
Tom Kinslow	C61,1B1	R	28	62	223	39	68	5	6	2	41	20	11	4	.305	.362	.408
Dave Foutz	1B72,P1	R	37	72	293	40	90	12	9	0	51	14	13	14	.307	.341	.410
Tom Daly	2B123	S	28	123	492	135	168	22	10	8	82	77	42	51	.341	.436	.476
Billy Shindle	3B116	R	30	116	476	94	141	22	9	4	96	29	20	19	.296	.344	.405
Tommy Corcoran	SS129	R	25	129	576	123	173	21	20	5	92	25	17	33	.300	.329	.432
Oyster Burns	OF125	R	29	125	505	106	179	32	14	5	107	44	18	30	.354	.409	.503
George Treadway	OF122,1B1	L	—	123	479	124	157	27	26	4	102	72	43	27	.328	.418	.518
Mike Griffin	OF106	L	29	107	402	122	144	28	4	5	75	78	14	39	.358	.467	.485
Candy LaChance	1B56,C10,OF3	S	24	68	257	48	83	13	8	5	52	16	32	20	.323	.365	.494
George Shoch	OF35,3B14,2B9*	R	35	64	239	47	77	6	5	1	37	26	6	16	.322	.400	.402
Con Daily	C60,1B7	L	29	67	234	40	60	14	7	0	32	31	22	8	.256	.351	.376
Dan Daub	P33,OF1	R	26	33	92	11	16	0	1	0	15	7	14	1	.174	.232	.196
John Anderson	OF16,3B1	S	20	17	63	14	19	1	3	1	19	3	3	7	.302	.333	.460
Billy Earle†	C12,2B1	R	26	14	50	13	17	6	0	0	6	6	2	4	.340	.421	.460
Pete Gilbert†	2B3,3B3	—	26	6	25	1	2	0	0	0	1	1	3	2	.080	.148	.080
Pete Browning†	OF1	R	33	1	2	1	2	0	0	0	2	1	0	0	1.000	1.000	1.000

G. Shoch, 6 G at SS

Pitcher	T	Age	G	GS	CG	ShO	IP	H	HR	BB	SO	W-L	Sv	ERA
Brickyard Kennedy	R	26	48	41	34	0	360.2	445	15	149	107	24-20	2	4.92
Ed Stein	R	24	45	41	38	2	359.0	396	10	171	84	27-14	1	4.54
Dan Daub	R	26	33	26	14	0	215.0	283	7	90	45	9-12	0	6.32
Con Lucid	—	20	10	9	7	0	71.1	87	6	44	15	5-3	0	6.56
Hank Gastright	R	29	16	8	6	1	93.0	135	1	55	20	2-6	2	6.39
Fred Underwood	—	25	7	6	5	0	47.0	80	1	30	10	2-4	0	7.85
George Sharrott	L	24	2	2	1	0	9.0	7	0	5	2	0-1	0	7.00
Andy Sommerville	—	18	1	1	0	0	0.1	1	0	5	0	0-1	0	162.00
Jim Korwan	R	20	1	0	0	0	5.0	9	1	5	2	0-0	0	14.40
Dave Foutz	R	37	1	0	0	0	2.0	4	0	1	0	0-0	0	13.50

1894 Cleveland Spiders 6th NL 68-61 .527 21.5 GB

Patsy Tebeau

Player	Gm by Position	B	Age	G	AB	R	H	2B	3B	HR	RBI	BB	SO	SB	Avg	OBP	Slg
Chief Zimmer	C89	R	33	90	341	55	97	20	5	4	65	17	31	14	.284	.328	.408
Patsy Tebeau	1B115,2B10,3B2*	R	29	125	523	82	158	23	7	3	89	35	35	30	.302	.347	.390
Cupid Childs	2B118	L	26	118	479	143	169	21	12	2	52	107	11	17	.353	.475	.459
Chippy McGarr	3B128	R	31	128	523	94	144	24	6	2	74	28	29	31	.275	.316	.356
Ed McKean	SS130	R	30	130	554	116	198	30	15	8	128	49	12	33	.357	.412	.509
Jesse Burkett	OF125,P1	L	25	125	523	138	187	27	14	8	94	84	27	28	.358	.447	.509
Harry Blake	OF73	R	20	73	296	51	78	15	4	1	51	30	22	1	.264	.335	.351
Jimmy McAleer	OF64	R	29	64	253	36	73	15	1	2	40	13	17	14	.289	.331	.379
Jack O'Connor	C45,OF33,1B7	R	25	86	330	67	104	23	7	2	51	15	7	15	.315	.345	.445
Buck Ewing	OF52,2B1	R	34	53	211	32	53	12	4	2	39	24	9	18	.251	.328	.374
W. Wings Tebeau†	OF27,1B12,3B1	R	32	40	150	32	47	9	4	0	25	25	18	9	.313	.411	.427
Nig Cuppy	P43,OF1	R	24	44	135	28	35	6	3	0	19	15	27	3	.259	.338	.348
Jake Virtue	OF21,2B3,1B2*	S	29	29	89	15	23	4	1	0	10	13	3	1	.258	.359	.326
Frank Griffith	P7,OF2	L	21	7	24	4	8	2	2	0	9	1	4	0	.333	.360	.583

P. Tebeau, 1 G at SS; J. Virtue, 1 G at P

Pitcher	T	Age	G	GS	CG	ShO	IP	H	HR	BB	SO	W-L	Sv	ERA
Cy Young	R	27	52	47	44	2	408.2	488	19	106	108	26-21	1	3.94
Nig Cuppy	R	24	43	33	29	3	316.0	381	11	128	65	24-15	0	4.56
John Clarkson	R	32	22	18	13	1	150.2	173	6	46	28	8-9	0	4.42
Mike Sullivan†	—	27	13	11	9	0	90.2	128	4	47	19	6-5	0	6.35
Frank Griffith	L	21	7	6	3	0	42.1	64	5	37	15	1-2	0	9.99
Tony Mullane†	R	35	4	4	3	0	33.0	46	3	10	3	1-2	0	7.64
Charlie Petty†	R	28	4	3	2	0	27.0	42	4	14	4	0-2	0	8.67
Bobby Wallace	R	20	4	3	2	0	26.0	28	1	20	10	2-1	0	5.19
Chauncey Fisher†	R	22	3	2	0	0	11.0	22	0	5	0	0-2	0	11.45
Frank Knauss	L	26	2	2	1	0	11.0	7	0	14	2	0-1	0	5.73
Bill Lyston	R	31	1	1	0	0	3.2	5	1	4	0	0-1	0	9.82
Jesse Burkett	L	25	1	0	0	0	4.0	6	0	1	0	0-0	0	4.50
Tom Thomas	R	20	1	0	0	0	0.1	0	0	2	0	0-0	0	27.00
Jake Virtue	L	29	1	0	0	0	0.0	0	0	1	0	0-0	0	—

1894 Pittsburgh Pirates 7th NL 65-65 .500 25.0 GB

Al Buckenberger (53-55)/Connie Mack (12-10)

Player	Gm by Position	B	Age	G	AB	R	H	2B	3B	HR	RBI	BB	SO	SB	Avg	OBP	Slg
Connie Mack	C69	R	31	69	228	32	57	7	1	1	21	20	14	8	.250	.321	.303
Jake Beckley	1B131	L	26	131	533	121	183	36	18	7	120	43	16	21	.343	.412	.518
Lou Bierbauer	2B130	L	28	130	525	86	159	19	13	3	107	26	9	19	.303	.337	.406
Denny Lyons	3B71	R	28	71	254	51	82	14	4	4	50	42	12	14	.323	.427	.457
Jack Glasscock	SS85	R	34	86	332	46	93	10	7	1	63	31	4	15	.280	.349	.361
Patsy Donovan	OF132	L	29	132	576	145	174	21	10	4	76	33	12	41	.302	.345	.394
Jake Stenzel	OF131	R	27	131	522	148	185	39	20	13	121	75	13	61	.354	.441	.580
Elmer Smith	OF125,P1	L	26	125	489	128	174	33	19	6	72	65	12	33	.356	.436	.538
Fred Hartman	3B49	R	26	49	182	41	58	4	7	2	20	16	11	12	.319	.389	.451
Joe Sugden	C31,3B4,SS3*	S	23	39	139	23	46	13	2	2	23	14	2	3	.331	.404	.496
Farmer Weaver†	C14,SS12,3B5*	L	29	30	115	16	40	7	2	0	24	6	1	4	.348	.405	.443
Bill Merritt†	C28,1B4,OF2	R	23	36	109	18	30	6	1	1	18	15	7	2	.275	.363	.349
Frank Scheibeck†	SS11,OF9,3B3*	R	29	28	102	20	36	2	3	1	10	11	9	7	.353	.416	.461
Monte Cross	SS13	R	24	13	43	14	19	1	5	2	13	5	4	6	.442	.520	.837
Gene Steere	SS10	—	21	10	39	3	8	0	0	0	4	2	1	2	.205	.244	.205
Gene DeMontreville	SS2	R	20	2	8	0	2	0	0	0	0	1	4	0	.250	.333	.250
Jim Ritz	3B1	—	20	1	4	1	0	0	0	0	0	0	0	1	.000	.200	.000

J. Sugden, 1 G at OF; F. Weaver, 1 G at OF; F. Scheibeck, 2 G at 2B

Pitcher	T	Age	G	GS	CG	ShO	IP	H	HR	BB	SO	W-L	Sv	ERA
Red Ehret	R	25	46	38	31	1	346.2	441	12	128	102	19-21	0	5.14
Ad Gumbert	R	25	37	31	26	0	269.2	372	14	84	65	15-14	0	6.02
Frank Killen	L	23	28	28	20	1	204.0	261	3	86	62	14-11	0	4.50
Tom Colcolough	R	23	22	14	11	0	148.2	207	5	70	29	8-5	0	7.08
Jock Menefee†	R	26	13	13	13	0	111.2	159	3	39	33	5-8	0	5.40
George Nicol†	L	23	8	5	3	0	44.1	57	2	33	11	3-4	0	6.50
Harry Jordan	—	21	1	1	1	0	9.0	10	0	2	1	1-0	0	4.00
Adonis Terry†	R	29	1	1	0	0	0.2	2	0	4	0	0-1	0	67.50
Jack Easton	—	27	3	1	1	0	19.2	26	0	4	1	0-1	0	4.12
Phil Knell†	L	29	1	0	0	0	7.0	11	0	6	0	0-0	0	11.57
Elmer Smith	L	26	1	0	0	0	4.0	6	0	1	0	0-0	0	4.50

1894 Chicago Colts 8th NL 57-75 .432 34.0 GB

Cap Anson

Player	Gm by Position	B	Age	G	AB	R	H	2B	3B	HR	RBI	BB	SO	SB	Avg	OBP	Slg
Pop Schriver	C88,3B3,SS3*	R	28	96	349	55	96	12	3	3	47	29	21	9	.275	.341	.352
Cap Anson	1B82,2B1	R	42	83	340	82	132	28	4	5	99	40	15	17	.388	.457	.538
Jiggs Parrott	2B123,3B1	—	22	124	517	82	128	17	9	3	64	16	35	30	.248	.274	.333
Charlie Irwin	3B67,SS61	L	25	128	498	84	144	24	9	8	95	63	23	35	.289	.379	.422
Bill Dahlen	SS66,3B55	R	24	121	502	149	179	32	14	15	107	76	33	42	.357	.444	.566
Walt Wilmot	OF133	S	30	133	597	134	197	45	12	5	130	35	23	74	.330	.368	.471
Bill Lange	OF109,SS2,3B1	R	23	111	442	84	145	16	9	6	90	56	18	65	.328	.405	.446
Jimmy Ryan	OF108	R	31	108	474	132	171	37	7	3	62	50	23	11	.361	.425	.487
George Decker	1B48,OF29,3B7*	L	25	91	384	74	120	17	6	8	92	24	17	23	.313	.361	.451
Malachi Kittridge	C51	R	24	51	168	36	53	8	2	0	23	26	20	2	.315	.407	.387
Clark Griffith	P36,OF7,SS1	R	24	46	142	27	33	5	4	0	15	23	9	6	.232	.339	.324
Bill Hutchison	P36,OF4	R	34	39	136	30	42	3	0	6	16	11	17	2	.309	.361	.463
Scott Stratton†	P15,OF5,1B2	L	24	23	96	29	36	5	4	3	23	6	1	3	.375	.417	.604
Adonis Terry†	P23,OF7,1B2	R	29	30	95	19	33	4	2	0	17	11	12	3	.347	.415	.432
Sam Dungan†	OF10	R	27	10	39	5	9	2	0	0	3	7	1	1	.231	.348	.282
Lew Camp	2B8	L	26	8	33	1	6	2	0	0	1	1	6	0	.182	.206	.242
John Houseman	SS3,2B1	—	24	4	15	5	6	3	1	0	4	5	3	2	.400	.571	.733

P. Schriver, 2 G at 1B; G. Decker, 2 G at 2B, 1 G at SS

Pitcher	T	Age	G	GS	CG	ShO	IP	H	HR	BB	SO	W-L	Sv	ERA
Bill Hutchison	R	34	36	34	28	0	277.2	373	9	140	59	14-16	0	6.06
Clark Griffith	R	24	36	30	28	0	261.1	328	12	85	71	21-14	0	4.92
Willie McGill	L	20	27	23	22	0	208.0	272	2	117	58	7-19	0	5.84
Adonis Terry†	R	29	23	21	16	0	163.1	232	12	123	39	5-11	0	5.84
Scott Stratton†	R	24	15	12	11	0	119.1	198	5	40	23	8-5	0	6.03
Bert Abbey	R	24	11	11	10	0	92.0	119	3	37	24	2-7	0	5.18
Kid Camp	R	24	3	2	2	0	22.0	34	0	12	6	0-1	0	6.55
Fritz Clausen	L	25	1	1	0	0	4.1	5	0	3	1	0-1	0	10.38

1894 St. Louis Browns 9th NL 56-76 .424 35.0 GB

Doggie Miller

Player	Gm by Position	B	Age	G	AB	R	H	2B	3B	HR	RBI	BB	SO	SB	Avg	OBP	Slg
Doggie Miller	3B52,C41,2B18*	R	29	127	481	93	163	9	11	8	86	58	9	17	.339	.414	.453
Roger Connor†	1B99	L	36	99	380	83	122	28	25	7	79	51	17	17	.321	.410	.582
Joe Quinn	2B106	R	29	106	405	59	116	18	1	4	61	24	8	25	.286	.328	.365
Heinie Peitz	3B47,C39,1B14*	R	23	99	338	52	89	19	9	3	49	43	21	14	.263	.348	.399
Bones Ely	SS126,P1,2B1	R	31	127	510	85	156	20	12	12	89	30	34	23	.306	.344	.463
Frank Shugart	OF122,3B7,SS7	S	27	133	527	103	154	19	18	7	72	38	37	21	.292	.349	.436
Tommy Dowd	OF117,2B7,3B1	R	25	123	524	92	142	16	8	4	62	54	23	74	.271	.341	.355
Charlie Frank	OF77,1B3,P2	—	24	80	319	52	89	12	7	4	42	44	13	14	.279	.372	.398
Duff Cooley	OF39,3B13,1B1*	L	21	54	206	35	61	3	1	1	21	12	16	7	.296	.335	.335
Ted Breitenstein	P56,OF7	L	25	63	182	27	40	7	2	0	13	31	19	3	.220	.340	.280
Pink Hawley	P53,OF1	L	21	53	163	16	43	6	6	2	23	5	16	2	.264	.298	.411
Art Twineham	C38	L	27	38	127	22	40	4	1	1	16	9	11	2	.315	.387	.386
Marty Hogan†	OF29	R	22	29	100	11	28	3	4	0	13	3	13	7	.280	.308	.390
Dick Buckley†	C27,1B1	—	35	29	89	5	16	1	2	1	3	6	3	0	.180	.240	.270
Tim O'Rourke†	3B18	L	30	18	71	10	20	4	1	0	10	8	3	2	.282	.354	.366
Kid Gleason†	P8,1B1	S	27	9	28	3	7	0	1	0	1	2	1	0	.250	.300	.321
Joe Peitz	OF7	—	24	7	26	10	11	2	3	0	3	6	1	2	.423	.531	.731
Ernie Mason	P4,OF1	—	—	4	12	0	3	0	0	0	0	1	1	0	.250	.308	.250
Paul Russell	2B1,3B1,OF1	—	24	3	10	1	1	0	0	0	0	0	2	0	.100	.100	.100
Willard Brown†	1B3	R	28	3	9	0	1	0	0	0	0	0	2	0	.111	.111	.111
Pete Browning†	OF2	R	33	2	7	1	1	0	0	0	0	0	0	0	.143	.143	.143
George Paynter	OF1	R	22	1	4	0	0	0	0	0	0	1	0	1	.000	.200	.000
Art Ball	2B1	—	18	1	3	0	1	0	0	0	0	0	1	0	.333	.333	.333
John Ricks	3B1	—	—	1	1	0	0	0	0	0	0	0	0	0	.000	.000	.000

D. Miller, 12 G at 1B, 4 G at OF, 1 G at SS; H. Peitz, 1 G at P; D. Cooley, 1 G at SS

Pitcher	T	Age	G	GS	CG	ShO	IP	H	HR	BB	SO	W-L	Sv	ERA
Ted Breitenstein	L	25	56	50	46	1	447.1	497	21	191	140	27-23	0	4.79
Pink Hawley	R	21	53	41	36	0	392.2	481	14	149	120	19-27	0	4.90
Dad Clarkson	R	27	32	32	24	1	233.1	318	9	117	46	8-17	0	6.36
Kid Gleason†	R	27	8	8	6	0	58.0	75	2	21	9	2-6	0	6.05
Ernie Mason	—	—	4	2	2	0	22.2	34	1	10	3	0-3	0	7.15
Charlie Frank	—	24	2	0	0	0	3.0	6	1	7	1	0-0	0	15.00
Heinie Peitz	R	23	1	0	0	0	3.0	7	0	2	0	0-0	0	9.00
Bones Ely	R	31	1	0	0	0	1.0	0	0	3	0	0-0	0	0.00

1894 Cincinnati Reds 10th NL 55-75 .423 35.0 GB

Charlie Comiskey

Player	Gm by Position	B	Age	G	AB	R	H	2B	3B	HR	RBI	BB	SO	SB	Avg	OBP	Slg
Morgan Murphy	C74,3B1,SS1	R	27	75	255	42	70	9	0	1	37	26	34	6	.275	.344	.322
Charlie Comiskey	1B60,OF1	R	34	61	220	26	58	8	0	0	33	5	5	10	.264	.289	.300
Bid McPhee	2B126	R	34	126	474	107	144	21	9	5	88	90	23	33	.304	.420	.418
Arlie Latham	3B127,2B2	R	34	129	524	129	164	23	6	4	60	60	24	59	.313	.393	.403
Germany Smith	SS127	R	31	127	482	73	127	33	5	3	76	41	28	15	.263	.324	.371
Dummy Hoy	OF126	L	32	126	495	114	148	22	13	5	70	87	18	27	.299	.416	.426
Bug Holliday	OF119,1B1	R	27	121	511	119	190	24	7	13	119	40	20	29	.372	.420	.523
Jim Canavan	OF95,SS3,3B2*	R	27	101	356	77	97	16	9	13	70	62	25	13	.272	.380	.478
Farmer Vaughn	C43,1B27,OF8*	R	30	72	284	50	88	15	5	8	64	12	11	5	.310	.338	.482
Tom Parrott	P41,OF13,1B12*	R	26	68	229	51	74	12	6	4	40	17	10	4	.323	.372	.480
Frank Dwyer	P45,OF10,SS2	R	26	54	172	31	46	9	2	2	28	15	13	0	.267	.326	.378
Jack McCarthy	OF25,1B15	L	25	40	167	29	45	9	1	0	21	17	6	3	.269	.348	.335
Bill Merritt†	C24,3B3,1B1*	R	23	29	113	17	37	6	1	1	21	9	3	4	.327	.387	.425
Frank Motz	1B18	—	24	18	69	8	14	4	0	0	12	9	1	2	.203	.304	.261
Bill Whitrock†	P10,OF7,3B1	—	24	18	60	8	13	1	0	0	8	2	4	1	.217	.242	.233
Bill Massey	1B10,2B2,3B1	R	23	13	53	7	15	3	0	0	5	3	2	0	.283	.321	.340
Marty Hogan†	OF6	R	22	6	23	4	3	0	0	0	3	1	4	2	.130	.167	.130
Connie Murphy	C1	L	23	1	4	0	0	0	0	0	0	1	1	0	.000	.200	.000

J. Canavan, 1 G at 1B, 1 G at 2B; F. Vaughn, 3 G at SS; T. Parrott, 1 G at 2B, 1 G at 3B, 1 G at SS; B. Merritt, 1 G at OF

Pitcher	T	Age	G	GS	CG	ShO	IP	H	HR	BB	SO	W-L	Sv	ERA
Frank Dwyer	R	26	45	40	34	1	348.0	471	27	106	49	19-22	1	5.07
Tom Parrott	R	26	41	36	31	1	308.2	402	19	126	61	17-19	1	5.60
Elton Chamberlin	R	26	22	21	18	1	177.2	220	10	91	57	10-9	0	5.77
Chauncey Fisher†	R	22	11	11	10	0	91.0	134	4	44	14	2-8	0	7.32
Bill Whitrock†	R	24	10	8	8	0	70.1	110	7	39	9	2-6	0	6.65
Lem Cross	R	22	8	8	4	0	53.0	94	8	21	11	3-4	0	8.49
Henry Fournier	L	28	6	4	4	0	45.0	71	4	20	5	1-3	0	5.40
Fred Blank	L	20	1	1	1	0	8.0	5	0	9	1	0-1	0	4.50
Carney Flynn	L	19	2	1	0	0	7.2	16	4	10	4	0-2	0	17.61
Bill Pfann	—	31	1	1	0	0	3.0	10	1	4	0	0-1	0	27.00
Jesse Tannehill	L	19	5	1	1	0	29.0	37	1	16	7	1-0	1	7.14
Murray McGuire	L	—	1	0	0	0	6.0	15	0	5	1	0-0	0	10.50

1894 Washington Senators 11th NL 45-87 .341 46.0 GB

Gus Schmelz

Player	Gm by Position	B	Age	G	AB	R	H	2B	3B	HR	RBI	BB	SO	SB	Avg	OBP	Slg
Deacon McGuire	C104	R	30	104	425	67	130	18	6	6	78	33	19	11	.306	.366	.419
Ed Cartwright	1B132	R	34	132	507	88	149	35	13	12	106	57	43	31	.294	.374	.485
Piggy Ward	2B79,OF12,SS3*	S	27	98	347	86	105	11	7	0	36	80	31	41	.303	.447	.375
Bill Joyce	3B99	L	28	99	355	103	126	25	14	17	89	87	33	21	.355	.496	.648
Frank Scheibeck†	SS52	R	29	52	196	49	45	2	4	0	17	45	24	11	.230	.384	.281
Charlie Abbey	OF129	L	27	129	523	95	164	26	18	7	101	58	38	31	.314	.389	.472
Kip Selbach	OF80,SS19	R	22	97	372	69	114	21	17	7	71	51	20	21	.306	.390	.511
Bill Hassamaer	OF68,3B31,2B14*	—	29	118	494	106	159	33	17	4	90	41	20	16	.322	.375	.482
Paul Radford	SS47,2B26,OF24	R	32	95	325	61	78	13	5	0	49	65	23	24	.240	.378	.311
W. Wings Tebeau†	OF61	R	32	61	222	41	50	10	6	0	28	37	20	17	.225	.341	.324
Win Mercer	P49,OF4	R	20	52	162	27	46	5	2	2	29	9	20	9	.284	.322	.377
Dan Dugdale	C33,3B3,OF2	—	29	38	134	19	32	4	2	0	16	13	14	7	.239	.306	.299
Al Maul	P28,OF12	R	28	41	124	23	30	3	3	2	20	14	11	1	.242	.352	.363
Otis Stocksdale	P18,OF4,2B2*	L	22	24	71	10	23	1	0	0	6	2	5	2	.324	.351	.338
Joe Sullivan†	2B8,SS6,3B1*	—	24	17	60	7	15	3	0	0	5	6	2	3	.250	.357	.300
Duke Esper†	P19,OF1	—	25	20	57	9	16	3	1	1	4	4	7	0	.281	.328	.421
Mike Sullivan†	P20,OF1	L	27	20	57	4	9	1	1	1	7	2	11	0	.158	.186	.263
Tim O'Rourke†	2B4,SS3	L	30	7	25	4	5	2	1	0	2	2	1	0	.200	.259	.360
Jake Boyd	P3,OF3	—	20	6	21	1	3	0	0	0	1	1	4	2	.143	.182	.143
George Haddock†	P4,OF1	R	27	5	16	4	3	2	0	0	3	1	2	1	.188	.235	.313
John Malarkey	P3,OF1	—	22	4	14	1	1	0	0	0	0	0	8	0	.071	.071	.071
Kid Mohler	2B3	L	19	3	9	0	1	0	0	0	0	2	4	0	.111	.273	.111
Count Campau	OF2	L	30	2	7	1	1	0	0	0	0	1	4	0	.143	.250	.143

P. Ward, 1 G at 3B; B. Hassamaer, 4 G at SS; O. Stocksdale, 1 G at 3B, 1 G at SS; J. Sullivan, 1 G at OF

Pitcher	T	Age	G	GS	CG	ShO	IP	H	HR	BB	SO	W-L	Sv	ERA
Win Mercer	R	20	49	38	30	0	333.0	431	9	125	69	17-23	3	3.76
Al Maul	R	28	28	26	21	0	201.2	272	12	73	34	11-15	0	5.98
Duke Esper†	L	25	19	15	7	0	122.1	191	8	40	27	5-10	0	7.50
Otis Stocksdale	R	22	18	14	11	0	117.1	176	10	42	10	5-9	0	5.06
Mike Sullivan†	—	27	20	12	11	0	117.2	166	10	74	21	2-10	1	6.58
Charlie Petty†	R	28	16	12	8	0	103.0	156	4	32	14	3-8	0	5.59
George Haddock†	R	27	4	4	4	0	29.0	50	2	17	1	0-4	0	8.69
John Malarkey	R	22	3	3	3	0	26.0	42	1	5	3	2-1	0	4.15
Jake Boyd	L	20	3	3	3	0	19.0	37	1	14	3	0-3	0	8.53
Varney Anderson	R	28	2	2	2	0	14.0	15	0	6	3	0-2	0	7.07
George Stephens	—	26	3	2	1	0	11.0	19	1	8	1	0-0	0	4.91
Bill Wynne	R	25	1	1	1	0	8.0	10	0	8	2	0-1	0	6.75
Rip Egan	R	22	1	0	0	0	5.0	8	1	2	2	0-0	0	10.80

1894 Louisville Colonels 12th NL 36-94 .277 54.0 GB

Billy Barnie

Player	Gm by Position	B	Age	G	AB	R	H	2B	3B	HR	RBI	BB	SO	SB	Avg	OBP	Slg
John Grim	C77,2B24,1B7*	R	26	108	410	66	122	27	7	7	70	16	15	14	.298	.339	.449
Luke Lutenberg	1B67,2B2	R	29	69	250	42	48	10	4	0	23	23	21	4	.192	.284	.264
Fred Pfeffer	2B90,SS15,P1	R	34	104	409	68	126	12	14	5	59	30	14	31	.308	.357	.443
Jerry Denny	3B60	R	35	60	221	26	61	11	7	0	32	13	12	10	.276	.325	.389
Danny Richardson	SS107,2B10	R	31	116	430	51	109	17	2	1	40	35	31	8	.253	.317	.309
Tom Brown	OF129	L	33	129	536	122	136	22	14	9	57	60	73	66	.254	.332	.397
Fred Clarke	OF75	L	21	75	310	54	83	11	7	7	48	25	27	25	.268	.330	.416
Larry Twitchell	OF51,P1	R	30	52	210	28	56	16	3	2	32	15	20	8	.267	.316	.400
Farmer Weaver†	OF35,C17,1B10*	L	29	64	244	19	54	5	2	3	24	7	11	3	.221	.249	.295
Tim O'Rourke†	1B30,OF18,3B3*	L	30	55	220	46	61	3	3	0	27	23	9	9	.277	.351	.318
Pat Flaherty	3B38	—	28	38	145	15	43	5	3	0	15	9	6	2	.297	.342	.372
Ollie Smith	OF38	L	26	38	134	26	40	6	1	3	20	27	15	13	.299	.427	.425
George Hemming†	P35,1B1	R	25	36	131	20	33	2	6	2	10	5	20	2	.252	.279	.405
George Nicol†	OF26,P1	—	23	27	108	12	38	6	4	0	19	2	3	4	.352	.375	.481
Pete Gilbert†	3B28	—	26	28	108	13	33	3	1	1	14	5	4	2	.306	.353	.380
Jock Menefee†	P28,2B1	R	26	29	79	7	13	1	0	0	4	8	7	2	.165	.250	.177
Billy Earle†	C18,1B1,2B1*	R	26	21	65	10	23	1	0	0	7	9	3	2	.354	.432	.369
Willard Brown†	1B13	R	28	13	48	5	10	2	0	0	9	5	7	1	.208	.283	.250
Fred Zahner	C10,OF2,1B1	—	24	13	45	7	9	0	1	0	3	3	5	2	.200	.250	.244
Fred Lake	2B6,C5,SS5	R	27	16	42	8	12	2	0	1	10	11	6	2	.286	.474	.405
Scott Stratton†	P7,OF5	L	24	13	37	9	12	1	2	0	4	4	2	1	.324	.390	.459
Sam Dungan†	OF8	R	27	8	32	6	11	1	0	0	3	4	1	2	.344	.417	.375
Henry Cote	C10	—	30	10	31	7	9	2	2	0	3	5	6	2	.290	.389	.484

J. Grim, 1 G at 3B; F. Weaver, 1 G at 2B; T. O'Rourke, 3 G at SS, 1 G at 2B; B. Earle, 1 G at 3B, 1 G at OF

Pitcher	T	Age	G	GS	CG	ShO	IP	H	HR	BB	SO	W-L	Sv	ERA
George Hemming†	R	25	35	32	32	1	294.1	358	7	133	66	13-19	1	4.37
Phil Knell†	L	29	32	28	25	0	247.0	330	9	104	67	7-21	0	5.32
Jock Menefee†	R	26	28	24	20	1	211.2	258	3	50	43	8-17	0	4.29
Jack Wadsworth	R	26	22	22	20	1	173.0	261	10	103	57	4-18	0	7.60
Bert Inks†	L	23	8	8	8	0	59.2	87	2	34	8	2-6	0	6.49
Matt Kilroy	L	28	8	7	3	0	37.0	46	2	20	11	0-5	0	3.89
Scott Stratton†	R	24	7	5	4	0	43.0	72	3	13	3	1-5	0	8.37
George Nicol†	L	23	1	1	1	0	9.0	19	2	5	3	0-1	0	15.00
Bill Peppers	—	27	2	1	0	0	8.0	10	0	4	0	0-1	0	6.75
Bill Whitrock†	R	24	1	1	0	0	4.0	8	0	2	0	0-1	0	9.00
Fred Pfeffer	R	34	1	0	0	0	7.0	8	0	6	0	0-0	0	2.57
Larry Twitchell	R	30	1	0	0	0	3.0	5	1	1	0	0-0	0	6.00

»1895 Baltimore Orioles 1st NL 87-43 .669 —

Ned Hanlon

Player	Gm by Position	B	Age	G	AB	R	H	2B	3B	HR	RBI	BB	SO	SB	Avg	OBP	Slg
Wilbert Robinson	C75	R	32	77	282	38	74	19	1	0	48	12	19	11	.262	.295	.337
Scoops Carey	1B123,3B1,SS1*	R	24	123	490	59	128	21	6	1	75	27	32	2	.261	.305	.335
Kid Gleason	2B85,3B12,P9*	S	28	112	421	90	130	14	12	0	74	33	18	19	.309	.366	.399
John McGraw	3B95,2B1	L	22	96	388	110	143	13	6	2	48	60	9	61	.369	.459	.448
Hughie Jennings	SS131	R	26	131	529	159	204	41	7	4	125	24	17	53	.386	.444	.512
Willie Keeler	OF131	L	23	131	565	162	213	24	15	4	78	37	12	47	.377	.429	.494
Steve Brodie	OF131	L	26	131	528	85	184	27	10	2	134	26	15	35	.348	.394	.449
Joe Kelley	OF131	R	23	131	518	148	189	26	19	10	134	77	29	54	.365	.456	.546
Heinie Reitz	2B48,3B18,SS1	L	28	71	245	45	72	15	5	0	29	18	11	15	.294	.350	.396
Boileryard Clarke	C60,1B6	R	26	67	241	38	70	15	3	0	35	13	18	8	.290	.350	.378
Frank Bonner†	3B11	R	25	11	42	9	14	1	1	0	7	5	1	4	.333	.404	.405
Dan Brouthers†	1B5	L	37	5	23	2	6	2	0	0	5	1	1	0	.261	.292	.348
Arlie Pond	P6,OF1	R	23	7	6	0	2	0	1	0	0	0	2	0	.333	.333	.667
Frank Bowerman	C1	R	26	1	1	0	0	0	0	0	0	0	0	0	.000	.000	.000

S. Carey, 1 G at OF; K. Gleason, 4 G at OF

Pitcher	T	Age	G	GS	CG	ShO	IP	H	HR	BB	SO	W-L	Sv	ERA
Bill Hoffer	R	24	41	38	32	4	314.0	296	9	124	80	31-6	0	3.21
George Hemming	R	26	34	31	26	1	262.1	288	10	96	43	20-13	0	4.05
Duke Esper	L	26	34	25	16	1	218.1	248	2	79	39	10-12	1	3.92
Sadie McMahon	R	27	15	15	15	4	122.1	110	1	32	37	10-4	0	2.94
Dad Clarkson†	R	28	20	14	10	0	142.0	169	5	64	23	12-3	0	3.87
Kid Gleason	R	28	9	5	3	0	50.1	77	4	21	6	2-4	1	6.97
Bill Kissinger†	R	23	2	2	1	0	11.1	18	0	2	3	1-0	0	3.97
Arlie Pond	R	23	6	1	1	0	13.2	10	0	12	13	0-1	2	5.93

1895 Cleveland Spiders 2nd NL 84-46 .646 3.0 GB

Patsy Tebeau

Player	Gm by Position	B	Age	G	AB	R	H	2B	3B	HR	RBI	BB	SO	SB	Avg	OBP	Slg
Chief Zimmer	C84,1B3	R	34	88	315	60	107	21	2	5	56	33	30	14	.340	.417	.467
Patsy Tebeau	1B49,2B9,3B6	R	30	63	264	50	84	13	2	2	52	16	18	8	.318	.362	.405
Cupid Childs	2B119	L	27	119	462	96	133	15	3	4	90	74	24	20	.288	.393	.359
Chippy McGarr	3B108,2B4	R	32	112	419	85	111	14	2	2	59	34	33	19	.265	.322	.322
Ed McKean	SS131	R	31	131	565	131	193	32	17	8	119	45	25	12	.342	.397	.501
Jesse Burkett	OF131	L	26	131	550	153	225	22	11	5	83	74	31	41	.409	.486	.524
Jimmy McAleer	OF131	R	30	131	528	84	143	17	2	0	68	38	37	32	.271	.327	.311
Harry Blake	OF83	R	21	84	315	50	87	10	1	3	45	30	33	11	.276	.341	.343
Jack O'Connor	C47,1B41,3B1	R	26	89	340	51	99	14	10	0	58	30	22	11	.291	.354	.391
W. Wings Tebeau	OF49,1B42	R	33	91	337	57	110	16	6	0	68	50	28	12	.326	.415	.409
Ed Gremminger	3B20	R	21	20	78	10	21	1	0	0	15	5	13	0	.269	.313	.282
Fred Donovan	C3	R	30	3	12	1	1	0	0	0	1	1	2	0	.083	.154	.083
Pussy Tebeau	OF2	L	25	2	6	3	3	0	0	0	0	2	1	1	.500	.625	.500
Tom O'Meara	C1	—	22	1	1	1	0	0	0	0	0	1	0	0	.000	.500	.000

Pitcher	T	Age	G	GS	CG	ShO	IP	H	HR	BB	SO	W-L	Sv	ERA
Cy Young	R	28	47	40	36	4	369.2	363	10	75	121	35-10	0	3.24
Nig Cuppy	R	25	47	40	36	1	353.0	384	9	95	91	26-14	2	3.54
Bobby Wallace	R	21	30	28	22	1	228.2	271	3	87	63	12-14	1	4.09
Phil Knell†	L	30	20	13	9	0	116.2	149	7	53	30	7-5	0	5.40
Zeke Wilson†	R	25	8	7	3	0	44.2	63	3	20	16	3-1	0	4.23
Mike Sullivan	—	28	4	3	2	0	31.0	42	1	16	5	1-2	0	8.42

1895 Philadelphia Phillies 3rd NL 78-53 .595 9.5 GB

Arthur Irwin

Player	Gm by Position	B	Age	G	AB	R	H	2B	3B	HR	RBI	BB	SO	SB	Avg	OBP	Slg
Jack Clements	C88	L	30	88	322	64	127	27	2	13	75	22	7	3	.394	.446	.612
Jack Boyle	1B133	R	29	133	565	90	143	17	4	0	67	35	23	13	.253	.302	.297
Bill Hallman	2B122,SS3	R	28	124	539	94	169	26	5	1	91	34	20	16	.314	.359	.386
Lave Cross	3B125	R	29	125	535	95	145	26	9	2	101	35	8	21	.271	.319	.364
Joe Sullivan	SS89,OF6	—	25	94	373	75	126	7	3	2	50	24	20	15	.338	.395	.389
Billy Hamilton	OF123	L	29	123	517	166	201	22	6	7	74	96	30	97	.389	.490	.495
Sam Thompson	OF118	L	35	119	538	131	211	45	21	18	165	31	11	27	.392	.430	.654
Ed Delahanty	OF103,SS9,2B6*	R	27	116	480	149	194	49	10	11	106	86	31	46	.404	.500	.617
Tuck Turner	OF55	S	22	59	210	51	81	8	6	2	43	25	11	14	.386	.453	.510
Charlie Reilly	SS34,3B11,2B3*	S	28	49	179	28	48	6	1	0	25	13	12	7	.268	.335	.313
Jack Taylor	P41,OF1	R	22	42	155	26	45	11	2	3	35	7	18	3	.290	.329	.445
Mike Grady	C38,OF5,1B1*	R	25	46	123	21	40	3	1	1	23	14	8	5	.325	.407	.390
Dick Buckley	C38	—	36	38	112	20	28	6	1	0	14	9	17	2	.250	.333	.321
Art Madison	SS6,2B3,3B2	R	24	11	34	6	12	3	0	0	8	1	1	4	.353	.371	.441
Ernie Beam	P9,OF1	—	28	10	11	2	2	0	0	0	0	0	4	1	.182	.250	.182

E. Delahanty, 1 G at 3B; C. Reilly, 1 G at OF; M. Grady, 1 G at 3B

Pitcher	T	Age	G	GS	CG	ShO	IP	H	HR	BB	SO	W-L	Sv	ERA
Kid Carsey	R	24	44	40	35	0	342.1	460	14	118	64	24-16	1	4.92
Jack Taylor	R	22	41	37	33	1	335.0	403	7	83	93	26-14	1	4.49
Willie McGill	L	21	20	20	13	0	146.0	177	2	81	70	10-8	0	5.55
Al Orth	R	22	11	10	9	0	88.0	103	0	22	25	8-1	1	3.89
Con Lucid†	—	21	10	10	7	1	69.2	80	3	35	19	6-3	0	5.94
Tom Smith	R	23	11	7	4	0	68.0	76	1	53	21	2-3	0	6.88
George Hodson	R	25	4	2	1	0	17.0	27	4	9	6	1-2	0	9.53
Gus Weyhing†	R	28	2	2	0	0	9.0	23	0	13	5	0-2	0	20.00
Ernie Beam	R	28	9	1	1	0	24.2	33	1	25	3	0-2	3	11.31
Henry Lampe	L	22	7	3	2	0	44.0	68	3	33	18	0-2	0	7.57
Deke White	L	22	3	1	1	0	17.1	17	1	13	6	1-0	1	9.87

1895 Chicago Colts 4th NL 72-58 .554 15.0 GB

Cap Anson

Player	Gm by Position	B	Age	G	AB	R	H	2B	3B	HR	RBI	BB	SO	SB	Avg	OBP	Slg
Tim Donahue	C63	L	25	63	219	29	59	9	1	2	36	20	25	5	.269	.339	.347
Cap Anson	1B122	R	43	122	474	87	159	23	6	2	91	55	23	12	.335	.408	.422
Ace Stewart	2B97,OF1	R	26	97	365	52	88	8	10	8	76	39	40	14	.241	.314	.384
Bill Everitt	3B130,2B3	L	26	133	550	129	197	16	10	3	88	33	42	47	.358	.399	.440
Bill Dahlen	SS129,OF1	R	25	129	516	106	131	19	10	7	62	61	51	38	.254	.344	.370
Bill Lange	OF123	R	24	123	478	120	186	27	16	10	98	55	24	67	.389	.456	.575
Walt Wilmot	OF108	S	31	108	466	86	132	16	6	8	72	30	19	28	.283	.327	.395
Jimmy Ryan	OF108	R	32	108	438	83	139	22	8	6	49	48	22	18	.317	.392	.445
George Decker	OF57,1B11,3B3*	L	26	73	297	51	82	9	7	2	41	17	22	11	.276	.324	.374
Malachi Kittridge	C59	R	25	60	212	30	48	6	3	3	29	16	9	6	.226	.284	.325
Clark Griffith	P42,OF1	R	25	43	144	20	46	3	0	1	27	16	9	2	.319	.391	.361
Adonis Terry	P38,SS1,OF1	R	30	40	137	18	30	3	2	1	10	2	17	1	.219	.236	.292
Harry Truby	2B33	—	25	33	119	17	40	3	0	0	16	10	7	7	.336	.402	.361
Bill Moran	C15	—	25	15	55	8	9	2	1	1	9	3	2	2	.164	.220	.291
Scott Stratton	P5,OF4	L	25	10	24	3	7	1	1	0	2	4	2	1	.292	.393	.417
Walter Thornton	P7,1B1	L	20	8	22	4	7	1	0	1	7	3	1	0	.318	.400	.500
Charlie Irwin	SS3	L	26	3	10	4	2	0	0	0	0	2	1	0	.200	.333	.200
Jiggs Parrott	1B1,SS1	—	23	3	4	0	1	0	0	0	0	0	0	0	.250	.250	.250

G. Decker, 1 G at 2B, 1 G at SS

Pitcher	T	Age	G	GS	CG	ShO	IP	H	HR	BB	SO	W-L	Sv	ERA
Clark Griffith	R	25	42	41	39	0	353.0	434	11	91	79	26-14	0	3.93
Bill Hutchison	R	35	38	35	30	2	291.0	371	13	129	85	13-21	0	4.73
Adonis Terry	R	30	38	34	31	0	311.1	346	4	131	88	21-14	0	4.80
Doc Parker	R	23	7	6	5	1	51.1	65	1	9	9	4-2	0	3.68
Danny Friend	L	22	5	5	5	0	41.0	50	5	14	10	2-2	0	5.27
Scott Stratton	R	25	5	5	3	0	30.0	51	1	14	4	2-3	0	9.60
Monte McFarland	—	22	2	2	2	0	14.0	21	0	5	5	2-0	0	5.14
John Dolan	R	27	2	2	1	0	11.0	16	0	6	1	0-1	0	6.55
Bert Abbey†	R	25	1	1	1	0	8.0	10	0	2	3	0-1	0	4.50
Walter Thornton	L	20	7	2	2	0	40.0	58	3	31	13	2-0	1	6.08

1895 Brooklyn Bridegrooms 5th NL 71-60 .542 16.5 GB

Dave Foutz

Player	Gm by Position	B	Age	G	AB	R	H	2B	3B	HR	RBI	BB	SO	SB	Avg	OBP	Slg
John Grim	C91,1B1,OF1	R	27	93	329	54	92	17	5	0	44	13	9	9	.280	.321	.362
Candy LaChance	1B125,OF3	S	25	127	536	99	167	22	8	8	108	29	48	37	.312	.356	.427
Tom Daly	2B120	S	29	120	455	89	128	17	7	2	68	52	52	28	.281	.359	.367
Billy Shindle	3B116	R	31	116	477	91	133	21	2	3	69	47	28	17	.279	.357	.350
Tommy Corcoran	SS127	R	26	127	535	81	142	17	10	2	69	23	11	17	.265	.299	.346
Mike Griffin	OF131,SS1	L	30	131	519	140	173	38	7	4	65	93	29	27	.333	.444	.457
John Anderson	OF101	S	21	102	419	76	120	11	14	9	87	12	29	24	.286	.314	.444
George Treadway	OF86	L	—	86	339	54	87	14	3	7	54	33	22	9	.257	.326	.378
George Shoch	OF39,2B13,SS6*	R	36	61	216	49	56	9	7	0	29	32	6	7	.259	.368	.366
Con Daily	C39,OF1	R	30	40	142	17	30	3	2	1	11	10	18	3	.211	.268	.282
Dave Foutz	OF20,1B8	R	38	31	115	14	34	4	1	0	21	4	2	1	.296	.319	.348
Ad Gumbert	P33,OF1	R	26	34	97	21	35	6	0	2	13	7	10	0	.361	.410	.485
Oyster Burns†	OF19	R	30	20	76	7	14	0	1	0	7	8	2	0	.184	.271	.211
Joe Mulvey	3B13	R	36	13	49	8	15	4	1	0	8	2	0	1	.306	.333	.429
Buster Burrell	C12	R	28	12	28	7	4	0	0	1	5	4	3	0	.143	.250	.250
Hunkey Hines	OF2	R	27	2	8	3	2	0	0	0	1	2	0	0	.250	.400	.250

G. Shoch, 3 G at 3B

Pitcher	T	Age	G	GS	CG	ShO	IP	H	HR	BB	SO	W-L	Sv	ERA
Brickyard Kennedy	R	27	39	33	26	2	279.2	335	13	93	39	19-12	1	5.12
Ed Stein	R	25	32	27	24	1	255.1	282	8	93	55	15-13	1	4.72
Ad Gumbert	R	26	33	26	20	0	234.0	288	11	69	45	11-16	1	5.08
Dan Daub	R	27	25	21	16	0	184.2	212	4	51	36	10-10	0	4.29
Con Lucid†	—	21	21	19	12	2	137.0	164	4	72	24	10-7	0	5.52
Bert Abbey†	R	25	8	6	5	0	52.0	66	0	9	14	5-2	0	4.33
Jack Cronin	R	21	2	0	0	0	5.0	10	0	3	1	0-0	2	10.80
Sandy McDougal	R	21	1	0	0	0	3.0	3	0	5	2	0-0	1	12.00

1895 Boston Beaneaters 5th NL 71-60 .542 16.5 GB

Frank Selee

Player	Gm by Position	B	Age	G	AB	R	H	2B	3B	HR	RBI	BB	SO	SB	Avg	OBP	Slg
Charlie Ganzel	C76,1B2	R	33	80	277	38	73	2	5	1	52	24	6	1	.264	.325	.318
Tommy Tucker	1B125	S	31	125	462	87	115	19	6	3	73	61	29	15	.249	.360	.335
Bobby Lowe	2B99	R	26	99	412	101	122	12	7	7	62	40	16	24	.296	.370	.410
Billy Nash	3B132	R	30	132	508	97	147	23	6	10	108	74	19	18	.289	.383	.417
Herman Long	SS122,2B2	L	29	124	535	109	169	23	10	9	75	31	12	35	.316	.357	.447
Hugh Duffy	OF130	R	28	130	531	110	187	30	6	9	100	63	16	42	.352	.425	.482
Jimmy Bannon	OF122,P1	R	24	123	489	101	171	35	5	6	74	54	31	28	.350	.420	.479
Tommy McCarthy	OF109,2B9	R	31	117	452	90	131	13	2	2	73	72	12	18	.290	.391	.341
Jack Ryan	C43,2B5,OF1	R	26	49	189	22	55	7	0	0	18	6	6	3	.291	.313	.328
Fred Tenney	OF28,C21	L	23	49	173	35	47	9	1	1	21	24	5	6	.272	.360	.353
Jack Stivetts	P38,1B5,OF2	R	27	46	158	20	30	6	4	0	24	6	18	1	.190	.220	.278
Kid Nichols	P47,OF1	S	25	49	157	23	37	3	2	0	18	14	28	0	.236	.298	.280
Jim Sullivan	P21,OF1	R	26	22	85	14	15	3	0	0	8	7	14	2	.176	.239	.212
Cozy Dolan	P25,OF1	L	22	26	83	12	20	4	1	0	7	6	7	3	.241	.300	.313
Joe Harrington	2B18	R	25	18	65	21	18	0	2	2	13	7	5	3	.277	.356	.431
Jimmy Collins†	OF10	R	25	11	38	10	8	3	0	1	8	4	4	0	.211	.302	.368
Charlie Nyce	SS9	—	24	9	35	7	8	5	0	2	9	4	2	0	.229	.325	.543
Frank Sexton	P7,2B1,OF1	—	22	9	22	2	5	0	0	0	2	1	1	0	.227	.261	.227
Otis Stocksdale†	P4,1B2	L	23	5	15	3	4	0	0	0	1	1	2	0	.267	.313	.267
John Warner†	C3	L	22	3	7	2	1	0	0	0	1	1	0	0	.143	.333	.143

Pitcher	T	Age	G	GS	CG	ShO	IP	H	HR	BB	SO	W-L	Sv	ERA
Kid Nichols	R	25	47	42	42	1	379.2	417	15	86	140	26-16	3	3.41
Jack Stivetts	R	27	38	34	30	0	291.0	341	15	89	111	17-17	0	4.64
Cozy Dolan	L	22	25	21	18	3	198.1	215	11	67	47	11-7	1	4.27
Jim Sullivan	R	26	21	19	16	0	179.1	236	10	58	46	11-9	0	4.82
Zeke Wilson†	R	25	6	6	4	0	45.0	54	1	27	5	2-4	0	5.20
Frank Sexton	—	22	7	5	4	0	49.0	59	2	22	14	1-5	0	5.69
Otis Stocksdale†	R	23	4	4	1	0	23.0	31	2	8	2	2-2	0	5.87
Bill Banks	R	21	1	1	1	0	7.0	7	0	4	4	1-0	0	0.00
Jimmy Bannon	R	24	1	0	0	0	3.0	4	0	2	1	0-0	0	6.00

1895 Pittsburgh Pirates 7th NL 71-61 .538 17.0 GB

Connie Mack

Player	Gm by Position	B	Age	G	AB	R	H	2B	3B	HR	RBI	BB	SO	SB	Avg	OBP	Slg
Bill Merritt†	C63,1B2	R	24	67	239	32	68	5	1	0	27	18	16	2	.285	.340	.314
Jake Beckley	1B129	L	27	129	530	104	174	31	19	5	110	24	20	20	.328	.381	.487
Lou Bierbauer	2B117	L	29	117	466	53	120	13	11	0	69	19	8	18	.258	.290	.333
Billy Clingman	3B106	S	25	106	382	69	99	16	4	0	45	41	43	19	.259	.334	.322
Monte Cross	SS107,2B1	R	25	108	393	67	101	14	13	3	54	38	38	39	.257	.327	.382
Jake Stenzel	OF129	R	28	129	514	114	192	38	13	7	97	57	25	53	.374	.447	.539
Patsy Donovan	OF125	L	30	125	519	114	160	17	16	1	58	47	19	36	.308	.375	.370
Elmer Smith	OF123	L	27	124	480	88	145	14	12	1	81	55	25	34	.302	.381	.388
Frank Genins	OF29,2B16,3B16*	—	28	73	252	43	63	8	0	2	24	22	14	19	.250	.315	.306
Joe Sugden	C49	S	24	49	155	28	48	4	1	1	17	16	12	4	.310	.385	.368
Bill Stuart	SS17,2B2	—	21	19	77	5	19	3	0	0	10	2	6	2	.247	.275	.286
Tom Kinslow	C18	R	29	19	62	10	14	2	0	0	5	2	2	1	.226	.250	.258
Connie Mack	C12,1B1	R	32	14	49	12	15	2	0	0	4	7	1	1	.306	.404	.347
Bill Niles	3B10,2B1	—	27	11	37	2	8	0	0	0	0	5	2	2	.216	.310	.216
John Corcoran	SS4,3B2	—	22	6	20	0	3	0	0	0	1	0	2	0	.150	.150	.150

F. Genins, 8 G at SS, 2 G at 1B

Pitcher	T	Age	G	GS	CG	ShO	IP	H	HR	BB	SO	W-L	Sv	ERA
Pink Hawley	R	22	56	50	44	4	444.1	449	7	122	142	31-22	1	3.18
Bill Hart	R	29	36	29	24	0	261.2	293	4	135	85	14-17	1	4.75
Brownie Foreman	L	19	19	16	12	0	139.2	131	0	64	54	8-6	2	3.22
Frank Killen	L	24	13	11	6	0	95.0	113	2	57	25	5-5	0	5.49
Jim Gardner	R	20	11	10	8	0	85.1	99	1	27	31	8-2	0	2.64
Sam Moran	L	24	10	6	6	0	62.2	78	2	51	19	2-4	0	7.47
Tom Colcolough	R	24	6	5	2	0	35.1	38	1	21	15	1-1	0	5.60
Harry Jordan	—	22	2	2	2	0	17.0	24	0	6	4	0-2	0	4.24
Jake Hewitt	L	25	4	2	1	0	13.0	13	0	2	4	1-0	0	4.15
Gus Weyhing†	R	28	1	1	1	0	9.0	10	0	5	3	1-0	0	1.00
Jock Menefee	R	27	2	1	0	0	1.2	2	0	7	0	0-1	0	16.20
Gussie Gannon	L	21	1	0	0	0	5.0	7	0	2	0	0-0	0	1.80
Dave Wright	R	19	1	0	0	0	2.0	6	0	1	0	0-0	0	27.00

1895 Cincinnati Reds 8th NL 66-64 .508 21.0 GB

Buck Ewing

Player	Gm by Position	B	Age	G	AB	R	H	2B	3B	HR	RBI	BB	SO	SB	Avg	OBP	Slg
Farmer Vaughn	C77,1B15,2B1*	R	31	92	334	60	102	23	5	1	48	17	10	15	.305	.339	.413
Buck Ewing	1B105	R	35	105	434	90	138	24	13	5	94	30	22	34	.318	.363	.468
Bid McPhee	2B115	R	35	115	432	107	129	24	12	1	75	73	30	30	.299	.409	.417
Arlie Latham	3B108,1B3,2B1	R	35	112	460	93	143	14	6	2	69	42	25	48	.311	.375	.380
Germany Smith	SS127	R	32	127	503	75	151	23	6	4	74	34	24	13	.300	.345	.394
Dusty Miller	OF132	L	26	132	529	103	177	31	16	10	112	33	34	43	.335	.378	.510
Dummy Hoy	OF107	L	33	107	429	93	119	21	11	3	55	52	8	50	.277	.363	.403
George Hogriever	OF66,2B3	R	26	69	239	61	65	8	7	2	34	36	17	41	.272	.374	.389
Eddie Burke†	OF56	L	28	56	228	52	61	8	6	1	25	22	14	19	.268	.343	.368
Tom Parrott	P41,1B14,OF9	R	27	64	201	35	69	13	7	3	41	11	8	10	.343	.377	.522
Bill Grey	3B27,2B16,C5*	—	24	52	181	24	55	17	4	1	29	15	8	4	.304	.364	.459
Bug Holliday	OF32	R	28	32	127	25	38	9	2	0	20	10	3	6	.299	.350	.402
Morgan Murphy	C25	R	28	25	82	15	22	2	0	0	16	11	8	6	.268	.355	.293
Bill Merritt†	C20,2B1	R	24	22	79	9	14	2	0	0	12	6	5	2	.177	.235	.203
Harry Spies†	C12,1B2	R	29	14	50	2	11	0	1	0	5	3	2	0	.220	.264	.260
Mike Kahoe	C3	R	21	3	4	0	0	0	0	0	0	0	0	0	.000	.000	.000

F. Vaughn, 1 G at 3B; B. Grey, 5 G at SS, 1 G at OF

Pitcher	T	Age	G	GS	CG	ShO	IP	H	HR	BB	SO	W-L	Sv	ERA
Billy Rhines	R	26	38	33	25	0	267.2	322	4	76	72	19-10	0	4.81
Frank Dwyer	R	27	37	31	23	2	280.1	355	10	74	46	18-15	0	4.24
Tom Parrott	R	27	41	31	23	0	263.1	382	8	76	57	11-18	3	5.47
Frank Foreman	L	32	32	27	19	0	219.0	253	11	92	55	11-14	1	4.11
Bill Phillips	R	26	18	9	6	0	109.0	126	6	44	15	6-7	2	6.03
King Bailey	L	24	1	1	1	0	8.0	13	0	0	0	1-0	0	5.63

1895 New York Giants 9th NL 66-65 .504 21.5 GB

George Davis (16-17)/Jack Doyle (32-31)/Harvey Watkins (18-17)

Player	Gm by Position	B	Age	G	AB	R	H	2B	3B	HR	RBI	BB	SO	SB	Avg	OBP	Slg
Duke Farrell	C62,3B24,1B2	S	28	90	312	38	90	16	9	1	58	38	18	11	.288	.371	.407
Jack Doyle	1B58,2B13,3B6*	R	25	82	319	52	100	21	3	1	66	24	12	35	.313	.365	.408
General Stafford	2B109,OF12,3B2	R	26	124	463	79	129	12	5	3	73	40	32	42	.279	.344	.346
George Davis	3B80,1B14,2B10*	S	24	110	430	108	146	36	9	5	101	55	12	48	.340	.417	.500
Shorty Fuller	SS126	R	27	126	458	82	103	11	3	0	32	64	34	15	.225	.323	.262
George Van Haltren	OF131,P1	L	29	131	521	113	177	23	19	8	103	57	29	32	.340	.408	.503
Mike Tiernan	OF119	L	28	120	476	127	165	23	21	7	70	66	19	36	.347	.427	.527
Eddie Burke†	OF39	L	28	39	167	38	43	6	2	1	12	7	9	14	.257	.299	.335
Parke Wilson	C53,1B11,3B3	R	27	67	238	32	56	9	0	0	30	14	16	11	.235	.281	.273
Yale Murphy	OF33,3B8,SS8*	L	25	51	184	35	37	6	2	0	16	27	13	7	.201	.303	.255
Amos Rusie	P49,OF1	R	24	53	179	14	44	3	1	1	19	0	28	2	.246	.246	.291
Tom Bannon	OF21,1B16	R	26	37	159	33	43	6	2	0	8	7	8	20	.270	.301	.333
Oyster Burns†	OF32,1B1	R	30	33	114	21	35	5	3	1	25	14	6	10	.307	.388	.430
Les German	P25,3B11	R	26	35	111	16	29	2	2	2	16	9	7	1	.261	.333	.369
Pop Schriver	C18,1B6	R	29	24	92	16	29	2	1	1	16	9	10	3	.315	.382	.391
Willie Clark	1B23	L	22	23	88	9	23	3	2	0	16	5	6	1	.261	.301	.341
Harry Davis	1B7	R	21	7	24	1	7	0	1	0	6	2	0	1	.292	.346	.375
Frank Butler	OF5	L	34	5	22	5	6	1	0	0	2	1	1	0	.273	.304	.318
Larry Battam	3B2	—	17	2	4	0	1	0	0	0	0	2	1	0	.250	.500	.250

J. Doyle, 4 G at C; G. Davis, 7 G at OF; Y. Murphy, 1 G at 2B

Pitcher	T	Age	G	GS	CG	ShO	IP	H	HR	BB	SO	W-L	Sv	ERA
Amos Rusie	R	24	49	47	42	4	393.1	384	9	159	201	23-23	0	3.73
Dad Clarke	R	30	37	30	27	1	281.2	336	5	60	67	18-15	1	3.39
Jouett Meekin	R	28	29	29	24	1	225.2	296	10	73	76	16-11	0	5.30
Les German	R	26	25	18	16	0	178.1	243	7	78	36	7-11	0	5.96
Andy Boswell†	R	20	5	4	3	0	34.0	41	1	22	18	2-2	0	5.82
Ed Doheny	L	21	3	3	3	0	25.2	37	2	19	9	0-3	0	6.66
Frank Knauss	L	27	1	1	0	0	3.2	9	0	2	1	0-0	0	17.18
George Van Haltren	L	29	1	0	0	0	5.0	13	0	2	1	0-0	0	12.60

1895 Washington Senators 10th NL 43-85 .336 43.0 GB

Gus Schmelz

Player	Gm by Position	B	Age	G	AB	R	H	2B	3B	HR	RBI	BB	SO	SB	Avg	OBP	Slg
Deacon McGuire	C132,SS1	R	31	132	533	89	179	30	8	10	97	40	18	16	.336	.388	.478
Ed Cartwright	1B122	R	35	122	472	95	156	34	17	3	90	54	41	50	.331	.400	.494
Jack Crooks	2B117	R	29	117	409	80	114	19	8	6	57	68	39	36	.279	.392	.408
Bill Joyce	3B126	L	29	126	474	110	148	25	13	17	95	96	54	29	.312	.442	.527
Frank Scheibeck	SS44,2B2,3B2	R	30	48	167	17	31	5	2	0	25	17	21	5	.186	.265	.240
Charlie Abbey	OF132	L	28	132	511	102	141	14	10	8	84	43	41	28	.276	.340	.389
Kip Selbach	OF118,SS6,2B5	R	23	129	516	115	166	21	22	6	55	69	28	31	.322	.403	.483
Bill Hassamaer†	OF75,1B9,3B1*	—	30	85	358	42	100	18	4	1	60	26	13	8	.279	.328	.360
Win Mercer	P43,SS7,OF5*	R	21	63	196	26	50	9	1	1	26	12	32	7	.255	.308	.327
Jake Boyd	OF21,P14,2B10*	—	21	51	157	29	42	5	1	1	16	20	28	2	.268	.375	.331
Tom Brown†	OF34	L	34	34	134	25	32	8	3	2	16	18	16	8	.239	.329	.388
Jack Glasscock†	SS25	R	35	25	100	20	23	2	0	0	10	7	3	3	.230	.300	.250
Varney Anderson	P29,OF1	R	29	35	97	22	28	2	3	0	16	10	9	0	.289	.361	.371
Dan Coogan	SS18,C5,OF2*	—	20	26	77	9	17	2	1	0	7	13	6	1	.221	.333	.273
Otis Stocksdale†	P20,OF2	L	23	25	74	12	23	4	2	0	15	3	8	1	.311	.338	.419
Al Maul	P16,OF4	R	29	22	72	9	18	5	2	0	16	6	7	0	.250	.308	.375
Gene DeMontreville	SS12	R	21	12	46	7	10	1	3	0	9	3	4	5	.217	.265	.370
Parson Nicholson	SS10	—	32	10	38	7	7	2	1	0	5	7	4	6	.184	.311	.289
John Gilroy	P8,OF3,3B1	—	25	12	29	8	7	1	0	0	4	1	4	0	.241	.267	.276
Billy Lush	OF5	S	21	5	18	2	6	0	0	0	2	2	1	0	.333	.400	.333
Joe Corbett	P3,SS2,OF2	R	19	7	15	1	2	0	0	0	1	0	5	0	.133	.133	.133
Andy Boswell†	P6,1B1	—	20	7	14	4	4	0	0	0	1	1	2	1	.286	.375	.286
Dan Mahoney	C2,1B1	R	31	6	12	2	2	0	0	0	1	0	0	0	.167	.167	.167
Joe Woerlin	SS1	—	30	1	3	1	1	0	0	0	0	0	0	0	.333	.333	.333
Bill McCauley	SS1	—	25	1	2	0	0	0	0	0	0	0	0	0	.000	.000	.000
Phil Wisner	SS1	—	25	1	0	0	0	0	0	0	0	0	0	0	—	—	—

B. Hassamaer, 1 G at SS; W. Mercer, 3 G at 3B, 1 G at 2B; J. Boyd, 8 G at SS, 1 G at 3B; D. Coogan, 1 G at 3B

Pitcher	T	Age	G	GS	CG	ShO	IP	H	HR	BB	SO	W-L	Sv	ERA
Win Mercer	R	21	43	38	32	0	311.0	430	17	96	84	13-23	2	4.46
Varney Anderson	R	29	29	25	18	0	204.2	288	13	97	35	9-16	0	5.89
Otis Stocksdale†	R	23	20	17	11	0	136.0	199	7	52	23	6-11	1	6.09
Al Maul	R	29	16	16	14	0	135.2	136	5	37	34	10-5	0	2.45
Jake Boyd	L	21	14	12	8	0	85.1	126	1	35	16	2-11	0	7.07
John Gilroy	—	25	8	4	2	0	41.1	63	3	24	2	1-4	0	6.53
Andy Boswell†	R	20	6	3	3	0	30.0	44	1	19	12	1-2	0	6.00
Joe Corbett	R	19	3	3	3	0	19.0	26	3	9	3	0-2	0	5.68
Carlton Molesworth	L	19	4	3	1	0	16.0	33	1	15	7	0-2	0	14.63
Doc McJames	R	21	2	2	2	0	17.0	17	0	16	9	1-1	0	1.59
Ed Buckingham	—	21	1	1	0	0	3.0	6	0	2	1	0-0	0	6.00
John Malarkey	R	23	22	8	5	0	100.2	135	3	60	32	0-8	2	5.99
Oscar Purner	—	22	1	0	0	0	2.0	4	1	3	0	0-0	0	9.00

1895 St. Louis Browns 11th NL 39-92 .298 48.5 GB

Al Buckenberger (16-34)/Chris Von Der Ahe (1-0)/Joe Quinn (11-28)/Lew Phelan (11-30)

Player	Gm by Position	B	Age	G	AB	R	H	2B	3B	HR	RBI	BB	SO	SB	Avg	OBP	Slg
Heinie Peitz	C71,1B11,3B10	R	24	90	334	44	95	14	12	2	65	29	20	9	.284	.345	.416
Roger Connor	1B103	L	37	103	398	78	131	29	9	8	77	63	10	9	.329	.423	.508
Joe Quinn	2B134	R	30	134	543	84	169	19	9	2	74	36	6	22	.311	.356	.390
Doggie Miller	C46,3B46,OF21*	R	30	121	490	81	143	15	4	5	74	25	12	18	.292	.334	.369
Bones Ely	SS117	R	32	117	467	68	121	16	2	1	46	19	17	28	.259	.288	.308
Duff Cooley	OF124,3B5,SS3*	L	22	132	563	106	191	9	20	7	75	36	29	27	.339	.382	.464
Tommy Dowd	OF115,3B17,2B2	R	26	129	505	95	163	19	17	7	74	30	31	30	.323	.364	.469
Tom Brown†	OF83	L	34	83	350	72	76	11	4	1	31	48	44	34	.217	.315	.280
Ted Breitenstein	P54,OF16	L	26	72	218	25	42	2	0	0	18	29	22	5	.193	.290	.202
Biff Sheehan	OF41,1B11	—	27	52	180	24	57	3	6	1	18	20	6	7	.317	.394	.417
Denny Lyons	3B33	R	29	33	129	24	38	6	0	2	25	14	5	3	.295	.377	.388
Bill Kissinger†	P24,SS4,OF4*	R	23	33	97	8	24	6	1	0	8	0	11	1	.247	.247	.330
Joe Otten	C24,OF2	—	—	26	87	8	21	0	0	0	8	5	8	2	.241	.283	.241
Ike Samuls	3B21,SS3	R	19	24	74	5	17	2	0	0	5	5	7	5	.230	.278	.257
Frank Bonner†	3B10,OF5,C1	R	25	15	59	3	8	0	1	1	8	1	8	2	.136	.164	.220
Marty Hogan	OF5	R	23	5	18	2	3	1	0	0	2	3	0	2	.167	.286	.222
Guy McFadden	1B4	—	22	4	14	1	3	0	0	0	2	0	2	0	.214	.214	.214
Joe Connor	3B2	R	20	2	7	0	0	0	0	0	1	0	2	0	.000	.000	.000
Henry Adkinson	OF1	—	20	1	5	1	2	0	0	0	0	0	2	0	.400	.400	.400
Walt Kinlock	3B1	—	17	1	3	0	1	0	0	0	0	0	2	0	.333	.333	.333
Fred Fagin	C1	—	—	1	3	0	1	0	0	0	2	0	0	0	.333	.333	.333
John Ryan	3B2	—	—	2	2	0	0	0	0	0	0	0	0	0	.000	.000	.000

D. Miller, 9 G at SS, 6 G at 1B; D. Cooley, 1 G at C; B. Kissinger, 1 G at 3B

Pitcher	T	Age	G	GS	CG	ShO	IP	H	HR	BB	SO	W-L	Sv	ERA
Ted Breitenstein	L	26	54	50	46	1	429.2	458	16	178	127	19-30	1	4.44
Red Ehret	R	26	37	32	18	0	231.2	360	11	88	55	6-19	0	6.02
Harry Staley	R	28	23	16	13	0	158.2	223	8	39	28	6-13	0	5.22
Bill Kissinger†	R	23	24	14	9	0	140.2	222	8	51	31	4-12	0	6.72
John McDougal	R	23	18	14	10	0	114.2	187	11	46	23	3-10	0	8.32
Dad Clarkson†	R	28	7	7	7	0	61.0	91	7	26	9	1-6	0	7.38
John Coleman	L	—	1	1	1	0	8.0	12	1	8	5	0-1	0	13.50
Red Donahue	R	22	1	1	1	0	8.0	9	2	3	2	0-1	0	6.75

1895 Louisville Colonels 12th NL 35-96 .267 52.5 GB

John McCloskey

Player	Gm by Position	B	Age	G	AB	R	H	2B	3B	HR	RBI	BB	SO	SB	Avg	OBP	Slg
John Warner†	C64,1B3,2B1	L	22	67	232	20	62	4	2	1	20	11	16	10	.267	.320	.315
Harry Spies†	1B47,C26,SS1	R	29	72	276	42	74	14	7	2	35	11	19	4	.268	.313	.391
John O'Brien	2B125,1B3	L	24	128	539	82	138	10	4	1	50	45	20	15	.256	.325	.295
Jimmy Collins†	3B77,OF18,2B2*	R	25	96	373	65	104	17	5	6	49	33	16	12	.279	.352	.399
Frank Shugart	SS88,OF27	S	28	113	473	61	125	14	13	4	70	31	25	14	.264	.315	.374
Fred Clarke	OF132	L	22	132	550	96	191	21	5	4	82	34	24	40	.347	.396	.425
Tom Gettinger	OF63,P2	L	26	63	260	28	70	11	5	2	32	8	15	6	.269	.296	.373
Joe Wright	OF59,C1	L	22	60	228	30	63	10	4	1	30	12	28	7	.276	.315	.368
Walt Preston	OF26,3B25	L	25	50	197	42	55	6	4	1	24	17	17	11	.279	.366	.365
Ducky Holmes	OF29,SS8,3B4*	L	26	40	161	33	60	10	2	3	20	12	9	9	.373	.426	.516
Tub Welsh	C28,1B20	—	28	47	153	18	37	4	1	1	8	13	7	2	.242	.310	.301
Tom McCreery	OF18,P8,SS4*	S	20	31	108	18	35	3	1	0	10	8	15	3	.324	.376	.370
Bert Cunningham	P31,OF1	R	29	32	100	14	30	7	3	0	13	9	20	0	.300	.358	.430
Dan Brouthers†	1B24	L	37	24	97	13	30	10	1	2	15	11	2	1	.309	.380	.495
Bill Hassamaer†	1B21,2B1,SS1	—	30	23	96	7	20	2	2	0	14	3	4	0	.208	.232	.271
Dan Sweeney	OF22	—	27	22	90	18	24	5	0	1	16	17	2	2	.267	.389	.356
Jack Glasscock†	SS13,1B5	R	35	18	74	9	25	3	1	1	6	3	1	1	.338	.388	.446
Ambrose McGann	SS8,3B6,OF5	—	20	20	73	9	21	5	2	0	9	8	6	6	.288	.358	.411
Pat Luby	P11,1B5,OF2	—	26	19	53	6	15	2	2	0	9	8	3	2	.283	.415	.396
Fred Zahner	C21	—	25	21	49	7	11	1	1	0	6	6	4	0	.224	.321	.286
Fred Pfeffer	SS5,1B3,2B3	R	35	11	45	8	13	1	0	0	5	5	3	2	.289	.360	.311
Bill Kemmer	3B9,1B2	R	21	11	38	5	7	0	0	1	3	2	4	0	.184	.225	.263
Dan Minnehan	3B7,OF2	R	29	8	34	6	13	0	0	0	6	1	1	0	.382	.400	.382
Henry Cote	C10	—	31	10	33	10	10	0	0	0	5	3	3	2	.303	.361	.303
Tom Morrison	3B3,SS3	—	20	6	22	3	6	0	2	0	4	1	1	0	.273	.304	.455
Hercules Burnett	OF4,1B1	R	25	5	17	6	7	0	1	2	3	2	2	2	.412	.474	.882
Gil Hatfield	3B3,SS2	—	40	5	16	3	3	0	0	0	1	1	1	0	.188	.278	.188
Barry McCormick	SS2,2B1	—	20	3	12	2	3	0	1	0	0	0	0	1	.250	.250	.417
Mike Trost	1B3	—	29	3	12	1	1	0	0	0	1	0	1	1	.083	.083	.083
Grant Briggs	C1	—	30	1	3	0	0	0	0	0	0	0	1	0	.000	.000	.000

J. Collins, 1 G at SS; D. Holmes, 2 G at P; T. McCreery, 1 G at 1B, 1 G at 3B

Pitcher	T	Age	G	GS	CG	ShO	IP	H	HR	BB	SO	W-L	Sv	ERA
Bert Cunningham	R	29	31	28	24	1	231.0	299	6	104	49	11-16	0	4.75
Bert Inks	L	24	28	27	21	0	205.1	294	3	78	42	7-20	0	6.40
Mike McDermott	R	32	33	26	18	0	207.1	258	8	103	42	4-19	0	5.99
Gus Weyhing†	R	28	28	25	22	1	213.0	285	9	66	53	7-19	0	5.41
Dan McFarlan	—	20	7	7	6	0	46.0	80	4	15	10	0-7	0	6.65
Pat Luby	R	26	11	6	5	0	71.1	115	5	19	12	1-5	0	6.81
Phil Knell†	L	30	10	6	3	0	56.2	75	3	21	19	0-6	0	6.51
Tom McCreery	R	20	8	4	3	1	48.2	51	0	38	14	3-1	1	5.36
Ducky Holmes	R	26	2	1	1	0	14.0	16	1	4	0	1-0	0	5.79
George Meakim	R	29	1	1	1	0	7.0	7	0	4	2	1-0	0	2.57
George Borchers	R	26	1	1	0	0	0.2	1	0	3	0	0-1	0	27.00
Jack Wadsworth	R	27	2	0	0	0	9.0	24	0	7	2	0-1	0	16.00
Tom Gettinger	L	26	2	0	0	0	6.1	13	1	1	0	0-0	0	7.11
Bill Kling	R	28	1	0	0	0	1.0	0	0	1	0	0-0	0	0.00
— Childers	—	—	1	0	0	0	0.0	2	0	5	0	0-0	0	—

»1896 Baltimore Orioles 1st NL 90-39 .698 —

Ned Hanlon

Player	Gm by Position	B	Age	G	AB	R	H	2B	3B	HR	RBI	BB	SO	SB	Avg	OBP	Slg
Boileryard Clarke	C67,1B14	R	27	80	300	48	89	14	7	2	71	14	12	7	.297	.345	.410
Jack Doyle	1B118,2B1	R	26	118	487	116	165	29	4	1	101	42	15	73	.339	.400	.421
Heinie Reitz	2B118,SS3	L	29	120	464	76	133	15	6	4	106	49	32	28	.287	.357	.371
Jim Donnelly	3B106	R	30	106	396	70	130	14	10	0	71	34	11	38	.328	.387	.414
Hughie Jennings	SS130	R	27	130	521	125	209	27	9	0	121	19	11	70	.401	.472	.488
Steve Brodie	OF132	L	27	132	516	98	153	19	11	2	87	36	17	25	.297	.363	.388
Joe Kelley	OF131	R	24	131	519	148	189	31	19	8	100	91	19	87	.364	.469	.543
Willie Keeler	OF126	L	24	126	544	153	210	22	13	4	82	37	9	67	.386	.432	.496
Wilbert Robinson	C67	R	33	67	245	43	85	9	6	2	38	14	13	9	.347	.385	.457
George Hemming	P25,OF2,1B1	R	27	30	97	16	25	6	5	0	11	4	7	4	.258	.294	.423
Joe Quinn†	2B8,OF8,3B5*	R	31	24	82	22	27	1	1	0	5	6	1	6	.329	.375	.366
John McGraw	3B18,1B1	L	23	23	77	20	25	2	2	0	14	11	4	13	.325	.422	.403
Bill Keister	2B8,3B6	L	21	15	58	8	14	3	0	0	5	3	5	4	.241	.302	.293
Joe Corbett	P8,3B1	R	20	9	22	0	6	1	1	0	3	0	4	0	.273	.273	.409
Frank Bowerman	C3,1B1	R	27	4	16	0	2	0	0	0	4	1	0	0	.125	.176	.125

J. Quinn, 1 G at SS

Pitcher	T	Age	G	GS	CG	ShO	IP	H	HR	BB	SO	W-L	Sv	ERA
Bill Hoffer	R	25	35	35	32	3	309.0	317	1	95	93	25-7	0	3.38
Arlie Pond	R	24	28	26	21	2	214.1	232	4	57	80	16-8	0	3.49
Sadie McMahon	R	28	22	22	19	0	175.2	195	4	55	33	11-9	0	3.48
George Hemming	R	27	25	21	20	3	202.0	233	9	54	33	15-6	0	4.19
Duke Esper	L	27	20	18	14	1	155.2	168	3	39	19	14-5	0	3.58
Dad Clarkson	R	29	7	4	3	0	47.0	72	1	18	7	4-2	0	4.98
Jerry Nops†	L	21	3	3	3	0	22.0	29	0	2	8	2-1	0	6.14
Joe Corbett	R	20	8	3	3	0	41.0	31	0	17	28	3-0	1	2.20
Otis Stocksdale	R	24	1	0	0	0	1.2	4	0	2	1	0-1	0	16.20

1896 Cleveland Spiders 2nd NL 80-48 .625 9.5 GB

Patsy Tebeau

Player	Gm by Position	B	Age	G	AB	R	H	2B	3B	HR	RBI	BB	SO	SB	Avg	OBP	Slg
Chief Zimmer	C91,3B1	R	35	91	336	46	93	18	3	3	46	31	48	4	.277	.354	.375
Patsy Tebeau	1B122,3B7,2B5*	R	31	132	543	56	146	22	6	2	94	21	22	20	.269	.300	.343
Cupid Childs	2B132	L	28	132	498	106	177	24	9	1	106	100	18	25	.355	.467	.446
Chippy McGarr	3B113,C1	R	33	113	455	68	122	16	4	1	53	22	30	16	.268	.302	.327
Ed McKean	SS133	R	32	133	571	100	193	29	12	7	112	45	9	13	.338	.388	.468
Jesse Burkett	OF133	L	27	133	586	160	240	27	16	6	72	49	19	34	.410	.461	.541
Jimmy McAleer	OF116	R	31	116	455	70	131	16	4	1	54	47	32	24	.288	.361	.347
Harry Blake	OF103,SS1	R	22	104	383	66	92	12	5	1	43	46	30	10	.240	.322	.305
Jack O'Connor	C37,1B17,OF12	R	27	68	256	41	76	11	1	1	43	15	12	15	.297	.343	.359
Cy Young	P51,1B3	R	29	53	180	31	52	11	3	3	28	4	15	1	.289	.304	.433
Bobby Wallace	OF23,P22,1B1	R	22	45	149	19	35	6	3	1	17	11	21	2	.235	.288	.336
Nig Cuppy	P46,OF1	R	26	47	141	29	38	5	2	1	20	20	21	1	.270	.364	.355
John Shearon	OF16	—	26	16	64	6	11	0	1	0	3	4	6	3	.172	.221	.203
Tom Delahanty†	3B16	L	24	16	56	11	13	4	0	0	4	8	4	4	.232	.338	.304
Tom O'Meara	C9,1B1	—	23	12	33	5	5	0	0	0	0	5	7	0	.152	.263	.152
Sport McAllister	OF4,C2,P1	S	21	8	27	2	6	2	0	0	1	0	2	1	.222	.250	.296
Dale Gear	P3,1B1	R	24	4	15	5	6	1	1	0	3	1	1	0	.400	.438	.600
Lou Criger	C1	R	24	2	5	0	0	0	0	0	0	1	0	1	.000	.167	.000

P. Tebeau, 1 G at P, 1 G at SS

Pitcher	T	Age	G	GS	CG	ShO	IP	H	HR	BB	SO	W-L	Sv	ERA
Cy Young	R	29	51	46	42	5	414.1	477	7	62	140	28-15	3	3.24
Nig Cuppy	R	26	46	40	35	1	358.0	388	8	75	86	25-14	1	3.12
Zeke Wilson	R	26	33	29	20	1	240.0	265	9	81	56	17-9	1	4.01
Bobby Wallace	R	22	22	16	13	2	145.1	167	2	49	46	10-7	0	3.34
Dale Gear	R	24	3	2	2	0	23.0	35	1	6	6	0-2	0	5.48
Elton Chamberlin	R	28	2	2	1	0	11.0	21	0	5	2	0-1	0	7.36
Sport McAllister	R	21	1	0	0	0	4.0	9	0	2	0	0-0	0	6.75
Patsy Tebeau	R	31	1	0	0	0	0.0	1	0	0	0	0-0	0	—

1896 Cincinnati Reds 3rd NL 77-50 .606 12.0 GB

Buck Ewing

Player	Gm by Position	B	Age	G	AB	R	H	2B	3B	HR	RBI	BB	SO	SB	Avg	OBP	Slg
Heinie Peitz	C67	R	25	68	211	33	63	12	5	2	34	30	15	7	.299	.386	.431
Buck Ewing	1B69	R	36	69	263	41	73	14	4	1	38	29	13	41	.278	.349	.373
Bid McPhee	2B117	R	36	117	433	81	132	18	7	1	87	51	18	48	.305	.391	.386
Charlie Irwin	3B127	L	27	127	476	77	141	16	6	1	67	26	17	31	.296	.338	.361
Germany Smith	SS120	R	33	120	456	65	131	22	9	2	71	28	22	22	.287	.330	.388
Dusty Miller	OF125	L	27	125	504	91	162	38	12	4	93	33	30	76	.321	.368	.468
Eddie Burke	OF122	L	29	122	521	120	177	24	9	1	52	41	29	53	.340	.392	.426
Dummy Hoy	OF120	L	34	121	443	120	132	23	7	4	57	65	13	50	.298	.403	.409
Farmer Vaughn	C57,1B57	R	32	114	433	71	127	20	9	2	66	16	7	7	.293	.320	.395
Bill Grey	2B12,C11,SS8*	—	25	46	121	15	25	2	1	0	17	19	11	6	.207	.314	.240
Red Ehret	P34,1B1	R	27	34	102	10	20	2	0	1	20	10	12	2	.196	.268	.245
Bug Holliday	OF16,1B5,P1*	R	29	29	84	17	27	4	0	0	8	9	4	1	.321	.394	.369

B. Grey, 3 G at OF, 2 G at 1B, 1 G at 3B; B. Holliday, 1 G at SS

Pitcher	T	Age	G	GS	CG	ShO	IP	H	HR	BB	SO	W-L	Sv	ERA
Frank Dwyer	R	28	36	34	30	3	288.2	321	8	60	57	24-11	1	3.15
Red Ehret	R	27	34	33	29	2	276.2	298	5	74	60	18-14	0	3.42
Frank Foreman	L	33	27	23	18	1	190.2	214	2	62	38	15-6	1	3.68
Billy Rhines	R	27	19	17	11	3	143.0	128	1	48	32	8-6	0	2.45
Chauncey Fisher	R	24	27	15	13	2	159.2	199	9	36	25	10-7	2	4.45
Bert Inks†	L	25	3	3	2	0	20.0	21	0	9	2	1-1	0	4.50
Brownie Foreman†	L	20	4	3	2	0	18.0	39	2	16	4	0-4	0	16.50
Wiley Davis	R	20	2	0	0	0	4.1	8	0	2	1	1-1	0	8.31
Hank Gastright	R	31	1	0	0	0	6.0	8	0	1	0	0-0	0	4.50
Bug Holliday	R	29	1	0	0	0	1.0	4	0	2	0	0-0	0	0.00

1896 Boston Beaneaters 4th NL 74-57 .565 17.0 GB

Frank Selee

Player	Gm by Position	B	Age	G	AB	R	H	2B	3B	HR	RBI	BB	SO	SB	Avg	OBP	Slg
Marty Bergen	C63,1B1	—	24	65	245	39	66	6	4	4	37	11	22	6	.269	.309	.376
Tommy Tucker	1B122	S	32	122	474	74	144	27	5	2	72	30	29	6	.304	.363	.395
Bobby Lowe	2B73	R	27	73	305	59	98	11	4	2	48	20	11	15	.321	.371	.403
Jimmy Collins	3B80,SS4	R	26	84	304	48	90	10	9	1	46	30	12	10	.296	.374	.398
Herman Long	SS120	L	30	120	501	105	172	26	8	6	100	26	16	36	.343	.382	.463
Billy Hamilton	OF131	L	30	131	523	152	191	24	9	3	52	110	29	83	.365	.477	.463
Hugh Duffy	OF120,2B9,SS2	R	29	131	527	97	158	16	8	5	113	52	19	39	.300	.365	.389
Jimmy Bannon	OF76,2B6,SS5*	R	25	89	343	52	86	9	5	0	50	32	23	16	.251	.316	.306
Fred Tenney	OF60,C27	L	24	88	348	64	117	14	3	2	49	36	12	18	.336	.400	.411
Jack Stivetts	P42,OF12,1B5*	R	28	67	221	42	76	9	6	3	49	12	10	4	.344	.380	.480
Joe Harrington	3B49,SS4,2B1	R	26	54	198	25	39	5	3	1	25	19	17	2	.197	.271	.268
Charlie Ganzel	C41,1B3,SS2	R	34	47	179	28	47	2	0	1	18	9	5	2	.263	.305	.291
Dan McGann	2B43	S	24	43	171	25	55	6	7	2	30	12	10	2	.322	.383	.474
Kid Nichols	P49,OF2	S	26	51	147	27	28	3	3	1	24	12	18	2	.190	.256	.272
Jack Ryan	C8	R	27	8	32	2	3	1	0	0	0	0	1	0	.094	.094	.125
George Yeager	1B2	R	23	2	5	1	1	0	0	0	0	0	1	0	.200	.200	.200

J. Bannon, 3 G at 3B; J. Stivetts, 1 G at 3B

Pitcher	T	Age	G	GS	CG	ShO	IP	H	HR	BB	SO	W-L	Sv	ERA
Kid Nichols	R	26	49	43	37	3	372.1	387	14	101	102	30-14	1	2.83
Jack Stivetts	R	28	42	36	31	2	329.0	353	20	99	71	22-14	0	4.10
Jim Sullivan	R	27	31	26	21	1	225.1	268	12	68	33	11-12	1	4.03
Fred Klobedanz	L	25	10	9	9	0	80.2	69	5	31	26	6-4	0	3.01
Willard Mains	R	27	8	5	3	0	42.2	43	1	31	13	3-2	1	5.48
Ted Lewis	R	23	6	5	4	0	41.2	37	2	27	12	1-4	0	3.24
Cozy Dolan	L	23	6	5	3	0	41.0	55	1	27	14	1-4	0	4.83
Bill Banks	R	22	4	3	2	0	23.0	42	2	13	6	0-3	0	10.57

1896 Chicago Colts 5th NL 71-57 .555 18.5 GB

Cap Anson

Player	Gm by Position	B	Age	G	AB	R	H	2B	3B	HR	RBI	BB	SO	SB	Avg	OBP	Slg
Malachi Kittridge	C64,P1	R	26	65	215	17	48	4	1	1	19	14	14	6	.223	.274	.265
Cap Anson	1B98,C10	R	44	108	402	72	133	18	2	2	90	49	10	24	.331	.407	.400
Fred Pfeffer†	2B94	R	36	94	360	45	88	16	7	2	52	23	20	22	.244	.294	.344
Bill Everitt	3B97,OF35	L	27	132	575	130	184	16	13	2	46	41	43	46	.320	.367	.403
Bill Dahlen	SS125	R	26	125	474	137	167	30	19	9	74	64	36	51	.352	.438	.553
Jimmy Ryan	OF128	R	33	128	489	83	149	24	10	3	86	46	16	29	.305	.369	.413
Bill Lange	OF121,C1	R	25	122	469	114	153	21	16	4	92	65	24	84	.326	.414	.465
George Decker	OF71,1B36	L	27	107	421	68	118	23	11	5	61	23	14	20	.280	.318	.423
Tim Donahue	C57	L	26	57	188	27	41	10	1	0	20	11	15	11	.218	.276	.282
Barry McCormick	3B35,SS6,2B3*	—	21	45	168	22	37	3	1	1	23	14	30	9	.220	.280	.268
Danny Friend	P36,OF1	—	23	37	126	12	30	3	3	1	10	3	5	2	.238	.256	.333
Harry Truby†	2B28	—	26	29	109	13	28	2	2	2	31	6	5	4	.257	.314	.367
George Flynn	OF29	—	25	29	106	15	27	1	2	0	4	11	9	12	.255	.336	.302
Josh Reilly	2B8,SS1	—	28	9	42	6	9	1	0	0	2	1	1	2	.214	.233	.238
Doc Parker	P9,OF1	R	24	10	36	4	10	0	1	0	4	1	5	0	.278	.297	.333
Algie McBride	OF9	L	27	9	29	2	7	1	1	1	7	7	3	0	.241	.389	.448
Con Daily	C9	L	31	9	27	1	2	0	0	0	1	1	2	1	.074	.107	.074
Walter Thornton	P5,OF3	L	21	9	22	6	8	0	1	0	1	5	2	2	.364	.481	.455

B. McCormick, 1 G at OF

Pitcher	T	Age	G	GS	CG	ShO	IP	H	HR	BB	SO	W-L	Sv	ERA
Clark Griffith	R	26	36	35	35	1	317.2	370	3	70	81	23-11	0	3.54
Danny Friend	L	23	36	33	28	1	290.2	298	11	139	86	18-14	0	4.74
Adonis Terry	R	31	30	28	25	1	235.1	268	6	88	74	15-14	0	4.28
Buttons Briggs	R	20	26	21	19	0	194.0	202	6	108	84	12-8	1	4.31
Doc Parker	R	24	9	7	7	0	73.0	100	3	27	15	1-5	0	6.16
Walter Thornton	L	21	5	5	2	0	23.2	30	1	13	10	2-1	0	5.70
Monte McFarland	—	23	4	3	2	0	25.0	32	0	21	3	0-4	0	7.20
Malachi Kittridge	R	26	1	0	0	0	1.2	2	0	1	0	0-0	0	5.40

1896 Pittsburgh Pirates 6th NL 66-63 .512 24.0 GB

Connie Mack

Player	Gm by Position	B	Age	G	AB	R	H	2B	3B	HR	RBI	BB	SO	SB	Avg	OBP	Slg
Joe Sugden	C70,1B7,OF4	S	25	80	301	42	89	5	7	0	36	19	9	5	.296	.348	.359
Jake Beckley†	1B56,OF3,2B1	L	28	59	217	44	55	7	5	3	32	22	28	8	.253	.349	.373
Dick Padden	2B61	R	25	61	219	33	53	4	8	2	24	14	9	8	.242	.294	.361
Denny Lyons	3B116	R	30	118	436	77	134	25	6	4	71	67	25	13	.307	.406	.420
Bones Ely	SS128	R	33	128	537	85	153	15	9	3	77	33	33	18	.285	.326	.363
Patsy Donovan	OF131	L	31	131	573	113	183	20	5	3	59	35	18	48	.319	.370	.387
Elmer Smith	OF122	L	28	122	484	121	175	21	14	6	94	74	18	33	.362	.454	.500
Jake Stenzel	OF114,1B1	R	29	114	479	104	173	26	14	2	82	32	13	57	.361	.409	.486
Bill Merritt	C62,3B5,1B3*	R	25	77	282	26	82	8	2	1	42	18	10	3	.291	.336	.344
Lou Bierbauer	2B59	L	30	59	258	33	74	10	6	0	39	5	7	7	.287	.300	.372
Harry Davis†	1B35,OF10,SS1	R	22	44	168	24	32	5	6	0	23	13	21	9	.190	.257	.292
Connie Mack	1B28,C5	R	33	33	120	9	26	4	1	0	16	5	8	0	.217	.248	.267
Joe Wright†	OF12,3B1	L	23	15	52	5	16	4	0	0	6	1	2	1	.308	.321	.385
Jud Smith	3B10	R	27	10	35	6	12	2	1	0	4	2	2	3	.343	.395	.457
Harry Truby†	2B8	—	26	8	32	1	5	0	0	0	3	2	4	1	.156	.206	.156
Abel Lizotte	1B7	—	26	7	29	3	3	0	0	0	3	2	2	1	.103	.161	.103
Eddie Boyle†	C2	R	22	2	5	0	0	0	0	0	0	0	1	0	.000	.000	.000
Tom Delahanty†	SS1	L	24	1	3	1	1	0	0	0	0	0	0	0	.333	.333	.333

B. Merritt, 3 G at 2B, 2 G at SS

Pitcher	T	Age	G	GS	CG	ShO	IP	H	HR	BB	SO	W-L	Sv	ERA
Frank Killen	L	25	52	50	44	5	432.1	476	7	119	134	30-18	0	3.41
Pink Hawley	R	23	49	43	37	2	378.0	382	2	157	137	22-21	0	3.57
Jim Hughey	R	27	25	14	11	0	155.0	171	3	67	48	6-8	0	4.99
Charlie Hastings	—	25	17	13	9	0	104.0	126	1	44	19	5-10	1	5.88
Brownie Foreman†	L	20	9	9	5	0	61.2	73	4	35	18	3-3	0	6.57
Elmer Horton	—	26	2	2	2	0	15.0	22	0	9	3	0-2	0	9.60
Jot Goar	R	26	3	0	0	0	13.1	36	1	8	3	0-1	0	16.88

1896 New York Giants 7th NL 64-67 .489 27.0 GB

Arthur Irwin (36-53)/Bill Joyce (28-14)

Player	Gm by Position	B	Age	G	AB	R	H	2B	3B	HR	RBI	BB	SO	SB	Avg	OBP	Slg
Parke Wilson	C71,1B2	R	28	75	253	33	60	2	0	0	23	13	14	9	.237	.277	.245
Willie Clark	1B65	L	23	72	247	38	72	12	4	0	33	15	12	8	.291	.352	.372
Kid Gleason	2B130,3B3,OF1	S	29	133	541	79	162	17	5	4	89	42	13	46	.299	.352	.372
George Davis	3B74,SS45,1B3*	S	25	124	494	98	158	25	12	6	99	50	24	48	.320	.387	.455
Frank Connaughton	SS54,OF30	R	27	88	315	53	82	3	2	2	43	25	7	22	.260	.319	.302
George Van Haltren	OF133,P2	L	30	133	562	136	197	18	21	5	74	55	36	39	.351	.410	.484
Mike Tiernan	OF133	L	29	133	521	132	192	24	16	7	89	77	18	35	.369	.452	.516
General Stafford	OF53,SS6	R	27	59	230	28	66	9	1	0	40	13	18	15	.287	.333	.335
Harry Davis†	OF40,1B23	R	22	64	233	43	64	11	10	2	50	31	20	16	.275	.372	.433
Duke Farrell†	C34,SS13,3B7	S	29	58	191	23	54	7	3	1	37	19	7	2	.283	.351	.366
Jake Beckley†	1B45,OF2	L	28	46	182	37	55	8	4	5	38	9	7	11	.302	.352	.473
Bill Joyce†	3B49	L	30	49	165	36	61	9	2	5	43	34	14	13	.370	.500	.539
Shorty Fuller	SS18	R	28	18	72	10	12	0	0	0	7	14	5	4	.167	.310	.167
Dave Zearfoss	C19	—	28	19	60	5	13	1	1	0	6	5	5	2	.217	.288	.267
John Warner†	C19	L	23	19	54	9	14	1	0	0	3	3	7	1	.259	.310	.278
George Ulrich	OF11,3B3	—	27	14	45	4	8	1	0	0	1	1	1	0	.178	.229	.200
Cy Seymour	P11,OF1	L	23	12	32	2	7	0	0	0	0	0	7	0	.219	.219	.219
Fred Pfeffer†	2B4	R	36	4	14	1	2	0	0	0	4	1	1	0	.143	.250	.143
Tom Bannon	OF2	R	27	2	7	1	1	1	0	0	0	1	1	0	.143	.250	.286
Reddy Foster		—	31	1	1	0	0	0	0	0	0	0	0	0	.000	.000	.000

G. Davis, 3 G at OF

Pitcher	T	Age	G	GS	CG	ShO	IP	H	HR	BB	SO	W-L	Sv	ERA
Jouett Meekin	R	29	42	41	34	0	334.1	378	8	127	110	26-14	0	3.82
Dad Clarke	R	31	48	40	33	1	351.0	431	9	60	66	17-24	1	4.26
Mike Sullivan	—	29	25	22	18	0	185.1	188	3	71	42	10-13	0	4.66
Ed Doheny	L	22	17	15	9	0	108.1	112	3	59	39	6-7	0	4.49
Cy Seymour	L	23	11	8	4	0	70.1	75	8	51	33	2-4	0	6.40
Carney Flynn†	L	21	3	2	1	0	10.2	18	0	8	4	0-2	0	11.81
Bill Reidy	R	22	2	1	1	0	13.0	24	0	2	1	0-1	0	7.62
Cy Bowen	R	25	2	1	1	0	12.0	12	0	9	3	0-1	0	6.00
Sal Campfield	R	28	6	2	2	0	27.0	31	1	6	6	1-1	0	4.00
Charlie Gettig	—	25	4	1	1	0	14.0	20	0	8	5	1-0	1	9.64
George Van Haltren	L	30	2	0	0	0	8.0	5	1	1	3	1-0	0	2.25
Les German†	R	27	1	0	0	0	2.2	9	0	1	0	0-0	0	13.50

1896 Philadelphia Phillies 8th NL 62-68 .477 28.5 GB

Billy Nash

Player	Gm by Position	B	Age	G	AB	R	H	2B	3B	HR	RBI	BB	SO	SB	Avg	OBP	Slg
Mike Grady	C61,3B7	R	26	72	242	49	77	20	7	1	44	16	19	10	.318	.382	.471
Dan Brouthers	1B57	L	38	57	218	42	75	13	3	1	41	44	11	7	.344	.462	.445
Bill Hallman	2B120,P1	R	29	120	469	82	150	21	3	2	83	45	23	16	.320	.382	.390
Billy Nash	3B65	R	31	65	227	29	56	9	1	3	30	34	21	3	.247	.355	.335
Billy Hulen	SS73,OF12,2B2	L	26	88	339	87	90	18	7	0	38	55	20	23	.265	.368	.360
Sam Thompson	OF119	L	36	119	517	103	154	28	7	12	100	28	13	12	.298	.341	.449
Ed Delahanty	OF99,1B22,2B1	R	28	123	499	131	198	44	17	13	126	62	22	37	.397	.472	.631
Duff Cooley†	OF64	L	23	64	287	63	88	6	4	2	22	18	16	18	.307	.348	.376
Lave Cross	3B61,SS37,2B6*	R	30	106	406	63	104	23	5	1	73	32	14	8	.256	.312	.345
Joe Sullivan†	OF45,SS2,3B1	—	26	48	191	45	48	5	3	2	24	18	12	9	.251	.347	.340
Jack Clements	C53	L	31	57	184	35	66	5	7	5	45	17	14	2	.359	.427	.543
Nap Lajoie	1B39	R	21	39	175	36	57	12	7	4	42	1	11	7	.326	.330	.543
Jack Taylor	P45,OF2	R	23	47	157	10	29	6	0	0	18	9	18	0	.185	.229	.223
Jack Boyle	C28,1B12	R	30	40	145	17	43	4	1	1	28	6	7	3	.297	.346	.359
Sam Mertes	OF35,2B1,SS1	R	23	37	143	20	34	4	4	0	14	8	10	19	.238	.288	.322
Phil Geier	OF12,2B3,C2	L	19	17	56	12	13	0	1	0	6	6	7	3	.232	.317	.268
William Gallagher	SS14	—	22	14	49	9	15	2	0	0	6	10	0	0	.306	.433	.347
Tuck Turner†	OF8	S	23	13	32	12	7	2	0	0	0	8	5	6	.219	.375	.281
Ben Ellis	3B2,SS2	—	25	4	16	0	1	0	0	0	0	3	6	0	.063	.211	.063
Dan Leahy	SS2	—	25	2	6	0	2	1	0	0	1	1	2	0	.333	.429	.500

L. Cross, 2 G at OF, 1 G at C

Pitcher	T	Age	G	GS	CG	ShO	IP	H	HR	BB	SO	W-L	Sv	ERA
Jack Taylor	R	23	45	41	35	1	359.0	459	17	112	97	20-21	1	4.79
Al Orth	R	23	25	23	19	0	196.0	244	10	46	23	15-10	0	4.41
Kid Carsey	R	25	27	21	18	1	187.1	273	4	72	36	11-11	1	5.62
Harry Keener	R	26	16	13	11	0	113.1	144	5	39	28	3-11	0	5.88
Willie McGill	L	22	12	11	7	0	79.2	87	0	53	29	5-4	0	5.31
Ad Gumbert†	R	27	11	10	7	1	77.1	99	0	23	14	5-3	0	4.54
Con Lucid	—	22	5	5	5	0	42.0	75	2	17	3	1-4	0	8.36
George Wheeler	—	26	3	2	2	0	16.1	18	0	5	2	1-1	0	3.86
Ned Garvin	R	22	2	1	1	0	13.0	19	0	7	4	0-1	0	7.62
Bill Whitrock	R	26	2	1	1	0	9.0	10	0	3	1	0-1	0	3.00
Jerry Nops†	L	21	1	1	1	0	7.0	11	0	1	1	1-0	0	5.14
Bert Inks†	L	25	3	1	0	0	10.1	21	1	5	2	0-1	0	7.84
Charlie Jordan	—	24	2	0	0	0	4.2	9	0	2	3	0-0	0	7.71
Bill Hallman	R	29	1	0	0	0	2.0	4	0	2	0	0-0	0	18.00

1896 Brooklyn Bridegrooms 9th NL 58-73 .443 33.0 GB

Dave Foutz

Player	Gm by Position	B	Age	G	AB	R	H	2B	3B	HR	RBI	BB	SO	SB	Avg	OBP	Slg
John Grim	C77,1B5	R	28	81	281	32	75	13	1	2	35	12	14	7	.267	.311	.342
Candy LaChance	1B89	S	26	89	348	60	99	10	13	7	58	23	32	17	.284	.331	.448
Tom Daly	2B66,C1	S	30	67	224	43	63	13	6	3	29	33	25	19	.281	.385	.433
Billy Shindle	3B131	R	32	131	516	75	144	24	9	1	61	24	20	24	.279	.316	.366
Tommy Corcoran	SS132	R	27	132	532	63	154	15	7	3	73	15	13	16	.289	.310	.361
Mike Griffin	OF122	L	31	122	493	101	152	27	9	4	51	48	25	23	.308	.380	.424
Fielder Jones	OF103	L	24	104	395	82	140	10	8	3	46	48	15	18	.354	.427	.443
Tommy McCarthy	OF103	R	32	104	377	62	94	8	4	3	47	34	17	22	.249	.316	.316
John Anderson	OF68,1B42	S	22	108	430	70	135	23	17	1	55	18	23	37	.314	.344	.453
George Shoch	2B62,OF10,3B3*	R	37	76	250	36	73	7	4	1	28	33	10	11	.292	.381	.364
Buster Burrell	C60	R	29	62	206	19	62	11	3	0	23	15	13	1	.301	.348	.383
Harley Payne	P34,OF1	S	28	38	98	5	21	4	1	0	10	9	3	0	.214	.280	.276
Frank Bonner	2B9	R	26	9	34	8	6	2	0	0	5	2	8	1	.176	.263	.235
Dave Foutz	1B1,OF1	R	39	2	8	0	2	1	0	0	0	1	0	0	.250	.333	.375

G. Shoch, 1 G at SS

Pitcher	T	Age	G	GS	CG	ShO	IP	H	HR	BB	SO	W-L	Sv	ERA
Brickyard Kennedy	R	28	42	38	28	1	305.2	334	12	130	76	17-20	1	4.42
Harley Payne	L	28	34	28	24	2	241.2	284	4	58	52	14-16	0	3.39
Dan Daub	R	28	32	24	18	0	225.0	255	4	63	53	12-11	0	3.60
Bert Abbey	R	26	25	18	12	0	164.1	210	7	48	37	8-8	0	5.15
George Harper	R	29	16	11	7	0	86.0	106	4	39	22	4-8	0	5.55
Ed Stein	R	26	17	10	6	0	90.1	130	6	51	16	3-6	0	4.88
Ad Gumbert†	R	27	5	4	2	0	31.0	34	2	11	3	0-4	0	3.77

1896 Washington Senators 9th NL 58-73 .443 33.0 GB

Gus Schmelz

Player	Gm by Position	B	Age	G	AB	R	H	2B	3B	HR	RBI	BB	SO	SB	Avg	OBP	Slg
Deacon McGuire	C98,1B1	R	32	108	389	60	125	25	3	2	70	30	14	12	.321	.379	.416
Ed Cartwright	1B133	R	36	133	499	76	138	15	10	1	62	54	44	28	.277	.350	.353
John O'Brien†	2B73	L	25	73	270	38	72	6	3	4	33	27	12	4	.267	.344	.356
Bill Joyce†	3B48,2B33	L	30	81	310	85	97	16	10	8	51	67	20	32	.313	.454	.506
Gene DeMontreville	SS133	R	22	133	533	94	183	24	5	8	77	29	27	28	.343	.381	.452
Kip Selbach	OF126	R	24	127	487	100	148	17	13	5	100	76	28	49	.304	.405	.423
Tom Brown	OF116	L	35	116	435	87	128	17	6	2	59	58	49	28	.294	.385	.375
Billy Lush	OF91,2B3	S	22	97	352	74	87	9	11	4	45	66	49	28	.247	.369	.369
Charlie Abbey	OF78,P1	L	29	79	301	47	79	12	6	1	49	27	20	16	.262	.331	.352
Win Mercer	P46,OF1	R	22	49	156	23	38	1	1	1	14	9	18	9	.244	.302	.282
Jim Rogers†	3B32,2B6,OF1	—	24	38	154	21	43	6	4	1	30	10	9	3	.279	.323	.390
Harvey Smith	3B36	L	24	36	131	21	36	7	2	0	17	12	7	9	.275	.345	.359
Duke Farrell†	C18,3B14	S	29	37	130	18	39	7	3	1	30	7	3	2	.300	.345	.423
Pat McCauley	C24,OF1	—	26	26	84	14	21	3	0	3	11	7	8	3	.250	.315	.393
Jack Crooks†	2B20,3B4	R	30	25	84	20	24	3	0	3	20	16	8	2	.286	.406	.429
Les German†	P28,3B1,OF1	R	27	30	70	11	16	1	0	1	6	5	5	3	.229	.299	.286
Zeke Wrigley	2B3,SS1	—	22	5	9	1	1	0	0	0	2	1	1	0	.111	.200	.111

Pitcher	T	Age	G	GS	CG	ShO	IP	H	HR	BB	SO	W-L	Sv	ERA
Win Mercer	R	22	46	45	38	2	366.1	456	10	117	94	25-18	0	4.13
Doc McJames	R	22	37	33	29	0	280.1	310	2	135	103	12-20	1	4.27
Les German†	R	27	28	20	14	0	166.2	240	6	74	20	2-20	1	6.32
Silver King	R	28	22	16	12	0	145.1	179	3	43	35	10-7	1	4.09
Al Maul	R	30	8	8	7	0	62.0	75	0	20	18	5-2	0	3.63
Elisha Norton	R	22	8	5	2	0	44.0	49	2	14	13	3-1	0	3.07
Jake Boyd	L	22	4	2	2	0	32.0	45	0	15	6	1-2	0	6.75
Varney Anderson	R	30	2	2	1	0	9.0	23	0	3	0	0-1	0	13.00
John Malarkey	R	24	1	1	0	0	7.0	9	1	3	0	0-1	0	1.29
Carney Flynn†	L	21	4	1	1	0	20.0	43	0	10	3	0-1	0	8.55
John Gilroy	—	26	1	0	0	0	2.0	0	0	1	0	0-0	0	0.00
Charlie Abbey	L	29	1	0	0	0	2.0	6	0	0	0	0-0	0	4.50

1896 St. Louis Browns 11th NL 40-90 .308 50.5 GB

H. Diddlebock (7-10)/A. Latham (0-3)/C. Von Der Ahe (0-2)/R. Connor (8-37)/T. Dowd (25-38)

Player	Gm by Position	B	Age	G	AB	R	H	2B	3B	HR	RBI	BB	SO	SB	Avg	OBP	Slg
Ed McFarland	C80,OF2	R	21	83	290	48	70	13	4	3	36	15	17	7	.241	.281	.345
Roger Connor	1B126	L	38	126	483	71	137	21	9	11	72	52	14	10	.284	.356	.433
Tommy Dowd	2B78,OF48	R	27	126	521	93	138	17	11	5	46	42	19	40	.265	.322	.369
Al Myers	3B120,2B1,SS1	R	22	122	454	47	116	12	8	0	37	40	32	8	.256	.320	.317
Monte Cross	SS125	R	26	125	427	66	104	10	6	6	52	58	48	40	.244	.342	.337
Tom Parrott	OF108,P7,1B6	R	28	118	474	62	138	13	12	7	70	11	24	12	.291	.307	.414
Klondike Douglass	OF74,C6,SS2	L	24	81	296	42	78	6	4	1	28	35	15	18	.264	.351	.321
Tuck Turner†	OF51	S	23	51	203	30	50	7	8	1	27	14	21	6	.246	.298	.374
Joe Sullivan†	OF45,2B7,3B1	—	26	51	212	25	62	4	2	2	21	9	12	5	.292	.351	.358
Joe Quinn†	2B48	R	31	48	191	19	40	6	1	1	17	9	5	8	.209	.252	.267
Morgan Murphy	C48	R	29	49	175	12	45	5	2	0	11	8	14	1	.257	.290	.309
Duff Cooley†	OF40	L	23	40	166	29	51	5	3	0	13	7	3	12	.307	.335	.373
Ted Breitenstein	P44,OF8	L	27	51	162	21	42	5	2	0	12	13	26	8	.259	.314	.315
Bill Hart	P42,OF8	—	30	49	161	9	30	4	5	0	15	3	15	7	.186	.206	.273
Red Donahue	P32,OF1	R	23	33	107	5	17	2	0	0	9	3	23	1	.159	.189	.178
Bill Kissinger	P20,OF3,3B1	R	24	23	73	8	22	4	0	0	12	0	4	0	.301	.301	.356
Tom Niland	OF13,SS5	R	26	18	68	3	12	0	1	0	3	5	4	0	.176	.243	.206
Arlie Latham	3B8	R	36	8	35	3	7	0	0	0	5	4	3	2	.200	.282	.200
Biff Sheehan	OF6	—	28	6	19	0	3	0	0	0	1	4	0	0	.158	.304	.158

Pitcher	T	Age	G	GS	CG	ShO	IP	H	HR	BB	SO	W-L	Sv	ERA
Ted Breitenstein	L	27	44	43	37	1	339.2	376	12	138	114	18-26	0	4.48
Bill Hart	R	30	42	41	37	0	336.0	411	11	141	65	12-29	0	5.12
Red Donahue	R	23	32	32	28	0	267.0	376	6	98	70	7-24	0	5.80
Bill Kissinger	R	24	20	12	11	0	136.0	209	5	55	22	2-9	1	6.49
Tom Parrott	R	28	7	2	2	0	42.0	62	4	18	8	1-1	0	6.21
John McDougal	R	24	3	1	0	0	10.0	13	2	4	0	0-1	0	8.10
John Wood	—	25	1	0	0	0	0.0	1	0	2	0	0-0	0	—

1896 Louisville Colonels 12th NL 38-93 .290 53.0 GB

John McCloskey (2-17)/Bill McGunnigle (36-76)

Player	Gm by Position	B	Age	G	AB	R	H	2B	3B	HR	RBI	BB	SO	SB	Avg	OBP	Slg
Charlie Dexter	C55,OF47	R	20	107	402	65	112	18	7	3	37	17	34	21	.279	.318	.381
Jim Rogers†	1B60,SS12	—	24	72	290	39	75	8	6	0	38	15	14	13	.259	.297	.328
John O'Brien†	2B49	L	25	49	186	24	63	9	1	2	24	13	7	4	.339	.385	.430
Billy Clingman	3B121	S	26	121	423	57	99	10	2	2	37	57	51	19	.234	.329	.281
Joe Dolan	SS44	—	23	44	165	14	35	2	1	3	18	9	12	6	.212	.253	.291
Fred Clarke	OF131	L	23	131	517	96	168	15	18	9	79	43	34	34	.325	.392	.476
Tom McCreery	OF111,P1,2B1	S	21	115	441	87	155	23	21	7	65	42	58	26	.351	.409	.546
Ollie Pickering	OF45	L	26	45	165	28	50	6	4	1	22	12	11	13	.303	.350	.406
Doggie Miller	C48,2B25,3B8*	R	31	98	324	54	89	17	4	1	33	27	9	16	.275	.334	.361
Pete Cassidy	1B38,SS11	R	23	49	184	16	39	1	1	0	12	7	7	5	.212	.256	.228
Chick Fraser	P43,OF2	R	25	45	146	12	22	3	2	0	6	7	34	1	.151	.195	.199
Ducky Holmes	OF33,P2,2B1*	L	27	47	141	22	38	3	2	0	18	13	5	8	.270	.360	.319
Jack Crooks†	2B39	R	30	39	122	19	29	5	1	2	15	20	8	8	.238	.354	.344
Frank Shannon	SS28,3B3	—	22	31	115	14	18	1	1	1	15	13	15	3	.157	.248	.209
Herm McFarland	OF28,C1	L	26	30	110	11	21	4	1	1	12	9	14	4	.191	.252	.273
John Warner†	C32,1B1	L	23	33	110	9	25	1	1	0	10	10	10	3	.227	.303	.255
Bill Hassamaer	1B29	—	31	30	106	8	26	5	0	2	14	14	7	1	.245	.333	.349
Frank Eustace	SS22,2B3	—	22	25	100	18	17	2	2	1	11	6	14	4	.170	.217	.260
Bert Cunningham	P27,SS1	R	30	29	88	11	22	3	2	2	15	5	14	0	.250	.290	.398
Abbie Johnson	2B25	—	23	25	87	10	20	2	1	0	14	4	6	0	.230	.264	.276
Sammy Strang	SS14	S	19	14	46	6	12	0	0	0	7	6	6	4	.261	.346	.261
Tom Smith	P11,1B4	R	24	15	39	3	8	1	1	0	1	4	5	0	.205	.279	.282
Tom Morrison	3B5,OF2,SS1	—	21	8	27	3	4	1	0	0	0	4	4	0	.148	.258	.185
Tom Kinslow	C5,1B1	R	30	8	25	4	7	0	1	0	7	1	5	0	.280	.308	.360
Eddie Boyle†	C3	R	22	3	9	0	0	0	0	0	0	2	2	0	.000	.182	.000
Joe Wright†	OF2	L	23	2	7	0	2	0	0	0	0	0	1	0	.286	.286	.286
George Treadway	1B1,OF1	L	—	2	7	0	1	0	0	0	1	1	0	0	.143	.250	.143
Frank Friend	C2	—	—	2	5	1	1	0	0	0	0	1	1	0	.200	.333	.200

D. Miller, 8 G at OF, 3 G at 1B, 2 G at SS; D. Holmes, 1 G at SS

Pitcher	T	Age	G	GS	CG	ShO	IP	H	HR	BB	SO	W-L	Sv	ERA
Bill Hill	L	21	43	39	32	0	319.2	353	14	155	104	9-28	2	4.31
Chick Fraser	R	25	43	38	36	0	349.1	396	9	166	91	12-27	1	4.87
Bert Cunningham	R	30	27	20	17	0	189.1	242	6	74	37	7-14	1	5.09
Art Herman	—	25	14	12	9	0	94.1	122	4	36	13	4-6	0	5.63
Mike McDermott	R	33	12	10	4	1	65.0	87	4	44	12	2-7	0	7.34
Gus Weyhing	R	29	5	5	4	0	42.0	62	6	15	9	2-3	0	6.64
Fritz Clausen	L	27	2	2	1	0	11.0	17	1	6	4	0-2	0	6.55
Ducky Holmes	R	27	2	1	0	0	12.0	26	0	8	3	0-1	0	7.50
Charlie Emig	L	21	1	1	1	0	8.0	12	1	7	1	0-1	0	7.88
Tom McCreery	R	21	1	1	0	0	1.0	4	1	5	0	0-1	0	36.00
Tom Smith	R	24	11	5	4	0	55.0	73	2	25	14	2-3	0	5.40
Joe Kostal	R	20	2	0	0	0	2.0	4	0	0	0	0-0	0	0.00

»1897 Boston Beaneaters 1st NL 93-39 .705 —

Frank Selee

Player	Gm by Position	B	Age	G	AB	R	H	2B	3B	HR	RBI	BB	SO	SB	Avg	OBP	Slg
Marty Bergen	C85,OF1	—	25	87	327	47	81	11	3	2	45	18	—	5	.248	.295	.318
Fred Tenney	1B128,OF4	L	25	132	566	125	180	24	3	1	85	49	—	34	.318	.376	.376
Bobby Lowe	2B123	R	28	123	499	87	154	24	8	5	106	32	—	16	.309	.355	.419
Jimmy Collins	3B134	R	27	134	529	103	183	28	13	6	132	41	—	14	.346	.400	.482
Herman Long	SS107,OF1	L	31	107	450	89	145	32	7	3	69	23	—	22	.322	.358	.444
Hugh Duffy	OF129,2B6,SS2	R	30	134	550	130	187	25	10	11	129	52	—	41	.340	.403	.482
Billy Hamilton	OF126	L	31	127	507	152	174	17	5	3	61	105	—	66	.343	.461	.414
Chick Stahl	OF111	L	24	114	469	112	166	30	13	4	97	38	—	18	.354	.406	.499
Jack Stivetts	OF29,P18,1B2*	R	29	61	199	41	73	9	9	2	37	15	—	2	.367	.417	.533
Fred Klobedanz	P38,OF2	L	26	48	148	29	48	8	5	1	20	5	—	1	.324	.363	.466
Bob Allen	SS32,2B1,OF1	R	29	34	119	33	38	5	0	1	24	18	—	1	.319	.409	.387
Charlie Ganzel	C27,1B2	R	35	30	105	15	28	4	3	0	14	4	—	2	.267	.300	.362
George Yeager	C13,OF10,2B4*	R	24	30	95	20	23	2	3	2	15	7	—	2	.242	.294	.389
Fred Lake	C18	R	30	19	62	2	15	4	0	0	5	1	—	2	.242	.254	.306
Tommy Tucker†	1B4	S	33	4	14	0	3	2	0	0	4	2	—	0	.214	.313	.357
Mike Mahoney	P1,C1	R	23	2	2	1	1	0	0	0	1	0	—	0	.500	.500	.500

J. Stivetts, 2 G at 2B; G. Yeager, 1 G at 3B

Pitcher	T	Age	G	GS	CG	ShO	IP	H	HR	BB	SO	W-L	Sv	ERA
Kid Nichols	R	27	46	40	37	2	368.0	362	9	68	127	31-11	3	2.64
Fred Klobedanz	L	26	38	37	30	2	309.1	344	13	125	92	26-7	0	4.60
Ted Lewis	R	24	38	34	30	2	290.0	316	11	125	65	21-12	1	3.85
Jack Stivetts	R	29	18	15	10	0	129.1	147	5	43	27	11-4	0	3.41
Jim Sullivan	R	28	13	9	8	1	89.0	91	1	26	17	4-5	2	3.94
Charlie Hickman	R	21	2	0	0	0	7.2	10	0	5	0	0-0	1	5.87
Mike Mahoney	—	23	1	0	0	0	1.0	3	0	1	1	0-0	0	18.00

1897 Baltimore Orioles 2nd NL 90-40 .692 2.0 GB

Ned Hanlon

Player	Gm by Position	B	Age	G	AB	R	H	2B	3B	HR	RBI	BB	SO	SB	Avg	OBP	Slg
Boileryard Clarke	C59,1B4	R	28	64	241	32	65	7	1	1	38	9	—	5	.270	.320	.320
Jack Doyle	1B114	R	27	114	460	91	163	29	4	2	87	29	—	62	.354	.394	.448
Heinie Reitz	2B128	L	30	128	477	76	138	15	6	2	84	50	—	23	.289	.370	.358
John McGraw	3B105	L	24	106	391	90	127	15	3	0	48	99	—	44	.325	.471	.379
Hughie Jennings	SS116	R	28	117	439	133	156	26	9	2	79	42	—	60	.355	.463	.469
Jake Stenzel	OF131	R	30	131	536	113	189	43	7	4	116	36	—	69	.353	.406	.481
Joe Kelley	OF130,SS3,3B2	R	25	131	505	113	183	31	9	5	118	70	—	44	.362	.447	.489
Willie Keeler	OF129	L	25	129	564	145	239	27	19	0	74	35	—	64	.424	.464	.539
Joe Quinn	3B37,SS21,2B11*	R	32	75	285	33	74	11	4	1	45	13	—	12	.260	.299	.337
Wilbert Robinson	C48	R	34	48	181	25	57	9	0	0	23	8	—	0	.315	.347	.365
Joe Corbett	P37,SS1,OF1	R	21	42	150	27	37	6	1	0	22	4	—	4	.247	.271	.300
Tom O'Brien	1B25,OF24	—	24	50	147	25	37	6	0	0	32	20	—	7	.252	.349	.293
Bill Hoffer	P38,OF4	R	26	42	139	20	33	8	1	1	16	6	—	2	.237	.279	.331
Frank Bowerman	C36	R	28	38	130	16	41	5	0	1	21	1	—	3	.315	.331	.377
Arlie Pond	P32,OF1	R	25	33	90	16	22	3	0	0	6	11	—	2	.244	.333	.278

J. Quinn, 6 G at OF, 2 G at 1B

Pitcher	T	Age	G	GS	CG	ShO	IP	H	HR	BB	SO	W-L	Sv	ERA
Joe Corbett	R	21	37	37	34	1	313.0	330	2	115	149	24-8	0	3.11
Bill Hoffer	R	26	38	33	29	1	303.1	350	5	104	62	22-11	0	4.30
Arlie Pond	R	25	32	28	23	0	248.0	267	4	72	59	18-9	0	3.52
Jerry Nops	L	22	30	25	23	1	220.2	235	5	52	69	20-6	0	2.81
Doc Amole	L	18	11	7	6	0	70.0	67	0	17	19	4-4	0	2.57
George Blackburn	R	25	5	4	3	0	33.0	34	2	12	1	2-2	0	6.82
Al Maul†	R	31	2	2	0	0	7.2	9	0	8	2	0-0	0	7.04
Dick Cogan	R	25	1	0	0	0	2.0	4	0	2	0	0-0	0	13.50

1897 New York Giants 3rd NL 83-48 .634 9.5 GB

Bill Joyce

Player	Gm by Position	B	Age	G	AB	R	H	2B	3B	HR	RBI	BB	SO	SB	Avg	OBP	Slg
John Warner	C110	L	24	110	397	50	109	6	3	2	51	26	—	8	.275	.344	.320
Willie Clark	1B107,OF7,3B1	L	24	116	431	63	122	17	12	1	75	37	—	18	.283	.352	.385
Kid Gleason	2B129,SS3	S	30	131	540	85	172	16	4	1	106	26	—	43	.319	.353	.369
Bill Joyce	3B106,1B2	L	31	109	388	109	118	15	13	3	64	78	—	33	.304	.441	.433
George Davis	SS129	S	26	130	519	112	183	31	10	10	136	41	—	65	.353	.406	.509
George Van Haltren	OF129	L	31	129	564	117	186	22	9	3	64	40	—	50	.330	.375	.417
Mike Tiernan	OF127	L	30	127	528	123	174	29	10	5	72	61	—	40	.330	.400	.451
Ducky Holmes†	OF77,SS1	L	28	79	306	51	82	8	6	1	44	18	—	30	.268	.317	.343
Tom McCreery†	OF45,2B3	S	22	49	177	36	53	8	5	1	28	22	—	15	.299	.380	.418
Parke Wilson	C30,1B10,OF4*	R	29	46	154	29	46	9	3	0	22	15	—	5	.299	.365	.396
Cy Seymour	P38,OF6	L	24	44	137	13	33	5	1	2	14	4	—	3	.241	.262	.336
Jim Donnelly†	3B23	R	31	23	85	19	16	3	0	0	11	9	—	6	.188	.266	.224
Charlie Gettig	3B7,2B6,P3*	R	26	22	75	8	15	6	0	0	12	6	—	3	.200	.277	.280
Jake Beckley†	1B17	L	29	17	68	8	17	2	3	1	11	2	—	2	.250	.301	.412
Walt Wilmot	OF9	S	33	11	34	8	9	2	0	1	4	2	—	1	.265	.306	.412
General Stafford†	OF5,SS2	R	28	7	23	0	2	0	0	0	3	3	—	0	.087	.192	.087
Dad Clarke†	P6,1B1	S	32	7	18	4	3	0	0	0	1	1	—	0	.167	.211	.167
Dave Zearfoss	C5	—	29	5	10	1	3	0	1	0	0	0	—	0	.300	.300	.500
Yale Murphy	SS3,2B2	L	27	5	8	1	0	0	0	0	1	2	—	0	.000	.200	.000

P. Wilson, 1 G at 2B; C. Gettig, 3 G at SS, 3 G at OF

Pitcher	T	Age	G	GS	CG	ShO	IP	H	HR	BB	SO	W-L	Sv	ERA
Amos Rusie	R	26	38	37	35	2	322.1	314	6	87	135	28-10	0	2.54
Jouett Meekin	R	30	37	34	30	2	303.2	328	9	99	83	20-11	0	3.76
Cy Seymour	L	24	38	33	28	2	277.2	254	4	164	149	18-14	1	3.37
Mike Sullivan	—	30	23	16	11	1	148.2	183	6	71	35	8-7	2	5.09
Ed Doheny	L	23	10	10	10	0	85.0	69	0	45	37	4-4	0	2.12
Dad Clarke†	R	32	6	4	2	0	31.0	43	1	11	10	2-1	0	6.10
Charlie Gettig	—	26	3	2	2	0	19.0	23	0	9	7	1-1	0	5.21

1897 Cincinnati Reds 4th NL 76-56 .576 17.0 GB

Buck Ewing

Player	Gm by Position	B	Age	G	AB	R	H	2B	3B	HR	RBI	BB	SO	SB	Avg	OBP	Slg
Heinie Peitz	C71,P2	R	26	77	266	35	78	11	7	1	44	18	—	3	.293	.340	.398
Jake Beckley†	1B97	L	29	97	365	76	126	17	9	7	76	18	—	23	.345	.395	.499
Bid McPhee	2B81	R	37	81	282	45	85	13	7	1	39	35	—	9	.301	.386	.408
Charlie Irwin	3B134	L	28	134	505	89	146	26	6	0	74	47	—	27	.289	.360	.364
Claude Ritchey	SS70,OF22,2B8	S	23	101	337	58	95	12	4	0	41	42	—	11	.282	.370	.341
Dummy Hoy	OF128	L	35	128	497	87	145	24	6	2	42	54	—	37	.292	.375	.376
Dusty Miller	OF119	L	28	119	440	83	139	27	1	4	70	48	—	29	.316	.393	.409
Eddie Burke	OF95	L	30	95	387	71	103	17	1	1	41	29	—	22	.266	.327	.323
Tommy Corcoran	SS63,2B47	R	28	109	445	76	128	30	5	3	57	13	—	15	.288	.311	.398
Farmer Vaughn	1B35,C15	R	33	54	199	21	58	13	5	0	30	2	—	2	.291	.299	.407
Bug Holliday	OF42,SS4,1B3*	R	30	61	195	50	61	9	4	2	20	27	—	6	.313	.399	.431
Pop Schriver	C53	R	31	61	178	29	54	12	4	1	30	19	—	3	.303	.374	.433
Buck Ewing	1B1	R	37	1	1	0	0	0	0	0	0	0	—	0	.000	.500	.000

B. Holliday, 3 G at 2B

Pitcher	T	Age	G	GS	CG	ShO	IP	H	HR	BB	SO	W-L	Sv	ERA
Ted Breitenstein	L	28	40	39	32	2	320.1	345	3	91	98	23-12	0	3.62
Billy Rhines	R	28	41	32	26	1	288.2	311	4	86	65	21-15	0	4.08
Frank Dwyer	R	29	37	31	22	0	247.1	315	5	56	41	18-13	0	3.78
Red Ehret	R	28	34	19	11	0	184.1	256	3	47	43	8-10	2	4.78
Bill Dammann	L	24	16	11	7	1	95.0	122	2	37	21	6-4	0	4.74
Stub Brown	L	26	2	1	1	0	13.0	17	1	8	2	0-1	0	4.15
Heinie Peitz	R	26	2	1	1	0	8.0	9	0	4	0	0-1	0	7.88

1897 Cleveland Spiders 5th NL 69-62 .527 23.5 GB

Patsy Tebeau

Player	Gm by Position	B	Age	G	AB	R	H	2B	3B	HR	RBI	BB	SO	SB	Avg	OBP	Slg
Chief Zimmer	C80	R	36	80	294	50	93	22	3	0	40	25	—	8	.316	.378	.412
Patsy Tebeau	1B92,2B18,3B2*	R	32	109	412	62	110	15	9	0	59	30	—	11	.267	.323	.347
Cupid Childs	2B114	L	29	114	444	105	150	15	9	1	61	74	—	25	.338	.435	.419
Bobby Wallace	3B130,OF1	R	23	130	516	99	173	33	21	4	112	48	—	14	.335	.394	.504
Ed McKean	SS125	R	33	125	523	83	143	21	14	2	78	40	—	15	.273	.330	.379
Jesse Burkett	OF127	L	28	127	517	129	198	28	7	2	60	76	—	28	.383	.468	.476
Louis Sockalexis	OF66	L	25	66	278	43	94	9	8	3	42	18	—	16	.338	.385	.460
Jack O'Connor	OF52,1B36,C13	R	28	103	397	49	115	21	4	2	69	26	—	20	.290	.338	.378
Ollie Pickering†	OF46,2B1	L	27	46	182	33	64	5	2	1	22	11	—	18	.352	.392	.418
Cy Young	P46,1B2	R	30	48	153	14	34	4	3	0	19	2	—	4	.222	.237	.288
Lou Criger	C37,1B2	R	25	39	138	15	31	4	1	0	22	23	—	5	.225	.340	.268
Sport McAllister	OF28,P4,SS4*	S	22	43	137	23	30	5	1	0	11	12	—	3	.219	.287	.270
Harry Blake	OF32	R	23	32	117	17	30	3	1	1	15	12	—	5	.256	.331	.325
Zeke Wilson	P34,OF2,1B1	R	27	37	116	16	26	0	1	0	9	8	—	3	.224	.274	.241
Jack Powell	P27,OF1	R	22	28	97	10	20	1	0	0	12	6	—	0	.206	.260	.216
Jimmy McAleer	OF24	R	32	24	91	6	20	2	0	0	10	7	—	4	.220	.283	.242
Ira Belden	OF8	L	23	8	30	5	8	0	2	0	4	2	—	0	.267	.333	.400
Henry Clarke	P5,OF2	R	21	7	25	3	7	0	0	0	3	2	—	0	.280	.333	.280
Dale Gear	OF6	R	25	7	24	3	4	1	0	0	2	3	—	2	.167	.286	.208
Fred Cooke	OF5	—	—	5	17	2	5	2	0	0	3	3	—	0	.294	.400	.412

P. Tebeau, 1 G at SS; S. McAllister, 3 G at 1B, 2 G at C, 1 G at 2B

Pitcher	T	Age	G	GS	CG	ShO	IP	H	HR	BB	SO	W-L	Sv	ERA
Cy Young	R	30	46	38	35	2	335.0	391	7	49	88	21-19	0	3.79
Zeke Wilson	R	27	34	30	26	1	263.2	323	9	83	69	16-11	0	4.16
Jack Powell	R	22	27	26	24	2	225.0	245	2	62	61	15-10	0	3.16
Nig Cuppy	R	27	19	17	13	1	138.2	150	3	26	23	10-6	0	3.18
Mike McDermott†	R	34	9	7	4	0	62.0	75	2	25	12	4-5	0	4.50
Henry Clarke	R	21	5	4	3	0	30.2	32	4	12	3	0-4	0	5.87
Charlie Brown	L	19	4	4	2	0	24.1	30	2	17	8	1-2	0	7.77
Sport McAllister	R	22	4	3	3	0	28.0	29	3	9	10	1-2	0	4.50
John Pappalau	R	22	2	1	1	0	12.0	22	0	6	3	0-1	0	10.50

1897 Brooklyn Bridegrooms 6th NL 61-71 .462 32.0 GB

Billy Barnie

Player	Gm by Position	B	Age	G	AB	R	H	2B	3B	HR	RBI	BB	SO	SB	Avg	OBP	Slg
John Grim	C77	R	29	80	290	26	72	10	1	0	25	1	—	3	.248	.259	.290
Candy LaChance	1B126	S	27	126	520	86	160	28	16	4	90	15	—	26	.308	.333	.446
George Shoch	2B68,SS13,OF4	R	38	85	284	42	79	9	2	0	38	49	—	6	.278	.393	.324
Billy Shindle	3B134	R	33	134	542	83	154	32	6	4	105	35	—	23	.284	.336	.387
Germany Smith	SS112	R	34	112	428	47	86	17	3	0	29	14	—	1	.201	.233	.255
Fielder Jones	OF135	L	25	135	548	134	172	15	10	1	49	61	—	48	.314	.392	.383
Mike Griffin	OF134	L	32	134	534	136	169	25	11	2	56	81	—	16	.316	.416	.416
John Anderson	OF115,1B3	S	23	117	492	93	160	28	12	4	85	17	—	29	.325	.357	.455
Jim Canavan	2B63	R	30	63	240	25	52	9	3	2	34	26	—	9	.217	.299	.304
Aleck Smith	C43,OF18,1B6	—	26	66	237	36	71	13	1	1	39	4	—	12	.300	.317	.376
Jack Dunn	P25,2B4,3B3*	R	24	36	131	20	29	4	0	0	17	4	—	2	.221	.244	.252
Harley Payne	P40,OF1	S	29	41	110	13	26	0	1	0	11	8	—	0	.236	.288	.255
Buster Burrell	C27,1B4	R	30	33	103	15	25	2	0	2	18	10	—	1	.243	.310	.320
Jimmy Sheckard	SS11,OF2	L	18	13	49	12	14	3	2	3	14	6	—	5	.286	.364	.612
Pat Hannifin	OF3,2B2	—	31	10	20	4	5	0	0	0	2	1	—	4	.250	.375	.250

J. Dunn, 3 G at OF, 1 G at SS

Pitcher	T	Age	G	GS	CG	ShO	IP	H	HR	BB	SO	W-L	Sv	ERA
Brickyard Kennedy	R	29	44	40	36	2	343.1	370	6	149	81	18-20	1	3.91
Harley Payne	L	29	40	38	30	1	280.0	350	8	71	86	14-17	0	4.63
Jack Dunn	R	24	25	21	21	0	216.2	251	6	66	26	14-9	0	4.57
Dan Daub	R	29	19	16	11	0	137.2	180	8	48	19	6-11	0	6.08
Chauncey Fisher	R	25	20	13	11	1	149.0	184	5	43	31	9-7	1	4.23
Sadie McMahon	R	29	9	7	5	0	63.0	75	1	29	13	0-6	0	5.86
John Brown	—	—	1	1	0	0	5.0	7	0	4	0	0-1	0	7.20

1897 Washington Senators 6th NL 61-71 .462 32.0 GB

Gus Schmelz (9-25)/Tom Brown (52-46)

Player	Gm by Position	B	Age	G	AB	R	H	2B	3B	HR	RBI	BB	SO	SB	Avg	OBP	Slg
Deacon McGuire	C73,1B6	R	33	93	327	51	112	17	7	4	53	21	—	9	.343	.386	.474
Tommy Tucker†	1B93	S	33	93	352	52	119	18	5	5	61	27	—	18	.338	.403	.460
John O'Brien	2B86	L	26	86	320	37	78	12	2	3	45	19	—	6	.244	.309	.322
Charlie Reilly	3B101	S	30	101	351	64	97	18	3	2	60	34	—	18	.276	.359	.362
Gene DeMontreville	SS99,2B33	R	23	133	566	92	193	27	8	3	93	21	—	30	.341	.366	.433
Kip Selbach	OF124	R	25	124	486	113	152	25	16	5	59	80	—	46	.313	.414	.461
Tom Brown	OF115	L	36	116	469	91	137	17	2	5	45	52	—	25	.292	.364	.369
Charlie Abbey	OF80	L	30	80	300	52	78	14	8	3	34	27	—	9	.260	.329	.390
Zeke Wrigley	OF36,SS33,3B30*	—	23	104	388	65	110	14	8	3	64	21	—	5	.284	.320	.384
Duke Farrell	C63,1B1	S	30	78	261	41	84	9	6	0	53	17	—	8	.322	.383	.402
Jake Gettman	OF36	S	20	36	143	28	45	7	3	3	29	7	—	8	.315	.359	.469
Ed Cartwright	1B33	R	37	33	124	19	29	4	0	0	15	8	—	9	.234	.286	.266
Tom Leahy†	OF10,3B5,2B3*	—	28	19	52	12	20	2	1	0	7	9	—	6	.385	.529	.462
Les German	P15,2B2,3B1	R	28	19	44	8	15	2	0	0	3	3	—	0	.341	.383	.386
Elisha Norton	P4,OF3	R	23	7	18	0	5	2	1	0	2	0	—	0	.278	.278	.500
Roger Bresnahan	P6,OF1	R	18	6	16	1	6	0	0	0	3	1	—	0	.375	.412	.375
Bill Fox	2B2,SS2	S	25	4	14	4	4	0	0	0	0	1	—	0	.286	.333	.286
Billy Lush	OF3	S	23	3	12	1	0	0	0	0	0	2	—	0	.000	.143	.000

Z. Wrigley, 9 G at 2B; T. Leahy, 1 G at C

Pitcher	T	Age	G	GS	CG	ShO	IP	H	HR	BB	SO	W-L	Sv	ERA
Win Mercer	R	23	45	42	34	3	332.0	395	5	102	88	20-20	2	3.25
Doc McJames	R	23	44	39	33	3	323.2	361	7	137	156	15-23	2	3.61
Cy Swaim	—	23	27	20	16	0	194.0	227	5	61	55	10-11	0	4.41
Silver King	R	29	23	19	12	0	154.0	196	7	45	32	6-9	1	4.79
Roger Bresnahan	R	18	6	5	3	1	41.0	52	1	10	12	4-0	0	3.95
Elisha Norton	R	23	4	2	1	0	17.0	31	0	11	3	2-1	0	6.88
Al Maul†	R	31	1	1	0	0	2.0	4	0	1	0	0-1	0	9.00
Les German	R	28	15	5	4	0	83.2	117	2	33	2	3-5	0	5.59
Joe Stanley	R	16	1	0	0	0	0.2	0	0	0	0	0-0	0	0.00

1897 Pittsburgh Pirates 8th NL 60-71 .458 32.5 GB

Patsy Donovan

Player	Gm by Position	B	Age	G	AB	R	H	2B	3B	HR	RBI	BB	SO	SB	Avg	OBP	Slg
Joe Sugden	C81,1B3	S	26	84	288	31	64	6	4	0	38	18	—	9	.222	.275	.271
Harry Davis	1B64,3B32,OF14*	R	23	111	429	70	131	10	28	2	63	26	—	21	.305	.359	.473
Dick Padden	2B134	R	26	134	517	84	146	16	10	2	58	38	—	18	.282	.350	.364
Jesse Hoffmeister	3B48	—	—	48	188	33	58	6	9	3	36	8	—	6	.309	.337	.484
Bones Ely	SS133	R	34	133	516	63	146	20	8	2	74	25	—	10	.283	.317	.364
Elmer Smith	OF123	L	29	123	467	99	145	19	17	6	54	70	—	25	.310	.408	.463
Patsy Donovan	OF120	L	32	120	479	82	154	16	7	0	57	25	—	34	.322	.360	.384
Steve Brodie	OF100	L	28	100	370	47	108	7	12	2	53	25	—	11	.292	.348	.392
Bill Merritt	C53,1B7	R	26	62	209	21	55	6	1	1	26	9	—	2	.263	.297	.316
Jesse Tannehill	OF33,P21	S	22	56	184	22	49	8	2	0	22	18	—	4	.266	.338	.332
Jim Donnelly†	3B44	R	31	44	161	22	31	4	0	0	14	16	—	14	.193	.270	.217
Denny Lyons	1B35,3B2	R	31	37	131	22	27	6	4	2	17	22	—	5	.206	.346	.359
Jack Rothfuss	1B32	R	25	35	115	20	36	3	1	2	18	5	—	3	.313	.352	.409
Tom Leahy†	OF13,C6,3B6	—	28	24	92	10	24	3	3	0	12	7	—	3	.261	.320	.359
Jim Gardner	P14,3B6,OF6*	—	22	27	76	13	12	2	1	1	8	9	—	3	.158	.264	.250
Charlie Kuhns	3B1	—	19	1	3	0	0	0	0	0	0	1	—	0	.000	.250	.000

H. Davis, 1 G at SS; J. Gardner, 1 G at 2B

Pitcher	T	Age	G	GS	CG	ShO	IP	H	HR	BB	SO	W-L	Sv	ERA
Frank Killen	L	26	42	41	38	1	337.1	417	4	76	99	17-23	0	4.46
Pink Hawley	R	24	40	39	33	0	311.1	362	7	94	88	18-18	0	4.80
Jim Hughey	R	28	25	17	13	0	149.1	193	3	45	38	6-10	1	5.06
Jesse Tannehill	L	22	21	16	11	1	142.0	172	1	24	40	9-9	1	4.25
Jim Gardner	R	22	14	11	8	0	95.1	115	4	32	35	5-5	0	5.19
Charlie Hastings	—	26	16	10	9	0	118.0	138	3	47	42	5-4	0	4.58

1897 Chicago Colts 9th NL 59-73 .447 34.0 GB

Cap Anson

Player	Gm by Position	B	Age	G	AB	R	H	2B	3B	HR	RBI	BB	SO	SB	Avg	OBP	Slg
Malachi Kittridge	C79	R	27	79	262	25	53	5	5	1	30	22	—	9	.202	.264	.271
Cap Anson	1B103,C11	R	45	114	424	67	121	17	3	3	75	60	—	11	.285	.379	.361
Jim Connor	2B76	R	34	77	285	40	83	10	5	3	38	24	—	10	.291	.355	.393
Bill Everitt	3B83,OF8	L	28	92	379	63	119	14	7	5	39	36	—	26	.314	.373	.427
Bill Dahlen	SS75	R	27	75	276	67	80	18	8	6	40	43	—	15	.290	.399	.478
Jimmy Ryan	OF136	R	34	136	520	103	156	33	17	5	85	50	—	27	.300	.369	.458
Bill Lange	OF118	R	26	118	479	119	163	24	14	5	83	48	—	73	.340	.406	.480
George Decker	OF75,1B38,2B1	L	28	111	428	72	124	12	7	5	63	24	—	11	.290	.333	.386
Barry McCormick	3B56,SS46,2B1	—	22	101	419	87	112	8	10	2	55	33	—	44	.267	.324	.348
Nixey Callahan	2B30,P23,OF21*	R	23	94	360	60	105	18	6	3	47	10	—	12	.292	.320	.400
Walter Thornton	OF59,P16	L	22	75	265	39	85	9	6	0	55	30	—	13	.321	.402	.400
Tim Donahue	C55,SS2,1B1	L	27	58	188	28	45	7	3	0	21	9	—	3	.239	.281	.309
Clark Griffith	P41,SS2,OF2*	R	27	46	162	27	38	8	4	0	21	18	—	2	.235	.311	.333
Fred Pfeffer	2B32	R	37	32	114	10	26	0	1	0	11	12	—	5	.228	.318	.246
Danny Friend	P24,OF1	—	24	25	88	12	25	5	0	0	9	5	—	1	.284	.323	.341
Tom Hernon	OF4	R	30	4	16	2	1	0	0	0	2	0	—	1	.063	.063	.063

N. Callahan, 18 G at SS, 2 G at 3B; C. Griffith, 1 G at 1B, 1 G at 3B

Pitcher	T	Age	G	GS	CG	ShO	IP	H	HR	BB	SO	W-L	Sv	ERA
Clark Griffith	R	27	41	38	38	1	343.2	410	3	86	102	21-18	1	3.72
Danny Friend	L	24	24	24	23	0	203.0	244	5	86	58	12-11	0	4.52
Nixey Callahan	R	23	23	22	21	1	189.2	221	6	55	52	12-9	0	4.03
Buttons Briggs	R	21	22	22	21	0	186.2	246	6	85	60	4-17	0	5.26
Walter Thornton	L	22	16	16	15	0	130.1	164	4	51	55	6-7	0	4.70
Roger Denzer	R	25	12	10	8	0	94.2	125	4	34	17	2-8	0	5.13
Jim Korwan	R	23	5	4	3	0	34.0	47	1	28	12	1-2	0	5.82
Adonis Terry	R	32	1	1	1	0	8.0	11	0	6	1	0-1	0	10.13
Dave Wright	R	21	1	1	1	0	7.0	17	1	2	4	1-0	0	15.43

1897 Philadelphia Phillies 10th NL 55-77 .417 38.0 GB

George Stallings

Player	Gm by Position	B	Age	G	AB	R	H	2B	3B	HR	RBI	BB	SO	SB	Avg	OBP	Slg
Jack Boyle	C50,1B24	R	31	75	288	37	73	9	1	2	36	19	—	3	.253	.306	.313
Nap Lajoie	1B108,OF19,3B2	R	22	127	545	107	197	40	23	9	127	15	—	20	.361	.392	.569
Lave Cross	3B47,2B38,OF2*	R	31	88	344	37	89	17	5	3	51	10	—	10	.259	.282	.363
Billy Nash	3B79,SS19,2B4	R	32	104	337	45	87	20	2	0	39	60	—	4	.258	.373	.329
Sam Gillen	SS69,3B6	—	26	75	270	32	70	10	3	0	27	35	—	2	.259	.353	.319
Duff Cooley	OF131,1B2	L	24	133	566	124	186	14	13	4	40	51	—	31	.329	.386	.420
Ed Delahanty	OF129,1B1	R	29	129	530	109	200	40	15	5	96	60	—	26	.377	.444	.538
Tommy Dowd†	OF73,2B19	R	28	91	391	68	114	14	4	0	43	19	—	30	.292	.324	.348
Phil Geier	OF45,2B37,SS6*	L	20	92	316	51	88	6	2	1	35	56	—	19	.278	.392	.320
Jack Clements	C49	L	32	55	185	18	44	4	2	6	36	12	—	3	.238	.305	.378
Frank Shugart	SS40	S	30	40	163	20	41	8	2	5	25	8	—	5	.252	.287	.417
Al Orth	P36,OF6	L	24	53	152	26	50	7	4	1	17	3	—	5	.329	.342	.447
Jack Taylor	P40,OF1	R	24	43	139	12	35	6	1	1	17	7	—	0	.252	.288	.331
Ed McFarland†	C37	R	22	38	130	18	29	3	5	1	16	14	—	2	.223	.308	.346
Bill Hallman†	2B31	R	30	31	126	16	33	3	0	0	15	8	—	1	.262	.326	.286
Mike Grady†	C3	R	27	4	13	1	2	0	0	0	0	1	—	0	.154	.214	.154
Sam Thompson	OF3	L	37	3	13	2	3	0	1	0	3	1	—	0	.231	.286	.385
Kohly Miller	2B3	—	—	3	11	2	2	0	0	0	1	2	—	0	.182	.308	.182
Ed Abbaticchio	2B3	R	20	3	10	0	3	0	0	0	0	1	—	0	.300	.364	.300
George Stallings	1B1,OF1	R	29	2	9	1	2	1	0	0	0	0	—	0	.222	.222	.333

L. Cross, 1 G at SS; P. Geier, 2 G at 3B

Pitcher	T	Age	G	GS	CG	ShO	IP	H	HR	BB	SO	W-L	Sv	ERA
Jack Taylor	R	24	40	37	35	2	317.1	376	5	76	88	16-20	2	4.23
Al Orth	R	24	36	34	29	2	282.1	349	12	82	64	14-19	0	4.62
Jack Fifield	R	25	27	26	21	0	210.2	263	8	80	38	5-18	0	5.51
George Wheeler	—	27	26	19	17	0	191.0	229	3	62	35	11-10	0	3.96
Davey Dunkle	R	24	7	7	7	0	62.0	72	0	23	9	5-2	0	3.48
Kid Carsey†	R	26	4	4	2	0	28.0	35	0	16	1	2-1	0	5.14
Tully Sparks	R	22	1	1	1	0	8.0	12	0	4	0	0-1	0	10.13
Tom Lipp	—	27	1	1	0	0	3.0	8	0	2	1	0-1	0	15.00
Youngy Johnson	R	19	5	2	1	0	29.0	39	0	12	7	1-2	0	4.66
Bob Becker	L	21	5	2	2	0	24.0	32	0	7	10	0-2	0	5.63

1897 Louisville Colonels 11th NL 52-78 .400 40.0 GB

Jim Rogers (17-24)/Fred Clarke (35-54)

Player	Gm by Position	B	Age	G	AB	R	H	2B	3B	HR	RBI	BB	SO	SB	Avg	OBP	Slg
Bill Wilson	C103,3B1	—	29	105	381	43	81	12	4	1	41	18	—	9	.213	.257	.273
Perry Werden	1B131	R	31	131	506	76	153	21	14	5	83	40	—	14	.302	.366	.429
Jim Rogers	2B39,1B3	—	25	41	150	22	22	3	2	2	22	22	—	4	.147	.260	.233
Billy Clingman	3B113	S	27	113	395	59	90	14	7	2	47	37	—	14	.228	.302	.314
General Stafford†	SS103,OF7,3B1	R	28	111	432	68	120	16	5	7	53	31	—	14	.278	.330	.387
Fred Clarke	OF127	L	24	128	518	120	202	30	13	6	67	45	—	57	.390	.462	.533
Tom McCreery†	OF89	S	22	89	338	55	96	5	6	4	40	38	—	13	.284	.356	.370
Ollie Pickering†	OF62	L	27	63	246	34	62	5	2	1	21	25	—	20	.252	.326	.301
Charlie Dexter	OF32,C23,3B14*	R	21	76	257	43	72	12	5	2	46	21	—	12	.280	.342	.389
Honus Wagner	OF52,2B9	R	23	61	237	37	80	17	4	2	39	15	—	19	.338	.379	.468
Abbie Johnson	2B33,SS12	—	24	48	161	16	39	6	1	0	23	13	—	2	.242	.303	.292
Joe Dolan	2B18,SS18	—	24	36	133	10	28	2	2	0	7	8	—	6	.211	.271	.256
Doc Nance	OF35	R	20	35	120	25	29	5	3	3	17	20	—	3	.242	.355	.408
Chick Fraser	P35,OF1	R	26	36	112	10	18	1	0	2	11	10	—	2	.161	.236	.223
Bert Cunningham	P29,OF2	R	31	31	93	13	22	0	1	2	10	1	—	1	.237	.253	.323
Heinie Smith	2B21	R	25	21	76	7	20	3	0	1	7	3	—	1	.263	.300	.342
Irv Hach	2B9,3B7	R	24	16	51	5	11	2	0	0	3	5	—	1	.216	.322	.255
Dick Butler	C10	—	—	10	38	3	7	0	0	0	2	0	—	1	.184	.184	.184
George Hemming	P9,1B1	R	28	10	28	5	5	1	0	0	2	2	—	0	.179	.233	.214
Bill Clark	P3,2B3,3B1	R	22	4	16	2	3	0	0	0	2	1	—	1	.188	.235	.188
Frank Martin	2B2	—	18	2	8	1	2	0	0	0	0	0	—	0	.250	.250	.250
Ducky Holmes†	SS1	L	28	2	4	0	0	0	0	0	0	1	—	0	.000	.200	.000
Tom Delahanty	2B1	L	25	1	4	1	1	1	0	0	2	0	—	0	.250	.250	.500
O. Schreckengost	C1	R	22	1	3	0	0	0	0	0	0	0	—	0	.000	.000	.000

C. Dexter, 2 G at SS

Pitcher	T	Age	G	GS	CG	ShO	IP	H	HR	BB	SO	W-L	Sv	ERA
Chick Fraser	R	26	35	34	32	0	286.1	332	11	133	70	15-19	0	4.09
Bert Cunningham	R	31	29	27	25	0	234.2	286	2	72	49	14-13	0	4.14
Bill Hill	L	22	27	26	20	1	199.0	209	6	69	55	7-17	0	3.62
Bill Magee	R	22	22	16	13	1	155.1	186	6	99	44	4-12	0	5.39
George Hemming	R	28	9	8	7	0	67.0	80	5	25	7	3-4	0	5.10
Roy Evans†	R	23	9	8	6	0	59.1	66	4	24	20	5-4	0	4.10
Dad Clarke†	R	32	7	6	6	0	54.2	74	3	10	7	2-4	0	3.95
Pete Dowling	L	—	4	4	2	0	26.0	39	0	8	3	1-2	0	5.88
Bill Clark	R	22	3	2	2	0	21.2	30	0	1	1	1-1	0	4.15
Art Herman	—	26	3	2	1	0	18.0	23	1	5	4	0-1	0	4.00
Rube Waddell	L	20	2	1	1	0	14.0	17	0	6	5	0-1	0	3.21
Burt Miller	—	21	4	1	1	0	17.0	32	0	3	3	0-1	0	7.94
Jim Jones	R	20	1	0	0	0	6.2	19	1	5	0	0-0	0	18.90

1897 St. Louis Browns 12th NL 29-102 .221 63.5 GB

Tommy Dowd (6-22)/Hugh Nicol (8-32)/Bill Hallman (13-36)/Chris Von Der Ahe (2-12)

Player	Gm by Position	B	Age	G	AB	R	H	2B	3B	HR	RBI	BB	SO	SB	Avg	OBP	Slg
Klondike Douglass	C61,OF43,1B17*	L	25	125	516	77	170	15	3	6	50	52	—	12	.329	.403	.405
Mike Grady†	1B83,OF1	R	27	83	322	48	90	11	3	7	55	26	—	7	.280	.352	.398
Bill Hallman†	2B77,1B3	R	30	79	298	31	66	6	2	0	26	24	—	12	.221	.288	.255
Fred Hartman	3B124	R	29	124	516	67	158	21	8	2	67	26	—	18	.306	.350	.390
Monte Cross	SS131	R	27	131	462	59	132	17	11	4	55	62	—	38	.286	.379	.396
Tuck Turner	OF102	S	24	103	416	58	121	17	12	2	41	35	—	8	.291	.350	.404
Dick Harley	OF89	L	24	89	330	43	96	6	4	3	35	36	—	23	.291	.379	.361
Dan Lally	OF84,1B3	L	29	87	355	56	99	15	5	2	42	9	—	12	.279	.310	.366
John Houseman	2B41,OF33,SS5*	—	27	80	278	34	68	6	6	0	21	28	—	16	.245	.329	.309
Morgan Murphy	C53,1B8	R	30	62	207	13	35	2	0	0	12	6	—	1	.169	.196	.179
Bill Hart	P39,OF6,1B1	R	31	46	156	14	39	1	2	2	14	1	—	4	.250	.255	.321
Red Donahue	P46,OF2,1B1	R	24	49	155	11	33	7	2	1	14	4	—	1	.213	.233	.303
Tommy Dowd†	OF30,2B5	R	28	35	145	25	38	9	1	0	9	6	—	11	.262	.291	.338
Ed McFarland†	C23,1B3,OF3*	R	22	31	107	14	35	5	2	1	17	8	—	2	.327	.374	.439
Roger Connor	1B22	L	39	22	83	13	19	3	1	1	12	13	—	3	.229	.333	.325
Lou Bierbauer	2B12	L	31	12	46	1	10	0	0	0	1	0	—	2	.217	.217	.217
Bill Kissinger	P7,OF7	R	25	14	39	7	13	3	2	0	6	3	—	0	.333	.381	.513
Ed Beecher	OF3	—	21	3	12	1	4	0	0	0	1	0	—	1	.333	.333	.333
Frank Huelsman	OF2	R	23	2	7	0	2	1	0	0	0	0	—	0	.286	.286	.429

K. Douglass, 7 G at 3B, 1 G at SS; J. Houseman, 3 G at 3B; E. McFarland, 1 G at 2B

Pitcher	T	Age	G	GS	CG	ShO	IP	H	HR	BB	SO	W-L	Sv	ERA
Red Donahue	R	24	46	42	38	1	348.0	484	16	106	64	10-35	1	6.13
Bill Hart	R	31	39	38	31	0	294.2	395	10	148	67	9-27	0	6.26
Kid Carsey†	R	26	12	11	11	0	99.0	133	5	31	14	3-8	0	6.00
Willie Sudhoff	R	22	11	9	9	0	92.2	126	8	21	19	2-7	0	4.47
Duke Esper	L	28	8	8	7	0	61.1	95	5	12	8	1-6	0	5.28
Con Lucid	—	23	6	6	5	0	49.0	66	0	26	4	1-5	0	3.67
Bill Hutchison	R	37	6	5	2	0	40.0	55	5	22	5	1-4	0	6.08
Bill Kissinger	R	25	7	4	2	0	31.1	51	2	15	5	0-4	0	11.49
Mike McDermott†	R	34	4	4	1	0	21.1	23	2	19	3	1-2	0	9.28
Percy Coleman	R	20	12	4	2	0	57.1	99	0	32	10	1-2	0	8.16
John Grimes	R	28	3	1	1	0	19.2	24	0	8	4	0-2	0	5.95
Roy Evans†	R	23	3	0	0	0	13.0	33	1	13	4	0-0	0	9.69

»1898 Boston Beaneaters 1st NL 102-47 .685 —

Frank Selee

Player	Gm by Position	B	Age	G	AB	R	H	2B	3B	HR	RBI	BB	SO	SB	Avg	OBP	Slg
Marty Bergen	C117,1B2	—	26	120	446	62	125	16	5	3	60	13	—	9	.280	.302	.359
Fred Tenney	1B117,C1	L	26	117	488	106	160	25	5	0	62	33	—	23	.328	.370	.400
Bobby Lowe	2B145,SS2	R	29	147	559	65	152	11	7	4	94	29	—	12	.272	.311	.338
Jimmy Collins	3B152	R	28	152	597	107	196	35	5	15	111	40	—	12	.328	.377	.479
Herman Long	SS142,2B2	L	32	144	589	99	156	21	10	6	99	39	—	20	.265	.311	.365
Hugh Duffy	OF152,C1,1B1*	R	31	152	568	97	169	13	3	8	108	59	—	29	.298	.365	.373
Chick Stahl	OF125	L	25	125	467	72	144	21	8	3	52	46	—	6	.308	.375	.407
Billy Hamilton	OF110	L	32	110	417	110	154	16	5	3	50	87	—	54	.369	.480	.453
George Yeager	C37,1B17,OF9*	R	25	68	221	37	59	13	1	3	24	16	—	1	.267	.328	.376
Kid Nichols	P50,1B1	S	28	51	158	26	38	3	3	2	23	4	—	0	.241	.268	.335
Ted Lewis	P41,2B1	R	25	42	131	17	37	6	0	0	18	6	—	0	.282	.314	.328
Fred Klobedanz	P35,1B6,OF2	L	27	43	127	12	27	2	1	3	15	1	—	0	.213	.237	.315
General Stafford†	OF35,1B1	R	29	37	123	21	32	2	0	1	8	4	—	3	.260	.289	.301
Jack Stivetts	OF14,1B10,SS4*	R	30	41	111	16	28	1	1	2	16	10	—	1	.252	.314	.333
Charlie Hickman	OF7,P6,1B6	R	22	19	58	4	15	2	0	0	7	1	—	2	.259	.283	.293
Dave Pickett	OF14	—	24	14	43	3	12	1	0	0	3	6	—	2	.279	.380	.302
Bill Keister	2B4,SS4,OF1	L	23	10	30	5	5	2	0	0	4	0	—	0	.167	.167	.233
Stub Smith	SS3	L	21	3	10	1	1	0	0	0	0	0	—	0	.100	.100	.100
Kitty Bransfield	C4,1B1	R	23	5	9	2	2	0	1	0	1	0	—	0	.222	.222	.444
Hi Ladd†	OF1	L	28	1	4	1	1	0	0	0	0	0	—	0	.250	.250	.250

H. Duffy, 1 G at 3B; G. Yeager, 2 G at SS; J. Stivetts, 2 G at P, 2 G at 2B

Pitcher	T	Age	G	GS	CG	ShO	IP	H	HR	BB	SO	W-L	Sv	ERA
Kid Nichols	R	28	50	42	40	5	388.0	316	7	85	138	31-12	4	2.13
Vic Willis	R	22	41	38	29	1	311.0	264	5	148	160	25-13	0	2.84
Ted Lewis	R	25	41	33	29	1	313.1	267	9	109	72	26-8	2	2.90
Fred Klobedanz	L	27	35	33	25	0	270.2	281	13	99	51	19-10	0	3.89
Charlie Hickman	R	22	6	3	3	1	33.0	22	0	13	9	1-2	2	2.18
Mike Sullivan	—	31	3	2	0	0	12.0	19	1	9	1	0-1	0	12.00
Jack Stivetts	R	30	2	1	1	0	12.0	17	2	7	1	0-1	0	8.25

1898 Baltimore Orioles 2nd NL 96-53 .644 6.0 GB

Ned Hanlon

Player	Gm by Position	B	Age	G	AB	R	H	2B	3B	HR	RBI	BB	SO	SB	Avg	OBP	Slg
Wilbert Robinson	C77	R	35	79	289	29	80	12	2	0	38	16	—	3	.277	.317	.332
Dan McGann	1B145	S	26	145	535	99	161	18	8	5	106	53	—	33	.301	.404	.393
Gene DeMontreville	2B123,SS28	R	24	151	567	93	186	19	2	0	86	52	—	49	.328	.394	.369
John McGraw	3B137,OF3	L	25	143	515	143	176	8	10	0	53	112	—	43	.342	.475	.396
Hughie Jennings	SS115,2B27,OF1	R	29	143	534	135	175	25	11	1	87	78	—	28	.328	.454	.421
Willie Keeler	OF128,3B1	L	26	129	561	126	216	7	2	1	44	31	—	28	.385	.420	.410
Joe Kelley	OF122,3B2	R	26	124	464	71	149	18	15	2	110	56	—	24	.321	.398	.438
Ducky Holmes†	OF113	L	29	113	442	54	126	10	9	1	64	23	—	25	.285	.333	.355
Boileryard Clarke	C70,1B10	R	29	82	285	26	69	5	2	0	27	4	—	2	.242	.289	.274
Jim Hughes	P38,OF15	R	24	52	164	23	37	7	4	2	20	12	—	2	.226	.278	.354
Jake Stenzel†	OF35	R	31	35	138	33	35	5	2	0	22	12	—	4	.254	.340	.319
Steve Brodie†	OF23	L	29	23	98	12	30	3	2	0	19	5	—	3	.306	.346	.378
Al Maul	P28,OF1	R	32	29	93	21	19	3	2	0	10	16	—	1	.204	.333	.280
Frank Kitson	P17,OF11	L	28	31	86	13	27	1	3	0	16	5	—	2	.314	.359	.395
Art Ball	3B15,SS14,2B2*	—	22	32	81	7	15	2	0	0	8	7	—	2	.185	.258	.210
Tom O'Brien†	OF16	—	25	18	60	9	13	0	0	0	14	10	—	0	.217	.338	.217
Joe Quinn†	3B8,2B1,OF1	R	33	12	32	5	8	1	0	0	5	1	—	0	.250	.273	.281
Bill Hoffer†	P4,OF4	R	27	8	24	2	5	1	0	0	4	4	—	0	.208	.321	.250
Frank Bowerman†	C4	R	29	5	16	5	7	1	0	0	1	2	—	1	.438	.526	.500
Mike Heydon	C3	L	23	3	9	2	1	0	0	0	1	2	—	0	.111	.333	.111
Henry Wilson	C1	—	21	1	2	0	0	0	0	0	0	1	—	0	.000	.333	.000

A. Ball, 1 G at OF

Pitcher	T	Age	G	GS	CG	ShO	IP	H	HR	BB	SO	W-L	Sv	ERA
Doc McJames	R	24	45	42	40	2	374.0	327	5	113	178	27-15	0	2.36
Jim Hughes	R	24	38	35	31	5	300.2	268	4	100	81	23-12	0	3.20
Jerry Nops	L	23	33	29	23	2	235.0	241	5	78	91	16-9	0	3.56
Al Maul	R	32	28	28	26	1	239.2	207	3	49	31	20-7	0	2.10
Frank Kitson	R	28	17	13	13	1	119.1	123	0	35	32	8-5	0	3.24
Bill Hoffer†	R	27	4	4	4	0	34.1	62	0	16	5	0-4	0	7.34
Arlie Pond	R	26	3	2	1	1	20.0	8	0	9	4	1-1	0	0.45

1898 Cincinnati Reds 3rd NL 92-60 .605 11.5 GB

Buck Ewing

Player	Gm by Position	B	Age	G	AB	R	H	2B	3B	HR	RBI	BB	SO	SB	Avg	OBP	Slg
Heinie Peitz	C101	R	27	105	330	49	90	15	5	1	43	35	—	9	.273	.348	.358
Jake Beckley	1B118	L	30	118	459	86	135	20	12	4	72	28	—	6	.294	.348	.416
Bid McPhee	2B130,OF3	R	38	133	486	72	121	26	9	1	60	66	—	21	.249	.341	.346
Charlie Irwin	3B136	L	29	136	501	77	120	14	5	3	55	31	—	18	.240	.297	.305
Tommy Corcoran	SS153	R	29	153	619	80	155	28	15	2	87	26	—	19	.250	.283	.354
Dusty Miller	OF152	L	29	152	586	99	175	24	12	3	90	38	—	32	.299	.351	.396
Elmer Smith	OF123,P1	L	30	123	486	79	166	21	10	1	66	69	—	20	.342	.425	.432
Algie McBride	OF120	L	29	120	486	94	147	14	12	2	43	51	—	16	.302	.383	.393
Harry Steinfeldt	2B31,OF29,3B22*	R	20	88	308	47	91	18	6	0	43	27	—	9	.295	.354	.393
Farmer Vaughn	1B39,C33	R	34	78	275	35	84	12	4	1	46	11	—	4	.305	.339	.389
Ted Breitenstein	P39,OF2	L	29	41	121	16	26	2	1	0	17	16	—	0	.215	.307	.248
Bob Wood	C29,1B1,OF1	R	32	39	109	14	30	6	0	0	16	9	—	1	.275	.331	.330
Bug Holliday	OF28	R	31	30	106	21	25	2	1	0	7	14	—	5	.236	.325	.274
Herm McFarland	OF17	L	28	19	64	10	18	1	3	0	11	7	—	3	.281	.361	.391

H. Steinfeldt, 5 G at SS, 4 G at 1B

Pitcher	T	Age	G	GS	CG	ShO	IP	H	HR	BB	SO	W-L	Sv	ERA
Pink Hawley	R	25	43	37	32	3	331.0	357	5	91	69	27-11	0	3.37
Ted Breitenstein	L	29	39	37	32	3	315.2	313	2	123	68	20-14	0	3.42
Bill Hill	L	23	33	32	26	2	262.0	261	3	119	75	13-14	0	3.98
Frank Dwyer	R	30	31	28	24	0	240.0	257	3	42	29	16-10	0	3.04
Bill Dammann	L	25	35	22	16	2	224.2	277	3	67	51	16-10	2	3.61
Percy Coleman	R	21	1	1	1	0	9.0	13	0	3	2	0-1	0	3.00
Jot Goar	R	28	1	0	0	0	2.0	4	0	1	0	0-0	0	9.00
Elmer Smith	L	30	1	0	0	0	1.0	2	0	3	0	0-0	0	18.00

1898 Chicago Orphans 4th NL 85-65 .567 17.5 GB

Tom Burns

Player	Gm by Position	B	Age	G	AB	R	H	2B	3B	HR	RBI	BB	SO	SB	Avg	OBP	Slg
Tim Donahue	C122	L	28	122	396	52	87	12	3	0	39	49	—	17	.220	.318	.265
Bill Everitt	1B149	L	29	149	596	102	190	15	6	0	69	53	—	28	.319	.377	.364
Jim Connor	2B138	R	35	138	505	51	114	9	9	0	67	42	—	11	.226	.289	.279
Barry McCormick	3B136,2B1,SS1	—	23	137	530	76	131	15	9	2	78	47	—	15	.247	.314	.321
Bill Dahlen	SS142	R	28	142	521	96	151	35	8	1	79	58	—	27	.290	.385	.393
Jimmy Ryan	OF144	R	35	144	572	122	185	32	13	4	79	73	—	29	.323	.405	.446
Bill Lange	OF111,1B2	R	27	113	442	79	141	16	11	5	69	36	—	22	.319	.377	.439
Sam Mertes	OF60,SS14,2B4*	R	25	83	269	45	80	4	8	1	47	34	—	27	.297	.388	.383
Walter Thornton	OF34,P28	L	23	62	210	34	62	5	2	0	14	22	—	8	.295	.362	.338
Danny Green	OF47	L	21	47	188	26	59	4	3	4	27	7	—	12	.314	.342	.431
Nixey Callahan	P31,OF9,1B1*	R	24	43	164	27	43	7	5	0	22	4	—	3	.262	.280	.366
Frank Isbell	OF27,P13,2B3*	L	22	45	159	17	37	4	0	0	8	3	—	3	.233	.252	.258
Walt Woods	P27,OF11,2B6*	R	23	48	154	16	27	1	0	0	8	4	—	3	.175	.201	.182
Frank Chance	C33,OF17,1B3	R	20	53	147	32	41	4	3	1	14	7	—	7	.279	.338	.367
Matt Kilroy	P13,OF12	L	32	26	96	20	22	4	1	0	10	13	—	0	.229	.321	.292
Harry Wolverton	3B13	L	24	13	49	4	16	1	0	0	2	1	—	1	.327	.353	.347
Art Nichols	C14	R	26	14	42	7	12	1	0	0	6	4	—	6	.286	.388	.310
Frank Martin	2B1	—	19	1	4	0	0	0	0	0	0	0	—	0	.000	.000	.000
Henry Clarke	P1,OF1	R	22	2	4	0	1	0	0	0	0	1	—	0	.250	.400	.250

S. Mertes, 2 G at 1B; N. Callahan, 1 G at 2B, 1 G at SS; F. Isbell, 3 G at 3B, 2 G at SS, 1 G at 1B; W. Woods, 3 G at 3B, 3 G at SS

Pitcher	T	Age	G	GS	CG	ShO	IP	H	HR	BB	SO	W-L	Sv	ERA
Clark Griffith	R	28	38	38	36	4	325.2	305	1	64	97	24-10	0	1.88
Nixey Callahan	R	24	31	31	30	2	274.1	267	2	71	73	20-10	0	2.46
Walter Thornton	L	23	28	25	21	2	215.1	226	4	56	56	13-10	0	3.34
Walt Woods	R	23	27	22	18	3	215.0	224	7	59	26	9-13	0	3.14
Matt Kilroy	L	32	13	11	10	0	100.1	119	2	30	18	6-7	0	4.31
Frank Isbell	R	22	13	9	7	0	81.0	86	0	42	16	4-7	0	3.56
Jack Taylor	R	24	5	5	5	0	41.0	32	0	10	11	5-0	0	2.20
Buttons Briggs	R	22	4	4	3	0	30.0	38	0	10	14	1-3	0	5.70
Bill Phyle	R	23	3	3	3	2	23.0	24	0	6	4	2-1	0	0.78
Danny Friend	L	25	2	2	2	0	17.0	20	1	10	4	0-2	0	5.29
John Katoll	R	26	2	1	1	0	11.0	8	0	1	3	0-1	0	0.82
Henry Clarke	R	22	1	1	1	0	9.0	8	0	5	1	1-0	0	2.00

1898 Cleveland Spiders 5th NL 81-68 .544 21.0 GB

Patsy Tebeau

Player	Gm by Position	B	Age	G	AB	R	H	2B	3B	HR	RBI	BB	SO	SB	Avg	OBP	Slg
Lou Criger	C82	R	26	84	287	43	80	13	4	1	32	40	—	2	.279	.377	.362
Patsy Tebeau	1B91,2B34,SS7*	R	33	131	477	53	123	11	4	1	63	53	—	5	.258	.341	.304
Cupid Childs	2B110	L	30	110	413	90	119	9	4	1	31	69	—	9	.288	.395	.337
Bobby Wallace	3B141,2B13	R	24	154	593	81	160	25	13	3	99	63	—	7	.270	.344	.371
Ed McKean	SS151	R	34	151	604	89	172	23	1	9	94	56	—	11	.285	.346	.371
Jesse Burkett	OF150	L	29	150	624	114	213	18	9	0	42	69	—	19	.341	.415	.399
Harry Blake	OF136,1B2	R	24	136	474	65	116	18	7	0	58	69	—	12	.245	.342	.312
Jimmy McAleer	OF104,2B2	R	33	106	366	47	87	3	0	0	48	46	—	7	.238	.331	.246
Jack O'Connor	1B69,C48,OF15	R	29	131	478	50	119	17	4	1	56	26	—	8	.249	.291	.308
Zeke Wilson	P33,OF3	R	28	37	118	11	21	2	1	0	9	5	—	0	.178	.224	.212
Emmett Heidrick	OF19	L	21	19	76	10	23	2	2	0	8	3	—	3	.303	.329	.382
Louis Sockalexis	OF16	L	26	21	67	11	15	2	0	0	10	1	—	0	.224	.246	.254
Chief Zimmer	C19	R	37	20	63	5	15	2	0	0	4	5	—	2	.238	.304	.270
Sport McAllister	P9,OF8	S	23	17	57	8	13	3	1	0	9	5	—	0	.228	.290	.316
Fred Frank	OF17	—	24	17	53	3	11	1	1	0	3	4	—	1	.208	.276	.264
Jimmy Burke	3B13	R	23	13	38	1	4	1	0	0	1	2	—	1	.105	.150	.132
O. Schreckengost	C9	R	23	10	35	5	11	2	3	0	10	0	—	1	.314	.314	.543
Ed Beecher	OF8	—	22	8	25	1	5	2	0	0	0	0	—	0	.200	.200	.280

P. Tebeau, 3 G at 3B

Pitcher	T	Age	G	GS	CG	ShO	IP	H	HR	BB	SO	W-L	Sv	ERA
Cy Young	R	31	46	41	40	1	377.2	387	6	41	101	25-13	0	2.53
Jack Powell	R	23	42	41	36	6	342.0	328	8	112	93	23-15	0	3.00
Zeke Wilson	R	28	33	31	28	1	254.2	307	4	51	45	13-18	0	3.60
Nig Cuppy	R	28	18	15	13	1	128.0	147	4	25	27	9-8	0	3.30
Cowboy Jones	L	23	9	9	7	0	72.0	76	0	29	26	4-4	0	3.00
Sport McAllister	R	23	9	7	6	0	65.1	73	2	23	9	3-4	0	4.55
Chick Fraser†	R	27	6	6	6	0	42.0	49	2	12	19	2-3	0	5.57
Frank Bates	R	—	4	4	4	0	29.0	30	0	11	5	2-1	0	3.10
Pete McBride	R	22	1	1	1	0	7.0	9	0	4	6	0-1	0	6.43
George Kelb	L	27	3	1	1	0	16.1	23	0	1	8	0-1	0	4.41

1898 Philadelphia Phillies 6th NL 78-71 .523 24.0 GB

George Stallings (19-27)/Bill Shettsline (59-44)

Player	Gm by Position	B	Age	G	AB	R	H	2B	3B	HR	RBI	BB	SO	SB	Avg	OBP	Slg
Ed McFarland	C121	R	23	121	429	65	121	21	5	3	71	44	—	4	.282	.352	.375
Klondike Douglass	1B146	L	26	146	582	105	150	26	4	2	48	55	—	18	.258	.333	.326
Nap Lajoie	2B146,1B1	R	23	147	608	113	197	43	11	6	127	21	—	25	.324	.354	.461
Billy Lauder	3B97	R	24	97	361	42	95	14	7	2	67	19	—	6	.263	.300	.357
Monte Cross	SS149	R	28	149	525	68	135	25	5	1	50	55	—	20	.257	.337	.330
Duff Cooley	OF149	L	25	149	629	123	196	24	12	4	55	48	—	17	.312	.364	.407
Ed Delahanty	OF144	R	30	144	548	115	183	36	9	4	92	77	—	58	.334	.426	.454
Elmer Flick	OF133	L	22	134	453	84	137	16	13	8	81	86	—	23	.302	.430	.448
Al Orth	P32,OF1	L	25	39	123	17	36	6	4	1	14	3	—	1	.293	.310	.431
Ed Abbaticchio	3B20,2B4,OF1	R	21	25	92	9	21	4	0	0	14	7	—	4	.228	.290	.272
Morgan Murphy†	C25	R	31	25	86	6	17	3	0	0	11	6	—	0	.198	.258	.233
Billy Nash	3B20	R	33	20	70	9	17	2	1	0	9	11	—	0	.243	.346	.300
Sam Thompson	OF14	L	38	14	63	14	22	5	3	1	15	4	—	2	.349	.388	.571
Dave Fultz	OF14,2B3,SS1	R	23	19	55	7	10	2	2	0	5	6	—	1	.182	.262	.291
Kid Elberfeld	3B14	R	23	14	38	1	9	4	0	0	7	5	—	0	.237	.420	.342
Newt Fisher	C8,3B1	R	27	9	26	0	3	1	0	0	0	0	—	0	.115	.148	.154
Jack Boyle	1B4,C3	R	32	6	22	0	2	0	1	0	3	1	—	0	.091	.130	.182
George Stallings		R	30	1	0	1	0	0	0	0	0	0	—	0	—	—	—

Pitcher	T	Age	G	GS	CG	ShO	IP	H	HR	BB	SO	W-L	Sv	ERA
Wiley Piatt	L	23	39	37	33	6	306.0	285	2	97	121	24-14	0	3.18
Red Donahue	R	25	35	35	33	1	284.1	327	7	80	57	16-17	0	3.55
Al Orth	R	25	32	28	25	1	250.0	290	2	53	52	15-13	0	3.02
Jack Fifield	R	26	21	21	18	2	171.1	170	2	60	31	11-9	0	3.31
George Wheeler	—	28	15	13	10	0	112.1	155	1	36	20	6-8	0	4.17
Davey Dunkle	R	25	12	7	4	0	68.1	83	1	38	21	1-4	0	6.98
Bill Duggleby	R	24	9	5	4	0	54.0	70	4	18	12	3-3	0	5.50
Bert Conn	R	18	1	1	0	0	7.0	13	1	2	3	0-1	0	6.43
Ed Murphy	R	21	7	3	2	0	30.0	41	3	10	8	1-2	0	5.10
Bob Becker	L	22	1	0	0	0	5.0	6	0	5	0	0-0	0	10.80

1898 New York Giants 7th NL 77-73 .513 25.5 GB

Bill Joyce (22-21)/Cap Anson (9-13)/Bill Joyce (46-39)

Player	Gm by Position	B	Age	G	AB	R	H	2B	3B	HR	RBI	BB	SO	SB	Avg	OBP	Slg
John Warner	C109,OF1	L	25	110	373	40	96	14	5	0	42	22	—	9	.257	.316	.322
Bill Joyce	1B130,3B14,2B2	L	32	145	508	91	131	20	9	10	91	88	—	34	.258	.386	.392
Kid Gleason	2B144,SS6	S	31	150	570	78	126	8	5	0	62	39	—	21	.221	.278	.253
Fred Hartman	3B123	R	30	123	475	57	129	16	11	2	88	25	—	11	.272	.313	.364
George Davis	SS121	S	27	121	486	80	149	20	5	2	86	32	—	26	.307	.351	.381
George Van Haltren	OF156	L	32	156	654	129	204	28	16	2	68	59	—	36	.312	.372	.413
Mike Tiernan	OF103	L	31	103	415	90	116	15	11	5	49	43	—	19	.280	.357	.405
Jack Doyle†	OF38,1B24,SS15*	R	28	82	297	42	84	15	3	1	43	12	—	14	.283	.317	.364
Cy Seymour	P45,OF35,2B1	L	25	80	297	41	82	5	2	4	23	9	—	8	.276	.300	.347
Mike Grady	C57,OF30,1B7*	R	28	93	287	64	85	19	5	3	49	38	—	20	.296	.399	.429
Charlie Gettig	OF21,P17,2B12*	R	27	64	196	30	49	6	2	0	26	15	—	5	.250	.310	.301
Amos Rusie	P37,1B1,OF1	R	27	41	138	23	29	2	4	0	8	1	—	2	.210	.216	.283
Walt Wilmot	OF34	S	34	35	138	16	33	4	2	2	22	9	—	4	.239	.286	.341
Tom McCreery†	OF35	S	23	35	121	15	24	4	3	1	17	19	—	3	.198	.307	.306
Pop Foster	OF21,3B10,SS2	R	20	32	112	10	30	6	1	0	9	0	—	0	.268	.268	.339
Tacks Latimer	C4,OF2	R	20	5	17	1	5	1	0	0	1	0	—	0	.294	.294	.353
John Puhl	3B2	—	21	2	9	1	2	0	0	0	1	0	—	0	.222	.222	.222
Joe Regan	OF2	R	25	2	5	1	1	0	0	0	2	0	—	0	.200	.200	.200
Jack Gilbert†	OF1	—	22	1	4	0	1	0	0	0	0	0	—	1	.250	.250	.250
Ed Glenn†	SS2	R	22	2	4	1	1	0	0	0	0	3	—	1	.250	.571	.250
Parke Wilson	OF1	R	30	1	4	0	0	0	0	0	0	0	—	0	.000	.000	.000
Dave Zearfoss	C1	—	30	1	1	0	1	0	0	0	0	0	—	0	1.000	1.000	1.000

J. Doyle, 5 G at 3B, 2 G at C; M. Grady, 3 G at SS; C. Gettig, 9 G at SS, 4 G at 3B, 2 G at 1B, 1 G at C

Pitcher	T	Age	G	GS	CG	ShO	IP	H	HR	BB	SO	W-L	Sv	ERA
Cy Seymour	L	25	45	43	39	4	356.2	313	4	213	239	25-19	0	3.18
Jouett Meekin	R	31	38	37	34	1	320.0	329	9	108	82	16-18	0	3.77
Amos Rusie	R	27	37	36	33	4	300.0	288	6	103	114	20-11	1	3.03
Ed Doheny	L	24	28	27	23	0	213.0	238	1	101	96	7-19	0	3.68
Bill Carrick	R	24	5	4	4	0	39.2	39	0	21	10	3-1	0	3.40
Jock Menefee	R	30	1	1	1	0	9.1	11	0	2	3	0-1	0	4.82
Charlie Gettig	—	27	17	8	7	0	115.0	141	1	39	14	6-3	0	3.83

1898 Pittsburgh Pirates 8th NL 72-76 .486 29.5 GB

Bill Watkins

Player	Gm by Position	B	Age	G	AB	R	H	2B	3B	HR	RBI	BB	SO	SB	Avg	OBP	Slg
Pop Schriver	C92,1B1	R	32	95	315	25	72	15	3	0	32	23	—	0	.229	.287	.295
Willie Clark	1B57	L	25	57	209	29	64	9	7	1	31	22	—	0	.306	.378	.431
Dick Padden	2B128	R	27	128	463	61	119	7	6	2	43	35	—	11	.257	.335	.311
Bill Grey	3B137	—	27	137	528	56	121	17	5	0	67	28	—	5	.229	.283	.280
Bones Ely	SS148	R	35	148	519	49	110	14	5	2	44	24	—	6	.212	.247	.270
Patsy Donovan	OF147	L	33	147	610	112	184	16	9	0	37	34	—	41	.302	.346	.357
Jack McCarthy	OF137	L	29	137	537	75	155	13	12	4	78	34	—	7	.289	.336	.380
Tom O'Brien†	OF69,1B21,3B8*	—	25	107	413	53	107	10	8	1	45	25	—	13	.259	.318	.329
Frank Bowerman†	C59,1B9	R	29	69	241	17	66	6	3	0	29	7	—	4	.274	.297	.324
Harry Davis†	1B53,OF6	R	24	58	222	31	65	9	13	1	24	12	—	7	.293	.332	.464
Tom McCreery†	OF51	S	23	53	190	33	59	5	7	2	20	26	—	3	.311	.394	.442
Steve Brodie†	OF42	L	29	42	156	15	41	5	0	0	21	6	—	3	.263	.303	.295
Jesse Tannehill	P43,OF7	S	23	60	152	25	44	9	3	1	17	7	—	4	.289	.321	.408
Jim Gardner	P25,3B8,2B1	—	23	35	91	8	14	0	0	0	3	14	—	1	.154	.274	.154
Bill Eagan	2B17	—	29	19	61	14	20	2	3	0	5	8	—	1	.328	.453	.459
John Ganzel	1B11	R	24	15	45	5	6	0	0	0	2	4	—	0	.133	.220	.133
Morgan Murphy†	C5	R	31	5	16	0	2	0	0	0	2	1	—	0	.125	.176	.125
Fred Lake	1B3	R	31	5	13	1	1	0	0	0	1	2	—	0	.077	.200	.077
Joe Rickert	OF2	R	21	2	6	0	1	0	0	0	0	0	—	0	.167	.167	.167
Hi Ladd†		L	28	1	1	0	0	0	0	0	0	0	—	0	.000	.000	.000

T. O'Brien, 7 G at 2B, 4 G at SS

Pitcher	T	Age	G	GS	CG	ShO	IP	H	HR	BB	SO	W-L	Sv	ERA
Jesse Tannehill	L	23	43	38	34	5	326.2	338	2	63	93	25-13	2	2.95
Billy Rhines	R	29	31	29	27	2	258.0	289	0	61	48	12-16	0	3.52
Frank Killen†	L	27	23	23	17	0	177.2	201	3	41	48	10-11	0	3.75
Jim Gardner	R	23	25	22	19	1	185.1	179	3	48	41	10-13	0	3.21
Bill Hart	R	32	16	15	13	1	125.0	141	4	44	19	5-9	1	4.82
Charlie Hastings	—	27	19	13	12	0	137.1	142	2	52	40	4-10	0	3.41
Jack Cronin	R	24	4	4	2	1	28.0	35	0	8	9	2-2	0	3.54
Sam Leever	R	26	5	3	2	0	33.0	26	0	5	15	1-0	0	2.45
Bill Hoffer†	R	27	4	3	3	0	31.0	26	0	15	11	3-0	0	1.74
Zeke Rosebraugh	L	27	4	2	2	0	21.2	23	0	9	6	0-2	0	3.32

1898 Louisville Colonels 9th NL 70-81 .464 33.0 GB

Fred Clarke

Player	Gm by Position	B	Age	G	AB	R	H	2B	3B	HR	RBI	BB	SO	SB	Avg	OBP	Slg
Malachi Kittridge	C86	R	28	86	287	27	70	8	5	1	31	15	—	9	.244	.281	.317
Honus Wagner	1B75,3B65,2B10	R	24	151	588	80	176	29	3	10	105	31	—	27	.299	.341	.410
Claude Ritchey	SS80,2B71	S	24	151	551	65	140	10	4	5	51	46	—	19	.254	.322	.314
Billy Clingman	3B79,SS74,2B1*	S	28	154	538	65	138	12	6	0	50	51	—	15	.257	.327	.301
Fred Clarke	OF149	L	25	149	599	116	184	23	12	3	47	48	—	40	.307	.373	.401
Dummy Hoy	OF148	L	36	148	582	104	177	15	16	6	66	49	—	37	.304	.367	.416
Charlie Dexter	OF95,2B8,C7	R	22	112	421	76	132	13	5	1	66	26	—	44	.314	.363	.375
General Stafford†	2B28,OF22,3B1	R	29	49	181	26	54	3	0	1	25	19	—	7	.298	.368	.331
George Decker†	1B32,OF6	L	29	42	148	27	44	4	3	0	19	9	—	9	.297	.342	.365
Harry Davis†	1B34,2B2,OF1	R	24	37	138	18	30	5	2	1	16	7	—	6	.217	.255	.304
Heinie Smith	2B33	R	26	35	121	14	23	4	0	0	13	6	—	6	.190	.246	.223
Bill Wilson	C28,1B1	—	30	29	102	5	17	1	2	1	13	5	—	3	.167	.213	.245
Mike Powers	C22,1B6,OF1	R	27	34	99	13	27	4	3	1	19	5	—	1	.273	.308	.404
Doc Nance	OF22	R	21	22	76	13	24	5	0	1	16	12	—	2	.316	.416	.421
Topsy Hartsel	OF21	L	24	22	71	11	23	0	0	0	9	11	—	2	.324	.422	.324
Cooney Snyder	C17	—	—	17	61	4	10	0	0	0	6	3	—	0	.164	.215	.164
Scoops Carey	1B8	R	27	8	32	1	6	1	1	0	1	1	—	0	.188	.212	.281
Billy Taylor	3B7,2B1	—	26	9	24	2	6	1	0	0	2	1	—	1	.250	.308	.292
Josh Clarke	OF5	L	19	6	18	0	3	0	0	0	0	1	—	0	.167	.211	.167
Tom Stouch	2B4	R	27	4	16	4	5	1	0	0	6	1	—	0	.313	.353	.375
John Richter	3B3	—	25	3	13	1	2	0	0	0	0	0	—	0	.154	.154	.154
Tommy Leach	3B3,2B1	R	20	3	10	0	1	0	0	0	0	0	—	0	.100	.100	.100

B. Clingman, 1 G at OF

Pitcher	T	Age	G	GS	CG	ShO	IP	H	HR	BB	SO	W-L	Sv	ERA
Bert Cunningham	R	32	44	42	41	0	362.0	387	8	65	34	28-15	0	3.16
Bill Magee	R	23	38	33	29	3	295.1	294	8	129	55	16-15	0	4.05
Pete Dowling	L	—	36	32	30	0	285.2	284	7	120	84	13-20	0	4.16
Chick Fraser†	R	27	26	26	20	1	203.0	230	4	100	58	7-17	0	5.32
Red Ehret	R	29	12	10	9	0	89.0	130	3	20	20	3-7	0	5.76
Nick Altrock	L	21	11	7	6	0	70.0	89	2	21	13	3-3	0	4.50
Frank Todd	L	28	4	2	0	0	11.0	23	0	8	5	0-2	0	13.91
Lou Mahaffey	—	24	1	1	1	0	9.0	10	0	5	1	0-1	0	3.00
Dad Clarke	R	33	1	1	1	0	9.0	10	1	2	1	0-1	0	5.00

1898 Brooklyn Bridegrooms 10th NL 54-91 .372 46.0 GB

Billy Barnie (15-20)/Mike Griffin (1-3)/Charlie Ebbets (38-68)

Player	Gm by Position	B	Age	G	AB	R	H	2B	3B	HR	RBI	BB	SO	SB	Avg	OBP	Slg
Jack Ryan	C84,3B4,1B1	R	29	87	301	39	57	11	4	0	24	15	—	5	.189	.233	.252
Candy LaChance	1B74,SS48,OF13	S	28	136	526	62	130	23	7	5	65	31	—	23	.247	.299	.346
Bill Hallman	2B124,3B10	R	31	134	509	57	124	10	7	2	63	29	—	9	.244	.291	.303
Billy Shindle	3B120	R	34	120	466	50	105	10	3	1	41	10	—	3	.225	.249	.266
George Magoon	SS93	R	23	93	343	35	77	7	0	1	39	30	—	7	.224	.293	.254
Fielder Jones	OF144,SS2	L	26	146	596	89	181	15	9	1	69	46	—	36	.304	.362	.364
Mike Griffin	OF134	L	33	134	537	88	161	18	6	2	40	60	—	15	.300	.379	.367
Jimmy Sheckard	OF105,3B1	L	19	105	408	51	113	17	9	4	64	37	—	8	.277	.349	.392
Tommy Tucker†	1B73	S	34	73	283	35	79	9	4	1	34	12	—	1	.279	.325	.350
Aleck Smith	OF26,C20,2B2*	—	27	52	199	25	52	6	5	0	23	3	—	7	.261	.276	.342
John Grim	C52	R	30	52	178	17	50	5	1	0	11	8	—	1	.281	.323	.320
Jack Dunn	P41,SS4,OF4*	R	25	51	167	21	41	0	1	0	19	7	—	3	.246	.280	.257
Joe Yeager	P36,OF4,SS2*	R	22	43	134	12	23	5	1	0	15	7	—	1	.172	.218	.224
John Anderson†	OF22,1B2	S	24	25	90	12	22	5	4	0	10	6	—	2	.244	.306	.389
Tom Daly	2B23	S	32	23	73	11	24	3	1	0	11	14	—	6	.329	.443	.397
Ralph Miller	P23,OF1	R	25	24	62	6	12	1	0	0	6	4	—	1	.194	.265	.210
Butts Wagner†	3B11	R	26	11	38	2	9	1	1	0	3	2	—	0	.237	.275	.316

A. Smith, 2 G at 3B, 1 G at 1B; J. Dunn, 2 G at 3B; J. Yeager, 1 G at 2B

Pitcher	T	Age	G	GS	CG	ShO	IP	H	HR	BB	SO	W-L	Sv	ERA
Brickyard Kennedy	R	30	40	39	38	0	339.1	360	12	123	73	16-22	0	3.37
Jack Dunn	R	25	41	37	31	0	322.2	352	10	82	66	16-21	0	3.60
Joe Yeager	R	22	36	33	32	0	291.1	333	4	80	70	12-22	0	3.65
Ralph Miller	R	25	23	21	16	0	151.2	161	4	86	43	4-14	0	5.34
Kit McKenna	R	25	14	9	7	0	100.2	118	4	57	27	2-6	0	5.63
Ed Stein	R	28	3	2	2	0	23.0	39	0	9	6	0-2	0	5.48
Harry Howell	R	21	2	2	2	0	18.0	15	0	11	2	2-0	0	5.00
Welcome Gaston	L	25	2	2	2	0	16.0	17	0	9	0	1-1	0	2.81
Lefty Hopper	L	24	2	2	2	0	11.0	14	0	5	5	0-2	0	4.91
Elmer Horton	—	28	1	1	1	0	9.0	16	0	6	0	0-1	0	10.00
Harley Payne	L	30	1	1	1	0	9.0	11	0	3	2	1-0	0	4.00
F.C. Hansford	L	—	1	0	0	0	7.0	10	0	5	0	0-0	0	3.86

1898 Washington Senators 11th NL 51-101 .336 52.5 GB

Tom Brown (12-26)/Jack Doyle (8-9)/Deacon McGuire (21-47)/Arthur Irwin (10-19)

Player	Gm by Position	B	Age	G	AB	R	H	2B	3B	HR	RBI	BB	SO	SB	Avg	OBP	Slg
Deacon McGuire	C93,1B37	R	34	131	489	59	131	18	3	1	57	24	—	10	.268	.310	.323
Jack Doyle†	1B38,2B5	R	28	43	177	26	54	2	2	2	26	7	—	9	.305	.335	.373
Heinie Reitz	2B132	L	31	132	489	62	148	20	2	2	47	32	—	11	.303	.357	.364
Jud Smith	3B47,SS10,1B7*	R	29	66	234	33	71	7	5	3	28	22	—	11	.303	.378	.415
Zeke Wrigley	SS97,2B11,OF3*	—	24	111	400	50	98	9	10	2	39	20	—	10	.245	.283	.333
Jake Gettman	OF139,1B3	S	21	142	567	75	157	16	5	5	47	29	—	32	.277	.319	.349
Kip Selbach	OF131,SS1	R	26	132	515	88	156	28	11	3	60	64	—	25	.303	.383	.417
John Anderson†	OF93,1B17	S	24	110	430	70	131	28	18	9	71	23	—	18	.305	.357	.516
Duke Farrell	C61,1B28	S	31	99	338	47	106	12	6	1	53	34	—	12	.314	.383	.393
Win Mercer	P33,SS23,OF19*	R	24	80	249	38	80	3	5	2	25	18	—	14	.321	.369	.398
Butts Wagner†	3B39,OF10,SS8*	R	26	63	223	20	50	11	2	1	31	14	—	4	.224	.279	.305
Gus Weyhing	P45,OF1	R	31	46	141	12	25	3	0	0	5	8	—	2	.177	.221	.199
Doc Casey	3B22,SS4,C3	S	28	28	112	13	31	2	0	0	15	3	—	15	.277	.302	.295
Al Myers	3B31	R	34	31	110	14	29	1	4	0	13	13	—	2	.264	.341	.345
Buck Freeman	OF29	L	26	29	107	19	39	2	3	3	21	7	—	2	.364	.424	.523
Wild Bill Donovan	OF20,P17,2B1*	R	21	39	103	11	17	2	3	2	8	4	—	2	.165	.211	.301
Bill Dinneen	P29,OF2	R	22	32	80	10	8	0	1	0	3	9	—	1	.100	.226	.125
Charlie Carr	1B20	R	21	20	73	6	14	2	0	0	4	2	—	2	.192	.213	.219
Frank Gatins	SS17	—	27	17	58	6	13	2	0	0	5	3	—	2	.224	.274	.259
Tom Leahy	3B12,2B3	—	29	15	55	10	10	2	0	0	5	8	—	6	.182	.297	.218
Frank Killen†	P17,OF4	L	27	21	55	7	15	2	0	0	7	12	—	1	.273	.403	.309
Tom Brown	OF15	L	37	16	55	8	9	1	0	0	2	5	—	3	.164	.233	.182
Bob McHale	OF9,1B1,SS1	—	28	11	33	5	6	2	0	0	7	1	—	1	.182	.270	.242
Jim Field	1B5	—	35	5	21	1	2	0	0	0	0	0	—	1	.095	.095	.095
Bill Eagle	OF4	—	20	4	13	0	4	1	0	0	2	0	—	0	.308	.308	.385
Tom Kinslow†	C3,1B1	R	32	3	9	0	1	0	0	0	0	0	—	0	.111	.111	.111
Jack Gilbert†	OF2	—	22	2	5	0	1	0	0	0	1	1	—	1	.200	.429	.200
Ed Glenn†	SS1	R	22	1	4	0	0	0	0	0	0	0	—	0	.000	.000	.000
Mart McQuaid	OF1	—	37	1	4	0	0	0	0	0	0	0	—	0	.000	.000	.000
Harry Davis†	1B1	R	24	1	3	0	0	0	0	0	0	0	—	0	.000	.000	.000

J. Smith, 1 G at 2B; Z. Wrigley, 1 G at 3B; W. Mercer, 5 G at 3B, 1 G at 2B; B. Wagner, 5 G at 2B; W. Donovan, 1 G at SS

Pitcher	T	Age	G	GS	CG	ShO	IP	H	HR	BB	SO	W-L	Sv	ERA
Gus Weyhing	R	31	45	42	39	0	361.0	428	10	84	92	15-26	0	4.51
Win Mercer	R	24	33	30	24	0	233.2	309	3	71	52	12-18	0	4.81
Bill Dinneen	R	22	29	27	22	0	218.1	238	6	88	83	9-16	0	4.00
Frank Killen†	L	27	17	16	15	0	128.1	149	4	29	43	6-9	0	3.58
Cy Swaim	—	24	16	13	9	0	101.1	119	4	28	30	3-11	1	4.26
Roy Evans	R	24	7	6	4	0	50.2	50	0	25	11	3-3	0	3.38
Doc Amole	L	19	7	5	4	0	49.1	83	0	22	11	0-6	0	7.84
Kirtley Baker	R	29	6	5	4	0	47.0	56	1	18	7	2-3	0	3.06
Pop Williams	L	24	2	2	2	0	17.0	32	0	7	3	0-2	0	8.47
Jack Sutthoff	R	25	2	1	0	0	8.1	16	1	8	3	0-0	0	12.96
Charlie Weber	—	29	1	1	0	0	4.0	9	0	1	0	0-1	0	15.75
Wild Bill Donovan	R	21	17	7	6	0	88.0	88	0	69	36	1-6	0	4.30

1898 St. Louis Browns 12th NL 39-111 .260 63.5 GB

Tim Hurst

Player	Gm by Position	B	Age	G	AB	R	H	2B	3B	HR	RBI	BB	SO	SB	Avg	OBP	Slg
Jack Clements	C86	L	33	99	335	39	86	19	5	3	41	21	—	1	.257	.314	.370
George Decker†	1B75	L	29	76	286	26	74	10	0	1	45	20	—	4	.259	.314	.304
Jack Crooks	2B66,3B3,SS2*	R	32	72	225	33	52	4	2	1	20	40	—	3	.231	.359	.280
Lave Cross	3B149,SS2	R	32	151	602	71	191	28	8	3	79	28	—	14	.317	.348	.405
Germany Smith	SS51	R	35	51	157	16	25	2	1	1	9	24	—	1	.159	.275	.204
Dick Harley	OF141	L	25	142	549	74	135	6	5	0	42	34	—	13	.246	.316	.275
Tommy Dowd	OF129,2B11	R	29	139	586	70	143	17	7	0	32	30	—	16	.244	.287	.297
Jake Stenzel†	OF108	R	31	108	404	64	114	15	11	1	33	41	—	21	.282	.367	.381
Joe Quinn†	2B62,SS41,OF1	R	33	103	375	35	94	10	5	0	36	24	—	13	.251	.301	.304
Joe Sugden	C60,OF15,1B8	S	27	89	289	29	73	7	1	0	34	23	—	5	.253	.314	.284
Tommy Tucker†	1B72	S	34	72	252	18	60	7	2	0	20	18	—	1	.238	.319	.282
Jack Taylor	P50,OF2	R	25	54	157	17	38	5	2	1	18	12	—	1	.242	.296	.318
Suter Sullivan	SS23,OF10,2B6*	—	25	42	144	10	32	3	0	0	12	13	—	1	.222	.300	.243
Russ Hall	SS35,3B3,OF1	—	26	39	143	13	35	2	1	0	10	7	—	1	.245	.285	.273
Tuck Turner	OF34	S	25	35	141	20	28	8	0	0	7	14	—	1	.199	.280	.255
Kid Carsey	P20,2B10,OF8	L	27	38	105	8	21	0	1	1	10	10	—	3	.200	.270	.248
Ducky Holmes†	OF22	L	29	23	101	9	24	1	1	0	0	2	—	4	.238	.260	.267
Tom Kinslow†	C14	R	32	14	53	5	15	2	1	0	4	1	—	0	.283	.309	.358
Lou Bierbauer	2B2,3B1,SS1	L	32	4	9	0	0	0	0	0	0	1	—	0	.000	.100	.000
Mike Mahoney	1B2	R	24	2	7	0	0	0	0	0	0	0	—	0	.000	.000	.000
Jim Donnelly	3B1	R	32	1	1	0	1	0	0	0	0	0	—	0	1.000	1.000	1.000

J. Crooks, 1 G at OF; S. Sullivan, 1 G at P, 1 G at 1B

Pitcher	T	Age	G	GS	CG	ShO	IP	H	HR	BB	SO	W-L	Sv	ERA
Jack Taylor	R	25	50	47	42	0	397.1	465	14	83	89	15-29	1	3.90
Willie Sudhoff	R	23	41	38	35	0	315.0	355	11	102	65	11-27	1	4.34
Jim Hughey	R	29	35	33	31	0	283.2	325	2	71	74	7-24	0	3.93
Kid Carsey	R	27	20	13	10	0	123.2	177	2	37	10	2-12	0	6.33
Duke Esper	L	29	10	8	6	0	64.2	86	1	22	14	3-5	0	5.98
Pete Daniels	L	34	10	6	3	0	54.2	62	0	14	13	1-6	0	3.62
Harry Maupin	R	25	2	2	2	0	18.0	22	0	3	3	0-2	0	5.50
Jim Callahan	—	—	2	2	1	0	8.1	18	2	7	2	0-2	0	16.20
Tom Smith	R	26	1	1	1	0	9.0	9	0	5	1	0-1	0	2.00
Joseph Gannon	—	—	1	1	1	0	9.0	13	0	5	2	0-1	0	11.00
George Gillpatrick	—	23	7	3	1	0	35.0	42	0	19	12	0-2	0	6.94
Suter Sullivan	—	25	1	0	0	0	6.0	10	0	4	3	0-0	0	1.50

»1899 Brooklyn Superbas 1st NL 101-47 .682 —

Ned Hanlon

Player	Gm by Position	B	Age	G	AB	R	H	2B	3B	HR	RBI	BB	SO	SB	Avg	OBP	Slg
Duke Farrell†	C78	S	32	80	254	40	76	10	7	2	55	35	—	6	.299	.399	.417
Dan McGann†	1B61	S	27	63	214	49	52	11	4	2	32	21	—	16	.243	.362	.360
Tom Daly	2B141	S	33	141	498	95	156	24	9	5	88	69	—	43	.313	.409	.428
Doc Casey†	3B134	S	29	134	525	75	141	14	8	1	43	25	—	27	.269	.313	.331
Bill Dahlen	SS110,3B11	R	29	121	428	87	121	22	7	4	76	67	—	29	.283	.398	.395
Joe Kelley	OF143	R	27	143	538	108	175	21	14	6	93	70	—	31	.325	.410	.450
Willie Keeler	OF141	L	27	141	570	140	216	12	13	1	61	37	—	45	.379	.425	.451
Fielder Jones	OF96	L	27	102	365	75	104	8	2	2	38	54	—	18	.285	.390	.334
John Anderson	OF76,1B41	S	25	117	439	65	118	18	7	4	92	27	—	25	.269	.317	.369
Hughie Jennings†	1B50,SS12,2B1	R	30	67	216	42	64	3	10	0	40	22	—	18	.296	.409	.403
Deacon McGuire†	C46	R	35	46	157	22	50	12	4	0	23	12	—	4	.318	.385	.446
Jack Dunn	P41,SS1	R	26	43	122	21	30	2	1	0	16	3	—	3	.246	.270	.279
Aleck Smith†	C17	—	28	17	61	6	11	0	1	0	6	2	—	0	.180	.206	.213
Zeke Wrigley†	SS14,3B1	—	25	15	49	4	10	2	2	0	11	3	—	2	.204	.250	.327
Joe Yeager	SS11,P10,3B1*	R	23	23	47	12	9	0	1	0	4	6	—	0	.191	.333	.234
John Grim	C12	R	31	15	47	3	13	1	0	0	7	1	—	0	.277	.320	.298
Erve Beck	2B6,SS2	R	20	8	24	2	4	2	0	0	2	0	—	0	.167	.167	.250
Pete Cassidy†	3B3,SS2	R	26	6	20	2	3	1	0	0	4	1	—	1	.150	.261	.200

J. Yeager, 1 G at OF

Pitcher	T	Age	G	GS	CG	ShO	IP	H	HR	BB	SO	W-L	Sv	ERA
Jim Hughes	R	25	35	35	30	3	291.2	250	6	119	99	28-6	0	2.68
Jack Dunn	R	26	41	34	29	2	299.1	323	8	86	48	23-13	2	3.70
Doc McJames	R	25	37	34	27	1	275.1	295	4	122	105	19-15	1	3.50
Brickyard Kennedy	R	31	40	33	27	2	277.1	297	11	86	55	22-9	2	2.79
Al Maul	R	33	4	4	2	0	26.0	35	1	6	2	2-0	0	4.50
Bill Hill†	L	24	2	1	1	0	11.0	11	0	6	3	1-0	1	0.82
Bill Reidy	R	25	2	1	1	0	7.0	9	0	2	2	1-0	1	2.57
Joe Yeager	R	23	10	4	2	1	47.2	56	1	16	6	2-2	1	4.72
Wild Bill Donovan	R	22	5	2	2	0	25.0	35	0	13	11	1-2	1	4.32
Dan McFarlan†	—	24	1	0	0	0	6.0	6	1	3	0	0-0	0	1.50
Welcome Gaston	L	26	1	0	0	0	3.0	3	0	4	0	0-0	0	3.00

1899 Boston Beaneaters 2nd NL 95-57 .625 8.0 GB

Frank Selee

Player	Gm by Position	B	Age	G	AB	R	H	2B	3B	HR	RBI	BB	SO	SB	Avg	OBP	Slg
Marty Bergen	C72	—	27	72	260	32	67	11	3	1	34	10	—	4	.258	.290	.335
Fred Tenney	1B150	L	27	150	603	115	209	19	17	1	67	63	—	28	.347	.411	.439
Bobby Lowe	2B148,SS4	R	30	152	559	81	152	5	9	4	88	35	—	17	.272	.316	.335
Jimmy Collins	3B151	R	29	151	599	98	166	28	11	5	92	40	—	12	.277	.335	.386
Herman Long	SS143,1B2	L	33	145	578	91	153	30	8	6	100	45	—	20	.265	.321	.375
Chick Stahl	OF148,P1	L	26	148	576	122	202	23	19	7	52	72	—	33	.351	.426	.493
Hugh Duffy	OF147	R	32	147	588	103	164	29	7	5	102	39	—	26	.279	.327	.378
Billy Hamilton	OF81	L	33	84	297	63	92	7	1	1	33	72	—	19	.310	.446	.350
Boileryard Clarke	C60	R	30	60	223	25	50	3	2	2	32	10	—	2	.224	.270	.283
General Stafford†	OF41,2B5,SS5	R	30	55	182	29	55	4	2	3	40	7	—	9	.302	.328	.396
Charlie Frisbee	OF40	S	25	42	152	22	50	4	2	0	20	9	—	10	.329	.374	.382
Billy Sullivan	C22	R	24	22	74	10	20	2	0	2	12	1	—	2	.270	.308	.378
Charlie Hickman	P11,OF7,1B1	R	23	19	63	15	25	2	7	0	15	2	—	1	.397	.433	.651
Charlie Kuhns	3B3,SS3	—	21	7	18	2	5	0	0	0	3	2	—	0	.278	.350	.278
George Yeager	OF2,C1	R	26	3	8	1	1	0	0	0	0	1	—	0	.125	.222	.125
Mike Hickey	2B1	R	27	1	3	0	1	0	0	0	0	0	—	0	.333	.333	.333
Bill Merritt	C1	R	28	1	2	0	0	0	0	0	0	0	—	0	.000	.333	.000

Pitcher	T	Age	G	GS	CG	ShO	IP	H	HR	BB	SO	W-L	Sv	ERA
Vic Willis	R	23	41	38	35	5	342.2	277	6	117	120	27-8	2	2.50
Kid Nichols	R	29	42	37	37	4	343.1	326	11	82	108	21-19	1	2.99
Ted Lewis	R	26	29	25	23	2	234.2	245	10	73	60	17-11	0	3.49
Jouett Meekin†	R	32	13	13	12	0	108.0	111	0	23	23	7-6	0	2.83
Frank Killen†	L	28	12	12	11	0	99.1	108	3	26	23	7-5	0	4.26
Harvey Bailey	L	22	12	11	8	0	86.2	83	7	35	26	6-4	0	3.95
Charlie Hickman	R	23	11	9	5	2	66.1	52	3	40	14	6-0	1	4.48
Fred Klobedanz	L	28	5	5	4	0	33.1	39	2	9	8	1-4	0	4.86
Oscar Streit	L	25	2	1	1	0	14.2	15	1	15	0	1-0	0	6.75
Mike Sullivan	—	32	1	1	1	0	9.0	10	1	4	1	1-0	0	5.00
Billy Ging	R	26	1	1	1	0	8.0	5	0	5	2	1-0	0	1.13
Chick Stahl	L	26	1	0	0	0	2.0	2	0	3	0	0-0	0	9.00

1899 Philadelphia Phillies 3rd NL 94-58 .618 9.0 GB

Bill Shettsline

Player	Gm by Position	B	Age	G	AB	R	H	2B	3B	HR	RBI	BB	SO	SB	Avg	OBP	Slg
Ed McFarland	C94	R	24	96	324	59	108	22	9	2	57	36	—	9	.333	.403	.475
Duff Cooley	1B79,OF14,2B1	L	26	94	406	75	112	15	8	1	31	29	—	15	.276	.330	.360
Nap Lajoie	2B67,OF5	R	24	77	312	70	118	19	9	6	70	12	—	13	.378	.419	.554
Billy Lauder	3B151	R	25	151	583	74	156	17	6	3	90	34	—	15	.268	.310	.333
Monte Cross	SS154	R	29	154	557	85	143	25	6	3	65	56	—	26	.257	.335	.339
Ed Delahanty	OF143	R	31	146	581	135	238	55	9	9	137	55	—	30	.410	.464	.582
Roy Thomas	OF135,1B14	L	25	150	547	137	178	12	4	0	47	115	—	42	.325	.457	.362
Elmer Flick	OF125	L	23	127	485	98	166	22	11	2	98	42	—	31	.342	.407	.445
Pearce Chiles	OF46,1B25,2B16	R	32	97	338	57	108	28	7	2	76	16	—	6	.320	.352	.462
Klondike Douglass	C66,1B4,3B4*	L	27	77	275	26	70	6	6	0	27	10	—	7	.255	.296	.320
Joe Dolan	2B61	—	26	61	222	27	57	6	3	1	30	11	—	3	.257	.298	.324
Billy Goeckel	1B36	R	27	37	141	17	37	3	1	0	16	1	—	6	.262	.283	.298
Chick Fraser	P35,3B3,OF2	R	28	40	117	19	21	4	1	0	11	6	—	2	.179	.226	.231
Al Orth	P21,OF1	L	26	22	62	5	13	3	1	1	5	1	—	2	.210	.222	.339
Red Owens	2B8	R	24	8	21	0	1	0	0	0	1	2	—	0	.048	.130	.048
Harry Croft†	2B2	—	23	2	7	0	1	0	0	0	0	1	—	0	.143	.250	.143
Dave Fultz†	2B1,SS1	R	24	2	5	0	2	0	0	0	0	0	—	1	.400	.400	.400

K. Douglass, 1 G at OF

Pitcher	T	Age	G	GS	CG	ShO	IP	H	HR	BB	SO	W-L	Sv	ERA
Wiley Piatt	L	24	39	38	31	2	305.0	323	6	86	89	23-15	0	3.45
Chick Fraser	R	28	35	33	29	4	270.2	278	1	85	68	21-12	0	3.36
Red Donahue	R	26	35	31	27	4	279.0	292	6	63	51	21-8	0	3.39
Al Orth	R	26	21	15	13	3	144.2	149	0	19	35	14-3	1	2.49
Bill Bernhard	R	28	21	12	10	1	132.1	120	3	36	23	6-6	0	2.65
Jack Fifield†	R	27	14	11	9	1	92.2	110	0	36	8	3-8	1	4.08
Bill Magee†	R	24	9	9	7	0	70.0	82	0	32	4	3-5	0	5.66
George Wheeler	—	29	6	5	3	0	39.0	44	1	13	3	3-1	0	6.00

1899 Baltimore Orioles 4th NL 86-62 .581 15.0 GB

John McGraw

Player	Gm by Position	B	Age	G	AB	R	H	2B	3B	HR	RBI	BB	SO	SB	Avg	OBP	Slg
Wilbert Robinson	C105	R	36	108	356	40	101	15	2	0	47	31	—	5	.284	.344	.337
Candy LaChance	1B125	S	29	125	472	65	145	23	10	1	75	21	—	31	.307	.350	.405
G. DeMontreville†	2B60	R	25	60	240	40	67	13	4	1	36	10	—	21	.279	.313	.379
John McGraw	3B117	L	26	117	399	140	156	13	3	1	33	124	—	73	.391	.547	.446
Bill Keister	SS90,2B46,OF1	L	24	136	523	96	172	22	16	3	73	16	—	33	.329	.368	.449
Jimmy Sheckard	OF146,1B1	L	20	147	536	104	158	18	10	3	75	56	—	77	.295	.380	.382
Ducky Holmes	OF138	L	30	138	553	80	177	31	7	4	66	39	—	50	.320	.381	.423
Steve Brodie	OF137	L	30	137	531	82	164	26	1	3	87	31	—	19	.309	.373	.379
Dave Fultz†	OF31,3B20,2B2*	R	24	57	210	31	62	3	2	0	18	13	—	17	.295	.342	.329
George Magoon†	SS62	R	24	62	207	26	53	8	3	0	31	26	—	7	.256	.353	.324
Pat Crisham	1B26,C22	—	22	53	172	23	50	5	3	0	20	4	—	4	.291	.311	.355
Joe McGinnity	P48,OF2	R	28	50	145	21	28	0	0	0	10	5	—	4	.193	.230	.193
John O'Brien†	2B39	L	28	39	135	14	26	4	0	1	17	15	—	4	.193	.283	.244
Aleck Smith†	C36,OF2,1B1	—	28	41	120	17	46	6	4	0	25	4	—	7	.383	.417	.500
Charlie Harris	3B21,OF3,2B2*	R	21	30	68	16	19	3	0	0	1	3	—	4	.279	.319	.324
Bobby Rothermel	2B5,3B2,SS1	—	28	10	21	1	2	0	0	0	3	1	—	0	.095	.136	.095
Kit McKenna	P8,OF1	—	26	9	17	1	1	1	0	0	0	3	—	0	.059	.238	.118
Hughie Jennings†	2B2	R	30	2	8	2	3	0	2	0	2	0	—	0	.375	.375	.875
Jack Ryan	C2	R	30	2	4	0	2	1	0	0	1	0	—	1	.500	.500	.750

D. Fultz, 1 G at 1B; C. Harris, 1 G at SS

Pitcher	T	Age	G	GS	CG	ShO	IP	H	HR	BB	SO	W-L	Sv	ERA
Joe McGinnity	R	28	48	41	38	4	366.1	358	3	93	74	28-16	2	2.68
Frank Kitson	R	29	40	37	34	3	327.2	329	6	66	75	22-16	0	2.77
Jerry Nops	L	24	33	33	26	2	259.0	296	1	71	60	17-11	0	4.03
Harry Howell	R	22	28	25	21	0	209.1	248	1	69	58	13-8	1	3.91
Bill Hill†	L	24	8	7	6	0	61.0	64	1	18	17	3-4	0	3.25
Kit McKenna	R	26	8	4	4	0	45.0	66	1	19	7	2-3	1	4.60
Ralph Miller	R	26	7	4	3	0	36.0	42	0	14	3	1-3	0	4.50

1899 St. Louis Perfectos 5th NL 84-67 .556 18.5 GB

Patsy Tebeau

Player	Gm by Position	B	Age	G	AB	R	H	2B	3B	HR	RBI	BB	SO	SB	Avg	OBP	Slg
Lou Criger	C75	R	27	77	258	39	66	4	5	2	44	28	—	14	.256	.333	.333
Patsy Tebeau	1B65,SS11,2B1*	R	34	77	281	27	69	10	3	1	26	18	—	5	.246	.303	.313
Cupid Childs	2B125	L	31	125	464	73	123	11	11	1	48	74	—	11	.265	.369	.343
Lave Cross†	3B103	R	33	103	403	61	122	14	5	4	64	17	—	11	.303	.333	.392
Bobby Wallace	SS100,3B52	R	25	151	577	91	170	28	14	12	108	54	—	17	.295	.357	.454
Emmett Heidrick	OF145	L	22	146	591	109	194	21	14	2	82	34	—	55	.328	.368	.421
Jesse Burkett	OF140,2B1	L	30	141	558	116	221	21	8	7	71	67	—	25	.396	.463	.500
Harry Blake	OF87,2B4,C1*	R	25	97	292	50	70	9	4	2	41	43	—	16	.240	.341	.318
Jack O'Connor	C57,1B26	R	30	84	289	33	73	5	6	0	43	15	—	7	.253	.299	.311
O. Schreckengost†	1B42,C25,2B1*	R	24	72	277	42	77	12	2	2	37	15	—	14	.278	.317	.357
Ed McKean	SS42,1B15,2B10	R	35	67	277	40	72	7	3	3	40	20	—	4	.260	.310	.339
Mike Donlin	OF51,1B13,P3*	L	21	66	266	49	86	9	6	6	27	17	—	20	.323	.366	.470
Jake Stenzel†	OF33	R	32	35	128	21	35	9	0	1	19	16	—	8	.273	.367	.367
Dusty Miller†	OF10	L	30	10	39	3	8	1	0	0	3	3	—	1	.205	.279	.231
Charlie Hemphill†	OF10	L	23	11	37	4	9	0	0	1	3	6	—	0	.243	.364	.324
Tim Flood	2B10	R	22	10	31	0	9	0	0	0	3	4	—	1	.290	.371	.290
Pete McBride	P11,2B1	R	23	12	27	2	5	1	0	1	5	2	—	0	.185	.241	.333
Fritz Buelow	C4,OF2	R	23	7	15	4	7	0	2	0	2	2	—	0	.467	.556	.733
Freddy Parent	2B2	R	23	2	8	0	1	0	0	0	1	0	—	0	.125	.125	.125
Jimmy Burke	2B2	R	24	2	6	1	2	0	0	0	0	1	—	0	.333	.429	.333

P. Tebeau, 1 G at 3B; H. Blake, 1 G at 1B, 1 G at SS; O. Schreckengost, 1 G at OF; M. Donlin, 3 G at SS

Pitcher	T	Age	G	GS	CG	ShO	IP	H	HR	BB	SO	W-L	Sv	ERA
Jack Powell	R	24	48	43	40	2	373.0	433	15	85	87	23-19	0	3.52
Cy Young	R	32	44	42	40	4	369.1	368	10	44	111	26-16	1	2.58
Willie Sudhoff†	R	24	26	24	18	0	189.1	203	6	67	33	13-10	0	3.61
Nig Cuppy	R	29	21	21	18	1	171.2	203	3	26	25	11-8	0	3.15
Cowboy Jones	L	24	12	12	9	0	85.1	111	1	22	28	6-5	0	3.59
Pete McBride	R	23	11	6	4	0	64.0	65	4	40	26	2-4	0	4.08
Tom Thomas	R	25	4	2	2	0	25.0	22	1	4	8	1-1	0	2.52
Jack Sutthoff	R	26	2	2	1	0	13.0	19	0	10	4	0-2	0	10.38
Zeke Wilson	R	29	5	2	2	0	26.0	30	0	4	3	1-1	0	4.50
Mike Donlin	L	21	3	1	0	0	15.1	15	1	14	6	0-1	0	7.63
Frank Bates†	R	—	2	0	0	0	8.2	7	0	5	0	0-0	0	1.04

1899 Cincinnati Reds 6th NL 83-67 .553 19.0 GB

Buck Ewing

Player	Gm by Position	B	Age	G	AB	R	H	2B	3B	HR	RBI	BB	SO	SB	Avg	OBP	Slg
Heinie Peitz	C91,P1	R	28	93	290	45	79	13	2	1	43	45	—	11	.272	.374	.341
Jake Beckley	1B134	L	31	134	513	87	171	27	16	3	99	40	—	20	.333	.393	.466
Bid McPhee	2B105,OF1	R	39	111	373	60	104	17	7	1	65	40	—	18	.279	.360	.370
Charlie Irwin	3B78,SS6,2B3*	L	30	90	314	42	73	4	8	1	52	26	—	26	.232	.295	.306
Tommy Corcoran	SS123,2B14	R	30	137	537	91	149	11	8	0	81	28	—	32	.277	.316	.328
Kip Selbach	OF140	R	27	140	521	104	154	27	11	3	87	70	—	38	.296	.384	.407
Elmer Smith	OF87	L	31	87	339	65	101	13	6	1	43	24	—	10	.298	.385	.381
Dusty Miller†	OF80	L	30	80	323	44	81	12	5	0	37	9	—	18	.251	.278	.319
Harry Steinfeldt	3B59,2B40,SS8*	R	21	107	386	62	94	16	8	0	43	40	—	19	.244	.324	.326
Algie McBride	OF64	L	30	64	251	57	87	12	5	1	23	30	—	5	.347	.431	.446
Bob Wood	C53,3B2,OF2*	R	33	62	194	34	61	11	7	0	24	25	—	3	.314	.406	.443
Kid Elberfeld	SS24,3B18	R	24	41	138	23	36	4	2	0	22	15	—	5	.261	.378	.319
Sam Crawford	OF31	L	19	31	127	25	39	3	7	1	20	2	—	6	.307	.318	.465
Farmer Vaughn	1B21,C7,OF1	R	35	31	108	9	19	1	0	0	2	3	—	2	.176	.198	.185
Ted Breitenstein	P26,OF7	L	30	33	105	18	37	4	1	1	11	10	—	1	.352	.409	.438
Jimmy Barrett	OF26	L	24	26	92	30	34	2	4	0	10	18	—	4	.370	.477	.478
Bill Phillips	P33,OF1	R	30	34	92	6	12	0	2	0	7	7	—	0	.130	.192	.174
Socks Seybold	OF22	R	28	22	85	13	19	5	1	0	8	6	—	2	.224	.283	.306
Mike Kahoe	C13	R	25	14	42	2	7	1	1	0	4	0	—	1	.167	.167	.238
Jake Stenzel†	OF7	R	32	9	29	5	9	1	0	0	3	4	—	2	.310	.412	.345
Lefty Houtz	OF5	L	23	5	17	1	4	0	1	0	0	4	—	1	.235	.381	.353

C. Irwin, 1 G at 1B; H. Steinfeldt, 2 G at OF; B. Wood, 1 G at 1B

Pitcher	T	Age	G	GS	CG	ShO	IP	H	HR	BB	SO	W-L	Sv	ERA
Noodles Hahn	L	20	38	34	32	4	309.0	280	3	68	145	23-8	0	2.68
Pink Hawley	R	26	34	29	25	0	250.1	289	7	65	46	14-17	1	4.24
Bill Phillips	R	30	33	27	18	1	227.2	234	3	71	43	17-9	1	3.32
Ted Breitenstein	L	30	26	24	21	0	210.2	219	2	71	59	13-9	0	3.59
Jack Taylor	R	26	24	18	15	2	168.1	197	7	41	34	9-10	2	4.12
Emil Frisk	R	24	9	9	9	0	68.1	81	1	17	17	3-6	0	3.95
Bill Dammann	L	26	9	5	3	1	48.0	74	0	11	2	2-1	1	4.88
Jack Cronin	R	25	5	5	5	0	41.0	56	2	16	9	2-2	0	5.49
Frank Dwyer	R	31	5	5	2	0	32.2	48	1	9	2	0-5	0	5.51
Heinie Peitz	R	28	1	0	0	0	5.0	6	0	1	3	0-0	0	5.40

1899 Pittsburgh Pirates 7th NL 76-73 .510 25.5 GB

Bill Watkins (7-15)/Patsy Donovan (69-58)

Player	Gm by Position	B	Age	G	AB	R	H	2B	3B	HR	RBI	BB	SO	SB	Avg	OBP	Slg
Frank Bowerman	C79,1B28	R	30	109	424	49	110	16	10	3	53	11	—	10	.259	.286	.366
Willie Clark	1B78	L	26	80	298	49	85	13	10	0	44	35	—	11	.285	.379	.396
John O'Brien†	2B79	L	28	79	279	26	63	2	4	1	33	21	—	8	.226	.285	.272
Jimmy Williams	3B152	R	22	152	617	126	219	28	27	9	116	60	—	26	.355	.417	.532
Bones Ely	SS132,2B6	R	36	138	522	66	145	18	6	3	72	22	—	8	.278	.313	.352
Jack McCarthy	OF138	L	30	138	560	108	171	22	17	3	67	39	—	28	.305	.355	.421
Patsy Donovan	OF121	L	34	121	531	82	156	11	7	1	55	17	—	26	.294	.322	.347
Ginger Beaumont	OF102,1B2	L	22	111	437	90	154	15	8	3	38	41	—	31	.352	.416	.444
Tom McCreery	OF97,SS9,2B7	S	24	118	455	76	147	21	9	2	64	47	—	11	.323	.390	.422
Pop Schriver	C78,1B8	R	33	91	301	31	85	19	5	1	49	23	—	4	.282	.343	.389
Jesse Tannehill	P40,OF1	S	24	47	132	17	34	5	3	0	10	8	—	2	.258	.310	.341
Heinie Reitz	2B34	L	32	34	130	11	34	4	2	0	15	10	—	3	.262	.314	.323
Pop Dillon	1B30	L	25	30	121	21	31	5	0	0	20	5	—	5	.256	.286	.298
Art Madison	2B19,SS15,3B2	R	28	42	118	20	32	2	4	0	19	11	—	1	.271	.338	.356
Bill Hoffer	P23,OF6,2B1	R	28	33	91	12	18	2	0	0	2	1	—	1	.198	.247	.220
Heinie Smith	2B15,SS1	R	27	15	53	9	15	3	1	0	12	5	—	2	.283	.345	.377
Paddy Fox	1B9,C3	—	30	13	41	4	10	0	1	1	3	3	—	2	.244	.311	.366

Pitcher	T	Age	G	GS	CG	ShO	IP	H	HR	BB	SO	W-L	Sv	ERA
Sam Leever	R	27	51	39	35	4	379.0	353	7	122	121	21-23	3	3.18
Jesse Tannehill	L	24	40	35	32	3	313.0	354	4	51	61	24-14	1	2.73
Bill Hoffer	R	28	23	19	15	2	163.2	169	5	64	44	8-10	0	3.63
Tully Sparks	R	24	28	17	8	0	170.0	180	1	82	53	8-6	0	3.86
Jack Chesbro	R	25	19	17	15	0	149.0	165	3	59	28	6-9	0	4.11
Billy Rhines	R	30	9	9	4	0	54.0	59	3	13	6	4-4	0	6.00
Chummy Gray	R	25	9	7	6	0	70.2	85	1	24	9	3-3	0	3.44
Harley Payne	L	31	5	5	2	0	26.1	33	2	4	8	1-3	0	3.76
Jim Gardner	R	24	6	3	0	0	32.1	52	1	13	2	1-0	0	7.52
Zeke Rosebraugh	L	28	2	2	0	0	6.0	14	0	3	2	0-1	0	9.00
Jay Parker	R	24	1	1	0	0	0.0	0	0	2	0	0-0	0	—

1899 Chicago Orphans 8th NL 75-73 .507 26.0 GB

Tom Burns

Player	Gm by Position	B	Age	G	AB	R	H	2B	3B	HR	RBI	BB	SO	SB	Avg	OBP	Slg
Tim Donahue	C91,1B1	L	29	92	278	39	69	9	3	0	29	34	—	10	.248	.345	.302
Bill Everitt	1B136	L	30	136	536	87	166	17	5	1	74	31	—	30	.310	.351	.366
Barry McCormick	2B99,SS3	—	24	102	376	48	97	15	2	2	52	25	—	14	.258	.311	.324
Harry Wolverton	3B98,SS1	L	25	99	389	50	111	14	11	1	49	30	—	14	.285	.350	.386
G. DeMontreville†	SS82	R	25	82	310	43	87	6	3	0	40	17	—	26	.281	.328	.319
Jimmy Ryan	OF125	R	36	125	525	91	158	20	10	3	68	43	—	9	.301	.357	.394
Danny Green	OF115	L	22	117	475	90	140	12	11	6	56	35	—	18	.295	.352	.404
Sam Mertes	OF108,1B3,SS1	R	26	117	426	83	127	13	16	9	81	33	—	45	.298	.349	.467
Bill Lange	OF94,1B14	R	28	107	416	81	135	21	7	1	58	38	—	41	.325	.382	.416
Jim Connor	2B44,3B25	R	36	69	234	26	48	7	1	0	24	18	—	6	.205	.265	.244
Frank Chance	C57,1B1,OF1	R	21	64	192	37	55	6	2	1	22	15	—	10	.286	.351	.354
George Magoon†	SS59	R	24	59	189	24	43	5	1	0	21	24	—	5	.228	.333	.265
Nixey Callahan	P35,OF9,SS2*	R	25	47	150	21	39	4	3	0	18	8	—	9	.260	.306	.327
Bill Bradley	3B30,SS5	R	21	35	129	26	40	6	1	2	18	12	—	4	.310	.378	.419
Clark Griffith	P38,SS1	R	29	39	120	15	31	5	0	0	14	14	—	2	.258	.346	.300
Art Nichols	C15	R	27	17	47	5	12	2	0	1	11	0	—	3	.255	.286	.362
Doc Curley	2B10	R	25	10	37	7	4	0	1	0	2	3	—	0	.108	.233	.162
Frank Quinn	OF10,2B1	—	23	12	34	6	6	0	1	0	1	6	—	1	.176	.300	.235
Dick Cogan	P5,OF3	R	27	8	25	4	5	1	2	0	4	2	—	0	.200	.286	.400

N. Callahan, 1 G at 2B

Pitcher	T	Age	G	GS	CG	ShO	IP	H	HR	BB	SO	W-L	Sv	ERA
Jack Taylor	R	25	41	39	39	1	354.2	380	6	84	67	18-21	0	3.76
Clark Griffith	R	29	38	38	35	0	319.2	329	5	65	73	22-14	0	2.79
Nixey Callahan	R	25	35	34	33	3	294.1	327	5	76	77	21-12	0	3.06
Ned Garvin	R	25	24	23	22	4	199.0	202	1	42	69	9-13	0	2.85
Bill Phyle	R	24	10	9	7	0	83.2	92	2	29	10	1-8	1	4.20
Dick Cogan	R	27	5	5	5	0	44.0	54	1	24	9	2-3	0	4.30
John Katoll	R	27	2	2	2	0	18.0	17	0	4	1	1-1	0	6.00
Skel Roach	R	27	1	1	1	0	9.0	13	0	1	0	1-0	0	3.00
John Malarkey	R	27	1	1	1	0	9.0	19	0	5	7	0-1	0	13.00

1899 Louisville Colonels 9th NL 75-77 .493 28.0 GB

Fred Clarke

Player	Gm by Position	B	Age	G	AB	R	H	2B	3B	HR	RBI	BB	SO	SB	Avg	OBP	Slg
Chief Zimmer†	C62,1B11	R	38	75	262	43	78	11	3	2	29	22	—	9	.298	.370	.385
Mike Kelley	1B76	R	23	76	282	48	68	11	2	3	33	21	—	10	.241	.307	.326
Claude Ritchey	2B137,SS11	S	25	147	536	65	161	15	7	4	71	49	—	21	.300	.370	.377
Tommy Leach	3B80,SS25,2B2	R	21	106	406	75	117	10	6	5	57	37	—	19	.288	.349	.379
Billy Clingman	SS109	S	29	109	366	67	96	15	4	2	44	46	—	13	.262	.349	.342
Dummy Hoy	OF154	L	37	154	633	116	194	17	13	5	49	61	—	32	.306	.376	.398
Fred Clarke	OF144,SS3	L	26	148	602	122	206	23	9	5	70	49	—	49	.342	.406	.435
Charlie Dexter	OF71,SS6	R	23	80	295	47	76	7	1	1	33	21	—	21	.258	.318	.298
Honus Wagner	3B75,OF61,2B7*	R	25	147	571	98	192	43	13	7	113	40	—	37	.336	.391	.494
Mike Powers†	C38,1B7	R	28	49	169	15	35	8	2	0	22	6	—	1	.207	.239	.278
Bert Cunningham	P39,OF3,SS1	R	33	44	154	17	40	2	0	2	17	5	—	1	.260	.283	.312
George Decker†	1B38	L	30	38	135	13	36	8	0	1	18	12	—	3	.267	.336	.348
Malachi Kittridge†	C43	R	29	45	129	11	26	2	1	0	12	26	—	3	.202	.340	.233
Deacon Phillippe	P42,OF2	R	27	44	128	17	26	5	0	0	10	8	—	3	.203	.255	.242
Walt Woods	P26,2B11,SS3*	R	24	42	126	15	19	1	1	1	14	10	—	5	.151	.213	.198
Dave Wills	1B24	L	22	24	94	15	21	3	1	0	12	2	—	1	.223	.240	.277
Topsy Hartsel	OF22	L	25	30	75	8	18	1	1	1	7	11	—	1	.240	.345	.320
Fred Ketcham	OF15	L	23	15	61	13	18	1	0	0	5	0	—	2	.295	.306	.311
Tacks Latimer	C8,1B1	R	21	9	29	3	8	1	0	0	4	2	—	1	.276	.323	.310
Patsy Flaherty	P5,OF2	L	23	7	24	3	5	1	1	0	6	3	—	0	.208	.296	.333
Farmer Steelman	C4	—	24	4	15	2	1	0	1	0	2	2	—	0	.067	.176	.200
Tom Messitt	C3	—	24	3	11	0	1	0	0	0	0	0	—	0	.091	.091	.091
Bob Langsford	SS1	R	33	1	4	0	0	0	0	0	0	0	—	0	.000	.000	.000
Burley Byers	SS1	—	23	1	3	0	0	0	0	0	0	0	—	0	.000	.000	.000
Harry Croft†		—	23	2	2	0	0	0	0	0	0	0	—	0	.000	.000	.000
Rudy Hulswitt	SS1	R	22	1	0	0	0	0	0	0	0	0	—	0	—	—	—

H. Wagner, 4 G at 1B; W. Woods, 2 G at OF

Pitcher	T	Age	G	GS	CG	ShO	IP	H	HR	BB	SO	W-L	Sv	ERA
Deacon Phillippe	R	27	42	38	33	2	321.0	331	10	64	68	21-17	1	3.17
Bert Cunningham	R	33	39	37	33	1	323.2	385	4	75	36	17-17	0	3.84
Pete Dowling	L	—	34	32	29	0	289.2	321	4	93	88	13-17	0	3.11
Walt Woods	R	24	26	21	17	0	186.1	216	9	37	21	9-13	0	3.28
Bill Magee†	R	24	12	10	6	1	71.0	91	1	28	13	3-7	0	5.20
Rube Waddell	L	22	10	9	9	1	79.0	69	4	14	44	7-2	1	3.08
Patsy Flaherty	L	23	5	4	4	0	39.0	41	0	5	5	2-3	0	2.31
Harry Wilhelm	R	25	5	3	2	0	25.0	36	1	3	6	1-1	0	6.12
Clay Fauver	R	26	1	1	1	0	9.0	11	0	2	1	1-0	0	0.00
Kitty Brashear	R	21	3	0	0	0	8.0	8	0	2	5	1-0	0	4.50

Seasons: Team Rosters 541

1899 New York Giants 10th NL 60-90 .400 42.0 GB

John Day (29-35)/Fred Hoey (31-55)

Player	Gm by Position	B	Age	G	AB	R	H	2B	3B	HR	RBI	BB	SO	SB	Avg	OBP	Slg
John Warner	C82,1B3	L	26	88	293	38	78	8	1	0	19	15	—	15	.266	.315	.300
Jack Doyle	1B113,C5	R	29	118	448	55	134	15	7	3	76	33	—	35	.299	.353	.384
Kid Gleason	2B146	S	32	146	576	72	152	14	4	0	59	24	—	29	.264	.293	.302
Fred Hartman	3B50	R	31	50	174	25	41	3	5	1	16	12	—	2	.236	.318	.328
George Davis	SS108	S	28	108	416	68	140	21	5	1	57	37	—	34	.337	.393	.418
George Van Haltren	OF151	L	33	151	604	117	182	21	3	2	58	74	—	31	.301	.378	.356
Tom O'Brien	OF127,3B21,SS2*	—	26	150	573	100	170	21	10	6	77	44	—	23	.297	.351	.400
Pop Foster	OF84,3B1,SS1	R	21	84	301	48	89	9	7	3	57	20	—	7	.296	.348	.402
Parke Wilson	C31,1B29,SS19*	R	31	97	328	49	88	8	6	0	42	43	—	16	.268	.360	.329
Mike Grady	C43,3B35,1B4*	R	29	86	311	47	104	18	8	2	54	29	—	20	.334	.403	.463
Cy Seymour	P32,OF8,1B3*	L	26	50	159	25	52	3	2	2	27	4	—	2	.327	.344	.409
Mike Tiernan	OF35	L	32	35	137	17	35	4	2	0	7	10	—	2	.255	.306	.314
Charlie Gettig	P18,3B8,1B3*	R	28	34	97	7	24	3	0	0	9	7	—	4	.247	.305	.278
Tom Fleming	OF22	L	25	22	77	9	16	1	1	0	4	1	—	1	.208	.218	.247
Scott Hardesty	SS20,1B2	—	29	22	72	4	16	0	0	0	4	1	—	2	.222	.243	.222
Pete Woodruff	OF19,1B1	R	—	20	61	11	15	1	1	2	7	9	—	3	.246	.343	.393
Frank Martin	3B17	—	20	17	54	5	14	2	0	0	1	2	—	0	.259	.298	.296
Tom Colcolough	P11,OF1	R	28	14	37	3	10	1	0	0	6	1	—	0	.270	.289	.297
Kid Carsey†	3B3,SS2	L	28	5	18	2	6	1	0	0	1	2	—	2	.333	.400	.389
Ira Davis	SS3,1B2	—	28	6	17	3	4	1	1	0	2	0	—	1	.235	.235	.412
Zeke Wrigley†	3B4	—	25	4	15	1	3	0	0	0	1	1	—	1	.200	.250	.200
John O'Neill	C2	—	—	2	7	0	0	0	0	0	0	0	—	0	.000	.000	.000
Bill Stuart	2B1	—	25	1	3	0	0	0	0	0	0	0	—	0	.000	.000	.000
Pete Cregan	OF1	R	24	1	2	0	0	0	0	0	0	0	—	0	.000	.000	.000
John Puhl	3B1	—	22	1	2	0	0	0	0	0	0	0	—	0	.000	.333	.000

T. O'Brien, 1 G at 1B, 1 G at 2B; P. Wilson, 15 G at 3B, 6 G at OF; M. Grady, 4 G at OF; C. Seymour, 1 G at 3B; C. Gettig, 3 G at 2B, 1 G at OF

Pitcher	T	Age	G	GS	CG	ShO	IP	H	HR	BB	SO	W-L	Sv	ERA
Bill Carrick	R	25	44	43	40	3	361.2	485	4	122	60	16-27	0	4.65
Ed Doheny	L	25	35	33	30	1	265.1	282	2	156	115	14-17	0	4.51
Cy Seymour	L	26	32	32	31	0	268.1	247	5	170	142	14-18	0	3.56
Jouett Meekin†	R	32	18	18	16	0	148.1	169	4	70	30	5-11	0	4.37
Charlie Gettig	—	28	18	15	12	0	128.0	161	3	54	25	7-8	0	4.43
Tom Colcolough	R	28	11	8	7	0	81.2	85	1	41	14	4-5	0	3.97
Leo Fishel	R	21	1	1	1	0	9.0	9	0	6	6	0-1	0	6.00
Willie Garoni	R	21	3	1	1	0	10.0	12	0	2	2	0-1	0	4.50
Frank McPartlin	R	27	1	0	0	0	4.0	4	0	3	2	0-0	0	4.50
Youngy Johnson	R	21	1	0	0	0	2.0	0	0	2	1	0-0	0	0.00
Doc Sechrist	R	23	1	0	0	0	0.0	0	0	2	0	0-0	0	—

1899 Washington Senators 11th NL 54-98 .355 49.0 GB

Arthur Irwin

Player	Gm by Position	B	Age	G	AB	R	H	2B	3B	HR	RBI	BB	SO	SB	Avg	OBP	Slg
Deacon McGuire†	C56,1B1	R	35	59	199	25	54	3	1	1	12	16	—	3	.271	.335	.312
Dan McGann†	1B76	S	27	76	280	65	96	9	8	5	58	14	—	11	.343	.410	.486
Frank Bonner	2B85	R	29	85	347	41	95	20	4	2	44	18	—	6	.274	.313	.372
Charlie Atherton	3B63,OF1	R	25	65	242	28	60	5	6	0	23	21	—	2	.248	.313	.318
Dick Padden	SS85,2B48	R	28	134	451	66	125	20	7	2	61	24	—	27	.277	.337	.366
Buck Freeman	OF155,P2	L	27	155	588	107	187	19	25	25	122	23	—	21	.318	.362	.563
Jimmy Slagle	OF146	L	25	147	599	92	163	15	8	0	41	55	—	22	.272	.338	.324
Jack O'Brien	OF121,3B4	L	26	127	468	68	132	11	5	6	51	31	—	17	.282	.331	.365
Win Mercer	3B62,P23,OF16*	R	25	108	375	73	112	6	7	1	35	32	—	16	.299	.360	.360
Shad Barry	OF23,1B22,3B13*	R	20	78	247	31	71	7	5	1	33	12	—	11	.287	.328	.368
Pete Cassidy†	1B37,3B6,SS3	R	26	46	178	21	56	13	0	3	32	9	—	5	.315	.365	.438
Malachi Kittridge†	C43	R	29	44	133	14	20	3	0	0	11	10	—	2	.150	.215	.173
Bill Dinneen	P37,OF1	R	23	37	119	9	36	2	0	0	4	8	—	0	.303	.346	.319
General Stafford†	2B17,SS13,3B2	R	30	31	118	11	29	5	1	1	14	5	—	4	.246	.276	.331
Frank Scheibeck	SS27	R	34	27	94	19	27	4	1	0	9	11	—	5	.287	.368	.351
Mike Roach	C20,1B3	—	25	24	78	7	17	1	0	0	7	3	—	3	.218	.265	.231
Billy Hulen	SS19	L	29	19	68	10	10	1	0	0	3	10	—	5	.147	.256	.162
Harry Davis	1B18	R	25	18	64	3	12	2	3	0	8	8	—	2	.188	.288	.313
Jake Gettman	OF16,1B2	S	22	19	62	5	13	1	0	0	2	4	—	4	.210	.258	.226
Jim Duncan†	C14	R	27	15	47	5	11	2	0	0	5	4	—	1	.234	.294	.277
Mike Powers†	C12,1B1	R	28	14	38	3	10	2	0	0	3	1	—	0	.263	.282	.316
Dick Butler	C11	—	—	12	36	4	10	0	1	0	1	2	—	1	.278	.316	.333
Doc Casey†	3B9	S	29	9	34	3	4	2	0	0	2	2	—	1	.118	.167	.176
Bill Coughlin	3B6	R	20	6	24	2	3	0	1	0	3	1	—	1	.125	.160	.208
Frank McManus	C7	—	23	7	21	3	8	1	0	0	2	2	—	3	.381	.435	.429
Jack Fifield†	P6,3B1	R	27	7	20	0	4	1	0	0	2	2	—	0	.200	.273	.250
Duke Farrell†	C4	S	32	5	12	2	4	1	0	0	1	2	—	1	.333	.429	.417
George Decker†	1B2,OF1	L	30	4	9	0	0	0	0	0	0	0	—	0	.000	.000	.000
Arlie Latham	2B1,OF1	R	39	6	6	1	1	0	0	0	0	1	—	0	.167	.286	.167
Mike Heydon	C2	L	24	3	3	0	0	0	0	0	0	2	—	0	.000	.400	.000

W. Mercer, 1 G at 1B, 1 G at SS; S. Barry, 13 G at SS, 7 G at 2B

Pitcher	T	Age	G	GS	CG	ShO	IP	H	HR	BB	SO	W-L	Sv	ERA
Gus Weyhing	R	32	43	38	34	2	334.2	414	8	76	96	17-21	0	4.54
Bill Dinneen	R	23	37	35	30	0	291.0	350	6	106	91	14-20	0	3.93
Dan McFarlan†	—	24	32	28	22	1	211.2	268	5	64	41	8-18	0	4.76
Win Mercer	R	25	23	21	21	0	186.0	234	2	53	28	7-14	0	4.60
Roy Evans	R	25	7	7	6	0	54.0	60	1	25	27	3-4	0	5.67
Bill Magee†	R	24	8	7	4	0	42.0	54	3	28	11	1-4	0	8.57
Kirtley Baker	R	30	11	6	3	0	54.0	79	3	22	6	1-7	0	6.83
Jack Fifield†	R	27	6	6	6	0	47.0	73	1	17	12	2-4	0	6.13
Kid Carsey†	R	28	4	3	2	0	29.0	27	0	4	3	1-2	0	3.72
Davey Dunkle	R	26	4	2	2	0	26.0	46	3	14	9	0-2	0	10.04
Frank Killen†	L	28	2	2	1	0	12.0	18	0	4	3	0-2	0	6.00
Buck Freeman	L	27	2	0	0	0	7.0	15	3	3	0	0-0	0	7.71
Lefty Herring	L	19	2	0	0	0	2.0	0	0	2	0	0-0	0	0.00
Bill Leith	L	26	1	0	0	0	2.0	4	0	2	1	0-0	0	18.00
Dorsey Riddlemoser	R	24	1	0	0	0	2.0	7	0	2	0	0-0	0	18.00

1899 Cleveland Spiders 12th NL 20-134 .130 84.0 GB

Lave Cross (8-30)/Joe Quinn (12-104)

Player	Gm by Position	B	Age	G	AB	R	H	2B	3B	HR	RBI	BB	SO	SB	Avg	OBP	Slg
Joe Sugden	C66,OF4,1B3*	S	28	76	250	19	69	5	1	0	14	11	—	2	.276	.307	.304
Tommy Tucker	1B127	S	35	127	456	40	110	19	3	0	40	24	—	3	.241	.297	.296
Joe Quinn	2B147	R	34	147	615	73	176	24	6	0	72	21	—	22	.286	.312	.345
Suter Sullivan	3B101,OF20,1B3*	—	26	127	473	37	116	16	3	0	55	25	—	16	.245	.297	.292
Harry Lochhead	SS146,P1,2B1	R	23	148	541	52	129	7	1	1	43	21	—	23	.238	.280	.261
Tommy Dowd	OF147	R	30	147	605	81	168	17	6	2	35	48	—	28	.278	.333	.336
Dick Harley	OF142	L	26	142	567	70	142	15	7	1	50	40	—	15	.250	.315	.307
Sport McAllister	OF79,C17,3B7*	S	24	113	418	29	99	6	8	1	31	19	—	5	.237	.273	.297
Charlie Hemphill†	OF54	L	23	55	202	23	56	3	5	2	23	6	—	3	.277	.301	.371
Lave Cross†	3B38	R	33	38	154	15	44	5	0	1	20	8	—	2	.286	.325	.338
O. Schreckengost†	C39,1B1,SS1*	R	24	43	150	15	47	8	3	0	10	6	—	4	.313	.348	.407
Jim Duncan†	1B17,C14	R	27	31	105	9	24	2	3	2	9	4	—	0	.229	.257	.362
Harry Colliflower	P14,OF6,1B4	L	30	23	76	5	23	4	0	0	9	2	—	0	.303	.321	.355
Chief Zimmer†	C20	R	38	20	73	9	25	2	1	2	14	5	—	1	.342	.407	.479
Crazy Schmit	P20,OF6	L	33	25	70	6	11	0	0	0	1	6	—	2	.157	.244	.157
Frank Bates†	P20,OF2	—	—	21	65	5	14	1	0	0	3	7	—	0	.215	.301	.231
Otto Krueger	3B9,2B2,SS2	R	22	13	44	4	10	1	0	0	2	8	—	1	.227	.358	.250
Jack Stivetts	P7,OF7,3B1*	R	31	18	39	8	8	1	1	0	2	6	—	0	.205	.326	.282
Kid Carsey†	P10,SS1	L	28	11	36	5	10	0	0	0	4	3	—	0	.278	.333	.278
Louis Sockalexis	OF5	L	27	7	22	0	6	1	0	0	3	1	—	0	.273	.304	.318
Jack Clements	C4	L	34	4	12	1	3	0	0	0	0	0	—	0	.250	.308	.250
Charlie Ziegler	2B1,SS1	—	24	2	8	2	2	0	0	0	0	0	—	0	.250	.250	.250
George Bristow	OF3	—	29	3	8	0	1	1	0	0	0	0	—	0	.125	.222	.250

J. Sugden, 1 G at 3B; S. Sullivan, 3 G at SS, 2 G at 2B; S. McAllister, 6 G at 1B, 3 G at P, 3 G at SS, 1 G at 2B; O. Schreckengost, 1 G at OF; J. Stivetts, 1 G at SS

Pitcher	T	Age	G	GS	CG	ShO	IP	H	HR	BB	SO	W-L	Sv	ERA
Jim Hughey	R	30	36	34	32	0	283.0	403	9	88	54	4-30	0	5.41
Charlie Knepper	R	28	27	26	26	0	219.2	307	11	77	43	4-22	0	5.78
Frank Bates†	R	—	20	19	17	0	153.0	239	6	105	13	1-18	0	7.24
Crazy Schmit	L	33	20	19	16	0	138.1	197	3	62	24	2-17	0	5.86
Harry Colliflower	L	30	14	12	11	0	98.0	152	6	41	8	1-11	0	8.17
Willie Sudhoff†	R	24	11	10	8	0	86.1	131	3	25	10	3-8	0	6.98
Bill Hill†	L	24	11	10	7	0	72.1	96	0	39	26	3-6	0	6.97
Kid Carsey†	R	28	10	9	8	0	77.2	109	2	24	11	1-8	0	5.68
Jack Harper	R	21	5	5	5	0	37.0	44	3	12	14	1-4	0	3.89
Jack Stivetts	R	31	7	4	3	0	38.0	48	0	25	5	0-4	0	5.68
Harry Maupin	R	26	5	3	2	0	25.0	55	0	7	3	0-3	0	12.60
Eddie Kolb	R	18	1	1	1	0	8.0	18	0	5	1	0-1	0	10.13
Highball Wilson	R	20	1	1	1	0	8.0	12	0	5	1	0-1	0	9.00
Sport McAllister	R	24	3	1	1	0	16.0	29	0	10	2	0-1	0	9.56
Harry Lochhead	R	23	1	0	0	0	3.2	4	0	2	0	0-0	0	0.00

»1900 Brooklyn Superbas 1st NL 82-54 .603 —

Ned Hanlon

Player	Gm by Position	B	Age	G	AB	R	H	2B	3B	HR	RBI	BB	SO	SB	Avg	OBP	Slg
Duke Farrell	C74	S	33	76	273	33	75	11	5	0	39	11	—	3	.275	.310	.352
Hughie Jennings	1B112,2B2	R	31	115	441	61	120	18	6	1	69	31	—	31	.272	.348	.347
Tom Daly	2B93,1B3,OF2	S	34	97	343	72	107	17	3	4	55	46	—	27	.312	.403	.414
Lave Cross†	3B117	R	34	117	461	73	135	14	6	4	67	25	—	20	.293	.332	.375
Bill Dahlen	SS133	R	30	133	483	87	125	16	11	1	69	73	—	31	.259	.364	.344
Willie Keeler	OF136,2B1	L	28	136	563	106	204	13	12	4	68	30	—	41	.362	.402	.449
Fielder Jones	OF136	L	28	136	552	106	171	26	4	4	54	57	—	33	.310	.383	.393
Jimmy Sheckard	OF78	L	21	85	273	74	82	19	10	1	39	42	—	30	.300	.416	.454
Joe Kelley	OF77,1B32,3B13	R	28	121	454	90	145	23	17	6	91	53	—	26	.319	.398	.485
Deacon McGuire	C69	R	36	71	241	20	69	15	2	0	34	19	—	2	.286	.348	.365
Gene DeMontreville	2B48,SS12,3B7*	R	26	69	234	34	57	8	1	0	28	10	—	21	.244	.283	.286
Joe McGinnity	P44,OF1	R	29	46	145	18	28	4	1	0	16	1	—	4	.193	.199	.234
Frank Kitson	P40,OF1	L	30	43	109	20	32	5	1	0	16	6	—	2	.294	.330	.358
Aleck Smith	3B6,C1	—	29	7	25	2	6	0	0	0	3	1	—	2	.240	.269	.240
Farmer Steelman	C1	—	25	1	4	0	0	0	0	0	0	0	—	0	.000	.000	.000
Doc Casey	3B1	S	30	1	3	0	1	0	0	0	1	0	—	0	.333	.500	.333

G. DeMontreville, 1 G at 1B, 1 G at OF

Pitcher	T	Age	G	GS	CG	ShO	IP	H	HR	BB	SO	W-L	Sv	ERA
Joe McGinnity	R	29	44	37	32	1	343.0	350	5	113	93	28-8	0	2.94
Brickyard Kennedy	R	32	42	35	26	2	292.0	316	5	111	75	20-13	0	3.91
Frank Kitson	R	30	40	30	21	2	253.1	283	12	56	55	15-13	4	4.19
Jerry Nops	L	25	9	8	6	1	68.0	79	1	18	22	4-4	0	3.84
Gus Weyhing†	R	33	8	8	3	0	48.0	66	1	20	8	3-4	0	4.31
Jack Dunn†	R	27	10	7	5	0	63.0	88	1	28	6	3-4	0	5.57
Wild Bill Donovan	R	23	5	4	2	0	31.0	36	0	18	13	1-2	0	6.68
Joe Yeager	R	24	2	2	2	0	17.0	21	1	5	2	1-1	0	6.88
Harry Howell	R	23	21	10	7	2	110.1	131	4	36	26	6-5	0	3.75

1900 Pittsburgh Pirates 2nd NL 79-60 .568 4.5 GB

Fred Clarke

Player	Gm by Position	B	Age	G	AB	R	H	2B	3B	HR	RBI	BB	SO	SB	Avg	OBP	Slg
Chief Zimmer	C78,1B2	R	39	82	271	27	80	7	10	0	35	17	—	4	.295	.361	.395
Duff Cooley	1B66	L	27	66	249	30	50	8	1	0	22	14	—	9	.201	.243	.241
Claude Ritchey	2B123	S	26	123	476	62	139	17	8	1	67	29	—	18	.292	.339	.368
Jimmy Williams	3B103,SS4	R	23	106	416	73	110	15	11	5	68	32	—	18	.264	.323	.389
Bones Ely	SS130	R	37	130	475	60	116	6	6	0	51	17	—	6	.244	.272	.282
Ginger Beaumont	OF138	L	23	138	567	105	158	14	9	5	50	40	—	27	.279	.331	.362
Honus Wagner	OF118,3B9,2B7*	R	26	135	527	107	201	45	22	4	100	41	—	38	.381	.434	.573
Fred Clarke	OF104	L	27	106	399	84	110	15	12	3	32	51	—	21	.276	.368	.396
Tom O'Brien	1B65,OF25,2B4*	—	27	102	376	61	109	22	6	3	61	21	—	12	.290	.349	.404
Tommy Leach	3B31,SS8,2B7*	R	22	51	160	20	34	1	2	1	16	21	—	8	.213	.304	.263
Jack O'Connor†	C40,1B2	R	31	43	147	15	35	4	1	0	19	3	—	5	.238	.263	.279
Tom McCreery	OF35,P1	S	25	43	132	20	29	4	3	1	13	16	—	2	.220	.304	.318
Jesse Tannehill	P29,OF4	S	25	34	110	19	37	7	0	0	17	5	—	2	.336	.365	.400
Pop Schriver	C24,1B1	R	34	37	92	12	27	7	0	1	12	10	—	0	.293	.381	.402
Jack Chesbro	P32,OF1	R	26	32	85	10	15	4	1	0	9	6	—	1	.176	.231	.247
Pop Dillon	1B5	L	26	5	18	3	2	1	0	0	1	0	—	0	.111	.111	.167
Tacks Latimer	C4	R	22	4	12	1	4	1	0	0	2	0	—	0	.333	.333	.417
Jiggs Donahue	C2,OF1	L	20	3	10	1	2	0	1	0	3	0	—	1	.200	.200	.400
Ed Poole	P1,OF1	R	25	2	4	1	2	0	1	1	3	0	—	0	.500	.500	1.750

H. Wagner, 3 G at 1B, 1 G at P; T. O'Brien, 2 G at SS; T. Leach, 4 G at OF

Pitcher	T	Age	G	GS	CG	ShO	IP	H	HR	BB	SO	W-L	Sv	ERA
Deacon Phillippe	R	28	38	33	29	1	279.0	274	7	42	75	20-13	0	2.84
Sam Leever	R	28	30	29	25	3	232.2	236	2	48	84	15-13	0	2.71
Jesse Tannehill	L	25	29	27	23	2	234.0	247	3	43	50	20-6	0	2.88
Jack Chesbro	R	26	32	26	20	3	215.2	220	4	79	56	15-13	1	3.67
Rube Waddell	L	23	29	22	16	2	208.2	176	3	55	130	8-13	0	2.37
Jouett Meekin	R	33	2	2	1	0	13.0	20	1	8	3	0-2	0	6.92
Patsy Flaherty	L	24	4	1	0	0	22.0	30	0	9	5	0-0	0	6.14
Bert Husting	R	22	2	0	0	0	8.0	10	2	5	7	0-0	0	5.63
Ed Poole	R	25	1	0	0	0	7.0	4	0	0	3	1-0	0	1.29
Walt Woods	R	25	1	0	0	0	3.0	9	0	1	1	0-0	0	21.00
Honus Wagner	R	26	1	0	0	0	3.0	3	0	4	1	0-0	0	0.00
Tom McCreery	R	25	1	0	0	0	3.0	3	2	1	0	0-0	0	12.00

1900 Philadelphia Phillies 3rd NL 75-63 .543 8.0 GB

Bill Shettsline

Player	Gm by Position	B	Age	G	AB	R	H	2B	3B	HR	RBI	BB	SO	SB	Avg	OBP	Slg
Ed McFarland	C93,3B1	R	25	94	344	50	105	14	8	0	38	29	—	9	.305	.364	.392
Ed Delahanty	1B130	R	32	131	539	82	174	32	10	2	109	41	—	16	.323	.378	.430
Nap Lajoie	2B102,3B1	R	25	102	451	95	152	33	12	7	92	10	—	22	.337	.362	.510
Harry Wolverton†	3B101	L	26	101	383	42	108	10	8	3	58	20	—	4	.282	.323	.373
Monte Cross	SS131	R	30	131	466	59	94	11	3	3	62	51	—	19	.202	.289	.258
Jimmy Slagle	OF141	L	26	141	574	115	165	16	9	0	45	60	—	34	.287	.358	.347
Roy Thomas	OF139,P1	L	26	140	531	132	168	4	3	0	33	115	—	37	.316	.451	.335
Elmer Flick	OF138	L	24	138	545	106	200	32	16	11	110	56	—	35	.367	.441	.545
Joe Dolan	3B31,2B29,SS12	—	27	74	257	39	51	7	3	1	27	16	—	10	.198	.259	.261
Klondike Douglass	C47,3B2	L	28	50	160	23	48	9	4	0	25	13	—	7	.300	.360	.406
Al Orth	P33,OF3	L	27	39	129	6	40	4	1	1	21	2	—	2	.310	.326	.380
Pearce Chiles	1B16,2B12,OF3	R	33	33	111	13	24	6	2	1	23	6	—	4	.216	.256	.333
Morgan Murphy	C11	R	33	11	36	2	10	0	1	0	3	0	—	0	.278	.278	.333
Al Myers	3B7	R	26	7	28	5	5	1	0	0	2	3	—	1	.179	.258	.214
Fred Jacklitsch	C3	R	24	5	11	0	2	1	0	0	3	0	—	0	.182	.182	.273
Charlie Ziegler	3B3	—	25	3	11	0	3	0	0	0	1	0	—	0	.273	.273	.273

Pitcher	T	Age	G	GS	CG	ShO	IP	H	HR	BB	SO	W-L	Sv	ERA
Al Orth	R	27	33	30	24	2	262.0	302	4	60	68	14-14	1	3.78
Bill Bernhard	R	29	32	27	20	0	218.2	284	3	74	49	15-10	2	4.77
Chick Fraser	R	29	29	26	22	1	223.1	250	7	93	58	15-9	0	3.14
Red Donahue	R	27	32	24	21	2	240.0	299	6	50	41	15-10	0	3.60
Wiley Piatt	L	25	22	20	16	1	160.2	194	5	71	47	9-10	0	4.65
Jack Dunn†	R	27	10	9	9	1	80.0	87	2	29	12	5-5	0	4.84
Al Maul	R	34	5	4	3	0	38.0	53	2	3	6	2-3	0	6.16
Bert Conn	R	20	4	1	1	0	17.1	29	0	16	2	0-2	0	8.31
Warren McLaughlin	L	24	1	0	0	0	6.0	4	0	6	1	0-0	0	4.50
Roy Thomas	L	26	1	0	0	0	2.2	4	0	0	0	0-0	0	3.38

1900 Boston Beaneaters 4th NL 66-72 .478 17.0 GB

Frank Selee

Player	Gm by Position	B	Age	G	AB	R	H	2B	3B	HR	RBI	BB	SO	SB	Avg	OBP	Slg
Boileryard Clarke	C67,1B8	R	31	81	270	35	85	5	2	1	30	9	—	0	.315	.344	.359
Fred Tenney	1B111	L	28	112	437	77	122	13	5	1	56	39	—	17	.279	.346	.339
Bobby Lowe	2B127	R	31	127	474	65	132	11	5	3	71	26	—	15	.278	.323	.342
Jimmy Collins	3B141,SS1	R	30	142	586	104	178	25	5	6	95	34	—	23	.304	.352	.394
Herman Long	SS125	L	34	125	486	80	127	19	4	12	66	44	—	26	.261	.325	.391
Billy Hamilton	OF136	L	34	136	520	103	173	20	5	1	47	107	—	32	.333	.449	.396
Chick Stahl	OF135	L	27	136	553	88	163	23	16	5	82	34	—	27	.295	.336	.421
Buck Freeman	OF91,1B19	L	28	117	418	58	126	19	13	6	65	25	—	10	.301	.355	.452
Shad Barry	OF24,SS18,2B16*	R	21	81	254	40	66	10	7	1	37	13	—	9	.260	.301	.366
Billy Sullivan	C66,2B1,SS1	R	25	72	238	36	65	6	0	8	41	9	—	4	.273	.302	.399
Hugh Duffy	OF49,2B1	R	33	55	181	27	55	5	4	2	31	16	—	11	.304	.360	.409
Jack Clements	C10	L	35	16	42	6	13	1	0	1	10	3	—	0	.310	.370	.405
Joe Connor	C7	R	25	7	19	2	4	0	0	0	4	2	—	1	.211	.286	.211

S. Barry, 10 G at 1B, 1 G at 3B

Pitcher	T	Age	G	GS	CG	ShO	IP	H	HR	BB	SO	W-L	Sv	ERA
Bill Dinneen	R	24	40	37	33	1	320.2	304	11	105	107	20-14	0	3.12
Vic Willis	R	24	32	29	22	2	236.0	258	11	106	53	10-17	1	4.19
Kid Nichols	R	30	29	27	25	4	231.1	215	11	72	53	13-16	0	3.07
Ted Lewis	R	27	30	22	19	1	209.0	215	11	86	66	13-12	0	4.13
Togie Pittinger	R	28	18	13	8	0	114.0	135	7	54	27	2-9	0	5.13
Nig Cuppy	R	30	17	13	9	0	105.1	107	8	24	23	8-4	1	3.08
Harvey Bailey	L	23	4	1	0	0	20.0	24	0	11	9	0-0	0	4.95
Rome Chambers	L	24	1	0	0	0	4.0	5	0	5	2	0-0	1	11.25

1900 Chicago Orphans 5th NL 65-75 .464 19.0 GB

Tom Loftus

Player	Gm by Position	B	Age	G	AB	R	H	2B	3B	HR	RBI	BB	SO	SB	Avg	OBP	Slg
Tim Donahue	C66,2B1	L	30	67	216	21	51	10	1	0	17	19	—	8	.236	.313	.292
John Ganzel	1B78	R	26	78	284	29	78	14	4	4	32	10	—	5	.275	.316	.394
Cupid Childs	2B137	L	32	137	531	67	128	14	5	0	44	57	—	15	.241	.323	.286
Bill Bradley	3B106,1B15	R	22	122	444	63	125	21	8	5	49	27	—	14	.282	.330	.399
Barry McCormick	SS84,3B21,2B5	—	25	110	379	35	83	13	5	3	48	38	—	8	.219	.292	.303
Jack McCarthy	OF123	L	31	124	503	68	148	16	7	0	48	24	—	22	.294	.329	.354
Jimmy Ryan	OF105	R	37	105	415	66	115	25	4	5	59	29	—	19	.277	.329	.393
Danny Green	OF101	L	23	103	389	63	116	21	5	5	49	17	—	28	.298	.339	.416
Sam Mertes	OF88,1B33,SS7	R	27	127	481	72	142	25	4	7	60	42	—	38	.295	.356	.407
Billy Clingman	SS47	S	30	47	159	15	33	6	0	0	11	17	—	6	.208	.292	.245
Frank Chance	C51,1B1	R	22	56	149	26	44	9	3	0	13	15	—	8	.295	.413	.396
Charlie Dexter	C22,OF13,2B1	R	24	40	125	7	25	5	0	2	20	1	—	2	.200	.213	.288
Sammy Strang	3B16,SS9,2B2	S	23	27	102	15	29	3	0	0	9	8	—	1	.284	.348	.314
Bill Everitt	1B23	L	31	23	91	10	24	4	0	0	17	3	—	2	.264	.287	.308
Johnny Kling	C15	R	25	15	51	8	15	3	1	0	7	2	—	0	.294	.321	.392
Cozy Dolan	OF13	L	27	13	48	5	13	1	0	0	2	2	—	2	.271	.300	.292
Art Nichols	C7	R	28	8	25	1	5	0	0	0	0	3	—	1	.200	.286	.200
Sam Dungan	OF3	R	33	6	15	1	4	0	0	0	1	1	—	0	.267	.313	.267
Harry Wolverton†	3B3	L	26	3	11	2	2	0	0	0	0	2	—	1	.182	.308	.182
Roger Bresnahan	C1	R	21	2	2	0	0	0	0	0	0	0	—	0	.000	.000	.000

Pitcher	T	Age	G	GS	CG	ShO	IP	H	HR	BB	SO	W-L	Sv	ERA
Nixey Callahan	R	26	32	32	32	2	285.1	347	5	74	77	13-16	0	3.82
Clark Griffith	R	30	30	30	27	4	248.0	245	6	51	61	14-13	0	3.05
Ned Garvin	R	26	30	28	25	1	246.1	225	4	63	107	10-18	0	2.41
Jack Taylor	R	26	28	26	25	2	222.1	226	4	58	57	10-17	1	2.55
Jock Menefee	R	32	16	13	11	0	117.0	140	1	35	30	9-4	0	3.85
Bert Cunningham	R	34	8	7	7	0	64.0	84	0	21	7	4-3	0	4.36
Frank Killen	L	29	6	6	6	0	54.0	65	1	11	4	3-3	0	4.67
Long Tom Hughes	R	21	3	3	3	0	21.0	31	0	7	12	1-1	0	5.14
Mal Eason	R	21	1	1	1	0	9.0	9	0	3	2	1-0	0	1.00
Erwin Harvey	L	21	1	0	0	0	4.0	3	0	1	0	0-0	0	0.00

1900 St. Louis Perfectos 5th NL 65-75 .464 19.0 GB

Patsy Tebeau (42-50)/Louie Heilbroner (23-25)

Player	Gm by Position	B	Age	G	AB	R	H	2B	3B	HR	RBI	BB	SO	SB	Avg	OBP	Slg
Lou Criger	C75,3B1	R	28	80	288	31	78	8	6	2	38	4	—	5	.271	.286	.361
Dan McGann	1B121,2B1	S	28	121	444	79	132	10	9	4	58	32	—	26	.297	.376	.387
Bill Keister	2B116,SS7,3B3	L	25	126	497	78	149	26	10	1	72	25	—	32	.300	.347	.398
John McGraw	3B99	L	27	99	334	84	115	10	4	2	33	85	—	29	.344	.505	.416
Bobby Wallace	SS126,3B1	R	26	126	485	70	130	25	9	4	70	40	—	7	.268	.328	.381
Jesse Burkett	OF141	L	31	141	559	88	203	11	15	7	68	62	—	32	.363	.429	.474
Patsy Donovan	OF124	L	35	126	503	78	159	11	1	0	61	38	—	45	.316	.368	.342
Emmett Heidrick	OF83	L	23	85	339	51	102	6	8	2	45	18	—	22	.301	.338	.383
Mike Donlin	OF47,1B21	L	22	78	276	40	90	8	6	10	48	14	—	14	.326	.361	.507
Wilbert Robinson	C54	R	37	60	210	26	52	5	1	0	28	11	—	7	.248	.291	.281
Pat Dillard	OF26,3B21,SS3	L	27	57	183	24	42	5	2	0	12	13	—	7	.230	.284	.279
Willie Sudhoff	P16,OF12,3B7	R	25	35	106	15	20	1	1	0	6	11	—	8	.189	.271	.217
Joe Quinn†	2B14,SS6,3B1	R	35	22	80	12	21	2	0	1	11	10	—	4	.263	.344	.325
Lave Cross†	3B16	R	34	16	61	6	18	1	0	0	6	1	—	1	.295	.306	.311
Otto Krueger	2B12	R	23	12	35	8	14	3	2	1	3	10	—	0	.400	.543	.686
Jack O'Connor†	C10	R	31	10	32	4	7	0	0	0	6	2	—	0	.219	.306	.219
Fritz Buelow	C4,OF1	R	24	6	17	2	4	0	0	0	3	0	—	0	.235	.235	.235
Patsy Tebeau	SS1	R	35	1	4	0	0	0	0	0	0	0	—	0	.000	.000	.000
Harry Stanton	C1	—	—	1	0	0	0	0	0	0	0	0	—	0	—	—	—

Pitcher	T	Age	G	GS	CG	ShO	IP	H	HR	BB	SO	W-L	Sv	ERA
Jack Powell	R	25	38	37	28	3	287.2	325	9	77	77	17-16	0	4.44
Cowboy Jones	L	25	39	36	29	3	292.2	334	10	82	68	13-19	0	3.54
Cy Young	R	33	41	35	32	4	321.1	337	7	36	115	19-19	0	3.00
Willie Sudhoff	R	25	16	14	13	2	127.0	128	3	37	29	6-8	0	2.76
Jim Hughey	R	31	20	12	11	0	112.2	147	4	40	23	5-7	0	5.19
Gus Weyhing†	R	33	7	5	3	0	46.2	60	2	21	6	3-2	0	4.63
Jack Harper	R	22	1	1	0	0	3.0	4	0	2	0	0-1	0	12.00
Tom Thomas	R	26	5	1	1	0	26.1	38	2	4	7	2-2	0	3.76

1900 Cincinnati Reds 7th NL 62-77 .446 21.5 GB

Bob Allen

Player	Gm by Position	B	Age	G	AB	R	H	2B	3B	HR	RBI	BB	SO	SB	Avg	OBP	Slg
Heinie Peitz	C80,1B8	R	29	91	294	34	75	14	1	2	34	20	—	5	.255	.318	.330
Jake Beckley	1B140	L	32	141	558	98	190	26	10	2	94	40	—	23	.341	.389	.434
Joe Quinn†	2B74	R	35	74	266	18	73	5	2	0	25	16	—	7	.274	.316	.308
Harry Steinfeldt	3B67,2B64,SS2*	R	22	134	510	57	125	29	7	2	66	27	—	14	.245	.292	.341
Tommy Corcoran	SS124,2B5	R	31	127	523	64	128	21	9	1	54	22	—	27	.245	.278	.325
Jimmy Barrett	OF137	L	25	137	545	114	172	11	7	5	42	72	—	44	.316	.400	.389
Algie McBride	OF109	L	31	112	436	59	120	15	8	4	59	25	—	12	.275	.320	.374
Sam Crawford	OF94	L	20	101	389	68	101	15	15	7	59	28	—	14	.260	.314	.429
Charlie Irwin	3B61,SS16,OF6*	L	31	87	333	59	91	15	6	1	44	14	—	9	.273	.314	.363
Mike Kahoe	C51,SS1	R	26	52	175	18	33	3	3	1	9	4	—	3	.189	.215	.257
Bob Wood	C18,3B15,OF1	R	34	45	139	17	37	8	1	0	22	10	—	3	.266	.320	.338
Ted Breitenstein	P24,OF12	L	31	41	126	12	24	1	1	2	12	9	—	0	.190	.244	.262
Phil Geier	OF27,3B2	L	23	30	113	18	29	1	4	0	10	7	—	3	.257	.306	.336
Elmer Smith†	OF27	L	32	29	111	14	31	4	4	1	18	18	—	5	.279	.389	.414
Topsy Hartsel	OF18	L	26	18	64	10	21	2	1	2	5	8	—	7	.328	.403	.484
Dick Harley	OF5	L	27	5	21	2	9	1	0	0	5	1	—	4	.429	.455	.476
Bob Allen	SS5	R	32	5	15	0	2	1	0	0	1	0	—	0	.133	.188	.200

H. Steinfeldt, 2 G at OF; C. Irwin, 3 G at 2B

Pitcher	T	Age	G	GS	CG	ShO	IP	H	HR	BB	SO	W-L	Sv	ERA
Noodles Hahn	L	21	39	37	29	4	311.1	306	4	89	132	16-20	0	3.27
Ed Scott	R	29	42	35	31	0	315.0	370	10	65	87	17-20	1	3.86
Doc Newton	L	22	36	27	22	1	234.2	255	4	100	88	9-15	0	4.14
Bill Phillips	R	31	29	24	17	3	208.1	229	5	67	51	9-11	0	4.28
Ted Breitenstein	L	31	24	20	18	1	192.1	205	4	79	39	10-10	0	3.65
Archie Stimmel	R	27	2	1	1	0	13.0	18	1	4	2	1-1	0	6.92

1900 New York Giants 8th NL 60-78 .435 23.0 GB

Buck Ewing (21-41)/George Davis (39-37)

Player	Gm by Position	B	Age	G	AB	R	H	2B	3B	HR	RBI	BB	SO	SB	Avg	OBP	Slg
Frank Bowerman	C75,SS2	R	31	80	270	25	65	5	3	1	42	6	—	10	.241	.268	.293
Jack Doyle	1B133	R	30	133	505	69	135	24	1	1	66	34	—	34	.267	.317	.325
Kid Gleason	2B111,SS1	S	33	111	420	60	104	11	3	1	29	17	—	23	.248	.280	.295
Charlie Hickman	3B120,OF7	R	24	127	473	65	148	19	17	9	91	17	—	10	.313	.359	.482
George Davis	SS114	S	29	114	426	69	136	20	4	3	61	35	—	29	.319	.376	.406
George Van Haltren	OF141,P1	L	34	141	571	114	180	30	7	1	51	50	—	45	.315	.371	.398
Kip Selbach	OF141	R	28	141	523	98	176	29	12	4	68	72	—	36	.337	.425	.461
Elmer Smith†	OF83	L	32	85	312	47	81	9	7	2	34	24	—	14	.260	.317	.353
Mike Grady	C41,1B12,SS11*	R	30	83	251	36	55	8	4	0	27	34	—	9	.219	.331	.283
Win Mercer	P33,3B19,OF14*	R	26	76	248	32	73	4	0	0	27	26	—	15	.294	.366	.310
John Warner	C31	L	27	34	108	15	27	4	0	0	13	8	—	1	.250	.319	.287
Pop Foster	OF12,SS7,2B5	R	22	31	84	19	22	3	1	0	11	11	—	0	.262	.347	.321
Danny Murphy	2B22	R	23	22	74	11	20	1	0	0	6	8	—	4	.270	.341	.284
Curt Bernard	OF19,SS1	L	22	20	71	9	18	2	0	0	8	6	—	1	.254	.329	.282
Cy Seymour	P13,OF3,1B1	L	27	23	40	9	12	0	0	0	2	3	—	0	.300	.349	.300
Charlie Frisbee	OF4	S	26	4	13	2	2	1	0	0	3	2	—	0	.154	.267	.231
Dick Cogan	P2,SS1	R	28	3	8	0	1	0	0	0	0	1	—	0	.125	.222	.125
Tommy Sheehan	SS1	R	22	1	2	0	0	0	0	0	0	1	—	0	.000	.000	.000

M. Grady, 7 G at 3B, 5 G at OF, 2 G at 2B; W. Mercer, 7 G at SS, 3 G at 2B

Pitcher	T	Age	G	GS	CG	ShO	IP	H	HR	BB	SO	W-L	Sv	ERA
Bill Carrick	R	26	45	41	32	1	341.2	415	7	92	63	19-22	0	3.53
Pink Hawley	R	27	41	38	34	2	329.1	377	7	89	80	18-18	0	3.53
Win Mercer	R	26	33	29	26	1	242.2	303	5	58	39	13-17	0	3.86
Ed Doheny	L	26	20	18	12	0	133.2	148	2	96	44	4-14	0	5.45
Luther Taylor	R	25	11	7	6	0	62.1	74	0	24	16	4-3	0	2.45
Cy Seymour	L	27	13	7	2	0	53.0	58	4	54	19	2-2	0	6.96
Christy Mathewson	R	21	6	1	1	0	33.2	37	1	20	15	0-3	0	5.08
Dick Cogan	R	28	2	0	0	0	8.0	10	0	6	1	0-0	0	6.75
George Van Haltren	L	34	1	0	0	0	3.0	1	0	3	0	0-0	0	0.00

»1901 Chicago White Stockings 1st AL 83-53 .610 —

Clark Griffith

Player	Gm by Position	B	Age	G	AB	R	H	2B	3B	HR	RBI	BB	SO	SB	Avg	OBP	Slg
Billy Sullivan	C97,3B1	R	26	98	367	54	90	15	6	4	56	10	—	12	.245	.271	.351
Frank Isbell	1B137,2B2,P1*	L	25	137	556	93	143	15	8	3	70	36	—	52	.257	.311	.329
Sam Mertes	2B132,OF5	R	28	137	545	94	151	16	17	5	98	52	—	46	.277	.347	.396
Fred Hartman	3B119	R	33	120	473	77	146	23	13	3	89	25	—	31	.309	.355	.431
Frank Shugart	SS107	S	34	107	415	62	104	9	12	2	47	28	—	12	.251	.301	.345
Fielder Jones	OF133	L	29	133	521	120	162	16	3	2	65	84	—	38	.311	.412	.365
Dummy Hoy	OF132	L	39	132	527	112	155	28	11	2	60	86	—	27	.294	.407	.400
Herm McFarland	OF132	L	31	132	473	83	130	21	9	4	59	75	—	33	.275	.384	.383
Joe Sugden	C42,1B5	S	30	48	153	21	42	7	1	0	19	13	—	4	.275	.339	.333
Jimmy Burke†	SS31,3B11	R	26	42	148	20	39	5	0	0	21	12	—	11	.264	.327	.297
Nixey Callahan	P27,3B6,2B2	R	27	45	118	15	39	7	3	1	19	10	—	10	.331	.383	.466
Pop Foster†	OF9	R	23	12	35	4	10	2	2	1	6	4	—	0	.286	.359	.543
Dave Brain	2B5	R	22	5	20	2	7	1	0	0	5	1	—	0	.350	.381	.400

F. Isbell, 1 G at 3B, 1 G at SS

Pitcher	T	Age	G	GS	CG	ShO	IP	H	HR	BB	SO	W-L	Sv	ERA
Roy Patterson	R	24	41	35	30	4	312.1	345	11	62	127	20-16	0	3.37
Clark Griffith	R	31	35	30	26	5	266.2	275	4	50	67	24-7	1	2.67
John Katoll	R	29	27	25	19	0	208.0	231	3	53	59	11-10	0	2.81
Nixey Callahan	R	27	27	22	20	1	215.1	195	4	50	70	15-8	0	2.42
Erwin Harvey	L	22	16	9	5	0	92.0	91	2	34	27	3-6	1	3.62
John Skopec	L	21	9	9	6	0	68.1	62	1	45	24	6-3	0	3.16
Wiley Piatt†	L	26	7	6	4	1	51.2	42	2	14	19	4-2	0	2.79
Frank Dupee	L	24	1	0	0	0	0.0	0	0	3	0	0-1	0	—
John McAleese	R	22	1	0	0	0	3.0	7	0	1	1	0-0	0	9.00
Frank Isbell	R	25	1	0	0	0	1.0	2	0	0	0	0-0	0	9.00

1901 Boston Americans 2nd AL 79-57 .581 4.0 GB

Jimmy Collins

Player	Gm by Position	B	Age	G	AB	R	H	2B	3B	HR	RBI	BB	SO	SB	Avg	OBP	Slg
O. Schreckengost	C72,1B4	R	26	86	280	37	85	13	5	0	38	19	—	6	.304	.356	.386
Buck Freeman	1B128,2B1,OF1	L	29	129	490	88	166	23	15	12	114	44	—	17	.339	.400	.520
Hobe Ferris	2B138	R	23	138	523	68	131	16	15	2	63	23	—	13	.250	.290	.350
Jimmy Collins	3B138	R	31	138	564	108	187	42	16	6	94	34	—	19	.332	.375	.495
Freddy Parent	SS138	R	25	138	517	87	158	23	9	4	59	41	—	16	.306	.367	.408
Tommy Dowd	OF137,1B2,3B1	R	32	138	594	104	159	18	7	3	52	38	—	33	.268	.315	.337
Charlie Hemphill	OF136	L	25	136	545	71	142	10	10	3	62	39	—	11	.261	.312	.332
Chick Stahl	OF131	L	28	131	515	105	156	20	16	6	72	54	—	29	.303	.377	.439
Lou Criger	C68,1B8	R	29	76	268	26	62	6	3	0	24	11	—	7	.231	.270	.276
Nig Cuppy	P13,OF4	R	31	17	49	4	10	3	0	0	6	4	—	0	.204	.264	.265
Fred Mitchell	P17,2B2,SS1	R	23	20	44	5	7	0	2	0	4	2	—	0	.159	.196	.250
Charlie Jones	OF10	R	25	10	41	6	6	2	0	0	6	1	—	2	.146	.167	.195
Larry McLean	1B5	R	19	9	19	4	4	1	0	0	2	0	—	1	.211	.211	.263
Ben Beville	P2,1B1	R	23	3	7	2	2	2	0	0	1	0	—	0	.286	.286	.571
Jack Slattery	C1	R	23	1	3	1	1	0	0	0	1	1	—	0	.333	.500	.333
Harry Gleason	3B1	R	26	1	1	0	1	0	0	0	0	0	—	1	1.000	1.000	1.000

Pitcher	T	Age	G	GS	CG	ShO	IP	H	HR	BB	SO	W-L	Sv	ERA
Cy Young	R	34	43	41	38	5	371.1	324	6	37	158	33-10	0	1.62
Ted Lewis	R	28	39	34	31	1	316.1	299	14	91	103	16-17	1	3.53
George Winter	R	23	28	28	26	1	241.0	234	4	66	63	16-12	0	2.80
Fred Mitchell	R	23	17	13	10	0	108.2	115	2	51	34	6-6	0	3.81
Nig Cuppy	R	31	13	11	9	0	93.1	111	1	14	22	4-6	0	4.15
Win Kellum	L	25	6	6	5	0	48.0	61	3	7	8	2-3	0	6.38
Ben Beville	R	23	2	2	1	0	9.0	8	0	9	1	0-2	0	4.00
George Prentiss	R	25	2	1	1	0	10.0	7	0	6	0	1-0	0	1.80
Frank Foreman†	L	38	1	1	1	0	8.0	8	1	2	1	0-1	0	9.00
Jake Volz	R	23	1	1	1	0	7.0	6	2	9	5	1-0	0	9.00
Deacon Morrissey	R	25	1	0	0	0	4.1	5	0	2	1	0-0	0	2.08

1901 Detroit Tigers 3rd AL 74-61 .548 8.5 GB

George Stallings

Player	Gm by Position	B	Age	G	AB	R	H	2B	3B	HR	RBI	BB	SO	SB	Avg	OBP	Slg
Fritz Buelow	C69	R	25	70	231	28	52	5	5	2	29	11	—	2	.225	.269	.316
Pop Dillon	1B74	L	27	74	281	40	81	14	6	1	42	15	—	14	.288	.324	.391
Kid Gleason	2B135	S	34	135	547	82	150	16	12	3	75	41	—	32	.274	.327	.364
Doc Casey	3B127	S	31	128	540	105	153	16	9	2	46	32	—	34	.283	.335	.357
Kid Elberfeld	SS121	R	26	121	432	76	133	21	11	3	76	57	—	23	.308	.397	.428
Jimmy Barrett	OF135	L	26	135	542	110	159	16	9	4	65	76	—	26	.293	.385	.378
Doc Nance	OF132	R	24	132	461	72	129	24	5	3	66	51	—	9	.280	.355	.373
Ducky Holmes	OF131	L	32	131	537	90	158	28	10	4	62	37	—	35	.294	.347	.406
Sport McAllister	C35,1B28,OF11*	S	26	90	306	45	92	9	4	3	57	15	—	17	.301	.344	.386
Al Shaw	C42,1B9,3B2*	R	26	55	171	20	46	7	0	1	23	10	—	2	.269	.321	.327
Joe Yeager	P26,SS12,2B1	R	25	41	125	18	37	7	1	2	17	4	—	3	.296	.343	.416
Davey Crockett	1B27	L	25	28	102	10	29	2	2	0	14	6	—	1	.284	.336	.343
Emil Frisk	P11,OF2	L	26	20	48	10	15	3	0	1	7	3	—	0	.313	.365	.438
Frank Owen	P8,OF1	S	21	9	20	1	1	1	0	0	1	1	—	0	.050	.095	.100
Harry Lochhead†	SS1	R	25	1	4	2	2	0	0	0	0	0	—	0	.500	.600	.500

S. McAllister, 10 G at 3B, 3 G at SS; A. Shaw, 1 G at SS

Pitcher	T	Age	G	GS	CG	ShO	IP	H	HR	BB	SO	W-L	Sv	ERA
Roscoe Miller	R	24	38	36	35	3	332.0	339	1	98	79	23-13	1	2.95
Ed Siever	L	24	38	33	30	2	288.2	334	9	65	85	18-15	0	3.24
Jack Cronin	R	27	30	28	21	1	219.2	261	6	42	62	13-15	0	3.89
Joe Yeager	R	25	26	25	22	2	199.2	209	4	46	38	12-11	1	2.61
Emil Frisk	R	26	11	7	6	0	74.2	94	1	26	22	5-4	0	4.34
Frank Owen	R	21	8	5	3	0	56.0	70	1	30	17	1-3	0	4.34
Ed High	L	24	4	1	1	0	18.0	21	0	6	4	1-0	0	3.50

1901 Philadelphia Athletics 4th AL 74-62 .544 9.0 GB

Connie Mack

Player	Gm by Position	B	Age	G	AB	R	H	2B	3B	HR	RBI	BB	SO	SB	Avg	OBP	Slg
Mike Powers	C111,1B3	R	30	116	431	53	108	26	5	1	47	18	—	10	.251	.292	.341
Harry Davis	1B117	R	27	117	496	92	152	28	10	8	76	23	—	21	.306	.340	.452
Nap Lajoie	2B119,SS12	R	26	131	544	145	232	48	14	14	125	24	—	27	.426	.463	.643
Lave Cross	3B100	R	35	100	424	82	139	28	12	2	73	19	—	23	.328	.358	.465
Joe Dolan†	SS61,3B35,2B1*	—	28	98	338	50	73	21	2	1	38	26	—	3	.216	.282	.299
Dave Fultz	OF106,2B18,SS9	R	26	132	561	95	164	17	9	0	52	32	—	36	.292	.334	.355
Socks Seybold	OF100,1B14	R	30	114	449	74	150	24	14	8	90	40	—	15	.334	.397	.503
Matty McIntyre	OF82	L	21	82	308	38	85	12	4	0	46	30	—	11	.276	.346	.341
Jack Hayden	OF50	L	20	51	211	35	56	6	4	0	17	18	—	4	.265	.323	.332
Phil Geier†	OF50,SS2,3B1	L	24	50	211	42	49	5	2	0	23	24	—	7	.232	.314	.275
Bones Ely†	SS45	R	38	45	171	11	37	6	2	0	16	3	—	6	.216	.230	.275
Chick Fraser	P40,OF2	R	30	43	139	17	26	2	3	0	8	6	—	4	.187	.226	.245
Farmer Steelman†	C14,OF12	—	26	27	88	5	23	2	0	0	7	10	—	4	.261	.350	.284
Harry Smith	C9,OF1	R	26	11	34	3	11	1	0	0	3	2	—	0	.324	.378	.353
Harry Lochhead†	SS9	R	25	9	34	3	3	0	0	0	2	3	—	0	.088	.184	.088
Morgan Murphy	C8,1B1	R	34	9	28	5	6	0	0	0	6	0	—	1	.214	.214	.250
Fred Ketcham	OF5	—	22	5	22	5	5	0	0	0	2	0	—	0	.227	.227	.227
Billy Milligan	P6,OF1	R	22	7	15	5	5	0	1	1	3	1	—	0	.333	.375	.667
Tom Leahy†	OF2,C1,SS1	—	32	5	15	1	5	1	0	0	1	1	—	0	.333	.375	.400
Bob Lindemann	OF3	S	20	3	9	0	1	0	0	0	0	0	—	0	.111	.111	.111
Charlie Carr	1B2	R	24	2	8	1	1	0	0	0	0	0	—	0	.125	.125	.125
Billy Lauder	3B2	R	27	2	8	1	1	0	0	0	0	0	—	0	.125	.125	.125
Bob McKinney	2B1,3B1	R	25	2	2	0	0	0	0	0	0	0	—	0	.000	.000	.000

J. Dolan, 1 G at OF

Pitcher	T	Age	G	GS	CG	ShO	IP	H	HR	BB	SO	W-L	Sv	ERA
Chick Fraser	R	30	40	37	35	2	331.0	344	6	132	110	22-16	0	3.81
Eddie Plank	L	25	33	32	28	1	260.2	254	3	68	90	17-13	0	3.31
Bill Bernhard	R	30	31	27	26	1	257.0	328	6	50	58	17-10	0	4.52
Snake Wiltse†	L	29	19	19	18	2	166.0	185	1	35	40	13-5	0	3.58
Wiley Piatt†	L	26	18	16	15	0	140.0	176	3	60	45	5-12	1	4.63
Billy Milligan	L	22	6	3	2	0	33.0	43	1	14	5	0-3	0	4.36
Bock Baker†	L	22	1	1	0	0	6.0	6	0	6	1	0-1	0	10.50
John McPherson	—	32	1	1	0	0	4.0	7	0	4	0	0-1	0	11.25
Pete Loos	R	23	1	1	0	0	1.0	2	0	4	0	0-1	0	27.00
Dummy Leitner†	R	30	1	0	0	0	2.0	1	0	1	1	0-0	0	0.00

1901 Baltimore Orioles 5th AL 68-65 .511 13.5 GB

John McGraw

Player	Gm by Position	B	Age	G	AB	R	H	2B	3B	HR	RBI	BB	SO	SB	Avg	OBP	Slg
Roger Bresnahan	C69,OF8,3B4*	R	22	86	295	40	79	9	9	1	32	23	—	10	.268	.323	.369
Burt Hart	1B58	S	31	58	206	33	64	3	5	0	23	20	—	7	.311	.383	.374
Jimmy Williams	2B130	R	24	130	501	113	159	26	21	7	96	56	—	21	.317	.388	.495
John McGraw	3B69	L	28	73	232	71	81	14	9	0	28	61	—	24	.349	.508	.487
Bill Keister	SS112	L	26	115	442	78	145	20	21	2	93	18	—	24	.328	.365	.482
Cy Seymour	OF133,1B1	L	28	134	547	84	166	19	8	1	77	28	—	38	.303	.337	.373
Jim Jackson	OF96	R	23	99	364	42	91	17	3	2	50	20	—	11	.250	.291	.330
Steve Brodie	OF83	L	32	83	306	41	95	6	6	2	41	25	—	9	.310	.378	.389
Mike Donlin	OF74,1B47	L	23	121	476	107	162	23	13	5	67	53	—	33	.340	.409	.475
Jack Dunn†	3B67,SS19,P9*	R	28	96	362	41	90	9	4	0	36	21	—	10	.249	.301	.296
Wilbert Robinson	C67	R	38	68	239	32	72	12	3	0	26	10	—	9	.301	.335	.377
Harry Howell	P37,OF9,SS6*	R	24	53	188	26	41	10	5	2	26	5	—	6	.218	.242	.356
Joe McGinnity	P48,3B1	R	30	48	148	12	31	2	1	0	6	4	—	3	.209	.235	.236
Frank Foutz	1B20	R	24	20	72	13	17	4	1	2	14	8	—	0	.236	.321	.403
George Rohe	1B8,3B6	R	25	14	36	7	10	2	0	0	4	5	—	1	.278	.381	.333
Chappie Snodgrass	OF2	R	31	3	10	0	1	0	0	0	1	0	—	0	.100	.100	.100
Tacks Latimer	C1	R	23	1	4	0	1	0	0	0	0	0	—	0	.250	.250	.250
Slats Jordan	1B1	L	21	1	3	0	0	0	0	0	0	0	—	0	.000	.000	.000

R. Bresnahan, 2 G at P, 2 G at 2B; J. Dunn, 1 G at 2B, 1 G at OF; H. Howell, 2 G at 1B, 1 G at 2B

Pitcher	T	Age	G	GS	CG	ShO	IP	H	HR	BB	SO	W-L	Sv	ERA
Joe McGinnity	R	30	48	43	39	1	382.0	412	7	96	75	26-20	1	3.56
Harry Howell	R	24	37	34	32	1	294.2	333	5	79	93	14-21	0	3.67
Jerry Nops	L	26	27	23	17	1	176.2	192	5	59	43	12-10	1	4.08
Frank Foreman†	L	38	24	22	18	1	191.1	225	2	58	41	12-6	1	3.67
Jack Dunn†	R	28	9	6	6	0	59.2	74	2	21	5	3-3	0	3.62
Crazy Schmit	L	35	4	3	1	0	22.2	25	0	16	2	0-2	0	1.99
Stan Yerkes†	R	26	1	1	1	0	8.0	12	0	2	4	0-1	0	6.75
Roger Bresnahan	R	22	2	1	0	0	6.0	10	0	4	3	0-1	0	6.00
Bill Karns	L	25	3	1	1	0	17.0	30	0	9	5	1-0	0	6.35

1901 Washington Senators 6th AL 61-72 .459 20.5 GB

Jimmy Manning

Player	Gm by Position	B	Age	G	AB	R	H	2B	3B	HR	RBI	BB	SO	SB	Avg	OBP	Slg
Boileryard Clarke	C107,1B3	R	32	110	422	58	118	15	5	3	54	23	—	7	.280	.335	.360
Mike Grady	1B59,C30,OF3	R	31	94	347	57	99	17	10	9	56	27	—	14	.285	.351	.470
John Farrell	2B72,OF62,3B1	R	24	135	555	100	151	32	11	3	63	52	—	25	.272	.336	.386
Bill Coughlin	3B137	R	22	137	506	75	139	17	13	6	68	25	—	16	.275	.317	.395
Billy Clingman	SS137	S	31	137	480	66	116	10	7	2	55	42	—	10	.242	.308	.304
Sam Dungan	OF104,1B35	R	34	138	559	70	179	26	12	1	72	40	—	9	.320	.368	.415
Pop Foster†	OF102,SS2	R	23	103	392	65	109	16	9	6	54	41	—	10	.278	.352	.411
Irv Waldron†	OF78	R	25	79	332	54	107	14	3	0	23	22	—	8	.322	.368	.383
Joe Quinn	2B66	R	36	66	266	33	67	11	2	2	34	11	—	7	.252	.287	.331
Dale Gear	OF34,P24	R	29	58	199	17	47	9	2	0	20	4	—	2	.236	.251	.302
Win Mercer	P24,OF16,1B7*	R	27	51	140	26	42	7	2	0	16	23	—	10	.300	.402	.379
Watty Lee	P36,OF7	L	21	43	129	15	33	6	3	0	12	7	—	0	.256	.304	.349
Bill Everitt	1B33	L	32	33	115	14	22	3	2	0	8	15	—	7	.191	.301	.252
Jack O'Brien†	OF11	L	28	11	45	5	8	0	0	0	5	3	—	2	.178	.245	.178
Charlie Luskey	OF8,C3	R	25	11	41	8	8	3	1	0	3	2	—	0	.195	.233	.317
Tim Jordan	1B6	L	22	6	20	2	4	1	0	0	2	3	—	0	.200	.304	.250
Ben Harrison	OF1	R	—	1	2	0	0	0	0	0	0	1	—	0	.000	.333	.000

W. Mercer, 1 G at 3B, 1 G at SS

Pitcher	T	Age	G	GS	CG	ShO	IP	H	HR	BB	SO	W-L	Sv	ERA
Bill Carrick	R	27	42	37	34	0	324.0	367	12	93	70	14-22	0	3.75
Watty Lee	L	21	36	33	25	2	262.0	328	14	45	63	16-16	0	4.40
Casey Patten	L	25	32	30	26	4	254.1	285	8	74	109	18-10	0	3.93
Win Mercer	R	27	24	22	19	1	179.2	217	8	50	31	9-13	1	4.56
Dale Gear	R	29	24	16	14	1	163.0	199	9	22	35	4-11	0	4.03

1901 Cleveland Blues 7th AL 54-82 .397 29.0 GB

Jimmy McAleer

Player	Gm by Position	B	Age	G	AB	R	H	2B	3B	HR	RBI	BB	SO	SB	Avg	OBP	Slg
Bob Wood	C84,OF3,1B1*	R	35	98	346	45	101	23	3	1	49	12	—	6	.292	.327	.384
Candy LaChance	1B133	S	31	133	548	81	166	22	9	1	75	7	—	11	.303	.314	.381
Erve Beck	2B132	R	22	135	539	78	156	26	8	6	79	23	—	7	.289	.320	.401
Bill Bradley	3B133,P1	R	23	133	516	95	151	28	13	1	55	26	—	15	.293	.336	.403
Frank Scheibeck	SS92	R	36	93	329	33	70	11	3	0	38	18	—	3	.213	.258	.264
Ollie Pickering	OF137	L	31	137	547	102	169	25	6	0	40	58	—	36	.309	.383	.377
Jack O'Brien†	OF92,3B1	L	28	92	375	54	106	14	5	0	39	22	—	13	.283	.329	.347
Jack McCarthy	OF86	L	32	86	343	60	110	14	7	0	32	30	—	9	.321	.382	.402
Erwin Harvey†	OF45	L	22	45	170	21	60	5	5	1	24	9	—	15	.353	.392	.459
George Yeager†	C25,1B5,2B2	R	28	39	139	13	31	5	0	0	14	4	—	2	.223	.250	.259
Joe Connor†	C32,OF4	R	26	37	121	13	17	3	1	0	6	7	—	2	.140	.200	.182
Frank Genins	OF26	—	34	26	101	15	23	5	0	0	9	8	—	3	.228	.284	.277
Danny Shay	SS19	—	24	19	75	4	17	2	2	0	10	2	—	0	.227	.266	.307
Tom Donovan	OF18,P1	R	28	18	71	9	18	3	1	0	5	0	—	1	.254	.254	.324
Jim McGuire	SS18	—	26	18	69	4	16	2	0	0	3	0	—	0	.232	.232	.261
Bill Hoffer	P16,SS1	R	30	17	44	3	6	0	2	0	2	3	—	0	.136	.208	.227
Bill Hallman†	SS5	R	34	5	19	2	4	0	0	0	3	2	—	0	.211	.286	.211
Truck Eagan†	2B5,3B1	R	23	5	18	2	3	0	1	0	2	1	—	0	.167	.211	.278
Jimmy McAleer	OF2,P1,3B1	R	36	3	7	0	1	0	0	0	0	0	—	0	.143	.143	.143
Frank Cross	OF1	—	28	1	5	0	3	0	0	0	0	0	—	0	.600	.600	.600
Ed Cermak	OF1	R	19	1	4	0	0	0	0	0	0	0	—	0	.000	.000	.000
Harry Hogan	OF1	—	25	1	4	0	0	0	0	0	0	0	—	0	.000	.000	.000
Shorty Gallagher	OF2	—	29	2	4	0	0	0	0	0	0	0	—	0	.000	.000	.000
Russ Hall	SS1	—	29	1	4	2	2	0	0	0	0	0	—	0	.500	.500	.500
Paddy Livingston	C1	R	21	1	2	0	0	0	0	0	0	0	—	0	.000	.333	.000

B. Wood, 1 G at 2B, 1 G at SS

Pitcher	T	Age	G	GS	CG	ShO	IP	H	HR	BB	SO	W-L	Sv	ERA
Pete Dowling†	L	—	33	30	28	2	256.1	269	1	104	99	11-22	0	3.86
Earl Moore	R	21	31	30	28	4	251.1	234	4	107	99	16-14	0	2.90
Bill Hart	R	35	20	19	16	0	157.2	180	3	57	48	7-11	0	3.77
Ed Scott	R	30	17	16	11	0	124.2	149	2	38	23	6-6	0	4.40
Jack Bracken	R	20	12	12	12	0	100.0	137	4	31	18	4-8	0	6.21
Bill Hoffer	R	30	16	10	10	0	99.0	113	2	35	19	3-8	3	4.55
Harry McNeal	R	23	12	10	9	0	85.1	120	4	30	15	5-5	0	4.43
Bill Cristall	L	22	6	6	5	1	48.1	54	1	30	12	1-5	0	4.84
Dick Braggins	R	21	4	3	2	0	32.0	44	1	15	1	1-2	0	4.78
Gus Weyhing†	R	34	2	1	0	0	11.1	20	0	5	0	0-0	0	7.94
Bock Baker†	L	22	1	1	1	0	8.0	23	0	6	0	0-1	0	5.63
Tom Donovan	R	28	1	0	0	0	7.0	16	0	3	0	0-0	0	5.14
Bill Bradley	R	23	1	0	0	0	1.0	4	0	0	0	0-0	0	0.00
Jimmy McAleer	R	36	1	0	0	0	0.1	2	0	3	0	0-0	0	0.00

1901 Milwaukee Brewers 8th AL 48-89 .350 35.5 GB

Hugh Duffy

Player	Gm by Position	B	Age	G	AB	R	H	2B	3B	HR	RBI	BB	SO	SB	Avg	OBP	Slg
Billy Maloney	C72,OF8	L	23	86	290	42	85	3	4	0	22	7	—	11	.293	.328	.331
John Anderson	1B125,OF13	S	27	138	576	90	190	46	7	8	99	24	—	35	.330	.360	.476
Billy Gilbert	2B127	R	25	127	492	77	133	14	7	0	43	31	—	19	.270	.320	.327
Jimmy Burke†	3B64	R	26	64	233	24	48	8	0	0	26	17	—	6	.206	.266	.240
Wid Conroy	SS118,3B12	R	24	131	503	74	129	20	6	5	64	36	—	21	.256	.316	.350
Bill Hallman	OF139	L	25	139	549	70	135	27	6	2	47	41	—	12	.246	.301	.328
Hugh Duffy	OF77	R	34	79	285	40	86	15	9	2	45	16	—	12	.302	.341	.439
Irv Waldron†	OF62	R	25	62	266	48	79	8	6	0	29	16	—	12	.297	.342	.372
Bill Friel	3B61,OF28,2B9*	L	25	106	376	51	100	13	7	4	35	23	—	15	.266	.310	.370
George Hogriever	OF54	R	32	54	221	25	52	10	2	0	16	30	—	7	.235	.329	.299
Jiggs Donahue†	C19,1B13	L	21	37	107	10	34	5	4	0	16	10	—	4	.318	.387	.439
Joe Connor†	C30,2B1,3B1*	R	26	38	102	10	28	3	1	1	9	6	—	4	.275	.321	.353
Tom Leahy†	C28,OF2,2B1	—	32	33	99	18	24	6	2	0	10	11	—	3	.242	.348	.343
Bert Husting	P34,1B1,3B1	R	23	36	94	12	19	2	1	1	9	1	—	1	.202	.211	.277
Ed Bruyette	OF21,2B3,3B1*	L	26	26	82	7	15	3	0	0	4	12	—	1	.183	.295	.220
Pink Hawley	P26,OF2	L	28	30	73	2	19	4	0	0	9	6	—	0	.260	.316	.315
Davy Jones	OF14	L	21	14	52	12	9	0	0	3	5	11	—	4	.173	.328	.346
George Bone	SS12	S	24	12	43	6	13	2	0	0	6	4	—	0	.302	.362	.349
Phil Geier†	OF8,3B3	L	24	11	39	4	7	1	1	0	1	5	—	4	.179	.273	.256
George McBride	SS3	R	20	3	12	0	2	0	0	0	0	1	—	0	.167	.231	.167
John Butler	C1	R	21	1	3	0	0	0	0	0	0	1	—	0	.000	.250	.000
Lou Gertenrich	OF1	R	26	2	3	1	1	0	0	0	0	0	—	0	.333	.333	.333

B. Friel, 6 G at SS; J. Connor, 1 G at OF; E. Bruyette, 1 G at SS

Pitcher	T	Age	G	GS	CG	ShO	IP	H	HR	BB	SO	W-L	Sv	ERA
Bill Reidy	R	27	37	33	28	2	301.1	364	14	62	50	16-20	0	4.21
Ned Garvin	R	27	37	27	22	1	257.1	258	4	90	122	7-20	2	3.46
Bert Husting	R	23	34	26	19	0	217.1	234	5	95	67	10-15	1	4.27
Tully Sparks	R	26	29	26	18	0	210.0	228	5	93	62	7-16	0	3.51
Pink Hawley	R	28	26	23	17	0	182.1	228	3	41	50	7-14	0	4.59
Pete Dowling†	L	—	10	4	3	0	49.2	71	1	14	25	1-4	1	5.62

»1901 Pittsburgh Pirates 1st NL 90-49 .647 —

Fred Clarke

Player	Gm by Position	B	Age	G	AB	R	H	2B	3B	HR	RBI	BB	SO	SB	Avg	OBP	Slg
Chief Zimmer	C68	R	40	69	236	17	52	7	3	0	21	20	—	6	.220	.292	.275
Kitty Bransfield	1B139	R	26	139	566	92	167	26	16	0	91	29	—	23	.295	.335	.398
Claude Ritchey	2B139,SS1	S	27	140	540	66	160	20	4	1	74	47	—	15	.296	.357	.354
Tommy Leach	3B92,SS4	R	23	98	374	64	114	12	13	1	44	20	—	16	.305	.347	.414
Bones Ely†	SS64,3B1	R	38	65	240	18	50	6	3	0	28	6	—	5	.208	.234	.258
Ginger Beaumont	OF133	L	24	133	558	120	185	14	5	8	72	44	—	36	.332	.382	.418
Fred Clarke	OF127,3B1,SS1	L	28	129	527	118	171	24	15	6	60	51	—	23	.324	.395	.461
Lefty Davis†	OF86	L	26	87	335	87	105	8	11	2	33	56	—	22	.313	.415	.421
Honus Wagner	SS61,OF54,3B24*	R	27	140	549	101	194	37	11	6	126	53	—	49	.353	.416	.494
Jack O'Connor	C59	R	32	61	202	16	39	7	3	0	22	10	—	2	.193	.238	.257
Jesse Tannehill	P32,OF10	S	26	42	135	19	33	3	3	1	12	6	—	0	.244	.277	.333
George Yeager†	C20,3B4,1B1	R	28	26	91	9	24	2	1	0	10	4	—	1	.264	.302	.308
Ed Poole	P12,OF12,2B1*	R	26	26	78	6	16	4	0	1	4	4	—	1	.205	.244	.295
Jimmy Burke†	3B14	R	26	14	51	4	10	0	0	0	4	4	—	0	.196	.268	.196
Lew Carr	SS9,3B1	R	28	9	28	2	7	1	1	0	4	2	—	0	.250	.344	.357
Jud Smith	3B6	R	32	6	21	1	3	1	0	0	0	3	—	0	.143	.250	.190
Truck Eagan†	SS3	R	23	4	12	0	1	0	0	0	2	0	—	1	.083	.083	.083
Terry Turner	3B2	R	20	2	7	0	3	0	0	0	1	0	—	0	.429	.429	.429
Elmer Smith†	OF1	L	33	4	4	0	0	0	0	0	0	2	—	0	.000	.333	.000
Jiggs Donahue†	C1	L	21	2	0	0	0	0	0	0	0	0	—	0	—	—	—

H. Wagner, 1 G at 2B; E. Poole, 1 G at 3B

Pitcher	T	Age	G	GS	CG	ShO	IP	H	HR	BB	SO	W-L	Sv	ERA
Deacon Phillippe	R	29	37	32	30	1	296.0	274	8	38	103	22-12	2	2.22
Jesse Tannehill	L	26	32	30	25	4	252.1	240	1	36	118	18-10	1	2.18
Jack Chesbro	R	27	36	28	26	6	287.2	261	4	52	129	21-10	1	2.38
Sam Leever	R	29	21	20	18	2	176.0	182	2	39	82	14-5	0	2.86
Ed Poole	R	26	12	10	8	1	80.0	78	3	30	26	5-4	0	3.60
Ed Doheny†	L	27	11	10	6	1	76.2	68	1	22	28	6-2	0	2.00
Snake Wiltse†	L	29	7	5	3	0	44.1	57	2	13	10	1-4	0	4.26
George Merritt	R	21	3	3	3	0	24.0	28	0	5	5	3-0	0	4.88
Rube Waddell†	L	24	2	2	0	0	7.2	10	0	9	4	0-2	0	9.39

Seasons: Team Rosters 545

1901 Philadelphia Phillies 2nd NL 83-57 .593 7.5 GB — Bill Shettsline

Player	Gm by Position	B	Age	G	AB	R	H	2B	3B	HR	RBI	BB	SO	SB	Avg	OBP	Slg
Ed McFarland	C74	R	26	74	295	33	84	14	2	1	32	18	—	11	.285	.326	.356
Hughie Jennings	1B80,2B1,SS1	R	32	82	302	38	79	21	2	1	39	25	—	13	.262	.342	.354
Bill Hallman†	2B90,3B33	R	34	123	445	46	82	13	5	0	38	26	—	13	.184	.236	.236
Harry Wolverton	3B93	L	27	93	379	42	117	15	4	0	43	22	—	13	.309	.356	.369
Monte Cross	SS139	R	31	139	483	49	95	14	1	1	44	52	—	24	.197	.281	.236
Elmer Flick	OF138	L	25	138	540	112	180	32	17	8	88	52	—	30	.333	.399	.500
Roy Thomas	OF129	L	27	129	479	102	148	5	2	1	28	100	—	27	.309	.437	.334
Ed Delahanty	OF84,1B58	R	33	139	542	106	192	38	16	8	108	65	—	29	.354	.427	.528
Shad Barry†	2B35,3B16,OF13*	R	22	67	252	35	62	10	0	1	22	15	—	13	.246	.294	.298
Jimmy Slagle†	OF48	L	27	48	183	20	37	6	2	1	20	16	—	5	.202	.277	.273
Klondike Douglass	C41,1B6,OF2	L	29	51	173	14	56	6	1	0	23	11	—	10	.324	.371	.370
Al Orth	P35,OF4	L	28	41	128	14	36	6	0	1	15	3	—	3	.281	.303	.352
Fred Jacklitsch	C30,3B1	R	25	33	120	14	30	4	3	0	24	12	—	2	.250	.328	.333
Doc White	P31,OF1	L	22	31	98	15	27	3	1	1	10	2	—	1	.276	.297	.357
Jack Townsend	P19,OF1	R	22	19	64	2	7	1	1	0	5	0	—	1	.109	.123	.156
Joe Dolan†	2B10	—	28	10	37	0	3	0	0	0	2	2	—	0	.081	.128	.081
George Browne	OF8	L	25	8	26	2	5	1	0	0	4	1	—	2	.192	.250	.231
Bert Conn	2B5	—	21	5	18	2	4	1	0	0	0	0	—	0	.222	.263	.278

S. Barry, 1 G at SS

Pitcher	T	Age	G	GS	CG	ShO	IP	H	HR	BB	SO	W-L	Sv	ERA
Red Donahue	R	28	34	33	33	1	295.1	299	2	59	88	20-13	0	2.59
Al Orth	R	28	35	33	30	6	281.2	250	3	32	92	20-12	0	2.27
Bill Duggleby	R	27	35	29	26	5	284.2	302	9	41	95	19-12	0	2.88
Doc White	L	22	31	27	22	0	236.2	241	2	56	132	14-13	0	3.19
Jack Townsend	R	22	19	16	14	2	143.2	118	3	64	72	9-6	0	3.45
Jack Dunn†	R	28	2	2	0	0	4.2	11	0	7	1	0-1	0	21.21

1901 Brooklyn Superbas 3rd NL 79-57 .581 9.5 GB — Ned Hanlon

Player	Gm by Position	B	Age	G	AB	R	H	2B	3B	HR	RBI	BB	SO	SB	Avg	OBP	Slg
Deacon McGuire	C81,1B3	R	37	85	301	28	89	16	4	0	40	18	—	4	.296	.342	.375
Joe Kelley	1B115,3B5	R	29	120	492	77	151	22	12	4	65	40	—	18	.307	.363	.425
Tom Daly	2B133	S	35	133	520	88	164	38	10	3	90	42	—	31	.315	.371	.444
Charlie Irwin†	3B65	L	32	65	242	25	52	13	2	0	20	14	—	4	.215	.269	.285
Bill Dahlen	SS129,2B2	R	31	131	511	69	136	17	9	4	82	30	—	23	.266	.313	.358
Willie Keeler	OF125,3B10,2B3	L	29	136	595	123	202	18	12	2	43	21	—	23	.339	.369	.420
Jimmy Sheckard	OF121,3B12	L	22	133	554	116	196	29	19	11	104	47	—	35	.354	.407	.534
Tom McCreery	OF82,1B4,SS2	S	26	91	335	47	97	11	14	3	53	32	—	13	.290	.355	.433
Duke Farrell	C59,1B17	S	34	80	284	38	84	10	6	1	31	7	—	7	.296	.320	.384
Cozy Dolan†	OF64	L	28	66	253	33	66	11	1	0	29	17	—	7	.261	.313	.312
Frank Gatins	3B46,SS5	—	30	50	197	21	45	7	2	1	21	5	—	6	.228	.255	.299
Frank Kitson	P38,OF2,1B1	L	31	47	133	22	35	5	2	1	16	4	—	0	.263	.290	.353
Lefty Davis†	OF24,2B1	L	26	25	91	11	19	2	0	0	7	10	—	4	.209	.287	.231
John Gochnauer	SS3	R	25	3	11	1	4	0	0	0	2	1	—	1	.364	.417	.364
Hughie Hearne	C2	R	28	2	5	1	2	0	0	0	3	0	—	0	.400	.400	.400
Farmer Steelman†	C1	—	26	1	3	0	1	0	0	0	0	0	—	0	.333	.333	.333

Pitcher	T	Age	G	GS	CG	ShO	IP	H	HR	BB	SO	W-L	Sv	ERA
Wild Bill Donovan	R	24	45	38	36	2	351.0	324	1	152	226	25-15	1	2.77
Frank Kitson	R	31	38	32	26	5	280.2	312	9	67	127	19-11	2	2.98
Jim Hughes	R	27	31	29	24	0	250.2	265	3	102	96	17-12	0	3.27
Doc Newton†	L	23	13	12	9	0	105.0	110	1	30	45	6-5	0	2.83
Doc McJames	R	27	13	12	6	0	91.0	104	1	40	42	5-6	0	4.75
Brickyard Kennedy	R	33	14	8	6	0	85.1	80	1	24	28	3-5	0	3.06
Gene McCann	R	25	6	5	3	0	34.0	34	1	16	9	2-3	0	3.44
Clarence Wright	R	22	1	1	1	0	9.0	6	0	1	6	1-0	0	1.00
Kid Carsey	R	30	2	0	0	0	7.0	9	1	3	4	1-0	0	10.29

1901 St. Louis Cardinals 4th NL 76-64 .543 14.5 GB — Patsy Donovan

Player	Gm by Position	B	Age	G	AB	R	H	2B	3B	HR	RBI	BB	SO	SB	Avg	OBP	Slg
Jack Ryan	C65,2B9,1B5*	R	32	83	300	27	59	6	5	0	31	7	—	5	.197	.218	.250
Dan McGann	1B103	S	29	103	423	73	115	15	9	6	56	16	—	17	.272	.333	.392
Dick Padden	2B115,SS8	R	30	123	489	71	125	17	7	2	62	31	—	26	.256	.315	.331
Otto Krueger	3B142	R	24	142	520	77	143	16	12	2	79	50	—	19	.275	.353	.363
Bobby Wallace	SS134	R	27	134	550	69	178	34	15	2	91	20	—	15	.324	.351	.451
Jesse Burkett	OF142	L	32	142	601	142	226	20	15	10	75	59	—	27	.376	.440	.509
Patsy Donovan	OF129	L	36	130	531	92	161	23	5	1	73	27	—	28	.303	.344	.371
Emmett Heidrick	OF118	L	24	118	502	94	170	24	12	6	67	21	—	32	.339	.366	.470
Art Nichols	C47,OF40	R	29	93	308	50	75	11	3	1	33	10	—	14	.244	.290	.308
Pop Schriver	C24,1B19	R	35	53	166	17	45	7	3	1	23	12	—	2	.271	.335	.367
Pete Childs†	2B19,OF2,SS1	—	29	29	79	12	21	1	0	0	8	14	—	0	.266	.389	.278
Bill Richardson	1B15	R	22	15	52	7	11	2	0	2	7	6	—	1	.212	.293	.365
Mike Heydon	C13,OF1	L	26	16	43	2	9	1	1	1	6	5	—	2	.209	.292	.349

J. Ryan, 3 G at OF

Pitcher	T	Age	G	GS	CG	ShO	IP	H	HR	BB	SO	W-L	Sv	ERA
Jack Powell	R	26	45	37	33	2	338.1	351	14	50	133	19-21	3	3.54
Jack Harper	R	23	39	37	28	1	308.2	294	7	99	128	23-12	0	3.62
Willie Sudhoff	R	26	38	26	25	1	276.1	281	4	92	78	17-10	2	3.52
Ed Murphy	R	24	23	21	16	0	165.0	201	5	32	42	10-9	0	4.20
Cowboy Jones	L	26	10	9	7	0	76.1	97	4	22	25	2-6	0	4.48
Mike O'Neill	R	23	5	4	4	1	41.0	29	2	10	16	2-2	0	1.32
Stan Yerkes†	R	26	4	4	4	0	34.0	35	2	6	15	3-1	0	3.18
Ted Breitenstein	L	32	3	3	1	0	15.0	24	1	14	3	0-3	0	6.60
Bill Magee†	R	26	1	1	0	0	8.0	8	0	4	3	0-0	0	4.50
Bob Wicker	R	23	1	0	0	0	3.0	4	0	1	2	0-0	0	0.00
Chauncey Fisher†	R	29	1	0	0	0	3.0	7	0	1	0	0-0	0	15.00
Farmer Burns	R	—	1	0	0	0	1.0	2	0	1	0	0-0	0	9.00

1901 Boston Beaneaters 5th NL 69-69 .500 20.5 GB — Frank Selee

Player	Gm by Position	B	Age	G	AB	R	H	2B	3B	HR	RBI	BB	SO	SB	Avg	OBP	Slg
Malachi Kittridge	C113	R	31	114	381	24	96	14	0	2	40	32	—	2	.252	.312	.304
Fred Tenney	1B113,C2	L	29	115	451	66	127	13	1	1	22	37	—	15	.282	.340	.322
Gene DeMontreville	2B120,3B20	R	27	140	577	83	173	14	4	5	72	17	—	25	.300	.321	.364
Bobby Lowe	3B111,2B18	R	32	129	491	47	125	11	1	3	47	17	—	22	.255	.284	.299
Herman Long	SS138	L	35	138	518	54	112	14	6	3	68	25	—	20	.216	.254	.284
Billy Hamilton	OF99	L	35	102	348	71	100	11	2	3	38	64	—	20	.287	.404	.356
Jimmy Slagle†	OF66	L	27	66	255	35	69	7	0	0	7	34	—	14	.271	.359	.298
Duff Cooley	OF53,1B10	L	28	63	240	27	62	13	3	0	27	14	—	5	.258	.302	.338
Fred Crolius	OF49	—	24	49	200	22	48	4	1	1	13	9	—	6	.240	.306	.285
Pat Moran	C28,1B13,3B4*	R	25	52	180	12	38	5	1	2	18	3	—	3	.211	.228	.283
Frank Murphy†	OF45	—	26	45	176	13	46	5	3	1	18	4	—	6	.261	.282	.341
Kid Nichols	P38,OF7,1B5	S	31	55	163	16	46	8	7	4	28	8	—	0	.282	.316	.491
Bill Dinneen	P37,OF3,1B2	R	25	54	147	12	31	5	0	1	6	8	—	8	.211	.256	.265
Daff Gammons	OF23,2B2,3B1	R	25	28	93	10	18	0	1	0	10	3	—	5	.194	.242	.215
Joe Rickert	OF13	R	24	13	60	6	10	1	2	0	1	6	—	1	.167	.206	.250
Elmer Smith†	OF15	L	33	16	57	5	10	2	1	0	3	6	—	2	.175	.254	.246
Pat Carney	OF13	L	24	13	55	6	16	2	1	0	6	3	—	0	.291	.339	.364
Shad Barry†	OF11	R	22	11	40	3	7	2	0	0	6	2	—	1	.175	.233	.225
Bob Lawson	P6,OF3,3B1	R	24	10	27	2	4	1	0	1	4	1	—	1	.148	.179	.296
Billy Lush	OF7	S	27	7	27	2	5	1	1	0	3	3	—	0	.185	.267	.296
George Grosart	OF7	—	21	7	26	4	3	0	0	0	1	0	—	0	.115	.115	.115
Fred Brown	OF5	R	22	7	14	1	2	0	0	0	2	0	—	0	.143	.143	.143
John Hinton	3B4	R	25	4	13	0	1	0	0	0	0	2	—	0	.077	.200	.077

P. Moran, 3 G at SS, 3 G at OF, 1 G at 2B

Pitcher	T	Age	G	GS	CG	ShO	IP	H	HR	BB	SO	W-L	Sv	ERA
Vic Willis	R	25	38	35	33	6	305.1	262	6	78	133	20-17	0	2.36
Kid Nichols	R	31	38	34	33	4	321.0	306	8	90	143	19-16	0	3.22
Bill Dinneen	R	25	37	34	31	0	309.1	295	9	77	141	15-18	0	2.94
Togie Pittinger	R	29	34	33	27	1	281.1	288	8	76	129	13-16	0	3.01
Bob Lawson	R	24	6	4	4	0	46.0	45	0	28	12	2-2	0	3.33

1901 Chicago Orphans 6th NL 53-86 .381 37.0 GB — Tom Loftus

Player	Gm by Position	B	Age	G	AB	R	H	2B	3B	HR	RBI	BB	SO	SB	Avg	OBP	Slg
Johnny Kling	C69,1B1,OF1	R	26	74	253	26	70	6	3	0	21	9	—	8	.277	.304	.324
Jack Doyle	1B75	R	31	75	285	21	66	9	2	0	39	7	—	8	.232	.263	.277
Cupid Childs	2B63	L	33	63	236	24	61	9	0	0	21	30	—	3	.258	.359	.297
Fred Raymer	3B82,SS29,1B5*	R	25	120	463	41	108	14	2	0	43	11	—	18	.233	.257	.272
Barry McCormick	SS112,3B3	—	26	115	427	45	100	13	4	1	32	31	—	12	.234	.288	.304
Topsy Hartsel	OF140	L	27	140	558	111	187	25	16	7	54	74	—	41	.335	.414	.475
Danny Green	OF133	L	24	133	537	82	168	16	12	6	61	40	—	31	.313	.364	.421
Frank Chance	OF50,C13,1B6	R	23	69	241	38	67	12	4	0	36	29	—	27	.278	.376	.361
Charlie Dexter	1B54,3B25,OF21*	R	25	116	460	46	123	9	5	1	66	16	—	22	.267	.302	.315
Mike Kahoe†	C63,1B6	R	27	67	237	21	53	12	2	1	21	8	—	5	.224	.249	.304
Pete Childs†	2B60	—	29	61	213	23	48	5	1	0	14	27	—	4	.225	.318	.258
Cozy Dolan†	OF41	L	28	43	171	29	45	1	2	0	16	7	—	3	.263	.296	.292
Jock Menefee	OF24,P21,1B2*	R	33	48	152	19	39	5	3	0	13	8	—	4	.257	.327	.329
Long Tom Hughes	P37,OF1	R	22	38	118	7	14	1	0	0	5	2	—	3	.119	.133	.127
Rube Waddell†	P29,1B1	R	24	30	98	16	25	3	3	2	14	2	—	2	.255	.270	.408
Jim Delahanty	3B17	R	22	17	63	4	12	2	0	0	4	3	—	5	.190	.239	.222
Bill Gannon	OF15	—	25	15	61	2	9	0	0	0	0	1	—	5	.148	.161	.148
Eddie Hickey	3B10	—	28	10	37	4	6	0	0	0	3	2	—	1	.162	.225	.162
Larry Hoffman	3B5,2B1	R	18	6	22	2	7	1	0	0	6	0	—	1	.318	.348	.364
Harry Croft	OF3	—	25	3	12	1	4	0	0	0	4	0	—	0	.333	.333	.333
Germany Schaefer	2B1,3B1	R	24	2	5	0	3	1	0	0	0	2	—	0	.600	.714	.800

F. Raymer, 3 G at 2B; C. Dexter, 13 G at 2B, 3 G at C; J. Menefee, 1 G at 2B

Pitcher	T	Age	G	GS	CG	ShO	IP	H	HR	BB	SO	W-L	Sv	ERA
Long Tom Hughes	R	22	37	35	32	1	308.1	309	6	115	225	10-23	0	3.24
Jack Taylor	R	27	33	31	30	0	275.2	341	5	44	68	13-19	0	3.36
Rube Waddell†	L	24	29	28	26	0	243.2	239	5	66	168	14-14	0	2.81
Mal Eason	R	22	27	25	23	1	220.2	246	9	60	68	8-17	0	3.59
Jock Menefee	R	33	21	20	19	0	182.1	201	4	34	55	8-12	0	3.80
Bert Cunningham	R	35	1	1	1	0	9.0	11	0	3	2	0-1	0	5.00
Charlie Ferguson	R	26	1	0	0	0	2.0	1	0	2	0	0-0	0	0.00

1901 New York Giants 7th NL 52-85 .380 37.0 GB

George Davis

Player	Gm by Position	B	Age	G	AB	R	H	2B	3B	HR	RBI	BB	SO	SB	Avg	OBP	Slg
John Warner	C84	L	28	87	291	19	70	6	1	0	20	3	—	3	.241	.268	.268
John Ganzel	1B138	R	27	138	526	42	113	13	3	2	66	20	—	6	.215	.255	.262
Ray Nelson	2B39	R	25	39	130	12	26	2	0	0	7	10	—	3	.200	.262	.215
Sammy Strang	3B91,2B37,OF5*	S	24	135	493	55	139	14	6	1	34	59	—	40	.282	.364	.341
George Davis	SS113,3B17	S	30	130	491	69	148	26	7	7	65	40	—	27	.301	.356	.426
George Van Haltren	OF135,P1	L	35	135	543	82	182	23	6	1	47	51	—	24	.335	.396	.405
Kip Selbach	OF125	R	29	125	502	89	145	29	6	1	56	45	—	8	.289	.350	.376
Algie McBride†	OF65	L	32	68	264	27	74	11	0	2	29	12	—	3	.280	.317	.345
Charlie Hickman	OF50,SS23,3B15*	R	25	112	406	44	113	20	6	4	62	15	—	5	.278	.315	.387
Frank Bowerman	C46,2B3,3B3*	R	32	59	191	20	38	5	3	0	14	7	—	3	.199	.235	.257
Frank Murphy†	2B23,OF12	—	26	35	130	10	21	3	0	0	8	6	—	2	.162	.199	.185
Jim Jones	OF20,P1	R	24	21	91	10	19	4	3	0	5	4	—	2	.209	.250	.319
Aleck Smith	C25	—	30	26	78	5	11	0	0	0	6	0	—	2	.141	.141	.141
Curt Bernard	OF15,2B4,SS2*	L	23	23	76	11	17	0	2	0	6	7	—	2	.224	.289	.276
Charlie Buelow	3B17,2B2	R	24	22	72	3	8	4	0	0	4	2	—	2	.111	.147	.167
Bill Phyle	P24,SS1	—	26	25	66	8	12	2	0	0	3	2	—	0	.182	.206	.212
Jim Miller	2B18	R	20	18	58	3	8	0	0	0	3	6	—	1	.138	.219	.138
Heinie Smith	2B7,P2	R	29	9	29	5	6	2	1	1	4	1	—	1	.207	.233	.448
Danny Murphy	2B5	R	24	5	20	0	4	0	0	0	0	1	—	0	.200	.238	.200
Joe Wall	C2,OF1	L	27	4	8	0	4	0	0	0	1	0	—	0	.500	.500	.500
Ike Van Zandt	P2,OF1	L	25	3	6	1	1	0	0	0	0	0	—	0	.167	.167	.167

S. Strang, 4 G at SS; C. Hickman, 9 G at P, 7 G at 2B, 2 G at 1B; F. Bowerman, 3 G at SS, 1 G at 1B; C. Bernard, 1 G at 3B

Pitcher	T	Age	G	GS	CG	ShO	IP	H	HR	BB	SO	W-L	Sv	ERA
Luther Taylor	R	26	45	43	37	4	353.1	377	8	112	136	18-27	0	3.18
Christy Mathewson	R	22	40	38	36	5	336.0	288	3	97	221	20-17	0	2.41
Bill Phyle	R	26	24	19	16	0	168.2	208	2	54	62	7-10	1	4.27
Charlie Hickman	R	25	9	9	6	0	65.0	76	1	26	11	3-5	0	4.57
Roger Denzer	R	29	11	9	3	1	61.2	69	2	5	22	2-6	0	3.36
Ed Doheny†	L	27	10	6	6	0	74.0	88	1	17	36	2-5	0	4.50
Bill Magee†	R	26	6	5	4	0	42.1	56	4	11	14	0-4	0	5.95
Al Maul	R	35	3	3	2	0	19.0	39	1	8	5	0-3	0	11.37
Dummy Leitner†	R	30	2	2	2	0	18.0	27	0	4	3	0-2	0	4.50
Willie Mills	R	23	2	2	2	0	16.0	21	2	4	3	0-2	0	8.44
Heinie Smith	R	29	2	1	1	0	13.1	24	0	5	5	0-1	0	8.10
Larry Hesterfer	L	23	1	1	1	0	6.0	15	0	3	2	0-1	0	7.50
Jim Jones	R	24	1	1	1	0	5.0	6	0	2	3	0-1	0	10.80
Chauncey Fisher†	R	29	1	1	0	0	4.0	11	0	2	1	0-0	0	15.75
Ike Van Zandt	—	25	2	0	0	0	12.2	16	0	8	2	0-0	0	7.11
Jake Livingstone	—	21	2	0	0	0	12.0	26	0	7	6	0-0	0	9.00
George Van Haltren	L	35	1	0	0	0	6.0	12	0	6	2	0-0	0	3.00
Harry Felix	R	31	1	0	0	0	2.0	3	0	0	0	0-0	0	0.00

1901 Cincinnati Reds 8th NL 52-87 .374 38.0 GB

Bid McPhee

Player	Gm by Position	B	Age	G	AB	R	H	2B	3B	HR	RBI	BB	SO	SB	Avg	OBP	Slg
Bill Bergen	C87	R	23	87	308	15	55	6	4	1	17	8	—	2	.179	.199	.234
Jake Beckley	1B140	R	33	140	580	78	178	36	13	3	79	28	—	4	.307	.346	.429
Harry Steinfeldt	3B55,2B50	R	23	105	382	40	95	18	7	6	47	28	—	10	.249	.303	.380
Charlie Irwin†	3B67	L	32	67	260	25	62	12	2	0	25	14	—	13	.238	.285	.300
George Magoon	SS112,2B15	R	26	127	460	47	116	16	7	1	53	52	—	15	.252	.331	.324
Dick Harley	OF133	L	28	133	535	69	146	13	2	4	27	31	—	37	.273	.323	.327
Sam Crawford	OF126	L	21	131	515	91	170	20	16	16	104	37	—	13	.330	.378	.524
John Dobbs	OF100,3B8	L	26	109	435	71	119	17	4	2	27	36	—	19	.274	.338	.345
Heinie Peitz	C49,2B21,3B6*	R	30	82	269	24	82	13	5	1	24	23	—	3	.305	.364	.401
Bill Fox	2B43	S	29	43	159	9	28	2	1	0	7	4	—	9	.176	.201	.201
Harry Bay	OF40	L	23	41	157	25	33	1	2	1	3	13	—	4	.210	.275	.261
Algie McBride†	OF28	L	32	30	123	19	29	7	0	2	18	7	—	0	.236	.282	.341
Tommy Corcoran	SS30	R	32	31	115	14	24	3	3	0	15	11	—	6	.209	.278	.287
Bill Phillips	P37,OF1	R	32	41	109	11	22	3	1	0	10	8	—	0	.202	.256	.248
Archie Stimmel	P20,OF2	R	28	22	62	1	5	1	0	0	0	3	—	0	.081	.123	.097
Pete O'Brien	2B15	L	24	16	54	1	11	1	0	1	3	2	—	0	.204	.232	.278
Jack Sutthoff	P10,OF1	L	28	11	28	0	3	0	0	0	1	0	—	0	.107	.107	.107
Jerry Hurley	C7	R	26	9	21	1	1	0	0	0	0	1	—	1	.048	.130	.048
Emil Haberer	3B3,1B2	R	23	6	18	2	3	0	1	0	1	3	—	0	.167	.286	.278
Chink Heileman	3B4,2B1	R	28	5	15	1	2	1	0	0	1	0	—	0	.133	.133	.200
Mike Kahoe†	C4	R	27	4	13	0	4	0	0	0	0	1	—	0	.308	.357	.308
Charlie Krause	2B1	—	27	1	4	0	1	0	0	0	0	0	—	0	.250	.250	.250

H. Peitz, 2 G at 1B

Pitcher	T	Age	G	GS	CG	ShO	IP	H	HR	BB	SO	W-L	Sv	ERA
Noodles Hahn	L	22	42	42	41	2	375.1	370	13	69	239	22-19	0	2.71
Bill Phillips	R	32	37	36	29	1	281.1	364	7	67	109	14-18	0	4.64
Doc Newton†	L	23	20	18	17	0	168.1	190	6	59	65	4-13	0	4.12
Archie Stimmel	R	28	20	18	14	1	153.1	170	10	44	55	4-14	0	4.11
Barney McFadden	R	27	8	5	4	0	46.0	54	3	40	11	3-4	0	6.07
Whitey Guese	R	29	6	5	4	0	44.1	62	5	14	11	1-4	0	6.09
Charlie Case	R	21	3	3	3	0	27.0	34	0	6	5	1-2	0	4.67
Len Swormstedt	R	22	3	3	3	0	26.0	19	2	5	13	2-1	0	1.73
Amos Rusie	R	30	3	2	2	0	22.0	43	2	3	6	0-1	0	8.59
Dick Scott	R	18	3	2	2	0	21.0	26	2	9	7	0-2	0	5.14
Crese Heismann	L	21	3	2	1	0	13.2	18	1	6	6	0-1	0	5.93
Gus Weyhing†	R	34	1	1	1	0	9.0	11	0	2	3	0-1	0	3.00
Doc Parker	R	29	1	1	1	0	8.0	26	1	2	0	0-1	0	15.75
Jack Sutthoff	R	28	10	4	4	0	70.1	82	2	39	12	1-6	0	5.50

>>1902 Philadelphia Athletics 1st AL 83-53 .610 —

Connie Mack

Player	Gm by Position	B	Age	G	AB	R	H	2B	3B	HR	RBI	BB	SO	SB	Avg	OBP	Slg
O. Schreckengost†	C71,1B7,OF1	R	27	79	284	45	92	17	2	2	43	9	—	3	.324	.347	.419
Harry Davis	1B128,OF5	R	28	133	561	89	172	43	8	6	92	30	—	28	.307	.343	.444
Danny Murphy	2B76	R	25	76	291	48	91	11	8	1	48	13	—	12	.313	.351	.416
Lave Cross	3B137	R	36	137	559	90	191	39	8	0	108	27	—	25	.342	.374	.440
Monte Cross	SS137	R	32	137	497	72	115	22	2	3	59	32	—	17	.231	.289	.302
Topsy Hartsel	OF137	L	28	137	545	109	154	20	8	5	58	87	—	47	.283	.383	.391
Socks Seybold	OF136	R	31	137	522	91	165	27	12	16	97	43	—	6	.316	.375	.506
Dave Fultz	OF114,2B16	R	27	129	506	109	153	20	5	1	49	62	—	44	.302	.381	.368
Mike Powers	C68,1B3	R	31	71	246	35	65	7	1	2	39	14	—	3	.264	.312	.325
Louis Castro	2B36,OF3,SS1	R	25	42	143	18	35	8	1	1	15	4	—	2	.245	.265	.336
Frank Bonner†	2B11	R	32	11	44	2	8	0	0	0	3	0	—	0	.182	.182	.182
Elmer Flick†	OF11	L	26	11	37	15	11	2	1	0	3	6	—	4	.297	.435	.405
Farmer Steelman	C5,OF5	—	27	10	32	1	6	1	0	0	6	2	—	2	.188	.235	.219
Nap Lajoie†	2B1	R	27	1	4	0	1	0	0	0	1	0	—	1	.250	.250	.250

Pitcher	T	Age	G	GS	CG	ShO	IP	H	HR	BB	SO	W-L	Sv	ERA
Eddie Plank	L	26	36	32	31	1	300.0	319	5	61	107	20-15	0	3.30
Rube Waddell	L	25	33	27	26	3	276.1	224	7	64	210	24-7	1	2.05
Bert Husting†	R	24	32	27	17	1	204.0	240	7	91	44	14-5	0	3.79
Snake Wiltse†	L	30	19	17	13	0	138.0	182	7	41	28	8-8	1	5.15
Fred Mitchell†	R	24	18	14	9	0	107.2	120	4	59	22	5-7	1	3.59
Highball Wilson	R	23	13	10	8	0	96.1	103	1	19	18	7-5	0	2.43
Andy Coakley	R	19	3	3	3	0	27.0	25	0	9	9	2-1	0	2.67
Bill Duggleby†	R	28	2	2	2	0	17.0	19	0	4	4	1-1	0	3.18
Ed Kenna	R	24	2	1	1	0	17.0	19	1	11	5	1-1	0	5.29
Bill Bernhard†	R	31	1	1	1	0	9.0	7	0	3	1	1-0	0	1.00
Tom Walker	R	20	1	1	1	0	8.0	10	0	0	2	0-1	0	5.63
Tad Quinn	R	19	1	1	1	0	8.0	12	1	1	3	0-1	0	4.50
Jim Porter	L	25	1	1	1	0	8.0	12	0	5	2	0-1	0	3.38

1902 St. Louis Browns 2nd AL 78-58 .574 5.0 GB

Jimmy McAleer

Player	Gm by Position	B	Age	G	AB	R	H	2B	3B	HR	RBI	BB	SO	SB	Avg	OBP	Slg
Joe Sugden	C61,1B4,P1	S	31	68	200	25	50	7	2	0	15	20	—	2	.250	.330	.305
John Anderson	1B126,OF3	S	28	126	524	60	149	29	6	4	85	21	—	15	.284	.316	.385
Dick Padden	2B117	R	31	117	413	54	109	26	3	1	40	30	—	11	.264	.327	.349
Barry McCormick	3B132,SS7,OF1	—	27	139	504	55	124	14	4	3	51	37	—	10	.246	.304	.308
Bobby Wallace	SS131,P1,OF1	R	28	133	494	71	141	32	9	1	63	45	—	18	.285	.350	.393
Jesse Burkett	OF137,P1,3B1*	L	33	138	553	97	169	29	9	5	52	71	—	23	.306	.390	.418
Emmett Heidrick	OF109,P1,3B1*	L	25	110	447	75	129	19	10	3	56	34	—	17	.289	.339	.396
Charlie Hemphill†	OF101,2B2	L	26	103	416	67	132	14	11	6	58	44	—	23	.317	.383	.447
Bill Friel	OF33,2B25,1B10*	L	26	80	267	26	64	9	2	2	20	14	—	4	.240	.283	.311
Mike Kahoe†	C53	R	28	55	197	21	48	9	2	2	28	6	—	4	.244	.270	.340
Jack Powell	P42,OF2,C1*	R	27	44	127	15	26	9	0	1	15	10	—	0	.205	.268	.299
Billy Maloney†	OF23,C7	L	24	30	112	8	23	3	0	0	11	6	—	0	.205	.258	.232
Jiggs Donahue	C23,1B5	L	22	30	89	11	21	1	1	1	7	12	—	2	.236	.327	.303
Willie Sudhoff	P30,OF1	R	27	31	77	6	13	2	0	0	5	4	—	3	.169	.220	.195
Davy Jones†	OF15	L	22	15	49	4	11	1	1	0	3	6	—	5	.224	.309	.286
Bill Reidy	P12,OF1	R	28	14	41	4	8	0	0	0	1	4	—	0	.195	.267	.195
Jimmy McAleer	OF2	R	37	2	3	0	2	0	0	0	0	0	—	0	.667	.667	.667

J. Burkett, 1 G at SS; E. Heidrick, 1 G at SS; B. Friel, 8 G at 3B, 3 G at SS, 1 G at P, 1 G at C; J. Powell, 1 G at 1B

Pitcher	T	Age	G	GS	CG	ShO	IP	H	HR	BB	SO	W-L	Sv	ERA
Jack Powell	R	27	42	39	36	3	328.1	320	12	93	137	22-17	3	3.21
Red Donahue	R	29	35	34	33	2	316.1	322	7	65	63	22-11	0	2.76
Jack Harper	R	24	29	26	20	2	222.1	224	8	81	74	15-11	0	4.13
Willie Sudhoff	R	27	30	25	20	0	220.0	213	6	67	42	12-12	2	2.86
Bill Reidy	R	28	12	9	7	0	95.0	111	0	13	16	3-5	0	4.45
Charlie Shields†	L	22	4	4	3	0	30.0	37	1	7	6	3-0	0	3.30
Bobby Wallace	R	28	1	1	0	0	2.0	3	0	0	1	0-0	0	0.00
Harry Kane	L	18	4	1	1	0	23.0	34	2	16	7	0-1	0	5.48
Bill Friel	R	26	1	0	0	0	4.0	4	0	0	0	0-0	0	4.50
Emmett Heidrick	R	25	1	0	0	0	1.0	0	0	0	0	0-0	0	0.00
Joe Sugden	R	31	1	0	0	0	1.0	1	0	0	0	0-0	0	0.00
Jesse Burkett	L	33	1	0	0	0	1.0	4	0	1	2	0-1	0	9.00

1902 Boston Pilgrims 3rd AL 77-60 .562 6.5 GB

Jimmy Collins

Player	Gm by Position	B	Age	G	AB	R	H	2B	3B	HR	RBI	BB	SO	SB	Avg	OBP	Slg
Lou Criger	C80,OF1	R	30	83	266	32	68	16	6	0	28	27	—	7	.256	.324	.361
Candy LaChance	1B138	S	32	138	541	60	151	13	4	6	56	18	—	8	.279	.309	.351
Hobe Ferris	2B134	R	24	134	499	57	122	16	14	8	63	21	—	11	.244	.276	.381
Jimmy Collins	3B107	R	32	108	429	71	138	21	10	6	61	24	—	18	.322	.360	.459
Freddy Parent	SS138	R	26	138	567	91	156	31	8	3	62	24	—	16	.275	.309	.374
Buck Freeman	OF138	L	30	138	564	75	174	38	19	11	121	32	—	17	.309	.352	.502
Chick Stahl	OF125	L	29	127	508	92	164	22	11	2	58	37	—	24	.323	.375	.421
Patsy Dougherty	OF102,3B1	L	25	108	438	77	150	12	6	0	34	42	—	20	.342	.407	.397
Harry Gleason	3B35,OF23,2B4	R	27	71	240	30	54	5	5	2	25	10	—	6	.225	.265	.313
John Warner	C64	L	29	65	222	19	52	5	7	0	12	13	—	0	.234	.286	.320
Bill Dinneen	P42,OF2	R	26	44	141	13	18	3	0	0	9	9	—	2	.128	.196	.149
Charlie Hickman†	OF27	R	26	28	108	13	32	5	2	3	16	3	—	1	.296	.339	.463
Long Tom Hughes†	P9,OF3	R	23	12	30	7	11	1	0	0	3	2	—	2	.367	.406	.400
Gary Wilson	2B2	R	25	2	8	0	1	0	0	0	1	0	—	0	.125	.125	.125

Pitcher	T	Age	G	GS	CG	ShO	IP	H	HR	BB	SO	W-L	Sv	ERA
Cy Young	R	35	45	43	41	3	384.2	350	6	53	160	32-11	0	2.15
Bill Dinneen	R	26	42	42	39	2	371.1	348	9	99	136	21-21	0	2.93
George Winter	R	24	20	20	18	0	168.1	149	2	53	51	11-9	0	2.99
Tully Sparks†	R	27	17	15	15	1	142.2	151	4	40	37	7-9	0	3.47
Long Tom Hughes†	R	23	9	8	4	0	49.1	51	0	24	15	3-3	0	3.28
George Prentiss†	R	26	7	4	3	0	41.0	55	0	10	9	2-2	0	5.27
Doc Adkins	R	29	4	2	1	0	20.0	30	2	7	3	1-1	0	4.05
Nick Altrock	L	25	3	2	1	0	18.0	19	0	7	5	0-2	1	2.00
Pep Deininger	L	24	2	1	0	0	12.0	19	3	9	2	0-0	0	9.75
Bert Husting†	R	24	1	1	1	0	8.0	15	0	8	4	0-1	0	9.00
Dave Williams	L	21	3	0	0	0	18.2	22	0	11	7	0-0	0	5.30
Fred Mitchell†	R	24	1	0	0	0	4.0	8	1	5	2	0-1	0	11.25

1902 Chicago White Sox 4th AL 74-60 .552 8.0 GB

Clark Griffith

Player	Gm by Position	B	Age	G	AB	R	H	2B	3B	HR	RBI	BB	SO	SB	Avg	OBP	Slg
Billy Sullivan	C70,1B2,OF2	R	27	76	263	36	64	12	3	1	26	6	—	11	.243	.268	.323
Frank Isbell	1B133,SS4,P1*	L	26	137	515	62	130	14	4	4	59	14	—	38	.252	.276	.318
Tom Daly	2B137	S	36	137	489	57	110	22	3	1	54	55	—	19	.225	.303	.288
Sammy Strang†	3B137	S	25	137	536	108	158	18	5	3	46	76	—	38	.295	.387	.364
George Davis	SS129,1B3	S	31	132	485	76	145	27	7	3	93	65	—	31	.299	.386	.402
Fielder Jones	OF135	L	30	135	532	98	171	16	5	0	54	57	—	33	.321	.390	.370
Danny Green	OF129	L	25	129	481	77	150	16	11	0	62	53	—	35	.312	.388	.391
Sam Mertes	OF120,SS5,C2*	R	29	129	497	60	140	23	7	1	79	37	—	46	.282	.334	.362
Ed McFarland	C69,OF2,1B1	R	27	75	246	29	56	9	2	1	25	19	—	8	.228	.291	.293
Nixey Callahan	P35,OF23,SS1	R	28	70	218	27	51	7	2	0	13	6	—	4	.234	.261	.284
Clark Griffith	P28,OF3	R	32	35	92	11	20	3	0	0	8	7	—	0	.217	.273	.250
Herm McFarland†	OF7	L	32	7	27	5	5	0	0	0	4	2	—	1	.185	.241	.185
John Durham	P3,OF2	R	20	5	15	3	1	0	0	0	0	2	—	0	.067	.176	.067
Ed Hughes	C1	R	21	1	4	0	1	0	0	0	0	0	—	0	.250	.250	.250

F. Isbell, 1 G at C; S. Mertes, 1 G at P, 1 G at 1B, 1 G at 2B, 1 G at 3B

Pitcher	T	Age	G	GS	CG	ShO	IP	H	HR	BB	SO	W-L	Sv	ERA
Nixey Callahan	R	28	35	31	29	2	282.1	287	8	89	75	16-14	0	3.60
Roy Patterson	R	25	34	30	26	2	268.0	262	5	67	61	19-14	0	3.06
Wiley Piatt	L	27	32	30	22	2	246.0	263	3	66	96	12-12	0	3.51
Clark Griffith	R	32	28	24	20	3	212.2	247	11	47	51	15-9	0	4.19
Ned Garvin†	R	28	23	19	16	2	175.1	169	3	43	55	10-10	0	2.21
John Durham	R	20	3	3	3	0	20.0	21	0	16	3	1-1	0	5.85
Frank Isbell	R	26	1	1	0	0	1.0	3	0	1	1	0-0	0	9.00
Sam Mertes	R	29	1	0	0	0	7.2	6	0	0	0	1-0	0	1.17
Dummy Leitner†	R	31	1	0	0	0	4.0	9	0	2	0	0-0	0	13.50
Samuel McMackin†	L	30	1	0	0	0	3.0	1	0	0	2	0-0	0	0.00
John Katoll†	R	30	1	0	0	0	1.0	1	0	0	2	0-0	0	0.00

1902 Cleveland Bronchos 5th AL 69-67 .507 14.0 GB

Bill Armour

Player	Gm by Position	B	Age	G	AB	R	H	2B	3B	HR	RBI	BB	SO	SB	Avg	OBP	Slg
Harry Bemis	C87,OF2,2B1	R	28	93	317	42	99	12	7	1	29	19	—	3	.312	.366	.404
Charlie Hickman†	1B98,2B3,P1	R	26	102	426	61	161	31	11	8	94	12	—	8	.378	.399	.559
Nap Lajoie†	2B86	R	27	86	348	81	132	35	5	7	64	19	—	19	.379	.421	.569
Bill Bradley	3B137	R	24	137	550	104	187	39	12	11	77	27	—	11	.340	.375	.515
John Gochnauer	SS127	R	26	127	459	45	85	16	4	0	37	38	—	7	.185	.247	.237
Elmer Flick†	OF110	L	26	110	424	70	126	19	11	2	61	47	—	20	.297	.371	.408
Harry Bay†	OF107	L	24	108	455	71	132	10	5	0	23	36	—	22	.290	.343	.334
Jack McCarthy	OF95	L	33	95	359	45	102	31	5	0	41	24	—	12	.284	.329	.398
Ollie Pickering	OF64,1B2	L	32	69	293	46	75	5	2	3	26	19	—	22	.256	.306	.317
Bob Wood	C52,1B16,OF2*	R	36	81	258	23	76	18	2	0	40	27	—	1	.295	.375	.380
Frank Bonner†	2B34	R	32	34	132	14	37	6	0	0	14	5	—	1	.280	.312	.326
Jack Thoney†	2B14,SS11,OF2	R	22	28	105	14	30	7	1	0	11	9	—	4	.286	.342	.371
Addie Joss	P32,1B1	R	22	33	103	8	12	3	1	0	10	5	—	0	.117	.157	.165
Charlie Hemphill†	OF19	L	26	25	94	14	25	2	0	0	11	5	—	4	.266	.303	.287
O. Schreckengost†	1B17	R	27	18	74	5	25	0	0	0	9	0	—	2	.338	.338	.338
Clarence Wright	P21,1B1	R	23	23	70	8	10	0	2	1	5	0	—	0	.143	.143	.243
Erwin Harvey	OF12	L	23	12	46	5	16	2	0	0	5	3	—	1	.348	.388	.391
Hal O'Hagen†	1B3	—	28	3	13	2	5	2	0	0	1	0	—	2	.385	.385	.538
Peaches Graham	2B1	R	25	2	6	0	2	0	0	0	1	1	—	0	.333	.429	.333
George Starnagle	C1	R	28	1	3	0	0	0	0	0	0	0	—	0	.000	.000	.000

B. Wood, 1 G at 2B, 1 G at 3B

Pitcher	T	Age	G	GS	CG	ShO	IP	H	HR	BB	SO	W-L	Sv	ERA
Earl Moore	R	22	36	34	29	4	293.0	304	8	101	84	17-17	1	2.95
Addie Joss	R	22	32	29	28	5	269.1	225	2	75	106	17-13	0	2.77
Bill Bernhard†	R	31	27	24	22	3	217.0	169	4	34	57	17-5	1	2.20
Clarence Wright	R	23	21	18	15	1	148.0	150	6	75	52	7-11	1	3.95
Oscar Streit	L	28	8	7	4	0	51.2	72	3	25	10	0-7	0	5.23
Otto Hess	L	23	7	4	4	0	43.2	67	0	23	13	2-4	0	5.98
Gus Dorner	R	25	4	4	4	1	36.0	33	1	13	5	3-1	0	1.25
Luther Taylor†	R	27	4	4	4	1	34.0	37	0	8	8	1-3	0	1.59
Charlie Smith	R	22	3	3	2	1	20.0	23	0	5	5	2-1	0	4.05
Dike Varney	L	21	3	3	0	0	14.2	14	0	12	7	1-1	0	6.14
Ed Walker	L	27	1	1	1	0	8.0	11	0	3	1	0-1	0	3.38
Lou Polchow	—	21	1	1	1	0	8.0	9	0	4	2	0-1	0	5.63
Dummy Leitner†	R	31	1	1	0	0	8.0	11	0	1	0	0-0	0	4.50
Charlie Hickman	R	26	1	1	1	0	8.0	11	0	5	1	0-1	0	7.88
Jack Lundbom	R	25	8	3	1	0	34.0	48	1	16	7	1-1	0	6.62
Moses Vasbinder	R	21	2	0	0	0	5.0	5	1	8	2	0-0	0	9.00
Ginger Clark	R	23	1	0	0	0	6.0	10	0	3	1	1-0	0	6.00

1902 Washington Senators 6th AL 61-75 .449 22.0 GB

Tom Loftus

Player	Gm by Position	B	Age	G	AB	R	H	2B	3B	HR	RBI	BB	SO	SB	Avg	OBP	Slg
Boileryard Clarke	C87	R	33	87	291	31	78	16	0	6	40	23	—	1	.268	.330	.385
Scoops Carey	1B120	R	31	120	452	46	142	35	11	0	60	20	—	3	.314	.350	.440
Jack Doyle†	2B68,1B7,OF4*	R	32	78	312	52	77	15	2	1	20	29	—	6	.247	.311	.317
Bill Coughlin	3B66,SS31,2B26	R	23	123	469	84	141	27	4	6	71	26	—	29	.301	.348	.414
Bones Ely	SS105	R	39	105	381	39	100	11	2	1	62	21	—	3	.262	.301	.310
Jimmy Ryan	OF120	R	39	120	484	92	155	32	6	6	44	43	—	10	.320	.384	.448
Ed Delahanty	OF111,1B13	R	34	123	473	103	178	43	14	10	93	62	—	16	.376	.453	.590
Watty Lee	OF95,P13	L	22	109	391	61	100	21	5	4	45	33	—	8	.256	.319	.366
Bill Keister	OF65,2B40,3B14*	L	27	119	483	82	145	33	9	9	90	14	—	27	.300	.329	.462
Harry Wolverton†	3B59	L	28	59	249	35	62	8	3	1	23	13	—	8	.249	.292	.317
Lew Drill†	C53,OF8,2B5*	R	25	71	221	33	58	10	4	1	29	26	—	5	.262	.351	.357
Al Orth	P38,OF13,1B1*	L	29	56	175	20	38	3	2	2	10	9	—	2	.217	.255	.291
Casey Patten	P36,OF3	S	26	39	125	6	12	0	0	0	1	6	—	0	.096	.137	.096
Bill Carrick	P31,OF2	—	28	33	108	9	20	2	3	0	6	2	—	2	.185	.200	.259
Joe Stanley	OF3	S	21	3	12	2	4	0	0	0	1	0	—	0	.333	.333	.333
Jake Atz	2B3	R	22	3	10	1	1	0	0	0	0	0	—	0	.100	.100	.100
Tim Donahue	C3	L	32	3	8	0	2	0	0	0	1	0	—	0	.250	.250	.250

J. Doyle, 1 G at C; B. Keister, 2 G at SS; L. Drill, 1 G at 3B; A. Orth, 1 G at SS

Pitcher	T	Age	G	GS	CG	ShO	IP	H	HR	BB	SO	W-L	Sv	ERA
Al Orth	R	29	38	37	36	1	324.0	367	18	40	76	19-18	0	3.97
Casey Patten	L	26	36	34	33	1	299.2	331	11	89	92	17-16	1	4.05
Bill Carrick	R	28	31	30	28	0	257.2	344	10	72	36	11-17	0	4.86
Jack Townsend	R	23	27	26	22	0	220.1	233	12	89	71	9-16	0	4.45
Watty Lee	L	22	13	10	10	0	98.0	118	5	20	24	5-7	1	5.05
Cy Vorhees†	—	27	1	1	1	0	8.0	10	0	2	1	0-1	0	4.50

1902 Detroit Tigers 7th AL 52-83 .385 30.5 GB

Frank Dwyer

Player	Gm by Position	B	Age	G	AB	R	H	2B	3B	HR	RBI	BB	SO	SB	Avg	OBP	Slg
Deacon McGuire	C70	R	38	73	229	27	52	14	1	2	23	24	—	0	.227	.300	.323
Pop Dillon†	1B66	L	28	66	243	21	50	6	3	0	22	16	—	2	.206	.255	.255
Kid Gleason	2B118	S	35	118	441	42	109	11	4	1	38	25	—	17	.247	.292	.297
Doc Casey	3B132	S	32	132	520	69	142	18	7	3	55	44	—	22	.273	.338	.352
Kid Elberfeld	SS130	R	27	130	488	70	127	17	6	1	64	55	—	19	.260	.348	.326
Jimmy Barrett	OF136	L	27	136	509	93	154	19	6	4	44	74	—	24	.303	.397	.387
Dick Harley	OF125	L	29	125	491	59	138	9	8	2	44	36	—	20	.281	.345	.344
Ducky Holmes	OF92	L	33	92	362	50	93	15	4	2	33	28	—	16	.257	.319	.337
Sport McAllister†	1B26,OF12,C9*	S	27	66	229	19	48	5	2	1	32	5	—	1	.210	.230	.262
Fritz Buelow	C63,1B2	R	26	66	224	23	50	5	2	2	29	9	—	3	.223	.256	.290
Erve Beck†	1B36,OF5	R	23	41	162	23	48	4	0	2	22	4	—	3	.296	.313	.358
George Mullin	P35,OF4	R	21	40	120	20	39	4	3	0	11	8	—	1	.325	.367	.408
Pete LePine	OF19,1B8	L	25	30	96	8	20	3	2	1	19	8	—	1	.208	.276	.313
Harry Arndt†	OF10,1B1	—	23	10	34	4	5	0	1	0	7	6	—	0	.147	.275	.206
John O'Connell	2B6,1B2	—	30	8	22	1	4	0	0	0	0	3	—	0	.182	.280	.182
Lew Post	OF3	—	27	3	12	2	1	0	0	0	2	0	—	0	.083	.083	.083
Lou Schiappacasse	OF2	R	21	2	5	0	0	0	0	0	1	1	—	0	.000	.167	.000

S. McAllister, 6 G at 3B, 6 G at SS, 3 G at 2B

Pitcher	T	Age	G	GS	CG	ShO	IP	H	HR	BB	SO	W-L	Sv	ERA
Win Mercer	R	28	35	33	28	4	281.2	282	5	80	40	15-18	1	3.04
George Mullin	R	21	35	30	25	0	260.0	282	4	95	78	13-16	0	3.67
Ed Siever	L	25	25	23	17	0	188.1	166	0	32	36	8-11	1	1.91
Roscoe Miller†	R	25	20	18	15	1	148.2	158	3	57	39	6-12	1	3.69
Joe Yeager	R	26	19	15	14	0	140.0	171	5	41	28	6-12	0	4.82
Arch McCarthy	R	21	10	8	8	0	72.0	90	2	31	10	2-7	0	6.13
Rube Kisinger	R	25	5	5	5	0	43.1	48	0	14	7	2-3	0	3.12
Wish Egan	R	21	3	3	2	0	22.0	23	0	6	0	0-2	0	2.86
Samuel McMackin†	L	30	1	1	1	0	8.1	9	0	4	2	0-1	0	3.24
John Terry	—	22	1	1	1	0	5.0	8	0	1	0	0-1	0	3.60
Jack Cronin†	R	28	4	0	0	0	17.1	26	1	8	5	0-0	0	9.35
Ed Fisher	R	25	1	0	0	0	4.0	4	0	1	0	0-0	0	0.00

1902 Baltimore Orioles 8th AL 50-88 .362 34.0 GB

John McGraw (26-31)/Wilbert Robinson (24-57)

Player	Gm by Position	B	Age	G	AB	R	H	2B	3B	HR	RBI	BB	SO	SB	Avg	OBP	Slg
Wilbert Robinson	C87	R	39	91	335	38	98	16	7	1	57	12	—	11	.293	.321	.391
Dan McGann†	1B68	S	30	68	250	40	79	10	8	0	42	19	—	17	.316	.378	.420
Jimmy Williams	2B104,3B19,1B1	R	25	125	498	83	156	27	21	8	83	36	—	14	.313	.361	.500
Roger Bresnahan†	3B30,C22,OF15	R	23	65	235	30	64	8	6	4	34	21	—	12	.272	.337	.409
Billy Gilbert	SS129	R	26	129	445	74	109	12	3	2	38	45	—	38	.245	.327	.299
Kip Selbach	OF127	R	30	128	503	86	161	27	9	3	60	58	—	22	.320	.393	.427
Cy Seymour†	OF72	L	29	72	280	38	75	8	8	3	41	18	—	12	.268	.317	.386
Harry Arndt†	OF62,2B4,3B2*	—	23	68	248	41	63	7	4	2	28	35	—	9	.254	.355	.339
Harry Howell	P26,2B26,OF18*	R	25	96	347	42	93	16	11	2	42	18	—	7	.268	.312	.395
Herm McFarland†	OF61	L	32	61	242	54	78	19	6	3	36	36	—	10	.322	.418	.488
Joe Kelley†	OF48,3B8,1B5	R	30	60	222	50	69	17	7	1	34	34	—	12	.311	.405	.464
Tom Jones	1B37,2B1	R	25	37	159	22	45	8	4	0	14	2	—	1	.283	.292	.384
Aleck Smith	C27,1B7,OF4*	—	31	41	145	10	34	3	0	0	21	8	—	5	.234	.275	.255
Snake Wiltse†	P19,1B12,OF4*	R	30	36	132	21	39	4	4	2	24	9	—	1	.295	.350	.432
Jimmy Mathison	3B28,SS1	—	23	29	91	12	24	2	1	0	7	9	—	2	.264	.368	.308
Joe McGinnity†	P25,OF2	R	31	27	87	10	25	2	4	0	8	2	—	2	.287	.303	.402
Andy Oyler	3B20,OF3,SS2*	R	22	27	77	9	17	1	0	1	6	8	—	3	.221	.318	.273
John McGraw†	3B19	L	29	20	63	14	18	3	2	1	3	17	—	5	.286	.451	.444
John Katoll†	P15,OF3	R	30	18	57	11	10	1	0	0	1	8	—	0	.175	.288	.193
Ike Butler	P16,OF3	—	28	19	53	7	6	1	0	0	5	4	—	1	.113	.175	.132
Charlie Shields†	P23,OF1	L	22	24	48	1	8	1	0	0	2	5	—	0	.167	.245	.188
George Yeager†	C11	R	29	11	38	3	7	1	0	0	1	2	—	0	.184	.225	.211
Bill Mellor	1B10	R	28	10	36	4	13	3	0	0	5	3	—	1	.361	.410	.444
Jimmy Sheckard†	OF4	L	23	4	15	3	4	1	0	0	0	1	—	2	.267	.313	.333
Jack Thoney†	3B3	R	22	3	11	1	0	0	0	0	0	1	—	1	.000	.083	.000
Sport McAllister†	2B2,1B1	S	27	3	11	0	1	0	0	0	1	1	—	0	.091	.167	.091
Lew Drill†	C1,1B1	R	25	2	8	2	2	0	0	0	0	0	—	0	.250	.250	.250
Pop Dillon†	1B2	L	28	2	7	1	2	0	1	0	0	2	—	0	.286	.444	.571
Ernie Courtney†	3B1	L	27	1	4	3	2	0	1	0	1	1	—	0	.500	.600	1.000
Slats Jordan	OF1	L	22	1	4	0	0	0	0	0	0	0	—	0	.000	.000	.000
C.B. Burns		R	23	1	1	0	1	0	0	0	0	0	—	0	1.000	1.000	1.000

H. Arndt, 1 G at SS; H. Howell, 15 G at 3B, 11 G at SS, 1 G at 1B; A. Smith, 3 G at 2B, 1 G at 3B; S. Wiltse, 1 G at 2B; A. Oyler, 1 G at 2B

Pitcher	T	Age	G	GS	CG	ShO	IP	H	HR	BB	SO	W-L	Sv	ERA
Harry Howell	R	25	26	23	19	1	199.0	243	5	48	33	9-15	0	4.12
Joe McGinnity†	R	31	25	23	19	0	198.2	219	3	46	39	13-10	0	3.44
Snake Wiltse†	L	30	19	18	18	0	164.0	215	4	51	37	7-11	0	5.10
Charlie Shields†	L	22	23	15	10	1	142.1	201	7	32	28	4-11	0	4.24
Ike Butler	R	28	16	14	12	1	116.1	168	1	45	13	1-10	0	5.34
John Katoll†	R	30	15	13	13	0	123.0	175	5	32	25	5-10	0	4.02
Long Tom Hughes†	R	23	13	13	12	1	108.1	120	2	32	45	7-5	0	3.90
Jack Cronin†	R	28	10	8	8	0	75.2	66	1	24	20	3-5	0	2.62
Crese Heismann†	L	22	3	3	2	0	16.0	20	1	12	2	0-3	0	8.44
Ernie Ross	L	22	2	2	2	0	17.0	20	0	12	2	1-1	0	7.41
Frank Foreman	L	39	2	2	2	0	16.1	28	0	6	2	0-2	0	6.06
Dad Hale†	R	22	3	2	1	0	14.0	21	0	6	6	0-1	0	4.50
Bob Lawson	R	25	3	2	1	0	13.0	21	0	3	5	0-2	0	4.85
George Prentiss†	R	26	2	2	0	0	6.2	14	1	5	1	0-1	0	10.80

»1902 Pittsburgh Pirates 1st NL 103-36 .741 —

Fred Clarke

Player	Gm by Position	B	Age	G	AB	R	H	2B	3B	HR	RBI	BB	SO	SB	Avg	OBP	Slg
Harry Smith	C50	R	27	50	185	14	35	4	1	0	12	4	—	4	.189	.211	.222
Kitty Bransfield	1B101	R	27	102	413	49	126	21	8	0	69	17	—	23	.305	.336	.395
Claude Ritchey	2B114,OF1	S	28	115	405	54	112	13	1	2	55	53	—	10	.277	.370	.328
Tommy Leach	3B134	R	24	135	514	97	143	14	22	6	85	45	—	25	.278	.341	.426
Wid Conroy	SS95,OF3	R	25	99	365	55	89	10	6	1	47	24	—	10	.244	.299	.312
Ginger Beaumont	OF130	L	25	130	541	100	193	21	6	0	67	39	—	33	.357	.404	.418
Fred Clarke	OF113	L	29	113	459	103	145	27	14	2	53	51	—	29	.316	.401	.449
Honus Wagner	OF61,SS44,1B32*	R	28	136	534	105	176	30	16	3	91	43	—	43	.330	.394	.463
Lefty Davis	OF59	L	27	59	232	52	65	7	3	0	20	35	—	19	.280	.377	.336
Jimmy Burke	2B27,OF18,3B9*	R	27	60	203	24	60	12	2	0	26	17	—	9	.296	.359	.374
Jack O'Connor	C42,1B6,OF1	R	33	49	170	13	50	1	2	1	28	3	—	2	.294	.306	.341
Jesse Tannehill	P26,OF16	S	27	44	148	27	43	6	1	1	17	12	—	3	.291	.348	.365
Chief Zimmer	C41,1B1	R	41	42	142	13	38	4	2	0	17	11	—	4	.268	.338	.324
Sam Leever	P28,OF1	R	30	29	90	7	16	3	2	0	8	3	—	1	.178	.204	.256
Jimmy Sebring	OF19	L	20	19	80	15	26	4	4	0	15	5	—	2	.325	.365	.475
Ed Phelps	C13,1B5	R	23	18	61	5	13	1	0	0	6	4	—	2	.213	.284	.230
Fred Crolius	OF9	—	25	9	38	4	10	2	1	0	7	0	—	0	.263	.263	.368
George Merritt	OF2	—	22	2	9	2	3	1	0	0	2	0	—	0	.333	.333	.444
Bill Miller	OF1	L	23	1	5	0	1	0	0	0	2	0	—	0	.200	.200	.200
Lee Fohl	C1	L	31	1	3	0	0	0	0	0	1	0	—	0	.000	.000	.000
Mike Hopkins	C1	R	29	1	2	0	2	1	0	0	0	0	—	0	1.000	1.000	1.500

H. Wagner, 1 G at P, 1 G at 2B; J. Burke, 4 G at SS

Pitcher	T	Age	G	GS	CG	ShO	IP	H	HR	BB	SO	W-L	Sv	ERA
Jack Chesbro	R	28	35	33	31	8	286.1	242	1	62	136	28-6	1	2.17
Deacon Phillippe	R	30	31	30	29	5	272.0	265	1	26	122	20-9	0	2.05
Sam Leever	R	30	28	26	23	4	222.0	203	2	31	86	16-7	2	2.39
Jesse Tannehill	L	27	26	24	23	2	231.0	203	0	25	100	20-6	0	1.95
Ed Doheny	L	28	22	21	19	2	188.1	161	0	61	88	16-4	0	2.53
Harvey Cushman	—	24	4	4	3	0	25.2	30	0	31	12	0-4	0	7.36
Warren McLaughlin	L	26	3	3	3	0	26.0	27	0	9	13	3-0	0	2.77
Ed Poole†	R	27	1	0	0	0	8.0	7	0	3	2	0-0	0	1.13
Honus Wagner	R	28	1	0	0	0	5.1	4	0	2	5	0-0	0	0.00

1902 Brooklyn Superbas 2nd NL 75-63 .543 27.5 GB

Ned Hanlon

Player	Gm by Position	B	Age	G	AB	R	H	2B	3B	HR	RBI	BB	SO	SB	Avg	OBP	Slg
Hughie Hearne	C65	R	29	66	231	22	65	10	0	0	28	16	—	3	.281	.336	.325
Tom McCreery	1B108,OF4	S	27	112	430	49	105	8	4	4	57	29	—	16	.244	.295	.309
Tim Flood	2B132,OF1	R	25	132	476	43	104	11	4	3	51	23	—	8	.218	.266	.277
Charlie Irwin	3B130,SS1	L	33	131	458	59	125	14	0	2	43	39	—	13	.273	.344	.317
Bill Dahlen	SS138	R	32	138	527	67	139	25	8	2	74	43	—	20	.264	.329	.353
Cozy Dolan	OF141	L	29	141	592	72	166	16	7	1	54	33	—	24	.280	.324	.336
Willie Keeler	OF133	L	30	133	559	86	186	20	5	0	38	21	—	19	.333	.365	.386
Jimmy Sheckard†	OF123	L	23	123	486	86	129	20	10	4	37	57	—	23	.265	.349	.372
Duke Farrell	C49,1B24	S	35	74	264	14	64	5	2	0	24	12	—	6	.242	.281	.277
Wild Bill Donovan	P35,1B8,OF4*	R	25	48	161	16	28	3	2	1	16	9	—	7	.174	.227	.236
Doc Newton	P31,1B2	L	24	33	109	7	19	2	0	0	10	9	—	3	.174	.237	.193
Ed Wheeler	3B11,2B10,SS5	S	24	30	96	4	12	0	0	0	5	3	—	1	.125	.152	.125
Jim Hughes	P31,OF1	R	28	32	94	12	20	4	3	1	13	7	—	0	.213	.275	.351
Lew Ritter	C16	R	26	16	57	5	12	1	0	0	2	1	—	2	.211	.237	.228
George Hildebrand	OF11	R	23	11	41	3	9	1	0	0	5	3	—	0	.220	.289	.244
Rube Ward	OF11	—	23	13	31	4	9	1	0	0	2	2	—	0	.290	.333	.323
Tacks Latimer	C8	R	24	8	24	0	1	0	0	0	0	0	—	0	.042	.042	.042
Joe Wall†	C5	L	28	5	18	0	3	0	0	0	0	3	—	0	.167	.318	.167
Nig Fuller	C3	R	23	3	9	0	0	0	0	0	1	0	—	0	.000	.000	.000
Pat Deisel	C1	R	26	1	3	0	2	0	0	0	1	1	—	0	.667	.800	.667

W. Donovan, 1 G at 2B

Pitcher	T	Age	G	GS	CG	ShO	IP	H	HR	BB	SO	W-L	Sv	ERA
Wild Bill Donovan	R	25	35	33	30	4	297.2	250	1	111	170	17-15	1	2.78
Frank Kitson	R	32	32	31	29	3	268.2	256	4	61	109	19-13	0	2.85
Jim Hughes	R	28	30	29	26	0	245.0	223	3	51	92	15-10	0	2.87
Doc Newton	L	24	31	28	26	4	264.1	208	2	87	107	15-14	0	2.42
Roy Evans†	R	28	13	11	11	2	97.1	91	0	33	35	5-6	0	2.68
John McMakin	L	24	4	4	4	0	32.0	34	0	11	6	2-2	0	3.09
Gene McCann	R	26	3	3	3	0	30.0	32	0	12	9	1-2	0	2.40
Ned Garvin†	R	28	2	2	2	1	18.0	15	0	4	7	1-1	0	1.00
Lave Winham	L	20	1	0	0	0	3.0	4	0	2	1	0-0	0	0.00

1902 Boston Beaneaters 3rd NL 73-64 .533 29.0 GB

Al Buckenberger

Player	Gm by Position	B	Age	G	AB	R	H	2B	3B	HR	RBI	BB	SO	SB	Avg	OBP	Slg
Malachi Kittridge	C72	R	32	80	255	18	60	7	0	2	30	24	—	4	.235	.304	.286
Fred Tenney	1B134	L	30	134	489	88	154	18	3	2	30	73	—	21	.315	.409	.376
Gene DeMontreville	2B112,SS10	R	28	124	481	51	125	16	5	0	53	12	—	23	.260	.279	.314
Ed Gremminger	3B140	R	28	140	522	55	134	20	12	1	65	39	—	7	.257	.314	.347
Herman Long	SS107,2B13	L	36	120	437	40	101	11	0	2	44	31	—	24	.231	.282	.270
Pat Carney	OF137,P2	L	25	137	522	75	141	17	4	2	65	42	—	27	.270	.339	.330
Duff Cooley	OF127,1B7	L	29	135	548	73	162	26	8	0	58	34	—	27	.296	.339	.372
Billy Lush	OF116,3B1	S	28	120	413	68	92	8	1	2	19	76	—	30	.223	.346	.262
Pat Moran	C71,1B3,OF1	R	26	80	251	22	60	5	5	1	24	17	—	6	.239	.303	.311
Charlie Dexter†	SS22,2B19,OF7*	R	26	48	183	33	47	3	0	1	18	16	—	16	.257	.323	.290
Ernie Courtney†	OF39,SS3	L	27	48	165	23	36	3	0	0	17	13	—	3	.218	.291	.236
John Malarkey	P21,2B1	—	30	22	62	3	13	4	0	1	7	5	—	1	.210	.269	.323
Fred Brown	OF2	R	23	2	6	1	2	1	0	0	0	0	—	0	.333	.333	.500

C. Dexter, 1 G at 3B

Pitcher	T	Age	G	GS	CG	ShO	IP	H	HR	BB	SO	W-L	Sv	ERA
Vic Willis	R	26	51	46	45	4	410.0	372	6	101	225	27-20	3	2.20
Togie Pittinger	R	30	46	40	36	7	389.1	360	4	128	174	27-16	0	2.52
Mal Eason†	R	23	27	26	20	2	213.1	237	4	59	50	9-11	0	2.66
John Malarkey	R	30	21	19	17	1	170.1	158	0	58	39	8-10	1	2.59
Dad Hale†	R	22	8	6	3	0	47.0	69	1	18	12	1-4	0	6.32
Bob Dresser	L	23	1	1	1	0	9.0	12	0	0	8	0-1	0	3.00
Red Long	R	25	1	1	1	0	8.0	4	0	3	5	0-0	0	1.13
Fred Klobedanz	L	31	1	1	1	0	8.0	9	0	2	4	1-0	0	1.13
Pat Carney	L	25	2	1	0	0	5.0	6	1	3	3	0-1	0	9.00
Sammy Curran	—	27	1	0	0	0	6.2	6	0	0	3	0-0	0	1.35

1902 Cincinnati Reds 4th NL 70-70 .500 33.5 GB

Bid McPhee (27-37)/Frank Bancroft (9-7)/Joe Kelley (34-26)

Player	Gm by Position	B	Age	G	AB	R	H	2B	3B	HR	RBI	BB	SO	SB	Avg	OBP	Slg
Bill Bergen	C89	R	24	89	322	19	58	8	3	0	36	14	—	2	.180	.214	.224
Jake Beckley	1B129,P1	L	34	129	531	82	175	23	7	5	69	34	—	15	.330	.377	.427
Heinie Peitz	2B48,C47,1B6*	R	31	112	387	54	122	22	5	1	60	24	—	7	.315	.369	.406
Harry Steinfeldt	3B129	R	24	129	479	53	133	20	7	1	49	24	—	12	.278	.316	.355
Tommy Corcoran	SS137,2B1	R	33	138	538	54	136	18	4	0	54	11	—	20	.253	.268	.301
Sam Crawford	OF140	L	22	140	555	92	185	18	22	3	78	47	—	16	.333	.386	.461
Dummy Hoy	OF72	L	40	72	279	48	81	15	2	2	20	41	—	11	.290	.389	.380
John Dobbs†	OF63	L	27	63	256	39	76	7	3	1	16	19	—	7	.297	.348	.359
Cy Seymour†	OF61,P1,3B1	L	29	62	244	27	83	8	2	2	37	12	—	8	.340	.378	.414
Erve Beck†	2B32,1B6,OF6	R	23	48	187	19	57	10	3	1	20	3	—	2	.305	.319	.406
George Magoon	2B41,SS3	R	27	45	162	29	44	9	2	0	23	13	—	7	.272	.344	.352
Joe Kelley†	OF20,2B10,3B9*	R	30	40	156	24	50	9	2	1	12	15	—	3	.321	.380	.423
Mike Donlin	OF32,P1	L	24	34	143	30	41	5	4	0	9	9	—	9	.287	.333	.378
Noodles Hahn	P36,1B1,OF1	L	23	37	119	10	22	3	3	0	9	10	—	2	.185	.248	.261
Henry Thielman†	P25,OF3	R	21	28	91	6	12	0	2	0	4	5	—	0	.132	.177	.176
Billy Maloney†	OF18,C7	L	24	27	89	13	22	4	0	1	7	2	—	8	.247	.272	.326
Ed Poole†	P16,OF1	R	27	17	61	7	7	2	0	0	1	0	—	0	.115	.115	.148
Jack Morrissey	2B11,OF1	S	26	12	39	5	11	1	1	0	3	4	—	0	.282	.349	.359
Harry Bay†	OF3	L	24	6	16	3	6	0	0	0	1	2	—	0	.375	.474	.375
Rube Vickers	P3,C1	L	24	4	11	0	4	1	0	0	3	0	—	0	.364	.364	.455

H. Peitz, 6 G at 3B; J. Kelley, 2 G at SS

Pitcher	T	Age	G	GS	CG	ShO	IP	H	HR	BB	SO	W-L	Sv	ERA
Noodles Hahn	L	23	36	36	35	6	321.0	282	2	58	142	23-12	0	1.77
Bill Phillips	R	33	33	33	30	0	269.0	267	3	55	85	16-16	0	2.51
Henry Thielman†	R	21	25	23	22	0	211.0	201	2	78	49	9-15	1	3.24
Ed Poole†	R	27	16	16	16	2	138.0	129	2	54	55	12-4	0	2.15
Bob Ewing	R	29	15	12	10	0	117.2	126	1	47	44	5-6	0	2.98
Clarence Currie†	R	23	10	7	6	1	65.1	70	1	17	20	3-4	0	3.72
Crese Heismann†	L	22	5	3	2	0	33.0	33	1	10	15	2-1	0	2.45
Archie Stimmel	R	29	4	3	3	0	26.0	37	1	12	7	0-4	0	3.46
Rube Vickers	R	24	3	3	3	0	21.0	31	0	8	6	0-3	0	6.00
Len Swormstedt	R	23	2	2	2	0	18.0	22	1	5	3	0-2	0	4.00
Buck Hooker	R	21	1	1	1	0	8.0	11	1	0	0	0-1	0	4.50
Jake Beckley	L	34	1	1	0	0	4.0	9	0	1	2	0-1	0	6.75
Martin Glendon	—	25	1	1	0	0	3.0	5	0	4	0	0-1	0	12.00
Cy Seymour	L	29	1	0	0	0	3.0	4	0	3	2	0-0	0	9.00
Mike Donlin	L	24	1	0	0	0	1.0	1	0	0	0	0-0	0	0.00

1902 Chicago Cubs 5th NL 68-69 .496 34.0 GB

Frank Selee

Player	Gm by Position	B	Age	G	AB	R	H	2B	3B	HR	RBI	BB	SO	SB	Avg	OBP	Slg
Johnny Kling	C112,SS1	R	27	114	431	49	123	19	3	0	57	29	—	24	.285	.330	.343
Frank Chance	1B38,C29,OF4	R	24	75	240	39	69	9	4	1	31	35	—	27	.288	.396	.371
Bobby Lowe	2B117,3B2	R	33	119	472	41	116	13	3	0	31	11	—	16	.246	.270	.286
Germany Schaefer	3B75,1B3,OF2*	R	25	81	291	32	57	2	3	0	14	19	—	12	.196	.250	.223
Joe Tinker	SS124,3B8	R	21	131	494	55	129	19	5	2	54	26	—	27	.261	.298	.332
Jimmy Slagle	OF112	L	28	115	454	64	143	11	4	0	28	53	—	40	.315	.387	.357
Davy Jones†	OF64	L	22	64	243	41	74	12	3	0	14	38	—	12	.305	.399	.379
John Dobbs†	OF59	L	27	59	235	31	71	8	2	0	35	18	—	3	.302	.352	.353
Charlie Dexter†	3B39,1B22,OF10	R	26	69	266	30	60	12	0	2	26	19	—	13	.226	.290	.293
Jock Menefee	OF23,P22,1B18*	R	34	65	216	24	50	4	1	0	15	15	—	4	.231	.303	.259
Dusty Miller	OF51	L	25	51	187	17	46	4	1	0	13	7	—	10	.246	.299	.278
Jack Taylor	P36,3B12,OF3*	R	28	55	186	18	44	6	1	0	17	8	—	6	.237	.272	.280
Bunk Congalton	OF45	L	27	45	179	14	40	3	0	1	24	7	—	3	.223	.253	.257
Art Williams	OF24,1B19	—	24	47	160	17	37	3	0	0	14	15	—	9	.231	.309	.250
Pop Williams	P31,OF6	L	28	38	116	14	23	1	2	0	13	11	—	0	.198	.285	.241
Hal O'Hagen†	1B31	—	28	31	108	10	21	1	3	0	10	11	—	8	.194	.269	.259
Johnny Evers	2B18,SS8	L	20	26	90	7	20	0	0	0	2	3	—	1	.222	.263	.222
Carl Lundgren	P18,SS2	R	22	20	66	3	7	1	0	0	5	2	—	2	.106	.132	.121
Jim Murray	OF12	R	24	12	47	3	8	0	0	0	1	2	—	0	.170	.204	.170
Dad Clark	1B12	L	28	12	43	1	8	1	0	0	2	4	—	1	.186	.255	.209
Harry Schlafly	OF5,2B4,3B2	R	23	10	31	5	10	0	3	0	5	6	—	2	.323	.432	.516
Mike Lynch	OF7	—	26	7	28	4	4	0	0	0	0	2	—	0	.143	.200	.143
Deacon Morrissey	P5,3B2	—	26	7	22	1	2	0	0	0	0	3	—	0	.091	.200	.091
Mike Jacobs	SS5	—	25	5	19	1	4	0	0	0	2	0	—	0	.211	.211	.211
Mike Kahoe†	C4,3B2,SS1	R	28	7	18	0	4	1	0	0	2	0	—	0	.222	.222	.278
Sammy Strang†	2B2,3B2	S	25	3	11	1	4	0	0	0	0	0	—	1	.364	.364	.364
Pete Lamer	C2	—	28	2	9	2	2	0	0	0	0	0	—	0	.222	.222	.222
Jack Hendricks†	OF2	L	27	2	7	0	4	0	1	0	0	0	—	0	.571	.571	.857
Ed Glenn	SS2	R	26	2	7	0	0	0	0	0	0	1	—	0	.000	.125	.000
Chick Pedroes	OF2	—	32	2	6	0	0	0	0	0	0	0	—	0	.000	.000	.000
Snapper Kennedy	OF1	S	23	1	5	0	0	0	0	0	0	0	—	0	.000	.000	.000
R.E. Hildebrand	OF1	—	—	1	4	1	0	0	0	0	0	1	—	0	.000	.200	.000
Joe Hughes	OF1	R	22	1	3	0	0	0	0	0	0	0	—	0	.000	.000	.000

G. Schaefer, 1 G at SS; J. Menefee, 2 G at 3B, 1 G at 2B; J. Taylor, 2 G at 1B, 1 G at 2B

Pitcher	T	Age	G	GS	CG	ShO	IP	H	HR	BB	SO	W-L	Sv	ERA
Jack Taylor	R	28	36	33	33	7	324.2	271	2	43	83	23-11	1	1.33
Pop Williams	L	28	31	31	26	1	254.1	259	1	63	94	11-16	0	2.51
Jock Menefee	R	34	22	21	20	4	197.1	202	1	26	60	12-10	0	2.42
Carl Lundgren	R	22	18	18	17	1	160.0	158	2	45	68	9-9	0	1.97
Bob Rhoads	R	22	16	12	12	1	118.0	131	1	42	43	4-8	1	3.20
Jim St. Vrain	L	19	12	11	10	1	95.0	88	0	25	51	4-6	0	2.08
Deacon Morrissey	R	26	5	5	5	0	40.0	40	0	8	13	1-3	0	2.25
Alex Hardy	L	24	4	4	4	1	35.0	29	0	12	12	2-2	0	3.60
Jim Gardner	R	27	3	3	2	0	25.0	23	0	10	6	1-2	0	2.88
Mal Eason†	R	23	2	2	2	0	18.0	21	0	2	4	1-1	0	1.00
Fred Glade	R	26	1	1	1	0	8.0	13	0	3	3	0-1	0	9.00

1902 St. Louis Cardinals 6th NL 56-78 .418 44.5 GB

Patsy Donovan

Player	Gm by Position	B	Age	G	AB	R	H	2B	3B	HR	RBI	BB	SO	SB	Avg	OBP	Slg
Jack Ryan	C66,1B4,3B4*	R	33	76	267	23	48	4	4	0	14	4	—	2	.180	.195	.225
Roy Brashear	1B67,2B21,OF16*	R	28	110	388	36	107	8	2	1	40	32	—	9	.276	.333	.314
John Farrell	2B118,SS21	R	25	138	565	68	141	13	5	0	25	43	—	9	.250	.308	.290
Fred Hartman	3B105,SS4,1B3	R	34	114	416	30	90	10	3	0	52	14	—	14	.216	.251	.255
Otto Krueger	SS107,3B18	R	25	128	467	55	124	7	8	0	46	29	—	14	.266	.313	.315
George Barclay	OF137	—	26	137	543	79	163	14	2	3	53	31	—	30	.300	.345	.350
Homer Smoot	OF129	L	24	129	518	58	161	19	4	3	48	23	—	20	.311	.350	.380
Patsy Donovan	OF126	L	37	126	502	70	158	12	4	0	35	28	—	34	.315	.363	.355
Art Nichols	1B56,C11,OF4	R	30	73	251	36	67	12	0	1	31	21	—	18	.267	.333	.327
Jack O'Neill	C59	R	29	63	192	13	27	1	1	0	12	13	—	2	.141	.214	.156
Mike O'Neill	P36,OF3	R	24	51	135	21	43	5	3	2	15	2	—	0	.319	.333	.444
Bob Wicker	P22,OF3	R	24	31	77	6	18	2	0	0	3	3	—	2	.234	.263	.260
Jack Calhoun	3B12,1B5,OF1	R	22	20	64	3	10	2	1	0	8	8	—	1	.156	.260	.219
Art Weaver	C11	—	23	11	33	2	6	2	0	0	3	1	—	0	.182	.206	.242
Doc Hazleton	1B7	—	25	7	23	0	3	0	0	0	0	2	—	0	.130	.231	.130
Jim Hackett	P4,OF2	R	24	6	21	2	6	1	0	0	4	2	—	1	.286	.348	.333
Rudy Kling	SS4	R	32	4	10	1	2	0	0	0	0	4	—	1	.200	.429	.200
Otto Williams	SS2	R	24	2	5	0	2	0	0	0	2	1	—	1	.400	.500	.400
John Murphy	3B1	—	23	1	3	1	2	1	0	0	1	1	—	0	.667	.750	1.000

J. Ryan, 2 G at 2B, 1 G at SS; R. Brashear, 3 G at SS

Pitcher	T	Age	G	GS	CG	ShO	IP	H	HR	BB	SO	W-L	Sv	ERA
Stan Yerkes	R	27	39	37	27	1	272.2	341	1	79	81	12-21	0	3.66
Mike O'Neill	R	24	36	32	29	2	288.1	297	3	66	105	16-15	0	2.90
Ed Murphy	R	25	23	17	12	1	164.0	187	7	31	37	10-6	1	3.02
Bob Wicker	R	24	22	16	14	1	152.1	159	1	45	78	5-12	0	3.19
Clarence Currie†	R	23	15	12	10	2	124.2	125	0	35	30	7-5	0	2.60
Alex Pearson	R	25	11	10	8	0	82.0	90	0	22	24	2-6	0	3.95
Bill Popp	R	25	9	7	5	0	60.1	87	2	26	20	2-6	0	4.92
Wiley Dunham	—	25	7	5	3	0	38.0	47	1	13	15	2-3	1	5.68
Jim Hackett	R	24	4	3	3	0	30.1	46	0	16	7	0-3	0	6.23
Chappie McFarland	R	27	2	1	1	0	11.0	11	1	3	3	0-1	0	5.73
Joe Adams	L	24	1	0	0	0	4.0	9	0	2	0	0-0	0	9.00

1902 Philadelphia Phillies 7th NL 56-81 .409 46.0 GB

Bill Shettsline

Player	Gm by Position	B	Age	G	AB	R	H	2B	3B	HR	RBI	BB	SO	SB	Avg	OBP	Slg
Red Dooin	C84,OF6	R	23	94	333	20	77	7	3	0	35	10	—	8	.231	.262	.270
Klondike Douglass	1B69,C29,OF10	L	30	109	408	37	95	12	3	0	37	23	—	6	.233	.274	.277
Pete Childs	2B123	—	30	123	403	25	78	5	0	0	25	34	—	6	.194	.256	.206
Bill Hallman	3B72	R	35	73	254	14	63	8	4	0	35	14	—	9	.248	.287	.311
Rudy Hulswitt	SS125,3B3	R	25	128	497	59	135	11	7	0	38	30	—	12	.272	.314	.322
Roy Thomas	OF138	L	28	138	500	89	143	4	7	0	24	107	—	17	.286	.414	.322
Shad Barry	OF137,1B1	R	23	138	543	65	156	20	6	3	58	44	—	14	.287	.343	.363
George Browne†	OF70	L	26	70	281	41	73	7	1	0	26	16	—	11	.260	.304	.292
Hughie Jennings	1B69,SS5,2B4	R	33	78	290	32	79	13	4	1	32	14	—	8	.272	.330	.355
Henry Krug	OF28,2B13,SS9*	R	25	53	198	20	45	3	3	0	14	7	—	2	.227	.261	.273
Doc White	P36,OF19	L	23	61	179	17	47	3	1	1	15	11	—	5	.263	.305	.307
Harry Wolverton†	3B34	L	28	34	136	12	40	3	2	0	16	9	—	3	.294	.347	.346
Fred Jacklitsch	C29,OF1	R	26	38	114	8	23	4	0	0	8	9	—	2	.202	.278	.237
Paddy Greene	3B19	R	27	19	65	6	11	1	0	0	1	2	—	2	.169	.206	.185
Harry Felix	P9,3B7	R	32	16	37	3	5	0	0	0	2	4	—	0	.135	.220	.135
Bill Thomas	OF3,1B1,2B1	R	24	6	17	1	2	0	0	0	0	1	—	0	.118	.167	.118
Tom Fleming	OF5	L	28	5	16	2	6	0	0	0	2	1	—	0	.375	.412	.375
Nap Shea	C3	R	28	3	8	1	1	0	0	0	0	1	—	0	.125	.300	.125
Bill Clay	OF3	—	27	3	8	1	2	0	0	0	1	0	—	0	.250	.250	.250
Joe Berry	C1	S	29	1	4	0	1	0	0	0	1	1	2	1	.250	.400	.250
Ed Watkins	OF1	—	25	1	3	0	0	0	0	0	0	1	—	0	.000	.250	.000
Frank Mahar		—	23	1	1	0	0	0	0	0	0	0	—	0	.000	.000	.000
Tom Maher		—	31	1	0	0	0	0	0	0	0	0	—	0	—	—	—

H. Krug, 6 G at 3B

Pitcher	T	Age	G	GS	CG	ShO	IP	H	HR	BB	SO	W-L	Sv	ERA
Doc White	L	23	36	35	34	3	306.0	277	3	72	185	14-20	1	2.53
Ham Iburg	R	24	30	29	20	1	236.0	286	1	62	106	11-18	0	3.89
Bill Duggleby†	R	28	33	27	25	0	258.2	282	2	57	60	12-16	0	3.38
Chick Fraser	R	31	27	26	24	3	224.0	238	2	74	97	13-14	0	3.42
Bill Magee†	R	27	8	7	6	0	53.2	61	1	18	15	2-4	0	3.69
Cy Vorhees†	—	27	10	5	3	1	53.2	63	1	20	24	3-3	0	3.86
Harry Felix	R	32	9	5	3	0	45.0	61	1	11	10	1-3	0	5.60
Jesse Whiting	—	23	1	1	1	0	9.0	13	0	6	0	0-1	0	5.00
Bill Wolfe	—	—	1	1	1	0	9.0	11	0	4	3	0-1	0	4.00
Barney McFadden	R	28	1	1	1	0	9.0	14	0	7	3	0-1	0	8.00
Solly Salisbury	R	25	2	1	0	0	6.0	15	1	2	0	0-0	0	13.50
Henry Fox	—	27	1	0	0	0	1.0	2	0	1	1	0-0	1	18.00

1902 New York Giants 8th NL 48-88 .353 53.5 GB

Horace Fogel (18-23)/Heinie Smith (5-27)/John McGraw (25-38)

Player	Gm by Position	B	Age	G	AB	R	H	2B	3B	HR	RBI	BB	SO	SB	Avg	OBP	Slg
Frank Bowerman	C98,1B3	R	33	107	367	38	93	14	6	0	26	13	—	12	.253	.279	.324
Dan McGann†	1B61	S	30	61	227	25	68	5	7	0	21	12	—	12	.300	.356	.383
Heinie Smith	2B138	R	30	138	511	46	129	19	2	0	33	17	—	32	.252	.278	.297
Billy Lauder	3B121,OF4	R	28	125	482	41	114	20	1	1	44	10	—	19	.237	.252	.288
Joe Bean	SS48	R	28	48	176	13	39	2	1	0	5	5	—	9	.222	.247	.244
Steve Brodie	OF109	L	33	109	416	37	117	8	2	3	42	22	—	11	.281	.327	.332
Jim Jones	OF67	R	25	67	249	16	59	11	1	0	19	13	—	7	.237	.275	.289
George Browne†	OF53	L	26	53	216	30	69	9	5	0	14	9	—	13	.319	.355	.407
Jack Dunn	OF43,SS36,3B18*	R	29	100	342	26	72	11	1	0	14	20	—	13	.211	.256	.249
Jack Doyle†	1B49	R	32	49	186	21	56	13	0	1	19	10	—	12	.301	.340	.387
Roger Bresnahan†	OF27,C16,1B4*	R	23	51	178	16	51	9	3	1	22	16	—	6	.287	.352	.388
Christy Mathewson	P34,OF4,1B3	R	23	42	127	10	26	3	0	2	12	6	—	2	.205	.252	.276
Jim Jackson	OF34	R	24	35	110	14	20	5	1	0	13	15	—	6	.182	.280	.245
George Yeager†	C27,1B3,OF1	R	29	38	108	6	22	2	1	0	9	11	—	1	.204	.277	.241
John McGraw†	SS34	L	29	35	107	13	25	0	0	0	5	26	—	7	.234	.397	.234
George Van Haltren	OF24	L	36	24	88	14	23	1	2	0	7	17	—	6	.261	.381	.318
Hal O'Hagen†	1B18,OF8	—	28	26	84	5	12	2	1	0	8	2	—	3	.143	.182	.190
Roy Clark	OF20	L	28	21	76	4	11	1	0	0	3	1	—	5	.145	.156	.158
Joe McGinnity†	P19,OF4,2B1	R	31	25	66	3	8	0	0	0	3	0	—	0	.121	.121	.121
Jack Cronin†	P13,OF7	R	28	20	65	1	11	3	0	0	5	1	—	2	.169	.194	.215
Heinie Wagner	SS17	R	21	17	56	4	12	1	0	0	2	0	—	3	.214	.214	.232
Jack Hendricks†	OF7	L	27	8	26	1	6	2	0	0	0	2	—	2	.231	.286	.308
Jim Delahanty	OF7	R	23	7	26	3	6	1	0	0	3	1	—	0	.231	.259	.269
Joe Wall†	OF3	L	28	6	14	2	5	2	0	0	0	2	—	0	.357	.438	.500
John Burke	P2,OF2	R	25	4	13	0	2	0	0	0	0	0	—	0	.154	.154	.154
Jack Robinson	C3	—	21	4	9	0	0	0	0	0	0	0	—	0	.000	.000	.000
Jim McDonald	OF2	R	—	2	9	0	3	0	0	0	1	0	—	0	.333	.333	.333
Libe Washburn	OF3	S	28	6	9	1	4	0	0	0	0	2	—	1	.444	.615	.444
Henry Thielman†	OF3,P2	R	21	6	9	0	1	0	0	0	0	2	—	1	.111	.273	.111
John O'Neill	C2	—	—	2	8	0	0	0	0	0	0	0	—	0	.000	.000	.000
Chick Hartley	OF1	R	21	1	4	0	0	0	0	0	0	0	—	0	.000	.000	.000
Jim Callahan	OF1	R	23	1	4	0	0	0	0	0	0	1	3	0	.000	.200	.000

J. Dunn, 3 G at P, 2 G at 2B; R. Bresnahan, 4 G at SS, 1 G at 3B

Pitcher	T	Age	G	GS	CG	ShO	IP	H	HR	BB	SO	W-L	Sv	ERA
Christy Mathewson	R	23	34	32	29	8	276.2	241	3	73	159	14-17	0	2.11
Luther Taylor†	R	27	26	25	18	0	200.2	194	4	55	87	7-15	0	2.29
Roy Evans†	R	28	23	17	17	0	176.0	186	2	58	48	8-13	0	3.17
Joe McGinnity†	R	31	19	16	16	1	153.0	122	1	32	67	8-8	0	2.06
Tully Sparks†	R	27	15	13	11	0	115.0	123	2	40	40	4-10	1	3.76
Jack Cronin†	R	28	13	12	11	0	114.0	105	3	18	52	5-6	0	2.45
Roscoe Miller†	R	25	10	9	7	0	72.2	77	1	11	15	1-8	0	4.58
Brickyard Kennedy	R	34	6	6	4	1	38.2	44	0	16	9	1-4	0	3.96
Bob Blewett	L	25	5	3	2	0	28.0	39	0	7	8	0-2	0	4.82
Jack Dunn	R	29	3	2	2	0	26.2	28	0	12	6	0-3	0	3.71
Henry Thielman†	R	21	2	2	0	0	6.0	8	0	6	5	0-1	0	1.50
John Burke	R	25	2	1	1	0	14.0	21	0	3	3	0-1	0	5.79
Bill Magee†	R	27	2	1	0	0	5.0	5	0	1	2	0-0	0	3.60

»1903 Boston Pilgrims 1st AL 91-47 .659 —

Jimmy Collins

Player	Gm by Position	B	Age	G	AB	R	H	2B	3B	HR	RBI	BB	SO	SB	Avg	OBP	Slg
Lou Criger	C96	R	31	96	317	41	61	7	10	3	31	26	—	5	.192	.256	.306
Candy LaChance	1B141	S	33	141	522	60	134	22	6	1	53	28	—	12	.257	.303	.328
Hobe Ferris	2B139,SS2	R	25	141	525	69	132	19	7	9	66	25	—	11	.251	.287	.366
Jimmy Collins	3B130	R	33	130	540	88	160	33	17	5	72	24	—	23	.296	.329	.448
Freddy Parent	SS139	R	27	139	560	83	170	31	17	4	80	13	—	24	.304	.326	.441
Buck Freeman	OF141	L	31	141	567	74	163	39	20	13	104	30	—	5	.287	.328	.496
Patsy Dougherty	OF139	L	26	139	590	106	195	19	12	4	59	33	—	35	.331	.372	.424
Chick Stahl	OF74	L	30	77	299	60	82	12	6	2	44	28	—	10	.274	.338	.375
Jack O'Brien	OF71,3B11,2B4*	L	30	96	338	44	71	14	4	3	38	21	—	10	.210	.262	.302
Jake Stahl	C28,OF1	R	24	40	92	14	22	3	5	2	8	4	—	1	.239	.286	.446
Duke Farrell	C17	S	36	17	52	5	21	5	1	0	8	5	—	1	.404	.466	.538
Aleck Smith	C10	—	32	11	33	4	10	1	0	0	4	0	—	0	.303	.303	.333
Harry Gleason	3B2	R	28	6	13	3	2	1	0	0	2	0	—	0	.154	.154	.231
George Stone		L	25	2	2	0	0	0	0	0	0	0	—	0	.000	.000	.000

J. O'Brien, 1 G at SS

Pitcher	T	Age	G	GS	CG	ShO	IP	H	HR	BB	SO	W-L	Sv	ERA
Cy Young	R	36	40	35	34	7	341.2	294	6	37	176	28-9	2	2.08
Bill Dinneen	R	27	37	34	32	6	299.0	255	6	66	148	21-13	2	2.26
Long Tom Hughes	R	24	33	31	25	5	244.2	232	5	60	112	20-7	0	2.57
Norwood Gibson	R	26	24	21	17	2	183.1	166	2	65	76	13-9	0	3.19
George Winter	R	25	24	19	14	0	178.1	182	4	37	64	9-8	0	3.08
Nick Altrock†	L	26	1	1	1	0	8.0	13	0	4	3	0-1	0	9.00

1903 Philadelphia Athletics 2nd AL 75-60 .556 14.5 GB

Connie Mack

Player	Gm by Position	B	Age	G	AB	R	H	2B	3B	HR	RBI	BB	SO	SB	Avg	OBP	Slg
O. Schreckengost	C77,1B10	R	28	92	306	26	78	13	4	3	30	11	—	0	.255	.285	.353
Harry Davis	1B104,OF2	R	29	106	420	77	125	28	7	6	55	24	—	24	.298	.343	.440
Danny Murphy	2B133	R	26	133	513	66	140	31	11	1	60	13	—	17	.273	.295	.382
Lave Cross	3B136,1B1	R	37	137	559	60	163	22	4	2	90	10	—	14	.292	.304	.356
Monte Cross	SS137,2B1	R	33	137	470	44	116	21	2	3	45	49	—	31	.247	.326	.319
Ollie Pickering	OF135	L	33	137	512	93	144	18	6	1	36	53	—	40	.281	.353	.346
Socks Seybold	OF120,1B18	R	32	137	522	76	156	45	8	8	84	38	—	5	.299	.353	.462
Topsy Hartsel	OF96	L	29	98	373	65	116	19	14	5	26	49	—	13	.311	.391	.477
Danny Hoffman	OF62,P1	L	23	74	248	29	61	5	7	2	22	6	—	7	.246	.267	.347
Mike Powers	C66,1B7	R	32	75	247	19	56	11	1	0	23	5	—	1	.227	.242	.279
Chief Bender	P36,1B3,OF1	R	19	43	120	10	22	4	1	0	8	3	—	3	.183	.216	.233
Bert Daly	2B4,3B3,SS1	R	22	10	21	2	4	0	2	0	4	1	—	0	.190	.227	.381
Connie McGeehan	P3,OF1	—	20	5	6	0	0	0	0	0	1	0	—	0	.000	.000	.000
John Kalahan	C1	R	24	1	5	0	0	0	0	0	0	0	—	0	.000	.000	.000
Ed Hilley	3B1	R	24	1	3	1	1	0	0	0	0	1	—	0	.333	.500	.333

Pitcher	T	Age	G	GS	CG	ShO	IP	H	HR	BB	SO	W-L	Sv	ERA
Eddie Plank	L	27	43	40	33	3	336.0	317	5	65	176	23-16	0	2.38
Rube Waddell	L	26	39	38	34	4	324.0	274	3	85	302	21-16	0	2.44
Chief Bender	R	19	36	33	29	2	270.0	239	6	65	127	17-14	0	3.07
Weldon Henley	R	22	29	21	13	1	186.1	186	3	67	86	12-10	0	3.91
Andy Coakley	R	20	6	3	2	0	37.2	48	2	11	20	0-3	0	5.50
Ed Pinnance	R	23	2	1	0	0	7.0	5	0	2	2	0-0	1	2.57
Jim Fairbank	R	22	4	1	1	0	24.0	33	1	12	10	1-1	0	4.88
Connie McGeehan	—	20	3	0	0	0	10.0	9	0	1	4	1-0	0	4.50
Tad Quinn	R	20	2	0	0	0	9.0	11	0	5	1	0-0	0	5.00
Danny Hoffman	L	23	1	0	0	0	3.1	2	0	2	0	0-0	0	2.70

550 Seasons: Team Rosters

1903 Cleveland Bronchos 3rd AL 77-63 .550 15.0 GB

Bill Armour

Player	Gm by Position	B	Age	G	AB	R	H	2B	3B	HR	RBI	BB	SO	SB	Avg	OBP	Slg
Harry Bemis	C74,1B10,2B1	R	29	92	314	31	82	20	3	1	41	8	—	5	.261	.295	.354
Charlie Hickman	1B125,2B7	R	27	131	522	64	154	31	11	12	97	17	—	14	.295	.325	.466
Nap Lajoie	2B122,1B1,3B1	R	28	125	485	90	167	41	11	7	93	24	—	21	.344	.379	.518
Bill Bradley	3B136	R	25	136	536	101	168	36	22	6	68	25	—	21	.313	.348	.496
John Gochnauer	SS134	R	27	134	438	48	81	16	4	0	48	48	—	10	.185	.265	.240
Harry Bay	OF140	L	25	140	579	94	169	15	12	1	35	29	—	45	.292	.329	.364
Elmer Flick	OF140	L	27	140	523	81	155	23	16	2	51	51	—	24	.296	.368	.413
Jack McCarthy†	OF108	L	34	108	415	47	110	20	8	0	43	19	—	15	.265	.299	.352
Fred Abbott	C71,1B3	R	28	77	255	25	60	11	3	1	25	7	—	8	.235	.270	.314
Jack Thoney	OF24,2B5,3B2	R	23	32	122	10	25	3	0	1	9	2	—	7	.205	.218	.254
Addie Joss	P33,1B1	R	23	34	114	8	22	5	1	0	6	1	—	0	.193	.200	.254
Billy Clingman	2B11,SS7,3B3	S	33	21	64	10	18	1	1	0	7	11	—	2	.281	.387	.328
Jack Hardy	OF5	R	26	5	19	1	3	1	0	0	1	1	—	1	.158	.200	.211
Jack Slattery†	1B2	R	25	4	11	1	0	0	0	0	0	0	—	0	.000	.000	.000
Happy Iott	OF3	R	26	3	10	1	2	0	0	0	0	2	—	1	.200	.333	.200
Hugh Hill		L	23	1	1	0	0	0	0	0	0	0	—	0	.000	.000	.000

Pitcher	T	Age	G	GS	CG	ShO	IP	H	HR	BB	SO	W-L	Sv	ERA
Addie Joss	R	23	32	31	31	3	283.2	232	3	37	120	18-13	0	2.19
Earl Moore	R	23	29	27	27	3	247.2	196	0	62	148	19-9	1	1.74
Bill Bernhard	R	32	20	19	18	3	165.2	151	1	21	60	14-6	0	2.12
Red Donahue†	R	30	16	15	14	4	136.2	142	3	12	45	7-9	0	2.44
Clarence Wright†	R	24	15	12	8	0	101.2	122	1	58	42	3-9	0	5.75
Gus Dorner	R	26	12	8	4	2	73.2	83	4	24	28	4-5	0	3.30
Ed Killian	L	26	9	8	7	3	61.2	61	1	13	18	3-4	0	2.48
Jesse Stovall	R	27	6	6	6	2	57.0	44	0	21	12	5-1	0	2.05
Bob Rhoads†	R	23	5	5	5	0	41.0	55	2	3	21	2-3	0	5.27
Alex Pearson	R	26	4	3	2	0	30.1	34	1	3	12	1-2	0	3.56
Martin Glendon	—	26	3	3	3	0	27.2	20	0	7	9	1-2	0	0.98
Ed Walker	L	28	3	3	0	0	12.1	13	0	10	4	0-0	0	5.11
Bill Pounds†	R	25	1	0	0	0	5.0	8	0	0	2	0-0	0	10.80

1903 New York Highlanders 4th AL 72-62 .537 17.0 GB

Clark Griffith

Player	Gm by Position	B	Age	G	AB	R	H	2B	3B	HR	RBI	BB	SO	SB	Avg	OBP	Slg
Monte Beville	C75,1B3	L	28	82	258	23	50	14	1	0	29	16	—	4	.194	.252	.256
John Ganzel	1B129	R	29	129	476	62	132	25	7	3	71	30	—	9	.277	.336	.378
Jimmy Williams	2B132	R	26	132	502	60	134	30	12	3	82	39	—	9	.267	.326	.392
Wid Conroy	3B123,SS4	R	26	126	503	74	137	23	12	1	45	32	—	33	.272	.322	.372
Kid Elberfeld†	SS90	R	28	90	349	49	100	18	5	0	45	22	—	16	.287	.346	.367
Willie Keeler	OF128,3B4	L	31	132	512	95	160	14	7	0	32	32	—	24	.313	.368	.367
Herm McFarland	OF103	L	33	103	362	41	88	16	9	5	45	46	—	13	.243	.333	.378
Lefty Davis	OF102,SS1	L	28	104	372	54	88	10	0	0	25	43	—	11	.237	.319	.263
Dave Fultz	OF77,3B2	R	28	79	295	39	66	12	1	0	25	25	—	29	.224	.295	.271
Jack O'Connor	C63,1B1	R	34	64	212	13	43	4	1	0	12	8	—	4	.203	.235	.231
Jesse Tannehill	P32,OF5	S	28	40	111	18	26	6	2	1	13	8	—	1	.234	.292	.351
Harry Howell	P25,3B7,SS5*	R	26	40	106	14	23	3	2	1	12	5	—	1	.217	.259	.311
Herman Long†	SS22	L	37	22	80	6	15	3	0	0	8	2	—	3	.188	.207	.225
Ernie Courtney†	SS19,2B4,1B1	L	28	25	79	7	21	3	3	1	8	7	—	1	.266	.341	.418
Pat McCauley	C6	—	33	6	19	0	1	0	0	0	1	0	—	0	.053	.053	.053
Jack Zalusky	C6,1B1	R	24	7	16	2	5	0	0	0	1	1	—	0	.313	.353	.313
Paddy Greene†	3B2,SS1	R	28	4	13	1	4	1	0	0	0	0	—	0	.308	.308	.385
Tim Jordan	1B2	L	24	2	8	2	1	0	0	0	0	0	—	0	.125	.125	.125
Fred Holmes	1B1	R	24	1	0	0	0	0	0	0	0	1	—	0	—	1.000	—

H. Howell, 1 G at 1B, 1 G at 2B

Pitcher	T	Age	G	GS	CG	ShO	IP	H	HR	BB	SO	W-L	Sv	ERA
Jack Chesbro	R	29	40	36	33	1	324.2	300	7	74	147	21-15	0	2.77
Jesse Tannehill	L	28	32	31	22	2	239.2	258	3	34	106	15-15	0	3.27
Clark Griffith	R	33	25	24	22	2	213.0	201	3	33	69	14-11	0	2.70
Bill Wolfe	R	27	20	16	12	1	148.1	143	1	26	48	6-9	0	2.97
Harry Howell	R	26	25	15	13	0	155.2	140	4	44	62	9-6	0	3.53
John Deering†	R	25	9	7	6	1	60.0	59	0	18	14	4-3	0	3.75
Snake Wiltse	L	31	4	3	2	0	25.0	35	1	6	6	0-3	1	5.40
Ambrose Puttmann	L	22	3	2	1	0	19.0	16	0	4	8	2-0	0	0.95
Doc Adkins	R	30	2	1	0	0	7.0	10	0	5	0	0-0	1	7.71
Ed Quick	R	—	1	1	0	0	2.0	5	0	1	0	0-0	0	9.00
Elmer Bliss	R	28	1	0	0	0	7.0	4	0	0	2	1-0	0	0.00

1903 Detroit Tigers 5th AL 65-71 .478 25.0 GB

Ed Barrow

Player	Gm by Position	B	Age	G	AB	R	H	2B	3B	HR	RBI	BB	SO	SB	Avg	OBP	Slg
Deacon McGuire	C69,1B1	R	39	72	248	15	62	12	1	0	21	19	—	3	.250	.306	.306
Charlie Carr	1B135	R	26	135	548	59	154	23	11	2	79	10	—	10	.281	.296	.374
Heinie Smith	2B93	R	31	93	336	36	75	11	3	1	22	19	—	12	.223	.271	.283
Joe Yeager	3B107,P1,SS1	R	27	109	402	36	103	15	6	0	43	18	—	9	.256	.303	.323
Sport McAllister	SS46,C18,OF5*	S	28	78	265	31	69	8	2	0	22	10	—	5	.260	.297	.306
Sam Crawford	OF137	L	23	137	550	88	184	23	25	4	89	25	—	18	.335	.366	.489
Jimmy Barrett	OF136	L	28	136	517	95	163	13	10	2	31	74	—	27	.315	.407	.391
Billy Lush	OF101,3B12,2B3*	S	29	119	423	71	116	18	14	1	33	70	—	14	.274	.379	.390
Herman Long†	SS38,2B31	L	37	69	239	21	53	12	0	0	23	10	—	11	.222	.256	.272
Fritz Buelow	C60,1B2	R	27	63	192	24	41	3	6	1	13	6	—	4	.214	.249	.307
Kid Elberfeld†	SS34,3B1	R	28	35	132	29	45	5	3	0	19	11	—	6	.341	.412	.424
George Mullin	P41,OF1	R	22	46	126	11	35	9	1	1	12	2	—	1	.278	.295	.389
Wild Bill Donovan	P35,OF1	R	26	40	124	11	30	3	2	0	12	4	—	3	.242	.266	.298
Frank Kitson	P31,OF5	L	33	36	116	12	21	0	2	0	4	2	—	2	.181	.195	.216
Doc Gessler†	OF28	L	22	29	105	9	25	5	4	0	12	3	—	1	.238	.273	.362
Ernie Courtney†	3B13,SS9	L	28	23	74	7	17	0	0	0	6	5	—	1	.230	.305	.230
Jack Burns	2B11	R	23	11	37	2	10	0	0	0	3	1	—	0	.270	.325	.270
John Murphy	SS5	—	24	5	22	1	4	1	0	0	1	0	—	0	.182	.182	.227
Simon Nicholls	SS2	L	20	2	8	0	3	0	0	0	0	0	—	0	.375	.375	.375
Paddy Greene†	3B1	R	28	1	3	0	0	0	0	0	0	0	—	0	.000	.000	.000

S. McAllister, 4 G at 3B, 1 G at 1B; B. Lush, 3 G at SS

Pitcher	T	Age	G	GS	CG	ShO	IP	H	HR	BB	SO	W-L	Sv	ERA
George Mullin	R	22	41	36	31	6	320.2	284	4	106	170	18-15	2	2.25
Wild Bill Donovan	R	26	35	34	34	4	307.0	247	3	95	187	17-16	0	2.29
Frank Kitson	R	33	31	28	28	2	257.2	277	8	38	102	15-16	0	2.58
Rube Kisinger	R	26	16	14	13	2	118.2	118	0	27	33	7-9	0	2.96
John Deering†	R	25	10	8	5	0	60.2	77	3	24	14	3-4	0	3.86
Mal Eason	R	24	7	6	6	1	56.1	60	1	19	21	2-5	0	3.36
John Skopec	L	23	6	5	3	0	39.1	46	0	13	14	3-2	0	3.43
Harry Kane	L	19	3	3	2	0	18.0	26	0	8	10	0-2	0	8.50
Alex Jones	L	33	2	2	0	0	8.2	19	0	6	2	0-1	0	12.46
Joe Yeager	R	27	1	1	1	0	9.1	15	0	0	1	0-1	0	3.86

1903 St. Louis Browns 6th AL 65-74 .468 26.5 GB

Jimmy McAleer

Player	Gm by Position	B	Age	G	AB	R	H	2B	3B	HR	RBI	BB	SO	SB	Avg	OBP	Slg
Mike Kahoe	C71	R	29	77	244	26	46	7	5	0	23	11	—	1	.189	.227	.258
John Anderson	1B133,OF7	S	29	138	550	65	156	34	8	2	78	23	—	16	.284	.312	.385
Bill Friel	2B63,3B24,OF9	L	27	97	351	46	80	11	8	0	25	23	—	4	.228	.279	.305
Hunter Hill	3B86	R	24	86	317	30	77	11	3	0	25	8	—	2	.243	.264	.297
Bobby Wallace	SS135	R	29	135	511	63	136	21	7	1	54	28	—	10	.266	.309	.341
Jesse Burkett	OF132	L	34	132	515	73	151	20	7	3	40	52	—	17	.293	.361	.377
Emmett Heidrick	OF119	L	26	120	461	55	129	20	15	1	42	19	—	19	.280	.310	.395
Charlie Hemphill	OF104	L	27	105	383	36	94	6	3	3	29	23	—	16	.245	.292	.300
Joe Sugden	C66,1B8	S	32	79	241	18	51	4	0	0	22	25	—	4	.212	.288	.228
Barry McCormick†	2B28,3B28,SS4	—	28	61	207	13	45	6	1	1	16	18	—	5	.217	.283	.271
Joe Martin†	OF38,2B6	L	27	44	173	18	37	6	4	0	7	6	—	0	.214	.249	.295
Willie Sudhoff	P38,OF1	R	28	41	110	12	20	1	2	0	6	3	—	1	.182	.204	.227
Dick Padden	2B29	R	32	29	94	7	19	3	0	0	6	9	—	5	.202	.306	.234
Pinky Swander	OF14	L	22	14	51	9	14	2	2	0	6	10	—	0	.275	.413	.392
Benny Bowcock	2B14	R	23	14	50	7	16	3	1	1	10	3	—	1	.320	.358	.480
Owen Shannon	C8,1B1	R	17	9	28	1	6	2	0	0	3	1	—	0	.214	.241	.286
Claude Gouzzie	2B1	R	30	1	1	0	0	0	0	0	0	0	—	0	.000	.000	.000

Pitcher	T	Age	G	GS	CG	ShO	IP	H	HR	BB	SO	W-L	Sv	ERA
Willie Sudhoff	R	28	38	35	30	5	293.2	262	4	56	104	21-15	0	2.27
Jack Powell	R	28	38	34	33	4	306.1	294	11	58	169	15-19	2	2.91
Ed Siever	L	26	31	27	24	1	254.0	245	6	39	90	13-14	0	2.48
Red Donahue†	R	30	16	15	14	0	131.0	145	0	22	51	8-7	1	2.75
Clarence Wright†	R	24	8	8	7	1	61.0	73	2	16	37	3-5	0	3.69
Roy Evans†	R	29	7	7	4	0	54.0	66	1	14	24	0-4	0	4.17
Barney Pelty	R	22	7	6	5	0	48.2	49	1	15	20	3-3	1	2.40
Bill Reidy†	R	29	5	5	5	1	43.0	53	1	7	8	1-4	0	3.98
Cy Morgan	R	24	2	1	1	0	13.0	12	0	6	6	0-2	0	4.15
John Terry	—	23	3	1	1	0	17.2	21	0	4	2	1-1	0	2.55

1903 Chicago White Sox 7th AL 60-77 .438 30.5 GB

Nixey Callahan

Player	Gm by Position	B	Age	G	AB	R	H	2B	3B	HR	RBI	BB	SO	SB	Avg	OBP	Slg
Jack Slattery†	C56,1B5	R	25	63	211	8	46	3	2	0	20	2	—	2	.218	.233	.251
Frank Isbell	1B117,3B19,2B2*	L	27	138	546	52	132	25	9	2	59	12	—	26	.242	.266	.332
George Magoon†	2B94	R	28	94	334	32	76	11	3	0	25	30	—	4	.228	.303	.278
Nixey Callahan	3B102,OF8,P3	R	29	118	439	47	128	26	5	2	56	20	—	24	.292	.324	.387
Lee Tannehill	SS138	R	22	138	503	48	113	14	3	2	50	25	—	10	.225	.263	.276
Fielder Jones	OF136	L	31	136	530	71	152	18	5	0	45	47	—	21	.287	.348	.340
Danny Green	OF133	L	26	135	499	75	154	26	7	6	62	47	—	29	.309	.375	.425
Ducky Holmes†	OF82,3B3	L	34	86	344	53	96	7	5	0	18	25	—	25	.279	.335	.328
Bill Hallman	OF57	L	27	63	207	29	43	7	4	0	18	31	—	11	.208	.320	.280
Ed McFarland	C56	R	28	61	201	15	42	7	2	1	19	14	—	3	.209	.264	.279
Tom Daly†	2B43	S	37	43	150	20	31	11	0	0	19	20	—	6	.207	.304	.280
Billy Sullivan	C31	R	28	32	111	10	21	4	0	1	7	5	—	3	.189	.224	.252
Cozy Dolan†	1B19,OF4	L	30	27	104	16	27	5	1	0	7	6	—	5	.260	.313	.327
Pep Clark	3B15	R	20	15	65	7	20	4	2	0	9	2	—	5	.308	.338	.431

F. Isbell, 1 G at SS, 1 G at OF

Pitcher	T	Age	G	GS	CG	ShO	IP	H	HR	BB	SO	W-L	Sv	ERA
Doc White	L	24	37	36	29	3	300.0	258	4	69	114	17-16	0	2.13
Patsy Flaherty	L	27	40	34	29	2	293.2	338	9	50	65	11-25	1	3.74
Roy Patterson	R	26	34	30	26	2	293.0	275	5	69	89	15-15	1	2.70
Frank Owen	R	23	26	20	15	1	167.1	167	1	44	66	8-12	1	3.50
Nick Altrock†	L	26	12	8	6	1	71.0	59	4	19	19	4-3	0	2.15
Davey Dunkle†	R	30	12	7	6	0	82.0	96	1	31	26	4-4	1	4.06
Nixey Callahan	R	29	3	3	3	0	28.0	40	0	5	12	1-2	0	4.50

1903 Washington Senators 8th AL 43-94 .314 47.5 GB

Tom Loftus

Player	Gm by Position	B	Age	G	AB	R	H	2B	3B	HR	RBI	BB	SO	SB	Avg	OBP	Slg
Malachi Kittridge†	C60	R	33	60	192	8	41	4	1	0	16	10	—	1	.214	.252	.245
Boileryard Clarke	1B88,C37	R	34	126	465	35	111	14	6	2	38	15	—	12	.239	.273	.308
Barry McCormick†	2B63	—	28	63	219	14	47	10	2	0	23	10	—	3	.215	.255	.279
Bill Coughlin	3B119,SS4,2B2	R	24	125	473	56	116	18	3	1	31	9	—	30	.245	.267	.302
Charles Moran	SS96,2B2	—	24	98	373	41	84	14	5	1	24	33	—	8	.225	.297	.298
Kip Selbach	OF140,3B1	R	31	140	533	68	134	23	12	3	49	41	—	20	.251	.305	.356
Jimmy Ryan	OF114	R	40	114	437	42	109	25	4	7	46	17	—	9	.249	.290	.373
Watty Lee	OF47,P22	L	23	75	231	17	48	8	4	0	13	18	—	5	.208	.265	.277
Rabbit Robinson	2B45,OF30,SS24*	R	21	103	373	41	79	10	8	1	20	33	—	16	.212	.279	.290
Scoops Carey	1B47	R	32	48	183	8	37	3	2	0	23	4	—	0	.202	.223	.240
Al Orth	P36,SS7,OF4*	L	30	55	162	19	49	9	7	0	11	4	—	3	.302	.323	.444
Ed Delahanty	OF40,1B1	R	35	42	156	22	52	11	1	1	21	12	—	3	.333	.388	.436
Lew Drill	C47,1B3	R	26	51	154	11	39	9	3	0	23	15	—	4	.253	.331	.351
Joe Martin†	2B15,3B13,OF7	L	27	35	119	11	27	4	5	0	7	5	—	2	.227	.258	.345
Jack Hendricks	OF32	L	28	32	112	10	20	1	3	0	4	13	—	3	.179	.264	.241
Highball Wilson	P30,OF1	—	24	31	85	8	17	3	3	0	2	5	—	1	.200	.253	.306
Ducky Holmes†	OF14,3B4,2B2	L	34	21	71	13	16	3	1	1	8	5	—	10	.225	.286	.338
Gene DeMontreville	2B11,SS1	R	29	12	44	0	12	2	0	0	3	0	—	0	.273	.273	.318
Champ Osteen	SS10	L	26	10	40	4	8	0	2	0	4	2	—	0	.200	.256	.300

R. Robinson, 5 G at 3B; A. Orth, 2 G at 1B

Pitcher	T	Age	G	GS	CG	ShO	IP	H	HR	BB	SO	W-L	Sv	ERA
Casey Patten	L	27	36	34	32	0	300.0	313	11	80	133	11-22	1	3.60
Al Orth	R	30	36	32	30	2	279.2	326	8	62	88	11-22	2	4.34
Highball Wilson	R	24	30	28	25	1	242.1	269	7	43	56	7-18	0	3.31
Watty Lee	L	23	22	20	15	2	166.2	169	5	40	70	8-12	0	3.08
Jack Townsend	R	24	20	13	10	0	126.2	145	3	48	54	1-11	0	4.76
Davey Dunkle†	R	30	14	13	10	0	108.1	111	4	33	51	5-9	0	4.24

»1903 Pittsburgh Pirates 1st NL 91-49 .650 —

Fred Clarke

Player	Gm by Position	B	Age	G	AB	R	H	2B	3B	HR	RBI	BB	SO	SB	Avg	OBP	Slg
Ed Phelps	C76,1B3	R	24	81	273	32	77	7	3	2	31	17	—	2	.282	.338	.352
Kitty Bransfield	1B127	R	28	127	505	69	134	23	7	2	57	33	—	13	.265	.314	.350
Claude Ritchey	2B137	S	29	138	506	66	145	28	10	0	59	55	—	15	.287	.360	.381
Tommy Leach	3B127	R	25	127	507	97	151	16	17	7	87	40	—	22	.298	.352	.438
Honus Wagner	SS111,OF12,1B6	R	29	129	512	97	182	30	19	5	101	44	—	46	.355	.414	.518
Ginger Beaumont	OF141	L	26	141	613	137	209	30	6	7	68	44	—	23	.341	.390	.444
Jimmy Sebring	OF124	L	21	124	506	71	140	16	13	4	64	32	—	20	.277	.325	.383
Fred Clarke	OF101,SS2	L	30	104	427	88	150	32	15	5	70	41	—	21	.351	.414	.532
Otto Krueger	SS29,OF28,3B13*	R	26	80	256	42	63	6	8	1	28	21	—	5	.246	.323	.344
Harry Smith	C60,OF1	R	28	61	212	15	37	3	2	0	19	12	—	2	.175	.222	.208
Deacon Phillippe	P36,OF1	R	31	37	124	20	26	4	2	0	16	5	—	0	.210	.246	.274
Art Weaver†	C11,1B5	—	24	16	48	8	11	0	1	0	3	2	—	0	.229	.260	.271
Kaiser Wilhelm	P12,OF1	R	29	13	34	1	3	0	0	0	0	2	—	0	.088	.162	.088
George Merritt	OF7,P1	—	23	9	27	4	4	0	1	0	3	2	—	1	.148	.233	.222
Joe Marshall	SS3,OF3,2B1	R	27	10	23	2	6	1	2	0	2	0	—	0	.261	.261	.478
Gene Curtis	OF5	R	20	5	19	2	8	1	0	0	3	1	—	0	.421	.450	.474
Fred Carisch	C4	R	21	5	18	4	6	4	0	1	5	0	—	0	.333	.333	.722
Hans Lobert	3B3,2B1,SS1	R	21	5	13	1	1	1	0	0	0	1	—	1	.077	.143	.154
Reddy Grey	OF1	L	28	2	6	1	2	0	0	0	1	1	—	0	.333	.429	.333
Ernie Diehl	OF1	R	25	1	3	0	1	0	0	0	0	0	—	0	.333	.333	.333
Lou Gertenrich	OF1	R	28	1	3	0	0	0	0	0	0	0	—	0	.000	.000	.000
Solly Hofman	OF2	R	20	3	2	1	0	0	0	0	0	0	—	0	.000	.000	.000

O. Krueger, 3 G at 2B

Pitcher	T	Age	G	GS	CG	ShO	IP	H	HR	BB	SO	W-L	Sv	ERA
Sam Leever	R	31	36	34	30	7	284.1	255	2	60	90	25-7	1	2.06
Deacon Phillippe	R	31	36	33	31	4	289.1	269	4	29	123	25-9	2	2.43
Ed Doheny	L	29	27	25	22	2	222.2	209	1	89	75	16-8	2	3.19
Brickyard Kennedy	R	35	18	15	10	1	125.1	130	0	57	39	9-6	0	3.45
Kaiser Wilhelm	R	29	12	9	7	1	86.1	88	0	25	20	5-3	0	3.23
Bucky Veil	R	21	12	6	4	0	70.2	70	1	36	20	5-3	0	3.82
Cy Falkenberg	R	22	10	6	3	0	56.1	65	0	32	24	1-5	0	3.83
Gus Thompson	R	26	5	4	3	0	43.0	52	1	16	22	2-2	0	3.56
Lave Winham	L	21	5	4	3	1	36.0	33	0	21	22	3-1	0	2.25
Jack Pfiester	L	25	3	3	2	0	19.0	26	0	10	15	0-3	0	6.16
Doc Scanlan	R	22	1	1	1	0	9.0	5	0	6	0	0-1	0	4.00
Lew Moren	R	19	1	1	1	0	6.0	9	0	2	2	0-1	0	9.00
George Merritt	R	23	1	0	0	0	4.0	4	0	1	2	0-0	0	2.25

1903 New York Giants 2nd NL 84-55 .604 6.5 GB

John McGraw

Player	Gm by Position	B	Age	G	AB	R	H	2B	3B	HR	RBI	BB	SO	SB	Avg	OBP	Slg
John Warner	C85	L	30	89	285	38	81	8	5	0	34	7	—	5	.284	.322	.347
Dan McGann	1B129	S	31	129	482	75	130	21	6	3	50	32	—	36	.270	.331	.357
Billy Gilbert	2B128	R	27	128	413	62	104	9	0	1	40	41	—	37	.252	.348	.281
Billy Lauder	3B108	R	29	108	395	52	111	13	0	0	53	14	—	19	.281	.307	.314
Charlie Babb	SS113,3B8	S	30	121	424	68	105	15	8	0	46	45	—	22	.248	.350	.321
George Browne	OF141	L	27	141	591	105	185	20	3	3	45	43	—	27	.313	.364	.372
Sam Mertes	OF137,C1,1B1	R	30	138	517	100	145	32	14	7	104	61	—	45	.280	.360	.437
Roger Bresnahan	OF84,1B13,C11*	R	24	113	406	87	142	30	8	4	55	61	—	34	.350	.443	.493
George Van Haltren	OF75	L	37	84	280	42	72	6	1	0	28	28	—	14	.257	.327	.286
Jack Dunn	SS27,3B25,2B19*	R	30	78	257	35	62	15	1	0	37	15	—	12	.241	.291	.307
Frank Bowerman	C55,1B4,OF1	R	34	64	210	22	58	6	2	1	31	6	—	5	.276	.306	.338
George Davis	SS4	S	32	4	15	2	4	0	0	0	1	1	—	0	.267	.313	.267
John McGraw	2B2,OF2,3B1*	L	30	12	11	2	3	0	0	0	1	1	—	1	.273	.429	.273

R. Bresnahan, 4 G at 3B; J. Dunn, 1 G at OF; J. McGraw, 1 G at SS

Pitcher	T	Age	G	GS	CG	ShO	IP	H	HR	BB	SO	W-L	Sv	ERA
Joe McGinnity	R	32	55	48	44	3	434.0	391	4	109	171	31-20	2	2.43
Christy Mathewson	R	24	45	42	37	3	366.1	321	4	100	267	30-13	2	2.26
Luther Taylor	R	28	33	31	18	1	244.2	306	6	89	94	13-13	0	4.19
Jack Cronin	R	29	20	11	8	0	115.2	130	5	37	50	6-4	1	3.81
Roscoe Miller	R	26	15	8	6	0	85.1	101	1	24	30	2-5	3	4.11
Red Ames	R	20	2	2	2	1	14.0	5	0	8	14	2-0	0	1.29
Bill Bartley	R	18	1	0	0	0	3.0	3	0	4	2	0-0	0	0.00

1903 Chicago Cubs 3rd NL 82-56 .594 8.0 GB

Frank Selee

Player	Gm by Position	B	Age	G	AB	R	H	2B	3B	HR	RBI	BB	SO	SB	Avg	OBP	Slg
Johnny Kling	C132	R	28	132	491	67	146	29	13	3	68	22	—	23	.297	.330	.428
Frank Chance	1B121,C2	R	25	125	441	83	144	24	10	2	81	78	—	67	.327	.439	.440
Johnny Evers	2B110,SS11,3B2	L	21	124	464	70	136	27	7	0	52	19	—	25	.293	.325	.381
Doc Casey	3B112	S	33	112	435	56	126	8	3	1	40	19	—	11	.290	.324	.329
Joe Tinker	SS107,3B19	R	22	124	460	67	134	21	7	2	70	37	—	27	.291	.345	.380
Jimmy Slagle	OF139	L	29	139	543	104	162	20	6	0	44	81	—	33	.298	.393	.357
Davy Jones	OF130	L	23	130	497	64	140	18	3	1	62	53	—	15	.282	.352	.336
Dick Harley	OF103	L	30	104	386	72	89	9	1	0	33	45	—	27	.231	.328	.259
Otto Williams†	SS26,2B7,1B3*	R	25	38	130	14	29	5	0	0	13	4	—	8	.223	.246	.262
Jack Taylor	P37,2B1,3B1	R	29	40	126	13	28	3	4	0	17	6	—	3	.222	.263	.310
Bobby Lowe	2B22,1B6,3B1	R	34	32	105	14	28	5	3	0	15	4	—	5	.267	.319	.371
Jack McCarthy†	OF24	L	34	24	101	11	28	5	0	0	14	4	—	8	.277	.305	.327
Tommy Raub	C12,1B6,OF5*	R	32	36	84	6	19	3	2	0	7	5	—	3	.226	.278	.310
Jock Menefee	P20,1B2	R	35	22	64	3	13	3	0	0	2	3	—	0	.203	.239	.250
John Dobbs†	OF16	L	28	16	61	8	14	1	1	0	4	7	—	0	.230	.329	.279
Jim Cook	OF5,2B1,1B1	R	23	8	26	3	4	1	0	0	2	2	—	1	.154	.241	.192
Bill Hanlon	1B8	—	27	8	21	4	2	0	0	0	2	6	—	1	.095	.296	.095
George Moriarty	3B1	R	19	1	5	1	0	0	0	0	0	0	—	0	.000	.000	.000
Larry McLean	C1	R	21	1	4	0	0	0	0	0	1	1	—	0	.000	.200	.000

O. Williams, 1 G at 3B; T. Raub, 4 G at 3B

Pitcher	T	Age	G	GS	CG	ShO	IP	H	HR	BB	SO	W-L	Sv	ERA
Jack Taylor	R	29	37	33	33	1	312.1	277	0	57	83	21-14	1	2.45
Jake Weimer	L	29	35	33	27	3	282.0	241	4	104	128	20-8	0	2.30
Bob Wicker†	R	25	32	27	24	1	246.2	236	3	74	110	20-9	1	3.03
Carl Lundgren	R	23	27	20	16	0	193.1	191	1	60	67	11-9	3	2.93
Jock Menefee	R	35	20	17	13	1	146.2	157	3	38	39	8-10	0	3.01
Clarence Currie†	R	24	6	3	2	0	33.1	35	1	9	9	1-2	1	2.97
Alex Hardy	L	25	3	3	1	0	12.2	21	0	7	4	1-1	0	6.39
Peaches Graham	R	26	1	1	0	0	5.0	9	0	3	4	0-1	0	5.40
Pop Williams†	L	29	1	1	1	0	5.0	9	0	0	2	0-1	0	5.40
Jack Doscher†	L	22	1	1	0	0	3.0	6	0	2	5	0-1	0	12.00

1903 Cincinnati Reds 4th NL 74-65 .532 16.5 GB

Joe Kelley

Player	Gm by Position	B	Age	G	AB	R	H	2B	3B	HR	RBI	BB	SO	SB	Avg	OBP	Slg
Heinie Peitz	C78,1B11,3B9*	R	32	105	358	45	93	15	3	0	42	37	—	7	.260	.331	.318
Jake Beckley	1B119	L	35	120	459	85	150	29	10	2	81	42	—	23	.327	.384	.447
Tom Daly†	2B79	S	37	80	307	42	90	14	9	1	38	16	—	5	.293	.332	.407
Harry Steinfeldt	3B104,SS14	R	25	118	439	71	137	32	12	6	83	47	—	6	.312	.386	.481
Tommy Corcoran	SS115	R	34	115	459	61	113	18	7	2	73	12	—	12	.246	.267	.329
Cy Seymour	OF135	L	30	135	558	85	191	25	15	7	72	33	—	25	.342	.382	.478
Mike Donlin	OF118,1B7	L	25	126	496	110	174	25	18	7	67	56	—	26	.351	.420	.516
Cozy Dolan†	OF93	L	30	93	385	64	111	20	3	0	58	28	—	11	.288	.340	.356
Joe Kelley	OF67,SS12,2B11*	R	31	105	383	85	121	22	4	3	45	51	—	18	.316	.402	.418
Bill Bergen	C58	R	25	58	207	21	47	4	2	0	19	7	—	2	.227	.252	.266
George Magoon†	2B32,3B9	R	28	42	139	6	30	6	0	0	9	19	—	2	.216	.314	.259
Bob Ewing	P29,OF3	R	30	32	95	17	24	3	2	0	6	10	—	0	.253	.330	.326
Jack Morrissey	2B17,OF8,SS2	S	27	29	89	14	22	1	0	0	9	14	—	3	.247	.350	.258
Charlie DeArmond	3B11	R	26	11	39	10	11	2	1	0	7	3	—	1	.282	.349	.385
Pete Cregan	OF6	R	28	6	19	0	2	0	0	0	0	1	—	0	.105	.190	.105
Lee Fohl	C4	L	32	4	14	3	5	1	1	0	2	0	—	0	.357	.400	.571
Emil Haberer	C4	R	25	5	13	1	1	0	0	0	0	2	—	0	.077	.200	.077
Dan Kerwin	OF2	L	23	2	6	1	4	1	0	0	1	2	—	0	.667	.778	.833
Harry Wood	OF2	L	18	2	3	0	0	0	0	0	0	1	—	0	.000	.250	.000
Pat Deisel	C1	R	27	2	0	0	0	0	0	0	0	1	—	0	—	1.000	—

H. Peitz, 4 G at 2B; J. Kelley, 8 G at 3B, 6 G at 1B

Pitcher	T	Age	G	GS	CG	ShO	IP	H	HR	BB	SO	W-L	Sv	ERA
Noodles Hahn	L	24	34	34	34	5	296.0	297	3	47	127	22-12	0	2.52
Bob Ewing	R	30	29	28	27	1	246.2	254	3	64	104	14-13	1	2.77
Jack Sutthoff	R	30	30	27	21	3	224.2	207	2	79	76	16-9	0	2.80
Ed Poole	R	28	25	21	18	1	184.1	188	4	77	73	7-13	0	3.27
Jack Harper	R	25	17	15	13	0	134.2	143	2	70	45	8-9	0	4.34
Bill Phillips	R	34	16	13	11	1	118.1	134	0	30	46	7-6	0	3.35
Rip Reagan	R	25	3	2	2	0	18.0	40	0	7	7	0-2	0	6.00
Jimmy Wiggs	R	26	2	1	0	0	5.0	12	0	2	2	0-1	0	5.40
Buck Hooker	R	22	1	0	0	0	2.1	2	0	2	0	0-0	0	0.00

552 Seasons: Team Rosters

1903 Brooklyn Superbas 5th NL 70-66 .515 19.0 GB

Ned Hanlon

Player	Gm by Position	B	Age	G	AB	R	H	2B	3B	HR	RBI	BB	SO	SB	Avg	OBP	Slg
Lew Ritter	C74,OF2	R	27	78	259	26	61	9	6	0	37	19	—	9	.236	.290	.317
Jack Doyle	1B139	R	33	139	524	84	164	27	6	0	91	54	—	34	.313	.383	.387
Tim Flood	2B84,SS2,OF1	R	26	89	309	27	77	15	2	0	32	15	—	14	.249	.291	.311
Sammy Strang	3B124,OF8,2B3	S	26	135	508	101	138	21	5	0	38	75	—	46	.272	.376	.333
Bill Dahlen	SS138	R	33	138	474	71	124	17	9	1	64	82	—	34	.262	.373	.342
Jimmy Sheckard	OF139	L	24	139	515	99	171	29	9	9	75	75	—	67	.332	.423	.476
John Dobbs†	OF110	L	28	111	414	61	98	15	7	2	59	48	—	23	.237	.323	.321
Judge McCredie	OF56	L	26	56	213	40	69	5	0	0	20	24	—	10	.324	.397	.347
Dutch Jordan	2B54,3B18,OF4*	R	23	78	267	27	63	11	1	0	21	19	—	9	.236	.289	.285
Fred Jacklitsch	C53,2B1,OF1	R	27	60	176	31	47	8	3	1	21	33	—	4	.267	.389	.364
Doc Gessler†	OF43	L	22	49	154	20	38	8	3	0	18	17	—	9	.247	.366	.338
Tom McCreery†	OF38	S	28	40	141	13	37	5	2	0	10	20	—	5	.262	.354	.326
Henry Schmidt	P40,OF1	R	30	41	107	17	21	1	1	1	10	13	—	3	.196	.283	.252
Hughie Hearne	C17,1B2	R	30	26	57	8	16	3	2	0	4	3	—	2	.281	.328	.404
Ed Householder	OF12	—	33	12	43	5	9	0	0	0	9	2	—	3	.209	.244	.209
Henry Thielman	OF5,P4	R	22	9	23	3	5	1	0	1	2	5	—	0	.217	.357	.391
Hughie Jennings	OF4	R	34	6	17	2	4	0	0	0	1	1	—	1	.235	.316	.235
Rube Vickers	P4,OF1	L	25	5	10	0	1	0	0	0	3	0	—	0	.100	.100	.100
Frank McManus	C2	—	27	2	7	0	0	0	0	0	0	0	—	0	.000	.000	.000
Matt Broderick	2B1	R	25	2	2	0	0	0	0	0	0	0	—	0	.000	.000	.000
Ed Hug	C1	R	22	1	0	0	0	0	0	0	0	1	—	0	—	1.000	—

D. Jordan, 1 G at 1B

Pitcher	T	Age	G	GS	CG	ShO	IP	H	HR	BB	SO	W-L	Sv	ERA
Oscar Jones	R	24	38	36	31	4	324.1	320	4	77	95	19-14	0	2.94
Henry Schmidt	R	30	40	36	29	5	301.0	321	5	120	96	22-13	2	3.83
Ned Garvin	R	29	38	34	30	2	298.0	277	2	84	154	15-18	2	3.08
Bill Reidy†	R	29	15	13	11	0	104.0	130	0	14	21	6-7	0	3.46
Roy Evans†	R	29	15	12	9	0	110.0	121	1	41	42	5-9	0	3.27
Grant Thatcher	R	26	4	4	4	0	28.0	33	1	7	9	3-1	0	2.89
Henry Thielman	R	22	4	3	3	0	29.0	31	3	14	10	0-3	0	4.66
Rube Vickers	R	25	4	1	1	0	14.0	27	0	9	5	0-1	0	10.93
Jack Doscher†	L	22	3	0	0	0	7.0	8	1	9	4	0-0	0	7.71
Bill Pounds†	R	25	1	0	0	0	6.0	8	1	2	2	0-0	0	6.00

1903 Boston Beaneaters 6th NL 58-80 .420 32.0 GB

Al Buckenberger

Player	Gm by Position	B	Age	G	AB	R	H	2B	3B	HR	RBI	BB	SO	SB	Avg	OBP	Slg
Pat Moran	C107,1B1	R	27	109	389	40	102	25	5	7	54	29	—	8	.262	.331	.406
Fred Tenney	1B122	L	31	122	447	79	140	22	3	3	41	70	—	21	.313	.415	.396
Ed Abbaticchio	2B116,SS17	R	26	133	489	61	111	18	5	1	46	52	—	23	.227	.306	.290
Ed Gremminger	3B140	R	29	140	511	57	135	24	9	5	56	31	—	12	.264	.313	.376
Harry Aubrey	SS94,2B1,OF1	—	22	96	325	26	69	8	2	0	27	18	—	7	.212	.264	.249
Duff Cooley	OF126,1B13	L	30	138	553	76	160	26	10	1	70	44	—	27	.289	.342	.378
Charlie Dexter	OF106,SS9,C6	R	27	123	457	82	102	15	1	3	34	61	—	32	.223	.323	.280
Pat Carney	OF92,P10,1B1	L	26	110	392	37	94	12	4	1	49	28	—	10	.240	.297	.298
Joe Stanley	OF77,P1,SS1	S	22	86	308	40	77	12	5	1	47	18	—	10	.250	.306	.331
Frank Bonner	2B24,SS22	R	33	48	173	11	38	5	0	1	10	7	—	2	.220	.262	.266
Vic Willis	P33,1B6	R	27	39	128	9	24	3	0	0	8	5	—	0	.188	.218	.211
Malachi Kittridge†	C30	R	33	32	99	10	21	2	0	0	6	11	—	1	.212	.291	.232
Tom McCreery†	OF23	S	28	23	83	15	18	2	1	1	10	9	—	6	.217	.293	.301
Pop Williams†	P10,OF2	L	29	14	42	4	10	0	0	0	3	0	—	0	.238	.238	.238

Pitcher	T	Age	G	GS	CG	ShO	IP	H	HR	BB	SO	W-L	Sv	ERA
Togie Pittinger	R	31	44	39	35	3	351.2	396	12	143	140	18-22	1	3.48
Vic Willis	R	27	33	32	29	2	278.0	256	3	88	125	12-18	0	2.98
John Malarkey	R	31	32	27	25	2	253.0	266	5	96	98	11-16	0	3.09
Wiley Piatt	L	28	25	23	18	0	181.0	198	5	61	100	9-14	0	3.18
Pop Williams†	L	29	10	10	9	1	83.0	97	3	37	20	4-5	0	4.12
Pat Carney	L	26	10	9	9	0	78.0	93	2	31	29	4-5	0	4.04
Joe Stanley	R	22	1	0	0	0	4.0	4	0	4	4	0-0	0	9.00

1903 Philadelphia Phillies 7th NL 49-86 .363 39.5 GB

Chief Zimmer

Player	Gm by Position	B	Age	G	AB	R	H	2B	3B	HR	RBI	BB	SO	SB	Avg	OBP	Slg
Frank Roth	C60,3B1	R	24	68	220	27	60	11	4	0	22	9	—	3	.273	.304	.359
Klondike Douglass	1B97	L	31	105	377	43	96	5	4	1	36	28	—	6	.255	.308	.297
Kid Gleason	2B102,OF4	S	36	106	412	65	117	19	6	1	49	23	—	12	.284	.326	.367
Harry Wolverton	3B123	L	29	123	494	72	152	13	12	0	53	18	—	10	.308	.342	.383
Rudy Hulswitt	SS138	R	26	138	519	56	128	22	9	1	58	28	—	10	.247	.288	.329
Roy Thomas	OF130	L	29	130	477	88	156	11	2	1	27	107	—	17	.327	.453	.365
Shad Barry	OF107,1B30,3B1	R	24	138	550	75	152	24	5	1	60	30	—	26	.276	.321	.344
Bill Keister	OF100	L	28	100	400	53	128	27	7	3	63	14	—	11	.320	.352	.445
John Titus	OF72	L	27	72	280	38	80	15	6	2	34	19	—	5	.286	.340	.404
Bill Hallman	2B22,3B19,1B9*	R	36	63	198	20	42	11	2	0	17	16	—	2	.212	.271	.288
Red Dooin	C51,1B1,OF1	R	24	62	188	18	41	5	1	0	14	8	—	9	.218	.254	.255
Chief Zimmer	C35	R	42	37	118	9	26	3	1	1	19	9	—	3	.220	.292	.288
Chick Fraser	P31,OF1	R	32	32	93	12	19	3	1	1	8	14	—	4	.204	.308	.290
Roy Brashear	2B18,1B2	R	29	20	75	9	17	3	0	0	4	6	—	2	.227	.284	.267
Libe Washburn	P4,OF2	S	29	8	18	1	3	0	0	0	1	1	—	0	.167	.211	.167
John Walsh	3B1	R	24	1	3	0	0	0	0	0	0	0	—	0	.000	.000	.000
Dutch Rudolph		L	20	1	1	0	0	0	0	0	0	0	—	0	.000	.000	.000

B. Hallman, 4 G at OF, 3 G at SS

Pitcher	T	Age	G	GS	CG	ShO	IP	H	HR	BB	SO	W-L	Sv	ERA
Bill Duggleby	R	29	36	30	28	3	264.1	318	4	79	57	13-16	2	3.75
Chick Fraser	R	32	31	29	26	1	250.0	260	8	97	104	12-17	1	4.50
Tully Sparks	R	28	28	28	27	0	248.0	248	3	56	88	11-15	0	2.72
Fred Mitchell	R	25	28	28	24	1	227.0	250	4	102	69	11-16	0	4.48
Jack McFetridge	—	33	14	13	11	0	102.2	120	2	49	31	1-11	0	4.91
Libe Washburn	L	29	4	4	4	0	35.0	44	0	11	9	0-4	0	4.37
Fred Burchell	L	23	6	3	2	0	44.0	48	0	14	12	0-3	0	2.86
Warren McLaughlin	L	27	3	2	2	0	23.0	38	0	11	3	0-3	0	7.04
Pop Williams†	L	29	2	2	2	0	18.0	21	0	6	8	1-1	0	3.00

1903 St. Louis Cardinals 8th NL 43-94 .314 46.5 GB

Patsy Donovan

Player	Gm by Position	B	Age	G	AB	R	H	2B	3B	HR	RBI	BB	SO	SB	Avg	OBP	Slg
Jack O'Neill	C74	R	30	75	246	23	58	9	1	0	27	13	—	11	.236	.288	.280
Jim Hackett	1B89,P7	R	25	99	351	24	80	13	8	0	36	19	—	2	.228	.272	.311
John Farrell	2B118,OF12	R	26	130	519	83	141	25	8	1	32	48	—	17	.272	.336	.356
Jimmy Burke	3B93,2B15,OF5	R	28	113	431	55	123	13	3	0	42	23	—	28	.285	.326	.329
Dave Brain	SS72,3B46	R	24	118	464	44	107	8	15	1	60	25	—	21	.231	.270	.319
Homer Smoot	OF129	L	25	129	500	67	148	22	8	4	49	32	—	17	.296	.342	.396
George Barclay	OF107	—	27	108	419	37	104	10	8	0	42	15	—	12	.248	.278	.310
Patsy Donovan	OF105	L	38	105	410	63	134	15	3	0	39	25	—	25	.327	.370	.378
Jack Ryan	C47,1B18,SS2	R	34	67	227	18	54	5	1	1	10	10	—	2	.238	.273	.282
Jack Dunleavy	OF38,P14	—	23	61	193	23	48	3	3	0	10	13	—	10	.249	.306	.295
Otto Williams†	SS52,2B1	R	25	53	187	10	38	4	2	0	9	9	—	6	.203	.240	.246
Art Nichols	1B25,OF7,C2	R	31	36	120	13	23	2	0	0	9	12	—	9	.192	.281	.208
Mike O'Neill	P19,OF13	R	25	41	110	12	25	2	2	0	6	8	—	3	.227	.303	.282
Lee DeMontreville	SS15,2B4,OF1	R	27	26	70	8	17	3	1	0	7	8	—	3	.243	.338	.314
Ed Murphy	P15,1B8,OF1	—	26	24	64	4	13	1	0	0	6	1	—	0	.203	.215	.219
Bob Rhoads†	P17,OF1	R	23	18	50	4	7	0	0	1	4	0	—	0	.140	.140	.200
Art Weaver†	C16	—	24	16	49	4	12	0	0	0	5	4	—	1	.245	.302	.245
Harry Berte	2B3,SS1	—	31	4	15	1	5	0	0	0	0	1	—	0	.333	.375	.333
Jack Coveney	C4	R	23	4	14	0	2	0	0	0	0	0	—	0	.143	.143	.143
Charlie Moran	P3,SS1	R	25	4	14	2	6	0	0	0	1	0	—	1	.429	.429	.429
Lon Ury	1B2	—	26	2	7	0	1	0	0	0	0	0	—	0	.143	.143	.143

Pitcher	T	Age	G	GS	CG	ShO	IP	H	HR	BB	SO	W-L	Sv	ERA
Chappie McFarland	R	28	28	26	25	1	229.0	253	2	48	76	9-19	0	3.07
Three Finger Brown	R	26	26	24	19	1	201.0	231	7	59	83	9-13	0	2.60
Mike O'Neill	R	25	19	17	12	0	145.0	184	2	43	39	4-13	0	3.79
Clarence Currie†	R	24	22	16	13	1	148.0	155	7	60	52	4-12	1	4.01
Bob Rhoads†	R	23	17	13	12	1	128.2	154	3	47	52	5-8	0	4.62
Jack Dunleavy	L	23	14	13	9	0	102.1	101	2	57	51	6-8	0	4.05
Ed Murphy	R	26	15	12	9	0	106.1	108	2	38	16	4-8	0	3.30
Jim Hackett	R	25	7	6	5	0	48.1	47	0	18	21	1-3	1	3.72
War Sanders	L	25	8	6	3	0	40.2	48	0	21	9	1-6	0	5.98
Charlie Moran	R	25	3	2	2	0	24.0	30	0	19	7	0-1	0	5.25
Pat Hynes	L	19	1	1	1	0	9.0	10	0	6	1	0-1	0	4.00
Harry Betts	R	22	1	1	1	0	9.0	11	0	5	2	0-1	0	10.00
Stan Yerkes	R	28	1	1	0	0	5.0	8	0	0	3	0-1	0	1.80
John Lovett	—	26	3	1	0	0	5.0	6	0	5	3	0-0	0	5.40
Bob Wicker†	R	25	1	0	0	0	5.0	4	0	3	3	0-0	0	0.00
Larry Milton	R	24	1	0	0	0	4.0	3	0	1	0	0-0	0	2.25
Rube Taylor	L	26	1	0	0	0	3.0	0	0	0	1	0-0	0	0.00

»1904 Boston Pilgrims 1st AL 95-59 .617 —

Jimmy Collins

Player	Gm by Position	B	Age	G	AB	R	H	2B	3B	HR	RBI	BB	SO	SB	Avg	OBP	Slg
Lou Criger	C95	R	32	98	299	34	63	10	5	2	34	27	—	1	.211	.283	.298
Candy LaChance	1B157	S	34	157	573	55	130	19	5	1	47	23	—	7	.227	.265	.283
Hobe Ferris	2B156	R	26	156	563	50	120	23	10	3	63	23	—	7	.213	.245	.306
Jimmy Collins	3B156	R	34	156	631	85	171	33	13	3	67	27	—	19	.271	.306	.379
Freddy Parent	SS155	R	28	155	591	85	172	22	9	6	77	28	—	20	.291	.330	.389
Buck Freeman	OF157	L	32	157	597	64	167	20	19	7	84	32	—	7	.280	.329	.412
Chick Stahl	OF157	L	31	157	587	83	170	27	19	3	67	64	—	11	.290	.366	.416
Kip Selbach†	OF98	R	32	98	376	50	97	19	8	0	30	48	—	10	.258	.347	.351
Duke Farrell	C56	S	37	68	198	11	42	9	2	0	15	15	—	1	.212	.281	.278
Patsy Dougherty†	OF49	L	27	49	195	33	53	5	4	0	4	25	—	10	.272	.355	.338
Jesse Tannehill	P33,OF2	S	29	45	122	14	24	2	6	0	6	9	—	1	.197	.252	.311
Bill O'Neill†	OF9,SS2	S	24	17	51	7	10	1	0	0	5	2	—	0	.196	.226	.216
Tom Doran	C11	L	23	12	32	1	4	0	1	0	0	4	—	1	.125	.243	.188
Bob Unglaub†	2B3,3B2,SS1	R	22	9	13	1	2	1	0	0	2	1	—	0	.154	.214	.231

Pitcher	T	Age	G	GS	CG	ShO	IP	H	HR	BB	SO	W-L	Sv	ERA
Cy Young	R	37	43	41	40	10	380.0	327	6	29	200	26-16	1	1.97
Bill Dinneen	R	28	37	37	37	5	335.2	283	8	63	153	23-14	0	2.20
Norwood Gibson	R	27	33	32	29	1	273.0	216	7	81	112	17-14	0	2.21
Jesse Tannehill	L	29	33	31	30	4	281.2	256	5	33	116	21-11	0	2.04
George Winter	R	26	20	16	12	1	135.2	126	4	27	31	8-4	0	2.32

1904 New York Highlanders 2nd AL 92-59 .609 1.5 GB

Clark Griffith

Player	Gm by Position	B	Age	G	AB	R	H	2B	3B	HR	RBI	BB	SO	SB	Avg	OBP	Slg
Deacon McGuire	C97,1B1	R	40	101	322	17	67	12	2	0	20	27	—	2	.208	.276	.258
John Ganzel	1B118,2B9,SS1	R	30	130	465	50	121	16	10	6	48	24	—	13	.260	.309	.376
Jimmy Williams	2B146	R	27	146	559	62	147	31	7	2	74	38	—	14	.263	.314	.354
Wid Conroy	3B110,SS27,OF3	R	27	140	489	58	119	18	12	1	52	43	—	30	.243	.314	.335
Kid Elberfeld	SS122	R	29	122	445	55	117	13	5	2	46	37	—	18	.263	.337	.328
Willie Keeler	OF142	L	32	143	543	78	186	14	8	2	40	35	—	21	.343	.390	.409
John Anderson	OF111,1B33	S	30	143	558	62	155	27	12	3	82	23	—	20	.278	.313	.385
Patsy Dougherty†	OF106	L	27	106	452	80	128	13	10	6	22	19	—	11	.283	.316	.396
Dave Fultz	OF90	R	29	97	339	39	93	17	4	2	32	24	—	17	.274	.324	.366
Red Kleinow	C62,3B2,OF1	R	24	68	209	12	43	8	4	0	16	15	—	4	.206	.259	.282
Jack Thoney†	3B26,OF10	R	24	36	128	17	24	4	2	0	12	8	—	9	.188	.241	.250
Champ Osteen	3B17,SS8,1B4	L	27	28	107	15	21	1	4	2	9	1	—	0	.196	.218	.336
Al Orth†	P20,OF2	L	31	26	64	6	19	1	1	0	7	0	—	2	.297	.308	.344
Long Tom Hughes†	P19,OF3	R	25	19	54	7	13	2	1	0	2	2	—	0	.241	.268	.315
Monte Beville†	1B4,C3	L	29	9	22	2	6	2	0	0	2	2	—	0	.273	.333	.364
Bob Unglaub†	3B4,SS1	R	22	6	19	2	4	0	0	0	2	0	—	0	.211	.211	.211
Orth Collins	OF5	L	24	5	17	3	6	1	1	0	1	1	—	0	.353	.389	.529
Frank McManus†	C4	—	28	4	7	0	0	0	0	0	0	0	—	0	.000	.000	.000
Elmer Bliss	OF1	L	29	1	1	0	0	0	0	0	0	0	—	0	.000	.000	.000

Pitcher	T	Age	G	GS	CG	ShO	IP	H	HR	BB	SO	W-L	Sv	ERA
Jack Chesbro	R	30	55	51	48	6	454.2	338	4	88	239	41-12	0	1.82
Jack Powell	R	29	47	45	38	3	390.1	340	15	92	202	23-19	0	2.44
Al Orth†	R	31	20	18	11	2	137.2	122	0	19	47	11-6	0	2.68
Long Tom Hughes†	R	25	19	18	12	1	136.1	141	3	48	75	7-11	0	3.70
Clark Griffith	R	34	16	11	8	1	100.1	91	3	16	36	7-5	1	2.87
Ned Garvin†	R	30	2	2	0	0	12.0	14	0	2	8	0-1	0	2.25
Walter Clarkson	R	25	13	4	2	0	66.1	63	3	25	43	1-2	1	5.02
Ambrose Puttmann	L	23	9	3	2	1	49.1	40	0	17	26	2-0	0	2.74
Bill Wolfe†	R	28	7	3	2	0	33.2	31	1	4	8	0-3	0	3.21

1904 Chicago White Sox 3rd AL 89-65 .578 6.0 GB

Nixey Callahan (23-18)/Fielder Jones (66-47)

Player	Gm by Position	B	Age	G	AB	R	H	2B	3B	HR	RBI	BB	SO	SB	Avg	OBP	Slg
Billy Sullivan	C107	R	29	108	371	29	85	18	4	1	44	12	—	11	.229	.255	.307
Jiggs Donahue	1B101	L	24	102	367	46	91	9	7	1	48	25	—	18	.248	.298	.319
Gus Dundon	2B103,3B3,SS2	R	29	108	373	40	85	9	3	0	36	30	—	19	.228	.292	.268
Lee Tannehill	3B153	R	23	153	547	50	125	31	5	0	61	20	—	14	.229	.260	.303
George Davis	SS152	S	33	152	563	75	142	27	15	1	69	43	—	32	.252	.311	.359
Fielder Jones	OF149	L	32	149	547	72	133	14	5	3	42	53	—	25	.243	.316	.303
Danny Green	OF146	L	27	147	536	83	142	16	10	2	62	63	—	28	.265	.352	.343
Nixey Callahan	OF104,2B28	R	30	132	482	66	126	23	2	0	54	39	—	29	.261	.318	.317
Frank Isbell	1B57,2B27,OF5*	L	28	96	314	27	66	10	3	1	34	16	—	19	.210	.255	.271
Ducky Holmes	OF63	L	35	68	251	42	78	11	9	1	19	14	—	13	.311	.354	.438
Ed McFarland	C49	R	29	50	160	22	44	11	3	0	20	17	—	2	.275	.348	.381
Doc White	P30,OF2	L	25	33	76	7	12	2	0	0	2	10	—	3	.158	.256	.184
Charlie Jones	OF5	R	28	5	17	2	4	0	1	0	1	1	—	0	.235	.278	.353
Mike Heydon	C4	L	29	4	10	0	1	1	0	0	1	1	—	0	.100	.250	.200
Frank Huelsman†	OF1	R	30	4	7	0	1	1	0	0	0	0	—	0	.143	.143	.286
Claude Berry	C3	R	24	3	1	1	0	0	0	0	0	1	—	0	.000	.500	.000

F. Isbell, 4 G at SS

Pitcher	T	Age	G	GS	CG	ShO	IP	H	HR	BB	SO	W-L	Sv	ERA
Frank Owen	R	24	37	36	34	4	315.0	243	2	61	103	21-15	1	1.94
Nick Altrock	L	27	38	36	31	6	307.0	274	2	48	87	19-14	0	2.96
Doc White	L	25	30	30	23	7	228.0	201	6	68	115	16-12	0	1.78
Frank Smith	R	24	26	23	22	4	202.1	157	0	58	107	16-9	0	2.09
Roy Patterson	R	27	22	17	14	4	165.0	148	1	24	64	9-9	0	2.29
Patsy Flaherty†	L	28	5	5	4	0	43.0	36	1	10	14	1-2	0	2.09
Elmer Stricklett	R	27	1	1	0	0	7.0	12	0	2	3	0-1	0	10.29
Ed Walsh	R	23	18	8	6	1	110.2	90	1	32	57	6-3	1	2.60
Tom Dougherty	R	23	1	0	0	0	2.0	0	0	0	0	1-0	0	0.00

1904 Cleveland Bronchos 4th AL 86-65 .570 7.5 GB

Bill Armour

Player	Gm by Position	B	Age	G	AB	R	H	2B	3B	HR	RBI	BB	SO	SB	Avg	OBP	Slg
Harry Bemis	C79,1B13,2B1	R	30	97	336	35	76	11	6	0	25	8	—	6	.226	.259	.295
Charlie Hickman†	2B45,1B40,OF1	R	28	86	337	34	97	22	10	4	45	13	—	9	.288	.318	.448
Nap Lajoie	2B95,SS44,1B2	R	29	140	553	92	208	49	15	5	102	27	—	29	.376	.413	.546
Bill Bradley	3B154	R	26	154	609	94	183	32	8	6	83	26	—	23	.300	.334	.409
Terry Turner	SS111	R	23	111	404	41	95	9	6	1	45	11	—	5	.235	.255	.295
Elmer Flick	OF144,2B6	L	28	150	579	97	177	31	17	6	56	51	—	38	.306	.371	.449
Billy Lush	OF138	S	30	138	477	76	123	13	8	1	50	72	—	12	.258	.359	.325
Harry Bay	OF132	L	26	132	506	69	122	12	9	3	36	43	—	38	.241	.307	.318
George Stovall	1B38,2B9,OF3*	R	25	52	181	18	54	10	1	1	31	2	—	4	.298	.317	.381
Fred Abbott	C33,1B7	R	29	41	130	14	22	4	2	0	12	6	—	2	.169	.206	.231
Charlie Carr†	1B32	R	27	32	120	9	27	5	1	0	7	4	—	0	.225	.250	.283
Fritz Buelow†	C42	R	28	42	119	11	21	4	1	0	5	11	—	2	.176	.252	.227
Otto Hess	P21,OF12	L	25	34	100	4	12	2	1	0	5	3	—	0	.120	.146	.160
Bob Rhoads	P22,OF5	R	24	29	92	5	18	2	2	0	14	1	—	0	.196	.204	.261
Bill Schwartz	1B22,3B1	R	20	24	86	5	13	2	0	0	0	0	—	4	.151	.151	.174
Addie Joss	P25,1B3	R	24	28	76	3	10	0	1	0	3	1	—	0	.132	.143	.158
Claude Rossman	OF17	L	23	18	62	5	13	5	0	0	6	0	—	0	.210	.210	.290
Rube Vinson	OF15	—	25	15	49	12	15	1	0	0	2	10	—	2	.306	.433	.327
Harry Ostdiek		R	23	7	18	1	3	0	1	0	3	3	—	1	.167	.318	.278
Mike Donovan	SS1	R	22	2	2	0	0	0	0	0	0	0	—	0	.000	.000	.000

G. Stovall, 1 G at 3B

Pitcher	T	Age	G	GS	CG	ShO	IP	H	HR	BB	SO	W-L	Sv	ERA
Bill Bernhard	R	33	38	37	35	4	320.2	323	3	55	137	23-13	0	2.13
Red Donahue	R	31	35	32	30	6	277.0	281	2	49	127	19-14	0	2.40
Earl Moore	R	24	26	24	22	1	227.2	186	2	61	139	12-11	0	2.25
Addie Joss	R	24	25	24	20	5	192.1	160	0	30	83	14-10	0	1.59
Bob Rhoads	R	24	22	19	18	0	175.1	175	1	48	72	10-9	0	2.87
Otto Hess	L	25	21	16	15	4	151.1	134	2	31	64	8-7	0	1.67
John Hickey	L	22	2	2	1	0	12.1	14	0	11	5	0-1	0	7.30

1904 Philadelphia Athletics 5th AL 81-70 .536 12.5 GB

Connie Mack

Player	Gm by Position	B	Age	G	AB	R	H	2B	3B	HR	RBI	BB	SO	SB	Avg	OBP	Slg
O. Schreckengost	C84,1B9	R	29	95	311	23	58	9	1	1	21	5	—	3	.186	.199	.232
Harry Davis	1B102	R	30	102	404	54	125	21	11	10	62	23	—	12	.309	.350	.490
Danny Murphy	2B150	R	27	150	557	78	160	30	17	7	77	22	—	22	.287	.320	.440
Lave Cross	3B155	R	38	155	607	73	176	31	10	1	71	13	—	10	.290	.310	.379
Monte Cross	SS153	R	34	153	503	33	95	23	4	1	38	46	—	19	.189	.266	.256
Topsy Hartsel	OF147	L	30	147	534	79	135	17	12	2	25	75	—	19	.253	.347	.341
Socks Seybold	OF129,1B13	R	33	143	510	56	149	26	9	3	64	42	—	12	.292	.351	.396
Ollie Pickering	OF121	L	34	124	455	56	103	10	3	0	30	45	—	17	.226	.299	.262
Danny Hoffman	OF51	L	24	53	204	31	61	7	5	3	24	5	—	9	.299	.329	.426
Mike Powers	C56,OF1	R	33	57	184	11	35	3	0	0	11	6	—	3	.190	.220	.207
Pete Noonan	C22,1B10	R	22	39	114	13	23	3	1	2	13	1	—	1	.202	.209	.298
Jim Mullin†	1B26,2B5,SS2*	R	20	41	110	9	24	1	0	1	9	5	—	4	.218	.277	.255
Lou Bruce	OF25,P2,2B1*	L	27	30	101	9	27	3	0	0	8	5	—	2	.267	.302	.297

J. Mullin, 1 G at OF; L. Bruce, 1 G at 3B

Pitcher	T	Age	G	GS	CG	ShO	IP	H	HR	BB	SO	W-L	Sv	ERA
Rube Waddell	L	27	46	46	39	8	383.0	307	5	91	349	25-19	0	1.62
Eddie Plank	L	28	44	43	37	7	357.1	311	2	86	201	26-17	0	2.17
Weldon Henley	R	23	36	34	31	5	295.2	245	3	76	130	15-17	0	2.53
Chief Bender	R	20	29	20	18	4	203.2	167	1	59	149	10-11	0	2.87
Andy Coakley	R	21	8	8	7	2	62.0	48	1	23	33	4-3	0	1.89
Fred Applegate	R	25	3	3	3	0	21.0	29	0	8	12	1-2	0	6.43
John Barthold	R	22	4	0	0	0	10.2	12	0	8	5	0-0	0	5.06
Jim Fairbank	R	23	3	1	1	0	17.0	19	0	13	6	0-1	0	6.35
Lou Bruce	R	27	2	0	0	0	11.0	11	1	2	2	0-0	0	4.91

1904 St. Louis Browns 6th AL 65-87 .428 29.0 GB

Jimmy McAleer

Player	Gm by Position	B	Age	G	AB	R	H	2B	3B	HR	RBI	BB	SO	SB	Avg	OBP	Slg
Joe Sugden	C79,1B28	S	33	105	348	25	93	6	3	0	30	28	—	6	.267	.331	.302
Tom Jones	1B134,2B23,OF4	R	27	156	625	53	152	15	10	2	68	15	—	16	.243	.270	.309
Dick Padden	2B132	R	33	132	453	42	108	19	4	0	36	40	—	23	.238	.325	.298
Charles Moran†	3B81,OF1	—	25	82	272	15	47	3	1	0	14	25	—	2	.173	.242	.191
Bobby Wallace	SS139	R	30	139	541	57	149	29	4	2	69	42	—	20	.275	.330	.355
Jesse Burkett	OF147	L	35	147	575	72	156	15	10	2	27	78	—	12	.271	.363	.343
Emmett Heidrick	OF130	L	27	133	538	66	147	14	10	1	36	16	—	35	.273	.294	.342
Charlie Hemphill	OF108,2B1	L	28	114	438	47	112	13	2	2	45	35	—	23	.256	.311	.308
Pat Hynes	OF63,P5	—	20	66	254	23	60	7	3	0	15	3	—	3	.236	.248	.287
Mike Kahoe	C69	R	30	72	236	9	51	6	1	0	12	8	—	4	.216	.242	.250
Hunter Hill†	3B56,OF1	R	25	58	219	19	47	3	0	0	14	6	—	4	.215	.246	.228
Harry Gleason	3B20,SS20,2B5	R	29	46	155	10	33	7	1	0	6	4	—	1	.213	.247	.271
Barney Pelty	P39,OF3	R	23	42	118	7	15	1	0	0	9	0	—	1	.127	.149	.136
Willie Sudhoff	P27,OF3	R	29	30	85	5	14	3	0	0	7	6	—	0	.165	.237	.200
Ed Siever	P29,OF1	L	27	30	71	6	11	0	0	0	1	5	—	0	.155	.221	.155
Frank Huelsman†	OF18	R	30	20	68	6	15	2	1	0	1	6	—	0	.221	.303	.279
Jack O'Connor	C14	R	35	14	47	4	10	1	0	0	2	2	—	4	.213	.245	.234
Gene DeMontreville	2B3	R	30	4	9	0	1	0	0	0	0	2	—	0	.111	.273	.111
Art Bader	OF1	R	17	2	3	0	0	0	0	0	0	1	—	0	.000	.250	.000
Harry Vahrenhorst		R	19	1	1	0	0	0	0	0	0	0	—	0	.000	.000	.000
Pinky Swander		L	23	1	1	0	0	0	0	0	0	0	—	0	.000	.000	.000

Pitcher	T	Age	G	GS	CG	ShO	IP	H	HR	BB	SO	W-L	Sv	ERA
Barney Pelty	R	23	39	35	31	2	301.0	270	7	77	126	15-18	0	2.84
Fred Glade	R	28	35	34	30	6	289.0	248	2	58	156	18-15	1	2.27
Harry Howell	R	27	34	33	32	2	299.2	254	1	60	122	13-21	0	2.19
Willie Sudhoff	R	29	27	24	20	1	222.1	232	8	54	63	8-15	0	3.76
Ed Siever	L	27	29	24	19	2	217.0	235	3	65	77	10-14	0	2.65
Clarence Wright	R	25	1	1	0	0	4.0	10	0	2	3	0-1	0	13.50
Cy Morgan	R	25	8	3	2	0	51.0	51	3	10	24	0-2	0	3.71
Pat Hynes	L	20	5	2	1	0	26.0	35	1	7	6	1-1	0	6.23

1904 Detroit Tigers 7th AL 62-90 .408 32.0 GB

Ed Barrow (32-46)/Bobby Lowe (30-44)

Player	Gm by Position	B	Age	G	AB	R	H	2B	3B	HR	RBI	BB	SO	SB	Avg	OBP	Slg
Lew Drill†	C49,1B2	R	27	51	160	7	39	6	1	0	13	20	—	2	.244	.335	.294
Charlie Carr†	1B92	R	27	92	360	29	77	13	3	0	40	14	—	6	.214	.245	.267
Bobby Lowe†	2B140	R	35	140	506	47	105	14	6	0	40	17	—	15	.208	.236	.259
Ed Gremminger	3B83	R	30	83	309	18	66	13	3	1	28	14	—	3	.214	.257	.285
Charley O'Leary	SS135	R	21	135	456	39	97	10	3	1	16	21	—	9	.213	.254	.254
Jimmy Barrett	OF162	L	29	162	624	83	167	10	5	0	31	79	—	15	.268	.353	.300
Matty McIntyre	OF152	L	24	152	578	74	146	11	10	2	46	44	—	11	.253	.310	.317
Sam Crawford	OF150	L	24	150	562	49	143	22	16	2	73	44	—	20	.254	.309	.361
Rabbit Robinson	SS30,3B26,OF20*	R	22	101	320	30	77	13	6	0	37	29	—	14	.241	.314	.319
Bill Coughlin†	3B56	R	25	56	206	22	47	6	0	0	17	5	—	1	.228	.257	.257
Bob Wood	C47	R	38	49	175	15	43	6	2	1	17	5	—	1	.246	.271	.320
Monte Beville†	C30,1B24	L	29	54	174	14	36	5	1	0	13	8	—	2	.207	.250	.247
George Mullin	P45,OF2	R	23	53	155	14	45	10	2	0	8	10	—	1	.290	.337	.381
Charlie Hickman†	1B39	R	28	42	144	18	35	6	6	2	22	11	—	3	.243	.297	.410
Wild Bill Donovan	P34,1B8,OF1	R	27	46	140	12	38	2	1	1	6	3	—	2	.271	.287	.321
Fritz Buelow†	C42	R	28	42	136	6	15	1	1	0	5	8	—	2	.110	.160	.132
Jesse Stovall	P22,1B3	L	28	25	56	5	11	0	1	0	2	3	—	2	.196	.237	.232
Frank Huelsman†	OF4	R	30	4	18	1	6	1	0	0	4	1	—	1	.333	.400	.389
Jack Burns	2B4	R	24	4	16	3	2	0	0	0	1	1	—	1	.125	.176	.125
Frank McManus†	C1	—	28	1	0	0	0	0	0	0	0	0	—	0	—	—	—

R. Robinson, 19 G at 2B

Pitcher	T	Age	G	GS	CG	ShO	IP	H	HR	BB	SO	W-L	Sv	ERA
George Mullin	R	23	45	44	42	7	382.1	345	1	131	161	17-23	0	2.40
Ed Killian	L	27	40	34	32	4	331.2	293	0	93	124	14-20	1	2.44
Wild Bill Donovan	R	27	34	34	30	3	293.0	251	5	94	137	17-16	0	2.46
Frank Kitson	R	34	26	24	19	0	199.2	211	7	38	69	8-13	1	3.07
Jesse Stovall	R	28	22	17	13	1	146.2	170	3	45	41	3-13	0	4.42
Charlie Jaeger	R	29	8	6	5	0	49.0	49	0	15	13	3-3	0	2.57
Bugs Raymond	R	22	5	2	1	0	14.2	14	0	6	7	0-1	0	3.07
Cy Ferry	R	25	3	1	1	0	13.0	12	0	11	4	0-1	0	6.23

1904 Washington Senators 8th AL 38-113 .252 55.5 GB

Mal Kittridge (1-16)/Patsy Donovan (37-97)

Player	Gm by Position	B	Age	G	AB	R	H	2B	3B	HR	RBI	BB	SO	SB	Avg	OBP	Slg
Malachi Kittridge	C79	R	34	81	265	11	64	7	0	0	24	8	—	2	.242	.266	.268
Jake Stahl	1B119,OF23	R	25	142	520	54	136	29	12	3	50	21	—	25	.262	.309	.381
Barry McCormick	2B113	—	29	113	404	36	88	11	1	0	39	27	—	9	.218	.274	.250
Hunter Hill†	3B71,OF5	R	25	77	290	18	57	6	1	0	17	11	—	10	.197	.228	.224
Joe Cassidy	SS99,OF32,3B23	R	21	152	581	63	140	12	19	1	33	15	—	17	.241	.265	.332
Patsy Donovan	OF122	L	39	125	436	30	100	6	0	0	19	24	—	17	.229	.271	.243
Bill O'Neill†	OF93,2B3	S	24	95	365	33	89	10	1	1	16	22	—	22	.244	.294	.285
Frank Huelsman†	OF84	R	30	84	303	21	75	19	4	2	30	24	—	6	.248	.313	.356
Boileryard Clarke	C52,1B29	R	35	85	275	23	58	8	1	0	17	17	—	5	.211	.269	.247
Bill Coughlin†	3B64	R	25	65	265	28	73	15	4	0	17	9	—	10	.275	.307	.362
Charles Moran†	SS61,3B1	—	25	62	243	27	54	10	0	0	7	23	—	7	.222	.289	.263
Kip Selbach†	OF48	R	32	48	178	15	49	8	4	0	14	24	—	9	.275	.361	.365
Lew Drill†	C29,OF14	R	27	46	142	17	38	7	2	1	11	21	—	3	.268	.385	.366
Jack Townsend	P36,OF2	R	25	38	119	6	20	4	0	1	8	2	—	0	.168	.189	.227
Jim Mullin†	2B27	R	20	27	102	10	19	2	2	0	4	4	—	3	.186	.224	.245
Al Orth†	OF18,P10	L	31	31	102	7	22	3	1	0	11	1	—	2	.216	.238	.265
Jack Thoney†	OF17	R	24	17	70	6	21	3	0	0	6	1	—	2	.300	.310	.343
Long Tom Hughes†	P16,OF2	R	25	18	57	5	13	3	2	1	10	1	—	0	.228	.241	.404
Rabbitt Nill	2B15	R	22	15	48	4	8	0	1	0	3	5	—	0	.167	.273	.208
Lefty Herring	1B10,OF5	L	24	15	46	3	8	1	0	0	2	7	—	0	.174	.283	.196
Izzy Hoffman	OF9	L	29	10	30	1	3	1	0	0	1	2	—	0	.100	.156	.133

Pitcher	T	Age	G	GS	CG	ShO	IP	H	HR	BB	SO	W-L	Sv	ERA
Casey Patten	L	28	45	39	37	2	357.2	367	2	79	150	14-23	3	3.07
Jack Townsend	R	25	36	34	31	2	291.1	319	3	100	143	5-26	0	3.58
Beany Jacobson	L	23	33	30	23	1	253.2	276	6	57	75	6-23	0	3.55
Bill Wolfe†	R	28	17	16	13	2	126.2	131	0	22	44	6-9	0	3.27
Long Tom Hughes†	R	25	16	14	14	0	124.1	133	4	34	48	2-13	1	3.47
Davey Dunkle	R	31	12	11	7	0	74.1	95	1	23	23	2-9	0	4.96
Al Orth†	R	31	10	7	7	0	73.2	88	2	15	23	3-4	0	4.76
Del Mason	R	20	5	3	2	0	33.0	45	1	13	16	0-3	0	6.00
Highball Wilson	R	25	3	3	3	0	25.0	33	0	4	11	0-3	0	4.68

»1904 New York Giants 1st NL 106-47 .693 —

John McGraw

Player	Gm by Position	B	Age	G	AB	R	H	2B	3B	HR	RBI	BB	SO	SB	Avg	OBP	Slg
John Warner	C86	L	31	86	287	29	57	5	1	1	15	14	—	7	.199	.253	.233
Dan McGann	1B141	S	32	141	517	81	148	22	6	6	71	36	—	42	.286	.354	.387
Billy Gilbert	2B146	R	28	146	478	57	121	13	3	1	54	46	—	33	.253	.340	.299
Art Devlin	3B130	R	24	130	474	81	133	16	8	1	66	62	—	33	.281	.371	.354
Bill Dahlen	SS145	R	34	145	523	70	140	26	2	2	80	44	—	47	.268	.326	.337
George Browne	OF149	L	28	150	596	99	169	16	5	4	39	39	—	24	.284	.332	.347
Sam Mertes	OF147,SS1	R	31	148	532	83	147	28	11	4	78	54	—	47	.276	.346	.393
Roger Bresnahan	OF93,1B10,SS4*	R	25	109	402	81	114	22	7	5	33	58	—	13	.284	.381	.410
Frank Bowerman	C79,1B9,2B2*	R	35	93	289	38	67	11	4	2	27	16	—	7	.232	.288	.318
Moose McCormick†	OF55	L	23	59	203	28	54	9	5	1	26	13	—	13	.266	.323	.374
Jack Dunn	3B28,SS10,2B9*	R	31	64	181	27	56	12	2	1	19	11	—	11	.309	.356	.414
Mike Donlin†	OF37	L	26	42	132	17	37	7	3	2	14	10	—	1	.280	.340	.424
Luther Taylor	P37,OF1	R	29	37	102	8	16	1	2	0	6	6	—	0	.157	.204	.206
Hooks Wiltse	P24,OF1	R	23	25	67	10	15	2	1	1	7	4	—	1	.224	.278	.328
Doc Marshall†	C3,OF2,2B1	R	28	11	17	3	6	1	0	0	2	1	—	0	.353	.389	.412
John McGraw	2B2,SS2	L	31	5	12	0	4	0	0	0	0	3	—	0	.333	.467	.333
Dan Brouthers	1B1	L	46	2	5	0	0	0	0	0	0	0	—	0	.000	.000	.000
Jim O'Rourke	C1	R	53	1	4	1	1	0	0	0	0	0	—	0	.250	.250	.250

R. Bresnahan, 1 G at 2B, 1 G at 3B; F. Bowerman, 1 G at P; J. Dunn, 7 G at OF, 1 G at P

Pitcher	T	Age	G	GS	CG	ShO	IP	H	HR	BB	SO	W-L	Sv	ERA
Christy Mathewson	R	25	48	46	33	4	367.2	306	7	78	212	33-12	1	2.03
Joe McGinnity	R	33	51	44	38	9	408.0	307	8	86	144	35-8	5	1.61
Luther Taylor	R	29	37	36	29	5	296.1	231	6	75	138	21-15	0	2.34
Hooks Wiltse	L	23	24	16	14	2	164.2	150	8	61	105	13-3	3	2.84
Red Ames	R	21	16	13	11	1	115.0	94	2	38	93	4-6	3	2.27
Billy Milligan	L	25	5	1	1	0	25.0	36	2	4	6	0-1	2	5.40
Claude Elliott†	R	24	3	1	1	0	15.0	21	2	3	8	0-1	0	3.00
Jack Dunn	R	31	1	0	0	0	4.0	3	1	3	1	0-0	1	4.50
Frank Bowerman	R	35	1	0	0	0	1.0	3	0	1	0	0-0	0	9.00

1904 Chicago Cubs 2nd NL 93-60 .608 13.0 GB

Frank Selee

Player	Gm by Position	B	Age	G	AB	R	H	2B	3B	HR	RBI	BB	SO	SB	Avg	OBP	Slg
Johnny Kling	C104,OF10,1B6	R	29	123	452	41	110	18	0	2	46	16	—	7	.243	.271	.296
Frank Chance	1B123,C1	R	26	124	451	89	140	16	10	6	49	36	—	42	.310	.382	.430
Johnny Evers	2B152	L	22	152	532	49	141	14	7	0	47	28	—	26	.265	.307	.318
Doc Casey	3B134,C2	S	34	136	548	71	147	20	4	1	43	18	—	21	.268	.300	.325
Joe Tinker	SS140,OF1	R	23	141	488	55	108	12	13	3	41	29	—	41	.221	.268	.318
Jimmy Slagle	OF120	L	30	120	481	73	125	12	10	1	31	41	—	28	.260	.322	.333
Jack McCarthy	OF115	L	35	115	432	36	114	14	2	0	51	23	—	14	.264	.307	.306
Davy Jones	OF97	L	24	98	336	44	82	11	5	3	39	41	—	14	.244	.330	.333
Shad Barry†	OF30,1B18,3B16*	R	25	73	263	29	69	7	2	1	26	17	—	12	.262	.310	.316
Otto Williams	OF21,1B11,SS10*	R	26	57	185	21	37	4	1	0	8	13	—	9	.200	.256	.232
Jack O'Neill	C49	R	31	51	168	8	36	5	0	1	19	6	—	1	.214	.258	.262
Bob Wicker	P30,OF20	R	26	50	155	17	34	1	0	0	9	4	—	4	.219	.244	.226
Three Finger Brown	P26,2B1,OF1	S	27	31	89	8	19	3	1	0	8	2	—	0	.213	.231	.270
Harry McChesney	OF22	R	24	22	88	9	23	6	2	0	11	4	—	2	.261	.293	.375
Wildfire Schulte	OF20	L	21	20	84	16	24	4	3	2	13	2	—	1	.286	.310	.476
Frank Corridon†	P12,1B5,OF2	R	23	19	58	3	13	1	0	0	1	1	—	0	.224	.237	.241
Aleck Smith	OF6,C1,3B1	—	33	10	29	2	6	1	0	0	1	3	—	1	.207	.281	.241
Solly Hofman	OF6,SS1	R	21	7	26	7	7	0	0	1	4	1	—	2	.269	.296	.385
George Moriarty	3B2,OF2	R	20	4	13	0	0	0	0	0	0	1	—	0	.000	.071	.000
Ike Van Zandt	OF3	L	28	3	11	0	0	0	0	0	0	0	—	0	.000	.000	.000
Bill Carney	OF2	S	30	2	7	0	0	0	0	0	0	1	—	0	.000	.125	.000
Tom Stanton	C1	S	29	1	3	0	0	0	0	0	0	0	—	0	.000	.000	.000
Fred Holmes	C1	R	25	1	3	1	1	1	0	0	0	0	—	0	.333	.333	.667
Dutch Rudolph	OF2	L	21	2	3	0	1	0	0	0	0	0	—	0	.333	.333	.333

S. Barry, 8 G at SS, 2 G at 2B; O. Williams, 6 G at 2B, 6 G at 3B

Pitcher	T	Age	G	GS	CG	ShO	IP	H	HR	BB	SO	W-L	Sv	ERA
Jake Weimer	L	30	37	37	31	5	307.0	229	1	97	177	20-14	0	1.91
Buttons Briggs	R	28	34	30	28	3	277.1	252	3	77	112	19-11	3	2.04
Carl Lundgren	R	24	31	27	25	2	242.0	203	2	77	106	17-9	1	2.60
Bob Wicker	R	26	30	27	23	4	229.0	201	6	58	99	17-9	0	2.67
Three Finger Brown	R	27	26	23	21	4	212.1	155	1	50	81	15-10	1	1.86
Frank Corridon†	R	23	12	10	9	0	100.1	88	2	37	34	5-5	0	3.05
Ernie Groth	R	19	3	2	2	0	16.0	22	1	6	9	0-2	1	5.63

1904 Cincinnati Reds 3rd NL 88-65 .575 18.0 GB

Joe Kelley

Player	Gm by Position	B	Age	G	AB	R	H	2B	3B	HR	RBI	BB	SO	SB	Avg	OBP	Slg
Admiral Schlei	C88	R	26	97	291	25	69	8	3	0	32	17	—	7	.237	.297	.285
Joe Kelley	1B117,OF6,2B1	R	32	123	449	75	126	21	13	0	63	49	—	15	.281	.359	.385
Miller Huggins	2B140	S	25	140	491	96	129	12	7	2	30	88	—	13	.263	.377	.328
Harry Steinfeldt	3B98	R	26	99	349	35	85	11	6	1	52	29	—	16	.244	.313	.318
Tommy Corcoran	SS150	R	35	150	578	55	133	17	9	2	74	19	—	19	.230	.257	.301
Cy Seymour	OF130	L	31	131	531	71	166	26	13	5	58	29	—	11	.313	.352	.439
Fred Odwell	OF126,2B1	L	31	129	468	75	133	22	10	1	58	26	—	30	.284	.333	.380
Cozy Dolan	OF102,1B24	L	31	129	465	88	132	8	10	6	51	39	—	19	.284	.342	.383
Sam Woodruff	3B61,2B17,SS8*	R	27	87	306	20	58	14	3	0	20	19	—	9	.190	.244	.255
Heinie Peitz	C64,1B18,3B1	R	33	84	272	32	66	13	2	1	30	14	—	1	.243	.282	.316
Mike Donlin†	OF53,1B6	L	26	60	236	42	84	11	7	1	38	18	—	21	.356	.406	.475
Jimmy Sebring†	OF56	L	22	56	222	22	50	9	2	0	24	14	—	8	.225	.271	.284
Bob Ewing	P26,OF4	R	31	30	97	9	25	6	1	1	6	5	—	2	.258	.301	.371
Win Kellum	P31,OF5	S	28	36	82	13	13	3	2	0	8	11	—	2	.159	.281	.244
Gabby Street	C11	R	21	11	33	1	4	1	0	0	0	1	—	2	.121	.147	.152
Peaches O'Neill	C5,1B1	R	24	8	15	0	4	0	0	0	1	1	—	0	.267	.313	.267

S. Woodruff, 1 G at OF

Pitcher	T	Age	G	GS	CG	ShO	IP	H	HR	BB	SO	W-L	Sv	ERA
Jack Harper	R	26	35	35	31	6	293.2	262	2	85	125	23-9	0	2.30
Noodles Hahn	L	25	35	34	33	2	297.2	258	3	35	98	16-18	0	2.06
Win Kellum	L	28	31	24	22	1	224.2	206	1	46	70	15-10	2	2.60
Tom Walker	R	22	24	24	22	2	217.0	196	2	53	64	15-8	0	2.24
Bob Ewing	R	31	26	24	22	0	212.0	198	3	58	99	11-13	0	2.46
Jack Sutthoff†	R	31	12	10	8	0	90.0	83	1	43	27	5-6	0	2.30
Claude Elliott†	R	24	9	6	4	1	57.2	53	1	23	19	3-1	0	2.97

1904 Pittsburgh Pirates 4th NL 87-66 .569 19.0 GB

Fred Clarke

Player	Gm by Position	B	Age	G	AB	R	H	2B	3B	HR	RBI	BB	SO	SB	Avg	OBP	Slg
Ed Phelps	C91,1B1	R	25	94	302	29	73	5	3	0	28	15	—	2	.242	.289	.278
Kitty Bransfield	1B139	R	29	139	520	47	116	17	9	0	60	22	—	11	.223	.259	.290
Claude Ritchey	2B156,SS2	S	30	156	544	79	143	22	12	0	51	59	—	12	.263	.338	.347
Tommy Leach	3B146	R	26	146	579	92	149	15	12	2	56	45	—	23	.257	.316	.335
Honus Wagner	SS121,OF8,1B3*	R	30	132	490	97	171	44	14	4	75	59	—	53	.349	.423	.520
Ginger Beaumont	OF153	L	27	153	615	97	185	12	12	3	54	34	—	28	.301	.338	.374
Jimmy Sebring†	OF80	L	22	80	305	28	82	11	7	0	32	17	—	8	.269	.307	.351
Fred Clarke	OF70	L	31	72	278	51	85	7	11	0	25	22	—	11	.306	.367	.410
Otto Krueger	OF33,SS32,3B10	R	27	86	268	34	52	6	2	1	26	29	—	8	.194	.282	.243
Moose McCormick†	OF66	L	23	66	238	25	69	10	6	2	23	13	—	6	.290	.332	.408
Harry Smith	C44,OF3	R	29	47	141	17	35	3	1	0	18	16	—	5	.248	.346	.284
Fred Carisch	C22,1B14	R	22	37	125	9	31	3	1	0	8	9	—	3	.248	.299	.288
Patsy Flaherty†	P29,OF2	L	28	36	104	9	22	3	4	2	19	8	—	0	.212	.268	.375
Jack Gilbert	OF25	—	28	25	87	13	21	0	0	0	3	12	—	3	.241	.353	.241
Harry Cassady	OF12	L	23	12	44	8	9	0	0	0	3	2	—	2	.205	.239	.205
Bull Smith	OF13	R	23	13	42	2	6	0	1	0	0	1	—	0	.143	.163	.190
Ernie Diehl	OF7,SS4	R	26	12	37	6	6	0	0	0	4	6	—	3	.162	.311	.162
Jimmy Archer	C7,OF1	R	21	7	20	1	3	0	0	0	1	0	—	0	.150	.150	.150
Jack Rafter	C1	R	29	1	3	0	0	0	0	0	0	0	—	0	.000	.000	.000
Tom Stankard	3B1,SS1	R	22	2	2	0	0	0	0	0	0	0	—	0	.000	.000	.000
Bobby Lowe†		R	35	1	1	0	0	0	0	0	0	0	—	0	.000	.000	.000

H. Wagner, 2 G at 2B

Pitcher	T	Age	G	GS	CG	ShO	IP	H	HR	BB	SO	W-L	Sv	ERA
Sam Leever	R	32	34	32	26	1	253.1	224	2	54	63	18-11	0	2.17
Patsy Flaherty†	L	28	29	28	28	5	242.0	210	3	59	54	19-9	0	2.05
Mike Lynch	R	24	27	24	24	1	222.2	200	1	91	95	15-11	0	2.71
Deacon Phillippe	R	32	21	19	17	3	166.2	183	1	26	82	10-10	1	3.24
Charlie Case	R	24	18	17	14	3	141.0	129	0	31	49	10-5	0	2.94
Roscoe Miller	R	27	19	17	11	2	134.1	133	4	39	35	7-7	0	3.35
Chick Robitaille	R	25	9	8	8	0	66.0	52	1	13	34	4-3	0	1.91
Watty Lee	L	24	5	3	1	0	22.2	34	0	9	5	1-2	0	8.74
Doc Scanlan†	R	23	4	3	1	0	22.0	21	0	20	10	1-3	0	4.91
Jack Pfiester	L	26	3	2	1	0	20.0	28	0	9	6	1-1	0	7.20
Bucky Veil	R	22	1	1	0	0	4.2	4	0	4	1	0-0	0	5.79
Howie Camnitz	R	22	10	2	2	0	49.0	48	0	20	21	1-4	0	4.22
Lew Moren	R	20	1	0	0	0	4.0	7	1	4	0	0-0	0	9.00

1904 St. Louis Cardinals 5th NL 75-79 .487 31.5 GB

Kid Nichols

Player	Gm by Position	B	Age	G	AB	R	H	2B	3B	HR	RBI	BB	SO	SB	Avg	OBP	Slg
Mike Grady	C77,1B11,2B3*	R	34	101	323	44	101	15	11	5	43	31	—	6	.313	.376	.474
Jake Beckley	1B142	L	36	142	551	72	179	22	9	1	67	35	—	17	.325	.375	.403
John Farrell	2B130	R	27	131	509	72	130	23	3	0	20	46	—	16	.255	.320	.312
Jimmy Burke	3B118	R	29	118	406	37	92	10	3	0	37	15	—	17	.227	.271	.266
Danny Shay	SS97,2B2	—	27	99	340	45	87	11	1	1	18	39	—	36	.256	.338	.303
Homer Smoot	OF137	L	26	137	520	58	146	23	6	3	66	37	—	23	.281	.331	.365
Spike Shannon	OF133	S	26	134	500	84	140	10	3	1	26	50	—	34	.280	.349	.318
George Barclay†	OF103	—	28	103	375	41	75	7	4	1	28	12	—	14	.200	.237	.248
Dave Brain	SS59,3B30,OF19*	R	25	125	488	57	130	24	12	7	72	17	—	18	.266	.291	.408
Jack Dunleavy	OF44,P7	—	24	51	172	23	40	7	3	1	14	16	—	8	.233	.305	.326
Hugh Hill	OF23	L	24	23	93	13	21	2	1	3	4	2	—	3	.226	.242	.366
Mike O'Neill	P25,OF3	R	26	28	91	9	21	7	2	0	16	5	—	0	.231	.286	.352
Larry McLean	C24	R	22	27	84	5	14	2	1	0	4	4	—	1	.167	.205	.214
Dave Zearfoss	C25	—	36	25	80	7	17	2	0	0	9	10	—	0	.213	.300	.238
Bill Byers	C16,1B1	R	26	17	60	3	13	0	0	0	4	1	—	0	.217	.230	.217
Simmy Murch	2B6,3B6,SS1	R	23	13	51	3	7	1	0	0	1	1	—	0	.137	.154	.157
John Butler	C12	R	24	12	37	0	6	1	0	0	1	4	—	0	.162	.262	.189
She Donahue†	2B3,SS1	R	27	4	15	1	4	0	0	0	2	0	—	3	.267	.267	.267
Charlie Swindells	C3	R	25	3	8	0	1	0	0	0	0	0	—	0	.125	.125	.125

M. Grady, 1 G at 3B; D. Brain, 13 G at 2B, 4 G at 1B

Pitcher	T	Age	G	GS	CG	ShO	IP	H	HR	BB	SO	W-L	Sv	ERA
Jack Taylor	R	30	41	39	39	2	352.0	297	5	82	103	20-19	1	2.22
Kid Nichols	R	34	36	35	35	3	317.0	268	3	50	134	21-13	1	2.02
Chappie McFarland	R	29	32	31	28	1	270.1	266	7	56	111	14-18	0	3.20
Mike O'Neill	R	26	25	24	23	1	220.0	229	1	50	68	10-14	0	2.09
Joe Corbett	R	28	14	14	12	0	108.2	110	2	51	68	5-8	0	4.39
Jack Dunleavy	L	24	7	5	5	0	55.0	63	4	23	28	1-4	0	4.42
Jim McGinley	R	25	3	3	3	0	27.0	28	0	6	6	2-1	0	2.00
War Sanders	L	26	4	3	1	0	19.0	25	1	1	11	1-2	0	4.74

1904 Brooklyn Superbas 6th NL 56-97 .366 50.0 GB

Ned Hanlon

Player	Gm by Position	B	Age	G	AB	R	H	2B	3B	HR	RBI	BB	SO	SB	Avg	OBP	Slg
Bill Bergen	C93,1B1	R	26	94	329	17	60	4	2	0	12	9	—	3	.182	.204	.207
Pop Dillon	1B134	L	30	135	511	60	132	18	6	0	31	40	—	13	.258	.313	.317
Dutch Jordan	2B70,3B11,1B4	R	24	87	252	21	45	10	2	0	19	13	—	7	.179	.225	.234
Mike McCormick	3B104,2B1	R	21	105	347	28	64	5	4	0	27	43	—	22	.184	.278	.222
Charlie Babb	SS151	S	31	151	521	49	138	18	3	0	53	53	—	34	.265	.345	.311
Harry Lumley	OF150	L	23	150	577	79	161	23	18	9	78	41	—	30	.279	.331	.428
Jimmy Sheckard	OF141,2B2	L	25	143	507	70	121	23	6	1	46	56	—	21	.239	.317	.314
John Dobbs	OF92,2B2,SS2	L	29	101	363	36	90	16	2	0	30	28	—	11	.248	.304	.303
Doc Gessler	OF88,1B1,2B1	L	23	104	341	41	99	18	4	2	28	30	—	13	.290	.355	.384
Sammy Strang	2B63,3B12,SS1	S	27	77	271	28	52	11	0	1	9	45	—	16	.192	.316	.244
Lew Ritter	C57,2B5,3B1	R	27	72	214	23	53	4	1	0	19	20	—	17	.248	.318	.276
Emil Batch	3B28	R	24	28	94	9	24	1	2	2	7	1	—	6	.255	.271	.372
Fred Jacklitsch	1B11,2B8,C5	R	28	26	77	8	18	3	1	0	8	7	—	7	.234	.322	.299
Bill Reidy	P6,2B5	R	30	11	32	2	5	0	0	0	1	3	—	0	.156	.250	.156
Jack Doyle†	1B8	R	34	8	22	2	5	1	0	0	2	6	—	1	.227	.414	.273
C. Loudenslager	2B1	—	23	1	2	0	0	0	0	0	0	0	—	0	.000	.000	.000
Deacon Van Buren†		L	33	1	1	0	1	0	0	0	0	0	—	0	1.000	1.000	1.000

Pitcher	T	Age	G	GS	CG	ShO	IP	H	HR	BB	SO	W-L	Sv	ERA
Oscar Jones	R	25	46	41	38	0	376.2	387	7	92	96	17-25	0	2.75
Jack Cronin	R	30	40	34	33	4	307.1	284	10	79	110	12-23	0	2.69
Ed Poole	R	29	25	23	19	1	178.0	178	4	74	67	8-14	1	3.39
Ned Garvin†	R	30	23	22	16	2	181.2	141	6	78	86	5-15	0	1.68
Doc Scanlan†	R	23	13	12	11	3	104.1	94	0	40	40	6-6	0	2.16
Fred Mitchell†	R	26	8	8	8	1	66.0	73	0	23	16	2-5	0	3.82
Doc Reisling	R	29	7	7	6	1	51.0	45	0	10	19	3-4	0	2.12
Bill Reidy	R	30	6	4	2	0	38.1	49	0	6	11	0-4	1	4.46
Bull Durham	R	27	2	2	1	0	11.0	10	0	5	1	2-0	0	3.27
Joe Koukalik	R	24	1	1	1	0	8.0	10	0	4	1	0-1	0	1.13
Jack Doscher	L	23	2	0	0	0	6.1	1	0	1	2	0-0	0	0.00
Grant Thatcher	R	27	1	0	0	0	9.0	9	0	2	4	1-0	0	4.00

1904 Boston Beaneaters 7th NL 55-98 .359 51.0 GB

Al Buckenberger

Player	Gm by Position	B	Age	G	AB	R	H	2B	3B	HR	RBI	BB	SO	SB	Avg	OBP	Slg
Tom Needham	C77,OF1	R	25	84	269	18	70	12	3	4	19	11	—	3	.260	.292	.372
Fred Tenney	1B144,OF4	L	32	147	533	76	144	17	9	1	37	57	—	17	.270	.351	.341
Fred Raymer	2B114	R	28	114	419	28	88	12	3	1	27	13	—	17	.210	.236	.260
Jim Delahanty	3B113,2B18,OF9*	R	25	142	499	56	142	27	8	3	60	27	—	16	.285	.333	.389
Ed Abbaticchio	SS154	R	27	154	579	76	148	18	10	3	54	40	—	24	.256	.309	.337
Phil Geier	OF137,3B7,2B5*	L	27	149	580	70	141	17	2	1	27	56	—	18	.243	.314	.284
Duff Cooley	OF116,1B6	L	31	122	467	41	127	18	7	5	70	24	—	14	.272	.312	.373
Rip Cannell	OF93	L	24	93	346	32	81	5	1	0	18	23	—	10	.234	.286	.254
Pat Moran	C72,3B39,1B2	R	28	113	398	26	90	11	3	4	34	18	—	10	.226	.267	.299
Pat Carney	OF71,P4,1B1	L	27	78	279	24	57	5	2	0	11	12	—	6	.204	.240	.237
Vic Willis	P43,1B6	R	28	52	148	9	27	3	0	0	8	14	—	0	.182	.258	.203
Tom Fisher	P31,OF6	R	23	36	99	8	21	1	0	2	8	7	—	0	.212	.264	.283
George Barclay†	OF24	—	28	24	93	5	21	3	1	0	10	2	—	3	.226	.258	.280
Bill Lauterborn	2B20	R	25	20	69	7	19	2	0	0	2	1	—	1	.275	.286	.304
Doc Marshall†	C10,OF1	R	28	13	43	3	9	0	1	0	2	2	—	2	.209	.244	.256
Kid O'Hara	OF8	S	28	8	29	3	6	0	0	0	0	4	—	1	.207	.303	.207
Joe Stanley	OF3	S	23	3	8	0	0	0	0	0	0	0	—	0	.000	.000	.000
Jack White	OF1	R	26	1	5	1	0	0	0	0	0	0	—	0	.000	.000	.000
Gene McAuliffe	C1	R	32	1	2	0	1	0	0	0	0	0	—	0	.500	.500	.500
Andy Sullivan	SS1	—	19	1	1	0	0	0	0	0	0	1	—	0	.000	.500	.000

J. Delahanty, 1 G at P; P. Geier, 1 G at SS

Pitcher	T	Age	G	GS	CG	ShO	IP	H	HR	BB	SO	W-L	Sv	ERA
Vic Willis	R	28	43	43	39	2	350.0	357	7	109	196	18-25	0	2.85
Togie Pittinger	R	32	38	37	35	5	335.1	298	1	144	146	15-21	0	2.66
Kaiser Wilhelm	R	30	39	36	30	3	288.0	316	8	74	73	14-20	0	3.69
Tom Fisher	R	23	31	21	19	2	214.0	257	5	82	84	6-16	0	4.25
Ed McNichol	R	25	17	15	12	1	122.0	120	3	74	39	2-12	0	4.28
Pat Carney	L	27	4	3	1	0	26.1	40	1	12	5	0-4	0	5.81
Joe Stewart	R	25	2	0	0	0	9.1	12	0	4	1	0-0	0	9.64
Jim Delahanty	R	25	1	0	0	0	3.1	5	0	1	0	0-0	0	0.00

1904 Philadelphia Phillies 8th NL 52-100 .342 53.5 GB

Hugh Duffy

Player	Gm by Position	B	Age	G	AB	R	H	2B	3B	HR	RBI	BB	SO	SB	Avg	OBP	Slg
Red Dooin	C96,1B4,OF3*	R	25	104	355	41	86	11	4	6	36	8	—	15	.242	.261	.346
Jack Doyle†	1B65,2B1	R	34	66	236	20	52	10	3	1	22	19	—	4	.220	.281	.301
Kid Gleason	2B152,3B1	S	37	153	587	61	161	23	6	0	42	37	—	17	.274	.319	.334
Harry Wolverton	3B102	L	30	102	398	43	106	15	5	0	49	26	—	18	.266	.321	.329
Rudy Hulswitt	SS113	R	27	113	406	36	99	11	4	1	36	16	—	8	.244	.276	.298
John Titus	OF140	L	28	146	504	60	148	25	5	4	55	46	—	15	.294	.362	.387
Roy Thomas	OF139	L	30	139	496	92	144	6	6	3	29	102	—	28	.290	.416	.345
Sherry Magee	OF94,1B1	R	19	95	364	51	101	15	12	3	57	14	—	11	.277	.308	.409
Johnny Lush	1B62,OF33,P7	L	18	106	369	39	102	22	3	2	42	27	—	12	.276	.336	.369
Frank Roth	C67,1B1,2B1	R	25	81	229	28	59	8	1	1	20	12	—	8	.258	.298	.314
She Donahue†	SS29,3B24,1B3*	R	27	58	200	21	43	4	0	0	14	3	—	7	.215	.227	.235
Bob Hall	3B20,SS15,1B11	—	25	46	163	11	26	4	0	0	17	14	—	5	.160	.226	.184
Shad Barry†	OF32,3B1	R	25	35	122	15	25	2	0	0	3	11	—	2	.205	.281	.221
Chick Fraser	P42,1B2	R	33	44	110	5	17	3	1	0	13	7	—	0	.155	.212	.200
Fred Mitchell†	P13,1B9,3B2*	R	26	25	82	9	17	3	1	0	3	5	—	1	.207	.253	.268
Hugh Duffy	OF14	R	37	18	46	10	13	1	1	0	5	13	—	3	.283	.441	.348
Deacon Van Buren†	OF12	L	33	12	43	2	10	2	0	0	3	3	—	2	.233	.283	.279
Doc Marshall†	C7	R	28	8	20	1	2	0	0	0	1	0	—	0	.100	.100	.100
Jesse Purnell	3B7	L	23	7	19	2	2	0	0	0	1	4	—	1	.105	.292	.105
Klondike Douglass	1B3	L	32	3	10	1	3	0	0	0	0	1	—	0	.300	.364	.300
Tom Fleming	OF1	L	30	3	6	0	0	0	0	0	0	0	—	0	.000	.000	.000
Herman Long	2B1	L	38	1	4	0	1	0	0	0	0	0	—	0	.250	.250	.250
Butch Rementer	C1	—	26	1	2	0	0	0	0	0	0	0	—	0	.000	.000	.000

R. Dooin, 1 G at 3B; S. Donahue, 2 G at 2B; F. Mitchell, 1 G at OF

Pitcher	T	Age	G	GS	CG	ShO	IP	H	HR	BB	SO	W-L	Sv	ERA
Chick Fraser	R	33	42	36	32	2	302.0	287	5	100	127	14-24	1	3.25
Bill Duggleby	R	30	32	27	22	2	223.2	265	3	53	55	12-13	1	3.78
Tully Sparks	R	29	26	25	19	3	200.2	208	1	43	67	7-16	0	2.65
Jack Sutthoff†	R	31	19	18	17	0	163.2	172	2	71	46	6-13	0	3.68
Fred Mitchell†	R	26	13	13	11	0	108.2	133	3	25	29	4-7	0	3.40
John McPherson	—	35	15	12	11	1	128.0	130	1	46	32	1-12	0	3.66
Frank Corridon†	R	23	12	11	11	1	94.1	88	2	28	44	6-5	0	2.19
Johnny Lush	L	18	7	6	3	0	42.2	52	0	27	27	0-6	0	3.59
Ralph Caldwell	L	20	6	5	5	0	41.0	40	1	15	30	2-2	0	4.17
Tom Barry	R	25	1	1	0	0	0.2	6	0	1	1	0-1	0	40.50
John Brackenridge	R	23	7	1	0	0	34.0	37	4	16	11	0-1	0	5.56

556 Seasons: Team Rosters

»1905 Philadelphia Athletics 1st AL 92-56 .622 —

Connie Mack

Player	Gm by Position	B	Age	G	AB	R	H	2B	3B	HR	RBI	BB	SO	SB	Avg	OBP	Slg
O. Schreckengost	C114,1B2	R	30	121	416	30	113	19	6	0	45	3	—	9	.272	.279	.346
Harry Davis	1B150	R	31	150	607	93	171	47	6	8	83	43	—	36	.282	.331	.418
Danny Murphy	2B150	R	28	150	533	71	148	34	4	6	71	42	—	23	.278	.340	.390
Lave Cross	3B147	R	39	147	583	68	155	29	5	0	77	26	—	8	.266	.300	.333
John Knight	SS81,3B2	R	19	88	325	28	66	12	1	3	29	9	—	4	.203	.227	.274
Topsy Hartsel	OF147	L	31	148	533	88	147	22	8	0	28	121	—	36	.276	.411	.347
Socks Seybold	OF132	R	34	132	488	64	132	37	4	6	59	42	—	5	.270	.338	.400
Danny Hoffman	OF119	L	25	119	454	64	119	10	10	1	35	33	—	46	.262	.314	.335
Monte Cross	SS76,2B2	R	35	78	248	28	67	17	2	0	24	19	—	8	.270	.337	.355
Bris Lord	OF60,3B1	R	21	66	238	38	57	14	0	0	13	14	—	3	.239	.285	.298
Mike Powers†	C40	R	34	40	121	8	18	0	0	0	10	3	—	4	.149	.176	.149
Harry Barton	C13,1B2,3B2*	S	30	29	60	5	10	2	1	0	3	3	—	2	.167	.206	.233

H. Barton, 1 G at OF

Pitcher	T	Age	G	GS	CG	ShO	IP	H	HR	BB	SO	W-L	Sv	ERA
Eddie Plank	L	29	41	41	35	4	346.2	287	3	75	210	24-12	0	2.26
Rube Waddell	L	28	46	34	27	7	328.2	231	5	90	287	27-10	4	1.48
Andy Coakley	R	22	35	31	21	3	255.0	227	2	73	145	18-8	0	1.84
Chief Bender	R	21	35	23	18	4	229.0	193	5	90	142	18-11	0	2.83
Weldon Henley	R	24	25	19	13	1	183.2	155	4	67	82	4-11	0	2.60
Jimmy Dygert	R	20	6	3	2	0	35.1	41	2	11	24	1-4	0	4.33
Joe Myers	R	23	1	1	1	0	5.0	3	0	3	5	0-0	0	3.60

1905 Chicago White Sox 2nd AL 92-60 .605 2.0 GB

Fielder Jones

Player	Gm by Position	B	Age	G	AB	R	H	2B	3B	HR	RBI	BB	SO	SB	Avg	OBP	Slg
Billy Sullivan	C92,1B2,3B1	R	30	99	323	25	65	10	3	2	26	13	—	14	.201	.239	.269
Jiggs Donahue	1B149	L	25	149	533	71	153	22	4	1	76	44	—	32	.287	.346	.349
Gus Dundon	2B104,SS2	R	30	106	364	30	70	7	3	0	22	23	—	14	.192	.248	.228
Lee Tannehill	3B142	R	24	142	480	38	96	17	2	0	39	45	—	8	.200	.274	.244
George Davis	SS151	S	34	151	550	74	153	29	1	1	55	60	—	31	.278	.353	.340
Fielder Jones	OF153	L	33	153	568	91	139	17	12	2	38	73	—	20	.245	.335	.327
Danny Green	OF107	L	28	112	379	56	92	13	6	0	44	53	—	11	.243	.345	.309
Nixey Callahan	OF93	R	31	96	345	50	94	18	6	1	43	29	—	26	.272	.336	.368
Frank Isbell	2B42,OF40,1B9*	L	29	94	341	55	101	21	11	2	45	15	—	15	.296	.335	.440
Ducky Holmes	OF89	L	36	92	328	42	66	15	2	0	22	19	—	11	.201	.258	.259
Ed McFarland	C70	R	30	80	250	24	70	13	4	0	31	23	—	5	.280	.345	.364
George Rohe	3B17,2B16	R	29	34	113	14	24	1	0	1	12	12	—	2	.212	.310	.248
Nick Altrock	P38,1B1	S	28	40	112	8	14	1	0	0	5	6	—	0	.125	.190	.134
Doc White	P36,OF1	L	26	37	86	7	14	4	1	0	7	4	—	3	.163	.200	.233
Ed Walsh	P22,OF5	R	24	29	58	5	9	2	0	0	2	4	—	0	.155	.222	.190
Hub Hart	C6	L	27	10	17	2	2	0	0	0	4	3	—	0	.118	.250	.118

F. Isbell, 2 G at SS

Pitcher	T	Age	G	GS	CG	ShO	IP	H	HR	BB	SO	W-L	Sv	ERA
Frank Owen	R	25	42	38	32	3	334.0	276	6	56	125	21-13	0	2.10
Nick Altrock	L	28	38	34	31	3	315.2	274	3	63	97	23-12	0	1.88
Doc White	L	26	36	33	25	4	260.1	204	2	58	120	17-13	0	1.76
Frank Smith	R	25	39	31	27	4	291.2	215	0	107	171	19-13	0	2.13
Ed Walsh	R	24	22	13	9	1	136.2	121	0	29	71	8-3	0	2.17
Roy Patterson	R	28	13	9	7	0	88.2	73	0	16	29	4-6	0	1.83

1905 Detroit Tigers 3rd AL 79-74 .516 15.5 GB

Bill Armour

Player	Gm by Position	B	Age	G	AB	R	H	2B	3B	HR	RBI	BB	SO	SB	Avg	OBP	Slg
Lew Drill	C71	R	28	71	211	17	55	9	0	0	24	32	—	7	.261	.366	.303
Chris Lindsay	1B88	R	26	88	329	38	88	14	1	0	31	18	—	10	.267	.315	.316
Germany Schaefer	2B151,SS3	R	28	153	554	64	135	17	9	2	47	45	—	19	.244	.302	.318
Bill Coughlin	3B137	R	26	138	489	48	123	20	6	0	44	34	—	16	.252	.309	.317
Charley O'Leary	SS148	R	22	148	512	47	109	13	1	0	33	29	—	13	.213	.259	.242
Matty McIntyre	OF131	L	25	131	495	59	130	21	5	0	30	48	—	9	.263	.330	.325
Sam Crawford	OF103,1B51	L	25	154	575	73	171	38	10	6	75	50	—	22	.297	.357	.430
Duff Cooley	OF97	L	32	99	377	25	93	11	9	1	32	26	—	7	.247	.297	.332
Charlie Hickman†	OF47,1B12	R	29	59	213	21	47	12	3	2	20	12	—	3	.221	.278	.333
Bobby Lowe	OF25,3B22,2B6*	R	36	60	181	17	35	7	2	0	9	13	—	3	.193	.255	.254
Ty Cobb	OF41	L	18	41	150	19	36	6	0	1	15	10	—	2	.240	.288	.300
Wild Bill Donovan	P34,OF8,2B2	R	28	46	130	16	25	4	0	0	5	12	—	8	.192	.266	.223
John Warner†	C36	L	32	36	119	12	24	2	3	0	7	8	—	2	.202	.252	.269
Tom Doran†	C32	L	24	34	94	8	15	3	0	0	4	8	—	2	.160	.248	.191
Jimmy Barrett	OF18	L	30	20	67	2	17	1	0	0	3	6	—	0	.254	.324	.269
John Sullivan	C12	R	32	12	31	4	5	0	0	0	4	4	—	0	.161	.257	.161
Bob Wood	C7	R	39	8	24	1	2	1	0	0	0	1	—	0	.083	.120	.125
John Eubank	P3,1B1	R	32	6	11	1	4	0	1	0	1	0	—	0	.364	.364	.545
Nig Clarke†	C2	L	22	3	7	1	3	0	0	1	1	0	—	0	.429	.500	.857

B. Lowe, 4 G at SS, 1 G at 1B

Pitcher	T	Age	G	GS	CG	ShO	IP	H	HR	BB	SO	W-L	Sv	ERA
George Mullin	R	24	44	41	35	1	347.2	303	4	138	168	21-21	0	2.51
Ed Killian	L	28	39	37	33	8	313.1	263	0	102	110	23-14	1	2.27
Wild Bill Donovan	R	28	34	32	27	5	280.2	236	2	101	135	18-15	0	2.60
Frank Kitson	R	35	33	27	21	3	225.2	230	3	57	78	12-14	1	3.47
Jimmy Wiggs	R	28	7	7	4	0	41.1	30	0	29	37	3-3	0	3.27
John Eubank	R	32	3	2	0	0	17.1	13	0	3	1	1-0	0	2.08
Charlie Jackson	R	28	2	2	1	0	11.0	14	1	7	3	0-2	0	5.73
Frosty Thomas	R	24	2	1	0	0	6.0	10	0	3	5	0-1	0	7.50
George Disch	—	26	8	3	1	0	47.2	43	1	8	14	0-2	0	2.64
Gene Ford	R	24	7	1	1	0	35.0	51	0	14	20	0-1	0	5.66
Eddie Cicotte	R	21	3	1	1	0	18.0	25	0	5	6	1-1	0	3.50
Walt Justis	R	21	2	0	0	0	3.1	4	0	6	0	0-0	0	8.10
Andy Bruckmiller	R	23	1	0	0	0	1.0	4	0	1	1	0-0	0	27.00

1905 Boston Pilgrims 4th AL 78-74 .513 16.0 GB

Jimmy Collins

Player	Gm by Position	B	Age	G	AB	R	H	2B	3B	HR	RBI	BB	SO	SB	Avg	OBP	Slg
Lou Criger	C109	R	33	109	313	33	62	6	7	1	36	54	—	5	.198	.322	.272
Moose Grimshaw	1B74	S	29	85	285	39	68	8	2	4	35	21	—	4	.239	.293	.323
Hobe Ferris	2B140,OF1	R	27	141	523	51	115	24	16	6	59	23	—	11	.220	.253	.361
Jimmy Collins	3B131	R	35	131	508	66	140	25	5	4	65	37	—	18	.276	.330	.368
Freddy Parent	SS153	R	29	153	602	55	141	16	5	0	33	47	—	25	.234	.296	.277
Jesse Burkett	OF149	L	36	149	573	78	147	13	13	4	47	67	—	13	.257	.339	.346
Chick Stahl	OF134	L	32	134	500	61	129	17	4	0	47	50	—	18	.258	.332	.308
Kip Selbach	OF116	R	33	124	418	54	103	16	6	4	47	67	—	12	.246	.355	.342
Buck Freeman	1B66,OF57,3B2	L	33	130	455	59	109	20	8	3	49	46	—	8	.240	.316	.338
Bob Unglaub	3B21,2B8,1B2	R	23	43	121	18	27	5	1	0	11	6	—	2	.223	.260	.281
Charlie Armbruster	C35	R	24	35	91	13	18	4	0	0	6	18	—	3	.198	.336	.242
Art McGovern	C15	R	23	15	44	1	5	1	0	0	1	4	—	0	.114	.204	.136
Candy LaChance	1B12	S	35	12	41	1	6	1	0	0	5	6	—	0	.146	.255	.171
John Godwin	OF6,2B5	R	28	13	37	4	13	1	0	0	10	3	—	3	.351	.442	.378
Duke Farrell	C7	S	38	7	21	2	6	1	0	0	2	1	—	0	.286	.318	.333
Pop Rising	OF3,3B1	—	33	8	18	2	2	1	1	0	2	2	—	0	.111	.200	.278
Frank Owens	C1	R	19	1	2	0	0	0	0	0	0	0	—	0	.000	.000	.000
Tom Doran†	C1	L	24	2	2	0	0	0	0	0	0	0	—	0	.000	.000	.000

Pitcher	T	Age	G	GS	CG	ShO	IP	H	HR	BB	SO	W-L	Sv	ERA
Cy Young	R	38	38	33	31	4	320.2	248	3	30	210	18-19	0	1.82
Jesse Tannehill	L	30	37	32	27	6	271.2	238	7	59	113	22-9	0	2.48
Bill Dinneen	R	29	31	29	23	2	243.2	235	7	50	97	12-14	1	3.73
George Winter	R	27	35	27	24	2	264.1	249	5	54	119	16-17	0	2.96
Norwood Gibson	R	28	23	17	9	0	134.0	118	9	55	67	4-7	0	3.69
Ed Barry	L	22	7	5	2	0	40.2	38	2	15	18	1-2	0	2.88
Ed Hughes	R	24	6	4	2	0	33.1	38	0	9	8	3-2	0	4.59
Hank Olmsted	R	26	3	3	3	0	25.0	18	0	12	6	1-2	0	3.24
Joe Harris	R	23	3	3	3	0	23.0	16	0	8	14	1-2	0	2.35

1905 Cleveland Bronchos 5th AL 76-78 .494 19.0 GB

Nap Lajoie (37-21)/Bill Bradley (20-21)/Nap Lajoie (19-36)

Player	Gm by Position	B	Age	G	AB	R	H	2B	3B	HR	RBI	BB	SO	SB	Avg	OBP	Slg
Fritz Buelow	C60,OF8,1B3*	R	29	74	236	11	41	4	1	1	18	6	—	7	.174	.201	.212
Charlie Carr	1B87	R	28	89	306	29	72	12	4	1	31	13	—	12	.235	.266	.310
Nap Lajoie	2B59,1B5	R	30	65	249	29	82	12	2	2	41	17	—	11	.329	.377	.418
Bill Bradley	3B145	R	27	145	537	63	144	34	6	0	51	27	—	22	.268	.321	.354
Terry Turner	SS154	R	24	154	582	48	153	16	14	4	72	14	—	17	.263	.287	.359
Harry Bay	OF143	L	27	143	550	90	164	18	10	0	22	36	—	36	.298	.347	.367
Elmer Flick	OF131,2B1	L	29	131	496	71	152	29	18	4	64	53	—	35	.306	.382	.462
Jim Jackson	OF105,3B3	R	27	108	421	58	108	12	4	2	31	34	—	15	.257	.318	.318
George Stovall	1B59,2B46,OF4	R	26	111	419	41	114	31	1	1	47	13	—	13	.272	.296	.358
Harry Bemis	C58,2B4,3B2*	R	31	69	226	27	66	13	3	0	28	13	—	3	.292	.344	.376
Otto Hess	OF27,P26	L	26	54	175	15	44	8	1	2	13	7	—	2	.251	.288	.343
Rube Vinson	OF36	—	26	38	133	12	26	3	1	0	9	7	—	4	.195	.246	.233
Nick Kahl	2B30,SS1,OF1	R	26	39	131	16	29	4	1	0	21	4	—	1	.221	.255	.267
Nig Clarke†	C42	L	22	42	123	11	24	6	1	0	9	11	—	0	.195	.261	.260
Addie Joss	P33,3B1	R	25	35	94	6	13	2	1	0	3	13	—	3	.138	.243	.181
Bunk Congalton	OF12	L	30	12	47	4	17	0	0	0	5	2	—	3	.362	.388	.362
Jap Barbeau	2B11	R	23	11	37	1	10	1	1	0	2	1	—	1	.270	.289	.351
Howard Wakefield	C8	R	21	9	25	3	4	0	0	0	1	0	—	0	.160	.192	.160
Eddie Grant	2B2	L	22	2	8	1	3	0	0	0	0	0	—	0	.375	.375	.375
Emil Leber	2B2	R	24	2	6	1	0	0	0	0	0	1	—	0	.000	.143	.000

F. Buelow, 2 G at 3B; H. Bemis, 1 G at 1B

Pitcher	T	Age	G	GS	CG	ShO	IP	H	HR	BB	SO	W-L	Sv	ERA
Addie Joss	R	25	33	32	31	3	286.0	246	4	46	132	20-12	0	2.01
Earl Moore	R	25	31	30	28	3	269.0	232	6	92	131	15-15	0	2.64
Bob Rhoads	R	25	28	26	24	4	235.0	219	4	55	61	16-9	0	2.83
Otto Hess	L	26	26	25	22	4	213.2	179	1	72	109	10-15	0	3.16
Bill Bernhard	R	34	22	19	17	0	174.1	185	5	34	56	7-13	0	3.36
Red Donahue	R	32	20	18	14	1	137.2	132	2	25	45	6-12	0	3.40
Hi West	R	20	6	4	4	1	33.0	43	0	10	15	2-2	0	4.09
Cy Ferry	R	26	1	1	0	0	2.0	3	1	0	2	0-0	0	13.50
John Halla	L	21	3	0	0	0	12.2	12	0	0	4	0-0	0	2.84

1905 New York Highlanders 6th AL 71-78 .477 21.5 GB — Clark Griffith

Player	Gm by Position	B	Age	G	AB	R	H	2B	3B	HR	RBI	BB	SO	SB	Avg	OBP	Slg
Red Kleinow	C83,1B3	R	25	88	253	23	56	6	3	1	24	20	—	7	.221	.284	.281
Hal Chase	1B124,2B1,SS1	R	22	126	465	60	116	16	6	3	49	15	—	22	.249	.277	.329
Jimmy Williams	2B129	R	28	129	470	54	107	20	8	6	62	50	—	14	.228	.306	.343
Joe Yeager	3B90,SS21	R	29	115	401	53	107	16	7	0	42	25	—	8	.267	.330	.342
Kid Elberfeld	SS108	R	30	111	390	48	102	18	2	0	53	23	—	18	.262	.329	.318
Willie Keeler	OF139,2B12,3B3	L	33	149	560	81	169	14	4	4	38	43	—	19	.302	.357	.363
Dave Fultz	OF122	R	30	130	422	49	98	13	3	0	42	39	—	44	.232	.308	.277
Patsy Dougherty	OF108,3B1	L	28	116	418	56	110	9	6	3	29	28	—	17	.263	.319	.335
Wid Conroy	3B48,OF25,SS17*	R	28	102	385	55	105	19	11	2	25	32	—	25	.273	.329	.395
Deacon McGuire	C71	R	41	72	228	9	50	7	2	0	33	18	—	3	.219	.291	.268
Ed Hahn	OF43	L	29	43	160	32	51	5	0	0	11	25	—	1	.319	.426	.350
Al Orth	P40,1B1,OF1	L	32	55	131	13	24	3	1	1	8	4	—	2	.183	.213	.244
John Anderson†	OF22,1B3	S	31	32	99	12	23	3	1	0	14	8	—	9	.232	.296	.283
Frank LaPorte	2B11	R	25	11	40	4	16	1	0	1	12	1	—	1	.400	.415	.500
Jim Cockman	3B13	R	32	13	38	5	4	0	0	0	2	4	—	2	.105	.190	.105
Mike Powers†	1B7,C4	R	34	11	33	3	6	1	0	0	2	1	—	0	.182	.206	.212
Rube Oldring	SS8	R	21	8	30	2	9	0	1	1	6	2	—	4	.300	.344	.467
Frank Delahanty	1B5,OF3	R	22	9	27	0	6	1	0	0	2	1	—	0	.222	.250	.259
Joe Connor	C6,1B2	R	30	8	22	4	5	1	0	0	2	3	—	1	.227	.320	.273
Fred Curtis	1B2	R	24	2	9	0	2	1	0	0	2	1	—	1	.222	.300	.333
Phil Cooney	3B1	L	22	1	3	0	0	0	0	0	0	0	—	0	.000	.000	.000
Fred Jacklitsch	C1	R	29	1	3	1	0	0	0	0	1	1	—	0	.000	.250	.000
Jack Doyle	1B1	R	35	1	3	0	0	0	0	0	0	0	—	0	.000	.000	.000
Joe McCarthy	C1	R	23	1	2	0	0	0	0	0	0	0	—	0	.000	.000	.000
Charlie Fallon		R	24	1	0	0	0	0	0	0	0	0	—	0	—	—	—

W. Conroy, 10 G at 1B, 3 G at 2B

Pitcher	T	Age	G	GS	CG	ShO	IP	H	HR	BB	SO	W-L	Sv	ERA
Jack Chesbro	R	31	41	38	24	3	303.1	262	5	71	156	19-15	0	2.20
Al Orth	R	32	40	37	26	6	305.1	273	8	61	121	18-16	0	2.86
Jack Powell†	R	30	36	23	13	1	203.0	214	4	57	84	8-13	1	3.50
Bill Hogg	R	23	39	22	9	3	205.0	178	1	101	125	9-13	1	3.20
Ambrose Puttmann	L	24	17	9	5	1	86.1	79	2	37	39	2-7	1	4.27
Doc Newton	L	27	11	7	2	0	59.2	61	1	24	15	2-2	1	2.11
Louis LeRoy	R	26	3	3	2	0	24.0	26	2	1	8	1-1	0	3.75
Clark Griffith	R	35	25	7	4	2	102.2	82	1	15	46	9-6	3	1.67
Walter Clarkson	R	26	9	4	3	0	46.0	40	1	13	35	3-3	0	3.91
Wilbur Good	L	19	5	2	0	0	19.0	18	1	14	13	0-2	0	4.74
Art Goodwin	R	29	1	0	0	0	0.1	2	0	2	0	0-0	0	81.00

1905 Washington Senators 7th AL 64-87 .424 29.5 GB — Jake Stahl

Player	Gm by Position	B	Age	G	AB	R	H	2B	3B	HR	RBI	BB	SO	SB	Avg	OBP	Slg
Mike Heydon	C77	L	30	77	245	20	47	7	4	1	26	21	—	5	.192	.261	.265
Jake Stahl	1B140	R	26	141	501	66	122	22	12	5	66	28	—	41	.244	.306	.365
Charlie Hickman†	2B85,1B3	R	29	88	360	48	112	25	9	2	46	9	—	3	.311	.332	.447
Hunter Hill	3B103	R	26	104	374	37	78	12	1	1	24	32	—	10	.209	.278	.254
Joe Cassidy	SS151	R	22	151	576	67	124	16	4	1	43	25	—	23	.215	.250	.262
Charlie Jones	OF142	R	29	142	544	68	113	18	4	2	41	31	—	24	.208	.254	.267
Frank Huelsman	OF123	R	31	126	421	48	114	28	8	3	62	31	—	11	.271	.333	.397
John Anderson†	OF89,1B4	S	31	101	400	50	116	21	6	1	38	22	—	22	.290	.330	.380
Rabbitt Nill	3B52,2B33,SS6	R	23	103	319	46	58	7	3	3	31	33	—	12	.182	.269	.251
Punch Knoll	OF70,C5,1B2	R	23	85	244	24	52	10	5	0	29	9	—	3	.213	.247	.295
Malachi Kittridge	C76	R	35	76	238	16	39	8	0	0	14	15	—	1	.164	.213	.197
Jim Mullin	2B39,1B7	R	21	50	163	18	31	7	6	0	13	5	—	5	.190	.214	.307
Joe Stanley	OF27	S	24	28	92	13	24	2	1	1	17	7	—	4	.261	.313	.337
Harry Cassady	OF9	L	24	9	30	1	4	0	0	0	1	0	—	0	.133	.133	.133
Claude Rothgeb	OF3	S	25	6	13	2	2	0	0	0	0	0	—	1	.154	.154	.154
Denny Sullivan	OF3	L	22	3	11	0	0	0	0	0	0	1	—	0	.000	.083	.000
Hughie Tate	OF3	R	25	4	10	1	3	0	1	0	2	0	—	1	.300	.300	.500
Shag Shaughnessy	OF1	R	22	1	3	0	0	0	0	0	0	1	—	0	.000	.250	.000

Pitcher	T	Age	G	GS	CG	ShO	IP	H	HR	BB	SO	W-L	Sv	ERA
Casey Patten	L	29	42	36	29	2	309.2	300	3	86	113	14-22	0	3.14
Long Tom Hughes	R	26	39	35	26	5	291.1	239	3	79	149	17-20	1	2.35
Jack Townsend	R	26	34	24	22	0	263.0	247	2	84	102	7-16	0	2.63
Bill Wolfe	R	29	28	23	17	1	182.0	162	1	37	52	9-13	2	2.57
Beany Jacobson	L	24	22	17	12	0	144.1	139	1	35	50	7-8	0	3.30
Cy Falkenberg	R	24	12	10	6	2	75.1	71	1	31	35	7-2	0	3.82
Rick Adams	L	26	11	6	3	1	62.2	63	1	24	25	2-4	0	3.59
Harry Hardy	L	29	3	2	2	0	24.0	20	0	6	10	1-1	0	1.88
Moxie Manuel	—	23	3	1	1	0	10.0	9	0	3	3	0-1	0	5.40

1905 St. Louis Browns 8th AL 54-99 .353 40.5 GB — Jimmy McAleer

Player	Gm by Position	B	Age	G	AB	R	H	2B	3B	HR	RBI	BB	SO	SB	Avg	OBP	Slg
Joe Sugden	C76,1B9	S	34	85	266	21	46	4	0	0	23	23	—	3	.173	.247	.188
Tom Jones	1B135	R	28	135	504	44	122	16	2	0	48	30	—	5	.242	.290	.282
Ike Rockenfield	2B95	R	28	95	322	40	70	12	0	0	16	46	—	11	.217	.340	.255
Harry Gleason	3B144,2B7	R	30	150	535	45	116	11	5	1	57	34	—	23	.217	.269	.262
Bobby Wallace	SS156	R	31	156	587	67	159	25	9	1	59	45	—	13	.271	.324	.349
George Stone	OF154	L	27	154	632	76	187	25	13	7	52	44	—	26	.296	.347	.410
Ben Koehler	OF124,1B12,2B6	R	28	142	536	55	127	14	6	2	47	32	—	22	.237	.285	.297
Emil Frisk	OF115	L	30	127	429	58	112	11	6	3	36	42	—	7	.261	.342	.336
Ike Van Zandt	OF74,P1,1B1	L	29	94	322	31	75	15	1	1	20	7	—	7	.233	.252	.295
Harry Howell	P38,OF3	R	28	41	135	9	26	6	2	1	10	3	—	0	.193	.216	.289
Tubby Spencer	C34	R	21	35	115	6	27	1	2	0	11	7	—	2	.235	.285	.278
Frank Roth	C29	R	26	35	107	9	25	3	0	0	7	6	—	1	.234	.274	.262
Charlie Starr	2B18,3B6	—	26	24	97	9	20	0	0	0	6	7	—	0	.206	.260	.206
Art Weaver	C28	—	26	28	92	5	11	2	1	0	3	1	—	0	.120	.129	.163
Charles Moran	2B20,3B5	—	26	28	82	6	16	1	0	0	5	10	—	3	.195	.290	.207
Dick Padden	2B16	R	34	16	58	5	10	1	1	0	4	3	—	3	.172	.213	.224
Charlie Gibson	C1	R	25	1	3	0	0	0	0	0	0	0	—	0	.000	.000	.000
Branch Rickey	C1	L	23	1	3	0	0	0	0	0	0	0	—	0	.000	.000	.000

Pitcher	T	Age	G	GS	CG	ShO	IP	H	HR	BB	SO	W-L	Sv	ERA
Harry Howell	R	28	38	37	35	4	323.0	252	2	101	198	15-22	0	1.98
Fred Glade	R	29	32	32	28	2	275.0	257	3	58	127	6-25	0	2.81
Willie Sudhoff	R	30	32	30	23	1	244.0	222	8	78	70	10-20	0	2.99
Barney Pelty	R	24	31	28	27	1	258.2	222	3	68	114	14-14	0	2.75
Jim Buchanan	R	28	22	15	12	1	141.1	149	2	27	54	5-9	2	3.50
Cy Morgan	R	26	13	8	5	1	77.1	82	1	37	44	2-5	0	3.61
Harry Ables	L	20	6	3	1	0	30.2	37	0	13	11	0-3	0	3.82
Jack Powell†	R	30	3	3	3	0	28.0	22	0	5	12	2-1	0	1.61
Ike Van Zandt	—	29	1	0	0	0	6.2	2	0	2	3	0-0	0	0.00

»1905 New York Giants 1st NL 105-48 .686 — — John McGraw

Player	Gm by Position	B	Age	G	AB	R	H	2B	3B	HR	RBI	BB	SO	SB	Avg	OBP	Slg
Roger Bresnahan	C87,OF8	R	26	104	331	58	100	18	3	0	46	50	—	11	.302	.411	.375
Dan McGann	1B136	S	33	136	491	88	147	23	14	5	75	55	—	22	.299	.391	.434
Billy Gilbert	2B115	R	29	115	376	45	93	11	3	0	24	41	—	11	.247	.331	.293
Art Devlin	3B153	R	25	153	525	74	129	14	7	2	61	66	—	59	.246	.344	.310
Bill Dahlen	SS147,OF1	R	35	148	520	67	126	20	4	7	81	62	—	37	.242	.337	.337
Mike Donlin	OF150	L	27	150	606	124	216	31	16	7	80	56	—	33	.356	.413	.495
Sam Mertes	OF150	R	32	150	551	81	154	27	17	5	108	56	—	52	.279	.351	.417
George Browne	OF127	L	29	127	536	95	157	16	14	4	43	20	—	26	.293	.321	.397
Frank Bowerman	C72,1B17,2B1	R	36	98	297	37	80	8	1	3	41	12	—	6	.269	.322	.333
Sammy Strang	2B47,OF38,SS9*	S	28	111	294	51	76	9	4	3	29	58	—	23	.259	.389	.347
Hooks Wiltse	P32,OF1	R	24	33	72	13	20	2	0	0	12	12	—	2	.278	.388	.306
Boileryard Clarke	1B15,C12	R	36	31	50	2	9	0	0	1	4	4	—	1	.180	.241	.240
Offa Neal	3B3,2B1	L	29	4	13	0	0	0	0	0	0	0	—	0	.000	.000	.000
Bob Hall†	OF1	—	26	1	3	1	1	0	0	0	0	0	—	0	.333	.333	.333
Moonlight Graham	OF1	L	28	1	0	0	0	0	0	0	0	0	—	0	—	—	—
John McGraw	OF1	L	32	3	0	0	0	0	0	0	0	0	—	1	—	—	—

S. Strang, 1 G at 1B, 1 G at 3B

Pitcher	T	Age	G	GS	CG	ShO	IP	H	HR	BB	SO	W-L	Sv	ERA
Joe McGinnity	R	34	46	38	26	2	320.1	289	6	71	125	21-15	3	2.87
Christy Mathewson	R	26	43	37	32	8	338.2	252	4	64	206	31-9	2	1.28
Red Ames	R	22	34	31	21	2	262.2	220	2	105	198	22-8	0	2.74
Luther Taylor	R	30	32	28	17	4	213.1	200	5	51	91	16-9	0	2.66
Hooks Wiltse	L	24	32	19	18	1	197.0	158	5	61	120	15-6	4	2.47
Claude Elliott	R	25	10	2	2	0	38.0	41	3	12	20	0-1	6	4.03

1905 Pittsburgh Pirates 2nd NL 96-57 .627 9.0 GB — Fred Clarke

Player	Gm by Position	B	Age	G	AB	R	H	2B	3B	HR	RBI	BB	SO	SB	Avg	OBP	Slg
Heinie Peitz	C87,2B1	R	34	88	278	18	62	10	0	0	27	24	—	2	.223	.289	.259
Del Howard	1B90,OF28,P1	L	27	123	435	56	127	18	5	2	63	27	—	19	.292	.345	.370
Claude Ritchey	2B153,SS2	S	31	153	533	54	136	29	6	0	52	51	—	12	.255	.324	.332
Dave Brain†	3B78,SS4	R	26	85	307	31	79	17	6	3	46	15	—	8	.257	.296	.381
Honus Wagner	SS145,OF2	R	31	147	548	114	199	32	14	6	101	54	—	57	.363	.427	.505
Fred Clarke	OF137	L	32	141	525	95	157	18	15	2	51	55	—	24	.299	.368	.402
Ginger Beaumont	OF97	L	28	103	384	60	126	12	8	3	40	22	—	21	.328	.365	.424
Otis Clymer	OF89,1B1	S	29	96	365	74	108	11	5	0	23	19	—	23	.296	.332	.353
Tommy Leach	OF71,3B58,2B2*	R	27	131	499	71	128	10	14	2	53	37	—	17	.257	.309	.345
Bill Clancy	1B52,OF4	L	26	56	227	23	52	11	3	2	34	4	—	3	.229	.246	.330
George Gibson	C44	R	24	46	135	14	24	2	2	2	14	15	—	2	.178	.270	.267
Bob Ganley	OF32	L	30	32	127	12	40	1	2	0	7	8	—	3	.315	.356	.354
Homer Hillebrand	1B16,P10,OF7*	R	25	39	110	9	26	3	2	0	7	6	—	1	.236	.282	.300
Fred Carisch	C30	R	23	32	107	7	22	0	3	0	8	2	—	1	.206	.227	.262
George McBride†	3B17,SS8	R	24	27	87	9	19	4	0	0	7	6	—	2	.218	.277	.264
Jim Wallace	OF7	L	23	7	29	3	6	1	0	0	3	1	—	2	.207	.281	.241
Steamer Flanagan	OF5	L	24	7	25	7	7	1	1	0	3	1	—	3	.280	.308	.400
Otto Knabe	3B3	R	21	3	10	0	3	1	0	0	2	3	—	0	.300	.462	.400
Harry Smith	C1	R	30	1	3	0	0	0	0	0	0	0	—	1	.000	.000	.000

T. Leach, 2 G at SS; H. Hillebrand, 3 G at C

Pitcher	T	Age	G	GS	CG	ShO	IP	H	HR	BB	SO	W-L	Sv	ERA
Deacon Phillippe	R	33	38	33	25	5	279.0	235	0	48	133	20-13	0	2.19
Sam Leever	R	33	33	29	20	3	229.2	199	3	54	81	20-5	1	2.70
Charlie Case	R	25	31	24	18	3	217.0	202	2	66	57	11-11	1	2.57
Mike Lynch	R	25	33	22	13	0	206.1	191	3	107	106	17-8	2	3.79
Patsy Flaherty	L	29	27	20	15	0	187.2	197	2	49	44	10-10	1	3.50
Chick Robitaille	R	26	17	12	10	0	120.1	126	1	28	32	8-5	0	2.92
Lefty Leifield	L	21	8	7	6	1	56.0	52	0	14	10	5-2	0	2.89
Homer Hillebrand	L	25	10	6	4	0	60.2	43	0	19	37	5-2	1	2.82
Ed Kinsella	R	23	3	2	2	0	17.0	19	0	3	11	0-1	0	2.65
Del Howard	R	27	1	0	0	0	6.0	4	1	1	0	0-0	0	0.00
George Moore	R	32	1	0	0	0	3.0	2	0	0	1	0-0	0	0.00

1905 Chicago Cubs 3rd NL 92-61 .601 13.0 GB

Frank Selee (37-28)/Frank Chance (55-33)

Player	Gm by Position	B	Age	G	AB	R	H	2B	3B	HR	RBI	BB	SO	SB	Avg	OBP	Slg
Johnny Kling	C106,OF4,1B1	R	30	111	380	26	83	8	6	1	52	28	—	13	.218	.272	.279
Frank Chance	1B115	R	27	118	392	92	124	16	12	2	70	78	—	38	.316	.450	.434
Johnny Evers	2B99	L	23	99	340	44	94	11	2	1	37	27	—	19	.276	.333	.329
Doc Casey	3B142,SS1	S	35	144	526	66	122	21	10	1	56	41	—	22	.232	.295	.316
Joe Tinker	SS149	R	24	149	547	70	135	18	8	2	66	34	—	31	.247	.292	.320
Jimmy Slagle	OF155	L	31	155	568	96	153	19	4	0	37	97	—	27	.269	.379	.317
Billy Maloney	OF145	L	27	145	558	78	145	17	14	2	56	43	—	59	.260	.325	.351
Wildfire Schulte	OF123	L	22	123	493	67	135	15	14	1	47	32	—	16	.274	.326	.367
Solly Hofman	2B59,1B9,SS9*	R	22	86	287	43	68	14	4	1	38	20	—	15	.237	.289	.324
Jack O'Neill	C50	R	32	53	172	16	34	4	2	0	12	8	—	6	.198	.277	.244
Jack McCarthy	OF37,1B6	L	36	59	170	16	47	4	3	0	14	10	—	8	.276	.320	.335
Shad Barry†	1B26	R	26	27	104	10	22	2	0	0	10	5	—	5	.212	.255	.231
Bob Wicker	P22,OF3	R	27	25	72	5	10	0	0	0	3	4	—	1	.139	.184	.139
Hans Lobert	3B13,OF1	R	23	14	46	7	9	2	0	0	1	3	—	4	.196	.260	.239

S. Hofman, 3 G at 3B, 3 G at OF

Pitcher	T	Age	G	GS	CG	ShO	IP	H	HR	BB	SO	W-L	Sv	ERA
Jake Weimer	L	31	33	30	26	2	250.1	212	1	80	107	18-12	1	2.26
Ed Reulbach	R	22	34	29	28	5	291.2	208	1	73	152	18-14	1	1.42
Three Finger Brown	R	28	30	24	24	4	249.0	219	3	44	89	18-12	0	2.17
Bob Wicker	R	27	22	22	17	4	178.0	139	3	47	86	13-6	0	2.02
Buttons Briggs	R	29	20	20	13	5	168.0	141	1	52	68	8-8	0	2.14
Carl Lundgren	R	25	23	19	16	3	169.1	132	3	53	69	13-5	0	2.23
Big Jeff Pfeffer	R	23	15	11	9	0	101.0	84	2	36	56	4-4	0	2.50

1905 Philadelphia Phillies 4th NL 83-69 .546 21.5 GB

Hugh Duffy

Player	Gm by Position	B	Age	G	AB	R	H	2B	3B	HR	RBI	BB	SO	SB	Avg	OBP	Slg
Red Dooin	C107,3B1	R	26	113	380	45	95	13	5	0	36	10	—	12	.250	.269	.311
Kitty Bransfield	1B151	R	30	151	580	55	150	23	9	3	76	27	—	27	.259	.294	.345
Kid Gleason	2B155	S	38	155	608	95	150	17	7	1	50	45	—	16	.247	.302	.303
Ernie Courtney	3B155	L	30	155	601	77	165	14	7	2	77	47	—	17	.275	.334	.331
Mickey Doolan	SS135	R	25	136	492	53	125	27	11	1	48	24	—	17	.254	.292	.360
Sherry Magee	OF155	R	20	155	603	100	180	24	17	5	98	44	—	48	.299	.354	.420
Roy Thomas	OF147	L	31	147	562	118	178	11	6	0	31	93	—	23	.317	.417	.358
John Titus	OF147	L	29	147	548	99	169	36	14	2	89	69	—	11	.308	.397	.436
Fred Abbott	C34,1B5	R	30	42	128	9	25	6	1	0	12	6	—	4	.195	.248	.258
Otto Krueger	SS23,OF6,3B1	R	28	46	114	10	21	1	1	0	12	13	—	1	.184	.273	.211
Mike Kahoe	C15	R	31	16	51	2	13	2	0	0	4	1	—	1	.255	.269	.294
Hugh Duffy	OF8	R	38	15	40	7	12	2	1	0	3	1	—	0	.300	.317	.400
Red Munson	C8	—	21	9	26	1	3	1	0	0	2	0	—	0	.115	.115	.154

Pitcher	T	Age	G	GS	CG	ShO	IP	H	HR	BB	SO	W-L	Sv	ERA
Togie Pittinger	R	33	46	37	29	4	337.1	311	3	104	136	23-14	2	3.09
Bill Duggleby	R	31	38	36	27	1	289.1	270	10	83	75	18-17	0	2.46
Tully Sparks	R	30	34	26	20	3	259.2	217	2	73	98	14-11	1	2.18
Frank Corridon	R	24	35	26	18	1	212.0	203	2	57	79	10-13	1	3.48
Kid Nichols†	R	35	17	16	15	1	138.2	129	1	28	50	10-6	0	2.27
Johnny Lush	L	19	2	2	1	0	17.0	12	0	8	8	2-0	0	1.59
Harry Kane	L	21	2	2	2	1	17.0	12	0	8	12	1-1	0	1.59
King Brady	R	24	2	2	2	0	13.0	19	0	2	3	1-1	0	3.46
Jack Sutthoff	R	32	13	6	4	1	77.2	82	2	36	26	3-4	0	3.82
Ralph Caldwell	L	21	7	2	1	0	34.0	44	1	7	29	1-2	1	4.24
Buck Washer	R	22	1	0	0	0	3.0	4	0	5	0	0-0	0	6.00

1905 Cincinnati Reds 5th NL 79-74 .516 26.0 GB

Joe Kelley

Player	Gm by Position	B	Age	G	AB	R	H	2B	3B	HR	RBI	BB	SO	SB	Avg	OBP	Slg
Admiral Schlei	C89,1B6	R	27	99	314	32	71	8	3	1	36	22	—	9	.226	.285	.280
Shad Barry†	1B124,OF2	R	26	125	494	90	160	11	12	1	56	33	—	16	.324	.372	.401
Miller Huggins	2B149	S	26	149	564	117	154	11	8	1	38	103	—	27	.273	.392	.326
Harry Steinfeldt	3B103,1B1,2B1*	R	27	114	384	49	104	16	9	1	39	30	—	15	.271	.329	.367
Tommy Corcoran	SS151	R	36	151	605	70	150	21	11	2	85	23	—	28	.248	.277	.329
Cy Seymour	OF149	L	32	149	581	95	219	40	21	8	121	51	—	21	.377	.429	.559
Fred Odwell	OF126	L	32	130	468	79	113	10	9	9	65	26	—	21	.241	.293	.359
Joe Kelley	OF85,1B2	R	33	90	321	43	89	7	6	1	37	27	—	8	.277	.346	.346
Al Bridwell	3B43,OF18,2B7*	L	21	82	254	17	64	3	1	0	17	19	—	8	.252	.309	.272
Jimmy Sebring	OF56	L	23	58	217	31	62	10	5	2	28	14	—	11	.286	.329	.406
Ed Phelps	C44	R	26	44	156	18	36	5	3	0	18	12	—	4	.231	.306	.301
Gabby Street†	C27	R	22	31	93	8	23	5	1	0	8	8	—	1	.247	.314	.323
Cozy Dolan†	1B13,OF9	L	32	22	77	7	18	2	1	0	4	7	—	2	.234	.306	.286
Johnny Siegle	OF16	R	30	17	56	9	17	1	2	1	8	7	—	0	.304	.391	.446
Cliff Blankenship	1B15	R	25	19	56	8	11	1	1	0	7	4	—	1	.196	.250	.250
Bill Hinchman	OF12,3B4,1B1	R	22	17	51	10	13	4	1	0	10	13	—	4	.255	.415	.373
Mike Mowrey	3B7	R	21	7	30	4	8	1	0	0	6	1	—	0	.267	.290	.300

H. Steinfeldt, 1 G at OF; A. Bridwell, 5 G at SS, 1 G at 1B

Pitcher	T	Age	G	GS	CG	ShO	IP	H	HR	BB	SO	W-L	Sv	ERA
Orval Overall	R	24	42	39	32	2	318.0	290	4	147	173	18-23	0	2.86
Bob Ewing	R	32	40	34	30	4	311.2	284	5	79	164	20-11	0	2.51
Charlie Chech	R	27	39	25	20	1	267.2	300	4	77	79	14-14	0	2.89
Jack Harper	R	27	26	23	15	1	179.1	189	2	69	70	9-13	1	3.86
Tom Walker	R	23	23	19	12	1	144.2	171	3	44	28	9-7	0	3.24
Noodles Hahn	L	26	13	8	5	1	77.0	85	0	9	17	5-3	0	2.81
Rip Vowinkel	R	20	6	6	4	0	45.1	52	2	10	7	3-3	0	4.17
Ollie Johns	L	25	4	1	1	0	18.0	31	1	4	8	1-0	1	3.50
Ernie Baker	R	29	1	0	0	0	4.0	7	1	0	1	0-0	0	4.50

1905 St. Louis Cardinals 6th NL 58-96 .377 47.5 GB

Kid Nichols (5-9)/Jimmy Burke (34-56)/Matt Robison (19-31)

Player	Gm by Position	B	Age	G	AB	R	H	2B	3B	HR	RBI	BB	SO	SB	Avg	OBP	Slg
Mike Grady	C71,1B20	R	35	100	311	41	89	20	7	4	41	33	—	15	.286	.360	.434
Jake Beckley	1B134	L	37	134	514	48	147	20	10	1	57	30	—	12	.286	.333	.370
Harry Arndt	2B90,OF9,3B7*	—	26	113	415	40	101	11	6	2	36	24	—	13	.243	.290	.313
Jimmy Burke	3B122	R	30	122	431	34	97	9	5	1	30	21	—	15	.225	.275	.276
George McBride†	SS80,1B1	R	24	81	281	22	61	1	2	2	34	14	—	10	.217	.264	.256
Spike Shannon	OF140	S	27	140	544	73	146	16	3	0	41	47	—	27	.268	.327	.309
Homer Smoot	OF138	L	27	139	534	73	166	21	16	4	58	33	—	21	.311	.359	.433
Jack Dunleavy	OF118,2B1	—	25	119	435	52	105	8	8	1	25	55	—	15	.241	.328	.303
Danny Shay	2B39,SS39	—	28	78	281	30	67	12	1	0	28	35	—	11	.238	.331	.288
Josh Clarke	OF26,2B16,SS4	L	26	50	167	31	43	3	2	3	18	27	—	8	.257	.361	.353
Dave Brain†	SS29,3B6,OF6	R	26	44	158	11	36	4	5	1	17	8	—	4	.228	.269	.335
John Warner†	C41	L	32	41	137	9	35	2	1	1	12	6	—	2	.255	.301	.321
Jack Taylor	P37,3B2	R	31	39	121	11	23	5	2	0	12	8	—	4	.190	.246	.264
Tom Leahy	C29	—	36	35	97	3	22	1	3	0	7	8	—	0	.227	.286	.299
Jake Thielman	P32,OF1	R	26	34	91	16	21	1	5	0	8	12	—	1	.231	.327	.352
Art Hoelskoetter	3B20,2B3,P1	R	22	24	83	7	20	2	1	0	5	3	—	1	.241	.267	.289
Rube DeGroff	OF15	L	25	15	56	3	14	2	1	0	5	5	—	1	.250	.311	.321
Dave Zearfoss	C19	—	37	20	51	2	8	0	1	0	2	4	—	0	.157	.218	.196
Jack Himes	OF11	L	26	12	41	3	6	0	0	0	0	1	—	0	.146	.167	.146
John Farrell	2B7	R	28	7	24	6	4	0	1	0	1	4	—	1	.167	.286	.250
Kid Nichols†	P7,OF1	S	35	8	22	0	5	0	0	0	0	0	—	0	.227	.227	.227
Simmy Murch	2B2,SS1	R	24	3	9	0	1	0	0	0	0	0	—	0	.111	.111	.111
Gerry Shea	C2	—	23	2	6	0	2	0	0	0	0	0	—	0	.333	.333	.333

H. Arndt, 5 G at SS

Pitcher	T	Age	G	GS	CG	ShO	IP	H	HR	BB	SO	W-L	Sv	ERA
Jack Taylor	R	31	37	34	34	3	309.0	302	0	85	102	15-21	1	3.44
Jake Thielman	R	26	32	29	26	0	242.0	265	4	62	87	15-16	0	3.50
Chappie McFarland	R	30	31	28	22	3	250.1	281	3	65	85	8-18	1	3.81
Buster Brown	R	23	23	21	17	3	178.2	172	0	62	57	8-11	0	2.97
Wish Egan	R	24	23	19	18	0	171.1	189	2	39	29	6-15	0	3.57
Win Kellum	L	29	11	7	5	1	74.0	70	1	10	19	3-3	0	2.92
Kid Nichols†	R	35	7	7	5	0	51.2	64	1	18	16	1-5	0	5.40
Sandy McDougal	R	31	5	5	5	0	44.2	50	0	12	10	1-4	0	3.43
Billy Campbell	L	31	2	2	2	0	17.0	27	0	7	2	1-1	0	7.41
Art Hoelskoetter	R	22	1	1	1	0	6.0	6	1	5	4	0-1	0	1.50
Jim McGinley	R	26	1	1	0	0	3.0	5	1	2	0	0-1	0	15.00

1905 Boston Beaneaters 7th NL 51-103 .331 54.5 GB

Fred Tenney

Player	Gm by Position	B	Age	G	AB	R	H	2B	3B	HR	RBI	BB	SO	SB	Avg	OBP	Slg
Pat Moran	C78	R	29	85	267	22	64	11	5	2	22	8	—	3	.240	.270	.341
Fred Tenney	1B148,P1	L	33	149	549	84	158	18	3	0	28	67	—	17	.288	.368	.332
Fred Raymer	2B134,1B1,OF1	R	29	137	498	26	105	14	2	0	31	8	—	15	.211	.232	.247
Harry Wolverton	3B122	L	31	122	463	38	104	15	7	2	55	23	—	10	.225	.276	.300
Ed Abbaticchio	SS152,OF1	R	28	153	610	70	170	25	12	3	41	35	—	30	.279	.326	.374
Rip Cannell	OF154	L	25	154	567	52	140	14	4	0	36	51	—	17	.247	.311	.286
Jim Delahanty	OF124,P1	R	26	125	461	50	119	11	8	5	55	28	—	12	.258	.315	.349
Cozy Dolan†	OF111,P2,1B2	L	32	112	433	44	119	11	7	3	48	27	—	21	.275	.322	.353
Tom Needham	C77,OF3,1B2	R	26	83	271	21	59	6	1	2	17	24	—	3	.218	.293	.269
Bill Lauterborn	3B29,2B23,SS3*	R	26	67	200	11	37	1	1	0	9	12	—	1	.185	.238	.200
Bud Sharpe	OF42,C3,1B1	L	23	46	170	8	31	3	2	0	11	7	—	0	.182	.215	.224
George Barclay	OF28	—	29	29	108	5	19	1	0	0	7	2	—	2	.176	.205	.185
Allie Strobel	3B4,OF1	R	21	5	19	1	2	0	0	0	2	0	—	0	.105	.105	.105
Gabby Street†	C3	R	22	3	12	0	2	0	0	0	0	0	—	1	.167	.167	.167
Dave Murphy	SS2,3B1	—	29	3	11	0	2	0	0	0	1	0	—	0	.182	.182	.182
Bill McCarthy	C1	—	19	1	3	0	0	0	0	0	0	0	—	0	.000	.000	.000

B. Lauterborn, 2 G at OF

Pitcher	T	Age	G	GS	CG	ShO	IP	H	HR	BB	SO	W-L	Sv	ERA
Irv Young	L	27	43	42	41	7	378.0	337	6	71	156	20-21	0	2.90
Vic Willis	R	29	41	41	36	4	342.0	340	7	107	149	12-29	0	3.21
Chick Fraser	R	34	39	37	35	2	334.1	320	8	149	130	14-21	0	3.28
Kaiser Wilhelm	R	31	34	28	23	0	242.1	287	7	75	76	3-23	0	4.53
Jake Volz	R	27	3	2	0	0	8.2	12	0	8	1	0-2	0	10.38
Frank Hershey	R	27	1	1	0	0	4.0	5	0	2	1	0-1	0	6.75
Jim Delahanty	R	26	1	1	0	0	2.0	5	1	0	0	0-0	0	4.50
Dick Harley	R	30	9	4	4	1	65.2	72	5	19	19	2-5	0	4.66
Cozy Dolan	L	32	2	0	0	0	4.0	7	2	1	1	0-1	0	9.00
Fred Tenney	L	33	1	0	0	0	2.0	5	0	1	0	0-0	0	4.50

1905 Brooklyn Dodgers 8th NL 48-104 .316 56.5 GB

Ned Hanlon

Player	Gm by Position	B	Age	G	AB	R	H	2B	3B	HR	RBI	BB	SO	SB	Avg	OBP	Slg
Lew Ritter	C84,OF4,3B2	R	29	92	311	32	68	10	5	1	28	15	—	16	.219	.255	.293
Doc Gessler	1B107,OF12	L	24	126	431	44	125	17	4	3	46	38	—	26	.290	.366	.369
Charlie Malay	2B75,OF25,SS1	S	26	102	349	33	88	7	2	1	31	22	—	13	.252	.300	.292
Emil Batch	3B145	R	25	145	568	64	143	20	11	5	49	26	—	21	.252	.285	.352
Phil Lewis	SS118	R	21	118	433	32	110	9	2	3	33	16	—	16	.254	.282	.305
Harry Lumley	OF129	L	24	130	505	50	148	19	10	7	47	36	—	22	.293	.340	.412
Jimmy Sheckard	OF129	L	26	130	480	58	140	20	11	3	41	61	—	23	.292	.380	.398
John Dobbs	OF123	L	30	123	460	59	117	21	4	2	36	31	—	15	.254	.304	.330
Bill Bergen	C76	R	27	79	247	12	47	3	2	0	22	7	—	4	.190	.213	.219
Charlie Babb	SS36,1B31,3B5*	S	32	75	235	27	44	8	2	0	17	27	—	10	.187	.303	.238
Bob Hall†	OF42,2B7,1B3	—	26	56	203	21	48	4	2	2	15	11	—	8	.236	.279	.296
Red Owens	2B43	R	30	43	168	14	36	6	2	1	20	6	—	1	.214	.241	.292
John Hummel	2B30	R	22	30	109	19	29	3	4	0	7	9	—	6	.266	.322	.367
Fred Mitchell	P12,1B7,3B4*	R	27	27	79	4	15	0	0	0	8	4	—	0	.190	.238	.190
Ed MacGamwell	1B4	L	26	4	16	0	4	0	0	0	0	1	—	0	.250	.294	.250
Ad Yale	1B4	—	35	4	13	1	1	0	0	0	1	1	—	0	.077	.143	.077

C. Babb, 2 G at 2B; F. Mitchell, 1 G at SS, 1 G at OF

Pitcher	T	Age	G	GS	CG	ShO	IP	H	HR	BB	SO	W-L	Sv	ERA
Harry McIntire	R	26	40	35	29	1	308.2	340	6	101	135	8-25	1	3.70
Doc Scanlan	R	24	33	28	22	2	249.2	220	4	104	135	14-12	0	2.92
Elmer Stricklett	R	28	33	28	25	1	237.1	259	0	71	77	9-18	1	3.34
Mal Eason	R	26	27	27	20	3	207.0	230	5	72	64	5-21	0	4.30
Oscar Jones	R	26	29	20	14	0	174.0	197	6	56	66	8-15	1	4.66
Fred Mitchell	R	27	12	10	9	0	96.1	107	2	38	44	3-7	0	4.76
Jack Doscher	L	24	12	7	6	0	71.0	60	1	30	33	1-5	0	3.17
Doc Reisling	R	30	2	0	0	0	3.0	3	0	4	2	0-1	0	3.00

»1906 Chicago White Sox 1st AL 93-58 .616 —

Fielder Jones

Player	Gm by Position	B	Age	G	AB	R	H	2B	3B	HR	RBI	BB	SO	SB	Avg	OBP	Slg
Billy Sullivan	C118	R	31	118	387	37	83	18	4	2	33	22	—	10	.214	.262	.297
Jiggs Donahue	1B154	L	26	154	556	70	143	17	7	1	57	48	—	36	.257	.320	.318
Frank Isbell	2B132,OF14,P1*	L	30	143	549	71	153	18	11	0	57	30	—	37	.279	.324	.352
Lee Tannehill	3B99,SS17	R	25	116	378	26	69	8	3	0	33	31	—	7	.183	.254	.220
George Davis	SS129,2B1	S	35	133	484	63	134	26	6	0	80	41	—	27	.277	.338	.355
Fielder Jones	OF144	L	34	144	496	77	114	22	4	2	34	83	—	26	.230	.346	.302
Ed Hahn†	OF130	L	30	130	484	80	110	7	5	0	27	69	—	19	.227	.335	.262
Bill O'Neill	OF93	S	26	94	330	37	82	4	1	1	21	22	—	19	.248	.301	.276
Patsy Dougherty†	OF74	L	29	75	253	30	59	9	4	1	27	19	—	11	.233	.295	.312
George Rohe	3B57,2B5,OF1	R	30	75	225	14	58	5	1	0	25	16	—	8	.258	.316	.289
Nick Altrock	P38,1B1	S	29	38	100	4	16	2	0	0	3	8	—	2	.160	.222	.180
Gus Dundon	2B18,SS14	R	31	33	96	7	13	1	0	0	4	11	—	4	.135	.224	.146
Doc White	P28,OF1	L	27	28	65	11	12	1	1	0	3	13	—	3	.185	.321	.231
Frank Roth	C15	R	27	16	51	4	10	1	1	0	7	3	—	1	.196	.241	.255
Frank Hemphill	OF13	R	28	13	40	0	3	0	0	0	2	9	—	1	.075	.275	.075
Hub Hart	C15	L	28	17	37	1	6	0	0	0	0	2	—	0	.162	.225	.162
Babe Towne	C12	R	26	13	36	3	10	0	0	0	6	7	—	0	.278	.395	.278
Rube Vinson	OF4	—	27	7	24	2	6	0	0	0	3	2	—	1	.250	.308	.250
Ed McFarland	C3	R	31	7	22	0	3	1	0	0	3	3	—	0	.136	.240	.182
Lee Quillen	SS3	R	24	4	9	1	3	0	0	0	0	0	—	1	.333	.333	.333

F. Isbell, 1 G at C

Pitcher	T	Age	G	GS	CG	ShO	IP	H	HR	BB	SO	W-L	Sv	ERA
Frank Owen	R	26	42	36	27	7	293.0	289	4	54	66	22-13	2	2.33
Ed Walsh	R	25	41	31	24	10	278.1	215	1	58	171	17-13	1	1.88
Nick Altrock	L	29	38	30	25	4	287.2	269	0	42	99	20-13	0	2.06
Doc White	L	27	28	24	20	7	219.1	160	2	38	95	18-6	0	1.52
Roy Patterson	R	29	21	18	12	3	142.0	119	1	17	45	10-7	1	2.09
Frank Smith	R	26	20	13	8	1	122.0	124	3	37	53	5-5	1	3.39
Lou Fiene	R	21	6	2	1	0	31.0	35	0	9	12	1-1	0	2.90
Frank Isbell	R	30	1	0	0	0	2.0	1	0	0	2	0-0	0	0.00

1906 New York Highlanders 2nd AL 90-61 .596 3.0 GB

Clark Griffith

Player	Gm by Position	B	Age	G	AB	R	H	2B	3B	HR	RBI	BB	SO	SB	Avg	OBP	Slg
Red Kleinow	C95,1B1	R	26	96	268	30	59	9	3	0	31	24	—	8	.220	.287	.276
Hal Chase	1B150,2B1	R	23	151	597	84	193	23	10	0	76	13	—	28	.323	.341	.395
Jimmy Williams	2B139	R	29	139	501	62	139	25	7	3	77	44	—	8	.277	.342	.373
Frank LaPorte	3B114,2B5,OF1	R	26	123	454	60	120	23	9	2	54	22	—	10	.264	.300	.368
Kid Elberfeld	SS98	R	31	99	346	59	106	11	5	2	31	30	—	19	.306	.378	.384
Willie Keeler	OF152	L	34	152	592	96	180	9	3	2	33	40	—	23	.304	.353	.340
Danny Hoffman†	OF98	L	26	100	320	34	82	10	6	0	23	27	—	32	.256	.318	.325
Wid Conroy	OF97,SS49,3B2	R	29	148	567	67	139	17	10	4	54	47	—	32	.245	.304	.332
Frank Delahanty	OF86	R	23	92	307	37	73	11	8	2	41	16	—	11	.238	.282	.345
George Moriarty	3B39,OF15,1B5*	R	22	65	197	22	46	7	7	0	23	17	—	8	.234	.298	.340
Deacon McGuire	C49,1B1	R	42	51	144	11	43	5	0	0	14	12	—	3	.299	.365	.333
Joe Yeager	SS22,2B13,3B3	R	30	57	123	20	37	6	1	0	12	13	—	3	.301	.407	.366
Ira Thomas	C42	R	25	44	115	12	23	1	2	0	15	8	—	2	.200	.258	.243
Patsy Dougherty†	OF12	L	29	12	52	3	10	2	0	0	4	0	—	0	.192	.192	.231
Ed Hahn†	OF7	L	30	11	22	2	2	1	0	0	1	3	—	2	.091	.259	.136

G. Moriarty, 1 G at 2B

Pitcher	T	Age	G	GS	CG	ShO	IP	H	HR	BB	SO	W-L	Sv	ERA
Jack Chesbro	R	32	49	42	24	4	325.0	314	2	75	152	23-17	1	2.96
Al Orth	R	33	45	39	36	3	338.2	317	2	66	133	27-17	0	2.34
Bill Hogg	R	24	28	25	15	3	206.0	171	5	72	107	14-13	0	2.93
Walter Clarkson	R	27	32	16	9	3	151.0	135	6	55	64	9-4	0	2.32
Doc Newton	L	28	21	15	6	2	125.0	118	3	33	52	7-5	0	3.17
Slow Joe Doyle	R	24	9	6	3	2	45.1	34	1	13	28	2-1	0	2.38
Noodles Hahn	L	27	6	6	3	1	42.0	38	0	6	17	3-2	0	3.86
Cy Barger	R	21	2	1	0	0	5.1	7	0	3	3	0-0	1	10.13
Clark Griffith	R	36	17	2	1	0	59.2	58	0	15	16	2-2	2	3.02
Louis LeRoy	R	27	11	2	1	0	44.2	33	0	12	28	2-0	1	2.22
Tom Hughes	R	22	3	1	1	0	15.0	11	0	1	5	1-0	0	4.20

1906 Cleveland Bronchos 3rd AL 89-64 .582 5.0 GB

Nap Lajoie

Player	Gm by Position	B	Age	G	AB	R	H	2B	3B	HR	RBI	BB	SO	SB	Avg	OBP	Slg
Harry Bemis	C81	R	32	93	297	28	82	13	5	2	30	12	—	8	.276	.311	.374
Claude Rossman	1B105,OF1	L	25	118	396	49	122	13	2	1	53	17	—	11	.308	.338	.359
Nap Lajoie	2B130,3B15,SS7	R	31	152	602	88	214	48	9	0	91	30	—	20	.355	.392	.465
Bill Bradley	3B82	R	28	82	302	32	83	15	2	2	25	18	—	13	.275	.324	.358
Terry Turner	SS147	R	25	147	584	85	170	27	7	2	62	35	—	27	.291	.338	.372
Elmer Flick	OF150,2B8	L	30	157	624	98	194	33	22	1	62	54	—	39	.311	.372	.439
Bunk Congalton	OF114	L	31	117	419	51	134	13	5	3	50	24	—	12	.320	.361	.396
Jim Jackson	OF104	R	28	105	374	44	80	13	2	0	38	38	—	25	.214	.290	.259
George Stovall	1B55,3B30,2B19	R	27	116	443	54	121	19	5	0	37	8	—	15	.273	.288	.339
Harry Bay	OF68	L	28	68	280	47	77	8	3	0	14	26	—	17	.275	.337	.325
Nig Clarke	C54	L	23	57	179	22	64	12	4	1	21	13	—	3	.358	.404	.486
Jap Barbeau	3B32,SS6	R	24	42	129	8	25	5	3	0	12	9	—	5	.194	.257	.279
Ben Caffyn	OF29	L	26	30	103	16	20	4	0	0	3	12	—	2	.194	.291	.233
Fritz Buelow	C33,1B1	R	30	34	86	7	14	2	0	0	7	9	—	0	.163	.250	.186
Joe Birmingham	OF9,3B1	R	21	10	41	5	13	2	1	0	6	1	—	2	.317	.333	.415
Malachi Kittridge†	C5	R	36	5	10	0	1	0	0	0	0	0	—	0	.100	.100	.100
Bill Shipke	2B2	R	23	2	6	0	0	0	0	0	0	0	—	0	.000	.000	.000

Pitcher	T	Age	G	GS	CG	ShO	IP	H	HR	BB	SO	W-L	Sv	ERA
Otto Hess	L	27	43	36	33	7	333.2	274	4	85	167	20-17	3	1.83
Bob Rhoads	R	26	38	34	31	7	315.0	259	5	92	89	22-10	0	1.80
Addie Joss	R	26	34	31	28	9	282.0	220	3	43	106	21-9	1	1.72
Bill Bernhard	R	35	31	30	23	2	255.1	235	1	47	85	16-15	0	2.54
Jack Townsend	R	27	17	12	8	1	92.2	92	1	31	31	3-7	0	2.91
Harry Eells	R	25	14	8	6	1	86.1	77	1	48	35	4-5	0	2.61
Earl Moore	R	26	5	4	2	0	29.2	27	1	18	8	1-1	0	3.94
Glenn Liebhardt	R	23	2	2	2	0	18.0	13	0	1	9	2-0	0	1.50

1906 Philadelphia Athletics 4th AL 78-67 .538 12.0 GB

Connie Mack

Player	Gm by Position	B	Age	G	AB	R	H	2B	3B	HR	RBI	BB	SO	SB	Avg	OBP	Slg
O. Schreckengost	C89,1B4	R	31	98	338	29	96	20	1	1	41	10	—	5	.284	.305	.358
Harry Davis	1B145	R	32	145	551	94	161	40	8	12	96	49	—	23	.292	.355	.459
Danny Murphy	2B119	R	29	119	448	48	135	24	7	2	60	21	—	17	.301	.341	.400
John Knight	3B67,2B7	R	20	74	253	29	49	7	2	3	20	19	—	6	.194	.250	.273
Monte Cross	SS134	R	36	134	445	32	89	23	3	1	40	50	—	22	.200	.291	.272
Topsy Hartsel	OF144	L	32	144	533	96	136	21	9	1	30	88	—	31	.255	.363	.334
Bris Lord	OF115	R	22	118	434	50	101	13	7	1	44	27	—	12	.233	.281	.302
Socks Seybold	OF114	R	35	116	411	41	130	23	2	5	59	30	—	9	.316	.367	.418
Harry Armbruster	OF74	L	24	91	265	40	63	6	3	2	24	43	—	13	.238	.353	.306
Mike Powers	C57,1B1	R	35	58	185	5	29	1	0	0	7	1	—	2	.157	.170	.162
Rube Oldring	3B49,SS3,2B2*	R	22	59	174	15	42	10	1	0	19	2	—	7	.241	.263	.310
Art Brouthers	3B33	—	23	36	144	18	30	5	1	0	14	5	—	4	.208	.240	.257
Dave Shean	2B22	R	22	22	75	7	16	3	2	0	3	5	—	6	.213	.280	.307
Simon Nicholls	SS12	L	23	12	44	1	8	1	0	0	1	3	—	0	.182	.234	.205
Claude Berry	C10	R	26	10	30	2	7	0	0	0	2	2	—	1	.233	.281	.233
Jim Byrnes	C8	R	26	10	23	2	4	0	1	0	0	0	—	0	.174	.174	.261
Danny Hoffman†	OF7	L	26	7	22	4	5	0	0	0	0	3	—	1	.227	.320	.227
Ed Lennox	3B6	R	20	6	17	1	1	1	0	0	0	1	—	0	.059	.111	.118
Eddie Collins	SS3,2B1,3B1	L	19	6	15	2	3	0	0	0	0	1	—	1	.200	.200	.200
Willy Fetzer		L	22	1	1	0	0	0	0	0	0	0	—	0	.000	.000	.000
Jack Hannifin†		R	23	1	1	0	1	0	0	0	0	0	—	0	1.000	1.000	1.000

R. Oldring, 1 G at 1B

Pitcher	T	Age	G	GS	CG	ShO	IP	H	HR	BB	SO	W-L	Sv	ERA
Rube Waddell	L	29	43	34	22	8	272.2	221	1	92	196	15-17	1	2.21
Chief Bender	R	22	36	27	24	0	238.1	208	5	48	159	15-10	3	2.53
Jimmy Dygert	R	21	35	25	15	4	213.2	175	1	91	106	11-13	0	2.70
Eddie Plank	L	30	26	25	21	5	211.2	173	1	51	108	19-6	0	2.25
Jack Coombs	R	23	23	18	13	1	173.0	144	0	68	90	10-10	0	2.50
Andy Coakley	R	23	22	16	10	0	149.0	144	0	44	59	7-8	0	3.14
Hack Schumann	R	21	4	2	1	0	18.0	21	0	8	9	0-2	0	4.00
Mike Cunningham	R	24	5	1	1	0	28.0	29	1	9	15	1-0	0	3.21
Jim Holmes	—	23	3	1	0	0	9.0	10	0	8	1	0-1	0	4.00
Bill Bartley	R	21	3	0	0	0	8.2	10	0	6	6	0-0	1	9.35

1906 St. Louis Browns 5th AL 76-73 .510 16.0 GB

Jimmy McAleer

Player	Gm by Position	B	Age	G	AB	R	H	2B	3B	HR	RBI	BB	SO	SB	Avg	OBP	Slg
Branch Rickey	C54,OF1	L	24	65	201	22	57	7	3	3	24	16	—	4	.284	.345	.393
Tom Jones	1B143	R	29	144	539	51	136	22	6	0	30	24	—	27	.252	.290	.315
Pete O'Brien	2B120,3B20,SS11	L	29	151	524	44	122	9	4	2	57	42	—	25	.233	.293	.277
Roy Hartzell	3B103,SS6,2B2	L	24	113	404	43	86	7	0	0	24	19	—	21	.213	.266	.230
Bobby Wallace	SS138	R	32	139	476	64	123	21	7	2	67	58	—	24	.258	.344	.345
Charlie Hemphill	OF154	L	30	154	585	90	169	19	12	4	62	43	—	33	.289	.338	.383
George Stone	OF154	L	28	154	581	91	208	25	20	6	71	52	—	35	.358	.417	.501
Harry Niles	OF108,3B34	R	25	142	541	71	124	14	4	2	31	46	—	30	.229	.297	.281
Tubby Spencer	C54	R	22	58	188	15	33	6	1	0	17	7	—	4	.176	.205	.218
Ben Koehler	OF52,2B7,3B1*	R	29	66	186	27	41	1	1	0	15	24	—	9	.220	.322	.237
Jack O'Connor	C51	R	37	55	174	8	33	0	0	0	11	2	—	4	.190	.199	.190
Ike Rockenfield	2B26	R	29	27	89	3	21	4	0	0	8	1	—	0	.236	.277	.281
Lou Nordyke	1B12	R	29	25	53	4	13	1	0	0	7	10	—	3	.245	.365	.264

B. Koehler, 1 G at SS

Pitcher	T	Age	G	GS	CG	ShO	IP	H	HR	BB	SO	W-L	Sv	ERA
Harry Howell	R	29	35	33	30	6	276.2	233	1	61	140	15-14	1	2.11
Fred Glade	R	30	35	32	28	4	266.2	215	4	59	96	15-14	1	2.36
Barney Pelty	R	25	34	30	25	4	260.2	189	1	59	92	16-11	2	1.59
Jack Powell	R	31	28	26	25	3	244.0	196	2	55	132	13-14	1	1.77
Ed Smith	R	27	19	18	13	0	154.2	153	3	53	45	8-11	0	3.72
Beany Jacobson	L	25	24	15	12	0	155.0	146	3	27	53	9-9	0	2.50

1906 Detroit Tigers 6th AL 71-78 .477 21.0 GB

Bill Armour

Player	Gm by Position	B	Age	G	AB	R	H	2B	3B	HR	RBI	BB	SO	SB	Avg	OBP	Slg
Boss Schmidt	C67	S	25	68	216	13	47	4	3	0	10	6	—	1	.218	.242	.264
Chris Lindsay	1B122,2B17,3B1	R	27	141	499	59	112	16	2	0	33	45	—	18	.224	.293	.265
Germany Schaefer	2B114,SS7	R	29	124	446	48	106	14	3	2	42	32	—	31	.238	.290	.296
Bill Coughlin	3B147	R	27	147	498	54	117	15	5	2	60	36	—	31	.235	.293	.297
Charley O'Leary	SS127	R	23	128	443	34	97	13	2	2	34	17	—	8	.219	.253	.271
Matty McIntyre	OF133	L	26	133	493	63	128	19	11	0	39	56	—	29	.260	.338	.343
Sam Crawford	OF116,1B32	L	26	145	563	65	166	25	16	2	72	38	—	24	.295	.341	.407
Ty Cobb	OF96	L	19	98	358	45	113	15	5	1	34	19	—	23	.316	.355	.394
Davy Jones	OF83	L	26	84	323	41	84	12	2	0	24	41	—	21	.260	.347	.310
Fred Payne	C47,OF17	R	25	72	222	23	60	5	5	0	20	13	—	4	.270	.316	.338
John Warner†	C49	L	33	50	153	15	37	4	2	0	10	12	—	4	.242	.326	.294
Bobby Lowe	SS19,2B17,3B5	R	37	41	145	11	30	3	0	1	12	4	—	3	.207	.233	.248
Wild Bill Donovan	P25,2B3,OF1	R	29	28	91	5	11	0	1	0	0	1	—	6	.121	.130	.143
Red Donahue	P28,OF1	R	33	29	81	2	10	0	1	0	1	3	—	0	.123	.155	.148
John Eubank	P24,OF2,2B1	R	33	26	60	8	12	1	1	0	1	0	—	1	.200	.213	.250
Sam Thompson	OF8	L	46	8	31	4	7	0	1	0	3	1	—	0	.226	.250	.290
Frank Scheibeck	2B3	R	41	3	10	1	1	0	0	0	0	2	—	0	.100	.250	.100
Gus Hetling	3B2	R	20	2	7	0	1	0	0	0	0	0	—	0	.143	.143	.143

Pitcher	T	Age	G	GS	CG	ShO	IP	H	HR	BB	SO	W-L	Sv	ERA
George Mullin	R	25	40	40	35	2	330.0	315	3	108	123	21-18	0	2.78
Red Donahue	R	33	28	28	26	3	241.0	260	1	54	82	13-14	0	2.73
Ed Siever	L	29	30	25	20	1	222.2	240	5	45	71	14-11	1	2.71
Wild Bill Donovan	R	29	25	25	22	0	211.2	221	4	72	85	9-15	0	3.15
Ed Killian	L	29	21	16	14	0	149.2	165	0	54	47	10-6	2	3.43
John Eubank	R	33	24	12	7	1	135.0	147	0	35	38	4-10	2	3.53
Ed Willett	R	22	3	3	3	0	25.0	24	0	8	16	0-3	0	3.96
Jack Rowan	R	19	1	1	1	0	9.0	15	0	6	0	0-1	0	11.00
Jimmy Wiggs	R	29	4	1	0	0	10.1	11	1	7	7	0-0	0	5.23

1906 Washington Senators 7th AL 55-95 .367 37.5 GB

Jake Stahl

Player	Gm by Position	B	Age	G	AB	R	H	2B	3B	HR	RBI	BB	SO	SB	Avg	OBP	Slg
Howard Wakefield	C60	R	22	77	211	17	59	9	2	1	21	7	—	6	.280	.303	.355
Jake Stahl	1B136	R	27	137	482	38	107	9	8	0	51	21	—	30	.222	.266	.274
Harry Schlafly	2B123	R	27	123	426	60	105	13	8	2	30	50	—	29	.246	.345	.329
Lave Cross	3B130	R	40	130	494	55	130	14	6	1	46	28	—	19	.263	.303	.322
Dave Altizer	SS113,OF2	L	29	115	433	56	111	9	5	1	27	35	—	37	.256	.324	.307
John Anderson	OF151	S	32	151	583	62	158	25	4	3	70	19	—	39	.271	.296	.343
Charlie Jones	OF128,2B1	R	30	131	497	56	120	11	11	3	42	24	—	34	.241	.283	.326
Charlie Hickman	OF95,1B18,3B5*	R	30	120	451	53	128	25	5	9	57	14	—	9	.284	.311	.421
Rabbitt Nill	SS31,2B25,3B15*	R	24	89	315	37	74	8	2	0	15	47	—	16	.235	.340	.273
Joe Stanley	OF63,P1	S	25	73	221	18	36	0	4	0	9	20	—	6	.163	.236	.199
Mike Heydon	C49	L	31	49	145	14	23	7	1	0	10	14	—	2	.159	.238	.221
John Warner†	C32	L	33	32	103	5	21	4	1	1	9	2	—	3	.204	.226	.291
Malachi Kittridge†	C22	R	36	22	68	5	13	0	0	0	3	1	—	0	.191	.203	.191
Otto Williams	SS8,2B6,1B2*	R	28	20	51	3	7	0	0	0	2	2	—	0	.137	.185	.137
W. Shannabrook	3B1	R	25	1	2	0	0	0	0	0	0	0	—	0	.000	.000	.000
Pat Duff		—	31	1	1	0	0	0	0	0	0	0	—	0	.000	.000	.000

C. Hickman, 1 G at 2B; R. Nill, 15 G at OF; O. Williams, 1 G at 3B

Pitcher	T	Age	G	GS	CG	ShO	IP	H	HR	BB	SO	W-L	Sv	ERA
Cy Falkenberg	R	25	40	36	30	2	298.2	277	1	108	178	14-20	1	2.86
Casey Patten	L	30	38	32	28	6	282.2	253	2	79	96	19-16	0	2.17
Long Tom Hughes	R	27	30	24	18	1	204.0	230	5	81	90	7-17	0	3.62
Charlie Smith	R	26	33	22	17	2	235.1	250	2	75	105	9-16	0	2.91
Frank Kitson	R	36	30	21	15	1	197.0	196	2	57	59	6-14	0	3.65
Willie Sudhoff	R	31	9	5	0	0	19.2	30	1	9	7	0-2	0	9.15
Clyde Goodwin	R	19	4	3	1	0	22.1	20	0	13	9	0-2	0	4.43
Harry Hardy	L	30	5	3	2	0	20.0	35	0	12	4	0-3	0	9.00
Bill Wolfe	R	30	4	3	2	0	20.0	17	0	10	8	0-3	0	4.05
Sam Edmondston	L	22	2	1	1	0	10.0	10	0	2	0	0-1	0	4.50
Chink Wilson	R	22	1	1	1	0	7.0	3	0	2	1	0-1	0	2.57
Con Starkel	R	25	1	0	0	0	3.0	7	1	2	1	0-0	0	18.00
Joe Stanley	R	25	1	0	0	0	3.0	3	1	1	0	0-0	0	12.00

1906 Boston Pilgrims 8th AL 49-105 .318 45.5 GB

Jimmy Collins (35-79)/Chick Stahl (14-26)

Player	Gm by Position	B	Age	G	AB	R	H	2B	3B	HR	RBI	BB	SO	SB	Avg	OBP	Slg
Charlie Armbruster	C66,1B1	R	25	72	201	9	29	6	1	0	6	25	—	2	.144	.242	.184
Moose Grimshaw	1B110	S	30	110	428	46	124	16	12	0	48	23	—	5	.290	.332	.383
Hobe Ferris	2B126,3B4	R	28	130	495	47	121	25	13	2	44	10	—	8	.244	.262	.360
Red Morgan	3B88	—	22	88	307	20	66	6	3	1	21	16	—	7	.215	.270	.264
Freddy Parent	SS143,2B6	R	30	149	600	67	141	14	10	1	49	31	—	16	.235	.277	.297
Chick Stahl	OF155	L	33	155	595	63	170	24	6	4	51	47	—	13	.286	.346	.366
Jack Hoey	OF94	L	24	94	361	27	88	8	4	0	24	14	—	10	.244	.274	.288
Jack Hayden	OF85	L	25	85	322	22	80	6	4	1	14	17	—	6	.248	.292	.301
Buck Freeman	OF65,1B43,3B4	L	34	121	392	42	98	18	9	1	30	28	—	5	.250	.302	.349
Kip Selbach	OF58	R	34	60	228	15	48	9	2	0	23	18	—	7	.211	.277	.268
John Godwin	3B27,SS14,OF10*	R	29	66	193	11	36	2	1	0	15	6	—	6	.187	.215	.207
Jimmy Collins	3B32	R	36	37	142	17	39	8	4	1	16	4	—	1	.275	.295	.408
Bob Peterson	C30,2B3,1B2*	R	21	39	118	10	24	1	1	1	9	11	—	1	.203	.277	.254
Bill Carrigan	C35	R	22	37	109	5	23	0	0	0	10	5	—	3	.211	.252	.211
Charlie Graham	C27	R	28	30	90	10	21	1	0	1	12	10	—	1	.233	.330	.278
Ralph Glaze	P19,3B1	R	24	22	55	4	10	4	0	0	6	3	—	0	.182	.224	.255
Chet Chadbourne	2B11,SS1	L	21	11	43	7	13	1	0	0	3	3	—	1	.302	.348	.326
Heinie Wagner	2B9	R	25	9	32	1	9	0	0	0	4	1	—	2	.281	.303	.281
Lou Criger	C6	R	34	7	17	0	3	1	0	0	1	1	—	1	.176	.222	.235
Tom Doran	C2	L	25	2	3	1	0	0	0	0	0	0	—	0	.000	.000	.000

J. Godwin, 3 G at 2B, 1 G at 1B; B. Peterson, 1 G at OF

Pitcher	T	Age	G	GS	CG	ShO	IP	H	HR	BB	SO	W-L	Sv	ERA
Cy Young	R	39	39	34	28	0	287.2	288	3	25	140	13-21	2	3.19
Bill Dinneen	R	30	28	27	22	1	218.2	209	4	52	60	8-19	0	2.92
Jesse Tannehill	L	31	27	26	18	2	196.1	207	9	39	82	13-11	0	3.16
Joe Harris	R	24	30	24	20	1	235.0	211	5	67	99	2-21	2	3.52
George Winter	R	28	29	22	18	1	207.2	215	8	38	72	6-18	2	4.12
Ralph Glaze	R	24	19	10	7	0	123.0	110	4	32	56	4-6	0	3.59
Frank Oberlin	R	30	4	4	4	0	34.0	38	0	13	13	1-3	0	3.18
Ed Barry	L	23	3	3	3	0	21.0	23	2	5	10	0-3	0	6.00
Len Swormstedt	R	27	3	2	2	0	21.0	17	0	0	6	1-1	0	1.29
Rube Kroh	L	19	1	1	1	1	9.0	2	0	4	5	1-0	0	0.00
Norwood Gibson	R	29	5	2	1	0	18.2	25	2	7	3	0-2	0	5.30
Ed Hughes	R	25	2	0	0	0	10.0	15	0	3	3	0-0	0	5.40

»1906 Chicago Cubs 1st NL 116-36 .763 —

Frank Chance

Player	Gm by Position	B	Age	G	AB	R	H	2B	3B	HR	RBI	BB	SO	SB	Avg	OBP	Slg
Johnny Kling	C96,OF3	R	31	107	343	45	107	15	8	2	46	23	—	14	.312	.357	.420
Frank Chance	1B136	R	28	136	474	103	151	24	10	3	71	70	—	57	.319	.419	.430
Johnny Evers	2B153,3B1	L	24	154	533	65	136	17	6	1	51	36	—	49	.255	.305	.315
Harry Steinfeldt	3B150,2B1	R	28	151	539	81	176	27	10	3	83	47	—	29	.327	.395	.430
Joe Tinker	SS147,3B1	R	25	148	523	75	122	18	4	1	64	43	—	30	.233	.293	.289
Jimmy Sheckard	OF149	L	27	149	549	90	144	27	10	1	45	67	—	30	.262	.349	.353
Wildfire Schulte	OF146	L	23	146	563	77	158	18	13	7	60	31	—	25	.281	.324	.396
Jimmy Slagle	OF127	L	32	127	498	71	119	8	6	0	33	63	—	25	.239	.324	.279
Pat Moran	C61	R	30	70	226	22	57	13	1	0	35	7	—	6	.252	.281	.319
Solly Hofman	OF23,1B21,SS9*	R	23	64	195	30	50	2	3	2	20	20	—	13	.256	.326	.328
Ed Reulbach	P33,OF1	R	23	34	83	4	13	0	0	0	4	2	—	0	.157	.176	.157
Doc Gessler†	OF21,1B1	L	25	34	83	8	21	3	0	0	10	12	—	4	.253	.354	.289
Carl Lundgren	P27,2B1	R	26	28	67	4	12	3	0	0	2	9	—	0	.179	.276	.224
Pete Noonan†	1B1	R	24	5	3	0	1	0	0	0	0	0	—	0	.333	.333	.333
Tom Walsh	C2	R	21	2	1	0	0	0	0	0	0	0	—	0	.000	.000	.000
Bull Smith		R	25	1	1	0	0	0	0	0	0	0	—	0	.000	.000	.000

S. Hofman, 4 G at 2B, 4 G at 3B

Pitcher	T	Age	G	GS	CG	ShO	IP	H	HR	BB	SO	W-L	Sv	ERA
Three Finger Brown	R	29	36	32	27	9	277.1	198	1	61	144	26-6	3	1.04
Jack Pfiester	L	28	31	29	20	4	250.2	173	3	63	153	20-8	0	1.51
Ed Reulbach	R	23	33	24	20	6	218.0	129	2	92	94	19-4	3	1.65
Carl Lundgren	R	26	27	24	21	5	207.2	160	3	89	103	17-6	2	2.21
Jack Taylor†	R	32	17	16	15	2	147.1	116	0	39	34	12-3	0	1.83
Orval Overall†	R	25	18	14	13	2	144.0	116	1	51	94	12-3	1	1.88
Bob Wicker†	R	28	10	8	5	0	72.1	70	0	19	25	3-5	0	2.99
Jack Harper†	R	28	1	1	0	0	1.0	0	0	0	0	0-0	0	0.00
Fred Beebe†	R	25	14	6	4	0	70.0	56	1	32	55	7-1	1	2.70

1906 New York Giants 2nd NL 96-56 .632 20.0 GB

John McGraw

Player	Gm by Position	B	Age	G	AB	R	H	2B	3B	HR	RBI	BB	SO	SB	Avg	OBP	Slg
Roger Bresnahan	C82,OF40	R	27	124	405	69	114	22	4	0	43	81	—	25	.281	.418	.356
Dan McGann	1B133	S	34	134	451	62	107	14	8	0	37	60	—	30	.237	.344	.304
Billy Gilbert	2B98	R	30	104	307	44	71	6	1	1	27	42	—	22	.231	.341	.267
Art Devlin	3B148	R	26	148	498	76	149	23	8	2	65	74	—	54	.299	.396	.390
Bill Dahlen	SS143	R	36	143	471	63	113	18	3	1	49	76	—	16	.240	.357	.297
George Browne	OF121	L	30	122	477	61	126	10	4	0	38	27	—	32	.264	.304	.302
Spike Shannon†	OF76	S	28	76	287	42	73	5	1	0	25	34	—	18	.254	.342	.279
Cy Seymour†	OF72	L	33	72	269	35	86	12	3	4	42	18	—	20	.320	.365	.431
Sammy Strang	2B57,OF39,SS4*	S	29	113	313	50	100	16	4	4	49	54	—	21	.319	.423	.435
Frank Bowerman	C67,1B20	R	37	103	285	23	65	7	3	1	42	15	—	5	.228	.274	.284
Sam Mertes†	OF71	R	33	71	253	37	60	9	6	1	33	29	—	21	.237	.323	.332
Mike Donlin	OF29,1B1	L	28	37	121	15	38	5	1	1	14	11	—	9	.314	.371	.397
Doc Marshall†	OF16,C13,1B2	R	30	38	102	8	17	3	2	0	7	7	—	7	.167	.234	.235
Jack Hannifin†	SS6,3B3,2B1	R	23	10	30	4	6	0	1	0	3	2	—	1	.200	.250	.267
Aleck Smith	C8,1B3,OF1	—	35	16	28	0	5	0	0	0	2	1	—	1	.179	.207	.179
Frank Burke	OF4	—	26	8	9	2	3	1	1	0	1	1	—	1	.333	.400	.667
Matty Fitzgerald	C3	R	25	4	6	2	4	0	0	0	2	0	—	1	.667	.667	.667
John McGraw	3B1	L	33	4	2	0	0	0	0	0	0	1	—	0	.000	.333	.000

S. Strang, 3 G at 3B, 1 G at 1B

Pitcher	T	Age	G	GS	CG	ShO	IP	H	HR	BB	SO	W-L	Sv	ERA
Joe McGinnity	R	35	45	37	32	3	339.2	316	1	71	105	27-12	2	2.25
Christy Mathewson	R	27	38	35	22	6	266.2	262	3	77	128	22-12	1	2.97
Luther Taylor	R	31	31	27	13	2	213.0	186	4	57	91	17-9	0	2.20
Hooks Wiltse	R	25	38	26	21	4	249.1	227	3	58	125	16-11	6	2.27
Red Ames	R	23	31	25	15	1	203.1	166	1	93	156	12-10	1	2.66
Henry Mathewson	R	19	2	1	1	0	10.0	7	0	14	2	0-1	1	5.40
George Ferguson	R	19	22	1	1	1	52.1	43	1	24	32	2-1	7	2.58

1906 Pittsburgh Pirates 3rd NL 93-60 .608 23.5 GB

Fred Clarke

Player	Gm by Position	B	Age	G	AB	R	H	2B	3B	HR	RBI	BB	SO	SB	Avg	OBP	Slg
George Gibson	C81	R	25	81	259	8	46	6	1	0	20	16	—	1	.178	.225	.208
Jim Nealon	1B154	R	21	154	556	82	142	21	12	3	83	53	—	15	.255	.327	.353
Claude Ritchey	2B151	S	32	152	484	46	130	21	5	1	62	68	—	6	.269	.369	.339
Tommy Sheehan	3B90	R	28	95	315	28	76	6	3	1	34	18	—	13	.241	.284	.289
Honus Wagner	SS137,OF2,3B1	R	32	142	516	103	175	38	9	2	71	58	—	53	.339	.416	.459
Bob Ganley	OF134	L	31	137	511	63	132	7	6	0	31	41	—	19	.258	.316	.295
Fred Clarke	OF110	L	33	118	417	69	129	14	13	1	39	40	—	18	.309	.371	.412
Ginger Beaumont	OF78	L	29	80	310	48	82	9	3	2	32	19	—	1	.265	.311	.332
Tommy Leach	3B65,OF60,SS1	R	28	133	476	66	136	10	7	1	39	33	—	21	.286	.333	.342
Dutch Meier	OF52,SS17	R	27	82	273	32	70	11	4	0	16	13	—	4	.256	.298	.326
Heinie Peitz	C38	R	35	40	125	13	30	8	0	0	20	13	—	1	.240	.321	.304
Ed Phelps†	C42	R	27	43	118	9	28	3	1	0	12	9	—	1	.237	.302	.280
Bill Hallman	OF23	L	30	23	89	12	24	3	1	1	6	15	—	3	.270	.375	.360
Otis Clymer	OF11	S	30	11	45	7	11	0	1	0	1	3	—	1	.244	.292	.289
Bill Abstein	2B3,OF2	R	23	8	20	2	4	0	0	0	3	0	—	2	.200	.200	.200
Alan Storke	3B2,SS1	R	21	5	12	1	3	1	0	0	1	1	—	1	.250	.308	.333
Fred Carisch	C4	R	24	4	12	0	1	0	0	0	0	1	—	1	.083	.154	.083
Harry Smith	C1	R	31	1	1	0	0	0	0	0	0	0	—	0	.000	.000	.000

Pitcher	T	Age	G	GS	CG	ShO	IP	H	HR	BB	SO	W-L	Sv	ERA
Vic Willis	R	30	41	36	32	6	322.0	295	0	76	124	23-13	1	1.73
Sam Leever	R	34	36	31	25	6	260.1	232	3	48	76	22-7	0	2.32
Lefty Leifield	L	22	37	31	24	8	255.2	214	3	68	111	18-13	1	1.87
Deacon Phillippe	R	34	33	24	19	3	218.2	216	3	26	90	15-10	0	2.47
Mike Lynch	R	26	18	12	7	0	119.0	101	2	31	48	6-5	0	2.42
Homer Hillebrand	L	26	7	5	4	1	53.0	42	1	21	32	3-2	0	2.21
C. McFarland†	R	31	6	5	2	1	35.1	39	0	7	11	1-3	0	2.55
King Brady	R	25	3	2	1	0	23.0	30	0	4	14	1-1	0	2.35
Charlie Case	R	26	2	2	1	0	11.0	8	0	5	3	1-1	0	5.73
Howie Camnitz	R	24	2	1	1	1	9.0	6	0	5	5	1-0	0	2.00
Bert Maxwell	R	19	1	1	0	0	8.0	8	0	2	1	0-1	0	5.63
Lou Manske	L	21	2	1	0	0	8.0	12	0	5	6	0-0	0	5.63
Irish McIlveen	L	25	2	1	0	0	7.0	10	1	2	3	0-1	0	6.43
Ed Karger†	L	23	6	2	0	0	28.0	21	0	9	8	2-3	0	1.93

1906 Philadelphia Phillies 4th NL 71-82 .464 45.5 GB

Hugh Duffy

Player	Gm by Position	B	Age	G	AB	R	H	2B	3B	HR	RBI	BB	SO	SB	Avg	OBP	Slg
Red Dooin	C107	R	27	113	351	25	86	19	1	0	32	13	—	15	.245	.274	.305
Kitty Bransfield	1B139	R	31	140	524	47	144	28	5	1	60	16	—	12	.275	.300	.353
Kid Gleason	2B135	S	39	135	494	47	112	17	2	0	34	36	—	17	.227	.281	.269
Ernie Courtney	3B96,1B13,OF3*	L	31	116	398	53	94	12	2	0	42	45	—	6	.236	.315	.276
Mickey Doolan	SS154	R	26	154	535	41	123	19	7	1	55	27	—	16	.230	.270	.297
Sherry Magee	OF154	R	21	154	563	77	159	36	8	6	67	52	—	55	.282	.348	.407
Roy Thomas	OF142	L	32	142	493	81	125	10	7	0	16	107	—	22	.254	.393	.302
John Titus	OF142	L	30	145	484	67	129	22	5	1	57	78	—	12	.267	.378	.339
Johnny Lush	P37,OF22,1B2	L	20	76	212	28	56	7	1	0	15	14	—	6	.264	.310	.307
Paul Sentell	3B33,2B19,OF2*	R	26	63	192	19	44	5	1	1	14	14	—	15	.229	.292	.281
Jerry Donovan	C53,SS1,OF1	R	29	61	166	11	33	4	0	0	15	6	—	2	.199	.236	.223
Joe Ward	3B27,2B3,SS1	—	21	35	129	12	38	8	6	0	11	5	—	2	.295	.321	.450
Ches Crist	C6	R	24	6	11	1	0	0	0	0	0	0	—	0	.000	.083	.000
Harry Huston	C2	R	22	2	4	0	0	0	0	0	0	1	—	0	.000	.200	.000
Hugh Duffy		R	39	1	1	0	0	0	0	0	0	0	—	0	.000	.000	.000

E. Courtney, 1 G at SS; P. Sentell, 1 G at SS

Pitcher	T	Age	G	GS	CG	ShO	IP	H	HR	BB	SO	W-L	Sv	ERA
Tully Sparks	R	31	42	37	29	6	316.2	244	4	62	114	19-16	3	2.16
Johnny Lush	L	20	37	35	24	4	281.0	254	2	119	151	18-15	0	2.37
Bill Duggleby	R	32	42	30	22	5	280.1	241	5	66	83	13-19	2	2.25
Lew Richie	R	22	33	22	14	3	205.2	170	3	79	65	9-11	0	2.41
Togie Pittinger	R	34	20	16	9	2	129.2	128	2	50	43	8-10	0	3.40
Walter Moser	R	25	6	4	4	0	42.2	49	0	15	17	0-4	0	3.59
Harry Kane	L	22	6	3	2	0	28.0	28	0	18	14	1-3	0	3.86
Kid Nichols	R	36	4	2	1	0	11.0	17	0	13	1	0-1	0	9.82
John McCloskey	—	23	9	4	3	0	41.0	46	2	9	6	3-2	0	2.85
Charlie Roy	R	22	7	1	0	0	18.1	24	0	5	6	0-1	0	4.91

1906 Brooklyn Dodgers 5th NL 66-86 .434 50.0 GB

Patsy Donovan

Player	Gm by Position	B	Age	G	AB	R	H	2B	3B	HR	RBI	BB	SO	SB	Avg	OBP	Slg
Bill Bergen	C103	R	28	103	353	9	56	3	3	0	19	7	—	2	.159	.175	.184
Tim Jordan	1B126	L	27	129	450	67	118	20	8	12	78	59	—	16	.262	.352	.422
Whitey Alperman	2B103,SS24,3B1	R	26	128	441	38	111	15	7	3	46	6	—	13	.252	.284	.338
Doc Casey	3B149	S	36	149	571	71	133	17	8	0	34	52	—	22	.233	.306	.291
Phil Lewis	SS135	R	22	136	452	40	110	8	4	0	37	43	—	14	.243	.309	.279
Billy Maloney	OF151	L	28	151	566	71	125	15	7	0	32	49	—	38	.221	.286	.272
Harry Lumley	OF131	L	25	133	484	72	157	23	12	9	61	48	—	35	.324	.386	.477
Jack McCarthy	OF86	L	37	91	322	23	98	13	1	0	35	20	—	9	.304	.347	.351
John Hummel	2B50,OF21,1B15	R	23	97	286	20	57	6	4	1	21	36	—	10	.199	.289	.259
Lew Ritter	C53,OF9,1B3*	R	30	73	226	22	47	1	3	0	15	16	—	6	.208	.263	.239
Emil Batch	OF50,3B2	R	26	59	203	23	52	7	6	0	11	15	—	3	.256	.311	.350
Doc Gessler†	1B9	L	25	9	33	3	8	1	2	0	4	3	—	3	.242	.324	.394
Patsy Donovan	OF6	L	41	7	21	1	5	0	0	0	0	0	—	0	.238	.238	.238
Phil Reardon	OF4	R	22	5	14	0	1	0	0	0	0	0	—	0	.071	.133	.071
John Butler	C1	R	26	1	0	0	0	0	0	0	0	0	—	0	—	—	—

L. Ritter, 2 G at 3B

Pitcher	T	Age	G	GS	CG	ShO	IP	H	HR	BB	SO	W-L	Sv	ERA
Elmer Stricklett	R	29	41	35	28	5	291.2	273	2	77	88	14-18	5	2.72
Doc Scanlan	R	25	38	33	28	6	288.0	230	5	127	120	18-13	2	3.19
Harry McIntire	R	27	39	31	25	4	276.0	254	2	89	121	13-21	3	2.97
Mal Eason	R	27	34	26	18	3	227.0	212	1	74	64	10-17	1	3.25
Jim Pastorius	L	24	29	24	16	3	211.2	225	4	69	58	10-14	0	3.61
Jesse Whiting	—	27	3	2	2	1	24.2	26	0	6	7	1-1	0	2.92
Jack Doscher	L	25	2	1	1	0	14.0	12	0	4	10	0-1	0	1.29
C. McFarland†	R	31	1	1	1	0	9.0	10	1	5	5	0-1	0	8.00
Hub Knolls	R	22	2	0	0	0	6.2	13	0	2	3	0-0	0	4.05

1906 Cincinnati Reds 6th NL 64-87 .424 51.5 GB

Ned Hanlon

Player	Gm by Position	B	Age	G	AB	R	H	2B	3B	HR	RBI	BB	SO	SB	Avg	OBP	Slg
Admiral Schlei	C91,1B21	R	28	116	388	44	95	13	8	4	54	29	—	7	.245	.304	.351
Snake Deal	1B65	R	27	65	231	13	48	4	3	0	21	6	—	15	.208	.228	.251
Miller Huggins	2B146	S	27	146	545	81	159	11	7	0	26	71	—	41	.292	.376	.338
Jim Delahanty	3B105,SS5,OF2	R	27	115	379	63	106	21	4	1	39	45	—	21	.280	.371	.364
Tommy Corcoran	SS117	R	37	117	430	29	89	13	1	1	33	19	—	8	.207	.242	.249
Joe Kelley	OF122,1B3,3B1*	R	34	129	465	43	106	19	11	1	53	44	—	9	.228	.300	.323
Frank Jude	OF80	R	22	80	308	31	64	6	4	1	31	16	—	7	.208	.261	.263
Cy Seymour†	OF79	L	33	79	307	35	79	7	2	4	38	24	—	9	.257	.317	.332
Shad Barry†	1B43,OF30	R	27	73	279	38	80	10	5	1	33	26	—	11	.287	.354	.369
Hans Lobert	3B35,SS31,2B10*	R	24	79	268	39	83	5	5	0	19	19	—	20	.310	.366	.366
Homer Smoot†	OF59	L	28	60	220	11	57	8	1	1	17	13	—	0	.259	.315	.318
Fred Odwell	OF57	L	33	58	202	20	45	5	4	0	21	15	—	11	.223	.286	.287
Paddy Livingston	C47	R	26	50	139	8	22	1	4	0	8	12	—	0	.158	.259	.223
Charlie Carr	1B22	R	29	22	94	9	18	2	3	0	10	2	—	0	.191	.216	.277
Johnny Siegle	OF21	R	31	22	68	4	8	2	2	0	7	3	—	0	.118	.178	.206
Bill Hinchman	OF16	R	23	18	54	7	11	1	1	0	1	8	—	2	.204	.306	.259
Mike Mowrey	3B15,2B1,SS1	R	22	21	53	3	17	3	0	0	6	5	—	2	.321	.379	.377
Ed Phelps†	C12	R	27	12	40	3	11	0	2	1	5	3	—	2	.275	.326	.450
Larry McLean	C12	R	24	12	35	3	7	2	0	0	2	4	—	0	.200	.282	.257
Jimmy Barrett	OF4	L	31	5	12	1	0	0	0	0	0	2	—	0	.000	.143	.000
Eddie Tiemeyer	3B3,P1	R	21	5	11	3	2	0	0	0	0	1	—	0	.182	.250	.182
Oscar Stanage	C1	R	23	1	1	0	0	0	0	0	0	0	—	0	.000	.000	.000

J. Kelley, 1 G at SS; H. Lobert, 1 G at OF

Pitcher	T	Age	G	GS	CG	ShO	IP	H	HR	BB	SO	W-L	Sv	ERA
Jake Weimer	L	32	41	39	31	6	304.2	263	0	99	141	20-14	1	2.22
Bob Ewing	R	33	33	32	26	2	287.2	248	4	60	145	13-14	0	2.38
Chick Fraser	R	35	31	28	25	2	236.0	221	1	80	58	10-20	0	2.67
Bob Wicker†	R	28	20	17	14	0	150.0	150	3	46	69	6-11	0	2.70
Orval Overall†	R	25	13	10	6	0	82.1	77	1	46	33	4-5	0	4.26
Sea Lion Hall	R	20	14	9	9	1	95.0	86	1	50	49	4-8	1	3.32
Jack Harper†	R	28	5	5	3	0	36.2	38	1	20	10	1-4	0	4.17
Bill Essick	R	24	6	4	3	0	39.1	39	1	16	16	2-2	0	2.97
Carl Druhot†	L	23	4	3	1	0	25.0	27	0	7	14	2-2	0	4.32
Gus Dorner†	R	29	2	1	1	0	15.0	16	0	4	5	0-1	0	1.20
Del Mason	R	22	2	1	1	0	12.0	10	1	6	4	0-1	0	4.50
Charlie Chech	R	28	11	5	5	0	66.0	59	1	24	17	1-4	3	2.32
Leo Hafford	R	22	3	1	1	0	19.0	13	0	11	5	1-1	0	0.95
Eddie Tiemeyer	R	21	1	0	0	0	1.0	1	0	1	1	0-0	0	0.00

1906 St. Louis Cardinals 7th NL 52-98 .347 63.0 GB

John McCloskey

Player	Gm by Position	B	Age	G	AB	R	H	2B	3B	HR	RBI	BB	SO	SB	Avg	OBP	Slg
Mike Grady	C60,1B38	R	36	97	280	33	70	11	3	3	27	48	—	5	.250	.369	.343
Jake Beckley	1B85	L	38	87	320	29	79	16	6	0	44	13	—	3	.247	.283	.334
Pug Bennett	2B153	R	32	153	595	66	156	16	7	1	34	56	—	20	.262	.334	.318
Harry Arndt	3B65,1B1,OF1	—	27	69	256	30	69	7	9	2	26	19	—	5	.270	.320	.391
George McBride	SS90	R	25	90	313	24	53	8	2	0	13	17	—	5	.169	.215	.208
Al Burch	OF91	L	22	91	335	40	89	5	1	0	11	37	—	15	.266	.339	.287
Homer Smoot†	OF86	L	28	86	343	41	85	9	10	0	31	11	—	3	.248	.289	.332
Spike Shannon†	OF80	S	28	80	302	36	78	4	0	0	25	36	—	15	.258	.337	.272
Art Hoelskoetter	3B53,SS16,P12*	R	23	94	317	21	71	6	3	0	14	4	—	2	.224	.238	.262
Shad Barry†	OF35,1B21,3B6	R	27	62	237	26	59	9	1	0	12	15	—	6	.249	.299	.295
Sam Mertes†	OF53	R	33	53	191	20	47	7	4	0	19	16	—	10	.246	.304	.325
Jack Himes	OF40	L	27	40	155	10	42	5	2	0	14	7	—	4	.271	.307	.329
Forrest Crawford	SS39,3B6	L	25	45	145	8	30	3	1	0	11	7	—	1	.207	.248	.241
Red Murray	OF34,C7	R	22	46	144	18	37	9	7	1	16	9	—	5	.257	.305	.438
Pete Noonan†	C23,1B16	R	24	44	125	8	21	1	3	1	9	11	—	1	.168	.235	.248
Doc Marshall†	C38	R	30	39	123	6	34	4	1	0	10	6	—	1	.276	.315	.325
Joe Marshall	OF23,1B4	R	30	33	95	2	15	1	2	0	7	6	—	0	.158	.216	.211
Tommy Raub	C22	R	35	24	78	9	22	2	4	0	2	4	—	2	.282	.325	.410
Bill Phyle	3B21	—	31	22	73	6	13	3	1	0	4	5	—	2	.178	.231	.247
Tom O'Hara	OF14	—	20	14	53	8	16	1	0	0	0	3	—	3	.302	.339	.321
Joe McCarthy	C14	R	24	15	37	3	9	2	0	0	2	2	—	0	.243	.282	.297
Ed Holly	SS10	R	26	10	34	1	2	0	0	0	7	5	—	0	.059	.179	.059
Ducky Holmes	C9	R	22	9	27	2	5	0	0	0	2	2	—	0	.185	.267	.185
Eddie Zimmerman	3B5	R	23	5	14	0	3	0	0	0	1	0	—	0	.214	.214	.214
Jack Slattery	C2	R	28	3	7	0	2	0	0	0	0	1	—	0	.286	.375	.286
Rube DeGroff	OF1	L	26	1	4	1	0	0	0	0	0	0	—	0	.000	.000	.000

A. Hoelskoetter, 12 G at OF, 1 G at 2B

Pitcher	T	Age	G	GS	CG	ShO	IP	H	HR	BB	SO	W-L	Sv	ERA
Buster Brown	R	24	32	27	21	0	238.1	208	0	112	109	8-16	0	2.64
Ed Karger†	L	23	25	20	17	0	191.2	193	0	43	73	5-16	1	2.72
Fred Beebe†	R	25	20	19	16	1	160.2	115	1	68	116	9-9	0	3.02
Jack Taylor†	R	32	17	17	17	1	155.0	133	0	47	27	8-9	0	2.15
Carl Druhot†	L	23	15	13	12	1	130.1	117	1	46	45	6-7	0	2.62
Gus Thompson	R	29	17	12	8	0	103.0	111	2	25	36	2-11	0	4.28
Wish Egan	R	25	16	12	7	0	86.1	97	3	27	23	2-9	0	4.59
Stoney McGlynn	R	34	6	6	6	0	48.0	43	0	15	25	2-2	0	2.44
Irv Higginbotham	R	24	7	6	4	0	47.1	50	1	11	14	1-4	0	3.23
Charlie Rhodes	R	21	9	6	3	0	45.0	37	0	20	32	3-4	0	3.40
C. McFarland†	R	31	6	4	2	0	37.1	33	1	8	16	2-1	1	1.93
Ambrose Puttmann	L	25	4	4	0	0	18.2	23	2	9	12	2-2	0	5.30
Art Fromme	R	22	3	3	3	1	25.0	19	0	10	11	1-2	0	1.44
Jake Thielman	R	27	1	1	0	0	5.0	5	0	2	0	0-1	0	3.60
Babe Adams	R	24	1	1	0	0	4.0	9	0	2	0	0-1	0	13.50
Art Hoelskoetter	R	23	12	3	2	0	58.1	53	1	34	20	1-4	0	4.63

1906 Boston Beaneaters 8th NL 49-102 .325 66.5 GB

Fred Tenney

Player	Gm by Position	B	Age	G	AB	R	H	2B	3B	HR	RBI	BB	SO	SB	Avg	OBP	Slg
Tom Needham	C76,2B5,1B2*	R	27	83	285	11	54	8	2	1	12	13	—	3	.189	.230	.242
Fred Tenney	1B143	L	34	143	544	61	154	12	8	1	28	58	—	17	.283	.357	.340
Allie Strobel	2B93,SS6,OF1	R	22	100	317	28	64	10	3	1	24	29	—	2	.202	.273	.262
Dave Brain	3B139	R	27	139	525	43	131	19	5	5	45	29	—	11	.250	.293	.333
Al Bridwell	SS119,OF1	L	22	120	459	41	104	9	1	0	22	44	—	6	.227	.297	.251
Cozy Dolan	OF144,2B7,P2*	L	33	152	549	54	136	20	4	0	39	55	—	17	.248	.318	.299
Johnny Bates	OF140	L	23	140	504	52	127	21	5	6	54	36	—	9	.252	.315	.349
Del Howard	OF87,2B45,SS14*	L	28	147	545	46	142	19	8	1	54	26	—	17	.261	.306	.330
Sam Brown	C35,OF13,3B12*	R	28	71	231	12	48	6	1	0	20	13	—	4	.208	.262	.242
Jack O'Neill	C48,1B2,OF1	R	33	61	167	14	30	5	1	0	4	12	—	0	.180	.243	.222
Big Jeff Pfeffer	P35,OF14	R	24	60	158	10	31	3	3	1	11	5	—	2	.196	.253	.272
Gene Good	OF34	L	23	34	119	4	18	0	0	0	0	13	—	2	.151	.246	.151
Jack Cameron	OF16,P2	—	21	18	61	3	11	0	0	0	4	2	—	0	.180	.206	.180
Frank Connaughton	SS11,2B1	R	37	12	44	3	9	0	0	0	1	3	—	1	.205	.271	.205
Chet Spencer	OF8	L	23	8	27	1	4	1	0	0	0	0	—	0	.148	.148	.185
Tommy Madden	OF4	L	22	4	15	1	4	0	0	0	0	1	—	0	.267	.313	.267
Ernie Diehl	OF2,SS1	R	28	3	11	1	5	0	1	0	0	0	—	0	.455	.455	.636
Jack Schulte	SS2	R	24	2	7	0	0	0	0	0	0	0	—	0	.000	.000	.000

T. Needham, 1 G at 3B, 1 G at OF; C. Dolan, 1 G at 1B; D. Howard, 2 G at 1B; S. Brown, 3 G at 1B, 2 G at 2B

Pitcher	T	Age	G	GS	CG	ShO	IP	H	HR	BB	SO	W-L	Sv	ERA
Irv Young	L	28	43	41	37	4	358.1	349	7	83	151	16-25	0	2.91
Vive Lindaman	R	28	39	36	32	2	307.1	303	4	90	115	12-23	0	2.43
Big Jeff Pfeffer	R	24	36	36	33	4	302.1	270	4	114	158	13-22	0	2.95
Gus Dorner†	R	29	34	32	29	0	273.1	264	5	103	104	8-25	0	3.65
Jim Moroney	L	22	3	3	3	0	27.0	28	1	12	11	0-3	0	5.33
Jack Cameron	—	21	2	1	0	0	6.0	4	0	6	2	0-0	0	0.00
Roy Witherup	R	19	8	3	3	0	46.0	59	2	19	14	0-3	0	6.26
Cozy Dolan	L	33	2	0	0	0	12.0	12	1	6	7	0-1	0	4.50
Bill McCarthy	R	24	1	0	0	0	2.0	2	0	3	0	0-0	0	9.00

»1907 Detroit Tigers 1st AL 92-58 .613 —

Hughie Jennings

Player	Gm by Position	B	Age	G	AB	R	H	2B	3B	HR	RBI	BB	SO	SB	Avg	OBP	Slg
Boss Schmidt	C103	S	26	104	349	32	85	6	6	0	23	5	—	8	.244	.259	.295
Claude Rossman	1B153	L	26	153	571	60	158	21	8	0	69	33	—	20	.277	.318	.342
Red Downs	2B80,OF20,3B1*	R	23	105	374	28	82	13	5	1	42	13	—	3	.219	.249	.289
Bill Coughlin	3B133	R	28	134	519	80	126	10	2	0	46	35	—	15	.243	.301	.270
Charley O'Leary	SS138	R	24	139	465	61	112	19	1	0	34	32	—	11	.241	.298	.286
Ty Cobb	OF150	L	20	150	605	97	212	29	15	5	119	24	—	49	.350	.380	.473
Sam Crawford	OF144,1B2	L	27	144	582	102	188	34	17	4	81	37	—	18	.323	.366	.460
Davy Jones	OF125	L	27	126	491	101	134	10	6	0	27	60	—	30	.273	.357	.318
Germany Schaefer	2B74,SS18,3B14*	R	30	109	372	45	96	12	3	1	32	30	—	21	.258	.313	.315
Fred Payne	C46,OF5	R	26	53	169	17	28	2	2	0	14	7	—	4	.166	.221	.201
Ed Killian	P41,OF2,1B1	L	30	46	122	16	39	5	3	0	11	4	—	3	.320	.346	.410
Matty McIntyre	OF20	L	27	20	81	6	23	1	1	0	9	7	—	3	.284	.341	.321
Jimmy Archer	C17,2B1	R	24	18	42	6	5	0	0	0	0	4	—	0	.119	.196	.119
Bobby Lowe	3B10,OF4,SS2	R	38	17	37	2	9	2	0	0	5	4	—	0	.243	.317	.297
Tex Erwin	C4	L	21	4	5	0	1	0	0	0	1	1	—	0	.200	.333	.200
Red Killefer	OF1	R	22	1	4	0	0	0	0	0	0	0	—	0	.000	.000	.000
Hughie Jennings	2B1,SS1	R	38	1	4	0	1	1	0	0	0	0	—	0	.250	.250	.500

R. Downs, 1 G at SS; G. Schaefer, 1 G at OF

Pitcher	T	Age	G	GS	CG	ShO	IP	H	HR	BB	SO	W-L	Sv	ERA
George Mullin	R	26	46	42	35	5	357.1	346	1	106	146	20-20	3	2.59
Ed Killian	L	30	41	34	29	3	314.0	286	2	91	96	25-13	0	1.78
Ed Siever	L	30	39	33	22	3	274.2	256	1	52	88	18-11	1	2.16
Wild Bill Donovan	R	30	32	28	27	3	271.0	222	3	82	123	25-4	1	2.19
John Eubank	R	34	15	8	4	1	81.0	88	0	20	17	3-3	0	2.67
Ed Willett	R	23	10	6	1	0	48.2	47	0	20	27	1-5	0	3.70
Herm Malloy	R	22	1	1	1	0	8.0	13	1	5	6	0-1	0	5.63
Elijah Jones	R	25	4	1	1	0	16.0	23	0	4	9	0-2	1	5.06

1907 Philadelphia Athletics 2nd AL 88-57 .607 2.5 GB

Connie Mack

Player	Gm by Position	B	Age	G	AB	R	H	2B	3B	HR	RBI	BB	SO	SB	Avg	OBP	Slg
O. Schreckengost	C99,1B2	R	32	101	356	30	97	16	3	0	38	17	—	4	.272	.306	.334
Harry Davis	1B149	R	33	149	582	84	155	37	8	8	87	42	—	20	.266	.318	.399
Danny Murphy	2B122	R	30	124	469	51	127	23	3	2	57	30	—	11	.271	.317	.345
Jimmy Collins†	3B98	R	37	102	372	39	102	21	1	0	35	24	—	4	.274	.332	.336
Simon Nicholls	SS82,2B28,3B13	L	24	126	460	75	139	12	2	0	23	24	—	13	.302	.338	.337
Socks Seybold	OF147	R	36	147	564	58	153	29	4	5	92	40	—	10	.271	.324	.363
Topsy Hartsel	OF143	L	33	143	507	93	142	23	6	3	29	106	—	20	.280	.405	.367
Rube Oldring	OF117	R	23	117	441	48	126	27	8	1	40	7	—	29	.286	.305	.390
Monte Cross	SS74	R	37	77	248	37	51	9	5	0	18	39	—	17	.206	.316	.282
Bris Lord	OF53,P1	R	23	57	170	12	31	3	0	1	11	14	—	2	.182	.249	.218
Mike Powers	C59	R	36	59	159	9	29	3	0	0	9	7	—	1	.182	.217	.201
John Knight†	3B38	R	21	40	139	9	29	6	1	0	12	10	—	1	.209	.272	.266
Eddie Collins	SS6	L	20	14	20	0	5	0	0	0	2	0	—	0	.250	.250	.250
Claude Berry	C8	R	27	8	19	2	4	2	0	0	1	2	—	0	.211	.286	.316

Pitcher	T	Age	G	GS	CG	ShO	IP	H	HR	BB	SO	W-L	Sv	ERA
Eddie Plank	L	31	43	40	33	8	343.2	282	5	85	183	24-16	0	2.20
Rube Waddell	L	30	44	33	20	7	284.2	234	2	73	232	19-13	0	2.15
Jimmy Dygert	R	22	42	28	18	5	261.2	200	2	85	151	20-8	1	2.34
Chief Bender	R	23	33	24	20	4	219.1	185	1	34	112	16-8	3	2.05
Jack Coombs	R	24	23	17	10	2	132.2	109	2	64	73	6-9	2	3.12
Charlie Fritz	L	25	1	1	0	0	3.0	0	0	3	1	1-0	0	3.00
Bill Bartley	R	22	15	3	2	0	56.1	44	0	19	16	0-2	0	2.24
Rube Vickers	R	29	10	4	3	1	50.1	44	1	12	21	2-2	0	3.40
George Craig	L	19	2	0	0	0	1.2	2	0	3	0	0-0	0	10.80
Bris Lord	R	23	1	0	0	0	1.0	3	0	0	0	0-0	0	9.00
Sam Hope	R	28	1	0	0	0	0.1	3	0	0	0	0-0	0	0.00

1907 Chicago White Sox 3rd AL 87-64 .576 5.5 GB

Fielder Jones

Player	Gm by Position	B	Age	G	AB	R	H	2B	3B	HR	RBI	BB	SO	SB	Avg	OBP	Slg
Billy Sullivan	C108,2B1	R	32	112	339	30	59	8	4	0	36	21	—	6	.174	.229	.221
Jiggs Donahue	1B157	L	27	157	609	75	158	16	4	0	68	28	—	27	.259	.295	.299
Frank Isbell	2B119,OF5,P1*	L	31	125	486	60	118	19	7	0	41	22	—	22	.243	.281	.311
George Rohe	3B76,2B39,SS30	R	31	144	494	46	105	11	2	2	51	39	—	16	.213	.274	.255
George Davis	SS132	S	36	132	466	59	111	16	2	1	52	47	—	15	.238	.313	.288
Ed Hahn	OF156	L	31	156	592	87	151	9	7	0	45	84	—	17	.255	.359	.294
Fielder Jones	OF154	L	35	154	559	72	146	18	1	0	47	67	—	17	.261	.345	.297
Patsy Dougherty	OF148	L	30	148	533	69	144	17	2	1	59	36	—	33	.270	.322	.315
Lee Quillen	3B48	R	25	49	151	17	29	5	0	0	14	10	—	8	.192	.256	.225
Ed McFarland	C43	R	32	52	138	11	39	9	1	0	8	12	—	3	.283	.340	.362
Lee Tannehill	3B31,SS2	R	26	33	108	9	26	2	0	0	11	8	—	3	.241	.293	.259
Hub Hart	C25	L	29	29	70	6	19	1	0	0	7	5	—	1	.271	.329	.286
Mike Welday	OF15	L	27	24	35	2	8	1	1	0	0	6	—	0	.229	.341	.314
Charlie Hickman†	OF3	R	31	21	23	1	6	2	0	0	1	4	—	0	.261	.370	.348
Jake Atz	3B2	R	27	3	7	0	1	0	0	0	0	0	—	0	.143	.143	.143
Charlie Armbruster†	C1	R	26	1	3	0	0	0	0	0	0	1	—	0	.000	.250	.000

F. Isbell, 1 G at SS

Pitcher	T	Age	G	GS	CG	ShO	IP	H	HR	BB	SO	W-L	Sv	ERA
Ed Walsh	R	26	56	46	37	5	422.1	341	3	87	206	24-18	4	1.60
Frank Smith	R	27	41	37	29	3	310.0	280	3	111	139	22-11	0	2.47
Doc White	L	28	46	35	24	7	291.0	270	3	38	141	27-13	1	2.26
Nick Altrock	L	30	30	21	15	1	213.2	210	3	31	61	8-12	2	2.57
Roy Patterson	R	30	19	13	4	1	96.0	105	0	18	27	4-6	0	2.63
Frank Owen	R	27	11	4	2	0	47.0	43	1	13	15	2-3	0	2.49
Lou Fiene	R	22	6	1	1	0	26.0	30	0	7	15	0-1	1	4.15
Frank Isbell	R	31	1	0	0	0	0.1	0	0	0	0	0-0	1	0.00

1907 Cleveland Bronchos 4th AL 85-67 .559 8.0 GB

Nap Lajoie

Player	Gm by Position	B	Age	G	AB	R	H	2B	3B	HR	RBI	BB	SO	SB	Avg	OBP	Slg
Nig Clarke	C115	L	24	120	390	44	105	19	6	3	33	35	—	3	.269	.333	.372
George Stovall	1B122,3B2	R	28	124	466	38	110	17	6	1	36	18	—	13	.236	.267	.305
Nap Lajoie	2B128,1B9	R	32	137	509	53	152	30	6	2	63	30	—	24	.299	.345	.393
Bill Bradley	3B139	R	29	139	498	48	111	20	1	0	34	35	—	20	.223	.286	.267
Terry Turner	SS139	R	26	148	524	57	127	20	7	0	46	19	—	27	.242	.272	.307
Bill Hinchman	OF148,1B4,2B1	R	24	152	514	62	117	19	9	1	50	47	—	15	.228	.311	.305
Elmer Flick	OF147	L	31	147	549	78	166	15	18	3	58	64	—	41	.302	.386	.412
Joe Birmingham	OF130,SS5	R	22	138	476	55	112	10	9	1	33	16	—	23	.235	.265	.300
Harry Bemis	C51,1B2	R	33	65	172	12	43	7	0	0	19	7	—	5	.250	.283	.291
Pete O'Brien†	2B17,3B12,SS11	L	30	43	145	9	33	5	2	0	6	7	—	1	.228	.263	.290
Harry Bay	OF31	L	29	34	95	14	17	1	1	0	7	10	—	7	.179	.271	.211
Pete Lister	1B22	R	25	22	65	5	18	2	0	0	4	3	—	2	.277	.319	.308
Frank Delahanty	OF15	R	24	15	52	3	9	0	1	0	4	4	—	2	.173	.232	.212
Harry Hinchman	2B15	S	28	15	51	3	11	3	1	0	9	5	—	2	.216	.286	.314
Rabbitt Nill†	3B7,SS4	R	25	12	43	5	12	1	0	0	2	3	—	2	.279	.326	.302
Howard Wakefield	C11	R	23	26	37	4	5	2	0	0	3	3	—	0	.135	.200	.189
Bunk Congalton†	OF6	L	32	9	22	2	4	0	0	0	2	4	—	0	.182	.308	.182

Pitcher	T	Age	G	GS	CG	ShO	IP	H	HR	BB	SO	W-L	Sv	ERA
Addie Joss	R	27	42	38	34	6	338.2	279	3	54	127	27-11	2	1.83
Glenn Liebhardt	R	24	38	34	27	4	280.1	254	1	85	110	18-14	0	2.09
Bob Rhoads	R	27	35	31	23	5	275.0	258	0	84	76	15-14	1	2.29
Jake Thielman	R	28	20	18	18	3	166.0	151	2	34	56	11-8	0	2.33
Otto Hess	L	28	17	14	7	0	93.1	84	1	37	36	6-6	1	2.89
Walter Clarkson†	R	28	17	10	9	1	90.2	77	1	29	32	4-6	0	1.99
Heinie Berger	R	25	14	7	5	1	87.1	74	0	20	50	3-3	0	2.99
Bill Bernhard	R	36	8	4	3	0	42.0	58	0	11	19	0-4	0	3.21
Earl Moore†	R	27	3	2	1	0	19.1	18	0	8	7	1-1	0	4.66

1907 New York Highlanders 5th AL 70-78 .473 21.0 GB

Clark Griffith

Player	Gm by Position	B	Age	G	AB	R	H	2B	3B	HR	RBI	BB	SO	SB	Avg	OBP	Slg
Red Kleinow	C86,1B1	R	27	90	269	30	71	6	4	0	26	24	—	5	.264	.327	.316
Hal Chase	1B121,OF4	R	24	125	498	72	143	23	3	2	68	19	—	32	.287	.315	.357
Jimmy Williams	2B139	R	30	139	504	53	136	17	11	2	63	35	—	14	.270	.319	.359
George Moriarty	3B91,1B22,OF9*	R	23	126	437	51	121	16	5	0	43	25	—	28	.277	.320	.336
Kid Elberfeld	SS118	R	32	120	447	61	121	17	6	0	51	36	—	22	.271	.343	.336
Danny Hoffman	OF135	L	27	136	517	81	131	10	3	5	46	42	—	30	.253	.325	.313
Willie Keeler	OF107	L	35	107	423	50	99	5	2	0	17	15	—	7	.234	.265	.255
Wid Conroy	OF100,SS38	R	30	140	530	58	124	12	11	3	51	30	—	41	.234	.279	.315
Frank LaPorte	3B64,OF63,1B1	R	27	130	470	56	127	20	11	0	48	27	—	10	.270	.317	.360
Ira Thomas	C61,1B2	R	26	80	208	20	40	5	4	1	24	10	—	5	.192	.240	.269
Branch Rickey	OF24,C11,1B7	L	25	52	137	16	25	1	3	0	15	11	—	4	.182	.253	.234
Al Orth	P36,OF1	L	34	44	105	11	34	6	0	1	13	4	—	1	.324	.355	.410
John Bell	OF17	R	26	17	52	4	11	2	1	0	3	3	—	4	.212	.268	.288
Neal Ball	SS11,2B5	R	26	15	44	5	9	1	1	0	4	1	—	2	.205	.222	.273
Walter Blair	C7	R	23	7	22	1	4	0	0	0	1	2	—	0	.182	.250	.182
Baldy Louden	3B3	R	21	4	9	4	1	0	0	0	0	2	—	1	.111	.273	.111
Deacon McGuire†	C1	R	43	1	1	0	0	0	0	0	0	0	—	1	.000	.000	.000

G. Moriarty, 8 G at 2B, 1 G at SS

Pitcher	T	Age	G	GS	CG	ShO	IP	H	HR	BB	SO	W-L	Sv	ERA
Al Orth	R	34	36	33	21	2	248.2	244	2	53	78	14-21	0	2.61
Jack Chesbro	R	33	30	25	17	1	206.0	192	0	46	78	10-10	0	2.53
Slow Joe Doyle	R	25	29	23	15	1	193.2	169	2	67	94	11-11	1	2.65
Bill Hogg	R	25	25	21	13	0	166.2	173	3	83	64	11-8	0	3.08
Doc Newton	L	29	19	15	10	0	133.0	132	0	31	70	7-10	0	3.18
Earl Moore†	R	27	12	9	3	0	64.0	72	1	30	28	2-6	1	3.94
Tex Neuer	L	30	7	6	6	3	54.0	40	1	19	22	4-2	0	2.17
Lew Brockett	R	26	8	4	1	0	46.1	58	1	26	13	1-3	0	6.22
Tom Hughes	R	23	4	3	2	0	27.0	16	0	11	10	2-1	0	2.67
Roy Castleton	L	21	3	2	1	0	16.0	11	1	3	3	1-1	0	2.81
Rube Manning	R	24	1	1	1	0	9.0	8	0	3	3	0-1	0	3.00
Bobby Keefe	R	25	19	3	0	0	57.2	60	1	20	20	4-2	3	2.50
Frank Kitson†	R	37	12	4	3	0	61.0	75	0	17	14	3-1	0	3.10
Walter Clarkson†	R	28	5	2	0	0	17.1	19	1	8	3	1-1	1	6.23
Ray Tift	L	23	4	1	0	0	19.0	33	0	4	6	0-0	0	4.74
Clark Griffith	R	37	4	0	0	0	8.1	15	0	6	5	0-0	0	8.64
Cy Barger	R	22	1	0	0	0	6.0	10	0	1	0	0-0	0	3.00

1907 St. Louis Browns 6th AL 69-83 .454 24.0 GB

Jimmy McAleer

Player	Gm by Position	B	Age	G	AB	R	H	2B	3B	HR	RBI	BB	SO	SB	Avg	OBP	Slg
Tubby Spencer	C63	R	23	71	230	27	61	11	1	1	25	7	—	1	.265	.299	.335
Tom Jones	1B155	R	30	155	549	53	137	17	3	0	34	34	—	24	.250	.298	.291
Harry Niles	2B116,OF1	R	26	120	492	65	142	9	5	2	35	28	—	19	.289	.331	.339
Joe Yeager	3B91,2B17,SS10	R	31	123	436	32	104	21	7	1	44	31	—	11	.239	.294	.326
Bobby Wallace	SS147	R	33	147	538	56	138	20	7	0	70	54	—	16	.257	.328	.320
George Stone	OF155	L	29	155	596	77	191	14	13	4	59	59	—	23	.320	.387	.408
Charlie Hemphill	OF153	L	31	153	603	66	156	20	9	0	38	51	—	14	.259	.319	.322
Ollie Pickering	OF151	L	37	151	576	63	159	15	10	0	60	35	—	15	.276	.321	.337
Roy Hartzell	3B38,2B12,SS2*	L	25	60	220	20	52	3	5	0	13	11	—	7	.236	.285	.295
Jim Stephens	C56	R	23	58	173	15	35	6	3	0	11	15	—	3	.202	.270	.272
Harry Howell	P42,OF2	R	30	44	114	12	27	5	0	2	7	7	—	2	.237	.281	.333
Jim Delahanty†	3B21,OF4,2B2	R	28	33	95	8	21	3	0	0	6	5	—	6	.221	.275	.253
Jack O'Connor	C25	R	38	25	89	2	14	2	0	0	4	0	—	0	.157	.176	.180
Fritz Buelow	C25	R	31	26	75	9	11	1	0	0	1	7	—	0	.147	.220	.160
Kid Butler	2B11,3B5,SS1	R	19	20	59	4	13	2	0	0	6	2	—	1	.220	.246	.254
Emil Frisk		L	32	5	4	0	1	0	0	0	0	1	—	0	.250	.400	.250
Jimmy McAleer		R	42	2	0	0	0	0	0	0	0	0	—	0	—	—	—

R. Hartzell, 2 G at OF

Pitcher	T	Age	G	GS	CG	ShO	IP	H	HR	BB	SO	W-L	Sv	ERA
Harry Howell	R	30	42	35	26	2	316.1	258	3	88	118	16-15	3	1.93
Barney Pelty	R	26	36	31	29	5	273.0	234	1	64	85	12-21	1	2.51
Jack Powell	R	32	32	31	27	4	255.2	229	4	62	96	13-16	0	2.68
Fred Glade	R	31	24	22	18	2	202.0	187	2	45	71	13-9	0	2.67
Bill Dinneen†	R	31	24	16	15	2	155.1	153	3	33	38	7-10	4	2.43
Beany Jacobson†	L	26	7	7	6	0	57.1	55	1	26	16	1-6	0	2.98
Cy Morgan†	R	28	10	6	4	0	55.0	77	3	17	14	2-5	0	6.05
Bill Bailey	L	18	6	5	3	0	48.1	39	0	15	17	4-1	0	2.42
Bill McGill	R	27	2	2	1	0	18.1	22	0	2	8	1-0	0	3.44

1907 Boston Pilgrims 7th AL 59-90 .396 32.5 GB

Cy Young (3-3)/George Huff (2-6)/Bob Unglaub (9-20)/Deacon McGuire (45-61)

Player	Gm by Position	B	Age	G	AB	R	H	2B	3B	HR	RBI	BB	SO	SB	Avg	OBP	Slg
Lou Criger	C75	R	35	75	226	12	41	4	0	0	14	19	—	2	.181	.251	.199
Bob Unglaub	1B139	R	25	139	544	49	138	17	13	1	62	23	—	14	.254	.284	.338
Hobe Ferris	2B150	R	29	150	561	41	135	25	2	4	60	10	—	11	.241	.254	.314
John Knight†	3B92,SS4	R	21	98	360	28	78	10	3	2	29	19	—	8	.217	.256	.278
Heinie Wagner	SS109,2B1,3B1	R	26	111	385	29	82	10	4	2	21	31	—	20	.213	.275	.275
Denny Sullivan	OF143	L	24	144	551	73	135	18	0	1	26	44	—	16	.245	.315	.283
Bunk Congalton†	OF123	L	32	127	496	44	142	11	8	2	47	20	—	13	.286	.318	.353
Jimmy Barrett	OF99	L	32	106	390	52	95	11	6	1	28	38	—	3	.244	.314	.310
Freddy Parent	OF47,SS43,3B7*	R	31	114	409	51	113	19	5	1	26	22	—	12	.276	.321	.355
Al Shaw	C73,1B1	R	32	76	198	10	38	1	3	0	7	18	—	4	.192	.269	.227
Moose Grimshaw	OF23,1B15,SS2	S	31	64	181	19	37	7	2	0	33	16	—	6	.204	.273	.265
Jimmy Collins†	3B41	R	37	41	158	13	46	8	0	0	10	10	—	4	.291	.333	.342
Jack Hoey	OF21	L	25	39	96	7	21	2	1	0	8	1	—	2	.219	.227	.260
Charlie Armbruster†	C21	R	26	23	60	2	6	1	0	0	0	8	—	1	.100	.206	.117
Harry Lord	3B10	L	25	10	38	4	6	1	0	0	3	1	—	1	.158	.179	.184
Chet Chadbourne	OF10	L	22	10	38	0	11	0	0	0	1	7	—	1	.289	.400	.289
Tris Speaker	OF4	L	19	7	19	0	3	0	0	0	1	1	—	0	.158	.200	.158
Bob Peterson	C4	R	22	4	13	1	1	0	0	0	0	0	—	0	.077	.077	.077
Buck Freeman	OF3	L	35	4	12	1	2	0	0	1	2	3	—	0	.167	.333	.417
George Whiteman	OF2	R	24	3	11	0	2	0	0	0	1	0	—	0	.182	.182	.182
Deacon McGuire†		R	43	6	4	1	3	0	0	1	1	0	—	0	.750	.750	1.500

F. Parent, 5 G at 2B

Pitcher	T	Age	G	GS	CG	ShO	IP	H	HR	BB	SO	W-L	Sv	ERA
Cy Young	R	40	43	37	33	6	343.1	286	3	51	147	21-15	2	1.99
George Winter	R	29	35	27	21	4	256.2	198	2	61	88	12-15	1	2.07
Ralph Glaze	R	25	32	21	11	1	182.1	150	4	48	68	9-13	0	2.32
Jesse Tannehill	L	32	18	16	10	2	131.0	131	3	20	29	6-7	1	2.47
Cy Morgan†	R	28	16	13	9	2	114.1	77	1	34	50	7-6	0	1.97
Rube Kroh	L	20	7	5	1	0	34.1	33	0	8	8	0-4	0	2.62
Bill Dinneen†	R	31	5	5	3	0	32.2	42	5	8	8	0-4	0	5.23
Ed Barry	L	24	2	2	1	0	17.1	13	1	5	6	0-1	0	2.08
Fred Burchell	L	27	2	1	0	0	10.0	8	0	2	6	0-1	0	2.70
Beany Jacobson†	L	26	2	1	0	0	2.0	2	0	3	1	0-1	0	9.00
Tex Pruiett	R	24	35	17	6	2	173.2	166	1	59	54	3-11	3	3.11
Joe Harris	R	25	12	5	3	0	59.0	57	0	13	24	0-7	0	3.05
Frank Oberlin†	R	31	12	4	2	0	46.0	48	2	24	18	1-4	0	4.30
Elmer Steele	R	21	4	1	0	0	11.1	11	0	1	10	0-1	0	1.59

1907 Washington Senators 8th AL 49-102 .325 43.5 GB

Joe Cantillon

Player	Gm by Position	B	Age	G	AB	R	H	2B	3B	HR	RBI	BB	SO	SB	Avg	OBP	Slg
John Warner	C64	L	34	72	207	11	53	5	0	0	17	12	—	3	.256	.306	.280
John Anderson	1B61,OF26	S	33	87	333	33	96	12	4	0	44	34	—	19	.288	.359	.348
Jim Delahanty†	2B68,3B27,OF9*	R	28	109	404	44	118	18	7	2	54	36	—	18	.292	.367	.386
Bill Shipke	3B63	R	24	64	189	17	37	3	2	1	9	15	—	6	.196	.262	.249
Dave Altizer	SS78,1B50,OF19	L	30	147	540	60	145	15	5	2	42	34	—	38	.269	.319	.326
Bob Ganley	OF154	L	32	154	605	73	167	10	5	1	35	54	—	40	.276	.337	.314
Charlie Jones	OF111,2B5,1B4*	R	31	121	437	48	116	14	10	0	37	22	—	26	.265	.304	.343
Otis Clymer†	OF51,1B1	S	31	57	206	30	65	5	5	1	16	18	—	18	.316	.382	.403
Rabbitt Nill†	2B39,OF18,3B1	R	25	66	215	21	47	7	3	0	25	15	—	6	.219	.282	.279
Charlie Hickman†	1B30,OF18,2B3*	R	31	60	198	20	55	9	4	1	23	14	—	4	.278	.338	.379
Clyde Milan	OF47	L	20	48	183	22	51	3	3	0	9	8	—	8	.279	.323	.328
Mike Heydon	C57	L	32	62	164	14	30	3	0	0	9	25	—	3	.183	.302	.201
Lave Cross	3B41	R	41	41	161	13	32	8	0	0	10	10	—	3	.199	.246	.248
Nig Perrine	2B24,SS18,3B2	R	22	44	146	13	25	4	1	0	15	13	—	10	.171	.253	.212
Tony Smith	SS51	R	23	51	139	12	26	3	1	0	8	18	—	3	.187	.285	.209
Pete O'Brien†	3B26,SS13,2B1	L	30	39	134	6	25	3	1	0	12	12	—	4	.187	.259	.224
Cliff Blankenship	C24,1B7	R	27	37	102	4	23	2	0	0	6	3	—	3	.225	.248	.245
Harry Schlafly	2B24	R	28	24	74	10	10	0	0	1	4	22	—	7	.135	.347	.176
Bill Kay	OF12	L	29	25	60	8	20	1	1	0	7	0	—	0	.333	.333	.383
Bruno Block	C21	R	22	24	57	3	8	2	1	0	2	2	—	0	.140	.169	.211
Mike Kahoe†	C15	R	33	17	47	3	9	1	0	0	1	0	—	0	.191	.191	.213
Owen Shannon	C4	R	21	4	7	0	1	0	0	0	0	0	—	0	.143	.143	.143

J. Delahanty, 4 G at 1B; C. Jones, 2 G at SS; C. Hickman, 1 G at P

Pitcher	T	Age	G	GS	CG	ShO	IP	H	HR	BB	SO	W-L	Sv	ERA
Charlie Smith	R	27	36	31	21	3	258.2	254	0	51	119	10-20	0	2.61
Casey Patten	L	31	36	29	20	1	237.1	272	3	63	58	12-16	0	3.56
Cy Falkenberg	R	26	32	24	17	1	233.2	195	0	77	108	6-17	1	2.35
Long Tom Hughes	R	28	34	23	18	2	211.0	206	1	47	102	8-13	3	3.11
Oscar Graham	L	28	20	14	6	0	104.0	116	3	29	44	4-9	0	3.98
Walter Johnson	R	19	14	12	11	2	110.1	100	1	20	71	5-9	0	1.88
Henry Gehring	R	26	15	9	8	2	87.0	92	1	14	31	3-7	0	3.31
Frank Oberlin†	R	31	11	8	3	0	48.2	57	0	12	18	2-6	0	4.62
Frank Kitson†	R	37	5	3	2	0	32.0	41	1	9	11	0-1	0	3.94
Sam Lanford	R	21	2	1	0	0	7.0	10	0	5	2	0-0	0	5.14
Bull Durham	R	30	2	0	0	0	5.0	10	0	4	1	0-0	0	12.60
John McDonald	R	24	1	0	0	0	6.0	12	0	2	3	0-0	0	9.00
Charlie Hickman	R	31	1	0	0	0	5.0	4	0	5	2	0-0	0	3.60
Sam Edmondston	L	23	1	0	0	0	3.0	8	0	1	0	0-0	0	9.00
Doc Tonkin	L	25	1	0	0	0	2.2	6	0	5	0	0-0	0	6.75

»1907 Chicago Cubs 1st NL 107-45 .704 —

Frank Chance

Player	Gm by Position	B	Age	G	AB	R	H	2B	3B	HR	RBI	BB	SO	SB	Avg	OBP	Slg
Johnny Kling	C98,1B2	R	32	104	334	44	95	15	8	1	43	27	—	9	.284	.342	.386
Frank Chance	1B109	R	29	111	382	58	112	19	2	1	49	51	—	35	.293	.395	.361
Johnny Evers	2B151	L	25	151	508	66	127	18	4	2	51	38	—	46	.250	.309	.313
Harry Steinfeldt	3B151	R	29	152	542	52	144	25	5	1	70	37	—	19	.266	.323	.336
Joe Tinker	SS113	R	26	117	402	36	89	11	3	1	36	25	—	20	.221	.269	.271
Jimmy Sheckard	OF142	L	28	143	484	76	129	23	1	1	36	76	—	31	.267	.373	.324
Jimmy Slagle	OF135	L	33	136	489	71	126	6	6	0	32	76	—	28	.258	.359	.294
Wildfire Schulte	OF91	L	24	97	342	44	98	14	7	2	32	22	—	7	.287	.339	.386
Solly Hofman	OF69,SS42,1B18*	R	24	134	470	67	126	11	3	1	36	41	—	29	.268	.328	.311
Pat Moran	C59	R	31	65	198	8	45	5	1	1	19	10	—	5	.227	.271	.278
Del Howard†	1B33,OF8	L	29	51	148	10	34	2	2	0	13	6	—	3	.230	.269	.270
Three Finger Brown	P34,OF1	S	30	36	85	6	13	0	2	1	7	1	—	0	.153	.163	.235
Newt Randall†	OF21	R	27	22	78	6	16	4	2	0	4	8	—	2	.205	.279	.308
Kid Durbin	P5,OF5	L	20	11	18	2	6	0	0	0	0	1	—	1	.333	.368	.333
Bill Sweeney†	SS3	R	21	3	10	1	1	0	0	0	1	1	—	1	.100	.182	.100
Mike Kahoe†	C3,1B1	R	33	5	10	0	4	0	0	0	1	0	—	0	.400	.400	.400
Heinie Zimmerman	2B4,SS1,OF1	R	20	5	9	0	2	1	0	0	1	0	—	0	.222	.222	.333
Jack Hardy	C1	R	30	1	4	0	1	0	0	0	0	0	—	0	.250	.250	.250

S. Hofman, 4 G at 3B, 3 G at 2B

Pitcher	T	Age	G	GS	CG	ShO	IP	H	HR	BB	SO	W-L	Sv	ERA
Orval Overall	R	26	36	30	25	8	268.1	201	3	69	141	23-8	3	1.68
Three Finger Brown	R	30	34	27	20	6	233.0	180	2	40	107	20-6	3	1.39
Carl Lundgren	R	27	28	25	21	7	207.0	130	0	92	84	18-7	0	1.17
Jack Pfiester	L	29	30	22	13	3	195.0	143	1	48	90	14-9	0	1.15
Ed Reulbach	R	24	27	22	16	4	192.0	147	1	64	96	17-4	0	1.69
Chick Fraser	R	36	22	15	9	2	138.1	112	1	46	41	8-5	0	2.28
Jack Taylor	R	33	18	13	8	0	123.0	127	0	33	22	7-5	0	3.29
Kid Durbin	L	20	5	1	1	0	16.2	14	0	10	5	0-1	1	5.40

1907 Pittsburgh Pirates 2nd NL 91-63 .591 17.0 GB

Fred Clarke

Player	Gm by Position	B	Age	G	AB	R	H	2B	3B	HR	RBI	BB	SO	SB	Avg	OBP	Slg
George Gibson	C109,1B1	R	26	113	382	28	84	8	7	3	35	18	—	2	.220	.261	.301
Jim Nealon	1B104	R	22	105	381	29	98	10	8	0	47	23	—	11	.257	.301	.325
Ed Abbaticchio	2B147	R	30	147	496	63	130	14	7	2	82	65	—	35	.262	.357	.331
Alan Storke	3B67,1B23,2B7*	R	22	112	357	24	92	6	6	1	39	16	—	6	.258	.295	.317
Honus Wagner	SS138,1B4	R	33	142	515	98	180	38	14	6	82	46	—	61	.350	.408	.513
Fred Clarke	OF144	L	34	148	501	97	145	18	13	2	59	68	—	37	.289	.383	.389
Goat Anderson	OF117,2B5	L	27	127	413	73	85	3	1	1	12	80	—	27	.206	.343	.225
Tommy Leach	OF111,3B33,SS6*	R	29	149	547	102	166	19	12	4	43	40	—	43	.303	.352	.404
Bill Hallman	OF84	L	31	94	302	39	67	6	2	0	15	33	—	21	.222	.305	.255
Tommy Sheehan	3B57,SS10	R	29	75	226	23	62	2	3	0	25	23	—	10	.274	.341	.310
Ed Phelps	C35,1B1	R	28	43	113	11	24	1	0	0	12	9	—	1	.212	.282	.221
Harry Swacina	1B26	R	25	26	95	9	19	1	1	0	10	4	—	1	.200	.240	.232
Otis Clymer†	OF15,1B1	S	31	22	66	8	15	2	0	0	4	5	—	4	.227	.311	.258
Danny Moeller	OF11	S	22	11	42	4	12	1	1	0	3	4	—	2	.286	.348	.357
Harry Smith	C18	R	32	18	38	4	10	1	0	0	1	4	—	0	.263	.364	.289
Bill McKechnie	3B2,2B1	S	20	3	8	0	1	0	0	0	0	0	—	0	.125	.125	.125
Harl Maggert	OF2	L	24	3	6	1	0	0	0	0	0	2	—	1	.000	.250	.000
Billy Kelsey	C2	R	25	2	5	1	2	0	0	0	0	0	—	0	.400	.400	.400
Marc Campbell	SS2	L	22	2	4	0	1	0	0	0	1	1	—	0	.250	.400	.250

A. Storke, 5 G at SS; T. Leach, 1 G at 2B

Pitcher	T	Age	G	GS	CG	ShO	IP	H	HR	BB	SO	W-L	Sv	ERA
Vic Willis	R	31	39	37	27	6	292.2	234	4	69	107	21-11	1	2.34
Lefty Leifield	L	23	40	33	24	6	286.0	270	1	100	112	20-16	1	2.33
Deacon Phillippe	R	35	35	26	17	1	214.0	214	2	36	61	14-11	2	2.61
Sam Leever	R	35	31	24	17	5	216.2	182	3	46	65	14-9	0	1.66
Howie Camnitz	R	25	31	19	15	4	180.0	135	0	59	85	13-8	1	2.15
Nick Maddox	R	20	6	6	6	1	54.0	32	0	13	38	5-1	0	0.83
Mike Lynch†	R	27	7	4	2	0	36.0	37	0	22	9	2-2	0	2.25
Babe Adams	R	25	4	3	1	0	22.0	40	1	3	11	0-2	0	6.95
Bill Otey	L	20	3	2	1	0	16.1	23	1	4	5	0-1	0	4.41
Bill Duggleby†	R	33	9	3	1	1	40.1	34	0	12	4	2-2	0	2.68
Harry Wolter†	R	22	1	0	0	0	2.0	3	0	2	0	0-0	0	4.50
King Brady	R	26	1	0	0	0	2.0	2	0	1	0	0-0	0	0.00
Connie Walsh	—	25	1	0	0	0	1.0	1	0	1	0	0-0	0	9.00

564 Seasons: Team Rosters

1907 Philadelphia Phillies 3rd NL 83-64 .565 21.5 GB — Billy Murray

Player	Gm by Position	B	Age	G	AB	R	H	2B	3B	HR	RBI	BB	SO	SB	Avg	OBP	Slg
Red Dooin	C94,2B1,OF1	R	28	101	313	18	66	8	4	0	14	15	—	10	.211	.252	.262
Kitty Bransfield	1B92	R	32	94	348	25	81	15	2	0	38	14	—	8	.233	.262	.287
Otto Knabe	2B121,OF5	R	23	129	444	67	113	16	9	1	34	52	—	18	.255	.339	.338
Ernie Courtney	3B75,1B48,OF4*	L	32	130	440	42	107	17	4	2	43	55	—	6	.243	.335	.314
Mickey Doolan	SS145	R	27	145	509	33	104	19	7	1	47	25	—	18	.204	.243	.275
John Titus	OF142	L	31	145	523	72	144	23	12	3	63	47	—	9	.275	.345	.382
Sherry Magee	OF139	R	22	140	503	75	165	28	12	4	85	53	—	46	.328	.396	.455
Roy Thomas	OF121	L	33	121	419	70	102	15	3	1	23	83	—	11	.243	.374	.301
Eddie Grant	3B74	L	24	74	268	26	65	4	3	0	19	10	—	10	.243	.272	.280
Fred Jacklitsch	C58,1B6,OF1	R	31	73	202	19	43	7	0	0	17	27	—	7	.213	.312	.248
Fred Osborn	OF36,1B1	L	23	56	163	22	45	2	3	0	9	3	—	4	.276	.298	.325
Kid Gleason	2B26,1B4,SS4*	S	40	36	126	11	18	3	0	0	6	7	—	3	.143	.200	.167
Johnny Lush†	P8,OF4	L	21	17	40	5	8	1	1	0	5	1	—	1	.200	.220	.275
Paul Sentell	SS2,OF1	R	27	3	3	0	0	0	0	0	0	1	—	0	.000	.250	.000

E. Courtney, 2 G at 2B, 2 G at SS; K. Gleason, 1 G at OF

Pitcher	T	Age	G	GS	CG	ShO	IP	H	HR	BB	SO	W-L	Sv	ERA
Frank Corridon	R	26	37	32	23	3	274.0	228	0	89	131	18-14	2	2.46
Tully Sparks	R	32	33	31	24	3	265.0	221	2	51	90	22-8	1	2.00
Lew Moren	R	23	37	31	21	3	255.0	202	3	101	98	11-18	1	2.54
Buster Brown†	R	25	21	16	13	4	130.0	118	0	56	38	9-6	0	2.42
Togie Pittinger	R	35	16	12	8	1	102.0	101	3	35	37	9-5	0	3.00
Johnny Lush†	L	21	8	8	5	2	57.1	48	0	21	20	3-5	0	2.98
George McQuillan	R	22	6	5	5	3	41.0	21	0	11	28	4-0	0	0.66
Lew Richie	R	23	25	12	9	2	117.0	88	0	38	40	6-6	0	1.77
Bill Duggleby†	R	33	5	2	2	0	29.0	43	2	11	8	0-2	0	7.45
Harry Coveleski	L	21	4	0	0	0	20.0	10	0	3	6	1-0	0	0.00
John McCloskey	—	24	3	0	0	0	9.0	15	0	6	3	0-0	0	7.00

1907 New York Giants 4th NL 82-71 .536 25.5 GB — John McGraw

Player	Gm by Position	B	Age	G	AB	R	H	2B	3B	HR	RBI	BB	SO	SB	Avg	OBP	Slg
Roger Bresnahan	C95,1B6,OF2*	R	28	110	328	57	83	9	7	4	38	61	—	15	.253	.380	.360
Dan McGann	1B81	S	35	81	262	29	78	9	1	2	36	29	—	9	.298	.383	.363
Larry Doyle	2B69	L	20	69	227	16	59	3	0	0	16	20	—	3	.260	.320	.273
Art Devlin	3B140,SS3	R	27	143	491	61	136	16	2	1	54	63	—	38	.277	.376	.324
Bill Dahlen	SS143	R	37	143	464	40	96	20	1	0	34	51	—	11	.207	.291	.254
Spike Shannon	OF155	S	29	155	585	104	155	12	5	1	33	82	—	33	.265	.363	.308
Cy Seymour	OF126	L	34	131	473	46	139	25	8	3	75	36	—	21	.294	.350	.400
George Browne	OF121	L	31	127	458	54	119	11	10	5	37	31	—	15	.260	.308	.360
Frank Bowerman	C62,1B29	R	38	96	311	31	81	8	2	0	32	17	—	11	.260	.309	.299
Sammy Strang	OF70,2B13,3B7*	S	30	123	306	56	77	20	4	4	30	60	—	21	.252	.388	.382
Tommy Corcoran	2B62	R	38	62	226	21	60	9	2	0	24	7	—	9	.265	.288	.323
Jack Hannifin	1B29,3B10,SS9*	R	24	56	149	16	34	7	3	1	15	15	—	6	.228	.303	.336
Danny Shay	2B13,SS9,OF2	—	30	35	79	10	15	1	1	1	6	12	—	5	.190	.304	.266
Fred Merkle	1B15	R	18	15	47	0	12	1	0	0	5	1	—	0	.255	.271	.277
Matty Fitzgerald	C6	R	26	7	15	1	2	1	0	0	1	0	—	0	.133	.133	.200
Harry Curtis	C6	—	24	6	9	2	2	0	0	0	1	2	—	2	.222	.364	.222
Ham Wade	OF1	R	26	1	0	0	0	0	0	0	0	0	—	0	—	1.000	—
Monte Pfyl	1B1	L	23	1	0	0	0	0	0	0	0	0	—	0	—	—	—

R. Bresnahan, 1 G at 3B; S. Strang, 5 G at 1B, 1 G at SS; J. Hannifin, 2 G at OF

Pitcher	T	Age	G	GS	CG	ShO	IP	H	HR	BB	SO	W-L	Sv	ERA
Christy Mathewson	R	28	41	36	31	8	315.0	250	5	53	178	24-12	2	2.00
Joe McGinnity	R	36	47	34	23	3	310.1	320	6	58	120	18-18	4	3.16
Red Ames	R	24	39	26	17	2	233.1	184	4	108	146	10-12	1	2.16
Hooks Wiltse	L	26	33	21	14	3	190.1	171	3	48	79	13-12	2	2.18
Luther Taylor	R	32	28	21	11	3	171.0	145	1	46	56	11-7	1	2.42
Mike Lynch†	R	27	12	10	7	0	72.0	68	3	30	34	3-6	1	3.38
Roy Beecher	R	23	2	2	2	0	14.0	17	0	6	5	0-2	0	2.57
George Ferguson	R	20	15	5	4	0	64.0	63	2	20	37	3-2	1	2.11
Henry Mathewson	R	20	1	0	0	0	1.0	1	0	0	0	0-0	1	0.00

1907 Brooklyn Dodgers 5th NL 65-83 .439 40.0 GB — Patsy Donovan

Player	Gm by Position	B	Age	G	AB	R	H	2B	3B	HR	RBI	BB	SO	SB	Avg	OBP	Slg
Lew Ritter	C89	R	31	93	271	15	55	6	1	0	17	18	—	5	.203	.255	.232
Tim Jordan	1B147	L	28	147	485	43	133	15	8	4	53	74	—	10	.274	.371	.363
Whitey Alperman	2B115,3B14,SS12	R	27	141	558	44	130	23	16	2	39	13	—	5	.233	.266	.342
Doc Casey	3B141	S	37	141	527	55	122	19	3	0	19	34	—	16	.231	.282	.279
Phil Lewis	SS136	R	23	136	475	52	118	11	1	0	30	23	—	16	.248	.286	.276
Billy Maloney	OF144	L	29	144	502	51	115	7	10	0	32	31	—	25	.229	.287	.283
Harry Lumley	OF118	L	26	127	454	47	121	23	11	9	66	31	—	18	.267	.316	.425
Emil Batch	OF102,3B2,2B1*	R	27	116	388	38	96	10	3	0	31	23	—	7	.247	.291	.289
John Hummel	2B44,OF33,1B12*	R	24	107	342	41	80	12	3	3	31	26	—	8	.234	.294	.313
Bill Bergen	C51	R	29	51	138	2	22	3	0	0	14	1	—	1	.159	.165	.181
Al Burch†	OF36,2B1	L	23	40	120	12	35	2	2	0	12	11	—	5	.292	.351	.342
Jack McCarthy	OF25	L	38	25	91	4	20	2	0	0	8	2	—	4	.220	.237	.242
John Butler	C28,OF1	R	27	30	79	6	10	1	0	0	2	9	—	0	.127	.216	.139
Ed McLane	OF1	—	25	1	2	0	0	0	0	0	0	0	—	0	.000	.333	.000
Jerry Hurley	C1	R	32	1	2	0	0	0	0	0	0	1	—	0	.000	.333	.000
Patsy Donovan	OF1	L	42	1	1	0	0	0	0	0	0	0	—	0	.000	.000	.000

E. Batch, 1 G at SS; J. Hummel, 8 G at SS

Pitcher	T	Age	G	GS	CG	ShO	IP	H	HR	BB	SO	W-L	Sv	ERA
Nap Rucker	L	22	37	30	26	4	275.1	242	3	80	131	15-13	0	2.06
George Bell	R	32	35	27	20	3	263.2	222	1	77	88	8-16	1	2.25
Elmer Stricklett	R	30	29	26	25	4	229.2	211	1	65	69	12-14	0	2.27
Jim Pastorius	L	25	28	26	20	4	222.0	218	2	77	70	16-12	0	2.35
Harry McIntire	R	28	28	22	19	3	199.2	178	6	79	49	7-15	0	2.39
Doc Scanlan	R	26	17	15	10	2	107.0	90	1	61	59	6-8	0	3.20
Weldon Henley	R	26	7	7	5	0	56.0	54	2	21	11	1-5	0	3.05
Jesse Whiting	—	28	1	0	0	0	3.0	3	0	3	2	0-0	0	12.00

1907 Cincinnati Reds 6th NL 66-87 .431 41.5 GB — Ned Hanlon

Player	Gm by Position	B	Age	G	AB	R	H	2B	3B	HR	RBI	BB	SO	SB	Avg	OBP	Slg
Larry McLean	C89,1B13	R	25	113	374	35	108	9	9	0	54	13	—	4	.289	.313	.361
John Ganzel	1B143	R	33	145	531	61	135	20	16	2	64	29	—	9	.254	.297	.363
Miller Huggins	2B156	S	28	156	561	64	139	12	4	1	31	83	—	28	.248	.346	.289
Mike Mowrey	3B127,SS11	R	23	138	448	43	113	16	6	1	44	35	—	10	.252	.308	.321
Hans Lobert	SS142,3B5	R	25	148	537	61	132	9	12	1	41	37	—	30	.246	.299	.313
Mike Mitchell	OF146,1B2	R	27	148	558	64	163	17	12	3	47	37	—	17	.292	.339	.382
Art Kruger	OF96	R	26	100	317	25	74	10	9	0	28	18	—	10	.233	.285	.322
Fred Odwell	OF84,2B1	L	34	94	274	24	74	5	7	0	24	22	—	10	.270	.336	.339
Lefty Davis	OF70	L	32	73	266	28	61	5	5	1	25	23	—	9	.229	.293	.297
John Kane	OF42,3B25,SS6*	R	24	79	262	40	65	9	4	3	19	22	—	20	.248	.325	.347
Admiral Schlei	C67,1B3,OF2	R	29	84	246	28	67	3	2	0	27	28	—	5	.272	.347	.301
Dode Paskert	OF16	R	25	16	50	10	14	4	0	1	8	2	—	2	.280	.333	.420
Mike O'Neill	OF9	R	29	9	29	5	2	0	2	0	2	2	—	1	.069	.129	.207
Chick Autry	OF7	L	22	7	25	3	5	0	0	0	0	1	—	0	.200	.231	.200
Harry Wolter†	OF4	L	22	4	15	1	2	0	0	0	1	0	—	0	.133	.133	.133
Bill McCarthy	C3	—	21	3	8	1	1	0	0	0	0	0	—	0	.125	.125	.125
Pete Lamer	C1	—	33	1	2	0	0	0	0	0	0	0	—	0	.000	.000	.000
Eddie Tiemeyer		R	22	1	0	1	0	0	0	0	0	1	—	0	—	1.000	—

J. Kane, 2 G at 2B

Pitcher	T	Age	G	GS	CG	ShO	IP	H	HR	BB	SO	W-L	Sv	ERA
Bob Ewing	R	34	41	37	32	2	332.2	279	2	85	147	17-19	0	1.73
Andy Coakley	R	24	37	30	21	1	265.1	269	1	79	89	17-16	1	2.34
Jake Weimer	L	33	29	26	19	3	209.0	165	6	63	67	11-14	0	2.41
Roy Hitt	L	20	21	18	14	2	153.1	143	2	56	63	6-10	0	3.40
Del Mason	R	23	25	17	13	1	146.0	144	2	55	45	5-12	0	3.14
Fred Smith	R	28	18	9	5	0	85.1	90	0	24	19	2-7	1	2.85
Sea Lion Hall	R	21	11	8	5	0	68.0	51	0	43	25	4-2	0	2.51
Bob Spade	R	30	3	3	3	1	27.0	21	0	9	7	1-2	0	1.00
Billy Campbell	L	33	3	3	3	0	21.0	19	0	3	4	3-0	0	2.14
Bill Essick	R	25	3	2	2	0	21.2	23	0	8	7	0-2	0	2.91
Cotton Minahan	R	24	2	2	1	0	14.0	12	0	13	4	0-2	0	1.29
Frank Leary	R	26	2	1	0	0	8.0	7	0	6	4	0-1	0	1.13

1907 Boston Beaneaters 7th NL 58-90 .392 47.0 GB — Fred Tenney

Player	Gm by Position	B	Age	G	AB	R	H	2B	3B	HR	RBI	BB	SO	SB	Avg	OBP	Slg
Tom Needham	C78,1B1	R	28	86	260	19	51	6	2	1	19	18	—	4	.196	.264	.246
Fred Tenney	1B149	L	35	150	554	83	151	18	8	0	26	82	—	15	.273	.371	.334
Claude Ritchey	2B144	S	33	144	499	45	127	17	4	2	51	50	—	8	.255	.329	.317
Dave Brain	3B130	R	28	133	509	60	142	24	9	10	56	29	—	10	.279	.324	.420
Al Bridwell	SS140	L	23	140	509	49	111	8	2	0	26	61	—	17	.218	.309	.242
Ginger Beaumont	OF149	L	30	150	580	67	187	19	14	4	62	37	—	25	.322	.366	.424
Johnny Bates	OF120	L	24	126	447	52	116	18	12	2	49	39	—	11	.260	.329	.367
Newt Randall†	OF73	R	27	75	258	16	55	6	3	0	15	19	—	4	.213	.285	.260
Sam Brown	C63,1B2	R	29	70	208	17	40	6	0	0	14	12	—	0	.192	.250	.221
Bill Sweeney†	3B23,SS15,OF11*	R	21	58	191	24	50	8	0	0	18	15	—	8	.262	.316	.272
Del Howard†	OF45,2B3	L	29	50	187	20	51	4	2	1	13	11	—	11	.273	.330	.332
Frank Burke	OF36	—	27	43	129	6	23	0	1	0	8	11	—	3	.178	.243	.194
Izzy Hoffman	OF19	L	32	19	86	17	24	3	1	0	3	6	—	2	.279	.326	.337
Jim Ball	C10	R	23	10	36	3	6	2	0	0	3	2	—	0	.167	.211	.222
Jess Orndorff	C5	S	26	5	17	0	2	0	0	0	0	0	—	0	.118	.118	.118
Joe Knotts	C3	R	23	3	8	0	0	0	0	0	0	1	—	0	.000	.111	.000
Oscar Westerberg	SS2	S	24	2	6	0	2	0	0	0	1	1	—	0	.333	.429	.333
Tom Asmussen	C2	—	30	2	5	0	0	0	0	0	0	0	—	0	.000	.000	.000
Bob Brush	1B1	—	32	2	2	0	0	0	0	0	0	0	—	0	.000	.000	.000

B. Sweeney, 5 G at 2B, 1 G at 1B

Pitcher	T	Age	G	GS	CG	ShO	IP	H	HR	BB	SO	W-L	Sv	ERA
Irv Young	L	29	40	32	22	3	245.1	287	5	58	86	10-23	1	3.96
Gus Dorner	R	30	36	31	24	2	271.1	253	4	92	85	12-16	0	3.12
Vive Lindaman	R	29	34	28	24	2	260.0	252	10	108	90	11-15	1	3.63
Patsy Flaherty	L	31	27	25	23	0	217.0	197	4	59	34	12-15	0	2.70
Big Jeff Pfeffer	R	25	19	16	12	1	144.0	129	3	61	65	6-8	0	3.00
Jake Boultes	R	22	24	12	11	0	139.2	140	1	50	49	5-9	0	2.71
Sam Frock	R	24	5	3	3	1	33.1	28	1	11	12	1-2	0	2.97
Frank Barberich	R	25	2	2	1	0	12.1	19	0	5	1	1-1	0	5.84
Rube Dessau	R	24	2	2	1	0	9.1	13	0	10	1	0-1	0	10.61
Ernie Lindemann	R	24	1	1	0	0	6.1	6	0	4	3	0-0	0	5.68

1907 St. Louis Cardinals 8th NL 52-101 .340 55.5 GB

John McCloskey

Player	Gm by Position	B	Age	G	AB	R	H	2B	3B	HR	RBI	BB	SO	SB	Avg	OBP	Slg
Doc Marshall	C83	R	31	84	268	19	54	8	2	2	18	12	—	2	.201	.246	.269
Ed Konetchy	1B91	R	21	91	331	34	83	11	8	3	30	26	—	13	.251	.317	.360
Pug Bennett	2B83,3B3	R	33	87	324	20	72	8	2	0	21	21	—	7	.222	.272	.259
Bobby Byrne	3B148,SS1	R	22	149	559	55	143	11	5	0	29	35	—	21	.256	.307	.293
Ed Holly	SS147,2B3	R	27	150	545	55	125	18	3	1	40	36	—	16	.229	.283	.279
Red Murray	OF131	R	23	132	485	46	127	10	10	7	46	24	—	23	.262	.301	.367
Shad Barry	OF81	R	28	81	294	30	73	5	2	0	19	28	—	4	.248	.320	.279
Jack Burnett	OF59	—	17	59	206	18	49	8	4	0	12	15	—	5	.238	.296	.316
Art Hoelskoetter	2B72,1B27,C8*	R	24	119	397	21	98	6	3	2	28	27	—	5	.247	.298	.292
Pete Noonan	C69	R	25	74	237	19	53	7	3	1	16	9	—	3	.224	.252	.291
John Kelly	OF52	—	28	53	197	12	37	5	0	0	6	13	—	7	.188	.245	.213
Tom O'Hara	OF47	—	21	48	173	11	41	2	1	0	5	12	—	1	.237	.286	.260
Al Burch†	OF48	L	23	48	154	18	35	3	1	0	5	17	—	7	.227	.304	.260
Jake Beckley	1B32	L	39	32	115	6	24	3	0	0	7	1	—	0	.209	.222	.235
Johnny Lush†	P20,OF7	L	21	27	82	6	23	2	3	0	5	5	—	4	.280	.322	.378
Harry Wolter†	OF12,P3	L	22	16	47	4	16	0	0	0	6	3	—	1	.340	.380	.340
Buck Hopkins	OF15	L	24	15	44	7	6	3	0	0	3	10	—	2	.136	.333	.205
Harry Arndt	1B4,3B3	—	28	11	32	3	6	1	0	0	2	1	—	0	.188	.212	.219
Al Shaw	OF8	L	26	9	25	2	7	0	0	0	1	3	—	1	.280	.379	.280
Joe Delahanty	OF6	R	31	7	22	3	7	0	0	1	2	0	—	3	.318	.318	.455
Forrest Crawford	SS7	L	26	7	22	0	5	0	0	0	3	2	—	0	.227	.292	.227
John Baxter	1B6	L	30	6	21	1	4	0	0	0	0	0	—	0	.190	.190	.190

A. Hoelskoetter, 8 G at OF, 2 G at P, 2 G at 3B

Pitcher	T	Age	G	GS	CG	ShO	IP	H	HR	BB	SO	W-L	Sv	ERA
Stoney McGlynn	R	35	45	39	33	3	352.1	329	6	112	109	14-25	1	2.91
Ed Karger	L	24	38	31	28	6	310.0	251	2	64	132	15-19	1	2.03
Fred Beebe	R	26	31	29	24	4	238.1	192	1	109	141	7-19	0	2.72
Johnny Lush†	L	21	20	19	15	4	144.0	132	2	42	71	7-10	0	2.50
Art Fromme	R	23	23	16	13	2	145.2	138	3	67	67	5-13	0	2.90
Buster Brown†	R	25	9	8	6	0	63.2	57	0	45	17	1-6	0	3.39
Bugs Raymond	R	25	8	6	6	1	64.2	56	3	21	34	2-4	0	1.67
Harry Wolter†	R	22	3	3	1	0	23.0	27	1	18	8	1-2	0	4.30
Charlie Shields	L	27	3	2	0	0	6.2	12	0	7	1	0-2	0	9.45
Carl Druhot	L	24	1	1	0	0	2.1	3	0	4	1	0-1	0	15.43
Art Hoelskoetter	R	24	2	0	0	0	11.0	9	0	10	8	0-0	0	5.73

»1908 Detroit Tigers 1st AL 90-63 .588 —

Hughie Jennings

Player	Gm by Position	B	Age	G	AB	R	H	2B	3B	HR	RBI	BB	SO	SB	Avg	OBP	Slg
Boss Schmidt	C121	S	27	122	419	45	111	14	3	1	38	16	—	5	.265	.297	.320
Claude Rossman	1B138	L	27	138	524	45	154	33	13	2	71	27	—	8	.294	.330	.418
Red Downs	2B82,3B1	R	24	84	289	29	64	10	3	1	35	5	—	2	.221	.237	.287
Bill Coughlin	3B119	R	29	119	405	32	87	5	1	0	23	23	—	10	.215	.269	.232
Germany Schaefer	SS68,2B58,3B29	R	31	153	584	96	151	20	10	3	52	37	—	40	.259	.304	.342
Matty McIntyre	OF151	L	28	151	569	105	168	24	13	0	28	83	—	20	.295	.392	.383
Ty Cobb	OF150	L	21	150	581	88	188	36	20	4	108	34	—	39	.324	.367	.475
Sam Crawford	OF134,1B17	L	28	152	591	102	184	33	16	7	80	37	—	15	.311	.355	.457
Charley O'Leary	SS64,2B1	R	25	65	211	21	53	9	3	0	17	9	—	4	.251	.295	.322
Davy Jones	OF32	L	28	56	121	17	25	2	1	0	10	13	—	11	.207	.284	.240
Ira Thomas	C29	R	27	40	101	6	31	1	0	0	8	5	—	0	.307	.346	.317
Red Killefer	2B16,SS7,3B4	R	23	28	75	9	16	1	0	0	11	3	—	4	.213	.253	.227
Donie Bush	SS20	S	20	20	68	13	20	1	1	0	4	7	—	2	.294	.360	.338
Fred Payne	C16,OF2	R	27	20	45	3	3	0	0	0	2	3	—	1	.067	.176	.067
Clay Perry	3B5	R	26	5	11	0	2	0	0	0	0	0	—	0	.182	.250	.182

Pitcher	T	Age	G	GS	CG	ShO	IP	H	HR	BB	SO	W-L	Sv	ERA
Ed Summers	R	23	40	32	23	5	301.0	271	3	55	103	24-12	1	1.64
George Mullin	R	27	39	30	26	1	290.2	301	1	71	121	17-13	0	3.10
Wild Bill Donovan	R	31	29	28	25	6	242.2	210	2	53	141	18-7	0	2.08
Ed Killian	L	31	27	23	15	0	180.2	170	3	53	47	12-9	1	2.99
Ed Willett	R	24	30	22	18	2	197.1	186	2	60	77	15-8	1	2.28
Ed Siever	L	31	11	9	4	1	61.2	74	0	13	23	2-6	0	3.50
George Winter†	R	30	7	6	5	0	56.1	49	0	7	25	1-5	1	1.60
Herm Malloy	R	23	3	2	2	0	17.0	20	1	4	8	0-2	0	3.71
George Suggs	R	25	6	1	1	0	27.0	32	0	2	8	1-1	1	1.67

1908 Cleveland Bronchos 2nd AL 90-64 .584 0.5 GB

Nap Lajoie

Player	Gm by Position	B	Age	G	AB	R	H	2B	3B	HR	RBI	BB	SO	SB	Avg	OBP	Slg
Nig Clarke	C90	L	25	97	290	34	70	8	6	1	27	30	—	6	.241	.315	.321
George Stovall	1B132,OF5,SS1	R	29	138	534	71	156	29	6	2	45	17	—	14	.292	.316	.380
Nap Lajoie	2B156,1B1	R	33	157	581	77	168	32	6	2	74	47	—	15	.289	.352	.375
Bill Bradley	3B118,SS30	R	30	148	548	70	133	24	7	1	46	29	—	18	.243	.297	.318
Bill Hinchman	OF75,SS51,1B4	R	25	137	464	55	107	23	8	6	59	38	—	9	.231	.301	.353
Josh Clarke	OF131	L	29	131	492	70	119	8	4	1	21	76	—	37	.242	.348	.280
Joe Birmingham	OF121,SS1	R	23	122	413	32	88	10	1	2	38	19	—	15	.213	.253	.257
Wilbur Good	OF42	L	22	46	154	23	43	1	3	1	14	13	—	7	.279	.351	.344
George Perring	SS48,3B41	R	23	89	310	23	67	8	5	0	19	16	—	8	.216	.255	.274
Harry Bemis	C76,1B2	R	34	91	277	23	62	9	1	0	33	7	—	14	.224	.253	.264
Terry Turner	OF36,SS17	R	27	60	201	21	48	11	1	0	19	15	—	18	.239	.298	.303
Charlie Hickman	OF28,1B20,2B1	R	32	65	197	16	46	6	1	2	16	9	—	2	.234	.271	.305
Dave Altizer†	OF24,SS3	L	31	29	89	11	19	1	2	0	5	7	—	7	.213	.278	.270
Elmer Flick	OF9	L	32	9	35	4	8	1	1	0	2	3	—	0	.229	.289	.314
Rabbitt Nill	SS6,OF3,2B1	R	26	10	23	3	5	0	0	0	1	0	—	0	.217	.217	.217
Grover Land	C8	R	23	8	16	1	3	0	0	0	2	0	—	0	.188	.188	.188
Otto Hess	P4,OF4	L	29	8	14	0	0	0	0	0	0	1	—	0	.000	.067	.000
Denny Sullivan†	OF2	L	25	3	6	0	0	0	0	0	0	0	—	0	.000	.000	.000
Homer Davidson	C5,OF1	R	23	9	4	2	0	0	0	0	0	0	—	1	.000	.000	.000
Deacon McGuire†	1B1	R	44	1	4	0	1	1	0	0	2	0	—	0	.250	.250	.500
Harry Bay		L	30	2	0	0	0	0	0	0	0	0	—	0	—	—	—

Pitcher	T	Age	G	GS	CG	ShO	IP	H	HR	BB	SO	W-L	Sv	ERA
Addie Joss	R	28	42	35	29	9	325.0	232	2	30	130	24-11	2	1.16
Bob Rhoads	R	28	37	30	20	1	270.0	229	2	73	62	18-12	0	1.77
Glenn Liebhardt	R	25	39	26	19	3	262.0	222	2	81	146	15-16	0	2.20
Heinie Berger	R	26	29	24	16	0	199.1	152	1	66	101	13-8	0	2.12
Charlie Chech	R	30	27	20	14	4	165.2	136	2	34	51	11-7	0	1.74
Jake Thielman†	R	29	11	8	5	0	61.2	59	2	9	15	4-3	0	3.65
Cy Falkenberg†	R	27	8	7	2	0	46.1	52	1	10	17	2-4	0	3.88
Bill Lattimore	L	24	4	4	1	1	24.0	24	0	7	5	1-2	0	4.50
Walter Clarkson	R	29	2	1	0	0	3.1	6	0	2	1	0-0	0	10.80
Jack Ryan	R	23	8	1	1	0	35.2	27	3	2	7	1-1	1	2.27
Slim Foster	R	—	6	1	1	0	21.0	16	1	12	11	1-0	2	2.14
Otto Hess	L	29	4	0	0	0	7.0	11	0	1	2	0-0	0	5.14
Jack Graney	L	22	2	0	0	0	3.1	6	0	1	0	0-0	0	5.40

1908 Chicago White Sox 3rd AL 88-64 .579 1.5 GB

Fielder Jones

Player	Gm by Position	B	Age	G	AB	R	H	2B	3B	HR	RBI	BB	SO	SB	Avg	OBP	Slg
Billy Sullivan	C137	R	33	137	430	40	82	8	4	0	29	22	—	15	.191	.235	.228
Jiggs Donahue	1B83	L	28	93	304	22	62	8	2	0	22	25	—	14	.204	.271	.243
George Davis	2B95,SS23,1B4	S	37	128	419	41	91	14	1	0	26	41	—	22	.217	.298	.255
Lee Tannehill	3B136,SS5	R	27	141	482	44	104	15	3	0	35	25	—	6	.216	.257	.259
Freddy Parent	SS118	R	32	119	391	28	81	7	5	0	35	50	—	9	.207	.300	.251
Fielder Jones	OF149	L	36	149	529	92	134	11	7	1	50	86	—	26	.253	.366	.306
Patsy Dougherty	OF128	L	31	138	482	68	134	11	6	0	45	58	—	47	.278	.367	.326
Ed Hahn	OF119	L	32	122	447	58	112	12	8	0	21	39	—	11	.251	.329	.313
John Anderson	OF90,1B9	S	34	123	355	36	93	17	1	0	47	30	—	21	.262	.321	.315
Frank Isbell	1B65,2B18	L	32	84	320	31	79	15	3	1	49	19	—	18	.247	.297	.322
Jake Atz	2B46,SS18,3B1	R	28	83	206	24	40	3	0	0	27	31	—	9	.194	.311	.209
Doc White	P41,OF3	L	29	51	109	12	25	1	0	0	10	12	—	4	.229	.306	.239
Billy Purtell	3B25	R	22	26	69	3	9	2	0	0	3	2	—	2	.130	.155	.159
Al Shaw	C29	R	33	32	49	0	4	1	0	0	2	2	—	0	.082	.118	.102
Art Weaver	C15	—	29	15	35	1	7	1	0	0	1	1	—	0	.200	.222	.229
O. Schreckengost†	C6	R	33	6	16	1	3	0	0	0	0	1	—	0	.188	.235	.188

Pitcher	T	Age	G	GS	CG	ShO	IP	H	HR	BB	SO	W-L	Sv	ERA
Ed Walsh	R	27	66	49	42	11	464.0	343	2	56	269	40-15	6	1.42
Doc White	L	29	41	37	24	5	296.0	267	3	69	126	18-13	0	2.55
Frank Smith	R	28	41	35	24	3	297.2	213	2	73	129	16-17	1	2.03
Frank Owen	R	28	25	14	5	1	140.0	142	2	37	48	6-7	0	3.41
Nick Altrock	L	31	23	13	8	1	136.0	127	2	18	21	5-7	2	2.71
Andy Nelson	L	—	2	1	0	0	9.0	11	0	4	1	0-0	0	2.00
Lou Fiene	R	23	1	1	1	0	9.0	9	0	1	3	0-1	0	4.00
Moxie Manuel	—	26	18	6	3	0	60.1	52	0	25	25	3-4	1	3.28
Fred Olmstead	R	26	1	0	0	0	2.0	6	0	1	1	0-0	0	13.50

1908 St. Louis Browns 4th AL 83-69 .546 6.5 GB

Jimmy McAleer

Player	Gm by Position	B	Age	G	AB	R	H	2B	3B	HR	RBI	BB	SO	SB	Avg	OBP	Slg
Tubby Spencer	C88	R	24	91	286	19	60	6	1	0	28	17	—	1	.210	.254	.238
Tom Jones	1B155	R	31	155	549	43	135	14	2	1	50	30	—	18	.246	.290	.284
Jimmy Williams	2B148	R	31	148	539	63	127	20	7	4	53	55	—	7	.236	.310	.321
Hobe Ferris	3B148	R	30	148	555	54	150	26	7	2	74	14	—	6	.270	.291	.353
Bobby Wallace	SS137	R	34	137	487	59	123	24	4	1	60	52	—	5	.253	.327	.324
George Stone	OF148	L	30	148	588	89	165	21	8	5	31	55	—	20	.281	.345	.369
Danny Hoffman	OF99	L	28	99	363	41	91	9	7	1	25	23	—	17	.251	.304	.322
Roy Hartzell	OF82,SS18,3B7*	L	26	115	422	41	112	5	6	2	32	19	—	24	.265	.302	.320
Charlie Jones	OF72	R	32	74	263	37	61	11	2	0	17	14	—	14	.232	.279	.289
Al Schweitzer	OF55	R	25	64	182	22	53	4	2	1	14	20	—	6	.291	.374	.352
Jim Stephens	C45	R	24	47	150	14	30	4	1	0	6	9	—	0	.200	.255	.240
Emmett Heidrick	OF25	L	31	26	93	8	20	2	2	1	6	1	—	3	.215	.223	.312
Dode Criss	OF11,P9,1B1	L	23	64	82	15	28	6	0	0	14	9	—	1	.341	.407	.415
Syd Smith†	C24	R	24	27	76	6	14	4	0	0	5	4	—	2	.184	.225	.237
Bert Blue†	C8	R	30	11	25	2	9	1	2	0	1	3	—	0	.360	.429	.560
Joe Yeager	2B4,SS1	R	32	10	15	3	5	1	0	0	1	1	—	2	.333	.474	.400

R. Hartzell, 4 G at 2B

Pitcher	T	Age	G	GS	CG	ShO	IP	H	HR	BB	SO	W-L	Sv	ERA
Rube Waddell	L	31	43	36	25	5	285.2	223	0	90	232	19-14	3	1.89
Harry Howell	R	31	41	32	27	2	324.1	279	1	70	117	18-18	1	1.89
Jack Powell	R	33	33	32	23	6	256.0	208	1	47	85	16-13	0	2.11
Bill Dinneen	R	32	27	16	11	1	167.0	133	2	53	39	14-7	0	2.10
Barney Pelty	R	27	20	13	7	2	122.0	104	0	32	36	7-4	0	1.99
Bill Graham	L	24	21	13	7	0	117.1	104	0	32	47	6-7	0	2.30
Bill Bailey	L	19	22	12	7	0	106.2	85	2	50	42	3-5	0	3.04
Dode Criss	R	23	9	1	0	0	18.0	15	1	13	9	0-1	0	6.50

566 Seasons: Team Rosters

1908 Boston Pilgrims 5th AL 75-79 .487 15.5 GB

Deacon McGuire (53-62)/Fred Lake (22-17)

Player	Gm by Position	B	Age	G	AB	R	H	2B	3B	HR	RBI	BB	SO	SB	Avg	OBP	Slg
Lou Criger	C84	R	36	84	237	12	45	4	2	0	25	13	—	1	.190	.232	.224
Jake Stahl†	1B78	R	29	78	258	29	64	9	11	0	23	20	—	14	.248	.338	.368
Amby McConnell	2B126,SS3	L	25	140	502	77	140	10	6	2	43	38	—	31	.279	.343	.335
Harry Lord	3B144	L	26	145	558	61	145	15	6	2	37	22	—	23	.260	.298	.319
Heinie Wagner	SS153	R	27	153	526	62	130	11	5	1	46	27	—	20	.247	.288	.293
Doc Gessler	OF126	L	27	128	435	55	134	13	14	3	63	51	—	19	.308	.394	.423
Jack Thoney	OF101	R	28	109	416	58	106	5	9	2	30	13	—	16	.255	.282	.325
Denny Sullivan†	OF97	L	25	101	355	33	85	7	8	0	25	14	—	14	.239	.276	.304
Gavy Cravath	OF77,1B5	R	27	94	277	43	71	10	11	1	34	38	—	6	.256	.354	.383
Bob Unglaub†	1B72	R	26	72	266	23	70	11	3	1	25	7	—	6	.263	.287	.338
Frank LaPorte†	2B27,3B12,OF5	R	28	62	156	14	37	1	3	0	15	12	—	3	.237	.296	.282
Bill Carrigan	C47,1B3	R	24	57	149	13	35	5	2	0	14	3	—	1	.235	.255	.295
Tris Speaker	OF31	L	20	31	116	12	26	2	2	0	9	4	—	3	.224	.262	.276
Pat Donahue	C32,1B3	L	23	35	86	8	17	2	0	1	6	9	—	0	.198	.289	.256
Jim McHale	OF19	R	32	21	67	9	15	2	2	0	7	4	—	4	.224	.278	.313
Ed McFarland	C13	R	33	19	48	5	10	2	1	0	4	1	—	0	.208	.224	.292
Jack Hoey	OF11	L	26	13	43	5	7	0	0	0	3	0	—	1	.163	.163	.163
Harry Niles†	2B8,SS2	R	27	17	33	4	9	0	0	1	3	6	—	3	.273	.400	.364
Walter Carlisle	OF3	S	24	3	10	0	1	0	0	0	0	1	—	1	.100	.182	.100
Jimmy Barrett	OF2	L	33	2	8	0	1	0	0	0	1	1	—	0	.125	.222	.125
Larry Gardner	3B2	L	22	2	6	0	3	0	0	0	1	0	—	0	.500	.500	.500
Harry Ostdiek	C1	R	27	1	3	0	0	0	0	0	0	0	—	0	.000	.000	.000
Deacon McGuire†		R	44	1	1	0	0	0	0	0	0	0	—	0	.000	.000	.000

Pitcher	T	Age	G	GS	CG	ShO	IP	H	HR	BB	SO	W-L	Sv	ERA
Cy Young	R	41	36	33	30	3	299.0	230	1	37	150	21-11	2	1.26
Cy Morgan	R	29	30	26	17	2	205.0	166	7	90	99	14-13	1	2.46
Eddie Cicotte	R	24	39	24	17	2	207.1	198	0	59	95	11-12	2	2.43
Fred Burchell	L	28	31	19	9	0	179.2	161	2	65	94	10-8	0	2.96
George Winter†	R	30	22	17	8	0	147.2	150	3	36	55	4-14	0	3.05
Elmer Steele	R	22	16	13	9	1	118.0	85	1	13	37	5-7	0	1.83
Frank Arellanes	R	26	11	8	6	1	79.0	60	1	18	33	4-3	0	1.82
Doc McMahon	—	21	1	1	1	0	9.0	14	0	0	3	1-0	0	3.00
King Brady	R	27	1	1	1	1	9.0	8	0	0	3	1-0	0	0.00
Jesse Tannehill†	L	33	1	1	0	0	5.0	4	0	3	2	0-0	0	3.60
Casey Patten†	L	32	1	1	0	0	3.0	8	0	1	0	0-1	0	15.00
Tex Pruiett	R	25	13	6	1	1	58.2	55	1	21	28	1-7	2	1.99
Ralph Glaze	R	26	10	3	2	0	34.2	43	1	5	13	2-2	0	3.38
Joe Wood	R	18	6	2	1	1	22.2	14	0	16	11	1-1	0	2.38
Charlie Hartman	—	19	1	0	0	0	2.0	1	0	2	1	0-0	0	4.50
Jake Thielman†	R	29	1	0	0	0	0.2	3	1	0	0	0-0	0	40.50

1908 Philadelphia Athletics 6th AL 68-85 .444 22.0 GB

Connie Mack

Player	Gm by Position	B	Age	G	AB	R	H	2B	3B	HR	RBI	BB	SO	SB	Avg	OBP	Slg
O. Schreckengost†	C65,1B1	R	33	71	207	16	46	7	1	0	16	6	—	1	.222	.248	.266
Harry Davis	1B147	R	34	147	513	65	127	23	9	5	62	61	—	20	.248	.332	.357
Danny Murphy	OF83,2B56,1B2	R	31	142	525	51	139	28	6	4	66	32	—	16	.265	.309	.364
Jimmy Collins	3B115	R	38	115	433	34	94	14	3	0	30	20	—	5	.217	.258	.263
Simon Nicholls	SS120,2B23,3B7	L	25	150	550	58	119	17	3	4	31	35	—	14	.216	.265	.280
Topsy Hartsel	OF129	L	34	129	460	73	112	16	6	4	29	93	—	15	.243	.371	.330
Rube Oldring	OF116	R	24	116	434	38	96	14	2	1	39	18	—	13	.221	.267	.270
Jack Coombs	OF47,P26	S	25	78	220	24	56	9	5	1	23	9	—	6	.255	.287	.355
Eddie Collins	2B47,SS28,OF10	L	21	102	330	39	90	18	7	1	40	16	—	8	.273	.312	.379
Mike Powers	C60,1B2	R	37	62	172	8	31	6	1	0	7	5	—	1	.180	.217	.227
Jack Barry	2B20,SS14,3B3	R	21	40	135	13	30	4	3	0	8	10	—	5	.222	.291	.296
Socks Seybold	OF34	R	37	48	130	5	28	2	0	0	3	12	—	2	.215	.287	.231
Syd Smith†	C31,1B6,OF1	R	24	46	128	8	26	8	0	1	10	4	—	0	.203	.233	.289
Frank Manush	3B20,2B2	R	24	23	77	6	12	2	1	0	0	2	—	2	.156	.188	.208
Herbie Moran†	OF19	L	24	19	59	4	9	0	0	0	4	6	—	1	.153	.242	.153
Scotty Barr	2B11,3B4,OF2*	R	21	19	56	4	8	2	0	0	1	3	—	0	.143	.200	.179
Jack Lapp	C13	L	23	13	35	4	5	0	1	0	1	5	—	0	.143	.268	.200
Amos Strunk	OF11	L	19	12	34	4	8	1	0	0	0	4	—	0	.235	.316	.265
Home Run Baker	3B9	L	22	9	31	5	9	3	0	0	2	0	—	0	.290	.290	.387
Jack Fox	OF8	R	23	9	30	2	6	0	0	0	0	0	—	2	.200	.200	.200
Shag Shaughnessy	OF8	R	25	8	29	2	9	0	0	0	1	2	—	3	.310	.355	.310
Joe Jackson	OF5	L	18	5	23	0	3	0	0	0	3	0	—	0	.130	.130	.130
Bert Blue†	C6	R	30	6	19	2	3	0	0	0	1	0	—	0	.158	.158	.158
Ben Egan	C2	R	24	2	6	1	1	1	0	0	0	1	—	0	.167	.286	.333

S. Barr, 1 G at 1B

Pitcher	T	Age	G	GS	CG	ShO	IP	H	HR	BB	SO	W-L	Sv	ERA
Rube Vickers	R	30	53	34	21	6	317.0	264	0	71	156	18-19	2	2.21
Eddie Plank	L	32	34	28	21	4	244.2	202	1	46	135	14-16	1	2.17
Jimmy Dygert	R	23	41	27	15	5	238.2	184	3	97	164	11-15	1	2.87
Jack Coombs	R	25	26	18	10	4	153.0	130	1	64	80	7-5	0	2.00
Biff Schlitzer	R	23	24	18	11	2	131.0	110	1	45	57	6-8	0	3.16
Chief Bender	R	24	18	17	14	2	138.2	121	1	21	85	8-9	1	1.75
Jack Flater	R	27	5	3	3	0	39.1	35	0	12	8	1-3	0	2.06
Al Kellogg	L	21	3	3	2	0	17.0	20	1	9	8	0-2	0	5.82
Harry Krause	L	20	4	2	2	0	21.0	20	0	4	10	1-1	0	2.57
Gus Salve	L	22	2	1	1	0	15.1	17	1	9	6	0-1	0	4.11
Doc Martin	R	20	1	1	0	0	2.0	2	0	3	2	0-1	0	13.50
Nick Carter	R	29	14	6	2	0	60.2	58	1	17	17	2-5	0	2.97
Bert Maxwell	R	21	4	0	0	0	13.0	23	0	9	7	0-0	0	11.08
Eddie Files	R	25	2	0	0	0	9.0	8	0	3	6	0-0	0	6.00

1908 Washington Senators 7th AL 67-85 .441 22.5 GB

Joe Cantillon

Player	Gm by Position	B	Age	G	AB	R	H	2B	3B	HR	RBI	BB	SO	SB	Avg	OBP	Slg
Gabby Street	C128	R	25	131	394	31	81	12	7	1	32	40	—	5	.206	.289	.279
Jerry Freeman	1B154	L	28	154	531	45	134	15	5	1	45	36	—	6	.252	.304	.305
Jim Delahanty	2B80	R	29	83	287	33	91	11	4	1	30	24	—	16	.317	.376	.394
Bill Shipke	3B110,2B1	R	25	111	341	40	71	7	8	0	20	38	—	15	.208	.297	.276
George McBride	SS155	R	27	155	518	47	120	10	6	0	34	41	—	12	.232	.292	.274
Bob Ganley	OF150	L	33	150	549	61	131	19	9	1	36	45	—	30	.239	.299	.311
Clyde Milan	OF122	L	21	130	485	55	116	10	12	1	32	38	—	29	.239	.304	.315
Ollie Pickering	OF98	L	38	113	373	45	84	7	4	2	30	28	—	13	.225	.285	.282
Otis Clymer	OF82,2B13,3B2	S	32	110	368	32	93	11	4	1	35	20	—	19	.253	.291	.313
Bob Unglaub†	3B39,2B27,1B4	R	26	72	276	23	85	10	5	0	29	8	—	8	.308	.327	.380
Dave Altizer†	2B38,3B16,1B4*	L	31	67	205	19	46	1	1	0	18	13	—	8	.224	.274	.239
John Warner	C41,1B1	L	35	51	116	8	28	2	1	0	8	8	—	7	.241	.313	.276
Bob Edmundson	OF24	R	29	26	80	5	15	4	1	0	2	7	—	0	.188	.261	.263
Eli Cates	P19,2B3	R	31	40	59	5	11	1	1	0	3	6	—	0	.186	.273	.237
Mike Kahoe	C11	R	34	17	27	1	5	1	0	0	0	0	—	0	.185	.185	.222

D. Altizer, 1 G at SS

Pitcher	T	Age	G	GS	CG	ShO	IP	H	HR	BB	SO	W-L	Sv	ERA
Long Tom Hughes	R	29	43	31	24	3	276.1	224	3	77	165	18-15	4	2.21
Walter Johnson	R	20	36	30	23	6	256.1	194	0	53	160	14-14	1	1.65
Charlie Smith	R	28	26	23	14	1	183.0	166	2	60	83	9-13	1	2.41
Bill Burns	L	28	23	19	11	2	164.0	135	3	18	55	6-11	0	1.70
Burt Keeley	R	28	28	15	12	1	169.2	173	3	48	68	6-11	1	2.97
Eli Cates	R	31	19	10	7	0	113.2	112	3	32	33	4-8	0	2.53
Jesse Tannehill†	L	33	10	9	5	0	71.2	77	0	23	14	2-4	0	3.77
Roy Witherup	R	21	6	6	4	0	48.1	51	0	8	31	2-4	0	2.98
Casey Patten†	L	32	4	3	1	0	18.0	25	0	6	6	0-2	0	3.50
Cy Falkenberg†	R	27	17	8	5	1	82.2	70	2	21	34	6-2	0	1.96
Henry Gehring	R	27	3	1	0	0	5.0	9	0	2	0	0-1	0	14.40

1908 New York Highlanders 8th AL 51-103 .331 39.5 GB

Clark Griffith (24-32)/Kid Elberfeld (27-71)

Player	Gm by Position	B	Age	G	AB	R	H	2B	3B	HR	RBI	BB	SO	SB	Avg	OBP	Slg
Red Kleinow	C89,2B2	R	28	96	279	16	47	3	2	1	13	22	—	5	.168	.237	.204
Hal Chase	1B98,2B3,OF3*	R	25	106	405	50	104	11	3	1	36	15	—	27	.257	.285	.306
Harry Niles†	2B85,OF7	R	27	96	361	43	90	14	6	4	24	25	—	18	.249	.305	.355
Wid Conroy	3B119,2B12,OF10	R	31	141	531	44	126	22	3	1	39	14	—	23	.237	.258	.296
Neal Ball	SS130,2B1	R	27	132	446	34	110	16	2	0	38	21	—	32	.247	.284	.291
Charlie Hemphill	OF142	L	32	142	505	62	150	12	9	0	44	59	—	42	.297	.374	.356
Willie Keeler	OF88	L	36	91	323	38	85	3	1	1	14	31	—	14	.263	.337	.288
Jake Stahl†	OF68,1B6	R	29	75	274	34	70	18	5	2	42	11	—	16	.255	.304	.380
George Moriarty	1B52,3B28,OF10*	R	24	101	348	25	82	12	1	0	27	11	—	22	.236	.269	.276
Walter Blair	C60,OF9,1B3	R	24	76	211	9	40	5	1	1	13	11	—	4	.190	.237	.237
Irish McIlveen	OF44	L	27	44	169	17	36	3	3	0	8	14	—	6	.213	.277	.266
Frank LaPorte†	2B26,OF11	R	28	39	145	7	38	3	4	1	15	8	—	3	.262	.301	.359
Frank Delahanty	OF36	R	25	37	125	12	32	1	2	0	10	10	—	9	.256	.316	.296
Queenie O'Rourke	OF14,SS11,2B4*	R	24	34	108	5	25	1	0	0	3	4	—	4	.231	.259	.241
Jack Chesbro	P45,1B1	R	34	45	102	8	18	2	1	0	6	0	—	0	.176	.184	.216
Jeff Sweeney	C25,1B1,OF1	R	19	32	82	4	12	2	0	0	2	5	—	0	.146	.195	.171
Birdie Cree	OF21	R	25	21	78	5	21	0	2	0	4	7	—	1	.269	.345	.321
Earle Gardner	2B20	R	24	20	75	7	16	2	0	0	4	1	—	0	.213	.234	.240
Kid Elberfeld	SS17	R	33	19	56	11	11	3	0	0	5	6	—	1	.196	.328	.250
Mike Donovan	3B5	R	26	5	19	2	5	1	0	0	2	0	—	0	.263	.263	.316

H. Chase, 1 G at P, 1 G at 3B; G. Moriarty, 8 G at 2B; Q. O'Rourke, 3 G at 3B

Pitcher	T	Age	G	GS	CG	ShO	IP	H	HR	BB	SO	W-L	Sv	ERA
Jack Chesbro	R	34	45	31	20	3	288.2	271	6	67	124	14-20	1	2.93
Joe Lake	R	27	38	27	19	2	269.1	252	6	77	118	9-22	0	3.17
Rube Manning	R	25	41	26	19	2	245.0	228	4	86	113	13-16	1	2.94
Bill Hogg	R	26	24	21	7	0	152.1	155	4	63	72	4-15	0	3.01
Al Orth	R	35	21	17	8	1	139.1	134	4	30	22	2-13	0	3.42
Doc Newton	L	30	23	13	6	1	88.1	78	0	41	49	4-6	1	2.95
Pete Wilson	L	22	6	6	4	1	39.0	27	0	33	28	3-3	0	3.46
Fred Glade	R	32	5	5	2	0	32.0	30	0	14	11	0-4	0	4.22
Jack Warhop	R	23	5	4	3	0	36.1	40	0	8	11	1-2	0	4.46
Andy O'Connor	R	23	1	1	1	0	8.0	15	0	7	5	0-1	0	10.13
Slow Joe Doyle	R	26	12	4	2	1	48.0	42	1	14	20	1-1	0	2.63
Harry Billiard	R	24	6	0	0	0	17.0	15	1	14	10	0-0	0	2.65
Hippo Vaughn	L	20	2	0	0	0	2.1	1	0	4	2	0-0	0	3.86
Hal Chase	L	25	1	0	0	0	0.1	0	0	0	0	0-0	0	0.00

»1908 Chicago Cubs 1st NL 99-55 .643 —

Frank Chance

Player	Gm by Position	B	Age	G	AB	R	H	2B	3B	HR	RBI	BB	SO	SB	Avg	OBP	Slg
Johnny Kling	C117,OF6,1B2	R	33	126	424	51	117	23	5	4	59	21	—	16	.276	.315	.382
Frank Chance	1B126	R	30	129	452	65	123	27	4	2	55	37	—	27	.272	.338	.363
Johnny Evers	2B122,OF1	L	26	126	416	83	125	19	6	0	37	66	—	36	.300	.402	.375
Harry Steinfeldt	3B150	R	30	150	539	63	130	20	6	1	62	36	—	12	.241	.294	.306
Joe Tinker	SS157	R	27	157	548	67	146	23	14	6	68	32	—	30	.266	.307	.392
Jimmy Sheckard	OF115	L	29	115	403	54	93	18	3	2	22	62	—	18	.231	.336	.305
Wildfire Schulte	OF102	L	25	102	386	42	91	20	2	1	43	29	—	15	.236	.294	.306
Jimmy Slagle	OF101	L	34	104	352	38	78	4	1	0	26	43	—	17	.222	.306	.239
Solly Hofman	OF50,1B37,2B22*	R	25	120	411	55	100	15	5	2	42	33	—	15	.243	.309	.319
Del Howard	OF81,1B5	L	30	96	315	42	88	7	3	1	26	23	—	11	.279	.338	.330
Pat Moran	C45	R	32	50	150	12	39	5	1	0	12	13	—	6	.260	.323	.307
Heinie Zimmerman	2B20,OF8,3B1*	R	21	46	113	17	33	4	1	0	9	1	—	2	.292	.298	.345
Jack Hayden	OF11	L	27	11	45	3	9	2	0	0	2	1	—	2	.200	.217	.244
Kid Durbin	OF11	L	21	14	28	3	7	1	0	0	0	2	—	0	.250	.323	.286
Doc Marshall†	C4,OF3	R	32	12	20	4	6	0	1	0	3	0	—	0	.300	.300	.400
Vin Campbell		L	20	1	1	0	0	0	0	0	0	0	—	0	.000	.000	.000

S. Hofman, 9 G at 3B; H. Zimmerman, 1 G at SS

Pitcher	T	Age	G	GS	CG	ShO	IP	H	HR	BB	SO	W-L	Sv	ERA
Ed Reulbach	R	25	46	35	25	7	297.2	227	4	106	133	24-7	1	2.03
Three Finger Brown	R	31	44	31	27	9	312.1	214	1	49	123	29-9	5	1.47
Jack Pfiester	L	30	33	29	18	3	252.0	204	1	70	117	12-10	0	2.00
Orval Overall	R	27	37	27	16	4	225.0	165	3	78	167	15-11	4	1.92
Chick Fraser	R	37	26	17	11	2	162.2	141	4	61	66	11-9	2	2.27
Carl Lundgren	R	28	23	15	9	1	138.2	149	5	56	38	6-9	0	4.22
Andy Coakley†	R	25	4	3	2	1	20.1	14	0	6	7	2-0	0	0.89
Rube Kroh	L	21	2	1	0	0	12.0	9	0	4	11	0-0	0	1.50
Bill Mack	L	23	2	0	0	0	6.1	5	1	1	2	0-0	0	2.84
Carl Spongberg	R	24	1	0	0	0	7.0	9	1	6	4	0-0	0	9.00

1908 Pittsburgh Pirates 2nd NL 98-56 .636 1.0 GB

Fred Clarke

Player	Gm by Position	B	Age	G	AB	R	H	2B	3B	HR	RBI	BB	SO	SB	Avg	OBP	Slg
George Gibson	C140	R	27	143	486	37	111	19	4	2	45	19	—	4	.228	.260	.296
Harry Swacina	1B50	R	26	53	176	7	38	6	1	0	13	5	—	4	.216	.238	.261
Ed Abbaticchio	2B144	R	31	146	500	43	125	16	7	1	61	58	—	22	.250	.336	.316
Tommy Leach	3B150,OF2	R	30	152	583	93	151	24	16	5	41	54	—	24	.259	.324	.381
Honus Wagner	SS151	R	34	151	568	100	201	39	19	10	109	54	—	53	.354	.415	.542
Fred Clarke	OF151	L	35	151	551	83	146	18	15	2	53	65	—	24	.265	.349	.363
Chief Wilson	OF144	L	24	144	529	47	120	8	7	3	43	22	—	12	.227	.260	.285
Roy Thomas†	OF101	L	34	102	386	52	99	11	10	1	24	49	—	11	.256	.348	.345
Alan Storke	1B49,3B6,2B1	R	23	64	202	20	51	5	3	1	12	9	—	4	.252	.284	.322
Jim Kane	1B40	L	26	55	145	16	35	3	3	0	22	12	—	5	.241	.299	.303
Spike Shannon†	OF32	S	30	32	127	10	25	0	2	0	12	9	—	5	.197	.250	.228
Danny Moeller	OF27	S	23	36	109	14	21	3	1	0	9	9	—	4	.193	.254	.239
Warren Gill	1B25	R	29	27	76	10	17	0	1	0	14	11	—	3	.224	.366	.250
Beals Becker†	OF17	L	21	20	65	4	10	0	1	0	0	2	—	2	.154	.191	.185
Ed Phelps	C20	R	29	34	64	3	15	2	2	0	11	2	—	0	.234	.269	.328
Charlie Starr	2B12,SS5,3B2	—	29	20	59	8	11	2	0	0	8	13	—	6	.186	.342	.220
Paddy O'Connor	C4	R	28	12	16	1	3	0	0	0	2	0	—	0	.188	.188	.188
Hunky Shaw		S	23	1	1	0	0	0	0	0	0	0	—	0	.000	.000	.000
John Sullivan	C1	R	35	1	1	0	0	0	0	0	0	0	—	0	.000	.000	.000
Cy Neighbors	OF1	R	27	1	0	0	0	0	0	0	0	0	—	0	—	—	—

Pitcher	T	Age	G	GS	CG	ShO	IP	H	HR	BB	SO	W-L	Sv	ERA
Vic Willis	R	32	41	38	25	7	304.2	239	2	69	97	23-11	0	2.07
Nick Maddox	R	21	36	32	22	4	260.2	209	5	90	70	23-8	1	2.28
Howie Camnitz	R	26	38	26	17	3	236.2	182	6	69	118	16-9	2	1.56
Lefty Leifield	L	24	34	26	18	5	218.2	168	1	86	87	15-14	2	2.10
Sam Leever	R	36	38	20	14	4	192.2	179	1	41	28	15-7	2	2.10
Tom McCarthy†	R	24	2	1	0	0	6.0	3	0	6	1	0-0	0	0.00
Irv Young†	L	30	16	7	3	1	89.2	73	1	21	31	4-3	1	2.01
Harley Young†	R	24	8	3	0	0	48.1	40	0	10	17	0-2	0	2.23
Deacon Phillippe	R	36	5	0	0	0	12.0	20	0	3	1	0-0	0	11.25
Bob Vail	R	26	4	1	0	0	15.0	15	0	7	9	1-2	0	6.00
Chick Brandom	R	21	3	1	1	0	17.0	13	0	4	8	1-0	1	0.53
Homer Hillebrand	L	28	1	0	0	0	1.0	1	0	0	1	0-0	0	0.00

1908 New York Giants 2nd NL 98-56 .636 1.0 GB

John McGraw

Player	Gm by Position	B	Age	G	AB	R	H	2B	3B	HR	RBI	BB	SO	SB	Avg	OBP	Slg
Roger Bresnahan	C139	R	29	140	449	70	127	25	3	1	54	83	—	14	.283	.401	.359
Fred Tenney	1B156	L	36	156	583	101	149	20	1	2	49	72	—	17	.256	.344	.304
Larry Doyle	2B102	L	21	104	377	65	116	16	9	0	33	22	—	17	.308	.354	.398
Art Devlin	3B157	R	28	157	534	59	135	18	4	2	45	62	—	19	.253	.346	.313
Al Bridwell	SS147	L	24	147	467	53	133	14	1	0	46	52	—	20	.285	.364	.319
Mike Donlin	OF155	L	30	155	593	71	198	26	13	6	106	23	—	30	.334	.364	.452
Cy Seymour	OF155	L	35	156	587	60	157	23	2	5	92	30	—	18	.267	.306	.339
Spike Shannon†	OF74	S	30	77	268	34	60	2	1	1	21	28	—	13	.224	.314	.250
Moose McCormick†	OF65	L	27	73	252	31	76	16	3	0	32	4	—	6	.302	.315	.389
Buck Herzog	2B42,SS12,3B4*	R	22	64	160	38	48	6	2	0	11	36	—	16	.300	.448	.363
Tom Needham	C47	R	29	54	91	8	19	3	0	0	11	12	—	0	.209	.339	.242
Shad Barry†	OF31	R	29	37	67	5	10	1	1	0	5	9	—	1	.149	.260	.194
Sammy Strang	2B14,OF5,SS3	S	31	28	53	8	5	0	0	0	2	23	—	5	.094	.385	.094
Fred Merkle	1B11,OF5,2B1*	R	19	38	41	6	11	2	1	1	7	4	—	0	.268	.333	.439
Dave Brain†	2B3,OF3,3B2*	R	29	11	17	2	3	0	0	0	1	2	—	1	.176	.263	.176
Josh Devore	OF2	L	20	5	6	1	1	0	0	0	2	1	—	1	.167	.286	.167
Fred Snodgrass	C3	R	20	6	4	2	1	0	0	0	1	0	—	1	.250	.250	.250
Steve Evans	OF1	L	23	2	2	0	1	0	0	0	0	0	—	0	.500	.500	.500
Jack Hannifin†	OF1	R	25	1	2	0	0	0	0	0	0	0	—	0	.000	.000	.000
Art Wilson		R	22	1	0	0	0	0	0	0	0	0	—	0	—	—	—

B. Herzog, 1 G at OF; F. Merkle, 1 G at 3B; D. Brain, 1 G at SS

Pitcher	T	Age	G	GS	CG	ShO	IP	H	HR	BB	SO	W-L	Sv	ERA
Christy Mathewson	R	29	56	44	34	11	390.2	285	5	42	259	37-11	5	1.43
Hooks Wiltse	L	27	44	38	30	7	330.0	266	4	73	118	23-14	2	2.24
Doc Crandall	R	20	32	24	13	0	214.2	198	3	59	77	12-12	2	2.93
Joe McGinnity	R	37	37	20	7	5	186.0	192	8	37	55	11-7	5	2.27
Luther Taylor	R	33	27	15	6	1	127.2	127	5	34	50	8-5	2	2.33
Red Ames	R	25	18	15	5	0	114.1	96	0	27	81	7-4	1	1.81
Rube Marquard	L	21	1	1	0	0	5.0	6	0	2	2	0-1	0	3.60
Bill Malarkey	R	29	15	0	0	0	35.0	31	1	10	12	0-2	2	2.57
Roy Beecher	R	24	2	0	0	0	5.2	11	0	3	0	0-0	1	7.94
Bull Durham	R	31	1	0	0	0	2.0	2	0	1	2	0-0	0	9.00

1908 Philadelphia Phillies 4th NL 83-71 .539 16.0 GB

Billy Murray

Player	Gm by Position	B	Age	G	AB	R	H	2B	3B	HR	RBI	BB	SO	SB	Avg	OBP	Slg
Red Dooin	C132	R	29	133	435	28	108	17	4	0	41	17	—	20	.248	.283	.306
Kitty Bransfield	1B143	R	33	144	527	53	160	25	7	3	71	23	—	30	.304	.335	.395
Otto Knabe	2B151	R	24	151	555	63	121	26	8	0	27	49	—	27	.218	.290	.294
Eddie Grant	3B134,SS13	L	25	147	598	69	146	13	8	0	32	35	—	27	.244	.289	.293
Mickey Doolan	SS129	R	28	129	445	29	104	25	4	2	49	17	—	5	.234	.267	.321
Fred Osborn	OF152	L	24	152	555	62	148	19	12	2	44	30	—	16	.267	.305	.355
John Titus	OF149	L	32	149	539	75	154	24	5	2	48	53	—	27	.286	.365	.360
Sherry Magee	OF142	R	23	143	508	79	144	30	16	2	57	49	—	40	.283	.359	.417
Ernie Courtney	3B22,1B13,2B5*	L	33	60	160	14	29	3	0	0	6	15	—	1	.181	.260	.200
Fred Jacklitsch	C30	R	32	37	86	6	19	3	0	0	7	14	—	3	.221	.337	.256
Dave Shean	SS14	R	24	14	48	4	7	2	0	0	2	1	—	1	.146	.180	.188
Wally Clement	OF8	L	26	16	36	0	8	3	0	0	1	0	—	2	.222	.222	.306
Roy Thomas†	OF6	L	34	6	24	2	4	0	0	0	0	2	—	0	.167	.231	.167
Moose McCormick†	OF5	L	27	11	22	0	2	0	0	0	2	2	—	0	.091	.167	.091
Charlie Johnson	OF4	L	23	6	16	2	4	0	1	0	2	1	—	0	.250	.333	.375
Kid Gleason	2B1,OF1	S	41	2	1	0	0	0	0	0	0	0	—	0	.000	.000	.000
Pep Deininger	OF1	L	30	1	0	0	0	0	0	0	0	0	—	0	—	—	—

E. Courtney, 2 G at SS

Pitcher	T	Age	G	GS	CG	ShO	IP	H	HR	BB	SO	W-L	Sv	ERA
George McQuillan	R	23	48	42	32	7	359.2	263	1	91	114	23-17	2	1.53
Tully Sparks	R	33	33	31	24	2	263.1	251	3	51	85	16-15	2	2.60
Frank Corridon	R	27	27	24	18	2	208.1	178	0	48	50	14-10	1	2.51
Lew Moren	R	24	28	16	9	4	154.0	146	1	49	72	8-9	0	2.92
Bill Foxen	L	24	22	16	10	2	147.1	126	2	53	52	7-7	0	1.95
Lew Richie	R	24	25	15	13	2	157.2	125	1	49	58	7-10	1	1.83
Harry Coveleski	L	22	6	5	5	2	43.2	29	0	12	22	4-1	0	1.24
Harry Hoch	R	21	3	3	2	0	26.0	20	0	13	4	2-1	0	2.77
Earl Moore	R	28	3	3	3	1	26.0	20	0	8	16	2-1	0	0.00
Buster Brown	R	26	3	0	0	0	7.0	9	0	5	3	0-0	0	2.57

1908 Cincinnati Reds 5th NL 73-81 .474 26.0 GB

John Ganzel

Player	Gm by Position	B	Age	G	AB	R	H	2B	3B	HR	RBI	BB	SO	SB	Avg	OBP	Slg
Admiral Schlei	C88	R	30	92	300	31	66	6	4	1	22	22	—	2	.220	.278	.277
John Ganzel	1B108	R	34	112	388	32	97	16	10	1	53	19	—	6	.250	.289	.351
Miller Huggins	2B135	S	29	135	498	65	119	14	5	0	23	58	—	30	.239	.321	.287
Hans Lobert	3B99,SS35,OF21	R	26	155	570	71	167	17	18	4	63	46	—	47	.293	.348	.407
Rudy Hulswitt	SS118,2B1	R	31	119	386	27	88	5	7	1	28	30	—	7	.228	.287	.285
John Kane	OF127,2B1	R	25	130	455	61	97	11	7	3	23	43	—	30	.213	.298	.288
Mike Mitchell	OF118,1B1	R	28	119	406	41	90	9	6	1	37	46	—	18	.222	.304	.281
Dode Paskert	OF116	R	26	118	395	40	96	14	4	1	36	27	—	25	.243	.298	.306
Larry McLean	C69,1B19	R	26	99	309	24	67	9	4	1	28	15	—	2	.217	.258	.282
Mike Mowrey	3B56,SS3,OF3*	R	24	77	227	17	50	9	1	0	23	12	—	5	.220	.266	.269
Doc Hoblitzell	1B32	R	19	32	114	8	29	3	2	0	8	7	—	2	.254	.309	.316
Bob Bescher	OF32	S	24	32	114	16	31	5	5	0	17	9	—	10	.272	.336	.404
Dick Bayless	OF19	L	24	19	71	7	16	1	0	1	3	6	—	0	.225	.304	.282
Dick Egan	2B18	R	24	18	68	8	14	3	1	0	5	2	—	7	.206	.229	.279
Dave Brain†	OF16	R	29	16	55	4	6	0	0	0	1	8	—	0	.109	.222	.109
Tom Daley	OF13	L	23	14	46	5	5	0	0	0	1	3	—	1	.109	.180	.109
Bob Coulson	OF6	R	21	8	18	3	6	1	1	0	1	3	—	0	.333	.429	.500
Ducky Pearce	C2	R	23	2	2	0	0	0	0	0	0	0	—	0	.000	.000	.000
Bill McGilvray		L	25	2	2	0	0	0	0	0	0	0	—	0	.000	.000	.000

M. Mowrey, 1 G at 2B

Pitcher	T	Age	G	GS	CG	ShO	IP	H	HR	BB	SO	W-L	Sv	ERA
Bob Ewing	R	35	37	32	23	4	293.2	247	5	57	95	17-15	3	2.21
Bob Spade	R	31	35	28	22	2	249.1	230	2	85	74	17-12	1	2.74
Andy Coakley†	R	25	32	28	20	4	242.1	219	3	64	61	8-18	2	1.86
Billy Campbell	L	34	35	24	19	2	221.1	203	3	44	73	12-13	2	2.60
Jake Weimer	L	34	15	15	9	2	116.2	110	2	50	36	8-7	0	2.39
Jean Dubuc	R	19	15	9	7	1	85.1	62	2	41	32	5-6	0	2.74
Jack Rowan	R	21	8	7	4	1	49.1	46	0	16	24	3-3	0	1.82
Jack Doscher	L	27	7	4	3	0	44.1	31	1	22	7	1-3	0	1.83
Jake Volz	R	30	7	4	1	0	22.2	16	1	12	6	1-2	0	3.57
Marty O'Toole	R	19	3	2	1	0	15.0	15	0	7	5	1-0	0	2.40
Tom McCarthy†	R	24	1	1	0	0	3.2	6	0	3	3	0-1	0	9.82
Ralph Savidge	R	29	4	1	1	0	21.0	18	0	8	7	0-1	0	2.57
Bill Tozer	R	25	4	0	0	0	10.2	11	0	4	5	0-0	0	1.69
Bert Sincock	L	20	1	0	0	0	4.2	3	0	0	1	0-0	0	3.86
Charlie Rhodes†	R	23	1	0	0	0	4.0	1	0	2	4	0-0	0	0.00

1908 Boston Beaneaters 6th NL 63-91 .409 36.0 GB

Joe Kelley

Player	Gm by Position	B	Age	G	AB	R	H	2B	3B	HR	RBI	BB	SO	SB	Avg	OBP	Slg
Frank Bowerman	C63,1B11	R	39	86	254	16	58	8	1	1	25	13	—	4	.228	.274	.280
Dan McGann	1B121,2B9	S	36	135	475	52	114	8	5	2	55	38	—	9	.240	.321	.291
Claude Ritchey	2B120	S	34	121	421	44	115	10	3	2	36	50	—	7	.273	.361	.325
Bill Sweeney	3B123,SS3,2B1	R	22	127	418	44	102	15	3	0	40	45	—	17	.244	.317	.294
Bill Dahlen	SS144	R	38	144	524	50	125	23	2	3	48	35	—	10	.239	.296	.307
George Browne	OF138	L	32	138	536	61	122	10	6	1	34	36	—	17	.228	.276	.274
Ginger Beaumont	OF121	L	31	125	476	66	127	20	6	2	52	42	—	13	.267	.328	.347
Johnny Bates	OF117	L	25	127	445	48	115	14	6	1	29	35	—	25	.258	.315	.324
Jack Hannifin†	3B35,2B22,SS15*	R	25	74	257	30	53	6	2	2	22	28	—	7	.206	.284	.268
Joe Kelley	OF51,1B11	R	36	62	228	25	59	8	2	2	17	27	—	5	.259	.342	.338
Peaches Graham	C62,2B5	R	31	75	215	22	59	5	0	0	22	23	—	4	.274	.361	.298
Beals Becker†	OF43	L	21	43	171	13	47	3	1	0	7	7	—	7	.275	.303	.304
Harry Smith	C38	R	33	41	130	13	32	2	2	1	16	7	—	2	.246	.295	.315
Fred Stem	1B18	L	22	19	72	9	20	0	1	0	3	2	—	1	.278	.297	.306
Herbie Moran†	OF8	L	24	8	29	3	8	0	0	0	2	2	—	1	.276	.364	.276
Jim Ball	C6	R	24	6	15	1	1	0	0	0	0	1	—	0	.067	.125	.067
Walt Thomas	SS5	R	24	5	13	2	2	0	0	0	1	3	—	2	.154	.313	.154

J. Hannifin, 8 G at OF, 1 G at 1B

Pitcher	T	Age	G	GS	CG	ShO	IP	H	HR	BB	SO	W-L	Sv	ERA
Patsy Flaherty	L	32	31	31	21	0	244.0	221	6	81	50	12-18	0	3.25
Vive Lindaman	R	30	43	30	21	2	270.2	246	7	70	68	12-16	1	2.36
Gus Dorner	R	31	38	28	14	3	216.1	176	3	77	41	8-19	0	3.54
George Ferguson	R	21	37	20	13	3	208.0	168	1	84	98	11-11	0	2.47
Tom McCarthy†	R	24	14	11	7	2	94.1	77	0	28	27	7-3	0	1.62
Irv Young†	L	30	16	11	7	1	85.0	94	2	19	32	4-9	0	2.86
Tom Tuckey	L	24	8	8	3	1	72.0	60	2	20	26	3-3	0	2.50
Bill Chappelle	R	24	13	7	3	1	70.1	60	0	17	23	2-4	0	1.79
Al Mattern	R	25	5	3	1	1	30.1	30	0	6	8	1-2	0	2.08
Jake Boultes	R	23	17	5	1	0	74.2	80	7	8	28	3-5	0	3.01
Harley Young†	R	24	6	2	1	0	27.1	29	0	4	12	0-1	0	3.29
Big Jeff Pfeffer	R	26	4	0	0	0	10.0	18	1	8	3	0-0	0	12.60
Charlie Maloney	R	22	1	0	0	0	2.0	3	0	1	0	0-0	0	4.50

568 Seasons: Team Rosters

1908 Brooklyn Dodgers 7th NL 53-101 .344 46.0 GB

Patsy Donovan

Player	Gm by Position	B	Age	G	AB	R	H	2B	3B	HR	RBI	BB	SO	SB	Avg	OBP	Slg
Bill Bergen	C99	R	30	99	302	8	53	8	2	0	15	5	—	1	.175	.189	.215
Tim Jordan	1B146	L	29	148	515	58	127	18	5	12	60	59	—	9	.247	.328	.371
Harry Pattee	2B74	L	26	80	264	19	57	5	2	0	9	25	—	24	.216	.286	.250
Tommy Sheehan	3B145	R	30	146	468	45	100	18	2	0	29	53	—	9	.214	.302	.261
Phil Lewis	SS116	R	24	118	415	22	91	5	6	1	30	13	—	9	.219	.243	.267
Al Burch	OF116	L	24	123	456	45	111	8	4	2	18	33	—	15	.243	.294	.292
Harry Lumley	OF116	L	27	127	440	36	95	13	12	4	39	29	—	4	.216	.266	.327
Billy Maloney	OF107,C4	L	30	113	359	31	70	5	7	3	17	24	—	14	.195	.255	.273
John Hummel	OF95,2B43,SS9*	R	25	154	594	51	143	11	12	4	41	34	—	20	.241	.284	.320
Whitey Alperman	2B42,3B9,OF5*	R	28	70	213	17	42	3	1	1	15	9	—	2	.197	.253	.235
Tommy McMillan	SS29,OF14	R	20	43	147	9	35	3	0	0	3	9	—	5	.238	.291	.259
Lew Ritter	C37	R	32	38	99	6	19	2	1	0	2	7	—	0	.192	.245	.232
Tom Catterson	OF18	L	23	19	68	5	13	1	1	1	2	5	—	0	.191	.257	.279
Joe Dunn	C20	R	23	20	64	3	11	3	0	0	5	0	—	0	.172	.172	.219
Alex Farmer	C11	R	28	12	30	1	5	1	0	0	2	1	—	0	.167	.194	.200
Simmy Murch	1B2	R	27	6	11	1	2	1	0	0	0	1	—	0	.182	.250	.273

J. Hummel, 8 G at 1B; W. Alperman, 2 G at SS

Pitcher	T	Age	G	GS	CG	ShO	IP	H	HR	BB	SO	W-L	Sv	ERA
Kaiser Wilhelm	R	34	42	36	33	6	332.0	266	3	83	99	16-22	0	1.87
Nap Rucker	L	23	42	35	30	6	333.1	265	1	125	199	17-19	1	2.08
Harry McIntire	R	29	40	35	26	4	288.0	259	5	90	108	11-20	2	2.69
Jim Pastorius	L	26	28	25	16	2	213.2	171	5	74	54	4-20	0	2.44
George Bell	R	33	29	21	12	2	155.1	162	3	45	63	4-15	1	3.59
Abe Kruger	R	23	2	1	0	0	6.1	5	0	3	2	0-1	0	4.26
Jim Holmes	—	25	13	1	1	0	40.0	37	0	20	10	1-4	0	3.38
Pembroke Finlayson	R	19	1	0	0	0	0.1	0	0	4	0	0-0	0	135.00

1908 St. Louis Cardinals 8th NL 49-105 .318 50.0 GB

John McCloskey

Player	Gm by Position	B	Age	G	AB	R	H	2B	3B	HR	RBI	BB	SO	SB	Avg	OBP	Slg
Bill Ludwig	C62	R	26	66	187	15	34	2	2	0	8	16	—	3	.182	.246	.214
Ed Konetchy	1B154	R	22	154	545	46	135	19	12	5	50	38	—	16	.248	.309	.354
Billy Gilbert	2B89	R	32	89	276	12	59	7	0	0	10	20	—	6	.214	.274	.239
Bobby Byrne	3B122,SS4	R	23	127	439	27	84	7	1	0	14	23	—	16	.191	.238	.212
Patsy O'Rourke	SS53	R	27	53	164	8	32	4	2	0	16	14	—	2	.195	.263	.244
Red Murray	OF154	R	24	154	593	64	167	19	15	7	62	37	—	48	.282	.332	.400
Joe Delahanty	OF138	R	32	140	499	37	127	14	11	1	44	32	—	11	.255	.309	.333
Al Shaw	OF91,SS4,3B1	L	27	107	367	40	97	13	4	1	19	25	—	9	.264	.311	.330
Chappy Charles	2B65,SS31,3B23	R	27	121	454	39	93	14	3	1	17	19	—	15	.205	.238	.256
Shad Barry†	OF69,SS2	R	29	74	268	24	61	8	1	0	11	19	—	9	.228	.286	.265
Art Hoelskoetter	C41,3B2,1B1*	R	25	62	155	10	36	7	1	0	6	6	—	1	.232	.265	.290
Jack Bliss	C43	R	26	44	136	9	29	4	0	1	5	8	—	3	.213	.267	.265
Champ Osteen	SS17,3B12	L	31	29	112	2	22	4	0	0	11	0	—	0	.196	.204	.232
Tom Reilly	SS29	R	23	29	81	5	14	1	0	1	3	2	—	4	.173	.193	.222
Walter Morris	SS23	R	28	23	73	1	13	1	1	0	2	0	—	1	.178	.178	.219
Charlie Moran	C16	R	30	21	63	2	11	1	2	0	2	0	—	0	.175	.175	.254
Wilbur Murdoch	OF16	—	33	27	62	5	16	3	0	0	5	3	—	4	.258	.292	.306
Ralph McLaurin	OF6	—	23	8	22	2	5	0	0	0	0	0	—	0	.227	.227	.227
Doc Marshall†	C6	R	32	6	14	0	1	0	0	0	1	0	—	0	.071	.071	.071

A. Hoelskoetter, 1 G at 2B

Pitcher	T	Age	G	GS	CG	ShO	IP	H	HR	BB	SO	W-L	Sv	ERA
Bugs Raymond	R	26	48	37	23	5	324.1	236	2	95	145	15-25	2	2.03
Johnny Lush	L	22	38	32	23	3	250.2	221	6	57	93	11-18	1	2.12
Fred Beebe	R	27	29	19	12	0	174.1	134	3	66	72	5-13	0	2.63
Ed Karger	L	25	22	15	9	1	141.1	148	1	50	34	4-9	0	3.06
Art Fromme	R	24	20	14	9	2	116.0	102	1	50	62	5-13	0	2.72
Irv Higginbotham	R	26	19	11	7	1	107.0	113	0	33	38	3-8	0	3.20
Charlie Rhodes†	R	23	4	4	3	0	33.0	23	2	12	15	1-2	0	3.00
O.F. Baldwin	R	26	4	4	0	0	14.2	16	0	11	5	1-3	0	6.14
Slim Sallee	L	23	25	12	7	1	128.2	144	1	36	39	3-8	0	3.15
Stoney McGlynn	R	36	16	6	4	0	75.2	76	0	17	23	1-6	1	3.45
Fred Gaiser	—	22	1	0	0	0	2.1	4	0	3	2	0-0	0	7.71

»1909 Detroit Tigers 1st AL 98-54 .645 —

Hughie Jennings

Player	Gm by Position	B	Age	G	AB	R	H	2B	3B	HR	RBI	BB	SO	SB	Avg	OBP	Slg
Boss Schmidt	C81,OF1	S	28	84	253	21	53	8	2	1	28	7	—	7	.209	.240	.269
Claude Rossman†	1B75	L	28	82	287	16	75	8	3	0	39	13	—	10	.261	.293	.310
Germany Schaefer†	2B86,OF1	R	32	87	280	26	70	10	3	0	22	14	—	12	.250	.286	.293
George Moriarty	3B106,1B24	R	25	133	473	43	129	20	4	1	39	24	—	34	.273	.309	.338
Donie Bush	SS157	S	21	157	532	114	145	18	2	0	33	88	—	53	.273	.380	.314
Ty Cobb	OF156	L	22	156	573	116	216	33	10	9	107	48	—	76	.377	.431	.517
Sam Crawford	OF139,1B17	L	29	156	589	83	185	35	14	6	97	47	—	30	.314	.366	.452
Matty McIntyre	OF122	L	29	125	476	65	116	18	9	1	34	54	—	13	.244	.325	.326
Charley O'Leary	3B54,2B15,SS4*	R	26	76	261	29	53	10	0	0	13	6	—	9	.203	.224	.241
Oscar Stanage	C77	R	26	77	252	17	66	8	6	0	21	11	—	2	.262	.298	.341
Davy Jones	OF57	L	29	69	204	44	57	2	2	0	10	28	—	12	.279	.369	.309
Tom Jones†	1B44	R	32	44	153	13	43	9	0	0	18	5	—	9	.281	.317	.340
Jim Delahanty†	2B46	R	30	46	150	29	38	10	1	0	20	17	—	9	.253	.364	.333
Red Killefer†	2B17,OF1	R	24	23	61	6	17	2	2	1	4	3	—	2	.279	.343	.426
Hennie Beckendorf	C15	R	25	15	27	1	7	1	0	0	1	2	—	0	.259	.310	.296
Del Gainer	1B2	R	22	2	5	0	1	0	0	0	0	0	—	0	.200	.200	.200
Joe Casey	C3	R	21	3	5	1	0	0	0	0	0	1	—	0	.000	.167	.000
Hughie Jennings	1B2	R	40	2	4	1	2	0	0	0	2	0	—	0	.500	.500	.500

C. O'Leary, 2 G at OF

Pitcher	T	Age	G	GS	CG	ShO	IP	H	HR	BB	SO	W-L	Sv	ERA
George Mullin	R	28	40	35	29	3	303.2	258	1	78	124	29-8	1	2.22
Ed Willett	R	25	41	34	25	3	292.2	239	5	76	89	21-10	1	2.34
Ed Summers	R	24	35	32	24	3	281.2	243	4	52	107	19-9	1	2.24
Ed Killian	L	32	25	19	14	3	173.1	150	1	49	54	11-9	1	1.71
Wild Bill Donovan	R	32	21	17	13	4	140.1	121	0	60	76	8-7	2	2.31
Kid Speer	L	23	12	8	4	0	76.1	88	2	13	12	4-4	1	2.83
Bill Lelivelt	R	24	4	2	1	0	20.0	27	0	2	4	0-1	1	4.50
Elijah Jones	R	27	2	2	0	0	10.0	10	0	0	2	1-1	0	2.70
Ralph Works	R	21	16	4	4	0	64.0	62	0	17	31	4-1	2	1.97
George Suggs	R	26	9	4	2	0	44.1	34	1	10	18	1-3	1	2.03
Ed Lafitte	R	23	3	1	1	0	14.0	22	2	2	11	0-1	1	3.86

1909 Philadelphia Athletics 2nd AL 95-58 .621 3.5 GB

Connie Mack

Player	Gm by Position	B	Age	G	AB	R	H	2B	3B	HR	RBI	BB	SO	SB	Avg	OBP	Slg
Ira Thomas	C84	R	28	84	256	22	57	9	3	0	31	18	—	4	.223	.292	.281
Harry Davis	1B149	R	35	149	530	73	142	22	11	4	75	51	—	20	.268	.338	.374
Eddie Collins	2B152,SS1	L	22	153	572	104	198	30	10	3	56	62	—	67	.346	.416	.449
Home Run Baker	3B146	L	23	148	541	73	165	27	19	4	85	26	—	20	.305	.343	.447
Jack Barry	SS124	R	22	124	409	56	88	11	2	1	23	44	—	17	.215	.307	.259
Danny Murphy	OF149	R	32	149	541	61	152	28	14	5	69	35	—	19	.281	.332	.412
Rube Oldring	OF89,1B1	R	25	90	326	39	75	13	8	1	28	20	—	17	.230	.287	.328
Bob Ganley†	OF77	L	34	80	274	32	54	4	2	0	9	28	—	16	.197	.272	.226
Topsy Hartsel	OF74	L	35	83	267	30	72	4	4	1	18	48	—	3	.270	.381	.326
Heine Heitmuller	OF60	R	26	64	210	36	60	9	8	0	15	18	—	7	.286	.351	.405
Paddy Livingston	C64	R	29	64	175	15	41	6	4	0	15	15	—	4	.234	.323	.314
Simon Nicholls	SS14,3B5,1B1	L	26	21	71	10	15	2	1	0	3	3	—	0	.211	.243	.268
Jack Lapp	C13	L	24	21	56	8	19	3	1	0	10	3	—	1	.339	.373	.429
Scotty Barr	OF15,1B7	R	22	22	51	5	4	1	0	0	1	11	—	2	.078	.254	.098
Stuffy McInnis	SS14	R	18	19	46	4	11	0	0	1	4	2	—	0	.239	.286	.304
Amos Strunk	OF9	L	20	11	35	1	4	0	0	0	2	1	—	2	.114	.139	.114
Morrie Rath	SS4,3B2	L	22	7	26	4	7	1	0	0	3	2	—	1	.269	.387	.308
Joe Jackson	OF4	L	19	5	17	3	5	0	0	0	3	1	—	0	.294	.333	.294
Ed Larkin	C2	R	23	2	6	0	1	0	0	0	1	1	—	0	.167	.286	.167
Jim Curry	2B1	R	16	1	4	1	1	0	0	0	0	0	—	0	.250	.250	.250
Mike Powers	C1	R	38	1	4	1	1	0	0	0	0	0	—	0	.250	.250	.250

Pitcher	T	Age	G	GS	CG	ShO	IP	H	HR	BB	SO	W-L	Sv	ERA
Eddie Plank	L	33	34	33	24	3	265.1	215	1	62	132	19-10	0	1.76
Chief Bender	R	25	34	29	24	5	250.0	196	1	45	161	18-8	1	1.66
Cy Morgan†	R	30	28	26	21	5	228.2	152	3	71	81	16-11	0	1.65
Jack Coombs	R	26	31	25	19	6	205.2	156	1	73	97	12-11	1	2.32
Harry Krause	L	21	32	21	16	7	213.0	151	2	49	139	18-8	0	1.39
Biff Schlitzer†	R	24	4	3	0	0	13.1	13	0	7	6	0-3	0	5.40
Tommy Atkins	L	21	1	1	0	0	6.0	6	0	5	4	0-0	0	4.50
Jimmy Dygert	R	24	32	12	6	1	137.1	117	1	50	79	9-5	0	2.42
Rube Vickers	R	31	18	3	1	0	55.2	60	0	19	25	3-2	1	3.40
John Kull	L	27	1	0	0	0	3.0	3	0	5	4	1-0	0	3.00

1909 Boston Red Sox 3rd AL 88-63 .583 9.5 GB

Fred Lake

Player	Gm by Position	B	Age	G	AB	R	H	2B	3B	HR	RBI	BB	SO	SB	Avg	OBP	Slg
Bill Carrigan	C77,1B8	R	25	94	280	27	83	13	2	1	36	17	—	2	.296	.341	.368
Jake Stahl	1B126	R	30	127	435	62	128	19	12	6	60	43	—	16	.294	.377	.434
Amby McConnell	2B121	L	26	121	453	61	108	7	8	0	36	34	—	26	.238	.300	.289
Harry Lord	3B134	L	27	136	534	86	166	12	7	0	31	20	—	36	.311	.345	.360
Heinie Wagner	SS123,2B1	R	28	124	430	53	110	16	7	1	49	35	—	18	.256	.316	.333
Tris Speaker	OF142	L	21	143	544	73	168	26	13	7	77	38	—	35	.309	.362	.443
Harry Niles	OF117,3B13,SS9*	R	28	145	546	64	134	12	5	1	38	39	—	27	.245	.311	.291
Doc Gessler†	OF109	L	28	111	386	56	115	24	1	0	46	31	—	16	.298	.362	.365
Harry Hooper	OF74	L	21	81	255	29	72	3	4	0	12	16	—	15	.282	.337	.325
Pat Donahue	C58	R	24	64	176	14	42	4	1	2	25	17	—	2	.239	.309	.307
Charlie French	2B28,SS23	L	25	51	167	15	42	3	1	0	13	15	—	8	.251	.324	.281
Harry Wolter	1B17,P10,OF9	L	24	54	119	14	29	2	4	2	10	9	—	2	.244	.297	.378
Tubby Spencer	C26	R	25	28	74	6	12	1	0	0	9	6	—	2	.162	.225	.176
Jack Thoney	OF10	R	29	13	40	1	5	1	0	0	3	2	—	2	.125	.167	.150
Larry Gardner	3B8,SS5	L	23	19	37	7	11	1	2	0	5	4	—	1	.297	.381	.432
Bunny Madden		R	26	10	17	0	4	0	0	0	1	0	—	0	.235	.235	.235
Paul Howard	OF6	R	25	6	15	2	3	1	0	0	2	3	—	0	.200	.368	.267
Babe Danzig	1B3	R	22	6	13	0	2	0	0	0	0	2	—	0	.154	.313	.154
Steve Yerkes		R	21	5	7	0	2	0	0	0	0	0	—	0	.286	.286	.286

H. Niles, 5 G at 2B

Pitcher	T	Age	G	GS	CG	ShO	IP	H	HR	BB	SO	W-L	Sv	ERA
Frank Arellanes	R	27	45	30	17	4	230.2	192	3	43	82	16-12	8	2.18
Joe Wood	R	19	24	19	13	4	160.2	121	1	43	88	11-7	0	2.18
Eddie Cicotte	R	25	27	15	10	1	161.2	117	3	56	84	14-5	1	1.95
Charlie Chech	R	31	17	13	6	1	106.2	107	3	27	40	7-5	0	2.95
Cy Morgan†	R	30	12	10	5	0	64.2	52	0	31	30	2-6	1	2.37
Biff Schlitzer†	R	24	13	8	5	0	75.2	81	0	19	24	4-4	1	3.21
Elmer Steele	R	23	16	8	2	0	75.2	75	1	15	32	4-4	1	2.85
Ray Collins	L	22	12	8	4	2	73.2	70	2	18	31	4-3	0	2.81
Jack Ryan	R	24	13	8	2	0	61.1	65	0	20	22	3-3	0	3.23
Sea Lion Hall	R	23	11	7	3	0	59.2	59	0	17	27	6-4	0	2.56
Ed Karger†	L	26	12	6	3	0	68.0	71	0	22	17	5-2	0	3.18
Harry Wolter	R	24	10	6	0	0	53.0	53	0	28	20	3-4	1	3.91
Fred Burchell	L	29	10	5	1	0	52.0	51	1	11	12	3-3	0	2.94
Charlie Smith†	R	29	3	3	2	0	25.0	23	2	2	11	3-0	0	2.16
Fred Anderson	R	23	1	1	0	0	8.0	3	0	1	5	0-0	0	1.13
Jack Chesbro†	R	35	1	1	0	0	6.0	7	1	4	3	0-1	0	4.50
Larry Pape	R	25	11	3	2	1	58.1	46	0	12	18	2-0	2	2.01
Bill Matthews	R	31	5	1	0	0	16.2	16	1	10	6	1-0	0	3.24
Chet Nourse	R	21	3	0	0	0	5.0	5	0	5	3	0-0	0	7.20

1909 Chicago White Sox 4th AL 78-74 .513 20.0 GB

Billy Sullivan

Player	Gm by Position	B	Age	G	AB	R	H	2B	3B	HR	RBI	BB	SO	SB	Avg	OBP	Slg
Billy Sullivan	C97	R	34	97	265	11	43	3	0	0	16	17	—	9	.162	.226	.174
Frank Isbell	1B101,OF9,2B5	L	33	120	433	33	97	17	6	0	33	23	—	23	.224	.265	.291
Jake Atz	2B118,OF3,SS1	R	29	119	381	39	90	18	3	0	22	38	—	14	.236	.309	.299
Lee Tannehill	3B91,SS64	R	28	155	531	39	118	21	5	0	47	31	—	12	.222	.269	.281
Freddy Parent	SS98,OF37,2B1	R	33	136	472	61	123	10	5	0	30	46	—	32	.261	.335	.303
Patsy Dougherty	OF138	L	32	139	491	71	140	23	13	1	55	51	—	36	.285	.359	.391
Ed Hahn	OF76	L	33	76	287	30	52	6	0	1	16	31	—	9	.181	.268	.213
Dave Altizer	OF62,1B45	L	32	116	382	47	89	6	7	1	20	39	—	27	.233	.330	.293
Billy Purtell	3B71,2B32	R	23	103	361	34	93	9	3	0	40	19	—	14	.258	.302	.299
Doc White	OF40,P24	L	30	72	192	24	45	1	5	0	7	33	—	7	.234	.347	.292
Frank Owens	C57	R	23	64	174	12	35	4	1	0	17	8	—	3	.201	.245	.236
Willis Cole	OF46	R	27	46	165	17	39	7	3	0	16	16	—	3	.236	.308	.315
Bobby Messenger	OF31	S	25	31	112	18	19	1	1	0	0	13	—	7	.170	.268	.196
Ed Walsh	P31,OF1	R	28	32	84	5	18	5	0	0	11	6	—	4	.214	.267	.274
Fred Payne	C27,OF3	R	28	32	82	8	20	2	0	0	12	5	—	0	.244	.295	.268
Mike Welday	OF20	L	29	29	74	3	14	0	0	0	5	4	—	2	.189	.231	.189
George Davis	1B17,2B2	S	38	28	68	5	9	1	0	0	2	10	—	4	.132	.253	.147
Gavy Cravath†	OF18	R	28	19	50	7	9	0	0	1	8	19	—	3	.180	.406	.240
Barney Reilly	2B11,OF1	R	25	12	25	3	5	0	0	0	3	3	—	2	.200	.286	.200
Cuke Barrows	OF5	R	25	5	20	1	3	0	0	0	2	0	—	0	.150	.190	.150
Jiggs Donahue†	1B2	L	29	2	4	0	0	0	0	0	2	1	—	0	.000	.200	.000
Ham Patterson†	1B1	R	31	1	3	2	0	0	0	0	0	1	—	0	.000	.250	.000

Pitcher	T	Age	G	GS	CG	ShO	IP	H	HR	BB	SO	W-L	Sv	ERA
Frank Smith	R	29	51	41	37	7	365.0	278	1	70	177	25-17	1	1.80
Jim Scott	R	21	36	29	20	4	250.1	194	0	93	135	12-12	1	2.30
Ed Walsh	R	28	31	28	20	8	230.1	166	0	50	127	15-11	2	1.41
Doc White	L	30	24	21	14	3	177.2	149	1	31	77	11-9	1	1.72
Bill Burns†	L	29	22	19	10	3	168.0	169	2	35	52	7-13	0	2.04
Fred Olmstead	R	27	8	6	5	0	54.2	52	1	12	21	3-2	0	1.81
Frank Owen	R	29	3	2	1	0	16.0	19	0	3	3	1-1	0	4.50
Nick Altrock†	L	32	1	1	1	0	9.0	16	0	1	2	0-1	0	5.00
Rube Suter	L	21	18	6	3	1	87.1	72	2	28	53	2-3	1	2.47
Lou Fiene	R	24	13	6	4	0	72.0	75	1	18	24	2-5	0	4.13

1909 New York Highlanders 5th AL 74-77 .490 23.5 GB

George Stallings

Player	Gm by Position	B	Age	G	AB	R	H	2B	3B	HR	RBI	BB	SO	SB	Avg	OBP	Slg
Red Kleinow	C77	R	29	78	206	24	47	11	4	0	15	25	—	7	.228	.315	.320
Hal Chase	1B118,SS1	R	26	118	474	60	134	17	3	4	63	20	—	25	.283	.317	.357
Frank LaPorte	2B83	R	29	89	309	35	92	19	3	0	31	18	—	5	.298	.340	.379
Jimmy Austin	3B111,SS23,2B1	S	29	136	437	37	101	11	5	1	39	32	—	30	.231	.285	.286
John Knight	SS77,1B19,2B17	R	23	116	360	46	85	8	5	0	40	37	—	15	.236	.311	.286
Clyde Engle	OF134	R	25	135	492	66	137	20	5	3	71	47	—	18	.278	.347	.358
Ray Demmitt	OF109	L	25	123	427	68	105	12	12	4	30	55	—	16	.246	.340	.358
Willie Keeler	OF95	L	37	99	360	44	95	7	5	1	32	24	—	10	.264	.327	.319
Kid Elberfeld	SS61,3B44	R	34	106	379	47	90	9	5	0	26	28	—	23	.237	.314	.288
Birdie Cree	OF79,SS6,2B4*	R	26	104	343	48	90	6	3	2	27	30	—	10	.262	.338	.315
Charlie Hemphill	OF45	L	33	73	181	23	44	5	1	0	10	32	—	10	.243	.357	.282
Jeff Sweeney	C62,1B3	R	20	67	176	19	47	3	0	0	21	16	—	3	.267	.328	.284
Walter Blair	C42	R	25	42	110	5	23	2	2	0	11	7	—	2	.209	.269	.264
Earle Gardner		R	25	22	85	12	28	4	0	0	15	3	—	4	.329	.352	.376
George McConnell	1B11,P2	R	31	13	43	4	9	0	1	0	5	1	—	1	.209	.227	.256
Al Orth	2B6,P1	L	36	22	34	3	9	0	1	0	5	5	—	1	.265	.359	.324
Neal Ball†	2B8	R	28	8	29	5	6	1	1	0	3	3	—	2	.207	.281	.310
Joe Ward†	2B7,1B1	—	24	9	28	3	5	0	0	0	0	1	—	2	.179	.233	.179
Bobby Vaughn	2B4,SS1	R	24	5	14	1	2	0	0	0	0	1	—	1	.143	.200	.143
Jack Wanner	SS2	R	23	3	8	0	1	0	0	0	0	2	—	1	.125	.300	.125
Eddie Tiemeyer	1B3	R	24	3	8	1	3	1	0	0	0	1	—	0	.375	.444	.500
Irish McIlveen		L	28	4	3	0	0	0	0	0	0	1	—	0	.000	.250	.000

B. Cree, 1 G at 3B

Pitcher	T	Age	G	GS	CG	ShO	IP	H	HR	BB	SO	W-L	Sv	ERA
Joe Lake	R	28	31	26	17	3	215.1	180	2	59	117	14-11	1	1.88
Jack Warhop	R	24	36	23	21	3	243.1	197	2	81	95	13-15	2	2.40
Rube Manning	R	26	26	21	11	2	173.0	167	2	48	71	7-11	1	3.17
Lew Brockett	R	28	26	18	10	3	170.0	148	3	59	70	10-8	1	2.12
Tom Hughes	R	25	24	16	9	2	118.2	109	3	37	69	7-8	1	2.65
Slow Joe Doyle	R	27	17	15	8	3	125.2	103	3	37	57	8-6	0	2.58
Pete Wilson	L	23	14	12	7	1	93.2	82	2	43	44	6-5	0	3.17
Doc Newton	L	31	4	4	1	0	22.1	27	0	11	11	0-3	0	2.82
Dick Carroll	R	24	2	1	0	0	5.0	7	1	1	1	0-0	0	3.60
George McConnell	R	31	2	1	0	0	4.0	3	0	3	4	0-1	0	2.25
Al Orth	R	36	1	1	0	0	3.0	6	0	1	1	0-0	0	12.00
Jack Quinn	R	25	23	11	8	0	118.2	110	1	24	36	9-5	1	1.97
Jack Chesbro†	R	35	9	4	2	0	49.2	70	2	13	17	0-4	0	6.34
Butch Schmidt	L	22	1	0	0	0	5.0	10	0	1	2	0-0	0	7.20
Russ Ford	R	26	1	0	0	0	3.0	4	0	4	2	0-0	0	9.00

1909 Cleveland Bronchos 6th AL 71-82 .464 27.5 GB

Nap Lajoie (57-57)/Deacon McGuire (14-25)

Player	Gm by Position	B	Age	G	AB	R	H	2B	3B	HR	RBI	BB	SO	SB	Avg	OBP	Slg
Ted Easterly	C76	L	24	98	287	32	75	14	10	1	27	13	—	8	.261	.293	.390
George Stovall	1B145	R	30	145	565	60	139	17	10	2	49	6	—	25	.246	.259	.322
Nap Lajoie	2B120,1B8	R	34	128	469	56	152	33	7	1	47	35	—	13	.324	.378	.431
Bill Bradley	3B87,1B3,2B3	R	31	95	334	30	62	6	3	0	22	19	—	8	.186	.236	.222
Neal Ball†	SS95	R	28	96	324	29	83	13	2	1	25	17	—	17	.256	.295	.318
Bill Hinchman	OF131,SS6	R	26	139	457	57	118	20	13	2	53	41	—	22	.258	.331	.372
Joe Birmingham	OF98	R	24	100	343	29	99	10	5	1	38	19	—	12	.289	.333	.356
Wilbur Good	OF80	L	23	94	318	33	68	6	5	0	17	28	—	13	.214	.296	.264
George Perring	3B67,SS11,2B4	R	24	88	283	26	63	10	9	0	20	19	—	6	.223	.283	.322
Bris Lord	OF67	R	25	69	249	26	67	7	3	1	25	8	—	10	.269	.295	.333
Elmer Flick	OF61	L	33	66	235	28	60	10	2	0	15	22	—	9	.255	.322	.315
Terry Turner	2B26,SS26	R	28	53	208	25	52	7	4	0	16	14	—	14	.250	.304	.322
Nig Clarke	C44	L	26	55	164	15	45	4	2	0	14	9	—	1	.274	.312	.323
Harry Bemis	C36	R	35	42	123	4	23	2	3	0	13	0	—	2	.187	.194	.252
Duke Reilley	OF18	S	24	20	62	10	13	0	0	0	0	4	—	5	.210	.258	.210
Dolly Stark	SS19	R	24	19	60	4	12	0	0	0	1	6	—	4	.200	.273	.200
Milo Netzel	3B6,OF3	L	23	10	37	2	7	1	0	0	3	3	—	1	.189	.250	.216
Tom Raftery	OF8	R	27	8	32	6	7	2	1	0	0	4	—	1	.219	.306	.344
Bob Higgins	C8	R	22	8	23	0	2	0	0	0	0	0	—	0	.087	.087	.087
Josh Clarke	OF4	L	30	4	12	1	0	0	0	0	0	2	—	0	.000	.200	.000
Walt Doane	OF2,P1	L	22	4	9	1	1	0	0	0	0	1	—	0	.111	.200	.111
Denny Sullivan	OF2	L	26	3	2	0	1	0	0	0	0	0	—	0	.500	.500	.500

Pitcher	T	Age	G	GS	CG	ShO	IP	H	HR	BB	SO	W-L	Sv	ERA
Cy Young	R	42	35	34	30	3	294.2	267	4	59	109	19-15	0	2.26
Heinie Berger	R	27	34	29	19	4	247.0	221	2	58	162	13-14	1	2.73
Addie Joss	R	29	33	28	24	4	242.2	198	0	31	67	14-13	0	1.71
Cy Falkenberg	R	28	24	18	13	2	165.0	135	0	50	82	10-9	0	2.40
Bob Rhoads	R	29	20	15	9	2	133.1	124	1	50	46	5-9	0	2.90
Jerry Upp	L	25	7	4	2	0	26.2	26	0	12	13	2-1	0	1.69
Lucky Wright	R	29	5	4	3	0	22.2	20	0	8	6	0-4	0	3.97
Harry Ables	L	24	5	3	3	0	29.2	26	1	10	24	1-1	0	2.12
Harry Otis	L	22	5	3	0	0	26.1	26	0	18	6	2-2	0	1.37
Willie Mitchell	L	19	3	3	3	0	23.0	18	0	10	8	1-2	0	1.57
Fred Winchell	R	27	4	3	0	0	14.1	16	0	2	7	0-3	1	6.28
Walt Doane	R	22	1	1	0	0	5.0	10	0	1	2	0-1	0	5.40
Carl Sitton	R	26	14	5	3	0	50.0	50	1	16	16	3-2	0	2.88
Glenn Liebhardt	R	26	12	4	1	0	52.1	54	0	16	15	1-5	0	2.92
Red Booles	L	28	4	1	0	0	22.2	20	0	8	6	0-1	0	1.99

1909 St. Louis Browns 7th AL 61-89 .407 36.0 GB

Jimmy McAleer

Player	Gm by Position	B	Age	G	AB	R	H	2B	3B	HR	RBI	BB	SO	SB	Avg	OBP	Slg
Lou Criger	C73	R	37	74	212	15	36	1	1	0	9	25	—	2	.170	.261	.184
Tom Jones†	1B95,3B2	R	32	97	337	30	84	9	3	0	29	18	—	13	.249	.299	.294
Jimmy Williams	2B109	R	32	110	374	32	73	3	6	0	22	29	—	6	.195	.257	.235
Hobe Ferris	3B114,2B34	R	31	148	556	36	120	18	5	4	58	12	—	11	.216	.232	.288
Bobby Wallace	SS87,3B29	R	35	116	403	36	96	12	2	0	35	38	—	7	.238	.310	.278
Danny Hoffman	OF110	L	29	110	387	44	104	6	7	2	26	41	—	24	.269	.349	.336
Roy Hartzell	OF85,SS65,2B1	L	27	152	595	64	161	12	5	0	32	29	—	14	.271	.312	.308
George Stone	OF81	L	31	83	310	33	89	5	4	1	15	24	—	8	.287	.340	.339
Art Griggs	1B49,OF41,2B8*	R	25	108	364	38	102	17	5	0	43	24	—	11	.280	.330	.354
John McAleese	OF79,3B2	R	30	85	267	33	57	7	0	0	12	32	—	18	.213	.318	.240
Jim Stephens	C72	R	25	79	223	18	49	5	0	3	18	13	—	5	.220	.278	.283
Bill Bailey	P32,OF3	L	20	38	77	1	22	1	1	0	7	3	—	1	.286	.313	.325
Al Schweitzer	OF22	R	26	27	76	7	17	2	0	0	2	5	—	3	.224	.298	.250
Walt Devoy	OF16,1B3	R	24	19	69	7	17	3	1	0	8	3	—	4	.246	.278	.319
Ned Crompton	OF17	L	20	17	63	7	10	2	1	0	2	7	—	1	.159	.254	.222
Burt Shotton	OF17	L	24	17	61	5	16	0	1	0	0	5	—	3	.262	.328	.295
Ham Patterson†	1B6,OF6	R	31	17	49	2	10	1	0	0	5	0	—	1	.204	.204	.224
Wib Smith	C13,1B1	L	22	17	42	3	8	0	0	0	2	0	—	0	.190	.190	.190
Harry Howell	P10,3B7,OF1	R	32	18	34	5	6	1	0	0	3	2	—	0	.176	.222	.206
Bill Killefer	C11	R	21	11	29	0	4	0	0	0	1	0	—	2	.138	.138	.138
Claude Rossman†	OF2	L	28	2	8	0	1	0	0	0	0	0	—	0	.125	.125	.125

A. Griggs, 1 G at SS

Pitcher	T	Age	G	GS	CG	ShO	IP	H	HR	BB	SO	W-L	Sv	ERA
Rube Waddell	L	32	31	28	16	5	220.1	204	1	57	141	11-14	1	2.37
Jack Powell	R	34	34	27	18	4	239.0	221	1	42	82	12-16	3	2.11
Barney Pelty	R	28	27	23	17	5	199.1	158	2	53	88	11-11	0	2.30
Bill Graham	L	25	34	21	13	3	187.1	171	3	60	82	8-14	1	3.12
Bill Bailey	L	20	32	20	17	1	199.0	174	2	75	114	9-10	0	2.44
Bill Dinneen	R	33	17	13	8	3	112.0	112	3	29	26	6-7	0	3.46
Dode Criss	R	24	11	6	3	0	55.1	53	0	32	43	1-5	0	3.42
Chuck Rose	L	23	3	3	3	0	25.0	32	1	7	6	1-2	0	5.40
Ed Kusel	R	23	3	3	3	0	24.0	41	1	1	2	0-3	0	7.13
Jack Gilligan	R	23	3	3	3	0	23.0	28	1	9	4	1-2	0	5.48
Phil Stremmel	R	29	2	2	2	0	18.0	22	0	4	6	0-2	0	4.50
Bill McCorry	R	21	2	2	2	0	15.0	29	1	6	10	0-2	0	9.00
Harry Howell	R	32	10	3	0	0	37.1	42	0	8	16	1-1	0	3.13

1909 Washington Senators 8th AL 42-110 .276 56.0 GB

Joe Cantillon

Player	Gm by Position	B	Age	G	AB	R	H	2B	3B	HR	RBI	BB	SO	SB	Avg	OBP	Slg
Gabby Street	C137	R	26	137	407	25	86	12	1	0	29	26	—	2	.211	.262	.246
Jiggs Donahue†	1B81	L	29	84	283	13	67	12	1	0	28	22	—	9	.237	.294	.286
Jim Delahanty†	2B85	R	30	90	302	18	67	13	5	1	21	23	—	4	.222	.290	.308
Wid Conroy	3B120,2B13,OF5*	R	32	139	488	44	119	13	4	1	20	37	—	24	.244	.298	.293
George McBride	SS156	R	28	156	504	38	118	16	0	0	34	36	—	17	.234	.294	.266
Clyde Milan	OF120	L	22	130	400	36	80	12	4	1	15	31	—	10	.200	.268	.258
George Browne†	OF101	L	33	103	393	40	107	15	5	1	16	17	—	13	.272	.308	.344
Jack Lelivelt	OF91	L	23	91	318	25	93	8	6	0	24	19	—	8	.292	.334	.355
Bob Unglaub	1B57,OF42,2B25*	R	27	130	480	43	127	14	9	3	41	22	—	15	.265	.301	.350
Otis Clymer	OF41	S	33	45	138	11	27	5	2	0	6	17	—	7	.196	.284	.261
Germany Schaefer†	2B32,3B1	R	32	37	128	13	31	5	1	1	4	6	—	2	.242	.281	.320
Red Killefer†	OF24,3B6,C3*	R	24	40	121	11	21	1	0	0	5	13	—	4	.174	.265	.182
Bob Groom	P44,OF2	R	24	46	88	1	8	1	0	0	2	0	—	0	.091	.091	.102
Bill Yohe	3B19	—	30	21	72	6	15	2	0	0	4	3	—	2	.208	.240	.236
Bob Ganley†	OF17	L	34	19	63	5	16	3	0	0	5	1	—	4	.254	.266	.302
Cliff Blankenship	C17,OF4	R	29	39	60	4	15	0	0	0	9	0	—	2	.250	.250	.250
Jack Slattery	1B11,C7	R	31	32	56	4	12	2	0	0	6	2	—	1	.214	.254	.250
Doc Gessler†	OF16,1B1	L	28	17	54	10	13	2	1	0	8	12	—	4	.241	.406	.315
Warren Miller	OF15	L	23	26	51	5	11	0	0	0	1	4	—	0	.216	.273	.216
Jerry Freeman	1B14,OF1	L	29	19	48	2	8	0	1	0	3	4	—	3	.167	.245	.208
Speed Kelly	3B10,2B3,OF1	R	24	17	42	3	6	2	1	0	1	3	—	1	.143	.200	.238
Jesse Tannehill	OF9,P3	S	34	16	36	2	6	1	0	0	1	5	—	0	.167	.286	.194
Jack Hardy	C9,2B1	R	32	10	24	3	4	0	0	0	4	1	—	0	.167	.200	.167
Bill Shipke	3B6,SS2	R	26	9	16	2	2	1	0	0	0	2	—	0	.125	.222	.188
Mike Kahoe	C3	R	35	4	8	0	1	0	0	0	0	0	—	2	.125	.125	.125
Tom Crooke	1B3	R	24	3	7	2	2	1	0	0	2	2	—	1	.286	.444	.429
Orth Collins	OF2,P1	L	29	8	7	0	0	0	0	0	0	0	—	0	.000	.000	.000
Gavy Cravath†	OF1	R	28	4	6	0	0	0	0	0	1	0	—	0	.000	.000	.000
Frank Hemphill	OF1	R	31	1	3	0	0	0	0	0	0	0	—	0	.000	.000	.000
Jimmy Sebring†	OF1	L	27	1	0	0	0	0	0	0	0	0	—	0	—	—	—

W. Conroy, 1 G at SS; B. Unglaub, 4 G at 3B; R. Killefer, 3 G at 2B, 1 G at SS

Pitcher	T	Age	G	GS	CG	ShO	IP	H	HR	BB	SO	W-L	Sv	ERA
Walter Johnson	R	21	40	36	27	4	296.1	247	1	84	164	13-25	1	2.22
Bob Groom	R	24	44	31	17	1	260.2	218	2	105	131	7-26	0	2.87
Dolly Gray	L	30	36	26	19	0	218.0	210	1	77	87	5-19	0	3.59
Charlie Smith†	R	29	23	15	7	1	145.2	140	4	37	72	3-12	0	3.27
Long Tom Hughes	R	30	22	13	7	2	120.1	113	1	33	77	4-7	1	2.69
Roy Witherup	R	22	12	8	5	0	68.0	79	1	20	26	1-5	0	4.24
Doc Reisling	R	34	10	6	6	1	66.2	70	0	17	22	2-4	0	2.43
Nick Altrock†	L	32	9	5	2	0	38.0	55	0	5	9	1-3	0	5.45
Dixie Walker	R	22	4	4	4	0	36.0	31	0	6	25	3-1	0	2.50
Bill Burns†	L	29	6	4	1	0	29.1	25	0	7	13	1-1	0	1.23
Jesse Tannehill	L	34	3	2	2	1	21.0	19	1	5	8	1-1	0	3.43
Bill Forman	R	22	2	2	1	0	11.0	8	0	7	2	0-2	0	4.91
Frank Oberlin	R	33	9	4	1	0	41.0	41	1	16	13	1-4	0	3.73
Joe Ohl	L	21	4	0	0	0	8.2	7	0	1	2	0-0	0	2.08
Joe Hovlik	R	24	3	0	0	0	6.0	13	0	3	1	0-0	0	4.50
Burt Keeley	R	29	2	0	0	0	7.0	12	0	1	0	0-0	0	11.57
Orth Collins	R	29	1	0	0	0	1.0	0	0	0	1	0-0	0	0.00

»1909 Pittsburgh Pirates 1st NL 110-42 .724 —

Fred Clarke

Player	Gm by Position	B	Age	G	AB	R	H	2B	3B	HR	RBI	BB	SO	SB	Avg	OBP	Slg
George Gibson	C150	R	28	150	510	42	135	25	9	2	52	44	—	9	.265	.326	.361
Bill Abstein	1B135	R	26	137	512	51	133	20	10	1	70	27	—	16	.260	.302	.344
Dots Miller	2B150	R	22	151	560	71	156	31	13	3	87	39	—	14	.279	.329	.396
Jap Barbeau†	3B85	R	27	91	350	60	77	16	3	0	25	37	—	19	.220	.302	.283
Honus Wagner	SS136,OF1	R	35	137	495	92	168	39	10	5	100	66	—	35	.339	.420	.489
Chief Wilson	OF154	L	25	154	569	64	155	22	12	4	59	19	—	17	.272	.303	.374
Fred Clarke	OF152	L	36	152	550	97	158	16	11	3	68	80	—	31	.287	.384	.373
Tommy Leach	OF138,3B13	R	31	151	587	126	153	29	8	6	43	66	—	27	.261	.337	.368
Bobby Byrne†	3B46	R	24	46	168	31	43	6	2	0	7	32	—	8	.256	.387	.315
Alan Storke†	1B18,3B14	R	24	37	118	12	30	5	2	0	12	7	—	1	.254	.302	.331
Ed Abbaticchio	SS18,2B4,OF1	R	32	36	87	13	20	0	0	1	16	19	—	2	.230	.368	.264
Ham Hyatt	OF6,1B2	L	24	48	67	9	20	3	4	0	7	3	—	1	.299	.329	.463
Ward Miller†	OF14	L	24	15	56	2	8	0	1	0	4	4	—	2	.143	.213	.179
Mike Simon	C9	R	26	12	18	2	3	0	0	0	2	1	—	0	.167	.211	.167
Paddy O'Connor	C3,3B1	R	29	9	16	1	5	1	0	0	3	0	—	0	.313	.313	.375
Kid Durbin†		L	22	1	0	0	0	0	0	0	0	0	—	0	—	—	—

Pitcher	T	Age	G	GS	CG	ShO	IP	H	HR	BB	SO	W-L	Sv	ERA
Vic Willis	R	33	39	35	24	4	289.2	243	3	83	95	22-11	1	2.24
Howie Camnitz	R	27	41	30	20	5	283.0	207	1	68	133	25-6	3	1.62
Nick Maddox	R	22	31	27	17	4	203.1	173	2	39	56	13-8	0	2.21
Lefty Leifield	L	25	32	27	13	3	201.2	172	4	54	43	19-8	0	2.37
Deacon Phillippe	R	37	22	12	7	1	131.2	121	2	14	38	8-3	0	2.32
Sam Frock	R	26	8	4	3	0	36.1	44	0	4	11	2-1	1	2.48
Babe Adams	R	27	25	12	7	3	130.0	88	0	23	65	12-3	2	1.11
Sam Leever	R	37	19	4	2	0	70.0	74	0	14	23	8-1	2	2.83
Chick Brandom	R	22	13	2	0	0	40.2	33	0	10	21	1-0	2	1.11
Bill Powell	R	24	3	1	0	0	7.1	7	0	6	2	0-1	0	3.68
Harry Camnitz	R	24	1	0	0	0	4.0	6	0	1	1	0-0	0	4.50
Gene Moore	L	23	1	0	0	0	2.0	4	0	3	2	0-0	0	18.00
Charlie Wacker	L	25	1	0	0	0	2.0	2	0	1	0	0-0	0	0.00

1909 Chicago Cubs 2nd NL 104-49 .680 6.5 GB

Frank Chance

Player	Gm by Position	B	Age	G	AB	R	H	2B	3B	HR	RBI	BB	SO	SB	Avg	OBP	Slg
Jimmy Archer	C80	R	26	80	261	31	60	9	2	1	30	12	—	5	.230	.266	.291
Frank Chance	1B92	R	31	93	324	53	88	16	4	0	46	30	—	29	.272	.341	.346
Johnny Evers	2B126	L	27	127	463	88	122	19	6	1	24	73	—	28	.263	.369	.337
Harry Steinfeldt	3B151	R	31	151	528	73	133	27	6	2	59	57	—	22	.252	.331	.337
Joe Tinker	SS143	R	28	143	516	56	132	26	11	4	57	17	—	23	.256	.280	.372
Solly Hofman	OF153	R	26	153	527	60	150	21	4	2	58	53	—	20	.285	.351	.351
Jimmy Sheckard	OF148	L	30	148	525	81	134	29	5	1	43	72	—	15	.255	.346	.335
Wildfire Schulte	OF140	L	26	140	538	57	142	16	11	4	60	24	—	23	.264	.298	.357
Pat Moran	C74	R	33	77	246	18	54	11	1	1	23	16	—	2	.220	.278	.285
Del Howard	1B57	L	31	69	203	25	40	4	2	1	24	18	—	6	.197	.282	.251
Heinie Zimmerman	2B27,3B16,SS12	R	22	65	183	23	50	9	2	0	21	3	—	7	.273	.285	.344
Joe Stanley	OF16	S	28	22	52	4	7	1	0	0	2	6	—	0	.135	.224	.154
John Kane	OF8,3B3,SS3*	R	26	20	45	6	4	1	0	0	5	2	—	1	.089	.146	.111
George Browne†	OF12	L	33	12	39	7	8	0	1	0	1	5	—	3	.205	.295	.256
Fred Luderus	1B11	L	23	11	37	8	11	1	1	1	9	3	—	0	.297	.366	.459
Tom Needham	C7	R	30	13	28	3	4	0	0	0	0	0	—	0	.143	.143	.143
Bill Davidson	OF2	R	22	2	7	2	1	0	0	0	0	1	—	1	.143	.250	.143

J. Kane, 2 G at 2B

Pitcher	T	Age	G	GS	CG	ShO	IP	H	HR	BB	SO	W-L	Sv	ERA
Three Finger Brown	R	32	50	34	32	8	342.2	246	1	53	172	27-9	7	1.31
Orval Overall	R	28	38	32	23	9	285.0	204	1	80	205	20-11	3	1.42
Ed Reulbach	R	26	35	32	23	6	262.2	194	1	82	105	19-10	0	1.78
Jack Pfiester	L	31	29	25	13	5	196.2	179	1	49	73	17-6	0	2.43
Rube Kroh	L	22	17	13	10	2	120.1	97	2	30	51	9-4	0	1.65
Rip Hagerman	R	21	13	7	4	1	79.0	64	0	28	32	4-4	0	1.82
Rudy Schwenck	L	25	3	2	0	0	4.0	16	0	3	3	1-1	0	13.50
King Cole	R	23	1	1	1	1	9.0	6	0	3	1	1-0	0	0.00
Ray Brown	R	20	1	1	1	0	9.0	5	0	4	2	1-0	0	2.00
Carl Lundgren	R	29	2	1	0	0	4.1	6	0	4	0	0-1	0	4.15
Andy Coakley	R	26	1	1	0	0	2.0	7	0	3	1	0-1	0	18.00
Irv Higginbotham†	R	27	19	6	4	0	78.0	64	0	20	32	5-2	1	2.19
Pat Ragan†	R	20	2	0	0	0	3.2	4	0	1	2	0-0	0	2.45
Chick Fraser	R	38	1	0	0	0	3.0	2	0	4	1	0-0	0	0.00

1909 New York Giants 3rd NL 92-61 .601 18.5 GB

John McGraw

Player	Gm by Position	B	Age	G	AB	R	H	2B	3B	HR	RBI	BB	SO	SB	Avg	OBP	Slg
Admiral Schlei	C89	R	31	92	279	25	68	12	0	0	30	40	—	4	.244	.343	.287
Fred Tenney	1B98	L	37	101	375	43	88	8	2	3	30	52	—	8	.235	.333	.291
Larry Doyle	2B144	L	22	147	570	86	172	27	11	6	49	45	—	31	.302	.360	.419
Art Devlin	3B143	R	29	143	491	61	130	19	8	0	56	65	—	26	.265	.362	.336
Al Bridwell	SS145	L	25	145	476	59	140	11	5	0	55	67	—	32	.294	.386	.338
Red Murray	OF149	R	25	149	570	74	150	15	12	7	91	45	—	48	.263	.319	.368
Bill O'Hara	OF111	L	25	115	360	48	85	9	3	1	30	41	—	31	.236	.318	.286
Moose McCormick	OF110	L	28	110	413	68	120	21	8	3	27	49	—	4	.291	.373	.402
Cy Seymour	OF74	L	36	80	280	37	87	12	5	1	30	25	—	14	.311	.369	.400
Fred Merkle	1B70,2B1	R	20	79	236	15	45	9	1	0	20	16	—	8	.191	.245	.237
Chief Meyers	C64	R	28	90	220	15	61	10	5	1	30	22	—	3	.277	.359	.382
Buck Herzog	OF29,2B6,3B4*	R	23	42	130	16	24	2	0	0	8	13	—	2	.185	.264	.200
Art Fletcher	SS22,2B7,3B6	R	24	33	98	7	21	0	1	0	6	1	—	0	.214	.238	.235
Tillie Shafer	3B16,2B13,OF2	S	20	38	84	11	15	2	1	0	7	14	—	6	.179	.296	.226
Fred Snodgrass	OF20,C2,1B1	R	21	28	70	10	21	5	0	1	6	7	—	10	.300	.388	.414
Art Wilson	C19	R	23	19	42	4	10	2	1	0	5	4	—	0	.238	.304	.333
Josh Devore	OF12	L	21	22	28	6	4	1	0	0	1	2	—	3	.143	.250	.179
Arlie Latham	2B2	R	49	4	2	1	0	0	0	0	0	0	—	1	.000	.000	.000

B. Herzog, 1 G at SS

Pitcher	T	Age	G	GS	CG	ShO	IP	H	HR	BB	SO	W-L	Sv	ERA
Christy Mathewson	R	30	37	33	26	8	275.1	192	2	36	149	25-6	2	1.14
Bugs Raymond	R	27	39	31	18	2	270.0	239	7	87	121	18-12	0	2.47
Hooks Wiltse	L	28	37	30	22	4	269.1	228	9	51	119	20-11	3	2.00
Red Ames	R	26	34	26	20	2	244.0	217	3	81	156	15-10	1	2.69
Rube Marquard	L	22	29	21	8	0	173.0	155	2	73	109	5-13	1	2.60
Al Klawitter	R	21	6	3	2	0	27.0	24	1	13	6	1-1	1	2.00
Louis Drucke	R	20	3	3	2	0	24.0	20	0	13	8	2-1	0	2.25
George Daly	R	21	3	3	3	0	21.0	31	0	8	8	0-3	0	6.00
Doc Crandall	R	21	30	7	4	0	122.0	117	5	33	55	6-4	6	2.88
Bull Durham	R	32	4	0	0	0	11.0	15	0	2	2	0-0	1	3.27
Jake Weimer	L	35	1	0	0	0	3.0	7	0	0	1	0-0	0	9.00
Red Waller	—	26	1	0	0	0	1.0	3	0	0	1	0-0	0	0.00

1909 Cincinnati Reds 4th NL 77-76 .503 33.5 GB

Clark Griffith

Player	Gm by Position	B	Age	G	AB	R	H	2B	3B	HR	RBI	BB	SO	SB	Avg	OBP	Slg
Larry McLean	C95	R	27	95	324	26	83	12	2	2	36	21	—	1	.256	.307	.324
Doc Hoblitzell	1B142	R	20	142	517	59	159	23	11	4	67	44	—	17	.308	.364	.418
Dick Egan	2B116,SS10	R	25	127	480	59	132	14	3	2	53	37	—	39	.275	.329	.329
Hans Lobert	3B122	R	27	122	425	50	90	13	5	4	52	48	—	30	.212	.304	.294
Tom Downey	SS119,C1	R	25	119	416	39	96	9	6	1	32	32	—	16	.231	.287	.288
Mike Mitchell	OF145	R	29	145	523	83	162	17	17	4	86	57	—	37	.310	.378	.430
Bob Bescher	OF117	S	25	124	446	73	107	17	6	1	34	56	—	54	.240	.335	.312
Rebel Oakes	OF113	L	22	120	415	55	112	10	5	3	31	40	—	23	.270	.341	.340
Dode Paskert	OF82,1B6	R	27	104	322	49	81	7	4	0	33	34	—	23	.252	.327	.298
Miller Huggins	2B31,3B15	S	30	57	159	18	34	3	1	0	6	28	—	11	.214	.335	.245
Frank Roth	C52	R	30	56	147	12	35	7	2	0	16	6	—	5	.238	.287	.313
Mike Mowrey†	3B22,SS13	R	25	38	115	10	22	5	0	0	5	20	—	2	.191	.311	.235
Ward Miller†	OF26	L	24	43	113	17	35	3	1	0	4	6	—	9	.310	.345	.354
Tommy Clarke	C17	R	21	18	52	8	13	3	2	0	10	6	—	3	.250	.328	.385
Chappy Charles†	2B10,SS3	R	28	13	43	3	11	2	0	0	5	4	—	2	.256	.319	.302
Chick Autry†	1B9	L	24	9	33	3	6	2	0	0	4	2	—	1	.182	.229	.242
Roy Ellam	SS9	R	23	10	21	4	4	0	1	1	4	7	—	1	.190	.393	.429
Bill Moriarty	SS6	R	26	6	20	1	4	1	0	0	1	0	—	2	.200	.200	.250
Emil Haberer	C4	R	31	5	16	1	3	1	0	0	2	0	—	0	.188	.188	.250
Swat McCabe	OF3	L	27	3	11	2	6	1	0	0	0	1	—	1	.545	.583	.636
Doc Johnston	1B3	L	21	3	10	1	0	0	0	0	1	0	—	0	.000	.000	.000
Si Pauxtis	C4	R	23	4	8	2	1	0	0	0	0	0	—	0	.125	.222	.125
Claire Patterson	OF2	L	21	4	8	0	1	0	0	0	1	0	—	0	.125	.125	.125
Del Young	OF2	L	23	2	7	0	2	0	0	0	1	1	—	0	.286	.375	.286
Cozy Dolan	3B3	R	19	3	6	2	1	0	0	0	0	2	—	0	.167	.375	.167
Mike Konnick	C2	R	20	2	5	0	2	1	0	0	1	0	—	0	.400	.400	.600
Kid Durbin†		L	22	6	5	1	1	0	0	0	0	1	—	0	.200	.333	.200
Ezra Midkiff	3B1	L	26	1	2	0	0	0	0	0	0	0	—	0	.000	.000	.000
Ducky Pearce	C2	R	24	2	2	0	0	0	0	0	0	0	—	0	.000	.000	.000

Pitcher	T	Age	G	GS	CG	ShO	IP	H	HR	BB	SO	W-L	Sv	ERA
Art Fromme	R	25	37	34	22	4	279.1	195	2	101	126	19-13	2	1.90
Harry Gaspar	R	26	44	29	19	4	260.0	228	0	57	65	19-11	2	2.01
Bob Ewing	R	36	31	29	14	2	218.1	195	1	63	86	11-12	0	2.43
Jack Rowan	R	22	38	23	14	0	225.2	185	0	104	81	11-12	0	2.79
Billy Campbell	L	35	30	15	7	0	148.1	162	0	39	37	7-11	2	2.67
Bob Spade	R	32	14	13	8	0	98.0	91	0	39	31	5-5	0	2.85
Ed Karger†	L	26	9	5	1	0	34.1	26	0	30	8	1-3	0	4.46
Jack Bushelman	R	23	1	1	1	0	7.0	7	1	4	3	0-1	0	2.57
Clark Griffith	R	39	1	1	1	0	6.0	11	0	2	3	0-1	0	6.00
Jean Dubuc	R	20	19	5	2	0	71.1	72	0	46	19	2-5	1	3.66
Tom Cantwell	R	20	6	1	1	0	21.2	16	0	7	7	1-0	0	1.66
Roy Castleton	L	23	4	1	1	0	14.0	14	0	6	5	1-1	0	1.93
Pat Ragan†	R	20	2	0	0	0	8.0	7	0	4	2	0-1	0	3.38
Chet Carmichael	R	21	2	0	0	0	7.0	9	0	3	2	0-0	0	0.00
Ralph Savidge	R	30	1	0	0	0	4.0	10	1	3	2	0-0	0	22.50
Bill Chappelle†	R	25	1	0	0	0	4.0	5	0	2	0	0-0	1	2.25

1909 Philadelphia Phillies 5th NL 74-79 .484 36.5 GB

Billy Murray

Player	Gm by Position	B	Age	G	AB	R	H	2B	3B	HR	RBI	BB	SO	SB	Avg	OBP	Slg
Red Dooin	C140	R	30	141	468	42	105	14	1	2	38	21	—	14	.224	.264	.271
Kitty Bransfield	1B138	R	34	140	527	47	154	27	6	1	59	18	—	17	.292	.319	.372
Otto Knabe	2B110,OF1	R	25	114	402	40	94	13	3	0	34	35	—	9	.234	.308	.281
Eddie Grant	3B154	L	26	154	631	75	170	18	4	1	37	35	—	28	.269	.311	.315
Mickey Doolan	SS147	R	29	147	493	39	108	12	10	1	35	37	—	10	.219	.276	.290
John Titus	OF149	L	33	151	540	69	146	22	6	3	46	66	—	23	.270	.367	.350
Sherry Magee	OF143	R	24	143	522	60	141	33	14	2	66	44	—	38	.270	.340	.398
Johnny Bates†	OF73	L	26	77	266	43	78	11	1	1	15	28	—	22	.293	.365	.353
Fred Osborn	OF54	L	25	58	189	14	35	4	1	0	19	12	—	6	.185	.238	.217
Joe Ward†	2B48,SS8,1B5*	—	24	74	184	21	49	8	2	0	23	9	—	7	.266	.304	.332
Pep Deininger	OF45,2B1	L	31	55	169	22	44	9	0	0	16	11	—	5	.260	.309	.314
Dave Shean†	2B14,1B11,OF3*	R	25	36	112	14	26	2	2	0	4	14	—	3	.232	.323	.286
Doc Martel	C13	R	26	24	41	1	11	3	1	0	7	4	—	0	.268	.333	.390
Fred Jacklitsch	C12,2B1	R	33	20	32	6	10	1	1	0	1	10	—	1	.313	.476	.406
Wally Clement†		L	27	3	3	0	0	0	0	0	0	0	—	0	.000	.000	.000
Charlie Starr†		—	30	3	3	0	0	0	0	0	0	0	—	0	.000	.000	.000
Ed McDonough	C1	R	22	1	1	0	0	0	0	0	0	0	—	0	.000	.000	.000
Ben Froelich	C1	R	21	1	1	0	0	0	0	0	0	0	—	0	.000	.000	.000

J. Ward, 2 G at OF; D. Shean, 1 G at SS

Pitcher	T	Age	G	GS	CG	ShO	IP	H	HR	BB	SO	W-L	Sv	ERA
Earl Moore	R	29	38	34	24	4	299.2	238	7	108	173	18-12	0	2.10
Lew Moren	R	25	40	31	19	2	257.2	226	6	93	110	16-15	1	2.65
George McQuillan	R	24	41	28	16	4	247.2	202	5	54	96	13-16	2	2.14
Frank Corridon	R	28	27	19	11	3	171.0	147	0	61	69	11-7	0	2.11
Harry Coveleski	L	23	24	17	8	2	121.2	109	0	49	56	6-10	1	2.74
Tully Sparks	R	34	24	16	6	1	121.2	126	4	32	40	6-11	0	2.96
Bill Foxen	L	25	18	7	5	1	83.1	65	2	32	37	3-7	0	3.35
Lew Richie†	R	25	11	1	0	0	45.0	40	0	18	11	1-1	1	2.00
Buster Brown†	R	27	7	1	0	0	25.0	22	1	16	10	0-0	0	3.24
Frank Scanlan	L	19	6	0	0	0	11.0	8	0	5	5	0-0	1	1.64
Ben Van Dyke	L	20	2	0	0	0	7.1	7	0	4	5	0-0	0	3.68

1909 Brooklyn Dodgers 6th NL 55-98 .359 55.5 GB

Harry Lumley

Player	Gm by Position	B	Age	G	AB	R	H	2B	3B	HR	RBI	BB	SO	SB	Avg	OBP	Slg
Bill Bergen	C112	R	31	112	346	16	48	1	1	1	15	10	—	4	.139	.163	.156
Tim Jordan	1B95	L	30	103	330	47	90	20	3	3	36	59	—	13	.273	.386	.379
Whitey Alperman	2B108	R	29	111	420	35	104	19	12	1	41	2	—	7	.248	.262	.357
Ed Lennox	3B121	R	23	126	435	33	114	18	9	2	44	47	—	11	.262	.337	.359
Tommy McMillan	SS105,2B2,3B1	R	21	108	373	18	79	15	1	0	24	20	—	11	.212	.254	.257
Al Burch	OF151,1B1	L	25	152	601	80	163	20	6	1	30	51	—	38	.271	.329	.329
Wally Clement†	OF88	L	27	92	340	35	87	8	4	0	17	18	—	11	.256	.293	.303
Harry Lumley	OF52	L	28	55	172	13	43	8	1	0	14	16	—	1	.250	.314	.331
John Hummel	1B54,2B38,SS36*	R	26	146	542	54	152	15	9	4	52	22	—	16	.280	.311	.363
Pryor McElveen	3B37,SS11,OF10*	R	27	81	258	22	51	8	1	3	25	14	—	6	.198	.242	.271
Jul Kustus	OF50	R	26	53	173	12	25	5	0	1	11	11	—	9	.145	.204	.191
Doc Marshall	C49,OF1	R	33	50	149	7	30	7	1	0	10	6	—	3	.201	.232	.262
George Hunter	OF23,P16	S	21	44	123	8	28	7	0	0	8	9	—	1	.228	.286	.285
Zack Wheat	OF26	L	21	26	102	15	31	7	3	0	4	6	—	1	.304	.343	.431
Jimmy Sebring†	OF25	L	27	25	81	11	8	1	1	0	5	11	—	3	.099	.207	.136
Red Downey	OF19	L	20	19	78	7	20	1	0	0	8	2	—	4	.256	.275	.269
Joe Dunn	C7	R	24	10	25	1	4	1	0	0	2	0	—	0	.160	.192	.200
Lee Meyer	SS7	—	21	7	23	1	3	0	0	0	0	2	—	0	.130	.200	.130
Hi Myers	OF6	R	20	6	22	1	5	1	0	0	6	2	—	1	.227	.292	.273
Harry Redmond	2B5	R	21	6	19	3	0	0	0	0	1	0	—	0	.000	.000	.000
Tom Catterson	OF6	L	24	9	18	0	4	0	0	0	1	3	—	0	.222	.333	.222

J. Hummel, 17 G at OF; P. McElveen, 5 G at 1B, 5 G at 2B

Pitcher	T	Age	G	GS	CG	ShO	IP	H	HR	BB	SO	W-L	Sv	ERA
Nap Rucker	L	24	38	33	28	6	309.1	245	6	101	201	13-19	1	2.24
George Bell	R	34	33	30	29	6	256.0	236	5	73	95	16-15	1	2.71
Harry McIntire	R	30	32	26	20	2	228.0	200	5	91	84	7-17	1	3.63
Kaiser Wilhelm	R	35	22	17	14	1	163.0	176	3	59	45	3-13	0	3.26
Doc Scanlan	R	28	19	17	12	2	141.1	125	2	65	72	8-7	0	2.93
George Hunter	L	21	16	13	10	0	113.1	104	2	38	43	4-10	0	2.46
Jim Pastorius	L	27	12	9	5	1	79.2	91	4	58	23	1-9	0	5.76
Eddie Dent	R	21	6	5	4	0	42.0	47	2	15	17	2-4	0	4.29
Elmer Knetzer	R	23	5	4	3	0	35.2	33	2	22	7	1-3	0	3.03
Sam Fletcher	R	—	1	1	1	0	9.0	13	0	2	5	0-1	0	8.00
Pembroke Finlayson	R	20	1	0	0	0	7.0	7	0	4	2	0-0	0	5.14

1909 St. Louis Cardinals 7th NL 54-98 .355 56.0 GB

Roger Bresnahan

Player	Gm by Position	B	Age	G	AB	R	H	2B	3B	HR	RBI	BB	SO	SB	Avg	OBP	Slg
Ed Phelps	C83	R	30	100	306	43	76	13	1	0	22	39	—	7	.248	.350	.297
Ed Konetchy	1B152	R	23	152	576	88	165	23	14	4	80	65	—	25	.286	.366	.396
Chappy Charles†	2B71,SS26,3B2	R	28	99	339	33	80	7	3	0	29	31	—	7	.236	.309	.274
Bobby Byrne†	3B105	R	24	105	421	61	90	13	6	1	33	46	—	21	.214	.302	.280
Rudy Hulswitt	SS65,2B12	R	32	82	289	21	81	8	3	0	29	19	—	7	.280	.329	.329
Rube Ellis	OF145	L	23	149	575	76	154	10	9	3	46	54	—	16	.268	.334	.332
Steve Evans	OF141,1B2	L	24	143	498	67	129	17	6	2	56	66	—	14	.259	.362	.329
Al Shaw	OF92	L	28	114	331	45	82	12	7	2	34	55	—	15	.248	.355	.344
Joe Delahanty	OF63,2B48	R	33	123	411	28	88	16	4	2	54	42	—	10	.214	.292	.287
Roger Bresnahan	C59,2B9,3B1	R	30	72	234	27	57	4	1	0	23	46	—	11	.244	.370	.269
Jap Barbeau†	3B47	R	27	47	175	23	44	3	0	0	5	28	—	14	.251	.370	.269
Alan Storke†	SS44,2B4,1B1	R	24	48	174	11	49	5	0	0	10	12	—	5	.282	.328	.310
Jack Bliss	C32	R	27	35	113	12	25	2	1	1	8	12	—	2	.221	.307	.283
Johnny Lush	P34,OF3	L	23	45	92	11	22	5	0	0	14	6	—	2	.239	.293	.293
Howard Murphy	OF19	L	27	25	60	3	12	0	0	0	3	4	—	1	.200	.250	.200
Champ Osteen	SS16	L	32	16	45	6	9	1	0	0	7	7	—	1	.200	.308	.222
Mike Mowrey†	2B7,3B2	R	25	12	29	3	7	1	0	0	4	4	—	1	.241	.333	.276
Billy Gilbert		R	33	12	29	4	5	0	0	0	1	4	—	1	.172	.333	.172
Bert James	OF6	L	22	6	21	1	6	0	0	0	0	4	—	1	.286	.400	.286
Charlie Enwright	SS2	L	21	3	7	1	1	0	0	0	1	2	—	0	.143	.333	.143
Tom Reilly	SS5	R	24	5	7	0	2	0	1	0	2	0	—	0	.286	.286	.571
Coonie Blank	C1	R	16	1	2	0	0	0	0	0	0	0	—	0	.000	.000	.000

Pitcher	T	Age	G	GS	CG	ShO	IP	H	HR	BB	SO	W-L	Sv	ERA
Fred Beebe	R	28	44	34	18	1	287.2	256	5	104	105	15-21	1	2.82
Johnny Lush	L	23	34	28	21	2	221.1	215	1	69	66	11-18	0	3.13
Slim Sallee	L	24	32	27	12	1	219.0	223	3	59	55	10-11	0	2.42
Bob Harmon	R	21	21	17	10	0	159.0	155	6	65	48	6-11	0	3.68
Les Backman	R	21	21	14	8	0	128.1	146	1	39	35	3-11	0	4.14
John Raleigh	L	19	15	10	3	0	80.2	85	0	21	26	1-10	0	3.79
Charlie Rhodes	R	24	12	10	4	0	61.0	55	0	33	25	3-5	0	3.98
Harry Sullivan	L	21	2	1	0	0	1.0	4	1	2	1	0-0	0	36.00
Steve Melter	R	23	23	1	0	0	64.1	79	1	20	24	0-1	3	3.50
Eddie Higgins	R	21	16	5	5	0	66.0	68	4	17	15	3-3	0	4.50
Forrest More†	R	25	15	3	1	0	50.0	48	0	20	17	1-5	0	5.04
Grover Lowdermilk	R	24	7	3	1	0	29.0	28	0	30	14	0-2	0	6.21
Irv Higginbotham†	R	27	3	1	1	0	11.1	5	0	2	2	1-0	0	1.59
Joe Bernard	R	27	1	0	0	0	1.0	1	0	2	2	0-0	0	0.00

1909 Boston Beaneaters 8th NL 45-108 .294 65.5 GB

Harry Smith (23-54)/Frank Bowerman (22-54)

Player	Gm by Position	B	Age	G	AB	R	H	2B	3B	HR	RBI	BB	SO	SB	Avg	OBP	Slg
Peaches Graham	C76,OF6,3B1*	R	32	92	267	27	64	6	3	0	17	24	—	7	.240	.302	.285
Fred Stem	1B68	L	23	73	245	13	51	2	3	0	11	12	—	5	.208	.254	.241
Dave Shean†	2B72	R	25	75	267	32	66	11	4	1	29	17	—	14	.247	.297	.330
Bill Sweeney	3B112,SS26	R	23	138	493	44	120	19	3	1	36	37	—	25	.243	.296	.300
Jack Coffey	SS73	R	22	73	257	21	48	4	4	0	20	11	—	2	.187	.229	.233
Beals Becker	OF152	L	22	152	562	60	138	15	6	6	24	47	—	21	.246	.305	.326
Ginger Beaumont	OF111	L	32	123	407	35	107	11	4	0	60	35	—	12	.263	.321	.310
Roy Thomas	OF76	L	35	83	281	36	74	9	1	0	11	47	—	5	.263	.369	.302
Fred Beck	OF57,1B33	L	22	96	334	20	66	4	6	3	27	17	—	5	.198	.245	.272
Johnny Bates†	OF60	L	26	63	236	27	68	15	3	1	23	20	—	15	.288	.354	.390
Charlie Starr†	2B54,SS6,3B3	—	30	61	216	16	48	2	3	0	6	31	—	7	.222	.333	.259
Chick Autry†	1B61,OF4	L	24	65	199	16	39	4	0	0	13	21	—	5	.196	.279	.216
Bill Dahlen	SS49,2B6,3B2	R	39	69	197	22	46	6	1	2	16	29	—	4	.234	.332	.305
Gus Getz	3B36,2B2,SS2	R	19	40	148	6	33	2	0	0	9	1	—	2	.223	.228	.236
Harry Smith	C31	R	34	43	113	9	19	4	1	0	4	5	—	3	.168	.203	.221
Frank Bowerman	C27	R	40	33	99	6	21	2	0	0	4	2	—	0	.212	.228	.232
Claude Ritchey	2B25	S	35	30	87	4	15	1	0	0	3	8	—	1	.172	.242	.184
Bill Rariden	C13	R	21	13	42	1	6	1	0	0	1	4	—	1	.143	.217	.167
Al Shaw	C14	R	34	17	41	1	4	0	0	0	0	5	—	0	.098	.213	.098
Herbie Moran	OF8	L	25	8	31	8	7	1	0	0	0	5	—	0	.226	.333	.258
Hosea Siner	3B5,2B1,SS1	R	24	10	23	1	3	0	0	0	1	2	—	0	.130	.200	.130
Ernie Diehl	OF1	R	31	1	4	1	2	1	0	0	0	0	—	0	.500	.500	.750
Bill Dam	OF1	—	24	1	2	1	1	1	0	0	0	1	—	0	.500	.667	1.000

P. Graham, 1 G at SS

Pitcher	T	Age	G	GS	CG	ShO	IP	H	HR	BB	SO	W-L	Sv	ERA
Al Mattern	R	26	47	32	24	2	316.1	322	4	108	98	15-21	3	2.85
George Ferguson	R	22	36	30	19	3	226.2	235	2	83	87	5-23	0	3.73
Kirby White	R	25	23	19	11	0	148.1	134	5	80	53	6-13	0	3.22
Buster Brown†	R	27	18	17	8	2	123.1	108	1	56	32	4-8	0	3.14
Lew Richie†	R	25	22	13	9	2	131.2	118	2	44	42	7-7	2	2.32
Tom Tuckey	L	25	17	10	4	0	90.2	104	1	22	16	0-9	0	4.27
Cliff Curtis	R	25	10	9	8	2	83.0	53	1	30	22	4-5	0	1.41
Tom McCarthy	R	25	8	7	3	0	46.1	47	3	28	11	0-5	0	3.50
Bill Chappelle†	R	25	5	3	2	0	29.0	31	0	11	8	1-1	0	1.86
Chick Evans	R	19	4	3	1	0	22.0	25	0	14	11	0-3	0	4.50
Vive Lindaman	R	31	15	6	6	1	66.0	75	1	28	13	1-6	0	4.64
Forrest More†	R	25	10	4	3	0	48.2	47	0	20	10	1-5	0	4.44
Gus Dorner	R	32	5	2	0	0	24.2	17	1	17	7	1-2	1	2.55
Bill Cooney	R	26	3	0	0	0	6.1	4	0	2	3	0-0	0	1.42
Jake Boultes	R	24	1	0	0	0	8.0	9	2	0	1	0-0	0	6.75

»1910 Philadelphia Athletics 1st AL 102-48 .680 —

Connie Mack

Player	Gm by Position	B	Age	G	AB	R	H	2B	3B	HR	RBI	BB	SO	SB	Avg	OBP	Slg
Jack Lapp	C63	L	25	71	192	18	45	4	3	0	17	20	—	0	.234	.310	.286
Harry Davis	1B139	R	36	139	492	61	122	19	4	1	41	53	—	17	.248	.332	.309
Eddie Collins	2B153	L	23	153	583	81	188	16	15	3	81	49	—	81	.322	.381	.417
Home Run Baker	3B146	L	24	146	561	83	159	25	15	2	74	34	—	21	.283	.329	.392
Jack Barry	SS145	R	23	145	487	64	126	19	5	3	60	52	—	14	.259	.336	.337
Danny Murphy	OF151	R	33	151	560	70	168	28	18	4	64	31	—	18	.300	.338	.436
Rube Oldring	OF134	R	26	134	546	79	168	27	14	4	57	23	—	17	.308	.340	.430
Topsy Hartsel	OF83	L	36	90	285	45	63	10	3	0	22	58	—	11	.221	.353	.277
Bris Lord†	OF70	R	26	72	288	53	80	16	12	1	20	23	—	6	.278	.333	.427
Ira Thomas	C60	R	29	60	180	14	50	8	1	1	19	6	—	2	.278	.301	.361
Paddy Livingston	C37	R	30	37	120	11	25	4	3	0	9	6	—	2	.208	.264	.292
Heine Heitmuller	OF28	R	27	31	111	11	27	2	2	0	7	6	—	6	.243	.288	.297
Stuffy McInnis	SS17,2B5,3B4*	R	19	38	73	10	22	2	4	0	12	7	—	3	.301	.363	.438
Ben Houser	1B26	L	26	34	69	9	13	3	2	0	7	7	—	0	.188	.263	.290
Amos Strunk	OF14	L	21	16	48	9	16	0	1	0	2	3	—	4	.333	.373	.375
Pat Donahue†	C14	R	25	15	35	2	5	0	0	0	4	3	—	1	.143	.231	.143
Morrie Rath†	3B11,2B3	L	23	18	26	3	4	0	0	0	1	5	—	0	.154	.290	.154
Earle Mack	C1	L	20	1	4	0	2	0	1	0	0	0	—	0	.500	.500	1.000
Claud Derrick	SS1	R	24	2	1	0	0	0	0	0	0	0	—	0	.000	.000	.000

S. McInnis, 1 G at OF

Pitcher	T	Age	G	GS	CG	ShO	IP	H	HR	BB	SO	W-L	Sv	ERA
Jack Coombs	R	27	45	38	35	13	353.0	248	0	115	224	31-9	1	1.30
Cy Morgan	R	31	36	34	23	3	290.2	214	0	117	134	18-12	0	1.55
Eddie Plank	L	34	38	32	22	1	250.1	218	3	55	123	16-10	2	2.01
Chief Bender	R	26	30	28	25	3	250.0	182	1	47	155	23-5	0	1.58
Harry Krause	L	22	16	11	9	2	112.1	99	4	42	60	6-6	0	2.88
Lefty Russell	L	19	1	1	1	1	9.0	8	0	2	5	1-0	0	0.00
Jimmy Dygert	R	25	19	8	6	1	99.1	81	0	49	59	4-4	0	2.54
Tommy Atkins	L	22	15	3	2	0	57.0	53	0	23	29	3-2	2	2.68

1910 New York Highlanders 2nd AL 88-63 .583 14.5 GB

George Stallings (78-59)/Hal Chase (10-4)

Player	Gm by Position	B	Age	G	AB	R	H	2B	3B	HR	RBI	BB	SO	SB	Avg	OBP	Slg
Jeff Sweeney	C77	R	21	78	215	25	43	4	4	0	13	17	—	12	.200	.271	.256
Hal Chase	1B130	R	27	130	524	67	152	20	5	3	73	16	—	40	.290	.312	.365
Frank LaPorte	2B79,OF23,3B15	R	30	124	432	43	114	14	6	2	67	33	—	16	.264	.321	.338
Jimmy Austin	3B133	S	30	133	432	46	94	11	4	2	36	47	—	22	.218	.305	.275
John Knight	SS79,1B23,2B7*	R	24	117	414	58	129	25	4	3	45	34	—	23	.312	.372	.413
Birdie Cree	OF134	R	27	134	467	58	134	19	16	4	73	40	—	28	.287	.353	.422
Harry Wolter	OF130	L	25	135	479	84	128	15	9	4	42	66	—	39	.267	.364	.361
Charlie Hemphill	OF94	L	34	102	351	45	84	9	4	0	21	55	—	19	.239	.350	.288
Bert Daniels	OF85,3B6,1B4	R	27	95	356	68	90	13	8	1	17	41	—	41	.253	.356	.343
Earle Gardner	2B70	R	26	86	271	36	66	4	2	1	24	21	—	9	.244	.303	.284
Roxey Roach	SS58,OF9	R	27	70	220	27	47	9	2	0	20	29	—	15	.214	.313	.273
Fred Mitchell	C68	R	32	68	196	16	45	7	2	0	18	9	—	6	.230	.274	.286
Eddie Foster	SS22	R	23	30	83	5	11	2	0	0	1	8	—	2	.133	.217	.157
Lou Criger	C27	R	38	27	69	3	13	2	0	0	4	10	—	0	.188	.291	.217
Walter Blair	C6	R	26	6	22	2	5	0	1	0	2	0	—	0	.227	.227	.318
Les Channell	OF6	L	24	6	19	3	6	0	0	0	3	2	—	2	.316	.381	.316
Clyde Engle†	OF3	R	26	5	13	0	3	0	0	0	0	2	—	1	.231	.333	.231
Red Kleinow†	C5	R	30	6	12	2	5	0	0	0	2	1	—	2	.417	.462	.417
Joe Walsh	C1	R	23	1	3	0	0	0	0	0	2	0	—	0	.000	.000	.000
Larry McClure	OF1	R	24	1	1	0	0	0	0	0	0	0	—	0	.000	.000	.000
Tommy Madden		L	26	1	1	0	0	0	0	0	0	0	—	0	.000	.000	.000

J. Knight, 4 G at 3B, 1 G at OF

Pitcher	T	Age	G	GS	CG	ShO	IP	H	HR	BB	SO	W-L	Sv	ERA
Russ Ford	R	27	36	33	29	8	299.2	194	4	70	209	26-6	1	1.65
Jack Quinn	R	26	35	31	20	0	235.2	214	2	58	82	18-12	0	2.44
Jack Warhop	R	25	37	27	20	0	243.0	219	1	79	75	14-14	2	3.00
Hippo Vaughn	L	22	30	25	18	5	221.2	190	1	58	107	13-11	1	1.83
Tom Hughes	R	26	23	15	11	0	151.2	153	0	37	64	7-9	1	3.50
Rube Manning	R	27	16	9	4	0	75.1	80	4	25	25	2-4	0	3.70
John Frill	L	31	10	5	3	1	48.1	55	1	5	27	2-2	1	4.47
Slow Joe Doyle†	R	28	3	2	1	0	12.1	19	0	5	6	0-2	0	8.03
Ray Fisher	R	22	17	7	3	0	92.1	95	0	18	42	5-3	1	2.92
Ray Caldwell	R	22	6	2	1	0	19.1	19	1	9	17	1-0	1	3.72

1910 Detroit Tigers 3rd AL 86-68 .558 18.0 GB

Hughie Jennings

Player	Gm by Position	B	Age	G	AB	R	H	2B	3B	HR	RBI	BB	SO	SB	Avg	OBP	Slg
Oscar Stanage	C84	R	27	88	275	24	57	7	4	2	25	20	—	1	.207	.266	.284
Tom Jones	1B135	R	33	135	432	32	110	12	4	1	45	35	—	22	.255	.325	.308
Jim Delahanty	2B106	R	31	106	378	67	111	16	2	3	45	43	—	15	.294	.379	.370
George Moriarty	3B134	R	26	136	490	53	123	24	3	2	60	33	—	33	.251	.308	.324
Donie Bush	SS141,3B1	S	22	142	496	90	130	13	4	3	34	78	—	49	.262	.365	.323
Sam Crawford	OF153,1B1	L	30	154	588	83	170	26	19	5	120	37	—	20	.289	.332	.423
Ty Cobb	OF137	L	23	140	506	106	194	35	13	8	91	64	—	65	.383	.456	.551
Davy Jones	OF101	L	30	113	377	77	100	6	6	0	24	51	—	25	.265	.362	.313
Matty McIntyre	OF77	L	30	83	305	40	72	15	5	0	25	39	—	4	.236	.323	.318
Charley O'Leary	2B38,SS16,3B6	R	27	65	211	23	51	7	1	0	9	9	—	7	.242	.276	.284
Boss Schmidt	C66	S	29	71	197	22	51	7	7	1	23	2	—	2	.259	.277	.381
George Mullin	P38,OF2	R	29	50	129	15	33	6	2	1	11	8	—	1	.256	.299	.357
Hack Simmons	1B22,3B7,OF2	R	25	42	110	12	25	3	1	0	9	10	—	1	.227	.303	.273
Ed Willett	P37,OF1	R	26	38	83	5	11	3	1	0	4	2	—	0	.133	.182	.193
Chick Lathers	3B13,2B7,SS4	L	21	41	82	4	19	2	0	0	3	8	—	0	.232	.300	.256
Joe Casey	C22	R	22	23	62	3	12	3	0	0	2	2	—	1	.194	.231	.242
Jay Kirke	2B7,OF1	L	22	8	25	3	5	1	0	0	3	1	—	1	.200	.231	.240
Hennie Beckendorf†	C2	R	26	3	13	0	3	0	0	0	2	1	—	0	.231	.286	.231

Pitcher	T	Age	G	GS	CG	ShO	IP	H	HR	BB	SO	W-L	Sv	ERA
George Mullin	R	29	38	32	27	5	289.0	260	7	102	98	21-12	0	2.87
Ed Willett	R	26	37	25	18	4	224.1	175	2	74	65	16-11	0	2.37
Ed Summers	R	25	30	25	18	1	220.1	211	8	60	82	13-12	0	2.53
Wild Bill Donovan	R	33	26	23	20	3	206.2	184	4	61	107	17-7	0	2.44
Sailor Stroud	R	25	28	15	7	3	130.1	123	9	41	63	5-9	1	3.25
Ralph Works	R	22	18	10	5	0	85.2	73	1	39	36	3-6	1	3.57
Ed Killian	L	33	11	9	5	1	74.0	75	2	27	20	4-3	0	3.04
Frank Browning	R	27	11	6	2	0	49.0	51	0	10	16	2-2	3	2.57
Marv Peasley	L	21	2	1	0	0	10.0	13	0	11	4	0-1	0	8.10
Bill Lelivelt	R	25	1	1	1	0	9.0	6	0	3	2	0-1	0	1.00
Dave Skeels	R	17	1	1	0	0	6.0	9	0	4	2	0-0	0	12.00
Hub Pernoll	L	22	11	5	4	0	54.2	54	1	14	25	4-3	0	2.96
Art Loudell	R	28	5	2	1	0	21.1	23	0	14	12	1-1	0	3.38

1910 Boston Red Sox 4th AL 81-72 .529 22.5 GB

Patsy Donovan

Player	Gm by Position	B	Age	G	AB	R	H	2B	3B	HR	RBI	BB	SO	SB	Avg	OBP	Slg
Bill Carrigan	C110	R	26	114	342	36	85	11	1	3	53	23	—	10	.249	.307	.313
Jake Stahl	1B142	R	31	144	531	68	144	19	16	10	77	42	—	22	.271	.334	.424
Larry Gardner	2B113	L	24	113	413	55	117	12	10	2	36	41	—	8	.283	.354	.375
Harry Lord†	3B70,SS1	L	28	77	288	25	72	5	5	1	32	14	—	17	.250	.294	.313
Heinie Wagner	SS140	R	29	142	491	61	134	26	7	1	52	44	—	26	.273	.335	.360
Harry Hooper	OF155	L	22	155	584	81	156	9	10	2	27	62	—	40	.267	.346	.327
Duffy Lewis	OF149	R	22	151	541	64	153	29	7	8	68	32	—	10	.283	.328	.407
Tris Speaker	OF140	L	22	141	538	92	183	20	14	7	65	52	—	35	.340	.404	.468
Clyde Engle†	3B51,2B27,OF15*	R	26	106	363	59	96	18	7	2	38	31	—	12	.264	.326	.369
Billy Purtell†	3B41,SS10	R	24	49	168	15	35	1	2	1	15	18	—	2	.208	.289	.256
Red Kleinow†	C49	R	30	50	147	9	22	1	0	1	8	20	—	3	.150	.251	.177
Hugh Bradley	1B21,C3,OF1	R	25	32	83	8	14	6	2	0	7	5	—	2	.169	.216	.289
Sea Lion Hall	P35,OF3	L	24	47	82	6	17	2	4	0	8	6	—	1	.207	.278	.329
Harry Niles†	OF15	R	29	18	57	6	12	3	0	1	3	4	—	1	.211	.262	.316
Charlie French†	2B8	L	26	9	40	4	8	1	0	0	3	1	—	0	.200	.220	.225
Amby McConnell†	2B10	L	27	12	36	6	6	0	0	0	1	5	—	4	.167	.302	.167
Bunny Madden	C12	R	27	14	35	4	13	3	0	0	4	3	—	0	.371	.436	.457
Dutch Lerchen	SS6	R	21	6	15	1	0	0	0	0	0	1	—	0	.000	.063	.000
Doc Moskiman	1B2,OF1	R	30	5	9	1	1	0	0	0	1	2	—	0	.111	.273	.111
Chris Mahoney	P2,OF1	R	25	3	7	1	1	0	0	0	0	0	—	0	.143	.143	.143
Hap Myers	OF2	R	22	3	6	0	2	0	0	0	0	0	—	0	.333	.333	.333
Ralph Pond	OF1	—	22	1	4	0	1	0	0	0	0	0	—	1	.250	.250	.250
Pat Donahue†	C1	R	25	2	4	0	0	0	0	0	0	0	—	0	.000	.000	.000
Ed Hearn	SS2	R	21	2	2	0	0	0	0	0	0	0	—	0	.000	.000	.000

C. Engle, 7 G at SS

Pitcher	T	Age	G	GS	CG	ShO	IP	H	HR	BB	SO	W-L	Sv	ERA
Eddie Cicotte	R	26	36	30	20	3	250.0	213	4	86	104	15-11	0	2.74
Ray Collins	L	23	35	26	18	4	244.2	205	1	41	109	13-11	1	1.62
Ed Karger	L	27	27	25	16	1	183.1	162	5	53	81	11-7	1	3.19
Charlie Smith	R	30	24	18	11	0	156.1	141	4	35	53	11-6	1	2.30
Frank Arellanes	R	28	18	13	2	0	100.0	106	1	24	33	4-7	0	2.88
Ben Hunt	L	21	7	7	3	0	46.2	45	4	20	19	2-3	0	4.05
Frank Smith†	R	30	4	3	2	0	28.0	22	0	11	8	1-2	0	4.82
Marty McHale	R	21	2	2	1	0	13.2	15	0	6	14	0-2	0	4.61
Chris Mahoney	R	25	2	1	0	0	11.0	16	1	5	6	0-1	1	3.27
Joe Wood	R	20	35	17	14	3	197.2	155	3	56	145	12-13	0	1.68
Sea Lion Hall	R	24	35	16	13	0	188.2	142	6	73	95	12-9	5	1.91
Frank Barberich	R	28	2	0	0	0	5.0	7	0	2	0	0-0	0	7.20
Louis LeRoy	R	31	1	0	0	0	4.0	7	1	2	3	0-0	0	11.25

1910 Cleveland Bronchos 5th AL 71-81 .467 32.0 GB

Deacon McGuire

Player	Gm by Position	B	Age	G	AB	R	H	2B	3B	HR	RBI	BB	SO	SB	Avg	OBP	Slg
Ted Easterly	C66,OF30	L	25	110	363	34	111	16	6	0	55	21	—	10	.306	.344	.383
George Stovall	1B132,2B2	R	31	142	521	49	136	19	4	0	52	14	—	16	.261	.284	.313
Nap Lajoie	2B149,1B10,SS4	R	35	159	591	94	227	51	7	4	76	60	—	26	.384	.445	.514
Bill Bradley	3B61	R	32	61	214	12	42	3	0	0	12	10	—	6	.196	.236	.210
Terry Turner	SS94,3B46,2B9	R	29	150	574	71	132	14	6	0	33	53	—	31	.230	.301	.275
Jack Graney	OF114	L	24	116	454	62	107	13	9	1	31	37	—	18	.236	.293	.311
Joe Birmingham	OF103,3B1	R	25	104	364	41	84	11	2	0	35	23	—	18	.231	.286	.272
Art Kruger†	OF62	R	29	62	223	19	38	6	3	0	14	20	—	12	.170	.251	.224
Harry Niles†	OF50,SS7,3B5	R	29	70	240	25	51	6	4	1	18	15	—	9	.213	.267	.283
Bris Lord†	OF56	R	26	56	201	23	44	5	6	0	17	12	—	4	.219	.270	.303
Harry Bemis	C46	R	36	61	167	12	36	5	1	1	16	5	—	3	.216	.238	.275
George Perring	3B33,1B4	R	25	39	122	14	27	6	3	0	8	3	—	3	.221	.240	.320
Neal Ball	SS27,2B6,OF6*	R	29	53	119	12	25	3	1	0	12	9	—	4	.210	.266	.252
Grover Land	C33	R	25	34	111	4	23	0	0	0	7	2	—	1	.207	.228	.207
Joe Jackson	OF20	L	20	20	75	15	29	2	5	1	11	8	—	4	.387	.446	.587
Elmer Flick	OF18	L	34	24	68	5	18	2	1	1	7	10	—	1	.265	.359	.368
Morrie Rath†	3B22,SS1	L	23	24	67	5	13	3	0	0	0	10	—	2	.194	.299	.239
Eddie Hohnhorst	1B17	L	25	17	62	8	20	3	1	0	6	4	—	3	.323	.364	.403
Cotton Knaupp	SS18	R	20	18	59	3	14	3	1	0	11	8	—	1	.237	.338	.322
Nig Clarke	C17	L	27	21	58	4	9	2	0	0	2	8	—	0	.155	.258	.190
Art Thomason	OF17	L	21	17	57	3	9	0	1	0	2	5	—	3	.158	.226	.193
Roger Peckinpaugh	SS14	R	19	15	45	1	9	0	0	0	6	1	—	3	.200	.234	.200
Dave Callahan	OF12	L	21	13	44	6	8	1	0	0	2	4	—	5	.182	.265	.205
Syd Smith	C9	R	26	9	27	1	9	1	0	0	3	3	—	0	.333	.400	.370
Bert Adams	C5	S	19	5	13	1	3	0	0	0	0	0	—	0	.231	.231	.231
Herman Bronkie	3B3,SS1	R	25	4	9	1	2	0	0	0	0	1	—	1	.222	.300	.222
Pat Donahue†	C2,1B1	R	25	2	6	0	1	0	0	0	0	0	—	0	.167	.167	.167
Deacon McGuire	C1	R	46	1	3	0	1	0	0	0	0	0	—	0	.333	.500	.333
Jim Rutherford	OF1	L	23	1	2	0	1	0	0	0	0	0	—	0	.500	.500	.500
Simon Nicholls	SS3	L	27	3	0	0	0	0	0	0	0	0	—	0	—	—	—

N. Ball, 3 G at 3B

Pitcher	T	Age	G	GS	CG	ShO	IP	H	HR	BB	SO	W-L	Sv	ERA
Cy Falkenberg	R	29	37	29	18	3	256.2	246	3	75	107	14-13	1	2.95
Cy Young	R	43	21	20	14	1	163.1	149	0	27	58	7-10	0	2.53
Willie Mitchell	L	20	35	18	11	1	183.2	155	2	55	102	12-8	0	2.60
Specs Harkness	R	22	26	16	6	1	136.1	132	2	55	60	10-7	1	3.04
Fred Link†	L	24	22	13	6	1	127.2	121	0	50	55	5-6	1	3.17
Addie Joss	R	30	13	12	9	1	107.1	96	2	18	49	5-5	0	2.26
George Kahler	R	20	12	12	8	2	95.1	80	0	46	38	6-4	0	1.60
Harry Fanwell	R	23	17	11	5	1	92.0	87	0	38	30	2-9	0	3.62
Heinie Berger	R	28	13	8	2	0	65.1	57	0	32	24	3-4	0	3.03
Fred Blanding	R	22	6	5	4	1	45.1	43	0	12	25	2-2	0	2.78
Ben DeMott	R	21	6	4	1	0	28.1	45	0	8	13	0-3	0	5.40
Elmer Koestner	R	24	27	13	8	1	145.0	145	0	63	44	5-10	2	3.04
Walt Doane	R	23	6	0	0	0	17.2	31	1	8	7	0-0	0	5.60
Harry Kirsch	R	22	2	0	0	0	3.0	5	0	1	5	0-0	0	6.00

1910 Chicago White Sox 6th AL 68-85 .444 35.5 GB

Hugh Duffy

Player	Gm by Position	B	Age	G	AB	R	H	2B	3B	HR	RBI	BB	SO	SB	Avg	OBP	Slg
Fred Payne	C78,OF2	R	29	91	257	17	56	5	4	0	19	11	—	6	.218	.256	.268
Chick Gandil	1B74,OF2	R	23	77	275	21	53	7	3	2	21	24	—	12	.193	.267	.262
Rollie Zeider	2B87,SS45,3B4	R	26	136	498	57	108	9	2	0	31	62	—	49	.217	.305	.243
Billy Purtell†	3B102	R	24	102	368	21	86	5	3	1	36	21	—	5	.234	.282	.272
Lena Blackburne	SS74	R	23	75	242	16	42	3	1	0	10	19	—	4	.174	.245	.194
Patsy Dougherty	OF121	L	33	127	443	45	110	8	6	1	43	41	—	22	.248	.318	.300
Shano Collins	OF65,1B27	R	24	97	315	29	62	10	8	1	24	25	—	10	.197	.258	.289
Paul Meloan	OF65	L	21	65	222	23	54	6	6	0	23	17	—	4	.243	.314	.324
Freddy Parent	OF62,2B11,SS4*	R	34	81	258	23	46	6	1	1	16	29	—	14	.178	.266	.221
Lee Tannehill	SS38,1B23,3B6	R	29	67	230	17	51	10	0	1	21	11	—	3	.222	.263	.278
Charlie French†	2B28,OF16	L	26	45	170	17	28	1	1	0	4	10	—	5	.165	.224	.182
Harry Lord†	3B44	L	28	44	165	26	49	6	3	0	10	14	—	17	.297	.352	.370
Bruno Block	C47	R	25	55	152	12	32	1	1	0	9	13	—	3	.211	.273	.230
Billy Sullivan	C45	R	35	45	142	10	26	4	1	0	6	7	—	0	.183	.227	.225
Doc White	P33,OF14	L	31	56	126	14	25	1	2	0	8	14	—	2	.198	.279	.238
Charlie Mullen	1B37,OF2	R	21	41	123	15	24	2	1	0	13	4	—	4	.195	.220	.228
Amby McConnell†	2B32	L	27	32	119	13	33	2	3	0	5	7	—	4	.277	.323	.345
George Browne†	OF29	L	34	30	112	17	27	4	1	0	4	12	—	5	.241	.315	.295
Dutch Zwilling	OF27	L	21	27	87	7	16	5	0	0	5	11	—	1	.184	.283	.241
Felix Chouinard	OF23,2B1	R	22	24	82	6	16	3	2	0	9	8	—	4	.195	.275	.280
Willis Cole	OF22	R	28	22	80	6	14	2	1	0	2	4	—	0	.175	.224	.225
Ed Hahn	OF15	L	34	15	53	2	6	2	0	0	1	7	—	0	.113	.217	.151
Red Kelly	OF14	R	25	14	45	6	7	0	1	0	1	7	—	0	.156	.296	.200
Bobby Messenger	OF9	S	26	9	26	7	6	0	1	0	4	4	—	3	.231	.375	.308
Cuke Barrows	OF6	R	26	6	20	0	4	0	0	0	1	3	—	0	.200	.304	.200
Red Bowser	OF1	—	28	1	2	0	0	0	0	0	0	0	—	0	.000	.000	.000

F. Parent, 1 G at 3B

Pitcher	T	Age	G	GS	CG	ShO	IP	H	HR	BB	SO	W-L	Sv	ERA
Ed Walsh	R	29	45	36	33	7	369.2	242	5	61	258	18-20	5	1.27
Doc White	L	31	33	29	20	2	236.2	219	2	50	111	15-13	1	2.66
Jim Scott	R	22	41	23	14	2	229.2	182	5	86	135	8-18	2	2.43
Fred Olmstead	R	28	32	20	14	4	184.1	174	1	50	68	10-12	0	1.95
Irv Young	L	32	27	17	7	4	135.2	122	0	39	64	4-8	0	2.72
Frank Lange	R	26	23	15	6	1	130.2	93	2	54	98	9-4	0	1.65
Frank Smith†	R	30	19	15	9	3	128.2	91	1	40	50	4-9	0	2.03
Chief Chouneau	R	20	1	1	0	0	5.1	7	0	0	1	0-1	0	3.38
Bill Burns†	L	30	1	0	0	0	0.1	0	0	1	0	0-0	0	0.00

1910 Washington Senators 7th AL 66-85 .437 36.5 GB

Jimmy McAleer

Player	Gm by Position	B	Age	G	AB	R	H	2B	3B	HR	RBI	BB	SO	SB	Avg	OBP	Slg
Gabby Street	C86	R	27	89	257	13	52	6	0	1	16	23	—	1	.202	.273	.237
Bob Unglaub	1B124	R	28	124	431	29	101	9	4	0	44	21	—	21	.234	.270	.274
Red Killefer	2B88,OF12	R	25	106	345	35	79	17	1	0	24	29	—	17	.229	.318	.284
Kid Elberfeld	3B113,2B10,SS3	R	35	127	455	53	114	9	2	2	42	35	—	19	.251	.322	.292
George McBride	SS154	R	29	154	514	54	118	19	4	1	55	61	—	11	.230	.321	.288
Doc Gessler	OF144	L	29	145	487	58	126	17	11	2	50	62	—	18	.259	.361	.351
Clyde Milan	OF142	L	23	142	531	89	148	17	6	0	16	71	—	44	.279	.379	.333
Jack Lelivelt	OF86,1B7	L	24	110	347	40	92	10	3	0	33	40	—	20	.265	.343	.311
Wid Conroy	3B46,OF46,2B5	R	33	103	351	36	89	11	3	1	27	30	—	11	.254	.314	.311
Germany Schaefer	2B35,OF26,3B2	R	33	74	229	27	63	6	5	0	14	25	—	17	.275	.352	.345
Eddie Ainsmith	C30	R	18	33	104	4	20	1	2	0	9	6	—	0	.192	.236	.240
Hennie Beckendorf†	C36	R	26	37	97	8	15	1	0	0	10	5	—	0	.155	.219	.165
John Henry	C18,1B10	R	20	28	87	2	13	1	1	0	5	2	—	2	.149	.169	.184
Bill Cunningham	2B21	R	22	22	74	3	22	5	1	0	14	12	—	4	.297	.402	.392
Doc Ralston	OF22	R	24	22	73	4	15	1	0	0	3	3	—	2	.205	.256	.219
Jock Somerlott	1B16	R	27	16	63	6	14	0	0	0	2	3	—	2	.222	.258	.222
George Browne†	OF5	L	34	7	22	1	4	0	0	0	0	1	—	0	.182	.217	.182
Tom Crooke	1B5	R	25	8	21	1	4	1	0	0	1	1	—	0	.190	.227	.238
Jack Hardy	C4,OF1	R	33	7	8	1	2	0	0	0	0	0	—	0	.250	.250	.250

Pitcher	T	Age	G	GS	CG	ShO	IP	H	HR	BB	SO	W-L	Sv	ERA
Walter Johnson	R	22	45	42	38	8	370.0	262	1	76	313	25-17	1	1.36
Bob Groom	R	25	34	30	22	3	257.2	255	8	77	98	12-17	0	2.76
Dolly Gray	L	31	34	29	21	3	229.0	216	3	64	84	8-19	0	2.63
Dixie Walker	R	23	29	26	16	3	199.1	167	2	68	85	11-11	0	3.30
Doc Reisling	R	35	30	20	13	2	191.0	185	3	44	57	10-10	1	2.54
Frank Oberlin	R	34	8	6	6	0	57.1	52	0	23	18	0-6	0	2.98
Charlie Moyer	—	24	6	3	2	0	25.0	22	1	13	3	0-3	0	3.24
Bill Otey	L	23	9	1	1	0	34.2	40	1	6	12	0-1	0	3.38
Dutch Hinrichs	R	21	3	0	0	0	7.0	10	0	3	5	0-1	1	2.57
Joe Hovlik	R	25	1	0	0	0	1.2	6	0	0	0	0-0	0	16.20
Bill Forman	R	23	1	0	0	0	0.2	1	0	0	0	0-0	0	13.50

1910 St. Louis Browns 8th AL 47-107 .305 57.0 GB

Jack O'Connor

Player	Gm by Position	B	Age	G	AB	R	H	2B	3B	HR	RBI	BB	SO	SB	Avg	OBP	Slg
Jim Stephens	C96	R	26	99	299	24	72	3	7	0	23	16	—	2	.241	.284	.298
Patrick Newnam	1B103	L	29	103	384	45	83	3	8	2	26	29	—	16	.216	.275	.281
Frank Truesdale	2B123	S	26	123	415	39	91	7	2	1	25	48	—	29	.219	.303	.253
Roy Hartzell	3B89,SS38,OF23	L	28	151	542	52	118	13	5	2	30	49	—	18	.218	.290	.271
Bobby Wallace	SS99,3B39	R	36	138	508	47	131	19	7	0	37	49	—	12	.258	.324	.323
George Stone	OF147	L	32	152	562	60	144	17	12	0	40	48	—	20	.256	.315	.329
Al Schweitzer	OF109	R	27	113	379	37	87	11	2	2	37	36	—	26	.230	.303	.285
Danny Hoffman	OF106	L	30	106	380	20	90	11	5	0	27	34	—	16	.237	.306	.292
Art Griggs	OF49,2B41,1B17*	R	26	123	416	28	98	22	5	2	30	25	—	11	.236	.281	.327
Bill Killefer	C73	R	22	74	193	14	24	2	2	0	7	12	—	0	.124	.184	.155
Hub Northen	OF26	L	24	26	96	6	19	1	0	0	16	5	—	2	.198	.238	.208
Dode Criss	1B12,P6	L	25	70	91	11	21	4	2	1	11	11	—	2	.231	.320	.352
Bill Abstein	1B23	R	27	25	87	1	13	2	0	0	3	2	—	3	.149	.169	.172
Red Corriden	SS14,3B12	R	22	26	84	19	13	3	0	1	4	13	—	5	.155	.297	.226
Red Fisher	OF19	L	23	23	72	5	9	2	1	0	3	8	—	5	.125	.222	.181
Barney Pelty	P27,3B1	R	29	28	56	2	5	0	0	0	2	2	—	0	.089	.121	.089
Joe McDonald	3B10	R	22	10	32	4	5	0	0	0	1	1	—	0	.156	.182	.156
Bert Graham	1B5,2B2	S	24	8	26	1	3	2	1	0	5	1	—	0	.115	.148	.269
Sled Allen	C12,1B1	R	23	14	23	3	3	1	0	0	1	1	—	0	.130	.231	.174
Ray Demmitt	OF8	L	26	10	23	4	4	1	0	0	2	3	—	0	.174	.296	.217
Tommy Mee	SS6,2B1,3B1	R	20	8	19	1	3	2	0	0	1	0	—	0	.158	.158	.263
Ray Jansen	3B1	R	21	1	5	0	4	0	0	0	0	0	—	0	.800	.800	.800
Joe Crisp	C1	R	20	1	1	0	0	0	0	0	0	0	—	0	.000	.000	.000
Jack O'Connor	C1	R	41	1	0	0	0	0	0	0	0	0	—	0	—	—	—

A. Griggs, 3 G at 3B, 3 G at SS

Pitcher	T	Age	G	GS	CG	ShO	IP	H	HR	BB	SO	W-L	Sv	ERA
Joe Lake	R	29	35	29	24	1	261.1	243	2	77	141	11-17	2	2.20
Bill Bailey	L	21	34	20	13	0	192.1	186	2	97	90	3-18	0	3.28
Barney Pelty	R	29	27	18	12	3	165.1	157	3	70	48	5-11	0	3.48
Jack Powell	R	35	21	18	8	3	129.1	121	0	28	52	7-11	0	2.30
Farmer Ray	R	23	21	16	11	0	140.2	146	3	49	35	4-10	0	3.58
Marc Hall	R	22	8	7	5	0	46.1	50	0	31	25	1-7	0	4.27
Red Nelson	R	24	7	6	6	1	60.0	57	0	14	30	5-1	0	2.55
Alex Malloy	R	23	7	6	4	0	52.2	47	0	17	27	0-6	0	2.56
Roy Mitchell	R	25	6	6	6	0	52.0	43	0	12	23	4-2	0	2.60
Bill Graham	L	26	9	6	1	0	43.0	46	2	13	12	0-8	0	3.56
Ed Kinsella	R	28	10	5	2	0	50.0	62	0	16	10	1-3	0	3.78
Jack Gilligan	R	24	9	5	2	0	39.1	37	0	28	10	0-3	0	3.66
Bob Spade†	R	33	7	5	2	1	34.2	34	1	17	8	1-3	0	4.41
Fred Link†	L	24	3	3	0	0	17.0	24	0	13	5	0-1	0	4.24
Ray Boyd	R	23	3	2	1	0	14.1	16	0	5	6	0-2	0	4.40
Bill Crouch	L	23	1	1	1	0	8.0	6	0	7	2	0-0	0	3.38
Rube Waddell	L	33	10	2	0	0	33.0	31	1	11	16	3-1	1	3.55
Dode Criss	R	25	6	0	0	0	19.1	12	0	9	9	2-1	0	1.40
Phil Stremmel	R	30	5	2	2	0	29.0	31	0	16	7	0-2	0	3.72
Harry Howell	R	33	1	0	0	0	3.1	7	0	2	1	0-0	0	10.80

»1910 Chicago Cubs 1st NL 104-50 .675 —

Frank Chance

Player	Gm by Position	B	Age	G	AB	R	H	2B	3B	HR	RBI	BB	SO	SB	Avg	OBP	Slg
Johnny Kling	C86	R	35	91	297	31	80	17	2	2	32	37	27	3	.269	.354	.360
Frank Chance	1B87	R	32	88	295	54	88	12	8	0	36	37	15	16	.298	.395	.393
Johnny Evers	2B125	L	28	125	433	87	114	11	7	0	28	108	18	28	.263	.413	.321
Harry Steinfeldt	3B128	R	32	129	448	70	113	21	1	2	58	36	29	10	.252	.323	.317
Joe Tinker	SS132	R	29	133	473	48	136	25	9	3	69	24	35	20	.288	.322	.397
Wildfire Schulte	OF150	L	27	151	559	93	168	29	15	10	68	39	57	22	.301	.349	.460
Jimmy Sheckard	OF143	L	31	144	507	82	130	27	6	5	51	83	53	22	.256	.366	.363
Solly Hofman	OF110,1B24,3B1	R	27	136	477	83	155	24	16	3	86	65	34	29	.325	.406	.461
Heinie Zimmerman	2B32,SS26,3B23*	R	23	99	335	35	95	16	6	3	38	20	36	7	.284	.326	.394
Jimmy Archer	C49,1B40	R	27	98	313	36	81	17	6	2	41	14	49	6	.259	.293	.371
Ginger Beaumont	OF56	L	33	76	172	30	46	5	1	2	22	28	14	4	.267	.373	.343
Tom Needham	C27,1B1	R	31	31	76	9	14	3	1	0	10	10	10	1	.184	.287	.250
John Kane	OF18,2B6,3B4*	R	27	32	62	11	15	0	0	1	12	9	10	2	.242	.338	.290
Fred Luderus†	1B17	L	24	24	54	5	11	1	1	0	3	4	3	0	.204	.259	.259
Orval Overall	P23,1B1,OF1	S	29	25	41	4	5	1	0	0	1	5	6	0	.122	.234	.146
Big Jeff Pfeffer	P13,OF1	R	28	14	17	1	3	1	1	0	2	1	1	0	.176	.222	.353
Doc Miller†		L	27	1	1	0	0	0	0	0	0	0	0	0	.000	.000	.000

H. Zimmerman, 4 G at OF, 1 G at 1B; J. Kane, 2 G at SS

Pitcher	T	Age	G	GS	CG	ShO	IP	H	HR	BB	SO	W-L	Sv	ERA
Three Finger Brown	R	33	46	31	27	7	295.1	256	3	64	143	25-13	7	1.86
King Cole	R	24	33	29	21	4	239.2	174	2	130	114	20-4	1	1.80
Ed Reulbach	R	27	24	23	13	1	173.1	161	1	49	55	12-8	0	3.12
Orval Overall	R	29	23	21	11	4	144.2	106	2	54	92	12-6	1	2.68
Harry McIntire	R	31	28	19	10	2	176.0	152	5	50	65	13-9	0	3.07
Jack Pfiester	L	32	14	13	5	2	100.1	82	0	26	34	6-3	0	1.79
Rube Kroh	L	23	6	4	1	0	34.1	33	1	15	16	3-1	0	4.46
Lew Richie†	R	26	30	11	8	3	130.0	117	1	51	53	11-4	4	2.70
Big Jeff Pfeffer	R	28	13	1	1	0	41.1	43	1	16	11	1-0	0	3.27
Orlie Weaver	R	24	7	2	2	0	32.0	34	2	15	22	1-2	0	3.66
Al Carson	R	27	2	0	0	0	6.2	6	0	1	2	0-0	0	4.05
Bill Foxen†	L	26	2	0	0	0	5.0	7	0	3	2	0-0	0	9.00

1910 New York Giants 2nd NL 91-63 .591 13.0 GB

John McGraw

Player	Gm by Position	B	Age	G	AB	R	H	2B	3B	HR	RBI	BB	SO	SB	Avg	OBP	Slg
Chief Meyers	C117	R	29	127	365	25	104	18	0	1	62	40	18	5	.285	.362	.342
Fred Merkle	1B144	R	21	144	506	75	148	35	14	4	70	44	59	23	.292	.353	.441
Larry Doyle	2B151	L	23	151	575	97	164	21	14	8	69	71	26	39	.285	.369	.412
Art Devlin	3B147	R	30	147	493	71	128	17	5	2	67	62	32	28	.260	.353	.327
Al Bridwell	SS141	L	26	142	492	74	136	15	7	0	48	73	23	14	.276	.374	.335
Red Murray	OF148	R	26	149	553	78	153	27	8	4	87	52	51	57	.277	.345	.376
Josh Devore	OF130	L	22	133	490	92	149	11	10	2	27	46	67	43	.304	.371	.380
Fred Snodgrass	OF101,1B9,C2*	R	22	123	396	69	127	22	8	2	44	71	52	33	.321	.440	.432
Cy Seymour	OF76	L	37	79	287	32	76	9	4	1	40	23	18	10	.265	.324	.334
Beals Becker	OF45,1B1	L	23	80	126	18	36	2	4	3	24	14	25	11	.286	.357	.437
Art Fletcher	SS22,2B11,3B11	R	25	51	125	12	28	2	1	0	13	4	9	9	.224	.248	.256
Admiral Schlei	C49	R	32	55	99	10	19	2	1	0	8	14	10	4	.192	.304	.232
Doc Crandall	P42,SS1	R	22	45	73	10	25	2	4	1	13	5	7	0	.342	.385	.521
Art Wilson	C25,1B1	R	24	26	52	10	14	4	1	0	5	9	6	2	.269	.387	.385
Tillie Shafer	3B8,2B2,SS2	S	21	29	21	5	4	1	0	0	1	0	6	0	.190	.190	.238
Hank Gowdy	1B5	R	20	7	14	1	3	1	0	0	2	2	3	1	.214	.313	.286
Willie Keeler	OF2	L	38	19	10	5	3	0	0	0	0	3	1	1	.300	.462	.300
Elmer Zacher†	OF1	R	26	1	0	0	0	0	0	0	0	0	0	0	—	—	—

F. Snodgrass, 1 G at 3B

Pitcher	T	Age	G	GS	CG	ShO	IP	H	HR	BB	SO	W-L	Sv	ERA
Christy Mathewson	R	31	38	35	27	2	318.1	292	5	60	184	27-9	0	1.89
Hooks Wiltse	L	29	36	30	18	2	235.1	232	4	52	88	14-12	2	2.72
Louis Drucke	R	21	34	27	15	0	215.1	174	3	82	151	12-10	0	2.47
Red Ames	R	27	33	23	13	3	190.1	161	3	63	94	12-11	0	2.22
Bugs Raymond	R	28	19	11	6	0	99.1	106	2	40	55	4-11	0	3.81
Rube Marquard	L	23	13	8	2	0	70.2	65	2	40	52	4-4	0	4.46
Doc Crandall	R	22	42	18	13	2	207.2	194	10	43	73	17-4	5	2.56
Walt Dickson	R	31	12	1	0	0	29.2	31	1	9	9	1-0	0	5.46
Ed Hendricks	L	25	4	1	1	0	12.0	12	0	4	2	0-1	1	3.75
Dick Rudolph	R	22	3	1	1	0	12.0	21	0	2	9	0-1	2	7.50
Al Klawitter	R	22	1	0	0	0	1.0	2	0	2	0	0-0	0	9.00

1910 Pittsburgh Pirates 3rd NL 86-67 .562 17.5 GB

Fred Clarke

Player	Gm by Position	B	Age	G	AB	R	H	2B	3B	HR	RBI	BB	SO	SB	Avg	OBP	Slg
George Gibson	C143	R	29	143	482	53	125	22	6	3	44	47	31	7	.259	.333	.349
John Flynn	1B93	R	26	96	332	32	91	10	2	6	52	30	47	6	.274	.336	.370
Dots Miller	2B119,1B1,SS1	R	23	120	444	45	101	13	10	1	48	33	41	11	.227	.284	.309
Bobby Byrne	3B148	R	25	148	602	101	178	43	12	2	52	66	27	36	.296	.366	.417
Honus Wagner	SS137,1B11,2B2	R	36	150	556	90	178	34	8	4	81	59	47	24	.320	.390	.432
Chief Wilson	OF146	L	26	146	536	59	148	14	13	4	50	21	68	8	.276	.312	.373
Tommy Leach	OF131,SS2,2B1	R	32	135	529	83	143	24	5	4	52	38	62	18	.270	.319	.357
Fred Clarke	OF118	L	37	123	429	57	113	23	9	2	63	53	23	12	.263	.350	.373
Vin Campbell	OF74	L	22	97	282	42	92	9	5	4	21	26	23	17	.326	.391	.436
Bill McKechnie	2B36,SS14,3B8*	S	23	71	212	23	46	1	2	0	12	11	23	4	.217	.256	.241
Ham Hyatt	1B38,OF4	L	25	74	175	19	46	5	6	1	30	8	14	3	.263	.306	.377
Mike Simon	C14	R	27	22	50	3	10	0	1	0	5	1	2	1	.200	.216	.240
Jack Kading	1B8	R	25	8	23	5	7	2	1	0	4	4	5	0	.304	.407	.478
Bud Sharpe†	1B4	L	28	4	16	2	3	0	1	0	1	0	2	0	.188	.188	.313
Alex McCarthy	SS3	R	22	3	12	1	1	0	1	0	0	0	2	0	.083	.083	.250
Max Carey	OF2	S	20	2	6	2	3	0	1	0	2	2	1	0	.500	.625	.833
Paddy O'Connor	C1	R	30	6	4	0	1	0	0	0	0	1	1	0	.250	.400	.250
Ed Abbaticchio†	SS1	R	33	3	3	0	0	0	0	0	0	0	0	0	.000	.000	.000

B. McKechnie, 4 G at 1B

Pitcher	T	Age	G	GS	CG	ShO	IP	H	HR	BB	SO	W-L	Sv	ERA
Howie Camnitz	R	28	38	31	16	1	260.0	246	1	61	120	12-13	2	3.22
Babe Adams	R	28	34	30	16	3	245.0	217	4	60	101	18-9	0	2.24
Lefty Leifield	L	26	40	30	13	3	218.1	197	6	67	64	15-13	2	2.64
Kirby White†	R	26	30	21	7	3	153.1	142	2	75	42	10-9	2	3.46
Bill Powell	R	25	12	9	4	2	75.0	65	0	34	23	4-6	0	2.40
Jack Ferry	R	23	6	3	2	0	31.0	26	0	8	12	1-2	0	2.32
Elmer Steele	R	24	3	3	2	0	24.0	19	0	3	7	0-3	0	2.25
Deacon Phillippe	R	38	31	8	5	1	121.2	111	4	9	30	14-2	4	2.29
Sam Leever	R	38	26	8	4	0	111.0	104	2	25	33	6-5	2	2.76
Nick Maddox	R	23	20	7	2	0	87.1	73	0	28	29	2-3	0	3.40
Lefty Webb	L	25	7	3	2	0	27.0	29	0	9	6	2-1	0	5.67
Gene Moore	L	24	4	1	0	0	17.1	19	1	7	9	2-1	0	3.12
Skip Dowd	R	21	1	0	0	0	2.0	4	0	2	1	0-0	0	0.00
Sam Frock†	R	27	1	0	0	0	2.0	2	0	2	1	0-0	0	4.50
Jack Mercer	—	21	1	0	0	0	1.0	0	0	2	1	0-0	0	0.00

1910 Philadelphia Phillies 4th NL 78-75 .510 25.5 GB

Red Dooin

Player	Gm by Position	B	Age	G	AB	R	H	2B	3B	HR	RBI	BB	SO	SB	Avg	OBP	Slg
Red Dooin	C91,OF3	R	31	103	331	30	80	13	4	0	30	22	17	10	.242	.289	.305
Kitty Bransfield	1B110	R	35	123	427	39	102	17	4	3	52	20	34	10	.239	.275	.319
Otto Knabe	2B136	R	26	137	510	73	133	18	6	1	44	47	42	15	.261	.327	.325
Eddie Grant	3B152	L	27	152	579	70	155	15	5	1	67	39	54	25	.268	.315	.316
Mickey Doolan	SS148	R	30	148	536	58	141	31	6	2	57	35	56	16	.263	.315	.354
Sherry Magee	OF154	R	25	154	519	110	172	39	17	6	123	94	36	49	.331	.445	.507
John Titus	OF142	L	34	143	535	91	129	26	5	3	35	93	44	20	.241	.358	.325
Johnny Bates	OF131	L	27	135	498	91	152	26	11	3	61	61	49	31	.305	.385	.420
Jimmy Walsh	2B26,OF26,SS9*	R	24	88	242	28	60	8	3	3	31	25	38	5	.248	.323	.343
Pat Moran	C56	R	34	68	199	13	47	7	1	0	11	17	16	6	.236	.306	.281
Joe Ward	1B32,3B1,SS1	—	25	48	124	11	18	2	1	0	13	3	11	1	.145	.178	.177
Roy Thomas	OF20	L	36	23	71	7	13	0	2	0	4	7	5	4	.183	.266	.239
Fred Luderus†	1B19	L	24	21	68	10	20	5	2	0	14	9	5	2	.294	.385	.426
Fred Jacklitsch	C13,1B2,2B1*	R	34	25	51	7	10	3	0	0	2	5	9	0	.196	.268	.255
Ad Brennan	P19,OF1	L	28	21	25	1	7	0	0	0	1	3	5	1	.280	.357	.280
Ed McDonough	C4	R	23	5	9	1	1	0	0	0	0	0	1	0	.111	.111	.111
Harry Cheek	C2	—	31	2	4	1	2	1	0	0	0	0	0	0	.500	.500	.750
John Castle	OF2	—	27	3	4	1	1	0	0	0	0	0	0	1	.250	.250	.250
Patsy Flaherty	P1,OF1	L	34	2	2	0	1	0	0	0	0	0	0	0	.500	.500	.500

J. Walsh, 5 G at 3B; F. Jacklitsch, 1 G at 3B

Pitcher	T	Age	G	GS	CG	ShO	IP	H	HR	BB	SO	W-L	Sv	ERA
Earl Moore	R	30	46	35	18	6	283.0	228	5	121	185	22-15	0	2.58
Bob Ewing	R	37	34	32	20	4	255.1	235	5	86	102	16-14	0	3.00
Lew Moren	R	26	34	26	12	1	205.1	207	6	82	74	13-14	1	3.55
George McQuillan	R	25	24	17	13	3	152.1	109	2	50	71	9-6	1	1.60
Eddie Stack	R	22	20	16	7	1	117.0	115	7	34	48	6-7	0	4.00
Bill Foxen†	L	26	16	9	5	0	77.2	73	2	40	33	5-5	0	2.55
George Chalmers	R	22	4	3	2	0	22.0	21	0	11	12	1-1	0	5.32
Tully Sparks	R	35	3	3	0	0	15.0	22	2	2	4	0-2	0	6.00
Lou Schettler	R	24	27	7	3	0	107.0	96	2	51	62	2-6	1	3.20
Ad Brennan	L	28	19	5	2	0	73.1	72	2	28	28	3-0	0	2.33
Jim Moroney	L	26	12	2	1	0	42.0	43	1	11	13	1-2	1	2.14
Barney Slaughter	R	25	8	1	0	0	18.0	21	0	11	7	0-1	1	5.50
Charlie Girard	R	25	7	1	0	0	26.2	33	2	12	11	0-2	1	6.41
Bert Humphries	R	29	5	0	0	0	9.2	13	0	3	3	0-0	2	4.66
Bill Culp	R	23	4	0	0	0	6.2	8	0	4	4	0-0	1	8.10
Patsy Flaherty	L	34	1	0	0	0	0.1	1	0	1	0	0-0	0	0.00

1910 Cincinnati Reds 5th NL 75-79 .487 29.0 GB

Clark Griffith

Player	Gm by Position	B	Age	G	AB	R	H	2B	3B	HR	RBI	BB	SO	SB	Avg	OBP	Slg
Larry McLean	C119	R	28	127	423	27	126	14	7	2	71	26	23	4	.298	.340	.378
Doc Hoblitzell	1B148,2B7	R	21	155	611	85	170	24	13	4	70	47	32	28	.278	.332	.380
Dick Egan	2B131,SS3	R	26	135	474	70	116	11	5	0	46	53	38	41	.245	.322	.289
Hans Lobert	3B90	R	28	93	314	43	97	6	6	3	40	30	9	41	.309	.369	.395
Tommy McMillan†	SS82	R	22	82	248	20	46	0	3	0	13	31	23	7	.185	.281	.210
Bob Bescher	OF150	S	26	150	589	95	147	20	10	4	48	81	75	70	.250	.344	.338
Mike Mitchell	OF149,1B7	R	30	156	583	79	167	16	18	5	88	59	56	35	.286	.356	.401
Dode Paskert	OF139,1B2	R	28	144	506	63	152	21	5	2	46	70	60	51	.300	.389	.374
Tom Downey	SS68,3B41	R	26	111	378	43	102	9	3	2	32	34	28	12	.270	.335	.325
Tommy Clarke	C56	R	22	64	151	19	42	6	5	1	20	19	17	1	.278	.370	.404
Ward Miller	OF26	L	25	81	126	21	30	6	0	0	10	22	13	10	.238	.356	.286
Sam Woodruff	3B17,2B4	R	33	21	61	6	9	1	0	0	2	7	8	2	.148	.235	.164
Mickey Corcoran	2B14	R	27	14	46	3	10	3	0	0	7	5	9	0	.217	.308	.283
Art Phelan	3B8,2B5,OF3*	R	22	23	42	7	9	0	0	0	4	7	6	5	.214	.327	.214
Swat McCabe	OF9	L	28	13	35	3	9	1	0	0	5	1	2	0	.257	.297	.286
Frank Roth	C4,OF1	R	31	26	29	3	7	2	0	0	3	0	2	1	.241	.267	.310
Chappy Charles	SS4	R	29	4	15	1	2	0	1	0	0	0	1	0	.133	.133	.267
Jim Doyle	3B5,OF1	R	28	7	13	1	2	2	0	0	1	0	2	0	.154	.154	.308
Dave Altizer	SS3	L	33	3	10	3	6	0	0	0	0	3	0	0	.600	.692	.600
Rabbit Robinson	3B2	R	28	2	7	0	0	0	0	0	1	1	0	0	.000	.125	.000
George Wheeler		L	28	3	3	0	0	0	0	0	0	0	2	0	.000	.000	.000
Mike Konnick	SS1	R	21	1	3	0	0	0	0	0	0	1	0	0	.000	.250	.000
Ned Crompton	OF1	L	21	1	2	0	0	0	0	0	0	0	2	0	.000	.000	.000
Bob Meinke	SS2	R	23	2	1	0	0	0	0	0	0	1	0	0	.000	.500	.000
Joe Burns		L	21	1	1	0	1	0	0	0	0	0	0	1	1.000	1.000	1.000
Clark Griffith		R	40	1	0	1	0	0	0	0	0	0	0	0	—	—	—

A. Phelan, 1 G at SS

Pitcher	T	Age	G	GS	CG	ShO	IP	H	HR	BB	SO	W-L	Sv	ERA
Harry Gaspar	R	27	48	31	16	4	275.0	257	6	75	74	15-17	7	2.59
George Suggs	R	27	35	30	23	2	266.0	248	6	48	91	20-12	3	2.40
Jack Rowan	R	23	42	30	18	4	261.0	242	4	105	108	14-13	1	2.93
Fred Beebe	R	29	35	26	11	2	214.1	193	3	94	93	12-14	0	3.07
Bill Burns†	L	30	31	21	13	2	178.2	183	3	49	57	8-13	0	3.48
Harry Coveleski	L	24	7	4	2	0	39.1	35	1	42	27	1-1	0	5.26
Bob Spade†	R	33	3	3	1	0	17.1	35	1	9	1	1-2	0	6.75
Roy Castleton	L	24	4	2	1	0	13.2	15	0	6	5	1-2	0	3.29
Rube Benton	L	23	12	2	0	0	38.0	44	1	23	15	0-1	1	4.74
Art Fromme	R	26	11	5	1	0	49.1	44	2	39	10	3-4	0	2.92
Wingo Anderson	L	23	7	2	0	0	17.1	16	0	17	11	0-0	0	4.67
Slow Joe Doyle†	R	28	5	0	0	0	11.1	16	0	11	4	0-0	0	6.35
Tom Cantwell	R	21	2	0	0	0	1.1	2	0	3	0	0-0	0	13.50
Mysterious Walker	R	26	1	0	0	0	3.0	4	0	4	1	0-0	0	3.00
Walt Slagle	R	31	1	0	0	0	1.0	0	0	3	0	0-0	0	9.00

1910 Brooklyn Dodgers 6th NL 64-90 .416 40.0 GB

Bill Dahlen

Player	Gm by Position	B	Age	G	AB	R	H	2B	3B	HR	RBI	BB	SO	SB	Avg	OBP	Slg
Bill Bergen	C89	R	32	89	249	11	40	2	1	0	14	6	39	0	.161	.180	.177
Jake Daubert	1B144	L	26	144	552	67	146	15	15	8	50	47	53	23	.264	.328	.389
John Hummel	2B153	R	27	153	578	67	141	21	13	5	74	57	81	21	.244	.314	.351
Ed Lennox	3B100	R	24	110	367	19	95	19	4	3	32	36	39	7	.259	.333	.357
Tony Smith	SS101,3B6	R	26	106	321	31	58	10	1	1	16	69	53	9	.181	.329	.227
Zack Wheat	OF156	L	22	156	606	78	172	36	15	2	55	47	80	16	.284	.341	.403
Bill Davidson	OF131	R	23	136	509	48	121	13	7	0	34	24	54	27	.238	.277	.291
Jack Dalton	OF72	R	24	77	273	33	62	9	4	1	21	26	30	5	.227	.304	.300
Al Burch	OF70,1B13	L	26	103	352	41	83	8	3	1	20	22	30	13	.236	.281	.284
Pryor McElveen	3B54,SS6,2B3*	R	28	74	213	19	48	8	3	1	26	22	47	6	.225	.307	.305
Tex Erwin	C68	L	24	81	202	15	38	3	1	1	10	24	12	3	.188	.278	.228
Dolly Stark	SS30	R	25	30	103	7	17	3	0	0	8	7	19	2	.165	.225	.194
Bob Coulson	OF25	R	23	25	89	14	22	3	4	1	13	6	14	9	.247	.302	.404
Happy Smith	OF16	L	26	35	76	6	18	2	0	0	5	4	14	4	.237	.275	.263
Tommy McMillan†	SS23	R	22	23	74	2	13	1	0	0	2	6	10	4	.176	.238	.189
Otto Miller	C28	R	21	31	66	5	11	3	0	0	2	2	19	1	.167	.203	.212
Harry Lumley	OF4	L	29	8	21	3	3	0	0	0	0	3	6	0	.143	.280	.143
Tim Jordan		L	31	5	5	1	1	0	0	1	3	0	2	0	.200	.200	.800
Bill Dahlen		R	40	3	2	0	0	0	0	0	0	1	0	0	.000	.000	.000
George Hunter	OF1	S	22	1	0	0	0	0	0	0	0	0	0	0	—	—	—

P. McElveen, 1 G at C

Pitcher	T	Age	G	GS	CG	ShO	IP	H	HR	BB	SO	W-L	Sv	ERA
Nap Rucker	L	25	41	39	27	6	320.1	293	5	84	147	17-18	0	2.58
George Bell	R	35	44	36	25	4	310.0	267	4	82	102	10-27	1	2.64
Cy Barger	R	25	35	30	25	2	271.2	267	2	107	87	15-15	1	2.88
Doc Scanlan	R	29	34	25	14	3	217.1	175	1	116	103	9-11	2	2.61
Elmer Knetzer	R	24	20	15	10	3	132.2	122	1	60	56	7-5	0	3.19
Sandy Burk	R	23	4	3	1	0	19.1	17	0	27	14	0-1	0	6.05
George Crable	L	24	2	1	1	0	7.1	5	0	5	3	0-0	0	4.91
Rube Dessau	R	27	19	0	0	0	51.1	67	0	29	24	2-3	1	5.79
Kaiser Wilhelm	R	36	15	5	0	0	68.1	88	3	18	17	3-7	0	4.74
Fred Miller	L	24	6	2	0	0	21.0	25	1	13	2	1-1	0	4.71
Frank Schneiberg	R	28	1	0	0	0	1.0	5	0	4	0	0-0	0	63.00

1910 St. Louis Cardinals 7th NL 63-90 .412 40.5 GB

Roger Bresnahan

Player	Gm by Position	B	Age	G	AB	R	H	2B	3B	HR	RBI	BB	SO	SB	Avg	OBP	Slg
Ed Phelps	C80	R	31	93	270	25	71	4	2	0	37	36	29	9	.263	.356	.293
Ed Konetchy	1B144,P1	R	24	144	520	87	157	23	16	3	78	78	59	18	.302	.397	.425
Miller Huggins	2B151	S	31	151	547	101	145	15	6	1	36	116	46	34	.265	.399	.320
Mike Mowrey	3B141	R	26	143	489	69	138	24	6	2	70	67	38	21	.282	.375	.368
Arnold Hauser	SS117,3B1	R	21	119	375	37	77	7	2	2	36	49	39	15	.205	.312	.251
Rube Ellis	OF141	L	24	142	550	87	142	18	8	4	54	62	70	25	.258	.339	.342
Steve Evans	OF141,1B10	L	25	151	506	73	122	21	8	2	73	78	63	10	.241	.376	.326
Rebel Oakes	OF127	L	23	131	468	50	118	14	6	0	43	38	38	18	.252	.315	.308
Roger Bresnahan	C77,OF2,P1	R	31	88	234	35	65	15	3	0	27	55	17	13	.278	.419	.368
Rudy Hulswitt	SS30,2B2	R	33	63	133	9	33	7	2	0	14	13	10	5	.248	.320	.331
Elmer Zacher†	OF36,2B1	R	26	47	132	7	28	5	1	0	10	10	19	3	.212	.278	.265
Frank Betcher	SS12,3B7,2B6*	S	22	35	89	7	18	2	0	0	6	7	14	1	.202	.276	.225
Ody Abbott	OF21	R	21	22	70	2	13	2	1	0	6	6	20	3	.186	.250	.243
Jack Bliss	C13	R	28	16	33	2	2	0	0	0	3	4	8	0	.061	.162	.061
Jap Barbeau	3B6,2B1	R	28	7	21	4	4	0	1	0	2	3	3	0	.190	.292	.286
Bill O'Hara	OF4,P1,1B1	L	26	9	20	1	3	0	0	0	1	2	3	0	.150	.227	.150
Ernie Lush	OF1	R	25	1	4	0	0	0	0	0	0	1	1	0	.000	.200	.000
Billy Kelly	C1	R	24	2	2	1	0	0	0	0	0	1	0	0	.000	.333	.000

F. Betcher, 2 G at OF

Pitcher	T	Age	G	GS	CG	ShO	IP	H	HR	BB	SO	W-L	Sv	ERA
Bob Harmon	R	22	43	33	15	0	236.0	227	1	133	87	13-15	2	4.46
Johnny Lush	L	24	36	24	13	1	225.1	235	6	70	54	14-13	1	3.20
Vic Willis	R	34	33	23	12	1	212.0	224	6	61	67	9-12	3	3.35
Frank Corridon	R	29	30	18	9	0	156.0	168	1	55	51	6-14	3	3.81
Slim Sallee	L	25	18	13	9	0	115.0	112	4	24	46	7-8	2	2.97
Bill Steele	R	24	9	9	8	0	71.2	71	1	24	25	4-4	1	3.27
Roy Golden	R	21	7	6	3	0	42.2	44	3	33	31	2-3	0	4.43
Ed Zmich	L	25	9	6	2	0	36.0	38	0	29	19	0-5	0	6.25
Bunny Hearn	L	19	5	5	4	0	39.0	49	2	16	14	1-3	0	5.08
Cy Alberts	R	28	4	3	2	0	27.2	35	1	20	10	1-2	0	6.18
Les Backman	R	22	26	11	6	0	116.0	117	4	53	41	6-7	2	3.03
Elmer Rieger	R	21	13	2	0	0	21.1	26	1	7	9	0-2	0	5.48
Rube Geyer	R	26	4	0	0	0	4.0	5	0	3	5	0-1	0	4.50
John Raleigh	L	20	3	1	0	0	5.0	8	0	0	2	0-0	0	9.00
Eddie Higgins	R	22	2	0	0	0	10.1	15	0	7	1	0-1	0	4.35
Charlie Pickett	R	27	2	0	0	0	6.0	7	0	2	2	0-0	0	1.50
Harry Patton	—	26	1	0	0	0	4.0	4	0	2	2	0-0	0	2.25
Ed Konetchy	R	24	1	0	0	0	4.0	4	0	1	2	0-0	0	4.50
Roger Bresnahan	R	31	1	0	0	0	3.1	6	0	1	0	0-0	0	0.00
Bill Chambers	R	20	1	0	0	0	1.0	1	0	0	0	0-0	0	0.00
Bill O'Hara	R	26	1	0	0	0	1.0	0	0	0	0	0-0	0	0.00

1910 Boston Beaneaters 8th NL 53-100 .346 50.5 GB

Fred Lake

Player	Gm by Position	B	Age	G	AB	R	H	2B	3B	HR	RBI	BB	SO	SB	Avg	OBP	Slg
Peaches Graham	C87,3B2,1B1*	R	33	110	291	31	82	13	2	0	21	33	15	5	.282	.359	.340
Bud Sharpe†	1B113	L	28	115	439	30	105	14	3	0	29	14	31	4	.239	.264	.285
Dave Shean	2B148	R	26	150	543	52	130	12	7	3	36	42	45	16	.239	.294	.304
Buck Herzog	3B105	R	24	106	380	51	95	20	3	3	32	30	34	13	.250	.329	.342
Bill Sweeney	SS110,3B21,1B17	R	24	150	499	43	133	22	4	5	46	61	28	25	.267	.349	.357
Bill Collins	OF151	S	28	151	584	67	141	6	7	3	40	43	48	36	.241	.308	.291
Fred Beck	OF134,1B19	L	23	154	571	52	157	32	9	10	64	19	55	8	.275	.307	.415
Doc Miller†	OF130	L	27	130	482	48	138	27	4	3	55	33	52	17	.286	.333	.378
Ed Abbaticchio†	SS46,2B1	R	33	52	178	20	44	4	2	0	10	12	16	2	.247	.295	.292
Harry Smith	C38	R	35	70	147	8	35	4	0	1	15	5	14	5	.238	.263	.286
Gus Getz	3B22,2B13,OF8*	R	20	54	144	14	28	0	1	0	7	6	10	2	.194	.232	.208
Bill Rariden	C49	R	22	49	137	15	31	5	1	1	14	12	22	1	.226	.293	.299
Wilbur Good	OF23	L	24	23	86	15	29	5	4	0	11	6	13	5	.337	.380	.488
Herbie Moran	OF20	L	26	20	67	11	8	0	0	0	3	13	14	6	.119	.280	.119
Pete Burg	3B11,SS2	R	28	13	46	7	15	0	1	0	10	7	12	5	.326	.415	.370
Rube Sellers	OF9	R	29	12	32	3	5	0	0	0	2	6	5	1	.156	.289	.156
Doc Martel	1B10	R	27	10	31	0	4	0	0	0	1	2	3	0	.129	.182	.129
Bill Cooney	OF2	—	27	8	12	2	3	0	0	0	1	2	0	0	.250	.357	.250
Fred Liese		L	24	5	4	0	0	0	0	0	0	1	2	0	.000	.200	.000
Rowdy Elliott	C1	R	19	3	2	0	0	0	0	0	0	0	0	0	.000	.000	.000
Jim Riley	OF1	R	23	1	1	0	0	0	0	0	0	1	1	0	.000	.500	.000
Art Kruger†		R	29	1	1	0	0	0	0	0	0	0	0	0	.000	.000	.000
Fred Lake		R	43	3	1	0	0	0	0	0	0	1	0	0	.000	.500	.000

P. Graham, 1 G at OF; G. Getz, 4 G at SS

Pitcher	T	Age	G	GS	CG	ShO	IP	H	HR	BB	SO	W-L	Sv	ERA
Al Mattern	R	27	51	37	17	6	305.0	288	5	121	94	16-19	1	2.98
Cliff Curtis	R	26	43	37	12	2	251.0	251	9	124	75	6-24	2	3.55
Buster Brown	R	28	46	29	16	1	263.0	251	0	94	88	9-23	2	2.67
Sam Frock†	R	27	45	29	13	2	255.1	245	8	91	170	12-19	2	3.21
George Ferguson	R	23	26	14	10	1	123.0	110	3	58	40	7-7	0	3.80
Kirby White†	R	26	3	3	3	0	26.0	15	2	12	6	1-2	0	1.38
Lew Richie†	R	26	4	2	0	0	16.1	20	0	9	7	0-3	0	2.76
Billy Burke	L	20	19	1	1	0	64.0	68	1	29	22	1-0	0	4.08
Chick Evans	R	20	13	1	0	0	31.0	28	1	27	12	1-1	2	5.23
Jiggs Parson	R	24	10	4	0	0	35.1	35	2	26	7	0-2	0	3.82
Lefty Tyler	L	20	2	2	0	0	11.1	11	1	6	6	0-0	0	2.38
Ralph Good	R	24	2	0	0	0	9.0	6	0	2	4	0-0	0	2.00

»1911 Philadelphia Athletics 1st AL 101-50 .669 —

Connie Mack

Player	Gm by Position	B	Age	G	AB	R	H	2B	3B	HR	RBI	BB	SO	SB	Avg	OBP	Slg
Ira Thomas	C103	R	30	103	297	33	81	14	3	0	39	23	—	4	.273	.341	.340
Stuffy McInnis	1B97,SS24	R	20	126	468	76	150	20	10	3	77	25	—	23	.321	.361	.425
Eddie Collins	2B132	L	24	132	493	92	180	22	13	3	73	62	—	38	.365	.451	.481
Home Run Baker	3B148	L	25	148	592	96	198	42	14	11	115	40	—	38	.334	.379	.508
Jack Barry	SS127	R	24	127	442	73	117	18	7	1	63	38	—	30	.265	.333	.344
Danny Murphy	OF136,2B4	R	34	141	508	104	167	27	11	6	66	50	—	22	.329	.398	.461
Bris Lord	OF132	R	27	134	574	92	178	37	11	3	55	35	—	15	.310	.355	.429
Rube Oldring	OF119	R	27	121	495	84	147	11	14	3	59	21	—	21	.297	.332	.394
Amos Strunk	OF62,1B2	L	22	74	215	42	55	7	2	1	21	35	—	13	.256	.363	.321
Harry Davis	1B53	R	37	57	183	27	36	9	1	1	22	24	—	2	.197	.297	.273
Jack Lapp	C57,1B4	L	26	68	167	35	59	10	3	1	26	24	—	4	.353	.435	.467
Claud Derrick	2B21,SS5,1B4*	R	25	36	100	14	23	1	2	0	5	7	—	7	.230	.294	.280
Paddy Livingston	C26	R	31	27	71	9	17	4	0	0	8	7	—	1	.239	.316	.296
Topsy Hartsel	OF10	L	37	25	38	8	9	2	0	0	1	8	—	0	.237	.396	.289
Willie Hogan†	OF6	R	26	7	19	1	2	1	0	0	2	0	—	0	.105	.105	.158
Chester Emerson	OF7	L	21	7	18	2	4	0	0	0	0	6	—	1	.222	.417	.222
Earle Mack	3B2	L	21	2	4	0	0	0	0	0	0	0	—	0	.000	.000	.000

C. Derrick, 2 G at 3B

Pitcher	T	Age	G	GS	CG	ShO	IP	H	HR	BB	SO	W-L	Sv	ERA
Jack Coombs	R	28	47	40	26	1	336.2	360	8	119	185	28-12	3	3.53
Eddie Plank	L	35	40	30	24	6	256.2	237	2	77	149	23-8	4	2.10
Cy Morgan	R	32	38	30	15	2	249.2	217	0	113	136	15-7	1	2.70
Chief Bender	R	27	31	24	16	3	216.1	198	2	58	114	17-5	2	2.16
Harry Krause	L	23	27	19	12	1	169.0	155	2	47	85	11-8	2	3.04
Boardwalk Brown	R	24	2	1	1	0	12.0	12	0	2	6	0-1	0	4.50
Dave Danforth	L	21	14	2	1	0	33.2	29	1	17	21	4-1	1	3.74
Doc Martin	R	23	11	3	1	0	38.0	40	1	17	21	1-1	0	4.50
Lefty Russell	L	20	7	2	0	0	31.2	45	1	18	7	0-3	0	7.67
Elmer Leonard	R	22	5	1	1	0	19.0	26	0	10	10	2-2	0	2.84
Lep Long	R	22	4	0	0	0	8.0	15	0	5	4	0-0	0	4.50
Allan Collamore	R	24	2	0	0	0	2.0	6	0	3	1	0-1	0	36.00
Howard Armstrong	R	21	1	0	0	0	3.0	3	0	1	0	0-1	0	0.00

1911 Detroit Tigers 2nd AL 89-65 .578 13.5 GB

Hughie Jennings

Player	Gm by Position	B	Age	G	AB	R	H	2B	3B	HR	RBI	BB	SO	SB	Avg	OBP	Slg
Oscar Stanage	C141	R	28	141	503	45	133	13	7	3	51	20	—	3	.264	.297	.336
Jim Delahanty	1B71,2B59,3B13	R	32	144	542	83	184	30	14	3	94	56	—	15	.339	.411	.463
Charley O'Leary	2B67,3B6	R	28	74	256	29	68	8	2	0	25	21	—	10	.266	.336	.313
George Moriarty	3B129,1B1	R	27	130	478	51	116	20	4	1	60	27	—	28	.243	.287	.308
Donie Bush	SS150	S	23	150	561	126	130	18	5	1	36	98	—	40	.232	.349	.287
Ty Cobb	OF146	L	24	146	591	147	248	47	24	8	127	44	—	83	.420	.467	.621
Sam Crawford	OF146	L	31	146	574	109	217	36	14	7	115	61	—	37	.378	.438	.526
Davy Jones	OF92	L	31	98	341	78	93	10	0	0	19	41	—	25	.273	.354	.302
Delos Drake	OF83,1B2	R	24	95	315	37	88	9	9	1	36	17	—	20	.279	.324	.375
Del Gainer	1B69	R	24	70	248	32	75	11	4	2	25	20	—	10	.302	.366	.403
Paddy Baumann	2B23,OF3	R	25	26	94	8	24	2	4	0	11	6	—	1	.255	.307	.362
Ed Lafitte	P29,OF2	R	25	31	70	6	11	2	0	1	6	1	—	0	.157	.169	.229
Biff Schaller	OF16,1B1	L	21	40	60	8	8	0	1	1	7	4	—	1	.133	.200	.217
Boss Schmidt	C9,OF1	S	30	28	46	4	13	2	1	0	2	0	—	0	.283	.298	.370
Chick Lathers	2B9,3B8,SS4*	L	22	29	45	5	10	1	0	0	4	5	—	0	.222	.314	.244
Jack Ness	1B12	R	25	12	39	6	6	0	0	0	2	2	—	0	.154	.195	.154
Joe Casey	C12,OF3	R	23	15	33	2	5	0	0	0	3	3	—	0	.152	.222	.152
Guy Tutwiler	2B6,OF3	L	21	13	32	3	6	2	0	0	3	2	—	0	.188	.235	.250
Squanto Wilson	C5	S	22	5	16	2	3	0	0	0	0	2	—	0	.188	.278	.188

C. Lathers, 3 G at 1B

Pitcher	T	Age	G	GS	CG	ShO	IP	H	HR	BB	SO	W-L	Sv	ERA
George Mullin	R	30	30	29	25	2	234.1	245	7	61	87	18-10	0	3.07
Ed Willett	R	27	38	27	15	2	231.1	261	5	80	86	13-14	1	3.66
Ed Summers	R	26	30	20	13	0	179.1	189	3	51	65	11-11	1	3.66
Ed Lafitte	R	25	29	20	15	2	172.1	205	2	52	63	11-8	1	3.92
Wild Bill Donovan	R	34	20	19	15	1	168.1	160	4	64	81	10-9	1	3.31
Ralph Works	R	23	30	15	9	3	167.1	173	3	67	68	11-5	1	3.87
Jack Lively	R	26	18	14	10	0	113.2	143	1	34	45	7-5	0	4.59
Wiley Taylor	R	23	3	2	1	0	19.0	18	0	10	9	0-2	0	3.79
Pug Cavet	L	21	1	1	0	0	4.0	6	0	1	1	0-1	0	4.50
Tex Covington	R	24	17	6	5	0	83.2	94	2	33	29	7-1	0	4.09
Clarence Mitchell	L	20	5	1	0	0	14.1	20	1	7	4	1-0	0	8.16

1911 Cleveland Bronchos 3rd AL 80-73 .523 22.0 GB

Deacon McGuire (6-11)/George Stovall (74-62)

Player	Gm by Position	B	Age	G	AB	R	H	2B	3B	HR	RBI	BB	SO	SB	Avg	OBP	Slg
Gus Fisher	C58,1B1	L	25	70	203	20	53	6	3	0	12	7	—	6	.261	.302	.320
George Stovall	1B118,2B2	R	32	128	458	48	124	17	7	0	79	21	—	11	.271	.306	.338
Neal Ball	2B94,3B17,SS1	R	30	116	412	45	122	14	9	3	45	27	—	21	.296	.339	.396
Terry Turner	3B92,2B14,SS10	R	30	117	417	59	105	16	9	0	28	34	—	29	.252	.310	.333
Ivy Olson	SS139	R	25	140	545	89	142	20	8	1	50	34	—	20	.261	.311	.332
Joe Jackson	OF147	L	21	147	571	126	233	45	19	7	83	56	—	41	.408	.468	.590
Jack Graney	OF142	L	25	146	527	84	142	25	5	1	45	66	—	21	.269	.363	.342
Joe Birmingham	OF102,3B16	R	26	125	447	55	136	18	5	2	51	15	—	16	.304	.334	.380
Nap Lajoie	1B41,2B37	R	36	90	315	36	115	20	1	2	60	26	—	13	.365	.420	.454
Ted Easterly	OF54,C23	L	26	99	287	34	93	19	5	1	37	8	—	6	.324	.345	.436
Syd Smith	C48,1B1,3B1	R	27	58	154	8	46	8	1	1	21	11	—	0	.299	.353	.383
Hank Butcher	OF34	R	24	38	133	21	32	7	3	1	11	11	—	9	.241	.303	.361
Grover Land	C34,1B1	R	26	35	107	5	15	1	2	0	10	3	—	2	.140	.164	.187
Art Griggs	2B11,OF4,3B3*	R	27	27	68	7	17	3	2	1	7	5	—	1	.250	.301	.397
Bill Lindsay	3B15,2B1	L	30	19	66	6	16	2	0	0	5	1	—	2	.242	.265	.273
Cotton Knaupp	SS13	R	21	13	39	2	4	1	0	0	0	0	—	3	.103	.103	.128
Steve O'Neill	C9	R	19	9	27	1	4	1	0	0	1	4	—	2	.148	.281	.185
Jack Mills	3B7	L	21	13	17	5	5	0	0	0	1	1	—	1	.294	.368	.294
Dave Callahan	OF3	L	22	5	12	1	4	0	1	0	0	1	—	0	.333	.385	.500
Herman Bronkie	3B2	R	26	2	6	0	1	0	0	0	0	0	—	0	.167	.167	.167
Bert Adams	C2	S	20	2	5	0	1	0	0	0	0	1	—	0	.200	.333	.200
Tim Hendryx	3B2	R	20	2	4	0	1	0	0	0	0	0	—	0	.250	.250	.250

A. Griggs, 1 G at 1B

Pitcher	T	Age	G	GS	CG	ShO	IP	H	HR	BB	SO	W-L	Sv	ERA
Vean Gregg	L	26	34	26	22	5	244.1	172	2	86	125	23-7	0	1.80
Gene Krapp	R	24	34	26	14	1	214.2	182	1	136	130	13-9	1	3.44
Willie Mitchell	L	21	30	22	9	0	177.1	190	1	60	78	7-14	0	3.76
George Kahler	R	21	30	17	10	0	154.1	153	1	66	97	9-8	1	3.27
Fred Blanding	R	23	29	16	11	0	176.0	190	5	60	80	7-11	2	3.68
Cy Falkenberg	R	30	15	13	7	0	106.2	117	0	24	46	8-5	1	3.29
Hi West	R	26	13	8	3	0	64.2	84	1	18	17	3-4	1	3.76
Cy Young†	R	44	7	7	4	0	46.1	54	2	13	20	3-4	0	3.88
Specs Harkness	R	23	12	6	3	0	53.1	62	1	21	25	2-2	0	4.22
Bill James	R	24	8	6	4	0	51.2	58	1	32	21	2-4	0	4.88
Earl Yingling	L	22	4	3	1	0	22.1	30	1	9	6	1-0	0	4.43
Jim Baskette	R	23	4	2	2	0	21.1	21	0	9	8	1-2	0	3.38
Pat Paige	R	29	2	1	1	0	16.0	21	0	7	6	1-0	0	4.50
Bugs Reisgl	R	23	2	1	1	0	13.0	13	1	3	6	0-1	0	6.23
Ben DeMott	R	22	1	1	0	0	3.2	10	0	2	2	0-1	0	12.27
Josh Swindell	R	25	4	1	1	0	17.1	19	0	4	6	0-1	0	2.08

1911 Chicago White Sox 4th AL 77-74 .510 24.0 GB

Hugh Duffy

Player	Gm by Position	B	Age	G	AB	R	H	2B	3B	HR	RBI	BB	SO	SB	Avg	OBP	Slg
Billy Sullivan	C89	R	36	89	256	26	55	9	3	0	31	16	—	1	.215	.266	.273
Shano Collins	1B98,2B3,OF3	R	25	106	370	48	97	16	12	4	48	20	—	14	.262	.309	.403
Amby McConnell	2B102	L	28	104	396	45	111	11	5	1	34	23	—	7	.280	.331	.341
Harry Lord	3B138	L	29	141	561	103	180	18	18	3	61	32	—	43	.321	.364	.433
Lee Tannehill	SS102,2B27,3B7*	R	30	141	516	60	131	17	6	0	49	32	—	0	.254	.300	.310
Matty McIntyre	OF146	L	31	146	569	102	184	19	11	1	52	64	—	17	.323	.397	.401
Ping Bodie	OF128,2B16	R	23	145	551	75	159	27	13	4	97	49	—	14	.289	.348	.407
Nixey Callahan	OF114	R	37	120	466	64	131	13	5	3	60	15	—	45	.281	.306	.350
Rollie Zeider	1B29,SS17,3B10*	R	27	73	217	39	55	3	0	2	21	29	—	28	.253	.347	.295
Patsy Dougherty	OF56	L	34	76	211	39	61	10	9	0	32	26	—	19	.289	.380	.422
Fred Payne	C56	R	30	66	133	14	27	2	1	1	19	8	—	6	.203	.259	.256
Roy Corhan	SS43	R	23	43	131	14	28	6	2	0	8	15	—	2	.214	.304	.290
Bruno Block	C38	R	26	39	115	11	35	6	1	1	18	6	—	0	.304	.339	.400
Charlie Mullen	1B20	R	22	20	59	7	12	2	1	0	5	5	—	0	.203	.266	.271
Cuke Barrows	OF13	R	27	13	46	5	9	2	0	0	4	7	—	2	.196	.315	.239
Tex Jones	1B9	R	25	9	31	4	6	1	0	0	4	3	—	1	.194	.265	.226
Ralph Kreitz	C7	R	25	7	17	0	4	1	0	0	0	2	—	0	.235	.316	.294
Felix Chouinard	2B4,OF4	R	23	14	17	3	3	0	0	0	0	0	—	0	.176	.176	.176
Bobby Messenger	OF4	S	27	13	17	4	2	0	0	0	0	3	—	0	.118	.250	.235
Freddy Parent	2B3	R	35	3	9	2	4	1	0	0	3	2	—	0	.444	.545	.556
Marty Berghammer	2B2	L	23	2	5	0	0	0	0	0	0	1	—	0	.000	.167	.000
Wally Mayer	C1	R	20	1	3	0	0	0	0	0	0	2	—	0	.000	.400	.000
Paul Meloan†	OF1	L	22	1	3	0	1	0	0	0	1	0	—	0	.333	.333	.333
Jimmy Johnston	OF1	R	21	1	2	0	0	0	0	0	2	0	—	0	.000	.000	.000

L. Tannehill, 5 G at 1B; R. Zeider, 9 G at 2B

Pitcher	T	Age	G	GS	CG	ShO	IP	H	HR	BB	SO	W-L	Sv	ERA
Ed Walsh	R	30	56	37	33	5	368.2	327	4	72	255	27-18	4	2.22
Doc White	L	32	34	29	16	3	214.1	219	2	35	72	10-14	2	2.98
Jim Scott	R	23	39	26	14	3	222.0	195	3	81	128	14-11	2	2.39
Frank Lange	R	27	29	22	8	1	161.2	151	3	77	104	8-8	0	3.23
Joe Benz	R	25	12	6	2	0	55.2	52	0	13	28	3-2	0	2.26
Fred Olmstead	R	29	25	11	7	1	117.2	146	3	30	45	6-6	2	4.21
Irv Young	L	33	24	11	3	1	92.2	99	2	25	40	5-6	2	4.37
Jesse Baker	L	23	22	8	3	0	94.0	101	3	30	51	2-7	1	3.93
Joe Hovlik	R	26	12	3	1	1	47.0	47	1	20	24	2-0	1	3.06
George Mogridge	L	22	4	1	0	0	12.2	12	1	1	5	0-2	0	5.68

1911 Boston Red Sox 5th AL 78-75 .510 24.0 GB

Patsy Donovan

Player	Gm by Position	B	Age	G	AB	R	H	2B	3B	HR	RBI	BB	SO	SB	Avg	OBP	Slg
Bill Carrigan	C62,1B6	R	27	72	232	29	67	6	1	1	30	26	—	5	.289	.373	.336
Clyde Engle	1B65,3B51,2B13*	R	27	146	514	58	139	13	3	2	48	51	—	24	.270	.343	.319
Larry Gardner	3B72,2B62	L	25	138	492	80	140	17	8	4	44	64	—	27	.285	.373	.376
Billy Purtell	3B15,2B3,SS3*	R	25	27	82	5	23	5	3	0	7	1	—	1	.280	.298	.415
Steve Yerkes	SS116,2B14,3B11	R	23	142	502	70	140	24	3	1	57	52	—	14	.279	.354	.345
Tris Speaker	OF138	L	23	141	500	88	167	34	13	8	80	59	—	25	.334	.418	.502
Harry Hooper	OF130	L	23	130	524	93	163	20	6	4	45	73	—	38	.311	.399	.395
Duffy Lewis	OF125	R	23	130	469	64	144	32	4	7	86	25	—	11	.307	.355	.437
Rip Williams	1B57,C38	R	29	95	284	36	68	8	5	0	31	24	—	9	.239	.314	.303
Heinie Wagner	2B40,SS32	R	30	80	261	34	67	13	8	1	38	29	—	15	.257	.340	.379
Les Nunamaker	C59	R	22	62	183	18	47	4	3	0	19	12	—	1	.257	.303	.311
Joe Riggert	OF39	R	24	50	146	19	31	4	4	2	13	12	—	5	.212	.290	.336
Olaf Henriksen	OF25	L	23	27	93	17	34	2	1	0	8	14	—	4	.366	.449	.409
Jack Lewis	2B18	R	27	18	59	7	16	0	0	0	6	7	—	2	.271	.368	.271
Hugh Bradley	1B12	R	26	12	41	9	13	2	0	1	4	2	—	1	.317	.364	.439
Hap Myers†	1B12	R	23	13	38	3	14	2	0	0	0	4	—	4	.368	.429	.421
Hal Janvrin	3B5,1B4	R	18	9	27	2	4	1	0	0	1	3	—	0	.148	.258	.185
Walter Lonergan	2B7,3B1,SS1	R	25	10	26	2	7	0	0	0	1	1	—	1	.269	.296	.269
Jack Thoney		R	31	26	20	5	5	0	0	0	2	0	—	1	.250	.250	.250
Bunny Madden†	C4	R	28	4	15	2	3	0	0	0	2	2	—	0	.200	.294	.200
Red Kleinow†	C8	R	31	8	14	0	3	0	0	0	0	2	—	1	.214	.313	.214
Hy Gunning	1B4	L	22	4	9	0	1	0	0	0	2	2	—	0	.111	.273	.111
Les Wilson	OF3	L	25	5	7	0	0	0	0	0	0	2	—	0	.000	.222	.000
Swede Carlstrom	SS2	R	24	2	6	0	1	0	0	0	0	0	—	0	.167	.167	.167
Tony Tonneman	C2	R	29	2	5	0	1	1	0	0	3	1	—	0	.200	.333	.400
Joe Giannini	SS1	L	22	1	2	0	1	1	0	0	0	0	—	0	.500	.500	1.000
Tracy Baker	1B1	R	19	1	0	0	0	0	0	0	0	0	—	0	—	—	—

C. Engle, 10 G at OF; B. Purtell, 1 G at OF

Pitcher	T	Age	G	GS	CG	ShO	IP	H	HR	BB	SO	W-L	Sv	ERA
Joe Wood	R	21	44	33	25	5	276.2	226	2	76	231	23-17	3	2.02
Eddie Cicotte	R	27	35	25	16	1	220.2	236	2	73	106	11-15	0	2.81
Ray Collins	L	24	31	24	14	0	194.2	184	1	44	86	11-12	1	2.50
Larry Pape	R	27	27	19	10	1	176.1	167	3	63	49	10-8	0	2.45
Ed Karger	L	28	25	18	6	1	131.0	134	4	42	57	5-8	0	3.37
Jack Killilay	R	24	14	7	1	0	61.0	65	0	36	28	4-2	0	3.54
Buck O'Brien	R	29	6	5	5	2	47.2	30	0	21	31	5-1	0	0.38
Walter Moser†	R	30	6	3	1	0	24.2	37	0	11	11	0-1	0	4.01
Casey Hageman	R	24	2	2	2	0	17.0	16	2	5	8	0-2	0	2.12
Blaine Thomas	R	22	2	2	0	0	4.2	3	0	7	0	0-0	0	0.00
Frank Smith†	R	31	1	1	0	0	2.1	6	0	3	1	0-0	0	15.43
Charlie Smith†	R	31	1	1	0	0	2.0	2	1	1	0	0-0	0	9.00
Sea Lion Hall	R	25	32	10	6	0	146.2	149	3	72	83	8-7	5	3.74
Judge Nagle†	R	31	5	1	0	0	27.0	27	2	6	12	1-1	0	3.33
Marty McHale	R	22	4	1	0	0	9.1	19	1	3	3	0-0	0	9.64
Jack Bushelman	R	25	3	1	1	0	12.0	8	0	10	5	0-1	0	3.00

1911 New York Highlanders 6th AL 76-76 .500 25.5 GB

Hal Chase

Player	Gm by Position	B	Age	G	AB	R	H	2B	3B	HR	RBI	BB	SO	SB	Avg	OBP	Slg
Walter Blair	C84,1B1	R	27	85	222	18	43	9	2	0	26	16	—	2	.194	.257	.252
Hal Chase	1B124,OF7,2B2*	R	28	133	527	82	166	32	7	3	62	21	—	36	.315	.342	.419
Earle Gardner	2B101	R	27	102	357	36	94	13	2	0	39	20	—	14	.263	.312	.311
Roy Hartzell	3B122,SS12,OF8	L	29	144	527	67	156	17	11	3	91	63	—	22	.296	.375	.387
John Knight	SS82,1B27,2B21*	R	25	132	470	69	126	16	7	3	62	42	—	18	.268	.342	.351
Birdie Cree	OF132,SS4,2B1	R	28	137	520	90	181	30	22	4	88	56	—	48	.348	.415	.513
Bert Daniels	OF120	R	28	131	462	74	132	16	9	2	31	48	—	40	.286	.375	.372
Harry Wolter	OF113,1B2	L	26	122	434	78	132	17	15	4	36	62	—	28	.304	.396	.440
Jeff Sweeney	C83	R	22	83	229	17	53	6	5	0	18	14	—	8	.231	.299	.301
Otis Johnson	SS46,2B15,3B3	S	27	71	209	21	49	9	6	3	36	39	—	12	.234	.363	.378
Charlie Hemphill	OF55	L	35	69	201	32	57	4	2	1	15	37	—	9	.284	.397	.338
Ray Caldwell	P41,OF11	L	23	59	147	14	40	4	1	0	17	11	—	5	.272	.323	.313
Cozy Dolan	3B18	R	21	19	69	19	21	1	2	0	6	8	—	12	.304	.385	.377
Bob Williams	C20	R	27	20	47	3	9	2	0	0	8	5	—	1	.191	.269	.234
Roxey Roach	SS8,2B5	R	28	13	40	4	10	2	1	0	2	6	—	0	.250	.348	.350
Mike Fitzgerald	OF9	L	21	16	37	6	10	1	0	0	6	4	—	4	.270	.341	.297
Stubby Magner	SS6,2B5	R	23	13	33	3	7	0	0	0	4	4	—	1	.212	.297	.212
Guy Zinn	OF8	L	24	9	27	5	4	0	2	0	1	4	—	0	.148	.281	.296
Johnny Priest	2B5,3B2	R	25	7	21	2	3	0	0	0	2	2	—	3	.143	.250	.143
Mike Handiboe	OF4	L	23	5	15	0	1	0	0	0	0	2	—	0	.067	.176	.067
Ed Wilkinson	OF3,2B1	R	21	10	13	2	3	0	0	0	1	0	—	0	.231	.231	.231
Gene Elliott	OF2,3B1	L	22	5	13	1	1	1	0	0	1	2	—	0	.077	.200	.154
Jim Curry	2B4	R	18	4	11	3	2	0	0	0	0	1	—	0	.182	.250	.182
Bill Bailey	OF2,3B1	L	29	5	9	1	1	0	0	0	0	0	—	0	.111	.111	.111
Joe Walsh	C3	R	24	4	9	2	2	1	0	0	0	0	—	0	.222	.222	.333

H. Chase, 1 G at SS; J. Knight, 1 G at 3B

Pitcher	T	Age	G	GS	CG	ShO	IP	H	HR	BB	SO	W-L	Sv	ERA
Russ Ford	R	28	37	33	26	1	281.1	251	3	76	158	22-11	0	2.27
Ray Caldwell	R	23	41	27	19	1	255.0	240	7	79	145	14-14	1	3.35
Jack Warhop	R	26	31	25	17	1	209.2	239	6	44	71	12-13	0	4.16
Ray Fisher	R	23	29	22	8	2	171.2	178	3	55	99	10-11	0	3.25
Hippo Vaughn	L	23	26	18	11	0	145.2	158	2	54	74	8-10	0	4.39
Lew Brockett	R	30	16	8	2	0	75.1	73	3	39	25	2-4	0	4.66
Harry Ables	L	26	3	2	0	0	11.0	16	0	7	6	0-1	0	9.82
Andy Coakley	R	28	2	1	1	0	11.2	20	0	2	4	0-1	0	5.40
Jack Quinn	R	27	40	16	7	0	174.2	203	2	41	71	8-10	2	3.76
Red Hoff	L	20	5	1	0	0	20.2	21	0	7	10	0-1	0	2.18
Ed Klepfer	R	23	2	0	0	0	4.0	5	0	2	4	0-0	0	6.75

1911 Washington Senators 7th AL 64-90 .416 38.5 GB

Jimmy McAleer

Player	Gm by Position	B	Age	G	AB	R	H	2B	3B	HR	RBI	BB	SO	SB	Avg	OBP	Slg
Gabby Street	C71	R	28	72	216	16	48	7	1	0	14	14	—	4	.222	.279	.264
Germany Schaefer	1B108,OF7	R	34	125	440	74	147	14	7	0	45	57	—	22	.334	.412	.398
Bill Cunningham	2B93	R	23	94	331	34	63	10	5	3	37	19	—	10	.190	.239	.278
Wid Conroy	3B85,OF15,2B1	R	34	106	349	40	81	11	4	2	28	20	—	12	.232	.282	.304
George McBride	SS154	R	30	154	557	58	131	11	4	0	59	52	—	15	.235	.312	.269
Clyde Milan	OF154	L	24	154	616	109	194	24	8	3	35	74	—	58	.315	.395	.394
Doc Gessler	OF126,1B1	L	30	128	450	65	127	19	5	4	78	74	—	29	.282	.406	.373
Tilly Walker	OF94	R	23	95	356	44	99	6	4	2	39	15	—	12	.278	.311	.334
Kid Elberfeld	2B68,3B52	R	36	127	404	58	110	19	4	0	47	65	—	24	.272	.405	.339
John Henry	C51,1B30	R	21	85	261	24	53	5	0	0	21	25	—	8	.203	.273	.222
Jack Lelivelt	OF49,1B7	L	25	72	225	29	72	12	4	0	22	22	—	7	.320	.386	.409
Eddie Ainsmith	C47	R	19	61	149	12	33	2	3	0	14	10	—	5	.221	.275	.275
Ray Morgan	3B25	R	22	25	89	11	19	2	0	0	5	4	—	2	.213	.247	.236
Tom Long	OF13	R	21	14	48	1	11	3	0	0	5	1	—	4	.229	.245	.292
Jock Somerlott	1B12	R	28	13	40	2	7	0	0	0	2	0	—	2	.175	.195	.175
Warren Miller	OF9	L	25	21	34	3	5	0	0	0	0	0	—	0	.147	.147	.147
Charlie Conway	OF2	R	25	2	3	0	1	0	1	0	0	0	—	0	.333	.333	1.000
Bull Smith		R	30	1	0	0	0	0	0	0	0	0	—	0	—	—	—

Pitcher	T	Age	G	GS	CG	ShO	IP	H	HR	BB	SO	W-L	Sv	ERA
Walter Johnson	R	23	40	37	36	6	322.1	292	8	70	207	25-13	1	1.90
Bob Groom	R	26	37	32	20	2	254.2	280	9	67	135	13-17	2	3.82
Long Tom Hughes	R	32	34	27	17	2	223.0	251	7	77	86	11-17	2	3.47
Dixie Walker	R	24	32	24	15	2	185.2	205	2	50	65	8-13	0	3.39
Dolly Gray	L	32	28	15	6	0	121.0	160	4	40	42	2-13	0	5.06
Carl Cashion	R	20	11	9	5	0	71.1	67	4	47	26	1-5	0	4.16
Bill Otey	L	24	12	2	0	0	49.2	68	2	15	16	1-3	0	6.34
Charlie Becker	L	22	11	5	5	1	71.1	80	2	23	31	3-5	0	4.04
Fred Sherry	R	22	10	3	2	0	52.1	63	1	19	20	0-4	0	4.30
Walt Herrell	—	22	1	0	0	0	2.0	5	0	2	0	0-0	0	18.00

1911 St. Louis Browns 8th AL 45-107 .296 56.5 GB

Bobby Wallace

Player	Gm by Position	B	Age	G	AB	R	H	2B	3B	HR	RBI	BB	SO	SB	Avg	OBP	Slg
Nig Clarke	C73,1B4	L	28	82	256	22	55	10	1	0	18	26	—	2	.215	.287	.262
John Black	1B54	R	21	54	186	13	28	4	0	0	7	10	—	4	.151	.202	.172
Frank LaPorte	2B133,3B3	R	31	136	507	71	159	37	12	2	82	34	—	4	.314	.361	.446
Jimmy Austin	3B148	S	31	148	541	84	141	25	11	2	45	69	—	26	.261	.351	.359
Bobby Wallace	SS124,2B1	R	37	125	410	35	95	12	2	0	31	46	—	8	.232	.312	.271
Burt Shotton	OF139	L	26	139	572	85	146	11	8	0	36	51	—	26	.255	.317	.302
Willie Hogan†	OF117,1B5	R	26	123	443	53	115	17	8	2	62	43	—	18	.260	.328	.348
Al Schweitzer	OF68	R	28	76	237	31	51	11	4	0	34	43	—	12	.215	.338	.295
Jim Stephens	C66	R	27	70	212	11	49	6	3	0	17	17	—	1	.231	.300	.302
Paul Meloan†	OF54	L	22	64	206	30	54	11	2	3	14	15	—	7	.262	.318	.379
Ed Hallinan	SS34,2B15,3B3	R	22	52	169	13	35	3	1	0	14	14	—	4	.207	.268	.237
Pete Compton	OF28	L	21	28	107	9	29	4	0	0	5	8	—	2	.271	.322	.308
Jim Murray	OF25	R	33	31	102	8	19	5	0	3	11	5	—	0	.186	.224	.324
Joe Kutina	1B26	R	26	26	101	12	26	6	2	3	15	2	—	2	.257	.279	.446
Dode Criss	1B14,P4	L	26	58	83	10	21	3	1	2	15	11	—	0	.253	.347	.386
Paul Krichell	C25	R	28	28	82	6	19	3	0	0	8	4	—	2	.232	.276	.268
Danny Hoffman	OF23	L	31	24	81	11	17	3	2	0	7	12	—	3	.210	.326	.296
Dave Rowan	1B18	L	28	18	65	7	25	1	1	0	11	4	—	0	.385	.420	.431
Barney Pelty	P28,2B1	R	30	29	65	5	9	1	1	0	4	2	—	0	.138	.164	.185
Patrick Newnam	1B20	L	30	20	62	11	12	4	0	0	5	12	—	4	.194	.351	.258
Hap Myers†	1B11	R	23	11	37	4	11	1	0	0	1	1	—	0	.297	.316	.324
Gus Williams	OF7	L	23	9	26	1	7	3	0	0	4	0	—	0	.269	.296	.385
Allie Moulton	2B4	R	25	4	15	4	1	0	0	0	1	4	—	0	.067	.263	.067
Clyde Southwick	C4	L	24	4	12	4	3	0	0	0	0	1	—	0	.250	.308	.250
Ernie Gust	1B3	R	23	3	12	0	0	0	0	0	0	0	—	0	.000	.000	.000
Al Clancy	3B2	R	22	3	5	0	0	0	0	0	0	1	—	0	.000	.167	.000
Jim Duggan	1B1	L	26	1	4	1	0	0	0	0	1	1	—	0	.000	.200	.000
Joe Crisp		R	21	1	1	0	1	0	0	0	0	0	—	0	1.000	1.000	1.000
Frank Truesdale		S	27	1	0	1	0	0	0	0	0	0	—	0	—	—	—

Pitcher	T	Age	G	GS	CG	ShO	IP	H	HR	BB	SO	W-L	Sv	ERA
Jack Powell	R	36	31	27	18	1	207.2	224	7	44	52	8-19	1	3.29
Joe Lake	R	30	30	25	14	2	215.1	245	3	40	69	10-15	0	3.30
Barney Pelty	R	30	28	22	18	1	197.0	197	4	69	59	7-15	0	2.97
Earl Hamilton	L	19	32	17	10	0	177.0	191	4	69	55	5-12	1	3.97
Red Nelson	R	25	16	13	6	0	81.0	103	1	44	24	3-9	0	5.22
Ed Hawk	R	21	5	4	4	0	37.2	38	1	8	14	0-4	0	3.35
Mack Allison	R	24	3	3	3	0	26.1	24	0	5	2	2-1	0	2.05
Elmer Brown	R	28	5	3	1	1	16.2	16	0	14	5	1-1	0	6.48
George Curry	R	22	3	3	0	0	15.2	19	0	24	2	0-3	0	7.47
Curly Brown	L	22	3	2	2	0	23.0	22	0	5	8	1-2	0	2.74
Dode Criss	R	26	4	2	0	0	18.1	24	0	10	9	0-2	0	8.35
Walter Moser†	R	30	2	2	0	0	3.1	11	0	4	2	0-2	0	21.60
Joe Willis†	L	21	1	1	0	0	7.0	8	0	3	0	0-1	0	5.14
Roy Mitchell	R	26	28	12	8	1	133.1	134	4	45	40	4-8	0	3.85
Lefty George	L	24	27	13	6	1	116.1	136	3	51	23	4-9	0	4.18
Bill Bailey	L	22	7	2	2	0	31.2	42	1	16	8	0-3	0	4.55
Howie Gregory	R	24	3	1	0	0	7.0	11	0	4	1	0-1	0	5.14
Jeff Pfeffer	R	23	2	0	0	0	10.0	11	0	4	4	0-0	0	7.20
Bill Harper	R	22	2	0	0	0	8.0	9	0	4	6	0-0	0	6.75

»1911 New York Giants 1st NL 99-54 .647 —

John McGraw

Player	Gm by Position	B	Age	G	AB	R	H	2B	3B	HR	RBI	BB	SO	SB	Avg	OBP	Slg
Chief Meyers	C128	R	30	133	391	48	130	18	9	1	61	25	33	7	.332	.392	.432
Fred Merkle	1B148	R	22	149	541	80	153	24	10	12	84	43	60	49	.283	.342	.431
Larry Doyle	2B141	L	24	143	526	102	163	25	25	13	77	71	39	38	.310	.397	.527
Art Devlin	3B79,1B6,2B6*	R	31	95	260	42	71	16	2	0	25	42	19	9	.273	.386	.350
Al Bridwell†	SS76	L	27	76	263	28	71	10	1	0	31	33	10	8	.270	.358	.316
Josh Devore	OF149	L	23	149	565	96	158	19	10	3	50	81	69	61	.280	.376	.365
Fred Snodgrass	OF149,1B1,3B1	R	23	151	534	83	157	27	10	1	77	72	59	51	.294	.393	.388
Red Murray	OF131	R	27	140	488	70	142	27	15	3	78	43	37	48	.291	.354	.426
Art Fletcher	SS74,3B21,2B13	R	26	112	326	73	104	17	8	1	37	30	27	20	.319	.400	.429
Buck Herzog†	3B65,2B3,SS1	R	25	69	247	37	66	14	4	1	26	14	19	22	.267	.325	.368
Beals Becker	OF55	L	24	88	172	28	45	11	1	1	20	26	22	19	.262	.359	.355
Doc Crandall	P41,SS6,2B3	R	23	61	113	12	27	1	4	2	21	8	16	2	.239	.295	.372
Art Wilson	C64	R	25	66	109	17	33	9	1	1	17	19	12	6	.303	.411	.431
Grover Hartley	C10	R	22	11	18	1	4	2	0	0	1	1	1	1	.222	.263	.333
George Burns	OF6	R	21	6	17	2	1	0	0	0	0	1	1	0	.059	.111	.059
Gene Paulette	1B7,3B1,SS1	R	20	10	12	1	2	0	0	0	1	0	1	0	.167	.167	.167
Mike Donlin†	OF3	L	33	12	12	3	4	0	0	1	1	0	1	2	.333	.333	.583
Hank Gowdy†	1B2	R	21	4	4	1	1	1	0	0	0	2	0	0	.250	.500	.500
Admiral Schlei		R	33	1	1	0	0	0	0	0	0	0	1	0	.000	.000	.000

A. Devlin, 6 G at SS

Pitcher	T	Age	G	GS	CG	ShO	IP	H	HR	BB	SO	W-L	Sv	ERA
Christy Mathewson	R	32	45	37	29	5	307.0	303	5	38	141	26-13	3	1.99
Rube Marquard	L	24	45	33	22	5	277.2	221	9	106	237	24-7	3	2.50
Hooks Wiltse	L	30	30	24	11	4	187.1	177	7	39	92	12-9	0	3.27
Red Ames	R	28	34	23	13	1	205.0	170	0	54	118	11-10	2	2.68
Louis Drucke	R	22	15	10	4	0	75.2	83	1	41	42	4-4	0	4.04
Bugs Raymond	R	29	17	9	4	1	81.2	73	1	33	39	6-4	0	3.31
Bert Maxwell	R	24	4	3	3	0	31.0	37	0	7	8	1-2	0	2.90
Doc Crandall	R	23	41	15	9	2	198.2	199	10	51	94	15-5	5	2.63
Charlie Faust	R	30	2	0	0	0	2.0	2	0	0	0	0-0	0	4.50
Dick Rudolph	R	23	1	0	0	0	2.0	2	0	0	0	0-0	0	9.00

1911 Chicago Cubs 2nd NL 92-62 .597 7.5 GB

Frank Chance

Player	Gm by Position	B	Age	G	AB	R	H	2B	3B	HR	RBI	BB	SO	SB	Avg	OBP	Slg
Jimmy Archer	C102,1B10,2B1	R	28	116	387	41	98	18	5	4	41	18	43	5	.253	.288	.357
Vic Saier	1B73	L	20	86	259	42	67	15	1	1	37	25	37	11	.259	.340	.336
Heinie Zimmerman	2B108,3B20,1B11	R	24	143	535	80	164	22	17	9	85	25	50	23	.307	.343	.462
Jim Doyle	3B127	R	29	130	472	69	133	23	12	5	62	40	54	19	.282	.340	.413
Joe Tinker	SS143	R	30	144	536	61	149	24	12	4	69	39	31	30	.278	.327	.390
Jimmy Sheckard	OF156	L	32	156	539	121	149	26	11	4	50	147	58	32	.276	.434	.388
Wildfire Schulte	OF154	L	28	154	577	105	173	30	21	21	107	76	68	23	.300	.384	.534
Solly Hofman	OF107,1B36	R	28	143	512	66	129	17	2	2	70	66	40	30	.252	.341	.305
Johnny Evers	2B33,3B11	L	29	46	155	29	35	4	3	0	7	34	10	6	.226	.372	.290
Dave Shean	2B23,SS19,3B1	R	27	54	145	17	28	4	0	0	15	8	15	4	.193	.240	.221
Wilbur Good†	OF40	L	25	58	145	27	39	5	4	2	21	11	17	10	.269	.329	.400
Frank Chance	1B29	R	33	31	88	23	21	6	3	1	17	25	13	9	.239	.432	.409
Al Kaiser†	OF23	R	24	26	84	16	21	0	5	0	7	7	12	6	.250	.308	.369
Johnny Kling†	C25	R	36	27	80	8	14	3	2	1	5	8	14	1	.175	.250	.300
Peaches Graham†	C28	R	34	36	71	6	17	3	0	0	8	11	8	2	.239	.365	.282
Tom Needham	C23	R	32	27	62	4	12	2	0	0	5	9	14	2	.194	.315	.226
Kitty Bransfield†	1B3	R	36	3	10	0	4	2	0	0	0	2	2	0	.400	.500	.600
Bill Collins†	OF4	S	29	7	3	2	1	1	0	0	0	1	3	0	.333	.500	.667

Pitcher	T	Age	G	GS	CG	ShO	IP	H	HR	BB	SO	W-L	Sv	ERA
Ed Reulbach	R	28	33	29	15	2	221.2	191	3	103	79	16-9	0	2.96
Lew Richie	R	27	36	28	18	4	253.0	213	6	103	78	15-11	1	2.31
Three Finger Brown	R	34	53	27	21	0	270.0	267	5	55	129	21-11	13	2.80
King Cole	R	25	32	27	13	2	221.1	188	3	99	101	18-7	0	3.13
Harry McIntire	R	32	25	17	9	1	149.0	147	5	33	56	11-7	0	4.11
Charlie Smith†	R	31	7	5	3	1	38.0	31	0	7	11	3-2	0	1.42
Jack Pfiester	L	33	6	5	3	0	33.2	34	0	18	15	0-4	0	4.01
Orlie Weaver†	R	25	6	4	1	1	43.2	29	0	17	20	3-2	0	2.06
Cy Slapnicka	R	25	3	2	1	0	24.0	21	0	7	10	0-2	0	3.38
Hank Griffin†	R	24	1	1	0	0	1.0	1	1	3	1	0-0	0	18.00
Reggie Richter	R	22	22	5	0	0	54.2	62	1	20	34	1-3	2	3.13
Fred Toney	R	22	18	4	1	0	67.0	55	2	35	27	1-1	0	2.42
Cliff Curtis†	R	27	4	1	0	0	7.0	7	0	5	4	1-2	0	3.86
Bill Foxen	L	27	3	1	0	0	13.0	12	0	12	6	1-1	0	2.08
Larry Cheney	R	25	3	1	0	0	10.0	8	0	3	11	1-0	0	0.00
Ernie Ovitz	R	25	1	0	0	0	2.0	3	0	3	0	0-0	0	4.50
Jack Rowan†	R	24	1	0	0	0	2.0	1	0	2	0	0-0	0	4.50

1911 Pittsburgh Pirates 3rd NL 85-69 .552 14.5 GB

Fred Clarke

Player	Gm by Position	B	Age	G	AB	R	H	2B	3B	HR	RBI	BB	SO	SB	Avg	OBP	Slg
George Gibson	C98	R	30	100	311	32	65	12	2	0	19	29	16	3	.209	.281	.260
Newt Hunter	1B61	R	31	65	209	35	53	10	6	2	24	25	43	9	.254	.345	.388
Dots Miller	2B129	R	24	137	470	82	126	17	8	6	78	51	48	17	.268	.345	.377
Bobby Byrne	3B152	R	26	153	598	96	155	24	17	2	52	67	41	23	.259	.342	.366
Honus Wagner	SS101,1B28,OF1	R	37	130	473	87	158	23	16	9	89	67	34	20	.334	.423	.507
Chief Wilson	OF146	L	27	148	544	72	163	34	12	12	107	41	55	10	.300	.353	.472
Max Carey	OF122	S	21	129	427	77	110	15	10	5	43	44	75	27	.258	.337	.375
Fred Clarke	OF101	L	38	110	392	73	127	25	13	5	49	53	27	10	.324	.407	.492
Tommy Leach	OF89,SS13,3B1	R	33	108	386	60	92	12	6	3	43	46	50	19	.238	.323	.324
Bill McKechnie	1B57,2B17,SS12*	S	24	104	321	40	73	8	7	2	37	28	18	9	.227	.293	.315
Mike Simon	C68	R	28	71	215	19	49	4	3	0	22	10	14	1	.228	.275	.274
Alex McCarthy	SS33,2B11,3B1*	R	23	50	150	18	36	5	1	2	31	14	24	4	.240	.305	.327
Vin Campbell	OF21	L	23	42	93	12	29	3	1	0	10	8	7	6	.312	.366	.366
John Flynn	1B13,OF1	R	27	33	59	5	12	0	1	0	3	9	8	0	.203	.309	.237
Billy Kelly	C1	R	25	6	8	0	1	0	0	0	0	0	2	0	.125	.125	.125
Mickey Keliher	1B2	L	21	3	7	0	0	0	0	0	0	0	5	0	.000	.000	.000
Bill Keen	1B1	R	18	6	7	0	0	0	0	0	0	1	4	0	.000	.125	.000
Jerry Dorsey	OF1	L	26	2	6	0	0	0	0	0	0	0	0	0	.000	.000	.000
John Shovlin		R	20	2	1	1	0	0	0	0	0	0	1	0	.000	.000	.000

B. McKechnie, 6 G at 3B; A. McCarthy, 1 G at OF

Pitcher	T	Age	G	GS	CG	ShO	IP	H	HR	BB	SO	W-L	Sv	ERA
Lefty Leifield	L	27	42	37	26	2	318.0	301	7	82	111	16-16	1	2.63
Babe Adams	R	29	40	37	24	6	293.1	253	5	42	133	22-12	0	2.33
Howie Camnitz	R	29	40	33	18	1	267.2	245	8	84	139	20-15	1	3.16
Elmer Steele†	R	25	31	16	7	2	166.0	153	5	31	52	9-9	2	2.60
Claude Hendrix	R	22	22	12	6	1	118.2	85	1	53	57	4-6	1	2.73
Marty O'Toole	R	22	5	5	3	0	38.0	28	1	20	34	3-2	0	2.37
Kirby White	R	27	2	1	0	0	3.0	3	1	1	1	0-1	0	9.00
Jack Ferry	R	24	26	8	4	1	85.2	83	3	27	32	6-4	3	3.15
Harry Gardner	R	22	13	3	2	0	42.0	39	2	20	24	1-1	2	4.50
Judge Nagle†	R	31	8	3	1	0	27.1	33	3	6	11	4-2	1	3.62
Hank Robinson	L	21	5	0	0	0	13.0	13	0	5	8	0-1	0	2.77
Deacon Phillippe	R	39	3	0	0	0	6.0	5	0	2	3	0-0	0	7.50
Ensign Cottrell	L	22	1	0	0	0	1.0	4	0	1	0	0-0	0	9.00
Sherry Smith	L	20	1	0	0	0	0.2	4	0	1	0	0-0	0	54.00

1911 Philadelphia Phillies 4th NL 79-73 .520 19.5 GB

Red Dooin

Player	Gm by Position	B	Age	G	AB	R	H	2B	3B	HR	RBI	BB	SO	SB	Avg	OBP	Slg
Red Dooin	C74	R	32	74	247	18	81	15	1	1	16	14	12	6	.328	.366	.409
Fred Luderus	1B146	L	25	146	551	69	166	24	11	16	99	40	76	6	.301	.353	.472
Otto Knabe	2B142	R	27	142	528	99	125	15	6	1	42	94	35	23	.237	.352	.294
Hans Lobert	3B147	R	29	147	541	94	154	20	9	9	72	66	31	40	.285	.368	.405
Mickey Doolan	SS145	R	31	146	512	51	122	23	6	1	49	44	65	14	.238	.301	.313
Dode Paskert	OF153	R	29	153	560	96	153	18	5	4	47	70	70	28	.273	.358	.345
Sherry Magee	OF120	R	26	121	445	79	128	32	5	15	94	49	33	22	.288	.366	.483
Fred Beck†	OF61	L	24	66	210	26	59	8	3	3	25	17	21	3	.281	.346	.390
Jimmy Walsh	OF48,2B14,SS9*	R	25	94	289	29	78	20	3	1	31	21	30	5	.270	.324	.370
John Titus	OF60	L	35	76	236	35	67	14	1	8	26	32	16	3	.284	.372	.453
Pat Moran	C32	R	35	34	103	2	19	3	0	0	8	3	13	0	.184	.208	.214
Bunny Madden†	C22	R	28	28	76	4	21	1	1	0	4	0	13	0	.276	.276	.316
Harry Welchonce	OF17	L	27	26	66	9	14	4	0	0	6	7	8	0	.212	.288	.273
Dick Cotter	C17	R	21	20	46	2	13	0	0	0	5	5	7	1	.283	.353	.283
Kitty Bransfield†	1B8	R	36	23	43	4	11	1	1	0	3	0	5	1	.256	.256	.326
Tubby Spencer	C11	R	27	11	32	2	5	1	0	1	3	3	7	0	.156	.229	.281
Roy Thomas	OF11	L	37	21	30	5	5	2	0	0	2	8	6	0	.167	.342	.233
Clarence Lehr	2B4,SS4,OF4	R	25	23	27	2	4	0	0	0	0	0	7	0	.148	.148	.148
Bill Killefer	C6	R	23	6	16	3	3	0	0	0	2	0	2	0	.188	.188	.188
Red Kleinow†	C4	R	31	4	8	0	1	1	0	0	0	0	1	0	.125	.125	.250
Paddy Mayes	OF2	L	26	5	5	1	0	0	0	0	0	1	2	0	.000	.286	.000
John Quinn	C1	R	25	1	2	0	0	0	0	0	0	0	0	0	.000	.000	.000
Hughie Miller		R	23	1	0	0	0	0	0	0	0	0	0	0	—	—	—

J. Walsh, 7 G at 3B, 4 G at C, 1 G at P, 1 G at 1B

Pitcher	T	Age	G	GS	CG	ShO	IP	H	HR	BB	SO	W-L	Sv	ERA
Pete Alexander	R	24	48	37	31	7	367.0	285	5	129	227	28-13	3	2.57
Earl Moore	R	31	42	36	21	5	308.1	265	11	164	174	15-19	1	2.63
George Chalmers	R	23	38	22	11	3	208.2	196	5	101	101	13-10	4	3.11
Bill Burns†	L	31	21	14	8	3	121.0	132	5	26	47	6-10	1	3.42
Eddie Stack	R	23	13	10	5	1	77.2	67	3	41	36	5-5	0	3.59
Fred Beebe	R	30	9	8	3	0	48.1	52	2	24	20	3-3	0	4.47
Jack Rowan†	R	24	12	6	2	0	45.2	59	3	20	17	2-4	0	4.73
Cliff Curtis†	R	27	8	5	3	1	45.0	45	0	15	13	2-1	0	2.60
Toots Shultz	R	22	5	3	2	0	25.0	30	5	15	9	0-3	0	9.36
Bob Ewing	R	38	4	3	1	0	24.0	29	2	14	12	0-1	0	7.88
Ad Brennan	L	29	5	3	1	0	22.2	22	0	12	12	2-1	0	3.57
Bert Humphries†	R	30	11	5	2	0	41.0	56	1	10	13	3-1	1	4.17
Bert Hall	R	22	7	1	0	0	18.0	19	0	13	8	0-1	0	4.00
Buck Stanley	L	24	4	0	0	0	11.1	14	0	9	5	0-0	0	6.35
Jake Smith	L	24	2	0	0	0	5.0	3	0	2	1	0-0	0	0.00
Jimmy Walsh	R	25	1	0	0	0	2.2	7	1	1	1	0-1	0	13.50
Troy Puckett	R	21	1	0	0	0	2.0	4	0	2	1	0-0	0	13.50

1911 St. Louis Cardinals 5th NL 75-74 .503 22.0 GB

Roger Bresnahan

Player	Gm by Position	B	Age	G	AB	R	H	2B	3B	HR	RBI	BB	SO	SB	Avg	OBP	Slg
Jack Bliss	C84,SS1	R	29	97	258	36	59	6	4	1	27	42	25	5	.229	.341	.295
Ed Konetchy	1B158	R	25	158	571	90	165	38	13	6	88	81	63	27	.289	.384	.433
Miller Huggins	2B136	S	32	138	509	106	133	19	2	1	24	96	52	37	.261	.385	.312
Mike Mowrey	3B134,SS1	R	27	137	471	59	126	29	7	0	61	59	46	15	.268	.355	.359
Arnold Hauser	SS134,3B2	R	22	136	515	61	124	11	8	3	46	26	67	24	.241	.286	.311
Rebel Oakes	OF151	L	24	154	551	69	145	13	6	2	59	41	35	25	.263	.320	.319
Steve Evans	OF150	L	26	154	547	74	161	24	13	5	71	46	52	13	.294	.369	.413
Rube Ellis	OF148	L	25	155	555	69	139	20	11	2	66	66	64	9	.250	.332	.337
Roger Bresnahan	C77,2B2	R	32	81	227	22	63	17	8	3	41	45	19	4	.278	.404	.463
Wally Smith	3B26,SS25,2B8*	R	22	81	194	23	42	6	5	2	19	21	33	5	.216	.303	.330
Lee Magee	2B18,SS3	S	22	26	69	9	18	1	1	0	8	8	8	4	.261	.338	.304
Otto McIvor	OF17	S	26	30	62	11	14	2	1	1	9	9	14	0	.226	.333	.339
Ivy Wingo	C18	L	20	25	57	4	12	2	0	0	3	3	7	0	.211	.250	.246
Denney Wilie	OF15	L	20	28	51	10	12	3	1	0	3	8	11	3	.235	.361	.333
Jim Clark	OF8	R	23	14	18	2	3	0	1	0	3	3	4	2	.167	.286	.278
Dan McGeehan	2B3	R	26	3	9	0	2	0	0	0	1	0	1	0	.222	.222	.222
Hap Morse	SS2,OF1	R	24	4	8	0	0	0	0	0	0	1	2	0	.000	.111	.000
Ed Conwell	3B1	R	21	1	1	0	0	0	0	0	0	0	0	0	.000	.000	.000
Milt Reed		L	20	1	1	0	0	0	0	0	0	0	0	0	.000	.000	.000
Frank Gilhooley	OF1	L	19	1	0	0	0	0	0	0	0	0	0	0	—	—	—

W. Smith, 1 G at OF

Pitcher	T	Age	G	GS	CG	ShO	IP	H	HR	BB	SO	W-L	Sv	ERA
Bob Harmon	R	23	51	41	28	2	348.0	290	10	181	144	23-16	4	3.13
Bill Steele	R	25	43	34	23	1	287.1	287	8	113	115	18-19	3	3.73
Slim Sallee	L	26	36	30	18	1	245.0	234	6	64	74	15-9	3	2.76
Roy Golden	R	22	30	25	6	0	148.2	127	6	129	81	4-9	0	5.02
Gene Woodburn	R	24	11	6	1	0	38.1	22	0	40	23	1-5	0	5.40
Joe Willis†	L	21	2	2	1	0	15.0	13	0	4	5	0-1	0	4.20
Roy Radebaugh	R	27	2	1	0	0	10.0	6	0	4	1	0-0	0	2.70
Rube Geyer	R	27	29	11	7	1	148.2	141	7	56	46	9-6	0	3.27
Lou Lowdermilk	L	24	16	3	3	0	65.0	72	0	29	20	3-4	0	3.46
Grover Lowdermilk	R	26	11	2	1	1	33.1	37	1	33	15	0-1	0	7.29
Jack McAdams	R	24	6	0	0	0	9.2	7	0	5	4	0-0	0	3.72
Gene Dale	R	22	5	2	0	0	14.2	13	0	16	13	0-2	0	6.75
Ed Zmich	L	26	4	0	0	0	12.2	8	0	8	4	1-0	0	2.13
George Zackert	L	26	4	1	0	0	7.1	17	0	6	6	0-2	0	11.05
Jack Heis	R	21	3	0	0	0	9.1	5	0	8	4	0-0	0	0.96
Pete Standridge	R	20	2	0	0	0	4.2	10	0	4	3	0-0	0	9.64
Bunny Hearn	L	20	2	0	0	0	2.2	7	1	0	1	0-0	0	13.50
Harry Camnitz	R	26	2	0	0	0	2.0	0	0	1	2	1-0	0	0.00

578 Seasons: Team Rosters

1911 Cincinnati Reds 6th NL 70-83 .458 29.0 GB

Clark Griffith

Player	Gm by Position	B	Age	G	AB	R	H	2B	3B	HR	RBI	BB	SO	SB	Avg	OBP	Slg
Larry McLean	C98	R	29	107	328	24	94	7	2	0	34	20	18	1	.287	.330	.320
Doc Hoblitzell	1B158	R	22	158	622	81	180	19	13	11	91	42	44	32	.289	.342	.415
Dick Egan	2B152	R	27	153	558	80	139	11	5	1	56	59	50	37	.249	.322	.292
Eddie Grant	3B122,SS11	L	28	136	458	49	102	12	7	1	53	51	47	28	.223	.301	.286
Tom Downey	SS92,2B6,3B5*	R	27	111	360	50	94	16	7	0	36	44	38	10	.261	.345	.344
Bob Bescher	OF153	S	27	153	599	106	165	32	10	1	45	102	78	80	.275	.385	.367
Johnny Bates	OF147	L	28	148	518	89	151	24	13	1	61	103	59	33	.292	.415	.394
Mike Mitchell	OF140	R	31	142	529	74	154	22	22	2	84	44	34	35	.291	.348	.427
Tommy Clarke	C81,1B1	R	23	86	203	20	49	6	7	1	25	25	22	4	.241	.328	.355
Jimmy Esmond	SS43,3B14,2B2	R	21	73	198	27	54	4	6	1	11	17	30	7	.273	.330	.369
Armando Marsans	OF34,1B1,3B1	R	23	58	138	17	36	2	2	0	11	15	11	11	.261	.346	.304
Rafael Almeida	3B27,2B1,SS1	R	23	36	96	9	30	5	1	0	15	9	16	3	.313	.383	.385
Fred Beck†	OF16,1B6	L	24	41	87	7	16	1	2	2	20	1	13	2	.184	.193	.310
Dave Altizer	SS23,1B1,2B1*	L	34	37	75	8	17	4	1	0	4	9	5	2	.227	.318	.307
Hank Severeid	C22	R	20	37	56	5	17	6	1	0	10	3	6	0	.304	.350	.446
Mike Balenti	SS2,OF1	R	24	8	8	2	2	0	0	0	0	0	1	3	.250	.250	.250
Danny Mahoney		R	22	1	0	0	0	0	0	0	0	0	0	0	—	—	—
Hub Northen†		L	25	1	0	0	0	0	0	0	0	0	0	0	—	—	—

T. Downey, 2 G at 1B, 1 G at OF; D. Altizer, 1 G at OF

Pitcher	T	Age	G	GS	CG	ShO	IP	H	HR	BB	SO	W-L	Sv	ERA
Harry Gaspar	R	28	44	32	11	2	253.2	272	9	69	76	11-17	4	3.30
George Suggs	R	28	36	29	17	1	260.2	258	3	79	91	15-13	0	3.00
Bobby Keefe	R	29	39	26	15	0	234.1	196	7	76	105	12-13	3	2.69
Art Fromme	R	27	38	26	11	1	208.0	190	8	79	107	10-11	0	3.46
Frank Smith†	R	31	34	18	10	0	176.1	198	1	55	67	10-14	1	3.98
Bert Humphries†	R	30	14	7	3	0	65.0	62	3	18	16	4-3	0	2.35
Rube Benton	L	24	6	6	5	0	44.2	44	0	23	28	3-3	0	2.01
Ray Boyd	R	24	7	4	3	0	44.0	34	0	19	20	2-2	1	2.66
Bill Burns†	L	31	6	3	0	0	17.2	17	1	3	5	1-0	1	3.06
George McQuillan	R	26	19	5	2	0	77.0	92	2	31	28	2-6	0	4.68
Jack Compton	R	29	8	3	0	0	25.1	19	0	15	6	0-1	1	3.91
Barney Schreiber	L	29	3	0	0	0	10.0	19	2	2	5	0-0	1	5.40
Jesse Tannehill	L	36	1	0	0	0	4.1	6	0	3	1	0-0	0	6.23
Herb Juul	L	25	1	0	0	0	4.0	3	0	4	2	0-0	0	4.50

1911 Brooklyn Dodgers 7th NL 64-86 .427 33.5 GB

Bill Dahlen

Player	Gm by Position	B	Age	G	AB	R	H	2B	3B	HR	RBI	BB	SO	SB	Avg	OBP	Slg
Bill Bergen	C84	R	33	84	227	8	30	3	1	0	10	14	42	2	.132	.183	.154
Jake Daubert	1B149	L	27	149	573	89	176	17	8	5	45	51	56	32	.307	.366	.391
John Hummel	2B127,1B4,SS2	R	28	137	477	54	129	21	11	5	58	67	66	16	.270	.360	.392
Eddie Zimmerman	3B122	R	28	122	417	31	77	10	7	3	36	34	37	9	.185	.249	.264
Bert Tooley	SS114	R	24	119	433	55	89	11	3	1	29	53	63	18	.206	.295	.252
Bob Coulson	OF145	R	24	146	521	52	122	23	7	0	50	42	78	32	.234	.301	.305
Zack Wheat	OF136	L	23	140	534	55	153	26	13	5	76	29	58	21	.287	.332	.412
Bill Davidson	OF74	R	24	87	292	33	68	3	4	1	26	16	21	18	.233	.275	.281
Tex Erwin	C74	L	25	91	218	30	59	13	2	7	34	31	23	5	.271	.367	.445
Dolly Stark	SS34,2B18,3B4	R	26	70	193	25	57	4	1	0	19	20	24	6	.295	.370	.326
Al Burch	OF43,2B3	L	27	54	167	18	38	2	3	0	7	15	22	3	.228	.291	.275
Cy Barger	P30,OF11,1B1	L	26	57	145	16	33	1	1	0	9	5	20	2	.228	.258	.248
Red Smith	3B28	R	21	28	111	10	29	6	1	0	19	5	13	5	.261	.299	.333
Hub Northen†	OF19	L	25	19	76	16	24	2	2	0	1	14	9	4	.316	.429	.395
Jud Daley	OF16	L	27	19	65	8	15	2	1	0	7	2	8	2	.231	.286	.292
Otto Miller	C22	R	22	25	62	7	13	2	2	0	8	0	4	2	.210	.210	.306
Hi Myers	OF13	R	22	13	43	2	7	1	0	0	0	2	3	1	.163	.200	.186
Tony Smith	SS10,2B3	R	27	13	40	3	6	1	0	0	2	8	7	1	.150	.292	.175
Pryor McElveen	2B5,SS1	R	29	16	31	1	6	0	0	0	5	0	3	0	.194	.194	.194
Al Humphrey	OF8	L	25	8	27	4	5	0	0	0	0	3	7	0	.185	.267	.185
Larry LeJeune	OF6	R	25	6	19	2	3	0	0	0	2	2	8	2	.158	.238	.158
George Browne	OF2	L	35	8	12	1	4	0	0	0	2	1	1	2	.333	.385	.333
Bob Higgins	C2,3B1	R	24	4	10	1	3	0	0	0	2	1	0	1	.300	.364	.300
Bill Dahlen	SS1	R	41	1	3	0	0	0	0	0	0	0	3	0	.000	.000	.000

Pitcher	T	Age	G	GS	CG	ShO	IP	H	HR	BB	SO	W-L	Sv	ERA
Nap Rucker	L	26	48	33	23	5	315.2	255	12	110	190	22-18	4	2.74
Cy Barger	R	26	30	30	21	1	217.1	224	4	71	60	11-15	0	3.52
Bill Schardt	R	25	39	22	10	1	195.1	190	4	91	77	5-15	4	3.59
Elmer Knetzer	R	25	35	20	11	3	204.0	202	1	93	66	11-12	0	3.49
Doc Scanlan	R	30	22	15	3	0	113.2	101	2	69	45	3-10	1	3.64
George Bell	R	36	19	12	6	2	101.0	123	2	28	28	5-6	0	4.28
Sandy Burk	R	24	13	7	1	0	58.0	54	1	47	15	1-3	0	5.12
Eddie Dent	R	23	5	3	1	0	31.2	30	0	10	3	2-1	0	3.69
Walt Miller	R	26	3	2	0	0	11.0	16	0	6	0	0-1	0	6.55
Pat Ragan	R	22	22	7	5	2	93.2	81	0	31	39	4-3	1	2.11
Elmer Steele†	R	25	5	2	0	0	23.0	24	0	5	9	0-0	0	3.13
Jack Ryan	R	26	3	1	0	0	6.0	9	1	4	1	0-1	0	3.00
Raleigh Aitchison	L	23	1	0	0	0	1.1	1	0	1	0	0-1	0	0.00

1911 Boston Beaneaters 8th NL 44-107 .291 54.0 GB

Fred Tenney

Player	Gm by Position	B	Age	G	AB	R	H	2B	3B	HR	RBI	BB	SO	SB	Avg	OBP	Slg
Johnny Kling†	C71,3B1	R	36	75	241	32	54	8	1	2	24	30	29	0	.224	.310	.290
Fred Tenney	1B96,OF2	L	39	102	369	52	97	13	4	1	36	50	17	5	.263	.352	.328
Bill Sweeney	2B136	R	25	137	523	92	164	33	6	3	63	77	26	33	.314	.404	.417
Scotty Ingerton	3B58,OF43,1B17*	R	25	136	521	63	130	24	4	5	61	39	68	6	.250	.304	.340
Buck Herzog†	SS74,3B4	R	25	79	294	53	91	19	5	5	41	33	21	26	.310	.398	.459
Doc Miller	OF146	L	28	146	577	69	192	36	3	7	91	43	43	32	.333	.379	.442
Al Kaiser†	OF58	R	24	66	197	20	40	5	2	2	15	10	26	4	.203	.249	.279
Mike Donlin†	OF56	L	33	56	222	33	70	16	1	2	34	22	17	7	.315	.377	.423
Bill Rariden	C65,3B3,2B1	R	23	70	246	22	56	9	0	0	21	21	18	3	.228	.288	.264
Al Bridwell†	SS51	L	27	51	182	29	53	5	0	0	10	33	8	2	.291	.403	.319
Ed McDonald	3B53	R	24	54	175	28	36	7	3	1	21	40	39	11	.206	.359	.297
Wilbur Good†	OF43	L	25	43	165	21	44	9	3	0	15	12	22	3	.267	.316	.358
Harry Spratt	SS26,2B5,3B4*	L	22	62	154	22	37	4	4	2	13	13	25	1	.240	.299	.357
George Jackson	OF39	R	28	39	147	28	51	11	2	0	25	12	21	12	.347	.404	.449
Josh Clarke	OF30	L	32	32	120	16	28	7	3	1	4	29	22	6	.233	.387	.367
Hank Gowdy†	1B26,C1	R	21	29	97	9	28	4	2	0	16	4	19	2	.289	.324	.371
Patsy Flaherty	OF19,P4	L	35	38	94	9	27	3	2	2	20	8	11	2	.287	.343	.426
Jay Kirke	OF14,1B3,2B1*	L	23	20	89	9	32	5	5	0	12	2	6	3	.360	.380	.528
Peaches Graham†	C26	R	34	33	88	7	24	6	1	0	12	14	5	2	.273	.373	.364
Ben Houser	1B20	L	27	20	71	11	18	1	0	1	9	8	6	2	.254	.329	.310
Art Butler	3B14,2B4,SS1	R	23	27	68	11	12	2	0	0	2	6	6	0	.176	.263	.206
Harry Steinfeldt	3B19	R	33	19	63	5	16	4	0	1	8	6	3	1	.254	.338	.365
Bill Jones	OF18	L	24	24	51	6	11	2	1	0	3	15	7	1	.216	.394	.294
Bill Collins†	OF13,3B1	S	29	17	44	8	6	1	1	0	8	1	8	4	.136	.156	.205
Herman Young	3B5,SS3	R	25	9	25	2	6	0	0	0	0	0	3	0	.240	.269	.240
Bert Weeden		L	28	1	1	0	0	0	0	0	0	0	0	0	.000	.000	.000

S. Ingerton, 11 G at 2B, 5 G at SS; H. Spratt, 4 G at OF; J. Kirke, 1 G at 3B, 1 G at SS

Pitcher	T	Age	G	GS	CG	ShO	IP	H	HR	BB	SO	W-L	Sv	ERA
Buster Brown	R	29	42	25	13	0	241.0	258	0	116	76	8-18	2	4.29
Al Mattern	R	28	33	21	11	0	186.1	228	13	63	51	4-15	0	4.97
Lefty Tyler	L	21	28	20	10	1	165.1	150	11	109	90	7-10	0	5.06
Hub Perdue	R	29	24	19	9	0	137.1	180	10	41	40	6-10	1	4.98
Orlie Weaver†	R	25	27	17	4	0	121.0	140	9	84	50	3-12	0	6.47
Cy Young†	R	44	11	11	8	2	80.0	83	4	15	35	4-5	0	3.71
Cliff Curtis†	R	27	12	9	5	0	77.0	79	4	34	23	1-8	1	4.44
Bill McTigue	L	20	14	8	0	0	37.0	37	3	49	23	0-5	0	7.05
Ed Donnelly	R	30	5	4	4	1	36.2	33	0	9	16	3-2	0	2.45
George Ferguson	R	24	6	3	0	0	24.0	40	3	12	4	1-3	0	9.75
Patsy Flaherty	L	35	4	2	1	0	14.0	21	0	8	0	0-2	0	7.07
Billy Burke	L	21	2	1	0	0	3.1	6	0	5	1	0-1	0	18.90
Big Jeff Pfeffer	R	29	26	6	4	1	97.0	116	3	57	24	7-5	2	4.73
Hank Griffin†	R	24	15	6	1	0	82.2	96	3	34	30	0-6	0	5.23
Brad Hogg	R	23	8	3	2	0	25.2	33	0	14	8	0-3	1	6.66
Jiggs Parson	R	25	7	0	0	0	25.0	36	2	15	7	0-1	0	6.48
Sam Frock	R	28	4	1	1	0	16.0	29	0	5	8	0-1	0	5.63
Fuller Thompson	R	22	3	0	0	0	4.2	5	0	2	0	0-0	0	3.86

»1912 Boston Red Sox 1st AL 105-47 .691 —

Jake Stahl

Player	Gm by Position	B	Age	G	AB	R	H	2B	3B	HR	RBI	BB	SO	SB	Avg	OBP	Slg
Bill Carrigan	C87	R	28	87	266	34	70	7	1	0	24	38	—	7	.263	.359	.297
Jake Stahl	1B92	R	33	95	326	40	98	21	6	3	60	31	—	13	.301	.372	.429
Steve Yerkes	2B131	R	24	131	523	73	132	22	6	0	42	41	—	4	.252	.312	.317
Larry Gardner	3B143	L	26	143	517	88	163	24	18	3	86	56	—	25	.315	.383	.449
Heinie Wagner	SS144	R	31	144	504	75	138	25	6	2	68	62	—	21	.274	.358	.359
Duffy Lewis	OF154	R	24	154	581	85	165	36	9	6	109	52	—	9	.284	.346	.408
Tris Speaker	OF153	L	24	153	580	136	222	53	12	10	90	82	—	52	.383	.464	.567
Harry Hooper	OF147	L	24	147	590	98	143	20	12	2	53	66	—	29	.242	.326	.327
Clyde Engle	1B25,2B15,3B11*	R	28	57	171	32	40	5	3	0	18	28	—	12	.234	.348	.298
Hugh Bradley	1B40	R	27	40	137	16	26	11	1	1	19	15	—	3	.190	.275	.307
Hick Cady	C43,1B4	R	26	47	135	19	35	13	2	0	9	10	—	0	.259	.324	.385
Les Nunamaker	C35	R	23	35	103	15	26	5	2	0	6	6	—	2	.252	.313	.340
Olaf Henriksen	OF11	L	24	37	56	20	18	3	1	0	8	14	—	0	.321	.457	.411
Neal Ball†	2B17	R	31	18	45	10	9	2	0	0	6	3	—	5	.200	.250	.244
Marty Krug	SS9,2B4	R	23	16	39	6	12	2	1	0	7	5	—	2	.308	.386	.410
Pinch Thomas	C12	L	24	12	30	0	6	0	0	0	5	2	—	1	.200	.250	.200

C. Engle, 2 G at SS, 1 G at OF

Pitcher	T	Age	G	GS	CG	ShO	IP	H	HR	BB	SO	W-L	Sv	ERA
Joe Wood	R	22	43	38	35	10	344.0	267	2	82	258	34-5	1	1.91
Buck O'Brien	R	30	37	34	25	2	275.2	237	3	90	115	20-13	0	2.58
Hugh Bedient	R	22	41	28	19	0	231.0	206	6	55	122	20-9	2	2.92
Ray Collins	L	25	27	24	17	4	199.1	192	4	42	82	13-8	0	2.53
Sea Lion Hall	R	26	34	20	9	2	191.0	178	3	70	83	15-8	2	3.02
Eddie Cicotte†	R	28	9	6	2	0	46.0	58	0	15	20	1-3	0	5.67
Casey Hageman	R	25	2	1	0	0	1.1	5	0	3	1	0-0	0	27.00
Larry Pape	R	28	13	2	1	0	48.2	74	0	16	17	1-1	1	4.99
Ben Van Dyke	L	23	3	1	0	0	14.1	13	0	7	8	0-0	0	3.14
Jack Bushelman	R	26	3	0	0	0	7.2	9	0	5	5	1-0	0	4.70
Doug Smith	L	20	1	0	0	0	3.0	4	0	0	1	0-0	0	3.00

1912 Washington Senators 2nd AL 91-61 .599 14.0 GB

Clark Griffith

Player	Gm by Position	B	Age	G	AB	R	H	2B	3B	HR	RBI	BB	SO	SB	Avg	OBP	Slg
John Henry	C63	R	22	63	191	23	37	4	1	0	9	31	—	10	.194	.309	.225
Chick Gandil	1B117	R	25	117	443	59	135	20	15	2	81	27	—	21	.305	.350	.431
Ray Morgan	2B76,SS4,3B1	R	23	80	273	40	65	10	7	1	30	29	—	11	.238	.318	.337
Eddie Foster	3B154	R	25	154	618	98	176	34	9	2	70	53	—	27	.285	.345	.379
George McBride	SS152	R	31	152	521	56	118	13	7	1	52	38	—	17	.226	.288	.284
Clyde Milan	OF154	L	25	154	601	105	184	19	11	1	79	63	—	88	.306	.377	.379
Danny Moeller	OF132	S	27	132	519	90	143	26	10	6	46	52	—	30	.276	.346	.399
Howard Shanks	OF113	R	21	116	399	52	92	14	7	1	48	40	—	21	.231	.305	.308
Eddie Ainsmith	C59	R	20	60	186	22	42	7	2	0	22	14	—	4	.226	.280	.285
Germany Schaefer	OF19,1B15,2B15*	R	35	60	166	21	41	7	3	0	19	23	—	11	.247	.342	.325
Rip Williams	C48	R	30	61	157	14	50	11	4	0	22	7	—	2	.318	.352	.439
Frank LaPorte†	2B37	R	32	39	136	13	42	9	1	0	17	12	—	3	.309	.365	.390
Tilly Walker	OF34,2B1	R	24	36	110	22	30	2	1	0	9	8	—	11	.273	.333	.309
Carl Cashion	P26,OF9	L	21	43	103	7	22	5	1	2	12	8	—	2	.214	.270	.340
John Knight	2B27,1B5	R	26	32	93	10	15	2	1	0	9	16	—	4	.161	.284	.204
John Flynn	1B20	R	28	20	71	9	12	4	1	0	5	7	—	2	.169	.253	.254
Duke Kenworthy	OF10	S	25	12	38	6	9	1	0	0	2	2	—	3	.237	.293	.263
Bill Cunningham	2B7	R	24	7	27	5	5	1	0	1	8	3	—	2	.185	.267	.333
Roy Moran	OF5	R	27	5	13	1	2	0	0	0	0	8	—	3	.154	.476	.154
Roxey Roach	SS2	R	29	2	2	1	1	0	0	1	1	0	—	0	.500	.500	2.000
Joe Agler		L	25	2	1	0	0	0	0	0	0	0	—	0	.000	.000	.000
Tom Long		R	22	1	1	0	0	0	0	0	0	0	—	0	.000	.000	.000
Jack Ryan	3B1	R	43	1	1	0	0	0	0	0	0	0	—	0	.000	.000	.000
Dave Howard		R	23	1	0	1	0	0	0	0	0	0	—	0	—	—	—

G. Schaefer, 1 G at P

Pitcher	T	Age	G	GS	CG	ShO	IP	H	HR	BB	SO	W-L	Sv	ERA
Bob Groom	R	27	43	40	29	2	316.0	287	3	94	179	24-13	1	2.62
Walter Johnson	R	24	50	37	34	7	369.0	259	2	76	303	33-12	2	1.39
Long Tom Hughes	R	33	31	26	11	1	196.0	201	8	78	108	13-10	1	2.94
Carl Cashion	R	21	26	17	13	1	170.1	150	4	103	84	10-6	1	3.17
Joe Engel	L	19	17	10	2	0	75.0	70	2	50	29	2-5	1	3.96
Hippo Vaughn†	L	24	12	8	4	0	81.0	75	0	43	49	4-3	0	2.89
Dixie Walker	R	25	9	8	5	0	60.0	72	2	18	29	3-6	0	5.25
Lefty Schegg	L	22	2	1	0	0	5.1	7	0	4	3	0-0	0	3.38
Barney Pelty†	R	31	11	4	1	0	43.2	40	0	10	15	1-4	0	3.30
Paul Musser	R	23	7	2	0	0	20.2	16	0	16	10	0-0	1	2.61
Jerry Akers	R	24	5	1	0	0	20.1	24	1	15	11	1-1	0	4.87
Charlie Becker	L	23	4	0	0	0	9.0	8	0	6	5	0-0	0	3.00
Joe Boehling	L	21	3	0	0	0	5.0	4	0	6	2	0-0	0	7.20
Bert Gallia	R	20	2	0	0	0	2.0	0	0	3	0	0-0	0	0.00
Herb Herring	R	20	1	0	0	0	1.0	1	0	1	0	0-0	0	0.00
Nick Altrock	L	35	1	0	0	0	1.0	1	0	2	0	0-1	0	18.00
Steve White†	R	27	1	0	0	0	0.2	2	1	0	1	0-0	0	0.00
Germany Schaefer	R	35	1	0	0	0	0.2	1	0	0	0	0-0	0	0.00

1912 Philadelphia Athletics 3rd AL 90-62 .592 15.0 GB

Connie Mack

Player	Gm by Position	B	Age	G	AB	R	H	2B	3B	HR	RBI	BB	SO	SB	Avg	OBP	Slg
Jack Lapp	C83	L	27	90	281	26	82	15	6	1	35	19	—	3	.292	.337	.399
Stuffy McInnis	1B153	R	21	153	568	83	186	25	13	3	101	49	—	27	.327	.384	.433
Eddie Collins	2B153	L	25	153	543	137	189	25	11	0	64	101	—	63	.348	.450	.435
Home Run Baker	3B149	L	26	149	577	116	200	40	21	10	130	50	—	40	.347	.404	.541
Jack Barry	SS139	R	25	139	483	76	126	19	9	0	55	47	—	22	.261	.335	.337
Amos Strunk	OF118	L	23	120	412	58	119	13	12	3	63	47	—	29	.289	.366	.400
Rube Oldring	OF97	R	28	98	395	61	119	14	5	1	24	10	—	17	.301	.324	.370
Bris Lord	OF96	R	28	96	378	63	90	12	9	0	25	34	—	15	.238	.309	.317
Harl Maggert	OF61	L	29	72	242	39	62	8	6	1	13	36	—	10	.256	.357	.351
Eddie Murphy	OF33	L	20	33	142	24	45	4	1	0	6	11	—	7	.317	.370	.359
Ira Thomas	C46	R	31	46	139	14	30	4	2	1	13	8	—	3	.216	.268	.295
Ben Egan	C46	R	28	48	138	9	24	3	4	0	13	6	—	3	.174	.208	.254
Danny Murphy	OF36	R	35	36	130	27	42	6	2	2	20	16	—	8	.323	.401	.446
Jimmy Walsh	OF30	L	26	31	107	11	27	8	2	0	15	12	—	7	.252	.328	.364
Claud Derrick	SS18	R	26	21	58	7	14	0	1	0	7	5	—	1	.241	.313	.276
Joe Mathes	3B4	S	20	4	14	0	2	0	0	0	0	0	—	0	.143	.200	.143
Howard Fahey	3B2,2B1,SS1	R	20	5	8	0	0	0	0	0	0	0	—	0	.000	.000	.000
Chester Emerson		L	22	1	1	0	0	0	0	0	0	0	—	0	.000	.000	.000

Pitcher	T	Age	G	GS	CG	ShO	IP	H	HR	BB	SO	W-L	Sv	ERA
Jack Coombs	R	29	40	32	23	1	262.1	227	5	94	120	21-10	3	3.29
Eddie Plank	L	36	37	30	24	5	259.2	234	1	83	110	26-6	2	2.22
Boardwalk Brown	R	25	34	24	16	3	199.0	204	2	87	64	13-11	1	3.66
Chief Bender	R	28	27	19	12	1	171.0	169	1	33	90	13-8	2	2.74
Byron Houck	R	20	30	17	12	0	180.2	148	1	74	75	8-8	1	2.94
Cy Morgan	R	33	16	14	5	0	93.2	75	0	51	47	3-8	0	3.75
Roy Crabb†	R	21	7	7	3	0	43.1	48	0	17	12	2-4	0	3.74
Harry Krause†	L	24	4	2	0	0	5.1	10	0	2	3	0-2	0	13.50
Joe Bush	R	19	1	1	0	0	8.0	14	0	4	3	0-0	0	7.88
Roger Salmon	L	21	2	1	0	0	5.0	7	0	4	5	1-0	0	9.00
Herb Pennock	L	18	17	2	1	0	50.0	48	1	30	38	1-2	2	4.50
Stan Coveleski	R	22	5	2	2	1	21.0	18	0	4	9	2-1	0	3.43
Lefty Russell	L	21	5	2	2	0	17.1	18	1	14	9	0-2	0	7.27
Dave Danforth	L	22	3	0	0	0	20.1	26	0	12	8	0-0	0	3.98
Hardin Barry	R	21	3	0	0	0	13.0	18	0	4	3	0-0	0	7.62
Doc Martin	R	24	2	0	0	0	4.1	5	0	5	4	0-0	0	10.38
Slim Harrell	R	21	1	0	0	0	3.0	4	0	0	1	0-0	0	0.00

1912 Chicago White Sox 4th AL 78-76 .506 28.0 GB

Nixey Callahan

Player	Gm by Position	B	Age	G	AB	R	H	2B	3B	HR	RBI	BB	SO	SB	Avg	OBP	Slg
Walt Kuhn	C75	R	28	75	178	16	36	7	0	0	10	20	—	5	.202	.286	.242
Rollie Zeider	1B69,3B59,SS1	R	28	129	420	57	103	12	10	1	42	50	—	47	.245	.330	.329
Morrie Rath	2B157	L	25	157	591	104	161	10	2	1	19	95	—	30	.272	.380	.301
Harry Lord	3B106,OF45	L	30	151	570	81	152	19	12	5	54	52	—	28	.267	.333	.368
Buck Weaver	SS147	R	21	147	523	55	117	21	8	1	43	9	—	12	.224	.245	.300
Ping Bodie	OF130	R	24	137	472	58	139	24	7	5	72	43	—	12	.294	.358	.407
Shano Collins	OF107,1B46	R	26	153	579	75	168	34	10	2	81	29	—	26	.290	.330	.394
Nixey Callahan	OF107	R	38	111	408	45	111	9	7	1	52	12	—	19	.272	.298	.336
Wally Mattick	OF78	R	25	88	285	45	74	7	9	1	35	27	—	15	.260	.334	.358
Bruno Block	C46	R	27	46	136	8	35	5	6	0	26	7	—	1	.257	.294	.382
Babe Borton	1B30	L	23	31	105	15	39	3	1	0	17	8	—	1	.371	.416	.419
Billy Sullivan	C39	R	37	39	91	9	19	2	1	0	15	9	—	0	.209	.287	.253
Matty McIntyre	OF45	L	32	45	84	10	14	0	0	0	10	14	—	3	.167	.300	.167
Jack Fournier	1B17	L	22	35	73	5	14	5	2	0	2	4	—	1	.192	.263	.315
Ray Schalk	C23	R	19	23	63	7	18	2	0	0	8	3	—	2	.286	.357	.317
Ted Easterly†	C10,OF1	L	27	30	55	5	20	2	0	0	14	2	—	1	.364	.386	.400
Ernie Johnson	SS16	L	24	18	42	7	11	0	1	0	5	1	—	0	.262	.279	.310
Cuke Barrows	OF3	R	28	8	13	0	3	0	0	0	2	2	—	1	.231	.333	.231
Wally Mayer	C6	R	21	7	9	1	0	0	0	0	0	1	—	0	.000	.100	.000
Mutz Ens	1B3	L	27	3	6	0	0	0	0	0	0	0	—	0	.000	.000	.000
Dennis Berran	OF2	L	24	2	4	1	1	0	0	0	0	0	—	0	.250	.250	.250
Lee Tannehill	3B3	R	31	4	3	0	0	0	0	0	0	1	—	0	.000	.400	.000
Polly McLarry		L	21	2	2	0	0	0	0	0	0	0	—	0	.000	.000	.000
Kid Gleason	2B1	S	45	1	2	0	1	0	0	0	0	0	—	0	.500	.500	.500
Polly Wolfe		L	23	1	1	0	0	0	0	0	0	0	—	0	.000	.000	.000
Del Paddock†		L	25	1	1	0	0	0	0	0	0	0	—	0	.000	.000	.000
Lena Blackburne	SS2,3B1	R	25	3	1	0	0	0	0	0	0	1	—	1	.000	.500	.000

Pitcher	T	Age	G	GS	CG	ShO	IP	H	HR	BB	SO	W-L	Sv	ERA
Ed Walsh	R	31	62	41	32	6	393.0	332	6	94	254	27-17	10	2.15
Joe Benz	R	26	41	31	11	3	238.2	230	5	70	96	13-17	0	2.90
Frank Lange	R	28	31	21	11	2	165.1	165	4	68	96	10-10	3	3.27
Doc White	L	33	32	19	9	1	172.0	172	1	47	57	8-10	0	3.24
Eddie Cicotte†	R	28	20	18	13	1	152.0	159	3	37	70	9-7	0	2.84
Jim Scott	R	24	6	4	2	1	37.2	36	0	15	23	2-2	0	2.15
Wiley Taylor	R	24	3	3	0	0	20.0	21	0	14	4	0-1	0	4.95
Roy Crabb†	R	21	2	1	0	0	8.2	6	0	4	3	0-1	0	1.04
Harry Smith	R	22	1	1	0	0	5.0	6	0	0	1	1-0	0	1.80
Rube Peters	R	27	28	11	4	0	108.2	134	2	33	39	5-6	0	4.14
George Mogridge	L	23	17	7	2	0	64.2	69	2	15	31	3-4	3	4.04
Walt Johnson	R	19	4	0	0	0	11.2	11	0	10	8	0-0	0	3.86
Phil Douglas	R	22	3	1	0	0	12.1	21	0	6	7	0-1	0	7.30
Rip Jordan	R	22	3	0	0	0	10.1	13	2	0	0	0-0	0	6.10
Ralph Bell	L	21	3	0	0	0	6.0	8	1	8	5	0-0	0	9.00
Flame Delhi	R	19	1	0	0	0	3.0	7	0	3	2	0-0	0	9.00
Fred Lamline	R	24	1	0	0	0	2.0	7	0	2	1	0-0	0	31.50

1912 Cleveland Bronchos 5th AL 75-78 .490 30.5 GB

Harry Davis (54-71)/Joe Birmingham (21-7)

Player	Gm by Position	B	Age	G	AB	R	H	2B	3B	HR	RBI	BB	SO	SB	Avg	OBP	Slg
Steve O'Neill	C68	R	20	68	215	17	49	4	0	0	14	12	—	2	.228	.272	.247
Art Griggs	1B71	R	28	89	273	29	83	16	7	0	39	33	—	10	.304	.381	.414
Nap Lajoie	2B97,1B20	R	37	117	448	66	165	34	4	0	90	28	—	18	.368	.414	.462
Terry Turner	3B103	R	31	103	370	54	114	14	4	0	33	31	—	19	.308	.363	.368
Roger Peckinpaugh	SS68	R	21	69	236	18	50	4	1	1	22	16	—	11	.212	.262	.250
Joe Jackson	OF150	L	22	152	572	121	226	44	26	3	90	54	—	35	.395	.458	.579
Joe Birmingham	OF96,1B9	R	27	107	369	49	94	19	3	1	45	26	—	15	.255	.311	.331
Buddy Ryan	OF90	L	26	93	328	53	89	12	9	1	31	30	—	12	.271	.343	.372
Ivy Olson	SS56,3B35,2B21*	R	26	123	467	68	118	13	1	0	33	21	—	16	.253	.291	.285
Jack Graney	OF75	L	26	78	264	44	64	13	2	0	20	50	—	9	.242	.367	.307
Ted Easterly†	C51	L	27	63	186	17	55	4	0	2	21	7	—	3	.296	.328	.349
Doc Johnston	1B41	L	24	43	164	22	46	7	4	1	11	11	—	8	.280	.326	.390
Neal Ball†	2B37	R	31	40	132	12	30	4	1	0	14	9	—	7	.227	.277	.273
Ray Chapman	SS31	R	21	31	109	29	34	6	3	0	19	10	—	10	.312	.375	.422
Hank Butcher	OF20	R	25	24	82	9	16	4	1	1	10	6	—	1	.195	.250	.305
Tim Hendryx	OF22	R	21	23	70	9	17	2	4	1	14	8	—	3	.243	.329	.429
Fred Carisch	C23	R	30	26	70	4	19	3	1	0	5	1	—	3	.271	.282	.343
Bill Hunter	OF16	L	24	21	55	6	9	2	0	0	2	10	—	0	.164	.303	.200
Eddie Hohnhorst	1B14	L	27	15	54	5	11	1	0	0	2	2	—	5	.204	.232	.222
Bert Adams	C20	S	21	20	54	5	11	2	1	0	6	4	—	0	.204	.259	.278
Paddy Livingston	C14	R	32	19	47	5	11	2	1	0	3	1	—	0	.234	.280	.319
Howard Baker	3B10	R	24	11	30	1	5	0	0	0	2	5	—	0	.167	.286	.167
Ken Nash	SS8	S	23	11	23	2	4	0	0	0	0	3	—	0	.174	.269	.174
Arthur Hauger	OF5	L	18	15	18	0	1	0	0	0	0	1	—	0	.056	.105	.056
Herman Bronkie	3B6	R	27	6	16	1	0	0	0	0	0	1	—	0	.000	.059	.000
Jack Kibble	3B4,2B1	S	20	5	8	1	0	0	0	0	0	0	—	0	.000	.111	.000
Harry Davis	1B2	R	38	2	5	0	0	0	0	0	0	0	—	0	.000	.000	.000
Lou Nagelsen	C2	R	25	2	3	0	0	0	0	0	0	0	—	0	.000	.000	.000
Hack Eibel	OF1	L	18	1	3	0	0	0	0	0	0	0	—	0	.000	.000	.000
Moxie Meixell		L	24	2	2	0	1	0	0	0	0	0	—	0	.500	.500	.500
Harvey Grubb	OF1	R	21	1	0	0	0	0	0	0	0	0	—	0	—	1.000	—

I. Olson, 3 G at OF

Pitcher	T	Age	G	GS	CG	ShO	IP	H	HR	BB	SO	W-L	Sv	ERA
Vean Gregg	L	27	37	34	26	1	271.1	242	4	90	184	20-13	2	2.59
George Kahler	R	22	41	32	17	3	246.1	263	1	121	104	12-19	1	3.69
Fred Blanding	R	24	39	31	23	1	262.0	259	4	79	75	18-14	1	2.95
Bill Steen	R	24	26	16	6	1	143.1	163	3	45	61	9-8	0	3.77
Willie Mitchell	L	22	29	15	8	0	163.2	149	0	56	94	5-8	1	2.80
Gene Krapp	R	25	9	7	4	0	58.2	57	0	42	22	2-5	0	4.60
Harry Krause†	L	24	2	2	0	0	4.2	11	0	2	1	0-1	0	11.57
Bert Brenner	R	24	2	1	1	0	13.0	14	0	4	3	1-0	0	2.77
Jim Baskette	R	24	29	11	7	1	116.0	109	2	46	51	8-4	1	3.18
Lefty George	L	25	11	5	2	0	44.1	69	1	18	18	0-5	0	4.87
Bill James	R	25	3	1	0	0	13.2	15	0	9	5	0-0	1	4.61
Lefty James	L	22	3	0	0	0	6.0	8	0	4	2	0-1	0	7.50
Ernie Wolf	R	23	1	0	0	0	5.2	8	0	4	1	0-0	0	6.35
Roy Walker	R	19	1	0	0	0	2.0	0	0	2	1	0-0	0	0.00
Jim Neher	R	23	1	0	0	0	1.0	0	0	0	0	0-0	0	0.00
Mysterious Walker	R	28	1	0	0	0	1.0	0	0	1	0	0-0	0	0.00

580 Seasons: Team Rosters

1912 Detroit Tigers 6th AL 69-84 .451 36.5 GB

Hughie Jennings

Player	Gm by Position	B	Age	G	AB	R	H	2B	3B	HR	RBI	BB	SO	SB	Avg	OBP	Slg
Oscar Stanage	C119	R	29	119	394	35	103	9	4	0	41	34	—	3	.261	.326	.305
George Moriarty	1B71,3B33	R	28	105	375	38	93	23	1	0	54	26	—	27	.248	.316	.315
Baldy Louden	2B86,3B26,SS5	R	26	121	403	57	97	12	4	1	36	58	—	28	.241	.352	.298
Charlie Deal	3B41	R	20	42	142	13	32	4	2	0	11	9	—	4	.225	.272	.282
Donie Bush	SS144	S	24	144	511	107	118	14	8	2	38	117	—	35	.231	.377	.301
Sam Crawford	OF149	L	32	149	581	81	189	30	21	4	109	42	—	41	.325	.373	.470
Ty Cobb	OF140	L	25	140	553	119	227	30	23	7	83	43	—	61	.410	.458	.586
Davy Jones	OF81	L	32	97	316	54	93	5	2	0	24	38	—	16	.294	.370	.323
Ossie Vitt	OF27,3B24,2B15	R	22	73	273	39	67	4	4	0	19	18	—	17	.245	.297	.289
Jim Delahanty	2B44,OF33	R	33	78	266	34	76	14	1	0	41	42	—	9	.286	.397	.346
Del Gainer	1B50,OF1	R	25	51	179	28	43	5	6	0	20	18	—	14	.240	.320	.335
Red Corriden	3B25,2B7,SS3	R	24	38	138	22	28	6	0	0	5	15	—	4	.203	.286	.246
Eddie Onslow	1B35	L	19	35	128	11	29	1	2	1	13	3	—	3	.227	.250	.289
Jean Dubuc	P37,OF2	R	23	40	108	16	29	6	2	1	9	3	—	0	.269	.295	.389
Bobby Veach	OF22	L	24	23	79	8	27	5	1	0	15	5	—	2	.342	.388	.430
Jack Onslow	C31	R	23	31	69	7	11	1	0	0	4	10	—	1	.159	.284	.174
Brad Kocher	C23	R	24	29	63	5	13	3	1	0	9	2	—	0	.206	.231	.286
Paddy Baumann	3B6,2B5,OF1	R	26	13	42	3	11	1	0	0	7	6	—	4	.262	.354	.286
Hank Perry	OF7	L	25	13	36	3	6	1	0	0	0	3	—	0	.167	.231	.194
Red McDermott	OF5	R	22	5	15	2	4	1	0	0	0	0	—	1	.267	.313	.333
Wild Bill Donovan	P3,1B2,OF2	R	35	6	13	3	1	0	0	0	0	1	—	0	.077	.143	.077
Al Bashang	OF5	S	23	5	12	3	1	0	0	0	0	3	—	0	.083	.267	.083
Charley O'Leary	2B3	R	29	3	10	1	2	0	0	0	1	0	—	0	.200	.200	.200
Ollie O'Mara	SS1	R	21	1	4	0	0	0	0	0	0	0	—	0	.000	.000	.000
Jim McGarr	2B1	R	23	1	4	0	0	0	0	0	0	0	—	0	.000	.000	.000
Bill Leinhauser	OF1	R	18	1	4	0	0	0	0	0	0	0	—	0	.000	.000	.000
Joe Sugden	1B1	S	41	1	4	1	1	0	0	0	0	0	—	0	.250	.250	.250
Dan McGarvey	OF1	R	24	1	3	0	0	0	0	0	0	1	—	0	.000	.400	.000
Ed Irvin	3B1	R	30	1	3	0	2	0	2	0	0	0	—	0	.667	.667	2.000
Hap Ward	OF1	R	26	1	2	0	0	0	0	0	0	0	—	0	.000	.000	.000
Pat Meaney	SS1	R	42	1	2	0	0	0	0	0	0	1	—	0	.000	.500	.000
Deacon McGuire	C1	R	48	1	2	1	1	0	0	0	0	0	—	0	.500	.500	.500
Billy Maharg	3B1	R	31	1	1	0	0	0	0	0	0	0	—	0	.000	.000	.000
Hughie Jennings		R	43	1	1	0	0	0	0	0	0	0	—	0	.000	.000	.000
Jack Smith	3B1	R	18	1	0	0	0	0	0	0	0	0	—	0	—	—	—

Pitcher	T	Age	G	GS	CG	ShO	IP	H	HR	BB	SO	W-L	Sv	ERA
Ed Willett	R	28	37	31	28	1	284.1	281	3	84	89	17-15	0	3.29
George Mullin	R	31	30	29	22	2	226.0	214	3	92	88	12-17	0	3.54
Jean Dubuc	R	23	37	26	23	2	250.0	217	2	109	97	17-10	3	2.77
Ralph Works†	R	24	27	17	9	1	157.0	185	1	66	64	5-10	1	4.24
Joe Lake†	R	31	26	14	11	0	162.2	190	3	39	86	9-11	1	3.10
Tex Covington	R	25	14	9	2	1	63.1	58	0	30	19	3-4	0	4.12
Bill Burns	L	32	6	5	2	0	38.2	52	0	9	6	1-4	0	5.35
Charlie Wheatley	R	19	5	5	2	0	35.0	45	1	17	14	1-4	0	6.17
George Boehler	R	20	4	4	2	0	31.0	49	0	14	13	0-2	0	6.68
Willie Jensen	R	23	4	3	1	0	25.0	30	1	14	4	1-2	0	5.40
Ed Summers	R	27	3	3	1	0	16.2	16	1	3	5	1-1	0	4.86
Hooks Dauss	R	22	2	2	2	0	17.0	11	0	9	7	1-1	0	3.18
Al Travers	R	20	1	1	1	0	8.0	26	0	7	1	0-1	0	15.75
Bun Troy	R	23	1	1	0	0	6.2	9	0	3	1	0-1	0	5.40
Pat McGehee	R	23	1	1	0	0	0.0	1	0	1	0	0-0	0	—
Harry Moran	L	23	5	2	1	0	14.2	19	1	12	3	0-1	0	4.91
Wild Bill Donovan	R	35	3	1	0	0	10.0	5	0	2	6	1-0	0	0.90
Hub Pernoll	L	24	3	0	0	0	9.0	9	0	4	3	0-0	0	6.00
Alex Remneas	R	26	1	0	0	0	1.2	5	0	0	0	0-0	0	27.00
Ed Lafitte	R	26	1	0	0	0	1.2	2	0	2	0	0-0	0	16.20

1912 St. Louis Browns 7th AL 53-101 .344 53.0 GB

Bobby Wallace (12-27)/George Stovall (41-74)

Player	Gm by Position	B	Age	G	AB	R	H	2B	3B	HR	RBI	BB	SO	SB	Avg	OBP	Slg
Jim Stephens	C66	R	28	74	205	13	51	7	5	0	22	7	—	3	.249	.274	.332
George Stovall	1B94	R	33	115	398	35	101	17	5	0	45	14	—	11	.254	.286	.322
Del Pratt	2B121,SS21,OF8*	R	24	151	570	76	172	26	15	5	69	36	—	24	.302	.348	.426
Jimmy Austin	3B149	S	32	149	536	57	135	14	8	2	44	38	—	28	.252	.306	.319
Bobby Wallace	SS87,3B10,2B2	R	38	100	323	39	78	14	5	0	31	43	—	3	.241	.332	.316
Burt Shotton	OF154	L	27	154	580	87	168	15	8	2	40	86	—	35	.290	.390	.353
Willie Hogan	OF99	R	27	107	360	32	77	10	2	1	36	34	—	17	.214	.284	.261
Pete Compton	OF72	L	22	103	268	26	75	6	4	2	30	22	—	11	.280	.339	.354
Frank LaPorte†	2B39,OF32	R	32	80	266	32	83	11	4	1	38	20	—	7	.312	.367	.395
Gus Williams	OF62	L	24	64	216	32	63	13	7	2	32	27	—	18	.292	.370	.444
Joe Kutina	1B51,OF1	R	27	67	205	18	42	9	3	1	18	13	—	0	.205	.262	.293
Paul Krichell	C57	R	29	57	161	19	35	6	0	0	8	19	—	2	.217	.304	.255
Heinie Jantzen	OF31	R	22	31	119	10	22	0	1	1	8	4	—	3	.185	.218	.227
Walt Alexander	C37	R	21	37	97	5	17	4	0	0	5	8	—	1	.175	.245	.216
Ed Hallinan	SS26	R	23	29	86	11	19	2	0	0	1	5	—	3	.221	.272	.244
John Daley	SS17	R	25	17	52	7	9	0	0	1	3	9	—	4	.173	.317	.231
Ed Miller	1B8,SS6	R	23	13	46	4	9	1	0	0	5	2	—	1	.196	.245	.217
Bunny Brief	OF9,1B4	R	19	15	42	9	13	3	0	0	5	6	—	2	.310	.408	.381
Frank Crossin	C8	R	21	8	22	2	5	0	0	0	2	1	—	1	.227	.261	.227
Bill Brown	OF7	L	18	9	20	0	4	0	0	0	1	0	—	0	.200	.200	.200
Charlie Snell	C8	R	18	8	19	0	4	1	0	0	0	3	—	0	.211	.348	.263
George Aiton	OF6	S	21	8	17	1	4	0	0	0	1	4	—	0	.235	.381	.235
Henry Smoyer	SS4,3B2	R	22	6	14	1	3	0	0	0	0	2	—	0	.214	.313	.214
Doc Shanley	SS4	R	23	5	8	1	0	0	0	0	1	2	—	0	.000	.200	.000
Phil Ketter	C2	—	28	2	6	1	2	0	0	0	0	0	—	0	.333	.333	.333
Tom Tennant		L	29	2	2	1	0	0	0	0	0	0	—	0	.000	.000	.000
Lou Criger	C1	R	40	1	2	1	0	0	0	0	0	0	—	0	.000	.000	.000
Charlie Miller	SS1	—	20	1	2	0	0	0	0	0	0	0	—	0	.000	.000	.000
Fred Walden	C1	R	22	1	0	0	0	0	0	0	0	0	—	0	—	—	—

D. Pratt, 1 G at 3B

Pitcher	T	Age	G	GS	CG	ShO	IP	H	HR	BB	SO	W-L	Sv	ERA
Jack Powell	R	37	32	27	19	0	235.1	248	5	52	67	9-17	0	3.10
Earl Hamilton	L	20	41	26	17	1	249.2	228	2	86	139	11-14	2	3.21
G. Baumgardner	R	20	30	26	19	2	218.1	222	1	79	102	11-13	0	3.38
Mack Allison	R	25	31	20	11	1	169.0	171	4	49	43	6-17	1	3.62
Roy Mitchell	R	27	13	8	5	0	62.0	81	2	17	22	3-4	0	4.65
Joe Lake†	R	31	11	6	4	0	57.0	70	0	16	28	1-7	0	4.42
Carl Weilman	L	22	9	6	5	2	48.1	42	0	3	24	2-4	1	2.79
Barney Pelty†	R	31	6	6	2	0	38.2	43	0	15	10	1-5	0	5.59
John Frill†	L	33	3	3	0	0	4.1	16	1	1	2	0-1	0	20.77
Bill Bailey	L	23	3	2	0	0	10.2	15	0	10	2	0-1	0	9.28
Elmer Brown	R	29	23	11	2	1	120.1	122	2	42	45	5-8	0	2.99
Curly Brown	L	23	16	5	2	1	64.2	69	0	35	28	1-3	0	4.87
Willie Adams	R	21	13	5	0	0	46.1	50	0	19	16	2-3	0	3.88
Red Nelson†	R	26	8	3	0	0	18.0	21	0	13	9	0-2	1	7.00
Buddy Napier	R	22	7	2	0	0	25.1	33	0	5	10	1-2	0	4.97
Hack Spencer	R	27	1	0	0	0	1.2	2	0	0	0	0-0	0	0.00

1912 New York Highlanders 8th AL 50-102 .329 55.0 GB

Harry Wolverton

Player	Gm by Position	B	Age	G	AB	R	H	2B	3B	HR	RBI	BB	SO	SB	Avg	OBP	Slg
Jeff Sweeney	C108	R	23	110	351	37	94	12	1	0	30	27	—	6	.268	.325	.308
Hal Chase	1B122,2B7	R	29	131	522	61	143	21	9	4	58	17	—	33	.274	.299	.372
Hack Simmons	2B88,1B13,SS4	R	27	110	401	45	96	17	2	0	41	33	—	19	.239	.308	.292
Roy Hartzell	3B56,OF55,SS10*	L	30	123	416	50	113	10	11	1	38	64	—	20	.272	.370	.356
Jack Martin	SS69	R	25	69	231	30	52	6	1	0	17	37	—	14	.225	.347	.260
Bert Daniels	OF133	R	29	133	496	72	136	25	11	2	41	51	—	37	.274	.363	.381
Guy Zinn	OF106	L	25	106	401	56	105	15	10	6	55	50	—	17	.262	.345	.394
Birdie Cree	OF50	R	29	50	190	25	63	11	6	0	22	20	—	12	.332	.409	.453
Dutch Sterrett	OF38,1B17,C10*	R	22	66	230	30	61	4	7	1	32	11	—	8	.265	.310	.357
Earle Gardner	2B43	R	28	43	160	14	45	3	1	0	26	5	—	11	.281	.303	.313
Del Paddock†	3B41,2B2,OF1	L	25	46	156	26	45	5	3	1	14	23	—	9	.288	.393	.378
Jack Lelivelt	OF36	L	26	36	149	12	54	6	7	2	23	4	—	7	.362	.383	.537
Tommy McMillan	SS41	R	24	41	149	24	34	2	0	0	12	15	—	18	.228	.303	.242
Bill Stumpf	SS27,2B8,3B4*	R	20	40	129	8	31	0	0	0	10	6	—	5	.240	.279	.240
Russ Ford	P36,2B2,OF2	R	29	40	112	15	32	8	0	1	8	6	—	2	.286	.322	.384
George McConnell	P23,1B2	R	34	42	91	11	27	4	2	0	8	4	—	0	.297	.333	.385
Gabby Street	C28	R	29	28	88	4	16	1	1	0	6	7	—	1	.182	.258	.216
Ezra Midkiff	3B21	L	29	21	86	9	21	1	0	0	9	7	—	4	.244	.301	.256
Pat Maloney	OF20	R	24	22	79	9	17	1	0	0	4	6	—	3	.215	.279	.228
Cozy Dolan†	3B13,SS4	R	22	18	60	15	12	1	3	0	11	5	—	5	.200	.273	.317
Harry Wolverton	3B7	L	38	33	50	6	15	1	1	0	4	2	—	1	.300	.340	.360
Bob Williams	C20	R	28	20	44	7	6	1	0	0	3	9	—	0	.136	.283	.159
Curt Coleman	3B10	L	25	12	37	8	9	4	0	0	4	7	—	0	.243	.364	.351
Harry Wolter	OF9	L	27	12	32	8	11	2	1	0	1	10	—	5	.344	.512	.469
John Dowd	SS10	R	21	10	31	1	6	1	0	0	0	6	—	0	.194	.342	.226
Klondike Smith	OF7	L	25	7	27	0	5	1	0	0	0	0	—	1	.185	.185	.222
Bill Otis	OF4	L	22	4	20	1	1	0	0	0	2	3	—	0	.050	.174	.050
Jack Little	OF3	R	21	3	12	2	3	0	0	0	0	1	—	2	.250	.357	.250
Benny Kauff	OF4	L	22	5	11	4	3	0	0	0	2	3	—	1	.273	.429	.273
Gus Fisher	C4	L	26	4	10	1	1	0	0	0	0	0	—	0	.100	.100	.100
George Batten	2B1	R	20	1	3	0	0	0	0	0	0	0	—	0	.000	.000	.000
Johnny Priest		R	26	2	2	1	1	0	0	0	1	0	—	0	.500	.500	.500
Homer Thompson	C1	R	21	1	0	0	0	0	0	0	0	0	—	0	—	—	—

R. Hartzell, 2 G at 2B; D. Sterrett, 1 G at 2B; B. Stumpf, 1 G at 1B

Pitcher	T	Age	G	GS	CG	ShO	IP	H	HR	BB	SO	W-L	Sv	ERA
Russ Ford	R	29	36	35	30	0	291.2	317	10	79	112	13-21	0	3.55
Ray Caldwell	R	24	30	26	13	3	183.1	196	1	67	95	8-16	0	4.47
Jack Warhop	R	27	39	22	16	0	258.0	256	3	59	110	10-19	3	2.86
George McConnell	R	34	23	20	19	0	176.2	172	3	52	91	8-12	0	2.75
Ray Fisher	R	24	17	13	5	0	90.1	107	2	32	47	2-8	0	5.88
Jack Quinn	R	28	18	11	7	0	102.2	139	4	23	47	5-7	0	5.79
Hippo Vaughn†	L	24	15	10	5	1	63.0	66	1	37	46	2-8	0	5.14
Iron Davis	R	22	10	7	5	0	54.0	61	3	28	22	1-4	0	6.50
Ray Keating	R	20	6	5	3	0	35.2	36	0	18	21	0-3	0	5.80
Tommy Thompson	R	22	7	2	1	0	32.2	43	0	13	15	0-2	0	6.06
Red Hoff	L	21	5	1	0	0	15.2	20	0	6	14	0-1	0	6.89
George Shears	L	22	4	0	0	0	15.0	24	1	11	9	0-0	0	5.40
Al Schulz	L	23	3	1	1	0	16.1	11	0	11	8	1-1	0	2.20

»1912 New York Giants 1st NL 103-48 .682 — John McGraw

Player	Gm by Position	B	Age	G	AB	R	H	2B	3B	HR	RBI	BB	SO	SB	Avg	OBP	Slg
Chief Meyers	C122	R	31	126	371	60	133	16	5	6	54	47	20	8	.358	.441	.477
Fred Merkle	1B129	R	23	129	479	82	148	22	6	11	84	42	70	37	.309	.374	.449
Larry Doyle	2B143	L	25	143	558	98	184	33	8	10	90	56	20	36	.330	.393	.471
Buck Herzog	3B140	R	26	140	482	72	127	20	9	2	47	57	34	37	.263	.350	.355
Art Fletcher	SS126,2B2,3B1	R	27	129	419	64	118	17	9	1	57	16	29	16	.282	.330	.372
Red Murray	OF143	R	28	143	549	83	152	26	20	3	92	27	45	38	.277	.320	.413
Beals Becker	OF117	L	25	125	402	66	106	18	8	6	58	54	35	30	.264	.354	.393
Fred Snodgrass	OF116,1B27,2B1	R	24	146	535	91	144	24	9	3	69	70	65	43	.269	.362	.364
Josh Devore	OF96	L	24	106	327	66	90	14	6	2	37	51	43	27	.275	.381	.373
Tillie Shafer	SS31,3B16,2B15	S	23	78	163	48	47	4	1	0	23	30	19	22	.288	.408	.325
Art Wilson	C61	R	26	65	121	17	35	6	0	3	19	13	14	2	.289	.358	.413
Doc Crandall	P37,1B1,2B1	R	24	50	80	9	25	6	2	0	19	6	7	0	.313	.360	.438
George Burns	OF23	R	22	29	51	11	15	4	0	0	3	8	8	7	.294	.400	.373
Heine Groh	2B12,SS7,3B6	R	22	27	48	8	13	2	1	0	3	8	7	6	.271	.375	.354
Moose McCormick	OF6,1B1	L	31	42	39	4	13	4	1	0	8	6	9	1	.333	.422	.487
Grover Hartley	C25	R	23	25	34	3	8	2	1	0	7	0	4	2	.235	.257	.353
Dave Robertson	1B1	L	22	3	2	0	1	0	0	0	1	0	1	1	.500	.500	.500

Pitcher	T	Age	G	GS	CG	ShO	IP	H	HR	BB	SO	W-L	Sv	ERA
Rube Marquard	L	25	43	38	22	1	294.2	286	9	80	175	26-11	1	2.57
Christy Mathewson	R	33	43	34	27	0	310.0	311	5	34	134	23-12	4	2.12
Jeff Tesreau	R	23	36	28	19	3	243.0	177	2	106	119	17-7	1	1.96
Red Ames	R	29	33	22	9	2	179.0	194	3	35	83	11-5	2	2.46
Hooks Wiltse	L	31	28	17	5	0	134.0	140	7	28	58	9-6	3	3.16
Al Demaree	R	27	2	2	1	1	16.0	17	0	2	11	1-0	0	1.69
Lore Bader	R	24	2	1	1	0	10.0	9	0	6	3	2-0	0	0.90
Ted Goulait	R	22	1	1	1	0	7.0	11	0	4	6	0-0	0	6.43
Doc Crandall	R	24	37	10	7	0	162.0	181	7	35	60	13-7	2	3.61
LaRue Kirby	R	22	3	1	1	0	11.0	13	1	6	2	1-0	0	5.73
Louis Drucke	R	23	1	0	0	0	2.0	5	0	1	0	0-0	1	13.50
Ernie Shore	R	21	1	0	0	0	1.0	8	1	1	1	0-0	1	27.00

1912 Pittsburgh Pirates 2nd NL 93-58 .616 10.0 GB Fred Clarke

Player	Gm by Position	B	Age	G	AB	R	H	2B	3B	HR	RBI	BB	SO	SB	Avg	OBP	Slg
George Gibson	C94	R	31	95	300	23	72	14	3	2	35	20	16	0	.240	.290	.327
Dots Miller	1B147	R	25	148	567	74	156	33	12	4	87	37	45	18	.275	.324	.397
Alex McCarthy	2B105,3B4	R	24	111	401	53	111	12	4	1	41	30	26	8	.277	.332	.334
Bobby Byrne	3B130	R	27	130	528	99	152	31	11	3	35	54	40	20	.288	.358	.405
Honus Wagner	SS143	R	38	145	558	91	181	35	20	7	102	59	38	26	.324	.395	.496
Chief Wilson	OF152	L	28	152	583	80	175	19	36	11	95	35	67	16	.300	.342	.513
Max Carey	OF150	S	22	150	587	114	177	23	8	5	66	61	79	45	.302	.372	.394
Mike Donlin	OF62	L	34	77	244	27	77	9	8	2	35	20	16	8	.316	.370	.443
Art Butler	2B43	R	24	43	154	19	42	4	2	1	17	15	13	2	.273	.337	.344
Billy Kelly	C39	R	26	48	132	20	42	3	2	1	11	2	16	8	.318	.328	.394
Mike Simon	C40	R	29	42	113	10	34	2	1	0	11	5	9	1	.301	.331	.336
Ed Mensor	OF32	S	22	39	99	19	26	3	2	0	1	23	12	10	.263	.402	.333
Ham Hyatt	OF15,1B3	L	27	46	97	13	28	3	1	0	22	6	8	2	.289	.330	.340
Tommy Leach†	OF24	R	34	28	97	24	29	4	2	0	19	12	9	6	.299	.376	.381
Bill McKechnie	3B13,SS4,2B3*	S	25	24	73	8	18	0	1	0	4	4	5	2	.247	.286	.274
Jim Viox	3B10,SS8,OF3*	R	21	33	70	8	13	2	3	1	7	3	9	2	.186	.219	.343
Stump Edington	OF14	L	20	15	53	4	16	0	2	0	12	3	1	0	.302	.339	.377
Solly Hofman†	OF15	R	29	17	53	7	15	4	1	0	2	5	6	0	.283	.345	.396
Stan Gray	1B4	R	23	6	20	4	5	0	1	0	2	0	3	0	.250	.250	.350
Ovid Nicholson	OF4	L	23	6	11	2	5	0	0	0	3	1	2	0	.455	.500	.455
Oran Dodd	2B4	R	25	5	9	0	0	0	0	0	1	1	3	0	.000	.100	.000
Wally Rehg	OF2	R	23	8	9	1	0	0	0	0	0	0	1	0	.000	.000	.000
Rivington Bisland		R	22	1	1	0	0	0	0	0	0	0	0	0	.000	.000	.000
Earl Blackburn†	C1	R	19	1	0	0	0	0	0	0	0	0	0	0	—	—	—
Ralph Capron		L	23	1	0	0	0	0	0	0	0	0	0	0	—	—	—
Mickey Keliher		L	22	2	0	1	0	0	0	0	0	0	0	0	—	—	—

B. McKechnie, 2 G at 1B; J. Viox, 1 G at 2B

Pitcher	T	Age	G	GS	CG	ShO	IP	H	HR	BB	SO	W-L	Sv	ERA
Marty O'Toole	R	23	37	36	17	5	275.1	237	4	159	150	15-17	0	2.71
Claude Hendrix	R	23	39	32	25	4	288.2	256	6	105	176	24-9	1	2.59
Howie Camnitz	R	30	41	32	22	2	276.2	256	8	82	121	22-12	2	2.83
Babe Adams	R	30	28	21	11	2	170.1	169	4	35	63	11-8	0	2.91
Wilbur Cooper	L	20	6	4	3	2	38.0	32	1	15	30	3-0	0	1.66
Hank Robinson	L	22	33	16	11	0	175.0	146	3	30	79	12-7	2	2.26
King Cole†	R	26	12	4	2	0	49.0	61	1	18	11	2-2	0	6.43
Ed Warner	L	23	11	3	1	1	45.0	40	0	18	13	1-1	0	3.60
Jack Ferry	R	25	11	3	1	1	39.0	33	1	23	10	2-0	1	3.00
Lefty Leifield†	L	28	6	1	1	1	23.2	29	0	10	8	1-2	0	4.18
Sherry Smith	L	21	3	0	0	0	4.0	6	0	1	3	0-0	1	6.75
Harry Gardner	R	23	1	0	0	0	0.1	3	0	1	0	0-0	0	0.00

1912 Chicago Cubs 3rd NL 91-59 .607 11.5 GB Frank Chance

Player	Gm by Position	B	Age	G	AB	R	H	2B	3B	HR	RBI	BB	SO	SB	Avg	OBP	Slg
Jimmy Archer	C118	R	29	120	385	35	109	20	2	5	58	22	36	7	.283	.330	.384
Vic Saier	1B120	L	21	122	451	74	130	25	14	2	61	34	65	11	.288	.340	.419
Johnny Evers	2B143	L	30	143	478	73	163	23	11	1	63	74	18	16	.341	.431	.441
Heinie Zimmerman	3B121,1B22	R	25	145	557	95	207	41	14	14	99	38	60	23	.372	.418	.571
Joe Tinker	SS142	R	31	142	550	80	155	24	7	0	75	38	21	25	.282	.331	.351
Jimmy Sheckard	OF146	L	33	146	523	85	128	22	10	3	47	122	81	15	.245	.392	.342
Wildfire Schulte	OF139	L	29	139	553	90	146	27	11	12	64	53	70	17	.264	.336	.418
Tommy Leach†	OF73,3B4	R	34	82	265	50	64	10	3	2	32	55	20	14	.242	.378	.325
Ward Miller	OF64	L	27	86	241	45	74	11	4	0	22	26	18	11	.307	.377	.386
Solly Hofman†	OF27,1B9	R	29	36	125	28	34	11	0	0	18	22	13	5	.272	.385	.360
Red Downs†	2B16,SS9,3B5	R	28	43	95	9	25	4	3	1	14	9	17	5	.263	.327	.400
Tom Needham	C32	R	33	33	90	12	16	5	0	0	10	7	13	3	.178	.260	.233
Ed Lennox	3B24	R	26	27	81	13	19	4	1	1	16	12	10	1	.235	.347	.346
Cy Williams	OF22	L	24	28	62	3	15	1	1	0	1	6	14	2	.242	.309	.290
Dick Cotter	C24	R	22	26	54	6	15	0	2	0	10	6	13	1	.278	.361	.352
Wilbur Good	OF10	L	26	39	35	7	5	0	0	0	1	3	7	3	.143	.211	.143
Tom Downey†	SS5,3B3,2B1	R	28	13	22	4	4	0	2	0	4	1	5	0	.182	.217	.364
Charley Moore	SS2,2B1,3B1	R	27	5	9	2	2	0	1	0	2	0	1	0	.222	.222	.444
Frank Chance	1B2	R	34	2	5	2	1	0	0	0	0	3	0	1	.200	.500	.200
Harry Chapman	C1	R	24	1	4	1	1	0	1	0	1	0	0	1	.250	.250	.750
Mike Hechinger	C2	R	22	2	3	0	0	0	0	0	0	2	0	0	.000	.400	.000
George Yantz	C1	R	25	1	1	1	1	0	0	0	0	0	0	0	1.000	1.000	1.000

Pitcher	T	Age	G	GS	CG	ShO	IP	H	HR	BB	SO	W-L	Sv	ERA
Larry Cheney	R	26	42	37	28	4	303.1	262	5	111	140	26-10	0	2.85
Jimmy Lavender	R	28	42	31	15	3	251.2	240	8	89	109	16-13	3	3.04
Lew Richie	R	28	39	27	15	4	238.0	222	5	74	69	16-8	0	2.95
Lefty Leifield†	L	28	13	9	4	1	70.2	68	0	21	23	7-2	0	2.42
Three Finger Brown	R	35	15	8	5	2	88.2	92	2	20	34	5-6	0	2.64
Harry McIntire	R	33	4	3	2	0	23.2	22	0	6	8	1-2	0	3.80
George Pearce	L	24	3	2	0	0	14.2	15	0	12	9	0-0	0	5.52
Grover Lowdermilk	R	27	2	1	1	0	13.0	17	1	14	8	0-1	0	9.69
Ed Reulbach	R	29	39	19	8	0	169.0	161	7	60	75	10-6	4	3.78
Charlie Smith	R	32	21	5	1	0	94.0	92	2	31	47	7-4	1	4.21
Jim Moroney	L	28	10	3	1	0	23.2	25	0	17	5	1-1	1	4.56
Fred Toney	R	23	9	2	0	0	24.0	21	0	11	9	1-2	0	5.25
King Cole†	R	26	8	3	0	0	19.0	36	2	8	9	1-2	0	10.89
Len Madden	L	21	6	2	0	0	12.1	16	1	9	5	0-1	0	2.92
Joe Vernon	R	22	1	0	0	0	4.0	4	0	6	1	0-0	0	11.25
Ensign Cottrell	L	23	1	0	0	0	4.0	8	0	1	1	0-0	0	9.00
Rudy Sommers	L	23	1	0	0	0	3.0	4	0	2	2	0-1	0	3.00
Bill Powell	R	27	1	0	0	0	2.0	2	0	1	0	0-0	0	9.00

1912 Cincinnati Reds 4th NL 75-78 .490 29.0 GB Hank O'Day

Player	Gm by Position	B	Age	G	AB	R	H	2B	3B	HR	RBI	BB	SO	SB	Avg	OBP	Slg
Larry McLean	C98	R	30	102	333	17	81	15	1	1	27	18	15	1	.243	.284	.303
Doc Hoblitzell	1B147	R	23	148	558	73	164	32	12	2	85	48	28	23	.294	.352	.405
Dick Egan	2B149	R	28	149	507	69	125	14	5	0	52	56	26	24	.247	.324	.294
Art Phelan	3B127,2B3	R	24	130	461	56	112	9	11	3	54	46	37	25	.243	.314	.330
Jimmy Esmond	SS74	R	22	82	231	24	45	5	3	1	40	20	31	11	.195	.259	.255
Mike Mitchell	OF144	R	32	147	552	60	156	14	13	4	78	41	43	23	.283	.333	.377
Bob Bescher	OF143	S	28	145	548	120	154	29	11	4	38	83	61	67	.281	.381	.396
Armando Marsans	OF98,1B6	R	24	110	416	59	132	19	7	1	38	20	17	35	.317	.353	.404
Eddie Grant	SS56,3B15	L	29	96	255	37	61	6	1	2	20	18	27	11	.239	.292	.294
Johnny Bates	OF65	L	29	81	239	45	69	12	7	1	29	47	16	10	.289	.406	.410
Tommy Clarke	C63	R	24	72	146	19	41	7	2	0	22	28	14	9	.281	.400	.356
Tex McDonald	SS42	L	21	61	140	16	36	3	4	1	15	13	24	5	.257	.329	.357
Hank Severeid	C20,1B7,OF6	R	21	50	114	10	27	0	3	0	13	8	11	0	.237	.287	.289
Pete Knisely	OF13,2B3,SS1	R	24	21	67	10	22	7	3	0	7	4	5	3	.328	.375	.522
Rafael Almeida	3B16	R	24	16	59	9	13	3	0	3	10	5	8	0	.220	.281	.390
Andy Kyle	OF7	L	22	9	21	3	7	1	0	0	4	4	2	0	.333	.440	.381
Earl Blackburn†	C1	R	19	1	0	0	0	0	0	0	0	1	0	0	—	1.000	—

Pitcher	T	Age	G	GS	CG	ShO	IP	H	HR	BB	SO	W-L	Sv	ERA
Rube Benton	L	25	50	39	22	2	302.0	316	2	118	162	18-21	2	3.10
Art Fromme	R	28	43	37	23	3	296.0	285	7	88	120	16-18	0	2.74
George Suggs	R	29	42	36	25	5	303.0	320	6	56	104	19-16	3	2.94
Bert Humphries	R	31	30	15	9	2	158.2	162	6	36	58	9-11	2	3.23
Harry Gaspar	R	29	7	6	2	0	36.2	38	0	16	13	1-3	0	4.17
Frank Harter	R	25	6	3	1	0	29.1	25	1	11	12	1-2	0	3.07
Frank Gregory	R	23	4	2	1	0	15.2	19	0	7	4	2-0	0	4.60
John Frill†	L	33	3	2	0	0	15.0	19	0	1	4	1-0	0	6.00
Gene Packard	L	24	1	1	1	0	9.0	7	0	4	2	1-0	0	3.00
Bill Doak	R	21	1	1	0	0	2.0	4	0	1	0	0-0	0	4.50
Bobby Keefe	R	30	17	6	0	0	68.2	78	0	33	29	1-3	2	5.24
Dixie Davis	R	21	7	0	0	0	26.2	25	0	16	12	0-1	0	2.70
Frank Smith	R	32	7	3	1	0	22.2	34	1	15	5	1-1	0	6.35
Jim Bagby	R	22	5	1	0	0	17.1	17	2	9	10	2-0	0	3.12
Gene Moore	L	26	5	2	0	0	14.2	17	0	11	6	0-1	1	4.91
Howard McGraner	L	22	4	0	0	0	19.0	22	2	7	5	1-0	0	7.11
Ralph Works†	R	24	3	1	1	0	9.2	4	0	5	5	1-1	0	2.79
Sam Fletcher	R	—	2	0	0	0	9.2	15	1	11	3	0-0	0	12.10
Ben Taylor	R	23	2	0	0	0	5.2	9	0	3	2	0-0	0	3.18
Ed Donalds	R	27	1	0	0	0	4.0	7	0	0	1	1-0	0	4.50
Hanson Horsey	R	22	1	0	0	0	4.0	14	0	3	0	0-0	0	22.50
Chuck Tompkins	R	22	1	0	0	0	3.0	5	0	0	1	0-0	0	0.00
Bill Prough	R	24	1	0	0	0	3.0	7	0	1	1	0-0	0	6.00
Bill Cramer	R	21	1	0	0	0	2.1	6	0	0	2	0-0	0	0.00

1912 Philadelphia Phillies 5th NL 73-79 .480 30.5 GB

Red Dooin

Player	Gm by Position	B	Age	G	AB	R	H	2B	3B	HR	RBI	BB	SO	SB	Avg	OBP	Slg
Bill Killefer	C85	R	24	85	268	18	60	6	3	1	21	4	14	6	.224	.241	.280
Fred Luderus	1B146	L	26	148	572	77	147	31	5	10	69	44	65	8	.257	.318	.381
Otto Knabe	2B123	R	28	126	426	56	120	11	4	0	46	55	20	16	.282	.366	.326
Hans Lobert	3B64	R	30	65	257	37	84	12	5	2	33	19	13	13	.327	.373	.436
Mickey Doolan	SS146	R	32	146	532	47	137	26	6	1	62	34	59	6	.258	.302	.335
Dode Paskert	OF141,2B2,3B1	R	30	145	540	102	170	37	5	2	43	91	67	36	.315	.420	.413
Sherry Magee	OF124,1B6	R	27	132	464	79	142	25	9	6	66	55	54	30	.306	.388	.438
Gavy Cravath	OF113	R	31	130	436	63	124	30	9	11	70	47	77	15	.284	.358	.470
Red Dooin	C58	R	33	69	184	20	43	9	0	0	22	5	12	8	.234	.262	.283
Doc Miller†	OF40	L	29	67	177	24	51	12	5	0	21	9	13	3	.288	.323	.412
Tom Downey†	3B46,SS3	R	28	54	171	27	50	6	3	1	23	21	20	3	.292	.370	.380
John Titus†	OF42	L	36	45	157	43	43	9	5	3	22	33	14	6	.274	.403	.452
Jimmy Walsh	2B31,3B12,C5	R	26	51	150	16	40	6	3	2	19	8	20	3	.267	.304	.387
John Dodge	3B23,2B5,SS1	R	23	30	92	3	11	1	0	0	3	4	11	2	.120	.156	.130
Peaches Graham	C19	R	35	24	59	6	17	1	0	1	4	8	5	1	.288	.373	.356
Cozy Dolan†	3B11	R	22	11	50	8	14	2	2	0	7	1	10	3	.280	.321	.400
Pat Moran	C13	R	36	13	26	1	3	1	0	0	1	1	7	0	.115	.148	.154
George Mangus	OF5	L	22	10	25	2	5	3	0	0	3	1	6	0	.200	.231	.320
Jack Boyle	3B6,SS2	L	22	15	25	4	7	1	0	0	2	1	5	0	.280	.308	.320
Bill Brinker	3B2,OF2	S	28	9	18	1	4	1	0	0	2	2	3	0	.222	.300	.278
Gene Steinbrenner	2B3	R	19	3	9	0	2	1	0	0	1	0	3	0	.222	.222	.333
George Browne	3B1	L	36	6	5	0	1	0	0	0	0	1	0	0	.200	.333	.200
Jimmie Savage	2B1	S	28	2	3	1	0	0	0	0	0	1	0	0	.000	.250	.000
Mike Loan	C1	R	17	1	2	1	1	0	0	0	0	0	0	0	.500	.500	.500

Pitcher	T	Age	G	GS	CG	ShO	IP	H	HR	BB	SO	W-L	Sv	ERA
Pete Alexander	R	25	46	34	25	3	310.1	289	11	105	195	19-17	3	2.81
Tom Seaton	R	24	44	27	16	2	255.0	246	8	106	118	16-12	2	3.28
Earl Moore	R	32	31	24	10	1	182.1	186	3	77	79	9-14	0	3.31
Eppa Rixey	L	21	23	20	10	3	162.0	147	2	54	59	10-10	0	2.50
Ad Brennan	L	30	27	19	13	1	174.0	185	4	49	78	11-9	2	3.57
George Chalmers	R	24	12	8	3	0	57.2	64	4	37	22	3-4	0	3.28
Cliff Curtis†	R	28	10	8	2	0	50.0	55	3	17	20	2-5	0	3.24
Red Nelson†	R	26	4	2	1	0	19.1	25	2	6	2	2-0	0	3.72
Rube Marshall	R	22	2	1	0	0	3.0	12	0	1	2	0-1	0	21.00
Toots Shultz	R	23	22	4	1	0	59.0	75	2	35	20	1-4	1	4.58
Happy Finneran	R	20	14	4	0	0	46.1	50	2	10	10	0-2	1	2.53
Erskine Mayer	R	23	7	1	0	0	21.1	27	1	7	5	0-1	0	6.33
Huck Wallace	L	29	4	0	0	0	4.2	7	0	4	4	0-0	0	0.00
Hank Ritter	R	18	3	0	0	0	6.0	5	0	7	1	0-0	0	4.50
Frank Nicholson	R	22	2	0	0	0	4.0	8	1	2	1	0-0	0	6.75

1912 St. Louis Cardinals 6th NL 63-90 .412 41.0 GB

Roger Bresnahan

Player	Gm by Position	B	Age	G	AB	R	H	2B	3B	HR	RBI	BB	SO	SB	Avg	OBP	Slg
Ivy Wingo	C92	L	21	100	310	38	82	18	8	2	44	23	45	8	.265	.317	.394
Ed Konetchy	1B142,OF1	R	26	143	538	81	169	26	13	8	82	62	66	25	.314	.389	.455
Miller Huggins	2B114	S	33	120	431	82	131	15	4	0	29	87	31	35	.304	.422	.357
Mike Mowrey	3B108	R	28	114	408	59	104	13	8	2	50	46	29	19	.255	.335	.341
Arnold Hauser	SS132	R	23	133	479	73	124	14	7	1	42	39	69	26	.259	.319	.324
Rebel Oakes	OF136	L	25	136	495	57	139	19	5	3	58	31	24	26	.281	.328	.358
Steve Evans	OF134	L	27	135	491	59	139	23	9	6	72	36	51	11	.283	.353	.403
Lee Magee	OF85,2B23,1B6*	S	23	128	458	60	133	13	8	0	40	39	29	16	.290	.347	.354
Rube Ellis	OF76	L	26	109	305	47	82	18	2	4	33	34	36	6	.269	.342	.380
Wally Smith	3B32,SS22,1B6	R	23	75	219	22	56	5	5	0	26	29	27	4	.256	.351	.324
Jack Bliss	C41	R	30	49	114	11	28	3	1	0	18	19	14	3	.246	.372	.289
Roger Bresnahan	C28	R	33	48	108	8	36	7	2	1	15	14	9	4	.333	.419	.463
Jim Galloway	2B16,SS1	S	24	21	54	4	10	2	0	0	4	5	8	2	.185	.254	.222
Frank Gilhooley	OF11	L	20	13	49	5	11	0	0	0	2	3	8	0	.224	.269	.224
Denney Wilie	OF16	L	21	30	48	2	11	0	1	0	6	7	9	0	.229	.351	.271
Possum Whitted	3B12	R	22	12	46	7	12	3	0	0	7	3	5	1	.261	.306	.326
Elmer Miller	OF11	R	21	12	37	5	7	1	0	0	3	4	9	1	.189	.268	.216
Ted Cather	OF5	R	23	5	19	4	8	1	1	0	2	0	4	1	.421	.421	.579
Frank Snyder	C11	R	19	11	18	2	2	0	0	0	0	2	7	1	.111	.200	.111
Ray Rolling	2B4	R	25	5	15	0	3	0	0	0	0	0	5	0	.200	.200	.200
John Kelleher	3B3	R	18	8	12	0	4	1	0	0	1	0	2	0	.333	.333	.417
John Mercer	1B1	L	20	1	1	0	0	0	0	0	0	0	0	0	.000	.000	.000
Ed Burns	C1	R	23	1	1	0	0	0	0	0	1	0	0	0	.000	.000	.000
Mike Murphy	C1	R	23	1	1	0	0	0	0	0	1	0	0	0	.000	.000	.000
Jim Clark		R	24	2	1	0	0	0	0	0	0	0	1	0	.000	.000	.000

L. Magee, 1 G at SS

Pitcher	T	Age	G	GS	CG	ShO	IP	H	HR	BB	SO	W-L	Sv	ERA
Bob Harmon	R	24	43	34	15	3	268.0	284	4	116	73	18-18	0	3.93
Slim Sallee	L	27	48	32	20	3	294.0	289	6	72	108	16-17	6	2.60
Bill Steele	R	26	40	25	7	0	194.0	245	5	66	67	9-13	2	4.69
Joe Willis	L	22	31	17	4	0	129.2	143	3	62	55	4-9	2	4.44
Dan Griner	R	24	12	7	2	0	54.0	59	3	15	20	3-4	0	3.17
Pol Perritt	R	19	6	3	1	0	31.0	25	0	10	13	1-1	0	3.19
Phil Redding	R	22	3	3	2	0	25.1	31	2	11	9	2-1	0	4.97
Bob Ewing	R	39	1	1	0	0	1.1	2	0	1	0	0-0	0	0.00
Rube Geyer	R	28	41	18	5	0	181.0	191	4	84	61	7-14	0	3.28
Gene Woodburn	R	25	20	5	1	0	48.1	60	0	42	25	1-4	0	5.59
Gene Dale	R	23	19	3	1	0	61.2	76	4	51	37	0-5	0	6.57
Sandy Burk†	R	25	12	4	2	0	44.2	37	0	12	17	1-3	1	2.42
Lou Lowdermilk	L	25	4	1	1	0	15.0	14	0	9	2	1-1	1	3.00
Wheezer Dell	R	25	3	0	0	0	2.1	3	0	3	0	0-0	0	11.57
Roland Howell	R	20	3	0	0	0	1.2	5	0	5	0	0-0	0	27.00
George Zackert	L	27	1	0	0	0	1.0	2	0	1	0	0-0	0	18.00

1912 Brooklyn Dodgers 7th NL 58-95 .379 46.0 GB

Bill Dahlen

Player	Gm by Position	B	Age	G	AB	R	H	2B	3B	HR	RBI	BB	SO	SB	Avg	OBP	Slg
Otto Miller	C94	R	23	98	316	35	88	18	1	1	31	18	50	11	.278	.325	.351
Jake Daubert	1B143	L	28	145	559	81	172	19	16	3	66	48	45	29	.308	.369	.415
George Cutshaw	2B91,3B5,SS1	R	24	102	357	41	100	14	4	0	28	31	16	16	.280	.341	.342
Red Smith	3B125	R	22	128	486	75	139	28	6	4	57	54	51	22	.286	.362	.393
Bert Tooley	SS76	R	25	77	265	34	62	6	5	2	37	19	21	12	.234	.285	.317
Herbie Moran	OF129	L	28	130	508	77	140	18	10	1	40	69	38	28	.276	.368	.356
Zack Wheat	OF120	L	24	123	453	70	138	28	7	8	65	39	40	16	.305	.367	.450
Hub Northen	OF102	L	26	118	412	54	116	26	6	3	46	41	46	8	.282	.352	.396
John Hummel	2B58,OF44,1B11	R	29	122	411	55	116	21	7	5	54	49	55	7	.282	.359	.404
Tom Fisher	SS74,2B1,3B1	R	25	82	257	27	60	10	3	0	26	14	32	7	.233	.273	.296
Jud Daley	OF55	L	28	61	199	22	51	9	1	1	13	24	17	2	.256	.342	.327
Tex Erwin	C41	L	26	59	133	14	28	3	0	2	14	18	16	1	.211	.305	.278
Ed Phelps	C32	R	33	52	111	8	32	4	3	0	23	16	15	1	.288	.388	.378
Enos Kirkpatrick	3B29,SS3	R	26	32	94	13	18	1	1	0	6	9	15	5	.191	.269	.223
Casey Stengel	OF17	L	21	17	57	9	18	1	0	1	13	15	9	5	.316	.466	.386
Red Downs†	2B9	R	28	9	32	2	8	3	0	0	3	1	5	3	.250	.273	.344
Dolly Stark	SS7	R	27	8	22	2	4	0	0	0	2	1	3	2	.182	.217	.182
Bob Higgins	C1	R	25	1	2	0	0	0	0	0	0	0	1	0	.000	.000	.000

Pitcher	T	Age	G	GS	CG	ShO	IP	H	HR	BB	SO	W-L	Sv	ERA
Nap Rucker	L	27	45	34	23	6	297.2	272	6	72	151	18-21	4	2.21
Pat Ragan	R	23	36	26	12	1	208.0	211	7	65	101	7-18	1	3.63
Eddie Stack	R	24	28	17	4	0	142.0	139	3	55	45	7-5	1	3.36
Earl Yingling	L	23	25	16	12	0	163.0	186	10	56	51	6-11	0	3.59
Frank Allen	L	22	20	15	5	1	109.0	119	1	57	58	3-9	0	3.63
Cy Barger	R	27	16	11	6	0	94.0	120	4	42	30	1-9	0	5.46
Elmer Knetzer	R	26	33	16	4	1	140.1	135	6	70	61	7-9	0	4.55
Maury Kent	R	26	20	9	2	1	93.0	107	3	46	24	5-5	0	4.84
Cliff Curtis†	R	28	19	9	3	0	80.0	72	4	37	22	4-7	1	3.94
Bill Schardt	R	26	7	0	0	0	20.2	25	1	6	7	0-1	1	4.35
Sandy Burk†	R	25	2	0	0	0	8.1	9	0	3	2	0-0	0	3.24
Eddie Dent	R	24	1	0	0	0	1.0	4	0	1	1	0-0	0	36.00

1912 Boston Beaneaters 8th NL 52-101 .340 52.0 GB

Johnny Kling

Player	Gm by Position	B	Age	G	AB	R	H	2B	3B	HR	RBI	BB	SO	SB	Avg	OBP	Slg
Johnny Kling	C74	R	37	81	252	26	80	10	3	2	30	15	30	3	.317	.356	.405
Ben Houser	1B83	L	28	108	332	38	95	17	3	8	52	22	29	1	.286	.332	.428
Bill Sweeney	2B153	R	26	153	593	84	204	31	13	1	100	68	34	27	.344	.416	.445
Ed McDonald	3B118	R	25	121	459	70	119	23	6	2	34	70	91	22	.259	.363	.349
Frank O'Rourke	SS59,3B1	R	17	61	196	11	24	3	1	0	16	11	50	1	.122	.177	.148
Vin Campbell	OF144	L	24	145	624	102	185	32	9	3	48	32	44	19	.296	.334	.391
George Jackson	OF107	R	29	110	397	55	104	13	5	4	48	38	72	22	.262	.342	.350
John Titus†	OF96	L	36	96	345	56	112	23	6	2	48	49	20	5	.325	.422	.443
Art Devlin	1B69,3B26,SS26*	R	32	124	436	59	126	18	8	0	54	51	37	11	.289	.367	.367
Jay Kirke	OF72,3B14,SS2*	L	24	103	359	53	115	11	4	4	62	9	46	7	.320	.339	.407
Bill Rariden	C73	R	24	79	247	27	55	3	1	1	14	18	35	3	.223	.281	.255
Doc Miller†	OF50	L	29	51	201	26	47	8	1	2	24	14	17	6	.234	.287	.313
Al Bridwell	SS31	L	28	31	106	6	25	5	1	0	14	5	5	2	.236	.270	.302
Hank Gowdy	C22,1B7	R	22	44	96	16	26	6	1	3	10	16	13	3	.271	.386	.448
Harry Spratt	SS23	L	23	27	89	6	23	3	2	3	15	7	11	2	.258	.313	.438
Rabbit Maranville	SS26	R	20	26	86	8	18	2	0	0	8	9	14	1	.209	.292	.233
Al Kaiser	OF4	R	25	4	13	0	0	0	0	0	0	0	3	0	.000	.000	.000
Joe Schultz	2B4	R	18	4	12	1	3	1	0	0	4	0	2	0	.250	.250	.333
Dave Shean	SS4	R	28	4	10	1	3	0	0	0	0	1	2	0	.300	.417	.300
Gil Whitehouse	C2	S	18	2	3	0	0	0	0	0	0	0	3	0	.000	.000	.000
Art Schwind	3B1	S	22	1	2	0	1	0	0	0	0	0	0	0	.500	.500	.500
Mike Gonzalez	C1	R	21	1	2	0	0	0	0	0	0	1	1	0	.000	.333	.000
Bill Jones		L	25	3	2	0	1	0	0	0	2	0	1	0	.500	.500	.500

A. Devlin, 1 G at OF; J. Kirke, 1 G at 1B

Pitcher	T	Age	G	GS	CG	ShO	IP	H	HR	BB	SO	W-L	Sv	ERA
Otto Hess	L	33	33	31	21	0	254.0	270	3	90	80	12-17	0	3.76
Hub Perdue	R	30	37	30	20	1	249.0	295	11	54	101	13-16	3	3.80
Lefty Tyler	L	22	42	29	15	1	256.1	262	8	126	144	12-22	0	4.18
Buster Brown	R	30	31	21	12	0	168.1	146	0	66	68	4-15	0	4.01
Walt Dickson	R	33	36	20	9	1	189.0	233	2	61	47	3-19	1	3.86
Al Mattern	R	29	2	1	0	0	6.1	10	0	1	3	0-1	0	7.11
Ed Donnelly	R	31	37	18	10	0	184.1	225	10	72	67	5-10	0	4.35
Bill McTigue	L	21	10	1	1	0	34.2	39	0	18	17	2-0	0	5.45
Brad Hogg	R	24	10	1	0	0	30.2	37	2	16	12	1-1	1	7.04
Rube Kroh	L	25	3	1	0	0	6.1	8	0	6	1	0-0	0	2.84
Steve White†	R	27	3	0	0	0	6.0	9	0	5	2	0-0	0	6.00
Hank Griffin	R	25	3	0	0	0	1.2	3	0	3	0	0-0	0	27.00
King Brady	R	31	1	0	0	0	2.2	5	0	3	0	0-0	0	20.25
Bill Brady	R	22	1	0	0	0	1.0	2	0	0	0	0-0	0	0.00

»1913 Philadelphia Athletics 1st AL 96-57 .627 —

Connie Mack

Player	Gm by Position	B	Age	G	AB	R	H	2B	3B	HR	RBI	BB	SO	SB	Avg	OBP	Slg
Jack Lapp	C78,1B1	L	28	82	238	23	54	4	4	1	20	37	26	1	.227	.336	.290
Stuffy McInnis	1B148	R	22	148	543	79	177	30	4	4	90	45	31	16	.326	.384	.418
Eddie Collins	2B148	L	26	148	534	125	184	23	13	3	73	85	37	55	.345	.441	.453
Home Run Baker	3B149	L	27	149	565	116	190	34	9	12	117	63	31	34	.336	.412	.492
Jack Barry	SS134	R	26	135	455	62	125	20	6	3	85	44	32	15	.275	.349	.365
Eddie Murphy	OF135	L	21	136	508	105	150	14	7	1	30	70	44	21	.295	.391	.356
Rube Oldring	OF131,SS5	R	29	137	538	101	152	27	9	5	71	34	37	40	.283	.328	.394
Jimmy Walsh	OF88	L	27	94	303	56	77	16	5	0	27	38	40	15	.254	.341	.340
Amos Strunk	OF80	L	24	93	292	30	89	11	12	0	46	29	23	14	.305	.368	.425
Wally Schang	C72	S	23	77	207	32	55	16	3	3	30	34	44	4	.266	.392	.415
Tom Daley	OF38	L	28	62	141	13	36	2	1	0	11	13	28	4	.255	.327	.284
Billy Orr	SS16,1B3,2B2*	R	22	27	67	6	13	1	1	0	7	4	10	1	.194	.239	.239
Danny Murphy	OF9	R	36	40	59	3	19	5	1	0	6	4	8	0	.322	.365	.441
Ira Thomas	C21	R	32	21	53	3	15	4	1	0	6	4	8	0	.283	.333	.396
Harry Davis	1B6	R	39	7	17	2	6	2	0	0	4	1	4	0	.353	.389	.471
Doc Lavan†	SS5	R	22	5	14	1	1	0	1	0	1	0	6	0	.071	.071	.214
Harry Fritz	3B5	R	22	5	13	1	0	0	0	0	0	2	4	0	.000	.188	.000
Press Cruthers	2B3	R	22	3	12	0	3	1	0	0	0	0	0	0	.250	.250	.333
George Brickley	OF4	R	18	5	12	0	2	0	1	0	0	0	4	0	.167	.231	.333
Wickey McAvoy	C4	R	18	4	9	0	1	0	0	0	0	0	4	0	.111	.200	.111
Joe Giebel	C1	R	21	1	3	0	1	0	0	0	0	0	1	0	.333	.333	.333
Monte Pfeffer	SS1	R	21	1	3	0	0	0	0	0	0	0	1	0	.000	.250	.000

B. Orr, 2 G at 3B

Pitcher	T	Age	G	GS	CG	ShO	IP	H	HR	BB	SO	W-L	Sv	ERA
Boardwalk Brown	R	26	43	35	11	3	235.1	200	6	87	70	17-11	1	2.94
Eddie Plank	L	37	41	30	18	7	242.2	211	3	57	151	18-10	4	2.60
Bob Shawkey	R	22	18	15	8	1	111.1	92	2	50	52	6-5	0	2.34
Charlie Boardman	L	20	2	2	1	0	9.0	10	0	6	4	0-2	0	2.00
Jack Coombs	R	30	2	2	0	0	5.1	5	0	6	0	0-0	0	10.13
Ensign Cottrell	L	24	2	1	1	0	10.0	15	0	2	3	1-0	0	5.40
Pat Bohen	R	21	1	1	1	0	8.0	3	0	2	5	0-1	0	1.13
Chief Bender	R	29	48	21	16	2	237.2	208	2	59	135	21-10	13	2.20
Byron Houck	R	21	41	19	4	1	175.2	147	3	122	71	14-6	0	4.15
Joe Bush	R	20	39	15	5	1	200.1	199	3	66	81	15-6	3	3.82
John Wyckoff	R	21	17	7	3	0	61.2	56	1	46	31	2-4	0	4.38
Herb Pennock	L	19	14	4	1	0	33.1	30	4	22	17	2-1	0	5.13
John Taff	R	23	7	1	0	0	17.2	22	0	5	9	0-1	1	6.62
Dave Morey	R	24	2	0	0	0	4.0	2	0	2	1	0-0	0	4.50

1913 Washington Senators 2nd AL 90-64 .584 6.5 GB

Clark Griffith

Player	Gm by Position	B	Age	G	AB	R	H	2B	3B	HR	RBI	BB	SO	SB	Avg	OBP	Slg
John Henry	C96	R	23	96	273	26	61	8	4	1	26	30	43	5	.223	.309	.293
Chick Gandil	1B145	R	26	148	550	61	175	25	8	1	72	36	33	22	.318	.363	.398
Ray Morgan	2B134,SS4	R	24	137	481	58	131	19	8	0	57	68	63	19	.272	.369	.345
Eddie Foster	3B105	R	26	106	409	56	101	11	5	1	41	36	31	22	.247	.309	.306
George McBride	SS150	R	32	150	499	52	107	18	7	1	52	43	46	12	.214	.286	.285
Clyde Milan	OF154	L	26	154	579	92	174	18	9	3	54	58	25	75	.301	.367	.378
Danny Moeller	OF153	S	28	153	589	88	139	15	10	5	42	72	103	62	.236	.322	.321
Howard Shanks	OF109	R	22	109	390	38	99	11	5	1	37	15	40	23	.254	.287	.315
Frank LaPorte	3B46,2B13,OF12	R	33	80	242	25	61	5	4	0	18	17	16	10	.252	.309	.306
Eddie Ainsmith	C79,P1	R	21	84	229	26	49	4	4	2	20	12	41	17	.214	.262	.293
Walter Johnson	P47,OF1	R	25	51	134	12	35	5	6	2	14	5	14	2	.261	.293	.433
Rip Williams	C18,1B9,OF5	R	31	66	106	9	30	6	2	1	12	9	16	3	.283	.339	.406
Germany Schaefer	2B16,1B6,3B2*	R	36	52	100	17	32	1	1	0	7	15	12	6	.320	.419	.350
Joe Gedeon	OF15,3B7,2B2*	R	19	29	71	3	13	1	3	0	6	1	6	3	.183	.205	.282
Jack Calvo	OF12	L	19	16	33	5	8	0	0	1	2	1	4	0	.242	.265	.333
Ben Spencer	OF8	L	23	8	21	2	6	1	1	0	2	2	4	2	.286	.348	.429
Merito Acosta	OF7	L	17	9	20	3	6	0	1	0	1	4	2	2	.300	.417	.400
Carl Cashion	P4,OF3	L	22	7	12	1	3	0	0	0	2	1	1	0	.250	.308	.250
Bill Morley	2B1	R	23	2	3	0	0	0	0	0	0	0	0	0	.000	.000	.000
Jack Ryan	C1	R	44	1	1	0	0	0	0	0	0	0	0	0	.000	.000	.000

G. Schaefer, 1 G at P, 1 G at OF; J. Gedeon, 2 G at SS, 1 G at P

Pitcher	T	Age	G	GS	CG	ShO	IP	H	HR	BB	SO	W-L	Sv	ERA
Walter Johnson	R	25	48	36	29	11	346.0	232	9	38	243	36-7	2	1.14
Bob Groom	R	28	37	36	18	4	264.2	258	8	81	156	16-16	0	3.23
Joe Boehling	L	22	38	25	18	3	235.1	197	3	82	110	17-7	4	2.07
Joe Engel	L	20	36	23	6	2	164.2	124	2	85	70	8-9	1	3.06
George Mullin†	R	32	12	9	3	0	57.1	69	1	25	14	3-5	0	5.02
Carl Cashion	R	22	4	3	0	0	8.2	7	0	14	3	1-1	0	6.23
Doc Ayers	R	23	4	2	1	1	17.2	12	0	4	17	1-1	1	1.53
Jim Shaw	R	19	2	1	0	0	13.0	8	0	7	14	0-1	0	2.08
Mutt Williams	R	21	1	1	0	0	4.0	4	1	2	1	1-0	0	4.50
Long Tom Hughes	R	34	36	13	4	0	129.2	129	6	61	59	4-12	7	4.03
Bert Gallia	R	21	31	4	0	0	96.0	85	2	46	46	1-5	3	4.13
Slim Love	L	22	5	1	0	0	16.2	14	0	6	5	1-0	1	1.62
Harry Harper	L	18	4	0	0	0	12.2	10	1	5	9	0-0	0	3.55
Nick Altrock	L	36	4	0	0	0	9.1	7	0	4	2	0-0	0	4.82
Jack Bentley	L	18	3	1	0	0	11.0	5	0	2	5	1-0	1	0.00
John Wilson	L	23	3	0	0	0	4.0	4	1	3	1	0-0	0	4.50
Tom Drohan	R	25	2	0	0	0	2.0	5	1	0	2	0-0	0	9.00
Harry Hedgpeth	L	24	1	0	0	0	1.0	1	0	0	0	0-0	0	0.00
Rex Dawson	R	24	1	0	0	0	1.0	1	0	0	1	0-0	0	0.00
Clark Griffith	R	43	1	0	0	0	1.0	1	0	0	0	0-0	0	0.00
Joe Gedeon	R	19	1	0	0	0	0.1	0	0	0	0	0-0	1	0.00
Eddie Ainsmith	R	21	1	0	0	0	0.1	2	0	0	0	0-0	0	54.00
Germany Schaefer	R	36	1	0	0	0	0.1	2	1	0	0	0-0	0	54.00

1913 Cleveland Bronchos 3rd AL 86-66 .566 9.5 GB

Joe Birmingham

Player	Gm by Position	B	Age	G	AB	R	H	2B	3B	HR	RBI	BB	SO	SB	Avg	OBP	Slg
Fred Carisch	C79	R	31	81	222	11	48	4	2	0	26	21	19	6	.216	.287	.252
Doc Johnston	1B133	L	25	133	530	74	135	19	12	2	39	35	65	19	.255	.309	.347
Nap Lajoie	2B126	R	38	137	465	66	156	25	2	1	68	33	17	17	.335	.398	.404
Ivy Olson	3B73,1B21,2B1	R	27	104	370	47	92	13	3	0	32	22	28	7	.249	.296	.300
Ray Chapman	SS138	R	22	141	508	78	131	19	7	3	39	46	51	29	.258	.322	.341
Joe Jackson	OF148	L	23	148	528	109	197	39	17	7	71	80	26	26	.373	.460	.551
Jack Graney	OF148	L	27	148	517	56	138	18	12	3	68	48	55	27	.267	.335	.366
Nemo Leibold	OF72	L	21	84	286	37	74	11	6	0	12	21	43	16	.259	.309	.339
Terry Turner	3B71,2B25,SS21	R	32	120	388	61	96	13	4	0	44	55	35	13	.247	.348	.302
Buddy Ryan	OF68,1B1	L	27	73	243	26	72	6	1	0	32	11	13	9	.296	.332	.329
Steve O'Neill	C78	R	21	78	234	19	69	13	3	0	29	10	24	5	.295	.329	.376
Joe Birmingham	OF36	R	28	47	131	16	37	9	1	0	15	8	22	7	.282	.324	.366
Grover Land	C17	R	28	17	47	3	11	1	0	0	9	4	1	1	.234	.321	.255
Ray Bates	3B12,OF2	R	23	27	30	4	5	0	2	0	4	3	9	3	.167	.265	.300
Jack Lelivelt†	OF1	L	27	23	23	0	9	2	0	0	7	0	3	1	.391	.391	.478
George Dunlop	SS4,3B3	R	24	7	17	3	4	1	0	0	0	0	5	0	.235	.235	.294
Larry Kopf	2B3,3B1	S	22	5	9	1	2	0	0	0	1	0	0	0	.222	.222	.222
Ernie Krueger	C4	R	22	5	6	0	0	0	0	0	0	0	2	0	.000	.000	.000
Johnny Beall†		L	31	6	6	0	1	0	0	0	1	0	2	0	.167	.167	.167
Eddie Edmonson	1B1,OF1	L	23	2	5	0	0	0	0	0	0	0	0	0	.000	.000	.000
Josh Billings	C1	R	21	1	3	0	0	0	0	0	0	0	3	0	.000	.000	.000
George Young		L	23	2	2	0	0	0	0	0	0	0	0	0	.000	.000	.000
Johnny Bassler	C1	L	18	1	2	0	0	0	0	0	0	0	0	0	.000	.000	.000
Billy Southworth	OF1	L	20	1	0	0	0	0	0	0	0	0	0	0	—	—	—
Josh Swindell		R	27	1	0	0	0	0	0	0	0	0	0	0	—	—	—
R. Peckinpaugh†		R	22	1	0	1	0	0	0	0	0	0	0	0	—	—	—

Pitcher	T	Age	G	GS	CG	ShO	IP	H	HR	BB	SO	W-L	Sv	ERA
Cy Falkenberg	R	32	39	36	23	6	275.2	238	2	88	166	23-10	0	2.22
Vean Gregg	L	28	44	34	23	3	285.1	258	2	124	166	20-13	3	2.24
Willie Mitchell	L	23	35	22	14	4	217.0	153	1	88	141	14-8	0	1.87
Fred Blanding	R	25	41	22	14	3	215.0	234	6	72	63	15-10	0	2.55
George Kahler	R	23	24	15	5	0	117.2	118	1	32	43	5-11	0	3.14
Bill Steen	R	25	22	13	8	2	128.1	113	3	49	57	4-5	2	2.45
Jim Baskette	R	25	2	1	0	0	4.2	8	1	2	0	0-0	0	5.79
Nick Cullop	L	25	23	8	4	0	97.2	105	3	35	30	3-7	0	4.42
Lefty James	L	23	11	4	4	0	39.0	42	0	9	18	2-2	0	3.00
Lynn Brenton	R	22	1	0	0	0	2.0	4	0	0	2	0-0	0	9.00
Lee Dashner	L	26	1	0	0	0	1.2	0	0	0	2	0-0	0	5.40
Dave Gregg	R	22	1	0	0	0	1.0	2	0	0	0	0-0	0	18.00
Luke Glavenich	R	20	1	0	0	0	1.0	3	0	3	1	0-0	0	9.00

1913 Boston Red Sox 4th AL 79-71 .527 15.5 GB

Jake Stahl (39-41)/Bill Carrigan (40-30)

Player	Gm by Position	B	Age	G	AB	R	H	2B	3B	HR	RBI	BB	SO	SB	Avg	OBP	Slg
Bill Carrigan	C82	R	29	85	256	17	62	15	5	0	28	27	26	6	.242	.319	.340
Clyde Engle	1B133,OF2	R	29	143	498	75	144	17	12	2	50	53	41	28	.289	.363	.384
Steve Yerkes	2B129	R	25	137	483	67	130	30	6	1	48	50	32	11	.269	.340	.362
Larry Gardner	3B130	L	27	131	473	64	133	17	10	0	63	47	34	18	.281	.347	.359
Heinie Wagner	SS105,2B4	R	32	110	365	43	83	14	8	2	34	40	29	9	.227	.316	.326
Harry Hooper	OF147,P1	L	25	148	586	100	169	29	12	4	40	60	51	26	.288	.359	.399
Duffy Lewis	OF142,P1	R	25	149	551	54	164	31	12	0	90	30	55	12	.298	.336	.397
Tris Speaker	OF139	L	25	141	520	94	189	35	22	3	71	65	22	46	.363	.441	.533
Hal Janvrin	SS48,3B19,2B8*	R	20	86	276	18	57	5	1	3	25	23	27	17	.207	.272	.264
Wally Rehg	OF27	R	24	30	101	14	28	3	2	0	9	2	7	4	.277	.291	.347
Hick Cady	C39	R	27	39	96	10	24	5	2	0	6	5	14	1	.250	.294	.344
Pinch Thomas	C31	L	25	37	91	6	26	1	2	1	15	2	11	1	.286	.309	.374
Les Nunamaker	C27	R	24	29	65	9	14	5	2	0	9	8	8	2	.215	.311	.354
Neal Ball	2B10,SS8,3B1	R	32	23	58	9	10	2	0	0	4	9	13	3	.172	.294	.207
Bill Mundy	1B16	L	24	16	47	4	12	0	0	0	4	4	12	0	.255	.314	.255
Sea Lion Hall	P35,3B1	L	27	43	42	2	9	1	1	0	2	1	10	0	.214	.233	.286
Olaf Henriksen	OF7	L	25	30	40	8	15	1	0	0	2	7	5	3	.375	.468	.400
Wally Snell	C1	R	24	5	8	1	3	0	0	0	0	0	0	1	.375	.375	.375
Jake Stahl		R	34	2	2	0	0	0	0	0	0	0	1	0	.000	.000	.000

H. Janvrin, 6 G at 1B

Pitcher	T	Age	G	GS	CG	ShO	IP	H	HR	BB	SO	W-L	Sv	ERA
Ray Collins	L	26	30	30	19	3	246.2	242	3	37	88	19-8	0	2.63
Hugh Bedient	R	23	43	28	15	1	259.2	255	1	67	122	15-14	5	2.77
Dutch Leonard	L	21	42	28	14	3	259.1	245	0	94	144	14-16	1	2.39
Joe Wood	R	23	23	18	12	1	145.2	120	0	61	123	11-5	2	2.29
Earl Moseley	R	28	24	15	7	3	120.2	105	1	49	62	8-5	0	3.13
Buck O'Brien†	R	31	15	12	6	0	90.1	103	0	35	54	4-9	0	3.69
Fred Anderson	R	27	10	8	4	0	57.1	84	0	21	32	0-6	0	5.97
Sea Lion Hall	R	27	35	4	2	0	105.0	97	1	46	48	5-4	2	3.43
Rube Foster	R	25	19	8	4	1	68.1	64	1	28	36	3-4	0	3.16
Paul Maloy	R	21	2	0	0	0	2.0	2	0	1	0	0-0	0	9.00
Harry Hooper	R	25	1	0	0	0	2.0	2	0	1	0	0-0	0	0.00
Esty Chaney	R	22	1	0	0	0	1.0	1	0	2	0	0-0	0	9.00
Duffy Lewis	R	25	1	0	0	0	1.0	3	0	0	1	0-0	0	18.00

1913 Chicago White Sox 5th AL 78-74 .513 17.5 GB

Nixey Callahan

Player	Gm by Position	B	Age	G	AB	R	H	2B	3B	HR	RBI	BB	SO	SB	Avg	OBP	Slg
Ray Schalk	C125	R	20	128	401	38	98	15	5	1	38	27	36	14	.244	.297	.314
Hal Chase†	1B102	R	30	102	384	49	110	11	10	2	39	16	41	9	.286	.320	.383
Morrie Rath	2B86	L	26	90	295	37	59	2	0	0	12	46	22	22	.200	.310	.207
Harry Lord	3B150	L	31	150	547	62	144	18	12	1	42	45	39	24	.263	.327	.346
Buck Weaver	SS151	R	22	151	533	51	145	17	8	4	52	15	60	20	.272	.302	.356
Shano Collins	OF147	R	27	148	535	53	128	26	9	1	47	32	60	22	.239	.286	.327
Ping Bodie	OF119	R	25	127	406	39	107	14	8	8	48	35	57	5	.264	.325	.397
Wally Mattick	OF63	R	26	68	207	15	39	8	1	0	11	18	16	3	.188	.253	.237
Joe Berger	2B69,SS4,3B1	R	26	79	223	27	48	6	2	2	20	36	28	5	.215	.330	.287
Larry Chappell	OF59	L	23	60	208	20	48	8	1	0	15	18	22	7	.231	.295	.279
Jack Fournier	1B29,OF23	L	23	68	172	20	40	8	5	1	23	21	23	9	.233	.323	.355
Ted Easterly	C19	L	28	60	97	3	23	1	0	0	8	4	9	2	.237	.267	.247
Biff Schaller	OF32	L	23	34	96	12	21	3	0	0	4	20	16	5	.219	.353	.250
Babe Borton†	1B26	L	24	28	80	9	22	5	0	0	13	23	5	1	.275	.442	.338
Johnny Beall†	OF17	L	31	17	60	10	16	0	1	2	3	0	0	1	.267	.279	.400
Walt Kuhn	C24	R	29	26	50	5	8	1	0	0	5	13	8	1	.160	.333	.180
Jim Breton	SS7,3B3	R	21	12	30	1	5	1	1	0	2	1	5	0	.167	.194	.267
Doc White	P19,1B1	L	34	20	25	1	3	0	0	0	0	3	1	0	.120	.214	.120
Davy Jones	OF8	L	33	10	21	2	6	0	0	0	0	9	0	1	.286	.500	.286
Rollie Zeider†	3B6,1B3,2B1	R	29	13	20	4	7	0	0	0	2	4	1	3	.350	.458	.350
Edd Roush	OF2	L	20	9	10	2	1	0	0	0	0	0	2	0	.100	.100	.100
Nixey Callahan	OF1	R	39	6	9	0	2	0	0	0	1	0	2	0	.222	.222	.222
Tom Daly	C1	R	21	1	3	0	0	0	0	0	0	0	0	0	.000	.000	.000
Don Rader	3B1,OF1	L	19	2	3	1	1	1	0	0	0	0	0	0	.333	.333	.667
Billy Meyer	C1	R	21	1	1	0	1	0	0	0	0	0	0	0	1.000	1.000	1.000

Pitcher	T	Age	G	GS	CG	ShO	IP	H	HR	BB	SO	W-L	Sv	ERA
Jim Scott	R	25	48	38	27	4	312.1	252	2	86	158	20-20	1	1.90
Reb Russell	L	24	51	36	26	8	316.1	249	2	79	122	22-16	4	1.91
Eddie Cicotte	R	29	41	30	18	3	267.1	224	2	73	121	18-12	1	1.58
Joe Benz	R	27	33	17	7	1	150.2	146	1	59	79	7-10	1	2.75
Ed Walsh	R	32	16	14	7	1	97.2	91	1	39	34	8-3	1	2.58
Buck O'Brien†	R	31	6	3	0	0	18.1	21	0	13	4	0-2	0	3.93
Frank Miller	R	27	1	1	0	0	1.2	4	0	3	2	0-1	0	27.00
Jim Scoggins	L	21	1	1	0	0	0.0	0	0	1	0	0-1	0	—
Doc White	L	34	19	8	2	0	103.0	106	2	39	39	2-4	0	3.50
Pop Boy Smith	R	21	15	2	0	0	32.0	31	0	11	13	0-1	0	3.38
Frank Lange	R	29	12	3	0	0	40.2	46	0	20	20	1-3	0	4.87
Bill Lathrop	R	21	6	0	0	0	17.0	16	0	12	9	0-1	0	4.24
Bob Smith	R	22	1	0	0	0	2.0	3	0	3	1	0-0	0	13.50

1913 Detroit Tigers 6th AL 66-87 .431 30.0 GB

Hughie Jennings

Player	Gm by Position	B	Age	G	AB	R	H	2B	3B	HR	RBI	BB	SO	SB	Avg	OBP	Slg
Oscar Stanage	C77	R	30	80	241	19	54	13	2	0	21	21	35	5	.224	.292	.295
Del Gainer	1B103	R	26	104	363	47	97	16	8	2	25	30	45	10	.267	.333	.372
Ossie Vitt	2B78,3B17,OF2	R	23	99	359	45	86	11	3	2	33	31	18	5	.240	.304	.304
George Moriarty	3B93,OF7	R	29	102	347	29	83	5	2	0	30	24	25	33	.239	.302	.265
Donie Bush	SS152	S	25	153	597	98	150	19	10	1	40	80	32	44	.251	.344	.322
Sam Crawford	OF140,1B13	L	33	153	610	78	193	32	23	9	83	52	28	13	.316	.370	.489
Bobby Veach	OF136	L	25	138	494	54	133	22	10	0	64	53	31	22	.269	.346	.354
Ty Cobb	OF118,2B1	L	26	122	428	70	167	18	16	4	67	58	31	52	.390	.467	.535
Paddy Baumann	2B48	R	27	50	191	31	57	7	4	1	22	16	18	4	.298	.353	.393
Baldy Louden	2B30,3B26,SS6*	R	27	72	191	28	46	4	5	0	23	24	22	6	.241	.344	.314
Red McKee	C62	L	22	67	187	18	53	3	4	1	20	21	21	7	.283	.359	.358
Hugh High	OF52	L	25	80	183	18	42	6	1	0	16	28	24	6	.230	.335	.273
Jean Dubuc	P36,OF3	R	24	68	135	17	36	5	3	2	11	2	17	1	.267	.277	.393
Henri Rondeau	C14,1B6	R	26	35	70	5	13	2	0	0	5	14	16	1	.186	.321	.214
Frank Gibson	C19,OF1	S	22	20	57	8	8	1	0	0	2	3	9	2	.140	.197	.158
Eddie Onslow	1B17	L	20	17	55	7	14	1	0	0	8	5	9	1	.255	.328	.273
Charlie Deal†	3B15	R	21	16	50	3	11	0	2	0	3	1	7	2	.220	.235	.300
Guy Tutwiler	1B14	L	23	14	47	4	10	0	1	0	7	4	12	2	.213	.275	.255
Wally Pipp	1B10	L	20	12	31	3	5	0	3	0	5	2	6	0	.161	.235	.355
Les Hennessy	2B9	R	19	14	22	2	3	0	0	0	0	3	6	2	.136	.240	.136
Al Platte	OF5	L	23	7	18	1	2	1	0	0	0	1	1	0	.111	.158	.167
Joe Burns	OF4	L	24	4	13	0	5	0	0	0	1	2	4	0	.385	.500	.385
Pepper Peploski	3B2	R	21	2	4	1	2	0	0	0	0	0	0	0	.500	.500	.500
Steve Partenheimer	3B1	R	21	1	2	0	0	0	0	0	0	1	0	0	.000	.333	.000
Ray Powell	OF1	L	24	2	0	0	0	0	0	0	0	0	0	0	—	—	—

B. Louden, 5 G at OF

Pitcher	T	Age	G	GS	CG	ShO	IP	H	HR	BB	SO	W-L	Sv	ERA
Ed Willett	R	29	34	30	19	0	241.2	237	0	89	59	13-14	0	3.09
Hooks Dauss	R	23	33	29	22	2	225.0	188	4	82	107	13-12	1	2.68
Jean Dubuc	R	24	36	28	22	1	242.2	228	1	91	73	15-14	2	2.89
Marc Hall	R	25	30	21	8	1	165.0	165	1	79	69	10-12	0	3.27
Ralph Comstock	R	22	10	7	1	0	60.1	90	0	16	37	2-5	1	5.37
George Mullin†	R	32	7	7	4	0	52.1	53	1	18	16	1-6	0	2.75
Lefty Williams	L	20	5	4	3	0	29.0	34	0	4	9	1-3	1	4.97
Charlie Grover	R	23	2	1	0	0	10.2	9	0	7	2	0-0	0	3.38
George Boehler	R	21	1	1	1	0	8.0	11	0	6	2	0-1	0	6.75
Erwin Renfer	R	17	1	1	0	0	6.0	5	0	3	1	0-1	0	6.00
Lou North	R	22	1	1	0	0	6.0	10	1	9	3	0-1	0	15.00
Joe Lake	R	32	28	12	6	0	137.0	149	3	24	35	8-7	1	3.28
Fred House	R	22	19	2	0	0	53.2	64	1	17	16	1-2	0	5.20
Carl Zamloch	R	23	17	5	3	0	69.2	66	1	23	28	1-6	1	2.45
Al Klawitter	R	25	8	3	1	0	32.0	39	0	15	10	1-2	0	5.91
Al Clauss	L	22	5	1	0	0	13.1	11	0	12	1	0-1	0	4.73
Heinie Elder	L	22	1	0	0	0	3.1	4	0	5	0	0-0	0	8.10
Charlie Harding	R	22	1	0	0	0	2.0	3	0	1	0	0-0	0	4.50
Lefty Lorenzen	L	20	1	0	0	0	2.0	4	0	3	0	0-0	0	18.00

1913 New York Yankees 7th AL 57-94 .377 38.0 GB

Frank Chance

Player	Gm by Position	B	Age	G	AB	R	H	2B	3B	HR	RBI	BB	SO	SB	Avg	OBP	Slg
Jeff Sweeney	C112,1B1,OF1	R	24	117	351	35	93	10	2	2	40	37	41	11	.265	.348	.322
John Knight	1B50,2B21	R	27	70	250	24	59	10	0	0	24	25	27	7	.236	.310	.276
Roy Hartzell	2B81,OF31,3B21*	L	31	141	490	60	127	18	1	0	38	67	40	26	.259	.353	.300
Ezra Midkiff	3B76,SS4,2B2	L	30	83	284	22	56	9	1	0	14	12	33	9	.197	.232	.236
R. Peckinpaugh†	SS93	R	22	95	340	35	91	10	7	1	32	24	47	19	.268	.316	.347
Birdie Cree	OF144	R	30	145	534	51	145	25	6	1	63	50	51	22	.272	.338	.346
Harry Wolter	OF121	L	28	126	425	53	108	18	6	2	43	80	50	13	.254	.377	.339
Bert Daniels	OF87	R	30	93	320	52	69	13	5	0	22	44	36	27	.216	.343	.288
Fritz Maisel	3B51	R	23	51	187	33	48	4	3	0	12	34	20	25	.257	.371	.310
Rollie Zeider†	SS24,2B19,1B4*	R	29	49	159	15	37	2	0	0	12	25	9	3	.233	.341	.245
Hal Chase†	1B29,2B5,OF5	R	30	39	146	15	31	2	4	0	9	11	13	5	.212	.268	.281
Bill McKechnie†	2B28,SS7,3B2	S	26	44	112	7	15	0	0	0	8	8	17	2	.134	.198	.134
Babe Borton†	1B33	L	24	33	108	8	14	2	0	0	11	18	19	1	.130	.260	.148
Dick Gossett	C38	R	21	39	105	9	17	2	0	0	9	10	22	1	.162	.254	.181
Ray Caldwell	P27,OF3	L	25	59	97	10	28	3	2	0	11	3	15	3	.289	.310	.361
Frank Gilhooley	OF24	L	21	24	85	10	29	2	1	0	14	4	9	6	.341	.378	.388
Harry Williams	1B27	R	23	27	82	18	21	3	1	1	12	15	10	6	.256	.378	.354
Doc Cook	OF20	L	27	20	72	9	19	2	1	0	1	10	4	1	.264	.369	.319
Claud Derrick	SS13,3B4,2B2	R	27	22	65	7	19	1	0	1	7	5	8	2	.292	.352	.354
Bill Holden	OF16	R	23	18	53	6	16	3	1	0	8	8	5	0	.302	.393	.396
Dutch Sterrett	1B6,C1,OF1	R	23	21	35	0	6	0	0	0	3	1	5	1	.171	.216	.171
Joe Smith	C13	R	19	13	32	1	5	0	0	0	2	1	14	1	.156	.182	.156
George Whiteman	OF11	R	30	11	32	8	11	3	1	0	2	7	2	2	.344	.462	.500
Bill Stumpf	SS6,2B5,OF1	R	21	12	29	5	6	1	0	0	1	3	3	0	.207	.281	.241
Jack Lelivelt†	OF5	L	27	18	28	2	6	0	1	0	4	2	2	1	.214	.267	.286
Frank Chance	1B7	R	35	11	24	3	5	0	0	0	6	8	1	1	.208	.406	.208
Bob Williams	C6	R	29	6	19	0	3	0	0	0	0	1	3	0	.158	.200	.158
Ralph Young	SS7	S	23	7	15	2	1	0	0	0	0	3	3	2	.067	.222	.067
Luke Boone	SS4	R	23	5	12	3	4	0	0	0	1	3	1	0	.333	.467	.333
Bill Reynolds	C5	R	28	5	5	0	0	0	0	0	0	0	1	0	.000	.000	.000
Joe Hanson	C1	—	17	1	2	0	0	0	0	0	0	0	0	0	.000	.000	.000
Dan Costello		L	21	2	2	1	1	0	0	0	0	0	0	0	.500	.500	.500

R. Hartzell, 4 G at SS; R. Zeider, 2 G at 3B

Pitcher	T	Age	G	GS	CG	ShO	IP	H	HR	BB	SO	W-L	Sv	ERA
Ray Fisher	R	25	43	31	15	1	246.1	244	3	71	92	12-16	1	3.18
Russ Ford	R	30	33	28	15	1	237.0	244	9	58	72	12-18	2	2.66
Al Schulz	L	24	38	22	9	0	192.2	197	4	69	77	7-13	0	3.74
Ray Keating	R	21	28	21	9	2	151.1	147	3	51	83	6-12	0	3.21
George McConnell	R	35	35	20	8	0	180.0	162	2	60	72	4-15	3	3.20
Ray Caldwell	R	25	27	16	15	2	164.1	131	5	60	87	9-8	1	2.41
Marty McHale	R	24	7	6	4	1	48.2	49	1	10	11	2-4	0	2.96
Jack Warhop	R	28	15	7	1	0	62.1	69	1	33	11	4-6	0	3.75
George Clark	L	22	11	1	0	0	19.0	22	1	19	5	0-1	0	9.00
Ed Klepfer	R	25	8	1	0	0	24.2	38	2	12	10	0-1	0	7.66
Cy Pieh	R	26	4	0	0	0	10.1	10	0	7	6	1-0	0	4.35
Red Hoff	L	22	2	0	0	0	3.0	0	0	1	2	0-0	0	0.00
Jim Hanley	L	27	1	0	0	0	4.0	5	0	4	2	0-0	0	6.75

1913 St. Louis Browns 8th AL 57-96 .373 39.0 GB

George Stovall (50-84)/Jimmy Austin (2-6)/Branch Rickey (5-6)

Player	Gm by Position	B	Age	G	AB	R	H	2B	3B	HR	RBI	BB	SO	SB	Avg	OBP	Slg
Sam Agnew	C103	R	26	104	307	27	64	9	5	2	24	20	49	11	.208	.272	.290
George Stovall	1B76	R	34	89	303	34	87	14	3	1	24	7	23	7	.287	.305	.363
Del Pratt	2B146,1B9	R	25	155	592	60	175	31	13	2	87	40	57	37	.296	.341	.402
Jimmy Austin	3B142	S	33	142	489	56	130	18	6	2	42	45	51	37	.266	.338	.339
Mike Balenti	SS56,OF8	R	26	70	211	17	38	2	4	0	11	6	32	3	.180	.206	.227
Burt Shotton	OF146	L	28	147	549	105	163	23	8	1	28	99	63	43	.297	.405	.373
Gus Williams	OF143	L	25	149	538	72	147	21	16	5	53	57	87	31	.273	.346	.400
Johnny Johnston	OF106	L	23	109	380	37	85	14	4	2	27	42	51	11	.224	.308	.297
Bunny Brief	1B62,OF8	R	20	84	258	24	56	11	6	1	26	22	46	3	.217	.286	.318
Doc Lavan†	SS46	R	22	46	149	8	21	2	1	0	4	10	46	3	.141	.210	.168
Bobby Wallace	SS39,3B7	R	39	55	147	11	31	5	0	0	21	14	16	1	.211	.293	.245
Walt Alexander	C43	R	22	43	110	5	15	2	1	0	7	5	36	1	.136	.181	.173
Pete Compton	OF21	L	23	63	100	14	18	5	2	2	17	13	13	2	.180	.274	.330
Bill McAllester	C37	R	24	47	85	3	13	4	0	0	6	11	12	2	.153	.250	.200
Tilly Walker	OF23	R	25	23	85	7	25	4	1	0	11	2	9	5	.294	.310	.365
Sam Covington	1B16	L	20	20	60	3	9	0	1	0	4	4	6	3	.150	.203	.183
Dee Walsh	SS22,3B1	S	23	23	53	8	9	0	1	0	5	6	11	3	.170	.302	.208
Rivington Bisland	SS12	R	23	12	44	3	6	0	0	0	3	2	5	0	.136	.191	.136
Buzzy Wares	2B9	R	27	11	35	5	10	2	0	0	1	1	3	2	.286	.306	.343
Tod Sloan	OF7	L	22	7	26	2	7	1	0	0	2	1	9	1	.269	.321	.308
George Maisel	OF5	R	21	11	18	2	3	1	0	0	1	1	7	0	.167	.211	.278
Ernie Walker	OF2	L	22	7	14	0	3	0	0	0	2	0	5	0	.214	.214	.214
Walt Meinert	OF2	L	22	4	8	1	3	0	0	0	1	1	1	0	.375	.444	.375
Fred Graff	3B4	R	23	4	5	1	2	1	0	0	2	3	3	0	.400	.625	.600
Frank Crossin	C2	R	22	4	4	1	1	0	0	0	0	1	1	0	.250	.500	.250
Charlie Flanagan	3B1,OF1	R	21	4	3	0	0	0	0	0	0	1	0	0	.000	.250	.000
George Tomer		L	17	1	1	0	0	0	0	0	0	0	1	0	.000	.000	.000
Luther Bonin		L	25	1	1	0	0	0	0	0	0	0	0	0	.000	.000	.000

Pitcher	T	Age	G	GS	CG	ShO	IP	H	HR	BB	SO	W-L	Sv	ERA
G. Baumgardner	R	21	38	31	22	2	253.1	267	6	84	78	10-19	1	3.13
Carl Weilman	L	23	39	28	17	2	251.2	262	2	60	79	10-20	0	3.40
Roy Mitchell	R	28	33	27	21	4	245.1	265	6	47	59	13-16	1	3.01
Walt Leverenz	L	25	30	27	13	2	202.2	159	3	89	87	6-17	1	2.58
Earl Hamilton	L	21	31	24	19	3	217.1	197	3	83	101	13-12	0	2.36
Wiley Taylor	R	25	5	4	1	0	31.2	33	0	16	12	0-2	0	4.83
Curly Brown	L	24	2	2	2	0	14.0	12	0	4	3	1-1	0	2.57
Hal Schwenk	L	22	1	1	1	0	11.0	12	0	4	3	1-0	0	3.27
Dwight Stone	R	26	18	7	4	1	91.0	94	0	46	37	2-6	0	3.56
Mack Allison	R	26	11	4	3	0	51.1	52	0	13	12	1-3	0	2.28
Willie Adams	R	22	4	0	0	0	9.0	12	1	4	5	0-0	0	10.00
Jack Powell	R	21	2	0	0	0	2.0	1	0	2	0	0-0	0	0.00
Pete Schmidt	R	22	1	0	0	0	2.0	3	0	2	0	0-0	1	4.50

»1913 New York Giants 1st NL 101-51 .664 —

John McGraw

Player	Gm by Position	B	Age	G	AB	R	H	2B	3B	HR	RBI	BB	SO	SB	Avg	OBP	Slg
Chief Meyers	C116	R	32	120	378	37	118	18	5	3	47	37	22	7	.312	.387	.410
Fred Merkle	1B153	R	24	153	563	78	147	30	13	2	69	41	60	35	.261	.315	.371
Larry Doyle	2B130	L	26	132	482	67	135	25	6	5	73	59	29	38	.280	.364	.388
Buck Herzog	3B84,2B2	R	27	96	290	46	83	15	3	3	31	22	12	23	.286	.349	.390
Art Fletcher	SS136	R	28	136	538	76	160	20	9	4	71	24	35	32	.297	.345	.390
George Burns	OF150	R	23	150	605	81	173	37	4	2	54	58	74	40	.286	.352	.370
Red Murray	OF147	R	29	147	520	70	139	21	3	2	59	34	28	35	.267	.320	.331
Fred Snodgrass	OF133,1B3,2B1	R	25	141	457	65	133	21	6	3	49	53	44	27	.291	.373	.383
Tillie Shafer	3B79,2B25,SS16*	S	24	138	508	74	146	17	12	5	52	61	55	32	.287	.369	.398
Moose McCormick	OF15	L	32	57	80	9	22	2	3	0	15	5	13	0	.275	.318	.375
Art Wilson	C49,1B2	R	27	54	79	5	15	0	1	0	8	11	11	1	.190	.289	.215
Larry McLean†	C28	R	31	30	75	3	24	4	0	0	9	4	4	1	.320	.354	.373
Doc Crandall†	P35,2B1	R	25	46	47	7	15	4	1	0	4	3	8	0	.319	.360	.447
Jim Thorpe	OF9	R	26	19	35	6	5	0	0	1	2	1	9	2	.143	.167	.229
Claude Cooper	OF15	L	21	27	30	11	9	4	0	0	4	4	6	3	.300	.382	.433
Hooks Wiltse	P17,1B3	R	32	20	24	2	5	1	0	0	2	0	1	1	.208	.208	.250
Josh Devore†	OF8	L	25	16	21	4	4	0	1	0	1	3	4	6	.190	.320	.286
Eddie Grant†	3B5,2B3,SS1	L	30	27	20	8	4	1	0	0	1	2	2	1	.200	.273	.250
Grover Hartley	C21,1B1	R	24	23	19	4	6	0	0	0	0	1	2	4	.316	.350	.316
Milt Stock	SS7	R	19	7	17	2	3	1	0	0	1	2	1	2	.176	.263	.235
Heine Groh†	3B2,SS1	R	23	4	2	0	0	0	0	0	0	0	1	0	.000	.000	.000
John Merritt	OF1	R	18	1	0	0	0	0	0	0	0	0	0	0	—	—	—
Joe Evers		R	21	1	0	0	0	0	0	0	0	0	0	0	—	—	—

T. Shafer, 15 G at OF

Pitcher	T	Age	G	GS	CG	ShO	IP	H	HR	BB	SO	W-L	Sv	ERA
Jeff Tesreau	R	24	41	38	17	1	282.0	222	7	119	167	22-13	0	2.17
Christy Mathewson	R	34	40	35	25	4	306.0	291	8	21	93	25-11	2	2.06
Rube Marquard	L	26	42	33	20	4	288.0	248	10	49	151	23-10	3	2.50
Al Demaree	R	28	31	24	11	2	199.2	176	4	38	76	13-4	2	2.21
Art Fromme†	R	29	26	13	3	0	112.1	112	5	29	50	11-6	0	4.01
Red Ames†	R	30	8	5	2	0	41.2	35	0	8	30	2-1	1	2.16
Bunny Hearn	L	22	2	2	1	0	13.0	13	0	7	8	1-1	0	2.77
Doc Crandall	R	25	35	2	2	0	97.2	102	3	24	42	4-4	6	2.86
Hooks Wiltse	L	32	17	2	0	0	57.2	53	1	8	25	0-0	3	1.56
Ferdie Schupp	L	22	5	1	0	0	12.0	10	0	3	2	0-0	0	0.75
Rube Schauer	R	22	3	1	1	0	12.0	14	0	9	7	0-1	0	7.50

1913 Philadelphia Phillies 2nd NL 88-63 .583 12.5 GB

Red Dooin

Player	Gm by Position	B	Age	G	AB	R	H	2B	3B	HR	RBI	BB	SO	SB	Avg	OBP	Slg
Bill Killefer	C118	R	25	120	360	25	88	14	3	0	24	4	17	2	.244	.255	.300
Fred Luderus	1B155	L	27	155	588	67	154	32	7	18	86	34	51	5	.262	.304	.432
Otto Knabe	2B148	R	29	148	571	70	150	25	7	2	53	45	26	14	.263	.320	.342
Hans Lobert	3B145,SS3,2B1	R	31	150	573	98	172	28	11	7	55	42	34	41	.300	.353	.424
Mickey Doolan	SS148,2B3	R	33	151	518	32	113	12	6	1	43	29	68	17	.218	.262	.270
Gavy Cravath	OF141	R	32	147	525	78	179	34	14	19	128	55	63	10	.341	.407	.568
Sherry Magee	OF123,1B4	R	28	138	470	92	144	36	6	11	70	38	36	23	.306	.369	.479
Dode Paskert	OF120	R	31	124	454	83	119	21	9	4	29	65	69	12	.262	.358	.374
Beals Becker†	OF77,1B1	L	26	88	306	53	99	19	10	9	44	22	30	11	.324	.369	.539
Red Dooin	C50	R	34	55	129	6	33	4	1	0	13	3	9	1	.256	.273	.302
Cozy Dolan†	OF12,SS10,2B9*	R	23	55	126	15	33	4	0	0	8	1	21	9	.262	.273	.294
Doc Miller	OF12	L	30	69	87	9	30	6	0	0	11	6	6	2	.345	.400	.414
Bobby Byrne†	3B15	R	28	19	58	9	13	1	0	1	4	5	3	2	.224	.308	.293
Josh Devore†	OF14	L	25	23	39	9	11	1	0	0	5	4	7	0	.282	.364	.308
Dan Howley	C22	R	27	26	32	5	4	2	0	0	2	4	4	3	.125	.222	.188
Ed Burns	C15	R	24	17	30	3	6	3	0	0	3	6	3	2	.200	.351	.300
Jimmy Walsh	2B6,SS3,3B1*	R	27	26	30	3	10	4	0	0	5	1	5	1	.333	.355	.467
Milt Reed	SS9,2B3	L	22	13	24	4	6	1	0	0	0	1	5	1	.250	.280	.292
Vern Duncan	OF3	L	23	8	12	3	5	1	0	0	1	0	3	0	.417	.417	.500
Doc Imlay	P9,1B1	R	24	9	3	0	0	0	0	0	0	0	1	0	.000	.000	.000
John Dodge†	SS3	R	24	3	3	0	1	0	0	0	0	2	0	0	.333	.600	.333
Ralph Capron	OF1	L	24	2	1	1	0	0	0	0	0	0	0	0	.000	.000	.000
Pat Moran		R	37	1	1	0	0	0	0	0	0	0	0	0	.000	.000	.000

C. Dolan, 4 G at 3B, 1 G at 1B; J. Walsh, 1 G at OF

Pitcher	T	Age	G	GS	CG	ShO	IP	H	HR	BB	SO	W-L	Sv	ERA
Pete Alexander	R	26	47	36	23	9	306.1	288	9	75	159	22-8	2	2.79
Tom Seaton	R	25	52	35	21	6	322.1	262	6	136	168	27-12	1	2.60
Ad Brennan	L	31	40	25	12	1	207.0	204	5	46	94	14-12	1	2.39
Eppa Rixey	L	22	35	19	9	2	155.2	148	4	56	75	9-5	2	3.12
George Chalmers	R	25	26	14	4	0	116.0	133	3	51	46	3-10	1	4.81
Howie Camnitz†	R	31	9	5	1	0	49.0	49	1	23	21	3-3	1	3.67
Erskine Mayer	R	24	39	19	7	2	170.2	172	6	46	51	9-9	1	3.11
Rube Marshall	R	23	14	1	0	0	45.1	54	2	22	18	0-1	1	4.57
Earl Moore†	R	33	12	5	0	0	52.0	50	3	40	24	1-3	1	5.02
Doc Imlay	R	24	9	0	0	0	13.2	19	1	7	7	0-0	0	7.24
Happy Finneran	R	21	3	0	0	0	5.0	12	0	2	0	0-0	0	7.20
Red Nelson†	R	27	2	0	0	0	8.1	9	0	4	3	0-0	0	2.16
Jim Haislip	R	21	1	0	0	0	3.0	4	0	3	0	0-0	0	6.00
Ray Hartranft	L	22	1	0	0	0	1.0	3	1	1	1	0-0	0	9.00

1913 Chicago Cubs 3rd NL 88-65 .575 13.5 GB

Johnny Evers

Player	Gm by Position	B	Age	G	AB	R	H	2B	3B	HR	RBI	BB	SO	SB	Avg	OBP	Slg
Jimmy Archer	C103,1B8	R	30	111	368	38	98	14	7	2	44	19	27	4	.266	.311	.359
Vic Saier	1B149	L	22	149	519	94	150	15	21	14	92	62	62	26	.289	.370	.480
Johnny Evers	2B136	L	31	136	446	81	127	20	5	3	49	50	14	11	.285	.361	.372
Heinie Zimmerman	3B125	R	26	127	447	69	140	28	12	9	95	41	40	18	.313	.379	.490
Al Bridwell	SS136	L	29	136	405	35	97	6	6	1	37	74	28	12	.240	.358	.291
Wildfire Schulte	OF130	L	30	132	497	85	138	28	6	9	68	39	68	21	.278	.336	.412
Tommy Leach	OF129,3B2	R	35	131	456	99	131	23	10	6	32	77	44	21	.287	.391	.421
Mike Mitchell†	OF81	R	33	82	279	37	73	11	6	4	35	32	33	15	.262	.340	.387
Art Phelan	2B46,3B38,SS1	R	25	91	261	41	65	11	6	2	35	29	26	8	.249	.331	.360
Ward Miller	OF63	L	28	80	203	23	48	5	7	1	16	34	33	13	.236	.349	.345
Roger Bresnahan	C58	R	34	69	162	20	37	5	2	1	21	21	11	7	.228	.324	.302
Cy Williams	OF44	L	25	49	156	17	35	3	3	4	32	5	26	5	.224	.262	.359
Otis Clymer†	OF26	S	37	30	105	16	24	5	1	0	7	14	18	9	.229	.319	.295
Red Corriden	SS36,2B2,3B1	R	25	46	97	13	17	3	0	2	9	10	14	4	.175	.252	.268
Wilbur Good	OF26	L	27	49	91	11	23	3	2	1	12	11	16	5	.253	.340	.363
Tom Needham	C14,1B1	R	34	20	42	5	10	4	1	0	11	4	8	0	.238	.304	.381
Tuffy Stewart	OF1	L	29	9	8	1	1	1	0	0	2	2	5	1	.125	.300	.250
Fritz Mollwitz	1B2	R	23	2	7	1	3	0	0	0	0	0	0	0	.429	.429	.429
Milo Allison	OF1	L	22	2	6	1	2	0	0	0	0	0	1	1	.333	.333	.333
Chick Keating	SS2	R	21	2	5	1	1	1	0	0	0	0	1	0	.200	.200	.400
Bubbles Hargrave	C2	R	20	3	3	0	1	0	0	0	1	0	0	0	.333	.333	.333
Mike Hechinger†		R	23	2	2	0	0	0	0	0	0	0	0	0	.000	.000	.000
Pete Knisely		R	25	2	2	0	0	0	0	0	0	0	1	0	.000	.000	.000
Ed McDonald		R	26	1	0	0	0	0	0	0	0	0	0	0	—	—	—

Pitcher	T	Age	G	GS	CG	ShO	IP	H	HR	BB	SO	W-L	Sv	ERA
Larry Cheney	R	27	54	36	25	2	305.0	271	7	98	136	21-14	11	2.57
George Pearce	L	25	25	21	14	3	163.2	137	4	59	73	13-5	0	2.31
Jimmy Lavender	R	29	40	20	10	0	204.0	206	6	98	91	10-14	2	3.66
Bert Humphries	R	32	28	20	13	2	181.0	169	10	24	61	16-4	1	2.69
Charlie Smith	R	33	20	17	8	1	137.2	138	2	34	47	7-9	0	2.55
Orval Overall	R	32	11	9	6	1	68.0	73	1	26	30	4-5	0	3.31
Eddie Stack†	R	25	11	7	3	1	51.0	56	1	15	28	4-2	1	4.24
Hippo Vaughn	L	25	7	6	5	2	56.0	37	0	27	36	5-1	0	1.45
Fred Toney	R	24	7	5	2	0	39.0	52	1	22	12	2-2	0	6.00
Doc Watson	L	27	1	1	1	0	9.0	8	0	6	1	1-0	0	1.00
Zip Zabel	R	22	1	1	0	0	5.0	3	0	1	0	1-0	0	0.00
Lew Richie	R	29	16	5	1	0	65.0	77	3	30	15	2-4	0	5.82
Ed Reulbach†	R	30	10	3	1	0	38.2	41	1	21	10	1-3	0	4.42
Earl Moore†	R	33	7	2	0	0	28.1	34	3	12	12	1-1	0	4.45
Lefty Leifield	L	29	6	1	0	0	21.1	28	0	5	4	0-1	0	5.48

1913 Pittsburgh Pirates 4th NL 78-71 .523 21.5 GB

Fred Clarke

Player	Gm by Position	B	Age	G	AB	R	H	2B	3B	HR	RBI	BB	SO	SB	Avg	OBP	Slg
Mike Simon	C92	R	30	92	255	23	63	6	2	1	17	10	15	3	.247	.281	.298
Dots Miller	1B150,SS3	R	26	154	580	75	158	24	20	7	90	37	52	20	.272	.317	.419
Jim Viox	2B124,SS10	R	22	137	492	86	156	32	8	2	65	64	28	14	.317	.399	.427
Bobby Byrne†	3B110	R	28	113	448	54	121	22	0	1	47	29	28	10	.270	.322	.326
Honus Wagner	SS105	R	39	114	413	51	124	18	4	3	56	26	40	21	.300	.349	.385
Chief Wilson	OF155	L	29	155	580	71	154	12	14	10	73	32	62	9	.266	.307	.386
Max Carey	OF154	S	23	154	620	99	172	23	10	5	49	55	67	61	.277	.339	.371
Mike Mitchell†	OF54	R	33	54	199	25	54	8	2	1	16	14	15	8	.271	.319	.347
Art Butler	2B28,SS26,3B2*	R	25	82	214	40	60	9	3	0	20	32	14	9	.280	.379	.350
Fred Kommers	OF40	L	27	40	155	14	36	5	4	0	22	10	29	1	.232	.279	.316
Cozy Dolan†	3B35	R	23	35	133	22	27	5	2	0	9	15	14	14	.203	.289	.271
George Gibson	C48	R	32	48	118	6	33	4	2	0	12	10	8	2	.280	.341	.347
Solly Hofman	OF24	R	30	28	83	11	19	5	2	0	7	8	6	3	.229	.297	.337
Billy Kelly	C40	R	27	48	82	11	22	2	2	0	9	2	12	1	.268	.302	.341
Ham Hyatt	1B5,OF5	L	28	63	81	8	27	6	2	4	16	3	8	0	.333	.372	.605
Everitt Booe	OF22	L	21	29	80	9	16	0	2	0	2	6	9	2	.200	.256	.250
Alex McCarthy	3B12,SS12,2B6	R	25	31	74	7	15	5	0	0	10	7	7	1	.203	.298	.270
Ed Mensor	OF18,2B1,SS1	S	26	44	56	9	10	1	0	0	1	8	13	2	.179	.292	.196
Bob Coleman	C24	R	22	24	50	5	9	2	0	0	9	7	8	0	.180	.281	.220
Roy Wood	OF8,1B1	R	20	14	35	4	10	4	0	0	2	1	8	0	.286	.306	.400
Fred Clarke	OF2	L	40	9	13	0	1	1	0	0	0	0	0	0	.077	.077	.154
Gil Britton	SS3	R	21	3	12	0	0	0	0	0	0	0	2	0	.000	.000	.000
Jake Kafora	C1	R	24	1	1	1	0	0	0	0	0	0	1	0	.000	.500	.000

A. Butler, 2 G at OF

Pitcher	T	Age	G	GS	CG	ShO	IP	H	HR	BB	SO	W-L	Sv	ERA
Babe Adams	R	31	43	37	24	4	313.2	271	8	49	144	21-10	0	2.15
Claude Hendrix	R	24	42	25	17	2	241.0	216	3	89	138	14-15	3	2.84
Hank Robinson	L	23	43	23	8	1	196.1	184	1	41	50	14-9	0	2.38
Howie Camnitz†	R	31	36	21	5	1	192.1	203	7	84	64	6-17	2	3.74
Marty O'Toole	R	24	26	16	7	0	144.2	148	3	55	58	6-8	1	3.30
George McQuillan	R	28	25	16	7	0	141.2	144	1	35	59	8-6	1	3.43
Wild Bill Luhrsen	R	29	5	3	2	0	29.0	25	3	16	11	3-1	0	2.48
Joe Conzelman	R	27	3	2	1	0	15.0	13	0	5	9	0-1	0	1.20
Bernie Duffy	R	19	3	2	0	0	11.1	18	0	3	8	0-0	0	5.56
John Scheneberg	R	25	1	1	0	0	6.0	10	0	2	1	0-1	0	6.00
Wilbur Cooper	L	21	30	9	3	1	93.0	98	0	45	39	5-3	0	3.29
Jack Ferry	R	26	4	0	0	0	5.0	4	0	2	2	1-0	0	5.40
Eddie Eayrs	L	22	2	0	0	0	8.0	8	0	6	5	0-0	0	2.25
Al Mamaux	R	19	1	0	0	0	3.0	2	0	2	2	0-0	0	3.00

586 Seasons: Team Rosters

1913 Boston Braves 5th NL 69-82 .457 31.5 GB

George Stallings

Player	Gm by Position	B	Age	G	AB	R	H	2B	3B	HR	RBI	BB	SO	SB	Avg	OBP	Slg
Bill Rariden	C87	R	25	95	246	31	58	9	2	3	30	30	21	5	.236	.324	.325
Hap Myers	1B135	R	25	140	524	74	143	20	1	2	50	38	48	57	.273	.333	.326
Bill Sweeney	2B137	R	27	139	502	65	129	17	6	0	47	66	50	18	.257	.347	.315
Art Devlin	3B69	R	33	73	210	19	48	7	5	0	12	29	17	8	.229	.328	.310
Rabbit Maranville	SS143	R	21	143	571	68	141	13	8	2	48	68	62	25	.247	.330	.308
Joe Connolly	OF124	L	25	126	427	79	120	18	11	5	57	66	47	18	.281	.379	.410
Les Mann	OF120	R	19	120	407	54	103	24	7	3	51	18	73	7	.253	.291	.369
John Titus	OF75	L	37	87	269	33	80	14	2	5	38	35	22	4	.297	.392	.420
Fred Smith	3B59,2B14,SS11*	R	21	92	285	35	65	9	3	0	27	29	55	7	.228	.302	.281
Bris Lord	OF62	R	29	73	235	22	59	12	1	6	26	8	22	7	.251	.276	.387
Bert Whaling	C77	R	25	79	211	22	51	8	2	0	25	10	32	3	.242	.283	.299
Tex McDonald†	3B31,2B6,OF1	L	22	62	145	24	52	4	4	0	18	15	17	4	.359	.422	.441
Guy Zinn	OF35	L	26	36	138	15	41	8	2	1	15	4	23	3	.297	.322	.406
Tommy Griffith	OF35	L	23	37	127	16	32	4	1	1	12	9	8	1	.252	.301	.323
Butch Schmidt	1B22	L	26	22	78	6	24	2	2	1	14	2	5	1	.308	.333	.423
Cy Seymour	OF18	L	40	39	73	2	13	2	0	0	10	7	7	2	.178	.259	.205
Jay Kirke	OF13	L	25	18	38	3	9	2	0	0	3	1	6	0	.237	.293	.289
Otis Clymer†	OF11	S	37	14	37	4	12	3	1	0	6	3	3	2	.324	.375	.459
Charlie Deal†	2B10	R	21	10	36	6	11	1	0	0	3	2	1	1	.306	.359	.333
Drummond Brown	C12	R	28	15	34	3	11	1	0	1	2	2	9	0	.324	.361	.441
Joe Schultz	OF5,2B1	R	19	9	18	2	4	0	0	0	1	2	7	0	.222	.333	.222
Bill Calhoun	1B3	L	23	6	13	0	1	0	0	0	0	0	3	0	.077	.077	.077
George Jackson	OF3	R	30	3	10	2	3	0	0	0	0	0	2	0	.300	.300	.300
Oscar Dugey	3B2,2B1,SS1	R	25	5	8	1	2	0	0	0	0	1	1	0	.250	.333	.250
Rex DeVogt	C3	R	25	3	6	0	0	0	0	0	0	0	3	0	.000	.000	.000
Hank Gowdy	C2	R	23	3	5	0	3	1	0	0	2	3	2	0	.600	.750	.800
Bill McKechnie†	OF1	S	26	1	4	1	0	0	0	0	0	0	1	0	.000	.200	.000
Jeff McCleskey	3B2	L	21	2	3	0	0	0	0	0	0	1	0	0	.000	.250	.000
Wilson Collins	OF9	R	24	16	3	3	1	0	0	0	0	0	1	0	.333	.333	.333
Fred Mitchell		R	35	4	3	0	1	0	0	0	0	0	2	0	.333	.333	.333
Art Bues		R	25	2	1	0	0	0	0	0	0	0	1	0	.000	.000	.000
Walt Tragesser	C2	R	26	2	0	0	0	0	0	0	0	0	0	0	—	—	—
Bill McTigue		L	22	1	0	0	0	0	0	0	0	0	0	0	—	—	—

F. Smith, 4 G at OF

Pitcher	T	Age	G	GS	CG	ShO	IP	H	HR	BB	SO	W-L	Sv	ERA
Lefty Tyler	L	23	39	34	28	4	290.1	245	2	108	143	16-17	2	2.79
Hub Perdue	R	31	38	32	16	3	212.1	201	7	39	91	16-13	1	3.26
Otto Hess	L	34	29	27	19	2	218.2	231	12	70	80	7-17	0	3.83
Dick Rudolph	R	25	33	22	17	2	249.1	258	4	59	109	14-13	0	2.92
Walt Dickson	R	34	19	15	8	0	128.0	118	4	45	47	6-7	0	3.23
Bill James	R	21	24	14	10	1	135.2	134	4	57	73	6-10	0	2.79
Jack Quinn	R	29	8	7	6	1	56.1	55	1	7	33	4-3	0	2.40
Gene Cocreham	R	28	1	1	0	0	8.1	13	0	4	3	0-1	0	7.56
Wynn Noyes	R	24	11	0	0	0	20.2	22	1	6	5	0-0	0	4.79
Paul Strand	L	19	7	0	0	0	17.0	22	1	12	6	0-0	0	2.12
Lefty Gervais	L	22	5	2	1	0	15.2	18	0	4	1	0-1	0	5.74
Buster Brown	R	31	2	0	0	0	13.1	19	0	3	3	0-0	0	4.73
Iron Davis	R	23	2	0	0	0	8.0	7	1	5	3	0-0	0	4.50

1913 Brooklyn Dodgers 6th NL 65-84 .436 34.5 GB

Bill Dahlen

Player	Gm by Position	B	Age	G	AB	R	H	2B	3B	HR	RBI	BB	SO	SB	Avg	OBP	Slg
Otto Miller	C103,1B1	R	24	104	320	26	87	11	7	0	26	10	31	7	.272	.294	.350
Jake Daubert	1B139	L	29	139	508	76	178	17	7	2	52	44	40	25	.350	.405	.423
George Cutshaw	2B147	R	25	147	592	72	158	23	13	7	80	39	22	39	.267	.315	.385
Red Smith	3B151	R	23	151	540	70	160	40	10	6	76	45	67	22	.296	.358	.441
Tom Fisher	SS131	R	26	132	474	42	124	11	10	4	54	10	43	16	.262	.278	.352
Zack Wheat	OF135	L	25	138	535	64	161	28	10	7	58	25	45	19	.301	.335	.430
Herbie Moran	OF129	L	29	132	515	71	137	15	5	0	26	45	29	21	.266	.333	.315
Casey Stengel	OF119	L	22	124	438	60	119	16	8	7	43	56	58	19	.272	.356	.393
John Hummel	OF28,SS17,1B6*	R	30	67	198	20	48	7	7	2	24	13	23	4	.242	.292	.379
William Fischer	C51	L	22	62	165	16	44	9	4	1	12	10	5	0	.267	.313	.388
Bill Collins	OF27	S	31	32	95	8	18	1	0	0	4	8	11	2	.189	.267	.200
Enos Kirkpatrick	SS10,1B8,2B6*	R	27	48	89	13	22	4	1	1	5	3	18	5	.247	.287	.348
Benny Meyer	OF26,C1	R	25	38	87	12	17	0	1	1	10	10	14	8	.195	.278	.253
Leo Callahan	OF8	L	22	33	41	6	7	3	1	0	3	4	5	0	.171	.244	.293
Tex Erwin	C13	L	27	20	31	6	8	1	0	0	3	4	5	0	.258	.343	.290
Lew McCarty	C9	R	24	9	26	1	6	0	0	0	2	2	2	0	.231	.286	.231
Al Scheer	OF6	L	24	6	22	3	5	0	0	0	0	2	4	1	.227	.292	.227
Ed Phelps	C4	R	34	15	18	0	4	0	0	0	0	1	2	0	.222	.263	.222
Mike Hechinger†	C4	R	23	9	11	1	2	1	0	0	0	0	2	0	.182	.182	.273
Ray Mowe	SS2	L	23	5	9	0	1	0	0	0	0	0	1	0	.111	.200	.111

J. Hummel, 3 G at 2B; E. Kirkpatrick, 4 G at 3B

Pitcher	T	Age	G	GS	CG	ShO	IP	H	HR	BB	SO	W-L	Sv	ERA
Nap Rucker	L	28	41	33	16	4	260.0	236	3	67	111	14-15	3	2.87
Pat Ragan	R	24	44	32	14	0	264.2	284	10	64	109	15-18	0	3.77
Frank Allen	L	23	34	25	11	0	174.2	144	6	81	82	4-18	2	2.83
Cliff Curtis	R	29	30	16	6	0	151.2	145	1	55	57	8-9	2	3.26
Earl Yingling	L	24	26	13	8	2	146.2	158	2	10	40	8-8	0	2.58
Ed Reulbach†	R	30	15	12	8	2	110.0	77	3	34	46	7-6	0	2.05
Mysterious Walker	R	29	11	8	3	0	58.1	44	3	35	35	1-3	0	3.55
Eddie Stack†	R	25	23	9	4	1	87.0	79	0	32	34	4-4	0	2.38
Bull Wagner	R	25	18	1	0	0	70.2	77	5	30	11	4-2	0	5.48
Jeff Pfeffer	R	25	5	2	1	0	24.1	28	0	13	13	0-1	0	3.33
Elmer Brown	R	30	3	1	0	0	13.0	6	0	10	6	0-0	0	2.08
Maury Kent	R	27	3	0	0	0	7.1	5	0	3	1	0-0	0	2.45
Bill Hall	R	19	3	0	0	0	4.2	4	0	5	3	0-0	0	5.79

1913 Cincinnati Reds 7th NL 64-89 .418 37.5 GB

Joe Tinker

Player	Gm by Position	B	Age	G	AB	R	H	2B	3B	HR	RBI	BB	SO	SB	Avg	OBP	Slg
Tommy Clarke	C100	R	25	114	330	29	87	11	8	1	38	39	40	2	.264	.345	.355
Doc Hoblitzell	1B134	R	24	137	502	59	143	23	7	3	62	35	26	18	.285	.334	.376
Heine Groh†	2B113,SS4	R	23	117	397	51	112	19	5	3	48	38	36	24	.282	.351	.378
John Dodge†	3B91	R	24	94	323	35	78	8	8	4	45	10	34	11	.241	.269	.353
Joe Tinker	SS101,3B9	R	32	110	382	47	121	20	13	1	57	20	26	10	.317	.352	.445
Bob Bescher	OF138	S	29	141	511	86	132	22	11	1	37	94	68	38	.258	.377	.350
Johnny Bates	OF111	L	30	131	407	63	113	13	7	6	51	67	30	21	.278	.388	.388
Armando Marsans	OF94,1B22,3B2*	R	25	118	435	49	129	7	6	0	38	17	25	37	.297	.327	.340
Josh Devore†	OF57	L	25	66	217	30	58	6	4	3	14	12	21	17	.267	.309	.373
Johnny Kling	C63	R	38	80	209	20	57	7	6	0	23	14	14	2	.273	.318	.364
Dick Egan	2B37,SS17,3B2	R	29	60	195	15	55	7	3	0	22	15	13	6	.282	.333	.349
Marty Berghammer	SS54,2B13	L	25	74	188	25	41	4	1	1	13	10	29	16	.218	.269	.266
Rafael Almeida	3B37,OF3,SS2*	R	25	50	130	14	34	4	2	3	21	11	16	4	.262	.324	.392
Jimmy Sheckard†	OF38	L	34	47	116	16	22	1	3	0	7	27	16	6	.190	.343	.250
Beals Becker†	OF28	L	26	30	108	11	32	5	3	0	14	6	12	0	.296	.333	.398
Eddie Grant†	3B26	L	30	27	94	12	20	1	0	0	9	11	10	7	.213	.295	.223
Al Wickland	OF24	L	25	26	79	7	17	5	5	0	8	6	19	3	.215	.279	.405
Earl Blackburn	C12	R	20	17	27	1	7	0	0	0	3	2	5	2	.259	.310	.259
Tex McDonald†	SS1	L	22	11	10	1	3	0	0	0	2	0	1	0	.300	.300	.300
Bert Niehoff	3B2	R	29	2	8	0	0	0	0	0	0	0	2	0	.000	.000	.000
Karl Meister	OF4	R	22	4	7	1	2	1	0	0	2	0	4	0	.286	.286	.429
Hank Severeid	C2,OF1	R	22	8	6	0	0	0	0	0	0	1	1	0	.000	.143	.000
Bill Hobbs	2B1,3B1	R	20	4	4	0	0	0	0	0	0	0	3	0	.000	.000	.000
Harry Chapman		R	25	2	2	0	1	0	0	0	0	0	1	0	.500	.500	.500
Mark Stewart	C1	L	23	1	1	0	0	0	0	0	0	0	0	0	.000	.000	.000

A. Marsans, 1 G at SS; R. Almeida, 1 G at 2B

Pitcher	T	Age	G	GS	CG	ShO	IP	H	HR	BB	SO	W-L	Sv	ERA
Chief Johnson	R	27	44	31	13	3	269.0	251	8	86	107	14-16	0	3.01
Red Ames†	R	30	31	24	12	1	187.1	185	7	70	80	11-13	2	2.88
George Suggs	R	30	36	22	9	2	199.0	220	6	35	73	8-15	2	4.03
Rube Benton	L	26	23	22	9	1	144.1	140	4	60	68	11-7	0	3.49
Gene Packard	L	25	39	21	9	2	190.2	208	2	64	73	7-11	0	2.97
Art Fromme†	R	29	9	7	2	0	56.0	55	1	21	24	1-4	0	4.18
Jack Rowan	R	26	5	5	5	0	39.0	37	0	9	21	0-4	0	3.00
Dick Robertson	R	22	2	1	1	0	10.0	13	0	9	1	0-1	0	7.20
Cy Morgan	R	34	1	1	0	0	2.1	5	0	1	2	0-1	0	15.43
Bill Powell	R	28	1	1	0	0	0.1	2	0	2	0	0-1	0	54.00
Three Finger Brown	R	36	39	16	11	1	173.1	174	7	44	41	11-12	6	2.91
Frank Harter	R	26	17	2	0	0	46.2	47	3	19	10	1-1	0	3.86
Ernie Herbert	R	26	6	0	0	0	17.1	12	0	5	5	0-0	0	2.08
Chick Smith	L	20	5	1	0	0	17.2	15	1	11	11	0-1	0	3.57
Ralph Works	R	25	5	2	0	0	15.0	15	0	8	4	0-1	0	7.80
Red Nelson†	R	27	2	0	0	0	1.2	6	1	4	0	0-0	0	37.80
Andy Harrington	R	24	1	0	0	0	4.0	6	0	1	1	0-0	0	9.00
Harry Betts	R	32	1	0	0	0	3.1	1	0	3	0	0-0	0	2.70
Joe McManus	R	25	1	0	0	0	2.0	3	0	4	1	0-0	0	18.00
Harry McIntire	R	34	1	0	0	0	1.0	3	0	0	0	0-1	0	27.00

1913 St. Louis Cardinals 8th NL 51-99 .340 49.0 GB

Miller Huggins

Player	Gm by Position	B	Age	G	AB	R	H	2B	3B	HR	RBI	BB	SO	SB	Avg	OBP	Slg
Ivy Wingo	C98,1B5,OF1	L	22	112	307	25	78	5	8	2	35	17	41	18	.254	.295	.342
Ed Konetchy	1B140,P1	R	27	140	504	75	139	18	17	8	68	53	41	27	.276	.353	.427
Miller Huggins	2B113	S	34	121	382	74	109	12	0	0	27	92	49	23	.285	.432	.317
Mike Mowrey	3B131	R	29	132	450	61	117	18	4	0	33	53	40	21	.260	.342	.318
Charley O'Leary	SS103,2B15	R	30	121	406	32	88	15	5	0	31	20	34	3	.217	.260	.278
Rebel Oakes	OF145	L	26	147	539	60	158	14	5	0	49	43	32	22	.293	.350	.338
Lee Magee	OF108,2B22,1B6*	S	24	137	531	54	142	13	7	2	31	34	30	23	.267	.314	.330
Steve Evans	OF74,1B1	L	28	97	245	18	61	15	6	1	31	20	28	5	.249	.321	.371
Possum Whitted	OF41,SS38,3B22*	R	23	123	404	44	89	10	5	0	38	31	44	9	.220	.282	.270
Ted Cather	OF57,P1,1B1	R	24	67	183	16	39	8	4	0	12	9	24	7	.213	.250	.301
Larry McLean†	C42	R	31	48	152	7	41	9	0	0	12	6	9	0	.270	.297	.329
Jimmy Sheckard†	OF46	L	34	52	136	18	27	2	1	0	17	41	25	5	.199	.388	.228
Palmer Hildebrand	C22,OF1	R	28	26	55	3	9	2	0	0	1	1	10	1	.164	.207	.200
Finners Quinlan	OF12	L	25	13	50	1	8	0	0	0	1	1	9	0	.160	.176	.160
Arnold Hauser	SS8,2B4	R	24	22	45	3	13	0	3	0	9	2	2	1	.289	.347	.422
Skipper Roberts	C16	L	25	26	41	4	6	2	0	0	3	3	13	1	.146	.205	.195
Zinn Beck	3B5,SS5	R	27	10	30	4	5	1	0	0	2	4	10	1	.167	.265	.200
Frank Snyder	C7	R	20	7	21	1	4	0	1	0	2	0	4	0	.190	.190	.286
Wesley Callahan	SS6	R	24	7	14	0	4	0	0	0	1	2	2	1	.286	.375	.286
Chuck Miller	OF3	L	23	4	12	0	2	0	0	0	1	0	2	0	.167	.167	.167
Heinie Peitz	C2,OF1	R	42	3	4	1	1	0	1	0	0	0	0	0	.250	.250	.750
Al Cabrera	SS1	—	30	1	2	0	0	0	0	0	0	0	0	0	.000	.000	.000
Doc Crandall†		R	25	2	2	0	0	0	0	0	0	0	2	0	.000	.000	.000
John Vann		R	20	1	1	0	0	0	0	0	0	0	1	0	.000	.000	.000
Jimmy Whelan		R	23	1	1	0	0	0	0	0	0	0	0	0	.000	.000	.000

L. Magee, 2 G at SS; P. Whitted, 7 G at 2B, 2 G at 1B

Pitcher	T	Age	G	GS	CG	ShO	IP	H	HR	BB	SO	W-L	Sv	ERA
Dan Griner	R	25	34	34	18	1	225.0	279	12	66	79	10-22	0	5.08
Slim Sallee	L	28	50	31	18	3	276.0	252	11	60	106	19-15	5	2.71
Bob Harmon	R	25	42	27	16	1	273.1	291	6	99	66	8-21	2	3.92
Pol Perritt	R	20	36	21	8	0	175.0	205	9	64	64	6-14	0	5.25
Bill Doak	R	22	15	12	5	1	93.0	79	4	39	51	2-8	1	3.10
Bill Steele	R	27	12	9	2	0	54.0	58	3	18	10	4-4	0	5.00
Bill Hopper	R	22	3	3	2	0	24.0	20	2	8	3	0-3	0	3.75
Dick Niehaus	L	20	3	3	2	0	24.0	20	1	13	4	0-2	0	4.13
Ben Hunt	L	24	2	1	0	0	8.1	6	0	9	6	0-1	0	3.24
Rube Geyer	R	29	30	4	2	0	78.2	83	6	38	21	1-5	1	5.26
Sandy Burk	R	26	19	5	0	0	70.0	81	1	33	29	0-2	1	5.14
Harry Trekell	R	20	7	1	1	0	30.0	25	2	8	15	0-1	0	4.50
Joe Willis	L	23	7	0	0	0	9.2	9	0	11	6	0-0	1	7.45
Walt Marbet	R	22	3	1	0	0	3.1	9	0	4	1	0-1	0	16.20
Ed Konetchy	R	27	1	0	0	0	4.2	1	0	4	3	1-0	0	0.00
Phil Redding	R	23	1	0	0	0	2.2	2	0	1	1	0-0	0	6.75
Ted Cather	R	24	1	0	0	0	0.1	1	0	2	0	0-0	0	54.00

Seasons: Team Rosters 587

»1914 Philadelphia Athletics 1st AL 99-53 .651 — Connie Mack

Player	Gm by Position	B	Age	G	AB	R	H	2B	3B	HR	RBI	BB	SO	SB	Avg	OBP	Slg
Wally Schang	C100	S	24	107	307	44	88	11	8	3	45	32	33	7	.287	.371	.404
Stuffy McInnis	1B149	R	23	149	576	74	181	12	8	1	95	19	27	25	.314	.341	.368
Eddie Collins	2B152	L	27	152	526	122	181	23	14	2	85	97	31	58	.344	.452	.452
Home Run Baker	3B149	L	28	150	570	84	182	23	10	9	89	53	37	19	.319	.380	.442
Jack Barry	SS140	R	27	140	467	57	113	12	0	0	42	53	34	22	.242	.324	.268
Eddie Murphy	OF148	L	22	148	573	101	156	12	9	3	43	87	46	36	.272	.379	.340
Amos Strunk	OF120	L	25	122	404	58	111	15	3	2	45	57	38	25	.275	.364	.342
Rube Oldring	OF117	R	30	119	466	68	129	21	7	3	49	18	35	14	.277	.308	.371
Jimmy Walsh†	OF56,1B3,3B3*	L	28	67	216	35	51	11	6	3	36	30	27	6	.236	.340	.384
Jack Lapp	C67	L	29	69	199	22	46	7	2	0	19	31	14	1	.231	.338	.286
Tom Daley†	OF24	L	29	29	86	17	22	1	3	0	7	12	14	4	.256	.347	.337
Larry Kopf	SS13,3B8,2B5	S	23	35	69	8	13	2	2	0	12	8	14	6	.188	.300	.275
Chick Davies	OF10,P1	L	22	19	46	6	11	3	1	0	5	5	13	1	.239	.314	.348
Shag Thompson	OF8	L	21	16	29	3	5	0	1	0	2	7	8	1	.172	.351	.241
Billy Orr	SS6,3B1	R	23	10	24	3	4	1	1	0	1	2	5	1	.167	.231	.292
Wickey McAvoy	C8	R	19	8	16	1	2	0	1	0	0	0	4	0	.125	.125	.250
Press Cruthers	2B4	R	23	4	15	1	3	0	1	0	0	0	4	0	.200	.200	.333
Jack Coombs	P2,OF2	S	31	5	11	0	3	1	0	0	2	1	1	0	.273	.333	.364
Earle Mack	1B2	L	24	2	8	0	0	0	0	0	1	0	0	1	.000	.000	.000
Harry Davis	1B1	R	40	5	7	0	3	0	0	0	2	1	0	0	.429	.556	.429
Sam Crane	SS2	R	19	2	6	0	0	0	0	0	0	2	3	0	.000	.250	.000
Ferdie Moore	1B2	—	18	2	4	1	2	0	0	0	1	0	2	0	.500	.500	.500
Dean Sturgis	C1	R	21	4	4	1	1	0	0	0	0	1	2	0	.250	.400	.250
Ira Thomas	C1	R	33	2	3	0	0	0	0	0	0	0	0	0	.000	.000	.000
Ben Rochefort		L	17	1	2	0	1	0	0	0	0	0	1	0	.500	.500	.500
Toots Coyne	3B1	—	19	1	2	0	0	0	0	0	0	0	2	0	.000	.000	.000
Buck Sweeney	OF1	—	24	1	1	0	0	0	0	0	0	0	1	0	.000	.000	.000

J. Walsh, 1 G at SS

Pitcher	T	Age	G	GS	CG	ShO	IP	H	HR	BB	SO	W-L	Sv	ERA
Bob Shawkey	R	23	38	30	18	5	237.0	223	4	75	89	16-8	2	2.73
Joe Bush	R	21	38	23	14	2	206.0	184	2	81	109	17-12	3	3.06
Eddie Plank	L	38	34	23	11	4	185.1	178	2	42	110	15-7	3	2.87
Chief Bender	R	30	28	23	14	7	179.0	159	4	55	107	17-3	2	2.26
John Wyckoff	R	22	32	20	11	0	185.0	153	2	103	86	11-7	2	3.02
Herb Pennock	L	20	28	14	8	3	151.2	136	1	65	90	11-4	3	2.79
Byron Houck†	R	22	3	3	0	0	11.0	14	0	6	4	0-0	0	3.27
Jack Coombs	R	31	2	2	0	0	8.0	8	0	3	1	0-1	0	4.50
Chick Davies	L	22	1	1	1	0	9.0	8	0	3	4	1-0	0	1.00
Willie Jensen	R	25	1	1	1	0	9.0	7	1	2	1	0-1	0	2.00
Rube Bressler	L	19	29	10	8	1	147.2	112	1	56	96	10-4	2	1.77
Boardwalk Brown†	R	27	15	7	2	0	66.0	64	1	26	20	1-6	0	4.09
Charlie Boardman	L	21	2	0	0	0	7.1	10	0	4	2	0-0	0	4.91
Fred Worden	R	19	1	0	0	0	2.0	8	0	0	1	0-0	0	18.00

1914 Boston Red Sox 2nd AL 91-62 .595 8.5 GB Bill Carrigan

Player	Gm by Position	B	Age	G	AB	R	H	2B	3B	HR	RBI	BB	SO	SB	Avg	OBP	Slg
Bill Carrigan	C78	R	30	81	178	18	45	5	1	1	22	40	18	1	.253	.395	.309
Doc Hoblitzell†	1B68	R	25	68	229	31	73	10	3	0	33	19	21	12	.319	.386	.389
Steve Yerkes†	2B91	R	26	92	293	23	64	17	2	1	23	14	23	5	.218	.259	.300
Larry Gardner	3B153	L	28	155	553	50	143	23	19	3	68	35	39	16	.259	.303	.385
Everett Scott	SS143	R	21	144	539	66	129	15	6	2	37	32	43	9	.239	.286	.301
Tris Speaker	OF156,P1,1B1	L	26	158	571	101	193	46	18	4	90	77	25	42	.338	.423	.503
Duffy Lewis	OF142	R	26	146	510	53	142	37	9	2	79	57	41	22	.278	.357	.398
Harry Hooper	OF140	L	26	141	530	85	137	23	15	1	41	58	47	19	.258	.336	.364
Hal Janvrin	2B57,1B56,SS20*	R	21	143	492	65	117	18	6	1	51	38	50	29	.238	.296	.305
Hick Cady	C58	R	28	61	159	14	41	6	1	0	8	12	22	2	.258	.310	.308
Wally Rehg	OF42	R	25	84	151	14	33	4	2	0	11	18	11	5	.219	.306	.272
Clyde Engle†	1B29,2B5,3B2	R	30	55	134	14	26	2	0	0	9	14	11	4	.194	.275	.209
Pinch Thomas	C61,1B1	L	26	63	130	9	25	1	0	0	5	18	17	1	.192	.291	.200
Olaf Henriksen	OF27	L	26	61	95	16	25	2	1	1	5	22	12	5	.263	.407	.337
Del Gainer†	1B18,2B11,OF1	R	27	38	84	11	20	9	2	2	13	8	14	2	.238	.312	.464
Bill Swanson	2B6,3B3,SS1	S	25	11	20	0	4	2	0	0	0	3	4	0	.200	.304	.300
Les Nunamaker†	C3,1B1	R	25	5	5	0	1	0	0	0	0	1	0	0	.200	.333	.200
Larry Pratt	C5	R	27	5	4	0	0	0	0	0	0	0	4	0	.000	.000	.000
Squanto Wilson	1B1	S	25	1	0	0	0	0	0	0	0	0	0	0	—	—	—

H. Janvrin, 6 G at 3B

Pitcher	T	Age	G	GS	CG	ShO	IP	H	HR	BB	SO	W-L	Sv	ERA
Ray Collins	L	27	39	30	16	6	272.1	252	3	56	72	20-13	0	2.51
Rube Foster	R	26	32	27	17	5	211.2	164	2	52	90	14-8	0	1.66
Dutch Leonard	L	22	36	25	17	7	224.2	139	3	60	176	19-5	3	1.00
Ernie Shore	R	23	20	16	10	1	139.2	103	1	35	52	10-5	1	2.00
Joe Wood	R	24	18	14	11	1	113.1	94	1	34	67	9-3	1	2.62
Rankin Johnson†	R	26	16	13	4	2	99.1	92	2	34	24	4-9	0	3.08
Vean Gregg†	L	29	12	9	4	0	68.1	71	0	37	24	3-4	0	3.95
Babe Ruth	L	19	4	3	1	0	23.0	21	1	7	3	2-1	0	3.91
Hugh Bedient	R	24	42	16	7	1	177.1	185	4	45	70	8-12	2	3.60
Fritz Coumbe†	L	24	17	5	1	0	62.1	49	0	16	17	1-2	1	1.44
Guy Cooper†	R	21	9	1	0	0	22.0	23	1	9	5	1-0	0	5.32
Ed Kelly	R	25	3	0	0	0	2.1	1	0	1	4	0-0	0	0.00
Matt Zeiser	R	25	2	0	0	0	10.0	9	0	8	0	0-0	0	1.80
Tris Speaker	L	26	1	0	0	0	1.0	2	0	0	0	0-0	0	9.00

1914 Washington Senators 3rd AL 81-73 .526 19.0 GB Clark Griffith

Player	Gm by Position	B	Age	G	AB	R	H	2B	3B	HR	RBI	BB	SO	SB	Avg	OBP	Slg
John Henry	C91	R	24	91	261	22	44	7	4	0	20	37	47	7	.169	.274	.226
Chick Gandil	1B145	R	27	145	526	48	136	24	10	3	75	44	44	30	.259	.324	.359
Ray Morgan	2B146	R	25	147	491	50	126	22	8	1	49	62	34	24	.257	.352	.340
Eddie Foster	3B156	R	27	157	616	82	174	16	10	2	50	60	47	31	.282	.348	.351
George McBride	SS156	R	33	156	503	49	102	12	4	0	24	43	70	12	.203	.274	.243
Danny Moeller	OF150	S	29	151	571	83	143	19	10	1	45	71	89	26	.250	.341	.324
Howard Shanks	OF139	R	23	143	500	44	112	22	10	4	64	29	51	18	.224	.269	.332
Clyde Milan	OF113	L	27	115	437	63	129	19	11	1	39	32	26	38	.295	.346	.396
Mike Mitchell†	OF53	R	34	55	193	20	55	5	3	1	20	22	19	9	.285	.361	.358
Rip Williams	C44,1B8,OF1	R	32	81	169	17	47	6	4	1	22	13	19	2	.278	.330	.379
Eddie Ainsmith	C51	R	22	58	151	11	34	7	0	0	13	9	28	8	.225	.273	.272
Walter Johnson	P51,OF1	R	26	54	136	23	30	4	1	3	16	10	27	2	.221	.274	.331
Wally Smith	2B12,1B7,SS7*	R	25	45	97	11	19	4	1	0	8	3	12	3	.196	.235	.258
Merito Acosta	OF22	L	18	38	74	10	19	2	2	0	4	11	18	3	.257	.353	.338
Germany Schaefer	2B3,OF3	R	37	25	29	6	7	1	0	0	2	3	5	4	.241	.313	.276
Charlie Pick	OF7	L	26	10	23	0	9	0	0	0	1	4	4	1	.391	.481	.391
Irish Meusel	OF1	R	21	1	2	0	0	0	0	0	0	0	0	0	.000	.000	.000
Doug Neff	SS3	R	22	3	2	0	0	0	0	0	0	0	0	0	.000	.000	.000
Joe Gedeon	OF3	R	20	4	2	0	0	0	0	0	1	0	1	0	.000	.333	.000
Tom Wilson	C1	S	24	1	1	0	0	0	0	0	0	0	0	0	.000	.000	.000

W. Smith, 5 G at 3B, 1 G at OF

Pitcher	T	Age	G	GS	CG	ShO	IP	H	HR	BB	SO	W-L	Sv	ERA
Walter Johnson	R	26	51	40	33	9	371.2	287	3	74	225	28-18	1	1.72
Doc Ayers	R	24	49	32	8	3	265.1	221	5	54	148	12-15	3	2.54
Jim Shaw	R	20	48	31	15	5	257.0	198	3	137	164	15-17	4	2.70
Joe Boehling	L	23	27	24	14	2	196.0	180	3	76	91	12-8	1	3.03
Carl Cashion	R	23	2	1	0	0	5.0	4	0	6	1	0-1	0	10.80
Joe Engel	L	21	35	15	1	0	124.1	108	2	75	41	7-5	2	2.97
Jack Bentley	L	19	30	11	3	2	125.1	110	3	53	55	5-7	4	2.37
Harry Harper	L	19	23	3	1	0	57.0	45	1	35	50	2-1	2	3.47
Mutt Williams	R	22	5	0	0	0	7.0	5	0	4	3	0-0	1	5.14
Bert Gallia	R	22	2	0	0	0	6.0	3	0	4	4	0-0	0	4.50
Jim Stevens	R	24	2	0	0	0	3.0	4	0	2	0	0-0	0	9.00
Frank Barron	L	23	1	0	0	0	1.0	1	0	0	1	0-0	0	0.00
Nick Altrock	L	37	1	0	0	0	1.0	3	0	0	0	0-0	0	0.00
Clark Griffith	R	44	1	0	0	0	1.0	1	0	0	1	0-0	1	0.00

1914 Detroit Tigers 4th AL 80-73 .523 19.5 GB Hughie Jennings

Player	Gm by Position	B	Age	G	AB	R	H	2B	3B	HR	RBI	BB	SO	SB	Avg	OBP	Slg
Oscar Stanage	C122	R	31	122	400	16	77	8	4	0	25	24	58	2	.193	.242	.233
George Burns	1B137	R	21	137	478	55	139	22	5	5	57	32	56	23	.291	.351	.389
Marty Kavanagh	2B115,1B4	R	23	127	439	60	109	21	6	4	35	41	42	16	.248	.318	.351
George Moriarty	3B126,1B3	R	30	132	465	56	118	19	5	1	40	39	27	34	.254	.318	.323
Donie Bush	SS157	S	26	157	596	97	150	18	4	0	32	112	54	35	.252	.373	.295
Sam Crawford	OF157	L	34	157	582	74	183	22	26	8	104	69	31	25	.314	.388	.483
Bobby Veach	OF145	L	26	149	531	56	146	19	14	1	72	50	29	20	.275	.341	.369
Ty Cobb	OF96	L	27	97	345	69	127	22	11	2	57	57	22	35	.368	.466	.513
Ossie Vitt	2B36,3B16,OF2*	R	24	66	195	35	49	7	0	0	8	31	8	10	.251	.354	.287
Hugh High	OF53	L	26	80	184	25	49	5	3	0	17	26	21	7	.266	.363	.326
Harry Heilmann	OF31,1B16,2B6	R	19	69	182	25	41	8	1	2	18	22	29	1	.225	.316	.313
Billy Purtell	3B16,2B1,SS1	R	28	26	76	4	13	4	0	0	3	2	7	0	.171	.203	.224
Del Baker	C38	R	22	43	70	4	15	2	1	0	1	6	9	0	.214	.276	.271
Red McKee	C27	L	23	32	64	7	12	1	1	0	8	14	16	1	.188	.342	.234
Paddy Baumann	2B3	R	28	3	11	1	0	0	0	0	0	2	1	0	.000	.154	.000
Fred McMullin	SS1	R	22	1	1	0	0	0	0	0	0	0	1	0	.000	.000	.000
Del Gainer†	1B1	R	27	1	0	0	0	0	0	0	0	0	0	0	—	—	—
Ray Demmitt†		L	30	1	0	0	0	0	0	0	0	0	0	0	—	—	—

O. Vitt, 1 G at SS

Pitcher	T	Age	G	GS	CG	ShO	IP	H	HR	BB	SO	W-L	Sv	ERA
Harry Coveleski	L	28	44	36	23	5	303.1	251	4	100	124	22-12	2	2.49
Hooks Dauss	R	24	45	35	22	3	302.0	286	3	87	150	18-15	4	2.86
Jean Dubuc	R	25	36	27	15	2	224.0	216	3	76	70	13-14	1	3.46
Red Oldham	L	20	9	7	3	0	45.1	42	1	8	23	2-4	0	3.38
John Williams	R	24	4	3	1	0	11.1	17	0	5	4	0-2	0	6.35
Lefty Williams	L	21	1	1	0	0	1.0	3	0	2	0	0-1	0	0.00
Alex Main	R	30	32	12	5	1	138.1	131	2	59	55	6-6	3	2.67
Pug Cavet	L	24	31	14	6	1	151.1	129	2	44	51	7-7	2	2.44
Ross Reynolds	R	26	26	7	3	1	78.0	62	0	39	31	5-3	0	2.08
Marc Hall	R	26	25	8	1	0	90.1	88	1	27	18	4-6	0	2.69
George Boehler	R	22	18	6	2	0	63.0	54	1	48	37	2-3	0	3.57
Ed McCreery	R	24	3	1	0	0	4.0	6	0	3	4	1-0	0	11.25

1914 St. Louis Browns 5th AL 71-82 .464 28.5 GB

Branch Rickey

Player	Gm by Position	B	Age	G	AB	R	H	2B	3B	HR	RBI	BB	SO	SB	Avg	OBP	Slg
Sam Agnew	C113	R	27	113	311	22	66	5	4	0	16	24	63	10	.212	.279	.254
John Leary	1B130,C15	R	23	144	533	35	141	28	7	0	45	10	71	9	.265	.282	.343
Del Pratt	2B152,OF5,SS1	R	26	158	584	85	165	34	13	5	65	50	45	37	.283	.341	.411
Jimmy Austin	3B127	S	34	130	466	55	111	16	4	0	30	40	59	20	.238	.300	.290
Doc Lavan	SS73	R	23	74	239	21	63	7	4	1	21	17	39	6	.264	.318	.339
Burt Shotton	OF152	L	29	154	579	82	156	19	9	0	38	64	66	40	.269	.344	.333
Tilly Walker	OF145	R	26	151	517	67	154	24	16	6	78	51	72	29	.298	.365	.441
Gus Williams	OF141	L	26	143	499	51	126	19	6	4	47	36	120	35	.253	.308	.339
Buzzy Wares	SS68,2B8	R	28	81	215	20	45	10	1	0	23	28	35	10	.209	.300	.265
Ivan Howard	3B34,1B28,OF3*	S	31	81	209	21	51	6	2	0	20	28	42	14	.244	.342	.292
Ernie Walker	OF36	L	23	71	131	19	39	5	3	1	14	13	26	6	.298	.366	.405
Frank Crossin	C41	R	23	43	90	5	11	1	1	0	5	10	10	3	.122	.225	.156
Bobby Wallace	SS19,3B2	R	40	26	73	3	16	2	1	0	5	5	13	1	.219	.269	.274
Ed Miller	1B8,2B5,OF5*	R	25	34	58	8	8	0	1	0	4	4	13	1	.138	.219	.172
William Rumler	C9,OF6	R	23	33	46	2	8	1	0	0	6	3	12	2	.174	.240	.196
Joe Jenkins	C9	R	23	19	32	0	4	1	1	0	0	1	11	2	.125	.152	.219
Dee Walsh	SS7	S	24	7	23	1	2	0	0	0	1	2	4	1	.087	.160	.087
Dick Kauffman	1B6	S	26	7	15	1	4	1	0	0	2	0	3	0	.267	.267	.333
Bob Clemens	OF5	R	27	7	13	1	3	0	1	0	3	2	1	0	.231	.375	.385
George Hale	C6	R	19	6	11	1	2	0	0	0	0	0	3	0	.182	.182	.182
Tim Bowden	OF4	L	22	7	9	0	2	0	0	0	0	1	6	0	.222	.300	.222
Jack Enzenroth†	C3	R	28	3	6	0	1	0	0	0	0	2	3	0	.167	.444	.167
Ed Hemingway	3B3	S	21	3	5	0	0	0	0	0	0	1	1	1	.000	.167	.000
Bobby Messenger	OF1	S	30	1	2	0	0	0	0	0	0	0	0	0	.000	.000	.000
Branch Rickey		L	32	2	2	0	0	0	0	0	0	0	1	0	.000	.000	.000
Charlie Bold	1B1	R	19	2	1	0	0	0	0	0	0	0	1	0	.000	.000	.000
Dutch Schirick		R	24	1	0	0	0	0	0	0	0	1	0	2	—	1.000	—

I. Howard, 1 G at SS; E. Miller, 2 G at 3B

Pitcher	T	Age	G	GS	CG	ShO	IP	H	HR	BB	SO	W-L	Sv	ERA
Carl Weilman	L	24	44	36	20	3	299.0	260	1	84	119	18-13	1	2.08
Earl Hamilton	L	22	44	35	20	5	302.1	265	5	100	111	17-18	2	2.50
Bill James	R	27	44	35	20	3	284.0	269	4	109	109	15-14	1	2.85
Walt Leverenz	L	26	27	16	5	0	111.1	107	5	63	41	1-12	0	3.80
Wiley Taylor	R	26	16	8	2	1	50.0	41	0	25	20	2-5	0	3.42
G. Baumgardner	R	22	45	18	9	3	183.2	152	3	84	93	14-13	3	2.79
Roy Mitchell	R	29	28	9	4	0	103.1	134	1	38	38	4-5	4	4.35
Harry Hoch	R	27	15	2	1	0	54.0	55	1	27	13	0-2	0	3.00
Ernie Manning	R	23	4	0	0	0	10.0	11	0	3	3	0-0	0	3.60
Grover Baichley	R	24	4	0	0	0	7.0	9	0	3	3	0-0	0	5.14
Allen Sothoron	R	21	1	0	0	0	6.0	6	0	4	3	0-0	0	6.00

1914 Chicago White Sox 6th AL 70-84 .455 30.0 GB

Nixey Callahan

Player	Gm by Position	B	Age	G	AB	R	H	2B	3B	HR	RBI	BB	SO	SB	Avg	OBP	Slg
Ray Schalk	C125	R	21	135	392	30	106	13	2	0	36	38	24	24	.270	.347	.314
Jack Fournier	1B97,OF6	L	24	109	379	44	118	14	9	6	44	31	44	10	.311	.368	.443
Lena Blackburne	2B143	R	27	144	474	52	105	10	5	1	35	66	58	25	.222	.324	.270
Jim Breton	3B79	R	22	81	231	21	49	7	2	0	24	24	42	9	.212	.292	.260
Buck Weaver	SS134	R	23	136	541	64	133	20	9	2	28	20	40	14	.246	.279	.327
Shano Collins	OF154	R	28	154	598	61	164	34	9	3	65	27	49	30	.274	.312	.376
Ray Demmitt†	OF142	L	30	146	515	63	133	13	12	2	46	61	48	12	.258	.344	.342
Ping Bodie	OF95	R	26	107	327	21	75	9	5	3	29	21	35	12	.229	.278	.315
Hal Chase†	1B58	R	31	58	206	27	55	10	5	0	20	23	19	9	.267	.343	.364
Scotty Alcock	3B48,2B1	R	28	54	156	12	27	4	2	0	7	7	14	4	.173	.213	.224
Joe Berger	SS27,2B12,3B7	R	27	48	148	11	23	3	1	0	3	13	9	2	.155	.224	.189
Tom Daly	OF23,3B5,C4*	R	22	61	133	13	31	2	0	0	8	7	13	3	.233	.271	.248
Braggo Roth	OF34	R	21	34	126	14	37	4	6	1	10	8	25	3	.294	.355	.444
Wally Mayer	C33,3B1	R	23	39	85	7	14	3	1	0	5	14	23	1	.165	.290	.224
Harry Lord	3B19,OF1	L	32	21	69	8	13	1	1	1	3	5	3	2	.188	.243	.275
Howard Baker	3B15	R	26	15	47	4	13	1	1	0	5	3	8	2	.277	.320	.340
Walt Kuhn	C16	R	30	17	40	4	11	1	0	0	0	8	11	2	.275	.396	.300
Larry Chappell	OF9	L	24	21	39	3	9	0	0	0	1	4	11	0	.231	.302	.231
Polly Wolfe	OF8	L	25	9	28	0	6	0	0	0	0	3	6	1	.214	.290	.214
Cecil Coombs	OF7	R	26	7	23	1	4	1	0	0	1	1	7	0	.174	.208	.217
Carl Manda	2B7	R	25	9	15	2	4	0	0	0	1	3	3	1	.267	.389	.267
Charlie Kavanagh		R	21	5	5	0	1	0	0	0	1	0	2	0	.200	.333	.200
Irv Porter	OF1	S	26	1	4	1	1	0	0	0	0	0	1	0	.250	.250	.250
Hank Schreiber	OF1	R	22	1	2	0	0	0	0	0	0	0	1	0	.000	.000	.000
Delos Brown		R	21	1	1	0	0	0	0	0	0	0	1	0	.000	.000	.000
Billy Sullivan	C1	R	39	1	0	0	0	0	0	0	0	0	0	0	—	—	—

T. Daly, 2 G at 1B

Pitcher	T	Age	G	GS	CG	ShO	IP	H	HR	BB	SO	W-L	Sv	ERA
Joe Benz	R	28	48	35	16	4	283.1	245	4	66	142	14-19	2	2.26
Jim Scott	R	26	43	33	11	2	253.1	227	5	75	138	14-18	2	2.84
Eddie Cicotte	R	30	45	30	15	4	269.1	220	0	72	122	11-16	3	2.04
Reb Russell	L	25	38	23	8	1	167.1	168	3	33	79	8-12	1	2.90
Ed Walsh	R	33	9	5	3	1	45.2	34	0	20	15	2-3	0	2.76
Red Faber	R	25	40	19	11	2	181.1	154	3	64	88	10-9	4	2.68
Mellie Wolfgang	R	24	24	11	9	2	119.1	96	0	32	50	9-5	0	1.89
Bill Lathrop	R	22	19	1	0	0	47.2	41	0	19	7	1-2	0	2.64
Hi Jasper	R	33	16	0	0	0	32.1	22	0	20	19	1-0	0	3.34

1914 New York Yankees 6th AL 70-84 .455 30.0 GB

Frank Chance (60-74)/Roger Peckinpaugh (10-10)

Player	Gm by Position	B	Age	G	AB	R	H	2B	3B	HR	RBI	BB	SO	SB	Avg	OBP	Slg
Jeff Sweeney	C78	R	25	87	258	25	55	8	1	1	22	35	30	19	.213	.316	.264
Charlie Mullen	1B93	R	25	93	323	33	84	8	0	0	44	33	55	11	.260	.332	.285
Luke Boone	2B90,3B9	R	24	106	370	34	82	8	2	0	21	31	41	10	.222	.285	.254
Fritz Maisel	3B148	R	24	149	548	78	131	23	9	2	28	76	69	74	.239	.334	.325
Roger Peckinpaugh	SS157	R	23	157	570	55	127	14	6	3	51	51	73	38	.223	.288	.284
Roy Hartzell	OF128,2B5	L	32	137	481	55	112	15	9	1	32	68	38	22	.233	.335	.308
Doc Cook	OF126	L	28	131	470	59	133	11	3	1	40	44	60	26	.283	.356	.326
Birdie Cree	OF76	R	31	77	275	45	85	18	5	0	40	30	24	4	.309	.389	.411
Les Nunamaker†	C70,1B5	R	25	87	257	19	68	10	3	2	29	22	34	11	.265	.327	.350
Frank Truesdale	2B67,3B4	S	30	77	217	23	46	4	0	0	13	39	35	11	.212	.340	.230
Tom Daley†	OF58	L	29	67	191	36	48	6	4	0	9	38	13	8	.251	.378	.325
Harry Williams	1B58	R	24	59	178	9	29	5	2	1	17	26	26	3	.163	.287	.230
Bill Holden†	OF45	R	24	50	165	12	30	3	2	0	12	16	26	2	.182	.254	.224
Jimmy Walsh†	OF41	L	28	43	136	13	26	1	3	1	11	29	21	6	.191	.333	.265
Ray Caldwell	P31,1B6	L	26	59	113	9	22	4	0	0	10	7	24	2	.195	.248	.230
Dick Gossett	C9	R	22	10	21	3	3	0	0	0	1	5	5	0	.143	.333	.143
Jay Rogers	C4	R	25	5	8	0	0	0	0	0	0	0	4	0	.000	.000	.000
Angel Aragon	OF1	R	23	6	7	1	1	0	0	0	0	1	2	0	.143	.333	.143
Charlie Meara	OF3	L	23	4	7	2	2	0	0	0	1	2	2	0	.286	.444	.286
Pi Schwert	C2	R	21	2	5	0	0	0	0	0	0	2	2	0	.000	.286	.000
Bill Reynolds	C1	R	29	4	5	0	2	0	0	0	0	0	3	0	.400	.400	.400
Harry Kingman	1B1	L	22	4	3	0	0	0	0	0	0	1	2	0	.000	.250	.000
Frank Gilhooley	OF1	L	22	1	3	0	2	0	0	0	0	1	0	0	.667	.750	.667
Bill Schwarz	C1	—	23	1	1	0	0	0	0	0	0	0	1	0	.000	.000	.000
Joe Harris	1B1,OF1	R	23	2	1	0	0	0	0	0	0	3	1	0	.000	.800	.000
Les Channell		L	28	1	1	0	1	1	0	0	0	0	0	0	1.000	1.000	2.000
Alex Burr	OF1	R	20	1	0	0	0	0	0	0	0	0	0	0	—	—	—
Frank Chance	1B1	R	36	1	0	0	0	0	0	0	0	0	0	0	—	—	—

Pitcher	T	Age	G	GS	CG	ShO	IP	H	HR	BB	SO	W-L	Sv	ERA
Ray Fisher	R	26	29	26	17	2	209.0	177	2	61	86	10-12	1	2.28
Ray Keating	R	22	34	25	14	0	210.0	198	1	67	109	7-11	1	2.96
Jack Warhop	R	29	37	23	15	0	216.2	182	8	44	56	8-15	0	2.37
Ray Caldwell	R	26	31	23	22	5	213.0	153	5	51	92	17-9	1	1.94
Marty McHale	R	25	31	23	12	0	191.0	195	3	33	75	7-16	1	2.97
Boardwalk Brown†	R	27	20	14	8	0	122.1	123	2	42	57	5-5	1	3.24
Al Schulz†	L	25	6	4	1	0	28.1	27	0	10	18	1-3	0	4.76
King Cole	R	28	33	15	8	2	141.2	151	3	51	43	11-9	0	3.30
Cy Pieh	R	27	18	4	1	0	62.1	68	6	29	24	4-4	0	5.05
Guy Cooper†	R	21	1	0	0	0	3.0	3	0	2	3	0-0	0	9.00

1914 Cleveland Bronchos 8th AL 51-102 .333 48.5 GB

Joe Birmingham

Player	Gm by Position	B	Age	G	AB	R	H	2B	3B	HR	RBI	BB	SO	SB	Avg	OBP	Slg
Steve O'Neill	C82,1B1	R	22	86	269	28	68	12	2	0	20	15	35	1	.253	.292	.312
Doc Johnston	1B90,OF2	L	26	103	340	43	83	15	1	0	23	28	46	14	.244	.311	.294
Nap Lajoie	2B80,1B31	R	39	121	419	37	108	14	3	0	50	32	15	14	.258	.313	.305
Terry Turner	3B104,2B17	R	33	120	428	43	105	14	9	1	33	44	36	17	.245	.319	.327
Ray Chapman	SS72,2B33	R	23	106	375	59	103	16	10	2	42	48	48	24	.275	.358	.387
Jack Graney	OF127	L	28	130	460	63	122	17	10	1	39	67	46	20	.265	.362	.352
Joe Jackson	OF119	L	24	122	453	61	153	22	13	3	53	41	34	22	.338	.399	.464
Nemo Leibold	OF107	L	22	114	402	46	106	13	3	0	32	54	56	12	.264	.354	.311
Ivy Olson	SS31,2B23,3B19*	R	28	89	310	22	75	6	2	1	20	13	24	15	.242	.275	.284
Jay Kirke	OF42,1B18	L	26	67	242	18	66	10	2	1	25	7	30	5	.273	.296	.343
Roy Wood	OF41,1B20	R	21	72	220	24	52	6	3	1	15	13	26	6	.236	.300	.305
Bill Wambsganss	SS36,2B4	R	20	43	143	12	31	6	2	0	12	8	24	2	.217	.277	.287
Fred Carisch	C38	R	32	40	102	8	22	3	2	0	5	12	18	2	.216	.298	.284
Ben Egan	C27	R	30	29	88	7	20	2	1	0	11	3	20	0	.227	.277	.273
Johnny Bassler	C25,3B1,OF1	L	19	43	77	5	14	1	1	0	6	15	8	3	.182	.323	.221
Larry Pezold	3B20,OF1	R	21	23	71	4	16	0	1	0	5	9	6	2	.225	.313	.254
Bill Steen	P30,3B1	R	26	31	70	4	14	2	0	0	5	2	26	0	.200	.233	.229
Jack Lelivelt	OF13,1B1	L	28	32	64	6	21	5	1	0	13	2	10	2	.328	.348	.438
Rivington Bisland	SS15,3B1	R	24	18	57	9	6	1	0	0	2	6	2	2	.105	.190	.123
Elmer Smith	OF13	L	21	13	53	5	17	3	0	0	8	2	11	1	.321	.345	.377
Walter Barbare	3B14,SS1	R	22	15	52	6	16	2	2	0	5	2	5	1	.308	.345	.423
Joe Birmingham	OF14	R	29	19	47	2	6	0	0	0	4	2	5	0	.128	.163	.128
Bruce Hartford	SS8	R	22	8	22	5	4	1	0	0	0	4	9	0	.182	.308	.227
Frank Mills	C2	L	19	4	8	0	1	0	0	0	0	1	2	0	.125	.222	.125
Josh Billings	C3	R	22	8	8	2	2	1	0	0	0	1	1	1	.250	.333	.375
George Dunlop	SS1	R	25	1	3	0	0	0	0	0	0	1	1	0	.000	.250	.000
Tinsley Ginn	OF2	L	22	2	1	0	0	0	0	0	0	0	0	0	.000	.000	.000
Al Cypert	3B1	R	24	1	1	0	0	0	0	0	0	0	0	0	.000	.000	.000
Tom Reilly		R	29	1	1	0	0	0	0	0	0	0	0	0	.000	.000	.000

I. Olson, 6 G at OF, 3 G at 1B

Pitcher	T	Age	G	GS	CG	ShO	IP	H	HR	BB	SO	W-L	Sv	ERA
Willie Mitchell	L	24	39	32	16	3	257.0	228	3	124	179	12-17	1	3.19
Rip Hagerman	R	26	37	26	12	3	198.0	189	3	118	112	9-15	0	3.09
Bill Steen	R	26	30	22	13	1	200.2	201	0	68	97	9-14	0	2.60
Guy Morton	R	21	25	13	5	0	128.0	116	1	55	80	1-13	1	3.02
Vean Gregg†	L	29	17	12	6	1	96.2	88	0	48	56	9-3	0	3.07
Paul Carter	R	20	5	4	1	0	24.2	35	0	5	9	1-3	0	2.92
Al Tedrow	R	23	4	3	1	1	22.1	19	0	14	4	1-2	0	1.21
George Kahler	R	24	2	1	1	0	14.0	17	0	7	3	0-1	0	3.86
Fred Blanding	R	26	29	12	5	0	116.0	133	0	54	35	3-9	1	3.96
Allan Collamore	R	27	27	8	3	0	105.1	100	3	49	32	3-7	0	3.25
Abe Bowman	R	21	22	10	2	1	72.2	74	0	45	27	2-7	0	4.46
Lefty James	L	24	17	6	1	0	50.2	44	0	32	16	0-3	0	3.20
Fritz Coumbe†	L	24	14	5	2	0	55.1	59	0	16	22	1-5	0	3.25
Harley Dillinger	L	19	11	2	1	0	33.2	41	0	25	11	0-1	0	4.54
Lloyd Bishop	R	24	3	1	0	0	8.0	14	0	3	1	0-1	0	5.63
Sad Sam Jones	R	21	1	0	0	0	3.1	2	0	2	0	0-0	0	2.70
Nick Cullop†	L	26	1	0	0	0	3.1	4	0	1	3	0-1	0	2.70
Henry Benn	R	24	1	0	0	0	1.0	0	0	0	1	0-0	0	0.00
George Beck	R	24	1	0	0	0	1.0	1	0	0	0	0-0	0	0.00

»1914 Boston Braves 1st NL 94-59 .614 —

George Stallings

Player	Gm by Position	B	Age	G	AB	R	H	2B	3B	HR	RBI	BB	SO	SB	Avg	OBP	Slg
Hank Gowdy	C115,1B9	R	24	128	366	42	89	17	6	3	46	48	40	14	.243	.337	.347
Butch Schmidt	1B147	L	27	147	537	67	153	17	9	1	71	43	55	14	.285	.350	.356
Johnny Evers	2B139	L	32	139	491	81	137	20	3	1	40	87	26	12	.279	.390	.338
Charlie Deal	3B74,SS1	R	22	79	257	17	54	13	2	0	23	20	23	4	.210	.270	.276
Rabbit Maranville	SS156	R	22	156	586	74	144	23	6	4	78	45	56	28	.246	.306	.326
Les Mann	OF123	R	20	126	389	44	96	16	11	4	40	24	50	9	.247	.292	.375
Joe Connolly	OF118	L	26	120	399	64	122	28	10	9	65	49	36	12	.306	.393	.494
Larry Gilbert	OF60	L	22	72	224	32	60	6	1	5	25	26	34	3	.268	.347	.371
Possum Whitted†	OF38,2B15,1B4*	R	24	66	218	36	57	11	4	2	31	18	18	10	.261	.326	.376
Red Smith†	3B60	R	24	60	207	30	65	17	1	3	37	28	24	4	.314	.401	.449
Bert Whaling	C59	R	26	60	172	18	36	7	0	0	12	21	28	2	.209	.303	.250
Herbie Moran†	OF41	L	30	41	154	24	41	3	1	0	4	17	11	4	.266	.347	.299
Ted Cather†	OF48	R	25	50	145	19	43	11	2	0	27	7	28	7	.297	.338	.400
Josh Devore†	OF42	L	26	51	128	22	29	4	0	1	5	18	14	2	.227	.327	.281
Jim Murray	OF32	R	36	39	112	10	26	4	2	0	12	6	24	2	.232	.277	.304
Oscar Dugey	2B16,OF16,3B1	R	26	58	109	17	21	2	0	1	10	10	15	10	.193	.267	.239
Jack Martin†	3B26,1B1,2B1	R	27	33	85	10	18	2	0	0	5	6	7	0	.212	.264	.235
Tommy Griffith	OF14	L	24	16	48	3	5	0	0	0	1	2	6	0	.104	.140	.104
Otto Hess	P14,1B5	L	35	31	47	5	11	1	0	1	6	1	11	0	.234	.250	.319
Wilson Collins	OF19	R	25	27	35	5	9	0	0	0	1	2	8	0	.257	.297	.257
Fred Tyler	C6	R	22	6	19	2	2	0	0	0	2	1	5	0	.105	.150	.105
Billy Martin	SS1	R	20	1	3	0	0	0	0	0	0	0	0	0	.000	.000	.000
Clarence Kraft	1B1	R	27	3	3	0	1	0	0	0	0	0	1	0	.333	.333	.333

P. Whitted, 4 G at 3B, 3 G at SS

Pitcher	T	Age	G	GS	CG	ShO	IP	H	HR	BB	SO	W-L	Sv	ERA
Bill James	R	22	46	37	30	4	332.1	261	0	118	156	26-7	2	1.90
Dick Rudolph	R	26	42	36	31	6	336.1	288	9	61	138	26-10	0	2.35
Lefty Tyler	L	24	38	34	21	5	271.1	247	7	101	140	16-13	2	2.69
Otto Hess	L	35	14	11	7	1	89.0	89	2	33	24	5-6	1	3.03
Hub Perdue†	R	32	9	9	2	0	51.0	60	5	11	13	2-5	0	5.82
Iron Davis	R	24	9	6	4	1	55.2	42	1	26	26	3-3	0	3.40
Tom Hughes	R	30	2	2	1	0	17.0	14	0	4	11	2-0	0	2.65
Dolf Luque	R	23	2	1	1	0	8.2	5	0	4	1	0-1	0	4.15
Ensign Cottrell	L	25	1	1	0	0	1.0	2	0	3	1	0-1	0	9.00
Dick Crutcher	R	24	33	15	5	1	158.2	169	4	66	48	5-7	0	3.46
Paul Strand	L	20	16	3	1	0	55.1	47	1	23	33	6-2	0	2.44
Gene Cocreham	R	29	15	3	1	0	44.2	48	2	27	15	3-4	0	4.84

1914 New York Giants 2nd NL 84-70 .545 10.5 GB

John McGraw

Player	Gm by Position	B	Age	G	AB	R	H	2B	3B	HR	RBI	BB	SO	SB	Avg	OBP	Slg
Chief Meyers	C126	R	33	134	381	33	109	13	5	1	55	34	25	4	.286	.357	.354
Fred Merkle	1B146	R	25	146	512	71	132	25	7	7	63	52	80	23	.258	.327	.375
Larry Doyle	2B145	L	27	145	539	87	140	19	8	5	63	58	25	17	.260	.343	.353
Milt Stock	3B113,SS1	R	20	115	365	52	96	17	1	3	41	34	21	11	.263	.333	.340
Art Fletcher	SS135	R	29	135	514	62	147	26	8	2	79	22	37	15	.286	.332	.379
George Burns	OF154	R	24	154	561	100	170	35	10	3	60	89	53	62	.303	.403	.417
Bob Bescher	OF126	S	30	135	512	82	138	23	4	6	35	45	48	36	.270	.336	.365
Fred Snodgrass	OF96,1B14,2B1*	R	26	113	392	54	103	20	4	0	44	37	43	25	.263	.336	.334
Eddie Grant	3B52,SS21,2B16	L	31	88	282	34	78	7	1	0	29	23	21	11	.277	.333	.309
Dave Robertson	OF71	L	24	82	256	25	68	12	3	2	32	70	26	9	.266	.427	.359
Larry McLean	C74	R	32	79	154	8	40	6	0	0	14	4	9	4	.260	.283	.299
Red Murray	OF49	R	30	86	139	19	31	6	3	0	23	9	7	11	.223	.270	.309
Jim Thorpe	OF4	R	27	30	31	5	6	1	0	0	2	0	4	1	.194	.194	.226
Mike Donlin		L	36	35	31	1	5	1	1	1	3	3	5	0	.161	.235	.355
Elmer Johnson	C11	R	30	11	12	0	2	1	0	0	0	1	3	0	.167	.231	.250
Sandy Piez	OF4	R	21	35	8	9	3	0	1	0	3	0	1	4	.375	.375	.625
Harry Smith	C4	R	24	5	7	0	3	0	0	0	2	3	1	1	.429	.600	.429
Walter Holke	1B2	S	21	2	6	0	2	0	0	0	0	0	0	0	.333	.333	.333
Fred Brainerd	2B2	R	22	2	5	1	1	0	0	0	0	1	0	0	.200	.333	.200
Ben Dyer	SS6,2B1	R	21	7	4	1	1	0	0	0	0	0	1	1	.250	.250	.250
Des Beatty	3B1,SS1	R	21	2	3	0	0	0	0	0	1	0	0	0	.000	.000	.000

F. Snodgrass, 1 G at 3B

Pitcher	T	Age	G	GS	CG	ShO	IP	H	HR	BB	SO	W-L	Sv	ERA
Jeff Tesreau	R	25	42	41	26	8	322.1	238	8	128	189	26-10	1	2.37
Christy Mathewson	R	35	41	35	29	5	312.0	314	16	23	80	24-13	2	3.00
Rube Marquard	L	27	39	33	15	4	268.0	261	9	47	92	12-22	2	3.06
Al Demaree	R	29	38	29	13	2	224.0	219	3	77	89	10-17	0	3.09
Marty O'Toole†	R	25	10	5	2	0	34.0	34	0	12	13	1-1	0	4.24
Eric Erickson	R	19	1	1	0	0	5.0	8	0	3	3	0-1	0	0.00
Art Fromme	R	30	38	12	3	1	138.0	142	7	44	57	9-5	2	3.20
Hooks Wiltse	L	33	20	0	0	0	38.0	41	2	12	19	1-1	1	2.84
Ferdie Schupp	L	23	8	0	0	0	17.0	19	0	9	9	0-0	1	5.82
Rube Schauer	R	23	6	0	0	0	22.1	16	2	8	6	0-0	0	3.22
Hank Ritter	R	20	1	0	0	0	8.0	4	0	4	4	1-0	0	1.13
Al Huenke	R	23	1	0	0	0	2.0	2	0	0	2	0-0	0	4.50

1914 St. Louis Cardinals 3rd NL 81-72 .529 13.0 GB

Miller Huggins

Player	Gm by Position	B	Age	G	AB	R	H	2B	3B	HR	RBI	BB	SO	SB	Avg	OBP	Slg
Frank Snyder	C98	R	21	100	326	19	75	15	4	1	25	13	28	1	.230	.262	.310
Dots Miller	1B91,SS60,2B5	R	27	155	573	67	166	27	10	4	88	34	52	16	.290	.339	.393
Miller Huggins	2B147	S	35	148	509	85	134	17	4	1	24	105	63	32	.263	.396	.318
Zinn Beck	3B122,SS16	R	28	137	457	42	106	15	11	3	45	28	32	14	.232	.282	.333
Art Butler	SS83,OF1	R	26	86	274	29	55	12	3	1	24	39	23	14	.201	.311	.277
Chief Wilson	OF154	L	30	154	580	64	150	27	12	9	73	32	66	14	.259	.302	.393
Lee Magee	OF102,1B39,2B6	S	25	142	529	59	150	23	4	2	40	42	24	36	.284	.337	.353
Cozy Dolan	OF96,3B27	R	24	126	421	76	101	16	3	4	32	55	74	42	.240	.335	.321
Walton Cruise	OF81	L	24	95	256	20	58	9	3	4	28	25	42	3	.227	.303	.332
Ivy Wingo	C70	L	23	80	237	24	71	8	5	4	26	18	17	15	.300	.352	.426
Lee Dressen	1B38	L	24	46	103	16	24	2	1	0	7	11	20	2	.233	.307	.272
Ted Cather†	OF28	R	25	39	99	11	27	7	0	0	13	3	15	4	.273	.294	.343
Joe Riggert†	OF30	R	27	34	89	9	19	5	2	0	8	5	14	4	.213	.255	.315
Ken Nash	3B10,2B6,SS3	S	25	24	51	4	14	3	1	0	6	6	10	0	.275	.351	.373
Chuck Miller		L	24	36	36	4	7	1	0	0	2	3	9	2	.194	.256	.222
Possum Whitted†	3B5,OF3,2B1	R	24	20	31	3	4	1	0	0	1	0	3	1	.129	.129	.161
Bruno Betzel	2B5	R	19	7	9	2	0	0	0	0	0	1	1	0	.000	.100	.000
Jack Roche	C5	R	23	12	9	1	6	2	1	0	3	0	1	1	.667	.700	1.111
Paddy O'Connor	C7	R	34	10	9	0	0	0	0	0	0	2	2	0	.000	.250	.000
Rolla Daringer	SS1	L	25	2	4	1	2	1	0	0	0	1	2	0	.500	.600	.750

Pitcher	T	Age	G	GS	CG	ShO	IP	H	HR	BB	SO	W-L	Sv	ERA
Bill Doak	R	23	36	33	16	7	256.0	193	2	87	118	19-6	0	1.72
Pol Perritt	R	21	41	32	18	3	286.0	248	7	93	115	16-13	2	2.36
Slim Sallee	L	29	46	29	18	3	282.1	252	5	72	105	18-17	6	2.10
Hub Perdue†	R	32	22	19	12	0	153.1	160	3	35	43	8-8	1	2.82
Hank Robinson	L	24	26	16	6	1	126.0	128	1	32	30	7-8	0	3.00
Casey Hageman†	R	27	12	7	1	0	55.1	43	0	20	21	1-4	0	2.44
Dan Griner	R	26	37	17	11	2	179.0	163	3	57	74	9-13	2	2.51
Bill Steele†	R	28	17	2	0	0	53.1	55	3	7	16	2-2	0	2.70
Dick Niehaus	L	21	8	1	1	0	17.1	18	1	8	6	1-0	0	3.12
Steamboat Williams	R	22	5	1	0	0	11.0	13	1	6	2	0-1	0	6.55
Bill Hopper	R	23	3	0	0	0	5.0	6	0	5	1	0-0	0	3.60

1914 Chicago Cubs 4th NL 78-76 .506 16.5 GB

Hank O'Day

Player	Gm by Position	B	Age	G	AB	R	H	2B	3B	HR	RBI	BB	SO	SB	Avg	OBP	Slg
Roger Bresnahan	C85,2B14,OF1	R	35	101	248	42	69	10	4	0	24	49	20	14	.278	.401	.351
Vic Saier	1B153	L	23	153	537	87	129	24	8	18	72	94	61	19	.240	.357	.415
Bill Sweeney	2B134	R	28	134	463	45	101	14	5	1	38	53	15	18	.218	.298	.276
Heinie Zimmerman	3B118,SS15,2B12	R	27	146	564	75	167	36	12	4	87	20	46	17	.296	.326	.424
Red Corriden	SS91,3B8,2B3	R	26	107	318	42	73	9	5	3	29	35	33	13	.230	.323	.318
Wilbur Good	OF154	L	28	154	580	70	158	24	7	2	43	53	74	31	.272	.341	.348
Tommy Leach	OF136,3B16	R	36	153	577	80	152	24	9	7	46	79	50	16	.263	.353	.373
Wildfire Schulte	OF134	L	31	137	465	54	112	22	7	5	61	39	55	16	.241	.306	.351
Jimmy Archer	C76	R	31	79	248	17	64	9	2	0	19	9	9	1	.258	.284	.310
Jimmy Johnston	OF28,2B4	R	24	50	101	9	23	3	2	1	8	4	9	3	.228	.264	.327
Claud Derrick†	SS28	R	28	28	96	5	21	3	1	0	13	5	13	2	.219	.257	.271
Cy Williams	OF27	L	26	55	94	12	19	2	2	0	5	13	13	2	.202	.312	.266
Pete Knisely	OF17	R	26	37	69	5	9	0	1	0	5	5	6	0	.130	.200	.159
Tom Fisher	SS15	R	27	15	50	5	15	2	2	0	5	3	4	2	.300	.340	.420
Art Phelan	3B7,2B3,SS2	R	26	25	46	5	13	2	1	0	3	4	3	0	.283	.340	.370
Art Bues	3B12	R	26	14	45	3	10	1	1	0	4	5	6	1	.222	.300	.289
Bubbles Hargrave	C16	R	21	23	36	3	8	2	0	0	2	0	4	2	.222	.222	.278
Chick Keating		R	22	20	30	3	3	0	1	0	0	6	9	0	.100	.250	.167
Fritz Mollwitz†	1B4,OF1	R	24	13	20	0	3	0	0	0	1	0	3	1	.150	.150	.150
Tom Needham	C7	R	35	9	17	3	2	1	0	0	3	1	4	1	.118	.167	.176
Johnny Bates†	OF3	L	31	9	8	2	1	0	0	0	1	1	1	0	.125	.300	.125
Earl Tyree	C1	R	24	1	4	1	0	0	0	0	0	0	0	0	.000	.000	.000
Milo Allison		L	23	1	1	0	1	0	0	0	0	0	0	0	1.000	1.000	1.000
Tuffy Stewart		L	30	2	1	0	0	0	0	0	0	0	0	0	.000	.000	.000
Herman Bronkie	3B1	R	29	1	1	1	1	1	0	0	1	0	0	0	1.000	1.000	2.000

Pitcher	T	Age	G	GS	CG	ShO	IP	H	HR	BB	SO	W-L	Sv	ERA
Larry Cheney	R	28	50	40	21	6	311.1	239	9	140	157	20-18	5	2.54
Hippo Vaughn	L	26	42	35	23	4	293.2	236	1	109	165	21-13	1	2.05
Jimmy Lavender	R	30	37	28	11	2	214.1	191	11	87	87	11-11	0	3.07
Bert Humphries	R	33	34	21	8	2	171.0	162	5	37	62	10-11	0	2.68
George Pearce	L	26	30	17	4	0	141.0	122	3	65	78	8-12	1	3.51
George McConnell	R	36	1	1	0	0	7.0	3	0	3	3	0-1	0	1.29
Zip Zabel	R	23	29	7	2	0	128.0	104	5	45	50	4-4	1	2.18
Charlie Smith	R	34	16	5	1	0	53.2	49	3	15	17	2-4	0	3.86
Casey Hageman†	R	27	16	1	0	0	46.2	44	0	12	17	2-1	1	3.47
Eddie Stack	R	26	7	1	0	0	16.1	13	0	11	9	0-1	0	4.96
Elmer Koestner†	R	28	4	0	0	0	6.1	6	0	4	6	0-0	0	2.84

1914 Brooklyn Dodgers 5th NL 75-79 .487 19.5 GB

Wilbert Robinson

Player	Gm by Position	B	Age	G	AB	R	H	2B	3B	HR	RBI	BB	SO	SB	Avg	OBP	Slg
Lew McCarty	C84	R	25	90	284	20	72	14	2	1	30	14	22	1	.254	.293	.327
Jake Daubert	1B126	L	30	126	474	89	156	17	7	6	45	30	34	25	.329	.375	.432
George Cutshaw	2B153	R	26	153	583	69	150	22	12	2	78	30	32	34	.257	.297	.346
Red Smith†	3B90	R	24	90	330	39	81	10	8	4	48	30	26	11	.245	.310	.361
Dick Egan	SS83,3B10,OF3*	R	30	106	337	30	76	10	3	1	21	22	25	8	.226	.273	.282
Zack Wheat	OF144	L	26	145	533	66	170	26	9	9	89	47	50	20	.319	.377	.452
Casey Stengel	OF121	L	23	126	412	55	130	13	10	4	60	56	55	19	.316	.404	.425
Jack Dalton	OF116	R	28	128	442	65	141	13	8	1	45	53	39	19	.319	.396	.391
Ollie O'Mara	SS63	R	23	67	247	41	65	10	2	1	7	16	26	14	.263	.316	.332
Hi Myers	OF60	R	25	70	227	35	65	3	9	0	17	7	24	2	.286	.316	.379
Gus Getz	3B55	R	24	55	210	13	52	8	1	0	20	2	15	9	.248	.255	.295
John Hummel	1B36,OF19,2B1*	R	31	73	208	25	55	8	9	0	20	16	25	5	.264	.317	.389
Otto Miller	C50	R	25	54	169	17	39	6	1	0	9	7	20	0	.231	.261	.278
William Fischer	C30	L	23	43	105	12	27	1	2	0	8	8	12	1	.257	.310	.305
Joe Riggert†	OF20	R	27	27	83	6	16	1	3	2	6	4	20	2	.193	.230	.349
Kid Elberfeld	SS18,2B1	R	39	30	62	7	14	1	0	0	1	2	4	0	.226	.304	.242
Tex Erwin†	C4	L	28	9	11	0	5	0	0	0	1	2	1	1	.455	.538	.455

D. Egan, 2 G at 2B, 1 G at 1B; J. Hummel, 1 G at SS

Pitcher	T	Age	G	GS	CG	ShO	IP	H	HR	BB	SO	W-L	Sv	ERA
Jeff Pfeffer	R	26	43	34	27	3	315.0	264	9	91	135	23-12	4	1.97
Ed Reulbach	R	31	44	29	14	3	256.0	228	5	83	119	11-18	3	2.64
Pat Ragan	R	25	38	25	14	1	208.1	214	5	85	106	10-15	3	2.98
Frank Allen†	L	24	36	21	10	1	171.1	165	6	57	68	8-14	0	3.10
Raleigh Aitchison	L	26	26	17	8	3	172.1	156	4	60	87	12-7	0	2.66
Nap Rucker	L	29	16	16	5	0	103.2	113	2	27	35	7-6	0	3.39
Charlie Schmutz	R	24	18	5	1	0	57.1	57	1	13	21	1-3	0	3.30
Elmer Brown	R	31	11	5	1	0	36.2	33	2	23	22	2-2	0	3.93
Bill Steele†	R	28	8	1	0	0	16.1	17	1	7	3	0-1	1	5.51
Johnny Enzmann	R	24	7	1	0	0	19.0	21	1	8	5	1-0	0	4.74
Bull Wagner	R	26	6	0	0	0	12.1	14	0	12	4	0-1	0	6.57

1914 Philadelphia Phillies 6th NL 74-80 .481 20.5 GB

Red Dooin

Player	Gm by Position	B	Age	G	AB	R	H	2B	3B	HR	RBI	BB	SO	SB	Avg	OBP	Slg
Bill Killefer	C90	R	26	98	299	27	70	10	1	0	27	8	17	3	.234	.261	.274
Fred Luderus	1B121	L	28	121	443	55	110	16	5	12	55	33	31	2	.248	.308	.388
Bobby Byrne	2B101,3B22	R	29	126	467	61	127	12	1	0	26	45	44	9	.272	.339	.302
Hans Lobert	3B133,SS2	R	32	135	505	83	139	24	5	1	52	49	32	31	.275	.343	.349
Jack Martin†	SS83	R	27	83	292	26	74	5	3	0	21	27	29	6	.253	.319	.291
Gavy Cravath	OF143	R	33	149	499	76	149	27	8	19	100	83	72	14	.299	.402	.499
Dode Paskert	OF128,SS4	R	32	132	451	59	119	25	6	3	44	56	68	23	.264	.349	.366
Beals Becker	OF126	L	27	138	514	76	167	25	5	9	66	37	59	16	.325	.370	.446
Sherry Magee	OF67,SS39,1B32*	R	29	146	544	96	171	39	11	15	103	55	42	25	.314	.380	.509
Hal Irelan	2B44,SS3,1B2*	S	23	67	165	16	39	8	0	1	16	21	22	3	.236	.326	.303
Ed Burns	C55	R	25	70	139	8	36	3	4	0	16	20	12	5	.259	.352	.338
Red Dooin	C40	R	35	53	118	10	21	2	0	1	8	4	14	4	.178	.205	.220
Milt Reed	SS22,2B11,3B1	L	23	44	107	10	22	2	1	0	2	10	13	4	.206	.280	.243
Josh Devore†	OF9	L	26	30	53	5	16	2	0	0	7	4	5	0	.302	.351	.340
Dummy Murphy	SS9	R	27	9	26	1	4	1	0	0	3	0	4	0	.154	.185	.192
Pat Hilly	OF4	R	27	8	10	2	3	0	0	0	1	1	5	0	.300	.364	.300
Fred Mollenkamp	1B3	—	24	3	8	0	1	0	0	0	0	2	0	0	.125	.300	.125
George McAvoy		—	30	1	1	0	0	0	0	0	0	0	0	0	.000	.000	.000
Frank Fletcher		R	23	1	1	0	0	0	0	0	0	0	1	0	.000	.000	.000
Pat Moran	C1	R	38	1	0	0	0	0	0	0	1	0	0	0	—	—	—

S. Magee, 8 G at 2B; H. Irelan, 2 G at 3B

Pitcher	T	Age	G	GS	CG	ShO	IP	H	HR	BB	SO	W-L	Sv	ERA
Pete Alexander	R	27	46	39	32	6	355.0	327	8	76	214	27-15	1	2.38
Erskine Mayer	R	25	48	38	24	4	321.0	308	8	91	116	21-19	2	2.58
Ben Tincup	R	23	28	17	9	3	155.0	165	0	62	108	8-10	2	2.61
Rube Marshall	R	24	27	17	7	0	134.1	144	2	50	49	6-7	1	3.75
Eppa Rixey	L	23	24	15	2	0	103.0	124	0	45	41	2-11	0	4.37
Elmer Jacobs	R	21	14	7	1	0	50.2	65	2	20	17	1-3	0	4.80
George Chalmers	R	26	3	2	1	0	18.0	23	0	15	6	0-3	0	5.50
Joe Oeschger	R	23	32	12	5	0	124.0	129	5	54	47	4-8	1	3.77
Stan Baumgartner	L	19	15	4	2	1	60.1	60	0	16	24	2-2	0	3.28
Henry Matteson	R	29	15	3	2	0	58.0	58	1	23	28	3-2	0	3.10

1914 Pittsburgh Pirates 7th NL 69-85 .448 25.5 GB

Fred Clarke

Player	Gm by Position	B	Age	G	AB	R	H	2B	3B	HR	RBI	BB	SO	SB	Avg	OBP	Slg
George Gibson	C101	R	33	102	274	19	78	9	5	0	30	27	27	4	.285	.359	.354
Ed Konetchy	1B154	R	28	154	563	56	140	23	9	4	51	32	48	20	.249	.291	.343
Jim Viox	2B138,SS2,OF2	R	23	143	506	52	134	18	5	1	57	63	33	9	.265	.351	.326
Mike Mowrey	3B78	R	30	79	284	24	72	7	5	1	25	22	20	8	.254	.316	.324
Honus Wagner	SS132,3B17,1B1	R	40	150	552	60	139	15	9	1	50	51	51	23	.252	.317	.317
Max Carey	OF154	S	24	156	593	76	144	25	17	1	31	59	56	38	.243	.313	.347
Joe Kelly	OF139	R	27	141	508	47	113	19	9	1	48	39	59	21	.222	.278	.301
Mike Mitchell†	OF76	R	34	76	273	31	64	11	5	2	23	16	16	5	.234	.279	.333
Zip Collins	OF49	L	22	49	182	14	44	2	0	0	15	8	10	3	.242	.277	.253
Alex McCarthy	3B36,2B10,SS6	R	26	57	173	14	26	0	1	1	14	6	17	2	.150	.192	.179
Bob Coleman	C72	R	23	73	150	11	40	4	1	1	14	15	32	3	.267	.333	.327
Joe Leonard	3B38,SS1	L	19	53	126	17	25	2	2	0	4	12	21	4	.198	.268	.246
Ed Mensor	OF25	S	27	44	89	15	18	2	1	1	6	22	13	2	.202	.372	.281
Ham Hyatt	1B7,C1	L	29	74	79	2	17	3	1	1	15	7	14	1	.215	.295	.316
Dan Costello	OF20	L	22	21	64	7	19	1	0	0	5	8	16	2	.297	.375	.313
Wally Gerber	SS17	R	22	17	54	5	13	1	1	0	5	2	8	0	.241	.281	.296
Jim Kelly	OF7	L	30	32	44	4	10	2	1	0	3	2	3	0	.227	.261	.318
Paddy Siglin	2B11	R	22	14	39	4	6	0	0	0	2	4	6	1	.154	.233	.154
Bobby Schang	C10	R	27	11	35	0	8	1	1	0	1	0	10	0	.229	.229	.314
Fritz Scheeren	OF10	R	22	11	31	4	9	0	1	1	2	1	6	1	.290	.313	.452
Ike McAuley	SS5,3B3,2B2	R	22	15	24	3	3	0	0	0	0	0	8	0	.125	.125	.125
Jake Kafora	C17	R	25	21	23	2	3	0	0	0	0	0	6	0	.130	.200	.130
Clarence Berger	OF5	L	19	6	13	2	1	0	0	0	0	1	4	0	.077	.143	.077
Syd Smith	C3	R	30	5	11	1	3	0	0	0	1	0	1	0	.273	.273	.273
Fred Clarke		L	41	2	2	0	0	0	0	0	0	0	0	0	.000	.000	.000
Pete Falsey		L	23	3	1	0	0	0	0	0	0	0	1	0	.000	.000	.000
Bill Wagner	C1	R	20	3	1	0	0	0	0	0	50	0	0	0	.000	.000	.000
Pat Kilhullen	C1	R	23	1	1	0	0	0	0	0	0	0	0	0	.000	.000	.000
Ralph Shafer		—	20	1	0	0	0	0	0	0	0	0	0	0	—	—	—
Sam Brenegan	C1	L	23	1	0	0	0	0	0	0	0	0	0	0	—	—	—

Pitcher	T	Age	G	GS	CG	ShO	IP	H	HR	BB	SO	W-L	Sv	ERA
Babe Adams	R	32	40	35	19	3	283.0	253	5	39	91	13-16	1	2.51
Wilbur Cooper	L	22	40	34	19	0	266.2	246	4	79	102	16-15	0	2.13
Bob Harmon	R	26	37	30	19	2	245.0	226	3	55	61	13-17	3	2.53
George McQuillan	R	29	45	28	15	0	259.1	248	8	60	96	13-17	4	2.98
Joe Conzelman	R	28	33	9	4	1	101.0	88	2	40	39	5-6	2	2.94
Erv Kantlehner	L	21	21	5	3	2	67.0	51	0	39	26	3-2	0	3.09
Marty O'Toole†	R	25	19	9	1	0	92.1	92	3	47	36	1-8	1	4.68
Al Mamaux	R	20	13	6	4	2	63.0	41	1	24	30	5-2	0	1.71
Herb Kelly	L	22	5	2	2	0	25.2	24	1	7	6	0-2	0	2.45
Dixie McArthur	R	22	1	0	0	0	1.0	1	0	0	1	0-0	0	0.00
Pat Bohen	R	22	1	0	0	0	1.0	2	0	2	0	0-0	0	18.00

1914 Cincinnati Reds 8th NL 60-94 .390 34.5 GB

Buck Herzog

Player	Gm by Position	B	Age	G	AB	R	H	2B	3B	HR	RBI	BB	SO	SB	Avg	OBP	Slg
Tommy Clarke	C106	R	26	113	313	30	82	13	7	2	25	31	30	6	.262	.332	.367
Doc Hoblitzell†	1B75	R	25	78	248	31	52	8	7	0	26	26	26	7	.210	.287	.298
Heine Groh	2B134,SS2	R	24	139	455	59	131	18	4	2	32	64	28	24	.288	.391	.358
Bert Niehoff	3B134,2B3	R	30	142	484	46	117	16	9	4	49	38	77	20	.242	.298	.337
Buck Herzog	SS137,1B2	R	28	138	498	54	140	14	8	1	40	42	27	46	.281	.348	.347
Herbie Moran†	OF107	L	30	107	395	43	93	10	5	1	35	41	29	26	.235	.312	.294
Bert Daniels	OF71	R	31	71	269	29	59	9	7	0	19	19	40	14	.219	.276	.305
George Twombly	OF68	R	22	68	240	22	56	0	5	0	19	14	27	12	.233	.284	.275
Doc Miller	OF47	L	31	93	192	8	49	7	2	0	33	16	18	4	.255	.313	.313
Mike Gonzalez	C83	R	23	95	176	19	41	6	0	0	10	13	16	2	.233	.293	.267
Johnny Bates†	OF54	L	31	58	155	29	39	7	5	2	15	28	17	4	.252	.380	.400
Red Killefer	OF37,2B5,3B1	R	29	42	141	16	39	6	1	0	12	20	18	11	.277	.386	.333
Bill Kellogg	1B38,2B11,OF2*	R	30	71	126	14	22	0	1	0	7	14	28	7	.175	.262	.190
Armando Marsans†	OF36	R	26	36	124	16	37	3	0	0	22	14	6	13	.298	.374	.323
Earl Yingling	P34,OF13	L	25	61	120	9	23	2	0	1	11	9	15	3	.192	.260	.233
Marty Berghammer	SS33,2B13	L	26	77	112	15	25	2	0	0	6	10	18	4	.223	.287	.241
Fritz Mollwitz†	1B32	R	24	32	111	12	18	2	0	0	5	3	9	2	.162	.198	.180
Fritz Von Kolnitz	3B20,OF11,1B1	R	21	41	104	8	23	2	0	0	6	6	16	4	.221	.270	.240
Tiny Graham	1B25	R	21	25	61	5	14	1	0	0	3	3	10	1	.230	.266	.246
Johnny Rawlings†	3B10,2B7,SS5	R	21	33	60	9	13	1	0	0	8	6	8	1	.217	.288	.233
Maury Uhler	OF36	R	27	46	56	12	12	2	0	0	3	5	11	4	.214	.279	.250
Harry LaRoss	OF20	R	26	22	48	7	11	1	0	0	5	2	10	4	.229	.260	.250
Howard Lohr	OF17	R	22	18	47	6	10	1	1	0	7	0	8	2	.213	.213	.277
Tex Erwin†	C12	L	28	12	35	5	11	3	0	1	7	2	3	0	.314	.351	.486
Bill Holden†	OF10	R	24	11	28	2	6	0	0	0	1	3	5	0	.214	.290	.214
Norm Glockson	C7	R	20	7	12	0	0	0	0	0	0	1	6	0	.000	.077	.000
Claud Derrick†	SS2	R	28	3	6	2	2	1	0	0	1	0	0	1	.333	.333	.500
Kid McLaughlin	OF2	L	26	3	2	1	0	0	0	0	0	0	0	0	.000	.000	.000
Ed Kippert	OF2	R	34	2	2	0	0	0	0	0	0	0	0	0	.000	.000	.000

B. Kellogg, 1 G at 3B

Pitcher	T	Age	G	GS	CG	ShO	IP	H	HR	BB	SO	W-L	Sv	ERA
Red Ames	R	31	47	37	18	4	297.0	274	7	94	128	15-23	6	2.64
Rube Benton	L	27	41	35	16	4	271.0	223	3	95	121	16-18	2	2.96
Earl Yingling	L	25	34	27	8	3	198.0	207	6	54	80	9-13	0	3.45
Phil Douglas	R	24	45	25	13	0	239.1	186	7	92	121	11-18	1	2.56
Pete Schneider	R	18	29	15	11	1	144.1	143	1	56	62	5-13	1	2.81
Dave Davenport†	R	24	10	6	3	1	54.0	38	1	30	22	2-2	2	2.50
Paul Fittery	L	26	8	4	2	0	43.2	41	0	12	21	0-2	0	3.09
Chief Johnson†	R	28	1	1	0	0	4.0	6	0	2	1	0-0	0	6.75
King Lear	R	23	17	4	3	1	55.2	55	3	19	20	1-2	1	3.07
Jack Rowan	R	27	12	2	0	0	39.0	38	1	10	16	1-3	2	3.46
Elmer Koestner†	R	28	5	1	0	0	18.1	18	0	9	6	0-0	0	4.42
Pete Fahrer	R	24	5	0	0	0	8.0	8	0	4	2	0-0	0	1.13
Karl Adams	R	22	4	0	0	0	8.0	14	1	5	5	0-0	0	9.00
Bob Ingersoll	R	31	4	0	0	0	6.0	5	0	5	2	0-0	0	3.00
Pat Griffin	R	21	1	0	0	0	1.0	3	0	2	0	0-0	0	9.00

»1914 Indianapolis Hoosiers 1st FL 88-65 .575 —

Bill Phillips

Player	Gm by Position	B	Age	G	AB	R	H	2B	3B	HR	RBI	BB	SO	SB	Avg	OBP	Slg
Bill Rariden	C130	R	26	131	396	44	93	15	5	0	47	61	43	12	.235	.337	.298
Charlie Carr	1B115	R	37	115	441	44	129	11	10	3	69	26	47	19	.293	.333	.383
Frank LaPorte	2B132	R	34	133	505	86	157	27	12	4	107	36	36	15	.311	.361	.436
Bill McKechnie	3B149	S	27	149	570	107	173	24	6	2	38	53	36	47	.304	.368	.377
Jimmy Esmond	SS151	R	24	151	542	74	160	23	15	2	49	40	48	25	.295	.344	.404
Benny Kauff	OF154	L	24	154	571	120	211	44	13	8	95	72	55	75	.370	.447	.534
Vin Campbell	OF132	L	26	134	544	92	173	23	11	7	44	37	47	26	.318	.368	.439
Al Scheer	OF102,2B4,SS1	L	25	120	363	63	111	23	6	3	45	49	39	9	.306	.396	.427
Al Kaiser	OF50,1B1	R	27	59	187	22	43	10	0	1	16	17	41	6	.230	.301	.299
Edd Roush	OF43,1B2	L	21	74	166	26	54	8	4	1	30	6	20	12	.325	.353	.440
Carl Vandagrift	2B28,3B12,SS5	R	31	43	136	25	34	4	0	0	9	9	15	7	.250	.306	.279
Biddy Dolan	1B31	R	32	32	103	13	23	4	2	1	15	12	13	5	.223	.316	.330
George Textor	C21	S	25	22	57	2	10	0	0	0	4	2	9	0	.175	.230	.175
Bill Warren	C23	L	27	26	50	5	12	2	0	0	5	5	7	2	.240	.309	.280
Frank Rooney	1B9	—	29	12	35	1	7	0	1	1	8	1	—	2	.200	.222	.343
Everitt Booe†	OF5,SS3	L	22	20	31	5	7	1	0	0	6	7	—	4	.226	.368	.258

Pitcher	T	Age	G	GS	CG	ShO	IP	H	HR	BB	SO	W-L	Sv	ERA
Cy Falkenberg	R	33	49	43	33	9	377.1	332	5	89	236	25-16	3	2.22
Earl Moseley	R	29	43	38	29	4	316.2	303	5	123	205	19-18	1	3.47
George Kaiserling	R	21	37	33	20	1	275.1	288	8	72	75	17-10	0	3.11
George Mullin	R	33	36	20	11	1	203.0	202	4	91	74	14-10	2	2.70
Harry Billiard	R	30	32	16	5	0	125.2	117	4	63	45	8-7	1	3.72
Ed Henderson†	L	29	2	1	1	0	10.0	8	0	4	1	1-0	0	4.50
Katsy Keifer	L	22	1	1	1	0	9.0	6	0	2	2	1-0	0	2.00
Charlie Whitehouse	L	20	8	2	2	0	26.0	34	0	5	10	2-0	0	4.85
R. McConnaughey	R	24	7	2	1	0	26.0	23	3	16	7	0-2	0	4.85
Frank Harter	R	27	6	1	1	0	24.2	33	0	7	8	1-2	0	4.01
Clarence Woods	R	22	2	0	0	0	2.0	1	0	2	1	0-0	1	4.50
Fred Ostendorf	L	23	1	0	0	0	2.0	5	0	2	0	0-0	0	22.50

1914 Chicago Whales 2nd FL 87-67 .565 1.5 GB

Joe Tinker

Player	Gm by Position	B	Age	G	AB	R	H	2B	3B	HR	RBI	BB	SO	SB	Avg	OBP	Slg
Art Wilson	C132	R	28	137	440	78	128	31	8	10	64	70	80	13	.291	.394	.466
Fred Beck	1B157	L	27	157	555	51	155	23	4	11	77	44	66	9	.279	.341	.395
Jack Farrell	2B155,SS3	S	25	156	524	58	123	23	4	0	35	52	65	12	.235	.307	.294
Rollie Zeider	3B117,SS1	R	30	119	452	60	124	13	2	1	36	44	28	35	.274	.344	.319
Joe Tinker	SS125	R	33	126	438	50	112	21	7	2	46	38	30	19	.256	.317	.349
Al Wickland	OF157	L	26	157	536	74	148	31	10	6	68	81	58	17	.276	.375	.405
Dutch Zwilling	OF154	L	25	154	592	91	185	38	8	16	95	46	68	21	.313	.363	.485
Max Flack	OF133	L	24	134	502	66	124	15	3	2	39	51	48	37	.247	.324	.301
Harry Fritz	3B46,SS9,2B1	R	23	65	174	16	37	5	1	0	13	18	18	2	.213	.297	.253
Austin Walsh	OF30	L	22	57	121	14	29	6	1	1	10	4	25	0	.240	.264	.331
Bruno Block	C33	R	29	45	106	8	21	4	1	0	14	11	17	1	.198	.274	.255
Jim Stanley	SS40,3B3,2B1*	S	25	54	98	13	19	3	0	0	4	19	14	2	.194	.347	.224
Tom McGuire	P24,OF5,2B3	R	22	43	70	5	19	4	1	1	11	7	17	0	.271	.338	.400
Clem Clemens	C8	R	27	13	27	4	4	0	0	0	2	3	—	0	.148	.233	.148
Bill Jackson	OF6,1B4	L	33	26	25	2	1	0	0	0	1	3	5	0	.040	.143	.040
Leo Kavanagh	SS5	R	19	5	11	0	3	0	0	0	1	1	—	0	.273	.333	.273
Dave Black	P8,C1	L	22	8	7	0	2	0	0	0	0	1	—	0	.286	.375	.286
Jimmy Smith	SS3	S	19	3	6	1	3	1	0	0	1	0	—	0	.500	.500	.667
Skipper Roberts†		L	26	4	3	0	1	0	0	0	1	1	—	0	.333	.500	.333
Jack Kading		R	29	3	3	0	0	0	0	0	0	0	—	0	.000	.000	.000

J. Stanley, 1 G at OF

Pitcher	T	Age	G	GS	CG	ShO	IP	H	HR	BB	SO	W-L	Sv	ERA
Claude Hendrix	R	25	49	37	34	6	362.0	262	6	77	189	29-11	5	1.69
Max Fiske	R	25	38	22	7	0	198.0	161	7	59	87	12-9	0	3.14
Erv Lange	R	26	36	22	10	2	190.0	162	3	55	87	12-10	2	2.23
Mike Prendergast	R	25	30	19	7	1	136.0	131	5	40	71	5-9	0	2.38
Doc Watson†	L	28	26	18	10	3	172.0	145	2	49	69	9-11	1	2.04
Rankin Johnson†	R	26	16	14	12	2	120.0	88	5	29	60	9-5	0	1.58
Tom McGuire	R	22	24	12	7	0	131.1	143	7	57	37	5-7	0	3.70
Ad Brennan	L	32	16	11	5	1	85.2	84	7	21	31	5-4	0	3.57
Babe Sherman	R	23	1	1	0	0	0.1	0	0	2	0	0-1	0	0.00
Dave Black	R	22	8	1	1	0	25.0	28	1	4	19	1-0	0	6.12

1914 Baltimore Terrapins 3rd FL 84-70 .545 4.5 GB

Otto Knabe

Player	Gm by Position	B	Age	G	AB	R	H	2B	3B	HR	RBI	BB	SO	SB	Avg	OBP	Slg
Fred Jacklitsch	C118	R	38	122	337	40	93	21	4	2	48	52	66	7	.276	.376	.380
Harry Swacina	1B158	R	32	158	617	70	173	26	8	0	90	14	23	15	.280	.297	.348
Otto Knabe	2B144	R	30	147	469	45	106	26	2	2	42	53	28	10	.226	.307	.303
Jimmy Walsh	3B113,2B1,SS1*	R	28	120	428	54	132	25	4	10	65	22	56	18	.308	.345	.456
Mickey Doolan	SS145	R	34	145	486	58	119	23	6	1	53	40	47	30	.245	.311	.323
Vern Duncan	OF148,3B8,2B1	L	24	157	557	99	160	20	8	2	53	67	55	13	.287	.375	.363
Benny Meyer	OF132,SS4	R	26	143	500	76	152	18	10	5	40	71	53	23	.304	.395	.410
Hack Simmons	OF73,2B26,1B4*	R	29	114	352	50	95	16	5	1	38	32	26	7	.270	.341	.352
Guy Zinn	OF57	L	27	61	225	30	63	10	6	3	25	16	26	6	.280	.336	.418
Johnny Bates†	OF59	L	31	59	190	24	58	6	3	1	29	38	18	6	.305	.429	.384
Enos Kirkpatrick	3B36,SS11,OF3*	R	28	55	174	22	44	7	2	2	16	18	30	10	.253	.330	.351
Harvey Russell	C47,SS1,OF1	L	27	81	168	18	39	3	2	0	13	18	17	2	.232	.310	.274
Jack Quinn	P46,OF2	R	30	48	121	10	33	6	1	2	10	8	21	1	.273	.318	.388
Frank Smith	P39,OF1	R	34	41	59	4	12	4	1	0	3	3	21	0	.203	.242	.305
Fred Kommers†	OF12	L	28	16	42	5	9	1	0	1	1	7	—	0	.214	.340	.310
Doc Kerr†	C13,1B1	S	32	14	34	4	9	1	1	0	1	1	—	1	.265	.286	.353
Jack McCandless	OF8	L	23	11	31	5	8	0	1	0	1	3	—	0	.258	.343	.323
Frank Lobert	3B7,2B1	R	30	11	30	3	6	0	1	0	2	0	—	0	.200	.200	.267
Medric Boucher†	C7,1B1,OF1	R	28	16	16	2	5	1	1	0	2	1	—	0	.313	.353	.500
Felix Chouinard†	OF2	R	26	5	9	3	4	0	0	0	1	0	—	0	.444	.444	.444

J. Walsh, 1 G at OF; H. Simmons, 2 G at SS, 1 G at 3B; E. Kirkpatrick, 1 G at 1B

Pitcher	T	Age	G	GS	CG	ShO	IP	H	HR	BB	SO	W-L	Sv	ERA
Jack Quinn	R	30	46	42	27	4	342.2	335	3	65	164	26-14	1	2.60
George Suggs	R	31	46	38	26	6	319.1	322	6	57	132	24-14	3	2.90
Kaiser Wilhelm	R	40	47	27	11	1	243.2	263	10	81	113	12-17	4	4.03
Frank Smith	R	34	39	22	9	1	174.2	180	8	47	83	10-8	2	2.99
Bill Bailey	L	25	19	18	10	1	128.2	106	2	68	131	7-9	0	3.08
Snipe Conley	R	20	35	11	4	2	125.0	112	2	47	86	4-6	0	2.52
Ducky Yount	R	28	13	1	1	0	41.1	44	2	19	19	1-1	0	4.14
Jack Ridgway	R	25	4	1	0	0	9.0	20	1	3	2	0-1	0	11.00
Vern Hughes	L	21	3	0	0	0	5.2	5	0	3	0	0-0	0	3.18
John Allen	R	23	1	0	0	0	2.0	2	0	2	2	0-0	0	18.00

1914 Buffalo Buffeds 4th FL 80-71 .530 7.0 GB

Harry Schlafly

Player	Gm by Position	B	Age	G	AB	R	H	2B	3B	HR	RBI	BB	SO	SB	Avg	OBP	Slg
Walter Blair	C128	R	30	128	378	22	92	11	2	0	33	32	64	6	.243	.304	.283
Joe Agler	1B76,OF54	L	27	135	463	82	126	17	6	0	20	77	78	21	.272	.376	.335
Tom Downey	2B129,SS16,3B5	R	30	151	541	69	118	20	3	2	42	40	55	35	.218	.273	.277
Fred Smith	3B127,SS19,1B1	R	22	145	473	48	104	12	10	2	45	49	78	24	.220	.297	.300
Baldy Louden	SS115	R	28	126	431	73	135	11	4	6	63	52	41	35	.313	.391	.399
Charlie Hanford	OF155	R	33	155	597	83	174	28	13	13	90	32	81	37	.291	.332	.447
Frank Delahanty†	OF78	R	31	79	274	29	55	4	7	2	27	23	—	21	.201	.265	.288
Tex McDonald†	OF61,2B10	L	23	69	250	32	74	13	6	3	32	20	—	11	.296	.353	.432
Hal Chase†	1B73	R	31	75	291	43	101	19	9	3	48	6	31	10	.347	.365	.505
Everitt Booe†	OF58,SS8,3B2*	L	22	76	241	29	54	6	2	0	14	21	—	8	.224	.289	.278
Del Young	OF41	L	28	80	174	17	48	5	5	4	22	3	13	0	.276	.288	.431
Harry Schlafly	2B23,1B7,C1*	R	35	51	127	16	33	7	1	2	19	12	22	3	.260	.338	.378
Clyde Engle†	3B23,OF9	R	30	32	110	12	28	4	1	0	12	11	18	5	.255	.328	.309
Art LaVigne	C34,1B3	R	29	51	90	10	14	2	0	0	4	7	25	0	.156	.216	.178
Luther Bonin	OF20	L	26	20	76	6	14	4	1	0	4	7	11	3	.184	.253	.263
Nick Allen	C26	R	25	32	63	3	15	1	0	0	4	3	12	4	.238	.273	.254
Bill Collins	OF15	S	32	21	47	6	7	2	2	0	2	1	8	0	.149	.167	.277
Ned Pettigrew		R	32	2	2	0	0	0	0	0	0	0	—	0	.000	.000	.000
Jack Snyder	C1	R	27	1	0	0	0	0	0	0	0	1	0	0	—	1.000	—
Del Wertz	SS1	R	25	3	0	1	0	0	0	0	0	0	0	0	—	—	—

E. Booe, 1 G at 2B; H. Schlafly, 1 G at 3B, 1 G at OF

Pitcher	T	Age	G	GS	CG	ShO	IP	H	HR	BB	SO	W-L	Sv	ERA
Gene Krapp	R	27	36	29	18	1	252.2	198	4	115	106	14-14	0	2.49
Fred Anderson	R	28	37	28	21	2	260.1	243	8	64	144	13-15	0	3.08
Earl Moore	R	34	36	27	14	2	194.2	184	3	99	96	11-15	2	4.30
Russ Ford	R	31	35	26	19	5	247.1	190	11	41	123	21-6	6	1.82
Al Schulz†	L	25	27	23	10	0	171.0	160	3	77	87	10-11	1	3.37
Ed Porray	R	25	3	3	0	0	10.1	18	2	7	0	0-1	0	4.35
Harry Moran	L	25	34	16	7	2	154.0	159	7	53	73	10-8	1	4.27
Bob Smith	R	23	15	1	0	0	36.2	39	3	16	13	1-0	2	3.44
Dan Woodman	R	20	13	0	0	0	33.2	30	1	11	13	0-0	1	2.41
Joe Houser	L	22	7	2	0	0	23.0	21	1	20	6	0-1	0	5.48
Biff Schlitzer	R	29	3	0	0	0	3.1	7	3	2	1	0-0	0	16.20

1914 Brooklyn Tip-Tops 5th FL 77-77 .500 11.5 GB

Bill Bradley

Player	Gm by Position	B	Age	G	AB	R	H	2B	3B	HR	RBI	BB	SO	SB	Avg	OBP	Slg
Grover Land	C97	R	29	102	335	24	92	6	2	0	29	12	23	7	.275	.306	.304
Hap Myers	1B88	R	26	92	305	61	67	10	5	1	29	44	43	43	.220	.322	.295
Solly Hofman	2B108,1B22,OF21*	R	31	147	515	65	148	25	12	5	83	54	41	34	.287	.357	.412
Tex Wisterzil	3B149	R	23	149	534	54	137	18	10	0	66	34	47	17	.257	.314	.328
Ed Gagnier	SS88,3B6	R	31	94	337	22	63	12	2	0	25	13	24	8	.187	.219	.234
Steve Evans	OF112,1B27	L	29	145	514	93	179	41	15	12	96	50	49	18	.348	.416	.556
Al Shaw	OF102	L	33	112	376	81	122	27	7	5	49	44	59	24	.324	.395	.473
Claude Cooper	OF101	L	22	113	399	56	96	14	11	2	25	26	60	25	.241	.294	.346
George Anderson	OF92	L	24	98	364	58	115	13	3	3	24	31	50	16	.316	.376	.393
Al Halt	SS71,2B3,OF1	R	23	80	261	26	61	6	3	3	25	13	39	11	.234	.270	.307
Jim Delahanty	2B55,1B5	R	35	74	214	28	62	13	5	0	15	25	21	4	.290	.372	.397
Danny Owens	C58	R	28	58	184	15	51	7	3	2	20	9	16	2	.277	.314	.380
Danny Murphy	OF46	R	37	52	161	16	49	9	0	4	32	17	16	4	.304	.374	.435
Art Griggs	1B27,OF1	R	30	40	112	10	32	6	1	1	15	5	11	1	.286	.328	.384
Felix Chouinard†	OF20	R	26	32	79	7	20	1	2	0	8	4	18	3	.253	.289	.316
Art Watson	C18	L	30	22	46	7	13	4	1	1	3	1	6	0	.283	.298	.478
Rinaldo Williams	3B4	L	20	4	15	1	4	0	0	0	0	0	4	0	.267	.267	.400
Bill Bradley		R	36	7	6	1	3	1	0	0	3	0	—	0	.500	.500	.667

S. Hofman, 1 G at SS

Pitcher	T	Age	G	GS	CG	ShO	IP	H	HR	BB	SO	W-L	Sv	ERA
Tom Seaton	R	26	44	38	26	7	302.2	299	6	102	172	25-14	2	3.03
Ed Lafitte	R	28	42	33	23	0	290.2	260	7	127	137	18-15	2	2.63
Happy Finneran	R	22	27	23	13	2	175.1	153	6	60	54	12-11	1	3.18
Byron Houck†	R	22	17	9	3	0	92.0	95	4	43	45	2-6	0	3.13
Dan Marion	R	23	17	9	4	0	89.1	97	1	38	41	3-2	0	3.93
Bert Maxwell	R	27	12	8	6	1	71.1	76	0	24	19	3-4	1	3.28
T. Finger Brown†	R	37	9	8	5	0	57.2	63	1	18	32	2-5	0	4.21
Fin Wilson	L	24	2	1	1	0	7.0	7	0	11	4	0-1	0	7.71
Joe Vernon	R	24	1	1	0	0	3.1	4	0	5	0	0-0	0	10.80
Rudy Sommers	L	25	23	8	2	0	82.0	88	2	34	40	2-7	0	4.06
Jim Bluejacket	R	26	17	7	3	1	67.0	77	2	19	29	4-5	1	3.76
Bill Chappelle	R	30	16	6	4	0	74.1	71	1	29	31	4-2	0	3.15
Rube Peters	R	29	11	3	1	0	37.2	52	1	16	13	2-2	0	3.82
Herold Juul	R	21	9	3	0	0	29.0	26	0	31	16	0-3	0	6.21
Esty Chaney	R	23	1	0	0	0	4.0	7	0	2	1	0-0	0	6.75
John McGraw	R	23	1	0	0	0	2.0	0	0	0	2	0-0	0	0.00

1914 Kansas City Packers 6th FL 67-84 .444 20.0 GB

George Stovall

Player	Gm by Position	B	Age	G	AB	R	H	2B	3B	HR	RBI	BB	SO	SB	Avg	OBP	Slg
Ted Easterly	C128	L	29	134	436	58	146	20	12	1	67	31	25	10	.335	.384	.443
George Stovall	1B116	R	35	124	450	51	128	20	5	7	75	23	35	6	.284	.325	.398
Duke Kenworthy	2B145	S	27	146	545	93	173	40	14	15	91	36	44	37	.317	.372	.525
George Perring	3B101,1B41,P1*	R	29	144	496	68	138	28	10	2	69	59	39	7	.278	.355	.387
Pep Goodwin	SS67,3B40,1B1	L	22	112	374	38	88	15	6	1	32	27	23	4	.235	.290	.316
Chet Chadbourne	OF146	L	29	147	581	92	161	22	8	1	37	69	49	42	.277	.359	.348
Grover Gilmore	OF132	L	25	139	530	91	152	25	5	1	32	37	108	23	.287	.337	.358
Art Kruger	OF120	R	33	122	441	45	114	24	7	4	47	23	59	11	.259	.297	.372
Cad Coles	OF39,1B3	L	28	78	194	17	49	7	3	1	25	5	30	6	.253	.271	.335
Johnny Rawlings†	SS61	R	21	61	193	19	41	3	0	0	15	22	25	6	.212	.296	.228
Cliff Daringer	SS24,3B19,2B14	L	29	64	160	12	42	2	1	0	16	11	7	9	.263	.322	.288
Gene Packard	P42,OF2	L	26	45	116	13	28	2	2	1	12	2	22	2	.241	.254	.319
John Potts	OF31	L	27	41	102	14	27	4	0	1	9	25	13	7	.265	.414	.333
Jack Enzenroth†	C24	R	28	26	67	7	12	4	1	0	5	5	19	0	.179	.236	.269
Drummond Brown	C23,1B2	R	29	31	58	4	11	3	0	0	5	7	6	1	.190	.277	.241
Walter Tappan	SS8,3B6,2B1	R	23	18	39	1	8	1	0	1	3	1	—	1	.205	.225	.308

G. Perring, 1 G at SS

Pitcher	T	Age	G	GS	CG	ShO	IP	H	HR	BB	SO	W-L	Sv	ERA
Nick Cullop†	L	26	44	36	22	4	295.2	256	6	87	149	14-17	1	2.34
Gene Packard	L	26	42	34	24	4	302.0	282	5	88	154	21-13	4	2.89
Dwight Stone	R	27	39	22	6	0	186.2	205	8	77	88	7-14	0	4.34
Chief Johnson†	R	28	20	19	12	2	134.0	157	2	33	78	9-10	0	3.16
Pete Henning	R	26	28	14	7	0	138.0	153	5	58	45	6-12	1	4.83
Dan Adams	R	25	36	14	6	0	135.0	141	3	52	38	3-9	3	3.51
Ben Harris	R	24	31	14	5	0	154.0	179	7	41	40	7-8	1	4.09
George Hogan	R	28	4	1	0	0	13.0	12	1	7	7	0-1	0	4.15
Ducky Swan	R	26	1	0	0	0	1.0	0	0	1	1	0-0	0	0.00
George Perring	R	29	1	0	0	0	0.2	2	0	1	0	0-0	0	13.50

1914 Pittsburgh Rebels 7th FL 64-86 .427 22.5 GB

Doc Gessler (3-8)/Rebel Oakes (61-78)

Player	Gm by Position	B	Age	G	AB	R	H	2B	3B	HR	RBI	BB	SO	SB	Avg	OBP	Slg
Claude Berry	C122	R	34	124	411	35	98	18	9	2	36	26	50	6	.238	.284	.341
Hugh Bradley	1B118	R	29	118	427	41	131	20	6	0	61	27	27	7	.307	.359	.382
Jack Lewis	2B115,SS1	R	30	117	394	32	92	14	5	1	48	17	46	9	.234	.276	.302
Ed Lennox	3B123	R	28	124	430	71	134	25	10	11	84	71	38	19	.312	.414	.493
Ed Holly	SS94,OF2,2B1	R	34	100	350	28	86	9	4	0	26	17	52	14	.246	.281	.294
Rebel Oakes	OF145	L	27	145	571	82	178	18	10	7	75	35	22	28	.312	.359	.415
Jimmie Savage	OF93,3B29,SS11*	S	30	132	479	81	136	9	9	1	26	67	32	17	.284	.372	.347
Davy Jones	OF93	L	34	97	352	58	96	9	8	2	24	42	16	15	.273	.355	.361
Tex McDonald†	OF29,2B27,SS5	L	23	67	223	27	71	16	7	3	29	13	—	9	.318	.361	.493
Cy Rheam	1B43,3B13,2B11*	R	20	73	214	15	45	5	3	0	20	9	33	6	.210	.242	.262
Frank Delahanty†	OF36,2B4	R	31	41	159	25	38	4	4	1	7	11	—	7	.239	.297	.333
Steve Yerkes†	SS39	R	26	39	142	18	48	9	5	1	25	11	13	2	.338	.386	.493
Mike Menosky	OF41	L	19	68	140	26	37	4	1	2	9	16	30	5	.264	.352	.350
Skipper Roberts†	C23,OF1	L	26	52	94	12	22	4	2	1	8	2	20	3	.234	.258	.351
Ralph Mattis	OF24	R	23	36	85	14	21	4	1	0	8	9	11	2	.247	.326	.318
Cy Barger	P33,SS1	L	29	38	83	4	17	1	2	0	9	2	5	0	.205	.224	.265
Doc Kerr†	C18	S	32	42	71	3	17	4	2	1	7	10	—	0	.239	.333	.394
Bob Coulson	OF18	R	27	18	64	7	13	1	0	0	3	7	10	2	.203	.282	.219
Mysterious Walker	P35,OF1	R	30	36	53	1	6	1	0	0	1	6	21	0	.113	.203	.132
Felix Chouinard†	2B4,OF3,SS1	R	26	9	30	2	9	1	0	1	3	0	—	1	.300	.300	.433
Jim Scott	SS8	R	25	8	24	2	6	1	0	0	1	5	—	1	.250	.379	.292
Frank Madden	C1	—	21	2	2	0	1	0	0	0	1	0	1	0	.500	.500	.500
Medric Boucher†		R	28	1	1	0	0	0	0	0	0	0	—	0	.000	.000	.000

J. Savage, 3 G at 2B; C. Rheam, 1 G at OF

Pitcher	T	Age	G	GS	CG	ShO	IP	H	HR	BB	SO	W-L	Sv	ERA
Howie Camnitz	R	32	36	34	20	1	262.0	256	8	90	82	14-18	1	3.23
Walt Dickson	R	35	40	32	19	3	256.2	262	5	74	63	9-21	1	3.16
Elmer Knetzer	R	28	37	30	20	3	272.0	257	9	88	146	20-11	1	2.88
Cy Barger	R	29	33	26	18	1	228.1	252	7	63	70	10-16	1	4.34
Mysterious Walker	R	30	35	21	12	0	169.1	197	3	74	79	4-16	0	4.31
Frank Allen†	L	24	1	1	1	0	7.0	9	0	0	3	1-0	0	5.14
George LaClaire	R	27	22	7	5	1	103.1	99	1	25	49	5-2	0	4.01
Willie Adams	R	23	15	2	1	0	55.1	70	4	22	14	1-1	0	3.74
Ed Henderson†	L	29	6	1	1	0	16.0	14	2	8	4	0-1	0	3.94

1914 St. Louis Terriers 8th FL 62-89 .411 25.0 GB

Three Finger Brown (50-63)/Fielder Jones (12-26)

Player	Gm by Position	B	Age	G	AB	R	H	2B	3B	HR	RBI	BB	SO	SB	Avg	OBP	Slg
Mike Simon	C78	R	31	93	276	21	57	11	2	0	21	18	21	2	.207	.263	.261
Hughie Miller	1B130	R	26	132	490	51	109	20	5	0	46	27	57	4	.222	.264	.284
Doc Crandall	2B63,P27,SS1*	R	26	118	278	40	86	16	5	2	41	58	32	3	.309	.429	.424
Al Boucher	3B147	R	32	147	516	62	119	26	4	2	49	52	88	13	.231	.304	.308
Al Bridwell	SS103,2B11	L	30	117	381	46	90	6	5	1	33	71	18	9	.236	.359	.286
Jack Tobin	OF132	L	22	139	529	81	143	24	10	7	35	51	53	20	.270	.340	.393
Delos Drake	OF116,1B18	R	27	138	514	51	129	18	8	3	42	31	57	17	.251	.295	.335
Ward Miller	OF111	L	29	121	402	49	118	17	7	4	50	59	36	18	.294	.397	.400
John Misse	2B50,SS48,3B2	R	29	99	306	28	60	8	1	0	22	36	52	3	.196	.281	.229
Fred Kommers†	OF67	L	28	76	244	33	75	9	8	3	41	24	—	7	.307	.376	.447
Grover Hartley	C32,2B13,1B9*	R	25	86	212	24	61	13	2	1	25	12	26	4	.288	.329	.382
LaRue Kirby	OF50	S	24	52	195	21	48	6	3	2	18	14	30	5	.246	.303	.338
Harry Chapman	C51,1B1,2B1*	R	26	64	181	16	38	2	1	0	14	13	27	2	.210	.270	.232
Joe Mathes	2B23	S	22	26	85	10	25	3	0	0	6	9	11	1	.294	.362	.329
Manuel Cueto	3B10,SS5,2B2	R	22	19	43	2	4	0	0	0	2	5	7	0	.093	.188	.093
Armando Marsans†	2B7,SS2	R	26	9	40	5	14	0	2	0	2	3	—	4	.350	.395	.450
Fielder Jones		L	42	5	3	0	1	0	0	0	0	1	—	0	.333	.500	.333

D. Crandall, 1 G at OF; G. Hartley, 3 G at 3B, 2 G at OF; H. Chapman, 1 G at OF

Pitcher	T	Age	G	GS	CG	ShO	IP	H	HR	BB	SO	W-L	Sv	ERA
Bob Groom	R	29	42	34	23	1	280.2	281	9	75	167	13-20	1	3.24
Dave Davenport†	R	24	33	26	13	2	215.2	204	3	80	142	8-13	4	3.46
Henry Keupper	L	27	42	25	12	1	213.0	256	3	49	70	8-20	0	4.27
Doc Crandall	R	26	27	21	18	1	196.0	194	8	52	84	13-9	0	3.54
Ed Willett	R	30	27	21	14	0	175.0	208	5	56	73	4-16	0	4.22
T. Finger Brown†	R	37	26	18	13	2	174.2	172	7	43	81	12-6	0	3.30
Doc Watson†	L	28	9	7	4	2	56.0	41	1	24	18	3-4	0	1.93
Ernie Herbert	R	27	18	2	0	0	50.1	56	2	27	24	1-1	1	3.75
Ted Welch	R	21	3	0	0	0	6.0	6	0	3	2	0-0	0	6.00

»1915 Boston Red Sox 1st AL 101-50 .669 —

Bill Carrigan

Player	Gm by Position	B	Age	G	AB	R	H	2B	3B	HR	RBI	BB	SO	SB	Avg	OBP	Slg
Pinch Thomas	C82	L	27	86	203	21	48	4	4	0	21	13	20	3	.236	.296	.296
Doc Hoblitzell	1B117	R	26	124	399	54	113	15	12	2	61	38	26	9	.283	.351	.396
Heinie Wagner	2B79,3B1,OF1	R	34	84	267	38	64	11	2	0	29	37	34	8	.240	.339	.296
Larry Gardner	3B127	L	29	127	430	51	111	14	6	1	55	39	24	11	.258	.327	.326
Everett Scott	SS100	R	22	100	359	25	72	11	0	0	28	17	21	4	.201	.237	.231
Duffy Lewis	OF152	R	27	152	557	69	162	31	7	2	76	45	63	14	.291	.348	.382
Tris Speaker	OF150	L	27	150	547	108	176	25	12	0	69	81	14	29	.322	.416	.411
Harry Hooper	OF149	L	27	149	566	90	133	20	13	2	51	89	36	22	.235	.342	.327
Hal Janvrin	SS64,3B20,2B8	R	22	99	316	41	85	9	1	0	37	14	27	8	.269	.317	.304
Jack Barry†	2B78	R	28	78	248	30	65	13	2	0	26	24	11	6	.262	.342	.331
Hick Cady	C77	R	29	78	205	25	57	10	2	0	17	19	25	0	.278	.342	.346
Del Gainer	1B56,OF6	R	28	82	200	30	59	5	8	1	29	21	31	7	.295	.371	.415
Bill Carrigan	C44	R	31	46	95	10	19	3	0	0	7	16	12	0	.200	.321	.232
Olaf Henriksen	OF25	L	27	73	92	9	18	2	2	0	13	18	7	1	.196	.333	.261
Mike McNally	3B18,2B5	R	22	23	53	7	8	0	1	0	0	3	7	0	.151	.196	.189
Chick Shorten	OF5	L	23	6	14	1	3	1	0	0	0	0	2	0	.214	.214	.286
Ray Haley	C4	R	24	5	7	2	1	1	0	0	0	1	0	0	.143	.250	.286
Bill Rodgers†	2B6	L	28	11	6	2	0	0	0	0	0	3	2	0	.000	.333	.000
Wally Rehg	OF1	R	26	5	5	2	1	0	0	0	0	0	1	1	.200	.200	.200

Pitcher	T	Age	G	GS	CG	ShO	IP	H	HR	BB	SO	W-L	Sv	ERA
Rube Foster	R	27	37	33	22	5	255.1	217	3	86	82	19-8	1	2.11
Ernie Shore	R	24	38	32	17	4	247.0	207	3	66	102	19-8	0	1.64
Babe Ruth	L	20	32	28	16	1	217.2	166	3	85	112	18-8	0	2.44
Dutch Leonard	L	23	32	21	10	2	183.1	130	3	67	116	15-7	0	2.36
Joe Wood	R	25	25	16	10	3	157.1	120	1	44	63	15-5	2	1.49
Vean Gregg	L	30	18	9	3	1	75.0	71	2	32	43	4-2	3	3.36
Carl Mays	R	23	38	6	2	0	131.2	119	0	21	65	6-5	7	2.60
Ray Collins	L	28	25	9	2	0	104.2	101	1	31	43	4-7	2	4.30
Herb Pennock†	L	21	5	1	0	0	14.0	23	0	10	7	0-0	0	9.64
Ralph Comstock†	R	24	3	0	0	0	9.0	10	2	2	1	1-0	0	2.00
Guy Cooper	R	22	1	0	0	0	2.0	0	0	2	0	0-0	0	0.00

1915 Detroit Tigers 2nd AL 100-54 .649 2.5 GB

Hughie Jennings

Player	Gm by Position	B	Age	G	AB	R	H	2B	3B	HR	RBI	BB	SO	SB	Avg	OBP	Slg
Oscar Stanage	C100	R	32	100	300	27	67	9	2	1	31	20	41	5	.223	.274	.277
George Burns	1B104	R	22	105	392	49	99	18	3	5	50	22	51	9	.253	.301	.352
Ralph Young	2B119	S	25	123	378	44	92	6	5	0	31	53	31	12	.243	.339	.286
Ossie Vitt	3B151,2B2	R	25	152	560	116	140	18	13	1	48	80	22	26	.250	.348	.334
Donie Bush	SS155	S	27	155	561	99	128	12	8	1	44	118	44	35	.228	.364	.283
Sam Crawford	OF156	L	35	156	612	81	183	31	19	4	112	66	29	24	.299	.367	.431
Ty Cobb	OF156	L	28	156	563	144	208	31	13	3	99	118	43	96	.369	.486	.487
Bobby Veach	OF152	L	27	152	569	81	178	40	10	3	112	68	43	16	.313	.390	.434
Marty Kavanagh	1B44,2B42,SS2*	R	24	113	332	55	98	14	13	4	49	42	44	8	.295	.378	.452
Del Baker	C61	R	23	68	134	16	33	3	3	0	15	15	15	3	.246	.327	.313
Red McKee	C35	L	24	55	106	10	29	5	0	1	17	13	16	1	.274	.353	.349
B. Doll Jacobson†	1B10,OF7	R	24	37	65	5	14	6	2	0	4	5	14	0	.215	.282	.369
George Moriarty	3B12,1B1,2B1*	R	31	31	38	2	8	1	0	0	0	5	7	1	.211	.318	.237
Frank Fuller	2B9,SS1	S	22	14	32	6	5	0	0	0	2	9	7	2	.156	.341	.156
John Peters	C1	R	21	1	3	0	0	0	0	0	0	0	1	0	.000	.000	.000

M. Kavanagh, 2 G at OF; G. Moriarty, 1 G at OF

Pitcher	T	Age	G	GS	CG	ShO	IP	H	HR	BB	SO	W-L	Sv	ERA
Harry Coveleski	L	29	50	38	20	1	312.2	271	2	87	150	22-13	4	2.45
Hooks Dauss	R	25	46	35	27	1	309.2	261	1	112	132	24-13	3	2.50
Jean Dubuc	R	26	39	33	22	5	258.0	231	5	88	74	17-12	2	3.21
Bill James†	R	28	11	9	3	1	67.0	57	1	33	24	7-3	0	2.42
Grover Lowdermilk†	R	30	7	5	0	0	28.0	17	0	24	18	4-1	0	4.18
Ross Reynolds	R	27	4	2	0	0	11.1	17	0	5	2	0-1	0	6.35
Bernie Boland	R	23	45	18	8	1	202.2	167	2	75	72	13-7	2	3.11
Bill Steen†	R	27	20	7	3	0	79.1	83	0	22	28	5-1	4	2.72
Pug Cavet	L	25	17	7	2	0	71.0	83	2	22	26	4-2	1	4.06
Red Oldham	L	21	17	2	1	0	57.2	52	1	17	17	3-0	4	2.81
George Boehler	R	23	8	0	0	0	15.0	19	0	4	7	1-1	0	1.80
Razor Ledbetter	R	20	1	0	0	0	1.0	1	0	0	0	0-0	0	0.00

1915 Chicago White Sox 3rd AL 93-61 .604 9.5 GB

Pants Rowland

Player	Gm by Position	B	Age	G	AB	R	H	2B	3B	HR	RBI	BB	SO	SB	Avg	OBP	Slg
Ray Schalk	C134	R	22	135	413	46	110	14	4	1	54	62	21	15	.266	.366	.327
Jack Fournier	1B65,OF57	L	25	126	422	86	136	20	18	5	77	64	37	21	.322	.429	.491
Eddie Collins	2B155	L	28	155	521	118	173	22	10	4	77	119	27	46	.332	.460	.436
Lena Blackburne	3B83,SS9	R	28	96	283	33	61	5	1	0	25	35	34	13	.216	.304	.240
Buck Weaver	SS148	R	24	148	563	83	151	18	11	3	49	32	58	24	.268	.316	.355
Happy Felsch	OF118	R	23	121	427	65	106	18	11	3	53	51	59	16	.248	.334	.363
Shano Collins	OF104,1B47	R	29	153	576	73	148	24	17	2	85	28	50	38	.257	.298	.368
Eddie Murphy†	OF70	L	23	70	273	51	86	11	5	0	26	39	12	20	.315	.410	.392
Braggo Roth†	3B35,OF30	R	22	70	240	44	60	6	10	3	35	29	50	12	.250	.338	.396
Joe Jackson†	OF46	L	25	46	162	21	43	4	5	2	36	24	12	6	.265	.370	.389
Bunny Brief	1B46	R	22	48	154	13	33	6	2	2	17	16	28	8	.214	.305	.318
Finners Quinlan	OF32	L	27	42	114	11	22	3	0	0	7	4	11	3	.193	.270	.219
Pete Johns	3B28	R	26	28	100	7	21	2	1	0	11	8	11	2	.210	.275	.250
Nemo Leibold†	OF22	L	23	36	74	10	17	1	0	0	11	15	11	1	.230	.360	.243
Wally Mayer	C20	R	24	22	54	3	12	3	1	0	5	5	8	0	.222	.288	.315
Tom Daly	C19,1B1	R	23	29	47	5	9	1	0	0	3	5	9	0	.191	.269	.213
Jim Breton	3B14,2B1,SS1	R	23	16	36	3	5	1	0	0	1	5	9	2	.139	.262	.167
Ray Demmitt	OF3	L	31	9	6	0	0	0	0	0	0	1	2	0	.000	.143	.000
Howard Baker†		R	27	2	2	0	0	0	0	0	0	0	2	0	.000	.000	.000
Charlie Jackson		L	21	1	1	0	0	0	0	0	0	0	1	0	.000	.000	.000
Larry Chappell		L	25	1	1	0	0	0	0	0	0	0	0	0	.000	.000	.000

Pitcher	T	Age	G	GS	CG	ShO	IP	H	HR	BB	SO	W-L	Sv	ERA
Jim Scott	R	27	48	35	23	7	296.1	256	3	78	120	24-11	2	2.03
Red Faber	R	26	50	32	22	3	299.2	264	3	99	182	24-14	2	2.55
Joe Benz	R	29	39	28	17	2	238.1	209	4	43	81	15-11	0	2.11
Eddie Cicotte	R	31	39	26	15	1	223.1	216	2	48	106	13-12	3	3.02
Reb Russell	L	26	41	25	10	3	229.1	215	0	47	90	11-10	2	2.59
Ed Walsh	R	34	3	3	3	1	27.0	19	0	7	12	3-0	0	1.33
Hi Jasper	R	34	3	2	1	0	15.2	8	2	9	15	0-1	0	4.60
Ed Klepfer†	R	27	3	2	1	0	12.2	11	0	5	3	1-0	0	2.84
Mellie Wolfgang	R	25	17	2	0	0	53.2	39	0	12	21	2-2	0	1.84
Dixie Davis	R	24	2	0	0	0	3.0	2	0	2	2	0-0	0	0.00
Walt Johnson	R	22	1	0	0	0	2.0	3	0	0	3	0-0	0	9.00

1915 Washington Senators 4th AL 85-68 .556 17.0 GB

Clark Griffith

Player	Gm by Position	B	Age	G	AB	R	H	2B	3B	HR	RBI	BB	SO	SB	Avg	OBP	Slg
John Henry	C94	R	25	95	277	20	61	9	2	1	22	36	28	10	.220	.323	.278
Chick Gandil	1B134	R	28	136	485	53	141	20	15	2	64	29	33	20	.291	.340	.406
Eddie Foster	3B79,2B75	R	28	154	618	75	170	25	10	0	52	48	30	20	.275	.329	.348
Howard Shanks	OF80,3B49,2B10	R	24	141	492	52	123	19	8	0	47	30	42	12	.250	.297	.321
George McBride	SS146	R	34	146	476	54	97	8	6	1	30	29	60	10	.204	.251	.252
Clyde Milan	OF151	L	28	153	573	83	165	13	7	2	66	53	32	40	.288	.353	.346
Danny Moeller	OF116	S	30	118	438	65	99	11	10	2	23	59	63	32	.226	.319	.311
Merito Acosta	OF53	L	19	72	163	20	34	4	1	0	18	28	15	8	.209	.338	.245
Rip Williams	C40,1B15,3B1	R	33	91	197	14	48	8	4	0	31	18	20	4	.244	.320	.325
Ray Morgan	2B57,3B2,SS2	R	26	62	193	21	45	5	4	0	21	30	15	6	.233	.342	.301
Walter Johnson	P49,OF4	R	27	64	147	14	34	7	4	2	17	8	34	0	.231	.276	.374
Tom Connolly	3B24,OF19,SS4	L	22	50	141	14	26	3	2	0	7	14	19	5	.184	.268	.234
Eddie Ainsmith	C42	R	23	47	120	13	24	4	2	0	6	10	18	7	.200	.267	.267
Charlie Jamieson	OF17	L	22	17	68	9	19	3	2	0	7	6	9	0	.279	.338	.382
Doug Neff	3B12,2B10,SS7	R	23	30	60	1	10	1	0	0	4	4	6	1	.167	.219	.183
Turner Barber	OF19	L	21	20	53	9	16	1	1	0	6	6	7	6	.302	.383	.358
Joe Judge	1B10,OF2	L	21	12	41	7	17	2	0	0	9	4	6	2	.415	.500	.463
Henri Rondeau	OF11	R	28	14	40	3	7	0	0	0	4	4	3	1	.175	.250	.175
Carl Sawyer	2B6,SS4	R	24	10	32	8	8	1	0	0	3	4	5	2	.250	.351	.281
Merlin Kopp	OF9	S	23	16	32	2	8	0	0	0	0	5	7	1	.250	.351	.250
Sam Mayer	OF10,P1,1B1	R	22	11	29	5	7	0	0	1	4	4	2	1	.241	.333	.345
Horace Milan	OF10	R	21	11	27	6	11	1	1	0	7	8	7	2	.407	.543	.519
Charlie Pick		L	27	3	2	0	0	0	0	0	0	0	0	0	.000	.000	.000

Pitcher	T	Age	G	GS	CG	ShO	IP	H	HR	BB	SO	W-L	Sv	ERA
Walter Johnson	R	27	47	39	35	7	336.2	258	1	56	203	27-13	4	1.55
Joe Boehling	L	24	40	32	14	2	229.1	217	5	119	108	14-13	0	3.22
Bert Gallia	R	23	43	29	14	3	259.2	220	2	64	130	17-11	1	2.29
Jim Shaw	R	21	25	18	7	1	133.0	102	2	76	78	6-11	2	2.50
Harry Harper	L	20	19	10	5	2	86.1	66	1	40	54	4-4	2	1.77
George Dumont	R	19	6	4	3	2	40.0	23	0	12	18	2-1	0	2.03
Sam Rice	R	25	4	2	1	0	18.0	13	0	9	9	1-0	0	2.00
Jack Bentley	L	20	4	2	0	0	11.1	8	0	3	0	0-2	0	0.79
Doc Ayers	R	25	40	16	8	2	211.1	178	1	38	96	14-9	3	2.21
Bill Hopper	R	24	13	0	0	0	31.1	39	0	16	8	0-1	1	4.60
Joe Engel	L	22	11	3	0	0	33.2	30	0	19	9	0-3	0	3.21
Nick Altrock	L	38	1	0	0	0	3.0	7	0	1	2	0-0	1	9.00
Sam Mayer	L	22	1	0	0	0	0.0	0	0	2	0	0-0	0	—

1915 New York Yankees 5th AL 69-83 .454 32.5 GB

Wild Bill Donovan

Player	Gm by Position	B	Age	G	AB	R	H	2B	3B	HR	RBI	BB	SO	SB	Avg	OBP	Slg
Les Nunamaker	C77,1B2	R	26	87	249	24	56	6	3	0	17	23	24	3	.225	.293	.273
Wally Pipp	1B134	L	22	136	479	59	118	20	13	4	60	66	81	18	.246	.339	.367
Luke Boone	2B115,SS11,3B4	R	25	130	431	44	88	12	2	5	43	41	53	14	.204	.285	.276
Fritz Maisel	3B134	R	25	135	530	77	149	16	6	4	46	48	35	51	.281	.342	.357
Roger Peckinpaugh	SS142	R	24	142	540	67	119	18	7	5	44	49	72	19	.220	.289	.307
Doc Cook	OF131	L	29	132	476	70	129	16	5	2	33	62	43	29	.271	.364	.338
Hugh High	OF117	L	27	119	427	51	110	19	7	1	43	62	47	22	.258	.356	.342
Roy Hartzell	OF107,2B5,3B2	L	33	119	387	39	97	11	2	3	60	57	37	7	.251	.351	.313
Paddy Baumann	2B43,3B19	R	29	76	219	30	64	13	1	2	28	28	32	9	.292	.380	.388
Birdie Cree	OF53	R	32	74	196	23	42	8	2	0	15	36	22	7	.214	.353	.276
Jeff Sweeney	C53	R	26	53	137	12	26	2	0	0	5	25	12	3	.190	.319	.204
Charlie Mullen	1B27	R	26	40	90	11	24	1	0	0	7	10	12	5	.267	.340	.278
Elmer Miller	OF26	R	24	26	83	4	12	1	0	0	3	4	14	0	.145	.193	.157
Walt Alexander†	C24	R	24	25	68	7	17	4	0	1	5	13	16	2	.250	.370	.353
Skeeter Shelton	OF10	R	27	10	40	1	1	0	0	0	0	2	10	0	.025	.071	.025
Tim Hendryx	OF12	R	24	13	40	4	8	2	0	0	1	4	2	0	.200	.289	.250
Ed Barney†	OF10	L	25	11	36	1	7	0	0	0	8	3	6	2	.194	.256	.194
Ernie Krueger	C8	R	24	10	29	3	5	1	0	0	0	0	5	0	.172	.200	.207
Pi Schwert	C9	R	22	9	18	6	5	3	0	0	6	1	6	0	.278	.316	.444
Tom Daley	OF2	L	30	10	8	2	2	0	0	0	1	2	2	1	.250	.400	.250
Gene Layden	OF2	L	21	3	7	2	2	0	0	0	0	0	1	0	.286	.286	.286
Frank Gilhooley	OF1	L	23	1	4	0	0	0	0	0	0	0	1	0	.000	.000	.000
Roxy Walters	C2	R	22	2	3	0	1	0	0	0	0	0	0	0	.333	.333	.333

Pitcher	T	Age	G	GS	CG	ShO	IP	H	HR	BB	SO	W-L	Sv	ERA
Ray Caldwell	R	27	36	35	31	3	305.0	266	6	107	130	19-16	0	2.89
Ray Fisher	R	27	30	28	19	4	247.2	219	7	62	97	18-11	0	2.11
Jack Warhop	R	30	21	19	12	0	143.1	164	7	52	34	7-9	0	3.96
Marty McHale	R	26	13	11	6	0	78.1	86	1	19	25	3-7	0	4.25
Boardwalk Brown	R	28	19	10	5	0	96.2	95	4	47	34	2-6	0	4.10
Ray Keating	R	23	11	10	8	1	79.1	66	3	45	37	3-6	0	3.63
Bob Shawkey†	R	24	16	9	5	1	85.2	78	2	35	31	4-7	0	3.26
King Cole	R	29	10	6	2	0	51.0	41	2	22	19	3-3	1	3.18
George Mogridge	L	26	6	6	3	1	41.0	33	0	11	11	2-3	0	1.76
Allan Russell	R	21	5	3	1	0	27.0	21	1	21	21	1-2	0	2.67
Cliff Markle	R	21	3	2	2	0	23.0	15	1	6	12	2-0	0	0.39
Dan Tipple	R	25	3	2	2	0	19.0	14	1	11	14	1-1	0	0.95
Neal Brady	R	18	2	1	0	0	8.2	9	0	7	6	0-0	0	3.12
Cy Pieh	R	28	21	8	3	2	94.0	78	2	39	46	4-5	1	2.87
Wild Bill Donovan	R	38	9	1	0	0	33.2	35	1	10	17	0-3	0	4.81
Dazzy Vance†	R	24	8	3	1	0	28.0	23	1	16	18	0-3	0	3.54
Ensign Cottrell	L	26	7	0	0	0	21.1	29	2	7	7	0-1	0	3.38

1915 St. Louis Browns 6th AL 63-91 .409 39.5 GB

Branch Rickey

Player	Gm by Position	B	Age	G	AB	R	H	2B	3B	HR	RBI	BB	SO	SB	Avg	OBP	Slg
Sam Agnew	C102	R	28	104	295	18	60	4	2	0	19	12	36	5	.203	.247	.231
John Leary	1B53,C11	R	24	75	227	19	55	10	0	0	15	5	36	2	.242	.268	.286
Del Pratt	2B158	R	27	159	602	61	175	31	11	3	78	26	43	32	.291	.323	.394
Jimmy Austin	3B141	S	35	141	477	61	127	6	6	1	30	64	60	18	.266	.355	.310
Doc Lavan	SS157	R	24	157	514	44	112	17	7	1	48	42	83	13	.218	.281	.284
Burt Shotton	OF154	L	30	156	559	93	158	18	11	1	30	118	62	43	.283	.409	.360
Tilly Walker	OF139	R	27	144	510	53	137	20	7	5	49	36	77	20	.269	.323	.365
Dee Walsh	OF45,3B2,P1*	S	25	59	150	13	33	5	0	0	6	14	25	6	.220	.308	.253
Ivan Howard	1B48,3B23,OF17*	S	32	113	324	43	90	10	7	2	43	43	48	29	.278	.368	.370
George Sisler	1B36,OF29,P15	L	22	81	274	28	78	10	2	3	29	7	27	10	.285	.307	.369
Hank Severeid	C64	R	24	80	203	12	45	6	1	1	22	16	25	2	.222	.279	.276
Dick Kauffman	1B32,OF1	S	27	37	124	9	32	8	2	0	14	5	27	0	.258	.298	.355
Gus Williams	OF35	L	27	45	119	15	24	2	2	1	11	6	16	11	.202	.246	.277
B. Doll Jacobson†	OF32	R	24	34	115	13	24	6	1	1	9	10	26	3	.209	.295	.304
Ernie Walker	OF33	L	24	50	109	15	23	4	2	0	9	23	32	5	.211	.348	.284
Billy Lee	OF15,3B1	R	23	18	59	2	11	1	0	0	4	6	5	1	.186	.262	.203
Muddy Ruel	C6	R	19	10	14	0	0	0	0	0	1	5	5	0	.000	.263	.000
Bobby Wallace	SS9	R	41	9	13	1	3	0	1	0	4	5	0	0	.231	.444	.385
George O'Brien	C3	R	25	3	9	1	2	0	0	0	0	1	2	0	.222	.300	.222
Pat Parker	OF2	R	22	3	6	0	1	0	0	0	1	0	3	0	.167	.167	.167
Ray Schmandt	1B1	R	19	3	4	0	0	0	0	0	0	0	1	0	.000	.000	.000
Shorty Dee	SS1	R	25	1	3	1	0	0	0	0	0	1	0	0	.000	.250	.000
Bill Dalrymple	3B1	—	24	2	2	0	0	0	0	0	0	0	0	0	.000	.000	.000
Bob Burkam		L	22	1	1	0	0	0	0	0	0	0	1	0	.000	.000	.000
Walt Alexander†	C1	R	24	1	1	0	0	0	0	0	0	0	0	0	.000	.000	.000

D. Walsh, 1 G at 2B, 1 G at SS; I. Howard, 2 G at 2B, 2 G at SS

Pitcher	T	Age	G	GS	CG	ShO	IP	H	HR	BB	SO	W-L	Sv	ERA
Carl Weilman	L	25	47	31	19	3	295.2	240	6	83	125	18-19	4	2.34
Grover Lowdermilk†	R	30	38	29	14	1	222.1	183	1	133	130	9-17	0	3.12
Earl Hamilton	L	23	35	27	13	1	204.0	203	4	69	63	9-17	0	2.87
Bill James†	R	28	34	23	8	0	170.1	155	2	92	58	7-10	1	3.59
George Sisler	L	22	15	8	6	0	70.0	62	0	38	41	4-4	0	2.83
Tim McCabe	R	20	7	4	4	1	41.2	25	1	9	17	3-1	0	1.30
Tom Phillips	R	26	5	4	1	0	27.1	28	0	12	5	1-3	0	2.96
Jim Park	R	22	3	3	1	0	22.2	18	1	9	5	2-0	0	1.19
Pete Sims	R	24	3	2	0	0	8.1	6	0	6	4	1-0	0	4.32
Johnny Tillman	R	21	2	1	0	0	10.0	6	0	4	6	1-0	0	0.90
Carl East	R	20	1	1	0	0	3.1	6	0	2	1	0-0	0	16.20
Scott Perry	R	24	1	1	0	0	2.0	5	0	1	0	0-0	0	13.50
Ernie Koob	L	22	28	13	6	0	133.2	119	2	50	37	4-5	1	2.36
Parson Perryman	R	26	24	3	0	0	50.1	52	2	16	19	2-4	0	3.93
Harry Hoch	R	28	12	3	1	0	40.0	52	2	26	9	0-4	0	7.20
Red Hoff	L	24	11	3	2	0	43.2	26	0	24	23	2-2	0	1.24
G. Baumgardner	R	23	7	1	1	0	22.1	29	0	11	6	0-2	0	4.43
Rollin Cook	R	24	5	0	0	0	13.2	16	0	9	7	0-2	0	7.24
Walt Leverenz	L	27	5	1	0	0	9.0	11	0	8	3	0-2	1	8.00
Allen Sothoron	R	22	3	1	0	0	3.2	8	0	5	2	0-1	0	7.36
Alex Remneas	R	29	2	0	0	0	6.0	3	0	3	5	0-0	0	1.50
Dee Walsh	R	25	1	0	0	0	2.0	2	0	2	0	0-0	0	13.50
Reeve McKay	R	33	1	0	0	0	1.0	1	0	0	0	0-0	0	9.00

1915 Cleveland Indians 7th AL 57-95 .375 44.5 GB

Joe Birmingham (12-16)/Lee Fohl (45-79)

Player	Gm by Position	B	Age	G	AB	R	H	2B	3B	HR	RBI	BB	SO	SB	Avg	OBP	Slg
Steve O'Neill	C115	R	23	121	386	32	91	14	2	2	34	26	41	2	.236	.293	.298
Jay Kirke	1B87	L	27	87	339	35	105	19	2	2	40	14	21	5	.310	.346	.395
Bill Wambsganss	2B78,3B35	R	21	121	375	30	73	4	4	0	21	36	50	8	.195	.272	.227
Walter Barbare	3B68,1B1	R	23	77	246	15	47	3	1	0	11	10	27	6	.191	.235	.211
Ray Chapman	SS154	R	24	154	570	101	154	14	17	3	67	70	82	36	.270	.353	.370
Elmer Smith	OF123	L	22	144	476	37	118	23	12	3	67	36	75	10	.248	.301	.366
Jack Graney	OF115	L	29	116	404	42	105	20	7	1	56	59	29	12	.260	.357	.351
Nemo Leibold†	OF52	L	23	57	207	28	53	5	4	0	4	24	16	5	.256	.339	.319
Joe Jackson†	OF49,1B30	L	25	82	299	42	99	16	9	3	45	28	11	10	.331	.394	.475
Terry Turner	2B51,3B20	R	34	75	262	35	66	14	1	0	14	29	13	12	.252	.329	.313
Billy Southworth	OF44	L	22	60	177	25	39	2	5	0	8	36	12	2	.220	.352	.288
Braggo Roth†	OF39	R	22	39	144	23	43	4	7	4	20	22	22	14	.299	.399	.507
Denney Wilie	OF35	L	24	45	131	14	33	4	1	2	10	26	18	2	.252	.384	.344
Ben Egan	C40	R	31	42	120	4	13	3	0	0	6	8	14	0	.108	.164	.133
Joe Evans	3B30,2B2	R	20	42	109	17	28	4	2	0	11	22	18	6	.257	.382	.330
Jack Hammond	2B19	R	24	35	84	9	18	2	1	0	4	1	19	0	.214	.224	.262
Roy Wood	1B21,OF2	R	22	33	78	5	15	2	1	0	3	2	13	1	.192	.232	.244
Pete Shields	1B23	R	23	23	72	4	15	6	0	0	6	4	14	3	.208	.250	.292
Bill Rodgers†	2B13	L	28	16	45	8	14	2	0	0	7	8	7	3	.311	.415	.356
Jim Eschen	OF10	R	23	15	42	11	10	1	0	0	2	5	9	0	.238	.319	.262
Josh Billings	C7,OF1	R	23	8	21	2	4	1	0	0	0	0	6	1	.190	.190	.238
Tex Hoffman	3B3	L	21	9	13	1	2	0	0	0	2	1	5	0	.154	.214	.154
Ben Paschal		R	19	9	9	0	1	0	0	0	0	0	3	0	.111	.111	.111
Howie Haworth	C5	L	21	7	7	0	1	0	0	0	1	2	2	0	.143	.333	.143
Lee Gooch		R	25	2	2	0	1	0	0	0	0	0	0	0	.500	.500	.500

Pitcher	T	Age	G	GS	CG	ShO	IP	H	HR	BB	SO	W-L	Sv	ERA
Willie Mitchell	L	25	36	30	12	1	236.0	210	1	84	149	11-14	1	2.82
Guy Morton	R	22	34	27	15	6	240.0	189	5	60	134	16-15	1	2.14
Rip Hagerman	R	27	29	22	7	0	151.0	156	4	77	69	6-14	0	3.52
Roy Walker	R	22	25	15	4	0	131.0	122	1	65	57	4-9	1	3.98
Bill Steen†	R	27	10	7	2	0	45.1	51	1	15	22	1-4	0	4.96
Ed Klepfer†	R	27	8	7	2	0	43.0	47	0	11	13	1-6	0	2.09
Allan Collamore	R	28	11	6	5	2	64.1	52	1	22	15	2-5	0	2.38
Clarence Garrett	R	24	4	4	2	0	23.1	19	1	6	5	2-2	0	2.31
Abe Bowman	R	22	2	1	0	0	1.1	1	0	3	0	0-1	0	20.25
Sad Sam Jones	R	22	48	9	2	0	145.2	131	0	63	42	4-9	5	3.65
Oscar Harstad	R	23	32	7	4	0	82.0	81	1	35	35	3-5	1	3.40
Fritz Coumbe	L	25	30	12	4	1	114.0	123	1	37	37	4-7	2	3.47
Lynn Brenton	R	24	11	5	1	0	51.0	60	1	20	18	2-3	0	3.35
Paul Carter	R	21	11	2	2	0	42.0	44	1	18	14	1-1	0	3.21
Herbert Hill	R	22	1	0	0	0	2.0	1	0	2	0	0-0	0	0.00

594 Seasons: Team Rosters

1915 Philadelphia Athletics 8th AL 43-109 .283 58.5 GB

Player	Gm by Position	B	Age	G	AB	R	H	2B	3B	HR	RBI	BB	SO	SB	Avg	OBP	Slg
Jack Lapp	C89,1B12	L	30	112	312	26	85	16	5	2	31	30	29	5	.272	.340	.375
Stuffy McInnis	1B119	R	24	119	456	44	143	14	4	0	49	14	17	8	.314	.337	.362
Nap Lajoie	2B110,SS10,1B5*	R	40	129	490	40	137	24	5	1	61	11	16	10	.280	.301	.355
Wally Schang	3B43,OF41,C26	S	25	116	359	64	89	9	11	1	44	66	47	18	.248	.385	.343
Larry Kopf	SS74,3B42,2B2	S	24	118	386	39	87	10	2	1	33	41	45	5	.225	.314	.269
Amos Strunk	OF111,1B19	L	26	132	485	76	144	28	16	1	45	56	45	17	.297	.371	.427
Jimmy Walsh	OF109,3B2,1B1	L	29	117	417	48	86	15	6	1	20	57	64	22	.206	.306	.278
Rube Oldring	OF96,3B8	R	31	107	408	49	101	23	3	6	42	22	21	11	.248	.293	.363
Eddie Murphy†	OF58,3B6	L	23	68	260	37	60	3	4	0	17	29	15	13	.231	.315	.273
Lew Malone	2B43,3B12,OF4*	R	18	76	201	17	41	4	4	1	17	21	40	7	.204	.283	.279
Jack Barry†	SS54	R	28	54	194	16	43	6	2	0	15	15	9	6	.222	.284	.273
Wickey McAvoy	C64	R	20	68	184	12	35	7	2	0	6	11	32	0	.190	.236	.250
Chick Davies	OF32,P4	L	23	56	132	13	24	5	3	0	11	14	31	2	.182	.270	.265
Thomas Healy	3B17,SS1	R	19	23	77	11	17	1	0	0	5	6	4	0	.221	.310	.234
Harry Damrau	3B16	R	24	16	56	4	11	1	0	0	3	5	17	1	.196	.262	.214
Bill Bankston	OF8	L	22	11	36	6	5	1	1	1	2	2	5	1	.139	.205	.306
Shag Thompson	OF7	L	22	17	33	5	11	2	0	0	2	4	6	0	.333	.405	.394
Socks Seibold	SS7	R	19	10	26	3	3	1	0	0	2	4	4	0	.115	.233	.154
Sam Crane	SS6,2B1	R	20	8	23	3	2	2	0	0	1	0	4	0	.087	.087	.174
Cy Perkins	C6	R	19	7	20	2	4	1	0	0	0	3	3	0	.200	.304	.250
Bruno Haas	P6,OF3	S	24	12	18	1	1	0	0	0	0	1	7	0	.056	.105	.056
Owen Conway	3B4	—	24	4	15	2	1	0	0	0	0	0	3	0	.067	.067	.067
Buck Danner	SS3	R	24	3	12	1	3	0	0	0	0	0	1	1	.250	.250	.250
Sam McConnell	3B5	L	20	6	11	1	2	1	0	0	0	1	3	0	.182	.250	.273
Henry Bostick	3B2	R	20	2	7	0	0	0	0	0	2	1	1	0	.000	.125	.000
Ralph Edwards	2B1	R	32	2	5	0	0	0	0	0	0	0	3	0	.000	.000	.000
Art Corcoran	3B1	—	20	1	4	0	0	0	0	0	0	0	2	0	.000	.000	.000
Bill Haeffner	C3	R	20	3	4	0	1	0	0	0	0	0	1	0	.250	.250	.250
Harry Davis	1B1	R	41	5	3	0	1	0	0	0	4	0	0	0	.333	.333	.333
Fred Lear	3B2	R	21	2	2	0	0	0	0	0	0	0	2	0	.000	.000	.000
Ira Thomas	C1	R	34	1	0	0	0	0	0	0	0	0	0	0	—	—	—

N. Lajoie, 2 G at 3B; L. Malone, 2 G at SS

Connie Mack

Pitcher	T	Age	G	GS	CG	ShO	IP	H	HR	BB	SO	W-L	Sv	ERA
John Wyckoff	R	23	43	34	20	1	276.0	238	1	165	157	10-22	0	3.52
Rube Bressler	L	20	32	20	7	1	178.1	183	3	118	69	4-17	0	5.20
Joe Bush	R	22	25	18	8	0	145.2	137	3	89	89	5-15	0	4.14
Tom Sheehan	R	21	15	13	8	1	102.0	131	1	38	22	4-9	0	4.15
Bob Shawkey†	R	24	17	13	7	1	100.0	103	3	38	56	6-6	0	4.05
Tom Knowlson	R	20	18	9	8	0	100.2	99	1	60	24	4-6	0	3.49
Cap Crowell	R	22	10	8	4	0	54.1	56	1	47	15	2-6	0	5.47
Herb Pennock†	L	21	11	8	3	1	44.0	46	2	29	24	3-6	1	5.32
Jack Nabors	R	27	10	7	2	0	54.0	58	1	35	18	0-5	0	5.50
Dana Fillingim	R	21	8	4	1	0	39.1	42	0	32	17	0-5	0	3.43
Jack Richardson	R	23	3	3	2	0	24.0	21	0	14	11	0-1	0	2.63
Harry Weaver	R	23	2	2	2	0	18.0	18	1	10	1	0-2	0	3.00
Chick Davies	L	23	4	2	0	0	15.1	20	0	12	2	1-2	0	8.80
Joe Sherman	R	24	2	1	1	0	15.0	15	0	1	5	1-0	0	2.40
Elmer Myers	R	21	1	1	1	1	9.0	2	0	5	12	1-0	0	0.00
Carl Ray	L	26	2	1	0	0	7.1	11	0	6	6	0-1	0	4.91
Bill Meehan	R	25	1	1	0	0	4.0	7	0	3	4	0-1	0	11.25
Tink Turner	R	25	1	1	0	0	2.0	5	1	3	0	0-1	0	22.50
Bob Cone	R	21	1	1	0	0	0.2	5	0	0	0	0-0	0	40.50
Bud Davis	R	18	18	2	2	0	66.2	65	0	59	18	0-2	0	4.05
Bruno Haas	L	24	6	2	1	0	14.1	23	0	28	7	0-1	0	11.93
Harry Eccles	L	21	5	1	0	0	21.0	18	2	6	13	0-1	1	4.71
Bill Morrisette	R	22	4	1	1	0	20.0	15	0	5	11	2-0	0	1.35
Walter Ancker	R	21	4	1	0	0	17.2	19	1	17	4	0-0	0	3.57
Jack Harper	R	21	3	0	0	0	8.2	5	0	1	3	0-0	0	3.12
Squiz Pillion	L	21	2	0	0	0	5.1	10	0	2	0	0-0	0	6.75
Bob Pepper	R	20	1	0	0	0	5.0	6	0	4	0	0-0	0	1.80

»1915 Philadelphia Phillies 1st NL 90-62 .592 —

Player	Gm by Position	B	Age	G	AB	R	H	2B	3B	HR	RBI	BB	SO	SB	Avg	OBP	Slg
Bill Killefer	C104	R	27	105	320	26	76	9	2	0	24	18	14	5	.238	.287	.278
Fred Luderus	1B141	L	29	141	499	55	157	36	7	7	62	42	36	9	.315	.376	.457
Bert Niehoff	2B148	R	31	148	529	61	126	27	2	2	49	30	63	21	.238	.280	.308
Bobby Byrne	3B105	R	30	105	387	50	81	6	4	0	21	39	28	4	.209	.290	.245
Dave Bancroft	SS153	S	24	153	563	85	143	18	2	7	30	77	62	15	.254	.346	.330
Gavy Cravath	OF149	R	34	150	522	89	149	31	7	24	115	86	77	11	.285	.393	.510
Possum Whitted	OF119,1B7	R	25	128	448	46	126	17	3	1	43	29	47	24	.281	.328	.339
Beals Becker	OF98	L	28	112	338	38	83	16	4	11	35	26	48	12	.246	.301	.414
Dode Paskert	OF92,1B5	R	33	109	328	51	80	17	4	3	39	35	38	9	.244	.319	.348
Milt Stock	3B55,SS4	R	21	69	227	37	59	7	3	1	15	22	26	6	.260	.325	.330
Ed Burns	C62	R	26	67	174	11	42	5	0	0	16	20	12	1	.241	.327	.270
Bud Weiser	OF20	R	24	37	64	6	9	2	0	0	8	7	12	2	.141	.236	.172
Oscar Dugey	2B14	R	27	42	39	4	6	1	0	0	0	7	5	2	.154	.283	.179
Bert Adams	C23,1B1	S	24	24	27	1	3	0	0	0	2	2	3	0	.111	.172	.111

Pat Moran

Pitcher	T	Age	G	GS	CG	ShO	IP	H	HR	BB	SO	W-L	Sv	ERA
Pete Alexander	R	28	49	42	36	12	376.1	253	3	64	241	31-10	3	1.22
Erskine Mayer	R	26	43	33	20	2	274.2	240	9	59	114	21-15	2	2.36
Al Demaree	R	30	32	26	13	3	209.2	201	4	58	69	14-11	1	3.05
Eppa Rixey	L	24	29	22	10	2	176.2	163	2	64	88	11-12	1	2.39
George Chalmers	R	27	26	20	13	1	170.1	159	3	45	82	8-9	1	2.48
George McQuillan†	R	30	9	8	5	0	63.2	60	1	11	13	4-3	0	2.12
Stan Baumgartner	L	20	16	1	0	0	48.1	38	2	23	27	0-2	0	2.42
Ben Tincup	R	24	10	0	0	0	31.0	26	1	9	10	0-0	0	2.03
Joe Oeschger	R	24	6	1	1	0	23.2	21	1	9	8	1-0	0	3.42

1915 Boston Braves 2nd NL 83-69 .546 7.0 GB

Player	Gm by Position	B	Age	G	AB	R	H	2B	3B	HR	RBI	BB	SO	SB	Avg	OBP	Slg
Hank Gowdy	C114	R	25	118	316	27	78	15	3	2	30	41	34	10	.247	.339	.332
Butch Schmidt	1B127	L	28	127	458	46	115	26	7	2	60	36	59	3	.251	.318	.352
Johnny Evers	2B82	L	33	83	278	38	73	4	1	1	22	50	16	7	.263	.375	.295
Red Smith	3B157	R	25	157	549	66	145	34	4	2	65	67	49	10	.264	.345	.352
Rabbit Maranville	SS149	R	23	149	509	51	124	23	6	2	43	45	65	18	.244	.308	.324
Sherry Magee	OF135,1B21	R	30	156	571	72	160	34	12	2	87	54	39	15	.280	.350	.392
Herbie Moran	OF123	L	31	130	419	59	84	13	5	0	21	66	41	16	.200	.320	.255
Joe Connolly	OF93	L	27	104	305	48	91	14	8	0	23	39	35	13	.298	.387	.397
Ed Fitzpatrick	2B71,OF29	R	25	105	303	54	67	19	3	0	24	43	36	13	.221	.344	.304
Dick Egan†	OF24,2B22,SS10*	R	31	83	220	20	57	9	1	0	21	28	18	3	.259	.343	.309
Bert Whaling	C69	R	27	72	190	10	42	6	2	0	13	8	38	0	.221	.264	.274
Pete Compton†	OF31	L	25	35	116	10	28	7	1	1	12	8	11	4	.241	.290	.345
Larry Gilbert	OF27	L	23	45	106	11	16	4	0	0	4	11	13	4	.151	.231	.189
Ted Cather	OF32	R	26	40	102	10	21	3	1	2	18	15	19	2	.206	.319	.314
Fred Snodgrass†	OF18,1B5	R	27	23	79	10	22	2	0	0	9	7	9	0	.278	.352	.304
Paul Strand	P6,OF5	L	21	24	22	3	2	0	0	0	2	0	4	0	.091	.091	.091
Zip Collins†	OF4	L	23	5	14	3	4	1	1	0	0	2	1	1	.286	.375	.500
Joe Shannon	OF2,2B1	R	18	5	10	3	2	0	0	0	1	0	3	0	.200	.200	.200
Walt Tragesser	C7	R	28	7	7	1	0	0	0	0	0	0	2	0	.000	.000	.000
Earl Blackburn	C3	R	22	3	6	0	1	0	0	0	0	2	1	0	.167	.375	.167
Otto Hess	P4,1B1	L	36	5	5	1	2	1	0	0	1	0	2	0	.400	.400	.600
Fletcher Low	3B1	R	22	1	4	1	1	0	1	0	1	0	0	0	.250	.250	.750
Red Shannon	2B1	S	18	1	3	0	0	0	0	0	0	0	0	0	.000	.000	.000

D. Egan, 9 G at 1B, 4 G at 3B

George Stallings

Pitcher	T	Age	G	GS	CG	ShO	IP	H	HR	BB	SO	W-L	Sv	ERA
Dick Rudolph	R	27	44	43	30	3	341.1	304	4	64	147	22-19	1	2.37
Pat Ragan†	R	26	33	26	13	3	227.0	208	2	59	81	16-12	0	2.46
Tom Hughes	R	31	50	25	17	4	280.1	208	0	58	171	16-14	9	2.12
Lefty Tyler	L	25	32	24	15	1	204.2	182	6	84	89	10-9	0	2.86
Art Nehf	L	22	12	10	6	4	78.1	60	0	21	39	5-4	0	2.53
Iron Davis	R	25	15	9	4	0	73.1	85	2	19	26	3-3	0	3.80
Bill James	R	23	13	9	4	0	68.1	68	0	22	23	5-4	0	3.03
Dolf Luque	R	24	2	1	0	0	5.0	6	0	4	3	0-0	0	3.60
Dick Crutcher	R	25	14	4	1	0	43.2	50	1	16	17	2-2	2	4.33
Jesse Barnes	R	22	9	3	2	0	45.1	41	1	10	16	3-0	0	1.39
Paul Strand	L	21	6	2	2	0	22.2	26	0	3	13	1-1	1	2.38
Otto Hess	L	36	4	1	1	0	14.0	16	0	6	5	0-1	0	3.86
Gene Cocreham	R	30	1	0	0	0	1.2	3	0	0	0	0-0	0	5.40

1915 Brooklyn Dodgers 3rd NL 80-72 .526 10.0 GB

Player	Gm by Position	B	Age	G	AB	R	H	2B	3B	HR	RBI	BB	SO	SB	Avg	OBP	Slg
Otto Miller	C83	R	26	84	254	20	57	4	6	0	25	6	28	3	.224	.245	.287
Jake Daubert	1B150	L	31	150	544	62	164	21	8	2	47	57	48	11	.301	.368	.381
George Cutshaw	2B154	R	27	154	566	68	139	18	9	0	62	34	35	28	.246	.293	.309
Gus Getz	3B128,SS2	R	25	130	477	39	123	10	5	2	46	8	14	19	.258	.275	.312
Ollie O'Mara	SS149	R	24	149	577	77	141	26	3	0	31	51	40	11	.244	.308	.300
Hi Myers	OF153	R	26	153	605	69	150	21	7	2	46	17	51	19	.248	.275	.316
Zack Wheat	OF144	L	27	146	528	64	136	15	12	5	66	52	42	21	.258	.324	.360
Casey Stengel	OF129	L	24	132	459	52	109	20	12	3	50	34	46	5	.237	.294	.353
Lew McCarty	C81	R	26	84	276	19	66	9	4	0	19	7	23	7	.239	.261	.301
Joe Schultz†	3B27,SS1	R	21	56	120	13	35	3	2	0	4	10	18	3	.292	.346	.350
John Hummel	OF21,1B11,SS1	R	32	53	100	6	23	2	3	0	8	6	11	1	.230	.274	.310
Bill Zimmerman	OF18	R	26	22	57	3	16	2	0	0	7	4	8	1	.281	.328	.316
Al Nixon	OF14	R	29	14	26	3	6	1	0	0	2	2	4	1	.231	.286	.269
Ivy Olson†	SS7,2B1,3B1*	R	29	18	26	2	2	0	1	0	3	1	0	0	.077	.111	.154
Red Smyth	OF9	L	22	19	22	3	3	1	0	0	3	4	2	1	.136	.269	.182
Mack Wheat	C8	R	22	8	14	0	1	0	0	0	0	0	5	0	.071	.316	.071
Dick Egan†		R	31	3	3	0	0	0	0	0	0	0	0	0	.000	.000	.000
Jack Karst	3B1	L	21	1	0	0	0	0	0	0	0	0	0	0	—	—	—

I. Olson, 1 G at OF

Wilbert Robinson

Pitcher	T	Age	G	GS	CG	ShO	IP	H	HR	BB	SO	W-L	Sv	ERA
Jeff Pfeffer	R	27	40	34	26	6	291.2	243	8	76	84	19-14	3	2.10
Wheezer Dell	R	28	40	24	12	4	215.0	166	5	100	94	11-10	1	2.34
Jack Coombs	R	32	29	24	17	2	195.2	166	1	91	56	15-10	0	2.58
Sherry Smith	L	24	29	20	11	2	173.2	169	3	42	52	14-8	2	2.59
Nap Rucker	L	30	19	15	7	1	122.2	134	3	28	38	9-4	1	2.42
Phil Douglas†	R	25	20	13	5	1	116.2	104	1	17	63	5-5	0	2.62
Raleigh Aitchison	L	27	7	5	2	0	32.2	36	3	6	14	0-4	0	4.96
Larry Cheney†	R	29	5	4	1	0	27.0	16	0	17	11	0-2	0	1.67
Rube Marquard†	L	28	6	3	0	0	24.2	29	0	5	13	2-2	1	6.20
Ed Appleton	R	23	34	10	5	0	138.1	133	3	66	50	4-10	0	3.32
Leon Cadore	R	24	7	2	1	0	21.0	28	0	8	12	0-2	0	5.57
Pat Ragan†	R	26	5	0	0	0	19.2	11	0	8	7	1-0	0	0.92
Duster Mails	L	20	2	0	0	0	5.0	6	2	5	3	0-1	0	3.60
Charlie Schmutz	R	25	1	0	0	0	4.0	7	0	1	1	0-0	0	6.75
Elmer Brown	R	32	1	0	0	0	2.0	4	0	3	1	0-0	0	9.00

1915 Chicago Cubs 4th NL 73-80 .477 17.5 GB

Player	Gm by Position	B	Age	G	AB	R	H	2B	3B	HR	RBI	BB	SO	SB	Avg	OBP	Slg
Jimmy Archer	C88	R	32	97	309	21	75	11	5	1	27	11	38	5	.243	.273	.320
Vic Saier	1B139	L	24	144	497	74	131	35	11	11	64	64	62	29	.264	.350	.445
Heinie Zimmerman	2B100,3B36,SS4	R	28	139	520	65	138	28	11	3	62	21	33	19	.265	.300	.379
Art Phelan	3B110,2B24	R	27	133	448	41	98	16	7	3	35	55	42	12	.219	.307	.306
Tom Fisher	SS145	R	28	147	568	70	163	22	5	5	53	30	51	9	.287	.326	.370
Cy Williams	OF149	L	27	151	518	59	133	22	6	13	64	26	49	15	.257	.305	.398
Wildfire Schulte	OF147	L	32	151	550	66	137	20	6	12	62	49	68	19	.249	.313	.373
Wilbur Good	OF125	L	29	128	498	66	126	18	9	2	27	34	65	19	.253	.307	.337
Roger Bresnahan	C68	R	36	77	221	19	45	8	1	1	19	29	23	19	.204	.296	.262
Red Murray†	OF40,2B1	R	31	51	144	20	43	6	1	0	11	8	8	6	.299	.340	.354
Pete Knisely	OF33,2B9	R	27	64	134	12	33	9	0	0	17	15	18	1	.246	.331	.313
Polly McLarry	2B21,1B18	L	24	68	127	16	25	3	0	1	12	14	20	2	.197	.277	.244
Alex McCarthy†	2B12,3B12,SS1	R	27	23	72	4	19	3	0	1	6	5	7	2	.264	.329	.347
Joe Mulligan	SS10,3B1	R	20	11	22	5	8	1	0	0	2	5	1	2	.364	.481	.409
Bubbles Hargrave	C9	R	22	15	19	2	3	0	1	0	2	1	5	0	.158	.200	.263
Chick Keating	SS2	R	23	4	8	1	0	0	0	0	0	0	3	1	.000	.000	.000
Joe Schultz†	2B2	R	21	7	8	1	2	0	0	0	3	0	2	0	.250	.250	.250
Jack Wallace	C2	R	24	2	7	1	2	0	0	0	1	0	2	0	.286	.375	.286
John Fluhrer	OF2	R	21	6	6	0	2	0	0	0	0	1	0	1	.333	.429	.333
Bob O'Farrell	C2	R	18	2	3	0	1	0	0	0	0	0	0	0	.333	.333	.333
Red Corriden	3B1,OF1	R	27	6	3	1	0	0	0	0	0	2	1	0	.000	.571	.000

Roger Bresnahan

Pitcher	T	Age	G	GS	CG	ShO	IP	H	HR	BB	SO	W-L	Sv	ERA
Hippo Vaughn	L	27	41	34	18	4	269.2	240	4	77	148	20-12	1	2.87
Jimmy Lavender	R	31	41	24	13	1	220.0	178	5	67	117	10-16	4	2.58
Bert Humphries	R	34	31	22	10	4	171.2	183	6	23	45	8-13	3	2.31
George Pearce	L	27	36	20	8	2	176.0	158	1	77	96	13-9	0	3.32
Larry Cheney†	R	29	25	18	6	2	131.1	120	1	55	68	8-9	0	3.56
Phil Douglas†	R	25	4	4	2	1	25.0	17	0	7	18	1-1	0	2.16
Brad Hogg	R	27	2	2	1	1	13.0	12	1	6	0	1-0	0	0.69
Zip Zabel	R	24	36	17	8	3	163.0	124	3	84	60	7-10	0	3.20
Pete Standridge	R	24	29	3	2	0	112.1	120	2	36	42	4-1	0	3.61
Karl Adams	R	23	26	12	3	0	107.0	105	5	43	57	1-9	0	4.71
Ed Schorr	R	24	2	0	0	0	6.0	9	0	5	3	0-0	0	7.50
Bob Wright	R	23	2	0	0	0	4.0	6	0	0	3	0-0	0	2.25

Seasons: Team Rosters

595

1915 Pittsburgh Pirates 5th NL 73-81 .474 18.0 GB

Fred Clarke

Player	Gm by Position	B	Age	G	AB	R	H	2B	3B	HR	RBI	BB	SO	SB	Avg	OBP	Slg
George Gibson	C118	R	34	120	351	28	88	15	6	1	30	31	25	5	.251	.313	.336
Doc Johnston	1B147	L	27	147	543	71	144	19	12	5	64	38	40	26	.265	.328	.372
Jim Viox	2B134,3B13,OF2	R	24	150	503	56	129	17	8	2	45	75	31	12	.256	.357	.334
Doug Baird	3B120,OF20,2B3	R	23	145	512	49	112	26	12	1	53	37	88	29	.219	.277	.322
Honus Wagner	SS131,2B12,1B10	R	41	156	566	68	155	32	17	6	78	39	64	22	.274	.325	.422
Bill Hinchman	OF156	R	32	156	577	72	177	33	14	5	77	48	75	17	.307	.368	.438
Max Carey	OF139	S	25	140	564	76	143	26	5	3	27	57	58	36	.254	.326	.333
Zip Collins†	OF89	L	23	101	354	51	104	8	5	1	23	24	38	6	.294	.340	.353
Wally Gerber	3B23,SS21,2B2	R	23	56	144	8	28	2	0	0	7	9	16	6	.194	.252	.208
Bobby Schang†	C45	R	28	56	125	13	23	6	3	0	4	14	32	2	.184	.271	.280
Dan Costello	OF22	L	23	71	125	16	27	4	1	0	11	7	23	7	.216	.258	.264
Ed Barney†	OF26	L	25	32	99	16	27	1	2	0	5	11	12	7	.273	.363	.323
Larry LeJeune	OF18	R	29	18	65	4	11	0	1	0	2	2	7	4	.169	.206	.200
Alex McCarthy†	2B9,SS5,3B4*	R	27	21	49	3	10	0	1	0	3	5	10	1	.204	.291	.245
Leo Murphy	C20	R	26	31	41	4	4	0	0	0	4	4	12	0	.098	.178	.098
Ike McAuley	SS5	R	23	5	15	0	2	1	0	0	0	0	6	0	.133	.133	.200
Paddy Siglin	2B1	R	23	6	7	1	2	0	0	0	0	1	2	1	.286	.375	.286
Pat Duncan	OF1	R	21	3	5	0	1	0	0	0	0	0	1	0	.200	.200	.200
Bill Wagner	C3	R	21	5	5	0	0	0	0	0	0	1	2	0	.000	.167	.000
Fritz Scheeren	OF1	R	23	4	3	0	0	0	0	0	0	0	0	0	.000	.000	.000
Fred Clarke	OF1	L	42	1	2	0	1	0	0	0	0	0	0	0	.500	.500	.500
Harry Daubert		R	23	1	1	0	0	0	0	0	0	0	1	0	.000	.500	.000
Syd Smith		R	31	1	1	0	0	0	0	0	0	0	0	0	.000	.000	.000

A. McCarthy, 1 G at 1B

Pitcher	T	Age	G	GS	CG	ShO	IP	H	HR	BB	SO	W-L	Sv	ERA
Bob Harmon	R	27	37	32	25	5	269.2	242	6	62	86	16-17	1	2.50
Al Mamaux	R	21	38	31	17	8	251.2	182	3	96	152	21-8	0	2.04
Babe Adams	R	33	40	30	17	2	245.0	229	6	34	62	14-14	2	2.87
George McQuillan†	R	30	30	20	9	0	149.0	160	1	39	56	8-10	1	2.84
Wilbur Cooper	L	23	38	19	11	1	185.2	180	4	52	71	5-16	4	3.30
Erv Kantlehner	L	22	29	18	10	1	163.0	135	1	58	64	5-12	3	2.26
Dazzy Vance†	R	24	1	1	0	0	2.2	3	0	5	0	0-1	0	10.13
Joe Conzelman	R	29	18	1	0	0	47.1	41	0	20	22	1-1	0	3.42
Carmen Hill	R	19	8	3	2	1	47.0	42	0	13	24	2-1	0	1.15
Herb Kelly	L	23	5	1	0	0	11.0	10	0	4	6	1-1	0	4.09
Phil Slattery	L	22	3	0	0	0	8.0	5	0	1	1	0-0	0	0.00

1915 St. Louis Cardinals 6th NL 72-81 .471 18.5 GB

Miller Huggins

Player	Gm by Position	B	Age	G	AB	R	H	2B	3B	HR	RBI	BB	SO	SB	Avg	OBP	Slg
Frank Snyder	C142	R	22	144	473	41	141	22	7	2	55	39	49	3	.298	.353	.387
Dots Miller	1B94,2B55,3B9*	R	28	150	553	73	146	17	10	2	72	43	48	27	.264	.324	.342
Miller Huggins	2B105	S	36	107	353	57	85	5	2	2	24	74	68	13	.241	.377	.283
Bruno Betzel	3B105,2B3,SS2	R	20	117	367	42	92	12	4	0	27	18	48	10	.251	.291	.305
Art Butler	SS125,2B2	R	27	130	469	73	119	12	5	1	31	47	34	26	.254	.323	.307
Tom Long	OF136	R	25	140	507	61	149	21	25	2	61	31	50	19	.294	.339	.446
Bob Bescher	OF129	S	31	130	486	71	128	15	7	4	34	52	53	27	.263	.342	.348
Chief Wilson	OF105	L	31	107	348	33	96	13	6	3	39	19	43	8	.276	.321	.374
Cozy Dolan	OF98	R	25	111	322	53	90	14	9	2	38	34	37	17	.280	.356	.398
Ham Hyatt	1B64,OF25	L	30	106	295	23	79	8	9	2	46	28	24	3	.268	.337	.376
Zinn Beck	3B62,SS4,2B2	R	29	70	223	21	52	9	4	0	15	12	31	3	.233	.282	.309
Mike Gonzalez	C32,1B8	R	24	51	97	12	22	2	2	0	10	8	9	4	.227	.306	.289
Rogers Hornsby	SS18	R	19	18	57	5	14	2	0	0	4	2	6	0	.246	.271	.281
Jack Roche	C4	R	24	46	39	2	8	0	1	0	6	4	8	1	.205	.295	.256
Rolla Daringer	SS10	L	26	10	23	3	2	0	0	0	0	9	5	0	.087	.344	.087
Jack Smith	OF4	L	20	4	16	2	3	0	1	0	0	1	5	0	.188	.235	.313
Harry Glenn	C5	L	25	6	16	1	5	0	0	0	1	3	0	0	.313	.421	.313
Jim Brown	OF1	R	18	1	2	0	1	0	0	0	0	2	1	0	.500	.750	.500

D. Miller, 3 G at SS

Pitcher	T	Age	G	GS	CG	ShO	IP	H	HR	BB	SO	W-L	Sv	ERA
Bill Doak	R	24	38	36	19	3	276.0	263	4	85	124	16-18	1	2.64
Slim Sallee	L	30	46	33	17	2	275.1	245	6	57	91	13-17	3	2.84
Lee Meadows	R	20	39	26	14	1	244.0	232	5	88	104	13-11	0	2.99
Red Ames†	R	32	15	14	8	2	113.1	93	1	32	48	9-3	1	2.46
Dan Griner	R	27	37	18	9	3	150.1	137	4	46	46	5-11	3	2.81
Hank Robinson	L	25	32	15	6	1	143.0	128	1	35	57	7-8	0	2.45
Hub Perdue	R	33	31	13	5	1	115.1	141	7	19	29	6-12	1	4.21
Dick Niehaus	L	22	15	2	0	0	45.1	48	2	22	21	2-1	0	3.97
Fred Lamline	R	27	4	0	0	0	19.0	21	0	3	11	0-0	0	2.84
Charlie Boardman	L	22	3	1	1	0	19.0	12	0	15	7	1-0	0	1.42

1915 Cincinnati Reds 7th NL 71-83 .461 20.0 GB

Buck Herzog

Player	Gm by Position	B	Age	G	AB	R	H	2B	3B	HR	RBI	BB	SO	SB	Avg	OBP	Slg
Ivy Wingo	C98,OF1	L	24	119	339	26	75	11	6	3	29	13	33	10	.221	.250	.316
Fritz Mollwitz	1B153	R	25	153	525	36	136	21	3	1	51	15	49	19	.259	.281	.316
Bill Rodgers†	2B56,SS6,3B1*	L	28	72	213	20	51	13	4	0	12	11	29	8	.239	.299	.338
Heine Groh	3B131,2B29	R	25	160	587	72	170	32	9	3	50	50	33	12	.290	.354	.390
Buck Herzog	SS153,1B2	R	29	155	579	61	153	14	10	1	42	34	21	35	.264	.314	.328
Tommy Griffith	OF160	L	25	160	583	59	179	31	16	4	85	41	34	6	.307	.355	.436
Red Killefer	OF150,1B2	R	30	155	555	75	151	25	11	1	41	38	33	12	.272	.340	.362
Tommy Leach	OF96	R	37	107	335	42	75	7	5	0	17	56	38	20	.224	.338	.275
Tommy Clarke	C72	R	27	96	226	23	65	7	2	0	21	33	22	7	.288	.381	.336
Ken Williams	OF62	L	25	71	219	22	53	10	4	0	16	15	20	4	.242	.297	.324
Ivy Olson†	2B39,3B15,1B7	R	29	63	207	18	48	5	4	0	14	12	13	10	.232	.274	.295
Joe Wagner	2B46,SS14,3B2	R	26	75	197	17	35	5	2	0	13	8	35	4	.178	.210	.223
Fritz Von Kolnitz	3B18,SS6,1B3*	R	22	50	78	6	15	4	1	0	6	7	11	1	.192	.259	.269
George Twombly	OF24	R	23	46	66	5	13	0	1	0	5	8	8	5	.197	.293	.227
Johnny Beall	OF10	L	33	10	34	3	8	1	0	0	3	5	10	0	.235	.350	.265
Red Dooin†	C10	R	36	10	31	2	10	0	0	0	0	2	5	1	.323	.364	.323

B. Rodgers, 1 G at OF; F. Von Kolnitz, 2 G at C, 1 G at OF

Pitcher	T	Age	G	GS	CG	ShO	IP	H	HR	BB	SO	W-L	Sv	ERA
Gene Dale	R	26	49	35	20	4	296.2	256	6	107	104	18-17	3	2.46
Pete Schneider	R	19	48	35	16	5	275.2	254	4	104	108	13-19	2	2.48
Fred Toney	R	26	36	23	18	6	222.2	160	1	73	108	15-6	2	1.58
Rube Benton†	L	28	35	21	6	2	176.1	165	2	67	83	9-13	4	3.32
Limb McKenry	R	26	21	11	5	0	110.1	94	2	39	37	5-5	0	2.94
Phil Douglas†	R	25	8	7	0	0	46.2	53	0	23	29	1-5	0	5.40
Lefty George	L	28	5	3	2	1	28.0	24	1	8	11	2-2	0	3.86
King Lear	R	24	40	15	9	0	167.2	169	7	45	46	6-10	0	3.01
Red Ames†	R	32	17	7	4	1	68.0	82	2	24	26	2-4	1	4.50
Curly Brown	L	26	7	3	0	0	27.0	26	0	6	13	0-2	0	4.67
Ray Callahan	L	23	3	0	0	0	6.1	12	1	1	4	0-0	0	8.53
Harry McCluskey	L	23	3	0	0	0	5.1	4	0	0	2	0-0	0	5.06
Goat Cochran	R	24	1	0	0	0	2.0	5	0	0	1	0-0	0	9.00

1915 New York Giants 8th NL 69-83 .454 21.0 GB

John McGraw

Player	Gm by Position	B	Age	G	AB	R	H	2B	3B	HR	RBI	BB	SO	SB	Avg	OBP	Slg
Chief Meyers	C96	R	34	110	289	24	67	10	5	1	26	26	18	4	.232	.311	.311
Fred Merkle	1B110,OF30	R	26	140	505	52	151	25	3	4	62	36	39	20	.299	.348	.384
Larry Doyle	2B147	L	28	150	591	86	189	40	10	4	70	32	28	22	.320	.358	.442
Hans Lobert	3B103	R	33	106	386	46	97	18	4	0	38	25	24	14	.251	.304	.319
Art Fletcher	SS149	R	30	149	562	59	143	17	7	3	74	6	36	12	.254	.280	.326
George Burns	OF155	R	25	155	622	83	169	27	14	3	51	56	57	27	.272	.333	.375
Dave Robertson	OF138	L	25	141	544	72	160	17	10	3	58	22	52	22	.294	.326	.379
Fred Snodgrass†	OF75	R	27	80	252	36	49	9	0	0	20	35	33	11	.194	.307	.230
Fred Brainerd	1B45,3B16,SS9*	R	23	91	249	31	50	7	2	1	21	21	44	6	.201	.266	.257
Eddie Grant	3B35,2B9,1B1*	L	32	87	192	18	40	2	1	0	10	9	20	5	.208	.248	.229
Red Murray†	OF34	R	31	45	127	12	28	1	2	3	11	7	15	2	.220	.261	.331
Red Dooin†	C46	R	36	46	124	9	27	2	2	0	9	3	15	0	.218	.236	.266
Marty Becker	OF16	S	21	17	52	5	13	2	0	0	3	2	9	3	.250	.278	.288
Jim Thorpe	OF15	R	28	17	52	8	12	3	1	0	1	2	16	4	.231	.259	.327
George Kelly	1B9,OF4	R	19	17	38	2	6	0	0	1	4	1	9	0	.158	.179	.237
Lew Wendell	C18	R	23	20	36	0	8	1	1	0	5	2	7	0	.222	.263	.306
Charlie Babington	OF12,1B1	R	20	28	33	5	8	3	1	0	2	0	4	1	.242	.265	.394
Larry McLean	C12	R	33	13	33	0	5	0	0	0	4	0	1	0	.152	.152	.152
Harry Smith†	C18	R	25	21	32	1	4	0	1	0	3	6	12	0	.125	.263	.188
Merwin Jacobson	OF5	L	21	8	24	0	2	0	0	0	0	1	5	0	.083	.120	.083
Bobby Schang†	C6	R	28	12	21	1	3	0	0	0	1	4	5	1	.143	.280	.143
Ben Dyer	3B6,SS1	R	22	7	19	4	4	0	1	0	0	4	3	0	.211	.375	.316
Brad Kocher	C3	R	27	4	11	3	5	0	1	0	2	0	1	0	.455	.455	.636
Howard Baker†	3B1	R	27	1	3	0	0	0	0	0	0	0	0	0	.000	.000	.000

F. Brainerd, 1 G at 2B, 1 G at OF; E. Grant, 1 G at SS

Pitcher	T	Age	G	GS	CG	ShO	IP	H	HR	BB	SO	W-L	Sv	ERA
Jeff Tesreau	R	26	43	39	24	8	306.0	235	4	75	176	19-16	3	2.29
Pol Perritt	R	22	35	29	16	4	220.0	226	6	59	91	12-18	0	2.66
Christy Mathewson	R	36	27	24	11	1	186.0	199	9	20	57	8-14	0	3.58
Sailor Stroud	R	30	32	22	8	0	184.0	194	3	35	62	11-9	1	2.79
Rube Marquard†	L	28	27	21	10	2	169.0	178	8	33	79	9-8	2	3.73
Rube Benton†	L	28	10	6	3	0	60.2	57	0	9	26	4-5	1	2.82
Fred Herbert	R	28	2	2	1	0	17.0	12	0	4	6	1-1	0	1.06
Emilio Palmero	L	20	3	2	1	0	11.2	10	0	9	8	0-2	0	3.09
Rube Schauer	R	24	32	7	4	0	105.1	101	4	35	65	2-8	0	3.50
Ferdie Schupp	L	24	23	1	0	0	54.2	57	1	29	28	1-0	0	5.10
Hank Ritter	R	21	22	1	0	0	58.1	66	4	15	35	2-1	2	4.63
Art Fromme	R	31	4	1	0	0	12.1	15	1	2	4	0-1	0	5.84

»1915 Chicago Whales 1st FL 86-66 .566 —

Joe Tinker

Player	Gm by Position	B	Age	G	AB	R	H	2B	3B	HR	RBI	BB	SO	SB	Avg	OBP	Slg
Art Wilson	C87	R	29	96	269	44	82	11	2	7	31	65	38	8	.305	.442	.439
Fred Beck	1B117	L	28	121	373	35	83	9	3	5	38	24	38	4	.223	.277	.303
Rollie Zeider	2B83,3B30,SS21	R	31	129	494	65	112	22	2	0	34	43	24	16	.227	.297	.279
Harry Fritz	3B70,2B6,SS1	R	24	79	236	27	59	8	4	3	26	13	27	4	.250	.298	.356
Jimmy Smith†	SS92,2B1	S	20	95	318	32	69	11	4	4	30	14	—	4	.217	.250	.314
Dutch Zwilling	OF148,1B3	L	26	150	548	65	157	32	7	13	94	67	65	24	.286	.366	.442
Max Flack	OF138	L	25	141	523	88	164	20	14	3	45	40	21	37	.314	.365	.423
Les Mann	OF130	R	21	135	470	75	144	12	19	4	58	36	40	18	.306	.357	.438
William Fischer	C80	L	24	105	292	30	96	15	4	4	50	24	19	5	.329	.384	.449
Jack Farrell	2B70,SS1	S	26	70	222	27	48	10	1	0	14	25	18	8	.216	.298	.270
Charlie Hanford	OF43	R	34	77	179	27	43	4	5	0	22	12	28	10	.240	.295	.318
Tex Wisterzil†	3B48	R	24	49	164	15	40	4	1	0	14	8	—	2	.244	.283	.280
Bill Jackson	1B36,OF1	L	34	50	98	15	16	1	0	1	12	14	15	3	.163	.268	.204
Al Wickland†	OF24	L	27	30	86	11	21	2	2	1	5	13	—	3	.244	.343	.349
Mickey Doolan†	SS24	R	35	24	86	9	23	1	1	0	9	2	—	5	.267	.292	.302
Joe Weiss	1B29	R	21	29	85	6	19	1	2	0	11	3	24	0	.224	.250	.282
Three Finger Brown	P35,OF1	S	38	36	82	10	24	2	1	0	6	3	14	0	.293	.318	.341
Joe Tinker	SS16,2B5,3B4	R	34	31	67	7	18	2	1	0	9	13	5	3	.269	.388	.328
Arnold Hauser	SS16,3B6	R	26	23	54	6	11	1	0	0	4	5	7	2	.204	.283	.222
Charlie Pechous	3B18	R	18	18	51	4	9	3	0	0	4	4	15	1	.176	.236	.235
Clem Clemens	C9,2B2	R	28	11	22	3	3	1	0	0	3	1	—	0	.136	.174	.182

Pitcher	T	Age	G	GS	CG	ShO	IP	H	HR	BB	SO	W-L	Sv	ERA
George McConnell	R	37	44	35	23	4	303.0	262	8	89	151	25-10	1	2.20
Claude Hendrix	R	26	40	31	26	5	285.0	256	7	84	107	16-15	4	3.00
Mike Prendergast	R	26	42	30	16	3	253.2	220	6	67	95	14-12	0	2.48
Three Finger Brown	R	38	35	25	17	3	236.1	189	2	64	95	17-8	4	2.09
Ad Brennan	L	33	19	13	7	2	106.0	117	4	30	40	3-9	0	3.74
Rankin Johnson†	R	27	11	6	3	0	57.0	58	2	23	19	2-4	1	4.42
Bill Bailey†	L	26	5	5	3	3	33.1	23	1	10	24	3-1	0	2.16
Dave Black†	R	23	25	10	2	0	121.1	104	4	33	43	6-7	0	2.45
Hans Rasmussen	R	20	2	0	0	0	2.0	3	0	2	2	0-0	0	13.50

1915 St. Louis Terriers 2nd FL 87-67 .565 0.0 GB

Fielder Jones

Player	Gm by Position	B	Age	G	AB	R	H	2B	3B	HR	RBI	BB	SO	SB	Avg	OBP	Slg
Grover Hartley	C113,1B1	R	26	120	394	47	108	21	6	1	50	42	21	10	.274	.356	.365
Babe Borton	1B159	L	26	159	549	97	157	20	14	3	83	92	64	17	.286	.395	.390
Bobby Vaughn	2B127,SS12,3B8	R	30	144	521	69	146	19	9	0	32	58	38	24	.280	.356	.351
Charlie Deal	3B65	R	23	65	223	21	72	12	4	1	27	12	16	10	.323	.357	.426
Ernie Johnson	SS152	L	27	152	512	58	123	18	10	7	67	46	35	32	.240	.305	.355
Jack Tobin	OF158	L	23	158	625	92	184	26	13	6	51	68	42	31	.294	.366	.406
Ward Miller	OF154	L	30	154	536	80	164	19	9	1	63	79	39	33	.306	.400	.381
Delos Drake	OF97,1B1	R	28	102	343	32	91	23	4	1	41	23	27	6	.265	.313	.364
Art Kores	3B60	R	28	60	201	18	47	9	2	1	22	21	13	6	.234	.306	.313
Harry Chapman	C53	R	27	62	186	19	37	6	3	1	29	22	24	4	.199	.284	.280
LaRue Kirby	OF52,P1	S	25	61	178	15	38	7	2	0	16	17	31	3	.213	.282	.275
Al Bridwell	2B42,3B15,1B1	L	31	65	175	20	40	3	2	0	9	25	6	6	.229	.328	.269
Armando Marsans	OF35	R	27	36	124	16	22	3	0	0	6	14	5	5	.177	.261	.202
Jimmy Walsh†	3B9	R	29	17	31	5	6	1	0	0	1	3	—	1	.194	.306	.226
Tex Wisterzil†	3B8	R	24	8	24	1	5	1	0	0	4	2	—	2	.208	.296	.250
Pete Compton†	OF2	L	25	2	8	0	2	0	0	0	3	0	—	0	.250	.250	.250
Hughie Miller	1B6	R	27	7	6	0	3	1	0	0	3	0	—	0	.500	.500	.667
Fielder Jones	OF3	L	43	7	6	1	0	0	0	0	0	0	—	0	.000	.000	.000

Pitcher	T	Age	G	GS	CG	ShO	IP	H	HR	BB	SO	W-L	Sv	ERA
Dave Davenport	R	25	55	46	30	10	392.2	300	5	96	229	22-18	1	2.20
Doc Crandall	R	27	51	33	22	4	312.2	307	5	77	117	21-15	0	2.59
Eddie Plank	L	39	42	31	23	6	268.1	212	1	54	147	21-11	3	2.08
Bob Groom	R	30	37	26	11	4	209.0	200	6	73	111	11-11	1	3.27
Doc Watson	L	29	33	20	6	0	135.2	132	1	58	45	9-9	0	3.98
Ed Willett	R	31	17	2	1	0	52.2	61	2	18	19	2-3	2	4.61
Ernie Herbert	R	28	11	1	1	0	48.0	48	1	18	23	1-0	0	3.38
LaRue Kirby	R	25	1	0	0	0	7.0	7	1	2	7	0-0	0	5.14

1915 Pittsburgh Rebels 3rd FL 86-67 .562 0.5 GB

Rebel Oakes

Player	Gm by Position	B	Age	G	AB	R	H	2B	3B	HR	RBI	BB	SO	SB	Avg	OBP	Slg
Claude Berry	C99	R	35	100	292	32	56	11	1	1	26	29	42	7	.192	.269	.247
Ed Konetchy	1B152	R	29	152	576	79	181	31	18	10	93	41	52	27	.314	.363	.483
Steve Yerkes	2B114,SS8	R	27	121	434	44	125	17	8	1	49	30	27	17	.288	.337	.371
Mike Mowrey	3B151	R	31	151	521	56	146	26	6	1	49	66	39	40	.280	.367	.359
Marty Berghammer	SS132	L	27	132	469	96	114	10	6	0	33	83	44	26	.243	.371	.290
Rebel Oakes	OF153	L	28	153	580	55	161	24	5	0	82	37	19	21	.278	.323	.336
Jim Kelly	OF148	L	31	148	524	68	154	12	17	4	50	35	46	38	.294	.340	.405
Al Wickland†	OF109	L	27	110	389	63	117	12	8	1	30	52	—	23	.301	.386	.380
Jack Lewis	2B45,SS11,OF6*	R	31	82	231	24	61	6	5	0	26	8	31	7	.264	.292	.333
Paddy O'Connor	C66	R	35	70	219	15	50	10	1	0	16	14	30	4	.228	.278	.283
Cy Rheam	OF22,1B1	R	21	34	69	10	12	0	0	1	5	1	7	4	.174	.186	.217
Hugh Bradley†	OF15	R	30	26	66	3	18	4	1	0	6	4	—	2	.273	.314	.364
Ed Lennox	3B3	R	29	55	53	1	16	3	1	1	9	7	12	0	.302	.383	.453
Davy Jones	OF13	L	35	14	49	6	16	0	1	0	4	6	—	1	.327	.400	.367
Ed Holly	SS11,3B3	R	35	16	42	8	11	2	0	0	5	5	6	3	.262	.354	.310
Frank Delahanty	OF11	R	32	14	42	3	10	1	0	0	3	1	—	0	.238	.256	.262
Mike Menosky	OF9	L	20	17	21	3	2	0	0	0	1	2	—	2	.095	.208	.095
Jimmie Savage	OF3,3B1	S	31	14	21	0	3	0	0	0	0	1	—	0	.143	.182	.143
Orie Kerlin	C3	L	24	3	1	0	0	0	0	0	0	0	—	0	.000	.000	.000

J. Lewis, 5 G at 1B, 1 G at 3B

Pitcher	T	Age	G	GS	CG	ShO	IP	H	HR	BB	SO	W-L	Sv	ERA
Frank Allen	L	25	41	37	24	6	283.1	230	9	100	127	23-12	0	2.51
Elmer Knetzer	R	29	41	33	22	3	279.0	256	5	89	120	18-15	3	2.58
Clint Rogge	R	25	37	31	17	5	254.1	240	6	93	93	17-12	0	2.55
Bunny Hearn	L	24	29	17	8	1	175.2	187	6	37	49	6-11	0	3.38
Ralph Comstock†	R	24	12	7	3	0	52.2	44	2	7	18	3-3	2	3.25
Howie Camnitz	R	33	4	2	0	0	20.0	19	1	11	6	0-2	0	4.50
Sandy Burk	R	28	2	2	1	0	18.0	8	0	11	9	2-0	0	1.00
Cy Barger	R	30	34	13	8	1	153.0	130	1	47	47	10-7	5	2.29
Walt Dickson	R	36	27	11	4	0	96.2	115	5	33	36	6-5	0	4.19
George LaClaire†	R	28	14	3	1	0	45.2	43	1	13	10	1-0	1	3.35
Al Braithwood	L	23	2	0	0	0	3.0	0	0	0	2	0-0	0	0.00
Johnny Miljus	R	20	1	0	0	0	1.0	1	0	0	0	0-0	0	0.00

1915 Kansas City Packers 4th FL 81-72 .529 5.5 GB

George Stovall

Player	Gm by Position	B	Age	G	AB	R	H	2B	3B	HR	RBI	BB	SO	SB	Avg	OBP	Slg
Ted Easterly	C88	L	30	110	309	32	84	12	5	3	32	21	15	2	.272	.320	.372
George Stovall	1B129	R	36	130	480	48	111	21	3	0	44	31	36	8	.231	.286	.288
Duke Kenworthy	2B108,OF7	S	28	122	396	59	118	30	7	3	52	28	32	20	.298	.355	.442
George Perring	3B102,1B31,2B31*	R	30	153	553	67	143	23	7	7	67	55	30	10	.259	.327	.363
Johnny Rawlings	SS120	R	22	120	399	40	86	9	2	2	24	27	40	17	.216	.269	.263
Chet Chadbourne	OF152	L	30	152	587	75	133	16	9	1	35	62	29	29	.227	.307	.290
Al Shaw	OF124	L	34	132	448	67	126	22	10	6	67	46	45	15	.281	.348	.415
Grover Gilmore	OF119	L	26	119	411	53	117	22	15	1	47	26	50	19	.285	.347	.418
Art Kruger	OF66	R	34	80	240	24	57	9	2	2	26	12	29	5	.238	.277	.317
Pep Goodwin	SS42,2B23	L	23	81	229	22	54	5	1	0	16	15	23	6	.236	.291	.266
Drummond Brown	C65,1B1	R	30	77	227	13	55	10	1	1	26	12	23	3	.242	.289	.308
Bill Bradley	3B61	R	37	66	203	15	38	9	1	0	9	9	18	6	.187	.225	.241
Jack Enzenroth	C8	R	29	14	19	3	3	0	0	0	3	6	—	0	.158	.360	.158

G. Perring, 1 G at SS

Pitcher	T	Age	G	GS	CG	ShO	IP	H	HR	BB	SO	W-L	Sv	ERA
Nick Cullop	L	27	44	36	22	3	302.1	278	8	67	111	22-11	2	2.44
Chief Johnson	R	29	46	34	19	4	281.1	253	5	71	118	18-17	1	2.75
Gene Packard	L	27	42	31	21	5	281.2	250	3	74	108	20-11	2	2.68
Alex Main	R	31	35	28	18	2	230.0	181	4	75	91	13-14	3	2.54
Pete Henning	R	27	40	20	15	1	207.0	181	5	76	73	8-16	2	3.17
Dan Adams	R	26	11	2	0	0	35.0	41	2	13	16	0-2	0	4.63
Charlie Blackburn	R	20	7	2	0	0	15.2	19	2	13	7	0-1	0	8.62
Joe Gingras	R	22	2	0	0	0	4.0	6	0	1	2	0-0	0	6.75
Ben Harris	R	25	1	0	0	0	2.0	1	0	0	0	0-0	0	0.00

1915 Newark Peppers 5th FL 80-72 .526 6.0 GB

Bill Phillips (26-27)/Bill McKechnie (54-45)

Player	Gm by Position	B	Age	G	AB	R	H	2B	3B	HR	RBI	BB	SO	SB	Avg	OBP	Slg
Bill Rariden	C142	R	27	142	444	49	120	30	7	0	40	60	29	8	.270	.361	.369
Emil Huhn	1B101,C16	R	23	124	415	34	94	18	1	1	41	28	40	13	.227	.279	.282
Frank LaPorte	2B146	R	35	148	550	55	139	28	10	2	56	48	33	14	.253	.314	.351
Bill McKechnie	3B117,OF1	S	28	127	451	49	113	22	5	1	43	41	31	28	.251	.316	.328
Jimmy Esmond	SS155	R	25	155	569	79	147	20	10	5	62	59	54	18	.258	.329	.355
Al Scheer	OF155	L	26	155	546	75	146	25	14	2	60	65	38	31	.267	.353	.375
Edd Roush	OF144	L	22	145	551	73	164	20	11	3	60	38	25	28	.298	.350	.390
Vin Campbell	OF126	L	27	127	525	78	163	18	10	1	44	29	35	24	.310	.352	.389
Germany Schaefer	OF17,1B13,3B9*	R	38	59	154	26	33	5	3	0	8	25	11	3	.214	.328	.286
Rupert Mills	1B37	R	22	41	134	12	27	5	1	0	16	6	21	6	.201	.241	.254
Gil Whitehouse	OF28,P1,C1	S	21	35	120	16	27	6	2	0	9	6	16	3	.225	.268	.308
Ted Reed	3B20	R	24	20	77	5	20	1	2	0	4	2	7	1	.260	.288	.325
Larry Strands	3B12,2B9,OF2	R	29	35	75	7	14	3	1	1	11	6	11	1	.187	.247	.293
Hugh Bradley†	1B8	R	30	12	33	0	5	0	0	0	2	2	—	2	.152	.243	.152
George Textor	C3	S	26	3	6	1	2	0	0	0	0	0	—	0	.333	.333	.333
Larry Pratt†	C3	R	28	5	4	2	2	2	0	0	0	3	—	2	.500	.714	1.000
Bill Warren	C1,1B1	L	28	5	3	0	1	0	0	0	0	0	—	0	.333	.333	.333

G. Schaefer, 2 G at 2B

Pitcher	T	Age	G	GS	CG	ShO	IP	H	HR	BB	SO	W-L	Sv	ERA
Earl Moseley	R	30	38	32	22	5	268.0	222	2	99	142	15-15	0	1.91
Ed Reulbach	R	32	33	30	23	4	270.0	233	3	69	117	21-10	1	2.23
George Kaiserling	R	22	41	29	16	5	261.1	246	1	73	75	15-15	2	2.24
Harry Moran	L	26	34	23	13	2	205.2	193	2	66	87	13-9	0	2.54
Cy Falkenberg†	R	34	25	21	14	0	172.0	175	6	47	76	9-11	1	3.24
Tom Seaton†	R	27	12	10	7	0	75.0	61	1	21	28	2-6	1	2.28
George Mullin	R	34	5	4	3	0	32.1	41	0	16	14	2-2	0	5.85
Chick Brandom	R	28	16	1	1	0	50.1	55	0	15	15	1-1	0	3.40
Harry Billiard	R	31	14	2	0	0	28.1	32	0	28	7	0-1	0	5.72
Charlie Whitehouse	L	21	11	3	1	0	39.2	46	0	17	18	2-2	0	4.31
Fred Trautman	R	23	1	0	0	0	3.0	4	0	1	2	0-0	0	6.00
Gil Whitehouse	R	21	1	0	0	0	1.0	0	0	1	0	0-0	0	0.00

1915 Buffalo Buffeds 6th FL 74-78 .487 12.0 GB

Harry Schlafly (13-28)/Walter Blair (1-1)/Harry Lord (60-49)

Player	Gm by Position	B	Age	G	AB	R	H	2B	3B	HR	RBI	BB	SO	SB	Avg	OBP	Slg
Walter Blair	C97	R	31	98	290	23	65	15	3	2	20	18	32	4	.224	.274	.317
Hal Chase	1B143,OF1	R	32	145	567	85	165	31	10	17	89	20	50	23	.291	.316	.471
Baldy Louden	2B88,SS27,3B19	R	29	141	469	67	132	18	5	4	48	64	45	30	.281	.372	.367
Harry Lord	3B92,OF1	L	33	97	359	50	97	12	6	1	21	21	15	15	.270	.311	.345
Roxey Roach	SS92	R	32	92	346	35	93	20	3	2	31	17	34	11	.269	.303	.361
Jack Dalton	OF119	R	29	132	437	68	128	17	8	2	46	50	38	28	.293	.368	.359
Clyde Engle	OF100,2B21,3B17*	R	31	141	501	56	131	22	8	3	71	34	43	24	.261	.312	.355
Benny Meyer†	OF88	R	27	93	333	37	77	8	6	1	29	40	—	9	.231	.316	.300
Solly Hofman	OF82,1B11,3B4*	R	32	109	346	29	81	10	6	0	27	30	28	12	.234	.295	.298
Tom Downey	2B48,3B35,SS2*	R	31	92	282	24	56	9	1	1	19	26	26	11	.199	.269	.248
Tex McDonald	OF65	L	24	87	251	31	68	9	6	6	39	27	34	5	.271	.346	.426
Nick Allen	C80	R	26	84	215	14	44	7	1	0	17	18	34	4	.205	.269	.247
Fred Smith†	SS32,3B1	R	23	35	114	8	27	2	4	0	11	13	—	2	.237	.320	.325
Joe Agler†	OF20,1B1	L	28	25	73	11	13	1	2	0	2	20	—	2	.178	.355	.247
Art Watson†	C6,OF1	L	31	22	30	6	14	1	0	1	13	0	—	0	.467	.467	.600
Del Young	OF3	L	29	12	15	0	2	0	0	0	0	1	—	1	.133	.188	.133
Ed Gagnier†	2B1	R	32	1	2	0	0	0	0	0	0	0	—	0	.000	.000	.000

C. Engle, 1 G at 1B; S. Hofman, 2 G at 2B, 1 G at SS; T. Downey, 1 G at 1B

Pitcher	T	Age	G	GS	CG	ShO	IP	H	HR	BB	SO	W-L	Sv	ERA
Al Schulz	L	26	42	38	25	5	309.2	264	8	149	160	21-14	0	3.08
Hugh Bedient	R	25	53	30	16	2	269.1	284	5	69	106	15-18	10	3.17
Gene Krapp	R	28	38	30	14	1	231.0	188	6	123	93	9-19	0	3.51
Fred Anderson	R	29	36	28	14	5	240.0	192	5	72	142	19-13	0	2.51
Russ Ford	R	32	21	15	7	0	127.1	140	7	48	34	5-9	0	4.52
Rube Marshall	R	25	21	4	2	0	59.1	62	1	33	21	3-1	0	3.94
Howard Ehmke	R	21	18	2	0	0	53.2	69	2	25	18	0-2	0	5.53
Ed Lafitte†	R	29	14	5	1	0	50.1	53	1	22	17	2-2	1	3.40
Dan Woodman	R	21	5	1	0	0	15.1	14	0	9	1	0-0	0	4.11
George LaClaire†	R	28	1	0	0	0	3.0	4	0	1	2	0-0	0	6.00
Bob Smith	R	24	1	0	0	0	1.0	1	0	2	0	0-0	0	18.00

1915 Brooklyn Tip-Tops 7th FL 70-82 .461 16.0 GB

Lee Magee (53-64)/John Ganzel (17-18)

Player	Gm by Position	B	Age	G	AB	R	H	2B	3B	HR	RBI	BB	SO	SB	Avg	OBP	Slg
Grover Land	C81	R	30	96	290	25	75	13	2	0	22	6	20	3	.259	.279	.317
Hap Myers	1B107	R	27	118	341	61	98	9	1	1	36	32	39	28	.287	.352	.328
Lee Magee	2B115,1B2	S	26	121	452	87	146	19	10	4	49	22	19	34	.323	.356	.436
Al Halt	3B111,SS40	R	24	151	524	41	131	22	7	3	64	39	79	20	.250	.307	.336
Fred Smith†	SS94,3B15	R	23	110	385	41	95	16	6	5	58	25	—	21	.247	.298	.358
Benny Kauff	OF136	L	25	136	483	92	165	23	11	12	83	85	50	55	.342	.446	.509
George Anderson	OF134	L	25	136	511	70	135	23	9	2	39	52	54	20	.264	.342	.356
Claude Cooper	OF121,1B32	L	23	153	527	75	155	26	12	2	63	77	78	31	.294	.388	.400
Steve Evans†	OF61,1B1	L	30	63	216	44	64	14	4	3	30	35	—	7	.296	.411	.440
Mike Simon	C45	R	32	47	142	7	25	5	1	0	12	9	12	1	.176	.225	.225
Hugh Bradley†	1B26,OF7,C1	R	30	37	126	7	31	3	2	0	18	4	—	6	.246	.269	.302
Tex Wisterzil†	3B31	R	24	36	106	13	33	3	3	0	21	21	—	8	.311	.438	.396
Ty Helfrich	2B34,OF1	R	24	43	104	12	25	6	0	0	5	15	21	2	.240	.336	.298
Harry Smith†	C19,OF1	R	25	28	65	5	13	0	0	1	4	7	16	2	.200	.278	.246
Ed Lafitte†	P17,OF2	R	29	20	53	3	14	4	0	0	6	2	—	0	.264	.291	.340
Ed Gagnier†	SS13,2B6	R	32	20	50	8	13	1	0	0	4	10	5	2	.260	.393	.280
Larry Pratt†	C17	R	28	20	49	5	9	1	0	1	2	2	—	2	.184	.216	.265
Art Griggs	1B5,OF1	R	31	27	38	4	11	1	0	1	2	3	7	0	.289	.372	.395
Dave Howard	2B12,OF2,3B1*	R	26	24	36	5	8	1	0	0	1	1	8	0	.222	.243	.250
Fin Wilson	P18,1B1	L	25	19	35	5	11	2	0	0	0	2	3	0	.314	.351	.371
Milt Reed	SS10	L	24	10	31	2	9	1	1	0	8	2	—	2	.290	.353	.387
Jim Delahanty	2B4	R	36	17	25	0	6	1	0	0	2	3	3	1	.240	.345	.280
Hooks Wiltse	P18,1B1	R	34	19	22	0	1	0	0	0	0	0	—	0	.045	.045	.045
Art Watson†	C7	L	31	9	19	4	5	0	3	0	1	3	—	0	.263	.364	.579
Frank Kane	OF2	L	20	3	10	2	2	0	1	0	2	0	—	0	.200	.200	.400
Al Tesch	2B3	S	24	8	7	2	2	1	0	0	2	0	—	0	.286	.286	.429
Danny Murphy	2B1,OF1	R	38	5	6	0	1	0	0	0	0	0	—	0	.167	.167	.167
Dick Wright	C3	R	25	4	5	0	0	0	0	0	0	0	—	0	.000	.000	.000
Felix Chouinard	OF2	R	27	4	4	1	2	0	0	0	2	0	—	0	.500	.500	.500

D. Howard, 1 G at SS

Pitcher	T	Age	G	GS	CG	ShO	IP	H	HR	BB	SO	W-L	Sv	ERA
Dan Marion	R	24	35	25	15	2	208.1	193	1	64	46	10-9	0	3.20
Happy Finneran	R	23	37	24	12	1	215.1	197	2	87	68	12-13	0	2.80
Tom Seaton†	R	27	32	23	13	0	189.1	199	6	99	86	12-11	3	4.56
Jim Bluejacket	R	27	24	21	10	2	162.2	155	2	75	48	9-11	0	3.15
Ed Lafitte†	R	29	17	16	7	0	117.2	126	6	57	34	6-9	0	3.98
Fin Wilson	L	25	18	11	5	0	102.1	85	2	53	47	1-7	0	3.78
Mysterious Walker	R	31	13	7	2	0	65.2	61	3	22	28	2-4	1	3.70
Cy Falkenberg†	R	34	7	7	5	1	48.0	31	1	12	20	3-3	0	1.50
Bill Upham	R	27	33	11	4	2	121.0	129	0	40	46	7-8	4	3.05
Hooks Wiltse	L	34	18	3	1	0	59.1	49	1	7	17	3-5	5	2.28
Frank Smith†	R	35	15	5	4	1	63.0	69	2	18	24	5-2	0	3.14
Bill Herring	R	21	3	0	0	0	3.0	5	1	2	3	0-0	0	15.00

1915 Baltimore Terrapins 8th FL 47-107 .305 40.0 GB

Otto Knabe

Player	Gm by Position	B	Age	G	AB	R	H	2B	3B	HR	RBI	BB	SO	SB	Avg	OBP	Slg
Frank Owens	C99	R	29	99	334	32	84	14	7	3	28	17	34	4	.251	.290	.362
Harry Swacina	1B75,2B1	R	33	85	301	24	74	13	1	1	38	9	11	9	.246	.268	.306
Otto Knabe	2B94	R	31	103	320	38	81	16	2	1	25	37	16	7	.253	.334	.325
Jimmy Walsh†	3B106	R	29	106	401	43	121	20	1	9	60	21	—	12	.302	.340	.424
Mickey Doolan†	SS119	R	35	119	404	41	75	13	7	2	21	24	—	10	.186	.238	.267
Vern Duncan	OF124,3B21,2B1	L	25	146	531	68	142	18	4	2	43	54	40	19	.267	.337	.328
Jack McCandless	OF105	L	24	117	406	47	87	6	7	5	34	41	99	9	.214	.296	.300
Steve Evans†	OF88,1B4	L	30	88	340	50	107	20	6	1	37	28	—	8	.315	.379	.418
Guy Zinn	OF88	L	28	102	312	30	84	18	3	5	43	35	28	2	.269	.343	.394
Joe Agler†	1B58,OF4,2B3	L	28	72	214	28	46	4	2	0	14	34	—	15	.215	.325	.252
Enos Kirkpatrick	3B28,2B21,1B5*	R	29	68	171	22	41	8	2	0	19	24	15	12	.240	.337	.310
Fred Jacklitsch	C45,SS1	R	39	49	135	20	32	9	0	2	13	31	25	2	.237	.387	.348
John Gallagher	2B37,SS5,3B1	R	23	40	126	11	25	4	0	0	4	5	22	1	.198	.229	.230
Benny Meyer†	OF34	R	27	35	120	20	29	2	0	0	5	37	—	6	.242	.424	.258
Jack Quinn	P44,OF1	R	31	56	110	12	29	4	1	0	10	8	24	0	.264	.314	.318
Jimmy Smith†	SS33	S	20	33	108	9	19	1	1	1	11	11	—	3	.176	.258	.231
Hack Simmons	2B13,OF13	R	30	39	88	8	18	7	1	1	14	10	9	1	.205	.293	.341
Ken Crawford	1B14,OF4	L	20	23	82	4	20	2	1	0	7	1	18	0	.244	.253	.293
Jim Hickman	OF20	R	23	20	81	7	17	4	1	1	7	4	14	5	.210	.256	.321
Harvey Russell	C21	L	28	53	73	5	19	1	2	0	11	14	5	1	.260	.407	.329
Karl Kolseth	1B6	L	22	6	23	1	6	1	1	0	1	1	—	0	.261	.292	.391
Wally Reinecker	3B3	R	25	3	8	0	1	0	0	0	0	0	—	0	.125	.222	.125
Charlie Eakle	2B2	—	27	2	7	0	2	1	0	0	0	0	—	1	.286	.286	.429
Doc Kerr	C2,1B1	S	33	3	6	1	2	0	0	0	0	1	—	0	.333	.429	.333
Charlie Maisel	C1	R	21	1	4	0	0	0	0	0	0	0	—	0	.000	.000	.000
Ed Forsyth	3B1	R	28	1	3	0	0	0	0	0	0	1	—	0	.000	.250	.000
Charlie Miller		R	37	1	1	0	0	0	0	0	0	0	—	0	.000	.000	.000

E. Kirkpatrick, 5 G at SS

Pitcher	T	Age	G	GS	CG	ShO	IP	H	HR	BB	SO	W-L	Sv	ERA
Jack Quinn	R	31	44	31	21	0	273.2	289	9	63	118	9-22	1	3.45
George Suggs	R	32	35	25	12	0	232.2	288	12	68	71	13-17	1	4.14
Bill Bailey†	L	26	36	23	11	2	190.1	179	8	115	98	5-19	0	4.63
Chief Bender	R	31	26	23	15	0	178.1	198	5	37	89	4-16	1	3.99
Rankin Johnson†	R	27	23	19	12	2	150.2	143	3	58	62	7-11	1	3.35
Frank Smith†	R	35	17	9	2	0	88.2	108	5	31	37	4-4	0	4.67
George LaClaire†	R	28	18	9	6	1	84.0	76	2	22	30	2-8	1	2.46
Charlie Young	R	22	9	5	1	0	35.0	39	0	21	13	1-3	0	5.91
Dave Black†	R	23	8	4	1	0	34.0	32	2	15	10	1-3	0	3.71
Snipe Conley	R	21	25	6	4	0	86.0	97	5	32	40	1-4	0	4.29
Tommy Vereker	—	21	2	0	0	0	3.0	3	1	2	1	0-0	0	15.00
Larry Douglas	R	25	2	0	0	0	3.0	3	0	2	1	0-0	0	3.00
Kaiser Wilhelm	R	41	1	0	0	0	1.0	0	0	0	0	0-0	0	0.00

»1916 Boston Red Sox 1st AL 91-63 .591 —

Bill Carrigan

Player	Gm by Position	B	Age	G	AB	R	H	2B	3B	HR	RBI	BB	SO	SB	Avg	OBP	Slg
Pinch Thomas	C90	L	28	99	216	21	57	10	1	1	21	33	13	4	.264	.364	.333
Doc Hoblitzell	1B126	R	27	130	417	57	108	17	1	0	39	47	28	10	.259	.338	.305
Jack Barry	2B94	R	29	94	330	28	67	6	1	0	20	17	24	8	.203	.277	.227
Larry Gardner	3B147	L	30	148	493	47	152	19	7	2	62	48	27	12	.308	.372	.387
Everett Scott	SS121,2B1,3B1	R	23	123	366	37	85	19	2	0	27	23	24	8	.232	.283	.295
Harry Hooper	OF151	L	28	151	575	75	156	20	11	1	37	80	35	27	.271	.361	.350
Duffy Lewis	OF151	R	28	152	563	56	151	29	5	1	56	33	56	16	.268	.313	.343
Tilly Walker	OF128	R	28	128	467	68	124	29	11	3	46	23	45	14	.266	.303	.394
Hal Janvrin	SS59,2B39,1B4*	R	23	117	310	32	69	11	4	0	26	32	32	6	.223	.299	.284
Hick Cady	C63,1B3	R	30	78	162	5	31	6	3	0	13	15	16	0	.191	.264	.265
Del Gainer	1B48,2B2	R	29	56	142	14	36	6	0	3	18	10	24	5	.254	.303	.359
Mike McNally	2B35,3B14,SS7*	R	23	87	135	28	23	0	0	0	9	10	19	9	.170	.228	.170
Chick Shorten	OF33	L	24	53	112	14	33	2	1	0	11	10	8	1	.295	.352	.330
Olaf Henriksen	OF31	L	28	68	99	13	20	2	2	0	11	19	15	2	.202	.331	.263
Sam Agnew	C38	R	29	40	67	4	14	2	1	0	7	6	4	0	.209	.293	.269
Bill Carrigan	C27	R	32	33	63	7	17	2	1	0	11	11	3	2	.270	.378	.333
Rube Foster	P33,OF1	R	28	38	62	3	11	3	0	0	2	3	10	0	.177	.215	.226
Jimmy Walsh†	OF6,3B2	L	30	13	16	5	2	0	0	0	2	4	2	3	.125	.300	.125
Heinie Wagner	3B4,2B1,SS1	R	35	6	8	2	4	1	0	0	0	3	0	2	.500	.636	.625
Sad Sam Jones	P12,OF1	R	23	13	6	0	2	0	0	0	0	0	2	0	.333	.333	.333
Ray Haley†		R	25	1	1	0	0	0	0	0	0	0	1	0	.000	.000	.000

H. Janvrin, 3 G at 3B; M. McNally, 1 G at OF

Pitcher	T	Age	G	GS	CG	ShO	IP	H	HR	BB	SO	W-L	Sv	ERA
Babe Ruth	L	21	44	41	23	9	323.2	230	0	118	170	23-12	1	1.75
Dutch Leonard	L	24	48	34	17	6	274.0	244	6	66	144	18-12	6	2.36
Ernie Shore	R	25	38	28	10	3	225.2	221	1	49	62	17-10	1	2.63
Carl Mays	R	24	44	24	14	2	245.0	208	3	74	76	18-13	3	2.39
Rube Foster	R	28	33	19	9	3	182.1	173	0	86	53	13-7	2	3.06
Marty McHale†	R	27	2	1	0	0	6.0	7	0	4	1	0-1	0	3.00
Vean Gregg	L	31	21	7	3	0	77.2	71	0	30	41	2-5	0	3.01
Sad Sam Jones	R	23	12	0	0	0	27.0	25	0	10	7	0-1	1	3.67
Herb Pennock	L	22	9	2	0	0	26.2	23	0	8	12	0-2	1	3.04
John Wyckoff†	R	24	8	0	0	0	22.2	19	0	18	18	0-0	1	4.76

1916 Chicago White Sox 2nd AL 89-65 .578 2.0 GB

Pants Rowland

Player	Gm by Position	B	Age	G	AB	R	H	2B	3B	HR	RBI	BB	SO	SB	Avg	OBP	Slg
Ray Schalk	C124	R	23	129	410	36	95	12	9	0	41	41	31	30	.232	.311	.305
Jack Fournier	1B85,OF1	L	26	105	313	36	75	13	9	3	44	36	40	19	.240	.328	.367
Eddie Collins	2B155	L	29	155	545	87	168	14	17	0	52	86	36	40	.308	.405	.396
Buck Weaver	3B85,SS66	R	25	151	582	78	132	27	6	3	38	30	48	22	.227	.280	.309
Zeb Terry	SS93	R	25	94	269	20	51	8	4	0	17	33	36	4	.190	.292	.249
Joe Jackson	OF155	L	26	155	592	91	202	40	21	3	78	46	25	24	.341	.393	.495
Happy Felsch	OF141	R	24	146	546	73	164	24	12	7	70	31	67	13	.300	.341	.427
Shano Collins	OF136,1B4	R	30	143	527	74	128	28	12	0	42	59	51	16	.243	.323	.342
Jack Ness	1B69	R	30	75	258	32	69	7	5	1	34	9	32	4	.267	.310	.345
Fred McMullin	3B63,SS2,2B1	R	24	68	187	8	48	3	0	0	10	19	30	9	.257	.332	.273
Eddie Murphy	OF24,3B1	L	24	51	105	14	22	5	1	0	4	9	5	3	.210	.284	.276
Jack Lapp	C34	L	31	40	101	6	21	0	1	0	7	8	10	1	.208	.266	.228
Nemo Leibold	OF24	L	24	45	82	5	20	1	2	0	13	7	7	7	.244	.303	.305
Fritz Von Kolnitz	3B13	R	23	24	44	1	10	3	0	0	7	2	6	0	.227	.261	.295
Byrd Lynn	C13	R	27	31	40	4	9	1	0	0	3	4	7	2	.225	.311	.250
Mellie Wolfgang	P28,3B1	R	26	28	40	2	9	1	0	0	3	0	8	0	.225	.225	.250
Cy Wright	SS8	L	22	8	18	0	0	0	0	0	0	1	7	0	.000	.053	.000
Ziggy Hasbrook	1B7	R	22	9	8	1	1	0	0	0	0	1	2	0	.125	.222	.125
George Moriarty	1B1,3B1	R	32	7	5	1	1	0	0	0	0	2	0	0	.200	.429	.200
Ted Jourdan		L	20	3	2	0	0	0	0	0	0	1	1	2	.000	.333	.000
Joe Fautsch		R	29	1	1	0	0	0	0	0	0	0	0	0	.000	.000	.000

Pitcher	T	Age	G	GS	CG	ShO	IP	H	HR	BB	SO	W-L	Sv	ERA
Lefty Williams	L	23	43	26	10	2	224.1	220	5	65	138	13-7	1	2.89
Red Faber	R	27	35	25	15	3	205.1	167	1	61	87	17-9	2	2.02
Jim Scott	R	28	32	20	8	1	165.1	155	3	53	71	7-14	2	2.72
Joe Benz	R	30	28	16	6	4	142.0	108	0	32	57	9-5	0	2.03
Mellie Wolfgang	R	26	27	14	6	1	127.0	103	2	42	36	4-6	0	1.98
Ed Walsh	R	35	2	1	0	0	3.1	4	0	3	3	0-1	0	2.70
Reb Russell	L	27	56	26	16	5	264.1	207	1	42	112	18-11	3	2.42
Eddie Cicotte	R	32	44	19	11	2	187.0	138	1	70	91	15-7	5	1.78
Dave Danforth	L	26	28	8	1	0	93.2	87	1	37	49	6-5	2	3.27

1916 Detroit Tigers 3rd AL 87-67 .565 4.0 GB

Hughie Jennings

Player	Gm by Position	B	Age	G	AB	R	H	2B	3B	HR	RBI	BB	SO	SB	Avg	OBP	Slg
Oscar Stanage	C94	R	33	94	291	16	69	17	3	0	30	17	48	3	.237	.286	.316
George Burns	1B124	R	23	135	479	60	137	22	6	4	73	22	30	12	.286	.327	.382
Ralph Young	2B146,SS6,3B1	S	26	153	528	60	139	16	6	1	45	62	43	20	.263	.342	.322
Ossie Vitt	3B151,SS2	R	26	153	597	88	135	17	12	0	42	75	28	18	.226	.314	.295
Donie Bush	SS144	S	28	145	550	73	124	5	9	0	34	75	42	19	.225	.319	.267
Bobby Veach	OF150	L	28	150	566	92	173	33	15	3	91	52	41	24	.306	.367	.433
Ty Cobb	OF143,1B1	L	29	145	542	113	201	31	10	5	68	78	39	68	.371	.452	.493
Sam Crawford	OF79,1B2	L	36	100	322	41	92	11	13	0	42	37	10	10	.286	.359	.401
Harry Heilmann	OF77,1B30,2B9	R	21	136	451	57	127	30	11	2	73	42	40	9	.282	.349	.410
Del Baker	C59	R	24	61	98	7	15	4	0	0	6	11	8	2	.153	.245	.194
Marty Kavanagh†	OF11,2B2,3B1	R	25	58	78	6	11	4	0	0	5	9	15	0	.141	.239	.192
Red McKee	C26	L	25	32	76	3	16	1	2	0	4	6	11	0	.211	.268	.276
George Harper	OF14	L	24	44	56	4	9	1	0	0	3	5	8	0	.161	.230	.179
Tubby Spencer	C19	R	32	19	54	7	20	1	1	1	10	6	6	2	.370	.443	.481
Ben Dyer	SS4	R	23	4	14	4	4	1	0	0	1	1	1	0	.286	.333	.357
Jack Dalton	OF4	R	30	8	11	1	2	0	0	0	0	0	5	0	.182	.182	.182
Frank Fuller	2B8,SS1	S	23	20	10	2	1	0	0	0	1	1	4	3	.100	.182	.100
Babe Ellison	3B2	R	20	2	7	0	1	0	0	0	1	0	1	0	.143	.143	.143
George Maisel	3B3	R	24	7	5	2	0	0	0	0	0	0	2	0	.000	.000	.000
Billy Sullivan	C1	R	41	1	0	0	0	0	0	0	0	0	0	0	—	—	—

Pitcher	T	Age	G	GS	CG	ShO	IP	H	HR	BB	SO	W-L	Sv	ERA
Harry Coveleski	L	30	44	39	22	3	324.1	278	6	63	108	21-11	2	1.97
Hooks Dauss	R	26	39	29	18	1	238.2	220	2	90	95	19-12	4	3.21
Bill James	R	29	30	20	8	0	151.2	141	1	79	61	8-12	1	3.68
Willie Mitchell†	L	26	23	17	7	2	127.2	119	1	48	60	7-5	0	3.31
Earl Hamilton†	L	24	5	5	3	1	37.1	34	0	22	7	1-2	0	2.65
Howard Ehmke	R	22	5	4	4	0	37.1	34	0	15	15	3-1	0	3.13
Bernie Boland	R	24	46	9	5	1	130.1	111	1	73	59	10-3	3	3.94
Jean Dubuc	R	27	36	16	8	1	170.1	134	1	84	40	10-10	1	2.96
G. Cunningham	R	21	35	14	5	0	150.1	146	0	74	68	7-10	2	2.75
Eric Erickson	R	21	8	0	0	0	16.0	13	0	8	7	0-0	0	2.81
George Boehler	R	24	5	2	1	0	13.1	12	0	9	8	1-1	0	4.73
Bill McTigue	L	25	3	0	0	0	5.1	5	0	5	1	0-0	0	5.06
Deacon Jones	R	23	1	0	0	0	7.0	7	0	5	2	0-0	0	2.57
Grover Lowdermilk†	R	31	1	0	0	0	0.1	0	0	3	0	0-0	0	0.00

1916 New York Yankees 4th AL 80-74 .519 11.0 GB

Wild Bill Donovan

Player	Gm by Position	B	Age	G	AB	R	H	2B	3B	HR	RBI	BB	SO	SB	Avg	OBP	Slg
Les Nunamaker	C79	R	27	91	260	25	77	14	7	0	28	34	21	4	.296	.380	.404
Wally Pipp	1B148	L	23	151	545	70	143	20	14	12	93	54	82	16	.262	.331	.417
Joe Gedeon	2B122	R	22	122	435	50	92	14	4	0	27	40	61	14	.211	.282	.262
Home Run Baker	3B96	L	30	100	360	46	97	23	2	10	52	36	30	15	.269	.344	.428
Roger Peckinpaugh	SS145	R	25	146	552	65	141	22	8	4	58	62	50	18	.255	.332	.346
Lee Magee	OF128,2B2	S	27	131	510	57	131	18	4	3	45	50	31	29	.257	.324	.325
Hugh High	OF109	L	28	115	377	44	99	13	4	1	28	47	44	13	.263	.349	.326
Frank Gilhooley	OF57	L	24	58	223	40	62	5	3	1	10	37	17	16	.278	.383	.341
Paddy Baumann	OF28,3B26,2B9	R	30	79	237	35	68	5	3	1	25	19	16	10	.287	.352	.346
Roxy Walters	C65	R	23	66	203	13	54	9	3	0	23	14	42	2	.266	.320	.340
Fritz Maisel	OF25,3B11,2B4	R	26	53	158	18	36	5	0	0	7	20	18	4	.228	.318	.259
Rube Oldring†	OF43	R	32	43	158	17	37	8	0	1	12	12	13	6	.234	.288	.304
Elmer Miller	OF42	R	25	43	152	12	34	3	2	1	18	11	18	8	.224	.280	.289
Charlie Mullen	2B20,1B17,OF6	R	27	59	146	11	39	9	1	0	18	9	13	7	.267	.310	.342
Luke Boone	3B25,SS12,2B8	R	26	46	124	14	23	4	0	1	8	8	10	7	.185	.252	.242
Ray Caldwell	P21,OF3	L	28	45	93	6	19	2	0	0	4	2	17	1	.204	.221	.226
Walt Alexander	C27	R	25	36	78	8	20	6	1	0	3	13	20	0	.256	.376	.359
Roy Hartzell	OF28	L	34	33	64	12	12	1	0	0	7	9	3	1	.188	.297	.203
Tim Hendryx	OF15	R	25	15	62	10	18	7	1	0	5	8	6	4	.290	.380	.435
Angel Aragon	3B8,OF3	R	25	13	27	1	5	0	0	0	3	2	2	2	.185	.241	.185
Solly Hofman†	OF6	R	33	6	27	0	8	1	1	0	2	1	1	1	.296	.321	.407
Doc Cook	OF3	L	30	3	10	0	1	0	0	0	1	0	2	0	.100	.100	.100
Germany Schaefer	OF1	R	39	1	1	0	0	0	0	0	0	0	0	0	.000	.000	.000

Pitcher	T	Age	G	GS	CG	ShO	IP	H	HR	BB	SO	W-L	Sv	ERA
Bob Shawkey	R	25	53	27	21	4	276.2	204	4	81	122	24-14	8	2.21
Nick Cullop	L	28	28	22	9	0	167.0	151	4	32	77	13-6	1	2.05
George Mogridge	L	27	30	21	9	2	194.2	174	3	45	66	6-12	0	2.31
Ray Fisher	R	28	31	21	9	1	179.0	191	4	51	56	11-8	2	3.17
Allan Russell	R	22	34	18	8	1	171.1	138	8	75	104	6-10	6	3.20
Ray Caldwell	R	28	21	18	14	1	165.2	142	6	65	76	5-12	0	2.99
Ray Keating	R	24	14	12	6	0	91.0	91	4	37	35	5-6	0	3.07
Urban Shocker	R	25	12	9	4	1	82.1	67	2	32	43	4-3	0	2.62
Cliff Markle	R	22	11	7	3	1	45.2	41	0	31	14	4-3	0	4.53
Slim Love	L	25	20	1	0	0	47.2	46	2	23	21	2-0	0	4.91
Jess Buckles	L	26	2	0	0	0	4.0	3	0	1	2	0-0	0	2.25
Mike Cantwell	L	20	1	0	0	0	2.0	0	0	2	0	0-0	0	0.00
Wild Bill Donovan	R	39	1	0	0	0	1.0	1	0	1	0	0-0	0	0.00

1916 St. Louis Browns 5th AL 79-75 .513 12.0 GB

Fielder Jones

Player	Gm by Position	B	Age	G	AB	R	H	2B	3B	HR	RBI	BB	SO	SB	Avg	OBP	Slg
Hank Severeid	C89,1B1,3B1	R	25	100	293	23	80	8	2	0	34	26	17	3	.273	.341	.314
George Sisler	1B141,P3,OF3*	L	23	151	580	83	177	21	11	4	76	40	37	34	.305	.355	.400
Del Pratt	2B158	R	28	158	596	64	159	35	12	5	103	54	56	26	.267	.331	.391
Jimmy Austin	3B124	S	36	129	411	55	85	15	6	1	28	74	59	19	.207	.333	.280
Doc Lavan	SS106	R	25	110	343	32	81	13	1	0	19	32	38	7	.236	.305	.280
Burt Shotton	OF157	L	31	156	614	97	174	23	6	1	36	110	65	41	.283	.392	.345
Armando Marsans	OF150	R	28	151	528	51	134	12	1	1	60	57	41	46	.254	.333	.286
Ward Miller	OF135,2B1	L	31	146	485	72	129	17	5	1	50	72	76	25	.266	.371	.328
Ernie Johnson	SS60,3B12	L	28	74	236	29	54	9	3	0	19	30	23	13	.229	.323	.292
Grover Hartley	C75	R	27	89	222	19	50	8	0	0	12	30	24	4	.225	.325	.261
Jack Tobin	OF41	L	24	77	150	16	32	4	1	0	10	12	13	7	.213	.272	.253
Babe Borton	1B22	L	27	66	98	10	22	1	2	1	12	19	13	1	.224	.350	.306
Charlie Deal†	3B22,2B1	R	24	23	74	7	10	1	0	0	10	6	8	4	.135	.200	.149
William Rumler	C9	R	25	27	37	6	12	3	0	0	10	3	7	0	.324	.375	.405
Harry Chapman	C14	R	28	18	31	2	3	0	0	0	0	2	5	0	.097	.152	.097
Bobby Wallace	3B9,SS5	R	42	14	18	0	5	0	0	0	1	2	1	0	.278	.350	.278
Billy Lee	OF3	R	24	7	11	1	2	0	0	0	0	1	0	0	.182	.250	.182
Verne Clemons	C2	R	24	4	7	0	1	1	0	0	0	0	1	0	.143	.143	.286
Gene Paulette		R	25	5	4	1	2	0	0	0	0	1	1	0	.500	.600	.500
Ray Kennedy		R	21	1	1	0	0	0	0	0	0	0	0	0	.000	.000	.000
George Hale	C3	R	21	4	1	0	0	0	0	0	0	0	1	0	.000	.500	.000

G. Sisler, 2 G at 3B

Pitcher	T	Age	G	GS	CG	ShO	IP	H	HR	BB	SO	W-L	Sv	ERA
Dave Davenport	R	26	59	31	13	1	290.2	267	4	100	129	12-11	1	2.85
Carl Weilman	L	26	46	31	19	1	276.0	237	3	76	91	17-18	2	2.15
Eddie Plank	L	40	37	26	17	3	235.2	203	2	67	88	16-15	3	2.33
Bob Groom	R	31	41	26	6	1	217.1	174	1	98	92	13-9	4	2.57
Ernie Koob	L	23	33	20	10	2	166.2	153	1	56	26	11-8	2	2.54
Earl Hamilton†	L	24	23	12	2	0	95.1	101	2	30	25	5-7	0	3.02
George Sisler	L	23	3	3	3	1	27.0	18	0	6	12	1-2	0	1.00
G. Baumgardner	R	24	4	2	0	0	8.0	12	0	5	4	1-0	0	7.88
Jim Park	R	23	26	6	1	0	79.0	69	2	25	26	1-4	0	2.62
Tim McCabe	R	21	13	0	0	0	25.2	29	0	7	7	2-0	0	3.16
Bill Fincher	R	22	12	1	0	0	21.0	22	0	7	5	0-1	0	2.14
Doc Crandall	R	28	2	0	0	0	1.1	7	0	1	0	0-0	0	27.00

1916 Cleveland Indians 6th AL 77-77 .500 14.0 GB

Lee Fohl

Player	Gm by Position	B	Age	G	AB	R	H	2B	3B	HR	RBI	BB	SO	SB	Avg	OBP	Slg
Steve O'Neill	C128	R	24	130	378	30	89	23	0	0	29	24	33	2	.235	.288	.296
Chick Gandil	1B145	R	29	146	533	51	138	26	9	0	72	36	48	13	.259	.312	.341
Ivan Howard	2B65,1B7	S	33	81	246	20	46	11	5	0	23	30	34	9	.187	.298	.272
Terry Turner	3B77,2B42	R	35	124	428	52	112	15	3	0	38	40	29	15	.262	.325	.311
Bill Wambsganss	SS106,2B24,3B5	R	22	136	475	57	117	14	4	0	45	41	40	13	.246	.313	.293
Jack Graney	OF154	L	30	155	589	106	142	41	14	5	54	102	72	10	.241	.355	.384
Tris Speaker	OF151	L	28	151	546	102	211	41	8	2	79	82	20	35	.386	.470	.502
Braggo Roth	OF112	R	23	125	409	50	117	19	7	4	72	38	48	29	.286	.350	.396
Ray Chapman	SS52,3B36,2B16	R	25	109	346	50	80	10	5	0	27	50	46	21	.231	.330	.289
Elmer Smith†	OF57	L	23	79	213	25	59	15	3	3	40	18	35	3	.277	.336	.418
Joe Evans	3B28	R	21	33	82	4	12	1	0	0	1	7	12	4	.146	.213	.159
Tom Daly	C25,OF1	R	24	31	73	3	16	1	1	0	8	1	2	0	.219	.230	.260
Walter Barbare	3B12	R	24	13	48	3	11	1	0	0	3	4	9	0	.229	.288	.250
Marty Kavanagh†	2B9,1B1,3B1	R	25	19	44	4	11	2	1	1	10	2	5	0	.250	.283	.409
Hank DeBerry	C14	R	21	15	33	7	9	4	0	0	4	6	9	0	.273	.385	.394
Josh Billings	C12	R	24	22	31	2	5	0	0	0	1	2	11	0	.161	.212	.161
Danny Moeller†	OF8,2B1	S	31	25	30	5	2	0	0	0	1	5	6	2	.067	.200	.067
Bob Coleman	C12	R	25	19	28	3	6	2	0	0	4	7	6	0	.214	.371	.286
Clyde Engle	3B7,1B2,OF1	R	32	11	26	1	4	0	0	0	1	0	6	0	.154	.154	.154
Lou Guisto	1B6	R	21	6	19	2	3	0	0	0	2	4	3	1	.158	.304	.158
Milo Allison	OF5	L	25	14	18	10	5	0	0	0	0	6	1	0	.278	.458	.278
Al Bergman	2B3	R	25	8	14	2	3	0	1	0	0	2	4	0	.214	.313	.357
Howard Lohr	OF3	R	24	3	7	0	1	0	0	0	1	0	1	1	.143	.143	.143
Jack Bradley	C1	R	22	2	3	0	0	0	0	0	0	0	1	0	.000	.000	.000
Joe Leonard†	2B1	L	21	3	2	1	0	0	0	0	0	0	1	0	.000	.000	.000
Larry Chappell†		L	26	3	2	0	0	0	0	0	0	1	0	1	.000	.333	.000
Ollie Welf		R	27	1	0	0	0	0	0	0	0	0	0	0	—	—	—

Pitcher	T	Age	G	GS	CG	ShO	IP	H	HR	BB	SO	W-L	Sv	ERA
Jim Bagby	R	26	48	27	14	3	272.2	253	2	67	88	16-16	5	2.61
Stan Coveleski	R	26	45	27	11	1	232.0	247	6	58	76	15-13	3	3.41
Guy Morton	R	23	27	18	9	0	149.2	139	1	42	88	12-8	0	2.89
Fred Beebe	R	35	20	12	5	1	100.2	92	1	37	32	5-3	2	2.41
Otis Lambeth	R	26	15	9	3	0	74.0	69	1	38	28	4-3	1	2.92
Joe Boehling†	L	25	12	9	3	0	60.2	63	0	23	18	2-4	0	2.67
Grover Lowdermilk†	R	31	10	9	2	0	51.1	52	0	45	28	1-5	0	3.16
Willie Mitchell†	L	26	12	6	1	0	43.2	55	1	19	24	2-5	1	5.15
Pop Boy Smith	R	24	5	3	0	0	25.2	25	1	11	4	1-2	1	3.86
Ken Penner	R	20	4	2	0	0	12.2	14	0	4	5	1-0	0	4.26
Ed Klepfer	R	28	31	13	4	1	143.0	136	0	46	62	6-6	2	2.52
Al Gould	R	23	30	9	6	1	106.2	101	0	40	41	5-7	1	2.53
Fritz Coumbe	L	26	29	13	7	2	120.1	121	1	27	39	7-5	0	2.02
Marty McHale†	R	27	5	0	0	0	11.1	10	1	6	2	0-0	0	5.56
Rip Hagerman	R	28	2	0	0	0	3.2	5	1	2	1	0-0	0	12.27
Red Gunkel	R	22	1	0	0	0	1.0	0	0	1	1	0-0	0	0.00
Shorty Desjardien	R	22	1	0	0	0	1.0	1	0	1	0	0-0	0	18.00

1916 Washington Senators 7th AL 76-77 .497 14.5 GB

Clark Griffith

Player	Gm by Position	B	Age	G	AB	R	H	2B	3B	HR	RBI	BB	SO	SB	Avg	OBP	Slg
John Henry	C116	R	26	117	305	28	76	12	3	0	46	49	40	12	.249	.364	.308
Joe Judge	1B103	L	22	103	336	42	74	10	8	0	28	54	44	18	.220	.333	.298
Ray Morgan	2B82,SS9,1B3*	R	27	99	315	41	84	12	4	1	29	59	29	14	.267	.398	.340
Eddie Foster	3B84,2B72	R	29	158	606	75	153	18	9	1	44	68	26	23	.252	.332	.317
George McBride	SS139	R	35	139	466	36	106	15	4	1	36	23	58	8	.227	.271	.283
Clyde Milan	OF149	L	29	150	565	58	154	14	3	1	45	56	31	34	.273	.343	.313
Howard Shanks	OF88,3B31,SS8*	R	25	140	471	51	119	15	7	1	48	41	34	23	.253	.317	.321
Danny Moeller†	OF63	S	31	78	240	30	59	8	1	1	23	30	35	13	.246	.335	.300
Rip Williams	1B34,C23,3B1	R	34	76	202	16	54	10	2	0	20	15	19	5	.267	.324	.337
Sam Rice	OF46,P5	L	26	58	197	26	59	8	3	1	17	15	13	4	.299	.352	.386
Elmer Smith†	OF45	L	23	45	168	12	36	10	3	2	27	18	28	4	.214	.298	.345
Joe Leonard†	3B42	L	21	42	168	20	46	7	0	0	14	22	23	4	.274	.358	.315
Henri Rondeau	OF48	R	29	50	162	20	36	5	3	1	28	18	18	7	.222	.311	.309
Charlie Jamieson	OF41,1B4,P1	L	23	64	145	16	36	4	0	0	13	18	18	5	.248	.331	.276
Eddie Ainsmith	C46	R	24	51	100	11	17	4	0	0	8	8	14	3	.170	.231	.210
Patsy Gharrity	C16,1B16	R	24	39	92	8	21	5	1	0	9	8	18	2	.228	.297	.304
Mike Menosky	OF9	L	21	10	37	5	6	1	1	0	3	1	10	1	.162	.184	.243
Turner Barber	OF9	L	22	15	33	3	7	0	1	1	5	2	3	0	.212	.257	.364
Carl Sawyer	2B6,SS5,3B1	R	25	16	31	3	6	1	0	0	2	4	4	3	.194	.306	.226
Merito Acosta	OF4	L	20	4	7	0	1	0	0	0	0	2	0	0	.143	.333	.143

R. Morgan, 1 G at 3B; H. Shanks, 7 G at 1B

Pitcher	T	Age	G	GS	CG	ShO	IP	H	HR	BB	SO	W-L	Sv	ERA
Walter Johnson	R	28	48	38	36	3	369.2	290	0	82	228	25-20	1	1.90
Harry Harper	L	21	36	34	12	2	249.2	209	4	101	149	14-10	0	2.45
Bert Gallia	R	24	49	31	13	1	283.2	278	3	99	120	17-12	2	2.76
Joe Boehling†	L	25	27	19	7	2	139.2	134	1	54	52	9-11	0	3.09
Claude Thomas	L	26	7	4	1	1	28.1	27	1	12	7	1-2	0	4.13
Molly Craft	R	20	2	1	1	0	11.0	12	0	6	9	0-1	0	3.27
Doc Ayers	R	26	43	17	7	0	157.0	173	4	52	69	5-9	2	3.78
Jim Shaw	R	22	26	9	5	2	106.1	86	1	50	44	3-8	1	2.62
George Dumont	R	20	17	5	2	0	53.0	37	0	17	21	2-3	1	3.06
Sam Rice	R	26	5	1	0	0	21.1	18	0	10	3	0-1	0	2.95
Marv Goodwin	R	25	3	0	0	0	5.2	5	0	3	1	0-0	0	3.18
Jack Bentley	L	21	2	0	0	0	1.1	0	0	1	1	0-0	0	0.00
Charlie Jamieson	L	23	1	0	0	0	4.0	2	0	3	2	0-0	0	4.50

1916 Philadelphia Athletics 8th AL 36-117 .235 54.5 GB

Connie Mack

Player	Gm by Position	B	Age	G	AB	R	H	2B	3B	HR	RBI	BB	SO	SB	Avg	OBP	Slg
Billy Meyer	C48	R	24	50	138	6	32	2	2	1	12	8	11	3	.232	.274	.297
Stuffy McInnis	1B140	R	25	140	512	42	151	25	3	1	60	25	19	7	.295	.331	.361
Nap Lajoie	2B105,1B5,OF2	R	41	113	426	33	105	14	4	2	35	14	26	15	.246	.272	.312
Charlie Pick	3B108,OF8	L	28	121	398	29	96	10	3	0	20	40	24	25	.241	.315	.281
Whitey Witt	SS142	L	20	143	563	64	138	16	15	2	36	55	71	19	.245	.315	.337
Amos Strunk	OF143,1B7	L	27	150	544	71	172	30	9	3	49	66	59	21	.316	.393	.421
Jimmy Walsh†	OF113,1B1	L	30	114	390	42	91	13	6	1	27	54	36	27	.233	.330	.305
Wally Schang	OF61,C36	S	26	110	338	41	90	15	8	7	38	38	44	14	.266	.358	.420
Lee McElwee	3B30,OF9,2B3*	R	22	54	155	9	41	3	0	0	10	8	17	0	.265	.301	.284
Rube Oldring†	OF40	R	32	40	146	10	36	8	3	0	14	9	9	1	.247	.290	.342
Lee King	OF22,SS11,3B5*	R	22	42	144	13	27	1	2	0	8	7	15	4	.188	.230	.222
Otis Lawry	2B29,OF5	L	22	41	123	10	25	0	0	0	4	9	21	4	.203	.263	.203
Val Picinich	C37	R	19	40	118	8	23	3	1	0	5	6	33	0	.195	.234	.237
Ray Haley†	C33	R	25	34	108	8	25	5	0	0	4	6	19	0	.231	.278	.278
Roy Grover	2B20	R	24	20	77	8	21	1	2	0	7	6	10	5	.273	.325	.338
Bill Stellbauer	OF14	R	22	25	48	2	13	2	1	0	5	6	7	2	.271	.352	.354
Jim Brown	OF12	R	19	14	42	6	10	2	1	1	5	4	9	0	.238	.304	.405
Ralph Mitterling	OF12	R	26	13	39	1	6	0	0	0	2	3	6	0	.154	.214	.154
Harland Rowe	3B7,OF1	L	20	17	36	2	5	1	0	0	3	2	8	0	.139	.184	.167
Red Lanning	OF9,P6	L	21	19	33	5	6	2	0	0	1	10	9	0	.182	.372	.242
Buck Thrasher	OF7	L	26	7	29	4	9	2	1	0	4	2	1	0	.310	.355	.448
Mike Murphy	C12	R	27	14	27	0	3	0	0	0	1	1	3	0	.111	.143	.111
Thomas Healy	3B6	R	20	6	23	4	6	1	1	0	2	1	2	1	.261	.320	.391
Charlie Grimm	OF7	L	17	12	22	0	2	0	0	0	0	2	4	0	.091	.167	.091
Doc Carroll	C10	R	24	10	22	1	2	0	0	0	0	1	8	0	.091	.167	.091
Shag Thompson	OF7	L	23	15	17	4	0	0	0	0	0	7	6	1	.000	.292	.000
Bill Johnson	OF4	L	23	4	15	1	4	1	0	0	1	0	4	0	.267	.267	.333
Socks Seibold	P3,OF1	R	20	5	12	0	2	1	0	0	1	0	4	0	.167	.167	.250
Moxie Divis	OF1	—	22	3	6	0	1	0	0	0	0	0	2	0	.167	.167	.167
Lew Malone	SS1	R	19	5	4	1	0	0	0	0	0	1	2	0	.000	.200	.000
Sam Crane	SS2	R	21	2	4	1	1	0	0	0	0	2	1	0	.250	.500	.250
Harry Davis		R	42	1	0	0	0	0	0	0	1	1	0	0	—	1.000	—

L. McElwee, 1 G at 1B, 1 G at SS; L. King, 2 G at 2B

Pitcher	T	Age	G	GS	CG	ShO	IP	H	HR	BB	SO	W-L	Sv	ERA
Elmer Myers	R	22	44	35	31	2	315.0	280	7	168	182	14-23	1	3.66
Joe Bush	R	23	40	33	25	8	286.2	222	3	130	157	15-24	0	2.57
Jack Nabors	R	28	40	30	11	0	212.2	206	2	95	74	1-20	1	3.47
Jing Johnson	R	21	12	12	8	0	84.1	90	3	39	25	2-8	0	3.74
Cap Crowell	R	23	9	6	1	0	39.2	43	0	34	15	0-5	0	4.76
G. Hesselbacher	R	21	6	4	2	0	26.0	37	3	22	6	0-4	0	7.27
Rube Parnham	R	22	4	3	2	0	24.2	27	0	13	8	2-1	0	4.01
Red Lanning	L	21	6	3	1	0	24.1	38	1	17	9	0-3	0	8.14
Socks Seibold	R	20	3	2	1	1	21.2	22	0	9	5	1-2	0	4.15
Rube Bressler	L	21	4	2	0	0	15.0	16	0	14	8	0-2	0	6.60
Tom Sheehan	R	22	38	17	8	0	188.0	197	2	94	54	1-16	0	3.69
Marsh Williams	R	23	10	4	3	0	51.1	71	4	31	17	0-6	0	7.89
John Wyckoff†	R	24	7	2	1	0	21.1	20	1	20	4	0-1	0	5.48
Carl Ray	L	27	3	1	0	0	9.1	9	0	14	5	0-1	0	4.82
Harry Weaver	R	24	3	0	0	0	8.0	14	0	5	2	0-0	0	10.13
Mike Driscoll	R	23	1	0	0	0	5.0	6	0	2	0	0-1	0	5.40
Axel Lindstrom	R	20	1	0	0	0	4.0	2	0	0	1	0-0	1	4.50
Bill Morrisette	R	23	1	0	0	0	4.0	6	0	5	2	0-0	0	6.75
Walt Whittaker	R	22	1	0	0	0	2.0	3	0	2	0	0-0	0	4.50
Jack Richardson	R	24	1	0	0	0	0.2	2	0	1	1	0-0	0	40.50

»1916 Brooklyn Dodgers 1st NL 94-60 .610 —

Wilbert Robinson

Player	Gm by Position	B	Age	G	AB	R	H	2B	3B	HR	RBI	BB	SO	SB	Avg	OBP	Slg
Chief Meyers	C74	R	35	80	239	21	59	10	3	0	21	26	15	2	.247	.336	.314
Jake Daubert	1B126	L	32	127	478	75	151	16	7	3	33	38	39	21	.316	.371	.397
George Cutshaw	2B154	R	28	154	581	58	151	21	4	2	63	25	32	27	.260	.292	.320
Mike Mowrey	3B144	R	32	144	495	57	121	22	6	0	60	50	60	16	.244	.320	.313
Ivy Olson	SS103,2B3,1B1	R	30	108	351	29	89	13	4	1	38	21	27	14	.254	.298	.322
Zack Wheat	OF149	L	28	149	568	76	177	32	13	9	73	43	49	19	.312	.366	.461
Casey Stengel	OF121	L	25	127	462	66	129	27	8	8	53	33	51	11	.279	.329	.424
Jimmy Johnston	OF106	R	26	118	425	58	107	13	8	1	26	35	38	22	.252	.313	.327
Hi Myers	OF106	R	27	113	412	54	108	12	14	3	36	21	35	17	.262	.308	.381
Otto Miller	C69	R	27	73	216	16	55	9	2	1	17	7	29	6	.255	.281	.329
Ollie O'Mara	SS51	R	25	72	193	18	39	5	2	0	15	12	20	10	.202	.249	.249
Lew McCarty†	C27,1B17	R	27	55	150	17	47	6	1	0	13	14	16	4	.313	.383	.367
Jeff Pfeffer	P41,OF2	R	28	43	122	5	34	2	2	0	12	4	32	2	.279	.302	.328
Gus Getz	3B20,SS7,1B3	R	26	40	96	9	21	1	2	0	8	0	5	9	.219	.219	.271
Fred Merkle†	1B15,OF4	R	27	23	69	6	16	1	0	0	2	7	4	2	.232	.312	.246
Jim Hickman	OF3	R	24	9	5	3	1	0	0	0	0	2	0	1	.200	.429	.200
Red Smyth	2B2	L	23	2	5	0	0	0	0	0	0	0	3	0	.000	.000	.000
Hack Miller	OF3	R	22	3	3	0	1	0	1	0	1	1	1	0	.333	.500	1.000
John Kelleher	3B1,SS1	R	22	2	3	0	0	0	0	0	0	0	0	0	.000	.000	.000
Bunny Fabrique	SS2	S	28	2	2	0	0	0	0	0	0	0	1	0	.000	.000	.000
Al Nixon	OF1	R	30	1	2	0	2	0	0	0	0	0	0	0	1.000	1.000	1.000
Mack Wheat	C2	R	23	2	2	0	0	0	0	0	0	0	1	0	.000	.000	.000
Artie Dede	C1	R	20	1	1	0	0	0	0	0	0	0	0	0	.000	.000	.000

Pitcher	T	Age	G	GS	CG	ShO	IP	H	HR	BB	SO	W-L	Sv	ERA
Jeff Pfeffer	R	28	41	36	30	6	328.2	274	5	63	128	25-11	1	1.92
Larry Cheney	R	30	41	32	15	5	253.0	178	5	105	166	18-12	0	1.92
Sherry Smith	L	25	36	25	15	4	219.0	193	5	45	67	14-10	1	2.34
Rube Marquard	L	29	36	20	15	2	205.0	169	2	38	107	13-6	5	1.58
Jack Coombs	R	33	27	20	10	3	159.0	136	3	44	47	13-8	0	2.66
Wheezer Dell	R	29	32	16	9	2	155.0	143	2	43	76	8-9	1	2.26
Ed Appleton	R	24	14	3	1	0	47.0	49	1	18	14	1-2	1	3.06
Duster Mails	L	21	11	0	0	0	17.1	15	1	9	13	0-1	0	3.63
Nap Rucker	L	31	9	4	1	0	37.1	34	0	7	14	2-1	0	1.69
Leon Cadore	R	25	1	0	0	0	6.0	10	0	0	2	0-0	0	4.50

1916 Philadelphia Phillies 2nd NL 91-62 .595 2.5 GB

Pat Moran

Player	Gm by Position	B	Age	G	AB	R	H	2B	3B	HR	RBI	BB	SO	SB	Avg	OBP	Slg
Bill Killefer	C91	R	28	97	286	22	62	5	4	3	27	8	14	2	.217	.246	.294
Fred Luderus	1B146	L	30	146	508	52	143	26	3	5	53	41	32	8	.281	.341	.374
Bert Niehoff	2B144,3B2	R	32	146	548	65	133	42	4	4	61	37	57	20	.243	.292	.356
Milt Stock	3B117,SS15	R	22	132	509	61	143	25	6	1	43	27	33	21	.281	.320	.360
Dave Bancroft	SS142	S	25	142	477	53	101	10	0	3	33	74	57	15	.212	.323	.252
Dode Paskert	OF146,SS1	R	34	149	555	82	155	30	7	8	46	54	76	22	.279	.346	.402
Possum Whitted	OF136,1B16	R	32	147	526	68	148	20	12	6	68	19	46	29	.281	.309	.399
Gavy Cravath	OF130	R	35	137	448	70	127	21	8	11	70	64	89	9	.283	.379	.440
Ed Burns	C75,SS1,OF1	R	27	78	219	14	51	8	1	0	14	16	18	3	.233	.294	.279
Bobby Byrne	3B40	R	31	48	141	22	33	10	1	0	9	14	7	6	.234	.308	.319
Wilbur Good	OF46	L	30	75	136	25	34	4	3	1	15	8	13	7	.250	.306	.346
Claude Cooper	OF29,1B1	L	24	56	104	9	20	2	0	0	11	7	15	1	.192	.250	.212
Oscar Dugey	2B12	R	28	41	50	9	11	3	0	0	1	9	8	3	.220	.339	.280
Chief Bender	P27,3B1	R	32	28	43	2	12	4	0	0	5	3	9	0	.279	.326	.372
Bert Adams	C11	S	25	11	13	2	3	0	0	0	1	0	3	0	.231	.231	.231
Bud Weiser	OF4	R	25	4	10	1	3	1	0	0	1	0	3	0	.300	.300	.400
Bob Gandy	OF1	L	22	1	2	0	0	0	0	0	0	0	1	0	.000	.000	.000
Ben Tincup		L	25	1	1	0	0	0	0	0	0	0	1	0	.000	.000	.000
Billy Maharg	OF1	R	35	1	1	0	0	0	0	0	0	0	0	0	.000	.000	.000

Pitcher	T	Age	G	GS	CG	ShO	IP	H	HR	BB	SO	W-L	Sv	ERA
Pete Alexander	R	29	48	45	38	16	389.0	323	6	50	167	33-12	3	1.55
Al Demaree	R	31	39	35	25	4	285.0	252	4	48	130	19-14	1	2.62
Eppa Rixey	L	25	38	33	20	3	287.0	239	2	74	134	22-10	0	1.85
Erskine Mayer	R	27	28	16	7	2	140.0	148	7	33	62	7-7	0	3.15
George Chalmers	R	28	12	8	2	0	53.2	49	2	19	21	1-4	0	3.19
Gary Fortune	R	21	1	1	0	0	5.0	2	0	4	3	0-1	0	3.60
Chief Bender	R	32	27	13	4	0	122.2	137	3	34	43	7-7	3	3.74
George McQuillan	R	31	21	3	1	0	62.0	58	2	15	22	1-7	2	2.76
Joe Oeschger	R	25	14	0	0	0	30.1	18	2	14	17	1-0	0	2.37
Erv Kantlehner†	L	23	3	0	0	0	4.0	7	0	3	2	0-0	0	9.00
Stan Baumgartner	L	21	1	0	0	0	4.0	5	0	1	0	0-0	0	2.25

1916 Boston Braves 3rd NL 89-63 .586 4.0 GB

George Stallings

Player	Gm by Position	B	Age	G	AB	R	H	2B	3B	HR	RBI	BB	SO	SB	Avg	OBP	Slg
Hank Gowdy	C116	R	26	118	349	32	88	14	1	1	34	24	33	8	.252	.311	.307
Ed Konetchy	1B158	R	30	158	566	76	147	29	13	3	70	43	46	13	.260	.320	.373
Johnny Evers	2B71	L	34	71	241	33	52	4	1	0	15	40	19	5	.216	.330	.241
Red Smith	3B150	R	26	150	509	48	132	16	10	3	60	53	55	13	.259	.333	.348
Rabbit Maranville	SS155	R	24	155	604	79	142	16	13	4	38	50	69	32	.235	.296	.325
Sherry Magee	OF120,1B2,SS1	R	31	122	419	44	101	17	5	3	54	44	52	10	.241	.322	.327
Fred Snodgrass	OF110	R	28	112	382	33	95	13	5	1	32	34	54	14	.249	.318	.317
Joe Wilhoit	OF108	L	30	116	383	44	88	13	4	2	38	27	45	18	.230	.282	.300
Zip Collins	OF78	L	24	93	268	39	56	1	6	1	18	18	42	4	.209	.261	.269
Dick Egan	2B59,SS12,3B8	R	32	83	238	23	53	8	3	0	16	19	21	2	.223	.280	.282
Ed Fitzpatrick	2B46,OF28	R	26	83	216	17	46	8	0	1	18	15	26	5	.213	.280	.264
Joe Connolly	OF31	L	28	62	110	11	25	5	2	0	12	14	13	5	.227	.320	.309
Earl Blackburn	C44	R	23	47	110	12	30	4	4	0	7	9	21	2	.273	.328	.382
Pete Compton†	OF30	L	26	34	98	13	20	2	0	0	8	7	7	5	.204	.264	.224
Walt Tragesser	C29	R	29	41	54	3	11	1	0	0	4	5	10	0	.204	.283	.222
Larry Chappell†	OF14	L	26	20	53	4	12	1	1	0	9	2	8	1	.226	.268	.283
Fred Bailey	OF2	L	20	6	10	0	1	0	0	0	1	0	3	0	.100	.100	.100
Art Rico	C4	R	19	4	4	0	0	0	0	0	0	0	0	0	.000	.000	.000
Joe Mathes	2B2	S	24	2	0	0	0	0	0	0	0	0	0	0	—	—	—

Pitcher	T	Age	G	GS	CG	ShO	IP	H	HR	BB	SO	W-L	Sv	ERA
Dick Rudolph	R	28	41	38	27	5	312.0	266	7	38	133	19-12	3	2.16
Lefty Tyler	L	26	34	28	21	6	249.1	200	6	58	117	17-9	1	2.02
Pat Ragan	R	27	28	23	14	3	182.0	143	3	47	94	9-9	0	2.08
Jesse Barnes	R	23	33	18	9	3	163.0	154	3	37	55	6-15	1	2.37
Frank Allen	L	26	19	14	7	2	113.0	102	1	31	63	8-2	1	2.07
Art Nehf	L	23	22	13	6	1	121.0	110	1	20	36	7-5	0	2.01
Ed Reulbach	R	33	21	11	6	0	109.1	99	1	41	47	7-6	0	2.47
Tom Hughes	R	32	40	13	7	1	161.0	121	0	51	97	16-3	5	2.35
Elmer Knetzer†	R	30	2	0	0	0	5.0	11	0	2	2	0-2	0	7.20

1916 New York Giants 4th NL 86-66 .566 7.0 GB

John McGraw

Player	Gm by Position	B	Age	G	AB	R	H	2B	3B	HR	RBI	BB	SO	SB	Avg	OBP	Slg
Bill Rariden	C119	R	28	120	351	23	78	9	3	1	29	55	32	4	.222	.333	.274
Fred Merkle†	1B112	R	27	112	401	45	95	19	3	7	44	33	46	17	.237	.308	.352
Larry Doyle†	2B113	L	29	113	441	55	118	24	10	2	47	27	23	17	.268	.316	.381
Bill McKechnie†	3B71	S	29	71	260	22	64	9	1	0	17	7	20	7	.246	.269	.288
Art Fletcher	SS133	R	31	133	500	53	143	23	8	3	66	13	36	15	.286	.323	.382
George Burns	OF155	R	26	155	623	105	174	24	8	5	41	63	47	37	.279	.346	.368
Benny Kauff	OF154	L	26	154	552	71	146	22	15	9	74	68	65	40	.264	.348	.408
Dave Robertson	OF144	L	26	150	587	88	180	18	8	12	69	14	56	21	.307	.326	.426
Buck Herzog†	2B44,3B27,SS9	R	30	77	280	40	73	10	4	0	25	22	24	19	.261	.326	.325
Heinie Zimmerman†	3B40,2B1	R	29	40	151	22	41	4	0	0	19	7	10	9	.272	.304	.298
Walter Holke	1B34	S	23	34	111	16	39	4	2	0	13	6	16	10	.351	.390	.423
George Kelly	1B13,OF12,3B1	R	20	49	76	4	12	2	1	0	3	6	24	1	.158	.220	.211
Hans Lobert	3B20	R	34	48	76	6	17	3	2	0	11	5	8	2	.224	.272	.316
Edd Roush†	OF15	L	23	39	69	4	13	0	1	0	5	1	4	4	.188	.200	.217
Lew McCarty†	C24	R	27	25	68	6	27	3	4	0	9	7	9	0	.397	.453	.559
Brad Kocher	C30	R	28	34	65	1	7	2	0	0	1	2	10	0	.108	.134	.138
Mickey Doolan†	SS16,2B2	R	36	18	51	4	12	3	1	1	3	2	4	1	.235	.264	.392
Herb Hunter†	3B5,1B2	L	19	21	28	3	7	0	0	1	4	0	5	0	.250	.250	.357
Red Dooin	C15	R	37	15	17	1	2	0	0	0	0	0	3	0	.118	.118	.118
Fred Brainerd	3B2	R	24	2	7	0	0	0	0	0	0	0	0	0	.000	.000	.000
Lew Wendell		R	24	2	2	0	0	0	0	0	0	0	2	0	.000	.000	.000
Heinie Stafford		R	24	1	1	0	0	0	0	0	0	0	0	0	.000	.000	.000
Red Killefer†		R	31	2	1	0	1	0	0	0	1	1	0	0	1.000	1.000	1.000
Jose Rodriguez		R	22	1	0	0	0	0	0	0	0	0	0	0	—	—	—
Duke Kelleher	C1	—	22	1	0	0	0	0	0	0	0	0	0	0	—	—	—

Pitcher	T	Age	G	GS	CG	ShO	IP	H	HR	BB	SO	W-L	Sv	ERA
Jeff Tesreau	R	27	40	32	23	5	268.1	249	9	65	113	14-14	2	2.92
Pol Perritt	R	23	40	29	17	5	251.0	243	11	56	115	18-11	2	2.62
Rube Benton	L	29	38	29	15	3	238.2	210	5	58	115	16-8	2	2.87
Fred Anderson	R	30	38	27	13	2	188.0	206	7	38	98	9-13	2	3.40
Slim Sallee†	L	31	15	11	7	2	111.2	96	2	10	35	9-4	0	1.37
Christy Mathewson†	R	37	12	6	4	1	65.2	59	3	7	16	3-4	2	2.33
Emilio Palmero	L	21	4	2	0	0	15.2	17	2	8	8	0-3	0	8.04
Ferdie Schupp	L	25	30	11	8	4	140.1	79	1	37	86	9-3	1	0.90
Rube Schauer	R	25	19	3	1	0	45.2	44	0	16	24	1-4	0	2.96
Sailor Stroud	R	31	10	4	0	0	46.2	47	1	9	16	3-2	1	2.70
George Smith	R	24	9	1	0	0	20.2	14	0	6	9	3-0	0	2.61
Hank Ritter	R	22	3	0	0	0	5.0	3	0	0	3	1-0	0	0.00

1916 Chicago Cubs 5th NL 67-86 .438 26.5 GB

Joe Tinker

Player	Gm by Position	B	Age	G	AB	R	H	2B	3B	HR	RBI	BB	SO	SB	Avg	OBP	Slg
Jimmy Archer	C61,3B1	R	33	77	205	11	45	6	2	1	30	12	24	3	.220	.269	.283
Vic Saier	1B147	L	25	147	498	60	126	25	3	7	50	79	68	20	.253	.356	.357
Otto Knabe†	2B42,3B1,SS1*	R	32	51	145	17	40	8	0	0	7	9	18	3	.276	.327	.331
Heinie Zimmerman†	3B85,2B14,SS4	R	29	107	398	54	116	25	5	6	64	16	33	15	.291	.324	.425
Chuck Wortman	SS69	R	24	69	234	17	47	4	2	2	16	18	22	4	.201	.258	.261
Max Flack	OF136	L	26	141	465	65	120	14	3	3	20	42	43	24	.258	.320	.320
Cy Williams	OF116	L	28	118	405	55	113	19	9	12	66	51	64	6	.279	.372	.459
Les Mann	OF115	R	22	127	415	46	113	13	9	2	29	19	31	11	.272	.307	.361
Rollie Zeider	3B55,2B33,OF7*	R	32	98	345	29	81	11	2	1	22	26	26	9	.235	.294	.287
Wildfire Schulte†	OF67	L	33	72	230	31	68	11	1	5	27	20	35	9	.296	.352	.417
Joe Mulligan	SS58	R	21	58	189	13	29	3	4	0	9	8	30	1	.153	.200	.212
William Fischer†	C56	L	25	65	179	15	35	9	2	1	14	11	8	2	.196	.246	.285
Joe Kelly	OF46	R	29	54	169	18	43	7	1	2	15	9	16	10	.254	.296	.343
Steve Yerkes	2B41	R	28	44	137	12	36	6	2	1	10	9	7	1	.263	.308	.358
Art Wilson†	C34	R	30	36	114	5	22	3	1	0	5	6	14	1	.193	.233	.237
Alex McCarthy†	2B34,SS3	R	28	37	107	10	26	2	3	0	6	11	7	1	.243	.341	.318
Fritz Mollwitz†	1B19,OF6	R	26	33	71	1	19	2	0	0	11	7	6	4	.268	.333	.296
Mickey Doolan†	SS24	R	36	28	70	4	15	2	1	0	5	8	7	0	.214	.295	.271
Charlie Pechous	3B22	R	19	22	69	5	10	1	1	0	4	3	21	1	.145	.181	.188
Rowdy Elliott	C18	R	25	23	55	5	14	3	0	0	3	3	5	1	.255	.293	.309
Gene Packard	P37,OF3	L	28	44	54	9	7	3	0	0	1	4	13	0	.130	.190	.185
Dutch Zwilling	OF10	L	27	35	53	4	6	1	0	1	8	4	6	0	.113	.175	.189
Larry Doyle†	2B9	L	29	9	38	6	15	5	1	1	7	1	1	2	.395	.410	.658
Earl Smith	OF7	S	25	14	27	2	7	1	1	0	4	2	5	1	.259	.310	.370
Nick Allen	C4	R	27	5	16	1	1	0	0	0	1	0	3	0	.063	.063	.063
Solly Hofman†	OF4	R	33	5	16	2	5	2	1	0	2	2	2	0	.313	.389	.563
Clem Clemens	C9	R	29	10	15	0	0	0	0	0	0	1	6	0	.000	.063	.000
Merwin Jacobson	OF4	L	22	4	13	2	3	0	0	0	0	1	4	2	.231	.286	.231
Joe Tinker	SS4,3B2	R	35	7	10	0	1	0	0	0	1	1	1	0	.100	.182	.100
Charlie Deal†	3B2	R	24	2	8	2	2	1	0	0	3	0	0	0	.250	.250	.375
Marty Shay	SS2	R	20	2	7	0	2	0	0	0	0	0	1	0	.286	.286	.286
Herb Hunter†	3B1	L	19	2	4	0	0	0	0	0	0	0	0	0	.000	.000	.000
Ed Sicking		R	19	1	1	0	0	0	0	0	0	0	0	0	.000	.000	.000
Johnny O'Connor	C1	R	24	1	0	0	0	0	0	0	0	0	0	0	—	—	—
Bob O'Farrell	C1	R	19	1	0	0	0	0	0	0	0	0	0	0	—	—	—

O. Knabe, 1 G at OF; R. Zeider, 5 G at SS, 2 G at 1B

Pitcher	T	Age	G	GS	CG	ShO	IP	H	HR	BB	SO	W-L	Sv	ERA
Hippo Vaughn	L	28	44	35	21	4	294.0	269	4	67	144	17-15	1	2.20
Jimmy Lavender	R	32	36	25	9	4	188.0	163	3	62	91	10-14	2	2.82
Claude Hendrix	R	27	36	24	15	3	218.0	193	4	67	117	8-16	2	2.68
George McConnell	R	38	28	21	8	1	171.1	137	8	35	82	4-12	0	2.57
Paul Carter	R	22	8	5	2	0	36.0	26	1	17	14	2-2	0	2.75
Scott Perry	R	25	4	3	2	1	28.1	30	0	3	10	2-1	0	2.54
Gene Packard	L	28	37	16	5	2	155.1	154	4	38	36	10-6	5	2.78
Mike Prendergast	R	27	35	10	4	2	152.0	127	5	23	56	6-11	2	2.31
Tom Seaton	R	28	31	12	4	0	121.0	108	3	43	45	6-6	1	3.27
Three Finger Brown	R	39	12	4	2	0	48.1	52	0	9	21	2-3	0	3.91
George Pearce	L	28	4	1	0	0	4.1	6	0	1	0	0-0	0	2.08

1916 Pittsburgh Pirates 6th NL 65-89 .422 29.0 GB

Nixey Callahan

Player	Gm by Position	B	Age	G	AB	R	H	2B	3B	HR	RBI	BB	SO	SB	Avg	OBP	Slg
Walter Schmidt	C57	R	29	64	184	16	35	1	2	2	15	10	13	3	.190	.236	.250
Doc Johnston	1B110	L	28	114	404	33	86	10	10	0	39	20	42	17	.213	.262	.287
Jack Farmer	2B31,OF15,SS5*	R	23	55	166	10	45	6	4	0	14	7	24	1	.271	.309	.355
Doug Baird	3B80,2B29,OF16	R	24	128	430	41	93	10	7	1	28	24	49	20	.216	.263	.279
Honus Wagner	SS92,1B24	R	42	123	432	45	124	15	9	1	39	34	36	11	.287	.350	.370
Max Carey	OF154	S	26	154	599	90	158	23	11	7	42	59	58	63	.264	.337	.374
Bill Hinchman	OF124,1B31	R	33	152	555	64	175	18	16	4	76	54	61	10	.315	.378	.427
Wildfire Schulte†	OF48	L	33	55	177	12	45	5	3	0	14	17	19	5	.254	.323	.316
Joe Schultz	2B24,3B24,OF6*	R	22	77	204	18	53	8	2	0	22	7	14	6	.260	.298	.319
Hooks Warner	3B42,2B1	L	22	44	168	12	40	1	1	2	14	6	19	6	.238	.264	.292
Carson Bigbee	2B23,OF19,3B1	L	21	43	164	17	41	3	6	0	3	7	14	8	.250	.285	.341
Dan Costello	OF41	L	24	60	159	11	38	1	3	0	8	6	23	3	.239	.267	.283
Alex McCarthy†	SS39,2B7,3B5	R	28	50	146	11	29	3	0	0	3	15	10	3	.199	.282	.219
Ed Barney	OF40	L	26	45	137	16	27	4	0	0	9	23	15	8	.197	.313	.226
Jim Viox	2B25,3B11	R	25	43	132	12	33	7	0	1	17	17	11	2	.250	.340	.326
Art Wilson†	C39	R	30	53	128	11	33	5	2	1	12	13	27	4	.258	.331	.352
William Fischer†	C35	L	25	42	113	11	29	7	1	1	6	10	3	1	.257	.323	.363
Jimmy Smith	SS27,3B6	S	21	36	96	4	18	1	1	0	5	6	22	0	.188	.257	.219
Otto Knabe†	2B28	R	32	28	89	4	17	3	1	0	9	6	6	1	.191	.258	.247
George Gibson	C29	R	35	33	84	4	17	2	2	0	4	3	7	0	.202	.239	.274
Ray O'Brien	OF14	L	23	16	57	5	12	3	2	0	3	1	14	0	.211	.224	.333
Bill Wagner	C15,2B4	R	22	19	38	2	9	0	2	0	2	5	8	0	.237	.326	.342
Lee King	OF8	R	23	8	18	0	2	0	0	0	1	0	7	0	.111	.111	.111
Pete Compton†	OF5	L	26	5	16	1	1	0	0	0	0	2	5	0	.063	.211	.063
Jesse Altenburg	OF8	L	23	8	14	2	6	1	1	0	0	1	1	0	.429	.467	.643
Frank Smykal	SS5,3B1	R	26	6	10	1	3	0	0	0	2	3	1	1	.300	.500	.300
Ike McAuley	SS4	R	24	4	8	1	2	0	0	0	1	0	1	0	.250	.250	.250
Paddy Siglin	2B3	R	24	3	4	0	1	0	0	0	0	0	2	0	.250	.250	.250
Billy Gleason	2B1	R	21	1	2	0	0	0	0	0	0	0	0	0	.000	.000	.000
Newt Halliday	1B1	R	20	1	1	0	0	0	0	0	0	0	1	0	.000	.000	.000
Wilbur Fisher		L	21	1	1	0	0	0	0	0	0	0	0	0	.000	.000	.000
Gene Madden		L	26	1	1	0	0	0	0	0	0	0	0	0	.000	.000	.000
Bill Batsch		R	24	1	0	0	0	0	0	0	0	1	0	0	—	1.000	—

J. Farmer, 1 G at 3B; J. Schultz, 1 G at SS

Pitcher	T	Age	G	GS	CG	ShO	IP	H	HR	BB	SO	W-L	Sv	ERA
Al Mamaux	R	22	45	37	26	1	310.0	264	3	136	163	21-15	2	2.53
Wilbur Cooper	L	24	42	23	16	2	246.0	189	4	74	111	12-11	2	1.87
Erv Kantlehner†	L	23	34	21	7	2	165.0	151	1	57	49	5-15	2	3.16
Frank Miller	R	30	30	20	10	2	173.0	135	4	49	88	7-10	1	2.29
Bob Harmon	R	28	31	17	10	2	172.2	175	4	39	62	8-11	0	2.81
Elmer Jacobs	R	23	34	17	8	0	153.0	151	2	38	46	6-10	0	2.94
Babe Adams	R	34	16	10	4	1	72.1	91	2	12	22	2-9	0	5.72
Bill Evans	R	22	13	7	3	0	63.0	57	2	16	21	2-5	0	3.00
Burleigh Grimes	R	22	6	5	4	0	45.2	40	1	10	20	2-3	0	2.36
Paul Carpenter	R	21	5	0	0	0	7.2	8	0	4	5	0-0	0	1.17
Carmen Hill	R	20	2	0	0	0	6.1	11	0	5	5	0-0	0	8.53
Jack Scott	R	24	1	0	0	0	5.0	5	1	3	4	0-0	0	10.80

1916 Cincinnati Reds 7th NL 60-93 .392 33.5 GB

Buck Herzog (34-49)/Ivy Wingo (1-1)/Christy Mathewson (25-43)

Player	Gm by Position	B	Age	G	AB	R	H	2B	3B	HR	RBI	BB	SO	SB	Avg	OBP	Slg
Ivy Wingo	C107	L	25	119	347	30	85	8	11	2	40	25	27	4	.245	.298	.349
Hal Chase	1B98,OF25,2B16	R	33	142	542	66	184	29	12	4	82	19	48	22	.339	.363	.459
Baldy Louden	2B108,SS23	R	30	134	439	38	96	16	4	1	32	54	54	12	.219	.313	.280
Heine Groh	3B110,2B33,SS5	R	26	149	553	85	149	24	14	2	28	84	34	13	.269	.370	.374
Buck Herzog†	SS65,3B12,OF1	R	30	79	281	30	75	14	2	1	24	21	12	15	.267	.329	.342
Tommy Griffith	OF155	L	26	155	595	50	158	28	7	2	61	36	37	16	.266	.310	.346
Greasy Neale	OF133	L	24	138	530	53	139	13	5	0	20	19	79	17	.262	.295	.306
Edd Roush†	OF69	L	23	69	272	34	78	7	14	0	15	13	19	15	.287	.336	.415
Red Killefer†	OF68	R	31	70	234	29	57	9	1	1	18	21	8	7	.244	.327	.303
Fritz Mollwitz†	1B54	R	26	65	183	12	41	4	4	0	16	5	12	6	.224	.245	.290
Tommy Clarke	C51	R	28	78	177	10	42	10	1	0	17	24	20	8	.237	.328	.305
Tom Fisher	SS29,2B6,OF1	R	29	61	136	9	37	4	3	0	11	8	14	7	.272	.313	.346
Bill McKechnie†	3B35	S	29	37	130	4	36	3	0	0	10	3	12	4	.277	.293	.300
Clarence Mitchell	P29,1B6,OF5	L	25	56	117	11	28	2	1	0	11	4	6	1	.239	.264	.274
Emil Huhn	C18,1B14,OF1	R	24	37	94	4	24	3	2	0	3	2	11	0	.255	.271	.330
Frank Emmer	SS29,OF2,2B1*	R	20	42	89	8	13	3	1	0	2	7	27	1	.146	.208	.202
Paul Smith	OF10	L	28	10	44	5	10	0	1	0	1	1	8	3	.227	.244	.273
Larry Kopf	SS11	S	25	11	40	2	11	2	0	0	5	1	8	1	.275	.293	.325
Ken Williams	OF10	L	26	10	27	1	3	0	0	0	1	2	5	1	.111	.172	.111
Johnny Beall	OF6	L	34	6	21	3	7	2	0	1	4	3	7	1	.333	.417	.571
Bill Hobbs	SS6	R	23	6	11	1	2	1	0	0	1	2	0	1	.182	.308	.273
George Twombly	OF1	R	24	3	5	0	0	0	0	0	0	1	1	0	.000	.167	.000
Bill Rodgers	SS1	L	29	3	4	0	0	0	0	0	0	0	2	0	.000	.000	.000

F. Emmer, 1 G at 3B

Pitcher	T	Age	G	GS	CG	ShO	IP	H	HR	BB	SO	W-L	Sv	ERA
Fred Toney	R	27	41	38	21	3	300.0	247	7	78	146	14-17	1	2.28
Pete Schneider	R	20	44	31	16	3	274.1	259	4	82	117	10-19	1	2.69
Clarence Mitchell	L	25	29	24	17	1	194.2	211	4	45	52	11-10	0	3.14
Al Schulz	L	27	44	22	10	0	215.0	208	4	93	95	8-19	2	3.14
Jim Bluejacket	R	28	3	2	0	0	7.2	12	0	3	1	0-1	0	7.04
Christy Mathewson†	R	37	1	1	1	0	9.0	15	1	1	3	1-0	0	8.00
Elmer Knetzer†	R	30	36	16	12	0	171.1	161	6	45	70	5-12	1	2.89
Earl Moseley	R	31	31	15	7	0	150.1	145	5	69	60	7-10	1	3.89
Gene Dale	R	27	17	5	2	0	69.2	80	3	33	23	3-4	0	5.17
Limb McKenry	R	27	6	1	0	0	14.2	14	0	8	2	1-1	0	4.30
Twink Twining	R	22	1	0	0	0	2.0	4	1	1	0	0-0	0	13.50

1916 St. Louis Cardinals 7th NL 60-93 .392 33.5 GB

Miller Huggins

Player	Gm by Position	B	Age	G	AB	R	H	2B	3B	HR	RBI	BB	SO	SB	Avg	OBP	Slg
Mike Gonzalez	C93,1B13	R	25	118	331	33	79	15	4	0	29	28	18	5	.239	.304	.308
Dots Miller	1B93,2B38,SS21*	R	29	143	505	47	120	22	7	1	46	40	49	18	.238	.300	.315
Bruno Betzel	2B113,3B33,OF7	R	21	142	510	49	119	15	11	1	37	39	77	22	.233	.288	.312
Rogers Hornsby	3B83,SS45,1B15*	R	20	139	495	63	155	17	15	6	65	40	63	17	.313	.369	.444
Roy Corhan	SS84	R	28	92	295	30	62	6	3	0	18	20	31	15	.210	.265	.251
Bob Bescher	OF151	S	32	151	561	78	132	24	8	6	43	60	50	39	.235	.316	.339
Jack Smith	OF120	L	21	130	357	43	87	6	5	6	34	20	50	24	.244	.291	.339
Chief Wilson	OF113	L	32	120	355	30	85	8	2	3	32	20	46	4	.239	.289	.299
Frank Snyder	C72,1B46,SS1	R	23	132	406	23	105	12	4	0	39	18	31	7	.259	.290	.308
Tom Long	OF106	R	26	119	403	37	118	11	10	1	33	10	43	21	.293	.312	.377
Zinn Beck	3B52,1B1	R	30	62	184	8	41	7	1	0	10	14	21	3	.223	.281	.272
Art Butler	OF15,2B8,3B1*	R	28	86	110	9	23	5	0	0	7	7	12	3	.209	.256	.255
Sammy Bohne	SS14	R	19	14	38	3	9	0	0	0	0	4	6	3	.237	.310	.237
Tony Brottem	C15,OF2	R	24	26	33	3	6	1	0	0	4	3	10	1	.182	.250	.212
Stuffy Stewart	2B8	R	22	9	17	0	3	0	0	0	1	0	3	0	.176	.176	.176
Miller Huggins	2B7	S	37	18	9	2	3	0	0	0	0	2	3	0	.333	.500	.333
Walton Cruise	OF2	L	26	3	3	0	2	0	0	0	0	1	0	0	.667	.750	.667

D. Miller, 1 G at 3B; R. Hornsby, 1 G at 2B; A. Butler, 1 G at SS

Pitcher	T	Age	G	GS	CG	ShO	IP	H	HR	BB	SO	W-L	Sv	ERA
Lee Meadows	R	21	51	36	11	1	289.0	261	3	119	120	12-23	2	2.58
Bill Doak	R	25	29	26	11	3	192.0	177	5	55	82	12-8	0	2.63
Red Ames	R	33	45	25	10	2	228.0	225	3	57	98	11-16	8	2.64
Bob Steele	L	22	29	21	7	1	148.0	156	6	42	67	5-15	0	3.41
Milt Watson	R	26	18	13	5	2	103.0	109	3	33	27	4-6	0	3.06
Sea Lion Hall	R	30	10	5	2	0	42.2	45	1	14	15	0-4	1	5.48
Steamboat Williams	R	24	36	8	5	0	105.0	121	6	27	25	6-7	1	4.20
Hi Jasper	R	35	21	9	2	0	107.0	97	0	42	37	5-6	1	3.28
Slim Sallee†	L	31	16	7	4	2	70.0	75	2	23	28	5-5	1	3.47
Joe Lotz	R	25	12	3	1	0	40.0	31	1	17	18	0-3	0	4.28
Murphy Currie	R	22	6	0	0	0	14.1	7	1	9	8	0-0	0	1.88
Dan Griner	R	28	4	0	0	0	11.0	15	0	3	3	0-0	1	4.09
Cy Warmoth	L	23	3	0	0	0	5.0	12	0	4	1	0-0	0	14.40

»1917 Chicago White Sox 1st AL 100-54 .649 —

Pants Rowland

Player	Gm by Position	B	Age	G	AB	R	H	2B	3B	HR	RBI	BB	SO	SB	Avg	OBP	Slg
Ray Schalk	C139	R	24	140	424	48	96	12	5	2	51	59	27	19	.226	.331	.292
Chick Gandil	1B149	R	30	149	553	53	151	9	7	0	57	30	36	16	.273	.316	.315
Eddie Collins	2B156	L	30	156	564	91	163	18	12	0	67	89	16	53	.289	.389	.363
Buck Weaver	3B107,SS10	R	26	118	447	64	127	16	5	3	32	27	29	19	.284	.332	.362
Swede Risberg	SS146	R	22	149	474	59	96	20	8	1	45	59	65	16	.203	.297	.285
Happy Felsch	OF152	R	25	152	575	75	177	17	10	6	102	33	52	26	.308	.352	.403
Joe Jackson	OF145	L	27	146	538	91	162	20	17	5	75	57	25	13	.301	.375	.429
Nemo Leibold	OF122	L	25	125	428	59	101	12	6	0	29	74	34	27	.236	.350	.292
Shano Collins	OF73	R	31	82	252	38	59	13	3	1	14	10	27	14	.234	.269	.321
Fred McMullin	3B52,SS2	R	25	59	194	35	46	2	1	0	12	27	17	9	.237	.339	.258
Byrd Lynn	C29	R	28	35	72	7	16	2	0	0	5	7	11	1	.222	.300	.250
Reb Russell	P35,OF1	L	28	39	68	5	19	3	3	0	9	2	10	0	.279	.300	.412
Eddie Murphy	OF9	L	25	53	51	9	16	2	1	0	16	5	1	4	.314	.386	.392
Ted Jourdan	1B14	L	21	17	34	2	5	0	1	0	2	1	3	0	.147	.171	.206
Joe Jenkins		R	26	10	9	0	1	0	0	0	2	0	5	0	.111	.111	.111
Ziggy Hasbrook	2B1	R	23	2	1	1	0	0	0	0	0	0	0	0	.000	.000	.000
Zeb Terry	SS1	R	26	2	1	0	0	0	0	0	0	2	0	0	.000	.667	.000
Jack Fournier		L	27	1	1	0	0	0	0	0	0	0	1	0	.000	.000	.000
Bobby Byrne†	2B1	R	32	1	1	0	0	0	0	0	0	0	0	0	.000	.000	.000

Pitcher	T	Age	G	GS	CG	ShO	IP	H	HR	BB	SO	W-L	Sv	ERA
Eddie Cicotte	R	33	49	35	29	7	346.2	246	2	70	150	28-12	4	1.53
Red Faber	R	28	41	29	16	3	248.0	224	1	85	84	16-13	3	1.92
Lefty Williams	L	24	45	29	8	1	230.0	221	3	81	85	17-8	1	2.97
Reb Russell	L	28	35	24	11	5	189.1	170	1	32	54	15-5	3	1.95
Jim Scott	R	29	24	17	6	2	125.0	126	0	42	37	6-7	0	1.87
Joe Benz	R	31	19	13	7	2	94.2	76	1	23	25	7-3	0	2.47
Dave Danforth	L	27	50	9	1	1	173.0	155	1	74	79	11-6	9	2.65
Mellie Wolfgang	R	27	5	0	0	0	17.2	18	1	6	3	0-0	0	5.09

1917 Boston Red Sox 2nd AL 90-62 .592 9.0 GB

Jack Barry

Player	Gm by Position	B	Age	G	AB	R	H	2B	3B	HR	RBI	BB	SO	SB	Avg	OBP	Slg
Sam Agnew	C85	R	30	85	260	17	54	6	2	0	16	19	30	2	.208	.267	.246
Doc Hoblitzell	1B118	R	28	120	420	49	108	19	7	1	47	46	22	12	.257	.336	.343
Jack Barry	2B116	R	30	116	388	45	83	9	0	2	30	47	27	12	.214	.305	.253
Larry Gardner	3B146	L	31	146	501	53	133	23	7	1	61	54	37	16	.265	.341	.345
Everett Scott	SS157	R	24	157	528	40	127	24	7	0	50	20	46	12	.241	.268	.313
Harry Hooper	OF151	L	29	151	559	89	143	21	11	3	45	80	40	21	.256	.355	.349
Duffy Lewis	OF150	R	29	150	553	55	167	29	9	1	65	29	54	8	.302	.342	.392
Tilly Walker	OF96	R	29	106	337	41	83	18	7	2	37	25	38	6	.246	.300	.359
Pinch Thomas	C77	L	29	83	202	24	48	7	0	0	24	27	9	2	.238	.333	.272
Jimmy Walsh	OF47	L	31	57	185	25	49	6	3	0	12	25	14	6	.265	.352	.330
Del Gainer	1B50	R	30	52	172	28	53	10	2	2	19	15	21	1	.308	.374	.424
Chick Shorten	OF43	L	25	69	168	12	30	4	2	0	16	10	10	2	.179	.229	.226
Hal Janvrin	2B38,SS10,1B1	R	24	55	127	21	25	3	0	0	8	11	13	2	.197	.266	.220
Mike McNally	3B14,SS9,2B6	R	24	42	50	9	15	1	0	0	2	6	3	3	.300	.375	.320
Hick Cady	C14	R	31	17	46	4	7	1	1	0	2	1	6	0	.152	.170	.217
Jimmy Cooney	2B10,SS1	R	22	11	36	4	8	1	0	0	3	6	2	0	.222	.333	.250
Wally Mayer	C4	R	26	4	12	2	2	0	0	0	0	5	2	0	.167	.412	.167
Olaf Henriksen		L	29	15	12	1	1	0	0	0	1	3	4	0	.083	.267	.083

Pitcher	T	Age	G	GS	CG	ShO	IP	H	HR	BB	SO	W-L	Sv	ERA
Babe Ruth	L	22	41	38	35	6	326.1	244	2	108	128	24-13	2	2.01
Dutch Leonard	L	25	37	36	26	4	294.1	257	4	72	144	16-17	1	2.17
Carl Mays	R	25	35	33	27	2	289.0	230	1	74	91	22-9	0	1.74
Ernie Shore	R	26	29	27	14	1	226.2	201	1	55	57	13-10	1	2.22
Rube Foster	R	29	17	16	9	1	124.2	108	0	53	34	8-7	0	2.53
Herb Pennock	L	23	24	5	4	1	100.2	90	2	23	35	5-5	1	3.31
Lore Bader	R	29	15	1	0	0	38.1	48	1	18	14	2-0	1	2.35
Sad Sam Jones	R	24	9	1	0	0	16.1	15	1	6	5	0-1	1	4.41
John Wyckoff	R	25	1	0	0	0	5.0	4	0	4	1	0-0	0	1.80

1917 Cleveland Indians 3rd AL 88-66 .571 12.0 GB

Lee Fohl

Player	Gm by Position	B	Age	G	AB	R	H	2B	3B	HR	RBI	BB	SO	SB	Avg	OBP	Slg
Steve O'Neill	C127	R	25	129	370	21	68	10	2	0	29	41	55	2	.184	.272	.222
Joe Harris	1B95,OF5,3B1	R	26	112	369	40	112	22	4	0	65	55	32	11	.304	.398	.385
Bill Wambsganss	2B137,1B3	R	23	141	499	52	127	17	6	0	43	37	42	16	.255	.315	.313
Joe Evans	3B127	R	22	132	385	36	73	4	5	2	33	42	44	12	.190	.271	.242
Ray Chapman	SS156	R	26	156	563	98	170	28	13	2	36	61	65	52	.302	.370	.409
Jack Graney	OF145	L	31	146	535	87	122	29	7	3	35	94	49	16	.228	.348	.325
Tris Speaker	OF142	L	29	142	523	90	184	42	11	2	60	67	14	30	.352	.432	.486
Braggo Roth	OF135	R	24	145	495	69	141	30	9	1	72	52	73	51	.285	.355	.388
Lou Guisto	1B59	R	22	73	200	9	37	4	2	0	29	25	18	3	.185	.282	.225
Terry Turner	3B40,2B23,SS1	R	36	69	180	16	37	7	0	0	15	14	19	4	.206	.263	.244
Elmer Smith†	OF40	L	24	64	161	21	42	5	1	3	22	13	18	6	.261	.316	.360
Josh Billings	C48	R	25	66	129	8	23	3	2	0	9	8	21	2	.178	.243	.233
Ivan Howard	3B6,2B4,OF4	S	34	27	39	7	4	0	0	0	0	3	5	1	.103	.167	.103
Milo Allison	OF11	L	26	32	35	4	5	0	0	0	0	9	7	3	.143	.318	.143
Hank DeBerry	C9	R	22	25	33	3	9	2	0	0	1	2	7	0	.273	.333	.333
Ray Miller†	1B4	L	29	19	21	1	4	1	0	0	2	8	3	0	.190	.414	.238
Marty Kavanagh	OF2	R	26	14	14	1	0	0	0	0	0	3	2	0	.000	.176	.000
Fred Eunick	3B1	R	25	1	2	0	0	0	0	0	0	0	0	0	.000	.000	.000

Pitcher	T	Age	G	GS	CG	ShO	IP	H	HR	BB	SO	W-L	Sv	ERA
Jim Bagby	R	27	49	37	26	8	320.2	277	6	73	83	23-13	7	1.96
Stan Coveleski	R	27	45	36	24	9	298.2	202	3	94	133	19-14	4	1.81
Ed Klepfer	R	29	41	27	9	0	213.0	208	0	55	66	14-4	1	2.37
Guy Morton	R	24	35	18	6	1	161.0	158	3	59	62	10-10	2	2.74
Joe Boehling	L	26	12	7	1	0	46.1	50	1	16	11	1-6	0	4.66
Red Torkelson	R	23	4	3	0	0	22.1	33	1	13	10	2-1	0	7.66
Fritz Coumbe	L	27	34	10	4	1	134.1	119	0	35	30	8-6	5	2.14
Al Gould	R	24	27	7	1	0	94.0	95	1	52	24	4-4	0	3.64
Otis Lambeth	R	27	26	10	2	0	97.1	97	2	30	27	7-6	2	3.14
Pop Boy Smith	R	25	6	0	0	0	8.2	14	0	4	3	0-1	0	8.31
Joe Wood	R	27	5	1	0	0	15.2	17	0	7	2	0-1	1	3.45
George Dickerson	R	24	1	0	0	0	1.0	0	0	0	0	0-0	0	0.00

1917 Detroit Tigers 4th AL 78-75 .510 21.5 GB

Hughie Jennings

Player	Gm by Position	B	Age	G	AB	R	H	2B	3B	HR	RBI	BB	SO	SB	Avg	OBP	Slg
Oscar Stanage	C95	R	34	99	297	19	61	14	1	0	30	20	35	3	.205	.263	.259
George Burns	1B104	R	24	119	407	42	92	14	10	1	40	15	33	3	.226	.264	.317
Ralph Young	2B141	S	27	141	503	64	116	18	2	1	35	61	35	8	.231	.317	.280
Ossie Vitt	3B140	R	27	140	512	65	130	13	6	0	47	56	15	18	.254	.329	.303
Donie Bush	SS147	S	29	147	581	112	163	18	3	0	24	80	40	34	.281	.370	.322
Bobby Veach	OF154	L	29	154	571	79	182	31	12	8	103	61	44	21	.319	.393	.457
Ty Cobb	OF152	L	30	152	588	107	225	44	24	6	102	61	34	55	.383	.444	.570
Harry Heilmann	OF123,1B27	R	22	150	556	57	156	22	11	5	86	41	54	11	.281	.333	.387
Tubby Spencer	C62	R	33	70	192	13	46	8	3	0	22	15	15	0	.240	.324	.313
George Harper	OF31	L	25	47	117	6	24	3	0	0	12	11	15	2	.205	.290	.231
Sam Crawford	1B15,OF3	L	37	61	104	6	18	4	0	2	12	4	6	0	.173	.204	.269
Hooks Dauss	P37,OF1	R	27	38	87	7	11	3	0	0	2	13	24	0	.126	.240	.161
Bob Jones	2B18,3B8	L	27	46	77	16	12	1	2	0	2	4	8	3	.156	.198	.221
Bernie Boland	P43,OF1	R	25	45	72	8	4	1	1	0	2	4	19	0	.056	.105	.097
Ben Dyer	SS14,3B8	R	24	30	67	6	14	5	0	0	2	2	17	3	.209	.232	.284
Willie Mitchell	P30,OF1	R	27	31	59	3	7	0	0	0	4	1	11	0	.119	.148	.119
Archie Yelle	C24	R	25	25	51	4	7	1	0	0	0	5	4	2	.137	.214	.157
Babe Ellison	1B9	R	21	9	29	2	5	1	2	1	4	6	3	0	.172	.333	.448
Fred Nicholson	OF3	R	22	13	14	4	4	1	0	0	1	1	2	0	.286	.333	.357
Ira Flagstead	OF2	R	23	4	4	0	0	0	0	0	0	0	0	0	.000	.000	.000
Frank Walker		R	22	2	2	0	0	0	0	0	0	0	1	0	.000	.000	.000
Tony DeFate†	2B1	R	22	3	2	1	0	0	0	0	0	0	1	0	.000	.000	.000

Pitcher	T	Age	G	GS	CG	ShO	IP	H	HR	BB	SO	W-L	Sv	ERA
Hooks Dauss	R	27	38	31	22	6	270.2	243	3	87	102	17-14	2	2.43
Bernie Boland	R	25	43	28	13	3	238.0	192	0	95	89	16-11	6	2.68
Howard Ehmke	R	23	35	25	13	4	206.0	174	3	88	90	10-15	2	2.97
Bill James	R	30	34	23	10	2	198.0	163	2	96	62	13-10	1	2.09
Willie Mitchell	L	27	30	22	12	5	185.1	172	2	46	80	12-8	0	2.19
Harry Coveleski	L	31	16	11	2	0	69.0	70	0	14	15	4-6	0	2.61
G. Cunningham	R	22	44	8	4	0	139.0	113	2	51	49	2-7	4	2.91
Deacon Jones	R	24	24	6	2	0	77.0	69	0	26	28	4-4	0	2.92
Johnny Couch	R	26	3	0	0	0	13.1	13	0	1	1	0-0	0	2.70

1917 Washington Senators 5th AL 74-79 .484 25.5 GB

Clark Griffith

Player	Gm by Position	B	Age	G	AB	R	H	2B	3B	HR	RBI	BB	SO	SB	Avg	OBP	Slg
Eddie Ainsmith	C119	R	25	125	350	38	67	17	4	0	42	40	48	16	.191	.280	.263
Joe Judge	1B100	L	23	102	393	62	112	15	15	2	30	50	40	17	.285	.369	.415
Ray Morgan	2B95,3B3	R	28	101	338	32	90	9	1	1	33	40	29	7	.266	.346	.308
Eddie Foster	3B86,2B57	R	30	143	554	66	130	16	8	0	43	46	23	11	.235	.293	.292
Howard Shanks	SS90,OF26,1B2	R	26	126	430	45	87	15	5	0	28	33	37	15	.202	.269	.260
Sam Rice	OF155	L	27	155	586	77	177	25	7	0	69	50	41	35	.302	.360	.369
Clyde Milan	OF153	L	30	155	579	60	170	15	4	0	48	58	26	20	.294	.364	.333
Mike Menosky	OF94	L	22	114	322	46	83	12	10	1	34	45	55	22	.258	.359	.366
Joe Leonard	3B67,1B19,SS1*	L	22	99	297	30	57	6	7	0	23	45	40	6	.192	.302	.259
Patsy Gharrity	1B46,C5,OF1	R	25	76	176	15	50	5	0	0	18	14	18	7	.284	.337	.313
John Henry	C59	R	27	65	163	10	31	6	0	0	18	24	16	1	.190	.302	.227
George McBride	SS41,3B6,2B2	R	36	50	141	6	27	3	0	0	9	10	17	1	.191	.265	.213
Elmer Smith†	OF29	L	24	35	117	8	26	4	3	0	17	5	14	1	.222	.260	.308
Sam Crane	SS32	R	22	32	95	6	17	2	0	0	4	4	14	0	.179	.212	.200
Horace Milan	OF23	R	23	31	73	8	21	3	1	0	9	4	9	4	.288	.342	.356
Charlie Jamieson†	OF9,P1	L	24	20	35	4	6	2	0	0	2	6	5	0	.171	.293	.229
Bill Murray	2B6,SS1	S	23	8	21	2	3	0	1	0	4	2	2	1	.143	.217	.238

J. Leonard, 1 G at OF

Pitcher	T	Age	G	GS	CG	ShO	IP	H	HR	BB	SO	W-L	Sv	ERA
Walter Johnson	R	29	47	34	30	8	326.0	248	3	68	188	23-16	3	2.21
Jim Shaw	R	23	47	31	15	2	266.1	233	1	123	118	15-14	1	3.21
Harry Harper	L	22	31	31	10	4	179.1	145	1	106	99	11-12	0	3.01
Bert Gallia	R	25	42	23	9	1	207.2	191	1	93	84	9-13	1	2.99
George Dumont	R	21	37	23	8	2	204.2	171	3	76	65	5-14	2	2.55
Doc Ayers	R	27	40	15	12	3	207.2	192	3	59	78	11-10	1	2.17
Molly Craft	R	21	8	0	0	0	14.0	17	0	8	2	0-0	1	3.86
Doc Waldbauer	R	25	2	0	0	0	5.0	10	0	2	2	0-0	1	7.20
Charlie Jamieson	L	24	1	0	0	0	2.1	10	0	2	1	0-0	0	38.57

1917 New York Yankees 6th AL 71-82 .464 28.5 GB

Wild Bill Donovan

Player	Gm by Position	B	Age	G	AB	R	H	2B	3B	HR	RBI	BB	SO	SB	Avg	OBP	Slg
Les Nunamaker	C91	R	28	104	310	22	81	9	2	0	33	21	25	5	.261	.310	.303
Wally Pipp	1B155	L	24	155	587	82	143	29	12	9	70	60	66	11	.244	.320	.380
Fritz Maisel	2B100,3B7	R	27	113	404	46	80	4	4	0	20	50	18	29	.198	.267	.228
Home Run Baker	3B146	L	31	146	553	57	156	24	2	6	71	48	27	18	.282	.345	.365
Roger Peckinpaugh	SS148	R	26	148	543	63	141	24	7	0	41	64	46	17	.260	.340	.330
Elmer Miller	OF112	R	26	114	379	43	95	11	3	3	35	40	44	11	.251	.336	.319
Tim Hendryx	OF107	R	26	125	393	43	98	14	7	5	44	62	45	6	.249	.359	.359
Hugh High	OF100	L	29	103	365	37	86	11	6	1	19	48	31	8	.236	.329	.307
Lee Magee†	OF50	S	28	51	173	17	38	4	1	0	8	13	18	3	.220	.278	.254
Roxy Walters	C57	R	24	61	171	16	45	2	0	0	14	9	22	2	.263	.304	.275
Frank Gilhooley	OF46	L	25	54	165	14	40	6	1	0	8	30	13	6	.242	.362	.291
Ray Caldwell	P32,OF8	L	29	63	124	12	32	6	1	2	12	16	16	2	.258	.343	.371
Joe Gedeon	2B31	R	23	33	117	15	28	7	0	0	8	7	13	4	.239	.288	.299
Paddy Baumann	2B18,OF7,3B1	R	31	49	110	10	24	2	1	0	8	4	9	2	.218	.246	.255
Armando Marsans†	OF25	R	29	25	88	10	20	4	0	0	15	8	3	6	.227	.292	.273
Walt Alexander	C20	R	26	20	51	1	7	2	1	0	4	4	11	1	.137	.200	.216
Angel Aragon	OF6,3B4,SS2	R	26	14	45	2	3	1	0	0	2	2	2	0	.067	.106	.089
Bill Lamar	OF11	L	20	11	41	2	10	0	0	0	3	0	2	1	.244	.244	.244
Sammy Vick	OF10	R	22	10	36	4	10	3	0	0	2	1	6	2	.278	.297	.361
Chick Fewster	2B11	R	21	11	36	2	8	0	0	0	1	5	5	1	.222	.317	.222
Aaron Ward	SS7	R	20	8	26	0	3	0	0	0	1	1	5	0	.115	.148	.115
Howie Camp	OF5	L	23	5	21	3	6	1	0	0	0	1	2	0	.286	.318	.333
Muddy Ruel	C6	R	21	6	17	1	2	0	0	0	1	2	2	1	.118	.211	.118

Pitcher	T	Age	G	GS	CG	ShO	IP	H	HR	BB	SO	W-L	Sv	ERA
Ray Caldwell	R	29	32	29	21	1	236.0	199	8	76	102	13-16	0	2.86
Bob Shawkey	R	26	32	26	16	2	236.1	207	2	72	97	13-15	1	2.44
George Mogridge	L	28	29	25	15	1	196.1	185	5	39	46	9-11	0	2.98
Nick Cullop	L	29	30	18	5	2	146.1	161	2	31	27	5-9	0	3.32
Ray Fisher	R	29	23	18	12	3	144.0	126	3	43	64	8-9	0	2.19
Urban Shocker	R	26	26	13	7	0	145.0	124	4	46	68	8-5	1	2.61
Bob McGraw	R	22	2	2	1	0	11.0	9	0	3	3	0-1	0	0.82
Bill Piercy	R	21	1	1	1	0	9.0	9	0	2	4	0-1	0	3.00
Neal Brady	R	20	2	1	0	0	9.0	6	0	5	4	1-0	0	2.00
Hank Thormahlen	L	20	1	1	0	0	8.0	9	0	4	5	0-1	0	2.25
Jack Enright	R	21	1	1	0	0	5.0	5	0	3	1	0-1	0	5.40
Slim Love	L	26	33	9	2	0	130.1	115	0	57	82	6-5	1	2.35
Allan Russell	R	23	25	10	6	0	104.1	89	3	39	55	7-8	2	2.24
Ed Monroe	R	22	9	1	1	0	28.2	35	1	6	12	1-0	1	3.45
Walt Smallwood	R	24	2	0	0	0	2.0	1	0	1	1	0-0	0	0.00

1917 St. Louis Browns 7th AL 57-97 .370 43.0 GB

Fielder Jones

Player	Gm by Position	B	Age	G	AB	R	H	2B	3B	HR	RBI	BB	SO	SB	Avg	OBP	Slg
Hank Severeid	C139,1B1	R	26	143	501	45	133	23	4	1	57	28	20	6	.265	.306	.333
George Sisler	1B133,2B2	L	24	135	539	60	190	30	9	2	52	30	19	37	.353	.390	.453
Del Pratt	2B119,1B4	R	29	123	450	40	111	22	8	1	53	33	36	18	.247	.301	.338
Jimmy Austin	3B121,SS6	S	37	127	455	61	109	18	8	0	19	50	46	13	.240	.319	.314
Doc Lavan	SS110,2B7	R	26	118	355	19	85	8	5	0	30	19	34	5	.239	.284	.290
Baby Doll Jacobson	OF131,1B11	R	26	148	529	53	131	23	7	4	55	31	67	10	.248	.294	.340
Burt Shotton	OF107	L	32	118	398	47	89	9	1	1	20	62	47	16	.224	.330	.259
Tod Sloan	OF77	L	26	109	313	32	72	6	2	2	25	28	34	8	.230	.307	.281
Armando Marsans†	OF67,3B5,2B1	R	29	75	257	31	59	12	0	0	20	20	6	11	.230	.285	.276
Earl Smith	OF51	S	26	52	199	31	56	7	7	0	10	15	21	5	.281	.332	.387
Ernie Johnson	SS39,2B18,3B14	L	29	80	199	28	49	6	2	2	20	12	16	13	.246	.296	.327
Lee Magee†	3B20,2B6,1B5*	S	28	36	112	11	19	1	0	0	4	6	6	3	.170	.212	.179
William Rumler	OF9	R	26	78	88	7	23	3	4	1	16	8	9	2	.261	.323	.420
Ward Miller	OF25	L	32	43	82	13	17	1	1	1	2	16	15	7	.207	.350	.280
George Hale	C28	R	22	38	61	4	12	2	1	0	8	10	12	0	.197	.310	.262
Ray Demmitt	OF14	L	33	14	53	6	15	1	2	0	7	0	8	1	.283	.296	.377
Wally Gerber	SS12,2B2	R	25	14	39	2	12	1	1	0	2	3	2	1	.308	.357	.385
Gene Paulette†	1B5,2B3,3B1	R	26	12	22	3	4	0	0	0	0	3	3	0	.182	.280	.182
Grover Hartley	C4,3B1,SS1	R	28	19	13	2	3	0	0	0	0	2	1	0	.231	.333	.231
Duke Kenworthy	2B4	S	30	5	10	1	1	0	0	0	1	1	1	1	.100	.182	.100
Scrappy Moore	3B2	R	24	4	8	1	1	0	0	0	0	1	0	0	.125	.222	.125
Ed Murray	SS1	R	22	1	1	0	0	0	0	0	0	0	1	0	.000	.000	.000
Tom Richardson		R	33	1	1	0	0	0	0	0	0	0	0	0	.000	.000	.000
Otto Neu	SS1	R	22	1	0	0	0	0	0	0	0	0	0	0	—	—	—
Ivan Bigler		R	24	1	0	0	0	0	0	0	0	0	0	0	—	—	—

L. Magee, 1 G at OF

Pitcher	T	Age	G	GS	CG	ShO	IP	H	HR	BB	SO	W-L	Sv	ERA
Dave Davenport	R	27	47	39	19	2	280.2	273	5	105	100	17-17	2	3.08
Allen Sothoron	R	24	48	32	17	3	276.2	259	2	96	85	14-19	4	2.83
Bob Groom	R	32	38	28	11	4	232.2	193	3	95	82	8-19	3	2.94
Eddie Plank	L	41	20	14	8	1	131.0	105	2	38	26	5-6	1	1.79
Carl Weilman	L	27	5	3	0	0	19.0	19	1	6	9	1-2	0	1.89
Grover Lowdermilk	R	32	3	2	2	1	19.0	16	0	4	9	2-1	0	1.42
Ernie Koob	L	24	39	18	3	1	133.2	139	1	57	47	6-14	1	3.91
Earl Hamilton	L	25	27	8	2	0	83.0	86	1	41	19	0-9	1	3.14
Tom Rogers	R	25	24	8	3	0	108.2	112	2	44	27	3-6	0	3.89
Rasty Wright	R	21	16	1	0	0	39.2	48	0	10	5	0-1	0	5.45
Jim Park	R	24	13	0	0	0	20.1	27	1	12	9	1-1	0	6.64
Speed Martin	R	23	9	2	0	0	15.2	20	0	5	5	0-2	0	5.74
Vince Molyneaux	R	28	7	0	0	0	22.0	18	0	20	4	0-0	0	4.91
Tim McCabe	R	22	1	0	0	0	2.1	4	1	4	2	0-0	0	23.14
Kewpie Pennington	R	20	1	0	0	0	1.0	1	0	0	0	0-0	0	0.00

1917 Philadelphia Athletics 8th AL 55-98 .359 44.5 GB

Connie Mack

Player	Gm by Position	B	Age	G	AB	R	H	2B	3B	HR	RBI	BB	SO	SB	Avg	OBP	Slg
Wally Schang	C80,3B12,OF6	S	27	118	316	41	90	14	9	3	36	29	24	6	.285	.362	.415
Stuffy McInnis	1B150	R	26	150	567	50	172	19	4	0	44	33	19	18	.303	.342	.351
Roy Grover	2B139	R	25	141	482	45	108	15	7	0	34	43	53	12	.224	.292	.284
Ray Bates	3B124	R	27	127	485	47	115	20	7	2	66	21	39	12	.237	.277	.320
Whitey Witt	SS111,OF7,3B6	L	21	128	452	62	114	13	4	0	28	65	45	12	.252	.346	.299
Amos Strunk	OF146	L	28	148	540	83	152	26	7	1	45	68	37	16	.281	.363	.361
Ping Bodie	OF145,1B1	R	29	148	557	51	162	28	11	7	74	53	40	13	.291	.356	.418
Charlie Jamieson†	OF83	L	24	85	345	41	92	6	2	0	27	37	36	8	.267	.341	.296
Billy Meyer	C55	R	25	62	162	9	38	5	1	0	9	7	14	0	.235	.271	.278
Joe Dugan	SS39,2B2	R	20	43	134	9	26	8	0	0	16	3	16	0	.194	.229	.254
Bill Johnson	OF30	L	24	48	109	7	19	2	2	1	8	8	14	4	.174	.237	.257
Ray Haley	C34	R	26	41	98	7	27	2	1	0	11	4	12	2	.276	.311	.316
Buck Thrasher	OF22	L	27	23	77	5	18	2	1	0	2	3	12	0	.234	.272	.286
Socks Seibold	P32,OF2	R	21	36	59	6	13	1	1	0	5	4	8	1	.220	.281	.271
Lee Gooch	OF16	R	27	17	59	4	17	2	0	1	8	4	10	0	.288	.333	.373
Otis Lawry	2B17,OF1	L	23	30	55	7	9	1	0	0	1	2	9	1	.164	.193	.182
Eddie Palmer	3B13,SS1	R	24	16	52	7	11	1	0	0	5	7	7	1	.212	.305	.231
Ralph Sharman	OF10	R	22	13	37	2	11	2	1	0	2	3	2	1	.297	.366	.405
Red Shannon		S	20	11	35	8	10	0	0	0	7	6	9	2	.286	.390	.286
Pug Griffin	1B3	R	21	18	25	4	5	1	0	1	3	1	9	1	.200	.231	.360
Wickey McAvoy	C8	R	22	10	24	1	6	1	0	1	4	0	3	0	.250	.250	.417
Cy Perkins	C6	R	21	6	18	1	3	0	0	0	2	2	1	0	.167	.250	.167
Gene Bailey	OF4	R	23	5	12	1	1	0	0	0	0	1	1	0	.083	.154	.083
Val Picinich	C2	R	20	2	6	0	2	0	0	0	0	1	2	0	.333	.429	.333
Dallas Bradshaw	2B1	L	21	2	4	0	0	0	0	0	0	0	1	0	.000	.000	.000
Pat French	OF1	R	23	3	2	0	0	0	0	0	0	0	0	0	.000	.000	.000
Harry Davis		R	43	1	1	0	0	0	0	0	0	0	0	0	.000	.000	.000

Pitcher	T	Age	G	GS	CG	ShO	IP	H	HR	BB	SO	W-L	Sv	ERA
Joe Bush	R	24	37	31	17	4	233.1	207	3	111	121	11-17	2	2.47
Elmer Myers	R	23	38	23	13	2	201.2	221	2	79	88	9-16	3	4.42
Jing Johnson	R	22	34	23	13	0	191.0	184	3	56	55	9-12	0	2.78
Wynn Noyes	R	28	27	22	11	1	171.0	156	5	77	64	10-10	1	2.95
Rube Schauer	R	26	33	21	10	0	215.0	209	6	69	62	7-16	1	3.14
Cy Falkenberg	R	36	15	8	4	0	80.2	86	1	26	35	2-6	0	3.35
Rollie Naylor	R	25	5	5	3	0	33.0	30	1	11	11	2-2	0	1.64
Walt Johnson	R	24	4	2	0	0	13.2	15	0	5	8	0-2	0	7.24
Rube Parnham	R	23	2	2	0	0	11.0	12	1	9	4	0-1	0	4.09
Socks Seibold	R	21	33	15	9	1	160.0	141	1	85	55	4-16	1	3.94
Walter Anderson	L	19	14	2	0	0	38.2	32	0	21	10	0-0	0	3.03
Dave Keefe	R	20	3	0	0	0	5.0	5	0	4	1	1-0	0	1.80
Jack Nabors	R	29	2	0	0	0	3.0	2	0	1	2	0-0	0	3.00
Eddie Bacon	—	22	1	0	0	0	6.0	5	0	7	0	0-0	0	6.00
Red Hill	L	24	1	0	0	0	2.2	5	0	1	0	0-0	0	6.75

»1917 New York Giants 1st NL 98-56 .636 —

John McGraw

Player	Gm by Position	B	Age	G	AB	R	H	2B	3B	HR	RBI	BB	SO	SB	Avg	OBP	Slg
Bill Rariden	C100	R	29	101	266	20	72	10	1	0	25	42	17	3	.271	.372	.316
Walter Holke	1B153	S	24	153	527	55	146	12	7	2	55	34	54	13	.277	.327	.338
Buck Herzog	2B113	R	31	114	417	69	98	10	8	2	31	31	36	12	.235	.308	.312
Heinie Zimmerman	3B149,2B5	R	30	150	585	61	174	22	9	5	102	16	43	13	.297	.317	.391
Art Fletcher	SS151	R	32	151	557	70	145	24	5	4	56	23	28	12	.260	.312	.343
Benny Kauff	OF153	L	27	153	559	89	172	22	4	5	68	59	54	30	.308	.379	.388
George Burns	OF152	R	27	152	597	103	180	25	13	5	45	75	55	40	.302	.380	.412
Dave Robertson	OF140	L	27	142	532	64	138	16	9	12	54	10	47	17	.259	.276	.391
Lew McCarty	C54	R	28	56	162	15	40	3	2	2	19	14	6	1	.247	.311	.327
Jimmy Smith	2B29,SS7	S	22	36	96	12	22	5	1	0	9	9	18	6	.229	.295	.302
George Gibson	C35	R	36	35	82	1	14	3	0	0	5	7	2	1	.171	.236	.207
Pete Kilduff†	2B21,SS5,3B1	R	24	31	78	12	16	3	0	1	12	4	11	2	.205	.253	.282
Jim Thorpe†	OF18	R	30	26	57	12	11	3	2	0	4	8	10	1	.193	.303	.316
Hans Lobert	3B21	R	35	50	52	4	10	1	0	1	5	5	5	2	.192	.276	.269
Joe Wilhoit†	OF11	L	31	34	50	9	17	2	2	0	8	8	5	0	.340	.431	.460
Ross Youngs	OF7	L	20	7	26	5	9	2	3	0	1	1	5	1	.346	.370	.654
Ed Hemingway	3B7	S	24	7	25	3	8	1	1	0	1	2	1	2	.320	.370	.440
Al Baird	2B7,SS3	R	22	10	24	1	7	0	0	0	4	2	2	2	.292	.346	.292
Red Murray	OF11,C1	R	33	22	22	1	1	1	0	0	3	4	3	0	.045	.192	.091
Jose Rodriguez	1B7	R	23	7	20	2	4	0	1	0	2	2	1	2	.200	.273	.300
Ernie Krueger†	C5	R	26	8	10	0	0	0	0	0	0	0	4	0	.000	.000	.000
Jack Onslow	C9	R	28	9	8	1	2	1	0	0	0	0	1	0	.250	.333	.375
George Kelly†	OF4,P1,1B1*	R	21	11	7	0	0	0	0	0	0	0	3	0	.000	.000	.000

G. Kelly, 1 G at 2B

Pitcher	T	Age	G	GS	CG	ShO	IP	H	HR	BB	SO	W-L	Sv	ERA
Ferdie Schupp	L	26	36	32	25	6	272.0	202	7	70	147	21-7	0	1.95
Pol Perritt	R	24	35	26	14	5	215.0	186	3	45	72	17-7	1	1.88
Rube Benton	L	30	35	25	14	3	215.0	190	5	41	70	15-9	3	2.72
Slim Sallee	L	32	34	24	18	1	215.1	199	4	34	54	18-7	4	2.17
Jeff Tesreau	R	28	33	20	11	1	183.2	168	6	58	85	13-8	2	3.09
Al Demaree†	R	32	15	11	1	0	78.1	70	1	17	23	4-5	0	2.64
Ad Swigler	R	21	1	1	0	0	6.0	7	0	8	4	0-1	0	6.00
Fred Anderson	R	31	38	18	8	1	162.0	122	1	34	69	8-8	3	1.44
George Smith	R	25	14	1	1	0	38.0	38	1	11	16	0-3	0	2.84
Jim Middleton	R	28	13	0	0	0	37.0	35	1	8	9	1-1	1	2.68
George Kelly	R	21	1	0	0	0	5.0	4	0	1	2	1-0	0	0.00

1917 Philadelphia Phillies 2nd NL 87-65 .572 10.0 GB

Pat Moran

Player	Gm by Position	B	Age	G	AB	R	H	2B	3B	HR	RBI	BB	SO	SB	Avg	OBP	Slg
Bill Killefer	C120	R	29	125	409	28	112	12	0	0	31	15	21	4	.274	.306	.303
Fred Luderus	1B154	L	31	154	522	57	136	24	4	5	72	65	35	5	.261	.349	.351
Bert Niehoff	2B96,1B7,3B6	R	33	116	361	30	92	17	4	2	42	23	29	8	.255	.303	.341
Milt Stock	3B133,SS19	R	23	150	564	76	149	27	6	3	53	51	34	25	.264	.326	.349
Dave Bancroft	SS120,2B3,OF2	S	26	127	478	56	116	22	5	4	43	44	42	14	.243	.307	.335
Possum Whitted	OF141,1B10,3B7*	R	27	149	553	69	155	24	9	3	70	30	56	10	.280	.317	.373
Gavy Cravath	OF139	R	36	141	503	70	141	29	16	12	83	70	57	6	.280	.369	.473
Dode Paskert	OF138	R	35	141	546	78	137	27	11	4	43	62	63	19	.251	.331	.363
Johnny Evers†	2B49,3B7	L	35	56	183	20	41	5	1	1	12	30	13	8	.224	.333	.279
Wildfire Schulte†	OF42	L	34	64	149	21	32	10	0	1	15	16	22	4	.215	.299	.302
Bert Adams	C38,1B1	S	26	43	107	4	22	4	1	1	7	0	20	0	.206	.206	.290
Oscar Dugey	2B15,OF4	R	29	44	72	12	14	4	1	0	9	4	9	2	.194	.237	.278
Patsy McGaffigan	SS17,OF1	R	28	19	60	5	10	1	0	0	6	0	7	1	.167	.167	.183
Ed Burns	C15	R	28	20	49	2	10	1	0	0	6	1	5	2	.204	.220	.224
Claude Cooper	OF12	L	25	24	29	5	3	1	0	0	1	5	4	0	.103	.235	.138
Harry Pearce	SS4	R	27	7	16	2	4	3	0	0	2	0	4	0	.250	.294	.438
Bobby Byrne†	3B4	R	32	13	14	1	5	0	0	0	0	1	2	0	.357	.400	.357

P. Whitted, 1 G at 2B

Pitcher	T	Age	G	GS	CG	ShO	IP	H	HR	BB	SO	W-L	Sv	ERA
Pete Alexander	R	30	45	44	35	8	388.0	336	4	56	200	30-13	0	1.83
Eppa Rixey	L	26	39	36	23	4	281.1	249	1	67	121	16-21	1	2.27
Joe Oeschger	R	26	42	30	18	5	262.0	241	7	72	123	15-14	1	2.75
Erskine Mayer	R	28	28	18	11	1	160.0	160	6	33	64	11-6	0	2.76
Jimmy Lavender	R	33	28	14	7	0	129.1	119	5	44	52	6-8	1	3.55
Chief Bender	R	33	20	10	8	4	113.0	84	1	26	43	8-2	2	1.67
Paul Fittery	L	29	17	2	1	0	55.2	69	1	27	13	1-1	0	4.53

1917 St. Louis Cardinals 3rd NL 82-70 .539 15.0 GB

Miller Huggins

Player	Gm by Position	B	Age	G	AB	R	H	2B	3B	HR	RBI	BB	SO	SB	Avg	OBP	Slg
Frank Snyder	C94	R	24	115	313	18	74	9	2	1	33	27	43	4	.236	.301	.288
Gene Paulette†	1B93	R	26	95	332	32	88	21	7	0	34	16	16	9	.265	.303	.370
Dots Miller	2B92,1B46,SS11	R	30	148	544	61	135	15	9	2	45	33	52	14	.248	.295	.320
Doug Baird†	3B103,OF2	R	25	104	364	38	92	19	12	0	24	23	52	18	.253	.301	.371
Rogers Hornsby	SS144	R	21	145	523	86	171	24	17	8	66	45	34	17	.327	.385	.484
Walton Cruise	OF152	L	27	153	529	70	156	20	10	5	59	38	73	16	.295	.343	.399
Tom Long	OF137	R	27	144	530	49	123	12	14	3	41	37	44	21	.232	.285	.325
Jack Smith	OF128	L	22	137	462	64	137	16	11	3	34	38	65	25	.297	.351	.398
Bruno Betzel	2B75,OF23,3B4	R	22	106	328	24	71	4	3	1	17	20	47	9	.216	.266	.256
Mike Gonzalez	C68,1B18,OF1	R	26	106	290	28	76	8	1	1	28	22	24	12	.262	.316	.307
Fred Smith	3B51,2B2,SS1	R	25	56	165	11	30	0	2	1	17	17	22	4	.182	.262	.224
Bob Bescher	OF32	S	33	42	110	10	17	1	1	1	8	20	13	3	.155	.290	.209
Red Smyth†	OF23	L	24	38	72	5	15	0	2	0	4	4	9	3	.208	.269	.264
Paddy Livingston	C6	R	37	7	20	0	4	0	0	0	2	0	1	2	.200	.200	.200
John Brock	C4	R	20	7	15	4	6	1	0	0	2	0	2	2	.400	.400	.467
Tony DeFate†	3B5,2B1	R	22	14	14	0	2	0	0	0	1	4	5	0	.143	.333	.143
Bobby Wallace	3B5,SS2	R	43	8	10	0	1	0	0	0	2	0	1	0	.100	.100	.100
Stuffy Stewart	2B2,OF2	R	23	13	9	4	0	0	0	0	0	0	4	0	.000	.000	.000
Ike McAuley	SS3	R	25	3	7	0	2	0	0	0	1	0	1	0	.286	.286	.286
Jack Roche	C1	R	26	1	1	0	0	0	0	0	0	0	0	0	.000	.000	.000

Pitcher	T	Age	G	GS	CG	ShO	IP	H	HR	BB	SO	W-L	Sv	ERA
Bill Doak	R	26	44	37	16	3	281.1	257	6	85	111	16-20	2	3.10
Lee Meadows	R	22	43	37	18	4	265.2	253	5	90	100	15-9	2	3.08
Marv Goodwin	R	26	14	12	6	3	85.1	70	1	19	38	6-4	0	2.21
Bob Steele†	L	23	12	6	1	0	42.0	33	1	19	23	1-3	0	3.21
Red Ames	R	34	43	19	10	2	209.0	189	2	57	62	15-10	3	2.71
Milt Watson	R	27	41	20	5	3	161.1	149	3	51	45	10-13	0	3.51
Oscar Horstmann	R	26	35	11	4	1	138.2	111	5	54	50	9-4	1	3.44
Gene Packard†	L	29	34	11	6	0	153.1	138	4	25	44	9-6	2	2.47
Jakie May	L	21	15	1	0	0	29.1	29	0	11	18	0-0	0	3.38
Lou North	R	26	5	0	0	0	11.1	14	1	4	4	0-0	0	3.97
George Pearce	L	29	5	0	0	0	10.2	7	0	3	4	1-1	0	3.38
Bruce Hitt	R	20	2	0	0	0	4.0	7	1	1	1	0-0	0	9.00
Tim Murchison	L	20	1	0	0	0	1.0	0	0	2	2	0-0	0	0.00

1917 Cincinnati Reds 4th NL 78-76 .506 20.0 GB

Christy Mathewson

Player	Gm by Position	B	Age	G	AB	R	H	2B	3B	HR	RBI	BB	SO	SB	Avg	OBP	Slg
Ivy Wingo	C120	L	26	121	399	37	106	16	11	2	39	25	13	9	.266	.311	.376
Hal Chase	1B151	R	34	152	602	71	167	28	15	4	86	15	49	21	.277	.296	.394
Dave Shean	2B131	R	33	131	442	36	93	9	5	2	35	22	39	10	.210	.249	.267
Heine Groh	3B154,2B2	R	27	156	599	91	182	39	11	1	53	71	30	15	.304	.385	.411
Larry Kopf	SS145	S	26	148	573	81	146	19	8	2	26	28	48	17	.255	.297	.326
Edd Roush	OF134	L	24	136	522	82	178	19	14	4	67	27	24	21	.341	.379	.454
Greasy Neale	OF119	L	25	121	385	40	113	14	9	3	33	24	36	25	.294	.343	.400
Tommy Griffith	OF100	L	27	115	363	45	98	18	7	1	45	19	23	5	.270	.308	.366
Jim Thorpe†	OF69	R	30	77	251	29	62	2	8	4	36	6	35	11	.247	.267	.367
Manuel Cueto	OF38,2B6,C5	R	25	56	140	10	28	3	0	1	11	16	17	4	.200	.287	.243
Sherry Magee†	OF41,1B2	R	32	45	137	17	44	8	4	0	23	16	7	4	.321	.400	.438
Bill McKechnie	2B26,SS13,3B4	S	30	48	134	11	34	3	1	0	15	7	7	5	.254	.296	.291
Tommy Clarke	C29	R	29	58	110	11	32	3	3	1	13	11	12	2	.291	.361	.400
Clarence Mitchell	P32,1B6,OF6	L	26	47	90	13	25	3	0	0	5	5	5	0	.278	.316	.311
Emil Huhn	C15	R	25	23	51	2	10	1	2	0	3	2	5	1	.196	.226	.294
Harry Smith	C7	R	27	8	17	0	2	0	0	0	1	2	7	0	.118	.211	.118
Gus Getz	2B4,3B3	R	27	7	14	2	4	0	0	0	3	3	0	0	.286	.412	.286

Pitcher	T	Age	G	GS	CG	ShO	IP	H	HR	BB	SO	W-L	Sv	ERA
Pete Schneider	R	21	46	42	25	0	341.2	316	4	119	142	20-19	0	1.98
Fred Toney	R	28	43	42	31	7	339.2	300	4	77	123	24-16	1	2.20
Mike Regan	R	29	32	26	16	1	216.0	228	4	41	50	11-10	0	2.71
Clarence Mitchell	L	26	32	20	10	2	159.1	166	4	34	37	9-15	1	3.22
Dutch Ruether†	L	23	7	4	1	1	35.2	43	0	14	12	1-2	0	3.53
Roy Sanders	R	24	2	2	1	0	14.1	12	0	16	3	0-1	0	4.40
Rube Bressler	L	22	2	1	0	0	9.0	15	0	5	2	0-0	0	6.00
Joe Engel	L	24	1	1	1	0	8.0	12	0	6	2	0-1	0	5.63
Hod Eller	R	22	37	11	7	1	152.1	131	2	37	77	10-5	1	2.36
Jimmy Ring	R	22	24	7	3	0	88.0	90	2	35	33	3-7	2	4.40
Elmer Knetzer	R	31	11	0	0	0	27.1	29	0	12	7	0-0	1	2.96
Scott Perry	R	26	4	1	0	0	13.1	17	0	8	4	0-0	0	6.75
Herman Pillette	R	21	1	0	0	0	1.0	4	0	0	0	0-0	0	18.00

1917 Chicago Cubs 5th NL 74-80 .481 24.0 GB

Fred Mitchell

Player	Gm by Position	B	Age	G	AB	R	H	2B	3B	HR	RBI	BB	SO	SB	Avg	OBP	Slg
Art Wilson	C75	R	31	81	211	17	45	9	2	2	25	32	36	6	.213	.322	.303
Fred Merkle†	1B140,OF6	R	28	146	549	65	146	30	9	3	57	42	60	13	.266	.323	.370
Larry Doyle	2B128	L	30	135	476	48	121	19	5	6	61	48	28	5	.254	.323	.353
Charlie Deal	3B130	R	25	135	449	46	114	11	3	0	47	19	18	10	.254	.284	.292
Chuck Wortman	SS65,2B1,3B1	R	25	75	190	24	33	4	1	0	9	18	23	6	.174	.245	.205
Cy Williams	OF136	L	29	138	468	53	113	22	4	5	42	38	78	8	.241	.308	.338
Max Flack	OF117	L	27	131	447	65	111	18	7	0	21	51	34	17	.248	.325	.320
Les Mann	OF116	R	23	117	444	63	121	19	10	1	44	27	46	14	.273	.316	.367
Rollie Zeider	SS48,3B26,2B24*	R	33	108	354	36	86	14	2	0	27	28	30	17	.243	.302	.294
Harry Wolter	OF97,1B1	L	32	117	353	44	88	15	7	0	28	38	40	7	.249	.324	.331
Rowdy Elliott	C73	R	26	85	223	18	56	8	5	0	28	11	11	4	.251	.292	.332
Pete Kilduff†	SS51,2B5	R	24	56	202	23	56	9	5	0	15	12	19	11	.277	.324	.371
Pickles Dillhoefer	C37	R	22	42	95	3	12	1	1	0	8	2	9	1	.126	.144	.158
Claude Hendrix	P40,OF2	R	28	48	86	7	22	3	1	0	7	5	20	1	.256	.304	.314
Dutch Ruether†	P10,1B5	L	23	31	44	3	12	1	3	0	11	8	11	0	.273	.385	.432
Charlie Pechous	3B7,SS5	R	20	13	41	2	10	0	0	0	1	2	9	1	.244	.295	.244
Morrie Schick	OF12	R	25	14	34	3	5	0	0	0	3	3	10	0	.147	.216	.147
Paddy Driscoll	2B8,3B2,SS1	R	22	13	28	2	3	1	0	0	3	2	6	2	.107	.167	.143
Turner Barber	OF7	L	23	7	28	2	6	1	0	0	2	2	8	1	.214	.267	.250
Vic Saier	1B6	L	26	6	21	5	5	1	0	0	2	2	1	0	.238	.304	.286
Roy Leslie	1B6	R	22	7	19	1	4	0	0	0	1	1	5	1	.211	.250	.211
Bob O'Farrell	C3	R	20	3	8	1	3	2	0	0	1	1	0	1	.375	.444	.625
William Marriott	OF1	L	23	3	6	0	0	0	0	0	0	0	1	0	.000	.000	.000
Harry Wolfe†	OF2,SS1	R	26	9	5	1	2	0	0	0	1	1	1	0	.400	.500	.400
Herb Hunter	2B1,3B1	L	20	3	3	0	0	0	0	0	0	0	0	0	.000	.000	.000
Earl Blackburn		R	24	2	2	0	0	0	0	0	0	0	0	0	.000	.000	.000
Jimmy Archer		R	34	2	2	0	0	0	0	0	0	0	1	0	.000	.000	.000

R. Zeider, 1 G at 1B, 1 G at OF

Pitcher	T	Age	G	GS	CG	ShO	IP	H	HR	BB	SO	W-L	Sv	ERA
Hippo Vaughn	L	29	41	38	27	5	295.2	255	3	91	195	23-13	0	2.01
Phil Douglas	R	27	51	37	20	5	293.1	269	13	50	151	14-20	1	2.55
Claude Hendrix	R	28	40	21	13	1	215.0	202	3	72	81	10-12	1	2.60
Al Demaree†	R	32	24	18	6	1	141.1	125	5	37	43	5-9	1	2.55
Paul Carter	R	23	23	13	6	0	113.1	115	2	19	34	5-8	2	3.26
Tom Seaton	R	29	16	9	3	1	74.2	60	0	23	27	5-4	1	2.53
Harry Weaver	R	25	4	2	1	0	19.2	17	0	7	8	1-1	0	2.75
Roy Walker	R	24	2	1	0	0	7.0	8	0	5	4	0-1	0	3.86
Mike Prendergast	R	28	35	8	1	0	99.2	112	6	21	43	3-6	1	3.34
Vic Aldridge	R	23	30	6	1	1	106.2	100	1	37	44	6-6	2	3.12
Dutch Ruether†	L	23	10	4	1	0	36.1	37	0	12	23	2-0	0	2.48
Gene Packard†	L	29	2	0	0	0	1.2	3	1	0	1	0-0	0	10.80

1917 Boston Braves 6th NL 72-81 .471 25.5 GB

George Stallings

Player	Gm by Position	B	Age	G	AB	R	H	2B	3B	HR	RBI	BB	SO	SB	Avg	OBP	Slg
Walt Tragesser	C94	R	30	98	297	23	66	10	2	0	25	15	36	5	.222	.264	.269
Ed Konetchy	1B129	R	31	130	474	56	129	19	13	2	54	36	40	16	.272	.330	.380
Johnny Rawlings	2B96,SS17,3B1*	R	24	122	371	37	95	9	4	2	31	38	32	12	.256	.337	.318
Red Smith	3B147	R	27	147	505	60	149	31	6	2	62	53	61	16	.295	.369	.392
Rabbit Maranville	SS142	R	25	142	561	69	146	19	13	3	43	40	47	27	.260	.312	.357
Joe Kelly	OF116	R	30	116	445	41	99	9	8	3	36	26	45	21	.222	.268	.299
Ray Powell	OF88	L	28	88	357	42	97	10	4	4	30	24	54	12	.272	.318	.356
Wally Rehg	OF86	R	28	87	341	48	92	12	6	1	31	24	32	13	.270	.320	.349
Sherry Magee†	OF65,1B2	R	32	72	246	24	63	8	4	1	29	13	23	7	.256	.302	.333
Joe Wilhoit†	OF52	L	31	54	186	20	51	5	0	1	10	17	15	5	.274	.335	.317
Ed Fitzpatrick	2B22,OF19,3B15	R	27	63	178	20	45	8	4	0	17	12	22	4	.253	.318	.343
Hank Gowdy	C49	R	27	49	154	12	33	7	0	0	14	15	13	2	.214	.288	.260
Lefty Tyler	P32,1B11	L	27	61	134	8	31	4	0	0	11	17	19	0	.231	.318	.261
Fred Bailey	OF27	L	21	50	110	9	21	2	1	1	5	9	25	3	.191	.270	.255
George Twombly	OF29,1B1	R	25	32	102	8	19	1	1	0	9	18	5	4	.186	.314	.216
Mike Massey	2B25	S	23	31	91	12	18	0	0	0	2	15	15	2	.198	.318	.198
Johnny Evers†	2B24	L	35	24	83	5	16	0	0	0	0	13	8	1	.193	.302	.193
Chief Meyers†	C24	R	36	25	68	5	17	4	4	0	4	4	4	0	.250	.311	.426
Sam Covington	1B17	L	24	17	66	8	13	2	0	1	10	5	5	1	.197	.264	.273
Zip Collins	OF5	L	25	9	27	3	4	0	1	0	2	0	4	0	.148	.148	.222
Art Rico	C11,OF1	R	20	13	14	1	4	1	0	0	2	0	2	0	.286	.286	.357
Hank Schreiber	3B1,SS1	R	25	2	7	1	2	0	0	0	0	0	1	0	.286	.286	.286
Larry Chappell		L	27	4	2	0	0	0	0	0	1	0	1	0	.000	.000	.000
Fred Jacklitsch	C1	R	41	1	0	0	0	0	0	0	0	0	0	0	—	—	—

J. Rawlings, 1 G at OF

Pitcher	T	Age	G	GS	CG	ShO	IP	H	HR	BB	SO	W-L	Sv	ERA
Jesse Barnes	R	24	50	33	27	2	295.0	261	3	50	107	13-21	1	2.68
Dick Rudolph	R	29	31	30	22	5	242.2	252	1	54	96	13-13	0	3.41
Lefty Tyler	L	27	32	28	22	4	239.0	203	1	86	98	14-12	1	2.52
Art Nehf	L	24	38	23	17	5	233.1	197	4	39	101	17-8	0	2.16
Tom Hughes	R	33	11	8	6	2	74.0	54	0	30	40	5-3	0	1.95
Ed Walsh	R	36	4	3	1	0	18.0	22	0	9	4	0-1	0	3.50
Pat Ragan	R	28	30	13	5	1	147.2	138	6	35	61	6-9	1	2.93
Frank Allen	L	27	29	14	2	0	112.0	124	3	47	56	3-11	0	3.94
Jack Scott	R	25	7	3	3	0	39.2	36	0	5	21	1-2	0	1.82
Ed Reulbach	R	34	5	2	0	0	22.1	21	0	15	9	0-1	0	2.82
Cal Crum	R	26	1	0	0	0	1.0	1	0	1	0	0-0	0	0.00

1917 Brooklyn Dodgers 7th NL 70-81 .464 26.5 GB

Wilbert Robinson

Player	Gm by Position	B	Age	G	AB	R	H	2B	3B	HR	RBI	BB	SO	SB	Avg	OBP	Slg
Otto Miller	C91	R	28	92	274	19	63	5	4	1	17	14	29	5	.230	.272	.288
Jake Daubert	1B125	L	33	125	468	59	122	4	4	2	30	51	30	11	.261	.341	.299
George Cutshaw	2B134	R	29	135	487	42	126	17	7	4	49	21	26	22	.259	.292	.347
Mike Mowrey	3B80,2B2	R	33	83	271	20	58	9	5	0	25	29	25	7	.214	.292	.284
Ivy Olson	SS133,3B6	R	31	139	580	64	156	18	5	2	38	14	34	6	.269	.291	.328
Casey Stengel	OF150	L	26	150	549	69	141	23	12	6	73	60	62	18	.257	.336	.375
Jim Hickman	OF101	R	25	114	370	46	81	15	4	6	36	17	66	14	.219	.253	.330
Zack Wheat	OF98	L	29	109	362	38	113	15	11	1	41	20	18	5	.312	.352	.423
Hi Myers	OF66,1B22,2B19*	R	28	120	471	37	126	15	10	1	41	18	25	5	.268	.294	.348
Jimmy Johnston	OF92,1B14,SS4*	R	27	103	330	33	89	10	4	0	25	23	28	16	.270	.321	.324
Frank O'Rourke	3B58	R	22	64	198	18	47	7	1	0	15	14	25	11	.237	.294	.283
Chief Meyers†	C44	R	36	47	132	8	28	3	0	0	3	13	7	4	.212	.283	.235
Bunny Fabrique	SS21	S	29	25	88	8	18	3	0	1	3	8	9	0	.205	.271	.273
Ernie Krueger†	C23	R	26	31	81	10	22	2	2	1	6	5	7	1	.272	.330	.383
Mack Wheat	C18,OF9	R	24	29	60	2	8	1	0	0	0	1	12	1	.133	.161	.150
Red Smyth†	3B4,OF2	L	24	29	24	5	3	0	0	0	1	4	6	0	.125	.250	.125
Jack Snyder	C5	R	30	7	11	1	3	0	0	0	1	0	2	0	.273	.273	.273
Fred Merkle†	1B2	R	28	2	8	1	1	1	0	0	0	0	1	0	.125	.125	.250
Bill Leard	2B1	R	31	3	3	0	0	0	0	0	0	0	1	0	.000	.000	.000
Lew Malone		R	20	1	0	1	0	0	0	0	0	0	0	0	—	—	—

H. Myers, 15 G at 3B; J. Johnston, 3 G at 2B, 3 G at 3B

Pitcher	T	Age	G	GS	CG	ShO	IP	H	HR	BB	SO	W-L	Sv	ERA
Jeff Pfeffer	R	29	30	30	24	3	266.0	225	4	66	115	11-15	0	2.23
Leon Cadore	R	26	37	30	21	1	264.0	231	3	63	115	13-13	3	2.45
Rube Marquard	L	30	37	29	14	2	232.2	200	5	60	117	19-12	0	2.55
Larry Cheney	R	31	35	24	14	1	210.1	185	4	73	102	8-12	2	2.35
Sherry Smith	L	26	38	23	15	0	211.2	210	5	51	58	12-12	3	3.32
Jack Coombs	R	34	31	14	9	0	141.0	147	7	49	34	7-11	0	3.96
Wheezer Dell	R	30	17	4	0	0	58.0	55	3	25	28	0-4	1	3.72
John Russell	L	21	5	1	1	0	16.0	12	1	6	1	0-1	0	4.50
Johnny Miljus	R	22	4	1	1	0	15.0	14	0	8	9	0-1	0	0.60
Paul Wachtel	R	29	2	0	0	0	6.0	9	0	4	3	0-0	0	10.50
Rich Durning	L	24	1	0	0	0	1.0	0	0	0	0	0-0	0	0.00

1917 Pittsburgh Pirates 8th NL 51-103 .331 47.0 GB

Nixey Callahan (20-40)/Honus Wagner (1-4)/Hugo Bezdek (30-59)

Player	Gm by Position	B	Age	G	AB	R	H	2B	3B	HR	RBI	BB	SO	SB	Avg	OBP	Slg
William Fischer	C69,1B2	L	26	95	245	25	70	9	2	3	25	27	19	11	.286	.359	.376
Honus Wagner	1B47,3B18,2B2*	R	43	74	230	15	61	7	1	0	24	24	17	5	.265	.337	.304
Jake Pitler	2B106,OF3	R	23	109	382	39	89	8	5	0	23	30	24	6	.233	.297	.280
Tony Boeckel	3B62	R	24	64	219	16	58	11	1	0	23	8	31	6	.265	.297	.324
Chuck Ward	SS112,2B8,3B5	R	22	125	423	25	100	12	3	0	43	32	43	5	.236	.302	.279
Max Carey	OF153	S	27	155	588	82	174	21	12	1	51	58	38	46	.296	.369	.378
Carson Bigbee	OF107,2B16,SS2	L	22	133	469	46	112	11	6	0	21	37	16	19	.239	.301	.288
Lee King	OF102	R	24	111	381	32	95	14	5	1	35	15	58	8	.249	.281	.320
Bill Hinchman	OF48,1B20	R	34	69	244	27	46	5	5	2	29	33	27	5	.189	.288	.275
Walter Schmidt	C61	R	30	72	183	9	45	7	0	0	17	11	11	4	.246	.296	.284
Bill Wagner	C37,1B12	R	23	53	151	15	31	7	2	0	9	11	22	1	.205	.264	.278
Alex McCarthy	3B26,2B13,SS9	R	29	49	151	15	33	4	0	0	8	11	13	1	.219	.276	.245
Fritz Mollwitz	1B36,2B1	R	27	36	140	15	36	4	1	0	12	8	8	4	.257	.297	.300
Doug Baird†	3B41,2B2	R	25	43	135	17	35	6	1	0	18	20	19	8	.259	.355	.319
Adam DeBus	SS21,3B18	R	24	38	131	9	30	5	4	0	7	7	14	2	.229	.279	.328
Charlie Jackson	OF36	L	23	41	121	7	29	3	2	0	1	10	22	4	.240	.303	.298
Bunny Brief	1B34	R	24	36	115	15	25	5	1	2	11	15	21	4	.217	.318	.330
Wildfire Schulte†	OF28	L	34	30	103	11	22	5	1	0	7	10	14	5	.214	.283	.282
Howdy Caton	SS14	R	20	14	57	6	12	1	2	0	4	6	7	0	.211	.286	.298
Billy Gleason	2B13	R	22	13	42	3	7	1	0	0	0	5	5	1	.167	.255	.190
Don Flinn	OF12	R	24	14	37	1	11	1	1	0	1	1	6	1	.297	.316	.378
Ray Miller†	1B6	L	29	6	27	1	4	1	0	0	0	2	3	0	.148	.207	.185
George Kelly†	1B8	R	21	8	23	2	2	0	1	0	0	1	9	0	.087	.125	.174
Red Smith	C6	R	25	11	21	1	3	1	0	0	2	3	4	1	.143	.250	.190
Jesse Altenburg	OF4	L	24	11	17	1	3	0	0	0	3	0	4	0	.176	.176	.176
Bill Webb	2B3,SS1	R	22	5	15	1	3	0	0	0	0	2	3	0	.200	.294	.200
Fred Blackwell	C3	L	25	3	10	1	2	0	0	0	2	0	3	0	.200	.200	.200
Joe Wilhoit†	OF3,1B1	L	31	9	10	0	2	0	0	0	0	1	1	0	.200	.273	.200
Harry Wolfe†	2B1,SS1	R	26	3	5	0	0	0	0	0	0	1	4	0	.000	.167	.000
Hooks Warner	3B1	L	23	3	5	0	1	0	0	0	0	0	1	0	.200	.200	.200
Ben Shaw		R	24	2	2	0	0	0	0	0	0	0	0	0	.000	.000	.000
Arch Reilly	3B1	R	25	1	0	0	0	0	0	0	0	0	0	0	—	—	—

H. Wagner, 1 G at SS

Pitcher	T	Age	G	GS	CG	ShO	IP	H	HR	BB	SO	W-L	Sv	ERA
Wilbur Cooper	L	25	40	34	23	7	297.2	276	4	54	99	17-11	1	2.36
Frank Miller	R	31	38	28	14	5	224.0	216	1	60	92	10-19	1	3.13
Elmer Jacobs	R	24	38	25	10	1	227.1	214	3	76	58	6-19	2	2.81
Bob Steele†	L	23	27	19	13	1	179.2	158	0	53	82	5-11	1	2.76
Hal Carlson	R	25	34	17	9	1	161.1	140	0	49	68	7-11	1	2.90
Al Mamaux	R	23	16	13	5	0	85.2	92	1	50	22	2-11	0	5.25
Elmer Ponder	R	24	3	2	1	1	21.1	12	0	6	11	1-1	0	1.69
Burleigh Grimes	R	23	37	17	8	1	194.0	186	5	70	72	3-16	0	3.53
Bill Evans	R	23	8	2	1	0	26.2	24	0	14	5	0-4	0	3.38

»1918 Boston Red Sox 1st AL 75-51 .595 —

Ed Barrow

Player	Gm by Position	B	Age	G	AB	R	H	2B	3B	HR	RBI	BB	SO	SB	Avg	OBP	Slg
Sam Agnew	C72	R	31	72	199	11	33	8	0	0	6	11	26	0	.166	.221	.206
Stuffy McInnis	1B94,3B23	R	27	117	423	40	115	11	5	0	56	19	10	10	.272	.306	.322
Dave Shean	2B115	R	34	115	425	58	112	16	3	0	34	40	25	11	.264	.331	.315
Fred Thomas	3B41,SS1	R	25	44	144	19	37	2	1	1	11	15	20	4	.257	.331	.306
Everett Scott	SS126	R	25	126	443	40	98	11	5	0	43	12	16	11	.221	.242	.269
Harry Hooper	OF126	L	30	126	474	81	137	26	13	1	44	75	25	24	.289	.391	.405
Amos Strunk	OF113	L	29	114	413	50	106	18	9	0	35	36	13	20	.257	.316	.344
George Whiteman	OF69	R	35	71	214	24	57	14	0	1	28	20	9	9	.266	.335	.346
Babe Ruth	OF59,P20,1B13	L	23	95	317	50	95	26	11	11	66	57	58	6	.300	.410	.555
Wally Schang	C57,OF16,3B5*	S	28	88	225	36	55	7	1	0	20	46	35	4	.244	.377	.284
Doc Hoblitzell	1B19	R	29	25	69	4	11	1	0	0	4	8	3	3	.159	.266	.174
George Cochran	3B23,SS1	—	29	25	63	8	8	0	0	0	3	11	7	3	.127	.276	.127
Wally Mayer	C23	R	27	26	49	7	11	4	0	0	5	7	7	0	.224	.321	.306
Jack Stansbury	3B18,OF2	R	32	20	47	3	6	1	0	0	2	6	3	0	.128	.241	.149
Jack Coffey†	3B14,2B1	R	31	15	44	5	7	1	0	1	2	3	2	2	.159	.213	.250
Frank Truesdale	2B10	S	34	15	36	6	10	1	0	0	2	4	5	1	.278	.350	.306
Hack Miller	OF10	R	24	12	29	2	8	2	0	0	4	0	4	0	.276	.276	.345
Walter Barbare	3B11,SS1	R	26	13	29	2	5	3	0	0	2	0	1	1	.172	.172	.276
Heinie Wagner	2B2,3B1	R	37	3	8	0	1	0	0	0	0	1	0	0	.125	.222	.125
Walt Kinney	P5,OF1	L	24	6	5	0	0	0	0	0	0	0	1	0	.000	.000	.000
Eusebio Gonzalez	SS2	R	25	3	5	2	2	0	1	0	0	1	1	0	.400	.571	.800
Red Bluhm		R	24	1	1	0	0	0	0	0	0	0	0	0	.000	.000	.000

W. Schang, 1 G at SS

Pitcher	T	Age	G	GS	CG	ShO	IP	H	HR	BB	SO	W-L	Sv	ERA
Carl Mays	R	26	35	33	30	8	293.1	230	2	81	114	21-13	0	2.21
Joe Bush	R	25	36	31	26	7	272.2	241	3	91	125	15-15	2	2.11
Sad Sam Jones	R	25	24	21	16	5	184.0	151	1	70	44	16-5	0	2.25
Babe Ruth	L	23	20	19	18	1	166.1	125	1	49	40	13-7	0	2.22
Dutch Leonard	L	26	16	16	12	3	125.2	119	0	53	47	8-6	0	2.72
Lore Bader	R	30	5	4	2	1	27.0	26	1	12	10	1-3	0	3.33
Jean Dubuc	R	29	2	1	1	0	10.2	11	1	5	1	0-1	0	4.22
Vince Molyneaux	R	29	6	0	0	0	10.2	3	0	8	1	1-0	0	3.38
Walt Kinney	L	24	5	0	0	0	15.0	5	0	8	4	0-0	0	1.80
Dick McCabe	R	22	3	1	0	0	9.2	13	0	2	3	0-1	0	2.79
Bill Pertica	R	21	1	0	0	0	3.0	3	0	0	1	0-0	0	3.00
John Wyckoff	R	26	1	0	0	0	2.0	4	0	1	2	0-0	0	0.00

1918 Cleveland Indians 2nd AL 73-54 .575 2.5 GB

Lee Fohl

Player	Gm by Position	B	Age	G	AB	R	H	2B	3B	HR	RBI	BB	SO	SB	Avg	OBP	Slg
Steve O'Neill	C113	R	26	114	359	34	87	8	7	1	35	48	22	5	.242	.343	.312
Doc Johnston	1B73	L	30	74	273	30	62	12	2	0	25	26	19	12	.227	.301	.286
Bill Wambsganss	2B87	R	24	87	315	34	93	15	2	0	40	21	21	16	.295	.345	.356
Joe Evans	3B74	R	23	79	243	38	64	6	7	1	22	30	29	7	.263	.344	.358
Ray Chapman	SS128	R	27	128	446	84	119	19	8	1	32	84	46	30	.267	.390	.352
Tris Speaker	OF127	L	30	127	471	73	150	33	11	0	61	64	9	27	.318	.403	.435
Braggo Roth	OF106	R	25	106	375	53	106	21	12	1	59	53	41	35	.283	.383	.411
Joe Wood	OF95,2B19	R	28	119	422	41	125	22	4	5	66	36	38	8	.296	.356	.403
Terry Turner	3B46,2B26	R	37	74	233	24	58	7	2	0	23	22	15	6	.249	.316	.296
Jack Graney	OF45	L	32	70	177	27	42	7	4	0	9	28	13	3	.237	.351	.322
Ed Miller	1B22	R	29	32	96	9	22	4	3	0	3	12	10	2	.229	.321	.333
Pinch Thomas	C24	L	30	32	73	2	18	0	1	0	5	6	6	0	.247	.304	.274
Rip Williams	1B21,C1	R	36	28	71	5	17	2	2	0	7	9	6	2	.239	.325	.324
Al Halt	3B14	R	27	26	69	9	12	2	0	0	1	9	12	4	.174	.269	.203
Bob Bescher	OF17	S	34	25	60	12	20	2	1	0	6	17	5	3	.333	.487	.400
Marty Kavanagh†	1B12	R	27	13	38	4	8	2	0	0	6	7	7	1	.211	.348	.263
Gus Getz†	OF3	R	28	6	15	2	2	1	0	0	0	4	1	0	.133	.350	.200
Jack Farmer		R	25	7	9	1	2	0	0	0	1	0	3	2	.222	.300	.222
Eddie Onslow	OF1	L	25	2	6	0	1	0	0	0	0	0	1	0	.167	.167	.167
Germany Schaefer	2B1	R	41	1	5	2	0	0	0	0	0	0	0	1	.000	.000	.000
Josh Billings	C1	R	26	2	3	0	1	0	0	0	0	0	0	0	.333	.333	.333
John Peters	C1	R	24	1	1	0	0	0	0	0	0	1	1	0	.000	.500	.000

Pitcher	T	Age	G	GS	CG	ShO	IP	H	HR	BB	SO	W-L	Sv	ERA
Stan Coveleski	R	28	38	33	25	2	311.0	261	2	76	87	22-13	1	1.82
Jim Bagby	R	28	45	31	23	2	271.1	274	0	78	57	17-16	6	2.72
Guy Morton	R	25	30	28	13	1	214.2	189	1	77	123	14-8	0	2.64
Fritz Coumbe	L	28	30	17	9	0	150.0	164	4	52	41	13-7	3	3.00
Johnny Enzmann	R	28	30	14	8	0	136.2	130	2	29	38	5-7	2	2.37
Bob Groom	R	33	14	5	0	0	43.1	70	0	18	8	2-2	0	7.06
George McQuillan	R	33	5	1	0	0	23.0	25	0	4	7	0-1	1	2.35
Otis Lambeth	R	28	2	0	0	0	7.0	10	0	6	3	0-0	0	6.43
Ad Brennan†	L	36	1	0	0	0	3.0	3	0	3	0	0-0	0	3.00
Roy Wilkinson	R	24	1	0	0	0	1.0	0	0	0	0	0-0	0	0.00

1918 Washington Senators 3rd AL 72-56 .563 4.0 GB

Clark Griffith

Player	Gm by Position	B	Age	G	AB	R	H	2B	3B	HR	RBI	BB	SO	SB	Avg	OBP	Slg
Eddie Ainsmith	C89	R	26	96	292	22	62	10	9	0	20	29	44	6	.212	.283	.308
Joe Judge	1B130	L	24	130	502	56	131	23	7	1	46	49	32	20	.261	.332	.341
Ray Morgan	2B80,OF2	R	29	88	300	25	70	11	1	0	30	28	14	4	.233	.311	.277
Eddie Foster	3B127,2B2	R	31	129	519	70	147	13	3	0	29	41	20	12	.283	.339	.320
Doc Lavan	SS117,OF1	R	27	117	464	44	129	17	2	0	45	14	21	12	.278	.302	.323
Clyde Milan	OF124	L	31	128	503	56	146	18	5	0	56	36	14	26	.290	.344	.346
Burt Shotton	OF122	L	33	126	505	68	132	16	7	0	21	67	28	25	.261	.349	.321
Wildfire Schulte	OF75	L	35	93	267	35	77	14	3	0	44	47	36	5	.288	.406	.363
Howard Shanks	OF64,2B48,3B3	R	27	120	436	42	112	19	4	1	56	31	21	23	.257	.312	.326
Walter Johnson	P39,OF4	R	30	65	150	10	40	4	4	1	18	9	18	2	.267	.321	.367
Val Picinich	C46	R	21	47	148	13	34	3	3	0	12	9	25	0	.230	.274	.291
George McBride	SS14,2B2	R	37	18	53	2	7	0	0	0	1	0	11	1	.132	.132	.132
Sam Rice	OF6	L	28	7	23	3	8	1	0	0	3	2	0	1	.348	.400	.391
Joe Casey	C8	R	30	9	17	3	4	0	0	0	2	2	2	0	.235	.316	.235
Patsy Gharrity		R	26	4	4	0	1	1	0	0	2	0	1	0	.250	.250	.500
Merito Acosta†		L	22	3	2	0	0	0	0	0	0	0	1	0	.000	.000	.000
Bob Berman	C1	R	19	2	0	0	0	0	0	0	0	0	0	0	—	—	—

Pitcher	T	Age	G	GS	CG	ShO	IP	H	HR	BB	SO	W-L	Sv	ERA
Harry Harper	L	23	35	32	14	3	244.0	182	1	104	78	11-10	1	2.18
Jim Shaw	R	24	41	30	14	4	241.1	201	2	90	129	16-12	1	2.42
Walter Johnson	R	30	39	29	29	8	326.0	241	2	70	162	23-13	3	1.27
Doc Ayers	R	28	40	24	11	4	219.2	215	2	63	67	10-12	3	2.83
Nick Altrock	L	41	5	3	1	0	24.0	24	1	6	5	1-2	0	3.00
Ad Brennan†	L	36	2	1	0	0	5.1	7	0	5	0	0-0	0	5.06
Henry Matteson	R	33	14	6	2	0	67.2	57	2	15	17	5-3	0	1.73
Ed Hovlik	R	26	8	2	1	0	28.0	25	0	10	10	2-1	0	1.29
Earl Yingling	L	29	5	2	2	0	38.0	30	0	12	15	1-2	0	2.13
Roy Hansen	R	20	5	0	0	0	9.0	10	0	3	2	1-0	0	3.00
George Dumont	R	22	4	1	1	0	14.0	18	0	6	12	1-1	0	5.14
Molly Craft	R	22	3	0	0	0	7.0	5	0	1	5	0-0	0	1.29
Stan Rees	L	19	2	0	0	0	2.0	3	0	4	1	1-0	0	0.00
Garland Buckeye	L	20	1	0	0	0	2.0	3	0	6	2	0-0	0	18.00

1918 New York Yankees 4th AL 60-63 .488 13.5 GB

Miller Huggins

Player	Gm by Position	B	Age	G	AB	R	H	2B	3B	HR	RBI	BB	SO	SB	Avg	OBP	Slg
Truck Hannah	C88	R	29	90	250	24	55	6	0	2	21	51	25	5	.220	.361	.268
Wally Pipp	1B91	L	25	91	349	48	106	15	9	2	44	22	34	11	.304	.345	.415
Del Pratt	2B126	R	30	126	477	65	131	19	7	2	55	35	26	12	.275	.327	.356
Home Run Baker	3B126	L	32	126	504	65	154	24	5	6	62	38	13	8	.306	.357	.409
Roger Peckinpaugh	SS122	R	27	122	446	59	103	15	3	0	43	43	41	12	.231	.303	.278
Frank Gilhooley	OF111	L	26	112	427	59	118	13	5	1	23	53	24	7	.276	.358	.337
Ping Bodie	OF90	R	30	91	324	36	83	12	6	3	46	27	24	6	.256	.319	.358
Elmer Miller	OF62	R	27	67	202	18	49	9	2	1	22	19	17	2	.243	.317	.322
Roxy Walters	C50,OF9	R	25	64	191	18	38	5	1	0	12	9	18	3	.199	.239	.236
Ray Caldwell	P24,OF19	L	30	65	151	14	44	10	0	1	18	13	23	2	.291	.352	.377
Ham Hyatt	OF25,1B5	L	33	53	131	11	30	8	0	2	10	8	8	1	.229	.273	.336
Armando Marsans	OF36	R	30	37	123	13	29	5	1	0	9	5	3	3	.236	.266	.293
Bill Lamar	OF27	L	21	28	110	12	25	3	0	0	2	6	2	2	.227	.267	.255
Jack Fournier	1B27	L	28	27	100	9	35	6	1	0	12	7	7	7	.350	.393	.430
John Hummel	OF15,1B3,2B1	R	35	22	61	9	18	1	2	0	4	11	8	3	.295	.411	.377
Aaron Ward	SS12,OF4,2B3	R	21	20	32	2	4	1	0	0	1	2	7	1	.125	.176	.156
Hugh High	OF4	L	30	7	10	1	0	0	0	0	0	1	1	0	.000	.091	.000
Zinn Beck	1B5	R	32	11	8	0	0	0	0	0	1	0	1	0	.000	.000	.000
Muddy Ruel	C2	R	22	3	6	0	2	0	0	0	0	2	1	1	.333	.500	.333
Sammy Vick	OF1	R	23	2	3	1	2	0	0	0	1	0	0	0	.667	.667	.667
Paddy O'Connor	C1	R	38	1	3	0	1	0	0	0	0	0	1	0	.333	.333	.333
Chick Fewster	2B2	R	22	5	2	1	1	0	0	0	0	0	0	0	.500	.500	.500

Pitcher	T	Age	G	GS	CG	ShO	IP	H	HR	BB	SO	W-L	Sv	ERA
Slim Love	L	27	38	29	13	1	228.2	207	3	116	95	13-12	1	3.07
Ray Caldwell	R	30	24	21	14	1	176.2	173	2	62	59	9-8	1	3.06
Allan Russell	R	24	27	18	7	2	141.0	139	6	73	54	7-11	4	3.26
Happy Finneran†	R	26	23	13	4	0	114.1	134	7	35	34	3-6	0	3.78
Hank Thormahlen	L	21	16	12	5	2	112.2	85	1	52	22	7-3	0	2.48
Bob Shawkey	R	27	3	2	1	1	16.0	7	0	10	3	1-1	0	1.13
Bob McGraw	R	23	1	1	0	0	0.0	0	0	4	0	0-1	0	—
George Mogridge	L	29	45	19	13	1	239.1	232	6	43	62	16-13	7	2.18
Ray Keating	R	26	15	6	1	0	48.1	39	0	30	16	2-2	0	3.91
Hank Robinson	L	28	11	3	1	0	48.0	47	0	16	14	2-4	0	3.00
Roy Sanders	R	24	6	2	0	0	25.2	28	0	16	8	0-2	0	4.21
Dazzy Vance	R	27	2	0	0	0	2.1	9	0	2	0	0-0	0	15.43
Ed Monroe	R	23	1	0	0	0	2.0	1	0	2	1	0-0	0	4.50
Alex Ferguson	R	21	1	0	0	0	1.2	2	0	2	1	0-0	0	0.00
Walter Bernhardt	R	25	1	0	0	0	0.2	0	0	0	0	0-0	0	0.00

1918 St. Louis Browns 5th AL 58-64 .475 15.0 GB

Fielder Jones (22-24)/Jimmy Austin (7-9)/Jimmy Burke (29-31)

Player	Gm by Position	B	Age	G	AB	R	H	2B	3B	HR	RBI	BB	SO	SB	Avg	OBP	Slg
Les Nunamaker	C81,1B1,OF1	R	29	85	274	22	71	9	2	0	22	28	16	6	.259	.339	.307
George Sisler	1B114,P2	L	25	114	452	69	154	21	9	2	41	40	17	45	.341	.400	.440
Joe Gedeon	2B123	R	24	123	441	39	94	14	3	1	41	27	29	7	.213	.271	.265
Fritz Maisel	3B79,OF1	R	28	90	284	43	66	4	2	0	16	46	17	11	.232	.341	.261
Jimmy Austin	SS57,3B48	S	38	110	367	42	97	14	4	0	20	53	32	18	.264	.359	.324
Jack Tobin	OF122	L	26	122	480	59	133	19	5	0	36	48	26	13	.277	.349	.338
Ray Demmitt	OF114	L	34	116	405	45	114	23	5	1	61	38	35	10	.281	.346	.370
Earl Smith	OF81	S	27	89	286	28	77	10	5	0	32	13	16	13	.269	.303	.339
Tim Hendryx	OF65	R	27	88	219	22	61	14	3	0	33	37	35	5	.279	.388	.370
Wally Gerber	SS56	R	26	56	171	10	41	4	0	0	10	19	11	2	.240	.316	.263
Hank Severeid	C42	R	27	51	133	8	34	4	0	0	11	18	4	4	.256	.357	.286
Pete Johns	1B10,3B4,SS4*	R	29	46	89	5	16	1	1	0	11	4	6	0	.180	.215	.213
Ernie Johnson	SS11,3B1	L	30	29	34	7	9	1	0	0	0	0	2	4	.265	.286	.294
George Hale	C11	R	23	12	30	0	4	1	0	0	1	1	5	0	.133	.161	.167
Ken Williams		L	28	2	1	0	0	0	0	0	1	1	0	0	.000	.500	.000

P. Johns, 4 G at OF, 2 G at 2B

Pitcher	T	Age	G	GS	CG	ShO	IP	H	HR	BB	SO	W-L	Sv	ERA
Allen Sothoron	R	25	29	24	14	2	209.0	152	3	67	71	12-12	0	1.94
Dave Davenport	R	28	31	22	12	2	180.0	182	0	69	60	10-11	1	3.25
Bert Gallia	R	26	19	17	10	1	124.0	126	1	61	48	8-6	0	3.48
Tom Rogers	R	26	29	16	11	0	154.0	148	3	49	29	8-10	2	3.27
Rasty Wright	R	22	18	13	6	1	111.1	99	1	18	25	8-2	0	2.51
Grover Lowdermilk	R	33	13	11	4	0	80.0	74	1	38	25	2-6	0	3.15
Urban Shocker	R	27	14	9	7	0	94.2	69	0	40	33	6-5	2	1.81
Bugs Bennett	R	26	4	2	0	0	10.1	12	1	7	0	0-2	0	3.48
George Sisler	L	25	2	1	0	0	8.0	10	0	4	4	0-0	1	4.50
Byron Houck	R	26	27	2	0	0	71.2	58	0	29	29	2-4	2	2.39
Lefty Leifield	L	34	15	6	3	1	67.0	61	1	19	22	2-6	0	2.55
Tim McCabe	R	23	1	0	0	0	1.1	2	0	1	0	0-0	0	13.50

1918 Chicago White Sox 6th AL 57-67 .460 17.0 GB

Pants Rowland

Player	Gm by Position	B	Age	G	AB	R	H	2B	3B	HR	RBI	BB	SO	SB	Avg	OBP	Slg
Ray Schalk	C106	R	25	108	333	35	73	6	3	0	22	36	22	12	.219	.301	.255
Chick Gandil	1B114	R	31	114	439	49	119	18	4	0	55	27	19	9	.271	.319	.330
Eddie Collins	2B96	L	31	97	330	51	91	8	2	2	30	73	13	22	.276	.407	.330
Fred McMullin	3B69,2B1	R	26	70	235	32	65	7	0	1	16	25	26	7	.277	.356	.319
Buck Weaver	SS98,3B11,2B1	R	27	112	420	37	126	12	5	0	29	11	24	20	.300	.323	.352
Nemo Leibold	OF114	L	26	116	440	57	110	14	7	0	31	63	32	13	.250	.344	.314
Shano Collins	OF92,1B5,2B1	R	32	103	365	30	100	18	11	1	56	17	19	7	.274	.310	.392
Eddie Murphy	OF63,2B8	L	26	91	286	36	85	9	3	0	23	22	18	6	.297	.350	.350
Swede Risberg	SS30,3B24,2B12*	R	23	82	273	36	70	12	3	1	27	23	32	5	.256	.321	.333
Happy Felsch	OF53	R	26	53	206	16	52	2	5	1	20	15	13	6	.252	.306	.325
Wilbur Good	OF35	L	32	35	148	24	37	9	4	0	11	11	16	1	.250	.315	.365
Babe Pinelli	3B24	R	22	24	78	7	18	1	1	1	7	7	8	3	.231	.302	.308
Otto Jacobs	C21	R	29	29	73	4	15	3	1	0	3	5	8	0	.205	.256	.274
Joe Jackson	OF17	L	28	17	65	9	23	2	2	1	20	8	1	3	.354	.425	.492
Frank Shellenback	P28,OF1	R	19	29	54	4	7	1	0	0	1	8	25	0	.130	.242	.148
Reb Russell	P19,OF1	L	29	27	50	2	7	3	0	0	3	0	6	0	.140	.157	.200
Johnny Mostil	2B9	R	22	10	33	4	9	2	2	0	4	1	6	1	.273	.294	.455
Al DeVormer	C6,OF1	R	26	8	19	2	5	2	0	0	0	0	4	1	.263	.263	.368
Ted Jourdan	1B2	L	22	7	10	1	1	0	0	0	1	0	0	0	.100	.100	.100
Byrd Lynn	C4	R	29	5	8	0	2	0	0	0	0	2	1	0	.250	.400	.250
Pat Hardgrove		R	23	2	2	0	0	0	0	0	0	0	0	0	.000	.000	.000
Mellie Wolfgang	P4,3B1	R	28	5	2	1	1	0	0	0	2	0	0	0	.500	.500	.500
Kid Willson		L	22	4	1	2	0	0	0	0	0	1	1	0	.000	.500	.000
Ray Shook		R	28	1	0	0	0	0	0	0	0	0	0	0	—	—	—

S. Risberg, 7 G at 1B, 3 G at OF

Pitcher	T	Age	G	GS	CG	ShO	IP	H	HR	BB	SO	W-L	Sv	ERA
Eddie Cicotte	R	34	38	30	24	1	266.0	275	2	40	104	12-19	2	2.64
Frank Shellenback	R	19	28	20	10	2	182.2	180	1	74	47	9-12	2	2.66
Joe Benz	R	32	29	17	10	1	154.0	156	1	28	30	8-8	0	2.51
Reb Russell	L	29	19	14	10	2	124.2	117	0	33	38	7-5	0	2.60
Lefty Williams	L	25	15	14	7	2	105.2	76	0	47	30	6-4	1	2.73
Red Faber	R	29	11	9	5	1	80.2	70	3	23	26	4-1	0	1.23
Jack Quinn	R	34	6	5	5	0	51.0	38	0	7	22	5-1	0	2.29
Roy Mitchell†	R	33	2	2	0	0	12.0	18	1	4	3	0-1	0	7.50
Dave Danforth	L	28	39	13	5	0	139.0	148	1	40	48	6-15	2	3.43
Mellie Wolfgang	R	28	4	0	0	0	8.1	12	0	3	1	0-1	0	5.40
Ed Corey	R	18	1	0	0	0	2.0	2	0	1	0	0-0	0	4.50

1918 Detroit Tigers 7th AL 55-71 .437 20.0 GB

Hughie Jennings

Player	Gm by Position	B	Age	G	AB	R	H	2B	3B	HR	RBI	BB	SO	SB	Avg	OBP	Slg
Archie Yelle	C52	R	26	56	144	7	25	3	0	0	7	9	15	0	.174	.227	.194
Harry Heilmann	OF40,1B37,2B2	R	23	79	286	34	79	10	6	5	39	35	10	13	.276	.359	.406
Ralph Young	2B91	S	28	91	298	31	56	7	1	0	21	54	17	15	.188	.313	.218
Ossie Vitt	3B66,2B9,OF3	R	28	81	267	29	64	5	2	0	17	32	6	5	.240	.321	.273
Donie Bush	SS128	S	30	128	500	74	117	10	3	0	22	79	31	9	.234	.340	.266
Bobby Veach	OF127,P1	L	30	127	499	59	139	21	13	3	78	35	23	21	.279	.331	.391
Ty Cobb	OF95,1B13,P2*	L	31	111	421	83	161	19	14	3	64	41	21	34	.382	.440	.515
George Harper	OF64	L	26	69	227	19	55	5	2	0	16	18	14	3	.242	.301	.282
Bob Jones	3B63,1B6	L	28	74	287	43	79	14	4	0	21	17	16	7	.275	.320	.352
Oscar Stanage	C47,1B5	R	35	54	186	9	47	4	0	1	14	11	18	2	.253	.294	.290
Frank Walker	OF45	R	23	55	167	10	33	10	3	1	20	7	29	3	.198	.234	.311
Tubby Spencer	C48,1B1	R	34	66	155	11	34	8	1	0	8	19	18	1	.219	.313	.284
G. Cunningham	P27,OF20	R	23	56	112	11	25	4	1	0	2	16	34	2	.223	.320	.277
Lee Dressen	1B30	L	28	31	107	10	19	1	2	0	3	21	10	2	.178	.323	.224
Art Griggs	1B25	R	34	28	99	11	36	8	0	0	16	10	5	2	.364	.422	.444
Jack Coffey†	2B22	R	31	22	67	7	14	0	2	0	4	8	6	2	.209	.303	.269
Rudy Kallio	P30,OF1	R	25	31	56	5	9	0	0	0	3	6	23	0	.161	.242	.161
Marty Kavanagh†	1B12	R	27	13	44	2	12	3	0	0	9	11	6	0	.273	.418	.341
Deacon Jones	P21,OF2	R	25	23	27	1	5	0	0	0	3	1	12	1	.185	.214	.185
Babe Ellison	OF4,2B3	R	22	7	23	1	6	1	0	0	2	3	1	1	.261	.346	.304
Jim Curry	2B5	R	25	5	20	1	5	1	0	0	0	0	0	0	.250	.286	.300
Ben Dyer	P2,1B2,OF2*	R	25	13	18	1	5	0	0	0	2	0	6	0	.278	.278	.278
Joe Cobb		R	23	1	0	0	0	0	0	0	0	1	0	0	—	1.000	—
Hughie Jennings	1B1	R	49	1	0	0	0	0	0	0	0	0	0	0	—	—	—

T. Cobb, 1 G at 2B, 1 G at 3B; B. Dyer, 1 G at 2B

Pitcher	T	Age	G	GS	CG	ShO	IP	H	HR	BB	SO	W-L	Sv	ERA
Hooks Dauss	R	28	33	26	21	1	249.2	243	3	58	73	12-16	3	2.99
Bernie Boland	R	26	29	25	14	4	204.0	176	1	67	63	14-10	0	2.65
Rudy Kallio	R	25	30	22	10	2	181.1	178	0	76	70	8-14	0	3.62
Bill James	R	31	19	18	8	1	122.0	127	3	68	42	6-11	0	3.76
G. Cunningham	R	23	27	14	10	0	140.0	131	0	38	39	6-7	1	3.15
Eric Erickson	R	23	12	9	8	0	94.1	81	2	29	48	4-5	1	2.48
Bill Bailey	L	29	8	4	1	0	37.2	53	0	26	13	1-2	0	5.97
Wild Bill Donovan	R	41	2	1	0	0	6.0	5	0	1	1	1-0	0	1.50
Willie Mitchell	L	28	1	1	0	0	4.0	3	0	5	2	0-1	0	9.00
Deacon Jones	R	25	21	4	1	0	67.0	60	0	38	15	3-1	0	3.09
Sea Lion Hall	R	32	6	1	0	0	13.1	14	1	6	2	0-1	0	6.75
Happy Finneran†	R	26	5	2	0	0	13.2	22	0	8	2	0-2	1	9.88
Harry Coveleski	L	32	3	1	1	0	14.0	17	0	6	3	0-1	0	3.86
Herb Hall	R	25	3	0	0	0	6.0	12	0	7	1	0-0	0	15.00
Ty Cobb	R	31	2	0	0	0	4.0	6	0	2	0	0-0	0	4.50
Ben Dyer	R	25	2	0	0	0	1.2	0	0	0	0	0-0	0	0.00
Bobby Veach	R	30	1	0	0	0	2.0	2	0	2	0	0-0	1	4.50

1918 Philadelphia Athletics 8th AL 52-76 .406 24.0 GB — Connie Mack

Player	Gm by Position	B	Age	G	AB	R	H	2B	3B	HR	RBI	BB	SO	SB	Avg	OBP	Slg
Wickey McAvoy	C74,P1,1B1*	R	23	83	271	14	66	5	3	0	32	13	23	5	.244	.283	.284
George Burns	1B128,OF2	R	25	130	505	61	178	22	9	6	70	23	25	8	.352	.390	.467
Jimmy Dykes	2B56,3B1	R	21	59	186	13	35	3	3	0	13	19	32	3	.188	.267	.237
Larry Gardner	3B127	L	32	127	463	50	132	22	6	1	52	43	22	9	.285	.346	.365
Joe Dugan	SS86,2B34	R	21	121	411	26	80	11	3	3	34	16	55	4	.195	.230	.258
Tilly Walker	OF109	R	30	114	414	56	122	20	0	11	48	41	44	8	.295	.360	.423
Charlie Jamieson	OF102,P5	L	25	110	416	50	84	11	2	0	11	54	30	11	.202	.297	.238
Merlin Kopp	OF96	S	26	96	363	60	85	7	7	0	18	42	55	22	.234	.320	.292
Red Shannon	SS45,2B26	S	21	72	225	23	54	6	5	0	16	42	52	5	.240	.367	.311
Cy Perkins	C60	R	22	68	218	9	41	4	1	1	14	8	15	1	.188	.217	.229
Merito Acosta†	OF45	L	22	49	169	23	51	3	3	0	14	18	10	4	.302	.369	.355
Rube Oldring	OF30,2B2,3B2	R	34	49	133	5	31	2	1	0	11	8	10	0	.233	.282	.263
Claude Davidson	2B15,OF8,3B1	L	21	31	81	4	15	1	0	0	4	5	9	0	.185	.233	.198
Jake Munch	1B2,OF2	L	27	22	30	3	8	0	1	0	0	0	5	0	.267	.267	.333
Frank Fahey	OF5,P3	S	22	10	17	2	3	1	0	0	1	0	3	0	.176	.176	.235

W. McAvoy, 1 G at OF

Pitcher	T	Age	G	GS	CG	ShO	IP	H	HR	BB	SO	W-L	Sv	ERA
Scott Perry	R	27	44	36	30	3	332.1	295	1	111	81	20-19	1	1.98
Vean Gregg	L	33	30	25	17	3	199.1	180	4	67	63	9-14	2	3.12
Mule Watson	R	21	21	19	11	3	141.2	139	0	44	30	7-10	0	3.37
Elmer Myers	R	24	18	15	5	1	95.1	101	4	42	17	4-8	1	4.63
Roy Johnson	R	22	10	8	3	0	50.0	47	0	32	11	1-5	0	3.42
Tom Zachary	L	22	2	2	0	0	8.0	9	0	7	1	2-0	0	5.63
Vic Keen	R	19	1	1	0	0	8.0	9	1	1	1	0-1	0	3.38
Willie Adams	R	27	32	14	7	0	169.0	164	2	97	39	5-12	0	4.42
Bob Geary	R	27	16	7	6	2	87.0	94	0	31	22	2-5	4	2.69
Bill Pierson	L	19	8	1	0	0	21.2	20	0	20	6	0-1	0	3.32
Charlie Jamieson	L	25	5	2	1	0	23.0	24	0	13	2	2-1	0	4.30
Red Shea	R	19	3	0	0	0	9.0	14	0	2	2	0-0	0	4.00
Frank Fahey	R	22	3	0	0	0	9.0	5	0	14	1	0-0	0	6.00
Chuck Holmes	R	22	2	0	0	0	2.0	4	0	1	0	0-0	0	13.50
Wickey McAvoy	R	23	1	0	0	0	0.2	1	1	0	0	0-0	0	0.00
Lou Bauer	R	19	1	0	0	0	0.0	0	0	2	0	0-0	0	—

»1918 Chicago Cubs 1st NL 84-45 .651 — — Fred Mitchell

Player	Gm by Position	B	Age	G	AB	R	H	2B	3B	HR	RBI	BB	SO	SB	Avg	OBP	Slg
Bill Killefer	C104	R	30	104	331	30	77	10	3	0	22	17	10	5	.233	.276	.281
Fred Merkle	1B129	R	29	129	482	55	143	25	5	3	65	35	36	21	.297	.349	.388
Rollie Zeider	2B79,1B1,3B1	R	34	82	251	31	56	3	2	0	26	23	20	16	.223	.288	.251
Charlie Deal	3B118	R	26	119	414	43	99	9	3	2	34	21	13	11	.239	.279	.290
Charlie Hollocher	SS131	L	22	131	509	72	161	23	6	2	38	47	30	26	.316	.379	.397
Les Mann	OF129	R	24	129	489	69	141	27	7	2	55	38	45	21	.288	.342	.384
Max Flack	OF121	L	28	123	478	74	123	17	10	4	41	56	19	17	.257	.343	.360
Dode Paskert	OF121,3B6	R	36	127	461	69	132	24	4	2	59	53	49	20	.286	.362	.369
Turner Barber	OF27,1B4	L	24	55	123	11	29	3	2	0	10	9	16	3	.236	.293	.293
Bob O'Farrell	C45	R	21	52	113	9	32	7	3	1	14	10	15	0	.283	.347	.425
Pete Kilduff	2B30	R	25	30	93	7	19	2	2	0	13	7	7	1	.204	.267	.269
Charlie Pick	2B20,3B8	L	30	29	89	13	29	4	1	0	12	14	4	7	.326	.417	.393
Bill McCabe	2B13,OF4	S	25	29	45	9	8	0	1	0	5	4	7	2	.178	.245	.222
Chuck Wortman	2B8,3B4	R	26	17	17	4	2	0	0	1	3	1	2	3	.118	.167	.294
Rowdy Elliott	C5	R	27	5	10	0	0	0	0	0	0	2	1	0	.000	.167	.000
Fred Lear		R	24	2	1	0	0	0	0	0	0	1	0	0	.000	.500	.000
Tom Daly	C1	R	26	1	1	0	0	0	0	0	0	0	0	0	.000	.000	.000
Tommy Clarke	C1	R	30	1	0	0	0	0	0	0	0	0	0	0	—	—	—

Pitcher	T	Age	G	GS	CG	ShO	IP	H	HR	BB	SO	W-L	Sv	ERA
Hippo Vaughn	L	30	35	33	27	8	290.1	216	4	76	148	22-10	0	1.74
Lefty Tyler	L	28	33	30	22	8	269.1	218	1	67	102	19-8	1	2.00
Claude Hendrix	R	29	32	27	21	3	233.0	229	2	54	86	20-7	0	2.78
Phil Douglas	R	28	25	19	11	2	156.2	145	2	31	51	10-9	2	2.13
Roy Walker	R	25	13	7	2	0	43.1	50	1	15	20	1-3	1	2.70
Speed Martin	R	24	9	5	4	1	53.2	47	0	14	16	5-2	1	1.84
Pete Alexander	R	31	3	3	3	0	26.0	19	0	3	15	2-1	0	1.73
Paul Carter	R	24	21	4	1	0	73.0	78	2	19	13	3-2	2	2.71
Harry Weaver	R	26	8	3	1	1	32.2	27	1	7	9	2-2	1	2.20
Vic Aldridge	R	24	3	0	0	0	12.1	11	0	6	10	0-1	0	1.46
Buddy Napier	R	28	1	0	0	0	6.2	10	0	4	2	0-0	0	5.40

1918 New York Giants 2nd NL 71-53 .573 10.5 GB — John McGraw

Player	Gm by Position	B	Age	G	AB	R	H	2B	3B	HR	RBI	BB	SO	SB	Avg	OBP	Slg
Lew McCarty	C75	R	29	86	257	16	69	7	3	0	24	17	13	3	.268	.321	.319
Walter Holke	1B88	S	25	88	326	38	82	17	4	1	27	10	26	10	.252	.276	.337
Larry Doyle	2B73	L	31	75	257	38	67	7	4	3	36	37	10	10	.261	.354	.354
Heinie Zimmerman	3B100,1B19	R	31	121	463	43	126	19	10	1	56	13	23	14	.272	.294	.363
Art Fletcher	SS124	R	33	124	468	51	123	20	2	0	47	18	26	12	.263	.311	.314
Ross Youngs	OF120,2B7	L	21	121	474	70	143	16	8	1	25	44	49	10	.302	.368	.376
George Burns	OF119	R	28	119	465	80	135	22	6	4	51	43	37	40	.290	.354	.389
Benny Kauff	OF67	L	28	67	270	41	85	19	4	2	39	16	30	9	.315	.355	.437
Bill Rariden	C63	R	30	69	183	15	41	5	1	0	17	15	15	1	.224	.283	.262
Joe Wilhoit	OF55	L	32	64	135	13	37	3	3	0	15	17	14	4	.274	.355	.341
Ed Sicking	3B24,2B18,SS3	R	21	46	132	9	33	4	0	0	12	6	11	2	.250	.283	.280
Jose Rodriguez	2B42,1B8,3B2	R	24	50	125	15	20	0	2	0	15	12	3	6	.160	.239	.192
Jim Thorpe	OF44	R	31	58	113	15	28	4	4	1	11	4	18	3	.248	.286	.381
Pete Compton	OF19	L	28	21	60	5	13	0	1	0	5	5	4	2	.217	.277	.250
Jay Kirke	1B16	L	30	17	56	1	14	1	0	0	3	1	3	0	.250	.263	.268
Bert Niehoff†	2B7	R	34	7	23	3	6	0	0	0	1	0	4	0	.261	.261	.261
George Gibson	C4	R	37	4	2	0	1	1	0	0	0	0	0	0	.500	.500	1.000

Pitcher	T	Age	G	GS	CG	ShO	IP	H	HR	BB	SO	W-L	Sv	ERA
Pol Perritt	R	25	35	31	19	6	233.0	212	5	38	60	18-13	0	2.74
Red Causey	R	24	29	18	10	2	158.1	143	2	42	48	11-6	2	2.79
Slim Sallee	L	33	18	16	12	1	132.0	122	3	12	33	8-8	2	2.25
Al Demaree	R	33	26	14	8	2	142.0	143	5	25	39	8-6	1	2.47
Fred Toney†	R	29	11	9	7	1	85.1	55	1	7	19	6-2	1	1.69
Jeff Tesreau	R	29	12	9	3	1	73.2	61	1	21	31	4-4	0	2.32
Jesse Barnes	R	25	9	9	4	2	54.2	53	0	13	12	6-1	0	1.81
Bob Steele†	L	24	12	7	5	1	66.0	56	1	11	24	3-5	1	2.59
Rube Benton	L	31	3	3	2	0	24.0	17	0	3	9	1-2	0	1.88
Fred Anderson	R	32	18	4	2	1	70.2	62	1	17	24	4-2	3	2.67
Ferdie Schupp	L	27	10	2	1	0	33.1	42	1	27	22	0-1	0	7.56
George Smith†	R	26	5	2	1	0	26.2	26	0	6	4	2-3	0	4.05
Jack Ogden	R	20	5	0	0	0	8.2	8	0	3	1	0-0	0	3.12
George Ross	L	26	1	0	0	0	2.1	2	0	3	2	0-0	1	0.00
Waite Hoyt	R	18	1	0	0	0	1.0	0	0	0	2	0-0	0	0.00

1918 Cincinnati Reds 3rd NL 68-60 .531 15.5 GB — Christy Mathewson (61-57)/Heine Groh (7-3)

Player	Gm by Position	B	Age	G	AB	R	H	2B	3B	HR	RBI	BB	SO	SB	Avg	OBP	Slg
Ivy Wingo	C93,OF5	L	27	100	323	36	82	15	6	0	31	19	18	6	.254	.297	.337
Hal Chase	1B67,OF1	R	35	74	259	30	78	12	6	2	38	13	15	5	.301	.339	.417
Lee Magee	2B114,3B3	S	29	119	459	62	133	22	13	0	28	28	19	19	.290	.331	.394
Heine Groh	3B126	R	28	126	493	88	158	28	3	1	37	54	24	11	.320	.395	.396
Lena Blackburne	SS125	R	31	125	435	35	99	8	10	1	45	25	30	6	.228	.271	.299
Tommy Griffith	OF118	L	28	118	427	47	113	10	4	2	48	39	30	10	.265	.326	.321
Edd Roush	OF113	L	25	113	435	61	145	18	10	5	62	22	10	24	.333	.368	.455
Greasy Neale	OF102	L	26	107	371	59	100	11	11	1	32	24	38	23	.270	.324	.367
Sherry Magee	1B66,OF38,2B6	R	33	115	400	46	129	15	13	2	76	37	18	14	.298	.370	.415
Manuel Cueto	OF20,2B9,SS9*	R	26	47	108	14	32	5	1	0	14	19	5	4	.296	.406	.361
Nick Allen	C31	R	29	37	96	6	25	2	2	0	5	4	7	0	.260	.297	.323
Harry Smith	C6,OF1	R	28	13	27	4	5	1	2	0	4	3	6	1	.185	.267	.370
Jimmy Archer†	C7,1B1	R	35	9	26	3	7	1	0	0	2	1	3	0	.269	.296	.308

M. Cueto, 6 G at C

Pitcher	T	Age	G	GS	CG	ShO	IP	H	HR	BB	SO	W-L	Sv	ERA
Pete Schneider	R	22	33	30	17	2	217.0	213	2	117	51	10-15	0	3.53
Hod Eller	R	23	37	22	14	0	217.2	205	1	59	84	16-12	1	2.36
Fred Toney†	R	29	21	19	9	1	136.2	148	2	31	32	6-10	2	2.90
Jimmy Ring	R	23	21	18	13	4	142.1	130	5	48	26	9-5	0	2.85
Rube Bressler	L	23	17	13	10	0	128.0	124	3	39	37	8-5	0	2.46
Dolf Luque	R	27	12	10	9	1	83.0	84	1	32	26	6-3	0	3.80
George Smith†	R	26	10	6	4	1	55.1	71	3	11	19	2-3	0	4.07
Roy Mitchell†	R	33	5	3	3	2	36.1	27	0	5	9	4-0	0	0.74
Dutch Ruether	L	24	2	2	1	0	10.0	10	0	3	10	0-1	0	2.70
Mike Regan	R	30	22	6	4	3	80.0	77	0	29	15	5-5	2	3.26
Larry Jacobus	R	24	5	0	0	0	17.1	25	0	1	8	0-1	0	5.71
Snipe Conley	R	24	5	0	0	0	13.2	17	2	5	2	2-0	1	5.27
Jesse Haines	R	24	1	0	0	0	5.0	5	0	1	2	0-0	1	1.80

1918 Pittsburgh Pirates 4th NL 65-60 .520 17.0 GB — Hugo Bezdek

Player	Gm by Position	B	Age	G	AB	R	H	2B	3B	HR	RBI	BB	SO	SB	Avg	OBP	Slg
Walter Schmidt	C104	R	31	105	323	31	77	6	3	0	27	17	19	7	.238	.281	.276
Fritz Mollwitz	1B119	R	28	119	432	43	116	12	7	0	45	23	24	23	.269	.305	.329
George Cutshaw	2B126	R	30	126	463	56	132	16	10	5	68	27	18	25	.285	.326	.395
Bill McKechnie	3B126	S	31	126	435	34	111	13	9	2	43	24	22	12	.255	.297	.340
Howdy Caton	SS79	R	21	80	303	37	71	5	7	0	17	32	16	12	.234	.312	.297
Max Carey	OF126	S	28	126	468	70	128	14	6	3	48	62	25	58	.274	.363	.348
Carson Bigbee	OF92	L	23	92	310	47	79	11	3	1	19	42	10	19	.255	.344	.319
Billy Southworth	OF64	L	25	64	246	37	84	5	7	2	43	26	9	19	.341	.409	.443
Casey Stengel	OF37	L	27	39	122	18	30	4	1	1	12	16	14	11	.246	.343	.320
Lee King	OF36	R	25	36	112	9	26	3	2	1	11	11	15	3	.232	.301	.321
Bill Hinchman	OF40,1B3	R	35	50	111	10	26	5	2	0	13	15	8	1	.234	.336	.315
Luke Boone	SS26,2B1	R	28	27	91	7	18	3	0	0	3	8	6	1	.198	.263	.231
Roy Ellam	SS26	R	32	26	77	9	10	1	1	0	2	17	17	2	.130	.302	.169
Tommy Leach	OF23,SS3	R	40	30	72	14	14	2	3	0	5	19	5	2	.194	.363	.306
Jimmy Archer†	C21,1B1	R	35	24	58	4	9	1	2	0	3	1	6	0	.155	.197	.241
Ben Shaw	1B9,C5	R	25	21	36	5	7	1	0	0	2	2	2	0	.194	.275	.222
Red Smith	C10	R	26	15	24	1	4	1	0	0	3	3	0	0	.167	.259	.208
Fred Blackwell	C8	L	26	8	13	1	2	0	0	0	4	3	4	0	.154	.313	.154
Gus Getz†	3B2	R	28	7	10	0	2	0	0	0	0	0	1	0	.200	.200	.200
Jake Pitler	2B1	R	24	2	1	1	0	0	0	0	0	1	0	2	.000	.500	.000

Pitcher	T	Age	G	GS	CG	ShO	IP	H	HR	BB	SO	W-L	Sv	ERA
Wilbur Cooper	L	26	38	29	26	3	273.1	219	2	65	117	19-14	3	2.11
Frank Miller	R	32	23	23	14	2	170.1	152	1	37	47	11-8	0	2.38
Roy Sanders	R	25	28	14	6	1	156.0	135	1	52	55	7-9	1	2.60
Erskine Mayer†	R	29	15	14	11	1	123.1	122	1	27	25	9-3	0	2.26
Bob Harmon	R	30	16	9	5	0	82.1	76	3	12	7	2-7	0	2.62
Ralph Comstock	R	27	15	8	6	0	81.0	78	0	14	44	5-6	1	3.00
Earl Hamilton	L	26	6	6	6	1	54.0	47	0	13	20	6-0	0	0.83
Cy Slapnicka	R	32	7	6	4	0	49.1	50	2	22	3	1-4	1	4.74
Carmen Hill	R	22	6	4	3	0	43.2	24	0	17	15	2-3	0	1.24
Elmer Jacobs†	R	25	8	4	0	0	23.1	31	0	14	2	0-1	0	5.79
Babe Adams	R	36	3	3	2	0	22.2	15	0	4	6	1-1	0	1.19
Hal Carlson	R	26	3	2	0	0	12.0	12	1	5	5	0-1	0	3.75
Bob Steele†	L	24	10	4	2	1	49.0	44	2	17	21	2-3	1	3.31

1918 Brooklyn Dodgers 5th NL 57-69 .452 25.5 GB

Wilbert Robinson

Player	Gm by Position	B	Age	G	AB	R	H	2B	3B	HR	RBI	BB	SO	SB	Avg	OBP	Slg
Otto Miller	C62,1B1	R	29	75	228	8	44	6	1	0	8	9	20	1	.193	.230	.228
Jake Daubert	1B105	L	34	108	396	50	122	12	15	2	47	27	18	10	.308	.360	.429
Mickey Doolan	2B91	R	38	92	308	14	55	8	2	0	18	22	24	8	.179	.233	.218
Ollie O'Mara	3B121	R	27	121	450	29	96	8	1	1	24	7	18	11	.213	.242	.242
Ivy Olson	SS126	R	32	126	506	63	121	16	4	1	17	27	18	21	.239	.286	.292
Hi Myers	OF107	R	29	107	407	36	104	9	8	4	40	20	26	17	.256	.292	.346
Zack Wheat	OF105	L	30	105	409	39	137	15	3	0	51	16	17	9	.335	.369	.386
Jimmy Johnston	OF96,1B21,3B4*	R	28	123	484	54	136	16	8	0	27	33	31	22	.281	.328	.347
Jim Hickman	OF46	R	26	53	167	14	39	4	7	1	16	8	31	5	.234	.281	.359
Mack Wheat	C38,OF7	R	25	57	157	11	34	7	1	1	3	8	24	2	.217	.255	.293
Ray Schmandt	2B34	R	22	34	114	11	35	5	4	0	18	7	7	1	.307	.347	.421
Jack Coombs	P27,OF13	S	35	46	113	6	19	3	2	0	3	7	5	1	.168	.223	.230
Ernie Krueger	C23	R	27	30	87	4	25	4	2	0	7	4	9	2	.287	.319	.379
Larry Cheney	P32,1B1	R	32	33	66	7	16	2	1	0	5	3	16	0	.242	.275	.303
Clarence Mitchell	OF9,P1	L	27	10	24	2	6	1	1	0	2	0	3	0	.250	.250	.375
Jimmy Archer†	C7	R	35	9	22	3	6	0	1	0	0	1	5	0	.273	.304	.364
Frank O'Rourke	2B2,OF1	R	23	4	12	0	2	0	0	0	2	1	3	0	.167	.231	.167
Al Nixon	OF4	R	32	6	11	1	5	0	0	0	0	0	0	0	.455	.455	.455
Chuck Ward	3B2	R	23	2	6	0	2	0	0	0	3	0	0	0	.333	.333	.333
Al Bashang	OF1	S	29	2	5	0	1	0	0	0	0	0	0	0	.200	.200	.200
Red Sheridan	2B2	R	21	2	4	0	1	0	0	0	0	1	0	1	.250	.400	.250

J. Johnston, 1 G at 2B

Pitcher	T	Age	G	GS	CG	ShO	IP	H	HR	BB	SO	W-L	Sv	ERA
Rube Marquard	L	31	34	29	19	4	239.0	231	7	59	89	9-18	0	2.64
Burleigh Grimes	R	24	40	28	19	7	269.2	210	3	76	113	19-9	1	2.14
Jack Coombs	R	35	27	22	16	2	189.0	191	10	49	44	8-14	0	3.81
Larry Cheney	R	32	32	21	15	0	200.2	177	2	74	83	11-13	1	3.00
Dick Robertson	R	27	13	9	7	1	87.0	87	0	28	18	3-6	0	2.59
Dan Griner	R	30	11	6	3	1	54.1	47	0	15	22	1-5	0	2.15
George Smith†	R	26	8	5	4	0	50.0	43	0	5	18	4-1	0	2.34
Leon Cadore	R	27	2	2	1	1	17.0	6	0	2	5	1-0	0	0.53
Jeff Pfeffer	R	30	1	1	1	1	9.0	2	0	3	1	1-0	0	0.00
Al Mamaux	R	24	2	1	0	0	8.0	14	0	2	2	0-1	0	6.75
Harry Heitmann	R	21	1	1	0	0	0.1	4	0	0	0	0-1	0	108.00
Clarence Mitchell	L	27	1	1	0	0	0.1	4	0	0	0	0-1	0	108.00
Norman Plitt	R	25	1	0	0	0	2.0	3	0	1	0	0-0	0	4.50
Rich Durning	L	25	1	0	0	0	2.0	3	0	4	0	0-0	0	13.50
Marty Herrmann	L	25	1	0	0	0	1.0	0	0	1	0	0-0	0	0.00
Jake Hehl	R	18	1	0	0	0	1.0	0	0	0	0	0-0	0	0.00
John Russell	L	22	1	0	0	0	1.0	2	0	1	0	0-0	0	18.00

1918 Philadelphia Phillies 6th NL 55-68 .447 26.0 GB

Pat Moran

Player	Gm by Position	B	Age	G	AB	R	H	2B	3B	HR	RBI	BB	SO	SB	Avg	OBP	Slg
Bert Adams	C76	S	27	84	227	10	40	4	0	0	12	10	26	5	.176	.214	.194
Fred Luderus	1B125	L	32	125	468	54	135	23	2	5	67	42	33	4	.288	.351	.378
Patsy McGaffigan	2B53,SS1	R	29	54	192	17	39	3	2	1	8	16	23	3	.203	.268	.255
Milt Stock	3B123	R	24	123	481	62	132	14	1	1	42	35	22	20	.274	.325	.314
Dave Bancroft	SS125	S	27	125	499	69	132	19	4	0	26	54	36	11	.265	.338	.319
Irish Meusel	OF120,2B4	R	25	124	473	48	132	25	6	4	62	30	21	18	.279	.323	.383
Gavy Cravath	OF118	R	37	121	426	43	99	27	5	8	54	54	46	7	.232	.320	.376
Cy Williams	OF91	L	30	94	351	49	97	14	1	6	39	27	30	10	.276	.337	.373
Ed Burns	C68	R	29	68	184	10	38	1	1	0	9	20	9	1	.207	.288	.223
Harry Pearce	2B46,SS2,1B1*	R	28	60	164	16	40	3	2	0	18	9	31	5	.244	.295	.287
Mike Fitzgerald	OF59	L	28	66	133	21	39	8	0	0	6	13	6	3	.293	.361	.353
Ed Hemingway	2B27,3B3,1B1	S	25	33	108	7	23	4	1	0	12	7	9	4	.213	.267	.269
Possum Whitted	OF22,1B1	R	28	24	86	7	21	4	0	0	3	4	10	4	.244	.278	.291
Pickles Dillhoefer	C6	R	23	8	11	0	1	0	0	0	0	1	1	2	.091	.167	.091
Mickey Devine	C3	R	26	4	8	0	1	1	0	0	0	0	1	0	.125	.125	.250
Ty Pickup	OF1	R	20	1	1	0	1	0	0	0	0	0	0	0	1.000	1.000	1.000

H. Pearce, 1 G at 3B

Pitcher	T	Age	G	GS	CG	ShO	IP	H	HR	BB	SO	W-L	Sv	ERA
Mike Prendergast	R	29	33	30	20	0	252.1	257	6	46	41	13-14	1	2.89
Brad Hogg	R	30	29	25	17	3	228.0	201	3	61	81	13-13	1	2.53
Joe Oeschger	R	27	30	23	13	2	184.0	159	3	83	60	6-18	3	3.03
Elmer Jacobs†	R	25	18	14	12	4	123.0	91	3	42	33	9-5	1	2.41
Erskine Mayer†	R	29	13	13	7	0	104.0	108	2	26	16	7-4	0	3.12
Alex Main	R	34	8	4	1	1	35.0	30	1	16	14	2-2	0	4.63
Milt Watson	R	28	23	11	6	0	112.2	126	1	36	29	5-7	0	3.43
Dixie Davis	R	27	17	2	1	0	47.0	43	1	30	18	0-2	0	3.06
Ben Tincup	R	27	8	1	0	0	16.2	24	0	6	6	0-1	0	7.56
Gary Fortune	R	23	5	2	1	0	30.2	41	2	19	10	0-2	0	8.22
Frank Woodward	R	24	2	0	0	0	6.0	6	0	4	4	0-0	0	6.00

1918 Boston Braves 7th NL 53-71 .427 28.5 GB

George Stallings

Player	Gm by Position	B	Age	G	AB	R	H	2B	3B	HR	RBI	BB	SO	SB	Avg	OBP	Slg
Art Wilson	C85	R	32	89	280	15	69	8	2	0	19	24	31	5	.246	.310	.289
Ed Konetchy	1B112,OF6,P1	R	32	119	437	33	103	15	5	2	56	32	35	5	.236	.291	.307
Buck Herzog	2B99,1B12,SS7	R	32	118	473	57	108	12	6	0	26	29	28	10	.228	.280	.279
Red Smith	3B119	R	28	119	429	55	128	20	3	2	65	45	47	8	.298	.373	.373
Johnny Rawlings	SS71,2B20,OF18	R	25	111	410	32	85	7	3	0	21	30	31	10	.207	.265	.239
Al Wickland	OF95	L	30	95	332	55	87	7	13	4	32	53	39	12	.262	.367	.398
Ray Powell	OF53	L	29	53	188	31	40	7	5	0	20	29	30	2	.213	.321	.303
Red Massey	OF45,1B1,3B1*	L	27	66	203	20	59	6	2	0	18	23	20	1	.291	.363	.340
Joe Kelly	OF45	R	31	47	155	20	36	2	4	0	15	6	12	12	.232	.265	.297
Jim Kelly	OF35	L	34	35	146	19	48	1	4	0	4	9	9	4	.329	.376	.390
Wally Rehg	OF38	R	29	40	133	6	32	5	1	1	12	5	14	3	.241	.268	.316
Zeb Terry	SS27	R	27	28	105	17	32	2	2	0	8	8	14	1	.305	.360	.362
Chet Chadbourne	OF27	L	33	27	104	9	27	2	1	0	6	5	5	5	.260	.300	.298
Jimmy Smith	2B10,SS9,OF6*	S	23	34	102	8	23	3	4	1	14	3	13	1	.225	.255	.363
John Henry	C38	R	28	43	102	6	21	2	0	0	4	10	15	0	.206	.283	.225
Bill Wagner	C13	R	24	13	47	2	10	0	0	1	7	4	5	0	.213	.275	.277
Rabbit Maranville	SS11	R	26	11	38	3	12	0	1	0	3	4	0	0	.316	.381	.368
Buzz Murphy	OF9	L	23	9	32	6	12	2	3	1	9	3	5	0	.375	.429	.719
Doc Crandall	P5,OF3	R	30	14	28	1	8	0	0	0	2	4	3	1	.286	.375	.286
Rip Conway	2B5,3B1	L	22	14	24	4	4	0	0	0	2	2	4	1	.167	.231	.167
Fred Bailey		L	22	4	4	1	1	0	0	0	0	0	1	0	.250	.250	.250
Sam Covington		L	25	3	3	0	1	0	0	0	0	0	0	0	.333	.333	.333
Tom Miller		L	20	2	2	0	0	0	0	0	0	0	0	1	.000	.000	.000
Doc Bass		—	18	2	1	1	1	0	0	0	0	0	0	1	1.000	1.000	1.000
Walt Tragesser	C7	R	31	7	1	0	0	0	0	0	0	0	0	0	.000	.000	.000

R. Massey, 1 G at SS; J. Smith, 5 G at 3B

Pitcher	T	Age	G	GS	CG	ShO	IP	H	HR	BB	SO	W-L	Sv	ERA
Art Nehf	L	25	32	31	28	2	284.1	274	2	76	96	15-15	0	2.69
Pat Ragan	R	29	30	25	15	2	206.1	212	4	54	68	8-17	0	3.23
Dick Rudolph	R	30	21	20	15	3	154.0	144	2	30	48	9-10	0	2.57
Dana Fillingim	R	24	14	13	10	4	113.0	99	0	28	29	7-6	0	2.23
Bunny Hearn	L	27	17	12	9	1	126.1	119	2	29	30	5-6	0	2.49
Lefty George	L	31	9	5	4	0	54.1	56	0	21	22	1-5	0	2.32
Jake Northrop	R	30	7	4	4	1	40.0	26	0	3	4	5-1	0	1.35
Doc Crandall	R	30	5	3	3	0	34.0	39	1	4	4	1-2	0	2.38
Tom Hughes	R	34	3	3	1	0	18.1	17	0	6	9	0-2	0	3.44
Bill Upham	R	30	3	2	2	0	20.2	28	2	1	8	1-1	0	5.23
Hugh McQuillan	R	20	1	1	1	0	9.0	7	0	5	1	1-0	0	3.00
Ed Konetchy	R	32	1	1	1	0	8.0	14	0	2	3	0-1	0	6.75
Cal Crum	R	27	1	1	0	0	2.1	6	0	3	0	0-1	0	15.43
Hugh Canavan	L	21	11	3	3	0	46.2	70	0	15	18	0-4	0	6.36

1918 St. Louis Cardinals 8th NL 51-78 .395 33.0 GB

Jack Hendricks

Player	Gm by Position	B	Age	G	AB	R	H	2B	3B	HR	RBI	BB	SO	SB	Avg	OBP	Slg
Mike Gonzalez	C100,OF5,1B2	R	27	117	349	33	88	13	4	3	20	39	30	14	.252	.327	.338
Gene Paulette	1B97,SS12,2B7*	R	27	125	461	33	126	15	3	0	52	27	16	11	.273	.316	.319
Tom Fisher	2B63	R	31	63	246	36	78	11	3	2	20	15	11	7	.317	.356	.411
Doug Baird	3B81,SS1,OF1	R	26	82	316	41	78	12	8	2	25	25	42	25	.247	.304	.354
Rogers Hornsby	SS109,OF2	R	22	115	416	51	117	19	11	5	60	40	43	8	.281	.349	.416
Cliff Heathcote	OF88	L	20	88	348	37	90	12	3	4	32	20	40	12	.259	.301	.345
Austin McHenry	OF80	R	22	80	272	32	71	12	6	1	29	21	24	8	.261	.319	.360
Walton Cruise	OF65	L	28	70	240	34	65	5	4	6	39	30	26	2	.271	.359	.400
Bruno Betzel	3B34,OF21,2B10	R	23	76	230	18	51	6	7	0	13	12	16	8	.222	.260	.309
Jack Smith	OF42	L	23	42	166	24	35	2	7	0	4	7	21	5	.211	.260	.235
Charlie Grimm	1B42,OF2,3B1	L	19	50	141	11	31	7	0	0	12	6	15	2	.220	.262	.270
George Anderson	OF35	L	28	35	132	20	39	4	5	0	6	15	7	0	.295	.380	.402
Red Smyth	OF25,2B11	L	25	40	113	19	24	1	2	0	4	16	11	3	.212	.315	.257
Frank Snyder	C27,1B3	R	25	39	112	5	28	7	1	0	10	6	13	4	.250	.288	.330
Bobby Wallace	2B17,SS12,3B1	R	44	32	98	3	15	1	0	0	4	6	9	1	.153	.202	.163
Bert Niehoff†	2B22	R	34	22	84	5	15	2	0	0	5	3	10	2	.179	.207	.202
Gene Packard	P30,1B1	L	30	36	69	3	12	2	1	0	6	2	9	0	.174	.197	.232
Herman Bronkie	3B18	R	33	18	68	7	15	3	0	1	7	2	4	0	.221	.243	.309
John Brock	C18,OF1	R	21	27	52	9	11	2	0	0	4	3	10	5	.212	.255	.250
Johnny Beall	OF18	L	36	19	49	2	11	1	0	0	6	3	6	0	.224	.269	.245
Marty Kavanagh†	OF8,2B4	R	27	12	44	6	8	1	0	1	8	3	1	1	.182	.234	.273
Dutch Distel	2B5,SS2,OF1	R	22	8	17	3	3	1	1	0	1	2	3	0	.176	.263	.353
Wally Mattick	OF3	R	31	8	14	0	2	0	0	0	1	2	3	0	.143	.333	.143
Bob Larmore	SS2	R	21	4	7	0	2	0	0	0	1	0	2	0	.286	.286	.286
Dick Wheeler	OF2	R	20	3	6	0	0	0	0	0	0	0	3	0	.000	.000	.000
Tony Brottem	1B2	R	26	2	4	0	0	0	0	0	0	1	0	0	.000	.200	.000
Ted Menze	OF1	R	20	1	3	0	0	0	0	0	0	0	2	0	.000	.000	.000

G. Paulette, 6 G at OF, 2 G at 3B, 1 G at P

Pitcher	T	Age	G	GS	CG	ShO	IP	H	HR	BB	SO	W-L	Sv	ERA
Red Ames	R	35	27	25	17	0	206.2	192	1	52	68	9-14	1	2.31
Bill Doak	R	27	31	23	16	1	211.0	191	3	60	74	9-15	1	2.43
Gene Packard	L	30	30	23	10	1	182.1	184	6	33	46	12-12	2	3.50
Lee Meadows	R	23	30	21	12	0	165.1	176	1	56	49	8-14	1	3.59
Jakie May	L	22	29	16	6	0	152.2	149	2	69	61	5-6	0	3.83
Bill Sherdel	L	21	35	17	9	1	182.1	174	3	49	40	6-12	0	2.71
Oscar Tuero	R	19	11	3	2	0	44.1	32	0	10	13	1-2	0	1.02
Oscar Horstmann	R	27	9	2	0	0	23.0	29	0	14	6	0-2	0	5.48
Rankin Johnson	R	30	6	1	0	0	23.0	20	0	7	4	1-1	0	2.74
Earl Howard	R	22	1	0	0	0	2.0	0	0	2	0	0-0	0	0.00
Gene Paulette	R	27	1	0	0	0	0.1	1	0	0	0	0-0	0	0.00

»1919 Chicago White Sox 1st AL 88-52 .629 —

Kid Gleason

Player	Gm by Position	B	Age	G	AB	R	H	2B	3B	HR	RBI	BB	SO	SB	Avg	OBP	Slg
Ray Schalk	C129	R	26	131	394	57	111	9	3	0	34	51	25	11	.282	.367	.320
Chick Gandil	1B115	R	32	115	441	54	128	24	7	1	60	20	20	10	.290	.325	.383
Eddie Collins	2B140	L	32	140	518	87	165	19	7	4	80	68	27	33	.319	.400	.405
Buck Weaver	3B97,SS43	R	28	140	571	89	169	33	9	3	75	11	21	22	.296	.315	.401
Swede Risberg	SS97,1B22	R	24	119	414	48	106	19	6	2	38	35	38	19	.256	.317	.345
Joe Jackson	OF139	L	29	139	516	79	181	31	14	7	96	60	10	9	.351	.422	.506
Happy Felsch	OF135	R	27	135	502	68	138	34	11	7	86	40	35	19	.275	.336	.428
Nemo Leibold	OF122	L	27	122	434	81	131	18	2	0	26	72	30	17	.302	.404	.353
Shano Collins	OF46,1B8	R	33	63	179	21	50	6	3	1	16	7	11	3	.279	.317	.363
Fred McMullin	3B46,2B5	R	27	60	170	31	50	8	4	0	19	11	18	4	.294	.355	.388
Byrd Lynn	C28	R	30	29	66	4	15	4	0	0	4	4	9	0	.227	.271	.288
Eddie Murphy	OF6	L	27	30	35	8	17	4	0	0	5	7	0	0	.486	.571	.600
Joe Jenkins	C4	R	28	11	19	0	3	1	0	0	1	1	1	0	.158	.200	.211
Harvey McClellan	3B3,SS2	R	24	7	12	2	4	0	0	0	1	1	1	0	.333	.385	.333

Pitcher	T	Age	G	GS	CG	ShO	IP	H	HR	BB	SO	W-L	Sv	ERA
Lefty Williams	L	26	41	40	27	5	297.0	265	7	58	125	23-11	1	2.64
Eddie Cicotte	R	35	40	35	30	5	306.2	256	5	49	110	29-7	1	1.82
Red Faber	R	30	25	20	9	0	162.1	185	7	45	45	11-9	0	3.83
Grover Lowdermilk†	R	34	20	11	5	0	96.2	95	0	43	43	5-5	0	2.79
Bill James†	R	32	5	5	3	2	39.1	39	0	14	11	3-2	0	2.52
Frank Shellenback	R	20	8	4	2	0	35.0	40	1	16	10	1-3	0	5.14
John Sullivan	L	25	4	2	1	0	15.0	24	0	8	9	0-1	0	4.20
Wynn Noyes†	R	30	1	1	0	0	6.0	10	0	0	4	0-0	0	7.50
Charlie Robertson	R	23	1	1	0	0	2.0	5	0	0	1	0-1	0	9.00
Dickie Kerr	L	25	39	17	10	1	212.1	208	2	64	79	13-7	0	2.88
Dave Danforth	L	29	15	1	0	0	41.2	58	1	20	17	1-2	1	7.78
Erskine Mayer†	R	30	6	2	0	0	23.2	30	1	11	9	1-3	0	8.37
Roy Wilkinson	R	25	4	1	1	1	22.0	21	0	10	5	1-1	0	2.05
Tom McGuire	R	27	1	0	0	0	3.0	5	0	3	0	0-0	0	9.00
Joe Benz	R	33	1	0	0	0	2.0	2	0	0	0	0-0	0	4.50
Pat Ragan†	R	30	1	0	0	0	1.0	1	0	0	0	0-0	0	0.00
Reb Russell	L	30	1	0	0	0	0.0	1	0	1	0	0-0	0	—

1919 Cleveland Indians 2nd AL 84-55 .604 3.5 GB

Lee Fohl (44-34)/Tris Speaker (40-21)

Player	Gm by Position	B	Age	G	AB	R	H	2B	3B	HR	RBI	BB	SO	SB	Avg	OBP	Slg
Steve O'Neill	C123	R	27	125	398	46	115	35	7	2	47	48	21	4	.289	.373	.427
Doc Johnston	1B98	L	31	102	331	42	101	17	3	1	33	25	18	21	.305	.359	.384
Bill Wambsganss	2B139	R	25	139	526	60	146	17	6	2	60	32	24	18	.278	.323	.344
Larry Gardner	3B139	L	33	139	524	67	157	29	7	2	79	39	29	7	.300	.352	.393
Ray Chapman	SS115	R	28	115	433	75	130	23	10	3	53	31	38	18	.300	.351	.420
Tris Speaker	OF134	L	31	134	494	83	146	38	12	2	63	73	12	15	.296	.395	.433
Jack Graney	OF125	L	33	128	461	79	108	22	8	1	30	105	39	7	.234	.380	.323
Elmer Smith	OF111	L	26	114	395	60	110	24	6	9	54	41	30	15	.278	.354	.438
Joe Wood	OF63,P1	R	29	72	192	30	49	10	6	0	27	32	21	3	.255	.367	.370
Joe Harris	1B46,SS4	R	28	62	184	30	69	16	1	1	46	33	21	2	.375	.472	.489
Harry Lunte	SS24	R	26	26	77	2	15	2	0	0	2	1	7	0	.195	.215	.221
Les Nunamaker	C16	R	30	26	56	6	14	1	1	0	7	2	6	0	.250	.276	.304
Pinch Thomas	C21	L	31	34	46	2	5	0	0	0	2	4	3	0	.109	.180	.109
Charlie Jamieson	P4,OF3	L	26	26	17	3	6	2	1	0	2	0	2	2	.353	.353	.588
Joe Evans	SS6	R	24	21	14	9	1	0	0	0	0	2	1	1	.071	.188	.071

Pitcher	T	Age	G	GS	CG	ShO	IP	H	HR	BB	SO	W-L	Sv	ERA
Stan Coveleski	R	29	43	34	24	4	296.0	286	2	60	118	24-12	4	2.52
Jim Bagby	R	29	35	32	21	0	241.1	258	3	44	61	17-11	3	2.80
Guy Morton	R	26	26	20	9	3	147.1	128	3	47	64	9-9	0	2.81
Elmer Myers	R	25	23	15	6	1	134.2	134	3	43	38	8-7	1	3.74
Hi Jasper	R	38	12	10	5	0	82.2	83	1	28	25	4-5	0	3.59
Ray Caldwell†	R	31	6	6	4	1	52.2	33	1	19	24	5-1	0	1.71
George Uhle	R	20	26	12	7	1	127.0	129	1	43	50	10-5	0	2.91
Tom Phillips	R	30	22	3	2	0	55.0	55	2	34	18	3-2	0	2.95
Johnny Enzmann	R	29	14	4	2	0	55.1	67	0	8	13	3-2	1	2.28
Fritz Coumbe	L	29	8	2	0	0	23.2	32	2	9	7	1-1	1	5.32
Tony Faeth	R	25	6	0	0	0	18.1	13	0	10	7	0-0	0	0.49
Ed Klepfer	R	31	5	0	0	0	7.1	12	1	6	7	0-0	0	7.36
Charlie Jamieson	L	26	4	1	0	0	13.0	12	0	8	0	0-0	0	5.54
Joe Wood	R	29	1	0	0	0	0.2	0	0	0	0	0-0	1	0.00
Joe Engel	L	26	1	0	0	0	0.0	0	0	3	0	0-0	0	—

1919 New York Yankees 3rd AL 80-59 .576 7.5 GB

Miller Huggins

Player	Gm by Position	B	Age	G	AB	R	H	2B	3B	HR	RBI	BB	SO	SB	Avg	OBP	Slg
Muddy Ruel	C81	R	23	81	233	18	56	6	0	0	31	34	26	4	.240	.340	.266
Wally Pipp	1B138	L	26	138	523	74	144	23	10	7	50	39	42	9	.275	.330	.398
Del Pratt	2B140	R	31	140	527	69	154	27	7	4	56	36	24	22	.292	.342	.393
Home Run Baker	3B141	L	33	141	567	70	166	22	1	10	83	44	18	13	.293	.346	.388
Roger Peckinpaugh	SS121	R	28	122	453	89	138	20	2	7	33	59	37	10	.305	.390	.404
Duffy Lewis	OF141	R	31	141	559	67	152	23	4	7	89	17	42	8	.272	.293	.365
Ping Bodie	OF134	R	31	134	475	45	132	27	8	6	59	36	46	15	.278	.334	.406
Sammy Vick	OF100	R	24	106	407	59	101	15	9	2	27	35	55	9	.248	.308	.344
Chick Fewster	OF41,SS24,2B4*	R	23	81	244	38	69	9	3	1	15	34	36	8	.283	.386	.357
Truck Hannah	C73,1B1	R	30	75	227	14	54	8	3	1	20	22	19	0	.238	.313	.313
Al Wickland	OF15	L	31	26	46	2	7	1	0	0	1	2	10	0	.152	.188	.174
Aaron Ward	1B5,3B3,SS2*	R	22	27	34	5	7	2	0	0	2	5	6	0	.206	.308	.265
George Halas	OF6	S	24	12	22	0	2	0	0	0	0	0	8	0	.091	.091	.091
Lefty O'Doul	P3,OF1	L	22	19	16	2	4	0	0	0	1	1	2	1	.250	.294	.250
Bill Lamar†	OF3,1B1	L	22	11	16	1	3	1	0	0	0	2	1	1	.188	.278	.250
Frank Gleich	OF4	L	25	5	4	0	1	0	0	0	1	1	0	0	.250	.400	.250
Fred Hofmann	C1	R	25	1	1	0	0	0	0	0	0	0	0	0	.000	.000	.000
Curt Walker		L	22	1	1	0	0	0	0	0	0	0	0	0	.000	.000	.000
Frank Kane		L	24	1	1	0	0	0	0	0	0	0	0	0	.000	.000	.000

C. Fewster, 2 G at 3B; A. Ward, 1 G at 2B

Pitcher	T	Age	G	GS	CG	ShO	IP	H	HR	BB	SO	W-L	Sv	ERA
Jack Quinn	R	35	38	31	18	4	266.0	242	8	65	97	15-14	0	2.61
Bob Shawkey	R	28	41	27	22	3	261.1	218	7	92	122	20-11	4	2.72
Hank Thormahlen	L	22	30	25	13	2	188.2	155	10	61	62	12-10	1	2.62
George Mogridge	L	30	35	18	13	3	169.0	159	6	46	58	10-7	0	2.82
Carl Mays†	R	27	13	13	12	1	120.0	96	3	37	54	9-3	0	1.65
Ernie Shore	R	28	20	13	3	0	95.0	105	4	44	24	5-8	0	4.17
Pete Schneider	R	23	7	4	0	0	29.0	19	1	22	11	0-1	0	3.41
Allan Russell†	R	25	23	9	4	1	90.2	89	6	32	50	5-5	1	3.47
Luke Nelson	R	25	9	1	0	0	24.1	22	1	11	11	3-0	0	2.96
Walt Smallwood	R	26	6	0	0	0	21.2	20	1	9	6	0-0	0	4.98
Bob McGraw†	R	24	6	0	0	0	16.1	11	1	10	3	1-0	0	3.31
Lefty O'Doul	L	22	3	0	0	0	5.0	7	0	4	2	0-0	0	3.60

1919 Detroit Tigers 4th AL 80-60 .571 8.0 GB

Hughie Jennings

Player	Gm by Position	B	Age	G	AB	R	H	2B	3B	HR	RBI	BB	SO	SB	Avg	OBP	Slg
Eddie Ainsmith	C106	R	27	114	364	42	99	17	12	3	32	45	30	9	.272	.354	.409
Harry Heilmann	1B140	R	24	140	537	74	172	30	15	8	93	37	41	7	.320	.366	.477
Ralph Young	2B121,SS4	S	29	125	456	63	96	13	5	1	25	53	32	8	.211	.294	.268
Bob Jones	3B127	L	29	127	439	37	114	18	6	1	57	34	39	11	.260	.314	.335
Donie Bush	SS129	S	31	129	509	82	124	11	6	0	26	75	36	22	.244	.343	.289
Bobby Veach	OF138	L	31	139	538	87	191	45	17	3	101	33	33	19	.355	.398	.519
Ty Cobb	OF123	L	32	124	497	92	191	36	13	1	70	38	22	28	.384	.429	.515
Ira Flagstead	OF83	R	25	97	287	43	95	22	3	5	41	35	39	6	.331	.416	.481
Chick Shorten	OF75	L	27	95	270	37	85	9	3	0	22	22	13	5	.315	.366	.370
Babe Ellison	2B25,OF10,SS1	R	23	56	134	18	29	4	0	0	11	13	24	4	.216	.291	.246
Oscar Stanage	C36,1B1	R	36	38	120	9	29	4	1	1	15	7	12	1	.242	.295	.317
Ben Dyer	3B23,SS11,OF1	R	26	44	85	11	21	4	0	0	15	8	19	0	.247	.312	.294
Archie Yelle	C5	R	27	6	4	1	0	0	0	0	0	1	0	0	.000	.200	.000
Snooks Dowd†		R	21	1	0	0	0	0	0	0	0	0	0	0	—	—	—

Pitcher	T	Age	G	GS	CG	ShO	IP	H	HR	BB	SO	W-L	Sv	ERA
Hooks Dauss	R	29	34	32	22	2	256.1	262	9	63	73	21-9	0	3.55
Howard Ehmke	R	25	33	31	20	2	248.2	255	5	107	79	17-10	0	3.18
Bernie Boland	R	27	35	30	18	1	242.2	222	7	80	71	14-16	1	3.04
Dutch Leonard	L	27	29	28	18	4	217.1	212	7	65	102	14-13	0	2.77
Eric Erickson†	R	24	3	2	0	0	14.2	17	0	10	4	0-2	0	6.75
Willie Mitchell	L	29	3	2	0	0	13.2	12	2	10	4	1-2	0	5.27
Bill James†	R	32	2	1	0	0	9.1	12	0	5	3	1-0	0	5.79
Doc Ayers†	R	29	24	5	3	1	93.2	88	2	28	32	5-3	0	2.69
Slim Love	L	28	22	8	4	0	89.2	92	3	40	46	6-4	1	3.01
G. Cunningham	R	24	17	0	0	0	47.2	54	0	15	11	1-1	1	4.91
Rudy Kallio	R	26	12	1	0	0	22.1	28	0	8	3	0-1	1	5.64

1919 St. Louis Browns 5th AL 67-72 .482 20.5 GB

Jimmy Burke

Player	Gm by Position	B	Age	G	AB	R	H	2B	3B	HR	RBI	BB	SO	SB	Avg	OBP	Slg
Hank Severeid	C103	R	28	112	351	16	87	12	2	0	36	21	13	2	.248	.298	.293
George Sisler	1B131	L	26	132	511	96	180	31	15	10	83	27	20	28	.352	.390	.530
Joe Gedeon	2B118	R	25	120	437	57	111	13	4	0	27	50	35	4	.254	.340	.302
Jimmy Austin	3B98	S	39	106	396	54	94	9	9	1	21	42	31	8	.237	.314	.313
Wally Gerber	SS140	R	27	140	462	43	105	14	6	1	37	49	36	1	.227	.308	.290
Jack Tobin	OF123	L	27	127	486	54	159	22	7	6	57	36	24	8	.327	.376	.438
Baby Doll Jacobson	OF106,1B8	R	28	120	455	70	147	31	8	4	51	24	27	9	.323	.362	.453
Earl Smith	OF68	S	28	88	252	21	63	12	5	1	36	18	27	1	.250	.300	.349
Ken Williams	OF63	L	29	65	227	32	68	10	5	6	35	26	25	7	.300	.376	.467
Ray Demmitt	OF49	L	35	79	202	19	48	11	2	1	19	14	27	3	.238	.290	.327
Herman Bronkie	3B34,2B16,1B2	R	34	67	196	23	50	6	4	0	14	23	23	2	.255	.336	.327
Josh Billings	C26,1B1	R	27	38	76	9	15	1	1	0	3	1	12	0	.197	.218	.237
Tod Sloan	OF20	L	28	27	63	9	15	1	3	0	6	12	3	0	.238	.368	.349
Wally Mayer	C25	R	28	30	62	2	14	4	1	0	5	8	11	0	.226	.314	.323
Joe Schepner	3B13	R	23	14	48	2	10	4	0	0	6	1	5	0	.208	.224	.292
John Shovlin	2B9	R	28	9	35	4	7	0	0	0	1	5	2	0	.200	.300	.200
Pat Collins	C5	R	22	11	21	2	3	1	0	0	1	4	2	0	.143	.280	.190
Gene Robertson	SS2	L	20	5	7	1	1	0	0	0	0	1	2	0	.143	.250	.143

Pitcher	T	Age	G	GS	CG	ShO	IP	H	HR	BB	SO	W-L	Sv	ERA
Allen Sothoron	R	26	40	30	21	3	270.0	256	4	87	106	20-13	3	2.20
Bert Gallia	R	27	34	25	14	1	222.1	220	10	92	83	12-14	2	3.60
Urban Shocker	R	28	30	25	14	5	211.0	193	6	55	86	13-11	0	2.69
Carl Weilman	L	29	20	20	12	3	148.0	133	3	45	44	10-6	0	2.07
Dave Davenport	R	29	24	16	4	0	123.1	135	4	41	37	2-11	1	3.94
Rolla Mapel	L	29	4	3	2	0	20.0	17	0	17	2	0-3	0	4.50
Bill Bayne	L	20	2	2	1	0	12.0	16	0	6	0	1-1	0	5.25
Ernie Koob	L	26	25	4	0	0	66.0	77	3	23	11	2-3	0	4.64
Rasty Wright	R	23	24	5	2	0	63.1	79	1	20	14	0-5	0	5.54
Lefty Leifield	L	35	19	9	6	2	92.0	96	4	25	18	6-4	0	2.93
Grover Lowdermilk†	R	34	7	0	0	0	12.0	6	0	4	6	0-0	0	0.75
Elam Vangilder	R	23	3	1	1	0	13.0	15	0	3	6	1-0	0	2.08
Tom Rogers†	R	27	2	0	0	0	1.0	7	0	0	1	0-1	0	27.00
Hal Haid	R	21	1	0	0	0	2.0	5	0	3	1	0-0	0	18.00

1919 Boston Red Sox 6th AL 66-71 .482 20.5 GB

Ed Barrow

Player	Gm by Position	B	Age	G	AB	R	H	2B	3B	HR	RBI	BB	SO	SB	Avg	OBP	Slg
Wally Schang	C103	S	29	113	330	43	101	16	3	0	55	71	42	15	.306	.436	.373
Stuffy McInnis	1B118	R	28	120	440	32	134	12	5	1	58	23	11	8	.305	.341	.361
Red Shannon†	2B79	S	22	80	290	36	75	11	7	0	17	17	42	7	.259	.313	.345
Ossie Vitt	3B133	R	29	133	469	64	114	10	3	0	40	44	11	9	.243	.309	.277
Everett Scott	SS138	R	26	138	507	41	141	19	0	0	38	19	26	8	.278	.306	.316
Harry Hooper	OF128	L	31	128	491	76	131	25	6	3	49	79	28	23	.267	.374	.360
Babe Ruth	OF111,P17,1B4	L	24	130	432	103	139	34	12	29	114	101	58	7	.322	.456	.657
Braggo Roth†	OF55	R	26	63	227	32	58	9	4	0	23	24	32	9	.256	.337	.330
Amos Strunk†	OF48	L	30	48	184	27	50	11	3	0	17	13	13	3	.272	.323	.364
Bill Lamar†	OF36	L	22	48	148	18	43	5	1	0	14	5	9	3	.291	.314	.338
Roxy Walters	C47	R	26	48	135	7	26	2	0	0	9	7	15	1	.193	.259	.207
Del Gainer	1B21,OF18	R	32	47	118	9	28	6	2	0	13	13	15	5	.237	.318	.322
Frank Gilhooley	OF33	L	27	48	112	14	27	4	0	0	1	12	8	2	.241	.315	.277
Jack Barry	2B31	R	32	31	108	13	26	5	0	0	2	5	4	2	.241	.293	.306
Dave Shean	2B29	R	35	29	100	4	14	0	0	0	8	5	7	1	.140	.189	.140
Ray Caldwell†	P18,OF2	L	31	33	48	5	13	1	1	0	4	0	9	0	.271	.271	.333
Mike McNally	3B11,SS11,2B3	R	26	33	42	10	11	4	0	0	6	1	2	4	.262	.279	.357
Joe Wilhoit	OF5	L	33	6	18	7	6	0	0	0	2	5	2	1	.333	.478	.333
Norm McNeil	C5	R	26	5	9	0	3	0	0	0	1	1	0	0	.333	.400	.333

Pitcher	T	Age	G	GS	CG	ShO	IP	H	HR	BB	SO	W-L	Sv	ERA
Sad Sam Jones	R	26	35	31	21	5	245.0	258	4	95	67	12-20	0	3.75
Herb Pennock	L	25	32	26	16	5	219.0	223	2	48	70	16-8	0	2.71
Carl Mays†	R	27	21	16	14	2	146.0	131	2	40	53	5-11	2	2.47
Babe Ruth	L	24	17	15	12	0	133.1	148	2	58	30	9-5	1	2.97
Ray Caldwell†	R	31	18	12	6	1	86.1	88	1	30	22	7-4	0	3.96
Allan Russell†	R	25	21	11	9	1	121.1	105	0	39	63	10-4	4	2.52
Waite Hoyt	R	19	13	11	6	1	105.1	99	1	22	28	4-6	0	3.25
Bill James†	R	32	13	7	4	0	72.2	74	2	39	12	3-5	0	4.09
Paul Musser	R	30	5	4	1	0	19.2	26	0	8	14	0-2	0	4.12
Joe Bush	R	26	3	2	0	0	9.0	11	0	4	3	0-0	0	5.00
George Dumont	R	23	13	2	0	0	35.1	45	1	19	12	0-4	0	4.33
Bob McGraw†	R	24	10	1	0	0	26.2	33	0	17	6	0-2	0	6.75
George Winn	L	21	3	0	0	0	4.2	6	0	1	0	0-0	0	7.71

610 Seasons: Team Rosters

1919 Washington Senators 7th AL 56-84 .400 32.0 GB

Clark Griffith

Player	Gm by Position	B	Age	G	AB	R	H	2B	3B	HR	RBI	BB	SO	SB	Avg	OBP	Slg
Val Picinich	C69	R	22	80	212	18	58	12	3	3	22	17	43	6	.274	.330	.401
Joe Judge	1B133	L	25	135	521	83	150	33	12	2	31	81	35	23	.288	.386	.409
Hal Janvrin†	2B56,SS2	R	26	61	208	17	37	4	1	1	13	19	17	8	.178	.253	.221
Eddie Foster	3B115	R	32	120	478	57	126	12	5	0	26	33	21	20	.264	.314	.310
Howard Shanks	SS94,2B34,OF6	R	28	135	491	33	122	8	7	1	54	25	48	13	.248	.289	.299
Sam Rice	OF141	L	29	141	557	80	179	23	9	3	71	42	26	26	.321	.376	.411
Mike Menosky	OF103	L	24	116	342	62	98	15	3	6	39	44	46	13	.287	.379	.401
Clyde Milan	OF86	L	32	88	321	43	92	12	6	0	37	40	16	11	.287	.371	.361
Patsy Gharrity	C60,OF33,1B7	R	27	111	347	35	94	19	4	2	43	25	39	4	.271	.325	.366
Buzz Murphy	OF73	L	24	79	252	19	66	7	4	0	28	19	32	5	.262	.326	.321
Joe Leonard	2B28,3B25,1B4*	L	24	71	198	26	51	8	3	2	20	20	28	3	.258	.329	.359
Walter Johnson	P39,OF1	R	31	56	125	13	24	1	3	1	8	12	17	1	.192	.263	.272
Frank Ellerbe	SS28	R	23	28	105	13	29	4	1	0	16	2	15	5	.276	.290	.333
Sam Agnew	C36	R	32	42	98	6	23	7	0	0	10	10	8	1	.235	.312	.306
Roy Grover†	2B24	R	27	24	75	6	14	0	0	0	7	6	10	2	.187	.256	.187
George McBride	SS15	R	38	15	40	3	8	1	1	0	4	3	6	0	.200	.256	.275
Bucky Harris	2B8	R	22	8	28	0	6	2	0	0	4	1	3	0	.214	.267	.286
Ike Davis	SS4	R	24	8	14	0	0	0	0	0	0	0	6	0	.000	.000	.000
Claude Davidson	3B2	L	22	2	7	1	3	0	0	0	0	1	1	0	.429	.500	.429
Danny Silva	3B1	R	22	1	4	0	1	0	0	0	0	0	0	0	.250	.250	.250
George Twombly	OF1	R	27	1	4	0	0	0	0	0	0	0	0	0	.000	.000	.000
Frank Kelliher		L	20	1	1	0	0	0	0	0	0	0	0	0	.000	.000	.000
Jesse Baker	SS1	R	24	1	0	0	0	0	0	0	0	0	0	0	—	—	—

J. Leonard, 1 G at OF

Pitcher	T	Age	G	GS	CG	ShO	IP	H	HR	BB	SO	W-L	Sv	ERA
Jim Shaw	R	25	45	38	23	3	306.2	274	5	101	128	16-17	4	2.67
Harry Harper	L	24	35	30	8	0	208.0	220	3	97	87	6-21	0	3.72
Walter Johnson	R	31	39	29	27	7	290.1	235	0	51	147	20-14	2	1.49
Eric Erickson†	R	24	20	15	7	1	132.0	130	7	63	86	6-11	0	3.95
Dick Robertson	R	28	7	4	0	0	27.2	25	1	9	7	0-1	0	2.28
Henry Courtney	L	20	4	3	3	1	26.1	25	0	19	6	3-0	0	2.73
Al Schacht	R	26	2	2	1	0	15.0	14	0	4	4	2-0	0	2.40
Bill Snyder	R	21	2	1	0	0	8.0	6	0	3	5	0-1	0	1.13
Rip Jordan	R	29	1	1	0	0	4.0	6	1	2	2	0-0	0	11.25
Tom Zachary	L	23	17	7	0	0	61.2	68	0	20	9	1-5	0	2.92
Molly Craft	R	23	16	2	0	0	48.2	59	2	18	17	0-3	0	3.88
Ed Gill	R	23	16	2	0	0	37.1	38	0	21	7	1-1	0	4.82
Harry Thompson†	L	29	12	2	0	0	43.1	48	0	8	10	0-3	1	3.53
Doc Ayers†	R	29	11	5	0	0	43.2	52	0	17	12	1-6	0	3.50
Charlie Whitehouse	L	25	6	1	0	0	12.0	13	1	6	5	0-1	0	4.50
Ed Hovlik	R	27	3	0	0	0	5.2	12	0	9	3	0-0	0	12.71
Clarence Fisher	R	20	2	0	0	0	4.0	8	0	3	1	0-0	0	13.50
Nick Altrock	L	42	1	0	0	0	0.0	4	0	0	0	0-0	0	—

1919 Philadelphia Athletics 8th AL 36-104 .257 52.0 GB

Connie Mack

Player	Gm by Position	B	Age	G	AB	R	H	2B	3B	HR	RBI	BB	SO	SB	Avg	OBP	Slg
Cy Perkins	C87,SS8	R	23	101	305	22	77	12	7	2	29	27	22	2	.252	.313	.357
George Burns	1B86,OF34	R	26	126	470	63	139	29	9	8	57	19	18	15	.296	.339	.447
Whitey Witt	OF59,2B56,3B2	L	23	122	460	56	123	15	6	0	33	46	26	11	.267	.334	.326
Fred Thomas	3B124	R	26	124	453	42	96	11	10	2	23	43	52	12	.212	.283	.294
Joe Dugan	SS98,2B4,3B2	R	22	104	387	25	105	17	2	1	30	11	30	9	.271	.300	.333
Tilly Walker	OF115	R	31	125	456	47	133	30	6	10	64	26	41	8	.292	.330	.450
Merlin Kopp	OF65	S	27	75	235	34	53	2	4	1	12	42	43	16	.226	.348	.281
Amos Strunk†	OF52	L	30	60	194	15	41	6	4	0	13	23	15	3	.211	.298	.284
Braggo Roth†	OF48	R	26	48	195	33	63	13	8	5	29	15	21	11	.323	.377	.549
Dick Burrus	1B38,OF10	L	21	70	194	17	50	3	4	0	8	9	25	2	.258	.294	.314
Wickey McAvoy	C57	R	24	62	170	10	24	5	2	0	11	14	21	1	.141	.207	.194
Red Shannon†	2B37	S	22	39	155	14	42	7	2	0	14	12	28	4	.271	.331	.342
Terry Turner	SS19,2B17,3B1	R	38	38	127	7	24	3	0	0	6	5	9	2	.189	.220	.213
Walt Kinney	P43,OF1	L	25	57	88	11	25	6	0	1	11	10	15	0	.284	.357	.386
Ivy Griffin	1B17	L	22	17	68	5	20	2	2	0	6	3	10	0	.294	.333	.382
Chick Galloway	SS17	R	22	17	63	2	9	0	0	0	4	1	8	0	.143	.156	.143
Al Wingo	OF15	L	21	15	59	9	18	1	3	0	2	4	12	0	.305	.349	.424
Roy Grover†	2B12,3B3	R	27	22	56	8	13	1	0	0	2	5	6	0	.232	.295	.250
Frank Welch	OF15	R	21	15	54	5	9	1	1	2	7	7	10	0	.167	.262	.333
Jimmy Dykes	2B16	R	22	17	49	4	9	1	0	0	1	7	11	0	.184	.286	.204
Art Ewoldt	3B9	R	25	9	32	2	7	1	0	0	2	1	5	0	.219	.242	.250
Charlie High	OF9	L	20	11	29	2	2	0	0	0	1	3	4	2	.069	.182	.069
Lena Styles	C8	R	19	8	22	0	6	1	0	0	5	1	6	0	.273	.304	.318
Bob Allen	OF6	R	24	9	22	3	3	1	0	0	0	3	7	0	.136	.269	.182
Snooks Dowd†	2B3,SS2,3B1*	R	21	13	18	4	3	0	0	0	6	0	5	2	.167	.167	.167
Johnny Walker	C3	R	22	3	9	0	0	0	0	0	0	0	2	0	.000	.000	.000
Harry Thompson†	P3,OF1	L	29	5	6	0	0	0	0	0	0	0	1	0	.000	.000	.000
Lew Groh	3B1	R	35	2	4	0	0	0	0	0	0	0	2	0	.000	.000	.000

S. Dowd, 1 G at OF

Pitcher	T	Age	G	GS	CG	ShO	IP	H	HR	BB	SO	W-L	Sv	ERA
Jing Johnson	R	24	34	25	12	0	202.0	222	8	62	67	9-15	0	3.61
Rollie Naylor	R	27	31	23	17	0	204.2	210	2	64	68	5-18	0	3.34
Scott Perry	R	28	25	21	12	0	183.2	193	4	72	38	4-17	1	3.58
Tom Rogers†	R	27	23	18	7	1	140.0	152	9	60	37	4-12	0	4.31
Wynn Noyes†	R	30	10	6	3	0	49.0	66	1	15	20	1-5	0	5.69
Jimmy Zinn	R	24	5	3	2	0	25.2	38	1	10	9	1-3	0	6.31
Danny Boone	R	24	3	2	0	0	14.2	24	0	10	1	0-1	0	6.75
Mule Watson	R	22	4	2	0	0	14.1	17	2	7	6	0-1	0	6.91
Ray Roberts	R	23	3	2	0	0	14.0	21	0	3	2	0-2	0	7.71
Bob Hasty	R	23	2	2	1	0	12.0	15	1	4	5	0-2	0	5.25
Pat Martin	L	25	2	2	1	0	11.0	11	0	8	6	0-2	0	4.09
Lefty York	L	26	2	2	0	0	4.1	13	0	5	2	0-2	0	24.92
Charlie Eckert	R	21	2	1	1	0	16.0	17	1	3	6	0-1	0	3.94
Dave Keefe	R	22	1	1	1	0	9.0	8	0	3	5	0-1	0	4.00
Bill Pierson	L	20	2	1	0	0	7.2	9	0	8	4	0-1	0	3.52
Walt Kinney	L	25	43	21	13	0	202.2	199	7	91	97	9-15	2	3.64
Socks Seibold	R	23	14	4	1	0	45.2	58	2	26	19	2-3	0	5.32
Bob Geary	R	28	9	2	1	0	32.1	32	1	18	9	0-3	0	4.73
Bill Grevell	R	21	5	2	0	0	12.0	15	0	18	3	0-0	0	14.25
Walter Anderson	L	21	3	0	0	0	14.0	13	0	8	10	1-0	0	3.86
Harry Thompson†	L	29	3	0	0	0	12.0	16	4	3	1	0-1	0	6.75
Mike Kircher	R	21	2	0	0	0	8.0	15	0	3	2	0-0	0	7.88
Willie Adams	R	28	1	0	0	0	4.2	7	1	2	0	0-0	0	3.86

»1919 Cincinnati Reds 1st NL 96-44 .686 —

Pat Moran

Player	Gm by Position	B	Age	G	AB	R	H	2B	3B	HR	RBI	BB	SO	SB	Avg	OBP	Slg
Ivy Wingo	C75	L	28	76	245	30	67	12	6	0	27	23	19	4	.273	.336	.371
Jake Daubert	1B140	L	35	140	537	79	148	10	12	2	44	35	23	11	.276	.322	.350
Morrie Rath	2B138	L	32	138	537	77	142	13	1	1	29	64	24	17	.264	.343	.298
Heine Groh	3B121	R	29	122	448	79	139	17	11	5	63	56	26	21	.310	.392	.431
Larry Kopf	SS135	S	28	135	503	51	136	18	5	0	58	28	27	18	.270	.313	.326
Greasy Neale	OF138	L	27	139	500	57	121	10	12	1	54	47	51	28	.242	.316	.316
Edd Roush	OF133	L	26	133	504	73	162	19	12	4	71	42	19	20	.321	.380	.431
Rube Bressler	OF48,P13	R	24	61	165	22	34	3	4	2	17	23	15	2	.206	.311	.309
Bill Rariden	C70	R	31	74	218	16	47	6	3	1	24	17	19	4	.216	.275	.284
Sherry Magee	OF47,2B1,3B1	R	34	56	163	11	35	6	1	0	21	26	19	4	.215	.337	.264
Pat Duncan	OF27	R	25	31	90	9	22	3	3	2	17	8	7	2	.244	.306	.411
Manuel Cueto	OF25,3B1	R	27	29	88	10	22	2	0	0	4	10	4	5	.250	.340	.273
Hank Schreiber	3B17,SS2	R	27	19	58	5	13	4	0	0	4	0	12	0	.224	.224	.293
Jimmy Smith	3B6,SS5,2B4*	S	24	28	40	9	11	1	3	1	10	4	8	1	.275	.341	.525
Dolf Luque	P30,3B1	R	28	31	32	3	4	1	1	0	2	3	1	0	.125	.200	.219
Nick Allen	C12	R	30	15	25	7	8	0	1	0	5	2	6	0	.320	.393	.400
Charlie See	OF4	L	22	8	14	1	4	0	0	0	1	1	0	0	.286	.333	.286
Wally Rehg	OF5	R	30	5	12	1	2	0	0	0	3	1	0	0	.167	.231	.167
Billy Zitzmann†	OF1	R	23	2	1	0	0	0	0	0	0	0	0	0	.000	.000	.000

J. Smith, 4 G at OF

Pitcher	T	Age	G	GS	CG	ShO	IP	H	HR	BB	SO	W-L	Sv	ERA
Hod Eller	R	24	38	30	16	7	248.1	216	7	50	137	20-9	2	2.39
Dutch Ruether	L	25	33	29	20	3	242.2	195	1	83	78	19-6	0	1.82
Slim Sallee	L	34	29	28	22	4	227.2	221	4	20	24	21-7	0	2.06
Ray Fisher	R	31	26	20	12	5	174.1	141	5	38	41	14-5	1	2.17
Jimmy Ring	R	24	32	18	12	2	183.0	150	1	51	61	10-9	3	2.26
Dolf Luque	R	28	30	9	6	2	106.0	89	2	36	40	9-3	3	2.63
Rube Bressler	L	24	13	4	1	0	41.2	37	1	8	13	2-4	0	3.46
Roy Mitchell	R	34	7	1	0	0	31.0	32	0	9	10	0-1	0	2.32
Ed Gerner	L	21	5	1	0	0	17.0	22	0	3	2	1-0	0	3.18
Mike Regan	R	31	1	0	0	0	2.1	1	0	0	1	0-0	0	0.00

1919 New York Giants 2nd NL 87-53 .621 9.0 GB

John McGraw

Player	Gm by Position	B	Age	G	AB	R	H	2B	3B	HR	RBI	BB	SO	SB	Avg	OBP	Slg
Lew McCarty	C59	R	30	85	210	17	59	5	4	2	21	18	15	2	.281	.341	.371
Hal Chase	1B107	R	36	110	408	58	116	17	7	5	45	17	40	16	.284	.318	.397
Larry Doyle	2B100	L	32	113	381	61	110	14	10	7	52	31	17	12	.289	.350	.433
Heinie Zimmerman	3B123	R	32	123	444	56	113	20	6	4	58	21	30	8	.255	.296	.354
Art Fletcher	SS127	R	34	127	488	54	135	20	5	3	54	9	28	6	.277	.300	.357
George Burns	OF139	R	29	139	534	86	162	30	9	2	46	82	37	40	.303	.396	.404
Benny Kauff	OF134	L	29	135	491	73	136	27	7	10	67	39	45	21	.277	.334	.422
Ross Youngs	OF130	L	22	130	489	73	152	31	7	2	43	51	47	24	.311	.384	.415
Frankie Frisch	2B29,3B20,SS1	S	20	54	190	21	43	3	2	2	24	4	14	15	.226	.242	.295
Mike Gonzalez	C52,1B4	R	28	58	158	18	30	6	0	0	8	20	9	3	.190	.293	.228
George Kelly	1B32	R	23	32	107	12	31	6	2	1	14	3	15	1	.290	.315	.411
Frank Snyder†	C31	R	26	32	92	7	21	6	0	0	11	8	9	1	.228	.297	.293
Al Baird	2B24,SS9,3B5	R	24	38	83	8	20	1	0	0	5	5	9	3	.241	.284	.253
Jigger Statz	OF18,2B5	R	21	21	60	7	18	2	1	0	6	3	8	2	.300	.333	.367
Earl Smith	C14,2B1	L	22	21	36	5	9	2	1	0	8	3	3	1	.250	.308	.361
Lee King	OF7	R	26	21	20	5	2	1	0	0	1	1	6	0	.100	.143	.150
Ed Sicking†	SS6	R	22	6	15	2	5	0	0	0	3	1	0	0	.333	.412	.333
Jimmy Cooney	SS4,2B1	R	24	5	14	3	3	0	0	0	1	0	0	0	.214	.214	.214
Bob Kinsella	OF3	L	20	3	9	1	2	0	0	0	0	0	3	0	.222	.222	.222
Chick Bowen	OF2	R	21	3	5	0	1	0	0	0	1	1	2	0	.200	.333	.200
Jim Thorpe†	OF2	R	32	2	3	0	1	0	0	0	1	0	0	0	.333	.333	.333
Dave Robertson†		L	29	1	0	0	0	0	0	0	0	0	0	0	—	—	—

Pitcher	T	Age	G	GS	CG	ShO	IP	H	HR	BB	SO	W-L	Sv	ERA
Jesse Barnes	R	26	38	34	23	4	295.2	263	8	35	92	25-9	1	2.40
Rube Benton	L	32	35	28	11	1	209.0	181	5	52	53	17-11	2	2.63
Fred Toney	R	30	24	20	14	4	181.0	157	6	35	40	13-6	1	1.84
Red Causey†	R	25	19	16	6	0	105.0	99	5	38	25	9-3	0	3.69
Art Nehf†	L	26	13	12	9	2	102.0	70	2	19	24	9-2	0	1.50
Phil Douglas†	R	29	8	6	4	0	51.1	53	0	6	21	2-4	0	2.10
Rosy Ryan	R	21	4	3	1	0	20.1	20	0	9	7	1-2	0	3.10
Bill Hubbell	R	22	2	2	2	0	18.1	19	0	2	3	1-1	0	1.96
George Smith†	R	27	3	2	0	0	11.0	18	1	4	0	0-2	0	5.73
Colonel Snover	L	24	2	1	0	0	9.0	7	0	3	4	0-1	0	1.00
Jean Dubuc	R	30	36	5	1	0	132.0	119	4	37	32	6-4	3	2.66
Jesse Winters	R	25	16	2	0	0	28.0	39	1	13	6	1-2	3	5.46
Pol Perritt	R	26	11	3	0	0	19.0	27	0	12	2	1-1	1	7.11
Ferdie Schupp†	L	28	9	4	0	0	32.0	32	2	18	17	1-3	1	5.63
Pat Ragan†	R	30	7	1	1	0	22.2	19	0	14	7	1-0	0	1.59
Joe Oeschger†	R	28	5	1	0	0	8.0	12	0	2	3	0-1	0	4.50
Johnny Jones	R	26	2	0	0	0	6.2	9	0	3	3	0-0	1	5.40
Bob Steele	L	25	1	0	0	0	3.0	3	0	2	0	0-1	0	6.00
Virgil Barnes	R	22	1	0	0	0	2.0	6	0	1	1	0-0	0	18.00

1919 Chicago Cubs 3rd NL 75-65 .536 21.0 GB

Fred Mitchell

Player	Gm by Position	B	Age	G	AB	R	H	2B	3B	HR	RBI	BB	SO	SB	Avg	OBP	Slg
Bill Killefer	C100	R	31	103	315	17	90	10	2	0	22	15	8	5	.286	.322	.330
Fred Merkle	1B132	R	30	133	498	52	133	20	6	3	62	33	35	20	.267	.315	.349
Charlie Pick†	2B71,3B3	L	31	75	269	27	65	8	6	0	18	14	12	17	.242	.292	.316
Charlie Deal	3B116	R	27	116	405	37	117	23	5	2	52	12	12	11	.289	.316	.385
Charlie Hollocher	SS115	L	23	115	430	51	116	14	5	3	26	44	19	16	.270	.347	.347
Max Flack	OF116	L	29	116	469	71	138	20	4	6	35	34	13	18	.294	.346	.392
Dode Paskert	OF80	R	37	88	270	21	53	11	3	2	29	28	33	7	.196	.274	.281
Les Mann†	OF78	R	25	80	299	31	68	8	8	1	22	11	29	12	.227	.257	.318
Lee Magee†	OF45,SS13,3B10*	S	30	79	267	36	78	12	4	1	17	18	16	14	.292	.339	.378
Turner Barber	OF68	L	25	76	230	26	72	9	4	0	21	14	17	7	.313	.355	.387
Buck Herzog†	2B52	R	33	52	193	15	53	4	4	0	17	10	7	12	.275	.336	.337
Bob O'Farrell	C38	R	22	49	125	11	27	4	2	0	9	7	10	2	.216	.258	.280
Dave Robertson†	OF25	L	29	27	96	8	20	2	0	1	10	1	10	3	.208	.224	.260
Pete Kilduff†	3B14,2B8,SS7	R	26	31	88	5	24	4	2	0	8	10	5	1	.273	.360	.364
Bill McCabe	OF19,SS4,3B1	S	26	33	84	8	13	3	1	0	5	9	15	3	.155	.253	.214
Fred Lear	1B9,2B9,SS3	R	25	40	76	8	17	3	1	1	11	8	11	2	.224	.306	.329
Tom Daly	C18	R	27	25	50	4	11	0	1	0	1	2	5	0	.220	.250	.260
Bernie Friberg	OF7	R	19	8	20	0	4	1	0	0	1	0	2	0	.200	.200	.250
Hal Reilly	OF1	L	25	1	3	0	0	0	0	0	0	0	1	0	.000	.000	.000

L. Magee, 7 G at 2B

Pitcher	T	Age	G	GS	CG	ShO	IP	H	HR	BB	SO	W-L	Sv	ERA
Hippo Vaughn	L	31	38	37	25	4	306.2	264	3	62	141	21-14	1	1.79
Pete Alexander	R	32	30	27	20	9	235.0	180	3	38	121	16-11	1	1.72
Claude Hendrix	R	30	33	25	15	2	206.1	208	3	42	69	10-14	0	2.62
Phil Douglas†	R	29	25	19	8	4	161.2	133	0	34	63	10-6	0	2.00
Lefty Tyler	L	29	6	5	3	0	30.0	20	0	13	9	2-2	0	2.10
Harry Weaver	R	27	2	1	0	0	3.1	6	0	2	1	0-1	0	10.80
Speed Martin	R	25	35	14	7	2	163.2	158	2	52	54	8-8	2	2.47
Paul Carter	R	25	28	7	2	0	85.0	81	1	28	17	5-4	1	2.65
Sweetbreads Bailey	R	24	21	5	0	0	71.1	75	2	20	19	3-5	0	3.15
Joel Newkirk	R	23	1	0	0	0	2.0	2	0	3	1	0-0	0	13.50

1919 Pittsburgh Pirates 4th NL 71-68 .511 24.5 GB

Hugo Bezdek

Player	Gm by Position	B	Age	G	AB	R	H	2B	3B	HR	RBI	BB	SO	SB	Avg	OBP	Slg
Walter Schmidt	C85	R	32	85	267	23	67	9	2	0	29	23	9	5	.251	.310	.300
Fritz Mollwitz†	1B52,OF2	R	29	56	168	11	29	2	4	0	12	15	18	9	.173	.249	.232
George Cutshaw	2B139	R	31	139	512	49	124	15	8	3	51	30	22	36	.242	.287	.320
Walter Barbare	3B80,2B1	R	27	85	293	34	80	11	5	1	34	18	18	11	.273	.317	.355
Zeb Terry	SS127	R	28	129	472	46	107	12	6	0	27	31	26	12	.227	.280	.278
Carson Bigbee	OF124	L	24	125	478	61	132	11	4	2	27	37	26	31	.276	.332	.328
Billy Southworth	OF121	L	26	121	453	56	127	14	14	4	61	32	22	23	.280	.329	.400
Casey Stengel	OF87	L	28	89	321	38	94	10	10	4	43	35	35	12	.293	.364	.424
Max Carey	OF63	S	29	66	244	41	75	10	2	0	9	25	24	18	.307	.376	.365
Vic Saier	1B51	L	28	58	166	19	37	3	3	2	17	18	13	5	.223	.306	.313
Tony Boeckel†	3B45	R	26	45	152	18	38	9	2	0	16	18	20	11	.250	.333	.336
Possum Whitted†	1B33,3B2,OF1	R	29	35	131	15	51	7	7	0	21	6	4	7	.389	.420	.550
Cliff Lee	C28,OF6	R	22	42	112	5	22	2	4	0	2	6	8	2	.196	.237	.286
Howdy Caton	SS17,3B14,OF1	R	22	39	102	13	18	1	2	0	5	12	10	2	.176	.263	.225
Fred Nicholson	OF17,1B1	R	24	30	66	8	18	2	2	1	6	6	11	2	.273	.333	.409
Fred Blackwell	C22	L	27	24	65	3	14	3	0	0	4	3	9	0	.215	.261	.262
Charlie Grimm	1B13	L	20	14	44	6	14	1	3	0	6	2	4	1	.318	.348	.477
Jeff Sweeney	C15	R	30	17	42	0	4	1	0	0	0	5	6	1	.095	.191	.119
Billy Zitzmann†	OF8	R	23	11	26	5	5	1	0	0	2	0	6	2	.192	.192	.231
Hooks Warner	3B3	L	25	6	8	0	1	0	0	0	2	3	1	0	.125	.364	.125

Pitcher	T	Age	G	GS	CG	ShO	IP	H	HR	BB	SO	W-L	Sv	ERA
Wilbur Cooper	L	27	35	32	27	4	286.2	229	10	74	106	19-13	1	2.67
Babe Adams	R	37	34	29	23	6	263.1	213	1	23	92	17-10	1	1.98
Frank Miller	R	33	32	26	16	3	201.2	170	6	34	59	13-12	0	3.03
Earl Hamilton	L	27	28	19	10	1	160.1	167	3	49	39	8-11	1	3.31
Hal Carlson	R	27	22	14	7	1	141.0	114	0	39	49	8-10	0	2.23
Erskine Mayer†	R	30	18	10	6	0	88.1	100	2	12	20	5-3	1	4.48
Elmer Ponder	R	26	9	5	0	0	47.1	55	0	6	6	0-5	0	3.99
Bill Evans	R	25	7	3	2	0	36.2	41	1	18	15	0-4	0	5.65
John Wisner	R	19	4	1	1	0	18.2	12	0	7	4	1-0	0	0.96
Carmen Hill	R	23	4	0	0	0	5.0	12	0	1	1	0-0	0	9.00

1919 Brooklyn Dodgers 5th NL 69-71 .493 27.0 GB

Wilbert Robinson

Player	Gm by Position	B	Age	G	AB	R	H	2B	3B	HR	RBI	BB	SO	SB	Avg	OBP	Slg
Ernie Krueger	C66	R	28	80	226	24	56	7	4	5	36	19	25	4	.248	.312	.381
Ed Konetchy	1B132	R	33	132	486	46	145	24	9	1	47	29	39	14	.298	.342	.391
Jimmy Johnston	2B87,OF14,1B2*	R	29	117	405	56	114	11	4	1	23	29	26	11	.281	.334	.336
Lew Malone	3B47,2B2,SS2	R	22	51	162	9	33	7	3	0	11	6	18	1	.204	.232	.284
Ivy Olson	SS140	R	33	140	590	73	164	14	9	1	38	30	12	26	.278	.316	.337
Zack Wheat	OF137	L	31	137	536	70	159	23	11	5	62	33	27	15	.297	.344	.409
Hi Myers	OF131	R	30	133	512	62	157	23	14	5	73	23	34	13	.307	.339	.436
Tommy Griffith	OF125	L	29	125	484	65	136	18	4	6	57	23	32	8	.281	.315	.372
Lee Magee†	2B36,3B9	S	30	45	181	16	43	7	2	0	7	5	8	5	.238	.262	.298
Otto Miller	C51	R	30	51	164	18	37	5	0	0	5	7	14	2	.226	.257	.256
Chuck Ward	3B45	R	24	45	150	7	35	1	2	0	8	7	11	0	.233	.277	.267
Ray Schmandt	2B18,1B12,3B6	R	23	47	127	8	21	4	0	0	10	4	13	0	.165	.191	.197
Mack Wheat	C38	R	26	41	112	5	23	3	0	0	8	2	22	1	.205	.246	.232
Jim Hickman	OF29	R	27	57	104	14	20	3	1	0	11	6	17	2	.192	.236	.240
Pete Kilduff†	3B26,2B1	R	26	32	73	9	22	3	1	0	8	12	11	5	.301	.407	.370
Doug Baird†	3B17	R	27	20	60	6	11	0	1	0	8	1	10	3	.183	.197	.217
Horace Allen	OF2	L	20	4	7	0	0	0	0	0	0	0	2	0	.000	.000	.000
Ollie O'Mara	3B2	R	28	2	7	1	0	0	0	0	0	0	0	0	.000	.000	.000
Tom Fitzsimmons	3B4	R	29	4	4	1	0	0	0	0	0	1	2	0	.000	.200	.000

J. Johnston, 1 G at SS

Pitcher	T	Age	G	GS	CG	ShO	IP	H	HR	BB	SO	W-L	Sv	ERA
Jeff Pfeffer	R	31	30	30	26	4	267.0	270	7	49	92	17-13	0	2.66
Leon Cadore	R	28	35	27	16	3	250.2	228	5	39	94	14-12	0	2.37
Al Mamaux	R	25	30	22	16	2	199.1	174	2	66	80	10-12	0	2.66
Burleigh Grimes	R	25	25	21	13	1	181.1	179	2	60	82	10-11	0	3.47
Sherry Smith	L	28	30	19	13	2	173.0	181	3	29	40	7-12	1	2.24
Rube Marquard	L	32	8	7	3	0	59.0	54	1	10	29	3-3	0	2.29
Clarence Mitchell	L	28	23	11	9	0	108.2	123	0	23	43	7-5	0	3.06
Larry Cheney†	R	33	9	4	2	0	39.0	45	1	14	14	1-3	0	4.15
Lafayette Henion	R	20	1	0	0	0	3.0	2	0	2	2	0-0	0	6.00

1919 Boston Braves 6th NL 57-82 .410 38.5 GB

George Stallings

Player	Gm by Position	B	Age	G	AB	R	H	2B	3B	HR	RBI	BB	SO	SB	Avg	OBP	Slg
Hank Gowdy	C74,1B1	R	29	78	219	18	61	8	1	1	22	19	16	5	.279	.339	.338
Walter Holke	1B136	S	26	137	518	48	151	14	6	0	48	21	25	19	.292	.325	.342
Buck Herzog†	2B70,1B1	R	33	73	275	27	77	8	5	1	25	13	11	16	.280	.327	.356
Tony Boeckel†	3B93	R	26	95	365	42	91	11	5	1	26	35	13	10	.249	.317	.315
Rabbit Maranville	SS131	R	27	131	480	44	128	18	10	5	43	36	23	12	.267	.319	.377
Ray Powell	OF122	L	30	123	470	51	111	12	12	2	33	41	79	16	.236	.303	.326
Walton Cruise†	OF66	L	29	73	241	23	52	7	0	1	21	17	29	8	.216	.267	.257
Joe Riggert	OF61	R	32	63	240	34	68	8	5	4	17	25	30	9	.283	.356	.408
Johnny Rawlings	2B58,OF10,SS5	R	26	77	275	30	70	8	2	1	16	16	20	10	.255	.298	.309
Red Smith	OF48,3B23	R	29	87	241	24	59	6	0	1	25	40	22	6	.245	.359	.282
Art Wilson	C64,1B1	R	33	71	191	14	49	8	1	0	16	25	19	2	.257	.346	.309
Jim Thorpe†	OF38,1B2	R	32	60	156	16	51	7	3	1	25	6	30	7	.327	.360	.429
Les Mann†	OF40	R	25	40	145	15	41	6	4	3	20	9	14	7	.283	.329	.441
Charlie Pick†	2B21,3B5,OF3*	L	31	34	114	12	29	1	1	1	7	7	5	4	.254	.325	.307
Lena Blackburne†	3B24,1B1,2B1*	R	32	31	80	5	21	3	1	0	4	6	7	3	.263	.322	.325
Joe Kelly	OF16	R	32	18	64	3	9	1	0	0	3	0	11	2	.141	.154	.156
Art Nehf†	P22,OF1	L	26	23	63	6	13	2	2	0	4	3	11	0	.206	.254	.302
Dizzy Nutter	OF12	L	25	18	52	4	11	0	0	0	3	4	5	1	.212	.268	.212
Dixie Carroll	OF13	L	28	15	49	10	13	3	1	0	7	7	1	5	.265	.379	.367
Jack Scott	P19,OF1	L	27	24	40	4	7	1	0	0	4	1	8	0	.175	.195	.200
Walt Tragesser†	C14	R	32	20	40	3	7	2	0	0	3	2	10	1	.175	.233	.225
Lloyd Christenbury	OF7	L	25	7	31	5	9	1	0	0	4	2	2	0	.290	.333	.323
Mickey O'Neil	C11	R	19	11	28	3	6	0	0	0	1	1	7	0	.214	.241	.214
Hod Ford	SS8,3B2	R	21	10	28	4	6	0	1	0	3	2	6	0	.214	.290	.286
Tom Miller		L	21	7	6	2	2	0	0	0	0	0	1	0	.333	.333	.333
Gene Bailey	OF3	R	25	4	6	0	2	0	0	0	1	0	2	1	.333	.333	.333
Sam White	C1	L	26	1	1	0	0	0	0	0	0	0	0	0	.000	.000	.000
Lee King		R	25	2	1	0	0	0	0	0	0	0	0	0	.000	.000	.000

C. Pick, 2 G at 1B; L. Blackburne, 1 G at SS

Pitcher	T	Age	G	GS	CG	ShO	IP	H	HR	BB	SO	W-L	Sv	ERA
Dick Rudolph	R	31	37	32	24	2	273.2	282	2	54	76	13-18	2	2.17
Art Nehf†	L	26	22	19	13	1	168.2	151	6	40	53	8-9	0	3.09
Dana Fillingim	R	25	32	18	9	0	186.1	185	2	39	50	6-13	2	3.38
Ray Keating	R	27	22	14	9	1	136.0	129	2	45	48	7-11	0	2.98
Al Demaree	R	34	25	13	6	0	128.0	147	8	35	34	6-6	3	3.80
Jack Scott	R	27	19	12	7	0	103.2	109	3	39	44	6-6	1	3.13
Red Causey†	R	25	10	10	3	0	69.0	81	1	20	14	4-5	0	4.57
Joe Oeschger†	R	28	7	7	4	1	56.2	63	0	21	16	4-2	0	2.54
Pat Ragan†	R	30	4	3	0	0	12.2	16	0	3	3	0-2	0	7.11
Hugh McQuillan	R	21	16	7	2	0	60.0	66	3	14	13	2-3	1	3.45
Jake Northrop	R	31	11	3	2	0	37.1	43	2	10	9	1-5	0	4.58
Larry Cheney†	R	33	8	2	0	0	33.0	35	0	15	13	0-2	0	3.55
Bill James	R	27	1	0	0	0	5.1	6	0	2	1	0-0	0	3.38

1919 St. Louis Cardinals 7th NL 54-83 .394 40.5 GB

Branch Rickey

Player	Gm by Position	B	Age	G	AB	R	H	2B	3B	HR	RBI	BB	SO	SB	Avg	OBP	Slg
Verne Clemons	C75	R	27	88	239	14	63	13	2	2	22	26	13	4	.264	.336	.360
Dots Miller	1B68,2B28	R	32	101	346	38	80	10	4	1	24	13	23	6	.231	.265	.292
Milt Stock	2B77,3B58	R	25	135	492	56	151	16	4	0	52	49	21	17	.307	.371	.356
Rogers Hornsby	3B72,SS37,2B25*	R	23	138	512	68	163	15	9	8	71	48	41	17	.318	.384	.430
Doc Lavan	SS99	R	28	100	356	25	86	12	2	1	25	11	30	4	.242	.264	.295
Jack Smith	OF111	L	24	119	408	47	91	16	3	0	15	26	29	30	.223	.271	.277
Austin McHenry	OF103	R	23	110	371	41	106	19	11	1	47	19	57	7	.286	.322	.404
Cliff Heathcote	OF101,1B2	L	21	114	401	53	112	13	4	1	29	20	41	27	.279	.315	.339
Burt Shotton	OF67	L	34	85	270	35	77	13	5	1	20	22	25	17	.285	.341	.381
Joe Schultz	OF49,2B5	R	25	88	229	24	58	9	1	2	21	11	7	4	.253	.288	.328
Frank Snyder†	C48,1B1	R	26	50	154	7	28	4	2	0	14	5	13	2	.182	.213	.234
Gene Paulette†	1B35,SS3	R	28	43	144	11	31	6	0	0	11	9	6	4	.215	.261	.257
Pickles Dillhoefer	C39	R	24	45	108	11	23	3	2	0	12	8	6	5	.213	.267	.278
Fritz Mollwitz†	1B25	R	29	25	83	7	19	3	0	0	5	7	3	2	.229	.289	.265
Doug Baird†	3B8,2B1,OF1	R	27	16	33	4	7	0	1	0	4	2	3	2	.212	.257	.273
Roy Leslie	1B9	R	24	12	24	2	5	1	0	0	4	4	3	0	.208	.321	.250
Walton Cruise†	OF5,1B2	L	29	9	21	0	2	1	0	0	0	1	6	0	.095	.136	.143
Hal Janvrin†	2B2,3B1,SS1	R	26	7	14	1	3	1	0	0	1	2	2	0	.214	.313	.286
Tom Fisher	2B3	R	32	3	11	0	3	1	0	0	1	0	2	0	.273	.273	.364
Sam Fishburn	1B1,2B1	R	26	9	6	0	2	1	0	0	2	0	0	0	.333	.333	.500
Wally Kimmick	SS1	R	22	2	1	1	0	0	0	0	0	1	0	1	.000	.500	.000
Mike Pasquariello†		R	20	1	1	0	0	0	0	0	0	0	1	0	.000	.000	.000

R. Hornsby, 5 G at 1B

Pitcher	T	Age	G	GS	CG	ShO	IP	H	HR	BB	SO	W-L	Sv	ERA
Bill Doak	R	28	31	29	13	3	202.2	182	5	55	69	13-14	0	3.11
Jakie May	L	23	28	19	8	1	125.2	99	1	87	58	3-12	0	3.22
Marv Goodwin	R	28	33	17	7	0	179.0	163	3	33	48	11-9	0	2.51
Lee Meadows†	R	24	22	12	3	1	92.0	100	3	30	28	4-10	0	3.03
Ferdie Schupp†	L	28	10	10	6	0	69.2	55	2	30	37	4-4	0	3.75
Oscar Tuero	R	20	45	16	4	0	154.2	137	4	42	45	5-7	4	3.20
Bill Sherdel	L	22	36	11	7	0	137.1	137	3	42	52	5-9	1	3.47
Red Ames†	R	36	23	6	1	0	70.0	88	1	25	19	3-5	1	4.89
Elmer Jacobs†	R	26	17	8	4	1	85.1	81	2	25	31	3-6	1	2.53
Frank Woodward†	R	25	17	7	2	0	72.0	65	1	28	18	3-5	1	2.63
Oscar Horstmann	R	28	6	2	0	0	15.0	14	0	12	5	0-1	0	3.00
Bill Bolden	R	26	3	1	0	0	12.0	17	0	4	4	0-1	0	5.25
Roy Parker	R	23	2	0	0	0	2.0	6	0	1	0	0-0	0	31.50
Will Koenigsmark	R	23	1	0	0	0	0.0	2	0	1	0	0-0	0	—
Art Reinhart	L	20	1	0	0	0	0.0	0	0	0	0	0-0	0	—

1919 Philadelphia Phillies 8th NL 47-90 .343 47.5 GB

Jack Coombs (18-44)/Gavvy Cravath (29-46)

Player	Gm by Position	B	Age	G	AB	R	H	2B	3B	HR	RBI	BB	SO	SB	Avg	OBP	Slg
Bert Adams	C73	S	28	78	232	14	54	7	2	1	17	6	27	4	.233	.252	.293
Fred Luderus	1B138	L	33	138	509	60	149	30	6	5	49	54	48	6	.293	.365	.405
Gene Paulette†	2B58,OF10,1B1	R	28	67	243	20	63	8	3	1	31	19	10	10	.259	.316	.329
Lena Blackburne†	3B72,1B1	R	32	72	291	32	58	10	5	2	19	10	22	2	.199	.228	.289
Dave Bancroft	SS88	S	28	92	335	45	91	13	7	0	25	31	30	8	.272	.333	.352
Irish Meusel	OF128	R	26	135	521	65	159	26	7	5	59	15	13	24	.305	.327	.411
Cy Williams	OF108	L	31	109	435	54	121	21	1	9	39	30	43	9	.278	.335	.393
Leo Callahan	OF58	L	28	81	235	26	54	14	4	1	9	29	19	5	.230	.317	.336
Possum Whitted†	OF47,2B26,1B2	R	29	78	287	32	72	14	1	3	32	14	20	5	.251	.286	.338
Harry Pearce	2B43,SS23,3B2	R	29	68	244	24	44	3	3	0	9	8	27	6	.180	.209	.217
Doug Baird†	3B66	R	27	66	242	33	61	13	3	2	30	22	28	13	.252	.317	.355
Gavy Cravath	OF56	R	38	83	214	34	73	18	5	12	45	35	21	8	.341	.438	.640
Ed Sicking†	SS41,2B22	R	22	61	185	16	40	2	1	0	15	8	17	4	.216	.253	.238
Walt Tragesser†	C34	R	32	35	114	7	27	7	0	0	8	9	31	4	.237	.298	.298
Hick Cady	C29	R	33	34	98	6	21	6	0	1	19	4	8	1	.214	.252	.306
Bevo LeBourveau	OF17	L	24	17	63	4	17	0	0	0	0	10	8	2	.270	.370	.270
Nig Clarke	C22	L	36	26	62	4	15	3	0	0	2	4	5	1	.242	.299	.290
Doc Wallace	SS2	R	25	2	4	0	1	0	0	0	0	0	1	0	.250	.250	.250
Lou Raymond	2B1	R	24	1	2	0	1	0	0	0	0	0	0	0	.500	.500	.500
Mike Pasquariello†	1B1	R	20	1	1	1	1	0	0	0	0	0	0	0	1.000	1.000	1.000
John Cavanaugh	3B1	R	19	1	1	0	0	0	0	0	0	0	1	0	.000	.000	.000
Bert Yeabsley		R	25	3	0	0	0	0	0	0	0	1	0	0	—	1.000	—

Pitcher	T	Age	G	GS	CG	ShO	IP	H	HR	BB	SO	W-L	Sv	ERA
George Smith†	R	27	31	19	11	1	184.2	194	7	46	42	5-11	0	3.22
Brad Hogg	R	31	22	19	13	0	150.1	163	7	55	48	5-12	0	4.43
Eppa Rixey	L	28	23	18	11	1	154.0	160	4	50	63	6-12	0	3.97
Lee Meadows†	R	24	18	17	15	3	149.1	128	2	49	88	8-10	0	2.47
Gene Packard	L	31	21	16	10	1	134.1	167	3	30	24	6-8	1	4.15
Elmer Jacobs†	R	26	17	15	13	0	128.2	150	5	44	37	6-10	0	3.85
Frank Woodward†	R	25	17	12	6	0	100.2	109	5	35	27	6-9	0	4.74
Larry Cheney†	R	33	9	6	5	0	57.1	69	2	28	25	2-5	0	4.55
Milt Watson	R	29	8	4	3	0	47.0	51	2	19	12	2-4	0	5.17
Joe Oeschger†	R	28	5	4	2	0	38.0	52	1	16	5	0-1	0	5.92
Mike Cantwell	L	23	5	3	2	0	27.1	36	1	9	6	1-3	0	5.60
Red Ames†	R	36	3	2	1	0	16.0	26	0	3	4	0-2	1	6.19
Pat Murray	L	21	8	2	1	0	34.1	50	0	12	11	0-2	0	6.29
Mike Prendergast	R	30	5	1	0	0	15.0	20	0	10	5	0-1	0	8.40
Rags Faircloth	R	26	2	0	0	0	2.0	5	0	0	0	0-0	0	9.00
Lefty Weinert	L	17	1	0	0	0	4.0	11	0	2	0	0-0	0	18.00

»1920 Cleveland Indians 1st AL 98-56 .636 —

Tris Speaker

Player	Gm by Position	B	Age	G	AB	R	H	2B	3B	HR	RBI	BB	SO	SB	Avg	OBP	Slg
Steve O'Neill	C148	R	28	149	489	63	157	39	5	3	55	69	39	3	.321	.408	.440
Doc Johnston	1B147	L	32	147	535	68	156	24	10	2	71	28	32	13	.292	.333	.385
Bill Wambsganss	2B153	R	26	153	565	83	138	16	11	1	55	54	26	9	.244	.316	.317
Larry Gardner	3B154	L	34	154	597	72	185	31	11	3	118	53	25	3	.310	.367	.414
Ray Chapman	SS111	R	29	111	435	97	132	27	8	3	49	52	38	13	.303	.380	.423
Tris Speaker	OF148	L	32	150	552	137	214	50	11	8	107	97	13	10	.388	.483	.562
Elmer Smith	OF129	L	27	129	456	82	144	37	10	12	103	53	35	5	.316	.391	.520
Charlie Jamieson	OF98,1B4	L	27	108	370	69	118	17	7	1	40	41	26	2	.319	.388	.411
Joe Evans	OF43,SS6	R	25	56	172	32	60	9	9	0	23	15	3	6	.349	.404	.506
Jack Graney	OF47	L	34	62	152	31	45	11	1	0	13	27	21	4	.296	.412	.382
Joe Wood	OF54,P1	R	30	61	137	25	37	11	2	1	30	25	16	1	.270	.390	.401
Harry Lunte	SS21,2B3	R	27	23	71	6	14	0	0	0	7	5	6	0	.197	.250	.197
Joe Sewell	SS22	L	21	22	70	14	23	4	1	0	12	9	4	1	.329	.413	.414
George Burns†	1B1,OF1	R	27	44	56	7	15	4	1	0	13	4	3	1	.268	.339	.375
Les Nunamaker	C17,1B6	R	31	34	54	10	18	3	0	3	14	4	5	1	.333	.379	.500
Pinch Thomas	C7	L	32	9	9	2	3	1	0	0	0	3	1	0	.333	.500	.444

Pitcher	T	Age	G	GS	CG	ShO	IP	H	HR	BB	SO	W-L	Sv	ERA
Jim Bagby	R	30	48	39	30	3	339.2	338	9	79	73	31-12	0	2.89
Stan Coveleski	R	30	41	37	26	3	315.0	284	6	65	133	24-14	2	2.49
Ray Caldwell	R	32	34	33	20	0	237.2	286	9	63	80	20-10	0	3.86
Guy Morton	R	27	29	17	5	1	137.0	140	2	57	72	8-6	1	4.47
Duster Mails	L	25	9	8	6	2	63.1	54	1	18	25	7-0	0	1.85
Joe Boehling	L	29	3	2	0	0	13.0	16	0	10	4	0-1	0	4.85
George Uhle	R	21	27	6	2	0	84.2	98	3	29	27	4-5	1	5.21
Dick Niehaus	L	27	19	3	0	0	40.0	42	0	16	12	1-2	2	3.60
Elmer Myers†	R	26	16	7	2	0	71.2	93	1	23	16	2-4	1	4.77
Tony Faeth	R	26	13	0	0	0	25.0	31	0	20	14	0-0	0	4.32
Bob Clark	R	22	11	2	2	1	42.0	59	0	13	8	1-2	0	3.43
Tim Murchison	L	23	2	0	0	0	5.0	3	0	4	0	0-0	0	0.00
Joe Wood	R	30	1	0	0	0	2.0	4	0	2	1	0-0	0	22.50
George Ellison	R	25	1	0	0	0	1.0	0	0	2	1	0-0	0	0.00

1920 Chicago White Sox 2nd AL 96-58 .623 2.0 GB

Kid Gleason

Player	Gm by Position	B	Age	G	AB	R	H	2B	3B	HR	RBI	BB	SO	SB	Avg	OBP	Slg
Ray Schalk	C151	R	27	151	485	64	131	25	5	1	61	68	19	10	.270	.362	.348
Shano Collins	1B117	R	34	133	495	70	150	21	10	1	63	23	24	12	.303	.339	.392
Eddie Collins	2B153,OF12	L	33	153	602	117	224	38	13	3	76	69	19	19	.372	.438	.493
Buck Weaver	3B126,SS25	R	29	151	629	102	208	34	8	2	74	28	23	19	.331	.365	.420
Swede Risberg	SS124	R	25	126	458	53	122	21	10	2	65	31	45	12	.266	.316	.369
Joe Jackson	OF145	L	30	146	570	105	218	42	20	12	121	56	14	9	.382	.444	.589
Happy Felsch	OF142	R	28	142	556	88	188	40	15	14	115	37	25	8	.338	.384	.540
Nemo Leibold	OF106	L	28	108	413	61	91	16	3	1	28	55	30	7	.220	.316	.281
Amos Strunk†	OF49	L	31	51	183	32	42	7	1	1	14	28	15	1	.230	.332	.295
Ted Jourdan	1B46	L	24	48	150	16	36	5	2	0	8	17	17	3	.240	.337	.300
Fred McMullin	3B29,2B3,SS1	R	28	46	127	14	25	1	4	0	13	9	13	1	.197	.255	.268
Eddie Murphy	OF19,3B3	L	28	58	118	22	40	2	1	0	19	12	4	1	.339	.405	.373
Byrd Lynn	C14	R	31	16	25	0	8	2	1	0	3	1	3	0	.320	.346	.480
Harvey McClellan	SS4,3B2	R	25	10	18	4	6	1	1	0	5	4	1	2	.333	.455	.500
Bibb Falk	OF4	L	21	7	17	1	5	1	1	0	2	0	5	0	.294	.294	.471
Bubber Jonnard	C1	R	22	2	5	0	0	0	0	0	0	0	1	0	.000	.000	.000

Pitcher	T	Age	G	GS	CG	ShO	IP	H	HR	BB	SO	W-L	Sv	ERA
Red Faber	R	31	40	39	28	2	319.0	332	8	88	108	23-13	1	2.99
Lefty Williams	L	27	39	38	26	0	299.0	302	15	90	128	22-14	0	3.91
Eddie Cicotte	R	36	37	35	28	4	303.1	316	6	74	87	21-10	2	3.26
Dickie Kerr	L	26	45	28	20	3	253.2	266	7	72	72	21-9	5	3.37
Shovel Hodge	R	26	4	2	1	0	19.2	15	0	12	5	1-1	0	2.29
Joe Kiefer	R	20	2	1	0	0	4.2	7	0	5	1	0-1	0	15.43
Roy Wilkinson	R	26	34	11	9	0	145.0	162	6	48	30	7-9	2	4.03
George Payne	R	30	12	0	0	0	29.2	39	2	9	7	1-1	0	5.46
Spencer Heath	R	25	4	0	0	0	7.0	19	1	2	0	0-0	0	15.43
Grover Lowdermilk	R	35	3	0	0	0	5.1	9	0	5	0	0-0	0	6.75

1920 New York Yankees 3rd AL 95-59 .617 3.0 GB

Miller Huggins

Player	Gm by Position	B	Age	G	AB	R	H	2B	3B	HR	RBI	BB	SO	SB	Avg	OBP	Slg
Muddy Ruel	C80	R	24	82	261	30	70	14	1	1	15	15	18	4	.268	.310	.341
Wally Pipp	1B153	L	27	153	610	109	171	30	14	11	76	48	54	4	.280	.339	.430
Del Pratt	2B154	R	32	154	574	84	180	37	8	4	97	50	24	12	.314	.372	.427
Aaron Ward	3B114,SS12	R	23	127	496	62	127	18	7	11	54	33	84	7	.256	.304	.387
Roger Peckinpaugh	SS137	R	29	139	534	109	144	26	6	8	54	72	47	8	.270	.356	.386
Babe Ruth	OF141,1B2,P1	L	25	142	458	158	172	36	9	54	137	148	80	14	.376	.530	.847
Ping Bodie	OF129	R	32	129	471	63	139	26	12	7	79	40	30	6	.295	.350	.446
Duffy Lewis	OF99	R	32	107	365	34	99	8	1	4	61	24	32	2	.271	.320	.332
Bob Meusel	OF64,3B45,1B2	R	23	119	460	75	151	40	7	11	83	20	72	4	.328	.359	.517
Truck Hannah	C78	R	31	79	259	24	64	11	1	2	25	24	35	2	.247	.313	.320
Sammy Vick	OF35	R	25	51	118	21	26	7	1	0	11	14	20	1	.220	.313	.297
Frank Gleich	OF15	L	26	24	41	6	5	0	0	0	3	6	10	0	.122	.234	.122
Fred Hofmann	C14	R	26	15	24	3	7	0	0	0	1	1	2	0	.292	.346	.292
Chick Fewster	SS5,2B3	R	24	21	21	8	6	1	0	0	1	7	2	0	.286	.464	.333
Joe Lucey	2B1,SS1	R	23	3	3	0	0	0	0	0	0	0	0	0	.000	.000	.000
Ray French	SS1	R	25	2	2	2	0	0	0	0	0	0	1	0	.000	.000	.000
Tom Connelly		L	22	1	1	0	0	0	0	0	0	0	0	0	.000	.000	.000

Pitcher	T	Age	G	GS	CG	ShO	IP	H	HR	BB	SO	W-L	Sv	ERA
Carl Mays	R	28	45	37	26	6	312.0	310	13	84	92	26-11	2	3.06
Bob Shawkey	R	29	38	31	20	5	267.2	246	10	85	126	20-13	2	2.45
Jack Quinn	R	36	41	31	16	2	253.1	271	8	48	101	18-10	3	3.20
Rip Collins	R	24	36	20	12	3	187.1	171	6	79	66	14-8	1	3.17
George Mogridge	L	31	26	15	7	0	125.1	146	4	36	35	5-9	1	4.31
Babe Ruth	L	25	1	1	0	0	4.0	3	0	2	0	1-0	0	4.50
Hank Thormahlen	L	23	29	14	5	0	143.1	178	5	43	35	9-6	1	4.14
Bob McGraw	R	25	15	0	0	0	27.0	24	1	20	11	0-0	0	4.67
Ernie Shore	R	29	14	5	2	0	44.1	61	1	21	12	2-2	1	4.87
Lefty O'Doul	L	23	2	0	0	0	3.2	4	0	2	2	0-0	0	4.91

1920 St. Louis Browns 4th AL 76-77 .497 21.5 GB

Jimmy Burke

Player	Gm by Position	B	Age	G	AB	R	H	2B	3B	HR	RBI	BB	SO	SB	Avg	OBP	Slg
Hank Severeid	C117	R	29	123	422	46	117	14	5	2	49	33	11	5	.277	.336	.348
George Sisler	1B154,P1	L	27	154	631	137	257	49	18	19	122	46	19	42	.407	.449	.632
Joe Gedeon	2B153	R	26	153	606	95	177	33	6	0	61	55	36	1	.292	.355	.366
Jimmy Austin	3B75	S	40	83	280	38	76	11	3	1	32	31	15	2	.271	.352	.343
Wally Gerber	SS154	R	28	154	584	70	163	26	2	2	60	58	32	4	.279	.346	.341
Baby Doll Jacobson	OF154,1B1	R	29	154	609	97	216	34	14	9	122	46	37	11	.355	.402	.501
Jack Tobin	OF147	L	28	147	593	94	202	34	10	4	62	39	23	21	.341	.383	.452
Ken Williams	OF138	L	30	141	521	90	160	34	13	10	72	41	26	18	.307	.362	.480
Earl Smith	3B70,OF15	S	29	103	353	45	108	21	8	3	55	13	18	11	.306	.336	.436
Josh Billings	C40	R	28	66	155	19	43	5	2	0	11	11	10	1	.277	.353	.335
Frank Thompson	3B14,2B2	R	24	22	53	7	9	0	0	0	5	13	10	1	.170	.343	.170
Pat Collins	C7	R	23	23	28	5	6	1	0	0	6	3	5	0	.214	.290	.250
Laymon Lamb	OF7	R	25	9	24	4	9	2	0	0	4	0	7	2	.375	.375	.458
Dutch Wetzel	OF5	R	26	6	19	5	9	1	1	0	5	4	1	0	.474	.565	.632
John Shovlin	SS5	R	29	7	7	2	2	0	0	0	2	0	0	0	.286	.286	.286
Marty McManus	3B1	R	20	1	3	0	1	0	1	0	1	0	0	0	.333	.333	1.000
Dud Lee	SS1	L	20	1	2	2	2	0	0	0	1	0	0	1	1.000	1.000	1.000
Paul Speraw	3B1	R	26	1	2	0	0	0	0	0	0	0	0	0	.000	.000	.000
Billy Mullen		R	24	1	1	0	0	0	0	0	0	0	0	0	.000	.000	.000
Johnny Heving		R	24	1	1	0	0	0	0	0	0	0	0	0	.000	.000	.000
Earl Pruess	OF1	R	25	1	0	1	0	0	0	0	0	1	0	1	—	1.000	—

Pitcher	T	Age	G	GS	CG	ShO	IP	H	HR	BB	SO	W-L	Sv	ERA
Dixie Davis	R	29	38	31	22	0	269.1	250	10	149	85	18-12	0	3.17
Urban Shocker	R	29	38	28	22	5	245.2	224	10	70	107	20-10	5	2.71
Allen Sothoron	R	27	36	26	12	1	218.1	263	6	89	81	8-15	2	4.70
Carl Weilman	L	30	30	24	13	1	183.1	201	6	61	45	9-13	2	4.47
Elam Vangilder	R	24	24	13	4	0	104.2	131	7	40	25	3-8	0	5.50
Bill Bayne	L	21	18	13	6	1	99.2	102	3	41	38	5-6	0	3.70
Joe DeBerry	R	23	10	7	3	1	54.2	65	2	20	12	2-4	0	4.94
Adrian Lynch	R	23	5	3	1	0	22.1	23	1	17	8	2-0	0	5.24
Ray Richmond	R	24	2	2	1	0	17.0	18	0	9	4	2-0	0	6.35
Hod Leverette	R	31	3	2	0	0	10.1	9	1	12	0	0-2	0	5.23
Bert Gallia†	R	28	2	1	0	0	3.2	8	0	3	0	0-1	0	7.36
Bill Burwell	R	25	33	2	0	0	113.1	133	5	42	30	6-4	4	3.65
Roy Sanders	R	26	8	1	0	0	17.1	20	0	17	2	1-1	0	5.19
Lefty Leifield	L	36	4	0	0	0	9.0	17	0	3	3	0-0	0	7.00
George Boehler	R	28	3	1	0	0	7.0	10	1	4	2	0-1	0	7.71
John Scheneberg	R	32	1	0	0	0	2.0	7	0	1	0	0-0	0	27.00
George Sisler	L	27	1	0	0	0	1.0	0	0	0	2	0-0	1	0.00

1920 Boston Red Sox 5th AL 72-81 .471 25.5 GB

Ed Barrow

Player	Gm by Position	B	Age	G	AB	R	H	2B	3B	HR	RBI	BB	SO	SB	Avg	OBP	Slg
Roxy Walters	C85,1B2	R	27	88	258	25	51	11	1	0	28	30	21	2	.198	.303	.248
Stuffy McInnis	1B148	R	29	148	559	50	166	21	3	2	71	18	19	6	.297	.321	.356
Mike McNally	2B76,SS8,1B6	R	27	93	312	42	80	5	1	0	23	31	24	13	.256	.326	.279
Eddie Foster	3B88,2B21	R	33	117	386	48	100	17	6	0	41	42	17	10	.259	.336	.334
Everett Scott	SS154	R	27	154	569	41	153	21	12	4	61	21	15	4	.269	.300	.369
Mike Menosky	OF141	L	25	141	532	80	158	24	9	3	64	65	52	23	.297	.383	.393
Harry Hooper	OF139	L	32	139	536	91	167	30	17	7	53	88	27	16	.312	.411	.470
Tim Hendryx	OF98	R	29	99	363	54	119	21	5	0	73	42	27	7	.328	.400	.413
Wally Schang	C73,OF40	S	30	122	387	58	118	30	7	4	51	64	37	7	.305	.413	.450
Ossie Vitt	3B64,2B21	R	30	87	296	50	65	10	4	1	28	43	10	5	.220	.321	.291
Cliff Brady	2B53	R	23	53	180	16	41	5	1	0	12	13	12	0	.228	.284	.267
Gene Bailey†	OF40	R	26	46	135	14	31	2	0	0	5	9	15	2	.230	.283	.244
Joe Bush	P35,OF2	R	27	45	102	14	25	2	0	0	7	9	15	0	.245	.306	.265
Hack Eibel	OF5,P3,1B1	L	26	29	43	4	8	2	0	0	6	3	6	1	.186	.239	.233
Hob Hiller	3B6,SS5,2B2*	R	27	17	29	4	5	1	1	0	2	2	5	0	.172	.226	.276
Ben Paschal	OF7	R	24	9	28	5	10	0	0	0	5	5	2	1	.357	.455	.357
Mickey Devine	C5	R	28	8	12	1	2	0	0	0	0	1	2	1	.167	.231	.167
Herb Hunter	OF4	L	23	4	12	2	1	0	0	0	0	1	1	0	.083	.154	.083
George Orme	OF3	R	28	4	6	4	2	0	0	0	1	3	0	0	.333	.556	.333
Ed Chaplin	C2	L	26	4	5	2	1	1	0	0	1	4	1	0	.200	.556	.400
Ray Grimes	1B1	R	26	1	4	1	1	0	0	0	0	1	0	0	.250	.400	.250
Jigger Statz†	OF2	R	22	2	3	0	0	0	0	0	0	0	0	0	.000	.000	.000
Paddy Smith	C1	L	26	2	2	0	0	0	0	0	0	0	1	0	.000	.000	.000

H. Hiller, 1 G at OF

Pitcher	T	Age	G	GS	CG	ShO	IP	H	HR	BB	SO	W-L	Sv	ERA
Sad Sam Jones	R	27	37	33	20	3	274.0	302	9	79	86	13-16	0	3.94
Joe Bush	R	27	35	32	18	0	243.2	287	3	94	88	15-15	1	4.25
Herb Pennock	L	26	37	31	19	4	242.1	244	9	61	68	16-13	2	3.68
Harry Harper	L	25	27	22	11	1	162.2	163	9	66	71	5-14	0	3.04
Waite Hoyt	R	20	22	11	6	2	121.1	123	2	47	45	6-6	1	4.38
Allan Russell	R	26	16	10	7	0	107.2	100	3	38	53	5-6	1	3.01
Elmer Myers†	R	26	12	10	9	1	97.0	90	1	24	34	9-1	0	2.13
Benn Karr	R	26	26	2	0	0	91.2	109	3	24	21	3-8	1	4.81
Gary Fortune	R	25	14	3	1	0	41.2	46	0	23	10	0-2	0	5.83
Hack Eibel	L	26	3	0	0	0	10.1	10	0	3	5	0-0	0	3.48
Hal Deviney	R	27	1	0	0	0	3.0	7	0	2	0	0-0	0	15.00

1920 Washington Senators 6th AL 68-84 .447 29.0 GB

Clark Griffith

Player	Gm by Position	B	Age	G	AB	R	H	2B	3B	HR	RBI	BB	SO	SB	Avg	OBP	Slg
Patsy Gharrity	C121,1B7,OF1	R	28	131	428	51	105	18	3	3	44	37	52	6	.245	.307	.322
Joe Judge	1B124	L	26	126	493	103	164	19	15	5	51	65	34	12	.333	.416	.462
Bucky Harris	2B135	R	23	137	506	76	152	26	6	1	68	41	36	16	.300	.377	.381
Frank Ellerbe	3B75,SS19,OF1	R	24	101	336	38	98	14	2	0	36	19	23	5	.292	.331	.345
Jim O'Neill	SS80,2B2	R	27	86	294	27	85	17	7	1	40	13	30	3	.289	.324	.405
Sam Rice	OF153	L	30	153	624	83	211	29	9	3	80	39	23	63	.338	.381	.428
Braggo Roth	OF128	R	27	138	468	80	136	23	8	9	92	75	57	24	.291	.395	.432
Clyde Milan	OF123	L	33	126	506	70	163	22	5	3	41	28	12	10	.322	.364	.403
Howard Shanks	3B63,OF35,1B14*	R	29	128	444	56	119	16	7	4	37	29	43	11	.268	.316	.363
Red Shannon†	SS31,2B16,3B15	S	23	62	222	30	64	8	7	0	30	22	32	2	.288	.352	.387
Val Picinich	C45	R	23	48	133	14	27	6	2	3	14	9	33	0	.203	.259	.346
Frank Brower	OF20,1B9,3B1	L	27	36	119	21	37	7	2	1	13	9	11	1	.311	.374	.429
Walter Johnson	P21,OF2	R	32	33	64	7	17	1	3	1	8	3	12	0	.266	.299	.422
Frank O'Rourke	SS13,3B1	R	25	14	54	8	16	1	0	0	5	2	5	2	.296	.321	.315
George McBride	SS13	R	39	13	41	6	9	1	0	0	3	2	3	0	.220	.256	.244
Ricardo Torres	1B7,C5	R	29	16	30	8	10	1	0	0	3	1	4	0	.333	.355	.367
Jack Calvo	OF10	L	26	17	23	5	1	0	1	0	2	2	2	0	.043	.120	.130
Doc Prothro	3B2,SS2	R	26	6	13	2	5	0	0	0	2	0	4	0	.385	.385	.385
Ed Johnson	OF2	L	21	2	8	0	2	0	0	0	1	0	0	0	.250	.250	.250
Fred Thomas†	3B2	R	27	3	7	0	1	0	0	0	0	0	1	0	.143	.333	.143
Bill Hollahan	3B3	R	23	3	4	0	1	0	0	0	1	1	2	1	.250	.400	.250
Bobby LaMotte	3B1,SS1	R	22	4	3	0	0	0	0	0	0	1	1	0	.000	.250	.000
Allie Watt	2B1	R	20	1	1	0	1	1	0	0	1	0	0	0	1.000	1.000	2.000
Elmer Bowman		R	23	2	1	1	0	0	0	0	0	1	0	0	.000	.500	.000

H. Shanks, 5 G at 2B, 1 G at SS

Pitcher	T	Age	G	GS	CG	ShO	IP	H	HR	BB	SO	W-L	Sv	ERA
Jim Shaw	R	26	38	32	17	0	236.1	285	12	87	88	11-18	1	4.27
Tom Zachary	L	24	44	30	18	3	262.2	289	7	78	53	15-16	2	3.77
Eric Erickson	R	25	39	28	12	0	239.1	231	13	128	87	12-16	1	3.84
Henry Courtney	L	21	37	24	10	1	188.0	223	6	77	48	8-11	0	4.74
Walter Johnson	R	32	21	15	12	4	143.2	135	5	27	78	8-10	3	3.13
Al Schacht	R	27	22	11	5	1	99.1	130	2	30	19	6-4	1	4.44
Duke Shirey	R	22	2	1	0	0	4.0	5	0	2	0	0-1	0	6.75
Jose Acosta	R	29	17	5	4	1	82.2	92	1	26	9	5-4	1	4.03
Bill Snyder	R	22	16	4	1	0	54.0	59	1	28	17	2-1	1	4.17
Harry Biemiller	R	22	5	2	1	0	17.0	21	1	13	10	1-0	0	4.76
Gus Bono	R	25	4	1	0	0	12.1	17	0	6	4	0-2	0	8.76
Leon Carlson	R	25	3	0	0	0	12.1	14	1	2	3	0-0	0	3.65
Joe Gleason	R	24	3	0	0	0	8.0	14	2	6	2	0-0	0	13.50
Clarence Fisher	R	21	2	0	0	0	3.2	5	0	5	0	0-1	0	9.82
Jerry Conway	L	19	1	0	0	0	2.0	1	0	1	0	0-0	0	0.00
Joe Engel	L	27	1	0	0	0	1.2	0	0	4	0	0-0	0	21.60

1920 Detroit Tigers 7th AL 61-93 .396 37.0 GB

Hughie Jennings

Player	Gm by Position	B	Age	G	AB	R	H	2B	3B	HR	RBI	BB	SO	SB	Avg	OBP	Slg
Oscar Stanage	C77	R	37	78	238	12	55	17	0	0	17	14	21	0	.231	.277	.303
Harry Heilmann	1B122,OF21	R	25	145	543	66	168	28	5	9	89	39	32	3	.309	.358	.429
Ralph Young	2B150	S	30	150	594	84	173	21	6	0	33	85	30	8	.291	.382	.347
Babe Pinelli	3B74,SS18,2B1	R	24	102	284	33	65	9	3	0	21	25	16	6	.229	.296	.282
Donie Bush	SS140	S	32	141	506	85	133	18	5	1	33	73	32	15	.263	.357	.324
Bobby Veach	OF154	L	32	154	612	92	188	39	15	11	113	36	22	11	.307	.353	.474
Ty Cobb	OF112	L	33	112	428	86	143	28	8	2	63	58	28	14	.334	.416	.451
Chick Shorten	OF99	L	28	116	364	35	105	9	6	1	40	28	14	2	.288	.339	.354
Ira Flagstead	OF82	R	26	110	311	40	73	13	5	3	35	37	27	3	.235	.318	.338
Bob Jones	3B67,2B5,SS1	L	30	81	265	35	66	6	3	1	18	22	13	3	.249	.309	.306
Eddie Ainsmith	C61	R	28	69	186	19	43	5	3	1	19	14	19	4	.231	.285	.306
Babe Ellison	1B33,OF4,3B1	R	24	61	155	11	34	7	2	0	21	8	26	4	.219	.258	.290
Sammy Hale	3B16,OF4,2B1	R	23	76	116	13	34	3	3	1	14	5	15	2	.293	.322	.397
Clyde Manion	C30	R	23	32	80	4	22	4	1	0	8	4	7	0	.275	.318	.350
Larry Woodall	C15	R	25	18	49	4	12	1	0	0	5	2	6	0	.245	.275	.265
Clarence Huber	3B11	R	23	11	42	4	9	2	1	0	5	0	5	0	.214	.214	.310
Danny Claire	SS3	R	22	3	7	1	1	0	0	0	0	0	0	0	.143	.143	.143

Pitcher	T	Age	G	GS	CG	ShO	IP	H	HR	BB	SO	W-L	Sv	ERA
Howard Ehmke	R	26	38	33	23	2	268.1	250	8	124	98	15-18	3	3.29
Hooks Dauss	R	30	38	32	18	0	270.1	308	11	84	82	13-21	0	3.56
Dutch Leonard	L	28	28	27	10	3	191.1	192	8	63	76	10-17	0	4.33
Red Oldham	L	26	39	23	11	1	215.1	248	5	91	62	8-13	1	3.85
John Bogart	R	19	4	3	0	0	23.2	16	0	18	5	2-1	0	3.04
Bernie Boland	R	28	4	3	1	0	17.1	23	0	14	4	0-2	0	7.79
Roy Crumpler	L	23	2	2	1	0	13.0	17	2	11	2	1-0	0	5.54
Mutt Wilson	R	23	3	2	1	0	13.0	12	0	5	4	1-1	0	3.46
Doc Ayers	R	30	46	22	9	3	208.2	217	6	62	103	7-14	1	3.88
Frank Okrie	L	23	21	1	1	0	41.0	44	2	18	9	1-2	0	5.27
Ernie Alten	L	25	14	1	0	0	23.0	40	2	9	4	0-1	0	9.00
Harry Baumgartner	R	27	9	0	0	0	18.0	18	1	6	7	0-1	0	4.00
John Glaiser	R	25	9	1	0	0	17.0	23	1	8	3	0-0	1	6.35
Bill Morrisette	R	27	8	3	1	0	27.0	25	0	19	15	1-1	0	4.33
Allen Conkwright	R	23	5	2	0	0	19.1	29	0	16	4	2-1	1	6.98
Red Cox	R	25	3	0	0	0	5.0	9	0	3	1	0-0	0	5.40
Jack Coombs	R	37	2	0	0	0	5.2	7	0	2	1	0-0	0	3.18
Cy Fried	L	22	2	0	0	0	1.2	3	0	4	0	0-0	0	16.20
Slim Love	L	29	1	0	0	0	4.1	6	0	4	2	0-0	0	8.31
Lou Vedder	R	23	1	0	0	0	2.0	0	0	0	1	0-0	0	0.00

1920 Philadelphia Athletics 8th AL 48-106 .312 50.0 GB

Connie Mack

Player	Gm by Position	B	Age	G	AB	R	H	2B	3B	HR	RBI	BB	SO	SB	Avg	OBP	Slg
Cy Perkins	C146,2B1	R	24	148	492	40	128	24	6	5	52	28	35	5	.260	.303	.364
Ivy Griffin	1B126,2B2	L	23	129	467	46	111	15	1	0	20	17	49	3	.238	.281	.274
Jimmy Dykes	2B108,3B34	R	23	142	546	81	140	25	4	8	35	55	73	6	.256	.334	.361
Fred Thomas†	3B61,SS12	R	27	76	255	27	59	6	3	1	11	26	17	8	.231	.307	.290
Chick Galloway	SS84,2B4,3B3	R	23	98	298	28	60	9	3	0	18	22	22	2	.201	.259	.252
Tilly Walker	OF149	R	32	149	585	79	157	23	7	17	82	41	59	9	.268	.321	.419
Frank Welch	OF97	R	22	100	360	43	93	17	5	4	40	26	41	2	.258	.312	.367
Amos Strunk†	OF53	L	31	58	202	23	60	9	3	0	20	21	9	0	.297	.363	.371
Joe Dugan	3B60,SS32,2B31	R	23	123	491	65	158	40	5	3	60	19	51	5	.322	.351	.442
Whitey Witt	OF50,2B10,SS2	L	24	65	218	29	70	11	3	1	25	27	16	2	.321	.396	.413
Glenn Myatt	OF37,C22	L	22	70	196	14	49	8	3	0	18	12	22	1	.250	.293	.321
Dick Burrus	1B31,OF2	L	22	71	135	11	25	8	0	0	10	5	7	0	.185	.225	.244
Frank Walker	OF24	R	25	24	91	10	21	2	2	0	10	5	14	0	.231	.278	.297
Red Shannon†	SS24	S	23	25	88	4	15	1	1	0	3	4	12	1	.170	.207	.205
Paul Johnson	OF18	R	23	18	72	6	15	0	0	0	5	4	8	1	.208	.250	.208
Lyle Bigbee	P12,OF12	L	26	37	70	4	13	1	0	1	8	8	10	1	.186	.269	.243
Charlie High	OF17	L	21	17	65	7	20	2	1	1	6	3	6	0	.308	.375	.415
George Burns†	OF13	R	27	22	60	1	14	3	0	1	7	6	7	4	.233	.313	.333
Lena Styles	C9,1B7	R	20	24	50	5	13	3	1	0	5	6	7	1	.260	.339	.360
Emmett McCann	SS11	R	18	13	34	4	9	1	1	0	3	3	1	0	.265	.342	.353
Johnny Walker	C6	R	23	9	22	0	5	1	0	0	5	0	1	0	.227	.227	.273
Bill Kelly	1B2	R	21	9	13	0	3	1	0	0	0	0	2	0	.231	.231	.308
Ed Wingo	C1	R	24	1	4	0	1	0	0	0	1	0	0	0	.250	.250	.250
Teddy Kearns		R	20	1	1	0	0	0	0	0	0	0	0	0	.000	.000	.000

Pitcher	T	Age	G	GS	CG	ShO	IP	H	HR	BB	SO	W-L	Sv	ERA
Rollie Naylor	R	28	42	36	20	0	251.1	306	7	86	90	10-23	0	3.47
Scott Perry	R	29	42	34	20	1	263.2	310	14	65	79	11-25	1	3.62
Slim Harriss	R	23	31	25	11	0	192.0	226	5	57	60	9-14	0	4.08
Roy Moore	L	21	24	14	7	0	132.2	161	6	64	45	1-13	0	4.68
Walt Kinney	L	26	10	8	5	1	61.0	59	3	28	19	2-4	0	3.10
Pat Martin	L	26	8	5	2	0	32.1	48	2	25	14	1-4	0	6.12
Bill Knowlton	R	27	1	1	0	0	5.2	9	0	3	5	0-1	0	4.76
Fred Heimach	L	19	1	1	0	0	5.0	13	0	1	0	0-1	0	14.40
Eddie Rommel	R	22	33	12	8	2	173.2	165	5	43	43	7-7	1	2.85
Dave Keefe	R	23	31	13	7	1	130.1	129	2	30	41	6-7	0	2.97
Bob Hasty	R	24	19	4	1	0	71.2	91	5	28	12	1-3	0	5.02
Lyle Bigbee	R	26	12	2	0	0	45.0	66	5	25	12	0-3	0	8.00
John Slappey	L	21	3	1	0	0	6.1	15	0	4	1	0-1	0	7.11
Charlie Eckert	R	22	2	0	0	0	5.2	8	0	1	1	0-0	0	4.76
Bill Shanner	R	25	1	0	0	0	4.0	6	2	1	1	0-0	0	6.75

»1920 Brooklyn Dodgers 1st NL 93-61 .604 —

Wilbert Robinson

Player	Gm by Position	B	Age	G	AB	R	H	2B	3B	HR	RBI	BB	SO	SB	Avg	OBP	Slg
Otto Miller	C89	R	31	90	301	16	87	9	2	0	33	9	18	0	.289	.312	.332
Ed Konetchy	1B130	R	34	131	497	62	153	22	12	5	63	33	18	3	.308	.352	.431
Pete Kilduff	2B134,3B5	R	27	141	478	62	130	26	8	0	58	58	43	2	.272	.351	.360
Jimmy Johnston	3B146,OF7,SS3	R	30	155	635	87	185	17	12	1	52	43	23	19	.291	.338	.361
Ivy Olson	SS125,2B21	R	34	143	637	71	162	13	11	1	46	20	19	4	.254	.278	.314
Hi Myers	OF152,3B2	R	31	154	582	83	177	36	22	4	80	35	54	9	.304	.345	.462
Zack Wheat	OF148	L	32	148	583	89	191	26	13	9	73	48	21	8	.328	.385	.463
Tommy Griffith	OF92	L	30	93	334	41	87	9	4	2	30	15	18	3	.260	.292	.329
Bernie Neis	OF83	S	24	95	249	38	63	11	2	2	22	26	35	9	.253	.329	.337
Ernie Krueger	C46	R	29	52	146	21	42	4	2	1	17	16	13	2	.288	.358	.363
Rowdy Elliott	C39	R	29	41	112	13	27	4	0	1	13	3	6	0	.241	.267	.304
Clarence Mitchell	P19,1B11,OF4	L	29	55	107	9	25	2	2	0	11	8	9	1	.234	.287	.290
Chuck Ward	SS19	R	25	19	71	7	11	1	0	0	4	3	3	1	.155	.200	.169
Bill McCabe†	SS12,OF6,2B5*	S	27	41	68	10	10	0	0	0	3	2	6	1	.147	.171	.147
Ray Schmandt	1B20	R	24	28	63	7	15	2	1	0	7	3	4	1	.238	.273	.302
Bill Lamar	OF12	L	23	24	44	5	12	4	0	0	4	0	1	0	.273	.273	.364
Wally Hood†	OF5	R	25	7	14	4	2	1	0	0	1	4	4	2	.143	.333	.214
Zack Taylor	C9	R	21	9	13	3	5	2	0	0	5	0	2	0	.385	.385	.538
Doug Baird†	3B2	R	28	6	6	1	2	0	0	0	1	2	1	0	.333	.556	.333
Jack Sheehan	SS2,3B1	S	27	3	5	0	2	1	0	0	0	1	0	0	.400	.500	.600
Red Sheridan	SS3	R	23	3	2	0	0	0	0	0	0	0	1	0	.000	.000	.000

B. McCabe, 1 G at 3B

Pitcher	T	Age	G	GS	CG	ShO	IP	H	HR	BB	SO	W-L	Sv	ERA
Burleigh Grimes	R	26	40	33	25	5	303.2	271	5	67	131	23-11	2	2.22
Leon Cadore	R	29	35	30	16	4	254.1	256	4	56	79	15-14	0	2.62
Jeff Pfeffer	R	32	30	28	20	2	215.0	225	5	45	80	16-9	0	3.01
Rube Marquard	L	33	28	26	10	1	189.2	181	5	35	89	10-7	0	3.23
Al Mamaux	R	26	41	18	9	2	190.2	172	2	63	101	12-8	4	2.69
Sherry Smith	L	29	33	12	6	2	136.1	134	1	27	33	11-9	3	1.85
Clarence Mitchell	L	29	19	7	3	1	78.2	85	1	23	18	5-2	1	3.09
George Mohart	R	28	13	1	0	0	35.2	33	0	7	13	0-1	0	1.77
Johnny Miljus	R	25	9	0	0	0	23.1	24	2	4	9	1-0	0	3.09

1920 New York Giants 2nd NL 86-68 .558 7.0 GB

John McGraw

Player	Gm by Position	B	Age	G	AB	R	H	2B	3B	HR	RBI	BB	SO	SB	Avg	OBP	Slg
Frank Snyder	C84	R	27	87	264	26	66	13	4	3	27	17	18	2	.250	.295	.364
George Kelly	1B155	R	24	155	590	69	157	22	11	11	94	41	92	6	.266	.320	.397
Larry Doyle	2B133	L	33	137	471	48	134	21	2	4	50	47	28	11	.285	.352	.363
Frankie Frisch	3B109,SS2	S	21	110	440	57	123	10	10	4	77	20	18	34	.280	.311	.375
Dave Bancroft†	SS108	S	29	108	442	79	132	29	7	0	31	33	32	7	.299	.349	.396
George Burns	OF154	R	30	154	631	115	181	35	9	6	46	76	48	22	.287	.365	.399
Ross Youngs	OF153	L	23	153	581	92	204	27	14	6	78	75	55	18	.351	.427	.477
Lee King	OF84	R	27	93	261	32	72	11	4	7	42	21	38	3	.276	.335	.429
Earl Smith	C82	L	23	91	262	20	77	7	1	1	30	18	16	5	.294	.344	.340
Art Fletcher†	SS41	R	35	41	171	21	44	7	2	0	24	1	15	3	.257	.282	.322
Benny Kauff	OF51	L	30	55	157	31	43	12	3	3	26	25	14	3	.274	.380	.446
Vern Spencer	OF40	L	26	45	140	15	28	2	3	0	19	11	17	4	.200	.258	.257
Ed Sicking†	3B28,2B15,SS3	R	23	46	134	11	23	3	1	0	9	10	10	6	.172	.234	.209
Fred Lear	3B24,2B1	R	26	31	87	12	22	0	1	1	7	8	15	0	.253	.323	.310
Roy Grimes	2B21	R	26	26	57	5	9	1	0	0	3	3	8	1	.158	.200	.175
Lew McCarty†	C5	R	31	36	38	2	5	0	0	0	0	4	2	2	.132	.214	.132
Jigger Statz†	OF12	R	22	16	30	0	4	0	1	0	5	2	9	0	.133	.188	.200
Al LeFevre	SS9,2B6,3B1	R	21	17	27	5	4	0	1	0	0	0	13	0	.148	.148	.222
Curt Walker	OF4	L	23	8	14	0	1	0	0	0	0	1	3	0	.071	.133	.071
Mike Gonzalez	C8	R	29	11	13	1	3	0	0	0	0	3	1	1	.231	.375	.231
Alex Gaston	C3	R	27	4	10	2	1	0	0	0	1	1	2	0	.100	.182	.100
Eddie Brown	OF2	R	28	3	8	1	1	1	0	0	0	0	3	0	.125	.125	.250
Doug Baird†	3B4	R	28	7	8	0	1	0	0	0	0	1	3	0	.125	.222	.125
Pug Griffin	OF2	R	24	5	4	0	1	0	0	0	0	1	2	0	.250	.400	.250
Bob Kinsella	OF1	L	21	1	3	0	1	0	0	0	1	0	2	0	.333	.333	.333

Pitcher	T	Age	G	GS	CG	ShO	IP	H	HR	BB	SO	W-L	Sv	ERA
Fred Toney	R	31	42	37	17	4	278.1	266	8	57	81	21-11	1	2.65
Jesse Barnes	R	27	43	35	23	2	292.2	271	9	56	63	20-15	0	2.64
Art Nehf	L	27	40	33	22	5	280.2	273	8	45	79	21-12	0	3.08
Rube Benton	L	33	33	25	12	4	193.1	222	8	31	52	9-16	2	3.03
Virgil Barnes	R	23	1	1	0	0	7.0	9	0	1	2	0-1	0	3.86
Tom Grubbs	R	26	1	1	0	0	5.0	9	0	0	0	0-1	0	7.20
Phil Douglas	R	30	46	21	10	3	226.0	225	6	55	71	14-10	2	2.71
Jesse Winters	R	26	21	0	0	0	46.1	37	1	28	14	0-0	0	3.50
Bill Hubbell†	R	23	14	0	0	0	30.0	26	2	15	8	0-1	2	2.10
Pol Perritt	R	27	8	0	0	0	15.0	9	0	4	3	0-0	2	1.80
Slim Sallee†	L	35	5	1	1	0	17.0	16	0	0	2	1-0	0	1.59
Rosy Ryan	R	22	3	1	1	0	15.1	14	1	4	5	0-1	0	1.76
Claude Davenport	R	22	1	0	0	0	2.0	2	1	1	0	0-0	0	4.50

1920 Cincinnati Reds 3rd NL 82-71 .536 10.5 GB

Pat Moran

Player	Gm by Position	B	Age	G	AB	R	H	2B	3B	HR	RBI	BB	SO	SB	Avg	OBP	Slg
Ivy Wingo	C107,2B2	L	29	108	364	32	96	11	5	2	38	19	13	6	.264	.300	.338
Jake Daubert	1B140	L	36	142	553	97	168	28	13	4	48	47	29	11	.304	.362	.423
Morrie Rath	2B126,3B1,OF1	L	33	129	506	61	135	7	4	2	28	36	24	10	.267	.319	.308
Heine Groh	3B144,SS1	R	30	145	550	86	164	28	12	0	49	60	29	16	.298	.375	.393
Larry Kopf	SS123,2B2,3B2*	S	29	126	458	56	112	15	6	0	59	35	24	14	.245	.305	.303
Pat Duncan	OF154	R	26	154	576	75	170	16	11	2	83	42	42	18	.295	.350	.372
Greasy Neale	OF150	L	28	150	530	55	135	10	7	3	46	45	48	29	.255	.322	.317
Edd Roush	OF139,1B11,2B1	L	27	149	579	81	196	22	16	4	90	42	22	36	.339	.386	.453
Sam Crane	SS25,3B10,2B4*	R	25	54	144	20	31	4	0	0	9	7	9	5	.215	.261	.243
Ed Sicking†	2B25,SS9,3B2	R	23	37	123	12	33	3	0	0	17	13	5	2	.268	.338	.293
Bill Rariden	C37	R	32	39	101	9	25	3	0	0	10	5	0	2	.248	.283	.277
Nick Allen	C36	R	31	43	85	10	23	3	1	0	4	6	11	0	.271	.340	.329
Charlie See	OF17,P1	L	23	47	82	9	25	4	0	0	15	1	7	2	.305	.329	.354
Rube Bressler	P10,OF3,1B2	R	25	21	30	4	8	1	0	0	3	1	4	1	.267	.290	.300

L. Kopf, 1 G at OF; S. Crane, 3 G at OF

Pitcher	T	Age	G	GS	CG	ShO	IP	H	HR	BB	SO	W-L	Sv	ERA
Jimmy Ring	R	25	42	33	18	1	266.2	268	4	92	73	17-16	1	3.54
Dutch Ruether	L	26	37	33	23	5	265.2	235	2	96	99	16-12	3	2.47
Dolf Luque	R	29	37	23	10	1	207.2	168	5	60	72	13-9	1	2.51
Hod Eller	R	25	35	22	15	2	210.1	208	6	52	76	13-12	0	2.95
Ray Fisher	R	32	33	22	10	1	201.0	189	5	50	56	10-11	1	2.73
Slim Sallee†	L	35	21	12	6	0	116.0	129	4	16	13	5-6	2	3.34
Buddy Napier	R	30	9	5	5	1	49.0	47	0	7	17	4-2	0	1.29
Dazzy Swartz	R	23	1	1	1	0	12.0	17	0	2	2	0-1	0	4.50
Rube Bressler	L	25	10	2	1	0	20.1	24	0	2	4	2-0	0	1.77
Lynn Brenton	R	29	5	1	1	0	18.1	17	0	4	13	2-1	1	4.91
Fritz Coumbe	L	30	3	0	0	0	14.2	17	0	4	7	0-1	0	4.91
Charlie See	R	23	1	0	0	0	6.0	6	0	4	3	0-0	0	6.00
George Lowe	R	25	1	0	0	0	2.0	1	0	1	0	0-0	0	0.00
Jack Theis	R	28	1	0	0	0	2.0	1	0	3	0	0-0	0	0.00

1920 Pittsburgh Pirates 4th NL 79-75 .513 14.0 GB

George Gibson

Player	Gm by Position	B	Age	G	AB	R	H	2B	3B	HR	RBI	BB	SO	SB	Avg	OBP	Slg
Walter Schmidt	C92	R	33	94	310	22	86	8	4	0	20	24	15	9	.277	.337	.329
Charlie Grimm	1B148	L	21	148	533	38	121	13	7	2	54	30	40	7	.227	.273	.289
George Cutshaw	2B129	R	32	131	488	56	123	16	8	0	47	23	10	17	.252	.287	.318
Possum Whitted	3B125,1B10,OF1	R	30	134	494	53	129	11	12	1	74	35	36	11	.261	.314	.338
Howdy Caton	SS96	R	23	98	352	29	83	11	5	0	27	33	19	4	.236	.305	.295
Billy Southworth	OF142	L	27	146	546	64	155	17	13	2	53	52	20	23	.284	.348	.374
Carson Bigbee	OF133	L	25	137	550	78	154	19	15	4	32	45	28	31	.280	.341	.391
Max Carey	OF129	S	30	130	485	74	140	18	4	1	35	59	31	52	.289	.369	.348
Fred Nicholson	OF58	R	25	99	247	33	89	16	7	4	30	18	31	9	.360	.404	.530
Walter Barbare	SS34,2B12,3B5	R	28	57	186	9	51	5	2	0	12	9	11	5	.274	.308	.323
Bill Haeffner	C52	R	25	54	175	8	34	4	1	0	14	8	14	1	.194	.230	.229
Bill McKechnie	3B20,SS10,2B6*	S	33	40	133	13	29	3	1	1	13	4	7	7	.218	.241	.278
Cliff Lee	C19,OF2	R	23	37	76	9	18	2	2	0	8	4	14	0	.237	.275	.316
Pie Traynor	SS17	R	20	17	52	6	11	3	1	0	2	3	6	1	.212	.268	.308
Cotton Tierney	2B10,SS2	R	26	12	46	4	11	5	0	0	8	3	4	1	.239	.286	.348
Clyde Barnhart	3B12	R	24	12	46	5	15	4	2	0	5	1	2	1	.326	.340	.500
Homer Summa	OF6	L	21	10	22	1	7	1	1	0	1	3	1	1	.318	.400	.455
Bill Hinchman		R	37	18	16	0	3	0	0	0	1	1	3	0	.188	.278	.188
Nig Clarke	C2	L	37	3	7	0	0	0	0	0	0	2	4	0	.000	.222	.000
Wally Hood†		R	25	2	1	1	0	0	0	0	0	1	0	1	.000	.500	.000

B. McKechnie, 1 G at 1B

Pitcher	T	Age	G	GS	CG	ShO	IP	H	HR	BB	SO	W-L	Sv	ERA
Wilbur Cooper	L	28	44	37	28	3	327.0	307	4	52	114	24-15	2	2.39
Babe Adams	R	38	35	33	19	8	263.0	240	6	18	84	17-13	2	2.16
Hal Carlson	R	28	39	31	16	3	246.2	262	4	63	62	14-13	3	3.36
Earl Hamilton	L	28	39	23	12	0	230.1	223	2	69	74	10-13	3	3.24
Elmer Ponder	R	27	33	23	13	2	196.0	182	3	40	62	11-15	0	2.62
Jimmy Zinn	R	25	6	3	2	0	31.0	32	2	5	18	1-1	0	3.48
Johnny Morrison	R	24	2	1	1	1	7.0	4	0	1	3	1-0	0	0.00
John Wisner	R	20	17	2	1	0	44.2	46	1	10	13	1-3	0	3.43
Johnny Meador	R	27	12	2	0	0	36.1	48	1	7	5	0-2	0	4.21
Sheriff Blake	R	20	6	0	0	0	13.1	21	0	6	7	0-0	0	8.10
Mule Watson†	R	23	5	0	0	0	11.1	15	2	7	1	0-0	0	8.74
Whitey Glazner	R	26	2	0	0	0	8.2	9	0	2	1	0-0	0	3.12

Seasons: Team Rosters

615

1920 Chicago Cubs 5th NL 75-79 .487 18.0 GB

Fred Mitchell

Player	Gm by Position	B	Age	G	AB	R	H	2B	3B	HR	RBI	BB	SO	SB	Avg	OBP	Slg
Bob O'Farrell	C86	R	23	94	270	29	67	11	4	3	19	34	23	1	.248	.332	.352
Fred Merkle	1B85,OF1	R	31	92	330	33	94	20	4	3	38	24	32	3	.285	.335	.397
Zeb Terry	SS70,2B63	R	29	133	496	56	139	26	9	0	52	44	22	12	.280	.341	.369
Charlie Deal	3B128	R	28	129	450	48	108	10	5	3	39	20	14	5	.240	.285	.304
Charlie Hollocher	SS80	L	24	80	301	53	96	17	2	0	22	41	15	20	.319	.406	.389
Dode Paskert	OF137	R	38	139	487	57	136	22	10	5	71	64	58	16	.279	.366	.396
Dave Robertson	OF134	L	30	134	500	68	150	29	11	10	75	40	44	17	.300	.353	.462
Max Flack	OF132	L	30	135	520	85	157	30	6	4	49	52	15	13	.302	.373	.406
Turner Barber	1B69,OF17,2B2	L	26	94	340	27	90	10	5	0	50	9	26	5	.265	.290	.324
Buck Herzog	2B59,3B28,1B1	R	34	91	305	39	59	9	2	0	19	20	21	8	.193	.261	.236
Bill Killefer	C61	R	32	62	191	16	42	7	1	0	16	8	5	2	.220	.280	.267
Babe Twombly	OF45,2B2	L	24	78	183	25	43	1	1	2	14	17	20	5	.235	.303	.284
Bernie Friberg	2B24,OF24	R	20	50	114	11	24	5	1	0	7	6	20	2	.211	.250	.272
Tom Daly	C29	R	28	44	90	12	28	6	0	0	13	2	6	1	.311	.333	.378
William Marriott	2B14	L	26	14	43	7	12	4	2	0	5	6	5	1	.279	.367	.465
Hal Leathers	SS6,2B3	L	21	9	23	3	7	1	0	1	0	1	1	1	.304	.333	.478
Sumpter Clarke	3B1	R	22	1	3	0	1	0	0	0	0	0	1	0	.333	.333	.333
Bill McCabe†		S	27	3	2	1	1	0	0	0	0	0	0	0	.500	.500	.500

Pitcher	T	Age	G	GS	CG	ShO	IP	H	HR	BB	SO	W-L	Sv	ERA
Pete Alexander	R	33	46	40	33	7	363.1	335	8	69	173	27-14	5	1.91
Hippo Vaughn	L	32	40	38	24	4	301.0	301	8	81	131	19-16	0	2.54
Lefty Tyler	L	30	27	27	18	2	193.0	193	6	57	57	11-12	0	3.31
Claude Hendrix	R	31	27	23	12	0	203.2	216	6	54	72	9-12	0	3.58
Joel Newkirk	R	24	2	1	0	0	6.2	8	1	6	2	0-1	0	5.40
Speed Martin	R	26	35	13	6	0	136.0	165	2	50	44	4-15	2	4.83
Paul Carter	R	26	31	8	2	0	106.0	131	3	36	14	3-6	2	4.67
Sweetbreads Bailey	R	25	21	1	0	0	36.2	55	1	11	8	1-2	0	7.12
Chippy Gaw	R	28	6	1	0	0	13.0	16	1	3	4	1-1	0	4.85
Virgil Cheeves	R	19	5	2	0	0	18.0	16	0	7	3	0-0	0	3.50
Percy Jones	L	20	4	0	0	0	7.0	15	1	3	0	0-0	0	11.57
Joe Jaeger	R	25	2	0	0	0	3.0	6	0	4	0	0-0	0	12.00
Ted Turner	R	28	1	0	0	0	1.1	2	0	1	0	0-0	0	13.50

1920 St. Louis Cardinals 5th NL 75-79 .487 18.0 GB

Branch Rickey

Player	Gm by Position	B	Age	G	AB	R	H	2B	3B	HR	RBI	BB	SO	SB	Avg	OBP	Slg
Verne Clemons	C103	R	28	112	338	17	95	10	6	1	36	30	12	1	.281	.340	.355
Jack Fournier	1B138	L	30	141	530	77	162	33	14	3	61	42	42	26	.306	.370	.438
Rogers Hornsby	2B149	R	24	149	589	96	218	44	20	9	94	60	50	12	.370	.431	.559
Milt Stock	3B155	R	26	155	639	85	204	28	6	0	76	40	27	15	.319	.360	.382
Doc Lavan	SS138	R	29	142	516	52	149	21	10	1	63	19	38	11	.289	.318	.374
Austin McHenry	OF133	R	24	137	504	66	142	19	11	10	65	25	73	8	.282	.316	.423
Cliff Heathcote	OF129	L	22	133	489	55	139	18	8	3	56	25	31	21	.284	.320	.372
Jack Smith	OF83	L	25	91	313	53	104	22	5	1	28	25	23	14	.332	.385	.444
Joe Schultz	OF80	R	26	99	320	38	84	5	5	0	32	21	11	5	.263	.308	.309
Hal Janvrin	SS27,1B25,OF20*	R	27	87	270	33	74	8	4	1	28	17	19	5	.274	.317	.344
Pickles Dillhoefer	C74	R	25	76	224	26	59	8	3	0	13	13	7	2	.263	.304	.326
Burt Shotton	OF51	L	35	62	180	28	41	5	0	1	12	18	14	5	.228	.305	.272
Mike Knode	OF9,2B4,3B2*	R	24	42	65	11	15	1	1	0	12	5	6	0	.231	.306	.277
Heinie Mueller	OF4	L	20	4	22	0	7	1	0	0	1	2	4	1	.318	.375	.364
Lew McCarty†	C3	R	31	5	7	0	2	0	0	0	0	5	0	0	.286	.583	.286
George Gilham	C1	R	20	1	3	0	0	0	0	0	0	0	1	0	.000	.000	.000
Tim Griesenbeck	C3	R	22	5	3	1	1	0	0	0	0	0	0	0	.333	.333	.333
Bill Schindler	C1	R	23	1	2	0	0	0	0	0	0	0	1	0	.000	.000	.000
Ed Hock	OF1	L	21	1	0	0	0	0	0	0	0	0	0	0	—	—	—

H. Janvrin, 6 G at 2B; M. Knode, 2 G at SS

Pitcher	T	Age	G	GS	CG	ShO	IP	H	HR	BB	SO	W-L	Sv	ERA
Jesse Haines	R	26	47	37	19	4	301.2	303	9	80	120	13-20	2	2.98
Bill Doak	R	29	39	37	20	5	270.0	256	7	80	90	20-12	1	2.53
Ferdie Schupp	L	29	38	37	17	0	250.2	246	5	127	119	16-13	0	3.52
Bill Sherdel	L	23	43	7	4	0	170.0	183	1	40	74	11-10	6	3.28
Marv Goodwin	R	29	32	12	3	0	116.1	153	1	28	23	3-8	1	4.95
Lou North	R	29	24	6	3	0	88.0	90	3	32	37	3-2	1	3.27
Elmer Jacobs	R	27	23	9	1	0	77.2	91	2	33	21	4-8	1	5.21
Jakie May	L	24	16	5	3	0	70.2	65	0	37	33	1-4	0	3.06
Mike Kircher	R	22	9	3	1	0	36.2	50	0	5	5	2-1	0	5.40
George Lyons	R	29	7	2	1	0	23.1	21	2	9	5	2-1	0	3.09
Hal Kime	L	21	4	0	0	0	7.0	9	0	2	1	0-0	0	2.57
Walt Schulz	R	19	2	0	0	0	6.0	10	0	2	0	0-0	0	6.00
George Scott	R	23	2	0	0	0	6.0	4	0	3	1	0-0	0	4.50
Bob Glenn	—	26	2	0	0	0	2.0	2	0	0	0	0-0	0	0.00
Oscar Tuero	R	21	2	0	0	0	0.2	5	0	1	0	0-0	0	54.00

1920 Boston Braves 7th NL 62-90 .408 30.0 GB

George Stallings

Player	Gm by Position	B	Age	G	AB	R	H	2B	3B	HR	RBI	BB	SO	SB	Avg	OBP	Slg
Mickey O'Neil	C105,2B1	R	20	112	304	19	86	5	4	0	28	21	20	4	.283	.339	.326
Walter Holke	1B143	S	27	144	551	53	162	15	11	3	64	28	31	4	.294	.329	.377
Charlie Pick	2B94	L	32	95	383	34	105	16	6	2	28	23	11	10	.274	.320	.363
Tony Boeckel	3B149,SS3,2B1	R	27	153	582	70	156	28	5	3	62	38	50	18	.268	.314	.349
Rabbit Maranville	SS133	R	28	134	493	48	131	19	15	1	43	28	24	14	.266	.305	.371
Ray Powell	OF147	L	31	147	609	69	137	12	12	6	29	44	83	10	.225	.282	.314
Les Mann	OF110	R	26	115	424	48	117	7	8	3	32	38	42	7	.276	.341	.351
Walton Cruise	OF82	L	30	91	288	40	80	7	5	1	21	31	26	5	.278	.352	.347
Hod Ford	2B59,SS18,1B4	R	22	88	257	16	62	12	5	1	30	18	25	3	.241	.296	.339
John Sullivan	OF66,1B6	R	30	81	250	36	74	14	4	1	28	29	29	3	.296	.374	.396
Eddie Eayrs	OF63,P7	L	29	87	244	31	80	5	2	1	24	30	18	4	.328	.410	.377
Hank Gowdy	C74	R	30	80	214	14	52	11	2	0	18	20	15	6	.243	.314	.313
Lloyd Christenbury	OF14,SS7,2B6*	L	26	65	106	17	22	2	2	0	14	13	12	0	.208	.300	.264
Gene Bailey†	OF8	R	26	13	24	2	2	0	0	0	0	3	3	0	.083	.185	.083
Art Wilson	3B6,C2	R	34	16	19	0	1	0	0	0	0	1	1	0	.053	.143	.053
Red Torphy	1B3	R	28	3	15	1	3	2	0	0	2	0	1	0	.200	.200	.333
Johnny Rawlings†	2B1	R	27	5	3	0	0	0	0	0	2	0	1	0	.000	.000	.000
Tom Whelan	1B1	R	26	1	1	0	0	0	0	0	0	1	1	0	.000	.500	.000
Oscar Dugey		R	32	5	0	2	0	0	0	0	0	0	0	0	—	—	—

L. Christenbury, 2 G at 3B

Pitcher	T	Age	G	GS	CG	ShO	IP	H	HR	BB	SO	W-L	Sv	ERA
Jack Scott	R	28	44	32	22	3	291.0	308	6	85	94	10-21	1	3.53
Joe Oeschger	R	29	38	30	20	5	299.0	294	10	99	80	15-13	0	3.46
Dana Fillingim	R	26	37	30	22	2	272.0	292	8	79	66	12-21	0	3.11
Hugh McQuillan	R	22	38	27	17	1	225.2	230	3	70	53	11-15	5	3.55
Dick Rudolph	R	32	18	12	3	0	89.0	104	4	24	24	4-8	0	4.04
Mule Watson†	R	23	13	10	4	2	74.2	79	0	17	16	5-4	0	3.62
Bunny Hearn	L	29	11	4	2	0	43.0	54	3	11	9	0-3	0	5.65
Eddie Eayrs	L	29	7	3	0	0	26.1	36	1	12	7	1-2	0	5.47
Leo Townsend	L	29	7	1	1	0	24.1	18	1	2	0	2-2	0	1.48
Al Pierotti	R	24	6	2	2	0	25.0	23	2	9	12	1-1	0	2.88
Ira Townsend	R	26	4	1	0	0	6.2	10	0	2	1	0-0	0	1.35
Johnny Jones	R	27	3	1	0	0	9.2	16	1	5	6	1-0	0	6.52

1920 Philadelphia Phillies 8th NL 62-91 .405 30.5 GB

Gavvy Cravath

Player	Gm by Position	B	Age	G	AB	R	H	2B	3B	HR	RBI	BB	SO	SB	Avg	OBP	Slg
Mack Wheat	C74	R	27	78	230	15	52	10	3	3	20	8	35	3	.226	.261	.335
Gene Paulette	1B139,SS2	R	29	143	562	59	162	16	6	1	36	33	16	9	.288	.332	.343
Johnny Rawlings†	2B97	R	27	98	384	39	90	19	2	3	30	22	25	9	.234	.278	.318
Ralph Miller	3B91,1B3,SS2*	R	24	97	338	28	74	14	1	0	28	11	32	3	.219	.246	.266
Art Fletcher†	SS102	R	35	102	379	36	112	25	7	4	38	15	28	4	.296	.329	.430
Cy Williams	OF147	L	32	148	590	88	192	36	10	15	72	32	45	18	.325	.364	.497
Irish Meusel	OF129,1B3	R	27	138	518	75	160	27	8	14	69	32	27	17	.309	.349	.473
Casey Stengel	OF118	L	29	129	445	53	130	25	6	9	50	38	35	7	.292	.356	.436
Dots Miller	2B59,3B17,SS12*	R	33	98	343	41	87	12	2	1	27	16	17	13	.254	.289	.309
Bevo LeBourveau	OF72	L	25	84	261	29	67	7	2	3	12	11	36	9	.257	.295	.333
Russ Wrightstone	3B56,SS2,2B1	L	27	76	206	23	54	6	1	3	17	10	25	3	.262	.303	.345
Walt Tragesser	C52	R	33	62	176	17	37	11	1	6	26	4	36	4	.210	.236	.386
Dave Bancroft†	SS42	S	29	42	171	23	51	7	2	0	5	9	12	1	.298	.337	.363
Frank Withrow	C48	R	29	48	132	8	24	4	1	0	12	8	26	0	.182	.239	.227
Gavy Cravath	OF5	R	39	46	45	2	13	5	0	1	11	9	12	0	.289	.407	.467
Fred Luderus	1B7	L	34	16	32	1	5	2	0	0	4	3	6	0	.156	.229	.219
Walt Walsh		R	23	2	0	0	0	0	0	0	0	0	0	0	—	—	—

R. Miller, 1 G at OF; D. Miller, 9 G at 1B, 1 G at OF

Pitcher	T	Age	G	GS	CG	ShO	IP	H	HR	BB	SO	W-L	Sv	ERA
Eppa Rixey	L	29	41	33	25	1	284.1	288	5	69	109	11-22	2	3.48
Lee Meadows	R	25	35	33	19	3	247.0	249	5	90	95	16-14	0	2.84
George Smith	R	28	43	28	10	2	250.2	265	10	51	51	13-18	2	3.45
Red Causey	R	26	35	26	11	1	181.1	203	4	79	30	7-14	3	4.32
Bill Hubbell†	R	23	24	20	9	1	150.0	176	3	42	26	9-9	2	3.84
Huck Betts	R	23	27	4	1	0	88.1	86	3	33	18	1-1	0	3.57
Bert Gallia†	R	28	18	5	1	0	72.0	79	2	29	35	2-6	2	4.50
Johnny Enzmann	R	30	16	1	1	0	58.2	79	1	16	35	2-3	0	3.84
Lefty Weinert	L	18	10	2	0	0	22.0	27	1	19	10	1-1	0	6.14
Mike Cantwell	L	24	5	1	0	0	23.1	25	1	15	8	0-3	0	3.86
Jim Keenan	L	21	1	0	0	0	3.0	3	0	1	2	0-0	0	3.00

»1921 New York Yankees 1st AL 98-55 .641 —

Miller Huggins

Player	Gm by Position	B	Age	G	AB	R	H	2B	3B	HR	RBI	BB	SO	SB	Avg	OBP	Slg
Wally Schang	C132	S	31	134	424	77	134	30	5	6	55	78	35	7	.316	.428	.453
Wally Pipp	1B153	L	28	153	588	96	174	35	9	8	97	45	28	17	.296	.347	.427
Aaron Ward	2B124,3B33	R	24	153	556	77	170	30	10	5	75	42	68	6	.306	.363	.423
Home Run Baker	3B83	L	35	94	330	46	97	16	2	9	71	26	12	8	.294	.353	.436
Roger Peckinpaugh	SS149	R	30	149	577	128	166	25	7	8	71	84	44	2	.288	.380	.397
Babe Ruth	OF152,P2,1B2	L	26	152	540	177	204	44	16	59	171	144	81	17	.378	.512	.846
Bob Meusel	OF147	R	24	149	598	104	190	40	16	24	135	34	88	17	.318	.356	.559
Elmer Miller	OF56	R	30	56	242	41	72	9	8	4	36	19	16	2	.298	.356	.450
Mike McNally	3B47,2B16	R	28	71	215	36	56	4	2	1	24	14	15	5	.260	.306	.312
Chick Fewster	OF43,2B15	R	25	66	207	44	58	19	0	1	19	28	43	4	.280	.382	.386
Braggo Roth	OF37	R	28	43	152	29	43	9	2	2	10	19	20	1	.283	.370	.408
Ping Bodie	OF25	R	33	31	87	5	15	2	2	0	12	8	8	0	.172	.242	.241
Chicken Hawks	OF15	L	25	41	73	16	21	2	3	2	15	5	12	0	.288	.333	.479
Fred Hofmann	C18,1B1	R	27	23	62	7	11	1	1	1	5	5	13	0	.177	.250	.274
Al DeVormer	C17	R	29	22	49	6	17	4	0	0	7	2	4	2	.347	.373	.429
Johnny Mitchell	SS7,2B5	S	26	13	42	4	11	1	0	0	2	4	4	1	.262	.326	.286
Tom Connelly	OF3	L	23	4	5	0	1	0	0	0	0	1	0	0	.200	.333	.200

Pitcher	T	Age	G	GS	CG	ShO	IP	H	HR	BB	SO	W-L	Sv	ERA
Carl Mays	R	29	49	38	30	1	336.2	332	11	76	70	27-9	7	3.05
Waite Hoyt	R	21	43	32	21	1	282.1	301	3	81	102	19-13	3	3.09
Bob Shawkey	R	30	38	31	18	3	245.0	245	15	86	126	18-12	2	4.08
Rip Collins	R	25	28	16	7	1	137.1	158	6	78	64	11-5	0	5.44
Bill Piercy	R	25	14	10	5	1	81.2	82	4	28	35	5-4	0	2.98
Harry Harper	L	26	8	7	4	0	52.2	52	3	25	22	4-3	0	3.76
Babe Ruth	L	26	2	1	0	0	9.0	14	1	9	2	2-0	0	9.00
Jack Quinn	R	37	33	13	6	0	119.0	158	2	32	44	8-7	0	3.78
Alex Ferguson	R	24	17	4	1	0	56.1	64	4	27	9	3-1	1	5.91
Tom Sheehan	R	27	12	1	0	0	33.0	43	1	19	7	1-0	1	5.45
Tom Rogers	R	29	5	0	0	0	11.0	12	1	9	0	0-1	1	7.36

616 Seasons: Team Rosters

1921 Cleveland Indians 2nd AL 94-60 .610 4.5 GB

Tris Speaker

Player	Gm by Position	B	Age	G	AB	R	H	2B	3B	HR	RBI	BB	SO	SB	Avg	OBP	Slg
Steve O'Neill	C105	R	29	106	335	39	108	22	1	1	50	57	22	0	.322	.424	.403
Doc Johnston	1B116	L	33	118	384	53	114	20	7	2	44	29	15	2	.297	.353	.401
Bill Wambsganss	2B103,3B2	R	27	107	410	80	117	28	5	2	46	44	27	13	.285	.359	.393
Larry Gardner	3B152	L	35	153	586	101	187	32	14	3	115	65	16	3	.319	.391	.437
Joe Sewell	SS154	L	22	154	572	101	182	36	12	4	91	80	17	7	.318	.412	.444
Charlie Jamieson	OF137	L	28	140	536	94	166	33	10	1	46	67	27	8	.310	.387	.414
Tris Speaker	OF128	L	33	132	506	107	183	52	14	3	74	68	12	2	.362	.439	.538
Elmer Smith	OF127	L	28	129	431	98	125	28	9	16	84	56	46	0	.290	.374	.508
George Burns	1B73	R	28	84	244	52	88	21	4	0	48	13	19	2	.361	.398	.480
Riggs Stephenson	2B54,3B2	R	23	65	206	45	68	17	2	2	34	23	15	4	.330	.408	.461
Joe Wood	OF64	R	31	66	194	32	71	16	5	4	60	25	17	2	.366	.438	.562
Joe Evans	OF47	R	26	57	153	36	51	11	0	0	21	19	5	4	.333	.410	.405
Les Nunamaker	C46	R	32	46	131	16	47	7	2	0	24	11	8	1	.359	.408	.443
Jack Graney	OF32	L	35	68	107	19	32	3	0	2	18	20	9	1	.299	.414	.383
George Uhle	P41,C1	R	22	48	94	21	23	2	3	1	18	6	9	0	.245	.290	.362
Pinch Thomas	C19	L	33	21	35	1	9	3	0	0	4	10	2	0	.257	.422	.343
Ginger Shinault	C20	R	28	22	29	5	11	1	0	0	3	6	5	1	.379	.486	.414
Luke Sewell	C3	R	20	3	6	0	0	0	0	0	1	0	3	0	.000	.000	.000
Tex Jeanes	OF4	R	20	4	2	2	1	0	0	0	2	1	0	0	.500	.667	.500
Lou Guisto	1B1	R	26	2	2	0	1	0	0	0	1	0	1	0	.500	.500	.500
Art Wilson	C2	R	35	2	1	0	0	0	0	0	0	0	0	0	.000	.000	.000

Pitcher	T	Age	G	GS	CG	ShO	IP	H	HR	BB	SO	W-L	Sv	ERA
Stan Coveleski	R	31	43	40	29	2	316.0	341	6	84	99	23-13	2	3.36
George Uhle	R	22	41	28	13	2	238.0	288	9	63	63	16-13	2	4.01
Jim Bagby	R	31	40	26	12	0	191.2	238	14	44	37	14-12	4	4.70
Duster Mails	L	26	34	24	10	2	194.1	210	4	89	87	14-8	2	3.94
Allen Sothoron†	R	28	22	16	10	2	144.2	146	0	58	61	12-4	0	3.24
Bernie Henderson	R	22	2	1	0	0	3.0	5	0	0	1	0-1	0	9.00
Ray Caldwell	R	33	37	13	5	1	147.0	159	7	49	76	6-6	4	4.90
Guy Morton	R	28	30	6	2	2	107.2	98	1	32	45	8-3	0	2.76
Ted Odenwald	L	19	10	0	0	0	17.1	16	0	6	4	1-0	0	1.56
Bob Clark	R	23	5	0	0	0	9.1	23	2	6	2	0-0	0	14.46
Jesse Petty	L	26	4	0	0	0	9.0	10	0	0	0	0-0	0	2.00

1921 St. Louis Browns 3rd AL 81-73 .526 17.5 GB

Lee Fohl

Player	Gm by Position	B	Age	G	AB	R	H	2B	3B	HR	RBI	BB	SO	SB	Avg	OBP	Slg
Hank Severeid	C126	R	30	143	472	66	153	23	7	2	78	42	9	7	.324	.379	.415
George Sisler	1B138	L	28	138	582	125	216	38	18	12	104	34	27	35	.371	.411	.560
Marty McManus	2B96,3B13,1B10*	R	21	121	412	49	107	19	8	3	64	27	30	5	.260	.308	.367
Frank Ellerbe†	3B105	R	25	105	430	65	124	20	12	2	48	22	42	1	.288	.326	.405
Wally Gerber	SS113	R	29	114	436	55	121	12	9	2	48	34	19	3	.278	.337	.360
Jack Tobin	OF150	L	29	150	671	132	236	31	18	8	59	35	22	7	.352	.386	.487
Ken Williams	OF145	L	31	146	547	115	190	31	7	24	117	74	42	20	.347	.429	.561
Baby Doll Jacobson	OF142,1B11	R	30	151	599	90	211	38	14	5	90	42	30	8	.352	.398	.487
Dud Lee	SS31,2B30,3B3	L	21	72	180	18	30	4	2	0	11	14	34	1	.167	.235	.211
Laymon Lamb	3B23,2B7,OF6	R	26	45	134	18	34	9	2	1	17	4	12	0	.254	.281	.373
Dutch Wetzel	OF27	R	27	61	119	16	25	2	0	2	10	9	20	0	.210	.271	.277
Pat Collins	C31	R	24	58	111	9	27	3	0	1	10	16	17	1	.243	.339	.297
Earl Smith†	3B13,OF4	S	30	25	78	7	26	4	2	2	14	3	4	0	.333	.366	.513
Billy Gleason	2B25	R	26	26	74	6	19	0	1	0	8	6	6	0	.257	.329	.284
Jimmy Austin	SS14,2B6,3B2	S	41	27	66	8	18	2	1	0	2	4	7	2	.273	.324	.333
Josh Billings	C12	R	29	20	46	2	10	0	0	0	4	0	7	0	.217	.217	.217
Jim Riley	2B4	L	26	4	11	0	0	0	0	0	0	1	3	0	.000	.083	.000
Billy Mullen	3B2	R	25	4	4	0	0	0	0	0	0	2	1	0	.000	.333	.000
Luke Stuart	2B3	R	29	3	3	2	1	0	0	1	2	0	1	0	.333	.333	1.333

M. McManus, 2 G at SS

Pitcher	T	Age	G	GS	CG	ShO	IP	H	HR	BB	SO	W-L	Sv	ERA
Urban Shocker	R	30	47	39	31	4	326.2	345	21	86	132	27-12	4	3.55
Dixie Davis	R	30	40	36	20	2	265.1	279	12	123	100	16-16	0	4.44
Elam Vangilder	R	25	31	21	10	1	180.1	196	10	67	48	11-12	0	3.94
Bernie Boland	R	29	8	6	0	0	27.0	34	2	28	6	1-4	0	9.33
Allen Sothoron†	R	28	5	4	1	0	27.2	33	0	8	9	1-2	0	5.20
Bill Bayne	L	22	47	14	7	1	164.0	167	8	80	82	11-5	3	4.72
Ray Kolp	R	26	37	18	5	1	166.2	208	12	51	43	8-7	0	4.97
Bill Burwell	R	26	33	3	1	0	84.1	102	2	29	17	2-4	2	5.12
Emilio Palmero	L	26	24	9	4	0	90.0	109	1	49	26	4-7	0	5.00
Joe DeBerry	R	24	10	1	0	0	12.1	15	0	10	1	0-1	0	6.57
Ray Richmond	R	25	7	1	0	0	14.2	23	1	14	7	0-1	0	11.66
Nick Cullop	L	33	4	1	0	0	11.2	18	1	6	3	0-2	0	8.49
Bugs Bennett†	R	29	3	1	0	0	5.2	11	1	6	3	0-0	0	14.29
Dutch Henry	L	19	1	0	0	0	2.0	2	0	0	1	0-0	0	4.50
George Boehler	R	29	1	0	0	0	1.0	1	0	0	0	0-0	0	0.00

1921 Washington Senators 4th AL 80-73 .523 18.0 GB

George McBride

Player	Gm by Position	B	Age	G	AB	R	H	2B	3B	HR	RBI	BB	SO	SB	Avg	OBP	Slg
Patsy Gharrity	C115	R	29	121	387	62	120	19	8	7	55	45	44	4	.310	.386	.455
Joe Judge	1B152	L	27	153	622	87	187	26	11	7	72	68	35	21	.301	.372	.412
Bucky Harris	2B154	R	24	154	584	82	169	22	8	0	54	54	39	29	.289	.367	.354
Howard Shanks	3B154	R	30	154	562	81	170	25	19	7	69	57	38	11	.302	.370	.452
Frank O'Rourke	SS122	R	26	123	444	51	104	17	8	3	54	26	56	6	.234	.287	.329
Sam Rice	OF141	L	31	143	561	83	185	39	13	4	79	38	10	25	.330	.382	.467
Bing Miller	OF109	R	26	114	420	57	121	28	8	9	71	25	50	3	.288	.334	.457
Clyde Milan	OF98	L	34	112	406	55	117	19	11	1	40	37	13	4	.288	.351	.397
Frank Brower	OF46,1B4	L	28	83	203	31	53	12	3	1	35	18	7	1	.261	.330	.365
Earl Smith†	OF43,3B1	S	30	59	180	20	39	5	2	2	12	10	19	1	.217	.266	.300
Val Picinich	C45	R	24	45	141	10	39	9	0	0	12	16	21	0	.277	.354	.340
Duffy Lewis	OF27	R	33	27	102	11	19	4	1	0	14	8	10	1	.186	.252	.245
Donie Bush†	SS21	S	33	23	84	15	18	1	0	0	2	12	4	2	.214	.313	.226
Goose Goslin	OF14	L	20	14	50	8	13	1	1	1	6	6	5	0	.260	.351	.380
Bobby LaMotte	SS12	R	23	16	41	5	8	0	0	0	2	5	0	0	.195	.283	.195
Frank Ellerbe†		R	25	10	10	1	2	0	1	0	2	0	2	0	.200	.200	.400
George Foss	3B2	R	24	4	7	0	0	0	0	0	0	0	1	0	.000	.000	.000
Tony Brottem†	C4	R	29	4	7	1	1	0	0	0	0	2	1	0	.143	.333	.143
Ricardo Torres	C2	R	30	2	3	1	1	0	0	0	0	1	1	0	.333	.500	.333

Pitcher	T	Age	G	GS	CG	ShO	IP	H	HR	BB	SO	W-L	Sv	ERA
George Mogridge	L	32	38	36	21	4	288.0	301	12	66	101	18-14	0	3.00
Walter Johnson	R	33	35	32	25	1	264.0	265	7	92	143	17-14	1	3.51
Tom Zachary	L	25	39	31	17	2	250.0	314	10	59	53	18-16	1	3.96
Eric Erickson	R	26	32	22	9	3	179.0	181	7	65	71	8-10	0	3.62
Henry Courtney	L	22	30	15	3	0	132.2	159	7	71	26	6-9	1	5.63
Tom Phillips	R	32	1	1	1	0	9.0	9	0	3	2	1-0	0	2.00
Jose Acosta	R	30	33	7	2	0	115.2	148	4	36	30	5-4	3	4.36
Al Schacht	R	28	29	5	2	0	82.2	110	2	27	15	6-6	1	4.90
Jim Shaw	R	27	15	4	0	0	40.1	59	2	17	4	1-0	3	7.36
Nemo Gaines	L	23	4	0	0	0	4.2	5	0	2	1	0-0	0	0.00
Frank Woodward	R	27	3	1	0	0	10.2	11	0	3	4	0-0	0	5.91
Red Bird	L	31	1	0	0	0	5.0	5	0	1	2	0-0	0	5.40
Ralph Miller	L	22	1	0	0	0	1.0	0	0	0	1	0-0	0	0.00
Vance McIlree	R	23	1	0	0	0	1.0	1	0	0	0	0-0	0	9.00

1921 Boston Red Sox 5th AL 75-79 .487 23.5 GB

Hugh Duffy

Player	Gm by Position	B	Age	G	AB	R	H	2B	3B	HR	RBI	BB	SO	SB	Avg	OBP	Slg
Muddy Ruel	C109	R	25	113	358	41	99	21	1	1	43	41	15	2	.277	.353	.349
Stuffy McInnis	1B152	R	30	152	584	72	179	31	10	0	74	21	9	2	.307	.335	.394
Del Pratt	2B134	R	33	135	521	80	169	36	10	5	100	44	10	8	.324	.378	.461
Eddie Foster	3B94,2B21	R	34	120	412	51	117	18	6	0	30	57	15	13	.284	.371	.357
Everett Scott	SS154	R	28	154	576	65	151	21	9	1	60	27	21	5	.262	.295	.335
Shano Collins	OF138,1B3	R	35	141	542	63	155	29	12	4	65	18	38	15	.286	.314	.406
Mike Menosky	OF133	L	26	133	477	77	143	18	5	3	43	60	45	12	.300	.383	.377
Nemo Leibold	OF117	L	29	123	467	88	143	26	6	0	31	41	27	13	.306	.363	.388
Ossie Vitt	3B71,OF3,1B2	R	31	78	232	29	44	11	1	0	12	45	13	1	.190	.321	.246
Roxy Walters	C54	R	28	54	169	17	34	4	1	0	13	10	11	3	.201	.254	.237
Tim Hendryx	OF41	R	30	49	137	10	33	8	2	0	21	24	13	1	.241	.362	.328
Joe Bush	P37,OF4	R	28	51	120	19	39	5	4	0	14	3	14	2	.325	.341	.433
Pinky Pittenger	OF27,3B3,SS2*	R	22	40	91	6	18	1	0	0	5	4	13	3	.198	.232	.209
Sammy Vick	OF14,C1	R	26	44	77	5	20	3	1	0	9	1	10	0	.260	.269	.325
Ernie Neitzke	OF8,P2	R	26	11	25	3	6	0	0	0	1	4	4	0	.240	.345	.240
John Perrin	OF4	L	23	4	13	3	3	0	0	0	1	0	3	0	.231	.231	.231
Ed Chaplin	C1	L	27	3	2	0	0	0	0	0	0	0	1	0	.000	.000	.000
Hob Hiller		R	28	1	1	0	0	0	0	0	0	0	0	0	.000	.000	.000

P. Pittenger, 1 G at 2B

Pitcher	T	Age	G	GS	CG	ShO	IP	H	HR	BB	SO	W-L	Sv	ERA
Sad Sam Jones	R	28	40	38	25	5	298.2	318	1	78	98	23-16	1	3.22
Joe Bush	R	28	37	32	21	3	254.1	244	10	93	96	16-9	1	3.50
Herb Pennock	L	27	32	31	15	1	222.2	268	7	59	91	13-14	0	4.04
Elmer Myers	R	27	30	20	11	0	172.0	217	11	53	40	8-12	0	4.87
Allen Sothoron†	R	28	2	2	0	0	6.0	15	0	5	2	0-2	0	13.50
Allan Russell	R	27	39	14	7	0	173.0	204	10	77	60	6-11	3	4.11
Benn Karr	R	27	26	7	5	0	117.2	123	8	38	37	8-7	0	3.67
Hank Thormahlen	L	24	23	9	3	0	96.1	101	3	34	17	1-7	0	4.48
Curt Fullerton	R	22	4	1	1	0	15.1	22	3	10	4	0-1	0	8.80
Ernie Neitzke	R	26	2	0	0	0	7.1	8	0	4	1	0-0	0	6.14
Sam Dodge	R	21	1	0	0	0	1.0	1	0	1	0	0-0	0	9.00

1921 Detroit Tigers 6th AL 71-82 .464 27.0 GB

Ty Cobb

Player	Gm by Position	B	Age	G	AB	R	H	2B	3B	HR	RBI	BB	SO	SB	Avg	OBP	Slg
Johnny Bassler	C115	L	26	119	388	37	119	18	5	0	56	58	16	2	.307	.401	.379
Lu Blue	1B152	S	24	153	585	103	180	33	11	5	75	103	47	13	.308	.416	.427
Ralph Young	2B106	S	31	107	401	70	120	8	3	0	29	69	23	11	.299	.406	.334
Bob Jones	3B141	L	31	141	554	82	168	23	9	1	72	37	24	8	.303	.348	.383
Donie Bush†	SS81,2B23	S	33	104	402	72	113	6	5	0	27	45	23	8	.281	.355	.321
Bobby Veach	OF149	L	33	150	612	110	207	43	13	16	128	48	31	14	.338	.387	.529
Harry Heilmann	OF145,1B3	R	26	149	602	114	237	43	14	19	139	53	37	2	.394	.444	.606
Ty Cobb	OF121	L	34	128	507	124	197	37	16	12	101	56	19	22	.389	.452	.596
Ira Flagstead	SS55,OF12,2B8*	R	27	85	259	40	79	16	2	0	31	21	21	7	.305	.371	.382
Chick Shorten	OF52	L	29	92	217	33	59	11	3	0	23	20	11	2	.272	.333	.350
Joe Sargent	2B24,3B23,SS18	R	27	66	178	21	45	8	5	2	22	24	26	2	.253	.342	.388
Eddie Ainsmith†	C34	R	29	35	98	6	27	5	2	0	12	13	7	1	.276	.360	.367
Larry Woodall	C25	R	26	46	80	10	29	4	1	0	14	6	7	1	.363	.407	.438
Herm Merritt	SS17	R	20	20	46	3	17	1	2	0	6	1	5	1	.370	.396	.478
Sam Barnes	2B2	L	21	7	11	2	2	1	0	0	0	2	1	0	.182	.357	.273
Clyde Manion	C4	R	24	12	10	0	2	0	0	0	2	2	2	0	.200	.385	.200
Jackie Tavener	SS2	L	23	2	4	0	0	0	0	0	0	0	1	0	.000	.000	.000
Sammy Hale		R	24	9	2	2	0	0	0	0	0	0	1	0	.000	.000	.000
Clarence Huber	3B1	R	24	1	0	0	0	0	0	0	0	0	0	0	—	—	—
G. Cunningham	OF1	R	26	1	0	0	0	0	0	0	0	0	0	0	—	—	—

I. Flagstead, 1 G at 3B

Pitcher	T	Age	G	GS	CG	ShO	IP	H	HR	BB	SO	W-L	Sv	ERA
Dutch Leonard	L	29	36	32	16	1	245.0	273	15	63	120	11-13	1	3.75
Hooks Dauss	R	31	32	28	16	0	233.0	275	11	81	68	10-15	1	4.33
Red Oldham	L	27	40	28	12	1	229.1	258	11	81	67	11-14	1	4.24
Howard Ehmke	R	27	30	22	13	1	196.1	220	15	81	68	13-14	0	4.54
Bert Cole	L	24	20	11	7	1	109.2	134	3	36	22	7-4	1	4.27
Suds Sutherland	R	27	13	8	3	0	58.0	80	1	18	18	6-2	0	4.97
Pol Perritt†	R	28	4	2	0	0	13.0	18	0	7	3	1-0	0	4.85
Doc Ayers	R	31	2	1	0	0	4.0	9	0	2	0	0-0	0	9.00
Jim Middleton	R	32	38	10	2	0	121.2	149	5	44	31	6-11	7	5.03
Carl Holling	R	24	35	11	4	0	136.0	162	8	58	38	3-7	4	4.30
Slicker Parks	R	25	10	1	0	0	25.1	33	2	16	10	3-2	0	5.68
Lefty Stewart	L	20	5	0	0	0	9.0	20	0	5	4	0-0	1	12.00
Jim Walsh	L	26	3	0	0	0	4.0	2	0	1	3	0-0	0	2.25
Danny Boone	R	26	1	0	0	0	2.0	1	0	2	0	0-0	1	4.50

1921 Chicago White Sox 7th AL 62-92 .403 36.5 GB

Kid Gleason

Player	Gm by Position	B	Age	G	AB	R	H	2B	3B	HR	RBI	BB	SO	SB	Avg	OBP	Slg
Ray Schalk	C126	R	28	128	416	32	105	24	4	0	47	40	36	3	.252	.328	.329
Earl Sheely	1B154	R	28	154	563	68	171	25	6	11	95	57	34	4	.304	.375	.428
Eddie Collins	2B136	L	34	139	526	79	177	20	10	2	58	66	11	12	.337	.412	.424
Joe Mulligan	3B152,SS1	R	26	152	609	82	153	21	12	1	45	32	53	13	.251	.293	.330
Ernie Johnson	SS141	L	33	142	613	93	181	28	7	1	51	29	24	22	.295	.328	.369
Bibb Falk	OF149	L	22	152	585	62	167	31	11	5	82	37	69	4	.285	.330	.402
Amos Strunk	OF111	L	32	121	401	68	133	19	10	3	69	38	27	7	.332	.391	.451
Harry Hooper	OF108	L	33	108	419	74	137	26	5	8	58	55	21	13	.327	.406	.470
Johnny Mostil	OF91,2B1	R	25	100	326	43	98	21	7	3	42	28	35	10	.301	.379	.436
Harvey McClellan	2B20,SS15,OF15*	R	26	63	196	20	35	4	1	1	14	14	18	2	.179	.237	.224
Yam Yaryan	C34	R	28	45	102	11	31	8	2	0	15	9	16	0	.304	.366	.422
George Lees	C16	R	26	20	42	3	9	2	0	0	4	0	3	0	.214	.214	.262
Fred Bratschi	OF5	R	29	16	28	0	8	1	0	0	3	0	2	0	.286	.286	.321
Red Ostergard		R	25	12	11	2	4	0	0	0	0	0	2	0	.364	.364	.364
Elmer Leifer	3B1,OF1	L	28	9	10	0	3	0	0	0	1	0	4	0	.300	.300	.300
Eddie Murphy		L	29	6	5	1	1	0	0	0	0	0	0	0	.200	.200	.200
Frank Pratt		L	23	1	1	0	0	0	0	0	0	0	0	0	.000	.000	.000

H. McClellan, 5 G at 3B

Pitcher	T	Age	G	GS	CG	ShO	IP	H	HR	BB	SO	W-L	Sv	ERA
Red Faber	R	32	43	39	32	4	330.2	293	10	87	124	25-15	1	2.48
Dickie Kerr	L	27	44	37	25	3	308.2	357	12	96	80	19-17	1	4.72
Roy Wilkinson	R	27	36	22	11	0	198.1	259	4	78	50	4-20	3	5.13
Dominic Mulrenan	R	27	12	10	3	0	56.0	84	2	36	10	2-8	0	7.23
John Russell	L	25	11	8	4	0	66.1	82	3	35	15	2-5	0	5.29
Cy Twombly	L	24	7	4	0	0	27.2	26	1	25	7	1-2	0	5.86
Lee Thompson	L	23	4	4	0	0	20.2	32	0	6	4	0-3	0	8.27
Bugs Bennett†	R	29	3	2	1	0	17.2	19	1	16	2	0-3	0	6.11
Hod Fenner	R	23	2	1	0	0	7.0	14	0	3	1	0-0	0	7.71
Shovel Hodge	R	27	36	11	6	0	142.2	191	7	54	25	6-8	2	6.56
Doug McWeeny	R	24	27	9	4	0	97.2	127	7	45	46	3-6	2	6.08
Lum Davenport	L	21	13	2	0	0	35.1	41	1	32	9	0-3	0	6.88
Jack Wieneke	L	27	10	3	0	0	25.1	39	4	17	10	0-1	0	8.17
Sarge Connally	R	22	5	2	0	0	22.1	29	0	10	6	0-1	0	6.45
Russ Pence	R	21	4	0	0	0	5.1	6	0	7	2	0-0	0	8.44
John Michaelson	R	27	2	0	0	0	2.2	4	0	1	1	0-0	0	10.13
Charlie Blackburn	R	26	1	0	0	0	1.0	0	0	1	0	0-0	0	0.00

1921 Philadelphia Athletics 8th AL 53-100 .346 45.0 GB

Connie Mack

Player	Gm by Position	B	Age	G	AB	R	H	2B	3B	HR	RBI	BB	SO	SB	Avg	OBP	Slg
Cy Perkins	C141	R	25	141	538	58	155	31	4	12	73	32	32	5	.288	.329	.428
Johnny Walker	1B99,C7	R	24	113	423	41	109	14	5	2	45	9	29	5	.258	.280	.329
Jimmy Dykes	2B155	R	24	155	613	88	168	32	13	16	77	60	75	6	.274	.348	.447
Joe Dugan	3B119	R	24	119	461	54	136	22	6	10	58	28	45	5	.295	.338	.434
Chick Galloway	SS110,3B20,2B1	R	24	131	465	42	123	28	5	3	47	29	43	12	.265	.309	.366
Whitey Witt	OF154	L	25	154	629	100	198	31	11	4	45	77	52	16	.315	.390	.418
Tilly Walker	OF142	R	33	142	556	89	169	32	5	23	101	73	41	3	.304	.385	.504
Frank Welch	OF104	R	23	115	403	48	115	18	6	7	45	34	43	6	.285	.344	.412
Frank Brazill	1B36,3B9	L	21	66	177	17	48	3	1	0	19	23	21	2	.271	.358	.299
Emmett McCann	SS32,3B9,2B2*	R	19	52	157	15	35	5	0	0	15	4	6	2	.223	.242	.255
Paul Johnson	OF32	R	24	48	127	17	40	6	2	1	10	9	17	0	.315	.360	.417
Ivy Griffin	1B28	L	24	39	103	14	33	4	2	0	13	5	6	1	.320	.358	.398
Zip Collins	OF20	L	29	24	71	14	20	5	1	0	5	6	5	1	.282	.354	.380
Glenn Myatt	C27	L	23	44	69	6	14	2	0	0	5	6	7	0	.203	.267	.232
Frank Walker	OF19	R	26	19	66	6	15	3	0	1	6	8	11	1	.227	.311	.318
Frank Callaway	SS14	R	23	14	50	7	12	1	1	0	2	2	11	1	.240	.309	.300
Bill Barrett	SS8,P4,3B2*	R	21	14	30	3	7	2	1	0	3	0	5	0	.233	.233	.367
Ben Mallonee	OF6	L	27	7	25	2	6	1	0	0	4	1	1	1	.240	.269	.280
Lena Styles	C2	R	21	4	5	0	1	0	0	0	0	0	2	0	.200	.200	.200
Elmer Yoter		R	21	3	3	0	0	0	0	0	0	0	0	0	.000	.000	.000
Dot Fulghum	SS1	R	20	2	2	0	0	0	0	0	0	1	1	0	.000	.333	.000
Red Shannon		S	24	1	1	0	0	0	0	0	0	0	0	0	.000	.000	.000

E. McCann, 1 G at C, 1 G at 1B; B. Barrett, 1 G at 1B

Pitcher	T	Age	G	GS	CG	ShO	IP	H	HR	BB	SO	W-L	Sv	ERA
Eddie Rommel	R	23	46	32	20	0	285.1	312	21	87	71	16-23	3	3.94
Slim Harriss	R	24	39	28	14	0	227.2	258	16	73	92	11-16	2	4.27
Roy Moore	L	22	29	26	12	0	191.2	206	4	122	64	10-10	0	4.51
Bob Hasty	R	25	35	22	9	0	179.1	238	8	40	46	5-16	0	4.87
Rollie Naylor	R	29	32	19	6	0	169.1	214	10	55	39	3-13	0	4.84
Scott Perry	R	30	12	8	5	0	70.0	77	4	24	19	3-6	1	4.11
Jim Sullivan	R	27	2	2	2	0	17.0	20	0	7	8	0-2	0	3.18
Fred Heimach	L	20	1	1	1	1	9.0	7	0	1	1	1-0	0	0.00
Arlas Taylor	L	25	1	1	0	0	2.0	7	1	2	1	0-1	0	22.50
Dave Keefe	R	24	44	12	4	0	173.0	214	19	64	68	2-9	1	4.68
Harvey Freeman	R	23	18	4	2	0	51.0	65	2	35	5	1-4	0	7.24
Lefty Wolf	R	21	8	0	0	0	15.0	15	0	16	11	0-0	0	7.20
Bill Barrett	R	21	4	0	0	0	5.0	2	0	9	2	1-0	0	7.20
Bill Bishop	L	20	2	0	0	0	7.0	8	0	10	4	0-0	0	9.00
Ray Miner	L	24	1	0	0	0	1.0	2	0	3	0	0-0	0	36.00

»1921 New York Giants 1st NL 94-59 .614 —

John McGraw

Player	Gm by Position	B	Age	G	AB	R	H	2B	3B	HR	RBI	BB	SO	SB	Avg	OBP	Slg
Frank Snyder	C101	R	28	108	309	36	99	13	2	8	45	27	24	3	.320	.382	.453
George Kelly	1B149	R	25	149	587	95	181	42	9	23	122	40	73	4	.308	.356	.528
Johnny Rawlings†	2B86,SS1	R	28	86	307	40	82	8	1	1	30	18	19	4	.267	.316	.309
Frankie Frisch	3B93,2B61	S	22	153	618	121	211	31	17	8	100	42	28	49	.341	.384	.485
Dave Bancroft	SS153	S	30	153	606	121	193	26	15	6	67	66	23	17	.318	.389	.441
George Burns	OF149,3B1	R	31	149	605	111	181	28	9	4	61	80	24	19	.299	.386	.395
Ross Youngs	OF137	L	24	141	504	90	165	24	16	3	102	71	47	21	.327	.411	.456
Irish Meusel†	OF62	R	28	62	243	37	80	12	6	2	36	15	12	5	.329	.373	.453
Earl Smith	C78	L	24	89	229	35	77	8	4	10	51	27	8	4	.336	.409	.537
Curt Walker†	OF58	L	24	64	192	30	55	13	5	3	35	15	8	4	.286	.338	.453
Goldie Rapp†	3B56	S	29	58	181	21	39	9	1	0	15	15	13	3	.215	.276	.276
Eddie Brown	OF30	R	29	70	128	16	36	6	2	0	12	4	11	1	.281	.324	.359
Lee King†	OF35,1B1	R	28	39	94	17	21	4	2	0	7	13	6	0	.223	.324	.309
Bill Cunningham	OF20	R	25	40	76	10	21	2	1	1	12	3	3	0	.276	.313	.368
Pat Patterson	3B14,SS7	R	20	23	35	5	14	0	0	1	5	2	5	0	.400	.432	.486
Mike Gonzalez	1B6,C2	R	30	13	24	3	9	1	0	0	0	1	0	0	.375	.400	.417
Alex Gaston	C11	R	28	20	22	1	5	1	1	0	3	1	9	0	.227	.261	.364
Casey Stengel†	OF8	L	30	18	22	4	5	1	0	0	2	1	5	0	.227	.261	.273
John Monroe†	2B8,SS1	L	22	19	21	4	3	0	0	1	3	3	6	0	.143	.280	.286
Joe Berry	2B7	S	26	9	6	0	2	0	1	0	2	1	1	0	.333	.429	.667
Hank Schreiber	2B2,SS2,3B1	R	29	4	6	2	2	0	0	0	2	1	1	0	.333	.429	.333
Joe Connolly	OF1	R	25	2	4	0	0	0	0	0	0	1	1	0	.000	.200	.000
Wally Kopf	3B2	S	21	2	3	0	1	0	0	0	0	1	1	0	.333	.500	.333
Bud Heine	2B1	L	20	1	2	0	0	0	0	0	0	0	1	0	.000	.000	.000
Butch Henline†		R	26	1	1	0	0	0	0	0	0	0	1	0	.000	.000	.000
Jim Mahady	2B1	R	20	1	0	0	0	0	0	0	0	0	0	0	—	—	—

Pitcher	T	Age	G	GS	CG	ShO	IP	H	HR	BB	SO	W-L	Sv	ERA
Art Nehf	L	28	41	34	18	2	260.2	266	18	55	67	20-10	1	3.63
Fred Toney	R	32	42	32	16	1	249.1	274	14	65	63	18-11	3	3.61
Jesse Barnes	R	28	42	31	15	1	258.2	298	13	44	56	15-9	6	3.10
Phil Douglas	R	31	40	27	13	3	221.2	266	17	55	55	15-10	2	4.22
Rube Benton	L	34	18	9	3	1	72.0	72	2	17	11	5-2	0	2.88
Slim Sallee	L	36	37	0	0	0	96.1	115	7	14	23	6-4	2	3.64
Rosy Ryan	R	23	36	16	5	0	147.1	140	6	32	58	7-10	3	3.73
Red Shea	R	22	9	2	1	0	32.0	28	2	2	10	5-2	0	3.09
Red Causey†	R	27	7	1	0	0	14.2	13	0	6	1	1-1	0	2.45
Pol Perritt†	R	28	5	1	0	0	11.2	17	0	2	5	2-0	0	3.86
Walt Zink	R	21	2	0	0	0	4.0	4	0	3	1	0-0	0	2.25
Claude Jonnard	R	23	1	0	0	0	4.0	4	0	0	7	0-0	1	0.00

1921 Pittsburgh Pirates 2nd NL 90-63 .588 4.0 GB

George Gibson

Player	Gm by Position	B	Age	G	AB	R	H	2B	3B	HR	RBI	BB	SO	SB	Avg	OBP	Slg
Walter Schmidt	C111	R	34	114	393	30	111	9	3	0	38	12	13	10	.282	.307	.321
Charlie Grimm	1B150	L	22	151	562	62	154	21	17	7	71	31	38	6	.274	.314	.409
George Cutshaw	2B84	R	33	98	350	46	119	18	4	0	53	11	11	14	.340	.362	.414
Clyde Barnhart	3B118	R	25	124	449	66	116	15	13	3	62	32	36	3	.258	.312	.370
Rabbit Maranville	SS153	R	29	153	612	90	180	25	12	1	70	47	38	25	.294	.347	.379
Carson Bigbee	OF146	L	26	147	632	100	204	23	17	3	42	41	19	21	.323	.364	.427
Max Carey	OF139	S	31	140	521	85	161	34	4	7	56	70	30	37	.309	.395	.430
Possum Whitted	OF102,1B7	R	31	108	403	60	114	23	7	7	63	26	21	5	.283	.328	.427
Cotton Tierney	2B72,3B32,OF4*	R	27	117	442	49	132	22	8	3	52	24	31	4	.299	.338	.405
Dave Robertson†	OF58	L	31	60	230	29	74	18	3	6	48	12	16	4	.322	.361	.504
Tony Brottem†	C29	R	29	30	91	6	22	2	0	0	9	3	11	0	.242	.266	.264
Johnny Mokan	OF15	R	25	19	52	7	14	3	2	0	9	5	3	0	.269	.333	.404
Bill Skiff	C13	R	25	16	45	7	13	2	0	0	11	0	4	1	.289	.289	.333
Ray Rohwer	OF10	L	26	30	40	6	10	3	2	0	6	4	8	0	.250	.318	.425
Johnny Gooch	C13	S	23	13	38	2	9	0	0	0	3	3	3	1	.237	.293	.237
Pie Traynor	3B3,SS1	R	21	7	19	0	5	0	0	0	2	1	2	0	.263	.300	.263
Mike Wilson	C5	R	24	5	4	0	0	0	0	0	0	0	0	0	.000	.000	.000
Kiki Cuyler	OF1	R	22	1	3	0	0	0	0	0	0	0	1	0	.000	.000	.000
Bill Warwick	C1	R	23	1	1	0	0	0	0	0	0	0	0	0	.000	.000	.000

C. Tierney, 3 G at SS

Pitcher	T	Age	G	GS	CG	ShO	IP	H	HR	BB	SO	W-L	Sv	ERA
Wilbur Cooper	L	29	38	38	29	2	327.0	341	9	80	134	22-14	0	3.25
Earl Hamilton	L	29	35	30	12	2	225.0	237	5	58	59	13-15	0	3.36
Whitey Glazner	R	27	36	25	15	0	234.0	214	5	58	88	14-5	1	2.77
Babe Adams	R	39	25	20	11	2	160.0	155	4	18	55	14-5	0	2.64
Johnny Morrison	R	25	21	17	11	3	144.0	131	3	33	52	9-7	0	2.88
Jimmy Zinn	R	26	32	9	5	1	127.1	159	3	30	49	7-6	4	3.68
Hal Carlson	R	29	31	10	3	0	109.2	121	6	23	37	4-8	4	4.27
Chief Yellowhorse	R	23	10	4	1	0	48.1	45	1	13	19	5-3	1	2.98
Elmer Ponder†	R	28	8	1	1	0	24.2	29	1	3	3	2-0	0	2.19
Lyle Bigbee	R	27	5	0	0	0	8.0	4	0	4	1	0-0	0	1.13
Rip Wheeler	R	23	1	0	0	0	3.0	6	0	1	0	0-0	0	9.00
Bill Hughes	R	24	1	0	0	0	2.0	3	0	1	2	0-0	0	4.50
Drew Rader	L	20	1	0	0	0	2.0	2	0	0	0	0-0	0	0.00
Phil Morrison	R	26	1	0	0	0	0.2	1	0	0	1	0-0	0	0.00

1921 St. Louis Cardinals 3rd NL 87-66 .569 7.0 GB

Branch Rickey

Player	Gm by Position	B	Age	G	AB	R	H	2B	3B	HR	RBI	BB	SO	SB	Avg	OBP	Slg
Verne Clemons	C107	R	29	117	341	29	109	16	2	2	48	33	17	0	.320	.380	.396
Jack Fournier	1B149	L	31	149	574	103	197	27	9	16	86	56	48	20	.343	.409	.505
Rogers Hornsby	2B142,OF6,3B3*	R	25	154	592	131	235	44	18	21	126	60	48	13	.397	.458	.639
Milt Stock	3B149	R	27	149	587	96	180	27	6	3	84	48	26	11	.307	.360	.388
Doc Lavan	SS150	R	30	150	560	58	145	23	11	2	82	23	30	7	.259	.291	.350
Austin McHenry	OF152	R	25	152	574	92	201	37	8	17	102	38	48	10	.350	.393	.531
Jack Smith	OF103	L	26	116	411	86	135	22	11	7	33	21	24	11	.328	.361	.477
Les Mann	OF79	R	27	97	256	57	84	12	7	7	30	23	28	5	.328	.390	.512
Joe Schultz	OF67,3B3,1B2	R	27	92	275	37	85	20	3	6	45	15	11	4	.309	.347	.469
Heinie Mueller	OF54	L	21	55	176	25	62	10	6	1	34	11	22	2	.352	.397	.494
Pickles Dillhoefer	C69	R	26	76	162	19	39	4	4	0	15	11	7	2	.241	.289	.315
Cliff Heathcote	OF51	L	23	62	156	18	38	6	2	0	9	10	9	7	.244	.293	.308
Eddie Ainsmith†	C23,1B2	R	29	27	62	5	18	0	0	0	5	3	4	0	.290	.323	.323
Specs Toporcer	2B12,SS2	L	22	22	53	4	14	1	0	0	2	3	4	1	.264	.304	.283
Burt Shotton	OF11	L	36	38	48	9	12	1	1	1	7	7	4	0	.250	.357	.375
Bill Sherdel	P38,1B1	L	24	39	44	2	5	0	0	0	4	4	7	0	.114	.188	.114
Hal Janvrin†	1B9,2B1	R	28	18	32	5	9	0	0	0	5	1	0	1	.281	.303	.313
Charlie Niebergall	C3	R	22	5	6	1	1	0	0	0	0	0	0	0	.167	.167	.167
Howie Jones	OF1	L	24	3	2	0	0	0	0	0	0	0	1	0	.000	.000	.000
Herb Hunter	1B1	L	24	9	2	3	0	0	0	0	0	1	0	0	.000	.333	.000
Reuben Ewing	SS1	R	21	3	1	0	0	0	0	0	0	0	1	0	.000	.000	.000
Walt Irwin		R	23	4	1	1	0	0	0	0	0	0	1	0	.000	.000	.000
George Gilham		R	21	1	1	0	0	0	0	0	0	0	0	0	.000	.000	.000
Lew McCarty		R	32	1	1	0	0	0	0	0	0	0	0	0	.000	.000	.000

R. Hornsby, 3 G at SS, 1 G at 1B

Pitcher	T	Age	G	GS	CG	ShO	IP	H	HR	BB	SO	W-L	Sv	ERA
Bill Pertica	R	24	38	31	15	2	208.1	212	9	70	67	14-10	2	3.37
Jesse Haines	R	27	37	29	14	3	244.1	261	15	56	84	18-12	0	3.50
Bill Doak	R	30	32	28	13	1	208.2	224	3	37	83	15-6	1	2.59
Roy Walker	R	28	38	24	11	0	170.2	194	10	53	52	11-12	3	4.22
Jeff Pfeffer†	R	33	18	13	7	1	98.2	115	3	28	22	9-3	0	4.29
Jakie May	L	25	5	5	1	0	21.0	29	0	12	5	1-3	0	4.71
Lou North	R	30	40	0	0	0	86.1	81	5	32	28	4-4	7	3.54
Bill Sherdel	L	24	38	8	5	1	144.1	137	7	38	57	9-8	1	3.18
Bill Bailey	L	32	19	6	3	1	74.0	95	1	22	20	2-5	0	4.26
Tink Riviere	R	21	18	2	0	0	38.1	45	2	20	15	1-0	0	6.10
Marv Goodwin	R	30	14	4	1	0	36.1	47	1	9	7	1-2	1	3.72
Ferdie Schupp†	L	30	9	4	1	0	37.1	42	5	21	22	2-0	1	4.10
Mike Kircher	R	23	3	0	0	0	3.1	4	0	1	2	0-1	0	8.10

1921 Boston Braves 4th NL 79-74 .516 15.0 GB

Fred Mitchell

Player	Gm by Position	B	Age	G	AB	R	H	2B	3B	HR	RBI	BB	SO	SB	Avg	OBP	Slg
Mickey O'Neil	C95	R	21	98	277	26	69	9	4	2	29	23	21	2	.249	.307	.332
Walter Holke	1B150	S	28	150	579	60	151	15	10	3	63	17	41	8	.261	.284	.337
Hod Ford	2B119,SS33	R	23	152	555	50	155	29	5	2	61	36	49	2	.279	.328	.360
Tony Boeckel	3B153	R	28	153	592	93	185	20	13	10	84	52	41	20	.313	.370	.441
Walter Barbare	SS121,2B8,3B2	R	29	134	550	66	166	22	7	0	49	24	28	11	.302	.331	.367
Ray Powell	OF149	L	32	149	624	114	191	25	18	12	74	58	85	6	.306	.369	.462
Billy Southworth	OF141	L	28	141	569	86	175	25	15	7	79	36	13	22	.308	.351	.441
Walton Cruise	OF102,1B2	L	31	108	344	47	119	16	7	8	55	48	24	10	.346	.429	.503
Fred Nicholson	OF59,1B4,2B2	R	26	83	245	36	80	11	7	5	41	17	29	5	.327	.370	.490
Hank Gowdy	C53	R	31	64	164	17	49	7	2	2	17	16	11	2	.299	.368	.402
Al Nixon	OF43	R	35	55	138	25	33	6	3	1	9	7	11	3	.239	.281	.348
Lloyd Christenbury	2B32,3B2,SS2	L	27	62	125	34	44	6	2	3	16	21	7	3	.352	.449	.504
Frank Gibson	C41	S	30	63	125	14	33	5	4	2	13	3	17	0	.264	.292	.416
John Sullivan†		R	31	5	5	0	0	0	0	0	0	0	0	0	.000	.000	.000

Pitcher	T	Age	G	GS	CG	ShO	IP	H	HR	BB	SO	W-L	Sv	ERA
Joe Oeschger	R	30	46	36	19	3	299.0	303	11	97	68	20-14	0	3.52
Mule Watson	R	24	44	31	15	1	259.1	269	11	57	48	14-13	2	3.85
Hugh McQuillan	R	23	45	31	13	2	250.0	284	9	90	94	13-17	5	4.00
Jack Scott	R	29	47	29	16	2	233.2	258	9	57	83	15-13	3	3.70
Dana Fillingim	R	27	44	22	11	3	239.2	249	10	56	54	15-10	1	3.45
Leo Townsend	L	30	1	1	0	0	1.1	2	0	3	0	0-1	0	27.00
Garland Braxton	L	21	17	2	0	0	37.1	44	0	17	16	1-3	0	4.82
Cy Morgan	R	25	17	0	0	0	30.1	37	0	17	8	1-1	1	6.53
Johnny Cooney	L	20	8	1	0	0	20.2	19	3	10	9	0-1	0	3.92
Ira Townsend	R	27	4	0	0	0	7.1	11	1	4	0	0-0	0	6.14
Eddie Eayrs	L	30	2	0	0	0	4.2	9	0	9	1	0-0	0	17.36
Al Pierotti	R	25	2	0	0	0	1.2	3	0	3	1	0-1	0	21.60

1921 Brooklyn Dodgers 5th NL 77-75 .507 16.5 GB

Wilbert Robinson

Player	Gm by Position	B	Age	G	AB	R	H	2B	3B	HR	RBI	BB	SO	SB	Avg	OBP	Slg
Otto Miller	C91	R	32	91	286	22	67	8	6	1	27	9	26	2	.234	.260	.315
Ray Schmandt	1B92	R	25	95	350	42	107	8	5	1	43	11	22	3	.306	.329	.366
Pete Kilduff	2B105,3B1	R	28	107	372	45	107	15	10	3	45	31	36	6	.288	.344	.406
Jimmy Johnston	3B150,SS3	R	31	152	624	104	203	41	14	5	56	45	26	28	.325	.372	.460
Ivy Olson	SS133,2B20	R	35	151	652	88	174	22	10	3	35	28	26	4	.267	.301	.345
Zack Wheat	OF148	L	33	148	568	91	182	31	10	14	85	44	19	11	.320	.372	.484
Hi Myers	OF124,2B21,3B1	R	32	144	549	51	158	14	4	4	68	22	51	8	.288	.318	.350
Tommy Griffith	OF124	L	31	129	455	66	142	21	6	12	71	36	13	3	.312	.364	.464
Bernie Neis	OF77,2B1	S	25	102	230	34	59	5	4	4	34	25	41	9	.257	.332	.365
Ed Konetchy†	1B54	R	35	55	197	25	53	6	5	3	23	19	21	3	.269	.336	.396
Ernie Krueger	C52	R	30	65	163	18	43	11	4	3	20	14	12	2	.264	.322	.436
Zack Taylor	C30	R	22	30	102	6	20	0	2	0	8	1	8	2	.196	.212	.235
Hal Janvrin†	SS17,2B10,1B8*	R	28	44	92	8	18	4	0	0	14	7	6	3	.196	.253	.239
Clarence Mitchell	P37,1B4	L	30	46	91	11	24	5	0	0	12	5	7	3	.264	.316	.319
Wally Hood	OF20	R	26	56	65	16	17	1	2	1	4	9	14	2	.262	.360	.385
Chuck Ward	SS12	R	26	12	28	1	2	1	0	0	0	4	2	0	.071	.188	.107
Jack Sheehan	2B2,3B1,SS1	S	28	5	12	2	0	0	0	0	0	0	1	0	.000	.000	.000
Eddie Eayrs†	OF1	L	30	8	6	1	1	0	0	0	1	2	0	0	.167	.375	.167
Bill Lamar	OF1	L	24	3	3	2	1	0	0	0	0	0	0	0	.333	.333	.333

H. Janvrin, 5 G at 3B, 1 G at OF

Pitcher	T	Age	G	GS	CG	ShO	IP	H	HR	BB	SO	W-L	Sv	ERA
Burleigh Grimes	R	27	37	35	30	2	302.1	313	6	76	136	22-13	0	2.83
Leon Cadore	R	30	35	30	12	1	211.2	243	17	46	79	13-14	0	4.17
Dutch Ruether	L	27	36	27	12	1	211.1	247	7	67	78	10-13	2	4.26
Jeff Pfeffer†	R	33	6	5	2	0	31.2	36	0	9	8	1-5	0	4.55
Ray Gordinier	R	29	3	3	0	0	12.0	10	0	8	4	1-0	0	5.25
Clarence Mitchell	L	30	37	18	13	3	190.0	206	7	46	39	11-9	2	2.89
Sherry Smith	L	30	35	17	9	0	175.1	232	4	34	36	7-11	4	3.90
Johnny Miljus	R	26	28	9	3	0	93.2	115	1	27	37	6-3	1	4.23
Ferdie Schupp†	L	30	20	7	1	0	61.0	75	2	27	26	3-4	2	4.57
Al Mamaux	R	27	12	1	0	0	43.0	36	1	13	21	3-3	1	3.14
S. Bailey†	R	26	7	0	0	0	24.1	35	1	7	6	0-0	0	5.18
George Mohart	R	29	2	0	0	0	7.0	8	0	1	1	0-0	0	3.86

1921 Cincinnati Reds 6th NL 70-83 .458 24.0 GB

Pat Moran

Player	Gm by Position	B	Age	G	AB	R	H	2B	3B	HR	RBI	BB	SO	SB	Avg	OBP	Slg
Ivy Wingo	C92,OF1	L	30	97	295	20	79	7	6	3	38	21	14	3	.268	.319	.363
Jake Daubert	1B136	L	37	136	516	69	158	18	12	2	64	24	16	12	.306	.341	.399
Sammy Bohne	2B102,3B53	R	24	153	613	98	175	28	16	3	44	54	38	26	.285	.347	.398
Heine Groh	3B97	R	31	97	357	54	118	19	6	0	48	36	17	22	.331	.398	.417
Larry Kopf	SS93,2B4,3B3*	S	30	107	367	36	80	8	3	1	25	43	20	3	.218	.310	.264
Pat Duncan	OF145	R	27	145	532	57	164	27	10	2	60	44	33	7	.308	.367	.408
Edd Roush	OF108	L	28	112	418	68	147	27	12	4	71	31	8	19	.352	.403	.502
Rube Bressler	OF85,1B6	R	26	109	323	41	99	18	6	1	54	39	20	5	.307	.385	.409
Lew Fonseca	2B50,1B16,OF16	R	22	82	297	38	82	10	3	1	41	8	13	2	.276	.304	.340
Bubbles Hargrave	C73	R	28	93	263	28	76	17	8	1	38	12	15	4	.289	.327	.426
Greasy Neale†	OF60	L	29	63	241	39	58	10	5	0	12	22	16	9	.241	.307	.324
Sam Crane	SS63,3B2,OF1	R	26	73	215	20	50	10	2	0	16	14	14	2	.233	.292	.298
Charlie See	OF30	L	24	37	106	11	26	5	1	1	7	7	5	3	.245	.298	.340
Dode Paskert	OF24	R	39	27	92	8	16	1	1	0	4	4	8	0	.174	.208	.207
Astyanax Douglass	C4	L	21	4	7	1	1	0	0	0	0	0	1	0	.143	.143	.143
Denny Williams	OF1	L	21	10	7	0	0	0	0	0	0	0	2	0	.000	.000	.000
Wally Kimmick	3B2	R	24	3	6	0	1	0	0	0	1	0	1	0	.167	.167	.167
Kenny Hogan	OF1	L	18	1	2	0	0	0	0	0	0	0	1	0	.000	.000	.000

L. Kopf, 1 G at OF

Pitcher	T	Age	G	GS	CG	ShO	IP	H	HR	BB	SO	W-L	Sv	ERA
Dolf Luque	R	30	41	36	25	3	304.0	318	13	64	102	17-19	3	3.38
Eppa Rixey	L	30	40	36	21	2	301.0	324	1	66	76	19-18	1	2.78
Rube Marquard	L	34	39	35	18	2	265.2	291	8	50	88	17-14	0	3.39
Pete Donohue	R	20	21	11	7	0	118.1	117	5	26	44	7-6	1	3.35
Lynn Brenton	R	30	17	9	2	0	60.0	80	0	17	19	1-8	1	4.05
Cliff Markle	R	27	10	6	5	0	67.0	75	0	20	23	2-6	0	3.76
Clint Rogge	R	31	6	3	0	0	35.1	43	2	9	12	1-2	0	4.08
Lefty Clarke	L	25	1	1	1	0	5.0	7	0	2	1	0-1	0	5.40
Fritz Coumbe	L	31	28	6	3	0	86.2	89	2	21	12	3-4	1	3.22
Buddy Napier	R	31	22	6	1	0	56.2	72	2	13	14	0-2	1	5.56
Hod Eller	R	26	13	3	0	0	34.1	46	3	15	7	2-2	1	4.98
Bob Geary	R	30	10	1	0	0	29.0	38	1	2	10	1-1	0	4.34

1921 Chicago Cubs 7th NL 64-89 .418 30.0 GB

Johnny Evers (41-55)/Bill Killefer (23-34)

Player	Gm by Position	B	Age	G	AB	R	H	2B	3B	HR	RBI	BB	SO	SB	Avg	OBP	Slg
Bob O'Farrell	C90	R	24	96	260	32	65	12	7	4	32	18	14	2	.250	.299	.396
Ray Grimes	1B147	R	27	147	530	91	170	38	6	6	79	70	55	5	.321	.406	.449
Zeb Terry	2B122	R	30	123	488	59	134	18	1	2	45	27	19	1	.275	.318	.328
Charlie Deal	3B112	R	29	115	422	52	122	19	8	3	66	13	9	3	.289	.310	.393
Charlie Hollocher	SS137	L	25	140	558	71	161	28	8	3	37	43	13	5	.289	.342	.384
Max Flack	OF130	L	31	133	572	80	172	31	4	6	37	32	15	17	.301	.342	.400
Turner Barber	OF123	L	27	127	452	73	142	14	4	1	54	41	24	5	.314	.379	.369
George Maisel	OF108	R	29	111	393	54	122	7	2	0	43	11	13	17	.310	.334	.338
John Kelleher	3B37,2B27,1B11*	R	27	95	301	31	93	11	7	4	47	16	16	2	.309	.346	.432
John Sullivan†	OF66	R	31	76	240	28	79	14	4	4	41	19	26	3	.329	.381	.471
Babe Twombly	OF45	L	25	87	175	22	66	8	1	1	18	11	10	4	.377	.414	.451
Tom Daly	C47	R	29	51	143	12	34	7	1	0	22	8	8	1	.238	.278	.301
Bill Killefer	C42	R	33	45	133	11	43	1	0	0	16	4	4	3	.323	.357	.331
William Marriott	2B6,3B1,SS1*	L	27	30	38	3	12	1	1	0	7	4	1	0	.316	.381	.395
Hooks Warner	3B10	L	27	14	38	4	8	1	0	0	3	2	1	1	.211	.268	.237
Dave Robertson†	OF7	L	31	22	36	7	8	3	0	0	14	1	3	0	.222	.243	.306
Red Thomas	OF8	R	23	8	30	5	8	3	0	1	5	4	5	0	.267	.371	.467
Carter Elliott	SS10	L	27	12	28	5	7	2	0	0	0	5	3	0	.250	.364	.321
Joe Klugmann	2B5	R	26	6	21	3	6	0	0	0	2	1	2	0	.286	.348	.286
Kettle Wirts	C5	R	23	7	11	0	2	0	0	0	1	0	3	0	.182	.182	.182

J. Kelleher, 11 G at SS, 1 G at OF; W. Marriott, 1 G at OF

Pitcher	T	Age	G	GS	CG	ShO	IP	H	HR	BB	SO	W-L	Sv	ERA
Pete Alexander	R	34	31	29	21	3	252.0	286	10	33	77	15-13	1	3.39
Speed Martin	R	27	37	28	13	1	217.1	245	12	68	86	11-15	1	4.35
Virgil Cheeves	R	20	37	22	9	1	163.0	192	8	47	39	11-12	0	4.64
Buck Freeman	R	24	38	20	6	0	177.1	189	12	70	42	9-10	3	4.11
Hippo Vaughn	L	33	17	14	7	0	109.1	153	8	31	30	3-11	0	6.01
Elmer Ponder†	R	28	16	11	5	0	89.1	117	7	17	31	3-6	0	4.74
Lefty Tyler	L	31	10	6	4	0	50.0	59	2	14	8	3-2	0	3.24
Vic Keen	R	22	5	4	1	0	25.0	29	0	9	9	0-3	0	4.68
Ollie Hanson	R	25	2	2	1	0	9.0	9	0	6	2	0-2	0	7.00
Tony Kaufmann	R	20	2	1	1	0	13.0	12	0	3	6	1-0	1	4.15
George Stueland	R	22	2	1	0	0	11.0	11	0	7	4	0-1	0	5.73
Lefty York	L	28	40	10	4	1	139.0	170	5	63	57	5-9	1	4.73
Percy Jones	L	21	32	5	1	0	98.2	116	2	39	46	3-5	0	4.56
S. Bailey†	R	26	3	0	0	0	5.0	6	0	2	2	0-0	0	3.60
Oscar Fuhr	L	27	1	0	0	0	4.0	11	1	0	2	0-0	0	9.00

1921 Philadelphia Phillies 8th NL 51-103 .331 43.5 GB

Wild Bill Donovan (25-62)/Kaiser Wilhelm (26-41)

Player	Gm by Position	B	Age	G	AB	R	H	2B	3B	HR	RBI	BB	SO	SB	Avg	OBP	Slg
Frank Bruggy	C86,1B2	R	30	96	277	28	86	11	2	5	28	23	37	6	.310	.370	.419
Ed Konetchy†	1B71	R	35	72	268	38	86	17	4	8	59	21	17	3	.321	.379	.504
Jimmy Smith	2B66	S	26	67	247	31	57	8	1	4	22	11	28	2	.231	.266	.320
Russ Wrightstone	3B54,OF37,2B4	L	28	109	372	59	110	13	4	9	51	18	20	4	.296	.332	.425
Frank Parkinson	SS105,3B1	R	26	108	391	36	99	20	2	5	32	13	81	3	.253	.277	.353
Cy Williams	OF146	L	33	146	562	67	180	28	6	18	75	30	32	5	.320	.357	.488
Irish Meusel†	OF84	R	28	84	343	59	121	21	7	12	51	18	17	8	.353	.385	.560
Bevo LeBourveau	OF76	L	26	93	281	42	83	12	5	6	35	29	51	4	.295	.361	.438
Dots Miller	3B41,1B38,2B6	R	34	84	320	37	95	11	3	0	23	15	27	3	.297	.330	.350
Cliff Lee	1B48,OF27,C2	R	24	88	286	31	88	14	4	4	29	13	34	5	.308	.338	.427
Johnny Rawlings†	2B60	R	28	60	254	20	74	14	2	1	16	8	12	4	.291	.318	.374
Lee King†	OF57	R	28	64	216	25	58	19	4	4	32	8	37	1	.269	.298	.449
Ralph Miller	SS46,3B10	R	25	57	204	19	62	10	0	3	26	6	10	3	.304	.327	.397
Goldie Rapp†	3B50,2B1	S	29	52	202	28	56	7	1	1	10	14	8	6	.277	.324	.337
John Peters	C44	R	27	55	155	7	45	4	0	3	23	6	13	1	.290	.329	.374
John Monroe†	2B28,3B9	L	22	41	133	13	38	4	2	1	8	11	9	2	.286	.345	.368
Butch Henline†	C32	R	26	33	111	8	34	2	0	0	8	2	6	1	.306	.319	.324
Curt Walker†	OF21	L	24	21	77	11	26	2	1	0	8	5	5	0	.338	.378	.390
Casey Stengel†	OF15	L	30	24	59	7	18	3	1	0	4	6	7	1	.305	.369	.390
Greasy Neale†	OF16	L	29	22	57	7	12	1	0	0	1	14	9	3	.211	.366	.228
Don Rader	SS9	L	27	9	32	4	9	2	0	0	3	3	5	0	.281	.343	.344
Mack Wheat	C9	R	28	10	27	1	5	2	1	0	4	0	3	0	.185	.241	.333
Lance Richbourg	2B4	L	23	10	5	2	1	1	0	0	0	0	3	1	.200	.200	.400

Pitcher	T	Age	G	GS	CG	ShO	IP	H	HR	BB	SO	W-L	Sv	ERA
Jimmy Ring	R	26	34	30	21	0	246.0	258	8	88	88	10-19	1	4.24
Bill Hubbell	R	24	36	30	15	1	220.1	269	18	38	43	9-16	2	4.33
George Smith	R	29	39	28	12	1	221.1	303	12	52	45	4-20	1	4.76
Lee Meadows	R	26	28	27	15	2	194.1	226	10	62	52	11-16	0	4.31
Jesse Winters	R	27	18	14	10	0	114.0	142	4	28	22	5-10	0	3.63
Red Causey†	R	27	7	7	4	0	50.2	58	4	11	8	3-3	0	2.84
Petie Behan	R	33	2	2	1	0	10.2	17	0	1	3	0-1	0	5.91
Huck Betts	R	24	32	2	1	0	100.2	141	8	14	28	3-7	4	4.47
Stan Baumgartner	L	26	22	7	2	0	66.2	103	8	22	13	3-6	0	7.02
Duke Sedgwick	R	23	16	5	1	0	71.1	81	3	32	21	1-3	0	4.92
Jim Keenan	L	22	15	2	0	0	32.1	48	3	15	7	1-2	0	6.68
Lefty Weinert	L	19	8	0	0	0	12.1	8	1	5	2	1-0	0	1.46
Kaiser Wilhelm	R	47	4	0	0	0	8.0	11	0	3	1	0-0	0	3.38

»1922 New York Yankees 1st AL 94-60 .610 —

Miller Huggins

Player	Gm by Position	B	Age	G	AB	R	H	2B	3B	HR	RBI	BB	SO	SB	Avg	OBP	Slg
Wally Schang	C119	S	32	124	408	46	130	21	7	1	53	53	36	12	.319	.405	.412
Wally Pipp	1B152	L	29	152	577	96	190	32	10	9	90	56	32	7	.329	.392	.466
Aaron Ward	2B152,3B2	R	25	154	558	69	149	19	5	7	68	45	64	7	.267	.328	.357
Joe Dugan†	3B60	R	25	60	252	44	72	9	1	3	25	13	21	1	.286	.331	.365
Everett Scott	SS154	R	29	154	557	64	150	23	5	3	45	23	22	2	.269	.304	.345
Whitey Witt	OF138	L	26	140	528	98	157	11	6	4	40	89	29	5	.297	.400	.364
Bob Meusel	OF121	R	25	121	473	61	151	26	11	16	84	40	58	13	.319	.376	.522
Babe Ruth	OF110,1B1	L	27	110	406	94	128	24	8	35	96	84	80	2	.315	.434	.672
Home Run Baker	3B60	L	36	69	234	30	65	12	3	7	36	15	14	1	.278	.327	.444
Elmer Miller†	OF51	R	31	51	172	31	46	7	2	3	18	11	12	2	.267	.311	.384
Mike McNally	3B34,2B9,SS4*	R	29	52	143	20	36	2	2	0	18	16	14	2	.252	.331	.294
Chick Fewster†	OF38,2B2	R	26	44	132	20	32	4	1	1	9	16	23	2	.242	.324	.311
Fred Hofmann	C29	R	28	37	91	13	27	5	3	2	10	9	12	0	.297	.360	.484
Norm McMillan	OF23,3B5	R	26	33	78	7	20	1	2	0	11	6	10	4	.256	.310	.321
Al DeVormer	C17,1B1	R	30	24	59	8	12	4	1	0	11	1	6	0	.203	.217	.305
Camp Skinner	OF4	L	25	27	33	1	6	0	0	0	2	0	4	1	.182	.206	.182
Elmer Smith†	OF11	L	29	21	27	1	5	0	0	1	5	3	5	0	.185	.267	.296
Johnny Mitchell†	SS4	S	27	4	4	1	0	0	0	0	0	0	1	0	.000	.000	.000

M. McNally, 1 G at 1B

Pitcher	T	Age	G	GS	CG	ShO	IP	H	HR	BB	SO	W-L	Sv	ERA
Bob Shawkey	R	31	39	33	19	3	299.2	286	16	98	130	20-12	1	2.91
Waite Hoyt	R	22	37	31	17	3	265.0	271	13	76	95	19-12	0	3.43
Joe Bush	R	29	39	30	20	0	255.1	240	16	85	92	26-7	3	3.31
Carl Mays	R	30	34	29	21	1	240.0	257	12	50	41	12-14	2	3.60
Sad Sam Jones	R	29	45	28	21	0	260.0	270	16	76	81	13-13	8	3.67
George Murray	R	23	22	3	0	0	56.2	53	0	26	14	4-2	0	3.97
Lefty O'Doul	L	25	6	0	0	0	16.0	24	0	12	5	0-0	0	3.38
Clem Llewellyn	R	26	1	0	0	0	1.0	1	0	0	0	0-0	0	0.00

1922 St. Louis Browns 2nd AL 93-61 .604 1.0 GB

Lee Fohl

Player	Gm by Position	B	Age	G	AB	R	H	2B	3B	HR	RBI	BB	SO	SB	Avg	OBP	Slg
Hank Severeid	C134	R	31	137	517	49	166	32	7	3	78	28	12	1	.321	.356	.427
George Sisler	1B141	L	29	142	586	134	246	42	18	8	105	49	14	51	.420	.467	.594
Marty McManus	2B153,1B1	R	22	154	606	88	189	34	11	11	109	38	41	9	.312	.358	.459
Frank Ellerbe	3B91	R	26	91	342	42	84	16	3	1	33	25	37	1	.246	.303	.319
Wally Gerber	SS152	R	30	153	604	81	161	22	8	1	51	52	34	6	.267	.326	.334
Ken Williams	OF153	L	32	153	585	128	194	34	11	39	155	74	31	37	.332	.413	.627
Jack Tobin	OF145	L	30	146	625	122	207	34	8	13	66	56	22	7	.331	.388	.474
Baby Doll Jacobson	OF137,1B7	R	31	145	555	88	176	22	16	9	102	46	36	19	.317	.379	.463
Eddie Foster†	3B37	R	35	37	144	29	44	4	0	0	12	20	8	3	.306	.394	.333
Chick Shorten	OF31	L	30	55	131	22	36	12	5	2	16	16	8	0	.275	.354	.489
Pat Collins	C27,1B5	R	25	63	127	14	39	6	0	8	23	21	21	0	.307	.405	.543
Herman Bronkie	3B18	R	37	23	64	7	18	4	1	0	2	6	7	0	.281	.343	.375
Jimmy Austin	3B9,2B2	S	42	15	31	6	9	3	1	0	1	3	2	0	.290	.353	.452
Gene Robertson	3B7,SS6,2B1	L	23	18	27	2	8	2	1	0	1	1	1	1	.296	.321	.444
Cedric Durst	OF6	L	25	15	12	5	4	1	0	0	0	0	1	0	.333	.333	.417
Josh Billings	C3	R	30	5	7	0	3	1	0	0	1	0	0	0	.429	.429	.571

Pitcher	T	Age	G	GS	CG	ShO	IP	H	HR	BB	SO	W-L	Sv	ERA
Urban Shocker	R	31	48	38	29	2	348.0	365	22	57	149	24-17	3	2.97
Elam Vangilder	R	26	43	30	19	3	245.0	248	13	48	63	19-13	4	3.42
Dixie Davis	R	31	25	25	7	2	174.1	162	10	87	65	11-6	0	4.08
Ray Kolp	R	27	32	18	9	1	169.2	199	10	36	54	14-4	0	3.93
Rasty Wright	R	26	31	16	5	0	154.0	148	7	50	44	9-7	5	2.92
Dave Danforth	L	32	20	10	3	0	79.2	93	1	38	48	5-2	1	3.28
Hub Pruett	L	21	39	8	4	0	119.2	99	2	59	70	7-7	7	2.33
Bill Bayne	L	23	26	9	3	0	92.2	86	5	37	38	4-5	2	4.56
Dutch Henry	L	20	4	0	0	0	5.0	7	0	5	3	0-0	0	5.40
Heinie Meine	R	26	1	0	0	0	4.0	5	1	2	0	0-0	0	4.50

1922 Detroit Tigers 3rd AL 79-75 .513 15.0 GB

Ty Cobb

Player	Gm by Position	B	Age	G	AB	R	H	2B	3B	HR	RBI	BB	SO	SB	Avg	OBP	Slg
Johnny Bassler	C117	L	27	121	372	41	120	14	0	0	41	62	12	2	.323	.422	.360
Lu Blue	1B144	S	25	145	584	131	175	31	9	6	45	82	48	8	.300	.392	.414
George Cutshaw	2B132	R	34	132	499	57	133	14	8	2	61	20	13	11	.267	.300	.339
Bob Jones	3B119	L	32	124	455	65	117	10	6	3	44	36	18	8	.257	.314	.325
Topper Rigney	SS155	R	25	155	536	68	161	17	7	2	63	68	44	17	.300	.380	.369
Bobby Veach	OF154	L	34	155	618	96	202	34	13	9	126	42	27	9	.327	.377	.468
Ty Cobb	OF134	L	35	137	526	99	211	42	16	4	99	55	24	9	.401	.462	.565
Harry Heilmann	OF115,1B5	R	27	118	455	92	162	27	10	21	92	58	28	8	.356	.432	.598
Fred Haney	3B53,1B11,SS2	R	24	81	213	41	75	7	4	0	25	32	14	3	.352	.439	.423
Danny Clark	2B38,OF5,3B1	L	28	83	185	31	54	11	3	3	26	15	11	1	.292	.345	.432
Bob Fothergill	OF39	R	24	42	152	20	49	12	4	0	29	8	9	1	.322	.356	.454
Larry Woodall	C40	R	27	50	125	19	43	2	2	0	18	8	11	0	.344	.388	.392
Ira Flagstead	OF31	R	28	44	91	21	28	5	3	3	8	14	16	0	.308	.411	.527
Clyde Manion	C22,1B1	R	25	42	69	9	19	4	1	0	12	4	6	0	.275	.315	.362
Chick Gagnon	3B1,SS1	R	24	10	4	2	1	0	0	0	0	0	2	0	.250	.250	.250
John Mohardt	OF3	R	24	5	1	2	1	0	0	0	0	1	0	0	1.000	1.000	1.000

Pitcher	T	Age	G	GS	CG	ShO	IP	H	HR	BB	SO	W-L	Sv	ERA
Herman Pillette	R	26	40	37	18	4	274.2	270	6	95	71	19-12	1	2.85
Howard Ehmke	R	28	45	30	16	1	279.2	299	12	101	108	17-17	1	4.22
Red Oldham	L	28	43	27	9	0	212.0	256	14	59	72	10-13	3	4.67
Hooks Dauss	R	32	39	25	12	1	218.2	251	7	59	78	13-13	4	4.20
Ole Olsen	R	27	37	15	5	0	137.0	147	8	40	52	7-6	3	4.53
Syl Johnson	R	21	29	8	3	0	97.0	99	7	30	29	7-3	1	3.71
Bert Cole	L	25	23	5	2	1	79.1	105	4	39	21	1-6	0	4.88
Lil Stoner	R	23	17	7	2	0	62.2	76	3	35	18	4-4	0	7.04
Roy Moore†	L	23	9	0	0	0	19.2	29	0	10	9	0-0	2	5.95
Carl Holling	R	25	5	1	0	0	9.1	21	1	5	2	1-1	0	15.43
Ken Holloway	R	24	1	0	0	0	1.0	1	0	0	1	0-0	0	0.00

1922 Cleveland Indians 4th AL 78-76 .506 16.0 GB

Tris Speaker

Player	Gm by Position	B	Age	G	AB	R	H	2B	3B	HR	RBI	BB	SO	SB	Avg	OBP	Slg
Steve O'Neill	C130	R	30	133	392	33	122	27	4	2	65	73	25	2	.311	.423	.416
Stuffy McInnis	1B140,C1	R	31	142	537	58	164	28	7	1	78	15	5	1	.305	.325	.389
Bill Wambsganss	2B124,SS16,C1	R	28	143	538	89	141	22	6	0	47	60	26	17	.262	.341	.325
Larry Gardner	3B128	L	36	137	470	74	134	31	3	2	68	49	21	9	.285	.355	.377
Joe Sewell	SS139,2B12	L	23	153	558	80	167	28	7	2	83	73	20	10	.299	.386	.385
Charlie Jamieson	OF144,P2	L	29	145	567	87	183	29	11	3	57	54	22	15	.323	.388	.429
Joe Wood	OF141,1B1	R	32	142	505	74	150	33	8	8	92	50	63	5	.297	.367	.442
Tris Speaker	OF110	L	34	131	426	85	161	48	8	11	71	77	11	8	.378	.474	.606
Riggs Stephenson	3B34,2B25,OF3	R	24	86	233	47	79	24	5	2	32	27	18	3	.339	.421	.511
Joe Evans	OF49	R	27	75	145	35	39	6	2	0	22	8	4	11	.269	.307	.338
Luke Sewell	C39	R	21	41	87	14	23	5	0	0	10	5	8	1	.264	.312	.322
Lou Guisto	1B24	R	27	35	84	7	21	10	1	0	9	2	7	0	.250	.276	.393
Pat McNulty	OF22	L	23	22	59	10	16	2	1	0	5	9	5	4	.271	.368	.339
Jack Graney	OF13	L	36	37	58	6	9	0	0	0	2	9	12	0	.155	.279	.155
Homer Summa	OF12	L	23	12	46	9	16	3	3	1	6	1	1	1	.348	.400	.609
Joe Connolly	OF12	R	26	12	45	6	11	2	1	0	6	5	8	1	.244	.320	.333
Les Nunamaker	C13	R	33	25	43	8	13	3	0	0	7	4	3	0	.302	.362	.372
Ginger Shinault	C11	R	29	13	15	1	2	1	0	0	0	0	2	0	.133	.133	.200
Jack Hammond†	2B1	R	31	1	4	1	1	0	0	0	0	0	0	0	.250	.250	.250
Joe Rabbitt	OF1	L	22	2	3	1	1	0	0	0	0	0	0	0	.333	.333	.333
Ike Kahdot	3B2	R	20	4	2	0	0	0	0	0	0	0	1	0	.000	.000	.000
Bill Doran	3B2	L	22	3	2	0	1	0	0	0	0	1	0	0	.500	.667	.500
Uke Clanton	1B1	L	24	1	1	0	0	0	0	0	0	0	1	0	.000	.000	.000
Chick Sorrells	SS1	R	25	2	0	0	0	0	0	0	0	0	0	0	.000	.000	.000

Pitcher	T	Age	G	GS	CG	ShO	IP	H	HR	BB	SO	W-L	Sv	ERA
George Uhle	R	23	50	40	23	5	287.1	328	6	89	82	22-16	3	4.07
Stan Coveleski	R	32	35	33	21	3	276.2	292	14	64	98	17-14	2	3.32
Guy Morton	R	29	38	23	13	3	202.2	218	7	85	102	14-9	0	4.00
Duster Mails	L	27	26	13	4	1	104.0	122	8	40	54	4-7	0	5.28
Danny Boone	R	27	11	10	4	2	75.1	87	3	19	9	4-6	0	4.06
Allen Sothoron	R	29	6	4	2	0	25.1	26	1	14	8	1-3	0	6.39
Dewey Metivier	R	24	2	2	2	0	18.0	18	1	3	1	2-0	0	4.50
Sherry Smith†	L	31	2	2	1	0	15.2	18	0	3	4	1-0	0	3.45
Phil Bedgood	R	24	1	1	1	0	9.0	7	0	4	5	1-0	0	4.00
John Middleton	L	22	2	1	0	0	7.1	8	1	6	2	0-1	0	7.36
Jim Lindsey	R	26	29	5	0	0	83.2	105	4	24	29	4-5	1	6.02
Jim Bagby	R	32	25	10	4	0	98.1	134	5	39	25	4-5	1	6.32
Jim Joe Edwards	L	27	25	7	0	0	92.2	113	1	40	44	3-8	0	4.47
Dave Keefe	R	25	18	1	0	0	36.1	47	2	12	11	0-0	0	6.19
George Winn	L	24	8	3	1	0	33.2	44	2	5	7	1-2	0	4.54
Charlie Jamieson	L	29	2	0	0	0	5.2	7	0	4	2	0-0	0	3.18
Joe Shaute	L	22	2	0	0	0	3.2	7	2	3	3	0-0	0	19.64
George Edmondson	R	26	2	0	0	0	2.0	4	0	0	0	0-0	0	9.00
Nellie Pott	L	22	2	0	0	0	2.0	7	1	2	0	0-0	0	31.50
Logan Drake	R	21	1	0	0	0	3.0	4	0	2	1	0-0	0	3.00
Ted Odenwald	L	20	1	0	0	0	1.1	6	0	2	2	0-0	0	40.50
Doc Hamann	R	21	1	0	0	0	0.0	3	0	3	0	0-0	0	—
Tex Jeanes	R	21	1	0	0	0	0.0	0	0	1	0	0-0	0	—

1922 Chicago White Sox 5th AL 77-77 .500 17.0 GB

Kid Gleason

Player	Gm by Position	B	Age	G	AB	R	H	2B	3B	HR	RBI	BB	SO	SB	Avg	OBP	Slg
Ray Schalk	C142	R	29	142	442	57	124	22	3	4	60	67	36	12	.281	.379	.371
Earl Sheely	1B149	R	29	149	526	72	167	37	4	6	80	60	27	4	.317	.393	.437
Eddie Collins	2B154	L	35	154	598	92	194	20	12	1	69	73	16	20	.324	.401	.403
Joe Mulligan	3B84,SS7	R	27	103	372	39	87	14	8	0	31	22	32	7	.234	.278	.315
Ernie Johnson	SS141	L	34	145	603	85	153	17	3	0	56	40	30	21	.254	.304	.292
Harry Hooper	OF149,2B1,SS1	L	34	152	602	111	183	35	8	11	80	68	33	16	.304	.379	.444
Bibb Falk	OF129	L	23	131	483	58	144	27	1	12	79	27	55	2	.298	.335	.433
Johnny Mostil	OF123	R	26	132	458	74	139	28	14	7	70	38	39	14	.303	.375	.472
Amos Strunk	OF75,1B9	L	33	92	311	36	90	11	4	0	33	33	28	9	.289	.358	.350
Harvey McClellan	3B71,SS8,2B2*	R	27	91	301	28	68	17	3	2	28	16	32	3	.226	.272	.322
Yam Yaryan	C25	R	29	36	71	9	14	2	0	2	9	6	10	1	.197	.269	.310
Jimmie Long	C2	R	24	3	3	0	0	0	0	0	0	1	0	0	.000	.250	.000
John Jenkins		R	25	5	3	0	0	0	0	0	1	0	2	0	.000	.000	.000
Roy Graham	C3	R	27	5	3	0	0	0	0	0	0	0	0	0	.000	.400	.000
Hal Bubser		R	26	3	3	0	0	0	0	0	0	0	2	0	.000	.000	.000
Johnny Evers	2B1	L	40	1	3	0	0	0	0	0	1	2	0	0	.000	.400	.000
Augie Swentor	C1	R	22	1	1	0	0	0	0	0	0	0	1	0	.000	.000	.000
Elmer Pence	OF1	R	21	1	0	0	0	0	0	0	0	0	0	0	—	—	—

H. McClellan, 1 G at OF

Pitcher	T	Age	G	GS	CG	ShO	IP	H	HR	BB	SO	W-L	Sv	ERA
Red Faber	R	33	43	38	31	4	353.0	334	10	83	148	21-17	2	2.80
Charlie Robertson	R	26	37	34	21	3	272.0	294	9	89	83	14-15	0	3.64
Dixie Leverett	R	28	33	27	16	4	224.2	224	11	79	60	13-10	2	3.32
Ted Blankenship	R	21	24	15	7	0	127.2	124	4	47	42	8-10	1	3.81
Ferdie Schupp	L	31	18	12	3	1	74.0	79	4	66	38	4-4	0	6.08
Henry Courtney†	R	23	18	11	5	0	86.2	100	5	37	28	5-6	0	4.98
Frank Mack	R	22	8	4	1	1	34.1	36	2	16	11	2-2	0	3.67
Shovel Hodge	R	28	35	8	2	0	139.0	154	3	65	37	7-6	1	4.14
Lum Davenport	L	22	9	1	0	0	16.2	14	2	13	9	1-1	0	10.80
Jose Acosta	R	31	5	1	0	0	15.0	25	4	6	2	0-2	0	8.40
Roy Wilkinson	R	28	4	1	0	0	14.1	24	1	6	3	0-1	1	8.79
Homer Blankenship	R	19	4	0	0	0	13.0	21	1	5	3	0-0	0	4.85
Doug McWeeny	R	25	4	1	0	0	10.2	13	0	7	5	0-1	0	5.91
John Russell	L	26	4	1	0	0	6.2	7	0	4	3	0-1	1	6.75
Larry Duff	R	27	3	1	0	0	12.2	16	1	3	7	1-1	0	4.97
Dick McCabe	R	26	3	0	0	0	3.1	4	0	0	1	1-0	0	5.40
Emmett Bowles	R	23	1	0	0	0	1.0	2	0	1	0	0-0	0	27.00
Ernie Cox	R	28	1	0	0	0	1.0	1	0	2	0	0-0	0	18.00

620 Seasons: Team Rosters

1922 Washington Senators 6th AL 69-85 .448 25.0 GB

Clyde Milan

Player	Gm by Position	B	Age	G	AB	R	H	2B	3B	HR	RBI	BB	SO	SB	Avg	OBP	Slg
Patsy Gharrity	C87	R	30	96	273	40	70	16	6	5	45	36	30	3	.256	.351	.414
Joe Judge	1B147	L	28	148	591	84	174	32	15	10	81	50	20	5	.294	.355	.450
Bucky Harris	2B154	R	25	154	602	95	162	24	8	2	40	52	38	25	.269	.341	.346
Bobby LaMotte	3B62,SS6	R	24	68	214	22	54	10	2	1	23	15	21	6	.252	.307	.332
Roger Peckinpaugh	SS147	R	31	147	520	62	132	14	4	2	48	55	36	11	.254	.329	.308
Sam Rice	OF154	L	32	154	633	91	187	37	13	6	69	48	13	20	.295	.347	.423
Frank Brower	OF121,1B7	L	29	139	471	61	138	20	6	9	71	52	25	8	.293	.375	.418
Goose Goslin	OF92	L	21	101	358	44	116	19	7	3	53	25	26	4	.324	.373	.441
Howard Shanks	3B54,OF27	R	31	84	272	35	77	10	9	1	32	25	25	6	.283	.352	.397
Val Picinich	C76	R	25	76	210	16	48	12	2	0	19	23	33	1	.229	.311	.305
Earl Smith	OF49,3B1	S	31	65	205	22	53	12	2	1	23	8	17	4	.259	.293	.351
Donie Bush	3B37,2B1	S	34	41	134	17	32	4	1	0	7	21	7	1	.239	.342	.284
Clyde Milan	OF12	L	35	42	74	8	17	5	0	0	5	2	2	0	.230	.250	.297
Ossie Bluege	3B17,SS2	R	21	19	61	5	12	1	0	0	2	7	7	1	.197	.300	.213
Ed Goebel	OF15	R	22	37	59	13	16	1	0	1	3	8	16	1	.271	.358	.339
Pete Lapan	C11	R	31	11	34	7	11	1	0	1	6	3	4	1	.324	.378	.441
George McNamara	OF3	L	21	3	11	3	3	0	0	0	1	1	2	0	.273	.333	.273
Ricardo Torres	C3	R	31	4	4	0	0	0	0	0	0	0	1	0	.000	.000	.000

Pitcher	T	Age	G	GS	CG	ShO	IP	H	HR	BB	SO	W-L	Sv	ERA
George Mogridge	L	33	34	32	18	3	251.2	300	12	72	61	18-13	0	3.58
Walter Johnson	R	34	41	31	23	4	280.0	283	8	99	105	15-16	4	2.99
Ray Francis	L	29	39	26	15	2	225.1	265	7	66	64	7-18	2	4.27
Tom Zachary	L	26	32	25	13	1	184.2	190	6	43	37	15-10	1	3.12
Eric Erickson	R	27	30	17	6	2	141.2	144	8	73	61	4-12	2	4.96
Joe Gleason	R	26	8	5	3	0	40.2	53	3	18	12	2-2	0	4.65
Jim Brillheart	L	18	31	10	3	0	119.2	120	3	72	47	4-6	1	3.61
Tom Phillips	R	33	17	7	2	1	70.0	72	2	22	19	3-7	0	4.89
Cy Warmoth	L	29	5	1	1	0	19.0	15	0	9	8	1-0	0	1.42
Lucas Turk	R	24	5	0	0	0	11.2	16	0	5	1	0-0	0	6.94
Henry Courtney†	L	23	5	0	0	0	10.0	11	0	9	4	0-1	0	3.60
Chief Youngblood	R	22	2	0	0	0	4.1	9	0	7	0	0-0	0	14.54
Frank Woodward	R	28	1	0	0	0	2.1	3	0	3	2	0-0	0	11.57
Slim McGrew	R	22	1	0	0	0	1.2	4	0	2	1	0-0	0	10.80

1922 Philadelphia Athletics 7th AL 65-89 .422 29.0 GB

Connie Mack

Player	Gm by Position	B	Age	G	AB	R	H	2B	3B	HR	RBI	BB	SO	SB	Avg	OBP	Slg
Cy Perkins	C141	R	26	148	505	58	135	20	6	6	69	40	30	1	.267	.322	.366
Joe Hauser	1B94	L	23	111	368	61	119	21	5	9	43	30	37	1	.323	.378	.481
Ralph Young	2B120	S	32	125	470	62	105	19	2	1	35	55	21	8	.223	.309	.279
Jimmy Dykes	3B141,2B5	R	25	145	501	66	138	23	7	12	68	55	98	6	.275	.359	.421
Chick Galloway	SS155	R	25	155	571	83	185	26	9	6	69	39	38	10	.324	.368	.433
Tilly Walker	OF148	R	34	153	565	111	160	31	4	37	99	61	64	4	.283	.357	.549
Bing Miller	OF139	R	27	143	535	90	180	29	12	21	90	24	42	10	.336	.373	.553
Frank Welch	OF104	R	24	114	375	43	97	17	3	11	49	40	40	3	.259	.335	.408
Beauty McGowan	OF82	L	20	99	300	36	69	10	5	1	20	40	46	6	.230	.323	.307
Doc Johnston	1B65	L	34	71	260	41	65	11	7	1	29	24	15	7	.250	.316	.358
Heinie Scheer	2B31,3B9	R	21	51	135	10	23	3	0	4	12	3	25	1	.170	.188	.281
Frank Bruggy	C31	R	31	53	111	10	31	7	0	0	9	6	11	1	.279	.322	.342
Frank Callaway	2B11,3B5,SS4	R	24	29	48	5	13	0	2	0	4	0	13	0	.271	.271	.354
Frank Brazill	3B2	L	22	6	13	0	1	0	0	0	1	0	1	0	.077	.077	.077
Ollie Fuhrman	C4	S	25	6	6	1	2	1	0	0	0	0	0	0	.333	.333	.500
Frank McCue	3B2	S	23	2	5	0	0	0	0	0	0	0	0	0	.000	.000	.000
Johnny Berger	C2	R	20	2	1	0	1	0	0	0	0	0	0	1	1.000	1.000	1.000

Pitcher	T	Age	G	GS	CG	ShO	IP	H	HR	BB	SO	W-L	Sv	ERA
Eddie Rommel	R	24	51	33	22	3	294.0	294	21	63	54	27-13	2	3.28
Slim Harriss	R	25	47	32	13	0	229.2	262	19	94	102	9-20	3	5.02
Bob Hasty	R	26	28	26	14	1	192.1	225	20	41	33	9-14	0	4.26
Rollie Naylor	R	30	35	26	11	0	171.1	212	7	51	37	10-15	0	4.73
Fred Heimach	L	21	37	19	7	0	171.2	220	18	63	47	7-11	1	5.03
Otto Rettig	R	28	4	4	1	0	18.1	18	0	12	3	1-2	0	4.91
Charlie Eckert	R	24	21	0	0	0	50.0	61	7	23	15	0-2	0	4.68
Jim Sullivan	R	28	20	2	1	0	51.1	76	3	25	15	0-2	0	5.44
Rube Yarrison	R	26	18	1	0	0	33.2	50	4	12	10	1-2	0	8.29
Curly Ogden	R	21	15	6	4	0	72.1	59	4	33	20	1-4	0	3.11
Roy Moore†	L	23	15	6	0	0	50.2	65	1	32	29	0-3	0	7.64
Gus Ketchum	R	25	6	0	0	0	16.0	19	2	8	4	0-1	0	5.63
Red Schillings	R	22	4	0	0	0	8.0	10	1	11	4	0-0	0	6.75
Harry O'Neill	R	25	1	0	0	0	3.0	2	0	1	0	0-0	0	3.00

1922 Boston Red Sox 8th AL 61-93 .396 33.0 GB

Hugh Duffy

Player	Gm by Position	B	Age	G	AB	R	H	2B	3B	HR	RBI	BB	SO	SB	Avg	OBP	Slg
Muddy Ruel	C112	R	26	116	361	34	92	15	1	0	28	41	26	4	.255	.333	.302
George Burns	1B140	R	29	147	558	71	171	32	5	12	73	20	28	8	.306	.341	.446
Del Pratt	2B154	R	34	154	607	73	183	44	7	6	86	53	20	7	.301	.361	.427
Joe Dugan†	3B64,SS20	R	25	84	341	45	98	22	3	3	38	9	28	2	.287	.308	.396
Johnny Mitchell†	SS58	S	27	59	203	20	51	4	1	1	8	16	17	1	.251	.318	.296
Shano Collins	OF117,1B1	R	36	135	472	33	128	24	7	1	52	7	30	7	.271	.289	.358
Mike Menosky	OF103	L	27	126	406	61	115	16	5	3	32	40	33	9	.283	.355	.369
Joe Harris	OF83,1B21	R	31	119	408	53	129	30	9	6	54	30	15	2	.316	.364	.478
Nemo Leibold	OF71	L	30	81	271	42	70	8	1	1	18	41	14	1	.258	.360	.306
Elmer Smith†	OF58	L	29	73	231	43	66	13	6	6	32	25	21	0	.286	.358	.472
Frank O'Rourke	SS48,3B20	R	27	67	216	28	57	14	3	1	17	20	28	6	.264	.335	.370
Pinky Pittenger	3B33,SS28	R	23	66	186	16	48	3	0	0	7	9	10	2	.258	.299	.274
Elmer Miller†	OF35	R	31	44	147	16	28	2	3	4	16	5	10	3	.190	.222	.327
Eddie Foster†	3B28,C2,SS2	R	35	48	109	11	23	3	0	0	3	9	10	1	.211	.277	.239
Roxy Walters	C36	R	29	38	98	4	19	2	0	0	6	6	8	0	.194	.240	.214
Chick Fewster†	3B23	R	26	23	83	8	24	4	1	0	9	6	10	8	.289	.344	.361
Ed Chaplin	C21	L	28	28	69	8	13	1	1	0	6	9	9	2	.188	.282	.232
Dick Reichle	OF6	L	25	6	24	3	6	1	0	0	0	0	2	0	.250	.280	.292
Chick Maynard	SS12	L	25	12	24	1	3	0	0	0	0	3	2	0	.125	.222	.125
Walt Lynch	C3	R	25	3	2	1	1	0	0	0	0	0	0	0	.500	.500	.500

Pitcher	T	Age	G	GS	CG	ShO	IP	H	HR	BB	SO	W-L	Sv	ERA
Jack Quinn	R	38	40	32	16	4	256.0	263	9	59	67	13-16	0	3.48
Rip Collins	R	26	32	29	15	3	210.2	219	4	103	69	14-11	0	3.76
Alex Ferguson	R	25	39	27	10	1	198.1	201	5	62	44	9-16	2	4.31
Herb Pennock	L	28	32	26	15	1	202.0	230	7	74	59	10-17	1	4.32
Benn Karr	R	28	41	13	7	0	183.1	212	10	45	41	5-12	1	4.47
Allan Russell	R	28	34	11	1	0	125.2	152	6	57	34	6-7	2	5.01
Curt Fullerton	R	23	31	3	0	0	64.1	70	4	35	17	1-4	0	5.46
Bill Piercy	R	26	29	12	7	1	121.1	140	2	62	24	3-9	0	4.67
Sam Dodge	R	22	3	0	0	0	6.0	11	0	3	3	0-0	0	4.50
Elmer Myers	R	28	3	1	0	0	5.2	10	1	3	1	0-1	0	17.47

»1922 New York Giants 1st NL 93-61 .604 —

John McGraw

Player	Gm by Position	B	Age	G	AB	R	H	2B	3B	HR	RBI	BB	SO	SB	Avg	OBP	Slg
Frank Snyder	C97	R	29	104	318	34	109	21	5	5	51	23	25	1	.343	.387	.487
George Kelly	1B151	R	26	151	592	96	194	33	8	17	107	30	65	12	.328	.363	.497
Frankie Frisch	2B85,3B53,SS1	S	23	132	514	101	168	16	13	5	51	47	13	31	.327	.387	.438
Heine Groh	3B110	R	32	115	426	63	113	21	3	3	51	53	21	5	.265	.353	.350
Dave Bancroft	SS156	S	31	156	651	117	209	41	5	4	60	79	27	16	.321	.397	.418
Irish Meusel	OF154	R	29	154	617	100	204	28	17	16	132	35	33	12	.331	.369	.509
Ross Youngs	OF147	L	25	149	559	105	185	34	10	7	86	55	50	17	.331	.398	.465
Casey Stengel	OF77	L	31	84	250	48	92	8	10	7	48	21	17	4	.368	.436	.564
Johnny Rawlings	2B77,3B5	R	29	88	308	46	87	13	8	1	30	23	15	7	.282	.342	.386
Earl Smith	C75	L	25	90	234	29	65	11	4	9	39	37	12	1	.278	.383	.474
Bill Cunningham	OF71,3B1	R	26	85	229	37	75	15	2	2	33	7	9	4	.328	.350	.437
Ralph Shinners	OF37	R	26	56	135	16	34	4	2	0	15	5	22	3	.252	.308	.311
Dave Robertson	OF8	L	32	42	47	5	13	2	0	1	3	3	7	0	.277	.320	.383
Lee King†	1B5,OF5	R	29	20	34	6	6	3	0	0	2	5	2	1	.176	.282	.265
Alex Gaston	C14	R	29	16	26	1	5	0	0	0	1	0	3	1	.192	.192	.192
Freddie Maguire	2B3	R	23	5	12	4	4	0	0	0	1	0	1	1	.333	.333	.333
Mahlon Higbee	OF3	R	20	3	10	2	4	0	0	1	5	0	2	0	.400	.400	.700
Travis Jackson	SS3	R	18	3	8	1	0	0	0	0	0	0	2	0	.000	.000	.000
Waddy MacPhee	3B2	R	22	2	7	2	2	0	1	0	0	1	0	0	.286	.375	.571
Ike Boone		L	25	2	2	0	1	0	0	0	0	0	1	0	.500	.500	.500
Joe Berry		S	27	6	0	0	0	0	0	0	0	0	0	0	—	—	—
Cozy Dolan		R	32	1	0	0	0	0	0	0	0	0	0	0	—	—	—

Pitcher	T	Age	G	GS	CG	ShO	IP	H	HR	BB	SO	W-L	Sv	ERA
Art Nehf	L	29	37	35	20	3	268.1	286	15	64	60	19-13	1	3.29
Jesse Barnes	R	29	37	30	14	2	212.2	236	10	38	52	13-8	0	3.51
Phil Douglas	R	32	24	21	9	1	157.2	154	6	35	33	11-4	0	2.63
Hugh McQuillan†	R	24	15	13	5	0	94.1	111	7	34	24	6-5	1	3.82
Fred Toney	R	33	13	12	6	0	86.1	91	5	31	10	5-6	0	4.17
Jack Scott†	R	30	17	10	5	0	79.2	83	7	23	37	8-2	2	4.41
Carmen Hill	R	26	8	4	0	0	28.1	33	0	5	6	2-1	0	4.76
Fred Johnson	R	28	2	2	1	0	18.0	20	3	1	8	0-2	0	4.00
Mike Cvengros	L	20	1	1	1	0	9.0	6	1	3	3	0-1	0	4.00
Clint Blume	R	23	1	1	1	0	9.0	7	0	1	2	1-0	0	1.00
Rosy Ryan	R	24	46	20	12	1	191.2	194	5	74	75	17-12	3	3.01
Claude Jonnard	R	24	33	0	0	0	96.0	96	7	28	44	6-1	5	3.84
Red Causey	R	28	24	2	1	0	70.2	69	2	34	13	4-3	1	3.18
Virgil Barnes	R	25	22	3	1	0	51.2	46	1	11	16	1-0	2	3.48
Red Shea	R	23	11	2	0	0	23.0	22	2	11	5	0-3	0	4.70

1922 Cincinnati Reds 2nd NL 86-68 .558 7.0 GB

Pat Moran

Player	Gm by Position	B	Age	G	AB	R	H	2B	3B	HR	RBI	BB	SO	SB	Avg	OBP	Slg
Bubbles Hargrave	C87	R	29	98	320	49	101	22	10	7	57	26	18	7	.316	.371	.513
Jake Daubert	1B156	L	38	156	610	114	205	15	22	12	66	56	21	14	.336	.395	.492
Sammy Bohne	2B85,SS20	R	25	112	383	53	105	14	5	3	51	39	18	13	.274	.344	.360
Babe Pinelli	3B156	R	26	156	547	77	167	19	7	1	72	48	37	17	.305	.368	.371
Ike Caveney	SS118	R	27	118	394	41	94	12	9	3	54	29	33	6	.239	.301	.338
George Burns	OF156	R	32	156	631	104	180	20	10	1	53	78	38	30	.285	.366	.353
Pat Duncan	OF151	R	28	151	607	94	199	44	12	8	94	40	31	12	.328	.370	.479
George Harper	OF109	L	30	128	430	67	146	22	8	2	68	35	22	11	.340	.397	.442
Lew Fonseca	2B71	R	23	81	291	55	105	20	3	4	45	14	18	7	.361	.390	.491
Ivy Wingo	C78	L	31	80	260	24	74	13	3	3	45	23	11	1	.285	.343	.392
Edd Roush	OF43	L	29	49	165	29	58	7	4	1	24	19	5	5	.352	.428	.461
Wally Kimmick	SS30,2B3,3B1	R	25	39	89	11	22	2	1	0	12	3	12	0	.247	.272	.292
Rube Bressler	1B3,OF2	R	27	52	53	7	14	0	2	0	8	4	4	1	.264	.316	.340
Greasy Neale	OF16	L	30	25	43	11	10	2	1	0	2	6	3	5	.233	.353	.326
Red Lutz	C1	R	23	1	1	0	1	1	0	0	0	0	0	0	1.000	1.000	2.000

Pitcher	T	Age	G	GS	CG	ShO	IP	H	HR	BB	SO	W-L	Sv	ERA
Eppa Rixey	L	31	40	38	26	2	313.1	337	13	45	80	25-13	0	3.53
Johnny Couch	R	31	43	34	18	2	264.0	301	13	56	45	16-9	1	3.89
Dolf Luque	R	31	39	32	18	0	261.0	266	7	72	79	13-23	0	3.31
Pete Donohue	R	21	33	30	18	2	242.0	257	7	43	66	18-9	1	3.12
Cactus Keck	R	23	27	15	5	1	131.0	138	4	29	27	7-6	1	3.37
John Gillespie	R	22	31	4	1	0	77.2	84	2	29	21	3-3	0	4.52
Cliff Markle	R	28	25	3	2	1	75.2	75	3	33	34	4-5	0	3.81
Karl Schnell	R	22	10	0	0	0	20.0	21	0	18	5	0-0	0	2.70
Jack Scott†	R	30	1	0	0	0	1.0	2	0	1	0	0-0	0	9.00

1922 Pittsburgh Pirates 3rd NL 85-69 .552 8.0 GB

George Gibson (32-33)/Bill McKechnie (53-36)

Player	Gm by Position	B	Age	G	AB	R	H	2B	3B	HR	RBI	BB	SO	SB	Avg	OBP	Slg
Johnny Gooch	C103	S	24	105	353	45	116	15	3	1	42	39	15	1	.329	.403	.397
Charlie Grimm	1B154	L	23	154	593	64	173	28	13	0	76	43	15	6	.292	.343	.383
Cotton Tierney	2B105,OF2,3B1*	R	28	122	441	58	152	26	14	7	86	22	40	7	.345	.378	.515
Pie Traynor	3B124,SS18	R	22	142	571	89	161	17	12	4	81	27	28	17	.282	.319	.375
Rabbit Maranville	SS138,2B18	R	30	155	672	115	198	26	15	0	63	61	43	24	.295	.355	.378
Max Carey	OF155	S	32	155	629	140	207	28	12	10	70	80	26	51	.329	.408	.459
Carson Bigbee	OF150	L	27	150	614	113	215	29	15	5	99	56	13	24	.350	.405	.471
Reb Russell	OF60	L	33	60	220	51	81	14	8	12	75	14	18	4	.368	.423	.668
Clyde Barnhart	3B30,OF26	R	26	75	209	30	69	7	5	1	38	25	7	3	.330	.402	.426
Walter Schmidt	C40	R	35	40	152	21	50	11	1	0	22	1	5	2	.329	.333	.414
Jewel Ens	2B29,3B3,1B2*	R	32	47	142	18	42	7	3	0	17	7	9	3	.296	.338	.387
Ray Rohwer	OF30	L	27	53	129	19	38	6	3	3	22	10	17	1	.295	.350	.457
Walter Mueller	OF31	R	27	32	122	21	33	5	1	2	18	5	7	1	.270	.305	.377
Johnny Mokan†	OF23	R	26	31	89	9	23	3	1	0	8	9	3	0	.258	.327	.315
Jim Mattox	C21	L	25	29	51	11	15	1	1	0	3	1	3	0	.294	.308	.353
Bubber Jonnard	C10	R	24	10	21	4	5	0	1	0	2	2	4	0	.238	.304	.333
Stuffy Stewart	2B3	R	28	3	13	3	2	0	0	0	0	0	1	0	.154	.154	.154
Jake Miller	OF3	R	26	3	11	0	1	0	0	0	0	2	0	1	.091	.231	.091
Jack Hammond†	2B4	R	31	9	11	3	3	0	0	0	0	1	0	0	.273	.333	.273
Tom Lovelace		R	24	1	1	0	0	0	0	0	0	0	0	0	.000	.000	.000
Art Merewether		R	19	1	1	0	0	0	0	0	0	0	0	0	.000	.000	.000
Tom McNamara		R	26	1	1	0	0	0	0	0	0	0	0	0	.000	.000	.000
Kiki Cuyler		R	23	1	0	0	0	0	0	0	0	0	0	0	—	—	—

C. Tierney, 1 G at SS; J. Ens, 1 G at SS

Pitcher	T	Age	G	GS	CG	ShO	IP	H	HR	BB	SO	W-L	Sv	ERA
Wilbur Cooper	L	30	41	37	27	4	294.2	330	13	61	129	23-14	0	3.18
Johnny Morrison	R	26	45	33	20	5	286.1	315	10	87	104	17-11	1	3.43
Whitey Glazner	R	28	34	26	10	1	193.0	238	9	52	77	11-12	1	4.38
Babe Adams	R	40	27	19	12	4	171.1	191	1	15	39	8-11	0	3.57
Myrl Brown	R	27	7	5	2	0	34.2	42	2	13	9	3-1	0	5.97
Hal Carlson	R	30	39	18	6	0	145.1	193	10	58	64	9-12	2	5.70
Earl Hamilton	L	30	33	14	9	1	160.0	183	6	40	34	11-7	2	3.99
Chief Yellowhorse	R	24	28	5	2	0	77.2	92	0	20	24	3-1	0	4.52
B. Hollingsworth	R	26	9	0	0	0	13.2	17	0	8	7	0-0	0	7.90
Jimmy Zinn	R	27	5	0	0	0	9.2	11	1	2	3	0-0	1	1.86
Rip Wheeler	R	24	1	0	0	0	1.0	1	0	2	0	0-0	0	0.00

1922 St. Louis Cardinals 3rd NL 85-69 .552 8.0 GB

Branch Rickey

Player	Gm by Position	B	Age	G	AB	R	H	2B	3B	HR	RBI	BB	SO	SB	Avg	OBP	Slg
Eddie Ainsmith	C116	R	30	119	379	46	111	14	4	13	59	28	43	2	.293	.343	.454
Jack Fournier	1B109,P1	L	32	128	404	64	119	23	9	10	61	40	21	6	.295	.368	.470
Rogers Hornsby	2B154	R	26	154	623	141	250	46	14	42	152	65	50	17	.401	.459	.722
Milt Stock	3B149,SS1	R	28	151	581	85	177	33	9	5	79	42	29	7	.305	.352	.418
Specs Toporcer	SS91,3B6,2B1*	L	23	116	352	56	114	25	6	3	36	24	18	2	.324	.370	.455
Jack Smith	OF136	L	27	143	510	117	158	23	12	8	46	50	30	18	.310	.375	.449
Joe Schultz	OF89	R	28	112	344	50	108	13	4	2	64	19	10	3	.314	.350	.392
Max Flack†	OF66	L	32	66	267	46	78	12	1	2	21	31	11	3	.292	.368	.367
Doc Lavan	SS82,3B5	R	31	89	264	24	60	8	1	0	27	13	10	3	.227	.271	.265
Austin McHenry	OF61	R	26	64	238	31	72	18	3	5	43	14	27	2	.303	.344	.466
Verne Clemons	C63	R	30	71	160	9	41	4	0	0	15	18	5	1	.256	.331	.281
Heinie Mueller	OF44	L	22	61	159	20	43	7	2	3	26	14	18	2	.270	.329	.396
Jim Bottomley	1B34	L	22	37	151	29	49	8	5	5	35	6	13	3	.325	.358	.543
Les Mann	OF57	R	28	84	147	42	51	14	1	2	20	16	12	0	.347	.415	.497
Ray Blades	OF29,SS4,3B1	R	25	37	130	27	39	2	4	3	21	25	21	3	.300	.428	.446
Cliff Heathcote†	OF32	L	24	34	98	11	24	5	2	0	14	9	4	0	.245	.315	.337
Del Gainer	1B26,OF10	R	35	43	97	19	26	7	4	2	23	14	6	1	.268	.360	.485
Jesse Haines	P29,1B1	R	28	30	72	6	12	1	1	0	3	1	16	1	.167	.178	.208
Bill Pertica	P34,SS1	R	25	35	33	3	6	1	1	0	0	0	13	0	.182	.182	.273
Burt Shotton	OF3	L	37	34	30	5	6	1	0	0	2	4	6	0	.200	.294	.233
Harry McCurdy	C9,1B2	L	22	13	27	3	8	2	2	0	5	1	1	0	.296	.321	.519
Ernie Vick	C3	R	21	3	6	1	2	2	0	0	0	0	0	0	.333	.333	.667
Howard Freigau	SS2,3B1	R	19	3	1	0	0	0	0	0	0	0	0	0	.000	.000	.000

S. Toporcer, 1 G at OF

Pitcher	T	Age	G	GS	CG	ShO	IP	H	HR	BB	SO	W-L	Sv	ERA
Jeff Pfeffer	R	34	44	32	19	1	261.1	286	12	58	83	19-12	2	3.58
Bill Sherdel	L	25	47	31	15	3	242.0	298	12	62	79	17-13	2	3.87
Bill Doak	R	31	37	29	8	2	180.1	222	12	69	73	11-13	2	5.54
Jesse Haines	R	28	29	26	11	2	183.0	207	10	45	62	11-9	0	3.84
Epp Sell	R	25	7	5	0	0	33.0	47	2	6	5	4-2	0	6.82
Jack Knight	R	27	1	1	0	0	4.0	9	0	3	1	0-0	0	9.00
Johnny Stuart	R	21	2	1	0	0	2.0	2	0	2	1	0-0	0	9.00
Lou North	R	31	53	11	4	0	149.2	164	4	64	84	10-3	4	4.45
Clyde Barfoot	R	30	42	2	1	0	117.2	139	2	30	19	4-5	2	4.21
Bill Pertica	R	25	34	14	2	0	117.1	153	5	65	30	8-8	0	5.91
Roy Walker	R	29	12	2	0	0	32.0	34	1	15	14	1-2	0	4.78
Bill Bailey	L	33	12	0	0	0	31.2	38	1	23	11	0-2	0	5.40
Marv Goodwin	R	31	2	0	0	0	4.0	3	0	3	0	0-0	0	2.25
Eddie Dyer	L	21	2	0	0	0	3.2	7	0	0	3	0-0	0	2.45
Jack Fournier	R	32	1	0	0	0	1.0	0	0	0	0	0-0	0	0.00
Sid Benton	R	26	1	0	0	0	0.0	0	0	2	0	0-0	0	—

1922 Chicago Cubs 5th NL 80-74 .519 13.0 GB

Bill Killefer

Player	Gm by Position	B	Age	G	AB	R	H	2B	3B	HR	RBI	BB	SO	SB	Avg	OBP	Slg
Bob O'Farrell	C125	R	25	128	392	68	127	18	8	4	60	79	34	5	.324	.439	.441
Ray Grimes	1B138	R	28	138	509	99	180	45	12	14	99	75	33	7	.354	.442	.572
Zeb Terry	2B125,SS4,3B3	R	31	131	496	56	142	24	2	0	67	34	16	2	.286	.335	.343
Marty Krug	3B104,2B23,SS1	R	33	127	450	67	124	23	4	4	60	43	43	7	.276	.343	.371
Charlie Hollocher	SS152	L	26	152	592	90	201	37	8	3	69	58	5	19	.340	.403	.444
Hack Miller	OF116	R	28	122	466	61	164	28	5	12	78	26	39	3	.352	.389	.511
Jigger Statz	OF110	R	24	110	462	77	137	19	5	1	34	41	31	16	.297	.355	.366
Bernie Friberg	OF74,1B6,3B5*	R	22	97	296	51	92	8	2	0	23	37	37	8	.311	.391	.351
Cliff Heathcote†	OF60	L	24	76	243	37	68	8	7	1	34	18	15	5	.280	.330	.383
Turner Barber	OF47,1B16	L	28	84	226	35	70	7	4	0	29	30	9	7	.310	.391	.376
John Kelleher	3B46,SS7,1B4	R	28	63	193	23	50	7	1	0	20	15	14	5	.259	.316	.306
Marty Callaghan	OF53	L	22	74	175	31	45	7	4	0	20	17	17	2	.257	.326	.343
George Maisel	OF26	R	30	38	84	9	16	1	1	0	6	8	2	1	.190	.261	.226
Gabby Hartnett	C27	R	21	31	72	4	14	1	1	0	4	6	8	1	.194	.256	.236
Kettle Wirts	C27	R	24	31	58	7	10	2	0	1	6	12	15	0	.172	.314	.259
Max Flack†	OF15	L	32	17	54	7	12	1	0	0	6	2	4	2	.222	.250	.241
Sparky Adams	2B11	R	27	11	44	5	11	0	1	0	3	4	3	1	.250	.313	.295
Howie Fitzgerald	OF6	L	20	10	24	3	8	1	0	0	4	3	2	1	.333	.407	.375
George Grantham	3B5	L	22	7	23	3	4	1	1	0	3	1	3	2	.174	.208	.304
Butch Weis		L	21	2	2	2	1	0	0	0	0	0	0	0	.500	.500	.500
Walt Golvin	1B2	L	28	2	2	0	0	0	0	0	1	0	0	0	.000	.000	.000
Joe Klugmann	2B2	R	27	2	2	0	0	0	0	0	0	0	0	0	.000	.000	.000
Hooks Cotter		L	22	1	1	0	1	1	0	0	0	0	0	0	1.000	1.000	2.000

B. Friberg, 3 G at 2B

Pitcher	T	Age	G	GS	CG	ShO	IP	H	HR	BB	SO	W-L	Sv	ERA
Vic Aldridge	R	28	36	34	20	2	258.1	287	14	56	66	16-15	0	3.52
Pete Alexander	R	35	33	31	20	1	245.2	283	7	34	48	16-13	1	3.63
Percy Jones	L	22	44	26	7	2	164.0	197	10	69	46	8-9	1	4.72
Virgil Cheeves	R	21	39	23	9	1	182.2	195	9	76	40	12-11	2	4.09
Fred Fussell	L	26	3	2	1	0	19.0	24	0	8	4	1-1	0	4.74
Speed Martin	R	28	1	1	0	0	6.0	10	0	2	2	1-0	0	7.50
Tiny Osborne	R	29	41	14	7	1	184.0	183	7	95	81	9-5	3	4.50
Tony Kaufmann	R	21	37	9	4	1	153.0	161	15	57	45	7-13	3	4.06
George Stueland	R	23	34	12	4	0	111.0	129	9	48	43	9-4	0	5.92
Buck Freeman	R	25	11	1	0	0	25.2	47	0	10	10	0-1	1	8.77
Vic Keen	R	23	7	3	2	0	34.2	36	4	10	11	1-2	1	3.89
Ed Morris	R	22	5	0	0	0	12.0	22	1	6	5	0-0	0	8.25
Uel Eubanks	R	19	2	0	0	0	1.2	5	0	4	1	0-0	0	27.00

1922 Brooklyn Dodgers 6th NL 76-78 .494 17.0 GB

Wilbert Robinson

Player	Gm by Position	B	Age	G	AB	R	H	2B	3B	HR	RBI	BB	SO	SB	Avg	OBP	Slg
Hank DeBerry	C81	R	27	85	259	29	78	10	1	3	35	20	9	4	.301	.354	.382
Ray Schmandt	1B110	R	26	110	396	54	106	17	3	2	44	21	28	6	.268	.306	.341
Ivy Olson	2B85,SS51	R	36	136	551	63	150	26	6	1	47	25	10	8	.272	.306	.347
Andy High	3B130,SS22,2B1	L	24	153	579	82	164	27	10	6	65	59	26	3	.283	.354	.396
Jimmy Johnston	2B62,SS50,3B26	R	32	138	567	110	181	20	7	4	49	38	17	18	.319	.364	.400
Hi Myers	OF152,2B1	R	33	153	618	82	196	20	9	6	89	13	26	9	.317	.331	.408
Zack Wheat	OF152	L	34	152	600	92	201	29	12	16	112	45	22	9	.335	.388	.503
Tommy Griffith	OF82	L	32	99	329	44	104	17	8	4	49	23	10	7	.316	.361	.453
Bert Griffith	OF77,1B6	R	26	106	325	45	100	22	8	2	35	5	11	5	.308	.322	.443
Otto Miller	C57	R	33	59	180	20	47	11	1	1	23	6	13	0	.261	.285	.350
Clarence Mitchell	1B42,P5	L	31	55	155	21	45	6	3	3	28	19	6	0	.290	.371	.426
Bernie Hungling	C36	R	26	39	102	9	23	1	2	1	13	6	20	2	.225	.269	.304
Chuck Ward	SS31,3B2	R	27	33	91	12	25	5	1	0	14	5	8	1	.275	.320	.352
Bernie Neis	OF27	S	26	61	70	15	16	4	1	1	9	13	8	3	.229	.349	.357
Hal Janvrin	2B15,SS4,3B2*	R	29	30	57	7	17	3	1	0	1	4	4	0	.298	.344	.386
Sam Post	1B8	L	25	9	25	3	7	0	0	0	4	1	4	1	.280	.308	.280
Zack Taylor	C6	R	23	7	14	0	3	0	0	0	2	1	1	0	.214	.267	.214
Sam Crane	SS3	R	27	3	8	1	2	1	0	0	0	0	1	0	.250	.333	.375
Possum Whitted		R	32	1	1	0	0	0	0	0	0	0	0	0	.000	.000	.000
Wally Hood		R	27	2	0	2	0	0	0	0	0	0	0	0	—	—	—

H. Janvrin, 1 G at 1B, 1 G at OF

Pitcher	T	Age	G	GS	CG	ShO	IP	H	HR	BB	SO	W-L	Sv	ERA
Dutch Ruether	L	28	35	35	26	2	267.1	290	11	92	89	21-12	0	3.53
Burleigh Grimes	R	28	36	34	18	1	259.0	324	17	84	99	17-14	1	4.69
Dazzy Vance	R	31	36	30	16	5	245.2	259	9	94	134	18-12	0	3.70
Leon Cadore	R	31	29	21	13	0	190.1	224	13	57	49	8-15	0	4.35
Harry Shriver	R	25	25	14	4	2	108.1	114	5	48	38	4-6	0	2.99
Clarence Mitchell	L	31	5	3	0	0	12.2	28	0	7	1	0-3	0	14.21
Al Mamaux	R	28	37	7	1	0	87.2	97	7	33	35	1-4	3	3.70
Art Decatur	R	28	29	2	1	0	87.2	87	3	29	31	3-4	1	2.77
Sherry Smith†	L	31	28	9	3	1	108.2	128	6	35	15	4-8	2	4.56
Ray Gordinier	R	30	5	0	0	0	11.1	13	3	8	5	0-0	0	8.74
Jim Murray	L	21	4	0	0	0	6.0	8	0	3	3	0-0	1	4.50
Paul Schreiber	R	19	1	0	0	0	1.0	2	0	0	0	0-0	0	0.00

1922 Philadelphia Phillies 7th NL 57-96 .373 35.5 GB

Kaiser Wilhelm

Player	Gm by Position	B	Age	G	AB	R	H	2B	3B	HR	RBI	BB	SO	SB	Avg	OBP	Slg
Butch Henline	C119	R	27	125	430	57	136	20	4	14	64	36	33	2	.316	.380	.479
Roy Leslie	1B139	R	27	141	513	44	139	23	2	6	50	37	49	3	.271	.320	.359
Frank Parkinson	2B139	R	27	141	545	86	150	18	6	15	70	55	93	3	.275	.344	.413
Goldie Rapp	3B117,SS2	S	30	119	502	58	127	26	3	0	38	32	29	6	.253	.299	.317
Art Fletcher	SS106	R	37	110	396	46	111	20	5	7	53	21	14	3	.280	.325	.409
Cy Williams	OF150	L	34	151	584	98	180	30	6	26	92	74	49	11	.308	.392	.514
Curt Walker	OF147	L	25	148	581	102	196	36	11	12	89	56	46	11	.337	.399	.499
Cliff Lee	OF89,1B18,3B1	R	25	122	422	65	136	29	6	17	77	32	43	2	.322	.371	.540
Russ Wrightstone	3B40,SS35,1B2	L	29	99	331	56	101	18	6	5	33	28	17	4	.305	.365	.441
Bevo LeBourveau	OF42	L	27	74	167	24	45	8	3	2	24	20	29	0	.269	.368	.389
Johnny Mokan†	OF37,3B2	R	26	47	151	20	38	7	1	3	27	16	25	1	.252	.327	.371
John Peters	C39	R	28	55	143	15	35	9	1	4	24	9	18	0	.245	.308	.406
Jimmy Smith	SS23,2B13,3B1	S	27	38	114	13	25	1	0	1	6	5	9	1	.219	.258	.254
Lee King†	OF15	R	29	19	53	8	12	5	1	2	13	8	6	0	.226	.328	.472
Frank Withrow	C8	R	31	10	21	3	7	2	0	0	3	3	5	0	.333	.417	.429
Rabbit Benton	2B5	R	20	6	19	1	4	1	0	0	3	2	1	0	.211	.286	.263

Pitcher	T	Age	G	GS	CG	ShO	IP	H	HR	BB	SO	W-L	Sv	ERA
Jimmy Ring	R	27	40	33	17	0	249.1	292	19	103	116	12-18	1	4.58
Lee Meadows	R	27	33	33	19	2	237.0	264	8	71	62	12-18	0	4.03
Bill Hubbell	R	25	35	24	11	1	189.0	257	14	41	33	7-15	1	5.00
Lefty Weinert	L	20	34	22	10	0	166.2	189	10	70	58	8-11	1	3.40
Petie Behan	R	34	7	5	3	1	47.1	49	3	14	13	4-2	0	2.47
George Smith	R	30	42	18	6	1	194.0	250	16	35	44	5-14	0	4.78
Jesse Winters	R	28	34	9	4	0	138.1	176	8	56	29	6-6	2	5.33
John Singleton	R	25	22	9	3	1	93.0	127	6	38	27	1-10	0	5.90
Lerton Pinto	L	23	9	0	0	0	24.2	31	1	14	4	0-1	0	5.11
Huck Betts	R	25	7	0	0	0	15.0	23	3	8	4	1-0	0	9.60
Stan Baumgartner	L	27	6	1	0	0	9.2	18	1	5	2	1-1	0	6.52
Tom Sullivan	L	26	3	0	0	0	8.0	16	0	5	2	0-0	0	11.25

622 Seasons: Team Rosters

1922 Boston Braves 8th NL 53-100 .346 39.5 GB

Fred Mitchell

Player	Gm by Position	B	Age	G	AB	R	H	2B	3B	HR	RBI	BB	SO	SB	Avg	OBP	Slg
Mickey O'Neil	C79	R	22	83	251	18	56	5	2	0	26	14	11	1	.223	.267	.259
Walter Holke	1B105	S	29	105	395	35	115	9	4	0	46	14	23	6	.291	.317	.334
Larry Kopf	2B78,SS33,3B13	S	31	126	466	59	124	6	3	1	37	45	22	8	.266	.332	.298
Tony Boeckel	3B106	R	29	119	402	61	116	19	6	6	47	35	32	14	.289	.349	.410
Hod Ford	SS115,2B28	R	24	143	515	58	140	23	9	2	60	30	36	2	.272	.317	.363
Ray Powell	OF136	L	33	142	550	82	163	22	11	6	37	59	66	3	.296	.369	.409
Walton Cruise	OF100,1B2	L	32	104	352	51	98	15	10	4	46	44	20	4	.278	.360	.412
Al Nixon	OF79	R	36	86	318	35	84	14	4	2	22	9	19	6	.264	.284	.352
Walter Barbare	2B45,3B38,1B14	R	30	106	373	38	86	5	4	0	40	21	22	2	.231	.272	.265
Fred Nicholson	OF63	R	27	78	222	31	56	4	5	2	29	23	24	5	.252	.336	.342
Hank Gowdy	C72,1B1	R	32	92	221	23	70	11	1	1	27	24	13	2	.317	.391	.389
Frank Gibson	C29,1B20	S	31	66	164	15	49	7	2	3	20	10	27	4	.299	.339	.421
Billy Southworth	OF41	L	29	43	158	27	51	4	4	4	18	18	1	4	.323	.392	.475
Lloyd Christenbury	OF32,2B5,3B2	L	28	71	152	22	38	5	2	1	13	18	11	2	.250	.337	.329
Bunny Roser	OF32	L	20	32	113	13	27	3	4	0	16	10	19	2	.239	.306	.336
Snake Henry	1B18	L	26	18	66	5	13	4	1	0	5	2	8	2	.197	.221	.288
Gil Gallagher	SS6	S	25	7	22	1	1	1	0	0	2	1	7	0	.045	.087	.091

Pitcher	T	Age	G	GS	CG	ShO	IP	H	HR	BB	SO	W-L	Sv	ERA
Mule Watson	R	25	41	29	8	1	201.0	262	9	59	53	8-14	1	4.70
Rube Marquard	L	35	39	24	7	0	198.0	255	12	66	57	11-15	1	5.09
Frank Miller	R	36	31	23	14	2	200.0	213	7	60	65	11-13	1	3.51
Joe Oeschger	R	31	46	23	10	1	195.2	234	8	81	51	6-21	1	5.06
Hugh McQuillan†	R	24	28	17	7	0	136.0	154	3	56	33	5-10	0	4.24
Harry Hulihan	L	23	7	6	2	0	40.0	40	0	26	16	2-3	0	3.15
Johnny Cooney	L	21	4	3	1	0	25.0	19	0	6	7	1-2	0	2.16
Dick Rudolph	R	34	3	3	1	0	16.0	22	2	5	3	0-2	0	5.06
Jim Yeargin	R	20	1	1	1	0	7.0	5	1	2	1	0-1	0	1.29
Dana Fillingim	R	28	25	12	5	1	117.0	143	6	37	25	5-9	2	4.54
Garland Braxton	L	22	25	4	2	0	66.2	75	3	24	15	1-2	0	3.38
Tim McNamara	R	23	24	5	4	2	70.2	55	2	26	16	3-4	0	2.42
Gene Lansing	R	24	15	1	0	0	40.2	46	1	22	14	0-1	0	5.98
Joe Genewich	R	25	6	2	1	0	23.0	29	2	11	4	0-2	0	7.04
Joe Matthews	L	23	3	1	0	0	10.0	5	1	6	0	0-1	0	3.60
Cy Morgan	R	26	2	0	0	0	1.1	8	0	2	0	0-0	0	27.00

»1923 New York Yankees 1st AL 98-54 .645 —

Miller Huggins

Player	Gm by Position	B	Age	G	AB	R	H	2B	3B	HR	RBI	BB	SO	SB	Avg	OBP	Slg
Wally Schang	C81	S	33	84	272	39	75	8	2	2	29	27	17	5	.276	.360	.342
Wally Pipp	1B144	L	30	144	569	79	173	19	8	6	108	36	28	6	.304	.352	.397
Aaron Ward	2B152	R	26	152	567	79	161	26	11	10	82	56	65	8	.284	.351	.422
Joe Dugan	3B146	R	26	146	644	111	182	30	7	7	67	25	41	4	.283	.311	.384
Everett Scott	SS152	R	30	152	533	48	131	16	4	6	60	13	19	1	.246	.266	.325
Babe Ruth	OF148,1B4	L	28	152	522	151	205	45	13	41	131	170	93	17	.393	.545	.764
Whitey Witt	OF144	L	27	146	596	113	187	18	10	6	56	67	42	2	.314	.386	.408
Bob Meusel	OF121	R	26	132	460	59	144	29	10	9	91	31	52	13	.313	.359	.478
Fred Hofmann	C70	R	29	72	238	24	69	10	4	3	26	18	27	2	.290	.350	.403
Elmer Smith	OF47	L	30	70	183	30	56	6	2	7	35	21	21	3	.306	.377	.475
Harvey Hendrick	OF13	L	25	37	66	9	18	3	1	3	12	2	8	3	.273	.294	.485
Benny Bengough	C19	R	24	19	53	1	7	2	0	0	3	4	2	0	.132	.193	.170
Mike McNally	3B7,SS6,2B5	R	30	30	38	5	8	0	0	0	1	3	4	2	.211	.268	.211
Ernie Johnson†	SS15,3B1	L	35	19	38	6	17	1	1	1	8	1	1	0	.447	.462	.605
Lou Gehrig	1B9	L	20	13	26	6	11	4	1	1	9	2	5	0	.423	.464	.769
Hinkey Haines	OF14	R	24	28	25	9	4	2	0	0	3	4	5	3	.160	.276	.240
Mike Gazella	SS4,2B2,3B2	R	26	8	13	2	1	0	0	0	1	2	3	0	.077	.200	.077

Pitcher	T	Age	G	GS	CG	ShO	IP	H	HR	BB	SO	W-L	Sv	ERA
Bob Shawkey	R	32	36	31	17	1	258.2	232	17	102	125	16-11	1	3.51
Joe Bush	R	30	37	30	23	3	275.2	263	7	117	125	19-15	0	3.43
Waite Hoyt	R	23	37	28	19	1	238.2	227	9	66	60	17-9	1	3.02
Sad Sam Jones	R	30	39	27	18	3	243.0	239	11	69	68	21-8	4	3.63
Herb Pennock	L	29	35	27	21	1	224.1	235	11	68	93	19-6	3	3.33
Carl Mays	R	31	23	7	2	0	81.1	119	8	32	16	5-2	0	6.20
George Pipgras	R	23	8	2	2	0	33.1	34	2	25	12	1-3	0	5.94
Oscar Roettger	R	23	5	0	0	0	11.2	16	3	12	7	0-0	1	8.49

1923 Detroit Tigers 2nd AL 83-71 .539 16.0 GB

Ty Cobb

Player	Gm by Position	B	Age	G	AB	R	H	2B	3B	HR	RBI	BB	SO	SB	Avg	OBP	Slg
Johnny Bassler	C128	L	28	135	383	45	114	12	3	0	49	76	13	2	.298	.414	.345
Lu Blue	1B129	S	26	129	504	100	143	27	7	1	46	96	40	9	.284	.402	.371
Fred Haney	2B69,3B55,SS16	R	25	142	503	85	142	13	4	4	67	45	23	12	.282	.347	.348
Bob Jones	3B97	L	33	100	372	51	93	15	4	1	40	29	13	7	.250	.306	.320
Topper Rigney	SS129	R	26	129	470	63	148	24	11	1	74	55	35	7	.315	.389	.419
Ty Cobb	OF141	L	36	145	556	103	189	40	7	6	88	66	14	9	.340	.413	.469
Harry Heilmann	OF130,1B12	R	28	144	524	121	211	44	11	18	115	74	40	8	.403	.481	.632
Bobby Veach	OF85,C1	L	35	114	293	45	94	13	3	2	39	29	21	10	.321	.388	.406
Heinie Manush	OF79	L	21	109	308	59	103	20	5	4	54	20	21	3	.334	.406	.471
Del Pratt	2B60,1B17,3B12	R	35	101	297	43	92	18	3	0	40	25	9	5	.310	.375	.391
Bob Fothergill	OF68	R	25	101	241	34	76	18	2	1	49	12	19	4	.315	.358	.419
Larry Woodall	C60	R	28	71	148	20	41	12	2	1	19	22	9	2	.277	.371	.405
George Cutshaw	2B43,3B2	R	35	45	143	15	32	1	2	0	13	9	5	2	.224	.279	.259
John Kerr	SS15	R	24	19	42	4	9	1	0	0	1	4	5	0	.214	.283	.238
Clyde Manion	C3,1B1	R	26	23	22	0	3	0	0	0	2	2	2	0	.136	.208	.136
Les Burke	3B2,C1,2B1	L	20	7	10	2	1	0	0	0	2	0	1	0	.100	.100	.100
Ira Flagstead†		R	29	1	1	0	0	0	0	0	0	0	0	0	.000	.000	.000
Fred Carisch	C2	R	41	2	0	0	0	0	0	0	0	0	0	0	—	—	—

Pitcher	T	Age	G	GS	CG	ShO	IP	H	HR	BB	SO	W-L	Sv	ERA
Hooks Dauss	R	33	50	39	22	4	316.0	331	10	78	105	21-13	3	3.62
Herman Pillette	R	27	47	37	14	0	250.1	280	7	83	64	14-19	1	3.85
Ken Holloway	R	25	42	24	7	1	194.0	232	12	75	55	11-10	1	4.45
Rip Collins	R	27	17	13	3	1	92.1	104	3	22	25	3-7	0	4.87
Bert Cole	L	26	52	13	5	1	163.0	183	9	61	32	13-5	5	4.14
Syl Johnson	R	22	37	18	7	1	176.1	181	12	47	93	12-7	0	3.98
Ray Francis	L	30	33	6	0	0	79.1	95	2	28	27	5-8	1	4.42
Ole Olsen	R	28	17	2	1	0	41.1	42	1	17	12	1-1	0	6.31
Earl Whitehill	L	23	8	3	2	1	33.0	22	2	15	19	2-0	0	2.73
Ed Wells	L	23	7	0	0	0	10.0	11	0	6	6	0-0	0	5.40
Rufe Clarke	R	23	5	0	0	0	6.0	6	0	6	2	1-1	0	4.50
Roy Moore	L	24	3	0	0	0	12.0	15	0	11	7	0-0	1	3.00

1923 Cleveland Indians 3rd AL 82-71 .536 16.5 GB

Tris Speaker

Player	Gm by Position	B	Age	G	AB	R	H	2B	3B	HR	RBI	BB	SO	SB	Avg	OBP	Slg
Steve O'Neill	C111	R	31	113	330	31	82	12	0	0	50	64	34	0	.248	.374	.285
Frank Brower	1B112,OF4	L	30	126	397	77	113	25	8	16	66	62	32	6	.285	.392	.509
Bill Wambsganss	2B88,3B4,SS2	R	29	101	345	59	100	20	4	1	59	43	15	12	.290	.373	.380
Rube Lutzke	3B143	R	25	143	511	71	131	20	6	3	65	59	57	10	.256	.338	.337
Joe Sewell	SS151	L	24	153	553	98	195	41	10	3	109	98	12	9	.353	.456	.479
Charlie Jamieson	OF152	L	30	152	644	130	222	36	12	2	51	80	37	19	.345	.422	.447
Tris Speaker	OF150	L	35	150	574	133	218	59	11	17	130	93	15	10	.380	.469	.610
Homer Summa	OF136	L	24	137	525	92	172	27	6	3	69	33	20	9	.328	.374	.419
Riggs Stephenson	2B66,OF3,3B2	R	25	91	301	48	96	20	6	5	65	15	25	6	.319	.357	.475
Glenn Myatt	C69	L	25	92	220	36	63	7	6	3	40	16	18	0	.286	.338	.414
Lou Guisto	1B40	R	28	40	144	17	26	5	0	0	18	15	15	1	.181	.263	.215
Joe Connolly	OF39	R	27	52	109	25	33	10	1	3	25	13	7	1	.303	.377	.495
Larry Gardner	3B19	L	37	52	79	4	20	5	1	0	12	12	7	0	.253	.352	.342
Ray Knode	1B21	L	22	22	38	7	11	0	0	2	4	2	4	1	.289	.325	.447
Luke Sewell	C7	R	22	10	10	2	2	0	1	0	1	1	0	0	.200	.273	.400
Wally Shaner	OF2,3B1	R	23	3	4	1	1	0	0	0	0	1	1	0	.250	.400	.250
Tom Gulley	OF1	L	23	2	3	1	1	1	0	0	0	0	0	0	.333	.333	.667
Sumpter Clarke	OF1	R	25	1	3	0	0	0	0	0	0	0	0	0	.000	.000	.000
Jackie Gallagher	OF1	L	21	1	1	0	1	0	0	0	1	0	0	0	1.000	1.000	1.000
Kenny Hogan		L	20	1	0	0	0	0	0	0	0	0	0	0	—	—	—

Pitcher	T	Age	G	GS	CG	ShO	IP	H	HR	BB	SO	W-L	Sv	ERA
George Uhle	R	24	54	44	29	1	357.2	378	8	102	109	26-16	5	3.77
Stan Coveleski	R	33	33	31	17	5	228.0	251	8	42	54	13-14	2	2.76
Jim Joe Edwards	L	28	38	21	8	1	179.1	200	5	75	68	10-10	1	3.71
Sherry Smith	L	32	30	16	10	1	124.0	129	4	37	23	9-6	1	3.27
Joe Shaute	L	23	33	16	7	0	172.0	176	4	53	61	10-8	0	3.51
Guy Morton	R	30	33	14	3	2	128.1	133	3	56	54	6-6	1	4.28
Danny Boone	R	28	27	4	2	0	70.1	93	3	31	15	4-6	0	6.01
Dewey Metivier	R	25	26	5	1	0	73.1	111	1	38	9	4-2	1	6.50
Phil Bedgood	R	25	9	2	0	0	18.2	16	0	14	7	0-2	0	5.30
Logan Drake	R	22	4	0	0	0	4.1	2	0	5	2	0-0	0	4.15
Jim Sullivan	R	29	3	0	0	0	5.0	10	0	5	4	0-1	0	14.40
Dutch Levsen	R	25	3	0	0	0	4.1	4	0	0	1	0-0	0	0.00
George Edmondson	R	27	1	0	0	0	4.0	8	0	3	0	0-0	0	11.25
Jay Fry	R	21	1	0	0	0	3.2	6	0	4	0	0-0	0	12.27
George Winn	L	25	1	0	0	0	2.0	0	0	1	0	0-0	0	0.00

1923 Washington Senators 4th AL 75-78 .490 23.5 GB

Donie Bush

Player	Gm by Position	B	Age	G	AB	R	H	2B	3B	HR	RBI	BB	SO	SB	Avg	OBP	Slg
Muddy Ruel	C133	R	27	136	449	63	142	24	3	0	54	55	21	4	.316	.394	.383
Joe Judge	1B112	L	29	113	405	56	127	24	6	2	63	58	20	11	.314	.406	.417
Bucky Harris	2B144,SS1	R	26	145	532	60	150	21	13	2	70	50	29	23	.282	.358	.382
Ossie Bluege	3B106,2B4	R	22	109	379	48	93	15	7	2	42	48	53	5	.245	.343	.338
Roger Peckinpaugh	SS154	R	32	154	568	73	150	18	4	2	62	64	30	10	.264	.340	.320
Goose Goslin	OF149	L	22	150	600	86	180	29	18	9	99	40	53	7	.300	.347	.453
Sam Rice	OF147	L	33	148	595	117	188	35	18	3	75	57	12	20	.316	.381	.450
Nemo Leibold†	OF84	L	31	95	315	68	96	13	4	1	22	53	16	7	.305	.408	.381
Joe Evans	OF72,3B21,1B5	R	28	106	372	42	98	15	3	0	38	27	18	6	.263	.313	.320
Patsy Gharrity	C35,1B33	R	31	93	251	26	52	9	4	3	33	22	27	6	.207	.276	.311
Rip Wade	OF19	L	25	33	69	8	16	2	2	2	14	5	10	0	.232	.284	.406
Bill Conroy	3B10,1B6,OF1	R	24	18	60	6	8	2	2	0	2	4	9	0	.133	.188	.233
Pinky Hargrave	3B8,C5,OF1	S	27	33	59	4	17	2	0	0	8	2	6	0	.288	.311	.322
Bobby Murray	3B10	L	24	10	37	2	7	1	0	0	2	1	4	1	.189	.211	.216
Jim O'Neill	2B8,3B4,SS1*	R	30	23	33	6	9	1	0	0	3	1	3	0	.273	.294	.303
Showboat Fisher	OF5	L	24	13	23	4	6	2	0	0	2	4	3	0	.261	.370	.348
Donie Bush	3B5,2B2	S	35	10	22	6	9	0	0	0	0	0	1	0	.409	.409	.409
Carr Smith	OF4	R	22	5	9	0	1	1	0	0	1	0	0	0	.111	.111	.222
Doc Prothro	3B6	R	29	6	8	2	2	0	1	0	3	1	3	0	.250	.333	.500
Jim Riley	1B2	L	28	2	3	1	0	0	0	0	0	2	0	0	.000	.400	.000
Pete Lapan		R	32	2	2	0	0	0	0	0	0	0	0	0	.000	.000	.000
Jake Propst		L	28	1	1	0	0	0	0	0	0	0	0	0	.000	.000	.000

J. O'Neill, 1 G at OF

Pitcher	T	Age	G	GS	CG	ShO	IP	H	HR	BB	SO	W-L	Sv	ERA
Walter Johnson	R	35	42	34	18	3	261.1	263	9	73	130	17-12	4	3.48
George Mogridge	L	34	33	30	17	3	211.0	228	10	56	62	13-13	1	3.11
Tom Zachary	L	27	35	29	10	0	204.1	270	9	63	40	10-16	0	4.49
Paul Zahniser	R	26	33	21	10	1	177.0	201	7	76	52	9-10	0	3.86
Cy Warmoth	L	30	21	13	3	0	105.0	103	4	76	45	7-5	0	4.29
Monroe Mitchell	R	21	10	6	3	1	41.2	57	0	22	8	2-4	2	6.48
Clay Roe	L	19	1	1	0	0	1.2	0	0	6	2	0-1	0	0.00
Allan Russell	R	29	52	5	4	0	181.1	177	9	77	67	10-7	9	3.03
B. Hollingsworth	R	27	17	8	1	0	72.2	72	3	50	26	3-7	0	4.09
Jim Brillheart	L	19	12	0	0	0	18.0	27	1	12	8	0-1	0	7.00
Firpo Marberry	R	24	11	4	2	0	44.2	42	1	17	18	4-0	0	2.82
Skipper Friday	R	25	7	2	1	0	30.0	35	2	22	9	0-1	0	6.90
Duke Sedgwick	R	25	5	2	1	0	16.0	27	1	6	4	0-1	0	7.88
Slim McGrew	R	23	3	0	0	0	5.0	11	0	3	1	0-0	0	12.60
Squire Potter	R	21	1	0	0	0	3.0	11	0	4	1	0-0	0	21.00
Ted Wingfield	R	23	1	0	0	0	1.0	0	0	0	1	0-0	0	0.00
Fred Schemanske	R	20	1	0	0	0	1.0	3	0	0	0	0-0	0	27.00

1923 St. Louis Browns 5th AL 74-78 .487 24.0 GB

Lee Fohl (52-49)/Jimmy Austin (22-29)

Player	Gm by Position	B	Age	G	AB	R	H	2B	3B	HR	RBI	BB	SO	SB	Avg	OBP	Slg
Hank Severeid	C116	R	32	122	432	50	133	27	6	3	51	31	11	3	.308	.356	.419
Dutch Schliebner†	1B127	R	32	127	444	50	122	19	6	4	52	39	60	3	.275	.339	.372
Marty McManus	2B133,1B20	R	23	154	582	86	180	35	10	15	94	49	50	14	.309	.367	.481
Gene Robertson	3B74,2B2	L	24	78	251	36	62	10	1	0	17	21	7	4	.247	.310	.295
Wally Gerber	SS154	R	31	154	605	85	170	26	3	1	62	54	50	4	.281	.342	.339
Jack Tobin	OF151	L	31	151	637	91	202	32	15	13	73	42	13	8	.317	.363	.476
Baby Doll Jacobson	OF146	R	32	147	592	76	183	29	6	8	81	29	27	6	.309	.343	.419
Ken Williams	OF145	L	33	147	555	106	198	37	12	29	91	79	32	18	.357	.439	.623
Homer Ezzell	3B73,2B8	R	27	88	275	31	68	6	0	0	14	15	20	4	.247	.291	.269
Pat Collins	C47	R	26	85	181	9	32	8	0	3	30	15	45	0	.177	.240	.271
Eddie Foster	2B20,3B7	R	36	27	100	9	18	2	0	0	4	7	7	0	.180	.241	.200
Cedric Durst	OF10,1B8	L	26	45	85	11	18	2	0	5	11	8	14	0	.212	.280	.412
Bill Whaley	OF13	R	24	23	50	5	12	2	1	0	1	4	2	0	.240	.309	.320
Frank Ellerbe	3B14	R	27	18	49	6	9	0	0	0	1	1	5	0	.184	.200	.184
Josh Billings	C4	R	31	4	9	0	0	0	0	0	0	0	2	0	.000	.000	.000
Herschel Bennett	OF1	L	26	5	4	0	0	0	0	0	0	1	1	0	.000	.200	.000
Johnny Schulte	C1,1B1	L	26	7	3	1	0	0	0	0	1	4	0	0	.000	.571	.000
Harry Rice		L	21	4	3	0	0	0	0	0	0	0	0	0	.000	.000	.000
Syl Simon		R	25	1	1	0	0	0	0	0	0	0	0	0	.000	.000	.000
Bill Mizeur		L	26	1	1	0	0	0	0	0	0	0	0	0	.000	.000	.000
Jimmy Austin	C1	S	43	1	0	0	0	0	0	0	0	0	0	0	—	—	—

Pitcher	T	Age	G	GS	CG	ShO	IP	H	HR	BB	SO	W-L	Sv	ERA
Elam Vangilder	R	27	41	35	20	4	282.1	276	11	120	74	16-17	1	3.06
Urban Shocker	R	32	43	35	24	3	277.1	292	12	49	109	20-12	5	3.41
Dave Danforth	L	33	38	29	16	1	226.1	221	4	87	96	16-14	1	3.94
Ray Kolp	R	28	34	17	11	1	171.1	178	11	54	44	5-12	1	3.89
Dixie Davis	R	32	19	17	5	1	109.1	106	4	63	36	4-6	0	3.62
Sloppy Thurston†	R	24	2	1	0	0	4.0	8	0	2	0	0-0	0	6.75
Hub Pruett	L	22	32	8	3	0	104.1	109	3	64	59	4-7	2	4.31
Charlie Root	R	24	27	2	0	0	60.0	68	4	18	27	0-4	0	5.70
Rasty Wright	R	27	20	8	4	0	82.2	107	6	34	26	7-4	0	6.42
Bill Bayne	L	24	19	2	0	0	46.0	49	4	31	15	2-2	0	4.50
George Grant	R	20	4	0	0	0	8.2	15	0	3	2	0-0	0	5.19
Jumbo Elliott	L	22	1	0	0	0	1.0	1	0	3	0	0-0	0	27.00

1923 Philadelphia Athletics 6th AL 69-83 .454 29.0 GB

Connie Mack

Player	Gm by Position	B	Age	G	AB	R	H	2B	3B	HR	RBI	BB	SO	SB	Avg	OBP	Slg
Cy Perkins	C137	R	27	143	500	53	135	34	5	2	65	65	30	1	.270	.356	.370
Joe Hauser	1B146	L	24	146	537	93	165	21	9	17	94	69	52	6	.307	.398	.475
Jimmy Dykes	2B102,SS20,3B2	R	26	124	416	50	105	28	1	4	43	35	40	6	.252	.318	.353
Sammy Hale	3B107	R	26	115	434	68	125	22	8	3	51	17	31	8	.288	.327	.396
Chick Galloway	SS134	R	26	134	504	64	140	18	9	2	62	37	30	12	.278	.327	.361
Wid Matthews	OF127	L	26	129	485	52	133	11	6	1	25	50	27	16	.274	.343	.328
Bing Miller	OF119	R	28	123	458	68	137	25	4	12	64	27	34	9	.299	.344	.450
Frank Welch	OF117	R	25	125	421	56	125	19	9	4	55	48	40	1	.297	.374	.413
Beauty McGowan	OF79	L	21	95	287	41	73	9	1	1	19	36	25	4	.254	.340	.303
Heinie Scheer	2B51	R	22	69	210	26	50	8	1	2	21	17	41	3	.238	.301	.314
Harry Riconda	3B47,SS2	R	26	55	175	23	46	11	4	0	12	12	18	4	.263	.317	.371
Fred Heimach	P40,1B6	L	22	63	118	14	30	4	1	1	11	4	18	0	.254	.279	.331
Tilly Walker	OF26	R	35	52	109	12	30	5	2	2	16	14	11	1	.275	.368	.413
Frank Bruggy	C44,1B5	R	32	54	105	4	22	3	0	1	6	4	9	1	.210	.245	.267
Walt French	OF10	L	23	16	39	7	9	3	0	0	2	5	7	0	.231	.318	.308
Chuck Rowland	C4	R	23	5	6	0	0	0	0	0	0	0	2	0	.000	.000	.000
John Jones	OF1	L	22	1	4	0	1	0	0	0	1	0	1	0	.250	.250	.250
Doc Wood	SS3	R	23	3	3	0	1	0	0	0	0	0	0	0	.333	.333	.333

Pitcher	T	Age	G	GS	CG	ShO	IP	H	HR	BB	SO	W-L	Sv	ERA
Bob Hasty	R	27	44	36	10	1	243.1	274	11	72	56	13-15	1	4.44
Eddie Rommel	R	25	56	31	19	3	297.2	306	14	108	76	18-19	5	3.27
Slim Harriss	R	26	46	28	9	0	209.1	221	9	95	89	10-16	6	4.00
Rollie Naylor	R	31	26	20	9	2	143.0	149	5	59	27	12-7	0	3.46
Dennis Burns	R	25	4	3	2	0	27.0	21	1	7	8	2-1	0	2.00
Hank Hulvey	R	25	1	1	0	0	7.0	10	1	2	2	0-1	0	7.71
Fred Heimach	L	22	40	19	10	0	208.1	238	14	69	63	6-12	0	4.32
Rube Walberg†	L	26	26	10	4	0	115.0	122	10	60	38	4-8	0	5.32
Curly Ogden	R	22	18	2	0	0	46.1	63	2	32	14	1-2	0	5.63
Roy Meeker	L	22	5	2	2	0	25.0	24	0	13	12	3-0	0	3.60
Walt Kinney	L	29	5	1	0	0	12.0	11	0	9	9	0-1	0	7.50
Al Kellett	R	21	5	0	0	0	10.0	11	0	8	1	0-1	0	6.30
Chuck Wolfe	R	26	3	0	0	0	9.2	6	1	8	1	0-0	0	3.72
Harry O'Neill	R	26	3	0	0	0	2.0	1	0	3	2	0-0	0	0.00
Ren Kelly	R	23	1	0	0	0	7.0	7	0	4	1	0-0	0	2.57
Doc Ozmer	R	22	1	0	0	0	2.0	1	0	1	1	0-0	0	4.50

1923 Chicago White Sox 7th AL 69-85 .448 30.0 GB

Kid Gleason

Player	Gm by Position	B	Age	G	AB	R	H	2B	3B	HR	RBI	BB	SO	SB	Avg	OBP	Slg
Ray Schalk	C121	R	30	123	382	42	87	12	2	1	44	39	28	6	.228	.306	.277
Earl Sheely	1B156	R	30	156	570	74	169	25	3	4	88	79	30	5	.296	.387	.372
Eddie Collins	2B142	L	36	145	505	89	182	22	5	5	67	84	8	49	.360	.455	.453
Willie Kamm	3B149	R	23	149	544	57	159	39	9	6	87	62	82	17	.292	.366	.430
Harvey McClellan	SS139,2B2	R	28	141	550	67	129	29	3	1	41	27	44	14	.235	.270	.304
Harry Hooper	OF143	L	35	145	576	87	166	32	4	10	65	68	22	18	.288	.370	.410
Johnny Mostil	OF143,3B6,SS1	R	27	153	546	91	159	37	15	3	64	62	51	41	.291	.376	.430
Bibb Falk	OF80	L	24	87	274	44	84	18	6	5	38	25	12	4	.307	.367	.471
Roy Elsh	OF57	R	31	81	209	28	52	7	2	0	24	16	23	15	.249	.305	.301
Bill Barrett	OF40,3B1	R	23	44	162	17	44	7	2	2	23	9	24	12	.272	.310	.377
M. Archdeacon	OF20	L	24	22	87	23	35	5	1	0	4	6	8	2	.402	.441	.483
John Happenny	2B20,SS8	R	22	32	86	7	19	5	0	0	10	3	13	0	.221	.256	.279
Roy Graham	C33	R	28	36	82	3	16	2	0	0	6	9	6	0	.195	.290	.220
Buck Crouse	C22	L	26	23	70	6	18	2	1	1	7	3	4	0	.257	.297	.357
Amos Strunk	OF4,1B3	L	34	54	54	7	17	0	0	0	8	8	5	1	.315	.403	.315
Ernie Johnson†	SS12	L	35	12	53	5	10	2	0	0	1	3	5	2	.189	.246	.226
Lou Rosenberg	2B2	R	19	3	4	0	1	0	0	0	0	0	1	0	.250	.250	.250
Charlie Dorman	C1	R	25	1	2	0	1	0	0	0	0	0	0	0	.500	.500	.500
Jess Cortazzo		R	18	1	1	0	0	0	0	0	0	0	0	0	.000	.000	.000
Roxy Snipes		L	26	1	1	0	0	0	0	0	0	0	0	0	.000	.000	.000
Leo Taylor		R	22	1	0	0	0	0	0	0	0	0	0	0	—	—	—

Pitcher	T	Age	G	GS	CG	ShO	IP	H	HR	BB	SO	W-L	Sv	ERA
Charlie Robertson	R	27	38	34	18	1	255.0	262	8	104	91	13-18	0	3.81
Red Faber	R	34	32	31	15	2	232.1	233	6	62	91	14-11	0	3.41
Mike Cvengros	L	21	40	26	14	0	214.1	216	6	107	86	12-13	3	4.41
Dixie Leverett	R	29	38	24	9	0	192.2	212	6	64	64	10-13	3	4.06
Ted Blankenship	R	22	44	23	9	1	208.2	219	8	100	57	9-14	0	4.27
Claral Gillenwater	R	23	5	3	1	1	21.1	28	2	6	2	1-3	0	5.48
Leon Cadore†	R	32	1	1	0	0	2.1	6	0	2	3	0-1	0	23.14
Frank Woodward	R	29	2	1	0	0	2.0	5	0	1	0	0-1	0	13.50
Sloppy Thurston†	R	24	44	12	8	0	191.2	223	11	36	55	7-8	4	3.05
Frank Mack	R	23	11	0	0	0	23.1	23	0	11	6	0-1	0	4.24
Ted Lyons	R	22	9	1	0	0	22.2	30	2	15	6	2-1	0	6.35
Paul Castner	L	26	6	0	0	0	10.0	14	0	5	0	0-0	0	6.30
Homer Blankenship	R	20	4	0	0	0	5.0	9	0	1	1	1-1	1	3.60
Sarge Connally	R	24	3	0	0	0	8.2	7	0	12	3	0-0	0	6.23
Lum Davenport	L	23	2	0	0	0	4.1	7	0	4	1	0-0	0	6.23
Red Proctor	R	22	2	0	0	0	4.0	11	0	2	0	0-0	0	13.50
Slim Embrey	R	21	1	0	0	0	2.2	7	0	2	1	0-0	0	10.13

1923 Boston Red Sox 8th AL 61-91 .401 37.0 GB

Frank Chance

Player	Gm by Position	B	Age	G	AB	R	H	2B	3B	HR	RBI	BB	SO	SB	Avg	OBP	Slg
Val Picinich	C81	R	26	87	268	33	74	21	1	2	31	46	32	3	.276	.386	.384
George Burns	1B146	R	30	146	551	91	181	47	5	7	82	45	33	9	.328	.386	.470
Chick Fewster	2B48,SS36	R	27	90	284	32	67	10	1	0	15	39	35	7	.236	.334	.278
Howard Shanks	3B83,2B37,OF6*	R	32	131	464	38	118	19	5	3	57	19	37	6	.254	.285	.336
Johnny Mitchell	SS87,2B5	S	28	92	347	40	78	15	4	0	19	34	18	7	.225	.296	.291
Joe Harris	OF132,1B9	R	32	142	483	82	162	28	11	13	76	52	27	7	.335	.406	.520
Ira Flagstead†	OF102	R	29	109	382	55	119	23	4	8	53	37	26	8	.312	.380	.455
Dick Reichle	OF93	L	26	122	361	40	93	17	3	1	39	22	34	3	.258	.315	.330
Norm McMillan	3B67,2B34,SS28	R	27	131	459	37	116	24	5	0	42	28	44	13	.253	.299	.327
Shano Collins	OF89	R	37	97	342	41	79	10	5	0	18	11	29	7	.231	.265	.289
Al DeVormer	C55,1B2	R	31	74	209	20	54	7	3	0	18	6	21	3	.258	.282	.321
Mike Menosky	OF49	L	28	84	188	22	43	8	4	0	25	22	19	3	.229	.310	.314
Pinky Pittenger	2B42,SS10,3B3	R	24	60	177	15	38	5	0	0	15	5	10	3	.215	.236	.243
Roxy Walters	C36,2B1	R	30	40	104	9	26	4	0	0	5	2	6	0	.250	.264	.288
John Donahue	OF9	S	29	10	36	5	10	4	0	0	1	4	5	0	.278	.350	.389
Frank Fuller	2B6	S	30	6	21	3	5	0	0	0	0	1	1	1	.238	.273	.238
Nemo Leibold†	OF10	L	31	12	18	1	2	0	0	0	0	1	2	0	.111	.158	.111
Ike Boone	OF4	L	26	5	15	1	4	0	1	0	2	1	0	0	.267	.313	.400
Camp Skinner	OF2	L	26	7	13	1	3	2	0	0	1	0	0	0	.231	.231	.385

H. Shanks, 2 G at SS

Pitcher	T	Age	G	GS	CG	ShO	IP	H	HR	BB	SO	W-L	Sv	ERA
Howard Ehmke	R	29	43	39	28	2	316.2	318	12	119	121	20-17	3	3.78
Jack Quinn	R	39	42	28	16	1	243.0	302	6	53	71	13-17	7	3.89
Alex Ferguson	R	26	34	27	11	0	198.1	229	5	67	72	9-13	0	4.04
Bill Piercy	R	27	30	24	11	0	187.1	193	5	73	51	8-17	0	3.41
George Murray	R	24	39	18	5	0	177.2	190	9	87	40	7-11	0	4.91
Curt Fullerton	R	24	37	16	7	0	143.1	167	9	71	37	2-15	1	5.09
Lefty O'Doul	L	26	23	0	0	0	53.0	69	2	31	10	1-1	0	5.43
Les Howe	R	27	12	2	0	0	30.0	23	0	7	7	1-0	0	2.40
Clarence Blethen	R	29	5	0	0	0	17.2	29	0	7	2	0-0	0	7.13
Carl Stimson	R	28	2	0	0	0	4.0	12	0	5	1	0-0	0	22.50
Dave Black	R	31	2	0	0	0	1.0	2	0	0	0	0-0	0	0.00

»1923 New York Giants 1st NL 95-58 .621 —

John McGraw

Player	Gm by Position	B	Age	G	AB	R	H	2B	3B	HR	RBI	BB	SO	SB	Avg	OBP	Slg
Frank Snyder	C112	R	30	120	402	37	103	13	6	5	63	24	29	5	.256	.298	.356
George Kelly	1B145	R	27	145	560	82	172	23	5	16	103	47	64	14	.307	.362	.452
Frankie Frisch	2B135,3B17	S	24	151	641	116	223	32	10	12	111	46	12	29	.348	.395	.485
Heine Groh	3B118	R	33	123	465	91	135	22	5	4	48	60	22	3	.290	.379	.385
Dave Bancroft	SS96,2B11	S	32	107	444	80	135	33	3	1	31	62	23	8	.304	.391	.399
Ross Youngs	OF152	L	26	152	596	121	200	33	12	3	87	73	36	13	.336	.412	.446
Irish Meusel	OF145	R	30	146	595	102	177	22	14	19	125	38	16	8	.297	.341	.477
Bill Cunningham	OF68,2B4	R	27	79	203	22	55	7	1	5	27	10	9	5	.271	.305	.389
Travis Jackson	SS60,3B31,2B1	R	19	96	327	45	90	12	7	4	37	22	40	3	.275	.321	.391
Jimmy O'Connell	OF64,1B8	L	22	87	252	42	63	9	2	6	39	34	32	7	.250	.351	.373
Casey Stengel	OF57	L	32	75	218	39	74	11	5	5	43	20	18	6	.339	.400	.505
Hank Gowdy†	C43	R	33	53	122	13	40	6	3	1	18	21	9	2	.328	.427	.451
Alex Gaston	C21	R	30	22	39	3	8	2	0	1	5	0	6	0	.205	.225	.333
Earl Smith†	C12	L	26	24	34	2	7	1	1	1	4	4	1	0	.206	.289	.382
Freddie Maguire	2B16,3B1	R	24	41	30	11	6	1	0	0	2	2	4	1	.200	.250	.233
Ralph Shinners	OF6	R	27	33	13	5	2	1	0	0	0	2	1	0	.154	.267	.231
Hack Wilson	OF3	R	23	3	10	0	2	0	0	0	0	0	1	0	.200	.200	.200
Mose Solomon	OF2	L	22	2	8	0	3	1	0	0	1	0	1	0	.375	.375	.500
Bill Terry	1B2	L	26	3	7	1	1	0	0	0	0	2	2	0	.143	.333	.143

Pitcher	T	Age	G	GS	CG	ShO	IP	H	HR	BB	SO	W-L	Sv	ERA
Hugh McQuillan	R	25	38	32	15	5	230.1	224	12	66	75	15-14	0	3.40
Art Nehf	L	30	34	27	7	1	196.0	219	14	49	50	13-10	2	4.50
Jack Bentley	L	28	31	26	12	1	183.0	198	10	67	80	13-8	3	4.48
Jack Scott	R	31	40	25	9	3	220.0	223	15	65	79	16-7	1	3.89
Mule Watson†	R	26	17	15	8	0	108.1	117	11	21	26	8-5	0	3.41
Fred Johnson	R	29	3	2	1	0	17.0	11	2	7	5	2-0	0	4.24
Walter Huntzinger	R	24	2	1	0	0	8.0	9	0	1	2	0-1	0	7.88
Rosy Ryan	R	25	45	15	7	0	172.2	169	8	46	58	16-5	4	3.49
Claude Jonnard	R	25	45	1	1	0	96.0	105	6	35	45	4-3	5	3.28
Virgil Barnes	R	26	22	2	0	0	53.0	59	2	19	6	2-3	1	3.91
Jesse Barnes†	R	30	12	4	1	0	36.0	48	1	13	12	3-1	1	6.25
Clint Blume	R	24	12	1	0	0	24.0	22	0	20	2	2-0	0	3.75
Dinty Gearin	L	25	6	2	1	0	24.0	23	1	10	9	1-1	0	3.38
Red Lucas	R	21	3	0	0	0	5.1	9	0	4	3	0-0	1	0.00
Rube Walberg†	L	26	2	0	0	0	5.0	4	0	1	1	0-0	0	1.80

1923 Cincinnati Reds 2nd NL 91-63 .591 4.5 GB

Pat Moran

Player	Gm by Position	B	Age	G	AB	R	H	2B	3B	HR	RBI	BB	SO	SB	Avg	OBP	Slg
Bubbles Hargrave	C109	R	30	118	378	54	126	23	9	10	78	44	22	4	.333	.419	.521
Jake Daubert	1B121	L	39	125	500	63	146	27	10	2	54	40	20	11	.292	.349	.398
Sammy Bohne	2B96,3B35,SS9*	R	26	139	539	77	136	18	10	3	47	48	37	16	.252	.316	.340
Babe Pinelli	3B116	R	27	117	423	44	117	14	5	0	51	27	29	10	.277	.320	.333
Ike Caveney	SS138	R	28	138	488	58	135	21	9	4	63	26	41	5	.277	.315	.381
George Burns	OF154	R	33	154	614	99	168	27	13	3	45	101	46	12	.274	.376	.375
Pat Duncan	OF146	R	29	147	566	92	185	26	8	7	83	30	27	15	.327	.363	.438
Edd Roush	OF137	L	30	138	527	88	185	41	18	6	88	46	16	10	.351	.406	.531
Lew Fonseca	2B45,1B14	R	24	65	237	33	66	11	4	3	28	9	16	4	.278	.310	.397
Ivy Wingo	C57	L	32	61	171	10	45	9	2	1	24	9	11	1	.263	.304	.357
George Harper	OF29	L	31	61	125	14	32	4	2	3	16	11	9	0	.256	.316	.392
Rube Bressler	1B22,OF6	R	28	54	119	25	33	3	1	0	18	20	4	3	.277	.399	.319
Wally Kimmick	2B17,3B4,SS1	R	26	29	80	11	18	2	1	0	6	5	15	3	.225	.271	.275
Boob Fowler	SS10	L	22	11	33	9	11	0	1	1	6	1	3	1	.333	.353	.485
Gus Sanberg	C5	R	27	7	17	1	3	1	0	0	1	1	1	0	.176	.222	.235
Eddie Pick	OF4	S	24	9	8	2	3	0	0	0	2	3	3	0	.375	.545	.375
Les Mann†		R	29	8	1	1	0	0	0	0	0	0	0	0	.000	.000	.000
Ed Hock		L	24	2	0	0	0	0	0	0	0	0	0	0	—	—	—

S. Bohne, 1 G at 1B

Pitcher	T	Age	G	GS	CG	ShO	IP	H	HR	BB	SO	W-L	Sv	ERA
Dolf Luque	R	32	41	37	28	6	322.0	279	2	88	151	27-8	2	1.93
Eppa Rixey	L	32	42	37	23	3	309.0	334	3	65	97	20-15	1	2.80
Pete Donohue	R	22	42	36	19	2	274.1	304	3	68	84	21-15	3	3.38
Rube Benton	L	36	33	26	15	0	219.0	243	10	57	59	14-10	1	3.66
Cactus Keck	R	24	35	6	1	0	87.0	84	5	32	16	3-6	2	3.72
Bill Harris	R	23	22	3	1	0	69.2	79	3	18	18	3-2	0	5.17
Johnny Couch†	R	32	19	8	1	0	69.1	98	2	15	14	2-7	0	5.97
Herb McQuaid	R	24	12	1	0	0	34.1	31	0	10	9	1-0	0	2.36
George Abrams	R	23	3	0	0	0	4.2	10	0	3	1	0-0	0	9.64
Haddie Gill	L	24	1	0	0	0	1.0	1	0	1	1	0-0	0	0.00
Karl Schnell	R	23	1	0	0	0	1.0	2	0	2	0	0-0	0	36.00

1923 Pittsburgh Pirates 3rd NL 87-67 .565 8.5 GB

Bill McKechnie

Player	Gm by Position	B	Age	G	AB	R	H	2B	3B	HR	RBI	BB	SO	SB	Avg	OBP	Slg
Walter Schmidt	C96	R	36	97	335	39	83	7	2	0	37	22	12	10	.248	.300	.281
Charlie Grimm	1B152	L	24	152	563	78	194	29	13	7	99	41	43	6	.345	.389	.480
Johnny Rawlings	2B119	R	30	119	461	53	131	18	4	1	45	25	29	9	.284	.322	.347
Pie Traynor	3B152,SS1	R	23	153	616	108	208	19	19	12	101	34	19	28	.338	.377	.489
Rabbit Maranville	SS141	R	31	141	581	78	161	19	9	1	41	42	34	14	.277	.327	.346
Max Carey	OF153	S	33	153	610	120	188	32	19	6	63	73	28	51	.308	.388	.452
Carson Bigbee	OF122	L	28	123	499	79	149	18	7	0	54	43	15	10	.299	.355	.363
Clyde Barnhart	OF92	R	27	114	327	60	106	25	13	9	72	47	21	5	.324	.409	.563
Reb Russell	OF76	L	34	94	291	49	84	18	7	9	58	20	21	3	.289	.341	.491
Johnny Gooch	C66	S	25	66	202	16	56	10	2	1	20	17	13	2	.277	.336	.361
Cotton Tierney†	2B29	R	29	29	120	22	35	5	2	2	23	2	10	2	.292	.309	.417
Walter Mueller	OF26	R	28	40	111	11	34	4	4	0	20	4	6	2	.306	.336	.414
Spencer Adams	2B11,SS6	L	25	25	56	11	14	0	1	0	4	6	6	2	.250	.323	.286
Kiki Cuyler	OF11	R	24	11	40	4	10	1	1	0	2	5	3	2	.250	.348	.325
Jim Mattox	C8	L	26	22	32	4	6	1	1	0	1	0	5	0	.188	.235	.281
Jewel Ens	1B4,3B3	R	33	12	29	3	8	1	1	0	5	0	3	2	.276	.276	.379
Eddie Moore	SS6	R	24	6	26	6	7	1	0	0	1	2	3	1	.269	.321	.308
Frank Luce	OF5	L	26	9	12	2	6	0	0	0	3	2	2	2	.500	.571	.500
Eppie Barnes	1B1	L	22	2	2	0	1	0	0	0	0	0	1	0	.500	.500	.500

Pitcher	T	Age	G	GS	CG	ShO	IP	H	HR	BB	SO	W-L	Sv	ERA
Wilbur Cooper	L	31	39	38	26	1	294.2	331	11	71	77	17-19	0	3.57
Johnny Morrison	R	27	42	37	27	2	301.2	287	6	110	114	25-13	2	3.49
Lee Meadows†	R	28	31	25	17	1	227.0	250	3	44	66	16-10	0	3.01
Babe Adams	R	41	26	22	11	0	158.2	196	8	25	38	13-7	1	4.42
Earl Hamilton	L	31	28	15	5	0	141.0	148	6	42	42	7-9	1	3.77
Whitey Glazner†	R	29	7	4	1	1	30.0	29	5	11	8	2-1	1	3.30
Jim Bagby	R	33	21	6	2	0	68.2	95	6	25	16	3-2	3	5.24
Earl Kunz	R	23	21	2	1	0	45.2	48	2	24	12	1-2	1	5.52
Ray Steineder	R	27	15	2	1	0	55.0	58	3	18	23	2-0	0	4.75
George Boehler	R	31	10	3	1	0	28.1	33	1	26	12	1-3	0	6.04
Arnie Stone	L	30	9	0	0	0	12.1	19	0	4	2	0-1	0	8.03
Hal Carlson	R	31	4	0	0	0	13.1	19	2	2	4	0-0	0	4.73

1923 Chicago Cubs 4th NL 83-71 .539 12.5 GB

Bill Killefer

Player	Gm by Position	B	Age	G	AB	R	H	2B	3B	HR	RBI	BB	SO	SB	Avg	OBP	Slg
Bob O'Farrell	C124	R	26	131	452	73	144	25	4	12	84	67	38	10	.319	.408	.471
Ray Grimes	1B62	R	29	64	216	32	71	7	2	2	36	24	17	5	.329	.401	.407
George Grantham	2B150	L	23	152	570	81	160	36	8	8	70	71	92	43	.281	.360	.414
Bernie Friberg	3B146	R	23	146	547	91	174	27	11	12	88	45	49	8	.318	.372	.473
Sparky Adams	SS79,OF1	R	28	95	311	40	90	12	0	4	35	26	10	20	.289	.346	.367
Jigger Statz	OF154	R	25	154	655	110	209	33	8	10	70	56	42	29	.319	.375	.440
Hack Miller	OF129	R	29	135	485	74	146	24	2	20	88	27	39	6	.301	.343	.482
Cliff Heathcote	OF112	L	25	117	393	48	98	14	3	1	27	25	22	32	.249	.298	.308
Charlie Hollocher	SS65	L	27	66	260	46	89	14	2	1	28	26	5	9	.342	.410	.423
Gabby Hartnett	C39,1B31	R	22	85	231	28	62	12	2	8	39	25	22	4	.268	.347	.442
John Kelleher	1B22,SS14,3B11*	R	29	66	193	27	59	10	0	6	21	14	9	2	.306	.353	.451
Allen Elliott	1B52	L	25	53	168	21	42	8	2	2	29	2	12	3	.250	.267	.357
Marty Callaghan	OF38	L	23	61	129	18	29	3	1	0	14	8	18	2	.225	.275	.279
Otto Vogel	OF24,3B1	R	23	41	81	10	17	0	1	1	6	7	11	2	.210	.297	.272
Denver Grigsby	OF22	L	22	24	72	8	21	5	2	0	5	7	5	1	.292	.363	.417
Butch Weis	OF6	L	22	22	26	2	6	1	0	0	2	5	8	0	.231	.355	.269
Pete Turgeon	SS2	R	26	3	6	1	1	0	0	0	0	0	0	0	.167	.167	.167
Kettle Wirts	C3	R	25	5	5	2	1	0	0	0	1	2	0	0	.200	.429	.200
Tony Murray	OF2	R	19	2	4	0	1	0	0	0	0	0	0	0	.250	.400	.250
Bob Barrett		R	24	3	3	0	1	0	0	0	0	0	0	0	.333	.333	.333

J. Kelleher, 6 G at 2B

Pitcher	T	Age	G	GS	CG	ShO	IP	H	HR	BB	SO	W-L	Sv	ERA
Pete Alexander	R	36	39	36	26	3	305.0	308	17	30	72	22-12	2	3.19
Vic Aldridge	R	29	30	30	15	2	217.0	209	17	67	64	16-9	0	3.48
Tiny Osborne	R	30	37	25	8	1	179.2	174	14	89	69	8-15	1	4.56
Tony Kaufmann	R	22	33	24	18	2	206.1	209	14	67	72	14-10	3	3.10
Rip Wheeler	R	25	3	3	1	0	24.0	28	2	5	5	1-2	0	4.88
Phil Collins	R	21	1	1	0	0	5.0	8	0	1	2	1-0	0	3.60
Vic Keen	R	24	35	17	10	0	177.0	169	8	57	46	12-8	1	3.00
Nick Dumovich	L	21	28	8	1	0	94.0	118	4	45	23	3-5	1	4.60
Fred Fussell	L	27	28	2	1	0	76.1	90	2	31	38	3-5	3	5.54
Virgil Cheeves	R	22	19	8	0	0	71.1	89	8	37	13	3-4	0	6.18
George Stueland	R	24	6	0	0	0	8.0	11	0	5	2	0-1	0	5.63
Ed Stauffer	R	25	1	0	0	0	2.0	5	0	1	0	0-0	0	13.50
Guy Bush	R	21	1	0	0	0	1.0	1	0	0	2	0-0	0	0.00

1923 St. Louis Cardinals 5th NL 79-74 .516 16.0 GB

Branch Rickey

Player	Gm by Position	B	Age	G	AB	R	H	2B	3B	HR	RBI	BB	SO	SB	Avg	OBP	Slg
Eddie Ainsmith†	C80	R	31	82	263	22	56	11	6	3	34	22	19	4	.213	.276	.335
Jim Bottomley	1B130	L	23	134	523	79	194	34	14	8	94	45	44	4	.371	.425	.535
Rogers Hornsby	2B96,1B10	R	27	107	424	89	163	32	10	17	83	55	29	3	.384	.459	.627
Milt Stock	3B150,2B1	R	29	151	603	63	174	33	3	2	96	40	21	9	.289	.334	.363
Howard Freigau	SS87,2B16,1B9*	R	20	113	358	30	94	18	1	1	35	25	36	5	.263	.314	.327
Max Flack	OF121	L	33	128	505	82	147	16	9	3	28	41	16	7	.291	.348	.376
Jack Smith	OF109	L	28	124	407	98	126	16	6	5	41	27	20	32	.310	.356	.415
Hi Myers	OF87	R	34	96	330	29	99	18	2	2	48	12	19	5	.300	.330	.385
Ray Blades	OF83,3B4	R	26	98	317	48	78	21	5	5	44	37	46	4	.246	.342	.391
Specs Toporcer	2B52,SS33,1B1*	L	24	97	303	45	77	11	3	3	35	41	14	4	.254	.349	.340
Heinie Mueller	OF74	L	23	78	265	39	91	16	9	5	41	18	16	4	.343	.392	.528
Harry McCurdy	C58	L	23	67	185	17	49	11	2	0	15	11	11	3	.265	.306	.346
Verne Clemons	C41	R	31	57	130	6	37	9	1	0	13	10	11	0	.285	.345	.369
Doc Lavan	SS40,3B4,1B3*	R	32	50	111	10	22	6	0	1	12	9	7	0	.198	.264	.279
Les Mann†	OF26	R	29	38	89	20	33	5	2	5	11	9	5	0	.371	.434	.640
Les Bell	SS15	R	21	15	51	5	19	2	1	0	9	9	7	1	.373	.467	.451
Eddie Dyer	OF8,P4	L	22	35	45	17	12	3	0	2	5	3	5	1	.267	.313	.467
Jake Flowers	SS7,2B2,3B2	R	21	13	32	0	3	1	0	0	2	2	7	1	.094	.147	.125
Charlie Niebergall	C7	R	24	9	28	2	3	1	0	0	1	2	2	0	.107	.167	.143
Taylor Douthit	OF7	R	22	9	27	3	5	0	2	0	0	0	4	1	.185	.185	.333
Jimmy Hudgens	1B3,2B1	L	20	6	12	2	3	1	0	0	0	3	3	0	.250	.400	.333
Speed Walker	1B2	R	25	2	7	1	2	0	0	0	0	0	1	0	.286	.286	.286
Joe Schultz	OF2	R	29	2	7	0	2	0	0	0	1	1	0	0	.286	.375	.286
George Kopshaw	C1	R	27	2	5	1	1	1	0	0	0	0	1	0	.200	.200	.400
Tige Stone	OF4,P1	R	21	5	1	0	1	0	0	0	0	2	0	0	1.000	1.000	1.000
Burt Shotton		L	38	1	0	1	0	0	0	0	0	0	0	0	—	—	—

H. Freigau, 1 G at 3B, 1 G at OF; S. Toporcer, 1 G at 3B; D. Lavan, 1 G at 2B

Pitcher	T	Age	G	GS	CG	ShO	IP	H	HR	BB	SO	W-L	Sv	ERA
Jesse Haines	R	29	37	36	23	1	266.0	283	7	75	73	20-13	0	3.11
Fred Toney	R	34	29	28	16	1	196.2	211	8	61	48	11-12	0	3.84
Bill Sherdel	L	26	39	26	14	0	225.0	270	15	59	78	15-13	2	4.32
Bill Doak	R	32	30	26	7	3	185.0	199	4	69	53	8-13	0	3.26
Jeff Pfeffer	R	35	26	18	7	1	152.1	171	8	40	32	8-9	0	4.02
Eddie Dyer	L	22	4	3	2	1	22.0	30	0	5	7	2-1	0	4.09
Bill Pertica	R	26	1	1	0	0	2.1	2	0	3	0	0-0	0	3.86
Johnny Stuart	R	22	37	10	7	1	149.2	139	11	70	55	9-5	3	4.27
Lou North	R	32	34	3	0	0	71.2	90	8	31	24	3-4	1	5.15
Clyde Barfoot	R	31	33	2	1	1	101.1	112	7	27	23	3-3	1	3.73
Epp Sell	R	26	5	1	0	0	15.0	16	1	8	2	0-1	0	6.00
Fred Wigington	R	25	4	0	0	0	8.1	11	0	5	2	0-0	0	3.24
Tige Stone	R	21	1	0	0	0	3.0	5	1	3	1	0-0	0	12.00

1923 Brooklyn Dodgers 6th NL 76-78 .494 19.5 GB

Wilbert Robinson

Player	Gm by Position	B	Age	G	AB	R	H	2B	3B	HR	RBI	BB	SO	SB	Avg	OBP	Slg
Zack Taylor	C84	R	24	96	337	29	97	11	6	0	46	9	13	2	.288	.312	.356
Jack Fournier	1B133	L	33	133	515	91	181	30	13	22	102	43	28	11	.351	.411	.588
Jimmy Johnston	2B84,SS52,3B14	R	33	151	625	111	203	29	11	4	60	53	15	16	.325	.378	.426
Andy High	3B80,SS45,2B5	L	25	123	426	51	115	23	9	3	37	47	13	4	.270	.344	.387
Moe Berg	SS47,2B1	R	21	49	129	9	24	3	2	0	6	2	5	1	.186	.198	.240
Tommy Griffith	OF127	L	33	131	481	70	141	21	9	8	66	50	19	8	.293	.361	.424
Bernie Neis	OF111	S	27	126	445	78	122	17	4	5	37	36	38	8	.274	.330	.364
Gene Bailey	OF100,1B5	R	29	127	411	71	109	11	7	1	42	43	34	9	.265	.343	.333
Zack Wheat	OF87	L	35	98	349	63	131	13	5	8	65	23	12	3	.375	.417	.510
Ivy Olson	2B72,3B4,1B2*	R	37	82	292	33	76	11	1	1	35	14	10	5	.260	.296	.315
Bert Griffith	OF62	R	27	79	248	23	73	8	4	2	37	13	16	1	.294	.332	.383
Hank DeBerry	C60	R	28	78	235	21	67	11	6	1	48	20	12	2	.285	.346	.396
Bill McCarren	3B66,OF1	R	27	69	216	28	53	10	1	3	27	22	39	0	.245	.326	.343
Dutch Ruether	P43,1B1	L	29	49	117	6	32	1	0	0	10	12	12	0	.274	.341	.282
Dutch Schliebner†	1B19	R	32	19	76	11	19	4	0	0	4	5	7	1	.250	.296	.303
Ray French	SS30	R	28	43	73	14	16	2	1	0	7	4	7	0	.219	.269	.274
Charlie Hargreaves	C15	R	26	20	57	5	16	0	0	0	4	1	2	0	.281	.293	.281
Turner Barber	OF12	L	29	13	46	3	10	2	0	0	8	2	2	0	.217	.250	.261
Billy Mullen	3B4	R	27	4	11	1	3	0	0	0	0	0	0	0	.273	.273	.273
Stuffy Stewart	2B3	R	29	4	11	3	4	1	0	1	1	1	1	0	.364	.417	.727
Eddie Ainsmith†	C2	R	31	2	10	0	2	0	0	0	2	0	0	0	.200	.200	.200
Bernie Hungling	C1	R	27	2	4	0	0	0	0	0	0	0	2	0	.000	.000	.000

I. Olson, 2 G at SS

Pitcher	T	Age	G	GS	CG	ShO	IP	H	HR	BB	SO	W-L	Sv	ERA
Burleigh Grimes	R	29	39	38	33	2	327.0	356	9	100	119	21-18	0	3.58
Dazzy Vance	R	32	37	35	21	3	280.1	263	10	100	197	18-15	0	3.50
Dutch Ruether	L	29	34	34	20	0	275.0	308	11	86	87	15-14	0	4.22
Leo Dickerman	R	26	35	20	7	1	159.2	180	4	72	58	8-12	0	3.72
Dutch Henry	L	21	17	9	5	2	94.1	105	9	28	28	4-6	0	3.91
Leon Cadore†	R	32	8	4	3	0	36.0	39	2	13	5	4-1	0	3.25
Harry Shriver	R	26	1	1	0	0	4.0	8	0	0	1	0-0	0	6.75
Harry Harper	L	28	1	1	0	0	3.2	8	2	3	4	0-1	0	14.73
Art Decatur	R	29	36	5	2	0	97.2	101	3	32	25	3-3	3	2.86
George Smith	R	31	25	7	3	0	91.0	99	4	28	15	3-6	1	3.66
Paul Schreiber	R	20	9	0	0	0	15.0	16	1	8	4	0-0	1	4.20
Al Mamaux	R	29	5	1	0	0	13.0	20	0	6	5	0-2	0	8.31

Seasons: Team Rosters 625

1923 Boston Braves 7th NL 54-100 .351 41.5 GB

Fred Mitchell

Player	Gm by Position	B	Age	G	AB	R	H	2B	3B	HR	RBI	BB	SO	SB	Avg	OBP	Slg
Mickey O'Neil	C95	R	23	96	306	29	65	7	4	0	20	17	14	3	.212	.258	.261
Stuffy McInnis	1B154	R	32	154	607	70	191	23	9	2	95	26	12	7	.315	.343	.392
Hod Ford	2B95,SS19	R	25	111	380	27	103	16	7	2	50	31	30	1	.271	.326	.366
Tony Boeckel	3B147,SS1	R	30	148	568	72	169	32	4	7	79	51	31	11	.298	.357	.405
Bob Smith	SS101,2B8	R	28	115	375	30	94	16	3	0	40	17	35	4	.251	.285	.309
Billy Southworth	OF151,2B2	L	30	153	611	95	195	29	16	6	78	61	23	14	.319	.383	.448
Gus Felix	OF123,2B5,3B4	R	28	139	506	64	138	17	2	6	44	51	65	8	.273	.348	.350
Ray Powell	OF84	L	34	97	338	57	102	20	4	4	38	45	36	1	.302	.385	.420
Al Nixon	OF80	R	37	88	321	53	88	12	4	0	19	24	14	2	.274	.334	.336
Earl Smith†	C54	L	26	72	191	22	55	15	1	3	19	22	10	0	.288	.364	.424
Jocko Conlon	2B36,SS6,3B4	R	25	59	147	23	32	3	0	0	17	11	11	0	.218	.299	.238
Larry Kopf	SS37,2B4	S	32	39	138	15	38	3	1	0	10	13	6	0	.275	.338	.312
Al Hermann	2B15,3B5,1B4	R	24	31	93	2	22	4	0	0	11	0	7	3	.237	.237	.280
Bill Bagwell	OF22	L	27	56	93	8	27	4	2	2	10	6	12	0	.290	.333	.441
Johnny Cooney	P23,OF11,1B1	R	22	42	66	7	25	1	0	0	3	4	2	0	.379	.414	.394
Frank Gibson	C20	S	32	41	50	13	15	1	0	0	5	7	7	0	.300	.386	.320
Hank Gowdy†	C15	R	33	23	48	5	6	1	1	0	5	15	5	1	.125	.354	.188
Walton Cruise	OF9	L	33	21	38	4	8	2	0	0	0	3	2	1	.211	.268	.263
Bob Emmerich	OF8	R	25	13	24	3	2	0	0	0	0	2	3	1	.083	.154	.083
Ernie Padgett	SS2,2B1	R	24	4	11	3	2	0	0	0	0	2	0	0	.182	.308	.182
Snake Henry		L	27	11	9	1	1	0	0	0	2	1	1	0	.111	.200	.111
Dee Cousineau	C1	R	24	1	2	1	2	0	0	0	2	0	0	0	1.000	1.000	1.000

Pitcher	T	Age	G	GS	CG	ShO	IP	H	HR	BB	SO	W-L	Sv	ERA
Rube Marquard	L	36	38	29	11	3	239.0	265	10	65	78	11-14	0	3.73
Joe Genewich	R	26	43	24	12	1	227.1	272	15	46	54	13-14	1	3.72
Jesse Barnes†	R	30	31	23	12	5	195.1	204	8	43	41	10-14	2	2.76
Tim McNamara	R	24	32	16	3	0	139.1	185	8	29	32	3-13	0	4.91
Frank Miller	R	37	8	6	0	0	39.1	54	2	11	6	0-3	1	4.58
Dick Rudolph	R	35	4	4	1	1	19.1	27	0	10	3	1-2	0	3.72
Joe Oeschger	R	32	44	19	6	1	166.1	227	4	54	33	5-15	2	5.68
Larry Benton	R	25	35	9	2	0	128.0	141	5	57	42	5-9	0	4.99
Dana Fillingim	R	29	35	12	1	0	100.1	141	6	36	27	1-9	0	5.20
Johnny Cooney	L	22	23	8	5	2	98.0	92	3	22	23	3-5	0	3.31
Mule Watson†	R	26	11	4	1	0	31.1	42	2	20	10	1-2	1	5.17
Joe Batchelder	L	24	4	1	1	0	9.0	12	2	1	2	1-0	0	7.00

1923 Philadelphia Phillies 8th NL 50-104 .325 45.5 GB

Art Fletcher

Player	Gm by Position	B	Age	G	AB	R	H	2B	3B	HR	RBI	BB	SO	SB	Avg	OBP	Slg
Butch Henline	C96,OF1	R	28	111	330	45	107	14	3	7	46	37	33	7	.324	.407	.448
Walter Holke	1B146,P1	S	30	147	562	64	175	31	4	7	70	16	37	7	.311	.330	.418
Cotton Tierney†	2B115,OF7,3B2	R	29	121	480	68	152	31	1	11	65	24	42	3	.317	.352	.454
Russ Wrightstone	3B72,SS21,2B9	L	30	119	392	59	107	21	7	7	57	21	19	5	.273	.315	.416
Heinie Sand	SS120,3B11	R	25	132	470	85	107	16	5	4	32	82	56	7	.228	.347	.309
Curt Walker	OF137,1B1	L	26	140	527	66	148	26	5	5	66	45	31	12	.281	.337	.378
Cy Williams	OF135	L	35	136	535	98	157	22	3	41	114	59	57	11	.293	.371	.576
Johnny Mokan	OF105,3B1	R	27	113	400	76	125	23	3	10	48	53	31	6	.313	.401	.460
Cliff Lee	OF83,1B16	R	26	107	355	54	114	20	4	11	47	20	39	3	.321	.357	.493
Jimmie Wilson	C69,OF2	R	22	85	252	27	66	9	0	1	25	4	17	4	.262	.276	.310
Frank Parkinson	2B37,SS15,3B11	R	28	67	219	21	53	12	0	3	28	13	31	0	.242	.288	.338
Goldie Rapp	3B45	S	31	47	179	27	47	5	0	1	10	14	14	1	.263	.320	.307
Freddy Leach	OF26	L	25	52	104	5	27	4	0	1	16	3	14	1	.260	.280	.327
Carlton Lord	3B14	R	23	17	47	3	11	2	0	0	2	2	3	0	.234	.265	.277
Andy Woehr	3B13	R	27	13	41	3	14	2	0	0	3	1	1	0	.341	.357	.390
Lenny Metz	2B6,SS6	R	23	12	37	4	8	0	0	0	3	4	3	0	.216	.310	.216
Tod Dennehey	OF9	L	24	9	24	4	7	2	0	0	2	1	3	0	.292	.320	.375
Mickey O'Brien	C9	R	28	15	21	3	7	2	0	0	0	2	1	0	.333	.391	.429
Dixie Parker	C2	L	28	4	5	0	1	0	0	0	1	0	1	0	.200	.200	.200
Joe Bennett	3B1	R	22	1	0	0	0	0	0	0	1	0	1	0	—	—	—

Pitcher	T	Age	G	GS	CG	ShO	IP	H	HR	BB	SO	W-L	Sv	ERA
Jimmy Ring	R	28	39	36	23	0	304.1	336	13	115	112	18-16	0	3.87
Whitey Glazner†	R	29	28	23	12	2	161.1	195	11	63	51	7-14	1	4.69
Lefty Weinert	L	21	38	20	8	1	156.0	207	10	81	46	4-17	1	5.42
Clarence Mitchell	L	32	29	19	8	1	139.1	170	8	46	41	9-10	0	4.72
Petie Behan	R	35	31	17	5	0	131.0	182	11	57	27	3-12	2	5.50
Johnny Couch†	R	32	11	7	2	0	65.0	91	4	21	18	2-4	0	5.26
Lee Meadows†	R	28	8	5	0	0	19.2	40	0	15	10	1-3	1	13.27
Ralph Head	R	29	35	13	5	0	132.1	185	13	57	24	2-9	0	6.66
Bill Hubbell	R	26	22	5	1	0	55.0	102	13	17	8	1-6	0	8.35
Jesse Winters	R	29	21	6	1	0	78.1	116	7	39	23	1-6	1	7.35
Huck Betts	R	26	19	4	3	0	84.1	100	7	14	18	2-4	1	3.09
Jim Bishop	R	25	15	0	0	0	32.2	48	2	11	5	0-3	1	6.34
Broadway Jones	R	24	3	0	0	0	8.0	5	0	7	1	0-0	0	9.00
Jim Grant	L	28	2	0	0	0	4.0	10	0	4	0	0-0	0	13.50
Pat Ragan	R	34	1	0	0	0	3.0	6	1	0	0	0-0	0	6.00
Red Miller	R	26	1	0	0	0	1.2	6	0	1	0	0-0	0	32.40
Walter Holke	L	30	1	0	0	0	0.1	1	0	0	0	0-0	0	0.00
Art Gardiner	R	23	1	0	0	0	0.0	1	0	1	0	0-0	0	—

»1924 Washington Senators 1st AL 92-62 .597 —

Bucky Harris

Player	Gm by Position	B	Age	G	AB	R	H	2B	3B	HR	RBI	BB	SO	SB	Avg	OBP	Slg
Muddy Ruel	C147	R	28	149	501	50	142	20	2	0	57	62	20	7	.283	.370	.331
Joe Judge	1B140	L	30	140	516	71	167	38	9	3	79	53	21	13	.324	.393	.450
Bucky Harris	2B143	R	27	143	544	88	146	28	9	1	58	56	41	19	.268	.344	.358
Ossie Bluege	3B102,2B10,SS4	R	23	117	402	59	113	15	4	2	49	39	36	7	.281	.358	.353
Roger Peckinpaugh	SS155	R	33	155	523	72	142	20	5	2	73	72	45	11	.272	.360	.340
Sam Rice	OF154	L	34	154	646	106	216	38	14	1	76	46	24	24	.334	.382	.441
Goose Goslin	OF154	L	23	154	579	100	199	30	17	12	129	68	29	16	.344	.421	.516
Nemo Leibold	OF70	L	32	84	246	41	72	6	4	0	20	42	10	6	.293	.398	.350
Earl McNeely	OF42	R	26	43	179	31	59	5	6	0	15	5	21	3	.330	.355	.425
Wid Matthews	OF44	L	27	53	169	25	51	10	4	0	13	11	4	3	.302	.355	.408
Doc Prothro	3B45	R	30	46	159	17	53	11	5	0	24	15	11	4	.333	.394	.465
Mule Shirley	1B25	L	23	30	77	12	18	2	2	0	16	3	7	0	.234	.263	.312
Tommy Taylor	3B16,2B2,OF1	R	31	26	73	11	19	3	1	0	10	2	8	2	.260	.289	.329
Bennie Tate	C14	L	22	21	43	2	13	2	0	0	7	1	2	0	.302	.318	.349
Showboat Fisher	OF11	L	25	15	41	7	9	1	0	0	6	1	6	2	.220	.319	.244
Pinky Hargrave	C8	S	28	24	33	3	5	1	1	0	5	1	4	0	.152	.176	.242
Lance Richbourg	OF7	L	26	15	32	3	9	2	1	0	1	2	6	0	.281	.324	.406
Ralph Miller	2B3	R	28	9	15	1	2	0	0	0	0	1	1	0	.133	.188	.133
Carr Smith	OF4	R	23	5	10	1	2	0	0	0	0	0	3	0	.200	.200	.200
Wade Lefler†	OF1	L	28	5	8	0	5	3	0	0	4	0	0	0	.625	.625	1.000
Bert Griffith	OF2	R	28	6	8	1	1	0	0	0	0	0	1	0	.125	.125	.125
Carl East	OF2	L	29	2	6	1	2	1	0	0	2	2	1	0	.333	.500	.500
Chick Gagnon	SS2	R	26	4	5	1	1	0	0	0	1	0	0	0	.200	.200	.200

Pitcher	T	Age	G	GS	CG	ShO	IP	H	HR	BB	SO	W-L	Sv	ERA
Walter Johnson	R	36	38	38	20	6	277.2	233	10	77	158	23-7	0	2.72
George Mogridge	L	35	30	30	13	2	213.0	217	2	61	48	16-11	0	3.76
Tom Zachary	L	28	33	27	13	1	202.2	198	5	53	45	15-9	2	2.75
Curly Ogden†	R	23	16	16	9	3	108.0	83	3	51	23	9-5	0	2.75
Paul Zahniser	R	27	24	14	5	1	92.0	98	2	49	28	5-7	0	4.40
Joe Martina	R	34	24	13	8	0	125.1	129	7	56	57	6-8	0	4.67
Firpo Marberry	R	25	50	15	6	0	195.1	190	3	70	68	11-12	15	3.09
Allan Russell	R	30	37	0	0	0	82.1	83	1	45	17	5-1	8	4.37
Byron Speece	R	27	21	1	0	0	54.1	60	0	27	15	2-1	0	2.65
Slim McGrew	R	24	6	2	0	0	23.1	25	1	12	8	0-1	0	5.01
Ted Wingfield†	R	24	4	0	0	0	7.0	9	0	4	2	0-0	0	2.57
Nick Altrock	L	47	1	0	0	0	2.0	4	0	0	0	0-0	0	0.00

1924 New York Yankees 2nd AL 89-63 .586 2.0 GB

Miller Huggins

Player	Gm by Position	B	Age	G	AB	R	H	2B	3B	HR	RBI	BB	SO	SB	Avg	OBP	Slg
Wally Schang	C108	S	34	114	356	46	104	19	7	5	52	48	43	2	.292	.382	.427
Wally Pipp	1B153	L	31	153	589	88	174	30	19	9	113	51	36	12	.295	.352	.457
Aaron Ward	2B120,SS1	R	27	120	400	42	101	13	10	8	66	40	45	1	.253	.324	.395
Joe Dugan	3B148,2B2	R	27	148	610	105	184	31	7	3	56	31	32	1	.302	.341	.390
Everett Scott	SS153	R	31	153	548	56	137	12	6	4	64	21	15	3	.250	.278	.316
Babe Ruth	OF152	L	29	153	529	143	200	39	7	46	121	142	81	9	.378	.513	.739
Whitey Witt	OF143	L	28	147	600	88	178	26	5	1	36	45	20	9	.297	.346	.362
Bob Meusel	OF143,3B2	R	27	143	579	93	188	40	11	12	120	32	43	26	.325	.365	.494
Fred Hofmann	C54	R	30	62	166	17	29	6	1	1	11	12	15	2	.175	.239	.241
Ernie Johnson	2B27,SS9,3B2	L	36	64	119	24	42	4	8	3	12	11	7	1	.353	.412	.597
Harvey Hendrick	OF17	L	26	40	76	7	20	0	0	1	11	2	7	1	.263	.291	.303
Mike McNally	2B25,3B13,SS6	R	31	49	69	11	17	0	0	0	2	7	5	1	.246	.316	.246
Earle Combs	OF11	L	25	24	35	10	14	5	0	0	2	4	2	0	.400	.462	.543
Shags Horan	OF13	R	28	22	31	4	9	1	0	0	7	1	5	0	.290	.313	.323
Benny Bengough	C11	R	25	11	16	4	5	1	1	0	3	2	0	0	.313	.389	.500
Lou Gehrig	1B2,OF1	L	21	10	12	2	6	1	0	0	5	1	3	0	.500	.538	.583
Ben Paschal	OF4	R	28	4	12	2	3	1	0	0	3	1	0	0	.250	.308	.333
Mack Hillis	2B1	R	22	1	1	1	0	0	0	0	0	0	0	0	.000	.000	.000
Chick Autry	C2	R	21	2	0	1	0	0	0	0	0	1	0	0	—	1.000	—

Pitcher	T	Age	G	GS	CG	ShO	IP	H	HR	BB	SO	W-L	Sv	ERA
Herb Pennock	L	30	40	34	25	4	286.1	302	13	64	101	21-9	3	2.83
Waite Hoyt	R	24	46	32	14	2	247.0	295	8	76	71	18-13	4	3.79
Joe Bush	R	31	39	31	19	3	252.0	262	9	109	80	17-16	1	3.57
Bob Shawkey	R	33	38	25	10	1	207.2	226	11	74	114	16-11	0	4.12
Sad Sam Jones	R	31	36	21	8	3	178.2	187	6	76	53	9-6	3	3.63
Walter Beall	R	24	4	2	0	0	23.0	19	2	17	18	2-0	0	3.52
Milt Gaston	R	28	29	2	0	0	86.0	92	3	44	24	5-3	1	4.50
Al Mamaux	R	30	14	2	0	0	38.0	44	2	20	12	1-1	0	5.68
George Pipgras	R	24	9	1	0	0	15.1	20	0	18	4	0-1	1	9.98
Cliff Markle	R	30	7	3	0	0	23.1	29	5	20	7	0-3	0	8.87
Ben Shields	L	21	1	0	0	0	2.0	6	0	2	3	0-0	0	27.00
Oscar Roettger	R	24	1	0	0	0	0.0	1	0	2	0	0-0	0	—

1924 Detroit Tigers 3rd AL 86-68 .558 6.0 GB

Ty Cobb

Player	Gm by Position	B	Age	G	AB	R	H	2B	3B	HR	RBI	BB	SO	SB	Avg	OBP	Slg
Johnny Bassler	C121	L	29	124	379	43	131	20	3	1	68	62	11	2	.346	.441	.422
Lu Blue	1B108	S	27	108	395	81	123	26	7	2	50	64	26	9	.311	.413	.428
Del Pratt	2B65,1B51,3B4	R	36	121	429	56	130	32	3	1	77	31	10	6	.303	.353	.399
Bob Jones	3B106	L	34	110	393	52	107	27	4	0	47	20	20	1	.272	.308	.361
Topper Rigney	SS146	R	27	147	499	81	144	29	9	4	93	102	39	11	.289	.410	.407
Ty Cobb	OF155	L	37	155	625	115	211	38	10	4	74	85	18	23	.338	.418	.450
Harry Heilmann	OF147,1B4	R	29	153	570	107	197	45	16	10	114	78	41	13	.346	.428	.533
Heinie Manush	OF106,1B1	L	22	120	422	83	122	24	8	9	68	27	30	14	.289	.355	.448
Fred Haney	3B59,SS4,2B3	R	26	86	256	54	79	11	1	1	30	39	13	7	.309	.400	.371
Les Burke	2B58,SS6	L	21	72	241	30	61	10	4	0	17	22	20	2	.253	.321	.328
Frank O'Rourke	2B40,SS7	R	29	47	181	28	50	11	2	0	19	12	19	7	.276	.332	.359
Bob Fothergill	OF45	R	26	54	166	28	50	8	3	0	15	5	13	2	.301	.326	.386
Larry Woodall	C62	R	29	67	165	23	51	9	2	0	24	21	5	0	.309	.387	.388
Al Wingo	OF43	L	26	78	150	21	43	12	2	1	26	21	13	2	.287	.374	.413
Charlie Gehringer	2B5	L	21	5	13	2	6	0	0	0	1	0	2	1	.462	.500	.462
Clyde Manion	C3,1B1	R	27	14	13	1	3	0	0	0	2	1	1	0	.231	.286	.231
John Kerr	3B3,OF2	R	25	17	11	3	3	0	0	0	1	0	0	0	.273	.273	.273

Pitcher	T	Age	G	GS	CG	ShO	IP	H	HR	BB	SO	W-L	Sv	ERA
Earl Whitehill	L	24	35	32	16	2	233.0	260	8	79	65	17-9	0	3.86
Rip Collins	R	28	34	30	11	1	216.0	199	6	63	75	14-7	0	3.21
Lil Stoner	R	25	36	25	10	1	215.2	271	13	65	66	11-11	0	4.72
Ed Wells	L	24	29	15	5	0	102.0	117	2	42	33	6-8	4	4.06
Dutch Leonard	L	32	9	7	3	0	51.1	68	1	18	26	3-2	1	4.56
Ken Holloway	R	26	49	14	5	1	181.1	209	6	61	46	14-6	3	4.07
Hooks Dauss	R	34	40	10	5	0	131.1	155	6	40	44	12-11	6	4.59
Syl Johnson	R	23	29	9	2	0	104.0	117	8	42	55	5-4	3	4.93
Bert Cole	L	27	28	11	2	1	109.1	135	4	35	16	3-9	2	4.69
Herman Pillette	R	28	19	3	1	0	37.2	46	1	14	13	1-1	1	4.78
Willie Ludolph	R	24	3	0	0	0	5.2	5	0	2	1	0-0	0	4.76
Rufe Clarke	R	24	2	0	0	0	5.1	3	0	5	1	0-0	0	3.38
Ken Jones	R	21	1	0	0	0	2.0	1	0	1	0	0-0	0	0.00

626 Seasons: Team Rosters

1924 St. Louis Browns 4th AL 74-78 .487 17.0 GB

George Sisler

Player	Gm by Position	B	Age	G	AB	R	H	2B	3B	HR	RBI	BB	SO	SB	Avg	OBP	Slg
Hank Severeid	C130	R	33	137	432	37	133	23	2	4	48	36	15	1	.308	.362	.398
George Sisler	1B151	L	31	151	636	94	194	27	10	9	74	31	29	19	.305	.340	.421
Marty McManus	2B119	R	24	123	442	71	147	23	5	5	80	55	40	13	.333	.409	.441
Gene Robertson	3B111,2B2	L	25	121	439	70	140	25	4	4	52	36	14	3	.319	.373	.421
Wally Gerber	SS147	R	32	148	496	61	135	20	4	0	55	43	34	4	.272	.341	.329
Baby Doll Jacobson	OF152	R	33	152	579	103	184	41	12	19	97	35	45	6	.318	.361	.528
Jack Tobin	OF131	L	32	136	569	87	170	30	8	2	48	50	12	6	.299	.357	.390
Ken Williams	OF108	L	34	114	398	78	129	21	4	18	84	69	17	20	.324	.425	.533
Joe Evans	OF49	R	29	77	209	30	53	3	3	0	19	24	12	1	.254	.330	.297
Norm McMillan	2B37,3B19,SS7	R	28	76	201	25	56	12	2	0	27	12	17	6	.279	.332	.358
Herschel Bennett	OF21	L	27	41	94	16	31	4	3	1	11	3	6	1	.330	.364	.468
Harry Rice	3B15,2B4,1B2*	L	22	54	93	19	26	7	0	0	15	7	5	1	.280	.350	.355
Frank Ellerbe†	3B21	R	28	21	61	7	12	3	0	0	2	2	3	0	.197	.222	.246
Tony Rego	C23	R	26	24	59	5	13	1	0	0	5	1	3	0	.220	.233	.237
Pat Collins	C20	R	27	32	54	9	17	2	0	1	11	11	14	0	.315	.431	.407
Syl Simon	3B6,SS5	R	26	23	32	5	8	1	1	0	6	3	5	0	.250	.314	.344
Verdo Elmore	OF3	L	24	7	17	2	3	3	0	0	0	1	3	0	.176	.222	.353
Pat Burke	3B1	R	23	1	3	0	0	0	0	0	1	0	0	0	.000	.000	.000
Bill Mizeur		L	27	1	1	0	0	0	0	0	0	0	0	0	.000	.000	.000

H. Rice, 2 G at SS, 2 G at OF

Pitcher	T	Age	G	GS	CG	ShO	IP	H	HR	BB	SO	W-L	Sv	ERA
Urban Shocker	R	33	39	33	17	4	246.1	270	11	52	88	16-13	1	4.06
Dave Danforth	L	34	41	27	12	1	219.2	246	16	69	65	15-12	4	4.51
Ernie Wingard	L	23	36	26	14	0	218.0	215	6	85	23	13-12	1	3.51
Dixie Davis	R	33	29	24	11	5	160.1	159	9	72	45	11-13	0	4.10
Elam Vangilder	R	28	43	18	5	0	145.1	183	10	55	49	5-10	1	5.76
Hub Pruett	L	23	33	1	0	0	65.0	64	1	42	27	3-4	0	4.57
George Lyons	R	33	26	6	2	0	77.2	97	2	45	25	3-2	0	5.21
Ray Kolp	R	29	25	12	5	1	96.2	131	4	25	29	5-7	0	5.68
Bill Bayne	L	25	22	3	0	0	50.2	47	4	29	20	1-3	0	4.09
George Grant	R	21	21	2	0	0	51.1	69	4	25	11	1-2	0	6.14
Ollie Voigt	R	24	8	1	0	0	16.1	21	1	13	4	1-0	0	5.51
Bill Lasley	R	21	2	0	0	0	4.0	7	0	2	0	0-0	0	6.75
Edgar Barnhart	R	19	1	0	0	0	1.0	0	0	2	0	0-0	0	0.00
Boom-Boom Beck	R	19	1	0	0	0	1.0	2	0	1	0	0-0	0	0.00

1924 Philadelphia Athletics 5th AL 71-81 .467 20.0 GB

Connie Mack

Player	Gm by Position	B	Age	G	AB	R	H	2B	3B	HR	RBI	BB	SO	SB	Avg	OBP	Slg
Cy Perkins	C128	R	28	128	392	31	95	19	4	0	32	31	20	3	.242	.304	.311
Joe Hauser	1B146	L	25	149	562	97	162	31	8	27	115	56	52	7	.288	.358	.516
Max Bishop	2B80	L	24	91	294	52	75	13	2	2	21	54	30	4	.255	.380	.333
Harry Riconda	3B73,SS2,C1	R	27	83	281	34	71	16	3	1	21	27	43	3	.253	.323	.342
Chick Galloway	SS129	R	27	129	464	41	128	16	4	2	48	23	23	11	.276	.311	.341
Al Simmons	OF152	R	22	152	594	69	183	31	9	8	102	30	60	16	.308	.343	.431
Bing Miller	OF94,1B7	R	29	113	398	62	136	22	4	6	62	12	24	11	.342	.376	.462
Bill Lamar	OF87	L	27	87	367	68	121	22	5	7	48	18	21	8	.330	.361	.474
Jimmy Dykes	2B77,3B27,SS4	R	27	110	410	68	128	26	6	3	50	38	59	1	.312	.372	.427
Frank Welch	OF74	R	26	94	293	47	85	13	2	5	31	35	27	2	.290	.372	.399
Sammy Hale	3B55,OF5,C1*	R	27	80	261	41	83	14	2	2	17	17	19	3	.318	.367	.410
Paul Strand	OF44	L	30	47	167	15	38	9	4	0	13	4	9	3	.228	.254	.329
Frank Bruggy	C44	R	33	50	113	9	30	6	0	0	8	8	15	4	.265	.314	.319
John Chapman	SS19	R	24	19	71	7	20	4	1	0	7	4	8	0	.282	.320	.366
Amos Strunk†	OF8	L	35	30	42	5	6	0	0	0	1	7	4	0	.143	.265	.143
Charlie Gibson	C12	R	24	12	15	1	2	0	0	0	1	2	0	0	.133	.235	.133
Ed Sherling		R	26	4	2	2	1	1	0	0	0	0	0	0	.500	.500	1.000
Joe Green		R	26	1	1	0	0	0	0	0	0	0	0	0	.000	.000	.000

S. Hale, 1 G at SS

Pitcher	T	Age	G	GS	CG	ShO	IP	H	HR	BB	SO	W-L	Sv	ERA
Eddie Rommel	R	26	43	34	21	3	278.0	302	8	94	72	18-15	1	3.95
Fred Heimach	L	23	40	26	10	0	198.0	243	2	60	60	14-12	0	4.73
Sam Gray	R	26	34	19	8	2	151.2	169	5	89	54	8-7	2	3.98
Rollie Naylor	R	32	10	7	1	0	38.1	53	2	20	10	0-5	0	6.34
Dennis Burns	R	26	37	17	7	0	154.0	191	3	68	26	6-8	1	5.08
Stan Baumgartner	L	29	36	16	12	1	181.0	181	6	73	45	13-6	4	2.88
Slim Harriss	R	27	36	12	4	1	123.0	138	5	62	45	6-10	2	4.68
Roy Meeker	L	23	30	14	5	1	146.0	166	7	81	37	5-12	0	4.68
Bob Hasty	R	28	18	4	0	0	52.2	57	4	30	15	1-3	0	5.64
Rube Walberg	L	27	6	2	0	0	7.0	10	0	10	3	0-0	0	12.86
Curly Ogden†	R	23	5	1	0	0	12.2	14	1	7	4	0-3	0	3.55
Bill Pierson	L	25	1	0	0	0	2.2	3	0	3	0	0-0	0	3.38

1924 Cleveland Indians 6th AL 67-86 .438 24.5 GB

Tris Speaker

Player	Gm by Position	B	Age	G	AB	R	H	2B	3B	HR	RBI	BB	SO	SB	Avg	OBP	Slg
Glenn Myatt	C95	L	26	105	342	55	117	22	7	8	73	33	12	6	.342	.402	.518
George Burns	1B127	R	31	129	462	64	143	37	5	4	66	29	27	14	.310	.370	.437
Chick Fewster	2B94,3B5	R	28	101	322	36	86	12	2	0	36	24	36	12	.267	.324	.317
Rube Lutzke	3B103,2B3	R	26	106	341	37	83	18	3	0	42	38	46	4	.243	.328	.314
Joe Sewell	SS153	L	25	153	594	99	188	45	5	4	104	67	13	3	.316	.388	.429
Charlie Jamieson	OF143	L	31	143	594	98	213	34	8	3	54	47	15	21	.359	.407	.458
Tris Speaker	OF128	L	36	135	486	94	167	36	9	9	65	72	13	5	.344	.432	.510
Homer Summa	OF95	L	25	111	390	55	113	21	6	2	38	11	16	4	.290	.311	.390
Pat McNulty	OF75	L	25	101	291	46	78	13	5	0	26	33	22	10	.268	.347	.347
Riggs Stephenson	2B58,OF7	R	26	71	240	33	89	20	0	4	44	27	10	1	.371	.439	.504
Luke Sewell	C57	R	23	63	165	27	48	9	1	0	17	22	13	1	.291	.387	.358
Frank Ellerbe†	3B39,2B2	R	28	46	120	7	31	1	3	1	14	1	10	0	.258	.270	.342
Frank Brower	1B26,P4,OF3	L	31	66	107	16	30	10	1	3	20	27	9	1	.280	.434	.477
Sumpter Clarke	OF33	R	26	45	104	17	24	6	1	0	11	6	12	0	.231	.273	.308
Roxy Walters	C25,2B7	R	31	32	74	10	19	2	0	0	5	10	6	0	.257	.345	.284
Elmer Yoter	3B19	R	24	19	66	3	18	1	1	0	7	5	8	0	.273	.324	.318
Larry Gardner	3B8,2B6	L	38	38	50	3	10	0	0	0	4	5	1	0	.200	.273	.200
Ray Knode	1B10	L	23	11	37	6	9	1	0	0	4	3	0	2	.243	.300	.270
Tom Gulley	OF5	L	24	8	20	4	3	0	1	0	1	3	2	0	.150	.292	.250
Joe Wyatt	OF4	R	24	4	12	1	2	0	0	0	1	2	1	0	.167	.286	.167
Freddy Spurgeon	2B3	R	23	3	7	0	1	1	0	0	0	0	0	0	.143	.250	.286
Kenny Hogan		L	21	2	1	0	0	0	0	0	0	0	0	0	.000	.000	.000

Pitcher	T	Age	G	GS	CG	ShO	IP	H	HR	BB	SO	W-L	Sv	ERA
Joe Shaute	L	24	46	34	21	2	283.0	317	8	83	68	20-17	2	3.75
Stan Coveleski	R	34	37	33	18	2	240.1	286	6	73	58	15-16	0	4.04
Sherry Smith	L	33	39	27	20	2	247.2	267	5	42	34	12-14	1	3.02
George Uhle	R	25	28	25	15	0	196.1	238	6	75	57	9-15	1	4.77
Jim Joe Edwards	L	29	10	7	5	1	57.0	64	3	34	15	4-3	0	2.84
Joe Dawson	R	27	4	4	0	0	20.1	24	0	21	7	1-2	0	6.64
Carl Yowell	L	21	4	2	2	0	27.0	37	1	13	8	1-1	0	6.67
Jake Miller	L	26	2	2	1	0	12.0	13	0	5	4	0-1	0	3.00
Frank Wayenberg	R	25	2	1	0	0	6.2	7	0	5	3	0-0	0	5.40
Dewey Metivier	R	26	26	6	1	0	76.1	110	3	34	14	1-5	3	5.31
Luther Roy	R	21	16	5	2	0	48.2	62	3	31	14	0-5	0	7.77
Watty Clark	L	22	12	1	0	0	25.2	38	0	14	6	1-3	0	7.01
Guy Morton	R	31	10	0	0	0	12.1	12	0	13	6	0-1	0	6.57
Virgil Cheeves	R	23	8	1	0	0	17.1	26	2	17	2	0-0	0	7.79
Bud Messenger	R	26	5	2	1	0	25.0	28	4	14	4	2-0	0	4.32
Logan Drake	R	23	5	1	0	0	11.1	18	0	10	8	0-1	0	10.32
George Edmondson	R	28	5	1	0	0	8.0	10	1	5	3	0-0	0	9.00
Dutch Levsen	R	26	4	1	1	0	16.1	22	0	4	3	1-1	0	4.41
Frank Brower	R	31	4	0	0	0	9.2	7	0	4	0	0-0	0	0.93
Jim Lindsey	R	28	3	0	0	0	3.0	8	0	3	0	0-0	0	21.00
Paul Fitzke	R	23	1	0	0	0	4.0	5	0	3	1	0-0	0	4.50
Bub Kuhn	R	24	1	0	0	0	1.0	4	1	0	0	0-1	0	27.00

1924 Boston Red Sox 7th AL 67-87 .435 25.0 GB

Lee Fohl

Player	Gm by Position	B	Age	G	AB	R	H	2B	3B	HR	RBI	BB	SO	SB	Avg	OBP	Slg
Steve O'Neill	C92	R	32	106	307	29	73	15	1	0	38	63	23	0	.238	.371	.293
Joe Harris	1B128,OF3	R	33	133	491	82	148	36	9	3	77	81	25	6	.301	.406	.430
Bill Wambsganss	2B155	R	30	156	636	93	174	41	5	0	49	54	33	14	.274	.334	.354
Danny Clark	3B94	L	30	104	325	36	90	23	3	2	54	51	19	4	.277	.378	.385
Dud Lee	SS90	L	24	94	288	36	73	9	4	0	29	40	17	8	.253	.350	.313
Ira Flagstead	OF144	R	30	149	560	106	172	35	7	5	43	77	41	10	.307	.401	.421
Bobby Veach	OF130	L	36	142	519	77	153	35	9	5	99	47	18	5	.295	.359	.426
Ike Boone	OF124	L	27	128	486	71	162	30	4	13	96	55	32	2	.333	.402	.492
Homer Ezzell	3B63,SS21,C1	R	28	90	277	35	75	8	4	0	32	14	21	12	.271	.311	.329
Shano Collins	OF56,1B12	R	38	89	240	37	70	17	5	0	28	18	17	4	.292	.349	.404
Howard Shanks	SS41,3B22,OF4*	R	33	72	193	22	50	16	3	0	25	21	12	1	.259	.332	.373
Val Picinich	C51	R	27	69	161	25	44	6	3	1	24	29	19	5	.273	.394	.366
Johnny Heving	C29	R	28	45	109	15	31	5	1	0	11	10	7	0	.284	.345	.349
Phil Todt	1B18,OF4	L	22	52	103	17	27	8	2	1	14	6	9	0	.262	.309	.408
Denny Williams	OF19	L	24	25	85	17	31	3	0	0	4	10	5	3	.365	.438	.400
Chappie Geygan	SS32	R	21	33	82	7	21	5	2	0	4	4	16	0	.256	.307	.366
Joe Connolly	OF3	R	28	14	10	1	1	0	0	0	1	2	2	0	.100	.250	.100

H. Shanks, 2 G at 1B, 2 G at 2B

Pitcher	T	Age	G	GS	CG	ShO	IP	H	HR	BB	SO	W-L	Sv	ERA
Howard Ehmke	R	30	45	36	26	4	315.0	324	9	81	119	19-17	4	3.46
Alex Ferguson	R	27	40	32	15	0	237.2	259	6	108	78	14-17	2	3.75
Jack Quinn	R	40	43	25	13	2	228.2	241	10	52	64	12-13	7	3.19
Curt Fullerton	R	25	33	20	9	0	152.0	166	1	73	33	7-12	2	4.32
Bill Piercy	R	28	22	18	3	0	121.0	156	4	66	20	5-7	0	5.88
Ted Wingfield†	R	24	4	3	2	0	25.2	23	0	8	4	0-2	0	2.45
Clarence Winters	R	25	4	2	0	0	7.0	22	0	4	3	0-1	0	20.57
Buster Ross	L	21	30	2	1	1	93.1	109	3	30	16	4-3	1	3.47
George Murray	R	25	28	7	0	0	80.1	97	6	32	27	2-9	0	6.72
Oscar Fuhr	L	30	23	10	4	1	80.1	100	1	39	30	3-6	0	5.94
Hoge Workman	R	24	11	0	0	0	18.0	25	2	11	7	0-0	0	8.50
Red Ruffing	R	20	8	2	0	0	23.0	29	0	9	10	0-0	0	6.65
Les Howe	R	28	4	0	0	0	7.1	11	1	2	3	1-0	0	7.36
John Woods	R	26	1	0	0	0	1.0	0	0	3	0	0-0	0	0.00
Charlie Jamerson	L	24	1	0	0	0	1.0	1	0	3	0	0-0	0	18.00
Al Kellett	R	22	1	0	0	0	0.0	0	0	2	0	0-0	0	—

1924 Chicago White Sox 8th AL 66-87 .431 25.5 GB

Johnny Evers (10-11)/Ed Walsh (1-2)/Eddie Collins (14-13)/Johnny Evers (41-61)

Player	Gm by Position	B	Age	G	AB	R	H	2B	3B	HR	RBI	BB	SO	SB	Avg	OBP	Slg
Buck Crouse	C90	L	27	94	305	30	79	10	1	1	44	23	12	3	.259	.319	.308
Earl Sheely	1B146	R	31	146	535	84	171	34	3	3	103	95	28	7	.320	.426	.411
Eddie Collins	2B150	L	37	152	556	108	194	27	7	6	86	89	16	42	.349	.441	.455
Willie Kamm	3B145	R	24	147	528	58	134	28	6	6	93	64	59	9	.254	.337	.364
Bill Barrett	SS77,OF27,3B8	R	24	119	406	52	110	18	5	2	56	30	38	15	.271	.326	.355
Bibb Falk	OF138	L	25	138	526	77	185	37	8	6	99	47	21	6	.352	.406	.487
Harry Hooper	OF123	L	36	130	476	107	156	27	8	10	62	65	26	16	.328	.413	.481
Johnny Mostil	OF105	R	28	118	385	75	125	22	5	4	49	45	41	7	.325	.401	.439
M. Archdeacon	OF95	L	25	95	288	59	92	9	3	0	25	40	30	11	.319	.410	.372
Ray Schalk	C56	R	31	57	153	15	30	4	2	1	11	21	10	1	.196	.301	.268
Roy Elsh	OF38,1B2	R	32	60	147	21	45	9	1	0	11	10	14	6	.306	.350	.381
Sloppy Thurston	P39,OF1	R	25	51	122	15	31	6	3	1	9	5	14	0	.254	.289	.377
Ray French	SS28,2B3	R	29	37	112	13	20	4	0	0	11	10	13	3	.179	.246	.214
Ray Morehart	SS27,2B2	L	24	31	100	10	20	4	2	0	8	17	7	3	.200	.316	.280
Harvey McClellan	SS21,2B7,3B1*	R	29	32	85	9	15	3	0	0	9	6	7	2	.176	.239	.212
Johnny Grabowski	C19	R	24	20	56	10	14	3	0	0	3	2	4	0	.250	.276	.304
Bud Clancy	1B8	L	23	13	35	5	9	1	0	0	6	3	2	3	.257	.316	.286
Ike Davis	SS10	R	29	10	33	5	8	1	1	0	4	2	5	0	.242	.286	.333
Joe Burns	C6	R	24	8	19	1	2	0	0	0	0	0	2	0	.105	.105	.105
Kettle Wirts	C5	R	26	6	12	0	1	0	0	0	0	2	2	1	.083	.214	.083
Bill Black	2B1	L	24	6	5	0	1	0	0	0	0	0	0	0	.200	.200	.200
Frank Naleway	SS1	R	21	1	2	0	0	0	0	0	0	1	0	0	.000	.333	.000
Wally Dashiell	SS1	R	22	1	2	0	0	0	0	0	0	0	0	0	.000	.000	.000
Bernie DeViveiros	2B1	R	23	1	1	0	0	0	0	0	0	0	0	0	.000	.000	.000
Amos Strunk†		L	35	1	1	0	0	0	0	0	0	0	0	0	.000	.000	.000

H. McClellan, 1 G at OF

Pitcher	T	Age	G	GS	CG	ShO	IP	H	HR	BB	SO	W-L	Sv	ERA
Sloppy Thurston	R	25	38	36	28	1	291.0	330	17	60	37	20-14	1	3.80
Ted Lyons	R	23	41	22	12	0	216.1	279	10	72	52	12-11	3	4.87
Red Faber	R	35	21	20	9	0	161.1	173	5	58	47	9-11	0	3.85
Mike Cvengros	L	22	26	15	2	0	105.2	119	5	67	36	3-12	0	5.88
Charlie Robertson	R	28	17	14	5	0	97.1	108	2	54	29	4-10	0	4.99
Dixie Leverett	R	30	21	11	4	0	99.0	123	2	41	29	2-3	0	5.82
Leo Mangum	R	28	13	7	1	0	47.0	69	3	25	12	1-4	0	7.09
Sarge Connally	R	25	44	13	6	0	160.0	177	4	68	55	7-13	6	4.05
Ted Blankenship	R	23	25	11	7	0	125.1	167	1	38	36	7-6	1	5.17
Doug McWeeny	R	27	13	5	2	0	43.1	47	2	17	18	1-3	0	4.57
Milt Steengrafe	R	24	3	0	0	0	5.2	15	0	4	3	0-0	0	12.71
Happy Foreman	L	26	3	0	0	0	4.0	7	0	4	1	0-0	0	2.25
Bob Barnes	L	22	2	0	0	0	4.2	14	1	0	1	0-0	0	19.29
John Dobb	L	22	2	0	0	0	2.0	4	0	1	2	0-0	0	9.00
Lum Davenport	L	24	1	0	0	0	2.0	1	0	2	1	0-0	0	0.00
Webb Schultz	R	26	1	0	0	0	1.0	1	0	0	0	0-0	0	9.00
Bob Lawrence	R	24	1	0	0	0	1.0	1	0	1	1	0-0	0	9.00

>>1924 New York Giants 1st NL 93-60 .608 — John McGraw (16-13)/Hughie Jennings (32-12)/John McGraw (45-35)

Player	Gm by Position	B	Age	G	AB	R	H	2B	3B	HR	RBI	BB	SO	SB	Avg	OBP	Slg
Frank Snyder	C110	R	31	118	354	37	107	18	3	5	53	30	43	3	.302	.357	.412
George Kelly	1B125,OF14,2B5*	R	28	144	571	91	185	37	9	21	136	38	52	7	.324	.371	.531
Frankie Frisch	2B143,SS10,3B2	S	25	145	603	121	198	33	15	7	69	56	24	22	.328	.387	.468
Heine Groh	3B145	R	34	145	559	82	157	32	3	2	46	52	29	8	.281	.354	.360
Travis Jackson	SS151	R	20	151	596	81	180	26	8	11	76	21	56	6	.302	.326	.428
Irish Meusel	OF138	R	31	139	549	75	170	26	9	6	102	33	18	11	.310	.351	.423
Ross Youngs	OF132,2B2	L	27	133	526	112	187	33	12	10	74	77	31	11	.356	.441	.521
Hack Wilson	OF103	R	24	107	383	62	113	19	12	10	57	44	46	4	.295	.369	.486
Billy Southworth	OF75	L	31	94	281	40	72	13	0	3	36	32	16	1	.256	.332	.335
Hank Gowdy	C78	R	34	87	191	25	62	9	1	4	37	26	11	1	.325	.411	.445
Bill Terry	1B35	L	27	77	163	26	39	7	2	5	24	17	18	1	.239	.311	.399
Jimmy O'Connell	OF29,2B1	L	23	52	104	24	33	4	2	2	18	11	16	2	.317	.388	.452
Freddy Lindstrom	2B23,3B11	R	18	52	79	19	20	3	1	0	4	6	10	3	.253	.314	.316
Art Nehf	P30,OF1	L	31	33	57	11	13	1	0	5	13	6	4	1	.228	.302	.509
Grover Hartley	C3	R	35	4	7	1	2	1	0	0	1	1	0	1	.286	.375	.429
Eddie Ainsmith	C9	R	32	10	5	0	3	0	0	0	0	0	0	0	.600	.600	.600
Buddy Crump	OF1	L	22	1	4	0	0	0	0	0	1	0	1	0	.000	.000	.000

G. Kelly, 1 G at 3B

Pitcher	T	Age	G	GS	CG	ShO	IP	H	HR	BB	SO	W-L	Sv	ERA
Virgil Barnes	R	27	35	29	15	1	229.1	239	10	57	59	16-10	3	3.06
Jack Bentley	L	29	28	24	13	1	188.0	196	11	56	60	16-5	1	3.78
Hugh McQuillan	R	26	27	23	14	1	184.0	179	8	43	49	14-8	3	2.69
Art Nehf	L	31	30	20	11	0	171.2	167	14	42	72	14-4	2	3.62
Wayland Dean	R	22	26	20	6	0	125.2	139	9	45	39	6-12	0	5.01
Mule Watson	R	27	22	16	6	1	99.2	122	7	24	18	7-4	0	3.79
Dinty Gearin†	L	26	6	3	2	0	29.0	30	3	16	4	1-2	0	2.48
Kent Greenfield	R	21	1	1	0	0	3.0	9	1	1	1	0-1	0	15.00
Rosy Ryan	R	26	37	9	2	0	124.2	137	1	37	36	8-6	5	4.26
Claude Jonnard	R	26	34	3	1	0	89.2	80	2	24	40	4-5	5	2.41
Ernie Maun	R	23	22	0	0	0	35.0	46	2	10	5	1-1	1	5.91
Walter Huntzinger	R	25	12	2	0	0	32.1	41	3	9	6	1-1	1	4.45
Harry Baldwin	R	24	10	2	1	0	33.2	42	5	11	5	3-1	0	4.28
Joe Oeschger†	R	33	10	2	0	0	29.0	35	1	14	10	2-0	0	3.10
Leon Cadore	R	33	2	0	0	0	4.0	2	0	3	2	0-0	0	0.00

1924 Brooklyn Dodgers 2nd NL 92-62 .597 1.5 GB — Wilbert Robinson

Player	Gm by Position	B	Age	G	AB	R	H	2B	3B	HR	RBI	BB	SO	SB	Avg	OBP	Slg
Zack Taylor	C93	R	25	99	345	36	100	9	4	1	39	14	14	0	.290	.319	.348
Jack Fournier	1B153	L	34	154	563	93	188	25	4	27	116	83	46	7	.334	.428	.536
Andy High	2B133,SS17,3B1	L	26	144	582	98	191	26	13	6	61	57	16	3	.328	.390	.448
Milt Stock	3B142	R	30	142	561	66	136	14	4	2	52	26	32	3	.242	.277	.292
Johnny Mitchell	SS64	S	29	64	243	42	64	10	0	1	16	37	22	3	.263	.361	.317
Zack Wheat	OF139	L	36	141	566	92	212	41	8	14	97	49	18	3	.375	.428	.549
Tommy Griffith	OF139	L	34	140	482	43	121	19	5	3	67	34	19	0	.251	.300	.330
Eddie Brown	OF114	R	32	114	455	56	140	30	4	5	78	26	15	3	.308	.345	.424
Jimmy Johnston	SS63,3B10,1B4*	R	34	86	315	51	94	11	2	2	29	27	10	5	.298	.356	.365
Hank DeBerry	C63	R	29	77	218	20	53	10	3	3	26	20	21	0	.243	.307	.358
Bernie Neis	OF62	S	28	80	211	43	64	8	3	4	26	27	17	4	.303	.385	.427
Dick Loftus	OF29,1B1	L	23	46	81	18	22	6	0	0	8	7	2	1	.272	.330	.346
Joe Klugmann	2B28,SS1	R	29	31	79	7	13	2	1	0	3	2	9	0	.165	.185	.215
Gene Bailey	OF17	R	30	18	46	7	11	3	0	1	4	7	6	1	.239	.340	.370
Binky Jones	SS10	R	24	10	37	0	4	1	0	0	2	0	3	0	.108	.108	.135
Charlie Hargreaves	C9	R	27	15	27	4	11	2	0	0	5	1	1	0	.407	.429	.481
Ivy Olson	SS8,2B2	R	38	10	27	0	6	1	0	0	0	3	1	0	.222	.300	.259
Fred Johnston	2B1,3B1	R	24	4	4	1	1	0	0	0	0	0	1	0	.250	.250	.250

J. Johnston, 1 G at OF

Pitcher	T	Age	G	GS	CG	ShO	IP	H	HR	BB	SO	W-L	Sv	ERA
Burleigh Grimes	R	30	38	36	30	1	310.2	351	15	91	135	22-13	1	3.82
Dazzy Vance	R	33	35	34	30	3	308.1	238	11	77	262	28-6	0	2.16
Dutch Ruether	L	30	30	21	13	2	166.2	189	4	45	63	8-13	3	3.94
Bill Doak†	R	33	21	16	8	2	149.1	130	8	35	32	11-5	0	3.07
Tiny Osborne†	R	31	21	13	6	0	104.1	123	1	54	52	6-5	0	5.18
Rube Ehrhardt	R	29	15	9	6	2	83.2	71	5	17	13	5-3	0	2.26
Rube Yarrison	R	28	3	2	0	0	11.0	12	0	3	2	0-2	0	6.55
Art Decatur	R	30	31	10	3	0	126.1	158	12	27	38	10-9	1	4.13
Dutch Henry	L	22	16	4	0	0	46.0	69	0	15	11	1-2	0	5.67
Jim Roberts	R	28	11	5	0	0	25.1	41	1	8	10	0-3	0	7.46
Leo Dickerman†	R	27	7	2	0	0	19.2	20	0	16	9	0-0	0	5.49
Nelson Greene	L	23	4	1	0	0	9.0	14	1	2	3	0-1	0	4.00
B. Hollingsworth	R	28	3	1	1	0	8.1	7	0	10	7	1-0	0	6.48
Tex Wilson	L	22	2	0	0	0	3.2	7	0	1	1	0-0	0	14.73
Tom Long	L	26	1	0	0	0	2.0	2	0	2	0	0-0	0	9.00

1924 Pittsburgh Pirates 3rd NL 90-63 .588 3.0 GB — Bill McKechnie

Player	Gm by Position	B	Age	G	AB	R	H	2B	3B	HR	RBI	BB	SO	SB	Avg	OBP	Slg
Johnny Gooch	C69	S	26	70	224	26	65	6	5	0	25	16	12	1	.290	.343	.362
Charlie Grimm	1B151	L	25	151	542	53	156	25	12	2	63	37	22	3	.288	.336	.389
Rabbit Maranville	2B152	R	32	152	594	62	158	33	20	2	71	35	53	18	.266	.307	.399
Pie Traynor	3B121	R	24	142	545	86	160	26	13	5	82	37	26	24	.294	.340	.417
Glenn Wright	SS153	R	23	153	616	80	177	28	18	7	111	27	52	14	.287	.318	.425
Max Carey	OF149	S	34	149	599	113	178	30	9	8	55	58	17	49	.297	.366	.417
Kiki Cuyler	OF114	R	25	117	466	94	165	27	16	9	85	30	62	32	.354	.402	.539
Clyde Barnhart	OF88	R	28	102	344	49	95	6	11	3	51	30	17	8	.276	.338	.384
Carson Bigbee	OF75	L	29	89	282	42	74	4	1	0	15	26	12	15	.262	.331	.284
Eddie Moore	OF35,3B13,2B4	R	25	72	209	47	75	8	4	2	13	27	12	6	.359	.437	.464
Walter Schmidt	C57	R	37	58	177	16	43	3	2	1	20	13	5	6	.243	.295	.299
Earl Smith†	C35	L	27	39	111	12	41	10	1	4	21	13	4	2	.369	.435	.586
Walter Mueller	OF15	R	29	30	50	6	13	1	1	0	8	4	4	1	.260	.327	.320
Cliff Knox	C6	S	22	6	18	1	4	0	0	0	2	2	0	0	.222	.300	.222
Jewel Ens	1B5	R	34	5	10	2	3	0	0	0	0	0	3	0	.300	.300	.300
Eppie Barnes	1B1	L	23	2	5	0	0	0	0	0	0	0	1	0	.000	.000	.000
Johnny Rawlings		R	31	3	3	0	1	0	0	0	2	0	0	0	.333	.333	.333

Pitcher	T	Age	G	GS	CG	ShO	IP	H	HR	BB	SO	W-L	Sv	ERA
Wilbur Cooper	L	32	38	35	25	4	268.2	296	13	40	62	20-14	1	3.28
Ray Kremer	R	31	41	30	17	4	259.1	262	7	51	64	18-10	1	3.19
Lee Meadows	R	29	36	30	15	3	229.1	240	7	51	61	13-12	0	3.26
Johnny Morrison	R	28	41	25	10	0	237.2	213	7	73	85	11-16	2	3.75
Emil Yde	L	24	33	22	14	4	194.0	171	3	62	53	16-3	0	2.83
Arnie Stone	L	31	26	2	1	0	64.0	57	0	15	7	4-2	0	2.95
Jeff Pfeffer†	R	36	15	4	1	0	58.2	68	3	17	19	5-3	0	3.07
Babe Adams	R	42	9	3	2	0	39.2	31	1	3	5	3-1	0	0.68
Del Lundgren	R	24	8	1	0	0	16.2	25	0	3	4	0-1	0	6.48
Ray Steineder†	R	28	5	0	0	0	2.2	6	0	5	0	0-1	0	13.50
Don Songer	L	24	4	1	0	0	9.1	14	1	3	3	0-0	1	6.75
Freddy Sale	R	22	1	0	0	0	1.0	2	0	0	0	0-0	0	0.00
Buckshot May	R	24	1	0	0	0	1.0	2	0	0	1	0-0	0	0.00

1924 Cincinnati Reds 4th NL 83-70 .542 10.0 GB — Jack Hendricks

Player	Gm by Position	B	Age	G	AB	R	H	2B	3B	HR	RBI	BB	SO	SB	Avg	OBP	Slg
Bubbles Hargrave	C91	R	31	98	312	42	94	19	10	3	33	30	20	2	.301	.370	.455
Jake Daubert	1B102	L	40	102	405	47	114	14	9	1	31	28	17	5	.281	.331	.368
Hughie Critz	2B96,SS1	R	23	102	413	67	133	15	14	3	35	19	18	19	.322	.352	.448
Babe Pinelli	3B143	R	28	144	510	61	156	16	7	0	70	32	32	23	.306	.353	.365
Ike Caveney	SS90,2B5	R	29	95	337	36	92	19	1	4	32	14	21	2	.273	.310	.371
Edd Roush	OF119	L	31	121	483	67	168	23	21	3	72	22	11	17	.348	.376	.501
Curt Walker†	OF109	L	27	109	397	55	119	21	10	4	46	44	15	7	.300	.371	.433
George Burns	OF90	R	34	93	336	43	86	19	2	2	33	29	21	3	.256	.315	.342
Rube Bressler	1B50,OF49	R	29	115	383	41	133	14	13	4	49	22	20	9	.347	.389	.483
Sammy Bohne	2B48,SS40,3B12	R	27	100	349	42	89	15	9	4	46	18	24	9	.255	.293	.384
Pat Duncan	OF83	R	30	96	319	34	86	21	6	2	37	20	23	1	.270	.313	.392
Ivy Wingo	C35,1B1	L	33	66	192	21	55	5	4	1	23	14	8	1	.286	.338	.370
Boob Fowler	SS32,2B4,3B2	L	23	59	129	20	43	6	1	0	9	5	15	2	.333	.358	.395
George Harper†	OF22	L	32	28	74	7	20	3	0	0	3	13	5	1	.270	.393	.311
Chick Shorten	OF15	L	32	41	69	7	19	3	0	0	6	4	2	0	.275	.315	.319
Lew Fonseca	2B10,1B6	R	25	20	57	5	13	2	1	0	9	4	4	1	.228	.279	.298
Gus Sanberg	C24	R	28	24	52	1	9	0	0	0	3	2	7	0	.173	.204	.173
Ed Hock	OF2	L	25	16	10	7	1	0	0	0	0	0	2	0	.100	.182	.100
Cliff Lee†	OF1	R	27	6	6	1	2	1	0	0	2	0	2	0	.333	.333	.500
Jim Begley	2B2	R	21	2	5	1	1	0	0	0	0	2	0	0	.200	.429	.200
Greasy Neale	OF2	L	32	3	4	0	0	0	0	0	0	0	1	0	.000	.000	.000
Eddie Pick	OF1	S	25	3	2	0	0	0	0	0	0	0	1	0	.000	.000	.000
Jack Blott	C1	R	21	2	1	0	0	0	0	0	0	0	0	0	.000	.000	.000

Pitcher	T	Age	G	GS	CG	ShO	IP	H	HR	BB	SO	W-L	Sv	ERA
Pete Donohue	R	23	35	32	16	3	222.1	248	9	36	72	16-9	0	3.60
Eppa Rixey	L	33	35	29	15	4	238.1	219	3	47	57	15-14	1	2.76
Dolf Luque	R	33	31	28	13	2	219.1	229	5	53	86	10-15	0	3.16
Carl Mays	R	32	37	27	15	2	226.0	238	3	36	63	20-9	0	3.15
Tom Sheehan	R	30	39	16	8	2	166.2	170	5	54	52	9-11	1	3.24
Jakie May	L	28	38	4	2	0	99.0	104	2	29	59	3-3	6	3.00
Rube Benton	L	37	32	15	6	1	162.2	166	2	24	42	7-9	1	2.77
Pedro Dibut	R	31	7	2	2	0	36.2	24	1	12	15	3-0	0	2.21
Bill Harris	R	24	3	0	0	0	7.0	10	0	2	5	0-0	0	9.00

1924 Chicago Cubs 5th NL 81-72 .529 12.0 GB — Bill Killefer

Player	Gm by Position	B	Age	G	AB	R	H	2B	3B	HR	RBI	BB	SO	SB	Avg	OBP	Slg
Gabby Hartnett	C105	R	23	111	354	56	106	17	7	16	67	39	37	10	.299	.377	.523
Hooks Cotter	1B90	L	24	98	310	39	81	16	4	4	33	36	31	3	.261	.338	.377
George Grantham	2B118,3B6	L	24	127	469	85	148	19	6	12	60	55	63	21	.316	.390	.458
Bernie Friberg	3B142	R	24	142	495	67	138	19	3	5	82	66	53	19	.279	.369	.360
Sparky Adams	SS89,2B19	R	29	117	418	66	117	11	5	1	27	40	20	15	.280	.344	.337
Jigger Statz	OF131,2B1	R	26	135	549	69	152	22	5	3	49	37	50	13	.277	.325	.352
Denver Grigsby	OF121	L	23	124	411	58	123	18	2	3	48	31	47	10	.299	.357	.375
Cliff Heathcote	OF111	L	26	113	392	66	121	19	7	0	30	28	28	26	.309	.356	.393
Charlie Hollocher	SS71	L	28	76	286	28	70	12	4	2	21	18	7	4	.245	.292	.336
Bob O'Farrell	C57	R	27	71	183	25	44	6	2	3	28	30	13	2	.240	.347	.344
Ray Grimes	1B50	R	30	51	177	33	53	6	5	5	34	28	15	4	.299	.401	.475
Otto Vogel	OF53,3B2	R	24	70	172	28	46	11	2	1	24	10	26	4	.267	.319	.372
Bob Barrett	2B25,1B10	R	25	54	133	12	32	2	3	5	21	7	29	1	.241	.279	.414
Butch Weis	OF36	L	23	37	133	19	37	8	1	0	23	15	14	4	.278	.356	.353
Hack Miller	OF30	R	30	53	131	17	44	8	1	4	25	8	11	1	.336	.379	.504
Howie Fitzgerald	OF5	L	22	7	19	1	3	0	0	0	2	0	2	0	.158	.158	.158
Teddy Kearns	1B4	R	24	4	16	0	4	0	1	0	1	1	1	0	.250	.294	.375
Allen Elliott	1B10	L	26	10	14	0	2	0	0	0	0	0	1	0	.143	.143	.143
Ralph Michaels	SS4	R	22	8	11	0	4	0	0	0	2	0	1	0	.364	.364	.364
John Churry	C3	R	23	6	7	0	1	1	0	0	0	2	0	0	.143	.333	.286

Pitcher	T	Age	G	GS	CG	ShO	IP	H	HR	BB	SO	W-L	Sv	ERA
Vic Aldridge	R	30	32	32	20	0	244.1	261	10	80	74	15-12	0	3.50
Vic Keen	R	25	40	28	15	0	234.2	242	17	80	75	15-14	3	3.80
Tony Kaufmann	R	23	34	26	16	3	208.1	218	21	66	79	16-11	0	4.02
Elmer Jacobs	R	31	38	22	13	1	190.1	181	9	72	50	11-12	1	3.74
Pete Alexander	R	37	21	20	12	0	169.1	183	9	25	33	12-5	0	3.03
Guy Bush	R	22	16	8	4	0	80.2	91	7	24	36	2-5	0	4.02
Herb Brett	R	24	1	1	0	0	5.1	6	0	7	1	0-0	0	5.06
Sheriff Blake	R	24	29	11	4	0	106.1	123	3	44	42	6-6	1	4.57
Rip Wheeler	R	26	29	4	0	0	101.1	103	8	21	16	3-6	0	3.91
George Milstead	L	21	13	2	1	0	29.2	41	3	13	6	1-1	0	6.07
Ray Pierce	L	27	6	0	0	0	7.1	7	2	4	2	0-0	0	7.36
Tiny Osborne†	R	31	2	0	0	0	3.0	3	0	2	2	0-0	1	3.00

1924 St. Louis Cardinals 6th NL 65-89 .422 28.5 GB

Branch Rickey

Player	Gm by Position	B	Age	G	AB	R	H	2B	3B	HR	RBI	BB	SO	SB	Avg	OBP	Slg
Mike Gonzalez	C119	R	33	120	402	34	119	27	1	3	53	24	22	1	.296	.337	.391
Jim Bottomley	1B133,2B1	L	24	137	528	87	167	31	12	14	111	35	35	5	.316	.362	.500
Rogers Hornsby	2B143	R	28	143	536	121	227	43	14	25	94	89	32	5	.424	.507	.696
Howard Freigau	3B98,SS2	R	21	98	376	35	101	17	6	2	39	19	24	10	.269	.306	.362
Jimmy Cooney	SS99,3B7,2B1	R	29	110	383	44	113	20	8	1	57	20	20	12	.295	.330	.397
Jack Smith	OF114	L	29	124	459	91	130	18	6	2	33	33	27	24	.283	.333	.362
Ray Blades	OF109,2B7,3B7	R	27	131	456	86	142	21	13	11	68	35	38	7	.311	.373	.487
Wattie Holm	OF64,C9,3B4	R	22	81	293	40	86	10	4	0	23	8	16	1	.294	.317	.355
Heinie Mueller	OF53,1B27	L	24	92	296	39	78	12	6	2	37	19	16	8	.264	.312	.365
Max Flack	OF52	L	34	67	209	31	55	11	3	2	21	21	5	3	.263	.330	.373
Specs Toporcer	3B33,SS25,2B3	L	25	70	198	30	62	10	3	1	24	11	14	2	.313	.362	.409
Taylor Douthit	OF50	R	23	53	173	24	48	13	1	0	13	16	19	4	.277	.349	.364
Hi Myers	OF22,3B12,2B3	R	35	43	124	12	26	5	1	1	15	3	10	1	.210	.228	.290
Chick Hafey	OF24	R	21	24	91	10	23	5	2	2	22	4	8	1	.253	.292	.418
Tommy Thevenow	SS23	R	20	23	89	4	18	4	1	0	7	1	6	1	.202	.211	.270
Eddie Dyer	P29,OF1	L	23	50	76	8	18	2	3	0	8	3	8	1	.237	.266	.342
Bill Sherdel	P35,OF2	L	27	49	75	4	15	4	0	0	8	13	9	0	.200	.318	.253
Charlie Niebergall	C34	R	25	40	58	6	17	6	0	0	7	3	9	0	.293	.339	.397
Les Bell	SS17	R	22	17	57	5	14	3	2	1	5	3	7	0	.246	.295	.421
Verne Clemons	C17	R	32	25	56	3	18	3	0	0	6	2	3	0	.321	.345	.375
Johnny Stuart	P28,3B1	R	23	30	54	5	11	1	0	0	3	2	6	0	.204	.232	.222
Ernie Vick	C16	R	23	16	23	2	8	1	0	0	0	3	3	0	.348	.423	.391
Ed Clough	OF6	L	17	7	14	0	1	0	0	0	1	0	3	0	.071	.071	.071
Joe Schultz†	OF2	R	30	12	12	0	2	0	0	0	2	3	0	0	.167	.333	.167
Ray Shepardson	C3	R	27	3	6	1	0	0	0	0	0	0	3	0	.000	.000	.000
Doc Lavan	2B2,SS2	R	33	4	6	0	0	0	0	0	0	0	0	0	.000	.000	.000
Joe Bratcher	OF1	L	25	4	1	1	0	0	0	0	0	0	0	0	.000	.000	.000

Pitcher	T	Age	G	GS	CG	ShO	IP	H	HR	BB	SO	W-L	Sv	ERA
Jesse Haines	R	30	35	31	16	1	222.2	275	14	66	69	8-19	0	4.41
Allen Sothoron	R	31	29	28	16	4	196.2	209	9	84	62	10-16	0	3.57
Johnny Stuart	R	23	28	22	13	0	159.0	167	12	60	54	9-11	0	4.75
Eddie Dyer	L	23	29	15	7	1	136.2	174	6	51	23	8-11	0	4.61
Leo Dickerman†	R	27	18	13	8	1	119.2	108	6	51	28	7-4	0	2.41
Jeff Pfeffer†	R	36	16	12	3	0	78.0	102	3	30	20	4-5	0	5.31
Flint Rhem	R	23	6	3	3	0	32.1	31	1	17	20	2-2	1	4.45
Pea Ridge Day	R	24	3	3	1	0	17.2	22	0	6	3	1-1	0	4.58
Vince Shields	R	23	2	1	0	0	12.0	10	1	3	4	1-1	0	3.00
Bill Sherdel	L	27	35	10	6	0	168.2	188	9	38	57	8-9	1	3.42
Hi Bell	R	26	28	11	5	0	113.1	124	5	29	29	3-8	1	4.92
Jesse Fowler	L	25	13	3	0	0	32.2	28	0	18	5	1-1	0	4.41
Bill Doak†	R	33	11	1	0	0	22.0	25	0	14	7	2-1	3	3.27
Art Delaney	R	27	8	1	1	0	20.0	19	0	6	2	1-0	0	1.80
Lou North†	R	33	6	0	0	0	14.2	15	1	9	8	0-0	0	6.75
Jack Berly	R	21	4	0	0	0	8.0	8	2	4	2	0-0	0	5.63
Bob Vines	R	27	2	0	0	0	10.2	23	1	0	0	0-0	0	9.28

1924 Philadelphia Phillies 7th NL 55-96 .364 37.0 GB

Art Fletcher

Player	Gm by Position	B	Age	G	AB	R	H	2B	3B	HR	RBI	BB	SO	SB	Avg	OBP	Slg
Butch Henline	C83,OF2	R	29	115	289	41	82	18	4	5	35	27	15	1	.284	.361	.426
Walter Holke	1B148	S	31	148	563	60	169	23	6	6	64	25	33	3	.300	.330	.394
Hod Ford	2B145	R	26	145	530	58	144	27	5	3	53	27	40	1	.272	.308	.358
Russ Wrightstone	3B97,2B9,SS5*	L	31	118	388	55	119	24	4	7	58	27	15	5	.307	.363	.443
Heinie Sand	SS137	R	26	137	539	79	132	21	6	6	40	52	57	5	.245	.316	.340
Cy Williams	OF145	L	36	148	558	101	183	31	11	24	93	67	49	7	.328	.403	.552
George Harper†	OF109	L	32	109	411	68	121	26	6	16	55	38	23	10	.294	.361	.504
Johnny Mokan	OF94	R	28	96	366	50	95	15	1	7	44	30	27	7	.260	.321	.363
Joe Schultz†	OF76	R	30	88	284	35	80	15	1	5	29	20	18	6	.282	.329	.394
Jimmie Wilson	C82,2B2,OF1	R	23	95	280	32	78	16	3	6	39	17	12	5	.279	.322	.421
Frank Parkinson	3B28,SS21	R	29	62	156	14	33	7	0	1	19	14	28	3	.212	.281	.276
Andy Woehr	3B44,2B1	R	28	50	152	11	33	4	5	0	17	5	8	2	.217	.252	.309
Fritz Henrich	OF32	L	25	36	90	4	19	4	0	0	4	2	12	0	.211	.228	.256
Curt Walker†	OF20	L	27	24	71	11	21	6	1	1	8	7	4	0	.296	.359	.451
Cliff Lee†	OF13,1B4	R	27	21	56	4	14	3	2	1	7	2	5	0	.250	.276	.429
Lew Wendell	C17	R	32	21	32	3	8	1	0	0	2	3	5	0	.250	.314	.281
Freddy Leach	OF7	L	26	8	28	6	13	2	1	2	7	2	1	0	.464	.500	.821
Lenny Metz	SS6	R	24	7	7	1	2	0	0	0	1	1	0	0	.286	.375	.286
Spoke Emery	OF1	R	25	5	3	3	2	0	0	0	0	0	0	0	.667	.667	.667

R. Wrightstone, 1 G at OF

Pitcher	T	Age	G	GS	CG	ShO	IP	H	HR	BB	SO	W-L	Sv	ERA
Jimmy Ring	R	29	32	31	16	1	215.1	236	9	108	72	10-12	0	3.97
Clarence Mitchell	L	33	30	26	9	1	165.0	223	10	58	36	6-13	1	5.62
Hal Carlson	R	32	38	24	12	1	203.2	267	9	55	66	8-17	2	4.86
Whitey Glazner	R	30	35	24	8	2	156.2	210	14	63	41	7-16	0	5.92
Bill Hubbell	R	27	36	22	9	2	179.0	233	9	45	30	10-9	2	4.83
Huck Betts	R	27	37	9	2	0	144.1	160	8	42	46	7-10	2	4.30
Johnny Couch	R	33	37	6	3	0	137.0	170	13	39	23	4-8	3	4.73
Joe Oeschger†	R	33	19	8	0	0	65.1	88	6	16	8	2-7	0	4.41
Burt Lewis	R	28	12	0	0	0	18.0	23	1	7	3	0-0	0	6.00
Ray Steineder†	R	28	9	0	0	0	28.2	29	1	16	11	1-1	0	4.40
Lefty Weinert	L	22	8	1	0	0	14.2	10	0	11	7	0-1	0	2.45
Jim Bishop	R	26	7	1	0	0	16.2	24	3	7	3	0-1	0	6.48
Earl Hamilton	L	32	3	0	0	0	6.0	9	0	2	2	0-1	0	10.50
Lerton Pinto	L	25	3	0	0	0	4.0	7	1	0	1	0-0	0	9.00

1924 Boston Braves 8th NL 53-100 .346 40.0 GB

Dave Bancroft (27-38)/Dick Rudolph (11-27)/Dave Bancroft (15-35)

Player	Gm by Position	B	Age	G	AB	R	H	2B	3B	HR	RBI	BB	SO	SB	Avg	OBP	Slg
Mickey O'Neil	C106	R	24	106	362	32	89	4	1	0	22	14	27	4	.246	.276	.262
Stuffy McInnis	1B146	R	33	146	581	57	169	23	7	1	59	15	6	9	.291	.311	.360
Cotton Tierney	2B115,3B22	R	30	136	505	38	131	16	1	6	58	22	37	11	.259	.296	.331
Ernie Padgett	3B113,2B29	R	25	138	502	42	128	25	9	1	46	37	56	4	.255	.310	.347
Bob Smith	SS80,3B23	R	29	106	347	32	79	12	3	2	38	15	26	5	.228	.260	.297
Casey Stengel	OF126	L	33	131	461	57	129	20	6	5	39	45	39	13	.280	.348	.382
Bill Cunningham	OF109	R	28	114	437	44	119	15	8	1	40	32	27	8	.272	.326	.350
Frank Wilson	OF55	L	23	61	215	20	51	7	0	1	15	23	22	3	.237	.311	.284
Dave Bancroft	SS79	S	33	79	319	49	89	11	1	2	21	37	24	4	.279	.356	.339
Frank Gibson	C46,1B10,3B2	S	33	90	229	25	71	15	6	1	30	10	23	1	.310	.342	.441
Gus Felix	OF51	R	29	59	204	25	43	7	1	1	10	18	16	0	.211	.275	.270
Ray Powell	OF46	L	35	74	188	21	49	9	1	1	15	21	28	1	.261	.338	.335
Johnny Cooney	P34,OF16,1B1	R	23	55	130	10	33	2	1	0	4	9	5	0	.254	.302	.285
Herb Thomas	OF32	R	22	32	127	12	28	4	1	1	8	9	8	5	.220	.288	.291
Les Mann	OF28	R	30	32	102	13	28	7	4	0	10	8	10	1	.275	.333	.422
Marty Shay	2B19,SS1	R	28	19	68	4	16	3	1	0	2	5	5	2	.235	.297	.309
Ed Sperber	OF17	L	29	24	59	8	17	2	0	1	12	10	9	3	.288	.400	.373
Earl Smith†	C13	L	27	33	59	1	16	3	0	0	8	6	3	0	.271	.338	.322
Hunter Lane	3B4,2B1	R	23	7	15	0	1	0	0	0	0	1	1	0	.067	.125	.067
Walton Cruise		L	34	9	9	4	4	1	0	1	3	0	2	0	.444	.444	.889
Eddie Phillips	C1	R	23	3	3	0	0	0	0	0	0	0	2	0	.000	.000	.000
Dee Cousineau	C3	R	25	3	2	0	0	0	0	0	0	0	0	0	.000	.000	.000
Wade Lefler†		L	28	1	1	0	0	0	0	0	0	0	1	0	.000	.000	.000
Al Hermann		R	25	1	1	0	0	0	0	0	0	0	1	0	.000	.000	.000
John Kelleher		R	30	1	1	0	0	0	0	0	0	0	1	0	.000	.000	.000

Pitcher	T	Age	G	GS	CG	ShO	IP	H	HR	BB	SO	W-L	Sv	ERA
Jesse Barnes	R	31	37	32	21	4	267.2	292	7	53	49	15-20	0	3.23
Joe Genewich	R	27	34	27	11	2	200.1	258	4	65	43	10-19	1	5.21
Tim McNamara	R	25	35	21	6	2	179.0	242	9	31	35	8-12	0	5.18
Johnny Cooney	L	23	34	19	12	2	181.0	176	4	50	67	8-9	2	3.18
Dutch Stryker	R	38	20	10	2	0	73.1	90	4	22	22	3-8	0	6.01
Rube Marquard	L	37	6	6	1	0	36.0	33	3	13	10	1-2	0	3.00
Skinny Graham	R	24	5	4	1	0	33.0	33	0	11	15	0-4	0	3.82
Ike Kamp	L	23	1	1	0	0	7.0	9	0	5	4	0-1	0	5.14
Dinty Gearin†	L	26	1	1	0	0	0.0	3	0	2	0	0-1	0	—
Jim Yeargin	R	22	32	12	6	0	141.1	162	7	42	34	1-11	0	5.09
Larry Benton	R	26	30	13	4	0	128.0	129	4	64	41	5-7	1	4.15
Red Lucas	R	22	27	4	1	0	83.2	112	5	18	30	1-4	0	5.16
Lou North†	R	33	9	4	1	0	35.1	45	1	19	11	1-2	0	5.35
Joe Muich	R	20	3	0	0	0	9.0	19	1	5	1	0-0	0	11.00
Joe Batchelder	L	25	3	0	0	0	4.2	4	0	2	2	0-0	0	3.86

»1925 Washington Senators 1st AL 96-55 .636 —

Bucky Harris

Player	Gm by Position	B	Age	G	AB	R	H	2B	3B	HR	RBI	BB	SO	SB	Avg	OBP	Slg
Muddy Ruel	C126,1B1	R	29	127	393	55	122	9	2	0	54	63	16	4	.310	.411	.344
Joe Judge	1B109	L	31	112	376	65	118	31	5	8	66	55	21	7	.314	.406	.487
Bucky Harris	2B144	R	28	144	551	91	158	30	3	1	66	64	21	14	.287	.370	.358
Ossie Bluege	3B144,SS4	R	24	145	522	77	150	27	4	4	79	59	56	16	.287	.362	.377
Roger Peckinpaugh	SS124,1B1	R	34	126	422	67	124	16	4	4	64	49	23	13	.294	.367	.379
Sam Rice	OF152	L	35	152	649	111	227	31	13	1	87	37	10	26	.350	.388	.442
Goose Goslin	OF150	L	24	150	601	116	201	34	20	18	113	53	50	26	.334	.394	.547
Earl McNeely	OF112,1B1	R	27	122	385	76	110	14	2	3	37	48	54	14	.286	.378	.356
Joe Harris†	1B58,OF41	R	34	100	300	60	97	21	9	12	59	51	28	5	.323	.430	.573
Hank Severeid†	C35	R	34	50	110	11	39	8	1	0	14	13	6	0	.355	.423	.445
Dutch Ruether	P30,1B1	L	31	55	108	18	36	3	2	1	15	10	8	0	.333	.390	.426
Everett Scott†	SS30,3B2	R	32	33	103	10	28	6	1	0	18	4	4	1	.272	.299	.350
Nemo Leibold	OF26,3B1	L	33	56	84	14	23	1	1	0	7	8	7	1	.274	.337	.310
Spencer Adams	2B15,SS8,3B3	L	27	39	55	11	15	4	1	0	4	5	4	1	.273	.333	.382
Bobby Veach†	OF11	L	37	18	37	4	9	3	0	0	8	3	3	0	.243	.300	.324
Bennie Tate	C14	L	23	16	27	0	13	3	0	0	7	2	2	0	.481	.517	.593
Mule Shirley	1B9	L	24	14	23	2	3	1	0	0	2	1	7	0	.130	.167	.174
Mike McNally	3B7,SS2,2B1	R	32	12	21	1	3	0	0	0	0	1	4	0	.143	.182	.143
Tex Jeanes	OF13	R	24	15	19	2	5	1	0	1	4	3	2	1	.263	.364	.474
Stuffy Stewart	3B5,2B1	R	31	7	17	3	6	1	0	0	3	1	2	1	.353	.389	.412
Wid Matthews	OF1	L	28	10	9	2	4	0	0	0	1	0	1	0	.444	.444	.444
Buddy Myer	SS4	L	21	4	8	1	2	0	0	0	0	0	1	0	.250	.250	.250
Pinky Hargrave†	C1	S	29	5	6	0	3	0	0	0	0	1	2	0	.500	.571	.500
Frank McGee	1B2	R	26	2	3	0	0	0	0	0	0	0	1	0	.000	.000	.000

Pitcher	T	Age	G	GS	CG	ShO	IP	H	HR	BB	SO	W-L	Sv	ERA
Tom Zachary	L	29	38	33	11	1	217.2	247	10	74	58	12-15	2	3.85
Stan Coveleski	R	35	32	32	15	3	241.0	230	7	73	58	20-5	0	2.84
Walter Johnson	R	37	30	29	16	3	229.0	211	7	78	108	20-7	0	3.07
Dutch Ruether	L	31	30	29	16	1	223.1	241	5	105	68	18-7	0	3.87
George Mogridge†	L	36	10	8	3	0	53.0	56	2	18	13	4-3	0	3.40
Alex Ferguson†	R	28	7	6	3	0	55.1	52	2	23	24	5-1	0	3.25
Lefty Thomas	L	21	2	2	1	0	13.0	14	0	7	10	0-2	0	2.08
Firpo Marberry	R	26	55	0	0	0	93.1	84	4	45	53	8-6	15	3.47
Allan Russell	R	31	32	2	0	0	68.2	85	6	37	25	2-4	2	5.77
Vean Gregg	L	40	26	5	1	0	74.1	87	3	38	18	2-2	2	4.12
Curly Ogden	R	24	17	4	2	1	42.0	45	1	18	6	3-1	0	4.50
Win Ballou	L	27	10	1	1	0	27.2	38	1	13	13	1-1	0	4.55
Harry Kelley	R	19	6	1	0	0	16.0	30	0	12	7	1-1	0	9.00
Jim Lyle	R	24	1	0	0	0	3.0	5	0	1	3	0-0	0	6.00
Spence Pumpelly	R	32	1	0	0	0	1.0	1	1	1	0	0-0	0	9.00

1925 Philadelphia Athletics 2nd AL 88-64 .579 8.5 GB

Connie Mack

Player	Gm by Position	B	Age	G	AB	R	H	2B	3B	HR	RBI	BB	SO	SB	Avg	OBP	Slg
Mickey Cochrane	C133	L	22	134	420	69	139	21	5	6	55	44	19	7	.331	.397	.448
Jim Poole	1B123	L	30	133	480	65	143	29	8	5	67	27	37	5	.298	.338	.423
Max Bishop	2B104	L	25	105	368	66	103	18	4	4	27	87	37	5	.280	.420	.383
Sammy Hale	3B96,2B1	R	28	110	391	62	135	30	11	8	63	17	27	7	.345	.376	.540
Chick Galloway	SS148	R	28	149	481	52	116	11	4	3	71	59	28	16	.241	.324	.299
Al Simmons	OF153	R	23	153	658	122	253	43	12	24	129	35	41	7	.384	.416	.596
Bill Lamar	OF131	L	28	138	568	85	202	39	8	3	77	21	17	2	.356	.379	.468
Bing Miller	OF115,1B12	R	30	124	474	78	151	29	10	10	81	19	14	11	.319	.355	.485
Jimmy Dykes	3B64,2B58,SS2	R	28	122	465	93	150	32	11	5	55	46	49	3	.323	.393	.471
Frank Welch	OF57	R	27	85	202	40	56	5	4	4	41	29	14	2	.277	.373	.401
Cy Perkins	C58,3B1	R	29	65	140	21	43	10	0	1	18	26	6	0	.307	.426	.400
Walt French	OF19	L	25	67	100	20	37	9	0	0	14	1	9	1	.370	.376	.460
Red Holt	1B25	L	30	27	88	13	24	7	0	1	8	12	9	0	.273	.360	.386
Bill Bagwell	OF4	L	29	36	50	4	15	2	1	0	10	2	2	0	.300	.327	.380
Carl Husta	SS6	R	23	6	22	2	3	0	0	0	2	2	3	0	.136	.208	.136
Charlie Berry	C4	R	22	10	14	1	3	1	0	0	3	0	2	0	.214	.214	.286
Red Smith	SS16,3B2	L	24	20	14	1	4	0	0	0	1	2	5	0	.286	.375	.286
Jimmie Foxx	C1	R	17	10	9	2	6	1	0	0	0	0	1	0	.667	.667	.778
Doc Gautreau†	2B4	R	23	4	7	0	0	0	0	0	0	0	3	0	.000	.000	.000
Jim Keesey	1B2	R	22	5	5	1	2	0	0	0	1	0	2	0	.400	.400	.400
Charlie Engle	SS1	R	21	1	0	0	0	0	0	0	0	0	0	0	—	—	—

Pitcher	T	Age	G	GS	CG	ShO	IP	H	HR	BB	SO	W-L	Sv	ERA
Slim Harriss	R	28	46	33	15	2	252.1	263	8	95	95	19-12	1	3.50
Eddie Rommel	R	27	52	28	14	1	261.0	285	10	95	67	21-10	3	3.69
Sam Gray	R	27	32	28	14	4	203.2	199	11	63	80	16-8	3	3.27
Jack Quinn†	R	41	18	14	4	0	99.2	119	3	16	19	6-3	0	3.88
Lefty Willis	L	19	1	1	0	0	5.0	9	2	2	3	0-0	0	10.80
Rube Walberg	L	28	53	20	7	0	191.2	197	11	77	82	8-14	7	3.99
Lefty Grove	L	25	45	18	5	0	197.0	207	11	131	116	10-12	1	4.75
Stan Baumgartner	L	30	37	11	2	1	113.1	120	2	35	18	6-3	3	3.57
Art Stokes	R	28	12	0	0	0	24.1	24	0	10	7	1-1	0	4.07
Fred Heimach	L	24	10	0	0	0	20.1	24	2	9	6	0-1	0	3.98
Elbert Andrews	R	23	6	0	0	0	8.0	12	0	11	0	0-0	0	10.13
Tom Glass	R	27	2	0	0	0	5.0	9	0	0	2	1-0	0	5.40

1925 St. Louis Browns 3rd AL 82-71 .536 15.0 GB

George Sisler

Player	Gm by Position	B	Age	G	AB	R	H	2B	3B	HR	RBI	BB	SO	SB	Avg	OBP	Slg
Leo Dixon	C75	R	30	76	205	27	46	11	1	1	19	24	42	3	.224	.318	.302
George Sisler	1B150,P1	L	32	150	649	100	224	21	15	12	105	27	24	11	.345	.371	.479
Marty McManus	2B154,OF1	R	25	154	587	108	169	44	8	13	90	73	69	5	.288	.371	.457
Gene Robertson	3B154,SS1	L	26	154	582	97	158	26	5	14	78	81	30	10	.271	.364	.405
Bobby LaMotte	SS93,3B3	R	27	97	356	61	97	20	4	2	51	34	22	5	.272	.338	.368
Baby Doll Jacobson	OF139	R	34	142	540	103	184	30	9	15	76	45	26	8	.341	.392	.513
Ken Williams	OF102	L	35	102	411	83	136	31	5	25	105	37	14	10	.331	.390	.613
Harry Rice	OF85,1B3,C1*	L	23	103	354	87	127	25	8	11	47	54	15	8	.359	.450	.568
Herschel Bennett	OF73	L	28	93	298	46	83	11	6	2	37	18	16	4	.279	.324	.376
Wally Gerber	SS71	R	33	72	246	29	67	13	1	0	19	26	15	1	.272	.344	.333
Pinky Hargrave†	C62	S	29	67	225	34	64	15	2	8	43	13	13	2	.284	.326	.476
Jack Tobin	OF39,1B3	L	33	77	193	25	58	11	0	2	27	9	5	8	.301	.335	.389
Joe Evans	OF47	R	30	55	159	27	50	12	0	0	20	16	6	6	.314	.377	.390
Hank Severeid†	C31	R	34	34	109	15	40	9	0	1	21	11	2	0	.367	.425	.477
Joe Bush	P33,OF1	R	32	57	102	10	26	12	0	2	18	6	8	2	.255	.296	.431
Tony Rego	C19	R	27	20	32	5	13	2	1	0	3	3	2	0	.406	.472	.531
Jimmy Austin	3B1	S	45	1	1	0	0	0	0	0	0	0	0	0	.000	.000	.000

H. Rice, 1 G at 2B, 1 G at 3B

Pitcher	T	Age	G	GS	CG	ShO	IP	H	HR	BB	SO	W-L	Sv	ERA
Milt Gaston	R	29	42	30	16	0	238.2	284	8	101	84	15-14	1	4.41
Joe Bush	R	32	33	28	15	2	208.2	239	18	91	63	14-14	0	5.09
Dixie Davis	R	34	35	23	9	0	180.1	192	10	106	58	12-7	1	4.59
Joe Giard	L	26	30	21	9	4	160.2	179	13	87	43	10-5	0	5.04
Ernie Wingard	L	24	32	18	8	0	145.0	184	10	77	20	9-10	0	5.34
George Mogridge†	L	36	2	2	1	0	15.1	17	2	5	8	1-1	0	5.87
Elam Vangilder	R	29	52	16	4	1	193.1	225	11	92	61	14-8	6	4.70
Dave Danforth	L	35	38	15	5	0	159.0	172	19	61	53	7-9	2	4.36
Ed Stauffer	R	27	20	1	0	0	30.1	34	1	21	13	0-1	0	5.34
Chet Falk	L	20	13	0	0	0	25.0	38	2	17	7	0-0	0	8.28
George Grant	R	22	12	0	0	0	16.1	26	2	8	7	0-2	0	6.06
Brad Springer	L	21	2	0	0	0	3.0	1	0	7	0	0-0	0	3.00
George Blaeholder	R	21	2	0	0	0	2.0	6	3	1	1	0-0	0	31.50
George Sisler	L	32	1	0	0	0	2.0	1	0	1	1	0-0	0	0.00

1925 Detroit Tigers 4th AL 81-73 .526 16.5 GB

Ty Cobb

Player	Gm by Position	B	Age	G	AB	R	H	2B	3B	HR	RBI	BB	SO	SB	Avg	OBP	Slg
Johnny Bassler	C118	L	30	121	344	40	96	19	3	0	52	74	6	1	.279	.408	.352
Lu Blue	1B148	S	28	150	532	91	163	18	9	3	94	83	29	19	.306	.403	.391
Frank O'Rourke	2B118,3B6	R	30	124	482	88	141	40	7	5	57	32	37	5	.293	.350	.436
Fred Haney	3B107	R	27	114	398	84	111	15	3	0	40	66	29	11	.279	.384	.332
Jackie Tavener	SS134	L	27	134	453	45	111	11	11	0	47	39	60	5	.245	.309	.318
Harry Heilmann	OF148	R	30	150	573	97	225	40	11	13	134	67	27	6	.393	.457	.569
Al Wingo	OF122	L	27	130	440	104	163	34	10	5	68	69	31	14	.370	.456	.527
Ty Cobb	OF105,P1	L	38	121	415	97	157	31	12	12	102	65	12	13	.378	.468	.598
Heinie Manush	OF73	L	23	99	277	46	84	14	3	5	47	24	21	8	.303	.363	.430
Bob Fothergill	OF59	R	27	71	204	38	72	14	0	2	28	6	3	2	.353	.377	.451
Les Burke	2B52	L	22	77	180	32	52	6	3	0	24	17	8	4	.289	.357	.356
Larry Woodall	C75	R	30	75	171	20	35	4	1	0	13	24	8	1	.205	.303	.240
Bob Jones	3B46	L	35	50	148	18	35	6	0	0	15	9	5	1	.236	.280	.277
Topper Rigney	SS51,3B4	R	28	62	146	21	36	5	2	2	18	21	15	2	.247	.341	.349
Johnny Neun	1B13	S	24	60	75	15	20	3	3	0	4	9	12	2	.267	.345	.387
Jack Warner	3B10	R	21	10	39	7	13	0	0	0	2	3	6	0	.333	.381	.333
Charlie Gehringer	2B6	L	22	8	18	3	3	0	0	0	0	2	0	0	.167	.250	.167
Oscar Stanage	C3	R	42	3	5	0	1	0	0	0	0	0	0	0	.200	.200	.200
Andy Harrington		R	22	1	1	0	0	0	0	0	0	0	0	0	.000	.000	.000

Pitcher	T	Age	G	GS	CG	ShO	IP	H	HR	BB	SO	W-L	Sv	ERA
Earl Whitehill	L	25	35	33	15	1	239.1	267	13	88	83	11-11	2	4.66
Hooks Dauss	R	35	35	30	16	1	228.0	238	11	85	58	16-11	1	3.16
Rip Collins	R	29	26	20	5	0	140.0	149	7	52	33	6-11	0	4.56
Lil Stoner	R	26	34	18	8	0	152.0	166	6	53	51	10-9	1	4.26
Dutch Leonard	L	33	18	18	9	0	125.2	143	7	43	65	11-4	0	4.51
Jess Doyle	R	27	45	3	0	0	118.1	158	6	50	31	4-7	8	5.93
Ken Holloway	R	27	38	14	6	0	157.2	170	8	67	29	13-4	2	4.62
Ed Wells	L	25	35	14	5	0	134.1	190	8	62	45	6-9	2	6.23
Bert Cole†	L	28	14	2	1	0	33.2	44	2	15	7	2-3	1	5.88
Ownie Carroll	R	22	10	4	1	0	40.2	46	1	28	12	2-2	0	3.76
Syl Johnson	R	24	6	0	0	0	13.0	11	1	10	5	0-2	0	3.46
Ty Cobb	R	38	1	0	0	0	1.0	0	0	0	0	0-0	1	0.00
Bill Moore	R	22	1	0	0	0	0.0	0	0	3	0	0-0	0	—

1925 Chicago White Sox 5th AL 79-75 .513 18.5 GB

Eddie Collins

Player	Gm by Position	B	Age	G	AB	R	H	2B	3B	HR	RBI	BB	SO	SB	Avg	OBP	Slg
Ray Schalk	C125	R	32	125	343	44	94	18	1	0	52	57	27	11	.274	.382	.332
Earl Sheely	1B153	R	32	153	600	93	189	43	3	9	111	68	23	3	.315	.389	.442
Eddie Collins	2B116	L	38	118	425	80	147	26	3	3	80	87	8	19	.346	.461	.442
Willie Kamm	3B152	R	25	152	509	82	142	32	4	6	83	90	36	11	.279	.391	.393
Ike Davis	SS144	R	30	146	562	105	135	31	9	0	61	71	58	19	.240	.333	.327
Bibb Falk	OF154	L	26	154	602	80	181	35	9	4	99	51	25	4	.301	.357	.409
Johnny Mostil	OF153	R	29	153	605	135	181	36	16	2	50	90	52	43	.299	.400	.421
Harry Hooper	OF124	L	37	127	442	62	117	23	5	6	55	54	21	12	.265	.351	.380
Bill Barrett	2B41,OF27,3B4*	R	25	81	245	44	89	23	3	3	40	24	27	5	.363	.420	.518
Buck Crouse	C48	L	28	54	131	18	46	7	0	2	25	12	4	1	.351	.410	.450
Spencer Harris	OF27	L	24	56	92	12	26	2	0	1	13	14	13	1	.283	.383	.337
John Kane	SS8,2B6	S	25	14	56	6	10	1	0	0	3	0	3	0	.179	.193	.196
Roy Elsh	1B3	R	33	32	48	6	9	1	0	0	4	5	7	2	.188	.264	.208
Johnny Grabowski	C21	R	25	21	46	5	14	4	1	0	10	2	4	0	.304	.333	.435
John Bischoff†	C4	R	30	7	11	1	1	0	0	0	0	1	5	0	.091	.167	.091
M. Archdeacon	OF1	L	26	10	9	2	1	0	0	0	0	2	1	0	.111	.273	.111
Jule Mallonee	OF1	L	25	2	3	1	0	0	0	0	0	1	0	0	.000	.250	.000
Leo Tankersley	C1	R	24	1	3	0	0	0	0	0	0	0	0	0	.000	.000	.000
Bud Clancy		L	24	4	3	0	0	0	0	0	0	1	0	0	.000	.250	.000

B. Barrett, 4 G at SS

Pitcher	T	Age	G	GS	CG	ShO	IP	H	HR	BB	SO	W-L	Sv	ERA
Ted Lyons	R	24	43	32	19	5	262.2	274	7	83	45	21-11	3	3.26
Red Faber	R	36	34	32	16	1	238.0	266	8	59	71	12-11	0	3.78
Sloppy Thurston	R	26	36	25	9	0	175.0	250	14	47	35	10-14	1	6.17
Ted Blankenship	R	24	40	23	16	3	222.0	218	11	69	81	17-8	1	3.16
Charlie Robertson	R	29	24	23	6	2	137.0	181	8	47	27	8-12	0	5.26
Mike Cvengros	L	23	22	11	4	0	104.2	109	7	55	32	3-9	0	4.30
Sarge Connally	R	26	40	2	0	0	104.2	122	2	58	45	6-7	8	4.90
Dickie Kerr	L	31	12	2	0	0	36.2	45	3	18	4	0-1	0	5.15
Jim Joe Edwards†	L	30	9	4	1	1	45.1	46	4	23	20	1-2	0	3.97
Frank Mack	R	25	8	0	0	0	13.1	24	1	13	6	0-0	0	9.45
Leo Mangum	R	29	7	0	0	0	15.0	25	0	6	6	1-0	0	7.80
Tink Riviere	R	25	3	0	0	0	4.2	6	0	7	1	0-0	0	7.71
Ken Ash	R	23	2	0	0	0	4.0	7	2	0	0	0-0	0	9.00
Jake Freeze	R	25	2	0	0	0	3.2	5	1	3	1	0-0	0	2.45
Chief Bender	R	41	1	0	0	0	1.0	1	1	1	0	0-0	0	18.00

1925 Cleveland Indians 6th AL 70-84 .455 27.5 GB

Tris Speaker

Player	Gm by Position	B	Age	G	AB	R	H	2B	3B	HR	RBI	BB	SO	SB	Avg	OBP	Slg
Glenn Myatt	C98,OF1	L	27	106	358	51	97	15	9	11	54	29	24	2	.271	.329	.455
George Burns	1B126	R	32	127	488	69	164	41	4	6	79	24	24	16	.336	.371	.473
Chick Fewster	2B86,3B10,OF1	R	29	93	294	39	73	16	1	1	38	36	25	6	.248	.330	.320
Rube Lutzke	3B69	R	27	81	238	31	52	9	0	1	16	26	29	2	.218	.295	.269
Joe Sewell	SS153,2B3	L	26	155	608	78	204	37	7	1	98	64	4	7	.336	.402	.424
Charlie Jamieson	OF135	L	32	138	557	109	165	24	5	4	42	72	26	14	.296	.380	.379
Pat McNulty	OF111	L	26	118	373	70	117	18	2	6	43	47	23	7	.314	.392	.421
Tris Speaker	OF109	L	37	117	429	79	167	35	5	12	87	70	12	5	.389	.479	.578
Freddy Spurgeon	3B56,2B46,SS3	R	24	107	376	50	108	9	3	0	32	15	21	8	.287	.315	.327
Cliff Lee	OF70	R	28	77	230	43	74	15	6	4	42	21	33	2	.322	.378	.491
Homer Summa	OF54,3B2	L	26	75	224	28	74	10	1	0	25	13	6	3	.330	.375	.384
Luke Sewell	C66,OF2	R	24	74	220	30	51	10	2	0	18	33	18	6	.232	.337	.295
Johnny Hodapp	3B37	R	19	37	130	12	31	5	1	0	14	11	7	2	.238	.298	.292
Ray Knode	1B34	L	24	45	108	13	27	5	0	0	11	10	4	3	.250	.314	.296
Joe Klugmann	2B29,1B4,3B2	R	30	38	85	12	28	9	2	0	12	8	4	3	.329	.387	.482
Riggs Stephenson	OF16	R	27	19	54	8	16	3	1	1	9	7	3	1	.296	.387	.444
Ike Eichrodt	OF13	R	22	15	52	4	12	3	1	0	4	2	7	0	.231	.259	.327
Harvey Hendrick	1B3	L	27	25	28	2	8	1	2	0	9	3	5	0	.286	.355	.464
Roxy Walters	C5	R	32	5	20	0	4	0	0	0	0	0	2	0	.200	.200	.200
Chick Tolson	1B3	R	30	3	12	0	3	0	0	0	0	2	1	0	.250	.357	.250
Frank McCrea	C1	R	28	1	5	1	1	0	0	0	0	0	0	0	.200	.200	.200
Gene Bedford	2B2	S	28	2	3	1	0	0	0	0	0	0	1	0	.000	.000	.000
Dutch Ussat	2B1	R	21	1	1	0	0	0	0	0	0	0	0	0	.000	.000	.000

Pitcher	T	Age	G	GS	CG	ShO	IP	H	HR	BB	SO	W-L	Sv	ERA
Sherry Smith	L	34	31	30	22	1	237.0	296	11	48	30	11-14	1	4.86
George Uhle	R	26	29	26	17	1	210.2	218	5	78	68	13-11	0	4.10
Benn Karr	R	31	32	24	12	1	197.2	248	8	80	41	11-12	0	4.78
Jake Miller	L	27	32	22	13	0	190.1	207	4	62	51	10-13	2	3.31
Garland Buckeye	L	27	30	18	11	1	153.0	161	3	58	49	13-8	0	3.65
Joe Shaute	L	25	26	17	10	1	131.0	160	6	44	34	4-12	4	5.43
Dutch Levsen	R	27	4	3	2	0	24.1	30	1	16	9	1-2	0	5.55
Ray Benge	R	23	2	2	1	1	11.2	9	0	3	3	1-0	0	1.54
Byron Speece	R	28	28	3	3	0	90.1	106	0	28	26	3-5	1	4.28
Bert Cole†	L	28	13	2	0	0	44.0	55	1	25	9	1-1	1	6.14
Jim Joe Edwards†	L	30	13	3	1	0	36.0	60	0	23	12	0-3	0	8.25
Carl Yowell	L	22	12	4	1	0	36.1	40	1	17	12	2-3	0	4.46
Luther Roy	R	22	6	1	0	0	10.0	14	1	11	1	0-0	0	3.60

630 Seasons: Team Rosters

1925 New York Yankees 7th AL 69-85 .448 28.5 GB

Miller Huggins

Player	Gm by Position	B	Age	G	AB	R	H	2B	3B	HR	RBI	BB	SO	SB	Avg	OBP	Slg
Benny Bengough	C94	R	26	95	283	17	73	14	2	0	23	19	9	0	.258	.305	.322
Lou Gehrig	1B120,OF6	L	22	126	437	73	129	23	10	20	68	46	49	6	.295	.365	.531
Aaron Ward	2B113,3B10	R	28	125	439	41	108	22	3	4	38	49	49	1	.246	.326	.337
Joe Dugan	3B96	R	28	102	404	50	118	19	4	0	31	19	20	2	.292	.330	.359
P. Wee Wanninger	SS111,3B3,2B1	L	22	117	403	35	95	13	6	1	22	11	34	3	.236	.256	.305
Earle Combs	OF150	L	26	150	593	117	203	36	13	3	61	65	43	12	.342	.411	.462
Bob Meusel	OF131,3B27	R	28	156	624	101	181	34	12	33	138	54	55	10	.290	.348	.542
Babe Ruth	OF98	L	30	98	359	61	104	12	2	25	66	59	68	2	.290	.393	.543
Ben Paschal	OF66	R	29	89	247	49	89	16	5	12	56	22	29	14	.360	.417	.611
Wally Pipp	1B47	L	32	62	178	19	41	6	3	3	24	13	12	3	.230	.286	.348
Ernie Johnson	2B34,SS28,3B2	L	37	76	170	30	48	5	1	5	17	8	10	6	.282	.315	.412
Wally Schang	C58	S	35	73	167	17	40	8	1	2	24	17	9	3	.240	.310	.335
Howard Shanks	3B26,2B21,OF4	R	34	66	155	15	40	3	1	1	18	20	15	1	.258	.343	.310
Bobby Veach†	OF33	L	37	56	116	13	41	10	2	0	15	8	0	1	.353	.400	.474
Mark Koenig	SS28	S	20	28	110	14	23	6	1	0	4	5	4	0	.209	.243	.282
Steve O'Neill	C31	R	33	35	91	7	26	5	0	1	13	10	3	0	.286	.363	.374
Everett Scott†	SS18	R	32	22	60	3	13	0	0	0	4	2	2	0	.217	.242	.217
Whitey Witt	OF10	L	29	31	40	9	8	2	1	0	0	6	2	1	.200	.304	.300
Roy Luebbe	C8	S	24	8	15	1	0	0	0	0	3	2	6	0	.000	.118	.000
Fred Merkle	1B5	R	36	7	13	4	5	1	0	0	1	1	1	1	.385	.429	.462
Fred Hofmann	C1	R	31	3	2	0	0	0	0	0	0	0	0	0	.000	.000	.000
Leo Durocher		R	19	2	1	1	0	0	0	0	0	0	0	0	.000	.000	.000
Heinie Odom	3B1	S	24	1	1	0	1	0	0	0	0	0	0	0	1.000	1.000	1.000

Pitcher	T	Age	G	GS	CG	ShO	IP	H	HR	BB	SO	W-L	Sv	ERA
Herb Pennock	L	31	47	31	21	2	277.0	267	11	71	88	16-17	2	2.96
Sad Sam Jones	R	32	43	31	14	1	246.2	267	14	104	92	15-21	2	4.63
Urban Shocker	R	34	41	30	15	2	244.1	278	17	58	74	12-12	2	3.65
Waite Hoyt	R	25	46	30	17	1	243.0	283	14	78	86	11-14	6	4.00
Bob Shawkey	R	34	33	20	9	1	186.0	209	12	67	81	6-14	0	4.11
Ben Shields	L	22	4	2	2	0	24.0	24	2	12	5	3-0	0	4.88
Garland Braxton	L	25	3	2	0	0	19.1	26	1	5	11	1-1	0	6.52
Hank Johnson	R	19	24	4	2	1	67.0	88	3	37	25	1-3	0	6.85
Alex Ferguson†	R	28	21	5	0	0	54.1	83	3	42	20	4-2	1	7.95
Walter Beall	R	25	8	1	0	0	11.1	11	0	19	8	0-1	0	12.71
Ray Francis†	L	32	4	0	0	0	4.2	5	0	3	1	0-0	0	7.71
Charlie Caldwell	R	23	3	0	0	0	2.2	7	0	3	1	0-0	0	16.88
Jim Marquis	R	24	2	0	0	0	7.1	12	1	6	0	0-0	0	9.82

1925 Boston Red Sox 8th AL 47-105 .309 49.5 GB

Lee Fohl

Player	Gm by Position	B	Age	G	AB	R	H	2B	3B	HR	RBI	BB	SO	SB	Avg	OBP	Slg
Val Picinich	C74,1B2	R	28	90	251	31	64	21	0	1	25	33	21	2	.255	.344	.351
Phil Todt	1B140	L	23	141	544	62	151	29	13	11	75	44	29	3	.278	.343	.439
Bill Wambsganss	2B103,1B6	R	31	111	360	50	83	12	4	1	41	52	21	3	.231	.329	.294
Doc Prothro	3B108,SS3	R	31	119	415	44	130	23	3	0	51	52	21	9	.313	.390	.383
Dud Lee	SS84	L	25	84	255	22	57	7	3	0	19	34	19	2	.224	.315	.275
Ira Flagstead	OF144	R	31	148	572	84	160	38	2	6	61	63	30	5	.280	.356	.385
Ike Boone	OF118	L	28	133	476	79	157	34	5	9	68	60	19	1	.330	.406	.479
Roy Carlyle	OF67	L	24	94	277	36	90	20	3	7	49	16	29	1	.325	.364	.495
Tex Vache	OF53	R	29	110	252	41	79	15	7	3	48	21	33	2	.313	.382	.464
Denny Williams	OF52	L	25	68	218	28	50	1	3	0	13	17	11	2	.229	.285	.261
Homer Ezzell	3B47,2B9	R	29	58	186	40	53	6	4	0	15	19	18	9	.285	.351	.360
Billy Rogell	2B49,SS6	S	20	58	169	12	33	5	1	0	17	11	17	0	.195	.244	.237
John Bischoff†	C40	R	30	41	133	13	37	9	1	1	16	6	11	1	.278	.309	.383
Johnny Heving	C34	R	29	45	119	14	20	7	0	0	6	12	7	0	.168	.244	.227
Bud Connolly	SS34,3B2	R	24	43	107	12	28	7	1	0	21	23	9	0	.262	.392	.346
Si Rosenthal	OF17	L	21	19	72	6	19	5	2	0	8	7	3	1	.264	.329	.389
Tom Jenkins	OF15	L	27	15	64	9	19	2	1	0	5	3	4	0	.297	.338	.359
Jack Rothrock	SS22	S	20	22	55	6	19	3	3	0	7	3	7	0	.345	.379	.509
Al Stokes	C17	R	25	17	52	7	11	0	1	0	1	4	8	0	.212	.268	.250
Mike Herrera	2B10	R	27	10	39	2	15	0	0	0	8	2	2	1	.385	.415	.385
Herb Welch	SS13	L	26	13	38	2	11	0	1	0	2	0	6	0	.289	.289	.342
Turkey Gross	SS9	R	29	9	32	2	3	0	1	0	2	2	2	0	.094	.171	.156
Joe Harris†	1B6	R	34	8	19	4	3	0	1	1	2	5	5	0	.158	.333	.421
Joe Lucey	P7,SS3	R	28	10	15	0	2	0	0	0	0	0	4	0	.133	.133	.133
Chappie Geygan	SS3	R	22	3	11	0	2	0	0	0	0	0	2	0	.182	.182	.182
Bobby Veach†	OF1	L	37	1	5	0	1	0	0	0	2	1	1	0	.200	.333	.200
Shano Collins	OF1	R	39	2	3	1	1	0	0	0	1	0	0	0	.333	.333	.333

Pitcher	T	Age	G	GS	CG	ShO	IP	H	HR	BB	SO	W-L	Sv	ERA
Howard Ehmke	R	31	34	31	22	0	260.2	285	8	85	95	9-20	1	3.73
Red Ruffing	R	21	37	27	13	3	217.1	253	10	75	64	9-18	1	5.01
Ted Wingfield	R	25	41	26	18	2	254.1	267	11	92	30	12-19	2	3.96
Paul Zahniser	R	28	37	21	7	1	176.2	232	6	89	30	5-12	1	5.15
Jack Quinn†	R	41	19	15	8	0	105.0	140	3	26	24	7-8	0	4.37
Ray Francis†	L	32	6	4	0	0	28.0	44	3	13	4	0-2	0	7.71
Rudy Kallio	R	32	7	4	0	0	18.2	28	0	9	2	1-4	0	7.71
Alex Ferguson†	R	28	5	4	0	0	15.2	22	6	5	5	0-2	1	10.91
Curt Fullerton	R	26	4	2	0	0	22.2	22	1	9	3	0-3	0	3.18
Joe Kiefer	R	25	2	2	0	0	15.0	20	0	9	4	0-2	0	6.00
Oscar Fuhr	L	31	39	6	0	0	91.1	138	7	30	27	0-6	0	6.60
Buster Ross	L	22	33	8	0	0	94.1	119	9	40	15	3-8	0	6.20
Joe Lucey	R	28	7	2	0	0	11.0	18	0	14	2	0-1	0	9.00
Hal Neubauer	R	23	7	0	0	0	10.1	17	2	11	4	1-0	0	12.19
Bob Adams	R	23	2	0	0	0	5.2	10	1	3	1	0-0	0	7.94

»1925 Pittsburgh Pirates 1st NL 95-58 .621 —

Bill McKechnie

Player	Gm by Position	B	Age	G	AB	R	H	2B	3B	HR	RBI	BB	SO	SB	Avg	OBP	Slg
Earl Smith	C96	L	28	109	329	34	103	22	3	8	64	31	13	4	.313	.374	.471
George Grantham	1B102	L	25	114	359	74	117	24	6	8	52	50	29	14	.326	.413	.493
Eddie Moore	2B122,OF15,3B3	R	26	142	547	106	163	29	8	6	77	73	26	19	.298	.383	.413
Pie Traynor	3B150,SS1	R	25	150	591	114	189	39	14	6	106	52	19	15	.320	.377	.464
Glenn Wright	SS153,3B1	R	24	153	614	97	189	32	10	18	121	31	32	3	.308	.341	.480
Kiki Cuyler	OF153	R	26	153	617	144	220	43	26	18	102	58	56	41	.357	.423	.598
Clyde Barnhart	OF138	R	29	142	539	85	175	32	11	4	114	59	25	9	.325	.391	.447
Max Carey	OF130	S	35	133	542	109	186	39	13	5	44	66	19	46	.343	.418	.491
Johnny Gooch	C76	S	27	79	215	24	64	8	4	0	30	20	16	1	.298	.357	.372
Stuffy McInnis	1B46	R	34	59	155	19	57	10	4	0	24	17	1	1	.368	.437	.484
Carson Bigbee	OF42	L	30	66	126	31	30	7	0	0	8	7	8	2	.238	.278	.294
Johnny Rawlings	2B29	R	32	36	110	17	31	7	0	2	13	8	8	0	.282	.336	.400
Al Niehaus†	1B15	R	26	17	64	7	14	8	0	0	7	1	5	0	.219	.242	.344
Fresco Thompson	2B12	R	23	14	37	4	9	2	1	0	8	4	1	2	.243	.317	.351
Roy Spencer	C11	R	25	14	28	1	6	1	0	0	2	1	3	1	.214	.241	.250
Jewel Ens	1B3	R	35	3	5	2	1	0	0	1	2	0	1	0	.200	.200	.800
Mule Haas	OF2	L	21	4	3	1	0	0	0	0	0	0	1	0	.000	.000	.000

Pitcher	T	Age	G	GS	CG	ShO	IP	H	HR	BB	SO	W-L	Sv	ERA
Lee Meadows	R	30	35	31	20	1	255.1	272	11	67	87	19-10	1	3.67
Emil Yde	L	25	33	28	13	0	207.0	254	11	75	41	17-9	4	4.13
Ray Kremer	R	32	40	27	14	0	214.2	232	19	47	62	17-8	2	3.69
Vic Aldridge	R	31	30	26	14	1	213.1	218	15	74	88	15-7	0	3.63
Johnny Morrison	R	29	44	26	10	0	211.0	245	12	60	60	17-14	0	3.88
Babe Adams	R	43	33	10	3	0	101.1	129	7	17	18	6-5	3	5.42
Tom Sheehan†	R	31	23	0	0	0	57.1	63	2	13	13	1-1	2	2.67
Red Oldham	L	31	11	4	3	0	53.0	66	2	18	10	3-2	1	3.91
Bud Culloton	R	29	9	1	0	0	21.0	19	1	1	3	0-1	0	2.57
Don Songer	L	25	8	0	0	0	11.2	14	0	8	4	0-1	0	2.31
Lou Koupal	R	26	6	0	0	0	9.0	14	1	7	0	0-0	0	9.00

1925 New York Giants 2nd NL 86-66 .566 8.5 GB

John McGraw (10-4)/Hughie Jennings (21-11)/John McGraw (55-51)

Player	Gm by Position	B	Age	G	AB	R	H	2B	3B	HR	RBI	BB	SO	SB	Avg	OBP	Slg
Frank Snyder	C96	R	32	107	325	21	78	9	1	11	51	20	49	0	.240	.286	.375
Bill Terry	1B126	L	28	133	489	75	156	31	6	11	70	42	52	4	.319	.374	.474
George Kelly	2B108,1B25,OF17	R	29	147	586	87	181	29	3	20	99	35	54	5	.309	.350	.471
Freddy Lindstrom	3B96,2B1,SS1	R	19	104	356	43	102	15	12	4	33	22	20	5	.287	.332	.430
Travis Jackson	SS110	R	21	112	411	51	117	15	2	9	59	24	43	8	.285	.327	.397
Ross Youngs	OF127,2B3	L	28	130	500	82	132	24	6	6	53	66	51	17	.264	.354	.372
Irish Meusel	OF126	R	32	135	516	82	169	35	8	21	111	26	19	5	.328	.363	.548
Billy Southworth	OF119	L	32	123	473	79	138	19	5	6	44	51	11	6	.292	.363	.391
Frankie Frisch	3B46,2B42,SS39	S	26	120	502	89	166	26	6	11	48	32	14	21	.331	.374	.472
Hack Wilson	OF50	R	25	62	180	28	43	7	4	6	30	21	33	5	.239	.322	.422
Hank Gowdy	C41	R	35	47	114	14	37	4	3	3	19	12	7	0	.325	.389	.491
Jack Bentley	P29,OF3,1B1	L	30	64	99	10	30	5	2	3	18	9	11	0	.303	.361	.485
Grover Hartley	C37,1B8	R	36	46	95	9	30	1	1	0	8	8	3	2	.316	.375	.347
Frank Walker	OF21	R	30	39	81	12	18	1	0	1	5	9	11	1	.222	.308	.272
Heine Groh	3B16,2B2	R	35	25	65	7	15	4	0	0	4	6	3	0	.231	.296	.292
Doc Farrell	SS13,3B7,2B1	R	23	27	56	6	12	1	0	0	4	4	6	0	.214	.267	.232
Mickey Devine	C11,3B1	R	33	21	33	6	9	3	0	0	4	2	3	0	.273	.314	.364
Hugh McMullen	C5	S	23	5	15	1	2	1	0	0	0	0	3	0	.133	.133	.200
Al Moore	OF2	R	22	2	8	0	1	0	0	0	0	1	2	0	.125	.222	.125
Chick Davies	P2,OF1	L	33	4	6	1	0	0	0	0	0	0	1	0	.000	.000	.000
Blackie Carter	OF1	R	22	1	4	0	0	0	0	0	0	0	1	0	.000	.000	.000
Earl Webb		L	27	4	3	0	0	0	0	0	0	1	1	0	.000	.250	.000
Pip Koehler	OF3	R	23	12	2	1	0	0	0	0	0	0	1	0	.000	.000	.000

Pitcher	T	Age	G	GS	CG	ShO	IP	H	HR	BB	SO	W-L	Sv	ERA
Jack Scott	R	33	36	28	18	2	239.2	251	10	55	87	14-15	3	3.15
Virgil Barnes	R	28	32	27	17	1	221.2	242	9	53	53	15-11	2	3.53
Jack Bentley	L	30	28	22	11	0	157.0	200	10	59	47	11-9	0	5.04
Kent Greenfield	R	22	29	21	12	0	171.2	195	4	64	66	12-8	0	3.88
Art Nehf	L	32	29	20	8	1	155.0	193	7	50	63	11-9	1	3.77
Hugh McQuillan	R	27	14	11	2	0	70.0	95	9	23	23	2-3	1	6.04
F. Fitzsimmons	R	23	10	8	6	1	74.2	70	4	18	17	6-3	0	2.65
Chick Davies	L	33	2	1	0	0	7.1	13	0	4	5	0-0	0	6.14
Wayland Dean	R	23	33	14	6	1	151.1	169	13	50	53	10-7	1	4.64
Walter Huntzinger	R	26	26	1	0	0	64.1	68	3	17	19	5-1	0	3.50
John Wisner	R	25	25	0	0	0	40.1	33	4	14	13	0-0	0	3.79
Harry Baldwin	R	25	1	0	0	0	1.0	3	0	1	0	0-0	0	9.00

1925 Cincinnati Reds 3rd NL 80-73 .523 15.0 GB

Jack Hendricks

Player	Gm by Position	B	Age	G	AB	R	H	2B	3B	HR	RBI	BB	SO	SB	Avg	OBP	Slg
Bubbles Hargrave	C84	R	32	87	273	28	82	13	6	2	33	25	23	4	.300	.361	.414
Walter Holke†	1B65	S	32	65	232	24	65	8	4	1	20	17	12	1	.280	.329	.362
Hughie Critz	2B144	R	24	144	541	74	150	14	8	2	51	34	17	13	.277	.321	.344
Babe Pinelli	3B109,SS17	R	29	130	492	68	139	33	6	2	49	22	28	8	.283	.316	.386
Ike Caveney	SS111	R	30	115	358	38	89	9	5	2	47	28	31	2	.249	.303	.318
Curt Walker	OF141	L	28	145	509	86	162	22	16	6	71	57	31	14	.318	.387	.460
Edd Roush	OF134	L	32	134	540	91	183	28	16	8	83	35	14	22	.339	.383	.494
Billy Zitzmann	OF89,SS1	R	29	104	301	53	76	13	3	0	21	35	22	11	.252	.342	.316
Rube Bressler	1B52,OF38	R	30	97	319	43	111	17	6	4	61	40	16	9	.348	.424	.476
Elmer Smith	OF80	L	32	96	284	47	77	13	7	8	46	28	20	6	.271	.339	.451
Chuck Dressen	3B47,2B5,OF4	R	26	76	215	35	59	8	2	3	19	12	4	5	.274	.319	.372
Sammy Bohne	SS49,2B10,OF4*	R	28	73	214	24	55	9	1	2	24	14	14	6	.257	.303	.336
Al Niehaus†	1B45	R	26	51	147	16	44	10	2	0	14	13	10	1	.299	.360	.395
Ivy Wingo	C55	L	34	55	146	6	30	7	0	0	12	11	8	1	.205	.261	.253
Ernie Krueger	C30	R	34	37	88	7	27	4	0	1	7	6	8	1	.307	.351	.386
Joe Schultz†	OF15	R	31	33	62	6	20	3	1	0	13	3	1	3	.323	.354	.403
Astyanax Douglass	C7	L	25	7	17	1	3	0	0	0	1	1	3	0	.176	.222	.176
Frank Bruggy	C6	R	34	6	14	2	3	0	0	0	1	2	0	0	.214	.313	.214
Jimmy Hudgens	1B3	L	22	3	7	0	3	1	1	0	0	1	1	0	.429	.500	.857
Hi Myers†	OF3	R	36	3	6	1	1	1	0	0	0	0	0	0	.167	.167	.333
Boob Fowler		L	24	6	5	0	2	1	0	0	2	0	1	0	.400	.400	.600
Ollie Klee	OF1	L	25	3	1	0	0	0	0	0	0	0	1	0	.000	.000	.000
Tom Sullivan	C1	R	18	1	1	0	0	0	0	0	0	0	0	0	.000	.000	.000

S. Bohne, 2 G at 1B, 2 G at 3B

Pitcher	T	Age	G	GS	CG	ShO	IP	H	HR	BB	SO	W-L	Sv	ERA
Pete Donohue	R	24	42	38	27	3	301.0	310	3	49	78	21-14	2	3.08
Dolf Luque	R	34	36	36	22	4	291.0	263	7	78	140	16-18	0	2.63
Eppa Rixey	L	34	39	36	22	2	287.1	302	8	47	69	21-11	1	2.88
Marv Goodwin	R	34	4	3	2	0	20.2	26	2	5	4	0-2	0	4.79
Jakie May	L	29	36	12	7	1	137.1	146	3	45	74	8-9	2	3.87
Rube Benton	L	38	33	16	6	1	146.2	182	3	34	36	9-10	1	4.05
Harry Biemiller	R	27	23	1	0	0	47.0	45	2	21	9	0-1	2	4.02
Neal Brady	R	28	20	3	2	0	63.2	73	4	20	12	1-3	1	4.66
Carl Mays	R	33	12	5	3	0	51.2	60	0	13	10	3-5	2	3.31
Tom Sheehan†	R	31	10	3	1	0	29.0	37	3	12	5	1-0	1	8.07
Pedro Dibut	R	32	1	0	0	0	0.0	3	0	0	0	0-0	0	—

1925 St. Louis Cardinals 4th NL 77-76 .503 18.0 GB

Branch Rickey (13-25)/Rogers Hornsby (64-51)

Player	Gm by Position	B	Age	G	AB	R	H	2B	3B	HR	RBI	BB	SO	SB	Avg	OBP	Slg
Bob O'Farrell†	C92	R	28	94	317	37	88	13	2	3	32	46	26	0	.278	.373	.360
Jim Bottomley	1B153	L	25	153	619	92	227	44	12	21	128	47	36	3	.367	.413	.578
Rogers Hornsby	2B136	R	29	138	504	133	203	41	10	39	143	83	39	5	.403	.489	.756
Les Bell	3B153,SS1	R	23	153	586	80	167	29	9	11	88	43	47	4	.285	.334	.422
Specs Toporcer	SS66,2B7	L	26	83	268	38	76	13	4	2	26	36	15	7	.284	.373	.384
Ray Blades	OF114,3B1	R	28	122	462	112	158	37	8	12	57	59	47	6	.342	.423	.535
Chick Hafey	OF88	R	22	93	358	36	108	25	2	5	57	10	29	3	.302	.321	.425
Heinie Mueller	OF72	L	25	78	243	33	76	16	4	1	26	17	11	0	.313	.365	.424
Ralph Shinners	OF66	R	29	74	251	39	74	9	2	7	36	12	19	8	.295	.330	.430
Jack Smith	OF64	L	30	80	243	53	61	11	4	4	31	19	13	20	.251	.308	.379
Max Flack	OF59	L	35	79	241	23	60	7	8	0	28	21	9	5	.249	.309	.344
Jimmy Cooney	SS37,2B15,OF1	R	30	54	187	27	51	11	2	0	18	4	5	1	.273	.292	.353
Tommy Thevenow	SS50	R	21	50	175	17	47	7	2	0	17	7	12	3	.269	.301	.331
Walter Schmidt	C31	R	38	37	87	9	22	2	1	0	9	4	3	1	.253	.293	.299
Taylor Douthit	OF21	R	24	30	73	13	20	3	1	1	8	2	6	0	.274	.312	.384
Mike Gonzalez†	C22	R	34	22	71	9	22	3	0	0	4	6	2	1	.310	.380	.352
Wattie Holm	OF13	R	23	13	58	10	12	1	1	0	2	3	1	1	.207	.246	.259
Bill Warwick	C13	R	27	13	41	8	12	1	2	1	6	5	5	0	.293	.370	.488
Ernie Vick	C9	R	24	14	32	3	6	2	1	0	3	3	1	0	.188	.257	.313
Howard Freigau†	SS7,2B1	R	22	9	26	2	4	0	0	0	0	2	1	0	.154	.214	.154
Hi Myers†		R	36	2	2	1	1	0	0	0	0	0	0	0	.500	.500	.500

Pitcher	T	Age	G	GS	CG	ShO	IP	H	HR	BB	SO	W-L	Sv	ERA
Jesse Haines	R	31	29	25	15	0	207.0	234	11	52	63	13-14	0	4.57
Flint Rhem	R	24	30	23	8	1	170.0	204	16	58	66	8-13	1	4.92
Allen Sothoron	R	32	28	23	8	2	155.2	173	7	63	67	10-10	0	4.05
Bill Sherdel	L	28	32	21	17	2	200.0	216	8	42	53	15-6	1	3.11
Leo Dickerman	R	28	29	20	7	2	130.2	135	10	79	40	4-11	1	5.58
Art Reinhart	L	26	20	16	15	1	144.2	149	7	47	26	11-5	0	3.05
Duster Mails	L	30	21	14	9	0	131.0	145	11	58	49	7-7	0	4.60
Eddie Dyer	L	24	27	5	1	0	82.1	93	4	24	25	4-3	3	4.15
Pea Ridge Day	R	25	17	4	1	0	40.0	53	5	7	13	2-4	1	6.30
Johnny Stuart	R	24	15	1	1	0	47.0	52	6	24	14	2-2	0	6.13
Wild Bill Hallahan	L	22	6	0	0	0	15.1	14	0	11	8	1-0	0	3.52
Ed Clough	L	18	3	1	0	0	10.0	11	1	5	3	0-1	0	8.10
Gil Paulsen	R	22	1	0	0	0	2.0	1	0	0	1	0-0	0	0.00

1925 Boston Braves 5th NL 70-83 .458 25.0 GB

Dave Bancroft

Player	Gm by Position	B	Age	G	AB	R	H	2B	3B	HR	RBI	BB	SO	SB	Avg	OBP	Slg
Frank Gibson	C86,1B2	S	34	104	316	36	88	23	5	2	50	15	28	3	.278	.313	.402
Dick Burrus	1B151	L	27	152	588	82	200	41	4	5	87	51	29	8	.340	.396	.449
Doc Gautreau†	2B68	R	23	68	279	45	73	13	3	0	23	35	13	11	.262	.346	.330
William Marriott	3B89,OF1	L	31	103	370	37	99	9	1	1	40	28	26	3	.268	.323	.305
Dave Bancroft	SS125	S	34	128	479	75	153	29	8	2	49	64	22	7	.319	.400	.426
Jimmy Welsh	OF116,2B3	L	22	122	484	69	151	25	8	7	63	20	24	7	.312	.350	.440
Gus Felix	OF114	R	30	121	459	60	141	25	7	2	66	30	34	5	.307	.356	.405
Dave Harris	OF90	R	24	92	340	49	90	8	7	5	36	27	44	6	.265	.321	.374
Bernie Neis	OF87	S	29	106	355	47	101	20	2	5	45	38	19	8	.285	.354	.394
Ernie Padgett	2B47,SS18,3B7	R	26	86	256	31	78	9	7	0	29	14	14	3	.305	.341	.395
Mickey O'Neil	C69	R	25	70	222	29	57	6	5	2	30	21	16	1	.257	.327	.356
Andy High†	3B60,2B1	L	27	60	219	31	63	11	1	4	28	24	2	3	.288	.361	.402
Les Mann	OF57	R	31	60	184	27	63	11	4	2	20	5	11	6	.342	.373	.478
Bob Smith	SS21,2B15,P13*	R	30	58	174	17	49	9	4	0	23	5	6	2	.282	.302	.379
Johnny Cooney	P31,1B3,OF1	R	24	54	103	17	33	7	0	0	13	3	6	1	.320	.346	.388
Oscar Siemer	C16	R	23	16	46	5	14	0	1	1	6	1	0	0	.304	.319	.413
Hod Kibbie	2B8,SS3	R	21	11	41	5	11	2	0	0	2	5	6	0	.268	.348	.317
Frank Wilson	OF10	L	24	12	31	3	13	1	1	0	0	4	1	2	.419	.486	.516
Abie Hood	2B5	L	22	5	21	2	6	2	0	1	2	1	0	0	.286	.318	.524
Shanty Hogan	OF5	R	19	9	21	2	6	1	1	0	3	1	3	0	.286	.318	.429
Red Lucas	2B6	L	23	6	20	1	3	0	0	0	2	2	4	0	.150	.227	.150
Herb Thomas	2B5	R	23	5	17	2	4	0	1	0	2	2	0	0	.235	.350	.353
Casey Stengel	OF1	L	34	12	13	0	1	0	0	0	2	1	2	0	.077	.143	.077
Ed Sperber		L	30	2	2	0	0	0	0	0	0	0	0	0	.000	.000	.000
Dee Cousineau	C1	R	26	1	0	0	0	0	0	0	0	0	0	0	—	—	—

B. Smith, 1 G at OF

Pitcher	T	Age	G	GS	CG	ShO	IP	H	HR	BB	SO	W-L	Sv	ERA
Johnny Cooney	L	24	31	29	20	2	245.2	267	18	50	65	14-14	0	3.48
Jesse Barnes	R	32	32	28	17	0	216.1	255	14	63	55	11-16	0	4.53
Skinny Graham	R	25	34	23	5	0	157.0	177	6	62	32	7-12	1	4.41
Larry Benton	R	27	31	21	16	2	183.1	170	5	70	49	14-7	1	3.09
Joe Genewich	R	28	34	21	10	0	169.0	185	4	41	34	12-10	0	3.99
Bob Smith	R	30	13	10	6	0	92.2	110	6	36	19	5-3	0	4.47
Rosy Ryan	R	27	37	7	1	0	122.2	152	7	52	48	2-8	2	6.31
Rube Marquard	L	38	26	8	0	0	72.0	105	5	27	19	2-8	0	5.75
Ike Kamp	L	24	24	4	1	0	58.1	68	0	35	20	2-4	0	5.09
Bill Vargus	L	25	11	2	1	0	36.1	45	1	13	5	1-1	0	3.96
Joe Batchelder	L	26	4	0	0	0	7.0	10	0	1	2	0-0	0	5.14
Bill Anderson	L	29	2	0	0	0	2.2	5	0	2	1	0-0	0	10.13
Foster Edwards	R	21	1	0	0	0	2.0	6	0	1	1	0-0	0	9.00
Joe Ogrodowski	R	18	1	0	0	0	1.0	6	0	3	0	0-0	0	54.00
Tim McNamara	R	26	1	0	0	0	0.2	6	0	2	1	0-0	0	81.00

1925 Philadelphia Phillies 6th NL 68-85 .444 27.0 GB

Art Fletcher

Player	Gm by Position	B	Age	G	AB	R	H	2B	3B	HR	RBI	BB	SO	SB	Avg	OBP	Slg
Jimmie Wilson	C89,OF1	R	24	108	335	42	110	19	3	3	54	32	25	5	.328	.390	.430
Chicken Hawks	1B90	L	29	105	320	52	103	15	5	5	45	32	33	3	.322	.387	.447
Bernie Friberg†	2B77,3B14,P1	R	25	91	304	41	82	12	1	5	22	39	35	1	.270	.353	.365
Clarence Huber	3B120	R	28	124	436	46	124	28	5	5	54	17	33	3	.284	.311	.406
Heinie Sand	SS143	R	27	148	496	69	138	30	7	3	55	64	65	1	.278	.364	.385
George Harper	OF126	L	33	132	495	86	173	35	7	18	97	28	32	10	.349	.391	.558
Cy Williams	OF96	L	37	107	314	78	104	11	5	13	60	53	34	4	.331	.435	.522
George Burns	OF88	R	35	88	349	65	102	29	1	1	22	33	20	4	.292	.353	.390
Lew Fonseca	2B69,1B55	R	26	126	467	78	149	30	5	7	60	21	42	6	.319	.352	.450
Freddy Leach	OF65	L	27	65	292	47	91	15	4	5	28	5	21	1	.312	.323	.442
Russ Wrightstone	OF45,SS12,3B11*	L	32	92	286	48	99	18	5	14	61	19	18	0	.346	.389	.591
Butch Henline	C68,OF1	R	30	93	263	43	80	12	5	8	48	24	16	3	.304	.380	.479
Johnny Mokan	OF68	R	29	75	209	30	69	11	2	6	42	27	9	3	.330	.417	.488
Wally Kimmick	SS28,3B21,2B13	R	28	70	141	16	43	3	2	1	10	22	26	0	.305	.399	.376
Clarence Mitchell	P32,1B2	L	34	52	92	7	18	2	0	0	13	5	9	2	.196	.237	.217
Walter Holke†	1B23	S	32	39	86	11	21	5	0	1	17	3	6	0	.244	.270	.337
Joe Schultz†	OF20	R	31	24	64	10	22	6	0	0	8	4	1	1	.344	.382	.438
Lew Wendell	C9	R	33	18	26	0	2	0	0	0	3	1	3	0	.077	.111	.077
George Durning	OF4	R	27	5	14	3	5	0	0	0	1	2	1	0	.357	.438	.357
Lenny Metz	SS9,2B2	R	25	11	14	1	0	0	0	0	0	0	2	0	.000	.000	.000
Benny Meyer	2B1	R	37	1	1	1	1	1	0	0	0	0	0	0	1.000	1.000	2.000

R. Wrightstone, 10 G at 2B, 6 G at 1B

Pitcher	T	Age	G	GS	CG	ShO	IP	H	HR	BB	SO	W-L	Sv	ERA
Jimmy Ring	R	30	38	37	21	1	270.0	325	14	119	93	14-16	0	4.37
Hal Carlson	R	33	35	32	18	4	234.0	281	19	52	80	13-14	0	4.23
Clarence Mitchell	L	34	32	26	12	1	199.1	245	23	51	46	10-17	1	5.28
Art Decatur†	R	31	25	15	4	0	128.0	170	13	35	31	4-13	2	5.27
Claude Willoughby	R	26	3	3	1	0	23.0	26	0	11	6	2-1	0	1.96
Huck Betts	R	28	35	7	1	0	97.1	146	10	38	28	4-5	1	5.55
Johnny Couch	R	34	34	7	2	1	94.1	112	9	39	11	5-6	2	5.44
Jack Knight	R	30	33	11	4	0	105.1	161	14	36	19	7-6	3	6.84
Ray Pierce	L	28	23	8	4	0	90.0	134	7	24	18	5-4	0	5.50
Dutch Ulrich	R	25	21	4	2	1	65.0	73	6	12	29	3-3	0	3.05
Skinny O'Neal	R	26	11	1	0	0	20.1	35	2	12	6	0-0	0	9.30
Dana Fillingim	R	31	5	1	0	0	8.2	19	0	6	2	1-0	0	10.38
Roy Crumpler	L	28	3	1	0	0	4.2	8	0	2	1	0-0	0	7.71
Bob Vines	R	28	3	0	0	0	4.0	9	0	3	0	0-0	0	11.25
Bill Hubbell†	R	28	2	0	0	0	2.2	5	0	1	0	0-0	0	0.00
Bernie Friberg	R	25	1	0	0	0	4.0	4	0	3	1	0-0	0	4.50

1925 Brooklyn Dodgers 6th NL 68-85 .444 27.0 GB

Wilbert Robinson

Player	Gm by Position	B	Age	G	AB	R	H	2B	3B	HR	RBI	BB	SO	SB	Avg	OBP	Slg
Zack Taylor	C96	R	26	109	352	33	109	16	4	3	44	17	19	0	.310	.343	.403
Jack Fournier	1B145	L	35	145	545	99	191	21	16	22	130	86	39	4	.350	.446	.569
Milt Stock	2B141,3B5	R	31	146	615	98	202	28	9	1	62	38	28	8	.328	.368	.408
Jimmy Johnston	3B81,OF20,1B8*	R	35	123	431	63	128	13	3	2	43	45	15	7	.297	.369	.355
Johnny Mitchell	SS90	S	30	97	336	45	84	8	3	0	18	28	19	2	.250	.308	.292
Eddie Brown	OF153	R	33	153	618	88	189	39	11	5	99	22	18	3	.306	.332	.429
Zack Wheat	OF149	L	37	150	616	125	221	42	14	14	103	45	22	3	.359	.403	.541
Dick Cox	OF111	R	27	122	434	68	143	23	10	7	64	37	29	4	.329	.382	.477
Cotton Tierney	3B61,1B1,2B1	R	31	93	265	27	68	14	4	2	39	12	23	0	.257	.294	.362
Hod Ford	SS66	R	27	66	216	32	59	11	0	1	15	26	15	0	.273	.357	.338
Hank DeBerry	C55	R	30	67	193	26	50	8	1	2	24	16	8	2	.259	.322	.342
Dick Loftus	OF38	L	24	51	131	16	31	6	0	0	13	5	5	2	.237	.275	.282
Andy High†	2B11,3B11,SS3	L	27	44	115	11	23	4	1	0	6	14	5	0	.200	.287	.252
Charlie Hargreaves	C18,1B2	R	28	45	83	9	23	3	1	0	13	6	1	1	.277	.326	.337
Chuck Corgan	SS14	S	22	14	47	4	8	1	1	0	0	3	9	0	.170	.220	.234
Roy Hutson	OF4	L	23	7	8	1	4	0	0	0	1	1	1	0	.500	.556	.500
Tommy Griffith†	OF2	L	35	7	4	2	0	0	0	0	0	3	2	1	.000	.429	.000
Jerry Standaert		R	23	1	1	0	0	0	0	0	0	0	1	0	.000	.000	.000
Bob Barrett†		R	26	1	1	0	0	0	0	0	1	0	0	0	.000	.000	.000

J. Johnston, 2 G at SS

Pitcher	T	Age	G	GS	CG	ShO	IP	H	HR	BB	SO	W-L	Sv	ERA
Dazzy Vance	R	34	31	31	26	4	265.1	247	8	66	221	22-9	0	3.53
Burleigh Grimes	R	31	33	31	19	0	246.2	305	15	102	73	12-19	0	5.04
Rube Ehrhardt	R	30	36	24	12	0	207.2	239	10	62	47	10-14	1	5.03
Tiny Osborne	R	32	41	22	10	0	175.0	210	9	75	59	8-15	1	4.94
Jesse Petty	L	30	28	22	7	0	153.0	188	15	47	39	9-9	0	4.88
Bob McGraw	R	30	2	2	2	0	19.2	14	0	13	3	0-2	0	3.20
Andy Rush	R	35	4	2	0	0	9.2	16	3	5	4	0-1	0	9.31
Bill Hubbell†	R	28	33	5	3	0	86.2	120	8	24	16	3-6	1	5.30
Joe Oeschger	R	34	21	3	1	0	37.0	60	2	19	6	1-2	0	6.08
Lloyd Brown	L	20	17	5	1	0	63.1	79	1	25	23	0-3	0	4.12
Guy Cantrell	R	21	14	3	1	0	36.0	42	0	14	13	1-0	0	3.00
Nelson Greene	L	24	11	0	0	0	22.0	45	4	7	4	2-0	1	10.64
Hank Thormahlen	L	28	5	2	0	0	16.0	22	0	9	7	0-3	0	3.94
Jumbo Elliott	L	24	3	1	0	0	10.2	17	0	9	3	0-2	0	8.44
Jim Roberts	R	29	1	0	0	0	1.0	1	0	0	0	0-0	0	0.00
Art Decatur†	R	31	1	0	0	0	1.0	3	0	0	0	0-0	0	18.00

1925 Chicago Cubs 8th NL 68-86 .442 27.5 GB

Bill Killefer (33-42)/Rabbit Maranville (23-30)/George Gibson (12-14)

Player	Gm by Position	B	Age	G	AB	R	H	2B	3B	HR	RBI	BB	SO	SB	Avg	OBP	Slg
Gabby Hartnett	C110	R	24	117	398	61	115	28	3	24	67	36	77	1	.289	.351	.555
Charlie Grimm	1B139	L	26	141	519	73	159	29	5	10	76	38	25	4	.306	.354	.439
Sparky Adams	2B144,SS5	R	30	149	627	95	180	29	8	2	48	44	15	26	.287	.341	.368
Howard Freigau†	3B96,SS17,1B7	R	22	117	476	77	146	22	10	8	71	30	31	10	.307	.349	.445
Rabbit Maranville	SS74	R	33	75	266	37	62	10	3	0	23	29	20	6	.233	.308	.293
Cliff Heathcote	OF99	L	27	109	380	57	100	14	5	5	39	39	26	15	.263	.343	.366
Mandy Brooks	OF89	R	27	90	349	55	98	25	7	14	72	19	28	10	.281	.322	.513
Tommy Griffith†	OF60	L	35	76	235	38	67	12	1	7	27	21	11	2	.285	.346	.434
Art Jahn	OF58	R	29	58	226	30	68	10	8	0	37	11	20	2	.301	.336	.416
Mike Gonzalez†	C50,1B9,2B1	R	34	70	197	26	52	13	1	3	18	13	15	2	.264	.316	.386
Butch Weis	OF47	L	24	67	180	16	48	5	3	2	25	23	22	2	.267	.350	.361
Pinky Pittenger	3B24,SS24	R	26	59	173	21	54	7	2	0	15	12	7	5	.312	.364	.376
Bernie Friberg†	3B26,OF12,1B6*	R	25	44	152	12	39	5	3	1	16	14	22	0	.257	.327	.349
Jigger Statz	OF37	R	27	38	148	21	38	6	3	2	14	11	16	4	.257	.317	.378
Denver Grigsby	OF39	L	24	51	137	20	35	5	0	0	20	19	12	1	.255	.346	.292
Ike McAuley	SS37	R	33	37	125	10	35	7	2	0	11	11	12	1	.280	.343	.368
Hack Miller	OF21	R	31	24	86	10	24	3	2	2	9	2	9	0	.279	.303	.430
Ralph Michaels	3B15,1B1,2B1*	R	23	22	50	10	14	1	0	0	6	6	9	1	.280	.357	.300
Alex Metzler	OF9	L	22	9	38	2	7	2	0	0	2	3	7	0	.184	.244	.237
Joe Munson	OF9	L	25	9	35	5	13	3	1	0	3	3	1	1	.371	.436	.514
Bob Barrett†	3B6,2B4	R	26	14	32	1	10	1	0	0	7	1	4	1	.313	.333	.344
Gale Staley	2B7	L	26	7	26	2	11	2	0	0	3	2	1	0	.423	.464	.500
Bob O'Farrell†	C3	R	28	17	22	2	4	0	1	0	3	2	5	0	.182	.250	.273
Chink Taylor	OF2	R	27	8	6	2	0	0	0	0	0	0	0	0	.000	.000	.000
John Churry	C3	R	24	3	6	1	3	0	0	0	1	0	0	0	.500	.500	.500
Teddy Kearns	1B3	R	25	3	2	0	1	0	0	0	0	0	0	0	.500	.500	.500
Mel Kerr		L	22	1	0	1	0	0	0	0	0	0	0	0	—	—	—

B. Friberg, 2 G at SS; R. Michaels, 1 G at SS

Pitcher	T	Age	G	GS	CG	ShO	IP	H	HR	BB	SO	W-L	Sv	ERA
Sheriff Blake	R	25	36	31	14	0	231.1	260	17	114	93	10-18	2	4.86
Pete Alexander	R	38	32	30	20	1	236.0	270	14	29	63	15-11	0	3.39
Wilbur Cooper	L	33	32	26	13	0	212.1	249	18	61	41	12-14	0	4.28
Tony Kaufmann	R	24	31	23	14	2	196.0	221	9	77	49	13-13	2	4.50
George Milstead	L	22	5	3	1	0	21.0	26	0	8	7	1-1	0	3.00
Guy Bush	R	23	42	15	5	0	182.0	213	15	52	76	6-13	4	4.30
Vic Keen	R	26	30	8	1	0	83.1	125	8	41	19	2-6	1	6.26
Percy Jones	L	25	28	13	6	1	124.0	123	12	71	60	6-6	0	4.65
Elmer Jacobs	R	32	18	4	1	1	55.2	63	9	22	19	2-3	1	5.17
Herb Brett	R	25	10	1	0	0	17.1	12	0	3	6	1-1	0	3.63
Jumbo Brown	R	18	2	0	0	0	6.0	5	0	4	0	0-0	0	3.00
George Stueland	R	26	2	0	0	0	3.0	2	0	3	2	0-0	0	3.00
Bob Osborn	R	22	1	0	0	0	2.0	6	0	0	0	0-0	0	0.00

»1926 New York Yankees 1st AL 91-63 .591 —

Miller Huggins

Player	Gm by Position	B	Age	G	AB	R	H	2B	3B	HR	RBI	BB	SO	SB	Avg	OBP	Slg
Pat Collins	C100	R	29	102	290	41	83	11	3	7	35	73	56	3	.286	.433	.417
Lou Gehrig	1B155	L	23	155	572	135	179	47	20	16	112	105	73	6	.313	.420	.549
Tony Lazzeri	2B145,SS5,3B1	R	22	155	589	79	162	28	14	18	114	54	96	16	.275	.338	.462
Joe Dugan	3B122	R	29	123	434	39	125	19	5	1	64	25	16	2	.288	.328	.362
Mark Koenig	SS141	S	21	147	617	93	167	26	8	5	62	43	37	4	.271	.319	.363
Babe Ruth	OF149,1B2	L	31	152	495	139	184	30	5	47	146	144	76	11	.372	.516	.737
Earle Combs	OF145	L	27	145	606	113	181	31	12	8	55	47	23	8	.299	.352	.429
Bob Meusel	OF107	R	29	108	413	73	130	22	3	12	81	37	32	16	.315	.373	.470
Ben Paschal	OF76	R	30	96	258	46	74	12	3	7	32	26	35	7	.287	.354	.438
Mike Gazella	3B45,SS11	R	29	66	168	21	39	6	0	0	20	25	24	2	.232	.335	.268
Hank Severeid†	C40	R	35	41	127	13	34	8	1	0	13	13	4	1	.268	.336	.346
Benny Bengough	C35	R	27	36	84	9	32	6	0	0	14	7	4	1	.381	.435	.452
Roy Carlyle†	OF15	L	25	35	53	3	20	5	1	0	11	4	9	0	.377	.431	.509
Aaron Ward	2B4,3B1	R	29	22	31	5	10	2	0	0	3	2	6	0	.323	.364	.387
Spencer Adams	2B4,3B1	L	28	28	25	7	3	1	0	0	1	3	7	1	.120	.214	.160
Bill Skiff	C6	R	30	6	11	0	1	0	0	0	0	0	1	0	.091	.091	.091
Nick Cullop		R	25	2	2	0	1	0	0	0	0	0	1	0	.500	.500	.500
Fred Merkle	1B1	R	37	1	2	0	0	0	0	0	0	0	1	0	.000	.000	.000
Kiddo Davis	OF1	R	24	1	0	0	0	0	0	0	0	0	0	0	—	—	—
Honey Barnes	C1	L	26	1	0	0	0	0	0	0	0	1	0	0	—	1.000	—

Pitcher	T	Age	G	GS	CG	ShO	IP	H	HR	BB	SO	W-L	Sv	ERA
Herb Pennock	L	32	40	33	19	1	266.1	294	11	43	78	23-11	2	3.62
Urban Shocker	R	35	41	33	19	0	258.1	272	13	71	59	19-11	2	3.38
Waite Hoyt	R	26	40	27	12	1	217.2	224	4	62	79	16-12	4	3.85
Sad Sam Jones	R	33	39	23	6	1	161.0	186	6	80	69	9-8	5	4.98
Dutch Ruether†	L	32	5	5	1	0	36.0	32	0	18	8	2-3	0	3.50
Garland Braxton	L	26	37	1	0	0	67.1	71	1	19	30	5-1	2	2.67
Myles Thomas	R	28	33	13	3	0	140.1	140	6	65	38	6-6	0	4.23
Bob Shawkey	R	35	29	10	3	1	104.1	102	8	37	63	8-7	3	3.62
Walter Beall	R	26	20	9	1	0	81.2	71	2	68	56	2-4	1	3.53
Herb McQuaid	R	27	17	1	0	0	38.1	48	5	13	6	1-0	0	6.10
Hank Johnson	R	20	1	0	0	0	1.0	2	0	2	0	0-0	1	18.00

1926 Cleveland Indians 2nd AL 88-66 .571 3.0 GB

Tris Speaker

Player	Gm by Position	B	Age	G	AB	R	H	2B	3B	HR	RBI	BB	SO	SB	Avg	OBP	Slg
Luke Sewell	C125	R	25	126	433	41	103	16	4	0	46	36	27	9	.238	.302	.293
George Burns	1B151	R	33	151	603	97	216	64	3	4	114	28	33	13	.358	.394	.494
Freddy Spurgeon	2B149	R	25	149	614	101	181	31	3	0	49	27	36	7	.295	.327	.355
Rube Lutzke	3B142	R	28	142	475	42	124	28	6	0	59	34	35	6	.261	.313	.345
Joe Sewell	SS154	L	27	154	578	91	187	41	5	4	85	65	6	17	.324	.399	.433
Homer Summa	OF154	L	27	154	581	74	179	31	6	4	76	47	9	15	.308	.368	.403
Tris Speaker	OF149	L	38	150	539	96	164	52	8	7	86	94	15	6	.304	.408	.469
Charlie Jamieson	OF143	L	33	143	555	89	166	33	7	2	45	53	22	9	.299	.361	.395
Glenn Myatt	C35	L	28	56	117	14	29	5	2	0	13	13	13	1	.248	.323	.325
Ike Eichrodt	OF27	R	23	37	80	14	25	7	1	0	7	2	11	1	.313	.329	.425
Ernie Padgett	3B29,SS2	R	27	36	62	7	13	0	1	0	6	8	3	1	.210	.300	.242
Pat McNulty		L	27	48	56	3	14	2	1	0	6	5	9	0	.250	.311	.321
Cliff Lee	OF9,C3	R	29	21	40	4	7	1	0	1	2	6	8	0	.175	.283	.275
Lee Lacy	2B11,3B2	R	29	13	24	2	4	0	0	1	2	2	6	0	.167	.259	.292
Ray Knode	1B11	L	25	31	24	6	8	1	1	0	2	2	3	0	.333	.385	.458
Chick Autry	C3	R	23	3	7	1	1	0	0	0	0	1	0	0	.143	.250	.143
Johnny Hodapp	3B3	R	20	3	5	0	1	0	0	0	0	0	1	0	.200	.200	.200

Pitcher	T	Age	G	GS	CG	ShO	IP	H	HR	BB	SO	W-L	Sv	ERA
George Uhle	R	27	39	36	32	3	318.1	300	7	118	159	27-11	1	2.83
Dutch Levsen	R	28	33	31	18	2	237.1	235	11	85	53	16-13	0	3.41
Joe Shaute	L	26	34	25	15	1	206.2	215	9	65	47	14-10	1	3.53
Sherry Smith	L	35	27	24	16	1	188.1	214	8	31	25	11-10	0	3.73
Garland Buckeye	L	28	32	18	5	1	165.2	160	3	69	36	6-9	0	3.10
Jake Miller	L	28	18	11	5	3	82.2	99	1	18	24	7-4	1	3.27
Benn Karr	R	32	30	7	4	0	113.1	137	9	41	23	5-6	1	5.00
Willis Hudlin	R	20	8	2	1	0	32.1	25	1	13	6	1-3	0	2.78
Ray Benge	R	24	8	0	0	0	12.2	15	0	4	3	1-0	0	3.55
Norm Lehr	R	25	4	0	0	0	14.2	11	0	4	4	0-0	0	3.07
Byron Speece	R	29	2	0	0	0	3.0	1	0	2	1	0-0	0	0.00

1926 Philadelphia Athletics 3rd AL 83-67 .553 6.0 GB

Connie Mack

Player	Gm by Position	B	Age	G	AB	R	H	2B	3B	HR	RBI	BB	SO	SB	Avg	OBP	Slg
Mickey Cochrane	C115	L	23	120	370	50	101	8	9	8	47	56	15	5	.273	.369	.408
Jim Poole	1B101	L	31	112	361	49	106	23	5	8	63	23	25	4	.294	.339	.452
Max Bishop	2B119	L	26	122	400	77	106	20	2	0	33	116	41	4	.265	.431	.325
Jimmy Dykes	3B77,2B44,SS1	R	29	124	429	54	123	32	5	1	44	49	34	6	.287	.370	.392
Chick Galloway	SS133	R	29	133	408	37	98	13	6	0	49	37	17	8	.240	.295	.301
Al Simmons	OF147	R	24	147	581	90	199	53	10	19	109	48	49	10	.343	.394	.566
Bill Lamar	OF107	L	29	116	419	62	119	17	6	5	50	18	15	4	.284	.315	.389
Walt French	OF98	L	26	112	397	51	121	18	7	1	36	18	24	2	.305	.340	.393
Sammy Hale	3B77,OF1	R	29	111	327	49	92	22	9	4	43	13	36	1	.281	.311	.440
Joe Hauser	1B65	L	27	91	229	31	44	10	0	8	36	39	34	1	.192	.312	.341
Frank Welch	OF49	R	28	75	174	26	49	8	1	4	23	26	9	2	.282	.381	.408
Cy Perkins	C55	R	30	63	148	14	43	6	0	0	19	18	7	0	.291	.371	.331
Bing Miller†	OF34,1B1	R	31	38	110	13	32	6	2	2	13	11	6	4	.291	.355	.436
Alex Metzler	OF17	L	23	20	67	8	16	3	0	0	12	7	5	1	.239	.311	.284
Bill Wambsganss	SS15,2B8	R	32	54	54	11	19	3	0	0	1	8	8	1	.352	.444	.407
Dave Barbee	OF10	R	21	19	47	7	8	1	1	1	5	2	4	0	.170	.220	.298
Frank Sigafoos	SS12	R	22	13	43	4	11	0	0	0	2	0	3	0	.256	.256	.256
Jimmie Foxx	C12,OF3	R	18	26	32	8	10	2	1	0	5	1	6	1	.313	.353	.438
Tom Jenkins†	OF6	L	28	6	23	3	4	2	0	0	0	0	2	0	.174	.174	.261
Charlie Engle	SS16	R	22	19	19	7	2	0	0	0	0	10	6	0	.105	.433	.105

Pitcher	T	Age	G	GS	CG	ShO	IP	H	HR	BB	SO	W-L	Sv	ERA
Lefty Grove	L	26	45	33	20	1	258.0	227	6	101	194	13-13	6	2.51
Eddie Rommel	R	28	37	26	12	3	219.0	225	10	54	52	11-11	0	3.08
Jack Quinn	R	42	31	21	8	3	163.2	191	4	36	58	10-11	1	3.41
Howard Ehmke†	R	32	20	18	10	1	147.1	125	1	50	55	12-4	0	2.81
Slim Harriss†	R	29	12	10	2	0	57.0	66	0	22	13	3-5	0	4.11
Joe Pate	L	34	47	2	0	0	113.0	109	3	51	24	9-0	6	2.71
Rube Walberg	L	29	40	19	5	2	151.0	168	4	60	72	12-10	2	2.80
Sam Gray	R	28	38	18	5	0	150.2	164	9	50	82	11-12	0	3.64
Lefty Willis	L	20	13	1	0	0	32.1	31	0	12	13	0-0	1	1.39
Fred Heimach†	L	25	13	1	0	0	31.2	28	1	5	8	1-0	0	2.84
Stan Baumgartner	L	31	10	1	0	0	22.1	28	0	10	0	1-1	0	4.03

Seasons: Team Rosters 633

1926 Washington Senators 4th AL 81-69 .540 8.0 GB

Bucky Harris

Player	Gm by Position	B	Age	G	AB	R	H	2B	3B	HR	RBI	BB	SO	SB	Avg	OBP	Slg
Muddy Ruel	C117	R	30	117	368	42	110	22	4	1	53	61	14	7	.299	.401	.389
Joe Judge	1B128	L	32	134	453	70	132	25	11	7	92	53	25	7	.291	.367	.442
Bucky Harris	2B141	R	29	141	537	94	152	39	9	1	63	58	41	16	.283	.363	.395
Ossie Bluege	3B134,SS8	R	25	139	487	69	132	19	8	3	65	70	46	12	.271	.368	.361
Buddy Myer	SS117,3B8	L	22	132	434	66	132	18	6	1	62	45	19	10	.304	.370	.380
Sam Rice	OF152	L	36	152	641	98	216	32	14	3	76	42	20	25	.337	.380	.445
Goose Goslin	OF147	L	25	147	568	105	201	26	15	17	108	63	38	8	.354	.425	.542
Earl McNeely	OF120	R	28	124	442	84	134	20	12	0	48	44	28	18	.303	.373	.403
Joe Harris	1B36,OF35	R	35	92	257	43	79	13	9	5	55	37	9	2	.307	.405	.486
Roger Peckinpaugh	SS46,1B1	R	35	57	147	19	35	4	1	1	14	28	12	3	.238	.360	.299
Bennie Tate	C45	L	24	59	142	17	38	5	2	1	13	15	1	0	.268	.338	.352
Stuffy Stewart	2B25	R	32	62	63	27	17	6	1	0	9	6	6	8	.270	.333	.397
Danny Taylor	OF12	R	25	21	50	10	15	0	1	1	5	5	7	1	.300	.364	.400
Bobby Reeves	3B16,2B1,SS1	R	22	20	49	4	11	0	1	0	7	6	9	1	.224	.321	.265
Hank Severeid†	C16	R	35	22	34	2	7	1	0	0	4	3	2	0	.206	.270	.235
Jack Tobin†	OF7	L	34	27	33	5	7	0	1	0	3	0	0	0	.212	.212	.273
Tex Jeanes	OF14	R	25	21	30	6	7	2	0	0	3	0	3	0	.233	.233	.300
Russ Ennis	C1	R	29	1	0	0	0	0	0	0	0	0	0	0	—	—	—

Pitcher	T	Age	G	GS	CG	ShO	IP	H	HR	BB	SO	W-L	Sv	ERA
Stan Coveleski	R	36	36	34	11	3	245.1	272	1	81	50	14-11	1	3.12
Walter Johnson	R	38	33	33	22	2	260.2	259	13	73	125	15-16	0	3.63
Dutch Ruether†	L	32	23	23	9	0	169.1	214	5	66	48	12-6	0	4.84
General Crowder	R	27	19	12	6	0	100.0	97	3	60	26	7-4	1	3.96
George Murray	R	27	12	12	5	0	81.1	89	1	37	28	6-3	0	5.64
Joe Bush†	R	33	12	11	3	0	71.1	83	6	35	27	1-8	0	6.69
Dick Jones	R	24	4	3	1	0	21.0	20	0	11	3	2-1	0	4.29
Firpo Marberry	R	27	64	5	3	0	138.0	120	4	66	43	12-7	22	3.00
Bill Morrell	R	33	26	2	1	0	69.2	83	5	29	16	3-3	1	5.30
Curly Ogden	R	25	22	9	4	0	96.1	114	2	45	21	4-4	0	4.30
Alex Ferguson	R	29	19	4	0	0	47.2	69	4	18	16	3-4	1	7.74
Emilio Palmero	L	31	7	3	0	0	17.0	22	1	15	6	2-2	0	4.76
Harry Kelley	R	20	7	1	0	0	10.0	17	0	8	6	0-0	0	8.10
Lefty Thomas	L	22	6	0	0	0	8.2	8	0	10	3	0-0	0	5.19
Jimmy Uchrinscko	R	25	3	0	0	0	8.0	13	0	8	0	0-0	0	10.13
Bump Hadley	R	21	1	0	0	0	3.0	6	0	2	0	0-0	0	12.00
Frank Loftus	R	28	1	0	0	0	1.0	3	0	2	0	0-0	0	9.00

1926 Chicago White Sox 5th AL 81-72 .529 9.5 GB

Eddie Collins

Player	Gm by Position	B	Age	G	AB	R	H	2B	3B	HR	RBI	BB	SO	SB	Avg	OBP	Slg
Ray Schalk	C80	R	33	82	226	26	60	9	1	0	32	27	11	5	.265	.349	.314
Earl Sheely	1B144	R	33	145	525	77	157	40	2	6	89	75	13	3	.299	.394	.417
Eddie Collins	2B101	L	39	106	375	66	129	32	4	1	62	62	8	13	.344	.441	.459
Willie Kamm	3B142	R	26	143	480	63	141	24	10	0	62	77	24	14	.294	.396	.385
Bill Hunnefield	SS98,3B17,2B15	S	27	131	470	81	129	26	4	3	48	37	28	24	.274	.329	.366
Bibb Falk	OF155	L	27	155	566	86	195	43	4	8	108	66	22	9	.345	.415	.477
Johnny Mostil	OF147	R	30	148	600	120	197	41	15	4	42	79	55	35	.328	.415	.467
Bill Barrett	OF102,1B2	R	26	111	368	46	113	31	4	6	61	25	26	9	.307	.353	.462
Spencer Harris	OF63	L	25	80	222	36	56	11	3	2	27	20	15	8	.252	.317	.356
Ray Morehart	2B48	L	26	73	192	27	61	10	3	0	21	11	15	3	.318	.358	.401
Everett Scott†	SS39	R	33	40	143	15	36	10	1	0	13	9	8	1	.252	.296	.336
Buck Crouse	C45	L	29	49	135	10	32	4	1	0	17	14	7	0	.237	.309	.281
Johnny Grabowski	C38,1B1	R	26	48	122	6	32	1	1	1	11	4	15	0	.262	.286	.311
Moe Berg	SS31,2B2,3B1	R	24	41	113	4	25	6	0	0	7	6	9	0	.221	.261	.274
Harry McCurdy	C25,1B8	L	26	44	86	16	28	7	2	1	11	6	10	0	.326	.370	.488
Bud Clancy	1B10	L	25	12	38	3	13	2	2	0	7	1	1	0	.342	.375	.500
Tom Gulley	OF12	L	26	16	35	5	8	3	1	0	8	5	2	0	.229	.325	.371
Pid Purdy	OF9	L	22	11	33	5	6	2	1	0	6	2	1	0	.182	.229	.303
Pat Veltman	SS1	R	20	5	4	1	1	0	0	0	0	1	1	0	.250	.400	.250

Pitcher	T	Age	G	GS	CG	ShO	IP	H	HR	BB	SO	W-L	Sv	ERA
Tommy Thomas	R	26	44	32	13	2	249.0	225	7	110	127	15-12	2	3.80
Ted Lyons	R	25	39	31	24	3	283.2	268	6	106	51	18-16	2	3.01
Ted Blankenship	R	25	29	26	15	1	209.1	217	13	65	66	13-10	1	3.61
Red Faber	R	37	27	25	13	1	184.2	203	3	57	65	15-9	0	3.56
Jim Joe Edwards	L	31	32	16	8	3	142.0	140	4	63	41	6-9	1	4.18
Dixie Leverett	R	32	6	3	1	0	24.0	31	1	7	12	1-1	0	6.00
Sloppy Thurston	R	27	31	13	6	1	134.1	164	10	36	35	6-8	3	5.02
Sarge Connally	R	27	31	8	5	0	108.1	128	0	35	47	6-5	3	3.16
Milt Steengrafe	R	26	13	1	0	0	38.1	43	1	19	10	1-1	0	3.99
Les Cox	R	20	2	0	0	0	5.0	6	2	5	3	0-1	0	5.40
Pryor McBee	L	25	1	0	0	0	1.1	1	0	3	1	0-0	0	6.75

1926 Detroit Tigers 6th AL 79-75 .513 12.0 GB

Ty Cobb

Player	Gm by Position	B	Age	G	AB	R	H	2B	3B	HR	RBI	BB	SO	SB	Avg	OBP	Slg
Clyde Manion	C74	R	29	75	176	15	35	4	0	0	14	24	16	1	.199	.295	.222
Lu Blue	1B109,OF1	S	29	128	429	92	123	24	14	1	52	90	18	13	.287	.413	.415
Charlie Gehringer	2B116,3B6	L	23	123	459	62	127	19	17	1	48	30	42	9	.277	.322	.399
Jack Warner	3B95,SS3	R	22	100	311	41	78	8	6	0	34	38	24	8	.251	.342	.315
Jackie Tavener	SS156	L	28	156	532	65	141	22	14	1	58	52	53	8	.265	.332	.365
Harry Heilmann	OF134	R	31	141	502	90	184	41	8	9	103	67	19	6	.367	.445	.534
Heinie Manush	OF120	L	24	136	498	95	188	35	8	14	86	31	28	11	.378	.421	.564
Bob Fothergill	OF103	R	28	110	387	63	142	31	7	3	73	33	23	4	.367	.421	.506
Frank O'Rourke	3B60,2B41,SS10	R	31	111	363	43	88	16	1	1	41	35	33	8	.242	.321	.300
Al Wingo	OF74,3B2	L	28	108	298	45	84	19	0	1	45	52	32	4	.282	.389	.356
Johnny Neun	1B49	S	25	97	242	47	72	14	4	0	15	27	26	4	.298	.370	.388
Ty Cobb	OF55	L	39	79	233	48	79	18	5	4	62	26	2	9	.339	.408	.511
Johnny Bassler	C63	L	31	66	174	20	53	8	1	0	22	45	6	0	.305	.447	.362
Larry Woodall	C59	R	31	67	146	18	34	5	0	0	15	15	2	0	.233	.304	.267
Les Burke	2B15,3B7,SS1	L	23	38	75	9	17	1	0	0	4	7	3	1	.227	.301	.240
Billy Mullen	3B9	R	30	11	13	2	1	0	0	0	0	5	1	1	.077	.333	.077
Ray Hayworth	C8	R	22	12	11	1	3	0	0	0	5	1	1	0	.273	.333	.273

Pitcher	T	Age	G	GS	CG	ShO	IP	H	HR	BB	SO	W-L	Sv	ERA
Earl Whitehill	L	26	36	34	13	0	252.1	271	7	79	109	16-13	0	3.99
Ed Wells	L	26	36	26	9	4	178.0	201	7	76	58	12-10	0	4.15
Sam Gibson	R	26	35	24	16	2	196.1	199	6	75	61	12-9	2	3.48
Lil Stoner	R	27	32	22	7	0	159.2	179	11	63	57	7-10	0	5.47
Rudy Kneisch	L	27	2	2	1	0	17.0	18	2	6	4	0-1	0	2.65
Ken Holloway	R	28	36	12	3	0	139.0	192	2	42	43	4-6	2	5.12
Augie Johns	L	26	35	14	3	1	112.2	117	6	69	40	6-4	1	5.35
Hooks Dauss	R	36	34	5	0	0	124.1	135	6	49	27	12-6	9	4.20
Rip Collins	R	30	30	13	5	3	122.0	128	4	44	44	8-8	1	2.73
George Smith	R	24	23	1	0	0	44.0	55	3	33	15	1-2	0	6.95
Clyde Barfoot	R	34	11	1	0	0	31.1	42	4	9	7	1-2	2	4.88
Wilbur Cooper†	L	34	8	3	0	0	13.2	27	0	9	2	0-4	0	11.20
Jess Doyle	R	28	2	0	0	0	4.1	6	0	1	2	0-0	1	4.15

1926 St. Louis Browns 7th AL 62-92 .403 29.0 GB

George Sisler

Player	Gm by Position	B	Age	G	AB	R	H	2B	3B	HR	RBI	BB	SO	SB	Avg	OBP	Slg
Wally Schang	C82	S	36	103	285	36	94	19	5	8	50	32	20	5	.330	.405	.516
George Sisler	1B149,P1	L	33	150	613	78	178	21	12	7	71	30	30	12	.290	.327	.398
Ski Melillo	2B88,3B11	R	26	99	385	54	98	18	5	1	30	32	31	6	.255	.315	.335
Marty McManus	3B84,2B61,1B4	R	26	149	549	102	156	30	10	9	68	55	62	5	.284	.350	.424
Wally Gerber	SS129	R	34	131	411	37	111	8	0	0	42	40	29	0	.270	.339	.290
Harry Rice	OF133,3B8,2B4*	L	24	148	578	86	181	27	10	9	59	63	40	10	.313	.384	.441
Bing Miller†	OF94	R	31	94	353	60	117	27	5	4	50	22	12	7	.331	.382	.470
Ken Williams	OF92	L	36	108	347	55	97	15	7	17	74	39	23	5	.280	.354	.510
Gene Robertson	3B55,SS10,2B3	L	27	78	247	23	62	12	6	1	19	17	10	5	.251	.302	.360
Pinky Hargrave	C58	S	30	92	235	20	66	16	3	7	37	10	38	3	.281	.319	.464
Herschel Bennett	OF50	L	29	80	225	33	60	14	2	1	26	22	21	2	.267	.337	.360
Cedric Durst	OF57,1B4	L	29	80	219	32	52	7	5	3	16	22	19	0	.237	.310	.356
B. Doll Jacobson†	OF50	R	35	50	182	18	52	15	1	2	21	9	14	1	.286	.319	.412
Leo Dixon	C33	R	31	33	89	7	17	3	1	0	8	11	14	1	.191	.294	.247
Bobby LaMotte	SS30,3B1	R	28	36	79	11	16	4	3	0	9	11	6	0	.203	.300	.329
Jimmy Austin	3B1	S	46	1	2	1	1	1	0	0	1	0	0	1	.500	.500	1.000

H. Rice, 2 G at SS

Pitcher	T	Age	G	GS	CG	ShO	IP	H	HR	BB	SO	W-L	Sv	ERA
Tom Zachary	L	30	34	31	18	3	247.1	264	14	97	53	14-15	0	3.60
Milt Gaston	R	30	32	28	14	1	214.1	227	13	101	39	10-18	0	4.33
Joe Giard	L	27	22	16	2	0	90.0	113	7	67	18	3-10	0	7.00
Ernie Nevers	R	24	11	7	4	0	74.2	82	4	24	16	2-4	0	4.46
Charlie Robertson	R	30	8	7	1	0	28.0	38	4	21	13	1-2	0	8.36
Win Ballou	L	28	43	13	5	0	154.0	186	12	71	59	11-10	2	4.79
Elam Vangilder	R	30	42	19	8	1	181.0	196	12	98	40	9-11	1	5.17
Ernie Wingard	L	25	39	16	7	0	169.0	188	9	76	30	5-8	3	3.57
Dixie Davis	R	35	27	7	2	0	83.0	93	7	40	39	3-8	1	4.66
Chet Falk	L	21	18	8	3	0	74.0	95	1	27	7	4-4	0	5.35
Claude Jonnard	R	28	12	3	0	0	36.0	46	1	24	13	0-2	1	6.00
Stew Bolen	L	23	5	0	0	0	14.2	21	2	6	7	0-0	0	6.14
George Sisler	L	33	1	0	0	0	2.0	0	0	2	3	0-0	1	0.00

1926 Boston Red Sox 8th AL 46-107 .301 44.5 GB

Lee Fohl

Player	Gm by Position	B	Age	G	AB	R	H	2B	3B	HR	RBI	BB	SO	SB	Avg	OBP	Slg
Alex Gaston	C98	R	33	98	301	37	67	5	3	0	21	21	28	3	.223	.282	.259
Phil Todt	1B154	L	24	154	599	56	153	19	12	7	69	40	38	3	.255	.306	.362
Bill Regan	2B106	R	27	108	403	40	106	21	3	4	34	23	37	6	.263	.309	.360
Fred Haney	3B137	R	28	138	462	47	102	15	7	0	52	74	28	13	.221	.330	.284
Topper Rigney	SS146	R	29	148	525	71	142	32	6	4	53	108	31	6	.270	.395	.377
Ira Flagstead	OF98	R	32	98	415	65	124	31	7	3	31	36	22	4	.299	.363	.429
B. Doll Jacobson†	OF98	R	35	98	394	44	120	36	1	6	69	22	22	4	.305	.344	.447
Si Rosenthal	OF67	L	22	104	285	34	76	12	3	4	34	19	18	4	.267	.317	.372
Mike Herrera	2B48,3B16,SS4	R	28	74	237	20	61	14	1	0	19	15	13	0	.257	.304	.325
Jack Tobin†	OF51	L	34	51	209	26	57	9	0	1	14	16	3	6	.273	.324	.330
Wally Shaner	OF48	R	26	69	191	20	54	12	2	0	21	17	13	1	.283	.348	.366
Fred Bratschi	OF37	R	34	72	167	12	46	10	1	0	19	14	15	0	.275	.335	.347
Roy Carlyle†	OF38	L	25	45	164	22	47	6	2	2	16	4	18	0	.287	.312	.384
John Bischoff	C46	R	31	59	127	6	33	11	2	0	19	15	16	1	.260	.343	.378
Howie Fitzgerald	OF23	L	24	31	97	11	25	2	0	0	8	5	7	1	.258	.294	.278
Al Stokes	C29	R	26	30	86	7	14	3	3	0	6	8	28	0	.163	.234	.267
Tom Jenkins†	OF13	L	28	21	50	3	9	1	1	0	6	3	7	0	.180	.226	.240
Bill Moore	C5	L	24	5	18	2	3	0	0	0	0	0	2	0	.167	.167	.167
Jack Rothrock	SS2	S	21	15	17	3	5	1	0	0	2	3	1	0	.294	.400	.353
Chappie Geygan	3B3	R	23	4	10	0	3	0	0	0	0	1	1	0	.300	.364	.300
Boob Fowler	3B2	L	25	2	8	1	1	0	0	0	1	0	0	0	.125	.125	.125
Dud Lee	SS2	L	26	2	7	2	1	0	0	0	0	0	0	0	.143	.250	.143
Emmett McCann	3B1,SS1	R	24	6	3	0	0	0	0	0	0	1	1	0	.000	.250	.000
Sam Langford		L	27	1	1	1	0	0	0	0	0	0	0	0	.000	.000	.000

Pitcher	T	Age	G	GS	CG	ShO	IP	H	HR	BB	SO	W-L	Sv	ERA
Hal Wiltse	L	22	37	29	9	1	196.1	201	6	99	59	8-15	0	4.22
Paul Zahniser	R	29	30	24	7	1	172.0	213	5	69	35	6-18	0	4.97
Red Ruffing	R	22	37	22	6	0	166.0	169	4	68	58	6-15	2	4.39
Slim Harriss†	R	29	21	18	6	1	113.0	135	0	33	34	6-10	0	4.46
Howard Ehmke†	R	32	14	14	7	1	97.1	115	3	45	38	3-10	0	5.46
Fred Heimach†	L	25	20	13	6	0	102.0	119	5	42	17	2-9	0	5.65
Ted Wingfield	R	26	43	20	9	1	190.2	220	11	50	30	11-16	3	4.44
Tony Welzer	R	27	39	6	1	1	141.0	167	5	57	30	4-3	0	4.79
Jack Russell	R	20	36	5	1	0	98.0	94	2	24	17	0-5	0	3.58
Del Lundgren	R	26	17	1	0	0	31.0	35	2	24	10	0-2	0	7.55
Joe Kiefer	R	26	11	1	0	0	30.0	29	2	16	4	0-2	0	4.80
Danny MacFayden	R	21	3	1	1	0	13.0	10	0	7	1	0-1	0	4.85
Happy Foreman	L	28	3	0	0	0	7.1	3	0	5	3	0-0	0	3.68
Rudy Sommers	L	37	2	0	0	0	2.0	3	0	3	0	0-0	0	13.50
Bill Clowers	L	27	2	0	0	0	1.2	2	0	0	0	0-0	0	0.00
Buster Ross	L	23	1	0	0	0	2.2	5	0	4	0	0-1	0	16.88

634 Seasons: Team Rosters

»1926 St. Louis Cardinals 1st NL 89-65 .578 —

Rogers Hornsby

Player	Gm by Position	B	Age	G	AB	R	H	2B	3B	HR	RBI	BB	SO	SB	Avg	OBP	Slg
Bob O'Farrell	C146	R	29	147	492	63	144	30	9	7	68	61	44	1	.293	.371	.433
Jim Bottomley	1B154	L	26	154	603	98	180	40	14	19	120	58	52	4	.299	.364	.506
Rogers Hornsby	2B134	R	30	134	527	96	167	34	5	11	93	61	39	3	.317	.388	.463
Les Bell	3B155	R	24	155	581	85	189	33	14	17	100	54	62	9	.325	.383	.518
Tommy Thevenow	SS156	R	22	156	563	64	144	15	5	2	63	27	26	8	.256	.291	.311
Taylor Douthit	OF138	R	25	139	530	96	163	20	4	3	52	55	46	23	.308	.375	.377
Ray Blades	OF105	R	29	107	416	81	127	17	12	8	43	62	57	6	.305	.409	.462
Billy Southworth†	OF99	L	33	99	391	76	124	22	6	11	69	26	9	13	.317	.364	.488
Chick Hafey	OF64	R	23	78	225	30	61	19	2	4	38	11	36	2	.271	.311	.427
Heinie Mueller†	OF51	L	26	52	191	36	51	7	5	3	28	11	6	8	.267	.330	.403
Wattie Holm	OF39	R	24	55	144	18	41	5	1	0	21	18	14	3	.285	.364	.333
Specs Toporcer	2B27,SS5,3B1	L	27	64	88	13	22	3	2	0	9	8	9	1	.250	.327	.330
Jake Flowers	2B11,1B3,SS1	R	24	40	74	13	20	1	0	3	9	5	9	1	.270	.325	.405
Ernie Vick	C23	R	25	24	51	6	10	2	0	0	4	3	4	0	.196	.241	.235
Bill Warwick	C9	R	28	9	14	0	5	0	0	0	2	0	2	0	.357	.357	.357
Jack Smith†		L	31	1	1	0	0	0	0	0	0	0	1	0	.000	.000	.000

Pitcher	T	Age	G	GS	CG	ShO	IP	H	HR	BB	SO	W-L	Sv	ERA
Flint Rhem	R	25	34	34	20	1	258.0	241	12	75	72	20-7	0	3.21
Bill Sherdel	L	29	34	29	17	3	234.2	255	15	49	59	16-12	0	3.49
Jesse Haines	R	32	33	21	14	3	183.0	186	10	48	46	13-4	1	3.25
Vic Keen	R	27	26	21	12	1	152.0	179	15	42	29	10-9	0	4.56
Pete Alexander†	R	39	23	16	11	2	148.1	136	8	24	35	9-7	2	2.91
Art Reinhart	L	27	27	11	9	0	143.0	159	5	47	26	10-5	0	4.22
Hi Bell	R	28	27	7	3	0	85.0	82	1	17	27	6-6	2	3.18
Wild Bill Hallahan	L	23	19	3	0	0	56.2	45	1	32	28	1-4	0	3.65
Syl Johnson	R	25	19	6	1	0	49.0	54	3	15	10	0-3	1	4.22
Allen Sothoron	R	33	15	4	1	0	42.2	37	2	16	19	3-3	0	4.22
Walter Huntzinger†	R	27	9	4	2	0	34.0	35	4	14	9	0-4	0	4.24
Eddie Dyer	L	25	6	0	0	0	9.1	7	0	14	4	1-0	0	11.57
Ed Clough	L	19	1	0	0	0	2.0	5	0	3	0	0-0	0	22.50
Duster Mails	L	31	1	0	0	0	1.0	2	0	1	1	0-1	0	0.00

1926 Cincinnati Reds 2nd NL 87-67 .565 2.0 GB

Jack Hendricks

Player	Gm by Position	B	Age	G	AB	R	H	2B	3B	HR	RBI	BB	SO	SB	Avg	OBP	Slg
Bubbles Hargrave	C93	R	33	105	326	42	115	22	8	6	62	25	17	2	.353	.406	.525
Wally Pipp	1B155	L	33	155	574	72	167	22	15	6	99	49	26	8	.291	.352	.413
Hughie Critz	2B155	R	25	155	607	96	164	24	14	3	79	39	25	7	.270	.316	.371
Chuck Dressen	3B123,SS1,OF1	R	27	127	474	76	126	27	11	4	48	49	31	0	.266	.338	.395
Frank Emmer	SS79	R	30	80	224	22	44	7	6	0	18	13	30	1	.196	.244	.281
Curt Walker	OF152	L	29	155	571	83	175	24	20	6	78	60	31	3	.306	.372	.450
Edd Roush	OF143,1B1	L	33	144	563	95	182	37	10	7	79	38	17	8	.323	.366	.462
Cuckoo Christensen	OF93	L	26	114	329	41	115	15	7	0	41	40	18	8	.350	.426	.438
Rube Bressler	OF80,1B4	R	31	86	297	58	106	15	9	1	51	37	20	3	.357	.433	.478
Val Picinich	C86	R	29	89	240	33	63	16	1	2	31	29	22	4	.263	.342	.363
Babe Pinelli	3B40,SS27,2B3	R	30	71	207	26	46	7	4	0	24	15	5	2	.222	.284	.295
Hod Ford	SS57	R	28	57	197	14	55	6	1	0	18	14	12	1	.279	.336	.320
Billy Zitzmann	OF31	R	30	53	94	21	23	2	1	0	3	6	7	3	.245	.304	.287
Red Lucas	P39,2B1	L	24	66	76	15	23	4	4	0	14	10	13	0	.303	.384	.461
Sammy Bohne†		R	29	25	54	8	11	0	2	0	5	4	8	1	.204	.259	.278
Jimmy Hudgens	1B6	L	23	17	20	2	5	1	0	0	1	1	0	0	.250	.286	.300
Ethan Allen	OF9	R	22	18	13	3	4	1	0	0	0	0	3	0	.308	.308	.385
Ivy Wingo	C7	L	35	7	10	0	2	0	0	0	1	1	0	0	.200	.333	.200
Everett Scott†	SS4	R	33	4	6	1	4	0	0	0	1	0	0	0	.667	.667	.667
Doc Prothro	3B2	R	32	3	5	1	1	0	1	0	1	1	1	0	.200	.333	.600
Howie Carter	2B3,SS1	R	21	5	1	0	0	0	0	0	0	0	0	0	.000	.000	.000
Clyde Sukeforth		L	24	1	1	0	0	0	0	0	0	0	1	0	.000	.000	.000

Pitcher	T	Age	G	GS	CG	ShO	IP	H	HR	BB	SO	W-L	Sv	ERA
Pete Donohue	R	25	47	38	17	5	285.2	298	6	39	73	20-14	2	3.37
Carl Mays	R	34	39	33	24	3	281.0	286	3	53	58	19-12	1	3.14
Dolf Luque	R	35	34	30	16	1	233.2	231	7	77	83	13-16	0	3.43
Eppa Rixey	L	35	37	29	14	3	233.0	231	12	58	61	14-8	0	3.40
Jakie May	L	30	45	15	9	1	167.2	175	4	44	103	13-9	3	3.22
Red Lucas	R	24	39	11	7	1	154.0	161	6	30	34	8-5	2	3.68
Roy Meeker	L	25	7	1	1	0	21.0	24	1	9	5	0-2	0	6.43
Art Nehf†	L	33	7	0	0	0	17.0	25	0	5	4	0-1	0	3.71
Pea Ridge Day	R	26	4	0	0	0	7.1	13	1	2	2	0-0	0	7.36
Mul Holland	R	23	3	0	0	0	6.2	3	0	5	0	0-0	0	1.35
Brad Springer	L	22	1	0	0	0	1.1	2	0	2	1	0-0	0	6.75
Rufe Meadows	L	18	1	0	0	0	0.1	0	0	0	0	0-0	0	0.00

1926 Pittsburgh Pirates 3rd NL 84-69 .549 4.5 GB

Bill McKechnie

Player	Gm by Position	B	Age	G	AB	R	H	2B	3B	HR	RBI	BB	SO	SB	Avg	OBP	Slg
Earl Smith	C98	L	29	105	292	29	101	17	2	2	46	28	7	1	.346	.407	.438
George Grantham	1B132	L	26	141	449	66	143	27	13	8	70	60	42	6	.318	.400	.490
Hal Rhyne	2B66,SS44,3B1	R	27	109	366	46	92	14	3	2	39	35	21	1	.251	.327	.322
Pie Traynor	3B148,SS3	R	26	152	574	83	182	25	17	3	92	38	14	8	.317	.361	.436
Glenn Wright	SS116	R	25	119	458	73	141	15	15	8	77	19	26	6	.308	.335	.459
Kiki Cuyler	OF157	R	27	157	614	113	197	31	15	8	92	50	66	35	.321	.380	.459
Paul Waner	OF139	L	23	144	536	101	180	35	22	8	79	66	19	11	.336	.413	.528
Max Carey†	OF82	S	36	86	324	46	72	14	5	0	28	30	14	10	.222	.288	.296
Johnny Gooch	C80	S	28	86	218	19	59	15	1	1	42	20	14	1	.271	.340	.362
Clyde Barnhart	OF61	R	30	76	203	26	39	3	0	0	10	23	13	1	.192	.278	.207
Johnny Rawlings	2B59	R	33	61	181	27	42	6	0	0	20	14	10	3	.232	.287	.265
Eddie Moore†	2B24,3B9,SS1	R	27	43	132	19	30	8	1	0	19	12	6	3	.227	.292	.303
Stuffy McInnis	1B40	R	35	47	127	12	38	6	1	0	13	7	3	1	.299	.336	.362
Joe Cronin	2B27,SS7	R	19	38	83	9	22	2	2	0	11	6	15	0	.265	.315	.337
Carson Bigbee	OF21	L	31	42	68	15	15	3	1	2	4	3	0	2	.221	.264	.382
Walter Mueller	OF15	R	31	19	62	8	15	0	1	0	3	0	2	0	.242	.242	.274
George Brickell	OF14	L	19	24	55	11	19	3	1	0	4	3	6	0	.345	.400	.436
Roy Spencer	C12	R	26	28	43	5	17	3	0	0	4	1	0	0	.395	.409	.465
Eddie Murphy	OF3	L	34	16	17	3	2	0	0	0	6	3	0	0	.118	.250	.118
Adam Comorosky	OF6	R	20	8	15	2	4	1	1	0	0	1	2	1	.267	.313	.467

Pitcher	T	Age	G	GS	CG	ShO	IP	H	HR	BB	SO	W-L	Sv	ERA
Lee Meadows	R	31	36	31	15	1	226.2	254	10	52	54	20-9	0	3.97
Ray Kremer	R	33	37	26	18	3	231.1	221	9	51	74	20-6	5	2.61
Vic Aldridge	R	32	30	26	12	1	190.0	204	7	73	61	10-13	1	4.07
Emil Yde	L	26	37	22	12	1	187.1	181	3	81	34	8-7	0	3.65
Johnny Morrison	R	30	26	13	6	2	122.1	119	2	44	39	6-8	2	3.38
Joe Bush†	R	33	19	11	9	2	110.2	97	7	35	38	6-6	3	3.01
Carmen Hill	R	30	6	6	4	1	39.2	42	2	9	8	3-3	0	3.40
Don Songer	L	26	35	14	5	1	126.1	118	4	52	27	7-8	2	3.13
Babe Adams	R	44	19	0	0	0	36.2	51	5	8	7	2-3	3	6.14
Red Oldham	L	32	17	2	0	0	41.2	56	1	18	16	2-2	2	5.62
Tom Sheehan	R	32	9	4	1	0	31.0	36	0	12	16	0-2	0	6.68
Lou Koupal	R	27	6	2	1	0	19.2	22	0	8	7	0-2	0	3.20
Roy Mahaffey	R	23	4	0	0	0	4.2	5	0	1	3	0-0	0	0.00
Bud Culloton	R	30	4	0	0	0	3.2	3	0	6	1	0-0	0	7.36
Chet Nichols	R	28	3	0	0	0	7.2	13	0	5	2	0-0	0	8.22

1926 Chicago Cubs 4th NL 82-72 .532 7.0 GB

Joe McCarthy

Player	Gm by Position	B	Age	G	AB	R	H	2B	3B	HR	RBI	BB	SO	SB	Avg	OBP	Slg
Gabby Hartnett	C88	R	25	93	284	35	78	25	3	8	41	32	37	0	.275	.352	.468
Charlie Grimm	1B147	L	27	147	524	58	145	30	6	8	82	49	25	3	.277	.342	.403
Sparky Adams	2B136,3B19,SS2	R	31	154	624	95	193	35	3	0	39	52	27	27	.309	.367	.375
Howard Freigau	3B135,SS2,OF1	R	23	140	508	51	137	27	7	3	51	43	42	6	.270	.327	.368
Jimmy Cooney	SS141	R	31	141	513	52	129	18	5	1	47	23	10	11	.251	.288	.312
Hack Wilson	OF140	R	26	142	529	97	170	36	8	21	109	69	61	10	.321	.406	.539
Cliff Heathcote	OF133	L	28	139	510	98	141	33	3	10	53	58	30	18	.276	.353	.412
Riggs Stephenson	OF74	R	28	82	281	40	95	18	3	3	44	31	16	2	.338	.404	.456
Mike Gonzalez	C78	R	35	80	253	24	63	13	3	1	23	13	17	3	.249	.288	.336
Pete Scott	OF60,3B1	R	27	77	189	34	54	13	1	3	34	22	31	3	.286	.363	.413
Joe Kelly	OF39	L	26	65	176	16	59	15	3	0	32	7	11	0	.335	.361	.455
Joe Munson	OF28	L	26	33	101	17	26	2	2	3	15	8	4	0	.257	.318	.406
Clyde Beck	2B30	R	26	30	81	10	16	0	0	1	4	7	15	0	.198	.261	.235
Chick Tolson	1B13	R	31	57	80	4	25	6	1	1	8	5	8	0	.313	.353	.450
Red Shannon	SS13	S	29	19	51	9	17	5	0	0	4	6	3	0	.333	.414	.431
Mandy Brooks	OF18	R	28	26	48	7	9	1	0	1	6	5	5	0	.188	.278	.271
Hank Schreiber	3B3,SS3,2B1	R	34	10	18	2	1	1	0	0	0	0	1	0	.056	.056	.111
Joe Graves	3B2	R	20	2	5	0	0	0	0	0	0	0	1	0	.000	.000	.000
John Churry	C1	R	25	2	4	0	0	0	0	0	0	1	2	0	.000	.200	.000
Ralph Michaels		R	24	2	0	1	0	0	0	0	0	0	0	0	—	—	—

Pitcher	T	Age	G	GS	CG	ShO	IP	H	HR	BB	SO	W-L	Sv	ERA
Charlie Root	R	27	42	32	21	2	271.1	267	10	62	127	18-17	2	2.82
Sheriff Blake	R	26	39	27	11	4	197.2	204	7	92	95	11-12	1	3.60
Tony Kaufmann	R	25	26	21	14	1	169.2	169	6	44	52	9-7	2	3.02
Percy Jones	L	26	30	20	10	2	160.1	151	3	90	80	12-7	2	3.09
Wilbur Cooper†	L	34	8	8	3	2	55.0	65	6	21	18	2-1	0	4.42
Pete Alexander†	R	39	7	7	4	0	52.0	55	0	7	12	3-3	0	3.46
Guy Bush	R	24	35	16	7	2	157.1	149	3	42	32	13-9	2	2.86
Bob Osborn	R	23	31	15	6	0	136.1	157	3	58	43	6-5	1	3.63
Bill Piercy	R	30	19	5	1	0	90.1	96	1	37	31	6-5	0	4.48
George Milstead	L	23	18	4	0	0	55.1	63	0	24	14	1-5	2	3.58
Walter Huntzinger†	R	27	11	0	0	0	28.2	26	0	8	4	1-1	2	0.94
Johnny Welch	R	19	3	0	0	0	4.1	5	0	1	0	0-0	0	2.08

1926 New York Giants 5th NL 74-77 .490 13.5 GB

John McGraw

Player	Gm by Position	B	Age	G	AB	R	H	2B	3B	HR	RBI	BB	SO	SB	Avg	OBP	Slg
Paul Florence	C76	S	26	76	188	19	43	4	3	2	14	23	12	2	.229	.322	.314
George Kelly	1B114,2B18	R	30	136	499	70	151	24	4	13	80	36	52	4	.303	.352	.445
Frankie Frisch	2B127,3B7	S	27	135	545	75	171	29	4	5	44	33	16	23	.314	.353	.409
Freddy Lindstrom	3B138,OF1	R	20	140	543	90	164	19	9	9	76	39	21	11	.302	.351	.420
Travis Jackson	SS108,OF1	R	22	111	385	64	126	24	8	8	51	20	26	2	.327	.362	.494
Irish Meusel	OF112	R	33	129	449	51	131	25	10	6	65	16	18	5	.292	.322	.432
Ross Youngs	OF94	L	29	95	372	62	114	12	5	4	43	37	19	21	.306	.372	.398
Ty Tyson	OF92	R	34	97	335	40	98	16	1	3	35	15	28	6	.293	.329	.373
Heinie Mueller†	OF82	L	26	85	305	36	76	6	2	4	29	21	17	7	.249	.300	.321
Bill Terry	1B38,OF14	L	29	98	225	26	65	12	5	5	43	22	17	3	.289	.352	.453
Doc Farrell	SS53,2B3	R	24	67	171	19	49	10	1	2	23	12	17	4	.287	.341	.392
Frank Snyder	C55	R	33	55	148	10	32	3	2	5	16	13	13	0	.216	.280	.365
Billy Southworth†	OF29	L	33	36	116	23	38	6	1	5	30	7	1	1	.328	.366	.526
Hugh McMullen	C56	S	24	57	91	5	17	2	0	0	6	2	18	1	.187	.204	.209
Al Moore	OF20	R	23	28	81	12	18	4	0	0	10	5	7	2	.222	.267	.272
Jimmy Johnston†	OF14	R	36	37	69	11	16	0	0	0	5	6	5	0	.232	.293	.232
Mel Ott	OF10	L	17	35	60	7	23	2	0	0	4	1	9	1	.383	.393	.417
Andy Cohen	2B10,SS10,3B2	R	21	32	35	4	9	0	1	0	8	1	2	0	.257	.278	.314
Heine Groh	3B7	R	36	12	35	2	8	2	0	0	3	2	3	0	.229	.270	.286
Grover Hartley	C13	R	37	13	21	0	1	0	0	0	0	5	0	0	.048	.231	.048
Blackie Carter	OF4	R	23	5	17	4	4	1	0	1	1	1	0	0	.235	.278	.471
Jack Cummings	C6	R	22	7	16	3	5	3	0	0	4	4	2	0	.313	.450	.500
Scottie Slayback	2B2	R	24	2	8	0	0	0	0	0	0	0	0	0	.000	.000	.000
Fresco Thompson	2B2	R	24	2	8	1	5	0	0	0	1	2	0	1	.625	.700	.625
Mike Smith	OF1	L	21	4	7	0	1	0	0	0	0	0	2	0	.143	.143	.143
Jim Hamby	C1	R	28	1	3	0	0	0	0	0	0	0	0	0	.000	.000	.000
Pete Cote		R	23	2	1	0	0	0	0	0	0	0	0	0	.000	.000	.000
Joe Connell		L	24	2	1	1	0	0	0	0	0	0	0	0	.000	.000	.000
Jim Boyle	C1	R	22	1	0	0	0	0	0	0	0	0	0	0	—	—	—

Pitcher	T	Age	G	GS	CG	ShO	IP	H	HR	BB	SO	W-L	Sv	ERA
Kent Greenfield	R	23	39	28	8	1	222.2	206	17	82	74	13-12	1	3.96
F. Fitzsimmons	R	24	37	26	12	0	219.0	224	7	58	48	14-10	0	2.88
Virgil Barnes	R	29	31	25	9	2	185.0	183	4	56	54	8-13	1	2.87
Jimmy Ring	R	31	39	23	5	0	183.1	207	12	74	76	11-10	2	4.57
Hugh McQuillan	R	28	33	22	12	1	167.0	171	7	42	47	11-10	0	3.72
John Wisner	R	26	5	3	2	0	28.0	21	4	10	5	2-2	0	3.54
Joe Poetz	R	26	2	1	0	0	8.0	5	2	8	0	0-1	0	3.38
Jack Scott	R	34	50	22	13	0	226.0	242	13	53	82	13-15	5	4.34
Chick Davies	L	34	38	1	0	0	89.0	96	3	35	27	2-4	6	3.94
Tim McNamara	R	27	6	0	0	0	6.0	7	0	4	4	0-0	0	9.00
Ned Porter	R	20	2	0	0	0	2.0	2	1	0	1	0-0	0	4.50
Art Nehf†	L	33	2	0	0	0	1.2	2	0	1	0	0-0	0	10.80
Al Smith	R	22	1	0	0	0	2.0	4	0	2	0	0-0	0	9.00
Jack Bentley†	L	31	1	0	0	0	2.0	0	0	2	1	0-0	0	0.00

Seasons: Team Rosters 635

1926 Brooklyn Dodgers 6th NL 71-82 .464 17.5 GB

Wilbert Robinson

Player	Gm by Position	B	Age	G	AB	R	H	2B	3B	HR	RBI	BB	SO	SB	Avg	OBP	Slg
Mickey O'Neil	C74	R	26	75	201	19	42	5	3	0	20	23	8	3	.209	.293	.264
Babe Herman	1B100,OF36	L	23	137	496	64	158	35	11	11	81	44	53	8	.319	.375	.500
Chick Fewster	2B103	R	30	105	337	53	82	16	3	2	24	45	49	9	.243	.341	.326
William Marriott	3B104	L	32	109	360	39	96	13	9	3	42	17	20	12	.267	.303	.378
Johnny Butler	SS102,3B42,2B8	R	33	147	501	54	135	27	5	1	68	54	44	6	.269	.346	.349
Gus Felix	OF125	R	31	134	432	64	121	21	7	3	53	51	32	9	.280	.360	.382
Dick Cox	OF117	R	28	124	398	53	118	17	4	1	45	46	20	6	.296	.375	.367
Zack Wheat	OF102	L	38	111	411	68	119	31	2	5	35	21	14	4	.290	.326	.411
Merwin Jacobson	OF86	L	32	110	288	41	71	9	2	0	23	36	24	5	.247	.330	.292
Jack Fournier	1B64	L	36	87	243	39	69	9	2	11	48	30	16	0	.284	.365	.473
Rabbit Maranville	SS60,2B18	R	34	78	234	32	55	8	5	0	24	26	24	7	.235	.312	.312
Charlie Hargreaves	C70	R	29	85	208	14	52	13	2	2	23	19	10	1	.250	.316	.361
Sammy Bohne†	2B31,SS20,3B15	R	29	47	125	4	25	3	2	1	11	12	9	1	.200	.270	.280
Hank DeBerry	C37	R	31	48	115	6	33	11	0	0	13	8	5	0	.287	.333	.383
Jerry Standaert	2B21,3B14,SS6	R	24	66	113	13	39	8	2	0	14	5	7	0	.345	.378	.451
Max Carey†	OF27	S	36	27	100	18	26	3	1	0	7	8	5	0	.260	.315	.310
Whitey Witt	OF23	L	30	63	85	13	22	1	1	0	3	12	6	1	.259	.351	.294
Moose Clabaugh	OF2	L	24	11	14	2	1	1	0	0	1	0	1	0	.071	.133	.143
Snooks Dowd	2B2	R	28	2	8	0	0	0	0	0	0	0	0	0	.000	.000	.000
Milt Stock	2B3	R	32	3	8	0	0	0	0	0	0	1	0	0	.000	.111	.000

Pitcher	T	Age	G	GS	CG	ShO	IP	H	HR	BB	SO	W-L	Sv	ERA
Jesse Petty	L	31	38	33	23	1	275.2	246	9	79	101	17-17	1	2.84
Burleigh Grimes	R	32	30	29	18	1	225.1	238	4	88	64	12-13	0	3.71
Doug McWeeny	R	29	42	24	10	1	216.1	213	6	84	96	11-13	1	3.04
Jesse Barnes	R	33	31	24	10	1	158.0	204	6	35	29	10-11	1	5.24
Dazzy Vance	R	35	24	22	12	1	169.0	172	7	58	140	9-10	1	3.89
Bob McGraw	R	31	33	21	10	0	174.1	197	12	67	49	9-13	1	4.59
Rube Ehrhardt	R	31	44	1	0	0	97.0	101	5	35	25	2-5	4	3.90
George Boehler	R	34	10	1	0	0	34.2	42	1	23	10	1-0	0	4.41
Leon Williams	L	20	8	0	0	0	8.1	16	0	2	3	0-0	0	5.40
Dutch Stryker	R	40	2	0	0	0	2.0	8	0	1	0	0-0	0	27.00
Ray Moss	R	24	1	0	0	0	1.0	3	0	0	0	0-0	0	9.00

1926 Boston Braves 7th NL 66-86 .434 22.0 GB

Dave Bancroft

Player	Gm by Position	B	Age	G	AB	R	H	2B	3B	HR	RBI	BB	SO	SB	Avg	OBP	Slg
Zack Taylor	C123	R	27	125	432	36	110	22	3	0	42	28	27	1	.255	.303	.319
Dick Burrus	1B128	L	28	131	486	59	131	21	1	3	61	37	16	4	.270	.324	.335
Doc Gautreau	2B74	R	24	79	266	36	71	9	4	0	8	35	24	17	.267	.356	.331
Andy High	3B81,2B49	L	28	130	476	55	141	17	10	2	66	39	9	4	.296	.351	.387
Dave Bancroft	SS123,3B2	S	35	127	453	70	141	18	6	1	44	64	29	3	.311	.399	.384
Eddie Brown	OF153	R	34	153	612	71	201	31	8	2	84	23	20	5	.328	.355	.415
Jimmy Welsh	OF129	L	23	134	490	69	136	18	11	3	57	33	28	6	.278	.333	.378
Jack Smith†	OF83	L	31	96	322	46	100	15	2	2	25	28	12	11	.311	.369	.388
Ed Taylor	3B62,SS33	R	24	92	272	37	73	8	2	0	33	38	26	4	.268	.368	.313
Frank Wilson	OF56	L	25	87	236	22	56	11	3	0	23	20	21	3	.237	.300	.309
Eddie Moore†	2B39,SS14,3B1	R	27	54	184	17	49	3	2	0	15	16	12	6	.266	.325	.304
Les Mann	OF46	R	32	50	129	23	39	8	2	1	20	9	9	5	.302	.348	.419
Johnny Cooney	1B31,P19,OF1	R	25	64	126	17	38	3	2	0	18	13	7	6	.302	.367	.357
Bernie Neis	OF23	S	30	30	93	16	20	5	2	0	8	8	10	4	.215	.277	.312
Oscar Siemer	C30	R	24	31	73	3	15	1	0	0	5	2	7	0	.205	.227	.219
Jimmy Johnston†	3B14,2B2,OF1	R	36	23	57	7	14	1	0	1	5	10	3	2	.246	.358	.316
Frank Gibson	C13	S	35	24	47	3	16	4	0	0	7	4	6	0	.340	.392	.426
Shanty Hogan	C4	R	20	4	14	1	4	1	1	0	5	0	0	0	.286	.286	.500
Harry Riconda	3B4	R	29	4	12	1	2	0	0	0	0	2	2	0	.167	.286	.167
Sid Womack	C1	R	29	1	3	0	0	0	0	0	1	0	0	0	.000	.000	.000

Pitcher	T	Age	G	GS	CG	ShO	IP	H	HR	BB	SO	W-L	Sv	ERA
Larry Benton	R	28	43	27	12	1	231.2	244	10	81	103	14-14	1	3.85
Joe Genewich	R	29	37	26	12	2	216.0	239	6	63	59	8-16	2	3.88
Bob Smith	R	31	33	23	14	4	201.1	199	10	75	44	10-13	1	3.75
Johnny Werts	R	28	32	23	7	1	189.1	212	6	47	65	11-9	0	3.28
Hal Goldsmith	R	27	19	15	5	0	101.0	135	2	28	16	5-7	0	4.37
Foster Edwards	R	22	3	3	1	0	25.0	20	0	13	4	2-0	0	0.72
George Mogridge	L	37	39	10	2	0	142.0	173	6	36	46	6-10	3	4.50
Bunny Hearn	L	22	34	12	3	0	117.1	121	2	56	40	4-9	2	4.22
Johnny Cooney	L	25	19	8	3	1	83.1	106	0	29	23	3-3	0	4.00
Skinny Graham	R	26	15	4	1	0	36.1	54	3	19	7	3-3	0	7.93
Rosy Ryan	R	28	7	2	0	0	19.0	29	1	7	1	0-2	0	7.58
Bill Vargus	L	26	4	0	0	0	3.0	4	0	1	0	0-0	0	3.00

1926 Philadelphia Phillies 8th NL 58-93 .384 29.5 GB

Art Fletcher

Player	Gm by Position	B	Age	G	AB	R	H	2B	3B	HR	RBI	BB	SO	SB	Avg	OBP	Slg
Jimmie Wilson	C79	R	25	90	279	40	85	10	2	4	32	25	20	3	.305	.362	.398
Jack Bentley†	1B56,P7	L	31	75	240	19	62	12	3	2	27	5	4	0	.258	.273	.358
Bernie Friberg	2B144	R	26	144	478	38	128	21	3	1	51	57	77	2	.268	.346	.331
Clarence Huber	3B115	R	29	118	376	45	92	17	7	1	34	42	29	9	.245	.324	.335
Heinie Sand	SS149	R	28	149	567	99	154	30	5	4	37	66	56	2	.272	.350	.363
Freddy Leach	OF123	L	28	129	492	73	162	29	7	11	71	16	33	6	.329	.352	.484
Johnny Mokan	OF123	R	30	127	456	68	138	23	5	6	62	41	31	4	.303	.365	.414
Cy Williams	OF93	L	38	107	336	63	116	13	4	18	53	38	35	2	.345	.418	.568
Russ Wrightstone	1B53,3B37,2B13*	L	33	112	368	55	113	23	1	7	57	27	11	5	.307	.356	.432
Al Nixon	OF88	R	40	93	311	38	91	18	2	4	41	13	20	5	.293	.323	.402
Butch Henline	C77,1B4,OF2	R	31	99	283	32	80	14	1	2	30	21	18	1	.283	.339	.360
George Harper	OF55	L	34	56	194	32	61	6	5	7	38	16	7	6	.314	.367	.505
Ray Grimes	1B28	R	32	32	101	13	30	5	0	0	15	6	13	0	.297	.343	.347
Clarence Mitchell	P28,1B4	L	35	39	78	8	19	4	0	0	6	5	5	0	.244	.289	.295
Dick Attreau	1B17	L	29	17	61	9	14	1	1	0	5	6	5	0	.230	.299	.279
Bob Rice	3B15,2B2,SS2	R	27	19	54	3	8	0	1	0	10	3	4	0	.148	.193	.185
Denny Sothern	OF13	R	22	14	53	5	13	1	0	3	10	4	10	0	.245	.310	.434
Bubber Jonnard	C15	R	28	19	34	3	4	1	0	0	2	3	4	0	.118	.189	.147
Wally Kimmick	1B5,3B4,SS4*	R	29	20	28	0	6	2	1	0	2	3	7	0	.214	.290	.357
Ed Cotter	3B8,SS5	R	21	17	26	3	8	0	1	0	1	1	4	1	.308	.333	.385
George Stutz	SS5	R	33	6	9	0	0	0	0	0	0	0	2	0	.000	.000	.000
Joe Buskey	SS5	R	23	5	8	1	0	0	0	0	0	1	1	0	.000	.111	.000
Lee Dunham	1B2	L	24	5	4	0	1	0	0	0	1	0	1	0	.250	.250	.250
Lew Wendell	C1	R	34	1	4	0	0	0	0	0	0	0	0	0	.000	.000	.000
Chick Keating	2B2,SS2,3B1	R	34	4	2	0	0	0	0	0	0	0	0	0	.000	.000	.000

R. Wrightstone, 5 G at OF; W. Kimmick, 1 G at 2B

Pitcher	T	Age	G	GS	CG	ShO	IP	H	HR	BB	SO	W-L	Sv	ERA
Hal Carlson	R	34	35	34	20	3	267.1	293	9	47	55	17-12	0	3.23
Wayland Dean	R	24	33	26	15	1	203.2	245	9	89	52	8-16	0	4.91
Clarence Mitchell	L	35	28	25	12	0	178.2	232	7	55	52	9-14	1	4.58
Art Decatur	R	32	2	1	0	0	3.0	6	0	2	0	0-0	0	6.00
Claude Willoughby	R	27	47	18	6	0	168.0	218	7	71	37	8-12	1	5.95
Dutch Ulrich	R	26	45	17	8	1	147.2	178	9	37	52	8-13	1	4.08
Ray Pierce	L	29	37	7	1	0	84.2	128	3	35	18	2-7	0	5.63
Jack Knight	R	31	35	15	5	0	142.2	206	14	48	29	3-12	2	6.62
Ed Baecht	R	19	28	1	1	0	56.0	73	4	28	14	2-0	0	6.11
Ernie Maun	R	25	14	5	0	0	37.2	57	4	18	9	1-4	0	6.45
Jack Bentley†	L	31	7	3	0	0	25.1	37	2	10	7	0-2	0	8.17
Lefty Taber	L	26	6	0	0	0	8.1	8	0	5	0	0-0	0	7.56
Mike Kelly	R	23	4	0	0	0	7.0	9	0	4	2	0-0	0	9.00
Pete Rambo	R	19	1	0	0	0	3.2	6	0	4	4	0-0	0	14.73
Rusty Yarnall	R	23	1	0	0	0	1.0	3	0	1	0	0-1	0	18.00

»1927 New York Yankees 1st AL 110-44 .714 —

Miller Huggins

Player	Gm by Position	B	Age	G	AB	R	H	2B	3B	HR	RBI	BB	SO	SB	Avg	OBP	Slg
Pat Collins	C89	R	30	92	251	38	69	9	3	7	36	54	24	0	.275	.407	.418
Lou Gehrig	1B155	L	24	155	584	149	218	52	18	47	175	109	84	10	.373	.474	.765
Tony Lazzeri	2B113,SS38,3B9	R	23	153	570	92	176	29	8	18	102	69	82	22	.309	.383	.482
Joe Dugan	3B111	R	30	112	387	44	104	24	3	2	43	27	37	1	.269	.321	.362
Mark Koenig	SS122	S	22	123	526	99	150	20	11	3	62	25	21	3	.285	.320	.382
Earle Combs	OF152	L	28	152	648	137	231	36	23	6	64	62	31	15	.356	.414	.511
Babe Ruth	OF151	L	32	151	540	158	192	29	8	60	164	138	89	7	.356	.487	.772
Bob Meusel	OF131	R	30	135	516	75	174	47	9	8	103	45	58	24	.337	.393	.510
Ray Morehart	2B53	L	27	73	195	45	50	7	2	1	20	29	18	4	.256	.353	.328
Johnny Grabowski	C68	R	27	70	195	29	54	2	4	0	25	20	15	0	.277	.350	.328
Cedric Durst	OF36,1B2	L	30	65	129	18	32	4	3	0	25	6	7	0	.248	.281	.326
Mike Gazella	3B44,SS6	R	30	54	115	17	32	8	4	0	9	23	16	4	.278	.403	.417
Benny Bengough	C30	R	28	31	85	6	21	3	3	0	10	4	4	0	.247	.281	.353
Ben Paschal	OF27	R	31	50	82	16	26	9	2	2	16	4	10	0	.317	.349	.549
Julie Wera	3B19	R	25	38	42	7	10	3	0	1	8	1	5	0	.238	.273	.381

Pitcher	T	Age	G	GS	CG	ShO	IP	H	HR	BB	SO	W-L	Sv	ERA
Waite Hoyt	R	27	36	32	23	3	256.1	242	10	54	86	22-7	1	2.63
Urban Shocker	R	36	31	27	13	2	200.0	207	8	41	35	18-6	0	2.84
Herb Pennock	L	33	34	26	18	1	209.2	225	5	48	51	19-8	2	3.00
Dutch Ruether	L	33	27	26	12	3	184.0	202	8	52	45	13-6	0	3.38
George Pipgras	R	27	29	21	9	1	166.1	148	2	77	81	10-3	0	4.11
Wilcy Moore	R	30	50	12	6	1	213.0	185	3	59	75	19-7	13	2.28
Myles Thomas	R	29	21	9	1	0	88.2	111	4	43	25	7-4	0	4.87
Bob Shawkey	R	36	19	2	0	0	43.2	44	1	16	23	2-3	4	2.89
Joe Giard	L	28	16	0	0	0	27.0	38	1	19	10	0-0	0	8.00
Walter Beall	R	27	1	0	0	0	1.0	1	0	1	0	0-0	0	9.00

1927 Philadelphia Athletics 2nd AL 91-63 .591 19.0 GB

Connie Mack

Player	Gm by Position	B	Age	G	AB	R	H	2B	3B	HR	RBI	BB	SO	SB	Avg	OBP	Slg
Mickey Cochrane	C123	L	24	126	432	80	146	20	6	12	80	50	7	9	.338	.409	.495
Jimmy Dykes	1B82,3B25,SS5*	R	30	121	417	61	135	33	6	3	60	44	23	2	.324	.394	.453
Max Bishop	2B106	L	27	117	372	80	103	15	1	0	22	105	28	8	.277	.442	.323
Sammy Hale	3B128	R	30	131	501	77	157	24	8	5	81	32	32	11	.313	.358	.423
Joe Boley	SS114	R	30	118	370	49	115	18	8	1	52	26	14	8	.311	.361	.411
Ty Cobb	OF127	L	40	134	490	104	175	32	7	5	93	67	12	22	.357	.440	.482
Al Simmons	OF105	R	25	106	406	86	159	36	11	15	108	31	30	10	.392	.436	.645
Walt French	OF94	L	27	109	326	48	99	10	5	0	41	16	14	9	.304	.338	.365
Bill Lamar	OF79	L	30	84	324	48	97	23	3	4	47	16	10	4	.299	.334	.426
Zack Wheat	OF62	L	39	88	247	34	80	12	1	1	38	18	5	2	.324	.379	.393
Eddie Collins	2B56,SS1	L	40	95	225	50	76	12	1	1	15	60	9	6	.338	.477	.413
Chick Galloway	SS61	R	30	77	181	25	48	10	4	0	22	18	9	1	.265	.332	.365
Cy Perkins	C54,1B1	R	31	59	137	11	35	7	2	1	15	12	8	0	.255	.315	.358
Jimmie Foxx	1B32,C5	R	19	61	130	23	42	6	5	3	20	14	11	2	.323	.393	.515
Jim Poole	1B31	L	32	38	99	4	22	2	0	0	10	9	6	0	.222	.287	.242
Dud Branom	1B26	L	29	30	94	8	22	1	0	0	13	2	5	1	.234	.250	.245
Charlie Bates	OF9	R	19	9	38	5	9	2	2	0	2	3	5	0	.237	.293	.395
B. Doll Jacobson†	OF14	R	36	17	35	3	8	3	0	1	5	0	3	0	.229	.229	.400
Rusty Saunders	OF4	R	21	5	15	2	2	0	0	0	2	3	2	0	.133	.278	.133
Joe Mellana	3B2	R	22	4	7	1	2	0	0	0	2	0	1	0	.286	.286	.286

J. Dykes, 5 G at OF, 3 G at 2B, 2 G at P

Pitcher	T	Age	G	GS	CG	ShO	IP	H	HR	BB	SO	W-L	Sv	ERA
Rube Walberg	L	30	46	34	15	0	249.1	257	18	91	136	16-12	4	3.97
Lefty Grove	L	27	51	28	14	1	262.1	251	6	79	174	20-13	9	3.19
Howard Ehmke	R	33	30	27	10	1	189.2	200	13	60	68	12-10	0	4.22
Jack Quinn	R	43	34	25	11	3	207.1	211	8	37	43	15-10	1	3.17
Eddie Rommel	R	29	30	17	8	2	146.2	166	6	48	33	11-3	1	4.36
Guy Cantrell†	R	23	2	2	0	0	18.0	25	0	7	7	0-2	0	5.00
Buzz Wetzel	R	32	2	1	0	0	4.2	8	0	5	0	0-0	0	7.71
Sam Gray	R	29	37	13	3	1	133.1	153	4	51	49	9-6	3	4.52
Joe Pate	L	35	32	0	0	0	53.2	67	3	21	14	0-3	6	5.20
Jing Johnson	R	32	17	3	2	0	51.2	42	2	16	16	4-2	0	3.48
Lefty Willis	L	21	15	2	1	0	27.0	32	2	11	7	3-1	0	5.67
Ike Powers	R	21	11	1	0	0	26.0	26	1	7	3	1-1	0	4.50
Neal Baker	R	23	5	2	0	0	17.1	27	2	7	3	0-0	0	5.71
Jimmy Dykes	R	30	2	0	0	0	2.0	2	0	1	0	0-0	0	4.50
Carroll Yerkes	L	24	1	0	0	0	1.0	0	0	1	0	0-0	0	0.00

1927 Washington Senators 3rd AL 85-69 .552 25.0 GB

Bucky Harris

Player	Gm by Position	B	Age	G	AB	R	H	2B	3B	HR	RBI	BB	SO	SB	Avg	OBP	Slg
Muddy Ruel	C128	R	31	131	428	61	132	16	5	1	52	63	18	9	.308	.403	.376
Joe Judge	1B137	L	33	137	522	68	161	29	11	2	71	45	22	10	.308	.366	.418
Bucky Harris	2B128	R	30	128	475	98	127	20	3	1	55	66	33	18	.267	.363	.328
Ossie Bluege	3B146	R	26	146	503	71	138	21	10	1	66	57	47	15	.274	.354	.362
Bobby Reeves	SS96,3B12,2B2	R	23	112	380	37	97	11	5	1	39	21	53	3	.255	.296	.318
Goose Goslin	OF148	L	26	148	581	96	194	37	15	13	120	50	28	21	.334	.392	.516
Sam Rice	OF139	L	37	142	603	98	179	33	14	2	65	36	11	19	.297	.336	.408
Tris Speaker	OF120,1B17	L	39	141	523	71	171	43	6	2	73	55	8	9	.327	.395	.444
Earl McNeely	OF47,1B4	R	29	73	185	40	51	10	4	0	16	11	13	11	.276	.320	.373
Topper Rigney†	SS32,3B6	R	30	45	132	20	36	5	4	0	13	22	10	1	.273	.381	.371
Bennie Tate	C39	L	25	61	131	12	41	5	1	1	24	8	4	0	.313	.357	.389
Stuffy Stewart	2B37,3B2	R	33	56	129	24	31	6	2	0	4	8	15	12	.240	.285	.318
Sammy West	OF18	L	22	38	67	9	16	4	1	0	6	8	8	1	.239	.320	.328
Buddy Myer†	SS15	L	23	15	51	7	11	1	0	0	7	8	3	3	.216	.322	.235
Babe Ganzel	OF13	R	26	13	48	7	21	4	2	1	13	7	3	0	.438	.509	.667
Grant Gillis	SS10	R	26	10	36	8	8	3	1	0	2	2	0	0	.222	.263	.361
Jackie Hayes	SS8,3B1	R	20	10	29	2	7	0	0	0	2	1	2	0	.241	.267	.241
Ollie Tucker	OF5	L	25	20	24	1	5	2	0	0	8	4	2	0	.208	.321	.292
Nick Cullop†	OF5,1B1	R	26	15	23	2	5	2	0	0	1	1	6	0	.217	.250	.304
Eddie Onslow	1B5	L	34	9	18	1	4	1	0	0	1	1	0	0	.222	.263	.278
Johnny Berger	C9	R	25	9	15	1	4	0	0	0	1	2	3	0	.267	.353	.267
Red Barnes	OF3	L	23	3	11	5	4	1	0	0	0	1	3	0	.364	.417	.455
Mickey O'Neil†	C4	R	27	5	6	0	0	0	0	0	0	0	1	0	.000	.000	.000
Buddy Dear	2B1	R	21	2	1	1	0	0	0	0	0	0	0	0	.000	.000	.000
Lefty Atkinson		L	23	1	1	1	0	0	0	0	0	0	0	0	.000	.000	.000

Pitcher	T	Age	G	GS	CG	ShO	IP	H	HR	BB	SO	W-L	Sv	ERA
Hod Lisenbee	R	28	39	34	17	4	242.0	221	6	78	105	18-9	0	3.57
Sloppy Thurston	R	28	29	28	13	2	205.1	254	16	60	38	13-13	0	4.47
Bump Hadley	R	22	30	27	13	0	198.2	177	2	86	60	14-6	0	2.85
Walter Johnson	R	39	18	15	7	1	107.2	113	7	26	48	5-6	0	5.10
Tom Zachary†	L	31	15	14	5	1	102.2	116	2	30	13	4-7	0	3.94
General Crowder†	R	28	15	11	4	2	67.1	58	3	42	22	4-7	0	4.54
Stan Coveleski	R	37	5	4	0	0	14.1	13	0	8	3	2-1	0	3.14
Paul Hopkins	R	22	2	1	0	0	9.0	13	1	4	5	1-0	0	5.00
Garland Braxton	L	27	58	2	0	0	155.1	144	5	33	96	10-9	13	2.95
Firpo Marberry	R	28	56	10	2	0	155.1	177	4	68	74	10-7	9	4.64
Bobby Burke	L	20	36	6	1	0	100.0	91	6	32	20	3-2	0	3.96
George Murray	R	28	7	3	0	0	18.0	18	1	15	5	1-1	0	7.00
Dick Coffman	R	20	5	2	0	0	16.0	20	0	2	5	0-1	0	3.38
Dick Jones	R	25	2	0	0	0	3.1	8	0	5	1	0-0	0	21.60
Clay Van Alstyne	R	27	2	0	0	0	3.0	3	0	0	0	0-0	0	3.00
Ralph Judd	R	25	1	0	0	0	4.0	8	0	2	2	0-0	1	6.75

1927 Detroit Tigers 4th AL 82-71 .536 27.5 GB

George Moriarty

Player	Gm by Position	B	Age	G	AB	R	H	2B	3B	HR	RBI	BB	SO	SB	Avg	OBP	Slg
Larry Woodall	C86	R	32	88	246	28	69	8	6	0	39	37	9	9	.280	.375	.362
Lu Blue	1B104	S	30	112	365	71	95	17	9	1	42	71	28	13	.260	.384	.364
Charlie Gehringer	2B121	L	24	133	508	110	161	29	11	4	61	52	31	17	.317	.383	.441
Jack Warner	3B138	R	23	139	559	78	149	22	9	1	45	47	45	15	.267	.330	.343
Jackie Tavener	SS114	L	29	116	419	60	115	22	9	5	59	36	38	20	.274	.333	.406
Heinie Manush	OF149	L	25	152	593	102	177	31	18	6	80	47	29	12	.298	.354	.442
Bob Fothergill	OF137	R	29	143	527	93	189	38	9	9	114	47	31	9	.359	.413	.516
Harry Heilmann	OF135	R	32	141	505	106	201	50	9	14	120	72	16	11	.398	.475	.616
Marty McManus	SS39,2B35,3B22*	R	27	108	369	60	99	19	7	9	69	34	38	8	.268	.332	.431
Johnny Neun	1B53	S	26	79	204	38	66	9	4	0	27	35	13	22	.324	.427	.407
Johnny Bassler	C67	L	32	81	200	19	57	7	0	0	24	45	9	1	.285	.416	.320
Al Wingo	OF34	L	29	75	137	15	32	8	2	0	20	25	14	1	.234	.352	.321
Art Ruble	OF43	L	24	56	91	16	15	4	2	0	11	14	15	2	.165	.283	.253
Merv Shea	C31	R	26	34	85	5	15	6	3	0	9	7	15	0	.176	.239	.318
Bernie DeViveiros	SS14,3B1	R	26	24	22	4	5	1	0	0	2	2	8	1	.227	.292	.273
Clyde Manion		R	30	1	0	0	0	0	0	0	0	1	0	0	—	1.000	—

M. McManus, 6 G at 1B

Pitcher	T	Age	G	GS	CG	ShO	IP	H	HR	BB	SO	W-L	Sv	ERA
Earl Whitehill	L	27	41	31	17	3	236.0	238	4	105	95	16-14	3	3.36
Sam Gibson	R	27	33	26	11	0	184.2	201	9	86	76	11-12	0	3.80
Rip Collins	R	31	30	25	10	1	172.2	207	5	59	37	13-7	0	4.69
Lil Stoner	R	28	38	24	13	0	215.0	251	9	77	63	10-13	5	3.98
Ken Holloway	R	29	36	23	11	1	183.1	210	10	61	36	11-12	6	4.07
Josh Billings	R	19	10	9	5	0	67.0	64	3	39	18	5-4	0	4.84
Rufus Smith	L	22	1	1	0	0	8.0	8	0	3	2	0-0	0	3.38
Ownie Carroll	R	24	31	15	8	0	172.0	186	5	73	41	10-6	0	3.98
George Smith	R	25	29	0	0	0	71.1	62	3	50	32	4-1	0	3.91
Don Hankins	R	25	20	1	0	0	42.1	67	1	13	10	2-1	2	6.38
Ed Wells	L	27	8	1	0	0	20.0	28	3	5	5	0-1	0	6.75
Jess Doyle	R	29	7	0	0	0	12.1	16	0	5	5	0-0	0	8.03
Jim Walkup	L	31	2	0	0	0	1.2	3	0	0	0	0-0	0	5.40
Augie Johns	L	27	1	0	0	0	1.0	1	0	1	1	0-0	0	9.00

1927 Chicago White Sox 5th AL 70-83 .458 39.5 GB

Ray Schalk

Player	Gm by Position	B	Age	G	AB	R	H	2B	3B	HR	RBI	BB	SO	SB	Avg	OBP	Slg
Harry McCurdy	C82	L	27	86	262	34	75	19	3	1	27	32	24	6	.286	.366	.393
Bud Clancy	1B123	L	26	130	464	46	139	21	2	3	53	24	24	4	.300	.337	.373
Aaron Ward	2B138,3B6	R	30	145	463	75	125	25	8	5	56	63	56	6	.270	.360	.391
Willie Kamm	3B146	R	27	148	540	85	146	32	13	0	59	70	18	7	.270	.354	.378
Bill Hunnefield	SS78,2B17,3B1	S	28	112	365	45	104	25	1	2	36	25	24	13	.285	.332	.375
Bill Barrett	OF147	R	27	147	556	62	159	35	9	4	83	52	46	20	.286	.347	.403
Bibb Falk	OF145	L	28	145	535	76	175	35	6	9	83	52	19	5	.327	.391	.465
Alex Metzler	OF134	L	24	134	543	87	173	29	11	3	61	61	39	15	.319	.396	.429
Buck Crouse	C81	L	30	85	222	22	53	11	0	0	20	21	10	4	.239	.307	.288
Roger Peckinpaugh	SS60	R	36	68	217	23	64	6	3	0	23	21	6	2	.295	.360	.350
Earl Sheely	1B36	R	34	45	129	11	27	3	0	2	16	20	5	1	.209	.320	.279
Roy Flaskamper	SS25	S	25	26	95	12	21	5	0	0	6	3	8	0	.221	.260	.274
Bernie Neis†	OF21	S	31	45	76	9	22	5	0	0	11	10	9	1	.289	.372	.355
Moe Berg	C10,2B10,SS6*	R	25	35	69	4	17	4	0	0	4	4	10	0	.246	.288	.304
Ike Boone	OF11	L	30	29	53	10	12	4	0	1	11	3	4	0	.226	.268	.358
Carl Reynolds	OF13	R	24	14	42	5	9	3	0	1	7	5	7	1	.214	.313	.357
Ray Schalk	C15	R	34	16	26	2	6	2	0	0	2	2	1	0	.231	.286	.308
Johnny Mostil	OF6	R	31	13	16	3	2	0	0	0	1	0	1	1	.125	.176	.125
Randy Moore	OF4	L	21	15	15	0	0	0	0	0	0	0	2	0	.000	.000	.000
Kid Willson	OF2	L	31	7	10	1	1	0	0	0	0	1	2	0	.100	.100	.100
Jim Battle	3B4,SS2	R	26	6	8	1	3	0	1	0	0	0	1	0	.375	.375	.625
Bob Way	2B1	R	21	5	3	3	1	0	0	0	1	0	0	0	.333	.333	.333
Lena Blackburne		R	40	1	1	1	1	0	0	0	1	0	0	0	1.000	1.000	1.000

M. Berg, 3 G at 3B

Pitcher	T	Age	G	GS	CG	ShO	IP	H	HR	BB	SO	W-L	Sv	ERA
Tommy Thomas	R	27	40	36	24	3	307.2	271	16	94	107	19-16	1	2.98
Ted Lyons	R	26	39	34	30	2	307.2	291	7	67	71	22-14	2	2.84
Ted Blankenship	R	26	37	34	11	3	236.2	280	14	74	51	12-17	0	5.06
Red Faber	R	38	18	15	6	0	110.2	131	2	41	39	4-7	0	4.55
Frank Stewart	R	20	1	1	0	0	4.0	5	0	4	0	0-1	0	9.00
Joe Brown	R	26	1	1	0	0	0.0	2	0	1	0	0-0	0	—
Sarge Connally	R	28	43	18	11	1	198.1	217	8	83	58	10-15	5	4.08
Bert Cole	L	30	27	2	0	0	66.2	79	3	19	12	1-4	0	4.73
Elmer Jacobs	R	34	25	8	2	1	74.1	105	3	37	22	2-4	0	4.60
Charlie Barnabe	L	27	17	4	1	0	61.0	86	2	20	5	0-5	0	5.31

1927 Cleveland Indians 6th AL 66-87 .431 43.5 GB

Jack McCallister

Player	Gm by Position	B	Age	G	AB	R	H	2B	3B	HR	RBI	BB	SO	SB	Avg	OBP	Slg
Luke Sewell	C126	R	26	128	470	52	138	27	6	0	53	20	23	4	.294	.328	.377
George Burns	1B139	R	34	140	549	84	175	51	2	3	78	42	27	13	.319	.375	.435
Lew Fonseca	2B96,1B13	R	28	112	428	60	133	20	7	2	40	12	17	12	.311	.333	.404
Rube Lutzke	3B98	R	29	100	311	35	78	12	3	0	41	22	29	2	.251	.307	.309
Joe Sewell	SS153	L	28	153	569	83	180	48	5	1	92	51	7	3	.316	.382	.424
Homer Summa	OF145	L	28	145	574	72	164	41	7	4	74	32	18	6	.286	.331	.402
Charlie Jamieson	OF127	L	34	127	489	73	151	23	6	0	36	64	14	7	.309	.394	.380
Ike Eichrodt	OF81	R	24	85	267	24	59	19	2	0	25	16	25	2	.221	.265	.307
Johnny Hodapp	3B67,1B4	R	21	79	240	25	73	15	3	5	40	14	23	2	.304	.343	.454
Freddy Spurgeon	2B52	R	26	57	179	30	45	6	1	1	19	18	14	8	.251	.323	.313
B. Doll Jacobson†	OF31	R	36	32	103	13	26	5	0	0	13	6	4	0	.252	.300	.301
Bernie Neis†	OF29	S	31	32	96	17	29	9	0	4	18	18	9	0	.302	.412	.521
Glenn Myatt	C26	L	29	55	94	15	23	6	0	2	8	12	7	1	.245	.336	.372
Nick Cullop†	OF20,P1	R	26	32	68	9	16	2	3	1	8	9	19	0	.235	.333	.397
Sam Langford	OF20	L	28	20	67	10	18	5	0	1	7	5	7	0	.269	.347	.388
Johnny Gill	OF17	L	22	21	60	8	13	3	0	1	4	7	13	1	.217	.319	.317
Chick Autry	C14	R	24	16	43	5	11	4	1	0	7	0	6	0	.256	.256	.395
Pat McNulty	OF12	L	28	19	41	3	13	1	0	0	4	4	3	1	.317	.378	.341
Carl Lind	2B11,SS1	R	23	12	37	2	5	0	0	0	1	5	7	1	.135	.256	.135
Dutch Ussat	3B4	R	23	4	16	4	3	0	1	0	2	2	1	0	.188	.278	.313
George Gerken	OF5	R	23	6	14	1	3	0	0	0	2	1	3	0	.214	.267	.214
Johnny Burnett	2B2	L	22	17	8	5	0	0	0	0	0	0	3	1	.000	.000	.000
Ernie Padgett	2B4	R	28	7	7	1	2	0	0	0	0	0	2	0	.286	.286	.286

Pitcher	T	Age	G	GS	CG	ShO	IP	H	HR	BB	SO	W-L	Sv	ERA
Willis Hudlin	R	21	43	30	18	1	264.2	291	3	83	65	18-12	0	4.01
Joe Shaute	L	27	45	28	14	0	230.1	255	9	75	63	9-16	2	4.22
Garland Buckeye	L	29	35	25	13	2	204.2	231	6	74	38	10-17	1	3.96
Jake Miller	L	29	34	23	11	0	185.1	189	4	48	53	10-8	0	3.21
George Uhle	R	28	25	22	10	1	153.1	187	3	59	69	8-9	1	4.34
Dutch Levsen	R	29	25	13	2	1	80.1	96	1	37	15	3-7	0	5.49
Hal McKain	R	20	2	1	0	0	11.0	18	0	4	5	0-1	0	4.09
George Grant	R	24	25	3	2	0	74.2	85	1	40	19	4-6	1	4.46
Benn Karr	R	33	22	5	1	0	76.2	92	5	32	17	3-3	2	5.05
Sherry Smith	L	36	11	2	1	0	38.0	53	2	14	8	1-4	1	5.45
Jumbo Brown	R	20	8	0	0	0	18.2	19	3	26	8	0-2	0	6.27
Willie Underhill	R	22	4	1	0	0	8.1	12	0	11	4	0-2	0	9.72
Hap Collard	R	28	4	0	0	0	5.1	8	0	3	2	0-0	0	5.06
Wes Ferrell	R	19	1	0	0	0	1.0	3	0	2	0	0-0	0	27.00
Nick Cullop	R	26	1	0	0	0	1.0	3	0	0	0	0-0	0	9.00

1927 St. Louis Browns 7th AL 59-94 .386 50.5 GB

Dan Howley

Player	Gm by Position	B	Age	G	AB	R	H	2B	3B	HR	RBI	BB	SO	SB	Avg	OBP	Slg
Wally Schang	C75	S	37	97	263	40	84	15	2	5	42	41	33	3	.319	.415	.449
George Sisler	1B149	L	34	149	614	87	201	32	8	5	97	24	15	27	.327	.357	.430
Ski Melillo	2B101	R	27	107	356	45	80	18	2	0	26	25	28	3	.225	.276	.287
Frank O'Rourke	3B121,2B16,1B3	R	32	140	538	85	144	25	3	1	39	64	43	19	.268	.358	.331
Wally Gerber	SS141,3B1	R	35	142	438	44	98	13	9	0	45	35	25	2	.224	.284	.295
Harry Rice	OF130	L	25	137	520	90	149	26	9	7	68	50	21	6	.287	.351	.412
Bing Miller	OF128	R	32	144	492	83	160	32	7	5	75	30	26	9	.325	.375	.449
Ken Williams	OF113	L	37	131	421	70	136	23	6	17	74	57	30	9	.323	.405	.527
Spencer Adams	2B54,3B28	L	29	88	259	32	69	11	3	0	29	24	33	1	.266	.333	.332
Herschel Bennett	OF55	L	30	93	256	40	68	12	2	3	30	14	21	6	.266	.311	.363
Steve O'Neill	C60	R	35	74	191	14	44	7	0	1	22	20	6	0	.230	.303	.283
Fred Schulte	OF49	R	26	60	189	32	60	16	5	3	34	20	14	5	.317	.383	.503
Leo Dixon	C35	R	32	36	103	6	20	3	1	0	12	7	6	0	.194	.245	.243
Otto Miller	SS35,3B11	R	26	51	76	8	17	5	0	0	8	8	5	0	.224	.306	.289
Red Kress	SS7	R	20	7	23	3	7	2	1	1	3	3	3	0	.304	.385	.609
Guy Sturdy	1B5	L	27	5	21	5	9	1	0	0	5	1	0	2	.429	.455	.476

Pitcher	T	Age	G	GS	CG	ShO	IP	H	HR	BB	SO	W-L	Sv	ERA
Milt Gaston	R	31	37	30	21	0	254.0	275	18	100	77	13-17	1	5.00
Sad Sam Jones	R	34	30	26	11	0	189.2	211	13	102	72	8-14	0	4.32
Elam Vangilder	R	31	44	23	12	3	203.0	245	13	102	62	10-12	1	4.79
Lefty Stewart	L	26	27	19	11	0	155.2	187	7	43	43	8-11	1	4.28
Tom Zachary†	L	31	13	12	6	0	78.1	110	4	27	13	4-6	0	4.37
Win Ballou	L	29	21	11	4	0	90.1	105	4	46	17	5-6	0	4.78
Jim Wright	R	26	2	1	1	0	12.0	8	0	4	4	1-0	0	4.50
George Blaeholder	R	23	1	1	1	0	9.0	8	1	4	2	0-1	0	5.00
Ernie Wingard	L	26	38	17	7	0	156.1	213	7	79	28	2-13	0	6.56
Ernie Nevers	R	25	27	5	2	0	94.2	105	8	35	22	3-8	2	4.94
General Crowder†	R	28	21	8	2	1	73.2	71	3	42	30	3-5	3	5.01
Chet Falk	L	22	9	0	0	0	15.2	25	1	10	2	1-0	0	5.74
Boom-Boom Beck	R	22	3	1	1	0	11.1	15	0	5	6	1-0	0	5.56
Stew Bolen	L	24	3	1	1	0	9.2	14	0	5	7	0-1	0	8.38

1927 Boston Red Sox 8th AL 51-103 .331 59.0 GB

Bill Carrigan

Player	Gm by Position	B	Age	G	AB	R	H	2B	3B	HR	RBI	BB	SO	SB	Avg	OBP	Slg
Grover Hartley	C86	R	38	103	244	23	67	11	0	1	31	22	14	1	.275	.337	.332
Phil Todt	1B139	L	25	140	516	55	122	22	6	6	52	28	23	6	.236	.280	.337
Bill Regan	2B121	R	28	129	468	43	128	37	10	2	66	26	51	10	.274	.315	.408
Billy Rogell	3B53,2B2,OF2	S	22	82	207	35	55	14	6	2	28	24	28	3	.266	.342	.420
Buddy Myer†	SS101,3B14,OF10*	L	23	133	469	59	135	22	11	2	47	48	15	9	.288	.359	.394
Ira Flagstead	OF129	R	33	131	466	63	133	26	8	4	69	57	25	12	.285	.374	.401
Wally Shaner	OF108,1B1	R	27	122	406	54	111	33	6	3	49	21	35	11	.273	.311	.406
Jack Tobin	OF93	L	35	111	374	52	116	18	3	2	40	36	9	5	.310	.371	.390
Jack Rothrock	SS40,2B36,3B20*	S	22	117	428	61	111	24	8	1	36	24	46	5	.259	.302	.360
Cleo Carlyle	OF52	L	24	95	278	31	65	12	8	1	28	36	40	4	.234	.324	.345
Fred Hofmann	C81	R	33	87	217	20	59	19	1	0	24	21	26	2	.272	.342	.369
Red Rollings	3B44,1B10,2B2	L	23	82	184	19	49	4	1	0	9	12	10	3	.266	.325	.299
B. Doll Jacobson†	OF39	R	36	45	155	11	38	9	3	0	24	5	12	1	.245	.278	.342
Fred Haney†	3B34,OF1	R	29	47	116	23	32	4	1	3	12	25	14	4	.276	.404	.405
Arlie Tarbert	OF27	R	22	33	69	5	13	1	0	0	5	3	12	0	.188	.253	.203
Bill Moore	C42	L	25	44	69	7	15	2	0	0	4	13	8	0	.217	.341	.246
P. Wee Wanninger†	SS15	L	24	18	60	4	12	0	0	0	1	6	2	2	.200	.284	.200
Frank Welch	OF6	R	29	15	28	2	5	2	0	0	4	5	1	0	.179	.303	.250
Topper Rigney†	3B4,SS1	R	30	8	18	0	2	1	0	0	0	1	2	0	.111	.158	.167
Marty Karow	SS3,3B2	R	22	6	10	0	2	1	0	0	0	0	2	0	.200	.200	.300
Elmer Eggert	2B1	R	25	5	3	0	0	0	0	0	0	1	1	0	.000	.250	.000
John Freeman	OF3	R	26	4	2	0	0	0	0	0	0	0	0	0	.000	.000	.000
Fred Bratschi		R	35	1	1	0	0	0	0	0	0	0	0	0	.000	.000	.000

B. Myer, 1 G at 2B; J. Rothrock, 13 G at 1B

Pitcher	T	Age	G	GS	CG	ShO	IP	H	HR	BB	SO	W-L	Sv	ERA
Hal Wiltse	L	23	36	29	13	1	219.0	276	5	76	47	10-18	1	5.10
Slim Harriss	R	30	44	27	11	1	217.2	253	8	66	77	14-21	1	4.18
Tony Welzer	R	28	37	19	8	0	171.2	214	10	71	56	6-11	1	4.72
Red Ruffing	R	23	26	18	10	0	158.1	160	7	87	77	5-13	2	4.66
Del Lundgren	R	27	30	17	5	2	136.1	160	7	87	39	5-12	0	6.27
Danny MacFayden	R	22	34	16	6	1	160.1	176	9	59	42	5-8	2	4.27
Jack Russell	R	21	34	15	4	1	147.0	172	5	40	25	4-9	0	4.10
Ted Wingfield	R	27	20	8	2	0	74.2	105	2	27	1	1-7	0	5.06
Rudy Sommers	L	38	7	0	0	0	14.0	18	2	14	2	0-0	0	8.36
Herb Bradley	R	24	6	2	2	0	23.0	16	0	7	6	1-1	0	3.13
John Wilson	R	22	5	2	2	0	25.1	31	1	13	8	0-2	0	3.55
Frank Bennett	R	22	4	1	0	0	12.1	15	0	6	1	0-1	0	2.92
Bob Cremins	L	21	4	0	0	0	5.1	5	0	3	0	0-0	0	5.06
Frank Bushey	R	20	1	0	0	0	1.1	2	0	2	0	0-0	0	6.75

»1927 Pittsburgh Pirates 1st NL 94-60 .610 —

Donie Bush

Player	Gm by Position	B	Age	G	AB	R	H	2B	3B	HR	RBI	BB	SO	SB	Avg	OBP	Slg
Johnny Gooch	C91	S	29	101	291	22	75	17	2	2	48	19	21	0	.258	.305	.351
Joe Harris	1B116,OF3	R	36	129	411	57	134	27	9	5	73	48	19	0	.326	.402	.472
George Grantham	2B124,1B29	L	27	151	531	96	162	33	11	8	66	74	39	9	.305	.396	.454
Pie Traynor	3B143	R	27	149	573	93	196	32	9	5	106	22	11	11	.342	.370	.455
Glenn Wright	SS143	R	26	143	570	78	160	26	4	9	105	39	46	4	.281	.328	.388
Lloyd Waner	OF150,2B1	L	21	150	629	133	223	17	6	2	27	37	23	14	.355	.396	.410
Paul Waner	OF143,1B14	L	24	155	623	113	237	40	17	9	131	60	14	5	.380	.437	.543
Clyde Barnhart	OF94	R	31	108	360	66	115	25	5	3	54	37	19	2	.319	.384	.442
Kiki Cuyler	OF73	R	28	85	285	60	88	13	7	3	31	37	36	20	.309	.394	.435
Earl Smith	C61	L	30	66	189	16	51	3	1	5	25	21	11	0	.270	.346	.376
Hal Rhyne	2B45,3B10,SS7	R	28	62	168	21	46	5	0	0	17	14	9	0	.274	.330	.304
Roy Spencer	C34	R	27	38	92	9	26	3	1	0	13	3	3	0	.283	.305	.337
Adam Comorosky	OF16	R	21	18	61	5	14	1	0	0	4	3	1	0	.230	.266	.246
Heine Groh	3B12	R	37	14	35	2	10	1	0	0	3	2	2	0	.286	.324	.314
Joe Cronin	2B7,SS4,1B1	R	20	12	22	2	5	1	0	0	3	2	3	0	.227	.292	.273
George Brickell	OF3	L	20	32	21	6	6	1	0	1	4	1	0	0	.286	.318	.476
Ed Sicking	2B5	R	30	6	7	1	1	1	0	0	3	1	0	0	.143	.250	.286
Herman Layne	OF2	R	26	11	6	3	0	0	0	0	0	1	0	0	.000	.143	.000
Dick Bartell	SS1	R	19	1	2	0	0	0	0	0	0	2	0	0	.000	.500	.000

Pitcher	T	Age	G	GS	CG	ShO	IP	H	HR	BB	SO	W-L	Sv	ERA
Lee Meadows	R	32	40	38	25	2	299.1	315	11	66	84	19-10	0	3.40
Vic Aldridge	R	33	35	34	17	1	239.1	248	16	74	86	15-10	1	4.25
Carmen Hill	R	31	43	31	22	2	277.2	260	12	80	95	22-11	3	3.24
Ray Kremer	R	34	35	28	18	3	226.0	205	9	53	63	19-8	2	2.47
Joe Bush†	R	34	5	3	0	0	6.2	14	1	5	1	1-2	0	13.50
Roy Mahaffey	R	24	2	1	0	0	9.1	9	0	9	4	1-0	0	7.71
Mike Cvengros	L	25	23	4	0	0	53.2	55	3	24	21	2-1	1	3.35
Johnny Morrison	R	31	21	2	1	0	53.2	63	2	21	21	3-2	3	4.19
Joe Dawson	R	30	20	7	4	0	80.2	80	2	32	17	3-7	0	4.46
Johnny Miljus	R	32	19	6	3	2	75.2	62	0	17	24	8-3	0	1.90
Emil Yde	L	27	9	2	0	0	29.2	45	1	15	9	1-3	0	9.71
Chet Nichols	R	29	8	0	0	0	27.2	34	1	17	9	0-3	0	5.86
Don Songer†	L	27	2	0	0	0	4.2	10	0	4	1	0-0	0	11.57
Red Peery	L	20	1	0	0	0	1.0	0	0	1	0	0-0	0	0.00

1927 St. Louis Cardinals 2nd NL 92-61 .601 1.5 GB

Bob O'Farrell

Player	Gm by Position	B	Age	G	AB	R	H	2B	3B	HR	RBI	BB	SO	SB	Avg	OBP	Slg
Frank Snyder	C62	R	34	63	194	7	50	5	0	1	30	9	18	0	.258	.291	.299
Jim Bottomley	1B152	L	27	152	574	95	174	31	15	19	124	74	49	8	.303	.387	.509
Frankie Frisch	2B153,SS1	S	28	153	617	112	208	31	11	10	78	43	10	48	.337	.387	.472
Les Bell	3B100,SS10	R	25	115	390	48	101	26	6	9	65	34	63	5	.259	.320	.426
Heinie Schuble	SS65	R	20	65	218	29	56	6	2	4	28	7	27	0	.257	.283	.358
Taylor Douthit	OF125	R	26	130	488	81	128	29	6	5	50	52	45	6	.262	.336	.377
Wattie Holm	OF97,3B9	R	25	110	419	55	120	27	8	3	66	24	29	4	.286	.327	.411
Chick Hafey	OF94	R	24	103	346	62	114	26	5	18	63	36	41	12	.329	.401	.590
Billy Southworth	OF83	L	34	92	306	52	92	15	5	2	39	23	7	10	.301	.350	.402
Specs Toporcer	3B54,SS27,2B2*	L	28	86	290	37	72	13	4	0	19	27	16	5	.248	.314	.321
Tommy Thevenow	SS59	R	23	59	191	23	37	6	1	0	4	14	8	2	.194	.249	.236
Ray Blades	OF50	R	30	61	180	33	57	8	5	2	29	28	22	3	.317	.414	.450
Bob O'Farrell	C53	R	30	61	178	19	47	10	1	0	18	23	22	3	.264	.348	.331
Johnny Schulte	C59	L	30	64	156	35	45	8	2	9	32	47	19	1	.288	.456	.538
Ernie Orsatti	OF26	L	24	27	92	15	29	7	3	0	12	11	12	2	.315	.388	.457
Danny Clark	OF9	L	33	58	72	8	17	2	2	0	13	8	7	0	.236	.313	.319
Art Reinhart	P21,1B1	L	28	27	32	8	10	1	0	0	0	2	6	0	.313	.353	.344
Rabbit Maranville	SS9	R	35	9	29	0	7	1	0	0	0	2	2	0	.241	.290	.276
Bobby Schang	C3	R	40	3	5	0	1	0	0	0	0	0	0	0	.200	.200	.200
Homer Peel	OF1	R	24	2	2	0	0	0	0	0	0	0	1	0	.000	.000	.000
Wally Roettger	OF3	R	24	5	1	0	0	0	0	0	0	1	0	0	.000	.500	.000

S. Toporcer, 1 G at 1B

Pitcher	T	Age	G	GS	CG	ShO	IP	H	HR	BB	SO	W-L	Sv	ERA
Jesse Haines	R	33	38	36	25	6	300.2	273	11	77	89	24-10	1	2.72
Pete Alexander	R	40	37	30	22	2	268.0	261	11	38	48	21-10	3	2.52
Bill Sherdel	L	30	39	28	18	0	232.1	241	17	48	59	17-12	6	3.53
Flint Rhem	R	26	27	26	9	2	169.1	189	6	54	51	10-12	0	4.41
Bob McGraw†	R	32	18	12	4	1	94.0	121	3	30	37	4-5	0	5.07
Fred Frankhouse	R	23	6	6	5	1	50.0	41	2	16	20	5-1	0	2.70
Hi Bell	R	29	25	1	0	0	57.1	71	5	22	31	1-3	0	3.92
Art Reinhart	L	28	21	9	4	2	81.2	82	5	36	15	5-2	1	4.19
Vic Keen	R	28	21	0	0	0	33.2	39	3	8	12	2-1	0	4.81
Carlisle Littlejohn	R	25	14	2	1	0	42.0	47	4	14	16	3-1	0	4.50
Jimmy Ring	R	32	13	3	1	0	33.0	39	3	17	13	0-4	0	6.55
Syl Johnson	R	26	2	0	0	0	3.0	3	1	0	2	0-0	0	6.00
Eddie Dyer	L	26	1	0	0	0	2.0	5	1	2	1	0-0	0	18.00
Tony Kaufmann†	R	26	1	0	0	0	0.2	4	0	1	0	0-0	0	40.50

1927 New York Giants 3rd NL 92-62 .597 2.0 GB

John McGraw (70-52)/Rogers Hornsby (22-10)

Player	Gm by Position	B	Age	G	AB	R	H	2B	3B	HR	RBI	BB	SO	SB	Avg	OBP	Slg
Zack Taylor†	C81	R	28	83	258	18	60	7	3	0	21	17	20	2	.233	.283	.283
Bill Terry	1B150	L	30	150	580	101	189	32	13	20	121	46	53	1	.326	.377	.529
Rogers Hornsby	2B155	R	31	155	568	133	205	32	9	26	125	86	38	9	.361	.448	.586
Freddy Lindstrom	3B87,OF51	R	21	138	562	107	172	36	8	7	58	40	40	10	.306	.354	.436
Travis Jackson	SS124,3B2	R	23	127	469	67	149	29	4	14	98	32	30	8	.318	.363	.486
George Harper	OF142	L	35	145	483	85	160	19	6	16	87	84	27	7	.331	.435	.495
Edd Roush	OF138	L	34	140	570	83	173	27	4	7	58	26	15	18	.304	.335	.402
Heinie Mueller	OF55,1B1	L	27	84	190	33	55	6	1	3	19	25	12	2	.289	.384	.379
Randy Reese	3B64,OF16,1B1	R	23	97	355	43	94	14	2	4	21	13	52	5	.265	.298	.349
Mel Ott	OF32	L	18	82	163	23	46	7	3	1	19	13	9	2	.282	.335	.380
Ty Tyson	OF41	R	35	43	159	24	42	7	2	1	17	10	19	5	.264	.308	.352
Doc Farrell†	SS36,3B2	R	25	42	142	13	55	10	1	3	34	12	11	0	.387	.442	.535
Al DeVormer	C54,1B3	R	35	68	141	14	35	3	1	2	21	11	11	1	.248	.312	.326
Jack Cummings	C34	R	23	43	80	8	29	6	1	2	14	5	10	0	.363	.407	.538
Les Mann†	OF22	R	33	29	67	13	22	4	1	2	10	8	7	2	.328	.400	.507
Jim Hamby	C19	R	29	21	52	6	10	0	1	0	5	7	7	1	.192	.288	.231
Mickey O'Neil†	C16	R	27	16	38	2	5	0	0	0	3	5	2	0	.132	.233	.132
Tex Jeanes	OF6,P1	R	26	11	20	5	6	0	0	0	0	2	2	0	.300	.364	.300
Herb Thomas†	OF3,SS1	R	25	13	17	2	3	1	1	0	1	1	1	0	.176	.263	.353
Buck Jordan		L	20	5	5	0	1	0	0	0	0	0	3	0	.200	.200	.200
Joe Klinger	OF1	R	24	3	5	0	2	0	0	0	0	0	2	0	.400	.400	.400
Red Smith	C1	R	23	1	0	0	0	0	0	0	0	0	0	0	—	—	—

Pitcher	T	Age	G	GS	CG	ShO	IP	H	HR	BB	SO	W-L	Sv	ERA
Burleigh Grimes	R	33	39	34	15	2	259.2	274	12	87	102	19-8	2	3.54
F. Fitzsimmons	R	25	42	31	14	1	244.2	260	15	67	78	17-10	3	3.72
Virgil Barnes	R	30	35	29	12	2	228.2	251	14	51	66	14-11	2	3.98
Larry Benton†	R	29	29	23	8	1	173.0	183	9	54	65	13-5	2	3.95
Hugh McQuillan†	R	29	11	9	5	0	58.0	73	4	22	17	5-4	0	4.50
Joe Bush†	R	34	3	2	1	0	12.0	18	1	5	6	1-1	0	7.50
Dutch Henry	L	25	45	15	7	1	163.2	184	6	31	40	11-6	4	4.23
Bill Clarkson	R	28	26	7	2	0	86.2	92	3	52	28	3-9	2	4.36
Don Songer†	L	27	22	1	0	0	50.1	48	4	31	9	3-5	1	2.86
Kent Greenfield†	R	24	12	1	0	0	20.0	39	3	13	4	2-2	0	9.45
Fay Thomas	R	22	9	0	0	0	16.1	19	3	4	11	0-0	0	3.31
Ben Cantwell	R	25	5	2	1	0	19.2	26	1	2	6	1-1	0	4.12
Jack Bentley	L	32	4	0	0	0	9.2	7	1	10	3	0-0	0	2.79
Jim Faulkner	L	27	3	1	0	0	9.2	13	0	5	2	1-0	0	3.72
Norman Plitt†	R	34	3	0	0	0	7.1	9	0	1	0	1-0	0	3.68
Virgil Cheeves	R	26	3	0	0	0	6.1	8	1	4	1	0-0	0	4.26
Bill Walker	L	23	3	0	0	0	4.0	6	0	5	4	0-0	0	9.00
Hank Boney	R	23	3	0	0	0	4.0	4	0	2	0	0-0	0	2.25
Mul Holland	R	24	2	0	0	0	2.0	0	0	3	0	1-0	0	0.00
Art Johnson	L	30	1	0	0	0	3.0	1	0	1	0	0-0	0	0.00
Ned Porter	R	21	1	0	0	0	2.0	3	0	1	0	0-0	0	0.00
Tex Jeanes	R	26	1	0	0	0	1.0	2	0	2	0	0-0	0	9.00

1927 Chicago Cubs 4th NL 85-68 .556 8.5 GB

Joe McCarthy

Player	Gm by Position	B	Age	G	AB	R	H	2B	3B	HR	RBI	BB	SO	SB	Avg	OBP	Slg
Gabby Hartnett	C126	R	26	127	449	56	132	32	5	10	80	44	42	2	.294	.361	.454
Charlie Grimm	1B147	L	28	147	543	68	169	29	6	2	74	45	21	3	.311	.367	.398
Clyde Beck	2B99,3B17,SS1	R	27	117	391	44	101	20	5	2	44	43	37	0	.258	.332	.350
Sparky Adams	2B60,3B53,SS40	R	32	146	647	100	189	17	7	0	49	42	26	26	.292	.335	.340
Woody English	SS84,3B1	R	20	87	334	46	97	14	4	1	28	16	26	1	.290	.325	.365
Riggs Stephenson	OF146	R	29	152	579	101	199	46	9	7	82	65	28	8	.344	.415	.491
Hack Wilson	OF146	R	27	146	551	119	175	30	12	30	129	71	70	13	.318	.401	.579
Earl Webb	OF86	L	29	102	332	58	100	18	4	14	52	48	31	3	.301	.391	.506
Cliff Heathcote	OF57	L	29	83	228	28	67	12	4	2	25	20	16	6	.294	.359	.408
Eddie Pick	3B49,2B1,OF1	S	28	54	181	23	31	5	2	2	15	20	26	0	.171	.254	.254
Pete Scott	OF36	R	28	71	156	28	49	18	1	0	21	19	18	1	.314	.392	.442
Jimmy Cooney†	SS33	R	32	33	132	16	32	2	0	0	6	8	7	1	.242	.286	.258
Mike Gonzalez	C35	R	36	39	108	15	26	4	1	1	15	10	8	1	.241	.311	.324
Howard Freigau	3B30	R	24	30	86	12	20	5	0	0	10	9	10	0	.233	.313	.291
Chick Tolson	1B8	R	32	39	54	6	16	4	0	2	17	4	9	0	.296	.345	.481
Elmer Yoter	3B11	R	27	13	27	2	6	1	1	0	5	4	4	0	.222	.323	.333
Harry Wilke	3B3	R	26	3	9	0	0	0	0	0	0	0	1	0	.000	.000	.000
Fred Haney†		R	29	4	3	0	0	0	0	0	0	0	0	0	.000	.000	.000
Tommy Sewell		L	21	1	1	0	0	0	0	0	0	0	0	0	.000	.000	.000
John Churry	C1	R	26	1	1	0	1	0	0	0	0	0	0	0	1.000	1.000	1.000

Pitcher	T	Age	G	GS	CG	ShO	IP	H	HR	BB	SO	W-L	Sv	ERA
Charlie Root	R	28	48	36	21	4	309.0	296	16	117	145	26-15	2	3.76
Sheriff Blake	R	27	32	27	13	2	224.1	238	3	82	64	13-14	0	3.29
Guy Bush	R	25	36	22	9	1	193.1	177	3	79	62	10-10	2	3.03
Hal Carlson†	R	35	27	22	15	2	184.1	201	9	27	27	12-8	0	3.17
Bob Osborn	R	24	24	12	2	0	107.2	125	2	48	45	5-5	0	4.18
Tony Kaufmann†	R	26	9	6	3	0	53.1	75	8	19	21	3-3	0	6.41
Lefty Weinert	L	25	5	3	1	0	19.2	21	2	6	5	1-1	0	4.58
Jim Brillheart	L	23	32	12	4	0	128.2	140	4	38	36	4-2	0	4.13
Percy Jones	L	27	30	11	5	1	112.2	123	3	72	37	7-8	0	4.07
Luther Roy	R	24	11	0	0	0	19.2	14	0	11	5	3-1	0	2.29
Art Nehf†	L	34	8	2	2	1	26.1	25	0	9	12	1-1	1	1.37
Hank Grampp	R	23	2	0	0	0	3.0	4	0	1	3	0-0	0	9.00
Wayland Dean†	R	25	2	0	0	0	2.0	0	0	2	2	0-0	0	0.00
Johnny Welch	R	20	1	0	0	0	1.0	0	0	3	1	0-0	0	9.00

1927 Cincinnati Reds 5th NL 75-78 .490 18.5 GB

Jack Hendricks

Player	Gm by Position	B	Age	G	AB	R	H	2B	3B	HR	RBI	BB	SO	SB	Avg	OBP	Slg
Bubbles Hargrave	C92	R	34	102	305	36	94	18	3	0	35	31	18	0	.308	.376	.387
Wally Pipp	1B114	L	34	122	443	49	115	19	6	2	41	32	11	2	.260	.309	.343
Hughie Critz	2B113	R	26	113	396	50	110	10	8	4	49	16	18	7	.278	.306	.374
Chuck Dressen	3B142,SS2	R	28	144	548	78	160	36	10	2	55	71	32	7	.292	.376	.405
Hod Ford	SS104,2B12	R	29	115	409	45	112	16	2	1	46	33	34	0	.274	.331	.330
Curt Walker	OF141	L	30	146	527	60	154	16	10	6	80	47	19	5	.292	.350	.395
Rube Bressler	OF120	R	32	124	467	43	136	14	8	3	77	32	22	4	.291	.338	.375
Ethan Allen	OF98	R	23	111	359	54	106	26	4	2	20	14	23	12	.295	.325	.407
Billy Zitzmann	OF60,SS8,3B3	R	31	88	232	47	66	10	4	0	24	20	18	9	.284	.352	.362
George Kelly	1B49,2B13,OF2	R	31	61	222	27	60	16	4	5	21	11	23	1	.270	.308	.446
Cuckoo Christensen	OF50	L	27	57	185	25	47	6	0	0	16	20	16	4	.254	.330	.286
Val Picinich	C61	R	30	65	173	16	44	8	3	0	12	24	15	3	.254	.345	.335
Red Lucas	P37,2B5,SS3*	L	25	80	150	14	47	5	2	0	28	12	10	0	.313	.368	.373
P. Wee Wanninger†	SS28	L	24	28	93	14	23	2	2	0	8	6	7	0	.247	.293	.312
Pinky Pittenger	2B20,SS9,3B2	R	28	31	84	17	23	5	0	1	10	2	5	4	.274	.291	.369
Babe Pinelli	3B15,SS9,2B5	R	31	30	76	11	15	2	0	1	4	6	7	2	.197	.265	.263
Pid Purdy	OF16	L	23	18	62	15	22	2	4	1	12	4	3	0	.355	.412	.565
Clyde Sukeforth	C24	L	25	38	58	12	11	2	0	0	2	7	2	2	.190	.277	.224
Jack White	2B3,SS2	S	21	5	4	1	0	0	0	0	0	0	0	0	.000	.000	.000
Ray Wolf	1B1	R	22	1	1	0	0	0	0	0	0	0	0	0	.000	.000	.000

R. Lucas, 1 G at OF

Pitcher	T	Age	G	GS	CG	ShO	IP	H	HR	BB	SO	W-L	Sv	ERA
Eppa Rixey	L	36	34	29	11	1	219.2	240	3	43	42	12-10	1	3.48
Jakie May	L	31	44	28	17	2	235.2	242	4	70	121	15-12	1	3.51
Dolf Luque	R	36	29	27	17	2	230.2	225	10	56	76	13-12	0	3.20
Pete Donohue	R	26	33	24	12	1	190.2	253	3	32	48	6-16	1	4.11
Red Lucas	R	25	37	23	19	4	239.2	231	6	39	51	18-11	2	3.38
Carl Mays	R	35	14	9	6	0	82.0	89	1	10	17	3-7	0	3.51
Ray Kolp	R	32	24	5	2	1	82.1	86	5	29	28	3-3	3	3.06
Art Nehf†	L	34	21	5	1	0	45.1	59	2	14	21	3-5	4	5.56
Pete Appleton	R	23	6	2	2	1	29.2	29	0	17	3	2-1	0	1.82
Jim Beckman	R	22	4	1	0	0	12.1	18	2	6	0	0-1	0	5.84

1927 Brooklyn Dodgers 6th NL 65-88 .425 28.5 GB

Wilbert Robinson

Player	Gm by Position	B	Age	G	AB	R	H	2B	3B	HR	RBI	BB	SO	SB	Avg	OBP	Slg
Hank DeBerry	C67	R	32	68	201	15	47	3	2	1	21	17	8	1	.234	.294	.284
Babe Herman	1B105,OF1	L	24	130	412	65	112	26	9	14	73	39	41	4	.272	.336	.481
Jay Partridge	2B140	L	24	146	572	72	149	17	6	7	40	20	36	9	.260	.289	.348
Bob Barrett	3B96	R	28	99	355	29	92	10	2	5	38	14	22	1	.259	.289	.341
Johnny Butler	SS90,3B60	R	34	149	521	39	124	13	6	2	57	34	33	9	.238	.292	.298
Max Carey	OF141	S	37	144	538	70	143	30	10	1	54	64	18	32	.266	.345	.364
Jigger Statz	OF122,2B1	R	29	130	507	64	139	24	7	1	21	26	43	10	.274	.310	.355
Gus Felix	OF119	R	32	130	445	43	118	21	8	0	57	39	47	6	.265	.327	.348
Harvey Hendrick	OF64,1B53,2B1	L	29	128	458	55	142	18	11	4	50	24	40	29	.310	.350	.424
Jake Flowers	SS65,2B1	R	25	67	231	26	54	5	5	2	20	21	25	3	.234	.300	.325
Butch Henline	C60	R	32	67	177	12	47	10	3	1	18	17	10	1	.266	.337	.373
Charlie Hargreaves	C44	R	30	46	133	9	38	3	1	0	11	14	7	1	.286	.362	.323
Irish Meusel	OF16	R	34	42	74	7	18	3	1	1	7	11	5	0	.243	.341	.351
Overton Tremper	OF18	R	21	26	60	4	14	0	0	0	4	0	2	0	.233	.246	.233
Chuck Corgan	2B13,SS3	S	24	19	57	3	15	1	0	0	1	4	4	0	.263	.311	.281
William Marriott	3B2	L	33	6	9	0	1	0	1	0	1	2	2	0	.111	.273	.333
Merwin Jacobson	OF3	L	33	11	6	4	0	0	0	0	1	0	1	0	.000	.000	.000
Oscar Roettger	OF1	R	27	5	4	0	0	0	0	0	0	1	1	0	.000	.333	.000
Chick Fewster		R	31	4	1	1	0	0	0	0	0	0	0	0	.000	.000	.000

Pitcher	T	Age	G	GS	CG	ShO	IP	H	HR	BB	SO	W-L	Sv	ERA
Jesse Petty	L	32	42	33	19	2	271.2	263	13	53	101	13-18	1	2.98
Dazzy Vance	R	36	34	32	25	2	273.1	242	12	69	184	16-15	1	2.70
Doug McWeeny	R	30	34	22	6	0	164.1	167	13	70	73	4-8	1	3.56
Jumbo Elliott	L	26	30	21	12	2	188.1	188	5	60	99	6-13	3	3.30
Bill Doak	R	36	27	20	6	1	145.0	153	6	40	32	11-8	1	3.48
Jesse Barnes	R	34	18	10	2	0	78.2	106	5	25	14	2-10	0	5.72
Ray Moss	R	25	1	1	0	0	8.1	11	0	1	1	1-0	0	3.24
Bob McGraw†	R	32	1	1	0	0	4.0	5	1	2	2	0-1	0	9.00
Rube Ehrhardt	R	32	46	3	2	0	95.2	90	3	37	22	3-7	2	3.57
Watty Clark	L	25	27	3	1	0	73.2	74	2	19	32	7-2	2	2.32
Norman Plitt†	R	34	19	8	1	0	62.1	73	3	36	9	2-6	0	4.91
Guy Cantrell†	R	23	6	0	0	0	10.0	10	0	6	5	0-0	0	2.70

1927 Boston Braves 7th NL 60-94 .390 34.0 GB

Dave Bancroft

Player	Gm by Position	B	Age	G	AB	R	H	2B	3B	HR	RBI	BB	SO	SB	Avg	OBP	Slg
Shanty Hogan	C61	R	21	71	229	24	66	17	1	3	32	9	23	2	.288	.324	.410
Jack Fournier	1B102	L	37	122	374	55	106	18	2	10	53	44	16	4	.283	.368	.422
Doc Gautreau	2B57	R	25	87	236	38	58	12	2	0	20	25	20	11	.246	.321	.314
Andy High	3B89,2B8,SS2	L	29	113	384	59	116	15	9	4	46	26	11	4	.302	.350	.419
Dave Bancroft	SS104	S	36	111	375	44	91	13	4	1	31	43	36	5	.243	.322	.307
Eddie Brown	OF153,1B1	R	35	155	558	64	171	35	6	2	75	28	20	11	.306	.340	.401
Jimmy Welsh	OF129,1B1	L	24	131	497	72	143	26	7	9	54	23	27	11	.288	.330	.423
Lance Richbourg	OF110	L	29	115	450	57	139	12	9	2	34	22	30	24	.309	.342	.389
Doc Farrell†	SS57,2B40,3B18	R	25	110	424	44	124	13	2	1	58	14	21	4	.292	.315	.340
Eddie Moore	3B52,2B39,OF16*	R	28	112	411	53	124	14	4	1	32	39	17	5	.302	.364	.363
Dick Burrus	1B61	L	29	72	220	22	70	8	3	0	32	17	10	3	.318	.370	.382
Jack Smith	OF48	L	32	84	183	27	58	6	4	1	24	16	12	8	.317	.375	.410
Frank Gibson	C47	S	36	60	167	7	37	1	2	0	19	3	10	2	.222	.235	.251
Luke Urban	C34	R	29	35	111	11	32	5	0	0	10	3	6	1	.288	.313	.333
Zack Taylor†	C27	R	28	30	96	8	23	2	1	1	14	8	5	0	.240	.298	.313
Herb Thomas†	2B17,SS2	R	25	24	74	11	17	6	1	0	6	3	9	2	.230	.269	.338
Les Mann†	OF24	R	33	29	66	8	17	3	1	0	6	8	3	2	.258	.338	.333
Earl Clark	OF13	R	19	13	44	6	12	1	0	0	3	2	4	0	.273	.304	.295
Sid Graves	OF5	R	25	7	20	5	5	1	1	0	2	0	1	1	.250	.250	.400
Dinny McNamara	OF3	L	21	11	9	3	0	0	0	0	0	0	3	0	.000	.000	.000
Johnny Cooney		R	26	10	1	3	0	0	0	0	0	0	0	0	.000	.000	.000

E. Moore, 1 G at SS

Pitcher	T	Age	G	GS	CG	ShO	IP	H	HR	BB	SO	W-L	Sv	ERA
Bob Smith	R	32	41	32	16	1	260.2	297	9	75	81	10-18	3	3.76
Kent Greenfield†	R	24	27	26	11	1	190.0	203	3	59	59	11-14	0	3.84
Charlie Robertson	R	31	28	22	6	0	154.1	188	2	46	49	7-17	0	4.72
Hugh McQuillan†	R	29	13	11	2	0	78.0	109	2	24	17	3-5	0	5.54
Larry Benton†	R	29	11	10	3	0	60.1	72	3	27	25	4-2	0	4.48
Johnny Werts	R	29	42	15	4	0	164.1	204	5	52	39	4-10	1	4.55
Joe Genewich	R	30	40	19	7	0	181.0	199	7	54	38	11-8	1	3.83
Foster Edwards	R	23	29	11	1	0	92.0	95	2	45	37	2-8	0	4.99
Hal Goldsmith	R	28	22	5	1	0	71.2	83	4	26	13	1-3	1	3.52
George Mogridge	L	38	20	1	0	0	48.2	48	4	15	26	6-4	5	3.70
Art Mills	R	24	15	1	0	0	37.2	41	1	18	7	0-1	0	3.82
Guy Morrison	R	31	11	3	1	0	34.1	40	1	15	6	1-2	0	4.46
Bunny Hearn	L	23	8	0	0	0	12.2	16	0	9	5	0-2	0	4.26
Jack Knight	R	32	3	0	0	0	3.0	6	0	2	0	0-0	0	15.00
Dick Rudolph	R	39	1	0	0	0	1.1	1	0	1	0	0-0	0	0.00

1927 Philadelphia Phillies 8th NL 51-103 .331 43.0 GB

Stuffy McInnis

Player	Gm by Position	B	Age	G	AB	R	H	2B	3B	HR	RBI	BB	SO	SB	Avg	OBP	Slg
Jimmie Wilson	C124	R	26	128	443	50	122	15	2	2	45	34	15	13	.275	.330	.332
Russ Wrightstone	1B136,2B1,3B1	L	34	141	533	62	163	24	5	6	75	48	20	9	.306	.365	.403
Fresco Thompson	2B153	R	25	153	597	78	181	32	14	1	70	34	36	19	.303	.343	.409
Bernie Friberg	3B103,2B5	R	27	111	335	31	78	8	1	1	28	41	49	3	.233	.322	.278
Heinie Sand	SS86,3B58	R	29	141	535	87	160	22	8	1	49	58	59	5	.299	.369	.376
Freddy Leach	OF140	L	29	140	536	69	164	30	4	12	83	21	32	2	.306	.342	.444
Cy Williams	OF130	L	39	131	492	86	135	18	2	30	98	61	57	0	.274	.365	.502
Dick Spalding	OF113	L	33	115	442	68	131	16	3	0	25	38	40	5	.296	.352	.346
Jimmy Cooney†	SS74	R	32	76	259	33	70	12	1	0	15	13	9	4	.270	.305	.324
Johnny Mokan	OF63	R	31	74	213	22	61	13	2	0	33	25	21	5	.286	.361	.366
Al Nixon	OF44	R	41	54	154	18	48	7	0	0	18	5	5	1	.312	.333	.357
Bubber Jonnard	C41	R	29	53	143	18	42	6	0	0	14	7	7	0	.294	.327	.336
Dick Attreau	1B26	L	30	44	83	17	17	1	1	1	11	14	18	1	.205	.320	.277
Bill Hohman	OF6	R	23	7	18	1	5	0	0	0	0	2	3	0	.278	.350	.278
Henry Baldwin	SS3,3B2	R	33	6	16	1	5	0	0	0	1	1	2	0	.313	.353	.313
Harry O'Donnell	C12	R	33	16	16	1	1	0	0	0	2	2	2	0	.063	.167	.063
Tony Kaufmann†	P5,OF1	R	26	8	7	1	1	0	0	1	2	0	1	0	.143	.143	.571
Bill Deitrick	SS5	R	25	5	6	1	1	0	0	0	0	0	0	0	.167	.167	.167
Stuffy McInnis	1B1	R	36	1	0	0	0	0	0	0	0	0	0	0	—	—	—

Pitcher	T	Age	G	GS	CG	ShO	IP	H	HR	BB	SO	W-L	Sv	ERA
Alex Ferguson	R	30	31	31	16	0	227.0	280	15	65	73	8-16	0	4.84
Hub Pruett	L	26	31	28	12	1	186.0	238	6	89	90	7-17	1	6.05
Jack Scott	R	35	48	25	17	1	233.1	304	15	69	69	9-21	1	5.09
Dutch Ulrich	R	27	32	18	14	1	193.1	201	6	40	42	8-11	1	3.17
Leo Sweetland	L	25	21	13	6	0	103.2	147	3	53	21	2-10	0	6.16
Clarence Mitchell	L	36	13	12	8	1	94.2	99	7	28	17	6-3	0	4.09
Hal Carlson†	R	35	11	9	4	0	63.2	80	7	18	13	4-5	1	5.23
Tony Kaufmann†	R	26	5	5	1	0	18.2	37	2	8	4	0-3	0	10.61
Russ Miller	R	27	2	2	1	1	15.1	21	2	3	4	1-1	0	5.28
Augie Walsh	R	22	1	1	1	0	10.0	12	3	5	0	0-1	0	4.50
Ed Baecht	R	20	1	1	0	0	6.0	12	0	2	0	0-1	0	12.00
Claude Willoughby	R	28	35	6	1	1	97.2	126	7	53	14	3-7	2	6.54
Art Decatur	R	33	29	3	0	0	94.2	130	11	20	27	3-5	0	7.42
Lefty Taber	L	27	3	1	0	0	3.1	8	0	5	0	0-1	0	18.90
Skinny O'Neal	R	28	2	0	0	0	5.0	9	0	2	2	0-0	0	9.00
Wayland Dean†	R	25	2	0	0	0	3.0	6	0	2	1	0-1	0	12.00

»1928 New York Yankees 1st AL 101-53 .656 —

Miller Huggins

Player	Gm by Position	B	Age	G	AB	R	H	2B	3B	HR	RBI	BB	SO	SB	Avg	OBP	Slg
Johnny Grabowski	C75	R	28	75	202	21	48	7	1	1	21	10	21	0	.238	.274	.297
Lou Gehrig	1B154	L	25	154	562	139	210	47	13	27	142	95	69	4	.374	.467	.648
Tony Lazzeri	2B110	R	24	116	404	62	134	30	11	10	82	43	50	15	.332	.397	.535
Joe Dugan	3B91	R	31	94	312	33	86	15	0	6	34	16	15	1	.276	.317	.381
Mark Koenig	SS125	S	23	132	533	89	170	19	10	4	63	32	19	3	.319	.360	.415
Babe Ruth	OF154	L	33	154	536	163	173	29	8	54	142	135	87	4	.323	.461	.709
Earle Combs	OF149	L	29	149	626	118	194	33	21	7	56	77	33	10	.310	.387	.463
Bob Meusel	OF131	R	31	131	518	77	154	45	5	11	113	39	56	6	.297	.349	.467
Leo Durocher	2B66,SS29	R	22	102	296	46	80	8	6	0	31	22	52	1	.270	.327	.338
Gene Robertson	3B70,2B3	L	29	83	251	29	73	9	0	1	36	14	6	2	.291	.328	.339
Benny Bengough	C58	R	29	58	161	12	43	3	1	0	9	7	8	0	.267	.302	.298
Pat Collins	C70	R	31	70	136	18	30	5	0	6	14	35	16	0	.221	.380	.390
Cedric Durst	OF33,1B3	L	31	74	135	18	34	2	1	2	10	7	9	1	.252	.289	.326
Ben Paschal	OF25	R	32	65	79	12	25	6	1	1	15	8	11	1	.316	.379	.456
Mike Gazella	3B16,2B4,SS3	R	31	32	56	11	13	0	0	0	2	6	7	2	.232	.317	.232
Bill Dickey	C6	L	21	10	15	1	3	1	1	0	2	0	2	0	.200	.200	.400
George Burns†	1B2	R	35	4	4	1	2	0	0	0	0	0	1	0	.500	.500	.500

Pitcher	T	Age	G	GS	CG	ShO	IP	H	HR	BB	SO	W-L	Sv	ERA
George Pipgras	R	28	46	38	22	4	300.2	314	4	103	139	24-13	3	3.38
Waite Hoyt	R	28	42	31	19	3	273.0	279	16	60	67	23-7	8	3.36
Herb Pennock	L	34	28	24	18	5	211.0	215	2	40	53	17-6	3	2.56
Hank Johnson	R	22	31	22	10	1	199.0	188	16	104	110	14-9	0	4.30
Al Shealy	R	28	23	12	3	0	96.0	124	4	42	39	8-6	2	5.06
Fred Heimach	L	27	13	9	5	0	68.0	66	3	16	25	2-3	0	3.31
Stan Coveleski	R	38	12	8	2	0	58.0	72	5	20	5	5-1	0	5.74
Tom Zachary†	L	32	7	6	3	0	45.2	54	1	15	7	3-3	1	3.94
Wilcy Moore	R	31	35	2	0	0	60.1	71	4	31	18	4-4	2	4.18
Archie Campbell	R	24	13	1	0	0	24.0	30	0	11	9	0-1	2	5.25
Myles Thomas	R	30	12	1	0	0	31.2	33	3	9	10	1-0	0	3.41
Rosy Ryan	R	30	3	0	0	0	6.0	17	1	1	5	0-0	0	16.50
Urban Shocker	R	37	1	0	0	0	2.0	3	0	0	0	0-0	0	0.00

1928 Philadelphia Athletics 2nd AL 98-55 .641 2.5 GB

Connie Mack

Player	Gm by Position	B	Age	G	AB	R	H	2B	3B	HR	RBI	BB	SO	SB	Avg	OBP	Slg
Mickey Cochrane	C130	L	25	131	468	92	137	26	12	10	57	76	25	7	.293	.395	.464
Joe Hauser	1B88	L	29	95	300	61	78	19	5	16	59	52	45	4	.260	.369	.517
Max Bishop	2B125	L	28	126	472	104	149	27	5	6	50	97	36	9	.316	.435	.432
Sammy Hale	3B79	R	31	88	314	38	97	20	9	4	58	9	21	2	.309	.334	.468
Joe Boley	SS132	R	31	132	425	49	112	20	3	0	49	32	11	5	.264	.317	.325
Bing Miller	OF133	R	33	139	510	76	168	34	7	8	85	27	24	10	.329	.372	.471
Al Simmons	OF114	R	26	119	464	78	163	33	9	15	107	31	30	1	.351	.396	.558
Ty Cobb	OF85	L	41	95	353	54	114	27	4	1	40	34	16	5	.323	.389	.431
Jimmie Foxx	3B60,1B30,C19	R	20	118	400	85	131	29	10	13	79	60	43	3	.328	.416	.548
Mule Haas	OF82	L	24	91	332	41	93	21	4	6	39	23	20	2	.280	.331	.422
Jimmy Dykes	2B32,SS21,3B20*	R	31	85	242	39	67	11	0	5	30	27	21	2	.277	.361	.384
Tris Speaker	OF50	L	40	64	191	28	51	22	2	3	29	10	5	5	.267	.310	.450
Ossie Orwoll	1B34,P27	L	27	64	170	28	52	13	2	0	22	16	24	3	.306	.366	.406
Walt French	OF20	L	28	49	74	9	19	4	0	0	7	2	5	1	.257	.286	.311
Joe Hassler	SS28	R	23	28	34	5	9	2	0	0	3	2	4	0	.265	.306	.324
Eddie Collins	2B2,SS1	L	41	36	33	3	10	3	0	0	7	4	4	0	.303	.378	.394
Cy Perkins	C19	R	32	19	29	1	5	0	0	0	1	1	1	0	.172	.200	.172
Joe Bush	P11,OF1	R	35	15	15	0	1	0	0	0	0	1	2	0	.067	.125	.067

J. Dykes, 8 G at 1B, 1 G at OF

Pitcher	T	Age	G	GS	CG	ShO	IP	H	HR	BB	SO	W-L	Sv	ERA
Lefty Grove	L	28	39	31	24	4	261.2	228	10	64	183	24-8	4	2.58
Rube Walberg	L	31	38	30	15	3	235.2	236	19	64	112	17-12	1	3.55
Jack Quinn	R	44	31	28	18	4	211.1	239	3	34	43	18-7	1	2.90
George Earnshaw	R	28	26	22	7	3	158.1	143	7	100	117	7-7	1	3.81
Howard Ehmke	R	34	23	18	5	1	139.1	135	6	44	34	9-8	0	3.62
Bill Shores	R	24	3	2	1	0	14.0	13	0	7	5	1-1	0	3.21
Carroll Yerkes	L	25	2	1	1	0	8.2	7	0	2	1	0-1	0	2.08
Eddie Rommel	R	30	43	11	6	0	173.2	177	11	26	37	13-5	4	3.06
Ossie Orwoll	L	27	27	8	3	0	106.0	110	7	50	53	6-5	2	4.58
Joe Bush	R	35	11	2	1	0	35.1	39	1	18	15	2-1	1	5.09
Ike Powers	R	22	9	0	0	0	12.0	8	1	10	4	1-0	2	4.50
Jing Johnson	R	33	3	0	0	0	10.2	13	1	5	3	0-0	0	5.06
Art Daney	R	23	1	0	0	0	1.0	1	0	0	0	0-0	0	0.00

1928 St. Louis Browns 3rd AL 82-72 .532 19.0 GB

Dan Howley

Player	Gm by Position	B	Age	G	AB	R	H	2B	3B	HR	RBI	BB	SO	SB	Avg	OBP	Slg
Wally Schang	C82	S	38	91	245	41	70	10	5	3	39	68	26	8	.286	.448	.404
Lu Blue	1B154	S	31	154	549	116	154	32	11	14	80	105	43	12	.281	.400	.455
Otis Brannan	2B135	L	29	135	483	68	118	18	3	10	66	60	19	3	.244	.333	.356
Frank O'Rourke	3B96,SS2	R	33	99	391	54	103	24	3	1	62	21	19	10	.263	.303	.348
Red Kress	SS150	R	21	150	560	78	153	26	10	3	81	48	70	5	.273	.332	.371
Heinie Manush	OF154	L	26	154	638	104	241	47	20	13	108	39	14	17	.378	.414	.575
Fred Schulte	OF143	R	27	146	556	90	159	44	6	7	85	51	60	6	.286	.347	.424
Earl McNeely	OF120	R	30	127	496	66	117	27	7	0	44	37	39	8	.236	.299	.319
Clyde Manion	C71	R	31	76	243	25	55	5	1	2	31	15	18	3	.226	.274	.280
Beauty McGowan	OF47	L	26	47	168	35	61	13	4	2	18	16	15	2	.363	.425	.524
Larry Bettencourt	3B41,OF2,C1	R	22	67	159	30	45	9	4	4	24	22	19	2	.283	.377	.465
Ski Melillo	2B28,3B19	R	28	51	132	9	25	2	0	0	9	9	11	2	.189	.241	.205
Guy Sturdy	1B1	L	28	54	45	3	10	1	0	1	8	8	4	1	.222	.340	.311
Steve O'Neill	C10	R	36	10	24	4	7	1	0	0	6	8	0	0	.292	.485	.333
Billy Mullen	3B6	R	32	15	18	2	7	1	0	0	2	3	4	0	.389	.476	.444
Wally Gerber†	SS6	R	36	6	18	1	5	1	0	0	0	1	3	0	.278	.316	.333
Ollie Sax	3B9	R	23	16	17	4	3	0	0	0	0	5	3	0	.176	.364	.176
Fred Bennett	OF1	R	26	7	8	0	2	1	0	0	0	0	2	0	.250	.250	.375
Ike Danning	C2	R	23	2	6	0	3	0	0	0	1	1	2	0	.500	.571	.500
Frank Wilson†	OF1	L	27	6	5	1	0	0	0	0	0	1	0	0	.000	.000	.000

Pitcher	T	Age	G	GS	CG	ShO	IP	H	HR	BB	SO	W-L	Sv	ERA
Sam Gray	R	30	35	31	21	2	262.2	256	11	86	102	20-12	3	3.19
General Crowder	R	29	41	31	19	1	244.0	238	11	91	99	21-5	2	3.69
Jack Ogden	R	30	38	31	18	1	242.2	257	23	80	67	15-16	2	4.15
George Blaeholder	R	24	38	26	9	1	214.1	235	23	52	87	10-15	3	4.37
Lefty Stewart	L	27	29	17	7	1	142.2	173	5	32	25	7-9	3	4.67
Dick Coffman	R	21	29	7	3	0	85.2	122	7	37	25	4-5	1	6.09
Hal Wiltse†	L	24	26	5	0	0	72.0	93	4	35	23	2-5	0	5.25
Ed Strelecki	R	23	22	2	1	0	50.1	49	4	17	8	0-2	1	4.29
Boom-Boom Beck	R	23	16	4	2	0	49.0	52	4	20	17	2-3	0	4.41
Ernie Nevers	R	26	6	0	0	0	9.0	9	1	2	1	1-0	0	3.00
Jim Wright	R	27	2	0	0	0	2.0	3	0	2	2	0-0	0	13.50

1928 Washington Senators 4th AL 75-79 .487 26.0 GB

Bucky Harris

Player	Gm by Position	B	Age	G	AB	R	H	2B	3B	HR	RBI	BB	SO	SB	Avg	OBP	Slg
Muddy Ruel	C101	R	32	108	350	31	90	18	2	0	55	44	14	12	.257	.342	.320
Joe Judge	1B149	L	34	153	542	78	166	31	10	3	93	80	19	16	.306	.396	.417
Bucky Harris	2B96,3B1,OF1	R	31	99	358	34	73	11	5	0	28	27	26	5	.204	.264	.263
Ossie Bluege	3B144	R	27	146	518	78	154	33	7	2	75	46	27	18	.297	.364	.400
Bobby Reeves	SS66,2B22,3B8*	R	24	102	353	44	107	16	8	3	42	24	47	4	.303	.351	.419
Sam Rice	OF147	L	38	148	616	95	202	32	15	2	55	49	15	16	.328	.379	.438
Goose Goslin	OF125	L	27	135	456	80	173	36	10	17	102	48	19	16	.379	.443	.614
Sammy West	OF116	L	23	125	378	59	114	30	7	3	40	20	23		.302	.338	.442
Red Barnes	OF104	L	24	114	417	82	127	22	15	6	51	55	38	7	.305	.391	.472
Joe Cronin	SS63	R	21	63	227	23	55	10	4	0	25	22	27	4	.242	.309	.322
Jackie Hayes	2B41,SS15,3B2	R	21	60	210	30	54	7	3	0	22	5	10	3	.257	.274	.319
Bennie Tate	C30	L	26	57	122	10	30	6	0	0	15	10	4	0	.246	.303	.295
Eddie Kenna	C34	R	30	41	118	14	35	4	2	1	20	14	8	1	.297	.376	.390
Grant Gillis	SS16,2B5,3B3	R	27	24	87	13	22	5	1	0	10	4	5	0	.253	.309	.333
George Sisler†	1B5,OF5	L	35	20	49	1	12	1	0	0	2	1	2	0	.245	.260	.265
Babe Ganzel	OF7	R	27	10	26	2	2	1	0	0	4	1	4	0	.077	.111	.115
Dick Spalding	OF11	L	34	16	23	1	8	0	0	0	0	0	4	0	.348	.348	.348
Harley Boss	1B5	L	19	12	12	1	3	0	0	0	2	3	1	0	.250	.400	.250
Pelham Ballenger	3B3	R	34	3	9	0	1	0	0	0	0	0	1	0	.111	.111	.111
Al Bool	C2	R	30	2	7	0	1	0	0	0	1	0	0	0	.143	.143	.143
Ed Crowley	3B1	R	21	2	1	0	0	0	0	0	0	0	0	0	.000	.000	.000
Hugh McMullen		S	26	1	1	0	0	0	0	0	0	0	1	0	.000	.000	.000

B. Reeves, 1 G at OF

Pitcher	T	Age	G	GS	CG	ShO	IP	H	HR	BB	SO	W-L	Sv	ERA
Bump Hadley	R	23	33	31	16	3	231.2	236	4	100	80	12-13	0	3.54
Sad Sam Jones	R	35	30	27	19	4	224.2	209	5	78	63	17-7	0	2.84
Garland Braxton	L	28	38	24	15	2	218.1	177	7	44	94	13-11	6	2.51
Milt Gaston	R	32	28	22	8	3	148.2	179	3	53	45	6-12	0	5.51
Tom Zachary†	L	32	20	14	5	1	102.2	130	5	40	19	6-9	0	5.44
Hod Lisenbee	R	29	16	9	3	0	77.0	102	4	32	13	2-6	0	6.08
Firpo Marberry	R	29	48	11	7	1	161.1	160	4	42	76	13-13	3	3.85
Lloyd Brown	L	23	27	10	2	0	107.0	112	7	40	38	4-4	1	4.04
Bobby Burke	L	21	26	7	2	1	85.1	87	1	18	27	2-4	0	3.90
Clay Van Alstyne	R	28	4	0	0	0	21.1	26	0	13	5	0-0	0	5.48
Jim Weaver	R	24	3	0	0	0	6.0	2	0	6	2	0-0	0	1.50

1928 Chicago White Sox 5th AL 72-82 .468 29.0 GB

Ray Schalk (32-42)/Lena Blackburne (40-40)

Player	Gm by Position	B	Age	G	AB	R	H	2B	3B	HR	RBI	BB	SO	SB	Avg	OBP	Slg
Buck Crouse	C76	L	31	78	218	17	55	5	2	2	20	19	14	3	.252	.315	.321
Bud Clancy	1B128	L	27	130	487	64	132	19	11	2	37	42	25	6	.271	.331	.368
Bill Hunnefield	2B83,SS3,3B1	S	29	94	333	42	98	8	3	2	24	26	24	16	.294	.351	.354
Willie Kamm	3B155	R	28	155	552	70	170	30	12	1	84	73	22	17	.308	.391	.411
Bill Cissell	SS123	R	24	125	443	66	115	22	3	1	60	29	41	18	.260	.307	.330
Alex Metzler	OF133	L	25	139	464	71	141	18	14	3	55	77	30	16	.304	.410	.422
Johnny Mostil	OF131	R	32	133	503	69	136	19	8	0	51	66	54	23	.270	.360	.340
Bibb Falk	OF78	L	29	98	286	42	83	18	4	1	37	25	16	5	.290	.347	.392
Carl Reynolds	OF74	R	25	84	291	51	94	21	11	2	36	17	13	15	.323	.371	.491
Buck Redfern	2B45,SS33,3B1	R	26	86	261	22	61	6	3	0	35	12	19	8	.234	.267	.280
Bill Barrett	OF37,2B25	R	28	76	235	34	65	11	2	3	26	14	30	8	.277	.320	.379
Moe Berg	C73	R	26	76	224	25	55	16	0	0	29	14	25	2	.246	.302	.317
Art Shires	1B32	L	20	33	123	20	42	6	1	1	11	13	10	0	.341	.409	.431
Harry McCurdy	C34	L	28	49	103	12	27	10	0	2	13	8	15	1	.262	.315	.417
George Blackerby	OF20	R	24	30	83	8	21	0	0	0	12	4	10	2	.253	.287	.253
Karl Swanson	2B21	L	24	22	64	2	9	1	0	0	6	4	7	3	.141	.191	.156
Randy Moore	OF16	L	22	24	61	6	13	4	1	0	5	3	5	0	.213	.250	.311
Johnny Mann	3B2	R	30	6	6	0	2	0	0	0	1	1	0	0	.333	.429	.333
Ray Schalk	C1	R	35	2	1	0	1	0	0	0	1	0	0	1	1.000	1.000	1.000

Pitcher	T	Age	G	GS	CG	ShO	IP	H	HR	BB	SO	W-L	Sv	ERA
Tommy Thomas	R	28	36	32	24	3	283.0	277	14	76	129	17-16	2	3.08
Ted Lyons	R	27	39	27	21	0	240.0	276	11	68	60	15-14	6	3.98
Grady Adkins	R	31	36	27	14	0	224.2	233	12	89	54	10-16	1	3.73
Red Faber	R	39	27	27	16	2	201.1	223	11	68	43	13-9	0	3.75
Ted Blankenship	R	27	27	22	8	0	158.0	186	9	80	36	9-11	0	4.61
Ed Walsh	R	23	14	10	3	0	78.0	86	2	42	32	4-7	0	4.96
Bob Weiland	L	22	1	1	1	1	9.0	7	0	5	9	1-0	0	0.00
Sarge Connally	R	29	28	5	1	0	74.1	89	1	29	28	2-5	2	4.84
George Cox	R	23	26	2	0	0	89.0	110	6	39	22	1-2	0	5.26
Charlie Barnabe	L	28	7	2	0	0	9.2	17	0	0	3	0-2	0	6.52
John Goodell	L	21	2	0	0	0	3.0	6	0	2	0	0-0	0	18.00
Rudy Leopold	L	22	2	0	0	0	2.1	3	0	0	0	0-0	0	3.86
Roy Wilson	L	31	1	0	0	0	3.1	2	0	3	2	0-0	0	0.00
Al Williamson	R	28	1	0	0	0	2.0	1	0	0	0	0-0	0	0.00
Dan Dugan	L	21	1	0	0	0	0.1	0	0	0	0	0-0	0	0.00

1928 Detroit Tigers 6th AL 68-86 .442 33.0 GB

George Moriarty

Player	Gm by Position	B	Age	G	AB	R	H	2B	3B	HR	RBI	BB	SO	SB	Avg	OBP	Slg
Pinky Hargrave	C88	S	32	121	320	38	88	13	5	10	63	32	28	4	.275	.343	.441
Bill Sweeney	1B75,OF3	R	23	89	309	47	78	15	5	0	19	15	28	12	.252	.287	.333
Charlie Gehringer	2B154	L	25	154	603	108	193	29	16	6	74	69	22	15	.320	.395	.451
Marty McManus	3B92,1B45,SS1	R	28	139	500	78	144	37	5	8	73	51	32	11	.288	.355	.430
Jackie Tavener	SS131	L	30	132	473	59	123	24	15	5	52	33	51	13	.260	.314	.406
Harry Rice	OF129,3B2	L	26	131	510	87	154	21	12	6	81	44	27	20	.302	.360	.425
Harry Heilmann	OF126,1B25	R	33	151	558	83	183	38	10	14	107	57	45	7	.328	.390	.507
Bob Fothergill	OF90	R	30	111	347	49	110	28	10	3	63	24	19	8	.317	.366	.481
Al Wingo	OF71	L	30	87	242	30	69	13	2	2	30	40	17	2	.285	.389	.380
Jack Warner	3B52,SS7	R	24	75	206	33	44	4	4	0	13	16	15	4	.214	.274	.272
Larry Woodall	C62	R	33	65	186	19	39	5	1	0	13	24	10	3	.210	.300	.247
Chick Galloway	SS22,3B21,1B1*	R	31	53	148	17	39	5	2	1	17	15	3	7	.264	.331	.345
Paul Easterling	OF34	R	22	43	114	17	37	7	1	3	12	8	24	2	.325	.374	.482
John Stone	OF26	L	22	26	113	20	40	10	3	2	21	5	8	1	.354	.387	.549
Johnny Neun	1B25	S	27	36	108	15	23	3	1	0	5	7	10	2	.213	.261	.259
Merv Shea	C30	R	27	39	85	8	20	2	3	0	9	9	11	2	.235	.316	.329

C. Galloway, 1 G at OF

Pitcher	T	Age	G	GS	CG	ShO	IP	H	HR	BB	SO	W-L	Sv	ERA
Earl Whitehill	L	28	31	30	12	1	196.1	214	8	78	93	11-16	0	4.31
Ownie Carroll	R	25	34	28	19	2	231.0	219	6	87	51	16-12	2	3.27
Vic Sorrell	R	27	29	23	8	0	171.0	182	9	83	67	8-11	0	4.79
Sam Gibson	R	28	20	18	5	1	119.2	155	4	52	29	5-8	0	5.42
Josh Billings	R	20	21	16	3	1	110.2	118	4	59	48	5-10	0	5.12
Phil Page	L	22	3	2	2	0	22.0	21	1	10	3	2-0	0	2.45
Charlie Sullivan	R	25	3	2	0	0	12.1	18	1	6	2	0-2	0	6.57
George Smith	R	26	39	2	0	0	106.0	103	3	50	54	1-1	3	4.42
Elam Vangilder	R	32	38	11	7	0	156.1	163	4	68	43	11-10	5	3.91
Lil Stoner	R	29	36	11	4	0	126.1	151	16	42	29	5-8	4	4.35
Ken Holloway	R	30	30	11	5	0	120.1	137	2	32	32	4-8	2	4.34

1928 Cleveland Indians 7th AL 62-92 .403 39.0 GB

Roger Peckinpaugh

Player	Gm by Position	B	Age	G	AB	R	H	2B	3B	HR	RBI	BB	SO	SB	Avg	OBP	Slg
Luke Sewell	C118	R	27	122	411	52	111	16	9	3	52	26	27	3	.270	.318	.375
Lew Fonseca	1B56,3B15,SS4*	R	29	75	263	38	86	19	4	3	36	13	17	4	.327	.361	.464
Carl Lind	2B154	R	24	154	650	102	191	42	4	1	54	36	48	8	.294	.331	.375
Johnny Hodapp	3B101,1B13	R	22	116	449	51	145	31	6	2	73	20	20	2	.323	.352	.432
Joe Sewell	SS137,3B19	L	29	155	588	79	190	40	2	4	70	58	9	7	.323	.391	.418
Homer Summa	OF132	L	29	134	504	60	143	26	3	3	57	20	15	4	.284	.319	.365
Charlie Jamieson	OF111	L	35	112	433	63	133	18	4	1	37	56	20	3	.307	.388	.374
Sam Langford	OF107	L	29	110	427	50	118	17	8	4	50	21	35	3	.276	.312	.382
Eddie Morgan	1B36,OF21,3B14	R	24	76	265	42	83	24	6	4	54	21	17	5	.313	.366	.494
George Burns†	1B53	R	35	82	209	29	52	12	1	5	30	17	11	2	.249	.323	.388
Luther Harvel	OF39	R	22	40	136	12	30	6	1	0	12	4	17	1	.221	.264	.279
Glenn Myatt	C30	L	30	58	125	9	36	7	2	1	15	13	13	0	.288	.355	.400
George Gerken	OF34	R	24	38	115	16	26	7	2	0	9	12	22	3	.226	.305	.322
Red Dorman	OF24	R	22	25	77	12	28	6	0	0	11	9	6	1	.364	.430	.442
Chick Autry	C18	R	25	22	60	6	18	6	1	1	9	1	7	0	.300	.311	.483
Ed Montague	SS15,3B9	R	22	32	51	12	12	0	1	0	3	6	7	0	.235	.339	.275
Ollie Tucker	OF14	L	26	14	47	5	6	0	0	1	2	7	3	0	.128	.255	.191
Bruce Caldwell	OF10,1B1	R	22	18	27	2	6	1	1	0	3	2	2	1	.222	.300	.333
Jonah Goldman	SS7	R	21	7	21	1	5	1	0	0	2	3	0	0	.238	.333	.286
Al Van Camp	1B5	R	24	5	17	0	4	1	0	0	2	0	1	1	.235	.235	.294
Cecil Bolton	1B4	L	24	4	13	1	2	0	2	0	0	2	2	0	.154	.267	.462
Johnny Burnett	SS2	L	23	3	10	3	5	0	0	0	1	0	1	0	.500	.500	.500
Aaron Ward	3B3,SS2,2B1	R	31	6	9	0	1	0	0	0	0	1	2	0	.111	.200	.111
Art Reinholz	3B2	R	25	2	3	0	1	0	0	0	0	1	0	0	.333	.500	.333
Johnny Gill		L	23	2	2	0	0	0	0	0	0	0	1	0	.000	.000	.000
Frank Wilson†		L	27	2	1	0	0	0	0	0	0	1	0	0	.000	.500	.000

L. Fonseca, 1 G at 2B

Pitcher	T	Age	G	GS	CG	ShO	IP	H	HR	BB	SO	W-L	Sv	ERA
Joe Shaute	L	28	36	32	21	1	253.2	295	9	68	81	13-17	2	4.04
George Uhle	R	29	31	28	18	2	214.1	252	8	48	74	12-17	1	4.07
Willis Hudlin	R	22	42	26	10	0	220.1	231	7	90	62	14-14	7	4.04
Jake Miller	L	30	25	23	7	0	158.0	203	6	43	37	8-9	0	4.44
George Grant	R	25	28	18	6	1	155.1	196	7	76	39	10-8	0	5.04
Garland Buckeye†	L	30	9	6	0	0	35.0	58	2	5	6	1-5	0	6.69
Wes Ferrell	R	20	2	2	1	0	16.0	15	0	5	4	0-2	0	2.25
Clint Brown	R	24	2	1	1	0	11.0	14	0	2	2	0-1	0	4.91
Les Barnhart	R	23	2	1	0	0	9.0	13	1	4	1	0-1	0	7.00
Jim Moore	R	24	1	1	1	0	9.0	5	0	5	1	0-1	0	2.00
Bill Bayne	L	29	37	6	3	0	108.2	128	3	43	39	2-5	3	5.13
Mel Harder	R	18	23	1	0	0	49.0	64	4	32	15	0-2	1	6.61
Johnny Miljus†	R	33	11	4	1	0	50.2	46	1	20	19	1-4	1	2.66
Dutch Levsen	R	30	11	3	0	0	41.1	39	4	31	7	0-3	0	5.44
Willie Underhill	R	23	11	3	1	0	28.0	33	0	20	16	1-2	0	4.50
Jumbo Brown	R	21	5	0	0	0	14.2	19	0	15	12	0-1	0	6.75
Hap Collard	R	29	1	0	0	0	4.0	4	0	4	1	0-0	0	2.25

1928 Boston Red Sox 8th AL 57-96 .373 43.5 GB

Bill Carrigan

Player	Gm by Position	B	Age	G	AB	R	H	2B	3B	HR	RBI	BB	SO	SB	Avg	OBP	Slg
Fred Hofmann	C71	R	34	78	199	14	45	8	1	0	16	11	25	0	.226	.270	.276
Phil Todt	1B144	L	26	144	539	61	136	31	8	12	73	26	47	6	.252	.290	.406
Bill Regan	2B137,OF1	R	29	138	511	53	135	30	6	7	75	21	40	9	.264	.296	.387
Buddy Myer	3B144	L	24	147	536	78	168	26	6	1	44	53	28	30	.313	.379	.390
Wally Gerber†	SS103	R	36	104	300	21	64	6	1	0	28	32	31	6	.213	.289	.240
Doug Taitt	OF139,P1	L	25	143	482	51	144	28	14	3	61	36	32	13	.299	.350	.434
Ira Flagstead	OF135	R	34	140	510	84	148	41	4	1	39	60	23	12	.290	.366	.392
Ken Williams	OF127	L	38	133	462	59	140	25	1	8	67	37	15	4	.303	.356	.413
Jack Rothrock	OF53,3B17,1B16*	S	23	117	344	52	92	9	4	3	22	33	40	12	.267	.333	.343
Billy Rogell	SS67,2B22,OF6*	S	23	102	296	33	69	10	4	0	29	22	47	2	.233	.295	.294
Charlie Berry	C63	R	25	80	177	18	46	7	3	1	19	21	19	1	.260	.342	.350
Johnny Heving	C62	R	32	82	158	11	41	7	2	0	11	11	10	1	.259	.308	.329
Danny MacFayden	P33,OF1	R	23	35	63	5	9	2	1	0	4	7	32	0	.143	.229	.206
George Loepp	OF14	R	26	15	51	6	9	3	1	0	3	5	12	0	.176	.250	.275
Red Rollings	1B5,2B4,OF4*	L	24	50	48	7	11	3	1	0	9	6	8	0	.229	.315	.333
Carl Sumner	OF10	L	19	16	29	6	8	1	1	0	3	5	6	0	.276	.382	.379
Denny Williams	OF6	L	28	16	18	1	4	0	0	0	1	1	1	0	.222	.263	.222
Arlie Tarbert	OF6	R	23	6	17	1	3	1	0	0	2	1	1	0	.176	.222	.235
Asby Asbjornson	C6	R	19	6	16	0	3	1	0	0	1	1	1	0	.188	.235	.250
Freddie Moncewicz	SS2	R	24	3	1	0	0	0	0	0	0	0	1	0	.000	.000	.000
Paul Hinson		R	24	3	0	1	0	0	0	0	0	0	0	0	—	—	—

J. Rothrock, 13 G at SS, 2 G at 2B, 1 G at P, 1 G at C; B. Rogell, 3 G at 3B; R. Rollings, 1 G at 3B

Pitcher	T	Age	G	GS	CG	ShO	IP	H	HR	BB	SO	W-L	Sv	ERA
Red Ruffing	R	24	42	34	25	1	289.1	303	8	96	118	10-25	2	3.89
Ed Morris	R	28	47	29	20	0	257.2	255	7	80	104	19-15	5	3.53
Danny MacFayden	R	23	33	28	9	0	195.0	215	12	78	61	9-15	0	4.75
Jack Russell	R	22	32	26	10	2	201.1	233	6	41	27	11-14	0	3.84
Slim Harriss	R	31	27	15	4	1	128.1	141	5	33	37	8-11	1	4.63
Hal Wiltse†	L	24	2	2	1	0	12.0	16	1	1	5	0-2	0	9.00
Pat Simmons	R	19	31	3	0	0	69.0	69	4	38	16	0-2	1	4.04
Merle Settlemire	L	25	30	9	0	0	82.1	116	2	34	12	0-6	0	5.47
Herb Bradley	R	25	15	5	1	1	47.1	64	2	16	14	0-3	0	7.23
Marty Griffin	R	26	11	3	0	0	37.2	42	0	17	9	0-3	0	5.02
Cliff Garrison	R	21	6	0	0	0	16.0	22	2	6	0	0-0	0	7.88
Steve Slayton	R	26	3	0	0	0	7.0	6	0	3	2	0-0	0	3.86
John Wilson	R	23	2	0	0	0	5.0	6	0	6	1	0-0	0	9.00
John Shea	L	23	1	0	0	0	1.0	1	0	1	0	0-0	0	18.00
Doug Taitt	R	25	1	0	0	0	1.0	2	0	2	1	0-0	0	27.00
Frank Bennett	R	23	1	0	0	0	1.0	1	0	0	0	0-0	0	0.00
Jack Rothrock	R	23	1	0	0	0	1.0	0	0	0	0	0-0	0	0.00

»1928 St. Louis Cardinals 1st NL 95-59 .617 —

Bill McKechnie

Player	Gm by Position	B	Age	G	AB	R	H	2B	3B	HR	RBI	BB	SO	SB	Avg	OBP	Slg
Jimmie Wilson†	C120	R	27	120	411	45	106	26	2	2	50	45	24	9	.258	.333	.345
Jim Bottomley	1B148	L	28	149	576	123	187	42	20	31	136	71	54	10	.325	.402	.628
Frankie Frisch	2B139	S	29	141	547	107	164	29	9	10	86	64	17	29	.300	.374	.441
Wattie Holm	3B83,OF7	R	26	102	386	61	107	24	6	3	47	32	17	1	.277	.334	.394
Rabbit Maranville	SS112	R	36	112	366	40	88	14	10	1	34	36	27	3	.240	.310	.342
Taylor Douthit	OF154	R	27	154	648	111	191	35	3	3	43	84	36	11	.295	.384	.372
Chick Hafey	OF133	R	25	138	520	101	175	46	6	27	111	40	53	8	.337	.386	.604
George Harper†	OF84	L	36	99	272	41	83	8	2	17	58	51	15	2	.305	.418	.537
Andy High	3B73,2B19	L	30	111	368	58	105	14	3	6	37	37	10	2	.285	.355	.389
Wally Roettger	OF66	R	25	68	261	27	89	17	4	6	44	10	22	2	.341	.372	.506
Tommy Thevenow	SS64,3B3,1B1	R	24	69	171	11	35	8	3	0	13	20	12	0	.205	.288	.287
Ray Blades	OF19	R	31	51	85	9	20	7	1	1	19	20	26	0	.235	.393	.376
Ernie Orsatti	OF17,1B5	L	25	27	69	10	21	6	0	3	15	10	11	0	.304	.400	.522
Earl Smith†	C18	L	31	24	58	3	13	2	0	0	7	5	4	0	.224	.286	.259
Bob O'Farrell†	C14	R	31	16	52	6	11	1	0	0	4	13	9	2	.212	.369	.231
Gus Mancuso	C11	R	22	11	38	2	7	0	1	0	3	0	5	0	.184	.184	.237
Specs Toporcer	1B1,2B1	L	29	8	14	0	0	0	0	0	0	0	3	0	.000	.000	.000
Pepper Martin	OF4	R	24	39	13	11	4	0	0	0	0	1	2	2	.308	.400	.308
Howie Williamson		L	23	10	9	0	2	0	0	0	0	1	4	0	.222	.300	.222
Spud Davis†	C2	R	23	2	5	1	1	0	0	0	1	1	0	0	.200	.333	.200

Pitcher	T	Age	G	GS	CG	ShO	IP	H	HR	BB	SO	W-L	Sv	ERA
Pete Alexander	R	41	34	31	18	1	243.2	262	16	37	59	16-9	2	3.36
Jesse Haines	R	34	33	28	20	1	240.1	238	14	72	77	20-8	0	3.18
Bill Sherdel	L	31	38	27	20	0	248.2	251	17	56	72	21-10	5	2.86
Flint Rhem	R	27	28	22	9	0	169.2	199	13	71	47	11-8	3	4.14
Clarence Mitchell†	L	37	19	18	9	1	150.0	149	8	38	31	8-9	0	3.30
Syl Johnson	R	27	34	6	2	0	120.0	117	6	33	66	8-4	3	3.90
Hal Haid	R	30	27	0	0	0	47.0	39	1	11	21	2-2	5	2.30
Art Reinhart	L	29	23	9	3	1	75.1	80	3	27	12	4-6	2	2.87
Fred Frankhouse	R	24	21	10	1	0	84.0	91	6	36	29	3-2	1	3.96
Carlisle Littlejohn	R	26	12	2	1	0	32.0	36	2	14	6	2-1	0	3.66
Tony Kaufmann	R	27	4	1	0	0	4.2	8	1	4	2	0-0	0	9.64

1928 New York Giants 2nd NL 93-61 .604 2.0 GB

John McGraw

Player	Gm by Position	B	Age	G	AB	R	H	2B	3B	HR	RBI	BB	SO	SB	Avg	OBP	Slg
Shanty Hogan	C124	R	22	131	411	48	137	25	2	10	71	42	25	0	.333	.406	.477
Bill Terry	1B149	L	31	149	568	100	185	36	11	17	101	64	36	7	.326	.394	.518
Andy Cohen	2B126,SS3,3B1	R	23	129	504	64	138	24	7	9	59	31	17	3	.274	.318	.403
Freddy Lindstrom	3B153	R	22	153	646	99	231	39	9	14	107	25	21	15	.358	.383	.511
Travis Jackson	SS149	R	24	150	537	73	145	35	6	14	77	56	46	8	.270	.339	.436
Jimmy Welsh	OF117	L	25	124	476	77	146	22	5	9	54	29	30	4	.307	.357	.431
Mel Ott	OF115,2B5,3B1	L	19	124	435	69	140	26	4	18	77	52	36	3	.322	.397	.524
Lefty O'Doul	OF94	L	31	114	354	67	113	19	4	8	46	30	8	9	.319	.372	.463
Randy Reese	OF64,2B26,1B6*	R	24	109	406	61	125	18	4	6	44	13	24	7	.308	.331	.416
Les Mann	OF68	R	34	82	193	29	51	7	1	2	25	18	9	2	.264	.330	.342
Edd Roush	OF39	L	35	46	163	20	41	5	3	2	13	14	8	1	.252	.315	.356
Bob O'Farrell†	C63	R	31	75	133	23	26	6	0	2	20	34	16	2	.195	.359	.286
George Harper†	OF18	L	36	19	57	11	13	1	0	2	7	10	4	1	.228	.353	.351
Art Jahn†	OF8	R	32	10	29	7	8	1	0	1	7	2	5	0	.276	.323	.414
Jack Cummings	C4	R	24	33	27	4	9	2	0	2	9	3	4	0	.333	.400	.630
Russ Wrightstone†	1B2	L	35	30	25	3	4	0	0	1	5	3	2	0	.160	.250	.280
Pat Veltman	OF1	R	22	1	3	1	1	0	1	0	0	1	0	0	.333	.500	1.000
Al Spohrer†	C2	R	25	2	2	0	0	0	0	0	0	0	0	0	.000	.000	.000
Joe Price		R	31	1	1	0	0	0	0	0	0	0	1	0	.000	.000	.000
Ray Foley		L	22	2	1	1	0	0	0	0	0	1	1	0	.000	.500	.000
Chick Fullis		R	24	11	1	5	0	0	0	0	0	1	1	0	.000	.500	.000
Bill Haeffner	C2	R	33	2	1	0	0	0	0	0	0	0	0	0	.000	.000	.000

R. Reese, 6 G at 3B, 6 G at SS

Pitcher	T	Age	G	GS	CG	ShO	IP	H	HR	BB	SO	W-L	Sv	ERA
Larry Benton	R	30	42	35	28	2	310.1	299	14	71	90	25-9	4	2.73
F. Fitzsimmons	R	26	40	32	16	1	261.1	264	13	65	67	20-9	1	3.68
Joe Genewich†	R	31	26	18	10	2	158.1	136	10	54	37	11-4	3	3.18
Vic Aldridge	R	34	22	17	3	1	119.1	133	7	45	33	4-7	2	4.83
Carl Hubbell	L	25	20	14	8	1	124.0	117	7	21	37	10-6	1	2.83
Virgil Barnes†	R	31	10	9	3	1	55.1	71	3	18	11	3-3	0	5.04
Leo Mangum	R	32	1	1	0	0	3.0	6	0	5	1	0-0	0	15.00
Jim Faulkner	L	28	38	8	3	0	117.1	131	5	41	32	9-8	2	3.53
Bill Walker	L	24	22	8	1	0	76.1	79	9	31	39	3-6	0	4.72
Dutch Henry	L	26	17	8	4	0	64.0	82	4	25	23	3-6	1	3.80
Jack Scott	R	36	16	3	3	0	50.1	59	3	11	17	4-1	1	3.58
Tiny Chaplin	R	22	12	1	0	0	24.0	27	0	8	5	0-2	0	4.50
Ben Cantwell†	R	26	7	1	0	0	18.1	20	1	4	0	1-0	1	4.42
Bill Clarkson†	R	29	4	0	0	0	5.2	10	0	1	3	0-0	0	7.94
Chet Nichols	R	30	3	0	0	0	2.2	11	0	3	1	0-0	0	23.63
Garland Buckeye†	L	30	1	0	0	0	3.2	9	1	2	3	0-0	0	14.73

1928 Chicago Cubs 3rd NL 91-63 .591 4.0 GB — Joe McCarthy

Player	Gm by Position	B	Age	G	AB	R	H	2B	3B	HR	RBI	BB	SO	SB	Avg	OBP	Slg
Gabby Hartnett	C118	R	27	120	388	61	117	26	9	14	57	65	32	3	.302	.404	.523
Charlie Grimm	1B147	L	29	147	547	67	161	25	5	5	62	39	20	7	.294	.342	.386
Freddie Maguire	2B138	R	29	140	574	67	160	24	7	1	41	25	38	6	.279	.312	.350
Clyde Beck	3B87,SS47,2B1	R	28	131	483	72	124	18	4	3	52	58	58	3	.257	.341	.329
Woody English	SS114,3B2	R	21	116	475	68	142	22	4	2	34	30	28	4	.299	.343	.375
Hack Wilson	OF143	R	28	145	520	89	163	32	9	31	120	77	94	4	.313	.404	.588
Riggs Stephenson	OF135	R	30	137	512	75	166	36	9	8	90	68	29	8	.324	.407	.477
Kiki Cuyler	OF127	R	29	133	499	92	142	25	9	17	79	51	61	37	.285	.359	.473
Johnny Butler	3B59,SS2	R	35	62	174	17	47	7	0	0	16	19	7	2	.270	.352	.310
Mike Gonzalez	C45	R	37	49	158	12	43	9	2	1	21	12	7	2	.272	.324	.373
Earl Webb	OF31	L	30	62	140	22	35	7	3	3	23	14	17	0	.250	.318	.407
Cliff Heathcote	OF39	L	30	67	137	26	39	8	0	3	18	17	12	6	.285	.364	.409
Norm McMillan	2B19,3B18	R	32	49	123	11	27	2	2	1	12	13	19	0	.220	.299	.293
Joe Kelly	1B10	L	28	32	52	3	11	1	0	1	7	1	3	0	.212	.255	.288
Johnny Moore		L	26	4	4	0	0	0	0	0	0	0	0	0	.000	.000	.000
Ray Jacobs		R	26	2	2	0	0	0	0	0	0	0	1	0	.000	.000	.000
Elmer Yoter	3B1	R	28	1	0	0	0	0	0	0	0	0	0	0	—	—	—

Pitcher	T	Age	G	GS	CG	ShO	IP	H	HR	BB	SO	W-L	Sv	ERA
Charlie Root	R	29	40	30	13	1	237.0	214	15	73	122	14-18	2	3.57
Sheriff Blake	R	28	34	29	16	4	240.2	209	4	101	78	17-11	1	2.47
Pat Malone	R	25	42	25	16	2	250.2	218	15	99	155	18-13	2	2.84
Guy Bush	R	26	42	24	9	2	204.1	229	10	86	61	15-6	2	3.83
Art Nehf	L	35	31	21	10	2	176.2	190	3	52	40	13-7	0	2.65
Percy Jones	L	28	39	18	9	1	154.0	167	4	56	41	10-6	3	4.03
Hal Carlson	R	36	20	5	2	0	56.1	74	4	15	11	3-2	4	5.91
Ed Holley	R	28	13	1	0	0	31.0	31	1	16	10	0-0	0	3.77
Lefty Weinert	L	26	10	1	0	0	17.0	24	0	9	8	1-0	0	5.29
Johnny Welch	R	21	3	0	0	0	4.0	13	0	0	2	0-0	0	15.75
Ben Tincup	R	37	2	0	0	0	9.0	14	0	1	3	0-0	0	7.00

1928 Pittsburgh Pirates 4th NL 85-67 .559 9.0 GB — Donie Bush

Player	Gm by Position	B	Age	G	AB	R	H	2B	3B	HR	RBI	BB	SO	SB	Avg	OBP	Slg
C. Hargreaves†	C77	R	31	79	260	15	74	8	2	1	32	12	9	1	.285	.319	.342
George Grantham	1B119	L	28	124	440	93	142	24	9	10	85	59	37	9	.323	.408	.486
Sparky Adams	2B107,SS27	R	33	135	539	91	149	14	6	0	38	64	18	8	.276	.357	.325
Pie Traynor	3B144	R	28	144	569	91	192	38	12	3	124	28	10	12	.337	.370	.462
Glenn Wright	SS101	R	27	108	407	63	126	20	8	8	66	21	53	3	.310	.343	.457
Lloyd Waner	OF152	L	22	152	659	121	221	22	14	5	61	40	13	8	.335	.377	.434
Paul Waner	OF131,1B24	L	25	152	602	142	223	50	19	6	86	77	16	6	.370	.446	.547
George Brickell	OF50	L	21	81	202	34	65	4	4	3	41	20	18	5	.322	.383	.426
Dick Bartell	2B39,SS27	R	20	72	233	27	71	8	4	1	36	21	18	4	.305	.377	.386
Clyde Barnhart	OF48	R	32	61	196	18	58	6	2	4	30	11	9	3	.296	.333	.408
Pete Scott	OF42,1B8	R	29	60	177	33	55	10	4	5	33	18	14	1	.311	.378	.497
Adam Comorosky	OF49	R	22	51	176	22	52	6	3	2	34	15	6	1	.295	.354	.398
Rollie Hemsley	C49	R	21	50	133	14	36	2	3	0	18	4	10	1	.271	.292	.331
Earl Smith†	C28	L	31	32	85	8	21	6	0	2	11	11	7	0	.247	.333	.388
Johnny Gooch†	C31	S	30	31	80	7	19	2	1	0	5	3	6	0	.238	.265	.288
Joe Mulligan	3B6,2B4	R	33	27	43	4	10	2	0	0	1	3	4	0	.233	.283	.279
Mack Hillis	2B8,3B1	R	26	11	36	6	9	2	3	1	7	0	6	1	.250	.250	.556
Joe Harris†	1B6	R	37	16	23	2	9	2	1	0	2	4	2	0	.391	.500	.565
Cobe Jones	SS2	S	20	2	2	0	1	0	0	0	0	0	0	0	.500	.500	.500
Bill Windle	1B1	L	23	1	1	1	1	1	0	0	0	0	0	0	1.000	1.000	2.000
John O'Connell	C1	R	24	1	1	0	0	0	0	0	0	0	0	0	.000	.000	.000

Pitcher	T	Age	G	GS	CG	ShO	IP	H	HR	BB	SO	W-L	Sv	ERA
Burleigh Grimes	R	34	48	37	28	4	330.2	311	11	77	97	25-14	3	2.99
Carmen Hill	R	32	36	31	16	1	237.0	229	16	81	73	16-10	2	3.53
Ray Kremer	R	35	34	31	17	1	219.0	253	15	68	61	15-13	0	4.64
Fred Fussell	L	32	28	20	9	2	159.2	183	6	41	43	8-9	1	3.61
Lee Meadows	R	33	4	2	1	0	10.0	18	0	5	3	1-1	0	8.10
Joe Dawson	R	31	31	7	1	0	128.2	116	6	56	36	7-7	3	3.29
Erv Brame	R	26	24	11	6	0	95.2	110	5	44	22	7-4	0	5.08
Johnny Miljus†	R	33	21	10	3	0	69.2	90	2	33	26	5-7	1	5.30
Walt Tauscher	R	26	17	0	0	0	29.1	28	0	12	7	0-0	1	4.91
Les Bartholomew	L	25	6	0	0	0	22.2	31	2	9	6	0-0	0	7.15
Homer Blankenship	R	25	5	2	1	0	21.2	27	1	9	6	0-2	0	5.82
Bill Burwell	R	33	4	1	0	0	20.2	18	2	8	2	1-0	0	5.23
Glenn Spencer	R	22	4	0	0	0	5.2	4	0	3	2	0-0	0	1.59
Elmer Tutwiler	R	22	2	0	0	0	3.2	4	0	0	1	0-0	0	4.91

1928 Cincinnati Reds 5th NL 78-74 .513 16.0 GB — Jack Hendricks

Player	Gm by Position	B	Age	G	AB	R	H	2B	3B	HR	RBI	BB	SO	SB	Avg	OBP	Slg
Val Picinich	C93	R	31	96	324	29	98	15	1	7	35	20	25	1	.302	.343	.420
George Kelly	1B99,OF13	R	32	116	402	46	119	23	7	3	58	28	35	2	.296	.345	.435
Hughie Critz	2B153	R	27	153	641	95	190	21	11	5	52	37	24	18	.296	.335	.387
Chuck Dressen	3B135	R	29	135	498	72	145	26	3	1	59	43	22	10	.291	.355	.361
Hod Ford	SS149	R	30	149	506	49	122	17	4	0	54	47	31	1	.241	.308	.291
Ethan Allen	OF129	R	24	129	485	55	148	30	7	1	62	27	29	6	.305	.343	.402
Curt Walker	OF122	L	31	123	427	64	119	15	12	6	73	49	14	19	.279	.354	.412
Billy Zitzmann	OF78	R	32	101	266	53	79	9	3	3	33	13	22	13	.297	.337	.387
Wally Pipp	1B72	L	35	95	272	30	77	11	3	2	26	23	13	1	.283	.341	.368
Marty Callaghan	OF69	L	28	81	238	29	69	11	4	0	24	27	10	5	.290	.362	.370
Pid Purdy	OF61	L	24	70	223	32	69	11	1	0	25	23	13	1	.309	.377	.368
Bubbles Hargrave	C57	R	35	65	190	19	56	12	3	0	23	13	14	4	.295	.353	.389
Joe Stripp	OF21,3B17	R	25	42	139	18	40	7	3	1	17	8	8	0	.288	.340	.403
Clyde Sukeforth	C26	L	26	33	53	5	7	2	1	0	3	3	5	0	.132	.179	.208
Pinky Pittenger	SS12,2B4,3B4	R	29	40	38	12	9	0	1	0	4	0	1	2	.237	.237	.289
Jack White	2B1	S	22	1	3	0	0	0	0	0	0	0	1	0	.000	.000	.000

Pitcher	T	Age	G	GS	CG	ShO	IP	H	HR	BB	SO	W-L	Sv	ERA
Eppa Rixey	L	37	43	37	17	3	291.1	317	4	67	58	19-18	2	3.43
Dolf Luque	R	37	33	29	11	1	234.1	254	12	84	72	11-10	1	3.57
Ray Kolp	R	33	44	24	12	1	209.0	219	9	55	61	13-10	3	3.19
Red Lucas	R	26	27	19	13	4	167.1	164	9	42	35	13-9	1	3.39
Pete Donohue	R	27	23	18	8	0	150.0	180	10	32	37	7-11	0	4.74
Jakie May	L	32	21	11	1	1	79.1	99	1	35	39	3-5	1	4.42
Carl Mays	R	36	14	7	4	1	62.2	67	3	22	10	4-1	1	3.88
Ken Ash	R	26	8	5	2	0	36.0	43	1	13	6	3-3	0	6.50
Harlan Pyle	R	22	2	1	0	0	1.1	1	0	4	1	0-0	0	20.25
Pete Appleton	R	24	31	1	0	0	82.2	101	7	22	20	3-4	0	4.68
Jim Joe Edwards	L	33	18	1	0	0	32.0	43	1	20	11	2-2	2	7.59
Jim Beckman	R	23	6	0	0	0	15.1	19	1	9	4	0-1	0	5.87
Si Johnson	R	21	3	0	0	0	10.1	9	0	5	1	0-0	0	4.35

1928 Brooklyn Dodgers 6th NL 77-76 .503 17.5 GB — Wilbert Robinson

Player	Gm by Position	B	Age	G	AB	R	H	2B	3B	HR	RBI	BB	SO	SB	Avg	OBP	Slg
Hank DeBerry	C80	R	33	82	258	19	65	8	2	0	23	18	15	3	.252	.301	.298
Del Bissonette	1B155	L	28	155	587	90	188	30	13	25	106	70	75	5	.320	.396	.543
Jake Flowers	2B94	R	26	103	339	51	93	11	6	2	44	47	30	10	.274	.366	.360
Harvey Hendrick	3B91,OF17	L	30	126	425	83	135	15	10	11	59	54	34	16	.318	.397	.478
Dave Bancroft	SS149	S	37	149	515	47	127	19	5	0	51	59	20	7	.247	.326	.303
Rube Bressler	OF137	R	33	145	501	78	148	29	13	4	70	80	33	2	.295	.398	.429
Babe Herman	OF127	L	25	134	486	64	165	37	6	12	91	38	36	1	.340	.390	.514
Max Carey	OF95	S	38	108	296	41	73	11	0	2	19	47	24	18	.247	.354	.304
Harry Riconda	2B53,3B21,SS16	R	31	92	281	22	63	15	4	3	35	20	28	6	.224	.285	.338
Ty Tyson	OF55	R	36	59	210	25	57	11	1	1	21	10	14	3	.271	.317	.348
Jigger Statz	OF52	R	30	77	171	28	40	8	1	0	16	18	12	3	.234	.311	.292
Wally Gilbert	3B39	R	27	39	153	26	31	4	0	0	3	14	8	2	.203	.274	.229
Butch Henline	C45	R	33	55	132	12	28	3	1	2	8	17	8	2	.212	.302	.295
Johnny Gooch†	C38	S	30	42	101	9	32	1	2	0	12	7	9	0	.317	.361	.366
Joe Harris†	OF16	R	37	55	89	8	21	6	1	1	8	14	4	0	.236	.340	.360
Jay Partridge	2B18,3B2	L	25	37	73	18	18	0	1	0	12	13	6	2	.247	.368	.274
C. Hargreaves†	C20	R	31	20	61	3	12	2	0	0	5	6	6	1	.197	.269	.230
Howard Freigau†	3B10,SS1	R	25	17	34	6	7	2	0	0	3	1	3	0	.206	.229	.265
Overton Tremper	OF10	R	22	10	31	1	6	2	1	0	1	0	1	0	.194	.194	.323
Max West	OF7	R	23	7	21	4	6	1	1	0	1	4	1	0	.286	.400	.429
Al Lopez	C3	R	19	3	12	0	0	0	0	0	0	0	0	0	.000	.000	.000

Pitcher	T	Age	G	GS	CG	ShO	IP	H	HR	BB	SO	W-L	Sv	ERA
Dazzy Vance	R	37	38	32	24	4	280.1	226	11	72	200	22-10	2	2.09
Doug McWeeny	R	31	42	32	12	4	244.0	218	11	114	79	14-14	1	3.17
Jesse Petty	L	33	40	31	15	2	234.0	264	18	56	74	15-15	1	4.04
Jumbo Elliott	L	27	41	21	7	2	192.0	194	8	64	74	9-14	1	3.89
Watty Clark	L	26	40	19	10	2	194.2	193	4	50	85	12-9	3	2.68
Bill Doak	R	37	28	12	4	1	99.1	104	1	35	12	3-8	3	3.26
Rube Ehrhardt	R	33	28	2	1	0	54.0	74	1	27	12	1-3	2	4.67
Ray Moss	R	26	22	5	1	1	60.1	62	5	35	5	0-3	1	4.92
Lou Koupal	R	29	17	1	1	0	37.1	43	0	15	10	1-0	1	2.41

1928 Boston Braves 7th NL 50-103 .327 44.5 GB — Jack Slattery (11-20)/Rogers Hornsby (39-83)

Player	Gm by Position	B	Age	G	AB	R	H	2B	3B	HR	RBI	BB	SO	SB	Avg	OBP	Slg
Zack Taylor	C124	R	29	125	399	36	100	15	1	2	30	33	29	2	.251	.313	.308
George Sisler†	1B118,P1	L	35	118	491	71	167	26	4	4	68	30	15	11	.340	.380	.434
Rogers Hornsby	2B140	R	32	140	486	99	188	42	7	21	94	107	41	5	.387	.498	.632
Les Bell	3B153	R	26	153	591	58	164	36	7	10	91	40	45	1	.277	.323	.413
Doc Farrell	SS132	R	26	134	483	36	104	14	2	3	43	26	26	3	.215	.263	.271
Lance Richbourg	OF148	L	30	148	612	105	206	26	12	2	52	62	39	11	.337	.399	.428
Eddie Brown	OF129,1B1	R	36	142	523	45	140	28	2	2	59	24	22	6	.268	.305	.340
Jack Smith	OF65	L	33	96	254	30	71	9	2	1	32	21	14	6	.280	.335	.343
Eddie Moore	OF54	R	29	68	215	27	51	9	0	2	18	19	12	7	.237	.299	.307
Heinie Mueller	OF41	L	28	42	151	25	34	3	1	0	19	17	9	1	.225	.316	.258
Dick Burrus	1B32	L	30	64	137	15	37	6	0	3	13	19	8	1	.270	.367	.380
Al Spohrer†	C48	R	25	51	124	15	27	3	0	0	9	5	11	1	.218	.254	.242
Earl Clark	OF27	R	20	28	112	18	34	9	1	0	10	4	8	0	.304	.339	.402
Howard Freigau†	SS14,2B11	R	25	52	109	11	28	8	1	1	17	9	14	1	.257	.319	.376
Jimmy Cooney	SS11,2B4	R	33	18	51	2	7	0	0	0	3	2	5	1	.137	.170	.137
Johnny Cooney	P24,1B3,OF2	R	27	33	41	2	7	0	0	0	2	4	3	0	.171	.244	.171
Doc Gautreau	2B4,SS1	R	26	23	18	3	5	0	1	0	0	4	3	1	.278	.409	.389
Luke Urban	C10	R	30	15	17	0	3	0	0	0	2	0	1	0	.176	.222	.176
Dave Harris	OF6	R	27	7	17	2	2	1	0	0	0	2	6	0	.118	.211	.176
Charlie Fitzberger		L	24	7	7	0	2	0	0	0	0	0	3	0	.286	.286	.286
Dinny McNamara	OF3	L	22	9	4	2	1	0	0	0	0	0	1	0	.250	.250	.250
Bill Cronin	C3	R	25	3	2	1	0	0	0	0	0	1	0	0	.000	.333	.000
Earl Williams	C1	R	25	3	2	0	0	0	0	0	0	0	1	0	.000	.000	.000

Pitcher	T	Age	G	GS	CG	ShO	IP	H	HR	BB	SO	W-L	Sv	ERA
Ed Brandt	L	23	38	31	12	1	225.1	234	22	109	84	9-21	0	5.07
Bob Smith	R	33	38	25	14	0	244.1	274	11	74	59	13-17	2	3.87
Kent Greenfield	R	25	32	23	5	0	143.2	173	6	60	30	3-11	0	5.32
Art Delaney	R	31	39	22	8	0	192.1	197	11	56	45	9-17	2	3.79
Joe Genewich†	R	31	13	11	4	0	80.2	88	14	18	15	3-7	0	4.13
Virgil Barnes†	R	31	16	10	1	0	60.1	86	3	26	7	2-7	0	5.82
Charlie Robertson	R	32	13	7	3	0	59.1	73	5	16	17	2-5	1	5.31
Johnny Cooney	L	27	24	6	2	0	89.2	106	7	31	18	3-7	1	4.32
Ben Cantwell†	R	26	22	9	3	0	90.0	112	7	36	18	3-3	0	5.10
Foster Edwards	R	24	21	3	2	0	49.1	67	2	23	17	2-1	0	5.66
Bill Clarkson†	R	29	19	1	0	0	34.2	53	2	22	8	0-2	0	6.75
Johnny Werts	R	30	10	2	0	0	18.1	31	2	8	5	0-2	0	10.31
B. Hollingsworth	R	32	7	2	0	0	22.1	30	2	13	10	0-2	0	5.24
Bunny Hearn	L	24	7	0	0	0	10.0	6	0	8	8	1-0	0	6.30
Clay Touchstone	R	25	5	0	0	0	8.0	15	0	2	1	0-0	0	4.50
Hal Goldsmith	R	29	4	0	0	0	8.1	14	2	1	1	0-0	0	3.24
Art Mills	R	25	4	0	0	0	7.2	17	3	8	0	0-0	0	12.91
Ray Boggs	L	23	4	0	0	0	5.0	2	0	7	0	0-0	0	5.40
Emilio Palmero	L	33	3	1	0	0	6.2	14	0	2	0	0-1	0	5.40
Guy Morrison	R	32	1	0	0	0	3.0	4	1	3	0	0-0	0	12.00
George Sisler	L	35	1	0	0	0	1.0	0	0	1	0	0-0	0	0.00

1928 Philadelphia Phillies 8th NL 43-109 .283 51.0 GB

Burt Shotton

Player	Gm by Position	B	Age	G	AB	R	H	2B	3B	HR	RBI	BB	SO	SB	Avg	OBP	Slg
Walt Lerian	C74	R	25	96	239	28	65	16	2	2	25	41	29	1	.272	.385	.381
Don Hurst	1B104	L	22	107	396	73	113	23	4	19	64	68	40	3	.285	.391	.508
Fresco Thompson	2B152	R	26	152	634	99	182	34	11	3	50	42	27	19	.287	.332	.390
Pinky Whitney	3B149	R	23	151	585	73	176	35	4	10	103	36	30	3	.301	.342	.426
Heinie Sand	SS137	R	30	141	426	38	90	26	1	0	38	60	47	1	.211	.310	.277
Denny Sothern	OF136	R	24	141	579	82	165	27	5	5	38	34	53	17	.285	.327	.375
Freddy Leach	OF120,1B25	L	30	145	588	83	179	36	11	13	96	30	30	4	.304	.342	.469
Cy Williams	OF69	L	40	99	238	31	61	9	0	12	37	54	34	0	.256	.400	.445
Chuck Klein	OF63	L	23	64	253	41	91	14	4	11	34	14	22	0	.360	.396	.577
Spud Davis†	C49	R	23	67	163	16	46	2	0	3	18	15	11	0	.282	.343	.350
Johnny Schulte	C34	L	31	65	113	14	28	2	2	4	17	15	12	0	.248	.336	.407
Bill Deitrick	OF21,SS8	R	26	52	100	13	20	6	0	0	7	17	10	1	.200	.322	.260
Art Jahn†	OF29	R	32	36	94	8	21	4	0	0	11	4	11	0	.223	.270	.266
Bernie Friberg	SS31,3B5,2B3*	R	28	52	94	11	19	3	0	1	7	12	16	0	.202	.292	.266
Russ Wrightstone†	OF26,1B4	L	35	33	91	7	19	5	1	1	11	14	5	0	.209	.321	.319
Bill Kelly	1B23	R	29	23	71	6	12	1	1	0	5	7	20	0	.169	.244	.211
Jimmie Wilson†	C20	R	27	21	70	11	21	4	1	0	13	9	8	3	.300	.380	.386
Al Nixon	OF20	R	42	25	64	7	15	2	0	0	7	6	4	1	.234	.300	.266
Harvey MacDonald	OF2	L	30	13	16	0	4	0	0	0	2	2	3	0	.250	.333	.250

B. Friberg, 3 G at OF, 2 G at 1B

Pitcher	T	Age	G	GS	CG	ShO	IP	H	HR	BB	SO	W-L	Sv	ERA
Ray Benge	R	26	40	28	12	1	201.2	219	16	88	68	8-18	1	4.55
Jimmy Ring	R	33	35	25	4	0	173.0	214	14	103	72	4-17	1	6.40
Alex Ferguson	R	31	34	19	5	1	134.2	162	14	48	50	5-10	2	5.55
Hub Pruett	L	27	13	9	4	0	71.1	78	2	49	35	2-4	0	4.54
John Milligan	L	24	13	7	3	0	68.0	69	2	32	22	2-5	0	4.37
Earl Caldwell	R	23	5	5	1	1	34.2	46	5	17	6	1-4	0	5.71
Marty Walker	L	29	1	1	0	0	0.0	2	0	3	0	0-1	0	—
Bob McGraw	R	33	39	3	0	0	120.0	148	7	56	28	7-8	1	5.18
Augie Walsh	R	23	38	11	2	0	122.1	160	13	40	38	4-9	2	6.18
Leo Sweetland	L	26	37	18	5	0	135.1	163	15	97	23	3-15	2	6.58
Claude Willoughby	R	29	35	13	5	1	130.2	180	6	83	26	6-5	1	5.30
Russ Miller	R	28	33	12	1	0	108.0	137	14	34	19	0-12	1	5.42
Ed Baecht	R	21	9	1	0	0	24.0	37	1	9	10	1-1	0	6.00
Ed Lennon	R	30	5	0	0	0	12.1	19	0	10	6	0-0	0	8.76
Clarence Mitchell†	L	37	3	0	0	0	5.2	13	0	2	0	0-0	0	9.53
June Greene	R	29	1	0	0	0	2.0	5	0	0	0	0-0	0	9.00

»1929 Philadelphia Athletics 1st AL 104-46 .693 —

Connie Mack

Player	Gm by Position	B	Age	G	AB	R	H	2B	3B	HR	RBI	BB	SO	SB	Avg	OBP	Slg
Mickey Cochrane	C135	L	26	135	514	113	170	37	8	7	95	69	8	7	.331	.412	.475
Jimmie Foxx	1B142,3B8	R	21	149	517	123	183	23	9	33	117	103	70	9	.354	.463	.625
Max Bishop	2B129	L	29	129	475	102	110	19	6	3	36	128	44	1	.232	.398	.316
Sammy Hale	3B99,2B1	R	32	101	379	51	105	14	3	1	40	12	18	6	.277	.303	.338
Joe Boley	SS88,3B1	R	32	91	303	36	76	17	6	2	47	24	16	1	.251	.310	.366
Bing Miller	OF145	R	34	147	556	84	186	32	16	8	93	40	25	24	.335	.383	.493
Al Simmons	OF142	R	27	143	581	114	212	41	9	34	157	31	38	4	.365	.398	.642
Mule Haas	OF139	L	25	139	578	115	181	41	9	16	82	34	38	0	.313	.356	.498
Jimmy Dykes	SS60,3B45,2B12	R	32	119	401	76	131	34	6	13	79	51	25	8	.327	.412	.539
Homer Summa	OF24	L	30	37	81	12	22	4	0	0	10	2	1	1	.272	.298	.321
Cy Perkins	C38	R	33	38	76	4	16	4	0	0	9	5	4	0	.211	.259	.263
Jim Cronin	2B10,SS9,3B4	S	23	25	56	7	13	2	1	0	4	5	7	0	.232	.295	.304
Ossie Orwoll	P12,OF9	L	28	30	51	6	13	2	1	0	6	2	11	0	.255	.283	.333
George Burns†	1B19	R	36	29	49	5	13	5	0	1	11	2	3	1	.265	.294	.429
Walt French		L	29	45	45	7	12	1	0	1	9	2	3	0	.267	.298	.356
Bud Morse	2B8	L	24	8	27	1	2	0	0	0	0	0	2	0	.074	.074	.074
Bevo LeBourveau	OF3	L	34	12	16	1	5	0	1	0	2	5	1	0	.313	.476	.438
Eric McNair	SS4	R	20	4	8	2	4	1	0	0	3	0	0	1	.500	.500	.625
Eddie Collins		L	42	9	7	0	0	0	0	0	0	2	0	0	.000	.222	.000
Doc Cramer	OF1	L	23	2	6	0	0	0	0	0	0	0	2	0	.000	.000	.000
Cloy Mattox	C3	L	26	3	6	0	1	0	0	0	0	1	1	0	.167	.286	.167
Rudy Miller	3B2	R	28	2	4	1	1	0	0	0	1	3	0	0	.250	.571	.250
Joe Hassler	SS2	R	24	4	4	1	0	0	0	0	0	0	2	0	.000	.000	.000

Pitcher	T	Age	G	GS	CG	ShO	IP	H	HR	BB	SO	W-L	Sv	ERA
Lefty Grove	L	29	42	37	21	2	275.0	278	8	81	170	20-6	4	2.81
Rube Walberg	L	32	40	33	20	3	267.2	256	22	99	94	18-11	4	3.60
George Earnshaw	R	29	44	33	13	3	254.2	233	8	125	149	24-8	1	3.29
Jack Quinn	R	45	35	18	7	0	161.0	182	8	39	41	11-9	2	3.97
Howard Ehmke	R	35	11	8	2	0	54.2	48	2	15	20	7-2	0	3.29
Bill Shores	R	25	39	13	5	1	152.2	150	9	59	49	11-6	7	3.60
Eddie Rommel	R	31	32	6	4	0	113.2	135	10	34	25	12-2	4	2.85
Carroll Yerkes	L	26	19	2	0	0	37.1	47	0	13	11	1-0	1	4.58
Ossie Orwoll	L	28	12	0	0	0	30.0	32	6	6	12	0-2	1	4.80
Bill Breckinridge	R	21	3	1	0	0	10.0	10	0	16	2	0-0	0	7.20

1929 New York Yankees 2nd AL 88-66 .571 18.0 GB

Miller Huggins (82-61)/Art Fletcher (6-5)

Player	Gm by Position	B	Age	G	AB	R	H	2B	3B	HR	RBI	BB	SO	SB	Avg	OBP	Slg
Bill Dickey	C127	L	22	130	447	60	145	30	6	10	65	14	16	4	.324	.346	.485
Lou Gehrig	1B154	L	26	154	553	127	166	33	9	35	126	122	68	4	.300	.431	.582
Tony Lazzeri	2B147	R	25	147	545	101	193	37	11	18	106	69	45	9	.354	.430	.561
Gene Robertson†	3B77	L	30	90	309	45	92	15	6	0	35	28	6	3	.298	.358	.385
Leo Durocher	SS93	R	23	106	341	53	84	4	5	0	32	34	33	3	.246	.320	.287
Earle Combs	OF141	L	30	142	586	119	202	33	15	3	65	69	32	11	.345	.414	.468
Babe Ruth	OF133	L	34	135	499	121	172	26	6	46	154	72	60	5	.345	.430	.697
Bob Meusel	OF96	R	32	100	391	46	102	15	3	10	57	17	42	1	.261	.292	.391
Mark Koenig	SS61,3B37,2B1	S	24	116	373	44	109	27	5	3	41	23	17	1	.292	.335	.416
Lyn Lary	3B55,SS14,2B2	R	23	80	236	48	73	9	2	5	26	24	15	4	.309	.380	.428
Cedric Durst	OF72,1B1	L	32	92	202	32	52	3	3	4	31	15	25	3	.257	.309	.361
Sammy Byrd	OF54	R	21	62	170	32	53	12	0	5	28	28	18	1	.312	.409	.471
Ben Paschal	OF20	R	33	42	72	13	15	3	0	2	11	6	3	1	.208	.269	.333
Benny Bengough	C23	R	30	23	62	5	12	2	1	0	7	0	2	0	.194	.194	.258
Johnny Grabowski	C22	R	29	22	59	4	12	1	0	0	2	3	6	1	.203	.242	.220
Art Jorgens	C15	R	24	18	34	6	11	3	0	0	4	6	7	0	.324	.425	.412
Julie Wera	3B4	R	27	5	12	1	5	0	0	0	2	1	1	0	.417	.462	.417
George Burns†		R	36	9	9	0	0	0	0	0	0	0	4	0	.000	.000	.000
Liz Funk		L	24	1	0	0	0	0	0	0	0	0	0	0	—	—	—

Pitcher	T	Age	G	GS	CG	ShO	IP	H	HR	BB	SO	W-L	Sv	ERA
George Pipgras	R	29	39	33	13	3	225.1	229	16	95	125	18-12	0	4.23
Waite Hoyt	R	29	30	25	12	0	201.2	219	9	69	57	10-9	1	4.24
Ed Wells	L	29	31	23	10	3	193.1	179	19	81	78	13-9	0	4.33
Herb Pennock	L	35	27	23	8	1	157.2	205	11	28	49	9-11	1	4.91
Hank Johnson	R	23	12	8	2	0	42.2	37	5	39	24	3-3	0	5.06
Wilcy Moore	R	32	41	0	0	0	62.0	64	4	19	21	6-4	8	4.06
Fred Heimach	L	28	35	10	3	3	134.2	141	4	29	26	11-6	4	4.01
Roy Sherid	R	22	33	15	9	0	154.2	165	6	55	51	6-6	1	3.61
Tom Zachary	L	33	26	11	7	2	119.2	131	5	30	35	12-0	2	2.48
Gordon Rhodes	R	21	10	4	0	0	42.2	57	3	16	13	0-4	0	4.85
Bots Nekola	L	22	9	1	0	0	18.2	21	0	15	2	0-0	0	4.34
Myles Thomas†	R	31	5	1	0	0	15.0	27	1	9	3	0-2	0	10.80

1929 Cleveland Indians 3rd AL 81-71 .533 24.0 GB

Roger Peckinpaugh

Player	Gm by Position	B	Age	G	AB	R	H	2B	3B	HR	RBI	BB	SO	SB	Avg	OBP	Slg
Luke Sewell	C123	R	28	124	406	41	96	16	3	1	39	29	26	6	.236	.287	.298
Lew Fonseca	1B147	R	30	148	566	97	209	44	15	6	103	50	23	19	.369	.426	.532
Johnny Hodapp	2B72	R	23	90	294	30	96	12	7	4	51	15	14	3	.327	.361	.456
Joe Sewell	3B152	L	30	152	578	90	182	38	3	7	73	48	4	6	.315	.372	.427
Jackie Tavener	SS89	L	31	92	250	25	53	9	4	2	27	26	28	1	.212	.286	.304
Earl Averill	OF152	L	27	152	603	110	199	43	13	18	97	64	53	13	.330	.397	.534
Bibb Falk	OF121	L	30	126	430	66	133	30	7	13	94	42	14	4	.309	.371	.502
Charlie Jamieson	OF93	L	36	102	364	56	106	22	1	0	26	50	12	2	.291	.377	.357
Eddie Morgan	OF81	R	25	93	318	60	101	19	10	3	37	37	24	4	.318	.392	.469
Ray Gardner	SS82	R	27	82	256	28	67	3	2	1	24	29	16	10	.262	.337	.301
Carl Lind	2B64,3B1	R	25	66	225	19	54	8	1	0	12	13	17	0	.240	.282	.284
Dick Porter	OF30,2B22	L	27	71	192	26	63	16	5	1	24	17	14	3	.328	.386	.479
Glenn Myatt	C41	L	31	59	129	14	30	4	1	1	17	7	5	0	.233	.277	.302
Joe Hauser	1B8	L	30	37	48	8	12	1	1	3	9	4	8	0	.250	.308	.500
Johnny Burnett	SS10,2B8	L	24	19	33	2	5	1	0	0	2	1	2	0	.152	.200	.182
Grover Hartley	C13	R	40	24	33	2	9	0	1	0	8	2	1	0	.273	.314	.333
Dan Jessee		L	28	1	0	0	0	0	0	0	0	0	0	0	—	—	—

Pitcher	T	Age	G	GS	CG	ShO	IP	H	HR	BB	SO	W-L	Sv	ERA
Willis Hudlin	R	23	40	33	22	2	280.1	299	7	73	60	17-15	1	3.34
Jake Miller	L	31	29	29	14	2	206.0	227	7	60	58	14-12	0	3.58
Wes Ferrell	R	21	43	25	18	1	242.2	256	7	109	100	21-10	5	3.60
Joe Shaute	L	29	26	24	8	1	162.0	211	6	52	43	8-8	0	4.28
Jimmy Zinn	R	34	18	11	6	1	105.1	150	8	33	29	4-6	2	5.04
Johnny Miljus	R	34	34	15	4	0	128.1	174	10	64	42	8-8	2	5.19
Ken Holloway	R	31	25	11	6	2	119.0	118	2	37	32	6-5	0	3.03
George Grant	R	26	12	0	0	0	24.0	41	2	23	5	0-2	0	10.50
Milt Shoffner	L	23	11	3	1	0	44.2	46	4	22	15	2-3	0	5.04
Mel Harder	R	19	11	0	0	0	17.2	24	2	5	4	1-0	0	5.60
Clint Brown	R	25	3	1	1	0	16.1	18	0	6	1	0-2	0	3.31
Jim Moore	R	25	2	0	0	0	5.2	6	1	4	0	0-0	0	9.53

1929 St. Louis Browns 4th AL 79-73 .520 26.0 GB

Dan Howley

Player	Gm by Position	B	Age	G	AB	R	H	2B	3B	HR	RBI	BB	SO	SB	Avg	OBP	Slg
Wally Schang	C85	S	39	94	249	43	59	10	5	5	36	74	22	1	.237	.424	.378
Lu Blue	1B151	S	32	151	573	111	168	40	10	6	61	126	32	12	.293	.422	.429
Ski Melillo	2B141	R	29	141	494	57	146	17	10	5	67	29	30	11	.296	.337	.401
Frank O'Rourke	3B151,2B3,SS2	R	34	154	585	81	147	23	9	2	62	41	28	14	.251	.306	.332
Red Kress	SS146	R	22	147	557	82	170	38	4	9	107	52	54	5	.305	.366	.436
Heinie Manush	OF141	L	27	142	574	85	204	45	10	6	81	43	24	9	.355	.401	.500
Beauty McGowan	OF117	L	27	125	441	62	112	26	6	2	51	61	34	5	.254	.346	.354
Fred Schulte	OF116	R	28	121	446	63	137	24	5	3	71	59	44	8	.307	.389	.404
Earl McNeely	OF62	R	31	69	230	27	56	8	1	1	18	7	13	2	.243	.272	.300
Red Badgro	OF37	L	26	54	148	27	42	12	0	1	18	11	15	1	.284	.342	.385
Rick Ferrell	C45	R	23	64	144	21	33	6	1	0	20	32	10	1	.229	.373	.285
Clyde Manion	C34	R	32	35	111	16	27	2	0	0	11	15	3	1	.243	.333	.261
Otis Brannan	2B19	L	30	23	51	4	15	1	0	1	8	4	4	0	.294	.345	.373
Ed Roetz	SS8,1B5,2B2*	R	23	16	45	7	11	4	1	0	5	4	6	0	.244	.306	.378
Len Dondero	3B10,2B5	R	25	19	31	2	6	0	0	1	8	0	4	0	.194	.194	.290
Tom Jenkins	OF3	L	31	21	22	1	4	0	1	0	0	4	8	0	.182	.308	.273
Jimmy Austin	3B1	S	49	1	1	0	0	0	0	0	0	0	1	0	.000	.000	.000

E. Roetz, 1 G at 3B

Pitcher	T	Age	G	GS	CG	ShO	IP	H	HR	BB	SO	W-L	Sv	ERA
Sam Gray	R	31	43	37	23	4	305.0	336	18	96	109	18-15	1	3.72
General Crowder	R	30	40	34	19	4	266.2	272	22	93	79	17-15	4	3.92
George Blaeholder	R	25	42	24	13	4	222.0	237	18	61	72	14-15	2	4.18
Rip Collins	R	33	26	20	10	1	155.1	162	16	73	47	11-6	1	4.00
Lefty Stewart	L	28	23	18	8	1	149.2	137	11	49	47	9-6	0	3.25
Fred Stiely	L	28	1	1	1	0	9.0	11	0	3	2	1-0	0	0.00
Jack Ogden	R	31	34	14	7	0	131.1	154	8	44	43	4-8	0	4.93
Dick Coffman	R	22	27	3	1	1	52.2	61	3	14	11	1-1	0	5.98
Chad Kimsey	R	22	24	3	1	0	64.1	88	2	19	13	3-6	1	5.04
Ed Strelecki	R	24	7	0	0	0	11.0	12	1	6	2	1-1	0	4.91
Paul Hopkins†	R	24	2	0	0	0	2.0	0	0	2	1	0-0	0	0.00
Oscar Estrada	L	25	1	0	0	0	1.0	1	0	1	0	0-0	0	0.00
Herb Cobb	R	24	1	0	0	0	1.0	3	1	1	0	0-0	0	36.00

1929 Washington Senators 5th AL 71-81 .467 34.0 GB — Walter Johnson

Player	Gm by Position	B	Age	G	AB	R	H	2B	3B	HR	RBI	BB	SO	SB	Avg	OBP	Slg
Bennie Tate	C74	L	27	81	265	26	78	12	3	0	30	16	8	2	.294	.335	.362
Joe Judge	1B142	L	35	143	543	83	171	35	8	6	71	73	33	12	.315	.396	.442
Buddy Myer	2B88,3B53	L	25	141	563	80	169	29	10	3	82	63	33	18	.300	.373	.403
Jackie Hayes	3B63,2B56,SS2	R	22	123	424	52	117	20	3	2	57	24	29	4	.276	.316	.351
Joe Cronin	SS143,2B1	R	22	145	494	72	139	29	8	8	61	85	37	5	.281	.388	.421
Sam Rice	OF147	L	39	150	616	119	199	39	10	1	62	55	9	16	.323	.381	.424
Goose Goslin	OF142	L	28	145	553	82	159	28	7	18	91	66	33	10	.288	.366	.461
Sammy West	OF139	L	24	142	510	60	136	16	8	3	75	45	41	9	.267	.326	.347
Ossie Bluege	3B34,2B14,SS10	R	28	64	220	35	65	6	0	5	31	19	15	6	.295	.354	.391
Muddy Ruel	C63	R	33	69	188	16	46	4	2	0	20	31	7	0	.245	.352	.287
Red Barnes	OF30	L	25	72	130	16	26	5	2	1	15	13	12	1	.200	.273	.292
Roy Spencer	C41	R	29	50	116	18	18	4	0	1	9	8	15	0	.155	.222	.216
Harley Boss	1B18	L	20	28	66	9	18	2	1	0	6	2	6	0	.273	.294	.333
Charlie Gooch	1B7,3B7,SS1	R	27	39	57	6	16	2	1	0	5	7	8	0	.281	.359	.351
Ira Flagstead†	OF11	R	35	18	39	5	7	1	0	0	9	4	5	1	.179	.256	.205
Spencer Harris	OF4	L	28	6	14	1	3	1	0	0	1	0	3	1	.214	.214	.286
Stuffy Stewart	2B3	R	35	22	6	10	0	0	0	0	0	1	0	0	.000	.143	.000
Doc Land	OF1	L	26	1	3	0	0	0	0	0	0	1	0	0	.000	.250	.000
Patsy Gharrity		R	37	3	2	0	0	0	0	0	0	1	2	0	.000	.333	.000
Nick Altrock	OF1	S	52	1	1	0	1	0	0	0	0	0	0	0	1.000	1.000	1.000

Pitcher	T	Age	G	GS	CG	ShO	IP	H	HR	BB	SO	W-L	Sv	ERA
Bump Hadley	R	24	37	27	7	1	195.1	196	10	85	98	6-16	0	5.62
Firpo Marberry	R	30	49	26	16	0	250.1	233	6	69	121	19-12	11	3.06
Sad Sam Jones	R	36	24	24	8	1	153.2	156	5	49	36	9-9	0	3.92
Garland Braxton	L	29	37	20	9	0	182.0	219	6	51	59	12-10	4	4.85
Myles Thomas†	R	31	22	14	7	0	125.1	139	3	48	33	7-8	2	3.52
Lloyd Brown	L	24	40	15	7	0	168.0	186	7	69	48	8-7	0	4.18
Bobby Burke	L	22	37	17	4	0	141.0	154	6	55	51	6-8	0	4.79
Ad Liska	R	22	24	10	4	0	94.1	87	1	42	33	3-9	0	4.77
Paul Hopkins†	R	24	7	0	0	0	16.1	15	1	9	5	0-1	0	2.20
Archie Campbell	R	25	4	0	0	0	4.0	10	1	5	1	0-1	0	15.75
Paul McCullough	R	30	3	0	0	0	7.1	7	1	2	3	0-0	0	8.59
Walter Beall	R	29	3	0	0	0	7.0	8	0	7	3	1-0	0	3.86
Don Savidge	R	20	3	0	0	0	6.0	12	1	2	2	0-0	0	9.00
Ed Wineapple	L	23	1	0	0	0	4.0	7	0	3	1	0-0	0	4.50

1929 Detroit Tigers 6th AL 70-84 .455 36.0 GB — Bucky Harris

Player	Gm by Position	B	Age	G	AB	R	H	2B	3B	HR	RBI	BB	SO	SB	Avg	OBP	Slg
Eddie Phillips	C63	R	28	68	221	24	52	13	1	2	21	20	16	0	.235	.302	.330
Dale Alexander	1B155	R	26	155	626	110	215	43	15	25	137	56	63	5	.343	.397	.580
Charlie Gehringer	2B154	L	26	155	634	131	215	45	19	13	106	64	19	27	.339	.405	.532
Marty McManus	3B150,SS8	R	29	154	599	99	168	32	8	18	90	60	52	16	.280	.347	.451
Heinie Schuble	SS86,3B2	R	22	92	258	35	60	11	7	2	28	19	23	3	.233	.288	.353
Roy Johnson	OF146	L	26	148	640	128	201	45	14	10	69	67	60	20	.314	.379	.475
Harry Rice	OF127	L	27	130	536	97	163	33	7	6	69	61	23	6	.304	.379	.425
Harry Heilmann	OF113,1B2	R	34	125	453	86	156	41	7	15	120	50	39	5	.344	.412	.565
Bob Fothergill	OF59	R	31	115	277	42	98	24	9	6	62	11	11	3	.354	.378	.570
Pinky Hargrave	C48	S	33	76	185	26	61	12	0	3	26	20	24	2	.330	.401	.443
Merv Shea	C46	R	28	50	162	23	47	6	0	3	24	19	18	2	.290	.365	.383
Yats Wuestling	SS52,2B1,3B1	R	25	54	150	13	30	4	1	0	16	9	24	1	.200	.250	.240
John Stone	OF36	L	23	51	150	23	39	11	2	2	15	11	13	1	.260	.311	.400
Bill Akers	SS24	R	24	24	83	15	22	4	1	1	9	10	9	2	.265	.351	.373
Ray Hayworth	C14	R	25	14	43	5	11	0	0	0	4	3	8	0	.256	.304	.256
Frank Sigafoos†	3B6,SS5	R	25	14	23	3	4	1	0	0	2	5	4	0	.174	.321	.217
Nolen Richardson	SS13	R	26	13	21	2	4	0	0	0	2	2	1	1	.190	.261	.190
Bucky Harris	2B4,SS1	R	32	7	11	3	1	0	0	0	0	2	2	1	.091	.231	.091
Larry Woodall		R	34	1	1	0	0	0	0	0	0	0	0	0	.000	.000	.000

Pitcher	T	Age	G	GS	CG	ShO	IP	H	HR	BB	SO	W-L	Sv	ERA
Vic Sorrell	R	28	36	31	13	1	226.0	270	15	106	81	14-15	1	5.18
George Uhle	R	30	32	30	23	1	249.0	283	9	58	100	15-11	0	4.08
Earl Whitehill	L	29	38	28	18	1	245.1	267	16	96	103	14-15	1	4.62
Ownie Carroll	R	26	34	26	12	0	202.0	249	10	86	54	9-17	1	4.63
Art Herring	R	23	4	4	2	0	32.0	38	0	19	15	2-1	0	4.78
Chief Hogsett	L	25	4	4	2	1	28.2	34	0	9	9	1-2	0	2.83
Whit Wyatt	R	21	4	4	1	0	25.1	30	1	18	14	0-1	0	6.75
Augie Prudhomme	R	26	34	6	2	0	94.0	119	7	53	26	1-6	1	6.22
Emil Yde	L	29	29	6	4	1	86.2	100	8	63	23	7-3	0	5.30
Lil Stoner	R	30	24	3	1	0	53.0	57	2	31	12	3-3	4	5.26
George Smith	R	27	14	2	1	0	35.2	42	1	36	13	3-2	0	5.80
Skinny Graham	R	29	13	6	2	0	51.2	70	2	33	7	1-3	1	5.57
Phil Page	L	23	10	4	1	0	25.1	29	1	19	6	0-2	0	8.17
Josh Billings	R	21	8	0	0	0	19.1	27	0	9	1	0-1	0	5.12
Elam Vangilder	R	33	6	0	0	0	11.1	16	1	7	3	0-1	0	6.35
Frank Barnes	L	29	4	1	0	0	5.0	10	0	3	0	0-1	0	7.20

1929 Chicago White Sox 7th AL 59-93 .388 46.0 GB — Lena Blackburne

Player	Gm by Position	B	Age	G	AB	R	H	2B	3B	HR	RBI	BB	SO	SB	Avg	OBP	Slg
Moe Berg	C106	R	27	107	352	32	101	7	0	0	47	17	16	5	.287	.323	.307
Art Shires	1B88,2B2	L	21	100	353	41	110	20	7	3	41	32	20	4	.312	.370	.433
John Kerr	2B122	R	30	127	419	50	108	20	4	1	39	31	24	9	.258	.310	.332
Willie Kamm	3B145	R	29	147	523	72	140	33	6	3	63	75	23	12	.268	.363	.371
Bill Cissell	SS152	R	25	152	618	83	173	27	12	5	62	28	53	26	.280	.312	.387
Alex Metzler	OF141	L	26	146	568	80	156	23	13	2	49	80	45	11	.275	.367	.371
Carl Reynolds	OF130	R	26	131	517	81	164	24	12	11	67	20	37	19	.317	.348	.474
Dutch Hoffman	OF89	R	25	107	337	27	87	16	5	3	37	24	28	6	.258	.307	.362
Bud Clancy	1B74	L	28	92	290	36	82	14	6	3	45	16	19	3	.283	.320	.403
Cliff Watwood	OF77	L	23	85	278	33	84	12	6	2	29	22	21	6	.302	.355	.410
Bill Hunnefield	2B26,3B4,SS2	S	30	47	127	13	23	5	0	0	9	7	3	7	.181	.224	.220
Doug Taitt†	OF30	L	26	47	124	11	21	7	0	0	12	8	13	0	.169	.220	.226
Buck Crouse	C40	L	32	45	107	11	29	7	0	2	12	5	7	2	.271	.316	.393
Chick Autry	C30	R	26	43	96	7	20	6	0	1	12	1	8	0	.208	.224	.302
Ted Lyons	P37,OF1	S	28	40	91	7	20	4	0	0	11	9	13	0	.220	.290	.264
Buck Redfern	2B11,3B5,SS4	R	27	21	46	0	6	0	0	0	3	3	3	1	.130	.184	.130
Johnny Mostil	OF11	R	33	12	35	4	8	3	0	0	3	6	2	1	.229	.341	.314
Frank Sigafoos†	2B6	R	25	7	3	1	1	0	0	0	1	2	1	0	.333	.600	.333
Karl Swanson		L	25	2	1	0	0	0	0	0	0	0	0	0	.000	.000	.000
Bill Barrett†		R	29	3	1	0	0	0	0	0	0	2	0	0	.000	.667	.000

Pitcher	T	Age	G	GS	CG	ShO	IP	H	HR	BB	SO	W-L	Sv	ERA
Tommy Thomas	R	29	36	31	24	2	259.2	270	17	60	62	14-18	1	3.19
Ted Lyons	R	28	37	31	21	1	259.1	276	11	76	57	14-20	2	4.10
Red Faber	R	40	31	31	15	1	234.0	241	10	61	68	13-13	0	3.88
Ed Walsh	R	24	24	20	7	0	129.0	156	9	64	31	6-11	0	5.65
Bob Weiland	L	23	15	9	1	0	62.0	62	3	43	25	2-4	1	5.81
Dutch Henry†	L	27	2	1	1	0	15.0	20	1	7	2	1-0	0	6.00
Hal McKain	R	22	34	10	4	1	158.0	158	10	85	33	6-9	1	3.65
Grady Adkins	R	32	31	15	5	0	138.1	168	12	67	24	2-11	0	5.33
Dan Dugan	L	22	19	2	0	0	65.0	77	8	19	15	1-4	1	6.65
Sarge Connally	R	30	11	0	0	0	11.1	13	0	8	3	0-0	1	4.76
Ted Blankenship	R	28	8	1	0	0	18.1	28	3	9	7	0-2	0	8.84
Jerry Byrne	R	22	3	1	0	0	7.1	11	0	6	1	0-1	0	7.36
Lena Blackburne	R	42	1	0	0	0	0.1	1	0	0	0	0-0	0	0.00

1929 Boston Red Sox 8th AL 58-96 .377 48.0 GB — Bill Carrigan

Player	Gm by Position	B	Age	G	AB	R	H	2B	3B	HR	RBI	BB	SO	SB	Avg	OBP	Slg
Charlie Berry	C72	R	26	77	207	19	50	11	4	1	21	15	29	2	.242	.302	.348
Phil Todt	1B153	L	27	153	534	49	140	38	10	4	64	31	28	6	.262	.305	.393
Bill Regan	2B91,3B10,1B1	R	30	104	371	38	107	27	7	1	54	22	38	7	.288	.328	.407
Bobby Reeves	3B132,2B2,SS2*	R	25	140	460	66	114	19	2	2	28	60	57	7	.248	.343	.311
Hal Rhyne	SS114,3B1,OF1	R	30	120	346	41	87	24	5	0	38	25	14	4	.251	.309	.350
Russ Scarritt	OF145	L	26	151	540	69	159	26	17	1	71	34	38	13	.294	.337	.411
Jack Rothrock	OF128	S	24	143	473	70	142	19	7	6	59	43	47	23	.300	.361	.408
Bill Barrett†	OF109,3B1	R	29	111	370	57	100	23	4	3	35	51	38	11	.270	.363	.378
Bill Narleski	SS51,2B28,3B10	R	30	96	260	30	72	16	1	0	25	21	22	4	.277	.333	.346
Elliott Bigelow	OF58	L	31	100	211	23	60	16	0	1	26	23	18	1	.284	.357	.374
Johnny Heving	C55	R	33	76	188	26	60	4	3	0	23	8	7	1	.319	.354	.372
Ken Williams	OF36,1B2	L	39	74	139	21	48	14	2	3	21	15	7	1	.345	.409	.540
Bob Barrett	3B34,1B4,2B2*	R	30	68	126	15	34	10	0	0	19	10	6	3	.270	.324	.349
Alex Gaston	C49	R	36	55	116	14	26	5	2	2	9	6	8	1	.224	.262	.353
Red Ruffing	P35,OF2	R	25	60	114	9	35	9	0	2	17	2	13	0	.307	.325	.439
Wally Gerber	SS30,2B22	R	37	61	91	6	15	3	1	0	5	8	12	1	.165	.232	.220
Grant Gillis	2B25	R	28	28	73	5	18	4	0	0	11	6	8	0	.247	.304	.301
Doug Taitt†	OF21	L	26	26	65	6	18	4	0	0	6	8	5	0	.277	.365	.338
Ira Flagstead†	OF13	R	35	14	36	9	11	2	0	0	3	5	1	1	.306	.390	.361
Joe Cicero	OF7	R	18	10	32	6	10	2	2	0	4	0	2	0	.313	.313	.500
Asby Asbjornson	C15	R	20	17	29	1	3	0	0	0	1	0	6	0	.103	.133	.103
Jerry Standaert	1B10	R	27	19	18	1	3	2	0	0	4	3	2	0	.167	.286	.278
Ed Connolly	C5	R	20	5	8	0	0	0	0	0	0	0	2	0	.000	.000	.000
Jack Ryan	OF2	R	24	2	3	0	0	0	0	0	0	0	0	0	.000	.000	.000

B. Reeves, 1 G at 1B; B. Barrett, 1 G at OF

Pitcher	T	Age	G	GS	CG	ShO	IP	H	HR	BB	SO	W-L	Sv	ERA
Jack Russell	R	23	35	32	13	0	227.1	263	12	40	37	6-18	0	3.92
Red Ruffing	R	25	35	30	18	1	244.1	280	17	118	109	9-22	1	4.86
Milt Gaston	R	33	39	29	20	1	243.2	265	15	81	83	12-19	2	3.73
Danny MacFayden	R	24	32	26	14	4	221.0	225	8	81	61	10-18	0	3.62
Ed Morris	R	29	33	26	17	2	208.1	227	7	95	73	14-14	1	4.45
Bill Bayne	L	30	27	6	2	0	84.1	111	9	29	26	5-5	0	6.72
Ed Carroll	R	21	24	3	0	0	67.1	77	6	20	13	1-0	0	5.61
Ed Durham	R	20	14	1	0	0	22.1	34	2	14	6	1-0	0	9.27
Ray Dobens	L	22	11	2	0	0	28.1	32	0	9	4	0-0	0	3.81
Hod Lisenbee	R	30	5	0	0	0	8.2	10	1	4	2	0-0	0	5.19
Herb Bradley	R	26	3	0	0	0	4.0	7	1	2	0	0-0	0	6.75
Pat Simmons	R	20	2	0	0	0	7.0	6	0	3	2	0-0	1	0.00

»1929 Chicago Cubs 1st NL 98-54 .645 — — Joe McCarthy

Player	Gm by Position	B	Age	G	AB	R	H	2B	3B	HR	RBI	BB	SO	SB	Avg	OBP	Slg
Zack Taylor†	C64	R	30	64	215	29	59	16	3	1	31	19	18	0	.274	.336	.391
Charlie Grimm	1B120	L	30	120	463	66	138	28	3	10	91	42	25	3	.298	.358	.436
Rogers Hornsby	2B156	R	33	156	602	156	229	47	8	39	149	87	65	2	.380	.459	.679
Norm McMillan	3B120	R	33	124	495	77	134	35	5	5	55	36	43	13	.271	.324	.392
Woody English	SS144	R	22	144	608	131	168	29	3	1	52	68	50	13	.276	.352	.339
Hack Wilson	OF150	R	29	150	574	135	198	30	5	39	159	78	83	3	.345	.425	.618
Riggs Stephenson	OF130	R	31	136	495	91	179	36	6	17	110	67	21	10	.362	.445	.562
Kiki Cuyler	OF129	R	30	139	509	111	183	29	7	15	102	66	56	43	.360	.438	.532
Cliff Heathcote	OF52	L	31	82	224	45	70	17	0	2	31	25	17	9	.313	.384	.415
Clyde Beck	3B33,SS14	R	29	54	190	28	40	7	0	0	9	19	24	3	.211	.282	.247
Mike Gonzalez	C60	R	38	60	167	15	40	3	0	0	18	18	14	1	.240	.317	.257
Chick Tolson	1B31	R	34	32	109	13	28	5	0	1	19	9	16	0	.257	.325	.330
Earl Grace	C27	L	22	27	80	7	20	1	0	2	17	9	7	0	.250	.333	.338
Footsie Blair	3B8,1B7,2B2	L	28	26	72	10	23	5	0	1	8	3	4	1	.319	.347	.431
Johnny Schulte	C30	L	32	31	69	6	18	3	0	0	9	7	11	0	.261	.329	.304
Johnny Moore	OF15	L	27	37	63	13	18	1	0	2	8	4	6	0	.286	.338	.397
Gabby Hartnett	C1	R	28	25	22	2	6	2	1	1	9	5	5	1	.273	.407	.591
Tom Angley	C5	L	24	5	16	1	4	1	0	0	6	2	2	0	.250	.333	.313
Danny Taylor	OF1	R	28	2	3	0	0	0	0	0	0	1	1	0	.000	.250	.000

Pitcher	T	Age	G	GS	CG	ShO	IP	H	HR	BB	SO	W-L	Sv	ERA
Charlie Root	R	30	43	31	19	4	272.0	286	12	83	124	19-6	5	3.47
Pat Malone	R	26	40	30	19	5	267.0	283	12	102	166	22-10	2	3.57
Sheriff Blake	R	29	35	30	13	1	218.1	244	8	130	70	14-13	1	4.29
Guy Bush	R	27	50	29	18	2	270.2	277	16	107	82	18-7	8	3.66
Hank Grampp	R	25	1	1	0	0	2.0	4	0	3	0	0-1	0	27.00
Art Nehf	L	36	32	15	4	0	120.2	148	11	39	27	8-5	1	5.59
Mike Cvengros	L	27	32	2	0	0	64.0	82	2	29	23	5-4	2	4.64
Hal Carlson	R	37	31	14	6	2	111.2	131	8	31	35	11-5	2	5.16
Claude Jonnard	R	31	12	2	0	0	27.2	41	4	11	11	0-1	0	7.48
Trader Horne	R	30	11	1	0	0	23.0	24	3	21	6	1-1	0	5.09
Ken Penner	R	33	5	0	0	0	12.2	14	1	6	3	0-1	0	2.84
Bob Osborn	R	26	3	1	0	0	9.0	8	0	2	1	0-0	0	3.00

1929 Pittsburgh Pirates 2nd NL 88-65 .575 10.5 GB

Donie Bush (67-51)/Jewel Ens (21-14)

Player	Gm by Position	B	Age	G	AB	R	H	2B	3B	HR	RBI	BB	SO	SB	Avg	OBP	Slg
Charlie Hargreaves	C101	R	32	102	328	33	88	12	5	1	44	16	12	1	.268	.306	.345
Earl Sheely	1B139	R	36	139	485	63	142	22	4	6	88	75	24	6	.293	.392	.392
George Grantham	2B76,OF19,1B12	L	29	110	349	85	107	23	10	12	90	93	38	10	.307	.454	.533
Pie Traynor	3B130	R	29	130	540	94	192	27	12	4	108	30	7	13	.356	.393	.472
Dick Bartell	SS97,2B70	R	21	143	610	101	184	40	13	2	57	40	29	11	.302	.347	.420
Lloyd Waner	OF151	L	23	151	662	134	234	28	20	5	74	37	20	6	.353	.395	.479
Paul Waner	OF143	L	26	151	596	131	200	43	15	15	100	89	24	15	.336	.424	.534
Adam Comorosky	OF121	R	23	127	473	86	152	26	11	6	97	40	22	19	.321	.377	.461
Rollie Hemsley	C80	R	22	88	235	31	68	13	7	0	37	11	22	1	.289	.321	.404
Sparky Adams	SS30,2B20,3B15*	R	34	74	196	37	51	8	1	0	11	15	5	3	.260	.316	.311
Stu Clarke	SS41,3B15,2B1	R	23	57	178	20	47	5	7	2	21	19	21	3	.264	.338	.404
George Brickell	OF27	L	22	60	118	13	37	4	2	0	17	7	12	3	.314	.352	.381
Cobe Jones	SS15	S	21	25	63	6	16	5	1	0	4	1	5	1	.254	.266	.365
Ira Flagstead†	OF9	R	35	26	50	8	14	2	1	0	6	4	2	1	.280	.333	.360
Bob Linton	C8	L	26	17	18	0	2	0	0	0	1	1	2	0	.111	.158	.111
Harry Riconda	SS4	R	32	8	15	3	7	2	0	0	2	0	0	0	.467	.467	.600
Jim Mosolf	OF3	L	23	8	13	3	6	1	1	0	2	1	1	0	.462	.500	.692
Jim Stroner	3B2	R	28	6	8	0	3	1	0	0	0	1	0	0	.375	.444	.500
Ben Sankey	SS2	R	21	2	7	1	1	0	0	0	0	0	1	0	.143	.143	.143
John O'Connell	C2	R	25	2	7	1	1	1	0	0	0	1	1	0	.143	.250	.286
Bill Windle	1B2	L	24	2	1	0	0	0	0	0	0	0	1	0	.000	.000	.000
Mel Ingram		R	24	3	0	1	0	0	0	0	0	0	0	0	—	—	—

S. Adams, 2 G at OF

Pitcher	T	Age	G	GS	CG	ShO	IP	H	HR	BB	SO	W-L	Sv	ERA
Burleigh Grimes	R	35	33	29	18	2	232.2	245	11	70	62	17-7	2	3.13
Erv Brame	R	27	37	28	19	1	229.2	250	17	71	68	16-11	0	4.55
Ray Kremer	R	36	34	27	14	0	221.2	226	21	60	66	18-10	0	4.26
Jesse Petty	L	34	36	25	12	1	184.1	197	12	42	58	11-10	0	3.71
Heinie Meine	R	33	22	13	7	1	108.0	120	4	34	19	7-6	1	4.50
Leon Chagnon	R	26	1	1	0	0	7.0	11	1	1	4	0-0	0	9.00
Steve Swetonic	R	25	41	12	3	0	143.2	172	6	50	35	8-10	5	4.82
Larry French	L	21	30	13	6	0	123.0	130	10	62	49	7-5	1	4.90
Carmen Hill†	R	33	27	3	0	0	79.0	94	4	35	28	2-3	3	3.99
Fred Fussell	L	33	21	3	0	0	39.2	68	8	8	18	2-2	1	8.62
Joe Dawson	R	32	4	0	0	0	8.2	13	2	3	2	0-1	0	8.31
Ralph Erickson	L	27	1	0	0	0	1.0	2	0	2	0	0-0	0	27.00
Lee Meadows	R	34	1	0	0	0	0.2	2	0	1	0	0-0	0	13.50

1929 New York Giants 3rd NL 84-67 .556 13.5 GB

John McGraw

Player	Gm by Position	B	Age	G	AB	R	H	2B	3B	HR	RBI	BB	SO	SB	Avg	OBP	Slg
Shanty Hogan	C93	R	23	102	317	19	95	13	0	5	45	25	22	1	.300	.362	.388
Bill Terry	1B149,OF1	L	32	150	607	103	226	39	5	14	117	48	35	10	.372	.418	.522
Andy Cohen	2B94,3B1,SS1	R	24	101	347	40	102	12	2	5	47	11	15	3	.294	.319	.383
Freddy Lindstrom	3B128	R	23	130	549	99	175	23	6	15	91	30	28	10	.319	.354	.464
Travis Jackson	SS149	R	25	149	551	92	162	21	12	21	94	64	56	10	.294	.367	.490
Mel Ott	OF149	L	20	150	545	138	179	37	2	42	151	113	38	6	.328	.449	.635
Edd Roush	OF107	L	36	115	450	76	146	19	7	8	52	45	16	6	.324	.390	.451
Freddy Leach	OF95	L	31	113	411	74	119	22	6	8	47	17	14	10	.290	.324	.431
Chick Fullis	OF78	R	25	86	274	67	79	11	1	7	29	30	26	7	.288	.365	.412
Bob O'Farrell	C84	R	32	91	248	35	76	14	3	4	42	28	30	3	.306	.384	.435
Randy Reese	2B44,OF8,3B4	R	25	58	209	36	55	11	3	0	21	15	19	8	.263	.316	.344
Doc Farrell†	3B28,2B25,SS4	R	27	63	178	18	38	6	0	0	16	9	17	2	.213	.251	.247
Jimmy Welsh†	OF35	L	26	38	129	25	32	7	0	2	8	9	3	3	.248	.331	.349
Pat Crawford	1B7,3B1	L	27	65	57	13	17	3	0	3	24	11	5	1	.298	.412	.509
Tony Kaufmann	OF16	R	28	39	32	18	1	0	0	0	1	6	4	3	.031	.184	.031
Ed Marshall	2B5	R	23	5	15	6	6	2	0	0	2	1	0	0	.400	.438	.533
Jack Cummings†	C1	R	25	3	3	0	1	0	0	0	0	0	0	0	.333	.333	.333
Buck Jordan	1B1	L	22	2	2	1	1	1	0	0	0	0	0	0	.500	.500	1.000
Ray Schalk	C5	R	36	5	2	0	0	0	0	0	0	0	1	0	.000	.000	.000
Sam Leslie	OF1	L	23	1	1	0	0	0	0	0	1	0	0	0	.000	.000	.000
Pat Veltman	C1	R	23	2	1	1	0	0	0	0	0	2	0	0	.000	.667	.000

Pitcher	T	Age	G	GS	CG	ShO	IP	H	HR	BB	SO	W-L	Sv	ERA
Carl Hubbell	L	26	39	35	19	1	268.0	273	17	67	106	18-11	1	3.69
F. Fitzsimmons	R	27	37	31	14	4	221.2	242	14	66	55	15-11	1	4.10
Larry Benton	R	31	39	30	14	3	237.0	276	16	61	63	11-17	3	4.14
Bill Walker	L	25	29	23	13	1	177.2	188	11	57	65	14-7	0	3.09
Roy Parmelee	R	22	2	1	0	0	7.0	13	1	3	1	1-0	0	9.00
Carl Mays	R	37	37	8	1	0	123.0	140	8	31	32	7-2	4	4.32
Jack Scott	R	37	30	6	2	0	91.2	89	12	27	40	7-6	1	3.53
Dutch Henry†	L	27	27	9	4	0	101.1	129	10	31	27	5-6	1	3.82
Joe Genewich	R	32	21	9	1	0	85.0	133	9	30	19	3-7	1	6.78
Ralph Judd	R	27	18	0	0	0	50.2	49	4	11	21	3-0	0	2.66
Ray Lucas	R	20	3	0	0	0	8.0	3	0	3	1	0-0	1	0.00
Jim Tennant	R	22	1	0	0	0	1.0	1	0	0	1	0-0	0	0.00

1929 St. Louis Cardinals 4th NL 78-74 .513 20.0 GB

Billy Southworth (43-45)/Gabby Street (1-0)/Bill McKechnie (34-29)

Player	Gm by Position	B	Age	G	AB	R	H	2B	3B	HR	RBI	BB	SO	SB	Avg	OBP	Slg
Jimmie Wilson	C119	R	28	120	394	59	128	27	8	4	71	43	19	4	.325	.394	.464
Jim Bottomley	1B145	L	29	146	560	108	176	31	12	29	137	70	54	3	.314	.391	.568
Frankie Frisch	2B121,3B13	S	30	138	527	93	176	40	12	5	74	53	12	24	.334	.397	.484
Andy High	3B123,2B22	L	31	146	603	95	178	32	4	10	63	38	18	7	.295	.340	.411
Charlie Gelbert	SS146	R	23	146	512	60	134	29	8	3	65	51	46	8	.262	.329	.367
Taylor Douthit	OF150	R	28	150	613	128	206	42	7	9	62	79	49	8	.336	.416	.471
Chick Hafey	OF130	R	26	134	517	101	175	47	9	29	125	45	42	7	.338	.394	.632
Ernie Orsatti	OF77,1B10	L	26	113	346	64	115	21	7	3	39	33	43	7	.332	.394	.460
Wally Roettger	OF69	R	26	79	269	27	68	11	3	3	42	13	27	0	.253	.287	.349
Wattie Holm	OF44	R	27	64	176	21	41	5	6	0	14	12	8	1	.233	.282	.330
Earl Smith	C50	L	32	57	145	9	50	8	0	1	22	18	6	0	.345	.417	.421
Johnny Butler	3B9,SS8	R	36	17	55	5	9	1	1	0	5	4	5	0	.164	.220	.218
Carey Selph	2B16	R	27	25	51	8	12	1	1	0	7	6	4	1	.235	.316	.294
Eddie Delker	SS9,2B7,3B3	R	23	22	40	5	6	0	1	0	3	2	12	0	.150	.227	.200
Billy Southworth	OF5	L	36	19	32	1	6	2	0	0	3	2	4	0	.188	.235	.250
Bubber Jonnard	C18	R	31	18	31	1	3	0	0	0	2	0	6	0	.097	.097	.097
Fred Haney	3B6	R	31	10	26	4	3	1	1	0	2	1	2	0	.115	.179	.231

Pitcher	T	Age	G	GS	CG	ShO	IP	H	HR	BB	SO	W-L	Sv	ERA
Jesse Haines	R	35	28	25	12	0	179.2	230	21	73	59	13-10	0	5.71
Bill Sherdel	L	32	33	22	11	1	195.2	278	14	58	69	10-15	0	5.93
Clarence Mitchell	L	38	25	22	16	1	173.0	221	13	60	39	8-11	0	4.27
Pete Alexander	R	42	22	19	8	1	132.0	149	10	23	33	9-8	0	3.89
Wild Bill Hallahan	L	26	20	12	5	0	93.2	94	6	60	52	4-4	0	4.42
Al Grabowski	L	27	6	6	4	2	50.0	44	0	8	22	3-2	0	2.52
Jim Lindsey	R	33	2	2	1	0	16.1	20	1	2	8	1-1	0	5.51
Bill Doak	R	38	3	2	0	0	9.0	17	1	5	3	1-2	0	12.00
Syl Johnson	R	28	42	19	12	3	182.1	186	11	56	80	13-7	3	3.60
Hal Haid	R	31	38	12	8	0	154.2	171	8	66	41	9-9	4	4.07
Fred Frankhouse	R	25	30	12	6	0	133.1	149	9	43	37	7-2	1	4.12
Mul Holland	R	26	8	0	0	0	14.1	13	3	7	5	0-1	0	9.42
Hi Bell	R	31	7	0	0	0	13.0	19	1	4	4	0-2	0	6.92
Carmen Hill†	R	33	3	1	0	0	8.2	10	2	8	1	0-0	0	8.31
Hal Goldsmith	R	30	2	0	0	0	4.0	3	1	1	0	0-0	0	6.75

1929 Philadelphia Phillies 5th NL 71-82 .464 27.5 GB

Burt Shotton

Player	Gm by Position	B	Age	G	AB	R	H	2B	3B	HR	RBI	BB	SO	SB	Avg	OBP	Slg
Walt Lerian	C103	R	26	105	273	28	61	13	2	6	25	53	37	0	.223	.354	.352
Don Hurst	1B154	L	23	154	589	100	179	29	4	31	125	80	36	10	.304	.390	.525
Fresco Thompson	2B148	R	27	148	623	115	202	41	3	4	53	75	34	16	.324	.398	.419
Pinky Whitney	3B154	R	24	154	612	89	200	43	14	8	115	61	35	7	.327	.390	.482
Tommy Thevenow	SS90	R	25	90	317	30	72	11	0	0	35	25	25	3	.227	.288	.262
Lefty O'Doul	OF154	L	32	154	638	152	254	35	6	32	122	76	19	2	.398	.465	.622
Chuck Klein	OF149	L	24	149	616	126	219	45	6	43	145	54	61	5	.356	.407	.657
Denny Sothern	OF71	R	25	76	294	52	90	21	3	5	27	16	24	13	.306	.346	.449
Bernie Friberg	SS73,OF40,2B8*	R	29	128	455	74	137	21	10	7	55	49	54	1	.301	.370	.437
Spud Davis	C89	R	24	98	263	31	90	18	0	7	48	19	17	1	.342	.391	.490
Homer Peel	OF39	R	26	53	156	16	42	12	1	0	19	12	7	1	.269	.329	.359
Cy Williams	OF11	L	41	66	65	11	19	2	0	5	21	22	9	0	.292	.471	.554
Elmer Miller	P8,OF4	L	26	31	38	3	9	1	0	1	4	1	5	0	.237	.256	.342
Tripp Sigman	OF10	L	30	10	29	8	15	1	0	2	9	3	1	0	.517	.563	.759
George Susce	C11	R	20	17	17	5	5	3	0	1	1	1	2	0	.294	.368	.647
Joe O'Rourke		L	24	3	3	0	0	0	0	0	0	0	1	0	.000	.000	.000
Terry Lyons	1B1	R	20	1	0	0	0	0	0	0	0	0	0	0	—	—	—

B. Friberg, 2 G at 1B

Pitcher	T	Age	G	GS	CG	ShO	IP	H	HR	BB	SO	W-L	Sv	ERA
Claude Willoughby	R	30	49	34	14	1	243.1	288	15	108	50	15-14	4	4.99
Ray Benge	R	27	38	27	9	2	199.0	255	24	77	78	11-15	4	6.29
Leo Sweetland	L	27	43	25	10	2	204.1	255	23	87	47	13-11	2	5.11
Luther Roy†	R	26	21	12	1	0	88.2	137	11	37	16	3-6	0	8.42
Lou Koupal†	R	30	15	12	3	0	86.2	106	5	29	18	5-5	2	4.78
Alex Ferguson†	R	32	5	4	1	0	12.2	19	2	10	3	1-2	0	12.08
Phil Collins	R	27	43	11	3	0	153.1	172	18	83	61	9-7	5	5.75
Bob McGraw	R	34	41	4	0	0	86.1	113	6	43	22	5-5	4	5.73
Hal Elliott	R	30	40	8	2	0	114.1	146	5	59	32	3-7	2	6.06
Sam Dailey	R	25	20	5	0	0	51.1	74	5	23	18	2-2	0	7.54
Harry Smythe	L	24	19	7	2	0	68.2	94	3	15	12	4-6	1	5.24
Elmer Miller	L	26	8	2	0	0	11.1	12	1	21	5	0-1	0	11.12
John Milligan	L	25	8	3	0	0	9.2	29	0	10	2	0-1	0	16.76
June Greene	R	30	5	0	0	0	13.2	33	2	9	4	0-0	0	19.76
Jim Holloway	R	20	3	0	0	0	4.2	10	2	5	1	0-0	0	13.50

1929 Brooklyn Dodgers 6th NL 70-83 .458 28.5 GB

Wilbert Robinson

Player	Gm by Position	B	Age	G	AB	R	H	2B	3B	HR	RBI	BB	SO	SB	Avg	OBP	Slg
Val Picinich	C85	R	32	93	273	28	71	16	6	4	31	34	24	3	.260	.342	.407
Del Bissonette	1B113	L	29	116	431	68	121	28	10	12	75	46	58	2	.281	.351	.476
Eddie Moore	2B74,SS36,OF2*	R	30	111	402	48	119	18	6	0	48	44	16	3	.296	.370	.371
Wally Gilbert	3B142	R	28	143	569	88	173	31	4	3	58	42	29	7	.304	.359	.388
Dave Bancroft	SS102	S	38	104	358	35	99	11	3	1	44	29	11	7	.277	.331	.332
Johnny Frederick	OF143	L	27	148	628	127	206	52	6	24	75	39	34	6	.328	.372	.545
Babe Herman	OF141	L	26	146	569	105	217	42	13	21	113	55	45	21	.381	.436	.612
Rube Bressler	OF122	R	34	136	456	72	145	22	8	9	77	67	27	4	.318	.406	.461
Harvey Hendrick	OF42,1B39,3B7*	L	31	110	384	69	136	25	6	14	82	31	20	14	.354	.404	.560
Hank DeBerry	C68	R	34	68	210	13	55	11	1	1	25	17	15	1	.262	.317	.338
Billy Rhiel	2B47,3B7,SS2	R	28	76	205	27	57	9	4	4	25	19	25	0	.278	.339	.420
Jake Flowers	2B39	R	27	46	130	16	26	6	0	1	16	22	6	9	.200	.316	.269
Jack Warner	SS17	R	25	17	62	3	17	2	0	0	4	7	6	3	.274	.348	.306
Butch Henline	C21	R	34	27	62	5	15	2	0	1	7	9	9	0	.242	.338	.323
Nick Cullop	OF11	R	28	13	41	7	8	2	2	1	5	8	7	0	.195	.327	.415
Glenn Wright	SS3	R	28	24	25	4	5	0	0	1	6	3	6	0	.200	.286	.320
Max Carey	OF4	S	39	19	23	2	7	0	0	0	1	3	2	0	.304	.407	.304
Max West	OF2	R	24	5	8	1	2	1	0	0	1	1	0	0	.250	.333	.375
Johnny Gooch†		S	31	1	1	0	0	0	0	0	0	0	0	0	.000	.000	.000

E. Moore, 1 G at 3B; H. Hendrick, 4 G at SS

Pitcher	T	Age	G	GS	CG	ShO	IP	H	HR	BB	SO	W-L	Sv	ERA
Watty Clark	L	27	41	36	19	3	279.0	295	14	71	140	16-19	1	3.74
Dazzy Vance	R	38	31	26	17	1	231.1	244	15	47	126	14-13	0	3.89
Doug McWeeny	R	32	36	24	4	0	146.0	167	17	93	59	4-10	1	6.10
Clise Dudley	R	25	35	21	8	1	156.2	202	9	64	33	6-14	0	5.69
Ray Moss	R	27	39	20	7	3	182.0	214	9	81	59	11-6	0	5.04
Jumbo Elliott	L	28	6	3	0	0	19.0	21	2	16	7	1-2	0	6.63
Alex Ferguson†	R	32	3	3	0	0	2.0	7	2	1	1	0-1	0	22.50
Bobo Newsom	R	21	3	2	0	0	9.1	15	0	5	6	0-3	0	10.61
Johnny Morrison	R	33	39	10	4	0	136.2	150	11	61	57	13-7	8	4.48
Cy Moore	R	24	32	4	0	0	68.0	87	3	31	17	3-3	2	5.56
Win Ballou	R	31	25	1	0	0	57.2	69	5	38	20	2-3	0	6.71
Lou Koupal†	R	30	18	3	0	0	40.1	49	3	25	17	0-1	4	5.36
Jimmy Pattison	L	20	6	0	0	0	11.2	9	1	4	5	0-1	0	4.63
Kent Greenfield†	R	26	6	0	0	0	8.2	13	1	3	1	0-0	0	8.31
Joe Bradshaw	R	31	2	0	0	0	4.0	3	0	4	1	0-0	0	4.50
Luther Roy†	R	26	2	0	0	0	3.2	4	0	2	0	0-0	0	4.91
Clarence Blethen	R	35	2	0	0	0	2.0	4	0	3	0	0-0	0	9.00

1929 Cincinnati Reds 7th NL 66-88 .429 33.0 GB

Jack Hendricks

Player	Gm by Position	B	Age	G	AB	R	H	2B	3B	HR	RBI	BB	SO	SB	Avg	OBP	Slg
Johnny Gooch†	C86	S	31	92	287	22	86	13	5	0	34	24	10	4	.300	.356	.380
George Kelly	1B147	R	33	147	577	73	169	45	9	5	103	33	61	7	.293	.332	.428
Hughie Critz	2B106	R	28	107	425	55	105	17	9	1	50	27	21	9	.247	.292	.336
Chuck Dressen	3B98	R	30	110	401	49	98	22	3	1	36	41	21	8	.244	.321	.322
Hod Ford	SS108,2B42	R	31	148	529	68	146	14	6	3	50	41	25	8	.276	.329	.342
Evar Swanson	OF142	R	26	148	574	100	172	35	12	4	43	41	47	33	.300	.353	.423
Ethan Allen	OF137	R	25	143	538	69	157	27	11	6	64	20	21	21	.292	.317	.416
Curt Walker	OF133	L	32	141	492	76	154	28	15	7	83	85	17	17	.313	.416	.474
Clyde Sukeforth	C76	L	27	84	237	31	84	16	2	1	33	17	6	8	.354	.398	.451
Pinky Pittenger	SS50,3B8,2B4	R	30	77	210	31	62	11	0	0	27	5	4	8	.295	.318	.348
Joe Stripp	3B55,2B2	R	26	64	187	24	40	3	2	3	20	24	15	2	.214	.313	.299
Pid Purdy	OF42	L	25	82	181	22	49	7	5	1	16	19	8	2	.271	.350	.381
Billy Zitzmann	OF22	R	33	47	84	18	19	3	0	0	6	9	10	4	.226	.309	.262
Leo Dixon	C14	R	34	14	30	0	5	2	0	0	2	3	7	0	.167	.242	.233
Wally Shaner	1B8,OF2	R	29	13	28	5	9	0	0	1	4	4	5	1	.321	.406	.429
Estel Crabtree		L	25	1	1	0	0	0	0	0	0	0	0	0	.000	.000	.000
Hugh McMullen	C1	S	27	1	1	0	0	0	0	0	0	0	0	0	.000	.000	.000
Ivy Wingo		L	38	1	1	0	0	0	0	0	0	0	0	0	.000	.000	.000

Pitcher	T	Age	G	GS	CG	ShO	IP	H	HR	BB	SO	W-L	Sv	ERA
Red Lucas	R	27	32	32	28	2	270.0	267	14	58	72	19-12	0	3.60
Eppa Rixey	L	38	35	24	11	0	201.0	235	6	60	37	10-13	1	4.16
Jakie May	L	33	41	24	10	0	199.0	219	7	75	92	10-14	3	4.61
Pete Donohue	R	28	32	24	7	0	177.2	243	12	51	30	10-13	0	5.42
Dolf Luque	R	38	32	22	8	1	176.0	213	7	56	43	5-16	0	4.50
Ray Kolp	R	34	30	16	4	1	145.1	151	8	39	27	8-10	0	4.03
Benny Frey	R	23	3	3	2	0	24.0	29	2	8	1	1-2	0	4.13
Ken Ash	R	27	29	7	2	0	82.0	91	2	30	26	1-5	2	4.83
Rube Ehrhardt	R	34	24	1	1	1	49.1	58	2	22	9	1-2	1	4.74
Dutch Kemner	R	30	9	0	0	0	15.1	19	0	8	10	0-0	1	7.63
Marv Gudat	L	23	7	2	2	0	26.2	29	0	4	0	1-1	0	3.38
Si Johnson	R	22	1	0	0	0	2.0	2	0	1	0	0-0	0	4.50
Paul Zahniser	R	32	1	0	0	0	1.0	2	1	1	0	0-0	0	27.00

1929 Boston Braves 8th NL 56-98 .364 43.0 GB

Judge Fuchs

Player	Gm by Position	B	Age	G	AB	R	H	2B	3B	HR	RBI	BB	SO	SB	Avg	OBP	Slg
Al Spohrer	C109	R	26	114	342	42	93	21	8	2	48	26	35	1	.272	.327	.398
George Sisler	1B154	L	36	154	629	67	205	40	8	2	79	33	17	6	.326	.363	.424
Freddie Maguire	2B138	R	30	138	496	54	125	26	8	0	41	19	40	8	.252	.284	.337
Les Bell	3B127,2B1	R	27	139	483	58	144	23	5	9	72	50	42	4	.298	.364	.422
Rabbit Maranville	SS145	R	37	146	560	87	159	26	10	0	55	47	33	13	.284	.344	.366
Lance Richbourg	OF134	L	31	139	557	76	170	24	13	3	56	42	26	7	.305	.355	.411
George Harper	OF130	L	37	136	457	65	133	25	5	10	68	69	27	5	.291	.389	.433
Earl Clark	OF74	R	21	84	279	43	88	13	3	1	30	12	30	6	.315	.346	.394
Jimmy Welsh†	OF51	L	26	53	186	24	54	8	7	2	16	13	9	1	.290	.350	.441
Joe Dugan	3B24	R	32	60	125	14	38	10	0	0	15	8	8	0	.304	.346	.384
Bernie James	2B32	S	23	46	101	12	31	3	2	0	9	9	13	3	.307	.369	.376
Zack Taylor†	C31	R	30	34	101	8	25	7	0	0	10	7	9	0	.248	.303	.317
Bob Smith	P34,SS5	R	34	39	99	12	17	4	2	1	8	2	8	1	.172	.188	.283
Heinie Mueller	OF24	L	29	46	93	10	19	2	1	0	11	12	12	2	.204	.302	.247
Lou Legett	C28	R	28	39	81	7	13	2	0	0	6	3	18	2	.160	.190	.185
Johnny Cooney	OF16,P14	R	28	41	72	10	23	4	1	0	6	3	3	1	.319	.355	.403
Phil Voyles	OF20	L	29	20	68	9	16	0	2	0	14	6	8	0	.235	.297	.294
Buzz Boyle	OF17	L	21	17	57	8	15	2	1	1	2	6	11	2	.263	.333	.386
Bill Dunlap	OF9	R	20	10	29	6	12	0	1	1	4	4	4	0	.414	.485	.586
Gene Robertson†	3B6,SS1	L	30	8	28	1	8	0	0	0	6	1	0	1	.286	.310	.286
Red Barron	OF6	R	29	10	21	3	4	1	0	0	1	1	4	2	.190	.227	.238
Jack Smith	OF9	L	34	19	20	2	5	0	0	0	2	2	2	0	.250	.318	.250
Hank Gowdy	C9	R	39	10	16	1	7	0	0	0	3	0	2	0	.438	.438	.438
Henry Peploski	3B2	L	23	6	10	1	2	0	0	0	1	1	3	0	.200	.273	.200
Bill Cronin	C6	R	26	6	9	0	1	0	0	0	0	0	0	0	.111	.111	.111
Doc Farrell†	SS1	R	27	5	8	0	1	0	0	0	2	0	1	0	.125	.125	.125
Jack Cummings†	C3	R	25	3	6	0	1	0	0	0	1	0	2	0	.167	.167	.167
Pat Collins	C6	R	32	7	5	1	0	0	0	0	2	3	1	0	.000	.375	.000
Al Weston		R	23	3	3	0	0	0	0	0	0	0	2	0	.000	.000	.000
Johnny Evers	2B1	L	47	1	0	0	0	0	0	0	0	0	0	0	—	—	—

Pitcher	T	Age	G	GS	CG	ShO	IP	H	HR	BB	SO	W-L	Sv	ERA
Bob Smith	R	34	34	29	19	1	231.0	256	20	71	65	11-17	3	4.68
Socks Seibold	R	33	33	27	16	1	205.2	228	17	80	54	12-17	1	4.73
Percy Jones	L	29	35	22	11	1	188.1	219	15	84	69	7-15	0	4.64
Ed Brandt	L	24	26	21	13	0	167.2	196	12	83	50	8-13	0	5.53
Ben Cantwell	R	27	27	20	8	0	157.0	171	11	52	25	4-13	2	4.47
Dixie Leverett	R	35	24	12	3	0	97.2	135	5	30	28	3-7	1	6.36
Bill Clarkson	R	30	2	1	0	0	7.0	16	0	4	0	0-1	0	10.29
Art Delaney	R	32	20	8	3	1	75.0	103	6	35	17	3-5	0	6.12
Bruce Cunningham	R	23	17	8	4	0	91.2	100	7	32	22	4-6	1	4.52
Johnny Cooney	L	28	14	2	1	0	45.0	57	4	22	11	2-3	3	5.00
Bunny Hearn	L	25	10	1	0	0	18.1	18	2	9	12	2-0	0	4.42
Red Peery	L	22	9	1	0	0	44.0	53	1	9	3	0-1	0	5.11
Kent Greenfield†	R	26	6	2	0	0	15.2	33	1	15	7	0-0	0	10.91
Johnny Werts	R	31	4	0	0	0	6.0	13	1	4	2	0-0	1	10.50
Clay Touchstone	R	26	1	0	0	0	2.2	6	1	0	1	0-0	0	16.88

»1930 Philadelphia Athletics 1st AL 102-52 .662 —

Connie Mack

Player	Gm by Position	B	Age	G	AB	R	H	2B	3B	HR	RBI	BB	SO	SB	Avg	OBP	Slg
Mickey Cochrane	C130	L	27	130	487	110	174	42	5	10	85	55	18	5	.357	.424	.526
Jimmie Foxx	1B153	R	22	153	562	127	188	33	13	37	156	93	66	7	.335	.429	.637
Max Bishop	2B127	L	30	130	441	117	111	27	6	10	38	128	60	3	.252	.426	.408
Jimmy Dykes	3B123,OF1	R	33	125	435	69	131	28	4	6	73	74	53	3	.301	.414	.425
Joe Boley	SS120	R	33	121	420	41	116	22	2	4	55	32	26	0	.276	.335	.367
Bing Miller	OF154	R	35	154	585	89	177	38	7	9	100	47	22	13	.303	.357	.438
Al Simmons	OF136	R	28	138	554	152	211	41	16	36	165	39	34	9	.381	.423	.708
Mule Haas	OF131	L	26	132	532	91	159	33	7	2	68	43	33	2	.299	.352	.398
Eric McNair	SS31,3B29,2B5*	R	21	78	237	27	63	12	2	0	34	9	19	5	.266	.293	.333
Dib Williams	2B39,SS19,3B1	R	20	67	191	24	50	10	3	3	22	15	19	2	.262	.322	.393
Wally Schang	C36	S	40	45	92	16	16	4	1	1	9	17	15	0	.174	.309	.272
Doc Cramer	OF21,SS1	L	24	30	82	12	19	1	1	0	6	2	8	0	.232	.250	.268
Homer Summa	OF15	L	31	25	54	10	15	2	1	1	5	4	1	0	.278	.339	.407
Jimmy Moore†	OF13	R	27	15	50	10	19	3	0	2	12	2	4	1	.380	.404	.560
Spencer Harris	OF13	L	29	22	49	4	9	1	0	0	5	5	2	0	.184	.259	.204
Cy Perkins	C19	R	34	20	38	1	6	2	0	0	4	2	3	0	.158	.200	.211
Mike Higgins	3B5,2B2,SS1	R	21	14	24	1	6	2	0	0	0	4	5	0	.250	.357	.333
Jim Keesey	1B3	R	27	11	12	2	3	1	0	0	2	1	2	0	.250	.308	.333
Charlie Perkins	P8,1B1	R	24	8	8	0	1	0	0	0	0	0	3	0	.125	.125	.125
Eddie Collins		L	43	3	2	1	1	0	0	0	0	0	0	0	.500	.500	.500

E. McNair, 1 G at OF

Pitcher	T	Age	G	GS	CG	ShO	IP	H	HR	BB	SO	W-L	Sv	ERA
George Earnshaw	R	30	49	39	20	3	296.0	299	20	139	193	22-13	2	4.44
Lefty Grove	L	30	50	32	22	2	291.0	273	8	60	209	28-5	9	2.54
Rube Walberg	L	33	38	30	12	2	205.1	207	6	85	100	13-12	1	4.69
Bill Shores	R	26	31	19	7	1	159.0	169	11	70	48	12-4	0	4.19
Eddie Rommel	R	32	35	9	5	0	130.1	142	11	27	35	9-4	3	4.28
Jack Quinn	R	46	35	7	0	0	89.2	109	6	22	28	9-7	6	4.42
Roy Mahaffey	R	27	33	16	6	0	152.2	186	16	53	38	9-5	0	5.01
Charlie Perkins	L	24	8	1	0	0	23.2	25	0	15	15	0-0	0	6.46
Glenn Liebhardt	R	19	5	0	0	0	9.0	14	2	8	2	0-1	0	11.00
Howard Ehmke	R	36	3	1	0	0	10.0	22	4	2	4	0-1	0	11.70
Al Mahon	L	20	2	0	0	0	4.1	11	0	7	0	0-0	0	22.85

1930 Washington Senators 2nd AL 94-60 .610 8.0 GB

Walter Johnson

Player	Gm by Position	B	Age	G	AB	R	H	2B	3B	HR	RBI	BB	SO	SB	Avg	OBP	Slg
Roy Spencer	C93	R	30	93	321	32	82	11	4	0	36	18	27	3	.255	.303	.315
Joe Judge	1B117	L	36	126	442	83	144	29	11	10	80	60	29	13	.326	.410	.509
Buddy Myer	2B134,OF2	L	26	138	541	97	164	18	8	2	61	58	31	14	.303	.372	.377
Ossie Bluege	3B134	R	29	134	476	64	138	27	7	3	69	51	40	15	.290	.368	.395
Joe Cronin	SS154	R	23	154	587	127	203	41	9	13	126	72	36	17	.346	.422	.513
Sam Rice	OF145	L	40	147	593	121	207	35	13	1	73	55	14	13	.349	.407	.457
Sammy West	OF118	L	25	120	411	75	135	22	10	6	67	37	34	5	.328	.385	.474
Heinie Manush†	OF86	L	28	88	356	74	129	33	8	7	65	26	17	4	.362	.406	.559
Dave Harris†	OF59	R	29	73	205	40	65	19	8	4	44	28	35	6	.317	.402	.546
Muddy Ruel	C60	R	34	66	198	18	50	3	4	0	26	24	13	1	.253	.342	.308
Goose Goslin†	OF47	L	29	47	188	34	51	11	5	7	38	19	19	3	.271	.344	.495
Jackie Hayes	2B29,3B9,1B8	R	23	51	166	25	47	7	2	1	20	7	8	2	.283	.312	.367
George Loepp	OF48	R	28	50	134	22	37	7	1	0	14	20	9	0	.276	.382	.343
Art Shires†	1B21	L	22	38	84	11	31	5	0	1	19	5	5	1	.369	.404	.464
Joe Kuhel	1B16	L	24	18	63	9	18	3	3	0	17	5	6	1	.286	.348	.429
Jim McLeod	3B10,SS7	R	21	18	34	3	9	1	0	0	1	1	5	1	.265	.306	.294
Pinky Hargrave†	C9	S	34	10	31	3	6	2	2	1	7	3	1	1	.194	.265	.484
Bennie Tate†	C9	L	28	14	20	1	5	0	0	0	2	0	1	0	.250	.250	.250
Ray Treadaway		L	22	6	19	1	4	2	0	0	1	0	3	0	.211	.211	.316
Red Barnes†		L	26	12	12	1	2	1	0	0	0	0	3	0	.167	.167	.250
Jake Powell	OF2	R	21	3	4	1	0	0	0	0	0	0	1	0	.000	.000	.000
Bill Barrett†	OF1	R	30	6	4	0	0	0	0	0	0	1	2	0	.000	.200	.000
Harley Boss	1B1	L	21	3	3	0	0	0	0	0	0	0	0	0	.000	.000	.000
Patsy Gharrity	1B1	R	38	2	1	0	0	0	0	0	0	0	0	0	.000	.000	.000

Pitcher	T	Age	G	GS	CG	ShO	IP	H	HR	BB	SO	W-L	Sv	ERA
Bump Hadley	R	25	42	34	15	1	260.1	242	6	105	162	15-11	2	3.73
General Crowder†	R	31	27	25	20	0	202.1	191	6	69	65	15-9	1	3.60
Sad Sam Jones	R	37	25	25	14	1	183.1	195	4	61	60	15-7	0	4.07
Lloyd Brown	L	25	38	22	10	1	197.0	220	6	65	59	16-12	0	4.25
Firpo Marberry	R	31	33	22	9	2	185.0	190	15	53	56	15-5	1	4.09
Ad Liska	R	23	32	16	7	1	150.2	140	6	71	40	9-7	1	3.29
Carl Fischer	L	24	8	4	1	0	33.1	37	0	18	21	1-1	1	4.86
Bobby Burke	L	23	24	4	2	0	74.1	62	2	29	35	3-4	3	3.63
Garland Braxton†	L	30	15	0	0	0	27.1	22	3	9	7	3-2	5	3.29
Myles Thomas	R	32	12	2	0	0	33.2	49	3	15	12	2-2	0	8.29
Harry Child	R	25	5	0	0	0	10.0	10	1	5	5	0-0	0	6.30
Carlos Moore	R	23	4	0	0	0	11.2	9	0	4	2	0-0	0	2.31

1930 New York Yankees 3rd AL 86-68 .558 16.0 GB

Bob Shawkey

Player	Gm by Position	B	Age	G	AB	R	H	2B	3B	HR	RBI	BB	SO	SB	Avg	OBP	Slg
Bill Dickey	C101	L	23	109	366	55	124	25	7	5	65	21	14	7	.339	.375	.486
Lou Gehrig	1B153	L	27	154	581	143	220	42	17	41	174	101	63	12	.379	.473	.721
Tony Lazzeri	2B77,3B60,SS8*	R	26	143	571	109	173	34	15	9	121	60	62	4	.303	.372	.462
Ben Chapman	3B91,2B45	R	21	138	513	74	162	31	10	10	81	43	58	14	.316	.370	.474
Lyn Lary	SS113	R	24	117	464	93	134	20	8	3	52	45	40	14	.289	.357	.386
Babe Ruth	OF144,P1	L	35	145	518	150	186	28	9	49	153	136	61	10	.359	.493	.732
Earle Combs	OF135	L	31	137	532	129	183	30	22	7	82	74	26	16	.344	.424	.523
Harry Rice†	OF87,1B6,3B1	L	28	100	346	62	103	17	5	7	74	31	21	3	.298	.361	.436
Sammy Byrd	OF85	R	22	92	218	46	62	12	2	6	31	30	18	5	.284	.371	.440
Dusty Cooke	OF73	L	23	92	216	43	55	12	3	6	29	32	61	4	.255	.353	.421
Jimmie Reese	2B48,3B5	L	28	77	188	44	65	14	2	3	18	11	8	1	.346	.382	.489
Bubbles Hargrave	C34	R	37	45	108	11	30	7	0	0	12	10	9	0	.278	.339	.343
Benny Bengough	C44	R	31	44	102	10	24	4	2	0	12	3	8	1	.235	.257	.314
Mark Koenig†	SS19	S	25	21	74	9	17	5	0	0	9	6	5	0	.230	.296	.297
Yats Wuestling†	SS21,3B3	R	26	25	58	5	11	0	1	0	3	4	14	0	.190	.242	.224
Art Jorgens	C16	R	25	16	30	7	11	3	0	0	1	2	4	0	.367	.406	.467
Cedric Durst†	OF6	L	33	8	19	0	3	1	0	0	5	0	1	0	.158	.158	.211
Bill Werber	SS3,3B1	R	22	4	14	5	4	0	0	0	2	3	1	0	.286	.412	.286
Bill Karlon	OF1	R	21	2	5	0	0	0	0	0	0	0	1	0	.000	.000	.000

T. Lazzeri, 1 G at 1B, 1 G at OF

Pitcher	T	Age	G	GS	CG	ShO	IP	H	HR	BB	SO	W-L	Sv	ERA
George Pipgras	R	30	44	30	15	3	221.0	230	9	70	111	15-15	4	4.11
Red Ruffing†	R	26	34	25	12	2	197.2	200	10	62	117	15-5	1	4.14
Roy Sherid	R	23	37	21	8	0	184.0	214	13	87	59	12-13	4	5.18
Ed Wells	L	30	27	21	7	0	150.2	185	11	49	46	12-3	0	5.20
Herb Pennock	L	36	25	19	11	1	156.1	194	8	20	46	11-7	0	4.32
Waite Hoyt†	R	30	8	7	2	0	47.2	64	7	9	10	2-2	0	4.53
Tom Zachary†	L	34	3	3	0	0	16.2	18	0	9	1	1-1	0	6.48
Frank Barnes	L	30	2	2	0	0	12.1	13	0	13	2	0-1	0	8.03
Sam Gibson	R	30	2	2	0	0	6.0	14	1	6	3	0-1	0	15.00
Babe Ruth	L	35	1	1	1	0	9.0	11	0	2	3	1-0	0	3.00
Hank Johnson	R	24	44	15	7	1	175.1	177	12	104	115	14-11	2	4.67
Lou McEvoy	R	28	28	1	0	0	52.1	64	4	29	14	1-3	3	6.71
Ken Holloway†	R	32	16	0	0	0	34.1	52	3	8	11	0-0	0	5.24
Lefty Gomez	L	21	15	6	2	0	60.0	66	12	28	22	2-5	1	5.55
Ownie Carroll†	R	27	10	1	0	0	32.2	49	2	18	8	0-1	0	6.61
Bill Henderson	R	28	3	0	0	0	8.0	7	1	4	2	0-0	0	4.50
Gordon Rhodes	R	22	3	0	0	0	2.0	3	0	4	1	0-0	0	9.00
Foster Edwards	R	26	2	0	0	0	1.2	5	0	2	1	0-0	0	21.60

1930 Cleveland Indians 4th AL 81-73 .526 21.0 GB

Roger Peckinpaugh

Player	Gm by Position	B	Age	G	AB	R	H	2B	3B	HR	RBI	BB	SO	SB	Avg	OBP	Slg
Luke Sewell	C76	R	29	76	292	40	75	21	2	1	43	14	9	5	.257	.293	.353
Eddie Morgan	1B129,OF19	R	26	150	584	122	204	47	11	26	136	62	66	8	.349	.413	.601
Johnny Hodapp	2B154	R	24	154	635	111	225	51	8	9	121	32	29	6	.354	.386	.502
Joe Sewell	3B97	L	31	109	353	44	102	17	6	0	48	42	3	1	.289	.374	.371
Jonah Goldman	SS93,3B20	R	23	111	306	32	74	18	0	1	44	28	25	3	.242	.312	.310
Earl Averill	OF134	L	28	139	534	102	181	33	8	19	119	56	48	10	.339	.404	.537
Dick Porter	OF118	L	28	119	480	100	168	43	8	4	57	55	31	3	.350	.420	.498
Charlie Jamieson	OF95	L	37	103	366	64	110	22	1	1	52	36	20	5	.301	.368	.374
Bob Seeds	OF70	R	23	85	277	37	79	11	3	3	32	12	22	1	.285	.315	.379
Glenn Myatt	C71	L	32	86	265	30	78	23	2	2	37	18	17	2	.294	.342	.419
Bibb Falk	OF42	L	31	82	191	34	62	12	1	4	36	23	8	2	.325	.397	.461
Ed Montague	SS46,3B13	R	24	58	179	37	47	5	2	1	16	37	38	1	.263	.392	.330
Johnny Burnett	3B27,SS19	L	25	54	170	28	53	13	0	0	20	17	8	2	.312	.378	.388
Lew Fonseca	1B28,3B6	R	31	40	129	20	36	9	2	0	17	7	7	1	.279	.316	.380
Carl Lind	SS22,2B1	R	26	24	69	8	17	3	0	0	6	3	7	0	.246	.278	.290
Joe Sprinz	C17	R	27	17	45	5	8	1	0	0	2	4	4	0	.178	.245	.200
Joe Vosmik	OF5	R	20	9	26	1	6	2	0	0	4	1	1	0	.231	.259	.308
Ralph Winegarner	3B5	R	20	5	22	5	10	1	0	0	2	1	7	0	.455	.478	.500
Ray Gardner	SS22	R	28	33	13	7	1	0	0	0	1	0	0	0	.077	.077	.077
George Detore	3B3	R	23	3	12	0	2	1	0	0	2	0	2	0	.167	.167	.250
Grover Hartley	C1	R	41	1	4	0	3	0	0	0	1	0	0	0	.750	.750	.750

Pitcher	T	Age	G	GS	CG	ShO	IP	H	HR	BB	SO	W-L	Sv	ERA
Wes Ferrell	R	22	43	35	25	1	296.2	299	14	106	143	25-13	3	3.31
Willis Hudlin	R	24	37	33	13	1	216.2	255	12	76	60	13-16	1	4.57
Clint Brown	R	26	35	31	16	3	213.2	271	14	51	54	11-13	1	4.97
Mel Harder	R	20	36	19	7	0	175.1	205	9	68	44	11-10	2	4.21
Roxie Lawson	R	24	7	4	2	0	33.2	46	1	23	10	1-2	0	6.15
Les Barnhart	R	25	1	1	0	0	8.1	12	0	4	1	1-0	0	6.48
Pete Appleton	R	26	39	7	2	0	118.2	122	8	53	45	8-7	1	4.02
Jake Miller	L	32	24	9	1	0	88.1	147	6	38	31	4-4	0	7.13
Milt Shoffner	L	24	24	10	1	0	84.2	129	8	50	17	3-4	0	7.97
Belve Bean	R	25	23	3	2	0	74.1	99	7	32	19	3-3	2	5.45
Ken Holloway†	R	32	12	2	0	0	30.0	49	5	14	8	1-1	2	8.40
Sal Gliatto	R	28	8	0	0	0	15.0	21	1	9	7	0-0	2	6.60
Joe Shaute	L	30	4	0	0	0	4.2	8	0	4	2	0-0	0	15.43

1930 Detroit Tigers 5th AL 75-79 .487 27.0 GB

Bucky Harris

Player	Gm by Position	B	Age	G	AB	R	H	2B	3B	HR	RBI	BB	SO	SB	Avg	OBP	Slg
Ray Hayworth	C76	R	26	77	227	24	63	15	4	0	22	20	19	0	.278	.336	.379
Dale Alexander	1B154	R	27	154	602	86	196	33	8	20	135	42	56	6	.326	.372	.507
Charlie Gehringer	2B154	L	27	154	610	144	201	47	15	16	98	69	17	19	.330	.404	.534
Marty McManus	3B130,SS3,1B1	R	30	132	484	74	155	40	4	9	89	59	28	23	.320	.396	.475
Mark Koenig†	SS70,P2	S	25	76	267	37	64	9	2	1	16	20	15	2	.240	.295	.300
Liz Funk	OF129	L	25	140	527	74	145	26	11	4	65	29	39	12	.275	.319	.389
Roy Johnson	OF118	L	27	125	462	84	127	30	13	2	35	40	46	17	.275	.333	.409
John Stone	OF108	L	24	126	422	60	132	29	11	3	56	32	49	6	.313	.363	.455
Bill Akers	SS49,3B26	R	25	85	233	36	65	8	5	9	40	36	34	5	.279	.375	.472
Billy Rogell	SS33,3B13,OF1	S	25	54	144	20	24	4	2	0	9	15	23	1	.167	.250	.222
Bob Fothergill†	OF38	R	32	55	143	14	37	9	3	2	14	6	10	1	.259	.289	.406
Pinky Hargrave†	C40	S	34	55	137	18	39	8	0	5	18	20	12	2	.285	.380	.453
Harry Rice†	OF35	L	28	37	128	16	39	6	0	2	24	19	8	0	.305	.403	.398
Gene Desautels	C42	R	23	42	126	13	24	4	2	0	9	7	9	2	.190	.239	.254
Paul Easterling	OF25	R	24	29	79	7	16	6	0	1	14	6	18	0	.203	.259	.316
Frank Doljack	OF20	R	22	20	74	10	19	5	1	3	17	2	11	0	.257	.286	.473
Tom Hughes	OF16	L	22	17	59	8	22	2	3	0	5	4	8	0	.373	.413	.508
Tony Rensa†	C18	R	28	20	37	6	10	2	1	1	3	6	7	1	.270	.386	.459
Jimmy Shevlin	1B25	L	20	28	14	4	2	0	0	0	2	2	3	0	.143	.250	.143
Johnny Watson	SS4,OF1	L	22	4	12	1	3	2	0	0	3	1	2	0	.250	.308	.417
Yats Wuestling†	SS4	R	26	4	9	0	0	0	0	0	0	2	3	0	.000	.182	.000
Hughie Wise	C2	S	24	2	6	0	2	0	0	0	0	0	0	0	.333	.333	.333
Hank Greenberg		R	19	1	1	0	0	0	0	0	0	0	0	0	.000	.000	.000

Pitcher	T	Age	G	GS	CG	ShO	IP	H	HR	BB	SO	W-L	Sv	ERA
Earl Whitehill	L	30	34	31	16	0	220.2	248	8	80	109	17-13	1	4.24
Vic Sorrell	R	29	35	30	14	2	233.1	245	13	106	97	16-11	1	3.86
George Uhle	R	31	33	29	18	1	239.0	239	18	75	117	12-12	3	3.65
Waite Hoyt†	R	30	26	20	8	1	135.2	176	7	47	25	9-8	4	4.78
Chief Hogsett	L	26	33	17	4	0	146.0	174	9	63	54	9-8	1	5.42
Tommy Bridges	R	23	8	5	2	0	37.2	28	4	23	17	3-2	0	4.06
Ownie Carroll†	R	27	6	3	0	0	20.1	30	3	9	4	0-5	0	10.62
Mark Koenig	R	25	2	1	0	0	9.0	11	0	8	6	0-1	0	10.00
Charlie Sullivan	R	27	40	3	2	0	93.2	112	9	53	38	1-5	5	6.53
Art Herring	R	24	23	6	1	0	77.2	97	2	36	16	3-3	0	5.33
Whit Wyatt	R	22	21	7	2	0	85.2	76	6	35	68	4-5	2	3.57
Guy Cantrell	R	26	16	2	1	0	35.0	38	5	20	20	1-5	0	5.66
Phil Page	L	24	12	0	0	0	12.0	23	1	9	2	0-1	0	9.75
Joe Samuels	R	25	2	0	0	0	6.0	10	1	6	1	0-0	0	16.50

1930 St. Louis Browns 6th AL 64-90 .416 38.0 GB

Bill Killefer

Player	Gm by Position	B	Age	G	AB	R	H	2B	3B	HR	RBI	BB	SO	SB	Avg	OBP	Slg
Rick Ferrell	C101	R	24	101	314	43	84	18	4	1	41	46	10	1	.268	.363	.360
Lu Blue	1B111	S	33	117	425	85	100	27	5	4	42	81	44	12	.235	.363	.351
Ski Melillo	2B148	R	30	149	574	61	147	30	10	5	59	23	44	15	.256	.287	.369
Frank O'Rourke	3B84,SS23,1B3	R	35	115	400	52	107	15	4	1	41	35	30	11	.268	.326	.333
Red Kress	SS123,3B31	R	23	154	614	94	192	43	8	16	112	50	56	3	.313	.366	.487
Goose Goslin†	OF101	L	29	101	396	81	129	25	7	30	100	48	35	14	.326	.400	.652
Fred Schulte	OF98,1B5	R	29	113	392	59	109	23	5	5	62	41	44	12	.278	.348	.401
Ted Gullic	OF82,1B3	R	23	92	308	39	77	7	5	4	44	27	43	4	.250	.310	.344
Earl McNeely	OF38,1B27	R	32	76	235	33	64	19	1	0	20	22	14	8	.272	.340	.362
Red Badgro	OF61	L	27	89	234	30	56	18	3	1	27	13	27	3	.239	.285	.355
Alex Metzler†	OF56	L	27	56	209	30	54	6	3	1	23	21	12	5	.258	.326	.330
Heinie Manush†	OF48	L	28	49	198	26	65	16	4	2	29	5	7	3	.328	.345	.480
Sammy Hale	3B47	R	33	62	190	21	52	8	1	2	25	8	18	1	.274	.303	.358
Clyde Manion	C56	R	33	57	148	12	32	1	0	1	11	24	17	0	.216	.326	.243
Jim Levey	SS8	S	23	8	37	7	9	2	0	0	3	3	2	0	.243	.300	.297
Bernie Hungling	C10	R	34	10	31	4	10	2	0	0	2	5	3	0	.323	.417	.387
Jack Burns	1B8	L	22	8	30	5	9	3	0	0	2	5	5	0	.300	.400	.400
Lin Storti	2B6	S	23	7	28	6	9	1	1	0	2	2	6	0	.321	.367	.429
Jack Crouch	C5	R	27	6	14	1	2	1	0	0	1	1	3	0	.143	.200	.214
Joe Hassler	SS3	R	25	5	8	3	2	0	0	0	1	0	1	0	.250	.250	.250
Tom Jenkins	OF2	L	32	2	8	1	2	1	1	0	3	0	1	0	.250	.250	.625

Pitcher	T	Age	G	GS	CG	ShO	IP	H	HR	BB	SO	W-L	Sv	ERA
Lefty Stewart	L	29	35	33	23	1	271.0	281	21	70	79	20-12	0	3.45
Dick Coffman	R	23	38	30	12	1	196.0	250	14	69	54	8-18	1	5.14
Sam Gray	R	32	27	24	7	0	167.2	215	17	52	51	4-15	0	6.28
George Blaeholder	R	26	37	23	10	1	191.1	235	20	46	70	11-13	4	4.61
Rip Collins	R	34	35	20	6	1	171.2	168	11	63	75	9-7	2	4.35
General Crowder†	R	31	13	10	5	1	77.1	85	11	27	42	3-7	1	4.66
Fred Stiely	L	29	4	2	1	0	19.0	27	4	8	5	0-1	0	8.53
Chad Kimsey	R	23	42	4	1	0	113.1	139	8	45	32	6-10	1	6.35
Herm Holshouser	R	23	25	1	0	0	62.1	103	8	28	37	0-1	1	7.80
Rollie Stiles	R	23	20	7	3	0	102.0	136	10	41	25	3-6	0	5.91

1930 Chicago White Sox 7th AL 62-92 .403 40.0 GB

Donie Bush

Player	Gm by Position	B	Age	G	AB	R	H	2B	3B	HR	RBI	BB	SO	SB	Avg	OBP	Slg
Bennie Tate†	C70	L	28	72	230	26	73	11	2	0	27	18	10	2	.317	.367	.383
Cliff Watwood	1B62,OF43	L	24	133	427	75	129	25	4	2	51	52	35	5	.302	.382	.393
Bill Cissell	2B106,3B24,SS10	R	26	141	562	82	152	28	9	2	48	28	32	16	.270	.307	.363
Willie Kamm	3B105	R	30	111	331	49	89	21	6	3	47	51	20	5	.269	.368	.396
Greg Mulleavy	SS73	R	24	77	289	27	76	14	5	0	28	20	23	5	.263	.311	.346
Smead Jolley	OF151	L	28	152	616	76	193	38	12	16	114	28	52	3	.313	.346	.492
Carl Reynolds	OF132	R	27	138	563	103	202	25	18	22	104	20	39	16	.359	.388	.584
Red Barnes†	OF72	L	26	85	266	48	66	12	7	1	31	26	20	4	.248	.317	.357
John Kerr	2B51,SS19	R	31	70	266	37	77	11	6	3	27	21	23	4	.289	.351	.410
Bud Clancy	1B60	L	29	68	234	28	57	8	3	3	27	12	18	3	.244	.286	.342
Bob Fothergill†	OF31	R	32	52	135	10	40	9	0	0	24	4	8	0	.296	.326	.363
Art Shires†	1B33	L	22	37	128	14	33	5	1	1	18	6	6	2	.258	.291	.336
Buck Crouse	C38	L	33	42	118	14	30	8	1	0	15	17	10	1	.254	.348	.339
Irv Jeffries	3B20,SS13	R	24	40	97	14	23	3	0	2	11	3	2	1	.237	.275	.330
Blondy Ryan	3B23,SS2,2B1	R	24	28	87	9	18	0	4	1	10	6	13	2	.207	.258	.333
Dave Harris†	OF23,2B1	R	29	33	86	16	21	2	1	5	13	7	22	0	.244	.309	.465
Bill Hunnefield	SS22,1B1	S	31	31	81	11	22	2	0	1	5	4	10	1	.272	.314	.333
Ernie Smith	SS21	R	30	24	79	5	19	3	0	0	3	5	6	2	.241	.286	.278
Alex Metzler†	OF27	L	27	56	76	12	14	4	0	0	5	11	6	0	.184	.287	.237
Chick Autry	C29	R	27	34	71	1	18	1	1	0	5	4	8	0	.254	.293	.296
Moe Berg	C20	R	28	20	61	4	7	3	0	0	7	1	5	0	.115	.129	.164
Johnny Riddle	C25	R	24	25	58	7	14	3	1	0	4	3	6	0	.241	.290	.328
Jimmy Moore†	OF11	R	27	16	39	4	8	2	0	0	2	6	3	0	.205	.326	.256
Luke Appling	SS6	R	23	6	26	2	8	2	0	0	2	0	0	2	.308	.308	.385
Jim Moore	P9,OF9	R	26	9	13	0	3	1	0	0	2	0	1	0	.231	.231	.308
Bruce Campbell	OF4	L	20	5	10	4	5	1	1	0	5	1	2	0	.500	.545	.800
Joe Klinger	C2,1B2	R	27	4	8	0	3	0	0	0	1	0	0	0	.375	.375	.375
Butch Henline	C3	R	35	3	8	1	1	0	0	0	2	0	3	0	.125	.125	.125
Hugh Willingham	2B1	R	24	3	4	2	1	0	0	0	0	2	1	0	.250	.500	.250

Pitcher	T	Age	G	GS	CG	ShO	IP	H	HR	BB	SO	W-L	Sv	ERA
Ted Lyons	R	29	42	36	29	1	297.2	331	12	57	69	22-15	1	3.78
Tommy Thomas	R	30	34	27	7	0	169.0	229	13	44	58	5-13	0	5.22
Red Faber	R	41	29	26	10	0	169.0	188	7	49	62	8-13	1	4.21
Pat Caraway	L	24	38	21	9	1	193.1	194	11	57	83	10-10	1	3.86
Garland Braxton†	L	30	19	10	2	0	90.2	127	9	33	44	4-10	1	6.45
Jim Moore	R	26	9	5	2	0	40.0	42	0	12	11	2-1	1	3.60
Ed Walsh	R	25	37	4	0	0	103.2	131	8	30	37	1-4	0	5.38
Dutch Henry	L	28	35	16	4	0	155.0	211	12	48	35	2-17	0	4.88
Hal McKain	R	23	32	5	0	0	89.0	108	0	42	52	6-4	5	5.56
Bob Weiland	L	24	14	3	0	0	32.2	38	1	21	15	0-4	0	6.61
Ted Blankenship	R	29	7	1	0	0	14.2	23	0	7	2	2-1	0	9.20
Biggs Wehde	R	23	4	0	0	0	6.1	7	1	7	3	0-0	0	9.95

1930 Boston Red Sox 8th AL 52-102 .338 50.0 GB

Heinie Wagner

Player	Gm by Position	B	Age	G	AB	R	H	2B	3B	HR	RBI	BB	SO	SB	Avg	OBP	Slg
Charlie Berry	C85	R	27	88	256	31	74	9	6	6	35	16	22	2	.289	.331	.441
Phil Todt	1B104	L	28	111	383	49	103	22	5	11	62	24	33	4	.269	.312	.439
Bill Regan	2B127,3B2	R	31	134	507	54	135	35	10	3	53	25	60	4	.266	.303	.393
Otto Miller	3B83,2B15	R	29	112	370	49	106	22	5	0	40	26	21	2	.286	.333	.373
Hal Rhyne	SS107	R	31	107	296	34	60	8	5	0	23	25	19	1	.203	.269	.264
Tom Oliver	OF154	R	27	154	646	86	189	34	2	0	46	42	25	6	.293	.339	.351
Earl Webb	OF116	L	32	127	449	61	145	30	6	16	66	44	56	2	.323	.385	.523
Russ Scarritt	OF110	L	27	113	447	48	129	17	8	2	48	12	49	4	.289	.312	.376
Cedric Durst†	OF75	L	33	102	302	29	74	19	5	1	24	17	24	3	.245	.290	.351
Bobby Reeves	3B62,SS15,2B11	R	26	92	272	41	59	7	4	2	18	50	36	6	.217	.345	.294
Bill Sweeney	1B56,3B1	R	25	88	243	32	75	13	0	4	30	9	15	5	.309	.333	.412
Johnny Heving	C71	R	34	75	220	15	61	5	3	0	17	11	14	2	.277	.312	.327
Rabbit Warstler	SS54	R	26	54	162	16	30	2	3	1	13	20	21	0	.185	.275	.253
Bill Narleski	SS19,3B14,2B5	R	31	39	98	11	23	9	0	0	7	7	5	0	.235	.306	.327
Jack Rothrock	OF9,3B1	S	25	45	65	4	18	3	1	0	4	2	9	0	.277	.299	.354
Ed Connolly	C26	R	21	27	48	1	9	2	0	0	7	4	3	0	.188	.250	.229
Joe Cicero	OF5,3B2	R	19	18	30	5	5	1	2	0	4	1	5	0	.167	.194	.333
Charlie Small	OF1	L	24	25	18	1	3	1	0	0	0	2	5	1	.167	.250	.222
Bill Barrett†	OF5	R	30	6	18	3	3	1	0	0	1	1	3	0	.167	.211	.222
Jim Galvin		R	22	2	2	0	0	0	0	0	0	0	0	0	.000	.000	.000
Tom Winsett		L	20	1	1	0	0	0	0	0	0	0	1	0	.000	.000	.000

Pitcher	T	Age	G	GS	CG	ShO	IP	H	HR	BB	SO	W-L	Sv	ERA
Milt Gaston	R	34	38	34	20	2	273.0	272	15	98	99	13-20	2	3.92
Danny MacFayden	R	25	36	33	18	1	269.1	293	9	93	76	11-14	2	4.21
Hod Lisenbee	R	31	37	31	15	0	237.1	254	20	86	47	10-17	0	4.40
Jack Russell	R	24	35	30	15	0	229.2	302	11	53	35	9-20	0	5.45
Ed Morris	R	30	18	9	3	0	65.1	67	1	38	28	4-9	0	4.13
Red Ruffing†	R	26	4	3	1	0	24.0	32	1	6	14	0-3	0	6.38
Ed Durham	R	21	33	12	6	1	140.0	144	9	43	28	4-15	1	4.69
George Smith	R	28	27	2	0	0	73.2	92	7	49	21	1-2	0	6.60
Frank Bushey	R	23	11	0	0	0	30.0	34	1	15	4	0-1	0	6.30
Ben Shields	L	27	3	0	0	0	10.0	16	0	6	1	0-0	0	9.00
Frank Mulroney	R	27	2	0	0	0	3.0	3	0	0	2	0-1	0	3.00
Bill Bayne	L	31	1	0	0	0	4.0	5	1	1	1	0-0	0	4.50
Bob Kline	R	20	1	0	0	0	1.0	1	0	0	0	0-0	0	0.00

»1930 St. Louis Cardinals 1st NL 92-62 .597 —

Gabby Street

Player	Gm by Position	B	Age	G	AB	R	H	2B	3B	HR	RBI	BB	SO	SB	Avg	OBP	Slg
Jimmie Wilson	C99	R	29	107	362	54	115	25	7	1	58	28	17	8	.318	.368	.434
Jim Bottomley	1B124	L	30	131	487	92	148	33	7	15	97	44	36	5	.304	.368	.493
Frankie Frisch	2B123,3B10	S	31	133	540	121	187	46	9	10	114	55	16	15	.346	.407	.520
Sparky Adams	3B104,2B25,SS7	R	35	137	570	98	179	36	9	0	55	45	27	7	.314	.365	.409
Charlie Gelbert	SS139	R	24	139	513	92	156	39	11	3	72	43	41	6	.304	.360	.441
Taylor Douthit	OF154	R	29	154	664	109	201	41	10	7	93	60	38	4	.303	.364	.426
Chick Hafey	OF116	R	27	120	446	108	150	39	12	26	107	46	51	12	.336	.407	.652
George Watkins	OF89,1B13,2B1	L	30	119	391	85	146	32	7	17	87	24	49	5	.373	.415	.621
Showboat Fisher	OF67	L	31	92	254	49	95	18	6	8	61	25	21	4	.374	.432	.587
Gus Mancuso	C61	R	24	76	227	39	83	17	2	7	59	18	16	1	.366	.415	.551
Andy High	3B48,2B3	L	32	72	215	34	60	12	2	2	29	23	6	1	.279	.349	.381
Ernie Orsatti	1B22,OF11	L	27	48	131	24	42	8	4	1	15	12	18	1	.321	.382	.466
Ray Blades	OF32	R	33	45	101	26	40	6	2	4	25	21	15	1	.396	.504	.614
Homer Peel	OF21	R	27	26	73	9	12	2	0	0	10	3	4	0	.164	.197	.192
Doc Farrell†	SS15,2B6,1B1	R	28	23	61	3	13	1	1	0	6	4	2	1	.213	.262	.262
George Puccinelli	OF3	R	23	11	16	5	9	1	0	3	8	0	1	0	.563	.563	1.188
Earl Smith	C6	L	33	8	10	0	0	0	0	0	0	3	1	0	.000	.231	.000
Pepper Martin		R	26	6	1	5	0	0	0	0	0	0	0	0	.000	.000	.000

Pitcher	T	Age	G	GS	CG	ShO	IP	H	HR	BB	SO	W-L	Sv	ERA
Wild Bill Hallahan	L	27	35	32	13	2	237.1	233	15	126	177	15-9	2	4.66
Syl Johnson	R	29	32	24	9	2	187.2	215	13	38	92	12-10	2	4.65
Jesse Haines	R	36	29	24	14	0	182.0	215	15	54	68	13-8	1	4.30
Burleigh Grimes†	R	36	22	19	10	1	152.1	174	5	43	58	13-6	0	3.01
Flint Rhem	R	29	26	19	9	0	139.2	173	11	37	47	12-8	0	4.45
Bill Sherdel†	L	33	13	7	1	0	64.0	86	5	13	29	3-2	0	4.64
Carmen Hill	R	34	4	2	0	0	14.2	12	2	13	8	0-1	0	4.30
Tony Kaufmann	R	29	2	1	0	0	10.1	15	2	4	2	0-1	0	7.84
Dizzy Dean	R	20	1	1	1	0	9.0	3	0	3	5	1-0	0	1.00
Clarence Mitchell†	L	39	1	1	0	0	3.0	5	0	2	1	1-0	0	6.00
Hi Bell	R	32	39	9	2	0	115.1	143	4	23	42	4-3	8	3.90
Jim Lindsey	R	34	39	6	3	0	105.2	131	6	46	50	7-5	5	4.43
Al Grabowski	L	28	33	8	1	0	106.0	121	7	50	45	6-4	1	4.84
Hal Haid	R	32	20	0	0	0	33.0	38	1	14	13	3-2	2	4.09
Fred Frankhouse†	R	26	8	1	0	0	19.2	31	1	11	4	2-3	0	7.32

1930 Chicago Cubs 2nd NL 90-64 .584 2.0 GB

Joe McCarthy (86-64)/Rogers Hornsby (4-0)

Player	Gm by Position	B	Age	G	AB	R	H	2B	3B	HR	RBI	BB	SO	SB	Avg	OBP	Slg
Gabby Hartnett	C136	R	29	141	508	84	172	31	3	37	122	55	62	0	.339	.404	.630
Charlie Grimm	1B113	L	31	114	429	58	124	27	2	6	66	41	26	1	.289	.359	.403
Footsie Blair	2B115,3B13	L	29	134	578	97	158	24	12	6	59	20	58	9	.273	.306	.388
Woody English	3B83,SS78	R	23	156	638	152	214	36	17	14	59	100	72	3	.335	.430	.511
Clyde Beck	SS57,2B24,3B2	R	30	83	244	32	52	7	0	6	34	36	32	2	.213	.314	.316
Kiki Cuyler	OF156	R	31	156	642	155	228	50	17	13	134	72	49	37	.355	.428	.547
Hack Wilson	OF155	R	30	155	585	146	208	35	6	56	190	105	84	3	.356	.454	.723
Riggs Stephenson	OF80	R	32	109	341	56	125	21	1	5	68	32	20	2	.367	.421	.478
Les Bell	3B70,1B2	R	28	74	248	35	69	15	4	5	47	24	27	1	.278	.342	.431
Danny Taylor	OF52	R	29	74	219	43	62	14	3	2	37	27	34	6	.283	.364	.402
George Kelly†	1B39	R	34	39	166	22	55	6	1	3	19	7	16	0	.331	.362	.434
Cliff Heathcote	OF35	L	32	70	150	30	39	10	1	9	18	18	15	4	.260	.343	.520
Doc Farrell†	SS38,2B1	R	28	46	113	21	33	6	0	1	16	9	5	0	.292	.344	.372
Rogers Hornsby	2B25	R	34	42	104	15	32	5	1	2	18	12	12	0	.308	.385	.433
Zack Taylor	C28	R	31	32	95	12	22	2	1	1	11	2	12	0	.232	.255	.305
Chick Tolson	1B5	R	35	13	20	0	6	1	0	0	1	6	5	1	.300	.462	.350

Pitcher	T	Age	G	GS	CG	ShO	IP	H	HR	BB	SO	W-L	Sv	ERA
Pat Malone	R	27	45	35	22	2	271.2	290	14	96	142	20-9	4	3.94
Charlie Root	R	31	37	30	15	4	220.1	247	17	63	124	16-14	3	4.33
Guy Bush	R	28	46	25	11	0	225.0	291	22	86	75	15-10	3	6.20
Sheriff Blake	R	30	34	24	7	0	186.2	213	14	99	80	10-14	0	4.82
Hal Carlson	R	38	8	6	3	0	51.2	68	5	14	14	4-2	0	5.05
Bud Teachout	L	26	40	16	6	0	153.0	178	16	48	59	11-4	0	4.06
Lynn Nelson	R	25	37	3	0	0	81.1	97	10	28	29	3-2	0	5.09
Bob Osborn	R	27	35	13	3	0	126.2	147	9	53	42	10-6	1	4.97
Al Shealy	R	30	24	0	0	0	27.0	37	2	14	14	0-0	0	8.00
Mal Moss	L	25	12	1	0	0	18.2	18	0	14	4	0-0	1	6.27
Jesse Petty†	L	35	9	3	0	0	39.1	51	2	6	18	1-3	0	2.97
Bill McAfee	R	22	2	0	0	0	1.0	3	0	2	0	0-0	0	0.00
Lon Warneke	R	21	1	0	0	0	1.1	2	0	5	0	0-0	0	33.75

1930 New York Giants 3rd NL 87-67 .565 5.0 GB

John McGraw

Player	Gm by Position	B	Age	G	AB	R	H	2B	3B	HR	RBI	BB	SO	SB	Avg	OBP	Slg
Shanty Hogan	C96	R	24	122	389	60	132	26	2	13	75	21	24	2	.339	.378	.517
Bill Terry	1B154	L	33	154	633	139	254	39	15	23	129	57	33	8	.401	.452	.619
Hughie Critz†	2B124	R	29	124	558	93	148	17	11	4	50	24	26	7	.265	.296	.357
Freddy Lindstrom	3B148	R	24	148	609	127	231	39	7	22	106	48	33	15	.379	.425	.575
Travis Jackson	SS115	R	26	116	431	70	146	27	8	13	82	32	25	6	.339	.386	.529
Mel Ott	OF146	L	21	148	521	122	182	34	5	25	119	103	35	9	.349	.458	.578
Freddy Leach	OF124	L	32	126	544	90	178	19	13	13	71	22	25	3	.327	.361	.482
Wally Roettger	OF114	R	27	121	420	51	119	15	5	5	51	25	29	1	.283	.330	.379
Bob O'Farrell	C69	R	33	94	249	37	75	16	4	4	54	31	21	1	.301	.381	.446
Ethan Allen†	OF62	R	26	76	238	48	73	9	2	7	31	12	23	5	.307	.340	.450
Ed Marshall	SS45,2B17,3B5	R	24	78	223	33	69	5	3	0	21	13	9	0	.309	.350	.359
Randy Reese	OF32,3B10,1B1	R	26	67	172	26	47	4	2	4	25	10	12	1	.273	.313	.390
Pat Crawford†	2B18,1B1	L	28	25	76	11	21	3	2	3	17	7	2	0	.276	.345	.487
Dave Bancroft	SS8	S	39	10	17	0	1	1	0	0	0	2	1	0	.059	.158	.118
Chick Fullis	OF2	R	26	13	6	2	0	0	0	0	0	0	1	1	.000	.000	.000
Jo-Jo Moore	OF1	L	21	3	5	1	1	0	0	0	0	0	1	0	.200	.200	.200
Harry Rosenberg	OF3	R	21	9	5	1	0	0	0	0	0	1	4	0	.000	.167	.000
Francis Healy	C1	R	19	7	2	2	0	0	0	0	0	0	0	0	.000	.000	.000
Sam Leslie		L	24	2	2	0	1	0	0	0	0	0	1	0	.500	.500	.500

Pitcher	T	Age	G	GS	CG	ShO	IP	H	HR	BB	SO	W-L	Sv	ERA
Bill Walker	L	26	39	34	13	2	245.1	258	19	88	105	17-15	1	3.93
Carl Hubbell	L	27	37	32	17	3	241.2	263	11	58	117	17-12	2	3.87
F. Fitzsimmons	R	28	41	29	17	1	224.1	230	26	59	76	19-7	1	4.25
Clarence Mitchell†	L	39	24	16	5	0	129.0	151	10	36	40	10-3	0	3.98
Pete Donohue†	R	29	18	11	4	0	86.2	135	6	18	26	7-6	1	6.13
Joe Genewich	R	33	18	9	3	0	61.0	71	6	20	13	2-5	3	5.61
Larry Benton†	R	32	8	4	1	0	30.0	42	8	14	16	1-3	1	7.80
Hub Pruett	L	29	45	8	1	0	135.2	152	11	63	49	5-4	3	4.78
Joe Heving	R	29	41	2	0	0	89.2	109	7	27	37	7-5	6	5.22
Tiny Chaplin	R	24	19	8	3	0	73.0	89	8	16	20	2-6	1	5.18
Roy Parmelee	R	23	11	1	0	0	21.0	18	3	26	19	0-1	0	9.43
Ray Lucas	R	21	6	0	0	0	10.1	9	2	10	1	0-0	0	6.97
Bill Morrell	R	37	2	0	0	0	8.0	6	0	1	3	0-0	0	1.13
Ralph Judd	R	28	2	0	0	0	7.2	13	0	3	0	0-0	0	5.87

648 Seasons: Team Rosters

1930 Brooklyn Dodgers 4th NL 86-68 .558 6.0 GB

Wilbert Robinson

Player	Gm by Position	B	Age	G	AB	R	H	2B	3B	HR	RBI	BB	SO	SB	Avg	OBP	Slg
Al Lopez	C126	R	21	128	421	60	130	20	4	6	57	33	35	3	.309	.362	.418
Del Bissonette	1B146	L	30	146	572	102	192	33	13	16	113	56	66	4	.336	.396	.523
Neal Finn	2B81	R	26	87	273	42	76	13	0	3	30	26	18	3	.278	.350	.359
Wally Gilbert	3B150	R	29	150	623	92	183	34	5	3	67	47	33	7	.294	.345	.379
Glenn Wright	SS134	R	29	135	532	83	171	28	12	22	126	32	70	2	.321	.360	.543
Babe Herman	OF153	L	27	153	614	143	241	48	11	35	130	66	56	18	.393	.455	.678
Johnny Frederick	OF142	L	28	142	616	120	206	44	11	17	76	46	34	1	.334	.383	.524
Rube Bressler	OF90,1B7	R	35	109	335	53	100	12	8	3	52	51	19	4	.299	.394	.409
Jake Flowers	2B65,OF1	R	28	89	253	37	81	18	3	2	50	21	18	5	.320	.372	.439
Eddie Moore	2B23,OF23,SS17*	R	31	76	196	24	55	13	1	1	20	21	7	1	.281	.356	.372
Harvey Hendrick	OF42,1B7	L	32	68	167	29	43	10	1	5	28	20	19	2	.257	.344	.419
Ike Boone	OF27	L	33	40	101	13	30	9	1	3	13	14	8	0	.297	.383	.495
Hank DeBerry	C35	R	35	35	95	11	28	3	0	0	14	4	10	0	.295	.323	.326
Val Picinich	C22	R	33	23	46	4	10	3	0	0	3	5	6	1	.217	.294	.283
Gordon Slade	SS21	R	25	25	37	8	8	2	0	1	2	3	5	0	.216	.275	.351
Hal Lee	OF12	R	25	22	37	5	6	0	0	1	4	4	5	0	.162	.244	.243
Jack Warner	3B6	R	26	21	25	4	8	1	0	0	0	2	7	1	.320	.370	.360

E. Moore, 1 G at 3B

Pitcher	T	Age	G	GS	CG	ShO	IP	H	HR	BB	SO	W-L	Sv	ERA
Dazzy Vance	R	39	35	31	20	4	258.2	241	15	55	173	17-15	0	2.61
Watty Clark	L	28	44	24	9	1	200.0	209	20	38	81	13-13	6	4.19
Dolf Luque	R	39	31	24	16	2	199.0	221	18	58	62	14-8	2	4.30
Ray Phelps	R	26	36	24	11	2	179.2	198	21	52	64	14-7	0	4.11
Jumbo Elliott	L	29	35	21	6	2	198.1	204	16	70	59	10-7	1	3.95
Jim Faulkner	L	30	2	1	0	0	0.1	2	1	1	0	0-0	1	81.00
Ray Moss	R	28	36	11	5	0	118.1	127	13	55	30	9-6	1	5.10
Sloppy Thurston	R	31	24	11	5	2	106.0	110	4	17	26	6-4	1	3.40
Clise Dudley	R	26	21	7	2	0	66.2	103	3	27	18	2-4	1	6.35
Johnny Morrison	R	34	16	0	0	0	34.2	47	4	16	11	1-2	1	5.45
Fred Heimach	L	29	9	0	0	0	7.1	14	0	3	1	0-2	1	4.91
Bobo Newsom	R	22	2	0	0	0	3.0	2	0	2	1	0-0	0	0.00
Cy Moore	R	25	1	0	0	0	0.0	2	0	0	0	0-0	0	—

1930 Pittsburgh Pirates 5th NL 80-74 .519 12.0 GB

Jewel Ens

Player	Gm by Position	B	Age	G	AB	R	H	2B	3B	HR	RBI	BB	SO	SB	Avg	OBP	Slg
Rollie Hemsley	C98	R	23	104	324	45	82	19	6	2	45	22	21	3	.253	.301	.367
Gus Suhr	1B151	L	24	151	542	93	155	26	14	17	107	80	56	11	.286	.380	.480
George Grantham	2B141,1B4	L	30	146	552	120	179	34	14	18	99	81	66	5	.324	.413	.534
Pie Traynor	3B130	R	30	130	497	90	182	22	11	9	119	48	19	7	.366	.423	.509
Dick Bartell	SS126	R	22	129	475	69	152	32	13	4	75	39	34	8	.320	.378	.467
Adam Comorosky	OF152	R	24	152	597	112	187	47	23	12	119	51	33	14	.313	.371	.529
Paul Waner	OF143	L	27	145	589	117	217	32	18	8	77	57	18	18	.368	.428	.525
Lloyd Waner	OF65	L	24	68	260	32	94	8	3	1	36	5	5	3	.362	.376	.427
George Brickell†	OF61	L	23	68	219	36	65	9	3	1	14	15	20	3	.297	.342	.379
Al Bool	C65	R	32	78	216	30	56	12	4	7	46	25	29	0	.259	.336	.449
Charlie Engle	3B24,SS23,2B10	R	26	67	216	34	57	10	1	0	15	22	20	1	.264	.335	.319
Ira Flagstead	OF40	R	36	44	156	21	39	7	4	2	21	17	9	1	.250	.324	.385
Jim Mosolf	OF12,P1	L	24	40	51	16	17	2	1	0	9	8	7	0	.333	.424	.412
Denny Sothern†	OF13	R	26	17	51	4	9	4	0	1	4	3	4	2	.176	.222	.314
Gus Dugas	OF9	L	23	9	31	8	9	2	0	0	1	7	4	0	.290	.421	.355
Charlie Hargreaves	C11	R	33	11	31	4	7	1	0	0	2	2	1	0	.226	.273	.258
Ben Sankey	SS6,2B4	R	22	13	30	6	5	0	0	0	0	2	3	0	.167	.219	.167
Stu Clarke	2B2	R	24	4	9	2	4	0	1	0	2	1	0	0	.444	.500	.667
Howdie Grosklos	SS1	R	23	2	3	0	1	0	0	0	1	0	0	0	.333	.333	.333

Pitcher	T	Age	G	GS	CG	ShO	IP	H	HR	BB	SO	W-L	Sv	ERA
Ray Kremer	R	37	39	38	18	1	276.0	366	29	63	58	20-12	0	5.02
Larry French	L	22	42	35	21	3	274.2	325	20	89	90	17-18	1	4.36
Erv Brame	R	28	32	29	22	0	235.2	291	21	56	55	17-8	1	4.74
Heinie Meine	R	34	20	16	4	0	117.1	168	6	44	18	6-8	1	6.14
Spades Wood	L	21	9	7	4	0	58.0	61	4	32	23	4-3	0	5.12
Jesse Petty†	L	35	10	7	0	0	41.1	67	8	13	16	1-6	1	8.27
Glenn Spencer	R	24	41	10	5	0	156.2	185	16	63	60	8-9	4	5.40
Steve Swetonic	R	26	23	6	3	1	96.2	107	7	27	35	6-6	5	4.47
Leon Chagnon	R	27	18	4	3	0	62.0	92	9	23	27	0-3	0	6.82
Percy Jones	L	30	9	2	0	0	19.0	26	3	11	3	0-1	0	6.63
Ralph Erickson	L	28	7	0	0	0	14.0	21	1	10	2	1-0	0	7.07
Lil Stoner	R	31	5	0	0	0	5.2	7	2	3	1	0-0	0	4.76
Marty Lang	L	24	2	0	0	0	1.2	9	2	3	2	0-0	0	54.00
Andy Bednar	R	21	2	0	0	0	1.1	4	0	1	1	0-0	0	27.00
Bernie Walter	R	21	1	0	0	0	1.0	0	0	0	1	0-0	0	0.00
Jim Mosolf	R	24	1	0	0	0	0.1	1	0	0	1	0-0	0	27.00

1930 Boston Braves 6th NL 70-84 .455 22.0 GB

Bill McKechnie

Player	Gm by Position	B	Age	G	AB	R	H	2B	3B	HR	RBI	BB	SO	SB	Avg	OBP	Slg
Al Spohrer	C108	R	27	112	356	44	113	22	8	2	37	22	24	3	.317	.361	.441
George Sisler	1B107	L	37	116	431	54	133	15	7	3	67	23	15	7	.309	.346	.397
Freddie Maguire	2B146	R	31	146	516	54	138	21	5	0	52	20	22	4	.267	.297	.328
Buster Chatham	3B92,SS17	R	28	112	404	48	108	20	11	5	56	37	41	8	.267	.332	.408
Rabbit Maranville	SS138,3B4	R	38	142	558	85	157	26	8	2	43	48	23	9	.281	.344	.367
Wally Berger	OF145	R	24	151	555	98	172	27	14	38	119	54	69	3	.310	.375	.614
Lance Richbourg	OF128	L	32	130	529	81	161	23	8	3	54	19	31	13	.304	.331	.395
Jimmy Welsh	OF110	L	27	113	422	51	116	21	9	3	36	29	23	5	.275	.327	.389
Earl Clark	OF63	R	22	82	233	29	69	11	3	3	28	7	22	3	.296	.320	.408
Johnny Neun	1B55	S	29	81	212	39	69	12	2	2	23	21	18	9	.325	.389	.429
Randy Moore	OF34,3B13	L	24	83	191	24	55	9	0	2	34	10	13	3	.288	.323	.366
Bill Cronin	C64	R	27	66	178	19	45	9	1	0	17	4	8	0	.253	.277	.315
Red Rollings	3B28,2B10	L	26	52	123	10	29	6	0	0	10	9	5	2	.236	.288	.285
Gene Robertson	3B17	L	31	21	59	7	11	1	0	0	7	5	3	0	.186	.250	.203
Billy Rhiel	3B13,2B2	R	29	20	47	3	8	4	0	0	4	2	5	0	.170	.204	.255
Bill Dunlap	OF7	R	21	16	29	3	2	1	0	0	0	0	6	0	.069	.069	.103
Hank Gowdy	C15	R	40	16	25	0	5	1	0	0	2	3	1	0	.200	.310	.240
Bernie James	2B7	S	24	8	11	1	2	1	0	0	1	0	1	0	.182	.182	.273
Buzz Boyle	OF1	L	22	1	1	0	0	0	0	0	0	0	1	0	.000	.000	.000
Owen Kahn		R	25	1	0	1	0	0	0	0	0	0	0	0	—	—	—

Pitcher	T	Age	G	GS	CG	ShO	IP	H	HR	BB	SO	W-L	Sv	ERA
Socks Seibold	R	34	36	33	20	1	251.0	288	16	85	70	15-16	2	4.12
Bob Smith	R	35	38	24	14	2	219.2	247	25	85	84	10-14	5	4.26
Tom Zachary†	L	34	24	22	10	1	151.1	192	9	50	57	11-5	0	4.58
Ben Cantwell	R	28	31	21	10	0	173.1	213	15	45	43	9-15	2	4.88
Bill Sherdel†	L	33	21	14	7	0	119.1	131	10	30	26	6-5	1	4.75
Burleigh Grimes†	R	36	11	9	1	0	49.0	72	4	22	15	3-5	0	7.35
Ed Brandt	L	25	41	13	4	1	147.1	168	15	59	65	4-11	1	5.01
Bruce Cunningham	R	24	36	6	2	0	106.2	121	7	41	28	5-6	0	5.48
Fred Frankhouse†	R	26	27	11	3	1	110.2	138	13	43	30	7-6	0	5.61
Ken Jones	R	27	8	1	0	0	19.2	28	1	4	4	0-1	0	5.95
Bob Brown	R	19	3	0	0	0	6.0	10	0	8	1	0-0	0	10.50
Johnny Cooney	L	29	2	0	0	0	7.0	16	2	3	1	0-0	0	18.00

1930 Cincinnati Reds 7th NL 59-95 .383 33.0 GB

Dan Howley

Player	Gm by Position	B	Age	G	AB	R	H	2B	3B	HR	RBI	BB	SO	SB	Avg	OBP	Slg
Clyde Sukeforth	C82	L	28	94	296	30	84	9	3	1	19	17	12	1	.284	.325	.345
Joe Stripp	1B75,3B48	R	27	130	464	74	142	37	6	3	64	51	37	15	.306	.377	.431
Hod Ford	SS74,2B66	R	32	132	424	36	98	16	7	1	34	24	28	2	.231	.272	.309
Tony Cuccinello	3B109,2B15,SS4	R	22	125	443	64	138	22	5	10	78	47	44	5	.312	.380	.451
Leo Durocher	SS103,2B13	R	24	119	354	31	86	15	3	3	32	20	45	0	.243	.287	.328
Curt Walker	OF120	L	33	134	472	74	145	26	11	8	51	64	30	4	.307	.391	.460
Bob Meusel	OF112	R	33	113	443	62	128	30	8	10	62	26	63	9	.289	.330	.460
Harry Heilmann	OF106,1B19	R	35	142	459	79	153	43	6	19	91	64	50	2	.333	.416	.577
Evar Swanson	OF71	R	27	95	301	43	93	15	3	2	22	11	17	4	.309	.335	.399
Johnny Gooch	C79	S	32	82	276	29	67	10	3	2	30	27	15	0	.243	.315	.322
Marty Callaghan	OF54	L	30	79	225	28	62	9	2	0	16	19	25	1	.276	.335	.333
Pat Crawford†	2B54,1B13	L	28	76	224	24	65	7	1	3	26	23	10	2	.290	.359	.371
George Kelly†	1B50	R	34	51	188	18	54	10	1	5	35	7	20	1	.287	.313	.431
Hughie Critz†	2B28	R	29	28	104	15	24	3	2	0	11	6	6	1	.231	.273	.298
Ethan Allen†	OF15	R	26	21	46	10	10	1	0	3	7	5	2	1	.217	.294	.435
Nick Cullop	OF5	R	29	7	22	2	4	0	0	1	5	1	9	0	.182	.217	.318
Chuck Dressen	3B10,2B3	R	31	33	19	0	4	0	0	0	1	1	3	0	.211	.250	.211
Lena Styles	C5,1B1	R	30	7	12	2	3	0	1	0	1	1	2	0	.250	.357	.417
Harry Riconda		R	33	1	1	0	0	0	0	0	0	0	0	0	.000	.000	.000

Pitcher	T	Age	G	GS	CG	ShO	IP	H	HR	BB	SO	W-L	Sv	ERA
Benny Frey	R	24	44	28	14	2	245.0	295	15	62	43	11-18	1	4.70
Red Lucas	R	28	33	28	18	1	210.2	270	15	44	53	14-16	1	5.38
Larry Benton†	R	32	35	22	9	0	177.2	246	7	45	47	7-12	1	5.12
Eppa Rixey	L	39	32	21	5	0	164.0	207	11	47	37	9-13	0	5.10
Ray Kolp	R	35	37	19	5	2	168.1	180	10	34	40	7-12	3	4.22
Jakie May	L	34	26	18	5	1	112.1	147	6	41	44	3-11	0	5.77
Pete Donohue†	R	29	8	5	2	0	34.1	53	0	13	4	1-3	1	6.29
Ownie Carroll†	R	27	3	2	1	0	14.0	17	3	3	0	0-1	0	4.50
Al Eckert	L	24	2	1	0	0	5.0	7	0	4	1	0-1	0	7.20
Biff Wysong	L	25	1	1	0	0	2.1	6	0	3	1	0-1	0	19.29
Si Johnson	R	23	35	3	0	0	78.1	86	5	31	47	3-1	0	4.94
Archie Campbell	R	26	23	3	1	0	58.0	71	2	31	19	2-4	4	5.43
Ken Ash	R	28	16	1	1	0	39.1	37	1	16	15	2-0	0	3.43
Doug McWeeny	R	33	8	2	0	0	25.2	28	0	20	10	0-2	0	7.36

1930 Philadelphia Phillies 8th NL 52-102 .338 40.0 GB

Burt Shotton

Player	Gm by Position	B	Age	G	AB	R	H	2B	3B	HR	RBI	BB	SO	SB	Avg	OBP	Slg
Spud Davis	C96	R	25	106	329	41	103	16	1	14	65	17	20	1	.313	.349	.495
Don Hurst	1B96,OF7	L	24	119	391	78	128	19	3	17	78	46	22	6	.327	.401	.522
Fresco Thompson	2B112	R	28	122	478	77	135	34	4	4	46	35	29	7	.282	.331	.395
Pinky Whitney	3B148	R	25	149	606	87	207	41	5	8	117	40	41	3	.342	.383	.465
Tommy Thevenow	SS156	R	26	156	573	57	164	21	1	0	78	23	26	1	.286	.316	.326
Chuck Klein	OF156	L	25	156	648	158	250	59	8	40	170	54	50	4	.386	.436	.687
Lefty O'Doul	OF131	L	33	140	528	122	202	37	7	22	97	63	21	3	.383	.453	.604
Denny Sothern†	OF84	R	26	90	347	66	97	26	1	5	36	22	37	6	.280	.326	.403
Bernie Friberg	2B44,OF35,SS12*	R	30	105	331	62	113	21	1	4	42	47	35	1	.341	.425	.447
Monk Sherlock	1B70,2B5,OF1	R	25	92	299	51	97	18	2	0	38	27	28	0	.324	.380	.398
George Brickell†	OF53	L	23	53	240	33	59	12	6	0	17	13	21	1	.246	.290	.346
Tony Rensa†	C49	R	28	54	172	31	49	11	2	3	31	10	18	0	.285	.328	.424
Harry McCurdy	C41	L	30	80	148	23	49	6	2	1	25	15	12	0	.331	.393	.419
Tripp Sigman	OF19	L	31	52	100	15	27	4	1	4	6	6	9	1	.270	.324	.450
Cy Williams	OF3	L	42	21	17	1	8	2	0	0	2	4	3	0	.471	.571	.588
Jim Spotts	C2	R	21	3	2	1	0	0	0	0	0	0	1	0	.000	.000	.000

B. Friberg, 8 G at 3B

Pitcher	T	Age	G	GS	CG	ShO	IP	H	HR	BB	SO	W-L	Sv	ERA
Ray Benge	R	28	38	29	14	0	225.2	305	21	81	70	11-15	1	5.70
Phil Collins	R	28	47	25	17	1	239.0	287	22	86	87	16-11	3	4.78
Leo Sweetland	L	28	34	25	8	1	167.0	271	24	60	36	7-15	0	7.71
Claude Willoughby	R	31	41	24	5	1	153.0	241	17	68	38	4-17	1	7.59
Hap Collard	R	31	30	15	4	0	127.0	188	15	39	25	6-12	0	6.80
Hal Elliott	R	31	48	11	2	0	117.1	191	7	58	37	6-11	0	7.67
Harry Smythe	L	25	25	3	0	0	49.2	84	3	31	9	0-3	2	7.79
Snipe Hansen	L	23	22	9	1	0	84.1	123	8	38	25	0-7	0	6.72
Chet Nichols	R	32	16	5	1	0	59.2	76	8	16	15	1-2	0	6.79
Buz Phillips	R	26	14	1	0	0	43.2	68	6	18	9	0-0	0	8.04
Lou Koupal	R	31	13	4	1	0	36.2	52	4	17	11	0-4	0	8.59
Byron Speece	R	33	11	0	0	0	19.2	41	1	4	9	0-0	0	13.27
John Milligan	L	26	9	2	1	0	28.1	26	0	21	7	1-2	0	3.18
Pete Alexander	R	43	9	3	0	0	21.2	40	5	6	6	0-3	0	9.14

»1931 Philadelphia Athletics 1st AL 107-45 .704 —

Connie Mack

Player	Gm by Position	B	Age	G	AB	R	H	2B	3B	HR	RBI	BB	SO	SB	Avg	OBP	Slg
Mickey Cochrane	C117	L	28	122	459	87	160	31	6	17	89	56	21	2	.349	.423	.553
Jimmie Foxx	1B112,3B26,OF1	R	23	139	515	93	150	32	10	30	120	73	84	4	.291	.380	.567
Max Bishop	2B130	L	31	130	497	115	146	30	4	5	37	112	51	3	.294	.426	.400
Jimmy Dykes	3B87,SS15	R	34	101	355	48	97	28	2	3	46	49	47	1	.273	.371	.389
Dib Williams	SS72,2B10,OF1	R	21	86	294	41	79	12	2	6	40	19	21	2	.269	.313	.384
Bing Miller	OF137	R	36	137	534	76	150	43	5	8	77	36	16	5	.281	.338	.425
Al Simmons	OF128	R	29	128	513	105	200	37	13	22	128	47	45	3	.390	.444	.641
Mule Haas	OF102	L	27	102	440	82	142	29	7	8	56	30	29	0	.323	.366	.475
Eric McNair	3B47,2B16,SS13	R	22	79	280	42	76	10	1	5	33	11	19	1	.271	.306	.368
Joe Boley	SS62,2B1	R	34	67	224	26	51	9	3	0	20	15	13	1	.228	.282	.295
Doc Cramer	OF55	L	25	65	223	37	58	8	2	2	20	11	15	2	.260	.301	.341
Phil Todt	1B52	L	29	62	197	23	48	14	2	5	44	8	22	1	.244	.273	.411
Jimmy Moore	OF36	R	28	49	143	18	32	5	1	2	21	11	13	0	.224	.284	.315
Johnny Heving	C40	R	35	42	113	8	27	3	2	1	12	6	8	0	.239	.277	.327
Joe Palmisano	C16,2B1	R	28	19	44	5	10	2	0	0	4	6	3	0	.227	.320	.273
Lou Finney	OF8	L	20	9	24	7	9	0	1	0	3	6	1	0	.375	.516	.458

Pitcher	T	Age	G	GS	CG	ShO	IP	H	HR	BB	SO	W-L	Sv	ERA
Rube Walberg	L	34	44	35	19	1	291.0	298	16	109	106	20-12	3	3.74
Lefty Grove	L	31	41	30	27	4	288.2	249	10	62	175	31-4	5	2.06
George Earnshaw	R	31	43	30	23	3	281.2	255	16	75	152	21-7	6	3.67
Roy Mahaffey	R	28	30	20	8	0	162.1	161	9	82	59	15-4	2	4.21
Waite Hoyt†	R	31	16	14	9	2	111.0	130	9	37	30	10-5	0	4.22
Hank McDonald	R	20	19	10	1	1	70.1	62	3	41	23	2-4	0	3.71
Eddie Rommel	R	33	25	10	8	1	118.0	136	5	27	18	7-5	0	2.97
Bill Shores	R	27	6	2	0	0	16.0	26	3	10	2	0-3	0	5.06
Jim Peterson	R	22	6	1	1	0	13.0	18	0	4	7	0-1	0	6.23
Lew Krausse	R	19	3	1	1	0	11.0	6	2	6	1	1-0	0	4.09
Sol Carter	R	22	2	0	0	0	2.1	1	0	4	1	0-0	0	19.29

1931 New York Yankees 2nd AL 94-59 .614 13.5 GB

Joe McCarthy

Player	Gm by Position	B	Age	G	AB	R	H	2B	3B	HR	RBI	BB	SO	SB	Avg	OBP	Slg
Bill Dickey	C125	L	24	130	477	65	156	17	10	6	78	39	20	2	.327	.378	.442
Lou Gehrig	1B154,OF1	L	28	155	619	163	211	31	15	46	184	117	56	17	.341	.446	.662
Tony Lazzeri	2B90,3B39	R	27	135	484	67	129	27	7	8	83	79	80	18	.267	.371	.401
Joe Sewell	3B121,2B1	L	32	130	484	102	146	22	1	6	64	62	8	1	.302	.391	.388
Lyn Lary	SS155	R	25	155	610	100	171	35	9	10	107	88	54	13	.280	.376	.416
Babe Ruth	OF142,1B1	L	36	145	534	149	199	31	3	46	163	128	51	5	.373	.494	.700
Ben Chapman	OF137,2B11	R	22	149	600	120	189	28	11	17	122	75	77	61	.315	.396	.483
Earle Combs	OF129	L	32	138	563	120	179	31	13	5	58	68	34	11	.318	.394	.446
Sammy Byrd	OF88	R	23	115	248	51	67	18	2	3	32	29	26	5	.270	.349	.395
Jimmie Reese	2B61	L	29	65	245	41	59	10	2	3	26	17	10	2	.241	.293	.335
Red Ruffing	P37,OF1	R	27	48	109	14	36	8	1	3	12	1	13	0	.330	.336	.505
Art Jorgens	C40	R	26	46	100	12	27	1	2	0	14	9	3	0	.270	.330	.320
Cy Perkins	C16	R	35	16	47	3	12	1	0	0	7	1	4	0	.255	.286	.277
Dusty Cooke	OF11	L	24	27	39	10	13	1	0	1	6	8	11	4	.333	.447	.436
Myril Hoag	OF23,3B1	R	23	44	28	6	4	2	0	0	3	1	8	0	.143	.172	.214
Dixie Walker	OF2	L	20	2	10	1	3	2	0	0	1	0	4	0	.300	.300	.500
Red Rolfe	SS1	L	22	1	0	0	0	0	0	0	0	0	0	0	—	—	—

Pitcher	T	Age	G	GS	CG	ShO	IP	H	HR	BB	SO	W-L	Sv	ERA
Red Ruffing	R	27	37	30	19	1	237.0	240	11	87	132	16-14	2	4.41
Lefty Gomez	L	22	40	26	17	1	243.0	206	7	85	150	21-9	3	2.63
Herb Pennock	L	37	25	25	12	1	189.1	247	7	30	65	11-6	0	4.28
Hank Johnson	R	25	40	23	8	0	196.1	176	13	102	106	13-8	4	4.72
Gordon Rhodes	R	23	18	11	4	0	87.0	82	3	52	36	6-3	0	3.41
George Pipgras	R	31	36	14	6	1	137.2	134	8	58	59	7-6	3	3.79
Ed Wells	L	31	27	10	6	0	116.2	130	7	37	34	9-5	2	4.32
Roy Sherid	R	24	17	8	3	0	74.1	94	4	24	39	5-5	2	5.69
Jim Weaver	R	27	17	5	2	0	57.2	66	1	29	28	2-1	0	5.31
Lefty Weinert	L	29	17	0	0	0	24.2	31	2	19	24	2-2	0	6.20
Ivy Andrews	R	24	7	3	1	0	34.1	36	3	8	10	2-0	0	4.19
Lou McEvoy	R	29	6	0	0	0	12.1	19	1	12	3	0-0	1	12.41

1931 Washington Senators 3rd AL 92-62 .597 16.0 GB

Walter Johnson

Player	Gm by Position	B	Age	G	AB	R	H	2B	3B	HR	RBI	BB	SO	SB	Avg	OBP	Slg
Roy Spencer	C145	R	31	145	483	48	133	16	3	1	60	35	21	0	.275	.327	.327
Joe Kuhel	1B139	L	25	139	524	70	141	34	8	8	85	47	45	7	.269	.335	.410
Buddy Myer	2B137	L	27	139	591	114	173	33	11	4	56	58	42	11	.293	.360	.406
Ossie Bluege	3B152,SS1	R	30	152	570	82	155	25	7	8	98	72	50	16	.272	.336	.382
Joe Cronin	SS155	R	24	156	611	103	187	44	13	12	126	81	52	10	.306	.391	.480
Heinie Manush	OF143	L	29	146	616	110	189	41	11	6	70	36	27	3	.307	.351	.438
Sammy West	OF127	L	26	132	526	77	175	43	13	3	91	30	37	6	.333	.369	.481
Sam Rice	OF105	L	41	120	413	81	128	21	8	0	42	35	11	6	.310	.365	.400
Dave Harris	OF60	R	30	77	231	49	72	14	8	5	50	49	38	7	.312	.434	.506
Harry Rice	OF42	L	29	47	162	32	43	5	6	0	15	12	10	2	.265	.320	.370
Jackie Hayes	2B19,3B8,SS3	R	24	38	108	11	24	2	1	0	8	6	4	2	.222	.263	.259
Pinky Hargrave	C25	S	35	40	80	6	26	8	0	1	19	9	12	1	.325	.393	.463
Joe Judge	1B15	L	37	35	74	11	21	3	0	0	9	8	8	0	.284	.354	.324
Cliff Bolton	C13	L	24	23	43	3	11	1	1	0	6	1	5	0	.256	.273	.326
Johnny Gill	OF8	L	26	8	30	2	8	2	1	0	5	1	6	0	.267	.313	.400
Buck Jordan	1B7	L	24	9	18	3	4	2	0	0	1	1	3	0	.222	.263	.333
Bill Andrus	3B2	R	23	3	7	0	0	0	0	0	1	0	1	0	.000	.000	.000
Babe Phelps		L	23	3	3	0	1	0	0	0	0	0	0	0	.333	.333	.333
Nick Altrock		S	54	1	0	0	0	0	0	0	0	1	0	0	—	1.000	—

Pitcher	T	Age	G	GS	CG	ShO	IP	H	HR	BB	SO	W-L	Sv	ERA
Lloyd Brown	L	26	42	32	15	1	258.2	256	13	79	79	15-14	0	3.20
General Crowder	R	32	44	26	13	1	234.1	255	13	72	85	18-11	2	3.88
Firpo Marberry	R	32	45	25	11	2	219.0	211	13	63	88	16-4	7	3.45
Sad Sam Jones	R	38	25	24	8	1	148.0	185	10	47	58	9-10	1	4.32
Carl Fischer	L	25	46	23	7	0	191.0	207	12	80	96	13-9	3	4.38
Ad Liska	R	24	2	1	0	0	4.0	9	0	1	2	0-1	0	6.75
Bump Hadley	R	26	55	11	2	1	179.2	145	4	92	124	11-10	8	3.06
Bobby Burke	L	24	30	13	3	1	128.2	124	6	50	38	8-3	2	4.27
Walt Tauscher	R	29	6	0	0	0	12.0	24	2	4	5	1-0	0	7.50
Montie Weaver	R	25	3	1	1	0	10.0	11	0	6	6	1-0	0	4.50
Walt Masters	R	24	3	0	0	0	9.0	7	0	4	1	0-0	1	2.00

1931 Cleveland Indians 4th AL 78-76 .506 30.0 GB

Roger Peckinpaugh

Player	Gm by Position	B	Age	G	AB	R	H	2B	3B	HR	RBI	BB	SO	SB	Avg	OBP	Slg
Luke Sewell	C105	R	30	108	375	45	103	30	4	1	53	36	17	1	.275	.341	.384
Eddie Morgan	1B117,3B3	R	27	131	462	87	162	33	4	11	86	83	46	4	.351	.451	.511
Johnny Hodapp	2B121	R	25	122	468	71	138	19	4	2	56	27	23	2	.295	.336	.365
Willie Kamm†	3B114	R	31	114	410	68	121	31	4	0	66	64	13	13	.295	.392	.390
Ed Montague	SS64	R	25	64	193	27	55	8	3	1	26	21	22	3	.285	.358	.373
Earl Averill	OF155	L	29	155	627	140	209	36	10	32	143	68	38	9	.333	.404	.576
Joe Vosmik	OF147	R	21	149	591	80	189	36	14	7	117	38	30	7	.320	.363	.464
Dick Porter	OF109,2B1	L	29	114	414	82	129	24	3	1	38	56	36	6	.312	.395	.391
Johnny Burnett	SS63,2B35,3B21*	L	26	111	427	85	128	25	5	1	52	39	25	5	.300	.360	.389
Glenn Myatt	C58	L	33	65	195	21	48	14	2	1	29	21	13	2	.246	.319	.354
Bibb Falk	OF33	L	32	79	161	30	49	13	1	2	28	17	13	1	.304	.371	.435
Bob Seeds	OF33,1B2	R	24	48	134	26	41	4	1	1	10	11	11	1	.306	.359	.373
Lew Fonseca†	1B26	R	32	26	108	21	40	9	1	1	14	8	7	3	.370	.419	.500
Odell Hale	3B15,2B10,SS1	R	22	25	92	14	26	2	4	1	5	8	8	2	.283	.340	.424
Bill Hunnefield†	SS21,2B1	S	32	21	71	13	17	4	1	0	4	9	4	3	.239	.325	.324
Jonah Goldman	SS30	R	24	30	62	0	8	1	0	0	3	4	6	1	.129	.182	.145
George Detore	3B13,SS10,2B3	R	24	30	56	3	15	6	0	0	7	8	2	0	.268	.359	.375
Bruce Connatser	1B12	R	28	12	49	5	14	3	0	0	4	2	3	0	.286	.327	.347
Charlie Jamieson	OF7	L	38	28	43	7	13	2	1	0	4	5	1	1	.302	.375	.395
Moe Berg	C8	R	29	10	13	1	1	1	0	0	0	1	1	0	.077	.143	.154
Joe Sprinz	C1	R	28	1	3	0	0	0	0	0	0	0	0	0	.000	.000	.000

J. Burnett, 1 G at OF

Pitcher	T	Age	G	GS	CG	ShO	IP	H	HR	BB	SO	W-L	Sv	ERA
Wes Ferrell	R	23	40	35	27	2	276.1	276	9	130	123	22-12	3	3.75
Willis Hudlin	R	25	44	34	15	1	254.1	313	14	88	83	15-14	4	4.60
Clint Brown	R	27	39	33	12	2	233.1	284	10	55	50	11-15	0	4.71
Mel Harder	R	21	40	24	9	0	194.0	229	8	72	63	13-14	1	4.36
Sarge Connally	R	32	17	9	5	0	85.2	87	7	50	37	5-5	1	4.20
Jake Miller	L	33	10	5	1	0	41.1	45	2	19	17	2-1	0	4.35
Pete Appleton	R	27	29	4	3	0	79.2	100	2	29	25	4-4	0	4.63
Roxie Lawson	R	25	17	3	0	0	55.2	72	5	36	20	0-2	0	7.60
Fay Thomas	R	26	16	2	0	0	48.2	63	2	32	25	2-4	0	5.18
Milt Shoffner	L	25	12	4	1	0	41.0	55	4	26	12	2-3	0	7.24
Oral Hildebrand	R	24	5	2	2	0	26.2	25	0	13	6	2-1	0	4.39
Belve Bean	R	26	4	0	0	0	7.0	11	0	4	3	0-1	0	6.43
Howard Craghead	R	23	4	0	0	0	5.2	8	0	2	2	0-0	0	6.35
Pete Donohue†	R	30	2	0	0	0	5.1	9	1	5	4	0-0	0	8.44

1931 St. Louis Browns 5th AL 63-91 .409 45.0 GB

Bill Killefer

Player	Gm by Position	B	Age	G	AB	R	H	2B	3B	HR	RBI	BB	SO	SB	Avg	OBP	Slg
Rick Ferrell	C108	R	25	117	386	47	118	30	4	3	57	56	12	2	.306	.394	.427
Jack Burns	1B143	L	23	144	570	75	148	27	7	4	70	42	58	19	.260	.312	.353
Ski Melillo	2B151	R	31	151	617	89	189	34	11	2	75	37	29	7	.306	.346	.407
Red Kress	3B84,OF40,SS38*	R	24	150	605	87	188	46	8	16	114	46	48	3	.311	.360	.493
Jim Levey	SS139	S	24	139	498	53	104	19	2	5	38	35	83	13	.209	.264	.285
Goose Goslin	OF151	L	30	151	591	114	194	42	10	24	105	80	41	9	.328	.412	.555
Fred Schulte	OF134	R	30	134	553	100	168	32	7	9	65	56	49	6	.304	.369	.436
Tom Jenkins	OF58	L	33	81	230	20	61	7	2	3	25	17	25	1	.265	.316	.352
Lin Storti	3B67,2B7	S	24	86	273	32	60	15	4	3	26	15	50	0	.220	.263	.337
Larry Bettencourt	OF58	R	25	74	206	27	53	9	2	3	26	31	35	4	.257	.357	.364
Benny Bengough	C37	R	32	40	140	6	35	4	1	0	12	4	4	0	.250	.271	.293
Earl McNeely	OF36	R	33	49	102	12	23	4	0	0	15	9	5	4	.225	.288	.265
Ed Grimes	3B22,2B4,SS3	R	25	43	57	9	15	1	2	0	5	9	3	1	.263	.364	.351
Russ Young	C16	S	28	16	34	2	4	0	0	1	2	2	4	0	.118	.167	.206
Frank Waddey	OF7	L	25	14	22	3	6	1	0	0	2	2	3	0	.273	.333	.318
Buck Stanton	OF1	L	25	13	15	3	3	2	0	0	0	0	6	0	.200	.200	.333
Jack Crouch	C7	R	28	8	12	0	0	0	0	0	1	0	4	0	.000	.000	.000
Frank O'Rourke	SS2,1B1	R	36	8	9	0	2	0	0	0	0	0	1	1	.222	.222	.222
Nap Kloza	OF3	R	27	3	7	1	1	0	0	0	0	1	4	0	.143	.250	.143

R. Kress, 10 G at 1B

Pitcher	T	Age	G	GS	CG	ShO	IP	H	HR	BB	SO	W-L	Sv	ERA
Sam Gray	R	33	43	37	13	0	258.0	323	20	54	88	11-24	2	5.09
Lefty Stewart	L	30	36	33	20	1	258.0	287	17	85	89	14-17	0	4.40
George Blaeholder	R	27	35	32	13	0	226.1	280	15	56	79	11-15	0	4.53
Dick Coffman	R	24	32	17	11	2	169.1	159	10	51	39	9-13	1	3.88
Rip Collins	R	35	17	14	2	0	107.0	130	5	38	34	5-5	0	3.79
Wally Hebert	L	23	23	13	5	1	103.0	128	11	43	26	6-7	0	5.07
Bob Cooney	R	23	5	4	1	0	39.1	46	1	20	13	0-3	0	4.12
Chad Kimsey	R	24	42	1	0	0	94.1	121	1	27	27	4-6	7	4.39
Rollie Stiles	R	24	34	2	0	0	81.0	112	2	60	32	3-1	0	7.22
Garland Braxton†	L	31	11	1	0	0	18.0	27	2	10	7	0-0	0	10.50
Fred Stiely	L	30	4	0	0	0	6.2	7	0	3	2	0-0	0	6.75
Jess Doyle	R	33	1	0	0	0	1.0	3	0	1	0	0-0	0	27.00

650 Seasons: Team Rosters

1931 Boston Red Sox 6th AL 62-90 .408 45.0 GB

Shano Collins

Player	Gm by Position	B	Age	G	AB	R	H	2B	3B	HR	RBI	BB	SO	SB	Avg	OBP	Slg
Charlie Berry	C102	R	28	111	357	41	101	16	2	6	49	29	38	4	.283	.337	.389
Bill Sweeney	1B124	R	26	131	498	48	147	30	3	1	58	20	30	5	.295	.322	.373
Rabbit Warstler	2B42,SS19	R	27	66	181	20	44	5	3	0	10	15	27	2	.243	.308	.304
Otto Miller	3B75,2B25	R	30	107	389	38	106	12	1	0	43	15	20	1	.272	.301	.308
Hal Rhyne	SS147	R	32	147	565	75	154	34	3	0	51	57	41	3	.273	.341	.343
Earl Webb	OF151	L	33	151	589	96	196	67	3	14	103	70	51	2	.333	.404	.528
Tom Oliver	OF148	R	28	148	586	52	162	35	5	0	70	25	17	4	.276	.307	.353
Jack Rothrock	OF79,2B23,1B8*	S	26	133	475	81	132	32	3	4	42	47	48	13	.278	.343	.383
Urbane Pickering	3B74,2B16	R	32	103	341	48	86	13	4	9	52	33	53	3	.252	.318	.393
Al Van Camp	OF59,1B25	R	27	101	324	34	89	15	4	0	33	20	24	3	.275	.319	.346
Ed Connolly	C41	R	22	42	93	3	7	1	0	0	3	5	18	0	.075	.131	.086
Bobby Reeves	2B29,P1	R	27	36	84	11	14	2	2	0	1	14	16	0	.167	.293	.238
Muddy Ruel†	C30	R	35	33	83	6	25	5	0	0	6	9	6	0	.301	.370	.361
Tom Winsett	OF8	L	21	64	76	6	15	1	0	1	7	4	21	0	.197	.247	.250
Marty McManus†	3B11,2B7	R	31	17	62	8	18	4	0	1	9	8	1	1	.290	.371	.403
Marv Olson	2B15	R	24	15	53	8	10	1	0	0	5	9	3	0	.189	.306	.208
Gene Rye	OF10	L	24	17	39	3	7	0	0	0	1	2	5	0	.179	.220	.179
Ollie Marquardt	2B13	R	28	17	39	4	7	1	0	0	2	3	4	0	.179	.238	.205
Russ Scarritt	OF9	L	28	10	39	2	6	1	0	0	1	2	2	0	.154	.195	.179
George Stumpf	OF7	L	20	7	28	2	7	1	1	0	4	1	2	0	.250	.276	.357
Howie Storie	C6	R	20	6	17	2	2	0	0	0	0	3	2	0	.118	.250	.118
John Smith	1B4	S	24	4	15	2	2	0	0	0	1	2	1	1	.133	.235	.133
Pat Creeden	2B2	L	25	5	8	0	0	0	0	0	0	1	3	0	.000	.111	.000
Bill McWilliams		R	20	2	2	0	0	0	0	0	0	0	1	0	.000	.000	.000
Johnny Lucas	OF2	R	28	3	2	0	0	0	0	0	0	0	1	0	.000	.000	.000
Bill Marshall		R	20	1	0	1	0	0	0	0	0	0	0	0	—	—	—

J. Rothrock, 2 G at 3B, 1 G at SS

Pitcher	T	Age	G	GS	CG	ShO	IP	H	HR	BB	SO	W-L	Sv	ERA
Danny MacFayden	R	26	35	32	17	2	230.2	263	4	79	74	16-12	0	4.02
Jack Russell	R	25	36	31	13	0	232.0	298	7	65	45	10-18	0	5.16
Milt Gaston	R	35	23	18	4	0	119.0	137	4	41	33	2-13	0	4.46
Wilcy Moore	R	34	53	15	8	1	185.1	195	7	55	37	11-13	10	3.88
Hod Lisenbee	R	32	41	17	6	0	164.2	190	13	49	42	5-12	0	5.19
Ed Durham	R	22	38	15	7	2	165.1	175	9	50	53	8-10	0	4.25
Ed Morris	R	31	37	14	3	0	130.2	131	4	74	46	5-7	0	4.75
Bob Kline	R	21	28	10	3	0	98.0	110	3	35	25	5-5	0	4.41
Jim Brillheart	L	27	11	1	0	0	19.2	27	2	15	7	0-0	0	5.49
Jud McLaughlin	L	19	9	0	0	0	12.0	23	1	8	3	0-0	0	12.00
Walter Murphy	R	23	2	0	0	0	2.0	4	0	1	0	0-0	0	9.00
Bobby Reeves	R	27	1	0	0	0	7.1	6	0	1	0	0-0	0	3.68

1931 Detroit Tigers 7th AL 61-93 .396 47.0 GB

Bucky Harris

Player	Gm by Position	B	Age	G	AB	R	H	2B	3B	HR	RBI	BB	SO	SB	Avg	OBP	Slg
Ray Hayworth	C88	R	27	88	273	28	70	10	3	0	25	19	27	0	.256	.307	.315
Dale Alexander	1B126,OF4	R	28	135	517	75	168	47	3	3	87	64	35	5	.325	.401	.445
Charlie Gehringer	2B78,1B9	L	28	101	383	67	119	24	5	4	53	29	15	13	.311	.359	.431
Marty McManus†	3B79,2B21,1B1	R	31	107	362	39	98	17	3	3	53	49	22	7	.271	.361	.359
Billy Rogell	SS48	S	26	48	185	21	56	12	3	2	24	24	17	8	.303	.383	.432
Roy Johnson	OF150	L	28	151	621	107	173	37	19	8	55	72	51	33	.279	.355	.438
John Stone	OF147	L	25	147	584	86	191	28	11	10	76	56	48	13	.327	.388	.464
Hub Walker	OF66	L	24	90	252	27	72	13	1	0	16	23	25	10	.286	.355	.345
Marv Owen	3B37,SS37,1B27*	R	25	105	377	35	84	11	6	3	39	29	38	2	.223	.282	.308
Mark Koenig	2B55,SS35,P3	S	26	106	364	33	92	24	4	1	39	14	12	8	.253	.282	.349
Gee Walker	OF44	R	23	59	189	20	56	17	2	1	28	14	21	10	.296	.345	.423
Frank Doljack	OF54	R	23	63	187	20	52	13	3	4	20	15	17	3	.278	.335	.444
Nolen Richardson	3B38	R	28	38	148	13	40	9	2	0	16	6	3	2	.270	.299	.358
Johnny Grabowski	C39	R	31	40	136	9	32	7	1	1	14	6	19	0	.235	.268	.324
Wally Schang	C30	S	41	30	76	9	14	2	0	0	2	14	11	1	.184	.311	.211
Bill Akers	SS21,2B2	R	26	29	66	5	13	2	0	2	3	7	6	0	.197	.274	.288
Louis Brower	SS20,2B2	R	30	21	62	3	10	1	0	0	6	8	5	1	.161	.278	.177
George Quellich	OF13	R	28	13	54	6	12	5	0	1	11	3	4	1	.222	.263	.370
Muddy Ruel†	C14	R	35	14	50	1	6	1	0	0	3	5	1	0	.120	.200	.140
Joe Dugan	3B5	R	34	8	17	1	4	0	0	0	0	0	3	0	.235	.235	.235
Gene Desautels	C3	R	24	3	11	1	1	0	0	0	1	0	1	0	.091	.091	.091
Ivey Shiver	OF2	R	24	2	9	2	1	0	0	0	0	0	3	0	.111	.111	.111
Bucky Harris	2B3	R	34	4	8	1	1	1	0	0	0	1	1	0	.125	.222	.250

M. Owen, 4 G at 2B

Pitcher	T	Age	G	GS	CG	ShO	IP	H	HR	BB	SO	W-L	Sv	ERA
Earl Whitehill	L	31	34	34	22	0	271.2	287	22	118	81	13-16	0	4.07
Vic Sorrell	R	30	35	32	19	1	245.0	267	8	114	99	13-14	1	4.15
Tommy Bridges	R	24	35	23	8	2	173.0	182	13	108	105	8-16	0	4.99
George Uhle	R	32	29	18	15	2	193.0	190	10	49	63	11-12	2	3.50
Chief Hogsett	L	27	22	12	5	0	112.1	150	8	33	47	3-9	2	5.93
Waite Hoyt†	R	31	16	12	5	0	92.0	124	2	32	10	3-8	0	5.87
Orlin Collier	R	24	2	2	0	0	10.1	17	0	7	3	0-1	0	7.84
Art Herring	R	25	35	16	9	0	165.0	186	8	67	64	7-13	1	4.31
Charlie Sullivan	R	28	31	4	2	0	99.0	109	6	46	28	3-2	0	4.73
Whit Wyatt	R	23	4	1	1	0	20.2	30	2	12	8	0-2	0	8.71
Mark Koenig	R	26	3	0	0	0	7.0	7	0	11	3	0-0	0	6.43

1931 Chicago White Sox 8th AL 56-97 .366 51.5 GB

Donie Bush

Player	Gm by Position	B	Age	G	AB	R	H	2B	3B	HR	RBI	BB	SO	SB	Avg	OBP	Slg
Bennie Tate	C85	L	29	89	273	27	73	12	3	0	22	26	10	1	.267	.331	.333
Lu Blue	1B155	S	34	155	589	119	179	23	15	1	62	127	60	13	.304	.430	.399
John Kerr	2B117,3B7,SS1	R	32	128	444	51	119	17	2	2	50	35	22	9	.268	.324	.329
Billy Sullivan	3B83,OF2,1B1	L	20	92	363	48	100	16	5	2	33	20	14	4	.275	.315	.364
Bill Cissell	SS83,2B23,3B1	R	27	109	409	42	90	13	5	1	46	16	26	18	.220	.256	.284
Carl Reynolds	OF109	R	28	118	462	71	134	24	14	6	77	24	26	17	.290	.333	.442
Cliff Watwood	OF102,1B4	L	25	128	367	51	104	16	6	1	47	56	30	9	.283	.380	.368
Lew Fonseca†	OF95,2B21,1B2*	R	32	121	465	65	139	26	5	2	71	32	22	4	.299	.348	.389
Bob Fothergill	OF74	R	33	108	312	25	88	9	4	3	56	17	17	2	.282	.323	.365
Luke Appling	SS76,2B1	R	24	96	297	36	69	13	4	1	28	29	27	9	.232	.303	.313
Frank Grube	C81	R	26	88	265	29	58	13	2	1	24	22	22	2	.219	.284	.294
Irv Jeffries	3B61,2B6,SS5	R	25	79	223	29	50	10	0	2	16	14	9	3	.224	.270	.296
Mel Simons	OF59	L	30	68	189	24	52	9	0	0	12	12	17	1	.275	.318	.323
Ike Eichrodt	OF32	R	28	34	117	9	25	5	1	0	15	1	8	0	.214	.220	.274
Smead Jolley	OF23	L	29	54	110	5	33	11	0	3	28	7	4	0	.300	.353	.482
Willie Kamm†	3B18	R	31	18	59	9	15	4	1	0	9	7	6	1	.254	.333	.356
Bill Norman	OF17	R	20	24	55	7	10	2	0	0	6	4	10	0	.182	.237	.218
Bruce Campbell	OF4	L	21	4	17	4	7	2	0	2	5	0	4	0	.412	.444	.882
Butch Henline	C4	R	36	11	15	2	1	1	0	0	2	2	4	0	.067	.176	.133
Hank Garrity	C7	R	23	8	14	0	3	1	0	0	2	1	2	0	.214	.267	.286

L. Fonseca, 1 G at 3B

Pitcher	T	Age	G	GS	CG	ShO	IP	H	HR	BB	SO	W-L	Sv	ERA
Tommy Thomas	R	31	42	36	11	2	245.1	296	17	69	71	10-14	2	4.73
Pat Caraway	L	25	51	32	11	1	220.0	268	17	101	55	10-24	2	6.22
Vic Frasier	R	26	46	29	13	2	254.0	258	11	127	87	13-15	4	4.46
Ted Lyons	R	30	22	12	7	0	101.0	117	6	33	16	4-6	0	4.01
Bob Weiland	L	25	15	8	3	0	75.0	75	3	46	38	2-7	0	5.16
Red Faber	R	42	44	19	5	1	184.0	210	11	57	49	10-14	1	3.82
Jim Moore	R	27	33	4	0	0	83.2	93	3	27	15	0-2	0	4.95
Hal McKain	R	24	27	8	3	0	112.0	134	10	57	39	6-9	0	5.71
Garland Braxton†	L	31	17	3	0	0	47.1	71	1	23	28	0-3	1	6.85
Grant Bowler	R	23	13	3	1	0	35.1	40	1	24	15	0-1	0	5.35
Biggs Wehde	R	24	8	0	0	0	16.0	19	0	10	3	1-0	0	6.75
Lou Garland	R	25	7	2	0	0	16.2	30	2	14	4	0-2	0	10.26

»1931 St. Louis Cardinals 1st NL 101-53 .656 —

Gabby Street

Player	Gm by Position	B	Age	G	AB	R	H	2B	3B	HR	RBI	BB	SO	SB	Avg	OBP	Slg
Jimmie Wilson	C110	R	30	115	383	45	105	20	2	0	51	28	15	5	.274	.332	.337
Jim Bottomley	1B93	L	31	108	382	73	133	34	5	9	75	34	24	3	.348	.403	.534
Frankie Frisch	2B129	S	32	131	518	96	161	24	4	4	82	45	13	28	.311	.368	.396
Sparky Adams	3B138,SS6	R	36	143	608	97	178	46	5	1	40	42	24	16	.293	.340	.390
Charlie Gelbert	SS130	R	25	131	447	61	129	29	5	1	62	54	31	7	.289	.365	.383
George Watkins	OF129	L	31	131	503	93	145	30	13	13	51	31	66	15	.288	.336	.477
Chick Hafey	OF118	R	28	122	450	94	157	35	8	16	95	39	43	11	.349	.404	.569
Pepper Martin	OF110	R	27	123	413	68	124	32	8	7	75	30	40	16	.300	.351	.467
Ripper Collins	1B68,OF3	S	27	89	279	34	84	20	10	4	59	18	24	1	.301	.350	.487
Gus Mancuso	C56	R	25	67	187	13	49	16	1	1	23	18	13	2	.262	.327	.374
Ernie Orsatti	OF45,1B1	L	28	70	158	27	46	16	6	0	19	14	16	1	.291	.349	.468
Wally Roettger†	OF42	R	28	45	151	16	43	12	2	0	17	9	14	0	.285	.337	.391
Jake Flowers†	SS24,2B21,3B1	R	29	45	137	19	34	11	1	2	19	9	6	7	.248	.295	.387
Taylor Douthit†	OF36	R	30	36	133	21	44	11	2	1	21	11	9	1	.331	.386	.466
Andy High	3B23,2B19	L	33	63	131	20	35	6	1	0	19	24	4	0	.267	.389	.328
Ray Blades	OF20	R	34	35	67	10	19	4	0	1	5	10	7	1	.284	.392	.388
Mike Gonzalez	C12	R	40	15	19	1	2	0	0	0	3	0	3	0	.105	.105	.105
Tony Kaufmann	P15,OF1	R	30	20	18	1	2	0	0	0	0	1	3	0	.111	.158	.111
Joe Benes	SS6,2B2,3B1	R	30	10	12	1	2	0	0	0	2	2	1	0	.167	.333	.167
Ray Cunningham	3B3	R	26	3	4	0	0	0	0	0	1	0	0	0	.000	.000	.000
Eddie Delker	3B1	R	25	1	2	0	1	1	0	0	2	0	0	0	.500	.500	1.000
Joel Hunt	OF1	R	25	4	1	2	0	0	0	0	0	0	1	0	.000	.000	.000
Gabby Street	C1	R	48	1	1	0	0	0	0	0	0	0	0	0	.000	.000	.000

Pitcher	T	Age	G	GS	CG	ShO	IP	H	HR	BB	SO	W-L	Sv	ERA
Wild Bill Hallahan	L	28	37	30	16	3	248.2	242	10	112	159	19-9	4	3.29
Burleigh Grimes	R	37	29	28	17	3	212.1	240	11	59	67	17-9	0	3.65
Flint Rhem	R	30	33	26	10	2	207.1	214	17	60	72	11-10	1	3.56
Syl Johnson	R	30	32	24	12	2	186.0	186	9	29	82	11-9	2	3.00
Paul Derringer	R	24	35	23	15	4	211.2	225	9	65	134	18-8	2	3.36
Jesse Haines	R	37	19	17	8	2	122.1	134	2	28	27	12-3	0	3.02
Jim Lindsey	R	35	35	2	1	1	74.2	77	2	45	32	6-4	7	2.77
Allyn Stout	R	26	30	3	1	0	72.2	87	2	34	40	6-0	3	4.21
Tony Kaufmann	R	30	15	1	0	0	49.0	65	3	17	13	1-1	1	6.06

1931 New York Giants 2nd NL 87-65 .572 13.0 GB

John McGraw

Player	Gm by Position	B	Age	G	AB	R	H	2B	3B	HR	RBI	BB	SO	SB	Avg	OBP	Slg
Shanty Hogan	C113	R	25	123	396	42	119	17	1	12	65	29	29	1	.301	.354	.439
Bill Terry	1B153	L	34	153	611	121	213	43	20	9	112	47	36	8	.349	.397	.529
Bill Hunnefield†	2B56,SS5	S	32	64	196	23	53	5	0	1	17	9	16	3	.270	.302	.311
Johnny Vergez	3B152	R	24	152	565	67	157	24	2	13	81	29	65	11	.278	.320	.396
Travis Jackson	SS145	R	27	145	555	65	172	26	10	5	71	36	23	13	.310	.353	.420
Mel Ott	OF137	L	22	138	497	104	145	23	8	29	115	80	44	10	.292	.392	.545
Freddy Leach	OF125	L	33	129	515	75	159	30	5	6	61	29	9	4	.309	.348	.421
Ethan Allen	OF77	R	27	94	298	58	98	18	2	5	43	15	15	6	.329	.363	.453
Freddy Lindstrom	OF73,2B4	R	25	78	303	38	91	12	6	5	36	26	12	5	.300	.356	.429
Chick Fullis	OF68,2B9	R	27	89	302	61	99	15	2	3	28	23	13	13	.328	.383	.421
Hughie Critz	2B54	R	30	66	238	33	69	7	2	4	17	8	17	4	.290	.313	.387
Ed Marshall	2B47,SS11,3B3	R	25	68	194	15	39	6	2	0	10	8	8	1	.201	.233	.253
Bob O'Farrell	C80	R	34	85	174	11	39	8	3	1	19	21	23	0	.224	.311	.322
Sam Leslie	1B6	L	25	53	53	11	16	4	0	3	5	1	2	3	.302	.315	.547
Gil English	3B3	R	21	3	8	0	0	0	0	0	0	1	3	0	.000	.111	.000
Jo-Jo Moore	OF1	L	22	4	8	0	2	1	0	0	3	0	1	1	.250	.250	.375
Francis Healy	C4	R	20	6	7	1	1	0	0	0	0	0	0	0	.143	.143	.143

Pitcher	T	Age	G	GS	CG	ShO	IP	H	HR	BB	SO	W-L	Sv	ERA
F. Fitzsimmons	R	29	35	33	19	4	253.2	242	16	62	78	18-11	0	3.05
Carl Hubbell	L	28	36	30	21	4	248.0	211	14	67	155	14-12	3	2.65
Bill Walker	L	27	37	28	19	6	239.1	212	6	64	121	16-9	3	2.26
Clarence Mitchell	L	40	27	25	13	0	190.1	221	12	52	39	13-11	0	4.07
Jim Mooney	L	24	10	8	6	2	71.2	71	1	16	38	7-1	0	2.01
Jack Berly	R	28	27	11	4	1	111.1	114	6	51	45	7-8	0	3.88
Joe Heving	R	30	22	0	0	0	42.1	48	4	11	26	1-6	3	4.89
Bill Morrell	R	38	20	7	2	0	66.0	83	4	27	16	5-3	1	4.36
Tiny Chaplin	R	25	16	3	1	0	42.1	39	2	16	7	3-0	1	3.19
Roy Parmelee	R	24	13	5	4	0	58.2	47	1	33	30	2-2	0	3.68
Hal Schumacher	R	20	8	2	1	0	18.1	31	3	14	11	1-1	1	10.80
Pete Donohue†	R	30	4	1	0	0	11.1	14	1	4	4	0-1	0	5.56
Emil Planeta	R	22	2	0	0	0	5.1	7	0	4	0	0-0	0	10.13
Ray Lucas	R	22	1	0	0	0	2.0	1	1	1	0	0-0	0	4.50

1931 Chicago Cubs 3rd NL 84-70 .545 17.0 GB

Rogers Hornsby

Player	Gm by Position	B	Age	G	AB	R	H	2B	3B	HR	RBI	BB	SO	SB	Avg	OBP	Slg
Gabby Hartnett	C105	R	30	116	380	53	107	32	1	8	70	52	48	3	.282	.370	.434
Charlie Grimm	1B144	L	32	146	531	65	176	33	11	4	66	53	29	1	.331	.393	.458
Rogers Hornsby	2B69,3B26	R	35	100	357	64	118	37	1	16	90	56	23	1	.331	.421	.574
Les Bell	3B70	R	29	75	252	30	71	17	1	4	32	19	22	0	.282	.332	.405
Woody English	SS138,3B18	R	24	156	634	117	202	38	8	2	53	68	80	12	.319	.391	.413
Kiki Cuyler	OF153	R	32	154	613	110	202	37	12	9	88	72	54	13	.330	.404	.473
Hack Wilson	OF103	R	31	112	395	66	103	22	4	13	61	63	69	1	.261	.362	.435
Danny Taylor	OF67	R	30	88	270	48	81	13	6	5	41	31	46	4	.300	.372	.448
Billy Jurges	3B54,2B33,SS3	R	23	88	293	34	59	15	5	0	23	25	41	2	.201	.264	.287
Riggs Stephenson	OF66	R	33	80	263	34	84	14	4	1	52	37	14	1	.319	.405	.414
Footsie Blair	2B44,1B23,3B1	L	30	86	240	31	62	19	5	3	29	14	26	1	.258	.302	.417
Vince Barton	OF61	L	23	66	239	45	57	10	1	13	50	21	40	1	.238	.323	.452
Rollie Hemsley†	C53	R	24	66	204	28	63	17	4	3	31	17	30	4	.309	.362	.475
Johnny Moore	OF22	L	29	39	104	19	25	3	1	2	16	7	5	1	.240	.288	.346
Billy Herman	2B25	R	21	25	98	14	32	7	0	0	16	13	6	2	.327	.405	.398
Jimmy Adair	SS18	R	24	18	76	9	21	3	1	0	3	1	8	1	.276	.286	.342
Mike Kreevich	OF4	R	23	5	12	0	2	0	0	0	0	0	6	1	.167	.167	.167
Earl Grace†	C2	L	24	7	9	2	1	0	0	0	1	4	1	0	.111	.385	.111
Zack Taylor	C5	R	32	8	4	0	1	0	0	0	0	2	1	0	.250	.500	.250

Pitcher	T	Age	G	GS	CG	ShO	IP	H	HR	BB	SO	W-L	Sv	ERA
Charlie Root	R	32	39	31	19	3	251.0	240	7	71	131	17-14	2	3.48
Pat Malone	R	28	36	30	12	2	228.1	229	9	88	112	16-9	0	3.90
Bob Smith	R	36	36	29	18	2	240.1	239	10	62	63	15-12	2	3.22
Guy Bush	R	29	39	24	14	1	180.1	190	9	66	54	16-8	2	4.49
Leo Sweetland	L	29	26	14	9	0	130.1	156	3	61	32	8-7	0	5.04
Jakie May	L	35	31	4	1	0	79.0	81	2	43	38	5-5	2	3.87
Bud Teachout	L	27	27	3	1	0	61.1	79	6	28	14	1-2	0	5.72
Ed Baecht	R	24	22	6	2	0	67.0	64	1	32	34	2-4	0	3.76
Lon Warneke	R	22	20	7	3	0	64.1	67	1	37	27	2-4	0	3.22
Sheriff Blake†	R	31	16	5	0	0	50.0	64	4	26	29	0-4	0	5.22
Johnny Welch	R	24	8	3	1	0	33.2	39	2	10	7	2-1	0	3.74

1931 Brooklyn Dodgers 4th NL 79-73 .520 21.0 GB

Wilbert Robinson

Player	Gm by Position	B	Age	G	AB	R	H	2B	3B	HR	RBI	BB	SO	SB	Avg	OBP	Slg
Al Lopez	C105	R	22	111	360	38	97	13	4	0	40	28	33	1	.269	.324	.328
Del Bissonette	1B152	L	31	152	587	90	170	19	14	12	87	59	53	4	.290	.354	.431
Neal Finn	2B112	R	27	118	413	46	113	22	2	0	45	21	42	2	.274	.314	.337
Wally Gilbert	3B145	R	30	145	552	60	147	25	6	0	46	39	38	3	.266	.322	.333
Gordon Slade	SS82,3B2	R	26	85	272	27	65	13	2	1	29	23	28	2	.239	.310	.313
Babe Herman	OF150	L	28	151	610	93	191	43	16	18	97	50	65	17	.313	.365	.525
Johnny Frederick	OF145	L	29	146	611	81	165	34	8	17	71	31	46	2	.270	.312	.435
Lefty O'Doul	OF132	L	34	134	512	85	172	32	11	7	75	48	16	5	.336	.396	.482
Glenn Wright	SS75	R	30	77	268	36	76	9	4	9	32	14	35	1	.284	.324	.448
Ernie Lombardi	C50	R	23	73	182	20	54	7	1	4	23	12	12	1	.297	.340	.412
Fresco Thompson	2B43,SS10,3B5	R	29	74	181	26	48	6	1	1	21	23	16	5	.265	.351	.326
Rube Bressler	OF35,1B1	R	36	67	153	22	43	4	5	0	26	11	10	0	.281	.329	.373
Val Picinich	C15	R	34	24	45	5	12	4	0	1	4	4	9	1	.267	.327	.422
Denny Sothern	OF10	R	27	19	31	10	5	1	0	0	0	4	8	0	.161	.257	.194
Jake Flowers†	2B6,SS1	R	29	22	31	3	7	0	0	0	1	7	4	1	.226	.368	.226
Bobby Reis	3B6	R	22	6	17	3	5	0	0	0	2	2	0	0	.294	.368	.294
Max Rosenfeld	OF3	R	28	3	9	0	2	1	0	0	0	1	1	0	.222	.300	.333
Ike Boone		L	34	6	5	0	1	0	0	0	0	1	1	0	.200	.333	.200
Jack Warner	SS2,3B1	R	27	9	4	2	2	0	0	0	0	1	1	0	.500	.600	.500
Alta Cohen	OF1	L	22	1	3	1	2	0	0	0	0	0	0	0	.667	.667	.667
Harvey Hendrick†		L	33	1	1	0	0	0	0	0	0	0	0	0	.000	.000	.000

Pitcher	T	Age	G	GS	CG	ShO	IP	H	HR	BB	SO	W-L	Sv	ERA
Dazzy Vance	R	40	30	29	12	2	218.2	221	12	53	150	11-13	0	3.38
Watty Clark	L	29	34	28	16	3	233.1	243	4	52	96	14-10	1	3.20
Ray Phelps	R	27	28	26	3	2	149.1	184	3	44	50	7-9	0	5.00
Joe Shaute	L	31	25	19	6	0	128.2	162	9	32	50	11-8	0	4.83
Sloppy Thurston	R	32	24	17	11	0	143.0	175	3	39	23	9-9	0	3.90
Dolf Luque	R	40	19	15	5	0	102.2	122	6	27	25	7-6	0	4.56
Van Lingle Mungo	R	20	5	4	2	1	31.0	27	0	13	12	3-1	0	2.32
Jack Quinn	R	47	39	1	0	0	64.1	65	1	24	25	5-4	15	2.66
Fred Heimach	L	30	31	10	7	1	135.1	145	6	23	43	9-7	1	3.46
Cy Moore	R	26	23	1	1	0	61.2	62	5	13	35	1-2	0	3.79
Pea Ridge Day	R	31	22	2	1	0	57.1	75	5	13	30	2-2	1	4.55
Earl Mattingly	R	26	8	0	0	0	14.1	15	0	10	6	0-1	0	2.51
Phil Gallivan	R	24	6	1	0	0	15.1	23	2	7	1	0-1	0	5.28
Ray Moss†	R	29	1	0	0	0	1.0	1	0	1	0	0-0	0	0.00

1931 Pittsburgh Pirates 5th NL 75-79 .487 26.0 GB

Jewel Ens

Player	Gm by Position	B	Age	G	AB	R	H	2B	3B	HR	RBI	BB	SO	SB	Avg	OBP	Slg
Eddie Phillips	C103	R	30	106	353	30	82	18	3	7	44	41	49	1	.232	.317	.360
George Grantham	1B78,2B51	L	31	127	465	91	142	26	6	10	46	71	50	5	.305	.400	.452
Tony Piet	2B44,SS1	R	24	44	167	22	50	12	4	0	24	13	24	10	.299	.354	.419
Pie Traynor	3B155	R	31	155	615	81	183	37	15	2	103	54	28	6	.298	.354	.416
Tommy Thevenow	SS120	R	27	120	404	35	86	12	1	0	38	28	22	0	.213	.266	.248
Lloyd Waner	OF153,2B1	L	25	154	681	90	214	25	13	4	57	39	16	7	.314	.352	.407
Paul Waner	OF138,1B10	L	28	150	559	88	180	35	10	6	70	73	21	6	.322	.404	.453
Adam Comorosky	OF90	R	25	99	350	37	85	12	1	1	48	34	28	11	.243	.310	.291
Gus Suhr	1B76	L	25	87	270	26	57	13	4	4	32	38	25	4	.211	.308	.333
Woody Jensen	OF67	L	23	73	267	43	65	5	4	3	17	10	18	4	.243	.276	.326
Howdie Groskloss	2B39,SS3	R	24	53	161	13	45	7	2	0	20	11	16	1	.280	.326	.348
Earl Grace†	C45	L	24	47	150	8	42	6	1	1	20	13	5	0	.280	.337	.353
Ben Sankey	SS49,2B2,3B2	R	23	57	132	14	30	2	5	0	14	14	10	0	.227	.301	.318
Bill Regan	2B28	R	32	28	104	8	21	8	0	1	10	5	19	2	.202	.239	.308
Fred Bennett	OF21	R	29	32	89	6	25	5	0	1	7	7	4	0	.281	.333	.371
Jim Mosolf	OF4	L	25	39	44	7	11	1	0	1	8	8	5	0	.250	.365	.341
Rollie Hemsley†	C9	R	24	10	35	3	6	3	0	0	1	3	3	0	.171	.237	.257
Hal Finney	C6	R	25	10	26	2	8	1	0	0	2	0	1	1	.308	.333	.346
Bill Steinecke	C1	R	24	4	4	0	0	0	0	0	0	0	1	0	.000	.000	.000
Pete McClanahan		R	24	7	4	2	2	0	0	0	0	2	0	0	.500	.667	.500

Pitcher	T	Age	G	GS	CG	ShO	IP	H	HR	BB	SO	W-L	Sv	ERA
Heinie Meine	R	35	36	35	22	3	284.0	278	8	87	58	19-13	1	2.98
Larry French	L	23	39	33	20	1	275.2	301	9	70	73	15-13	1	3.26
Ray Kremer	R	38	30	30	15	1	230.0	246	6	65	58	11-15	0	3.33
Erv Brame	R	29	26	21	15	2	179.2	211	14	45	33	9-13	0	4.21
Spades Wood	L	22	15	10	2	0	64.0	69	2	46	33	2-6	0	6.05
Bill Harris	R	31	4	4	3	1	31.0	21	0	9	10	2-2	0	0.87
Glenn Spencer	R	25	38	18	11	1	186.2	180	8	65	51	11-12	3	3.42
Bob Osborn	R	28	27	2	0	0	64.2	85	3	20	9	6-1	0	5.01
Steve Swetonic	R	27	14	0	0	0	27.2	28	0	16	8	0-2	1	3.90
George Grant	R	28	11	0	0	0	17.0	28	0	7	6	0-0	0	7.41
Claude Willoughby	R	32	9	2	1	0	25.2	32	4	12	4	0-2	0	6.31
Andy Bednar	R	22	3	0	0	0	4.0	10	1	0	2	0-0	0	11.25

1931 Philadelphia Phillies 6th NL 66-88 .429 35.0 GB

Burt Shotton

Player	Gm by Position	B	Age	G	AB	R	H	2B	3B	HR	RBI	BB	SO	SB	Avg	OBP	Slg
Spud Davis	C114	R	26	120	393	30	128	32	1	4	51	36	28	0	.326	.382	.443
Don Hurst	1B135	L	25	137	489	63	149	37	5	11	91	64	28	8	.305	.386	.468
Les Mallon	2B97,1B5,3B3*	R	25	122	375	41	116	19	2	1	45	29	40	0	.309	.359	.379
Pinky Whitney	3B128	R	26	130	501	64	144	36	5	9	74	30	38	6	.287	.331	.433
Dick Bartell	SS133	R	23	135	554	88	160	43	7	0	34	27	38	6	.289	.325	.392
Chuck Klein	OF148	L	26	148	594	121	200	34	10	31	121	59	49	7	.337	.398	.584
George Brickell	OF122	L	24	130	514	77	130	14	5	1	31	42	39	5	.253	.316	.305
Buzz Arlett	OF94,1B13	S	32	121	418	65	131	26	7	18	72	45	39	3	.313	.387	.538
Bernie Friberg	2B64,3B25,1B5*	R	31	103	353	33	92	19	5	1	26	33	25	1	.261	.324	.351
Fred Koster	OF41	L	25	76	151	21	34	2	2	0	8	14	21	4	.225	.291	.265
Doug Taitt	OF38	L	28	38	151	13	34	4	2	1	15	4	14	0	.225	.245	.298
Harry McCurdy	C45	L	31	66	150	21	43	9	0	1	25	23	16	2	.287	.382	.367
Hal Lee	OF38	R	26	44	131	13	29	10	0	2	12	10	18	0	.221	.282	.344
Bobby Stevens	SS10	L	24	12	35	3	12	0	0	0	4	2	2	0	.343	.410	.343
Hugh Willingham	SS8,3B2,OF1	R	25	23	35	5	9	2	1	1	3	2	9	0	.257	.297	.457
Tony Rensa	C17	R	29	19	29	2	3	1	0	0	2	6	2	0	.103	.257	.138
Gene Connell	C6	R	25	6	12	1	3	0	0	0	0	0	3	0	.250	.250	.250

L. Mallon, 3 G at SS; B. Friberg, 3 G at SS

Pitcher	T	Age	G	GS	CG	ShO	IP	H	HR	BB	SO	W-L	Sv	ERA
Ray Benge	R	29	38	31	16	2	247.0	251	12	61	117	14-18	2	3.17
Jumbo Elliott	L	30	52	30	12	2	249.0	288	15	83	99	19-14	5	4.27
Phil Collins	R	29	42	27	16	2	240.1	268	14	83	73	12-16	4	3.86
Clise Dudley	R	27	30	24	8	0	179.0	206	10	56	50	8-14	0	3.52
Stew Bolen	L	28	28	16	2	0	98.2	117	5	63	55	3-12	0	6.39
Sheriff Blake†	R	31	14	9	1	0	71.0	90	2	35	31	4-5	1	5.58
Bob Adams	R	24	1	1	0	0	6.0	14	0	1	3	0-1	0	9.00
Frank Watt	R	28	38	12	5	0	122.2	147	5	49	25	5-5	2	4.84
Ed Fallenstein	R	22	24	0	0	0	41.2	56	2	26	15	0-0	0	7.13
Dutch Schesler	R	31	17	0	0	0	38.1	65	4	18	14	0-0	0	7.28
Hal Elliott	R	32	16	4	0	0	33.0	46	5	19	8	0-2	2	9.55
Lil Stoner	R	32	7	1	0	0	13.2	22	0	5	2	0-0	0	6.59
Ben Shields	L	28	4	0	0	0	5.1	9	1	7	0	1-0	0	15.19
John Milligan	L	27	3	0	0	0	8.0	11	0	4	6	0-0	0	3.38
Chet Nichols	R	33	3	0	0	0	5.2	10	0	1	1	0-1	0	9.53
Hal Wiltse	L	27	1	0	0	0	1.0	3	0	0	0	0-0	0	9.00

652 Seasons: Team Rosters

1931 Boston Braves 7th NL 64-90 .416 37.0 GB

Bill McKechnie

Player	Gm by Position	B	Age	G	AB	R	H	2B	3B	HR	RBI	BB	SO	SB	Avg	OBP	Slg
Al Spohrer	C111	R	28	114	350	23	84	17	5	0	27	22	27	2	.240	.285	.317
Earl Sheely	1B143	R	38	147	538	30	147	15	2	1	77	34	21	0	.273	.319	.314
Freddie Maguire	2B148	R	32	148	492	36	112	18	2	0	26	16	26	3	.228	.259	.272
Billy Urbanski	3B68,SS19	R	28	82	303	22	72	13	4	0	17	10	32	3	.238	.274	.307
Rabbit Maranville	SS137,2B11	R	39	145	562	69	146	22	5	0	33	56	34	9	.260	.329	.317
Wally Berger	OF156,1B1	R	25	156	617	94	199	44	8	19	84	55	70	13	.323	.380	.512
Red Worthington	OF124	R	25	128	491	47	143	25	10	4	44	26	38	1	.291	.328	.407
Wes Schulmerich	OF87	R	30	95	327	36	101	17	7	2	43	28	30	0	.309	.363	.422
Lance Richbourg	OF71	L	33	97	286	32	82	11	6	2	29	19	14	9	.287	.331	.388
Randy Moore	OF29,3B22,2B1	L	25	83	192	19	50	8	1	3	34	13	3	1	.260	.311	.359
Bill Dreesen	3B47	L	26	48	180	38	40	10	4	1	10	23	23	1	.222	.310	.339
Bill Cronin	C50	R	28	51	107	8	22	6	1	0	10	7	5	0	.206	.267	.280
Johnny Neun	1B36	S	30	79	104	17	23	1	3	0	11	11	14	2	.221	.302	.288
Al Bool	C37	R	33	49	85	5	16	1	0	0	6	9	13	0	.188	.266	.200
Charlie Wilson	3B14	S	26	16	58	7	11	4	0	1	11	3	5	0	.190	.230	.310
Earl Clark	OF14	R	23	16	50	8	11	2	0	0	4	7	4	1	.220	.316	.260
Buster Chatham	3B6,SS6	R	29	17	44	4	10	1	0	1	3	6	6	0	.227	.320	.318
Bucky Walters	3B6,2B3	R	22	9	38	2	8	2	0	0	0	0	3	0	.211	.211	.263
Bill Hunnefield†	2B4	S	32	11	21	2	6	0	0	0	1	0	2	0	.286	.286	.286
Johnny Scalzi		R	24	2	1	0	0	0	0	0	0	0	1	0	.000	.000	.000
Pat Veltman		R	25	1	1	0	0	0	0	0	0	0	0	0	.000	.000	.000

Pitcher	T	Age	G	GS	CG	ShO	IP	H	HR	BB	SO	W-L	Sv	ERA
Ed Brandt	L	26	33	29	23	3	250.0	228	11	77	112	18-11	2	2.92
Socks Seibold	R	35	33	29	10	3	206.1	226	12	65	50	10-18	0	4.67
Tom Zachary	L	35	33	28	16	3	229.0	243	8	53	64	11-15	2	3.10
Bill Sherdel	L	34	27	16	8	0	137.2	163	13	35	34	6-10	0	4.25
Fred Frankhouse	R	27	26	15	6	0	127.1	125	4	43	50	8-8	1	4.03
Ben Cantwell	R	29	33	16	9	2	156.1	160	4	34	32	7-9	2	3.63
Bruce Cunningham	R	25	33	16	6	1	136.2	157	7	54	32	3-12	1	4.48
Hal Haid	R	33	27	0	0	0	56.0	59	3	16	20	0-2	1	4.50
Bill McAfee	R	23	18	1	0	0	29.2	39	2	10	9	0-1	0	6.37
Ray Moss†	R	29	12	5	0	0	45.0	56	2	16	14	1-3	0	4.60
Bob Brown	R	20	3	1	0	0	6.1	9	0	3	2	0-1	0	8.53

1931 Cincinnati Reds 8th NL 58-96 .377 43.0 GB

Dan Howley

Player	Gm by Position	B	Age	G	AB	R	H	2B	3B	HR	RBI	BB	SO	SB	Avg	OBP	Slg
Clyde Sukeforth	C106	L	29	112	351	22	90	15	4	0	25	38	13	0	.256	.334	.322
Harvey Hendrick†	1B137	L	33	137	530	74	167	32	9	1	75	53	40	3	.315	.379	.415
Tony Cuccinello	2B154	R	23	154	575	67	181	39	11	2	93	54	28	1	.315	.374	.431
Joe Stripp	3B96,1B9	R	28	105	426	71	138	26	2	3	42	21	31	5	.324	.359	.415
Leo Durocher	SS120	R	25	121	361	26	82	11	5	1	29	18	32	0	.227	.264	.294
Estel Crabtree	OF101,3B4,1B2	L	27	117	443	70	119	12	12	4	37	23	33	3	.269	.309	.377
Taylor Douthit†	OF95	R	30	95	374	42	98	9	1	0	24	42	24	4	.262	.340	.291
Edd Roush	OF88	L	38	101	376	46	102	12	5	1	41	17	5	2	.271	.308	.338
Nick Cullop	OF83	R	30	104	334	29	88	23	7	8	48	21	86	1	.263	.309	.446
Cliff Heathcote	OF59	L	33	90	252	34	65	15	6	0	28	32	16	3	.258	.342	.365
Wally Roettger†	OF44	R	28	44	185	25	65	11	4	1	20	7	9	1	.351	.378	.470
Hod Ford	SS73,2B3,3B1	R	33	84	175	18	40	8	1	0	13	13	13	0	.229	.286	.286
Clyde Beck	3B38	R	31	53	136	17	21	4	2	0	19	21	14	1	.154	.272	.213
Asby Asbjornson	C31	R	22	45	118	13	36	7	1	0	22	7	23	0	.305	.349	.381
Lena Styles	C31	R	31	34	87	7	21	3	0	0	5	8	7	0	.241	.313	.276
Frank Sigafoos	3B15,SS2	R	27	21	65	6	11	2	0	0	8	0	6	0	.169	.182	.200
Mickey Heath	1B7	L	27	7	26	2	7	0	0	0	3	2	5	0	.269	.321	.269
Chuck Dressen	3B4	R	32	5	15	0	1	0	0	0	0	1	1	0	.067	.125	.067
Gene Moore	OF3	L	21	4	14	2	2	1	0	0	1	0	0	0	.143	.143	.214
Ray Fitzgerald		R	26	1	1	0	0	0	0	0	0	0	0	0	.000	.000	.000

Pitcher	T	Age	G	GS	CG	ShO	IP	H	HR	BB	SO	W-L	Sv	ERA
Si Johnson	R	24	42	33	14	0	262.1	273	5	74	95	11-19	0	3.77
Red Lucas	R	29	29	29	24	3	238.0	261	10	39	56	14-13	0	3.59
Larry Benton	R	33	38	23	12	2	204.1	240	6	53	35	10-15	2	3.35
Benny Frey	R	25	34	17	7	1	133.2	166	2	36	19	8-12	2	4.92
Eppa Rixey	L	40	22	17	4	0	126.2	143	4	30	22	4-7	0	3.91
Whitey Hilcher	R	22	2	1	0	0	12.0	16	0	4	5	0-1	0	3.00
Ray Kolp	R	36	30	10	2	0	107.0	144	8	39	24	4-9	1	4.96
Ownie Carroll	R	28	29	12	4	0	107.1	135	6	51	24	3-9	0	5.53
Jack Ogden	R	33	22	9	3	1	89.0	79	3	32	24	4-8	1	2.93
Al Eckert	L	25	14	1	0	0	18.2	26	3	9	5	0-1	0	9.16
Ed Strelecki	R	26	13	0	0	0	24.1	37	2	9	3	0-0	0	9.25
Biff Wysong	L	26	12	2	0	0	21.2	25	2	23	5	0-2	0	7.89

»1932 New York Yankees 1st AL 107-47 .695 —

Joe McCarthy

Player	Gm by Position	B	Age	G	AB	R	H	2B	3B	HR	RBI	BB	SO	SB	Avg	OBP	Slg
Bill Dickey	C108	L	25	108	423	66	131	20	4	15	84	34	13	2	.310	.361	.482
Lou Gehrig	1B155	L	29	156	596	138	208	42	9	34	151	108	38	4	.349	.451	.621
Tony Lazzeri	2B133,3B5	R	28	142	510	79	153	28	16	15	113	82	64	11	.300	.399	.506
Joe Sewell	3B122	L	33	125	503	95	137	21	3	11	68	56	3	0	.272	.349	.392
Frankie Crosetti	SS83,3B33,2B1	R	21	116	398	47	96	20	9	5	57	51	51	3	.241	.335	.374
Ben Chapman	OF149	R	23	151	581	101	174	41	15	10	107	71	55	38	.299	.381	.473
Earle Combs	OF138	L	33	144	591	143	190	32	10	9	65	81	16	3	.321	.405	.455
Babe Ruth	OF127,1B1	L	37	133	457	120	156	13	5	41	137	130	62	2	.341	.489	.661
Lyn Lary	SS80,1B5,2B2*	R	26	91	280	56	65	14	4	3	39	52	28	9	.232	.358	.343
Sammy Byrd	OF90	R	24	105	209	49	62	12	1	8	30	30	20	1	.297	.385	.478
Art Jorgens	C55	R	27	56	151	13	33	7	1	2	19	14	11	0	.219	.285	.318
Doc Farrell	2B16,SS5,1B2*	R	30	26	63	4	11	1	1	0	4	2	8	0	.175	.212	.222
Myril Hoag	OF35,1B1	R	24	46	54	18	20	5	0	1	7	7	13	1	.370	.443	.519
Jack Saltzgaver	2B16	L	29	20	47	10	6	2	1	0	5	10	10	1	.128	.281	.213
Eddie Phillips	C9	R	31	9	31	4	9	1	0	2	4	2	3	1	.290	.333	.516
Joe Glenn	C5	R	23	6	16	0	2	0	0	0	0	1	5	0	.125	.222	.125
Roy Schalk	2B3	R	23	3	12	3	3	1	0	0	0	2	2	0	.250	.357	.333
Dusty Cooke		L	25	3	0	1	0	0	0	0	0	1	0	0	—	1.000	—

L. Lary, 2 G at 3B, 1 G at OF; D. Farrell, 1 G at 3B

Pitcher	T	Age	G	GS	CG	ShO	IP	H	HR	BB	SO	W-L	Sv	ERA
Lefty Gomez	L	23	37	31	21	1	265.1	266	23	105	176	24-7	1	4.21
Red Ruffing	R	28	35	29	22	3	259.0	219	16	115	190	18-7	2	3.09
George Pipgras	R	32	32	27	14	2	219.0	235	15	87	111	16-9	0	4.19
Johnny Allen	R	26	33	21	13	3	192.0	162	10	76	109	17-4	4	3.70
Herb Pennock	L	38	22	21	9	1	146.2	191	8	38	54	9-5	0	4.60
Danny MacFayden†	R	27	17	15	8	0	121.1	137	11	37	33	7-5	1	3.93
Hank Johnson	R	26	5	4	2	0	31.1	34	7	15	27	2-2	0	4.88
Charlie Devens	R	22	1	1	1	0	9.0	6	0	7	4	1-0	0	2.00
Ed Wells	L	32	22	0	0	0	31.2	38	1	12	13	3-3	2	4.26
Jumbo Brown	R	25	19	3	3	1	55.2	58	1	30	31	5-2	1	4.53
Wilcy Moore†	R	35	10	1	0	0	25.0	27	1	6	8	2-0	4	2.52
Gordon Rhodes†	R	24	10	2	1	0	24.0	25	0	21	15	1-2	0	7.88
Ivy Andrews†	R	25	4	1	1	0	24.2	20	0	9	7	2-1	0	1.82
Johnny Murphy	R	23	2	0	0	0	3.1	7	0	3	2	0-0	0	16.20

1932 Philadelphia Athletics 2nd AL 94-60 .610 13.0 GB

Connie Mack

Player	Gm by Position	B	Age	G	AB	R	H	2B	3B	HR	RBI	BB	SO	SB	Avg	OBP	Slg
Mickey Cochrane	C137,OF1	L	29	139	518	118	152	35	4	23	112	100	22	0	.293	.412	.510
Jimmie Foxx	1B141,3B13	R	24	154	585	151	213	33	9	58	169	116	96	3	.364	.469	.749
Max Bishop	2B106	L	32	114	409	89	104	24	2	5	37	110	43	2	.254	.412	.359
Jimmy Dykes	3B141,SS10,2B1	R	35	153	558	71	148	29	5	7	90	77	65	8	.265	.358	.373
Eric McNair	SS133	R	23	135	554	87	158	47	3	18	95	28	29	8	.285	.323	.478
Al Simmons	OF154	R	30	154	670	144	216	28	9	35	151	47	76	4	.322	.368	.548
Mule Haas	OF137	L	28	143	558	91	170	28	5	6	65	62	49	1	.305	.376	.405
Doc Cramer	OF86	L	26	92	384	73	129	27	6	3	46	17	27	3	.336	.367	.461
Bing Miller	OF84	R	37	95	305	40	90	17	3	8	58	20	11	7	.295	.343	.449
Dib Williams	2B53,SS3	R	22	62	215	30	54	10	1	4	24	22	23	0	.251	.329	.363
Johnny Heving	C28	R	36	33	77	14	21	6	1	0	10	7	6	0	.273	.333	.377
Ed Coleman	OF16	L	30	26	73	13	25	7	1	1	13	1	6	1	.342	.351	.507
Oscar Roettger	1B15	R	32	26	60	7	14	1	0	0	6	5	4	0	.233	.292	.250
Ed Madjeski	C8	R	23	17	35	4	8	0	0	0	3	3	6	0	.229	.289	.229
Joe Boley†	SS10	R	35	10	34	2	7	2	0	0	4	1	4	0	.206	.229	.265
John Jones	OF1	L	31	4	6	0	1	0	0	0	0	0	3	0	.167	.167	.167
Al Reiss	SS6	S	23	9	5	0	1	0	0	0	1	1	1	0	.200	.333	.200
Ed Cihocki		R	25	1	1	0	0	0	0	0	0	0	0	0	.000	.000	.000

Pitcher	T	Age	G	GS	CG	ShO	IP	H	HR	BB	SO	W-L	Sv	ERA
Rube Walberg	L	35	41	34	19	3	272.0	305	16	103	96	17-10	1	4.73
George Earnshaw	R	32	36	33	21	1	245.1	262	28	94	109	19-13	0	4.77
Lefty Grove	L	32	44	30	27	4	291.2	269	13	79	188	25-10	7	2.84
Roy Mahaffey	R	29	37	28	13	1	222.2	245	27	96	106	13-13	0	5.09
Tony Freitas	L	24	23	18	10	1	150.1	150	11	48	31	12-5	0	3.83
Sugar Cain	R	25	10	6	3	0	45.0	42	1	28	24	3-4	0	5.00
Tim McKeithan	R	25	4	2	0	0	12.2	18	0	5	0	0-1	0	7.11
Lew Krausse	R	20	20	3	2	1	57.0	64	3	24	16	4-1	0	4.58
Eddie Rommel	R	34	17	0	0	0	65.1	84	6	18	16	1-2	2	5.51
Joe Bowman	R	22	7	0	0	0	11.0	14	2	6	4	0-1	0	8.18
Jimmie DeShong	R	22	6	0	0	0	10.0	17	3	9	5	0-0	0	11.70
Irv Stein	R	21	1	0	0	0	3.0	7	2	1	0	0-0	0	12.00

1932 Washington Senators 3rd AL 93-61 .604 14.0 GB

Walter Johnson

Player	Gm by Position	B	Age	G	AB	R	H	2B	3B	HR	RBI	BB	SO	SB	Avg	OBP	Slg
Roy Spencer	C98	R	32	102	317	28	78	9	0	1	41	24	17	0	.246	.301	.284
Joe Kuhel	1B85	L	26	101	347	52	101	21	5	4	52	32	19	5	.291	.353	.415
Buddy Myer	2B139	L	28	143	577	120	161	38	16	5	52	69	33	12	.279	.360	.426
Ossie Bluege	3B149	R	31	149	507	64	131	22	4	5	64	84	41	9	.258	.367	.347
Joe Cronin	SS141	R	25	143	557	95	177	43	18	6	116	66	45	7	.318	.393	.492
Heinie Manush	OF146	L	30	149	625	121	214	41	14	14	116	36	29	7	.342	.383	.520
Sammy West	OF143	L	27	146	554	88	159	27	12	6	83	48	57	4	.287	.345	.412
Carl Reynolds	OF95	R	29	102	406	53	124	28	7	9	63	14	19	8	.305	.332	.475
Joe Judge	1B78	L	38	82	291	45	75	16	3	3	29	37	19	3	.258	.343	.364
Sam Rice	OF69	L	42	106	288	58	93	16	7	1	34	32	6	7	.323	.391	.438
Moe Berg	C75	R	30	75	195	16	46	8	1	1	26	8	13	1	.236	.266	.303
Dave Harris	OF34	R	31	81	156	26	51	7	4	6	29	19	34	4	.327	.400	.538
John Kerr	2B17,SS14,3B8	R	33	51	132	14	36	6	1	0	15	13	3	3	.273	.338	.333
Howard Maple	C41	L	28	44	41	6	10	0	1	0	7	7	7	0	.244	.367	.293
Wes Kingdon	3B8,SS4	R	31	18	34	10	11	3	1	0	3	5	2	0	.324	.410	.471
Danny Musser	3B1	L	26	1	2	0	1	0	0	0	0	0	0	0	.500	.500	.500
Jim McLeod	SS1	R	23	7	0	1	0	0	0	0	0	1	0	0	—	1.000	—

Pitcher	T	Age	G	GS	CG	ShO	IP	H	HR	BB	SO	W-L	Sv	ERA
General Crowder	R	33	50	39	21	3	327.0	319	17	77	103	26-13	1	3.33
Montie Weaver	R	26	43	30	13	1	234.0	236	9	112	83	22-10	2	4.08
Lloyd Brown	L	27	46	24	10	2	202.2	239	11	55	53	15-12	5	4.44
Tommy Thomas†	R	32	18	14	7	1	117.0	114	5	46	36	8-7	0	3.54
Carl Fischer†	L	26	12	7	1	1	50.2	57	4	31	23	3-2	1	4.97
Bill McAfee	R	24	8	5	2	0	41.1	47	3	22	10	6-1	0	3.92
Firpo Marberry	R	33	54	15	8	1	197.2	202	13	72	66	8-4	13	4.01
Bobby Burke	L	25	22	10	2	0	91.0	98	4	44	32	3-6	0	5.14
Dick Coffman†	R	25	22	9	2	0	76.1	92	2	31	17	1-6	0	4.83
Frank Ragland	R	28	12	1	0	0	37.2	54	5	21	11	1-0	0	7.41
Bob Friedrichs	R	25	2	0	0	0	4.0	4	0	7	2	0-0	0	11.25
Bud Thomas	R	21	2	0	0	0	3.0	1	0	2	1	0-0	0	0.00
Ed Edelen	R	20	2	0	0	0	1.0	0	0	6	0	0-0	0	27.00

1932 Cleveland Indians 4th AL 87-65 .572 19.0 GB

Roger Peckinpaugh

Player	Gm by Position	B	Age	G	AB	R	H	2B	3B	HR	RBI	BB	SO	SB	Avg	OBP	Slg
Luke Sewell	C84	R	31	87	300	36	76	20	2	2	52	38	24	4	.253	.337	.353
Eddie Morgan	1B142	R	28	144	532	96	156	32	7	4	68	94	44	7	.293	.402	.402
Bill Cissell†	2B129,SS6	R	28	131	541	78	173	35	6	6	93	28	25	18	.320	.354	.440
Willie Kamm	3B148	R	32	148	524	76	150	34	9	3	83	75	36	6	.286	.379	.403
Johnny Burnett	SS103,2B26	L	27	129	512	81	152	23	5	4	53	46	27	2	.297	.359	.385
Earl Averill	OF153	L	30	153	631	116	198	37	14	32	124	75	40	5	.314	.392	.569
Joe Vosmik	OF153	R	22	153	621	106	194	39	12	10	97	58	42	2	.312	.376	.462
Dick Porter	OF145	L	30	146	621	106	191	42	8	4	60	64	43	2	.308	.373	.420
Glenn Myatt	C65	L	34	82	252	45	62	12	1	8	46	28	21	2	.246	.326	.397
Ed Montague	SS57,3B11	R	26	66	192	29	47	5	1	0	24	21	24	3	.245	.326	.281
Bruce Connatser	1B14	R	29	23	60	8	14	3	1	0	4	4	8	1	.233	.281	.317
Mike Powers	OF8	L	26	14	33	4	6	4	0	0	5	2	2	0	.182	.229	.303
Frankie Pytlak	C12	R	23	12	29	5	7	1	1	0	4	3	2	0	.241	.333	.345
Johnny Hodapp†	2B7	R	26	7	16	2	2	1	0	0	0	0	2	0	.125	.125	.188
Charlie Jamieson	OF2	L	39	16	16	0	1	1	0	0	0	2	3	0	.063	.211	.125
Bob Seeds†	OF1	R	25	2	4	0	0	0	0	0	0	0	0	0	.000	.000	.000
Joe Boley†	SS1	R	35	1	4	0	1	0	0	0	0	0	0	0	.250	.250	.250
Boze Berger	SS1	R	22	1	1	0	0	0	0	0	0	0	1	0	.000	.000	.000

Pitcher	T	Age	G	GS	CG	ShO	IP	H	HR	BB	SO	W-L	Sv	ERA
Wes Ferrell	R	24	38	34	26	3	287.2	299	17	104	105	23-13	1	3.66
Clint Brown	R	28	37	32	21	1	262.2	298	14	50	59	15-12	1	4.08
Mel Harder	R	22	39	32	17	1	254.2	277	9	68	90	15-13	0	3.75
Willis Hudlin	R	26	33	21	12	0	181.2	204	10	59	65	12-8	2	4.71
Oral Hildebrand	R	25	27	15	7	0	129.1	124	7	62	49	8-6	0	3.69
Jack Russell†	R	26	18	11	6	0	113.0	146	5	27	27	5-7	1	4.70
Sarge Connally	R	33	35	7	4	1	112.1	119	6	42	32	8-6	3	4.33
Monte Pearson	R	22	8	0	0	0	8.0	10	1	11	5	0-0	0	10.13
Ralph Winegarner	R	22	5	1	1	0	17.1	7	0	13	5	1-0	0	1.04
Pete Appleton†	R	28	4	0	0	0	5.0	11	1	3	1	0-0	0	16.20
Leo Moon	L	33	1	0	0	0	5.2	11	0	7	1	0-0	0	11.12

1932 Detroit Tigers 5th AL 76-75 .503 29.5 GB

Bucky Harris

Player	Gm by Position	B	Age	G	AB	R	H	2B	3B	HR	RBI	BB	SO	SB	Avg	OBP	Slg
Ray Hayworth	C105	R	28	109	338	41	99	20	2	2	44	31	22	1	.293	.354	.382
Harry Davis	1B140	L	24	141	590	92	159	32	13	4	74	60	53	12	.269	.339	.388
Charlie Gehringer	2B151	L	29	152	618	112	184	44	11	19	107	68	34	9	.298	.370	.497
Heinie Schuble	3B76,SS15	R	25	102	340	58	92	20	6	5	52	24	37	14	.271	.319	.409
Billy Rogell	SS139,3B4	S	27	144	554	88	150	29	6	9	61	50	38	14	.271	.332	.394
John Stone	OF141	L	26	145	582	106	173	35	12	17	108	58	64	2	.297	.361	.486
Gee Walker	OF116	R	24	127	480	71	155	32	6	8	78	13	38	30	.323	.345	.465
Earl Webb†	OF84	L	34	88	338	49	97	19	8	3	51	39	18	1	.287	.361	.417
Billy Rhiel	3B36,1B12,OF8*	R	31	85	250	30	70	13	3	3	38	17	23	2	.280	.328	.392
Jo-Jo White	OF47	L	23	80	208	25	54	6	3	2	21	22	19	6	.260	.330	.346
Roy Johnson†	OF48	L	29	49	195	33	49	14	2	3	22	20	26	7	.251	.324	.390
Nolen Richardson	3B65,SS4	R	29	69	155	13	34	5	2	0	12	9	13	5	.219	.262	.277
Muddy Ruel	C48	R	36	51	136	10	32	4	2	0	18	17	6	1	.235	.320	.294
Gene Desautels	C24	R	25	28	72	8	17	2	0	0	2	13	11	0	.236	.360	.264
Bill Lawrence	OF15	R	26	25	46	10	10	1	0	0	3	5	5	0	.217	.294	.239
Frank Doljack	OF6	R	24	8	26	5	10	1	0	1	7	2	2	1	.385	.429	.538
Dale Alexander†	1B2	R	29	23	16	0	4	0	0	0	4	6	2	0	.250	.455	.250
George Susce	C2	R	23	2	0	0	0	0	0	0	0	0	0	0	—	—	—

B. Rhiel, 1 G at 2B

Pitcher	T	Age	G	GS	CG	ShO	IP	H	HR	BB	SO	W-L	Sv	ERA
Earl Whitehill	L	32	33	31	17	3	244.0	255	17	93	81	16-12	0	4.54
Vic Sorrell	R	31	32	31	13	1	234.1	234	11	77	84	14-14	0	4.03
Tommy Bridges	R	25	34	26	10	4	201.0	174	14	119	108	14-12	1	3.36
Whit Wyatt	R	24	43	22	10	0	205.2	228	12	102	82	9-13	1	5.03
Chief Hogsett	L	28	47	15	7	0	178.0	201	8	66	56	11-9	7	3.54
George Uhle	R	33	33	15	6	1	146.2	152	15	42	51	6-6	5	4.48
Buck Marrow	R	22	18	7	2	0	63.2	70	6	29	31	2-5	1	4.81
Izzy Goldstein	R	24	16	6	2	0	56.1	63	2	41	14	3-2	0	4.47
Art Herring	R	26	12	0	0	0	22.1	25	2	15	12	1-2	2	5.24
Rip Sewell	R	25	5	0	0	0	10.2	19	2	8	2	0-0	0	12.66

1932 St. Louis Browns 6th AL 63-91 .409 44.0 GB

Bill Killefer

Player	Gm by Position	B	Age	G	AB	R	H	2B	3B	HR	RBI	BB	SO	SB	Avg	OBP	Slg
Rick Ferrell	C120	R	26	126	438	67	138	30	5	2	65	66	18	5	.315	.406	.420
Jack Burns	1B150	L	24	150	617	111	188	33	8	11	70	61	43	17	.305	.368	.438
Ski Melillo	2B153	R	32	154	612	71	148	19	11	3	66	36	42	6	.242	.286	.324
Art Scharein	3B77,SS3,2B2	R	27	81	303	43	92	19	2	0	42	25	10	4	.304	.363	.380
Jim Levey	SS152	S	25	152	568	59	159	30	8	4	63	21	48	6	.280	.310	.382
Goose Goslin	OF149,3B1	L	31	150	572	88	171	28	9	17	104	92	35	12	.299	.398	.469
Bruce Campbell†	OF139	L	22	137	585	83	169	35	11	14	85	40	100	7	.289	.341	.458
Fred Schulte	OF129,1B5	R	31	146	565	106	166	35	6	9	73	71	44	5	.294	.373	.425
Lin Storti	3B51	S	25	53	193	19	50	11	2	3	26	5	20	1	.259	.278	.383
Benny Bengough	C47	R	33	54	139	13	35	7	1	0	15	12	4	0	.252	.311	.317
Debs Garms	OF33	L	24	34	134	20	38	7	1	1	8	17	7	4	.284	.364	.373
Ed Grimes	3B18,2B2,SS1	R	26	31	68	7	16	0	1	0	13	6	12	0	.235	.297	.265
Tom Jenkins	OF12	L	34	25	62	5	20	1	0	0	5	1	6	0	.323	.333	.339
Red Kress†	3B14	R	25	14	52	2	9	0	1	2	9	4	6	1	.173	.232	.327
Larry Bettencourt	OF4,3B2	R	26	27	30	4	4	1	0	1	3	7	6	1	.133	.297	.267
Johnny Schulte†	C6	L	35	15	24	2	5	2	0	0	3	1	6	0	.208	.240	.292
Showboat Fisher	OF5	L	33	18	22	2	4	0	0	0	2	2	5	0	.182	.250	.182
Nap Kloza	OF3	R	28	19	13	4	2	0	1	0	2	4	4	0	.154	.353	.308
Jim McLaughlin	3B1	R	30	1	1	0	0	0	0	0	1	0	0	0	.000	.000	.000

Pitcher	T	Age	G	GS	CG	ShO	IP	H	HR	BB	SO	W-L	Sv	ERA
George Blaeholder	R	28	42	36	16	1	258.1	304	19	76	80	14-14	0	4.70
Bump Hadley†	R	27	40	33	12	1	229.2	244	21	163	132	13-20	1	5.53
Lefty Stewart	L	31	41	32	18	2	259.2	269	22	99	86	15-19	0	4.61
Dick Coffman†	R	25	9	6	3	1	61.0	66	3	21	14	5-3	0	3.10
Sam Gray	R	34	52	18	7	3	206.2	250	9	53	79	7-12	4	4.53
Wally Hebert	L	24	35	15	2	0	108.1	145	6	45	29	1-12	1	6.48
Chad Kimsey†	R	25	33	0	0	0	78.1	85	3	33	13	4-2	3	4.02
Carl Fischer†	L	26	24	11	4	0	97.0	122	12	45	35	3-7	0	5.57
Bob Cooney	R	24	23	3	1	0	71.0	94	8	36	23	1-2	1	6.97
Lou Polli	R	30	5	0	0	0	6.2	13	0	3	5	0-0	0	5.40

1932 Chicago White Sox 7th AL 49-102 .325 56.5 GB

Lew Fonseca

Player	Gm by Position	B	Age	G	AB	R	H	2B	3B	HR	RBI	BB	SO	SB	Avg	OBP	Slg
Frank Grube	C92	R	27	93	277	36	78	16	2	0	31	33	13	6	.282	.362	.354
Lu Blue	1B105	S	35	112	373	51	93	21	2	0	43	64	21	17	.249	.364	.316
Jackie Hayes	2B97,3B10,SS10	R	25	117	475	53	122	20	5	2	54	30	28	7	.257	.302	.333
Carey Selph	3B71,2B26	R	30	116	396	50	112	19	8	0	51	31	9	7	.283	.341	.371
Luke Appling	SS85,2B30,3B14	R	25	139	489	66	134	20	10	3	63	40	36	9	.274	.329	.374
Liz Funk	OF120	L	27	122	440	59	114	21	5	2	40	43	19	17	.259	.325	.343
Bob Seeds†	OF112	R	25	116	434	53	126	18	6	2	45	31	37	5	.290	.340	.373
Bob Fothergill	OF86	R	34	116	346	36	102	24	1	7	50	27	10	4	.295	.348	.431
Red Kress†	OF64,SS53,3B19	R	25	135	515	83	147	42	4	9	57	47	36	6	.285	.346	.435
Billy Sullivan	1B52,3B17,C5	L	21	93	307	31	97	16	1	1	45	20	9	1	.316	.358	.384
Charlie Berry†	C70	R	29	72	226	33	69	15	6	4	31	21	23	3	.305	.364	.478
Johnny Hodapp†	OF31,2B5,3B4	R	26	68	176	21	40	8	0	3	20	11	3	1	.227	.273	.324
Jack Rothrock†	OF19,3B8,1B1	S	27	39	64	8	12	2	1	0	6	5	9	1	.188	.246	.250
Charlie English	3B13,SS1	R	22	24	63	7	20	3	1	1	8	3	7	0	.317	.348	.444
Evar Swanson	OF14	R	29	14	52	9	16	3	1	0	8	8	3	3	.308	.400	.404
Cliff Watwood†	OF13	L	26	13	49	5	15	2	0	0	0	1	3	0	.306	.333	.347
Bill Norman	OF13	R	21	13	48	6	11	3	1	0	2	2	3	0	.229	.260	.333
Bill Cissell†	SS12	R	28	12	43	7	11	1	1	1	5	1	0	0	.256	.273	.395
Smead Jolley†	OF11	L	30	12	42	3	15	3	0	0	7	3	0	1	.357	.413	.429
Lew Fonseca	OF8,P1	R	33	18	37	0	5	1	0	0	6	1	7	0	.135	.158	.162
Hal Anderson	OF9	R	28	9	32	4	8	0	0	0	2	0	1	0	.250	.250	.250
Bruce Campbell†	OF4	L	22	9	26	3	4	1	0	0	2	0	4	0	.154	.154	.192
Fabian Kowalik	P2,3B2	S	24	6	13	2	5	2	0	0	2	1	0	0	.385	.429	.538
Bennie Tate†	C4	L	30	4	10	1	1	0	0	0	0	1	0	0	.100	.182	.100
Mel Simons	OF6	L	31	7	5	0	0	0	0	0	0	0	1	0	.000	.000	.000
Greg Mulleavy	2B1	R	26	1	3	0	0	0	0	0	0	0	0	0	.000	.000	.000

Pitcher	T	Age	G	GS	CG	ShO	IP	H	HR	BB	SO	W-L	Sv	ERA
Sad Sam Jones	R	39	30	28	10	0	200.1	217	9	75	64	10-15	0	4.22
Ted Lyons	R	31	33	26	19	1	230.2	243	10	71	58	10-15	2	3.28
Milt Gaston	R	36	28	25	7	1	166.2	183	10	73	44	7-17	1	4.00
Vic Frasier	R	27	29	21	4	0	146.0	180	14	70	33	3-13	0	6.23
Charlie Biggs	R	25	6	4	0	0	24.2	32	2	12	1	1-1	0	6.93
Ed Walsh	R	27	4	4	1	0	20.1	26	3	13	7	0-2	0	8.41
Bump Hadley†	R	27	3	2	1	0	18.2	17	2	8	13	1-1	1	3.86
Art Smith	R	26	3	2	0	0	7.0	17	1	4	1	0-1	0	11.57
Fabian Kowalik	R	24	2	1	0	0	10.1	16	2	4	2	0-1	0	6.97
Red Faber	R	43	42	5	0	0	106.0	123	0	38	26	2-11	6	3.74
Paul Gregory	R	24	33	9	3	0	117.2	125	8	51	39	5-3	0	4.51
Pat Caraway	L	26	19	9	1	0	64.2	80	6	37	13	2-6	0	6.82
Phil Gallivan	R	25	13	3	1	0	33.1	49	4	24	12	1-3	0	7.56
Pete Daglia	R	26	12	5	2	0	50.0	67	4	20	16	2-4	0	5.76
Tommy Thomas†	R	32	12	3	1	0	43.2	55	6	15	11	3-3	0	6.18
Bill Chamberlain	L	23	12	5	0	0	41.1	39	3	25	11	0-5	0	4.57
Hal McKain	R	25	8	0	0	0	11.1	17	1	5	7	0-0	0	11.12
Art Evans	L	20	7	0	0	0	18.0	19	0	10	6	0-0	0	3.00
Chad Kimsey†	R	25	7	0	0	0	11.0	8	0	5	6	1-1	2	2.45
Grant Bowler	R	24	4	0	0	0	6.1	15	1	3	2	0-0	0	15.63
Clarence Fieber	L	18	3	0	0	0	5.1	6	0	3	1	1-0	0	1.69
Les Bartholomew	L	29	3	0	0	0	5.1	5	0	6	1	0-0	0	5.06
Archie Wise	R	19	2	0	0	0	7.1	8	1	5	2	0-0	0	4.91
Jim Moore	R	28	1	0	0	0	1.0	1	0	1	2	0-0	0	0.00
Lew Fonseca	R	33	1	0	0	0	1.0	0	0	0	0	0-0	0	0.00
Bob Poser	R	22	1	0	0	0	0.2	3	0	2	1	0-0	0	27.00

1932 Boston Red Sox 8th AL 43-111 .279 64.0 GB

Shano Collins (11-44)/Marty McManus (32-67)

Player	Gm by Position	B	Age	G	AB	R	H	2B	3B	HR	RBI	BB	SO	SB	Avg	OBP	Slg
Bennie Tate†	C76	L	30	81	273	21	67	12	5	2	26	20	6	0	.245	.297	.348
Dale Alexander†	1B101	R	29	101	376	58	140	27	3	8	56	55	19	4	.372	.454	.524
Marv Olson	2B106,3B1	R	25	115	403	58	100	14	6	0	25	61	26	1	.248	.347	.313
Urbane Pickering	3B126,C1	R	33	132	457	47	119	28	5	2	40	39	71	3	.260	.320	.357
Rabbit Warstler	SS107	R	28	115	388	26	82	15	5	0	34	22	43	9	.211	.259	.276
Smead Jolley†	OF126,C6	L	30	137	531	57	164	27	5	18	99	27	29	0	.309	.345	.480
Tom Oliver	OF116	R	29	122	455	39	120	23	3	0	37	25	12	1	.264	.305	.327
Roy Johnson†	OF85	L	29	94	348	70	104	24	4	11	47	44	41	13	.299	.379	.486
Marty McManus	2B49,3B30,SS2*	R	32	93	302	39	71	19	4	5	24	36	30	1	.235	.317	.374
Cliff Watwood†	OF46,1B18	L	26	95	266	26	66	11	0	0	30	20	11	7	.248	.301	.289
Ed Connolly	C75	R	23	75	222	9	50	8	4	0	21	20	27	0	.225	.289	.297
Hal Rhyne	SS55,3B4,2B1	R	33	71	207	26	47	12	5	0	14	23	14	3	.227	.310	.333
Earl Webb†	OF50,1B2	L	34	52	192	23	54	9	1	5	27	25	15	0	.281	.364	.417
George Stumpf	OF51	L	21	79	169	18	34	2	2	1	18	18	21	1	.201	.278	.254
Al Van Camp	1B25	R	28	34	103	10	23	4	2	0	6	4	17	0	.223	.252	.301
Jack Rothrock†	OF12	S	27	12	48	3	10	1	0	0	0	5	5	3	.208	.283	.229
Johnny Reder	1B10,3B1	R	22	17	37	4	5	1	0	0	3	6	6	0	.135	.256	.162
Andy Spognardi	2B9,SS3,3B2	R	23	17	34	9	10	1	0	0	1	6	6	0	.294	.400	.324
Charlie Berry†	C10	R	29	10	32	0	6	3	0	0	6	3	2	0	.188	.257	.281
Howie Storie	C5	R	21	6	8	0	3	0	0	0	0	0	0	0	.375	.375	.375
Otto Miller		R	31	2	2	0	0	0	0	0	0	0	0	0	.000	.000	.000
Hank Patterson	C1	R	24	1	1	0	0	0	0	0	0	0	0	0	.000	.000	.000
Johnny Lucas		R	29	1	1	0	0	0	0	0	0	0	0	0	.000	.000	.000

M. McManus, 1 G at 1B

Pitcher	T	Age	G	GS	CG	ShO	IP	H	HR	BB	SO	W-L	Sv	ERA
Bob Weiland	L	26	43	27	7	0	195.2	231	11	97	63	6-16	1	4.51
Ed Durham	R	23	34	22	4	0	175.1	187	13	49	52	6-13	0	3.80
Ivy Andrews†	R	25	25	19	8	0	141.2	144	4	53	30	8-6	0	3.81
Gordon Rhodes†	R	24	12	11	4	0	79.1	79	5	31	22	1-8	0	5.11
Danny MacFayden†	R	27	12	11	6	0	77.2	91	3	33	29	1-10	0	5.10
Jack Russell†	R	26	11	6	1	0	39.2	61	2	15	7	1-7	0	6.81
Pete Donohue	R	31	4	2	0	0	12.2	18	2	6	1	0-1	0	7.82
Bob Kline	R	22	47	19	4	1	172.0	203	10	76	31	11-13	2	5.28
Wilcy Moore†	R	35	37	2	0	0	84.1	98	5	42	28	4-10	4	5.23
John Michaels	L	24	28	8	2	0	80.2	101	4	27	16	1-6	0	5.13
Larry Boerner	R	27	21	5	0	0	61.0	71	2	37	19	0-4	0	5.02
Johnny Welch	R	25	20	8	3	1	72.1	93	3	38	26	4-6	0	5.23
Hod Lisenbee	R	33	19	6	3	0	73.1	87	9	25	13	0-4	0	5.65
Pete Appleton†	R	28	11	3	0	0	46.0	49	2	26	15	0-3	0	4.11
Ed Gallagher	L	21	9	3	0	0	23.2	30	3	28	6	0-3	0	12.55
G. McNaughton	R	21	6	2	0	0	21.0	21	1	22	6	0-1	0	6.43
Regis Leheny	L	24	2	0	0	0	2.2	5	0	3	1	0-0	0	16.88
Jud McLaughlin	L	20	1	0	0	0	3.0	5	0	4	0	0-0	0	15.00

»1932 Chicago Cubs 1st NL 90-64 .584 —

Rogers Hornsby (53-46)/Charlie Grimm (37-18)

Player	Gm by Position	B	Age	G	AB	R	H	2B	3B	HR	RBI	BB	SO	SB	Avg	OBP	Slg
Gabby Hartnett	C117,1B1	R	31	121	406	52	110	25	3	12	52	51	59	0	.271	.354	.436
Charlie Grimm	1B149	L	33	149	570	66	175	42	2	7	80	35	22	2	.307	.349	.425
Billy Herman	2B154	R	22	154	656	102	206	42	7	1	51	40	33	14	.314	.358	.404
Woody English	3B93,SS38	R	25	127	522	70	142	23	7	3	47	55	73	5	.272	.344	.360
Billy Jurges	SS108,3B5	R	24	115	396	40	100	24	4	2	52	19	26	1	.253	.288	.348
Riggs Stephenson	OF147	R	34	147	583	86	189	49	4	4	85	54	27	3	.324	.383	.443
Kiki Cuyler	OF109	R	33	110	446	58	130	19	9	10	77	29	43	9	.291	.340	.442
Johnny Moore	OF109	L	30	119	443	59	135	24	5	13	64	22	38	4	.305	.342	.470
Stan Hack	3B51	L	22	72	178	32	42	5	6	2	19	17	16	5	.236	.306	.365
Rollie Hemsley	C47,OF1	R	25	60	151	27	36	10	3	4	20	10	16	2	.238	.286	.424
Lance Richbourg	OF33	L	34	44	148	22	38	2	2	1	21	8	4	0	.257	.295	.318
Vince Barton	OF34	L	24	36	134	19	30	2	3	3	15	8	22	0	.224	.273	.351
Mark Koenig	SS31	S	27	33	102	15	36	5	1	3	11	3	5	0	.353	.377	.510
Marv Gudat	OF14,1B8,P1	L	26	60	94	15	24	4	1	1	15	16	10	0	.255	.369	.351
Rogers Hornsby	OF10,3B6	R	36	19	58	10	13	2	0	1	7	10	4	0	.224	.357	.310
Frank Demaree	OF17	R	22	23	56	4	14	3	0	0	6	2	7	0	.250	.288	.304
Bob Smith	P34,2B2	R	37	36	42	5	10	4	1	0	4	0	2	1	.238	.238	.381
Zack Taylor	C14	R	33	21	30	2	6	1	0	0	3	1	4	0	.200	.226	.233
Danny Taylor†	OF6	R	31	6	22	3	5	2	0	0	3	3	1	1	.227	.320	.318
Harry Taylor	1B1	L	24	10	8	1	1	0	0	0	0	1	1	0	.125	.222	.125

Pitcher	T	Age	G	GS	CG	ShO	IP	H	HR	BB	SO	W-L	Sv	ERA
Pat Malone	R	29	37	33	17	2	237.0	222	13	78	120	15-17	0	3.38
Lon Warneke	R	23	35	32	25	4	277.0	247	12	64	106	22-6	0	2.37
Guy Bush	R	30	40	30	15	1	238.2	262	13	70	73	19-11	0	3.21
Charlie Root	R	33	39	23	11	0	216.1	211	10	55	96	15-10	3	3.58
Burleigh Grimes	R	38	30	18	5	1	141.1	174	8	50	36	6-11	1	4.78
Jakie May	L	36	35	0	0	0	53.2	61	3	19	20	2-2	1	4.36
Bob Smith	R	37	34	11	4	1	119.0	148	4	36	35	4-3	2	4.61
Bud Tinning	R	26	24	7	2	0	93.1	93	3	24	30	5-3	0	2.80
LeRoy Herrmann	R	26	7	0	0	0	12.2	18	0	9	5	2-1	0	6.39
Carroll Yerkes	L	29	2	0	0	0	9.0	5	2	3	4	0-0	0	3.00
Bobo Newsom	R	24	1	0	0	0	1.0	1	0	0	0	0-0	0	0.00
Marv Gudat	L	26	1	0	0	0	1.0	1	0	0	2	0-0	0	0.00
Ed Baecht	R	25	1	0	0	0	1.0	1	0	1	0	0-0	0	0.00

1932 Pittsburgh Pirates 2nd NL 86-68 .558 4.0 GB

George Gibson

Player	Gm by Position	B	Age	G	AB	R	H	2B	3B	HR	RBI	BB	SO	SB	Avg	OBP	Slg
Earl Grace	C114	L	25	115	390	41	107	17	5	7	55	14	23	0	.274	.305	.397
Gus Suhr	1B154	L	26	154	581	78	153	31	16	5	81	63	39	7	.263	.337	.398
Tony Piet	2B154	R	25	154	574	66	162	25	8	7	85	46	56	19	.282	.343	.390
Pie Traynor	3B127	R	32	135	513	74	169	27	10	2	68	32	20	6	.329	.373	.433
Arky Vaughan	SS128	L	20	129	497	71	158	15	10	4	61	39	26	10	.318	.375	.412
Paul Waner	OF154	L	29	154	630	107	215	62	10	8	82	56	24	13	.341	.397	.510
Lloyd Waner	OF131	L	26	134	565	90	188	27	11	2	38	31	11	6	.333	.367	.430
Adam Comorosky	OF92	R	26	108	370	54	106	18	4	4	46	25	20	7	.286	.337	.389
Dave Barbee	OF78	R	27	97	327	37	84	22	6	5	55	18	38	1	.257	.300	.407
Tommy Thevenow	SS29,3B22	R	28	59	194	12	46	3	3	0	26	7	12	0	.237	.264	.284
Tom Padden	C43	R	23	47	118	13	31	6	1	0	10	9	7	0	.263	.315	.331
Gus Dugas	OF20	L	25	55	97	13	23	3	3	3	12	7	11	0	.237	.288	.423
Hal Finney	C11	R	26	31	33	14	7	3	0	0	4	3	4	0	.212	.297	.303
Bill Brubaker	3B7	R	21	7	24	3	10	3	0	0	4	3	4	1	.417	.481	.542
Bill Brenzel	C9	R	22	9	24	0	1	1	0	0	2	0	4	0	.042	.042	.083
Howdie Grosklos	SS1	R	25	17	20	1	2	0	0	0	0	0	3	0	.100	.100	.100
Woody Jensen		L	24	7	5	2	0	0	0	0	0	0	2	0	.000	.000	.000

Pitcher	T	Age	G	GS	CG	ShO	IP	H	HR	BB	SO	W-L	Sv	ERA
Larry French	L	24	47	33	19	3	274.1	301	17	62	72	18-16	4	3.02
Heinie Meine	R	36	28	25	13	1	172.1	193	6	45	32	12-9	1	3.86
Bill Swift	R	24	39	23	11	0	214.1	205	15	26	64	14-10	4	3.61
Steve Swetonic	R	28	24	19	11	4	162.2	134	11	55	39	11-6	0	2.82
Ray Kremer	R	39	11	10	3	1	56.2	61	5	16	6	4-3	0	4.29
Hal Smith	R	30	2	1	1	1	12.0	9	0	2	4	1-0	0	0.75
Glenn Spencer	R	26	39	13	5	1	137.2	167	10	44	35	4-8	1	4.97
Bill Harris	R	32	37	17	4	0	168.0	178	6	38	63	10-9	2	3.64
Leon Chagnon	R	29	30	10	4	1	128.0	140	10	34	52	9-6	0	3.94
Erv Brame	R	30	23	3	0	0	51.0	84	6	16	10	3-1	0	7.41

1932 Brooklyn Dodgers 3rd NL 81-73 .526 9.0 GB

Max Carey

Player	Gm by Position	B	Age	G	AB	R	H	2B	3B	HR	RBI	BB	SO	SB	Avg	OBP	Slg
Al Lopez	C125	R	23	126	404	44	111	18	6	1	43	34	35	3	.275	.331	.356
George Kelly	1B62,OF1	R	36	64	202	23	49	9	1	4	22	22	27	0	.243	.317	.356
Tony Cuccinello	2B154	R	24	154	597	76	168	32	6	12	77	46	47	5	.281	.337	.415
Joe Stripp	3B93,1B43	R	29	138	534	94	162	36	9	6	64	36	30	14	.303	.350	.438
Glenn Wright	SS122,1B2	R	31	127	446	50	122	31	5	11	60	12	57	4	.274	.293	.439
Lefty O'Doul	OF148	L	35	148	595	120	219	32	8	21	90	50	20	11	.368	.423	.555
Hack Wilson	OF125	R	32	135	481	77	143	37	5	23	123	51	85	2	.297	.366	.538
Danny Taylor†	OF96	R	31	105	395	84	128	22	7	11	48	33	41	13	.324	.378	.499
Johnny Frederick	OF88	L	30	118	384	54	115	28	2	16	56	25	35	1	.299	.349	.508
Gordon Slade	SS55,3B23	R	27	79	250	23	60	15	1	1	23	11	26	3	.240	.280	.320
Bud Clancy	1B53	L	31	53	196	14	60	4	2	0	16	6	13	0	.306	.327	.347
Neal Finn	3B50,2B2,SS1	R	28	65	189	22	45	5	2	0	14	11	15	2	.238	.284	.286
Clyde Sukeforth	C36	L	30	59	111	14	26	4	4	0	12	6	10	1	.234	.280	.342
Val Picinich	C24	R	35	41	70	8	18	6	0	1	11	4	8	0	.257	.297	.386
Max Rosenfeld	OF30	R	29	34	39	8	14	3	0	2	7	0	10	2	.359	.359	.590
Alta Cohen	OF8	L	23	9	32	1	5	1	0	0	1	3	7	0	.156	.229	.188
Ike Boone	OF8	L	35	13	21	2	3	1	0	0	2	5	2	0	.143	.308	.190
Bruce Caldwell	1B6	R	26	7	11	2	1	0	0	0	2	2	2	0	.091	.231	.091
Paul Richards	C3	R	23	3	8	0	0	0	0	0	0	0	2	0	.000	.000	.000
Dick Siebert	1B2	L	20	6	7	1	2	0	0	0	0	2	2	0	.286	.444	.286
Bobby Reis	3B1	R	23	1	4	0	1	0	0	0	0	0	1	0	.250	.250	.250
Fresco Thompson		R	30	3	1	0	0	0	0	0	0	0	0	0	.000	.000	.000

Pitcher	T	Age	G	GS	CG	ShO	IP	H	HR	BB	SO	W-L	Sv	ERA
Watty Clark	L	30	40	36	19	2	273.0	282	10	49	99	20-12	0	3.49
Van Lingle Mungo	R	21	39	33	11	1	223.1	224	9	115	107	13-11	2	4.43
Dazzy Vance	R	41	27	24	9	1	175.2	171	10	57	103	12-11	1	4.20
Sloppy Thurston	R	33	28	20	10	2	153.0	174	14	38	35	12-8	0	4.06
Waite Hoyt†	R	32	8	4	0	0	26.2	38	3	12	7	1-3	1	7.76
Jack Quinn	R	48	42	0	0	0	87.1	102	1	24	28	3-7	8	3.30
Fred Heimach	L	31	36	15	7	0	167.2	203	7	28	30	9-4	0	3.97
Joe Shaute	L	32	34	9	1	0	117.0	147	8	21	32	7-7	4	4.54
Ray Phelps	R	28	20	8	4	1	79.1	101	5	27	21	4-5	0	5.90
Cy Moore	R	27	20	2	0	0	48.2	56	3	17	21	0-3	0	4.81
Fay Thomas	R	27	7	2	0	0	17.0	22	0	8	9	0-1	0	7.41
Ed Pipgras	R	28	5	1	0	0	10.0	16	2	6	5	0-1	0	5.40
Art Jones	R	26	1	0	0	0	1.0	2	0	1	0	0-0	0	18.00

1932 Philadelphia Phillies 4th NL 78-76 .506 12.0 GB

Burt Shotton

Player	Gm by Position	B	Age	G	AB	R	H	2B	3B	HR	RBI	BB	SO	SB	Avg	OBP	Slg
Spud Davis	C120	R	27	125	402	44	135	23	5	14	70	40	39	1	.336	.399	.522
Don Hurst	1B150	L	26	150	579	109	196	41	4	24	143	65	27	10	.339	.412	.547
Les Mallon	2B88,3B5	R	26	103	347	44	90	16	0	5	31	28	28	1	.259	.318	.349
Pinky Whitney	3B151,2B5	R	27	154	624	93	186	33	11	13	124	35	66	6	.298	.335	.449
Dick Bartell	SS154	R	24	154	614	118	189	48	7	1	53	64	47	8	.308	.379	.414
Chuck Klein	OF154	L	27	154	650	152	226	50	15	38	137	60	49	20	.348	.404	.646
Hal Lee	OF148	R	27	149	595	76	180	42	10	18	85	36	45	6	.303	.343	.497
Kiddo Davis	OF133	R	30	137	576	100	178	39	6	5	57	44	56	16	.309	.359	.424
Bernie Friberg	2B56	R	32	61	154	17	37	8	2	0	14	19	23	0	.240	.324	.318
Harry McCurdy	C42	L	32	62	136	13	32	6	1	1	14	17	13	0	.235	.325	.316
Rube Bressler†	OF18	R	37	27	83	9	19	6	1	0	6	2	5	0	.229	.247	.325
Al Todd	C25	R	30	33	70	8	16	5	0	0	9	1	9	1	.229	.260	.300
George Brickell	OF12	L	25	45	66	9	22	6	1	0	2	4	5	2	.333	.389	.455
Eddie Delker†	2B27	R	26	30	62	7	10	1	1	1	7	6	14	0	.161	.235	.258
Cliff Heathcote†	1B7	L	34	30	39	7	11	2	0	1	5	3	3	0	.282	.333	.410
George Knothe	2B5	R	34	6	12	2	1	1	0	0	0	0	0	0	.083	.083	.167
Russ Scarritt	OF1	L	29	11	11	0	2	0	0	0	0	1	2	0	.182	.250	.182
Hugh Willingham		R	26	4	2	0	0	0	0	0	0	0	0	0	.000	.000	.000
Doug Taitt		L	29	4	2	0	0	0	0	0	1	2	0	0	.000	.500	.000

Pitcher	T	Age	G	GS	CG	ShO	IP	H	HR	BB	SO	W-L	Sv	ERA
Ed Holley	R	32	34	30	16	2	228.0	247	15	55	87	11-14	0	3.95
Ray Benge	R	30	41	28	13	2	222.1	247	15	58	89	13-12	6	4.05
Snipe Hansen	L	25	39	23	5	0	191.0	215	13	51	56	10-10	2	3.72
Jumbo Elliott	L	31	39	22	8	0	166.0	210	14	47	62	11-10	0	5.42
Flint Rhem†	R	31	26	20	10	0	168.2	177	13	49	35	11-7	1	3.74
Phil Collins	R	30	43	21	6	0	184.1	231	21	65	66	14-12	3	5.27
Jack Berly	R	29	21	1	1	0	46.0	61	4	21	15	1-2	2	7.63
Hal Elliott	R	33	16	7	0	0	57.2	70	5	38	13	2-4	0	5.77
Reggie Grabowski	R	24	14	2	0	0	34.1	38	2	22	15	2-2	0	3.67
Clise Dudley	R	28	13	0	0	0	17.2	23	3	8	5	1-1	1	7.13
Chet Nichols	R	34	11	0	0	0	19.1	23	2	14	5	0-2	1	6.98
Ad Liska	R	25	8	0	0	0	26.2	22	0	10	6	2-0	1	1.69
Stew Bolen	L	29	5	0	0	0	16.0	18	0	10	3	0-0	0	2.81
Bob Adams	R	25	4	0	0	0	6.0	7	0	2	2	0-0	0	1.50

1932 Boston Braves 5th NL 77-77 .500 13.0 GB

Bill McKechnie

Player	Gm by Position	B	Age	G	AB	R	H	2B	3B	HR	RBI	BB	SO	SB	Avg	OBP	Slg
Al Spohrer	C100	R	29	104	335	31	90	12	2	0	33	15	26	2	.269	.300	.316
Art Shires	1B80	L	24	82	298	32	71	9	3	5	30	25	21	1	.238	.299	.339
Rabbit Maranville	2B149	R	40	149	571	67	134	20	4	0	37	46	28	4	.235	.295	.284
Fritz Knothe	3B87	R	29	89	344	45	82	19	1	1	36	39	37	5	.238	.318	.308
Billy Urbanski	SS136	R	29	136	563	80	153	25	8	8	46	28	60	8	.272	.307	.387
Wally Berger	OF134,1B11	R	26	145	602	90	185	34	6	17	73	33	66	5	.307	.346	.468
Red Worthington	OF104	R	26	105	435	62	132	35	8	8	61	15	24	1	.303	.330	.476
Wes Schulmerich	OF101	R	31	119	404	47	105	22	5	11	57	27	61	5	.260	.314	.421
Randy Moore	OF41,3B31,1B22	L	26	107	351	41	103	21	2	3	43	15	11	1	.293	.322	.390
Freddy Leach	OF50	L	34	84	223	21	55	9	2	1	29	18	10	1	.247	.306	.318
Pinky Hargrave	C73	S	36	82	217	20	57	14	3	4	33	24	18	1	.263	.336	.410
Buck Jordan	1B49	L	25	49	212	27	68	12	3	2	29	4	5	1	.321	.333	.434
Dutch Holland	OF39	R	28	39	156	15	46	11	1	1	18	12	20	0	.295	.345	.397
Hod Ford†	2B20,SS16,3B2	R	34	40	95	9	26	5	2	0	6	6	9	0	.274	.324	.368
Bill Akers	3B20,2B5,SS5	R	27	36	93	8	24	3	1	1	17	10	15	0	.258	.330	.344
Bucky Walters	3B22	R	23	22	75	8	14	3	1	0	4	2	18	0	.187	.208	.253
Earl Clark	OF16	R	24	50	44	11	11	2	0	0	4	2	7	1	.250	.283	.295
Johnny Schulte†	C10	L	35	10	9	1	2	0	0	1	2	2	1	0	.222	.364	.556
Ox Eckhardt		L	30	8	8	1	2	0	0	0	1	0	1	0	.250	.250	.250

Pitcher	T	Age	G	GS	CG	ShO	IP	H	HR	BB	SO	W-L	Sv	ERA
Ed Brandt	L	27	35	31	19	2	254.0	271	11	57	79	16-16	1	3.97
Bob Brown	R	21	35	28	9	0	213.0	187	6	104	110	14-7	1	3.30
Huck Betts	R	35	31	27	16	3	221.2	229	9	35	32	13-11	1	2.80
Tom Zachary	L	36	32	24	12	1	212.0	231	5	55	67	12-11	0	3.10
Socks Seibold	R	36	28	20	6	1	136.2	173	12	41	33	3-10	0	4.68
Ben Cantwell	R	30	37	9	3	1	146.0	133	6	33	33	13-11	5	2.96
Fred Frankhouse	R	28	37	6	3	0	108.2	113	7	45	35	4-6	0	3.56
Hub Pruett	L	31	18	7	4	0	63.0	76	3	30	27	1-5	0	5.14
Bruce Cunningham	R	26	18	3	0	0	47.0	50	1	19	21	1-0	0	3.45
Leo Mangum	R	36	7	0	0	0	10.1	17	1	0	3	0-0	0	5.23
Bill Sherdel†	L	35	1	0	0	0	1.2	3	0	1	0	0-0	0	0.00

1932 St. Louis Cardinals 6th NL 72-82 .468 18.0 GB

Gabby Street

Player	Gm by Position	B	Age	G	AB	R	H	2B	3B	HR	RBI	BB	SO	SB	Avg	OBP	Slg
Gus Mancuso	C82	R	26	103	310	25	88	23	1	5	43	30	15	0	.284	.347	.413
Ripper Collins	1B81,OF60	S	28	149	549	82	153	28	8	21	91	38	67	4	.279	.329	.474
Jimmie Reese	2B77	L	30	90	309	38	82	15	0	2	26	20	19	4	.265	.314	.333
Jake Flowers	3B54,SS7,2B2	R	30	67	247	35	63	11	1	2	18	31	18	7	.255	.341	.332
Charlie Gelbert	SS122	R	26	122	455	60	122	28	9	1	45	39	30	8	.268	.330	.376
George Watkins	OF120	L	32	127	458	67	143	35	3	9	63	45	46	18	.312	.384	.461
Ernie Orsatti	OF96,1B1	L	29	101	375	44	126	27	6	2	44	18	29	5	.336	.368	.456
Pepper Martin	OF69,3B15	R	28	85	323	47	77	19	6	4	34	30	31	9	.238	.305	.372
Frankie Frisch	2B75,3B37,SS4	S	33	115	486	59	142	26	2	3	60	25	13	18	.292	.327	.372
Jim Bottomley	1B74	L	32	91	311	45	92	16	3	11	48	25	32	2	.296	.350	.473
Jimmie Wilson	C75,1B3,2B1	R	31	92	274	36	68	16	2	2	28	15	18	9	.248	.290	.343
Ray Blades	OF62	R	35	80	201	35	46	10	1	3	29	34	31	2	.229	.340	.333
Sparky Adams	3B30	R	37	31	127	22	35	3	1	0	13	14	5	0	.276	.352	.315
George Puccinelli	OF30	R	25	31	108	17	30	8	0	3	11	12	13	1	.278	.350	.435
Joe Medwick	OF26	R	20	26	106	13	37	12	1	2	12	2	10	3	.349	.367	.538
Charlie Wilson	SS24	S	27	24	96	7	19	3	3	1	2	3	8	0	.198	.222	.323
Harvey Hendrick†	3B12,OF5	L	34	28	72	8	18	2	0	1	5	5	9	0	.250	.299	.319
Roy Pepper	OF17	R	26	21	57	3	14	2	1	0	7	5	13	1	.246	.306	.316
Eddie Delker†	2B10,3B5,SS4	R	26	20	42	1	5	4	0	0	2	8	7	0	.119	.260	.214
Bill Delancey	C8	L	20	8	26	1	5	0	2	0	2	2	1	0	.192	.250	.346
Ray Cunningham	3B8,2B2	R	27	11	22	4	4	1	0	0	0	3	4	0	.182	.280	.227
Joel Hunt	OF5	R	26	12	21	0	4	1	0	0	3	4	3	0	.190	.320	.238
Rube Bressler†	OF4	R	37	10	19	0	3	0	0	0	2	0	1	0	.158	.158	.158
Wattie Holm	OF4	R	30	11	17	2	3	1	0	0	1	3	1	0	.176	.333	.235
Mike Gonzalez	C7	R	41	17	14	0	2	0	0	0	3	0	2	0	.143	.143	.143
Hod Ford†	SS1	R	34	1	2	0	0	0	0	0	0	0	0	0	.000	.000	.000
Skeeter Webb		R	22	1	0	0	0	0	0	0	0	0	0	0	—	—	—

Pitcher	T	Age	G	GS	CG	ShO	IP	H	HR	BB	SO	W-L	Sv	ERA
Dizzy Dean	R	22	46	33	16	4	286.0	280	14	102	191	18-15	2	3.30
Paul Derringer	R	25	39	30	14	1	233.1	296	6	67	78	11-14	0	4.05
Tex Carleton	R	25	44	22	9	3	196.1	198	12	70	113	10-13	0	4.08
Wild Bill Hallahan	L	29	25	22	13	1	176.1	169	10	69	108	12-7	1	3.11
Syl Johnson	R	31	32	22	7	1	164.2	199	14	35	70	5-14	2	4.92
Jesse Haines	R	38	20	10	4	1	85.1	116	4	16	27	3-5	0	4.75
Flint Rhem†	R	31	6	6	5	1	50.0	48	3	10	18	4-2	0	3.06
Ray Starr	R	26	3	2	1	1	20.0	19	2	10	6	1-1	0	2.70
Allyn Stout	R	27	36	3	1	0	73.2	87	5	28	32	4-5	1	4.40
Jim Lindsey	R	36	33	5	0	0	89.1	96	6	38	31	3-3	3	4.94
Jim Winford	R	22	4	1	0	0	8.1	9	0	5	4	1-1	0	6.48
Bill Sherdel†	L	35	3	0	0	0	5.2	7	0	1	1	0-0	0	4.76
Benny Frey†	R	26	2	0	0	0	3.0	6	0	2	0	0-2	0	12.00
Dick Terwilliger	R	26	1	0	0	0	3.0	1	0	2	2	0-0	0	0.00
Bud Teachout	L	28	1	0	0	0	1.0	2	0	0	0	0-0	0	0.00

1932 New York Giants 6th NL 72-82 .468 18.0 GB

John McGraw (17-23)/Bill Terry (55-59)

Player	Gm by Position	B	Age	G	AB	R	H	2B	3B	HR	RBI	BB	SO	SB	Avg	OBP	Slg
Shanty Hogan	C136	R	26	140	502	36	144	18	2	8	77	26	22	0	.287	.323	.378
Bill Terry	1B154	L	35	154	643	124	225	42	11	28	117	32	23	4	.350	.382	.580
Hughie Critz	2B151	R	31	151	659	90	182	32	7	2	50	34	27	3	.276	.313	.355
Johnny Vergez	3B111,SS1	R	25	118	376	42	98	21	3	6	43	25	36	1	.261	.310	.380
Ed Marshall	SS63	R	26	68	226	18	56	8	1	0	28	6	11	1	.248	.270	.292
Mel Ott	OF154	L	23	154	566	119	180	30	8	38	123	100	39	6	.318	.424	.601
Freddy Lindstrom	OF128,3B15	R	26	144	595	83	161	26	5	15	92	27	28	6	.271	.303	.407
Jo-Jo Moore	OF86	L	23	86	361	53	110	15	2	2	27	20	18	4	.305	.341	.374
Chick Fullis	OF55,2B1	R	28	96	235	35	70	14	3	1	21	11	12	1	.298	.332	.396
Gil English	3B39,SS23	R	22	59	204	22	46	7	5	2	19	5	20	0	.225	.244	.338
Travis Jackson	SS52	R	28	52	195	23	50	17	1	4	38	13	16	1	.256	.310	.415
Len Koenecke	OF35	L	28	42	137	33	35	5	0	4	14	11	13	3	.255	.320	.380
Ethan Allen	OF24	R	28	54	103	13	18	6	2	1	7	1	12	0	.175	.198	.301
Eddie Moore	SS21,3B6,2B5	R	33	37	87	9	23	3	0	1	6	9	6	1	.264	.340	.333
Sam Leslie	1B2	L	26	77	75	5	22	4	0	1	15	2	5	0	.293	.329	.387
Bob O'Farrell	C41	R	35	50	67	7	16	3	0	0	8	11	10	0	.239	.354	.284
Francis Healy	C11	R	21	14	32	5	8	2	0	0	4	2	8	0	.250	.294	.313
Art McLarney	SS9	S	23	9	23	2	3	1	0	0	3	1	3	0	.130	.167	.174
Tip Tobin		R	25	1	1	0	0	0	0	0	0	0	0	0	.000	.000	.000
Pat Veltman		R	26	2	1	0	0	0	0	0	0	0	1	0	.000	.000	.000

Pitcher	T	Age	G	GS	CG	ShO	IP	H	HR	BB	SO	W-L	Sv	ERA
Carl Hubbell	L	29	40	32	22	0	284.0	260	20	40	137	18-11	2	2.50
F. Fitzsimmons	R	30	35	31	11	0	237.2	287	18	83	65	11-11	0	4.43
Bill Walker	L	28	31	22	9	0	163.0	177	23	55	74	8-12	2	4.14
Jim Mooney	L	25	29	18	4	1	124.2	154	18	42	37	6-10	0	5.05
Waite Hoyt†	R	32	18	12	3	0	97.1	103	6	25	29	5-7	0	3.42
Sam Gibson	R	32	41	5	1	1	81.2	107	7	30	39	4-8	3	4.85
Dolf Luque	R	41	38	5	1	0	110.0	128	4	32	32	6-7	5	4.01
Hi Bell	R	34	35	10	3	0	120.0	132	12	16	25	8-4	2	3.68
Hal Schumacher	R	21	27	13	2	1	101.1	119	3	39	38	5-6	0	3.55
Clarence Mitchell	L	41	8	3	1	0	30.1	41	1	11	7	1-3	2	4.15
Roy Parmelee	R	25	8	3	0	0	25.1	25	0	14	23	0-3	0	3.91

1932 Cincinnati Reds 8th NL 60-94 .390 30.0 GB

Dan Howley

Player	Gm by Position	B	Age	G	AB	R	H	2B	3B	HR	RBI	BB	SO	SB	Avg	OBP	Slg
Ernie Lombardi	C110	R	24	118	413	43	125	22	9	11	68	41	19	0	.303	.371	.479
Harvey Hendrick†	1B94	L	34	94	398	56	120	30	3	4	40	23	29	3	.302	.341	.422
George Grantham	2B115,1B10	L	32	126	493	81	144	29	6	6	39	56	40	4	.292	.364	.412
Wally Gilbert	3B111	R	31	114	420	35	90	18	2	1	40	20	23	2	.214	.252	.274
Leo Durocher	SS142	R	26	143	457	43	99	22	5	1	33	36	40	3	.217	.275	.293
Babe Herman	OF146	L	29	148	577	87	188	38	19	16	87	60	45	7	.326	.389	.541
Estel Crabtree	OF95	L	28	108	402	38	110	14	9	2	35	23	26	2	.274	.316	.368
Wally Roettger	OF94	R	29	106	347	26	96	18	3	3	43	23	24	0	.277	.323	.372
Taylor Douthit	OF88	R	31	96	333	28	81	12	1	0	25	31	29	3	.243	.311	.285
Jo-Jo Morrissey	SS45,2B42,3B12	R	28	89	269	15	65	10	1	0	13	14	15	2	.242	.282	.286
Chick Hafey	OF65	R	29	83	253	34	87	19	3	2	36	22	20	4	.344	.403	.466
Andy High	3B46,2B12	L	34	84	191	16	36	4	2	0	12	23	6	1	.188	.276	.230
Clyde Manion	C47	R	35	49	135	7	28	4	0	0	12	14	16	0	.207	.282	.237
Mickey Heath	1B39	L	28	39	134	14	27	1	3	0	15	20	23	0	.201	.310	.254
Asby Asbjornson	C16	R	23	29	58	5	10	2	0	1	4	0	15	0	.172	.186	.259
Harry Heilmann	1B6	R	37	15	31	3	8	2	0	0	6	0	2	0	.258	.258	.323
Jimmy Shevlin	1B7	L	22	7	24	3	5	2	0	0	4	4	0	4	.208	.345	.292
Cliff Heathcote†		L	34	8	3	3	0	0	0	0	0	0	0	0	.000	.000	.000
Otto Bluege		R	22	1	0	1	0	0	0	0	0	0	0	0	—	—	—

Pitcher	T	Age	G	GS	CG	ShO	IP	H	HR	BB	SO	W-L	Sv	ERA
Red Lucas	R	30	31	31	28	0	269.1	261	10	35	63	13-17	0	2.84
Si Johnson	R	25	42	27	14	2	245.0	246	8	57	94	13-15	2	3.27
Ownie Carroll	R	29	32	26	15	0	210.0	245	7	44	55	10-19	1	4.50
Larry Benton	R	34	35	21	7	0	179.2	201	10	27	35	6-13	2	4.31
Ray Kolp	R	37	32	19	7	2	159.2	176	13	27	42	6-10	1	3.89
Benny Frey†	R	26	28	15	5	0	131.1	159	10	30	27	4-10	0	4.32
Eppa Rixey	L	41	25	11	6	2	111.2	108	3	16	14	5-5	0	2.66
Jack Ogden	R	34	24	3	1	0	57.0	72	5	22	20	2-2	0	5.21
Whitey Hilcher	R	23	11	2	0	0	18.2	24	3	10	4	0-3	0	7.71
Biff Wysong	L	27	7	0	0	0	12.1	13	0	8	5	1-0	0	3.65

»1933 Washington Senators 1st AL 99-53 .651 —

Joe Cronin

Player	Gm by Position	B	Age	G	AB	R	H	2B	3B	HR	RBI	BB	SO	SB	Avg	OBP	Slg
Luke Sewell	C141	R	32	141	474	65	125	30	4	2	61	48	24	7	.264	.335	.357
Joe Kuhel	1B153	L	27	153	602	89	194	34	10	11	107	59	48	17	.322	.385	.467
Buddy Myer	2B129	L	29	131	530	95	160	29	15	4	61	60	29	6	.302	.374	.436
Ossie Bluege	3B138	R	32	140	501	63	131	14	0	6	71	55	34	6	.261	.338	.325
Joe Cronin	SS152	R	26	152	602	89	186	45	11	5	118	87	49	5	.309	.398	.445
Heinie Manush	OF150	L	31	153	658	115	221	32	17	5	95	36	18	6	.336	.372	.459
Fred Schulte	OF142	R	32	144	550	98	162	30	7	5	87	61	27	10	.295	.366	.402
Goose Goslin	OF128	L	32	132	549	97	163	35	10	10	64	42	32	5	.297	.348	.452
Dave Harris	OF45,1B6,3B2	R	32	82	177	33	46	9	2	5	38	25	26	3	.260	.358	.418
Bob Boken	2B31,3B19,SS10	R	25	55	133	19	37	5	2	3	26	9	16	0	.278	.324	.414
Sam Rice	OF39	L	43	73	85	19	25	4	3	1	12	3	7	0	.294	.326	.447
Moe Berg	C35	R	31	40	65	8	12	3	0	2	9	4	5	0	.185	.232	.323
Cecil Travis	3B15	L	19	18	43	7	13	1	0	0	2	2	5	0	.302	.348	.326
John Kerr	2B16,OF1	R	34	28	40	5	8	0	0	0	0	3	2	0	.200	.256	.200
Cliff Bolton	C9,OF1	L	26	33	39	4	16	1	1	0	6	6	3	0	.410	.500	.487
Nick Altrock		S	56	1	1	0	0	0	0	0	0	0	0	0	.000	.000	.000

Pitcher	T	Age	G	GS	CG	ShO	IP	H	HR	BB	SO	W-L	Sv	ERA
Earl Whitehill	L	33	39	37	19	2	270.0	271	9	100	96	22-8	1	3.33
General Crowder	R	34	52	35	17	0	299.1	311	14	81	110	24-15	4	3.97
Lefty Stewart	L	32	34	31	11	1	230.2	227	19	60	69	15-6	0	3.82
Montie Weaver	R	27	23	21	12	1	152.1	147	3	53	45	10-5	0	3.25
Ed Linke	R	21	3	2	0	0	16.0	15	0	11	6	1-0	0	5.06
Ray Prim	L	26	2	1	0	0	14.1	13	0	2	6	0-1	0	3.14
Jack Russell	R	27	50	3	2	0	124.0	119	3	32	28	12-6	13	2.69
Tommy Thomas	R	33	35	14	2	0	135.0	149	9	49	35	7-7	3	4.80
Bill McAfee	R	25	27	1	0	0	53.0	64	3	21	14	3-2	5	6.62
Bobby Burke	L	26	25	6	4	1	64.0	64	1	31	28	4-3	0	3.23
Ed Chapman	R	27	6	1	0	0	9.0	10	2	2	4	0-0	0	8.00
Alex McColl	R	39	4	1	1	0	17.0	13	0	7	5	1-0	0	2.65
Bud Thomas	R	22	2	0	0	0	4.0	11	1	2	1	0-0	0	15.75
John Campbell	R	25	1	0	0	0	1.0	1	0	1	0	0-0	0	0.00

1933 New York Yankees 2nd AL 91-59 .607 7.0 GB

Joe McCarthy

Player	Gm by Position	B	Age	G	AB	R	H	2B	3B	HR	RBI	BB	SO	SB	Avg	OBP	Slg
Bill Dickey	C127	L	26	130	478	58	152	24	8	14	97	47	14	3	.318	.381	.490
Lou Gehrig	1B152	L	30	152	593	138	198	41	12	32	139	92	42	9	.334	.424	.605
Tony Lazzeri	2B138	R	29	139	523	94	154	22	12	18	104	73	62	15	.294	.383	.486
Joe Sewell	3B131	L	34	135	524	87	143	18	1	2	54	71	4	2	.273	.361	.323
Frankie Crosetti	SS133	R	22	136	451	71	114	20	5	9	60	55	40	4	.253	.337	.379
Ben Chapman	OF147	R	24	147	565	112	176	36	4	9	98	72	45	27	.312	.393	.437
Babe Ruth	OF132,P1,1B1	L	38	137	459	97	138	21	3	34	103	114	90	4	.301	.442	.582
Earle Combs	OF104	L	34	122	419	86	125	22	16	5	60	47	19	6	.298	.370	.463
Dixie Walker	OF77	L	22	98	328	68	90	15	7	15	51	26	28	2	.274	.330	.500
Lyn Lary	3B28,SS16,1B3*	R	27	52	127	25	28	3	3	0	13	28	17	2	.220	.361	.291
Sammy Byrd	OF71	R	25	85	107	26	30	6	1	2	11	15	12	0	.280	.369	.411
Doc Farrell	SS22,2B20	R	31	44	93	16	25	0	0	0	6	16	6	0	.269	.376	.269
Art Jorgens	C19	R	28	21	50	9	11	3	0	2	13	12	3	1	.220	.371	.400
Tony Rensa	C8	R	31	8	29	4	9	2	1	0	3	1	3	0	.310	.333	.448
Joe Glenn	C5	R	24	5	21	1	3	0	0	0	1	0	3	0	.143	.143	.143
Bill Werber†	3B1	R	25	3	2	0	0	0	0	0	0	0	0	0	.000	.000	.000

L. Lary, 1 G at OF

Pitcher	T	Age	G	GS	CG	ShO	IP	H	HR	BB	SO	W-L	Sv	ERA
Lefty Gomez	L	24	35	30	14	4	234.2	218	16	106	163	16-10	2	3.18
Red Ruffing	R	29	35	28	18	0	235.0	230	7	93	122	9-14	3	3.91
Johnny Allen	R	27	25	24	10	1	184.2	171	9	87	119	15-7	1	4.39
Russ Van Atta	L	27	26	22	10	2	157.0	160	8	63	76	12-4	1	4.18
Don Brennan	R	29	18	10	3	0	85.0	92	4	47	46	5-1	3	4.98
Charlie Devens	R	23	14	8	2	0	62.0	59	1	50	23	3-3	0	4.35
George Uhle†	R	34	12	6	4	0	61.0	63	4	20	26	6-1	0	5.16
George Pipgras†	R	33	4	4	3	0	33.0	32	1	12	14	2-2	0	3.27
Babe Ruth	L	38	1	1	1	0	9.0	12	0	3	0	1-0	0	5.00
Wilcy Moore	R	36	35	0	0	0	62.0	92	1	20	17	5-6	8	5.52
Danny MacFayden	R	28	25	6	2	0	90.1	120	8	37	28	3-2	0	5.88
Herb Pennock	L	39	23	5	2	1	65.0	96	4	21	22	7-4	4	5.54
Jumbo Brown	R	26	21	8	1	0	74.0	78	3	52	55	7-5	0	5.23
Pete Appleton	R	29	1	0	0	0	2.0	3	0	1	0	0-0	0	0.00

656 Seasons: Team Rosters

1933 Philadelphia Athletics 3rd AL 79-72 .523 19.5 GB

Connie Mack

Player	Gm by Position	B	Age	G	AB	R	H	2B	3B	HR	RBI	BB	SO	SB	Avg	OBP	Slg
Mickey Cochrane	C128	L	30	130	429	104	138	30	4	15	60	106	22	8	.322	.459	.515
Jimmie Foxx	1B149,SS1	R	25	149	573	125	204	37	9	48	163	96	93	2	.356	.449	.703
Max Bishop	2B113	L	33	117	391	80	115	27	1	4	42	106	46	1	.294	.446	.399
Mike Higgins	3B152	R	24	152	567	85	178	35	11	13	99	61	53	2	.314	.383	.483
Dib Williams	SS84,2B29,1B2	R	23	115	408	52	118	20	5	11	73	32	35	1	.289	.342	.444
Doc Cramer	OF152	L	27	152	661	109	195	27	8	8	75	36	24	5	.295	.331	.396
Bob Johnson	OF142	R	26	142	535	103	155	44	4	21	93	85	74	8	.290	.387	.505
Ed Coleman	OF89	L	31	102	388	48	109	26	3	6	68	19	51	0	.281	.318	.410
Eric McNair	SS46,2B27	R	24	89	310	57	81	15	4	7	48	15	32	2	.261	.302	.403
Lou Finney	OF63	L	22	74	240	26	64	12	2	3	32	13	17	1	.267	.304	.371
Ed Madjeski	C41	R	24	51	142	17	40	4	0	0	17	4	21	0	.282	.301	.310
Bing Miller	OF30,1B6	R	38	67	120	22	33	7	1	2	17	12	7	4	.275	.346	.400
Ed Cihocki	SS28,2B1,3B1	R	26	33	97	6	14	2	3	0	9	7	16	0	.144	.202	.227
Joe Zapustas	OF2	R	25	2	5	0	1	0	0	0	0	0	0	0	.200	.200	.200
Frankie Hayes	C3	R	18	3	5	0	0	0	0	0	0	0	2	0	.000	.000	.000

Pitcher	T	Age	G	GS	CG	ShO	IP	H	HR	BB	SO	W-L	Sv	ERA
Sugar Cain	R	26	38	32	16	1	218.0	244	18	137	43	13-12	1	4.25
Lefty Grove	L	33	45	28	21	2	275.1	280	12	83	114	24-8	6	3.20
Roy Mahaffey	R	30	33	23	9	0	179.1	198	5	74	66	13-10	0	5.17
Rube Walberg	L	36	40	20	10	1	201.0	224	12	95	68	9-13	4	4.88
George Earnshaw	R	33	21	18	4	0	117.2	153	8	58	37	5-10	0	5.97
Johnny Marcum	R	23	5	5	4	2	37.0	28	0	20	14	3-2	0	1.95
Emil Roy	R	26	1	1	0	0	2.1	4	0	3	0	0-1	0	27.00
Jim Peterson	R	24	32	5	0	0	90.2	114	6	36	18	2-5	0	4.96
Bobby Coombs	R	25	21	0	0	0	31.1	47	4	20	8	0-1	2	7.47
Tony Freitas	L	25	19	9	2	0	64.1	90	8	24	15	2-4	1	7.27
Dick Barrett	R	26	15	7	3	0	70.1	74	2	49	26	4-4	0	5.76
Bill Dietrich	R	23	8	1	0	0	17.0	13	1	19	4	0-1	0	5.82
Gowell Claset	L	25	8	1	0	0	11.1	23	1	11	1	2-0	0	9.53
Hank McDonald†	R	22	4	1	0	0	12.1	14	0	4	1	1-1	0	5.11
Tim McKeithan	R	26	3	1	0	0	9.0	10	0	4	3	1-0	0	4.00
Hank Winston	R	29	1	0	0	0	6.2	7	0	6	2	0-0	0	6.75

1933 Cleveland Indians 4th AL 75-76 .497 23.5 GB

Roger Peckinpaugh (26-25)/Bibb Falk (1-0)/Walter Johnson (48-51)

Player	Gm by Position	B	Age	G	AB	R	H	2B	3B	HR	RBI	BB	SO	SB	Avg	OBP	Slg
Roy Spencer	C72	R	33	75	227	26	46	5	2	0	23	23	17	0	.203	.282	.242
Harley Boss	1B110	L	24	112	438	54	118	17	7	1	53	25	27	2	.269	.310	.347
Odell Hale	2B73,3B21	R	24	98	351	49	97	19	8	10	64	30	37	2	.276	.333	.462
Willie Kamm	3B131	R	33	133	447	59	126	17	2	1	47	54	27	7	.282	.359	.336
Bill Knickerbocker	SS80	R	21	80	279	20	63	16	3	2	32	11	30	1	.226	.255	.326
Earl Averill	OF149	L	31	151	599	83	180	39	16	11	92	54	29	3	.301	.363	.474
Dick Porter	OF124	L	31	132	499	73	133	19	6	0	41	51	42	4	.267	.335	.329
Joe Vosmik	OF113	R	23	119	438	53	115	20	10	4	56	42	13	0	.263	.331	.381
Bill Cissell	2B62,SS46,3B1	R	29	112	409	53	94	21	3	6	33	31	29	6	.230	.284	.340
Johnny Burnett	SS41,2B17,3B12	L	28	83	261	39	71	11	2	1	29	23	14	3	.272	.333	.341
Frankie Pytlak	C69	R	24	80	248	36	77	10	6	2	33	17	10	3	.310	.355	.423
Milt Galatzer	OF40,1B5	L	26	57	160	19	38	2	1	1	17	23	21	2	.238	.333	.281
Wes Ferrell	P28,OF13	R	25	61	140	26	38	7	0	7	26	20	22	0	.271	.363	.471
Eddie Morgan	1B32,OF1	R	29	39	121	10	32	3	3	1	13	7	9	1	.264	.305	.364
Glenn Myatt	C27	L	35	40	77	10	18	4	0	0	7	15	8	0	.234	.372	.286
Johnny Oulliber	OF18	R	22	22	75	9	20	1	0	0	3	4	5	0	.267	.313	.280
Mike Powers	OF11	L	27	24	47	6	13	2	1	0	2	6	6	2	.277	.358	.362
Hal Trosky	1B11	L	20	11	44	6	13	1	2	1	8	2	12	0	.295	.340	.477

Pitcher	T	Age	G	GS	CG	ShO	IP	H	HR	BB	SO	W-L	Sv	ERA
Mel Harder	R	23	43	31	14	2	253.0	254	10	67	81	15-17	4	2.95
Oral Hildebrand	R	26	36	31	15	6	220.1	205	8	88	90	16-11	0	3.76
Wes Ferrell	R	25	28	26	16	1	201.0	225	8	70	41	11-12	0	4.21
Clint Brown	R	29	33	23	10	2	185.0	202	10	34	47	11-12	1	3.41
Willis Hudlin	R	27	34	17	6	0	147.1	161	7	61	44	5-13	1	3.97
Monte Pearson	R	23	19	16	10	0	135.1	111	5	55	54	10-5	0	2.33
Thornton Lee	L	26	3	2	2	0	17.1	13	1	11	7	1-1	0	4.15
Sarge Connally	R	34	41	3	1	0	103.0	112	4	49	30	5-3	1	4.89
Belve Bean	R	28	27	2	0	0	70.1	80	6	20	41	1-2	0	5.25
Howard Craghead	R	25	11	0	0	0	17.1	19	1	10	2	0-0	0	6.23

1933 Detroit Tigers 5th AL 75-79 .487 25.0 GB

Bucky Harris (73-79)/Del Baker (2-0)

Player	Gm by Position	B	Age	G	AB	R	H	2B	3B	HR	RBI	BB	SO	SB	Avg	OBP	Slg
Ray Hayworth	C133	R	29	134	425	37	104	14	3	1	45	35	28	0	.245	.302	.299
Hank Greenberg	1B117	R	22	117	449	59	135	33	3	12	87	46	78	6	.301	.367	.468
Charlie Gehringer	2B155	L	30	155	628	103	204	42	6	12	105	68	27	5	.325	.393	.468
Marv Owen	3B136	R	27	138	550	77	144	24	9	2	65	44	56	2	.262	.320	.349
Billy Rogell	SS155	S	28	155	587	67	173	42	11	0	57	79	33	6	.295	.381	.404
John Stone	OF141	L	27	148	574	86	161	33	11	11	80	54	37	1	.280	.344	.434
Pete Fox	OF124	R	24	128	535	82	154	26	13	7	57	23	38	9	.288	.320	.424
Gee Walker	OF113	R	25	127	483	68	135	29	7	9	64	15	49	26	.280	.304	.424
Jo-Jo White	OF54	L	24	91	234	43	59	9	5	2	34	27	26	5	.252	.337	.359
Harry Davis	1B44	L	25	66	173	24	37	8	2	0	14	22	8	2	.214	.303	.283
Frank Doljack	OF37	R	25	42	147	18	42	5	2	0	22	14	13	2	.286	.348	.347
Heinie Schuble	3B23,SS2,2B1	R	26	49	96	12	21	4	1	0	6	5	17	2	.219	.257	.281
Johnny Pasek	C28	R	28	28	61	6	15	4	0	0	4	7	7	2	.246	.324	.311
Gene Desautels	C30	R	26	30	42	5	6	1	0	0	4	4	6	0	.143	.234	.167
Frank Reiber	C6	R	23	13	18	3	5	0	1	1	3	2	3	0	.278	.350	.556
Billy Rhiel	OF2	R	32	19	17	1	3	0	1	0	1	5	4	0	.176	.364	.294
Earl Webb†	OF2	L	35	6	11	1	3	0	0	0	3	3	0	0	.273	.429	.273

Pitcher	T	Age	G	GS	CG	ShO	IP	H	HR	BB	SO	W-L	Sv	ERA
Firpo Marberry	R	34	37	32	15	1	238.1	232	13	61	84	16-11	2	3.29
Tommy Bridges	R	26	33	28	17	2	233.0	192	8	110	120	14-12	2	3.09
Vic Sorrell	R	32	36	28	13	1	232.2	233	18	78	75	11-15	1	3.79
Carl Fischer	L	27	35	22	9	0	182.2	176	5	84	93	11-15	3	3.55
Schoolboy Rowe	R	23	19	15	8	1	123.1	129	7	31	75	7-4	0	3.58
Vic Frasier†	R	28	20	14	4	0	104.1	129	9	59	26	5-5	0	6.64
Luke Hamlin	R	28	3	3	0	0	16.2	20	3	10	10	1-0	0	4.86
Roxie Lawson	R	27	4	2	0	0	16.0	17	2	17	6	0-1	0	7.31
Chief Hogsett	L	29	45	2	0	0	116.0	137	7	56	39	6-10	9	4.50
Art Herring	R	27	24	3	1	0	61.0	61	6	20	20	1-2	0	3.84
Eldon Auker	R	22	15	6	2	1	55.0	63	3	25	17	3-3	0	5.24
Whit Wyatt†	R	25	10	0	0	0	17.0	20	1	9	9	0-1	0	4.24
Bots Nekola	L	26	2	0	0	0	1.1	4	1	1	0	0-0	0	27.00
George Uhle†	R	34	1	0	0	0	0.2	2	1	0	1	0-0	0	27.00

1933 Chicago White Sox 6th AL 67-83 .447 31.0 GB

Lew Fonseca

Player	Gm by Position	B	Age	G	AB	R	H	2B	3B	HR	RBI	BB	SO	SB	Avg	OBP	Slg
Charlie Berry	C83	R	30	86	271	25	69	8	3	2	28	17	16	0	.255	.301	.328
Red Kress	1B111,OF8	R	26	129	467	47	116	20	5	10	78	37	40	4	.248	.304	.377
Jackie Hayes	2B138	R	26	138	535	65	138	23	5	2	47	55	36	2	.258	.331	.331
Jimmy Dykes	3B151	R	36	151	554	49	144	22	6	1	68	69	37	3	.260	.354	.327
Luke Appling	SS151	R	26	151	612	90	197	36	10	6	85	56	29	6	.322	.379	.443
Mule Haas	OF146	L	29	146	585	97	168	33	4	1	51	65	41	0	.287	.360	.362
Al Simmons	OF145	R	31	146	605	85	200	29	10	14	119	39	49	5	.331	.373	.481
Evar Swanson	OF139	R	30	144	539	102	165	25	7	1	63	93	35	19	.306	.411	.384
Frank Grube	C83	R	28	85	256	23	59	13	0	0	23	38	20	1	.230	.334	.281
Billy Sullivan	1B22,C8	L	22	54	125	9	24	0	1	0	13	10	5	0	.192	.252	.208
Earl Webb†	OF16,1B10	L	35	58	107	16	31	5	0	1	8	16	13	0	.290	.382	.364
Hal Rhyne	2B19,3B13,SS2	R	34	39	83	9	22	1	1	0	10	5	9	1	.265	.315	.301
Lew Fonseca	1B12	R	34	23	59	8	12	2	0	2	15	7	6	1	.203	.288	.339
John Stoneham	OF9	L	24	10	25	4	3	0	0	1	3	2	2	0	.120	.185	.240
Milt Bocek	OF6	R	20	11	22	3	8	1	0	1	3	4	6	0	.364	.462	.545
Charlie English	2B3	R	23	3	9	2	4	2	0	0	1	1	1	0	.444	.500	.667
Liz Funk	OF2	L	28	10	9	1	2	0	0	0	0	1	0	0	.222	.300	.222
Mem Lovett		R	21	1	1	0	0	0	0	0	0	0	0	0	.000	.000	.000

Pitcher	T	Age	G	GS	CG	ShO	IP	H	HR	BB	SO	W-L	Sv	ERA
Ted Lyons	R	32	36	27	14	2	228.0	260	10	74	74	10-21	1	4.38
Sad Sam Jones	R	40	27	25	11	2	176.2	181	13	65	60	10-12	0	3.36
Milt Gaston	R	37	30	25	7	1	167.0	177	9	60	39	8-12	0	4.85
Ed Durham	R	24	24	21	6	0	138.2	137	12	46	65	10-6	0	4.48
Paul Gregory	R	25	23	17	5	0	103.2	124	10	47	18	4-11	0	4.95
Jake Miller	L	35	26	14	4	2	105.2	130	3	47	30	5-6	0	5.62
Les Tietje	R	21	3	3	1	0	22.1	16	1	15	9	2-0	0	2.42
Ira Hutchinson	R	22	1	1	0	0	4.0	7	1	3	2	0-0	0	13.50
Joe Heving	R	32	40	6	3	1	118.0	113	6	27	47	7-5	6	2.67
Red Faber	R	44	36	2	0	0	86.1	92	2	28	18	3-4	5	3.44
Chad Kimsey	R	26	28	2	0	0	96.0	124	7	36	19	4-1	0	5.53
Whit Wyatt†	R	25	26	7	2	0	87.2	91	7	45	31	3-4	1	4.62
Vic Frasier†	R	28	10	1	0	0	20.1	32	2	11	4	1-1	0	8.85
Hal Haid	R	35	6	0	0	0	14.2	18	2	13	7	0-0	0	7.98
George Murray	R	34	2	0	0	0	2.1	3	0	2	0	0-0	0	7.71

1933 Boston Red Sox 7th AL 63-86 .423 34.5 GB

Marty McManus

Player	Gm by Position	B	Age	G	AB	R	H	2B	3B	HR	RBI	BB	SO	SB	Avg	OBP	Slg
Rick Ferrell†	C116	R	27	118	421	50	125	19	4	3	72	58	19	2	.297	.385	.382
Dale Alexander	1B79	R	30	94	313	40	88	14	1	5	40	25	22	0	.281	.336	.380
Johnny Hodapp	2B101,1B10	R	27	115	413	55	129	27	5	3	54	33	14	1	.312	.365	.424
Marty McManus	3B76,2B26,1B4	R	33	106	366	51	104	30	4	3	36	49	21	3	.284	.369	.413
Rabbit Warstler	SS87	R	29	92	322	44	70	13	1	1	17	42	36	2	.217	.308	.273
Roy Johnson	OF125	L	30	133	483	88	151	30	7	10	95	55	36	13	.313	.387	.466
Dusty Cooke	OF118	L	26	119	454	86	132	35	10	5	54	67	71	7	.291	.384	.445
Smead Jolley	OF102	L	31	118	411	47	116	32	4	9	65	24	20	1	.282	.325	.445
Bill Werber†	SS71,3B38,2B2	R	25	108	425	64	110	30	6	3	39	33	39	15	.259	.312	.379
Tom Oliver	OF86	R	30	90	244	25	63	9	1	0	23	13	7	1	.258	.296	.303
Bob Seeds	1B41,OF32	R	26	82	230	26	56	13	4	0	23	21	20	1	.243	.310	.335
Bucky Walters	3B43,2B7	R	24	52	195	27	50	8	3	4	28	19	24	1	.256	.326	.390
Joe Judge†	1B28	L	39	35	108	20	32	8	1	0	22	13	4	2	.296	.372	.389
Johnny Gooch	C26	S	35	37	77	6	14	1	1	0	2	11	7	0	.182	.284	.221
Merv Shea†	C16	R	32	16	56	1	8	3	0	0	8	4	7	0	.143	.200	.196
Freddie Muller	2B14	R	25	15	48	6	9	1	1	0	3	5	5	1	.188	.264	.250
Mel Almada	OF13	L	20	14	44	11	15	0	0	1	3	11	3	3	.341	.473	.409
George Stumpf	OF15	L	22	22	41	8	14	3	0	0	5	4	2	4	.341	.400	.415
Bernie Friberg	2B6,3B5,SS2	R	33	17	41	5	13	3	0	0	9	6	1	0	.317	.404	.390
Bob Fothergill	OF4	R	35	28	32	1	11	1	0	0	5	2	4	0	.344	.382	.375
Cliff Watwood	OF9	L	27	13	30	2	4	0	0	0	2	3	3	0	.133	.212	.133
Tom Winsett	OF4	L	23	6	12	1	1	0	0	0	0	1	6	0	.083	.154	.083
Lou Legett	C2	R	32	8	5	1	1	1	0	0	1	0	0	0	.200	.200	.400
Marv Olson	2B1	R	26	3	1	1	0	0	0	0	0	0	1	0	.000	.000	.000
Greg Mulleavy		R	27	1	0	1	0	0	0	0	0	0	0	0	—	—	—

Pitcher	T	Age	G	GS	CG	ShO	IP	H	HR	BB	SO	W-L	Sv	ERA
Gordon Rhodes	R	25	34	29	14	0	232.0	242	13	93	85	12-15	0	4.03
Bob Weiland	L	27	39	27	12	0	216.1	197	19	100	97	8-14	3	3.87
Lloyd Brown†	L	28	33	21	9	2	163.1	180	4	64	37	8-11	1	4.02
Hank Johnson	R	27	25	21	7	0	155.1	156	13	74	65	8-6	1	4.11
Ivy Andrews	R	26	34	17	5	0	140.0	157	8	61	37	7-13	1	4.95
George Pipgras†	R	33	22	17	9	2	128.1	140	5	45	56	9-8	1	4.07
Johnny Welch	R	26	47	7	1	0	129.0	142	6	67	68	4-9	3	4.60
Bob Kline	R	23	46	8	1	0	127.0	127	5	67	16	7-8	4	4.54
Curt Fullerton	R	34	6	2	2	0	25.1	36	1	13	10	0-2	0	8.53
Jud McLaughlin	L	21	6	0	0	0	8.2	14	1	5	1	0-0	0	6.23
Mike Meola	R	27	3	0	0	0	2.1	5	0	2	1	0-0	0	23.14

1933 St. Louis Browns 8th AL 55-96 .364 43.5 GB

Bill Killefer (34-57)/Allen Sothoron (2-6)/Rogers Hornsby (19-33)

Player	Gm by Position	B	Age	G	AB	R	H	2B	3B	HR	RBI	BB	SO	SB	Avg	OBP	Slg
Merv Shea†	C85	R	32	94	279	26	73	11	1	1	27	43	26	2	.262	.360	.319
Jack Burns	1B143	L	25	144	556	89	160	43	4	7	71	56	51	11	.288	.353	.417
Ski Melillo	2B130	R	33	132	496	50	145	23	6	3	79	29	18	12	.292	.333	.381
Art Scharein	3B95,SS24,2B7	R	28	123	471	49	96	13	3	0	26	41	21	7	.204	.269	.244
Jim Levey	SS138	S	26	141	529	43	103	10	4	2	36	26	68	4	.195	.237	.240
Bruce Campbell	OF144	L	23	148	567	87	157	38	8	16	106	69	77	10	.277	.357	.457
Sammy West	OF127	L	28	133	517	93	155	25	12	11	48	59	49	10	.300	.373	.458
Carl Reynolds	OF124	R	30	135	475	81	136	26	14	8	71	50	25	5	.286	.357	.451
Ted Gullic	OF36,3B33,1B14	R	26	104	304	34	74	18	3	5	35	15	38	3	.243	.281	.372
Lin Storti	2B29,3B27	S	26	70	210	26	41	7	4	3	21	25	31	2	.195	.281	.310
Debs Garms	OF47	L	25	78	189	35	60	10	2	4	24	30	21	2	.317	.416	.455
Rollie Hemsley†	C27	R	26	32	95	7	23	2	1	1	15	11	12	0	.242	.321	.316
Rick Ferrell†	C21	R	27	22	72	8	18	2	0	1	5	12	4	2	.250	.357	.319
Muddy Ruel	C28	R	37	36	63	13	12	2	0	0	8	24	4	0	.190	.414	.222
Jack Crouch†	C9	R	30	19	30	1	5	0	0	1	5	2	6	0	.167	.219	.267
Rogers Hornsby†		R	37	11	9	2	3	1	0	1	2	2	1	0	.333	.455	.778

Pitcher	T	Age	G	GS	CG	ShO	IP	H	HR	BB	SO	W-L	Sv	ERA
Bump Hadley	R	28	45	36	19	2	316.2	309	17	141	149	15-20	3	3.92
George Blaeholder	R	29	38	36	14	3	255.2	283	24	69	63	15-19	0	4.72
Ed Wells	L	33	36	22	10	0	203.2	230	13	63	58	6-14	1	4.20
Dick Coffman	R	26	21	13	3	1	81.0	114	9	39	19	3-7	1	5.89
Lloyd Brown†	L	28	8	6	0	0	39.0	57	1	17	7	1-6	0	7.15
Sam Gray	R	35	38	6	0	0	112.0	131	7	45	36	7-4	4	4.10
Wally Hebert	L	25	33	10	3	0	88.1	114	4	35	19	4-6	0	5.30
Rollie Stiles	R	26	31	9	6	1	115.0	154	4	47	29	3-7	1	5.01
Hank McDonald†	R	22	25	5	0	0	58.1	83	6	34	22	0-4	0	8.64
Jack Knott	R	26	20	9	0	0	82.2	88	11	33	19	1-8	0	5.01
Garland Braxton	L	33	5	1	0	0	8.1	11	0	8	5	0-1	0	9.72

»1933 New York Giants 1st NL 91-61 .599 —

Bill Terry

Player	Gm by Position	B	Age	G	AB	R	H	2B	3B	HR	RBI	BB	SO	SB	Avg	OBP	Slg
Gus Mancuso	C142	R	27	144	481	39	127	17	2	6	56	48	21	0	.264	.331	.345
Bill Terry	1B117	L	36	123	475	68	153	20	5	6	58	40	23	3	.322	.375	.423
Hughie Critz	2B133	R	32	133	558	68	137	18	5	2	33	23	24	4	.246	.279	.306
Johnny Vergez	3B123	R	26	123	458	57	124	21	6	16	72	39	66	1	.271	.332	.448
Blondy Ryan	SS146	R	27	146	525	47	125	10	5	3	48	15	62	0	.238	.259	.293
Mel Ott	OF152	L	24	152	580	98	164	36	1	23	103	75	48	1	.283	.367	.467
Jo-Jo Moore	OF132	L	24	132	524	56	153	16	5	0	42	21	27	4	.292	.323	.342
Kiddo Davis	OF120	R	31	126	434	61	112	20	4	7	37	25	30	10	.258	.298	.371
Lefty O'Doul†	OF63	L	36	78	229	31	70	9	1	9	35	29	17	1	.306	.388	.472
Homer Peel	OF45	R	30	84	148	16	38	1	1	1	12	14	10	0	.257	.325	.297
Sam Leslie†	1B35	L	27	40	137	21	44	12	3	3	27	12	9	0	.321	.380	.518
Bernie James	2B26,SS6,3B5	S	27	60	125	22	28	2	1	1	10	8	12	5	.224	.271	.280
Travis Jackson	3B21,SS21	R	29	53	122	11	30	5	0	0	12	8	11	2	.246	.292	.287
Paul Richards	C36	R	24	51	87	4	17	3	0	0	10	3	12	0	.195	.222	.230
Chuck Dressen	3B16	R	34	16	45	3	10	4	0	0	3	1	4	0	.222	.239	.311
Joe Malay	1B8	L	27	8	24	0	3	0	0	0	2	0	0	0	.125	.125	.125
Phil Weintraub	OF6	L	25	8	15	3	3	0	0	1	1	3	2	0	.200	.333	.400
Hank Leiber	OF1	R	22	6	10	1	2	0	0	0	0	0	2	0	.200	.200	.200
Harry Danning	C1	R	21	3	2	0	0	0	0	0	0	1	0	0	.000	.333	.000

Pitcher	T	Age	G	GS	CG	ShO	IP	H	HR	BB	SO	W-L	Sv	ERA
F. Fitzsimmons	R	31	36	35	13	1	251.2	243	14	72	65	16-11	0	2.90
Carl Hubbell	L	30	45	33	22	10	308.2	256	6	47	156	23-12	5	1.66
Hal Schumacher	R	22	35	33	21	7	258.2	199	9	84	96	19-12	1	2.16
Roy Parmelee	R	26	32	32	14	3	218.1	191	9	77	132	13-8	0	3.17
Hi Bell	R	35	38	7	1	1	105.1	100	4	20	24	6-5	5	2.05
Dolf Luque	R	42	35	0	0	0	80.1	75	4	19	23	8-2	4	2.69
Glenn Spencer	R	27	17	3	1	0	47.1	52	3	26	14	0-2	0	5.13
Watty Clark†	L	31	16	5	0	0	44.0	58	3	11	11	3-4	0	4.70
Bill Shores	R	29	8	3	1	0	36.2	41	4	14	20	2-1	0	3.93
Jack Salveson	R	19	8	2	2	0	30.2	30	4	14	8	0-2	0	3.82
George Uhle†	R	34	6	1	0	0	13.2	16	1	6	4	1-1	0	7.90
Ray Starr†	R	27	6	2	0	0	13.1	19	0	10	2	0-1	0	5.40

1933 Pittsburgh Pirates 2nd NL 87-67 .565 5.0 GB

George Gibson

Player	Gm by Position	B	Age	G	AB	R	H	2B	3B	HR	RBI	BB	SO	SB	Avg	OBP	Slg
Earl Grace	C88	L	26	93	291	22	84	13	1	3	44	26	23	0	.289	.349	.371
Gus Suhr	1B154	L	27	154	566	72	151	31	11	10	75	72	52	2	.267	.350	.413
Tony Piet	2B97	R	26	107	362	45	117	21	5	1	42	19	28	12	.323	.367	.417
Pie Traynor	3B154	R	33	154	624	85	190	27	6	1	82	35	24	5	.304	.342	.372
Arky Vaughan	SS152	L	21	152	573	85	180	29	19	9	97	64	23	3	.314	.388	.478
Paul Waner	OF154	L	30	154	618	101	191	38	16	7	70	60	20	3	.309	.372	.456
Freddy Lindstrom	OF130	R	27	138	538	70	167	39	10	5	55	33	22	1	.310	.350	.448
Lloyd Waner	OF114	L	27	121	500	59	138	14	5	0	26	22	8	3	.276	.307	.324
Tommy Thevenow	2B61,SS3,3B1	R	29	73	253	20	79	5	1	0	34	3	5	2	.312	.320	.340
Woody Jensen	OF40	L	25	70	196	29	58	7	3	0	15	8	2	1	.296	.330	.362
Adam Comorosky	OF30	R	27	64	162	18	46	8	1	1	15	4	9	2	.284	.301	.364
Hal Finney	C47	R	27	56	133	17	31	4	1	1	18	3	19	0	.233	.250	.301
Tom Padden	C27	R	24	30	90	5	19	2	0	0	8	2	6	0	.211	.237	.233
Val Picinich†	C16	R	36	16	52	6	13	4	0	1	7	5	10	0	.250	.316	.385
Pep Young	2B1,SS1	R	25	25	20	3	6	1	1	0	0	0	5	0	.300	.300	.450
Bill Brubaker	3B1	R	22	2	2	0	0	0	0	0	0	0	0	0	.000	.000	.000
Red Nonnenkamp		L	21	1	2	1	0	0	0	0	0	0	1	0	.000	.000	.000

Pitcher	T	Age	G	GS	CG	ShO	IP	H	HR	BB	SO	W-L	Sv	ERA
Larry French	L	25	47	35	21	5	291.1	290	9	55	88	18-13	1	2.72
Bill Swift	R	25	37	29	13	2	218.1	214	11	36	64	14-10	0	3.13
Heinie Meine	R	37	32	29	12	2	207.1	227	10	50	50	15-8	0	3.65
Steve Swetonic	R	29	31	21	8	3	164.2	166	10	64	37	12-12	0	3.50
Hal Smith	R	31	28	19	8	2	145.0	149	5	31	40	8-7	1	2.86
Ralph Birkofer	L	24	9	8	3	1	50.2	43	1	17	20	4-2	0	2.31
Leon Chagnon	R	30	39	5	1	0	100.0	100	2	17	35	6-4	1	3.69
Waite Hoyt	R	33	36	8	4	1	117.0	118	3	19	44	5-7	4	2.92
Bill Harris	R	33	31	0	0	0	58.2	68	1	14	19	4-4	5	3.22
Ray Kremer	R	40	7	0	0	0	20.0	36	2	9	4	1-0	0	10.35
Clise Dudley	R	29	1	0	0	0	0.1	6	0	1	0	0-0	0	135.00

1933 Chicago Cubs 3rd NL 86-68 .558 6.0 GB

Charlie Grimm

Player	Gm by Position	B	Age	G	AB	R	H	2B	3B	HR	RBI	BB	SO	SB	Avg	OBP	Slg
Gabby Hartnett	C140	R	32	140	490	55	135	21	4	16	88	37	51	1	.276	.326	.433
Charlie Grimm	1B104	L	34	107	384	38	95	15	2	3	37	23	15	1	.247	.290	.320
Billy Herman	2B153	R	23	153	619	82	173	35	2	0	44	45	34	5	.279	.332	.342
Woody English	3B103,SS1	R	26	105	398	54	104	19	2	3	41	53	44	5	.261	.348	.342
Billy Jurges	SS143	R	25	143	487	49	131	17	6	5	50	26	39	3	.269	.313	.359
Frank Demaree	OF133	R	23	134	515	68	140	24	6	6	51	22	42	4	.272	.304	.377
Babe Herman	OF131	L	30	137	508	77	147	36	12	16	93	50	57	6	.289	.353	.502
Riggs Stephenson	OF91	R	35	97	346	45	114	17	4	4	51	34	16	5	.329	.397	.436
Kiki Cuyler	OF69	R	34	70	262	37	83	13	3	5	35	21	29	4	.317	.376	.447
Mark Koenig	3B37,SS26,2B2	S	28	80	218	32	62	12	1	3	25	15	9	5	.284	.330	.390
Harvey Hendrick	1B38,OF8,3B1	L	35	69	189	30	55	13	3	4	23	13	17	4	.291	.346	.455
Gilly Campbell	C20	L	25	46	89	11	25	3	1	1	10	7	4	0	.281	.347	.371
Jim Mosolf	OF22	L	27	31	82	13	22	5	1	1	9	5	8	0	.268	.326	.390
Taylor Douthit†	OF18	R	32	27	71	8	16	5	0	0	5	11	7	2	.225	.329	.296
Stan Hack	2B17	L	23	20	60	10	21	3	1	1	2	8	3	4	.350	.451	.483
Dolph Camilli	1B16	L	26	16	58	8	13	2	1	2	7	4	11	3	.224	.274	.397
Zack Taylor	C12	R	34	16	11	0	0	0	0	0	0	0	1	0	.000	.000	.000
Babe Phelps	C2	L	25	3	7	0	2	0	0	0	2	0	1	0	.286	.286	.286

Pitcher	T	Age	G	GS	CG	ShO	IP	H	HR	BB	SO	W-L	Sv	ERA
Lon Warneke	R	24	36	34	26	4	287.1	262	8	75	133	18-13	1	2.00
Guy Bush	R	31	41	32	20	4	258.2	261	9	68	84	20-12	2	2.75
Charlie Root	R	34	35	30	20	2	242.1	232	14	61	86	15-10	0	2.60
Pat Malone	R	30	31	26	13	2	186.1	186	10	59	72	10-14	0	3.91
Bud Tinning	R	27	32	21	10	3	175.1	169	3	60	59	13-6	1	3.18
Lynn Nelson	R	28	24	3	3	0	75.2	65	2	30	20	5-5	1	3.21
Roy Henshaw	L	21	21	0	0	0	38.2	32	0	20	16	2-1	0	4.19
Burleigh Grimes†	R	39	17	7	3	1	69.2	71	2	29	12	3-6	3	3.49
LeRoy Herrmann	R	27	9	1	0	0	21.0	26	3	8	4	0-1	1	5.57
Beryl Richmond	L	25	4	0	0	0	4.2	10	0	2	2	0-0	0	1.93
Carroll Yerkes	L	30	1	0	0	0	2.0	2	0	1	0	0-0	0	4.50

1933 Boston Braves 4th NL 83-71 .539 9.0 GB

Bill McKechnie

Player	Gm by Position	B	Age	G	AB	R	H	2B	3B	HR	RBI	BB	SO	SB	Avg	OBP	Slg
Shanty Hogan	C95	R	27	96	328	15	83	7	0	3	30	13	9	0	.253	.288	.302
Buck Jordan	1B150	L	26	152	588	77	168	29	9	4	46	34	22	4	.286	.327	.386
Rabbit Maranville	2B142	R	41	143	478	46	104	15	4	0	38	36	34	2	.218	.274	.266
Pinky Whitney†	3B85,2B18	R	28	100	382	42	94	17	2	8	49	25	23	2	.246	.296	.364
Billy Urbanski	SS143	R	30	144	566	65	142	21	4	0	35	33	48	4	.251	.298	.302
Wally Berger	OF136	R	27	137	528	84	165	37	8	27	106	41	77	2	.313	.365	.566
Randy Moore	OF122,1B10	L	27	135	497	64	150	23	7	8	70	40	16	3	.302	.356	.425
Hal Lee†	OF87	R	28	88	312	32	69	15	9	1	28	18	26	1	.221	.266	.337
Joe Mowry	OF64	S	25	86	249	25	55	8	5	0	20	15	22	1	.221	.273	.293
Al Spohrer	C65	R	30	67	184	11	46	6	1	0	12	11	13	3	.250	.292	.310
Fritz Knothe†	3B33,SS9	R	30	44	158	15	36	5	2	1	6	13	25	1	.228	.291	.304
Dick Gyselman	3B42,2B5,SS1	R	25	58	155	10	37	6	2	0	12	7	21	0	.239	.272	.303
Tommy Thompson	OF24	L	23	24	97	6	18	1	0	0	6	4	6	0	.186	.218	.196
Wes Schulmerich†	OF21	R	32	29	85	10	21	6	1	1	13	5	10	0	.247	.289	.376
Pinky Hargrave	C25	S	37	45	73	5	13	0	0	0	6	5	7	1	.178	.241	.178
Red Worthington	OF10	R	27	17	45	3	7	4	0	0	0	1	3	0	.156	.174	.244
Dutch Holland	OF7	R	29	13	31	3	8	3	0	0	3	3	8	1	.258	.324	.355
Earl Clark	OF6	R	25	7	23	3	8	1	0	0	1	2	1	0	.348	.400	.391
Hod Ford	SS5	R	35	5	15	0	1	0	0	0	1	3	1	0	.067	.222	.067
Al Wright	2B3	R	20	4	1	0	1	0	0	0	0	0	0	0	1.000	1.000	1.000

Pitcher	T	Age	G	GS	CG	ShO	IP	H	HR	BB	SO	W-L	Sv	ERA
Ed Brandt	L	28	41	32	23	3	287.2	256	10	77	104	18-14	4	2.60
Fred Frankhouse	R	29	43	30	14	2	244.2	249	12	77	83	16-15	2	3.16
Ben Cantwell	R	31	40	29	18	2	254.2	242	12	54	57	20-10	2	2.62
Huck Betts	R	36	35	26	17	2	242.0	225	9	55	40	11-11	4	2.79
Tom Zachary	L	37	26	20	6	2	125.0	134	1	35	22	7-9	2	3.53
Leo Mangum	R	37	25	5	2	1	84.0	93	2	11	28	4-3	0	3.32
Bob Smith†	R	38	14	4	3	1	58.2	68	3	7	16	4-3	1	3.22
Socks Seibold	R	37	11	5	1	0	36.2	43	0	14	10	1-4	1	3.68
Ed Fallenstein	R	24	9	4	1	1	35.0	43	1	13	5	2-1	0	3.60
Ray Starr†	R	27	9	1	0	0	28.0	32	4	9	15	0-1	0	3.86
Bob Brown	R	22	5	0	0	0	6.2	6	0	3	3	0-0	0	2.70

1933 St. Louis Cardinals 5th NL 82-71 .536 9.5 GB

Gabby Street (46-45)/Frank Frisch (36-26)

Player	Gm by Position	B	Age	G	AB	R	H	2B	3B	HR	RBI	BB	SO	SB	Avg	OBP	Slg
Jimmie Wilson	C107	R	32	113	369	34	94	17	0	1	45	23	33	6	.255	.300	.309
Ripper Collins	1B123	S	29	132	493	66	153	26	7	10	68	38	49	7	.310	.363	.452
Frankie Frisch	2B132,SS15	S	34	147	585	74	177	32	6	4	66	48	16	18	.303	.358	.398
Pepper Martin	3B145	R	29	145	599	122	189	36	12	8	57	67	46	26	.316	.387	.456
Leo Durocher†	SS123	R	27	123	395	45	102	18	4	2	41	26	32	3	.258	.306	.339
Joe Medwick	OF147	R	21	148	595	92	182	40	10	18	98	26	56	5	.306	.337	.497
George Watkins	OF135	L	33	138	525	66	146	24	5	5	62	39	62	11	.278	.342	.371
Ernie Orsatti	OF107,1B3	L	30	120	436	55	130	21	6	0	38	33	33	14	.298	.348	.374
Ethan Allen	OF67	R	29	91	261	25	63	7	3	0	36	13	22	3	.241	.280	.291
Pat Crawford	1B29,2B15,3B7	L	31	91	224	24	60	8	2	0	21	14	9	1	.268	.317	.321
Bob O'Farrell	C50	R	36	55	163	16	39	4	2	2	20	15	25	0	.239	.303	.325
Rogers Hornsby†	2B17	R	37	46	83	9	27	6	0	2	21	12	6	1	.325	.423	.470
Gordon Slade	SS31	R	28	39	62	6	7	1	0	0	3	6	7	1	.113	.191	.129
Gene Moore	OF10	L	23	11	38	6	15	3	2	0	8	4	10	1	.395	.452	.579
Bill Lewis	C8	R	28	15	35	8	14	1	0	1	8	2	3	0	.400	.432	.514
Estel Crabtree	OF7	L	29	23	34	6	9	3	0	0	3	2	3	1	.265	.306	.353
Sparky Adams†	SS5,3B3	R	38	8	30	1	5	1	0	0	0	1	3	0	.167	.219	.200
Roy Pepper	OF2	R	27	3	9	2	2	0	0	1	2	0	1	0	.222	.222	.556
Burgess Whitehead	SS9,2B3	R	23	12	7	2	2	0	0	0	1	0	1	0	.286	.286	.286
Joe Sprinz	C3	R	30	3	5	1	1	0	0	0	0	1	1	0	.200	.333	.200
Charlie Wilson	SS1	S	28	1	1	0	0	0	0	0	0	0	1	0	.000	.000	.000

Pitcher	T	Age	G	GS	CG	ShO	IP	H	HR	BB	SO	W-L	Sv	ERA
Dizzy Dean	R	23	48	34	26	3	293.0	279	11	64	199	20-18	4	3.04
Tex Carleton	R	26	44	33	15	4	277.0	263	15	97	147	17-11	3	3.38
Wild Bill Hallahan	L	30	36	32	16	2	244.1	245	6	98	93	16-13	0	3.50
Bill Walker	L	29	29	20	6	2	158.0	168	8	67	41	9-10	0	3.42
Burleigh Grimes†	R	39	4	3	0	0	13.2	15	1	8	4	0-1	1	5.27
Paul Derringer†	R	26	3	2	1	0	17.0	24	0	9	3	0-2	0	4.24
Syl Johnson	R	32	35	1	0	0	84.0	89	7	16	28	3-3	3	4.29
Jesse Haines	R	39	32	10	5	0	115.1	113	3	37	37	9-6	1	2.50
Dazzy Vance	R	42	28	11	2	0	99.0	105	3	28	67	6-2	3	3.55
Jim Mooney	L	26	21	8	2	0	77.1	87	1	26	14	2-5	1	3.72
Allyn Stout†	R	28	1	0	0	0	2.0	1	0	1	1	0-0	0	0.00
Jim Lindsey	R	37	1	0	0	0	2.0	2	0	1	1	0-0	0	4.50

1933 Brooklyn Dodgers 6th NL 65-88 .425 26.5 GB

Max Carey

Player	Gm by Position	B	Age	G	AB	R	H	2B	3B	HR	RBI	BB	SO	SB	Avg	OBP	Slg
Al Lopez	C124,2B1	R	24	126	372	39	112	11	4	3	41	21	39	10	.301	.338	.376
Sam Leslie†	1B95	L	27	96	364	41	104	11	4	5	46	23	14	1	.286	.340	.379
Tony Cuccinello	2B120,3B14	R	25	134	485	58	122	31	4	9	65	44	40	4	.252	.316	.388
Joe Stripp	3B140	R	30	141	537	69	149	20	7	1	51	26	23	5	.277	.312	.346
Jimmy Jordan	SS51,2B11	R	25	70	211	16	54	12	1	0	17	4	6	3	.256	.270	.322
Johnny Frederick	OF138	L	31	147	556	65	171	22	7	7	64	36	14	9	.308	.355	.410
Danny Taylor	OF91	R	32	103	358	75	102	21	9	9	40	47	45	11	.285	.368	.469
Hack Wilson	OF90,2B5	R	33	117	360	41	96	13	2	9	54	52	50	7	.267	.359	.389
Buzz Boyle	OF90	L	25	93	338	38	101	13	4	0	31	16	24	7	.299	.331	.361
Jake Flowers	SS36,2B19,3B8*	R	31	78	210	28	49	11	2	2	22	24	15	13	.233	.312	.333
Glenn Wright	SS51,1B9,3B2	R	32	71	192	19	49	13	0	1	18	11	24	1	.255	.299	.339
Joe Hutcheson	OF45	L	28	55	184	19	43	4	1	6	21	15	13	1	.234	.295	.364
Lefty O'Doul†	OF41	L	36	43	159	14	40	5	1	5	21	15	6	2	.252	.320	.390
Chink Outen	C56	L	28	93	153	20	38	10	0	4	17	20	15	1	.248	.335	.392
Lonny Frey	SS34	L	22	34	135	25	43	5	3	0	12	13	13	4	.319	.378	.400
Del Bissonette	1B32	L	33	35	114	9	28	7	0	1	10	2	17	2	.246	.259	.333
Joe Judge†	1B28	L	39	42	112	7	24	2	1	0	9	7	10	1	.214	.261	.250
Clyde Sukeforth	C18	L	31	20	36	1	2	0	0	0	0	2	1	0	.056	.105	.056
Bert Delmas	2B10	L	22	12	28	4	7	0	0	0	0	1	7	0	.250	.276	.250
Max Rosenfeld	OF2	R	30	5	9	0	1	0	0	0	0	1	1	0	.111	.200	.111
Val Picinich†	C6	R	36	6	6	1	1	1	0	0	0	0	1	0	.167	.167	.333
Lu Blue	1B1	S	36	1	1	0	0	0	0	0	0	0	0	0	.000	.000	.000

J. Flowers, 1 G at OF

Pitcher	T	Age	G	GS	CG	ShO	IP	H	HR	BB	SO	W-L	Sv	ERA
Boom-Boom Beck	R	28	43	35	15	3	257.0	270	9	69	89	12-20	1	3.54
Ownie Carroll	R	30	33	31	11	0	226.1	248	9	54	45	13-15	0	3.78
Ray Benge	R	31	37	30	16	2	228.2	238	11	55	74	10-17	1	3.42
Van Lingle Mungo	R	22	41	28	18	3	248.0	223	7	84	110	16-15	0	2.72
Watty Clark†	L	31	11	8	4	1	50.2	61	2	6	14	2-4	1	4.80
Joe Shaute	L	33	41	4	0	0	108.1	125	4	31	26	3-4	2	3.49
Sloppy Thurston	R	34	32	15	5	0	131.1	171	4	34	22	6-8	3	4.52
Rosy Ryan	R	35	30	0	0	0	61.1	69	3	16	22	1-1	2	4.26
Dutch Leonard	R	24	10	3	2	0	40.0	42	0	10	6	2-3	0	2.93
Fred Heimach	L	32	10	3	0	0	29.2	49	2	11	7	0-1	0	10.01
Ray Lucas	R	24	2	0	0	0	5.0	6	0	4	0	0-0	0	7.20

1933 Philadelphia Phillies 7th NL 60-92 .395 31.0 GB

Burt Shotton

Player	Gm by Position	B	Age	G	AB	R	H	2B	3B	HR	RBI	BB	SO	SB	Avg	OBP	Slg
Spud Davis	C132	R	28	141	495	51	173	28	3	9	65	32	24	2	.349	.395	.473
Don Hurst	1B142	L	27	147	550	58	147	27	8	8	76	48	32	3	.267	.327	.389
Jack Warner	2B71,3B30,SS1	R	29	107	340	31	76	15	1	0	22	28	33	1	.224	.285	.274
Jim McLeod	3B67	R	24	67	232	20	45	6	1	0	15	12	25	1	.194	.237	.228
Dick Bartell	SS152	R	25	152	587	78	159	25	5	1	37	56	46	6	.271	.340	.336
Chuck Klein	OF152	L	28	152	606	101	223	44	7	28	120	56	36	15	.368	.422	.602
Chick Fullis	OF151	R	29	151	647	91	200	31	6	1	45	36	34	18	.309	.350	.380
Wes Schulmerich†	OF97	R	32	97	365	53	122	19	4	8	59	32	45	1	.334	.394	.474
Neal Finn	2B51	R	29	51	169	15	40	4	1	0	13	10	14	2	.237	.287	.272
Hal Lee†	OF45	R	28	46	167	25	48	12	2	0	12	18	13	1	.287	.360	.383
Al Todd	C34,OF2	R	31	73	136	13	28	4	0	0	10	4	18	1	.206	.239	.235
Pinky Whitney†	3B30	R	28	31	121	12	32	4	0	3	19	8	8	1	.264	.310	.372
Fritz Knothe†	3B32,2B4	R	30	41	113	10	17	2	0	0	11	6	19	2	.150	.193	.168
Mickey Haslin	2B26	R	22	26	89	3	21	2	0	0	9	3	5	1	.236	.261	.258
Gus Dugas	1B11,OF1	L	26	37	71	4	12	3	0	0	9	1	9	0	.169	.181	.211
Harry McCurdy	C2	L	33	73	54	9	15	1	0	2	12	16	6	0	.278	.451	.407
Eddie Delker	2B17,3B4	R	27	25	41	6	7	3	1	0	1	0	12	0	.171	.171	.293
Alta Cohen	OF7	L	24	19	32	6	6	1	0	0	1	6	4	0	.188	.316	.219
George Brickell	OF4	L	26	8	13	2	4	1	1	0	1	1	0	0	.308	.357	.538
Hugh Willingham		R	27	1	1	0	0	0	0	0	0	0	0	0	.000	.000	.000

Pitcher	T	Age	G	GS	CG	ShO	IP	H	HR	BB	SO	W-L	Sv	ERA
Ed Holley	R	33	30	28	12	3	206.2	219	18	62	56	13-15	0	3.53
Snipe Hansen	L	26	32	22	8	0	168.1	199	12	30	47	6-14	1	4.44
Jumbo Elliott	L	32	35	21	6	0	161.2	188	8	49	43	6-10	2	3.84
Flint Rhem	R	32	28	19	3	0	125.0	182	10	33	27	5-14	2	6.62
Cy Moore	R	28	36	18	9	3	161.1	177	7	42	53	8-9	1	3.74
John Jackson	R	23	10	7	1	0	54.0	74	3	35	11	2-2	0	6.00
Reggie Grabowski	R	25	10	5	4	1	48.0	38	4	10	9	1-3	0	2.44
Ad Liska	R	26	45	1	0	0	75.2	96	5	26	23	3-1	1	4.52
Phil Collins	R	31	42	13	5	1	151.0	178	9	57	40	8-13	6	4.11
Frank Pearce	R	27	20	7	3	1	82.0	78	5	29	18	5-4	0	3.62
Jack Berly	R	30	13	6	1	1	50.0	62	5	22	4	2-3	0	5.04
Frank Ragland	R	29	11	5	0	0	38.1	51	1	10	4	0-4	0	6.81
Clarence Pickrel	R	22	9	0	0	0	13.2	20	0	3	6	1-0	0	3.95
Charlie Butler	L	27	1	0	0	0	1.0	1	0	2	0	0-0	0	9.00

1933 Cincinnati Reds 8th NL 58-94 .382 33.0 GB

Donie Bush

Player	Gm by Position	B	Age	G	AB	R	H	2B	3B	HR	RBI	BB	SO	SB	Avg	OBP	Slg
Ernie Lombardi	C95	R	25	107	350	30	99	21	1	4	47	16	17	2	.283	.322	.383
Jim Bottomley	1B145	L	33	145	549	57	137	23	9	13	83	42	28	3	.250	.311	.395
Jo-Jo Morrissey	2B88,SS63,3B15	R	29	148	534	43	123	20	0	0	26	20	22	5	.230	.261	.268
Sparky Adams†	3B132,SS8	R	38	137	538	59	141	21	1	1	22	44	30	3	.262	.320	.310
Otto Bluege	SS95,2B10,3B1	R	23	108	291	17	62	6	2	0	18	26	29	0	.213	.278	.247
Chick Hafey	OF144	R	30	144	568	77	172	34	6	7	62	40	44	3	.303	.351	.421
Harry Rice	OF141	L	31	143	510	44	133	19	6	0	54	35	24	4	.261	.316	.322
Johnny Moore	OF132	L	31	133	514	60	135	19	5	1	44	29	16	4	.263	.306	.325
George Grantham	2B72,1B12	L	33	87	260	32	53	14	3	4	28	38	21	4	.204	.310	.327
Wally Roettger	OF55	R	30	84	209	13	50	7	1	1	17	8	10	0	.239	.267	.297
Rollie Hemsley†	C41	R	26	49	116	9	22	8	0	0	7	6	8	0	.190	.230	.259
Clyde Manion	C34	R	36	36	84	3	14	1	0	0	3	8	7	0	.167	.239	.179
Leo Durocher†	SS16	R	27	16	51	6	11	1	0	1	3	4	5	0	.216	.273	.294
Andy High	3B11,2B2	L	35	24	43	4	9	2	0	1	6	5	1	0	.209	.292	.326
Tommy Robello	2B11,3B2	R	20	14	30	1	7	3	0	0	3	1	5	0	.233	.258	.333
Bob Smith†	P16,SS1	R	38	23	25	2	5	1	0	0	1	1	0	1	.200	.231	.240
Jack Crouch†	C6	R	30	10	16	5	2	0	0	0	1	0	0	1	.125	.222	.125
Eddie Hunter		R	28	1	0	0	0	0	0	0	0	0	0	0	—	—	—
Taylor Douthit†		R	32	1	0	1	0	0	0	0	0	0	0	0	—	—	—

Pitcher	T	Age	G	GS	CG	ShO	IP	H	HR	BB	SO	W-L	Sv	ERA
Paul Derringer†	R	26	33	31	16	2	231.0	240	4	51	86	7-25	1	3.23
Red Lucas	R	31	29	29	21	3	219.2	248	13	18	40	10-16	0	3.40
Si Johnson	R	26	34	28	14	4	211.1	212	7	54	51	7-18	1	3.49
Larry Benton	R	35	34	19	7	2	152.2	160	5	36	33	10-11	2	3.71
Eppa Rixey	L	42	16	12	5	1	94.1	118	1	12	10	6-3	0	3.15
Benny Frey	R	27	37	9	1	1	132.0	144	4	21	12	6-4	0	3.82
Ray Kolp	R	38	30	14	4	0	150.1	168	7	23	28	6-9	3	3.53
Allyn Stout†	R	28	23	5	2	0	71.1	85	3	26	29	2-3	0	3.79
Bob Smith†	R	38	16	6	4	0	73.2	75	3	11	18	4-4	0	2.20
Jack Quinn	R	49	14	0	0	0	15.2	20	0	5	3	0-1	1	4.02

»1934 Detroit Tigers 1st AL 101-53 .656 —

Mickey Cochrane

Player	Gm by Position	B	Age	G	AB	R	H	2B	3B	HR	RBI	BB	SO	SB	Avg	OBP	Slg
Mickey Cochrane	C124	L	31	129	437	74	140	32	1	2	76	78	26	8	.320	.428	.412
Hank Greenberg	1B153	R	23	153	593	118	201	63	7	26	139	63	93	9	.339	.404	.600
Charlie Gehringer	2B154	L	31	154	601	134	214	50	7	11	127	99	25	11	.356	.450	.517
Marv Owen	3B154	R	28	154	565	79	179	34	9	8	96	59	37	3	.317	.385	.451
Billy Rogell	SS154	S	29	154	592	114	175	32	8	3	100	74	36	13	.296	.374	.392
Goose Goslin	OF149	L	33	151	614	106	187	38	7	13	100	65	38	5	.305	.373	.453
Pete Fox	OF121	R	25	128	516	101	147	31	2	2	45	49	53	25	.285	.351	.364
Jo-Jo White	OF100	L	25	115	384	97	120	18	5	0	44	69	39	28	.313	.419	.385
Gee Walker	OF80	R	26	98	347	54	104	19	2	6	39	19	20	20	.300	.340	.418
Ray Hayworth	C54	R	30	54	167	20	49	5	2	0	27	16	22	0	.293	.355	.347
Frank Doljack	OF30,1B3	R	26	56	120	15	28	7	1	1	19	13	15	2	.233	.313	.333
Flea Clifton	3B4,2B1	R	24	16	16	3	1	0	0	0	1	1	2	0	.063	.118	.063
Heinie Schuble	SS3,3B2,2B1	R	27	11	15	2	4	2	0	0	2	1	4	0	.267	.313	.400
Rudy York	C2	R	20	3	6	0	1	0	0	0	0	1	3	0	.167	.286	.167
Icehouse Wilson		R	21	1	1	0	0	0	0	0	0	0	0	0	.000	.000	.000
Frank Reiber		R	24	3	1	0	0	0	0	0	0	2	0	0	.000	.667	.000
Cy Perkins		R	38	1	1	0	0	0	0	0	0	0	0	0	.000	.000	.000

Pitcher	T	Age	G	GS	CG	ShO	IP	H	HR	BB	SO	W-L	Sv	ERA
Tommy Bridges	R	27	36	35	23	3	275.0	249	16	104	151	22-11	1	3.67
Schoolboy Rowe	R	24	45	30	20	3	266.0	259	12	81	149	24-8	1	3.45
Firpo Marberry	R	35	38	19	6	1	155.2	174	12	48	64	15-5	3	4.57
Vic Sorrell	R	33	28	19	6	1	129.2	146	13	45	46	6-9	2	4.79
Carl Fischer	L	28	20	15	4	1	95.0	107	5	38	39	6-4	1	4.36
General Crowder†	R	35	9	9	3	1	66.2	81	3	20	30	5-1	0	4.19
Steve Larkin	R	23	2	1	0	0	6.0	8	0	5	8	0-0	0	1.50
Eldon Auker	R	23	43	18	10	2	205.0	234	9	56	86	15-7	1	3.42
Chief Hogsett	L	30	26	0	0	0	50.1	61	4	19	23	3-2	3	4.29
Luke Hamlin	R	29	20	5	1	0	75.1	87	11	44	30	2-3	1	5.38
Vic Frasier	R	29	8	2	0	0	22.2	30	0	12	11	1-3	0	5.96
Red Phillips	R	25	7	1	1	0	23.1	31	1	16	3	2-0	1	6.17

1934 New York Yankees 2nd AL 94-60 .610 7.0 GB

Joe McCarthy

Player	Gm by Position	B	Age	G	AB	R	H	2B	3B	HR	RBI	BB	SO	SB	Avg	OBP	Slg
Bill Dickey	C104	L	27	104	395	56	127	24	4	12	72	38	18	0	.322	.384	.494
Lou Gehrig	1B153,SS1	L	31	154	579	128	210	40	6	49	165	109	31	9	.363	.465	.706
Tony Lazzeri	2B92,3B30	R	30	123	438	59	117	24	6	14	67	71	64	11	.267	.369	.445
Jack Saltzgaver	3B84,1B4	L	31	94	350	64	95	8	1	6	36	48	28	8	.271	.359	.351
Frankie Crosetti	SS119,3B23,2B1	R	23	138	554	85	147	22	10	11	67	61	58	5	.265	.344	.401
Ben Chapman	OF149	R	25	149	588	82	181	21	13	5	86	67	68	26	.308	.381	.413
Babe Ruth	OF111	L	39	125	365	78	105	17	4	22	84	103	63	1	.288	.447	.537
Sammy Byrd	OF104	R	26	106	191	32	47	8	0	3	23	18	22	1	.246	.318	.335
Red Rolfe	SS46,3B26	L	25	89	279	54	80	13	2	0	18	26	16	2	.287	.348	.348
Myril Hoag	OF86	R	26	97	251	45	67	8	2	3	34	21	21	1	.267	.324	.351
Earle Combs	OF62	L	35	63	251	47	80	13	5	2	25	40	9	3	.319	.412	.434
Don Heffner	2B68	R	23	72	241	29	63	8	3	0	25	25	18	1	.261	.331	.320
Art Jorgens	C56	R	29	58	183	14	38	6	1	0	20	23	24	2	.208	.296	.251
George Selkirk	OF46	L	26	46	176	23	55	7	1	5	38	15	17	1	.313	.370	.449
Dixie Walker	OF1	L	23	17	17	2	2	0	0	0	0	1	3	0	.118	.167	.118
Zack Taylor	C3	R	35	4	7	0	1	0	0	0	0	0	1	0	.143	.143	.143
Lyn Lary†	1B1	R	28	1	0	0	0	0	0	0	0	1	0	0	—	1.000	—

Pitcher	T	Age	G	GS	CG	ShO	IP	H	HR	BB	SO	W-L	Sv	ERA
Lefty Gomez	L	25	38	33	25	6	281.2	223	12	96	158	26-5	1	2.33
Red Ruffing	R	30	36	31	19	5	256.1	232	18	104	149	19-11	0	3.93
Johnny Broaca	R	24	26	24	13	1	177.1	203	9	65	74	12-9	0	4.16
Johnny Murphy	R	25	40	20	10	0	207.2	193	11	76	70	14-10	4	3.12
Danny MacFayden	R	29	22	11	4	0	96.0	110	5	31	41	4-3	0	4.50
Johnny Allen	R	28	13	10	4	0	71.2	62	3	32	54	5-2	0	2.89
Charlie Devens	R	24	1	1	1	0	11.0	9	0	5	4	1-0	0	1.64
Vito Tamulis	L	22	1	1	1	1	9.0	7	0	1	5	1-0	0	0.00
Jimmie DeShong	R	24	31	12	6	0	133.2	126	6	56	40	6-7	3	4.11
Russ Van Atta	L	28	28	9	0	0	88.0	107	3	46	39	3-5	0	6.34
Burleigh Grimes†	R	40	10	0	0	0	18.0	22	0	14	5	1-2	1	5.50
George Uhle	R	35	10	2	0	0	16.1	30	3	7	10	2-4	0	9.92
Harry Smythe†	L	29	8	0	0	0	15.0	24	1	8	7	0-2	1	7.80
Floyd Newkirk	R	25	1	0	0	0	1.0	1	0	1	0	0-0	0	0.00

1934 Cleveland Indians 3rd AL 85-69 .552 16.0 GB

Walter Johnson

Player	Gm by Position	B	Age	G	AB	R	H	2B	3B	HR	RBI	BB	SO	SB	Avg	OBP	Slg
Frankie Pytlak	C88	R	25	91	289	46	75	12	4	0	35	36	11	11	.260	.352	.329
Hal Trosky	1B154	L	21	154	625	117	206	45	9	35	142	58	49	2	.330	.388	.598
Odell Hale	2B137,3B5	R	25	143	563	82	170	44	6	13	101	48	50	8	.302	.357	.471
Willie Kamm	3B118	R	34	121	386	52	104	23	3	0	42	62	38	7	.269	.372	.345
Bill Knickerbocker	SS146	R	22	146	593	82	188	32	5	4	67	25	40	6	.317	.347	.408
Earl Averill	OF154	L	32	154	598	128	187	48	6	31	113	99	44	4	.313	.414	.569
Joe Vosmik	OF104	R	24	104	405	71	138	33	2	6	78	35	10	1	.341	.393	.477
Sam Rice	OF78	L	44	97	335	48	98	19	1	1	33	28	9	5	.293	.351	.364
Johnny Burnett	3B42,SS9,2B3*	L	29	72	208	28	61	11	2	3	30	18	11	1	.293	.352	.409
Milt Galatzer	OF49	L	27	49	196	29	53	10	2	0	15	21	8	3	.270	.344	.342
Bob Seeds†	OF48	R	27	61	186	28	46	8	1	0	18	21	13	2	.247	.327	.301
Dutch Holland	OF31	R	30	50	128	19	32	12	1	2	13	13	11	0	.250	.319	.406
Glenn Myatt	C34	L	36	36	107	18	34	6	1	0	12	13	5	1	.318	.392	.393
Moe Berg†	C28	R	32	29	97	4	25	3	1	0	9	1	7	0	.258	.265	.309
Eddie Moore	2B18,3B3,SS2	R	35	27	65	4	10	2	0	0	8	10	4	0	.154	.267	.185
Bill Brenzel	C15	R	24	15	51	4	11	3	0	0	3	2	1	0	.216	.245	.275
Ralph Winegarner	P22,OF1	R	24	32	51	9	10	2	0	1	5	3	11	0	.196	.241	.294
Dick Porter†	OF10	L	32	13	44	9	10	2	1	1	6	4	5	0	.227	.292	.386
Kit Carson	OF4	L	21	5	18	4	5	2	1	0	1	2	3	0	.278	.350	.500
Bob Garbark	C5	R	24	5	11	1	0	0	0	0	0	1	3	0	.000	.083	.000
Roy Spencer	C4	R	34	5	7	0	1	1	0	0	2	0	1	0	.143	.143	.286

J. Burnett, 2 G at OF

Pitcher	T	Age	G	GS	CG	ShO	IP	H	HR	BB	SO	W-L	Sv	ERA
Monte Pearson	R	24	39	33	19	0	254.2	257	16	130	140	18-13	2	4.52
Mel Harder	R	24	44	29	17	6	255.1	246	6	81	91	20-12	4	2.61
Oral Hildebrand	R	27	33	28	10	1	198.0	225	14	99	72	11-9	1	4.50
Willis Hudlin	R	28	36	26	15	1	195.0	210	8	65	58	15-10	4	4.75
Bill Perrin	L	24	1	1	0	0	5.0	13	0	2	3	0-1	0	14.40
Lloyd Brown	L	29	38	15	5	0	117.0	116	7	51	39	5-10	6	3.85
Thornton Lee	L	27	24	6	0	0	85.2	105	8	44	41	1-1	0	5.04
Ralph Winegarner	R	24	22	6	4	0	78.1	91	1	39	32	5-4	0	5.51
Belve Bean	R	29	21	1	0	0	51.1	53	2	21	20	5-1	0	3.86
Clint Brown	R	30	17	2	0	0	50.1	83	3	14	15	4-3	1	5.90
Bob Weiland†	L	28	16	7	2	0	70.0	71	5	30	42	1-5	0	4.11
Sarge Connally	R	35	5	0	0	0	5.1	4	0	5	1	0-0	1	5.06
Denny Galehouse	R	22	1	0	0	0	1.0	2	0	1	0	0-0	0	18.00

1934 Boston Red Sox 4th AL 76-76 .500 24.0 GB

Bucky Harris

Player	Gm by Position	B	Age	G	AB	R	H	2B	3B	HR	RBI	BB	SO	SB	Avg	OBP	Slg
Rick Ferrell	C128	R	28	132	437	50	130	29	4	1	48	66	20	0	.297	.390	.389
Eddie Morgan	1B137	R	30	138	528	95	141	28	4	3	79	81	46	7	.267	.367	.352
Bill Cissell	2B96,SS7,3B2	R	30	102	416	71	111	13	4	4	44	28	23	11	.267	.315	.346
Bill Werber	3B130,SS22	R	26	152	623	129	200	41	10	11	67	77	37	40	.321	.397	.472
Lyn Lary†	SS129	R	28	129	419	58	101	20	4	2	54	66	51	12	.241	.344	.322
Roy Johnson	OF137	L	31	143	569	85	182	43	10	7	119	54	36	11	.320	.379	.467
Carl Reynolds	OF100	R	31	113	413	61	125	26	9	4	86	27	28	5	.303	.350	.438
Moose Solters	OF89	R	28	101	365	61	109	25	4	7	58	18	50	9	.299	.333	.447
Dick Porter†	OF65	L	32	80	265	30	80	13	6	0	56	21	15	5	.302	.355	.396
Max Bishop	2B57,1B15	L	34	97	253	65	66	13	1	1	22	82	22	3	.261	.445	.332
Dusty Cooke	OF44	L	27	74	168	34	41	8	5	1	26	36	25	7	.244	.377	.369
Mel Almada	OF23	L	21	23	90	7	21	2	1	0	10	6	8	3	.233	.281	.278
Bucky Walters†	3B23	R	25	23	88	10	19	4	4	4	18	3	12	0	.216	.242	.489
Gordie Hinkle	C26	R	29	27	75	7	13	6	1	0	9	7	23	0	.173	.244	.280
Skinny Graham	OF13	L	24	13	47	7	11	2	1	0	3	6	13	2	.234	.321	.319
Lou Legett	C17	R	33	19	38	4	11	0	0	0	1	2	4	0	.289	.325	.289
Al Niemiec	2B9	R	23	9	32	2	7	0	0	0	3	3	4	0	.219	.286	.219
Joe Judge	1B2	L	40	10	15	3	5	2	0	0	2	2	1	0	.333	.412	.467
Red Kellett	SS4,2B2,3B1	R	24	9	9	0	0	0	0	0	0	1	5	0	.000	.100	.000
Bob Seeds†	OF1	R	27	8	6	0	1	0	0	0	1	0	1	0	.167	.167	.167
Freddie Muller	2B1,3B1	R	26	2	1	1	0	0	0	0	0	1	0	0	.000	.500	.000

Pitcher	T	Age	G	GS	CG	ShO	IP	H	HR	BB	SO	W-L	Sv	ERA
Gordon Rhodes	R	26	44	31	10	0	219.0	247	10	98	79	12-12	2	4.56
Fritz Ostermueller	L	26	33	23	10	0	198.2	200	7	99	75	10-13	3	3.49
Wes Ferrell	R	26	26	23	17	3	181.0	205	4	49	67	14-5	1	3.63
Johnny Welch	R	27	41	22	8	1	206.1	223	14	76	91	13-15	0	4.49
Lefty Grove	L	34	22	12	5	0	109.1	149	5	32	43	8-8	0	6.50
Bob Weiland†	L	28	11	7	2	0	55.2	63	4	27	29	1-5	0	5.50
George Hockette	L	26	3	3	3	2	27.1	22	3	6	14	2-1	0	1.65
Spike Merena	L	24	4	3	2	1	24.2	20	2	16	7	1-2	0	2.92
George Pipgras	R	34	2	1	0	0	3.1	4	1	3	0	0-0	0	8.10
Hank Johnson	R	28	31	14	7	1	124.1	162	12	53	66	6-8	1	5.36
Rube Walberg	L	37	30	10	2	0	104.2	118	5	41	38	6-7	1	4.04
Herb Pennock	L	40	30	2	1	0	62.0	68	2	16	16	2-0	1	3.05
Joe Mulligan	R	20	14	2	1	0	44.2	46	1	27	13	1-0	0	3.63

1934 Philadelphia Athletics 5th AL 68-82 .453 31.0 GB

Connie Mack

Player	Gm by Position	B	Age	G	AB	R	H	2B	3B	HR	RBI	BB	SO	SB	Avg	OBP	Slg
Charlie Berry	C99	R	31	99	269	14	72	10	2	0	34	22	23	1	.268	.323	.320
Jimmie Foxx	1B140,3B9	R	26	150	539	120	180	28	6	44	130	111	75	11	.334	.449	.653
Rabbit Warstler	2B107,SS2	R	30	117	419	56	99	19	3	1	36	51	30	9	.236	.321	.303
Mike Higgins	3B144	R	25	144	543	89	179	37	6	16	90	56	70	9	.330	.392	.508
Eric McNair	SS151	R	25	151	599	80	168	20	4	17	82	35	42	7	.280	.321	.412
Doc Cramer	OF152	L	28	153	649	99	202	29	9	6	46	40	35	1	.311	.353	.411
Bob Johnson	OF139	R	27	141	547	111	168	26	6	34	92	58	60	12	.307	.375	.563
Ed Coleman	OF86	L	32	101	329	53	92	14	6	14	60	29	34	0	.280	.342	.486
Lou Finney	OF54,1B15	L	23	92	272	32	76	11	4	1	28	14	17	4	.279	.315	.360
Frankie Hayes	C89	R	19	92	248	24	56	10	0	6	30	20	44	2	.226	.286	.339
Dib Williams	2B53,SS2	R	24	66	205	25	56	10	1	2	17	21	18	0	.273	.341	.361
Bing Miller	OF46	R	39	81	177	22	43	10	2	1	22	16	14	1	.243	.309	.339
Jerry McQuaig	OF6	R	22	7	16	2	1	0	0	0	1	2	4	0	.063	.167	.063
Charlie Moss	C6	R	23	10	10	3	2	0	0	0	1	0	0	0	.200	.200	.200
Ed Madjeski†	C1	R	25	8	8	1	3	1	0	0	2	0	1	0	.375	.375	.500

Pitcher	T	Age	G	GS	CG	ShO	IP	H	HR	BB	SO	W-L	Sv	ERA
Sugar Cain	R	27	36	32	15	0	230.2	235	15	128	66	9-17	0	4.41
Johnny Marcum	R	24	37	31	17	2	232.0	257	13	88	92	14-11	0	4.50
Bill Dietrich	R	24	39	23	14	4	207.2	201	12	114	88	11-12	3	4.68
Joe Cascarella	R	27	42	22	9	2	194.1	214	8	104	71	12-15	1	4.68
Al Benton	R	23	32	21	7	0	155.0	145	7	88	58	7-9	1	4.88
George Caster	R	26	5	3	2	0	37.0	32	3	14	15	3-2	0	3.41
Jack Wilson	R	22	2	2	1	0	9.0	15	1	9	2	0-1	0	12.00
Roy Mahaffey	R	31	37	14	3	0	129.0	142	10	55	37	6-7	2	5.37
Bob Kline†	R	24	20	0	0	0	39.2	50	6	13	14	6-2	1	6.35
Mort Flohr	L	22	14	3	0	0	30.2	34	3	33	6	0-2	0	5.87
Harry Matuzak	R	24	11	0	0	0	24.0	28	2	10	9	0-3	0	4.88
Whitey Wilshere	L	21	9	2	0	0	21.2	39	0	15	19	0-1	0	12.05
Ed Lagger	R	21	8	0	0	0	18.0	27	1	14	2	0-0	0	11.00
Tim McKeithan	R	27	3	0	0	0	4.0	7	2	5	0	0-0	0	15.75
Clarence Vaughn	R	22	2	0	0	0	4.1	3	1	3	1	0-0	0	2.08

1934 St. Louis Browns 6th AL 67-85 .441 33.0 GB

Rogers Hornsby

Player	Gm by Position	B	Age	G	AB	R	H	2B	3B	HR	RBI	BB	SO	SB	Avg	OBP	Slg
Rollie Hemsley	C114,OF6	R	27	123	431	47	133	31	7	2	52	29	37	6	.309	.355	.427
Jack Burns	1B154	L	26	154	612	86	157	28	8	13	73	62	47	9	.257	.327	.392
Ski Melillo	2B141	R	34	144	552	54	133	19	3	2	55	28	27	4	.241	.279	.297
Harlond Clift	3B141	R	21	147	572	104	149	30	10	14	56	84	100	7	.260	.357	.421
Alan Strange	SS125	R	27	127	430	39	100	17	2	1	45	48	28	3	.233	.310	.288
Roy Pepper	OF136	R	28	148	564	71	168	24	6	7	101	29	67	1	.298	.333	.399
Bruce Campbell	OF123	L	24	138	481	62	134	25	6	9	74	51	64	5	.279	.350	.412
Sammy West	OF120	L	29	122	482	90	157	22	10	9	55	62	55	3	.326	.403	.469
Ollie Bejma	SS32,2B14,3B13*	R	26	95	262	39	71	16	3	2	29	40	36	3	.271	.376	.378
Debs Garms	OF56	L	26	91	232	25	68	14	4	0	31	27	19	0	.293	.372	.388
Frank Grube	C55	R	29	65	170	22	49	10	0	0	11	24	11	2	.288	.379	.347
Earl Clark	OF9	R	26	13	41	4	7	2	0	0	1	1	3	0	.171	.190	.220
George Puccinelli	OF6	R	27	10	26	4	6	1	0	2	5	1	8	0	.231	.286	.500
Rogers Hornsby	3B1,OF1	R	38	24	23	2	7	2	0	1	11	7	4	0	.304	.484	.522
Grover Hartley	C2	R	45	5	3	0	1	1	0	0	0	1	0	0	.333	.500	.667
Art Scharein		R	29	1	2	0	1	0	0	0	2	0	0	0	.500	.500	.500
Charley O'Leary		R	51	1	1	1	1	0	0	0	0	0	0	0	1.000	1.000	1.000

O. Bejma, 9 G at OF

Pitcher	T	Age	G	GS	CG	ShO	IP	H	HR	BB	SO	W-L	Sv	ERA
George Blaeholder	R	30	39	33	14	1	234.1	276	16	68	66	14-18	3	4.22
Bobo Newsom	R	26	47	32	15	2	262.1	259	15	149	135	16-20	5	4.01
Bump Hadley	R	29	39	32	7	2	213.0	212	14	127	79	10-16	1	4.35
Dick Coffman	R	27	40	21	6	1	173.0	212	11	59	55	9-10	3	4.53
Jim Weaver†	R	30	5	5	2	0	19.2	17	3	20	11	2-0	0	6.41
Jack Knott	R	27	45	10	2	0	138.0	149	17	67	56	10-3	4	4.96
Ivy Andrews	R	27	43	13	2	0	139.0	166	7	65	51	4-11	3	4.66
Ed Wells	L	34	33	8	2	0	92.0	108	7	35	27	1-7	1	4.79
Bill McAfee	R	26	28	0	0	0	61.2	84	4	26	11	1-0	0	5.84
Lefty Mills	L	24	4	0	0	0	8.2	10	0	11	2	0-0	0	4.15
Jim Walkup	R	24	3	0	0	0	8.1	6	0	5	6	0-0	0	2.16

1934 Washington Senators 7th AL 66-86 .434 34.0 GB

Joe Cronin

Player	Gm by Position	B	Age	G	AB	R	H	2B	3B	HR	RBI	BB	SO	SB	Avg	OBP	Slg
Eddie Phillips	C53	R	33	56	169	6	33	6	1	2	16	26	24	1	.195	.306	.278
Joe Kuhel	1B63	L	28	63	263	49	76	12	3	3	25	30	14	2	.289	.364	.392
Buddy Myer	2B135	L	30	139	524	103	160	33	8	3	57	102	32	6	.305	.419	.416
Cecil Travis	3B99	L	20	109	392	48	125	22	4	1	53	24	37	1	.319	.361	.403
Joe Cronin	SS127	R	27	127	504	68	143	30	9	7	101	53	28	8	.284	.353	.421
Fred Schulte	OF134	R	33	136	524	72	156	32	6	3	73	53	34	3	.298	.363	.399
Heinie Manush	OF131	L	32	137	556	88	194	42	11	11	89	36	23	7	.349	.392	.523
John Stone	OF112	L	28	113	419	77	132	28	7	7	67	52	26	1	.315	.395	.465
Ossie Bluege	3B41,SS30,2B5*	R	33	99	285	39	70	9	2	0	11	23	15	2	.246	.306	.291
Dave Harris	OF64,3B5	R	33	97	235	28	59	14	3	2	37	39	40	2	.251	.358	.362
Pete Susko	1B58	L	29	58	224	25	64	5	3	2	25	18	10	3	.286	.342	.362
Luke Sewell	C50,OF7,1B6*	R	33	72	207	21	49	7	3	2	21	22	10	0	.237	.313	.329
Red Kress†	1B30,OF10,2B6*	R	27	56	171	18	39	4	3	4	24	17	19	3	.228	.298	.357
Cliff Bolton	C39	L	27	42	148	12	40	9	1	1	17	11	9	2	.270	.321	.365
John Kerr	3B17,2B13	R	35	31	103	8	28	4	0	0	12	8	13	1	.272	.324	.311
Moe Berg†	C31	R	32	33	86	5	21	4	0	0	6	6	4	2	.244	.301	.291
Johnny Gill	OF13	L	29	13	53	7	13	3	0	2	7	2	3	0	.245	.286	.415
Fred Sington	OF9	R	24	9	35	2	10	2	0	0	6	4	3	0	.286	.359	.343
Jake Powell	OF9	R	25	9	35	6	10	2	0	0	1	4	2	1	.286	.359	.343
Bob Boken†	3B6,2B1	R	26	11	27	5	6	1	1	0	6	3	1	2	.222	.300	.333
Gus Dugas	OF2	L	27	24	19	2	1	1	0	0	1	3	3	0	.053	.182	.105
Elmer Klumpp	C11	R	27	12	15	2	2	0	0	0	0	0	1	0	.133	.188	.133
Syd Cohen	P3,OF1	S	28	4	11	1	3	0	0	0	2	0	1	0	.273	.273	.273

O. Bluege, 5 G at OF; L. Sewell, 1 G at 2B, 1 G at 3B; R. Kress, 1 G at 3B, 1 G at SS

Pitcher	T	Age	G	GS	CG	ShO	IP	H	HR	BB	SO	W-L	Sv	ERA
Earl Whitehill	L	34	32	31	15	0	235.0	269	10	94	96	14-11	0	4.52
Monte Weaver	R	28	31	31	11	0	204.2	255	16	63	51	11-15	0	4.79
Lefty Stewart	L	33	24	22	7	1	152.0	184	8	36	36	7-11	0	4.03
Tommy Thomas	R	34	33	18	7	1	133.1	154	9	58	42	8-9	1	5.47
Ed Linke	R	22	7	4	2	0	34.2	38	1	9	9	2-2	0	4.15
Reese Diggs	R	18	4	3	2	0	21.1	26	3	15	2	1-2	0	6.75
Syd Cohen	L	28	3	2	2	0	18.0	25	2	6	6	1-1	0	7.50
Orville Armbrust	R	24	3	2	0	0	12.2	10	1	3	3	1-0	0	2.13
Allen Benson	R	25	2	2	0	0	9.2	19	0	5	4	0-1	0	12.10
Jack Russell	R	28	54	9	3	0	157.2	179	6	56	38	5-10	7	4.17
Alex McColl	R	40	42	2	1	0	112.0	129	6	36	29	3-4	1	3.86
Bobby Burke	L	27	37	15	7	1	168.0	155	2	72	52	8-8	0	3.21
General Crowder†	R	35	29	13	4	0	100.2	142	9	38	39	4-10	3	6.79
Ray Prim	L	27	8	1	0	0	14.2	19	1	8	3	0-2	0	6.75
Bob Kline†	R	24	6	0	0	0	4.0	10	0	4	1	1-0	0	15.75
John Milligan	L	30	2	0	0	0	2.2	6	0	0	1	0-0	0	10.13
Marc Filley	R	22	1	0	0	0	0.1	2	0	0	0	0-0	0	27.00

1934 Chicago White Sox 8th AL 53-99 .349 47.0 GB

Lew Fonseca (4-11)/Jimmy Dykes (49-88)

Player	Gm by Position	B	Age	G	AB	R	H	2B	3B	HR	RBI	BB	SO	SB	Avg	OBP	Slg
Ed Madjeski†	C79	R	25	85	281	36	62	14	2	5	32	14	31	2	.221	.260	.338
Zeke Bonura	1B127	R	25	127	510	86	154	35	4	27	110	64	31	0	.302	.380	.545
Jackie Hayes	2B61	R	27	62	226	19	58	9	1	1	31	23	20	3	.257	.325	.319
Jimmy Dykes	3B74,1B27,2B27	R	37	127	456	52	122	17	4	7	82	64	28	1	.268	.363	.368
Luke Appling	SS110,2B8	R	27	118	452	75	137	28	6	2	61	59	27	3	.303	.384	.405
Al Simmons	OF138	R	32	138	558	102	192	36	7	18	104	53	58	3	.344	.403	.530
Evar Swanson	OF105	R	31	117	426	71	127	9	5	0	34	59	31	10	.298	.385	.343
Mule Haas	OF89	L	30	106	351	54	94	16	3	2	22	47	22	1	.268	.354	.348
Bob Boken†	2B57,SS22	R	26	81	297	30	70	9	1	3	40	15	32	2	.236	.275	.303
Jocko Conlan	OF54	L	34	63	225	35	56	11	3	0	16	19	7	2	.249	.310	.324
Marty Hopkins†	3B63	R	27	67	210	22	45	7	0	2	28	42	26	0	.214	.348	.276
Merv Shea	C60	R	33	62	176	8	28	3	0	0	5	24	19	0	.159	.260	.176
Frenchy Uhalt	OF40	L	24	57	165	28	40	5	1	0	16	29	12	6	.242	.359	.285
Joe Chamberlain	SS26,3B14	R	24	43	141	13	34	5	1	2	17	6	38	1	.241	.272	.333
Frenchy Bordagaray	OF17	R	24	29	87	12	28	3	1	0	2	3	8	1	.322	.344	.379
Muddy Ruel	C21	R	38	22	57	4	12	3	0	0	7	8	5	0	.211	.308	.263
Rip Radcliff	OF14	L	28	14	56	7	15	2	1	0	5	0	2	1	.268	.268	.339
Mark Mauldin	3B10	R	19	10	38	3	10	2	0	1	3	0	3	0	.263	.263	.395
Milt Bocek	OF10	R	21	19	38	3	8	1	0	0	3	5	5	0	.211	.302	.237
Charlie Uhlir	OF6	L	21	14	27	3	4	0	0	0	3	2	6	0	.148	.207	.148
George Caithamer	C5	R	23	5	19	1	6	1	0	0	3	1	5	0	.316	.350	.368
Red Kress†	2B3	R	27	8	14	3	4	0	0	0	1	3	3	0	.286	.412	.286
Johnny Pasek	C4	R	29	4	9	1	3	0	0	0	0	1	1	0	.333	.400	.333
Bill Fehring	C1	S	22	1	1	0	0	0	0	0	0	0	1	0	.000	.000	.000

Pitcher	T	Age	G	GS	CG	ShO	IP	H	HR	BB	SO	W-L	Sv	ERA
George Earnshaw	R	34	33	30	16	2	227.0	242	28	104	97	14-11	0	4.52
Milt Gaston	R	38	29	28	10	1	194.0	247	16	84	48	6-19	0	5.85
Sad Sam Jones	R	41	27	26	11	1	183.1	217	16	60	60	8-12	0	5.11
Ted Lyons	R	33	30	24	21	0	205.1	249	15	66	53	11-13	1	4.87
Les Tietje	R	22	34	22	6	0	176.0	174	20	96	81	5-14	0	4.81
Vern Kennedy	R	27	3	3	1	0	19.1	21	1	9	7	0-2	0	3.72
Hugo Klaerner	R	25	3	3	1	0	17.1	24	4	16	9	0-2	0	10.90
Phil Gallivan	R	27	35	7	3	0	126.2	155	14	64	55	4-7	1	5.61
Joe Heving	R	33	33	2	0	0	88.0	133	12	48	40	1-7	4	7.26
Whit Wyatt	R	26	23	6	2	0	67.2	83	10	37	36	4-11	2	7.18
Harry Kinzy	R	23	13	2	1	0	34.1	38	1	31	12	0-1	0	4.98
Lee Stine	R	20	4	0	0	0	11.0	11	2	10	8	0-0	0	8.18
John Pomorski	R	28	3	0	0	0	1.2	1	0	2	0	0-0	0	5.40
Monty Stratton	R	22	1	0	0	0	3.1	4	0	1	0	0-0	0	5.40

»1934 St. Louis Cardinals 1st NL 95-58 .621 —

Frank Frisch

Player	Gm by Position	B	Age	G	AB	R	H	2B	3B	HR	RBI	BB	SO	SB	Avg	OBP	Slg
Spud Davis	C94	R	29	107	347	45	104	22	4	9	65	34	27	0	.300	.366	.464
Ripper Collins	1B154	S	30	154	600	116	200	40	12	35	128	57	50	2	.333	.393	.615
Frankie Frisch	2B115,3B25	S	35	140	550	74	168	30	6	3	75	45	10	11	.305	.359	.398
Pepper Martin	3B107,P1	R	30	110	454	76	131	25	11	5	49	32	41	23	.289	.337	.425
Leo Durocher	SS146	R	28	146	500	62	130	26	5	3	70	33	40	2	.260	.308	.350
Jack Rothrock	OF154,2B1	S	29	154	647	106	184	35	3	11	72	49	56	10	.284	.336	.399
Joe Medwick	OF149	R	22	149	620	110	198	40	18	18	106	21	83	3	.319	.343	.529
Ernie Orsatti	OF90	L	31	105	337	39	101	14	4	0	31	27	31	6	.300	.353	.365
Burgess Whitehead	2B48,SS29,3B28	R	24	100	332	55	92	13	5	1	24	12	19	5	.277	.310	.355
Bill Delancey	C77	L	22	93	253	41	80	18	3	13	40	41	37	1	.316	.414	.565
Chick Fullis†	OF56	R	30	69	199	21	52	9	1	0	26	14	11	4	.261	.310	.317
Buster Mills	OF18	R	25	29	72	7	17	4	1	1	8	4	11	0	.236	.295	.361
Pat Crawford	3B9,2B4	L	32	61	70	3	19	2	0	0	16	5	3	0	.271	.320	.300
Kiddo Davis†	OF9	R	32	16	33	6	10	3	0	1	4	3	1	1	.303	.361	.485
Gene Moore	OF3	L	24	9	18	2	5	1	0	0	1	2	2	0	.278	.350	.333
Francis Healy	C2,3B1,OF1	R	23	15	13	1	4	1	0	0	1	0	2	0	.308	.308	.385
Lew Riggs		L	24	2	1	0	0	0	0	0	0	0	1	0	.000	.000	.000
Red Worthington†		R	28	1	1	0	0	0	0	0	0	0	1	0	.000	.000	.000

Pitcher	T	Age	G	GS	CG	ShO	IP	H	HR	BB	SO	W-L	Sv	ERA
Dizzy Dean	R	24	50	33	24	7	311.2	288	14	75	195	30-7	7	2.66
Tex Carleton	R	27	40	31	16	0	240.2	260	14	52	103	16-11	2	4.26
Paul Dean	R	20	39	26	16	5	233.1	225	19	52	150	19-11	2	3.43
Wild Bill Hallahan	L	31	32	26	10	2	162.2	195	2	66	70	8-12	0	4.26
Bill Walker	L	30	24	19	10	1	153.0	160	11	66	76	12-4	0	3.12
Jesse Haines	R	40	37	6	0	0	90.0	86	6	19	17	4-4	1	3.50
Jim Mooney	L	27	32	7	1	0	82.1	114	3	49	27	2-4	1	5.47
Dazzy Vance†	R	43	19	4	1	0	59.0	62	4	14	33	1-1	1	3.66
Jim Lindsey†	R	38	11	0	0	0	14.0	21	2	3	7	0-1	1	6.43
Flint Rhem†	R	33	5	1	0	0	15.2	26	0	7	6	1-0	1	4.60
Jim Winford	R	24	5	1	0	0	12.2	17	0	6	3	0-2	0	7.82
Burleigh Grimes†	R	40	4	0	0	0	7.2	5	1	2	1	2-1	0	3.52
Clarence Heise	L	26	1	0	0	0	2.0	3	1	0	1	0-0	0	4.50
Pepper Martin	R	30	1	0	0	0	2.0	1	0	0	0	0-0	0	4.50

1934 New York Giants 2nd NL 93-60 .608 2.0 GB

Bill Terry

Player	Gm by Position	B	Age	G	AB	R	H	2B	3B	HR	RBI	BB	SO	SB	Avg	OBP	Slg
Gus Mancuso	C122	R	28	122	383	32	94	14	0	7	46	27	19	0	.245	.295	.337
Bill Terry	1B153	L	37	153	602	109	213	30	6	8	83	60	47	0	.354	.414	.463
Hughie Critz	2B137	R	33	137	571	77	138	17	1	6	40	19	24	3	.242	.269	.306
Johnny Vergez	3B104	R	27	108	320	31	64	18	1	7	27	28	55	1	.200	.269	.328
Travis Jackson	SS130,3B9	R	30	137	523	75	140	26	7	16	101	37	71	1	.268	.316	.436
Mel Ott	OF153	L	25	153	582	119	190	29	10	35	135	85	43	0	.326	.415	.591
Jo-Jo Moore	OF131	L	25	139	580	106	192	37	4	15	61	31	23	5	.331	.370	.486
George Watkins	OF81	L	34	105	296	38	73	18	3	6	33	24	34	1	.247	.316	.389
Blondy Ryan	3B65,SS30,2B25	R	28	110	385	35	93	19	0	2	41	19	68	3	.242	.277	.306
Hank Leiber	OF51	R	23	63	187	17	45	5	3	2	25	4	13	1	.241	.257	.332
Lefty O'Doul	OF38	L	37	83	177	27	56	4	3	9	46	18	7	2	.316	.383	.525
Harry Danning	C37	R	22	53	97	8	32	7	0	1	7	1	9	1	.330	.337	.433
Paul Richards	C37	R	25	42	75	10	12	1	0	0	3	13	8	0	.160	.284	.173
Phil Weintraub	OF20	L	26	31	74	13	26	2	0	0	15	15	10	0	.351	.461	.378
Homer Peel	OF10	R	31	21	41	7	8	0	0	1	3	1	2	0	.195	.214	.268
George Grantham	1B4,3B2	L	34	32	29	5	7	2	0	1	4	8	6	0	.241	.405	.414
Fresco Thompson		R	32	1	1	0	0	0	0	0	0	0	0	0	.000	.000	.000

Pitcher	T	Age	G	GS	CG	ShO	IP	H	HR	BB	SO	W-L	Sv	ERA
F. Fitzsimmons	R	32	38	37	14	3	263.1	266	12	51	73	18-14	1	3.04
Hal Schumacher	R	23	41	36	18	2	297.0	299	16	89	112	23-10	0	3.18
Carl Hubbell	L	31	49	34	25	5	313.0	286	17	37	118	21-12	8	2.30
Roy Parmelee	R	27	22	20	7	2	152.2	134	6	60	83	10-6	0	3.42
Watty Clark†	L	32	5	4	1	0	18.2	23	5	5	6	1-2	0	6.75
Joe Bowman	R	24	30	10	3	0	107.1	119	9	36	36	5-4	3	3.61
Al Smith	L	26	30	5	0	0	66.2	70	2	21	27	3-5	5	4.32
Dolf Luque	R	43	26	0	0	0	42.1	54	3	17	12	4-3	7	3.83
Hi Bell	R	36	22	2	0	0	54.0	72	2	12	9	4-3	6	3.67
Jack Salveson	R	20	12	4	0	0	38.1	43	2	13	18	3-1	0	3.52
Slick Castleman	R	20	7	1	0	0	16.2	18	1	10	5	1-0	0	5.40

1934 Chicago Cubs 3rd NL 86-65 .570 8.0 GB

Charlie Grimm

Player	Gm by Position	B	Age	G	AB	R	H	2B	3B	HR	RBI	BB	SO	SB	Avg	OBP	Slg
Gabby Hartnett	C129	R	33	130	438	58	131	21	1	22	90	37	46	0	.299	.358	.502
Charlie Grimm	1B74	L	35	75	267	24	79	8	1	5	47	16	12	1	.296	.338	.390
Billy Herman	2B111	R	24	113	456	79	138	21	6	3	42	34	31	6	.303	.355	.395
Stan Hack	3B109	L	24	111	402	54	116	16	6	1	21	45	42	11	.289	.363	.366
Billy Jurges	SS98	R	26	100	358	43	88	15	2	8	33	19	34	1	.246	.289	.366
Kiki Cuyler	OF142	R	35	142	559	80	189	42	8	6	69	31	62	15	.338	.377	.474
Babe Herman	OF113,1B7	L	31	125	467	65	142	34	5	14	84	35	71	1	.304	.353	.488
Chuck Klein	OF110	L	29	115	435	78	131	27	2	20	80	47	38	3	.301	.372	.510
Woody English	SS56,3B46,2B7	R	27	109	421	65	117	26	5	3	31	48	65	6	.278	.353	.385
Tuck Stainback	OF96,3B1	R	22	104	359	47	110	14	3	2	46	8	42	7	.306	.327	.379
Augie Galan	2B43,3B3,SS1	S	22	66	192	31	50	6	2	5	22	16	15	4	.260	.317	.391
Don Hurst†	1B48	L	28	51	151	13	30	5	0	3	12	8	18	0	.199	.239	.291
Dolph Camilli†	1B32	L	27	32	120	17	33	8	0	4	19	5	25	1	.275	.315	.442
Riggs Stephenson	OF15	R	36	38	74	5	16	0	0	0	7	7	5	0	.216	.293	.216
Babe Phelps	C18	L	26	44	70	7	20	5	2	2	12	1	8	0	.286	.296	.500
Bob O'Farrell†	C22	R	37	22	67	3	15	3	0	0	5	3	11	0	.224	.257	.269
Bennie Tate	C8	L	32	11	24	1	3	0	0	0	1	0	1	0	.125	.160	.125
Phil Cavarretta	1B5	L	17	7	21	5	8	0	1	1	6	2	3	1	.381	.435	.619

Pitcher	T	Age	G	GS	CG	ShO	IP	H	HR	BB	SO	W-L	Sv	ERA
Lon Warneke	R	25	43	35	23	3	291.1	273	16	66	143	22-10	3	3.21
Bill Lee	R	24	35	29	16	4	214.1	218	9	74	104	13-14	1	3.40
Guy Bush	R	32	40	27	15	1	209.1	213	15	54	75	18-10	2	3.83
Pat Malone	R	31	34	21	8	1	191.0	200	14	55	111	14-7	0	3.53
Jim Weaver†	R	30	27	20	8	1	159.0	163	5	54	98	11-9	0	3.91
Lynn Nelson	R	29	2	1	0	0	1.0	4	1	1	0	0-1	0	36.00
Bud Tinning	R	28	39	7	1	1	129.1	134	9	46	44	4-6	3	3.34
Charlie Root	R	35	34	9	2	0	117.2	141	8	53	46	4-7	0	4.28
Roy Joiner	L	27	20	2	0	0	34.0	61	3	8	9	0-1	0	8.21
Charlie Wiedemeyer	L	20	4	1	0	0	8.0	16	0	4	2	0-0	0	10.13
Dick Ward	R	25	3	0	0	0	6.0	9	0	2	1	0-0	0	3.00

1934 Boston Braves 4th NL 78-73 .517 16.0 GB — Bill McKechnie

Player	Gm by Position	B	Age	G	AB	R	H	2B	3B	HR	RBI	BB	SO	SB	Avg	OBP	Slg
Al Spohrer	C98	R	31	100	265	25	59	15	0	0	17	14	18	1	.223	.262	.279
Buck Jordan	1B117	L	27	124	489	68	152	26	9	2	58	35	19	3	.311	.358	.413
Marty McManus	2B73,3B37	R	34	119	435	56	120	18	0	8	47	32	42	5	.276	.330	.372
Pinky Whitney	3B111,2B36,SS2	R	29	146	563	58	146	26	2	12	79	25	54	7	.259	.294	.377
Billy Urbanski	SS146	R	31	146	605	104	177	30	6	7	53	56	37	4	.293	.357	.397
Wally Berger	OF150	R	28	150	615	92	183	35	8	34	121	49	65	2	.298	.352	.546
Hal Lee	OF128,2B4	R	29	139	521	70	152	23	6	8	79	47	43	3	.292	.353	.405
Tommy Thompson	OF82	L	24	105	343	40	91	12	3	0	37	13	19	2	.265	.300	.318
Randy Moore	OF72,1B37	L	28	123	422	55	120	21	2	7	64	40	16	2	.284	.346	.393
Shanty Hogan	C90	R	28	92	279	20	73	5	2	4	34	16	13	0	.262	.316	.337
Les Mallon	2B42	R	28	42	166	23	49	6	1	0	18	15	12	0	.295	.354	.343
Joe Mowry	OF20,2B1	S	26	25	79	9	17	3	0	1	4	3	13	0	.215	.244	.291
Red Worthington†	OF11	R	28	41	65	6	16	5	0	0	6	6	5	0	.246	.319	.323
Dick Gyselman	3B15,2B2	R	26	24	36	7	6	1	1	0	4	2	11	0	.167	.211	.250
Dan McGee	SS7	R	22	7	22	2	3	0	0	0	1	3	6	0	.136	.240	.136
Johnnie Tyler	OF1	S	27	3	6	0	1	0	0	0	1	0	3	0	.167	.167	.167
Elbie Fletcher	1B1	L	18	8	4	4	2	0	0	0	0	0	2	1	.500	.500	.500

Pitcher	T	Age	G	GS	CG	ShO	IP	H	HR	BB	SO	W-L	Sv	ERA
Fred Frankhouse	R	30	37	31	13	2	233.2	239	10	77	78	17-9	1	3.20
Ed Brandt	L	29	40	28	20	3	255.0	249	13	83	106	16-14	5	3.53
Huck Betts	R	37	40	27	10	2	213.0	258	17	42	69	17-10	3	4.06
Flint Rhem†	R	33	25	20	5	1	152.2	164	5	38	56	8-8	0	3.60
Ben Cantwell	R	32	27	19	6	1	143.1	163	8	34	45	5-11	5	4.33
Bob Brown	R	23	16	8	2	1	58.1	59	2	36	21	1-3	0	5.71
Tom Zachary†	L	38	5	4	2	1	24.0	27	1	8	4	1-2	0	3.38
Bob Smith	R	39	39	5	3	0	121.2	133	9	36	26	6-9	5	4.66
Leo Mangum	R	38	29	3	1	0	94.1	127	9	23	28	5-3	1	5.72
Dick Barrett	R	27	15	3	0	0	32.1	50	2	12	14	1-3	0	6.68
Clarence Pickrel	R	23	10	1	0	0	16.0	24	0	7	9	0-0	0	5.06
Jumbo Elliott†	L	33	7	3	0	0	15.1	19	2	9	6	1-1	0	5.87

1934 Pittsburgh Pirates 5th NL 74-76 .493 19.5 GB — George Gibson (27-24)/Pie Traynor (47-52)

Player	Gm by Position	B	Age	G	AB	R	H	2B	3B	HR	RBI	BB	SO	SB	Avg	OBP	Slg
Earl Grace	C83,1B1	L	27	95	289	27	78	17	1	4	24	20	19	0	.270	.317	.377
Gus Suhr	1B151	L	28	151	573	67	162	36	13	13	103	66	52	4	.283	.360	.459
Cookie Lavagetto	2B83	R	21	87	304	41	67	16	3	3	46	32	39	6	.220	.295	.322
Pie Traynor	3B110	R	34	119	444	62	137	22	10	1	61	21	27	3	.309	.341	.410
Arky Vaughan	SS149	L	22	149	558	115	186	41	11	12	94	94	38	10	.333	.431	.511
Paul Waner	OF145	L	31	146	599	122	217	32	16	14	90	68	24	8	.362	.429	.539
Lloyd Waner	OF139	L	28	140	611	95	173	27	6	1	48	38	12	6	.283	.326	.352
Freddy Lindstrom	OF92	R	28	97	383	59	111	24	4	4	49	23	21	1	.290	.333	.405
Tommy Thevenow	2B75,3B44,SS1	R	30	122	446	37	121	16	2	0	54	20	20	0	.271	.306	.316
Woody Jensen	OF66	L	26	88	283	34	82	13	4	0	27	4	13	2	.290	.304	.364
Tom Padden	C76	R	25	82	237	27	76	12	2	0	22	30	23	3	.321	.399	.388
Wally Roettger	OF23	R	31	47	106	7	26	5	1	0	11	3	8	0	.245	.266	.311
Pat Veltman	C11	R	28	12	28	1	3	0	0	0	2	0	1	0	.107	.107	.107
Pep Young	2B2,SS2	R	26	19	17	3	4	0	0	0	2	0	6	0	.235	.235	.235
Bill Brubaker	3B3	R	23	3	6	0	2	1	0	0	1	1	0	0	.333	.429	.500
Hal Finney	C5	R	28	5	0	3	0	0	0	0	0	0	0	0	—	1.000	—

Pitcher	T	Age	G	GS	CG	ShO	IP	H	HR	BB	SO	W-L	Sv	ERA
Larry French	L	26	49	35	16	3	263.2	299	8	59	103	12-18	1	3.58
Bill Swift	R	26	37	24	13	1	212.2	244	15	46	81	11-13	0	3.98
Ralph Birkofer	L	25	41	24	11	0	204.0	227	11	66	71	11-12	1	4.10
Red Lucas	R	32	29	21	12	1	172.2	198	14	40	44	10-9	0	4.38
Heinie Meine	R	38	26	14	2	0	106.1	134	12	25	22	7-6	0	4.32
Burleigh Grimes†	R	40	8	4	0	0	27.1	36	0	10	9	1-2	0	7.24
Ed Holley†	R	34	5	4	0	0	9.1	20	1	6	2	0-3	0	15.43
Cy Blanton	R	25	1	1	0	0	8.0	5	1	4	5	0-1	0	3.38
Steamboat Struss	R	25	1	1	0	0	7.0	7	0	6	3	0-1	0	6.43
Waite Hoyt	R	34	48	15	8	3	190.2	184	6	43	105	15-6	5	2.93
Leon Chagnon	R	31	33	1	0	0	58.0	68	5	24	19	4-1	1	4.81
Hal Smith	R	32	20	5	1	0	50.0	72	3	18	15	3-4	0	7.20
Bill Harris	R	34	11	2	0	0	19.0	28	2	7	8	0-0	0	6.63
Lloyd Johnson	L	23	1	0	0	0	1.0	1	0	0	0	0-0	0	0.00

1934 Brooklyn Dodgers 6th NL 71-81 .467 23.5 GB — Casey Stengel

Player	Gm by Position	B	Age	G	AB	R	H	2B	3B	HR	RBI	BB	SO	SB	Avg	OBP	Slg
Al Lopez	C137,2B2,3B2	R	25	140	439	58	120	23	2	7	54	49	44	2	.273	.349	.383
Sam Leslie	1B138	L	28	146	546	75	181	29	6	9	102	69	34	5	.332	.409	.456
Tony Cuccinello	2B101,3B43	R	26	140	528	59	138	32	2	14	94	49	45	0	.261	.325	.409
Joe Stripp	3B96,1B7,SS1	R	31	104	384	50	121	19	6	1	40	22	20	2	.315	.354	.404
Lonny Frey	SS109,3B13	L	23	125	490	77	139	24	5	8	57	52	54	11	.284	.358	.402
Buzz Boyle	OF121	L	26	128	472	88	144	26	10	7	48	51	44	8	.305	.376	.447
Len Koenecke	OF121	L	30	123	460	79	147	31	7	14	73	70	38	8	.320	.411	.509
Danny Taylor	OF108	R	33	120	405	62	121	24	6	7	57	63	47	12	.299	.396	.440
Jimmy Jordan	SS51,2B41,3B9	R	26	97	369	34	98	17	2	0	43	9	32	1	.266	.285	.322
Johnny Frederick	OF77,1B1	L	32	104	307	51	91	20	1	4	35	33	13	4	.296	.370	.407
Hack Wilson†	OF43	R	34	67	172	24	45	5	0	6	27	40	33	0	.262	.401	.395
Glenn Chapman	OF40,2B14	R	28	67	93	19	26	5	1	1	10	7	19	1	.280	.330	.387
Jim Bucher	2B20,3B6	L	23	47	84	12	19	5	2	0	8	4	7	1	.226	.261	.333
Ray Berres	C37	R	26	39	79	7	17	4	0	0	3	1	16	0	.215	.225	.266
Clyde Sukeforth	C18	L	32	27	43	5	7	1	0	0	1	1	6	0	.163	.182	.186
Johnny McCarthy	1B13	L	24	17	39	7	7	2	0	1	5	2	2	0	.179	.220	.308
Nick Tremark	OF9	L	21	17	28	3	7	1	0	0	6	2	2	0	.250	.300	.286
Wally Millies	C2	R	27	2	7	0	0	0	0	0	0	0	0	0	.000	.000	.000
Bert Hogg		R	21	2	1	0	0	0	0	0	0	0	0	0	.000	.000	.000

Pitcher	T	Age	G	GS	CG	ShO	IP	H	HR	BB	SO	W-L	Sv	ERA
Van Lingle Mungo	R	23	45	38	22	3	315.1	300	15	104	184	18-16	3	3.37
Ray Benge	R	32	36	32	14	1	227.0	252	11	61	64	14-12	0	4.32
Johnny Babich	R	21	25	19	7	0	135.0	148	5	51	62	7-11	1	4.20
Tom Zachary†	L	38	22	12	4	0	101.2	122	5	21	28	5-6	2	4.43
Dutch Leonard	R	25	44	20	11	2	183.2	210	12	33	58	14-11	5	3.28
Les Munns	R	25	33	9	4	0	99.1	106	7	60	41	3-7	0	4.71
Ownie Carroll	R	31	26	5	0	0	74.1	108	9	33	17	1-3	1	6.42
Boom-Boom Beck	R	29	22	9	2	0	57.0	72	6	32	24	2-6	0	7.42
Watty Clark†	L	32	17	1	0	0	25.1	40	0	9	10	2-0	0	5.33
Art Herring	R	28	14	4	2	0	49.1	63	2	29	15	2-4	0	6.20
Charlie Perkins	L	28	11	2	0	0	24.1	37	3	14	5	0-3	0	8.51
Ray Lucas	R	25	10	2	0	0	30.2	39	2	14	3	1-1	0	6.75
Harry Smythe†	L	29	8	0	0	0	21.1	30	3	8	5	1-1	0	5.91
Phil Page	L	28	6	0	0	0	10.0	13	1	6	4	1-0	0	5.40

1934 Philadelphia Phillies 7th NL 56-93 .376 37.0 GB — Jimmie Wilson

Player	Gm by Position	B	Age	G	AB	R	H	2B	3B	HR	RBI	BB	SO	SB	Avg	OBP	Slg
Al Todd	C82	R	32	91	302	33	96	22	2	4	41	10	39	3	.318	.344	.444
Dolph Camilli†	1B102	L	27	102	378	52	100	20	3	12	68	48	69	3	.265	.350	.429
Lou Chiozza	2B85,3B26,OF17	L	24	134	484	66	147	28	5	0	44	34	35	9	.304	.357	.382
Bucky Walters†	3B80,2B3,P2	R	25	83	300	36	78	20	3	4	38	19	54	1	.260	.308	.387
Dick Bartell	SS146	R	26	146	604	102	187	30	4	0	37	64	59	13	.310	.384	.373
Ethan Allen	OF145	R	30	145	581	87	192	42	4	10	85	33	47	6	.330	.370	.468
Johnny Moore†	OF115	L	32	116	458	68	157	34	6	11	93	40	18	7	.343	.397	.515
Kiddo Davis†	OF100	R	32	100	393	50	115	25	5	3	48	27	28	1	.293	.338	.405
Jimmie Wilson	C77	R	33	91	277	25	81	11	0	3	35	14	10	1	.292	.326	.365
Irv Jeffries	2B52,3B1	R	28	56	175	28	43	6	0	4	19	15	10	2	.246	.305	.349
Mickey Haslin	3B26,2B21,SS4	R	23	72	166	28	44	8	2	1	11	16	13	1	.265	.330	.355
Don Hurst†	1B34	L	28	40	130	16	34	9	0	2	21	12	7	1	.262	.324	.377
Harvey Hendrick	OF12,1B7,3B7	L	36	59	116	12	34	8	0	0	19	9	15	0	.293	.344	.362
Chick Fullis†	OF27	R	30	28	102	8	23	6	0	0	12	10	4	2	.225	.301	.284
Andy High	3B14,2B2	L	36	47	68	4	14	2	0	0	7	9	3	1	.206	.299	.235
Art Ruble	OF14	L	31	19	54	7	15	4	0	0	8	7	3	0	.278	.361	.352
Wes Schulmerich†	OF13	R	33	15	52	2	13	1	0	0	1	4	8	0	.250	.316	.269
Bud Clancy	1B10	L	33	20	49	8	12	0	0	1	7	6	4	0	.245	.339	.306
Ed Boland	OF7	L	26	8	30	2	9	1	1	0	5	0	2	1	.300	.300	.400
Marty Hopkins†	3B9	R	27	10	25	6	3	2	0	0	3	7	5	0	.120	.313	.200
Prince Oana	OF4	R	26	6	21	3	5	1	0	0	3	0	1	0	.238	.238	.286
Hack Wilson†	OF6	R	34	7	20	0	2	0	0	0	3	3	4	0	.100	.217	.100
Joe Holden	C6	L	21	10	14	1	1	0	0	0	0	0	2	0	.071	.071	.071
Fred Frink	OF1	R	22	2	0	0	0	0	0	0	0	0	0	0	—	—	—

Pitcher	T	Age	G	GS	CG	ShO	IP	H	HR	BB	SO	W-L	Sv	ERA
Phil Collins	R	32	45	32	15	0	254.0	277	30	87	72	13-18	1	4.18
Curt Davis	R	30	51	31	18	3	274.1	283	14	60	99	19-17	5	2.95
Euel Moore	R	26	20	16	3	0	122.1	145	9	41	38	5-7	1	4.05
Ed Holley†	R	34	15	13	0	0	72.2	85	10	31	14	1-8	0	7.18
Bucky Walters	R	25	2	1	0	0	7.0	8	1	2	7	0-0	0	1.29
Snipe Hansen	L	27	50	16	5	2	151.0	194	15	61	40	6-12	3	5.42
Syl Johnson†	R	33	42	10	4	3	133.2	122	14	24	54	5-9	3	3.50
Cy Moore	R	29	35	15	3	0	126.2	163	11	65	55	4-9	0	6.47
Reggie Grabowski	R	26	27	5	0	0	65.1	114	13	23	13	1-3	0	9.23
George Darrow	L	30	17	8	2	0	49.0	57	4	28	14	2-6	1	5.51
Frank Pearce	R	28	7	1	0	0	20.0	25	4	5	4	0-2	0	7.20
Ted Kleinhans†	L	35	5	0	0	0	6.0	11	1	3	2	0-0	0	9.00
Bill Lohrman	R	21	4	0	0	0	6.0	5	0	1	2	0-1	0	4.50
Jumbo Elliott†	L	33	3	1	0	0	5.1	8	0	4	1	0-1	0	10.13
Cy Malis	R	27	1	0	0	0	3.2	4	0	2	1	0-0	0	4.91

1934 Cincinnati Reds 8th NL 52-99 .344 42.0 GB — Bob O'Farrell (30-60)/Burt Shotton (1-0)/Chuck Dressen (21-39)

Player	Gm by Position	B	Age	G	AB	R	H	2B	3B	HR	RBI	BB	SO	SB	Avg	OBP	Slg
Ernie Lombardi	C111	R	26	132	417	42	127	19	4	9	62	16	22	0	.305	.335	.434
Jim Bottomley	1B139	L	34	142	556	72	158	31	11	11	78	33	40	1	.284	.324	.439
Tony Piet	3B51,2B49	R	27	106	421	58	109	20	5	1	38	23	44	6	.259	.307	.337
Mark Koenig	3B64,SS58,2B26*	S	29	151	633	60	172	26	6	1	67	15	24	5	.272	.289	.336
Gordon Slade	SS97,2B39	R	29	138	555	61	158	19	8	4	52	25	34	6	.285	.320	.369
Chick Hafey	OF140	R	31	140	535	75	157	29	6	18	67	52	63	4	.293	.359	.471
Adam Comorosky	OF122	R	28	127	446	46	115	12	6	0	40	34	23	1	.258	.315	.312
Harlin Pool	OF94	L	26	99	358	38	117	22	5	2	50	17	18	3	.327	.369	.433
Sparky Adams	3B38,2B29	R	39	87	278	38	70	16	1	0	14	20	10	2	.252	.307	.317
Wes Schulmerich†	OF56	R	33	74	209	21	55	8	3	5	19	22	43	1	.263	.333	.402
Bob O'Farrell†	C42	R	37	44	123	10	30	8	3	1	9	11	19	0	.244	.306	.382
Link Blakely	OF28	R	22	34	102	11	23	1	1	0	10	5	14	1	.225	.269	.255
Alex Kampouris	2B16	R	21	19	66	6	13	1	0	0	3	3	18	2	.197	.254	.212
Ivey Shiver	OF15	R	27	19	59	6	12	1	0	2	6	3	15	1	.203	.242	.322
Clyde Manion	C24	R	37	25	54	4	10	0	0	0	4	4	7	0	.185	.241	.185
Johnny Moore†	OF10	L	32	16	42	5	8	1	1	0	5	3	2	0	.190	.244	.262
Jimmy Shevlin	1B10	L	24	18	39	6	12	2	0	0	6	6	5	0	.308	.400	.359
Frank McCormick	1B2	R	23	12	16	1	5	2	1	0	5	0	1	0	.313	.313	.563
Jake Flowers		R	32	13	9	1	3	0	0	0	0	1	1	1	.333	.455	.333
Bill Marshall	2B2	R	23	6	8	0	1	0	0	0	0	0	2	0	.125	.125	.125
Ted Petoskey	OF2	R	23	6	7	0	0	0	0	0	1	0	5	0	.000	.000	.000
Harry McCurdy	1B3	L	34	3	6	0	0	0	0	0	1	0	1	0	.000	.000	.000
Tommy Robello		R	21	2	2	0	0	0	0	0	0	0	0	0	.000	.000	.000

M. Koenig, 4 G at 1B

Pitcher	T	Age	G	GS	CG	ShO	IP	H	HR	BB	SO	W-L	Sv	ERA
Paul Derringer	R	27	47	31	18	1	261.0	297	8	59	122	15-21	4	3.59
Si Johnson	R	27	46	31	9	0	215.2	264	15	84	89	7-22	3	5.22
Benny Frey	R	28	39	30	12	2	245.1	288	10	42	33	11-16	2	3.52
Tony Freitas	L	26	30	18	5	0	152.2	194	6	25	37	6-12	1	4.01
Whitey Wistert	R	22	2	1	0	0	8.0	5	1	5	1	0-1	0	1.13
Allyn Stout	R	29	41	16	4	0	140.2	170	10	47	51	6-8	1	4.86
Don Brennan	R	30	28	7	2	0	78.0	89	3	35	31	4-3	2	3.81
Ray Kolp	R	39	28	2	0	0	61.2	78	1	12	19	0-2	3	4.52
Ted Kleinhans†	L	35	24	9	0	0	80.0	107	2	38	23	2-6	0	5.74
Larry Benton	R	36	16	1	0	0	29.0	53	1	7	5	0-1	2	6.52
Joe Shaute	L	34	8	1	0	0	17.1	19	1	3	2	0-1	0	4.15
Beryl Richmond	L	26	6	2	1	0	19.1	23	0	10	9	1-2	0	3.72
Dazzy Vance†	R	43	6	2	0	0	18.0	28	1	11	9	0-2	0	7.50
Lee Grissom	L	26	4	1	0	0	7.0	13	0	7	4	0-1	0	15.43
Jim Lindsey†	R	38	4	0	0	0	4.0	4	0	2	2	0-0	0	4.50
Syl Johnson†	R	33	2	0	0	0	6.2	9	2	0	0	0-0	0	2.70
Junie Barnes	L	22	2	0	0	0	0.1	0	0	1	0	0-0	0	0.00
Sherman Edwards	R	24	1	0	0	0	3.0	4	0	1	1	0-0	0	3.00

662 Seasons: Team Rosters

»1935 Detroit Tigers 1st AL 93-58 .616 —

Mickey Cochrane

Player	Gm by Position	B	Age	G	AB	R	H	2B	3B	HR	RBI	BB	SO	SB	Avg	OBP	Slg
Mickey Cochrane	C110	L	32	115	411	93	131	33	3	5	47	96	15	5	.319	.452	.450
Hank Greenberg	1B152	R	24	152	619	121	203	46	16	36	170	87	91	4	.328	.411	.628
Charlie Gehringer	2B149	L	32	150	610	123	201	32	8	19	108	79	16	11	.330	.409	.502
Marv Owen	3B131	R	29	134	483	52	127	24	5	2	71	43	37	1	.263	.326	.346
Billy Rogell	SS150	S	30	150	560	88	154	23	11	6	71	80	29	3	.275	.367	.388
Goose Goslin	OF144	L	34	147	590	88	172	34	6	9	109	56	31	5	.292	.355	.415
Pete Fox	OF125	R	26	131	517	116	166	38	8	15	73	45	52	14	.321	.382	.513
Jo-Jo White	OF98	L	26	114	412	82	99	13	12	2	32	68	42	19	.240	.348	.345
Gee Walker	OF85	R	27	98	362	52	109	22	6	7	53	15	21	6	.301	.329	.453
Ray Hayworth	C48	R	31	51	175	22	54	14	2	0	22	9	14	0	.309	.342	.411
Flea Clifton	3B21,2B5,SS4	R	25	43	110	15	28	5	0	0	9	5	13	2	.255	.293	.300
Hub Walker	OF7	L	28	9	25	4	4	3	0	0	1	3	4	0	.160	.250	.280
Chet Morgan	OF4	L	25	14	23	2	4	1	0	0	1	5	0	0	.174	.321	.217
Frank Reiber	C5	R	25	8	11	3	3	0	0	0	1	3	3	0	.273	.429	.273
Hugh Shelley	OF5	R	24	7	8	1	2	0	0	0	1	2	1	0	.250	.400	.250
Heinie Schuble	3B2,2B1	R	28	11	8	3	2	0	0	0	0	1	0	0	.250	.333	.250

Pitcher	T	Age	G	GS	CG	ShO	IP	H	HR	BB	SO	W-L	Sv	ERA
Schoolboy Rowe	R	25	42	34	21	6	275.2	272	11	68	140	19-13	3	3.69
Tommy Bridges	R	28	36	34	23	4	274.1	277	22	113	163	21-10	1	3.51
General Crowder	R	36	33	32	16	2	241.0	269	16	67	59	16-10	0	4.26
Eldon Auker	R	24	36	25	13	2	195.0	213	13	61	63	18-7	0	3.83
Vic Sorrell	R	34	12	6	4	0	51.1	65	2	25	22	4-3	0	4.03
Roxie Lawson	R	29	7	4	4	2	40.0	34	3	24	16	3-1	2	1.58
Chief Hogsett	L	31	40	0	0	0	96.2	109	1	49	39	6-6	5	3.54
Joe Sullivan	L	24	25	12	5	0	125.2	119	4	71	53	6-6	0	3.51
Clyde Hatter	L	26	8	2	0	0	33.1	44	2	30	15	0-0	0	7.56
Firpo Marberry	R	36	5	2	1	0	19.0	22	2	9	7	0-1	0	4.26
Carl Fischer†	L	29	3	1	0	0	12.0	16	2	5	7	0-1	0	6.00

1935 New York Yankees 2nd AL 89-60 .597 3.0 GB

Joe McCarthy

Player	Gm by Position	B	Age	G	AB	R	H	2B	3B	HR	RBI	BB	SO	SB	Avg	OBP	Slg
Bill Dickey	C118	L	28	120	448	54	125	26	6	14	81	35	11	1	.279	.339	.458
Lou Gehrig	1B149	L	32	149	535	125	176	26	10	30	119	132	38	8	.329	.466	.583
Tony Lazzeri	2B118,SS9	R	31	130	477	72	130	18	6	13	83	63	75	11	.273	.361	.417
Red Rolfe	3B136,SS17	L	26	149	639	108	192	33	9	5	67	57	39	7	.300	.361	.404
Frankie Crosetti	SS87	R	24	87	305	49	78	17	6	8	50	41	27	3	.256	.351	.430
Ben Chapman	OF138	R	26	140	553	118	160	38	8	8	74	61	39	17	.289	.361	.430
George Selkirk	OF127	L	27	128	491	64	153	29	12	11	94	44	36	2	.312	.372	.487
Jesse Hill	OF94	R	28	107	392	69	115	20	3	4	33	42	32	14	.293	.362	.390
Earle Combs	OF70	L	36	89	298	47	84	7	4	3	35	36	10	1	.282	.359	.362
Jack Saltzgaver	2B25,3B18,1B6	L	32	61	149	17	39	6	0	3	18	23	12	0	.262	.368	.362
Myril Hoag	OF37	R	27	48	110	13	28	4	1	1	13	12	19	4	.255	.328	.336
Blondy Ryan†	SS30	R	29	30	105	12	25	1	3	0	11	3	10	0	.238	.259	.305
Art Jorgens	C33	R	30	36	84	6	20	2	0	0	8	12	10	0	.238	.333	.262
Nolen Richardson	SS12	R	32	12	46	3	10	1	1	0	5	3	1	0	.217	.265	.283
Joe Glenn	C16	R	26	17	43	7	10	4	0	0	6	4	1	0	.233	.298	.326
Don Heffner	2B10	R	24	10	36	3	11	3	1	0	8	4	1	0	.306	.375	.444
Dixie Walker	OF2	L	24	8	13	1	2	1	0	0	1	0	1	0	.154	.154	.231

Pitcher	T	Age	G	GS	CG	ShO	IP	H	HR	BB	SO	W-L	Sv	ERA
Lefty Gomez	L	26	34	30	15	2	246.0	223	18	86	138	12-15	1	3.18
Red Ruffing	R	31	30	29	19	2	222.0	201	17	76	81	16-11	0	3.12
Johnny Broaca	R	25	29	27	14	2	201.0	199	16	79	78	15-7	0	3.58
Johnny Allen	R	29	23	23	12	2	167.0	149	11	58	113	13-6	0	3.61
Vito Tamulis	L	23	30	19	9	3	160.2	178	7	55	57	10-5	1	4.09
Johnny Murphy	R	26	40	8	4	0	117.0	110	7	55	28	10-5	5	4.08
Jimmie DeShong	R	25	29	3	0	0	69.0	64	6	33	30	4-1	3	3.26
Pat Malone	R	32	29	2	0	0	56.1	53	7	33	25	3-5	3	5.43
Jumbo Brown	R	28	20	8	3	0	87.1	94	2	37	41	6-5	0	3.61
Russ Van Atta†	L	29	5	0	0	0	4.2	5	0	4	3	0-0	0	3.86

1935 Cleveland Indians 3rd AL 82-71 .536 12.0 GB

Walter Johnson (46-48)/Steve O'Neill (36-23)

Player	Gm by Position	B	Age	G	AB	R	H	2B	3B	HR	RBI	BB	SO	SB	Avg	OBP	Slg
Eddie Phillips	C69	R	34	70	220	18	60	16	1	1	41	15	21	0	.273	.319	.368
Hal Trosky	1B153	L	22	154	632	84	171	33	7	26	113	46	60	1	.271	.321	.468
Boze Berger	2B120,SS3,1B2*	R	25	124	461	62	119	27	5	5	43	34	97	7	.258	.310	.371
Odell Hale	3B149,2B1	R	26	150	589	80	179	37	11	16	101	52	55	15	.304	.361	.486
Bill Knickerbocker	SS128	R	23	132	540	77	161	34	5	0	55	27	31	2	.298	.332	.380
Joe Vosmik	OF150	R	25	152	620	93	216	47	20	10	110	59	30	2	.348	.408	.537
Earl Averill	OF139	L	33	140	563	109	162	34	13	19	79	70	58	8	.288	.368	.496
Milt Galatzer	OF81	L	28	93	259	45	78	9	3	0	19	35	8	4	.301	.389	.359
Bruce Campbell	OF75	L	25	80	308	56	100	26	3	7	54	31	33	2	.325	.390	.497
Roy Hughes	2B40,SS29,3B1	R	24	82	266	40	78	15	3	0	14	18	17	13	.293	.340	.372
Ab Wright	OF47	R	29	67	160	17	38	11	1	2	18	10	17	2	.238	.291	.356
Frankie Pytlak	C48	R	26	55	149	14	44	6	1	1	12	11	4	3	.295	.348	.369
Bill Brenzel	C51	R	25	52	142	12	31	5	1	0	14	6	10	2	.218	.250	.268
Ralph Winegarner	P25,OF4,3B3*	R	25	65	84	11	26	4	1	3	17	9	12	1	.310	.376	.488
Glenn Myatt†	C10	L	37	10	36	1	3	1	0	0	2	4	3	0	.083	.175	.111
Kit Carson		L	22	16	22	1	5	2	0	0	1	2	6	0	.227	.292	.318
Bob Garbark	C6	R	25	6	18	4	6	1	0	0	4	5	1	0	.333	.478	.389
Willie Kamm	3B4	R	35	6	18	2	6	0	0	0	1	0	1	0	.333	.333	.333
Greek George	C1	R	22	2	0	0	0	0	0	0	0	0	0	0	—	—	—

B. Berger, 1 G at 3B; R. Winegarner, 1 G at 1B

Pitcher	T	Age	G	GS	CG	ShO	IP	H	HR	BB	SO	W-L	Sv	ERA
Mel Harder	R	25	42	35	17	4	287.1	313	6	53	95	22-11	2	3.29
Willis Hudlin	R	29	36	29	14	3	231.2	252	8	61	45	15-11	5	3.69
Monte Pearson	R	25	30	24	10	1	181.2	199	9	103	90	8-13	0	4.90
Thornton Lee	L	28	32	20	8	1	180.2	179	6	71	81	7-10	1	4.04
Oral Hildebrand	R	28	34	20	8	0	171.1	171	12	63	49	9-8	5	3.94
Lloyd Brown	L	30	42	8	4	2	122.0	123	6	37	45	8-7	4	3.61
Ralph Winegarner	R	25	25	4	2	0	67.1	89	10	29	41	2-2	0	5.75
Lefty Stewart†	L	34	24	10	2	1	91.0	122	6	17	24	6-6	2	5.44
Clint Brown	R	31	23	5	1	0	49.0	61	3	14	20	4-3	2	5.14
Denny Galehouse	R	23	5	1	1	0	13.0	16	1	9	8	1-0	0	9.00
Belve Bean†	R	30	1	0	0	0	1.0	2	1	0	0	0-0	0	9.00

1935 Boston Red Sox 4th AL 78-75 .510 16.0 GB

Joe Cronin

Player	Gm by Position	B	Age	G	AB	R	H	2B	3B	HR	RBI	BB	SO	SB	Avg	OBP	Slg
Rick Ferrell	C131	R	29	133	458	54	138	34	4	3	61	65	15	5	.301	.388	.413
Babe Dahlgren	1B149	R	23	149	525	77	138	27	7	9	63	56	67	6	.263	.337	.392
Ski Melillo†	2B105	R	35	106	399	45	104	13	2	1	39	38	22	3	.261	.328	.311
Bill Werber	3B123	R	27	124	462	84	118	30	3	14	61	69	41	29	.255	.357	.424
Joe Cronin	SS139	R	28	144	556	70	164	37	14	9	95	63	40	3	.295	.370	.460
Mel Almada	OF149,1B3	L	22	151	607	85	176	27	9	3	59	55	34	20	.290	.350	.379
Roy Johnson	OF142	L	32	145	553	70	174	33	9	3	66	74	34	11	.315	.398	.423
Dusty Cooke	OF82	L	28	100	294	51	90	18	6	3	34	46	24	6	.306	.400	.439
Dib Williams†	3B30,2B29,SS15*	R	25	75	251	26	63	12	0	3	25	24	23	2	.251	.319	.335
Carl Reynolds	OF64	R	32	78	244	33	66	13	4	6	35	24	20	4	.270	.336	.430
Bing Miller	OF29	R	40	78	138	18	42	8	1	3	26	10	8	0	.304	.356	.442
Max Bishop	2B34,1B11,SS2	L	35	60	122	19	28	3	1	1	14	28	14	0	.230	.377	.295
Moe Berg	C37	R	33	38	98	13	28	5	0	2	12	5	3	0	.286	.320	.398
Moose Solters†	OF21	R	29	24	79	15	19	6	1	0	8	2	7	1	.241	.268	.342
George Dickey	C4	S	19	5	11	1	0	0	0	0	1	1	3	0	.000	.083	.000
Skinny Graham	OF2	L	25	8	10	1	3	0	0	0	1	1	3	1	.300	.364	.300
Doc Farrell	2B4	R	33	4	7	1	2	1	0	0	1	1	0	0	.286	.375	.429
John Kroner	3B2	R	26	2	4	1	1	0	0	0	0	1	1	0	.250	.400	.250
Lou Legett		R	34	2	0	1	0	0	0	0	0	0	0	0	—	—	—

D. Williams, 1 G at 1B

Pitcher	T	Age	G	GS	CG	ShO	IP	H	HR	BB	SO	W-L	Sv	ERA
Wes Ferrell	R	27	41	38	31	3	322.1	336	16	108	110	25-14	0	3.52
Lefty Grove	L	35	35	30	23	2	273.0	269	6	65	121	20-12	1	2.70
Gordon Rhodes	R	27	34	19	1	0	146.1	195	14	60	44	2-10	2	5.41
Johnny Welch	R	28	31	19	10	1	143.0	155	4	53	48	10-9	2	4.47
Fritz Ostermueller	L	27	22	19	10	0	137.2	135	0	78	41	7-8	1	3.92
Joe Cascarella†	R	28	6	4	0	0	17.0	25	3	11	9	0-3	0	6.88
Rube Walberg	L	38	44	10	4	0	142.2	152	10	54	44	5-9	3	3.91
Jack Wilson	R	23	23	6	2	0	64.0	72		36	19	3-4	1	4.22
George Hockette	L	27	23	4	0	0	61.0	83	6	12	11	2-3	0	5.16
Hank Johnson	R	29	13	2	0	0	31.0	41	3	14	14	2-1	1	5.52
Stew Bowers	R	20	10	2	1	0	23.2	26	1	17	5	2-1	0	3.42
George Pipgras	R	35	5	1	0	0	5.0	9	3	5	2	0-1	0	14.40
Hy Vandenberg	R	28	3	0	0	0	5.1	15	1	4	2	0-0	0	20.25
Walt Ripley	R	18	2	0	0	0	4.0	7	0	3	0	0-0	0	9.00

1935 Chicago White Sox 5th AL 74-78 .487 19.5 GB

Jimmy Dykes

Player	Gm by Position	B	Age	G	AB	R	H	2B	3B	HR	RBI	BB	SO	SB	Avg	OBP	Slg
Luke Sewell	C112	R	34	118	421	52	120	19	3	2	67	32	18	3	.285	.336	.359
Zeke Bonura	1B138	R	26	138	550	107	162	34	4	21	92	57	28	4	.295	.364	.485
Jackie Hayes	2B85	R	28	89	329	45	88	14	0	4	45	29	15	3	.267	.327	.347
Jimmy Dykes	3B98,1B16,2B3	R	38	117	403	45	116	24	2	4	61	59	28	4	.288	.381	.387
Luke Appling	SS153	R	28	153	525	94	161	28	6	1	71	122	40	12	.307	.437	.389
Rip Radcliff	OF142	L	29	146	623	95	178	28	8	10	68	53	21	4	.286	.346	.404
Al Simmons	OF126	R	33	128	525	68	140	22	7	16	79	33	43	4	.267	.313	.427
Mule Haas	OF84	L	31	92	327	44	95	22	1	2	40	37	17	4	.291	.363	.382
George Washington	OF79	L	28	108	339	40	96	22	3	8	47	10	18	1	.283	.310	.437
Tony Piet†	2B59,3B17	R	28	77	292	47	87	17	5	3	27	33	27	2	.298	.375	.421
Marty Hopkins	3B49,2B5	R	28	59	144	20	32	3	0	2	17	36	23	1	.222	.378	.285
Jocko Conlan	OF37	L	35	65	140	20	40	7	1	0	15	14	6	3	.286	.355	.350
Merv Shea	C43	R	34	46	122	8	28	2	0	0	13	30	9	0	.230	.382	.246
Fred Tauby	OF7	R	29	13	32	5	4	1	0	0	2	2	3	0	.125	.176	.156
Glenn Wright	2B7	R	34	9	25	1	3	1	0	0	1	0	6	0	.120	.120	.160
Mike Kreevich	3B6	R	27	6	23	3	10	2	0	0	2	1	0	1	.435	.458	.522
Frank Grube†	C9	R	30	9	19	1	7	2	0	0	6	3	2	0	.368	.455	.474
Bud Hafey†		R	22	2	0	1	0	0	0	0	0	0	0	0	—	—	—

Pitcher	T	Age	G	GS	CG	ShO	IP	H	HR	BB	SO	W-L	Sv	ERA
John Whitehead	R	26	28	27	18	1	222.1	209	17	101	72	13-13	0	3.72
Vern Kennedy	R	28	31	25	16	2	211.2	211	17	95	65	11-11	1	3.91
Ted Lyons	R	34	23	22	19	3	190.2	194	15	56	54	15-8	0	3.02
Les Tietje	R	23	30	21	9	1	169.2	184	14	81	64	9-15	0	4.30
Sad Sam Jones	R	42	21	19	7	0	140.0	162	8	51	38	8-7	0	4.05
Ray Phelps	R	31	27	17	4	0	125.0	126	10	55	38	4-8	1	4.82
Monty Stratton	R	23	5	5	2	0	38.0	40	0	9	8	1-2	0	4.03
George Earnshaw†	R	35	3	3	0	0	18.0	26	2	11	8	1-2	0	9.00
Whit Wyatt	R	27	30	1	0	0	52.0	65	6	25	22	4-3	5	6.75
Carl Fischer†	L	29	24	11	3	1	88.2	102	7	39	31	5-5	0	6.19
Jack Salveson†	R	21	20	2	2	0	66.2	79	6	23	22	1-2	1	4.86
Joe Vance	R	29	10	0	0	0	31.0	36	1	21	12	2-2	0	6.68
Italo Chelini	L	20	2	0	0	0	5.0	7	1	4	1	0-0	0	12.60
Lee Stine	R	21	1	0	0	0	2.0	2	1	3	1	0-0	0	9.00

1935 Washington Senators 6th AL 67-86 .438 27.0 GB

Bucky Harris

Player	Gm by Position	B	Age	G	AB	R	H	2B	3B	HR	RBI	BB	SO	SB	Avg	OBP	Slg
Cliff Bolton	C106	L	28	110	375	47	114	18	11	2	55	56	13	0	.304	.396	.427
Joe Kuhel	1B151	L	29	151	633	99	165	25	9	2	74	78	44	5	.261	.345	.338
Buddy Myer	2B151	L	31	151	616	115	215	36	11	5	100	96	40	7	.349	.440	.468
Cecil Travis	3B114,OF16	L	21	138	534	85	170	27	8	0	61	41	28	4	.318	.377	.399
Ossie Bluege	SS58,3B25,2B4	R	34	100	320	44	84	14	3	0	34	37	21	2	.263	.341	.325
Jake Powell	OF136,2B2	R	26	139	551	88	172	26	10	6	98	37	37	15	.312	.360	.428
John Stone	OF114	L	29	125	455	78	143	27	18	1	78	39	29	4	.314	.372	.459
Heinie Manush	OF111	L	33	119	479	68	131	26	9	4	56	35	17	2	.273	.328	.390
Red Kress	SS53,1B5,P3*	R	28	84	252	32	75	13	4	2	42	25	16	3	.298	.361	.405
Fred Schulte	OF55	R	34	75	224	33	60	6	4	2	23	26	22	0	.268	.347	.357
Dee Miles	OF45	L	26	60	216	28	57	5	2	0	29	7	13	6	.264	.290	.306
Sammy Holbrook	C47	R	24	52	135	20	35	2	2	2	25	30	16	0	.259	.408	.348
Lyn Lary†	SS30	R	29	39	103	8	20	4	0	0	7	12	10	3	.194	.278	.233
Alan Strange†	SS16	R	28	20	54	3	10	2	1	0	5	4	1	0	.185	.241	.259
Bobby Estalella	3B15	R	24	15	51	7	16	2	0	2	10	17	7	1	.314	.485	.471
Jack Redmond	C15	L	24	22	34	8	6	1	0	1	7	3	1	0	.176	.243	.294
Buddy Lewis	3B6	L	18	8	28	0	3	0	0	0	2	0	5	0	.107	.107	.107
Chick Starr	C12	R	24	12	24	1	5	0	0	0	1	0	1	0	.208	.208	.208
John Mihalic	SS6	R	23	6	22	4	5	3	0	0	6	2	3	1	.227	.292	.364
Fred Sington	OF4	R	25	20	22	1	4	0	0	0	3	5	1	0	.182	.333	.182
Red Marion	OF3	R	21	4	11	1	2	1	0	1	1	0	2	0	.182	.182	.545

R. Kress, 2 G at OF, 1 G at 2B

Pitcher	T	Age	G	GS	CG	ShO	IP	H	HR	BB	SO	W-L	Sv	ERA
Earl Whitehill	L	35	34	34	19	1	279.1	318	16	104	102	14-13	0	4.29
Bump Hadley	R	30	35	32	13	0	230.1	268	18	102	77	10-15	0	4.92
Bobo Newsom†	R	27	28	23	17	2	198.1	222	9	84	65	11-12	2	4.45
Ed Linke	R	23	40	22	10	0	178.0	211	6	80	51	11-7	3	5.01
Bobby Burke	L	28	15	10	2	0	66.1	90	7	27	16	1-8	0	7.46
Jim Hayes	R	22	7	4	1	0	28.0	38	0	23	9	2-4	0	8.36
Dick Lanahan	L	23	3	3	0	0	20.2	27	2	17	10	0-3	0	5.66
Buck Rogers	L	22	2	1	0	0	10.0	16	0	6	7	0-1	0	7.20
Lefty Stewart†	L	34	1	1	0	0	2.2	8	1	2	1	0-1	0	13.50
Jack Russell	R	29	43	7	2	0	126.0	170	10	37	30	4-9	3	5.71
Leon Pettit	L	33	41	7	1	0	109.0	129	6	58	45	8-5	3	4.95
Henry Coppola	R	22	19	5	2	1	59.1	72	6	29	19	3-4	0	5.92
Belve Bean†	R	30	10	2	0	0	31.0	43	5	19	6	2-0	0	7.26
Phil Hensiek	R	33	6	1	0	0	13.0	21	2	9	6	0-3	1	9.69
Montie Weaver	R	29	5	2	0	0	12.0	16	1	6	4	1-1	0	5.25
Mac McLean	R	22	4	0	0	0	8.2	12	0	5	3	0-0	0	7.27
Red Kress	R	28	3	0	0	0	5.2	8	0	5	5	0-0	0	12.71
Tommy Thomas†	R	35	1	0	0	0	0.1	3	0	0	0	0-0	0	54.00

1935 St. Louis Browns 7th AL 65-87 .428 28.5 GB

Rogers Hornsby

Player	Gm by Position	B	Age	G	AB	R	H	2B	3B	HR	RBI	BB	SO	SB	Avg	OBP	Slg
Rollie Hemsley	C141	R	28	144	504	57	146	32	7	0	48	44	41	3	.290	.349	.381
Jack Burns	1B141	L	27	143	549	77	157	28	1	5	67	68	49	3	.286	.366	.368
Tom Carey	2B76	R	28	76	296	29	86	18	4	0	42	13	11	0	.291	.320	.378
Harlond Clift	3B127,2B6	R	22	137	475	101	140	26	4	11	69	83	39	0	.295	.406	.436
Lyn Lary†	SS93	R	29	93	371	78	107	25	7	2	35	64	43	25	.288	.396	.410
Sammy West	OF135	L	30	138	527	93	158	37	4	10	70	75	46	1	.300	.388	.442
Moose Solters†	OF127	R	29	127	552	79	182	39	6	18	104	34	35	10	.330	.369	.520
Ed Coleman†	OF102	L	33	108	397	66	114	15	9	17	71	53	41	0	.287	.373	.499
Roy Pepper	OF57	R	29	92	261	20	66	15	3	4	37	20	32	0	.253	.306	.379
Beau Bell	OF37,1B15,3B3	R	27	76	220	20	55	8	2	3	17	16	16	1	.250	.304	.345
Johnny Burnett	3B31,SS18,2B12	L	30	70	206	17	46	10	1	0	26	19	16	1	.223	.289	.282
Ollie Bejma	2B47,SS8,3B2	R	27	64	198	18	38	8	2	2	26	27	21	1	.192	.289	.283
Alan Strange†	SS49	R	28	49	147	8	34	6	1	0	17	17	7	0	.231	.311	.286
Tommy Heath	C37	R	21	47	93	10	22	3	0	0	9	20	13	0	.237	.372	.269
Ski Melillo†	2B18	R	35	19	63	8	13	3	0	0	5	8	4	0	.206	.296	.254
Mel Mazzera	OF10	L	21	12	30	4	7	2	0	1	2	4	9	0	.233	.324	.400
Heinie Mueller	1B3,OF2	L	35	16	27	0	5	1	0	0	1	1	4	0	.185	.214	.222
Rogers Hornsby	1B3,2B2,3B1	R	39	10	24	1	5	3	0	0	3	3	6	0	.208	.296	.333
Debs Garms	OF2	L	27	10	15	1	4	0	0	0	0	2	2	0	.267	.353	.267
Hal Warnock	OF2	L	23	6	7	1	2	2	0	0	0	0	3	0	.286	.286	.571
Frank Grube†	C3	R	30	3	6	3	2	1	0	0	0	0	1	0	.333	.333	.500

Pitcher	T	Age	G	GS	CG	ShO	IP	H	HR	BB	SO	W-L	Sv	ERA
Sugar Cain†	R	28	31	24	8	0	167.2	197	7	104	68	9-8	0	5.26
Bobo Newsom†	R	27	7	6	1	0	42.2	54	2	13	22	0-6	1	4.85
Earl Caldwell	R	30	6	5	2	1	36.2	34	2	17	5	3-2	0	3.68
Jim Walkup	R	25	55	20	4	1	181.1	226	17	104	44	6-9	0	6.25
Russ Van Atta†	L	29	53	17	1	0	170.1	201	10	86	87	9-16	3	5.34
Ivy Andrews	R	28	50	20	10	0	213.1	231	10	53	43	13-7	1	3.54
Fay Thomas	R	30	49	19	4	0	147.0	165	11	89	67	7-15	1	4.78
Jack Knott	R	28	48	19	7	2	187.2	219	8	78	45	11-8	7	4.60
Dick Coffman	R	28	41	18	5	0	143.2	206	14	46	34	5-11	2	6.14
Bob Weiland	L	29	14	4	0	0	32.0	39	6	31	11	0-2	0	9.56
Snipe Hansen†	L	28	10	0	0	0	26.2	44	2	9	8	0-1	0	8.78
George Blaeholder†	R	31	6	2	0	0	17.2	25	3	6	0	1-1	0	7.13
Bob Poser	R	25	4	1	0	0	13.2	26	0	4	1	1-1	0	9.22

1935 Philadelphia Athletics 8th AL 58-91 .389 34.0 GB

Connie Mack

Player	Gm by Position	B	Age	G	AB	R	H	2B	3B	HR	RBI	BB	SO	SB	Avg	OBP	Slg
Paul Richards†	C79	R	26	85	257	31	63	10	1	4	29	24	12	0	.245	.310	.339
Jimmie Foxx	1B121,C26,3B2	R	27	147	535	118	185	33	7	36	115	114	99	6	.346	.461	.636
Rabbit Warstler	2B136,3B2	R	31	138	496	62	124	20	7	3	59	56	53	8	.250	.326	.337
Mike Higgins	3B131	R	26	133	524	69	155	32	4	23	94	42	62	6	.296	.350	.504
Eric McNair	SS121,3B11,1B2	R	26	137	526	55	142	22	2	4	57	35	33	3	.270	.319	.342
Doc Cramer	OF149	L	29	149	644	96	214	37	4	3	70	37	34	6	.332	.373	.416
Bob Johnson	OF147	R	28	147	582	103	174	29	5	28	109	78	76	2	.299	.384	.510
Wally Moses	OF80	L	24	85	345	60	112	21	3	5	35	25	18	3	.325	.375	.446
Lou Finney	OF75,1B18	L	24	109	410	45	112	11	6	0	31	18	18	7	.273	.307	.329
Charlie Berry	C56	R	32	62	190	14	48	7	3	3	29	10	20	0	.253	.290	.368
Skeeter Newsome	SS24,2B13,3B4*	R	24	59	145	18	30	7	1	1	10	5	9	2	.207	.233	.290
Alex Hooks	1B10	L	28	15	44	4	10	3	0	0	4	3	10	0	.227	.277	.295
Bernie Snyder	2B5,SS4	R	21	10	32	5	11	1	0	0	3	1	2	0	.344	.364	.375
Jack Peerson	SS4	R	24	10	19	3	6	1	0	0	1	1	1	0	.316	.350	.368
Ed Coleman†	OF1	L	33	10	13	0	1	0	0	0	0	0	3	0	.077	.077	.077
Bill Patton	C3	R	22	9	10	1	3	1	0	0	2	2	3	0	.300	.417	.400
Dib Williams†	2B2	R	25	4	10	0	1	0	0	0	0	0	1	0	.100	.100	.100
Jack Owens	C2	R	27	2	8	0	2	0	0	0	1	0	1	0	.250	.250	.250
Bill Conroy	C1	R	20	1	4	0	1	1	0	0	0	1	0	0	.250	.400	.500
Charlie Moss	C1	R	24	4	3	1	1	0	0	0	1	1	0	0	.333	.500	.333

S. Newsome, 1 G at OF

Pitcher	T	Age	G	GS	CG	ShO	IP	H	HR	BB	SO	W-L	Sv	ERA
Johnny Marcum	R	25	39	27	19	2	242.2	256	9	83	99	17-12	3	4.08
George Blaeholder†	R	31	23	22	10	1	149.0	173	10	49	22	6-10	0	3.99
Whitey Wilshere	L	22	27	18	7	3	142.1	136	8	78	80	9-9	1	4.05
Roy Mahaffey	R	32	27	17	5	0	136.0	153	11	42	39	8-4	0	3.90
Carl Doyle	R	22	14	9	3	0	79.2	86	3	72	34	2-7	0	5.99
Sugar Cain†	R	28	6	5	0	0	26.0	39	1	19	5	0-5	0	6.58
Woody Upchurch	L	24	3	3	1	0	21.1	23	3	12	2	0-2	0	5.06
Herman Fink	R	23	5	3	0	0	15.2	18	0	10	2	0-3	0	9.19
Vallie Eaves	R	23	3	3	1	0	14.0	12	0	15	6	1-2	0	5.14
Al Veach	R	25	2	2	1	0	10.0	20	1	9	3	0-2	0	11.70
Bill Ferrazzi	R	28	3	2	0	0	7.0	7	0	5	0	1-2	0	5.14
Wedo Martini	R	21	3	2	0	0	6.1	8	0	11	1	0-2	0	17.05
Earl Huckleberry	R	25	1	1	0	0	6.2	8	1	4	2	1-0	0	9.45
Bill Dietrich	R	25	43	15	8	1	185.1	203	7	101	59	7-13	3	5.39
Al Benton	R	24	27	9	0	0	78.1	110	7	47	42	3-4	0	7.70
George Caster	R	27	25	1	0	0	63.1	86	8	37	24	1-4	1	6.25
George Turbeville	L	20	19	6	2	0	63.2	74	2	69	20	0-3	0	7.63
Dutch Lieber	R	25	18	1	0	0	46.2	45	1	19	14	1-1	2	3.09
Joe Cascarella†	R	28	9	3	1	0	32.1	29	1	22	15	1-6	0	5.29

»1935 Chicago Cubs 1st NL 100-54 .649 —

Charlie Grimm

Player	Gm by Position	B	Age	G	AB	R	H	2B	3B	HR	RBI	BB	SO	SB	Avg	OBP	Slg
Gabby Hartnett	C110	R	34	116	413	67	142	32	6	13	91	41	46	1	.344	.404	.545
Phil Cavarretta	1B145	L	18	146	589	85	162	28	12	8	82	39	61	4	.275	.322	.404
Billy Herman	2B154	R	25	154	666	113	227	57	6	7	83	42	29	6	.341	.383	.476
Stan Hack	3B111,1B7	L	25	124	427	75	133	23	9	4	64	65	17	14	.311	.406	.436
Billy Jurges	SS146	R	27	146	519	69	125	33	1	1	59	42	39	3	.241	.304	.314
Augie Galan	OF154	S	23	154	646	133	203	41	11	12	79	87	53	22	.314	.399	.467
Chuck Klein	OF111	L	30	119	434	71	127	14	4	21	73	41	42	4	.293	.355	.488
Frank Demaree	OF98	R	25	107	385	60	125	19	4	2	66	26	23	6	.325	.369	.410
Freddy Lindstrom	OF50,3B33	R	29	90	342	49	94	22	4	3	62	10	13	1	.275	.297	.389
Ken O'Dea	C63	L	22	76	202	30	52	13	2	6	38	26	18	0	.257	.345	.431
Kiki Cuyler†	OF42	R	36	45	157	22	42	5	1	4	18	10	16	3	.268	.331	.389
Tuck Stainback	OF28	R	23	47	94	16	24	4	0	3	11	0	13	1	.255	.271	.394
Woody English	3B16,SS12	R	28	34	84	11	17	2	0	2	8	20	4	1	.202	.368	.298
Walter Stephenson	C6	R	24	16	26	2	10	1	1	0	2	1	5	0	.385	.407	.500
Charlie Grimm	1B2	L	36	2	8	0	0	0	0	0	0	0	1	0	.000	.000	.000
Johnny Gill		L	30	3	3	2	1	1	0	0	1	0	1	0	.333	.333	.667

Pitcher	T	Age	G	GS	CG	ShO	IP	H	HR	BB	SO	W-L	Sv	ERA
Bill Lee	R	25	39	32	18	3	252.0	241	11	84	100	20-6	1	2.96
Lon Warneke	R	26	42	30	20	1	261.2	257	19	50	120	20-13	4	3.06
Larry French	L	27	42	30	16	4	246.1	279	10	44	90	17-10	2	2.96
Tex Carleton	R	28	31	22	8	0	171.0	169	17	60	84	11-8	1	3.89
Roy Henshaw	L	23	31	18	7	3	142.2	135	6	68	53	13-5	1	3.28
Charlie Root	R	36	38	18	11	1	201.1	193	15	47	94	15-8	2	3.08
Fabian Kowalik	R	27	20	2	1	0	55.0	60	2	19	20	2-2	1	4.42
Hugh Casey	R	21	13	0	0	0	25.2	29	2	14	10	0-0	0	3.86
Clay Bryant	R	23	9	1	0	0	22.2	34	1	7	13	1-2	2	5.16
Clyde Shoun	L	23	5	1	0	0	12.2	14	2	5	5	1-0	0	2.84
Roy Joiner	L	28	2	0	0	0	3.1	6	0	2	0	0-0	0	5.40

1935 St. Louis Cardinals 2nd NL 96-58 .623 4.0 GB

Frank Frisch

Player	Gm by Position	B	Age	G	AB	R	H	2B	3B	HR	RBI	BB	SO	SB	Avg	OBP	Slg
Bill Delancey	C83	L	23	103	301	37	84	14	5	6	41	42	34	0	.279	.369	.419
Ripper Collins	1B150	S	31	150	578	109	181	36	10	23	122	65	45	0	.313	.385	.529
Frankie Frisch	2B89,3B5	S	36	103	354	52	104	16	2	1	55	33	16	2	.294	.356	.359
Pepper Martin	3B114,OF16	R	31	135	539	121	161	41	6	9	54	33	58	20	.299	.341	.447
Leo Durocher	SS142	R	29	143	513	62	136	23	5	8	78	29	46	4	.265	.304	.376
Joe Medwick	OF154	R	23	154	634	132	224	46	13	23	126	30	59	4	.353	.386	.576
Jack Rothrock	OF127	S	30	129	502	76	137	18	5	3	56	57	29	7	.273	.347	.347
Terry Moore	OF117	R	23	119	456	63	131	34	3	6	53	15	40	13	.287	.314	.414
Burgess Whitehead	2B80,3B8,SS6	R	25	107	338	45	89	10	2	0	33	11	14	5	.263	.289	.305
Spud Davis	C81,1B5	R	30	102	315	28	100	24	2	1	60	33	30	0	.317	.386	.416
Ernie Orsatti	OF60	L	32	90	221	28	53	9	3	1	24	18	25	10	.240	.297	.321
Charlie Gelbert	3B37,SS21,2B3	R	29	62	168	24	49	7	2	2	21	17	18	0	.292	.357	.393
Charlie Wilson	3B8	S	30	16	31	1	10	0	0	0	1	2	2	0	.323	.364	.323
Lynn King	OF6	L	27	8	22	6	4	0	0	0	0	4	1	2	.182	.308	.182
Tom Winsett		L	25	7	12	2	6	1	0	0	2	2	3	0	.500	.571	.583
Lyle Judy	2B5	R	21	8	11	2	0	0	0	0	0	2	2	2	.000	.154	.000
Bob O'Farrell	C8	R	38	14	10	0	0	0	0	0	0	2	0	0	.000	.167	.000
Sam Narron	C1	R	21	4	7	0	3	0	0	0	0	0	0	0	.429	.429	.429
Gene Moore		L	25	3	3	0	0	0	0	0	0	0	1	0	.000	.000	.000

Pitcher	T	Age	G	GS	CG	ShO	IP	H	HR	BB	SO	W-L	Sv	ERA
Dizzy Dean	R	25	50	36	29	3	325.1	324	16	77	190	28-12	5	3.04
Paul Dean	R	21	46	33	19	2	269.2	261	16	55	143	19-12	5	3.37
Bill Walker	L	31	37	25	8	2	193.1	222	7	78	79	13-8	1	3.82
Wild Bill Hallahan	L	32	40	23	8	3	181.1	196	7	57	73	15-8	1	3.42
Nub Kleinke	R	24	4	2	0	0	12.2	19	1	3	5	0-0	0	4.97
Mike Ryba	R	32	2	1	1	0	16.0	15	0	1	6	1-1	0	3.38
Jim Winford	R	25	2	1	0	0	11.1	13	1	5	7	0-0	0	3.97
Bill McGee	R	25	1	1	1	0	9.0	3	0	1	2	1-0	0	1.00
Ed Heusser	R	26	33	11	2	0	123.1	125	5	27	39	5-5	2	2.92
Jesse Haines	R	41	30	12	3	0	115.1	110	4	28	24	6-5	2	3.59
Phil Collins†	R	33	26	8	2	0	82.2	96	6	26	18	7-6	2	4.57
Ray Harrell	R	23	11	1	0	0	29.2	39	4	11	13	1-1	0	6.67
Bud Tinning	R	29	4	0	0	0	7.2	9	1	5	2	0-0	0	5.87
Tony Kaufmann	R	34	3	0	0	0	3.2	4	0	1	0	0-0	0	2.45
Al Eckert	L	29	2	0	0	0	3.0	7	0	1	1	0-0	0	12.00
Mays Copeland	R	21	1	0	0	0	0.2	2	1	0	0	0-0	0	13.50
Dick Ward	R	26	1	0	0	0	0.0	0	0	1	0	0-0	0	—

1935 New York Giants 3rd NL 91-62 .595 8.5 GB

Bill Terry

Player	Gm by Position	B	Age	G	AB	R	H	2B	3B	HR	RBI	BB	SO	SB	Avg	OBP	Slg
Gus Mancuso	C126	R	29	128	447	33	133	18	2	5	56	30	16	1	.298	.342	.380
Bill Terry	1B143	L	38	145	596	91	203	32	8	6	64	41	55	7	.341	.383	.451
Mark Koenig	2B64,SS21,3B15	S	30	107	396	40	112	12	0	3	37	13	18	0	.283	.306	.336
Travis Jackson	3B128	R	31	128	511	74	154	20	12	9	80	29	64	3	.301	.340	.440
Dick Bartell	SS137	R	27	137	539	60	141	28	4	14	53	37	52	5	.262	.316	.406
Jo-Jo Moore	OF155	L	26	155	681	108	201	28	9	15	71	53	24	5	.295	.353	.429
Hank Leiber	OF154	R	24	154	613	110	203	37	4	22	107	48	29	0	.331	.389	.512
Mel Ott	OF137,3B15	L	26	152	593	113	191	33	6	31	114	82	58	7	.322	.407	.555
Hughie Critz	2B59	R	34	65	219	19	41	0	3	2	14	3	10	2	.187	.198	.242
Al Cuccinello	2B48,3B2	R	20	54	165	27	41	7	1	4	20	1	20	0	.248	.262	.376
Harry Danning	C44	R	23	65	152	16	37	11	1	2	20	9	16	0	.243	.286	.368
Phil Weintraub	1B19,OF7	L	27	64	112	18	27	3	3	1	6	17	13	0	.241	.341	.348
Kiddo Davis	OF21	R	33	47	91	16	24	7	1	2	6	10	4	2	.264	.343	.429
Glenn Myatt†	C4	L	37	13	18	2	4	0	1	1	6	0	3	0	.222	.222	.500
Paul Richards†	C4	R	26	7	4	0	1	0	0	0	0	2	1	0	.250	.500	.250
Joe Malay		L	29	1	1	0	1	0	0	0	0	0	0	0	1.000	1.000	1.000

Pitcher	T	Age	G	GS	CG	ShO	IP	H	HR	BB	SO	W-L	Sv	ERA
Carl Hubbell	L	32	42	35	24	1	302.2	314	27	49	150	23-12	0	3.27
Hal Schumacher	R	24	33	33	19	3	261.2	235	11	70	79	19-9	0	2.89
Roy Parmelee	R	28	34	31	13	0	226.0	214	20	97	79	14-10	0	4.22
Slick Castleman	R	21	29	25	9	1	173.2	186	14	64	64	15-6	0	4.09
F. Fitzsimmons	R	33	18	15	6	4	94.0	104	7	22	23	4-8	0	4.02
Harry Gumbert	R	25	6	3	1	0	23.2	35	1	10	11	1-2	0	6.08
Al Smith	L	27	40	10	4	1	124.0	125	6	32	44	10-8	5	3.41
Allyn Stout	R	30	40	2	0	0	88.0	99	7	37	29	1-4	5	4.91
Frank Gabler	R	23	26	1	0	0	60.0	79	6	20	24	2-1	0	5.70
Leon Chagnon	R	32	14	1	0	0	38.1	32	1	5	16	0-2	1	3.52
Euel Moore†	R	27	6	0	0	0	8.0	9	0	4	3	1-0	0	5.63
Dolf Luque	R	44	2	0	0	0	3.2	1	0	1	2	1-0	0	0.00

1935 Pittsburgh Pirates 4th NL 86-67 .562 13.5 GB

Pie Traynor

Player	Gm by Position	B	Age	G	AB	R	H	2B	3B	HR	RBI	BB	SO	SB	Avg	OBP	Slg
Tom Padden	C94	R	26	97	302	35	82	9	1	1	30	48	26	1	.272	.371	.318
Gus Suhr	1B149,OF2	L	29	153	529	68	144	33	12	10	81	70	54	6	.272	.357	.437
Pep Young	2B107,3B6,OF6*	R	27	128	494	60	131	25	10	7	82	21	59	2	.265	.298	.399
Tommy Thevenow	3B82,SS13,2B8	R	31	110	408	38	97	9	9	0	47	12	23	1	.238	.261	.304
Arky Vaughan	SS137	L	23	137	499	108	192	34	10	19	99	97	18	4	.385	.491	.607
Woody Jensen	OF140	L	27	143	627	97	203	28	7	8	62	15	14	9	.324	.344	.429
Paul Waner	OF136	L	32	139	549	98	176	29	12	11	78	61	22	2	.321	.392	.477
Lloyd Waner	OF121	L	29	122	537	83	166	22	14	0	46	22	10	1	.309	.336	.402
Cookie Lavagetto	2B42,3B15	R	22	78	231	27	67	9	4	0	19	18	15	1	.290	.341	.364
Earl Grace	C69	L	28	77	224	19	59	8	1	3	29	32	17	1	.263	.355	.348
Pie Traynor	3B49	R	35	57	204	24	57	10	3	1	36	10	17	2	.279	.323	.373
Bud Hafey†	OF47	R	22	58	184	29	42	11	2	6	16	16	48	0	.228	.290	.408
Babe Herman†	OF15,1B3	L	32	26	81	8	19	8	1	0	7	3	10	0	.235	.271	.358
Earl Browne	1B9	L	24	9	32	6	8	2	0	0	6	2	8	0	.250	.294	.313
Bill Brubaker	3B5	R	24	6	11	1	0	0	0	0	0	2	5	0	.000	.154	.000
Aubrey Epps	C1	R	23	1	4	1	3	0	1	0	3	0	0	0	.750	.750	1.250
Steve Swetonic		R	31	1	0	1	0	0	0	0	0	0	0	0	—	—	—

P. Young, 4 G at SS

Pitcher	T	Age	G	GS	CG	ShO	IP	H	HR	BB	SO	W-L	Sv	ERA
Cy Blanton	R	26	35	31	23	4	254.1	220	3	55	142	18-13	1	2.58
Guy Bush	R	33	41	25	8	1	204.1	237	16	40	42	11-11	2	4.32
Jim Weaver	R	31	33	22	11	4	176.1	177	9	58	87	14-8	0	3.42
Bill Swift	R	27	39	21	11	3	203.2	193	6	37	74	15-8	1	2.70
Red Lucas	R	33	20	19	8	2	125.2	136	10	23	29	8-6	0	3.44
Claude Passeau	R	26	1	1	0	0	3.0	7	0	2	1	0-1	0	12.00
Waite Hoyt	R	35	39	11	5	0	164.0	187	8	27	63	7-11	6	3.40
Ralph Birkofer	L	26	37	18	8	1	150.1	173	5	42	80	9-7	1	4.07
Mace Brown	R	26	18	5	2	0	72.2	84	5	22	28	4-1	0	3.59
Jack Salveson†	R	21	5	0	0	0	7.0	11	1	5	2	0-1	0	9.00
Wayne Osborne	R	22	2	0	0	0	1.1	1	0	0	1	0-0	0	6.75
Hal Smith	R	33	1	0	0	0	3.0	2	0	1	0	0-0	0	3.00

1935 Brooklyn Dodgers 5th NL 70-83 .458 29.5 GB

Casey Stengel

Player	Gm by Position	B	Age	G	AB	R	H	2B	3B	HR	RBI	BB	SO	SB	Avg	OBP	Slg
Al Lopez	C126	R	26	128	379	50	95	12	4	3	39	35	36	2	.251	.316	.327
Sam Leslie	1B138	L	29	142	520	72	160	30	7	5	93	55	19	4	.308	.379	.421
Tony Cuccinello	2B64,3B36	R	27	102	360	49	105	20	3	8	53	40	35	3	.292	.366	.431
Joe Stripp	3B88,1B15	R	32	109	373	44	114	13	5	3	43	22	15	2	.306	.344	.391
Lonny Frey	SS127,2B4	L	24	131	515	88	135	35	11	11	77	66	68	6	.262	.352	.437
Buzz Boyle	OF124	L	27	127	475	51	129	17	9	4	44	43	45	7	.272	.332	.371
Frenchy Bordagaray	OF105	R	25	120	422	69	119	19	6	1	39	17	29	18	.282	.319	.363
Danny Taylor	OF99	R	34	112	352	51	102	19	5	7	59	46	32	6	.290	.372	.432
Jim Bucher	2B41,3B39,OF37	L	24	123	473	72	143	22	1	7	58	10	33	4	.302	.317	.397
Len Koenecke	OF91	L	31	100	325	43	92	13	2	4	27	43	45	0	.283	.369	.372
Jimmy Jordan	2B46,SS28,3B5	R	27	94	295	26	82	7	0	0	30	9	17	3	.278	.302	.302
Babe Phelps	C34	L	27	47	121	17	44	7	2	5	22	9	10	0	.364	.408	.579
Bobby Reis	OF21,P14,2B4*	R	26	52	85	10	21	3	2	0	4	6	13	2	.247	.297	.329
Buster Mills	OF17	R	26	17	56	12	12	2	1	1	7	5	11	0	.214	.323	.339
Zack Taylor	C26	R	36	26	54	2	7	3	0	0	5	2	8	0	.130	.175	.185
Johnny McCarthy	1B19	L	25	22	48	9	12	1	1	0	4	2	9	1	.250	.280	.313
Johnny Cooney	OF10	R	34	10	29	3	9	0	1	0	1	3	2	0	.310	.375	.379
Vince Sherlock	2B8	R	25	9	26	4	12	1	0	0	6	1	2	1	.462	.481	.500
Nick Tremark	OF4	L	22	10	13	1	3	1	0	0	3	1	1	0	.231	.286	.308
Frank Skaff	3B3	R	21	6	11	4	6	1	1	0	3	0	2	0	.545	.545	.818
Rod Dedeaux	SS2	R	20	2	4	0	1	0	0	0	1	0	0	0	.250	.250	.250
Whitey Ock	C1	R	23	1	3	0	0	0	0	0	0	1	2	0	.000	.250	.000
Ralph Onis	C1	R	26	1	1	0	1	0	0	0	0	0	0	0	1.000	1.000	1.000

B. Reis, 1 G at 1B, 1 G at 3B

Pitcher	T	Age	G	GS	CG	ShO	IP	H	HR	BB	SO	W-L	Sv	ERA
Van Lingle Mungo	R	24	37	26	18	4	214.1	205	13	90	143	16-10	2	3.65
Watty Clark	L	33	33	25	11	1	207.0	215	11	28	35	13-8	0	3.30
Johnny Babich	R	22	37	24	7	2	143.1	191	7	52	55	7-14	0	6.66
George Earnshaw†	R	35	25	22	6	2	166.0	175	14	53	72	8-12	0	4.12
Tom Zachary	L	39	25	21	9	1	158.0	193	10	35	33	7-12	4	3.59
Ray Benge	R	33	23	17	5	1	124.2	142	12	47	39	9-9	1	4.48
Dutch Leonard	R	26	43	11	4	0	137.2	152	11	29	41	2-9	8	3.92
Les Munns	R	26	21	5	0	0	58.1	74	5	33	13	1-3	1	5.55
Dazzy Vance	R	44	20	0	0	0	51.0	55	3	16	28	3-2	2	4.41
Bobby Reis	R	26	14	2	1	0	41.1	46	0	24	7	3-2	2	2.83
Tom Baker	R	22	11	1	1	0	42.0	48	2	20	10	1-0	0	4.29
Harry Eisenstat	L	19	2	0	0	0	4.2	9	0	2	2	0-1	0	13.50
Frank Lamanske	L	28	2	0	0	0	3.2	5	0	1	1	0-0	0	7.36
Bob Logan	L	25	2	0	0	0	2.2	2	0	1	1	0-1	0	3.38
Bob Barr	R	27	2	0	0	0	2.1	5	0	2	0	0-0	0	3.86
Harvey Green	R	20	2	0	0	0	1.0	2	0	3	0	0-0	0	9.00

1935 Cincinnati Reds 6th NL 68-85 .444 31.5 GB

Chuck Dressen

Player	Gm by Position	B	Age	G	AB	R	H	2B	3B	HR	RBI	BB	SO	SB	Avg	OBP	Slg
Ernie Lombardi	C82	R	27	120	332	36	114	23	3	12	64	16	6	0	.343	.379	.539
Jim Bottomley	1B97	L	35	107	399	44	103	21	1	1	49	18	24	3	.258	.294	.323
Alex Kampouris	2B141,SS6	R	22	148	499	46	123	26	5	7	62	32	84	8	.246	.295	.361
Lew Riggs	3B135	L	25	142	532	73	148	26	8	5	46	43	32	8	.278	.334	.385
Billy Myers	SS112	R	24	117	445	60	119	15	10	5	36	29	81	10	.267	.315	.380
Ival Goodman	OF146	L	26	148	592	86	159	23	18	12	72	35	50	14	.269	.314	.429
Sammy Byrd	OF115	R	27	121	416	51	109	25	4	9	52	37	51	4	.262	.322	.406
Babe Herman†	OF76,1B14	L	32	92	349	44	117	23	5	10	58	35	25	5	.335	.396	.516
Billy Sullivan	1B40,3B15,2B6	L	24	85	241	29	64	9	4	2	36	19	16	4	.266	.324	.361
Kiki Cuyler†	OF57	R	36	62	223	36	56	8	3	2	22	27	18	5	.251	.337	.341
Gilly Campbell	C66,1B5,OF1	L	27	88	218	26	56	7	0	3	30	42	7	3	.257	.379	.330
Gordon Slade	SS30,2B19,OF8*	R	30	71	196	22	55	10	0	1	14	16	16	0	.281	.341	.347
Adam Comorosky	OF40	R	29	59	137	22	34	3	1	2	14	7	14	1	.248	.290	.328
Hank Erickson	C25	R	27	37	88	9	23	3	2	1	4	6	4	0	.261	.323	.375
Harlin Pool	OF18	L	27	28	68	8	12	6	2	0	11	2	2	0	.176	.200	.324
Chick Hafey	OF15	R	32	15	59	10	20	6	1	1	9	4	5	1	.339	.400	.525
Calvin Chapman	SS12,2B4	L	24	15	53	6	18	1	0	0	3	4	5	2	.340	.386	.358
Les Scarsella	1B2	L	21	6	10	4	2	1	0	0	0	3	1	0	.200	.385	.300
Ted Petoskey	OF2	R	24	4	5	0	2	0	0	0	0	0	1	1	.400	.400	.400
Tony Piet†	OF1	R	28	6	5	2	1	1	0	0	2	0	0	0	.200	.200	.400
Lee Gamble	OF2	L	25	2	4	2	2	1	0	0	2	1	0	1	.500	.600	.750

G. Slade, 7 G at 3B

Pitcher	T	Age	G	GS	CG	ShO	IP	H	HR	BB	SO	W-L	Sv	ERA
Paul Derringer	R	28	45	33	20	3	276.2	295	13	49	120	22-13	2	3.51
Al Hollingsworth	L	27	38	22	8	0	173.1	165	5	76	89	6-13	0	3.89
Si Johnson	R	28	30	20	4	1	130.0	155	14	59	40	5-11	0	6.23
Gene Schott	R	21	33	19	9	1	159.0	153	5	64	49	8-11	0	3.91
Tony Freitas	L	27	31	18	5	1	143.2	174	6	38	51	5-10	2	4.57
Danny MacFayden†	R	30	7	4	1	0	36.0	39	1	13	13	1-2	0	4.75
Lee Grissom	L	27	3	3	1	1	21.0	31	0	4	13	1-1	0	3.86
Whitey Hilcher	R	26	4	2	1	1	19.1	19	0	5	9	2-0	0	2.79
Don Brennan	R	31	38	5	2	1	114.1	101	4	44	48	5-5	5	3.15
Benny Frey	R	29	38	13	3	1	114.1	164	6	32	24	6-10	2	6.85
LeRoy Herrmann	R	29	29	8	2	0	108.0	124	9	31	30	3-5	0	3.58
Emmett Nelson	R	30	19	7	3	1	60.1	70	2	23	14	4-4	1	4.33

1935 Philadelphia Phillies 7th NL 64-89 .418 35.5 GB

Jimmie Wilson

Player	Gm by Position	B	Age	G	AB	R	H	2B	3B	HR	RBI	BB	SO	SB	Avg	OBP	Slg
Al Todd	C87	R	33	107	328	40	95	18	3	3	42	19	35	3	.290	.334	.390
Dolph Camilli	1B156	L	28	156	602	88	157	23	5	25	83	65	113	9	.261	.336	.440
Lou Chiozza	2B120,3B2	L	25	124	472	71	134	26	6	3	47	33	44	5	.284	.333	.383
Johnny Vergez	3B148,SS2	R	28	148	546	56	136	27	4	9	63	46	67	8	.249	.312	.363
Mickey Haslin	SS87,3B11,2B9	R	24	110	407	53	108	17	3	3	52	19	25	5	.265	.300	.344
Ethan Allen	OF156	R	31	156	645	90	198	46	1	8	63	43	54	5	.307	.351	.419
Johnny Moore	OF150	L	33	153	600	84	194	33	3	19	93	45	50	4	.323	.375	.483
George Watkins	OF148	L	35	150	600	80	162	25	5	17	76	40	78	3	.270	.320	.413
Jimmie Wilson	C78,2B1	R	34	93	290	38	81	20	0	1	37	19	19	4	.279	.326	.359
Chile Gomez	SS36,2B32	R	26	67	222	24	51	3	0	0	16	17	34	2	.230	.285	.243
Blondy Ryan†	SS35,2B1,3B1	R	29	39	129	13	34	3	0	1	10	7	20	1	.264	.312	.310
Bucky Walters	P24,OF5,2B2*	R	26	49	96	14	24	2	1	0	6	9	12	0	.250	.314	.292
Joe Bowman	P33,OF1	L	25	49	67	6	13	1	1	1	7	4	7	1	.194	.239	.284
Ed Boland	OF10	L	27	30	47	5	10	0	0	0	4	4	6	1	.213	.275	.213
Fred Lucas	OF10	R	32	20	34	1	9	0	0	0	2	3	6	0	.265	.324	.265
Hugh Mulcahy	P18,OF1	R	21	19	17	0	0	0	0	0	0	0	7	0	.000	.000	.000
Joe Holden	C4	L	22	6	9	0	1	0	0	0	0	0	3	1	.111	.111	.111
Art Bramhall	3B1,SS1	R	26	2	1	0	0	0	0	0	0	0	0	0	.000	.000	.000
Bubber Jonnard	C1	R	37	1	1	0	0	0	0	0	0	0	0	0	.000	.000	.000
Dino Chiozza	SS2	L	23	2	0	1	0	0	0	0	0	0	0	0	—	—	—

B. Walters, 1 G at 3B

Pitcher	T	Age	G	GS	CG	ShO	IP	H	HR	BB	SO	W-L	Sv	ERA
Curt Davis	R	31	44	27	19	3	231.0	264	14	47	74	16-14	2	3.66
Bucky Walters	R	26	24	22	8	2	151.0	168	9	68	40	9-9	0	4.17
Joe Bowman	R	25	33	17	6	1	148.1	157	13	56	58	7-10	1	4.25
Euel Moore†	R	27	15	8	1	0	40.1	63	5	20	15	1-6	1	7.81
Hal Kelleher	R	21	3	3	2	1	25.0	26	0	12	12	2-0	0	1.80
Phil Collins†	R	33	3	3	0	0	14.2	24	5	9	4	0-2	0	11.66
Snipe Hansen†	L	28	2	1	0	0	4.1	8	0	5	0	0-1	0	12.46
Orville Jorgens	R	27	53	24	6	0	188.1	216	12	96	57	10-15	2	4.83
Jim Bivin	R	25	47	14	0	0	161.2	220	20	65	54	2-9	1	5.79
Pretzels Pezzullo	L	24	41	7	2	0	84.1	115	5	45	24	3-5	1	6.40
Syl Johnson	R	34	37	18	8	1	174.2	182	15	31	89	10-8	6	3.56
Ray Prim	L	28	29	6	1	0	73.1	110	4	15	27	3-4	0	5.77
Hugh Mulcahy	R	21	18	5	0	0	52.2	62	2	25	11	1-5	1	4.78
Frank Pearce	R	29	5	0	0	0	13.0	22	0	6	7	0-0	0	8.31
Tommy Thomas†	R	35	4	1	0	0	12.0	15	2	5	3	0-1	0	5.25

1935 Boston Braves 8th NL 38-115 .248 61.5 GB

Bill McKechnie

Player	Gm by Position	B	Age	G	AB	R	H	2B	3B	HR	RBI	BB	SO	SB	Avg	OBP	Slg
Al Spohrer	C90	R	32	92	260	22	63	7	1	1	16	9	12	0	.242	.273	.288
Buck Jordan	1B95,3B8,OF2	L	28	130	470	62	131	24	5	5	35	19	17	3	.279	.307	.383
Les Mallon	2B73,3B36,OF1	R	29	116	412	48	113	24	2	2	25	28	37	3	.274	.322	.357
Pinky Whitney	3B74,2B49	R	30	126	458	41	125	23	4	4	60	24	36	2	.273	.312	.367
Billy Urbanski	SS129	R	32	132	514	53	118	17	0	4	30	40	32	3	.230	.286	.286
Wally Berger	OF149	R	29	150	589	91	174	39	4	34	130	50	80	3	.295	.355	.548
Hal Lee	OF110	R	30	112	422	49	128	18	6	0	39	18	25	0	.303	.333	.374
Tommy Thompson	OF85	L	25	112	297	34	81	7	1	4	30	36	17	2	.273	.353	.343
Randy Moore	OF78,1B21	L	29	125	407	42	112	20	4	4	42	26	16	1	.275	.319	.373
Joe Coscarart	3B41,SS27,2B15	R	25	86	284	30	67	11	2	1	29	16	28	2	.236	.277	.299
Shanty Hogan	C56	R	29	59	163	9	49	8	0	2	25	21	8	0	.301	.394	.387
Elbie Fletcher	1B39	L	19	39	148	12	35	7	1	1	9	7	13	1	.236	.271	.318
Joe Mowry	OF45	S	27	81	136	17	36	8	1	1	13	11	13	0	.265	.324	.360
Ray Mueller	C40	R	23	42	97	10	22	5	0	3	11	3	11	0	.227	.250	.371
Babe Ruth	OF26	L	40	28	72	13	13	0	0	6	12	20	24	0	.181	.359	.431
Rabbit Maranville	2B20	R	43	23	67	3	10	2	0	0	5	3	3	0	.149	.186	.179
Johnnie Tyler	OF11	S	28	13	47	7	16	2	1	2	11	4	3	0	.340	.404	.553
Ed Moriarty	2B8	R	22	8	34	4	11	2	1	1	1	0	6	0	.324	.324	.529
Art Doll	C3	R	22	3	10	0	1	0	0	0	0	0	1	0	.100	.100	.100
Bill Lewis		R	30	6	4	1	0	0	0	0	0	1	1	0	.000	.200	.000

Pitcher	T	Age	G	GS	CG	ShO	IP	H	HR	BB	SO	W-L	Sv	ERA
Fred Frankhouse	R	31	40	29	10	1	230.2	278	12	81	64	11-15	0	4.76
Ed Brandt	L	30	29	25	12	0	174.2	224	12	66	61	5-19	0	5.00
Ben Cantwell	R	33	39	24	13	0	210.2	235	15	44	34	4-25	0	4.61
Danny MacFayden†	R	30	28	20	7	1	151.2	200	8	34	46	5-13	0	5.10
Bob Brown	R	24	15	10	2	1	65.0	79	2	36	17	1-8	0	6.37
Flint Rhem	R	34	10	6	0	0	40.1	61	4	11	10	0-5	0	5.36
Bob Smith	R	40	46	20	8	2	203.1	232	13	61	58	8-18	5	3.94
Huck Betts	R	38	44	19	2	1	159.2	213	9	40	40	2-9	0	5.47
Larry Benton	R	37	29	0	0	0	72.0	103	6	24	21	2-3	0	6.88
Al Blanche	R	25	6	0	0	0	17.1	14	0	5	4	0-0	0	1.56
Leo Mangum	R	39	3	0	0	0	4.2	6	0	2	0	0-0	0	3.86

»1936 New York Yankees 1st AL 102-51 .667 —

Joe McCarthy

Player	Gm by Position	B	Age	G	AB	R	H	2B	3B	HR	RBI	BB	SO	SB	Avg	OBP	Slg
Bill Dickey	C107	L	29	112	423	99	153	26	8	22	107	46	16	0	.362	.428	.617
Lou Gehrig	1B155	L	33	155	579	167	205	37	7	49	152	130	46	3	.354	.478	.696
Tony Lazzeri	2B148,SS2	R	32	150	537	82	154	29	6	14	109	97	65	8	.287	.397	.441
Red Rolfe	3B133	L	27	135	568	116	181	39	15	10	70	68	38	3	.319	.392	.493
Frankie Crosetti	SS151	R	25	151	632	137	182	35	7	15	78	90	83	18	.288	.387	.437
Joe DiMaggio	OF138	R	21	138	637	132	206	44	15	29	125	24	39	4	.323	.352	.576
George Selkirk	OF135	L	28	137	493	93	152	28	9	18	107	94	60	13	.308	.420	.511
Jake Powell†	OF84	R	27	87	324	62	99	13	3	7	48	33	30	16	.306	.370	.429
Myril Hoag	OF39	R	28	45	156	23	47	9	4	3	34	7	16	3	.301	.343	.468
Roy Johnson	OF33	L	33	63	147	21	39	8	2	1	19	21	14	3	.265	.361	.367
Ben Chapman†	OF36	R	27	36	139	19	37	14	3	1	21	15	20	1	.266	.338	.432
Joe Glenn	C44	R	27	44	129	21	35	7	0	1	20	20	10	1	.271	.373	.349
Jack Saltzgaver	3B16,2B6,1B4	L	33	34	90	14	19	5	0	1	13	13	18	0	.211	.311	.300
Art Jorgens	C30	R	31	31	66	5	18	3	1	0	5	2	3	0	.273	.294	.348
Don Heffner	3B8,2B5,SS3	R	25	19	48	7	11	2	1	0	6	6	5	0	.229	.315	.313
Bob Seeds	OF9,3B3	R	29	13	42	12	11	1	0	4	10	5	3	3	.262	.340	.571
Dixie Walker†	OF5	L	25	6	20	3	7	0	2	1	5	1	3	1	.350	.381	.700

Pitcher	T	Age	G	GS	CG	ShO	IP	H	HR	BB	SO	W-L	Sv	ERA
Red Ruffing	R	32	33	33	25	3	271.0	274	22	90	102	20-12	0	3.85
Monte Pearson	R	26	33	31	15	1	223.0	191	13	135	118	19-7	1	3.71
Lefty Gomez	L	27	31	30	10	0	188.2	184	6	122	105	13-7	0	4.39
Johnny Broaca	R	26	37	27	12	1	206.0	235	16	66	84	12-7	3	4.24
Bump Hadley	R	31	31	17	8	1	173.2	194	12	89	74	14-4	1	4.35
Pat Malone	R	33	35	9	5	0	134.2	144	4	60	72	12-4	9	3.81
Johnny Murphy	R	27	27	5	2	0	88.0	90	5	36	34	9-3	5	3.38
Jumbo Brown	R	29	20	3	0	0	64.0	93	4	29	19	1-4	1	5.91
Ted Kleinhans	L	37	19	0	0	0	29.1	36	0	23	10	1-1	1	5.83
Kemp Wicker	L	29	7	0	0	0	20.0	31	2	11	5	1-2	0	7.65
Steve Sundra	R	26	1	0	0	0	2.0	2	0	2	1	0-0	0	0.00

1936 Detroit Tigers 2nd AL 83-71 .539 19.5 GB

Mickey Cochrane (29-24)/Del Baker (18-16)/Mickey Cochrane (36-31)

Player	Gm by Position	B	Age	G	AB	R	H	2B	3B	HR	RBI	BB	SO	SB	Avg	OBP	Slg
Ray Hayworth	C81	R	32	81	250	31	60	10	0	1	30	39	18	0	.240	.347	.292
Jack Burns†	1B138	L	28	138	558	96	158	36	3	4	63	79	45	4	.283	.375	.380
Charlie Gehringer	2B154	L	33	154	641	144	227	60	12	15	116	83	13	4	.354	.431	.555
Marv Owen	3B153,1B2	R	30	154	583	72	172	20	4	9	105	53	41	9	.295	.361	.389
Billy Rogell	SS146,3B1	S	31	146	585	85	160	27	5	6	68	73	41	14	.274	.357	.368
Goose Goslin	OF144	L	35	147	572	122	180	33	8	24	125	85	50	14	.315	.403	.526
Al Simmons	OF138,1B1	R	34	143	568	96	186	38	6	13	112	49	35	6	.327	.383	.484
Gee Walker	OF125	R	28	134	550	105	194	55	5	12	93	23	30	17	.353	.387	.536
Pete Fox	OF55	R	27	73	220	46	67	12	1	4	26	34	23	1	.305	.405	.423
Mickey Cochrane	C42	L	33	44	126	24	34	8	0	2	17	46	15	1	.270	.465	.381
Glenn Myatt	C27	L	38	27	78	5	17	1	0	0	5	9	4	0	.218	.299	.231
Frank Reiber	C17,OF1	R	26	20	55	7	15	2	0	1	5	2	7	0	.273	.333	.364
Jo-Jo White	OF18	L	27	58	51	11	14	3	0	0	6	9	10	2	.275	.383	.333
Hank Greenberg	1B12	R	25	12	46	10	16	6	2	1	16	9	6	1	.348	.455	.630
Birdie Tebbetts	C10	R	23	10	33	7	10	1	2	1	4	5	3	0	.303	.395	.545
Flea Clifton	SS6,3B2,2B1	R	26	13	26	5	5	1	0	0	1	4	3	0	.192	.300	.231
Salty Parker	SS7,1B2	R	22	11	25	6	7	2	0	0	4	2	3	0	.280	.333	.360
Gil English	3B1	R	26	1	1	0	0	0	0	0	0	0	1	0	.000	.000	.000

Pitcher	T	Age	G	GS	CG	ShO	IP	H	HR	BB	SO	W-L	Sv	ERA
Tommy Bridges	R	29	39	38	26	5	294.2	289	21	115	175	23-11	0	3.60
Schoolboy Rowe	R	26	41	35	19	4	245.1	266	15	64	115	19-10	3	4.51
Eldon Auker	R	25	35	31	14	2	215.1	263	11	83	66	13-16	0	4.89
Jake Wade	L	24	13	11	4	1	78.1	93	7	52	30	4-5	0	5.29
General Crowder	R	37	9	7	1	0	44.0	64	5	21	10	4-3	0	8.39
Roxie Lawson	R	30	41	8	3	0	128.0	139	13	71	34	8-6	3	5.48
Vic Sorrell	R	35	30	14	5	1	131.1	153	9	64	37	6-7	3	5.28
Joe Sullivan	L	25	26	4	1	0	79.2	111	4	40	32	2-5	1	6.78
Red Phillips	R	27	22	6	3	0	87.1	124	12	22	15	2-4	0	6.49
Chad Kimsey	R	29	22	0	0	0	52.0	58	2	29	11	2-3	3	4.85
Chief Hogsett†	L	32	3	0	0	0	4.0	8	1	1	1	0-1	0	9.00

1936 Chicago White Sox 3rd AL 81-70 .536 20.0 GB

Jimmy Dykes

Player	Gm by Position	B	Age	G	AB	R	H	2B	3B	HR	RBI	BB	SO	SB	Avg	OBP	Slg
Luke Sewell	C126	R	35	128	451	59	113	20	5	5	73	54	16	11	.251	.332	.350
Zeke Bonura	1B146	R	27	148	587	120	194	39	7	12	138	94	29	4	.330	.426	.482
Jackie Hayes	2B89,SS13,3B2	R	29	108	417	53	130	34	3	5	84	35	25	4	.312	.366	.444
Jimmy Dykes	3B125	R	39	127	435	62	116	16	3	7	60	61	36	1	.267	.362	.366
Luke Appling	SS137	R	29	138	526	111	204	31	7	6	128	85	25	10	.388	.473	.508
Mike Kreevich	OF133	R	28	137	550	99	169	32	11	5	69	61	46	10	.307	.378	.433
Rip Radcliff	OF132	L	30	138	618	120	207	31	7	8	82	44	12	6	.335	.381	.447
Mule Haas	OF96,1B7	L	32	119	408	75	116	26	2	0	46	64	29	1	.284	.383	.358
Tony Piet	2B68,3B32	R	29	109	352	69	96	15	2	7	42	66	48	15	.273	.400	.386
Larry Rosenthal	OF80	L	26	85	317	71	89	15	8	3	46	59	37	2	.281	.394	.407
Frank Grube	C32	R	31	33	93	6	15	2	1	0	11	9	15	1	.161	.235	.204
Dixie Walker†	OF17	L	25	26	70	12	19	2	0	0	11	14	6	1	.271	.400	.300
George Washington	OF12	L	29	20	49	6	8	2	0	1	5	1	4	0	.163	.180	.265
Jo-Jo Morrissey	3B9,SS4,2B1	R	32	17	38	3	7	1	0	0	6	2	3	0	.184	.225	.211
Merv Shea	C14	R	35	14	24	3	3	0	0	0	2	6	5	0	.125	.300	.125
George Stumpf	OF4	L	25	10	22	3	6	1	0	0	2	5	2	1	.273	.333	.318
Les Rock	1B2	L	23	2	1	0	0	0	0	0	1	0	0	0	.000	.000	.000

Pitcher	T	Age	G	GS	CG	ShO	IP	H	HR	BB	SO	W-L	Sv	ERA
Vern Kennedy	R	29	35	34	20	1	274.1	282	13	147	99	21-9	0	4.63
John Whitehead	R	27	34	32	15	1	230.2	254	9	98	70	13-13	1	4.64
Sugar Cain†	R	29	30	26	14	1	195.1	228	18	75	42	14-10	0	4.75
Ted Lyons	R	35	26	24	15	1	182.0	227	21	45	48	10-13	0	5.14
Monty Stratton	R	24	16	14	3	0	95.0	117	8	46	37	5-7	0	5.21
Bill Dietrich†	R	26	14	11	6	1	82.2	93	8	36	39	4-4	0	4.68
Clint Brown	R	32	38	2	0	0	83.0	106	5	24	19	6-2	5	4.99
Italo Chelini	L	21	18	6	5	0	83.2	100	8	30	16	4-3	0	4.95
Red Evans	R	29	17	0	0	0	47.1	70	4	22	19	0-3	1	7.61
Ray Phelps	R	32	15	4	2	0	68.2	91	9	42	17	4-6	0	6.03
Bill Shores	R	32	9	0	0	0	17.0	26	1	8	5	0-0	0	9.53
Whit Wyatt	R	28	3	0	0	0	3.0	3	0	0	0	0-0	1	0.00
Les Tietje†	R	24	2	0	0	0	2.1	6	0	5	3	0-0	0	27.00

1936 Washington Senators 4th AL 82-71 .536 20.0 GB

Bucky Harris

Player	Gm by Position	B	Age	G	AB	R	H	2B	3B	HR	RBI	BB	SO	SB	Avg	OBP	Slg
Cliff Bolton	C83	L	29	86	289	41	84	18	4	2	51	25	12	1	.291	.349	.401
Joe Kuhel	1B149,3B1	L	30	149	588	107	189	42	8	16	118	64	30	15	.321	.392	.502
Ossie Bluege	2B52,SS23,3B15	R	35	90	319	43	92	12	1	1	55	38	16	5	.288	.375	.342
Buddy Lewis	3B139	L	19	143	601	100	175	21	13	6	67	47	46	6	.291	.347	.399
Cecil Travis	SS71,OF53,2B4*	L	22	138	517	77	164	34	10	2	92	39	21	4	.317	.366	.433
John Stone	OF114	L	30	123	437	95	149	22	11	15	90	60	26	8	.341	.421	.545
Ben Chapman†	OF97	R	27	97	401	91	133	36	7	4	60	69	18	19	.332	.431	.486
Carl Reynolds	OF72	R	33	89	293	41	81	18	2	4	41	21	22	8	.276	.329	.392
Red Kress	SS64,2B33,1B5	R	29	109	391	51	111	20	6	8	51	39	25	6	.284	.349	.427
Jesse Hill	OF60	R	29	85	233	50	71	19	5	0	34	29	23	11	.305	.384	.429
Wally Millies	C72	R	29	74	215	26	67	10	2	0	25	11	8	1	.312	.345	.377
Jake Powell†	OF53	R	27	53	214	40	62	11	5	1	30	19	21	10	.290	.348	.402
Buddy Myer	2B43	L	32	51	156	31	42	5	2	0	15	42	11	7	.269	.427	.327
Fred Sington	OF25	R	26	25	94	13	30	8	0	1	28	15	9	0	.319	.413	.436
John Mihalic	2B25	R	24	25	88	15	21	2	1	0	8	14	14	2	.239	.343	.284
Shanty Hogan	C10	R	30	19	65	8	21	4	0	1	7	11	2	0	.323	.421	.431
Dee Miles	OF10	L	27	25	59	8	14	1	2	0	7	1	5	0	.237	.250	.322
Bobby Estalella		R	25	13	9	2	2	0	2	0	0	4	5	0	.222	.462	.667
Alex Sabo	C4	R	26	4	8	1	3	0	0	0	1	0	2	0	.375	.375	.375
Chick Starr	C1	R	25	1	0	0	0	0	0	0	0	0	0	0	—	—	—

C. Travis, 2 G at 3B

Pitcher	T	Age	G	GS	CG	ShO	IP	H	HR	BB	SO	W-L	Sv	ERA
Bobo Newsom	R	28	43	38	24	4	285.1	294	13	146	156	17-15	2	4.32
Jimmie DeShong	R	26	34	31	16	2	223.2	255	11	96	59	18-10	2	4.63
Earl Whitehill	L	36	28	28	14	0	212.1	252	17	89	63	14-11	0	4.87
Pete Appleton	R	32	38	20	12	1	201.2	199	7	77	77	14-9	3	3.53
Joe Cascarella†	R	29	22	16	7	1	139.1	147	7	54	34	9-8	1	4.07
Bill Phebus	R	26	2	1	0	0	7.1	4	1	4	4	0-0	0	2.45
Monte Weaver	R	30	26	5	3	0	91.0	92	3	38	15	6-4	1	4.35
Syd Cohen	L	30	19	1	0	0	36.0	44	4	14	21	0-2	1	5.25
Jack Russell†	R	30	18	5	1	0	49.2	66	3	25	6	3-2	3	6.34
Ed Linke	R	24	13	6	1	0	52.0	73	4	14	11	1-5	0	7.10
Henry Coppola	R	23	6	0	0	0	14.0	17	1	12	2	0-0	1	4.50
Firpo Marberry†	R	37	5	1	0	0	14.0	11	2	3	4	0-2	0	3.86
Bill Dietrich†	R	26	5	0	0	0	8.1	13	0	6	4	0-1	0	9.72
Joe Bokina	R	26	5	1	0	0	8.0	15	0	6	5	0-2	0	9.00
Ken Chase	L	22	1	0	0	0	2.1	2	0	4	1	0-0	0	11.57

1936 Cleveland Indians 5th AL 80-74 .519 22.5 GB

Steve O'Neill

Player	Gm by Position	B	Age	G	AB	R	H	2B	3B	HR	RBI	BB	SO	SB	Avg	OBP	Slg
Billy Sullivan	C72,3B5,1B3*	L	25	93	319	39	112	32	6	2	48	16	9	5	.351	.382	.508
Hal Trosky	1B151,2B1	L	23	151	629	124	216	45	9	42	162	36	58	6	.343	.382	.644
Roy Hughes	2B152	R	25	152	638	112	188	35	9	0	63	57	40	20	.295	.356	.378
Odell Hale	3B148,2B3	R	27	153	620	126	196	50	13	14	87	64	43	8	.316	.380	.506
Bill Knickerbocker	SS155	R	24	155	618	81	182	35	3	8	73	56	30	5	.294	.354	.400
Earl Averill	OF150	L	34	152	614	136	232	39	15	28	126	65	35	3	.378	.438	.627
Joe Vosmik	OF136	R	26	138	506	76	145	29	7	7	94	79	21	5	.287	.383	.413
Roy Weatherly	OF84	L	21	84	349	64	117	28	6	8	53	16	29	3	.335	.364	.519
Frankie Pytlak	C58	R	27	75	224	35	72	15	4	0	31	24	11	5	.321	.394	.424
Bruce Campbell	OF47	L	26	76	172	35	64	15	2	6	30	19	17	2	.372	.440	.587
Jim Gleeson	OF33	S	24	41	139	26	36	9	2	4	12	18	17	2	.259	.344	.439
Milt Galatzer	OF42,P1,1B1	L	29	49	97	12	23	4	1	0	6	13	8	1	.237	.333	.299
Greek George	C22	R	23	23	77	3	15	3	0	0	5	9	16	0	.195	.279	.234
Boze Berger	1B8,2B8,3B7*	R	26	28	52	1	9	2	0	0	3	1	14	0	.173	.189	.212
Joe Becker	C15	R	28	22	50	5	9	3	1	1	11	5	4	0	.180	.255	.340
Jeff Heath	OF12	L	21	12	41	6	14	3	3	1	8	3	4	1	.341	.386	.634

B. Sullivan, 1 G at OF; B. Berger, 2 G at SS

Pitcher	T	Age	G	GS	CG	ShO	IP	H	HR	BB	SO	W-L	Sv	ERA
Johnny Allen	R	30	36	31	19	4	243.0	234	5	97	165	20-10	1	3.44
Mel Harder	R	26	36	30	13	0	224.2	294	13	71	84	15-15	1	5.17
Oral Hildebrand	R	29	36	21	9	0	174.2	197	10	83	65	10-11	4	4.90
Lloyd Brown	L	31	24	16	12	1	140.1	166	13	45	34	8-10	1	4.17
Bob Feller	R	17	14	8	5	0	62.0	52	1	47	76	5-3	1	3.34
Al Milnar	L	22	4	3	1	0	22.0	26	0	18	9	1-2	0	7.36
Bill Zuber	R	23	2	2	1	0	13.2	14	0	15	5	1-1	0	6.59
Thornton Lee	L	29	43	8	2	0	127.0	138	2	67	49	3-5	3	4.89
Denny Galehouse	R	24	36	15	5	0	148.1	161	5	68	71	8-7	1	4.85
George Blaeholder	R	32	35	16	6	0	134.1	158	21	47	30	8-4	0	5.09
Willis Hudlin	R	30	27	7	1	0	64.0	112	1	31	20	1-5	0	9.00
Ralph Winegarner	R	26	9	0	0	0	14.2	18	0	6	3	0-0	0	4.91
George Uhle	R	37	7	0	0	0	12.2	26	2	5	5	0-1	0	8.53
Paul Kardow	R	20	2	0	0	0	2.0	1	0	2	0	0-0	0	4.50
Milt Galatzer	L	29	1	0	0	0	6.0	7	0	5	3	0-0	0	4.50

1936 Boston Red Sox 6th AL 74-80 .481 28.5 GB

Joe Cronin

Player	Gm by Position	B	Age	G	AB	R	H	2B	3B	HR	RBI	BB	SO	SB	Avg	OBP	Slg
Rick Ferrell	C121	R	30	121	410	59	128	27	5	8	55	65	17	0	.312	.406	.461
Jimmie Foxx	1B139,OF16,3B1	R	28	155	585	130	198	32	8	41	143	105	119	13	.338	.440	.631
Ski Melillo	2B93	R	36	98	327	39	74	12	4	0	32	28	16	0	.226	.287	.287
Bill Werber	3B101,OF45,2B1	R	28	145	535	89	147	29	6	10	67	89	37	23	.275	.382	.407
Eric McNair	SS84,2B35,3B11	R	27	128	494	68	141	36	2	4	74	27	34	3	.285	.329	.391
Doc Cramer	OF154	L	30	154	643	99	188	31	7	0	41	49	20	4	.292	.347	.362
Dusty Cooke	OF91	L	29	111	341	58	93	20	3	6	47	72	48	4	.273	.401	.402
Mel Almada	OF81	L	23	96	320	40	81	16	4	1	21	24	15	2	.253	.305	.338
Heinie Manush	OF72	L	34	82	313	43	91	15	5	0	45	17	11	1	.291	.329	.371
John Kroner	2B38,3B28,SS18*	R	27	84	298	40	87	17	8	4	62	26	24	2	.292	.349	.443
Joe Cronin	SS60,3B21	R	29	81	295	36	83	22	4	2	43	32	21	1	.281	.354	.403
Moe Berg	C39	R	34	39	125	9	30	4	1	0	19	2	6	0	.240	.264	.288
Babe Dahlgren	1B16	R	24	16	57	6	16	3	1	1	7	7	1	2	.281	.359	.421
Fabian Gaffke	OF15	R	22	15	55	5	7	2	0	1	3	4	5	0	.127	.200	.218
Bing Miller	OF13	R	41	30	47	9	14	2	1	1	6	5	5	0	.298	.377	.447
George Dickey	C10	S	20	10	23	0	1	1	0	0	0	2	3	0	.043	.120	.087

J. Kroner, 1 G at OF

Pitcher	T	Age	G	GS	CG	ShO	IP	H	HR	BB	SO	W-L	Sv	ERA
Wes Ferrell	R	28	39	38	28	3	301.0	330	11	119	106	20-15	0	4.19
Lefty Grove	L	36	35	30	22	6	253.1	237	14	65	130	17-12	2	2.81
Fritz Ostermueller	L	28	43	23	7	1	180.2	210	8	84	90	10-16	2	4.88
Johnny Marcum	R	26	31	23	9	1	174.0	194	14	52	57	8-13	1	4.81
Mike Meola†	R	30	6	3	1	0	21.1	29	0	10	8	0-2	1	5.48
Ted Olson	R	23	5	3	1	0	18.1	24	3	8	5	1-1	0	7.36
Jennings Poindexter	L	25	3	3	0	0	10.2	13	0	16	2	0-2	0	6.75
Jack Wilson	R	24	43	9	2	0	136.1	152	4	86	74	6-8	3	4.42
Rube Walberg	L	39	24	9	5	0	100.1	98	7	36	49	5-4	0	4.40
Jack Russell†	R	30	23	2	0	0	40.0	57	2	16	9	0-3	0	5.63
Jim Henry	R	26	21	8	2	0	76.1	75	10	40	36	5-1	0	4.60
Joe Cascarella†	R	29	10	1	0	0	20.2	27	0	9	7	0-2	0	6.97
Johnny Welch†	R	29	9	3	1	0	32.2	43	4	8	9	2-1	0	5.51
Stew Bowers	R	21	5	0	0	0	5.2	10	1	2	0	0-0	0	9.53
Emerson Dickman	R	21	1	0	0	0	1.0	2	0	1	2	0-0	0	9.00

1936 St. Louis Browns 7th AL 57-95 .375 44.5 GB

Rogers Hornsby

Player	Gm by Position	B	Age	G	AB	R	H	2B	3B	HR	RBI	BB	SO	SB	Avg	OBP	Slg
Rollie Hemsley	C114	R	29	116	377	43	99	24	2	2	39	46	30	2	.263	.343	.353
Jim Bottomley	1B140	L	36	140	544	72	162	39	11	12	95	44	55	0	.298	.354	.476
Tom Carey	2B128,SS1	R	29	134	488	58	133	27	6	1	57	27	25	2	.273	.315	.359
Harlond Clift	3B152	R	23	152	576	145	174	40	11	20	73	115	68	12	.302	.424	.514
Lyn Lary	SS155	R	30	155	620	112	179	30	6	2	52	117	54	37	.289	.403	.366
Sammy West	OF148	L	31	152	533	78	148	26	4	7	70	94	70	2	.278	.386	.381
Moose Solters	OF147	R	30	152	628	100	183	45	7	17	134	41	76	3	.291	.336	.467
Beau Bell	OF142,1B17	R	28	155	616	100	212	40	12	11	123	60	55	4	.344	.403	.502
Tony Giuliani	C66	R	23	71	198	17	43	3	0	0	13	11	13	0	.217	.258	.232
Ollie Bejma	2B32,3B7,SS1	R	28	67	139	19	36	6	2	2	18	27	21	0	.259	.380	.360
Ed Coleman	OF18	L	34	92	137	13	40	5	4	2	34	15	17	0	.292	.366	.431
Roy Pepper	OF18	R	30	75	124	13	35	5	0	2	23	5	23	0	.282	.310	.371
Jack Burns†	1B2	L	28	9	14	2	3	1	0	0	1	3	1	0	.214	.353	.286
Rogers Hornsby	1B1	R	40	2	5	1	2	0	0	0	2	1	0	0	.400	.500	.400

Pitcher	T	Age	G	GS	CG	ShO	IP	H	HR	BB	SO	W-L	Sv	ERA
Chief Hogsett†	L	32	39	29	10	0	215.1	278	15	90	67	13-15	1	5.52
Ivy Andrews	R	29	36	25	11	0	191.1	221	19	50	33	7-12	1	4.84
Earl Caldwell	R	31	41	25	10	2	189.0	252	15	83	59	7-16	2	6.00
Tommy Thomas	R	36	36	21	8	1	179.2	219	25	72	40	11-9	0	5.26
Les Tietje†	R	24	14	7	2	0	50.1	65	2	30	16	3-5	0	6.62
Sugar Cain†	R	29	4	3	1	0	16.1	20	0	9	8	1-1	0	6.61
Russ Van Atta	L	30	52	9	2	0	122.2	164	9	68	59	4-7	2	6.60
Jack Knott	R	29	47	23	9	0	192.2	272	15	93	60	9-17	6	7.29
Glenn Liebhardt	R	25	24	0	0	0	55.1	98	4	27	20	0-0	0	8.78
Roy Mahaffey	R	33	21	9	1	0	60.0	82	6	40	13	2-6	1	8.10
Harry Kimberlin	R	27	13	0	0	0	20.0	24	3	16	4	0-0	0	5.40
Mike Meola†	R	30	9	0	0	0	19.1	29	0	13	6	0-1	0	9.31
Sig Jakucki	R	26	7	2	0	0	20.2	32	2	12	9	0-3	0	8.71
Jim Walkup	R	26	5	2	0	0	15.2	20	0	6	5	0-3	0	8.04

1936 Philadelphia Athletics 8th AL 53-100 .346 49.0 GB

Connie Mack

Player	Gm by Position	B	Age	G	AB	R	H	2B	3B	HR	RBI	BB	SO	SB	Avg	OBP	Slg
Frankie Hayes	C143	R	21	144	505	59	137	25	2	10	67	46	58	3	.271	.335	.388
Lou Finney	1B78,OF73	L	25	151	653	100	197	26	10	1	41	47	22	7	.302	.351	.377
Rabbit Warstler†	2B66	R	32	66	236	27	59	8	6	1	24	36	16	0	.250	.354	.347
Mike Higgins	3B145	R	27	146	550	89	159	32	2	12	80	67	61	7	.289	.366	.420
Skeeter Newsome	SS123,2B2,3B1*	R	25	127	471	41	106	15	2	0	46	25	27	13	.225	.266	.265
Wally Moses	OF144	L	25	146	585	98	202	35	11	7	66	62	32	12	.345	.410	.479
Bob Johnson	OF131,2B22,1B1	R	29	153	566	91	165	29	14	25	121	88	71	6	.292	.389	.525
George Puccinelli	OF117	R	29	135	457	83	127	30	3	11	78	65	70	2	.278	.369	.429
Chubby Dean	1B77	L	19	111	342	41	98	21	3	1	48	24	24	3	.287	.337	.374
Al Niemiec	2B52,SS5	R	25	69	203	22	40	3	2	1	20	26	16	2	.197	.291	.246
Rusty Peters	SS25,3B10,OF2*	R	21	45	119	12	26	3	2	3	16	4	28	1	.218	.244	.353
Charlie Moss	C19	R	25	33	44	2	11	1	1	0	10	6	5	1	.250	.340	.318
Dick Culler	2B7,SS2	R	21	9	38	3	9	0	0	0	1	1	3	0	.237	.256	.237
Hal Luby	2B9	R	23	9	38	3	7	1	0	0	3	0	7	2	.184	.205	.211
Jack Peerson	SS7,2B1	R	25	8	34	7	11	1	1	0	5	0	3	0	.324	.324	.412
Emil Mailho	OF1	L	26	21	18	5	1	0	0	0	0	5	3	0	.056	.261	.056
Charlie Berry	C12	R	33	13	17	0	1	1	0	0	1	6	2	0	.059	.304	.118
Bill Nicholson	OF1	L	21	11	12	2	0	0	0	0	0	0	5	0	.000	.000	.000
Jim Oglesby	1B3	L	30	3	11	0	2	0	0	0	2	2	0	0	.182	.308	.182
Bill Conroy	C1	R	21	1	2	0	1	0	0	0	0	0	1	0	.500	.500	.500

S. Newsome, 1 G at OF; R. Peters, 1 G at 2B

Pitcher	T	Age	G	GS	CG	ShO	IP	H	HR	BB	SO	W-L	Sv	ERA
Gordon Rhodes	R	28	35	28	13	1	216.1	266	26	102	61	9-20	1	5.74
Harry Kelley	R	30	35	27	20	1	235.1	250	21	75	82	15-12	3	3.86
Buck Ross	R	21	30	27	12	1	200.2	253	17	83	47	9-14	0	5.83
Herman Fink	R	24	34	24	9	0	188.2	222	18	78	53	8-16	3	5.39
George Turbeville	L	21	12	6	2	0	43.2	42	6	32	10	2-5	0	6.39
Carl Doyle	R	23	8	6	1	0	38.2	66	4	29	12	0-3	0	10.94
Fred Archer	L	26	6	5	2	0	36.2	41	3	15	9	2-3	0	6.38
Whitey Wilshere	L	23	5	3	0	0	18.1	21	1	19	4	1-2	0	6.87
Hank Johnson	R	30	3	3	0	0	11.2	16	4	10	6	0-2	0	7.71
Eddie Smith	L	22	2	2	2	0	19.0	22	3	8	7	1-1	0	1.89
Randy Gumpert	R	18	22	3	2	0	62.1	74	2	32	9	1-2	2	4.76
Bill Dietrich†	R	26	21	4	0	0	71.2	91	4	40	34	4-6	3	6.53
Hod Lisenbee	R	37	19	7	4	0	85.2	115	9	24	17	1-7	0	6.20
Stu Flythe	R	24	17	3	0	0	39.1	49	4	61	14	0-0	0	13.04
Red Bullock	L	24	12	2	0	0	16.2	19	0	37	7	0-2	0	14.04
Woody Upchurch	L	25	7	2	1	0	22.1	36	7	14	6	0-2	0	9.67
Pete Naktenis	L	22	7	1	0	0	18.2	24	2	27	18	0-1	0	12.54
Harry Matuzak	R	26	6	1	0	0	15.0	21	0	4	8	0-1	0	7.20
Dutch Lieber	R	26	3	0	0	0	11.2	17	0	6	1	0-1	0	7.71

»1936 New York Giants 1st NL 92-62 .597 —

Bill Terry

Player	Gm by Position	B	Age	G	AB	R	H	2B	3B	HR	RBI	BB	SO	SB	Avg	OBP	Slg
Gus Mancuso	C138	R	30	139	519	55	156	21	3	9	63	39	28	0	.301	.351	.405
Sam Leslie	1B99	L	30	117	417	49	123	19	5	6	54	23	16	0	.295	.335	.408
Burgess Whitehead	2B153	R	26	154	632	99	176	31	3	4	47	29	32	14	.278	.317	.356
Travis Jackson	3B116,SS9	R	32	126	465	41	107	8	1	7	53	18	56	0	.230	.260	.297
Dick Bartell	SS144	R	28	145	510	71	152	31	3	8	42	40	36	6	.298	.355	.418
Jo-Jo Moore	OF149	L	27	152	649	110	205	29	9	7	63	37	27	2	.316	.358	.421
Mel Ott	OF148	L	27	150	534	120	175	28	6	33	135	111	41	6	.328	.448	.588
Hank Leiber	OF86	R	25	101	337	44	94	19	7	9	67	37	41	1	.279	.352	.457
Jimmy Ripple	OF76	L	26	96	311	42	95	17	2	7	47	28	15	1	.305	.365	.441
Bill Terry	1B56	L	39	79	229	36	71	10	5	2	39	19	19	0	.310	.363	.424
Eddie Mayo	3B40	L	26	46	141	11	28	4	1	1	8	11	12	0	.199	.257	.262
Harry Danning	C24	R	24	32	69	3	11	2	2	0	4	1	5	0	.159	.183	.246
Kiddo Davis	OF22	R	34	47	67	6	16	1	0	0	5	5	6	0	.239	.301	.254
Mark Koenig	SS10,2B8,3B3	S	31	42	58	7	16	4	0	1	7	8	4	0	.276	.373	.397
Roy Spencer	C14	R	36	19	18	3	5	1	0	0	3	2	3	0	.278	.350	.333
Johnny McCarthy	1B4	L	26	4	16	1	7	0	0	1	2	0	1	1	.438	.438	.625
Joe Martin	3B7	R	24	7	15	0	4	1	0	0	2	0	4	0	.267	.313	.333
Jim Sheehan	C1	R	22	1	4	0	0	0	0	0	0	0	0	0	.000	.000	.000
Babe Young		L	20	1	1	0	0	0	0	0	0	0	0	0	.000	.000	.000
Charlie English	2B1	R	26	6	1	0	0	0	0	0	0	0	0	0	.000	.000	.000

Pitcher	T	Age	G	GS	CG	ShO	IP	H	HR	BB	SO	W-L	Sv	ERA
Carl Hubbell	L	33	42	34	25	3	304.0	265	7	57	123	26-6	3	2.31
Hal Schumacher	R	25	35	30	9	3	215.1	234	15	69	75	11-13	1	3.47
Al Smith	L	28	43	30	9	4	209.1	217	16	69	89	14-13	2	3.78
F. Fitzsimmons	R	34	28	17	7	0	141.0	147	6	39	35	10-7	2	3.32
Frank Gabler	R	24	43	14	5	0	161.2	170	11	34	46	9-8	6	3.12
Dick Coffman	R	29	42	2	0	0	101.2	119	7	23	26	7-5	7	3.90
Harry Gumbert	R	26	39	15	3	0	140.2	157	7	54	52	11-3	0	3.90
Slick Castleman	R	22	29	12	2	1	111.2	148	6	56	54	4-7	1	5.64
Firpo Marberry†	R	37	1	0	0	0	0.1	1	0	0	0	0-0	0	0.00

1936 Chicago Cubs 2nd NL 87-67 .565 5.0 GB

Charlie Grimm

Player	Gm by Position	B	Age	G	AB	R	H	2B	3B	HR	RBI	BB	SO	SB	Avg	OBP	Slg
Gabby Hartnett	C114	R	35	121	424	49	130	25	6	7	64	30	36	0	.307	.361	.443
Phil Cavarretta	1B115	L	19	124	458	55	125	18	1	9	56	17	36	8	.273	.306	.376
Billy Herman	2B153	R	26	153	632	101	211	57	7	5	93	59	30	5	.334	.392	.470
Stan Hack	3B140,1B11	L	26	149	561	102	167	27	4	6	78	89	39	17	.298	.396	.392
Billy Jurges	SS116	R	28	118	429	51	120	25	1	1	42	23	25	4	.280	.321	.350
Frank Demaree	OF154	R	26	154	605	93	212	34	3	16	96	49	30	4	.350	.400	.496
Augie Galan	OF145	S	24	145	575	74	152	26	4	8	81	67	50	16	.264	.344	.365
Ethan Allen†	OF89	R	32	91	373	47	110	18	6	3	39	13	30	12	.295	.322	.399
Ken O'Dea	C55	L	23	80	189	36	58	10	3	2	38	38	18	0	.307	.423	.423
Woody English	SS42,3B17,2B1	R	29	64	182	33	45	9	0	0	20	40	28	1	.247	.394	.297
Johnny Gill	OF41	L	31	71	174	20	44	8	0	7	28	13	19	0	.253	.309	.420
Charlie Grimm	1B35	L	37	39	132	13	33	4	0	1	16	5	8	0	.250	.277	.303
Chuck Klein†	OF29	L	31	29	109	19	32	5	0	5	18	16	14	0	.294	.384	.477
Tuck Stainback	OF26	R	24	44	75	13	13	3	0	1	5	6	14	1	.173	.235	.253
Gene Lillard	SS4,3B3	R	22	19	34	6	7	1	0	0	2	3	8	0	.206	.270	.235
Walter Stephenson	C4	R	25	6	12	0	1	0	0	0	1	0	5	0	.083	.083	.083

Pitcher	T	Age	G	GS	CG	ShO	IP	H	HR	BB	SO	W-L	Sv	ERA
Bill Lee	R	26	43	33	20	4	258.2	238	14	93	102	18-11	1	3.31
Lon Warneke	R	27	40	29	13	4	240.1	246	10	76	113	16-13	1	3.45
Larry French	L	28	43	28	16	4	252.1	262	16	54	104	18-9	3	3.39
Tex Carleton	R	29	35	26	12	4	197.1	204	14	67	88	14-10	1	3.65
Curt Davis†	R	32	24	20	10	0	153.0	146	11	31	52	11-9	1	3.00
Roy Henshaw	L	24	39	14	6	2	129.1	152	8	56	69	6-5	1	3.97
Charlie Root	R	37	33	4	0	0	73.2	81	3	20	32	3-6	1	4.15
Clay Bryant	R	24	26	0	0	0	57.1	57	0	24	35	1-2	0	3.30
Fabian Kowalik†	R	28	6	0	0	0	16.0	24	1	7	1	0-2	1	6.75
Clyde Shoun	L	24	4	0	0	0	4.1	3	0	6	1	0-0	0	12.46

1936 St. Louis Cardinals 2nd NL 87-67 .565 5.0 GB — Frank Frisch

Player	Gm by Position	B	Age	G	AB	R	H	2B	3B	HR	RBI	BB	SO	SB	Avg	OBP	Slg
Spud Davis	C103,3B2	R	31	112	363	24	99	26	2	4	59	35	34	0	.273	.342	.388
Johnny Mize	1B97,OF8	L	23	126	414	76	136	30	8	19	93	50	32	1	.329	.402	.577
Stu Martin	2B83,SS3	L	22	92	332	63	99	21	4	6	41	29	27	17	.298	.356	.440
Charlie Gelbert	3B60,SS28,2B8	R	30	93	280	33	64	15	2	3	27	25	26	2	.229	.292	.329
Leo Durocher	SS136	R	30	136	510	57	146	22	3	1	58	29	47	3	.286	.327	.347
Joe Medwick	OF155	R	24	155	636	115	223	64	13	18	138	34	33	3	.351	.387	.577
Terry Moore	OF133	R	24	143	590	85	156	39	4	5	47	37	52	9	.264	.309	.369
Pepper Martin	OF127,3B15,P1	R	32	143	572	121	177	36	11	11	76	58	66	23	.309	.373	.469
Frankie Frisch	2B60,3B22,SS1	S	37	93	303	40	83	10	0	1	26	36	10	2	.274	.353	.317
Ripper Collins	1B61,OF9	S	32	103	277	48	81	15	3	13	48	48	30	1	.292	.399	.509
Bruce Ogrodowski	C85	R	24	94	237	28	54	15	1	1	20	10	20	0	.228	.259	.312
Art Garibaldi	3B46,2B24	R	28	71	232	30	64	12	0	1	20	16	30	3	.276	.323	.341
Lynn King	OF34	L	28	78	100	12	19	2	1	0	10	9	14	2	.190	.257	.230
Don Gutteridge	3B23	R	24	23	91	13	29	3	4	3	16	1	14	3	.319	.326	.538
Chick Fullis	OF26	R	32	47	89	15	25	6	1	0	6	7	11	0	.281	.333	.371
Eddie Morgan	OF4	L	21	8	18	4	5	0	0	1	3	2	4	0	.278	.350	.444
Mike Ryba	P14,C4	R	33	18	18	2	3	0	0	0	3	1	7	0	.167	.211	.167
Johnny Vergez†	3B8	R	29	8	18	1	3	1	0	0	1	1	3	0	.167	.211	.222
Lou Scoffic	OF3	R	23	4	7	2	3	0	0	0	2	1	2	0	.429	.500	.429
Pat Ankenman	SS1	R	23	1	3	0	0	0	0	0	0	0	3	0	.000	.000	.000
Walter Alston	1B1	R	24	1	1	0	0	0	0	0	0	0	1	0	.000	.000	.000
Heinie Schuble	3B1	R	29	2	0	0	0	0	0	0	0	0	0	0	—	—	—

Pitcher	T	Age	G	GS	CG	ShO	IP	H	HR	BB	SO	W-L	Sv	ERA
Dizzy Dean	R	26	51	34	28	2	315.0	310	21	53	195	24-13	11	3.17
Roy Parmelee	R	29	37	28	9	0	221.0	226	13	107	79	11-11	2	4.56
Jim Winford	R	26	39	23	10	1	192.0	203	10	68	72	11-10	3	3.80
Paul Dean	R	22	17	14	5	0	92.0	113	3	20	28	5-5	1	4.60
Bill Walker	L	32	21	13	4	1	79.2	106	5	27	22	5-6	1	5.87
Si Johnson†	R	29	12	9	3	1	61.2	82	4	11	21	5-3	0	4.38
Wild Bill Hallahan†	L	33	9	6	1	0	37.0	58	4	17	16	2-2	0	6.32
Cotton Pippen	R	25	6	3	0	0	21.0	37	5	8	8	0-2	0	7.71
Ed Heusser	R	27	42	3	0	0	104.1	130	6	38	26	7-3	3	5.43
Jesse Haines	R	42	25	9	4	0	99.1	110	4	21	19	7-5	1	3.90
George Earnshaw†	R	36	20	6	1	0	57.2	80	4	20	28	2-1	1	6.40
Mike Ryba	R	33	14	0	0	0	45.0	55	3	16	25	5-1	0	5.40
Flint Rhem	R	35	10	4	0	0	26.2	49	2	9	7	2-1	0	6.75
Les Munns	R	27	7	1	0	0	24.0	23	2	12	4	0-3	1	4.50
Bill McGee	R	26	7	2	0	0	16.0	23	3	4	8	1-1	0	7.88
Bill Cox	R	23	2	0	0	0	2.2	4	0	1	1	0-0	0	6.75
Pepper Martin	R	32	1	0	0	0	2.0	1	0	2	0	0-0	0	0.00
Nels Potter	R	24	1	0	0	0	1.0	0	0	0	0	0-0	0	0.00

1936 Pittsburgh Pirates 4th NL 84-70 .545 8.0 GB — Pie Traynor

Player	Gm by Position	B	Age	G	AB	R	H	2B	3B	HR	RBI	BB	SO	SB	Avg	OBP	Slg
Tom Padden	C87	R	27	88	281	22	70	9	2	1	31	22	41	0	.249	.304	.306
Gus Suhr	1B156	L	30	156	583	111	182	33	12	11	118	95	34	8	.312	.410	.467
Pep Young	2B123	R	28	125	475	47	118	23	10	6	77	29	52	3	.248	.293	.377
Bill Brubaker	3B145	R	25	145	554	77	160	27	4	6	102	50	96	5	.289	.352	.384
Arky Vaughan	SS156	L	24	156	568	122	190	30	11	9	78	118	21	6	.335	.453	.474
Woody Jensen	OF153	L	28	153	696	98	197	34	10	10	58	16	19	2	.283	.305	.404
Paul Waner	OF145	L	33	148	585	107	218	53	9	5	94	74	29	7	.373	.446	.520
Lloyd Waner	OF92	L	30	106	414	67	133	13	8	1	31	31	5	1	.321	.369	.399
Al Todd	C70	R	34	76	267	28	73	10	5	2	28	11	24	4	.273	.307	.371
Fred Schulte	OF55	R	35	74	238	28	62	7	3	1	17	20	20	1	.261	.320	.328
Cookie Lavagetto	2B37,3B13,SS1	R	23	60	197	21	48	15	2	2	26	15	13	0	.244	.300	.371
Bud Hafey	OF29	R	23	39	118	19	25	6	1	4	13	10	27	0	.212	.273	.381
Hal Finney	C14	R	30	21	35	3	0	0	0	0	3	0	8	0	.000	.000	.000
Earl Browne	OF4,1B1	L	25	8	23	7	7	1	2	0	3	1	4	0	.304	.333	.522
Johnny Dickshot	OF1	R	26	9	9	2	2	0	0	0	1	1	2	0	.222	.300	.222

Pitcher	T	Age	G	GS	CG	ShO	IP	H	HR	BB	SO	W-L	Sv	ERA
Cy Blanton	R	27	44	32	15	4	235.2	235	9	55	127	13-15	3	3.51
Bill Swift	R	28	45	31	17	0	262.1	275	18	63	92	16-16	2	4.01
Jim Weaver	R	32	38	31	11	1	225.2	239	12	74	108	14-8	0	4.31
Red Lucas	R	34	27	22	12	0	175.2	178	7	26	53	15-4	0	3.18
Jack Tising	R	32	10	6	1	0	47.0	52	5	24	27	1-3	0	4.21
Russ Bauers	R	22	1	1	0	0	1.1	2	0	4	0	0-0	0	33.75
Mace Brown	R	27	47	10	3	0	165.0	178	8	55	56	10-11	3	3.87
Ralph Birkofer	L	27	34	13	2	0	109.1	130	4	41	44	7-5	0	4.69
Waite Hoyt	R	36	22	9	6	0	116.2	115	5	20	37	7-5	1	2.70
Guy Bush†	R	34	16	0	0	0	34.2	49	3	11	10	1-3	2	5.97
Johnny Welch†	R	29	9	1	0	0	22.0	22	3	6	5	0-0	1	4.50

1936 Cincinnati Reds 5th NL 74-80 .481 18.0 GB — Chuck Dressen

Player	Gm by Position	B	Age	G	AB	R	H	2B	3B	HR	RBI	BB	SO	SB	Avg	OBP	Slg
Ernie Lombardi	C105	R	28	121	387	42	129	23	2	12	68	19	16	1	.333	.375	.496
Les Scarsella	1B115	L	22	115	485	63	152	21	9	3	65	14	36	6	.313	.335	.412
Alex Kampouris	2B119,OF1	R	23	122	355	43	85	10	4	5	46	24	46	3	.239	.289	.332
Lew Riggs	3B140	L	26	141	538	69	138	20	12	6	57	38	33	5	.257	.314	.372
Billy Myers	SS98	R	25	98	323	45	87	9	6	6	27	28	56	6	.269	.328	.390
Kiki Cuyler	OF140	R	37	144	567	96	185	29	11	7	74	47	67	16	.326	.380	.453
Ival Goodman	OF120	L	27	136	489	81	139	15	14	17	71	38	53	6	.284	.347	.476
Babe Herman	OF92,1B4	L	33	119	380	59	106	25	2	13	71	39	36	4	.279	.348	.458
Tommy Thevenow	SS68,2B33,3B12	R	32	106	321	25	75	7	2	0	36	15	23	2	.234	.268	.268
Hub Walker	OF73,C1,1B1	L	29	92	258	49	71	18	1	4	23	35	32	8	.275	.366	.399
Gilly Campbell	C71,1B1	L	28	89	235	28	63	13	1	1	40	43	14	2	.268	.384	.345
Calvin Chapman	OF31,2B23	L	25	96	219	35	54	7	3	1	22	16	19	5	.247	.301	.320
Sammy Byrd	OF37	R	28	59	141	17	35	8	0	2	13	11	11	0	.248	.303	.348
George McQuinn	1B38	L	26	38	134	5	27	3	4	0	13	10	22	0	.201	.262	.284
Lee Handley	2B16,3B7	R	22	24	78	10	24	1	0	2	8	7	16	3	.308	.365	.397
Eddie Joost	SS7,2B5	R	20	13	26	1	4	1	0	0	1	2	5	0	.154	.214	.192
Dee Moore	P2,C1	R	22	6	10	4	4	2	1	0	1	0	3	0	.400	.400	.800
Eddie Miller	SS4,2B1	R	19	5	10	0	1	0	0	0	0	1	1	0	.100	.182	.100

Pitcher	T	Age	G	GS	CG	ShO	IP	H	HR	BB	SO	W-L	Sv	ERA
Paul Derringer	R	29	51	37	13	2	282.1	331	11	42	121	19-19	5	4.02
Al Hollingsworth	L	28	29	25	9	0	184.0	204	4	66	76	9-10	0	4.16
Gene Schott	R	22	31	22	8	1	180.0	184	7	73	65	11-11	1	3.80
Wild Bill Hallahan†	L	33	23	19	5	2	135.0	150	3	57	32	5-9	0	4.33
Peaches Davis	R	31	26	15	5	0	125.2	139	7	36	32	8-8	5	3.58
Lee Grissom	L	28	6	4	0	0	24.1	33	1	9	13	1-1	0	6.29
Dee Moore	R	22	2	1	0	0	7.0	3	0	2	3	0-0	0	0.00
Don Brennan	R	32	41	4	0	0	94.1	117	2	35	40	5-2	9	4.39
Lee Stine	R	22	40	13	5	1	121.2	157	6	41	26	3-8	2	5.03
Benny Frey	R	30	31	12	5	0	131.1	164	5	30	20	10-8	0	4.25
Whitey Hilcher	R	27	14	1	0	0	35.0	44	3	14	10	1-2	0	6.17
Jake Mooty	R	23	8	0	0	0	13.2	10	0	4	11	0-1	1	3.95
Emmett Nelson	R	31	6	1	0	0	17.0	24	1	4	3	1-0	0	3.18
Tony Freitas	L	28	4	0	0	0	7.0	6	0	2	1	0-2	0	1.29
Si Johnson†	R	29	2	0	0	0	4.0	7	1	0	2	0-0	0	13.50
Whitey Moore	R	24	1	0	0	0	5.0	3	0	3	4	1-0	0	5.40

1936 Boston Braves 6th NL 71-83 .461 21.0 GB — Bill McKechnie

Player	Gm by Position	B	Age	G	AB	R	H	2B	3B	HR	RBI	BB	SO	SB	Avg	OBP	Slg
Al Lopez	C127,1B1	R	27	128	426	46	103	12	5	7	50	41	41	1	.242	.311	.343
Buck Jordan	1B136	L	29	138	555	81	179	27	5	3	66	45	22	2	.323	.375	.405
Tony Cuccinello	2B150	R	28	150	565	68	174	26	3	7	86	58	49	1	.308	.374	.402
Joe Coscarart	3B97,SS6,2B1	R	26	104	367	28	90	11	2	2	44	19	37	0	.245	.292	.302
Billy Urbanski	SS80,3B38	R	33	122	494	55	129	17	5	0	26	31	42	2	.261	.310	.316
Gene Moore	OF151	L	26	151	637	91	185	38	12	13	67	40	80	6	.290	.335	.449
Hal Lee	OF150	R	31	152	565	46	143	24	7	3	64	52	50	4	.253	.318	.336
Wally Berger	OF133	R	30	138	534	88	154	23	3	25	91	53	84	1	.288	.361	.483
Rabbit Warstler†	SS74	R	32	74	304	27	64	6	0	0	17	22	33	2	.211	.266	.230
Tommy Thompson	OF39,1B25	L	26	106	266	37	76	9	0	4	36	31	12	3	.286	.362	.365
Mickey Haslin†	3B17,2B7	R	25	36	104	14	29	1	2	2	11	5	9	0	.279	.312	.385
Ray Mueller	C23	R	24	24	71	5	14	4	0	0	5	5	17	0	.197	.250	.254
Bill Lewis	C21	R	31	29	62	11	19	2	0	0	3	12	7	0	.306	.419	.339
Bobby Reis	P35,OF2	R	27	37	60	3	13	2	0	0	5	3	6	0	.217	.254	.250
Pinky Whitney†	3B10	R	31	10	40	1	7	0	0	0	5	2	4	0	.175	.233	.175
Ed Moriarty		R	23	6	6	1	1	0	0	0	0	0	1	0	.167	.167	.167
Fabian Kowalik†	P1,OF1	S	28	2	5	0	2	0	0	0	1	0	1	0	.400	.400	.400
Andy Pilney		R	23	3	2	0	0	0	0	0	0	0	1	0	.000	.000	.000
Swede Larsen	2B2	R	22	3	3	1	0	0	0	0	0	0	0	0	.000	.000	.000

Pitcher	T	Age	G	GS	CG	ShO	IP	H	HR	BB	SO	W-L	Sv	ERA
Danny MacFayden	R	31	37	31	21	2	266.2	268	5	66	86	17-13	0	2.87
Tiny Chaplin	R	30	40	31	14	0	231.2	273	21	62	86	10-15	2	4.12
Johnny Lanning	R	25	28	20	3	1	153.0	154	9	55	33	7-11	0	3.65
Ray Benge†	R	34	21	19	2	0	115.0	161	6	38	32	7-9	0	5.79
Guy Bush†	R	34	15	11	5	0	90.1	98	2	20	28	4-5	0	3.39
Roy Weir	L	25	12	7	3	2	57.1	53	0	24	29	4-3	0	2.83
Wayne Osborne	R	23	5	3	0	0	20.0	31	1	9	8	1-1	0	5.85
Bob Brown	R	25	2	2	0	0	8.1	10	1	3	5	0-2	0	5.40
Fabian Kowalik†	R	28	1	1	1	0	9.0	18	0	2	0	0-1	0	8.00
Art Doll	R	23	1	1	0	0	8.0	11	1	2	2	0-1	0	3.38
Gene Ford	R	24	2	1	0	0	2.0	2	0	3	0	0-0	0	13.50
Bobby Reis	R	27	35	5	3	0	138.2	152	7	74	25	6-5	0	4.48
Bob Smith	R	41	35	11	5	2	136.0	142	3	35	36	6-7	8	3.77
Ben Cantwell	R	34	34	12	4	0	133.1	127	8	35	42	9-9	2	3.04
Al Blanche	R	26	11	0	0	0	16.0	20	1	8	4	0-1	1	6.19
Amby Murray	L	23	4	1	0	0	11.0	15	1	3	2	0-0	0	4.09
Jim McCloskey	L	26	4	1	0	0	8.0	14	0	3	2	0-0	0	11.25
Johnny Babich	R	23	3	0	0	0	6.0	11	1	6	1	0-0	0	10.50
Hal Weafer	R	22	1	0	0	0	3.0	6	1	3	0	0-0	0	12.00

1936 Brooklyn Dodgers 7th NL 67-87 .435 25.0 GB — Casey Stengel

Player	Gm by Position	B	Age	G	AB	R	H	2B	3B	HR	RBI	BB	SO	SB	Avg	OBP	Slg
Ray Berres	C105	R	28	105	267	16	64	10	1	1	13	14	35	1	.240	.280	.296
Buddy Hassett	1B156	L	24	156	635	79	197	29	11	3	82	35	17	5	.310	.350	.405
Jimmy Jordan	2B98,SS9,3B6	R	28	115	398	26	93	15	1	2	28	15	21	2	.234	.262	.291
Joe Stripp	3B106	R	33	110	439	51	139	31	1	1	60	22	12	2	.317	.351	.399
Lonny Frey	SS117,2B30,OF1	L	25	148	524	63	146	29	4	4	60	71	56	7	.279	.369	.372
Johnny Cooney	OF130	R	35	130	507	71	143	17	5	0	30	24	15	3	.282	.315	.335
George Watkins†	OF98	L	36	105	364	54	93	24	6	4	43	38	34	5	.255	.334	.387
Frenchy Bordagaray	OF92,2B11,3B6	R	26	125	372	63	117	21	3	4	31	17	42	12	.315	.346	.419
Jim Bucher	3B39,2B32,OF30	L	25	110	370	49	93	12	8	2	41	29	27	5	.251	.306	.343
Babe Phelps	C98,OF1	L	28	115	319	36	117	23	2	5	57	27	18	1	.367	.421	.498
Eddie Wilson	OF47	L	26	52	173	28	60	8	1	3	25	14	25	3	.347	.402	.457
Ben Geraghty	SS31,2B9,3B5	R	23	51	129	11	25	4	0	0	9	8	16	4	.194	.241	.225
Danny Taylor	OF31	R	35	43	116	12	34	6	0	2	15	11	14	2	.293	.359	.397
Freddy Lindstrom	OF26	R	30	26	106	12	28	4	0	0	10	5	7	1	.264	.297	.302
Randy Moore	OF21	L	30	42	88	4	21	3	0	0	14	8	1	0	.239	.302	.273
Tom Winsett	OF21	L	26	22	85	13	20	7	0	1	18	11	14	0	.235	.330	.353
Sid Gautreaux	C15	S	24	75	71	8	19	3	0	0	16	9	7	0	.268	.358	.310
Ox Eckhardt	OF10	L	34	16	44	5	8	1	0	1	6	5	2	0	.182	.265	.273
Nick Tremark	OF8	L	23	8	32	6	8	2	0	0	1	3	2	0	.250	.333	.313
Jack Radtke	2B14,3B5,SS4	S	23	33	31	8	3	0	0	0	2	4	9	3	.097	.200	.097
Johnny Hudson	SS4,2B1	R	24	6	12	1	2	0	0	0	0	2	1	0	.167	.286	.167
Dick Siebert	OF1	L	24	2	2	0	0	0	0	0	0	0	0	0	.000	.000	.000

Pitcher	T	Age	G	GS	CG	ShO	IP	H	HR	BB	SO	W-L	Sv	ERA
Van Lingle Mungo	R	25	45	37	22	2	311.2	275	8	118	238	18-19	3	3.35
Fred Frankhouse	R	32	41	31	9	1	234.1	236	18	89	84	13-10	2	3.65
Ed Brandt	L	31	38	29	12	1	234.0	246	14	65	104	11-13	2	3.50
George Earnshaw†	R	36	19	13	4	1	93.0	113	7	30	40	4-9	1	5.32
George Jeffcoat	R	22	40	5	3	0	95.2	84	7	63	46	5-6	3	4.52
Max Butcher	R	25	38	15	5	0	147.2	154	11	59	55	6-6	2	3.96
Tom Baker	R	23	35	8	2	0	87.2	98	3	48	35	1-8	2	4.72
Watty Clark	L	34	33	16	1	1	120.0	162	11	28	28	7-11	2	4.43
Dutch Leonard	R	27	16	0	0	0	32.0	34	2	5	8	0-0	1	3.66
Hank Winston	R	32	14	0	0	0	32.1	40	2	16	8	1-3	0	6.12
Harry Eisenstat	L	20	5	2	1	0	14.1	22	1	6	5	1-2	0	5.65
Tom Zachary†	L	40	1	0	0	0	0.1	2	0	1	0	0-0	0	54.00

1936 Philadelphia Phillies 8th NL 54-100 .351 38.0 GB — Jimmie Wilson

Player	Gm by Position	B	Age	G	AB	R	H	2B	3B	HR	RBI	BB	SO	SB	Avg	OBP	Slg
Earl Grace	C65	L	29	86	221	24	55	11	0	4	32	34	20	0	.249	.352	.353
Dolph Camilli	1B150	L	29	151	530	106	167	29	13	28	102	116	84	5	.315	.441	.577
Chile Gomez	2B71,SS40	R	27	108	332	24	77	4	1	0	28	14	32	0	.232	.265	.250
Pinky Whitney†	3B111	R	31	114	411	44	121	17	3	6	59	37	33	2	.294	.354	.394
Leo Norris	SS121,2B38	R	28	154	581	64	154	27	4	11	76	39	79	4	.265	.315	.382
Chuck Klein†	OF117	L	31	117	492	83	152	30	7	20	86	33	45	6	.309	.352	.520
Johnny Moore	OF112	L	34	124	472	85	155	24	3	16	68	26	22	1	.328	.365	.494
Ernie Sulik	OF105	L	25	122	404	69	116	14	4	6	36	40	22	4	.287	.353	.386
Lou Chiozza	OF90,2B33,3B26	L	26	144	572	83	170	32	6	1	48	37	39	17	.297	.346	.379
Jimmie Wilson	C63,1B1	R	35	85	230	25	64	12	0	1	27	12	21	5	.278	.314	.343
Bill Atwood	C53	R	24	71	192	21	58	9	2	2	29	11	15	0	.302	.346	.401
Ethan Allen†	OF30	R	32	30	125	21	37	3	1	1	9	4	8	4	.296	.318	.360
Bucky Walters	P40,2B1,3B1	R	27	64	121	12	29	10	1	1	16	7	15	0	.240	.281	.364
Chuck Sheerin	2B17,3B13,SS5	R	27	39	72	4	19	4	0	0	4	7	18	0	.264	.329	.319
George Watkins†	OF17	L	36	19	70	7	17	4	0	2	5	5	13	2	.243	.293	.386
Mickey Haslin†	2B12,3B5	R	25	16	64	6	22	1	1	0	6	3	5	0	.344	.373	.391
Fabian Kowalik†	P22,OF3	S	28	42	57	2	13	1	0	0	7	2	8	0	.228	.254	.246
Morrie Arnovich	OF13	R	25	13	48	4	15	3	0	1	7	1	3	0	.313	.353	.438
Johnny Vergez†	3B12	R	29	15	40	4	11	2	0	1	5	3	11	0	.275	.326	.400
Stan Sperry	2B15	L	22	20	37	2	5	3	0	0	4	3	5	0	.135	.200	.216
Gene Corbett	1B6	L	22	6	21	1	3	0	0	0	2	2	3	0	.143	.217	.143
Walt Bashore	OF6,3B1	R	26	10	10	1	2	0	0	0	0	1	3	0	.200	.273	.200
Joe Holden		L	23	1	1	0	0	0	0	0	0	0	0	0	.000	.000	.000

Pitcher	T	Age	G	GS	CG	ShO	IP	H	HR	BB	SO	W-L	Sv	ERA
Bucky Walters	R	27	40	33	15	4	258.0	284	11	115	66	11-21	0	4.26
Joe Bowman	R	26	40	28	12	0	203.2	243	14	53	80	9-20	1	5.04
Orville Jorgens	R	28	39	21	4	0	167.1	196	16	69	58	8-8	0	4.79
Curt Davis†	R	32	10	8	3	0	60.1	71	6	19	18	2-4	0	4.62
Hugh Mulcahy	R	22	3	2	2	0	22.2	20	0	12	2	1-1	0	3.18
Elmer Burkart	R	19	2	2	0	0	7.2	4	0	12	2	0-0	0	3.52
Claude Passeau	R	27	49	21	8	2	217.1	247	7	55	85	11-15	3	3.48
Syl Johnson	R	35	39	8	1	0	111.0	129	10	29	48	5-7	7	4.30
Fabian Kowalik†	R	28	22	8	2	0	77.0	100	5	31	19	1-5	0	5.38
Euel Moore	R	28	20	5	1	0	54.1	76	4	12	19	2-3	1	6.96
Pete Sivess	R	22	17	6	2	0	65.0	84	6	36	22	3-4	0	4.57
Ray Benge†	R	34	15	6	0	0	45.2	70	3	19	13	1-4	1	4.73
Hal Kelleher	R	22	14	4	1	0	44.0	60	2	29	13	0-5	0	5.32
Tom Zachary†	L	40	7	2	0	0	20.1	28	2	11	8	0-3	1	7.97
Herb Harris	L	23	4	0	0	0	7.0	14	0	5	0	0-0	0	10.29
Lefty Bertrand	L	27	1	0	0	0	2.0	3	1	2	1	0-0	0	9.00
Pretzels Pezzullo	L	25	1	0	0	0	2.0	1	0	6	0	0-0	0	4.50

»1937 New York Yankees 1st AL 102-52 .662 — Joe McCarthy

Player	Gm by Position	B	Age	G	AB	R	H	2B	3B	HR	RBI	BB	SO	SB	Avg	OBP	Slg
Bill Dickey	C137	L	30	140	530	87	176	35	2	29	133	73	22	3	.332	.417	.570
Lou Gehrig	1B157	L	34	157	569	138	200	37	9	37	159	127	49	4	.351	.473	.643
Tony Lazzeri	2B125	R	33	126	446	56	109	21	3	14	70	71	76	7	.244	.348	.399
Red Rolfe	3B154	L	28	154	648	143	179	34	10	4	62	90	53	4	.276	.365	.378
Frankie Crosetti	SS147	R	26	149	611	127	143	29	5	11	49	86	105	13	.234	.340	.352
Joe DiMaggio	OF150	R	22	151	621	151	215	35	15	46	167	64	37	3	.346	.412	.673
Myril Hoag	OF99	R	29	106	362	48	109	19	8	3	46	33	33	4	.301	.364	.423
Jake Powell	OF94	R	28	97	365	54	96	22	3	3	45	25	36	7	.263	.314	.364
George Selkirk	OF69	L	29	78	256	49	84	13	5	18	68	34	24	8	.328	.411	.629
Tommy Henrich	OF59	L	24	67	206	39	66	14	5	8	42	35	17	4	.320	.419	.553
Don Heffner	2B38,SS13,3B3*	R	26	60	201	23	50	6	5	0	21	19	19	1	.249	.314	.328
Joe Glenn	C24	R	28	25	53	6	15	2	2	0	4	10	11	0	.283	.397	.396
Roy Johnson†	OF12	L	34	12	51	5	15	3	0	0	6	3	2	1	.294	.333	.353
Art Jorgens	C11	R	32	13	23	3	3	1	0	0	3	2	5	0	.130	.200	.174
Jack Saltzgaver	1B4	L	34	17	11	6	2	0	0	0	0	3	4	0	.182	.357	.182
Babe Dahlgren		R	25	1	1	0	0	0	0	0	0	0	0	0	.000	.000	.000

D. Heffner, 1 G at 1B, 1 G at OF

Pitcher	T	Age	G	GS	CG	ShO	IP	H	HR	BB	SO	W-L	Sv	ERA
Lefty Gomez	L	28	34	34	25	6	278.1	233	10	93	194	21-11	0	2.33
Red Ruffing	R	33	31	31	22	4	256.1	242	17	68	131	20-7	0	2.98
Bump Hadley	R	32	29	25	6	0	178.1	199	16	83	70	11-8	0	5.30
Monte Pearson	R	27	22	20	7	1	144.2	145	6	64	71	9-3	1	3.17
Kemp Wicker	L	30	16	10	6	1	88.0	107	8	26	14	7-3	0	4.40
Spud Chandler	R	29	12	10	6	2	82.1	79	8	20	31	7-4	0	2.84
Johnny Broaca	R	27	7	6	3	0	44.0	58	5	17	9	1-4	0	4.70
Joe Vance	R	31	2	2	0	0	15.0	11	2	9	3	1-0	0	3.00
Johnny Murphy	R	28	39	4	0	0	110.0	121	7	50	36	13-4	10	4.17
Pat Malone	R	34	28	9	3	0	92.0	109	5	35	49	4-4	6	5.48
Frank Makosky	R	27	26	1	1	0	58.0	64	6	24	27	5-2	3	4.97
Ivy Andrews†	R	30	11	5	3	1	49.0	49	2	17	17	3-2	1	3.12

1937 Detroit Tigers 2nd AL 89-65 .578 13.0 GB — Mickey Cochrane (16-13)/Del Baker (34-20)/Mickey Cochrane (39-32)

Player	Gm by Position	B	Age	G	AB	R	H	2B	3B	HR	RBI	BB	SO	SB	Avg	OBP	Slg
Rudy York	C54,3B41	R	23	104	375	72	115	18	3	35	103	41	52	3	.307	.375	.651
Hank Greenberg	1B154	R	26	154	594	137	200	49	14	40	183	102	101	8	.337	.436	.668
Charlie Gehringer	2B142	L	34	144	564	133	209	40	1	14	96	90	25	11	.371	.458	.520
Marv Owen	3B106	R	31	107	396	48	114	22	5	1	45	41	24	3	.288	.358	.376
Billy Rogell	SS146	S	32	146	536	85	148	30	7	8	64	83	48	5	.276	.376	.403
Gee Walker	OF151	R	29	151	635	105	213	42	4	18	113	41	74	23	.335	.380	.499
Pete Fox	OF143	R	28	148	628	116	208	39	8	12	82	41	43	12	.331	.372	.476
Jo-Jo White	OF82	L	28	94	305	50	75	5	7	0	21	50	40	12	.246	.354	.308
Chet Laabs	OF62	R	25	72	242	31	58	13	5	8	37	24	66	6	.240	.308	.434
Goose Goslin	OF40,1B1	L	36	79	181	30	43	11	1	4	35	35	18	0	.238	.367	.376
Birdie Tebbetts	C48	R	24	50	162	15	31	4	3	2	16	10	13	0	.191	.238	.290
Mickey Cochrane	C27	L	34	27	98	27	30	10	1	2	12	25	4	0	.306	.452	.490
Ray Hayworth	C28	R	33	30	78	9	21	2	0	1	8	14	15	0	.269	.394	.333
Gil English†	2B12,3B6	R	27	18	65	6	17	1	0	1	6	6	4	1	.262	.333	.323
Cliff Bolton	C13	L	30	27	57	6	15	2	0	1	7	8	6	0	.263	.354	.351
Charlie Gelbert†	SS16	R	31	20	47	4	4	2	0	0	1	4	11	0	.085	.157	.128
Flea Clifton	3B7,SS4,2B3	R	27	15	43	4	5	1	0	0	2	7	10	3	.116	.240	.140
Babe Herman	OF2	L	34	17	20	2	6	3	0	0	3	1	6	2	.300	.364	.450

Pitcher	T	Age	G	GS	CG	ShO	IP	H	HR	BB	SO	W-L	Sv	ERA
Eldon Auker	R	26	39	32	19	1	252.2	250	13	97	73	17-9	1	3.88
Tommy Bridges	R	30	34	31	18	3	245.1	267	15	91	138	15-12	0	4.07
Roxie Lawson	R	31	37	29	15	0	217.1	236	17	115	68	18-7	1	5.26
Jake Wade	L	25	33	25	7	1	165.1	160	13	107	69	7-10	0	5.39
Boots Poffenberger	R	21	29	16	5	0	137.1	147	8	79	35	10-5	3	4.65
George Gill	R	28	31	10	4	1	127.2	146	11	42	40	11-4	1	4.51
Slick Coffman	R	26	28	5	1	0	101.0	121	8	39	22	7-5	0	4.37
Jack Russell	R	31	25	0	0	0	40.1	63	4	20	10	2-5	4	7.59
Pat McLaughlin	R	26	10	3	0	0	32.2	39	3	16	8	0-2	0	6.34
Schoolboy Rowe	R	27	10	2	1	0	31.1	49	7	9	6	1-4	0	8.62
Vic Sorrell	R	36	7	2	0	0	17.0	25	3	8	11	0-2	1	9.00
Clyde Hatter	L	28	3	0	0	0	9.1	17	0	11	4	1-0	0	11.57
Bob Logan†	L	27	1	0	0	0	0.2	1	0	1	1	0-0	0	0.00

1937 Chicago White Sox 3rd AL 86-68 .558 16.0 GB — Jimmy Dykes

Player	Gm by Position	B	Age	G	AB	R	H	2B	3B	HR	RBI	BB	SO	SB	Avg	OBP	Slg
Luke Sewell	C118	R	36	122	412	51	111	21	6	1	61	46	18	4	.269	.343	.357
Zeke Bonura	1B115	R	28	116	447	79	154	41	2	19	100	49	24	5	.345	.412	.573
Jackie Hayes	2B143	R	30	143	573	63	131	27	4	2	79	41	37	4	.229	.282	.300
Tony Piet	3B86,2B13	R	30	100	332	34	78	15	1	4	38	32	36	14	.235	.314	.322
Luke Appling	SS154	R	30	154	574	98	182	42	8	4	77	86	28	18	.317	.407	.439
Dixie Walker	OF154	L	26	154	593	105	179	28	16	9	95	78	26	1	.302	.383	.449
Rip Radcliff	OF139	L	31	144	584	105	190	38	10	4	79	53	25	6	.325	.383	.445
Mike Kreevich	OF138	R	29	144	583	94	176	29	16	12	73	43	45	10	.302	.350	.468
Boze Berger	3B40,2B1,SS1	R	27	52	130	19	31	5	0	5	13	15	24	1	.238	.322	.392
Mule Haas	1B32,OF2	L	33	54	111	8	23	3	3	0	15	16	10	1	.207	.313	.288
Merv Connors	3B28	R	23	28	103	12	24	4	1	2	12	14	19	2	.233	.325	.350
Larry Rosenthal	OF25	L	27	58	97	20	28	5	3	0	9	9	20	1	.289	.355	.402
Jimmy Dykes	1B15,3B11	R	40	30	85	10	26	5	0	1	23	9	7	0	.306	.372	.400
Hank Steinbacher	OF15	L	24	26	73	13	19	4	1	1	9	4	7	2	.260	.299	.384
Merv Shea	C25	R	36	25	71	7	15	1	0	0	5	15	10	1	.211	.349	.225
Tony Rensa	C23	R	35	26	57	10	17	5	1	0	5	8	6	3	.298	.385	.421

Pitcher	T	Age	G	GS	CG	ShO	IP	H	HR	BB	SO	W-L	Sv	ERA
Vern Kennedy	R	30	32	30	15	1	221.0	238	16	124	114	14-13	0	5.09
Thornton Lee	L	30	30	25	13	2	204.2	209	17	60	80	12-10	0	3.52
John Whitehead	R	28	26	24	8	3	165.2	191	14	56	45	11-8	0	4.07
Ted Lyons	R	36	22	22	11	0	169.1	182	21	45	45	12-7	0	4.15
Monty Stratton	R	25	22	21	14	5	164.2	142	6	37	69	15-5	0	2.40
Bill Dietrich	R	27	29	20	7	1	143.1	162	15	72	62	8-10	1	4.90
Bill Cox	R	24	3	2	1	0	12.2	9	0	5	8	1-0	0	0.71
Clint Brown	R	33	53	0	0	0	100.0	92	7	36	51	7-7	18	3.42
Johnny Rigney	R	22	22	4	0	0	90.2	107	10	46	38	2-5	1	4.96
Sugar Cain	R	30	18	6	1	0	68.2	88	7	51	17	4-2	0	6.16
Italo Chelini	L	22	4	0	0	0	8.2	15	2	0	3	0-1	0	10.38
George Gick	R	21	1	0	0	0	2.0	0	0	0	1	0-0	1	0.00

1937 Cleveland Indians 4th AL 83-71 .539 19.0 GB — Steve O'Neill

Player	Gm by Position	B	Age	G	AB	R	H	2B	3B	HR	RBI	BB	SO	SB	Avg	OBP	Slg
Frankie Pytlak	C115	R	28	125	397	60	125	15	6	1	44	52	15	16	.315	.404	.390
Hal Trosky	1B152	L	24	153	601	104	179	36	9	32	128	65	60	3	.298	.367	.547
Odell Hale	3B90,2B64	R	28	154	561	74	150	32	4	6	82	56	41	9	.267	.335	.371
Roy Hughes	3B58,2B32	R	26	104	346	57	96	12	6	1	40	40	22	11	.277	.352	.355
Lyn Lary	SS156	R	31	156	644	110	187	46	7	8	77	88	64	18	.290	.377	.421
Earl Averill	OF156	L	35	156	609	121	182	33	11	21	92	88	65	5	.299	.387	.493
Moose Solters	OF149	R	31	152	589	90	190	42	11	20	109	42	56	6	.323	.372	.533
Bruce Campbell	OF123	L	27	134	448	82	135	42	11	4	61	67	49	4	.301	.392	.471
John Kroner	2B64,3B11	R	28	86	283	29	67	14	1	2	26	22	25	1	.237	.292	.314
Billy Sullivan	C38,1B5,3B1	L	26	72	168	26	48	12	3	3	22	17	7	1	.286	.355	.446
Roy Weatherly	OF38,3B1	L	22	53	134	19	27	4	0	5	13	6	14	1	.201	.246	.343
Jeff Heath	OF14	L	22	20	61	8	14	1	4	0	8	0	9	0	.230	.230	.377
Joe Becker	C12	R	29	18	33	3	11	2	1	0	2	3	4	0	.333	.405	.455
Hugh Alexander	OF3	R	19	7	11	0	1	0	0	0	0	0	5	1	.091	.091	.091
Blas Monaco	2B3	S	21	5	7	0	2	0	1	0	2	0	2	0	.286	.375	.571
Ken Keltner	3B1	R	20	1	1	0	0	0	0	0	1	0	0	0	.000	.000	.000
Bill Sodd		R	22	1	1	0	0	0	0	0	0	0	1	0	.000	.000	.000

Pitcher	T	Age	G	GS	CG	ShO	IP	H	HR	BB	SO	W-L	Sv	ERA
Mel Harder	R	27	38	30	13	0	233.2	269	9	86	95	15-12	2	4.28
Denny Galehouse	R	25	36	29	7	0	200.2	238	11	83	78	9-14	3	4.57
Willis Hudlin	R	31	35	23	10	2	175.2	213	8	43	31	12-11	2	4.10
Earl Whitehill	L	37	33	22	6	1	147.0	189	9	80	53	8-8	2	6.49
Johnny Allen	R	31	24	20	14	0	173.0	157	4	60	87	15-1	0	2.55
Bob Feller	R	18	26	19	9	0	148.2	116	4	106	150	9-7	1	3.39
Joe Heving	R	36	40	0	0	0	72.2	92	6	30	35	8-4	5	4.83
Lloyd Brown	L	32	31	5	2	0	77.0	107	4	27	32	2-6	0	6.55
Whit Wyatt	R	29	29	4	2	0	73.0	67	3	40	52	2-3	0	4.44
Ivy Andrews†	R	30	20	4	1	1	59.2	76	3	9	16	3-4	0	4.37
Ken Jungels	R	21	2	0	0	0	3.0	3	0	1	0	0-0	0	0.00
Carl Fischer†	L	31	2	0	0	0	0.2	2	0	1	1	0-1	0	27.00

1937 Boston Red Sox 5th AL 80-72 .526 21.0 GB

Joe Cronin

Player	Gm by Position	B	Age	G	AB	R	H	2B	3B	HR	RBI	BB	SO	SB	Avg	OBP	Slg
Gene Desautels	C94	R	30	96	305	33	74	10	3	0	27	36	26	1	.243	.325	.295
Jimmie Foxx	1B150,C1	R	29	150	569	111	162	24	6	36	127	99	96	10	.285	.392	.538
Eric McNair	2B106,SS9,3B4*	R	28	126	455	60	133	29	4	12	76	30	33	10	.292	.340	.453
Mike Higgins	3B152	R	28	153	570	88	172	33	5	9	106	76	51	2	.302	.385	.425
Joe Cronin	SS148	R	30	148	570	102	175	40	4	18	110	84	73	5	.307	.402	.486
Doc Cramer	OF133	L	31	133	560	90	171	22	11	0	51	35	14	8	.305	.351	.384
Buster Mills	OF120	R	28	123	505	85	149	25	8	7	58	46	41	11	.295	.361	.418
Ben Chapman†	OF112,SS1	R	28	113	423	76	130	23	11	7	57	57	35	27	.307	.391	.463
Fabian Gaffke	OF50	R	23	54	184	32	53	10	4	6	34	15	25	1	.288	.342	.484
Dom Dallessandro	OF35	L	23	68	147	18	34	7	1	0	11	27	16	2	.231	.351	.293
Bobby Doerr	2B47	R	19	55	147	22	33	5	1	2	14	18	25	2	.224	.313	.313
Moe Berg	C47	R	35	47	141	13	36	3	1	0	20	5	4	0	.255	.281	.291
Mel Almada†	OF27,1B4	L	24	32	110	17	26	6	2	1	9	15	6	0	.236	.328	.355
Rick Ferrell†	C18	R	31	18	65	8	20	2	0	1	4	15	4	0	.308	.438	.385
Ski Melillo	2B19,3B2,SS2	R	37	26	56	8	14	2	0	0	6	5	4	0	.250	.311	.286
Johnny Peacock	C9	L	27	9	32	3	10	2	1	0	6	1	0	0	.313	.333	.438
Bob Daughters		R	22	1	0	1	0	0	0	0	0	0	0	0	—	—	—
Stew Bowers		S	22	1	0	1	0	0	0	0	0	0	0	0	—	—	—

E. McNair, 1 G at 1B

Pitcher	T	Age	G	GS	CG	ShO	IP	H	HR	BB	SO	W-L	Sv	ERA
Lefty Grove	L	37	32	32	21	3	262.0	269	9	83	153	17-9	0	3.02
Bobo Newsom†	R	29	30	27	14	1	207.2	193	14	119	127	13-10	0	4.46
Johnny Marcum	R	27	37	23	9	1	183.2	230	17	47	59	13-11	3	4.85
Archie McKain	L	26	36	18	3	0	137.0	152	7	64	66	8-8	2	4.66
Wes Ferrell†	R	29	12	11	5	0	73.1	111	14	34	31	3-6	0	7.61
Jim Henry	R	27	3	2	1	0	15.1	15	2	11	8	1-0	0	5.28
Jack Wilson	R	25	51	21	14	1	221.1	209	13	119	137	16-10	7	3.70
Rube Walberg	L	40	32	11	3	0	104.2	143	7	46	46	5-7	1	5.59
Fritz Ostermueller	L	29	25	7	2	0	86.2	101	2	44	29	3-7	1	4.98
Ted Olson	R	24	11	0	0	0	32.1	42	4	15	11	0-0	0	7.24
Tommy Thomas†	R	37	9	0	0	0	11.0	16	2	4	4	0-2	0	4.09
Joe Gonzales	R	22	8	2	2	0	31.0	37	1	11	11	1-2	0	4.35

1937 Washington Senators 6th AL 73-80 .477 28.5 GB

Bucky Harris

Player	Gm by Position	B	Age	G	AB	R	H	2B	3B	HR	RBI	BB	SO	SB	Avg	OBP	Slg
Rick Ferrell†	C84	R	31	86	279	31	64	6	0	1	32	50	18	1	.229	.348	.262
Joe Kuhel	1B136	L	31	136	547	73	155	24	11	6	61	63	39	6	.283	.357	.400
Buddy Myer	2B119,OF1	L	33	125	430	54	126	16	10	1	65	78	41	2	.293	.407	.384
Buddy Lewis	3B156	L	20	156	668	107	210	32	6	10	79	52	44	11	.314	.367	.425
Cecil Travis	SS129	L	23	135	526	72	181	27	7	3	66	39	34	3	.344	.395	.439
John Stone	OF137	L	31	139	542	84	179	33	15	6	88	66	36	6	.330	.403	.480
Al Simmons	OF102	R	35	103	419	60	117	21	10	8	84	27	35	3	.279	.329	.434
Mel Almada†	OF100	L	24	100	433	74	134	21	4	4	33	38	21	12	.309	.365	.404
Fred Sington	OF64	R	27	78	228	27	54	15	4	3	36	37	33	1	.237	.348	.377
Wally Millies	C56	R	30	59	179	21	40	7	1	0	28	9	15	1	.223	.261	.274
Ben Chapman†	OF32	R	28	35	130	23	34	7	1	0	12	26	7	8	.262	.385	.331
Ossie Bluege	SS28,1B2,3B2	R	36	42	127	12	36	4	2	1	13	13	19	1	.283	.355	.370
Jimmy Wasdell	1B21,OF7	L	23	32	110	13	28	4	4	2	12	7	13	0	.255	.299	.418
John Mihalic	2B28,SS3	R	25	38	107	13	27	5	2	0	8	17	9	2	.252	.355	.336
Jesse Hill†	OF21	R	30	33	92	24	20	2	1	1	4	13	16	2	.217	.314	.293
George Case	OF22	R	21	22	90	14	26	6	2	0	11	3	5	2	.289	.312	.400
Shanty Hogan	C21	R	31	21	66	4	10	4	0	0	5	6	8	0	.152	.222	.212
Jimmy Bloodworth	2B14	R	19	15	50	3	11	2	1	0	8	5	8	0	.220	.291	.300
Johnny Riddle†	C8	R	31	8	26	2	7	0	0	0	3	0	2	0	.269	.296	.269
Milt Gray	C2	R	23	2	6	0	0	0	0	0	0	0	1	0	.000	.000	.000
Frank Trechock	SS1	R	21	1	4	0	2	0	0	0	0	0	1	0	.500	.500	.500
Jerry Lynn	2B1	R	21	1	3	0	2	1	0	0	0	0	0	0	.667	.667	1.000
Mike Guerra	C1	R	24	1	3	0	0	0	0	0	0	0	2	0	.000	.000	.000
Herb Crompton	C2	R	25	2	3	0	1	0	0	0	0	0	0	0	.333	.333	.333
Alex Sabo	C1	R	27	1	0	0	0	0	0	0	0	0	0	0	—	—	—

Pitcher	T	Age	G	GS	CG	ShO	IP	H	HR	BB	SO	W-L	Sv	ERA
Jimmie DeShong	R	27	37	34	20	0	264.1	290	15	124	86	14-15	1	4.90
Montie Weaver	R	31	30	26	9	0	188.2	197	21	70	44	12-9	0	4.20
Wes Ferrell†	R	29	25	24	21	0	207.2	214	11	88	92	11-13	0	3.94
Pete Appleton	R	33	35	18	7	4	168.0	167	16	72	62	8-15	2	4.45
Carl Fischer†	L	31	17	11	2	0	72.0	74	6	31	30	4-5	2	4.38
Bobo Newsom†	R	29	11	10	3	0	67.2	76	4	48	39	3-4	0	5.85
Ken Chase	L	23	14	9	4	0	76.1	74	4	60	43	4-3	0	4.13
Bill Phebus	R	27	6	5	4	1	40.2	33	2	24	12	3-2	1	2.21
Joe Krakauskas	L	22	5	4	3	0	40.0	33	0	22	18	4-1	0	2.70
Joe Kohlman	R	24	2	2	1	0	13.0	15	0	3	3	1-0	0	4.15
Red Anderson	R	25	2	1	0	0	10.2	11	0	11	3	0-1	0	6.75
Ed Linke	R	25	36	7	0	0	128.2	158	11	59	61	6-1	3	5.60
Syd Cohen	L	31	33	0	0	0	55.0	64	1	17	22	2-4	4	3.11
Bucky Jacobs	R	24	11	1	0	0	22.1	26	0	11	8	1-1	0	4.84
Joe Cascarella†	R	30	10	4	1	0	32.1	50	3	23	10	0-5	1	8.07
Dick Lanahan	L	25	6	2	0	0	11.1	16	2	13	2	0-1	0	12.71

1937 Philadelphia Athletics 7th AL 54-97 .358 46.5 GB

Connie Mack (39-80)/Earle Mack (15-17)

Player	Gm by Position	B	Age	G	AB	R	H	2B	3B	HR	RBI	BB	SO	SB	Avg	OBP	Slg
Earle Brucker	C92	R	36	102	317	40	82	16	5	6	37	48	30	1	.259	.356	.397
Chubby Dean	1B78,P2	L	20	104	309	36	81	14	4	2	31	42	10	2	.262	.350	.353
Rusty Peters	2B70,3B31,SS13	R	22	116	339	39	88	17	6	3	43	41	59	4	.260	.339	.372
Bill Werber	3B125,OF3	R	29	128	493	85	144	31	4	7	70	74	39	35	.292	.386	.414
Skeeter Newsome	SS122	R	26	122	438	53	111	22	1	1	30	37	22	11	.253	.312	.315
Wally Moses	OF154	L	26	154	649	113	208	48	13	25	86	54	38	9	.320	.374	.550
Bob Johnson	OF133,2B2	R	30	138	477	91	146	32	6	25	108	98	65	9	.306	.425	.556
Jesse Hill†	OF68	R	30	70	242	32	71	12	3	1	37	31	20	16	.293	.374	.380
Lou Finney	1B50,OF39,2B1	L	26	92	379	53	95	14	9	1	20	20	16	2	.251	.288	.343
Jack Rothrock	OF58,2B1	S	32	88	232	28	62	15	0	0	21	28	15	1	.267	.346	.332
Frankie Hayes	C56	R	22	60	188	24	49	11	1	10	38	29	34	0	.261	.359	.489
Wayne Ambler	2B56	R	21	56	162	3	35	5	0	0	11	13	8	1	.216	.274	.247
Bill Cissell	2B33	R	33	34	117	15	31	7	0	1	14	17	10	0	.265	.358	.350
Lynn Nelson	P30,OF6	L	32	74	113	18	40	6	2	4	29	6	13	1	.354	.387	.549
Gene Hasson	1B28	L	21	28	98	12	30	6	3	3	14	13	14	0	.306	.387	.520
Ace Parker	SS19,2B9,OF5	R	25	38	94	8	11	0	1	2	13	4	17	0	.117	.153	.202
Bill Conroy	C18,1B1	R	22	26	60	4	12	1	1	0	3	7	9	1	.200	.284	.250
Warren Huston	2B16,SS15,3B2	R	23	38	54	5	7	3	0	0	3	2	9	0	.130	.161	.185
Babe Barna	OF9,1B1	L	22	14	36	10	14	2	0	2	9	2	6	1	.389	.421	.611
Doyt Morris	OF3	R	20	6	13	0	2	0	0	0	0	0	3	0	.154	.154	.154
Eddie Yount	OF2	R	20	4	7	1	2	0	0	0	1	0	1	0	.286	.286	.286
Hal Wagner	C1	L	21	1	0	0	0	0	0	0	0	0	0	0	—	—	—

Pitcher	T	Age	G	GS	CG	ShO	IP	H	HR	BB	SO	W-L	Sv	ERA
George Caster	R	29	34	33	19	3	231.2	227	23	107	100	12-19	0	4.43
Harry Kelley	R	31	41	29	14	0	205.0	267	16	79	68	13-21	0	5.36
Bud Thomas	R	26	35	26	6	0	169.2	208	15	52	54	8-15	0	4.99
Eddie Smith	L	23	38	23	14	0	196.2	178	18	90	79	4-17	5	3.94
Buck Ross	R	22	28	22	7	1	147.1	183	12	63	37	5-10	0	4.89
Al Williams	R	23	16	8	2	0	75.1	88	0	49	27	4-1	1	5.38
Chubby Dean	L	20	2	1	0	0	9.0	7	0	6	4	1-0	0	4.00
George Turbeville	L	22	31	3	0	0	77.1	80	2	56	17	0-4	0	4.77
Lynn Nelson	R	32	30	4	1	0	116.0	140	12	51	49	4-9	2	5.90
Herman Fink	R	25	28	3	1	0	80.0	82	6	35	18	2-1	1	4.05
Randy Gumpert	R	19	10	1	0	0	12.0	16	1	15	5	0-0	0	12.00
Bill Kalfass	L	21	3	1	1	0	12.0	10	0	10	9	1-0	0	3.00
Fred Archer	L	27	1	0	0	0	3.0	4	0	0	2	0-0	0	6.00

1937 St. Louis Browns 8th AL 46-108 .299 56.0 GB

Rogers Hornsby (25-52)/Jim Bottomley (21-56)

Player	Gm by Position	B	Age	G	AB	R	H	2B	3B	HR	RBI	BB	SO	SB	Avg	OBP	Slg
Rollie Hemsley	C94,1B2	R	30	100	334	30	74	12	3	3	28	25	29	0	.222	.276	.302
Harry Davis	1B112,OF1	L	29	120	450	89	124	25	3	3	35	71	26	7	.276	.374	.364
Tom Carey	2B87,SS44,3B1	R	30	130	487	54	134	24	1	1	40	21	26	1	.275	.306	.335
Harlond Clift	3B155	R	24	155	571	103	175	36	7	29	118	98	80	8	.306	.413	.546
Bill Knickerbocker	SS115,2B6	R	25	121	491	53	128	29	5	4	61	30	32	3	.261	.303	.365
Joe Vosmik	OF143	R	27	144	594	81	193	47	9	4	93	49	38	2	.325	.377	.455
Beau Bell	OF131,1B26,3B2	R	29	156	642	82	218	51	8	14	117	53	54	2	.340	.391	.509
Sammy West	OF105	L	32	122	457	68	150	37	4	7	58	46	28	1	.328	.390	.473
Ethan Allen	OF78	R	33	103	320	39	101	18	1	0	31	21	17	3	.316	.360	.378
Ben Huffman	C42	L	22	76	176	18	48	9	0	1	24	10	7	1	.273	.323	.341
Jim Bottomley	1B24	L	37	65	109	11	26	7	0	1	12	18	15	1	.239	.346	.330
Red Barkley	2B31	R	23	31	101	9	27	6	0	0	14	14	17	1	.267	.357	.327
Nig Lipscomb	2B27,P3,3B1	R	26	36	96	11	31	9	1	0	8	11	10	0	.323	.398	.438
Eddie Silber	OF21	R	23	22	83	10	26	2	0	0	4	5	13	0	.313	.352	.337
Rogers Hornsby	2B17	R	41	20	56	7	18	3	0	1	11	7	5	0	.321	.397	.429
Tony Giuliani	C19	R	24	19	53	6	16	1	0	0	3	3	3	0	.302	.339	.321
Tommy Heath	C14	R	23	17	43	4	10	0	2	1	3	10	3	0	.233	.377	.395
Sam Harshany	C4	R	27	5	11	0	1	1	0	0	0	3	0	0	.091	.286	.182
Mel Mazzera		L	23	7	7	1	2	2	0	0	0	0	2	0	.286	.286	.571
Tom Cafego	OF1	L	25	4	4	1	0	0	0	0	0	0	1	0	.000	.000	.000

Pitcher	T	Age	G	GS	CG	ShO	IP	H	HR	BB	SO	W-L	Sv	ERA
Oral Hildebrand	R	30	30	27	12	1	201.1	228	18	87	75	8-17	1	5.14
Chief Hogsett	L	33	37	26	8	1	177.1	245	19	75	68	6-19	2	6.29
Jack Knott	R	30	38	22	8	0	191.1	220	25	91	74	8-18	2	4.89
Jim Walkup	R	27	27	18	6	0	150.1	218	16	83	46	9-12	0	7.36
Julio Bonetti	R	25	28	16	7	0	143.1	190	13	60	43	4-11	1	5.84
Lou Koupal	R	38	26	13	6	0	105.2	150	10	55	24	4-9	0	6.56
Les Tietje	R	25	5	4	2	0	30.0	32	0	17	5	1-2	0	4.20
Harry Kimberlin	R	28	3	2	1	0	15.1	16	2	9	5	0-2	0	2.35
Lefty Mills	L	27	2	2	1	0	12.2	16	1	10	10	1-1	0	6.39
Bill Miller	R	27	1	1	0	0	4.0	7	1	4	1	0-1	0	13.50
Bob Muncrief	R	21	1	1	0	0	2.0	3	1	2	0	0-0	0	4.50
Bill Trotter	R	28	34	12	3	0	122.1	150	14	50	37	2-9	1	5.81
Tommy Thomas†	R	37	17	2	0	0	30.2	46	2	10	10	0-1	0	7.04
Russ Van Atta	L	31	16	6	1	0	58.2	74	2	32	34	1-2	0	5.52
Sheriff Blake†	R	37	15	1	0	0	36.2	55	5	20	12	2-2	1	7.61
Earl Caldwell	R	32	9	2	0	0	29.0	39	3	13	8	0-0	0	6.83
Bill Strickland	R	29	9	0	0	0	21.1	28	2	15	6	0-0	0	5.91
George Hennessey	R	29	5	0	0	0	7.0	15	2	6	4	0-1	0	10.29
Emil Bildilli	L	24	4	1	0	0	8.0	12	1	3	2	0-1	0	10.13
Nig Lipscomb	R	26	3	0	0	0	9.2	13	3	5	1	0-0	0	6.52
Ed Baecht	R	30	3	0	0	0	6.1	13	3	6	3	0-0	1	12.79

»1937 New York Giants 1st NL 95-57 .625 —

Bill Terry

Player	Gm by Position	B	Age	G	AB	R	H	2B	3B	HR	RBI	BB	SO	SB	Avg	OBP	Slg
Harry Danning	C86	R	25	93	292	30	84	12	4	8	51	18	20	0	.288	.331	.438
Johnny McCarthy	1B110	L	27	114	420	53	117	19	3	10	65	24	37	2	.279	.322	.410
Burgess Whitehead	2B152	R	27	152	574	64	164	15	6	5	52	28	20	7	.286	.323	.359
Lou Chiozza	3B93,OF12	L	27	117	439	49	102	11	2	4	29	20	30	6	.232	.266	.294
Dick Bartell	SS128	R	29	128	516	91	158	38	2	14	62	40	38	5	.306	.367	.469
Jo-Jo Moore	OF140	L	28	142	580	89	180	37	10	6	57	46	37	7	.310	.364	.440
Jimmy Ripple	OF111	L	27	121	426	70	135	23	3	5	66	29	20	3	.317	.362	.420
Mel Ott	OF91,3B60	L	28	151	545	99	160	28	2	31	95	102	69	7	.294	.408	.523
Gus Mancuso	C81	R	31	86	287	30	80	17	1	4	39	17	20	1	.279	.319	.387
Wally Berger†	OF52	R	31	59	199	40	58	11	2	12	43	18	30	3	.291	.359	.548
Sam Leslie	1B44	L	31	72	191	25	59	7	2	3	30	20	12	1	.309	.380	.414
Hank Leiber	OF46	R	26	51	184	24	54	7	3	4	32	15	27	1	.293	.347	.429
Kiddo Davis†	OF37	R	35	56	76	20	20	10	0	0	9	10	7	0	.263	.356	.395
Blondy Ryan	SS19	R	31	21	75	10	18	3	1	1	13	6	8	0	.240	.296	.347
Mickey Haslin	SS9,2B4,3B4	R	26	27	42	8	8	1	0	0	5	9	3	1	.190	.333	.214
Ed Madjeski	C5	R	28	5	15	0	3	0	0	0	2	0	2	0	.200	.200	.200
Phil Weintraub†	OF1	L	29	6	9	3	3	2	0	0	1	1	1	0	.333	.400	.556

Pitcher	T	Age	G	GS	CG	ShO	IP	H	HR	BB	SO	W-L	Sv	ERA
Carl Hubbell	L	34	39	32	18	4	261.2	261	18	55	159	22-8	4	3.20
Hal Schumacher	R	26	38	29	10	1	217.2	222	11	89	100	13-12	1	3.60
Cliff Melton	L	25	46	27	14	2	248.0	216	9	55	142	20-9	7	2.61
Harry Gumbert	R	27	34	24	10	1	200.1	194	11	62	65	10-11	1	3.68
Slick Castleman	R	23	23	23	10	2	160.1	148	19	33	78	11-6	0	3.31
F. Fitzsimmons†	R	35	6	4	1	1	27.1	28	3	8	13	2-2	0	4.61
Bill Lohrman	R	24	2	1	1	0	10.0	5	0	2	3	1-0	1	0.90
Hy Vandenberg	R	30	1	1	1	0	8.0	10	0	6	2	0-1	0	7.88
Ben Cantwell†	R	35	1	1	0	0	4.0	6	1	1	0	0-1	0	9.00
Dick Coffman	R	30	42	1	0	0	80.0	93	4	31	30	8-3	3	3.04
Al Smith	L	29	33	9	2	0	85.2	91	8	30	41	5-4	0	4.20
Tom Baker†	R	24	13	0	0	0	31.0	30	0	16	11	1-0	0	4.06
Don Brennan†	R	33	6	0	0	0	9.1	12	0	9	1	1-0	0	6.75
Frank Gabler†	R	25	6	0	0	0	9.0	20	1	2	3	0-0	0	10.00
Jumbo Brown†	R	30	4	0	0	0	8.2	5	0	5	4	1-0	0	1.04

670 Seasons: Team Rosters

1937 Chicago Cubs 2nd NL 93-61 .604 3.0 GB

Charlie Grimm

Player	Gm by Position	B	Age	G	AB	R	H	2B	3B	HR	RBI	BB	SO	SB	Avg	OBP	Slg
Gabby Hartnett	C103	R	36	110	356	47	126	21	6	12	82	43	19	0	.354	.424	.548
Ripper Collins	1B111	S	33	115	456	77	125	16	5	16	71	32	46	2	.274	.329	.436
Billy Herman	2B137	R	27	138	564	106	189	35	11	8	65	56	22	2	.335	.396	.479
Stan Hack	3B150	L	27	154	582	106	173	27	6	2	63	83	42	16	.297	.388	.375
Billy Jurges	SS128	R	29	129	450	53	134	18	10	1	65	42	41	2	.298	.365	.389
Frank Demaree	OF154	R	27	154	615	104	199	36	6	17	115	57	31	6	.324	.382	.485
Augie Galan	OF140,2B8,SS2	S	25	147	611	104	154	24	10	18	78	79	48	23	.252	.339	.412
Joe Marty	OF84	R	23	88	290	41	84	17	2	5	44	28	30	3	.290	.356	.414
Phil Cavarretta	OF55,1B43	L	20	106	329	43	94	18	7	5	56	32	35	7	.286	.349	.429
Ken O'Dea	C64	L	24	83	219	31	66	7	5	4	32	24	26	1	.301	.370	.434
Lonny Frey	SS30,2B13,3B9*	L	26	78	198	33	55	9	3	1	22	33	15	6	.278	.381	.369
Tuck Stainback	OF49	R	25	72	160	18	37	7	1	0	14	7	16	3	.231	.268	.288
John Bottarini	C18,OF1	R	28	26	40	3	11	3	0	1	7	5	10	0	.275	.370	.425
Carl Reynolds	OF2	R	34	7	11	0	3	1	0	0	1	2	2	0	.273	.385	.364
Bob Garbark		R	27	1	1	0	0	0	0	0	0	0	0	0	.000	.000	.000
Dutch Meyer		R	21	1	0	0	0	0	0	0	0	0	0	0	—	—	—

L. Frey, 5 G at OF

Pitcher	T	Age	G	GS	CG	ShO	IP	H	HR	BB	SO	W-L	Sv	ERA
Bill Lee	R	27	42	33	17	2	272.1	289	14	73	108	14-15	3	3.54
Larry French	L	29	42	28	11	4	208.0	229	17	65	100	16-10	0	3.98
Tex Carleton	R	30	32	27	18	4	208.1	183	10	94	105	16-8	0	3.15
Roy Parmelee	R	30	33	18	8	0	145.2	165	13	79	55	7-8	0	5.13
Curt Davis	R	33	28	14	8	0	123.2	138	7	30	32	10-5	1	4.08
Charlie Root	R	38	43	15	5	0	178.2	173	18	32	74	13-5	5	3.38
Clay Bryant	R	25	38	10	4	1	135.1	117	1	78	75	9-3	3	4.26
Clyde Shoun	L	25	37	9	2	0	93.0	118	9	45	43	7-7	0	5.61
Bob Logan†	L	27	4	0	0	0	6.1	6	0	4	2	0-0	1	1.42
Newt Kimball	R	22	2	0	0	0	5.0	12	1	1	0	0-0	0	10.80
Kirby Higbe	R	22	1	0	0	0	5.0	4	1	1	2	1-0	0	5.40

1937 Pittsburgh Pirates 3rd NL 86-68 .558 10.0 GB

Pie Traynor

Player	Gm by Position	B	Age	G	AB	R	H	2B	3B	HR	RBI	BB	SO	SB	Avg	OBP	Slg
Al Todd	C128	R	35	133	514	51	158	18	10	8	86	16	36	2	.307	.330	.428
Gus Suhr	1B151	L	31	151	575	69	160	28	14	5	97	83	42	2	.278	.369	.402
Lee Handley	2B126	R	23	127	480	59	120	21	12	3	37	37	40	5	.250	.305	.363
Bill Brubaker	3B115	R	26	120	413	57	105	20	4	6	48	47	51	2	.254	.335	.366
Arky Vaughan	SS108,OF12	L	25	126	469	71	151	17	17	5	72	54	22	7	.322	.394	.463
Paul Waner	OF150	L	34	154	619	94	219	30	9	2	74	63	34	4	.354	.413	.441
Lloyd Waner	OF123	L	31	129	537	80	177	23	4	1	45	34	12	3	.330	.370	.393
Woody Jensen	OF120	L	29	124	509	77	142	23	9	5	45	15	29	2	.279	.301	.389
Pep Young	SS45,3B39,2B30	R	29	113	408	43	106	20	3	9	54	26	63	4	.260	.306	.390
Johnny Dickshot	OF64	R	27	82	264	42	67	8	4	3	33	26	36	0	.254	.323	.348
Tom Padden	C34	R	28	35	98	14	28	2	0	0	8	13	11	1	.286	.369	.306
Fred Schulte	OF4	R	36	29	20	5	2	0	0	0	3	4	3	0	.100	.280	.100
Pie Traynor	3B3	R	37	5	12	3	2	0	0	0	0	0	1	0	.167	.167	.167
Bill Schuster	SS2	R	24	3	6	2	3	0	0	0	1	1	0	0	.500	.571	.500
Ray Berres	C2	R	29	2	6	0	1	0	0	0	0	0	0	0	.167	.167	.167

Pitcher	T	Age	G	GS	CG	ShO	IP	H	HR	BB	SO	W-L	Sv	ERA
Cy Blanton	R	28	36	34	14	4	242.2	250	13	76	143	14-12	0	3.30
Ed Brandt	L	32	33	25	7	3	176.1	177	11	67	74	11-10	2	3.11
Red Lucas	R	35	20	20	9	1	126.1	150	12	23	20	8-10	0	4.27
Russ Bauers	R	23	34	19	11	2	187.2	174	2	80	118	13-6	1	2.88
Joe Bowman	R	27	30	19	7	0	128.0	161	11	35	38	8-8	1	4.57
Ken Heintzelman	L	21	1	1	1	0	9.0	6	0	3	4	1-0	0	2.00
Mace Brown	R	28	50	2	0	0	107.2	109	2	45	60	7-2	7	4.18
Bill Swift	R	29	36	17	9	0	164.0	160	14	34	84	9-10	3	3.95
Jim Weaver	R	33	32	9	2	1	109.2	106	2	31	44	8-5	0	3.20
Jim Tobin	R	24	20	8	7	0	87.0	74	1	28	37	6-3	1	3.00
Waite Hoyt†	R	37	11	0	0	0	28.0	31	3	6	21	1-2	2	4.50

1937 St. Louis Cardinals 4th NL 81-73 .526 15.0 GB

Frank Frisch

Player	Gm by Position	B	Age	G	AB	R	H	2B	3B	HR	RBI	BB	SO	SB	Avg	OBP	Slg
Bruce Ogrodowski	C87	R	25	90	279	37	65	10	3	3	31	11	17	2	.233	.267	.323
Johnny Mize	1B144	L	24	145	560	103	204	40	7	25	113	56	57	2	.364	.427	.595
Jimmy Brown	2B112,SS25,3B1	S	27	138	525	86	145	20	9	2	53	27	29	10	.276	.313	.360
Don Gutteridge	3B105,SS8	R	25	119	447	66	121	26	10	7	61	25	66	12	.271	.311	.421
Leo Durocher	SS134	R	31	135	477	46	97	11	3	1	47	38	36	6	.203	.262	.245
Joe Medwick	OF156	R	25	156	633	111	237	56	10	31	154	41	50	4	.374	.414	.641
Don Padgett	OF109	L	25	123	446	62	140	22	6	10	74	30	43	4	.314	.357	.457
Terry Moore	OF106	R	25	115	461	76	123	17	3	5	43	32	41	13	.267	.317	.349
Pepper Martin	OF82,3B5	R	33	98	339	60	103	27	8	5	38	33	50	9	.304	.366	.475
Frenchy Bordagaray	3B50,OF27	R	27	96	300	43	88	11	4	1	37	15	25	11	.293	.331	.367
Mickey Owen	C78	R	21	80	234	17	54	4	2	0	20	15	13	1	.231	.277	.265
Stu Martin	2B48,1B9,SS1	L	23	90	223	34	58	6	1	1	17	32	18	3	.260	.353	.309
Mike Ryba	P38,C3	R	34	41	48	6	15	2	0	0	7	5	5	0	.313	.377	.354
Dick Siebert	1B7	L	25	22	38	3	7	2	0	0	2	4	8	1	.184	.279	.237
Herb Bremer	C10	R	23	11	33	2	7	1	0	0	3	2	4	0	.212	.257	.242
Frankie Frisch	2B17	S	38	17	32	3	7	2	0	0	4	1	0	0	.219	.242	.281
Randy Moore†	OF1	L	31	8	7	0	0	0	0	0	0	0	0	0	.000	.000	.000

Pitcher	T	Age	G	GS	CG	ShO	IP	H	HR	BB	SO	W-L	Sv	ERA
Bob Weiland	L	31	41	34	21	2	264.1	283	14	94	105	15-14	0	3.54
Lon Warneke	R	28	36	33	18	2	238.2	280	32	69	87	18-11	0	4.53
Dizzy Dean	R	27	27	25	17	4	197.1	200	9	33	120	13-10	1	2.69
Si Johnson	R	30	38	21	12	1	192.1	222	14	43	64	12-12	1	3.32
Howie Krist	R	21	6	4	1	0	27.2	34	0	10	6	3-1	0	4.23
Mike Ryba	R	34	38	8	5	0	135.0	152	8	40	57	9-6	0	4.13
Ray Harrell	R	25	35	15	1	1	96.2	99	7	59	41	3-7	1	5.87
Jesse Haines	R	43	16	6	2	0	65.2	81	5	23	18	3-3	0	4.52
Jim Winford	R	27	16	4	0	0	46.1	56	2	27	17	2-4	0	5.83
Sheriff Blake†	R	37	14	2	2	0	43.2	45	1	18	20	0-3	0	3.71
Tom Sunkel	L	24	9	1	0	0	29.1	24	0	11	9	0-0	1	2.76
Nub Kleinke	R	26	5	2	1	0	20.2	25	0	7	9	1-1	0	4.79
Ade White	L	33	5	0	0	0	9.1	14	1	3	2	0-1	0	6.75
Bill McGee	R	27	4	1	1	0	14.0	13	1	4	9	1-0	0	2.57
Nate Andrews	R	23	4	0	0	0	9.0	12	1	3	6	0-0	0	4.00
John Chambers	R	25	2	0	0	0	2.0	5	0	2	1	0-0	0	18.00
Paul Dean	R	23	1	0	0	0	0.0	1	0	2	0	0-0	0	—

1937 Boston Braves 5th NL 79-73 .520 16.0 GB

Bill McKechnie

Player	Gm by Position	B	Age	G	AB	R	H	2B	3B	HR	RBI	BB	SO	SB	Avg	OBP	Slg
Al Lopez	C102	R	28	105	334	31	68	11	1	3	38	35	57	3	.204	.281	.269
Elbie Fletcher	1B148	L	21	148	539	56	133	22	4	1	38	56	64	3	.247	.321	.308
Tony Cuccinello	2B151	R	29	152	575	77	156	36	4	11	80	61	40	2	.271	.341	.405
Gil English†	3B71	R	27	79	269	25	78	5	2	2	37	23	27	3	.290	.348	.346
Rabbit Warstler	SS149	R	33	149	555	57	124	20	0	3	36	51	62	4	.223	.291	.276
Gene Moore	OF148	L	27	148	561	88	159	29	10	16	70	61	73	11	.283	.358	.456
Vince DiMaggio	OF130	R	24	132	493	56	126	18	4	13	69	39	111	8	.256	.311	.387
Debs Garms	OF81,3B36	L	29	125	478	60	124	15	8	2	37	37	33	2	.259	.317	.337
Roy Johnson†	OF63	L	34	85	260	24	72	8	3	3	22	38	29	5	.277	.369	.365
Ray Mueller	C57	R	25	64	187	21	47	9	2	2	26	18	36	1	.251	.317	.353
Eddie Mayo	3B50	L	27	65	172	19	39	6	1	1	18	15	20	1	.227	.293	.291
Wally Berger†	OF28	R	31	30	113	14	31	9	1	5	22	11	33	0	.274	.344	.504
Bobby Reis	OF18,P4,1B4	R	28	45	86	10	21	5	0	0	6	13	12	2	.244	.343	.302
Tommy Thevenow	SS12,3B6,2B2	R	33	21	34	5	4	0	1	0	2	4	2	0	.118	.211	.176
Beauty McGowan	OF2	L	35	9	12	0	1	0	0	0	0	1	2	0	.083	.154	.083
Buck Jordan†		L	30	8	8	1	2	0	0	0	0	0	0	0	.250	.250	.250
Johnny Riddle†	C2	R	31	2	3	0	0	0	0	0	0	1	0	0	.000	.250	.000
Link Wasem	C2	R	26	2	1	0	0	0	0	0	0	0	0	0	.000	.000	.000
Billy Urbanski		R	34	1	1	0	0	0	0	0	0	0	1	0	.000	.000	.000

Pitcher	T	Age	G	GS	CG	ShO	IP	H	HR	BB	SO	W-L	Sv	ERA
Lou Fette	R	30	35	33	23	5	259.0	243	5	81	70	20-10	0	2.88
Danny MacFayden	R	32	32	32	16	2	246.0	250	5	60	70	14-14	0	2.93
Jim Turner	R	33	33	30	24	5	256.2	228	13	52	69	20-11	1	2.38
Guy Bush	R	35	32	20	11	1	180.2	201	8	48	56	8-15	1	3.54
Milt Shoffner	L	31	6	5	3	1	42.2	38	1	9	13	3-1	1	2.53
Johnny Lanning	R	26	32	11	4	1	116.2	107	10	40	37	5-7	2	3.93
Ira Hutchinson	R	26	31	8	1	0	91.2	99	4	35	29	4-6	0	3.73
Frank Gabler†	R	25	19	9	2	1	76.0	84	7	16	19	4-7	2	5.09
Bob Smith	R	42	18	0	0	0	44.0	52	6	6	14	0-1	3	4.09
Roy Weir	L	26	10	4	1	0	33.0	27	0	19	8	1-1	0	3.82
Bobby Reis	R	28	4	0	0	0	5.0	3	0	5	0	0-0	0	1.80
Vic Frasier	R	32	3	0	0	0	8.0	12	1	1	2	0-0	0	5.63

1937 Brooklyn Dodgers 6th NL 62-91 .405 33.5 GB

Burleigh Grimes

Player	Gm by Position	B	Age	G	AB	R	H	2B	3B	HR	RBI	BB	SO	SB	Avg	OBP	Slg
Babe Phelps	C111	L	29	121	409	42	128	37	3	7	58	25	28	2	.313	.357	.469
Buddy Hassett	1B131	L	25	137	556	71	169	31	6	1	53	20	19	13	.304	.334	.387
Cookie Lavagetto	2B100,3B45	R	24	149	503	64	142	26	6	8	70	74	41	13	.282	.375	.406
Joe Stripp	3B66,1B14,SS3	R	34	90	300	37	73	10	2	1	26	20	18	1	.243	.291	.300
Woody English	SS116,2B11	R	30	129	378	45	90	16	2	1	42	65	55	4	.238	.350	.299
Heinie Manush	OF123	L	35	132	466	57	155	25	7	4	73	40	24	6	.333	.389	.442
Johnny Cooney	OF111	R	36	120	430	61	126	18	5	0	37	22	10	5	.293	.327	.358
Gibby Brack	OF101	R	29	112	372	60	102	27	9	5	38	44	93	9	.274	.351	.435
Jim Bucher	2B49,3B43,OF6	L	26	125	380	44	96	11	2	4	37	20	18	5	.253	.295	.324
Tom Winsett	OF101,P1	L	27	118	350	32	83	15	5	5	42	45	64	3	.237	.329	.351
Roy Spencer	C45	R	37	51	117	5	24	2	2	0	4	8	17	0	.205	.256	.256
Lindsay Brown	SS45	R	25	48	115	16	31	3	1	0	6	3	17	1	.270	.288	.313
Tony Malinosky	3B13,SS11	R	27	35	79	7	18	2	0	0	3	9	11	0	.228	.307	.253
Goody Rosen	OF21	L	24	22	77	10	24	5	1	0	6	6	6	2	.312	.361	.403
Eddie Wilson	OF21	L	27	36	54	11	12	4	1	1	8	17	14	1	.222	.408	.389
Paul Chervinko	C26	R	26	30	48	1	7	0	1	0	2	3	16	0	.146	.196	.188
Eddie Morgan	1B7,OF7	L	22	31	48	4	9	3	0	0	5	9	7	0	.188	.316	.250
George Cisar	OF13	R	24	20	29	8	6	0	0	0	4	2	6	3	.207	.258	.207
Jake Daniel	1B7	L	25	12	27	3	5	1	0	0	3	3	4	0	.185	.267	.222
Johnny Hudson	SS11	R	25	13	27	3	5	4	0	0	2	3	9	0	.185	.267	.333
Bert Haas	OF4,1B3	R	23	16	25	2	10	3	0	0	2	1	1	0	.400	.423	.520
Randy Moore†	C10	L	31	13	22	3	3	1	0	0	2	3	2	0	.136	.240	.182
Nick Polly	3B7	R	20	10	18	2	4	0	0	0	2	0	1	0	.222	.222	.222
Art Parks	OF4	L	25	7	16	2	5	2	0	0	0	2	2	0	.313	.389	.438
Elmer Klumpp	C3	R	30	5	11	0	1	0	0	0	2	1	4	0	.091	.167	.091
Sid Gautreaux		S	25	11	10	0	1	1	0	0	2	1	1	0	.100	.182	.200
George Fallon	2B4	R	22	4	8	0	2	1	0	0	0	1	1	0	.250	.333	.375

Pitcher	T	Age	G	GS	CG	ShO	IP	H	HR	BB	SO	W-L	Sv	ERA
Fred Frankhouse	R	33	33	26	9	1	179.1	214	8	78	64	10-13	0	4.27
Luke Hamlin	R	32	39	25	11	1	185.2	183	4	48	93	11-13	1	3.59
Max Butcher	R	26	39	24	8	1	191.2	203	12	75	57	11-15	0	4.27
Van Lingle Mungo	R	26	25	21	14	0	161.0	136	3	56	122	9-11	3	2.91
Waite Hoyt†	R	37	27	19	10	1	167.0	180	5	30	44	7-7	0	3.23
F. Fitzsimmons†	R	35	13	13	4	0	90.2	91	2	32	29	4-8	0	4.27
Buck Marrow	R	27	6	3	0	0	16.1	19	2	9	2	1-2	0	6.61
Roy Henshaw	L	25	42	16	5	0	156.1	176	14	69	98	5-12	2	5.07
George Jeffcoat	R	23	21	3	1	1	54.1	58	4	27	29	1-3	0	5.13
Jim Lindsey	R	41	20	0	0	0	38.1	43	4	12	15	0-1	2	3.52
Harry Eisenstat	L	21	13	4	0	0	47.2	61	2	11	12	3-3	0	3.97
Ben Cantwell†	R	35	13	0	0	0	27.1	32	1	8	12	0-0	0	4.61
Ralph Birkofer	L	28	11	1	0	0	29.2	45	3	9	9	0-2	0	6.67
Tom Baker†	R	24	7	0	0	0	8.1	14	1	5	2	0-1	0	8.64
Jim Peterson	R	28	3	0	0	0	5.2	8	3	2	4	0-0	0	7.94
Watty Clark	L	35	2	0	0	0	2.1	4	0	3	0	0-0	0	7.71
Tom Winsett	R	27	1	0	0	0	1.0	3	0	2	0	0-0	0	18.00

1937 Philadelphia Phillies 7th NL 61-92 .399 34.5 GB

Jimmie Wilson

Player	Gm by Position	B	Age	G	AB	R	H	2B	3B	HR	RBI	BB	SO	SB	Avg	OBP	Slg
Bill Atwood	C80	R	25	87	279	27	68	15	1	2	32	30	27	3	.244	.317	.326
Dolph Camilli	1B131	L	30	131	475	101	161	23	7	27	80	90	82	6	.339	.446	.587
Del Young	2B108	S	25	109	360	36	70	9	2	0	24	18	55	6	.194	.235	.231
Pinky Whitney	3B130	R	32	138	487	56	166	19	4	8	79	43	44	6	.341	.395	.446
George Scharein	SS146	R	22	146	511	44	123	20	1	0	57	36	47	13	.241	.293	.284
Hersh Martin	OF139	S	27	141	579	102	164	35	7	8	49	69	66	11	.283	.362	.409
Morrie Arnovich	OF107	R	26	117	410	60	119	27	4	10	60	34	32	5	.290	.349	.449
Chuck Klein	OF103	L	32	115	406	74	132	20	2	15	57	39	21	3	.325	.386	.495
Leo Norris	2B74,3B24,SS20	R	29	116	381	45	98	24	3	9	36	21	53	3	.257	.296	.407
Earl Browne	OF54,1B23	L	26	105	332	42	97	19	3	6	52	21	41	4	.292	.342	.422
Johnny Moore	OF74	L	35	96	307	46	98	16	2	9	59	18	18	2	.319	.357	.472
Earl Grace	C64	L	30	80	223	19	47	10	1	6	29	33	15	0	.211	.313	.345
Jimmie Wilson	C22	R	36	39	87	15	24	3	0	1	8	6	4	1	.276	.323	.345
Walter Stephenson	C7	R	26	10	23	1	6	0	0	0	2	2	3	0	.261	.320	.261
Fred Tauby	OF10	R	31	11	20	2	0	0	0	0	3	0	5	1	.000	.000	.000
Howie Gorman	OF7	L	24	13	19	3	4	1	0	0	1	1	1	1	.211	.250	.263
Gene Corbett	3B3,2B1	L	23	7	12	4	4	2	0	0	1	0	0	0	.333	.333	.500
Bill Andrus		R	29	3	2	0	0	0	0	0	0	0	2	0	.000	.000	.000

Pitcher	T	Age	G	GS	CG	ShO	IP	H	HR	BB	SO	W-L	Sv	ERA
Claude Passeau	R	28	50	34	18	1	292.1	348	16	79	135	14-18	2	4.34
Bucky Walters	R	28	37	34	15	3	246.1	292	14	86	87	14-15	0	4.75
Wayne LaMaster	L	30	50	30	10	1	220.1	255	24	82	135	15-19	4	5.31
Hugh Mulcahy	R	23	56	25	9	1	215.2	256	17	97	54	8-18	3	5.13
Orville Jorgens	R	29	52	11	1	0	140.2	159	12	68	34	3-4	3	4.41
Syl Johnson	R	36	32	15	4	0	138.0	155	20	22	46	4-10	3	5.02
Hal Kelleher	R	23	27	2	1	0	58.1	72	3	31	20	2-4	0	6.63
Elmer Burkart	R	20	7	0	0	0	16.0	20	0	9	4	0-0	0	6.19
Pete Sivess	R	23	6	2	1	0	23.0	30	5	11	4	1-1	0	7.04
Larry Crawford	L	23	6	0	0	0	6.0	12	2	1	2	0-0	0	15.00
Bob Allen	R	22	3	1	0	0	12.0	18	2	8	8	0-1	0	6.75
Leon Pettit	L	35	3	1	0	0	4.0	6	1	4	0	0-1	0	11.25
Bobby Burke	L	30	2	0	0	0	0.0	1	0	2	0	0-0	0	—
Walt Masters	R	30	1	0	0	0	1.0	5	0	1	0	0-0	0	36.00

1937 Cincinnati Reds 8th NL 56-98 .364 40.0 GB

Chuck Dressen (51-78)/Bobby Wallace (5-20)

Player	Gm by Position	B	Age	G	AB	R	H	2B	3B	HR	RBI	BB	SO	SB	Avg	OBP	Slg
Ernie Lombardi	C90	R	29	120	368	41	123	22	1	9	59	14	17	1	.334	.362	.473
Buck Jordan†	1B76	L	30	98	316	45	89	14	3	1	28	25	14	6	.282	.334	.354
Alex Kampouris	2B146	R	24	146	458	62	114	21	4	17	71	60	65	2	.249	.342	.424
Lew Riggs	3B100	L	27	122	384	43	93	17	5	6	45	24	17	4	.242	.289	.359
Billy Myers	SS121	R	26	124	335	35	84	13	3	7	43	44	57	0	.251	.339	.370
Ival Goodman	OF141	L	28	147	549	86	150	25	12	12	55	55	58	10	.273	.347	.428
Kiki Cuyler	OF106	R	38	117	406	48	110	12	4	0	32	36	50	10	.271	.333	.320
Chick Hafey	OF64	R	34	89	257	39	67	11	5	9	41	23	42	2	.261	.324	.447
Les Scarsella	1B65,OF14	L	23	110	329	35	81	11	4	3	34	17	26	5	.246	.285	.331
Hub Walker	OF58	L	30	78	221	33	55	9	4	1	19	34	24	7	.249	.349	.339
Spud Davis	C59	R	32	76	209	19	56	10	1	3	33	23	15	0	.268	.341	.368
Phil Weintraub†	OF47	L	29	49	177	27	48	10	4	3	20	19	25	1	.271	.345	.424
Jimmy Outlaw	3B41	R	24	49	165	18	45	7	3	0	11	3	31	2	.273	.290	.352
Kiddo Davis†	OF35	R	35	40	136	19	35	6	0	1	5	16	6	1	.257	.340	.324
Charlie Gelbert†	SS37	R	31	43	114	12	22	4	0	1	13	15	12	1	.193	.287	.254
Frank McCormick	1B20	R	26	24	83	5	27	5	0	0	9	2	4	1	.325	.341	.386
Charlie English	3B15	R	27	17	63	1	15	3	1	0	4	0	2	0	.238	.238	.317
Eddie Miller	SS30	R	20	36	60	3	9	3	1	0	5	3	8	0	.150	.190	.233
Harry Craft	OF10	R	22	10	42	7	13	2	1	0	4	1	3	0	.310	.326	.405
Gilly Campbell	C17	L	29	18	40	3	11	2	0	0	2	5	1	0	.275	.356	.325
Dutch Mele	OF5	L	22	6	14	1	2	1	0	0	1	1	1	0	.143	.200	.214
Pinky Jorgensen	OF4	R	22	6	14	1	4	0	0	0	1	1	2	0	.286	.333	.286
Dee Moore	C6	R	23	7	13	2	1	0	0	0	0	1	2	0	.077	.200	.077
Eddie Joost	2B6	R	21	6	12	0	1	0	0	0	0	0	0	0	.083	.083	.083
Double Joe Dwyer		L	34	12	11	2	3	0	0	0	1	1	0	0	.273	.333	.273
Gus Brittain	C1	R	27	3	6	0	1	0	0	0	0	0	3	0	.167	.167	.167
Arnie Moser		R	21	5	5	0	0	0	0	0	0	0	2	0	.000	.000	.000
Harry Chozen	C1	R	21	1	4	0	1	0	0	0	0	0	0	0	.250	.250	.250

Pitcher	T	Age	G	GS	CG	ShO	IP	H	HR	BB	SO	W-L	Sv	ERA
Lee Grissom	L	29	50	30	14	5	223.2	193	7	93	149	12-17	6	3.26
Paul Derringer	R	30	43	26	12	1	222.2	240	7	55	94	10-14	1	4.04
Peaches Davis	R	32	42	24	11	1	218.0	252	5	51	59	11-13	3	3.59
Al Hollingsworth	L	29	43	24	11	1	202.1	224	8	73	74	9-15	5	3.91
Paul Gehrman	R	25	2	1	0	0	9.1	11	0	5	1	0-1	0	2.89
Gene Schott	R	23	37	17	7	2	154.1	150	2	48	56	4-13	1	2.97
Wild Bill Hallahan	L	34	21	9	2	0	63.0	90	3	29	18	3-9	0	6.14
J. Vander Meer	L	22	19	9	4	0	84.1	63	0	69	52	3-5	0	3.84
Jake Mooty	R	24	14	2	0	0	39.0	54	2	22	11	0-3	1	8.31
Whitey Moore	R	25	13	6	0	0	38.2	32	1	39	27	0-3	0	4.89
Joe Cascarella†	R	30	11	3	2	0	43.2	44	1	22	16	1-2	1	3.92
Don Brennan†	R	33	10	0	0	0	16.0	25	1	10	6	1-1	0	6.75
Ted Kleinhans	L	38	7	3	1	0	27.1	29	1	12	13	1-2	0	2.30
Jumbo Brown†	R	30	4	1	0	0	9.2	16	0	3	4	1-0	0	8.38
Red Barrett	R	22	1	0	0	0	6.1	5	0	2	1	0-0	0	1.42

»1938 New York Yankees 1st AL 99-53 .651 —

Joe McCarthy

Player	Gm by Position	B	Age	G	AB	R	H	2B	3B	HR	RBI	BB	SO	SB	Avg	OBP	Slg
Bill Dickey	C126	L	31	132	454	84	142	27	4	27	115	75	22	3	.313	.412	.568
Lou Gehrig	1B157	L	35	157	576	115	170	32	6	29	114	107	75	6	.295	.410	.523
Joe Gordon	2B126	R	23	127	458	83	117	24	7	25	97	56	72	11	.255	.340	.502
Red Rolfe	3B151	L	29	151	631	132	196	36	8	10	80	74	44	13	.311	.386	.441
Frankie Crosetti	SS157	R	27	157	631	113	166	35	3	9	55	106	97	27	.263	.382	.371
Joe DiMaggio	OF145	R	23	145	599	129	194	32	13	32	140	59	21	6	.324	.386	.581
Tommy Henrich	OF130	L	25	131	471	109	127	24	7	22	91	92	32	6	.270	.391	.490
George Selkirk	OF95	L	30	99	335	58	85	12	5	10	62	68	52	9	.254	.384	.409
Myril Hoag	OF70	R	30	85	267	28	74	14	3	0	48	25	31	4	.277	.344	.352
Jake Powell	OF43	R	29	45	164	27	42	12	1	2	20	15	20	3	.256	.326	.378
Bill Knickerbocker	2B34,SS3	R	26	46	128	15	32	8	3	1	21	11	10	0	.250	.309	.383
Joe Glenn	C40	R	29	41	123	10	32	7	2	0	25	10	14	1	.260	.316	.350
Babe Dahlgren	3B8,1B6	R	26	27	43	8	8	1	0	0	1	1	7	0	.186	.205	.209
Art Jorgens	C8	R	33	9	17	3	4	2	0	0	2	3	3	0	.235	.350	.353

Pitcher	T	Age	G	GS	CG	ShO	IP	H	HR	BB	SO	W-L	Sv	ERA
Lefty Gomez	L	29	32	32	20	4	239.0	239	7	99	129	18-12	0	3.35
Red Ruffing	R	34	31	31	22	3	247.1	246	16	82	127	21-7	0	3.31
Monte Pearson	R	28	28	27	17	1	202.0	198	12	113	98	16-7	0	3.97
Spud Chandler	R	30	23	23	14	2	172.0	183	7	47	36	14-5	0	4.03
Bump Hadley	R	33	29	17	8	1	167.1	165	13	66	61	9-8	1	3.60
Joe Beggs	R	27	14	9	4	0	58.1	69	7	20	8	3-2	0	5.40
Wes Ferrell†	R	30	5	4	1	0	30.0	52	6	18	7	2-2	0	8.10
Atley Donald	R	27	2	2	0	0	12.0	7	0	14	6	0-1	0	5.25
Johnny Murphy	R	29	32	2	1	0	91.1	90	5	41	43	8-2	11	4.24
Steve Sundra	R	28	25	8	3	0	93.2	107	7	43	33	6-4	0	4.80
Ivy Andrews	R	31	19	1	1	0	48.0	51	3	17	13	1-3	1	3.00
Lee Stine	R	24	4	0	0	0	8.2	9	0	1	4	0-0	0	1.04
Joe Vance	R	32	3	1	0	0	11.1	20	2	4	2	0-0	0	7.15
Kemp Wicker	L	31	1	0	0	0	1.0	0	0	1	0	1-0	0	0.00

1938 Boston Red Sox 2nd AL 88-61 .591 9.5 GB

Joe Cronin

Player	Gm by Position	B	Age	G	AB	R	H	2B	3B	HR	RBI	BB	SO	SB	Avg	OBP	Slg
Gene Desautels	C108	R	31	108	333	47	97	16	2	2	48	57	31	1	.291	.396	.369
Jimmie Foxx	1B149	R	30	149	565	139	197	33	9	50	175	119	76	5	.349	.462	.704
Bobby Doerr	2B145	R	20	145	509	70	147	26	7	5	80	59	39	5	.289	.363	.397
Mike Higgins	3B138	R	29	139	524	77	159	29	5	5	106	71	55	10	.303	.388	.406
Joe Cronin	SS142	R	31	143	530	98	172	51	5	17	94	91	60	7	.325	.428	.536
Doc Cramer	OF148,P1	L	32	148	658	116	198	36	8	0	71	51	19	4	.301	.354	.380
Joe Vosmik	OF146	R	28	146	621	121	201	37	6	9	86	59	26	0	.324	.384	.446
Ben Chapman	OF126,3B1	R	29	127	480	92	163	40	8	6	80	65	33	13	.340	.418	.494
Johnny Peacock	C57,1B1,OF1	L	28	72	195	29	59	7	1	1	39	17	4	4	.303	.358	.364
Red Nonnenkamp	OF39,1B5	L	26	87	180	37	51	4	1	0	18	21	13	6	.283	.358	.317
Eric McNair	SS15,2B14,3B3	R	29	46	96	9	15	1	1	0	7	3	6	0	.156	.182	.188
Jim Tabor	3B11,SS2	R	21	19	57	8	18	3	2	1	8	1	6	0	.316	.328	.491
Moe Berg	C7,1B1	R	36	10	12	0	4	0	0	0	0	0	1	0	.333	.333	.333
Fabian Gaffke	OF2,C1	R	24	15	10	2	1	0	0	0	1	3	2	0	.100	.308	.100

Pitcher	T	Age	G	GS	CG	ShO	IP	H	HR	BB	SO	W-L	Sv	ERA
Jack Wilson	R	26	37	27	11	3	194.2	200	16	91	96	15-15	1	4.30
Jim Bagby Jr.	R	21	43	25	10	1	198.2	218	9	90	73	15-11	2	4.21
Lefty Grove	L	38	24	21	12	1	163.2	169	8	52	99	14-4	1	3.08
Fritz Ostermueller	L	30	31	18	10	1	176.2	199	15	58	46	13-5	2	4.58
Johnny Marcum	R	28	15	11	7	0	92.1	113	11	25	25	5-6	0	4.09
Joe Heving†	R	37	16	11	7	1	82.0	94	5	22	34	8-1	2	3.73
Bill Harris	R	38	13	11	5	1	80.1	83	5	21	26	5-5	1	4.03
Archie McKain	L	27	37	5	1	0	99.2	119	6	44	27	5-4	6	4.52
Emerson Dickman	R	23	32	11	3	1	104.0	117	9	54	22	5-5	0	5.28
Lee Rogers†	L	24	14	2	0	0	27.2	32	4	18	7	1-1	0	6.51
Charlie Wagner	R	25	13	6	1	0	36.2	47	5	24	14	1-3	0	8.35
Dick Midkiff	R	23	13	2	0	0	35.1	43	5	21	10	1-1	0	5.09
Al Baker	R	32	3	0	0	0	7.2	13	2	2	2	0-0	0	9.39
Ted Olson	R	25	2	0	0	0	7.0	9	0	2	2	0-0	0	6.43
Bill Humphrey	R	27	2	0	0	0	2.0	5	0	1	0	0-0	0	9.00
Bill LeFebvre	L	22	1	0	0	0	4.0	8	2	0	0	0-0	0	13.50
Doc Cramer	R	32	1	0	0	0	4.0	3	0	3	1	0-0	0	4.50

1938 Cleveland Indians 3rd AL 86-66 .566 13.0 GB

Ossie Vitt

Player	Gm by Position	B	Age	G	AB	R	H	2B	3B	HR	RBI	BB	SO	SB	Avg	OBP	Slg
Frankie Pytlak	C99	R	29	113	364	46	112	14	7	1	43	36	15	9	.308	.376	.393
Hal Trosky	1B148	L	25	150	554	106	185	40	9	19	110	67	40	5	.334	.407	.542
Odell Hale	2B127	R	29	130	496	69	138	32	2	8	69	44	39	8	.278	.338	.399
Ken Keltner	3B149	R	21	149	576	86	159	31	9	26	113	33	75	4	.276	.319	.497
Lyn Lary	SS141	R	32	141	568	94	152	36	4	3	51	88	65	23	.268	.366	.361
Earl Averill	OF131	L	36	134	482	101	159	27	15	14	93	81	48	5	.330	.429	.535
Bruce Campbell	OF122	L	28	133	511	90	148	27	12	12	72	53	57	11	.290	.360	.460
Jeff Heath	OF122	L	23	126	502	104	172	31	18	21	112	33	55	3	.343	.383	.602
Roy Weatherly	OF55	L	23	83	210	32	55	14	3	2	18	14	14	8	.262	.308	.386
Rollie Hemsley	C58	R	31	66	203	27	60	11	3	2	28	23	14	1	.296	.367	.409
Moose Solters	OF46	R	32	67	199	30	40	6	3	2	22	13	28	4	.201	.250	.291
John Kroner	2B31,1B7,3B3*	R	29	51	117	13	29	16	0	1	17	19	6	0	.248	.353	.410
Skeeter Webb	SS13,3B3,2B2	R	28	20	58	11	16	2	0	0	2	8	7	1	.276	.364	.310
Hank Helf		R	24	6	13	1	1	0	0	0	1	1	1	0	.077	.143	.077
Oscar Grimes	2B2,1B1	R	23	4	10	2	2	0	1	0	2	2	0	0	.200	.333	.400
Tommy Irwin	SS3	R	25	3	9	1	1	0	0	0	0	3	1	0	.111	.333	.111
Ray Mack	2B2	R	21	2	6	2	2	0	1	0	2	0	1	0	.333	.333	.667
Chuck Workman	OF1	L	23	2	5	1	2	0	0	0	0	0	0	0	.400	.400	.400
Lou Boudreau	1B1	R	20	1	1	0	0	0	0	0	0	1	0	0	.000	.500	.000
Lloyd Russell		R	25	2	0	0	0	0	0	0	0	0	0	0	—	—	—

J. Kroner, 1 G at SS

Pitcher	T	Age	G	GS	CG	ShO	IP	H	HR	BB	SO	W-L	Sv	ERA
Bob Feller	R	19	39	36	20	2	277.2	225	13	208	240	17-11	1	4.08
Mel Harder	R	28	38	29	15	2	240.0	257	16	62	102	17-10	4	3.83
Johnny Allen	R	32	30	27	13	0	200.0	189	15	81	112	14-8	0	4.19
Earl Whitehill	L	38	26	23	4	0	160.1	187	18	83	60	9-8	0	5.56
Willis Hudlin	R	32	29	15	8	0	127.0	158	13	45	27	8-8	1	4.89
Johnny Humphries	R	23	45	6	1	0	103.0	105	6	63	56	9-8	6	5.24
Denny Galehouse	R	26	36	12	5	1	114.0	119	12	65	66	7-8	3	4.34
Al Milnar	L	24	23	5	2	0	68.1	90	5	26	29	3-1	1	5.00
Bill Zuber	R	25	15	0	0	0	28.2	33	0	20	14	0-3	1	5.02
Ken Jungels	R	22	9	0	0	0	15.1	21	1	18	7	1-0	0	8.80
Clay Smith	R	23	4	0	0	0	11.0	18	1	2	3	0-0	0	6.55
Joe Heving†	R	37	3	0	0	0	6.0	10	0	5	0	1-1	0	9.00
Charley Suche	L	22	1	0	0	0	1.1	4	0	3	1	0-0	0	27.00

1938 Detroit Tigers 4th AL 84-70 .545 16.0 GB

Mickey Cochrane (47-51)/Del Baker (37-19)

Player	Gm by Position	B	Age	G	AB	R	H	2B	3B	HR	RBI	BB	SO	SB	Avg	OBP	Slg
Rudy York	C116,OF14,1B1	R	24	135	463	85	138	27	2	33	127	92	74	1	.298	.417	.579
Hank Greenberg	1B155	R	27	155	556	144	175	23	4	58	146	119	92	7	.315	.438	.683
Charlie Gehringer	2B152	L	35	152	568	133	174	32	5	20	107	112	21	14	.306	.424	.486
Don Ross	3B75	R	23	77	265	22	69	7	1	1	30	28	11	1	.260	.331	.306
Billy Rogell	SS134	S	33	136	501	76	130	22	8	3	55	86	37	9	.259	.372	.353
Pete Fox	OF155	R	29	155	634	91	186	35	10	7	96	31	39	16	.293	.328	.413
Dixie Walker	OF114	L	27	127	454	84	140	27	6	6	43	65	32	5	.308	.396	.434
Chet Morgan	OF74	L	28	74	306	50	87	6	1	0	27	20	12	5	.284	.330	.310
Mark Christman	3B69,SS21	R	24	95	318	35	79	6	4	1	44	27	21	5	.248	.307	.302
Chet Laabs	OF53	R	26	64	211	26	50	7	3	7	37	15	52	3	.237	.288	.398
Jo-Jo White	OF55	L	29	78	206	40	54	6	1	0	15	30	15	3	.262	.359	.301
Birdie Tebbetts	C53	R	25	53	143	16	42	6	2	1	25	12	13	1	.294	.348	.385
Tony Piet	3B18,2B1	R	31	41	80	9	17	6	0	0	14	15	11	2	.213	.351	.288
Roy Cullenbine	OF17	S	24	25	67	12	19	1	3	0	9	12	9	2	.284	.392	.388
Ray Hayworth†	C7	R	34	8	19	1	4	0	0	0	5	3	4	1	.211	.318	.211
Benny McCoy	2B6,3B1	L	22	7	15	2	3	1	0	0	0	1	2	0	.200	.250	.267
George Archie		R	24	3	2	1	0	0	0	0	0	0	1	0	.000	.000	.000

Pitcher	T	Age	G	GS	CG	ShO	IP	H	HR	BB	SO	W-L	Sv	ERA
Vern Kennedy	R	31	33	26	11	0	190.1	215	13	113	53	12-9	2	5.06
Eldon Auker	R	27	27	24	12	1	160.2	184	14	56	46	11-10	0	5.27
George Gill	R	29	24	23	13	1	164.0	195	15	50	30	12-9	0	4.12
Tommy Bridges	R	31	25	20	13	0	151.0	171	14	58	101	13-9	1	4.59
Roxie Lawson	R	32	27	16	5	0	127.0	154	13	82	39	8-9	1	5.46
Boots Poffenberger	R	22	25	15	8	0	125.0	147	8	66	28	6-7	1	4.82
Al Benton	R	27	19	10	6	0	95.1	93	10	39	33	5-3	0	3.30
Schoolboy Rowe	R	28	4	3	0	0	21.0	20	1	11	4	0-2	0	3.00
Slick Coffman	R	27	39	6	1	0	95.2	120	6	48	31	4-4	2	6.02
Harry Eisenstat	L	22	32	9	5	0	125.1	131	7	29	37	9-6	4	3.73
Jake Wade	L	26	27	2	0	0	70.0	73	9	48	23	3-2	0	6.56
Bob Harris	R	21	3	1	1	0	10.0	14	0	4	7	1-0	0	7.20
Joe Rogalski	R	25	2	0	0	0	7.0	12	0	0	2	0-0	0	2.57
Woody Davis	R	25	2	0	0	0	6.0	3	0	4	1	0-0	0	1.50

1938 Washington Senators 5th AL 75-76 .497 23.5 GB

Bucky Harris

Player	Gm by Position	B	Age	G	AB	R	H	2B	3B	HR	RBI	BB	SO	SB	Avg	OBP	Slg
Rick Ferrell	C131	R	32	135	411	55	120	24	5	1	58	75	17	1	.292	.401	.382
Zeke Bonura	1B129	R	29	137	540	72	156	27	3	22	114	44	29	2	.289	.346	.472
Buddy Myer	2B121	L	34	127	437	79	147	22	8	6	71	93	32	9	.336	.454	.465
Buddy Lewis	3B151	L	21	151	656	122	194	35	9	12	91	58	35	17	.296	.354	.431
Cecil Travis	SS143	L	24	146	567	96	190	30	5	5	67	58	22	6	.335	.401	.432
Al Simmons	OF117	R	36	125	470	79	142	23	6	21	95	38	40	2	.302	.357	.511
George Case	OF101	R	22	107	433	69	132	27	3	2	40	39	28	11	.305	.362	.395
Sammy West†	OF85	L	33	92	344	51	104	19	5	5	47	33	21	1	.302	.363	.430
Taffy Wright	OF60	L	26	100	263	37	92	18	10	2	36	13	17	1	.350	.389	.517
John Stone	OF53	L	32	56	213	24	52	12	4	3	28	30	16	2	.244	.337	.380
Mel Almada†	OF47	L	25	47	197	24	48	7	4	1	15	8	16	4	.244	.277	.335
Ossie Bluege	2B38,SS10,1B1*	R	37	58	184	25	48	12	1	0	21	21	11	3	.261	.340	.337
Jimmy Wasdell	1B26,OF6	L	24	53	140	19	33	2	1	2	16	12	12	5	.236	.296	.307
Tony Giuliani	C46	R	25	46	115	10	25	4	0	0	15	8	3	1	.217	.268	.252
Goose Goslin	OF13	L	37	38	57	6	9	3	0	2	8	8	5	0	.158	.262	.316
Mickey Livingston	C2	R	23	2	4	0	3	2	0	0	1	0	1	0	.750	.750	1.250

O. Bluege, 1 G at 3B

Pitcher	T	Age	G	GS	CG	ShO	IP	H	HR	BB	SO	W-L	Sv	ERA
Dutch Leonard	R	29	33	31	15	3	223.1	221	11	53	68	12-15	0	3.43
Wes Ferrell†	R	30	23	22	9	0	149.0	193	12	68	36	13-8	0	5.92
Ken Chase	L	24	32	21	7	0	150.0	151	4	113	64	9-10	1	5.58
Montie Weaver	R	32	31	18	7	0	139.0	157	9	74	43	7-6	0	5.24
Rene Monteagudo	L	22	5	3	2	0	22.0	26	3	15	13	1-1	0	5.73
Pete Appleton	R	34	43	10	5	0	164.1	175	12	61	62	7-9	5	4.60
Harry Kelley†	R	32	38	14	7	2	148.1	162	12	46	44	9-8	1	4.49
Jimmie DeShong	R	28	31	14	1	0	131.1	160	11	83	41	5-8	0	6.58
Chief Hogsett	L	34	31	9	1	0	91.0	107	12	36	33	5-6	3	6.03
Joe Krakauskas	L	23	29	10	5	1	121.1	99	4	88	104	7-5	0	3.12
Joe Kohlman	R	25	7	0	0	0	14.1	12	1	11	5	0-0	0	6.28
Bill Phebus	R	28	5	0	0	0	6.1	9	1	7	2	0-0	1	11.37

1938 Chicago White Sox 6th AL 65-83 .439 32.0 GB

Jimmy Dykes

Player	Gm by Position	B	Age	G	AB	R	H	2B	3B	HR	RBI	BB	SO	SB	Avg	OBP	Slg
Luke Sewell	C65	R	37	65	211	23	45	4	1	0	27	20	20	0	.213	.284	.242
Joe Kuhel	1B111	L	32	117	412	67	110	27	4	8	51	72	35	9	.267	.376	.410
Jackie Hayes	2B61	R	31	62	238	40	78	21	2	1	20	24	6	3	.328	.389	.445
Marv Owen	3B140	R	32	141	577	84	162	23	6	6	55	45	31	6	.281	.337	.373
Luke Appling	SS78	R	31	81	294	41	89	14	0	0	44	42	17	1	.303	.392	.350
Mike Kreevich	OF127	R	30	129	489	73	145	26	12	6	73	55	23	13	.297	.371	.436
Gee Walker	OF107	R	30	120	442	69	135	23	6	16	87	38	32	9	.305	.360	.493
Hank Steinbacher	OF101	L	25	106	399	59	132	23	8	4	61	41	19	1	.331	.393	.459
Rip Radcliff	OF99,1B23	L	32	129	503	64	166	23	6	5	81	36	17	5	.330	.376	.429
Boze Berger	SS67,2B42,3B9	R	28	118	470	60	102	15	3	3	36	43	80	4	.217	.284	.281
Tony Rensa	C57	R	36	59	165	15	41	5	0	3	19	25	16	1	.248	.351	.333
Norm Schlueter	C34	R	21	35	118	11	27	5	1	0	7	4	15	1	.229	.254	.288
Larry Rosenthal	OF22	L	28	61	105	14	30	5	1	1	12	12	13	0	.286	.359	.381
Jimmy Dykes	2B23,3B1	R	41	26	89	9	27	4	2	2	13	10	8	0	.303	.374	.461
George Meyer	2B24	R	28	24	81	10	24	2	2	0	9	11	17	3	.296	.387	.370
Merv Connors	1B16	R	24	24	62	14	22	4	0	6	13	9	17	0	.355	.437	.710
Mike Tresh	C10	R	24	10	29	3	7	2	0	0	2	8	4	0	.241	.405	.310
Johnny Gerlach	SS8	R	21	9	25	2	7	0	0	0	1	4	2	0	.280	.379	.280
Tommy Thompson	1B1	L	28	19	18	2	2	0	0	0	2	1	2	0	.111	.158	.111
Jesse Landrum	2B3	R	25	4	6	0	0	0	0	0	1	0	2	0	.000	.000	.000
Joe Martin		R	26	1	0	0	0	0	0	0	0	0	0	0	—	—	—

Pitcher	T	Age	G	GS	CG	ShO	IP	H	HR	BB	SO	W-L	Sv	ERA
Thornton Lee	L	31	33	30	18	1	245.1	252	12	94	77	13-12	1	3.49
John Whitehead	R	29	32	24	10	1	183.1	218	12	80	38	10-11	2	4.76
Ted Lyons	R	37	23	23	17	1	194.2	238	13	52	54	9-11	0	3.70
Monty Stratton	R	26	26	22	17	0	186.1	186	18	56	82	15-9	2	4.01
Jack Knott†	R	31	20	18	9	0	131.0	135	8	54	35	5-10	0	4.05
Bill Dietrich	R	28	8	7	1	0	48.0	49	7	31	11	2-4	0	5.44
Sugar Cain	R	31	5	3	0	0	19.2	26	0	18	6	0-1	0	4.58
Johnny Rigney	R	23	38	12	7	0	167.0	164	16	72	84	9-9	1	3.56
Frank Gabler†	R	26	18	7	3	0	69.1	101	12	34	17	1-7	0	9.09
Harry Boyles	R	26	9	2	1	0	29.1	31	2	25	18	0-4	1	5.22
Clint Brown	R	34	8	0	0	0	13.2	16	0	9	2	1-3	2	4.61
Bill Cox†	R	25	7	1	0	0	11.2	11	0	13	5	0-2	0	6.94
Gene Ford	R	26	4	0	0	0	14.0	21	1	12	2	0-0	0	10.29
Bob Uhl	L	24	1	0	0	0	2.0	1	0	0	0	0-0	0	0.00
George Gick	R	22	1	0	0	0	1.0	0	0	0	1	0-0	0	0.00

1938 St. Louis Browns 7th AL 55-97 .362 44.0 GB

Gabby Street (53-90)/Oscar Melillo (2-7)

Player	Gm by Position	B	Age	G	AB	R	H	2B	3B	HR	RBI	BB	SO	SB	Avg	OBP	Slg
Billy Sullivan	C99	L	27	111	375	35	104	16	1	7	49	20	10	8	.277	.316	.381
George McQuinn	1B148	L	28	148	602	100	195	42	7	12	82	58	49	4	.324	.384	.477
Don Heffner	2B141	R	27	141	473	47	116	23	3	2	69	65	53	1	.245	.341	.319
Harlond Clift	3B149	R	25	149	534	119	155	25	7	34	118	118	67	10	.290	.423	.554
Red Kress	SS150	R	31	150	566	74	171	33	3	7	79	69	47	5	.302	.378	.408
Beau Bell	OF132,1B4	R	30	147	526	91	138	35	3	13	84	71	46	1	.262	.350	.414
Buster Mills	OF113	R	29	123	466	66	133	24	4	3	46	43	46	7	.285	.350	.373
Mel Almada†	OF101	L	25	102	436	77	149	22	2	3	37	38	22	9	.342	.398	.422
Mel Mazzera	OF47	L	24	86	204	33	57	8	2	6	29	12	25	1	.279	.329	.426
Tommy Heath	C65	R	24	70	194	22	44	13	0	2	22	35	24	0	.227	.345	.325
Sammy West†	OF41	L	33	44	165	17	51	8	2	1	27	14	9	1	.309	.363	.400
Glenn McQuillen	OF30	R	23	43	116	14	33	4	0	0	13	4	12	0	.284	.308	.319
Roy Hughes	2B21,3B5,SS2	R	27	58	96	16	27	3	0	2	13	12	11	3	.281	.361	.375
Joe Grace	OF12	L	24	12	47	7	16	1	0	0	4	2	3	0	.340	.367	.362
Ethan Allen	OF7	R	34	19	33	4	10	3	1	0	4	2	4	0	.303	.343	.455
Sam Harshany	C10	R	28	11	24	2	7	0	0	0	0	3	2	0	.292	.370	.292
Sig Gryska	SS7	R	22	7	21	3	10	2	1	0	4	3	3	0	.476	.542	.667
Johnny Lucadello	3B6	R	19	7	20	1	3	1	0	0	0	0	0	0	.150	.150	.200

Pitcher	T	Age	G	GS	CG	ShO	IP	H	HR	BB	SO	W-L	Sv	ERA
Bobo Newsom	R	30	44	40	31	0	329.2	334	30	192	226	20-16	1	5.08
Lefty Mills	L	28	30	27	15	1	210.1	216	16	116	134	10-12	0	5.31
Oral Hildebrand	R	31	23	23	10	0	163.0	194	18	73	66	8-10	0	5.69
Jim Walkup	R	28	18	13	1	0	94.0	127	13	53	28	1-12	0	6.80
Jack Knott†	R	31	7	4	0	0	30.0	35	3	15	8	1-2	0	4.80
Emil Bildilli	L	25	5	3	2	0	21.2	33	3	11	11	1-2	0	7.06
Vito Tamulis†	L	26	3	2	0	0	15.1	26	2	10	11	0-3	0	7.63
Bill Trotter	R	29	1	1	1	0	8.0	8	0	0	1	0-1	0	5.63
Harry Kimberlin	R	29	1	1	1	0	8.0	8	1	3	1	0-0	0	3.38
Jim Weaver†	R	34	1	1	0	0	7.0	9	0	9	4	0-1	0	9.00
Ed Cole	R	29	36	6	1	0	88.2	116	8	48	26	1-5	3	5.18
Russ Van Atta	L	32	25	12	3	1	104.0	118	7	61	35	4-7	0	6.06
Bill Cox†	R	25	22	7	1	0	63.0	81	8	35	16	1-4	0	7.00
Ed Linke	R	26	21	2	0	0	39.2	60	6	33	18	1-7	0	7.94
Fred Johnson	R	44	17	6	3	0	69.0	91	7	27	24	3-7	3	5.61
Les Tietje	R	26	17	8	2	1	62.0	83	8	38	15	2-5	0	7.55
Julio Bonetti	R	26	17	0	0	0	28.1	41	1	13	7	2-3	0	6.35
Glenn Liebhardt	R	27	2	0	0	0	3.0	4	1	0	1	0-0	0	6.00

1938 Philadelphia Athletics 8th AL 53-99 .349 46.0 GB

Connie Mack

Player	Gm by Position	B	Age	G	AB	R	H	2B	3B	HR	RBI	BB	SO	SB	Avg	OBP	Slg
Frankie Hayes	C90	R	23	99	316	56	92	19	3	11	55	54	51	2	.291	.396	.475
Lou Finney	1B64,OF46	L	27	122	454	61	125	21	12	10	48	39	25	5	.275	.333	.441
Dario Lodigiani	2B80,3B13	R	21	93	325	36	91	15	1	6	44	34	25	3	.280	.361	.388
Bill Werber	3B134	R	30	134	499	92	129	22	7	11	69	93	37	19	.259	.377	.397
Wayne Ambler	SS116,2B4	R	22	120	393	42	92	21	2	0	38	48	31	2	.234	.317	.298
Bob Johnson	OF150,2B3,3B1	R	31	152	563	114	176	27	9	30	113	87	73	9	.313	.406	.552
Wally Moses	OF139	L	27	142	589	86	181	29	8	8	49	58	31	15	.307	.369	.424
Sam Chapman	OF110	R	22	114	406	60	105	17	7	17	63	55	94	3	.259	.353	.461
Stan Sperry	2B60	L	24	60	253	28	69	6	3	0	27	15	9	1	.273	.313	.320
Dick Siebert†	1B46	L	26	48	194	24	55	8	3	0	28	10	9	2	.284	.329	.356
Earle Brucker	C44,1B1	R	37	53	171	26	64	21	1	3	35	19	16	1	.374	.437	.561
Ace Parker	SS26,2B9,3B9	R	26	56	113	12	26	5	0	0	12	10	16	1	.230	.293	.274
Hal Wagner	C30	L	22	33	88	10	20	2	1	0	8	8	9	0	.227	.299	.273
Nick Etten	1B22	L	24	22	81	6	21	6	2	0	11	9	7	1	.259	.333	.383
Mule Haas	OF12,1B6	L	34	40	78	7	16	2	0	0	12	12	10	0	.205	.311	.231
Gene Hasson	1B19	L	22	19	69	10	19	6	2	1	12	12	7	0	.275	.383	.464
Skeeter Newsome	SS15	R	27	17	48	7	13	4	0	0	7	1	4	1	.271	.286	.354
Irv Bartling	SS13,3B1	R	24	14	46	5	8	1	1	0	5	3	7	0	.174	.224	.239
Babe Barna	OF7	L	23	9	30	4	4	0	0	0	2	3	5	0	.133	.212	.133
Rusty Peters	SS2	R	23	2	7	0	0	0	0	0	0	0	1	0	.000	.000	.000
Paul Easterling	OF1	R	32	4	7	1	2	0	0	0	0	1	2	0	.286	.375	.286
Charlie Berry	C1	R	35	1	2	0	0	0	0	0	0	0	0	0	.000	.000	.000

Pitcher	T	Age	G	GS	CG	ShO	IP	H	HR	BB	SO	W-L	Sv	ERA
George Caster	R	30	42	40	20	2	281.1	310	25	117	112	16-20	1	4.35
Bud Thomas	R	27	42	29	7	0	212.1	259	23	62	48	9-14	0	4.92
Buck Ross	R	23	29	28	10	0	184.1	218	23	80	54	9-16	0	5.32
Lynn Nelson	R	33	32	23	13	0	191.0	215	29	79	75	10-11	2	5.65
Jim Reninger	R	23	4	4	1	0	22.2	28	3	14	9	0-2	0	7.15
Harry Kelley†	R	32	4	3	0	0	8.0	17	0	10	3	0-2	0	16.88
Randy Gumpert	R	20	4	2	0	0	12.1	24	1	10	1	0-2	0	10.95
Eddie Smith	L	24	43	7	0	0	130.2	151	13	76	78	3-10	4	5.92
Nels Potter	R	26	35	9	4	0	111.1	139	15	49	43	2-12	5	6.47
Al Williams	R	24	30	8	1	0	93.1	128	6	54	25	0-7	0	6.94
Dave Smith	R	23	21	0	0	0	44.1	50	0	28	13	2-1	0	5.08
Chubby Dean	L	21	6	1	0	0	23.0	22	3	15	3	2-1	0	3.52
Ralph Buxton	R	27	5	0	0	0	9.1	12	1	5	9	0-1	0	4.82

Seasons: Team Rosters 673

»1938 Chicago Cubs 1st NL 89-63 .586 —

Charlie Grimm (45-36)/Gabby Hartnett (44-27)

Player	Gm by Position	B	Age	G	AB	R	H	2B	3B	HR	RBI	BB	SO	SB	Avg	OBP	Slg
Gabby Hartnett	C83	R	37	88	299	40	82	19	1	10	59	48	17	1	.274	.380	.445
Ripper Collins	1B135	S	34	143	490	78	131	22	8	13	61	54	48	1	.267	.344	.424
Billy Herman	2B151	R	28	152	624	86	173	34	7	1	56	59	31	3	.277	.342	.359
Stan Hack	3B152	L	28	152	609	109	195	34	11	4	67	94	39	16	.320	.411	.432
Billy Jurges	SS136	R	30	137	465	53	114	18	3	1	47	58	53	3	.245	.335	.303
Carl Reynolds	OF125	R	35	125	497	59	150	28	10	3	67	22	32	9	.302	.335	.416
Frank Demaree	OF125	R	28	129	476	63	130	15	7	8	62	45	34	1	.273	.341	.384
Augie Galan	OF103	S	26	110	395	52	113	16	9	6	69	49	17	8	.286	.368	.418
Phil Cavarretta	OF52,1B28	L	21	92	268	29	64	11	4	1	28	14	27	4	.239	.287	.321
Ken O'Dea	C71	L	25	86	247	22	65	12	1	3	33	12	18	1	.263	.297	.356
Joe Marty	OF68	R	24	76	235	32	57	8	3	7	35	18	26	0	.243	.305	.391
Tony Lazzeri	SS25,3B7,2B4*	R	34	54	120	21	32	5	0	5	23	22	30	0	.267	.380	.433
Bob Garbark	C20,1B1	R	28	23	54	2	14	0	0	0	5	1	0	0	.259	.273	.259
Coaker Triplett	OF9	R	26	12	36	4	9	2	1	0	2	0	1	0	.250	.250	.361
Jim Asbell	OF10	R	24	17	33	6	6	2	0	0	3	3	9	0	.182	.250	.242
Steve Mesner	SS1	R	20	2	4	2	1	0	0	0	0	1	1	0	.250	.400	.250
Bobby Mattick	SS1	R	22	1	1	0	1	0	0	0	1	0	0	0	1.000	1.000	1.000

T. Lazzeri, 1 G at OF

Pitcher	T	Age	G	GS	CG	ShO	IP	H	HR	BB	SO	W-L	Sv	ERA
Bill Lee	R	28	44	37	19	9	291.0	281	18	74	121	22-9	2	2.66
Clay Bryant	R	26	44	30	17	3	270.1	235	6	125	135	19-11	2	3.10
Larry French	L	30	43	27	10	3	201.1	210	17	62	83	10-19	0	3.80
Tex Carleton	R	31	33	24	9	0	167.2	213	11	74	80	10-9	0	5.42
Dizzy Dean	R	28	13	10	3	1	74.2	63	2	8	22	7-1	0	1.81
Vance Page	R	32	13	9	3	0	68.0	90	4	13	18	5-4	1	3.84
Kirby Higbe	R	23	2	2	0	0	10.0	10	1	6	4	0-0	0	5.40
Charlie Root	R	39	44	11	5	0	160.2	163	10	30	70	8-7	8	2.86
Jack Russell	R	32	42	0	0	0	102.1	100	1	30	29	6-1	3	3.34
Bob Logan	L	28	14	0	0	0	22.2	18	0	17	10	0-2	2	2.78
Al Epperly	R	20	9	4	1	0	27.0	28	1	15	10	2-0	0	3.67
Newt Kimball	R	23	1	0	0	0	1.0	3	0	0	1	0-0	0	9.00

1938 Pittsburgh Pirates 2nd NL 86-64 .573 2.0 GB

Pie Traynor

Player	Gm by Position	B	Age	G	AB	R	H	2B	3B	HR	RBI	BB	SO	SB	Avg	OBP	Slg
Al Todd	C132	R	36	133	491	52	130	19	7	7	75	18	31	2	.265	.296	.375
Gus Suhr	1B145	L	32	145	530	82	156	35	14	3	64	87	37	4	.294	.394	.430
Pep Young	2B149	R	30	149	562	58	156	36	5	4	79	40	64	7	.278	.329	.381
Lee Handley	3B136	R	24	139	570	91	153	25	8	6	51	53	31	7	.268	.332	.372
Arky Vaughan	SS147	L	26	148	541	88	174	35	5	7	68	104	21	14	.322	.433	.444
Paul Waner	OF147	L	35	148	625	77	175	31	6	6	69	47	28	2	.280	.331	.378
Lloyd Waner	OF144	L	32	147	619	79	194	25	7	5	57	28	11	5	.313	.343	.401
Johnny Rizzo	OF140	R	25	143	555	97	167	31	9	23	111	54	61	1	.301	.368	.514
Woody Jensen	OF38	L	30	68	125	12	25	4	0	0	10	1	3	0	.200	.213	.232
Bill Brubaker	3B18,1B9,SS3*	R	27	45	112	18	33	5	0	3	19	9	14	2	.295	.347	.420
Ray Berres	C40	R	30	40	100	7	23	2	0	0	6	8	10	0	.230	.287	.250
Johnny Dickshot	OF10	R	28	29	35	3	8	0	0	0	4	8	5	3	.229	.372	.229
Tommy Thevenow	2B9,SS4,3B1	R	34	15	25	2	5	0	0	0	2	4	0	0	.200	.333	.200
Heinie Manush†		L	36	15	13	2	4	1	1	0	4	2	0	0	.308	.400	.538

B. Brubaker, 1 G at OF

Pitcher	T	Age	G	GS	CG	ShO	IP	H	HR	BB	SO	W-L	Sv	ERA
Russ Bauers	R	24	40	34	12	3	243.0	207	7	99	117	13-14	3	3.07
Jim Tobin	R	25	40	33	14	2	241.1	254	17	66	70	14-12	0	3.47
Cy Blanton	R	29	29	25	10	1	172.2	190	13	46	80	11-7	0	3.70
Bob Klinger	R	30	28	21	10	1	159.1	152	7	42	58	12-5	1	2.99
Ed Brandt	L	33	24	14	5	1	96.1	93	3	35	38	5-4	0	3.46
Red Lucas	R	36	13	13	4	0	84.0	90	5	16	19	6-3	0	3.54
Mace Brown	R	29	51	2	0	0	132.2	155	5	44	55	15-9	5	3.80
Bill Swift	R	30	36	9	2	0	150.0	155	9	40	77	7-5	4	3.24
Joe Bowman	R	28	17	1	0	0	60.0	68	2	20	25	3-4	1	4.65
Rip Sewell	R	31	17	0	0	0	38.1	41	3	21	17	0-1	1	4.23
Ken Heintzelman	L	22	1	0	0	0	2.0	1	0	3	1	0-0	0	9.00

1938 New York Giants 3rd NL 83-67 .553 5.0 GB

Bill Terry

Player	Gm by Position	B	Age	G	AB	R	H	2B	3B	HR	RBI	BB	SO	SB	Avg	OBP	Slg
Harry Danning	C114	R	26	120	448	59	137	26	3	9	60	23	40	1	.306	.345	.438
Johnny McCarthy	1B125	L	28	134	470	55	128	13	4	8	59	39	28	3	.272	.329	.368
Alex Kampouris†	2B79	R	25	82	268	35	66	9	1	5	37	27	50	0	.246	.318	.343
Mel Ott	3B113,OF37	L	29	150	527	116	164	23	6	36	116	118	47	2	.311	.442	.583
Dick Bartell	SS127	R	30	127	481	67	126	26	1	9	49	55	60	4	.262	.347	.376
Jimmy Ripple	OF131	L	28	134	501	68	131	21	3	10	60	49	21	2	.261	.333	.375
Jo-Jo Moore	OF114	L	29	125	506	76	153	23	6	11	56	22	27	2	.302	.335	.437
Hank Leiber	OF89	R	27	98	360	50	97	18	4	12	65	31	45	0	.269	.327	.442
Bob Seeds	OF76	R	31	81	296	35	86	12	3	9	52	20	33	0	.291	.338	.443
Lou Chiozza	2B34,OF16,3B1	L	28	57	179	15	42	7	2	3	17	12	7	5	.235	.283	.346
George Myatt	SS24,3B19	L	24	43	170	27	52	2	1	3	10	14	13	10	.306	.362	.382
Gus Mancuso	C44	R	32	52	158	19	55	8	0	2	15	17	13	0	.348	.411	.437
Sam Leslie	1B32	L	32	76	154	12	39	7	1	1	16	11	6	0	.253	.307	.331
Bill Cissell	2B33,3B6	R	34	38	149	19	40	6	0	2	18	6	11	1	.268	.297	.349
Mickey Haslin	3B15,2B13	R	27	31	102	13	33	3	0	3	15	4	4	0	.324	.361	.441
Wally Berger†	OF9	R	32	16	32	5	6	0	0	0	4	2	4	0	.188	.235	.188
Blondy Ryan	2B5,3B3,SS2	R	32	12	24	1	5	0	0	0	0	1	3	0	.208	.240	.208
Les Powers		L	28	2	3	0	0	0	0	0	0	0	1	0	.000	.000	.000

Pitcher	T	Age	G	GS	CG	ShO	IP	H	HR	BB	SO	W-L	Sv	ERA
Harry Gumbert	R	28	38	33	14	1	235.2	238	13	84	84	15-13	0	4.01
Cliff Melton	L	26	36	31	10	1	243.0	266	19	61	101	14-14	0	3.89
Hal Schumacher	R	27	28	28	12	4	185.0	178	12	50	54	13-8	0	3.50
Carl Hubbell	L	35	24	22	13	1	179.0	171	16	33	104	13-10	1	3.07
Slick Castleman	R	24	21	14	4	0	90.2	108	4	37	18	4-5	0	4.17
Dick Coffman	R	31	51	3	1	1	111.1	116	3	21	21	8-4	12	3.48
Jumbo Brown	R	31	43	0	0	0	90.0	65	5	28	42	5-3	5	1.80
Bill Lohrman	R	25	31	14	3	0	152.0	152	9	33	52	9-6	0	3.32
Johnnie Wittig	R	24	13	6	2	0	39.1	41	4	26	14	2-3	0	4.81
Hy Vandenberg	R	31	6	1	0	0	18.0	28	2	12	7	0-1	0	7.50
Tom Baker	R	25	2	0	0	0	4.0	5	0	3	0	0-0	0	6.75
Oscar Georgy	R	21	1	0	0	0	1.0	2	0	1	0	0-0	0	18.00

1938 Cincinnati Reds 4th NL 82-68 .547 6.0 GB

Bill McKechnie

Player	Gm by Position	B	Age	G	AB	R	H	2B	3B	HR	RBI	BB	SO	SB	Avg	OBP	Slg
Ernie Lombardi	C123	R	30	129	489	60	167	30	1	19	95	40	14	0	.342	.391	.524
Frank McCormick	1B151	R	27	151	640	89	209	40	4	5	106	18	17	1	.327	.348	.425
Lonny Frey	2B121,SS3	L	27	124	501	76	133	26	6	4	36	49	50	4	.265	.331	.365
Lew Riggs	3B140	L	28	142	531	53	134	21	13	2	55	40	28	3	.252	.311	.352
Billy Myers	SS123,2B11	R	27	134	442	57	112	18	6	12	47	41	80	2	.253	.317	.403
Harry Craft	OF151	R	23	151	612	70	165	28	9	15	83	29	46	3	.270	.305	.418
Ival Goodman	OF142	L	29	145	568	103	166	27	10	30	92	53	51	3	.292	.368	.533
Wally Berger†	OF98	R	32	99	407	74	125	23	4	16	56	29	44	2	.307	.356	.501
Dusty Cooke	OF51	L	31	82	233	41	64	15	1	2	33	28	36	0	.275	.355	.373
Willard Hershberger	C39,2B1	R	28	49	105	12	29	3	1	0	12	5	6	1	.276	.315	.324
Nolen Richardson	SS35	R	35	35	100	8	29	4	0	0	10	3	4	0	.290	.311	.330
Lee Gamble	OF9	L	28	53	75	13	24	3	1	0	5	0	6	0	.320	.320	.387
Alex Kampouris†	2B21	R	25	21	74	13	19	1	0	2	7	10	13	0	.257	.353	.351
Don Lang	3B15,2B1,SS1	R	23	21	50	5	13	3	1	1	11	2	7	0	.260	.288	.420
Spud Davis†	C11	R	33	12	36	3	6	1	0	0	1	5	6	0	.167	.286	.194
Justin Stein†	SS7,2B2	R	26	11	18	3	6	1	0	0	1	0	1	0	.333	.333	.389
Kiddo Davis	OF5	R	36	5	18	3	5	1	0	0	0	1	4	0	.278	.316	.333
Nino Bongiovanni	OF2	L	26	2	7	0	2	1	0	0	0	0	0	0	.286	.286	.429
Buck Jordan†		L	31	9	7	0	2	0	0	0	0	2	0	0	.286	.444	.286
Dick West		R	22	1	1	0	0	0	0	0	0	0	0	0	.000	.000	.000
Jimmy Outlaw		R	25	4	0	1	0	0	0	0	0	0	0	0	—	—	—

Pitcher	T	Age	G	GS	CG	ShO	IP	H	HR	BB	SO	W-L	Sv	ERA
Paul Derringer	R	31	41	37	26	4	307.0	315	20	49	132	21-14	3	2.93
J. Vander Meer	L	23	32	29	16	3	225.1	177	12	103	125	15-10	0	3.12
Bucky Walters†	R	29	27	22	11	2	168.1	168	5	66	65	11-6	1	3.69
Peaches Davis	R	33	29	19	11	1	167.2	193	9	40	28	7-12	1	3.97
Jim Weaver†	R	34	30	15	2	0	129.1	109	6	54	64	6-4	3	3.13
Whitey Moore	R	26	19	11	3	1	90.1	66	4	42	38	6-4	0	3.49
Lee Grissom	L	30	14	7	0	0	51.0	60	4	22	16	2-3	0	5.29
Joe Cascarella	R	31	33	1	0	0	61.0	66	2	22	30	4-7	4	4.57
Gene Schott	R	24	31	4	0	0	83.0	89	8	32	21	5-5	2	4.45
Al Hollingsworth†	L	30	9	4	1	0	34.0	43	2	12	13	2-2	0	7.15
Ray Benge	R	36	9	0	0	0	15.1	13	1	6	5	1-1	2	4.11
Red Barrett	R	23	6	2	2	0	28.2	28	2	15	5	2-0	0	3.14
Ted Kleinhans	L	39	1	0	0	0	1.0	2	0	0	0	0-0	0	9.00

1938 Boston Braves 5th NL 77-75 .507 12.0 GB

Casey Stengel

Player	Gm by Position	B	Age	G	AB	R	H	2B	3B	HR	RBI	BB	SO	SB	Avg	OBP	Slg
Ray Mueller	C75	R	26	83	274	23	65	8	6	4	35	16	28	3	.237	.282	.354
Elbie Fletcher	1B146	L	22	147	529	71	144	24	7	6	48	60	40	5	.272	.351	.378
Tony Cuccinello	2B147	R	30	147	555	62	147	25	2	9	76	52	32	4	.265	.331	.366
Joe Stripp†	3B58	R	35	59	229	19	63	10	0	1	19	10	7	2	.275	.305	.332
Rabbit Warstler	SS135,2B7	R	34	142	467	37	108	10	4	0	40	48	38	3	.231	.303	.270
Vince DiMaggio	OF149,2B1	R	25	150	540	71	123	28	3	14	61	65	134	11	.228	.313	.369
Johnny Cooney	OF110,1B13	R	37	120	432	45	117	25	5	0	17	22	12	2	.271	.308	.352
Max West	OF109,1B7	L	21	123	418	47	98	16	5	10	63	38	38	5	.234	.300	.368
Debs Garms	OF63,3B54	L	30	117	428	62	135	19	1	0	47	34	22	4	.315	.371	.364
Al Lopez	C71	R	29	71	236	19	63	6	1	1	14	11	24	5	.267	.305	.314
Gene Moore	OF47	L	28	54	180	27	49	8	3	3	19	16	20	1	.272	.338	.400
Gil English	3B43,OF3,2B2*	R	28	53	165	17	41	6	0	2	21	15	16	1	.248	.315	.321
Harl Maggert	OF10,3B8	R	24	66	89	12	25	3	0	3	19	10	20	0	.281	.354	.416
Jim Hitchcock	SS24,3B2	R	27	28	76	2	13	0	0	0	7	2	11	1	.171	.192	.171
Johnny Riddle	C19	R	32	19	57	6	16	1	0	0	2	4	2	0	.281	.328	.298
Bobby Reis	P16,OF10,SS3*	R	29	34	49	6	9	0	0	0	4	1	3	1	.184	.200	.184
Roy Johnson	OF7	L	35	7	29	2	5	0	0	0	1	1	5	1	.172	.200	.172
Eddie Mayo	3B6,SS2	L	28	8	14	2	3	0	0	1	4	1	0	0	.214	.267	.429
Joe Walsh	SS4	R	21	4	8	0	0	0	0	0	0	0	2	0	.000	.000	.000
Ralph McLeod	OF1	L	21	6	7	1	2	1	0	0	0	0	2	0	.286	.286	.429
Butch Sutcliffe	C3	R	22	4	4	1	1	0	0	0	2	2	1	0	.250	.500	.250
Bob Kahle		R	22	8	3	2	1	0	0	0	0	0	0	0	.333	.333	.333
Tom Kane	2B2	R	31	2	2	0	0	0	0	0	0	2	0	0	.000	.500	.000

G. English, 2 G at SS; B. Reis, 1 G at C, 1 G at 2B

Pitcher	T	Age	G	GS	CG	ShO	IP	H	HR	BB	SO	W-L	Sv	ERA
Jim Turner	R	34	35	34	22	3	268.0	267	21	54	71	14-18	0	3.46
Lou Fette	R	31	33	32	17	3	239.2	235	11	79	83	11-13	1	3.15
Danny MacFayden	R	33	29	29	19	5	219.2	208	6	64	58	14-9	0	2.95
Johnny Lanning	R	27	32	18	4	1	138.0	146	5	52	39	8-7	0	3.72
Milt Shoffner	L	32	26	15	9	1	139.2	147	7	36	49	8-7	1	3.54
Tom Earley	R	21	2	1	1	0	11.0	8	2	1	4	1-0	0	3.27
Ira Hutchinson	R	27	36	12	4	1	151.0	150	3	61	38	9-8	4	2.74
Dick Errickson	R	24	34	10	6	1	122.2	113	1	56	40	9-7	6	3.15
Bobby Reis	R	29	16	2	1	0	57.2	61	5	41	20	1-6	0	4.99
Roy Weir	L	27	5	0	0	0	13.1	14	4	6	3	1-0	0	6.75
Tommy Reis†	R	23	4	0	0	0	6.1	8	1	1	4	0-0	0	7.11
Art Doll	R	25	3	0	0	0	4.0	4	0	3	1	0-0	0	2.25
Art Kenney	L	22	2	0	0	0	2.1	3	0	8	2	0-0	0	15.43
Johnny Niggeling	R	34	2	0	0	0	2.0	4	0	1	1	1-0	0	9.00
Hiker Moran	R	26	1	0	0	0	3.0	1	0	1	0	0-0	0	0.00
Mike Balas	R	28	1	0	0	0	1.1	3	0	0	0	0-0	0	6.75
Frank Gabler†	R	26	1	0	0	0	0.1	3	0	1	0	0-0	0	81.00

1938 St. Louis Cardinals 6th NL 71-80 .470 17.5 GB

Frank Frisch (63-72)/Mike Gonzalez (8-8)

Player	Gm by Position	B	Age	G	AB	R	H	2B	3B	HR	RBI	BB	SO	SB	Avg	OBP	Slg
Mickey Owen	C116	R	22	122	397	45	106	25	2	4	36	32	14	2	.267	.325	.370
Johnny Mize	1B140	L	25	149	531	85	179	34	16	27	102	74	47	0	.337	.422	.614
Stu Martin	2B99	L	24	114	417	54	116	26	2	1	27	30	28	4	.278	.328	.357
Don Gutteridge	3B73,SS68	R	26	142	552	61	141	21	15	9	64	29	49	14	.255	.293	.397
Lynn Myers	SS69	R	24	70	227	18	55	10	2	1	19	9	25	9	.242	.271	.317
Joe Medwick	OF144	R	26	146	590	100	190	47	8	21	122	42	41	0	.322	.369	.536
Enos Slaughter	OF92	L	22	112	395	59	109	20	10	8	58	32	38	1	.276	.330	.438
Terry Moore	OF75,3B6	R	26	94	312	49	85	21	3	4	21	46	19	9	.272	.366	.397
Don Padgett	OF71,1B16,C6	L	26	110	388	59	105	26	5	8	65	18	28	0	.271	.303	.425
Jimmy Brown	2B49,SS30,3B24	S	28	108	382	50	115	12	6	0	38	27	9	7	.301	.350	.364
Pepper Martin	OF62,3B4	R	34	91	269	34	79	18	2	2	38	18	34	4	.294	.340	.398
Joe Stripp†	3B51	R	35	54	199	24	57	7	0	0	18	18	10	0	.286	.349	.322
Frenchy Bordagaray	OF29,3B4	R	28	81	156	19	44	5	1	0	21	8	9	2	.282	.325	.327
Herb Bremer	C50	R	24	50	151	14	33	5	1	2	14	9	36	1	.219	.263	.305
Jim Bucher	2B14,3B1	L	27	17	57	7	13	3	1	0	7	2	2	0	.228	.254	.316
Hal Epps	OF10	L	24	17	50	8	15	0	0	1	3	2	4	2	.300	.327	.360
Creepy Crespi	SS7	R	20	7	19	2	5	2	0	0	1	2	7	0	.263	.333	.368
Tuck Stainback†	OF2	R	26	6	10	2	0	0	0	0	0	0	3	0	.000	.000	.000
Dick Siebert†		L	26	1	1	0	1	0	0	0	0	0	0	0	1.000	1.000	1.000

Pitcher	T	Age	G	GS	CG	ShO	IP	H	HR	BB	SO	W-L	Sv	ERA
Bob Weiland	L	32	35	29	11	1	228.1	248	14	67	117	16-11	1	3.59
Lon Warneke	R	29	31	26	12	4	197.0	199	14	64	89	13-8	0	3.97
Bill McGee	R	28	47	25	10	1	216.0	216	4	78	104	7-12	5	3.21
Curt Davis	R	34	40	21	8	2	173.1	187	9	27	36	12-8	3	3.63
Roy Henshaw	L	26	27	15	4	0	130.0	132	7	48	34	5-11	0	4.02
Paul Dean	R	24	5	4	2	1	31.0	37	3	5	14	3-1	0	2.61
Mort Cooper	R	25	4	3	1	0	23.2	17	1	12	11	2-1	1	3.04
Si Johnson	R	31	6	3	0	0	15.2	27	0	6	4	0-3	0	7.47
Clyde Shoun	L	26	40	12	3	0	117.1	130	8	43	37	6-6	1	4.14
Max Macon	L	22	38	12	5	1	129.1	133	9	61	39	4-11	2	4.11
Ray Harrell	R	26	32	3	1	0	63.0	78	6	29	32	2-3	2	4.86
Max Lanier	L	22	18	3	1	0	45.0	57	1	28	14	0-3	0	4.20
Guy Bush	R	36	6	0	0	0	6.0	6	1	3	1	0-1	1	4.50
Mike Ryba	R	35	3	0	0	0	5.0	8	0	1	0	1-1	0	5.40
Howie Krist	R	22	2	0	0	0	1.1	1	0	0	1	0-0	0	0.00
Preacher Roe	L	23	1	0	0	0	2.2	6	0	2	1	0-0	0	13.50

1938 Brooklyn Dodgers 7th NL 69-80 .463 18.5 GB

Burleigh Grimes

Player	Gm by Position	B	Age	G	AB	R	H	2B	3B	HR	RBI	BB	SO	SB	Avg	OBP	Slg
Babe Phelps	C55	L	30	66	208	33	64	12	2	5	46	23	15	2	.308	.379	.457
Dolph Camilli	1B145	L	31	146	509	106	128	25	11	24	100	119	101	6	.251	.393	.485
Johnny Hudson	2B132,SS3	R	26	135	498	59	130	21	5	2	37	39	76	7	.261	.315	.335
Cookie Lavagetto	3B132,2B4	R	25	137	487	68	133	34	6	6	79	68	31	15	.273	.364	.405
Leo Durocher	SS141	R	32	141	479	41	105	18	5	1	56	47	30	3	.219	.293	.284
Ernie Koy	OF135	R	28	142	521	78	156	29	13	11	76	38	76	15	.299	.352	.468
Goody Rosen	OF113	L	25	138	473	75	133	17	11	4	51	65	43	0	.281	.368	.389
Buddy Hassett	OF71,1B8	L	26	115	335	49	98	11	6	0	40	32	19	3	.293	.356	.361
Kiki Cuyler	OF68	R	39	82	253	45	69	10	8	2	23	34	23	6	.273	.363	.399
Gilly Campbell	C44	L	30	54	126	10	31	5	0	0	11	19	9	0	.246	.354	.286
Merv Shea	C47	R	37	48	120	14	22	5	0	0	12	28	20	1	.183	.338	.225
Tuck Stainback†	OF23	R	26	35	104	15	34	6	3	0	20	2	4	1	.327	.346	.442
Pete Coscarart	2B27	R	25	32	79	10	12	3	0	0	6	9	18	0	.152	.256	.190
Woody English	3B21,2B3,SS3	R	31	34	72	9	18	2	0	0	7	8	11	2	.250	.333	.278
Oris Hockett	OF17	L	28	21	70	8	23	5	1	1	8	4	9	0	.329	.365	.471
Gibby Brack†	OF13	R	30	40	56	10	12	2	1	1	6	4	14	1	.214	.267	.339
Fred Sington	OF17	R	28	17	53	10	19	6	1	2	5	13	5	1	.358	.493	.623
Woody Williams	SS18,3B1	R	25	20	51	6	17	1	1	0	6	4	1	1	.333	.382	.392
Heinie Manush†	OF12	L	36	17	51	9	12	3	1	0	6	5	4	1	.235	.304	.333
Roy Spencer	C16	R	38	16	45	2	12	1	1	0	6	5	6	0	.267	.340	.333
Packy Rogers	SS9,3B8,2B3*	R	25	23	37	3	7	1	1	0	5	6	6	0	.189	.302	.270
Tom Winsett	OF9	L	28	12	30	6	9	1	0	1	7	6	4	0	.300	.417	.433
Paul Chervinko	C12	R	27	12	27	0	4	0	0	0	3	2	0	0	.148	.207	.148
Greek George	C7	R	25	7	20	0	4	0	1	0	2	0	4	0	.200	.200	.300
Ray Hayworth†	C3	R	34	5	4	0	0	0	0	0	0	1	1	0	.000	.200	.000
Ray Thomas	C1	R	27	1	3	1	1	0	0	0	0	0	0	0	.333	.333	.333
Bert Haas		R	24	1	0	0	0	0	0	0	0	0	0	0	—	—	—

P. Rogers, 1 G at OF

Pitcher	T	Age	G	GS	CG	ShO	IP	H	HR	BB	SO	W-L	Sv	ERA
Luke Hamlin	R	33	44	30	10	3	237.1	243	14	65	97	12-15	6	3.68
F. Fitzsimmons	R	36	27	26	12	3	202.2	205	8	43	38	11-8	0	3.02
Van Lingle Mungo	R	27	24	18	6	2	133.1	133	11	72	72	4-11	0	3.92
Bill Posedel	R	31	33	17	6	1	140.0	178	14	46	49	8-9	1	5.66
John Gaddy	R	24	2	2	1	0	13.0	13	0	4	3	2-0	0	0.69
Sam Nahem	R	22	1	1	1	0	9.0	6	0	4	2	1-0	0	3.00
Jim Winford	R	28	2	1	0	0	5.2	9	1	4	4	0-1	0	11.12
Tot Pressnell	R	31	43	19	6	1	192.0	209	11	56	57	11-14	3	3.56
Vito Tamulis†	L	26	38	18	9	0	159.2	181	11	40	70	12-6	2	3.83
Fred Frankhouse	R	34	30	8	2	1	93.2	92	6	44	32	3-5	0	4.04
Max Butcher†	R	27	24	8	3	1	72.2	104	9	39	21	5-4	2	6.56
Buck Marrow	R	28	15	0	0	0	19.2	23	1	11	6	0-1	0	4.58
Lee Rogers†	L	24	12	2	0	0	23.2	23	0	10	11	0-2	0	5.70
Waite Hoyt	R	38	6	1	0	0	16.1	24	1	5	3	0-3	0	4.96
Wayne LaMaster†	L	31	3	0	0	0	11.1	17	0	3	3	0-1	0	4.76
Dykes Potter	R	27	2	0	0	0	2.0	4	1	0	1	0-0	0	4.50

1938 Philadelphia Phillies 8th NL 45-105 .300 43.0 GB

Jimmie Wilson (45-103)/Hans Lobert (0-2)

Player	Gm by Position	B	Age	G	AB	R	H	2B	3B	HR	RBI	BB	SO	SB	Avg	OBP	Slg
Bill Atwood	C94	R	26	102	281	27	55	8	1	3	28	25	26	0	.196	.261	.263
Phil Weintraub	1B98	L	30	100	351	51	109	23	2	4	45	64	43	1	.311	.422	.422
Heinie Mueller	2B111,3B21	S	25	136	444	53	111	12	4	4	34	64	43	2	.250	.346	.322
Pinky Whitney	3B75,1B4,2B2	R	33	102	300	27	83	9	1	3	38	27	22	0	.277	.336	.343
Del Young	SS87,2B17	S	26	108	340	27	78	13	2	0	31	20	35	0	.229	.276	.279
Morrie Arnovich	OF133	R	27	139	502	47	138	29	0	4	72	42	37	2	.275	.333	.357
Chuck Klein	OF119	L	33	129	458	53	113	22	2	8	61	38	30	7	.247	.304	.356
Hersh Martin	OF116	S	28	120	466	58	139	36	6	3	39	34	48	8	.298	.347	.421
George Scharein	SS77,2B39	R	23	117	390	47	93	16	4	1	29	16	33	11	.238	.268	.308
Buck Jordan†	3B58,1B17	L	31	87	310	31	93	18	1	0	18	17	4	1	.300	.336	.365
Gibby Brack†	OF68	R	30	72	282	40	81	20	4	4	28	18	30	2	.287	.332	.429
Spud Davis†	C63	R	33	70	215	11	53	7	0	2	23	14	14	1	.247	.293	.307
Tuck Stainback†	OF25	R	26	30	81	9	21	3	0	1	11	3	3	1	.259	.294	.333
Gene Corbett	1B22	L	24	24	75	7	6	1	0	2	7	6	11	0	.080	.148	.173
Cap Clark	C29	L	31	52	74	11	19	1	1	0	4	9	10	0	.257	.337	.297
Earl Browne	1B16,OF2	L	27	21	74	4	19	4	0	0	8	5	11	0	.257	.304	.311
Justin Stein†	3B7,2B3	R	26	11	39	6	10	0	1	0	2	2	4	0	.256	.293	.308
Eddie Feinberg	SS4,OF2	S	19	10	20	0	3	0	0	0	0	0	1	0	.150	.150	.150
Alex Pitko	OF7	R	23	7	19	2	6	1	0	0	2	3	3	1	.316	.409	.368
Ray Stoviak	OF4	L	23	10	10	1	0	0	0	0	0	0	3	0	.000	.000	.000
Art Rebel	OF3	L	23	7	9	2	2	0	0	0	1	1	1	0	.222	.300	.222
Jimmie Wilson	C1	R	37	3	2	0	0	0	0	0	0	0	1	0	.000	.000	.000
Howie Gorman		L	25	1	1	0	0	0	0	0	0	0	1	0	.000	.000	.000

Pitcher	T	Age	G	GS	CG	ShO	IP	H	HR	BB	SO	W-L	Sv	ERA
Hugh Mulcahy	R	24	46	34	15	0	267.1	294	14	120	90	10-20	1	4.61
Claude Passeau	R	29	44	33	15	0	239.0	281	8	93	100	11-18	1	4.52
Al Hollingsworth†	L	30	24	21	11	1	174.1	177	4	77	80	5-16	0	3.82
Max Butcher†	R	27	12	12	11	0	98.1	94	6	31	29	4-8	0	2.93
Bucky Walters†	R	29	12	12	9	1	82.2	91	7	42	28	4-8	0	5.23
Wayne LaMaster†	L	31	18	12	1	0	63.2	80	8	31	35	4-7	0	7.77
Elmer Burkart	R	21	2	1	1	0	10.0	12	0	3	1	0-1	0	4.50
Pete Sivess	R	24	39	8	2	0	116.0	143	12	69	32	3-6	3	5.51
Al Smith	L	30	37	1	0	0	86.0	115	7	40	46	1-4	1	6.28
Syl Johnson	R	37	22	6	2	0	83.0	87	4	11	21	2-7	0	4.23
Wild Bill Hallahan	L	35	21	10	1	0	89.0	107	4	45	22	1-8	0	5.46
Hal Kelleher	R	24	6	0	0	0	7.1	16	0	9	4	0-0	0	18.41
Tommy Reis†	R	23	4	0	0	0	4.2	8	0	8	2	0-1	0	19.29
Tom Lanning	L	31	3	1	0	0	7.0	9	0	2	2	0-1	0	6.43
Ed Heusser	R	29	1	0	0	0	1.0	2	1	1	0	0-0	0	27.00

»1939 New York Yankees 1st AL 106-45 .702 —

Joe McCarthy

Player	Gm by Position	B	Age	G	AB	R	H	2B	3B	HR	RBI	BB	SO	SB	Avg	OBP	Slg
Bill Dickey	C126	L	32	128	480	98	145	23	3	24	105	77	37	5	.302	.403	.513
Babe Dahlgren	1B144	R	27	144	531	71	125	18	6	15	89	57	54	2	.235	.312	.377
Joe Gordon	2B151	R	24	151	567	92	161	32	5	28	111	75	57	11	.284	.370	.506
Red Rolfe	3B152	L	30	152	648	139	213	46	10	14	80	81	41	7	.329	.404	.495
Frankie Crosetti	SS152	R	28	152	656	109	153	25	5	10	56	65	81	11	.233	.315	.332
George Selkirk	OF124	L	31	128	418	103	128	17	4	21	101	103	49	12	.306	.452	.517
Joe DiMaggio	OF117	R	24	120	462	108	176	32	6	30	126	52	20	3	.381	.448	.671
Charlie Keller	OF105	L	22	111	398	87	133	21	6	11	83	81	49	6	.334	.447	.500
Tommy Henrich	OF88,1B1	L	26	99	347	64	96	18	4	9	57	51	23	7	.277	.371	.429
Buddy Rosar	C35	R	24	43	105	18	29	5	1	0	12	13	10	4	.276	.356	.343
Jake Powell	OF23	R	30	31	86	12	21	4	1	1	9	3	8	1	.244	.270	.349
Joe Gallagher†	OF12	R	25	14	41	8	10	0	1	2	9	3	8	1	.244	.311	.439
Lou Gehrig	1B8	L	36	8	28	2	4	0	0	0	1	5	1	0	.143	.273	.143
Bill Knickerbocker	2B2,SS2	R	27	6	13	2	2	1	0	0	1	0	0	0	.154	.154	.231
Art Jorgens	C2	R	34	3	0	1	0	0	0	0	0	0	0	0	—	—	—

Pitcher	T	Age	G	GS	CG	ShO	IP	H	HR	BB	SO	W-L	Sv	ERA
Red Ruffing	R	35	28	28	22	5	233.1	211	15	75	95	21-7	0	2.93
Lefty Gomez	L	30	26	26	14	2	198.0	173	11	84	102	12-8	0	3.41
Atley Donald	R	28	24	20	11	1	153.0	144	12	60	55	13-3	1	3.71
Monte Pearson	R	29	22	20	8	0	146.1	151	9	70	76	12-5	0	4.49
Bump Hadley	R	34	26	18	7	1	154.0	132	10	85	65	12-6	2	2.98
Oral Hildebrand	R	32	21	15	7	1	126.2	102	11	41	50	10-4	2	3.06
Marius Russo	L	24	21	11	9	2	116.0	86	6	41	55	8-3	2	2.41
Wes Ferrell	R	31	3	3	1	0	19.1	14	2	17	6	1-2	0	4.66
Johnny Murphy	R	30	38	0	0	0	61.1	57	2	28	30	3-6	19	4.40
Steve Sundra	R	29	24	11	8	1	120.2	110	7	56	27	11-1	0	2.76
Spud Chandler	R	31	11	0	0	0	19.0	26	0	9	4	3-0	0	2.84
Marv Breuer	R	25	1	0	0	0	1.0	2	0	1	0	0-0	0	9.00

1939 Boston Red Sox 2nd AL 89-62 .589 17.0 GB

Joe Cronin

Player	Gm by Position	B	Age	G	AB	R	H	2B	3B	HR	RBI	BB	SO	SB	Avg	OBP	Slg
Johnny Peacock	C84	L	29	92	274	33	76	11	4	0	36	29	11	1	.277	.347	.347
Jimmie Foxx	1B123,P1	R	31	124	467	130	168	31	10	35	105	89	72	4	.360	.464	.694
Bobby Doerr	2B126	R	21	127	525	75	167	28	2	12	73	38	32	1	.318	.365	.448
Jim Tabor	3B148	R	22	149	577	76	167	33	8	14	95	40	54	16	.289	.337	.447
Joe Cronin	SS142	R	32	143	520	97	160	33	3	19	107	87	48	6	.308	.407	.492
Ted Williams	OF149	L	20	149	565	131	185	44	11	31	145	107	64	2	.327	.436	.609
Joe Vosmik	OF144	R	29	145	554	89	153	29	6	7	84	66	33	4	.276	.356	.388
Doc Cramer	OF135	L	33	137	589	110	183	30	6	0	56	36	17	3	.311	.352	.382
Lou Finney†	1B32,OF24	L	28	95	249	43	81	18	3	1	46	24	11	2	.325	.385	.434
Gene Desautels	C73	R	32	76	226	26	55	14	0	0	21	33	13	3	.243	.340	.305
Tom Carey	2B35,SS10	R	32	54	161	17	39	6	2	0	20	3	9	0	.242	.265	.304
Red Nonnenkamp	OF15	L	27	58	75	12	18	2	1	0	5	12	6	0	.240	.345	.293
Moe Berg	C13	R	37	14	33	3	9	1	0	1	5	2	3	0	.273	.314	.394
Boze Berger	SS10,3B5,2B2	R	29	20	30	4	9	2	0	0	2	1	10	0	.300	.323	.367
Fabian Gaffke		R	25	1	1	0	0	0	0	0	1	0	0	0	.000	.000	.000

Pitcher	T	Age	G	GS	CG	ShO	IP	H	HR	BB	SO	W-L	Sv	ERA
Eldon Auker	R	28	31	25	6	1	151.0	183	13	61	43	9-10	0	5.36
Lefty Grove	L	39	23	23	17	2	191.0	180	8	58	81	15-4	0	2.54
Jack Wilson	R	27	36	22	6	0	177.1	198	10	75	80	11-11	2	4.67
Fritz Ostermueller	L	31	34	20	8	0	159.1	173	6	58	61	11-7	4	4.24
Denny Galehouse	R	27	30	18	6	1	146.2	160	6	52	68	9-10	0	4.54
Woody Rich	R	23	21	12	3	0	77.0	78	2	35	24	4-3	1	4.91
Jim Bagby Jr.	R	22	21	11	3	0	80.0	119	7	36	35	5-5	0	7.09
Charlie Wagner	R	26	9	5	0	0	38.1	49	3	14	13	3-1	0	4.23
Bill LeFebvre	L	23	5	3	0	0	26.1	35	2	14	8	1-1	0	5.81
Emerson Dickman	R	24	48	1	0	0	113.2	126	10	43	46	8-3	5	4.43
Joe Heving	R	38	46	5	1	0	107.0	124	8	34	43	11-3	7	3.70
Jake Wade†	L	27	20	6	1	0	47.2	68	1	37	21	1-4	0	6.23
Montie Weaver	R	33	9	1	1	0	20.1	26	0	13	6	1-0	1	6.64
Bill Sayles	R	21	5	0	0	0	14.0	14	1	13	9	0-0	0	7.07
Jimmie Foxx	R	31	1	0	0	0	1.0	0	0	0	1	0-0	0	0.00

1939 Cleveland Indians 3rd AL 87-67 .565 20.5 GB

Ossie Vitt

Player	Gm by Position	B	Age	G	AB	R	H	2B	3B	HR	RBI	BB	SO	SB	Avg	OBP	Slg
Rollie Hemsley	C106	R	32	107	395	58	104	17	4	2	36	26	26	2	.263	.309	.342
Hal Trosky	1B118	L	26	122	448	89	150	31	4	25	104	52	28	2	.335	.405	.589
Odell Hale	2B73,3B2	R	30	108	253	36	79	16	2	4	48	25	18	4	.312	.374	.439
Ken Keltner	3B154	R	22	154	587	84	191	35	11	13	97	51	41	6	.325	.379	.489
Skeeter Webb	SS81	R	29	81	269	28	71	14	1	2	26	15	24	1	.264	.305	.346
Ben Chapman	OF146	R	30	149	545	101	158	31	9	6	82	87	30	18	.290	.390	.413
Bruce Campbell	OF115	L	29	130	450	84	129	23	13	8	72	67	48	7	.287	.383	.449
Jeff Heath	OF108	L	24	121	431	64	126	31	7	14	69	41	64	8	.292	.354	.494
Oscar Grimes	2B48,1B43,SS37*	R	24	119	364	51	98	20	5	4	56	56	61	8	.269	.368	.385
Roy Weatherly	OF76	L	24	95	323	43	100	16	6	1	32	19	23	7	.310	.348	.406
Lou Boudreau	SS53	R	21	53	225	42	58	15	4	0	19	28	24	2	.258	.340	.360
Frankie Pytlak	C51	R	30	63	183	20	49	2	5	0	14	20	5	4	.268	.343	.333
Ray Mack	2B34,3B1	R	22	36	112	12	17	4	1	1	6	12	19	0	.152	.240	.232
Moose Solters†	OF25	R	33	41	102	19	28	7	2	2	19	9	15	2	.275	.333	.441
Jim Shilling†	2B27,SS3	R	25	31	98	8	27	7	2	0	12	7	9	1	.276	.324	.388
Earl Averill†	OF11	L	37	24	55	8	15	8	0	1	7	6	12	0	.273	.344	.473
Luke Sewell	C15,1B1	R	38	16	20	1	3	1	0	0	1	3	1	0	.150	.261	.200
Lyn Lary†	SS2	R	33	3	2	0	0	0	0	0	0	0	1	0	.000	.000	.000

O. Grimes, 3 G at 3B

Pitcher	T	Age	G	GS	CG	ShO	IP	H	HR	BB	SO	W-L	Sv	ERA
Bob Feller	R	20	39	35	24	4	296.2	227	13	142	246	24-9	1	2.85
Al Milnar	L	25	37	26	12	2	209.0	212	11	99	76	14-12	3	3.79
Mel Harder	R	29	29	26	12	1	208.0	213	15	64	67	15-9	1	3.50
Johnny Allen	R	33	28	26	9	2	175.0	199	9	56	79	9-7	0	4.58
Willis Hudlin	R	33	27	20	7	0	143.0	175	6	42	28	9-10	3	4.91
Mike Naymick	R	21	2	1	1	0	4.2	3	0	5	3	0-1	0	1.93
Joe Dobson	R	22	35	3	0	0	78.0	87	3	51	27	2-3	1	5.88
Harry Eisenstat†	L	23	26	11	4	1	103.2	109	8	28	38	6-7	2	3.30
Johnny Broaca	R	29	22	2	0	0	46.0	53	5	28	13	4-2	0	4.70
Bill Zuber	R	26	16	1	0	0	31.2	41	2	19	16	2-0	0	5.97
Johnny Humphries	R	24	15	1	0	0	28.0	30	0	32	12	2-4	2	8.36
Tom Drake	R	26	8	1	0	0	15.0	23	2	19	1	0-1	0	9.00
Lefty Sullivan	L	22	7	1	0	0	12.2	9	0	9	4	0-1	0	4.26
Floyd Stromme	R	22	5	0	0	0	13.0	13	1	13	4	0-1	0	4.85

1939 Chicago White Sox 4th AL 85-69 .552 22.5 GB

Jimmy Dykes

Player	Gm by Position	B	Age	G	AB	R	H	2B	3B	HR	RBI	BB	SO	SB	Avg	OBP	Slg
Mike Tresh	C119	R	25	119	352	49	91	5	2	0	38	64	30	3	.259	.377	.284
Joe Kuhel	1B136	L	33	139	546	107	164	24	9	15	56	64	51	18	.300	.376	.460
Ollie Bejma	2B81,3B1,SS1	R	31	90	307	52	77	9	3	8	44	36	27	1	.251	.331	.378
Eric McNair	3B103,2B19,SS9	R	30	129	479	62	155	18	5	7	82	38	41	17	.324	.375	.426
Luke Appling	SS148	R	32	148	516	82	162	16	6	0	56	105	37	16	.314	.430	.368
Gee Walker	OF147	R	31	149	598	95	174	30	11	13	111	28	43	17	.291	.330	.443
Mike Kreevich	OF139	R	31	145	541	85	175	30	8	5	77	59	40	23	.323	.390	.436
Larry Rosenthal	OF93	L	29	107	324	50	86	21	5	10	51	53	46	6	.265	.369	.454
Rip Radcliff	OF78,1B20	L	33	113	397	49	105	25	2	2	53	26	21	6	.264	.313	.353
Jackie Hayes	2B69	R	32	72	269	34	67	12	3	0	23	27	10	0	.249	.320	.316
Marv Owen	3B55	R	33	58	194	22	46	9	0	0	15	16	15	4	.237	.302	.284
Hank Steinbacher	OF22	L	26	71	111	16	19	2	1	1	15	21	8	0	.171	.303	.234
Ken Silvestri	C20	S	23	22	75	6	13	3	0	2	5	6	13	0	.173	.244	.293
Norm Schlueter	C32	R	22	34	56	5	13	2	1	0	8	1	11	2	.232	.246	.304
Tony Rensa	C13	R	37	14	25	3	5	0	0	0	2	1	2	0	.200	.231	.200
Bob Kennedy	3B2	R	18	3	8	0	2	0	0	0	1	0	0	0	.250	.250	.250
Johnny Gerlach	3B1	R	22	3	2	0	2	0	0	0	0	0	0	0	1.000	1.000	1.000
Jimmy Dykes	3B2	R	42	2	1	0	0	0	0	0	0	0	0	0	.000	.000	.000
Tommy Thompson†		L	29	1	0	0	0	0	0	0	1	0	0	0	—	—	—

Pitcher	T	Age	G	GS	CG	ShO	IP	H	HR	BB	SO	W-L	Sv	ERA
Thornton Lee	L	32	33	29	15	2	235.0	260	14	70	81	15-11	3	4.21
Johnny Rigney	R	24	35	29	11	2	218.2	208	10	84	119	15-8	3	3.70
Jack Knott	R	32	25	23	8	0	149.2	157	13	41	56	11-6	0	4.15
Eddie Smith†	L	25	29	22	7	1	176.2	161	11	90	67	9-11	0	3.67
Ted Lyons	R	38	21	21	16	0	172.2	162	7	26	65	14-6	0	2.76
Bill Dietrich	R	29	25	19	2	0	127.2	134	14	56	43	7-8	0	5.22
John Whitehead†	R	30	7	4	0	0	32.0	60	4	5	9	0-3	0	8.16
Vallie Eaves	R	27	2	1	1	0	11.2	11	1	8	5	0-1	0	4.63
Clint Brown	R	35	61	0	0	0	118.1	127	8	27	41	11-10	18	3.88
Johnny Marcum†	R	29	19	6	2	0	90.0	125	15	19	32	3-3	0	6.00
Vic Frasier	R	34	10	1	0	0	23.2	45	0	11	7	0-1	0	10.27
Art Herring	R	33	7	0	0	0	14.1	13	2	5	8	0-0	0	5.65
Jess Dobernic	R	21	4	0	0	0	3.1	3	0	6	1	0-1	0	13.50
Harry Boyles	R	27	2	0	0	0	3.1	4	0	6	1	0-0	0	10.80

1939 Detroit Tigers 5th AL 81-73 .526 26.5 GB

Del Baker

Player	Gm by Position	B	Age	G	AB	R	H	2B	3B	HR	RBI	BB	SO	SB	Avg	OBP	Slg
Birdie Tebbetts	C100	R	26	106	341	37	89	22	2	4	53	25	20	2	.261	.315	.372
Hank Greenberg	1B136	R	28	138	500	112	156	42	7	33	112	91	95	8	.312	.420	.622
Charlie Gehringer	2B107	L	36	118	406	86	132	29	6	16	86	68	16	4	.325	.423	.544
Mike Higgins	3B130	R	30	132	489	57	135	23	2	8	76	56	41	7	.276	.353	.380
Frank Croucher	SS93,2B3	R	24	97	324	38	87	15	0	5	40	16	42	2	.269	.303	.361
Barney McCosky	OF145	L	22	147	611	120	190	33	14	4	58	70	45	20	.311	.384	.430
Pete Fox	OF126	R	30	141	519	69	153	24	6	7	66	35	41	23	.295	.342	.405
Earl Averill†	OF80	L	37	87	309	58	81	20	6	10	58	43	30	4	.262	.354	.463
Rudy York	C67,1B19	R	25	102	329	66	101	16	1	20	68	41	50	5	.307	.387	.544
Benny McCoy	2B34,SS16	L	23	55	192	38	58	13	6	1	33	29	26	3	.302	.394	.448
Roy Cullenbine	OF46,1B2	S	25	75	179	31	43	9	2	6	23	34	29	0	.240	.362	.413
Billy Rogell	SS43,3B21,2B2	S	34	74	174	24	40	6	3	2	23	26	14	3	.230	.330	.333
Red Kress†	SS25,2B16,3B4	R	32	51	157	19	38	7	0	1	22	17	16	2	.242	.316	.306
Dixie Walker†	OF37	L	28	43	154	30	47	4	5	4	19	15	8	4	.305	.367	.474
Beau Bell†	OF37	R	31	54	134	14	32	4	2	0	24	24	16	0	.239	.358	.299
Les Fleming	OF3	L	23	8	16	0	0	0	0	0	1	0	4	0	.000	.000	.000
Mark Christman†	3B5	R	25	6	16	0	4	2	0	0	0	0	2	0	.250	.250	.375
Chet Laabs†	OF5	R	27	5	16	1	5	1	1	0	2	2	0	0	.313	.389	.500
Merv Shea	C4	R	38	4	2	0	0	0	0	0	0	0	1	0	.000	.000	.000
Dixie Parsons	C4	R	23	5	1	0	0	0	0	0	0	1	1	0	.000	.500	.000

Pitcher	T	Age	G	GS	CG	ShO	IP	H	HR	BB	SO	W-L	Sv	ERA
Bobo Newsom†	R	31	35	31	21	2	246.0	222	14	104	164	17-10	2	3.37
Tommy Bridges	R	32	29	26	16	2	198.0	186	11	61	129	17-7	2	3.50
Schoolboy Rowe	R	29	28	24	8	1	164.0	192	17	61	51	10-12	0	4.99
Dizzy Trout	R	24	33	22	6	0	162.0	168	5	74	72	9-10	2	3.61
Fred Hutchinson	R	19	13	12	3	0	84.2	95	9	51	22	3-6	0	5.21
Vern Kennedy†	R	32	4	4	1	0	21.0	25	4	9	9	0-3	0	6.43
Cotton Pippen†	R	28	3	2	0	0	14.0	18	1	6	5	0-1	0	7.07
Roxie Lawson†	R	33	2	1	0	0	11.1	7	1	7	4	1-1	0	4.76
Hal Newhouser	L	18	1	1	1	0	5.0	3	0	4	4	0-1	0	5.40
Al Benton	R	28	37	16	3	0	150.0	182	11	58	67	6-8	5	4.56
Archie McKain	L	28	32	11	4	1	129.2	120	6	54	49	5-6	4	3.68
Bud Thomas†	R	28	27	0	0	0	47.1	45	7	20	14	7-0	1	4.18
Slick Coffman	R	28	23	1	0	0	42.1	51	4	22	10	2-1	0	6.38
Harry Eisenstat†	L	23	10	2	1	0	29.2	39	3	9	6	2-2	0	6.98
Floyd Giebell	R	29	9	0	0	0	15.1	19	1	12	9	1-1	0	2.93
Jim Walkup†	R	29	7	0	0	0	12.0	15	3	8	5	0-1	0	7.50
Bob Harris†	R	22	5	1	0	0	18.0	18	4	8	9	1-1	0	4.00
Red Lynn†	R	25	4	0	0	0	8.1	11	2	3	3	0-1	0	8.64
George Gill†	R	30	3	1	0	0	8.2	14	1	3	1	0-1	0	8.31

1939 Washington Senators 6th AL 65-87 .428 41.5 GB

Bucky Harris

Player	Gm by Position	B	Age	G	AB	R	H	2B	3B	HR	RBI	BB	SO	SB	Avg	OBP	Slg
Rick Ferrell	C83	R	33	87	274	32	77	13	1	0	31	41	12	1	.281	.377	.336
Mickey Vernon	1B75	L	21	76	276	23	71	15	4	1	30	24	28	1	.257	.317	.351
Jimmy Bloodworth	2B73,OF5	R	21	83	318	34	92	24	1	4	40	10	26	3	.289	.313	.409
Buddy Lewis	3B134	L	22	140	536	87	171	23	16	10	75	72	27	10	.319	.402	.478
Cecil Travis	SS118	L	25	130	476	55	139	20	9	5	63	34	25	0	.292	.342	.403
George Case	OF123	R	23	128	530	103	160	20	7	2	35	56	36	51	.302	.369	.377
Taffy Wright	OF123	L	27	129	499	77	154	29	11	4	93	38	19	1	.309	.359	.435
Sammy West	OF89,1B17	L	34	115	390	52	110	20	8	3	52	67	29	1	.282	.387	.397
Bobby Estalella	OF74	R	28	82	280	51	77	18	6	8	41	40	27	2	.275	.368	.468
Buddy Myer	2B65	L	35	83	258	33	78	10	3	1	32	40	18	4	.302	.396	.376
Johnny Welaj	OF55	R	25	63	201	23	55	11	2	1	33	13	20	13	.274	.318	.363
Charlie Gelbert	SS28,3B20,2B1	R	33	68	188	36	48	7	5	3	29	30	11	2	.255	.361	.394
Tony Giuliani	C50	R	26	54	172	20	43	6	2	0	18	4	7	0	.250	.267	.308
Jimmy Wasdell	1B28	L	25	29	109	12	33	5	1	0	13	9	16	3	.303	.361	.367
Bob Prichard	1B26	L	21	26	85	8	20	5	0	0	8	19	16	0	.235	.375	.294
Jake Early	C24	L	24	32	84	8	22	7	2	0	14	5	14	0	.262	.303	.393
Ossie Bluege	1B11,2B2,3B2*	R	38	18	59	5	9	0	0	0	3	7	2	1	.153	.242	.153
Hal Quick	SS10	R	21	12	41	3	10	1	0	0	2	1	1	1	.244	.279	.268
Ed Leip	2B8	R	28	9	32	4	11	1	0	0	2	2	4	0	.344	.382	.375
Morrie Aderholt	2B7	L	23	7	25	5	5	0	0	1	4	2	6	0	.200	.259	.320
Al Evans	C6	R	22	7	21	2	7	0	0	0	1	5	2	0	.333	.462	.333
Elmer Gedeon	OF5	R	22	5	15	1	3	0	0	0	1	2	5	0	.200	.294	.200
Bob Loane	OF3	R	24	3	9	2	0	0	0	0	1	4	4	0	.000	.308	.000
Alex Pitko	OF3	R	24	4	8	0	1	0	0	0	1	1	3	0	.125	.222	.125

O. Bluege, 2 G at SS

Pitcher	T	Age	G	GS	CG	ShO	IP	H	HR	BB	SO	W-L	Sv	ERA
Dutch Leonard	R	30	34	34	21	2	269.1	273	16	59	88	20-8	0	3.54
Ken Chase	L	25	32	31	15	1	232.0	215	10	114	118	10-19	0	3.80
Joe Krakauskas	L	24	39	29	12	0	217.1	230	13	114	110	11-17	1	4.60
Joe Haynes	R	21	27	20	10	1	173.0	186	10	78	64	8-12	0	5.36
Jimmie DeShong	R	29	7	6	1	0	40.2	56	7	31	12	0-3	0	8.63
Early Wynn	R	19	3	3	1	0	20.1	26	0	10	1	0-2	0	5.75
Dick Bass	R	32	1	1	0	0	8.0	7	0	6	1	0-1	0	6.75
Alex Carrasquel	R	26	40	17	7	0	159.1	165	7	68	41	5-9	2	4.69
Pete Appleton	R	35	40	4	2	0	102.2	104	7	48	50	5-10	6	4.56
Walt Masterson	R	19	24	5	1	0	58.1	66	2	48	12	2-2	0	5.55
Harry Kelley	R	33	15	3	2	0	53.2	69	2	14	20	4-3	1	4.70
Bud Thomas†	R	28	4	0	0	0	9.0	11	0	2	0	0-0	0	6.00
Bill Holland	L	24	3	0	0	0	4.0	6	1	5	2	0-1	0	11.25
Lou Thuman	R	22	3	0	0	0	4.0	5	0	2	1	0-0	0	9.00
Bucky Jacobs	R	26	2	0	0	0	3.0	1	0	0	1	0-0	0	0.00
Mike Palagyi	R	21	1	0	0	0	0.0	0	0	3	0	0-0	0	—

1939 Philadelphia Athletics 7th AL 55-97 .362 51.5 GB

Connie Mack (25-37)/Earle Mack (30-60)

Player	Gm by Position	B	Age	G	AB	R	H	2B	3B	HR	RBI	BB	SO	SB	Avg	OBP	Slg
Frankie Hayes	C114	R	24	124	431	66	122	28	5	20	83	40	55	4	.283	.348	.510
Dick Siebert	1B99	L	27	101	402	58	118	28	3	6	47	21	22	4	.294	.329	.423
Joe Gantenbein	2B76,3B14,SS5	L	23	111	348	47	101	14	4	4	36	32	22	1	.290	.353	.388
Dario Lodigiani	3B89,2B28	R	22	121	393	46	102	22	4	6	44	42	18	2	.260	.337	.382
Skeeter Newsome	SS93,2B2	R	28	99	248	22	55	9	1	0	17	19	12	5	.222	.277	.266
Bob Johnson	OF150,2B1	R	32	150	544	115	184	30	9	23	114	99	59	15	.338	.440	.553
Sam Chapman	OF117,1B19	R	23	140	498	74	134	24	6	15	64	51	62	11	.269	.338	.432
Wally Moses	OF103	L	28	115	437	68	134	28	7	3	33	44	23	7	.307	.370	.423
Bill Nagel	2B56,3B43,P1	R	23	105	341	39	86	19	4	12	39	25	86	2	.252	.307	.437
Dee Miles	OF77	L	30	106	320	49	96	17	6	1	37	15	17	3	.300	.331	.400
Wayne Ambler	SS77,2B19	R	23	95	227	15	48	13	0	0	24	22	25	1	.211	.281	.269
Earle Brucker	C47	R	38	62	172	18	50	15	1	3	31	24	16	0	.291	.381	.442
Nick Etten	1B41	L	25	43	155	20	39	11	2	3	29	16	11	0	.252	.322	.406
Eric Tipton	OF34	R	24	47	104	12	24	4	2	1	14	13	7	2	.231	.316	.337
Al Brancato	3B20,SS1	R	20	21	68	12	14	5	0	1	8	8	4	1	.206	.299	.324
Fred Chapman	SS15	R	22	15	49	5	14	1	1	0	1	1	3	1	.286	.300	.347
Lou Finney†	OF4	L	28	9	22	1	3	0	0	0	1	2	0	0	.136	.208	.136
Eddie Collins	OF6,2B1	L	22	32	21	6	5	1	0	0	0	0	3	1	.238	.238	.286
Bill Lillard	SS7	R	21	7	19	4	6	1	0	0	1	3	1	0	.316	.409	.368
Bob McNamara	3B5,SS2,1B1*	R	22	9	9	0	2	1	0	0	3	1	1	0	.222	.300	.333
Hal Wagner	C5	L	23	5	8	0	1	0	0	0	0	0	3	0	.125	.125	.125
Harry O'Neill	C1	R	22	1	0	0	0	0	0	0	0	0	0	0	—	—	—

B. McNamara, 1 G at 2B

Pitcher	T	Age	G	GS	CG	ShO	IP	H	HR	BB	SO	W-L	Sv	ERA
Buck Ross	R	24	29	28	6	1	174.0	216	17	95	43	6-14	0	6.00
Nels Potter	R	27	41	25	9	0	196.1	258	26	88	60	8-12	2	6.60
Lynn Nelson	R	34	35	24	12	1	197.2	233	27	64	75	10-13	1	4.78
Bill Beckmann	R	31	27	19	7	2	155.1	198	15	41	20	7-11	0	5.39
George Caster	R	31	28	17	7	1	136.0	144	16	45	59	9-9	0	4.90
Cotton Pippen†	R	28	25	17	5	0	118.2	169	13	40	33	4-11	1	5.99
Les McCrabb	R	24	5	4	2	0	35.2	42	4	10	11	1-2	0	4.04
Sam Page	R	23	4	3	1	0	22.0	34	1	15	11	0-3	0	6.95
Jim Reninger	R	24	4	2	0	0	16.1	24	3	12	3	0-2	0	7.71
Bud Thomas†	R	28	2	2	0	0	4.0	8	2	1	0	0-1	0	15.75
Chubby Dean	L	22	54	1	0	0	116.2	132	8	80	39	5-8	7	5.25
Bob Joyce	R	24	30	6	1	0	107.2	156	13	37	25	3-5	0	6.69
Roy Parmelee	R	32	14	5	0	0	44.2	42	2	35	13	1-6	1	6.45
Walt Masters	R	32	4	0	0	0	11.0	15	0	8	2	0-0	0	6.55
Eddie Smith†	L	25	3	0	0	0	3.2	7	0	2	3	1-0	0	9.82
Bill Nagel	R	23	1	0	0	0	3.0	7	1	1	0	0-0	0	12.00
Jim Schelle	R	22	1	0	0	0	0.0	1	0	3	0	0-0	0	—
Dave Smith	R	24	1	0	0	0	0.0	1	0	2	0	0-0	0	—

676 Seasons: Team Rosters

1939 St. Louis Browns 8th AL 43-111 .279 64.5 GB

Fred Haney

Player	Gm by Position	B	Age	G	AB	R	H	2B	3B	HR	RBI	BB	SO	SB	Avg	OBP	Slg
Joe Glenn	C82	R	30	88	286	29	78	13	1	4	29	31	40	4	.273	.344	.367
George McQuinn	1B154	L	29	154	617	101	195	37	13	20	94	65	42	6	.316	.383	.515
Johnny Berardino	2B114,3B8,SS2	R	22	126	468	42	120	24	5	5	58	37	36	6	.256	.314	.361
Harlond Clift	3B149	R	26	151	526	90	142	25	2	15	84	111	55	4	.270	.402	.411
Don Heffner	SS73,2B32	R	28	110	375	45	100	10	2	1	35	48	39	1	.267	.350	.312
Myril Hoag	OF117,P1	R	31	129	482	58	142	23	4	10	75	24	35	9	.295	.329	.421
Chet Laabs†	OF79	R	27	95	317	52	95	20	5	10	62	33	62	4	.300	.368	.489
Joe Gallagher†	OF67	R	25	71	266	41	75	17	2	9	40	17	42	0	.282	.327	.462
Billy Sullivan	OF59,C19,1B4	L	28	118	332	53	96	17	5	5	50	34	18	3	.289	.362	.416
Mark Christman†	SS64,2B1	R	25	79	222	27	48	6	3	0	20	20	10	2	.216	.281	.270
Joe Grace	OF53	L	25	74	207	35	63	11	2	3	22	19	24	3	.304	.363	.420
Sam Harshany	C36	R	29	42	145	15	35	2	0	0	15	9	8	0	.241	.290	.255
Mel Almada†	OF34	L	26	42	134	17	32	2	1	1	7	10	8	1	.239	.292	.291
Moose Solters†	OF30	R	33	40	131	14	27	6	1	0	14	10	20	1	.206	.262	.267
Hal Spindel	C32	R	26	48	119	13	32	3	1	0	11	8	7	0	.269	.315	.311
Mel Mazzera	OF25	L	25	34	111	21	33	5	2	3	22	10	20	0	.297	.361	.459
Tommy Thompson†	OF23	L	29	30	86	23	26	5	0	1	7	23	7	0	.302	.455	.395
Sig Gryska	SS14	R	23	18	49	4	13	2	0	0	8	6	10	3	.265	.345	.306
Red Kress†	SS13	R	32	13	43	5	12	1	0	0	8	6	2	1	.279	.367	.302
Beau Bell†	OF9	R	31	11	32	4	7	1	0	1	5	4	3	0	.219	.324	.344
Johnny Lucadello	2B7	R	20	9	30	0	7	2	0	0	4	2	4	0	.233	.281	.300
Roy Hughes†	2B6,SS1	R	28	17	23	6	2	0	0	0	1	4	4	0	.087	.222	.087
Bob Neighbors	SS5	R	21	7	11	3	2	0	0	1	1	0	1	0	.182	.182	.455
Eddie Silber		R	25	1	1	0	0	0	0	0	0	0	1	0	.000	.000	.000

Pitcher	T	Age	G	GS	CG	ShO	IP	H	HR	BB	SO	W-L	Sv	ERA
Jack Kramer	R	21	40	31	10	2	211.2	269	18	127	68	9-16	0	5.83
Vern Kennedy†	R	32	33	27	12	1	191.2	229	18	115	55	9-17	0	5.73
Bob Harris†	R	22	28	16	6	0	126.0	162	5	71	48	3-12	0	5.71
Johnny Marcum†	R	29	12	6	2	0	47.2	66	12	10	14	2-5	0	7.74
Bobo Newsom†	R	31	6	6	3	0	45.2	50	5	22	28	3-1	0	4.73
Emil Bildilli	L	26	2	2	2	0	19.0	21	0	6	8	1-1	0	3.32
Jake Wade†	L	27	4	2	1	0	16.1	26	1	19	9	0-2	0	11.02
Bill Cox	R	26	4	2	1	0	9.1	10	0	8	8	0-2	0	9.64
Russ Van Atta	L	33	2	1	0	0	7.0	9	0	7	6	0-0	0	11.57
Bill Trotter	R	30	41	13	4	0	156.2	205	16	54	61	6-13	0	5.34
Roxie Lawson†	R	33	36	14	5	0	150.2	181	10	83	43	3-7	0	5.32
Lefty Mills	L	29	34	14	4	0	144.1	147	16	113	103	4-11	2	6.55
George Gill†	R	30	27	11	5	0	95.0	139	10	34	24	1-12	0	7.11
John Whitehead†	R	30	26	4	0	0	66.0	88	10	17	9	1-3	1	5.86
Harry Kimberlin	R	30	17	3	0	0	41.0	59	6	19	11	1-2	0	5.49
Ewald Pyle	L	28	6	1	0	0	8.1	17	3	11	5	0-2	0	12.96
Ed Cole	R	30	6	0	0	0	6.1	8	1	6	5	0-2	0	7.11
Fred Johnson	R	45	5	2	1	0	14.0	23	0	9	2	0-1	0	6.43
Loy Hanning	R	21	4	1	0	0	10.0	6	1	4	8	0-1	0	3.60
Bob Muncrief	R	23	2	0	0	0	3.0	7	1	3	1	0-0	0	15.00
Myril Hoag	R	31	1	0	0	0	1.0	0	0	0	0	0-0	0	0.00
Jim Walkup†	R	29	1	0	0	0	0.2	2	0	1	0	0-1	0	0.00

»1939 Cincinnati Reds 1st NL 97-57 .630 —

Bill McKechnie

Player	Gm by Position	B	Age	G	AB	R	H	2B	3B	HR	RBI	BB	SO	SB	Avg	OBP	Slg
Ernie Lombardi	C120	R	31	130	450	43	129	26	2	20	85	35	19	0	.287	.342	.487
Frank McCormick	1B156	R	28	156	630	99	209	41	4	18	128	40	16	1	.332	.374	.495
Lonny Frey	2B124	L	28	125	484	95	141	27	9	11	55	72	46	5	.291	.388	.452
Bill Werber	3B147	R	31	147	599	115	173	35	5	5	57	91	46	15	.289	.388	.389
Billy Myers	SS151	R	28	151	509	79	143	18	6	9	56	71	90	4	.281	.369	.393
Harry Craft	OF134	R	24	134	502	58	129	20	7	13	67	27	54	5	.257	.299	.402
Ival Goodman	OF123	L	30	124	470	85	152	37	16	7	84	54	32	2	.323	.401	.515
Wally Berger	OF95	R	33	97	329	36	85	15	1	14	44	36	63	1	.258	.341	.438
Lee Gamble	OF56	L	29	72	221	24	59	7	2	0	14	9	14	5	.267	.296	.317
Willard Hershberger	C60	R	29	63	174	23	60	9	2	0	32	9	4	1	.345	.384	.420
Nino Bongiovanni	OF39	L	27	66	159	17	41	6	0	0	16	9	8	0	.258	.298	.296
Eddie Joost	2B32,SS6	R	23	42	143	23	36	6	3	0	14	12	15	1	.252	.310	.336
Frenchy Bordagaray	OF43,2B2	R	29	63	122	19	24	5	1	0	12	9	10	3	.197	.252	.254
Lew Riggs	3B11	L	29	22	38	5	6	1	0	0	1	5	4	1	.158	.256	.184
Al Simmons†	OF5	R	37	9	21	0	3	0	0	0	1	2	3	0	.143	.217	.143
Dick West	OF5,C1	R	23	8	19	1	4	0	0	0	4	1	4	0	.211	.250	.211
Vince DiMaggio	OF7	R	26	8	14	1	1	1	0	0	2	2	10	0	.071	.188	.143
Les Scarsella		L	25	16	14	0	2	0	0	0	2	0	2	0	.143	.143	.143
Bud Hafey†	OF4	R	26	6	13	1	2	1	0	0	1	1	4	1	.154	.214	.231
Milt Galatzer	1B2	L	32	3	5	0	0	0	0	0	0	1	1	0	.000	.000	.000
Nolen Richardson	SS1	R	36	1	3	0	0	0	0	0	0	0	0	0	.000	.000	.000
Jimmie Wilson	C1	R	38	4	3	0	1	0	0	0	0	0	1	0	.333	.333	.333

Pitcher	T	Age	G	GS	CG	ShO	IP	H	HR	BB	SO	W-L	Sv	ERA
Bucky Walters	R	30	39	36	31	2	319.0	250	15	109	137	27-11	0	2.29
Paul Derringer	R	32	38	35	28	5	301.0	321	15	35	128	25-7	0	2.93
Whitey Moore	R	27	42	24	9	2	187.2	177	10	95	81	13-12	0	3.45
Lee Grissom	L	31	33	21	3	0	153.2	145	14	56	53	9-7	0	4.10
J. Vander Meer	L	24	30	21	8	0	129.0	128	7	95	102	5-9	0	4.67
Johnny Niggeling	R	35	10	5	2	1	40.1	51	2	13	20	2-1	0	5.80
Junior Thompson	R	22	42	11	5	3	152.1	130	6	55	87	13-5	0	2.54
Hank Johnson	R	33	20	0	0	0	31.1	30	1	13	10	0-3	1	2.01
Peaches Davis	R	34	20	0	0	0	30.2	43	5	11	4	1-0	2	6.46
Milt Shoffner†	L	33	10	3	0	0	37.2	43	3	11	6	2-2	0	3.35
Wes Livengood	R	28	5	0	0	0	6.0	9	3	3	4	0-0	0	9.00
Pete Naktenis	L	25	3	0	0	0	4.0	2	0	0	1	0-0	0	2.25
Jim Weaver	R	35	3	0	0	0	3.0	3	0	1	3	0-0	0	3.00
Red Barrett	R	24	2	0	0	0	5.1	5	0	1	1	0-0	0	1.69
Elmer Riddle	R	24	1	0	0	0	2.0	1	0	0	0	0-0	0	0.00
Art Jacobs	L	36	1	0	0	0	1.0	2	0	1	0	0-0	1	9.00

1939 St. Louis Cardinals 2nd NL 92-61 .601 4.5 GB

Ray Blades

Player	Gm by Position	B	Age	G	AB	R	H	2B	3B	HR	RBI	BB	SO	SB	Avg	OBP	Slg
Mickey Owen	C126	R	23	131	344	32	89	18	2	3	35	43	28	6	.259	.344	.349
Johnny Mize	1B152	L	26	153	564	104	197	44	14	28	108	92	49	0	.349	.444	.626
Stu Martin	2B107,1B1	L	25	120	425	60	114	26	7	3	30	33	40	4	.268	.325	.384
Don Gutteridge	3B143,SS2	R	27	148	524	71	141	27	4	7	54	27	70	5	.269	.309	.376
Jimmy Brown	SS104,2B50	S	29	147	645	88	192	31	8	3	51	32	18	4	.298	.335	.384
Joe Medwick	OF149	R	27	150	606	98	201	48	8	14	117	45	44	6	.332	.380	.507
Enos Slaughter	OF149	L	23	149	604	95	193	52	5	12	86	44	53	2	.320	.371	.482
Terry Moore	OF121,P1	R	27	130	417	65	123	25	2	17	77	43	38	6	.295	.362	.487
Pepper Martin	OF51,3B22	R	35	88	281	48	86	17	7	3	37	30	35	6	.306	.375	.448
Don Padgett	C61,1B6	L	27	92	233	38	93	15	3	5	53	18	11	1	.399	.444	.554
Lynn Myers	SS36,3B13,2B5	R	25	74	117	24	28	6	1	0	10	12	23	1	.239	.310	.308
Lynn King	OF44	L	31	89	85	10	20	2	0	0	11	15	3	2	.235	.350	.259
Lyn Lary†	SS30,3B3	R	33	34	75	11	14	3	0	0	9	16	15	1	.187	.330	.227
Creepy Crespi	2B6,SS4	R	21	15	29	3	5	1	0	0	6	3	6	0	.172	.250	.207
Herman Franks	C13	L	25	17	17	1	1	0	0	0	3	3	3	0	.059	.200	.059
Herb Bremer	C8	R	25	9	9	0	1	0	0	0	1	0	2	0	.111	.111	.111
Bob Repass	2B2	R	21	3	6	0	2	1	0	0	1	0	2	0	.333	.333	.500
Eddie Lake	SS2	R	23	2	4	0	1	0	0	0	0	1	2	0	.250	.400	.250
Johnny Hopp	1B1	L	22	6	4	1	2	1	0	0	2	1	1	0	.500	.600	.750
Joe Orengo	SS7	R	24	7	3	0	0	0	0	0	0	0	1	0	.000	.000	.000
Buster Adams		R	24	2	1	1	0	0	0	0	0	0	0	0	.000	.000	.000
Johnny Echols		R	22	2	0	0	0	0	0	0	0	0	0	0	—	—	—

Pitcher	T	Age	G	GS	CG	ShO	IP	H	HR	BB	SO	W-L	Sv	ERA
Curt Davis	R	35	49	31	13	3	248.0	279	16	48	70	22-16	7	3.63
Mort Cooper	R	26	45	26	7	2	210.2	208	6	97	130	12-6	4	3.25
Bob Weiland	L	33	32	23	6	3	146.1	146	4	50	63	10-12	1	3.57
Lon Warneke	R	30	34	21	6	2	162.0	160	14	49	59	13-7	2	3.78
Tom Sunkel	L	26	20	11	2	1	85.1	79	4	56	54	4-4	0	4.22
Max Lanier	L	23	7	6	2	0	37.2	29	1	13	14	2-1	0	2.39
Clyde Shoun	L	27	53	2	0	0	103.0	98	4	42	50	3-1	9	3.76
Bob Bowman	R	28	51	15	4	1	169.1	141	8	60	78	13-5	9	2.60
Bill McGee	R	29	43	17	5	4	156.0	155	13	59	56	12-5	0	3.81
Paul Dean	R	25	16	2	0	0	43.0	54	4	10	16	0-1	0	6.07
Nate Andrews	R	25	11	1	0	0	16.0	24	0	12	6	1-2	0	6.75
Murry Dickson	R	22	1	0	0	0	3.2	1	0	1	2	0-0	0	0.00
Frank Barrett	R	25	1	0	0	0	1.2	1	0	1	3	0-1	0	5.40
Ken Raffensberger	L	21	1	0	0	0	1.0	2	0	0	1	0-0	0	0.00
Terry Moore	R	27	1	0	0	0	1.0	0	0	0	1	0-0	0	0.00

1939 Brooklyn Dodgers 3rd NL 84-69 .549 12.5 GB

Leo Durocher

Player	Gm by Position	B	Age	G	AB	R	H	2B	3B	HR	RBI	BB	SO	SB	Avg	OBP	Slg
Babe Phelps	C92	L	31	98	323	33	92	21	2	6	42	24	24	0	.285	.336	.418
Dolph Camilli	1B157	L	32	157	565	105	164	30	12	26	104	110	107	1	.290	.409	.524
Pete Coscarart	2B107,3B4,SS2	R	26	115	419	59	116	22	2	4	43	46	56	10	.277	.354	.368
Cookie Lavagetto	3B149	R	26	153	587	93	176	28	5	10	87	78	30	14	.300	.387	.416
Leo Durocher	SS113,3B1	R	33	116	390	42	108	21	6	1	34	27	24	2	.277	.325	.369
Ernie Koy	OF114	R	29	125	425	57	118	37	5	8	67	39	64	11	.278	.338	.445
Gene Moore	OF86,1B1	L	29	107	306	45	69	13	6	3	39	40	50	4	.225	.315	.337
Art Parks	OF65	L	27	71	239	27	65	13	2	1	19	28	14	2	.272	.348	.356
Johnny Hudson	SS50,2B45,3B1	R	27	109	343	46	87	17	3	2	32	30	36	5	.254	.317	.338
Al Todd	C73	R	37	86	245	28	68	10	5	5	32	13	16	1	.278	.317	.380
Dixie Walker†	OF59	L	28	61	225	27	63	6	4	2	38	20	10	1	.280	.339	.369
Tuck Stainback	OF55	R	27	68	201	22	54	7	0	3	19	4	23	0	.269	.290	.348
Goody Rosen	OF47	L	26	54	183	22	46	6	4	1	12	23	21	4	.251	.335	.344
Mel Almada†	OF32	L	26	39	112	11	24	4	0	0	3	9	17	2	.214	.273	.250
Jimmy Ripple†	OF28	L	29	28	106	18	35	8	4	0	22	11	8	0	.330	.398	.481
Fred Sington	OF22	R	29	32	84	13	23	5	0	1	7	15	15	0	.274	.384	.369
Tony Lazzeri†	2B11,3B2	R	35	14	39	6	11	2	0	3	6	10	7	1	.282	.451	.564
Lyn Lary†	SS12,3B7	R	33	29	31	7	5	1	1	0	1	12	6	1	.161	.409	.258
Ray Hayworth†	C18	R	35	21	26	0	4	2	0	0	1	4	7	0	.154	.267	.231
Chris Hartje	C8	R	24	9	16	2	5	1	0	0	5	1	0	0	.313	.353	.375
Oris Hockett	OF1	L	29	9	13	3	3	0	0	0	1	1	1	0	.231	.286	.231
Lindsay Deal	OF1	L	27	4	7	0	0	0	0	0	0	0	2	0	.000	.000	.000
Gene Schott†		R	25	1	0	0	0	0	0	0	0	0	0	0	—	—	—

Pitcher	T	Age	G	GS	CG	ShO	IP	H	HR	BB	SO	W-L	Sv	ERA
Luke Hamlin	R	34	40	36	19	2	269.2	255	27	54	88	20-13	0	3.64
Hugh Casey	R	25	40	25	15	0	227.1	228	13	54	79	15-10	1	2.93
F. Fitzsimmons	R	37	27	20	5	0	151.1	178	6	28	44	7-9	3	3.87
Tot Pressnell	R	32	31	18	10	2	156.2	171	8	33	43	9-7	2	4.02
Whit Wyatt	R	31	16	14	6	2	109.0	88	3	39	52	8-3	0	2.31
Van Lingle Mungo	R	28	14	10	1	0	77.1	70	7	33	34	4-5	0	3.26
Al Hollingsworth†	L	31	8	5	1	0	27.1	33	1	11	11	1-2	0	5.27
Bill Crouch	R	28	6	3	3	0	38.1	37	3	14	10	4-0	0	2.58
Ira Hutchinson	R	28	41	1	0	0	105.2	103	9	51	46	5-2	1	4.34
Vito Tamulis	L	27	39	17	8	1	158.2	177	10	45	83	9-8	4	4.37
Red Evans	R	32	24	6	0	0	64.1	74	4	26	28	1-8	1	5.18
Carl Doyle	R	26	5	1	1	0	17.2	8	1	7	7	1-2	1	1.02
Boots Poffenberger	R	23	3	1	0	0	5.0	7	1	4	2	0-0	0	5.40
George Jeffcoat	R	25	1	0	0	0	2.0	2	0	0	1	0-0	0	0.00

1939 Chicago Cubs 4th NL 84-70 .545 13.0 GB

Gabby Hartnett

Player	Gm by Position	B	Age	G	AB	R	H	2B	3B	HR	RBI	BB	SO	SB	Avg	OBP	Slg
Gabby Hartnett	C86	R	38	97	306	36	85	18	2	12	59	37	32	0	.278	.358	.467
Rip Russell	1B143	R	24	143	542	55	148	24	5	9	79	36	56	2	.273	.318	.386
Billy Herman	2B156	R	29	156	623	111	191	34	18	7	70	66	31	9	.307	.378	.453
Stan Hack	3B156	L	29	156	641	112	191	28	6	8	56	65	35	17	.298	.364	.398
Dick Bartell	SS101	R	31	105	336	37	80	24	2	3	34	42	25	6	.238	.335	.348
Augie Galan	OF145	S	27	148	549	104	167	36	8	6	71	75	26	8	.304	.392	.432
Hank Leiber	OF98	R	28	112	365	65	113	16	1	24	88	59	42	1	.310	.411	.556
Jim Gleeson	OF91	S	27	111	332	43	74	19	6	4	45	39	46	7	.223	.308	.352
Carl Reynolds	OF72	R	36	88	281	33	69	10	6	4	44	16	38	5	.246	.298	.367
Gus Mancuso	C76	R	33	80	251	17	58	10	0	2	17	24	19	0	.231	.298	.295
Bill Nicholson	OF58	L	24	58	220	37	65	12	5	5	38	20	29	0	.295	.354	.464
Bobby Mattick	SS48	R	23	51	178	16	51	12	1	0	23	6	19	1	.287	.314	.365
Joe Marty†	OF21	R	25	23	76	6	10	1	0	2	10	4	13	2	.132	.175	.224
Phil Cavarretta	1B13	L	22	22	55	4	15	3	1	0	0	4	3	2	.273	.322	.364
Steve Mesner	SS12,2B1,3B1	R	21	17	43	7	12	4	0	0	6	3	4	0	.279	.340	.372
Bob Garbark	C21	R	29	24	21	1	3	0	0	0	0	0	3	0	.143	.143	.143

Pitcher	T	Age	G	GS	CG	ShO	IP	H	HR	BB	SO	W-L	Sv	ERA
Bill Lee	R	29	37	36	20	1	282.1	295	18	85	105	19-15	0	3.44
Claude Passeau†	R	30	34	27	13	1	221.0	215	8	48	108	13-9	3	3.05
Larry French	L	31	36	21	10	2	194.0	205	7	50	98	15-8	1	3.29
Vance Page	R	33	27	17	8	1	139.1	169	8	37	43	7-7	1	3.88
Dizzy Dean	R	29	19	13	7	2	96.1	98	4	17	27	6-4	0	3.36
Clay Bryant	R	27	4	4	2	0	31.1	42	3	14	9	2-1	0	5.74
Ray Harrell†	R	27	4	2	0	0	17.1	29	2	6	5	0-2	0	8.31
Jack Russell	R	33	39	0	0	0	68.2	78	3	24	32	4-3	3	3.67
Charlie Root	R	40	35	16	8	0	167.1	189	11	34	65	8-8	4	4.03
Earl Whitehill	L	39	24	11	2	1	89.1	102	8	50	42	4-7	1	5.14
Gene Lillard	R	25	20	7	2	0	55.0	68	2	36	31	3-5	0	6.55
Kirby Higbe†	R	24	9	2	0	0	22.2	12	0	22	16	2-1	0	3.18
Vern Olsen	L	21	4	0	0	0	7.2	2	0	7	3	1-0	0	0.00

1939 New York Giants 5th NL 77-74 .510 18.5 GB

Bill Terry

Player	Gm by Position	B	Age	G	AB	R	H	2B	3B	HR	RBI	BB	SO	SB	Avg	OBP	Slg
Harry Danning	C132	R	27	135	520	79	163	28	5	16	74	35	42	4	.313	.359	.479
Zeke Bonura	1B122	R	30	123	455	75	146	26	6	11	85	46	22	1	.321	.388	.477
Burgess Whitehead	2B91,SS4,3B1	R	29	95	335	31	80	6	3	2	24	24	19	1	.239	.299	.293
Tom Hafey	3B70	R	25	70	256	37	62	10	1	6	26	10	44	1	.242	.271	.359
Billy Jurges	SS137	R	31	138	543	84	155	21	11	6	63	47	34	3	.285	.349	.398
Frank Demaree	OF150	R	29	150	560	68	170	27	2	11	79	66	40	2	.304	.381	.418
Jo-Jo Moore	OF136	L	30	138	562	80	151	23	2	10	47	45	17	5	.269	.324	.370
Mel Ott	OF96,3B20	L	30	125	396	85	122	23	2	27	80	100	50	2	.308	.449	.581
Alex Kampouris	2B62,3B11	R	26	74	201	23	50	12	2	5	29	30	41	0	.249	.349	.403
Bob Seeds	OF50	R	32	63	173	33	46	5	1	5	26	22	31	1	.266	.352	.393
Lou Chiozza	3B30,SS8	L	29	40	142	19	38	3	1	3	12	9	10	3	.268	.311	.366
Jimmy Ripple†	OF23	L	29	66	123	10	28	4	0	1	12	8	7	0	.228	.286	.285
Ken O'Dea	C30	L	26	52	97	7	17	1	0	3	11	10	16	0	.175	.252	.278
Johnny McCarthy	1B12,OF4,P1	L	29	50	80	12	21	6	1	1	11	3	8	0	.263	.298	.400
Babe Young	1B22	L	23	22	75	8	23	4	0	3	14	5	6	0	.307	.373	.480
George Myatt	3B14	L	25	22	53	7	10	2	0	0	3	6	6	2	.189	.271	.226
Tony Lazzeri†	3B13	R	35	13	44	7	13	0	0	1	8	7	6	0	.295	.392	.364
Johnny Dickshot	OF10	R	29	10	34	3	8	0	0	0	5	5	3	0	.235	.333	.235
Al Glossop	2B10	S	23	10	32	3	6	0	0	1	3	4	2	0	.188	.278	.281
Skeeter Scalzi	SS5	R	26	11	18	3	6	0	0	0	0	3	2	1	.333	.429	.333
Ray Hayworth†	C2	R	35	5	13	1	3	0	0	0	0	0	1	0	.231	.231	.231

Pitcher	T	Age	G	GS	CG	ShO	IP	H	HR	BB	SO	W-L	Sv	ERA
Harry Gumbert	R	29	36	34	14	2	243.2	257	21	81	81	18-11	0	4.32
Hal Schumacher	R	28	29	27	8	1	181.2	199	14	89	58	13-10	0	4.81
Bill Lohrman	R	26	38	24	9	1	185.2	200	15	45	70	12-13	1	4.07
Cliff Melton	L	27	41	23	9	2	207.1	214	7	65	95	12-15	5	3.56
Carl Hubbell	L	36	29	18	10	0	154.0	150	11	24	62	11-9	2	2.75
Manny Salvo	R	26	32	18	4	0	136.0	150	11	75	69	4-10	1	4.63
Hy Vandenberg	R	32	2	1	0	0	6.1	10	0	6	3	0-0	0	5.68
Jumbo Brown	R	32	31	0	0	0	56.1	69	1	25	24	4-0	7	4.15
Dick Coffman	R	32	28	0	0	0	38.0	50	1	6	9	1-2	3	3.08
Red Lynn†	R	25	26	0	0	0	49.2	44	3	21	22	1-0	1	3.08
Slick Castleman	R	25	12	4	0	0	33.2	36	1	23	6	1-2	0	4.54
Johnnie Wittig	R	25	5	2	1	0	16.2	18	0	14	4	0-2	0	7.56
Tom Gorman	L	23	4	0	0	0	5.0	7	0	1	2	0-0	0	7.20
Johnny McCarthy	L	29	1	0	0	0	5.0	8	1	2	0	0-0	0	7.20

1939 Pittsburgh Pirates 6th NL 68-85 .444 28.5 GB

Pie Traynor

Player	Gm by Position	B	Age	G	AB	R	H	2B	3B	HR	RBI	BB	SO	SB	Avg	OBP	Slg
Ray Mueller	C81	R	27	86	180	14	42	8	1	2	18	14	22	0	.233	.289	.322
Elbie Fletcher†	1B101	L	23	102	370	49	112	23	4	12	71	48	28	3	.303	.386	.484
Pep Young	2B84	R	31	84	293	34	81	14	3	3	29	23	29	1	.276	.333	.375
Lee Handley	3B100	R	25	101	376	43	107	14	5	1	42	32	20	17	.285	.341	.356
Arky Vaughan	SS152	L	27	152	595	94	182	30	11	6	62	70	20	12	.306	.385	.424
Paul Waner	OF106	L	36	125	461	62	151	30	6	3	45	35	18	0	.328	.375	.438
Lloyd Waner	OF92,3B1	L	33	112	379	49	108	15	3	0	24	17	13	0	.285	.321	.340
Johnny Rizzo	OF86	R	26	94	330	49	86	23	3	6	55	42	27	0	.261	.349	.403
Bill Brubaker	2B65,3B32,SS1	R	28	100	345	41	80	23	1	7	43	29	51	3	.232	.297	.365
Chuck Klein†	OF66	L	34	85	270	37	81	16	4	11	47	26	17	1	.300	.361	.511
Fern Bell	OF67,3B1	R	26	83	262	44	75	5	8	2	34	42	18	2	.286	.385	.389
Ray Berres	C80	R	31	81	231	22	53	6	1	0	16	11	25	1	.229	.267	.264
Gus Suhr†	1B52	L	33	63	204	23	59	10	2	1	31	25	23	4	.289	.367	.373
Bob Elliott	OF30	R	22	32	129	18	43	10	3	3	19	9	4	0	.333	.377	.527
M. Van Robays	OF25,3B1	R	24	27	105	13	33	9	0	2	16	6	10	0	.314	.351	.457
George Susce	C31	R	30	31	75	8	17	3	1	1	4	12	5	0	.227	.333	.333
Frankie Gustine	3B22	R	19	22	70	5	13	3	0	0	3	9	4	0	.186	.278	.229
Red Juelich	2B10,3B2	R	22	17	46	5	11	0	2	0	4	2	4	0	.239	.271	.326
Joe Schultz	C4	L	20	4	14	3	4	2	0	0	2	2	0	0	.286	.375	.429
Woody Jensen	OF3	L	31	12	12	0	2	0	0	0	1	0	0	0	.167	.167	.167
Heinie Manush	OF1	L	37	10	12	0	0	0	0	0	1	1	1	0	.000	.077	.000
Eddie Yount		R	22	2	2	0	0	0	0	0	0	0	2	0	.000	.000	.000

Pitcher	T	Age	G	GS	CG	ShO	IP	H	HR	BB	SO	W-L	Sv	ERA
Bob Klinger	R	31	37	33	10	2	225.0	251	11	81	64	14-17	0	4.36
Joe Bowman	R	29	37	27	10	1	184.2	217	15	43	58	10-14	1	4.48
Jim Tobin	R	26	25	19	8	0	145.1	194	7	33	43	9-9	0	4.52
Max Butcher†	R	28	14	12	5	2	86.2	104	2	23	21	4-4	0	3.43
Russ Bauers	R	25	15	8	1	0	53.2	46	4	25	12	2-4	0	3.35
Cy Blanton	R	30	10	6	1	0	42.0	45	4	10	11	2-3	1	4.29
Oad Swigart	R	24	3	3	1	1	24.1	27	1	6	8	1-1	0	4.44
Johnny Gee	L	23	3	3	1	0	19.2	20	0	10	16	1-2	0	4.12
Rip Sewell	R	32	52	12	5	1	176.1	177	11	73	69	10-9	2	4.08
Mace Brown	R	30	47	19	8	1	200.1	232	8	52	71	9-13	7	3.37
Bill Swift	R	31	36	8	2	1	129.2	150	6	28	56	5-7	4	3.89
Ken Heintzelman	L	23	17	2	1	1	35.2	35	2	18	18	1-1	0	5.05
Bill Clemensen	R	20	12	1	0	0	27.0	32	0	20	13	0-1	0	7.33
Pep Rambert	R	22	2	0	0	0	3.2	7	0	1	4	0-0	0	9.82

1939 Boston Braves 7th NL 63-88 .417 32.5 GB

Casey Stengel

Player	Gm by Position	B	Age	G	AB	R	H	2B	3B	HR	RBI	BB	SO	SB	Avg	OBP	Slg
Al Lopez	C129	R	30	131	412	32	104	22	1	8	49	40	45	1	.252	.319	.369
Buddy Hassett	1B123,OF23	L	27	147	590	72	182	15	3	2	60	29	14	13	.308	.342	.354
Tony Cuccinello	2B80	R	31	81	310	42	95	17	1	2	40	26	26	5	.306	.360	.387
Hank Majeski	3B99	R	22	106	367	35	100	16	1	7	54	18	30	2	.272	.310	.379
Eddie Miller	SS77	R	22	77	296	32	79	12	2	4	31	16	21	4	.267	.315	.361
Max West	OF124	L	22	130	449	67	128	26	6	19	82	51	55	1	.285	.364	.497
Johnny Cooney	OF116,1B2	R	38	118	368	39	101	8	1	2	27	21	8	2	.274	.317	.318
Debs Garms	OF96,3B37	L	31	132	513	68	153	24	9	2	37	39	20	2	.298	.350	.392
Rabbit Warstler	SS49,2B43,3B21	R	35	114	342	34	83	11	3	0	24	24	31	2	.243	.292	.292
Al Simmons†	OF82	R	37	93	330	39	93	17	5	7	43	22	40	0	.282	.331	.427
Sibby Sisti	2B34,3B17,SS10	R	18	63	215	19	49	7	1	1	11	12	38	4	.228	.269	.284
Jimmy Outlaw	OF39,SS2	R	26	65	133	15	35	2	0	0	5	10	14	1	.263	.315	.278
Phil Masi	C42	R	23	46	114	14	29	7	2	1	14	9	15	0	.254	.315	.377
Elbie Fletcher†	1B31	L	23	35	106	14	26	2	0	0	6	19	5	1	.245	.365	.264
Whitey Wietelmann	SS22,2B1	S	20	23	69	2	14	1	0	0	5	2	9	1	.203	.225	.217
Bama Rowell	OF16	L	23	21	59	5	11	2	2	0	6	1	4	0	.186	.200	.288
Ralph Hodgin	OF9	L	23	32	48	4	10	1	0	0	4	3	4	0	.208	.255	.229
Chet Ross	OF8	R	22	11	31	4	10	1	1	0	4	2	10	0	.323	.364	.419
Stan Andrews	C10	R	22	13	26	1	6	0	0	0	1	1	2	0	.231	.259	.231
Chet Clemens	OF7	R	22	9	23	2	5	0	0	0	1	1	3	1	.217	.250	.217
Otto Huber	2B4,3B4	R	25	11	22	2	6	1	0	0	3	0	1	0	.273	.273	.318
Red Barkley	SS7,3B4	R	25	12	11	1	0	0	0	0	0	1	2	0	.000	.083	.000
Bill Schuster	3B1,SS1	R	26	2	3	0	0	0	0	0	0	0	1	0	.000	.000	.000
Oliver Hill		L	26	2	2	1	1	1	0	0	0	0	0	0	.500	.500	1.000

Pitcher	T	Age	G	GS	CG	ShO	IP	H	HR	BB	SO	W-L	Sv	ERA
Bill Posedel	R	32	33	29	18	5	220.2	221	8	78	73	15-13	0	3.92
Danny MacFayden	R	34	33	28	8	0	191.2	221	11	59	46	8-14	2	3.90
Lou Fette	R	32	27	26	11	6	146.0	123	7	61	35	10-10	0	2.96
Jim Turner	R	35	25	22	9	0	157.2	181	10	51	50	4-11	0	4.28
Al Veigel	R	22	2	2	0	0	2.2	3	0	5	1	0-1	0	6.75
Johnny Lanning	R	28	37	6	3	0	129.0	120	6	53	45	5-6	4	3.14
Joe Sullivan	L	28	31	11	7	0	113.2	114	3	50	46	6-9	1	3.64
Dick Errickson	R	25	28	11	3	0	128.1	143	6	54	33	6-9	1	4.00
Milt Shoffner†	L	33	25	11	7	0	132.1	133	4	42	51	4-6	1	3.13
Fred Frankhouse	R	35	23	0	0	0	38.0	37	3	18	12	0-2	4	2.61
Tom Earley	R	22	14	2	0	0	40.0	49	1	19	9	1-4	1	4.73
Hiker Moran	R	27	6	2	1	0	20.0	21	3	11	4	1-1	0	4.50
George Barnicle	R	21	6	1	0	0	18.1	16	1	8	15	2-2	0	4.91
Joe Callahan	R	22	4	1	1	0	17.1	17	0	3	8	1-0	0	3.12
Roy Weir	L	28	2	0	0	0	2.2	1	0	1	2	0-0	0	0.00

1939 Philadelphia Phillies 8th NL 45-106 .298 50.5 GB

Doc Prothro

Player	Gm by Position	B	Age	G	AB	R	H	2B	3B	HR	RBI	BB	SO	SB	Avg	OBP	Slg
Spud Davis	C85	R	34	87	202	10	62	8	1	0	23	24	20	0	.307	.383	.356
Gus Suhr†	1B60	L	33	60	198	21	63	12	2	3	24	34	14	1	.318	.421	.444
Roy Hughes†	2B65	R	28	65	237	22	54	5	1	1	16	21	18	4	.228	.291	.270
Pinky May	3B132	R	28	135	464	49	133	27	3	2	62	41	20	4	.287	.346	.371
George Scharein	SS117	R	24	118	399	35	95	17	1	1	33	13	40	4	.238	.262	.293
Morrie Arnovich	OF132	R	28	134	491	68	159	25	2	5	67	58	28	7	.324	.397	.413
Hersh Martin	OF95	S	29	111	393	59	111	28	5	1	22	42	27	4	.282	.355	.387
Joe Marty†	OF79,P1	R	25	91	299	32	76	12	6	9	44	24	27	1	.254	.310	.425
Heinie Mueller	2B51,3B17,OF17*	S	26	115	341	46	95	19	4	9	43	33	34	4	.279	.342	.437
Gibby Brack	OF48,1B19	R	31	91	270	40	78	21	4	6	41	26	49	1	.289	.351	.463
LeGrant Scott	OF55	L	28	76	232	31	65	15	1	1	26	22	14	5	.280	.343	.366
Del Young	SS55,2B17	S	27	77	217	22	57	9	2	3	20	8	24	1	.263	.289	.364
Jack Bolling	1B48	L	22	69	211	27	61	11	0	3	13	11	10	6	.289	.324	.384
Wally Millies	C84	R	32	84	205	12	48	3	0	0	12	9	5	0	.234	.270	.249
Pinky Whitney	1B12,2B8,3B2	R	34	34	75	9	14	0	1	1	6	7	4	0	.187	.256	.253
Bud Bates	OF14	R	27	15	58	8	15	2	0	1	2	2	8	1	.259	.283	.345
Bennie Warren	C17	R	27	18	56	4	13	0	0	1	7	7	7	0	.232	.317	.286
Les Powers	1B13	L	29	19	52	7	18	1	1	0	2	4	6	0	.346	.393	.404
Bud Hafey†	OF13,P2	R	26	18	51	3	9	1	0	0	3	3	12	1	.176	.222	.196
Stan Benjamin	OF7,3B5	R	25	12	50	4	7	2	1	0	2	1	6	1	.140	.157	.220
Chuck Klein†	OF11,1B1	L	34	25	47	8	9	2	1	1	9	10	4	1	.191	.333	.340
Charlie Letchas	2B12	R	23	12	44	2	10	2	0	1	3	1	2	0	.227	.244	.341
Jim Shilling†	2B5,3B3,SS3*	R	25	11	33	3	10	1	3	0	4	1	4	0	.303	.324	.515
Dave Coble	C13	R	26	15	25	2	7	1	0	0	0	0	3	0	.280	.280	.320
Len Gabrielson	1B5	L	23	5	18	3	4	0	0	0	1	2	3	0	.222	.300	.222
Eddie Feinberg	2B4,SS1	S	20	6	18	2	4	1	0	0	0	2	0	0	.222	.300	.278
Bill Atwood	C2	R	27	4	6	0	0	0	0	0	1	2	3	1	.000	.250	.000
Cliff Watwood	1B2	L	33	2	6	0	1	0	0	0	0	0	0	0	.167	.167	.167
Joe Kracher	C2	R	23	5	5	1	1	0	0	0	0	2	1	0	.200	.429	.200

H. Mueller, 1 G at SS; J. Shilling, 1 G at OF

Pitcher	T	Age	G	GS	CG	ShO	IP	H	HR	BB	SO	W-L	Sv	ERA
Hugh Mulcahy	R	25	38	31	14	1	225.2	246	19	93	59	9-16	4	4.99
Kirby Higbe†	R	24	34	26	14	1	187.1	208	10	101	79	10-14	2	4.85
Max Butcher†	R	28	19	16	3	0	104.1	131	10	51	27	2-13	0	5.61
Syl Johnson	R	38	22	14	6	0	111.0	112	10	15	37	8-8	2	3.81
Ike Pearson	R	22	26	13	4	0	125.0	144	15	56	29	2-13	0	5.76
Al Hollingsworth†	L	31	15	10	3	0	60.0	78	2	27	24	1-9	0	5.85
Claude Passeau†	R	30	8	8	4	1	53.1	54	1	25	29	2-4	0	4.22
Roy Bruner	R	22	4	4	2	0	27.0	38	3	13	11	0-4	0	6.67
Boom-Boom Beck	R	34	34	16	12	0	182.2	203	11	64	77	7-14	3	4.73
Bill Kerksieck	R	25	23	2	1	0	63.0	81	13	32	13	0-2	0	7.14
Ray Harrell†	R	27	22	10	4	0	94.2	101	6	56	35	3-7	0	5.42
Jennings Poindexter	L	28	11	1	0	0	30.1	29	0	15	12	0-0	0	4.15
Jim Henry	R	29	9	1	0	0	23.0	24	3	8	7	0-1	1	5.09
Al Smith	L	31	5	0	0	0	9.0	11	1	5	2	0-0	0	4.00
Elmer Burkart	R	22	5	0	0	0	8.1	11	0	2	2	1-0	0	4.32
Gene Schott	R	25	4	0	0	0	11.0	14	0	5	1	0-1	0	4.91
Bill Hoffman	L	21	3	0	0	0	6.0	8	1	7	1	0-0	0	13.50
Bud Hafey	R	26	2	0	0	0	1.1	7	0	1	1	0-0	0	33.75
Joe Marty	R	25	1	0	0	0	4.0	2	0	3	1	0-0	0	4.50

»1940 Detroit Tigers 1st AL 90-64 .584 —

Del Baker

Player	Gm by Position	B	Age	G	AB	R	H	2B	3B	HR	RBI	BB	SO	SB	Avg	OBP	Slg
Birdie Tebbetts	C107	R	27	111	379	46	112	24	4	4	46	35	14	4	.296	.357	.412
Rudy York	1B155	R	26	155	588	105	186	46	6	33	134	89	88	3	.316	.410	.583
Charlie Gehringer	2B138	L	37	139	515	108	161	33	3	10	81	101	17	10	.313	.428	.447
Mike Higgins	3B129	R	31	131	480	70	130	24	3	13	76	61	31	4	.271	.357	.415
Dick Bartell	SS139	R	32	139	528	76	123	24	3	7	53	76	53	12	.233	.335	.330
Hank Greenberg	OF148	R	29	148	573	129	195	50	8	41	150	93	75	6	.340	.433	.670
Barney McCosky	OF141	L	23	143	589	123	200	39	19	4	57	67	41	13	.340	.408	.491
Pete Fox	OF85	R	31	93	350	49	101	17	4	5	48	21	30	7	.289	.329	.403
Bruce Campbell	OF74	L	30	103	297	56	84	15	5	8	44	45	28	2	.283	.381	.448
Billy Sullivan	C57	L	29	78	220	36	68	14	4	3	41	31	11	2	.309	.399	.450
Earl Averill	OF22	L	38	64	118	10	33	4	1	2	20	5	14	0	.280	.309	.381
Red Kress	3B17,SS12	R	33	33	99	13	22	3	1	1	11	10	12	0	.222	.294	.303
Dutch Meyer	2B21	R	24	23	58	12	15	3	0	0	6	4	10	2	.259	.317	.310
Frank Croucher	SS26,2B7,3B1	R	25	37	57	3	6	0	0	0	2	4	5	0	.105	.164	.105
Tuck Stainback	OF9	R	28	15	40	4	9	2	0	0	1	1	9	0	.225	.244	.275
Scat Metha	2B10,3B6	R	26	26	37	6	9	0	1	0	3	2	8	0	.243	.282	.297
Pat Mullin	OF1	L	22	4	4	0	0	0	0	0	0	0	0	0	.000	.000	.000
Frank Secory		R	27	1	1	0	0	0	0	0	0	0	1	0	.000	.000	.000

Pitcher	T	Age	G	GS	CG	ShO	IP	H	HR	BB	SO	W-L	Sv	ERA
Bobo Newsom	R	32	36	34	20	3	264.0	235	19	100	164	21-5	0	2.83
Tommy Bridges	R	33	29	28	12	2	197.2	171	11	88	133	12-9	0	3.37
Schoolboy Rowe	R	30	27	23	11	1	169.0	170	15	43	61	16-3	0	3.46
Johnny Gorsica	R	25	29	20	5	2	160.0	170	10	57	68	7-7	0	4.33
Hal Newhouser	L	19	28	20	7	0	133.1	149	12	76	89	9-9	0	4.86
Fred Hutchinson	R	20	17	10	1	0	76.0	85	6	26	32	3-7	0	5.68
Cotton Pippen	R	29	4	3	0	0	21.1	29	3	10	9	1-2	0	6.75
Floyd Giebell	R	30	2	2	2	1	18.0	14	2	4	11	2-0	0	1.00
Al Benton	R	29	42	0	0	0	79.1	93	5	36	50	6-10	17	4.42
Dizzy Trout	R	25	33	10	1	0	100.2	125	4	54	64	3-7	2	4.47
Archie McKain	L	29	27	0	0	0	51.0	48	2	25	24	5-0	3	2.82
Tom Seats	L	29	26	2	0	0	55.2	67	4	21	25	2-2	1	4.69
Clay Smith	R	25	14	1	0	0	28.1	32	3	13	14	1-1	0	5.08
Lynn Nelson	R	35	6	2	0	0	14.0	23	5	9	7	1-1	0	10.93
Bud Thomas	R	29	3	0	0	0	4.0	8	1	3	0	0-1	0	9.00
Dick Conger	R	19	2	0	0	0	3.0	2	0	3	1	1-0	0	3.00
Bob Uhl	L	26	1	0	0	0	0.0	4	0	2	0	0-0	0	—

1940 Cleveland Indians 2nd AL 89-65 .578 1.0 GB

Ossie Vitt

Player	Gm by Position	B	Age	G	AB	R	H	2B	3B	HR	RBI	BB	SO	SB	Avg	OBP	Slg
Rollie Hemsley	C117	R	33	119	416	46	111	20	5	4	42	22	25	1	.267	.304	.368
Hal Trosky	1B139	L	27	140	522	85	154	39	4	25	93	79	45	1	.295	.392	.529
Ray Mack	2B146	R	23	146	530	60	150	21	5	12	69	51	77	4	.283	.346	.409
Ken Keltner	3B148	R	23	149	543	67	138	24	10	15	77	51	56	10	.254	.322	.418
Lou Boudreau	SS155	R	22	155	627	97	185	46	10	9	101	73	39	6	.295	.370	.443
Ben Chapman	OF140	R	31	143	548	82	157	40	6	4	50	78	45	13	.286	.377	.403
Roy Weatherly	OF135	L	25	135	578	90	175	35	11	12	59	27	26	9	.303	.335	.464
Beau Bell	OF97,1B14	R	32	120	444	55	124	22	2	4	58	34	41	2	.279	.332	.365
Jeff Heath	OF90	L	25	100	356	55	78	16	3	14	50	40	62	5	.219	.298	.399
Frankie Pytlak	C58,OF1	R	31	62	149	16	21	2	1	0	16	17	5	0	.141	.234	.168
Rusty Peters	2B9,3B6,SS6*	R	25	30	71	5	17	3	2	0	7	4	14	1	.239	.280	.338
Soup Campbell	OF16	L	25	35	62	8	14	1	0	0	2	7	12	0	.226	.304	.242
Odell Hale	3B3	R	31	48	50	3	11	3	1	0	6	5	7	0	.220	.291	.320
Oscar Grimes	1B4,3B1	R	25	11	13	3	0	0	0	0	0	0	5	0	.000	.000	.000
Hank Helf	C1	R	26	1	1	0	0	0	0	0	0	0	0	0	.000	.000	.000

R. Peters, 1 G at 1B

Pitcher	T	Age	G	GS	CG	ShO	IP	H	HR	BB	SO	W-L	Sv	ERA
Bob Feller	R	21	43	37	31	4	320.1	245	13	118	261	27-11	4	2.61
Al Milnar	L	26	37	33	15	4	242.1	242	14	99	99	18-10	3	3.27
Mel Harder	R	30	31	25	5	0	186.1	200	16	59	76	12-11	0	4.06
Al Smith	L	32	31	24	11	1	183.0	187	12	55	46	15-7	2	3.44
Johnny Allen	R	34	32	17	5	3	138.2	126	3	48	62	9-8	5	3.44
Willis Hudlin†	R	34	4	4	2	0	23.2	31	3	2	8	2-1	0	4.94
Joe Dobson	R	23	40	7	2	1	100.0	101	8	48	57	3-7	3	4.95
Harry Eisenstat	L	24	27	3	0	0	71.2	78	6	12	27	1-4	4	3.14
Johnny Humphries	R	25	19	1	1	0	33.2	35	5	29	17	0-2	1	8.29
Bill Zuber	R	27	17	0	0	0	24.0	25	3	14	12	1-1	0	5.63
Mike Naymick	R	22	13	4	0	0	30.0	36	1	17	15	1-2	0	5.10
Nate Andrews	R	26	6	0	0	0	12.0	16	1	6	3	0-1	0	6.00
Dixie Howell	R	20	3	0	0	0	5.0	2	0	4	2	0-0	0	1.80
Ken Jungels	R	24	2	0	0	0	3.1	3	0	1	1	0-0	0	2.70
Cal Dorsett	R	27	1	0	0	0	1.0	1	1	0	0	0-0	0	9.00

1940 New York Yankees 3rd AL 88-66 .571 2.0 GB

Joe McCarthy

Player	Gm by Position	B	Age	G	AB	R	H	2B	3B	HR	RBI	BB	SO	SB	Avg	OBP	Slg
Bill Dickey	C102	L	33	106	372	45	92	11	1	9	54	48	32	0	.247	.336	.355
Babe Dahlgren	1B155	R	28	155	568	51	150	24	4	12	73	46	54	1	.264	.325	.384
Joe Gordon	2B155	R	25	155	616	112	173	32	10	30	103	52	57	18	.281	.340	.511
Red Rolfe	3B138	L	31	139	588	102	147	26	6	10	53	50	48	4	.250	.311	.366
Frankie Crosetti	SS145	R	29	145	546	84	106	23	4	4	31	72	77	14	.194	.299	.273
Charlie Keller	OF136	L	23	138	500	102	143	18	15	21	93	106	65	8	.286	.411	.508
Joe DiMaggio	OF130	R	25	132	508	93	179	28	9	31	133	61	30	1	.352	.425	.626
George Selkirk	OF111	L	32	118	379	68	102	17	5	19	71	84	43	3	.269	.406	.491
Tommy Henrich	OF76,1B2	L	27	90	293	57	90	28	5	10	53	48	30	1	.307	.408	.539
Buddy Rosar	C63	R	25	73	228	34	68	11	3	4	37	19	11	7	.298	.357	.425
Bill Knickerbocker	SS19,3B17	R	28	45	124	17	30	8	1	1	10	14	8	1	.242	.333	.347
Buster Mills	OF14	R	31	34	63	10	25	3	3	1	15	7	5	0	.397	.457	.587
Jake Powell	OF7	R	31	12	27	3	5	0	0	0	2	1	4	0	.185	.214	.185
Mike Chartak	OF3	L	24	11	15	2	2	1	0	0	3	5	5	0	.133	.350	.200

Pitcher	T	Age	G	GS	CG	ShO	IP	H	HR	BB	SO	W-L	Sv	ERA
Red Ruffing	R	36	30	30	20	3	226.0	218	24	76	97	15-12	0	3.38
Marius Russo	L	25	30	24	15	0	189.1	181	17	55	87	14-8	1	3.28
Spud Chandler	R	32	27	24	6	1	172.0	184	12	60	56	8-7	0	4.60
Marv Breuer	R	26	27	22	10	0	164.0	175	20	61	71	8-9	0	4.55
Monte Pearson	R	30	16	16	7	1	109.2	108	8	44	43	7-5	0	3.69
Tiny Bonham	R	26	12	12	10	3	99.1	83	4	13	37	9-3	0	1.90
Lefty Gomez	L	31	9	5	0	0	27.1	37	2	18	14	3-3	0	6.59
Johnny Murphy	R	31	35	1	0	0	63.1	58	5	15	23	8-4	9	3.69
Steve Sundra	R	30	27	8	2	0	99.1	121	11	42	26	4-6	2	5.53
Bump Hadley	R	35	25	2	0	0	80.0	88	4	52	39	3-5	2	5.74
Atley Donald	R	29	24	11	6	1	118.2	113	11	59	60	8-3	0	3.03
Oral Hildebrand	R	33	13	0	0	0	19.1	19	1	14	5	1-1	0	1.86
Lee Grissom†	L	32	5	0	0	0	4.2	4	0	2	1	0-0	0	0.00

1940 Boston Red Sox 4th AL 82-72 .532 8.0 GB

Joe Cronin

Player	Gm by Position	B	Age	G	AB	R	H	2B	3B	HR	RBI	BB	SO	SB	Avg	OBP	Slg
Gene Desautels	C70	R	33	71	222	19	50	7	1	0	17	32	13	0	.225	.328	.266
Jimmie Foxx	1B95,C42,3B1	R	32	144	515	106	153	30	4	36	119	101	87	4	.297	.412	.581
Bobby Doerr	2B151	R	22	151	595	87	173	37	10	22	105	57	53	10	.291	.353	.497
Jim Tabor	3B120	R	23	120	459	73	131	28	6	21	81	42	58	14	.285	.345	.510
Joe Cronin	SS146,3B2	R	33	149	548	104	156	35	6	24	111	83	65	7	.285	.380	.502
Doc Cramer	OF149	L	34	150	661	94	200	27	12	1	51	36	29	3	.303	.340	.384
Ted Williams	OF143,P1	L	21	144	561	134	193	43	14	23	113	96	54	4	.344	.442	.594
Dom DiMaggio	OF94	R	23	108	418	81	126	32	6	8	46	41	46	7	.301	.367	.464
Lou Finney	OF69,1B51	L	29	130	534	73	171	31	15	5	73	33	13	5	.320	.360	.463
Johnny Peacock	C48	L	30	63	131	20	37	4	1	0	13	23	10	1	.282	.390	.328
Charlie Gelbert†	3B29,SS1	R	34	30	91	9	18	2	0	0	8	8	16	0	.198	.263	.220
Stan Spence	OF15	L	25	51	68	5	19	2	1	2	13	4	9	0	.279	.319	.426
Tom Carey	SS20,2B4,3B4	R	33	43	62	4	20	4	0	0	7	2	1	0	.323	.344	.387
Marv Owen	3B9,1B8	R	34	20	57	4	12	0	0	0	6	8	4	0	.211	.308	.211
Joe Glenn	C19	R	31	22	47	3	6	1	0	0	4	5	7	0	.128	.212	.149
Tony Lupien	1B8	L	23	10	19	5	9	3	2	0	4	1	1	0	.474	.500	.842
Red Nonnenkamp		L	28	9	7	0	0	0	0	0	1	1	4	0	.000	.125	.000

Pitcher	T	Age	G	GS	CG	ShO	IP	H	HR	BB	SO	W-L	Sv	ERA
Jim Bagby Jr.	R	23	36	21	6	1	182.2	217	15	83	57	10-16	2	4.73
Lefty Grove	L	40	22	21	9	1	153.1	159	20	50	62	7-6	0	3.99
Denny Galehouse	R	28	25	20	5	0	120.0	155	10	41	53	6-6	0	5.18
Fritz Ostermueller	L	32	31	16	5	0	143.2	166	7	70	80	5-9	0	4.95
Earl Johnson	L	21	17	10	2	0	70.1	69	0	39	26	6-2	0	4.09
Mickey Harris	L	23	13	9	3	0	68.1	83	8	26	36	4-2	0	5.00
Bill Fleming	R	26	10	6	1	0	46.1	53	4	20	24	1-2	0	4.86
Bill Butland	R	22	3	3	1	0	21.0	27	0	10	5	1-2	0	5.57
Jack Wilson	R	28	41	16	9	0	157.2	170	17	87	102	12-6	5	5.08
Joe Heving	R	39	39	7	4	0	119.0	129	7	42	55	12-7	3	4.01
Emerson Dickman	R	25	35	9	2	0	100.0	121	15	38	40	8-6	3	6.03
Herb Hash	R	29	34	12	3	1	120.0	123	11	84	36	7-7	3	4.95
Charlie Wagner	R	27	12	1	0	0	29.1	45	5	8	13	1-0	0	5.52
Alex Mustaikis	R	31	6	1	0	0	15.0	15	1	15	6	0-1	0	9.00
Yank Terry	R	29	4	1	0	0	19.1	24	2	11	9	1-0	0	8.84
Woody Rich	R	24	3	1	1	0	11.2	9	2	1	8	1-0	0	0.77
Ted Williams	R	21	1	0	0	0	2.0	3	0	0	1	0-0	0	4.50

1940 Chicago White Sox 4th AL 82-72 .532 8.0 GB

Jimmy Dykes

Player	Gm by Position	B	Age	G	AB	R	H	2B	3B	HR	RBI	BB	SO	SB	Avg	OBP	Slg
Mike Tresh	C135	R	26	135	480	62	135	15	5	1	64	49	40	3	.281	.349	.340
Joe Kuhel	1B155	L	34	155	603	111	169	28	8	27	94	87	59	12	.280	.374	.488
Skeeter Webb	2B74,SS7,3B1	R	30	84	334	33	79	11	2	1	29	30	33	3	.237	.299	.290
Bob Kennedy	3B154	R	19	154	606	74	153	23	3	3	52	42	58	3	.252	.301	.315
Luke Appling	SS150	R	33	150	566	96	197	27	13	0	79	69	35	3	.348	.420	.442
Mike Kreevich	OF144	R	32	144	582	86	154	27	10	8	55	34	49	15	.265	.305	.387
Taffy Wright	OF144	L	28	147	581	79	196	31	9	5	88	43	25	4	.337	.385	.448
Moose Solters	OF107	R	34	116	428	65	132	28	3	12	80	27	54	3	.308	.351	.472
Larry Rosenthal	OF92	L	30	107	276	46	83	14	5	6	42	64	32	2	.301	.432	.453
Eric McNair	2B65,3B1	R	31	66	251	26	57	13	1	7	31	12	26	1	.227	.265	.371
Tom Turner	C29	R	23	37	96	11	20	1	2	0	6	3	12	1	.208	.240	.260
Jackie Hayes	2B15	R	33	18	41	2	8	0	1	0	1	2	11	0	.195	.233	.244
Don Kolloway	2B10	R	21	10	40	5	9	1	0	0	3	0	3	1	.225	.225	.250
Ken Silvestri	C1	S	24	28	24	5	6	2	0	2	10	4	7	0	.250	.357	.583
Dave Short		L	23	4	3	1	1	0	0	0	0	1	2	0	.333	.500	.333

Pitcher	T	Age	G	GS	CG	ShO	IP	H	HR	BB	SO	W-L	Sv	ERA
Johnny Rigney	R	25	39	33	19	2	280.2	240	22	90	141	14-18	3	3.11
Eddie Smith	L	26	32	28	12	0	207.1	179	16	95	119	14-9	0	3.21
Thornton Lee	L	33	28	27	24	1	228.0	223	13	56	87	12-13	0	3.47
Jack Knott	R	33	25	23	4	2	158.0	166	12	52	44	11-9	0	4.56
Ted Lyons	R	39	22	22	17	4	186.1	188	17	37	72	12-8	0	3.24
Bill Dietrich	R	30	23	17	6	1	149.2	154	10	65	43	10-6	0	4.03
Vallie Eaves	R	28	5	3	0	0	18.2	22	2	24	11	0-2	0	6.75
Jack Hallett	R	25	2	2	1	0	14.0	15	1	6	9	1-1	0	6.43
Clint Brown	R	36	37	0	0	0	66.0	75	5	16	23	4-6	10	3.68
Pete Appleton	R	36	25	0	0	0	57.2	54	8	28	21	4-0	5	5.62
Ed Weiland	R	25	5	0	0	0	14.1	15	5	7	3	0-0	0	8.79
Orval Grove	R	20	3	0	0	0	6.0	4	0	4	1	0-0	0	3.00

1940 St. Louis Browns 6th AL 67-87 .435 23.0 GB

Fred Haney

Player	Gm by Position	B	Age	G	AB	R	H	2B	3B	HR	RBI	BB	SO	SB	Avg	OBP	Slg
Bob Swift	C128	R	25	130	398	37	97	20	1	0	39	28	39	1	.244	.295	.299
George McQuinn	1B150	L	30	151	594	78	166	39	10	16	84	57	58	3	.279	.343	.460
Don Heffner	2B125	R	29	126	487	52	115	23	2	3	53	39	37	5	.236	.295	.310
Harlond Clift	3B147	R	27	150	523	92	143	29	5	20	87	104	62	9	.273	.396	.463
Johnny Berardino	SS112,2B13,3B9	R	23	142	523	71	135	31	4	16	85	32	46	6	.258	.301	.424
Rip Radcliff	OF139,1B4	L	34	150	584	83	200	33	9	7	81	47	20	6	.342	.392	.466
Wally Judnich	OF133	L	23	137	519	97	157	27	7	24	89	54	71	8	.303	.368	.520
Chet Laabs	OF63	R	28	105	218	32	59	11	5	10	40	34	59	3	.271	.372	.505
Roy Cullenbine†	OF57,1B6	S	26	86	257	41	59	11	2	7	31	50	34	0	.230	.359	.370
Joe Grace	OF51,C12	L	26	80	229	45	59	14	2	5	25	26	23	2	.258	.336	.402
Myril Hoag	OF46	R	32	76	191	20	50	11	0	3	26	13	30	6	.262	.309	.366
Alan Strange	SS35,2B4	R	33	54	167	26	31	8	3	0	6	22	12	2	.186	.284	.269
George Susce	C61	R	31	61	113	6	24	4	0	0	13	9	9	1	.212	.282	.248
Joe Gallagher†	OF15	R	26	23	70	14	19	3	1	2	8	4	12	2	.271	.311	.429
Johnny Lucadello	2B16	R	21	17	63	15	20	4	2	2	10	6	4	1	.317	.394	.540
Lyn Lary	SS12,2B1	R	34	27	54	5	3	1	1	0	3	4	7	0	.056	.136	.111
Fuzz White		L	22	2	2	0	0	0	0	0	0	0	0	0	.000	.000	.000
Sam Harshany	C2	R	30	3	1	0	0	0	0	0	0	1	0	0	.000	.500	.000

Pitcher	T	Age	G	GS	CG	ShO	IP	H	HR	BB	SO	W-L	Sv	ERA
Eldon Auker	R	29	38	35	20	2	263.2	299	17	96	78	16-11	0	3.96
Vern Kennedy	R	33	34	32	18	0	222.1	263	18	122	70	12-17	0	5.59
Bob Harris	R	23	35	28	8	1	194.0	225	24	85	49	11-15	1	4.92
Johnny Niggeling	R	36	28	20	10	0	153.2	148	9	69	82	7-11	2	4.45
Jack Kramer	R	22	16	9	1	0	64.2	86	4	26	12	3-7	0	6.26
Maury Newlin	R	26	1	1	0	0	6.0	4	1	2	3	1-0	0	6.00
Bill Trotter	R	31	36	4	1	0	98.0	117	5	31	29	7-6	0	3.77
Slick Coffman	R	29	31	4	1	0	74.2	108	5	23	26	2-2	1	6.27
Roxie Lawson	R	34	30	2	0	0	72.0	77	5	54	18	5-3	4	5.13
Emil Bildilli	L	27	28	11	3	0	97.0	113	12	52	32	2-4	1	5.57
Lefty Mills	L	30	26	5	1	0	59.0	64	7	52	18	0-6	0	7.78
John Whitehead	R	31	15	4	1	1	40.0	46	3	14	11	1-3	0	5.40
Bill Cox	R	27	12	0	0	0	17.1	23	3	12	7	0-1	0	7.27
Willis Hudlin†	R	34	6	1	0	0	11.1	19	0	8	4	0-1	0	11.12

Seasons: Team Rosters 679

1940 Washington Senators 7th AL 64-90 .416 26.0 GB

Bucky Harris

Player	Gm by Position	B	Age	G	AB	R	H	2B	3B	HR	RBI	BB	SO	SB	Avg	OBP	Slg
Rick Ferrell	C99	R	34	103	326	35	89	18	2	0	28	47	15	1	.273	.365	.340
Zeke Bonura†	1B79	R	31	79	311	41	85	16	3	3	45	40	13	2	.273	.358	.373
Jimmy Bloodworth	2B96,1B17,3B6	R	22	119	469	47	115	17	8	11	70	16	71	3	.245	.272	.386
Cecil Travis	3B113,SS23	L	26	136	528	60	170	37	11	2	76	48	23	0	.322	.381	.445
Jimmy Pofahl	SS112,2B4	R	23	119	406	34	95	23	5	2	36	37	55	2	.234	.298	.330
George Case	OF154	R	24	154	656	109	192	29	5	5	56	52	39	35	.293	.349	.375
Gee Walker	OF140	R	32	140	595	87	175	29	7	13	96	24	58	21	.294	.325	.432
Buddy Lewis	OF112,3B36	L	23	148	600	101	190	38	10	6	63	74	36	15	.317	.393	.443
Johnny Welaj	OF53	R	26	88	215	31	55	9	0	3	21	19	20	8	.256	.322	.340
Buddy Myer	2B54	L	36	71	210	28	61	14	4	0	29	34	10	6	.290	.389	.395
Jake Early	C56	L	25	80	206	26	53	8	4	5	14	23	22	0	.257	.335	.408
Jack Sanford	1B34	R	23	34	122	5	24	4	2	0	10	6	17	0	.197	.234	.262
Sammy West	1B12,OF9	L	35	57	99	7	25	6	1	1	18	16	13	0	.253	.357	.364
Charlie Gelbert†	SS12,P2,2B1	R	34	22	54	7	20	7	1	0	7	4	3	0	.370	.424	.537
Jimmy Wasdell†	1B8	L	26	10	35	3	3	1	0	0	0	2	7	0	.086	.135	.114
Sherry Robertson	SS10	L	21	10	33	4	7	0	1	0	0	5	6	0	.212	.316	.273
Al Evans	C9	R	23	14	25	1	8	2	0	0	7	6	7	1	.320	.452	.400
Mickey Vernon	1B4	L	22	5	19	0	3	0	0	0	0	0	3	0	.158	.158	.158
Jim Mallory	OF3	R	21	4	12	2	2	0	0	0	0	1	1	0	.167	.231	.167
Dick Hahn	C1	R	23	1	3	0	0	0	0	0	0	0	0	0	.000	.000	.000
Morrie Aderholt	2B1	L	24	1	2	0	0	0	0	0	0	0	0	0	.000	.000	.000

Pitcher	T	Age	G	GS	CG	ShO	IP	H	HR	BB	SO	W-L	Sv	ERA
Dutch Leonard	R	31	35	35	23	2	289.0	328	19	78	124	14-19	0	3.49
Ken Chase	L	26	35	34	20	1	261.2	260	14	143	129	15-17	0	3.23
Sid Hudson	R	25	38	31	19	3	252.0	272	20	81	96	17-16	1	4.57
Walt Masterson	R	20	31	19	3	0	130.1	128	6	88	68	3-13	2	4.90
Willis Hudlin†	R	34	8	6	1	0	37.1	50	9	5	9	1-2	0	6.51
Al Hollingsworth	L	32	3	2	0	0	18.0	18	0	11	7	1-0	0	5.50
Red Anderson	R	28	2	2	2	0	14.0	12	0	5	3	1-1	0	3.86
Joe Krakauskas	L	25	32	10	2	0	109.0	137	7	73	68	1-6	2	6.44
Alex Carrasquel	R	27	28	0	0	0	48.0	42	4	29	19	6-2	0	4.88
Rene Monteagudo	L	24	27	8	3	0	100.2	128	7	52	64	2-6	2	6.08
Joe Haynes	R	22	22	7	1	0	63.1	85	4	34	23	3-6	0	6.54
Bucky Jacobs	R	27	9	0	0	0	15.0	16	1	9	6	0-1	0	6.00
Lou Thuman	R	23	2	0	0	0	5.0	10	0	7	0	0-1	0	14.40
Charlie Gelbert	R	34	2	0	0	0	4.0	5	2	3	1	0-0	0	9.00
Gil Torres	R	24	2	0	0	0	2.2	3	0	0	1	0-0	0	0.00

1940 Philadelphia Athletics 8th AL 54-100 .351 36.0 GB

Connie Mack

Player	Gm by Position	B	Age	G	AB	R	H	2B	3B	HR	RBI	BB	SO	SB	Avg	OBP	Slg
Frankie Hayes	C134,1B2	R	25	136	465	73	143	23	4	16	70	61	59	9	.308	.389	.477
Dick Siebert	1B154	L	28	154	595	69	170	31	6	5	77	33	34	8	.286	.325	.383
Benny McCoy	2B130,3B1	L	24	134	490	56	126	26	5	7	62	65	44	2	.257	.345	.373
Al Rubeling	3B98,2B10	R	27	108	376	49	92	16	6	4	38	48	58	4	.245	.330	.351
Al Brancato	SS80,3B25	R	21	107	298	42	57	11	2	1	23	28	36	3	.191	.265	.252
Bob Johnson	OF136	R	33	138	512	93	137	25	4	31	103	83	64	8	.268	.374	.514
Wally Moses	OF133	L	29	142	537	91	166	41	9	9	50	75	44	6	.309	.396	.469
Sam Chapman	OF129	R	24	134	508	88	140	26	3	23	75	46	96	2	.276	.337	.474
Dee Miles	OF50	L	31	88	236	26	71	9	6	1	23	8	18	1	.301	.327	.403
Bill Lillard	SS69,2B1	R	22	73	206	26	49	8	2	1	21	28	28	0	.238	.332	.311
Joe Gantenbein	3B45,1B6,SS3*	L	24	75	197	21	47	6	2	4	23	11	21	1	.239	.282	.350
Chubby Dean	P30,1B1	L	23	67	90	6	26	2	0	0	6	16	9	0	.289	.396	.311
Al Simmons	OF18	R	38	37	81	7	25	4	0	1	19	4	8	0	.309	.341	.395
Hal Wagner	C28	L	24	34	75	9	19	5	1	0	10	11	6	0	.253	.356	.347
Fred Chapman	SS25	R	23	26	69	6	11	1	0	0	4	6	10	1	.159	.227	.174
Crash Davis	2B19,SS1	R	20	23	67	4	18	1	1	0	9	3	10	1	.269	.310	.313
Earle Brucker	C13	R	39	23	46	3	9	1	1	0	2	6	3	0	.196	.288	.261
Elmer Valo	OF6	L	19	6	23	6	8	0	0	0	0	3	0	2	.348	.423	.348
Jack Wallaesa	SS6	S	20	6	20	0	3	0	0	0	2	0	2	0	.150	.150	.150
Eric Tipton	OF2	R	25	2	8	2	1	0	1	0	0	1	1	0	.125	.222	.375
Dario Lodigiani		R	23	1	1	0	0	0	0	0	0	0	0	0	.000	.000	.000
Buddy Hancken	C1	R	25	1	0	0	0	0	0	0	0	0	0	0	—	—	—

J. Gantenbein, 1 G at OF

Pitcher	T	Age	G	GS	CG	ShO	IP	H	HR	BB	SO	W-L	Sv	ERA
Johnny Babich	R	27	31	30	16	1	229.1	222	16	80	94	14-13	0	3.73
Nels Potter	R	28	31	25	13	0	200.2	213	18	71	73	9-14	0	4.44
George Caster	R	32	36	24	11	0	178.1	234	18	69	75	4-19	2	6.56
Chubby Dean	L	23	30	19	8	1	159.1	220	21	63	38	6-13	1	6.61
Buck Ross	R	25	24	19	10	0	156.1	160	15	60	43	5-10	1	4.38
Porter Vaughan	L	21	18	15	5	0	99.1	104	9	61	46	2-9	2	5.35
Phil Marchildon	R	26	2	2	1	0	10.0	12	1	8	4	0-2	0	7.20
Ed Heusser	R	31	41	6	2	0	110.0	144	11	42	39	6-13	5	4.99
Bill Beckmann	R	32	34	9	6	2	127.1	132	11	35	47	8-4	1	4.17
Herman Besse	L	28	17	5	0	0	53.0	70	10	34	19	0-3	0	8.83
Les McCrabb	R	25	4	0	0	0	11.2	19	2	2	4	0-0	0	6.94
Carl Miles	L	22	2	0	0	0	8.0	9	2	8	6	0-0	0	13.50
Pat McLaughlin	R	29	1	0	0	0	1.2	4	1	1	0	0-0	0	16.20

»1940 Cincinnati Reds 1st NL 100-53 .654 —

Bill McKechnie

Player	Gm by Position	B	Age	G	AB	R	H	2B	3B	HR	RBI	BB	SO	SB	Avg	OBP	Slg
Ernie Lombardi	C101	R	32	109	376	50	120	22	0	14	74	31	14	0	.319	.382	.489
Frank McCormick	1B155	R	29	155	618	93	191	44	3	19	127	52	26	2	.309	.367	.482
Lonny Frey	2B150	L	29	150	563	102	150	23	6	8	54	80	48	22	.266	.361	.371
Bill Werber	3B143	R	32	143	584	105	162	35	5	12	48	68	40	16	.277	.361	.416
Billy Myers	SS88	R	29	90	282	33	57	14	2	5	30	30	56	0	.202	.283	.319
Ival Goodman	OF135	L	31	136	519	78	134	20	6	12	63	60	54	9	.258	.335	.389
Harry Craft	OF109,1B2	R	25	115	422	47	103	18	5	6	48	17	46	2	.244	.277	.353
Mike McCormick	OF107	R	23	110	417	48	125	20	0	1	30	13	36	8	.300	.326	.355
Eddie Joost	SS78,2B7,3B4	R	24	88	278	24	60	7	2	1	24	32	40	4	.216	.301	.266
Morrie Arnovich†	OF60	R	29	62	211	17	60	10	2	0	21	13	10	1	.284	.326	.351
Willard Hershberger	C37	R	30	48	123	6	38	4	2	0	26	6	6	0	.309	.351	.374
Johnny Rizzo†	OF30	R	27	31	110	17	31	6	0	4	17	14	14	1	.282	.363	.445
Jimmy Ripple†	OF30	L	30	32	101	15	31	10	0	4	20	13	5	1	.307	.397	.525
Lew Riggs	3B11	L	30	41	72	8	21	7	1	1	9	2	4	0	.292	.311	.458
Bill Baker	C24	R	29	27	69	5	15	1	1	0	7	4	8	2	.217	.260	.261
Lee Gamble	OF10	L	30	38	42	12	6	1	0	0	0	0	1	0	.143	.143	.167
Jimmie Wilson	C16	R	39	16	37	2	9	2	0	0	3	2	1	1	.243	.282	.297
Dick West	C7	R	24	7	28	4	11	2	1	1	6	0	2	1	.393	.393	.571
Mike Dejan	OF2	L	25	12	16	1	3	0	1	0	1	2	3	0	.188	.316	.313
Vince DiMaggio†	OF1	R	27	2	4	2	1	0	0	0	0	1	0	0	.250	.400	.250
Wally Berger†		R	34	2	2	0	0	0	0	0	0	0	0	0	.000	.000	.000

Pitcher	T	Age	G	GS	CG	ShO	IP	H	HR	BB	SO	W-L	Sv	ERA
Paul Derringer	R	33	37	37	26	3	296.2	280	17	48	115	20-12	0	3.06
Bucky Walters	R	31	36	36	29	3	305.0	241	19	92	115	22-10	0	2.48
Junior Thompson	R	23	33	31	17	3	225.1	197	10	96	103	16-9	0	3.32
Jim Turner	R	36	24	23	11	0	187.0	187	9	32	53	14-7	0	2.89
Whitey Moore	R	28	25	15	5	1	116.2	100	8	56	60	8-8	1	3.63
J. Vander Meer	L	25	10	7	2	0	48.0	38	3	41	41	3-1	1	3.75
Joe Beggs	R	29	37	1	0	0	76.2	68	1	21	25	12-3	7	2.00
Milt Shoffner	L	34	20	0	0	0	54.1	56	3	18	17	1-0	0	5.63
Johnny Hutchings	R	24	19	4	0	0	54.0	53	2	18	18	2-1	0	3.50
Elmer Riddle	R	25	15	1	1	0	33.2	30	0	17	9	1-2	2	1.87
Red Barrett	R	25	3	0	0	0	2.2	5	0	1	0	1-0	0	6.75
Witt Guise	L	30	2	0	0	0	7.2	8	0	5	1	0-0	0	1.17

1940 Brooklyn Dodgers 2nd NL 88-65 .575 12.0 GB

Leo Durocher

Player	Gm by Position	B	Age	G	AB	R	H	2B	3B	HR	RBI	BB	SO	SB	Avg	OBP	Slg
Babe Phelps	C99	L	32	118	370	47	109	24	5	13	61	30	27	2	.295	.349	.492
Dolph Camilli	1B140	L	33	142	512	92	147	29	13	23	96	89	83	9	.287	.397	.529
Pete Coscarart	2B140	R	27	143	506	55	120	24	4	9	58	53	59	5	.237	.311	.354
Cookie Lavagetto	3B116	R	27	118	448	56	115	21	3	4	43	70	32	4	.257	.361	.344
Pee Wee Reese	SS83	R	21	84	312	58	85	8	4	5	28	45	42	15	.272	.366	.372
Dixie Walker	OF136	L	29	143	556	75	171	37	8	6	66	42	21	3	.308	.357	.435
Joe Medwick†	OF103	R	28	106	423	62	127	18	12	14	66	26	28	2	.300	.345	.499
Joe Vosmik	OF99	R	30	116	404	45	114	14	6	1	42	22	21	0	.282	.321	.354
Jimmy Wasdell†	OF42,1B17	L	26	77	230	35	64	14	3	3	37	18	24	6	.278	.333	.413
Pete Reiser	3B30,OF17,SS5	L	21	58	225	34	66	11	4	3	20	15	33	2	.293	.338	.418
Johnny Hudson	SS38,2B27	R	28	85	179	13	39	4	3	0	19	9	26	2	.218	.255	.274
Leo Durocher	SS53,2B4	R	34	62	160	10	37	9	1	1	14	12	13	1	.231	.285	.319
Gus Mancuso	C56	R	34	60	144	16	33	8	0	0	16	13	7	0	.229	.293	.285
Charlie Gilbert	OF43	L	20	57	142	23	35	9	1	2	8	8	13	0	.246	.287	.366
Herman Franks	C43	L	26	65	131	11	24	4	0	1	14	20	6	2	.183	.296	.237
Joe Gallagher†	OF20	R	26	57	110	10	29	6	1	3	16	2	14	1	.264	.283	.418
Roy Cullenbine†	OF19	S	26	22	61	8	11	1	0	1	9	23	11	2	.180	.405	.246
Ernie Koy†	OF19	R	30	24	48	9	11	2	1	1	8	3	5	1	.229	.275	.375
Don Ross	3B10	R	25	10	38	4	11	2	0	1	8	3	3	1	.289	.341	.421
Gene Moore†	OF6	L	30	10	26	3	7	2	0	0	2	1	3	0	.269	.296	.346
Jimmy Ripple†	OF3	L	30	7	13	0	3	0	0	0	0	2	2	0	.231	.333	.231
Tony Giuliani	C1	R	27	1	1	0	0	0	0	0	0	0	0	1	.000	.000	.000

Pitcher	T	Age	G	GS	CG	ShO	IP	H	HR	BB	SO	W-L	Sv	ERA
Whit Wyatt	R	32	37	34	16	5	239.1	233	19	62	124	15-14	0	3.46
Luke Hamlin	R	35	33	25	9	2	182.1	183	17	34	91	9-8	0	3.06
Curt Davis†	R	36	22	18	9	2	137.0	135	13	19	46	8-7	2	3.81
F. Fitzsimmons	R	38	20	18	11	4	134.1	120	5	25	35	16-2	1	2.81
Tex Carleton	R	33	34	17	4	1	149.0	140	12	47	88	6-6	2	3.81
Lee Grissom†	R	32	14	10	3	1	73.2	59	3	34	56	2-5	0	2.81
Steve Rachunok	R	23	2	1	1	0	10.0	9	0	5	10	0-1	0	4.50
Hugh Casey	R	26	44	10	5	2	154.0	136	13	51	53	11-8	2	3.62
Vito Tamulis	L	28	41	12	4	1	154.1	147	5	34	55	8-5	2	3.09
Tot Pressnell	R	33	24	4	1	1	68.1	58	4	17	21	6-5	2	3.69
Newt Kimball†	R	25	21	0	0	0	33.2	29	2	15	21	3-1	1	3.21
Ed Head	R	22	13	5	2	0	39.1	40	0	18	13	1-2	0	4.12
Van Lingle Mungo	R	29	7	0	0	0	22.0	24	1	10	9	1-0	1	2.45
Wes Flowers	L	26	5	2	0	0	21.0	23	2	10	8	1-1	0	3.43
Carl Doyle†	R	27	3	0	0	0	5.2	18	3	6	4	0-0	1	27.00
Lou Fette†	R	33	2	0	0	0	3.0	3	0	2	0	1-0	0	0.00
Max Macon	L	24	2	0	0	0	2.0	5	2	0	1	1-0	0	22.50
Wes Ferrell	R	32	1	0	0	0	4.0	4	0	4	4	0-0	0	6.75

1940 St. Louis Cardinals 3rd NL 84-69 .549 16.0 GB

Ray Blades (14-24)/Mike Gonzalez (1-5)/Billy Southworth (69-40)

Player	Gm by Position	B	Age	G	AB	R	H	2B	3B	HR	RBI	BB	SO	SB	Avg	OBP	Slg
Mickey Owen	C113	R	24	117	307	27	81	16	2	0	27	34	13	4	.264	.341	.329
Johnny Mize	1B153	L	27	155	579	111	182	31	13	43	137	82	49	7	.314	.404	.636
Joe Orengo	2B77,3B34,SS19	R	25	129	415	58	119	23	4	7	56	65	90	9	.287	.383	.412
Stu Martin	3B73,2B33	L	26	112	369	45	88	12	6	4	32	33	35	4	.238	.301	.336
Marty Marion	SS125	R	22	125	435	44	121	18	1	3	46	21	34	9	.278	.311	.345
Terry Moore	OF133	R	28	136	537	92	163	33	4	17	64	42	44	18	.304	.356	.475
Enos Slaughter	OF132	L	24	140	516	96	158	25	13	17	73	50	35	8	.306	.370	.504
Ernie Koy†	OF91	R	30	93	348	44	108	19	5	8	52	28	59	12	.310	.368	.463
Jimmy Brown	2B48,3B41,SS28	S	30	107	454	56	127	17	4	0	30	24	15	9	.280	.317	.335
Don Padgett	C72,1B2	L	28	93	240	24	58	15	1	6	41	26	14	1	.242	.321	.388
Pepper Martin	OF63,3B2	R	36	86	228	28	72	15	4	3	39	22	24	6	.316	.378	.456
Joe Medwick†	OF37	R	28	37	158	21	48	12	0	3	20	6	8	0	.304	.329	.437
Johnny Hopp	OF39,1B10	L	23	80	152	24	41	7	4	1	14	9	21	3	.270	.315	.388
Don Gutteridge	3B39	R	28	69	108	19	29	5	0	3	14	5	15	3	.269	.301	.398
Eddie Lake	2B17,SS6	R	24	32	66	12	14	3	0	2	7	12	17	1	.212	.342	.348
Harry Walker	OF7	L	23	7	27	2	5	1	0	0	6	0	2	0	.185	.185	.259
Carden Gillenwater	OF7	R	22	7	25	1	4	1	0	0	5	0	2	0	.160	.160	.200
Walker Cooper	C6	R	25	6	19	3	6	1	0	0	2	2	1	0	.316	.381	.368
Bill Delancey	C12	L	28	15	18	0	4	0	0	0	2	0	2	0	.222	.222	.222
Hal Epps	OF3	L	26	11	15	6	3	0	0	0	0	0	3	0	.200	.200	.200
Red Jones	OF1	L	25	12	11	0	1	0	0	0	1	1	3	0	.091	.167	.091
Creepy Crespi	3B2,SS1	R	22	3	11	2	3	1	0	0	0	1	2	1	.273	.333	.364

Pitcher	T	Age	G	GS	CG	ShO	IP	H	HR	BB	SO	W-L	Sv	ERA
Lon Warneke	R	31	33	31	17	1	232.0	235	17	47	85	16-10	0	3.14
Bill McGee	R	30	38	31	11	3	218.0	222	13	96	78	16-10	0	3.80
Mort Cooper	R	27	38	29	16	3	230.2	225	12	86	95	11-12	3	3.63
Bob Bowman	R	29	28	17	7	0	114.1	118	9	43	43	7-5	0	4.33
Curt Davis†	R	36	14	7	0	0	54.0	73	4	19	12	0-4	1	5.17
Newt Kimball†	R	25	2	1	1	0	14.0	11	1	6	6	1-0	0	2.57
Gene Lillard	R	26	2	1	0	0	4.2	8	1	4	2	0-1	0	13.50
Murry Dickson	R	23	1	1	0	0	1.2	5	0	1	0	0-0	0	16.20
Clyde Shoun	L	28	54	19	13	1	197.1	193	13	46	82	13-11	5	3.92
Max Lanier	L	24	35	11	4	2	105.0	113	1	38	49	9-6	3	3.34
Jack Russell	R	34	26	0	0	0	54.0	53	1	26	16	3-4	1	2.50
Carl Doyle†	R	27	21	5	1	0	81.0	99	7	41	44	3-3	0	5.89
Ira Hutchinson	R	29	20	2	1	0	63.1	68	3	19	19	4-2	1	3.13
Ernie White	L	23	8	1	0	0	21.2	29	0	14	15	1-1	0	4.15
Harry Brecheen	L	25	3	0	0	0	3.1	2	0	2	4	0-0	0	0.00
Bob Weiland	L	34	1	0	0	0	0.2	3	1	0	0	0-0	0	40.50

680 Seasons: Team Rosters

1940 Pittsburgh Pirates 4th NL 78-76 .506 22.5 GB

Frank Frisch

Player	Gm by Position	B	Age	G	AB	R	H	2B	3B	HR	RBI	BB	SO	SB	Avg	OBP	Slg
Spud Davis	C87	R	35	99	285	23	93	14	1	5	39	35	20	0	.326	.404	.435
Elbie Fletcher	1B147	L	24	147	510	94	139	22	7	16	104	119	54	5	.273	.418	.437
Frankie Gustine	2B130	R	20	133	524	59	147	32	7	1	55	35	39	7	.281	.328	.374
Lee Handley	3B80,2B2	R	26	98	302	50	85	7	4	1	19	27	16	7	.281	.340	.341
Arky Vaughan	SS155,3B2	L	28	156	594	113	178	40	15	7	95	88	25	12	.300	.393	.453
Bob Elliott	OF147	R	23	148	551	88	161	34	11	5	64	45	28	13	.292	.348	.421
M. Van Robays	OF143,1B1	R	25	145	572	82	156	27	7	11	116	33	58	2	.273	.316	.402
Vince DiMaggio†	OF108	R	27	110	356	59	103	26	0	19	54	37	83	11	.289	.364	.522
Debs Garms	3B64,OF19	L	32	103	358	76	127	23	7	5	57	23	6	3	.355	.395	.500
Paul Waner	OF45,1B8	L	37	89	238	32	69	16	1	1	32	23	14	0	.290	.352	.378
Al Lopez†	C59	R	31	59	174	15	45	6	2	1	24	13	13	5	.259	.310	.333
Lloyd Waner	OF42	L	34	72	166	30	43	3	0	0	3	5	5	2	.259	.285	.277
Pep Young	2B33,SS7,3B5	R	32	54	136	19	34	8	2	2	20	12	23	1	.250	.320	.382
Bill Brubaker	3B19,SS8,1B4	R	29	38	78	8	15	3	1	0	7	8	16	0	.192	.267	.256
Joe Schultz	C13	L	21	16	36	2	7	0	1	0	4	2	1	0	.194	.237	.250
Ed Fernandes	C27	S	22	28	33	1	4	1	0	0	2	7	6	0	.121	.275	.152
Ray Berres†	C21	R	32	21	32	2	6	0	0	0	2	1	1	0	.188	.212	.188
Johnny Rizzo†	OF7	R	27	9	28	1	5	1	0	0	2	5	5	0	.179	.324	.214
Ed Leip	2B2	R	29	3	5	2	1	0	0	0	0	0	0	0	.200	.200	.200
Frank Kalin	OF2	R	22	3	3	0	0	0	0	0	1	2	0	0	.000	.400	.000
Fern Bell		R	27	6	3	0	0	0	0	0	1	1	1	0	.000	.250	.000
Ray Mueller	C4	R	28	4	3	1	1	0	0	0	1	2	0	0	.333	.600	.333

Pitcher	T	Age	G	GS	CG	ShO	IP	H	HR	BB	SO	W-L	Sv	ERA
Joe Bowman	R	30	32	24	10	0	187.2	209	10	66	57	9-10	2	4.46
Max Butcher	R	29	35	24	6	2	136.1	161	13	46	40	8-9	2	6.01
Rip Sewell	R	33	33	23	14	2	189.2	169	6	67	60	16-5	1	2.80
Bob Klinger	R	32	39	22	3	0	142.0	196	5	53	48	8-13	3	5.39
Dutch Dietz	R	28	4	2	0	0	15.1	22	2	4	8	0-1	0	5.87
Mace Brown	R	31	48	17	5	2	173.0	181	5	49	73	10-9	7	3.49
Dick Lanahan	L	28	40	8	4	0	108.0	121	8	42	45	6-8	2	4.25
Ken Heintzelman	L	24	39	16	5	2	165.0	193	7	65	71	8-8	3	4.47
Johnny Lanning	R	29	38	7	2	0	115.2	119	8	39	42	8-4	2	4.05
Danny MacFayden	R	35	35	8	0	0	91.1	112	5	27	24	5-4	2	3.55
Russ Bauers	R	26	15	2	0	0	30.2	42	2	18	11	0-2	0	7.63
Oad Swigart	R	25	7	2	0	0	22.1	27	1	10	9	0-2	0	4.43
Pep Rambert	R	23	3	1	0	0	8.1	12	0	4	0	0-1	0	7.56
Ray Harrell	R	28	3	0	0	0	3.1	5	0	2	3	0-0	0	8.10

1940 Chicago Cubs 5th NL 75-79 .487 25.5 GB

Gabby Hartnett

Player	Gm by Position	B	Age	G	AB	R	H	2B	3B	HR	RBI	BB	SO	SB	Avg	OBP	Slg
Al Todd	C104	R	38	104	381	31	97	13	2	6	42	11	29	1	.255	.283	.346
Phil Cavarretta	1B52	L	23	65	193	34	54	11	4	2	22	31	18	3	.280	.388	.409
Billy Herman	2B135	R	30	135	558	77	163	24	4	5	57	47	30	1	.292	.347	.376
Stan Hack	3B148,1B1	L	30	149	603	101	191	38	6	8	40	75	24	21	.317	.395	.439
Bobby Mattick	SS126,3B1	R	24	128	441	30	96	15	0	0	33	19	33	5	.218	.250	.252
Bill Nicholson	OF123	L	25	135	491	78	146	27	7	25	98	50	67	2	.297	.366	.534
Jim Gleeson	OF123	S	28	129	485	76	152	39	11	5	61	54	52	4	.313	.389	.470
Hank Leiber	OF103,1B12	R	29	117	440	68	133	24	2	17	86	45	68	1	.302	.371	.482
Dom Dallessandro	OF74	L	26	107	287	33	77	19	6	1	36	34	13	4	.268	.348	.387
Rip Russell	1B51,3B3	R	25	68	215	15	53	7	2	5	33	8	23	1	.247	.277	.367
Augie Galan	OF54,2B2	S	28	68	209	33	48	14	2	3	22	37	23	9	.230	.346	.359
Zeke Bonura†	1B44	R	31	49	182	20	48	14	0	4	20	10	4	1	.264	.302	.407
Rabbit Warstler†	SS28,2B17	R	36	45	159	19	36	4	1	1	18	8	19	1	.226	.263	.283
Rip Collins	C42	R	30	47	120	11	25	3	0	1	14	14	18	4	.208	.296	.258
Gabby Hartnett	C22,1B1	R	39	37	64	3	17	3	0	1	12	8	7	0	.266	.347	.359
Billy Rogell	SS14,3B9,2B3	S	35	33	59	7	8	0	0	1	3	2	8	1	.136	.164	.186
Clyde McCullough	C7	R	23	9	26	4	4	1	0	0	1	5	5	0	.154	.290	.192
Bobby Sturgeon	SS7	R	20	7	21	1	4	1	0	0	2	0	1	0	.190	.190	.238

Pitcher	T	Age	G	GS	CG	ShO	IP	H	HR	BB	SO	W-L	Sv	ERA
Larry French	L	32	40	33	18	3	246.0	240	12	64	107	14-14	2	3.29
Claude Passeau	R	31	46	31	20	4	280.2	259	8	59	124	20-13	5	2.50
Bill Lee	R	30	37	30	9	1	211.1	246	12	70	70	9-17	0	5.03
Vern Olsen	L	22	34	20	9	4	172.2	172	5	62	71	13-9	0	2.97
Jake Mooty	R	27	20	12	6	0	114.0	101	11	49	42	6-6	1	2.92
Dizzy Dean	R	30	10	9	3	0	54.0	68	4	20	18	3-3	0	5.17
Ken Raffensberger	L	22	43	10	3	0	114.2	120	10	29	55	7-9	3	3.38
Charlie Root	R	41	36	8	1	0	112.0	118	9	33	50	2-4	1	3.86
Vance Page	R	34	30	1	0	0	59.0	65	1	26	22	1-3	2	4.42
Clay Bryant	R	28	8	0	0	0	26.1	26	2	14	5	0-1	0	4.78
Julio Bonetti	R	28	1	0	0	0	1.1	3	0	4	0	0-0	0	20.25

1940 New York Giants 6th NL 72-80 .474 27.5 GB

Bill Terry

Player	Gm by Position	B	Age	G	AB	R	H	2B	3B	HR	RBI	BB	SO	SB	Avg	OBP	Slg
Harry Danning	C131	R	28	140	524	65	157	34	4	13	91	35	31	3	.300	.349	.454
Babe Young	1B147	L	24	149	556	75	159	27	4	17	101	69	28	4	.286	.367	.441
Burgess Whitehead	3B74,2B57,SS4	R	30	133	568	68	160	9	6	4	36	26	17	9	.282	.319	.340
Mel Ott	OF111,3B42	L	31	151	536	89	155	27	3	19	79	100	50	6	.289	.407	.457
Mickey Witek	SS89,2B32	R	24	119	433	34	111	7	0	3	31	24	17	2	.256	.295	.293
Jo-Jo Moore	OF133	L	31	138	543	83	150	33	4	6	46	43	30	7	.276	.337	.385
Frank Demaree	OF119	R	30	121	460	68	139	18	6	7	61	45	39	5	.302	.364	.413
Johnny Rucker	OF57	L	23	86	277	38	82	7	5	4	23	7	32	4	.296	.313	.401
Tony Cuccinello†	2B47,3B37	R	32	88	307	26	64	9	2	5	36	16	42	1	.208	.248	.300
Billy Jurges	SS63	R	32	63	214	23	54	3	3	2	36	25	14	2	.252	.347	.322
Bob Seeds	OF40	R	33	56	155	18	45	5	2	4	16	17	19	0	.290	.371	.426
Ken O'Dea	C31	L	27	48	96	9	23	4	1	0	12	16	15	0	.240	.348	.302
Al Glossop†	2B24	S	24	27	91	16	19	3	0	4	8	10	16	1	.209	.294	.374
Johnny McCarthy	1B6	L	30	51	67	6	16	4	0	0	5	2	8	0	.239	.261	.299
Buster Maynard	OF7	R	27	7	29	6	8	2	2	1	2	2	6	0	.276	.323	.586
Glen Stewart	3B6,SS5	R	27	15	29	1	4	1	0	0	0	1	2	0	.138	.167	.172
Red Tramback	OF1	L	24	2	4	0	1	0	0	0	0	1	1	1	.250	.400	.250

Pitcher	T	Age	G	GS	CG	ShO	IP	H	HR	BB	SO	W-L	Sv	ERA
Harry Gumbert	R	30	35	30	14	2	237.0	230	17	81	77	12-14	2	3.76
Hal Schumacher	R	29	34	30	12	1	227.0	218	14	96	123	13-13	1	3.25
Bill Lohrman	R	27	31	28	11	5	195.0	200	19	43	73	10-15	1	3.78
Carl Hubbell	L	37	31	27	11	2	214.1	220	22	59	86	11-12	0	3.65
Cliff Melton	L	28	37	21	4	1	166.2	185	9	68	91	10-11	2	4.91
Bob Carpenter	R	22	5	3	2	0	33.0	29	2	14	25	2-0	0	2.73
Willis Hudlin†	R	34	1	1	0	0	5.0	9	1	1	1	0-1	0	10.80
Jumbo Brown	R	33	41	0	0	0	55.1	49	5	25	31	2-4	7	3.42
Red Lynn	R	26	33	0	0	0	42.1	40	3	24	25	4-3	3	3.83
Roy Joiner	L	33	30	2	0	0	53.0	66	8	17	25	3-2	1	3.40
Paul Dean	R	26	27	7	2	0	99.1	110	8	29	32	4-4	0	3.90
Hy Vandenberg	R	33	13	3	1	0	32.1	27	2	16	17	1-1	1	3.90

1940 Boston Braves 7th NL 65-87 .428 34.5 GB

Casey Stengel

Player	Gm by Position	B	Age	G	AB	R	H	2B	3B	HR	RBI	BB	SO	SB	Avg	OBP	Slg
Ray Berres†	C85	R	32	85	229	12	44	4	1	0	14	18	19	0	.192	.251	.218
Buddy Hassett	1B98,OF13	L	28	124	458	59	107	19	4	0	27	25	16	4	.234	.273	.293
Bama Rowell	2B115,OF7	L	24	130	486	46	148	19	8	3	58	18	22	12	.305	.331	.395
Sibby Sisti	3B102,2B16	R	19	123	459	73	115	19	5	6	34	36	64	4	.251	.311	.353
Eddie Miller	SS151	R	23	151	569	78	157	33	3	14	79	41	43	8	.276	.330	.418
Chet Ross	OF149	R	23	149	569	84	160	23	14	17	89	59	127	4	.281	.352	.460
Max West	OF102,1B36	L	23	139	524	72	137	27	5	7	72	65	54	2	.261	.344	.372
Johnny Cooney	OF99,1B7	R	39	108	365	40	116	14	3	0	21	25	9	4	.318	.363	.373
Gene Moore†	OF94	L	30	103	363	46	106	24	1	5	39	25	32	2	.292	.338	.405
Al Glossop†	2B18,3B18,SS1	S	24	60	148	17	35	2	1	3	14	17	22	1	.236	.315	.324
Phil Masi	C52	R	24	63	138	11	27	4	1	1	14	14	14	0	.196	.270	.261
Tony Cuccinello†	3B33	R	32	34	126	14	34	9	0	0	19	8	9	1	.270	.319	.341
Al Lopez†	C36	R	31	36	119	20	35	3	1	2	17	6	8	1	.294	.328	.387
Les Scarsella	1B15	L	26	18	60	7	18	1	3	0	8	3	5	2	.300	.344	.417
Rabbit Warstler†	2B24,3B2,SS1	R	36	33	57	6	12	0	0	0	4	10	5	0	.211	.328	.211
Whitey Wietelmann	2B15,3B9,SS3	S	21	35	41	3	8	1	0	0	1	5	5	0	.195	.283	.220
Mel Preibisch	OF11	R	25	11	40	3	9	2	0	0	5	2	4	0	.225	.262	.275
Stan Andrews	C14	R	23	19	33	1	6	0	0	0	2	0	3	1	.182	.182	.182
Sig Broskie	C11	R	29	11	22	1	6	1	0	0	4	1	2	0	.273	.304	.318
Bob Loane	OF10	R	25	13	22	4	5	3	0	0	1	2	5	2	.227	.292	.364
Buddy Gremp	1B3	R	20	4	9	0	2	0	0	0	2	0	0	0	.222	.222	.222
Don Manno	OF2	R	25	3	7	1	2	0	0	1	4	0	2	0	.286	.286	.714
Claude Wilborn	OF3	L	27	5	7	0	0	0	0	0	0	0	1	0	.000	.000	.000
Hank Majeski		R	23	3	3	0	0	0	0	0	0	0	0	0	.000	.000	.000

Pitcher	T	Age	G	GS	CG	ShO	IP	H	HR	BB	SO	W-L	Sv	ERA
Bill Posedel	R	33	35	32	18	0	233.0	263	16	81	86	12-17	1	4.13
Dick Errickson	R	26	34	29	17	3	236.1	241	8	90	34	12-13	3	3.16
Joe Sullivan	L	29	36	22	7	0	177.1	157	9	89	64	10-14	1	3.55
Manny Salvo	R	27	21	20	14	5	160.2	151	9	43	60	10-9	0	3.08
Jim Tobin	R	27	15	11	9	0	96.1	102	8	24	29	7-3	0	3.83
Lou Fette†	R	33	7	5	0	0	32.1	38	0	18	2	0-5	0	5.57
Art Johnson	L	23	2	1	0	0	6.0	10	0	3	1	0-1	0	10.50
Nick Strincevich	R	25	32	14	5	0	128.2	142	17	63	54	4-8	1	5.53
Dick Coffman	R	33	31	0	0	0	48.1	63	4	11	11	1-5	3	5.40
Al Javery	R	22	29	4	1	0	83.1	99	2	36	42	2-4	1	5.51
Al Piechota	R	26	21	8	2	0	61.0	68	6	41	18	2-5	0	5.75
George Barnicle	R	22	13	2	1	0	32.2	28	1	31	11	1-0	0	7.44
Joe Callahan	R	23	6	2	0	0	15.0	20	1	13	3	0-2	0	10.20
Hank LaManna	R	20	5	1	1	0	13.1	13	1	8	3	1-0	0	4.73
Ace Williams	L	23	5	0	0	0	9.0	21	0	12	5	0-0	0	16.00
Tom Earley	R	23	4	1	1	1	16.1	16	1	3	5	2-0	0	3.86
Bill Swift	R	32	4	0	0	0	9.1	12	0	7	7	1-1	1	2.89

1940 Philadelphia Phillies 8th NL 50-103 .327 50.0 GB

Doc Prothro

Player	Gm by Position	B	Age	G	AB	R	H	2B	3B	HR	RBI	BB	SO	SB	Avg	OBP	Slg
Bennie Warren	C97,1B1	R	28	106	289	33	71	6	1	12	34	40	46	1	.246	.339	.398
Art Mahan	1B145,P1	L	27	146	544	55	133	24	5	2	39	40	37	4	.244	.297	.318
Ham Schulte	2B119,SS1	R	27	120	436	44	103	18	2	1	21	32	30	3	.236	.288	.294
Pinky May	3B135,SS1	R	29	136	501	59	147	24	2	1	48	58	33	2	.293	.371	.355
Bobby Bragan	SS132,3B2	R	22	132	474	36	105	14	1	7	44	28	34	2	.222	.265	.300
Joe Marty	OF118	R	26	123	455	52	123	21	8	13	50	17	50	2	.270	.298	.437
Chuck Klein	OF96	L	35	116	354	39	77	16	2	7	37	44	30	2	.218	.304	.333
Johnny Rizzo†	OF91,3B7	R	27	103	367	53	107	12	2	20	53	37	31	2	.292	.358	.499
Heinie Mueller	2B34,OF31,3B13*	S	27	97	263	24	65	13	2	3	28	37	23	2	.247	.344	.346
Bill Atwood	C69	R	28	78	203	7	39	9	0	0	22	25	18	0	.192	.284	.236
Mel Mazzera	OF42,1B11	L	26	69	156	16	37	5	4	0	13	19	15	1	.237	.320	.321
Danny Litwhiler	OF34	R	23	36	142	10	49	2	2	5	17	3	13	1	.345	.363	.493
Morrie Arnovich†	OF37	R	29	39	141	13	28	2	1	0	12	14	15	0	.199	.276	.227
Hersh Martin	OF23	S	30	33	83	10	21	6	1	0	5	9	9	1	.253	.326	.349
Wally Millies	C24	R	33	26	43	1	3	0	0	0	0	4	4	0	.070	.149	.070
Wally Berger†	OF11,1B1	R	34	20	41	3	13	2	0	1	5	4	7	1	.317	.378	.439
Hal Marnie	2B11	R	21	11	34	4	6	0	0	0	4	4	2	0	.176	.263	.176
George Jumonville	SS10,3B1	R	23	11	34	0	3	0	0	0	0	1	6	0	.088	.139	.088
Del Young	SS6,2B5	S	28	15	33	2	8	0	1	0	1	2	1	0	.242	.286	.303
Neb Stewart	OF9	R	22	10	31	3	4	0	0	0	0	1	5	0	.129	.156	.129
Gus Suhr	1B7	L	34	10	25	4	4	0	0	2	5	5	5	0	.160	.300	.400
George Scharein	SS7	R	25	7	17	0	5	0	0	0	0	0	3	0	.294	.294	.294
Alex Monchak	SS9,2B1	R	23	19	14	1	2	0	0	0	0	0	6	1	.143	.143	.143
Sam File	SS6,3B1	R	18	7	13	0	1	0	0	0	1	0	2	0	.077	.077	.077
Stan Benjamin	OF2	R	26	8	9	1	2	0	0	0	1	1	1	0	.222	.300	.222
Ed Levy		R	23	1	1	0	0	0	0	0	0	0	0	0	.000	.000	.000
Roy Hughes	2B1	R	29	1	0	0	0	0	0	0	0	0	0	0	—	—	—

H. Mueller, 2 G at 1B

Pitcher	T	Age	G	GS	CG	ShO	IP	H	HR	BB	SO	W-L	Sv	ERA
Kirby Higbe	R	25	41	36	20	1	283.0	242	12	121	137	14-19	1	3.72
Hugh Mulcahy	R	26	36	36	21	3	280.0	283	12	91	82	13-22	0	3.60
Ike Pearson	R	23	29	20	5	1	145.1	160	13	57	43	3-14	1	5.45
Boom-Boom Beck	R	35	29	15	4	0	129.1	147	13	41	38	4-9	0	4.31
Cy Blanton	R	31	13	10	5	0	77.0	82	7	21	24	4-3	0	4.32
Johnny Podgajny	R	20	4	4	3	0	35.0	33	0	1	12	1-3	0	2.83
Si Johnson	R	33	37	14	5	0	138.1	145	15	42	58	5-14	1	4.88
Lefty Smoll	L	26	33	9	0	0	109.0	145	6	36	31	2-8	0	5.37
Lloyd Brown	L	35	18	2	0	0	37.2	58	3	16	16	1-3	3	6.21
Syl Johnson	R	39	17	2	2	0	40.2	37	6	5	13	2-2	2	4.20
Charlie Frye	R	25	15	5	1	0	50.1	58	3	26	18	0-6	0	4.65
Frank Hoerst	L	22	6	0	0	0	12.0	12	1	8	3	1-0	0	5.25
Max Wilson	L	24	3	0	0	0	7.0	16	1	2	3	0-0	0	12.86
Roy Bruner	R	23	2	0	0	0	6.1	5	2	6	4	0-0	0	5.68
Paul Masterson	L	24	2	0	0	0	5.0	5	0	2	3	0-0	0	7.20
Art Mahan	L	27	1	0	0	0	1.0	1	0	0	0	0-0	0	0.00

»1941 New York Yankees 1st AL 101-53 .656 —

Joe McCarthy

Player	Gm by Position	B	Age	G	AB	R	H	2B	3B	HR	RBI	BB	SO	SB	Avg	OBP	Slg
Bill Dickey	C104	L	34	109	348	35	99	15	5	7	71	45	17	2	.284	.371	.417
Johnny Sturm	1B124	L	25	124	524	58	125	17	3	3	36	37	50	3	.239	.293	.300
Joe Gordon	2B131,1B30	R	26	156	588	104	162	26	7	24	87	72	80	10	.276	.358	.466
Red Rolfe	3B134	L	32	136	561	106	148	22	5	8	42	57	38	3	.264	.332	.364
Phil Rizzuto	SS128	R	23	133	515	65	158	20	9	3	46	27	36	14	.307	.343	.398
Joe DiMaggio	OF139	R	26	139	541	122	193	43	11	30	125	76	13	4	.357	.440	.643
Tommy Henrich	OF139	L	28	144	538	106	149	27	5	31	85	81	40	3	.277	.377	.519
Charlie Keller	OF137	L	24	140	507	102	151	24	10	33	122	102	65	6	.298	.416	.580
Buddy Rosar	C60	R	26	67	209	25	60	17	2	1	36	22	10	0	.287	.355	.402
Jerry Priddy	2B31,3B14,1B10	R	21	56	174	18	37	7	0	1	26	18	16	4	.213	.290	.270
George Selkirk	OF47	L	33	70	164	30	36	5	0	6	25	28	30	1	.220	.340	.360
Frankie Crosetti	SS32,3B13	R	30	50	148	13	33	2	2	1	22	18	14	0	.223	.320	.284
Frenchy Bordagaray	OF19	R	31	36	73	10	19	1	0	0	4	6	8	1	.260	.325	.274
Ken Silvestri	C13	S	25	17	40	6	10	5	0	1	4	7	6	0	.250	.362	.450
Johnny Lindell		R	24	1	1	0	0	0	0	0	0	0	0	0	.000	.000	.000

Pitcher	T	Age	G	GS	CG	ShO	IP	H	HR	BB	SO	W-L	Sv	ERA
Marius Russo	L	26	28	27	17	3	209.2	195	8	87	105	14-10	1	3.09
Red Ruffing	R	37	23	23	13	2	185.2	177	13	54	60	15-6	0	3.54
Lefty Gomez	L	32	23	23	8	2	156.1	151	10	103	76	15-5	0	3.74
Spud Chandler	R	33	28	20	11	4	163.2	146	5	60	60	10-4	4	3.19
Atley Donald	R	30	22	20	10	0	159.0	141	11	69	71	9-5	0	3.57
Marv Breuer	R	27	26	18	7	1	141.0	131	10	49	77	9-7	2	4.09
Tiny Bonham	R	27	23	14	7	1	126.2	118	12	31	43	9-6	2	2.98
George Washburn	R	26	1	1	0	0	2.0	2	0	5	1	0-1	0	13.50
Johnny Murphy	R	32	35	0	0	0	77.1	68	1	40	29	8-3	15	1.98
Norm Branch	R	26	27	0	0	0	47.0	37	2	26	28	5-1	2	2.87
Charley Stanceu	R	25	22	2	0	0	48.0	58	3	35	21	3-3	0	5.63
Steve Peek	R	26	17	8	2	0	80.0	85	6	39	18	4-2	0	5.06

1941 Boston Red Sox 2nd AL 84-70 .545 17.0 GB

Joe Cronin

Player	Gm by Position	B	Age	G	AB	R	H	2B	3B	HR	RBI	BB	SO	SB	Avg	OBP	Slg
Frankie Pytlak	C91	R	32	106	336	36	91	23	1	2	39	28	19	5	.271	.329	.363
Jimmie Foxx	1B124,3B5,OF1	R	33	135	487	87	146	27	8	19	105	93	103	2	.300	.412	.505
Bobby Doerr	2B132	R	23	132	500	74	141	28	4	16	93	43	43	1	.282	.339	.450
Jim Tabor	3B125	R	24	126	498	65	139	29	3	16	101	36	48	17	.279	.328	.446
Joe Cronin	SS119,3B22,OF1	R	34	143	518	98	161	38	8	16	95	82	55	1	.311	.406	.508
Dom DiMaggio	OF144	R	24	144	584	117	165	37	6	8	58	90	57	13	.283	.385	.408
Ted Williams	OF133	L	22	143	456	135	185	33	3	37	120	145	27	2	.406	.551	.735
Lou Finney	OF92,1B24	L	30	127	497	83	143	24	10	4	53	38	17	2	.288	.340	.400
Pete Fox	OF62	R	32	73	268	38	81	12	7	0	31	21	32	9	.302	.357	.399
Johnny Peacock	C70	L	31	79	261	28	74	20	1	0	27	21	3	2	.284	.339	.368
Skeeter Newsome	SS69,2B23	R	30	93	227	28	51	6	0	2	17	22	11	10	.225	.296	.278
Stan Spence	OF52,1B1	L	26	86	203	22	47	10	3	2	28	18	14	1	.232	.304	.340
Al Flair	1B8	L	24	10	30	3	6	2	1	0	2	1	1	1	.200	.226	.333
Odell Hale†	3B6,2B1	R	32	12	24	5	5	2	0	1	1	3	4	0	.208	.296	.417
Tom Carey	2B9,SS8	R	34	25	21	7	4	0	0	0	2	0	2	0	.190	.190	.190
Paul Campbell		L	23	1	0	0	0	0	0	0	0	0	0	0	—	—	—

Pitcher	T	Age	G	GS	CG	ShO	IP	H	HR	BB	SO	W-L	Sv	ERA
Dick Newsome	R	31	36	29	17	2	213.2	235	13	79	58	19-10	0	4.13
Charlie Wagner	R	28	29	25	12	3	187.1	175	14	85	51	12-8	0	3.07
Mickey Harris	L	24	35	22	11	1	194.0	189	6	86	111	8-14	1	3.25
Lefty Grove	L	41	21	21	10	0	134.0	155	8	42	54	7-7	0	4.37
Joe Dobson	R	24	27	18	7	1	134.1	136	8	67	69	12-5	0	4.49
Earl Johnson	L	22	17	12	4	0	93.2	90	4	51	46	4-5	0	4.52
Tex Hughson	R	25	12	8	4	0	61.0	70	3	13	22	5-3	0	4.13
Woody Rich	R	25	2	1	0	0	3.2	8	1	2	4	0-0	0	17.18
Mike Ryba	R	38	40	3	0	0	121.0	143	14	42	54	7-3	6	4.46
Jack Wilson	R	29	27	12	4	1	116.1	140	7	70	55	4-13	1	5.03
Bill Fleming	R	27	16	1	0	0	41.1	32	4	24	20	1-1	1	3.92
Nels Potter†	R	29	10	0	0	0	20.0	21	0	16	6	2-0	0	4.50
Emerson Dickman	R	26	9	3	1	0	31.0	37	4	17	16	1-1	0	6.39
Oscar Judd	L	33	7	0	0	0	12.1	15	1	10	5	0-0	1	8.76
Herb Hash	R	30	4	0	0	0	8.1	7	1	7	3	1-0	1	5.40

1941 Chicago White Sox 3rd AL 77-77 .500 24.0 GB

Jimmy Dykes

Player	Gm by Position	B	Age	G	AB	R	H	2B	3B	HR	RBI	BB	SO	SB	Avg	OBP	Slg
Mike Tresh	C115	R	27	115	390	38	98	10	1	0	33	38	27	1	.251	.319	.282
Joe Kuhel	1B151	L	35	153	600	99	150	39	5	12	63	70	55	20	.250	.331	.392
Bill Knickerbocker	2B88	R	29	89	343	51	84	23	2	7	29	41	27	6	.245	.329	.385
Dario Lodigiani	3B86	R	24	87	322	39	77	19	2	4	40	31	19	0	.239	.316	.348
Luke Appling	SS154	R	34	154	592	93	186	26	8	1	57	82	32	12	.314	.399	.390
Taffy Wright	OF134	L	29	136	513	71	165	35	5	10	97	60	27	5	.322	.399	.468
Mike Kreevich	OF113	R	33	121	436	44	101	16	8	0	37	35	26	17	.232	.289	.305
Myril Hoag†	OF99	R	33	106	380	30	97	13	3	1	44	27	28	6	.255	.306	.313
Don Kolloway	2B62,1B4	R	22	71	280	33	76	8	3	3	24	6	12	11	.271	.292	.354
Bob Kennedy	3B71	R	20	76	257	16	53	9	3	1	29	17	23	5	.206	.255	.276
Moose Solters	OF63	R	35	76	251	24	65	9	4	4	43	18	31	3	.259	.311	.375
Ben Chapman†	OF49	R	32	57	190	26	43	9	1	2	19	19	14	2	.226	.297	.316
Tom Turner	C35	R	24	38	126	7	30	5	0	0	8	9	15	2	.238	.289	.278
Skeeter Webb	2B18,SS5,3B3	R	31	29	84	7	16	2	0	0	6	3	9	1	.190	.227	.214
Larry Rosenthal†	OF18	L	31	20	59	9	14	4	0	0	1	12	5	0	.237	.366	.305
George Dickey	C17	S	25	32	55	6	11	1	0	2	8	5	7	0	.200	.267	.327
Jake Jones	1B3	R	20	3	11	0	0	0	0	0	0	0	4	0	.000	.000	.000
Dave Philley	OF2	S	21	7	9	4	2	1	0	0	0	3	3	0	.222	.417	.333
Dave Short	OF2	L	24	3	8	0	0	0	0	0	0	2	1	0	.000	.200	.000
Stan Goletz		L	23	5	5	0	3	0	0	0	0	0	2	0	.600	.600	.600
Chet Hajduk		R	22	1	1	0	0	0	0	0	0	0	0	0	.000	.000	.000

Pitcher	T	Age	G	GS	CG	ShO	IP	H	HR	BB	SO	W-L	Sv	ERA
Thornton Lee	L	34	35	34	30	3	300.1	258	18	92	130	22-11	1	2.37
Eddie Smith	L	27	34	33	21	1	263.1	243	13	114	111	13-17	1	3.18
Johnny Rigney	R	26	30	29	18	3	237.0	224	21	92	119	13-13	0	3.84
Ted Lyons	R	40	22	22	19	2	187.1	199	9	37	63	12-10	0	3.70
Bill Dietrich	R	31	19	15	4	1	109.1	114	7	50	26	5-8	0	5.35
Buck Ross†	R	26	20	11	7	0	108.1	99	6	43	30	3-8	0	3.16
Jack Hallett	R	26	22	6	3	0	74.2	96	7	38	25	5-5	0	6.03
Johnny Humphries	R	26	14	6	4	4	73.0	63	2	22	25	4-2	1	1.85
Pete Appleton	R	37	13	0	0	0	27.1	27	4	17	12	0-3	1	5.27
Joe Haynes	R	23	8	0	0	0	28.0	30	0	11	18	0-0	0	3.86
Orval Grove	R	21	2	0	0	0	7.0	9	2	5	5	0-0	0	10.29

1941 Cleveland Indians 4th AL 75-79 .487 26.0 GB

Roger Peckinpaugh

Player	Gm by Position	B	Age	G	AB	R	H	2B	3B	HR	RBI	BB	SO	SB	Avg	OBP	Slg
Rollie Hemsley	C96	R	34	98	288	29	69	10	5	2	24	18	19	2	.240	.284	.330
Hal Trosky	1B85	L	28	89	310	43	91	17	0	11	51	44	21	1	.294	.383	.455
Ray Mack	2B145	R	24	145	501	54	114	22	4	9	44	54	69	8	.228	.303	.341
Ken Keltner	3B149	R	24	149	581	83	156	31	13	23	84	51	56	2	.269	.330	.485
Lou Boudreau	SS147	R	23	148	579	95	149	45	8	10	56	85	57	9	.257	.355	.415
Jeff Heath	OF151	L	26	151	585	89	199	32	20	24	123	50	69	18	.340	.396	.586
Gee Walker	OF105	R	33	121	445	56	126	26	11	6	48	18	46	12	.283	.313	.431
Roy Weatherly	OF88	L	26	102	363	59	105	21	5	3	37	32	20	2	.289	.350	.399
Soup Campbell	OF78	L	26	104	328	36	82	10	4	3	35	31	21	1	.250	.317	.332
Oscar Grimes	1B62,2B13,3B1	R	26	77	244	28	58	9	3	4	24	39	47	4	.238	.345	.348
Gene Desautels	C66	R	34	66	189	20	38	5	1	1	17	14	12	1	.201	.260	.254
Beau Bell	OF14,1B10	R	33	48	104	12	20	4	3	0	9	10	8	1	.192	.270	.288
Larry Rosenthal†	OF14,1B1	L	31	45	75	10	14	3	1	1	8	9	10	1	.187	.274	.293
Hank Edwards	OF16	L	22	16	68	10	15	1	1	1	6	2	4	0	.221	.243	.309
Rusty Peters	SS11,3B9,2B3	R	26	29	63	6	13	2	0	0	2	7	10	0	.206	.286	.238
Jim Hegan	C16	R	20	16	47	4	15	2	0	1	5	4	7	0	.319	.373	.426
Buck Frierson	OF3	R	23	5	11	2	3	1	0	0	2	1	1	0	.273	.333	.364
Vern Freiburger	1B2	R	17	2	8	0	1	0	0	0	1	0	2	0	.125	.125	.125
Les Fleming	1B2	L	25	2	8	0	2	1	0	0	2	0	0	0	.250	.250	.375
Red Howell		R	32	11	7	0	2	0	0	0	2	4	2	0	.286	.545	.286
Oris Hockett	OF2	L	31	2	6	0	2	0	0	0	1	2	0	0	.333	.500	.333
Bob Lemon	3B1	L	20	5	4	0	1	0	0	0	0	1	0	0	.250	.250	.250
Chuck Workman		L	26	9	4	2	0	0	0	0	0	1	1	0	.000	.200	.000
Fabian Gaffke	OF2	R	27	4	4	0	1	0	0	0	0	2	2	0	.250	.500	.250
Jack Conway	SS2	R	21	2	2	0	1	0	0	0	1	0	0	0	.500	.500	.500
George Susce	C1	R	32	1	0	0	0	0	0	0	0	0	0	0	—	—	—

Pitcher	T	Age	G	GS	CG	ShO	IP	H	HR	BB	SO	W-L	Sv	ERA
Bob Feller	R	22	44	40	28	6	343.0	284	15	194	260	25-13	2	3.15
Al Milnar	L	27	35	30	9	1	229.1	236	9	116	82	12-19	0	4.36
Al Smith	L	33	29	27	13	2	206.2	204	12	75	76	12-13	0	3.83
Jim Bagby Jr.	R	24	33	27	12	0	200.2	214	10	76	53	9-15	2	4.04
Mel Harder	R	31	15	10	1	0	68.2	76	8	37	21	5-4	1	5.24
Chubby Dean†	L	24	8	8	2	0	53.1	57	3	24	14	1-4	0	4.39
Red Embree	R	23	1	1	0	0	4.0	7	0	3	4	0-1	0	6.75
Clint Brown	R	37	41	0	0	0	74.1	77	3	28	22	3-3	5	3.27
Joe Heving	R	40	27	3	2	1	70.2	63	2	31	18	5-2	5	2.29
Harry Eisenstat	L	25	21	0	0	0	34.0	43	2	16	11	1-1	2	4.24
Joe Krakauskas	L	26	12	5	0	0	41.2	39	3	29	25	1-2	0	4.10
Steve Gromek	R	21	9	2	1	0	23.1	25	0	11	19	1-1	2	4.24
Ken Jungels	R	25	6	0	0	0	13.2	17	4	8	6	0-0	0	7.24
Cal Dorsett	R	28	5	2	0	0	11.1	21	0	10	5	0-1	0	10.32
Nate Andrews	R	27	2	0	0	0	2.1	3	0	2	1	0-0	0	11.57

1941 Detroit Tigers 4th AL 75-79 .487 26.0 GB

Del Baker

Player	Gm by Position	B	Age	G	AB	R	H	2B	3B	HR	RBI	BB	SO	SB	Avg	OBP	Slg
Birdie Tebbetts	C98	R	28	110	359	28	102	19	4	2	47	38	29	1	.284	.354	.376
Rudy York	1B155	R	27	155	590	91	153	29	3	27	111	92	88	3	.259	.360	.456
Charlie Gehringer	2B116	L	38	127	436	65	96	19	4	3	46	95	26	1	.220	.363	.303
Mike Higgins	3B145	R	32	147	540	79	161	28	3	11	73	67	45	5	.298	.378	.422
Frank Croucher	SS136	R	26	136	489	51	124	21	4	2	39	33	72	2	.254	.305	.325
Bruce Campbell	OF133	L	31	141	512	72	141	28	10	15	93	68	67	3	.275	.364	.457
Barney McCosky	OF122	L	24	127	494	80	160	25	8	3	55	61	33	8	.324	.401	.425
Rip Radcliff†	OF87	L	35	96	379	47	120	14	5	3	39	19	13	4	.317	.351	.404
Billy Sullivan	C63	L	30	85	234	29	66	15	1	3	29	35	11	0	.282	.375	.393
Pat Mullin	OF51	L	23	54	220	42	76	11	5	5	23	18	18	5	.345	.400	.509
Tuck Stainback	OF80	R	29	94	200	19	49	8	1	2	10	3	21	6	.245	.260	.325
Dutch Meyer	2B40	R	25	46	153	12	29	9	1	1	14	8	13	1	.190	.230	.281
Boyd Perry	SS25,2B11	R	27	36	83	9	15	5	0	0	11	10	9	1	.181	.269	.241
Hank Greenberg	OF19	R	30	19	67	12	18	5	1	2	12	16	12	1	.269	.410	.463
Ned Harris	OF12	L	24	26	61	11	13	3	1	1	4	6	13	1	.213	.284	.344
Eric McNair	3B11,SS3	R	32	23	59	5	11	1	0	0	3	4	4	0	.186	.250	.203
Dick Bartell†	SS5	R	33	5	12	0	2	0	0	0	1	2	2	0	.167	.333	.250
Murray Franklin	SS4,3B1	R	27	13	10	1	3	1	0	0	2	2	0	0	.300	.417	.400
Bob Patrick	OF3	R	23	5	7	2	2	0	0	0	0	0	1	0	.286	.286	.286
Dick Wakefield	OF1	L	20	7	7	0	1	0	0	0	0	0	1	0	.143	.143	.143
Hoot Evers	OF1	R	20	1	4	0	0	0	0	0	0	0	2	0	.000	.000	.000
Fred Hutchinson		L	21	2	2	0	0	0	0	0	0	0	2	0	.000	.000	.000

Pitcher	T	Age	G	GS	CG	ShO	IP	H	HR	BB	SO	W-L	Sv	ERA
Bobo Newsom	R	33	43	36	12	2	250.1	265	15	118	175	12-20	2	4.60
Hal Newhouser	L	20	33	27	5	1	173.0	166	6	137	106	9-11	0	4.79
Tommy Bridges	R	34	25	22	10	1	147.2	128	10	70	90	9-12	0	3.41
Johnny Gorsica	R	26	33	21	8	1	171.0	193	14	55	59	9-11	2	4.47
Schoolboy Rowe	R	31	27	14	4	0	139.0	155	6	33	54	8-6	1	4.14
Al Benton	R	30	38	14	7	1	157.2	130	11	65	63	15-6	7	2.97
Dizzy Trout	R	26	37	18	6	1	151.2	144	7	84	88	9-9	2	3.74
Bud Thomas	R	30	26	1	0	0	72.2	74	4	22	17	1-3	2	4.21
Floyd Giebell	R	31	17	2	0	0	34.1	45	3	26	10	0-0	0	6.03
Archie McKain†	L	30	15	0	0	0	43.0	58	3	11	14	2-1	0	5.02
Hal Manders	R	24	8	0	0	0	15.1	13	0	8	7	1-0	0	2.35
Les Mueller	R	22	4	0	0	0	13.0	9	1	10	8	0-0	0	4.85
Hal White	R	22	4	0	0	0	9.0	11	0	6	2	0-0	0	6.00
Virgil Trucks	R	24	1	0	0	0	2.0	4	0	0	3	0-0	0	9.00
Earl Cook	R	32	1	0	0	0	2.0	4	0	0	1	0-0	0	4.50

1941 St. Louis Browns 6th AL 70-84 .455 31.0 GB

Fred Haney (15-29)/Luke Sewell (55-55)

Player	Gm by Position	B	Age	G	AB	R	H	2B	3B	HR	RBI	BB	SO	SB	Avg	OBP	Slg
Rick Ferrell†	C98	R	35	100	321	30	81	14	3	2	23	52	22	2	.252	.357	.333
George McQuinn	1B125	L	31	130	495	93	147	28	4	18	80	74	30	5	.297	.388	.479
Don Heffner	2B105	R	30	110	399	48	93	14	2	0	17	38	27	5	.233	.303	.278
Harlond Clift	3B154	R	28	154	584	108	149	33	9	17	84	113	93	6	.255	.376	.430
Johnny Berardino	SS123,3B1	R	24	128	469	48	127	30	4	5	89	41	27	3	.271	.332	.384
Wally Judnich	OF140	L	24	146	546	90	155	40	6	14	83	80	45	5	.284	.377	.456
Roy Cullenbine	OF120,1B22	S	27	149	501	82	159	29	9	9	98	121	43	6	.317	.452	.465
Chet Laabs	OF100	R	29	118	392	64	109	23	6	15	59	51	59	5	.278	.361	.482
Joe Grace	OF88,C9	L	27	115	362	53	112	17	4	6	60	57	31	1	.309	.410	.428
Johnny Lucadello	2B70,SS12,3B6*	R	22	107	351	58	98	22	4	2	31	48	23	5	.279	.366	.382
Bob Swift	C58	R	26	63	170	13	44	7	0	0	21	22	11	2	.259	.344	.300
Alan Strange	SS32,1B2,3B1	R	34	45	112	14	26	4	0	0	11	15	5	1	.232	.323	.268
Bobby Estalella	OF17	R	30	46	83	7	20	6	1	0	14	18	13	0	.241	.376	.337
Rip Radcliff†	OF14,1B3	L	35	19	71	12	20	2	2	2	14	10	1	1	.282	.370	.451
Frank Grube	C18	R	36	18	39	1	6	2	0	0	1	2	4	0	.154	.195	.205
George Archie†	1B8	R	27	9	29	3	11	3	0	0	5	7	3	2	.379	.500	.483
Glenn McQuillen	OF6	R	26	7	21	4	7	2	1	0	3	1	2	0	.333	.364	.524
Chuck Stevens	1B4	S	22	4	13	2	2	0	0	0	2	0	1	0	.154	.154	.154
Vern Stephens	SS1	R	20	3	2	0	1	0	0	0	0	0	0	0	.500	.500	.500
Myril Hoag†		R	33	1	1	0	0	0	0	0	0	0	0	0	.000	.000	.000

J. Lucadello, 1 G at OF

Pitcher	T	Age	G	GS	CG	ShO	IP	H	HR	BB	SO	W-L	Sv	ERA
Eldon Auker	R	30	34	31	13	0	216.0	268	20	85	60	14-15	0	5.50
Bob Harris	R	24	34	29	9	2	186.2	237	18	85	57	12-14	1	5.21
Bob Muncrief	R	25	36	24	12	2	214.1	221	18	53	67	13-9	1	3.65
Denny Galehouse	R	29	30	24	11	2	190.1	183	10	68	61	9-10	0	3.64
Johnny Niggeling	R	37	24	20	13	1	168.1	168	17	63	68	7-9	0	3.80
Vern Kennedy†	R	34	6	6	2	0	45.0	44	5	27	6	2-4	0	4.40
George Caster	R	33	32	9	3	0	104.1	105	12	37	36	3-7	3	5.00
Jack Kramer	R	23	29	3	0	0	59.1	69	5	40	20	4-3	2	5.16
Bill Trotter	R	32	29	0	0	0	49.2	68	2	19	17	4-2	0	5.98
Johnny Allen†	R	35	20	9	2	0	67.0	89	4	29	27	2-5	1	6.58
Fritz Ostermueller	L	33	15	2	0	0	46.0	45	3	23	20	0-3	0	4.50
Maury Newlin	R	27	14	0	0	0	27.2	43	4	12	10	0-2	1	6.51
Archie McKain†	L	30	8	0	0	0	10.0	16	2	4	2	0-1	1	8.10
Emil Bildilli	L	28	2	0	0	0	2.1	5	0	3	2	0-0	0	11.57
Hooks Iott	L	21	2	0	0	0	2.0	2	0	1	1	0-0	0	9.00

1941 Washington Senators 6th AL 70-84 .455 31.0 GB

Bucky Harris

Player	Gm by Position	B	Age	G	AB	R	H	2B	3B	HR	RBI	BB	SO	SB	Avg	OBP	Slg
Jake Early	C100	L	26	104	355	42	102	20	7	10	54	24	38	0	.287	.338	.468
Mickey Vernon	1B132	L	23	138	531	73	159	27	11	9	93	43	51	9	.299	.352	.443
Jimmy Bloodworth	2B132,3B6,SS1	R	23	142	506	59	124	24	3	7	66	41	58	1	.245	.303	.346
George Archie†	3B73,1B23	R	27	105	379	45	102	20	4	3	48	30	42	8	.269	.324	.367
Cecil Travis	SS136,3B16	L	27	152	608	106	218	39	19	7	101	52	25	2	.359	.410	.520
Doc Cramer	OF152	L	35	154	660	93	180	25	6	2	66	37	15	4	.273	.317	.338
George Case	OF151	R	25	153	649	95	176	32	8	2	53	51	37	33	.271	.325	.354
Buddy Lewis	OF96,3B49	L	24	149	569	97	169	29	11	9	72	82	30	10	.297	.386	.434
Al Evans	C51	R	24	53	159	16	44	8	4	1	19	9	18	0	.277	.315	.396
Ben Chapman†	OF26	R	32	28	110	9	28	6	0	1	10	10	6	2	.255	.317	.336
Buddy Myer	2B24	L	37	53	107	14	27	3	1	0	9	18	10	2	.252	.360	.299
Johnny Welaj	OF19	R	27	49	96	16	20	4	0	0	5	6	16	3	.208	.255	.250
Roberto Ortiz	OF21	R	26	22	79	10	26	1	2	1	17	3	10	0	.329	.354	.430
Jimmy Pofahl	SS21	R	24	22	75	9	14	3	2	0	6	10	11	1	.187	.282	.280
Rick Ferrell†	C21	R	35	21	66	8	18	5	0	0	13	15	4	1	.273	.407	.348
Hillis Layne	3B13	L	23	13	50	8	14	2	0	0	6	4	5	1	.280	.333	.320
Sammy West	OF8	L	36	26	37	3	10	0	0	0	6	11	2	1	.270	.438	.270
Morrie Aderholt	2B2,3B1	L	25	11	14	3	2	0	0	0	1	1	3	0	.143	.200	.143
Cliff Bolton	C3	L	34	14	11	0	0	0	0	0	1	1	2	0	.000	.083	.000
Charlie Letchas	2B2	R	25	2	8	0	1	0	0	0	1	1	1	0	.125	.222	.125
Jack Sanford	1B1	R	24	3	5	1	2	0	1	0	0	1	1	0	.400	.500	.800
Sherry Robertson	3B1	L	22	1	3	0	0	0	0	0	0	0	3	0	.000	.000	.000

Pitcher	T	Age	G	GS	CG	ShO	IP	H	HR	BB	SO	W-L	Sv	ERA
Dutch Leonard	R	32	34	33	19	4	256.0	271	6	54	91	18-13	0	3.45
Sid Hudson	R	26	33	33	17	3	249.2	242	12	97	108	13-14	0	3.46
Ken Chase	L	27	33	30	8	1	205.2	228	11	115	98	6-18	0	5.08
Steve Sundra	R	31	28	23	11	0	168.1	203	11	61	50	9-13	0	5.29
Early Wynn	R	21	5	5	4	0	40.0	35	1	10	15	3-1	0	1.58
Dick Mulligan	L	23	1	1	1	0	9.0	11	0	2	2	0-1	0	5.00
Bill Zuber	R	28	36	7	1	0	96.1	110	5	61	51	6-4	2	5.42
Alex Carrasquel	R	28	35	5	4	0	96.2	103	7	49	30	6-2	2	3.44
Walt Masterson	R	21	34	6	1	0	78.1	101	3	53	40	4-3	3	5.97
Red Anderson	R	29	32	6	1	0	112.0	127	7	53	34	4-6	0	4.18
Vern Kennedy†	R	34	17	7	2	0	66.1	77	5	39	22	1-7	0	5.70
Danny MacFayden	R	36	5	0	0	0	7.0	12	1	5	3	0-1	0	10.29
Harry Dean	R	26	2	0	0	0	2.0	2	0	3	0	0-0	0	4.50
Ronnie Miller	R	22	1	0	0	0	2.0	2	0	1	0	0-0	0	4.50

1941 Philadelphia Athletics 8th AL 64-90 .416 37.0 GB

Connie Mack

Player	Gm by Position	B	Age	G	AB	R	H	2B	3B	HR	RBI	BB	SO	SB	Avg	OBP	Slg
Frankie Hayes	C123	R	26	126	439	66	123	27	4	12	63	62	56	2	.280	.369	.442
Dick Siebert	1B123	L	29	123	467	63	156	28	8	5	79	37	22	1	.334	.385	.460
Benny McCoy	2B135	L	25	141	517	86	140	12	7	8	61	95	50	3	.271	.384	.368
Pete Suder	3B136,SS3	R	25	139	531	45	130	20	9	4	52	19	47	1	.245	.271	.339
Al Brancato	SS139,3B7	R	22	144	530	60	124	20	9	2	49	59	49	1	.234	.311	.317
Sam Chapman	OF141	R	25	143	552	97	178	29	9	25	106	47	49	6	.322	.378	.543
Bob Johnson	OF122,1B28	R	34	149	552	98	152	30	8	22	107	95	75	6	.275	.385	.478
Wally Moses	OF109	L	30	116	438	78	132	31	4	4	35	62	27	3	.301	.388	.418
Eddie Collins	OF50	L	24	80	219	29	53	6	3	0	12	20	24	2	.242	.305	.297
Dee Miles	OF35	L	32	80	170	14	53	7	1	0	15	4	8	0	.312	.331	.365
Hal Wagner	C42	L	25	46	131	18	29	8	2	1	15	19	9	1	.221	.320	.336
Crash Davis	2B20,1B12	R	21	39	105	8	23	3	0	0	8	11	16	0	.219	.293	.248
Fred Chapman	SS28,3B2,2B1	R	24	35	69	1	11	1	0	0	4	4	15	1	.159	.205	.174
Elmer Valo	OF10	L	20	15	50	13	21	0	1	2	6	4	2	0	.420	.463	.580
Chubby Dean†	P18,1B1	L	24	27	38	0	9	2	0	0	9	4	3	0	.237	.310	.289
Don Richmond	3B9	L	21	9	35	3	7	1	1	0	5	0	1	0	.200	.200	.286
Al Simmons	OF5	R	39	9	24	1	3	1	0	0	1	1	2	0	.125	.160	.167
Al Rubeling	3B6	R	28	6	19	0	5	0	0	0	2	2	1	0	.263	.333	.263
Felix Mackiewicz	OF3	R	23	5	14	3	4	0	1	0	0	1	0	0	.286	.333	.429
Eric Tipton	OF1	R	26	1	4	0	2	0	0	0	0	0	0	0	.500	.500	.500
Ray Poole		L	21	2	2	0	0	0	0	0	0	0	1	0	.000	.000	.000
John Leovich	C1	R	23	1	2	0	1	1	0	0	0	0	0	0	.500	.500	1.000

Pitcher	T	Age	G	GS	CG	ShO	IP	H	HR	BB	SO	W-L	Sv	ERA
Phil Marchildon	R	27	30	27	14	1	204.1	188	15	118	74	10-15	0	3.57
Jack Knott	R	34	27	26	11	0	194.1	212	20	81	54	13-11	0	4.40
Les McCrabb	R	26	26	23	11	1	157.1	188	16	49	40	9-13	2	5.49
Bill Beckmann	R	33	22	15	4	0	130.0	141	11	33	28	5-9	1	4.57
Johnny Babich	R	28	16	14	4	0	78.1	85	9	31	19	2-7	0	6.09
Fred Caligiuri	R	22	5	5	4	0	43.0	45	2	14	7	2-2	0	2.93
Dick Fowler	R	20	4	3	1	0	24.0	26	4	8	8	1-2	0	3.38
Porter Vaughan	L	22	5	3	1	0	22.2	32	3	12	6	0-2	0	7.94
Roger Wolff	R	30	2	2	2	0	17.0	15	0	4	2	0-2	0	3.18
Buck Ross†	R	26	1	1	0	0	4.0	10	2	2	0	0-1	0	18.00
Tom Ferrick	R	26	36	4	2	1	119.1	130	8	33	30	8-10	7	3.77
Lum Harris	R	26	33	10	5	0	131.2	134	16	51	49	4-4	2	4.78
Bump Hadley†	R	36	25	9	1	0	102.1	131	13	47	31	4-6	3	5.01
Chubby Dean†	L	24	18	7	2	0	75.2	90	9	35	22	2-4	0	6.19
Nels Potter†	R	29	10	3	1	0	23.1	35	3	16	7	1-1	2	9.26
Rankin Johnson	R	24	7	0	0	0	10.0	14	0	3	0	1-0	0	3.60
Herman Besse	L	29	6	2	1	0	19.2	28	4	12	8	2-0	0	10.07
Tex Shirley	R	23	5	0	0	0	7.1	8	1	6	1	0-1	1	2.45
Pat Tobin	R	25	1	0	0	0	1.0	4	0	2	0	0-0	0	36.00

»1941 Brooklyn Dodgers 1st NL 100-54 .649 —

Leo Durocher

Player	Gm by Position	B	Age	G	AB	R	H	2B	3B	HR	RBI	BB	SO	SB	Avg	OBP	Slg
Mickey Owen	C128	R	25	128	386	32	89	15	2	1	44	34	14	1	.231	.296	.288
Dolph Camilli	1B148	L	34	149	529	92	151	29	6	34	120	104	115	3	.285	.407	.556
Billy Herman†	2B133	R	31	133	536	77	156	30	4	3	41	58	38	1	.291	.361	.379
Cookie Lavagetto	3B120	R	28	132	441	75	122	24	7	1	78	80	21	7	.277	.388	.370
Pee Wee Reese	SS151	R	22	152	595	76	136	23	5	2	46	68	56	10	.229	.311	.294
Dixie Walker	OF146	L	30	148	531	88	165	32	8	9	71	70	18	4	.311	.391	.452
Pete Reiser	OF133	L	22	137	536	117	184	39	17	14	76	46	71	4	.343	.406	.558
Joe Medwick	OF131	R	29	133	538	100	171	33	10	18	88	38	35	2	.318	.364	.517
Jimmy Wasdell	OF54,1B15	L	27	94	265	39	79	14	3	4	48	16	15	2	.298	.345	.419
Lew Riggs	3B43,1B1,2B1	L	31	77	197	27	60	13	4	5	36	16	12	1	.305	.357	.487
Herman Franks	C54,OF1	L	27	57	139	10	28	7	0	1	11	14	13	0	.201	.275	.273
Pete Coscarart	2B19,SS1	R	28	43	62	13	8	1	0	0	5	7	12	1	.129	.217	.145
Joe Vosmik	OF18	R	31	25	56	0	11	0	0	0	4	4	4	0	.196	.250	.196
Alex Kampouris	2B15	R	28	16	51	8	16	4	2	2	9	11	8	0	.314	.444	.588
Leo Durocher	SS12,2B1	R	35	18	42	2	12	1	0	0	6	1	3	0	.286	.302	.310
Paul Waner†	OF9	L	38	11	35	5	6	0	0	0	4	8	0	0	.171	.326	.171
Babe Phelps	C11	L	33	16	30	3	7	3	0	2	4	1	2	0	.233	.258	.533
Augie Galan†	OF6	S	29	17	27	3	7	3	0	0	4	3	1	0	.259	.333	.370
Tommy Tatum	OF4	R	21	8	12	1	2	1	0	0	1	1	3	0	.167	.231	.250
Tom Drake	P10,OF1	R	28	11	5	0	2	0	0	0	0	0	1	0	.400	.400	.400
Tony Giuliani	C3	R	28	3	2	0	0	0	0	0	0	0	0	0	.000	.000	.000
George Pfister	C1	R	22	1	2	0	0	0	0	0	0	0	0	0	.000	.000	.000

Pitcher	T	Age	G	GS	CG	ShO	IP	H	HR	BB	SO	W-L	Sv	ERA
Kirby Higbe	R	26	48	39	19	2	298.0	244	16	132	121	22-9	3	3.14
Whit Wyatt	R	33	38	35	23	7	288.1	223	10	82	176	22-10	1	2.34
Luke Hamlin	R	36	30	20	5	1	136.0	139	14	41	58	8-8	1	4.24
Curt Davis	R	37	28	16	10	5	154.1	141	7	27	50	13-7	2	2.97
F. Fitzsimmons	R	39	13	12	3	1	82.2	78	3	26	19	6-1	0	2.07
Ed Albosta	R	22	2	2	0	0	13.0	11	1	8	5	0-2	0	6.23
Hugh Casey	R	27	45	18	4	1	162.0	155	8	57	61	14-11	7	3.89
Mace Brown†	R	32	24	0	0	0	42.2	31	3	26	22	3-2	3	3.16
Kemp Wicker	L	34	16	2	0	0	32.0	30	3	14	8	1-2	1	3.66
Newt Kimball	R	26	15	5	1	0	52.0	43	0	29	17	3-1	1	3.63
Vito Tamulis†	L	29	12	0	0	0	22.0	21	1	10	8	0-0	1	3.68
Johnny Allen†	R	35	11	4	1	0	57.1	38	6	12	21	3-0	0	2.51
Tom Drake	R	28	10	2	0	0	24.2	26	2	9	12	1-1	0	4.38
Bill Swift	R	33	9	0	0	0	22.0	26	4	7	9	3-0	1	3.27
Larry French†	L	33	6	1	0	0	15.2	16	1	4	8	0-0	0	3.45
Lee Grissom†	L	33	4	1	0	0	11.1	10	2	8	5	0-0	1	2.38
Van Lingle Mungo	R	30	2	0	0	0	2.0	1	0	2	0	0-0	0	4.50
Bob Chipman	L	22	1	0	0	0	5.0	3	0	1	3	1-0	0	0.00

1941 St. Louis Cardinals 2nd NL 97-56 .634 2.5 GB

Billy Southworth

Player	Gm by Position	B	Age	G	AB	R	H	2B	3B	HR	RBI	BB	SO	SB	Avg	OBP	Slg
Gus Mancuso	C105	R	35	106	328	25	75	13	1	2	37	37	19	0	.229	.309	.293
Johnny Mize	1B122	L	28	126	473	67	150	39	8	16	100	70	45	4	.317	.406	.535
Creepy Crespi	2B145	R	23	146	560	85	156	24	2	4	46	57	58	3	.279	.355	.350
Jimmy Brown	3B123,2B11	S	31	132	549	81	168	28	9	3	56	45	22	2	.306	.363	.406
Marty Marion	SS155	R	23	155	547	50	138	22	3	3	58	42	48	8	.252	.308	.320
Terry Moore	OF121	R	29	122	493	86	145	26	4	6	68	52	31	3	.294	.364	.400
Enos Slaughter	OF108	L	25	113	425	71	132	22	9	13	76	53	28	4	.311	.390	.496
Johnny Hopp	OF91,1B39	L	24	134	445	83	135	25	11	4	50	50	63	15	.303	.378	.436
Don Padgett	OF62,C18,1B2	L	29	107	324	39	80	18	0	5	44	21	16	0	.247	.293	.349
Walker Cooper	C63	R	26	68	200	19	49	9	1	1	20	13	14	1	.245	.291	.315
Coaker Triplett	OF46	R	29	76	185	29	53	6	3	3	21	18	27	0	.286	.350	.400
Estel Crabtree	OF50,3B1	L	37	77	167	27	57	6	3	5	28	26	24	1	.341	.439	.503
Eddie Lake	3B15,SS15,2B5	R	25	45	76	9	8	2	0	0	0	15	22	3	.105	.253	.132
Steve Mesner	3B22	R	23	24	69	8	10	1	0	0	10	5	6	0	.145	.203	.159
Stan Musial	OF11	L	20	12	47	8	20	4	0	1	7	2	1	1	.426	.449	.574
Ernie Koy†	OF12	R	31	13	40	5	8	1	0	2	4	1	8	0	.200	.220	.375
Harry Walker	OF5	L	24	7	15	3	4	1	0	0	1	2	1	0	.267	.353	.333
Erv Dusak	OF4	R	20	6	14	1	2	0	0	0	3	2	6	1	.143	.250	.143
Walter Sessi	OF3	L	22	5	13	2	0	0	0	0	0	1	2	0	.000	.071	.000
Whitey Kurowski	3B4	R	23	5	9	1	3	2	0	0	2	0	2	0	.333	.400	.556
Pep Young†		R	33	2	2	0	0	0	0	0	0	0	2	0	.000	.000	.000
Charlie Marshall	C1	R	21	1	0	0	0	0	0	0	0	0	0	0	—	—	—

Pitcher	T	Age	G	GS	CG	ShO	IP	H	HR	BB	SO	W-L	Sv	ERA
Lon Warneke	R	32	37	30	12	4	246.0	227	19	82	83	17-9	0	3.15
Ernie White	L	24	32	25	12	3	210.0	169	12	70	117	17-7	2	2.40
Mort Cooper	R	28	29	25	12	0	186.2	175	15	69	118	13-9	0	3.91
Max Lanier	L	25	35	18	8	2	153.0	126	4	59	93	10-8	3	2.82
Harry Gumbert†	R	31	33	17	8	3	144.1	139	7	30	53	11-5	1	2.74
Howie Pollet	L	20	9	8	6	2	70.0	55	1	27	37	5-2	0	1.93
Bill McGee†	R	31	4	3	0	0	14.0	17	1	13	2	0-1	0	5.14
Johnny Beazley	R	23	1	1	1	0	9.0	10	0	3	4	1-0	0	1.00
Howie Krist	R	25	37	8	2	0	114.0	107	10	35	36	10-0	2	4.03
Ira Hutchinson	R	30	29	0	0	0	46.2	32	3	19	19	1-5	5	3.86
Sam Nahem	R	25	26	8	2	0	81.2	76	2	38	31	5-2	1	2.98
Clyde Shoun	L	29	26	6	0	0	70.0	98	9	20	34	3-5	0	5.66
Bill Crouch†	R	30	18	4	0	0	45.0	45	2	14	15	1-2	6	3.00
Johnny Grodzicki	R	24	5	1	0	0	13.1	6	0	11	10	2-1	0	1.35
Hank Gornicki†	R	30	4	1	1	1	11.1	6	0	9	6	1-0	0	3.18
Hersh Lyons	R	25	1	0	0	0	1.1	1	0	3	1	0-0	0	0.00

Seasons: Team Rosters

683

1941 Cincinnati Reds 3rd NL 88-66 .571 12.0 GB

Bill McKechnie

Player	Gm by Position	B	Age	G	AB	R	H	2B	3B	HR	RBI	BB	SO	SB	Avg	OBP	Slg
Ernie Lombardi	C116	R	33	117	398	33	105	12	1	10	60	36	14	1	.264	.325	.374
Frank McCormick	1B154	R	30	154	603	77	162	31	5	17	97	40	13	2	.269	.318	.421
Lonny Frey	2B145	L	30	146	543	78	138	29	5	6	59	72	37	16	.254	.345	.359
Bill Werber	3B107	R	33	109	418	56	100	9	2	4	46	53	24	14	.239	.328	.299
Eddie Joost	SS147,2B4,1B2*	R	25	152	537	67	136	25	4	4	40	69	59	9	.253	.340	.337
Harry Craft	OF115	R	26	119	413	48	103	15	2	10	59	33	43	4	.249	.308	.368
Mike McCormick	OF101	R	24	110	369	52	106	17	3	4	31	30	24	4	.287	.341	.382
Jim Gleeson	OF84	S	29	102	301	47	70	10	0	3	34	45	30	7	.233	.340	.296
Ernie Koy†	OF49	R	31	67	204	24	51	11	2	2	27	14	22	1	.250	.301	.353
Dick West	C64	R	25	67	172	15	37	5	2	1	17	6	23	4	.215	.246	.285
Chuck Aleno	3B40,1B2	R	24	54	169	23	41	7	3	1	18	11	16	3	.243	.289	.337
Lloyd Waner†	OF44	L	35	55	164	17	42	4	1	0	6	8	0	0	.256	.291	.293
Ival Goodman	OF40	L	32	42	149	14	40	5	2	1	12	16	15	1	.268	.343	.349
Jimmy Ripple	OF25	L	31	38	102	10	22	6	1	1	9	9	4	0	.216	.279	.324
Eddie Lukon	OF22	L	20	23	86	6	23	3	0	0	3	6	6	1	.267	.315	.302
Bobby Mattick	SS12,3B5,2B1	R	25	20	60	8	11	3	0	0	7	8	7	1	.183	.279	.233
Hank Sauer	OF8	R	24	9	33	4	10	4	0	0	5	1	4	0	.303	.324	.424
Benny Zientara	2B6	R	21	9	21	3	6	0	0	0	2	1	3	0	.286	.318	.286
Pep Young†	3B3	R	33	4	12	2	2	0	0	0	0	0	1	0	.167	.231	.167
Johnny Riddle	C10	R	35	10	10	2	3	0	0	0	0	0	1	0	.300	.300	.300
Eddie Shokes		L	21	1	1	0	0	0	0	0	0	0	1	0	.000	.000	.000
Bill Baker†	C1	R	30	2	1	0	0	0	0	0	0	1	1	0	.000	.500	.000
Ray Lamanno	C1	R	21	1	0	0	0	0	0	0	0	0	0	0	—	1.000	—

E. Joost, 1 G at 3B

Pitcher	T	Age	G	GS	CG	ShO	IP	H	HR	BB	SO	W-L	Sv	ERA
Bucky Walters	R	32	37	35	27	5	302.0	292	10	88	129	19-15	2	2.83
J. Vander Meer	L	26	33	32	18	6	226.1	172	8	126	202	16-13	0	2.82
Paul Derringer	R	34	29	28	17	2	228.1	233	17	54	76	12-14	1	3.31
Elmer Riddle	R	26	33	22	15	4	216.2	180	8	59	80	19-4	1	2.24
Junior Thompson	R	24	27	15	4	0	109.0	117	6	57	46	6-6	1	4.87
Ray Starr	R	35	7	4	3	2	34.0	28	1	6	11	3-2	0	2.65
Monte Pearson	R	31	7	4	1	0	24.1	22	3	15	8	1-3	0	5.18
Joe Beggs	R	30	37	0	0	0	57.0	57	2	27	19	4-3	5	3.79
Jim Turner	R	37	23	10	3	0	113.0	120	5	24	34	6-4	0	3.11
Whitey Moore	R	29	23	4	1	0	61.2	62	2	45	17	2-1	0	4.38
Johnny Hutchings†	R	25	8	0	0	0	11.0	12	0	4	5	0-0	0	4.09
Bob Logan	L	31	2	0	0	0	3.1	5	0	5	0	0-1	0	8.10

1941 Pittsburgh Pirates 4th NL 81-73 .526 19.0 GB

Frank Frisch

Player	Gm by Position	B	Age	G	AB	R	H	2B	3B	HR	RBI	BB	SO	SB	Avg	OBP	Slg
Al Lopez	C114	R	32	114	317	33	84	9	1	5	43	31	23	0	.265	.330	.347
Elbie Fletcher	1B151	L	25	151	521	95	150	29	13	11	74	118	54	5	.288	.421	.457
Frankie Gustine	2B104,3B15	R	21	121	463	46	125	24	7	1	46	28	38	5	.270	.313	.359
Lee Handley	3B114	R	27	124	459	59	132	18	4	0	33	35	22	16	.288	.338	.344
Arky Vaughan	SS97,3B3	L	29	106	374	69	118	20	7	6	38	50	13	8	.316	.399	.455
Vince DiMaggio	OF151	R	28	151	528	73	141	27	5	21	100	68	100	10	.267	.354	.456
Bob Elliott	OF139	R	24	141	527	74	144	24	10	3	76	64	52	6	.273	.353	.374
M. Van Robays	OF121	R	26	129	457	62	129	23	5	4	78	41	29	0	.282	.343	.381
Stu Martin	2B53,3B2,1B1	L	27	88	233	37	71	13	2	0	19	10	17	2	.305	.341	.378
Alf Anderson	SS58	R	27	70	223	32	48	7	2	1	10	14	30	2	.215	.265	.278
Debs Garms	3B29,OF24	L	33	83	220	25	58	9	3	3	42	22	12	0	.264	.331	.373
Bud Stewart	OF41	L	25	73	172	27	46	7	0	0	10	12	17	3	.267	.315	.308
Spud Davis	C49	R	36	57	107	3	27	4	1	0	6	11	11	0	.252	.322	.308
Bill Baker†	C33	R	30	35	67	5	15	3	0	0	6	11	0	0	.224	.333	.269
Ripper Collins	1B11,OF3	S	37	49	62	5	13	2	2	0	11	6	14	0	.210	.279	.306
Billy Cox	SS10	R	21	10	37	4	10	3	1	0	2	3	2	1	.270	.325	.405
Vinnie Smith	C9	R	25	9	33	3	10	1	0	0	5	1	5	0	.303	.324	.333
Ed Leip	2B7,SS1	R	30	15	25	1	5	0	2	0	3	1	2	1	.200	.231	.360
Culley Rikard	OF5	L	27	6	20	1	4	1	0	0	0	1	1	0	.200	.238	.250
Lloyd Waner†	OF1	L	35	3	4	2	1	0	0	0	1	2	0	0	.250	.500	.250
Joe Schultz	C2	L	22	2	2	1	1	0	0	0	0	0	0	0	.500	.500	.500

Pitcher	T	Age	G	GS	CG	ShO	IP	H	HR	BB	SO	W-L	Sv	ERA
Rip Sewell	R	34	39	32	18	2	249.0	225	18	84	76	14-17	2	3.72
Max Butcher	R	30	33	32	19	0	236.0	249	11	66	61	17-12	0	3.05
Ken Heintzelman	L	25	35	24	13	2	196.0	206	8	83	81	11-11	0	3.44
Johnny Lanning	R	30	34	23	9	0	175.2	175	6	47	41	11-11	1	3.13
Russ Bauers	R	27	8	5	1	0	37.1	40	1	25	20	1-3	0	5.54
Johnny Gee	L	25	3	2	0	0	7.1	10	0	5	2	0-2	0	6.14
Bill Clemensen	R	22	2	1	1	0	13.0	7	0	7	4	1-0	0	2.77
Bill Brandt	R	26	2	1	0	0	7.0	5	0	3	0	0-1	0	3.86
Dick Conger	R	20	2	1	0	0	4.0	3	0	3	2	0-0	0	0.00
Bob Klinger	R	33	35	9	3	0	116.2	127	5	30	36	9-4	4	3.93
Dutch Dietz	R	29	33	6	4	1	100.1	88	6	33	22	7-2	1	2.33
Lefty Wilkie	L	26	26	6	2	1	79.0	90	1	40	16	2-4	2	4.56
Joe Bowman	R	31	18	7	1	1	69.1	77	3	28	22	3-2	1	2.99
Joe Sullivan†	L	30	16	4	0	0	39.1	40	2	22	10	4-1	1	2.97
Nick Strincevich†	R	26	12	3	0	0	31.0	35	4	13	12	1-2	0	5.23
Dick Lanahan	L	29	7	0	0	0	12.0	13	1	3	5	0-1	0	5.25
Mace Brown†	R	32	1	0	0	0	1.1	2	0	0	0	0-0	0	0.00

1941 New York Giants 5th NL 74-79 .484 25.5 GB

Bill Terry

Player	Gm by Position	B	Age	G	AB	R	H	2B	3B	HR	RBI	BB	SO	SB	Avg	OBP	Slg
Harry Danning	C116,1B1	R	29	130	459	58	112	22	4	7	56	30	25	1	.244	.292	.355
Babe Young	1B150	L	25	152	574	90	152	28	5	25	104	66	39	1	.265	.346	.462
Burgess Whitehead	2B104,SS1	R	31	116	403	41	92	15	4	1	23	14	10	7	.228	.258	.293
Dick Bartell†	3B84,SS21	R	33	104	373	44	113	20	0	5	35	52	29	6	.303	.394	.397
Billy Jurges	SS134	R	33	134	471	50	138	25	2	5	61	47	36	0	.293	.361	.386
Mel Ott	OF145	L	32	148	525	89	150	29	0	27	90	100	68	5	.286	.403	.495
Johnny Rucker	OF142	L	24	143	622	95	179	38	9	1	42	29	61	8	.288	.320	.383
Jo-Jo Moore	OF116	L	32	121	428	47	117	16	2	7	40	30	15	4	.273	.322	.369
Joe Orengo	3B59,SS9,2B6	R	26	77	252	23	54	11	2	4	25	28	49	1	.214	.298	.321
Morrie Arnovich	OF61	R	30	85	207	25	58	8	3	2	22	23	14	2	.280	.352	.377
Gabby Hartnett	C34	R	40	64	150	20	45	5	0	5	26	12	14	0	.300	.356	.433
Odell Hale†	2B29	R	32	41	102	13	20	3	0	0	9	18	13	1	.196	.317	.225
Mickey Witek	2B23	R	25	26	94	11	34	5	0	1	16	4	2	0	.362	.388	.447
Ken O'Dea	C14	L	28	59	89	13	19	5	1	3	17	8	20	0	.213	.278	.393
John Davis	3B21	R	25	21	70	8	15	3	0	0	5	8	12	0	.214	.295	.257
Hal Schumacher	P30,OF1	R	30	38	66	6	10	1	0	0	4	6	13	0	.152	.222	.167
Babe Barna	OF10	L	26	10	42	5	9	3	0	1	5	2	6	0	.214	.250	.357
Johnny McCarthy	1B8,OF1	L	31	14	40	1	13	3	0	0	12	3	0	0	.325	.372	.400
Frank Demaree†	OF10	R	31	16	35	3	6	0	0	0	1	4	1	0	.171	.256	.171
Sid Gordon	OF9	R	23	9	31	4	8	1	1	0	4	6	1	0	.258	.378	.355
Rae Blaemire	C2	R	30	2	5	0	2	0	0	0	0	0	0	0	.400	.400	.400
Jack Aragon		R	25	1	0	0	0	0	0	0	0	0	0	0	—	—	—

Pitcher	T	Age	G	GS	CG	ShO	IP	H	HR	BB	SO	W-L	Sv	ERA
Hal Schumacher	R	30	30	26	12	3	206.0	187	11	79	63	12-10	1	3.36
Cliff Melton	L	29	42	22	9	3	194.1	181	14	61	100	8-11	1	3.01
Carl Hubbell	L	38	26	22	11	1	164.0	169	10	53	75	11-9	1	3.57
Bill Lohrman	R	28	33	20	6	2	159.0	184	7	40	61	9-10	3	4.02
Bob Carpenter	R	23	29	19	8	1	131.2	138	15	42	42	11-6	2	3.83
Bill McGee†	R	31	22	14	1	0	106.0	117	9	54	41	2-9	0	4.92
Harry Gumbert†	R	31	5	5	1	0	32.1	34	3	18	9	1-1	0	4.45
Dave Koslo	L	21	4	3	2	0	23.2	17	0	10	12	1-2	0	1.90
Harry Feldman	R	21	3	3	1	1	20.1	21	0	6	9	1-1	0	3.98
Hugh East	R	21	2	2	0	0	15.2	19	0	9	4	1-1	0	3.45
Tom Sunkel	L	28	2	2	1	1	15.1	7	0	12	14	1-1	0	2.93
Bump Hadley†	R	36	3	2	0	0	13.0	19	1	9	4	1-0	0	6.23
Rube Fischer	R	24	2	1	1	0	11.0	10	0	6	9	1-0	0	2.45
Ace Adams	R	29	38	0	0	0	71.0	84	3	35	18	4-1	1	4.82
Jumbo Brown	R	34	31	0	0	0	57.0	49	2	21	30	1-5	8	3.32
Bob Bowman	R	30	29	6	2	0	80.1	100	10	36	25	6-7	1	5.71
Johnnie Wittig	R	27	25	9	0	0	85.1	111	5	45	47	3-5	0	5.59
Paul Dean	R	27	5	0	0	0	5.2	8	0	3	3	0-0	0	3.18

1941 Chicago Cubs 6th NL 70-84 .455 30.0 GB

Jimmie Wilson

Player	Gm by Position	B	Age	G	AB	R	H	2B	3B	HR	RBI	BB	SO	SB	Avg	OBP	Slg
Clyde McCullough	C119	R	24	125	418	41	95	9	2	9	53	34	67	5	.227	.289	.323
Babe Dahlgren†	1B99	R	29	99	359	50	101	20	1	16	59	43	39	2	.281	.360	.476
Lou Stringer	2B137,SS7	R	24	145	512	59	126	31	4	5	53	59	86	3	.246	.324	.352
Stan Hack	3B150,1B1	L	31	151	586	111	186	33	5	7	45	99	40	10	.317	.417	.427
Bobby Sturgeon	SS126,2B1,3B1	R	21	129	433	45	106	15	3	0	25	9	30	5	.245	.260	.293
Bill Nicholson	OF143	L	26	147	532	74	135	26	1	26	98	82	91	1	.254	.357	.453
Dom Dallessandro	OF131	L	27	140	486	73	132	36	2	6	85	68	37	3	.272	.362	.391
Phil Cavarretta	OF66,1B33	L	24	107	346	46	99	18	4	6	40	53	28	2	.286	.384	.413
Lou Novikoff	OF54	R	25	62	203	22	49	8	0	5	24	11	15	0	.241	.284	.355
Hank Leiber	OF29,1B15	R	30	53	162	20	35	5	0	7	25	16	25	0	.216	.291	.377
Bob Scheffing	C34	R	27	51	132	9	32	8	0	1	20	5	19	2	.242	.270	.326
Augie Galan†	OF31	S	29	65	120	18	25	3	0	1	13	22	10	0	.208	.331	.258
Johnny Hudson	SS17,2B13,3B10	R	29	50	99	8	20	4	0	0	6	3	15	3	.202	.225	.242
Charlie Gilbert	OF22	L	21	39	86	11	24	2	1	0	12	11	6	1	.279	.361	.326
Barney Olsen	OF23	R	21	24	73	13	21	6	1	1	4	4	11	0	.288	.325	.438
Greek George	C18	R	28	35	64	4	10	2	0	0	6	2	10	0	.156	.182	.188
Billy Myers	SS19,2B1	R	30	24	63	10	14	1	0	1	4	7	25	1	.222	.310	.286
Billy Herman†	2B11	R	31	11	36	4	7	0	1	0	0	9	5	0	.194	.356	.250
Eddie Waitkus	1B9	L	21	12	28	1	5	0	0	0	0	0	3	0	.179	.207	.179
Lennie Merullo	SS7	R	24	7	17	3	6	1	0	0	1	2	0	1	.353	.421	.412
Rip Russell	1B5	R	26	6	17	1	5	1	0	0	1	1	5	0	.294	.333	.353
Frank Jelinich	OF2	R	21	4	8	0	1	0	0	0	2	1	2	0	.125	.222	.125
Al Todd		R	39	6	6	1	1	0	0	0	0	0	1	0	.167	.167	.167

Pitcher	T	Age	G	GS	CG	ShO	IP	H	HR	BB	SO	W-L	Sv	ERA
Claude Passeau	R	32	34	30	20	3	231.0	262	10	52	80	14-14	0	3.35
Vern Olsen	L	23	37	23	10	2	185.2	202	7	59	73	10-8	1	3.15
Bill Lee	R	31	28	22	12	0	167.1	179	6	43	62	8-14	1	3.76
Larry French†	L	33	26	18	6	1	138.0	161	10	43	60	5-14	0	4.63
Charlie Root	R	42	19	15	6	0	106.2	133	8	37	46	8-7	0	5.40
Vallie Eaves	R	29	12	7	4	0	58.2	56	4	21	24	3-3	0	3.53
Johnny Schmitz	L	20	5	3	1	0	20.2	12	0	9	11	2-0	0	1.31
Russ Meers	L	22	1	1	0	0	8.0	5	0	0	5	0-1	0	1.13
Walt Lanfranconi	R	24	2	1	0	0	6.0	7	0	2	1	0-1	0	3.00
Dizzy Dean	R	31	1	1	0	0	1.0	3	0	0	1	0-0	0	18.00
Jake Mooty	R	28	33	14	7	1	153.1	143	9	56	45	8-9	4	3.35
Paul Erickson	R	25	32	15	7	1	141.0	126	2	64	85	5-7	1	3.70
Tot Pressnell	R	34	29	1	0	0	70.0	69	2	23	27	5-3	1	3.09
Vance Page	R	35	25	3	1	0	48.1	48	2	30	17	2-2	1	4.28
Ken Raffensberger	L	23	10	1	0	0	18.0	17	0	7	5	0-1	0	4.50
Wimpy Quinn	R	23	3	0	0	0	5.0	3	0	3	2	0-0	0	7.20
Emil Kush	R	24	2	0	0	0	4.0	2	0	0	2	0-0	0	2.25
Hank Gornicki†	R	30	1	0	0	0	2.0	3	0	0	2	0-0	0	4.50

1941 Boston Braves 7th NL 62-92 .403 38.0 GB — Casey Stengel

Player	Gm by Position	B	Age	G	AB	R	H	2B	3B	HR	RBI	BB	SO	SB	Avg	OBP	Slg
Ray Berres	C120	R	33	120	279	21	56	10	0	1	19	17	20	2	.201	.247	.247
Buddy Hassett	1B99	L	29	118	405	59	120	9	4	1	33	36	15	10	.296	.354	.346
Bama Rowell	2B112,OF14,3B2	L	25	138	483	49	129	23	6	7	60	39	36	11	.267	.322	.383
Sibby Sisti	3B137,2B2,SS2	R	20	140	541	72	140	24	3	1	45	38	76	7	.259	.309	.320
Eddie Miller	SS154	R	24	154	585	54	140	27	3	6	68	35	72	8	.239	.288	.326
Max West	OF132	L	24	138	484	63	134	28	4	12	68	72	68	5	.277	.373	.426
Johnny Cooney	OF111,1B4	R	40	123	442	52	141	25	2	0	29	27	15	3	.319	.358	.385
Gene Moore	OF110	L	31	129	397	42	108	17	8	5	43	45	37	5	.272	.349	.393
Paul Waner†	OF77,1B7	L	38	95	294	40	82	10	2	2	46	47	14	1	.279	.378	.347
Phil Masi	C83	R	25	87	180	17	40	8	2	3	18	16	13	4	.222	.286	.339
Skippy Roberge	2B46,3B5,SS2	R	24	55	167	12	36	6	0	0	15	9	18	0	.216	.256	.251
Babe Dahlgren†	1B39,3B5	R	29	44	166	20	39	8	1	7	30	16	13	0	.235	.306	.422
Frank Demaree†	OF28	R	31	48	113	20	26	5	2	2	15	12	5	2	.230	.304	.363
Buddy Gremp	1B21,2B6,C3	R	21	37	75	7	18	3	0	0	10	5	3	0	.240	.288	.280
Hank Majeski	3B11	R	24	19	55	5	8	5	0	0	3	1	13	0	.145	.161	.236
Al Montgomery	C30	R	20	42	52	4	10	1	0	0	4	9	8	0	.192	.323	.212
Lloyd Waner†	OF15	L	35	19	51	7	21	1	0	0	4	2	0	1	.412	.434	.431
Chet Ross	OF29	R	24	29	50	1	6	1	0	0	4	9	17	0	.120	.254	.140
Whitey Wietelmann	2B10,SS5,3B2	S	22	16	33	1	3	0	0	0	0	1	2	0	.091	.118	.091
Hank LaManna	P35,OF4	R	21	47	32	6	9	2	0	0	1	0	11	0	.281	.281	.344
Don Manno	OF5,3B3,1B1	R	26	22	30	2	5	1	0	0	4	3	7	0	.167	.242	.200
John Dudra	2B5,3B5,1B1*	R	25	14	25	3	9	3	1	0	3	3	4	0	.360	.429	.560
Earl Averill	OF4	L	39	8	17	2	2	0	0	0	2	1	4	0	.118	.211	.118
Buster Bray	OF3	L	28	4	11	2	1	1	0	0	1	1	2	0	.091	.167	.182
Mel Preibisch	OF2	R	26	5	4	0	0	0	0	0	0	1	2	0	.000	.200	.000

J. Dudra, 1 G at SS

Pitcher	T	Age	G	GS	CG	ShO	IP	H	HR	BB	SO	W-L	Sv	ERA
Manny Salvo	R	28	35	27	11	2	195.0	192	9	93	67	7-16	0	4.06
Jim Tobin	R	28	33	26	20	3	238.0	229	12	60	61	12-12	0	3.10
Dick Errickson	R	27	38	23	5	2	165.2	192	12	62	45	6-12	1	4.78
Al Javery	R	23	34	23	9	1	160.2	181	5	65	54	10-11	1	4.31
Bill Posedel	R	34	18	9	3	0	57.1	61	6	30	10	4-4	0	4.87
Wes Ferrell	R	33	4	3	1	0	14.0	13	1	9	10	2-1	0	5.14
George Barnicle	R	23	1	1	0	0	6.2	5	0	4	2	0-1	0	6.75
Art Johnson	L	24	43	18	6	0	183.1	189	7	71	70	7-15	1	3.53
Johnny Hutchings†	R	25	36	7	1	1	95.2	110	7	22	36	1-6	2	4.14
Hank LaManna	R	21	35	4	0	0	72.2	77	5	56	23	5-4	1	5.33
Tom Earley	R	24	33	13	6	1	138.2	120	9	46	54	6-8	3	2.53
Joe Sullivan†	L	30	16	2	0	0	52.1	60	3	26	11	2-2	0	4.13
Nick Strincevich†	R	26	3	0	0	0	3.1	7	0	6	1	0-0	0	10.80
Eddie Carnett	L	24	2	0	0	0	1.1	4	0	3	2	0-0	0	20.25
Al Piechota	R	27	1	0	0	0	1.0	0	0	1	0	0-0	0	0.00

1941 Philadelphia Phillies 8th NL 43-111 .279 57.0 GB — Doc Prothro

Player	Gm by Position	B	Age	G	AB	R	H	2B	3B	HR	RBI	BB	SO	SB	Avg	OBP	Slg
Bennie Warren	C110	R	29	121	345	34	74	13	2	9	35	44	66	0	.214	.309	.342
Nick Etten	1B150	L	27	151	540	78	168	27	4	14	79	82	33	9	.311	.405	.454
Danny Murtaugh	2B85,SS1	R	23	85	347	34	76	8	1	0	11	26	31	18	.219	.275	.248
Pinky May	3B140	R	30	142	490	46	131	17	4	0	39	55	30	2	.267	.344	.318
Bobby Bragan	SS154,2B2,3B1	R	23	154	557	37	140	19	3	4	69	26	29	7	.251	.285	.318
Danny Litwhiler	OF150	R	24	151	590	72	180	29	6	18	66	39	43	1	.305	.350	.466
Joe Marty	OF132	R	27	137	477	60	128	19	3	8	39	51	41	6	.268	.344	.371
Stan Benjamin	OF110,1B8,2B2*	R	27	129	480	47	113	20	7	3	27	20	81	17	.235	.266	.325
Johnny Rizzo	OF62,SS2	R	28	99	235	20	51	9	2	4	24	24	34	1	.217	.295	.323
Heinie Mueller	2B29,OF21,3B19	S	28	93	233	21	53	11	1	1	22	22	24	2	.227	.302	.296
Mickey Livingston	C71,1B1	R	26	95	207	16	42	6	1	0	18	20	38	2	.203	.276	.242
Hal Marnie	2B39,SS16,3B3	R	22	61	158	12	38	3	3	0	11	13	25	0	.241	.298	.297
Chuck Klein	OF14	L	36	50	73	6	9	0	0	1	3	10	6	0	.123	.229	.164
Bill Nagel	2B12,OF2,3B1	R	25	17	56	2	8	1	1	0	6	3	14	0	.143	.186	.196
Jim Carlin	OF9,3B2	R	23	16	21	2	3	1	0	1	2	3	4	0	.143	.250	.333
Paul Busby	OF3	L	22	10	16	3	5	0	0	0	2	0	1	0	.313	.313	.313
Bill Harman	P5,C5	R	22	15	14	1	1	0	0	0	0	0	3	0	.071	.071	.071
George Jumonville	2B1,SS1	R	24	6	7	1	3	0	0	1	2	0	0	0	.429	.429	.857
Wally Millies	C1	R	34	1	2	0	0	0	0	0	0	0	0	0	.000	.000	.000

S. Benjamin, 1 G at SS

Pitcher	T	Age	G	GS	CG	ShO	IP	H	HR	BB	SO	W-L	Sv	ERA
Cy Blanton	R	32	28	25	7	1	163.2	186	11	57	64	6-13	0	4.51
Johnny Podgajny	R	21	34	24	8	0	181.1	191	8	70	53	9-12	0	4.62
Tommy Hughes	R	21	34	24	5	2	170.0	187	12	82	59	9-14	0	4.45
Si Johnson	R	34	39	21	6	1	163.1	207	8	54	80	5-12	2	4.52
Lee Grissom†	L	33	29	18	2	0	131.1	120	4	70	74	2-13	0	3.97
Paul Masterson	L	25	2	1	1	0	11.1	11	0	6	8	1-0	0	4.76
Gene Lambert	R	20	2	1	0	0	9.0	11	0	2	3	0-1	0	2.00
Dale Jones	R	22	2	1	0	0	8.1	13	0	6	2	0-1	0	7.56
Ike Pearson	R	24	46	10	0	0	136.0	139	8	70	38	4-14	6	3.57
Frank Hoerst	L	23	37	11	1	0	105.2	111	7	50	33	3-10	0	5.20
Boom-Boom Beck	R	36	34	7	2	0	95.1	104	8	35	34	1-9	0	4.63
Rube Melton	R	24	25	5	2	0	83.2	81	7	47	57	1-5	0	4.73
Bill Crouch†	R	30	20	5	1	0	59.0	65	4	17	26	2-3	1	4.42
Roy Bruner	R	24	13	1	0	0	29.1	37	1	25	13	0-3	0	4.91
Vito Tamulis†	L	29	6	1	0	0	12.0	21	1	7	5	0-1	0	9.00
Bill Harman	R	22	5	0	0	0	13.0	15	0	8	3	0-0	0	4.85

»1942 New York Yankees 1st AL 103-51 .669 — — Joe McCarthy

Player	Gm by Position	B	Age	G	AB	R	H	2B	3B	HR	RBI	BB	SO	SB	Avg	OBP	Slg
Bill Dickey	C80	L	35	82	268	28	79	13	1	2	37	26	11	2	.295	.359	.373
Buddy Hassett	1B132	L	30	132	538	80	153	16	6	5	48	32	16	5	.284	.325	.364
Joe Gordon	2B147	R	27	147	538	88	173	29	4	18	103	79	95	12	.322	.409	.491
Frankie Crosetti	3B62,SS8,2B2	R	31	74	285	50	69	5	5	4	23	31	31	1	.242	.335	.337
Phil Rizzuto	SS144	R	24	144	553	79	157	24	7	4	68	44	40	22	.284	.343	.374
Joe DiMaggio	OF154	R	27	154	610	123	186	29	13	21	114	68	36	4	.305	.376	.498
Charlie Keller	OF152	L	25	152	544	106	159	24	9	26	108	114	61	14	.292	.417	.513
Tommy Henrich	OF119,1B7	L	29	127	483	77	129	30	5	13	67	58	42	4	.267	.352	.431
Red Rolfe	3B60	L	33	69	265	42	58	8	2	8	25	23	18	1	.219	.281	.355
Buddy Rosar	C58	R	27	69	209	18	48	10	0	2	34	17	20	1	.230	.288	.306
Jerry Priddy	3B35,1B11,2B8*	R	22	59	189	23	53	9	2	2	28	31	27	0	.280	.385	.381
Rollie Hemsley†	C29	R	35	31	85	12	25	3	1	0	15	5	9	1	.294	.333	.353
George Selkirk	OF19	L	34	42	78	15	15	3	0	0	10	16	8	0	.192	.330	.231
Roy Cullenbine†	OF19,1B1	S	28	21	77	16	28	7	0	2	17	18	2	0	.364	.484	.532
Ed Levy	1B13	R	25	13	41	5	5	0	0	0	3	4	5	1	.122	.200	.122
Eddie Kearse	C11	R	26	11	26	2	5	0	0	0	2	3	1	1	.192	.276	.192
Tuck Stainback	OF3	R	30	15	10	0	2	0	0	0	0	0	2	0	.200	.200	.200
Mike Chartak†		L	26	5	5	0	0	0	0	0	0	0	0	0	.000	.000	.000

J. Priddy, 3 G at SS

Pitcher	T	Age	G	GS	CG	ShO	IP	H	HR	BB	SO	W-L	Sv	ERA
Tiny Bonham	R	28	28	27	22	6	226.0	199	11	24	71	21-5	0	2.27
Spud Chandler	R	34	24	24	17	3	200.2	176	13	74	74	16-5	0	2.38
Red Ruffing	R	38	24	24	16	4	193.2	183	10	41	80	14-7	0	3.21
Hank Borowy	R	26	25	21	13	4	178.1	157	6	66	85	15-4	1	2.52
Marv Breuer	R	28	27	19	6	0	164.1	157	11	37	72	8-9	1	3.07
Atley Donald	R	31	20	19	10	1	147.2	133	6	45	53	11-3	0	3.11
Lefty Gomez	L	33	13	13	2	0	80.0	67	4	65	41	6-4	0	4.28
Marius Russo	L	27	9	5	2	0	45.1	41	2	14	15	4-1	0	2.78
Johnny Murphy	R	33	31	0	0	0	58.0	66	2	23	24	4-10	11	3.41
Johnny Lindell	R	25	23	2	0	0	52.2	52	3	22	28	2-1	1	3.76
Norm Branch	R	27	10	0	0	0	15.2	18	3	16	13	0-1	2	6.32
Jim Turner†	R	38	5	0	0	0	7.0	4	0	1	2	1-1	1	1.29
Mel Queen	R	24	4	0	0	0	5.2	6	0	3	0	1-0	0	0.00

1942 Boston Red Sox 2nd AL 93-59 .612 9.0 GB — Joe Cronin

Player	Gm by Position	B	Age	G	AB	R	H	2B	3B	HR	RBI	BB	SO	SB	Avg	OBP	Slg
Bill Conroy	C83	R	27	83	250	22	50	4	2	4	20	40	47	2	.200	.315	.280
Tony Lupien	1B121	L	25	128	463	63	130	25	7	3	70	50	20	10	.281	.351	.384
Bobby Doerr	2B142	R	24	144	545	71	158	35	5	15	102	67	55	4	.290	.369	.455
Jim Tabor	3B138	R	25	139	508	56	128	18	2	12	75	37	47	6	.252	.303	.366
Johnny Pesky	SS147	L	22	147	620	105	205	29	9	2	51	42	36	12	.331	.375	.416
Dom DiMaggio	OF151	R	25	151	622	110	178	36	8	14	48	70	52	16	.286	.364	.437
Ted Williams	OF150	L	23	150	522	141	186	34	5	36	137	145	51	3	.356	.499	.648
Lou Finney	OF95,1B2	L	31	113	397	58	113	16	7	3	61	29	11	3	.285	.335	.383
Johnny Peacock	C82	L	32	88	286	17	76	7	3	0	25	21	11	1	.266	.316	.311
Pete Fox	OF71	R	33	77	256	42	67	15	5	3	42	20	28	8	.262	.323	.395
Jimmie Foxx†	1B27	R	34	30	100	18	27	4	0	5	14	18	15	0	.270	.392	.460
Skeeter Newsome	3B12,2B10,SS7	R	31	29	95	7	26	6	0	0	9	9	5	2	.274	.337	.337
Joe Cronin	3B11,1B5,SS1	R	35	45	79	7	24	3	0	4	24	15	21	0	.304	.415	.494
Mike Ryba	P18,C3	R	39	21	17	1	5	0	0	0	1	0	1	0	.294	.294	.294
Paul Campbell	OF4	L	24	26	15	4	1	0	0	0	0	1	5	1	.067	.125	.067
Andy Gilbert	OF5	R	27	6	11	0	1	0	0	0	1	1	3	0	.091	.167	.091
Tom Carey	2B1	R	35	1	1	0	1	0	0	0	1	0	0	0	1.000	1.000	1.000

Pitcher	T	Age	G	GS	CG	ShO	IP	H	HR	BB	SO	W-L	Sv	ERA
Tex Hughson	R	26	38	30	22	4	281.0	258	10	75	113	22-6	4	2.59
Charlie Wagner	R	29	29	26	17	2	205.1	184	5	95	52	14-11	0	3.29
Joe Dobson	R	25	30	23	10	3	182.2	155	9	68	72	11-9	0	3.30
Dick Newsome	R	32	24	23	11	0	158.0	174	11	67	40	8-10	0	5.01
Oscar Judd	L	34	31	19	11	0	150.1	135	3	90	70	8-10	2	3.89
Yank Terry	R	31	20	11	3	0	85.0	82	5	43	37	6-5	1	3.92
Ken Chase	L	28	13	10	4	0	80.1	82	5	41	34	5-1	0	3.81
Mace Brown	R	33	34	0	0	0	60.1	56	4	28	20	9-3	6	3.43
Bill Butland	L	24	23	10	6	2	111.1	85	8	33	46	7-1	1	2.51
Mike Ryba	R	39	18	0	0	0	44.1	49	5	13	16	3-3	3	3.86

1942 St. Louis Browns 3rd AL 82-69 .543 19.5 GB — Luke Sewell

Player	Gm by Position	B	Age	G	AB	R	H	2B	3B	HR	RBI	BB	SO	SB	Avg	OBP	Slg
Rick Ferrell	C95	R	36	99	273	20	61	6	1	0	26	33	13	0	.223	.307	.253
George McQuinn	1B144	L	32	145	554	86	145	32	5	12	78	60	77	1	.262	.335	.403
Don Gutteridge	2B145,3B2	R	30	147	616	90	157	27	11	1	50	59	54	16	.255	.320	.339
Harlond Clift	3B141,SS1	R	29	143	541	108	148	39	4	7	55	106	48	6	.274	.394	.399
Vern Stephens	SS144	R	21	145	575	84	169	26	6	14	92	41	53	1	.294	.341	.433
Chet Laabs	OF139	R	30	144	520	90	143	21	7	27	99	88	88	0	.275	.380	.498
Wally Judnich	OF122	L	25	132	457	78	143	22	6	17	82	74	41	3	.313	.413	.499
Glenn McQuillen	OF77	R	27	100	339	40	96	15	12	3	47	10	17	1	.283	.306	.425
Mike Chartak†	OF64	L	26	73	237	37	59	11	2	9	43	40	27	3	.249	.362	.426
Frankie Hayes†	C51	R	27	56	159	14	40	6	0	2	17	28	39	0	.252	.364	.327
Tony Criscola	OF52	L	26	91	158	17	47	9	2	1	13	8	13	2	.297	.331	.399
Roy Cullenbine†	OF27,1B5	S	28	38	109	15	21	7	1	2	14	30	20	0	.193	.367	.330
Bob Swift†	C28	R	27	29	76	3	15	4	0	1	8	3	5	0	.197	.228	.289
Johnny Berardino	3B6,SS6,1B5*	R	25	29	74	11	21	6	0	1	10	4	2	3	.284	.329	.405
Alan Strange	3B10,SS3,2B1	R	35	19	37	3	10	2	0	0	5	3	1	0	.270	.325	.324
Don Heffner	2B6,1B4	R	31	19	36	2	6	2	0	0	3	1	4	1	.167	.189	.222
Luke Sewell	C6	R	41	6	12	1	1	0	0	0	1	1	5	0	.083	.154	.083
Babe Dahlgren†		R	30	2	2	0	0	0	0	0	0	0	0	0	.000	.000	.000
Ray Hayworth		R	38	1	1	0	1	0	0	0	0	0	0	0	1.000	1.000	1.000

J. Berardino, 4 G at 2B

Pitcher	T	Age	G	GS	CG	ShO	IP	H	HR	BB	SO	W-L	Sv	ERA
Eldon Auker	R	31	35	34	17	2	249.0	273	16	86	62	14-13	0	4.08
Denny Galehouse	R	30	32	28	12	3	192.1	193	5	79	75	12-12	1	3.60
Johnny Niggeling	R	38	28	27	16	3	206.1	173	10	93	107	15-11	0	2.66
Al Hollingsworth	L	34	33	18	7	1	161.0	173	4	52	60	10-6	4	2.96
Bob Muncrief	R	26	24	18	7	0	134.1	149	11	31	39	6-8	0	3.89
Steve Sundra†	R	32	20	13	6	0	110.2	122	2	29	26	8-3	0	3.82
Bob Harris†	R	25	6	6	0	0	33.2	37	2	17	9	1-5	0	5.61
George Caster	R	34	39	0	0	0	80.0	62	3	39	34	8-2	5	2.81
Stan Ferens	L	27	19	3	1	0	69.0	76	2	21	23	3-4	0	3.78
Pete Appleton†	R	38	14	0	0	0	27.1	25	1	11	12	1-1	2	2.96
Frank Biscan	L	22	11	0	0	0	27.0	13	1	11	10	0-1	1	2.33
Loy Hanning	R	24	11	0	0	0	17.1	26	2	12	9	1-1	0	7.79
Fritz Ostermueller	L	34	10	4	2	0	43.2	46	4	17	21	3-1	0	3.71
John Whitehead	R	33	4	0	0	0	4.0	8	0	1	0	0-0	0	6.75
Bill Trotter†	R	33	3	0	0	0	2.0	5	0	2	0	0-1	0	18.00
Ewald Pyle	L	31	2	0	0	0	5.1	6	0	4	1	0-0	0	6.75

1942 Cleveland Indians 4th AL 75-79 .487 28.0 GB

Lou Boudreau

Player	Gm by Position	B	Age	G	AB	R	H	2B	3B	HR	RBI	BB	SO	SB	Avg	OBP	Slg
Otto Denning	C78,OF2	R	29	92	214	15	45	14	0	1	19	18	14	0	.210	.275	.290
Les Fleming	1B156	L	26	156	548	71	160	27	4	14	82	106	57	6	.292	.412	.432
Ray Mack	2B143	R	25	143	481	43	108	14	6	2	45	41	51	9	.225	.288	.291
Ken Keltner	3B151	R	25	152	624	72	179	34	4	6	78	20	36	4	.287	.312	.383
Lou Boudreau	SS146	R	24	147	506	57	143	18	10	2	58	75	39	7	.283	.379	.370
Jeff Heath	OF146	L	27	147	568	82	158	37	13	10	76	62	66	9	.278	.350	.442
Oris Hockett	OF145	L	32	148	601	85	150	22	7	7	48	45	45	12	.250	.305	.344
Roy Weatherly	OF117	L	27	128	473	61	122	23	7	5	39	35	25	8	.258	.310	.368
Buster Mills	OF53	R	33	80	195	19	54	4	2	1	26	23	18	5	.277	.353	.333
Jim Hegan	C66	R	21	68	170	10	33	5	0	0	11	11	31	1	.194	.243	.224
Gene Desautels	C61	R	35	62	162	14	40	5	0	0	9	12	13	1	.247	.303	.278
Oscar Grimes	2B24,3B8,1B1*	R	27	51	84	10	15	2	0	0	2	13	17	3	.179	.289	.202
Fabian Gaffke	OF16	R	28	40	67	4	11	2	0	0	3	6	13	1	.164	.243	.194
Rusty Peters	SS24,2B1,3B1	R	27	34	58	6	13	5	1	0	2	2	14	0	.224	.250	.345
Hank Edwards	OF12	L	23	13	48	6	12	2	1	0	7	5	8	2	.250	.321	.333
Ted Sepkowski	2B2	L	18	5	10	0	1	0	0	0	0	0	3	0	.100	.100	.100
Eddie Robinson	1B1	L	21	8	8	1	1	0	0	0	2	1	0	0	.125	.222	.125
Bob Lemon	3B1	L	21	5	5	0	0	0	0	0	0	0	3	0	.000	.000	.000
George Susce	C2	R	33	2	1	1	1	0	0	0	0	1	0	0	1.000	1.000	1.000

O. Grimes, 1 G at SS

Pitcher	T	Age	G	GS	CG	ShO	IP	H	HR	BB	SO	W-L	Sv	ERA
Jim Bagby Jr.	R	25	38	35	16	4	270.2	267	19	64	54	17-9	1	2.96
Mel Harder	R	32	29	29	13	4	198.2	179	8	82	74	13-14	0	3.44
Al Smith	L	34	30	24	7	1	168.1	163	9	71	66	10-15	0	3.96
Chubby Dean	L	25	27	22	8	0	172.2	170	7	66	46	8-11	1	3.81
Al Milnar	L	28	28	19	8	2	157.0	146	3	85	35	6-8	0	4.13
Ray Poat	R	24	4	4	1	1	18.1	24	1	9	8	1-3	0	5.40
Tom Ferrick	R	27	31	2	2	0	81.1	56	3	32	28	3-2	3	1.99
Harry Eisenstat	L	26	29	1	0	0	47.2	58	1	6	19	2-1	2	2.45
Vern Kennedy	R	35	28	12	4	0	108.0	99	1	50	37	4-8	1	4.08
Joe Heving	R	41	27	2	0	0	46.1	52	4	25	13	5-3	3	4.86
Red Embree	R	24	19	6	2	0	63.0	58	0	31	44	3-4	0	3.86
Steve Gromek	R	22	14	0	0	0	44.1	46	2	23	14	2-0	0	3.65
Clint Brown	R	38	7	0	0	0	9.0	16	2	2	4	1-1	0	6.00
Joe Krakauskas	L	27	3	0	0	0	7.0	7	1	4	2	0-0	0	3.86
Allie Reynolds	R	27	2	0	0	0	5.0	5	0	4	2	0-0	0	0.00
Pete Center	R	30	1	0	0	0	3.1	7	0	4	0	0-0	0	16.20
Paul Calvert	R	24	1	0	0	0	2.0	0	0	2	2	0-0	0	0.00

1942 Detroit Tigers 5th AL 73-81 .474 30.0 GB

Del Baker

Player	Gm by Position	B	Age	G	AB	R	H	2B	3B	HR	RBI	BB	SO	SB	Avg	OBP	Slg
Birdie Tebbetts	C97	R	29	99	308	24	76	11	0	1	27	39	17	4	.247	.335	.292
Rudy York	1B152	R	28	153	577	81	150	26	4	21	90	73	71	3	.260	.343	.428
Jimmy Bloodworth	2B134,SS2	R	24	137	533	62	129	23	1	13	57	35	63	2	.242	.295	.362
Mike Higgins	3B137	R	33	143	499	65	133	34	2	11	79	72	21	3	.267	.362	.409
Billy Hitchcock	SS80,3B1	R	25	85	280	27	59	8	1	0	29	26	21	2	.211	.280	.246
Barney McCosky	OF154	L	25	154	600	75	176	28	11	7	50	68	37	11	.293	.365	.412
Doc Cramer	OF150	L	36	151	630	71	166	26	4	0	43	43	18	4	.263	.314	.317
Ned Harris	OF104	L	25	121	398	53	108	16	10	9	45	49	35	5	.271	.351	.430
Don Ross	OF38,3B20	R	27	87	226	29	62	10	2	3	30	36	16	2	.274	.379	.376
Dixie Parsons	C62	R	26	63	188	8	37	4	0	2	11	13	22	1	.197	.249	.250
Murray Franklin	SS32,2B7	R	28	48	154	24	40	7	0	2	16	7	5	0	.260	.301	.344
Rip Radcliff	OF24,1B4	L	36	62	144	13	36	5	0	1	20	9	6	0	.250	.294	.306
Johnny Lipon	SS34	R	19	34	131	5	25	2	0	0	9	7	7	1	.191	.232	.206
Eric McNair†	SS21	R	33	26	68	5	11	2	0	1	4	3	5	0	.162	.197	.235
Dutch Meyer	2B14	R	26	14	52	5	17	3	0	2	9	4	4	0	.327	.386	.500
Charlie Gehringer	2B3	L	39	45	45	6	12	0	0	1	7	7	4	0	.267	.365	.333
Hank Riebe	C11	R	20	11	35	1	11	2	0	0	2	0	6	0	.314	.314	.371
Al Unser	C4	R	29	4	8	2	3	0	0	0	0	0	2	0	.375	.375	.375
Bob Patrick	OF3	R	24	4	8	1	2	1	0	1	3	1	0	0	.250	.333	.750

Pitcher	T	Age	G	GS	CG	ShO	IP	H	HR	BB	SO	W-L	Sv	ERA
Al Benton	R	31	35	30	9	1	226.2	210	9	84	110	7-13	2	2.90
Dizzy Trout	R	27	35	29	13	1	223.0	214	14	89	91	12-18	0	3.43
Hal White	R	23	34	25	12	4	216.2	212	6	82	93	12-12	1	2.91
Hal Newhouser	L	21	38	23	11	1	183.2	137	4	114	103	8-14	5	2.45
Tommy Bridges	R	35	23	22	11	2	174.0	164	6	61	97	9-7	1	2.74
Virgil Trucks	R	25	28	20	8	2	167.2	147	3	74	91	14-8	0	2.74
Schoolboy Rowe†	R	32	2	1	0	0	10.1	9	0	2	7	1-0	0	0.00
Johnny Gorsica	R	27	28	0	0	0	53.0	63	2	26	19	3-2	4	4.75
Roy Henshaw	L	30	23	2	0	0	61.2	63	3	27	24	2-4	1	4.09
Hal Manders	R	25	18	0	0	0	33.0	39	4	15	14	2-0	0	4.09
Charlie Fuchs	R	28	9	4	1	1	36.2	43	5	19	15	3-3	0	6.63
Jack Wilson†	R	30	9	0	0	0	13.0	20	3	5	7	0-0	0	4.85

1942 Chicago White Sox 6th AL 66-82 .446 34.0 GB

Jimmy Dykes

Player	Gm by Position	B	Age	G	AB	R	H	2B	3B	HR	RBI	BB	SO	SB	Avg	OBP	Slg
Mike Tresh	C72	R	28	72	233	21	54	8	1	0	15	28	24	2	.232	.314	.275
Joe Kuhel	1B112	L	36	115	413	60	103	14	4	4	52	60	22	22	.249	.347	.332
Don Kolloway	2B116,1B33	R	23	147	601	72	164	40	4	3	60	30	39	16	.273	.311	.368
Bob Kennedy	3B96,OF16	R	21	113	412	37	95	18	5	0	38	22	41	11	.231	.270	.299
Luke Appling	SS141	R	35	142	543	78	142	26	4	3	53	63	23	17	.262	.342	.341
Wally Moses	OF145	L	31	146	577	73	156	28	4	7	49	74	27	16	.270	.353	.369
Myril Hoag	OF112	R	34	113	412	47	99	18	2	2	37	36	21	17	.240	.301	.308
Taffy Wright	OF81	L	30	85	300	43	100	13	5	0	47	48	9	1	.333	.432	.410
Tom Turner	C54	R	25	56	182	18	44	9	1	3	21	19	15	0	.242	.313	.352
Dario Lodigiani	3B43,2B7	R	25	59	168	9	47	7	0	0	15	18	10	3	.280	.353	.321
Sammy West	OF45	L	37	49	151	14	35	5	0	0	25	31	18	2	.232	.363	.265
George Dickey	C29	S	26	59	116	6	27	3	0	1	17	9	11	0	.233	.288	.284
Skeeter Webb	2B29	R	32	32	94	5	16	2	1	0	4	4	13	1	.170	.204	.213
Bill Mueller	OF26	R	21	26	85	5	14	1	0	0	5	12	9	2	.165	.276	.176
Leo Wells	SS12,3B6	R	24	35	62	8	12	2	0	1	4	4	5	1	.194	.242	.274
Val Heim	OF12	L	21	13	45	6	9	1	1	0	7	5	3	1	.200	.294	.267
Jimmy Grant	3B10	L	23	12	36	0	6	1	1	0	1	5	6	0	.167	.268	.250
Bud Sketchley	OF12	L	23	13	36	1	7	1	0	0	3	7	4	0	.194	.326	.222
Thurman Tucker	OF5	L	24	7	24	2	3	0	1	0	1	0	4	0	.125	.125	.208
Jake Jones	1B5	R	21	7	20	2	3	1	0	0	1	2	2	1	.150	.227	.200

Pitcher	T	Age	G	GS	CG	ShO	IP	H	HR	BB	SO	W-L	Sv	ERA
Johnny Humphries	R	27	28	28	17	2	228.0	227	9	59	71	12-12	0	2.68
Eddie Smith	L	28	29	28	18	2	215.0	223	17	86	78	7-20	1	3.98
Bill Dietrich	R	32	26	23	6	0	160.0	173	16	70	39	6-11	0	4.89
Ted Lyons	R	41	20	20	20	1	180.1	167	11	26	50	14-6	0	2.10
Buck Ross	R	27	22	14	4	2	113.1	118	6	39	37	5-7	1	5.00
Jake Wade	L	30	15	10	3	0	85.2	84	2	56	32	5-5	0	4.10
Thornton Lee	L	35	11	8	6	1	76.0	82	4	31	25	2-6	0	3.32
Orval Grove	R	22	12	8	4	0	66.1	77	1	33	21	4-6	0	5.16
Johnny Rigney	R	27	7	7	6	0	59.0	40	2	16	34	3-3	0	3.20
Joe Haynes	R	24	40	1	1	0	103.0	88	6	47	35	8-5	6	2.62
Ed Weiland	R	27	5	0	0	0	9.2	18	0	3	4	0-0	0	7.45
Len Perme	L	24	4	1	1	0	13.0	5	0	4	4	0-1	0	1.38
Pete Appleton†	R	38	4	0	0	0	4.2	2	0	3	2	0-0	0	3.86

1942 Washington Senators 7th AL 62-89 .411 39.5 GB

Bucky Harris

Player	Gm by Position	B	Age	G	AB	R	H	2B	3B	HR	RBI	BB	SO	SB	Avg	OBP	Slg
Jake Early	C98	L	27	104	353	31	72	14	2	3	46	37	37	0	.204	.281	.280
Mickey Vernon	1B151	L	24	151	621	76	168	34	6	9	86	59	63	25	.271	.337	.388
Ellis Clary	2B69,3B2	R	25	76	240	34	66	9	0	0	16	45	25	2	.275	.394	.313
Bobby Estalella	3B78,OF36	R	31	133	429	68	119	24	5	8	65	85	42	5	.277	.400	.413
John Sullivan	SS92	R	21	94	357	38	84	16	1	0	42	25	30	2	.235	.285	.286
Stan Spence	OF149	L	27	149	629	94	203	27	15	4	79	62	16	5	.323	.384	.432
George Case	OF120	R	26	125	513	101	164	26	2	5	43	44	30	44	.320	.377	.407
Bruce Campbell	OF87	L	32	122	378	41	105	17	5	5	63	37	34	0	.278	.344	.389
Jimmy Pofahl	SS49,2B15,3B14	R	25	84	283	22	59	7	2	0	28	29	30	4	.208	.282	.247
Bob Repass	2B33,3B29,SS11	R	24	81	259	30	62	11	1	2	23	33	30	6	.239	.328	.313
Roy Cullenbine†	OF35,3B28	S	28	64	241	30	69	19	0	2	35	44	18	1	.286	.396	.390
Al Evans	C67	R	25	74	223	22	51	4	1	0	10	25	36	3	.229	.309	.256
Mike Chartak†	OF24	L	26	24	92	11	20	4	2	1	8	14	16	0	.217	.321	.337
Chile Gomez	2B23,3B1	R	33	25	73	8	14	2	2	0	6	9	7	1	.192	.289	.274
Frank Croucher	2B18	R	27	26	65	2	18	1	1	0	5	3	9	0	.277	.309	.323
Roberto Ortiz	OF9	R	27	20	42	4	7	1	3	1	4	5	11	0	.167	.271	.405
Ray Hoffman	3B6	L	25	7	19	2	1	0	0	0	2	1	1	0	.053	.100	.053
Stan Galle	3B3	R	23	13	18	3	2	0	0	0	1	1	0	0	.111	.158	.111
Al Kvasnak	OF3	R	21	5	11	3	2	0	0	0	0	2	1	0	.182	.308	.182
Gene Moore	OF1	L	32	1	2	0	0	0	0	0	0	0	1	0	.000	.000	.000

Pitcher	T	Age	G	GS	CG	ShO	IP	H	HR	BB	SO	W-L	Sv	ERA
Sid Hudson	R	27	35	31	19	1	239.1	266	9	70	72	10-17	2	4.36
Bobo Newsom†	R	34	30	29	15	2	213.2	236	5	92	113	11-17	0	4.93
Early Wynn	R	22	30	28	10	1	190.0	246	6	73	58	10-16	0	5.12
Walt Masterson	R	22	25	15	8	4	142.2	138	6	54	63	5-9	2	3.34
Jack Wilson†	R	30	12	6	1	0	42.0	57	2	23	18	1-4	0	6.64
Dutch Leonard	R	33	6	5	1	1	35.0	28	1	5	15	2-2	0	4.11
Steve Sundra†	R	32	6	4	2	0	33.2	43	1	15	5	1-3	0	5.61
Dewey Adkins	R	24	1	1	0	0	6.1	7	0	6	3	0-0	0	9.95
Bill Zuber	R	29	37	7	3	1	126.2	115	5	82	64	9-9	1	3.84
Alex Carrasquel	R	29	35	15	7	1	152.1	161	7	53	40	7-7	4	3.43
Ray Scarborough	R	24	17	5	1	1	63.1	68	2	32	16	2-1	0	4.12
Bill Trotter†	R	33	17	0	0	0	40.2	52	4	14	13	3-1	0	5.75
Hardin Cathey	R	22	12	2	0	0	30.1	44	1	16	8	1-1	0	7.42
Bill Kennedy	L	23	8	2	1	0	18.0	21	1	10	4	0-1	2	8.00
Lou Bevil	R	19	4	1	0	0	10.0	9	0	11	2	0-1	0	6.30
Phil McCullough	R	24	1	0	0	0	3.0	5	0	2	2	0-0	0	6.00

1942 Philadelphia Athletics 8th AL 55-99 .357 48.0 GB

Connie Mack

Player	Gm by Position	B	Age	G	AB	R	H	2B	3B	HR	RBI	BB	SO	SB	Avg	OBP	Slg
Hal Wagner	C94	L	26	104	288	26	68	17	1	1	30	24	29	1	.236	.304	.313
Dick Siebert	1B152	L	30	153	612	57	159	25	7	2	74	24	17	4	.260	.291	.333
Bill Knickerbocker	2B81,SS1	R	30	87	289	25	73	12	0	1	19	29	30	1	.253	.323	.304
Buddy Blair	3B126	L	31	137	484	48	135	26	8	5	66	30	30	1	.279	.325	.397
Pete Suder	SS69,3B34,2B31	R	26	128	476	46	122	20	4	4	54	24	39	4	.256	.293	.340
Bob Johnson	OF149	R	35	149	550	78	160	35	7	13	80	82	61	3	.291	.384	.451
Elmer Valo	OF122	L	21	133	459	64	115	13	10	2	40	70	21	13	.251	.355	.336
Mike Kreevich	OF107	R	34	116	444	57	113	19	1	1	30	47	31	7	.255	.326	.309
Dee Miles	OF81	L	33	99	346	41	94	12	5	0	22	12	10	5	.272	.300	.335
Crash Davis	2B57,SS26,1B3	R	22	86	272	31	61	8	1	2	26	21	30	1	.224	.282	.283
Bob Swift†	C60	R	27	60	192	9	44	3	0	0	15	13	17	1	.229	.278	.245
Jack Wallaesa	SS36	S	22	36	117	13	30	4	1	2	13	8	26	0	.256	.315	.359
Eric McNair†	SS29,2B1	R	33	34	103	8	25	2	0	0	4	11	5	1	.243	.316	.262
Frankie Hayes†	C20	R	27	21	63	8	15	4	0	0	5	5	8	1	.238	.333	.302
Eddie Collins	OF9	L	25	20	34	6	8	2	0	0	4	4	2	1	.235	.316	.294
Jim Castiglia	C3	L	23	16	18	2	7	0	0	0	2	1	3	0	.389	.421	.389
Ken Richardson	OF3,1B1,3B1	R	27	6	15	1	1	0	0	0	0	2	0	0	.067	.176	.067
Felix Mackiewicz	OF3	R	24	6	14	3	3	2	0	0	2	0	4	0	.214	.214	.357
George Yankowski	C6	R	19	6	13	0	2	1	0	0	2	0	2	0	.154	.154	.231
Larry Eschen	SS7,2B1	R	21	12	11	0	0	0	0	0	0	4	6	0	.000	.267	.000
Bruce Konopka	1B3	L	22	5	10	2	3	0	0	0	1	1	0	0	.300	.364	.300
Dick Adkins	SS3	R	22	3	7	2	1	0	0	0	0	2	2	0	.143	.333	.143

Pitcher	T	Age	G	GS	CG	ShO	IP	H	HR	BB	SO	W-L	Sv	ERA
Phil Marchildon	R	28	38	31	18	1	244.0	215	14	140	110	17-14	1	4.20
Roger Wolff	R	31	32	25	15	2	214.1	206	16	69	94	12-15	3	3.32
Lum Harris	R	27	26	20	10	1	166.0	146	14	70	60	11-15	0	3.74
Russ Christopher	R	24	30	18	10	0	165.0	154	8	99	58	4-13	1	3.82
Dick Fowler	R	21	31	17	4	0	140.0	159	13	45	38	6-11	1	4.95
Jack Knott	R	35	20	14	4	0	95.1	127	7	36	31	2-10	0	5.57
Bob Harris†	R	25	16	8	2	1	78.0	77	5	24	26	1-5	0	2.88
Herman Besse	L	30	30	14	4	0	133.0	163	7	69	78	2-9	1	6.16
Tex Shirley	R	24	15	1	0	0	35.2	37	0	22	10	0-1	1	5.30
Fred Caligiuri	R	23	13	2	0	0	36.2	45	2	18	20	0-3	1	6.38
Bob Savage	R	20	8	3	0	0	30.2	24	0	31	10	0-1	0	3.23
Bill Beckmann†	R	34	5	1	0	0	20.1	24	1	9	10	0-1	0	7.08
Joe Coleman	R	19	1	0	0	0	6.0	8	0	1	0	0-1	0	3.00
Les McCrabb	R	27	1	0	0	0	4.0	14	2	2	0	0-0	0	31.50
Sam Lowry	R	22	1	0	0	0	3.0	3	0	1	0	0-0	0	6.00
Ted Abernathy	L	20	1	0	0	0	2.2	2	0	3	1	0-0	0	10.13

>>1942 St. Louis Cardinals 1st NL 106-48 .688 —

Billy Southworth

Player	Gm by Position	B	Age	G	AB	R	H	2B	3B	HR	RBI	BB	SO	SB	Avg	OBP	Slg
Walker Cooper	C115	R	27	125	438	58	123	32	7	7	65	29	29	4	.281	.327	.434
Johnny Hopp	1B88	L	25	95	314	41	81	16	7	3	37	36	40	14	.258	.334	.382
Creepy Crespi	2B83,SS5	R	24	93	292	33	71	4	2	0	35	27	29	4	.243	.309	.271
Whitey Kurowski	3B104,SS1,OF1	R	24	115	366	51	93	17	3	9	42	33	60	7	.254	.326	.391
Marty Marion	SS147	R	24	147	485	66	134	38	5	0	54	48	50	8	.276	.343	.375
Enos Slaughter	OF151	L	26	152	591	100	188	31	17	13	98	88	30	9	.318	.412	.494
Stan Musial	OF135	L	21	140	467	87	147	32	10	10	72	62	25	6	.315	.397	.490
Terry Moore	OF126,3B1	R	30	130	489	80	141	26	3	6	49	56	26	10	.288	.364	.391
Jimmy Brown	2B82,3B66,SS12	S	32	145	606	75	155	28	4	1	71	52	11	4	.256	.315	.320
Ray Sanders	1B77	L	25	95	282	37	71	17	2	5	39	42	31	2	.252	.351	.379
Ken O'Dea	C49	L	29	58	192	22	45	7	1	5	32	17	23	0	.234	.297	.359
Harry Walker	OF56,2B2	L	25	74	191	38	60	12	2	0	16	11	14	2	.314	.355	.398
Coaker Triplett	OF46	R	30	64	154	18	42	7	4	1	23	17	15	1	.273	.345	.390
Erv Dusak	OF8,3B1	R	21	12	27	4	5	3	0	0	3	3	7	0	.185	.267	.296
Buddy Blattner	SS13,2B3	R	22	19	23	3	1	0	0	0	1	3	6	0	.043	.185	.043
Gus Mancuso†	C3	R	36	5	13	0	1	0	0	0	1	0	0	0	.077	.077	.077
Sam Narron	C2	R	28	10	10	0	4	0	0	0	1	0	0	0	.400	.400	.400
Estel Crabtree		L	38	10	9	1	3	2	0	0	2	1	3	0	.333	.400	.556
Jeff Cross	SS1	R	23	1	4	0	1	0	0	0	1	0	0	0	.250	.250	.250

Pitcher	T	Age	G	GS	CG	ShO	IP	H	HR	BB	SO	W-L	Sv	ERA
Mort Cooper	R	29	37	35	22	10	278.2	207	9	68	152	22-7	0	1.78
Johnny Beazley	R	24	43	23	13	3	215.1	181	4	73	91	21-6	3	2.13
Max Lanier	L	26	34	20	8	2	161.0	137	4	60	93	13-8	2	2.96
Harry Gumbert	R	32	38	19	5	0	163.0	156	3	59	52	9-5	5	3.26
Ernie White	L	25	26	19	7	1	128.1	113	11	41	67	7-5	2	2.52
Lon Warneke†	R	33	12	12	5	0	82.0	76	8	15	31	6-4	0	3.29
Murry Dickson	R	25	36	7	2	0	120.2	91	1	61	66	6-3	2	2.91
Howie Krist	R	26	34	8	3	0	118.1	103	2	43	47	13-3	1	2.51
Howie Pollet	L	21	27	13	5	2	109.1	102	7	39	42	7-5	0	2.88
Whitey Moore†	R	30	9	0	0	0	12.1	10	0	11	1	0-1	0	4.38
Bill Lohrman†	R	29	5	0	0	0	12.2	11	0	2	6	1-1	0	1.42
Bill Beckmann†	R	34	2	0	0	0	7.0	4	0	1	3	1-0	0	0.00
Clyde Shoun†	L	30	2	0	0	0	1.2	1	0	0	0	0-0	0	0.00

1942 Brooklyn Dodgers 2nd NL 104-50 .675 2.0 GB

Leo Durocher

Player	Gm by Position	B	Age	G	AB	R	H	2B	3B	HR	RBI	BB	SO	SB	Avg	OBP	Slg
Mickey Owen	C133	R	26	133	421	53	109	16	3	0	44	44	17	10	.259	.330	.311
Dolph Camilli	1B150	L	35	150	524	89	132	23	7	26	109	97	85	10	.252	.372	.471
Billy Herman	2B153,1B3	R	32	155	571	76	146	34	2	2	65	72	52	6	.256	.339	.333
Arky Vaughan	3B119,SS5,2B1	L	30	128	495	82	137	18	4	2	49	51	17	8	.277	.348	.341
Pee Wee Reese	SS151	R	23	151	564	87	144	24	5	3	53	82	55	15	.255	.350	.332
Joe Medwick	OF140	R	30	142	553	69	166	37	4	4	96	32	25	2	.300	.338	.403
Pete Reiser	OF125	L	23	125	480	89	149	33	5	10	64	48	45	20	.310	.375	.463
Dixie Walker	OF110	L	31	118	393	57	114	28	1	6	54	47	15	1	.290	.367	.412
Johnny Rizzo	OF70	R	29	78	217	31	50	8	0	4	27	24	25	2	.230	.307	.323
Augie Galan	OF55,1B4,2B3	S	30	69	209	24	55	16	0	0	22	24	12	2	.263	.339	.340
Lew Riggs	3B46,1B1	L	32	70	180	20	50	5	0	3	22	13	9	0	.278	.333	.356
Billy Sullivan	C41	L	31	43	101	11	27	2	1	1	14	12	6	1	.267	.345	.337
Frenchy Bordagaray	OF17	R	32	48	58	11	14	2	0	0	5	3	3	2	.241	.279	.276
Alex Kampouris	2B9	R	29	10	21	3	5	2	1	0	3	0	4	0	.238	.238	.429
Babe Dahlgren†	1B10	R	30	17	19	2	1	0	0	0	0	4	5	0	.053	.217	.053
Cliff Dapper	C8	R	22	8	17	2	8	1	0	1	9	2	2	0	.471	.526	.706
Stan Rojek		R	23	1	0	1	0	0	0	0	0	0	0	0	—	—	—

Pitcher	T	Age	G	GS	CG	ShO	IP	H	HR	BB	SO	W-L	Sv	ERA
Kirby Higbe	R	27	38	32	13	2	221.2	180	17	106	115	16-11	0	3.25
Whit Wyatt	R	34	31	30	16	0	217.1	185	9	63	104	19-7	0	2.73
Curt Davis	R	38	32	26	13	5	206.0	179	10	51	60	15-6	2	2.36
Johnny Allen	R	36	27	15	5	1	118.0	106	11	39	50	10-6	3	3.20
Max Macon	L	26	14	8	4	1	84.0	67	3	33	27	5-3	1	1.93
Bobo Newsom†	R	34	6	5	2	1	32.0	28	1	14	21	2-2	0	3.38
F. Fitzsimmons	R	40	1	1	0	0	3.0	6	1	1	0	0-0	0	15.00
Hugh Casey	R	28	50	2	0	0	112.0	91	3	44	54	6-3	13	2.25
Larry French	L	34	38	14	8	4	147.2	127	1	36	62	15-4	0	1.83
Ed Head	R	24	36	15	5	1	136.2	118	11	47	78	10-6	4	3.56
Les Webber	R	27	19	3	1	0	51.2	46	2	22	23	3-2	1	2.96
Newt Kimball	R	27	14	1	0	0	29.1	27	0	19	8	2-0	0	3.68
Schoolboy Rowe†	R	32	9	2	0	0	30.1	36	2	12	6	1-0	0	5.34
Chet Kehn	R	20	3	1	0	0	7.2	8	2	4	3	0-0	0	7.04
Bob Chipman	L	23	2	0	0	0	1.1	1	0	2	1	0-0	0	0.00

1942 New York Giants 3rd NL 85-67 .559 20.0 GB

Mel Ott

Player	Gm by Position	B	Age	G	AB	R	H	2B	3B	HR	RBI	BB	SO	SB	Avg	OBP	Slg
Harry Danning	C116	R	30	119	408	45	114	20	3	1	34	34	29	3	.279	.335	.350
Johnny Mize	1B138	L	29	142	541	97	165	25	7	26	110	60	39	3	.305	.380	.521
Mickey Witek	2B147	R	26	148	553	72	144	19	6	5	48	36	20	2	.260	.306	.344
Bill Werber	3B93	R	34	98	370	51	76	9	2	1	13	51	22	9	.205	.308	.249
Billy Jurges	SS124	R	34	127	464	45	119	7	1	2	30	43	42	1	.256	.324	.289
Mel Ott	OF152	L	33	152	549	118	162	21	0	30	93	109	61	6	.295	.415	.497
Willard Marshall	OF107	L	21	116	401	41	103	9	2	11	59	26	20	1	.257	.307	.372
Babe Barna	OF89	L	27	104	331	39	85	8	7	6	58	38	48	3	.257	.333	.378
Dick Bartell	3B52,SS31	R	34	90	316	53	77	10	3	5	24	44	34	4	.244	.351	.342
Babe Young	OF54,1B18	L	26	101	287	37	80	17	1	11	59	34	22	1	.279	.365	.460
Buster Maynard	OF58,3B10,2B1	R	29	89	190	17	47	4	1	4	32	19	19	3	.247	.319	.342
Hank Leiber	OF41,P1	R	31	58	147	11	32	6	0	4	23	19	27	0	.218	.315	.340
Gus Mancuso†	C38	R	36	39	109	4	21	1	1	0	8	14	7	1	.193	.285	.220
Ray Berres	C12	R	34	12	32	0	6	0	0	0	1	2	3	0	.188	.235	.188
Connie Ryan	2B11	R	22	11	27	4	5	0	0	0	2	4	3	1	.185	.290	.185
Sid Gordon	3B6	R	24	6	19	4	6	0	1	0	2	3	2	0	.316	.409	.421
Howie Moss	OF3	R	22	7	14	0	0	0	0	0	0	0	4	0	.000	.000	.000
Charlie Fox	C3	R	20	3	7	1	3	0	0	0	1	1	2	0	.429	.500	.429

Pitcher	T	Age	G	GS	CG	ShO	IP	H	HR	BB	SO	W-L	Sv	ERA
Hal Schumacher	R	31	29	29	12	3	216.0	208	12	82	49	12-13	0	3.04
Bob Carpenter	R	24	28	25	12	2	185.2	192	13	51	53	11-10	0	3.15
Carl Hubbell	L	39	24	20	11	0	157.1	158	17	34	61	11-8	0	3.95
Bill Lohrman†	R	29	26	19	12	2	158.0	143	11	33	41	13-4	0	2.56
Cliff Melton	L	30	23	17	12	2	143.2	122	9	33	61	11-5	1	2.63
Dave Koslo	L	22	19	11	3	1	78.0	79	6	32	42	3-6	0	5.08
Tom Sunkel	L	29	19	11	3	0	63.2	65	5	41	29	3-6	0	4.81
Van Lingle Mungo	R	31	9	5	0	0	36.1	38	4	21	27	1-2	0	5.94
Bill Voiselle	R	23	2	1	0	0	9.0	6	1	4	5	0-1	0	2.00
Hank Leiber	R	31	1	1	1	0	9.0	9	0	5	5	0-1	0	6.00
Ace Adams	R	30	61	0	0	0	88.0	69	1	31	33	7-4	11	1.84
Harry Feldman	R	22	31	6	2	1	114.0	100	5	73	49	7-1	0	3.16
Bill McGee	R	32	31	8	2	1	104.0	95	9	46	40	6-3	1	2.94
Hugh East	R	22	4	1	0	0	7.1	15	1	7	2	0-2	0	9.82

1942 Pittsburgh Pirates 5th NL 66-81 .449 36.5 GB

Frank Frisch

Player	Gm by Position	B	Age	G	AB	R	H	2B	3B	HR	RBI	BB	SO	SB	Avg	OBP	Slg
Al Lopez	C99	R	33	103	289	17	74	8	2	1	26	34	17	0	.256	.338	.308
Elbie Fletcher	1B144	L	26	145	506	86	146	22	5	7	57	105	60	0	.289	.417	.393
Frankie Gustine	2B108,3B2,SS2*	R	22	115	388	34	89	11	4	2	35	29	27	5	.229	.286	.294
Bob Elliott	3B142,OF1	R	25	143	560	75	166	26	7	9	89	52	35	2	.296	.358	.416
Pete Coscarart	SS108,2B25	R	29	133	487	57	111	12	4	3	29	38	56	2	.228	.288	.287
Vince DiMaggio	OF138	R	29	143	496	57	118	22	3	15	75	52	87	10	.238	.311	.385
Jimmy Wasdell	OF97,1B7	L	28	122	409	44	106	11	2	3	38	47	22	1	.259	.337	.318
Johnny Barrett	OF94	L	26	111	332	56	82	11	6	0	26	48	42	10	.247	.347	.316
M. Van Robays	OF84	R	27	100	328	29	76	13	5	1	46	30	24	0	.232	.298	.311
Babe Phelps	C72	L	34	95	257	21	73	11	1	9	41	20	24	2	.284	.345	.440
Bud Stewart	OF34,3B10,2B6	L	26	82	183	21	40	8	4	0	20	22	16	2	.219	.302	.306
Alf Anderson	SS48	R	28	54	166	24	45	4	1	0	7	18	19	4	.271	.342	.307
Stu Martin	2B30,1B1,SS1	L	28	42	120	16	27	4	2	1	12	8	10	1	.225	.273	.317
Culley Rikard	OF16	L	28	38	52	6	10	2	1	0	5	7	8	0	.192	.288	.269
Frank Colman	OF8	L	24	10	37	2	5	0	0	1	2	2	2	0	.135	.179	.216
Johnny Wyrostek	OF8	L	22	9	35	0	4	0	1	0	3	3	2	0	.114	.184	.171
Huck Geary	SS8	L	25	9	22	3	5	0	0	0	2	2	3	0	.227	.292	.227
Bill Baker	C11	R	31	18	17	1	2	0	0	0	2	1	0	0	.118	.167	.118
Jim Russell	OF3	S	23	5	14	2	1	0	0	0	0	1	4	0	.071	.133	.071
Ed Leip		R	31	3	0	0	0	0	0	0	0	0	0	0	—	—	—

F. Gustine, 1 G at C

Pitcher	T	Age	G	GS	CG	ShO	IP	H	HR	BB	SO	W-L	Sv	ERA
Rip Sewell	R	35	40	33	18	5	248.0	259	12	72	69	17-15	2	3.41
Bob Klinger	R	34	37	19	8	1	152.2	151	6	45	58	8-11	1	3.24
Max Butcher	R	31	24	18	9	0	150.2	144	7	44	49	5-8	1	2.93
Ken Heintzelman	L	26	27	18	5	3	130.0	143	9	63	39	8-11	0	4.57
Hank Gornicki	R	31	25	14	7	2	112.0	89	2	40	48	5-6	2	2.57
Luke Hamlin	R	37	23	14	6	1	112.0	128	3	19	38	4-4	0	3.94
Jack Hallett	R	27	3	3	2	0	22.1	23	0	8	16	0-1	0	4.84
Bill Brandt	R	27	3	3	1	0	16.1	23	1	5	4	1-1	0	4.96
Dick Conger	R	21	2	1	0	0	8.1	9	0	5	3	0-0	0	2.16
Dutch Dietz	R	30	40	13	3	0	134.1	139	8	57	35	6-9	3	3.95
Lefty Wilkie	L	27	35	6	3	0	107.1	112	4	37	18	6-7	1	4.19
Johnny Lanning	R	31	34	8	2	1	119.1	125	7	26	31	6-8	1	3.32
Nick Strincevich	R	27	7	1	0	0	22.1	19	2	9	10	0-0	0	2.82
Ken Jungels	R	26	6	0	0	0	13.2	12	0	4	7	0-0	0	6.59
Harry Shuman	R	27	1	0	0	0	2.0	0	0	1	1	0-0	0	0.00

1942 Chicago Cubs 6th NL 68-86 .442 38.0 GB

Jimmie Wilson

Player	Gm by Position	B	Age	G	AB	R	H	2B	3B	HR	RBI	BB	SO	SB	Avg	OBP	Slg
Clyde McCullough	C97	R	25	109	337	39	95	22	1	5	31	25	47	7	.282	.331	.398
Phil Cavarretta	OF70,1B61	L	25	136	482	59	130	28	4	3	54	71	42	7	.270	.365	.363
Lou Stringer	2B113,3B1	R	25	121	406	45	96	10	5	9	41	31	55	3	.236	.292	.352
Stan Hack	3B139	L	32	140	553	91	166	36	3	6	39	94	40	9	.300	.402	.409
Lennie Merullo	SS143	R	25	143	515	53	132	23	3	2	37	35	45	14	.256	.310	.324
Bill Nicholson	OF151	L	27	152	588	83	173	22	11	21	78	76	80	8	.294	.382	.476
Lou Novikoff	OF120	R	26	128	483	48	145	25	5	7	64	24	28	3	.300	.337	.416
Dom Dallessandro	OF66	L	28	96	264	30	69	12	4	4	43	36	18	4	.261	.350	.383
Rip Russell	1B35,2B24,3B10*	R	27	102	302	32	73	9	0	8	41	17	21	0	.242	.282	.351
Jimmie Foxx†	1B52,C1	R	34	70	205	25	42	8	0	3	19	22	55	1	.205	.282	.288
Charlie Gilbert	OF47	L	22	74	179	18	33	6	3	0	7	25	24	1	.184	.284	.251
Bobby Sturgeon	2B32,SS29,3B2	R	22	63	162	8	40	7	1	0	7	4	13	2	.247	.269	.302
Chico Hernandez	C43	R	26	47	118	6	27	5	0	0	7	11	13	0	.229	.295	.271
Bob Scheffing	C32	R	28	44	102	7	20	3	0	2	12	7	11	2	.196	.248	.284
Peanuts Lowrey	OF19	R	23	27	58	4	11	0	0	1	4	4	4	0	.190	.242	.241
Babe Dahlgren†	1B14	R	30	17	56	4	12	1	0	0	6	4	2	0	.214	.267	.232
Cy Block	3B8,2B1	R	23	9	33	6	12	1	1	0	4	3	3	2	.364	.417	.455
Marv Rickert	OF6	L	21	8	26	5	7	0	0	0	1	1	5	0	.269	.296	.269
Whitey Platt	OF4	R	21	4	16	1	1	0	0	0	2	0	3	0	.063	.063	.063
Paul Gillespie	C4	L	21	5	16	3	4	0	0	2	4	1	2	0	.250	.294	.625
Marv Felderman	C2	R	26	3	6	0	1	0	0	0	0	1	4	0	.167	.286	.167

R. Russell, 3 G at OF

Pitcher	T	Age	G	GS	CG	ShO	IP	H	HR	BB	SO	W-L	Sv	ERA
Claude Passeau	R	33	35	34	24	3	278.1	284	13	74	89	19-14	0	2.68
Bill Lee	R	32	32	30	18	1	219.2	221	4	67	75	13-13	0	3.85
Vern Olsen	L	24	32	17	4	1	140.1	161	6	55	46	6-9	1	4.49
Lon Warneke†	R	33	15	12	8	1	99.0	97	2	21	28	5-7	2	2.27
Jake Mooty	R	29	19	10	1	0	84.1	89	11	44	28	2-5	1	4.70
Hank Wyse	R	24	4	4	1	1	28.0	33	1	6	8	2-1	0	1.93
Hi Bithorn	R	26	38	16	9	0	171.1	191	8	81	65	9-14	2	3.68
Bill Fleming	R	28	33	14	4	2	134.1	117	9	63	59	5-6	2	3.01
Tot Pressnell	R	35	27	0	0	0	39.1	40	5	5	9	1-1	4	5.49
Johnny Schmitz	L	21	23	10	1	0	86.2	70	3	45	51	3-7	2	3.43
Paul Erickson	R	26	18	7	1	0	63.0	70	4	41	26	1-6	0	5.43
Dick Errickson†	R	28	13	0	0	0	24.0	39	1	8	9	1-1	0	4.13
Ed Hanyzewski	R	21	6	1	0	0	19.0	17	2	8	6	1-1	0	3.79
Jesse Flores	R	27	4	0	0	0	5.1	5	1	2	6	0-1	0	3.38
Vallie Eaves	R	30	2	0	0	0	3.0	4	0	2	0	0-0	0	9.00
Joe Berry	R	37	2	0	0	0	2.0	7	0	2	1	0-0	0	18.00
Emil Kush	R	25	1	0	0	0	2.0	1	0	1	1	0-0	0	0.00
Bob Bowman	R	31	1	0	0	0	1.0	1	0	0	0	0-0	0	0.00

1942 Boston Braves 7th NL 59-89 .399 44.0 GB

Casey Stengel

Player	Gm by Position	B	Age	G	AB	R	H	2B	3B	HR	RBI	BB	SO	SB	Avg	OBP	Slg
Ernie Lombardi	C85	R	34	105	309	32	102	14	0	11	46	37	12	1	.330	.403	.482
Max West	1B85,OF50	L	25	134	452	54	115	22	0	16	56	68	59	4	.254	.354	.409
Sibby Sisti	2B124,OF1	R	21	129	407	50	86	11	4	4	35	45	55	5	.211	.296	.287
Nanny Fernandez	3B98,OF44	R	23	145	577	63	147	29	3	6	55	38	61	15	.255	.303	.347
Eddie Miller	SS142	R	25	142	534	47	130	28	2	6	47	22	42	11	.243	.279	.337
Tommy Holmes	OF140	L	25	141	558	56	155	24	4	4	41	64	10	2	.278	.353	.357
Paul Waner	OF94	L	39	114	333	43	86	17	1	1	39	62	20	2	.258	.376	.324
Chet Ross	OF57	R	25	76	220	20	43	7	2	5	19	16	37	0	.195	.250	.314
Clyde Kluttz	C57	R	24	72	210	21	56	10	1	1	31	7	13	0	.267	.294	.338
Buddy Gremp	1B62,3B1	R	22	72	207	12	45	11	0	3	19	13	21	1	.217	.267	.314
Johnny Cooney	OF54,1B23	R	41	74	198	23	41	6	0	0	7	23	5	2	.207	.290	.237
Frank Demaree	OF49	R	32	64	187	18	42	5	0	3	24	17	10	2	.225	.289	.299
Skippy Roberge	2B29,3B27,SS6	R	25	74	172	10	37	7	0	1	12	9	19	1	.215	.258	.273
Tony Cuccinello	3B20,2B14	R	34	40	104	8	21	3	0	1	8	9	11	1	.202	.265	.260
Phil Masi	C39,OF4	R	26	57	87	14	19	3	1	0	9	12	4	2	.218	.313	.276
Ducky Detweiler	3B12	R	23	12	44	3	14	2	1	0	5	2	7	0	.318	.348	.409
Whitey Wietelmann	SS11,2B1	S	23	13	34	4	7	2	0	0	0	4	5	0	.206	.289	.265
Frank McElyea	OF1	R	23	7	4	2	0	0	0	0	0	0	0	0	.000	.000	.000
Mike Sandlock	SS2	S	26	2	1	1	1	0	0	0	0	0	0	0	1.000	1.000	1.000

Pitcher	T	Age	G	GS	CG	ShO	IP	H	HR	BB	SO	W-L	Sv	ERA
Al Javery	R	24	42	37	19	5	261.0	251	8	78	85	12-16	0	3.03
Jim Tobin	R	29	37	33	28	1	287.2	283	20	96	71	12-21	0	3.97
Lou Tost	L	31	35	22	5	1	147.2	146	12	52	43	10-10	0	3.53
Tom Earley	R	25	27	18	6	0	112.2	120	10	55	28	6-11	1	4.71
Manny Salvo	R	29	25	14	6	1	130.2	129	7	41	25	7-8	0	3.03
Warren Spahn	L	21	4	2	1	0	15.2	25	0	11	7	0-0	0	5.74
Jim Hickey	R	21	1	1	0	0	1.1	4	1	2	0	0-1	0	20.25
Johnny Sain	R	24	40	3	0	0	97.0	79	8	63	68	4-7	6	3.90
Bill Donovan	L	25	31	10	2	1	89.1	97	2	32	23	3-6	0	3.43
Dick Errickson†	R	28	21	4	0	0	59.1	76	8	20	15	2-5	1	5.01
Johnny Hutchings	R	26	20	3	0	0	65.2	66	2	34	27	1-0	0	4.39
Lefty Wallace	L	20	19	3	1	0	49.1	39	3	24	20	1-3	0	3.83
Hank LaManna	R	22	5	0	0	0	6.2	5	1	3	2	0-1	0	5.40
Art Johnson	L	25	4	0	0	0	6.1	4	0	5	0	0-0	0	1.42
George Diehl	R	24	1	0	0	0	3.2	2	0	2	0	0-0	0	2.45

1942 Philadelphia Phillies 8th NL 42-109 .278 62.5 GB

Hans Lobert

Player	Gm by Position	B	Age	G	AB	R	H	2B	3B	HR	RBI	BB	SO	SB	Avg	OBP	Slg
Mickey Livingston	C78,1B6	R	27	89	239	20	49	6	1	2	22	25	20	0	.205	.283	.264
Nick Etten	1B135	L	28	139	459	37	121	21	3	8	41	67	26	3	.264	.357	.375
Al Glossop	2B118,3B1	S	26	121	454	33	102	15	1	4	40	29	35	3	.225	.273	.289
Pinky May	3B107	R	31	115	345	25	82	15	0	0	18	51	17	3	.238	.338	.281
Bobby Bragan	SS78,C22,2B4*	R	24	109	335	17	73	12	2	2	15	20	21	0	.218	.264	.284
Danny Litwhiler	OF151	R	25	151	591	59	160	25	9	9	56	27	42	2	.271	.310	.389
Ron Northey	OF109	L	22	127	402	31	101	13	2	5	31	28	33	2	.251	.300	.331
Ernie Koy†	OF78	R	32	91	258	21	63	9	3	4	26	14	50	0	.244	.283	.349
Danny Murtaugh	SS60,3B53,2B32	R	24	144	506	48	122	16	4	0	27	49	39	13	.241	.311	.289
Lloyd Waner	OF75	L	36	101	287	23	75	7	3	0	10	16	6	1	.261	.300	.307
Bennie Warren	C78,1B1	R	30	90	225	19	47	6	3	7	20	24	36	0	.209	.288	.356
Stan Benjamin	OF45,1B15	R	28	78	210	24	47	8	3	2	8	10	27	5	.224	.262	.319
Earl Naylor	OF34,P20	R	23	76	168	9	33	4	1	0	14	11	18	1	.196	.246	.232
Bill Burich	SS19,3B3	R	24	25	80	3	23	1	0	0	7	6	13	2	.288	.337	.300
Ed Freed	OF11	R	22	13	33	3	10	3	1	0	1	4	3	1	.303	.378	.455
Hal Marnie	2B11,SS7,3B1	R	23	24	30	3	5	0	0	0	0	1	2	1	.167	.194	.167
Ed Murphy	1B8	R	23	13	28	2	7	2	0	0	4	2	4	0	.250	.300	.321
Chuck Klein		L	37	14	14	0	1	0	0	0	0	0	2	0	.071	.071	.071
Bert Hodge	3B2	L	25	8	11	0	2	0	0	0	0	1	0	0	.182	.250	.182
Bill Peterman	C1	R	21	1	1	0	1	0	0	0	0	0	0	0	1.000	1.000	1.000
Benny Culp	C1	R	28	1	0	0	0	0	0	0	0	0	0	0	—	—	—

B. Bragan, 3 G at 3B

Pitcher	T	Age	G	GS	CG	ShO	IP	H	HR	BB	SO	W-L	Sv	ERA
Tommy Hughes	R	22	40	31	19	0	253.0	224	8	99	77	12-18	1	3.06
Rube Melton	R	25	42	29	10	1	209.1	180	7	114	107	9-20	4	3.70
Si Johnson	R	35	39	26	10	1	195.1	198	6	72	78	8-19	0	3.69
Johnny Podgajny	R	22	43	23	6	0	186.2	191	9	63	40	6-14	0	3.91
Frank Hoerst	L	24	33	22	5	0	150.2	162	11	78	52	4-16	1	5.20
Cy Blanton	R	33	6	3	0	0	22.1	30	3	13	15	0-4	0	5.64
Andy Lapihuska	R	19	3	2	0	0	20.2	17	0	13	8	0-2	0	5.23
Ike Pearson	R	25	35	7	0	0	85.1	87	5	50	21	1-6	0	4.54
Sam Nahem	R	26	35	2	0	0	74.2	72	2	40	38	1-3	0	4.94
Boom-Boom Beck	R	37	26	1	0	0	53.0	69	4	17	10	0-1	0	4.75
Earl Naylor	R	23	20	4	1	0	60.1	68	5	29	19	0-5	0	6.12
George Hennessey	R	34	5	1	0	0	17.0	11	1	10	2	1-1	0	2.65
Paul Masterson	L	26	4	0	0	0	8.1	10	1	5	3	0-0	0	6.48
Hilly Flitcraft	L	18	3	0	0	0	3.1	6	0	2	1	0-0	0	8.10
Gene Lambert	R	21	1	0	0	0	1.0	3	0	0	1	0-0	0	9.00

1942 Cincinnati Reds 17th NL 76-76 .500 29.0 GB

Bill McKechnie

Player	Gm by Position	B	Age	G	AB	R	H	2B	3B	HR	RBI	BB	SO	SB	Avg	OBP	Slg
Ray Lamanno	C104	R	22	111	371	40	98	12	2	12	43	31	54	0	.264	.324	.404
Frank McCormick	1B144	R	31	145	564	58	156	24	0	13	89	45	18	1	.277	.332	.388
Lonny Frey	2B140	L	31	141	523	66	139	23	6	2	39	87	38	9	.266	.373	.344
Bert Haas	3B146,1B6,OF2	R	28	154	585	59	140	21	6	6	54	59	54	6	.239	.310	.326
Eddie Joost	SS130,2B15	R	26	142	562	65	126	30	3	6	41	62	57	9	.224	.307	.320
Max Marshall	OF129	L	28	131	530	49	135	17	6	7	43	34	38	4	.255	.301	.349
Gee Walker	OF110	R	34	119	422	40	97	20	2	5	50	31	44	11	.230	.290	.322
Eric Tipton	OF58	R	27	63	207	22	46	5	5	4	18	25	14	1	.222	.309	.353
Ival Goodman	OF57	L	33	87	226	21	55	18	1	0	15	24	32	0	.243	.319	.332
Mike McCormick	OF38	R	25	40	135	18	32	2	3	1	11	13	7	0	.237	.304	.319
Rollie Hemsley†	C34	R	35	36	115	7	13	1	2	0	7	4	11	0	.113	.143	.157
Harry Craft	OF33	R	27	37	113	7	20	2	1	0	6	3	11	0	.177	.205	.212
Frankie Kelleher	OF30	R	25	38	110	13	20	3	1	3	12	16	20	0	.182	.286	.309
Bucky Walters	P34,OF1	R	33	40	99	13	24	6	1	2	13	3	13	0	.242	.265	.384
Damon Phillips	SS27	R	23	28	84	4	17	2	0	0	6	7	5	0	.202	.264	.226
Dick West	C17,OF6	R	26	33	79	9	14	3	0	1	8	5	13	1	.177	.226	.253
Clyde Vollmer	OF11	R	20	12	43	2	4	0	0	1	4	1	5	0	.093	.114	.163
Al Lakeman	C17	R	23	20	38	0	6	1	0	0	2	3	10	0	.158	.238	.184
Joe Abreu	3B6,2B2	R	29	9	28	4	6	1	0	1	3	4	4	0	.214	.313	.357
Hank Sauer	1B4	R	25	7	20	4	5	0	0	2	4	2	2	0	.250	.318	.550
Jim Gleeson	OF5	S	30	9	20	3	4	0	0	0	2	2	2	0	.200	.304	.200
Chuck Aleno	3B2,2B1	R	25	7	14	1	2	1	0	0	0	3	3	0	.143	.294	.214
Bobby Mattick	SS3	R	26	6	10	0	2	1	0	0	0	0	1	0	.200	.200	.300
Frank Secory	OF2	R	29	2	5	1	0	0	0	0	1	3	2	0	.000	.375	.000
Ernie Koy†		R	32	3	2	0	0	0	0	0	0	0	2	0	.000	.000	.000

Pitcher	T	Age	G	GS	CG	ShO	IP	H	HR	BB	SO	W-L	Sv	ERA
Ray Starr	R	36	37	33	17	4	276.2	228	10	106	83	15-13	0	2.67
J. Vander Meer	L	27	33	33	21	4	244.0	188	6	102	186	18-12	0	2.43
Bucky Walters	R	33	34	32	21	2	253.2	223	8	73	109	15-14	0	2.66
Paul Derringer	R	35	29	27	13	1	208.2	203	4	49	68	10-11	0	3.06
Elmer Riddle	R	27	29	19	7	1	158.1	157	7	79	78	7-11	0	3.69
Joe Beggs	R	31	38	0	0	0	88.2	65	4	33	24	6-5	8	2.13
Clyde Shoun†	L	30	34	0	0	0	72.2	55	2	24	32	1-3	0	2.23
Junior Thompson	R	25	29	10	1	0	101.2	86	5	53	35	4-7	0	3.36
Jim Turner†	R	38	3	0	0	0	3.1	5	1	3	0	0-0	0	10.80
Ewell Blackwell	R	19	2	0	0	0	3.0	3	0	3	1	0-0	0	6.00
Whitey Moore†	R	30	1	0	0	0	1.0	0	0	1	0	0-0	0	0.00

»1943 New York Yankees 1st AL 98-56 .636 —

Joe McCarthy

Player	Gm by Position	B	Age	G	AB	R	H	2B	3B	HR	RBI	BB	SO	SB	Avg	OBP	Slg
Bill Dickey	C71	L	36	85	242	29	85	18	2	4	33	41	12	2	.351	.445	.492
Nick Etten	1B154	L	29	154	583	78	158	35	5	14	107	76	31	3	.271	.355	.420
Joe Gordon	2B152	R	28	152	543	82	135	28	5	17	69	98	75	4	.249	.365	.413
Bill Johnson	3B155	R	24	155	592	70	166	24	6	5	94	53	30	3	.280	.344	.367
Frankie Crosetti	SS90	R	32	95	348	36	81	8	1	2	20	36	47	4	.233	.317	.279
Charlie Keller	OF141	L	26	141	512	97	139	15	11	31	86	106	60	7	.271	.396	.525
Johnny Lindell	OF122	R	26	122	441	53	108	17	12	4	51	51	55	2	.245	.329	.365
Bud Metheny	OF91	L	28	103	360	51	94	18	2	9	36	39	34	2	.261	.333	.397
Roy Weatherly	OF68	L	28	77	280	37	74	8	3	7	28	18	9	4	.264	.311	.389
Snuffy Stirnweiss	SS68,2B4	R	24	83	274	34	60	8	4	1	25	47	37	11	.219	.333	.288
Tuck Stainback	OF61	R	31	71	231	31	60	11	2	0	10	7	16	3	.260	.285	.325
Ken Sears	C50	L	25	60	187	22	52	7	0	2	22	11	18	1	.278	.328	.348
Rollie Hemsley	C52	R	36	62	180	12	43	6	3	2	24	13	9	0	.239	.290	.339
Oscar Grimes	SS3,1B1	R	28	9	20	4	3	0	0	0	1	3	7	0	.150	.261	.150
Aaron Robinson		L	28	1	1	0	0	0	0	0	0	0	1	0	.000	.000	.000

Pitcher	T	Age	G	GS	CG	ShO	IP	H	HR	BB	SO	W-L	Sv	ERA
Spud Chandler	R	35	30	30	20	5	253.0	197	5	54	134	20-4	0	1.64
Butch Wensloff	R	27	29	27	18	1	223.1	179	7	70	105	13-11	1	2.54
Hank Borowy	R	27	29	27	14	3	217.1	195	11	72	113	14-9	0	2.82
Tiny Bonham	R	29	28	26	17	4	225.2	197	13	52	71	15-8	1	2.27
Atley Donald	R	32	22	15	2	0	119.1	134	10	38	57	6-4	0	4.60
Marius Russo	L	28	24	14	5	1	101.2	89	7	45	42	5-10	1	3.72
Bill Zuber	R	30	20	13	7	0	118.0	100	3	74	57	8-4	1	3.89
Johnny Murphy	R	34	37	0	0	0	68.0	44	2	30	31	12-4	8	2.51
Jim Turner	R	39	18	0	0	0	43.1	44	1	13	15	3-0	1	3.53
Tommy Byrne	L	23	11	2	0	0	31.2	28	1	35	22	2-1	0	6.54
Marv Breuer	R	29	5	1	0	0	14.0	22	0	6	6	0-1	0	8.36

1943 Washington Senators 2nd AL 84-69 .549 13.5 GB

Ossie Bluege

Player	Gm by Position	B	Age	G	AB	R	H	2B	3B	HR	RBI	BB	SO	SB	Avg	OBP	Slg
Jake Early	C122	L	28	126	423	37	109	23	3	5	60	53	43	5	.258	.346	.362
Mickey Vernon	1B143	L	25	145	553	89	148	29	8	7	70	67	55	24	.268	.357	.387
Jerry Priddy	2B134,SS15,3B1	R	23	149	560	68	152	31	3	4	62	67	76	5	.271	.350	.359
Ellis Clary†	3B68,2B3,SS1	R	26	73	254	36	65	19	1	0	19	44	31	8	.256	.370	.339
John Sullivan	SS133	R	22	134	456	49	95	12	2	1	55	57	59	6	.208	.298	.250
Stan Spence	OF148	L	28	149	570	72	152	23	10	12	88	84	39	8	.267	.366	.405
George Case	OF140	R	27	141	613	102	180	36	5	1	52	41	27	61	.294	.341	.374
Bob Johnson	OF88,3B19,1B10	R	36	117	438	65	116	22	8	7	63	64	50	11	.265	.362	.400
Gene Moore	OF57,1B1	L	33	92	254	41	68	14	3	2	39	19	29	0	.268	.321	.370
Alex Kampouris†	3B33,2B10,OF1	R	30	51	145	24	30	4	0	2	13	30	25	7	.207	.361	.276
Tony Giuliani	C49	R	30	49	133	5	30	4	1	0	20	12	14	0	.226	.290	.271
Jake Powell	OF33	R	34	37	132	14	35	10	2	0	20	5	13	3	.265	.297	.371
Sherry Robertson	3B27,SS1	L	24	59	120	22	26	4	1	3	14	17	19	0	.217	.319	.342
George Myatt	2B11,3B2,SS2	L	29	42	53	11	13	3	0	0	3	13	7	3	.245	.394	.302
Harlond Clift†	3B8	R	30	8	30	4	9	0	0	0	4	5	3	0	.300	.417	.300
Red Roberts	SS6,3B1	R	24	9	23	1	6	1	0	1	3	4	2	0	.261	.370	.435
Red Marion	OF4	R	29	14	17	2	3	0	0	0	1	3	1	0	.176	.300	.176
Ed Butka	1B3	R	27	3	9	0	3	1	0	0	1	0	3	0	.333	.333	.444
Roberto Ortiz	OF1	R	28	1	4	0	1	0	0	0	0	0	0	0	.250	.250	.250
Tom Padden†	C2	R	34	3	3	1	0	0	0	0	0	1	1	0	.000	.250	.000
Red Barbary		R	23	1	1	0	0	0	0	0	0	0	0	0	.000	.000	.000

Pitcher	T	Age	G	GS	CG	ShO	IP	H	HR	BB	SO	W-L	Sv	ERA
Early Wynn	R	23	37	33	12	3	256.2	232	15	83	89	18-12	0	2.91
Dutch Leonard	R	34	31	30	15	2	219.2	218	9	46	51	11-13	1	3.28
Milo Candini	R	25	28	21	8	3	166.0	144	3	65	67	11-7	1	2.49
Ewald Pyle	L	32	18	11	2	1	72.2	70	0	45	25	4-8	1	4.09
Johnny Niggeling†	R	39	6	6	5	3	51.0	27	0	17	24	4-2	0	0.88
Bobo Newsom†	R	35	6	6	2	0	40.0	38	1	21	11	3-3	0	3.83
Bill LeFebvre	L	27	6	3	1	0	32.1	33	3	16	10	2-0	0	4.45
Lefty Gomez	L	34	1	1	0	0	4.2	4	0	5	0	0-1	0	5.79
Alex Carrasquel	R	30	39	13	4	1	144.1	160	3	54	48	11-7	5	3.68
Mickey Haefner	L	30	36	13	8	1	165.1	126	4	60	65	11-5	6	2.29
Jim Mertz	R	26	33	10	2	0	116.2	109	7	58	53	5-7	3	4.63
Ray Scarborough	R	25	24	6	2	0	86.0	93	2	46	43	4-4	3	2.83
Dewey Adkins	R	25	7	0	0	0	10.1	9	0	5	1	0-0	0	2.61
Owen Scheetz	R	29	6	0	0	0	9.0	16	0	4	5	0-0	1	7.00
Lew Carpenter	R	29	4	0	0	0	3.1	1	0	4	1	0-0	0	0.00
Ox Miller†	R	28	3	0	0	0	6.0	10	1	5	1	0-0	0	10.50
Vern Curtis	R	23	2	0	0	0	4.0	3	0	6	1	0-0	0	6.75

1943 Cleveland Indians 3rd AL 82-71 .536 15.5 GB

Lou Boudreau

Player	Gm by Position	B	Age	G	AB	R	H	2B	3B	HR	RBI	BB	SO	SB	Avg	OBP	Slg
Buddy Rosar	C114	R	28	115	382	53	108	17	1	1	41	33	12	0	.283	.340	.340
Mike Rocco	1B108	L	27	108	405	43	97	14	4	5	46	51	40	1	.240	.328	.331
Ray Mack	2B153	R	26	153	545	56	120	25	2	7	62	47	61	8	.220	.285	.312
Ken Keltner	3B107	R	26	110	427	47	111	31	3	4	39	36	20	2	.260	.317	.375
Lou Boudreau	SS152,C1	R	25	152	539	69	154	32	7	3	67	90	31	4	.286	.388	.388
Oris Hockett	OF139	L	33	141	601	70	166	33	4	2	51	45	45	13	.276	.331	.354
Roy Cullenbine	OF121,1B13	S	29	138	488	66	141	24	4	8	56	96	58	3	.289	.407	.404
Jeff Heath	OF111	L	28	118	424	58	116	22	6	18	79	63	58	5	.274	.369	.481
Hank Edwards	OF74	L	24	92	297	38	82	18	6	3	28	30	34	4	.276	.343	.407
Rusty Peters	3B46,SS14,2B6*	R	28	79	215	22	47	6	2	1	19	18	29	1	.219	.282	.279
Gene Desautels	C66	R	36	68	185	14	38	6	1	0	19	11	16	2	.205	.250	.249
Otto Denning	1B34	R	30	37	129	8	31	6	0	0	13	5	1	3	.240	.269	.287
Jim Bagby Jr.	P36,SS1	R	26	41	112	7	30	1	1	0	11	1	10	1	.268	.274	.295
Pat Seerey	OF16	R	20	26	72	8	16	3	0	1	5	4	19	0	.222	.263	.306
Gene Woodling	OF6	L	20	8	25	5	8	2	1	1	5	1	3	0	.320	.346	.600
Jimmy Grant†	3B5	L	24	15	22	3	3	2	0	0	1	4	7	0	.136	.269	.227
Eddie Turchin	3B4,SS2	R	26	11	13	4	3	0	0	0	1	3	1	0	.231	.375	.231
Frank Doljack	OF2	R	35	3	7	0	0	0	0	0	0	1	2	0	.000	.125	.000
Jim McDonnell	C1	L	20	2	1	1	0	0	0	0	0	2	1	0	.000	.667	.000
George Susce	C3	R	34	3	1	0	0	0	0	0	0	0	0	0	.000	.000	.000

R. Peters, 2 G at OF

Pitcher	T	Age	G	GS	CG	ShO	IP	H	HR	BB	SO	W-L	Sv	ERA
Jim Bagby Jr.	R	26	36	33	16	3	273.0	248	15	80	70	17-14	1	3.10
Al Smith	L	35	29	27	14	3	208.1	186	7	72	72	17-7	1	2.55
Allie Reynolds	R	28	34	21	11	3	198.2	140	3	109	151	11-12	3	2.99
Mel Harder	R	33	19	18	6	1	135.1	126	7	61	40	8-7	0	3.06
Vern Kennedy	R	36	28	17	8	1	146.2	130	4	59	63	10-7	0	2.45
Chubby Dean	L	26	17	9	3	0	76.0	83	1	34	29	5-5	0	4.50
Ed Klieman	R	25	1	1	1	0	9.0	8	0	5	2	0-1	0	1.00
Joe Heving	R	42	30	1	0	0	72.0	58	1	34	34	1-1	9	2.75
Mike Naymick	R	25	29	4	0	0	62.2	32	3	47	41	4-4	2	2.30
Pete Center	R	31	24	1	0	0	42.1	29	3	18	10	1-2	1	2.76
Jack Salveson	R	29	23	11	4	3	86.0	87	5	26	24	5-3	3	3.35
Ray Poat	R	25	17	4	1	0	45.0	44	3	20	31	2-5	0	4.40
Al Milnar†	L	29	16	6	0	0	39.0	51	0	35	12	1-3	0	8.08
Paul Calvert	R	25	5	0	0	0	8.1	6	0	6	2	0-0	0	4.32
Steve Gromek	R	23	3	0	0	0	4.0	6	0	0	4	0-0	0	9.00

1943 Chicago White Sox 4th AL 82-72 .532 16.0 GB

Jimmy Dykes

Player	Gm by Position	B	Age	G	AB	R	H	2B	3B	HR	RBI	BB	SO	SB	Avg	OBP	Slg
Mike Tresh	C85	R	29	86	279	20	60	3	0	0	20	37	20	2	.215	.307	.226
Joe Kuhel	1B153	L	37	153	531	55	113	21	1	5	46	76	45	14	.213	.319	.284
Don Kolloway	2B85	R	24	85	348	29	75	14	4	1	33	9	30	11	.216	.235	.287
Ralph Hodgin	3B56,OF42	L	27	117	407	52	128	22	8	1	50	20	24	3	.314	.356	.415
Luke Appling	SS155	R	36	155	585	63	192	33	2	3	80	90	29	27	.328	.419	.407
Wally Moses	OF148	L	32	150	599	82	147	22	12	3	48	55	47	56	.245	.310	.337
Thurman Tucker	OF132	L	25	139	528	81	124	15	6	3	39	79	72	29	.235	.336	.303
Guy Curtright	OF128	R	30	138	488	67	142	20	7	3	48	69	60	13	.291	.382	.379
Skeeter Webb	2B54	R	33	58	213	15	50	5	2	0	22	6	19	5	.235	.256	.277
Jimmy Grant†	3B51	L	24	58	197	23	51	9	2	4	22	18	34	4	.259	.321	.386
Tom Turner	C49	R	26	51	154	16	37	7	1	2	11	13	21	1	.240	.299	.338
Dick Culler	3B26,2B19,SS3	R	28	53	148	9	32	5	1	0	11	16	11	4	.216	.297	.264
Tony Cuccinello†	3B30	R	35	34	103	5	28	5	0	2	11	13	13	3	.272	.353	.379
Vince Castino	C30	R	25	33	101	14	23	1	0	2	16	12	11	0	.228	.310	.297
Moose Solters	OF21	R	37	42	97	6	15	0	0	1	8	7	5	0	.155	.212	.186
Don Hanski	1B5,P1	L	27	9	21	1	5	1	0	0	2	0	5	0	.238	.238	.286
Cass Michaels	3B2	R	17	2	7	0	0	0	0	0	0	0	0	0	.000	.000	.000
Frank Kalin		R	25	4	4	0	0	0	0	0	0	0	0	0	.000	.000	.000

Pitcher	T	Age	G	GS	CG	ShO	IP	H	HR	BB	SO	W-L	Sv	ERA
Johnny Humphries	R	28	28	27	8	2	188.0	198	7	54	51	11-11	1	3.30
Bill Dietrich	R	33	26	26	12	2	186.2	180	4	53	52	12-10	0	2.80
Orval Grove	R	23	32	25	18	3	216.1	192	9	72	76	15-9	2	2.75
Eddie Smith	L	29	25	25	14	2	187.2	197	2	76	66	11-11	0	3.69
Buck Ross	R	28	21	21	7	1	149.1	140	6	56	41	11-7	0	3.19
Thornton Lee	L	36	19	19	7	1	127.0	129	8	50	35	5-9	0	4.18
Gordon Maltzberger	R	30	37	0	0	0	98.2	86	8	24	48	7-4	14	2.46
Joe Haynes	R	25	35	2	1	0	109.1	114	2	32	37	7-2	3	2.96
Jake Wade	L	31	21	9	3	1	83.2	66	3	54	41	3-7	0	3.01
Bill Swift	R	35	18	1	0	0	51.1	48	5	27	28	0-2	0	4.21
Don Hanski	L	27	1	0	0	0	1.0	1	0	1	0	0-0	0	0.00
Floyd Speer	R	30	1	0	0	0	1.0	1	0	2	1	0-0	0	9.00

1943 Detroit Tigers 5th AL 78-76 .506 20.0 GB

Steve O'Neill

Player	Gm by Position	B	Age	G	AB	R	H	2B	3B	HR	RBI	BB	SO	SB	Avg	OBP	Slg
Paul Richards	C100	R	34	100	313	32	69	7	1	5	33	38	35	1	.220	.307	.297
Rudy York	1B155	R	29	155	571	90	155	22	11	34	118	84	88	5	.271	.366	.527
Jimmy Bloodworth	2B129	R	25	129	474	41	114	23	4	6	52	29	59	4	.241	.289	.344
Mike Higgins	3B138	R	34	138	523	62	145	20	1	10	84	57	31	2	.277	.349	.377
Joe Hoover	SS144	R	28	144	575	78	140	15	8	4	38	36	101	6	.243	.289	.318
Dick Wakefield	OF155	L	22	155	633	91	200	38	8	7	79	62	60	4	.316	.377	.434
Doc Cramer	OF138	L	37	140	606	79	182	18	4	1	43	31	13	4	.300	.335	.348
Ned Harris	OF96	L	26	114	354	43	90	14	3	6	32	47	29	6	.254	.343	.362
Don Ross	OF38,SS18,2B7*	R	28	89	247	19	66	13	0	0	18	20	3	2	.267	.325	.320
Joe Wood	2B22,3B18	R	23	60	164	22	53	4	4	1	17	6	13	2	.323	.347	.415
Rip Radcliff	OF19,1B1	L	37	70	115	3	30	4	0	0	10	13	3	1	.261	.341	.296
Dixie Parsons	C40	R	27	40	106	2	15	3	0	0	4	6	16	0	.142	.188	.170
Al Unser	C37	R	30	38	101	14	25	5	0	0	4	15	15	0	.248	.350	.297
Jimmy Outlaw	OF16	R	30	20	67	8	18	1	0	1	6	8	4	0	.269	.347	.328
Charlie Metro	OF14	R	24	44	40	12	8	0	0	0	2	3	6	1	.200	.256	.200
John McHale		L	21	4	3	0	0	0	0	0	0	1	1	0	.000	.250	.000

D. Ross, 1 G at 3B

Pitcher	T	Age	G	GS	CG	ShO	IP	H	HR	BB	SO	W-L	Sv	ERA
Dizzy Trout	R	28	44	30	18	5	246.2	204	6	101	111	20-12	6	2.48
Virgil Trucks	R	26	33	25	10	2	202.2	170	11	52	118	16-10	2	2.84
Hal Newhouser	L	22	37	25	10	1	195.2	163	3	111	144	8-17	1	3.04
Hal White	R	24	32	24	7	2	177.2	150	6	71	58	7-12	2	3.39
Tommy Bridges	R	36	25	22	11	3	191.2	159	9	61	124	12-7	0	2.39
Stubby Overmire	L	24	29	18	8	3	147.0	135	5	38	48	7-6	1	3.18
Rufe Gentry	R	25	4	4	2	0	29.1	30	2	12	8	1-3	0	3.68
Johnny Gorsica	R	28	35	4	1	0	96.1	88	3	40	45	4-5	5	3.36
Roy Henshaw	L	31	26	3	0	0	71.1	75	2	33	33	0-2	2	3.79
Prince Oana	R	35	10	0	0	0	34.0	34	4	19	15	3-2	0	4.50
Joe Orrell	R	25	10	0	0	0	19.1	18	0	11	2	0-0	1	3.72

1943 St. Louis Browns 6th AL 72-80 .474 25.0 GB

Luke Sewell

Player	Gm by Position	B	Age	G	AB	R	H	2B	3B	HR	RBI	BB	SO	SB	Avg	OBP	Slg
Frankie Hayes	C76,1B1	R	28	88	250	16	47	7	0	5	30	37	36	1	.188	.295	.276
George McQuinn	1B122	L	33	125	449	53	109	19	2	12	74	56	65	4	.243	.327	.374
Don Gutteridge	2B132	R	31	132	538	77	147	35	6	1	36	50	46	10	.273	.335	.366
Harlond Clift†	3B104	R	30	105	379	43	88	11	3	3	25	54	37	5	.232	.329	.301
Vern Stephens	SS123,OF11	R	22	137	512	75	148	27	3	22	91	54	73	3	.289	.357	.482
Chet Laabs	OF150	R	31	151	580	83	145	27	7	17	85	73	105	5	.250	.338	.409
Milt Byrnes	OF114	L	26	129	429	58	120	28	7	4	50	54	49	1	.280	.362	.406
Mike Chartak	OF77,1B18	L	27	108	344	38	88	16	2	10	37	39	55	1	.256	.333	.401
Mark Christman	3B37,SS24,1B20*	R	29	98	336	31	91	11	5	2	35	19	19	0	.271	.318	.351
Al Zarilla	OF60	L	24	70	228	27	58	7	1	2	17	17	20	1	.254	.309	.320
Rick Ferrell	C70	R	37	74	209	12	50	7	0	0	20	34	14	0	.239	.348	.273
Mike Kreevich	OF51	R	35	60	161	24	41	6	0	0	10	26	13	4	.255	.358	.292
Joe Schultz	C26	L	24	46	92	6	22	5	0	0	8	9	8	0	.239	.307	.293
Ellis Clary†	3B14	R	26	23	69	15	19	2	0	0	5	12	6	1	.275	.383	.304
Tony Criscola	OF13	L	27	29	52	4	8	0	0	0	1	8	7	0	.154	.267	.154
Floyd Baker	SS10,3B1	L	26	22	46	5	8	2	0	0	4	6	4	0	.174	.269	.217
Hal Epps	OF8	L	29	8	35	2	10	4	0	0	1	3	4	1	.286	.342	.400
Don Heffner†	2B13,1B1	R	32	18	33	2	4	1	0	0	2	2	2	0	.121	.171	.152
Hank Schmulbach		L	18	1	0	1	0	0	0	0	0	0	0	0	—	—	—

M. Christman, 14 G at 2B

Pitcher	T	Age	G	GS	CG	ShO	IP	H	HR	BB	SO	W-L	Sv	ERA
Steve Sundra	R	33	32	29	13	3	208.0	212	10	66	44	15-11	0	3.25
Denny Galehouse	R	31	31	28	14	2	224.0	217	8	74	114	11-11	1	2.77
Bob Muncrief	R	27	35	27	12	3	205.0	211	13	48	80	13-12	1	2.81
Al Hollingsworth	L	35	35	20	9	1	154.0	169	7	51	63	6-13	3	4.21
Johnny Niggeling†	R	39	20	20	7	0	150.1	122	7	57	73	6-8	0	3.17
Bobo Newsom†	R	35	10	9	0	0	52.1	69	7	35	37	1-6	0	7.39
Al Milnar†	L	29	3	2	1	0	14.2	23	0	9	7	1-2	0	5.52
Al LaMacchia	R	21	1	1	0	0	4.0	9	0	2	2	0-1	0	11.25
George Caster	R	35	35	0	0	0	76.1	69	4	41	43	6-8	8	2.12
Nels Potter	R	31	33	13	8	0	168.1	146	11	54	80	10-5	1	2.78
Charlie Fuchs†	R	29	13	0	0	0	35.2	42	4	11	9	0-0	0	4.04
Fritz Ostermueller†	L	35	11	3	0	0	28.2	36	1	13	4	0-2	0	5.02
Archie McKain	L	32	10	0	0	0	16.0	16	0	6	6	1-1	0	3.94
Paul Dean	R	29	3	1	0	0	13.1	16	0	3	1	0-0	0	3.38
Sid Peterson	R	25	3	0	0	0	10.0	15	0	3	0	2-0	0	2.70
Fred Sanford	R	23	3	0	0	0	9.1	7	0	4	2	0-0	0	1.93
Jack Kramer	R	25	3	0	0	0	9.0	11	0	8	4	0-0	0	8.00
Ox Miller†	R	28	2	0	0	0	6.0	7	2	3	3	0-0	0	12.00

1943 Boston Red Sox 7th AL 68-84 .447 29.0 GB

Joe Cronin

Player	Gm by Position	B	Age	G	AB	R	H	2B	3B	HR	RBI	BB	SO	SB	Avg	OBP	Slg
Roy Partee	C91	R	25	96	299	30	84	14	2	0	31	39	33	0	.281	.368	.341
Tony Lupien	1B153	L	26	154	608	65	155	21	9	4	47	54	23	16	.255	.317	.339
Bobby Doerr	2B155	R	25	155	604	78	163	32	3	16	75	62	59	8	.270	.339	.412
Jim Tabor	3B133,OF2	R	26	137	537	57	130	26	3	13	85	43	54	7	.242	.299	.374
Skeeter Newsome	SS98,3B15	R	32	114	449	48	119	21	2	1	22	21	21	5	.265	.301	.327
Pete Fox	OF125	R	34	127	489	54	141	24	4	2	44	34	40	22	.288	.337	.366
Leon Culberson	OF79	R	23	81	312	36	85	16	6	3	34	31	35	14	.272	.338	.391
Catfish Metkovich	OF76,1B2	L	22	78	321	34	79	14	4	5	27	19	38	1	.246	.294	.361
Eddie Lake	SS63	R	27	75	216	26	43	10	0	3	16	47	35	3	.199	.345	.287
Johnny Lazor	OF63	L	30	83	208	21	47	10	2	0	13	21	25	5	.226	.297	.293
Al Simmons	OF33	R	41	40	133	9	27	5	0	1	12	8	21	0	.203	.248	.263
Ford Garrison	OF32	R	27	36	129	13	36	5	1	1	11	5	14	0	.279	.306	.357
Dee Miles	OF25	L	34	45	121	9	26	2	2	0	10	3	3	0	.215	.234	.264
Johnny Peacock	C32	L	33	48	114	7	23	3	1	0	7	10	9	1	.202	.266	.246
Babe Barna†	OF29	L	28	30	112	19	19	4	1	2	10	15	24	2	.170	.268	.277
Tom McBride	OF24	R	28	26	96	11	23	3	1	0	7	7	3	2	.240	.291	.292
Bill Conroy	C38	R	28	39	89	13	16	5	0	1	6	18	19	0	.180	.336	.270
Joe Cronin	3B10	R	36	59	77	8	24	4	0	5	29	11	4	0	.312	.398	.558
Danny Doyle	C13	S	26	13	43	2	9	1	0	0	6	7	9	0	.209	.320	.233

Pitcher	T	Age	G	GS	CG	ShO	IP	H	HR	BB	SO	W-L	Sv	ERA
Tex Hughson	R	27	35	32	20	4	266.0	242	23	73	114	12-15	2	2.64
Yank Terry	R	32	30	22	7	0	163.2	147	8	63	63	7-9	1	3.52
Dick Newsome	R	33	25	22	8	2	154.1	166	8	68	40	8-13	0	4.49
Joe Dobson	R	26	25	20	9	3	164.1	144	4	57	63	7-11	0	3.12
Oscar Judd	L	35	23	20	8	1	155.1	131	2	69	53	11-6	0	2.90
Pinky Woods	R	28	23	12	2	0	100.2	109	6	55	32	5-6	1	4.92
Lou Lucier	R	25	16	9	3	0	74.0	94	1	33	23	3-4	0	3.89
Ken Chase†	R	29	7	5	0	0	27.1	36	0	30	9	0-4	0	6.91
Mace Brown	R	34	49	0	0	0	93.1	71	2	51	40	6-6	9	2.12
Mike Ryba	R	40	40	8	4	1	143.2	142	4	57	50	7-5	2	3.26
Emmett O'Neill	R	25	11	5	1	0	57.2	56	3	46	20	1-4	0	4.53
Andy Karl†	R	29	11	0	0	0	26.0	31	0	13	6	1-1	1	3.46

1943 Philadelphia Athletics 8th AL 49-105 .318 49.0 GB

Connie Mack

Player	Gm by Position	B	Age	G	AB	R	H	2B	3B	HR	RBI	BB	SO	SB	Avg	OBP	Slg
Hal Wagner	C99	L	27	111	289	22	69	17	1	1	26	36	17	3	.239	.327	.315
Dick Siebert	1B145	L	31	146	558	50	140	26	7	1	72	33	21	6	.251	.295	.328
Pete Suder	2B95,3B32,SS5	R	27	131	475	30	105	14	5	3	41	14	40	1	.221	.243	.291
Eddie Mayo	3B123	L	33	128	471	49	103	10	1	0	28	34	32	2	.219	.278	.244
Irv Hall	SS148,2B1,3B1	R	24	151	544	37	139	15	4	0	54	22	42	10	.256	.292	.298
Jo-Jo White	OF133	L	34	139	500	69	124	17	7	1	30	61	51	12	.248	.335	.316
Bobby Estalella	OF97	R	32	117	367	43	95	14	4	11	63	52	44	1	.259	.352	.409
Johnny Welaj	OF72	R	29	93	281	45	68	16	1	0	15	15	17	12	.242	.280	.306
Elmer Valo	OF63	L	22	77	249	31	55	6	2	3	18	35	13	2	.221	.319	.297
Bob Swift	C77	R	28	77	224	16	43	5	1	1	11	35	16	0	.192	.301	.237
Don Heffner†	2B47,1B1	R	32	52	178	17	37	6	0	0	8	18	12	3	.208	.284	.242
Jim Tyack	OF38	L	32	54	155	11	40	8	1	0	23	14	9	1	.258	.320	.323
Jimmy Ripple	OF31	L	33	32	126	8	30	3	1	0	15	7	7	0	.238	.284	.278
George Staller	OF20	L	27	21	85	14	23	1	3	3	12	5	6	1	.271	.326	.459
Bill Burgo	OF17	R	23	17	70	12	26	4	2	1	9	4	1	0	.371	.421	.529
Frank Skaff	1B18,3B3,SS1	R	29	32	64	8	18	2	1	1	8	6	11	0	.281	.343	.391
Joe Rullo	2B16	R	27	16	55	2	16	3	0	0	6	8	7	0	.291	.381	.345
Woody Wheaton	OF7	L	28	7	30	2	6	2	0	0	2	3	2	0	.200	.294	.267
Ed Busch	SS4	R	25	4	17	2	5	0	0	0	0	1	2	0	.294	.368	.294
Tony Parisse	C5	R	32	6	17	0	3	0	0	0	1	2	2	0	.176	.263	.176
Felix Mackiewicz	OF3	R	25	9	16	1	1	0	0	0	0	2	8	0	.063	.167	.063
George Kell	3B1	R	20	1	5	1	1	0	1	0	1	0	0	0	.200	.200	.600
Lew Flick	OF1	L	28	1	5	2	3	0	0	0	0	0	0	0	.600	.600	.600
Vern Benson		L	18	2	2	0	0	0	0	0	0	0	0	0	.000	.000	.000
Bruce Konopka		L	23	2	2	0	0	0	0	0	0	0	1	0	.000	.000	.000
Earle Brucker		R	42	1	1	0	0	0	0	0	0	0	0	0	.000	.000	.000

Pitcher	T	Age	G	GS	CG	ShO	IP	H	HR	BB	SO	W-L	Sv	ERA
Jesse Flores	R	28	31	27	13	0	231.1	208	13	70	113	12-14	0	3.11
Lum Harris	R	28	32	27	15	1	216.1	241	17	63	55	7-21	1	4.20
Roger Wolff	R	32	41	26	13	2	221.0	232	11	72	91	10-15	6	3.54
Don Black	R	26	33	26	12	1	208.0	193	8	110	65	6-16	1	4.20
Orie Arntzen	R	33	32	20	9	0	164.1	172	5	69	66	4-13	0	4.22
Russ Christopher	R	25	24	15	5	0	133.0	120	3	58	56	5-8	2	3.45
Charlie Bowles	R	26	2	2	2	0	18.0	17	0	4	6	1-1	0	3.00
Jim Mains	R	21	1	1	1	0	8.0	9	0	3	4	0-1	0	5.63
Norm Brown	R	24	1	1	0	0	7.0	5	0	0	1	0-0	0	0.00
Everett Fagan	R	25	18	2	0	0	37.1	41	4	14	9	2-6	3	6.27
Lou Ciola	R	20	12	3	2	0	43.2	48	2	22	7	1-3	0	5.56
Bert Kuczynski	R	23	6	1	0	0	24.2	36	2	9	8	0-1	0	4.01
Carl Scheib	R	16	6	0	0	0	18.2	24	4	3	3	0-1	0	4.34
Sam Lowry	R	23	5	0	0	0	18.0	18	1	9	3	0-0	0	5.00
Herman Besse	L	31	5	1	0	0	16.1	18	2	4	3	1-1	0	3.31
Ted Abernathy	L	21	5	2	1	0	14.2	24	0	13	10	0-3	0	12.89
John Burrows†	L	29	4	1	0	0	7.2	8	0	9	3	0-1	0	8.22
Tom Clyde	R	19	4	0	0	0	6.0	7	1	4	0	0-0	0	9.00

»1943 St. Louis Cardinals 1st NL 105-49 .682 —

Billy Southworth

Player	Gm by Position	B	Age	G	AB	R	H	2B	3B	HR	RBI	BB	SO	SB	Avg	OBP	Slg
Walker Cooper	C112	R	28	122	449	52	143	30	4	9	81	19	19	1	.318	.349	.463
Ray Sanders	1B141	L	26	144	478	69	134	21	5	11	73	77	33	1	.280	.381	.414
Lou Klein	2B126,SS51	R	24	154	627	91	180	28	14	7	62	50	70	9	.287	.342	.410
Whitey Kurowski	3B137,SS2	R	25	139	522	69	150	24	8	13	70	31	54	3	.287	.330	.439
Marty Marion	SS128	R	25	129	418	38	117	15	3	1	52	32	37	1	.280	.334	.337
Stan Musial	OF155	L	22	157	617	108	220	48	20	13	81	72	18	9	.357	.425	.562
Harry Walker	OF144,2B1	L	26	148	564	76	166	28	6	2	53	40	24	5	.294	.341	.376
Danny Litwhiler†	OF70	R	26	80	258	40	72	14	3	7	31	19	31	1	.279	.333	.438
Debs Garms	OF47,3B23,SS1	L	35	90	249	26	64	10	2	0	22	13	8	1	.257	.299	.313
Johnny Hopp	OF52,1B27	L	26	91	241	33	54	10	2	2	25	24	22	8	.224	.297	.307
Ken O'Dea	C56	L	30	71	203	15	57	11	2	3	25	19	25	0	.281	.345	.399
Jimmy Brown	2B19,3B9,SS6	S	33	34	110	6	20	4	2	0	8	6	1	0	.182	.224	.255
Frank Demaree	OF23	R	33	39	86	5	25	2	0	0	9	8	4	1	.291	.351	.314
George Fallon	2B36	R	28	36	78	6	18	1	0	0	5	2	9	0	.231	.259	.244
Coaker Triplett†	OF6	R	31	9	25	1	2	0	0	1	4	1	6	0	.080	.115	.200
Buster Adams†	OF6	R	28	8	11	1	1	1	0	0	1	4	4	0	.091	.333	.182
Sam Narron	C3	R	29	10	11	0	1	0	0	0	0	1	2	0	.091	.167	.091

Pitcher	T	Age	G	GS	CG	ShO	IP	H	HR	BB	SO	W-L	Sv	ERA
Mort Cooper	R	30	37	32	24	6	274.0	228	5	79	141	21-8	3	2.30
Max Lanier	L	27	32	25	14	2	213.1	195	3	75	123	15-7	3	1.90
Harry Gumbert	R	33	21	19	7	2	133.0	115	4	32	40	10-5	0	2.84
Howie Krist	R	27	34	17	9	2	164.1	141	5	62	57	11-5	3	2.90
Howie Pollet	L	22	16	14	12	5	118.1	83	2	32	61	8-4	0	1.75
Ernie White	L	26	14	10	5	1	78.2	78	4	33	28	5-5	0	3.78
Al Brazle	L	29	13	9	8	1	88.0	74	0	29	26	8-2	0	1.53
Bud Byerly	R	22	2	2	0	0	13.0	14	0	5	6	1-0	0	3.46
George Munger	R	24	32	9	5	0	93.1	101	2	42	45	9-5	2	3.95
Murry Dickson	R	26	31	7	2	0	115.2	114	4	49	44	8-2	0	3.58
Harry Brecheen	L	28	29	13	8	1	135.1	98	4	39	68	9-6	4	2.26

1943 Cincinnati Reds 2nd NL 87-67 .565 18.0 GB

Bill McKechnie

Player	Gm by Position	B	Age	G	AB	R	H	2B	3B	HR	RBI	BB	SO	SB	Avg	OBP	Slg
Ray Mueller	C140	R	31	141	427	50	111	19	4	8	52	56	42	1	.260	.347	.379
Frank McCormick	1B120	R	32	126	472	56	143	28	0	8	59	29	15	2	.303	.345	.413
Lonny Frey	2B144	L	32	144	586	78	154	20	8	2	43	76	56	7	.263	.347	.334
Steve Mesner	3B130	R	25	137	504	53	137	26	1	0	52	26	20	6	.272	.309	.327
Eddie Miller	SS154	R	26	154	576	49	129	26	4	2	71	33	43	8	.224	.271	.293
Eric Tipton	OF139	R	28	140	493	82	142	26	7	9	49	85	36	1	.288	.395	.424
Max Marshall	OF129	L	29	132	508	55	120	11	8	4	39	34	52	8	.236	.287	.313
Gee Walker	OF106	R	35	114	429	48	105	23	2	3	54	12	38	6	.245	.270	.329
Bert Haas	1B44,3B23,OF18	R	29	101	332	39	87	17	6	4	44	22	26	6	.262	.308	.386
Estel Crabtree	OF65	L	39	95	254	25	70	12	0	2	26	25	17	1	.276	.345	.346
Dain Clay	OF33	R	23	49	93	19	25	2	4	0	9	8	14	1	.269	.333	.376
Woody Williams	2B12,3B7,SS5	R	30	30	69	8	26	2	1	0	11	1	3	0	.377	.386	.435
Al Lakeman	C21	R	24	22	55	5	14	2	1	0	6	3	11	0	.255	.293	.327
Tony DePhillips	C35	R	30	35	20	0	2	1	0	0	2	1	5	0	.100	.143	.150
Mike McCormick	OF4	R	26	4	15	0	2	0	0	0	0	2	0	0	.133	.235	.133
Frankie Kelleher	OF1	R	26	9	10	1	0	0	0	0	0	2	0	0	.000	.167	.000
Chuck Aleno	OF2	R	26	7	10	0	3	0	0	0	1	2	1	0	.300	.417	.300
Charlie Brewster†	2B2	R	26	7	8	0	1	0	0	0	0	0	1	0	.125	.125	.125
Lonnie Goldstein	1B2	L	25	5	5	1	1	0	0	0	0	2	1	0	.200	.429	.200
Dick West		R	27	3	0	1	0	0	0	0	0	0	0	0	—	—	—

Pitcher	T	Age	G	GS	CG	ShO	IP	H	HR	BB	SO	W-L	Sv	ERA
J. Vander Meer	L	28	36	36	21	3	289.0	228	5	162	174	15-16	0	2.87
Bucky Walters	R	34	34	34	21	5	246.1	244	8	109	80	15-15	0	3.54
Elmer Riddle	R	28	36	33	19	5	260.1	235	6	107	69	21-11	3	2.66
Ray Starr	R	37	36	33	9	2	217.1	201	9	91	42	11-10	1	3.64
Clyde Shoun	L	31	45	5	2	0	147.0	131	5	46	61	14-5	7	3.06
Joe Beggs	R	32	39	4	4	2	115.1	121	0	25	28	7-6	6	2.34
Ed Heusser	R	34	26	10	2	1	91.0	97	4	23	28	4-3	0	3.46
Rocky Stone	R	24	13	0	0	0	25.0	23	0	8	11	0-1	0	4.32
Bob Malloy	R	25	6	0	0	0	10.0	14	1	8	4	0-0	0	6.30
Jack Niemes	L	23	3	0	0	0	3.0	5	0	2	1	0-0	0	6.00

1943 Brooklyn Dodgers 3rd NL 81-72 .529 23.5 GB

Leo Durocher

Player	Gm by Position	B	Age	G	AB	R	H	2B	3B	HR	RBI	BB	SO	SB	Avg	OBP	Slg
Mickey Owen	C100,3B3,SS1	R	27	106	365	31	95	11	2	0	54	25	15	4	.260	.309	.301
Dolph Camilli	1B95	L	36	95	353	56	87	15	6	6	43	65	48	2	.246	.365	.374
Billy Herman	2B117,3B37	R	33	153	585	76	193	41	2	2	100	66	26	4	.330	.398	.417
Arky Vaughan	SS99,3B55	L	31	149	610	112	186	39	6	5	66	60	13	20	.305	.370	.413
Al Glossop	SS33,2B24,3B17*	S	27	87	217	28	37	9	0	3	21	28	27	0	.171	.268	.253
Dixie Walker	OF136	L	32	138	540	83	163	32	6	5	71	49	24	3	.302	.363	.411
Augie Galan	OF124,1B13	S	31	139	495	83	142	26	3	9	67	103	39	6	.287	.412	.406
Luis Olmo	OF57	R	23	57	238	39	72	6	4	4	37	8	20	3	.303	.325	.412
Frenchy Bordagaray	OF53,3B25	R	33	89	268	47	81	18	2	0	19	30	15	6	.302	.379	.384
Paul Waner	OF57	L	40	82	225	29	70	16	0	1	26	35	9	0	.311	.406	.396
Bobby Bragan	C57,3B12	R	25	74	220	17	58	7	2	2	24	15	16	0	.264	.311	.341
Howie Schultz	1B45	R	20	45	182	20	49	12	0	1	34	6	24	3	.269	.300	.352
Joe Medwick†	OF42	R	31	48	173	13	47	10	0	0	25	10	8	1	.272	.315	.329
Dee Moore†	C15,3B9	R	29	37	79	8	20	3	0	0	12	11	8	1	.253	.344	.291
Gene Hermanski	OF17	L	23	18	60	6	18	2	1	0	12	11	7	1	.300	.417	.367
Max Macon	P25,1B3	L	27	45	55	7	9	0	0	0	6	0	1	1	.164	.164	.164
Red Barkley	SS18	R	29	20	51	6	16	3	0	0	7	4	7	1	.314	.364	.373
Alex Kampouris†	2B18	R	30	19	44	9	10	4	1	0	4	17	6	0	.227	.452	.364
Johnny Cooney	1B3,OF2	R	42	37	34	7	7	0	0	0	2	4	3	1	.206	.289	.206
Boyd Bartley	SS9	R	23	9	21	0	1	0	0	0	1	1	3	0	.048	.091	.048
Al Campanis	2B7	S	26	7	20	3	2	0	0	0	0	4	5	0	.100	.250	.100
Bill Hart	3B6,SS1	R	30	8	19	0	3	0	0	0	1	1	2	0	.158	.200	.158
Leo Durocher	SS6	R	37	6	18	1	4	0	0	0	1	1	2	0	.222	.263	.222
Carden Gillenwater	OF4	R	25	8	17	1	3	0	0	0	2	2	3	0	.176	.263	.176
Joe Orengo†	3B6	R	28	7	15	1	3	2	0	0	1	4	2	0	.200	.368	.333
Gil Hodges	3B1	R	19	1	2	0	0	0	0	0	0	1	2	1	.000	.333	.000
Pat Ankenman	SS1	R	30	1	2	1	1	0	0	0	0	0	0	0	.500	.500	.500
Hal Peck		L	26	1	1	0	0	0	0	0	0	0	0	0	.000	.000	.000

A. Glossop, 1 G at OF

Pitcher	T	Age	G	GS	CG	ShO	IP	H	HR	BB	SO	W-L	Sv	ERA
Kirby Higbe	R	28	35	27	8	1	185.0	189	4	95	108	13-10	0	3.70
Whit Wyatt	R	35	26	26	13	3	180.2	139	5	43	80	14-5	0	2.49
Curt Davis	R	39	31	21	8	2	164.1	182	8	39	47	10-13	3	3.78
Rube Melton	R	26	30	17	4	2	119.1	106	3	79	63	5-8	0	3.92
Bobo Newsom†	R	35	22	12	6	1	125.0	113	4	57	75	9-4	1	3.02
Rex Barney	R	18	9	8	1	0	45.1	36	4	41	23	2-2	0	6.35
F. Fitzsimmons	R	41	9	7	1	0	44.2	50	6	21	12	3-4	0	5.44
Hal Gregg	R	21	5	4	0	0	18.2	21	2	21	7	0-3	0	9.64
Les Webber	R	28	54	0	0	0	115.2	112	6	69	24	2-2	10	3.81
Ed Head	R	25	47	18	7	3	169.2	166	8	66	83	9-10	6	3.66
Max Macon	L	27	25	9	0	0	77.0	89	4	32	21	7-5	0	5.96
Johnny Allen†	R	37	17	1	0	0	38.0	42	3	25	15	5-1	1	4.26
Fritz Ostermueller†	L	35	7	1	0	0	27.1	21	0	12	15	1-1	0	3.29
Bill Lohrman†	R	30	6	2	2	0	27.2	29	2	10	5	0-2	0	3.58
Bill Sayles†	R	25	5	0	0	0	11.2	13	0	10	5	0-0	0	7.71
Newt Kimball†	R	28	5	0	0	0	11.0	9	0	5	2	1-1	1	1.64
Chris Haughey	R	17	1	0	0	0	7.0	5	0	10	0	0-1	0	3.86
Bob Chipman	L	24	1	0	0	0	1.2	2	0	2	0	0-0	0	0.00

690 Seasons: Team Rosters

1943 Pittsburgh Pirates 4th NL 80-74 .519 25.0 GB

Player	Gm by Position	B	Age	G	AB	R	H	2B	3B	HR	RBI	BB	SO	SB	Avg	OBP	Slg
Al Lopez	C116,3B1	R	34	118	372	40	98	9	4	1	39	44	25	2	.263	.341	.317
Elbie Fletcher	1B154	L	27	154	544	91	154	24	5	9	70	95	49	1	.283	.395	.395
Pete Coscarart	2B85,SS47,3B1	R	30	133	491	57	119	19	6	0	48	46	48	4	.242	.307	.305
Bob Elliott	3B151,2B2,SS1	R	26	156	581	82	183	30	12	7	101	56	24	4	.315	.376	.444
Frankie Gustine	SS68,2B40,1B1	R	23	112	414	40	120	21	3	0	43	32	36	12	.290	.341	.355
Vince DiMaggio	OF156,SS1	R	30	157	580	64	144	41	2	15	88	70	126	11	.248	.329	.403
Jim Russell	OF134,1B6	S	24	146	533	79	138	19	11	4	44	77	67	12	.259	.354	.358
Johnny Barrett	OF99	L	27	130	290	41	67	12	3	1	32	32	23	5	.231	.316	.303
M. Van Robays	OF60	R	28	69	236	32	68	17	7	1	35	18	19	0	.288	.344	.432
Tommy O'Brien	OF48,3B9	R	24	89	232	35	72	12	7	2	26	15	24	0	.310	.352	.448
Bill Baker	C56	R	32	63	172	12	47	6	3	1	26	22	6	3	.273	.365	.360
Al Rubeling	2B44,3B1	R	30	47	168	23	44	8	4	0	9	8	17	0	.262	.295	.357
Huck Geary	SS46	L	26	46	166	17	25	4	0	1	13	18	6	3	.151	.234	.193
Johnny Wyrostek	OF20,3B2,1B1*	L	23	51	79	7	12	3	0	0	1	3	15	0	.152	.183	.190
Frank Colman	OF11	L	25	32	59	9	16	2	2	0	4	8	7	0	.271	.358	.373
Tony Ordenana	SS1	R	24	1	4	0	2	0	0	0	3	0	0	0	.500	.500	.500
Hank Camelli	C1	R	28	1	3	1	0	0	0	0	0	1	0	0	.000	.250	.000
Jimmy Wasdell†		L	29	4	2	0	1	0	0	0	1	2	0	0	.500	.750	.500

J. Wyrostek, 1 G at 2B

Frank Frisch

Pitcher	T	Age	G	GS	CG	ShO	IP	H	HR	BB	SO	W-L	Sv	ERA
Rip Sewell	R	36	35	31	25	2	265.1	267	6	75	65	21-9	3	2.54
Bob Klinger	R	35	33	25	14	3	195.0	185	6	58	65	11-8	0	2.72
Wally Hebert	L	35	34	23	12	1	184.0	197	3	45	41	10-11	0	2.98
Max Butcher	R	32	33	21	10	2	193.2	191	4	57	45	10-8	1	2.60
Johnny Gee	L	27	15	10	2	0	82.0	89	5	27	18	4-4	0	4.28
Cookie Cuccurullo	L	25	1	1	0	0	7.0	10	0	3	3	0-1	0	6.43
Hank Gornicki	R	32	42	18	4	1	147.0	165	10	47	63	9-13	4	3.98
Xavier Rescigno	R	29	37	14	5	1	132.2	125	6	45	41	6-9	2	3.12
Bill Brandt	R	28	29	3	0	0	57.1	57	3	19	17	4-1	0	3.14
Johnny Podgajny†	R	23	15	5	0	0	34.1	37	1	13	7	0-4	0	4.72
Johnny Lanning	R	32	12	2	0	0	27.0	23	0	9	11	4-1	2	2.33
Harry Shuman	R	28	11	0	0	0	22.0	30	0	8	5	0-0	0	5.32
Jack Hallett	R	28	9	4	2	1	47.2	36	0	11	11	1-2	0	1.70
Dutch Dietz†	R	31	8	0	0	0	9.0	12	0	4	4	0-3	0	6.00

1943 Chicago Cubs 5th NL 74-79 .484 30.5 GB

Player	Gm by Position	B	Age	G	AB	R	H	2B	3B	HR	RBI	BB	SO	SB	Avg	OBP	Slg
Clyde McCullough	C81	R	26	87	266	20	63	5	2	2	23	24	33	6	.237	.302	.293
Phil Cavarretta	1B134,OF7	L	26	143	530	93	154	27	9	8	73	75	42	3	.291	.382	.421
Eddie Stanky	2B131,SS12,3B2	R	26	142	510	92	125	15	1	0	47	92	42	4	.245	.363	.278
Stan Hack	3B136	L	33	144	533	78	154	24	4	3	35	82	27	5	.289	.384	.366
Lennie Merullo	SS125	R	26	129	453	37	115	18	3	1	25	26	42	7	.254	.297	.313
Bill Nicholson	OF154	L	28	154	608	95	188	30	9	29	128	71	86	4	.309	.386	.531
Peanuts Lowrey	OF113,SS16,2B3	R	24	130	480	59	140	25	12	1	63	35	24	13	.292	.340	.400
Lou Novikoff	OF61	R	27	78	233	22	65	7	3	0	28	18	15	0	.279	.333	.335
Ival Goodman	OF61	L	34	80	225	31	72	10	5	3	45	24	20	4	.320	.390	.449
Dom Dallessandro	OF45	L	29	87	176	13	39	8	3	1	31	40	14	1	.222	.369	.318
Chico Hernandez	C41	R	27	43	126	10	34	4	0	0	9	9	9	0	.270	.324	.302
Stu Martin	2B22,3B8,1B2	L	29	64	118	13	26	4	0	0	5	15	10	1	.220	.308	.254
Mickey Livingston†	C31,1B4	R	28	36	111	11	29	5	1	4	16	12	8	1	.261	.333	.432
Heinz Becker	1B18	S	27	24	69	5	10	0	0	0	2	9	6	0	.145	.244	.145
Andy Pafko	OF13	R	22	13	58	7	22	3	0	0	10	2	5	1	.379	.400	.431
Eddie Sauer	OF13	R	24	14	55	3	15	3	0	0	9	3	6	1	.273	.322	.327
Bill Schuster	SS13	R	30	13	51	3	15	2	1	0	0	3	2	0	.294	.333	.373
Al Todd	C17	R	41	21	45	1	6	0	0	0	1	1	5	0	.133	.152	.133
Don Johnson	2B10	R	31	10	42	5	8	2	0	0	1	2	4	0	.190	.227	.238
Whitey Platt	OF14	R	22	20	41	2	7	3	0	0	2	1	7	0	.171	.190	.244
Pete Elko	3B9	R	25	9	30	1	4	0	0	0	0	4	5	0	.133	.235	.133
Johnny Ostrowski	OF5,3B4	R	25	10	29	2	6	0	1	0	3	3	8	0	.207	.303	.276
Charlie Gilbert	OF6	L	23	8	20	1	3	0	0	0	0	3	3	1	.150	.261	.150
Billy Holm	C7	R	30	7	15	0	1	0	0	0	0	2	4	0	.067	.176	.067
Mickey Kreitner	C3	R	20	3	8	0	3	0	0	0	2	1	2	0	.375	.444	.375

Jimmie Wilson

Pitcher	T	Age	G	GS	CG	ShO	IP	H	HR	BB	SO	W-L	Sv	ERA
Claude Passeau	R	34	35	31	18	1	257.0	245	10	66	93	15-12	1	2.91
Hi Bithorn	R	27	39	30	19	7	249.2	226	8	65	86	18-12	2	2.60
Paul Derringer	R	36	32	22	10	2	174.0	184	7	39	75	10-14	3	3.57
Bill Lee†	R	33	13	12	4	0	78.1	83	4	27	18	3-7	0	3.56
Walter Signer	R	32	4	2	1	0	25.0	24	3	4	5	2-1	0	2.88
Dale Alderson	R	25	4	2	0	0	14.0	21	2	3	4	0-1	0	6.43
Hank Wyse	R	25	38	15	8	2	156.0	160	4	34	45	9-7	5	2.94
Ed Hanyzewski	R	22	33	16	3	0	130.0	120	2	45	55	8-7	0	2.56
Ray Prim	L	36	29	5	0	0	60.0	67	2	14	27	4-3	1	2.55
John Burrows†	L	29	23	1	0	0	32.2	25	0	16	18	0-2	2	3.86
Lon Warneke	R	34	21	10	4	0	88.1	82	3	18	30	4-5	0	3.16
Dick Barrett†	R	36	15	4	0	0	45.0	52	2	28	20	0-4	0	4.80
Paul Erickson	R	27	15	4	0	0	42.2	47	4	22	24	1-3	0	6.12
Bill Fleming	R	29	11	0	0	0	32.1	40	2	12	12	0-1	0	6.40
Jake Mooty	R	30	2	0	0	0	1.0	2	0	1	1	0-0	0	0.00

1943 Boston Braves 6th NL 68-85 .444 36.5 GB

Player	Gm by Position	B	Age	G	AB	R	H	2B	3B	HR	RBI	BB	SO	SB	Avg	OBP	Slg
Phil Masi	C73	R	27	80	238	27	65	9	1	2	28	27	20	7	.273	.347	.345
Johnny McCarthy	1B78	L	33	78	313	32	95	24	6	2	33	10	19	1	.304	.327	.438
Connie Ryan	2B100,3B30	R	23	132	457	52	97	10	2	1	24	58	56	7	.212	.301	.249
Eddie Joost	3B67,2B60,SS1	R	27	124	421	34	78	16	3	2	20	68	80	5	.185	.299	.252
Whitey Wietelmann	SS153	S	24	153	534	33	115	14	1	0	39	46	40	9	.215	.281	.245
Tommy Holmes	OF152	L	26	152	629	75	170	33	10	5	41	58	20	7	.270	.334	.378
Chuck Workman	OF149,1B3,3B1	L	28	153	615	71	153	17	1	10	67	53	72	12	.249	.311	.328
Butch Nieman	OF93	L	25	101	335	39	84	15	8	7	46	39	39	4	.251	.331	.406
Chet Ross	OF73	R	26	94	285	27	62	12	2	7	32	26	67	1	.218	.285	.347
Kerby Farrell	1B69,P5	L	29	85	280	11	75	14	1	0	21	16	15	1	.268	.307	.325
Clyde Kluttz	C55	R	25	66	207	13	51	7	0	0	20	15	9	0	.246	.297	.280
Hugh Poland†	C38	L	30	44	141	5	27	7	0	0	13	4	11	0	.191	.214	.241
Joe Burns	3B34,OF4	R	27	52	135	12	28	3	0	1	5	8	25	2	.207	.262	.252
Jim Tobin	P33,1B1	R	30	46	107	8	30	4	0	2	12	6	16	0	.280	.319	.374
Heinie Heltzel	3B29	R	29	29	86	6	13	3	0	0	5	7	13	0	.151	.215	.186
Buck Etchison	1B6	L	28	10	19	2	6	3	0	0	2	2	2	0	.316	.381	.474
Bill Brubaker	3B5,1B3	R	32	13	19	3	8	3	0	0	1	2	2	0	.421	.476	.579
Tony Cuccinello†	3B4,2B2,SS1	R	35	13	19	0	0	0	0	0	2	3	1	0	.000	.136	.000
Connie Creeden		L	27	5	4	0	1	0	0	0	1	1	0	0	.250	.400	.250
Sam Gentile		L	26	8	4	1	1	1	0	0	0	1	0	0	.250	.400	.500
Ben Geraghty	2B1,3B1,SS1	R	30	8	1	2	0	0	0	0	0	0	0	0	.000	.000	.000

Bob Coleman (21-25)/Casey Stengel (47-60)

Pitcher	T	Age	G	GS	CG	ShO	IP	H	HR	BB	SO	W-L	Sv	ERA
Al Javery	R	25	41	35	19	5	303.0	288	13	99	134	17-16	0	3.21
Nate Andrews	R	29	36	34	23	3	283.2	253	11	75	80	14-20	0	2.57
Red Barrett	R	28	38	31	14	3	255.0	240	11	63	64	12-18	0	3.18
Jim Tobin	R	30	33	30	24	1	250.0	241	12	69	52	14-14	0	2.74
Manny Salvo†	R	30	21	14	5	1	98.2	99	6	31	26	5-7	0	3.47
Carl Lindquist	R	24	2	2	0	0	13.0	17	3	4	1	0-2	0	6.23
John Dagenhard	R	26	2	1	1	0	11.0	9	0	4	2	1-0	0	0.00
Dave Odom	R	25	22	3	1	0	54.2	54	3	30	17	0-3	2	5.27
Ben Cardoni	R	22	11	0	0	0	28.0	38	1	14	5	0-0	1	6.43
Danny MacFayden	R	38	10	1	0	0	21.1	31	1	9	5	2-1	0	5.91
Allyn Stout	R	38	9	0	0	0	9.1	17	1	4	3	1-0	1	6.75
George Jeffcoat	R	29	8	1	0	0	17.2	15	1	10	10	1-2	0	3.06
Bill Donovan	L	26	7	0	0	0	14.2	17	0	9	1	1-0	0	1.84
Kerby Farrell	L	29	5	0	0	0	23.0	24	1	9	4	0-1	0	4.30
Lou Tost	L	32	3	1	0	0	6.2	10	2	4	3	0-1	0	5.40
Ray Martin	R	18	2	0	0	0	3.1	3	0	1	1	0-0	0	8.10
George Diehl	R	25	1	0	0	0	4.0	4	0	3	1	0-0	0	4.50
Roy Talcott	R	23	1	0	0	0	0.2	1	0	2	0	0-0	0	27.00

1943 Philadelphia Phillies 7th NL 64-90 .416 41.0 GB

Player	Gm by Position	B	Age	G	AB	R	H	2B	3B	HR	RBI	BB	SO	SB	Avg	OBP	Slg
Mickey Livingston†	C84,1B2	R	28	84	265	25	66	9	2	3	18	19	18	1	.249	.304	.332
Jimmy Wasdell†	1B82,OF56	L	29	141	522	54	136	19	6	4	67	46	22	6	.261	.323	.343
Danny Murtaugh	2B113	R	25	113	451	65	123	17	4	1	35	57	23	4	.273	.357	.335
Pinky May	3B132	R	32	137	415	31	117	19	2	1	48	56	21	2	.282	.369	.345
Glen Stewart	SS77,2B18,1B8*	R	30	110	336	23	71	10	1	2	24	32	41	1	.211	.284	.265
Ron Northey	OF145	L	23	147	586	72	163	31	5	16	68	51	52	2	.278	.339	.430
Buster Adams†	OF107	R	28	111	418	48	107	14	7	4	38	39	67	2	.256	.319	.352
Coaker Triplett†	OF90	R	31	105	360	45	98	16	4	14	52	28	28	2	.272	.325	.456
Babe Dahlgren	1B73,3B35,SS25*	R	31	136	508	55	146	19	2	5	56	50	39	2	.287	.354	.362
Ray Hamrick	2B31,SS12	R	21	44	160	12	32	3	1	0	9	8	28	0	.200	.238	.231
Charlie Brewster†	SS46	R	26	49	159	13	35	2	0	0	12	10	19	1	.220	.275	.233
Danny Litwhiler†	OF34	R	26	36	139	23	36	6	0	5	17	11	14	1	.259	.313	.410
Earl Naylor	OF33	R	24	33	120	12	21	2	0	3	14	12	16	1	.175	.256	.267
Dee Moore†	C21,OF6,3B5*	R	29	37	113	13	27	4	1	1	8	15	8	0	.239	.328	.319
Bob Finley	C24	R	27	28	81	9	21	2	0	1	7	4	10	0	.259	.294	.321
Andy Seminick	C22,OF1	R	22	22	72	9	13	2	0	2	5	7	22	0	.181	.253	.292
Tom Padden†	C16	R	34	17	41	5	12	0	0	0	1	2	6	0	.293	.341	.293
Paul Busby	OF10	L	24	26	40	13	10	1	0	0	5	2	1	2	.250	.286	.275
Benny Culp	C10	R	29	10	24	4	5	1	0	0	2	3	3	0	.208	.296	.250
Chuck Klein	C2	L	38	12	20	0	2	0	0	0	3	0	3	1	.100	.100	.100
Garton Del Savio	SS4	R	29	4	11	0	1	0	0	0	0	1	0	0	.091	.167	.091

G. Stewart, 1 G at C; B. Dahlgren, 1 G at C; D. Moore, 1 G at 1B

Bucky Harris (38-52)/Freddie Fitzsimmons (26-38)

Pitcher	T	Age	G	GS	CG	ShO	IP	H	HR	BB	SO	W-L	Sv	ERA
Al Gerheauser	L	26	38	31	11	2	215.0	222	10	70	92	10-19	0	3.60
Jack Kraus	L	25	34	25	10	1	199.2	197	7	78	48	9-15	2	3.16
Schoolboy Rowe	R	33	27	25	11	3	199.0	194	7	29	52	14-8	1	2.94
Dick Barrett†	R	36	23	20	10	2	169.1	137	5	51	65	10-9	1	2.39
Si Johnson	R	36	21	14	9	1	113.0	110	4	25	46	8-3	2	3.27
Dick Conger	R	22	13	10	2	0	54.2	72	3	24	18	2-7	0	6.09
Charlie Fuchs†	R	29	17	9	4	1	77.2	76	4	34	12	2-7	1	4.29
Bill Lee†	R	33	13	7	2	0	60.2	70	4	21	17	1-5	3	4.60
Ken Raffensberger	L	25	1	1	1	0	8.0	7	0	2	3	0-1	0	1.13
Newt Kimball†	R	28	34	6	2	0	89.2	85	4	42	33	1-6	2	4.12
Dutch Dietz†	R	31	21	0	0	0	36.0	42	2	15	10	1-1	2	6.50
Johnny Podgajny†	R	23	13	5	3	0	64.0	77	4	16	13	4-4	0	4.22
Dale Matthewson	R	20	11	1	0	0	26.0	26	1	8	8	0-3	0	4.85
Andy Karl†	R	29	9	2	0	0	26.2	44	0	11	4	1-2	0	7.09
George Eyrich	R	18	9	0	0	0	18.2	23	1	9	5	0-0	0	3.38
Boom-Boom Beck	R	38	4	0	0	0	13.2	24	1	5	3	0-0	0	9.88
Rogers McKee	L	16	4	1	1	0	13.1	12	0	5	1	1-0	0	6.08
Deacon Donahue	R	23	2	0	0	0	4.0	4	0	1	1	0-0	0	4.50
Andy Lapihuska	R	20	1	0	0	0	2.1	5	1	3	0	0-0	0	23.14
Bill Webb	R	29	1	0	0	0	1.0	1	1	1	0	0-0	0	9.00
Manny Salvo†	R	30	1	0	0	0	0.1	2	0	1	0	0-0	0	27.00

1943 New York Giants 8th NL 55-98 .359 49.5 GB

Player	Gm by Position	B	Age	G	AB	R	H	2B	3B	HR	RBI	BB	SO	SB	Avg	OBP	Slg
Gus Mancuso	C77	R	37	94	252	11	50	5	0	2	20	28	16	0	.198	.284	.242
Joe Orengo†	1B82	R	28	83	266	28	58	8	2	6	29	36	46	1	.218	.311	.331
Mickey Witek	2B153	R	27	153	622	68	195	17	0	6	55	41	23	1	.314	.356	.370
Dick Bartell	3B54,SS33	R	35	99	337	48	91	14	0	5	28	47	27	5	.270	.371	.356
Billy Jurges	SS99,3B28	R	35	136	481	46	110	8	2	4	29	53	38	2	.229	.310	.279
Johnny Rucker	OF117	L	26	132	505	56	138	19	4	2	46	22	44	4	.273	.304	.339
Mel Ott	OF111,3B1	L	34	125	380	65	89	12	2	18	47	95	48	7	.234	.391	.418
Buster Maynard	OF74,3B22	R	30	121	393	43	81	8	2	9	32	24	27	3	.206	.252	.305
Sid Gordon	3B53,1B41,OF28*	R	25	131	474	50	119	9	11	9	63	43	32	2	.251	.315	.373
Joe Medwick†	OF74,1B3	R	31	78	324	41	91	20	3	5	45	9	14	0	.281	.300	.407
Ernie Lombardi	C73	R	35	104	295	19	90	7	0	10	51	16	11	1	.305	.343	.431
Charlie Mead	OF37	L	22	37	146	9	40	6	1	1	13	10	15	3	.274	.321	.349
Nap Reyes	1B38,3B1	R	23	40	125	13	32	4	2	0	13	4	12	2	.256	.290	.320
Babe Barna†	OF31	L	28	40	113	11	23	5	1	1	12	16	9	3	.204	.302	.292
Buddy Kerr	SS27	R	20	27	98	14	28	3	0	2	12	8	5	1	.286	.352	.378
Ray Berres	C17	R	35	20	28	1	4	1	0	0	0	1	2	0	.143	.172	.179
Joe Stephenson	C6	R	22	9	24	4	6	1	0	0	1	0	5	0	.250	.250	.292
Hugh Poland†	C4	L	30	4	12	1	1	0	1	0	2	1	0	0	.083	.154	.250
Vic Bradford	OF1	R	28	6	5	1	1	0	0	0	1	1	1	0	.200	.333	.200

S. Gordon, 3 G at 2B

Mel Ott

Pitcher	T	Age	G	GS	CG	ShO	IP	H	HR	BB	SO	W-L	Sv	ERA
Cliff Melton	L	31	34	28	6	2	186.1	184	7	69	55	9-13	0	3.19
Johnnie Wittig	R	29	40	22	4	1	164.0	171	14	76	56	5-15	4	4.23
Ken Chase†	L	29	21	20	4	1	129.1	140	7	74	86	4-12	0	4.11
Rube Fischer	R	26	22	17	4	0	130.2	140	4	59	47	5-10	1	4.61
Bill Lohrman†	R	30	17	12	3	0	80.1	110	7	25	16	5-6	1	5.15
Carl Hubbell	L	40	12	11	3	0	66.0	87	7	24	31	4-4	0	4.91
Ken Trinkle	R	23	11	6	1	0	45.2	51	3	15	10	1-5	0	3.74
Bill Voiselle	R	24	4	4	3	0	31.0	18	1	14	19	1-2	0	2.03
Frank Seward	R	22	1	1	1	0	9.0	12	0	5	2	0-1	0	3.00
Tom Sunkel	L	30	1	1	0	0	2.2	4	1	3	0	0-1	0	10.13
Ace Adams	R	31	70	3	1	0	140.1	121	5	55	46	11-7	9	2.82
Van Lingle Mungo	R	32	45	13	2	2	154.1	140	7	79	83	3-7	2	3.91
Harry Feldman	R	23	31	10	1	0	104.2	114	7	58	49	4-5	0	4.30
Bill Sayles†	R	25	18	3	1	0	53.0	60	1	23	38	1-3	0	4.75
Johnny Allen†	R	37	15	0	0	0	41.0	37	4	14	24	1-3	2	3.07
Hugh East	R	23	13	5	1	0	40.1	51	4	25	21	1-3	0	5.36
Bobby Coombs	R	35	9	0	0	0	16.0	33	1	8	5	0-1	0	12.94

Seasons: Team Rosters

691

»1944 St. Louis Browns 1st AL 89-65 .578 —

Luke Sewell

Player	Gm by Position	B	Age	G	AB	R	H	2B	3B	HR	RBI	BB	SO	SB	Avg	OBP	Slg
Frank Mancuso	C87	R	26	88	244	19	50	11	0	1	24	20	32	1	.205	.271	.262
George McQuinn	1B146	L	34	146	516	83	129	26	3	11	72	85	74	4	.250	.357	.376
Don Gutteridge	2B146	R	32	148	603	89	148	27	11	3	36	51	63	20	.245	.304	.342
Mark Christman	3B145,1B3	R	30	148	547	56	148	25	1	6	83	47	37	5	.271	.332	.353
Vern Stephens	SS143	R	23	145	559	91	164	32	1	20	109	62	54	2	.293	.365	.462
Milt Byrnes	OF122	L	27	128	407	63	120	20	4	4	45	68	50	1	.295	.396	.393
Mike Kreevich	OF100	R	36	105	402	55	121	15	6	5	44	27	24	3	.301	.348	.405
Gene Moore	OF98,1B1	L	34	110	390	56	93	13	6	6	58	24	37	0	.238	.284	.349
Al Zarilla	OF79	L	25	100	288	43	86	13	6	6	45	29	33	1	.299	.375	.448
Red Hayworth	C86	R	29	89	269	20	60	11	1	1	25	10	13	0	.223	.254	.283
Chet Laabs	OF55	R	32	66	201	28	47	10	2	5	23	29	33	3	.234	.330	.378
Floyd Baker	2B17,SS16	L	27	44	97	10	17	3	0	0	5	11	5	2	.175	.259	.206
Mike Chartak	1B12,OF7	L	28	35	72	8	17	2	1	1	7	6	9	0	.236	.304	.333
Hal Epps†	OF18	L	30	22	62	15	11	1	1	0	3	14	14	0	.177	.338	.226
Frank Demaree	OF16	R	34	16	51	4	13	2	0	0	6	6	3	0	.255	.333	.294
Ellis Clary	3B11,2B6	R	27	25	49	6	13	1	1	0	4	12	9	1	.265	.410	.327
Tom Turner†	C11	R	27	15	25	2	8	1	0	0	4	2	5	0	.320	.370	.360
Tom Hafey	OF4,1B1	R	30	8	14	1	5	2	0	0	2	1	4	0	.357	.400	.500
Joe Schultz	C3	L	25	3	8	1	2	0	0	0	0	0	1	0	.250	.250	.250
Babe Martin	OF1	R	24	2	4	0	3	1	0	0	1	0	0	0	.750	.750	1.000
Len Schulte		R	27	1	0	0	0	0	0	0	0	0	0	1	—	—	—

Pitcher	T	Age	G	GS	CG	ShO	IP	H	HR	BB	SO	W-L	Sv	ERA
Jack Kramer	R	26	33	31	18	1	257.0	233	3	75	124	17-13	0	2.49
Nels Potter	R	32	32	29	16	3	232.0	211	6	70	91	19-7	0	2.83
Bob Muncrief	R	28	33	27	12	3	219.1	216	11	50	88	13-8	1	3.08
Sig Jakucki	R	34	35	24	12	4	198.0	211	17	54	67	13-9	3	3.55
Denny Galehouse	R	32	24	19	6	2	153.0	162	6	44	80	9-10	0	3.12
Steve Sundra	R	34	3	3	2	0	19.0	15	1	4	1	2-0	0	1.42
George Caster	R	36	42	0	0	0	81.0	91	5	33	46	6-6	12	2.44
Al Hollingsworth	L	36	26	10	3	2	92.2	108	3	37	22	5-7	1	4.47
Tex Shirley	R	26	23	11	2	1	80.1	59	4	64	35	5-4	0	4.15
Sam Zoldak	L	25	18	0	0	0	38.2	49	1	19	15	0-0	0	3.72
Lefty West	L	28	11	0	0	0	24.1	34	1	19	11	0-0	0	6.29
Willis Hudlin	R	38	1	0	0	0	2.0	3	0	0	1	0-1	0	4.50

1944 Detroit Tigers 2nd AL 88-66 .571 1.0 GB

Steve O'Neill

Player	Gm by Position	B	Age	G	AB	R	H	2B	3B	HR	RBI	BB	SO	SB	Avg	OBP	Slg
Paul Richards	C90	R	35	95	300	24	71	13	0	3	37	35	30	8	.237	.318	.310
Rudy York	1B151	R	30	151	583	77	161	27	7	18	98	68	73	5	.276	.353	.439
Eddie Mayo	2B143,SS11	L	34	154	607	76	151	18	3	5	63	57	23	9	.249	.317	.313
Mike Higgins	3B146	R	35	148	543	79	161	32	4	7	76	81	34	4	.297	.392	.409
Joe Hoover	SS119,2B1	R	29	120	441	67	104	20	2	0	29	35	66	7	.236	.301	.290
Doc Cramer	OF141	L	38	143	578	69	169	20	9	2	42	37	21	6	.292	.337	.369
Jimmy Outlaw	OF137	R	31	139	535	69	146	20	6	3	57	41	40	7	.273	.327	.350
Dick Wakefield	OF78	L	23	78	276	53	98	15	5	12	53	55	29	2	.355	.464	.576
Chuck Hostetler	OF65	L	40	90	265	42	79	9	2	0	20	21	31	4	.298	.350	.347
Bob Swift	C76	R	29	80	247	15	63	11	1	1	19	27	27	2	.255	.331	.320
Don Ross	OF37,SS2,1B1	R	29	66	167	14	35	5	0	2	15	14	9	2	.210	.275	.275
Joe Orengo	SS29,3B11,1B5*	R	29	46	154	14	31	10	0	0	10	20	29	1	.201	.297	.266
Charlie Metro†	OF20	R	25	38	78	8	15	0	1	0	5	3	10	1	.192	.222	.218
Al Unser	2B5,C1	R	31	11	25	2	3	0	1	1	5	3	2	0	.120	.214	.320
Don Heffner	2B5	R	33	6	19	0	4	1	0	0	1	5	1	0	.211	.375	.263
Red Borom	2B4,SS1	L	28	7	14	1	1	0	0	0	1	2	2	0	.071	.188	.071
Bubba Floyd	SS3	R	27	3	9	1	4	1	0	0	0	1	0	0	.444	.500	.556
Hack Miller	C5	R	31	5	5	1	1	0	0	1	3	1	1	0	.200	.333	.800
Jack Sullivan	2B1	R	26	1	1	0	0	0	0	0	0	1	0	0	.000	.000	.000
John McHale		L	22	1	1	0	0	0	0	0	0	0	0	0	.000	.000	.000

J. Orengo, 2 G at 2B

Pitcher	T	Age	G	GS	CG	ShO	IP	H	HR	BB	SO	W-L	Sv	ERA
Dizzy Trout	R	29	49	40	33	7	352.1	314	9	83	144	27-14	0	2.12
Hal Newhouser	L	23	47	34	25	6	312.1	264	6	102	187	29-9	2	2.22
Rufe Gentry	R	26	37	30	10	3	203.1	211	9	108	68	12-14	0	4.25
Stubby Overmire	L	25	32	28	11	3	199.2	214	2	41	57	11-11	1	3.07
Johnny Gorsica	R	29	34	19	8	1	162.0	192	5	32	47	6-14	4	4.11
Boom-Boom Beck	R	39	28	2	0	0	74.0	67	5	27	25	1-2	1	3.89
Jake Mooty	R	31	15	0	0	0	28.1	35	0	18	7	0-0	0	4.45
Joe Orrell	R	26	10	2	0	0	22.1	26	0	11	10	2-1	0	2.42
Roy Henshaw	L	32	7	1	0	0	12.1	17	0	6	10	0-0	0	8.76
Bob Gillespie	R	25	7	0	0	0	11.0	7	0	12	4	0-1	0	6.55
Zeb Eaton	R	24	6	0	0	0	15.2	19	2	8	4	0-0	0	5.74
Chief Hogsett	L	40	3	0	0	0	6.1	7	1	4	5	0-0	0	0.00

1944 New York Yankees 3rd AL 83-71 .539 6.0 GB

Joe McCarthy

Player	Gm by Position	B	Age	G	AB	R	H	2B	3B	HR	RBI	BB	SO	SB	Avg	OBP	Slg
Mike Garbark	C85	R	28	89	299	23	78	9	4	1	33	25	27	0	.261	.320	.328
Nick Etten	1B154	L	30	154	573	88	168	25	4	22	91	97	29	4	.293	.399	.466
Snuffy Stirnweiss	2B154	R	25	154	643	125	205	35	16	8	43	73	87	55	.319	.389	.460
Oscar Grimes	3B97,SS20	R	29	116	387	44	108	17	8	5	46	59	57	6	.279	.377	.403
Mike Milosevich	SS91	R	29	94	312	27	77	11	4	0	32	30	37	1	.247	.313	.308
Johnny Lindell	OF149	R	27	149	594	91	178	33	16	18	103	44	56	5	.300	.351	.500
Bud Metheny	OF132	L	29	137	518	72	124	16	1	14	67	56	57	5	.239	.316	.355
Hersh Martin	OF80	S	34	85	328	49	99	12	4	9	47	34	26	5	.302	.371	.445
Rollie Hemsley	C76	R	37	81	284	23	76	12	5	2	26	9	13	0	.268	.290	.366
Don Savage	3B60	R	25	71	239	31	63	7	5	4	24	20	41	1	.264	.323	.385
Frankie Crosetti	SS55	R	33	55	197	20	47	4	2	5	30	11	21	3	.239	.299	.355
Ed Levy	OF36	R	27	40	153	12	37	11	2	4	29	6	19	1	.242	.270	.418
Russ Derry	OF28	L	27	38	114	14	29	3	0	4	14	20	19	1	.254	.366	.386
Larry Rosenthal†	OF26	L	34	36	101	9	20	3	0	0	9	19	15	1	.198	.325	.228
Tuck Stainback	OF24	R	32	30	78	13	17	3	0	0	5	3	7	1	.218	.247	.256
Johnny Cooney†	OF2	R	43	10	8	1	1	0	0	0	1	1	0	0	.125	.222	.125
Bill Drescher	C1	L	23	4	7	0	1	0	0	0	0	0	0	0	.143	.143	.143
Paul Waner†		L	41	9	7	1	1	0	0	0	1	2	1	1	.143	.333	.143
Rip Collins	C3	R	34	3	3	0	1	0	0	0	0	1	0	0	.333	.500	.333

Pitcher	T	Age	G	GS	CG	ShO	IP	H	HR	BB	SO	W-L	Sv	ERA
Hank Borowy	R	28	35	30	19	3	252.2	224	15	88	107	17-12	2	2.64
Monk Dubiel	R	26	30	28	19	3	232.0	217	12	86	79	13-13	0	3.38
Tiny Bonham	R	30	26	25	17	1	213.2	228	14	41	54	12-9	0	2.99
Atley Donald	R	33	30	19	9	0	159.0	173	13	59	48	13-10	0	3.34
Joe Page	L	26	19	16	4	0	102.2	100	3	52	63	5-7	0	4.56
Bill Zuber	R	31	22	13	2	1	107.0	101	5	54	59	5-7	0	4.21
Mel Queen	R	26	10	10	4	1	81.2	68	7	34	30	6-3	0	3.31
Bill Bevens	R	27	8	5	3	0	43.2	44	4	13	16	4-1	0	2.68
Spud Chandler	R	36	1	1	0	0	6.0	6	1	1	1	0-0	0	4.50
Jim Turner	R	40	35	0	0	0	41.2	42	3	22	13	4-4	7	3.46
Johnny Johnson	L	29	22	1	0	0	26.2	25	0	24	11	0-2	3	4.05
Steve Roser	R	26	16	6	1	0	84.0	80	3	34	34	4-3	1	3.86
Al Lyons	R	25	11	0	0	0	39.2	43	2	24	14	0-0	0	4.54

1944 Boston Red Sox 4th AL 77-77 .500 12.0 GB

Joe Cronin

Player	Gm by Position	B	Age	G	AB	R	H	2B	3B	HR	RBI	BB	SO	SB	Avg	OBP	Slg
Roy Partee	C85	R	26	89	280	18	68	12	0	2	41	37	29	0	.243	.333	.307
Lou Finney	1B59,OF2	L	33	68	251	37	72	11	2	0	32	23	7	1	.287	.347	.347
Bobby Doerr	2B125	R	26	125	468	95	152	30	10	15	81	58	31	5	.325	.399	.528
Jim Tabor	3B114	R	27	116	438	58	125	25	3	13	72	31	38	4	.285	.334	.445
Skeeter Newsome	SS126,2B8,3B1	R	33	136	472	41	114	26	3	0	41	33	21	4	.242	.291	.309
Bob Johnson	OF142	R	37	144	525	106	170	40	8	17	106	95	67	2	.324	.431	.528
Pete Fox	OF119	R	35	121	496	70	156	38	6	1	64	27	34	10	.315	.354	.421
Catfish Metkovich	OF82,1B50	L	23	134	549	94	152	28	8	9	59	31	57	13	.277	.319	.406
Leon Culberson	OF72	R	24	75	282	41	67	11	5	2	21	20	26	0	.238	.288	.333
Jim Bucher	3B44,2B21	L	33	80	277	39	76	9	2	4	31	19	13	3	.274	.326	.365
Hal Wagner†	C64	L	28	66	223	21	74	13	4	1	38	29	14	1	.332	.418	.439
Tom McBride	OF57,1B5	R	29	71	216	29	53	7	3	0	24	8	13	4	.245	.276	.306
Joe Cronin	1B49	R	37	76	191	24	46	7	0	5	28	34	19	1	.241	.358	.356
Eddie Lake	SS41,P6,2B3*	R	28	57	126	21	26	5	0	0	8	23	22	5	.206	.329	.246
Ford Garrison†	OF12	R	28	13	49	5	12	3	0	0	2	6	4	0	.245	.327	.306
Bill Conroy	C19	R	29	19	47	6	10	2	0	0	4	11	9	0	.213	.362	.255
Johnny Lazor	OF6,C1	L	31	16	24	0	2	1	0	0	0	1	0	0	.083	.120	.125
Johnny Peacock†	C2	L	34	4	4	0	0	0	0	0	0	0	0	0	.000	.000	.000

E. Lake, 1 G at 3B

Pitcher	T	Age	G	GS	CG	ShO	IP	H	HR	BB	SO	W-L	Sv	ERA
Joe Bowman	R	34	26	24	10	1	168.1	175	14	64	53	12-8	0	4.81
Tex Hughson	R	28	28	23	19	2	203.1	172	4	41	112	18-5	5	2.26
Emmett O'Neill	R	26	28	22	8	1	151.2	154	6	89	68	6-11	0	4.63
Pinky Woods	R	29	38	20	5	1	170.2	171	4	88	56	4-8	0	3.27
Yank Terry	R	33	27	17	3	0	132.2	142	10	65	30	6-10	0	4.21
Rex Cecil	R	27	11	9	4	0	61.0	72	5	33	33	4-5	0	5.16
Clem Dreisewerd	L	28	7	7	3	0	48.2	52	2	9	9	2-4	0	4.07
Oscar Judd	L	36	9	6	1	0	30.0	30	1	15	9	1-1	0	3.60
Vic Johnson	L	23	7	5	0	0	27.1	42	0	15	7	0-3	0	6.26
Stan Partenheimer	L	21	1	1	0	0	1.0	3	0	2	0	0-0	0	18.00
Mike Ryba	R	41	42	7	2	0	138.0	119	7	39	50	12-7	2	3.33
Frank Barrett	R	30	38	2	0	0	90.1	93	5	42	40	8-7	8	3.69
Clem Hausmann	R	24	32	12	3	0	137.0	139	6	69	43	4-7	2	3.42
Eddie Lake	R	28	6	0	0	0	19.1	20	2	11	7	0-0	0	4.19
Joe Wood	R	28	3	1	0	0	9.2	13	0	3	5	0-1	0	6.52
Lou Lucier†	R	26	3	0	0	0	5.1	7	0	7	2	0-0	0	5.06

1944 Cleveland Indians 5th AL 72-82 .468 17.0 GB

Lou Boudreau

Player	Gm by Position	B	Age	G	AB	R	H	2B	3B	HR	RBI	BB	SO	SB	Avg	OBP	Slg
Buddy Rosar	C98	R	29	99	331	29	87	9	3	0	30	34	17	1	.263	.339	.308
Mike Rocco	1B155	L	28	155	653	87	174	29	7	13	70	56	51	4	.266	.325	.392
Ray Mack	2B83	R	27	83	284	24	66	15	3	0	29	28	45	4	.232	.301	.306
Ken Keltner	3B149	R	27	149	573	74	169	41	9	13	91	53	29	4	.295	.355	.466
Lou Boudreau	SS149,C1	R	26	150	584	91	191	45	5	3	67	73	39	11	.327	.406	.437
Roy Cullenbine	OF151	S	30	154	571	98	162	34	5	16	80	87	49	4	.284	.380	.445
Oris Hockett	OF110	L	34	124	457	47	132	29	5	1	50	35	27	8	.289	.339	.381
Pat Seerey	OF86	R	21	101	342	39	80	16	0	15	39	19	99	0	.234	.276	.412
Rusty Peters	2B63,SS13,3B8	R	29	88	282	23	63	13	3	1	24	15	35	2	.223	.268	.301
Myril Hoag†	OF66	R	36	67	277	33	79	9	3	1	27	25	23	6	.285	.347	.350
Paul O'Dea	OF41,P3,1B3	L	23	76	173	25	55	9	0	0	13	23	21	2	.318	.401	.370
Jeff Heath	OF37	L	29	60	151	20	50	5	2	5	33	18	12	0	.331	.402	.490
Norm Schlueter	C43	R	27	49	122	2	15	4	0	0	11	12	22	0	.123	.201	.156
Jimmy Grant	2B20,3B4	L	25	61	99	12	27	4	3	1	12	11	20	1	.273	.357	.404
George Susce	C29	R	35	29	61	3	14	1	0	0	4	2	5	0	.230	.254	.246
Jim McDonnell	C13	L	21	20	43	5	10	0	0	0	4	4	3	0	.233	.298	.233
Russ Lyon	C3	R	31	7	11	1	2	0	0	0	0	1	1	0	.182	.250	.182
Hank Ruszkowski	C2	R	18	3	8	1	3	0	0	0	1	0	1	0	.375	.375	.375
Steve Biras	2B1	R	22	2	2	0	2	0	0	0	2	0	0	0	1.000	1.000	1.000
Jim Devlin	C1	L	21	1	1	0	0	0	0	0	0	0	0	0	.000	.000	.000

Pitcher	T	Age	G	GS	CG	ShO	IP	H	HR	BB	SO	W-L	Sv	ERA
Mel Harder	R	34	30	27	12	2	196.1	211	5	69	64	12-10	0	3.71
Al Smith	L	36	28	26	7	1	181.2	197	6	69	44	7-13	0	3.42
Steve Gromek	R	24	35	21	12	2	203.2	160	5	70	115	10-9	1	2.56
Allie Reynolds	R	29	28	21	5	1	158.0	141	2	91	84	11-8	1	3.30
Jim Bagby Jr.	R	27	13	10	2	0	79.0	101	2	34	12	4-5	0	4.33
Vern Kennedy†	R	37	12	10	2	0	59.0	66	0	37	17	2-5	0	5.03
Hal Kleine	L	21	11	6	1	0	40.2	38	0	36	13	1-2	0	5.75
Earl Henry	L	27	2	2	1	0	17.2	18	0	3	5	1-1	0	4.58
Bill Bonness	L	20	2	1	0	0	7.0	11	0	5	1	0-1	0	7.71
Joe Heving	R	43	63	1	0	0	119.2	106	2	41	46	8-3	10	1.96
Ed Klieman	R	26	47	19	5	1	178.1	185	4	70	44	11-13	5	3.38
Ray Poat	R	26	36	6	1	0	80.2	82	9	37	40	4-8	1	5.13
Paul Calvert	R	26	35	4	0	0	77.0	89	4	38	31	1-3	0	4.56
Mike Naymick†	R	26	7	0	0	0	13.0	16	1	10	4	0-0	0	9.69
Paul O'Dea	L	23	3	0	0	0	4.1	5	0	6	0	0-0	0	2.08
Red Embree	R	26	3	1	0	0	3.1	2	0	5	4	0-1	0	13.50

1944 Philadelphia Athletics 5th AL 72-82 .468 17.0 GB

Connie Mack

Player	Gm by Position	B	Age	G	AB	R	H	2B	3B	HR	RBI	BB	SO	SB	Avg	OBP	Slg
Frankie Hayes	C155,1B1	R	29	155	581	62	144	18	6	13	78	57	59	2	.248	.315	.367
Bill McGhee	1B75	L	38	77	287	27	83	12	0	1	19	21	20	2	.289	.338	.341
Irv Hall	2B97,SS40,1B4	R	25	143	559	60	150	20	8	0	45	31	46	2	.268	.309	.333
George Kell	3B139	R	21	139	514	51	138	15	3	0	44	22	23	5	.268	.300	.309
Ed Busch	SS111,2B27,3B4	R	26	140	484	41	131	11	3	0	40	29	17	5	.271	.313	.306
Bobby Estalella	OF128,1B6	R	33	140	506	54	151	17	9	7	60	59	60	3	.298	.374	.409
Ford Garrison†	OF119	R	28	121	449	58	121	13	2	4	37	22	40	10	.269	.307	.334
Jo-Jo White†	OF74,SS1	L	35	85	267	30	59	4	2	1	21	40	27	5	.221	.329	.262
Dick Siebert	1B74,OF58	L	32	132	468	52	143	27	5	6	52	62	17	2	.306	.387	.423
Hal Epps†	OF60	L	30	67	229	27	60	8	8	0	13	18	18	2	.262	.316	.367
Joe Rullo	2B33,1B1	R	28	35	96	5	16	0	0	0	5	6	19	1	.167	.223	.167
Bill Burgo	OF22	R	24	27	88	6	21	2	0	1	3	7	3	1	.239	.316	.295
Joe Burns	3B17,2B9	R	28	28	75	5	18	2	0	1	8	4	8	0	.240	.278	.307
Woody Wheaton	P11,OF8	L	29	30	59	1	11	2	0	0	5	5	3	1	.186	.250	.220
Larry Rosenthal†	OF19	L	34	32	54	5	11	2	0	1	6	5	9	0	.204	.271	.296
Charlie Metro†	OF11,3B5,2B2	R	25	24	40	4	4	0	0	0	1	7	6	0	.100	.234	.100
Lew Flick	OF6	L	29	19	35	1	4	0	0	0	2	1	2	1	.114	.139	.114
Bobby Wilkins	SS9	R	21	24	25	7	6	0	0	0	3	1	4	0	.240	.296	.240
Bob Garbark	C15	R	34	18	23	2	6	2	0	0	2	1	0	0	.261	.292	.348
Hal Peck	OF2	L	27	2	8	0	2	0	0	0	1	0	2	0	.250	.250	.250
Al Simmons	OF2	R	42	4	6	1	3	0	0	0	2	0	0	0	.500	.500	.500
Jim Pruett	C2	R	26	3	4	1	1	0	0	0	0	1	0	0	.250	.500	.250
Bill Mills	C1	R	23	5	4	0	1	0	0	0	0	1	1	0	.250	.400	.250
Tony Parisse	C2	R	33	4	4	0	0	0	0	0	0	0	1	0	.000	.000	.000
Hal Wagner†	C1	L	28	5	4	0	1	0	0	0	0	0	0	0	.250	.250	.250

Pitcher	T	Age	G	GS	CG	ShO	IP	H	HR	BB	SO	W-L	Sv	ERA
Bobo Newsom	R	36	37	33	18	2	265.0	243	11	82	142	13-15	1	2.82
Don Black	R	27	29	27	8	0	177.1	177	6	75	78	10-12	0	4.06
Jesse Flores	R	29	27	25	11	2	185.2	172	8	49	65	9-11	0	3.39
Russ Christopher	R	26	35	24	13	1	215.1	200	6	63	84	14-14	1	2.97
Luke Hamlin	R	39	29	23	9	2	190.0	204	13	38	58	6-12	0	3.74
Lum Harris	R	29	23	22	12	2	174.1	193	8	26	33	10-9	0	3.30
Joe Berry	R	39	53	0	0	0	111.1	78	4	23	44	10-8	12	1.94
Carl Scheib	R	17	15	0	0	0	36.1	36	1	11	13	0-0	0	4.21
Woody Wheaton	L	29	11	1	1	0	38.0	36	1	20	15	0-1	0	3.55
John McGillen	L	26	2	0	0	0	1.0	1	0	2	0	0-0	0	18.00
Ted Abernathy	L	22	1	0	0	0	3.0	5	0	1	2	0-0	0	3.00

1944 Chicago White Sox 7th AL 71-83 .461 18.0 GB

Jimmy Dykes

Player	Gm by Position	B	Age	G	AB	R	H	2B	3B	HR	RBI	BB	SO	SB	Avg	OBP	Slg
Mike Tresh	C93	R	30	93	312	22	81	8	1	0	25	37	15	0	.260	.342	.292
Hal Trosky	1B130	L	31	135	497	55	120	32	2	10	70	62	30	3	.241	.327	.374
Roy Schalk	2B142,SS5	R	35	146	587	47	129	14	4	1	44	45	52	5	.220	.276	.262
Ralph Hodgin	3B82,OF33	L	28	121	465	56	137	25	7	1	51	21	14	3	.295	.333	.385
Skeeter Webb	SS135,2B5	R	34	139	513	44	108	19	6	0	30	20	39	7	.211	.242	.271
Wally Moses	OF134	L	33	136	535	82	150	26	9	3	34	52	22	21	.280	.345	.379
Thurman Tucker	OF120	L	26	124	446	59	128	15	6	2	46	57	40	13	.287	.368	.361
Eddie Carnett	OF88,1B25,P2	L	27	126	457	51	126	18	8	1	60	26	35	5	.276	.322	.357
Guy Curtright	OF51	R	31	72	198	22	50	8	2	2	23	23	21	4	.253	.330	.343
Grey Clarke	3B45	R	31	63	169	14	44	10	1	0	27	22	6	0	.260	.352	.331
Johnny Dickshot	OF40	R	34	62	162	18	41	8	5	0	15	13	10	2	.253	.313	.364
Tony Cuccinello	3B30,2B6	R	36	38	130	5	34	3	0	0	17	8	16	0	.262	.304	.285
Tom Turner†	C36	R	27	36	113	9	26	6	0	2	13	5	16	0	.230	.263	.336
Vince Castino	C26	R	26	29	78	8	18	5	0	0	3	10	13	0	.231	.326	.295
Cass Michaels	SS21,3B3	R	18	27	68	4	12	4	1	0	5	2	5	0	.176	.200	.265
Myril Hoag†	OF14	R	36	17	48	5	11	1	0	0	4	10	1	1	.229	.362	.250
Tom Jordan	C14	R	24	14	45	2	12	1	1	0	3	1	0	0	.267	.283	.333
William Metzig	2B5	R	25	5	16	1	2	0	0	0	1	1	4	0	.125	.176	.125

Pitcher	T	Age	G	GS	CG	ShO	IP	H	HR	BB	SO	W-L	Sv	ERA
Bill Dietrich	R	34	36	36	15	2	246.0	269	15	68	70	16-17	0	3.62
Orval Grove	R	24	34	33	11	2	234.2	237	11	71	105	14-15	0	3.72
Ed Lopat	L	26	27	25	13	1	210.0	217	12	59	75	11-10	0	3.26
Johnny Humphries	R	29	30	20	8	0	169.0	170	9	57	42	8-10	1	3.67
Thornton Lee	L	37	15	14	6	0	113.1	105	3	25	39	3-9	0	3.02
Gordon Maltzberger	R	31	46	0	0	0	91.1	81	2	19	49	10-5	12	2.96
Joe Haynes	R	26	33	12	8	0	154.1	148	5	43	44	5-6	2	2.57
Buck Ross	R	29	20	9	2	0	90.1	97	7	35	20	2-7	0	5.18
Jake Wade	L	32	19	5	1	0	74.2	75	3	41	35	2-4	2	4.82
Don Hanski	L	28	2	0	0	0	3.0	5	0	2	0	0-0	0	12.00
Floyd Speer	R	31	2	0	0	0	2.0	4	0	0	1	0-0	0	9.00
Eddie Carnett	L	27	2	0	0	0	2.0	3	1	0	1	0-0	0	9.00

1944 Washington Senators 8th AL 64-90 .416 25.0 GB

Ossie Bluege

Player	Gm by Position	B	Age	G	AB	R	H	2B	3B	HR	RBI	BB	SO	SB	Avg	OBP	Slg
Rick Ferrell	C96	R	38	99	339	14	94	11	1	0	25	46	13	2	.277	.364	.316
Joe Kuhel	1B138	L	38	139	518	90	144	26	7	4	51	68	40	11	.278	.364	.378
George Myatt	2B121,SS15,OF3	L	30	140	538	86	153	19	6	0	40	54	44	26	.284	.357	.342
Gil Torres	3B123,2B10,1B4	R	28	134	524	42	140	20	6	0	58	21	24	10	.267	.297	.328
John Sullivan	SS138	R	23	138	471	49	118	12	1	0	30	52	43	3	.251	.325	.280
Stan Spence	OF150,1B3	L	29	153	592	83	187	31	8	18	100	69	28	3	.316	.391	.486
George Case	OF114	R	28	119	465	63	116	14	2	2	32	49	22	49	.249	.325	.301
Jake Powell	OF92,3B1	R	35	96	367	29	88	9	1	1	37	16	26	7	.240	.272	.278
Roberto Ortiz	OF80	R	29	85	316	36	80	11	4	5	35	19	47	4	.253	.312	.361
Mike Guerra	C58,OF1	R	31	75	210	29	59	7	2	1	29	13	14	8	.281	.323	.348
Fred Vaughn	2B26,3B3	R	25	30	109	10	28	2	1	1	21	9	24	2	.257	.319	.321
Hillis Layne	3B18,2B3	L	26	33	87	6	17	2	0	0	8	6	10	2	.195	.263	.218
Bill LeFebvre	P24,1B2	L	28	60	62	4	16	2	2	0	8	12	9	0	.258	.378	.355
Ed Boland	OF14	L	36	19	59	4	16	4	0	0	14	0	6	0	.271	.271	.339
Harlond Clift	3B12	R	31	12	44	4	7	3	0	0	3	3	3	0	.159	.213	.227
Ed Butka	1B14	R	28	15	41	1	8	1	0	0	1	2	11	0	.195	.233	.220
Rene Monteagudo	OF9	L	28	10	38	2	11	2	0	0	4	0	1	0	.289	.289	.342
Joe Vosmik	OF12	R	34	14	36	2	7	2	0	0	9	2	3	0	.194	.237	.250
Al Evans	C8	R	27	14	22	5	2	0	0	0	0	2	6	0	.091	.167	.091
Eddie Yost	3B3,SS2	R	17	7	14	3	2	0	0	0	0	1	2	0	.143	.200	.143
George Binks	OF3	L	27	5	12	0	3	0	0	0	0	0	1	0	.250	.250	.250
Preston Gomez	2B2,SS2	R	21	8	7	2	2	1	0	0	2	0	4	0	.286	.286	.429
Luis Suarez	3B1	R	27	1	2	0	0	0	0	0	0	0	0	0	.000	.000	.000
Roy Valdes		R	24	1	1	0	0	0	0	0	0	0	0	0	.000	.000	.000

Pitcher	T	Age	G	GS	CG	ShO	IP	H	HR	BB	SO	W-L	Sv	ERA
Dutch Leonard	R	35	32	31	17	3	229.1	222	8	37	62	14-14	0	3.06
Mickey Haefner	L	31	31	28	18	3	228.0	221	7	71	86	12-15	1	3.04
Early Wynn	R	24	33	25	19	2	207.2	221	3	67	65	8-17	2	3.38
Johnny Niggeling	R	40	24	24	14	2	206.0	164	5	88	121	10-8	0	2.32
Roger Wolff	R	33	33	21	5	0	155.0	186	9	60	73	4-15	2	4.99
Baby Ortiz	R	24	2	2	1	0	13.0	13	0	6	4	0-2	0	6.23
Alex Carrasquel	R	31	43	7	3	0	134.0	143	8	50	35	8-7	2	3.43
Milo Candini	R	26	28	10	4	2	103.0	110	3	49	31	6-7	1	4.11
Bill LeFebvre	L	28	24	4	2	0	69.2	86	3	21	18	2-4	3	4.52
Jug Thesenga	R	30	5	1	0	0	12.1	18	0	12	2	0-0	0	5.11
Sandy Ullrich	R	22	3	0	0	0	9.2	17	2	4	2	0-0	0	9.31
Vern Curtis	R	24	3	1	0	0	9.2	8	0	3	2	0-1	0	2.79
Bill Zinser	R	26	2	0	0	0	0.2	1	0	5	1	0-0	0	27.00
Wally Holborow	R	30	1	0	0	0	3.0	0	0	2	1	0-0	0	0.00

»1944 St. Louis Cardinals 1st NL 105-49 .682 —

Billy Southworth

Player	Gm by Position	B	Age	G	AB	R	H	2B	3B	HR	RBI	BB	SO	SB	Avg	OBP	Slg
Walker Cooper	C97	R	29	112	397	56	126	25	5	13	72	20	19	4	.317	.352	.504
Ray Sanders	1B152	L	27	154	601	87	177	34	9	12	102	71	50	2	.295	.371	.441
Emil Verban	2B146	R	28	146	498	51	128	14	2	0	43	19	14	0	.257	.287	.293
Whitey Kurowski	3B146,2B9,SS1	R	26	149	555	95	150	25	7	20	87	58	40	2	.270	.341	.449
Marty Marion	SS144	R	26	144	506	50	135	26	2	6	63	43	50	1	.267	.324	.362
Stan Musial	OF146	L	23	146	568	112	197	51	14	12	94	90	28	7	.347	.440	.549
Danny Litwhiler	OF136	R	27	140	492	53	130	25	5	15	82	37	56	2	.264	.328	.427
Johnny Hopp	OF131,1B6	L	27	139	527	106	177	35	9	11	72	58	47	15	.336	.404	.499
Ken O'Dea	C69	L	31	85	265	35	66	11	2	6	37	37	29	1	.249	.343	.374
Augie Bergamo	OF50,1B2	L	27	80	192	35	55	6	3	2	19	35	23	0	.286	.399	.380
Debs Garms	OF23,3B21	L	36	73	149	17	30	3	0	0	5	13	8	0	.201	.265	.221
George Fallon	2B38,SS24,3B6	R	29	69	141	16	28	6	0	1	9	16	11	1	.199	.285	.262
Pepper Martin	OF29	R	40	40	86	15	24	4	0	2	4	15	11	2	.279	.386	.395
John Antonelli	1B3,3B3,2B2	R	28	8	21	0	4	1	0	0	1	0	4	0	.190	.190	.238
Bob Keely	C1	R	34	1	0	0	0	0	0	0	0	0	0	0	—	—	—

Pitcher	T	Age	G	GS	CG	ShO	IP	H	HR	BB	SO	W-L	Sv	ERA
Mort Cooper	R	31	34	33	22	7	252.1	227	6	60	97	22-7	1	2.46
Max Lanier	L	28	33	30	16	5	224.1	192	5	71	141	17-12	0	2.65
Harry Brecheen	L	29	30	22	13	3	189.1	174	8	46	88	16-5	0	2.85
Ted Wilks	R	28	36	21	16	4	207.2	173	12	49	70	17-4	0	2.64
George Munger	R	25	21	12	7	2	121.0	92	2	41	55	11-3	2	1.34
Harry Gumbert†	R	34	10	7	3	0	61.1	60	1	19	16	4-2	1	2.49
Bill Trotter	R	35	2	1	0	0	6.0	14	5	4	0	0-1	0	13.50
Freddy Schmidt	R	28	37	9	3	2	114.1	94	5	58	58	7-3	5	3.15
Al Jurisich	R	22	30	14	5	2	130.0	102	7	65	53	7-9	1	3.39
Blix Donnelly	R	30	27	4	2	1	76.1	61	2	34	45	2-1	2	2.12
Bud Byerly	R	23	9	4	2	0	42.1	37	2	20	13	2-2	0	3.40
Mike Naymick†	R	26	1	0	0	0	2.0	2	0	1	1	0-0	0	4.50

1944 Pittsburgh Pirates 2nd NL 90-63 .588 14.5 GB

Frank Frisch

Player	Gm by Position	B	Age	G	AB	R	H	2B	3B	HR	RBI	BB	SO	SB	Avg	OBP	Slg
Al Lopez	C115	R	35	115	331	27	76	12	1	1	34	34	24	4	.230	.303	.281
Babe Dahlgren	1B158	R	32	158	599	67	173	28	7	12	101	47	56	2	.289	.347	.419
Pete Coscarart	2B136,SS4,OF1	R	31	139	554	89	146	30	4	4	42	41	57	10	.264	.315	.354
Bob Elliott	3B140,SS1	R	27	143	538	85	160	28	16	10	108	75	42	9	.297	.383	.465
Frankie Gustine	SS116,2B11,3B1	R	24	127	405	42	93	18	3	2	42	33	41	8	.230	.288	.304
Jim Russell	OF149	S	25	152	580	109	181	34	14	8	66	79	63	6	.312	.399	.460
Johnny Barrett	OF147	L	28	149	568	99	153	24	19	7	83	86	56	28	.269	.366	.415
Vince DiMaggio	OF101,3B1	R	31	109	342	41	82	20	4	9	50	33	83	6	.240	.307	.401
Frank Colman	OF53,1B6	L	26	99	226	30	61	9	5	6	53	25	27	0	.270	.345	.434
Al Rubeling	OF18,2B17,3B16	R	31	92	184	22	45	7	2	4	30	19	19	4	.245	.322	.370
Frankie Zak	SS67	R	22	87	160	33	48	3	1	0	11	22	18	6	.300	.385	.331
Tommy O'Brien	OF48,3B1	R	25	85	156	27	39	6	2	3	20	21	12	1	.250	.343	.372
Hank Camelli	C61	R	29	63	125	14	37	5	1	1	10	18	12	0	.296	.385	.376
Spud Davis	C35	R	39	54	93	6	28	7	0	2	14	10	8	0	.301	.369	.441
Lee Handley	2B19,3B11,SS3	R	30	40	86	7	19	2	0	0	5	3	5	1	.221	.247	.244
Lloyd Waner†	OF7	L	38	19	14	2	5	0	0	0	2	2	0	0	.357	.438	.357
Al Gionfriddo	OF1	L	22	4	6	0	1	0	0	0	0	1	1	0	.167	.286	.167
Bill Rodgers	OF1	L	21	2	4	1	1	0	0	0	0	0	1	0	.250	.250	.250
Hank Sweeney	1B1	L	28	1	2	0	0	0	0	0	0	0	1	0	.000	.000	.000
Vic Barnhart	SS1	R	21	1	2	0	1	0	0	0	0	1	1	0	.500	.667	.500

Pitcher	T	Age	G	GS	CG	ShO	IP	H	HR	BB	SO	W-L	Sv	ERA
Rip Sewell	R	37	38	33	24	3	286.0	263	15	99	87	21-12	2	3.18
Max Butcher	R	33	35	27	13	5	199.0	216	8	46	43	13-11	1	3.12
Nick Strincevich	R	29	40	26	11	0	190.0	190	5	37	47	14-7	2	3.08
Preacher Roe	L	29	39	25	7	1	185.1	182	7	59	88	13-11	1	3.11
Fritz Ostermueller†	L	36	28	24	14	1	204.2	201	7	65	80	11-7	1	2.73
Len Gilmore	R	26	1	1	1	0	8.0	13	2	0	0	0-1	0	7.88
Xavier Rescigno	R	30	48	6	2	0	124.0	146	9	34	45	10-8	5	4.35
Cookie Cuccurullo	L	26	32	4	0	0	106.1	110	5	44	31	2-1	4	4.06
Ray Starr	R	38	27	12	5	0	89.2	116	6	36	25	6-5	3	5.02
Johnny Gee†	L	28	4	0	0	0	11.1	20	0	5	3	0-0	0	7.15
Joe Vitelli	R	36	4	0	0	0	7.0	5	1	7	2	0-0	0	2.57
Roy Wise	R	19	2	0	0	0	3.0	4	0	3	1	0-0	0	9.00

1944 Cincinnati Reds 3rd NL 89-65 .578 16.0 GB

Bill McKechnie

Player	Gm by Position	B	Age	G	AB	R	H	2B	3B	HR	RBI	BB	SO	SB	Avg	OBP	Slg
Ray Mueller	C155	R	32	155	555	54	159	24	4	10	73	53	47	4	.286	.353	.398
Frank McCormick	1B153	R	33	153	581	85	177	37	3	20	102	57	17	7	.305	.371	.482
Woody Williams	2B155	R	31	155	653	73	157	23	3	1	35	44	24	7	.240	.290	.289
Steve Mesner	3B120	R	26	121	414	31	100	17	4	1	47	34	20	1	.242	.301	.309
Eddie Miller	SS155	R	27	155	536	48	112	21	5	4	55	41	41	9	.209	.269	.289
Eric Tipton	OF139	R	29	140	479	62	144	28	3	3	36	59	32	5	.301	.380	.390
Gee Walker	OF117	R	36	121	478	56	133	21	3	5	62	23	48	7	.278	.318	.366
Dain Clay	OF98	R	24	110	356	51	89	15	0	0	17	17	18	8	.250	.290	.292
Max Marshall	OF59	L	30	66	229	36	56	13	2	4	23	21	10	3	.245	.308	.371
Tony Criscola	OF35	L	28	64	157	14	36	3	2	0	14	14	12	0	.229	.297	.274
Chuck Aleno	3B42,1B3,SS3	R	27	50	127	10	21	3	0	1	15	15	15	0	.165	.259	.213
Estel Crabtree	OF19,1B2	L	40	58	98	7	28	4	1	0	11	13	3	0	.286	.369	.347
Jo-Jo White†	OF23	L	35	24	85	9	20	2	0	0	5	10	7	0	.235	.316	.259
Buck Fausett	3B6,P2	L	36	13	31	2	3	0	1	0	1	1	2	0	.097	.125	.161
Joe Just	C10	R	28	11	11	0	2	0	0	0	0	0	2	0	.182	.250	.182
Chucho Ramos	OF3	R	26	4	10	1	5	1	0	0	0	0	0	0	.500	.500	.600
Len Rice	C5	R	25	10	4	1	0	0	0	0	0	0	0	0	.000	.000	.000
Jodie Beeler	2B1,3B1	R	22	3	3	0	0	0	0	0	0	0	2	0	.000	.000	.000
Kermit Wahl	3B1	R	21	4	1	0	0	0	0	0	0	0	0	0	.000	.000	.000
Al Lakeman		R	25	1	1	0	0	0	0	0	0	0	1	0	.000	.000	.000
Mike Kosman		R	26	1	0	0	0	0	0	0	0	0	0	0	—	—	—
Johnny Riddle	C1	R	38	1	0	0	0	0	0	0	0	0	0	0	—	—	—

Pitcher	T	Age	G	GS	CG	ShO	IP	H	HR	BB	SO	W-L	Sv	ERA
Bucky Walters	R	35	34	32	27	6	285.0	233	10	87	77	23-8	1	2.40
Ed Heusser	R	35	30	23	17	4	192.2	165	9	42	42	13-11	2	2.38
Clyde Shoun	L	32	38	21	12	1	202.2	193	10	42	55	13-10	2	3.02
Tommy de la Cruz	R	32	34	20	9	0	191.1	170	9	45	65	9-9	1	3.25
Harry Gumbert†	R	34	24	19	11	2	155.1	157	7	40	40	10-8	2	3.30
Arnold Carter	L	26	33	18	9	3	148.2	143	1	40	33	11-7	3	2.60
Jim Konstanty	R	27	20	12	5	1	112.2	113	11	33	19	6-4	0	2.80
Elmer Riddle	R	29	4	4	2	0	26.2	25	0	12	6	2-2	0	4.05
Joe Beggs	R	33	1	1	1	0	9.0	8	0	0	2	1-0	0	2.00
Bill Lohrman†	R	31	2	1	0	0	1.2	5	0	2	0	0-1	0	27.00
Bob Malloy	R	26	9	0	0	0	23.1	22	0	11	4	1-1	0	3.09
Bob Ferguson	R	25	9	2	0	0	16.0	24	3	10	9	0-3	1	9.00
Bob Katz	R	33	6	2	0	0	18.1	17	0	7	4	0-1	0	3.93
Buck Fausett	R	36	2	0	0	0	10.2	13	0	7	3	0-0	0	5.91
Howie Fox	R	23	2	0	0	0	2.1	2	0	0	0	0-0	0	0.00
Kent Peterson	L	18	1	0	0	0	1.0	0	0	0	0	0-0	0	0.00
Joe Nuxhall	L	15	1	0	0	0	0.2	2	0	5	0	0-0	0	67.50
Jake Eisenhart	L	21	1	0	0	0	0.1	0	0	1	0	0-0	0	0.00

1944 Chicago Cubs 4th NL 75-79 .487 30.0 GB

Jimmie Wilson (1-9)/Roy Johnson (0-1)/Charlie Grimm (74-69)

Player	Gm by Position	B	Age	G	AB	R	H	2B	3B	HR	RBI	BB	SO	SB	Avg	OBP	Slg
Dewey Williams	C77	R	28	79	262	23	63	7	2	0	27	23	18	2	.240	.302	.282
Phil Cavarretta	1B139,OF13	L	27	152	614	106	197	35	15	5	82	67	42	4	.321	.390	.451
Don Johnson	2B154	R	32	154	608	50	169	37	1	2	71	28	48	8	.278	.311	.352
Stan Hack	3B75,1B18	L	34	98	383	65	108	16	1	3	32	53	21	5	.282	.369	.352
Lennie Merullo	SS56,1B1	R	27	66	193	20	41	8	1	1	16	16	18	3	.212	.276	.280
Bill Nicholson	OF156	L	29	156	582	116	167	35	8	33	122	93	71	3	.287	.391	.545
Andy Pafko	OF123	R	23	128	469	47	126	16	2	6	62	28	23	2	.269	.315	.350
Dom Dallessandro	OF106	L	30	117	381	53	116	19	4	8	74	61	29	1	.304	.400	.438
Roy Hughes	3B66,SS52	R	33	126	478	86	137	16	6	1	28	35	30	16	.287	.337	.351
Bill Schuster	SS38,2B6	R	31	60	154	14	34	7	1	1	14	12	16	4	.221	.277	.299
Ival Goodman	OF35	L	35	62	141	24	37	8	1	1	16	23	15	0	.262	.377	.355
Lou Novikoff	OF29	R	28	71	139	15	39	4	2	3	19	10	11	1	.281	.329	.403
Billy Holm	C50	R	31	54	132	10	18	2	0	0	6	16	19	1	.136	.235	.152
Tony York	SS15,3B12	R	31	28	85	4	20	1	0	0	7	4	11	0	.235	.270	.247
Mickey Kreitner	C39	R	21	39	85	3	13	2	0	0	1	8	16	0	.153	.234	.176
Frank Secory	OF17	R	31	22	56	10	18	1	0	4	17	6	8	1	.321	.387	.554
Eddie Sauer	OF12	R	25	23	50	3	11	4	0	0	5	2	6	0	.220	.250	.300
Charlie Brewster	SS10	R	27	10	44	4	11	2	0	0	2	5	7	0	.250	.327	.295
Roy Easterwood	C12	R	29	17	33	1	7	2	0	1	2	1	11	0	.212	.235	.364
Paul Gillespie	C7	L	23	9	26	2	7	1	0	1	2	3	3	0	.269	.345	.423
Eddie Stanky†	2B3,3B3,SS3	R	27	13	25	4	6	0	1	0	0	2	2	1	.240	.296	.320
Pete Elko	3B6	R	26	7	22	2	5	1	0	0	0	0	1	0	.227	.227	.273
Jimmie Foxx	3B2,C1	R	36	15	20	0	1	1	0	0	2	2	5	0	.050	.136	.100
Johnny Ostrowski	OF2	R	26	8	13	2	2	1	0	0	2	1	4	0	.154	.214	.231
Joe Stephenson	C3	R	23	4	8	1	1	0	0	0	0	1	3	1	.125	.222	.125
Garth Mann		R	28	1	0	1	0	0	0	0	0	0	0	0	—	—	—

Pitcher	T	Age	G	GS	CG	ShO	IP	H	HR	BB	SO	W-L	Sv	ERA
Hank Wyse	R	26	41	34	14	3	257.1	277	9	57	86	16-15	1	3.15
Claude Passeau	R	35	34	27	18	2	227.0	234	8	50	89	15-9	3	2.89
Bob Chipman†	L	25	26	21	8	1	129.0	147	9	40	41	9-9	2	3.49
Ed Hanyzewski	R	23	14	7	3	0	58.1	61	6	20	19	2-5	0	4.47
Charlie Gassaway	L	25	2	2	0	0	11.2	20	3	10	7	0-1	0	7.71
Paul Derringer	R	37	42	16	7	0	180.0	205	13	39	69	7-13	3	4.15
Bill Fleming	R	30	39	18	9	1	158.1	163	6	62	42	9-10	0	3.13
Hy Vandenberg	R	37	35	9	2	0	126.1	123	8	51	54	7-4	2	3.63
Paul Erickson	R	28	33	15	5	3	124.1	113	5	67	82	5-9	1	3.55
Red Lynn	R	30	22	7	4	1	84.1	80	4	37	35	5-4	1	4.06
Dale Alderson	R	26	12	1	0	0	21.2	31	2	9	7	0-0	0	6.65
Mack Stewart	R	29	8	0	0	0	12.1	11	1	4	3	0-0	0	1.46
John Burrows	L	30	3	0	0	0	3.0	7	0	3	1	0-0	0	18.00
John Miklos	L	33	2	0	0	0	7.0	9	1	3	0	0-0	0	7.71

1944 New York Giants 5th NL 67-87 .435 38.0 GB

Mel Ott

Player	Gm by Position	B	Age	G	AB	R	H	2B	3B	HR	RBI	BB	SO	SB	Avg	OBP	Slg
Ernie Lombardi	C100	R	36	117	373	37	95	13	0	10	58	33	25	0	.255	.317	.370
Phil Weintraub	1B99	L	36	104	361	55	114	18	9	13	77	59	59	0	.316	.412	.524
George Hausmann	2B122	R	28	131	466	70	124	20	4	1	30	40	25	3	.266	.324	.333
Hal Luby	3B65,2B45,1B1	R	31	111	323	30	82	10	2	2	35	52	15	2	.254	.364	.316
Buddy Kerr	SS149	R	21	150	548	68	146	31	4	9	63	37	32	14	.266	.316	.387
Johnny Rucker	OF139	L	27	144	587	79	143	14	8	6	39	24	48	8	.244	.275	.325
Joe Medwick	OF122	R	32	128	490	64	165	24	3	7	85	38	24	2	.337	.386	.441
Mel Ott	OF103,3B4	L	35	120	399	91	115	16	4	26	82	90	47	2	.288	.423	.544
Nap Reyes	1B63,3B37,OF3	R	24	116	374	38	108	16	5	8	53	15	24	2	.289	.325	.422
Billy Jurges	3B61,SS10,2B1	R	36	85	246	28	52	2	1	1	23	23	20	4	.211	.279	.240
Gus Mancuso	C72	R	38	78	195	15	49	4	1	1	25	30	20	0	.251	.351	.297
Red Treadway	OF38	L	24	50	170	23	51	5	2	0	5	13	11	2	.300	.350	.353
Danny Gardella	OF25	L	24	47	112	20	28	2	2	6	14	11	13	0	.250	.323	.464
Bruce Sloan	OF21	L	29	59	104	7	28	4	1	1	9	13	8	0	.269	.350	.356
Charlie Mead	OF23	L	23	39	78	5	14	1	0	1	8	5	7	0	.179	.229	.231
Steve Filipowicz	OF10,C1	R	23	15	41	10	8	2	1	0	7	3	7	0	.195	.250	.293
Ray Berres	C12	R	36	16	17	4	8	0	0	1	2	1	0	0	.471	.526	.647
Roy Nichols	2B1,3B1	R	23	11	9	3	2	1	0	0	0	2	2	0	.222	.364	.333

Pitcher	T	Age	G	GS	CG	ShO	IP	H	HR	BB	SO	W-L	Sv	ERA
Bill Voiselle	R	25	43	41	25	1	312.2	276	31	118	161	21-16	0	3.02
Harry Feldman	R	24	40	27	8	1	205.1	214	18	91	70	11-13	2	4.16
Ewald Pyle	L	33	31	21	3	0	164.0	152	12	68	79	7-10	0	4.34
Johnny Allen	R	38	18	13	2	1	84.0	88	7	24	33	4-7	0	4.07
Cliff Melton	L	32	13	10	1	0	64.1	78	5	19	15	2-2	0	4.06
Jack Brewer	R	24	14	7	2	0	55.0	66	8	16	21	1-4	0	5.56
Ace Adams	R	32	65	4	1	0	137.2	149	8	58	32	8-11	13	4.25
Rube Fischer	R	27	38	18	2	1	128.2	128	7	87	39	6-14	2	5.18
Frank Seward	R	23	25	7	2	0	78.1	98	8	32	16	3-2	0	5.40
Andy Hansen	R	19	23	4	0	0	52.2	63	3	32	15	3-3	1	6.49
Lou Polli	R	42	19	0	0	0	35.2	42	3	20	6	0-2	3	4.54
Ken Brondell	R	22	7	2	1	0	19.1	27	3	8	1	0-1	0	8.38
Bob Barthelson	R	19	7	1	0	0	9.2	13	2	5	4	1-1	0	4.66
Ken Miller	R	29	4	0	0	0	5.0	1	0	4	2	0-1	0	0.00
Johnny Gee†	L	28	4	0	0	0	4.2	5	0	0	3	0-0	0	0.00
Frank Rosso	R	23	2	0	0	0	4.0	11	0	3	1	0-0	0	9.00
Walter Ockey	R	24	2	0	0	0	2.2	2	1	2	1	0-0	0	3.38

1944 Boston Braves 6th NL 65-89 .422 40.0 GB

Bob Coleman

Player	Gm by Position	B	Age	G	AB	R	H	2B	3B	HR	RBI	BB	SO	SB	Avg	OBP	Slg
Phil Masi	C63,1B12,3B2	R	28	89	251	33	69	13	5	3	23	31	20	4	.275	.355	.402
Buck Etchison	1B85	L	29	109	308	30	66	16	0	8	33	33	50	1	.214	.292	.344
Connie Ryan	2B80,3B14	R	24	88	332	56	98	18	5	4	25	36	40	13	.295	.364	.416
Damon Phillips	3B90,SS60	R	25	140	489	35	126	30	1	1	53	28	34	1	.258	.301	.329
Whitey Wietelmann	SS103,2B23,3B1	S	25	125	417	46	100	18	1	2	32	33	25	0	.240	.300	.302
Tommy Holmes	OF155	L	27	155	631	93	195	42	6	13	73	61	11	4	.309	.372	.456
Butch Nieman	OF126	L	26	134	468	65	124	16	6	16	65	47	47	5	.265	.332	.427
Chuck Workman	OF103,3B19	L	29	140	418	46	87	18	3	11	53	42	41	1	.208	.287	.344
Max Macon	1B72,OF22,P1	L	28	106	366	38	100	15	3	3	36	12	23	7	.273	.296	.355
Clyde Kluttz	C58	R	26	81	229	20	64	12	2	2	19	13	14	0	.279	.318	.376
Ab Wright	OF47	R	38	71	195	20	50	9	0	7	35	18	31	0	.256	.326	.410
Stew Hofferth	C47	R	31	66	180	14	36	8	0	1	26	11	5	0	.200	.246	.261
Chet Ross	OF38	R	27	54	154	20	35	9	2	5	26	12	23	1	.227	.287	.409
Frank Drews	2B46	R	28	46	141	14	29	9	1	0	10	25	14	0	.206	.329	.284
Roland Gladu	3B15,OF3	L	33	21	66	5	16	2	1	1	7	3	8	0	.242	.275	.348
Warren Huston	3B20,2B5,SS4	R	30	33	55	7	11	1	0	0	1	8	5	0	.200	.313	.218
Steve Shemo	2B16,3B2	R	29	18	31	3	9	2	0	0	1	1	3	0	.290	.313	.355
Mike Sandlock	3B22,SS7	S	28	30	30	1	3	0	0	0	2	5	3	0	.100	.250	.100
Dick Culler	SS8	R	29	8	28	2	2	0	0	0	0	4	2	0	.071	.188	.071
Hugh Poland	C6	L	31	8	23	1	3	1	0	0	2	0	1	0	.130	.130	.174
Chet Clemens	OF7	R	27	19	17	7	3	1	1	0	2	2	2	0	.176	.263	.353
Ben Geraghty	2B4,3B3	R	31	11	16	3	4	0	0	0	0	1	2	0	.250	.294	.250
Pat Capri	2B1	R	25	7	1	1	0	0	0	0	0	0	1	0	.000	.000	.000
Gene Patton		L	17	1	0	0	0	0	0	0	0	0	0	0	—	—	—

Pitcher	T	Age	G	GS	CG	ShO	IP	H	HR	BB	SO	W-L	Sv	ERA
Jim Tobin	R	31	43	36	28	5	299.1	271	18	97	83	18-19	3	3.01
Nate Andrews	R	30	37	34	16	2	257.1	263	14	74	76	16-15	2	3.22
Al Javery	R	26	40	33	11	3	254.0	248	12	118	137	10-19	3	3.54
Red Barrett	R	29	42	30	11	1	230.1	257	13	63	54	9-16	2	4.06
Johnny Hutchings	R	28	14	7	1	0	56.2	55	3	26	26	1-4	1	3.97
Ira Hutchinson	R	33	40	8	1	1	119.2	136	8	53	22	9-7	1	4.21
Stan Klopp	R	33	24	0	0	0	46.1	47	1	33	17	1-2	0	4.27
Ben Cardoni	R	23	22	5	1	0	75.2	83	5	37	24	0-6	0	3.93
Jim Hickey	R	23	8	0	0	0	9.0	15	0	5	3	0-0	0	5.00
Woody Rich	R	28	7	2	1	0	25.0	32	3	12	6	1-1	0	5.76
Carl Lindquist	R	25	5	0	0	0	8.2	8	1	2	4	0-0	0	3.12
George Woodend	R	26	3	0	0	0	2.0	5	0	5	0	0-0	0	13.50
Max Macon	L	28	1	0	0	0	3.0	10	2	1	1	0-0	0	21.00
Harry MacPherson	R	17	1	0	0	0	1.0	0	0	1	1	0-0	0	0.00

694 Seasons: Team Rosters

1944 Brooklyn Dodgers 7th NL 63-91 .409 42.0 GB

Leo Durocher

Player	Gm by Position	B	Age	G	AB	R	H	2B	3B	HR	RBI	BB	SO	SB	Avg	OBP	Slg
Mickey Owen	C125,2B1	R	28	130	461	43	126	20	3	1	42	36	17	4	.273	.326	.336
Howie Schultz	1B136	R	21	138	526	59	134	32	3	11	83	24	67	6	.255	.290	.390
Eddie Stanky†	2B58,SS35,3B1	R	27	89	261	32	72	9	2	0	16	44	13	3	.276	.382	.326
Frenchy Bordagaray	3B98,OF25	R	34	130	501	85	141	26	4	6	51	36	22	2	.281	.331	.385
Bobby Bragan	SS51,C35,3B6*	R	26	94	266	26	71	8	4	0	17	13	14	2	.267	.304	.327
Augie Galan	OF147,2B2	S	32	151	547	96	174	43	9	12	93	101	23	4	.318	.426	.495
Dixie Walker	OF140	L	33	147	535	77	191	37	8	13	91	72	27	6	.357	.434	.529
Goody Rosen	OF65	L	31	89	264	38	69	8	3	0	23	26	27	0	.261	.330	.314
Luis Olmo	OF64,2B42,3B31	R	24	136	520	65	134	20	5	9	85	17	37	10	.258	.284	.367
Tommy Brown	SS46	R	16	46	146	17	24	4	0	0	8	8	17	0	.164	.208	.192
Paul Waner†	OF32	L	41	83	136	16	39	4	1	0	16	27	7	0	.287	.405	.331
Jack Bolling	1B27	L	27	56	131	21	46	14	1	1	25	14	4	0	.351	.418	.496
Eddie Basinski	2B37,SS3	R	21	39	105	13	27	4	1	0	9	6	10	1	.257	.310	.314
Barney Koch	2B29,SS1	R	21	33	96	11	21	2	0	0	1	3	9	0	.219	.242	.240
Eddie Miksis	3B15,SS10	R	17	26	91	12	20	2	0	0	11	6	11	4	.220	.268	.242
Bill Hart	SS25,3B2	R	31	29	90	8	16	4	2	0	4	9	7	1	.178	.253	.267
Gil English	SS13,3B11,2B2	R	34	27	79	4	12	3	0	1	7	6	7	0	.152	.212	.228
Morrie Aderholt	OF13	L	28	17	59	9	16	2	3	0	10	4	4	0	.271	.317	.407
Red Durrett	OF9	L	23	11	32	3	5	1	0	1	1	7	10	0	.156	.308	.281
Pat Ankenman	2B11,SS2	R	31	13	24	1	6	1	0	0	3	0	2	0	.250	.250	.292
Lou Rochelli	2B5	R	25	5	17	0	3	0	1	0	2	2	6	0	.176	.263	.294
Gene Mauch	SS5	R	18	5	15	2	2	1	0	0	2	2	3	0	.133	.235	.200
Lloyd Waner†	OF4	L	38	15	14	3	4	0	0	0	1	3	0	0	.286	.412	.286
Ray Hayworth	C6	R	40	7	10	1	0	0	0	0	0	2	1	0	.000	.167	.000
Stan Andrews	C4	R	27	4	8	1	1	0	0	0	1	1	2	0	.125	.222	.125
Fats Dantonio	C3	R	25	3	7	0	1	0	0	0	0	0	1	0	.143	.143	.143
Johnny Cooney†	OF2	R	43	7	4	0	3	0	0	0	1	0	0	0	.750	.750	.750
Clancy Smyres		S	22	5	2	1	0	0	0	0	0	0	0	0	.000	.000	.000
Roy Jarvis	C1	R	18	1	1	0	0	0	0	0	0	0	1	0	.000	.000	.000

B. Bragan, 1 G at 2B

Pitcher	T	Age	G	GS	CG	ShO	IP	H	HR	BB	SO	W-L	Sv	ERA
Hal Gregg	R	22	39	31	6	0	197.2	201	12	137	92	9-16	2	5.46
Curt Davis	R	40	31	23	12	1	194.0	207	12	39	49	10-11	4	3.34
Rube Melton	R	27	37	23	6	1	187.1	178	1	96	91	9-13	0	3.46
Cal McLish	R	18	23	13	3	0	84.0	110	10	48	24	3-10	0	7.82
Ben Chapman	R	35	11	9	6	0	79.1	75	4	33	37	5-3	0	3.40
Whit Wyatt	R	36	9	9	1	0	37.2	51	1	16	4	2-6	0	7.17
Ed Head	R	26	9	8	5	1	63.1	54	2	19	17	4-3	0	2.70
Art Herring	R	38	12	6	3	1	55.1	59	3	17	19	3-4	1	3.42
John Wells	R	21	4	2	0	0	15.0	18	1	11	7	0-2	0	5.40
Chink Zachary	R	26	4	2	0	0	10.1	10	2	7	3	0-2	0	9.58
Frank Wurm	L	20	1	1	0	0	0.1	1	0	5	1	0-0	0	108.00
Les Webber	R	29	48	9	1	0	140.1	157	9	64	42	7-8	3	4.94
Tommy Warren	L	26	22	4	2	0	68.2	74	4	40	18	1-4	0	4.98
Ralph Branca	R	18	21	1	0	0	44.2	46	2	32	16	0-2	1	7.05
Clyde King	R	19	14	3	1	0	43.2	42	1	12	14	2-1	0	3.09
Tom Sunkel	L	31	12	3	0	0	24.0	39	1	10	6	1-3	1	7.50
Bob Chipman†	L	25	11	3	1	0	36.1	38	1	24	20	3-1	0	4.21
Fritz Ostermueller†	L	36	10	4	3	0	41.2	46	3	12	17	2-1	1	3.24
Wes Flowers	L	30	9	1	0	0	17.1	26	3	13	3	1-1	0	7.79
Charlie Fuchs	R	30	8	0	0	0	15.2	25	2	9	5	1-0	0	5.74
Bill Lohrman†	R	31	3	0	0	0	2.2	4	0	4	1	0-0	0	0.00
Claude Crocker	R	19	2	0	0	0	3.1	6	0	5	1	0-0	0	10.80
Charlie Osgood	R	17	1	0	0	0	3.0	2	0	3	0	0-0	0	3.00
Jack Franklin	R	24	1	0	0	0	2.0	2	1	4	0	0-0	0	13.50

1944 Philadelphia Phillies 8th NL 61-92 .399 43.5 GB

Freddie Fitzsimmons

Player	Gm by Position	B	Age	G	AB	R	H	2B	3B	HR	RBI	BB	SO	SB	Avg	OBP	Slg
Bob Finley	C74	R	28	94	281	18	70	11	1	1	21	12	25	1	.249	.292	.306
Tony Lupien	1B151	L	27	153	597	82	169	23	9	5	52	56	29	18	.283	.347	.377
Moon Mullen	2B114,3B1	L	27	118	464	51	124	9	4	0	31	28	32	4	.267	.315	.304
Glen Stewart	3B83,SS32,2B1	R	31	118	377	32	83	11	5	0	29	28	40	0	.220	.274	.276
Ray Hamrick	SS74	R	22	74	292	22	60	10	1	1	23	23	34	1	.205	.268	.257
Buster Adams	OF151	R	29	151	584	86	165	35	3	17	64	74	74	2	.283	.370	.440
Ron Northey	OF151	L	24	152	570	72	164	35	9	22	104	67	51	1	.288	.367	.496
Jimmy Wasdell	OF121,1B4	L	30	133	451	47	125	20	3	3	40	45	17	0	.277	.344	.355
Charlie Letchas	2B47,3B32,SS29	R	28	116	396	29	94	8	1	0	33	32	27	0	.237	.298	.258
Johnny Peacock†	C73,2B1	L	34	83	253	21	57	9	3	0	21	31	15	1	.225	.310	.285
Ted Cieslak	3B48,OF5	R	27	85	220	18	54	10	0	2	11	21	17	1	.245	.314	.318
Coaker Triplett	OF44	R	32	84	184	15	43	5	1	1	25	19	10	1	.234	.305	.288
Granny Hamner	SS21	R	17	21	77	6	19	1	0	0	5	3	7	0	.247	.275	.260
Andy Seminick	C11,OF7	R	23	22	63	9	14	2	1	0	4	6	17	2	.222	.300	.286
Heinie Heltzel	SS10	R	30	11	22	1	4	1	0	0	0	2	3	0	.182	.280	.227
Merv Shea	C6	R	43	7	15	2	4	0	0	1	1	4	4	0	.267	.421	.467
Lee Riley	OF3	L	37	4	12	1	1	1	0	0	1	0	0	0	.083	.083	.167
Chuck Klein	OF1	L	39	4	7	1	1	0	0	0	0	0	2	0	.143	.143	.143
Joe Antolick	C3	R	28	4	6	1	2	0	0	0	0	1	0	0	.333	.429	.333
Putsy Caballero	3B2	R	16	4	4	0	0	0	0	0	0	0	1	0	.000	.000	.000
Benny Culp	C1	R	30	4	2	1	0	0	0	0	0	0	0	0	.000	.000	.000
Turkey Tyson		L	29	1	1	0	0	0	0	0	0	0	0	0	.000	.000	.000
Nick Goulish		L	26	1	1	0	0	0	0	0	0	0	0	0	.000	.000	.000

Pitcher	T	Age	G	GS	CG	ShO	IP	H	HR	BB	SO	W-L	Sv	ERA
Ken Raffensberger	L	26	37	31	18	3	258.2	257	9	45	136	13-20	0	3.06
Charley Schanz	R	25	40	30	13	1	241.1	231	6	103	84	13-16	3	3.32
Al Gerheauser	L	27	30	29	10	2	182.2	210	8	65	66	8-16	0	4.58
Bill Lee	R	34	31	28	11	3	208.1	199	9	57	50	10-11	1	3.15
Dick Barrett	R	37	37	27	11	1	221.1	223	7	88	74	12-18	0	3.86
Vern Kennedy†	R	37	12	7	3	0	55.1	60	3	20	23	1-5	0	4.23
Charlie Ripple	L	22	1	1	0	0	2.1	6	0	4	2	0-0	0	15.43
Andy Karl	R	30	38	0	0	0	89.0	76	1	21	26	3-2	2	2.33
Chet Covington	L	33	19	0	0	0	38.2	46	2	8	13	1-1	0	4.66
Harry Shuman	R	29	18	0	0	0	26.2	26	1	11	4	0-0	0	4.05
Dale Matthewson	R	21	17	1	0	0	32.0	27	1	16	8	0-0	0	3.94
Barney Mussill	L	24	16	0	0	0	19.1	20	1	13	5	0-1	0	6.05
Deacon Donahue	R	24	6	0	0	0	9.1	18	0	2	2	0-2	0	7.71
John Fick	L	23	4	0	0	0	5.1	3	0	3	2	0-0	0	3.38
Rogers McKee	L	17	1	0	0	0	2.0	2	1	1	0	0-0	0	4.50
Lou Lucier†	R	26	1	0	0	0	2.0	3	0	2	1	0-0	0	13.50
Al Verdel	R	23	1	0	0	0	1.0	0	0	0	0	0-0	0	0.00

»1945 Detroit Tigers 1st AL 88-65 .575 —

Steve O'Neill

Player	Gm by Position	B	Age	G	AB	R	H	2B	3B	HR	RBI	BB	SO	SB	Avg	OBP	Slg
Bob Swift	C94	R	30	95	279	19	65	5	0	0	24	25	22	1	.233	.296	.251
Rudy York	1B155	R	31	155	595	71	157	25	5	18	87	59	85	6	.264	.330	.413
Eddie Mayo	2B124	L	35	134	501	71	143	24	3	10	54	48	29	7	.285	.348	.405
Bob Maier	3B124,OF5	R	29	132	486	58	128	25	7	1	34	37	32	7	.263	.315	.350
Skeeter Webb	SS104,2B11	R	35	118	407	43	81	12	2	0	21	30	35	8	.199	.254	.238
Roy Cullenbine†	OF146	S	31	146	523	80	145	27	5	18	93	101	36	2	.277	.397	.451
Doc Cramer	OF140	L	39	141	541	62	149	22	8	6	58	35	21	2	.275	.323	.379
Jimmy Outlaw	OF105,3B21	R	32	132	446	56	121	16	5	0	34	45	33	6	.271	.338	.330
Hank Greenberg	OF72	R	34	78	270	47	84	20	2	13	60	42	40	3	.311	.404	.544
Paul Richards	C83	R	36	83	234	26	60	12	1	3	32	19	31	4	.256	.315	.355
Joe Hoover	SS68	R	30	74	222	33	57	10	5	1	17	21	35	6	.257	.324	.360
Red Borom	2B28,3B4,SS2	L	29	55	130	19	35	4	0	0	9	7	8	4	.269	.307	.300
Chuck Hostetler	OF8	L	41	42	44	3	7	3	0	0	2	7	8	0	.159	.275	.227
Don Ross†	3B8	R	30	8	29	3	11	4	0	0	4	5	1	2	.379	.471	.517
Hub Walker	OF7	L	38	28	23	4	3	0	0	0	1	9	4	1	.130	.375	.130
Ed Mierkowicz	OF6	R	21	10	15	0	2	2	0	0	2	1	3	0	.133	.188	.267
John McHale	1B3	L	23	19	14	0	2	0	0	0	1	1	4	0	.143	.250	.143
Hack Miller	C2	R	32	2	4	0	3	0	0	0	1	0	0	0	.750	.750	.750
Milt Welch	C1	R	20	1	2	0	0	0	0	0	0	0	1	0	.000	.000	.000
Russ Kerns		L	24	1	1	0	0	0	0	0	0	0	0	0	.000	.000	.000
Carl McNabb		R	28	1	1	0	0	0	0	0	0	0	1	0	.000	.000	.000

Pitcher	T	Age	G	GS	CG	ShO	IP	H	HR	BB	SO	W-L	Sv	ERA
Hal Newhouser	L	24	40	36	29	8	313.1	239	5	110	212	25-9	2	1.81
Dizzy Trout	R	30	41	31	18	4	246.1	252	8	79	97	18-15	2	3.14
Al Benton	R	34	31	27	12	5	191.2	175	7	63	76	13-8	3	2.02
Stubby Overmire	L	26	31	22	9	0	162.1	189	6	42	36	9-9	4	3.88
Les Mueller	R	26	26	18	6	2	134.2	117	8	58	42	6-8	1	3.68
Virgil Trucks	R	28	1	1	0	0	5.1	3	0	2	3	0-0	0	1.69
Walter Wilson	R	31	25	4	1	0	70.1	76	4	35	28	1-3	0	4.61
George Caster†	R	37	22	0	0	0	51.1	47	3	27	23	5-1	2	3.86
Zeb Eaton	R	25	17	3	0	0	53.1	48	0	40	15	4-2	0	4.05
Jim Tobin†	R	32	14	6	2	0	58.1	61	2	28	14	4-5	1	3.55
Art Houtteman	R	17	13	0	0	0	25.1	27	1	11	9	0-2	0	5.33
Joe Orrell	R	27	12	5	1	0	48.0	46	1	24	14	2-3	0	3.00
Billy Pierce	L	18	5	0	0	0	10.0	6	1	10	10	0-0	0	1.80
Tommy Bridges	R	38	4	1	0	0	11.0	14	2	2	6	1-0	0	3.27
Prince Oana	R	37	3	1	0	0	11.1	3	0	7	3	0-0	1	1.59
Pat McLaughlin	R	34	1	0	0	0	1.0	2	0	0	0	0-0	0	9.00

1945 Washington Senators 2nd AL 87-67 .565 1.5 GB

Ossie Bluege

Player	Gm by Position	B	Age	G	AB	R	H	2B	3B	HR	RBI	BB	SO	SB	Avg	OBP	Slg
Rick Ferrell	C83	R	39	91	286	33	76	12	1	1	38	43	13	2	.266	.366	.325
Joe Kuhel	1B141	L	39	142	533	73	152	29	13	2	75	79	31	10	.285	.378	.400
George Myatt	2B94,OF32,3B6*	L	31	133	490	81	145	17	7	1	39	63	43	30	.296	.378	.365
Harlond Clift	3B111	R	32	119	375	49	79	12	0	8	53	76	58	2	.211	.349	.307
Gil Torres	SS145,3B2	R	29	147	562	39	133	12	5	0	48	21	29	7	.237	.264	.276
George Binks	OF128,1B20	L	28	145	550	62	153	32	6	6	81	34	52	11	.278	.324	.391
George Case	OF123	R	29	123	504	72	148	19	5	1	31	49	27	30	.294	.360	.357
Buddy Lewis	OF69	L	28	69	258	42	86	14	7	2	37	37	15	1	.333	.423	.465
Fred Vaughn	2B76,SS1	R	26	80	268	28	63	7	4	1	25	23	48	0	.235	.298	.302
Mike Kreevich†	OF40	R	37	45	158	22	44	8	2	1	23	21	11	7	.278	.363	.373
Al Evans	C41	R	28	51	150	19	39	11	2	2	19	17	22	2	.260	.339	.400
Hillis Layne	3B33	L	27	61	147	23	44	5	4	1	14	10	7	2	.299	.352	.408
Mike Guerra	C38	R	32	56	138	11	29	1	1	1	15	10	12	4	.210	.268	.254
Jose Zardon	OF43	R	22	54	131	13	38	5	3	0	13	7	11	3	.290	.326	.374
Jake Powell†	OF27	R	36	31	98	4	19	2	0	0	3	8	8	1	.194	.255	.214
Vince Ventura	OF15	R	28	18	58	4	12	0	0	0	2	4	8	1	.207	.258	.207
Cecil Travis	3B14	L	31	15	54	4	13	2	1	0	10	4	5	0	.241	.293	.315
Dick Kimble	SS15	L	29	20	49	5	12	1	1	0	1	5	2	0	.245	.315	.306
Walt Chipple	OF13	R	26	18	44	4	6	0	0	0	5	5	6	0	.136	.224	.136
Howie McFarland	OF3	R	35	6	11	0	1	0	0	0	2	0	3	0	.091	.091	.091

G. Myatt, 1 G at SS

Pitcher	T	Age	G	GS	CG	ShO	IP	H	HR	BB	SO	W-L	Sv	ERA
Roger Wolff	R	34	33	29	21	4	250.0	200	7	53	108	20-10	2	2.12
Dutch Leonard	R	36	31	29	12	4	216.0	208	5	35	96	17-7	1	2.13
Mickey Haefner	L	32	37	28	19	1	238.1	226	10	69	83	16-14	3	3.47
Marino Pieretti	R	24	44	27	14	3	233.0	235	3	91	66	14-13	2	3.32
Johnny Niggeling	R	41	26	25	8	2	176.2	161	7	73	90	7-12	0	3.16
Walt Masterson	R	25	4	2	1	1	25.0	21	1	10	14	1-2	0	1.08
Alex Carrasquel	R	32	35	7	5	2	122.2	105	5	40	38	7-5	1	2.71
Sandy Ullrich	R	23	28	6	0	0	81.1	91	3	34	26	3-3	1	4.54
Wally Holborow	R	31	15	1	1	1	31.1	20	0	16	14	1-1	0	2.30
Pete Appleton†	R	41	6	2	1	0	21.1	16	1	11	12	1-0	1	3.38
Dick Stone	L	33	3	0	0	0	5.0	6	0	2	0	0-0	0	0.00
Armando Roche	R	18	2	0	0	0	6.0	10	0	2	0	0-0	0	6.00
Bert Shepard	L	25	1	0	0	0	5.1	3	0	1	2	0-0	0	1.69
Joe Cleary	R	26	1	0	0	0	0.1	5	0	3	1	0-0	0	189.00

1945 St. Louis Browns 3rd AL 81-70 .536 6.0 GB

Luke Sewell

Player	Gm by Position	B	Age	G	AB	R	H	2B	3B	HR	RBI	BB	SO	SB	Avg	OBP	Slg
Frank Mancuso	C115	R	27	119	365	39	98	13	3	1	38	46	44	0	.268	.354	.329
George McQuinn	1B136	L	35	139	483	69	134	31	3	7	61	65	51	1	.277	.364	.398
Don Gutteridge	2B128,OF14	R	33	143	543	72	129	24	3	2	49	43	46	9	.238	.295	.304
Mark Christman	3B77	R	31	78	289	32	80	7	4	4	34	19	19	1	.277	.328	.370
Vern Stephens	SS144,3B4	R	24	149	571	90	165	27	3	24	89	55	70	2	.289	.352	.473
Milt Byrnes	OF125,1B2	L	28	133	442	53	110	29	4	8	59	78	84	1	.249	.363	.387
Gene Moore	OF100	L	35	110	354	48	92	16	2	5	50	40	26	1	.260	.337	.359
Mike Kreevich†	OF81	R	37	84	295	34	70	11	1	2	21	37	27	4	.237	.322	.302
Len Schulte	3B71,2B37,SS14	R	28	119	430	37	106	16	1	0	36	24	35	0	.247	.286	.288
Pete Gray	OF61	L	30	77	234	26	51	6	2	0	13	13	11	5	.218	.259	.261
Lou Finney†	OF36,1B22,3B1	L	34	57	213	24	59	8	4	2	22	21	6	0	.277	.345	.380
Babe Martin	OF48,1B6	R	25	54	185	13	37	5	2	2	16	11	24	0	.200	.245	.281
Red Hayworth	C55	R	30	56	160	7	31	4	0	0	17	7	6	0	.194	.228	.219
Chet Laabs	OF35	R	33	35	109	15	26	4	3	1	8	16	17	0	.239	.352	.358
Joe Schultz	C4	L	26	41	44	1	13	2	0	0	8	3	1	0	.295	.340	.341
Ellis Clary	3B16,2B3	R	28	26	38	6	8	1	0	1	2	2	3	0	.211	.250	.316

Pitcher	T	Age	G	GS	CG	ShO	IP	H	HR	BB	SO	W-L	Sv	ERA
Nels Potter	R	33	32	32	21	3	255.1	212	10	68	129	15-11	0	2.47
Jack Kramer	R	27	29	25	15	3	193.0	190	13	73	99	10-15	2	3.36
Sig Jakucki	R	35	30	24	15	1	192.1	188	9	65	55	12-10	2	3.51
Tex Shirley	R	27	32	24	10	2	183.2	191	8	93	77	8-12	0	3.63
Al Hollingsworth	L	37	26	22	15	1	173.1	164	4	68	64	12-9	1	2.70
Bob Muncrief	R	29	27	15	10	0	145.2	132	8	44	54	13-4	1	2.72
Ox Miller	R	30	4	3	3	0	28.1	23	2	5	4	2-1	0	1.59
Sam Zoldak	L	26	26	1	1	0	69.2	74	3	18	19	3-2	0	3.36
Lefty West	L	29	24	8	1	0	74.1	71	2	31	38	3-4	0	3.63
Earl Jones	L	26	10	0	0	0	28.1	18	0	18	13	0-0	1	2.54
George Caster†	R	37	10	0	0	0	15.2	20	0	7	9	1-2	1	6.89
Cliff Fannin	R	21	5	0	0	0	10.1	8	0	5	5	0-0	0	2.61
Al LaMacchia	R	23	5	0	0	0	9.0	6	0	3	2	2-0	0	2.00
Pete Appleton†	R	41	2	0	0	0	2.1	3	0	7	1	0-0	0	15.43
Dee Sanders	R	24	2	0	0	0	1.1	7	0	1	1	0-0	0	40.50

1945 New York Yankees 4th AL 81-71 .533 6.5 GB

Joe McCarthy

Player	Gm by Position	B	Age	G	AB	R	H	2B	3B	HR	RBI	BB	SO	SB	Avg	OBP	Slg
Mike Garbark	C59	R	29	60	176	23	38	5	3	1	26	23	12	0	.216	.310	.295
Nick Etten	1B152	L	31	152	565	77	161	24	4	18	111	90	23	2	.285	.387	.437
Snuffy Stirnweiss	2B152	R	26	152	632	107	195	32	22	10	64	78	62	33	.309	.385	.476
Oscar Grimes	3B141,1B1	R	30	142	480	64	127	19	7	4	45	97	73	7	.265	.395	.358
Frankie Crosetti	SS126	R	34	130	441	57	105	12	0	4	48	59	65	7	.238	.341	.293
Bud Metheny	OF128	L	30	133	509	64	126	18	2	8	53	54	31	5	.248	.325	.338
Hersh Martin	OF102	S	35	117	408	53	109	18	6	7	53	65	31	4	.267	.368	.392
Tuck Stainback	OF83	R	33	95	327	40	84	12	2	5	32	13	20	0	.257	.289	.352
Russ Derry	OF68	L	28	78	253	37	57	6	2	13	45	31	49	1	.225	.312	.419
Charlie Keller	OF44	L	28	44	163	26	49	7	4	10	34	31	21	0	.301	.412	.577
Aaron Robinson	C45	L	30	50	160	19	45	6	1	8	24	21	23	0	.281	.368	.481
Johnny Lindell	OF41	R	28	41	159	26	45	6	3	1	20	17	10	2	.283	.363	.377
Bill Drescher	C33	L	24	48	126	10	34	3	1	0	15	8	5	0	.270	.313	.310
Herb Crompton	C33	R	33	36	99	6	19	3	0	0	12	2	7	0	.192	.208	.222
Mike Milosevich	SS22,2B1	R	30	30	69	5	15	2	0	0	7	6	6	0	.217	.289	.246
Joe Buzas	SS12	R	25	30	65	8	17	2	1	0	6	2	5	2	.262	.284	.323
Don Savage	3B14,OF2	R	26	34	58	5	13	1	0	0	3	3	14	1	.224	.262	.241
Paul Waner		L	42	1	0	0	0	0	0	0	0	1	0	0	—	1.000	—

Pitcher	T	Age	G	GS	CG	ShO	IP	H	HR	BB	SO	W-L	Sv	ERA
Bill Bevens	R	28	29	25	14	2	184.0	174	12	68	76	13-9	0	3.67
Tiny Bonham	R	31	23	23	12	0	180.2	186	11	22	42	8-11	0	3.29
Monk Dubiel	R	27	26	20	9	1	151.1	157	9	62	45	10-9	0	4.64
Hank Borowy†	R	29	18	18	7	1	132.1	107	6	58	35	10-5	0	3.13
Al Gettel	R	27	27	17	9	0	154.2	141	11	53	67	9-8	3	3.90
Bill Zuber	R	32	21	14	7	0	127.0	121	2	56	50	5-11	1	3.19
Red Ruffing	R	41	11	11	8	1	87.1	85	2	20	24	7-3	0	2.89
Atley Donald	R	34	9	9	6	2	63.2	62	3	25	19	5-4	0	2.97
Spud Chandler	R	37	4	4	2	1	31.0	30	2	7	12	2-1	0	4.65
Jim Turner	R	41	30	0	0	0	54.1	45	4	31	22	3-4	10	3.64
Ken Holcombe	R	26	23	2	0	0	55.1	43	2	27	20	3-3	0	1.79
Joe Page	L	27	20	9	4	0	102.0	95	1	46	50	6-3	0	2.82
Steve Roser	R	27	11	0	0	0	27.0	27	1	8	11	0-0	0	3.67
Paul Schreiber	R	42	2	0	0	0	4.1	4	0	2	1	0-0	0	4.15

1945 Cleveland Indians 5th AL 73-72 .503 11.0 GB

Lou Boudreau

Player	Gm by Position	B	Age	G	AB	R	H	2B	3B	HR	RBI	BB	SO	SB	Avg	OBP	Slg
Frankie Hayes†	C119	R	30	119	385	39	91	15	6	6	43	53	52	1	.236	.335	.353
Mike Rocco	1B141	L	29	143	565	81	149	28	6	10	56	52	40	0	.264	.326	.388
Dutch Meyer	2B130	R	29	130	524	71	153	29	8	7	48	40	32	2	.292	.342	.418
Don Ross†	3B106	R	30	106	363	26	95	15	1	2	43	42	15	0	.262	.340	.325
Lou Boudreau	SS97	R	27	97	345	50	106	24	1	3	48	35	20	0	.307	.374	.409
Pat Seerey	OF117	R	22	126	414	56	98	22	2	14	56	66	97	1	.237	.342	.401
Felix Mackiewicz	OF112	R	27	120	359	42	98	14	7	2	37	44	41	5	.273	.356	.368
Jeff Heath	OF101	L	30	102	370	60	113	16	7	15	61	56	39	3	.305	.398	.508
Al Cihocki	SS41,3B29,2B23	R	21	92	283	21	60	9	3	0	24	11	48	2	.212	.241	.265
Paul O'Dea	OF53,P1	L	24	87	221	21	52	2	2	1	21	20	26	3	.235	.299	.276
Les Fleming	OF33,1B5	L	29	42	140	18	46	10	2	3	22	11	5	0	.329	.382	.493
Myril Hoag	OF33,P2	R	37	40	128	10	27	5	3	0	3	11	18	1	.211	.279	.297
Eddie Carnett	OF16,P2	L	28	30	73	5	16	7	0	0	7	2	9	0	.219	.250	.315
Ed Wheeler	3B14,SS11,2B3	R	30	46	72	12	14	2	0	0	2	8	13	1	.194	.275	.222
Jim McDonnell	C23	L	22	28	51	3	10	2	0	0	8	2	4	0	.196	.226	.235
Hank Ruszkowski	C14	R	19	14	49	2	10	0	0	0	5	4	9	0	.204	.264	.204
Elmer Weingartner	SS20	R	26	20	39	5	9	1	0	0	1	4	11	0	.231	.302	.256
Red Steiner†	C4	L	29	12	21	0	3	0	0	0	2	1	4	0	.143	.182	.143
Stan Benjamin	OF4	R	31	14	21	1	7	2	0	0	3	0	0	0	.333	.333	.429
Papa Williams	1B3	R	31	16	19	0	4	0	0	0	0	1	2	0	.211	.250	.211
Roy Cullenbine†	OF4,3B3	S	31	8	13	3	1	1	0	0	0	11	0	0	.077	.500	.154
Bob Rothel	3B4	R	21	4	10	0	2	0	0	0	0	3	1	0	.200	.385	.200
Gene Desautels	C10	R	38	10	9	1	1	0	0	0	0	1	1	0	.111	.200	.111

Pitcher	T	Age	G	GS	CG	ShO	IP	H	HR	BB	SO	W-L	Sv	ERA
Steve Gromek	R	25	33	30	21	3	251.0	229	6	66	101	19-9	1	2.55
Allie Reynolds	R	30	44	30	16	2	247.1	227	7	130	112	18-12	4	3.20
Jim Bagby Jr.	R	28	25	19	11	3	159.1	171	3	59	38	8-11	1	3.73
Al Smith	L	37	21	19	8	3	133.2	141	8	48	34	5-12	1	3.84
Mel Harder	R	35	11	11	2	0	76.0	93	3	23	16	3-7	0	3.67
Bob Feller	R	26	9	9	7	1	72.0	50	1	35	59	5-3	0	2.50
Red Embree	R	27	8	8	5	1	70.0	56	3	26	42	4-4	0	1.93
Ed Klieman	R	27	38	12	4	1	126.1	123	3	49	33	5-8	4	3.85
Pete Center	R	33	31	8	2	0	85.2	89	2	28	34	6-3	1	3.99
Jack Salveson	R	31	19	0	0	0	44.0	52	3	6	11	0-0	0	3.68
Earl Henry	L	28	15	1	0	0	21.2	20	0	20	10	0-3	0	5.40
Hal Kleine	L	22	3	0	0	0	7.0	8	0	7	5	0-0	0	3.86
Myril Hoag	R	37	2	0	0	0	3.0	3	0	1	0	0-0	0	0.00
Eddie Carnett	L	28	2	0	0	0	2.0	0	0	0	1	0-0	0	0.00
Paul O'Dea	L	24	1	0	0	0	2.0	4	0	2	0	0-0	0	13.50
Paul Calvert	R	27	1	0	0	0	1.1	3	0	1	1	0-0	0	13.50

1945 Chicago White Sox 6th AL 71-78 .477 15.0 GB

Jimmy Dykes

Player	Gm by Position	B	Age	G	AB	R	H	2B	3B	HR	RBI	BB	SO	SB	Avg	OBP	Slg
Mike Tresh	C150	R	31	150	458	50	114	11	0	0	47	65	37	6	.249	.342	.273
Kerby Farrell	1B97	L	31	103	396	44	102	11	3	0	34	24	18	4	.258	.300	.301
Roy Schalk	2B133	R	36	133	513	50	127	23	1	1	65	32	41	3	.248	.293	.302
Tony Cuccinello	3B112	R	37	118	402	50	124	25	3	2	49	45	19	6	.308	.379	.400
Cass Michaels	SS126,2B1	R	19	129	445	47	109	8	5	2	54	37	28	8	.245	.307	.299
Wally Moses	OF139	L	34	140	569	79	168	35	15	2	50	69	33	11	.295	.373	.420
Johnny Dickshot	OF124	R	35	130	486	74	147	19	10	4	58	48	41	18	.302	.366	.407
Oris Hockett	OF106	L	35	106	417	46	122	23	4	2	55	27	30	10	.293	.340	.381
Guy Curtright	OF84	R	32	98	324	51	91	15	7	4	32	39	29	3	.281	.358	.407
Bill Nagel	1B57,3B1	R	29	67	220	21	46	10	3	3	27	15	41	3	.209	.263	.323
Floyd Baker	3B58,2B11	L	28	82	208	22	52	8	0	0	19	23	12	3	.250	.325	.288
Danny Reynolds	SS14,2B11	R	25	29	72	6	12	2	1	0	4	3	8	1	.167	.200	.222
Luke Appling	SS17	R	38	18	58	12	21	2	2	1	10	12	7	1	.362	.471	.517
Vince Castino	C25	R	27	26	37	2	8	1	0	0	4	3	7	0	.216	.275	.243
Joe Orengo	3B7,2B1	R	30	17	15	5	1	0	0	0	1	3	2	0	.067	.222	.067
Bill Mueller	OF7	R	24	13	9	3	0	0	0	0	0	2	1	1	.000	.182	.000

Pitcher	T	Age	G	GS	CG	ShO	IP	H	HR	BB	SO	W-L	Sv	ERA
Orval Grove	R	25	33	30	16	4	217.0	233	12	68	54	14-12	1	3.44
Thornton Lee	L	38	29	28	19	1	228.1	208	6	76	108	15-12	0	2.44
Ed Lopat	L	27	26	24	17	1	199.1	226	8	56	74	10-13	1	4.11
Johnny Humphries	R	30	22	21	10	1	153.0	172	11	48	33	6-14	1	4.24
Bill Dietrich	R	35	18	16	6	3	122.1	136	4	36	43	7-10	0	4.19
Joe Haynes	R	27	14	13	8	1	104.0	92	5	29	34	5-5	1	3.55
Johnny Johnson	L	30	29	0	0	0	69.2	85	2	35	38	3-0	4	4.26
Earl Caldwell	R	40	27	11	5	1	105.1	108	8	37	45	6-7	4	3.59
Frank Papish	L	27	19	5	3	0	84.1	75	3	40	45	4-4	1	3.74
Buck Ross	R	30	13	2	0	0	37.1	51	3	17	8	1-1	0	5.79
Clay Touchstone	R	42	6	0	0	0	10.0	14	1	6	4	0-0	0	5.40

1945 Boston Red Sox 7th AL 71-83 .461 17.5 GB

Joe Cronin

Player	Gm by Position	B	Age	G	AB	R	H	2B	3B	HR	RBI	BB	SO	SB	Avg	OBP	Slg
Bob Garbark	C67	R	35	68	199	21	52	6	0	0	17	18	10	0	.261	.329	.291
Catfish Metkovich	1B97,OF42	L	24	138	539	65	140	26	3	5	62	51	70	19	.260	.331	.347
Skeeter Newsome	2B82,SS33,3B11	R	34	125	438	45	127	30	1	1	48	20	15	6	.290	.322	.370
Johnny Tobin	3B72,2B5,OF1	L	24	84	278	25	70	6	2	0	21	26	24	2	.252	.320	.288
Eddie Lake	SS130,2B1	R	29	133	473	81	132	27	1	11	51	106	37	9	.279	.412	.410
Bob Johnson	OF140	R	38	143	529	71	148	27	7	12	74	63	56	5	.280	.358	.425
Leon Culberson	OF91	R	25	97	331	26	91	21	6	6	45	20	37	4	.275	.316	.429
Tom McBride	OF81,1B11	R	30	100	344	38	105	11	7	1	47	26	17	2	.305	.354	.387
Johnny Lazor	OF81	L	32	101	335	35	104	19	2	5	45	18	17	3	.310	.346	.424
Ben Steiner	2B77	L	23	78	304	39	78	8	3	3	20	31	29	10	.257	.327	.332
Pete Fox	OF57	R	36	66	208	21	51	4	1	0	20	11	18	2	.245	.296	.274
Ty LaForest	3B45,OF5	R	28	52	204	25	51	7	4	2	16	10	35	4	.250	.285	.353
Dolph Camilli	1B54	L	38	63	198	24	42	5	2	2	19	35	38	2	.212	.330	.288
Jim Bucher	3B32,2B2	L	34	52	151	19	34	4	3	0	11	7	13	1	.225	.264	.291
Billy Holm	C57	R	32	58	135	12	25	2	1	0	9	23	17	1	.185	.317	.215
Fred Walters	C38	R	32	40	93	2	16	2	0	0	5	10	9	1	.172	.252	.194
Red Steiner†	C24	L	29	20	58	6	12	1	0	0	4	14	2	0	.207	.361	.224
Frankie Pytlak	C6	R	36	9	17	1	2	0	0	0	0	3	0	0	.118	.250	.118
Loyd Christopher†	OF3	R	25	8	14	4	4	0	0	0	4	3	2	0	.286	.412	.286
Joe Cronin	3B3	R	38	3	8	1	3	0	0	0	1	3	2	0	.375	.545	.375
Nick Polly	3B2	R	28	4	7	0	1	0	0	0	1	0	0	0	.143	.143	.143
Lou Finney†		L	34	2	2	0	0	0	0	0	0	0	1	0	.000	.000	.000

Pitcher	T	Age	G	GS	CG	ShO	IP	H	HR	BB	SO	W-L	Sv	ERA
Boo Ferriss	R	23	35	31	26	5	264.2	263	6	85	94	21-10	2	2.96
Emmett O'Neill	R	27	24	22	10	1	141.2	134	5	117	55	8-11	0	5.15
Jim Wilson	R	23	23	21	8	2	144.1	121	7	88	50	6-8	0	3.30
Randy Heflin	R	26	20	14	6	2	102.0	102	3	61	39	4-10	0	4.06
Pinky Woods	R	30	24	12	3	0	107.1	108	3	63	36	4-7	2	4.19
Otie Clark	R	27	12	9	4	1	82.0	86	0	19	20	4-4	0	3.07
Rex Cecil	R	28	7	7	1	0	45.0	46	4	27	30	2-5	0	5.20
Joe Bowman†	R	35	3	3	0	0	11.2	18	1	9	0	0-2	0	9.26
Clem Dreisewerd	L	29	2	2	0	0	9.2	13	0	2	3	0-1	0	4.66
Oscar Judd†	L	37	2	1	0	0	6.1	10	1	3	5	0-1	0	8.53
Frank Barrett	R	31	37	0	0	0	86.0	77	0	29	35	4-3	3	2.62
Mike Ryba	R	42	34	9	4	1	123.0	122	5	33	44	7-6	2	2.49
Clem Hausmann	R	25	31	13	4	2	125.0	131	5	60	30	5-7	2	5.04
Vic Johnson	L	24	26	9	4	1	85.1	90	4	46	21	6-4	2	4.01
Yank Terry	R	34	12	4	1	0	56.2	68	8	14	28	0-4	0	4.13

696 Seasons: Team Rosters

1945 Philadelphia Athletics 8th AL 52-98 .347 34.5 GB

Connie Mack

Player	Gm by Position	B	Age	G	AB	R	H	2B	3B	HR	RBI	BB	SO	SB	Avg	OBP	Slg
Buddy Rosar	C85	R	30	92	300	23	63	12	1	1	25	20	16	2	.210	.262	.267
Dick Siebert	1B147	L	33	147	573	62	153	29	1	7	51	50	33	2	.267	.327	.358
Irv Hall	2B151	R	26	151	616	62	161	17	5	0	50	35	42	3	.261	.307	.305
George Kell	3B147	R	22	147	567	50	154	30	3	4	56	27	15	2	.272	.306	.356
Ed Busch	SS116,2B2,3B2*	R	27	126	416	37	104	10	3	0	35	32	9	2	.250	.305	.288
Bobby Estalella	OF124	R	34	126	451	45	135	25	6	8	52	74	46	1	.299	.399	.435
Hal Peck	OF110	L	28	112	449	51	124	22	9	5	39	37	28	5	.276	.331	.399
Mayo Smith	OF65	L	30	73	203	18	43	5	0	0	11	36	13	0	.212	.333	.236
Bill McGhee	OF48,1B8	L	39	93	250	24	63	6	1	0	19	24	16	3	.252	.320	.284
Charlie Metro	OF57	R	26	65	200	18	42	10	1	3	15	23	33	1	.210	.291	.315
Bobby Wilkins	SS40,OF4	R	22	62	154	22	40	6	0	0	4	10	17	2	.260	.305	.299
Greek George	C46	R	32	51	138	8	24	4	1	0	11	17	29	0	.174	.265	.217
Ernie Kish	OF30	L	27	43	110	10	27	5	1	0	10	9	9	0	.245	.320	.309
Frankie Hayes†	C32	R	30	32	110	12	25	2	1	3	14	18	14	1	.227	.336	.345
Joe Burns	OF19,3B5,1B1	R	29	31	90	7	23	1	1	0	3	4	17	0	.256	.287	.289
Larry Rosenthal	OF21	L	35	28	75	6	15	3	2	0	5	9	8	0	.200	.286	.293
Al Brancato	SS10	R	26	10	34	3	4	1	0	0	0	1	3	0	.118	.143	.147
Sam Chapman	OF8	R	29	9	30	3	6	2	0	0	1	2	4	0	.200	.250	.267
Ford Garrison	OF5	R	29	6	23	3	7	1	0	1	6	4	3	1	.304	.407	.478
Joe Cicero	OF7	R	34	12	19	3	3	0	0	0	0	1	6	0	.158	.238	.158
Joe Astroth	C8	R	22	10	17	1	1	0	0	0	1	0	1	0	.059	.111	.059
Jim Pruett	C4	R	27	6	9	1	2	0	0	0	0	1	2	0	.222	.300	.222
Larry Drake	OF1	L	24	1	2	0	0	0	0	0	0	0	2	0	.000	.000	.000

E. Busch, 1 G at 1B

Pitcher	T	Age	G	GS	CG	ShO	IP	H	HR	BB	SO	W-L	Sv	ERA
Bobo Newsom	R	37	36	34	16	3	257.1	255	12	103	127	8-20	0	3.29
Russ Christopher	R	27	33	27	17	2	227.1	213	9	75	100	13-13	2	3.17
Jesse Flores	R	30	29	24	9	4	191.1	180	6	63	52	7-10	1	3.43
Don Black	R	28	26	18	8	0	125.1	154	5	69	47	5-11	0	5.17
Lou Knerr	R	23	27	17	5	0	130.0	142	6	74	41	5-11	0	4.22
Steve Gerkin	R	32	21	12	3	0	102.0	112	4	27	25	0-12	0	3.62
Charlie Bowles	R	28	8	4	1	0	33.1	35	3	23	11	0-3	0	5.13
Phil Marchildon	R	31	3	2	0	0	9.0	5	0	11	2	0-1	0	4.00
Bill Connelly	R	20	2	1	0	0	8.0	7	0	8	0	1-1	0	4.50
Joe Berry	R	40	52	0	0	0	130.1	114	5	38	51	8-7	5	2.35
Charlie Gassaway	L	26	24	11	4	0	118.0	114	4	55	50	4-7	0	3.74
Dick Fowler	R	24	7	3	2	1	37.1	41	1	18	21	1-2	0	4.82
Carl Scheib	R	18	4	0	0	0	8.2	6	0	4	2	0-0	0	3.12
Woody Crowson	R	26	1	0	0	0	3.0	2	0	3	2	0-0	0	6.00

»1945 Chicago Cubs 1st NL 98-56 .636 —

Charlie Grimm

Player	Gm by Position	B	Age	G	AB	R	H	2B	3B	HR	RBI	BB	SO	SB	Avg	OBP	Slg
Mickey Livingston	C68,1B1	R	30	71	224	19	57	4	2	2	23	19	6	2	.254	.324	.317
Phil Cavarretta	1B120,OF11	L	28	132	498	94	177	34	10	6	97	81	34	5	.355	.449	.500
Don Johnson	2B138	R	33	138	557	94	168	23	2	2	58	32	34	9	.302	.343	.361
Stan Hack	3B146,1B5	L	35	150	597	110	193	29	7	2	43	99	30	12	.323	.420	.405
Lennie Merullo	SS118	R	28	121	394	40	94	18	0	2	37	31	30	7	.239	.297	.299
Bill Nicholson	OF151	L	30	151	559	82	136	28	4	13	88	92	73	4	.243	.356	.377
Andy Pafko	OF140	R	24	144	534	64	159	24	12	12	110	45	36	5	.298	.361	.455
Peanuts Lowrey	OF138,SS2	R	26	143	523	72	148	22	7	7	89	48	27	11	.283	.343	.392
Roy Hughes	SS36,2B21,3B9*	R	34	69	222	34	58	8	1	0	8	16	18	6	.261	.311	.306
Paul Gillespie	C45,OF1	L	24	75	163	12	47	6	0	3	25	18	9	2	.288	.366	.380
Heinz Becker	1B28	S	29	67	133	25	38	8	2	2	27	17	16	0	.286	.375	.421
Dewey Williams	C54	R	29	59	100	16	28	2	2	2	5	13	13	0	.280	.363	.400
Len Rice	C29	R	26	32	99	10	23	3	0	0	7	5	8	2	.232	.269	.263
Eddie Sauer	OF26	R	26	49	93	8	24	4	1	2	11	8	23	2	.258	.317	.387
Frank Secory	OF12	R	32	35	57	4	9	1	0	0	6	2	7	0	.158	.186	.175
Bill Schuster	SS22,2B3,3B1	R	32	45	47	8	9	2	1	0	2	7	4	2	.191	.296	.277
Reggie Otero	1B8	L	29	14	23	1	9	0	0	0	5	2	2	0	.391	.440	.391
Johnny Ostrowski	3B4	R	27	7	10	4	3	2	0	0	1	0	0	0	.300	.300	.500
Cy Block	2B1,3B1	R	26	2	7	1	1	0	0	0	1	0	0	0	.143	.143	.143
Johnny Moore		L	43	7	6	0	1	0	0	0	2	1	1	0	.167	.286	.167
Loyd Christopher†	OF1	R	25	1	0	0	0	0	0	0	0	0	0	0	—	—	—

R. Hughes, 2 G at 1B

Pitcher	T	Age	G	GS	CG	ShO	IP	H	HR	BB	SO	W-L	Sv	ERA
Hank Wyse	R	27	38	34	23	2	278.1	272	17	55	77	22-10	0	2.68
Paul Derringer	R	38	35	30	15	1	213.2	223	7	51	86	16-11	4	3.45
Claude Passeau	R	36	34	27	19	5	227.0	205	4	59	98	17-9	1	2.46
Ray Prim	L	38	34	19	9	2	165.1	142	9	23	88	13-8	2	2.40
Hank Borowy†	R	29	15	14	11	1	122.1	105	2	47	47	11-2	1	2.13
Ed Hanyzewski	R	24	2	1	0	0	4.2	7	1	1	0	0-0	0	5.79
Hy Vandenberg	R	38	30	7	3	1	95.1	91	4	33	35	7-3	2	3.49
Paul Erickson	R	29	28	9	3	0	108.1	94	5	48	53	7-4	3	3.32
Bob Chipman	L	26	25	10	3	1	72.0	63	4	34	29	4-5	0	3.50
Mack Stewart	R	30	16	1	0	0	28.1	37	0	14	9	0-1	0	4.76
Lon Warneke	R	36	9	1	0	0	14.0	16	0	1	6	0-1	0	3.86
Ray Starr†	R	39	9	1	0	0	13.1	17	1	7	5	1-0	0	7.43
Jorge Comellas	R	28	7	1	0	0	12.0	11	1	6	6	0-2	0	4.50
Walter Signer	R	34	6	0	0	0	8.0	11	1	5	0	0-0	1	3.38
George Hennessey	R	37	2	0	0	0	3.2	7	0	1	2	0-0	0	7.36

1945 St. Louis Cardinals 2nd NL 95-59 .617 3.0 GB

Billy Southworth

Player	Gm by Position	B	Age	G	AB	R	H	2B	3B	HR	RBI	BB	SO	SB	Avg	OBP	Slg
Ken O'Dea	C91	L	32	100	307	36	78	18	2	4	43	50	31	0	.254	.359	.365
Ray Sanders	1B142	L	28	143	537	85	148	29	3	8	78	83	55	3	.276	.375	.385
Emil Verban	2B155	R	29	155	597	59	166	22	8	0	72	19	15	4	.278	.304	.342
Whitey Kurowski	3B131,SS6	R	27	133	511	84	165	27	3	21	102	45	45	1	.323	.383	.511
Marty Marion	SS122	R	27	123	430	63	119	27	5	1	59	39	39	2	.277	.340	.370
Buster Adams†	OF140	R	30	140	578	98	169	26	0	20	101	57	75	3	.292	.359	.441
Red Schoendienst	OF118,SS10,2B1	S	22	137	565	89	157	22	6	1	47	21	17	26	.278	.305	.343
Johnny Hopp	OF104,1B15	L	28	124	446	67	129	22	8	3	44	49	24	14	.289	.363	.395
Augie Bergamo	OF77,1B2	L	28	94	304	51	96	17	2	3	44	43	21	0	.316	.401	.414
Del Rice	C77	R	22	83	253	27	66	17	3	1	28	16	33	0	.261	.313	.364
Debs Garms	3B32,OF10	L	37	74	146	23	49	7	2	0	18	31	3	0	.336	.452	.411
Art Rebel	OF18	L	30	26	72	12	25	4	0	0	5	6	4	1	.347	.397	.403
Lou Klein	SS7,OF7,3B4*	R	26	19	57	12	13	4	1	1	6	14	9	0	.228	.389	.386
George Fallon	SS20,2B4	R	30	24	55	4	13	2	1	0	7	6	6	1	.236	.311	.309
Dave Bartosch	OF11	R	28	24	47	9	12	1	0	0	1	6	3	0	.255	.340	.277
Pep Young	SS11,3B9,2B3	R	37	27	47	5	7	1	0	1	4	1	8	0	.149	.167	.234
Jim Mallory†	OF11	R	26	13	43	3	10	2	0	0	5	0	2	0	.233	.233	.279
Walker Cooper	C4	R	30	4	18	3	7	0	0	0	1	0	1	0	.389	.389	.389
Gene Crumling	C6	R	23	6	12	0	1	0	0	0	1	0	1	0	.083	.083	.083
Glenn Crawford†	OF1	L	31	4	3	0	0	0	0	0	0	1	0	0	.000	.250	.000
John Antonelli†	3B1	R	29	2	3	0	0	0	0	0	0	0	1	0	.000	.000	.000
Bob Keely	C1	R	35	1	1	0	0	0	0	0	0	0	0	0	.000	.000	.000

L. Klein, 2 G at 2B

Pitcher	T	Age	G	GS	CG	ShO	IP	H	HR	BB	SO	W-L	Sv	ERA
Red Barrett†	R	30	36	29	22	3	246.2	244	12	38	63	21-9	0	2.74
Blix Donnelly	R	31	31	23	9	1	166.1	157	10	87	76	8-10	2	3.52
Ken Burkhart	R	28	42	22	12	4	217.1	206	10	66	67	18-8	2	2.90
Harry Brecheen	L	30	24	18	13	3	157.1	136	5	44	63	15-4	2	2.52
Ted Wilks	R	29	18	16	4	1	98.1	103	9	29	28	4-7	0	2.93
Max Lanier	L	29	4	3	3	0	26.0	22	0	8	16	2-2	0	1.73
Mort Cooper†	R	32	4	3	1	0	23.2	20	1	7	14	2-0	0	1.52
Bud Byerly	R	24	33	8	2	0	95.0	111	3	41	39	4-5	0	4.74
George Dockins	L	28	31	12	5	2	126.1	132	4	38	33	8-6	0	3.21
Al Jurisich	R	23	27	6	1	0	71.2	61	7	41	42	3-3	0	5.15
Jack Creel	R	29	26	8	2	0	87.0	78	5	45	34	5-4	2	4.14
Glenn Gardner	R	29	17	4	2	1	54.2	50	2	27	20	3-1	1	3.29
Stan Partenheimer	L	22	8	2	0	0	13.1	12	2	16	6	0-0	0	6.08
Bill Crouch	R	34	6	0	0	0	13.1	12	1	7	4	1-0	0	3.38
Art Lopatka	L	26	4	1	1	0	11.2	7	0	3	5	1-0	0	1.54

1945 Brooklyn Dodgers 3rd NL 87-67 .565 11.0 GB

Leo Durocher

Player	Gm by Position	B	Age	G	AB	R	H	2B	3B	HR	RBI	BB	SO	SB	Avg	OBP	Slg
Mike Sandlock	C47,SS22,2B4*	S	29	80	195	21	55	14	2	2	17	18	19	2	.282	.346	.405
Augie Galan	1B66,OF49,3B40	S	33	152	576	114	177	36	7	9	92	114	27	13	.307	.423	.441
Eddie Stanky	2B153,SS1	R	28	153	555	128	143	29	5	1	39	148	42	6	.258	.417	.333
Frenchy Bordagaray	3B57,OF22	R	35	113	273	32	70	9	6	2	49	29	15	7	.256	.328	.355
Eddie Basinski	SS101,2B6	R	22	108	336	30	88	9	4	0	33	11	33	0	.262	.293	.313
Dixie Walker	OF153	L	34	154	607	102	182	42	9	8	124	75	16	6	.300	.381	.438
Goody Rosen	OF141	L	32	145	606	126	197	24	11	12	75	50	36	4	.325	.379	.460
Luis Olmo	OF106,3B31,2B1	R	25	141	556	62	174	27	13	10	110	36	33	15	.313	.356	.462
Ed Stevens	1B55	L	20	55	201	29	55	14	3	4	29	32	20	0	.274	.376	.433
Tommy Brown	SS55,OF1	R	17	57	196	13	48	3	4	2	19	6	16	3	.245	.267	.332
Bill Hart	3B39,SS8	R	32	58	161	27	37	6	2	3	27	14	21	7	.230	.291	.348
Howie Schultz	1B38	R	22	39	142	18	34	8	2	1	19	10	14	2	.239	.294	.345
Fats Dantonio	C45	R	26	47	128	12	32	6	1	0	12	11	6	3	.250	.309	.313
Johnny Peacock†	C38	L	35	48	110	11	28	5	1	0	14	24	10	2	.255	.388	.318
Mickey Owen	C24	R	29	24	84	5	24	9	0	0	11	10	2	0	.286	.368	.393
Morrie Aderholt†	OF8	L	29	39	60	4	13	1	0	0	6	3	10	0	.217	.254	.233
Clyde Sukeforth	C13	L	43	18	51	2	15	1	0	0	1	4	1	0	.294	.345	.314
Stan Andrews†	C21	R	28	21	49	5	8	0	1	0	2	5	4	0	.163	.255	.204
Babe Herman	OF3	L	42	37	34	6	9	1	0	1	9	5	7	0	.265	.359	.382
Red Durrett	OF4	L	24	8	16	2	2	0	0	0	0	3	3	0	.125	.263	.125
John Douglas	1B4	L	27	5	9	0	0	0	0	0	0	2	4	0	.000	.182	.000
Leo Durocher	2B2	R	39	2	5	1	1	0	0	0	2	0	0	0	.200	.200	.200
Claude Corbitt	3B2	R	29	2	4	1	2	0	0	0	0	1	0	0	.500	.600	.500
Don Lund		R	22	4	3	0	0	0	0	0	0	1	1	0	.000	.250	.000
Ray Hayworth	C2	R	41	2	2	0	0	0	0	0	0	1	0	0	.000	.333	.000
Barney White	3B1,SS1	R	22	4	1	2	0	0	0	0	0	1	1	0	.000	.500	.000
Erv Palica		R	17	2	0	0	0	0	0	0	0	0	0	0	—	—	—

M. Sandlock, 2 G at 3B

Pitcher	T	Age	G	GS	CG	ShO	IP	H	HR	BB	SO	W-L	Sv	ERA
Hal Gregg	R	23	42	34	13	2	254.1	221	5	120	139	18-13	2	3.47
Vic Lombardi	L	22	38	24	9	0	203.2	195	11	86	64	10-11	4	3.31
Curt Davis	R	41	24	18	10	0	149.2	171	10	21	39	10-10	0	3.25
Tom Seats	L	34	31	18	6	2	121.2	127	8	37	44	10-7	0	4.36
Art Herring	R	39	22	15	7	2	124.0	103	11	43	34	7-4	2	3.48
Ralph Branca	R	19	16	15	7	0	109.2	73	4	79	69	5-6	1	3.04
Lee Pfund	R	26	15	10	2	0	62.1	69	4	35	27	3-2	0	5.20
Ben Chapman†	R	36	10	7	2	0	53.2	64	3	32	23	3-3	0	5.53
Clyde King	R	20	42	2	0	0	112.1	131	8	48	29	5-5	3	4.09
Cy Buker	R	26	42	4	0	0	87.1	90	2	45	48	7-2	5	3.30
Les Webber	R	30	17	7	5	0	75.1	69	3	25	30	7-3	0	3.58
Otho Nitcholas	R	36	7	0	0	0	18.2	19	4	1	4	1-0	0	5.30
Ernie Rudolph	R	36	7	0	0	0	8.2	12	1	7	3	1-0	0	5.19
Ray Hathaway	R	28	4	1	0	0	9.0	11	1	6	3	0-1	0	4.00
Claude Crocker	R	20	1	0	0	0	2.0	2	0	1	1	0-0	1	0.00

1945 Pittsburgh Pirates 4th NL 82-72 .532 16.0 GB

Frank Frisch

Player	Gm by Position	B	Age	G	AB	R	H	2B	3B	HR	RBI	BB	SO	SB	Avg	OBP	Slg
Al Lopez	C91	R	36	91	243	22	53	8	0	0	18	35	12	1	.218	.317	.251
Babe Dahlgren	1B144	R	33	144	531	57	133	24	8	5	75	51	51	1	.250	.318	.354
Pete Coscarart	2B122,SS1	R	32	123	392	59	95	17	2	8	38	55	55	2	.242	.341	.357
Bob Elliott	3B81,OF61	R	28	144	541	80	157	36	6	8	108	64	38	5	.290	.366	.423
Frankie Gustine	SS104,2B29,C1	R	25	128	478	67	134	27	5	2	66	37	33	8	.280	.335	.370
Jim Russell	OF140	S	26	146	510	88	145	24	8	12	77	71	40	15	.284	.377	.433
Johnny Barrett	OF132	L	29	142	507	97	130	29	4	15	67	79	68	25	.256	.357	.418
Al Gionfriddo	OF106	L	23	122	409	74	116	18	9	2	42	60	22	12	.284	.377	.386
Lee Handley	3B79	R	31	98	312	39	93	16	2	1	32	20	16	7	.298	.340	.372
Bill Salkeld	C86	L	28	95	267	45	83	16	1	15	52	50	16	2	.311	.420	.547
Vic Barnhart	SS60,3B4	R	22	71	201	21	54	7	0	0	19	9	11	2	.269	.300	.303
Tommy O'Brien	OF45	R	26	58	161	23	54	6	5	0	18	9	13	0	.335	.374	.435
Frank Colman	1B22,OF12	L	27	77	153	18	32	11	1	4	30	9	16	0	.209	.253	.373
Jack Saltzgaver	2B31,3B1	L	42	52	117	20	38	5	3	0	10	8	8	0	.325	.368	.419
Spud Davis	C13	R	40	23	33	2	8	2	0	0	6	2	2	0	.242	.306	.303
Frankie Zak	SS10,2B1	R	23	15	28	2	4	2	0	0	3	3	5	0	.143	.226	.214
Lloyd Waner	OF3	L	39	23	19	5	5	0	0	0	1	1	3	0	.263	.300	.263
Hank Camelli	C1	R	30	1	2	0	0	0	0	0	0	1	0	0	.000	.333	.000
Bill Rodgers		L	22	1	1	0	1	0	0	0	0	0	0	0	1.000	1.000	1.000
Joe Vitelli		R	37	1	0	1	0	0	0	0	0	0	0	0	—	—	—

Pitcher	T	Age	G	GS	CG	ShO	IP	H	HR	BB	SO	W-L	Sv	ERA
Preacher Roe	L	30	33	31	15	3	235.0	228	11	46	148	14-13	1	2.87
Nick Strincevich	R	30	36	29	18	1	228.1	235	7	49	74	16-10	2	3.31
Rip Sewell	R	38	33	24	9	1	188.0	212	9	91	60	11-9	1	4.07
Max Butcher	R	34	28	20	12	2	169.1	184	7	46	37	10-8	0	3.03
Ken Gables	R	26	29	16	6	0	138.2	139	5	46	49	11-7	1	4.15
Fritz Ostermueller	L	37	14	11	4	1	80.2	74	6	37	29	5-4	0	4.57
Xavier Rescigno	R	31	44	1	0	0	78.2	95	6	34	29	3-5	9	5.72
Al Gerheauser	L	28	32	14	5	0	140.1	170	5	54	55	5-10	1	3.91
Cookie Cuccurullo	L	27	29	4	0	0	56.2	68	2	34	17	1-3	1	5.24
Boom-Boom Beck†	R	40	14	5	4	0	63.0	54	2	14	20	6-1	0	2.14
Ray Starr†	R	39	4	0	0	0	6.2	10	0	4	0	0-2	0	9.45
Johnny Lanning	R	34	1	0	0	0	2.0	8	1	0	0	0-0	0	36.00

1945 New York Giants 5th NL 78-74 .513 19.0 GB

Mel Ott

Player	Gm by Position	B	Age	G	AB	R	H	2B	3B	HR	RBI	BB	SO	SB	Avg	OBP	Slg
Ernie Lombardi	C96	R	37	115	368	46	113	7	1	19	70	43	11	0	.307	.387	.486
Phil Weintraub	1B77	L	37	82	283	45	77	9	1	10	42	54	29	2	.272	.389	.417
George Hausmann	2B154	R	29	154	623	98	174	15	8	2	45	73	46	7	.279	.356	.339
Nap Reyes	3B115,1B5	R	25	122	431	39	124	15	4	5	44	25	26	1	.288	.338	.376
Buddy Kerr	SS148	R	22	149	546	53	136	20	3	4	40	41	34	5	.249	.304	.319
Mel Ott	OF118	L	36	135	451	73	139	23	0	21	79	71	41	1	.308	.411	.499
Johnny Rucker	OF98	L	28	105	429	58	117	19	11	7	51	20	36	7	.273	.305	.417
Danny Gardella	OF94,1B15	L	25	121	430	54	117	10	1	18	71	46	55	2	.272	.349	.426
Red Treadway	OF60	L	25	88	224	31	54	4	2	4	23	20	13	3	.241	.303	.330
Clyde Kluttz†	C57	R	27	73	222	25	62	14	0	4	21	15	10	1	.279	.331	.396
Billy Jurges	3B44,SS8	R	37	61	176	22	57	3	1	3	24	24	11	2	.324	.405	.403
Whitey Lockman	OF32	L	18	32	129	16	44	9	0	3	18	13	10	1	.341	.410	.481
Steve Filipowicz	OF31	R	24	35	112	14	23	5	0	2	16	4	13	0	.205	.239	.304
Mike Schemer	1B27	L	27	31	108	10	36	3	1	1	10	6	1	2	.333	.368	.407
Roy Zimmerman	1B25,OF1	L	28	27	98	14	27	1	0	5	15	5	16	1	.276	.330	.439
Jim Mallory†	OF21	R	26	37	94	10	28	1	0	0	9	6	7	1	.298	.340	.309
Joe Medwick†	OF23	R	33	26	92	14	28	4	0	3	11	2	2	2	.304	.319	.446
Charlie Mead	OF11	L	24	11	37	4	10	1	0	1	6	5	2	0	.270	.357	.378
Ray Berres	C20	R	37	20	30	4	5	0	0	0	2	2	3	0	.167	.219	.167
Al Gardella	1B8,OF1	L	27	16	26	2	2	0	0	0	1	4	3	0	.077	.226	.077
Johnny Hudson	3B5,2B2	R	33	28	11	8	0	0	0	0	0	1	1	0	.000	.083	.000
Bill DeKoning	C2	R	25	3	1	0	0	0	0	0	0	0	1	0	.000	.000	.000

Pitcher	T	Age	G	GS	CG	ShO	IP	H	HR	BB	SO	W-L	Sv	ERA
Bill Voiselle	R	26	41	35	14	4	232.1	249	15	97	115	14-14	0	4.49
Harry Feldman	R	25	35	30	10	3	217.2	213	14	69	74	12-13	1	3.27
Van Lingle Mungo	R	34	26	26	7	2	183.0	161	4	71	101	14-7	0	3.20
Jack Brewer	R	25	28	21	8	0	159.2	162	14	58	49	8-6	0	3.83
Andy Hansen	R	20	23	13	4	0	92.2	98	7	28	37	4-3	3	4.66
Sal Maglie	R	28	13	10	7	3	84.1	72	2	22	32	5-4	0	2.35
Don Fisher	R	29	2	1	1	1	18.0	12	1	7	4	1-0	0	2.00
Ace Adams	R	33	65	0	0	0	113.0	109	7	44	39	11-9	15	3.42
Slim Emmerich	R	25	31	7	1	0	100.0	111	8	33	27	4-4	0	4.86
Rube Fischer	R	28	31	4	0	0	76.2	90	5	49	27	3-8	1	5.63
Ray Harrell	R	33	12	0	0	0	25.1	34	1	14	7	0-0	0	4.97
Adrian Zabala	L	28	11	5	1	0	43.1	46	2	20	14	2-4	0	4.78
Ewald Pyle†	L	34	6	1	0	0	6.1	16	0	4	2	0-0	0	17.05
Loren Bain	R	22	3	0	0	0	8.0	10	0	4	1	0-0	0	7.88
Roy Lee	L	27	3	1	0	0	7.0	8	3	3	0	0-2	0	11.57
Johnny Gee	L	29	2	0	0	0	3.0	5	0	2	1	0-0	1	9.00
John Phillips	R	26	1	0	0	0	4.1	5	1	4	0	0-0	0	10.38

1945 Boston Braves 6th NL 67-85 .441 30.0 GB

Bob Coleman (42-51)/Del Bissonette (25-34)

Player	Gm by Position	B	Age	G	AB	R	H	2B	3B	HR	RBI	BB	SO	SB	Avg	OBP	Slg
Phil Masi	C95,1B7	R	29	114	371	55	101	25	4	7	46	42	32	9	.272	.348	.418
Vince Shupe	1B77	L	23	78	283	22	76	8	0	0	15	17	16	3	.269	.312	.297
Whitey Wietelmann	2B87,SS39,3B2*	S	26	123	428	53	116	15	3	4	33	39	27	4	.271	.335	.348
Chuck Workman	3B107,OF24	L	30	139	514	77	141	16	2	25	87	51	58	9	.274	.347	.459
Dick Culler	SS126,3B6	R	30	136	527	87	138	12	1	2	30	50	35	7	.262	.328	.300
Tommy Holmes	OF154	L	28	154	636	125	224	47	6	28	117	70	9	15	.352	.420	.577
Carden Gillenwater	OF140	R	27	144	517	74	149	20	2	7	72	73	70	13	.288	.379	.375
Butch Nieman	OF57	L	27	97	247	43	61	15	0	14	56	43	33	11	.247	.361	.478
Joe Mack	1B65	S	33	66	260	30	60	13	1	3	44	34	39	1	.231	.320	.323
Joe Medwick†	OF38,1B15	R	33	66	218	17	62	13	0	0	26	12	12	3	.284	.325	.344
Stew Hofferth	C45	R	32	50	170	13	40	2	0	3	15	14	11	1	.235	.297	.300
Frank Drews	2B48	R	29	49	147	13	30	4	1	0	19	16	18	0	.204	.282	.245
Eddie Joost	2B19,3B16	R	29	35	141	16	35	7	1	0	9	13	7	0	.248	.312	.312
Bill Ramsey	OF43	R	25	78	137	16	40	8	0	1	12	4	22	1	.292	.326	.372
Tommy Nelson	3B20,2B12	R	28	40	121	6	20	2	0	0	6	4	13	1	.165	.192	.182
Morrie Aderholt†	OF24,2B1	L	29	31	102	15	34	4	0	2	11	9	6	3	.333	.387	.431
Clyde Kluttz†	C19	R	27	25	81	9	24	4	1	0	10	2	6	0	.296	.313	.370
Steve Shemo	2B12,3B3,SS1	R	30	17	46	4	11	1	0	0	7	1	3	0	.239	.255	.261
Stan Wentzel	OF4	R	28	4	19	3	4	0	1	0	6	0	3	1	.211	.211	.316
Mike Ulisney	C4	R	27	11	18	4	7	1	0	1	4	1	0	0	.389	.421	.611
Norm Wallen	3B4	R	28	4	15	1	2	0	1	0	1	1	1	0	.133	.188	.267

W. Wietelmann, 1 G at P

Pitcher	T	Age	G	GS	CG	ShO	IP	H	HR	BB	SO	W-L	Sv	ERA
Jim Tobin†	R	32	27	25	16	0	196.2	220	10	56	38	9-14	0	3.84
Bob Logan	L	35	34	25	5	1	187.0	213	9	53	53	7-11	1	3.18
Nate Andrews	R	31	21	19	8	0	137.2	160	9	52	26	7-12	0	4.58
Al Javery	R	27	17	14	2	1	77.1	92	4	51	18	2-7	0	6.28
Bill Lee†	R	35	16	13	6	1	106.1	112	6	36	12	6-3	0	2.79
Ed Wright	R	26	15	12	7	1	111.1	104	7	33	24	8-3	0	2.51
Mort Cooper†	R	32	20	11	4	1	78.0	77	4	27	45	7-4	1	3.35
Red Barrett†	R	30	9	5	2	0	38.0	43	6	16	13	2-3	2	4.74
Elmer Singleton	R	27	7	5	1	0	37.1	35	1	14	14	1-4	0	4.82
Lefty Wallace	L	23	5	3	1	0	20.0	18	1	9	4	1-0	0	4.50
Bob Whitcher	L	28	6	3	0	0	15.2	12	1	12	6	0-2	0	2.87
Ewald Pyle†	L	34	4	2	0	0	13.2	16	1	18	10	0-1	0	7.24
Johnny Hutchings	R	29	57	12	3	2	185.0	173	21	75	99	7-6	3	3.75
Don Hendrickson	R	31	37	2	1	0	73.1	74	8	39	14	4-8	5	4.91
Tom Earley	R	28	11	2	1	0	41.0	36	4	19	4	2-1	0	4.61
Ira Hutchinson	R	34	11	0	0	0	28.2	33	2	8	4	2-3	1	5.02
Hal Schacker	R	20	6	0	0	0	15.1	14	2	9	6	0-1	0	5.28
Lou Fette	R	38	5	1	0	0	11.0	16	1	7	4	0-2	0	5.73
Charlie Cozart	L	25	5	0	0	0	8.0	10	2	15	4	1-0	0	10.13
Joe Heving	R	44	3	0	0	0	5.1	5	0	3	1	1-0	0	3.38
Ben Cardoni	R	24	3	0	0	0	4.0	6	0	3	5	0-0	0	9.00
Whitey Wietelmann	R	26	1	0	0	0	1.0	6	0	2	0	0-0	0	54.00

1945 Cincinnati Reds 7th NL 61-93 .396 37.0 GB

Bill McKechnie

Player	Gm by Position	B	Age	G	AB	R	H	2B	3B	HR	RBI	BB	SO	SB	Avg	OBP	Slg
Al Lakeman	C74	R	26	76	258	22	66	9	4	8	31	17	45	0	.256	.304	.415
Frank McCormick	1B151	R	34	152	580	68	160	33	0	10	81	56	22	6	.276	.345	.384
Woody Williams	2B133	R	32	133	482	46	114	14	0	0	27	39	24	6	.237	.296	.266
Steve Mesner	3B148,2B3	R	27	150	540	52	137	19	1	1	52	52	18	4	.254	.322	.298
Eddie Miller	SS115	R	28	115	421	46	100	27	2	13	49	18	38	4	.238	.275	.404
Dain Clay	OF152	R	25	153	656	81	184	29	2	1	50	37	58	19	.280	.321	.335
Al Libke	OF108,P4,1B2	L	26	130	449	41	127	23	5	4	53	34	62	6	.283	.336	.383
Eric Tipton	OF83	R	30	108	331	32	80	17	1	5	34	40	37	11	.242	.327	.344
Gee Walker	OF67,3B3	R	37	106	316	28	80	11	2	2	21	16	38	8	.253	.289	.320
Al Unser	C61	R	32	67	204	23	54	10	3	3	21	14	24	0	.265	.318	.387
Kermit Wahl	2B32,SS31,3B7	R	22	71	194	18	39	8	2	0	10	23	22	2	.201	.286	.263
Dick Sipek	OF31	L	22	82	156	14	38	6	2	0	13	9	15	0	.244	.302	.308
Hank Sauer	OF28,1B3	R	28	31	116	18	34	1	0	5	20	6	16	2	.293	.328	.431
Wally Flager†	SS15	L	23	21	52	5	11	1	0	0	6	8	5	0	.212	.317	.231
Johnny Riddle	C23	R	39	23	45	0	8	0	0	0	2	4	6	0	.178	.245	.178
Joe Just	C14	R	29	14	34	2	5	0	0	0	2	4	7	0	.147	.237	.147
Eddie Lukon	OF2	L	24	2	8	1	1	0	0	0	0	0	1	0	.125	.125	.125
Ray Medeiros		R	19	1	0	0	0	0	0	0	0	0	0	0	—	—	—

Pitcher	T	Age	G	GS	CG	ShO	IP	H	HR	BB	SO	W-L	Sv	ERA
Ed Heusser	R	36	31	30	18	4	223.0	248	10	60	56	11-16	1	3.71
Joe Bowman†	R	35	25	24	15	1	185.2	198	8	68	71	11-13	0	3.59
Bucky Walters	R	36	22	22	12	3	168.0	166	6	51	45	10-10	0	2.68
Vern Kennedy†	R	38	24	20	11	1	157.2	170	10	69	38	5-12	1	4.00
Frank Dasso	R	27	16	12	6	0	95.2	89	9	53	39	4-5	0	3.67
Herm Wehmeier	R	18	2	2	0	0	5.0	10	0	4	0	0-1	0	12.60
Howie Fox	R	24	45	15	7	0	164.1	169	6	77	54	8-13	0	4.93
Hod Lisenbee	R	46	31	3	0	0	80.1	97	12	16	14	1-3	1	5.49
Mike Modak	R	23	20	3	1	1	42.1	52	0	23	7	1-2	1	5.74
Earl Harrist	R	26	14	5	1	0	62.1	60	2	27	15	2-4	0	3.61
Arnold Carter	L	27	13	6	2	1	46.2	54	2	13	4	2-4	0	3.09
Elmer Riddle	R	30	12	3	0	0	29.2	39	4	27	5	1-4	0	8.19
Boom-Boom Beck†	R	40	11	5	2	0	47.2	42	0	12	9	2-4	1	3.40
Mel Bosser	R	31	7	2	0	0	16.0	9	0	17	3	2-0	0	3.38
Johnny Hetki	R	23	5	2	2	0	32.2	28	1	11	9	1-2	0	3.58
Al Libke	R	26	4	0	0	0	4.1	3	0	3	2	0-0	0	0.00
Guy Bush	R	43	4	0	0	0	4.1	5	0	3	1	0-0	1	8.31

1945 Philadelphia Phillies 8th NL 46-108 .299 52.0 GB

Freddie Fitzsimmons (18-51)/Ben Chapman (28-57)

Player	Gm by Position	B	Age	G	AB	R	H	2B	3B	HR	RBI	BB	SO	SB	Avg	OBP	Slg
Andy Seminick	C70,3B4,OF1	R	24	80	188	18	45	7	2	6	26	18	38	3	.239	.313	.394
Jimmy Wasdell	OF65,1B63	L	31	134	500	65	150	19	8	7	60	32	11	7	.300	.346	.412
Tony Daniels	2B75,3B1	R	20	76	230	15	46	3	2	0	10	12	22	1	.200	.249	.230
John Antonelli†	3B108,2B23,1B1*	R	29	125	504	50	129	27	2	1	28	24	24	1	.256	.292	.323
Bitsy Mott	SS63,2B27,3B7	R	27	90	289	21	64	8	0	0	22	27	25	2	.221	.290	.249
Vince DiMaggio	OF121	R	32	127	452	64	116	25	3	19	84	43	91	12	.257	.321	.451
Coaker Triplett	OF92	R	33	120	363	36	87	11	1	7	46	40	27	6	.240	.315	.333
Vance Dinges	OF65,1B42	L	30	109	397	46	114	15	4	1	36	35	17	5	.287	.346	.353
Glenn Crawford†	OF38,SS34,2B14	L	31	82	302	41	89	13	2	2	24	36	15	5	.295	.372	.371
Jimmie Foxx	1B40,3B14,P9	R	37	89	224	30	60	11	1	7	38	23	39	0	.268	.336	.420
Rene Monteagudo	OF35,P14	L	29	114	193	26	58	6	0	0	15	28	7	2	.301	.389	.332
Gus Mancuso	C70	R	39	70	176	11	35	5	0	0	16	28	10	2	.199	.309	.227
Jake Powell†	OF44	R	36	48	173	13	40	5	0	1	14	8	13	1	.231	.265	.277
Wally Flager†	SS48,2B1	L	23	49	168	21	42	4	1	2	15	17	15	1	.250	.323	.321
Garvin Hamner	2B21,SS9,3B1	R	21	32	101	12	20	3	0	0	5	7	9	2	.198	.250	.228
Nick Picciuto	3B30,2B4	R	23	36	89	7	12	6	0	0	6	6	17	0	.135	.189	.202
Hal Spindel	C31	R	32	36	87	7	20	3	0	0	8	6	7	0	.230	.280	.264
Johnny Peacock†	C23	L	35	33	74	6	15	6	0	0	6	6	0	1	.203	.263	.284
Ed Walczak	2B17,SS2	R	26	20	57	6	12	3	0	0	2	6	9	0	.211	.286	.263
Buster Adams†	OF14	R	30	14	56	6	13	3	1	2	8	5	5	0	.232	.295	.429
Tony Lupien	1B15	L	28	15	54	1	17	1	0	0	3	6	0	2	.315	.383	.333
Ben Chapman†	OF10,3B4,P3	R	36	24	51	4	16	2	0	0	4	2	1	0	.314	.340	.353
Granny Hamner	SS13	R	18	14	41	3	7	2	0	0	6	1	3	0	.171	.190	.220
Stan Andrews†	C12	R	28	13	33	3	11	2	0	1	6	1	5	1	.333	.353	.485
Don Hasenmayer	2B4,3B1	R	18	5	18	1	2	0	0	0	1	2	1	0	.111	.200	.111
Nick Goulish	OF2	L	27	13	11	4	3	0	0	0	2	1	3	0	.273	.333	.273
Putsy Caballero	3B5	R	17	9	1	1	0	0	0	0	1	0	0	0	.000	.000	.000

J. Antonelli, 1 G at SS

Pitcher	T	Age	G	GS	CG	ShO	IP	H	HR	BB	SO	W-L	Sv	ERA
Dick Barrett	R	38	36	30	8	0	190.2	216	11	92	72	8-20	1	5.43
Charley Schanz	R	26	35	21	5	1	144.2	165	5	87	56	4-15	5	4.35
Charlie Sproull	R	26	34	19	2	0	130.1	158	10	80	47	4-10	1	5.94
Dick Mauney	R	25	20	16	6	2	122.2	127	7	27	35	6-10	1	3.08
Jack Kraus	L	27	19	13	0	0	81.2	96	3	40	28	4-9	0	5.40
Bill Lee†	R	35	13	13	2	0	77.1	107	0	30	13	3-6	0	4.66
Whit Wyatt	R	37	10	10	2	0	51.1	72	3	14	10	0-7	0	5.26
Hugh Mulcahy	R	31	5	4	1	0	28.1	33	1	9	2	1-3	0	3.81
Ken Raffensberger	L	27	5	4	1	0	24.1	28	3	14	6	0-3	0	4.44
Don Grate	R	21	4	2	0	0	8.1	18	0	12	6	0-1	0	17.28
Andy Karl	R	31	67	2	1	0	180.2	175	7	50	51	8-8	15	2.99
Oscar Judd†	L	37	23	9	3	1	82.2	80	3	40	36	5-4	2	3.81
Rene Monteagudo	L	29	14	0	0	0	45.2	67	1	28	16	0-0	0	7.49
Izzy Leon	R	34	14	4	0	0	38.2	49	3	19	11	0-4	0	5.35
Dick Coffman	R	38	14	0	0	0	26.1	39	0	2	2	2-1	0	5.13
Lou Lucier	R	27	13	0	0	0	20.1	14	1	5	5	0-1	1	2.21
Vern Kennedy†	R	38	12	3	0	0	36.0	43	2	14	13	0-3	0	5.50
Jimmie Foxx	R	37	9	2	0	0	22.2	13	0	14	10	1-0	0	1.59
Lefty Scott	L	29	8	2	0	0	22.1	29	1	12	5	0-2	0	4.43
Charlie Ripple	L	23	4	0	0	0	7.2	7	0	10	5	0-1	0	7.04
Mitch Chetkovich	R	27	4	0	0	0	3.0	2	0	3	0	0-0	0	0.00
Ben Chapman†	R	36	3	0	0	0	7.0	7	0	6	4	0-0	0	7.71

»1946 Boston Red Sox 1st AL 104-50 .675 —

Joe Cronin

Player	Gm by Position	B	Age	G	AB	R	H	2B	3B	HR	RBI	BB	SO	SB	Avg	OBP	Slg
Hal Wagner	C116	L	30	117	370	39	85	12	2	6	52	69	32	3	.230	.354	.322
Rudy York	1B154	R	32	154	579	78	160	30	6	17	119	86	93	3	.276	.371	.437
Bobby Doerr	2B151	R	28	151	583	95	158	34	9	18	116	66	67	5	.271	.346	.453
Rip Russell	3B70,2B3	R	31	80	274	22	57	10	1	6	35	13	30	1	.208	.247	.318
Johnny Pesky	SS153	L	26	153	621	115	208	43	4	2	55	65	29	9	.335	.401	.427
Ted Williams	OF150	L	27	150	514	142	176	37	8	38	123	156	44	0	.342	.497	.667
Dom DiMaggio	OF142	R	29	142	534	85	169	24	7	7	73	66	58	10	.316	.393	.427
Catfish Metkovich	OF81	L	25	86	281	42	69	15	2	4	25	36	39	8	.246	.333	.356
Mike Higgins†	3B59	R	37	64	200	18	55	11	1	2	28	24	24	0	.275	.356	.370
Leon Culberson	OF49,3B4	R	26	59	179	34	56	10	1	3	18	16	19	3	.313	.369	.430
Wally Moses†	OF44	L	35	48	175	13	36	11	3	2	17	14	15	2	.206	.268	.337
Tom McBride	OF43	R	31	61	153	21	46	5	2	0	19	9	6	0	.301	.340	.359
Roy Partee	C38	R	28	40	111	13	35	5	2	0	9	13	14	0	.315	.387	.396
Eddie Pellagrini	3B14,SS9	R	28	22	71	7	15	3	1	2	4	3	18	1	.211	.253	.366
Don Gutteridge	2B9,3B8	R	34	22	47	8	11	3	0	1	6	2	7	0	.234	.265	.362
Ernie Andres	3B15	R	28	15	41	0	4	2	0	0	1	3	5	0	.098	.159	.146
Eddie McGah	C14	R	24	15	37	2	8	1	1	0	1	7	7	0	.216	.341	.297
Johnny Lazor	OF7	L	33	23	29	1	4	0	0	1	4	2	11	0	.138	.194	.241
Paul Campbell	1B5	L	28	28	26	3	3	1	0	0	0	2	7	0	.115	.179	.154
Frankie Pytlak	C4	R	37	4	14	1	2	0	0	0	1	0	0	0	.143	.143	.143
Tom Carey	2B3	R	39	3	5	0	1	0	0	0	0	0	1	0	.200	.200	.200
Ben Steiner	3B1	L	24	3	4	1	1	0	0	0	0	0	0	0	.250	.250	.250
Andy Gilbert	OF1	R	31	2	1	1	0	0	0	0	0	0	0	0	.000	.000	.000

Pitcher	T	Age	G	GS	CG	ShO	IP	H	HR	BB	SO	W-L	Sv	ERA
Tex Hughson	R	30	39	35	21	6	278.0	252	15	51	172	20-11	3	2.75
Boo Ferriss	R	24	40	35	26	6	274.0	274	14	71	106	25-6	3	3.25
Mickey Harris	L	29	34	30	15	0	222.2	236	18	76	131	17-9	0	3.64
Joe Dobson	R	29	32	24	9	1	166.2	148	11	68	91	13-7	0	3.24
Jim Bagby Jr.	R	29	21	11	6	1	106.2	117	4	49	16	7-6	0	3.71
Charlie Wagner	R	33	8	4	0	0	30.2	32	6	19	14	1-0	0	5.87
Earl Johnson	L	27	29	5	0	0	80.0	78	5	39	40	5-4	3	3.71
Bob Klinger	R	38	28	1	0	0	57.0	49	1	25	16	3-2	9	2.37
Clem Dreisewerd	L	30	20	1	0	0	47.1	50	3	15	19	4-1	0	4.18
Mace Brown	R	37	18	0	0	0	26.1	26	2	16	10	3-1	1	2.05
Bill Zuber†	R	33	15	7	2	1	56.2	37	4	39	29	5-1	0	2.54
Mike Ryba	R	43	9	0	0	0	12.2	12	1	5	5	0-1	1	3.55
Bill Butland	L	28	5	2	0	0	16.1	23	3	13	10	1-0	0	11.02
Randy Heflin	R	27	5	1	0	0	14.2	16	0	12	6	0-1	0	2.45
Mel Deutsch	R	30	3	0	0	0	6.1	7	1	3	2	0-0	0	5.68
Jim Wilson	R	24	1	0	0	0	0.2	2	1	0	0	0-0	0	27.00

1946 Detroit Tigers 2nd AL 92-62 .597 12.0 GB

Steve O'Neill

Player	Gm by Position	B	Age	G	AB	R	H	2B	3B	HR	RBI	BB	SO	SB	Avg	OBP	Slg
Birdie Tebbetts	C87	R	33	87	280	20	68	11	2	1	34	28	23	1	.243	.312	.307
Hank Greenberg	1B140	R	35	142	523	91	145	29	5	44	127	80	88	5	.277	.373	.604
Jimmy Bloodworth	2B71	R	28	76	249	26	61	8	1	5	36	12	26	3	.245	.285	.345
George Kell†	3B105,1B1	R	23	105	434	67	142	19	9	4	41	30	14	3	.327	.371	.440
Eddie Lake	SS155	R	30	155	587	105	149	24	1	8	31	103	69	15	.254	.369	.339
Dick Wakefield	OF104	L	25	111	396	64	106	11	5	12	59	59	55	3	.268	.364	.412
Roy Cullenbine	OF81,1B21	S	32	113	328	63	110	21	0	15	56	88	39	3	.335	.477	.537
Hoot Evers	OF76	R	25	81	304	42	81	8	4	4	33	34	43	7	.266	.344	.359
Jimmy Outlaw	OF43,3B38	R	33	92	299	36	78	14	2	2	31	29	24	5	.261	.328	.341
Pat Mullin	OF75	L	28	93	276	34	68	13	4	3	35	25	36	3	.246	.311	.355
Doc Cramer	OF50	L	40	68	204	26	60	8	2	1	26	15	8	3	.294	.342	.368
Eddie Mayo	2B49	L	36	51	202	21	51	9	2	0	22	14	12	6	.252	.301	.317
Skeeter Webb	2B50,SS8	R	36	64	169	12	37	1	1	0	17	9	18	3	.219	.258	.237
Paul Richards	C54	R	37	57	139	13	28	5	2	0	11	23	18	2	.201	.315	.266
Anse Moore	OF32	L	28	51	134	16	28	4	0	1	8	12	9	1	.209	.279	.261
Bob Swift	C42	R	31	42	107	13	25	2	0	2	10	14	7	0	.234	.322	.308
Barney McCosky†	OF24	L	29	25	91	11	18	5	0	1	11	17	9	0	.198	.324	.286
Mike Higgins†	3B17	R	37	18	60	2	13	3	1	0	8	5	6	0	.217	.277	.300
Johnny Lipon	SS8,3B1	R	23	14	20	4	6	0	0	0	1	5	3	0	.300	.440	.300
Johnny Groth	OF4	R	19	4	9	1	0	0	0	0	0	0	3	0	.000	.000	.000
Billy Hitchcock†	2B1	R	29	3	3	0	0	0	0	0	0	1	0	0	.000	.250	.000
Ned Harris		L	29	1	1	0	0	0	0	0	0	0	0	0	.000	.000	.000

Pitcher	T	Age	G	GS	CG	ShO	IP	H	HR	BB	SO	W-L	Sv	ERA
Hal Newhouser	L	25	37	34	29	6	292.2	215	10	98	275	26-9	1	1.94
Dizzy Trout	R	31	38	32	23	5	276.1	244	11	97	151	17-13	3	2.34
Virgil Trucks	R	29	32	29	15	2	236.2	217	23	75	161	14-9	0	3.23
Fred Hutchinson	R	26	28	26	16	3	207.0	184	14	66	138	14-11	2	3.09
Al Benton	R	35	28	15	6	1	140.2	132	9	58	60	11-7	1	3.65
Stubby Overmire	L	27	24	13	3	0	97.1	106	6	29	34	5-7	1	4.62
Ted Gray	L	21	3	2	0	0	11.2	17	4	5	5	0-2	1	8.49
Lou Kretlow	R	25	1	1	1	0	9.0	7	2	2	4	1-0	0	3.00
Art Houtteman	R	18	1	1	0	0	8.0	15	1	0	2	0-1	0	9.00
George Caster	R	38	26	0	0	0	41.1	42	1	24	19	2-1	4	5.66
Johnny Gorsica	R	31	14	0	0	0	23.2	28	5	11	14	0-0	1	4.56
Hal White	R	27	11	1	1	0	27.1	34	5	15	12	1-1	0	5.60
Tommy Bridges	R	39	9	1	0	0	21.1	24	5	8	17	1-1	1	5.91
Hal Manders†	R	29	2	0	0	0	6.0	8	1	2	3	0-0	0	10.50
Rufe Gentry	R	28	2	0	0	0	3.0	4	0	7	1	0-0	0	15.00

1946 New York Yankees 3rd AL 87-67 .565 17.0 GB

Joe McCarthy (22-13)/Bill Dickey (57-48)/Johnny Neun (8-6)

Player	Gm by Position	B	Age	G	AB	R	H	2B	3B	HR	RBI	BB	SO	SB	Avg	OBP	Slg
Aaron Robinson	C95	L	31	100	330	32	98	17	2	16	64	48	39	0	.297	.388	.506
Nick Etten	1B84	L	32	108	323	37	75	14	1	9	49	38	35	0	.232	.315	.365
Joe Gordon	2B108	R	31	112	376	35	79	15	0	11	47	49	72	2	.210	.308	.338
Snuffy Stirnweiss	3B79,2B46,SS4	R	27	129	487	75	122	19	7	0	37	66	58	18	.251	.340	.318
Phil Rizzuto	SS125	R	28	126	471	53	121	17	1	2	38	34	39	14	.257	.315	.310
Charlie Keller	OF149	L	29	150	538	98	148	29	10	30	101	113	101	1	.275	.405	.533
Joe DiMaggio	OF131	R	31	132	503	81	146	20	8	25	95	59	24	1	.290	.367	.511
Tommy Henrich	OF111,1B41	L	33	150	565	92	142	25	4	19	83	87	63	5	.251	.358	.411
Johnny Lindell	OF74,1B14	R	29	102	332	41	86	10	5	10	40	32	47	4	.259	.328	.410
Bill Johnson	3B74	R	27	85	296	51	77	14	5	4	35	31	42	1	.260	.334	.382
Bill Dickey	C39	L	39	54	134	10	35	8	0	2	10	19	12	0	.261	.357	.366
Steve Souchock	1B20	R	27	47	86	15	26	3	3	2	10	7	13	0	.302	.362	.477
Frankie Crosetti	SS24	R	35	28	59	4	17	3	0	0	3	8	2	0	.288	.382	.339
Gus Niarhos	C29	R	25	37	40	11	9	1	1	0	2	11	2	1	.225	.392	.300
Oscar Grimes†	SS7,2B5	R	31	14	39	1	8	1	0	0	4	1	7	0	.205	.225	.231
Bobby Brown	SS5,3B2	L	21	7	24	1	8	1	0	0	1	4	0	0	.333	.429	.375
Yogi Berra	C6	L	21	7	22	3	8	1	0	2	4	1	1	0	.364	.391	.682
Ken Silvestri	C12	S	30	13	21	4	6	1	0	0	1	3	7	0	.286	.375	.333
Frank Colman†	OF5	L	28	5	15	2	4	0	0	1	5	1	1	0	.267	.313	.467
Eddie Bockman	3B4	R	25	4	12	2	1	1	0	0	0	1	4	0	.083	.154	.167
Hank Majeski†	3B2	R	29	8	12	1	1	0	1	0	0	0	3	0	.083	.083	.250
Bill Drescher	C3	L	25	5	6	0	2	1	0	0	1	0	0	0	.333	.333	.500
Bud Metheny		L	31	3	3	0	0	0	0	0	0	0	0	0	.000	.000	.000
Roy Weatherly		L	31	2	2	0	1	0	0	0	0	0	0	0	.500	.500	.500

Pitcher	T	Age	G	GS	CG	ShO	IP	H	HR	BB	SO	W-L	Sv	ERA
Spud Chandler	R	38	34	32	20	6	257.1	200	7	90	138	20-8	2	2.10
Bill Bevens	R	29	31	31	18	3	249.2	213	11	78	120	16-13	0	2.23
Joe Page	L	28	31	17	6	1	136.0	126	7	72	77	9-8	3	3.57
Tiny Bonham	R	32	18	14	6	2	104.2	97	6	23	30	5-8	3	3.70
Red Ruffing	R	42	8	8	4	2	61.0	37	2	23	19	5-1	0	1.77
Vic Raschi	R	27	2	2	2	0	16.0	14	0	5	11	2-0	0	3.94
Al Lyons	R	27	2	1	0	0	8.1	11	0	6	4	0-1	0	5.40
Randy Gumpert	R	28	33	12	4	0	132.2	113	8	32	63	11-3	1	2.31
Johnny Murphy	R	37	27	0	0	0	45.0	40	4	19	19	4-2	7	3.40
Al Gettel	R	28	26	11	5	2	103.0	89	6	40	54	6-7	0	2.97
Cuddles Marshall	R	21	23	11	1	0	81.0	96	4	56	32	3-4	0	5.33
Bill Wight	L	24	14	4	1	0	40.1	44	1	30	11	2-2	0	4.46
Mel Queen	R	28	14	3	1	0	30.1	40	2	21	26	1-1	0	6.53
Jake Wade†	L	34	13	1	0	0	35.1	33	2	14	22	2-1	1	2.29
Marius Russo	L	31	8	3	0	0	18.2	26	1	11	7	0-2	0	4.34
Tommy Byrne	L	26	4	1	0	0	9.1	7	1	8	5	0-1	0	5.79
Steve Roser†	R	28	4	1	0	0	3.1	7	0	4	1	1-1	0	16.20
Frank Hiller	R	25	3	1	0	0	11.1	13	2	6	4	0-2	0	4.76
Karl Drews	R	26	3	1	0	0	6.1	6	0	6	4	0-1	0	8.53
Bill Zuber†	R	33	3	0	0	0	5.2	10	2	3	3	0-1	0	12.71
Charley Stanceu†	R	30	3	0	0	0	4.0	6	0	5	3	0-0	0	9.00
Herb Karpel	L	28	2	0	0	0	1.2	4	0	0	0	0-0	0	10.80

1946 Washington Senators 4th AL 76-78 .494 28.0 GB

Ossie Bluege

Player	Gm by Position	B	Age	G	AB	R	H	2B	3B	HR	RBI	BB	SO	SB	Avg	OBP	Slg
Al Evans	C81	R	29	88	272	30	69	10	4	2	30	30	28	1	.254	.332	.342
Mickey Vernon	1B147	L	28	148	587	88	207	51	8	8	85	49	64	14	.353	.403	.508
Jerry Priddy	2B138	R	26	138	511	54	130	22	8	6	58	57	73	9	.254	.332	.364
Cecil Travis	SS75,3B56	L	32	137	465	45	117	22	3	1	56	45	47	2	.252	.323	.318
Billy Hitchcock†	SS53,3B46	R	29	98	354	27	75	8	3	0	25	26	52	2	.212	.268	.251
Stan Spence	OF150	L	31	152	578	83	169	50	10	16	87	62	31	1	.292	.365	.497
Buddy Lewis	OF145	L	29	150	582	82	170	28	13	7	45	59	26	5	.292	.359	.421
Joe Grace†	OF74	L	32	77	321	39	97	17	4	2	31	24	19	1	.302	.358	.399
Sherry Robertson	3B38,2B14,SS12*	L	27	74	230	30	46	6	3	6	19	30	42	6	.200	.292	.330
Jake Early	C64	L	31	64	189	13	38	6	0	4	18	23	27	0	.201	.288	.296
Gil Torres	SS31,3B18,2B7*	R	30	63	185	18	47	8	0	0	13	11	12	3	.254	.296	.297
Jeff Heath†	OF47	L	31	48	166	23	47	12	3	4	27	36	36	0	.283	.411	.464
Gil Coan	OF29	L	24	59	134	17	28	3	2	3	9	7	37	2	.209	.269	.328
George Binks	OF28	L	29	65	134	13	26	3	0	0	12	6	16	1	.194	.229	.216
Mike Guerra	C27	R	33	41	83	3	21	2	1	0	4	5	6	1	.253	.295	.301
George Myatt	3B7,2B2	L	32	15	34	7	8	1	0	0	4	2	3	1	.235	.297	.265
Jack Sanford	1B6	R	29	10	26	7	6	0	1	0	1	2	6	0	.231	.286	.308
Eddie Yost	3B7	R	19	8	25	2	2	1	0	0	1	5	5	2	.080	.233	.120
Joe Kuhel†	1B5	L	40	14	20	2	3	0	0	0	2	5	2	0	.150	.320	.150
Ray Goolsby	OF1	R	26	3	4	0	0	0	0	0	0	1	1	0	.000	.200	.000

S. Robertson, 1 G at OF; G. Torres, 3 G at P

Pitcher	T	Age	G	GS	CG	ShO	IP	H	HR	BB	SO	W-L	Sv	ERA
Mickey Haefner	L	33	33	27	17	2	227.2	220	10	80	85	14-11	1	2.85
Dutch Leonard	R	37	26	23	7	2	161.2	182	9	36	62	10-10	0	3.56
Bobo Newsom†	R	38	24	22	14	2	178.0	163	5	60	82	11-8	1	2.78
Ray Scarborough	R	28	32	20	6	1	155.2	176	8	74	46	7-11	1	4.05
Roger Wolff	R	35	21	17	6	0	122.0	115	8	30	50	5-8	0	2.58
Early Wynn	R	26	17	12	9	0	107.0	112	8	33	36	8-5	0	3.11
Johnny Niggeling†	R	42	8	6	3	0	38.0	39	1	21	10	3-2	0	4.03
Sid Hudson	R	31	31	15	6	1	142.1	160	9	37	35	8-11	1	3.60
Marino Pieretti	R	25	30	2	1	0	62.0	70	9	40	20	2-2	0	5.95
Walt Masterson	R	26	29	9	2	0	91.1	105	8	67	61	5-6	1	6.01
Bill Kennedy	L	27	21	2	0	0	39.0	40	1	29	18	1-2	3	6.00
Vern Curtis	R	26	11	0	0	0	16.1	19	1	10	7	0-0	0	7.16
Milo Candini	R	28	9	0	0	0	21.2	15	1	4	6	2-0	1	2.08
Max Wilson	L	30	9	0	0	0	12.2	16	1	9	8	0-1	0	7.11
Jake Wade†	L	34	6	0	0	0	11.1	12	1	12	9	0-0	0	4.76
Gil Torres	R	30	3	0	0	0	7.0	9	0	3	2	0-0	1	7.71
Al LaMacchia†	R	24	2	0	0	0	2.2	6	1	2	0	0-1	0	16.88

Seasons: Team Rosters 699

1946 Chicago White Sox 5th AL 74-80 .481 30.0 GB

Jimmy Dykes (10-20)/Ted Lyons (64-60)

Player	Gm by Position	B	Age	G	AB	R	H	2B	3B	HR	RBI	BB	SO	SB	Avg	OBP	Slg
Mike Tresh	C79	R	32	80	217	28	47	5	2	0	21	36	24	0	.217	.336	.258
Hal Trosky	1B80	L	33	88	299	22	76	12	3	2	31	34	37	4	.254	.330	.334
Don Kolloway	2B90,3B31	R	27	123	482	45	135	23	4	3	53	9	29	14	.280	.293	.363
Dario Lodigiani	3B44	R	29	44	155	12	38	8	0	0	13	16	14	4	.245	.324	.297
Luke Appling	SS149	R	39	149	582	59	180	27	5	1	55	71	41	6	.309	.384	.378
Thurman Tucker	OF110	L	28	121	438	62	126	20	3	1	36	54	45	9	.288	.367	.354
Taffy Wright	OF107	L	34	115	422	46	116	19	4	7	52	42	17	10	.275	.342	.389
Bob Kennedy	OF75,3B29	R	25	113	411	43	106	13	5	5	34	24	42	6	.258	.300	.350
Cass Michaels	2B66,3B13,SS6	R	20	91	291	37	75	8	0	1	22	29	36	9	.258	.333	.296
Ralph Hodgin	OF57	L	30	87	258	32	65	10	1	0	25	19	6	0	.252	.308	.298
Whitey Platt	OF61	R	25	84	247	28	62	8	5	3	32	17	34	1	.251	.307	.360
Joe Kuhel†	1B63	L	40	64	238	24	65	9	3	4	20	21	24	4	.273	.335	.387
Frankie Hayes†	C52	R	31	53	179	15	38	6	0	2	16	29	33	1	.212	.322	.279
Wally Moses†	OF36	L	35	56	168	20	46	9	1	4	16	17	20	2	.274	.344	.411
Leo Wells	3B38,SS2	R	28	45	127	11	24	4	1	1	11	12	34	3	.189	.259	.260
Jake Jones	1B20	R	25	24	79	10	21	5	1	3	13	2	13	0	.266	.284	.468
George Dickey	C30	S	30	37	78	8	15	1	0	0	1	12	13	0	.192	.300	.205
Dave Philley	OF17	S	26	17	68	10	24	2	3	0	17	4	4	5	.353	.389	.471
Guy Curtright	OF15	R	33	23	55	7	11	2	0	0	5	11	14	0	.200	.333	.236
Ed Fernandes	C12	S	28	14	32	4	8	2	0	0	4	8	7	0	.250	.400	.313
Floyd Baker	3B6	L	29	9	24	2	6	1	0	0	3	2	3	0	.250	.308	.292
Frank Whitman	SS6,1B1,2B1	R	21	17	16	7	1	0	0	0	1	2	6	0	.063	.211	.063
Tom Jordan†	C2	R	26	10	15	1	4	2	1	0	0	0	1	0	.267	.267	.533
Joe Smaza	OF1	L	22	2	5	2	1	0	0	0	0	0	0	0	.200	.200	.200

Pitcher	T	Age	G	GS	CG	ShO	IP	H	HR	BB	SO	W-L	Sv	ERA
Ed Lopat	L	28	29	29	20	2	231.0	216	18	48	89	13-13	0	2.73
Orval Grove	R	26	33	26	10	1	205.1	213	10	78	60	8-13	0	3.02
Joe Haynes	R	28	32	23	9	0	177.1	203	14	60	60	7-9	2	3.76
Eddie Smith	L	32	24	21	3	1	145.1	135	9	60	59	8-11	1	2.85
Johnny Rigney	R	31	15	11	3	2	82.2	76	6	35	51	5-5	0	4.03
Bill Dietrich	R	36	11	9	3	0	62.0	63	4	24	20	3-3	1	2.61
Thornton Lee	L	39	7	7	2	0	43.1	39	1	23	23	2-4	0	3.53
Ted Lyons	R	45	5	5	5	0	42.2	38	2	9	10	1-4	0	2.32
Earl Caldwell	R	41	39	0	0	0	90.2	60	2	29	42	13-4	8	2.08
Frank Papish	L	28	31	15	6	2	138.0	122	7	63	66	7-5	0	2.74
Ralph Hamner	R	29	25	7	1	0	71.1	80	2	39	29	2-7	1	4.42
Al Hollingsworth†	L	38	21	2	0	0	55.0	63	2	22	22	3-2	1	4.58
Gordon Maltzberger	R	33	19	0	0	0	39.2	30	3	6	17	2-0	2	1.59
Len Perme	L	28	4	0	0	0	4.1	6	0	7	2	0-0	0	8.31
Emmett O'Neill†	R	28	2	0	0	0	3.2	4	0	5	0	0-0	0	0.00

1946 Cleveland Indians 6th AL 68-86 .442 36.0 GB

Lou Boudreau

Player	Gm by Position	B	Age	G	AB	R	H	2B	3B	HR	RBI	BB	SO	SB	Avg	OBP	Slg
Jim Hegan	C87	R	25	88	271	29	64	11	5	0	17	17	44	1	.236	.284	.314
Les Fleming	1B80,OF1	L	30	99	306	40	85	17	5	8	42	50	42	1	.278	.383	.444
Dutch Meyer	2B64	R	30	72	207	13	48	5	3	0	16	26	16	0	.232	.321	.285
Ken Keltner	3B112	R	29	116	398	47	96	17	1	13	45	30	38	0	.241	.294	.387
Lou Boudreau	SS139	R	28	140	515	51	151	30	6	6	62	40	14	6	.293	.345	.410
Hank Edwards	OF123	L	27	124	458	62	138	33	16	10	54	43	48	1	.301	.361	.509
George Case	OF118	R	30	118	484	46	109	23	4	1	22	34	38	28	.225	.280	.295
Pat Seerey	OF115	R	23	117	404	57	91	17	2	26	62	65	101	2	.225	.334	.470
Jack Conway	2B50,SS14,3B3	R	26	68	258	24	58	6	2	0	18	20	36	2	.225	.281	.264
Felix Mackiewicz	OF72	R	28	78	258	35	67	15	4	0	16	16	32	5	.260	.305	.349
Ray Mack	2B61	R	29	61	171	13	35	6	2	1	9	23	27	2	.205	.299	.281
Frankie Hayes†	C50	R	31	51	156	11	40	12	0	3	18	21	26	1	.256	.345	.391
Don Ross	3B41,OF2	R	31	55	153	12	41	7	0	3	14	17	12	0	.268	.341	.373
Heinz Becker†	1B44	S	30	50	147	15	44	10	1	0	17	23	18	1	.299	.401	.381
Gene Woodling	OF37	L	23	61	133	8	25	1	4	0	9	16	13	1	.188	.280	.256
Mike Rocco	1B27	L	30	34	98	8	24	2	0	2	14	15	15	1	.245	.345	.327
Bob Lemon	P32,OF12	L	25	55	89	9	16	3	0	1	4	7	18	0	.180	.240	.247
Sherm Lollar	C24	R	21	28	62	7	15	6	0	1	9	5	9	0	.242	.299	.387
Dale Mitchell	OF11	L	24	11	44	7	19	3	0	0	5	1	2	1	.432	.444	.500
Jimmy Wasdell†	1B4,OF3	L	32	32	41	1	11	0	0	0	4	4	4	1	.268	.333	.268
Tom Jordan†	C13	R	26	14	35	2	7	1	0	1	3	3	1	1	.200	.263	.314
Howie Moss†	3B8	R	26	8	32	2	2	0	0	0	0	3	9	0	.063	.143	.063
Eddie Robinson	1B7	L	25	8	30	6	12	1	0	3	4	2	4	0	.400	.438	.733
Buster Mills	OF6	R	37	9	22	1	6	0	0	0	3	3	5	0	.273	.360	.273
Rusty Peters	SS7	R	31	9	21	0	6	0	0	0	2	1	1	0	.286	.318	.286
Jackie Price	SS4	L	33	7	13	1	3	0	0	0	0	0	0	0	.231	.231	.231
Ralph Weigel	C6	R	24	6	12	0	2	0	0	0	0	0	2	1	.167	.167	.167
Ted Sepkowski	3B2	L	22	2	8	2	4	1	0	0	1	0	0	0	.500	.500	.625
Blas Monaco		S	30	12	6	2	0	0	0	0	0	1	1	0	.000	.143	.000
Charlie Brewster	SS1	R	29	3	2	0	0	0	0	0	0	1	1	0	.000	.333	.000

Pitcher	T	Age	G	GS	CG	ShO	IP	H	HR	BB	SO	W-L	Sv	ERA
Bob Feller	R	27	48	42	36	10	371.1	277	11	153	348	26-15	4	2.18
Allie Reynolds	R	31	31	28	9	3	183.1	180	10	108	107	11-15	0	3.88
Red Embree	R	28	28	26	8	4	200.0	170	15	79	87	8-12	0	3.47
Steve Gromek	R	26	29	21	5	2	153.2	159	20	47	75	5-15	4	4.33
Mel Harder	R	36	13	12	4	1	92.1	85	4	31	21	5-4	0	3.41
Bob Kuzava	L	23	2	2	0	0	12.0	9	0	11	4	1-0	0	3.00
Les Webber†	R	31	4	2	0	0	5.1	13	0	5	5	1-1	0	23.63
Ralph McCabe	R	27	1	1	0	0	4.0	5	3	2	3	0-1	0	11.25
Bob Lemon	R	25	32	5	1	0	94.0	77	1	68	39	4-5	1	2.49
Joe Krakauskas	L	31	29	5	0	0	47.1	60	2	25	20	2-5	1	5.51
Joe Berry†	R	41	21	0	0	0	37.1	32	4	21	16	3-6	1	3.38
Pete Center	R	34	21	0	0	0	29.0	29	2	20	6	0-2	1	4.97
Don Black	R	29	18	4	0	0	43.2	45	5	21	15	1-2	0	4.53
Charlie Gassaway	L	27	13	6	0	0	50.2	54	2	26	23	1-1	0	3.91
Tom Ferrick†	R	31	9	0	0	0	18.0	25	3	4	9	0-0	1	5.00
Ed Klieman	R	28	9	0	0	0	15.0	18	0	10	2	0-0	0	6.60
Vic Johnson	L	25	9	1	0	0	13.2	20	1	8	3	0-1	0	9.22
Johnny Podgajny	R	26	6	0	0	0	9.0	13	0	2	4	0-0	0	5.00
Ray Flanigan	R	23	3	1	0	0	9.0	11	1	8	2	0-1	0	11.00

1946 St. Louis Browns 7th AL 66-88 .429 38.0 GB

Luke Sewell (53-71)/Zack Taylor (13-17)

Player	Gm by Position	B	Age	G	AB	R	H	2B	3B	HR	RBI	BB	SO	SB	Avg	OBP	Slg
Frank Mancuso	C85	R	28	87	262	22	63	8	3	3	23	30	31	1	.240	.323	.328
Chuck Stevens	1B120	S	27	122	432	53	107	17	4	3	27	47	62	4	.248	.324	.326
Johnny Berardino	2B143	R	29	144	582	70	154	29	5	5	68	34	58	2	.265	.306	.357
Mark Christman	3B77,SS47	R	32	128	458	40	118	22	2	1	41	22	29	0	.258	.295	.321
Vern Stephens	SS112	R	25	115	450	67	138	19	4	14	64	35	49	0	.307	.357	.460
Wally Judnich	OF137	L	29	142	511	60	134	23	4	15	72	60	54	0	.262	.340	.411
Al Zarilla	OF107	L	27	125	371	46	96	14	9	4	43	27	37	3	.259	.311	.377
Jeff Heath†	OF83	L	31	86	316	46	87	20	4	12	57	37	37	0	.275	.353	.478
Chet Laabs	OF72	R	34	80	264	40	69	13	0	16	52	20	50	3	.261	.316	.492
Bob Dillinger	3B54,SS1	R	27	83	225	33	63	6	3	0	11	19	32	8	.280	.341	.333
Johnny Lucadello	3B37,2B19	R	27	87	210	21	52	7	1	1	15	36	20	0	.248	.358	.305
Hank Helf	C69	R	32	71	182	17	35	11	0	6	21	9	40	0	.192	.234	.352
Glenn McQuillen	OF48	R	31	59	166	24	40	3	3	1	12	19	18	0	.241	.319	.313
Joe Grace†	OF43	L	32	48	161	21	37	7	2	1	13	16	20	1	.230	.307	.317
Babe Dahlgren	1B24	R	34	28	80	2	14	1	0	0	9	8	13	0	.175	.250	.188
Jerry Witte	1B18	R	30	18	73	7	14	2	0	2	4	0	18	0	.192	.192	.301
Joe Schultz	C17	L	27	42	57	1	22	4	0	0	14	11	2	0	.386	.485	.456
Paul Lehner	OF12	L	25	16	45	6	10	1	2	0	5	1	5	0	.222	.239	.333
Les Moss	C12	R	21	12	35	4	13	3	0	0	5	3	5	1	.371	.436	.457
Lou Finney	OF7	L	35	16	30	0	9	0	0	0	3	2	4	0	.300	.344	.300
Ken Sears	C4	L	28	7	15	1	5	0	0	0	1	3	0	0	.333	.444	.333
George Bradley	OF3	R	32	4	12	2	2	1	0	0	3	0	1	0	.167	.167	.250
George Archie	1B3	R	32	4	11	1	2	1	0	0	0	0	1	0	.182	.182	.273
Babe Martin	C2	R	26	3	9	0	2	0	0	0	1	1	2	0	.222	.300	.222
Len Schulte	2B1,3B1	R	29	4	5	1	2	0	0	0	2	0	0	0	.400	.400	.400

Pitcher	T	Age	G	GS	CG	ShO	IP	H	HR	BB	SO	W-L	Sv	ERA
Jack Kramer	R	28	31	28	13	3	194.2	190	6	68	69	13-11	0	3.19
Denny Galehouse	R	34	30	24	11	2	180.0	194	9	52	90	8-12	0	3.65
Sam Zoldak	L	27	35	21	9	2	170.1	166	11	57	51	9-11	2	3.43
Nels Potter	R	34	23	19	10	0	145.0	152	9	59	72	8-9	0	3.72
Tex Shirley	R	28	27	18	7	0	139.2	148	7	105	45	6-12	0	4.96
Fred Sanford	R	26	3	3	2	2	22.0	19	0	9	8	2-1	0	2.05
Chet Johnson	L	28	5	3	0	0	18.0	20	0	13	8	0-0	0	5.00
Al Milnar†	L	32	4	2	1	1	14.2	15	1	6	1	1-1	0	2.45
Stan Ferens	L	31	34	6	1	0	88.0	100	3	38	28	2-9	0	4.50
Ellis Kinder	R	31	33	7	1	0	86.2	78	8	36	59	3-3	1	3.32
Bob Muncrief	R	30	29	14	4	1	115.1	149	6	31	49	3-12	0	4.99
Cliff Fannin	R	22	27	7	4	1	86.2	76	4	42	52	5-2	2	3.01
Tom Ferrick†	R	31	25	1	0	0	32.1	26	1	5	13	4-1	5	2.78
Frank Biscan	L	26	16	0	0	0	22.2	28	0	22	9	1-1	1	5.16
Ox Miller	R	31	11	3	0	0	35.1	52	5	15	12	1-3	1	6.88
Al LaMacchia†	R	24	8	0	0	0	15.0	17	2	7	3	0-0	0	6.00
Al Hollingsworth†	L	38	5	0	0	0	11.0	23	1	4	3	0-0	0	6.55
Steve Sundra	R	36	2	0	0	0	4.0	9	0	3	1	0-0	0	11.25
Ray Shore	R	25	1	0	0	0	1.0	3	0	1	1	0-0	0	18.00

1946 Philadelphia Athletics 8th AL 49-105 .318 55.0 GB

Connie Mack

Player	Gm by Position	B	Age	G	AB	R	H	2B	3B	HR	RBI	BB	SO	SB	Avg	OBP	Slg
Buddy Rosar	C117	R	31	121	424	34	120	22	2	2	47	36	17	1	.283	.339	.358
George McQuinn	1B134	L	36	136	484	47	109	23	6	3	35	64	62	4	.225	.317	.316
Gene Handley	2B68,3B4,SS1	R	31	89	251	31	63	8	5	0	21	22	25	8	.251	.311	.323
Hank Majeski†	3B72	R	29	78	264	25	66	14	3	1	25	26	13	3	.250	.320	.337
Pete Suder	SS67,3B33,2B12*	R	30	128	455	38	128	20	3	2	50	18	37	1	.281	.309	.352
Sam Chapman	OF145	R	30	146	545	77	142	22	5	20	67	54	66	1	.261	.327	.429
Elmer Valo	OF90	L	25	108	348	59	107	21	6	1	31	60	18	9	.307	.411	.411
Barney McCosky†	OF85	L	29	92	308	33	109	17	4	1	34	43	13	2	.354	.433	.445
Tuck Stainback	OF66	R	34	91	291	35	71	10	2	0	20	7	20	3	.244	.264	.292
Jack Wallaesa	SS59	S	26	63	194	16	38	4	2	5	11	14	47	1	.196	.250	.314
Oscar Grimes†	2B43,3B6,SS4	R	31	59	191	28	50	5	0	1	20	27	29	2	.262	.356	.304
Irv Hall	2B40,SS7	R	27	63	185	19	46	6	2	0	19	9	18	1	.249	.287	.303
Russ Derry	OF50	L	29	69	184	17	38	8	5	4	14	27	54	0	.207	.311	.304
Hal Peck	OF35	L	29	48	150	14	37	8	2	2	11	16	14	1	.247	.319	.367
Gene Desautels	C52	R	39	52	130	10	28	3	1	0	13	12	16	1	.215	.282	.254
Jake Caulfield	SS31,3B1	R	28	44	94	13	26	8	0	0	10	4	11	0	.277	.306	.362
Bruce Konopka	1B20,OF1	L	26	38	93	7	22	4	1	0	9	4	8	0	.237	.268	.301
George Kell†	3B26	R	23	26	87	3	26	6	1	0	11	10	6	0	.299	.378	.391
Don Richmond	3B16	L	26	16	62	3	18	3	0	1	9	0	10	1	.290	.290	.387
Ford Garrison	OF8	R	30	9	37	1	4	0	0	0	0	0	6	0	.108	.108	.108
Joe Astroth	C4	R	23	4	7	0	1	0	0	0	0	0	2	0	.143	.143	.143
George Armstrong	C4	R	22	8	6	0	1	1	0	0	0	1	1	0	.167	.286	.333
Vern Benson	OF2	L	21	7	5	1	0	0	0	0	0	1	3	0	.000	.167	.000

P. Suder, 3 G at 1B, 2 G at OF

Pitcher	T	Age	G	GS	CG	ShO	IP	H	HR	BB	SO	W-L	Sv	ERA
Phil Marchildon	R	32	36	29	16	1	226.2	197	14	114	95	13-16	1	3.49
Dick Fowler	R	25	32	28	14	1	205.2	213	16	75	89	9-16	0	3.28
Lou Knerr	R	24	30	22	6	0	148.1	171	13	67	58	3-16	0	5.40
Jesse Flores	R	31	29	15	8	4	155.0	147	8	38	48	9-7	1	2.32
Bobo Newsom†	R	38	10	9	3	1	58.2	61	2	30	32	3-5	0	3.38
Bill McCahan	R	25	4	2	2	1	18.0	16	0	9	6	1-1	0	1.00
Joe Coleman	R	23	4	2	0	0	13.0	19	1	8	8	0-2	0	5.54
Bob Savage	R	24	40	19	7	1	164.0	164	5	93	78	3-15	2	4.06
Lum Harris	R	31	34	12	4	0	125.1	153	11	48	33	3-14	0	5.24
Russ Christopher	R	28	30	13	1	0	119.1	119	5	44	79	5-7	0	4.30
Everett Fagan	R	28	20	0	0	0	45.0	47	2	24	12	0-1	0	4.80
Lee Griffeth	L	21	10	0	0	0	15.1	13	1	6	4	0-0	0	2.93
Herman Besse	L	34	7	3	0	0	20.2	19	1	9	10	0-2	1	5.23
Joe Berry†	R	41	5	0	0	0	13.0	15	1	3	5	0-1	0	2.77
Norm Brown	R	27	4	0	0	0	7.1	8	2	6	3	0-1	0	6.14
Jack Knott	R	39	3	1	0	0	6.1	7	1	1	2	0-1	0	5.68
Pat Cooper	R	28	1	0	0	0	1.0	1	0	1	0	0-0	0	0.00
Porter Vaughan	L	27	1	0	0	0	0.0	1	0	1	0	0-0	0	—

»1946 St. Louis Cardinals 1st NL 98-58 .628 —

Eddie Dyer

Player	Gm by Position	B	Age	G	AB	R	H	2B	3B	HR	RBI	BB	SO	SB	Avg	OBP	Slg
Joe Garagiola	C70	L	20	74	211	21	50	4	1	3	22	23	25	0	.237	.312	.308
Stan Musial	1B114,OF42	L	25	156	624	124	228	50	20	16	103	73	31	7	.365	.434	.587
Red Schoendienst	2B128,3B12,SS4	S	23	142	606	94	170	28	5	0	34	37	27	12	.281	.322	.343
Whitey Kurowski	3B138	R	28	142	519	76	156	32	5	14	89	72	47	2	.301	.391	.462
Marty Marion	SS145	R	28	146	498	51	116	29	4	3	46	59	53	1	.233	.318	.325
Enos Slaughter	OF156	L	30	156	609	100	183	30	8	18	130	69	41	9	.300	.374	.465
Harry Walker	OF92,1B8	L	29	112	346	53	82	14	6	3	27	30	29	12	.237	.300	.338
Erv Dusak	OF77,3B11,2B2	R	25	100	275	38	66	9	1	9	42	33	63	7	.240	.321	.378
Terry Moore	OF66	R	34	91	278	32	73	14	1	3	28	18	26	0	.263	.312	.353
Dick Sisler	1B37,OF29	L	25	83	235	17	61	11	2	3	42	14	28	0	.260	.307	.362
Buster Adams	OF58	R	31	81	173	21	32	6	0	5	22	29	27	3	.185	.312	.306
Del Rice	C53	R	23	55	139	10	38	8	1	1	12	8	16	0	.273	.313	.367
Clyde Kluttz†	C49	R	28	52	136	8	36	7	0	0	14	10	10	0	.265	.315	.316
Lou Klein	2B23	R	27	23	93	12	18	3	0	1	4	9	7	1	.194	.265	.258
Jeff Cross	SS17,2B8,3B1	R	27	49	69	17	15	3	0	0	6	10	8	4	.217	.316	.261
Ken O'Dea†	C22	L	33	22	57	2	7	2	0	1	3	8	8	0	.123	.231	.211
Bill Endicott	OF2	L	27	20	20	2	4	3	0	0	3	4	4	0	.200	.333	.350
Walter Sessi		L	27	15	14	2	2	0	0	1	2	1	4	0	.143	.200	.357
Nippy Jones	2B3	R	21	16	12	3	4	0	0	0	1	2	2	0	.333	.429	.333
Danny Litwhiler†		R	29	6	5	0	0	0	0	0	0	1	1	0	.000	.167	.000
Del Wilber	C4	R	27	4	4	0	0	0	0	0	0	1	0	0	.000	.200	.000
Emil Verban†		R	30	1	1	0	0	0	0	0	0	0	0	0	.000	.000	.000

Pitcher	T	Age	G	GS	CG	ShO	IP	H	HR	BB	SO	W-L	Sv	ERA
Howie Pollet	L	25	40	32	22	4	266.0	228	12	86	107	21-10	5	2.10
Harry Brecheen	L	31	36	30	14	5	231.1	212	8	67	117	15-15	3	2.49
Johnny Beazley	R	28	19	18	5	0	103.0	109	6	55	36	7-5	0	4.46
Ken Burkhart	R	29	25	13	5	2	100.0	111	4	36	32	6-3	2	2.88
George Munger	R	27	10	7	2	0	48.2	47	0	12	28	2-2	1	3.33
Max Lanier	L	30	6	6	6	2	56.0	45	1	19	36	6-0	0	1.93
Freddie Martin	R	31	6	3	2	0	28.2	29	0	8	19	2-1	0	4.08
Murry Dickson	R	29	47	19	12	2	184.1	160	8	56	82	15-6	1	2.88
Ted Wilks	R	30	40	4	0	0	95.0	88	13	38	40	8-0	1	3.41
Al Brazle	L	32	37	15	6	2	153.1	152	1	55	58	11-10	0	3.29
Red Barrett	R	31	23	9	1	1	67.0	75	5	24	22	3-2	2	4.03
Freddy Schmidt	R	30	16	0	0	0	27.1	27	0	15	14	1-0	0	3.29
Howie Krist	R	30	15	0	0	0	18.2	22	3	8	3	0-2	0	6.75
Blix Donnelly†	R	32	13	0	0	0	13.2	17	1	10	11	1-2	0	3.95
Johnny Grodzicki	R	29	3	0	0	0	4.0	4	1	4	2	0-0	0	9.00

1946 Brooklyn Dodgers 2nd NL 96-60 .615 2.0 GB

Leo Durocher

Player	Gm by Position	B	Age	G	AB	R	H	2B	3B	HR	RBI	BB	SO	SB	Avg	OBP	Slg
Bruce Edwards	C91	R	22	92	292	24	78	13	5	1	25	34	20	1	.267	.348	.356
Ed Stevens	1B99	L	21	103	310	34	75	13	7	10	60	27	44	2	.242	.303	.426
Eddie Stanky	2B141	R	29	144	483	98	132	24	7	0	36	137	56	8	.273	.436	.352
Cookie Lavagetto	3B67	R	33	88	242	36	57	9	1	3	27	38	17	3	.236	.339	.318
Pee Wee Reese	SS152	R	27	152	542	79	154	16	10	5	60	87	71	10	.284	.384	.378
Dixie Walker	OF149	L	35	150	576	80	184	29	9	9	116	67	28	14	.319	.391	.448
Carl Furillo	OF112	R	24	117	335	29	95	18	6	3	35	31	20	6	.284	.346	.400
Pete Reiser	OF97,3B15	L	27	122	423	75	117	21	5	11	73	55	58	34	.277	.361	.428
Augie Galan	OF60,3B19,1B12	S	34	99	274	53	85	22	5	3	38	68	21	8	.310	.451	.460
Dick Whitman	OF85	L	25	104	265	39	69	15	3	2	31	22	19	5	.260	.317	.362
Howie Schultz	1B87	R	23	90	249	27	63	14	1	3	27	16	34	2	.253	.298	.353
Ferrell Anderson	C70	R	28	79	199	19	51	10	0	2	14	18	21	1	.256	.330	.337
Billy Herman†	3B29,2B16	R	36	47	184	24	53	8	4	0	28	26	10	2	.288	.376	.375
Bob Ramazzotti	3B30,2B16	R	29	62	120	10	25	4	0	0	7	9	13	0	.208	.264	.242
Gene Hermanski	OF34	L	26	64	110	15	22	2	2	0	8	17	10	2	.200	.313	.255
Joe Medwick	OF18,1B1	R	34	41	77	7	24	4	0	2	18	6	5	0	.312	.369	.442
Eddie Miksis	3B13,2B1	R	19	23	48	3	7	0	0	0	5	3	3	0	.146	.212	.146
Stan Rojek	SS15,2B6,3B4	R	27	45	47	11	13	2	1	0	2	4	1	1	.277	.333	.362
Mike Sandlock	C17,3B1	S	30	19	34	1	5	0	0	0	0	3	4	0	.147	.216	.147
Don Padgett†	C10	L	34	19	30	2	5	1	0	1	9	4	4	0	.167	.265	.300
Joe Tepsic	OF1	R	22	15	5	2	0	0	0	0	0	1	1	0	.000	.167	.000
Jack Graham†	1B2	L	29	2	5	0	1	0	0	0	0	0	0	0	.200	.200	.200
Lew Riggs	3B1	L	36	1	4	0	0	0	0	0	0	0	0	0	.000	.000	.000
Goody Rosen†	OF1	L	33	3	3	0	1	0	0	0	0	0	1	0	.333	.333	.333
Earl Naylor		R	27	3	2	1	0	0	0	0	0	0	1	0	.000	.000	.000
Otis Davis		L	25	1	0	1	0	0	0	0	0	0	0	0	—	—	—
John Corriden		S	27	1	0	1	0	0	0	0	0	0	0	0	—	—	—

Pitcher	T	Age	G	GS	CG	ShO	IP	H	HR	BB	SO	W-L	Sv	ERA
Joe Hatten	L	29	42	30	13	1	222.0	207	10	110	85	14-11	2	2.84
Kirby Higbe	R	31	42	29	11	3	210.2	178	6	107	134	17-8	1	3.03
Vic Lombardi	L	23	41	25	13	2	193.0	170	10	84	60	13-10	3	2.89
Hal Gregg	R	24	26	16	4	2	117.1	103	3	44	54	6-4	2	2.99
Rube Melton	R	29	24	12	3	2	99.2	72	3	52	44	6-3	1	1.99
Rex Barney	R	21	16	9	1	0	53.2	46	2	51	36	2-5	0	5.87
Ed Head	R	28	13	7	3	1	56.0	56	3	24	17	3-2	1	3.21
Hank Behrman	R	25	47	11	2	0	150.2	138	3	69	78	11-5	4	2.93
Hugh Casey	R	32	46	1	0	0	99.2	101	2	33	31	11-5	5	1.99
Art Herring	R	40	35	2	0	0	86.0	91	2	29	34	7-2	5	3.35
Ralph Branca	R	20	24	10	2	2	67.1	62	4	41	42	3-1	3	3.88
Les Webber†	R	31	11	4	0	0	43.0	34	5	15	16	3-3	0	2.30
Harry Taylor	R	27	4	0	0	0	4.2	5	0	1	6	0-0	1	3.86
Jean-Pierre Roy	R	26	3	1	0	0	6.1	5	2	5	6	0-0	0	9.95
Paul Minner	L	22	3	0	0	0	4.0	6	1	3	3	0-1	0	6.75
Glen Moulder	R	28	1	0	0	0	2.0	2	1	1	1	0-0	0	4.50
Curt Davis	R	42	1	0	0	0	2.0	3	1	2	0	0-0	0	13.50
Cal McLish	R	20	1	0	0	0	0.0	1	0	0	0	0-0	0	—

1946 Chicago Cubs 3rd NL 82-71 .536 14.5 GB

Charlie Grimm

Player	Gm by Position	B	Age	G	AB	R	H	2B	3B	HR	RBI	BB	SO	SB	Avg	OBP	Slg
Clyde McCullough	C89	R	29	95	307	38	88	18	5	4	34	22	39	2	.287	.338	.417
Eddie Waitkus	1B106	L	26	113	441	50	134	24	5	4	55	23	14	3	.304	.340	.408
Don Johnson	2B83	R	34	83	314	37	76	10	1	1	19	26	39	6	.242	.306	.290
Stan Hack	3B90	L	36	92	323	55	92	13	4	0	26	83	32	3	.285	.431	.350
Billy Jurges	SS73,3B7,2B2	R	38	82	221	26	49	9	2	0	17	43	28	3	.222	.351	.281
Peanuts Lowrey	OF126,3B20	R	27	144	540	75	139	24	5	4	54	56	22	10	.257	.328	.343
Marv Rickert	OF104	L	25	111	392	44	103	18	3	7	47	28	54	3	.263	.314	.378
Phil Cavarretta	OF86,1B51	L	29	139	510	89	150	28	10	8	78	88	54	2	.294	.401	.435
Bill Nicholson	OF80	L	31	105	296	36	65	13	2	8	41	44	44	1	.220	.325	.358
Bobby Sturgeon	SS72,2B21	R	26	100	294	26	87	12	2	1	21	10	18	0	.296	.319	.361
Andy Pafko	OF64	R	25	65	234	18	66	6	4	3	39	27	15	4	.282	.366	.380
Lou Stringer	2B62,3B1,SS1	R	29	80	209	26	51	3	1	3	19	26	34	0	.244	.328	.311
Mickey Livingston	C56	R	31	66	176	14	45	14	0	2	20	20	19	0	.256	.338	.369
Johnny Ostrowski	3B50,2B1	R	28	64	160	20	34	4	2	3	12	20	31	1	.213	.300	.319
Lennie Merullo	SS44	R	29	65	126	14	19	8	0	0	7	11	13	2	.151	.219	.214
Bob Scheffing	C40	R	32	63	115	8	32	4	1	0	18	12	18	0	.278	.346	.330
Dom Dallessandro	OF20	L	32	65	89	4	20	2	2	1	9	23	12	1	.225	.384	.326
Frank Secory	OF9	R	33	33	43	6	10	3	0	3	12	6	6	0	.233	.327	.512
Cy Block	3B4	R	27	6	13	2	3	0	0	0	0	4	0	0	.231	.412	.231
Charlie Gilbert†	OF2	L	26	15	13	2	1	0	0	0	1	1	4	0	.077	.143	.077
Hank Schenz	3B5	R	27	6	11	0	2	0	0	0	1	0	0	1	.182	.182	.182
Al Glossop	2B2,SS2	S	30	4	10	2	0	0	0	0	0	1	3	0	.000	.231	.000
Heinz Becker†		S	30	9	7	0	2	0	0	0	1	1	1	0	.286	.375	.286
Cecil Garriott		L	29	6	5	1	0	0	0	0	0	0	2	0	.000	.167	.000
Dewey Williams	C2	R	30	4	5	0	1	0	0	0	0	0	2	0	.200	.200	.200
Ted Pawelek	C1	L	26	4	4	0	1	1	0	0	0	0	0	0	.250	.250	.500
Clarence Maddern	OF2	R	24	3	3	0	0	0	0	0	0	0	0	0	.000	.250	.000

Pitcher	T	Age	G	GS	CG	ShO	IP	H	HR	BB	SO	W-L	Sv	ERA
Johnny Schmitz	L	25	41	31	14	2	224.1	184	6	94	135	11-11	2	2.61
Hank Borowy	R	30	32	28	8	1	201.0	220	9	61	95	12-10	0	3.76
Hank Wyse	R	28	40	27	12	2	201.1	206	7	52	52	14-12	1	2.68
Claude Passeau	R	37	21	21	10	2	129.1	118	5	42	47	9-8	0	3.13
Doyle Lade	R	25	3	2	0	0	15.1	15	0	3	8	0-2	0	4.11
Hal Manders†	R	29	2	1	0	0	6.0	11	1	3	4	0-1	0	9.00
Emil Kush	R	29	40	6	1	1	129.2	120	4	43	50	9-2	2	3.05
Bob Chipman	L	27	34	10	5	3	109.1	103	8	54	42	6-5	2	3.13
Paul Erickson	R	30	32	14	5	1	137.0	119	2	65	70	9-7	0	2.43
Hi Bithorn	R	30	26	7	2	1	86.2	97	5	25	34	6-5	1	3.84
Russ Bauers	R	32	15	2	2	0	43.1	45	1	19	22	2-1	1	3.53
Bill Fleming	R	32	14	1	0	0	29.1	37	2	12	10	0-1	0	6.14
Ray Prim	L	39	14	2	0	0	23.1	28	5	10	10	2-3	1	5.79
Red Adams	R	24	8	0	0	0	12.0	18	1	7	8	0-1	0	8.25
Russ Meers	L	27	7	2	0	0	11.1	10	0	10	2	1-2	0	3.18
Vern Olsen	L	28	5	0	0	0	9.2	10	0	9	8	0-0	0	2.79
Russ Meyer	R	22	4	1	0	0	17.0	21	2	10	10	0-0	1	3.18
Ed Hanyzewski	R	25	3	0	0	0	6.0	8	0	5	1	1-0	0	4.50
Emmett O'Neill†	R	28	1	0	0	0	1.0	0	0	3	1	0-0	0	0.00

1946 Boston Braves 4th NL 81-72 .529 15.5 GB

Billy Southworth

Player	Gm by Position	B	Age	G	AB	R	H	2B	3B	HR	RBI	BB	SO	SB	Avg	OBP	Slg
Phil Masi	C124	R	30	133	397	52	106	17	5	3	62	55	41	5	.267	.358	.358
Ray Sanders	1B77	L	29	80	259	43	63	12	0	6	35	50	38	0	.243	.368	.359
Connie Ryan	2B120,3B24	R	26	143	502	55	121	28	8	1	48	55	63	7	.241	.317	.335
Nanny Fernandez	3B81,SS18,OF14	R	27	115	372	37	95	15	2	2	42	30	44	1	.255	.313	.323
Dick Culler	SS132	R	31	134	482	70	123	15	3	0	33	62	18	7	.255	.342	.299
Tommy Holmes	OF146	L	29	149	568	80	176	35	6	6	79	58	14	7	.310	.377	.424
Bama Rowell	OF85	L	30	95	293	37	82	12	6	3	31	29	15	5	.280	.345	.392
Carden Gillenwater	OF78	R	28	99	224	30	51	10	1	1	14	39	27	3	.228	.342	.295
Johnny Hopp	1B68,OF58	L	29	129	445	71	148	23	8	3	48	34	34	21	.333	.386	.440
Billy Herman†	2B44,1B22,3B5	R	36	75	252	32	77	23	1	3	22	43	13	1	.306	.409	.440
Danny Litwhiler†	OF65,3B2	R	29	79	247	29	72	12	2	8	38	19	23	1	.291	.347	.453
Skippy Roberge	3B48	R	29	48	169	13	39	6	2	2	20	7	12	1	.231	.270	.325
Mike McCormick†	OF48	R	29	59	164	23	43	6	2	1	16	11	7	0	.262	.309	.341
Don Padgett†	C26	L	34	44	98	6	25	3	0	2	21	5	7	0	.255	.291	.347
Whitey Wietelmann	SS16,3B8,2B4*	S	27	44	78	7	16	0	0	0	5	14	8	0	.205	.326	.205
Stew Hofferth	C15	R	33	20	58	3	12	1	1	0	10	3	6	0	.207	.246	.259
Chuck Workman†	OF12	L	31	25	48	5	8	2	0	2	7	3	11	0	.167	.231	.333
Tommy Neill	OF13	L	26	13	45	8	12	2	0	0	7	2	1	0	.267	.298	.311
Johnny Barrett†	OF17	L	30	24	43	3	10	3	0	0	6	12	1	0	.233	.400	.302
Ken O'Dea†	C12	L	33	12	32	4	7	0	0	0	2	8	4	0	.219	.375	.219
Al Dark	SS12,OF1	R	24	15	13	0	3	3	0	0	1	0	3	0	.231	.231	.462
Johnny McCarthy	1B2	L	36	2	7	0	1	0	0	0	1	2	0	0	.143	.333	.143
Hugh Poland	C2	L	33	4	6	0	1	1	0	0	0	0	0	0	.167	.167	.333
Bob Brady	C1	L	23	3	5	0	1	0	0	0	0	1	1	0	.200	.333	.200
Damon Phillips		R	27	2	2	0	1	0	0	0	0	0	0	0	.500	.500	.500
Ducky Detweiler		R	27	1	1	0	0	0	0	0	0	0	0	0	.000	.000	.000
Max West†	1B1	L	29	1	1	0	0	0	0	0	0	0	1	0	.000	.000	.000
Sibby Sisti	3B1	R	25	1	0	0	0	0	0	0	0	0	0	0	—	—	—

W. Wietelmann, 3 G at P

Pitcher	T	Age	G	GS	CG	ShO	IP	H	HR	BB	SO	W-L	Sv	ERA
Johnny Sain	R	28	37	34	24	3	265.0	225	8	87	129	20-14	2	2.21
Mort Cooper	R	33	28	27	15	3	199.0	181	17	39	83	13-11	1	3.12
Ed Wright	R	27	36	21	9	2	176.1	164	8	71	44	12-9	0	3.52
Bill Lee	R	36	25	21	8	0	140.0	148	7	45	32	10-9	0	4.18
Warren Spahn	L	25	24	16	8	0	125.2	107	6	36	67	8-5	1	2.94
Johnny Niggeling†	R	42	8	8	3	0	58.0	54	2	21	24	2-5	0	3.26
Al Javery	R	28	2	1	0	0	3.1	5	0	5	0	0-1	0	13.50
Johnny Hutchings	R	30	1	1	0	0	3.0	5	1	1	1	0-1	0	9.00
Si Johnson†	R	39	28	12	5	1	127.0	134	8	35	41	6-5	1	2.76
Lefty Wallace	L	24	27	8	2	0	75.1	76	5	31	27	3-3	0	4.18
Frank Barrett	R	32	23	0	0	0	35.1	35	2	17	12	2-4	1	5.09
Bill Posedel	R	39	19	0	0	0	28.1	34	4	13	9	2-0	4	6.99
Elmer Singleton	R	28	15	2	0	0	33.2	27	3	21	17	0-1	1	3.74
Steve Roser†	R	28	14	1	0	0	35.0	33	1	18	18	1-1	1	3.60
Ernie White	L	29	12	1	0	0	23.2	22	1	12	8	0-1	0	4.18
Jim Konstanty	R	29	10	1	0	0	15.1	17	2	7	9	0-1	0	5.28
Dick Mulligan†	L	28	4	0	0	0	15.1	6	1	9	4	1-0	0	2.35
Whitey Wietelmann	R	27	3	0	0	0	6.2	9	1	4	2	0-0	0	8.10
Earl Reid	R	33	2	0	0	0	3.0	4	0	3	2	1-0	0	3.00
Don Hendrickson	R	32	2	0	0	0	2.0	4	0	2	2	0-1	0	4.50
Ace Williams	L	29	1	0	0	0	0.0	1	0	1	0	0-0	0	—

Seasons: Team Rosters 701

1946 Philadelphia Phillies 5th NL 69-85 .448 28.0 GB

Ben Chapman

Player	Gm by Position	B	Age	G	AB	R	H	2B	3B	HR	RBI	BB	SO	SB	Avg	OBP	Slg
Andy Seminick	C118	R	25	124	406	55	107	15	5	12	52	39	86	2	.264	.334	.414
Frank McCormick	1B134	R	35	135	504	46	143	20	2	11	66	36	21	2	.284	.333	.397
Emil Verban†	2B138	R	30	138	473	44	130	17	5	0	34	21	18	5	.275	.306	.332
Jim Tabor	3B124	R	29	124	463	53	124	15	2	10	50	36	51	3	.268	.322	.374
Skeeter Newsome	SS107,2B3,3B2	R	35	112	375	35	87	10	2	1	23	30	23	4	.232	.289	.277
Johnny Wyrostek	OF142	L	26	145	545	73	153	30	4	6	45	70	42	7	.281	.366	.383
Del Ennis	OF138	R	21	141	540	70	169	30	6	17	73	39	65	5	.313	.364	.485
Ron Northey	OF111	L	26	128	438	55	109	24	6	16	62	39	59	1	.249	.313	.441
Roy Hughes	SS34,3B31,2B7*	R	35	89	276	23	65	11	1	0	22	19	15	7	.236	.287	.283
Charlie Gilbert†	OF69	L	26	88	260	34	63	5	2	1	17	25	18	3	.242	.314	.288
Rollie Hemsley	C45	R	39	49	139	7	31	4	1	0	11	9	10	0	.223	.270	.266
Vance Dinges	1B26,OF1	L	31	50	104	7	32	5	1	1	10	9	12	2	.308	.363	.404
John O'Neil	SS32	R	26	46	94	12	25	3	0	0	9	5	12	0	.266	.303	.298
Jimmy Wasdell†	OF11,1B2	L	32	26	51	7	13	0	2	1	5	3	2	0	.255	.309	.392
Lou Novikoff	OF3	R	30	17	23	0	7	1	0	0	3	1	2	0	.304	.333	.348
Ken Richardson	2B6	R	31	6	20	1	3	1	0	0	2	0	2	0	.150	.150	.200
Danny Murtaugh	2B6	R	28	6	19	1	4	1	0	1	3	2	2	0	.211	.286	.421
Vince DiMaggio†	OF6	R	33	6	19	1	4	1	0	0	1	0	7	0	.211	.211	.263
Charlie Letchas	2B4	R	30	6	13	1	3	0	0	0	0	1	1	0	.231	.286	.231
Dee Moore	C6,1B2	R	32	11	13	2	1	0	0	0	1	7	3	0	.077	.400	.077
Don Hasenmayer	3B3	R	19	6	12	0	1	1	0	0	0	0	2	0	.083	.083	.167
Granny Hamner	SS2	R	19	2	7	0	1	0	0	0	0	0	3	0	.143	.143	.143
Hal Spindel	C1	R	33	1	3	0	1	0	0	0	1	0	0	0	.333	.333	.333
Glenn Crawford		L	32	1	1	0	0	0	0	0	0	0	0	0	.000	.000	.000
Bill Burich	3B1	R	28	2	1	1	0	0	0	0	0	0	0	0	.000	.000	.000

R. Hughes, 1 G at 1B

Pitcher	T	Age	G	GS	CG	ShO	IP	H	HR	BB	SO	W-L	Sv	ERA
Oscar Judd	L	38	30	24	12	1	173.1	169	6	90	65	11-12	2	3.53
Ken Raffensberger	L	28	39	23	14	2	196.0	203	9	39	73	8-15	6	3.63
Schoolboy Rowe	R	36	17	16	9	2	136.0	112	3	21	51	11-4	0	2.12
Charley Stanceu†	R	30	14	11	1	0	70.1	71	4	39	23	2-4	0	4.22
Al Jurisich	R	24	13	10	2	1	68.1	71	9	31	34	4-3	1	3.69
Blix Donnelly†	R	32	12	8	2	0	76.1	64	7	24	38	3-4	1	2.95
Lou Possehl	R	20	4	4	0	0	13.2	19	0	10	4	1-2	0	5.93
Eli Hodkey	L	28	2	1	0	0	4.1	9	0	5	0	0-1	0	12.46
Dick Koecher	L	20	1	1	0	0	2.2	7	0	1	2	0-1	0	10.13
Al Milnar†	L	32	1	1	0	0	0.0	2	0	2	0	0-0	0	—
Andy Karl	R	32	39	0	0	0	65.1	84	6	22	15	3-7	5	4.96
Charley Schanz	R	27	32	15	4	0	116.1	130	8	71	47	6-6	4	5.80
Tommy Hughes	R	26	29	13	3	2	111.0	123	5	44	34	6-9	1	4.38
Dick Mauney	R	26	24	7	3	1	90.0	98	4	18	31	6-4	2	2.70
Dick Mulligan†	L	28	19	5	1	0	54.2	61	0	27	16	2-2	1	4.77
Frank Hoerst	L	28	18	7	2	0	68.1	77	4	36	17	1-6	0	4.61
Hugh Mulcahy	R	32	16	5	1	0	62.2	69	3	33	12	2-4	0	4.45
Johnny Humphries	R	31	10	1	0	0	25.0	24	1	9	10	0-0	0	3.96
Charlie Ripple	L	24	6	0	0	0	3.1	5	0	6	3	1-0	0	10.80
Ike Pearson	R	29	5	2	1	1	14.1	16	1	8	6	1-0	0	3.77
Art Lopatka	L	27	4	1	0	0	5.1	13	1	4	4	0-1	0	16.88
Don Grate	R	22	3	0	0	0	8.0	4	0	2	2	1-0	0	1.13
Si Johnson†	R	39	1	0	0	0	3.0	7	1	0	2	0-0	0	3.00
Ben Chapman	R	37	1	0	0	0	1.0	1	0	0	1	0-0	0	0.00

1946 Cincinnati Reds 6th NL 67-87 .435 30.0 GB

Bill McKechnie (64-86)/Hank Gowdy (3-1)

Player	Gm by Position	B	Age	G	AB	R	H	2B	3B	HR	RBI	BB	SO	SB	Avg	OBP	Slg
Ray Mueller	C100	R	34	114	378	35	96	18	4	8	48	27	37	0	.254	.309	.386
Bert Haas	1B140,3B6	R	32	140	535	57	141	24	7	3	50	33	42	22	.264	.310	.351
Bobby Adams	2B74,OF2,3B1	R	24	94	311	35	76	13	3	4	24	18	32	16	.244	.292	.344
Grady Hatton	3B116,OF2	L	23	116	436	56	118	18	3	14	69	66	53	6	.271	.369	.422
Eddie Miller	SS88	R	29	91	299	30	58	10	0	6	36	25	34	5	.194	.258	.288
Dain Clay	OF120	R	26	121	435	52	99	17	0	2	22	53	40	11	.228	.318	.280
Al Libke	OF115,P1	L	27	124	431	32	109	22	1	5	42	43	50	0	.253	.322	.343
Eddie Lukon	OF83	L	25	102	312	31	78	8	8	12	34	26	29	3	.250	.310	.442
Lonny Frey	2B65,OF28	L	35	111	333	46	82	10	3	3	24	63	31	5	.246	.368	.321
Benny Zientara	2B39,3B36	R	26	78	280	26	81	10	2	0	16	14	11	3	.289	.323	.339
Claude Corbitt	SS77	R	30	82	274	25	68	10	1	1	16	23	13	3	.248	.309	.303
Ray Lamanno	C61	R	26	85	239	18	58	12	0	1	30	11	26	0	.243	.285	.305
Max West†	OF58	L	29	72	202	16	43	13	0	5	18	32	36	1	.213	.323	.351
Bob Usher	OF80,3B1	R	21	92	152	16	31	5	1	1	14	13	27	2	.204	.271	.270
Eddie Shokes	1B29	L	26	31	83	3	10	1	0	0	5	18	21	1	.120	.277	.133
Mike McCormick†	OF21	R	29	23	74	10	16	2	0	0	5	8	4	0	.216	.293	.243
Al Lakeman	C6	R	27	23	30	0	4	0	0	0	4	2	7	0	.133	.188	.133
Howie Moss†	OF6	R	26	7	26	1	5	0	0	0	1	0	4	0	.192	.222	.192
Clyde Vollmer	OF7	R	24	9	22	1	4	0	0	0	1	1	3	2	.182	.217	.182
Lonnie Goldstein		L	28	6	5	1	0	0	0	0	0	1	1	0	.000	.167	.000
Garland Lawing†	OF1	R	26	2	3	0	0	0	0	0	0	0	2	0	.000	.000	.000

Pitcher	T	Age	G	GS	CG	ShO	IP	H	HR	BB	SO	W-L	Sv	ERA
J. Vander Meer	L	31	29	25	11	5	204.1	175	11	78	94	10-12	0	3.17
Ewell Blackwell	R	23	33	25	10	6	194.1	160	1	79	100	9-13	0	2.45
Joe Beggs	R	35	28	22	14	3	190.0	175	15	39	38	12-10	1	2.32
Bucky Walters	R	37	22	22	10	2	151.1	146	9	64	60	10-7	0	2.56
Ed Heusser	R	37	29	21	9	1	167.2	167	11	39	47	7-14	2	3.22
Nate Andrews†	R	32	7	7	3	0	43.1	50	2	8	13	2-4	0	3.95
Al Libke	R	27	1	1	0	0	5.0	4	0	3	2	0-0	0	3.60
Harry Gumbert	R	36	36	10	5	0	119.0	112	8	42	44	6-8	4	3.25
Johnny Hetki	R	24	32	11	4	0	126.1	121	3	31	41	6-6	1	2.99
Clyde Shoun	L	34	27	5	0	0	79.0	87	3	26	20	1-6	0	4.10
Bob Malloy	R	28	27	3	1	0	72.0	71	2	26	24	2-5	2	2.75
Clayton Lambert	R	29	23	4	2	0	52.2	48	3	20	20	2-2	1	4.27
Howie Fox	R	25	4	0	0	0	5.0	12	1	5	1	0-0	0	18.00
George Burpo	L	24	2	0	0	0	2.1	4	0	5	1	0-0	0	15.43
Frank Dasso	R	28	2	0	0	0	1.0	2	0	2	1	0-0	0	27.00

1946 Pittsburgh Pirates 7th NL 63-91 .409 34.0 GB

Frank Frisch (62-89)/Spud Davis (1-2)

Player	Gm by Position	B	Age	G	AB	R	H	2B	3B	HR	RBI	BB	SO	SB	Avg	OBP	Slg
Al Lopez	C56	R	37	56	150	13	46	2	0	1	12	23	14	1	.307	.399	.340
Elbie Fletcher	1B147	L	30	148	532	72	136	25	8	4	66	111	37	4	.256	.384	.355
Frankie Gustine	2B113,SS13,3B7	R	26	131	495	60	128	23	6	8	52	40	52	2	.259	.318	.378
Lee Handley	3B102,2B3	R	32	116	416	43	99	8	7	1	28	29	20	4	.238	.289	.298
Billy Cox	SS114	R	26	121	411	32	119	22	6	2	36	26	15	4	.290	.333	.387
Ralph Kiner	OF140	R	23	144	502	63	124	17	3	23	81	74	109	3	.247	.345	.430
Jim Russell	OF134,1B5	S	27	146	516	68	143	29	6	8	50	67	54	11	.277	.362	.403
Bob Elliott	OF92,3B43	R	29	140	486	50	128	25	3	5	68	64	44	6	.263	.351	.358
Jimmy Brown	SS30,2B21,3B9	S	36	79	241	23	58	6	0	0	12	18	5	3	.241	.293	.266
Bill Salkeld	C51	L	29	69	160	18	47	8	0	3	19	39	16	2	.294	.432	.400
M. Van Robays	OF37,1B2	R	31	59	146	14	31	5	3	1	12	11	15	0	.212	.272	.308
Chuck Workman†	OF40,3B1	L	31	58	145	11	32	4	1	2	16	11	19	2	.221	.280	.303
Burgess Whitehead	2B30,3B4,SS1	R	36	55	127	10	28	1	2	0	5	6	6	3	.220	.261	.260
Bill Baker	C41,1B1	R	35	53	113	7	27	4	0	1	8	12	6	0	.239	.312	.301
Al Gionfriddo	OF33	L	24	64	102	11	26	2	2	0	10	14	5	1	.255	.345	.314
Hank Camelli	C39	R	31	42	96	8	20	2	2	0	5	8	9	0	.208	.269	.271
Johnny Barrett†	OF21	L	30	32	71	7	12	3	0	0	6	8	11	1	.169	.253	.211
Frank Colman†	OF8,1B2	L	28	26	53	3	9	3	0	1	6	2	7	0	.170	.214	.283
Al Gerheauser	P35,OF1	L	29	36	21	3	7	2	0	0	1	0	11	0	.333	.333	.429
Vinnie Smith	C7	R	30	7	21	2	4	0	0	0	0	1	5	0	.190	.227	.190
Frankie Zak	SS10	R	24	21	20	8	4	0	0	0	0	1	0	0	.200	.238	.200
Roy Jarvis	C1	R	20	2	4	0	1	0	0	0	0	1	1	0	.250	.400	.250
Ben Guintini	OF1	R	26	2	3	0	0	0	0	0	0	0	0	0	.000	.000	.000
Pete Coscarart		R	33	3	2	0	1	1	0	0	0	0	0	0	.500	.500	1.000
Vic Barnhart		R	23	2	1	0	0	0	0	0	0	0	0	0	.000	.000	.000
Alf Anderson		R	32	2	1	0	0	0	0	0	0	1	0	0	.000	.500	.000

Pitcher	T	Age	G	GS	CG	ShO	IP	H	HR	BB	SO	W-L	Sv	ERA
Fritz Ostermueller	L	38	27	25	16	2	193.1	193	5	56	57	13-10	0	2.84
Ken Heintzelman	L	30	32	24	6	2	157.2	165	7	86	57	8-12	1	3.77
Nick Strincevich	R	31	32	22	11	3	176.0	185	7	44	49	10-15	1	3.58
Rip Sewell	R	39	25	20	11	2	149.1	140	6	53	33	8-12	0	3.68
Ed Bahr	R	26	27	14	7	0	136.2	128	8	52	44	8-6	0	2.63
Lee Howard	L	22	3	2	1	0	13.1	14	0	9	6	0-1	0	2.03
Junior Walsh	R	27	4	2	0	0	10.1	9	0	10	2	0-1	0	5.23
Al Tate	R	27	2	1	1	0	9.0	8	0	7	2	0-1	0	5.00
Jim Hopper	R	26	2	1	0	0	4.0	6	1	3	1	0-1	0	11.25
Jack Hallett	R	31	35	9	3	1	115.0	107	0	39	64	5-7	0	3.29
Al Gerheauser	L	29	35	3	1	0	81.2	92	2	25	32	2-2	0	3.97
Ken Gables	R	27	32	7	0	0	100.2	113	3	52	39	2-4	1	5.27
Johnny Lanning	R	35	27	9	3	0	91.0	97	3	31	16	4-5	1	3.07
Preacher Roe	L	31	21	10	1	0	70.0	83	5	25	28	3-8	2	5.14
Ed Albosta	R	27	17	6	0	0	39.2	41	3	35	19	0-6	0	6.13
Hank Gornicki	R	35	7	0	0	0	12.2	12	0	11	4	0-0	0	3.55
Lefty Wilkie	L	31	7	0	0	0	7.2	13	0	3	3	0-0	0	10.57
Bill Clemensen	R	27	1	0	0	0	2.0	0	0	0	2	0-0	0	0.00

1946 New York Giants 8th NL 61-93 .396 36.0 GB

Mel Ott

Player	Gm by Position	B	Age	G	AB	R	H	2B	3B	HR	RBI	BB	SO	SB	Avg	OBP	Slg
Walker Cooper	C73	R	31	87	280	29	75	10	1	8	46	17	12	0	.268	.310	.396
Johnny Mize	1B101	L	33	101	377	70	127	18	3	22	70	62	26	3	.337	.437	.576
Buddy Blattner	2B114,1B1	R	26	126	420	63	107	18	6	11	49	56	52	12	.255	.351	.405
Bill Rigney	3B73,SS33	R	28	110	360	38	85	9	1	3	31	36	29	9	.236	.307	.292
Buddy Kerr	SS126,3B18	R	23	145	497	50	124	20	3	6	40	53	31	7	.249	.324	.338
Willard Marshall	OF125	L	25	131	510	63	144	18	3	13	48	33	29	3	.282	.327	.406
Sid Gordon	OF101,3B30	R	28	135	450	64	132	15	4	5	45	60	27	1	.293	.380	.378
Goody Rosen†	OF84	L	33	100	310	39	87	11	4	5	30	48	32	2	.281	.377	.390
Babe Young	1B49,OF24	L	30	104	291	30	81	11	0	7	33	30	21	3	.278	.346	.388
Mickey Witek	2B42,3B35	R	30	82	284	32	75	13	2	4	29	28	10	1	.264	.330	.366
Jack Graham†	OF62,1B7	L	29	100	270	34	59	6	4	14	47	23	37	1	.219	.282	.426
Ernie Lombardi	C63	R	38	88	238	19	69	4	1	12	39	18	24	0	.290	.347	.466
Johnny Rucker	OF54	L	29	95	197	28	52	8	2	1	13	7	27	4	.264	.300	.340
Bennie Warren	C30	R	34	39	69	7	11	1	1	4	8	14	21	0	.159	.301	.377
Mel Ott	OF16	L	37	31	68	2	5	1	0	1	4	8	15	0	.074	.171	.132
Bobby Thomson	3B16	R	22	18	54	8	17	4	1	2	9	4	5	0	.315	.362	.537
Jess Pike	OF10	L	30	16	41	4	7	1	1	1	6	6	9	0	.171	.277	.317
Vince DiMaggio†	OF13	R	33	15	25	2	0	0	0	0	0	2	5	0	.000	.074	.000
Mickey Grasso	C7	R	26	7	22	1	3	0	0	0	1	0	3	0	.136	.136	.136
Garland Lawing†	OF4	R	26	8	12	2	2	0	0	0	0	0	3	0	.167	.167	.167
Jim Gladd	C4	R	23	4	11	0	1	0	0	0	0	1	4	0	.091	.167	.091
Dick Lajeskie	2B4	R	20	6	10	3	2	0	0	0	0	3	2	0	.200	.429	.200
Clyde Kluttz†	C2	R	28	5	8	0	3	0	0	0	1	0	1	0	.375	.375	.375
Buster Maynard	OF3	R	33	7	4	2	0	0	0	0	0	1	1	0	.000	.200	.000
Morrie Arnovich	OF1	R	35	1	3	0	0	0	0	0	0	0	0	0	.000	.000	.000
Dick Bartell	3B4,2B2	R	38	5	2	0	0	0	0	0	0	0	0	0	.000	.000	.000
Mike Schemer		L	28	1	1	0	0	0	0	0	0	0	0	0	.000	.000	.000

Pitcher	T	Age	G	GS	CG	ShO	IP	H	HR	BB	SO	W-L	Sv	ERA
Dave Koslo	L	26	40	35	17	3	265.1	251	16	101	121	14-19	1	3.63
Monte Kennedy	L	24	38	27	10	1	186.2	153	14	116	71	9-10	1	3.42
Bill Voiselle	R	27	36	25	10	2	178.0	171	14	85	89	9-15	0	3.74
Hal Schumacher	R	35	24	13	2	0	96.2	95	8	52	48	4-4	1	3.91
Bob Joyce	R	31	14	7	2	0	60.2	79	3	20	24	3-4	0	5.34
Bob Carpenter	R	28	12	6	1	1	39.0	37	7	18	13	1-3	0	4.85
Sheldon Jones	R	24	6	4	1	0	28.0	21	4	17	24	1-2	0	3.21
Marv Grissom	R	28	4	3	0	0	18.2	17	1	13	9	0-2	0	4.34
Nate Andrews†	R	32	3	2	0	0	12.0	17	2	4	5	1-0	0	6.00
Harry Feldman	R	26	3	2	0	0	4.0	9	1	3	3	0-2	0	18.00
Ken Trinkle	R	26	48	13	2	0	151.0	146	8	74	49	7-14	2	3.87
Junior Thompson	R	29	39	1	0	0	62.2	36	5	40	31	4-6	4	1.29
Mike Budnick	R	26	35	7	1	1	88.1	75	13	48	36	2-3	3	3.16
Jack Kraus	L	28	17	1	0	0	25.0	25	4	15	7	2-1	0	6.12
Woody Abernathy	L	31	15	1	0	0	40.0	32	5	10	6	1-1	1	3.38
Rube Fischer	R	29	15	1	0	0	35.2	48	2	21	14	1-2	0	6.31
Johnny Gee	L	30	13	6	1	0	47.1	60	3	15	22	2-4	0	3.99
Ace Adams	R	34	3	0	0	0	2.2	9	2	1	3	0-1	0	16.88
Slim Emmerich	R	26	2	0	0	0	4.0	6	1	0	1	0-0	0	4.50
Red Kress	R	39	1	0	0	0	3.2	5	1	1	1	0-0	0	12.27
John Carden	R	25	1	0	0	0	2.0	4	0	4	1	0-0	0	22.50
Jack Brewer	R	26	1	0	0	0	2.0	3	0	2	3	0-0	0	13.50

702 Seasons: Team Rosters

»1947 New York Yankees 1st AL 97-57 .630 —

Bucky Harris

Player	Gm by Position	B	Age	G	AB	R	H	2B	3B	HR	RBI	BB	SO	SB	Avg	OBP	Slg
Aaron Robinson	C74	L	32	82	252	23	68	11	5	5	36	40	26	0	.270	.370	.413
George McQuinn	1B142	L	37	144	517	84	157	24	3	13	80	78	66	0	.304	.395	.437
Snuffy Stirnweiss	2B148	R	28	148	571	102	146	18	8	5	41	89	47	5	.256	.358	.342
Bill Johnson	3B132	R	28	132	494	67	141	19	8	10	95	44	43	1	.285	.351	.417
Phil Rizzuto	SS151	R	29	153	549	78	150	26	9	2	60	57	31	11	.273	.350	.364
Joe DiMaggio	OF139	R	32	141	534	97	168	31	10	20	97	64	32	3	.315	.391	.522
Tommy Henrich	OF132,1B6	L	34	142	550	109	158	35	13	16	98	71	54	3	.287	.372	.485
Johnny Lindell	OF118	R	30	127	476	66	131	18	7	11	67	32	70	1	.275	.322	.412
Yogi Berra	C51,OF24	L	22	83	293	41	82	15	3	11	54	13	12	0	.280	.310	.464
Charlie Keller	OF43	L	30	45	151	36	36	6	1	13	36	41	18	0	.238	.404	.550
Bobby Brown	3B27,SS11,OF3	L	22	69	150	21	45	6	1	1	18	21	9	0	.300	.390	.373
Ralph Houk	C41	R	27	41	92	7	25	3	1	0	12	11	5	0	.272	.350	.326
Allie Clark	OF16	R	24	24	67	9	25	5	0	1	14	5	2	0	.373	.417	.493
Jack Phillips	1B10	R	25	16	36	5	10	0	1	1	2	3	5	0	.278	.333	.417
Sherm Lollar	C9	R	22	11	32	4	7	0	1	1	6	1	5	0	.219	.242	.375
Frank Colman	OF6	L	29	22	28	2	3	0	0	2	6	2	6	0	.107	.167	.321
Lonny Frey†	2B8	L	36	24	28	10	5	2	0	0	2	10	1	3	.179	.410	.250
Johnny Lucadello	2B5	R	28	12	12	0	1	0	0	0	0	1	5	0	.083	.154	.083
Ken Silvestri	C3	S	31	3	10	0	2	0	0	0	0	2	2	0	.200	.333	.200
Al Lyons†	P6,OF1	R	28	8	6	1	4	1	0	0	3	0	1	0	.667	.667	.833
Frankie Crosetti	2B1,SS1	R	36	3	1	0	0	0	0	0	0	0	0	0	.000	.000	.000
Ted Sepkowski†		L	23	2	0	1	0	0	0	0	0	0	0	0	—	—	—
Ray Mack†		R	30	1	0	0	0	0	0	0	0	0	0	0	—	—	—

Pitcher	T	Age	G	GS	CG	ShO	IP	H	HR	BB	SO	W-L	Sv	ERA
Allie Reynolds	R	32	34	30	17	4	241.2	207	23	123	129	19-8	2	3.20
Spec Shea	R	26	27	23	13	3	178.2	127	10	89	89	14-5	1	3.07
Bill Bevens	R	30	28	23	11	1	165.0	167	13	77	77	7-13	0	3.82
Spud Chandler	R	39	17	16	13	2	128.0	100	4	41	68	9-5	0	2.46
Bobo Newsom†	R	39	17	15	6	2	115.2	109	8	30	42	7-5	0	2.80
Vic Raschi	R	28	15	14	6	1	104.2	89	11	38	51	7-2	0	3.87
Don Johnson	R	20	15	8	2	0	54.1	57	2	23	16	4-3	0	3.64
Bill Wight	L	25	1	1	1	0	9.0	8	0	2	3	1-0	0	1.00
Joe Page	L	29	56	2	0	0	141.1	105	5	72	116	14-8	17	2.48
Karl Drews	R	27	30	10	0	0	91.2	92	6	55	45	6-6	1	4.91
Randy Gumpert	R	29	24	6	2	0	56.1	71	4	28	25	4-1	0	5.43
Butch Wensloff	R	31	11	5	1	0	51.2	41	3	22	18	3-1	0	2.61
Al Lyons†	R	28	6	0	0	0	11.0	18	2	9	7	1-0	0	9.00
Mel Queen†	R	29	5	0	0	0	6.2	9	2	4	2	0-0	0	9.45
Dick Starr	R	26	4	1	1	0	12.1	12	1	8	1	1-0	0	1.46
Tommy Byrne	L	27	4	1	0	0	4.1	5	0	6	2	0-0	0	4.15
Rugger Ardizoia	R	27	1	0	0	0	2.0	4	1	1	0	0-0	0	9.00

1947 Detroit Tigers 2nd AL 85-69 .552 12.0 GB

Steve O'Neill

Player	Gm by Position	B	Age	G	AB	R	H	2B	3B	HR	RBI	BB	SO	SB	Avg	OBP	Slg
Bob Swift	C97	R	32	97	279	23	70	11	0	1	21	33	16	2	.251	.330	.301
Roy Cullenbine	1B138	S	33	142	464	82	104	18	1	24	78	137	51	3	.224	.401	.422
Eddie Mayo	2B142	L	37	142	535	66	149	28	4	6	48	48	28	3	.279	.338	.379
George Kell	3B152	R	24	152	588	75	188	29	5	5	93	61	16	9	.320	.387	.412
Eddie Lake	SS158	R	31	158	602	96	127	19	6	12	46	120	54	11	.211	.343	.322
Hoot Evers	OF123	R	26	126	460	67	136	24	5	10	67	45	49	8	.296	.366	.435
Pat Mullin	OF106	L	29	116	398	62	102	28	6	15	62	63	66	3	.256	.359	.470
Dick Wakefield	OF101	L	26	112	368	59	104	15	5	8	51	80	44	1	.283	.412	.416
Vic Wertz	OF82	L	22	102	333	60	96	22	4	6	44	47	66	2	.288	.376	.432
Hal Wagner†	C71	L	31	71	191	19	55	10	0	5	33	28	16	0	.288	.382	.419
Doc Cramer	OF35	L	41	73	157	21	42	2	2	2	30	20	5	0	.268	.350	.344
Jimmy Outlaw	OF37,3B9	R	34	70	127	20	29	7	1	0	15	21	14	3	.228	.338	.299
John McHale	1B25	L	25	39	95	10	20	1	0	3	11	7	24	1	.211	.265	.316
Skeeter Webb	2B30,SS6	R	37	50	79	13	16	3	0	0	6	7	9	3	.203	.267	.241
Birdie Tebbetts†	C20	R	34	20	53	1	5	1	0	0	2	3	3	0	.094	.143	.113
Ed Mierkowicz	OF10	R	23	21	42	6	8	1	0	1	1	1	12	1	.190	.209	.286
Hank Riebe	C3	R	25	8	7	0	0	0	0	0	2	0	2	0	.000	.000	.000
Johnny Groth	OF1	R	20	2	4	1	1	0	0	0	0	2	1	0	.250	.500	.250
Ben Steiner		L	25	1	0	1	0	0	0	0	0	0	0	0	—	—	—

Pitcher	T	Age	G	GS	CG	ShO	IP	H	HR	BB	SO	W-L	Sv	ERA
Hal Newhouser	L	26	40	36	24	3	285.0	268	9	110	176	17-17	2	2.87
Dizzy Trout	R	32	32	26	9	2	186.1	186	6	65	74	10-11	2	3.48
Virgil Trucks	R	30	36	26	8	2	180.2	186	15	79	108	10-12	2	4.53
Fred Hutchinson	R	27	33	25	18	3	219.2	211	14	61	113	18-10	2	3.03
Stubby Overmire	L	28	28	17	7	3	140.2	142	9	44	33	11-5	0	3.77
Al Benton	R	36	36	14	4	0	133.0	147	11	61	33	6-7	7	4.40
Hal White	R	28	35	5	0	0	84.2	91	5	47	33	4-5	2	3.61
Johnny Gorsica	R	32	31	0	0	0	57.2	44	5	26	20	2-0	1	3.75
Art Houtteman	R	19	23	9	7	2	110.2	106	6	36	58	7-2	0	3.42
Rufe Gentry	R	29	1	0	0	0	0.1	1	0	2	0	0-0	0	81.00

1947 Boston Red Sox 3rd AL 83-71 .539 14.0 GB

Joe Cronin

Player	Gm by Position	B	Age	G	AB	R	H	2B	3B	HR	RBI	BB	SO	SB	Avg	OBP	Slg
Birdie Tebbetts†	C89	R	34	90	291	22	87	10	0	1	28	21	30	2	.299	.346	.344
Jake Jones†	1B109	R	26	109	404	50	95	14	3	16	76	41	60	5	.235	.310	.403
Bobby Doerr	2B146	R	29	146	561	79	145	23	10	17	95	59	47	3	.258	.329	.426
Sam Dente	3B46	R	25	46	168	14	39	4	2	0	11	19	15	0	.232	.310	.280
Johnny Pesky	SS133,3B22	L	27	155	638	106	207	27	8	0	39	72	22	12	.324	.393	.392
Ted Williams	OF156	L	28	156	528	125	181	40	9	32	114	162	47	0	.343	.499	.634
Dom DiMaggio	OF134	R	30	136	513	75	145	21	5	8	71	74	62	10	.283	.376	.390
Sam Mele	OF115,1B1	R	24	123	453	71	137	14	8	12	73	37	35	0	.302	.356	.448
Wally Moses	OF58	L	36	90	255	32	70	18	2	2	27	27	16	3	.275	.344	.384
Eddie Pellagrini	3B42,SS26	R	29	74	231	29	47	8	1	4	19	23	35	2	.203	.281	.299
Rudy York†	1B48	R	33	48	184	16	39	7	0	6	27	22	32	0	.212	.296	.348
Roy Partee	C54	R	29	60	169	14	39	2	0	0	16	18	23	0	.231	.305	.243
Don Gutteridge	2B20,3B19	R	35	54	131	20	22	2	0	2	5	17	13	3	.168	.264	.229
Leon Culberson	OF25,3B4	R	27	47	84	10	20	1	0	0	11	12	10	1	.238	.354	.250
Merrill Combs	3B17	L	27	17	68	8	15	1	0	1	6	9	9	0	.221	.329	.279
Hal Wagner†	C21	L	31	21	65	5	15	3	0	0	6	9	5	0	.231	.324	.277
Rip Russell	3B13	R	32	26	52	8	8	1	0	1	3	8	7	0	.154	.267	.231
Matt Batts	C6	R	25	7	16	3	8	1	0	1	5	1	1	0	.500	.529	.750
Eddie McGah	C7	R	25	9	14	1	0	0	0	0	2	3	0	0	.000	.176	.000
Strick Shofner	3B4	L	27	5	13	1	2	0	1	0	0	0	3	0	.154	.154	.308
Frankie Hayes	C4	R	32	5	13	0	2	0	0	0	1	0	1	0	.154	.154	.154
Billy Goodman	OF1	L	21	12	11	1	2	0	0	0	1	1	2	0	.182	.250	.182
Tom McBride†	OF1	R	32	2	5	0	1	0	0	0	0	0	0	0	.200	.200	.200
Tex Aulds	C3	R	26	3	4	0	1	0	0	0	0	0	1	0	.250	.250	.250

Pitcher	T	Age	G	GS	CG	ShO	IP	H	HR	BB	SO	W-L	Sv	ERA
Joe Dobson	R	30	33	31	15	1	228.2	203	15	73	110	18-8	1	2.95
Boo Ferriss	R	25	33	28	14	1	218.1	241	14	92	64	12-11	0	4.04
Tex Hughson	R	31	29	26	13	3	189.1	173	17	71	119	12-11	0	3.33
Denny Galehouse†	R	35	21	21	11	3	149.0	150	7	34	38	11-7	0	3.32
Tommy Fine	R	32	9	7	1	0	36.0	41	0	19	10	1-2	0	5.50
Earl Johnson	L	28	45	17	6	3	142.1	129	5	62	65	12-11	8	2.97
Harry Dorish	R	25	41	9	2	0	136.0	149	6	54	50	7-8	2	4.70
Johnny Murphy	R	38	32	0	0	0	54.2	41	1	28	9	0-0	3	2.80
Bob Klinger	R	39	28	0	0	0	42.0	42	5	24	12	1-1	5	3.86
Bill Zuber	R	34	20	1	0	0	50.2	60	4	31	23	1-0	0	5.33
Mickey Harris	L	30	15	6	1	0	51.2	42	3	23	35	5-4	0	2.44
Mel Parnell	L	25	15	5	1	0	50.2	60	1	27	23	2-3	0	6.39
Eddie Smith†	L	33	8	3	0	0	17.0	18	3	18	15	1-3	0	7.41
Cot Deal	R	24	5	2	0	0	12.2	20	0	7	6	0-1	0	9.24
Chuck Stobbs	L	17	4	1	0	0	9.0	10	0	10	5	0-1	0	6.00
Al Widmar	R	22	2	0	0	0	1.1	1	1	2	1	0-0	0	13.50
Bill Butland	L	29	1	0	0	0	2.0	3	0	0	1	0-0	0	4.50

1947 Cleveland Indians 4th AL 80-74 .519 17.0 GB

Lou Boudreau

Player	Gm by Position	B	Age	G	AB	R	H	2B	3B	HR	RBI	BB	SO	SB	Avg	OBP	Slg
Jim Hegan	C133	R	26	135	378	38	94	14	5	4	42	41	49	3	.249	.324	.344
Eddie Robinson	1B87	L	26	95	318	52	78	10	1	14	52	30	18	1	.245	.314	.415
Joe Gordon	2B155	R	32	155	562	89	153	27	6	29	93	62	49	7	.272	.346	.496
Ken Keltner	3B150	R	30	151	541	49	139	29	3	11	76	59	45	5	.257	.331	.383
Lou Boudreau	SS148	R	29	150	538	79	165	45	3	4	67	67	10	1	.307	.388	.424
Catfish Metkovich	OF119,1B1	L	26	126	473	68	120	22	7	5	40	32	51	5	.254	.302	.362
Dale Mitchell	OF115	L	25	123	493	69	156	16	10	1	34	23	14	2	.316	.347	.396
Hank Edwards	OF100	L	28	108	393	54	102	12	3	15	59	31	55	1	.260	.315	.420
Hal Peck	OF97	L	30	114	392	58	115	18	2	8	44	27	31	3	.293	.342	.411
Les Fleming	1B77	L	31	103	281	39	68	14	2	4	43	53	42	0	.242	.362	.349
Pat Seerey	OF68	R	24	82	216	24	37	4	1	11	29	34	66	0	.171	.284	.352
Al Lopez	C57	R	38	61	126	9	33	1	0	0	14	9	13	1	.262	.311	.270
Eddie Bockman	3B12,2B4,SS1*	R	26	46	66	8	17	2	2	1	14	5	17	0	.258	.310	.394
Bob Lemon	P37,OF2	L	26	47	56	11	18	4	3	2	5	6	9	0	.321	.387	.607
Jack Conway	SS24,2B5,3B1	R	27	34	50	3	9	2	0	0	5	3	8	0	.180	.226	.220
Larry Doby	2B4,1B1,SS1	L	23	29	32	3	5	1	0	0	2	1	11	0	.156	.182	.188
Hank Ruszkowski	C16	R	21	23	27	5	7	2	0	3	4	2	6	0	.259	.310	.667
Joe Frazier	OF5	L	24	9	14	1	1	1	0	0	0	1	1	0	.071	.133	.143
Al Rosen	3B2,OF1	R	23	7	9	1	1	0	0	0	0	0	3	0	.111	.111	.111
Ted Sepkowski†	OF1	L	23	10	8	0	1	1	0	0	0	1	1	0	.125	.222	.250
Felix Mackiewicz†	OF2	R	29	2	5	0	0	0	0	0	0	0	2	0	.000	.000	.000
Heinz Becker		S	31	2	2	0	0	0	0	0	0	0	1	0	.000	.000	.000
Jimmy Wasdell		L	33	1	1	0	0	0	0	0	0	0	0	0	.000	.000	.000

E. Bockman, 1 G at OF

Pitcher	T	Age	G	GS	CG	ShO	IP	H	HR	BB	SO	W-L	Sv	ERA
Bob Feller	R	28	42	37	20	5	299.0	230	17	127	196	20-11	3	2.68
Don Black	R	30	30	28	8	3	190.2	177	17	85	72	10-12	0	3.92
Red Embree	R	29	27	21	6	0	162.2	137	13	67	56	8-10	0	3.15
Al Gettel	R	29	31	21	9	2	149.0	122	12	62	64	11-10	0	3.20
Mel Harder	R	37	15	15	4	1	80.0	91	3	27	17	6-4	0	4.50
Bob Kuzava	L	24	4	4	1	1	21.2	22	1	9	9	1-1	0	4.15
Ed Klieman	R	29	58	0	0	0	92.0	78	5	39	21	5-4	17	3.03
Bob Lemon	R	26	37	15	6	1	167.1	150	7	97	65	11-5	3	3.44
Bryan Stephens	R	26	31	5	1	0	92.0	79	6	39	34	5-10	1	4.01
Steve Gromek	R	27	29	7	0	0	84.1	77	8	36	39	3-5	4	3.74
Les Willis	L	39	22	2	0	0	44.0	58	3	24	10	0-2	1	3.48
Roger Wolff†	R	36	7	2	0	0	16.0	15	1	10	5	0-0	0	3.94
Ernest Groth	R	25	2	0	0	0	1.1	0	0	1	1	0-0	0	0.00
Cal Dorsett	R	34	2	0	0	0	1.1	3	1	3	1	0-0	0	27.00
Lymie Linde	R	26	1	0	0	0	0.2	3	0	1	0	0-0	0	27.00
Gene Bearden	L	26	1	0	0	0	0.1	2	0	1	0	0-0	0	81.00

Seasons: Team Rosters 703

1947 Philadelphia Athletics 5th AL 78-76 .506 19.0 GB

Connie Mack

Player	Gm by Position	B	Age	G	AB	R	H	2B	3B	HR	RBI	BB	SO	SB	Avg	OBP	Slg
Buddy Rosar	C102	R	32	102	359	40	93	20	2	1	33	40	13	1	.259	.335	.334
Ferris Fain	1B132	L	26	136	461	70	134	28	6	7	71	95	34	4	.291	.414	.423
Pete Suder	2B140,SS3,3B2	R	31	145	528	45	127	28	4	5	60	35	44	0	.241	.290	.337
Hank Majeski	3B134,SS4,2B1	R	30	141	479	54	134	26	5	8	72	53	31	1	.280	.358	.405
Eddie Joost	SS151	R	31	151	540	76	111	22	3	13	64	114	110	6	.206	.348	.330
Sam Chapman	OF146	R	31	149	551	84	139	18	5	14	83	65	70	3	.252	.331	.379
Barney McCosky	OF136	L	30	137	546	77	179	22	7	1	52	57	29	1	.328	.395	.399
Elmer Valo	OF104	L	26	112	370	60	111	12	6	5	36	64	21	11	.300	.406	.405
George Binks	OF75,1B13	L	30	104	333	33	86	19	4	2	34	23	36	8	.258	.308	.357
Mike Guerra	C62	R	34	72	209	20	45	2	2	0	18	10	15	1	.215	.251	.244
Gene Handley	2B17,3B10,SS1	R	32	36	90	10	23	2	1	0	8	10	2	1	.256	.330	.300
Dick Adams	1B24,OF3	R	27	37	89	9	18	2	3	2	11	2	18	0	.202	.220	.360
Mickey Rutner	3B11	R	27	12	48	4	12	1	0	1	4	3	2	0	.250	.294	.333
A. Knickerbocker	OF14	R	28	21	48	8	12	3	2	0	2	3	4	0	.250	.294	.396
Chet Laabs	OF7	R	35	15	32	5	7	1	0	1	5	4	4	0	.219	.306	.344
Don Richmond	3B4,2B1	L	27	19	21	2	4	1	1	0	4	3	3	0	.190	.292	.333
Pat Cooper	1B1	R	29	13	16	0	4	2	0	0	3	0	5	0	.250	.250	.375
Herman Franks	C4	L	33	8	15	2	3	0	1	0	1	4	4	0	.200	.368	.333
Ray Poole		L	27	13	13	1	3	0	0	0	1	1	4	0	.231	.286	.231
Nellie Fox	2B1	L	19	7	3	2	0	0	0	0	0	1	0	0	.000	.250	.000
Tom Kirk		L	19	1	1	0	0	0	0	0	0	0	0	0	.000	.000	.000

Pitcher	T	Age	G	GS	CG	ShO	IP	H	HR	BB	SO	W-L	Sv	ERA
Phil Marchildon	R	33	35	35	21	2	276.2	228	15	141	128	19-9	0	3.22
Dick Fowler	R	26	36	31	16	3	227.1	210	12	85	75	12-11	0	2.81
Joe Coleman	R	24	32	21	9	2	160.1	171	17	62	65	6-12	1	4.32
Jesse Flores	R	32	28	20	4	0	151.1	139	10	59	41	4-13	0	3.39
Bill McCahan	R	26	29	19	10	1	165.1	160	7	62	47	10-5	0	3.32
Carl Scheib	R	20	21	12	6	2	116.0	121	12	55	26	4-6	0	5.04
Bill Dietrich	R	37	11	9	2	1	60.2	48	0	40	18	5-2	0	3.12
Lou Brissie	L	23	1	1	0	0	7.0	9	1	5	4	0-1	0	6.43
Bob Savage	R	25	44	8	2	1	146.0	135	8	55	56	8-10	2	3.76
Russ Christopher	R	29	44	0	0	0	80.2	70	4	33	33	10-7	12	2.90

1947 Chicago White Sox 6th AL 70-84 .455 27.0 GB

Ted Lyons

Player	Gm by Position	B	Age	G	AB	R	H	2B	3B	HR	RBI	BB	SO	SB	Avg	OBP	Slg
Mike Tresh	C89	R	33	90	274	19	66	6	2	0	20	26	26	2	.241	.309	.277
Rudy York†	1B102	R	33	102	400	40	97	18	4	15	64	36	55	1	.243	.305	.420
Don Kolloway	2B99,1B11,3B8	R	28	124	485	49	135	25	4	2	35	17	34	11	.278	.303	.359
Floyd Baker	3B101,2B1,SS1	L	30	105	371	61	98	12	3	0	22	66	28	9	.264	.375	.313
Luke Appling	SS129,3B2	R	40	139	503	67	154	29	0	8	49	64	28	8	.306	.386	.412
Dave Philley	OF133,3B4	S	27	143	551	55	142	25	11	2	45	35	39	21	.258	.303	.354
Bob Kennedy	OF106,3B1	R	26	115	428	47	112	19	3	6	48	18	38	3	.262	.291	.362
Taffy Wright	OF100	L	35	124	401	48	130	13	0	4	54	48	17	8	.324	.398	.387
Cass Michaels	2B60,3B44,SS2	R	21	110	355	31	97	15	4	3	34	39	28	10	.273	.350	.363
Thurman Tucker	OF65	L	29	89	254	28	60	9	4	1	17	38	25	10	.236	.336	.315
George Dickey	C80	S	31	83	211	15	47	6	0	1	27	34	25	4	.223	.331	.265
Jack Wallaesa	SS27,OF22,3B1	S	27	81	205	25	40	9	1	7	32	23	51	2	.195	.279	.351
Ralph Hodgin	OF41	L	31	59	180	26	53	10	3	1	24	13	4	1	.294	.352	.400
Jake Jones†	1B43	R	26	45	171	15	41	7	1	3	20	13	25	1	.240	.297	.345
Joe Stephenson	C13	R	26	16	35	3	5	0	0	0	3	1	7	0	.143	.211	.143
Loyd Christopher	OF7	R	27	7	23	1	5	0	1	0	0	2	4	0	.217	.280	.304
Joe Kuhel		L	41	3	3	0	0	0	0	0	0	0	3	0	.000	.000	.000

Pitcher	T	Age	G	GS	CG	ShO	IP	H	HR	BB	SO	W-L	Sv	ERA
Ed Lopat	L	29	31	31	22	3	252.2	241	17	73	109	16-13	0	2.81
Frank Papish	L	29	38	26	6	1	199.0	185	6	98	79	12-12	3	3.26
Joe Haynes	R	29	29	22	7	2	182.0	174	5	61	50	14-6	0	2.42
Orval Grove	R	27	25	19	6	1	135.2	158	10	70	33	6-8	0	4.44
Bob Gillespie	R	28	25	17	1	0	118.0	133	4	53	36	5-8	0	4.73
Thornton Lee	L	40	21	11	2	1	86.2	86	5	56	57	3-7	1	4.47
Red Ruffing	R	43	9	9	1	0	53.0	63	7	16	11	3-5	0	6.11
Johnny Rigney	R	32	11	7	2	0	50.2	42	3	15	19	2-3	0	1.95
Earl Caldwell	R	42	40	0	0	0	54.1	53	4	30	22	1-4	8	3.64
Earl Harrist	R	28	33	4	0	0	93.2	85	3	49	55	3-8	5	3.56
Gordon Maltzberger	R	34	33	0	0	0	63.2	61	4	25	22	1-4	5	3.39
Pete Gebrian	R	23	27	4	0	0	66.1	61	7	33	17	2-3	5	4.48
Eddie Smith†	L	33	15	5	0	0	33.1	40	1	24	12	1-3	0	7.29
Hi Bithorn	R	31	2	0	0	0	2.0	2	0	0	0	1-0	0	0.00

1947 Washington Senators 7th AL 64-90 .416 33.0 GB

Ossie Bluege

Player	Gm by Position	B	Age	G	AB	R	H	2B	3B	HR	RBI	BB	SO	SB	Avg	OBP	Slg
Al Evans	C94	R	30	99	319	17	77	8	3	2	23	28	25	2	.241	.303	.304
Mickey Vernon	1B154	L	29	154	600	77	159	29	12	7	85	49	42	12	.265	.320	.388
Jerry Priddy	2B146	R	27	147	505	42	108	20	3	3	49	62	79	7	.214	.301	.283
Eddie Yost	3B114	R	20	115	428	52	102	17	3	0	14	45	57	3	.238	.314	.292
Mark Christman	SS106,2B1	R	33	110	374	27	83	15	2	1	33	33	16	4	.222	.287	.281
Stan Spence	OF142	L	32	147	506	62	141	22	6	16	73	81	41	2	.279	.378	.441
Buddy Lewis	OF130	L	30	140	506	67	132	15	4	6	48	51	27	6	.261	.330	.342
Joe Grace	OF67	L	33	78	234	25	58	9	4	3	17	35	15	1	.248	.348	.359
Sherry Robertson	OF55,3B10,2B4	L	28	95	266	25	62	9	3	1	23	32	52	4	.233	.318	.301
Cecil Travis	3B39,SS15	L	33	74	204	10	44	4	1	1	10	16	19	1	.216	.273	.260
Tom McBride†	OF51,3B1	R	32	56	166	19	45	4	2	0	15	15	9	3	.271	.331	.319
John Sullivan	SS40,2B1	R	26	49	133	13	34	0	1	0	5	22	14	0	.256	.361	.271
Frank Mancuso	C35	R	29	43	131	5	30	5	1	0	13	5	11	0	.229	.257	.282
Rick Ferrell	C37	R	41	37	99	10	30	11	0	0	12	14	7	0	.303	.389	.414
George Case	OF21	R	31	36	80	11	12	1	0	0	2	8	8	5	.150	.227	.163
Gil Coan	OF11	L	25	11	42	5	21	3	2	0	3	5	6	2	.500	.553	.667
Ed Lyons	2B7	R	24	7	26	2	4	0	0	0	0	2	2	0	.154	.214	.154
Junior Wooten	OF6	R	23	6	24	0	2	0	0	0	1	0	4	1	.083	.083	.083
George Myatt	2B1	L	33	12	7	1	0	0	0	0	0	4	4	0	.000	.364	.000
Felix Mackiewicz†	OF3	R	29	3	6	1	1	1	0	0	0	0	1	0	.167	.167	.333
Cal Ermer	2B1	R	23	1	3	0	0	0	0	0	0	0	0	0	.000	.000	.000

Pitcher	T	Age	G	GS	CG	ShO	IP	H	HR	BB	SO	W-L	Sv	ERA
Walt Masterson	R	27	35	31	14	4	253.0	215	11	97	135	12-16	1	3.13
Early Wynn	R	27	33	31	22	2	247.0	251	13	90	73	17-15	0	3.64
Mickey Haefner	L	34	31	28	14	4	193.0	195	8	85	77	10-14	1	3.64
Ray Scarborough	R	29	33	18	8	2	161.0	165	6	67	63	6-13	0	3.41
Sid Hudson	R	32	20	17	5	1	106.0	113	8	58	37	6-9	0	5.60
Bobo Newsom†	R	39	14	13	1	0	83.2	99	2	37	40	4-6	0	4.09
Milo Candini	R	29	38	2	0	0	87.0	96	5	35	31	3-4	1	5.17
Tom Ferrick	R	32	31	0	0	0	60.0	57	1	20	23	1-7	9	3.15
Marino Pieretti	R	26	23	10	2	1	83.0	97	3	47	32	2-4	0	4.23
Scott Cary	L	24	23	3	1	0	54.2	73	5	20	25	3-1	0	5.93
Lou Knerr	R	25	6	0	0	0	9.0	17	1	8	5	0-0	0	11.00
Hal Toenes	R	29	3	1	0	0	6.2	11	0	2	5	0-1	0	6.75
Lum Harris	R	32	3	0	0	0	6.1	7	0	7	2	0-0	0	2.84
Bill Kennedy	L	28	2	0	0	0	6.2	10	1	5	1	0-0	0	8.10
Buzz Dozier	R	19	2	0	0	0	4.2	2	0	1	2	0-0	0	0.00

1947 St. Louis Browns 8th AL 59-95 .383 38.0 GB

Muddy Ruel

Player	Gm by Position	B	Age	G	AB	R	H	2B	3B	HR	RBI	BB	SO	SB	Avg	OBP	Slg
Les Moss	C96	R	22	96	274	17	43	5	2	6	27	35	48	0	.157	.255	.255
Wally Judnich	1B129,OF15	L	30	144	500	58	129	24	3	18	64	60	62	2	.258	.338	.426
Johnny Berardino	2B86	R	30	90	306	29	80	22	1	1	20	44	26	6	.261	.358	.350
Bob Dillinger	3B137	R	28	137	571	70	168	23	6	3	37	56	38	34	.294	.361	.371
Vern Stephens	SS149	R	26	150	562	74	157	18	4	15	83	70	61	8	.279	.359	.406
Jeff Heath	OF140	L	32	141	491	81	123	20	7	27	85	88	87	2	.251	.366	.485
Paul Lehner	OF127	L	26	135	483	59	120	25	9	7	48	28	29	5	.248	.294	.381
Al Zarilla	OF110	L	28	127	380	34	85	15	6	3	38	40	45	3	.224	.303	.318
Ray Coleman	OF93	L	25	110	343	34	89	9	7	2	30	26	32	2	.259	.314	.344
Billy Hitchcock	2B46,3B17,SS7*	R	30	80	275	25	61	2	2	1	28	21	34	3	.222	.277	.255
Jake Early	C85	L	32	87	214	25	48	9	3	3	19	54	34	0	.224	.381	.336
Jerry Witte	1B27	R	31	34	99	4	14	2	1	2	12	11	22	0	.141	.227	.242
Hank Thompson	2B19	L	21	27	78	10	20	1	1	0	5	10	7	2	.256	.341	.295
Willard Brown	OF18	R	32	21	67	4	12	3	0	1	6	0	7	2	.179	.179	.269
Rusty Peters	2B13,SS2	R	32	39	47	10	16	4	0	0	2	6	8	0	.340	.415	.426
Joe Schultz		L	28	43	38	3	7	0	0	1	1	4	5	0	.184	.262	.263
Perry Currin	SS1	L	18	3	2	0	0	0	0	0	0	1	0	0	.000	.333	.000
Glenn McQuillen		R	32	1	1	0	0	0	0	0	0	0	0	0	.000	.000	.000

B. Hitchcock, 5 G at 1B

Pitcher	T	Age	G	GS	CG	ShO	IP	H	HR	BB	SO	W-L	Sv	ERA
Jack Kramer	R	29	33	28	9	1	199.1	206	16	89	77	11-16	1	4.97
Ellis Kinder	R	32	34	26	10	2	194.1	201	11	82	110	8-15	1	4.49
Fred Sanford	R	27	34	23	9	0	186.1	186	17	76	62	7-16	4	3.72
Bob Muncrief	R	31	31	23	7	0	176.1	210	14	51	74	8-14	0	4.90
Sam Zoldak	L	28	35	19	6	1	171.0	162	7	76	36	9-10	1	3.47
Cliff Fannin	R	23	26	18	6	2	145.2	134	10	77	77	6-8	1	3.58
Dizzy Dean	R	37	1	1	0	0	4.0	3	0	1	0	0-0	0	0.00
Nels Potter	R	35	32	10	3	0	122.2	130	13	44	65	4-10	2	4.04
Glen Moulder	R	29	32	2	0	0	73.0	78	4	43	23	4-2	2	3.82
Walter Brown	R	32	19	0	0	0	46.0	50	3	28	10	1-0	0	4.89
Denny Galehouse†	R	35	9	4	0	0	32.1	42	3	16	11	1-3	1	6.12
Bud Swartz	L	18	5	0	0	0	5.1	9	1	7	1	0-0	0	6.75
Hooks Iott†	L	27	4	0	0	0	8.1	15	4	14	6	0-1	0	16.20

»1947 Brooklyn Dodgers 1st NL 94-60 .610 —

Clyde Sukeforth (2-0)/Burt Shotton (92-60)

Player	Gm by Position	B	Age	G	AB	R	H	2B	3B	HR	RBI	BB	SO	SB	Avg	OBP	Slg
Bruce Edwards	C128	R	23	130	471	53	139	15	8	9	80	49	55	2	.295	.364	.418
Jackie Robinson	1B151	R	28	151	590	125	175	31	5	12	48	74	36	29	.297	.383	.427
Eddie Stanky	2B146	R	30	146	559	97	141	24	5	3	53	103	39	3	.252	.373	.329
Spider Jorgensen	3B128	L	27	129	441	57	121	29	8	5	67	58	45	4	.274	.360	.410
Pee Wee Reese	SS142	R	28	142	476	81	135	24	4	12	73	104	67	7	.284	.414	.426
Dixie Walker	OF147	L	36	148	529	77	162	31	3	9	94	97	26	6	.306	.415	.427
Carl Furillo	OF121	R	25	124	437	61	129	24	7	8	88	34	24	7	.295	.347	.437
Pete Reiser	OF108	L	28	110	388	68	120	23	2	5	46	68	41	14	.309	.415	.418
Gene Hermanski	OF66	L	27	79	189	36	52	7	1	7	39	28	7	5	.275	.377	.434
Arky Vaughan	OF22,3B10	L	35	64	126	24	41	5	2	2	25	27	11	4	.325	.444	.444
Eddie Miksis	2B13,OF11,3B5*	R	20	45	86	18	23	1	0	4	10	9	8	0	.267	.337	.419
Duke Snider	OF25	L	20	40	83	6	20	3	1	0	5	3	24	2	.241	.276	.301
Stan Rojek	SS17,3B9,2B7	R	28	32	80	7	21	0	1	0	7	7	3	1	.263	.322	.288
Gil Hodges	C24	R	23	28	77	9	12	3	1	1	7	14	19	0	.156	.286	.260
Cookie Lavagetto	3B18,1B3	R	34	41	69	6	18	1	0	3	11	12	5	0	.261	.370	.406
Al Gionfriddo†	OF17	L	25	37	62	10	11	2	1	0	6	16	11	2	.177	.346	.242
Bobby Bragan	C21	R	29	25	36	3	7	2	0	0	3	7	3	1	.194	.326	.250
Tommy Brown	3B6,OF3,SS1	R	19	15	34	3	8	1	0	0	2	1	6	0	.235	.257	.265
Don Lund	OF5	R	24	11	20	5	6	2	0	2	5	3	7	0	.300	.391	.700
Ed Stevens	1B4	L	22	5	13	0	2	1	0	0	0	1	5	0	.154	.214	.231
Dick Whitman	OF3	L	26	4	10	1	4	0	0	0	2	1	0	0	.400	.455	.400
Marv Rackley	OF2	L	25	18	9	2	2	0	0	0	2	1	0	0	.222	.300	.222
Tommy Tatum†	OF3	R	27	4	6	0	0	0	0	0	0	0	1	0	.000	.000	.000
Howie Schultz†	1B1	R	24	2	1	0	0	0	0	0	0	0	0	0	.000	.000	.000

E. Miksis, 2 G at SS

Pitcher	T	Age	G	GS	CG	ShO	IP	H	HR	BB	SO	W-L	Sv	ERA
Ralph Branca	R	21	43	36	15	5	280.0	251	22	98	148	21-12	1	2.67
Joe Hatten	L	30	42	32	11	3	225.1	211	9	105	76	17-8	0	3.63
Vic Lombardi	L	24	33	20	7	3	174.2	156	12	65	72	12-11	3	2.99
Harry Taylor	R	28	33	20	10	2	162.0	130	10	83	58	10-5	1	3.11
Kirby Higbe†	R	32	4	3	0	0	15.2	18	0	12	10	2-0	0	5.17
Hugh Casey	R	33	46	0	0	0	76.2	75	7	29	40	10-4	18	3.99
Hank Behrman†	R	26	40	6	0	0	92.0	97	10	48	33	5-3	8	5.48
Hal Gregg	R	25	37	16	2	1	104.1	115	6	55	59	4-5	1	5.87
Clyde King	R	22	29	9	2	0	87.2	85	11	29	31	6-5	0	2.77
Rex Barney	R	22	28	9	0	0	77.2	66	4	59	36	5-2	0	4.98
Ed Chandler	R	25	15	1	0	0	29.2	31	7	12	8	0-1	1	6.37
Phil Haugstad	R	23	6	1	0	0	12.2	14	1	4	4	1-0	0	2.84
Dan Bankhead	R	27	4	0	0	0	10.0	15	1	8	6	0-0	1	7.20
George Dockins	L	30	4	0	0	0	5.1	10	2	2	1	0-0	0	11.81
Rube Melton	R	30	4	1	0	0	4.2	7	1	7	1	0-1	0	13.50
Jack Banta	R	22	3	1	0	0	7.2	7	1	4	3	0-1	0	7.04
Erv Palica	R	19	3	0	0	0	3.0	2	0	2	1	0-1	0	3.00
Johnny Van Cuyk	L	25	2	0	0	0	3.1	5	0	1	2	0-0	0	5.40
Willie Ramsdell	R	31	2	0	0	0	2.2	4	0	3	3	1-1	0	6.75

1947 St. Louis Cardinals 2nd NL 89-65 .578 5.0 GB

Eddie Dyer

Player	Gm by Position	B	Age	G	AB	R	H	2B	3B	HR	RBI	BB	SO	SB	Avg	OBP	Slg
Del Rice	C94	R	24	97	261	28	57	7	3	12	44	36	40	1	.218	.315	.406
Stan Musial	1B149	L	26	149	587	113	183	30	13	19	95	80	24	4	.312	.398	.504
Red Schoendienst	2B142,3B5,OF1	S	24	151	659	91	167	25	9	3	48	48	27	6	.253	.304	.332
Whitey Kurowski	3B141	R	29	146	513	108	159	27	6	27	104	87	56	4	.310	.420	.544
Marty Marion	SS141	R	29	149	540	57	147	19	6	4	74	49	58	3	.272	.334	.352
Enos Slaughter	OF142	L	31	147	551	100	162	31	13	10	86	59	27	4	.294	.366	.452
Terry Moore	OF120	R	35	127	460	61	130	17	1	7	45	38	39	1	.283	.339	.370
Ron Northey†	OF94,3B2	L	27	110	311	52	91	19	3	15	63	48	29	0	.293	.391	.518
Erv Dusak	OF89,3B7	R	26	111	328	56	93	7	3	6	28	50	34	1	.284	.378	.378
Joe Garagiola	C74	L	21	77	183	20	47	10	2	5	25	40	14	0	.257	.398	.415
Joe Medwick	OF43	R	35	75	150	19	46	12	0	4	28	16	12	0	.307	.373	.467
Del Wilber	C34	R	28	51	99	7	23	8	1	0	12	5	13	0	.232	.269	.333
Chuck Diering	OF75	R	24	105	74	22	16	3	1	2	11	19	22	3	.216	.383	.365
Dick Sisler	1B10,OF5	L	26	46	74	4	15	2	1	0	9	3	8	0	.203	.234	.257
Nippy Jones	2B13,OF2	R	22	23	73	6	18	4	0	1	5	2	10	0	.247	.267	.342
Jeff Cross	3B15,SS14,2B2	R	28	51	49	4	5	1	0	0	3	10	6	0	.102	.254	.122
Harry Walker†	OF10	L	30	10	25	2	5	1	0	0	0	4	2	0	.200	.310	.240
Bernie Creger	SS13	R	20	15	16	3	3	1	0	0	0	1	3	1	.188	.235	.250

Pitcher	T	Age	G	GS	CG	ShO	IP	H	HR	BB	SO	W-L	Sv	ERA
George Munger	R	28	40	31	13	6	224.1	218	12	76	123	16-5	3	3.37
Harry Brecheen	L	32	29	28	18	1	223.1	220	20	66	89	16-11	1	3.30
Murry Dickson	R	30	47	25	11	4	231.2	211	16	88	111	13-16	3	3.07
Howie Pollet	L	26	37	24	9	0	176.1	195	11	87	73	9-11	2	4.34
Jim Hearn	R	26	37	21	4	1	162.0	151	8	63	57	12-7	1	3.22
Ken Johnson	L	24	2	1	1	0	10.0	2	0	5	8	1-0	0	0.00
Al Brazle	L	33	44	19	7	0	168.0	186	7	48	85	14-8	4	2.84
Ted Wilks	R	31	37	0	0	0	50.1	57	10	11	28	4-0	5	5.01
Ken Burkhart	R	30	34	6	1	0	95.0	108	14	23	44	3-6	1	5.21
Gerry Staley	R	26	18	1	1	0	29.1	33	2	8	14	1-0	0	2.76
Johnny Grodzicki	R	30	16	0	0	0	23.1	21	5	19	8	0-1	0	5.40
Freddy Schmidt†	R	31	2	0	0	0	4.0	5	1	1	2	0-0	0	2.25

1947 Boston Braves 3rd NL 86-68 .558 8.0 GB

Billy Southworth

Player	Gm by Position	B	Age	G	AB	R	H	2B	3B	HR	RBI	BB	SO	SB	Avg	OBP	Slg
Phil Masi	C123	R	31	126	411	54	125	22	4	9	50	47	27	7	.304	.377	.443
Earl Torgeson	1B117	L	23	128	399	73	112	20	6	16	78	82	59	11	.281	.403	.481
Connie Ryan	2B150,SS1	R	27	150	544	60	144	33	5	5	69	71	60	5	.265	.351	.371
Bob Elliott	3B148	R	30	150	555	93	176	35	5	22	113	87	60	3	.317	.410	.517
Dick Culler	SS77	R	32	77	214	20	53	5	1	0	19	19	15	1	.248	.309	.280
Tommy Holmes	OF147	L	30	150	618	90	191	33	3	9	53	44	16	3	.309	.360	.416
Johnny Hopp	OF125	L	30	134	430	74	124	20	2	2	32	58	30	13	.288	.376	.358
Bama Rowell	OF100,2B7,3B4	L	31	113	384	48	106	23	2	5	40	18	14	7	.276	.310	.385
Mike McCormick	OF79	R	30	92	284	42	81	13	7	3	36	20	21	1	.285	.332	.412
Danny Litwhiler	OF66	R	30	91	226	38	59	5	2	7	31	25	43	1	.261	.337	.394
Frank McCormick†	1B46	R	36	81	212	24	75	18	2	2	43	11	8	2	.354	.386	.486
Nanny Fernandez	SS62,OF8,3B6	R	28	83	209	16	43	4	0	2	21	22	20	2	.206	.281	.254
Sibby Sisti	SS51,2B1	R	26	56	153	22	43	8	0	2	15	20	17	2	.281	.371	.373
Hank Camelli	C51	R	32	52	150	10	29	8	1	1	11	18	18	0	.193	.280	.280
Tommy Neill	OF2	L	27	7	10	1	2	0	1	0	0	1	2	0	.200	.333	.400
Danny Murtaugh	2B2,3B2	R	29	3	8	0	1	0	0	0	0	1	2	0	.125	.222	.125
Bob Brady		L	24	1	1	0	0	0	0	0	0	0	0	0	.000	.000	.000

Pitcher	T	Age	G	GS	CG	ShO	IP	H	HR	BB	SO	W-L	Sv	ERA
Warren Spahn	L	26	40	35	22	7	289.2	245	15	84	123	21-10	3	2.33
Johnny Sain	R	29	38	35	22	3	266.0	265	19	79	132	21-12	1	3.52
Red Barrett	R	32	36	30	12	3	210.2	200	16	53	53	11-12	1	3.55
Bill Voiselle†	R	28	22	20	7	0	131.1	146	10	51	59	8-7	0	4.32
Mort Cooper†	R	34	10	7	2	0	46.2	48	1	13	15	2-5	0	4.05
Ray Martin	R	22	1	1	1	0	9.0	7	0	4	2	1-0	0	1.00
Ernie White	L	30	1	1	0	0	4.0	1	0	1	1	0-0	0	0.00
Si Johnson	R	40	36	10	3	0	112.2	124	7	34	27	6-8	2	4.23
Walt Lanfranconi	R	30	36	4	1	0	64.0	65	2	27	18	4-4	1	2.95
Andy Karl	R	33	27	0	0	0	35.0	41	2	13	5	2-3	3	3.86
Clyde Shoun†	L	35	26	3	1	1	73.2	73	6	21	23	5-3	1	4.40
Ed Wright	R	28	23	6	1	0	64.2	80	9	35	14	3-3	0	6.40
Glenn Elliott	L	27	11	0	0	0	19.0	18	4	11	8	0-1	1	4.74
Johnny Beazley	R	29	9	2	2	0	28.2	30	1	19	12	2-0	0	4.40
Johnny Lanning	R	36	3	0	0	0	3.2	4	0	6	0	0-0	0	9.82
Dick Mulligan	L	29	1	0	0	0	2.0	4	0	1	1	0-0	0	9.00
Max Macon	L	31	1	0	0	0	2.0	1	0	1	1	0-0	0	0.00

1947 New York Giants 4th NL 81-73 .526 13.0 GB

Mel Ott

Player	Gm by Position	B	Age	G	AB	R	H	2B	3B	HR	RBI	BB	SO	SB	Avg	OBP	Slg
Walker Cooper	C132	R	32	140	515	79	157	24	8	35	122	24	43	2	.305	.339	.586
Johnny Mize	1B154	L	34	154	586	137	177	26	2	51	138	74	42	2	.302	.384	.614
Bill Rigney	2B72,3B41,SS24	R	29	130	531	84	142	24	3	17	59	51	54	7	.267	.337	.420
Jack Lohrke	3B111	R	23	112	329	44	79	12	4	11	35	46	29	3	.240	.337	.401
Buddy Kerr	SS138	R	24	138	547	73	157	23	5	7	49	36	49	2	.287	.331	.386
Willard Marshall	OF155	L	26	155	587	102	171	19	6	36	107	67	30	3	.291	.366	.528
Bobby Thomson	OF127,2B9	R	23	138	545	105	154	26	5	29	85	40	78	1	.283	.336	.508
Sid Gordon	OF124,3B2	R	29	130	437	57	119	19	8	13	57	50	21	2	.272	.347	.442
Gary Gearhart	OF44	R	23	73	179	26	44	9	0	6	17	17	30	1	.246	.315	.397
Mickey Witek	2B40,3B3	R	31	51	160	22	35	4	1	3	17	15	12	1	.219	.286	.313
Buddy Blattner	2B34,3B11	R	27	55	153	28	40	9	2	0	13	21	19	4	.261	.351	.346
Ernie Lombardi	C24	R	39	48	110	8	31	5	0	4	21	7	9	0	.282	.325	.436
Joe Lafata	OF19,1B2	L	25	62	95	13	21	1	0	2	18	15	18	1	.221	.333	.295
Clint Hartung	P23,OF7	R	24	34	94	13	29	4	3	4	13	3	21	0	.309	.330	.543
Rocky Rhawn	2B8,3B5	R	28	13	45	7	14	3	0	1	3	8	1	0	.311	.415	.444
Babe Young†		L	31	14	14	0	1	1	0	0	0	0	1	0	.071	.071	.143
Fuzz White	OF5	L	29	7	13	3	3	0	0	0	0	0	0	0	.231	.231	.231
Wes Westrum	C2	R	24	6	12	1	5	1	0	0	2	0	2	0	.417	.417	.500
Mickey Livingston†	C1	R	32	5	6	0	1	0	0	0	0	1	2	0	.167	.286	.167
Sal Yvars	C1	R	23	1	5	0	1	0	0	0	0	0	2	0	.200	.200	.200
Bennie Warren	C3	R	35	3	5	0	1	0	0	0	0	0	1	0	.200	.200	.200
Mel Ott		L	38	4	4	0	0	0	0	0	0	0	0	0	.000	.000	.000
Whitey Lockman		L	20	2	2	0	1	0	0	0	1	0	0	0	.500	.500	.500

Pitcher	T	Age	G	GS	CG	ShO	IP	H	HR	BB	SO	W-L	Sv	ERA
Dave Koslo	L	27	39	31	10	3	217.1	223	23	82	86	15-10	0	4.39
Larry Jansen	R	26	42	30	20	1	248.0	241	23	57	104	21-5	1	3.16
Monte Kennedy	L	25	34	24	9	0	148.1	158	8	88	60	9-12	0	4.85
Clint Hartung	R	24	23	20	8	1	138.0	140	15	69	54	9-7	0	4.57
Mort Cooper†	R	34	8	8	2	0	36.2	51	7	13	12	1-5	0	7.12
Ray Poat	R	29	7	7	5	0	60.0	53	8	13	25	4-3	0	2.55
Mario Picone	R	20	2	1	0	0	7.0	10	1	2	1	0-0	0	7.71
Ken Trinkle	R	27	62	0	0	0	93.2	100	3	48	37	8-4	10	3.75
Joe Beggs†	R	36	32	0	0	0	66.0	81	6	18	23	3-3	2	4.23
Andy Hansen	R	22	27	9	1	0	82.1	78	8	38	18	1-5	0	4.37
Hooks Iott†	L	27	20	9	2	1	71.1	67	3	52	46	3-8	0	5.93
Sheldon Jones	R	25	15	6	0	0	55.2	51	2	29	24	2-2	0	3.88
Junior Thompson	R	30	15	0	0	0	35.2	36	3	27	13	4-2	0	4.29
Bill Ayers	R	27	13	4	0	0	35.1	46	6	14	22	0-3	1	8.15
Bill Voiselle†	R	28	11	5	1	0	42.2	44	4	22	20	1-4	0	4.64
Mike Budnick	R	27	7	1	0	0	12.0	16	0	10	6	0-0	0	10.50
Hub Andrews	R	24	7	0	0	0	8.2	14	1	4	2	0-0	0	6.23
Bob Carpenter†	R	29	2	0	0	0	3.0	5	0	3	0	0-0	0	12.00
Woody Abernathy	L	32	1	0	0	0	2.0	4	0	1	0	0-0	0	9.00

1947 Cincinnati Reds 5th NL 73-81 .474 21.0 GB

Johnny Neun

Player	Gm by Position	B	Age	G	AB	R	H	2B	3B	HR	RBI	BB	SO	SB	Avg	OBP	Slg
Ray Lamanno	C109	R	27	118	413	33	106	21	3	5	50	28	39	0	.257	.307	.358
Babe Young†	1B93	L	31	95	364	55	103	21	3	14	79	35	26	0	.283	.349	.473
Benny Zientara	2B100,3B13	R	27	117	418	60	108	18	1	2	24	23	23	2	.258	.297	.321
Grady Hatton	3B136	L	24	146	524	91	147	24	8	16	77	81	50	7	.281	.377	.448
Eddie Miller	SS151	R	30	151	545	69	146	38	4	19	87	49	40	5	.268	.333	.457
Frankie Baumholtz	OF150	L	28	151	643	96	182	32	9	5	45	56	53	6	.283	.341	.384
Augie Galan	OF118	S	35	124	392	60	123	18	2	6	61	94	19	0	.314	.449	.416
Bert Haas	OF69,1B53	R	33	135	482	58	138	17	7	3	67	42	27	9	.286	.346	.369
Bobby Adams	2B69	R	25	81	217	39	59	11	2	4	20	25	23	9	.272	.358	.396
Eddie Lukon	OF55	L	26	86	200	26	41	6	1	11	33	28	36	0	.205	.306	.410
Ray Mueller	C55	R	35	71	192	17	48	11	0	6	33	16	25	1	.250	.311	.401
Tommy Tatum†	OF49,2B1	R	27	69	176	19	48	5	2	1	16	16	16	7	.273	.333	.341
Clyde Vollmer	OF66	R	25	78	155	19	34	10	0	1	13	9	18	0	.219	.267	.303
Kermit Wahl	3B20,SS9,2B2	R	24	39	81	8	14	0	0	1	4	6	12	0	.173	.239	.210
Chuck Kress	1B8	L	25	11	27	4	4	0	0	0	0	6	4	0	.148	.303	.148
Bob Usher	OF8	R	22	9	22	2	4	0	0	1	1	2	2	0	.182	.250	.318
Hugh Poland†	C3	L	34	16	18	1	6	1	0	0	2	1	4	0	.333	.368	.389
Ted Kluszewski	1B2	L	22	9	10	1	1	0	0	0	1	1	2	0	.100	.182	.100
Al Lakeman†		R	28	2	2	0	0	0	0	0	0	0	1	0	.000	.000	.000
Virgil Stallcup	SS1	R	25	8	1	1	0	0	0	0	0	0	1	0	.000	.000	.000

Pitcher	T	Age	G	GS	CG	ShO	IP	H	HR	BB	SO	W-L	Sv	ERA
Ewell Blackwell	R	24	33	33	23	6	273.0	227	10	95	193	22-8	0	2.47
J. Vander Meer	L	32	30	29	9	3	186.0	186	11	87	79	9-14	0	4.40
Bucky Walters	R	38	20	20	5	2	122.0	137	15	49	43	8-8	0	5.75
Ken Raffensberger†	L	29	19	15	7	0	106.2	132	11	29	38	6-5	1	4.13
Harry Gumbert	R	37	46	0	0	0	90.1	88	3	47	43	10-10	10	3.89
Buddy Lively	R	22	38	17	3	1	123.0	126	16	63	52	4-7	0	4.68
Kent Peterson	L	21	37	17	3	1	152.1	156	9	62	78	6-13	2	4.25
Johnny Hetki	R	25	37	5	2	0	96.0	110	7	48	33	3-4	0	5.81
Eddie Erautt	R	22	36	10	2	0	119.0	146	5	53	43	4-9	0	5.07
Elmer Riddle	R	32	16	3	0	0	30.1	42	5	31	8	1-0	0	8.31
Joe Beggs†	R	36	11	4	0	0	32.1	42	4	6	11	0-3	0	5.29
Clyde Shoun†	L	35	10	0	0	0	14.1	16	2	5	7	0-0	0	5.02
Harry Perkowski	L	24	3	1	0	0	7.1	12	1	3	2	0-0	0	3.68
Clayton Lambert	R	30	3	0	0	0	5.2	12	3	6	1	0-0	0	15.88
Ken Polivka	L	26	2	0	0	0	3.0	3	0	3	1	0-0	0	3.00
Mike Schultz	L	26	1	0	0	0	2.0	4	0	2	0	0-0	0	4.50
Herm Wehmeier	R	20	1	0	0	0	1.0	0	0	0	0	0-0	0	0.00
Bob Malloy	R	29	1	0	0	0	1.0	3	1	0	1	0-0	0	18.00

1947 Chicago Cubs 6th NL 69-85 .448 25.0 GB

Charlie Grimm

Player	Gm by Position	B	Age	G	AB	R	H	2B	3B	HR	RBI	BB	SO	SB	Avg	OBP	Slg
Bob Scheffing	C97	R	33	110	363	33	96	11	5	5	50	25	25	2	.264	.312	.364
Eddie Waitkus	1B126	L	27	130	514	60	150	28	6	2	35	32	17	3	.292	.336	.381
Don Johnson	2B108,3B6	R	35	120	402	33	104	17	2	3	26	24	45	2	.259	.302	.333
Peanuts Lowrey	3B91,OF25,2B6	R	28	115	448	56	126	17	5	5	37	38	26	2	.281	.339	.375
Lennie Merullo	SS108	R	30	108	373	24	90	16	1	0	29	15	26	4	.241	.274	.290
Bill Nicholson	OF140	L	32	148	487	69	119	28	1	26	75	87	83	1	.244	.364	.466
Andy Pafko	OF127	R	26	129	513	68	155	25	7	13	66	31	39	4	.302	.346	.454
Phil Cavarretta	OF100,1B24	L	30	127	459	56	144	22	5	2	63	58	35	2	.314	.391	.397
Stan Hack	3B66	L	37	76	240	28	65	11	2	0	12	41	19	0	.271	.377	.333
Clyde McCullough	C64	R	30	86	234	25	59	12	4	3	30	20	20	1	.252	.314	.376
Bobby Sturgeon	SS45,2B30,3B5	R	27	87	232	16	59	10	5	0	21	7	12	0	.254	.276	.341
Cliff Aberson	OF40	R	25	47	140	24	39	6	3	4	20	20	32	0	.279	.369	.450
Marv Rickert	OF30,1B7	L	26	71	137	7	20	0	0	2	15	15	17	0	.146	.230	.190
Dom Dallessandro	OF28	L	33	66	115	18	33	7	1	1	14	21	11	0	.287	.397	.391
Ray Mack†	2B21	R	30	21	78	9	17	6	0	2	12	5	15	0	.218	.274	.372
Lonny Frey†	2B9	L	36	24	43	4	9	0	0	0	3	4	6	0	.209	.277	.209
Billy Jurges	SS14	R	39	14	40	5	8	2	0	1	2	9	9	0	.200	.347	.325
Mickey Livingston†	C7	R	32	19	33	2	7	2	0	0	3	1	5	0	.212	.235	.273
Sal Madrid	SS8	R	27	8	24	0	3	1	0	0	0	1	6	0	.125	.160	.167
Hank Schenz	3B5	R	28	7	14	2	1	0	0	0	0	2	1	0	.071	.235	.071
Dewey Williams	C1	R	31	3	2	0	0	0	0	0	0	0	1	0	.000	.000	.000

Pitcher	T	Age	G	GS	CG	ShO	IP	H	HR	BB	SO	W-L	Sv	ERA
Johnny Schmitz	L	26	38	28	10	3	207.0	209	8	80	97	13-18	4	3.22
Doyle Lade	R	26	34	25	7	1	187.1	202	15	79	62	11-10	0	3.94
Hank Borowy	R	31	40	25	7	1	183.0	190	19	63	75	8-12	2	4.38
Paul Erickson	R	31	40	20	6	0	174.0	179	17	93	82	7-12	1	4.34
Hank Wyse	R	29	37	19	5	1	142.0	158	12	64	53	6-9	1	4.31
Bob Chipman	L	28	32	17	5	1	134.2	135	6	66	51	7-6	0	3.68
Ox Miller	R	32	4	4	1	0	16.0	31	2	5	7	1-2	0	10.13
Ralph Hamner	R	30	3	3	2	0	25.0	24	0	16	14	1-2	0	2.52
Freddy Schmidt†	R	31	1	1	0	0	3.0	4	0	5	0	0-0	0	9.00
Emil Kush	R	30	47	1	1	0	91.0	80	8	53	44	8-3	5	3.36
Russ Meers	L	28	35	1	0	0	64.1	61	5	38	28	2-0	0	4.48
Russ Meyer	R	23	23	2	1	0	45.0	43	4	14	22	3-2	0	3.40
Claude Passeau	R	38	19	6	1	0	63.1	97	7	24	26	2-6	2	6.25
Bill Lee	R	37	14	2	0	0	24.0	26	2	14	9	0-2	0	4.50
Bob Carpenter†	R	29	4	1	0	0	7.1	10	1	4	1	0-1	0	4.91

1947 Philadelphia Phillies 7th NL 62-92 .403 32.0 GB

Ben Chapman

Player	Gm by Position	B	Age	G	AB	R	H	2B	3B	HR	RBI	BB	SO	SB	Avg	OBP	Slg
Andy Seminick	C107	R	26	111	337	48	85	16	2	13	50	58	69	4	.252	.370	.427
Howie Schultz†	1B114	R	24	114	403	30	90	19	1	6	35	21	70	0	.223	.264	.320
Emil Verban	2B155	R	31	155	540	50	154	14	8	0	42	23	8	5	.285	.316	.341
Lee Handley	3B83,2B3,SS1	R	33	101	277	17	70	10	3	0	42	24	18	1	.253	.312	.310
Skeeter Newsome	SS85,2B6,3B3	R	36	95	310	36	71	8	2	2	22	24	24	4	.229	.284	.287
Del Ennis	OF135	R	22	139	541	71	149	25	6	12	81	37	51	9	.275	.325	.410
Harry Walker†	OF127,1B4	L	30	130	488	79	181	28	16	1	41	59	37	13	.371	.443	.500
Johnny Wyrostek	OF126	L	27	128	454	68	124	24	7	5	51	61	45	7	.273	.364	.390
Jim Tabor	3B67	R	30	75	251	27	59	14	0	4	31	20	21	2	.235	.297	.339
Ralph Lapointe	SS54	R	25	56	211	33	65	7	0	1	15	17	15	8	.308	.362	.355
Al Lakeman†	1B29,C23	R	28	55	182	11	29	3	0	6	19	5	39	0	.159	.186	.275
Buster Adams	OF51	R	32	69	182	21	45	11	1	2	15	26	29	2	.247	.341	.352
Don Padgett	C39	L	35	75	158	14	50	8	1	0	24	16	5	0	.316	.383	.380
Charlie Gilbert	OF37	L	27	83	152	20	36	5	2	2	10	13	14	1	.237	.301	.336
Jack Albright	SS33	R	26	41	99	9	23	4	0	2	5	10	11	1	.232	.303	.333
Puddin' Head Jones	3B17	R	21	18	62	5	14	0	1	0	10	7	0	2	.226	.304	.258
Ron Northey†	OF13	L	27	13	47	7	12	3	0	0	3	6	3	1	.255	.340	.319
Nick Etten	1B11	L	33	14	41	5	10	4	0	1	8	5	4	0	.244	.326	.415
Frank McCormick†	1B12	R	36	15	40	7	9	2	0	1	8	3	2	0	.225	.279	.350
Jesse Levan	OF2	L	20	2	9	3	4	0	0	0	1	0	0	0	.444	.444	.444
Hugh Poland†	C2	L	34	4	8	0	0	0	0	0	0	0	0	0	.000	.000	.000
Granny Hamner	SS2	R	20	2	7	1	2	0	0	0	0	1	0	0	.286	.375	.286
Putsy Caballero	2B2,3B1	R	19	2	7	2	1	0	0	0	0	1	0	0	.143	.250	.143
Lou Finney		L	36	4	4	0	0	0	0	0	0	0	0	0	.000	.000	.000
Rollie Hemsley	C2	R	40	2	3	0	1	0	0	0	1	0	0	0	.333	.333	.333

Pitcher	T	Age	G	GS	CG	ShO	IP	H	HR	BB	SO	W-L	Sv	ERA
Dutch Leonard	R	38	32	29	19	3	235.0	224	14	57	103	17-12	0	2.68
Schoolboy Rowe	R	37	31	28	15	1	195.2	232	22	45	74	14-10	1	4.32
Oscar Judd	L	39	32	19	8	1	146.2	155	6	69	54	4-15	0	4.60
Ken Heintzelman†	L	31	24	19	8	0	136.0	144	12	46	55	7-10	1	4.04
Tommy Hughes	R	27	29	15	4	1	127.0	121	5	59	44	4-11	1	3.47
Ken Raffensberger†	L	29	10	7	3	1	41.0	50	4	8	16	2-6	0	5.49
Dick Koecher	L	21	3	2	1	0	17.0	20	1	10	4	0-2	0	4.76
Curt Simmons	L	18	1	1	1	0	9.0	5	0	6	9	1-0	0	1.00
Blix Donnelly	R	33	38	10	5	1	120.2	113	6	46	31	4-6	5	2.98
Al Jurisich	R	25	34	12	5	0	118.1	110	15	52	48	1-7	3	4.94
Charley Schanz	R	28	34	6	1	0	101.2	107	7	47	42	2-4	2	4.16
Freddy Schmidt†	R	31	29	5	0	0	76.2	76	4	43	24	5-8	0	4.70
Dick Mauney	R	27	9	1	0	0	16.1	15	1	7	6	0-0	1	3.86
Frank Hoerst	L	29	4	1	0	0	11.1	19	1	3	0	1-1	0	7.94
Homer Spragins	R	26	4	0	0	0	5.1	3	0	3	3	0-0	0	6.75
Lou Possehl	R	21	2	0	0	0	4.1	5	0	0	1	0-0	0	4.15

1947 Pittsburgh Pirates 7th NL 62-92 .403 32.0 GB

Billy Herman (61-92)/Bill Burwell (1-0)

Player	Gm by Position	B	Age	G	AB	R	H	2B	3B	HR	RBI	BB	SO	SB	Avg	OBP	Slg
Dixie Howell	C74	R	27	76	214	23	59	11	0	4	25	27	34	1	.276	.357	.383
Hank Greenberg	1B119	R	36	125	402	71	100	13	2	25	74	104	73	0	.249	.408	.478
Jimmy Bloodworth	2B87	R	29	88	316	27	79	9	0	7	48	16	39	1	.250	.290	.345
Frankie Gustine	3B156	R	27	156	616	102	183	30	6	9	67	63	65	5	.297	.364	.409
Billy Cox	SS129	R	27	132	529	75	145	30	7	15	54	29	28	5	.274	.313	.442
Ralph Kiner	OF152	R	24	152	565	118	177	23	4	51	127	98	81	1	.313	.417	.639
Jim Russell	OF119	S	28	128	478	68	121	21	8	8	51	63	58	7	.253	.343	.381
Wally Westlake	OF109	R	26	112	407	59	111	17	4	17	69	27	63	5	.273	.324	.459
Culley Rikard	OF79	L	33	109	324	57	93	16	4	4	32	50	39	1	.287	.384	.398
Clyde Kluttz	C69	R	29	73	232	26	70	9	2	6	42	17	18	1	.302	.355	.435
Eddie Basinski	2B56	R	24	56	161	15	32	6	2	4	17	18	27	0	.199	.279	.335
Elbie Fletcher	1B50	L	31	69	157	22	38	9	1	1	22	29	24	2	.242	.364	.331
Whitey Wietelmann	SS22,2B14,3B6*	S	28	48	128	21	30	4	1	1	7	12	10	0	.234	.300	.305
Gene Woodling	OF21	L	24	22	79	7	21	2	2	0	10	7	5	0	.266	.326	.342
Bill Salkeld	C15	L	30	47	61	5	13	2	0	0	8	6	8	0	.213	.284	.246
Billy Sullivan	C12	L	36	38	55	1	14	3	0	0	8	6	3	1	.255	.328	.309
Pete Castiglione	SS13	R	26	13	50	6	14	0	0	0	1	2	5	0	.280	.308	.280
Billy Herman	2B10,1B2	R	37	15	47	3	10	4	0	0	6	2	7	0	.213	.245	.298
Roy Jarvis	C15	R	21	18	45	4	7	1	0	1	4	6	5	0	.156	.255	.244
Gene Mauch	2B6,SS4	R	21	16	30	8	9	0	0	0	1	7	6	0	.300	.432	.300
Al Gionfriddo†		L	25	1	1	0	0	0	0	0	0	0	0	0	.000	.000	.000

W. Wietelmann, 1 G at 1B

Pitcher	T	Age	G	GS	CG	ShO	IP	H	HR	BB	SO	W-L	Sv	ERA
Kirby Higbe†	R	32	46	30	10	1	225.0	204	22	110	99	11-17	5	3.72
Fritz Ostermueller	L	39	26	24	12	3	183.0	181	18	68	66	12-10	0	3.84
Preacher Roe	L	32	38	22	4	1	144.0	156	19	63	59	4-15	2	5.25
Tiny Bonham	R	33	33	18	7	3	149.2	167	17	35	63	11-8	3	3.85
Rip Sewell	R	40	24	12	4	1	121.0	121	11	36	36	6-4	0	3.57
Mel Queen†	R	29	14	12	2	0	74.0	70	8	51	34	3-7	0	4.01
Ed Bahr	R	27	19	11	1	0	82.1	82	5	43	25	3-5	0	4.59
Hugh Mulcahy	R	33	2	1	0	0	6.2	8	1	7	2	0-0	0	4.05
Ken Heintzelman†	L	31	2	1	0	0	4.0	9	2	6	2	0-0	0	20.25
Jim Bagby Jr.	R	30	37	6	2	0	115.2	143	14	37	23	5-4	0	4.67
Elmer Singleton	R	29	36	3	0	0	67.0	70	8	39	24	2-2	1	6.31
Nick Strincevich	R	32	32	7	1	0	89.0	111	9	37	22	1-6	0	5.26
Roger Wolff†	R	36	13	6	1	0	30.0	49	4	18	7	1-4	0	8.70
Al Lyons†	R	28	13	0	0	0	28.1	36	4	12	16	1-2	0	7.31
Art Herring	R	41	11	0	0	0	10.2	18	3	4	6	1-3	2	8.44
Hank Behrman†	R	26	10	2	0	0	24.2	33	6	17	11	0-2	0	9.12
Steve Nagy	L	28	6	1	0	0	14.0	18	1	9	4	1-3	0	5.79
Lee Howard	L	23	2	0	0	0	2.2	4	1	0	2	0-0	0	3.38
Cal McLish	R	21	1	0	0	0	1.0	2	0	0	0	0-0	0	18.00
Lou Tost	L	36	1	0	0	0	1.0	3	0	0	0	0-0	0	9.00
Ken Gables	R	28	1	0	0	0	0.1	3	1	0	0	0-0	0	54.00

»1948 Cleveland Indians 1st AL 97-58 .626 —

Lou Boudreau

Player	Gm by Position	B	Age	G	AB	R	H	2B	3B	HR	RBI	BB	SO	SB	Avg	OBP	Slg
Jim Hegan	C142	R	27	144	472	60	117	21	6	14	61	48	74	6	.248	.317	.407
Eddie Robinson	1B131	L	27	134	493	53	125	18	5	16	83	36	42	1	.254	.307	.408
Joe Gordon	2B144,SS2	R	33	144	550	96	154	21	4	32	124	77	68	5	.280	.371	.507
Ken Keltner	3B153	R	31	153	558	91	166	24	4	31	119	89	52	2	.297	.395	.522
Lou Boudreau	SS151,C1	R	30	152	560	116	199	34	6	18	106	98	9	3	.355	.453	.534
Dale Mitchell	OF140	L	26	141	608	82	204	30	8	4	56	45	17	13	.336	.383	.431
Larry Doby	OF114	L	24	121	439	83	132	23	9	14	66	54	77	9	.301	.384	.490
Thurman Tucker	OF66	L	30	83	242	52	63	13	2	1	19	31	17	11	.260	.347	.343
Allie Clark	OF65,3B5,1B1	R	25	81	271	43	84	5	2	9	38	23	13	0	.310	.364	.443
Wally Judnich	OF49,1B20	L	31	79	218	36	56	13	3	2	29	56	23	2	.257	.411	.372
Hank Edwards	OF41	L	29	55	160	27	43	9	2	3	18	18	18	1	.269	.346	.406
Johnny Berardino	2B20,1B18,SS12*	R	31	66	147	19	28	5	1	2	10	27	16	0	.190	.328	.279
Joe Tipton	C40	R	26	47	90	11	26	3	0	1	13	4	10	0	.289	.333	.356
Bob Kennedy†	OF50,2B2,1B1	R	27	66	73	10	22	3	2	0	5	4	6	0	.301	.338	.397
Hal Peck	OF9	L	31	45	63	12	18	3	0	0	8	4	8	1	.286	.328	.333
Pat Seerey†	OF7	R	25	10	23	7	6	0	0	1	6	7	8	0	.261	.433	.391
Ray Boone	SS4	R	24	6	5	0	2	1	0	0	1	0	1	0	.400	.400	.600
Al Rosen	3B2	R	24	5	5	0	1	0	0	0	0	0	2	0	.200	.200	.200
Ray Murray		R	30	4	4	0	0	0	0	0	0	0	3	0	.000	.000	.000

J. Berardino, 3 G at 3B

Pitcher	T	Age	G	GS	CG	ShO	IP	H	HR	BB	SO	W-L	Sv	ERA
Bob Feller	R	29	44	38	18	2	280.1	255	20	116	164	19-15	3	3.56
Bob Lemon	R	27	43	37	20	10	293.2	231	12	129	147	20-14	2	2.82
Gene Bearden	L	27	37	29	15	6	229.2	187	9	106	80	20-7	1	2.43
Sam Zoldak†	L	29	23	12	4	1	105.2	104	6	24	17	9-6	0	2.81
Don Black	R	31	18	10	1	0	52.0	57	5	40	16	2-2	0	5.37
Bill Kennedy†	L	27	6	3	0	0	11.1	16	0	13	12	1-0	0	11.12
Russ Christopher	R	30	45	0	0	0	59.0	55	3	27	14	3-2	17	2.90
Ed Klieman	R	30	44	0	0	0	79.2	62	3	46	18	3-2	4	2.60
Steve Gromek	R	28	38	9	4	1	130.0	109	10	51	50	9-3	2	2.84
Satchel Paige	R	41	21	7	3	2	72.2	61	2	22	43	6-1	1	2.48
Bob Muncrief	R	32	21	9	1	1	72.1	76	8	31	24	5-4	0	3.98
Al Gettel†	R	30	5	2	0	0	7.2	15	2	10	4	0-1	0	17.61
Lymie Linde	R	27	3	0	0	0	10.0	9	1	4	0	0-0	0	5.40
Mike Garcia	R	24	1	0	0	0	2.0	3	0	0	1	0-0	0	0.00
Butch Wensloff	R	32	1	0	0	0	1.2	2	1	3	2	0-1	0	10.80
Ernest Groth	R	26	1	0	0	0	1.0	1	0	2	0	0-0	0	9.00
Les Webber	R	33	1	0	0	0	0.2	3	0	1	1	0-0	0	40.50

1948 Boston Red Sox 2nd AL 96-59 .619 1.0 GB

Joe McCarthy

Player	Gm by Position	B	Age	G	AB	R	H	2B	3B	HR	RBI	BB	SO	SB	Avg	OBP	Slg
Birdie Tebbetts	C126	R	35	128	446	54	125	26	2	5	68	62	32	5	.280	.371	.381
Billy Goodman	1B117,2B2,3B2	L	22	127	445	65	138	27	2	1	66	74	44	5	.310	.414	.387
Bobby Doerr	2B138	R	30	140	527	94	150	23	6	27	111	83	49	3	.285	.386	.505
Johnny Pesky	3B141	L	28	143	565	124	159	26	6	3	55	99	32	3	.281	.394	.365
Vern Stephens	SS155	R	27	155	635	114	171	25	8	29	137	77	56	1	.269	.350	.471
Dom DiMaggio	OF155	R	31	155	648	127	185	40	4	9	87	101	58	10	.285	.383	.401
Ted Williams	OF134	L	29	137	509	124	188	44	3	25	127	126	41	4	.369	.497	.615
Stan Spence	OF92,1B14	L	33	114	391	71	92	17	4	12	61	82	33	0	.235	.368	.391
Wally Moses	OF45	L	37	78	189	26	49	12	1	2	29	21	19	5	.259	.340	.365
Sam Mele	OF55	R	25	66	180	25	42	12	1	2	25	13	21	1	.233	.292	.344
Billy Hitchcock	2B15,3B15	R	31	49	124	15	37	3	2	1	20	7	9	0	.298	.341	.379
Matt Batts	C41	R	26	46	118	13	37	12	0	1	24	15	9	0	.314	.391	.441
Jake Jones	1B31	R	27	36	105	3	21	4	0	1	8	11	26	1	.200	.276	.267
Lou Stringer	2B2	R	31	4	11	1	1	0	0	1	1	0	3	0	.091	.091	.364
Babe Martin	C1	R	28	4	4	0	2	0	0	0	0	0	1	0	.500	.500	.500
Tom Wright		L	24	3	2	1	1	0	1	0	0	0	0	0	.500	.500	1.500
Neill Sheridan		R	26	2	1	0	0	0	0	0	0	0	1	0	.000	.000	.000
Johnny Ostrowski		R	30	1	1	0	0	0	0	0	0	0	1	0	.000	.000	.000

Pitcher	T	Age	G	GS	CG	ShO	IP	H	HR	BB	SO	W-L	Sv	ERA
Joe Dobson	R	31	38	32	16	5	245.1	237	14	92	116	16-10	2	3.56
Jack Kramer	R	30	29	29	14	2	205.0	233	12	64	72	18-5	0	4.35
Mel Parnell	L	26	35	27	16	1	212.0	205	7	90	77	15-8	0	3.14
Ellis Kinder	R	33	28	22	10	1	178.0	183	10	63	53	10-7	0	3.74
Mickey Harris	L	31	20	17	6	1	113.2	120	10	59	42	7-10	0	5.30
Denny Galehouse	R	36	27	15	6	1	137.1	152	10	46	38	8-8	3	4.00
Windy McCall	L	22	1	1	0	0	1.1	6	1	1	0	0-1	0	20.25
Earl Johnson	L	29	35	3	1	0	91.1	98	7	42	45	10-4	5	4.53
Boo Ferriss	R	26	31	9	1	0	115.1	127	7	61	30	7-3	3	5.23
Tex Hughson	R	32	15	0	0	0	19.1	21	0	7	6	3-1	0	5.12
Harry Dorish	R	26	9	0	0	0	14.1	18	1	6	5	0-1	0	5.65
Earl Caldwell†	R	43	8	0	0	0	9.0	11	2	11	5	1-1	0	13.00
Mickey McDermott	L	20	7	0	0	0	23.1	16	2	35	17	0-0	0	6.17
Chuck Stobbs	L	18	6	0	0	0	7.0	9	0	7	4	0-0	0	6.43
Cot Deal	R	25	4	0	0	0	4.0	3	0	3	2	1-0	0	0.00
Mike Palm	R	23	3	0	0	0	3.0	6	0	5	1	0-0	0	6.00

1948 New York Yankees 3rd AL 94-60 .610 2.5 GB

Bucky Harris

Player	Gm by Position	B	Age	G	AB	R	H	2B	3B	HR	RBI	BB	SO	SB	Avg	OBP	Slg
Gus Niarhos	C82	R	27	83	228	41	61	12	2	0	19	52	15	1	.268	.404	.338
George McQuinn	1B90	L	38	94	302	33	75	11	4	11	41	40	38	0	.248	.336	.421
Snuffy Stirnweiss	2B141	R	29	141	515	90	130	20	7	3	32	86	62	5	.252	.360	.336
Bill Johnson	3B118	R	29	127	446	59	131	20	6	12	64	41	30	0	.294	.358	.446
Phil Rizzuto	SS128	R	30	128	464	65	117	13	2	6	50	60	24	6	.252	.340	.328
Joe DiMaggio	OF152	R	33	153	594	110	190	26	11	39	155	67	30	1	.320	.396	.598
Tommy Henrich	OF102,1B46	L	35	146	588	138	181	42	14	25	100	76	42	2	.308	.391	.554
Johnny Lindell	OF79	R	31	88	309	58	98	17	2	13	55	35	50	0	.317	.387	.511
Yogi Berra	C71,OF50	L	23	125	469	70	143	24	10	14	98	25	24	3	.305	.341	.488
Bobby Brown	3B41,SS26,2B17*	L	23	113	363	62	109	19	5	3	48	48	16	0	.300	.383	.405
Charlie Keller	OF66	L	31	83	247	41	66	15	2	6	44	41	25	1	.267	.372	.417
Steve Souchock	1B32	R	29	44	118	11	24	3	1	3	11	7	13	3	.203	.248	.322
Cliff Mapes	OF21	L	26	53	88	19	22	11	1	1	12	6	13	1	.250	.298	.432
Hank Bauer	OF14	R	25	19	50	6	9	1	1	1	9	6	13	1	.180	.268	.300
Sherm Lollar	C10	R	23	22	38	0	8	0	0	0	4	1	6	0	.211	.231	.211
Ralph Houk	C14	R	28	14	29	3	8	2	0	0	3	0	0	0	.276	.276	.345
Charlie Silvera	C4	R	23	4	14	1	8	0	1	0	1	0	1	0	.571	.571	.714
Frankie Crosetti	2B6,SS5	R	37	17	14	4	4	0	1	0	0	2	0	0	.286	.375	.429
Joe Collins		L	25	5	5	0	1	1	0	0	2	0	1	0	.200	.200	.400
Bud Stewart†		L	32	6	5	1	1	1	0	0	0	0	0	0	.200	.200	.400
Jack Phillips	1B1	R	26	1	2	0	0	0	0	0	0	0	1	0	.000	.000	.000
Lonny Frey†		L	37	1	0	1	0	0	0	0	0	0	0	0	—	—	—

B. Brown, 4 G at OF

Pitcher	T	Age	G	GS	CG	ShO	IP	H	HR	BB	SO	W-L	Sv	ERA
Allie Reynolds	R	33	39	31	11	1	236.1	240	17	111	101	16-7	3	3.77
Ed Lopat	L	30	33	31	13	3	226.2	246	16	66	83	17-11	0	3.65
Vic Raschi	R	29	36	31	18	6	222.2	208	15	74	124	19-8	1	3.84
Spec Shea	R	27	28	22	8	3	155.2	117	10	87	71	9-10	1	3.41
Bob Porterfield	R	24	16	12	2	1	78.0	85	5	34	30	5-3	0	4.50
Joe Page	L	30	55	1	0	0	107.2	116	8	66	77	7-8	16	4.26
Tommy Byrne	L	28	31	11	5	1	133.2	79	8	101	93	8-5	2	3.30
Frank Hiller	R	27	22	5	1	0	62.1	59	8	30	25	5-2	0	4.04
Red Embree	R	30	20	8	4	0	76.2	77	6	30	25	5-3	0	3.76
Karl Drews†	R	28	19	2	0	0	38.0	35	3	31	11	2-3	1	3.79
Randy Gumpert†	R	30	15	0	0	0	25.0	27	0	6	12	1-0	0	2.88
Dick Starr	R	27	1	0	0	0	2.0	0	0	2	2	0-0	0	4.50
Cuddles Marshall	R	23	1	0	0	0	1.0	0	0	3	0	0-0	0	0.00

706 Seasons: Team Rosters

1948 Philadelphia Athletics 4th AL 84-70 .545 12.5 GB

Connie Mack

Player	Gm by Position	B	Age	G	AB	R	H	2B	3B	HR	RBI	BB	SO	SB	Avg	OBP	Slg
Buddy Rosar	C90	R	33	90	302	30	77	13	0	4	41	39	12	0	.255	.344	.338
Ferris Fain	1B145	L	27	145	520	81	146	27	6	7	88	113	37	10	.281	.412	.396
Pete Suder	2B148	R	32	148	519	64	125	23	5	7	60	60	60	1	.241	.321	.345
Hank Majeski	3B142,SS8	R	31	148	590	88	183	41	4	12	120	48	43	2	.310	.368	.454
Eddie Joost	SS135	R	32	135	509	99	127	22	2	16	55	119	87	2	.250	.393	.395
Barney McCosky	OF134	L	31	135	515	95	168	21	5	0	46	68	22	1	.326	.405	.386
Sam Chapman	OF118	R	32	123	445	58	115	18	6	13	70	55	50	6	.258	.341	.413
Elmer Valo	OF109	L	27	113	383	72	117	17	4	3	46	81	13	10	.305	.432	.394
Don White	OF54,3B17	R	29	86	253	29	62	14	2	1	28	19	16	0	.245	.303	.328
Ray Coleman†	OF53	L	26	68	210	32	51	6	6	0	21	31	17	4	.243	.340	.329
Mike Guerra	C47	R	35	53	142	18	30	4	2	1	23	18	13	2	.211	.300	.289
Carl Scheib	P32,OF2	R	21	52	104	14	31	8	3	2	21	8	17	0	.298	.348	.490
Herman Franks	C27	L	34	40	98	10	22	7	1	1	14	16	11	0	.224	.345	.347
Skeeter Webb	2B9,SS8	R	38	23	54	5	8	2	0	0	3	0	9	0	.148	.148	.185
Rudy York	1B14	R	34	31	51	4	8	0	0	0	6	7	15	0	.157	.259	.157
George Binks†	OF14	L	31	17	41	2	4	1	0	0	2	2	2	1	.098	.140	.122
Billy DeMars	SS9,2B1,3B1	R	22	18	29	3	5	0	0	0	1	5	3	0	.172	.294	.172
Nellie Fox	2B3	L	20	3	13	0	2	0	0	0	0	1	0	1	.154	.214	.154
Bob Wellman	1B2,OF1	R	22	4	10	1	2	0	1	0	0	3	2	0	.200	.385	.400
Earle Brucker	C2	L	22	2	6	0	1	1	0	0	0	1	1	0	.167	.286	.333

Pitcher	T	Age	G	GS	CG	ShO	IP	H	HR	BB	SO	W-L	Sv	ERA
Phil Marchildon	R	34	33	30	12	1	226.1	214	19	131	66	9-15	0	4.53
Joe Coleman	R	25	33	29	13	3	215.2	224	11	90	86	14-13	0	4.09
Dick Fowler	R	27	29	26	16	2	204.2	221	15	76	50	15-8	2	3.78
Lou Brissie	L	24	39	25	11	0	194.0	202	6	95	127	14-10	5	4.13
Carl Scheib	R	21	32	24	15	1	198.2	219	14	76	44	14-8	0	3.94
Bill McCahan	R	27	17	15	5	0	86.2	98	8	65	20	4-7	0	5.71
Bill Dietrich	R	38	4	2	0	0	15.1	21	0	9	5	1-2	0	5.87
Charlie Harris	R	22	45	0	0	0	93.2	89	2	35	32	5-2	5	4.13
Bob Savage	R	26	33	1	1	0	75.1	98	9	33	26	5-1	5	6.21
Alex Kellner	L	23	13	1	0	0	23.0	21	0	16	14	0-0	0	7.83
Nels Potter†	R	36	8	0	0	0	18.0	17	1	5	13	2-2	1	4.00
Wally Holborow	R	34	5	1	1	0	17.1	32	1	7	3	1-2	0	5.71

1948 Detroit Tigers 5th AL 78-76 .506 18.5 GB

Steve O'Neill

Player	Gm by Position	B	Age	G	AB	R	H	2B	3B	HR	RBI	BB	SO	SB	Avg	OBP	Slg
Bob Swift	C112	R	33	113	292	23	65	6	0	4	33	51	29	1	.223	.338	.284
Sam Vico	1B142	L	24	144	521	50	139	23	9	8	58	39	39	2	.267	.326	.392
Eddie Mayo	2B86,3B10	L	38	106	370	35	92	20	1	2	42	30	19	1	.249	.310	.324
George Kell	3B92	R	25	92	368	47	112	24	3	2	44	33	15	2	.304	.369	.402
Johnny Lipon	SS117,2B1,3B1	R	25	121	458	65	133	18	8	5	52	68	22	4	.290	.384	.397
Hoot Evers	OF138	R	27	139	538	81	169	33	6	10	103	51	31	3	.314	.378	.454
Pat Mullin	OF131	L	30	138	496	91	143	16	11	23	80	77	57	1	.288	.385	.504
Vic Wertz	OF98	L	23	119	391	49	97	19	9	7	67	48	70	0	.248	.335	.396
Dick Wakefield	OF86	L	27	110	322	50	89	20	5	11	53	70	55	0	.276	.406	.472
Neil Berry	SS41,2B26	R	26	87	256	46	68	8	1	0	16	37	23	1	.266	.358	.305
Eddie Lake	2B45,3B17	R	32	64	198	51	52	6	0	2	18	57	20	3	.263	.427	.323
Jimmy Outlaw	3B47,OF13	R	35	74	198	33	56	12	0	0	25	31	15	0	.283	.383	.343
Hal Wagner†	C52	L	32	54	109	10	22	3	0	0	10	20	11	1	.202	.326	.229
Paul Campbell	1B27	L	30	59	83	15	22	1	1	1	11	1	10	0	.265	.274	.337
Hank Riebe	C24	R	26	25	62	0	12	0	0	0	5	3	5	0	.194	.231	.194
Joe Ginsberg	C11	L	21	11	36	7	13	0	0	0	1	3	1	0	.361	.410	.361
Johnny Groth	OF4	R	21	6	17	3	8	3	0	1	5	1	1	0	.471	.500	.824
Johnny Bero	2B2	L	25	4	9	2	0	0	0	0	0	1	1	0	.000	.100	.000
Ed Mierkowicz	OF1	R	24	3	5	0	1	0	0	0	1	2	2	0	.200	.429	.200
Doc Cramer	OF1	L	42	4	4	1	0	0	0	0	1	3	0	0	.000	.429	.000
John McHale		L	26	1	1	0	0	0	0	0	0	0	0	0	.000	.000	.000

Pitcher	T	Age	G	GS	CG	ShO	IP	H	HR	BB	SO	W-L	Sv	ERA
Hal Newhouser	L	27	39	35	19	2	272.1	249	10	99	143	21-12	1	3.01
Fred Hutchinson	R	28	33	28	15	0	221.0	223	32	48	92	13-11	0	4.32
Virgil Trucks	R	31	43	26	7	0	211.2	190	13	85	123	14-13	2	3.78
Dizzy Trout	R	33	32	23	11	2	183.2	193	7	73	91	10-14	2	3.43
Art Houtteman	R	20	43	20	4	0	164.1	186	11	52	74	2-16	10	4.66
Stubby Overmire	L	29	37	4	0	0	66.1	89	5	31	14	3-4	3	5.97
Al Benton	R	37	30	0	0	0	44.1	45	4	36	18	2-2	3	5.68
Hal White	R	29	27	0	0	0	42.2	46	2	26	17	2-1	1	6.12
Ted Gray	L	23	26	11	3	1	85.1	73	2	72	60	6-2	0	4.22
Billy Pierce	L	21	22	5	0	0	55.1	47	5	51	36	3-0	0	6.34
Lou Kretlow	R	27	5	2	1	0	23.1	21	1	11	9	2-1	0	4.63
Rufe Gentry	R	30	4	0	0	0	6.2	5	0	5	1	0-0	0	2.70

1948 St. Louis Browns 6th AL 59-94 .386 37.0 GB

Zack Taylor

Player	Gm by Position	B	Age	G	AB	R	H	2B	3B	HR	RBI	BB	SO	SB	Avg	OBP	Slg
Les Moss	C103	R	23	107	335	35	86	12	1	14	46	39	50	0	.257	.334	.424
Chuck Stevens	1B85	S	29	85	288	34	75	12	4	1	26	41	26	2	.260	.353	.340
Jerry Priddy	2B146	R	28	151	560	96	166	40	9	8	79	86	71	6	.296	.391	.443
Bob Dillinger	3B153	R	29	153	644	110	207	34	10	2	44	65	34	28	.321	.385	.415
Eddie Pellagrini	SS98	R	30	105	290	31	69	8	3	2	27	34	40	1	.238	.320	.307
Al Zarilla	OF136	L	29	144	529	77	174	39	3	12	74	48	48	11	.329	.389	.482
Whitey Platt	OF114	R	27	123	454	57	123	22	10	7	82	39	51	1	.271	.331	.410
Paul Lehner	OF89,1B2	L	27	103	333	23	92	15	4	2	46	30	19	0	.276	.336	.363
Sam Dente	SS76,3B6	R	26	98	267	26	72	11	2	0	22	22	8	1	.270	.328	.326
Dick Kokos	OF71	L	20	71	258	40	77	15	3	4	40	28	32	4	.298	.374	.426
Hank Arft	1B69	L	26	69	248	25	59	10	3	5	38	45	43	1	.238	.355	.363
Roy Partee	C76	R	30	82	231	14	47	8	1	0	17	25	21	2	.203	.284	.247
Don Lund†	OF45	R	25	63	161	21	40	7	4	3	25	10	17	0	.248	.305	.398
Pete Layden	OF30	R	28	41	104	11	26	2	1	0	4	6	10	4	.250	.297	.288
Andy Anderson	2B21,SS10,1B2	R	25	51	87	13	24	5	1	1	12	8	15	0	.276	.337	.391
Joe Schultz		L	29	43	37	0	7	0	0	0	9	6	3	0	.189	.302	.189
Ray Coleman†	OF5	L	26	17	29	2	5	0	1	0	2	2	5	1	.172	.226	.241
Ken Wood	OF5	R	23	10	24	2	2	0	1	0	2	1	4	0	.083	.120	.167
George Binks†	OF5,1B4	L	31	15	23	2	5	0	0	0	1	2	1	0	.217	.280	.217
Jerry McCarthy	1B2	L	25	2	3	0	1	0	0	0	0	0	0	0	.333	.333	.333
Tom Jordan		R	28	1	1	0	0	0	0	0	0	0	0	0	.000	.000	.000

Pitcher	T	Age	G	GS	CG	ShO	IP	H	HR	BB	SO	W-L	Sv	ERA
Fred Sanford	R	28	42	33	9	1	227.0	250	19	91	79	12-21	2	4.64
Cliff Fannin	R	24	34	29	10	3	213.2	198	14	104	102	10-14	1	4.17
Ned Garver	R	22	38	24	7	0	198.0	200	14	95	75	7-11	5	3.41
Bill Kennedy†	L	27	26	20	3	0	132.0	132	10	104	77	7-8	0	4.70
Sam Zoldak†	L	29	11	9	0	0	54.0	64	4	19	13	2-4	0	4.67
Nels Potter†	R	36	2	2	0	0	10.1	11	1	4	4	1-1	0	5.23
Al Widmar	R	23	49	0	0	0	82.2	88	4	48	34	2-6	1	4.46
Frank Biscan	L	28	47	4	1	0	98.2	129	3	71	45	6-7	2	6.11
Bryan Stephens	R	27	43	12	2	0	122.2	141	14	67	35	3-6	3	6.02
Joe Ostrowski	L	31	26	9	3	0	78.1	108	6	17	20	4-6	3	5.97
Karl Drews†	R	28	20	2	0	0	38.0	43	3	38	11	3-2	2	8.05
Ray Shore	R	27	17	4	0	0	38.0	40	3	35	12	1-2	0	6.39
Al Gerheauser	L	31	14	2	0	0	23.1	32	0	10	10	0-3	0	7.33
Clem Dreisewerd†	L	32	13	0	0	0	22.1	28	6	8	6	0-2	1	5.64
Blackie Schwamb	R	21	12	5	0	0	31.2	44	3	21	7	1-1	0	8.53
Jim Wilson	R	26	4	0	0	0	2.2	5	0	5	1	0-0	0	13.50

1948 Washington Senators 7th AL 56-97 .366 40.0 GB

Joe Kuhel

Player	Gm by Position	B	Age	G	AB	R	H	2B	3B	HR	RBI	BB	SO	SB	Avg	OBP	Slg
Jake Early	C92	L	33	97	246	22	54	7	2	1	28	36	33	2	.220	.322	.276
Mickey Vernon	1B150	L	30	150	558	78	135	27	7	3	48	54	43	15	.242	.310	.332
Al Kozar	2B149	R	26	150	577	61	144	25	8	1	58	66	52	6	.250	.327	.326
Eddie Yost	3B145	R	21	145	555	74	138	32	11	2	50	82	51	4	.249	.349	.357
Mark Christman	SS102,3B9,2B3	R	34	120	409	38	106	17	2	1	40	25	19	0	.259	.303	.318
Gil Coan	OF131	L	26	138	513	56	119	13	9	7	60	41	78	23	.232	.298	.333
Bud Stewart†	OF114	L	32	118	401	56	112	17	13	7	69	49	27	8	.279	.361	.439
Junior Wooten	OF73,1B6,P1	R	24	88	258	34	66	8	3	1	23	24	21	2	.256	.324	.322
Al Evans	C85	R	31	93	228	19	59	6	3	2	28	38	20	1	.259	.367	.338
Carden Gillenwater	OF67	R	30	77	221	23	54	10	4	3	21	39	36	4	.244	.358	.367
Tom McBride	OF55	R	33	92	206	22	53	9	1	1	29	28	15	2	.257	.346	.325
Sherry Robertson	OF51	L	29	71	187	19	46	11	3	2	22	24	26	8	.246	.335	.369
John Sullivan	SS57,2B4	R	27	85	173	25	36	4	1	0	12	22	25	2	.208	.297	.243
Len Okrie	C17	R	24	19	42	1	10	0	1	0	1	1	7	0	.238	.256	.286
Sammy Meeks	SS10,2B1	R	25	24	33	4	4	1	0	0	2	1	12	0	.121	.147	.152
Leon Culberson	OF11	R	28	12	29	1	5	0	0	0	2	8	5	0	.172	.351	.172
Angel Fleitas	SS7	R	33	15	13	1	1	0	0	0	1	3	5	0	.077	.250	.077
Jim Clark	3B1,SS1	R	20	9	12	1	3	0	0	0	0	0	2	0	.250	.250	.250
Larry Drake	OF2	L	27	4	7	0	2	0	0	0	1	1	3	0	.286	.375	.286
Clyde Vollmer†	OF1	R	26	1	5	1	2	0	0	0	0	0	1	0	.400	.400	.400
Jay Difani		R	24	2	2	0	0	0	0	0	0	0	2	0	.000	.000	.000

Pitcher	T	Age	G	GS	CG	ShO	IP	H	HR	BB	SO	W-L	Sv	ERA
Early Wynn	R	28	33	31	15	1	198.0	236	18	94	49	8-19	0	5.82
Sid Hudson	R	33	39	29	4	0	182.0	217	11	107	53	4-16	1	5.88
Walt Masterson	R	28	33	27	9	2	188.0	171	12	122	72	8-15	2	3.83
Ray Scarborough	R	30	31	26	9	0	185.1	166	9	72	76	15-8	1	2.82
Mickey Haefner	L	35	28	20	4	0	147.2	151	7	61	45	5-13	0	4.02
Dick Weik	R	20	3	3	0	0	12.2	14	1	22	8	1-2	0	5.68
Dave Thompson	L	30	46	7	0	0	131.1	134	9	54	40	6-10	4	3.84
Tom Ferrick	R	33	37	0	0	0	73.2	75	3	38	34	2-5	10	4.15
Milo Candini	R	30	35	4	1	0	94.1	96	1	63	23	2-3	3	5.15
Dick Welteroth	R	20	33	2	0	0	65.1	73	6	50	16	2-1	1	5.51
Earl Harrist†	R	29	23	4	0	0	60.2	70	1	37	21	3-3	0	4.60
Marino Pieretti†	R	27	8	1	0	0	12.0	18	1	7	6	0-2	0	10.50
Ramon Garcia	R	24	4	0	0	0	3.2	11	0	4	2	0-0	0	17.18
Junior Wooten	L	24	1	0	0	0	2.0	2	0	2	1	0-0	0	9.00
Cal Cooper	R	25	1	0	0	0	1.0	5	1	1	0	0-0	0	45.00

1948 Chicago White Sox 8th AL 51-101 .336 44.5 GB

Ted Lyons

Player	Gm by Position	B	Age	G	AB	R	H	2B	3B	HR	RBI	BB	SO	SB	Avg	OBP	Slg
Aaron Robinson	C92	L	33	98	326	47	82	14	2	8	39	46	30	0	.252	.344	.380
Tony Lupien	1B154	L	31	154	617	69	152	19	3	6	54	74	38	11	.246	.327	.316
Don Kolloway	2B83,3B18	R	29	119	417	60	114	14	4	6	38	18	18	2	.273	.303	.369
Luke Appling	3B72,SS64	R	41	139	497	63	156	16	2	0	47	94	35	10	.314	.423	.354
Cass Michaels	SS85,2B55,OF1	R	22	145	484	47	120	12	6	5	56	69	42	8	.248	.344	.329
Dave Philley	OF128	S	28	137	488	51	140	28	3	5	42	50	33	8	.287	.353	.387
Taffy Wright	OF114	L	36	134	455	50	127	15	6	4	61	39	18	2	.279	.341	.365
Pat Seerey†	OF93	R	25	95	340	44	78	11	0	18	64	83	94	0	.229	.381	.421
Floyd Baker	3B71,2B18,SS1	L	31	104	335	47	72	8	3	0	18	73	26	4	.215	.359	.257
Ralph Hodgin	OF79	L	32	114	331	28	88	11	5	1	34	21	11	0	.266	.310	.338
Ralph Weigel	C39,OF2	R	26	66	163	8	38	7	3	0	26	13	18	1	.233	.294	.313
Bob Kennedy†	OF30	R	27	30	113	4	28	8	1	0	14	4	17	0	.248	.274	.336
Mike Tresh	C34	R	34	39	108	10	27	1	0	1	11	9	9	0	.250	.308	.287
Jim Delsing	OF15	L	22	20	63	5	12	0	0	0	5	5	12	0	.190	.261	.190
Al Gettel†	P22,2B1	R	30	24	54	4	13	2	0	0	3	0	6	0	.241	.241	.278
Jack Wallaesa	SS5,OF1	S	28	33	48	2	9	0	0	1	3	1	12	0	.188	.204	.250
Herb Adams	OF4	L	20	5	11	1	3	1	0	0	1	1	0	0	.273	.333	.364
Jerry Scala	OF2	L	23	3	6	1	0	0	0	0	0	0	3	0	.000	.000	.000
Frank Whitman	SS1	R	23	3	6	0	0	0	0	0	0	0	3	0	.000	.000	.000

Pitcher	T	Age	G	GS	CG	ShO	IP	H	HR	BB	SO	W-L	Sv	ERA
Bill Wight	L	26	34	32	7	1	223.1	238	9	135	68	9-20	1	4.80
Joe Haynes	R	30	27	22	6	0	149.2	167	13	52	40	9-10	0	3.97
Al Gettel†	R	30	22	19	7	0	148.0	154	7	60	49	8-10	1	4.01
Marino Pieretti†	R	27	21	18	4	0	120.0	117	6	52	28	8-10	1	4.95
Randy Gumpert†	R	30	16	11	6	1	97.1	103	6	13	31	2-6	0	3.79
Howie Judson	R	22	40	5	1	0	107.1	102	7	56	38	4-5	8	4.78
Glen Moulder	R	30	33	9	0	0	85.2	108	8	54	26	3-6	2	6.41
Frank Papish	L	30	32	14	2	0	95.1	97	7	75	41	2-8	4	5.00
Orval Grove	R	28	32	11	1	0	87.2	110	6	42	18	2-10	1	6.16
Bob Gillespie	R	29	25	6	1	0	72.0	81	3	33	19	0-4	0	5.13
Earl Caldwell†	R	43	25	1	0	0	39.0	53	3	22	10	1-5	3	5.31
Ike Pearson	R	31	23	2	0	0	53.0	62	7	27	12	2-3	1	4.92
Earl Harrist†	R	29	11	1	0	0	23.0	23	4	13	14	1-3	0	5.87
Fred Bradley	R	27	8	0	0	0	15.2	11	2	4	2	0-0	0	4.60
Jim Goodwin	L	21	8	1	0	0	10.1	9	0	12	3	0-1	0	8.71
Marv Rotblatt	L	20	7	2	0	0	18.1	19	0	23	4	0-1	0	7.85

»1948 Boston Braves 1st NL 91-62 .595 —

Billy Southworth

Player	Gm by Position	B	Age	G	AB	R	H	2B	3B	HR	RBI	BB	SO	SB	Avg	OBP	Slg
Phil Masi	C109	R	32	113	376	43	95	19	0	5	44	35	26	2	.253	.318	.343
Earl Torgeson	1B129	L	24	134	438	70	111	23	5	10	67	81	54	19	.253	.372	.397
Eddie Stanky	2B66	R	31	67	247	49	79	14	2	2	29	61	13	3	.320	.455	.417
Bob Elliott	3B150	R	31	151	540	99	153	24	5	23	100	131	57	6	.283	.423	.474
Al Dark	SS133	R	26	137	543	85	175	39	6	3	48	24	36	4	.322	.353	.433
Tommy Holmes	OF137	L	31	139	585	85	190	35	7	6	61	46	20	1	.325	.375	.439
Jeff Heath	OF106	L	33	115	364	64	116	26	5	20	76	51	46	2	.319	.404	.582
Mike McCormick	OF100	R	31	115	343	45	104	22	7	1	39	32	34	1	.303	.363	.417
Jim Russell	OF84	S	29	89	322	44	85	18	1	9	54	46	31	4	.264	.361	.410
Clint Conatser	OF76	R	26	90	224	30	62	9	3	3	23	32	27	0	.277	.370	.384
Sibby Sisti	2B44,SS26	R	27	83	221	30	54	6	2	0	21	31	34	0	.244	.340	.290
Bill Salkeld	C59	L	31	78	198	26	48	8	1	8	28	42	37	1	.242	.378	.414
Frank McCormick	1B50	R	37	75	180	14	45	9	2	4	34	10	9	0	.250	.289	.389
Connie Ryan	2B40,3B4	R	28	51	122	14	26	3	0	0	10	21	16	0	.213	.333	.238
Bobby Sturgeon	2B18,3B4,SS4	R	28	34	78	10	17	3	1	0	4	4	5	0	.218	.256	.282
Danny Litwhiler†	OF8	R	31	13	33	0	9	2	0	0	6	4	2	0	.273	.385	.333
Marv Rickert†	OF3	L	27	3	13	1	3	0	1	0	2	0	1	0	.231	.286	.385
Al Lyons	P7,OF4	R	29	16	12	2	2	0	0	0	0	2	4	0	.167	.286	.167
Paul Burris	C2	R	24	2	4	0	2	0	0	0	0	0	0	0	.500	.500	.500
Ray Sanders		L	31	5	4	0	1	0	0	0	2	1	0	0	.250	.400	.250

Pitcher	T	Age	G	GS	CG	ShO	IP	H	HR	BB	SO	W-L	Sv	ERA
Johnny Sain	R	30	42	39	28	4	314.2	297	19	83	137	24-15	1	2.60
Warren Spahn	L	27	36	35	16	3	257.0	237	19	77	114	15-12	1	3.71
Bill Voiselle	R	29	37	30	9	2	215.2	226	18	90	89	13-13	2	3.63
Vern Bickford	R	27	33	22	10	1	146.0	125	9	63	60	11-5	1	3.27
Johnny Beazley	R	30	3	2	0	0	16.0	19	2	7	4	0-1	0	4.50
Glenn Elliott	L	28	1	1	0	0	3.0	5	0	1	2	1-0	0	3.00
Bobby Hogue	R	27	40	1	0	0	86.1	88	4	19	43	8-2	2	3.23
Clyde Shoun	L	36	36	2	1	0	74.0	77	7	20	25	5-1	4	4.01
Red Barrett	R	33	34	13	3	0	128.1	132	9	26	40	7-8	0	3.65
Nels Potter†	R	36	18	7	3	0	85.0	77	4	8	47	5-2	2	2.33
Ernie White	L	31	15	0	0	0	23.0	13	0	17	8	0-2	2	1.96
Jim Prendergast	L	30	10	2	0	0	16.2	30	1	5	3	1-1	1	10.26
Al Lyons	R	29	7	0	0	0	12.2	17	1	8	5	1-0	0	7.82
Johnny Antonelli	L	18	4	0	0	0	4.0	2	0	3	0	0-0	1	2.25
Ed Wright	R	29	3	0	0	0	4.2	9	0	2	2	0-0	0	1.93
Ray Martin	R	23	2	0	0	0	2.1	0	0	1	0	0-0	0	0.00

1948 St. Louis Cardinals 2nd NL 85-69 .552 6.5 GB

Eddie Dyer

Player	Gm by Position	B	Age	G	AB	R	H	2B	3B	HR	RBI	BB	SO	SB	Avg	OBP	Slg
Del Rice	C99	R	25	100	290	24	57	10	1	4	34	37	46	1	.197	.298	.279
Nippy Jones	1B128	R	23	132	481	58	122	21	9	10	81	36	45	2	.254	.307	.397
Red Schoendienst	2B96	S	25	119	408	64	111	21	4	4	36	28	16	1	.272	.319	.373
Don Lang	3B95,2B2	R	33	117	323	30	87	14	1	4	31	47	38	2	.269	.364	.356
Marty Marion	SS142	R	30	144	567	70	143	26	4	4	43	37	54	1	.252	.298	.333
Stan Musial	OF155,1B2	L	27	155	611	135	230	46	18	39	131	79	34	7	.376	.450	.702
Enos Slaughter	OF146	L	32	146	549	91	176	27	11	11	90	81	29	4	.321	.409	.470
Terry Moore	OF71	R	36	91	207	30	48	11	0	4	18	27	12	0	.232	.321	.343
Erv Dusak	OF68,2B29,3B9*	R	27	114	311	60	65	9	2	6	19	49	55	3	.209	.317	.309
Ron Northey	OF67	L	28	96	246	40	79	10	1	13	64	38	25	0	.321	.420	.528
Ralph Lapointe	2B44,SS25,3B1	R	26	87	222	27	50	3	0	0	15	18	19	1	.225	.283	.239
Whitey Kurowski	3B65	R	30	77	220	34	47	8	0	2	33	42	28	0	.214	.352	.277
Bill Baker	C36	R	37	45	119	13	35	10	1	0	15	15	7	1	.294	.373	.395
Babe Young†	1B35	L	32	41	111	14	27	5	2	1	13	16	6	0	.243	.339	.351
Del Wilber	C26	R	29	27	58	5	11	2	0	0	10	4	9	0	.190	.242	.224
Joe Garagiola	C23	L	22	24	56	9	6	1	0	2	7	12	9	0	.107	.275	.232
Hal Rice	OF8	L	24	8	31	3	10	1	2	0	3	2	4	0	.323	.364	.484
Eddie Kazak	3B6	R	27	6	22	1	6	3	0	0	2	0	2	0	.273	.273	.409
Joe Medwick	OF1	R	36	20	19	0	4	0	0	0	2	1	2	0	.211	.250	.211
Chuck Diering	OF5	R	25	7	7	2	0	0	0	0	0	2	2	1	.000	.222	.000
Larry Miggins		R	22	1	1	1	0	0	0	0	0	0	0	0	.000	.000	.000
Bobby Young	3B1	L	23	3	1	0	0	0	0	0	0	0	1	0	.000	.000	.000
Johnny Bucha	C1	R	23	2	1	0	0	0	0	0	0	1	0	0	.000	.500	.000
Jeff Cross†		R	29	2	0	0	0	0	0	0	0	0	0	0	—	—	—

E. Dusak, 1 G at P, 1 G at SS

Pitcher	T	Age	G	GS	CG	ShO	IP	H	HR	BB	SO	W-L	Sv	ERA
Harry Brecheen	L	33	33	30	21	7	233.1	193	6	49	149	20-7	1	2.24
Murry Dickson	R	31	42	29	11	1	252.1	257	39	85	113	12-16	1	4.14
Howie Pollet	L	27	36	26	11	0	186.1	216	10	67	80	13-8	0	4.54
George Munger	R	29	39	25	7	2	166.0	179	13	74	72	10-11	0	4.50
Al Brazle	L	34	42	23	6	3	156.1	171	8	50	55	10-6	1	3.80
Ted Wilks	R	32	57	2	1	0	130.2	113	4	39	71	6-6	13	2.62
Jim Hearn	R	27	34	13	3	0	89.2	92	9	35	27	8-6	1	4.22
Gerry Staley	R	27	31	3	0	0	52.0	61	5	21	23	4-4	0	6.92
Ken Burkhart†	R	31	20	0	0	0	37.1	50	4	14	16	0-0	1	5.54
Ken Johnson	L	25	13	4	0	0	45.1	43	1	30	20	2-4	0	4.76
Al Papai	R	31	10	0	0	0	16.0	14	3	7	8	0-1	0	5.06
Ray Yochim	R	25	1	0	0	0	1.0	0	0	3	1	0-0	0	0.00
Erv Dusak	R	27	1	0	0	0	1.0	0	0	1	0	0-0	0	0.00
Clarence Beers	R	29	1	0	0	0	0.2	3	0	1	0	0-0	0	13.50

1948 Brooklyn Dodgers 3rd NL 84-70 .545 7.5 GB

Leo Durocher (35-37)/Ray Blades (1-0)/Burt Shotton (48-33)

Player	Gm by Position	B	Age	G	AB	R	H	2B	3B	HR	RBI	BB	SO	SB	Avg	OBP	Slg
Roy Campanella	C78	R	26	83	279	32	72	11	3	9	45	36	45	3	.258	.345	.416
Gil Hodges	1B96,C38	R	24	134	481	48	120	18	5	11	70	43	61	7	.249	.311	.376
Jackie Robinson	2B116,1B30,3B6	R	29	147	574	108	170	38	8	12	85	57	37	22	.296	.367	.453
Billy Cox	3B70,SS6,2B1	R	28	88	237	36	59	13	2	3	15	38	19	3	.249	.353	.359
Pee Wee Reese	SS149	R	29	151	566	96	155	31	4	9	75	79	63	25	.274	.363	.390
Gene Hermanski	OF119	L	28	133	400	63	116	22	7	15	60	64	46	15	.290	.391	.493
Carl Furillo	OF104	R	26	108	364	55	108	20	4	4	44	43	32	6	.297	.374	.407
Marv Rackley	OF74	L	26	88	281	55	92	13	5	0	15	19	25	8	.327	.370	.409
Bruce Edwards	C48,OF21,3B14*	R	24	96	286	36	79	17	2	8	54	26	28	4	.276	.341	.434
Eddie Miksis	2B54,3B22,SS5	R	21	86	221	28	47	7	1	2	16	19	27	5	.213	.278	.281
Dick Whitman	OF48	L	27	60	165	24	48	13	0	0	20	14	12	4	.291	.346	.370
George Shuba	OF56	L	23	63	161	21	43	6	0	4	32	34	31	1	.267	.395	.379
Duke Snider	OF47	L	21	53	160	22	39	6	6	5	21	12	27	4	.244	.297	.450
Preston Ward	1B38	L	20	42	146	9	38	9	2	1	21	15	23	0	.260	.329	.370
Tommy Brown	3B43,1B1	R	20	54	145	18	35	4	0	2	20	7	17	1	.241	.281	.310
Pete Reiser	OF30,3B4	L	29	64	127	17	30	8	2	1	19	29	21	4	.236	.382	.354
Arky Vaughan	OF26,3B8	L	36	65	123	19	30	3	0	3	22	21	8	0	.244	.354	.341
Spider Jorgensen	3B24	L	28	31	90	15	27	6	2	1	13	16	13	1	.300	.411	.444
Don Lund†	OF25	R	25	27	69	9	13	4	0	1	5	5	16	1	.188	.243	.290
Gene Mauch†	2B7,SS1	R	22	12	13	1	2	0	0	0	0	1	4	0	.154	.214	.154
Bobby Bragan	C5	R	30	9	12	0	2	0	0	0	0	1	0	0	.167	.231	.167
Bob Ramazzotti	3B2,2B1	R	31	4	3	0	0	0	0	0	0	0	1	0	.000	.000	.000

B. Edwards, 1 G at 1B

Pitcher	T	Age	G	GS	CG	ShO	IP	H	HR	BB	SO	W-L	Sv	ERA
Rex Barney	R	23	44	34	12	4	246.2	193	17	122	138	15-13	0	3.10
Joe Hatten	L	31	42	30	11	1	208.2	228	9	94	73	13-10	0	3.58
Ralph Branca	R	22	36	28	11	1	215.2	189	24	80	122	14-9	1	3.51
Preacher Roe	L	33	34	22	8	2	177.2	156	14	33	86	12-8	2	2.63
Harry Taylor	R	29	17	13	2	0	80.2	90	8	61	32	2-7	0	5.36
Carl Erskine	R	21	17	9	3	0	64.0	51	5	35	29	6-3	0	3.23
Jack Banta	R	23	2	1	0	0	3.1	5	0	5	1	0-1	0	8.10
Erv Palica	R	20	41	10	3	0	125.1	111	13	58	74	6-6	3	4.45
Hank Behrman	R	27	34	4	2	1	91.0	95	7	42	42	5-4	7	4.05
Paul Minner	L	24	28	2	0	0	62.2	61	5	26	23	4-3	1	2.44
Willie Ramsdell	R	32	27	1	0	0	50.1	48	6	41	34	4-4	4	5.19
Hugh Casey	R	34	22	0	0	0	36.0	59	6	17	7	3-0	4	8.00
Clyde King	R	23	9	0	0	0	12.1	14	3	6	5	0-1	0	8.03
Dwain Sloat	L	29	4	1	0	0	7.1	7	0	8	1	0-1	0	6.14
Johnny Van Cuyk	L	26	3	0	0	0	5.0	4	1	1	1	0-0	0	3.60
John Hall	R	24	3	0	0	0	4.1	4	1	2	2	0-0	0	6.23
Elmer Sexauer	R	22	2	0	0	0	0.2	0	0	2	0	0-0	0	13.50
Phil Haugstad	R	24	1	0	0	0	1.0	1	0	0	0	0-0	0	0.00

1948 Pittsburgh Pirates 4th NL 83-71 .539 8.5 GB

Billy Meyer

Player	Gm by Position	B	Age	G	AB	R	H	2B	3B	HR	RBI	BB	SO	SB	Avg	OBP	Slg
Ed Fitz Gerald	C96	R	24	102	262	31	70	9	3	1	35	32	37	3	.267	.349	.336
Ed Stevens	1B117	L	23	128	429	47	109	19	6	10	69	35	53	4	.254	.313	.396
Danny Murtaugh	2B146	R	30	146	514	56	149	21	5	1	71	60	40	10	.290	.365	.356
Frankie Gustine	3B118	R	28	131	449	68	120	19	2	9	42	42	62	5	.267	.333	.379
Stan Rojek	SS156	R	29	156	641	85	186	27	5	4	51	61	41	24	.290	.355	.367
Ralph Kiner	OF154	R	25	156	555	104	147	19	5	40	123	112	61	1	.265	.391	.533
Wally Westlake	OF125	R	27	132	428	78	122	10	6	17	65	46	40	2	.285	.360	.456
Dixie Walker	OF112	L	37	129	408	39	129	19	3	2	54	52	18	1	.316	.393	.392
Johnny Hopp	OF80,1B25	L	31	120	392	64	109	15	12	1	31	40	25	5	.278	.345	.385
Clyde Kluttz	C91	R	30	94	271	26	60	12	2	4	20	20	19	3	.221	.275	.325
Eddie Bockman	3B51,2B1	R	27	70	176	23	42	7	1	4	23	17	35	2	.239	.309	.358
Max West	1B32,OF16	L	31	87	146	19	26	4	0	8	21	27	29	1	.178	.310	.370
Ted Beard	OF22	L	27	25	81	15	16	1	3	0	7	12	18	5	.198	.316	.284
Monty Basgall	2B22	R	26	38	51	12	11	1	0	2	6	3	5	0	.216	.259	.353
Johnny Riddle	C10	R	42	10	15	1	3	0	0	0	0	1	2	0	.200	.250	.200
Grady Wilson	SS7	R	25	12	10	1	1	1	0	0	1	0	3	0	.100	.100	.200
Pete Castiglione	SS1	R	27	4	2	0	0	0	0	0	0	0	0	1	.000	.000	.000
Don Gutteridge		R	36	4	2	0	0	0	0	0	0	0	1	0	.000	.000	.000
Earl Turner	C1	R	25	2	1	0	0	0	0	0	0	0	0	0	.000	.000	.000

Pitcher	T	Age	G	GS	CG	ShO	IP	H	HR	BB	SO	W-L	Sv	ERA
Elmer Riddle	R	33	28	27	12	3	191.0	184	20	81	63	12-10	1	3.49
Bob Chesnes	R	27	25	23	15	0	194.1	180	13	90	69	14-6	0	3.57
Fritz Ostermueller	L	40	23	22	10	2	134.1	143	13	41	43	8-11	0	4.42
Tiny Bonham	R	34	22	20	7	0	135.2	145	18	23	42	6-10	0	4.31
Rip Sewell	R	41	21	17	7	0	121.2	126	9	37	36	13-3	0	3.48
Cal McLish	R	22	2	1	0	0	5.0	8	0	2	1	0-0	0	9.00
Kirby Higbe	R	33	56	8	3	0	158.0	140	11	83	86	8-7	10	3.36
Vic Lombardi	L	25	38	17	9	0	163.0	156	9	67	54	10-9	4	3.70
Elmer Singleton	R	30	38	5	1	0	92.1	90	12	40	53	4-6	2	4.97
Mel Queen	R	30	25	8	0	0	66.1	82	8	40	34	4-4	1	6.65
Hal Gregg	R	26	22	8	1	0	74.1	72	3	34	25	2-4	1	4.60
Woody Main	R	26	17	0	0	0	27.0	35	4	19	12	1-1	0	8.33
Nick Strincevich†	R	33	3	0	0	0	4.1	8	0	2	1	0-0	0	8.31
Junior Walsh	R	29	2	0	0	0	4.1	4	1	5	0	1-0	0	10.38

1948 New York Giants 5th NL 78-76 .506 13.5 GB

Mel Ott (37-38)/Leo Durocher (41-38)

Player	Gm by Position	B	Age	G	AB	R	H	2B	3B	HR	RBI	BB	SO	SB	Avg	OBP	Slg
Walker Cooper	C79	R	33	91	290	40	77	12	0	16	54	28	29	1	.266	.332	.472
Johnny Mize	1B152	L	35	152	560	110	162	26	4	40	125	94	37	4	.289	.395	.564
Bill Rigney	2B105,SS7	R	30	113	424	72	112	17	3	10	43	47	54	4	.264	.342	.389
Sid Gordon	3B115,OF23	R	30	142	521	100	156	26	4	30	107	74	39	8	.299	.390	.537
Buddy Kerr	SS143	R	25	144	496	41	119	16	4	0	46	56	36	9	.240	.317	.288
Whitey Lockman	OF144	L	21	146	584	117	167	24	10	18	59	68	63	8	.286	.361	.454
Willard Marshall	OF142	L	27	143	537	72	146	21	8	14	86	64	34	2	.272	.350	.419
Bobby Thomson	OF125	R	24	138	471	75	117	20	2	16	63	30	77	2	.248	.296	.401
Jack Lohrke	3B50,2B36	R	24	97	280	35	70	15	1	5	31	30	30	3	.250	.323	.364
Wes Westrum	C63	R	25	66	125	14	20	3	1	4	16	20	36	3	.160	.276	.296
Mickey Livingston	C42	R	33	45	99	9	21	4	1	2	12	21	12	0	.212	.350	.333
Les Layton	OF20	R	26	63	91	14	21	4	4	2	12	6	21	1	.231	.286	.429
Don Mueller	OF22	L	21	36	81	12	29	4	1	1	9	0	3	0	.358	.358	.469
Johnny McCarthy	1B6	L	38	56	57	6	15	0	1	2	12	3	2	0	.263	.300	.404
Lonny Frey†	2B13	L	37	29	51	6	13	1	0	1	6	4	6	0	.255	.309	.333
Jack Conway	2B13,SS6,3B3	R	28	24	49	8	12	2	1	1	3	5	10	0	.245	.315	.388
Rocky Rhawn	SS14,3B7	R	29	36	44	11	12	2	1	2	8	8	6	3	.273	.385	.432
Sal Yvars	C15	R	24	15	38	4	8	1	0	1	6	3	0	0	.211	.286	.316
Pete Milne	OF9	L	23	12	27	0	6	0	1	0	2	1	6	0	.222	.250	.296
Buddy Blattner	2B7	R	28	8	20	3	4	1	0	0	0	3	2	0	.200	.304	.250
Hal Bamberger	OF3	L	23	7	12	0	1	0	0	0	0	1	2	0	.083	.154	.083
Jack Harshman	1B3	L	20	5	8	0	2	0	0	0	1	1	3	0	.250	.333	.250
Joe Lafata		L	26	1	1	0	0	0	0	0	0	0	1	0	.000	.000	.000

Pitcher	T	Age	G	GS	CG	ShO	IP	H	HR	BB	SO	W-L	Sv	ERA
Larry Jansen	R	27	42	36	15	4	277.0	283	25	54	126	18-12	2	3.61
Ray Poat	R	30	39	24	7	3	157.2	162	21	67	57	11-10	0	4.34
Clint Hartung	R	25	36	19	6	2	153.1	146	15	72	42	8-8	1	4.75
Dave Koslo	L	28	35	18	5	3	149.0	168	7	62	58	8-10	3	3.87
Monte Kennedy	L	26	25	16	7	1	114.1	118	10	57	63	3-9	0	4.01
Red Webb	R	23	5	3	2	0	28.0	27	2	10	9	2-1	0	3.21
Sheldon Jones	R	26	55	21	8	2	201.1	204	16	90	82	16-8	5	3.35
Ken Trinkle	R	28	53	0	0	0	70.2	66	6	41	20	4-5	7	3.18
Andy Hansen	R	23	36	9	3	0	100.0	96	4	36	27	5-3	1	2.97
Alex Konikowski	R	20	22	1	0	0	33.1	46	7	17	9	2-3	1	7.56
Thornton Lee	L	41	11	4	1	0	32.2	41	3	12	17	1-3	0	4.41
Bobo Newsom	R	40	11	4	0	0	25.2	35	1	13	9	0-4	0	4.21
Clem Dreisewerd†	L	32	4	0	0	0	12.2	17	3	5	2	0-1	1	5.68
Mickey McGowan	L	26	3	0	0	0	3.2	3	1	4	2	0-0	0	7.36
Lou Lombardo	L	19	2	0	0	0	5.1	5	1	5	0	0-0	0	6.75
Jack Hallett	R	33	2	0	0	0	4.0	3	0	4	3	0-0	0	4.50
Paul Erickson†	R	32	2	0	0	0	1.0	0	0	2	1	0-0	0	0.00
Hub Andrews	R	25	1	0	0	0	3.0	3	0	0	0	0-0	0	0.00
Joe Beggs	R	37	1	0	0	0	0.1	2	0	0	0	0-0	0	0.00

708 Seasons: Team Rosters

1948 Philadelphia Phillies 6th NL 66-88 .429 25.5 GB

Ben Chapman (37-42)/Dusty Cooke (6-6)/Eddie Sawyer (23-40)

Player	Gm by Position	B	Age	G	AB	R	H	2B	3B	HR	RBI	BB	SO	SB	Avg	OBP	Slg
Andy Seminick	C124	R	27	125	391	49	88	11	3	13	44	58	68	4	.225	.328	.368
Dick Sisler	1B120	L	27	121	446	60	122	21	3	11	56	47	46	1	.274	.344	.408
Granny Hamner	2B87,SS37,3B3	R	21	129	446	42	116	21	5	3	48	22	39	2	.260	.298	.350
Putsy Caballero	3B79,2B23	R	20	113	351	33	86	12	1	0	19	24	18	7	.245	.293	.285
Eddie Miller	SS122	R	31	130	468	45	115	20	1	14	61	19	40	1	.246	.281	.382
Del Ennis	OF151	R	23	152	589	86	171	40	4	30	95	47	58	2	.290	.345	.525
Richie Ashburn	OF116	L	21	117	463	78	154	17	4	2	40	60	22	32	.333	.410	.400
Johnny Blatnik	OF105	R	27	121	415	56	108	27	8	6	45	31	77	3	.260	.315	.407
Bert Haas	3B54,1B35	R	34	95	333	35	94	9	2	4	34	36	25	8	.282	.354	.357
Harry Walker	OF81,1B4,3B1	L	31	112	332	34	97	11	2	2	23	33	30	4	.292	.358	.355
Bama Rowell	3B18,OF17,2B12	L	32	77	196	15	47	16	2	1	22	8	14	2	.240	.270	.357
Emil Verban†	2B54	R	32	55	169	14	39	5	1	0	11	11	5	0	.231	.282	.272
Don Padgett	C19	L	36	36	74	3	17	3	0	0	7	3	2	0	.230	.260	.270
Al Lakeman	C22,P1	R	29	32	68	2	11	2	0	1	4	5	22	0	.162	.219	.235
Puddin' Head Jones	3B17	R	22	17	60	9	20	2	0	2	9	3	5	0	.333	.365	.467
Jackie Mayo	OF11	L	22	12	35	7	8	2	1	0	3	7	7	1	.229	.386	.343
Stan Lopata	C4	R	22	6	15	2	2	1	0	0	2	0	4	0	.133	.133	.200
Howie Schultz†	1B3	R	25	6	13	0	1	0	0	0	1	1	2	0	.077	.143	.077
Hal Wagner†	C1	L	32	3	4	0	0	0	0	0	0	0	0	0	.000	.000	.000

Pitcher	T	Age	G	GS	CG	ShO	IP	H	HR	BB	SO	W-L	Sv	ERA
Dutch Leonard	R	39	34	31	16	1	225.2	226	9	54	92	12-17	0	2.51
Curt Simmons	L	19	31	22	7	0	170.0	169	8	108	86	7-13	0	4.87
Schoolboy Rowe	R	38	30	20	8	0	148.0	167	5	31	46	10-10	2	4.07
Robin Roberts	R	21	20	20	9	0	146.2	148	10	61	84	7-9	0	3.19
Blix Donnelly	R	34	26	19	8	1	131.2	125	13	49	46	5-7	2	3.69
Ken Heintzelman	L	32	27	16	5	2	130.0	117	10	45	57	6-11	2	4.29
Paul Erickson†	R	32	4	2	0	0	17.1	19	2	17	5	2-0	0	5.19
Lou Possehl	R	22	3	2	1	0	14.2	17	3	4	7	1-1	0	4.91
Jocko Thompson	L	31	2	2	1	0	13.0	10	0	9	7	1-0	0	2.77
Monk Dubiel	R	30	37	17	6	2	150.1	139	13	58	42	8-10	4	3.89
Ed Heusser	R	39	33	0	0	0	74.0	89	9	28	22	3-2	3	4.99
Sam Nahem	R	32	28	1	0	0	59.0	68	4	45	30	3-3	0	7.02
Charlie Bicknell	R	19	17	1	0	0	25.2	29	5	17	5	0-1	0	5.96
Nick Strincevich†	R	33	6	1	0	0	16.2	26	1	10	4	0-1	0	9.18
Jim Konstanty	R	31	6	0	0	0	9.2	7	0	2	7	1-0	2	0.93
Oscar Judd	L	40	4	1	0	0	14.1	19	1	11	7	0-2	0	6.91
Dick Koecher	L	22	3	0	0	0	6.0	4	0	3	2	0-1	0	3.00
Al Porto	L	22	3	0	0	0	4.0	2	0	1	1	0-0	0	0.00
Lou Grasmick	R	23	2	0	0	0	5.0	3	1	8	2	0-0	0	7.20
Al Lakeman	R	29	1	0	0	0	0.2	1	1	0	0	0-0	0	13.50

1948 Cincinnati Reds 7th NL 64-89 .418 27.0 GB

Johnny Neun (44-56)/Bucky Walters (20-33)

Player	Gm by Position	B	Age	G	AB	R	H	2B	3B	HR	RBI	BB	SO	SB	Avg	OBP	Slg
Ray Lamanno	C125	R	28	127	385	31	93	12	0	0	27	48	32	2	.242	.329	.273
Ted Kluszewski	1B98	L	23	113	379	49	104	23	4	12	57	18	32	1	.274	.307	.451
Bobby Adams	2B64,3B7	R	26	87	262	33	78	20	3	1	21	25	23	6	.298	.361	.408
Grady Hatton	3B123,2B3,SS2*	L	25	133	458	58	110	17	2	9	44	72	50	7	.240	.343	.345
Virgil Stallcup	SS148	R	26	149	539	40	123	30	4	3	65	18	52	2	.228	.253	.315
Hank Sauer	OF132,1B12	R	31	145	530	78	138	22	1	35	97	60	85	2	.260	.340	.504
Johnny Wyrostek	OF130	L	28	136	512	74	140	24	9	17	76	52	63	7	.273	.344	.455
Frankie Baumholtz	OF110	L	29	128	415	57	123	19	5	4	30	27	32	8	.296	.344	.395
Danny Litwhiler†	OF83,3B15	R	31	106	338	51	93	19	2	14	44	48	41	1	.275	.365	.467
Claude Corbitt	2B52,3B16,SS11	R	32	87	258	24	66	11	0	0	18	14	16	4	.256	.297	.298
Benny Zientara	2B60,3B3,SS2	R	28	74	187	17	35	1	2	0	7	12	11	0	.187	.236	.214
Babe Young†	1B31,OF1	L	32	49	130	11	30	7	2	1	12	19	12	0	.231	.329	.338
Dewey Williams	C47	R	32	48	95	9	16	2	0	1	5	10	18	0	.168	.248	.221
Augie Galan	OF18	S	36	54	77	18	22	3	2	2	16	26	4	0	.286	.471	.455
Howie Schultz†	1B26	R	25	36	72	9	12	0	0	2	9	4	7	2	.167	.211	.250
Ray Mueller	C10	R	36	14	34	2	7	1	0	0	2	4	3	0	.206	.289	.235
Steve Filipowicz	OF7	R	27	7	26	0	9	0	1	0	3	2	1	0	.346	.393	.423
Clyde Vollmer†	OF2	R	26	7	9	0	1	0	0	0	0	1	1	0	.111	.200	.111
Marv Rickert†		L	27	8	6	0	1	0	0	0	0	0	0	0	.167	.167	.167
Hugh Poland		L	35	3	3	0	1	0	0	0	0	0	0	0	.333	.333	.333

G. Hatton, 1 G at OF

Pitcher	T	Age	G	GS	CG	ShO	IP	H	HR	BB	SO	W-L	Sv	ERA
J. Vander Meer	L	33	33	33	14	3	232.0	204	15	124	120	17-14	0	3.41
Ken Raffensberger	L	30	40	24	7	4	180.1	187	15	37	57	11-12	0	3.84
Howie Fox	R	27	34	24	5	0	171.0	185	11	62	63	6-9	1	4.53
Herm Wehmeier	R	21	33	24	6	0	147.1	179	21	75	56	11-8	0	5.86
Ewell Blackwell	R	25	22	20	4	1	138.2	134	12	52	114	7-9	1	4.54
Bucky Walters	R	39	7	5	1	0	35.0	42	7	18	19	0-3	0	4.63
Harry Gumbert	R	38	61	0	0	0	106.1	123	5	34	25	10-8	17	3.47
Kent Peterson	L	22	43	17	2	0	137.0	146	10	59	64	2-15	1	4.60
Walker Cress	R	31	30	2	1	0	60.0	60	2	42	33	0-1	0	4.50
Bud Burkhart†	R	31	16	0	0	0	41.2	42	3	16	14	0-3	0	6.91
Jim Blackburn	R	24	16	0	0	0	32.1	38	1	14	10	0-2	0	4.18
Tommy Hughes	R	28	12	4	0	0	27.0	43	3	24	7	0-4	0	9.00
Buddy Lively	R	23	10	0	0	0	22.2	13	0	11	12	0-0	0	2.38
Johnny Hetki	R	26	3	0	0	0	6.2	8	0	3	3	0-1	0	9.45
Eddie Erautt	R	23	2	0	0	0	3.0	3	0	1	0	0-0	0	6.00
Ken Holcombe	R	29	2	0	0	0	2.1	3	0	0	2	0-0	0	7.71

1948 Chicago Cubs 8th NL 64-90 .416 27.5 GB

Charlie Grimm

Player	Gm by Position	B	Age	G	AB	R	H	2B	3B	HR	RBI	BB	SO	SB	Avg	OBP	Slg
Bob Scheffing	C78	R	34	102	293	23	88	18	2	5	45	22	27	0	.300	.351	.427
Eddie Waitkus	1B116,OF20	L	28	139	562	87	166	27	10	7	44	43	19	11	.295	.348	.416
Hank Schenz	2B78,3B5	R	29	96	337	43	88	17	1	1	14	18	15	3	.261	.306	.326
Andy Pafko	3B139	R	27	142	548	82	171	30	2	26	101	50	50	3	.312	.375	.516
Roy Smalley	SS124	R	22	124	361	25	78	11	4	4	36	23	76	0	.216	.265	.302
Bill Nicholson	OF136	L	33	143	494	68	129	24	5	19	67	81	60	2	.261	.371	.445
Hal Jeffcoat	OF119	R	23	134	473	53	132	16	4	4	42	24	68	8	.279	.315	.355
Peanuts Lowrey	OF103,3B9,2B2*	R	29	129	435	47	128	12	3	2	54	34	31	2	.294	.347	.349
Phil Cavarretta	1B41,OF40	L	31	111	334	41	93	16	5	3	40	35	29	4	.278	.349	.383
Emil Verban†	2B56	R	32	56	248	37	73	15	1	1	16	4	7	4	.294	.308	.375
Clarence Maddern	OF55	R	26	80	214	16	54	12	1	4	27	10	25	0	.252	.301	.374
Clyde McCullough	C51	R	31	69	172	10	36	4	2	1	7	15	25	0	.209	.273	.273
Rube Walker	C44	L	22	79	171	17	47	8	0	5	26	24	17	0	.275	.371	.409
Gene Mauch†	2B26,SS19	R	22	53	138	18	28	3	2	1	7	26	10	1	.203	.329	.275
Dick Culler	SS43,2B2	R	33	48	89	4	15	2	0	0	5	13	3	0	.169	.275	.191
Cliff Aberson	OF8	R	26	12	32	1	6	1	0	1	6	5	10	0	.188	.297	.313
Jeff Cross†	SS9,2B1	R	29	16	20	1	2	0	0	0	0	0	4	0	.100	.100	.100
Don Johnson	2B2,3B2	R	36	6	12	0	3	0	0	0	0	0	1	1	.250	.250	.250
Danny Lynch	2B1	R	22	7	7	3	2	0	0	1	1	1	1	0	.286	.375	.714
Carmen Mauro	OF2	L	21	3	5	2	1	0	0	1	1	2	0	0	.200	.429	.800
Carl Sawatski		L	20	2	2	0	0	0	0	0	0	0	0	0	.000	.000	.000

P. Lowrey, 1 G at SS

Pitcher	T	Age	G	GS	CG	ShO	IP	H	HR	BB	SO	W-L	Sv	ERA
Johnny Schmitz	L	27	34	30	18	2	242.0	186	11	97	100	18-13	1	2.64
Russ Meyer	R	24	29	26	8	3	164.2	157	8	77	89	10-10	0	3.66
Dutch McCall	L	27	30	20	5	0	151.1	158	14	85	89	4-13	0	4.82
Ralph Hamner	R	31	27	17	5	0	111.1	110	12	69	53	5-9	0	4.69
Doyle Lade	R	27	19	12	6	0	87.1	99	4	31	29	5-6	0	4.02
Jess Dobernic	R	30	54	0	0	0	85.2	67	8	40	48	7-2	1	3.15
Hank Borowy	R	32	39	17	2	1	127.0	156	9	49	50	5-10	1	4.89
Bob Rush	R	22	36	16	4	0	133.1	153	8	37	72	5-11	0	3.92
Emil Kush	R	31	34	1	0	0	72.0	70	4	37	31	1-4	3	4.38
Bob Chipman	L	29	34	3	0	0	60.1	73	5	24	16	2-1	4	3.58
Cliff Chambers	L	26	29	12	3	1	103.2	100	4	48	51	2-9	0	4.43
Paul Erickson†	R	32	3	0	0	0	5.2	7	0	6	4	0-0	0	6.35
Warren Hacker	R	23	3	1	0	0	3.0	7	0	3	0	0-1	0	21.00
Ben Wade	R	25	2	0	0	0	5.0	4	0	4	1	0-1	0	7.20
Tony Jacobs	R	22	1	0	0	0	2.0	3	1	0	2	0-0	0	4.50
Don Carlsen	R	21	1	0	0	0	1.0	5	0	2	1	0-0	0	36.00

»1949 New York Yankees 1st AL 97-57 .630 —

Casey Stengel

Player	Gm by Position	B	Age	G	AB	R	H	2B	3B	HR	RBI	BB	SO	SB	Avg	OBP	Slg
Yogi Berra	C109	L	24	116	415	59	115	20	2	20	91	22	25	2	.277	.323	.480
Tommy Henrich	OF61,1B52	L	36	115	411	90	118	20	3	24	85	86	34	2	.287	.416	.526
Jerry Coleman	2B122,SS4	R	24	128	447	54	123	21	5	2	42	63	44	8	.275	.367	.358
Bobby Brown	3B86,OF3	L	24	104	343	61	97	14	4	6	61	38	18	4	.283	.359	.399
Phil Rizzuto	SS152	R	31	153	614	110	169	22	7	5	65	72	34	18	.275	.352	.358
Cliff Mapes	OF108	L	27	111	304	56	75	13	3	7	38	58	50	6	.247	.369	.378
Gene Woodling	OF98	L	26	112	296	60	80	13	7	5	44	52	21	2	.270	.381	.412
Hank Bauer	OF95	R	26	103	301	56	82	6	6	10	45	37	42	2	.272	.354	.432
Bill Johnson	3B81,1B21,2B1	R	30	113	329	48	82	11	3	8	56	48	44	1	.249	.348	.374
Joe DiMaggio	OF76	R	34	76	272	58	94	14	6	14	67	55	18	0	.346	.459	.596
Johnny Lindell	OF65	R	32	78	211	33	51	10	6	6	27	35	27	3	.242	.350	.374
Dick Kryhoski	1B51	L	24	54	177	18	52	10	3	1	27	9	17	2	.294	.335	.401
Snuffy Stirnweiss	2B51,3B4	R	30	70	157	29	41	8	2	0	11	29	20	3	.261	.380	.338
Charlie Silvera	C51	R	24	58	130	8	41	2	0	0	13	18	5	2	.315	.403	.331
Charlie Keller	OF31	L	32	60	116	17	29	4	1	3	16	25	15	2	.250	.392	.379
Jack Phillips†	1B38	R	27	45	91	16	28	4	1	1	10	12	9	1	.308	.388	.407
Gus Niarhos	C30	R	28	32	43	7	12	2	1	0	6	13	8	0	.279	.456	.372
Fenton Mole	1B8	L	24	10	27	2	5	2	1	0	2	3	5	0	.185	.267	.333
Johnny Mize†	1B6	L	36	13	23	4	6	1	0	1	2	4	2	0	.261	.393	.435
Jim Delsing	OF5	L	23	9	20	5	7	1	0	1	3	1	2	0	.350	.381	.550
Joe Collins	1B5	L	26	7	10	2	1	0	0	0	4	6	2	0	.100	.438	.100
Ralph Houk	C5	R	29	5	7	0	4	0	0	0	0	1	0	0	.571	.571	.571
Mickey Witek		R	33	1	1	0	1	0	0	0	0	0	0	0	1.000	1.000	1.000

Pitcher	T	Age	G	GS	CG	ShO	IP	H	HR	BB	SO	W-L	Sv	ERA
Vic Raschi	R	30	38	37	21	3	274.2	247	16	138	124	21-10	0	3.34
Allie Reynolds	R	34	35	31	4	2	213.2	200	15	123	105	17-6	1	4.00
Ed Lopat	L	31	31	30	14	2	215.1	222	19	69	70	15-10	1	3.26
Tommy Byrne	L	29	32	30	12	3	196.0	125	11	179	129	15-7	0	3.72
Bob Porterfield	R	25	12	8	3	0	57.2	53	3	29	25	2-5	0	4.06
Joe Page	L	31	60	0	0	0	135.1	103	8	75	99	13-8	27	2.59
Fred Sanford	R	29	29	11	3	0	95.1	100	9	57	51	7-3	0	3.87
Cuddles Marshall	R	24	21	2	0	0	49.1	48	3	48	13	3-0	3	5.11
Spec Shea	R	28	20	3	0	0	52.1	48	5	43	22	1-1	1	5.33
Ralph Buxton	R	38	14	0	0	0	26.2	22	3	16	14	0-1	2	4.05
Duane Pillette	R	26	12	3	2	0	37.1	43	6	19	9	2-4	0	4.34
Frank Hiller	R	28	4	0	0	0	7.2	9	0	7	3	0-2	1	5.87
Hugh Casey†	R	35	4	0	0	0	7.2	11	0	8	5	1-0	0	8.22
Wally Hood	R	23	2	0	0	0	2.1	0	0	1	2	0-0	0	0.00

1949 Boston Red Sox 2nd AL 96-58 .623 1.0 GB

Joe McCarthy

Player	Gm by Position	B	Age	G	AB	R	H	2B	3B	HR	RBI	BB	SO	SB	Avg	OBP	Slg
Birdie Tebbetts	C118	R	36	122	403	42	109	14	0	5	48	62	22	8	.270	.369	.342
Billy Goodman	1B117	L	23	122	443	54	132	23	3	0	56	58	21	2	.298	.382	.363
Bobby Doerr	2B139	R	31	139	541	91	167	30	9	18	109	75	33	2	.309	.393	.497
Johnny Pesky	3B148	L	29	148	604	111	185	27	7	2	69	100	19	8	.306	.408	.384
Vern Stephens	SS155	R	28	155	610	113	177	31	2	39	159	101	73	2	.290	.391	.539
Ted Williams	OF155	L	30	155	566	150	194	39	3	43	159	162	48	1	.343	.490	.650
Dom DiMaggio	OF144	R	32	145	605	126	186	34	5	8	60	96	55	9	.307	.404	.420
Al Zarilla†	OF122	L	30	124	474	68	133	32	4	9	71	48	51	4	.281	.352	.422
Matt Batts	C50	R	27	60	157	23	38	9	1	3	31	25	22	1	.242	.350	.369
Billy Hitchcock	1B29,2B8	R	32	55	147	22	30	6	1	0	9	17	11	2	.204	.291	.259
Tommy O'Brien	OF32	R	30	49	125	24	28	5	0	3	10	21	12	1	.224	.336	.336
Sam Mele†	OF11	R	26	18	46	1	9	1	1	0	7	7	14	2	.196	.302	.261
Walt Dropo	1B11	R	26	11	41	3	6	2	0	0	1	3	7	0	.146	.205	.195
Lou Stringer	2B9	R	32	35	41	10	11	4	0	1	6	5	10	0	.268	.348	.439
Merrill Combs	3B9,SS1	L	29	14	24	5	5	1	0	0	1	9	0	0	.208	.424	.250
Stan Spence†	OF5	L	34	7	20	3	3	1	0	0	1	6	1	0	.150	.346	.200
Tom Wright		L	25	5	4	1	1	0	0	0	1	1	0	0	.250	.400	.500
Babe Martin	C1	R	29	2	2	0	0	0	0	0	0	0	0	0	.000	.000	.000

Pitcher	T	Age	G	GS	CG	ShO	IP	H	HR	BB	SO	W-L	Sv	ERA
Mel Parnell	L	27	39	33	27	4	295.1	258	8	134	122	25-7	2	2.77
Ellis Kinder	R	34	43	30	19	6	252.0	251	21	99	138	23-6	4	3.36
Joe Dobson	R	32	33	27	12	2	212.2	219	12	97	87	14-12	2	3.85
Chuck Stobbs	L	19	26	19	10	0	152.0	145	10	75	70	11-6	0	4.03
Jack Kramer	R	31	21	18	7	2	111.2	126	8	49	24	6-8	1	5.16
Mickey McDermott	L	21	12	12	6	2	80.0	63	5	52	50	5-4	0	4.05
Mickey Harris†	L	32	7	6	2	0	37.2	53	3	20	14	2-3	0	5.02
Tex Hughson	R	33	29	2	0	2	77.2	82	5	41	35	4-2	3	5.33
Earl Johnson	L	30	19	3	0	0	49.1	65	1	29	20	3-6	0	7.48
Walt Masterson†	R	29	18	5	1	0	55.0	58	2	35	19	3-4	4	4.25
Frank Quinn	R	21	8	0	0	0	21.0	18	2	9	4	0-0	0	3.00
Windy McCall	L	23	5	0	0	0	9.1	13	2	10	8	0-0	0	11.57
Harry Dorish	R	27	5	0	0	0	7.2	7	1	1	5	0-0	0	2.35
Boo Ferriss	R	27	4	0	0	0	6.2	7	1	4	1	0-0	0	4.05
Jack Robinson	R	28	3	0	0	0	4.0	4	0	1	1	0-0	0	2.25
Denny Galehouse	R	37	2	0	0	0	2.0	4	1	3	0	0-0	0	13.50
Johnnie Wittig	R	35	1	0	0	0	2.0	2	0	2	0	0-0	0	9.00

Seasons: Team Rosters 709

1949 Cleveland Indians 3rd AL 89-65 .578 8.0 GB

Lou Boudreau

Player	Gm by Position	B	Age	G	AB	R	H	2B	3B	HR	RBI	BB	SO	SB	Avg	OBP	Slg
Jim Hegan	C152	R	28	152	468	54	105	19	5	8	55	49	89	1	.224	.298	.338
Mickey Vernon	1B153	L	31	153	584	72	170	27	4	18	83	58	51	9	.291	.357	.443
Joe Gordon	2B145	R	34	148	541	74	136	18	3	20	84	83	33	5	.251	.355	.407
Ken Keltner	3B69	R	32	80	246	35	57	9	2	8	30	38	26	0	.232	.335	.382
Lou Boudreau	SS88,3B38,1B6*	R	31	134	475	53	135	20	3	4	60	70	10	0	.284	.381	.364
Dale Mitchell	OF149	L	27	149	640	81	203	16	23	3	56	43	11	10	.317	.360	.428
Larry Doby	OF147	L	25	147	547	106	153	25	3	24	85	91	90	10	.280	.389	.468
Bob Kennedy	OF98,3B21	R	28	121	424	49	117	23	5	9	57	37	40	5	.276	.334	.417
Ray Boone	SS76	R	25	86	258	39	65	4	4	4	26	38	17	0	.252	.352	.345
Thurman Tucker	OF42	L	31	80	197	28	48	5	2	0	14	18	19	4	.244	.307	.289
Johnny Berardino	3B25,2B8,SS3	R	32	50	116	11	23	6	1	0	13	14	14	0	.198	.295	.267
Allie Clark	OF17,1B1	R	26	35	74	8	13	4	0	1	9	4	7	0	.176	.218	.270
Luke Easter	OF12	L	33	21	45	6	10	3	0	0	2	8	6	0	.222	.340	.289
Al Rosen	3B10	R	25	23	44	3	7	2	0	0	5	7	4	0	.159	.275	.205
Mike Tresh	C38	R	35	38	37	4	8	0	0	0	1	5	7	0	.216	.310	.216
Hal Peck	OF2	L	32	33	29	1	9	1	0	0	9	3	3	0	.310	.375	.345
Minnie Minoso	OF7	R	26	9	16	2	3	0	0	1	1	2	2	0	.188	.350	.375
Hank Edwards†	OF5	L	30	5	15	3	4	0	0	1	1	1	2	0	.267	.313	.467
Bobby Avila	2B5	R	25	31	14	3	3	0	0	0	3	1	3	0	.214	.267	.214
Milt Nielsen	OF3	L	24	3	9	1	1	0	0	0	0	2	4	0	.111	.273	.111
Herman Reich†	OF1	R	31	1	2	0	1	0	0	0	0	1	0	0	.500	.667	.500
Fred Marsh		R	25	1	0	0	0	0	0	0	0	0	0	0	—	—	—

L. Boudreau, 1 G at 2B

Pitcher	T	Age	G	GS	CG	ShO	IP	H	HR	BB	SO	W-L	Sv	ERA
Bob Lemon	R	28	37	33	22	2	279.2	211	19	137	138	22-10	1	2.99
Bob Feller	R	30	36	28	15	0	211.0	198	18	84	108	15-14	0	3.75
Early Wynn	R	29	26	23	6	0	164.2	186	8	57	62	11-7	0	4.15
Gene Bearden	L	28	32	19	5	0	127.0	140	6	92	41	8-8	0	5.10
Mike Garcia	R	25	41	20	8	5	175.2	154	6	60	94	14-5	2	2.36
Al Benton	R	38	40	11	4	2	135.2	116	7	51	41	9-6	10	2.12
Satchel Paige	R	42	31	5	1	0	83.0	70	4	33	54	4-7	5	3.04
Steve Gromek	R	29	27	12	3	0	92.0	86	8	40	22	4-6	0	3.33
Sam Zoldak	L	30	27	0	0	0	53.0	60	4	18	11	1-2	0	4.25
Frank Papish	L	31	25	3	1	0	62.0	54	2	39	23	1-0	1	3.19

1949 Detroit Tigers 4th AL 87-67 .565 10.0 GB

Red Rolfe

Player	Gm by Position	B	Age	G	AB	R	H	2B	3B	HR	RBI	BB	SO	SB	Avg	OBP	Slg
Aaron Robinson	C108	L	34	110	331	38	89	12	0	13	56	73	21	0	.269	.402	.423
Paul Campbell	1B74	L	31	87	255	38	71	15	4	3	30	24	32	3	.278	.343	.404
Neil Berry	2B95,SS4	R	27	109	329	38	78	9	1	0	18	27	24	4	.237	.299	.271
George Kell	3B134	R	26	134	522	97	179	38	9	3	59	71	13	7	.343	.424	.467
Johnny Lipon	SS120	R	26	127	439	57	110	14	6	3	59	75	24	2	.251	.362	.330
Vic Wertz	OF155	L	24	155	608	96	185	26	6	20	133	80	61	2	.304	.385	.465
Hoot Evers	OF123	R	28	132	432	68	131	21	6	7	72	70	38	6	.303	.403	.428
Johnny Groth	OF99	R	22	103	348	60	102	19	5	11	73	65	27	3	.293	.407	.471
Don Kolloway†	2B62,1B57,3B7	R	30	126	483	71	142	19	3	2	47	49	25	7	.294	.361	.358
Pat Mullin	OF79	L	31	104	310	55	83	8	6	12	59	42	29	1	.268	.357	.448
Eddie Lake	SS38,2B19,3B18	R	33	94	240	38	47	9	1	1	15	61	33	2	.196	.359	.254
Bob Swift	C69	R	34	74	189	16	45	6	0	2	18	26	20	0	.238	.330	.302
Sam Vico	1B53	L	25	67	142	15	27	5	2	4	18	21	17	0	.190	.311	.338
Dick Wakefield	OF32	L	28	59	126	17	26	3	1	6	19	32	24	0	.206	.367	.389
Hank Riebe	C11	R	27	17	33	1	6	2	0	0	2	0	5	1	.182	.182	.242
Jimmy Outlaw		R	36	5	4	1	1	0	0	0	0	0	1	0	.250	.250	.250
Don Lund		R	26	2	2	0	0	0	0	0	0	0	1	0	.000	.000	.000
Bob Mavis		L	31	1	0	0	0	0	0	0	0	0	0	0	—	—	—
Earl Rapp†		L	28	1	0	0	0	0	0	0	0	1	0	0	—	1.000	—

Pitcher	T	Age	G	GS	CG	ShO	IP	H	HR	BB	SO	W-L	Sv	ERA
Hal Newhouser	L	28	38	35	22	3	292.0	277	19	111	144	18-11	1	3.36
Virgil Trucks	R	32	41	32	17	6	275.0	209	16	124	153	19-11	4	2.81
Ted Gray	L	24	34	27	8	3	195.0	163	11	103	96	10-10	1	3.51
Art Houtteman	R	21	34	25	13	2	203.2	227	19	59	85	15-10	0	3.71
Fred Hutchinson	R	29	33	21	9	4	188.2	167	18	52	54	15-7	1	2.96
Dizzy Trout	R	34	33	0	0	0	59.1	68	2	21	19	3-6	3	4.40
Marv Grissom	R	31	27	2	0	0	39.1	56	6	34	17	2-4	0	6.41
Lou Kretlow	R	28	25	10	1	0	76.0	85	5	69	40	3-2	0	6.16
Marlin Stuart	R	30	14	2	0	0	29.2	39	3	35	14	0-2	0	9.10
Stubby Overmire	L	30	14	1	0	0	17.1	29	2	9	3	1-3	0	9.87
Hal White	R	30	9	0	0	0	12.0	5	0	4	4	1-0	2	0.00
Saul Rogovin	R	25	5	0	0	0	5.2	13	1	7	2	0-1	0	14.29

1949 Philadelphia Athletics 5th AL 81-73 .526 16.0 GB

Connie Mack

Player	Gm by Position	B	Age	G	AB	R	H	2B	3B	HR	RBI	BB	SO	SB	Avg	OBP	Slg
Mike Guerra	C95	R	36	98	298	41	79	14	1	3	31	37	26	3	.265	.346	.349
Ferris Fain	1B150	L	28	150	525	81	138	21	5	3	78	136	51	8	.263	.415	.339
Pete Suder	2B89,3B36,SS2	R	33	118	445	44	119	24	6	10	75	23	35	0	.267	.306	.416
Hank Majeski	3B113	R	32	114	448	62	124	26	5	9	67	29	23	0	.277	.326	.417
Eddie Joost	SS144	R	33	144	525	128	138	25	3	23	81	149	80	2	.263	.429	.453
Sam Chapman	OF154	R	33	154	589	89	164	24	4	24	108	80	68	3	.278	.367	.455
Elmer Valo	OF150	L	28	150	547	86	155	27	12	5	85	119	32	14	.283	.413	.404
Wally Moses	OF92	L	38	110	308	49	85	19	3	1	25	51	19	1	.276	.381	.367
Nellie Fox	2B77	L	21	88	247	42	63	6	2	0	21	32	9	2	.255	.354	.296
Don White	OF47,3B4	R	30	57	169	12	36	6	0	0	10	14	12	2	.213	.273	.249
Taffy Wright	OF35	L	37	59	149	14	35	2	5	2	25	16	6	0	.235	.321	.356
Joe Astroth	C44	R	26	55	148	18	36	4	3	0	12	21	13	1	.243	.337	.284
Buddy Rosar	C31	R	34	32	95	7	19	2	0	0	6	16	5	0	.200	.315	.221
Tod Davis	SS14,3B12,2B1	R	24	31	75	7	20	0	1	1	6	9	16	0	.267	.345	.333
Augie Galan†	OF9	S	37	12	26	4	8	2	0	0	0	9	2	0	.308	.486	.385
Hank Biasatti	1B8	L	27	21	24	6	2	2	0	0	2	8	5	0	.083	.313	.167
Bobby Estalella	OF6	R	38	8	20	2	5	0	0	0	3	1	2	0	.250	.286	.250

Pitcher	T	Age	G	GS	CG	ShO	IP	H	HR	BB	SO	W-L	Sv	ERA
Joe Coleman	R	26	33	30	18	1	240.1	249	12	127	109	13-14	1	3.86
Lou Brissie	L	25	34	29	18	0	229.1	220	20	118	118	16-11	3	4.28
Dick Fowler	R	28	31	28	15	4	213.2	210	13	115	43	15-11	1	3.75
Alex Kellner	L	24	38	27	19	0	245.0	243	18	129	94	20-12	1	3.75
Carl Scheib	R	22	38	23	11	2	182.2	191	15	118	43	9-12	0	5.12
Phil Marchildon	R	35	7	6	0	0	16.0	24	3	19	2	0-3	0	11.81
Bill McCahan	R	28	7	4	0	0	20.2	23	0	9	3	1-1	0	2.61
Charlie Harris	R	23	37	0	0	0	84.1	92	12	42	18	1-1	3	5.44
Bobby Shantz	L	23	33	7	4	1	127.0	100	9	74	58	6-8	2	3.40
Jim Wilson	R	27	2	0	0	0	5.0	7	2	5	2	0-0	0	14.40
Clem Hausmann	R	29	1	0	0	0	1.0	0	0	2	0	0-0	0	9.00

1949 Chicago White Sox 6th AL 63-91 .409 34.0 GB

Jack Onslow

Player	Gm by Position	B	Age	G	AB	R	H	2B	3B	HR	RBI	BB	SO	SB	Avg	OBP	Slg
Don Wheeler	C58	R	26	67	192	17	46	9	2	1	22	27	19	2	.240	.333	.323
Chuck Kress†	1B95	L	27	97	353	45	98	17	6	1	44	39	44	6	.278	.349	.368
Cass Michaels	2B154	R	23	154	561	73	173	27	9	6	83	101	50	5	.308	.417	.421
Floyd Baker	3B122,SS3,2B1	L	32	125	388	38	101	15	4	1	40	84	32	3	.260	.392	.327
Luke Appling	SS141	R	42	142	492	82	148	21	5	5	58	121	24	7	.301	.439	.394
Dave Philley	OF145	S	29	146	598	84	171	20	8	0	44	54	51	13	.286	.347	.346
Catfish Metkovich	OF87	L	28	93	338	50	80	9	4	5	45	41	24	5	.237	.321	.331
Herb Adams	OF48	L	21	56	208	26	61	5	3	0	16	9	16	1	.293	.323	.346
Steve Souchock	OF39,1B30	R	30	84	252	29	59	13	5	7	37	25	38	5	.234	.303	.409
Gus Zernial	OF46	R	26	73	198	29	63	17	2	5	38	15	26	0	.318	.366	.500
Joe Tipton	C53	R	27	67	191	20	39	5	3	3	19	27	17	1	.204	.306	.309
Eddie Malone	C51	R	29	55	170	17	46	7	2	1	16	29	19	2	.271	.377	.353
Johnny Ostrowski	OF41,3B8	R	31	49	158	19	42	9	4	5	31	15	41	4	.266	.333	.468
Gordon Goldsberry	1B38	L	21	39	145	25	36	3	2	1	13	18	9	2	.248	.331	.317
Jerry Scala	OF37	L	24	37	120	17	30	7	1	1	13	17	19	3	.250	.348	.350
Billy Bowers	OF20	L	27	26	78	5	15	2	1	0	6	4	5	1	.192	.232	.244
Rocky Rhawn†	3B19,SS3	R	30	24	73	12	15	4	1	0	5	12	8	0	.205	.318	.288
Rocky Krsnich	3B16	R	21	16	55	7	12	3	1	1	9	6	4	0	.218	.295	.364
Earl Rapp†	OF13	L	28	19	54	3	14	1	1	0	11	5	6	1	.259	.322	.315
Fred Hancock	SS27,3B3,OF1	R	29	39	52	7	7	2	1	0	9	8	9	0	.135	.262	.212
Dick Lane	OF11	R	22	12	42	4	5	0	0	0	4	5	3	0	.119	.213	.119
Bill Higdon	OF6	L	25	11	23	3	7	3	0	0	1	6	3	1	.304	.448	.435
George Yankowski	C6	R	26	12	18	0	3	1	0	0	2	0	2	0	.167	.167	.222
Jim Baumer	SS7	R	18	8	10	2	4	1	1	0	2	2	1	0	.400	.571	.700
Pat Seerey	OF2	R	26	4	4	1	0	0	0	0	0	3	1	0	.000	.429	.000
Don Kolloway†	3B2	R	30	4	4	0	0	0	0	0	0	0	1	0	.000	.000	.000

Pitcher	T	Age	G	GS	CG	ShO	IP	H	HR	BB	SO	W-L	Sv	ERA
Bill Wight	L	27	35	33	14	3	245.0	254	9	96	78	15-13	1	3.31
Randy Gumpert	R	31	34	32	18	3	234.0	223	22	83	78	13-16	1	3.81
Billy Pierce	L	22	32	26	8	0	171.2	145	11	112	95	7-15	0	3.88
Bob Kuzava	L	26	29	18	9	1	156.2	139	6	91	83	10-6	0	4.02
Mickey Haefner†	L	36	14	12	4	1	80.1	84	9	41	17	4-6	1	4.37
Jack Bruner	L	24	4	2	0	0	7.2	10	0	8	4	1-2	0	8.22
Fred Bradley	R	28	1	1	0	0	2.0	4	0	3	0	0-0	0	13.50
Max Surkont	R	27	44	2	0	0	96.0	92	9	60	38	3-5	4	4.78
Marino Pieretti	R	28	39	9	0	0	116.0	131	10	54	25	4-6	4	5.51
Howie Judson	R	23	26	12	3	0	108.0	114	13	70	36	1-14	1	4.58
Al Gettel†	R	31	19	7	1	1	63.0	69	12	26	22	2-5	1	6.43
Ed Klieman†	R	31	18	0	0	0	33.0	33	2	15	9	2-0	3	3.00
Clyde Shoun†	L	37	16	0	0	0	23.1	37	1	13	8	1-1	0	5.79
Bob Cain	L	24	6	0	0	0	11.0	7	0	5	5	0-0	1	2.45
Bill Evans	R	30	4	0	0	0	6.1	6	0	8	1	0-1	0	7.11
Ernest Groth	R	27	3	0	0	0	5.0	2	0	3	1	0-1	0	5.40
Alex Carrasquel	R	36	3	0	0	0	3.2	8	1	4	1	0-0	0	14.73
Orval Grove	R	29	1	0	0	0	0.2	4	1	1	1	0-0	0	54.00

1949 St. Louis Browns 7th AL 53-101 .344 44.0 GB

Zack Taylor

Player	Gm by Position	B	Age	G	AB	R	H	2B	3B	HR	RBI	BB	SO	SB	Avg	OBP	Slg
Sherm Lollar	C93	R	24	109	284	28	74	9	1	8	49	32	22	0	.261	.340	.384
Jack Graham	1B136	L	32	137	500	71	119	22	1	24	79	61	62	0	.238	.326	.430
Jerry Priddy	2B145	R	29	145	544	83	158	26	4	11	63	80	81	5	.290	.382	.414
Bob Dillinger	3B133	R	30	137	544	68	176	22	13	1	51	51	40	20	.324	.385	.417
Eddie Pellagrini	SS76	R	31	79	235	26	56	8	1	2	15	14	24	2	.238	.284	.306
Dick Kokos	OF138	L	21	143	501	80	131	28	1	23	77	66	91	3	.261	.351	.459
Roy Sievers	OF125,3B7	R	22	140	471	84	144	28	1	16	91	70	75	1	.306	.398	.471
Stan Spence†	OF85,1B1	L	34	104	314	46	77	13	3	13	45	52	36	1	.245	.356	.430
Paul Lehner	OF55,1B18	L	28	104	297	25	68	13	0	3	37	16	20	0	.229	.271	.303
Les Moss	C83	R	24	97	278	28	81	11	0	10	39	49	32	0	.291	.399	.439
Whitey Platt	OF59,1B2	R	28	102	244	29	63	8	2	3	29	24	27	0	.258	.325	.344
John Sullivan	SS71,3B23,2B6	R	28	105	243	29	55	8	3	0	18	38	35	0	.226	.331	.284
Andy Anderson	SS44,2B8,3B8	R	26	71	136	10	17	3	0	1	5	14	21	0	.125	.207	.169
Al Zarilla†	OF15	L	30	15	56	10	14	1	0	1	6	8	2	1	.250	.354	.321
George Elder	OF10	L	28	41	44	9	11	3	0	0	2	4	11	0	.250	.313	.318
Owen Friend	2B2	R	22	2	8	1	3	0	0	0	1	0	0	0	.375	.375	.375
Al Naples	SS2	R	21	2	7	0	1	1	0	0	0	0	1	0	.143	.143	.286
Ken Wood	OF3	R	24	7	6	0	0	0	0	0	0	1	2	0	.000	.143	.000
Hank Arft		L	27	6	5	1	1	1	0	0	0	0	1	0	.200	.200	.400
Frankie Pack		L	21	1	1	0	0	0	0	0	0	0	1	0	.000	.000	.000

Pitcher	T	Age	G	GS	CG	ShO	IP	H	HR	BB	SO	W-L	Sv	ERA
Ned Garver	R	23	41	32	16	1	223.2	245	14	102	70	12-17	3	3.98
Cliff Fannin	R	25	30	25	5	0	143.0	177	15	93	57	8-14	1	6.17
Karl Drews	R	29	31	23	3	1	139.2	180	11	66	35	4-12	0	6.64
Red Embree	R	31	35	19	4	0	127.1	146	13	89	24	3-13	1	5.37
Ribs Raney	R	26	3	3	1	0	16.1	23	2	12	5	1-2	0	7.71
Ed Albrecht	R	20	1	1	1	0	5.0	1	0	4	1	1-0	0	5.40
Tom Ferrick	R	34	50	0	0	0	104.1	102	9	41	34	6-4	6	3.88
Bill Kennedy	L	28	48	16	2	0	153.2	172	12	73	69	4-11	1	4.69
Al Papai	R	32	42	15	6	0	142.1	175	8	81	31	4-11	2	5.06
Joe Ostrowski	L	32	40	13	4	0	141.0	185	16	27	34	8-8	2	4.79
Dick Starr	R	28	30	8	1	1	83.1	96	6	48	44	1-7	0	4.32
Ray Shore	R	28	13	0	0	0	23.1	27	2	31	13	0-1	0	10.80
Ralph Winegarner	R	39	9	0	0	0	16.2	24	2	2	8	0-0	0	7.56
Bob Malloy	R	31	5	0	0	0	9.2	6	0	7	2	1-1	0	2.79
Bob Savage	R	27	4	0	0	0	7.0	12	1	3	1	0-0	0	6.43
Irv Medlinger	L	22	3	0	0	0	4.0	11	1	3	4	0-0	0	27.00
Jim Bilbrey	R	25	1	0	0	0	1.0	1	0	3	0	0-0	0	18.00

710 Seasons: Team Rosters

1949 Washington Senators 8th AL 50-104 .325 47.0 GB

Joe Kuhel

Player	Gm by Position	B	Age	G	AB	R	H	2B	3B	HR	RBI	BB	SO	SB	Avg	OBP	Slg
Al Evans	C107	R	32	109	321	32	87	12	3	2	42	50	19	4	.271	.369	.346
Eddie Robinson	1B143	L	28	143	527	66	155	27	3	18	78	67	30	3	.294	.381	.459
Al Kozar	2B102	R	27	105	350	46	94	15	2	4	31	25	23	2	.269	.321	.357
Eddie Yost	3B122	R	22	124	435	57	110	19	7	9	45	91	41	3	.253	.383	.391
Sam Dente	SS153	R	27	153	590	48	161	24	4	1	53	31	24	4	.273	.309	.332
Clyde Vollmer	OF114	R	27	129	443	58	112	17	1	14	59	53	62	1	.253	.335	.391
Bud Stewart	OF105	L	33	118	388	58	110	23	4	8	43	49	33	6	.284	.368	.425
Gil Coan	OF97	L	27	111	358	36	78	7	8	3	25	29	58	9	.218	.278	.307
Sherry Robertson	2B71,3B19,OF13	L	30	110	374	59	94	17	3	11	42	42	35	10	.251	.329	.401
Sam Mele†	OF63,1B11	R	26	78	264	21	64	12	2	3	25	17	34	2	.242	.288	.337
Buddy Lewis	OF67	L	32	95	257	25	63	14	4	3	28	41	12	2	.245	.355	.366
Jake Early	C53	L	34	53	138	12	34	4	0	1	11	26	11	0	.246	.370	.297
Roberto Ortiz	OF32	R	34	40	129	12	36	3	0	1	11	9	12	0	.279	.326	.326
Mark Christman	3B23,1B6,SS4*	R	35	49	112	8	24	2	0	3	18	8	7	0	.214	.273	.313
John Simmons	OF26	R	24	62	93	12	20	0	0	0	5	11	6	0	.215	.298	.215
Ralph Weigel	C21	R	27	34	60	4	14	2	0	0	4	8	6	0	.233	.324	.267
Hal Keller		L	21	3	3	1	1	0	0	0	0	0	0	0	.333	.333	.333
Herman Reich†		R	31	2	2	0	0	0	0	0	0	0	1	0	.000	.000	.000
Jay Difani	2B1	R	25	2	1	0	1	1	0	0	0	0	0	0	1.000	1.000	2.000

M. Christman, 1 G at 2B

Pitcher	T	Age	G	GS	CG	ShO	IP	H	HR	BB	SO	W-L	Sv	ERA
Sid Hudson	R	34	40	27	11	2	209.0	234	11	91	54	8-17	1	4.22
Ray Scarborough	R	31	34	27	11	1	199.2	204	10	88	81	13-11	0	4.60
Paul Calvert	R	31	34	23	5	0	160.2	175	11	86	52	6-17	1	5.43
Mickey Harris†	L	32	23	19	4	0	129.0	151	8	55	54	2-12	0	5.16
Dick Weik	R	21	27	14	2	2	95.1	78	5	103	58	3-12	1	5.38
Mickey Haefner†	L	36	19	12	4	1	91.2	85	7	53	23	5-5	0	4.42
Walt Masterson†	R	29	10	7	3	0	53.0	42	4	21	17	3-2	0	3.23
Jim Pearce	R	24	2	1	0	0	5.1	9	1	5	1	0-1	0	8.44
Dizzy Sutherland	L	27	1	1	0	0	1.0	2	0	6	0	0-1	0	45.00
Dick Welteroth	R	21	52	2	0	0	95.1	107	6	89	37	2-5	2	7.36
Joe Haynes	R	31	37	10	0	0	96.1	106	6	55	19	2-9	2	6.26
Lloyd Hittle	L	25	36	9	3	2	109.0	123	2	57	32	5-7	0	4.21
Al Gettel†	R	31	16	1	0	0	34.2	43	4	24	7	0-2	1	5.45
Julio Gonzales	R	28	13	0	0	0	34.1	33	3	27	5	0-0	0	4.72
Dave Thompson	L	31	9	1	1	0	16.1	22	1	9	8	1-3	0	4.41
Milo Candini	R	31	3	0	0	0	5.2	4	0	1	1	0-0	1	4.76
Buzz Dozier	R	21	2	0	0	0	6.1	12	0	6	1	0-0	0	11.37
Ed Klieman†	R	31	2	0	0	0	3.0	8	0	3	1	0-0	0	18.00

»1949 Brooklyn Dodgers 1st NL 97-57 .630 —

Burt Shotton

Player	Gm by Position	B	Age	G	AB	R	H	2B	3B	HR	RBI	BB	SO	SB	Avg	OBP	Slg
Roy Campanella	C127	R	27	130	436	65	125	22	2	22	82	67	36	3	.287	.385	.498
Gil Hodges	1B156	R	25	156	596	94	170	23	4	23	115	66	64	10	.285	.360	.453
Jackie Robinson	2B156	R	30	156	593	122	203	38	12	16	124	86	27	37	.342	.432	.528
Billy Cox	3B100	R	29	100	390	48	91	18	2	8	40	30	18	5	.233	.290	.351
Pee Wee Reese	SS155	R	30	155	617	132	172	27	3	16	73	116	59	26	.279	.396	.410
Duke Snider	OF145	L	22	146	552	100	161	28	7	23	92	56	92	12	.292	.361	.493
Carl Furillo	OF142	R	27	142	549	95	177	27	10	18	106	37	29	4	.322	.368	.506
Gene Hermanski	OF77	L	29	87	224	48	67	12	3	8	42	47	21	12	.299	.431	.487
Marv Rackley†	OF47	L	27	63	150	25	45	5	1	1	15	14	8	1	.300	.360	.367
Bruce Edwards	C41,OF4,3B1	R	25	64	148	24	31	3	0	8	25	25	15	0	.209	.324	.392
Mike McCormick	OF49	R	32	55	139	17	29	5	1	2	14	14	12	1	.209	.281	.302
Spider Jorgensen	3B36	L	29	53	134	15	36	5	1	1	14	23	13	0	.269	.376	.343
Eddie Miksis	3B29,SS4,2B3*	R	22	50	113	17	25	5	0	1	6	7	8	3	.221	.267	.292
Luis Olmo	OF34	R	29	38	105	15	32	4	1	1	14	5	11	2	.305	.336	.390
Tommy Brown	OF27	R	21	41	89	14	27	2	0	3	18	6	8	0	.303	.347	.427
Dick Whitman	OF11	L	28	23	49	8	9	2	0	0	2	4	4	0	.184	.245	.224
Cal Abrams	OF7	L	25	8	24	6	2	1	0	0	0	7	6	1	.083	.290	.125
Johnny Hopp†	OF4,1B2	L	32	8	14	0	0	0	0	0	0	0	3	0	.000	.000	.000
Bob Ramazzotti†	3B3	R	32	5	13	1	2	0	0	1	3	0	3	0	.154	.154	.385
Chuck Connors		L	28	1	1	0	0	0	0	0	0	0	0	0	.000	.000	.000
George Shuba		L	24	1	1	0	0	0	0	0	0	0	0	0	.000	.000	.000

E. Miksis, 1 G at 1B

Pitcher	T	Age	G	GS	CG	ShO	IP	H	HR	BB	SO	W-L	Sv	ERA
Don Newcombe	R	23	38	31	19	5	244.1	223	17	73	149	17-8	1	3.17
Joe Hatten	L	32	37	29	11	2	187.1	194	15	69	58	12-8	2	4.18
Preacher Roe	L	34	30	27	13	3	212.2	201	25	44	109	15-6	1	2.79
Ralph Branca	R	23	34	27	9	2	186.2	181	21	91	109	13-5	1	4.39
Rex Barney	R	24	38	20	6	2	140.2	108	15	89	80	9-8	1	4.41
Erv Palica	R	21	49	1	0	0	97.0	93	6	49	44	8-9	6	3.62
Jack Banta	R	24	48	12	2	1	152.1	125	12	68	97	10-6	3	3.37
Paul Minner	L	25	27	1	0	0	47.1	49	7	18	17	3-1	2	3.80
Carl Erskine	R	22	22	3	2	0	79.2	68	6	51	49	8-1	0	4.63
Morrie Martin	L	26	10	4	0	0	30.2	39	5	15	15	1-3	0	7.04
Pat McGlothin	R	28	7	0	0	0	15.2	13	2	5	11	1-1	0	4.60
Bud Podbielan	R	25	7	1	0	0	12.1	9	1	9	5	0-1	0	3.65
Johnny Van Cuyk	L	27	2	0	0	0	2.0	3	0	1	0	0-0	0	9.00

1949 St. Louis Cardinals 2nd NL 96-58 .623 1.0 GB

Eddie Dyer

Player	Gm by Position	B	Age	G	AB	R	H	2B	3B	HR	RBI	BB	SO	SB	Avg	OBP	Slg
Del Rice	C92	R	26	92	284	25	67	16	1	4	29	30	40	0	.236	.320	.342
Nippy Jones	1B98	R	24	110	380	51	114	20	2	8	62	16	20	1	.300	.330	.426
Red Schoendienst	2B138,SS14,3B6*	S	26	151	640	102	190	25	2	3	54	51	18	8	.297	.351	.356
Eddie Kazak	3B80,2B5	R	28	92	326	43	99	15	3	6	42	29	17	0	.304	.362	.423
Marty Marion	SS134	R	31	134	515	61	140	31	2	5	70	37	42	0	.272	.323	.369
Stan Musial	OF156,1B1	L	28	157	612	128	207	41	13	36	123	107	38	3	.338	.438	.624
Enos Slaughter	OF150	L	33	151	568	92	191	34	13	13	96	79	37	3	.336	.418	.511
Chuck Diering	OF124	R	26	131	369	60	97	21	8	3	38	35	49	1	.263	.328	.388
Ron Northey	OF73	L	29	90	265	28	69	18	2	7	50	31	15	0	.260	.338	.423
Tommy Glaviano	3B73,2B7	R	25	87	258	32	69	16	1	6	36	41	35	0	.267	.380	.407
Rocky Nelson	1B70	L	24	82	244	28	54	8	4	4	32	11	12	1	.221	.258	.336
Joe Garagiola	C80	L	23	81	241	25	63	14	0	3	26	31	19	0	.261	.348	.357
Lou Klein	SS21,2B9,3B7	R	30	58	114	25	25	6	0	2	12	22	20	0	.219	.355	.325
Hal Rice	OF10	L	25	40	46	3	9	2	1	1	9	3	7	0	.196	.245	.348
Eddie Sauer†	OF10	R	30	24	45	5	10	2	1	0	1	3	8	0	.222	.271	.311
Solly Hemus	2B16	L	26	20	33	8	11	1	0	0	2	7	3	0	.333	.450	.364
Bill Baker	C10	R	38	20	30	2	4	1	0	0	4	2	2	0	.133	.188	.167
Steve Bilko	1B5	R	20	6	17	3	5	2	0	0	2	5	6	0	.294	.455	.412
Whitey Kurowski	3B2	R	31	10	14	0	2	0	0	0	0	1	0	0	.143	.200	.143
Bill Howerton	OF6	L	27	9	13	1	4	1	0	0	1	0	2	0	.308	.308	.385
Del Wilber	C2	R	30	2	4	0	1	0	0	0	0	0	0	0	.250	.250	.250
Russ Derry		L	32	2	2	0	0	0	0	0	0	0	2	0	.000	.000	.000
Erv Dusak		R	28	1	0	1	0	0	0	0	0	0	0	0	—	—	—

R. Schoendienst, 2 G at OF

Pitcher	T	Age	G	GS	CG	ShO	IP	H	HR	BB	SO	W-L	Sv	ERA
Harry Brecheen	L	34	32	31	14	2	214.2	207	18	65	88	14-11	1	3.35
Howie Pollet	L	28	39	28	17	5	230.2	228	9	59	108	20-9	1	2.77
George Munger	R	30	35	28	12	2	188.1	179	13	87	82	15-8	2	3.87
Al Brazle	L	35	39	25	9	1	206.1	208	18	61	75	14-8	0	3.18
Max Lanier	L	33	15	15	4	1	92.0	92	5	35	37	5-4	0	3.82
Ted Wilks	R	33	59	0	0	0	118.1	105	7	38	71	10-3	9	3.73
Gerry Staley	R	28	45	17	5	2	171.1	154	7	41	55	10-10	6	2.73
Freddie Martin	R	34	21	5	3	0	70.0	65	3	20	30	6-0	0	2.44
Bill Reeder	R	27	21	1	0	0	33.2	33	2	30	21	1-1	0	5.08
Jim Hearn	R	28	17	4	0	0	42.0	48	3	23	18	1-3	0	5.14
Ken Johnson	L	26	14	2	0	0	33.2	29	1	35	18	0-1	0	6.42
Cloyd Boyer	R	21	4	1	0	0	3.1	5	0	7	0	0-0	0	10.80
Ray Yochim	R	26	3	0	0	0	2.1	3	1	4	3	0-0	0	15.43
Kurt Krieger	R	22	1	0	0	0	1.0	0	0	1	0	0-0	0	0.00

1949 Philadelphia Phillies 3rd NL 81-73 .526 16.0 GB

Eddie Sawyer

Player	Gm by Position	B	Age	G	AB	R	H	2B	3B	HR	RBI	BB	SO	SB	Avg	OBP	Slg
Andy Seminick	C98	R	28	109	334	52	81	11	2	24	68	69	74	0	.243	.380	.503
Dick Sisler	1B96	L	28	121	412	42	119	19	6	7	50	25	38	0	.289	.333	.415
Eddie Miller	2B82,SS1	R	32	85	266	21	55	10	1	6	29	29	21	1	.207	.294	.320
Puddin' Head Jones	3B145	R	23	149	532	71	130	35	1	19	77	65	66	3	.244	.328	.421
Granny Hamner	SS154	R	22	154	662	83	174	32	5	6	53	25	47	6	.263	.290	.353
Richie Ashburn	OF154	L	22	154	662	84	188	18	11	1	37	58	38	9	.284	.343	.349
Del Ennis	OF154	R	24	154	610	92	184	39	11	25	110	59	61	2	.302	.367	.525
Bill Nicholson	OF91	L	34	98	299	42	70	8	3	11	40	45	53	1	.234	.344	.391
Stan Hollmig	OF66	R	23	81	251	28	64	11	6	2	26	20	43	1	.255	.315	.371
Stan Lopata	C58	R	23	83	240	31	65	9	2	8	27	21	44	1	.271	.330	.425
Eddie Waitkus	1B54	L	29	54	209	41	64	16	3	1	28	33	12	3	.306	.403	.426
Mike Goliat	2B50,1B5	R	23	55	189	24	40	6	3	3	19	20	32	0	.212	.290	.323
Buddy Blattner	2B15,3B12,SS1	R	29	64	97	15	24	6	0	5	21	19	17	0	.247	.371	.464
Putsy Caballero	2B21,SS1	R	21	29	68	8	19	3	0	0	3	0	3	0	.279	.279	.324
Jackie Mayo	OF25	L	23	45	39	3	5	0	0	0	2	4	5	0	.128	.209	.128
Ed Sanicki	OF6	R	25	7	13	4	3	0	0	3	7	1	4	0	.231	.286	.923
Bill Glynn	1B1	L	23	8	10	0	2	0	0	0	1	0	3	0	.200	.200	.200
Johnny Blatnik	OF2	R	28	6	8	3	1	0	0	0	0	4	1	0	.125	.417	.125
Ken Silvestri	C1,2B1,SS1	S	33	4	4	1	0	0	0	0	0	2	1	0	.000	.333	.000
Hal Wagner	C1	L	33	1	4	0	0	0	0	0	0	0	1	0	.000	.000	.000
Bert Haas†		R	35	2	1	0	0	0	0	0	0	1	1	0	.000	.500	.000

Pitcher	T	Age	G	GS	CG	ShO	IP	H	HR	BB	SO	W-L	Sv	ERA
Ken Heintzelman	L	33	33	32	15	5	250.0	239	19	93	65	17-10	0	3.02
Robin Roberts	R	22	43	31	11	3	226.2	229	15	75	95	15-15	4	3.69
Russ Meyer	R	25	37	28	14	2	213.0	199	14	70	78	17-8	1	3.08
Hank Borowy	R	33	28	28	12	2	193.1	188	19	63	43	12-12	0	4.19
Jocko Thompson	L	32	8	5	1	0	31.1	38	6	11	12	1-3	0	6.89
Jim Konstanty	R	32	53	0	0	0	97.0	98	9	29	43	9-5	7	3.25
Ken Trinkle	R	29	42	0	0	0	74.1	79	3	30	14	1-1	2	4.00
Curt Simmons	L	20	38	14	2	0	131.1	133	7	55	83	4-10	1	4.59
Blix Donnelly	R	35	23	10	1	0	78.1	84	7	40	36	2-1	0	5.06
Schoolboy Rowe	R	39	23	6	2	0	65.1	68	2	17	22	3-7	0	4.82
Charlie Bicknell	R	20	13	0	0	0	28.1	32	3	17	4	0-0	0	7.62
Bob Miller	R	23	3	0	0	0	2.2	2	0	2	0	0-0	0	0.00

1949 Boston Braves 4th NL 75-79 .487 22.0 GB

Billy Southworth (55-54)/Johnny Cooney (20-25)

Player	Gm by Position	B	Age	G	AB	R	H	2B	3B	HR	RBI	BB	SO	SB	Avg	OBP	Slg
Del Crandall	C63	R	19	67	228	21	60	10	1	4	34	9	18	2	.263	.291	.368
Elbie Fletcher	1B121	L	33	122	413	57	108	19	3	11	51	84	65	1	.262	.396	.402
Eddie Stanky	2B135	R	32	138	506	90	144	24	5	1	42	113	41	3	.285	.417	.358
Bob Elliott	3B130	R	32	139	482	77	135	29	5	17	76	90	38	0	.280	.395	.467
Al Dark	SS125,3B4	R	27	130	529	74	146	23	5	3	53	31	43	5	.276	.317	.355
Jim Russell	OF120	S	30	130	415	57	96	22	1	8	54	64	68	3	.231	.337	.347
Tommy Holmes	OF103	L	32	117	380	47	101	20	4	8	59	39	6	1	.266	.337	.403
Marv Rickert	OF75,1B12	L	28	100	277	44	81	18	3	6	49	23	38	1	.292	.347	.444
Sibby Sisti	OF48,2B21,SS18*	R	28	101	268	39	69	12	0	5	22	34	42	1	.257	.343	.358
Pete Reiser	OF63,3B4	L	30	84	221	32	60	8	3	8	40	33	42	3	.271	.369	.443
Eddie Sauer†	OF71	R	30	79	214	26	57	12	0	3	31	17	34	0	.266	.323	.364
Connie Ryan	3B25,SS18,2B16*	R	29	85	208	28	52	13	1	6	20	21	30	1	.250	.319	.409
Bill Salkeld	C63	L	32	66	161	17	41	5	0	5	25	44	24	1	.255	.417	.379
Clint Conatser	OF44	R	27	53	152	10	40	6	0	3	16	14	19	0	.263	.325	.362
Jeff Heath	OF31	L	34	36	111	17	34	7	0	9	23	15	26	0	.306	.389	.613
Phil Masi†	C37	R	33	37	105	13	22	2	0	0	6	14	10	1	.210	.303	.229
Earl Torgeson	1B25	L	25	25	100	17	26	5	1	4	19	13	4	4	.260	.345	.450
Mickey Livingston†	C22	R	34	28	64	6	15	2	1	0	6	3	5	0	.234	.290	.297
Ray Sanders	1B7	L	32	9	21	0	3	1	0	0	0	4	9	0	.143	.280	.190
Don Thompson	OF2	L	25	7	11	0	2	0	0	0	0	0	2	0	.182	.182	.182
Al Lakeman	1B2	R	30	3	6	0	1	0	0	0	0	1	0	0	.167	.286	.167
Steve Kuczek		R	24	1	1	0	1	1	0	0	0	0	0	0	1.000	1.000	2.000

S. Sisti, 1 G at 3B; C. Ryan, 3 G at 1B

Pitcher	T	Age	G	GS	CG	ShO	IP	H	HR	BB	SO	W-L	Sv	ERA
Warren Spahn	L	28	38	38	25	4	302.1	283	27	86	151	21-14	0	3.07
Johnny Sain	R	31	37	36	16	1	243.0	285	15	75	73	10-17	0	4.81
Vern Bickford	R	28	37	36	15	2	230.2	246	20	106	101	16-11	0	4.25
Bill Voiselle	R	30	30	22	5	4	169.1	170	14	78	63	7-8	1	4.04
Nels Potter	R	37	41	3	1	0	96.2	99	6	30	57	6-11	7	4.19
Bobby Hogue	R	28	33	0	0	0	72.0	78	4	25	23	2-2	3	3.13
Bob Hall	R	25	31	6	2	0	74.1	77	7	41	43	6-4	0	4.36
Red Barrett	R	34	23	0	0	0	44.1	58	4	10	17	1-1	0	5.68
Johnny Antonelli	L	19	22	10	3	1	96.0	99	6	42	48	3-7	0	3.56
Glenn Elliott	L	29	22	6	1	0	68.1	70	7	27	15	3-4	0	3.95
Johnny Beazley	R	31	1	0	0	0	2.0	0	0	0	0	0-0	0	0.00
Clyde Shoun†	L	37	1	0	0	0	1.0	1	0	0	0	0-0	0	0.00

Seasons: Team Rosters 711

1949 New York Giants 5th NL 73-81 .474 24.0 GB

Leo Durocher

Player	Gm by Position	B	Age	G	AB	R	H	2B	3B	HR	RBI	BB	SO	SB	Avg	OBP	Slg
Wes Westrum	C62	R	26	64	169	23	41	4	1	7	28	37	39	1	.243	.385	.402
Johnny Mize†	1B101	L	36	106	388	59	102	15	0	18	62	50	19	1	.263	.351	.441
Hank Thompson	2B69,3B1	L	23	75	275	51	77	10	4	9	34	42	30	5	.280	.377	.444
Sid Gordon	3B123,OF15,1B1	R	31	141	489	87	139	26	2	26	90	95	37	1	.284	.404	.505
Buddy Kerr	SS89	R	26	90	220	16	46	4	0	0	19	21	23	0	.209	.284	.227
Bobby Thomson	OF156	R	25	156	641	99	198	35	9	27	109	44	45	10	.309	.355	.518
Whitey Lockman	OF151	L	22	151	617	97	186	32	7	11	65	62	31	12	.301	.368	.429
Willard Marshall	OF138	L	28	141	499	81	153	19	3	12	70	78	20	4	.307	.401	.429
Bill Rigney	SS81,2B26,3B14	R	31	122	389	53	108	19	6	6	47	47	38	3	.278	.356	.404
Jack Lohrke	2B23,3B19,SS15	R	25	55	180	32	48	11	4	5	22	16	12	3	.267	.333	.456
Ray Mueller†	C56	R	37	56	170	17	38	2	2	5	23	13	14	1	.224	.279	.347
Walker Cooper†	C40	R	34	42	147	14	31	4	2	4	21	7	8	0	.211	.261	.347
Joe Lafata	1B47	L	27	64	140	18	33	2	2	3	16	9	23	1	.236	.282	.343
Bert Haas†	1B23,3B11	R	35	54	104	12	27	2	3	1	10	5	8	0	.260	.294	.365
Monte Irvin	OF10,1B5,3B5	R	30	36	76	7	17	3	2	0	7	17	11	0	.224	.366	.316
Mickey Livingston†	C19	R	34	19	57	6	17	2	0	4	12	2	8	0	.298	.333	.544
Don Mueller	OF6	L	22	51	56	5	13	4	0	0	1	5	6	0	.232	.295	.304
Davey Williams	2B13	R	21	13	50	7	12	1	1	1	5	7	4	0	.240	.333	.360
Bobby Hofman	2B16	R	23	19	48	4	10	0	0	0	3	5	6	0	.208	.296	.208
George Hausmann	2B13	R	33	16	47	5	6	0	1	0	3	7	6	0	.128	.241	.170
Pete Milne	OF1	L	24	31	29	5	7	1	0	1	6	3	6	0	.241	.313	.379
Rocky Rhawn†	2B8	R	30	14	29	8	5	0	0	0	2	7	2	1	.172	.333	.172
Augie Galan†	1B3,OF1	S	37	22	17	0	1	1	0	0	2	5	3	0	.059	.273	.118
Rudy Rufer	SS7	R	22	7	15	1	1	0	0	0	2	2	0	0	.067	.176	.067
Sal Yvars	C2	R	25	3	8	0	0	0	0	0	0	1	1	0	.000	.111	.000
Herman Franks	C1	L	35	1	3	1	2	0	0	0	0	0	0	0	.667	.667	.667
Dick Culler	SS7	R	34	7	1	0	0	0	0	0	0	1	0	0	.000	.500	.000

Pitcher	T	Age	G	GS	CG	ShO	IP	H	HR	BB	SO	W-L	Sv	ERA
Larry Jansen	R	28	37	35	17	3	259.2	271	36	62	113	15-16	0	3.85
Monte Kennedy	L	27	38	32	14	4	223.1	208	13	100	95	12-14	1	3.43
Sheldon Jones	R	27	42	27	11	1	207.1	198	19	88	79	15-12	0	3.34
Clint Hartung	R	26	33	25	8	0	154.2	156	16	86	48	9-11	0	5.00
Dave Koslo	L	29	38	23	15	0	212.0	193	13	43	64	11-14	4	2.50
Roger Bowman	L	21	2	2	0	0	6.1	6	1	7	4	0-0	0	4.26
Hank Behrman	R	28	43	4	1	1	71.1	64	5	52	25	3-3	0	4.92
Kirby Higbe†	R	34	37	2	0	0	80.1	72	12	41	38	2-0	2	3.47
Andy Hansen	R	24	33	2	0	0	66.1	58	7	28	26	2-6	1	4.61
Red Webb	R	24	20	0	0	0	44.2	41	3	21	9	1-1	0	4.03
Adrian Zabala	L	32	15	4	2	1	41.0	44	5	10	13	2-3	1	5.27
Andy Tomasic	R	29	2	0	0	0	5.0	9	2	5	2	0-1	0	18.00
Ray Poat†	R	31	2	0	0	0	2.1	8	0	1	0	0-0	0	19.29

1949 Pittsburgh Pirates 6th NL 71-83 .461 26.0 GB

Billy Meyer

Player	Gm by Position	B	Age	G	AB	R	H	2B	3B	HR	RBI	BB	SO	SB	Avg	OBP	Slg
Clyde McCullough	C90	R	32	91	241	30	57	9	3	4	21	24	30	1	.237	.316	.349
Johnny Hopp†	1B77,OF16	L	32	105	371	55	118	14	5	5	39	37	29	9	.318	.380	.423
Monty Basgall	2B98,3B3	R	27	107	308	25	67	9	1	2	26	31	32	1	.218	.291	.273
Pete Castiglione	3B98,SS17,OF2	R	28	118	448	57	120	20	2	6	43	20	43	2	.268	.299	.362
Stan Rojek	SS144	R	30	144	557	72	136	19	2	0	31	50	31	4	.244	.309	.285
Ralph Kiner	OF152	R	26	152	549	116	170	19	5	54	127	117	61	6	.310	.432	.658
Wally Westlake	OF143	R	28	147	525	77	148	24	8	23	104	45	69	6	.282	.345	.490
Dino Restelli	OF61,1B1	R	24	72	232	41	58	11	0	12	40	35	26	3	.250	.358	.453
Danny Murtaugh	2B74	R	31	75	236	16	48	7	2	2	24	29	17	2	.203	.291	.275
Ed Stevens	1B58	L	24	67	221	22	58	10	1	4	32	22	24	1	.262	.332	.371
Eddie Bockman	3B68,2B5	R	28	79	220	21	49	6	1	6	19	23	31	3	.223	.296	.341
Tom Saffell	OF53	L	27	73	205	36	66	7	1	2	25	21	27	5	.322	.385	.395
Dixie Walker	OF39,1B3	L	38	88	181	26	51	4	1	1	18	26	11	0	.282	.372	.331
Ed Fitz Gerald	C56	R	25	75	160	16	42	7	0	2	18	8	27	1	.263	.302	.344
Phil Masi†	C44,1B2	R	33	48	135	16	37	6	1	2	13	17	16	1	.274	.355	.378
Jack Phillips†	1B16,3B1	R	27	18	56	6	13	3	1	0	3	3	4	6	.232	.283	.321
Marv Rackley†	OF8	L	27	11	35	5	11	2	0	0	2	2	3	1	.314	.351	.371
Wally Judnich	OF8	L	32	10	35	5	8	1	0	0	1	1	2	0	.229	.250	.257
Les Fleming	1B5	L	33	24	31	0	8	0	2	0	7	6	2	0	.258	.395	.387
Ted Beard	OF10	L	28	14	24	1	2	0	0	0	1	2	2	0	.083	.154	.083
Rocky Rhawn†	3B2	R	30	3	7	0	1	0	0	0	0	0	0	0	.143	.143	.143
Jack Cassini		R	29	8	0	3	0	0	0	0	0	0	0	0	—	—	—

Pitcher	T	Age	G	GS	CG	ShO	IP	H	HR	BB	SO	W-L	Sv	ERA
Bill Werle	L	28	35	29	10	2	221.0	243	22	51	106	12-13	0	4.24
Bob Chesnes	R	28	27	25	8	1	145.1	153	15	82	49	7-13	1	5.88
Cliff Chambers	L	27	34	21	10	1	177.1	186	15	58	93	13-7	0	3.96
Tiny Bonham	R	35	18	14	5	1	89.0	81	11	23	25	7-4	0	4.25
Elmer Riddle	R	34	16	12	1	0	74.1	81	9	45	24	1-8	1	5.33
Junior Walsh	R	30	9	7	1	1	42.2	40	5	16	24	1-4	0	5.06
Murry Dickson	R	32	44	20	11	2	224.1	216	17	80	89	12-14	0	3.29
Vic Lombardi	L	26	34	12	4	0	134.0	149	14	68	64	5-5	1	4.57
Hugh Casey†	R	35	33	0	0	0	38.2	50	4	14	9	4-1	5	4.66
Rip Sewell	R	42	28	6	2	1	76.0	82	8	32	26	6-1	1	3.91
Harry Gumbert†	R	39	16	0	0	0	27.2	30	5	18	5	1-4	3	5.86
Bob Muncrief†	R	33	13	4	1	0	35.2	44	8	13	11	1-5	3	6.31
Ray Poat†	R	31	11	2	0	0	36.0	52	6	15	17	0-1	0	6.25
Hal Gregg	R	27	8	1	0	0	18.2	20	1	8	9	1-1	0	3.38
Kirby Higbe†	R	34	7	1	0	0	15.2	25	2	12	5	0-2	0	13.21

1949 Cincinnati Reds 7th NL 62-92 .403 35.0 GB

Bucky Walters (61-90)/Luke Sewell (1-2)

Player	Gm by Position	B	Age	G	AB	R	H	2B	3B	HR	RBI	BB	SO	SB	Avg	OBP	Slg
Walker Cooper†	C77	R	34	82	307	34	86	9	2	16	62	21	24	0	.280	.330	.479
Ted Kluszewski	1B134	L	24	136	531	63	164	26	2	8	68	19	24	3	.309	.333	.411
Jimmy Bloodworth	2B92,1B23,3B8	R	31	134	452	40	118	27	1	9	59	27	36	1	.261	.304	.385
Grady Hatton	3B136	L	26	137	537	71	141	38	5	11	69	62	48	4	.263	.342	.413
Virgil Stallcup	SS141	R	27	141	575	49	146	28	5	3	45	9	44	1	.254	.268	.336
Johnny Wyrostek	OF129	L	29	134	474	54	118	20	4	9	46	58	63	7	.249	.333	.365
Lloyd Merriman	OF86	L	24	103	287	35	66	12	5	4	26	21	36	2	.230	.285	.348
Danny Litwhiler	OF82,3B3	R	32	102	292	35	85	18	1	11	48	44	42	0	.291	.384	.473
Harry Walker†	OF77,1B1	L	32	86	314	53	100	15	2	1	23	34	17	4	.318	.385	.389
Peanuts Lowrey†	OF78	R	30	89	309	48	85	16	2	2	25	37	11	1	.275	.354	.359
Bobby Adams	2B63,3B14	R	27	107	277	32	70	16	2	0	25	26	36	4	.253	.317	.325
Dixie Howell	C56	R	29	64	172	17	42	6	1	2	18	8	21	0	.244	.286	.326
Hank Sauer†	OF39,1B1	R	32	42	152	22	36	6	0	4	16	18	19	0	.237	.318	.355
Ray Mueller†	C31	R	37	32	106	7	29	4	0	1	13	5	13	1	.274	.319	.340
Claude Corbitt	SS18,2B17,3B1	R	33	44	94	10	17	1	0	0	3	9	1	1	.181	.252	.191
Frankie Baumholtz†	OF20	L	30	27	81	12	19	5	3	1	8	6	8	0	.235	.295	.407
Sammy Meeks	2B8,SS3	R	26	16	36	10	11	2	0	2	6	2	6	1	.306	.342	.528
Chuck Kress†	1B16	L	27	27	29	3	6	3	0	0	3	3	5	0	.207	.281	.310
Johnny Pramesa	C13	R	23	17	25	2	6	1	0	1	2	3	5	0	.240	.321	.400
Wally Post	OF3	R	19	6	8	1	2	0	0	0	1	0	3	0	.250	.250	.250

Pitcher	T	Age	G	GS	CG	ShO	IP	H	HR	BB	SO	W-L	Sv	ERA
Ken Raffensberger	L	31	41	38	20	5	284.0	289	23	80	103	18-17	0	3.39
Howie Fox	R	28	38	30	9	0	215.0	221	13	77	60	6-19	0	3.98
Herm Wehmeier	R	22	33	29	11	1	213.1	202	20	117	80	11-12	0	4.68
J. Vander Meer	L	34	28	24	7	3	159.2	172	12	85	76	5-10	0	4.90
Harry Perkowski	L	26	5	3	2	0	23.2	21	2	14	3	1-1	0	4.56
Eddie Erautt	R	24	39	9	1	0	112.2	99	9	61	43	4-11	1	3.36
Buddy Lively	R	24	31	10	3	1	103.1	91	11	53	30	4-6	1	3.92
Ewell Blackwell	R	26	30	4	0	0	76.2	80	7	34	55	5-5	1	4.23
Kent Peterson	L	23	30	7	2	0	66.1	66	7	46	28	4-5	0	6.24
Frank Fanovich	L	27	29	1	0	0	43.1	44	2	28	27	0-2	0	5.40
Harry Gumbert†	R	39	29	0	0	0	40.2	58	5	8	12	4-3	2	5.53
Jess Dobernic†	R	31	14	0	0	0	19.1	28	7	16	6	0-0	0	9.78
Ken Burkhart	R	32	11	0	0	0	28.1	29	2	10	8	0-0	1	3.18
Dixie Howell	R	29	5	1	0	0	13.1	21	3	8	7	0-1	0	8.10
Walker Cress	R	32	3	0	0	0	2.0	2	0	3	0	0-0	0	0.00

1949 Chicago Cubs 8th NL 61-93 .396 36.0 GB

Charlie Grimm (19-31)/Frank Frisch (42-62)

Player	Gm by Position	B	Age	G	AB	R	H	2B	3B	HR	RBI	BB	SO	SB	Avg	OBP	Slg
Mickey Owen	C59	R	33	62	198	15	54	9	3	2	18	12	13	1	.273	.318	.379
Herman Reich†	1B85,OF16	R	31	108	386	43	108	18	2	3	34	13	32	4	.280	.305	.360
Emil Verban	2B88	R	33	98	343	38	99	11	1	0	22	8	2	3	.289	.309	.327
Frankie Gustine	3B55,2B16	R	29	76	261	29	59	13	4	4	27	18	22	3	.226	.279	.352
Roy Smalley	SS132	R	23	135	477	57	117	21	10	8	35	36	77	2	.245	.304	.382
Hal Jeffcoat	OF101	R	24	108	363	43	89	18	6	2	26	20	48	12	.245	.286	.344
Andy Pafko	OF98,3B49	R	28	144	519	79	146	29	2	18	69	63	33	4	.281	.369	.449
Hank Sauer†	OF96	R	32	96	357	59	104	17	1	27	83	37	47	0	.291	.363	.571
Phil Cavarretta	1B70,OF25	L	32	105	360	46	106	22	4	8	49	45	31	2	.294	.374	.444
Bob Ramazzotti†	3B36,SS12,2B4	R	32	65	190	14	34	3	1	0	6	5	33	9	.179	.200	.205
Hank Edwards†	OF51	L	30	58	176	25	51	8	4	7	21	19	22	0	.290	.359	.500
Rube Walker	C43	L	23	56	172	11	42	4	1	3	22	9	18	0	.244	.282	.331
Frankie Baumholtz†	OF43	L	30	58	164	15	37	4	2	1	15	9	21	2	.226	.270	.293
Harry Walker†	OF39	L	32	42	159	20	42	6	3	1	14	11	6	2	.264	.312	.358
Gene Mauch	2B25,SS19,3B7	R	23	72	150	15	37	6	2	1	7	21	15	3	.247	.339	.333
Bob Scheffing	C40	R	35	55	149	12	40	6	1	3	19	9	9	0	.268	.314	.383
Wayne Terwilliger	2B34	R	24	36	112	11	25	2	1	2	10	16	22	0	.223	.326	.313
Peanuts Lowrey†	OF31,3B1	R	30	38	111	18	30	5	0	2	10	9	8	3	.270	.325	.369
Rube Novotney	C20	R	24	22	67	4	18	2	1	0	6	3	11	0	.269	.300	.328
Smoky Burgess	C8	L	22	46	56	4	15	0	0	1	12	4	4	0	.268	.317	.321
Bill Serena	3B11	R	24	12	37	3	8	3	0	1	7	7	9	0	.216	.341	.378
Hank Schenz	3B5	R	30	7	14	2	6	0	0	0	1	1	0	2	.429	.467	.429
Clarence Maddern	1B1	R	27	10	9	1	3	0	0	1	2	2	0	0	.333	.455	.667
Cliff Aberson	OF1	R	27	4	7	0	0	0	0	0	0	0	2	0	.000	.000	.000
Jim Kirby		R	26	3	2	0	1	0	0	0	0	0	0	0	.500	.500	.500

Pitcher	T	Age	G	GS	CG	ShO	IP	H	HR	BB	SO	W-L	Sv	ERA
Johnny Schmitz	L	28	36	31	9	3	207.0	227	11	92	75	11-13	3	4.35
Dutch Leonard	R	40	33	28	10	1	180.0	198	4	43	83	7-16	0	4.15
Bob Rush	R	23	35	27	9	1	201.0	197	10	79	80	10-18	4	4.07
Monk Dubiel	R	31	32	20	3	1	147.2	142	16	54	52	6-9	4	4.14
Bob Chipman	L	30	38	11	3	1	113.1	110	7	63	46	7-8	1	3.97
Doyle Lade	R	28	36	13	5	1	129.2	141	14	58	43	4-5	1	5.00
Bob Muncrief†	R	33	34	3	1	0	75.0	80	9	31	36	5-6	2	4.56
Warren Hacker	R	24	30	12	3	0	125.2	141	7	53	40	5-8	0	4.23
Dewey Adkins	R	31	30	5	1	0	82.1	98	10	39	43	2-4	0	5.68
Emil Kush	R	32	26	0	0	0	47.2	51	7	24	22	3-3	2	3.78
Cal McLish	R	23	8	2	0	0	23.0	31	5	12	6	1-1	0	5.87
Ralph Hamner	R	32	6	1	0	0	12.1	22	1	8	3	0-2	0	8.76
Dwain Sloat	L	30	5	1	0	0	9.0	14	0	3	3	0-0	0	7.00
Jess Dobernic†	R	31	4	0	0	0	4.0	9	2	4	0	0-0	0	20.25
Mort Cooper	R	36	1	0	0	0	0.0	2	1	1	0	0-0	0	—

»1950 New York Yankees 1st AL 98-56 .636 —

Casey Stengel

Player	Gm by Position	B	Age	G	AB	R	H	2B	3B	HR	RBI	BB	SO	SB	Avg	OBP	Slg
Yogi Berra	C148	L	25	151	597	116	192	30	6	28	124	55	12	4	.322	.380	.533
Joe Collins	1B99,OF2	L	27	108	205	47	48	8	3	8	28	31	34	5	.234	.335	.420
Jerry Coleman	2B152,SS6	R	25	153	522	69	150	19	6	6	69	67	38	3	.287	.372	.381
Bill Johnson	3B100,1B5	R	31	108	327	44	85	16	2	6	40	42	30	1	.260	.346	.376
Phil Rizzuto	SS155	R	32	155	617	125	200	36	7	7	66	91	38	12	.324	.417	.439
Joe DiMaggio	OF137,1B1	R	35	139	525	114	158	33	10	32	122	80	33	0	.301	.394	.585
Gene Woodling	OF118	L	27	122	449	81	127	20	10	6	60	69	31	5	.283	.380	.412
Hank Bauer	OF110	R	27	113	415	72	133	16	2	13	70	35	41	2	.320	.380	.463
Cliff Mapes	OF102	L	28	108	356	60	88	14	6	12	61	47	61	1	.247	.338	.421
Bobby Brown	3B82	L	25	95	277	33	74	4	2	4	37	39	18	3	.267	.360	.339
Johnny Mize	1B72	L	37	90	274	43	76	12	0	25	72	29	24	0	.277	.351	.595
Tommy Henrich	1B34	L	37	73	151	20	41	6	8	6	34	27	6	0	.272	.382	.536
Jackie Jensen	OF23	R	23	45	70	13	12	2	2	1	5	7	8	4	.171	.247	.300
Billy Martin	2B22,3B1	R	22	34	36	10	9	1	0	1	8	3	3	0	.250	.308	.361
Johnny Hopp†	1B12,OF6	L	33	19	27	9	9	2	1	1	8	9	1	0	.333	.500	.593
Charlie Silvera	C15	R	25	18	25	2	4	0	0	0	1	1	2	0	.160	.192	.160
Johnny Lindell†	OF6	R	33	7	21	2	4	0	0	0	2	4	2	0	.190	.320	.190
Jim Delsing†		L	24	12	10	2	4	0	0	0	2	2	0	0	.400	.500	.400
Ralph Houk	C9	R	30	10	9	0	1	1	0	0	1	0	2	0	.111	.111	.222
Hank Workman	1B1	L	24	2	5	1	1	0	0	0	0	1	0	0	.200	.200	.200
Snuffy Stirnweiss†	2B4	R	31	7	2	0	0	0	0	0	0	0	0	0	.000	.000	.000
Dick Wakefield		L	29	3	2	0	1	0	0	0	1	1	1	0	.500	.667	.500
Gus Niarhos†		R	29	1	0	0	0	0	0	0	0	0	0	0	—	—	—

Pitcher	T	Age	G	GS	CG	ShO	IP	H	HR	BB	SO	W-L	Sv	ERA
Vic Raschi	R	31	33	32	17	2	256.2	232	19	116	155	21-8	1	4.00
Ed Lopat	L	32	35	32	15	3	236.1	244	19	65	72	18-8	1	3.47
Tommy Byrne	L	30	31	31	10	2	203.1	188	23	160	118	15-9	0	4.74
Allie Reynolds	R	35	35	29	14	2	240.2	215	12	138	160	16-12	2	3.74
Whitey Ford	L	21	20	12	7	2	112.0	87	7	52	59	9-1	1	2.81
Joe Page	L	32	37	0	0	0	55.1	66	8	31	33	3-7	13	5.04
Tom Ferrick†	R	35	30	0	0	0	56.2	49	5	22	20	8-4	9	3.65
Fred Sanford	R	30	26	12	2	0	112.2	103	9	79	54	5-4	0	4.55
Joe Ostrowski†	L	33	21	4	1	0	43.2	50	11	15	15	1-1	3	5.15
Bob Porterfield	R	26	10	2	0	0	19.2	28	2	8	9	1-1	1	8.69
Don Johnson†	R	23	8	0	0	0	18.0	35	2	12	9	1-0	0	10.00
Duane Pillette†	R	27	4	0	0	0	7.0	9	0	3	4	0-0	0	1.29
Ernie Nevel	R	30	3	1	0	0	6.1	10	0	6	3	0-1	0	9.95
Lew Burdette	R	23	2	0	0	0	1.1	3	0	0	0	0-0	0	6.75
Dave Madison	R	29	1	0	0	0	3.0	3	1	1	1	0-0	0	6.00

1950 Detroit Tigers 2nd AL 95-59 .617 3.0 GB

Red Rolfe

Player	Gm by Position	B	Age	G	AB	R	H	2B	3B	HR	RBI	BB	SO	SB	Avg	OBP	Slg
Aaron Robinson	C103	L	35	107	283	37	64	7	0	9	37	75	35	0	.226	.388	.346
Don Kolloway	1B118,2B1	R	31	125	467	55	135	20	4	6	62	29	28	1	.289	.331	.388
Jerry Priddy	2B157	R	30	157	618	104	171	26	6	13	75	95	95	2	.277	.376	.401
George Kell	3B157	R	27	157	641	114	218	56	6	8	101	66	18	3	.340	.403	.484
Johnny Lipon	SS147	R	27	147	601	104	176	27	6	2	63	81	26	9	.293	.378	.368
Johnny Groth	OF157	R	23	157	566	95	173	30	8	12	85	95	27	1	.306	.407	.451
Vic Wertz	OF145	L	25	149	559	99	172	37	4	27	123	91	55	0	.308	.408	.533
Hoot Evers	OF139	R	29	143	526	100	170	35	11	21	103	71	40	5	.323	.408	.551
Dick Kryhoski	1B47	L	25	53	169	20	37	10	0	4	19	8	11	0	.219	.258	.349
Pat Mullin	OF32	L	32	69	142	16	31	5	0	6	23	20	23	1	.218	.315	.380
Bob Swift	C66	R	35	67	132	14	30	4	0	2	9	25	6	0	.227	.350	.303
Joe Ginsberg	C31	L	23	36	95	12	22	6	0	0	12	11	6	1	.232	.318	.295
Charlie Keller	OF6	L	33	50	51	7	16	1	3	2	16	13	6	0	.314	.453	.569
Neil Berry	SS11,2B2,3B1	R	28	38	39	9	10	1	0	0	7	6	11	0	.256	.356	.282
Eddie Lake	3B1,SS1	R	34	20	7	3	0	0	0	0	0	1	3	0	.000	.125	.000
Frank House	C5	L	20	5	5	1	2	1	0	0	0	0	1	0	.400	.400	.600
Paul Campbell		L	32	3	1	1	0	0	0	0	0	0	1	0	.000	.000	.000

Pitcher	T	Age	G	GS	CG	ShO	IP	H	HR	BB	SO	W-L	Sv	ERA
Art Houtteman	R	22	41	34	21	4	274.2	257	29	99	88	19-12	4	3.54
Hal Newhouser	L	29	35	30	15	1	213.2	232	23	81	87	15-13	3	4.34
Fred Hutchinson	R	30	39	26	10	1	231.2	269	18	48	71	17-8	0	3.96
Ted Gray	L	25	27	21	7	0	149.1	139	22	72	102	10-7	1	4.40
Dizzy Trout	R	35	34	20	11	1	184.2	190	13	64	88	13-5	4	3.75
Virgil Trucks	R	33	7	7	2	1	48.1	45	6	21	25	3-1	0	3.54
Hal White	R	31	42	8	3	1	111.0	96	7	65	53	9-6	1	4.54
Paul Calvert	R	32	32	0	0	0	51.1	71	7	25	14	2-2	4	6.31
Marlin Stuart	R	31	19	1	0	0	43.2	59	6	22	19	3-1	2	5.56
Hank Borowy†	R	34	13	2	1	0	32.2	23	3	16	12	1-1	0	3.31
Saul Rogovin	R	26	11	5	1	0	40.0	39	5	26	11	2-1	0	4.50
Ray Herbert	R	20	8	3	1	0	22.1	20	1	12	5	1-2	1	3.63
Bill Connelly†	R	25	2	0	0	0	4.0	4	1	2	1	0-0	0	6.75

1950 Boston Red Sox 3rd AL 94-60 .610 4.0 GB

Joe McCarthy (31-28)/Steve O'Neill (63-32)

Player	Gm by Position	B	Age	G	AB	R	H	2B	3B	HR	RBI	BB	SO	SB	Avg	OBP	Slg
Birdie Tebbetts	C74	R	37	79	268	33	83	10	1	8	45	29	26	1	.310	.377	.444
Walt Dropo	1B134	R	27	136	559	101	180	28	8	34	144	45	75	0	.322	.378	.583
Bobby Doerr	2B149	R	32	149	586	103	172	29	11	27	120	67	42	3	.294	.367	.519
Johnny Pesky	3B116,SS8	L	30	127	490	112	153	22	6	1	49	104	31	2	.312	.437	.388
Vern Stephens	SS146	R	29	149	628	125	185	34	6	30	144	65	43	1	.295	.361	.511
Dom DiMaggio	OF140	R	33	141	588	131	193	30	11	7	70	82	68	15	.328	.414	.452
Al Zarilla	OF128	L	31	130	471	92	153	32	10	9	74	76	47	2	.325	.423	.493
Ted Williams	OF86	L	31	89	334	82	106	24	1	28	97	82	21	3	.317	.452	.647
Billy Goodman	OF45,3B27,1B21*	L	24	110	424	91	150	25	3	4	68	52	25	2	.354	.427	.455
Matt Batts	C73	R	28	75	238	27	65	15	3	4	34	18	19	0	.273	.327	.412
Clyde Vollmer†	OF39	R	28	57	169	35	48	10	0	7	37	21	35	1	.284	.363	.467
Tom Wright	OF24	L	26	54	107	17	34	7	0	0	20	6	18	0	.318	.360	.383
Buddy Rosar	C25	R	35	27	84	13	25	2	0	1	12	7	4	0	.298	.352	.357
Tommy O'Brien†	OF9	R	31	9	31	0	4	1	0	0	3	3	5	0	.129	.206	.161
Ken Keltner	3B8,1B1	R	33	13	28	2	9	2	0	0	2	3	6	0	.321	.387	.393
Lou Stringer	3B3,2B1,SS1	R	33	24	17	7	5	1	0	0	2	0	4	1	.294	.294	.353
Fred Hatfield	3B3	L	25	10	12	3	3	0	0	0	2	3	1	0	.250	.400	.250
Charlie Maxwell	OF1	L	23	3	8	1	0	0	0	0	0	1	3	0	.000	.111	.000
Jimmy Piersall	OF2	R	20	6	7	4	2	0	0	0	0	4	0	0	.286	.545	.286
Bob Scherbarth	C1	R	24	1	0	0	0	0	0	0	0	0	0	0	—	—	—
Merrill Combs†		L	30	1	0	0	0	0	0	0	0	1	0	0	—	1.000	—

B. Goodman, 5 G at 2B, 1 G at SS

Pitcher	T	Age	G	GS	CG	ShO	IP	H	HR	BB	SO	W-L	Sv	ERA
Mel Parnell	L	28	40	31	21	2	249.0	244	17	106	93	18-10	3	3.61
Joe Dobson	R	33	39	27	12	1	206.2	217	15	81	81	15-10	4	4.18
Chuck Stobbs	L	20	32	21	6	0	169.1	158	17	88	78	12-7	1	5.10
Willard Nixon	R	22	22	15	2	0	101.1	126	8	58	57	8-6	2	6.04
Harry Taylor	R	31	3	2	2	1	19.0	13	0	8	8	2-0	0	1.42
Ellis Kinder	R	35	48	23	11	1	207.0	212	23	78	95	14-12	9	4.26
Mickey McDermott	L	22	38	15	4	0	130.0	119	8	124	96	7-3	5	5.19
Walt Masterson	R	30	33	15	6	1	129.1	145	15	82	60	8-6	1	5.64
Al Papai†	R	33	16	3	2	0	50.2	61	5	28	19	4-2	2	6.75
Dick Littlefield	L	24	15	2	0	0	23.1	27	6	24	13	2-2	1	9.26
Charley Schanz	R	31	14	0	0	0	22.2	25	3	24	14	3-2	0	8.34
Earl Johnson	L	31	11	0	0	0	13.2	18	0	8	6	0-0	0	7.24
Jim McDonald	R	23	9	0	0	0	19.0	23	1	10	5	1-0	0	3.79
Gordy Mueller	R	27	8	0	0	0	7.0	11	1	13	1	0-0	0	10.29
Jim Suchecki	R	22	4	0	0	0	4.0	3	0	4	3	0-0	0	4.50
James Atkins	R	29	1	0	0	0	4.2	4	1	4	0	0-0	0	3.86
Frank Quinn	R	22	1	0	0	0	2.0	2	0	1	0	0-0	0	9.00
Bob Gillespie	R	31	1	0	0	0	1.1	2	1	4	0	0-0	0	20.25
Phil Marchildon	R	36	1	0	0	0	1.1	1	0	2	0	0-0	0	6.75
Boo Ferriss	R	28	1	0	0	0	1.0	2	0	1	1	0-0	0	18.00

1950 Cleveland Indians 4th AL 92-62 .597 6.0 GB

Lou Boudreau

Player	Gm by Position	B	Age	G	AB	R	H	2B	3B	HR	RBI	BB	SO	SB	Avg	OBP	Slg
Jim Hegan	C129	R	29	131	415	53	91	16	5	14	58	42	52	1	.219	.291	.383
Luke Easter	1B128,OF13	L	34	141	540	96	151	20	4	28	107	70	95	0	.280	.373	.487
Joe Gordon	2B105	R	35	119	368	59	87	12	1	19	57	56	44	4	.236	.340	.429
Al Rosen	3B154	R	26	155	554	100	159	23	4	37	116	100	72	5	.287	.405	.543
Ray Boone	SS102	R	26	109	365	53	110	14	6	7	58	56	27	4	.301	.397	.430
Bob Kennedy	OF144	R	29	146	540	79	157	27	5	9	54	53	31	3	.291	.355	.409
Larry Doby	OF140	L	26	142	503	110	164	25	5	25	102	98	71	8	.326	.442	.545
Dale Mitchell	OF127	L	28	130	506	81	156	27	5	3	49	67	21	3	.308	.390	.399
Lou Boudreau	SS61,1B8,2B2*	R	32	81	260	23	70	13	2	1	29	31	5	1	.269	.349	.346
Bobby Avila	2B62,SS2	R	26	80	201	39	60	10	2	1	21	29	17	5	.299	.390	.383
Allie Clark	OF41	R	27	59	163	19	35	6	1	6	21	11	10	0	.215	.264	.374
Ray Murray	C45	R	32	55	139	16	38	8	2	1	13	12	13	1	.273	.331	.381
Thurman Tucker	OF34	L	32	57	101	13	18	2	0	1	7	14	14	1	.178	.284	.228
Mickey Vernon†	1B25	L	32	28	90	8	17	0	0	0	10	12	10	2	.189	.284	.189
Jim Lemon	OF10	R	22	12	34	4	6	1	0	1	1	3	12	0	.176	.243	.294
Herb Conyers	1B1	L	29	7	9	2	3	0	0	1	1	1	2	1	.333	.400	.667
Johnny Berardino†	2B1,3B1	R	33	4	5	1	2	0	0	0	3	1	0	0	.400	.500	.400

L. Boudreau, 2 G at 3B

Pitcher	T	Age	G	GS	CG	ShO	IP	H	HR	BB	SO	W-L	Sv	ERA
Bob Lemon	R	29	44	37	22	3	288.0	281	28	146	170	23-11	3	3.84
Bob Feller	R	31	35	34	16	3	247.0	230	20	103	119	16-11	0	3.43
Mike Garcia	R	26	33	29	11	0	184.0	191	15	74	76	11-11	0	3.86
Early Wynn	R	30	32	28	14	2	213.2	166	20	101	143	18-8	0	3.20
Al Aber	L	22	1	1	1	0	9.0	5	0	4	4	1-0	0	2.00
Al Benton	R	39	36	0	0	0	63.0	57	7	30	26	4-2	4	3.57
Sam Zoldak	L	31	33	3	0	0	63.2	64	6	21	15	4-2	4	3.96
Steve Gromek	R	30	31	13	4	1	113.1	94	10	36	43	10-7	0	3.65
Marino Pieretti	R	29	29	1	0	0	47.0	45	2	30	11	0-1	1	4.21
Jesse Flores	R	35	28	2	1	1	53.0	53	3	25	27	3-3	4	3.74
Gene Bearden†	L	29	14	3	0	0	45.1	57	5	32	10	1-3	0	6.15
Dick Rozek	L	23	12	2	0	0	25.1	28	3	19	14	0-0	0	4.97
Dick Weik†	R	22	11	2	0	0	26.0	18	1	26	16	1-3	0	3.81

1950 Washington Senators 5th AL 67-87 .435 31.0 GB

Bucky Harris

Player	Gm by Position	B	Age	G	AB	R	H	2B	3B	HR	RBI	BB	SO	SB	Avg	OBP	Slg
Al Evans	C88	R	33	90	289	24	68	8	3	2	30	29	21	0	.235	.309	.304
Mickey Vernon†	1B85	L	32	90	327	47	100	17	3	9	65	50	29	6	.306	.404	.459
Cass Michaels†	2B104	R	24	106	388	48	97	8	4	4	47	55	39	2	.250	.345	.322
Eddie Yost	3B155	R	23	155	573	114	169	26	2	11	58	141	63	6	.295	.440	.405
Sam Dente	SS128,2B29	R	28	155	603	56	144	20	5	2	59	39	19	1	.239	.286	.299
Irv Noren	OF121,1B17	L	25	138	542	80	160	27	10	14	98	67	77	5	.295	.375	.459
Bud Stewart	OF100	L	34	118	378	46	101	15	6	4	35	46	33	5	.267	.348	.370
Sam Mele	OF99,1B16	R	27	126	435	57	119	21	6	12	86	51	40	2	.274	.351	.432
Gil Coan	OF98	L	28	104	366	58	111	17	4	7	50	28	46	10	.303	.359	.429
Mickey Grasso	C69	R	30	75	195	25	56	4	1	1	22	25	31	1	.287	.374	.333
Johnny Ostrowski†	OF45	R	32	55	141	16	32	2	1	4	23	20	31	2	.227	.327	.340
Eddie Robinson†	1B36	L	29	36	125	21	30	4	2	1	13	25	14	0	.240	.375	.328
Sherry Robertson	OF14,2B12,3B1	L	31	71	123	19	32	3	3	2	16	22	18	1	.260	.372	.382
Merrill Combs†	SS30	L	30	37	102	19	25	1	0	0	6	22	16	0	.245	.379	.255
Roberto Ortiz†	OF19	R	35	39	75	4	17	2	1	0	8	7	12	0	.227	.301	.280
Al Kozar†	2B15	R	28	20	55	7	11	1	0	0	3	5	8	0	.200	.267	.218
Hal Keller	C8	L	22	11	28	1	6	3	0	1	5	2	6	0	.214	.267	.429
Len Okrie	C17	R	26	17	27	2	6	0	0	0	2	6	7	0	.222	.382	.222
Gene Bearden†	P12,1B1	L	29	14	22	1	5	1	0	0	2	3	2	0	.227	.320	.273
Fred Taylor	1B3	L	25	6	16	1	2	0	0	0	0	1	2	0	.125	.176	.125
Clyde Vollmer†	OF6	R	28	6	14	4	4	0	0	0	1	2	3	1	.286	.375	.286
Tommy O'Brien†	OF3	R	31	3	9	1	1	0	0	0	1	1	1	0	.111	.200	.111
George Genovese		L	28	3	1	1	0	0	0	0	0	1	0	0	.000	.500	.000

Pitcher	T	Age	G	GS	CG	ShO	IP	H	HR	BB	SO	W-L	Sv	ERA
Sid Hudson	R	35	30	30	17	0	237.2	261	17	98	75	14-14	0	4.09
Bob Kuzava†	L	27	22	22	8	1	155.0	156	8	75	84	8-7	0	3.95
Connie Marrero	R	39	27	19	8	1	152.0	159	17	55	63	6-10	1	4.50
Sandy Consuegra	R	29	21	18	8	2	124.2	132	6	57	38	7-8	2	4.40
Al Sima	L	28	17	9	1	0	77.0	89	9	26	23	4-5	0	4.79
Gene Bearden†	L	29	12	9	4	0	68.1	81	1	33	20	3-5	0	4.21
Steve Nagy	L	31	9	9	2	0	53.1	69	5	29	17	2-5	0	6.58
Ray Scarborough†	R	32	8	8	4	2	58.1	62	1	22	24	3-5	0	4.01
Julio Moreno	R	29	4	3	1	0	21.1	22	1	12	7	1-1	0	4.64
Carlos Pascual	R	19	2	2	2	0	17.0	12	0	8	3	1-1	0	2.12
Rogelio Martinez	R	31	2	1	0	0	1.1	4	0	2	0	0-1	0	27.00
Mickey Harris	L	33	53	0	0	0	98.0	93	10	46	41	5-9	15	4.78
Joe Haynes	R	32	27	10	1	1	101.2	124	14	46	15	7-5	0	5.84
Elmer Singleton	R	32	21	1	0	0	36.1	39	4	17	19	1-2	0	5.20
Jim Pearce	R	25	20	3	1	0	56.2	58	2	37	18	2-1	0	6.04
Dick Weik†	R	22	14	5	1	0	44.0	38	2	47	26	1-3	0	4.30
Lloyd Hittle	L	26	11	4	1	0	43.1	60	1	17	9	2-4	0	4.98
Bob Ross	L	21	6	2	0	0	12.2	15	1	15	2	0-1	0	8.53
Dick Welteroth	R	22	5	0	0	0	6.0	5	0	6	2	0-0	0	3.00

Seasons: Team Rosters 713

1950 Chicago White Sox 6th AL 60-94 .390 38.0 GB

Jack Onslow (8-22)/Red Corriden (52-72)

Player	Gm by Position	B	Age	G	AB	R	H	2B	3B	HR	RBI	BB	SO	SB	Avg	OBP	Slg
Phil Masi	C114	R	34	122	377	38	105	17	2	7	55	49	36	2	.279	.366	.390
Eddie Robinson†	1B119	L	29	119	428	62	133	11	2	20	73	60	28	0	.311	.402	.486
Nellie Fox	2B121	L	22	130	457	45	113	12	7	0	30	35	17	4	.247	.304	.304
Hank Majeski	3B112	R	33	122	414	47	128	18	2	6	46	42	34	1	.309	.377	.406
Chico Carrasquel	SS141	R	24	141	524	72	148	21	5	4	46	66	46	0	.282	.368	.365
Dave Philley	OF154	S	30	156	619	69	150	21	5	14	80	52	57	6	.242	.302	.360
Gus Zernial	OF137	R	27	143	543	75	152	16	4	29	93	38	110	0	.280	.330	.484
Marv Rickert†	OF78,1B1	L	29	84	278	38	66	9	2	4	27	21	42	0	.237	.291	.327
Floyd Baker	3B53,2B3,OF2	L	33	83	186	26	59	7	0	0	11	32	10	1	.317	.417	.355
Cass Michaels†	2B35	R	24	36	138	21	43	6	3	4	19	13	8	0	.312	.375	.486
Mike McCormick†	OF44	R	33	55	138	16	32	4	3	0	10	16	6	0	.232	.312	.304
Luke Appling	SS20,1B13,2B1	R	43	50	128	11	30	3	4	0	13	12	8	2	.234	.300	.320
Gordon Goldsberry	1B40,OF3	L	22	82	127	19	34	8	2	2	25	26	18	0	.268	.392	.409
Herb Adams	OF33	L	22	34	118	12	24	2	3	0	2	12	7	3	.203	.288	.271
Gus Niarhos†	C36	R	29	41	105	17	34	4	0	0	16	14	6	0	.324	.408	.362
Eddie Malone	C21	R	30	31	71	2	16	2	0	0	10	10	8	0	.225	.321	.254
Jerry Scala	OF23	L	25	40	67	8	13	2	1	0	6	10	10	0	.194	.299	.254
Johnny Ostrowski†	OF15	R	32	22	49	10	12	2	1	2	2	9	9	0	.245	.373	.449
Jim Busby	OF12	R	23	18	48	5	10	0	0	0	4	1	5	0	.208	.224	.208
Joe Erautt	C5	R	28	16	18	0	4	0	0	0	1	1	3	0	.222	.263	.222
Al Kozar†	2B4,3B1	R	28	10	10	4	3	0	0	1	2	0	3	0	.300	.300	.600
Chuck Kress	1B2	L	28	3	8	0	0	0	0	0	0	0	0	0	.000	.000	.000
Bill Wilson	OF2	R	21	3	6	0	0	0	0	0	0	2	2	0	.000	.250	.000
Ed McGhee	OF1	R	25	3	6	0	1	0	1	0	0	0	1	0	.167	.167	.500
Joe Kirrene	3B1	R	18	1	4	0	1	0	0	0	0	0	1	0	.250	.250	.250
Bill Salkeld	C1	L	33	1	3	0	0	0	0	0	0	1	0	0	.000	.250	.000

Pitcher	T	Age	G	GS	CG	ShO	IP	H	HR	BB	SO	W-L	Sv	ERA
Billy Pierce	L	23	33	29	15	1	219.1	189	11	137	118	12-16	1	3.98
Bill Wight	L	28	30	28	13	3	206.0	213	10	79	62	10-16	0	3.58
Bob Cain	L	25	34	23	11	1	171.2	153	12	109	77	9-12	2	3.93
Ray Scarborough†	R	32	27	23	8	1	149.1	160	10	62	70	10-13	1	5.30
Ken Holcombe	R	31	24	15	5	0	96.0	122	10	45	37	3-10	1	4.59
Bob Kuzava†	L	27	10	7	1	0	44.1	43	5	27	21	1-3	0	5.68
Gus Keriazakos	R	18	1	1	0	0	2.1	7	0	5	1	0-1	0	19.29
Howie Judson	R	24	46	3	1	0	112.0	105	10	63	34	2-3	0	3.94
Luis Aloma	R	26	42	0	0	0	87.2	77	6	53	49	7-2	4	3.80
Randy Gumpert	R	32	40	17	6	1	155.1	165	15	58	48	5-12	0	4.75
Mickey Haefner†	L	37	24	9	2	0	70.2	83	11	45	17	1-6	0	5.73
Lou Kretlow†	R	29	11	1	0	0	21.1	17	1	27	14	0-0	0	3.80
Jack Bruner†	L	25	9	0	0	0	12.1	7	0	14	8	0-0	0	3.65
Marv Rotblatt	L	22	2	0	0	0	8.2	11	2	5	6	0-0	0	6.23
Bill Connelly†	R	25	2	0	0	0	2.1	5	1	1	0	0-0	0	11.57
Charlie Cuellar	R	32	2	0	0	0	1.1	6	0	3	1	0-0	0	33.75
John Perkovich	R	26	1	0	0	0	5.0	7	3	1	3	0-0	0	7.20

1950 St. Louis Browns 7th AL 58-96 .377 40.0 GB

Zack Taylor

Player	Gm by Position	B	Age	G	AB	R	H	2B	3B	HR	RBI	BB	SO	SB	Avg	OBP	Slg
Sherm Lollar	C109	R	25	126	396	55	111	22	3	13	65	64	25	2	.280	.391	.449
Don Lenhardt	1B86,OF39,3B10	R	27	139	480	75	131	22	6	22	81	90	94	3	.273	.390	.481
Owen Friend	2B93,3B24,SS3	R	23	119	372	48	88	15	2	8	50	40	68	2	.237	.312	.352
Bill Sommers	3B37,2B21	R	27	65	137	24	35	5	1	0	14	25	14	0	.255	.370	.307
Tom Upton	SS115,2B2,3B1	R	23	124	389	50	92	5	6	2	30	52	45	7	.237	.328	.296
Dick Kokos	OF127	L	22	143	490	77	128	27	5	18	67	88	73	8	.261	.375	.447
Ray Coleman	OF98	L	28	117	384	54	104	25	6	8	55	32	37	7	.271	.330	.430
Ken Wood	OF94	R	25	128	369	42	83	24	0	13	62	38	58	0	.225	.299	.396
Roy Sievers	OF78,3B21	R	23	113	370	46	88	20	4	10	57	34	42	1	.238	.305	.395
Snuffy Stirnweiss†	2B62,3B31,SS5	R	31	93	326	32	71	16	2	1	24	51	49	3	.218	.324	.288
Hank Arft	1B84	L	28	98	280	45	75	16	4	1	32	46	48	3	.268	.375	.364
Les Moss	C60	R	25	84	222	24	59	6	0	8	34	26	32	0	.266	.343	.401
Jim Delsing†	OF53	L	24	69	209	25	55	5	2	0	15	20	23	1	.263	.328	.306
Billy DeMars	SS54,3B5	R	24	61	178	25	44	5	1	0	13	22	13	0	.247	.330	.287
Leo Thomas	3B35	R	26	35	121	19	24	6	0	1	9	20	14	0	.198	.312	.273
Ned Garver	P37,OF1	R	24	51	91	13	26	4	0	1	10	8	9	0	.286	.343	.363
Frankie Gustine	3B6	R	30	9	19	1	3	1	0	0	2	3	8	0	.158	.273	.211

Pitcher	T	Age	G	GS	CG	ShO	IP	H	HR	BB	SO	W-L	Sv	ERA
Ned Garver	R	24	37	31	22	2	260.0	264	18	108	85	13-18	0	3.39
Al Widmar	R	25	36	26	8	1	194.2	211	16	74	78	7-15	4	4.76
Stubby Overmire	L	31	31	19	8	2	161.0	200	11	45	39	9-12	0	4.19
Dick Starr	R	29	32	16	4	1	123.2	140	11	74	30	7-5	2	5.02
Cliff Fannin	R	26	25	16	3	0	102.0	116	18	58	42	5-9	1	6.53
Joe Ostrowski†	L	33	9	7	2	0	57.1	57	2	7	15	2-4	0	2.51
Ed Albrecht	R	21	2	1	0	0	6.2	6	0	7	1	0-1	0	5.40
Harry Dorish	R	28	29	13	4	0	109.0	162	13	36	36	4-9	0	6.44
Cuddles Marshall	R	25	28	2	0	0	53.2	72	1	51	24	1-3	1	7.88
Don Johnson†	R	23	25	12	4	0	96.0	126	14	55	31	5-6	1	6.09
Duane Pillette†	R	27	24	7	1	0	73.2	104	6	44	18	3-5	2	7.09
Tom Ferrick†	R	35	16	0	0	0	24.0	24	2	7	6	1-3	2	4.13
Tommy Fine	R	35	14	0	0	0	36.2	53	6	25	6	0-1	0	8.10
Jack Bruner†	L	25	13	1	0	0	35.0	36	4	23	16	1-2	1	4.63
Lou Kretlow†	R	29	9	2	0	0	14.1	25	2	18	10	0-2	0	11.93
Sid Schacht	R	32	8	1	0	0	10.2	24	5	14	7	0-0	0	16.03
Ribs Raney	R	27	1	0	0	0	2.0	2	0	2	2	0-1	0	4.50
Bill Kennedy	L	29	1	0	0	0	2.0	1	0	2	1	0-0	0	0.00
Russ Bauers	R	36	1	0	0	0	2.0	6	0	1	0	0-0	0	4.50
Lou Sleater	L	23	1	0	0	0	1.0	0	0	0	1	0-0	0	0.00

1950 Philadelphia Athletics 8th AL 52-102 .338 46.0 GB

Connie Mack

Player	Gm by Position	B	Age	G	AB	R	H	2B	3B	HR	RBI	BB	SO	SB	Avg	OBP	Slg
Mike Guerra	C78	R	37	87	252	25	71	10	4	2	26	16	12	1	.282	.325	.377
Ferris Fain	1B151	L	29	151	522	83	147	25	4	10	83	133	26	8	.282	.430	.402
Billy Hitchcock	2B107,SS1	R	33	115	399	35	109	22	5	1	54	45	32	3	.273	.347	.361
Bob Dillinger†	3B84	R	31	84	356	55	110	21	9	3	41	31	20	5	.309	.366	.444
Eddie Joost	SS131	R	34	131	476	79	111	12	3	18	58	103	68	5	.233	.373	.384
Sam Chapman	OF140	R	34	144	553	93	139	20	6	23	95	67	79	3	.251	.337	.434
Elmer Valo	OF117	L	29	129	446	62	125	16	5	10	46	83	22	12	.280	.401	.406
Paul Lehner	OF101	L	29	114	427	48	132	17	5	9	52	32	33	1	.309	.357	.436
Kermit Wahl	3B61,SS18,2B2	R	27	89	280	26	72	12	3	2	27	30	30	1	.257	.331	.343
Wally Moses	OF62	L	39	88	265	47	70	16	5	2	21	40	17	0	.264	.365	.385
Pete Suder	2B47,3B11,SS10*	R	34	77	248	34	61	10	0	8	35	23	31	2	.246	.310	.383
Joe Tipton	C59	R	28	64	184	15	49	5	1	6	20	19	16	0	.266	.335	.402
Barney McCosky	OF42	L	33	66	179	19	43	10	1	0	11	22	12	0	.240	.323	.307
Joe Astroth	C38	R	27	39	110	11	36	3	1	1	18	18	3	0	.327	.422	.400
Bob Wellman	OF2	R	24	11	15	1	5	0	0	1	1	0	3	0	.333	.333	.533
Roberto Ortiz†	OF3	R	35	6	14	1	1	0	0	0	3	0	3	0	.071	.071	.071
Gene Markland	2B5	R	30	5	8	2	1	0	0	0	0	3	0	0	.125	.364	.125
Ben Guintini	OF1	R	30	3	4	0	0	0	0	0	0	0	1	0	.000	.000	.000
Bob Rinker	C1	R	29	3	3	0	1	0	0	0	0	0	0	0	.333	.333	.333

P. Suder, 4 G at 1B

Pitcher	T	Age	G	GS	CG	ShO	IP	H	HR	BB	SO	W-L	Sv	ERA
Lou Brissie	L	26	46	31	15	2	246.0	237	22	117	101	7-19	8	4.02
Alex Kellner	L	25	36	29	15	0	225.1	253	28	112	85	8-20	2	5.47
Bobby Shantz	L	24	36	23	6	1	214.2	251	18	85	93	8-14	0	4.61
Hank Wyse	R	32	41	23	4	0	170.2	192	16	87	33	9-14	0	5.85
Dick Fowler	R	29	11	9	2	0	66.2	75	7	56	15	1-5	0	6.48
Johnny Kucab	R	30	4	2	2	0	26.0	29	4	8	8	1-1	0	3.46
Bob Hooper	R	28	45	20	3	0	170.1	181	15	91	58	15-10	5	5.02
Carl Scheib	R	23	43	8	1	0	106.0	138	13	70	37	3-10	3	7.22
Joe Coleman	R	27	15	6	2	0	54.0	74	9	50	12	0-5	0	8.50
Moe Burtschy	R	28	9	1	0	0	19.0	22	2	21	12	0-1	0	7.11
Joe Murray	L	29	8	2	0	0	30.0	34	1	21	8	0-3	0	5.70
Harry Byrd	R	25	6	0	0	0	10.2	25	3	9	2	0-0	0	16.88
Ed Klieman	R	32	5	0	0	0	5.2	10	0	2	0	0-0	0	9.53
Les McCrabb	R	35	2	0	0	0	1.1	7	0	0	2	0-0	0	27.00

»1950 Philadelphia Phillies 1st NL 91-63 .591 —

Eddie Sawyer

Player	Gm by Position	B	Age	G	AB	R	H	2B	3B	HR	RBI	BB	SO	SB	Avg	OBP	Slg
Andy Seminick	C124	R	29	130	393	55	113	15	3	24	68	68	50	0	.288	.400	.524
Eddie Waitkus	1B154	L	30	154	641	102	182	32	5	2	44	55	29	3	.284	.341	.359
Mike Goliat	2B145	R	24	145	483	49	113	13	6	13	64	53	75	3	.234	.314	.366
Puddin' Head Jones	3B157	R	24	157	610	100	163	28	6	25	88	61	40	5	.267	.337	.456
Granny Hamner	SS157	R	23	157	637	78	172	27	5	11	82	39	35	2	.270	.314	.380
Del Ennis	OF149	R	25	153	595	92	185	34	8	31	126	56	59	2	.311	.372	.551
Richie Ashburn	OF147	L	23	151	594	84	180	25	14	2	41	63	32	14	.303	.372	.402
Dick Sisler	OF137	L	29	141	523	79	155	29	4	13	83	64	50	1	.296	.373	.442
Dick Whitman	OF32	L	29	75	132	21	33	7	0	0	12	10	10	1	.250	.317	.303
Stan Lopata	C51	R	24	58	129	10	27	2	2	1	11	22	25	1	.209	.325	.279
Jimmy Bloodworth†	2B27,1B7,3B2	R	32	54	96	6	22	2	0	0	13	6	12	0	.229	.275	.250
Bill Nicholson	OF15	L	35	41	58	3	13	2	1	3	10	8	16	0	.224	.318	.448
Jackie Mayo	OF15	L	24	18	36	1	8	3	0	0	3	2	5	0	.222	.263	.306
Putsy Caballero	2B5,3B4,SS2	R	22	46	24	12	4	0	0	0	0	2	2	1	.167	.231	.167
Ken Silvestri	C9	S	34	11	20	2	5	0	1	0	4	4	3	0	.250	.400	.350
Stan Hollmig	OF3	R	24	11	12	1	3	2	0	0	1	0	3	0	.250	.250	.417
Johnny Blatnik†	OF1	R	29	4	4	0	1	0	0	0	0	2	3	0	.250	.500	.250

Pitcher	T	Age	G	GS	CG	ShO	IP	H	HR	BB	SO	W-L	Sv	ERA
Robin Roberts	R	23	40	39	21	5	304.1	282	29	77	146	20-11	1	3.02
Curt Simmons	L	21	31	27	11	2	214.2	178	19	88	146	17-8	1	3.40
Russ Meyer	R	26	32	25	3	0	159.2	193	21	67	74	9-11	1	5.30
Bob Miller	R	24	35	22	7	2	174.0	190	9	57	44	11-6	1	3.57
Bubba Church	R	25	31	18	8	2	142.0	113	12	56	50	8-6	1	2.73
Ken Heintzelman	L	34	23	17	4	1	125.1	122	10	54	39	3-9	0	4.09
Ken Johnson†	L	27	14	8	3	1	60.2	61	3	43	32	4-1	0	4.01
Jim Konstanty	R	33	74	0	0	0	152.0	108	11	50	56	16-7	22	2.66
Milo Candini	R	32	18	0	0	0	30.0	32	2	15	10	1-0	0	2.70
Blix Donnelly	R	36	14	1	0	0	21.0	30	5	10	10	2-4	0	4.29
Hank Borowy†	R	34	3	0	0	0	6.1	5	0	4	3	0-0	0	5.68
Paul Stuffel	R	23	3	0	0	0	5.0	4	0	1	3	0-0	0	1.80
Jack Brittin	R	26	3	0	0	0	4.0	2	0	3	3	0-0	0	4.50
Jocko Thompson	L	33	2	0	0	0	4.0	1	0	4	2	0-0	0	0.00
Steve Ridzik	R	21	1	0	0	0	3.0	3	1	1	2	0-0	0	6.00

1950 Brooklyn Dodgers 2nd NL 89-65 .578 2.0 GB

Burt Shotton

Player	Gm by Position	B	Age	G	AB	R	H	2B	3B	HR	RBI	BB	SO	SB	Avg	OBP	Slg
Roy Campanella	C123	R	28	126	437	70	123	19	3	31	89	55	51	1	.281	.364	.551
Gil Hodges	1B153	R	26	153	561	98	159	26	2	32	113	73	73	6	.283	.367	.508
Jackie Robinson	2B144	R	31	144	518	99	170	39	4	14	81	80	24	12	.328	.423	.500
Billy Cox	3B107,2B13,SS9	R	30	119	451	62	116	17	2	8	44	35	24	6	.257	.311	.357
Pee Wee Reese	SS134,3B7	R	31	141	531	97	138	21	5	11	52	91	62	17	.260	.369	.380
Carl Furillo	OF153	R	28	153	620	99	189	30	6	18	106	41	40	8	.305	.353	.460
Duke Snider	OF151	L	23	152	620	109	199	31	10	31	107	58	79	16	.321	.379	.553
Gene Hermanski	OF78	L	30	94	289	36	86	17	3	7	34	36	26	2	.298	.381	.450
Jim Russell	OF55	S	31	77	214	37	49	8	2	10	32	31	36	1	.229	.329	.425
Bobby Morgan	3B52,SS10	R	24	67	199	38	45	10	3	7	21	32	43	0	.226	.342	.412
Bruce Edwards	C38,1B2	R	26	50	142	16	26	4	1	8	16	13	22	1	.183	.256	.394
George Shuba	OF27	L	25	34	111	15	23	8	2	3	12	13	22	2	.207	.302	.396
Tommy Brown	OF16	R	22	48	86	15	25	2	1	8	20	11	9	0	.291	.378	.616
Eddie Miksis	2B15,SS15,3B7	R	23	51	76	13	19	2	1	2	10	5	10	3	.250	.296	.382
Cal Abrams	OF15	L	26	38	44	5	9	1	0	0	4	9	13	0	.205	.340	.227
Wayne Belardi	1B1	L	19	10	10	0	0	0	0	0	0	0	4	0	.000	.000	.000
Steve Lembo	C5	R	23	5	6	0	1	0	0	0	0	1	0	0	.167	.286	.167
Spider Jorgensen†	3B1	L	30	2	2	0	0	0	0	0	1	1	0	0	.000	.333	.000

Pitcher	T	Age	G	GS	CG	ShO	IP	H	HR	BB	SO	W-L	Sv	ERA
Don Newcombe	R	24	40	35	20	4	267.1	258	22	75	130	19-11	3	3.70
Preacher Roe	L	35	36	32	16	2	250.2	245	34	66	125	19-11	1	3.30
Carl Erskine	R	23	22	13	3	0	103.0	109	15	35	50	7-6	1	4.72
Bud Podbielan	R	26	20	10	2	0	72.2	93	10	29	28	5-4	1	5.33
Erv Palica	R	22	43	19	10	2	201.1	176	13	98	131	13-8	1	3.58
Ralph Branca	R	24	43	15	5	0	142.0	152	24	55	100	7-9	7	4.69
Dan Bankhead	R	30	41	12	2	1	129.1	119	16	88	96	9-4	3	5.50
Joe Hatten	L	33	23	8	2	1	68.2	82	10	31	29	2-2	0	4.59
Rex Barney	R	25	20	1	0	0	33.2	25	6	48	23	2-1	0	6.42
Jack Banta	R	25	16	5	1	0	41.1	39	2	36	15	4-4	2	4.35
Chris Van Cuyk	L	23	12	4	1	0	33.1	33	3	12	21	1-3	0	4.86
Billy Loes	R	20	10	0	0	0	12.2	16	5	5	2	0-0	0	7.82
Joe Landrum	R	21	7	0	0	0	6.2	12	2	1	5	0-1	0	8.10
Al Epperly	R	32	5	0	0	0	9.0	14	1	5	3	0-0	0	5.00
Willie Ramsdell†	R	34	5	0	0	0	6.1	7	0	2	2	1-2	1	2.84
Jim Romano	R	23	3	1	0	0	6.1	8	0	2	8	0-0	0	5.68
Mal Mallette	L	28	2	0	0	0	1.1	2	0	1	2	0-0	0	0.00
Clem Labine	R	23	1	0	0	0	2.0	2	0	1	0	0-0	0	4.50
Pat McGlothin	R	29	1	0	0	0	2.0	5	0	1	2	0-0	0	13.50

1950 New York Giants 3rd NL 86-68 .558 5.0 GB

Leo Durocher

Player	Gm by Position	B	Age	G	AB	R	H	2B	3B	HR	RBI	BB	SO	SB	Avg	OBP	Slg
Wes Westrum	C139	R	27	140	437	68	103	13	3	23	71	92	73	2	.236	.371	.437
Tookie Gilbert	1B111	L	21	113	322	40	71	12	2	4	32	43	36	3	.220	.314	.307
Eddie Stanky	2B151	R	33	152	527	115	158	25	5	8	51	144	50	9	.300	.460	.412
Hank Thompson	3B138,OF10	L	24	148	512	82	148	17	6	20	91	83	60	8	.289	.391	.463
Al Dark	SS154	R	28	154	587	79	164	36	5	16	67	39	60	9	.279	.331	.440
Bobby Thomson	OF149	R	26	149	563	79	142	22	7	25	85	55	45	3	.252	.324	.449
Whitey Lockman	OF128	L	23	129	532	72	157	28	5	6	52	42	29	1	.295	.349	.400
Don Mueller	OF125	L	23	132	525	60	153	15	6	7	84	10	26	1	.291	.309	.383
Monte Irvin	1B59,OF49,3B1	R	31	110	374	61	112	19	5	15	66	52	41	3	.299	.392	.497
Bill Rigney	2B23,3B11	R	32	56	83	8	15	2	0	0	8	8	13	0	.181	.253	.205
Roy Weatherly	OF15	L	35	52	69	10	18	3	3	0	11	13	10	0	.261	.378	.391
Sam Calderone	C33	R	24	34	67	9	20	1	0	1	12	2	5	0	.299	.319	.358
Jack Lohrke	3B16,2B1	R	26	30	43	4	8	0	0	0	4	4	8	0	.186	.255	.186
Clint Hartung	P20,OF2,1B1	R	27	32	43	7	13	2	1	3	10	1	13	0	.302	.318	.605
Jack Maguire	OF9,1B2	R	25	29	40	3	7	2	0	0	3	3	13	0	.175	.233	.225
Spider Jorgensen†	3B5	L	30	24	37	5	5	0	0	0	4	5	2	0	.135	.238	.135
Jack Harshman	1B9	L	22	9	32	3	4	0	0	2	4	3	6	0	.125	.200	.313
Sal Yvars	C9	R	26	9	14	0	2	0	0	0	0	1	2	0	.143	.200	.143
Rudy Rufer	SS8	R	23	15	11	1	1	0	0	0	0	0	1	1	.091	.091	.091
Ray Mueller†	C4	R	38	4	11	0	1	1	0	0	0	0	2	0	.091	.091	.182
Pete Milne		L	25	4	4	1	1	0	1	0	1	0	1	0	.250	.250	.750
Mike McCormick†		R	33	4	4	0	0	0	0	0	0	0	2	0	.000	.000	.000
Marv Blaylock		L	20	1	1	0	0	0	0	0	0	0	0	0	.000	.000	.000
Nap Reyes	1B1	R	30	1	1	0	0	0	0	0	0	0	0	0	.000	.000	.000

Pitcher	T	Age	G	GS	CG	ShO	IP	H	HR	BB	SO	W-L	Sv	ERA
Larry Jansen	R	29	40	35	21	5	275.0	238	31	55	161	19-13	3	3.01
Sheldon Jones	R	28	40	28	11	2	199.0	188	26	90	97	13-16	2	4.61
Dave Koslo	L	30	40	22	7	2	186.2	190	18	68	56	13-15	3	3.91
Jim Hearn†	R	29	16	16	11	5	125.0	72	8	38	54	11-3	0	1.94
Sal Maglie	R	33	47	16	12	5	206.0	169	14	86	96	18-4	1	2.71
Monte Kennedy	L	28	36	17	5	0	114.1	120	14	53	41	5-4	2	4.72
Jack Kramer	R	32	35	9	1	0	86.2	91	6	39	27	3-6	1	3.53
Andy Hansen	R	25	31	1	0	0	57.0	64	8	26	19	0-1	3	5.53
Clint Hartung	R	27	20	8	1	0	65.1	87	10	44	23	3-3	0	6.61
Kirby Higbe	R	35	18	1	0	0	34.2	37	2	30	17	0-3	0	4.93
George Spencer	R	23	10	1	1	0	25.1	12	3	7	5	1-0	0	2.49

1950 Boston Braves 4th NL 83-71 .539 8.0 GB

Billy Southworth

Player	Gm by Position	B	Age	G	AB	R	H	2B	3B	HR	RBI	BB	SO	SB	Avg	OBP	Slg
Walker Cooper†	C88	R	35	102	337	52	111	19	3	14	60	30	26	1	.329	.389	.528
Earl Torgeson	1B156	L	26	156	576	120	167	30	3	23	87	119	69	15	.290	.412	.472
Roy Hartsfield	2B96	R	24	107	419	62	116	15	2	7	24	27	61	7	.277	.322	.372
Bob Elliott	3B137	R	33	142	531	94	162	28	5	24	107	68	67	2	.305	.386	.512
Buddy Kerr	SS155	R	27	155	507	45	115	24	6	2	46	50	50	0	.227	.296	.310
Sam Jethroe	OF141	S	32	141	582	100	159	28	8	18	58	52	93	35	.273	.338	.442
Sid Gordon	OF123,3B10	R	32	134	481	78	146	33	4	27	103	78	31	2	.304	.403	.557
Tommy Holmes	OF88	L	33	105	322	44	96	20	1	9	51	33	8	0	.298	.370	.450
Willard Marshall	OF85	L	29	105	298	38	70	10	2	5	40	36	5	1	.235	.319	.332
Del Crandall	C75,1B1	R	20	79	255	21	56	11	0	4	37	13	24	0	.220	.257	.310
Luis Olmo	OF55,3B1	R	30	69	154	23	35	7	1	5	22	18	23	3	.227	.308	.383
Gene Mauch	2B28,3B7,SS5	R	24	48	121	17	28	5	0	1	15	14	9	1	.231	.316	.298
Sibby Sisti	SS23,2B19,3B13*	R	29	69	105	21	18	3	1	2	11	16	19	1	.171	.287	.276
Pete Reiser	OF24,3B1	L	31	53	78	12	16	2	0	1	10	18	22	1	.205	.367	.269
Connie Ryan†	2B20	R	30	20	72	12	14	2	0	3	6	12	9	0	.194	.326	.347
Bob Addis	OF7	L	24	16	28	7	7	1	0	0	2	3	5	1	.250	.323	.286
Paul Burris	C8	R	26	10	23	1	4	1	0	0	3	1	2	0	.174	.208	.217
Walt Linden	C3	R	26	3	5	0	2	1	0	0	0	1	0	0	.400	.500	.600
Emil Verban†	2B2	R	34	4	5	1	0	0	0	0	0	0	0	0	.000	.000	.000

S. Sisti, 1 G at 1B, 1 G at OF

Pitcher	T	Age	G	GS	CG	ShO	IP	H	HR	BB	SO	W-L	Sv	ERA
Vern Bickford	R	29	40	39	27	2	311.2	293	25	122	126	19-14	0	3.47
Warren Spahn	L	29	41	39	25	1	293.0	248	22	111	191	21-17	1	3.16
Johnny Sain	R	32	37	37	25	3	278.1	294	34	70	96	20-13	0	3.94
Max Surkont	R	28	9	6	2	0	55.2	63	5	20	21	5-2	0	3.23
Bobby Hogue	R	29	36	1	0	0	62.2	69	8	31	15	3-5	7	5.03
Bob Chipman	L	31	27	12	4	0	124.0	127	10	37	40	7-7	1	4.43
Bob Hall	R	26	21	4	0	0	50.1	58	8	33	22	0-2	0	6.97
Johnny Antonelli	L	20	20	6	2	1	58.2	81	2	22	33	2-3	0	5.83
Norm Roy	R	21	19	6	2	0	59.2	72	7	39	25	4-3	1	5.13
Ernie Johnson	R	26	16	1	0	0	20.2	37	1	13	15	2-0	0	6.97
Dick Donovan	R	22	10	3	0	0	29.2	28	4	34	9	0-2	0	8.19
Mickey Haefner†	L	37	8	2	1	0	24.0	23	3	12	10	0-2	0	5.63
Dave Cole	R	19	4	0	0	0	8.0	7	0	3	8	0-1	0	1.13
Murray Wall	R	23	1	0	0	0	4.0	6	0	2	2	0-0	0	9.00
Bucky Walters	R	41	1	0	0	0	4.0	5	0	2	0	0-0	0	4.50
Dick Manville	R	23	1	0	0	0	2.0	0	0	3	2	0-0	0	0.00

1950 St. Louis Cardinals 5th NL 78-75 .510 12.5 GB

Eddie Dyer

Player	Gm by Position	B	Age	G	AB	R	H	2B	3B	HR	RBI	BB	SO	SB	Avg	OBP	Slg
Del Rice	C130	R	27	130	414	39	101	20	3	9	54	43	65	0	.244	.323	.372
Rocky Nelson	1B70	L	25	76	235	27	58	10	4	1	20	26	9	4	.247	.324	.336
Red Schoendienst	2B143,SS10,3B1	S	27	153	642	81	177	43	9	7	63	33	32	3	.276	.313	.403
Tommy Glaviano	3B106,2B5,SS1	R	26	115	410	92	117	29	2	11	44	90	74	6	.285	.421	.446
Marty Marion	SS101	R	32	106	372	36	92	10	2	4	40	44	55	1	.247	.327	.317
Enos Slaughter	OF145	L	34	148	556	82	161	26	7	10	101	66	33	3	.290	.367	.415
Bill Howerton	OF94	L	28	110	313	50	88	20	8	10	59	47	60	0	.281	.375	.492
Chuck Diering	OF81	R	27	89	204	34	51	12	0	3	18	35	38	1	.250	.360	.353
Stan Musial	OF77,1B69	L	29	146	555	105	192	41	7	28	109	87	36	5	.346	.437	.596
Eddie Kazak	3B48	R	29	93	207	21	53	2	2	5	23	18	19	0	.256	.319	.357
Eddie Miller	SS51,2B1	R	33	64	172	17	39	8	0	3	22	19	21	0	.227	.307	.326
Harry Walker	OF46,1B2	L	33	60	150	17	31	5	0	0	7	18	12	0	.207	.292	.240
Hal Rice	OF37	L	26	44	128	12	27	3	1	2	11	10	10	0	.211	.268	.297
Johnny Lindell†	OF33	R	33	36	113	16	21	5	2	5	16	15	24	0	.186	.287	.398
Joe Garagiola	C30	L	24	34	88	8	28	6	1	2	20	10	7	0	.318	.388	.477
Peanuts Lowrey†	2B6,3B5,OF4	R	31	17	56	10	15	0	0	1	4	6	1	0	.268	.349	.321
Johnny Bucha	C17	R	25	22	36	1	5	1	0	0	1	4	7	0	.139	.225	.167
Steve Bilko	1B9	R	21	10	33	1	6	1	0	0	2	4	10	0	.182	.270	.212
Nippy Jones	1B8	R	25	13	26	0	6	1	0	0	6	3	1	0	.231	.310	.269
Johnny Blatnik†	OF7	R	29	7	20	0	3	0	0	0	1	3	2	0	.150	.261	.150
Solly Hemus	3B5	L	27	11	15	1	2	1	0	0	0	2	4	0	.133	.235	.200
Erv Dusak	P14,OF2	R	29	23	12	0	1	1	0	0	0	0	3	0	.083	.083	.167
Don Bollweg	1B4	L	29	4	11	1	2	0	0	0	1	1	1	0	.182	.250	.182
Ed Mickelson	1B4	R	23	5	10	1	1	0	0	0	0	2	3	0	.100	.250	.100
Ed Mierkowicz		R	26	1	1	0	0	0	0	0	0	0	1	0	.000	.000	.000
Danny Gardella		L	30	1	1	0	0	0	0	0	0	0	0	0	.000	.000	.000

Pitcher	T	Age	G	GS	CG	ShO	IP	H	HR	BB	SO	W-L	Sv	ERA
Howie Pollet	L	29	37	30	14	2	232.1	228	19	68	117	14-13	2	3.29
Max Lanier	L	34	27	27	10	2	181.1	173	13	68	89	11-9	0	3.13
Harry Brecheen	L	35	27	23	12	2	163.1	151	18	45	80	8-11	1	3.80
Gerry Staley	R	29	42	22	7	1	169.2	201	14	61	62	13-13	3	4.99
George Munger	R	31	32	20	5	1	154.2	158	15	70	61	7-8	0	3.90
Al Brazle	L	36	46	12	3	0	164.2	188	12	80	47	11-9	6	4.10
Cloyd Boyer	R	22	36	14	6	2	120.1	105	15	49	82	7-7	1	3.52
Freddie Martin	R	35	30	2	0	0	63.1	87	4	30	19	4-2	0	5.12
Ted Wilks	R	34	18	0	0	0	24.1	27	4	9	15	2-0	0	6.66
Erv Dusak	R	29	14	2	0	0	36.1	27	2	27	16	0-2	1	3.72
Al Papai†	R	33	13	0	0	0	19.0	21	0	14	7	1-0	0	5.21
Jim Hearn†	R	29	6	0	0	0	9.0	12	1	6	4	0-1	0	10.00
Tom Poholsky	R	20	5	1	0	0	14.2	16	2	3	2	0-0	0	3.68
Cot Deal	R	27	3	0	0	0	1.0	3	0	2	1	0-0	0	18.00
Ken Johnson†	L	27	2	0	0	0	2.0	1	0	3	1	0-0	0	0.00

1950 Cincinnati Reds 6th NL 66-87 .431 24.5 GB

Luke Sewell

Player	Gm by Position	B	Age	G	AB	R	H	2B	3B	HR	RBI	BB	SO	SB	Avg	OBP	Slg
Dixie Howell	C81	R	30	82	224	30	50	9	1	2	22	32	31	0	.223	.326	.299
Ted Kluszewski	1B131	L	25	134	538	76	165	37	0	25	111	33	28	3	.307	.348	.515
Connie Ryan†	2B103	R	30	106	367	45	95	18	5	3	43	52	46	4	.259	.352	.360
Grady Hatton	3B126,2B1,SS1	L	27	130	438	67	114	17	1	11	54	70	39	6	.260	.366	.379
Virgil Stallcup	SS136	R	28	136	483	44	121	23	2	8	54	17	39	4	.251	.276	.356
Johnny Wyrostek	OF129,1B4	L	30	131	509	70	145	34	5	8	76	52	38	1	.285	.357	.418
Bob Usher	OF93	R	25	106	321	51	83	17	0	6	35	27	38	3	.259	.316	.368
Lloyd Merriman	OF84	L	25	92	298	44	77	15	3	2	31	30	23	6	.258	.330	.349
Joe Adcock	OF75,1B24	R	22	102	372	46	109	16	1	8	55	24	24	2	.293	.336	.406
Bobby Adams	2B53,3B42	R	28	115	348	57	98	21	8	3	25	43	29	7	.282	.361	.414
Peanuts Lowrey†	OF72,2B1	R	31	91	264	34	60	14	0	1	11	36	7	0	.227	.320	.292
Johnny Pramesa	C73	R	24	74	228	14	70	10	1	5	30	19	15	0	.307	.363	.425
Danny Litwhiler	OF29	R	33	54	112	15	29	4	0	6	12	20	21	0	.259	.371	.455
Sammy Meeks	SS29,3B2	R	27	39	95	7	27	5	0	1	8	6	14	1	.284	.327	.368
Ron Northey†	OF24	L	30	27	77	11	20	5	0	5	9	15	6	0	.260	.380	.519
Bob Scheffing†	C11	R	36	21	47	4	13	0	0	2	6	4	2	0	.277	.333	.404
Walker Cooper†	C13	R	35	15	47	3	9	3	0	0	4	0	5	0	.191	.191	.255
Hobie Landrith	C4	L	20	4	14	1	3	0	0	0	1	2	1	0	.214	.313	.214
Jimmy Bloodworth†	2B4	R	32	4	14	1	3	1	0	0	1	2	0	0	.214	.313	.286
Ted Tappe		L	19	7	5	1	1	0	0	1	1	1	1	0	.200	.333	.800
Marv Rackley		L	28	5	2	0	1	0	0	0	1	0	0	0	.500	.500	.500
Jim Bolger	OF2	R	18	2	1	0	0	0	0	0	0	0	0	0	.000	.000	.000

Pitcher	T	Age	G	GS	CG	ShO	IP	H	HR	BB	SO	W-L	Sv	ERA
Ken Raffensberger	L	32	38	35	18	4	239.0	271	34	40	87	14-19	0	4.26
Ewell Blackwell	R	27	40	32	18	1	261.0	203	12	112	188	17-15	4	2.97
Herm Wehmeier	R	23	41	32	12	0	230.0	255	27	135	121	10-18	4	5.67
Howie Fox	R	29	34	22	10	1	187.0	196	14	85	64	11-8	1	4.33
Willie Ramsdell†	R	34	27	22	8	1	157.1	151	17	75	83	7-12	0	3.72
Frank Smith	R	22	38	4	0	0	90.2	73	12	39	55	2-7	3	3.87
Eddie Erautt	R	25	33	2	1	0	65.1	82	9	22	35	4-2	1	5.65
Johnny Hetki	R	28	22	1	0	0	53.0	53	9	37	21	1-2	0	5.09
Harry Perkowski	L	27	22	0	0	0	34.1	36	6	23	19	0-0	0	5.24
Kent Peterson	L	24	9	2	0	0	20.0	25	4	17	6	0-3	0	7.20
Bud Byerly	R	29	4	1	0	0	14.2	12	1	4	5	0-1	0	2.45
Jim Avrea	R	29	2	0	0	0	5.1	6	0	3	2	0-0	0	3.38

1950 Chicago Cubs 7th NL 64-89 .418 26.5 GB

Frank Frisch

Player	Gm by Position	B	Age	G	AB	R	H	2B	3B	HR	RBI	BB	SO	SB	Avg	OBP	Slg
Mickey Owen	C86	R	34	86	259	22	63	11	0	2	21	13	16	2	.243	.282	.309
Preston Ward	1B76	L	22	80	285	31	72	11	2	6	33	27	42	3	.253	.317	.368
Wayne Terwilliger	2B126,1B1,3B1*	R	25	133	480	63	116	22	3	10	32	43	63	13	.242	.311	.363
Bill Serena	3B125	R	25	127	435	56	104	20	4	17	61	65	75	1	.239	.339	.421
Roy Smalley	SS154	R	24	154	557	58	128	21	9	21	85	49	114	2	.230	.297	.413
Andy Pafko	OF144	R	29	146	514	95	156	24	8	36	92	69	32	4	.304	.397	.591
Hank Sauer	OF125,1B18	R	33	145	540	85	148	32	2	32	103	60	67	1	.274	.350	.519
Bob Borkowski	OF65,1B1	R	24	85	256	27	70	7	4	4	29	16	30	1	.273	.319	.379
Phil Cavarretta	1B67,OF3	L	33	82	256	49	70	11	1	10	31	40	31	1	.273	.376	.441
Rube Walker	C62	L	24	74	213	19	49	7	1	6	16	18	34	0	.230	.290	.357
Carmen Mauro	OF49	L	23	62	185	19	42	4	3	1	10	13	31	3	.227	.285	.297
Hal Jeffcoat	OF53	R	25	66	179	21	42	13	1	2	18	6	23	7	.235	.259	.352
Bob Ramazzotti	2B31,3B10,SS3	R	33	61	145	19	38	3	3	1	6	4	16	3	.262	.287	.345
Ron Northey†	OF27	L	30	53	114	11	32	9	0	4	20	10	9	0	.281	.339	.465
Randy Jackson	3B27	R	24	34	111	13	25	4	3	3	6	7	25	4	.225	.271	.396
Hank Edwards	OF29	L	31	41	110	13	40	11	1	2	21	10	13	0	.364	.417	.536
Carl Sawatski	C32	L	22	38	103	4	18	1	0	1	7	11	19	0	.175	.254	.214
Emil Verban†	2B8,SS3,3B1*	R	34	45	37	7	4	1	0	0	1	3	5	0	.108	.175	.135
Bob Scheffing†	C3	R	36	12	16	0	3	1	0	0	1	0	2	0	.188	.188	.250
Harry Chiti	C1	R	17	3	6	0	2	0	0	0	0	0	0	0	.333	.333	.333

W. Terwilliger, 1 G at OF; E. Verban, 1 G at OF

Pitcher	T	Age	G	GS	CG	ShO	IP	H	HR	BB	SO	W-L	Sv	ERA
Bob Rush	R	24	39	34	19	1	254.2	261	11	93	93	13-20	1	3.71
Johnny Schmitz	L	29	39	27	8	3	193.0	217	23	91	75	10-16	0	4.99
Paul Minner	L	26	39	24	9	1	190.1	217	18	72	99	8-13	4	4.11
Warren Hacker	R	25	5	3	1	0	15.1	20	3	8	5	0-1	1	5.28
Monk Dubiel	R	32	39	12	4	2	142.2	152	12	67	51	6-10	2	4.16
Frank Hiller	R	29	38	17	9	2	153.0	153	16	32	55	12-5	1	3.53
Dutch Leonard	R	41	35	1	0	0	74.0	70	7	27	28	5-1	6	3.77
Doyle Lade	R	29	34	12	2	0	117.2	126	14	50	36	5-6	2	4.74
Johnny Klippstein	R	22	33	11	3	0	104.2	112	9	64	51	2-9	1	5.25
J. Vander Meer	L	35	32	6	0	0	73.2	60	10	59	41	3-4	1	3.79
Bill Voiselle	R	31	19	7	0	0	51.1	64	7	29	25	0-4	0	5.79
Andy Varga	L	19	1	0	0	0	1.0	0	0	1	0	0-0	0	0.00

1950 Pittsburgh Pirates 8th NL 57-96 .373 33.5 GB

Billy Meyer

Player	Gm by Position	B	Age	G	AB	R	H	2B	3B	HR	RBI	BB	SO	SB	Avg	OBP	Slg
Clyde McCullough	C100	R	33	103	279	28	71	16	4	6	34	31	35	3	.254	.340	.405
Johnny Hopp†	1B70,OF7	L	33	106	318	51	108	24	5	8	47	43	17	7	.340	.420	.522
Danny Murtaugh	2B108	R	32	118	367	34	108	20	5	2	37	47	42	2	.294	.376	.392
Nanny Fernandez	3B52	R	31	65	198	23	51	11	0	6	27	19	17	2	.258	.326	.404
Stan Rojek	SS68,2B3	R	31	76	230	28	59	12	1	0	17	18	13	2	.257	.313	.317
Ralph Kiner	OF150	R	27	150	547	112	149	21	6	47	118	122	79	2	.272	.408	.590
Wally Westlake	OF123	R	29	139	477	69	136	15	6	24	95	48	78	1	.285	.359	.493
Gus Bell	OF104	L	21	111	422	62	119	22	11	8	53	28	46	4	.282	.333	.443
Danny O'Connell	SS65,3B12	R	23	79	315	39	92	16	1	8	32	24	33	7	.292	.342	.425
Pete Castiglione	3B35,SS29,2B9*	R	29	94	263	29	67	10	3	3	22	23	23	1	.255	.317	.350
Bob Dillinger†	3B51	R	31	58	222	23	64	8	2	1	9	13	22	4	.288	.328	.356
Jack Phillips	1B54,3B3,P1	R	28	69	208	25	61	7	6	5	34	20	17	1	.293	.355	.457
Tom Saffell	OF43	L	28	67	182	18	37	7	0	2	6	14	34	1	.203	.264	.275
Ted Beard	OF49	L	29	61	177	32	41	6	2	4	12	27	45	3	.232	.333	.356
Ray Mueller†	C63	R	38	67	156	17	42	7	0	6	24	11	14	2	.269	.321	.429
Johnny Berardino†	2B36,3B3	R	33	40	131	12	27	3	1	1	12	19	11	0	.206	.307	.267
Dale Coogan	1B32	L	19	53	129	19	31	6	1	1	13	17	24	0	.240	.338	.326
Hank Schenz	2B21,3B12,SS4	R	31	58	101	17	23	4	2	1	5	6	7	0	.228	.271	.337
Earl Turner	C34	R	27	40	74	10	18	0	0	3	5	4	13	1	.243	.282	.365
Ed Stevens	1B12	L	25	17	46	2	9	2	0	0	3	4	5	0	.196	.260	.239
George Strickland	SS19,3B1	R	24	23	27	0	3	0	0	0	2	3	8	0	.111	.226	.111
Marv Rickert†	OF3	L	29	17	20	0	3	0	0	0	4	0	4	0	.150	.150	.150
Ed Fitz Gerald	C5	R	26	6	15	1	1	1	0	0	0	0	3	0	.067	.067	.133

P. Castiglione, 3 G at 1B

Pitcher	T	Age	G	GS	CG	ShO	IP	H	HR	BB	SO	W-L	Sv	ERA
Cliff Chambers	L	28	37	33	11	2	249.1	262	18	92	93	12-15	0	4.30
Mel Queen	R	32	33	21	4	1	120.1	135	18	73	76	5-14	0	5.98
Bill MacDonald	R	21	32	20	6	2	153.0	138	17	88	60	8-10	1	4.29
Vern Law	R	20	27	17	5	1	128.0	137	11	49	57	7-9	0	4.92
Bob Chesnes	R	29	9	7	2	0	39.0	44	7	17	12	3-3	0	5.54
Murry Dickson	R	33	51	22	8	0	225.0	227	20	83	76	10-15	3	3.80
Bill Werle	L	29	48	22	6	0	215.1	249	25	65	78	8-16	8	4.60
Vic Lombardi	L	27	39	2	0	0	76.1	93	14	48	26	0-5	1	6.60
Junior Walsh	R	31	38	2	0	0	62.1	56	6	34	33	1-1	2	5.05
Bill Pierro	R	24	12	3	0	0	29.0	33	2	28	13	0-2	0	10.55
Woody Main	R	28	12	0	0	0	20.1	21	2	11	12	1-0	1	4.87
Hank Borowy†	R	34	11	3	0	0	25.1	32	6	9	9	1-3	0	6.39
Hal Gregg	R	28	5	1	0	0	5.1	10	2	7	3	0-1	0	13.50
Frank Barrett	R	36	5	0	0	0	4.1	5	1	1	0	1-2	0	4.15
Frank Papish	L	32	4	1	0	0	2.1	8	1	4	1	0-0	0	27.00
Windy McCall	L	24	2	0	0	0	6.2	12	2	4	5	0-0	0	9.45
Jack Phillips	R	28	1	0	0	0	5.0	7	0	1	2	0-0	0	7.20
Harry Gumbert	R	40	1	0	0	0	1.2	3	0	2	0	0-0	0	5.40

»1951 New York Yankees 1st AL 98-56 .636 —

Casey Stengel

Player	Gm by Position	B	Age	G	AB	R	H	2B	3B	HR	RBI	BB	SO	SB	Avg	OBP	Slg
Yogi Berra	C141	L	26	141	547	92	161	19	4	27	88	44	20	5	.294	.350	.492
Joe Collins	1B114,OF15	L	28	125	262	52	75	8	5	9	48	34	23	9	.286	.368	.458
Jerry Coleman	2B102,SS18	R	26	121	362	48	90	11	2	3	43	31	36	6	.249	.315	.315
Bobby Brown	3B90	L	26	103	313	44	84	15	2	6	51	47	18	1	.268	.369	.387
Phil Rizzuto	SS144	R	33	144	540	87	148	21	6	2	43	58	27	18	.274	.350	.346
Gene Woodling	OF116	L	28	120	420	65	118	15	8	15	71	62	37	0	.281	.373	.462
Joe DiMaggio	OF113	R	36	116	415	72	109	22	4	12	71	61	36	0	.263	.365	.422
Hank Bauer	OF107	R	28	118	348	53	103	19	3	10	54	42	39	5	.296	.373	.454
Gil McDougald	3B82,2B55	R	23	131	402	72	123	23	4	14	63	56	54	14	.306	.396	.488
Mickey Mantle	OF86	S	19	96	341	61	91	11	5	13	65	43	74	8	.267	.349	.443
Johnny Mize	1B93	L	38	113	332	37	86	14	1	10	49	36	24	1	.259	.339	.398
Jackie Jensen	OF48	R	24	56	168	30	50	8	1	8	25	18	18	8	.298	.369	.500
Johnny Hopp	1B25	L	34	46	63	10	13	1	0	2	4	9	11	2	.206	.306	.317
Billy Martin	2B23,SS6,3B2*	R	23	51	58	10	15	1	2	0	2	4	9	0	.259	.328	.345
Charlie Silvera	C18	R	26	18	51	5	14	3	0	1	7	5	3	0	.275	.339	.392
Cliff Mapes†	OF34	L	29	45	51	6	11	3	1	2	8	4	14	0	.216	.273	.431
Bill Johnson†	3B13	R	32	15	40	5	12	3	0	0	4	7	0	0	.300	.404	.375
Bob Cerv	OF9	R	25	12	28	4	6	1	0	0	2	4	6	0	.214	.313	.250
Jim Brideweser	SS2	R	24	2	8	1	3	0	0	0	0	0	1	0	.375	.375	.375
Ralph Houk	C3	R	31	3	5	0	1	0	0	0	2	0	1	0	.200	.200	.200
Archie Wilson	OF2	R	27	4	4	0	0	0	0	0	0	0	0	0	.000	.200	.000
Clint Courtney	C1	L	24	1	2	0	0	0	0	0	0	1	1	0	.000	.333	.000

B. Martin, 1 G at OF

Pitcher	T	Age	G	GS	CG	ShO	IP	H	HR	BB	SO	W-L	Sv	ERA
Vic Raschi	R	32	35	34	15	4	258.1	233	20	103	164	21-10	0	3.27
Ed Lopat	L	33	31	31	20	4	234.2	209	12	71	93	21-9	0	2.91
Allie Reynolds	R	36	40	26	16	7	221.0	171	12	100	126	17-8	7	3.05
Tom Morgan	R	21	27	16	4	2	124.2	119	11	36	57	9-3	2	3.68
Art Schallock	L	27	11	6	1	0	46.1	50	3	20	19	3-1	0	3.88
Johnny Sain†	R	33	7	4	1	0	37.0	41	5	8	21	2-1	1	4.14
Bob Wiesler	L	20	4	3	0	0	9.1	13	0	11	3	0-2	0	13.50
Joe Ostrowski	L	34	34	3	2	0	95.1	103	4	18	30	6-4	5	3.49
Spec Shea	R	30	25	11	2	2	95.2	112	11	50	38	5-5	0	4.33
Bob Kuzava†	L	28	23	8	4	1	82.1	76	5	27	50	8-4	5	2.40
Jack Kramer†	R	33	19	3	0	0	40.2	46	1	21	15	1-3	0	4.65
Stubby Overmire†	L	32	15	4	1	0	44.2	50	2	18	14	1-1	0	4.63
Fred Sanford†	R	31	11	2	0	0	26.2	15	2	25	10	0-3	0	3.71
Tommy Byrne†	L	31	9	3	0	0	21.0	16	0	36	14	2-1	0	6.86
Tom Ferrick†	R	36	9	0	0	0	12.0	21	4	7	3	1-1	1	7.50
Bobby Hogue†	R	30	7	0	0	0	7.1	4	0	3	2	1-0	0	0.00
Bob Porterfield†	R	27	2	0	0	0	3.0	5	0	3	2	0-0	0	15.00
Bob Muncrief	R	35	2	0	0	0	3.0	5	0	4	2	0-0	0	9.00
Ernie Nevel	R	31	1	0	0	0	4.0	1	0	1	1	0-0	1	0.00

1951 Cleveland Indians 2nd AL 93-61 .604 5.0 GB

Al Lopez

Player	Gm by Position	B	Age	G	AB	R	H	2B	3B	HR	RBI	BB	SO	SB	Avg	OBP	Slg
Jim Hegan	C129	R	30	133	416	60	99	17	5	6	43	38	72	0	.238	.302	.346
Luke Easter	1B125	L	35	128	486	65	131	12	5	27	103	37	71	0	.270	.333	.481
Bobby Avila	2B136	R	27	141	542	76	165	21	3	10	58	60	31	14	.304	.374	.410
Al Rosen	3B154	R	27	154	573	82	152	30	1	24	102	85	71	7	.265	.362	.447
Ray Boone	SS151	R	27	151	544	65	127	14	1	12	51	48	36	5	.233	.302	.329
Larry Doby	OF132	L	27	134	447	84	132	27	5	20	69	101	81	4	.295	.428	.512
Dale Mitchell	OF124	L	29	134	510	83	148	21	7	11	62	53	16	7	.290	.358	.424
Bob Kennedy	OF106	R	30	108	321	30	79	15	4	7	29	34	33	4	.246	.320	.383
Harry Simpson	OF68,1B50	L	25	122	332	51	76	7	0	7	24	45	48	6	.229	.325	.313
Sam Chapman†	OF84,1B1	R	35	94	246	24	56	9	1	6	36	27	32	3	.228	.304	.346
Birdie Tebbetts	C44	R	38	55	137	8	36	6	0	2	18	8	7	0	.263	.308	.350
Snuffy Stirnweiss	2B25,3B2	R	32	50	88	10	19	1	0	1	4	22	25	1	.216	.373	.261
Barney McCosky†	OF16	L	34	31	61	8	13	3	0	0	2	8	5	1	.213	.304	.262
Merrill Combs	SS16	L	31	19	28	2	5	2	0	0	2	2	3	0	.179	.233	.250
Minnie Minoso†	1B7	R	28	8	14	3	6	2	0	0	2	1	1	0	.429	.529	.571
Paul Lehner†	OF1	L	30	12	13	2	3	0	0	0	1	1	2	0	.231	.286	.231
Clarence Maddern	OF1	R	29	11	12	0	2	0	0	0	0	0	1	0	.167	.167	.167
Allie Clark†	OF3	R	28	3	10	3	3	2	0	1	3	1	2	0	.300	.364	.800
Hal Naragon	C2	L	22	3	8	0	2	0	0	0	0	1	0	0	.250	.400	.250
Milt Nielsen		L	26	16	6	1	0	0	0	0	0	1	1	0	.000	.143	.000
Lou Klein†		R	32	2	2	0	0	0	0	0	0	0	1	0	.000	.000	.000
Ray Murray†	C1	R	33	1	1	0	1	0	0	0	1	0	0	0	1.000	1.000	1.000
Thurman Tucker		L	33	1	1	0	0	0	0	0	0	0	1	0	.000	.000	.000
Doug Hansen		R	22	3	0	2	0	0	0	0	0	0	0	0	—	—	—

Pitcher	T	Age	G	GS	CG	ShO	IP	H	HR	BB	SO	W-L	Sv	ERA
Early Wynn	R	31	37	34	21	3	274.1	227	18	107	133	20-13	1	3.02
Bob Lemon	R	30	42	34	17	1	263.1	244	19	124	132	17-14	2	3.52
Bob Feller	R	32	33	32	16	4	249.2	239	22	95	111	22-8	0	3.50
Mike Garcia	R	27	47	30	15	1	254.0	239	10	82	118	20-13	6	3.15
Bob Chakales	R	23	17	10	2	1	68.1	80	3	43	32	3-4	0	4.74
Sam Jones	R	25	2	1	0	0	8.2	4	0	5	4	0-1	0	2.08
J. Vander Meer	L	36	1	1	0	0	3.0	8	0	1	2	0-1	0	18.00
Lou Brissie†	L	27	54	4	1	0	112.1	90	5	61	50	4-3	9	3.20
Steve Gromek	R	31	27	8	4	0	107.1	98	6	29	40	7-4	1	2.77
George Zuverink	R	26	16	0	0	0	25.1	24	2	13	14	0-0	0	5.33
Dick Rozek	L	24	7	1	0	0	15.1	18	1	11	5	0-0	0	2.93
Red Fahr	R	26	5	0	0	0	5.2	11	0	2	0	0-0	0	4.76
Charlie Harris†	R	25	2	0	0	0	4.0	5	0	4	1	0-0	0	4.50

716 Seasons: Team Rosters

1951 Boston Red Sox 3rd AL 87-67 .565 11.0 GB

Steve O'Neill

Player	Gm by Position	B	Age	G	AB	R	H	2B	3B	HR	RBI	BB	SO	SB	Avg	OBP	Slg
Les Moss†	C69	R	26	71	202	18	40	6	0	3	26	25	34	0	.198	.289	.272
Walt Dropo	1B93	R	28	99	360	37	86	14	0	11	57	38	52	0	.239	.312	.369
Bobby Doerr	2B106	R	33	106	402	60	116	21	2	13	73	57	33	2	.289	.378	.448
Vern Stephens	3B89,SS2	R	30	109	377	62	113	21	2	17	78	38	33	1	.300	.364	.501
Johnny Pesky	SS106,3B11,2B5	L	31	131	480	93	150	20	6	3	41	84	15	2	.313	.417	.398
Ted Williams	OF147	L	32	148	531	109	169	28	4	30	126	144	45	1	.318	.464	.556
Dom DiMaggio	OF146	R	34	146	639	113	189	34	4	12	72	73	53	4	.296	.370	.418
Clyde Vollmer	OF106	R	29	115	386	66	97	9	2	22	85	54	66	0	.251	.345	.456
Billy Goodman	1B62,2B44,OF38*	L	25	141	546	92	162	34	4	0	50	79	37	7	.297	.388	.374
Lou Boudreau	SS52,3B15,1B2	R	33	82	273	37	73	18	1	5	47	30	12	1	.267	.353	.396
Buddy Rosar	C56	R	36	58	170	11	39	7	0	1	13	19	14	0	.229	.307	.288
Fred Hatfield	3B49	L	26	80	163	23	28	4	2	2	14	22	27	1	.172	.274	.258
Charlie Maxwell	OF13	L	24	49	80	8	15	1	0	3	12	9	18	0	.188	.270	.313
Aaron Robinson†	C25	L	36	26	74	9	15	1	1	2	7	17	10	0	.203	.352	.324
Tom Wright	OF18	L	27	28	63	8	14	1	1	1	9	11	8	0	.222	.347	.317
Mike Guerra†	C10	R	38	10	32	1	5	0	0	0	2	6	5	1	.156	.289	.156
Matt Batts†	C11	R	29	11	29	1	4	1	0	0	2	1	2	0	.138	.167	.172
Al Evans	C10	R	34	12	24	1	3	1	0	0	2	4	2	0	.125	.250	.167
Mel Hoderlein	2B3,3B3	S	28	9	14	1	5	1	1	0	1	6	2	0	.357	.550	.571
Norm Zauchin	1B4	R	21	5	12	0	2	1	0	0	0	0	4	0	.167	.167	.250
Sammy White	C4	R	22	4	11	0	2	0	0	0	0	0	3	0	.182	.182	.182
Al Richter	SS3	R	24	5	11	1	1	0	0	0	0	3	0	0	.091	.286	.091
Bob DiPietro	OF3	R	23	4	11	0	1	0	0	0	0	1	1	0	.091	.167	.091
Karl Olson	OF5	R	20	5	10	0	1	0	0	0	0	0	3	0	.100	.100	.100

B. Goodman, 1 G at 3B

Pitcher	T	Age	G	GS	CG	ShO	IP	H	HR	BB	SO	W-L	Sv	ERA
Mel Parnell	L	29	36	29	11	3	221.0	229	11	77	77	18-11	2	3.26
Chuck Stobbs	L	21	34	25	6	0	170.0	180	15	74	75	10-9	0	4.76
Ray Scarborough	R	33	37	22	8	0	184.0	201	21	61	71	12-9	0	5.09
Mickey McDermott	L	23	34	19	9	1	172.0	141	10	92	127	8-8	3	3.35
Bill Wight	L	29	34	17	4	2	118.1	128	5	63	38	7-7	0	5.10
Leo Kiely	L	21	17	16	4	0	113.1	106	9	39	46	7-7	0	3.34
Harley Hisner	R	24	1	1	0	0	6.0	7	0	4	3	0-1	0	4.50
Ellis Kinder	R	36	63	2	1	0	127.0	108	9	46	84	11-2	14	2.55
Willard Nixon	R	23	33	14	2	1	125.0	136	12	56	70	7-4	1	4.90
Harry Taylor	R	32	31	8	1	0	81.1	100	6	42	22	4-9	2	5.75
Walt Masterson	R	31	30	1	0	0	59.1	53	1	32	39	3-0	2	3.34
Bill Evans	R	32	9	0	0	0	15.1	15	0	8	3	0-0	0	4.11
Paul Hinrichs	R	25	4	0	0	0	3.1	7	1	4	1	0-0	0	21.60
Ben Flowers	R	24	1	0	0	0	3.0	2	0	1	2	0-0	0	0.00

1951 Chicago White Sox 4th AL 81-73 .526 17.0 GB

Paul Richards

Player	Gm by Position	B	Age	G	AB	R	H	2B	3B	HR	RBI	BB	SO	SB	Avg	OBP	Slg
Phil Masi	C78	R	35	84	225	24	61	11	2	4	28	32	27	1	.271	.367	.391
Eddie Robinson	1B147	L	30	151	564	85	159	23	5	29	117	77	54	2	.282	.371	.495
Nellie Fox	2B147	L	23	147	604	93	189	32	12	4	55	43	11	9	.313	.372	.425
Bob Dillinger†	3B70	R	32	89	299	39	90	6	4	0	20	15	17	5	.301	.337	.348
Chico Carrasquel	SS147	R	25	147	538	41	142	22	4	2	58	46	39	14	.264	.325	.331
Jim Busby	OF139	R	24	143	477	59	135	15	2	5	68	40	46	26	.283	.344	.354
Al Zarilla	OF117	L	32	120	382	56	98	21	2	10	60	60	57	2	.257	.363	.401
Minnie Minoso†	OF82,3B68,SS1	R	28	138	516	109	167	32	14	10	74	71	41	31	.324	.419	.498
Bud Stewart	OF63	L	35	95	217	40	60	13	5	6	40	29	9	1	.276	.367	.465
Don Lenhardt†	OF53,1B2	R	28	64	199	23	53	9	1	10	45	24	25	1	.266	.351	.472
Ray Coleman†	OF51	L	29	51	181	21	50	8	7	3	21	15	14	2	.276	.332	.448
Gus Niarhos	C59	R	30	66	168	27	43	6	0	1	10	47	9	4	.256	.419	.310
Floyd Baker	3B44,2B5,SS3	L	34	82	133	24	35	6	1	0	14	25	12	0	.263	.380	.323
Bud Sheely	C33	L	30	34	89	2	16	2	0	0	7	6	7	0	.180	.240	.202
Joe DeMaestri	SS27,2B11,3B8	R	22	56	74	8	15	0	2	1	3	5	11	0	.203	.253	.297
Paul Lehner†	OF20	L	30	23	72	9	15	3	1	0	3	10	4	0	.208	.305	.278
Bert Haas	1B7,OF4,3B1	R	37	23	43	1	7	0	1	1	2	5	4	0	.163	.250	.279
Hank Majeski†	3B9	R	34	12	35	4	9	4	0	0	6	1	0	0	.257	.278	.371
Harry Dorish	P32,3B1	R	29	32	31	2	8	2	0	0	0	0	3	0	.258	.258	.323
Joe Erautt	C12	R	29	16	25	3	4	1	0	0	0	3	2	0	.160	.276	.200
Dave Philley†	OF6	S	31	7	25	0	6	2	0	0	2	2	3	0	.240	.296	.320
Gus Zernial†	OF4	R	28	4	19	2	2	0	0	0	4	2	2	0	.105	.190	.105
Bob Boyd	1B6	L	25	12	18	3	3	0	1	0	4	3	3	0	.167	.286	.278
Red Wilson	C4	R	22	4	11	1	3	1	0	0	0	1	2	0	.273	.333	.364
Gordon Goldsberry	1B8	L	23	10	11	4	1	0	0	0	1	2	2	0	.091	.231	.091
Sammy Hairston	C2	R	31	4	5	1	2	1	0	0	1	2	0	0	.400	.571	.600
Rocky Nelson†		L	26	6	5	0	0	0	0	0	0	1	0	0	.000	.167	.000

Pitcher	T	Age	G	GS	CG	ShO	IP	H	HR	BB	SO	W-L	Sv	ERA
Billy Pierce	L	24	37	28	18	1	240.1	237	14	73	113	15-14	2	3.03
Ken Holcombe	R	32	28	23	12	2	159.1	142	9	68	39	11-12	0	3.78
Saul Rogovin†	R	27	22	22	17	3	192.2	166	11	67	77	11-7	0	2.48
Joe Dobson	R	34	28	21	6	0	146.2	136	17	51	67	7-6	3	3.62
Lou Kretlow	R	30	26	18	7	1	137.0	129	7	74	89	6-9	0	4.20
Howie Judson	R	25	27	14	3	0	121.2	124	9	55	43	5-6	1	3.77
Bob Cain†	L	26	4	4	1	0	26.1	25	3	13	3	1-2	0	3.76
Dick Littlefield	L	25	4	2	0	0	9.2	9	1	17	7	1-1	0	8.38
Randy Gumpert	R	33	33	16	7	1	141.2	156	20	34	45	9-8	2	4.32
Harry Dorish	R	29	32	4	2	1	96.2	101	6	31	29	5-6	0	3.54
Marv Rotblatt	L	23	26	2	0	0	47.2	44	4	23	20	4-2	2	3.40
Luis Aloma	R	27	25	1	1	1	69.1	52	3	24	25	6-0	3	1.82
Ross Grimsley	L	29	7	0	0	0	14.0	12	1	10	8	0-0	0	3.86
Hal Brown	R	26	3	0	0	0	8.2	15	3	4	4	0-0	1	9.35
Bob Mahoney†	R	23	3	0	0	0	6.2	5	1	5	3	0-0	0	5.40

1951 Detroit Tigers 5th AL 73-81 .474 25.0 GB

Red Rolfe

Player	Gm by Position	B	Age	G	AB	R	H	2B	3B	HR	RBI	BB	SO	SB	Avg	OBP	Slg
Joe Ginsberg	C95	L	24	102	304	44	79	10	2	8	37	43	21	0	.260	.355	.385
Dick Kryhoski	1B112	L	26	119	421	58	121	19	4	12	57	28	29	1	.287	.335	.437
Jerry Priddy	2B154,SS1	R	31	154	584	73	152	22	6	8	57	69	73	4	.260	.338	.360
George Kell	3B147	R	28	147	598	92	191	36	3	2	59	61	18	10	.319	.386	.400
Johnny Lipon	SS125	R	28	129	487	56	129	15	1	0	38	49	27	7	.265	.335	.300
Vic Wertz	OF131	L	26	138	501	86	143	24	4	27	94	78	61	0	.285	.383	.511
Johnny Groth	OF112	R	24	118	428	41	128	29	1	3	49	31	32	1	.299	.349	.393
Hoot Evers	OF108	R	30	116	393	47	88	15	2	11	46	40	47	5	.224	.297	.356
Pat Mullin	OF83	L	33	110	295	41	83	11	6	12	51	40	38	2	.281	.367	.481
Don Kolloway	1B59	R	32	78	212	28	54	7	0	1	17	15	12	2	.255	.307	.302
Steve Souchock	OF59,3B3,1B1*	R	32	91	188	33	46	10	3	11	28	18	27	0	.245	.314	.505
Neil Berry	SS38,2B10,3B7	R	29	67	157	17	36	5	2	0	9	10	15	4	.229	.275	.287
Bob Swift	C43	R	36	44	104	8	20	0	0	0	5	12	10	0	.192	.276	.192
Aaron Robinson†	C35	L	36	36	82	3	17	6	0	0	9	17	9	0	.207	.343	.280
Charlie Keller	OF8	L	34	54	62	6	16	2	0	3	21	11	12	0	.258	.370	.435
Frank House	C18	L	21	18	41	3	9	2	0	1	4	6	2	1	.220	.319	.341
Russ Sullivan	OF7	L	28	7	26	2	5	1	0	1	1	2	1	0	.192	.250	.346
Al Federoff	2B1	R	26	2	4	0	0	0	0	0	0	0	0	0	.000	.000	.000
Doc Daugherty		R	23	1	1	0	0	0	0	0	0	0	1	0	.000	.000	.000

S. Souchock, 1 G at 2B

Pitcher	T	Age	G	GS	CG	ShO	IP	H	HR	BB	SO	W-L	Sv	ERA
Ted Gray	L	26	34	28	9	1	197.1	194	17	95	131	7-14	1	4.06
Dizzy Trout	R	36	42	22	7	0	191.2	172	13	75	89	9-14	5	4.04
Bob Cain†	L	26	35	22	6	1	149.1	135	12	82	58	11-10	2	4.70
Fred Hutchinson	R	31	31	20	9	2	188.1	204	11	27	53	10-10	2	3.68
Marlin Stuart	R	32	29	15	5	0	124.0	119	9	71	46	4-6	1	3.77
Hal Newhouser	L	30	15	14	7	1	96.1	98	10	19	37	6-6	0	3.92
Saul Rogovin†	R	27	5	4	0	0	24.0	23	4	7	5	1-1	0	5.25
Dick Marlowe	R	22	2	1	0	0	1.2	5	0	2	1	0-1	0	32.40
Hal White	R	32	38	4	0	0	76.0	74	7	49	23	3-4	4	4.74
Virgil Trucks	R	34	37	18	6	1	153.2	153	9	75	89	13-8	1	4.33
Gene Bearden†	L	30	37	4	2	1	106.0	112	6	58	38	3-4	0	4.33
Hank Borowy	R	35	26	1	0	0	45.1	58	3	27	16	2-2	0	6.95
Wayne McLeland	R	26	6	1	0	0	11.0	20	1	4	0	0-1	0	8.18
Earl Johnson	L	32	6	0	0	0	5.2	9	0	2	2	0-0	1	6.35
Ray Herbert	R	21	5	0	0	0	12.2	8	0	9	9	4-0	0	1.42
Paul Calvert	R	33	1	0	0	0	1.0	1	0	0	0	0-0	0	0.00

1951 Philadelphia Athletics 6th AL 70-84 .455 28.0 GB

Jimmy Dykes

Player	Gm by Position	B	Age	G	AB	R	H	2B	3B	HR	RBI	BB	SO	SB	Avg	OBP	Slg
Joe Tipton	C72	R	29	72	213	23	51	9	0	3	20	51	25	1	.239	.389	.324
Ferris Fain	1B108,OF11	L	30	117	425	63	146	30	3	6	57	80	20	0	.344	.451	.471
Pete Suder	2B103,SS18,3B3	R	35	123	440	46	108	18	1	1	42	30	42	5	.245	.295	.298
Hank Majeski†	3B88	R	34	89	323	41	92	19	4	5	42	35	24	1	.285	.358	.415
Eddie Joost	SS140	R	35	140	553	107	160	28	5	19	78	106	70	10	.289	.409	.461
Gus Zernial†	OF138	R	28	139	552	90	151	30	5	33	125	61	99	2	.274	.350	.525
Dave Philley†	OF120,3B2	S	31	125	468	71	123	18	7	7	59	63	38	9	.263	.354	.376
Elmer Valo	OF116	L	30	123	444	75	134	27	8	7	55	75	20	11	.302	.412	.446
Billy Hitchcock	3B45,2B23,1B1	R	34	77	222	27	68	10	4	1	36	21	23	2	.306	.371	.401
Lou Limmer	1B58	L	26	94	214	25	34	9	1	5	30	28	40	1	.159	.256	.280
Joe Astroth	C57	R	28	64	187	30	46	10	2	2	19	18	13	0	.246	.312	.353
Allie Clark†	OF32,3B10	R	28	56	161	20	40	10	1	4	22	15	7	2	.248	.320	.398
Lou Klein†	2B42	R	32	49	144	22	33	7	0	5	17	10	12	0	.229	.279	.382
Wally Moses	OF27	L	40	70	136	17	26	6	0	0	9	21	9	2	.191	.304	.235
Ray Murray†	C39	R	33	40	122	10	26	6	0	0	13	14	8	0	.213	.294	.262
Sam Chapman†	OF17	R	35	18	65	7	11	1	0	0	5	12	12	0	.169	.299	.185
Kermit Wahl†	3B18	R	28	20	59	4	11	2	0	0	6	9	5	0	.186	.294	.220
Paul Lehner†	OF7	L	30	9	28	1	4	1	0	0	1	1	1	0	.143	.172	.179
Barney McCosky†	OF7	L	34	12	27	4	8	2	0	1	1	3	4	0	.296	.367	.481
Tod Davis	2B2,3B1	R	26	11	15	0	1	0	0	0	0	1	3	0	.067	.125	.067
Ed Samcoff	2B3	R	26	4	11	0	0	0	0	0	0	1	2	0	.000	.083	.000

Pitcher	T	Age	G	GS	CG	ShO	IP	H	HR	BB	SO	W-L	Sv	ERA
Alex Kellner	L	26	33	29	11	1	209.2	218	20	93	94	11-14	2	4.46
Bobby Shantz	L	25	32	25	13	3	205.1	213	15	70	77	18-10	0	3.94
Bob Hooper	R	29	38	23	9	0	189.0	192	13	61	64	12-10	5	4.38
Dick Fowler	R	30	22	22	4	0	125.0	141	11	72	29	5-11	0	5.62
Sam Zoldak	L	32	26	18	8	1	128.0	127	9	24	18	6-10	0	3.16
Lou Brissie†	L	27	2	2	0	0	13.1	20	0	8	3	0-2	0	6.75
Carl Scheib	R	24	46	11	3	0	143.0	132	7	71	49	1-12	10	4.47
Morrie Martin	L	28	35	13	3	1	138.0	139	13	63	35	11-4	0	3.78
Johnny Kucab	R	31	30	1	0	0	74.2	76	9	23	23	4-3	4	4.22
Joe Coleman	R	28	28	9	1	0	96.1	117	12	59	34	1-6	1	5.98
Hank Wyse†	R	33	9	1	0	0	14.2	24	0	8	5	1-2	0	7.98
Moe Burtschy	R	29	7	0	0	0	17.0	18	0	12	4	0-0	0	5.29
Charlie Harris†	R	25	3	0	0	0	4.0	4	0	5	2	0-0	0	9.00

1951 Washington Senators 7th AL 62-92 .403 36.0 GB

Bucky Harris

Player	Gm by Position	B	Age	G	AB	R	H	2B	3B	HR	RBI	BB	SO	SB	Avg	OBP	Slg
Mike Guerra†	C66	R	38	72	214	20	43	2	1	1	20	16	18	4	.201	.257	.234
Mickey Vernon	1B137	L	33	141	546	69	160	30	7	9	87	53	45	7	.293	.358	.423
Cass Michaels	2B128	R	25	138	485	59	125	20	4	4	45	61	41	1	.258	.342	.340
Eddie Yost	3B152,OF3	R	24	154	568	109	161	36	4	12	65	126	55	6	.283	.423	.424
Pete Runnels	SS73	L	23	78	273	31	76	12	2	0	25	31	24	0	.278	.354	.337
Gil Coan	OF132	L	29	135	538	85	163	25	7	9	62	39	62	8	.303	.357	.426
Irv Noren	OF126	L	26	129	509	82	142	33	5	8	86	51	35	10	.279	.345	.411
Sam Mele	OF124,1B15	R	28	143	558	58	153	36	7	5	94	32	31	2	.274	.315	.391
Sam Dente	SS65,2B10,3B5	R	29	88	273	21	65	8	1	0	29	25	10	3	.238	.302	.275
Mike McCormick	OF62	R	34	81	243	31	70	9	3	1	23	29	20	1	.288	.364	.362
Gene Verble	SS28,2B19,3B1	R	23	68	177	16	36	3	2	0	15	18	10	1	.203	.277	.243
Mickey Grasso	C49	R	31	52	175	16	36	3	0	1	14	14	17	0	.206	.268	.240
Clyde Kluttz†	C46	R	33	53	159	15	49	9	0	1	22	20	8	0	.308	.389	.384
Sherry Robertson	OF22	L	32	62	111	14	21	2	1	1	10	9	22	2	.189	.256	.252
Frank Campos	OF7	L	27	8	26	4	11	3	1	0	3	0	1	0	.423	.423	.615
Dan Porter	OF3	L	19	13	19	2	4	0	0	0	0	2	4	0	.211	.286	.211
Frank Sacka	C6	R	26	7	16	1	4	0	0	0	3	0	5	0	.250	.250	.250
Fred Taylor	1B2	L	26	6	12	1	2	1	0	0	0	0	4	0	.167	.167	.250
Willie Miranda	SS2,1B1	S	25	7	9	2	4	0	0	0	0	0	0	0	.444	.444	.444
Len Okrie	C5	R	27	5	8	1	1	1	0	0	0	2	1	0	.125	.300	.250
Roy Hawes	1B1	L	24	3	6	0	1	0	0	0	0	0	1	0	.167	.167	.167

Pitcher	T	Age	G	GS	CG	ShO	IP	H	HR	BB	SO	W-L	Sv	ERA
Connie Marrero	R	40	25	25	16	2	187.0	198	8	71	66	11-9	0	3.90
Don Johnson†	R	24	21	20	8	1	143.2	138	9	58	52	7-11	0	3.95
Sid Hudson	R	36	23	19	8	0	138.2	168	8	52	43	5-12	0	5.13
Bob Porterfield†	R	27	19	19	10	3	133.1	109	8	54	53	9-8	0	3.24
Julio Moreno	R	30	31	18	5	0	132.2	132	18	80	37	5-11	2	4.88
Dick Starr†	R	30	11	11	1	0	61.1	76	12	24	17	1-7	0	5.58
Bob Kuzava†	L	28	8	8	3	0	52.1	57	5	28	22	3-3	0	5.50
Fred Sanford†	R	31	7	7	0	0	37.0	51	5	27	12	2-3	0	6.57
Hank Wyse†	R	33	3	2	0	0	9.1	17	0	10	3	0-0	0	9.64
Gene Bearden†	L	30	1	1	0	0	2.2	6	0	2	1	0-0	0	16.88
Mickey Harris	L	34	41	0	0	0	87.1	87	6	43	47	6-8	4	3.81
Sandy Consuegra	R	30	40	12	5	0	146.0	140	10	63	31	7-8	3	4.01
Joe Haynes	R	33	26	3	1	0	73.0	85	9	37	18	1-4	2	4.56
Tom Ferrick†	R	36	22	0	0	0	41.2	36	3	7	17	2-0	2	2.38
Al Sima	L	29	18	8	1	0	77.0	79	5	41	26	3-7	0	4.79
Bob Ross	L	22	11	1	0	0	31.2	36	3	21	23	0-1	0	6.54
Alton Brown	R	26	7	0	0	0	11.2	14	1	12	7	0-0	0	9.26

1951 St. Louis Browns 8th AL 52-102 .338 46.0 GB

Zack Taylor

Player	Gm by Position	B	Age	G	AB	R	H	2B	3B	HR	RBI	BB	SO	SB	Avg	OBP	Slg
Sherm Lollar	C85,3B1	R	26	98	310	44	78	21	0	8	44	43	26	1	.252	.350	.397
Hank Arft	1B97	L	29	112	345	44	90	16	5	7	42	41	34	4	.261	.339	.397
Bobby Young	2B147	L	26	147	611	75	159	13	9	1	31	44	51	8	.260	.310	.316
Fred Marsh	3B117,SS3,2B2	R	27	130	445	44	108	21	4	4	43	36	56	4	.243	.299	.335
Bill Jennings	SS64	R	25	64	195	20	35	10	2	0	13	26	42	1	.179	.276	.251
Jim Delsing	OF124	L	25	131	449	59	112	20	2	8	45	56	39	2	.249	.338	.356
Ken Wood	OF100	R	26	109	333	40	79	19	0	15	44	27	49	1	.237	.296	.429
Ray Coleman†	OF87	L	29	91	341	41	96	16	5	5	55	24	32	3	.282	.329	.402
Matt Batts†	C64	R	29	79	248	26	75	17	1	5	31	21	22	1	.302	.357	.440
Cliff Mapes†	OF53	L	29	56	201	32	55	7	2	7	30	26	33	0	.274	.360	.433
Johnny Bero	SS55,2B1	L	28	61	160	24	34	5	0	5	17	26	30	1	.213	.323	.338
Tom Upton	SS47	R	24	52	131	9	26	4	3	0	12	12	22	1	.198	.271	.275
Jack Maguire†	OF26,3B5,2B2	R	26	41	127	15	31	2	1	1	14	12	21	1	.244	.309	.299
Johnny Berardino	3B31,2B2,1B1*	R	34	39	119	13	27	7	1	0	13	17	18	1	.227	.324	.303
Dale Long†	1B28,OF1	L	25	34	105	11	25	5	1	2	11	10	22	0	.238	.310	.362
Don Lenhardt†	OF27,1B1	R	28	31	103	9	27	3	0	5	18	6	13	1	.262	.303	.437
Earl Rapp†	OF25	L	30	26	98	14	32	5	3	2	14	11	11	1	.327	.394	.500
Ben Taylor	1B25	L	23	33	93	14	24	2	1	3	6	9	22	1	.258	.337	.398
Roy Sievers	OF25	R	24	31	89	10	20	2	1	1	11	9	21	0	.225	.303	.303
Paul Lehner†	OF18	L	30	21	67	2	9	5	0	1	2	6	5	0	.134	.205	.254
Les Moss†	C12	R	26	16	47	5	8	2	0	1	7	6	8	0	.170	.264	.277
Bob Nieman	OF11	R	24	12	43	6	16	3	1	2	8	3	5	0	.372	.413	.628
Joe Lutz	1B11	L	26	14	36	7	6	0	1	0	5	6	9	0	.167	.286	.222
Kermit Wahl†	3B6	R	28	8	27	2	9	1	1	0	3	0	3	0	.333	.333	.444
Bud Thomas	SS14	R	22	14	20	3	7	0	0	1	1	0	3	2	.350	.350	.500
Jim Dyck	3B4	R	29	4	15	1	1	0	0	0	0	1	1	0	.067	.125	.067
Frank Saucier	OF3	L	25	18	14	4	1	1	0	0	1	3	4	0	.071	.278	.143
Mike Goliat†	2B2	R	25	5	11	0	2	0	0	0	0	0	1	0	.182	.182	.182
Billy DeMars	SS1	R	25	1	4	1	1	0	0	0	0	1	0	0	.250	.400	.250
Clyde Kluttz†	C1	R	33	4	4	2	2	1	0	0	1	1	0	0	.500	.600	.750
Eddie Gaedel		R	26	1	0	0	0	0	0	0	0	1	0	0	—	1.000	—

J. Berardino, 1 G at OF

Pitcher	T	Age	G	GS	CG	ShO	IP	H	HR	BB	SO	W-L	Sv	ERA
Ned Garver	R	25	33	30	24	1	246.0	237	17	96	84	20-12	0	3.73
Duane Pillette	R	28	35	24	6	1	191.0	205	14	115	65	6-14	0	4.99
Tommy Byrne†	L	31	19	17	7	2	122.2	104	5	114	57	4-10	0	3.82
Al Widmar	R	26	26	16	4	0	107.2	157	19	52	28	4-9	0	6.52
Jim McDonald	R	24	16	11	5	0	84.0	84	5	46	28	4-7	1	4.07
Dick Starr†	R	30	15	9	0	0	62.0	66	10	42	26	2-5	0	7.40
Stubby Overmire†	L	32	8	7	3	0	53.1	61	5	21	13	1-6	0	3.54
Fred Sanford†	R	31	9	7	1	0	27.1	37	6	23	7	2-4	0	10.21
Don Johnson†	R	24	6	3	0	0	15.0	27	4	18	8	0-1	0	12.60
Bob Turley	R	20	1	1	0	0	7.1	11	0	3	5	0-1	0	7.36
Bob Mahoney†	R	23	30	4	0	0	81.0	86	7	41	30	2-5	0	4.44
Jim Suchecki	R	23	29	6	0	0	89.2	113	8	42	47	0-6	0	5.42
Satchel Paige	R	44	23	3	0	0	62.0	67	6	29	48	3-4	5	4.79
Lou Sleater	L	24	20	8	4	0	81.0	88	7	53	33	1-9	1	5.11
Bill Kennedy	L	30	19	5	1	0	56.0	76	4	37	29	1-5	0	5.79
Bobby Hogue†	R	30	18	0	0	0	29.2	31	1	23	11	1-1	1	5.16
Cliff Fannin	R	27	7	1	0	0	15.1	20	6	5	11	0-2	0	6.46
Irv Medlinger	L	24	6	0	0	0	9.2	10	1	12	5	0-0	0	8.38
Sid Schacht†	R	33	6	0	0	0	6.0	14	1	5	4	0-0	1	21.00
Duke Markell	R	27	5	2	1	0	21.1	25	3	20	10	1-1	0	6.33
Tito Herrera	R	24	3	0	0	0	2.1	6	2	4	1	0-0	0	27.00

>>1951 New York Giants 1st NL 98-59 .624 —

Leo Durocher

Player	Gm by Position	B	Age	G	AB	R	H	2B	3B	HR	RBI	BB	SO	SB	Avg	OBP	Slg
Wes Westrum	C122	R	28	124	361	59	79	12	0	20	70	104	93	1	.219	.400	.418
Whitey Lockman	1B119,OF34	L	24	153	614	85	173	27	7	12	73	50	32	4	.282	.339	.407
Eddie Stanky	2B140	R	34	145	515	88	127	17	2	14	43	127	63	8	.247	.401	.369
Hank Thompson	3B71	L	25	87	264	37	62	8	4	8	33	43	23	1	.235	.342	.386
Al Dark	SS156	R	29	156	646	114	196	41	7	14	69	42	39	12	.303	.352	.454
Willie Mays	OF121	R	20	121	464	59	127	22	5	20	68	56	60	7	.274	.354	.472
Don Mueller	OF115	L	24	122	469	58	130	10	7	16	69	19	13	1	.277	.307	.431
Monte Irvin	OF112,1B39	R	32	151	558	94	174	19	11	24	121	89	44	12	.312	.415	.514
Bobby Thomson	OF77,3B69	R	27	148	518	89	152	27	8	32	101	73	57	5	.293	.385	.562
Ray Noble	C41	R	32	55	141	16	33	6	0	5	26	6	26	0	.234	.265	.383
Bill Rigney	3B12,2B9	R	33	44	69	9	16	2	0	4	9	8	7	0	.232	.321	.435
Davey Williams	2B22	R	23	30	64	17	17	1	0	2	8	5	8	1	.266	.319	.375
Spider Jorgensen	OF11,3B1	L	31	28	51	5	12	0	0	2	8	3	2	0	.235	.291	.353
Clint Hartung	OF12	R	28	21	44	4	9	1	0	0	2	1	9	0	.205	.222	.227
Sal Yvars	C23	R	27	25	41	9	13	2	0	2	3	5	7	0	.317	.417	.512
Jack Lohrke	3B17,SS1	R	27	23	40	3	8	0	0	1	3	10	2	0	.200	.360	.275
Artie Wilson	2B3,SS3,1B2	L	30	19	22	2	4	0	0	0	1	2	1	2	.182	.250	.182
Jack Maguire†	OF8	R	26	16	20	6	8	1	1	1	4	2	2	0	.400	.455	.700
Earl Rapp†		L	30	13	11	0	1	0	0	0	1	2	3	0	.091	.231	.091
Hank Schenz†		R	32	8	0	1	0	0	0	0	0	0	0	0	—	—	—

Pitcher	T	Age	G	GS	CG	ShO	IP	H	HR	BB	SO	W-L	Sv	ERA
Sal Maglie	R	34	42	37	22	3	298.0	254	27	86	146	23-6	4	2.93
Larry Jansen	R	30	39	34	18	3	278.2	254	26	56	145	23-11	0	3.04
Jim Hearn	R	30	34	34	11	0	211.1	204	22	82	66	17-9	0	3.62
Al Corwin	R	24	15	8	3	1	59.0	49	7	21	30	5-1	1	3.66
Roger Bowman	L	23	9	5	0	0	26.1	35	2	22	24	2-4	0	6.15
George Spencer	R	24	57	4	2	0	132.0	125	21	56	36	10-4	6	3.75
Sheldon Jones	R	29	41	12	2	0	120.1	119	12	52	58	6-11	4	4.26
Dave Koslo	L	31	39	16	5	2	149.2	153	18	45	54	10-9	3	3.31
Al Gettel	R	33	30	1	0	0	57.1	52	12	25	36	1-2	0	4.87
Monte Kennedy	L	29	29	5	1	0	68.0	68	0	31	22	1-2	0	2.25
Jack Kramer†	R	33	4	1	0	0	4.2	11	0	3	2	0-0	0	15.43
Alex Konikowski	R	23	3	0	0	0	4.0	2	0	0	5	0-0	0	0.00
George Bamberger	R	25	2	0	0	0	2.0	4	2	2	1	0-0	0	18.00
Red Hardy	R	28	2	0	0	0	1.1	4	0	1	0	0-0	0	6.75

1951 Brooklyn Dodgers 2nd NL 97-60 .618 1.0 GB

Chuck Dressen

Player	Gm by Position	B	Age	G	AB	R	H	2B	3B	HR	RBI	BB	SO	SB	Avg	OBP	Slg
Roy Campanella	C140	R	29	143	505	90	164	33	1	33	108	53	51	1	.325	.393	.590
Gil Hodges	1B158	R	27	158	582	118	156	25	3	40	103	93	99	9	.268	.374	.527
Jackie Robinson	2B150	R	32	153	548	106	185	33	7	19	88	79	27	25	.338	.429	.527
Billy Cox	3B139,SS1	R	31	142	455	62	127	25	4	9	51	37	50	5	.279	.336	.411
Pee Wee Reese	SS154	R	32	154	616	94	176	20	8	10	84	81	57	20	.286	.371	.393
Carl Furillo	OF157	R	29	158	667	93	197	32	4	16	91	43	33	8	.295	.344	.427
Duke Snider	OF150	L	24	150	606	96	168	26	6	29	101	62	97	14	.277	.344	.483
Andy Pafko†	OF76	R	30	84	277	42	69	11	0	18	58	35	27	1	.249	.350	.484
Cal Abrams	OF34	L	27	67	150	27	42	8	0	3	19	36	26	3	.280	.419	.393
Rocky Bridges	3B40,2B10,SS9	R	23	63	134	13	34	7	0	1	15	10	10	0	.254	.306	.328
Don Thompson	OF61	L	27	80	118	25	27	3	0	0	6	12	12	2	.229	.305	.254
Gene Hermanski†	OF19	L	31	31	80	8	20	4	0	1	5	10	12	0	.250	.333	.338
Rube Walker†	C23	L	25	36	74	6	18	4	0	2	9	6	14	0	.243	.300	.378
ick Williams	OF15	R	22	23	60	5	12	3	1	1	5	4	10	0	.200	.250	.333
Wayne Terwilliger†	2B24,3B1	R	26	37	50	11	14	1	0	0	4	8	7	1	.280	.390	.300
Bruce Edwards†	C9	R	27	17	36	6	9	2	0	1	8	1	3	0	.250	.270	.389
Hank Edwards†		L	32	35	31	1	7	3	0	0	3	4	9	0	.226	.314	.323
Tommy Brown†	OF5	R	23	11	25	2	4	2	0	0	1	2	4	0	.160	.222	.240
Jim Russell	OF4	S	32	16	13	2	0	0	0	0	0	4	6	0	.000	.278	.000
Eddie Miksis†	3B6,2B1	R	24	19	10	6	2	1	0	0	0	1	2	0	.200	.333	.300
Mickey Livingston	C2	R	36	2	5	0	2	0	0	0	2	1	0	0	.400	.500	.400
Wayne Belardi		L	20	3	3	1	1	0	1	0	0	0	2	0	.333	.333	1.000

Pitcher	T	Age	G	GS	CG	ShO	IP	H	HR	BB	SO	W-L	Sv	ERA
Don Newcombe	R	25	40	36	18	3	272.0	235	19	91	164	20-9	0	3.28
Preacher Roe	L	36	34	33	19	2	257.2	247	30	64	113	22-3	0	3.04
Ralph Branca	R	25	42	27	13	3	204.0	180	19	85	118	13-12	3	3.26
Joe Hatten†	L	34	11	6	0	0	49.1	55	3	21	22	1-0	0	4.56
Chris Van Cuyk	L	24	9	6	0	0	29.1	33	4	11	16	1-2	0	5.52
Clyde King	R	26	48	3	1	0	121.1	118	15	50	33	14-7	6	4.15
Carl Erskine	R	24	46	19	7	0	189.2	206	23	78	95	16-12	4	4.46
Bud Podbielan	R	27	27	5	1	0	79.2	67	9	36	26	2-2	0	3.50
Phil Haugstad	R	27	21	1	0	0	30.2	28	4	24	22	0-1	0	6.46
Erv Palica	R	23	19	8	0	0	53.0	55	10	20	15	2-6	0	4.75
Johnny Schmitz†	L	30	16	7	0	0	55.2	55	4	28	24	1-4	0	5.34
Clem Labine	R	24	14	6	5	2	65.1	52	4	20	39	5-1	0	2.20
Dan Bankhead	R	31	7	1	0	0	14.0	27	5	14	9	0-1	0	15.43
Earl Mossor	R	25	3	0	0	0	1.2	2	1	7	1	0-0	0	32.40

718 Seasons: Team Rosters

1951 St. Louis Cardinals 3rd NL 81-73 .526 15.5 GB

Marty Marion

Player	Gm by Position	B	Age	G	AB	R	H	2B	3B	HR	RBI	BB	SO	SB	Avg	OBP	Slg
Del Rice	C120	R	28	122	374	34	94	13	1	9	47	34	26	0	.251	.319	.364
Nippy Jones	1B71	R	26	80	300	20	79	12	0	3	41	9	13	1	.263	.287	.333
Red Schoendienst	2B124,SS8	S	28	135	553	88	160	32	7	6	54	35	23	0	.289	.335	.405
Bill Johnson†	3B124	R	32	124	442	52	116	23	1	14	64	46	49	5	.262	.340	.414
Solly Hemus	SS105,2B12	L	28	120	420	68	118	18	9	2	32	75	31	7	.281	.395	.381
Enos Slaughter	OF106	L	35	123	409	48	115	17	8	4	64	67	25	7	.281	.386	.391
Stan Musial	OF91,1B60	L	30	152	578	124	205	30	12	32	108	98	40	4	.355	.449	.614
Peanuts Lowrey	OF85,3B11,2B3	R	32	114	370	52	112	19	5	5	40	35	12	0	.303	.366	.422
Wally Westlake†	OF68	R	30	73	267	36	68	8	5	6	39	24	42	1	.255	.325	.390
Hal Rice	OF63	L	27	69	236	20	60	12	1	4	38	24	22	0	.254	.323	.364
Stan Rojek†	SS51	R	32	51	186	21	51	7	3	0	14	10	10	0	.274	.318	.344
Tommy Glaviano	OF17,2B9	R	27	54	104	20	19	4	0	1	4	26	18	3	.183	.356	.250
Bill Sarni	C35	R	23	36	86	7	15	1	0	0	2	9	13	1	.174	.253	.186
Chuck Diering	OF44	R	28	64	85	9	22	5	1	0	8	6	15	0	.259	.308	.341
Steve Bilko	1B19	R	22	21	72	5	16	4	0	2	12	9	10	0	.222	.309	.361
Joe Garagiola†	C23	L	25	27	72	9	14	3	2	2	9	9	7	0	.194	.284	.375
Bill Howerton†	OF17	L	29	24	65	10	17	4	1	1	4	10	12	0	.262	.360	.400
Vern Benson	3B9,OF4	L	26	13	46	8	12	3	1	1	7	6	8	0	.261	.346	.435
Dick Cole†	2B14	R	25	15	36	4	7	1	0	0	3	6	5	0	.194	.310	.222
Don Richmond	3B11	L	31	12	34	3	3	1	0	1	4	3	3	0	.088	.162	.206
Eddie Kazak	3B10	R	30	11	33	2	6	2	0	0	4	5	5	0	.182	.289	.242
Harry Walker	OF6,1B1	L	34	8	26	6	8	1	0	0	2	2	1	0	.308	.357	.346
Rocky Nelson†	1B4,OF1	L	26	9	18	3	4	1	0	0	1	1	0	0	.222	.263	.278
Bob Scheffing†	C11	R	37	12	18	0	2	0	0	0	2	3	5	0	.111	.238	.111
Don Bollweg	1B2	L	30	6	9	1	1	1	0	0	2	0	1	0	.111	.111	.222
Jay Van Noy	OF1	L	22	6	7	1	0	0	0	0	0	1	6	0	.000	.125	.000
Larry Ciaffone	OF1	R	26	5	5	0	0	0	0	0	0	1	2	0	.000	.167	.000

Pitcher	T	Age	G	GS	CG	ShO	IP	H	HR	BB	SO	W-L	Sv	ERA
Gerry Staley	R	30	42	30	10	4	227.0	244	14	74	67	19-13	3	3.81
Tom Poholsky	R	21	38	26	10	1	195.0	204	15	68	70	7-13	1	4.43
Max Lanier	L	35	31	23	9	2	160.0	149	13	50	59	11-9	1	3.26
Harry Brecheen	L	36	24	16	5	0	138.2	134	11	54	57	8-4	2	3.25
Cliff Chambers†	L	29	21	16	9	1	129.1	120	13	56	45	11-6	0	3.83
Joe Presko	R	22	15	12	5	0	88.2	86	10	20	38	7-4	2	3.45
Jackie Collum	L	24	3	2	1	1	17.0	11	0	10	5	2-1	0	1.59
Al Brazle	L	37	56	8	5	0	154.1	139	13	60	66	6-5	7	3.09
George Munger	R	32	23	11	3	0	94.2	106	13	46	44	4-6	0	5.32
Dick Bokelmann	R	24	20	1	0	0	52.1	49	2	31	22	3-3	3	3.78
Cloyd Boyer	R	23	19	8	1	0	63.1	68	9	46	40	2-5	1	5.26
Ted Wilks†	R	35	17	0	0	0	18.0	19	1	5	5	0-0	1	3.00
Jack Crimian	R	25	11	0	0	0	17.0	24	3	8	5	1-0	1	9.00
Howie Pollet†	L	30	6	2	0	0	12.1	10	1	8	10	0-3	1	4.38
Erv Dusak†	R	30	5	0	0	0	10.0	14	0	7	8	0-0	0	7.20
Bob Habenicht	R	25	3	0	0	0	5.0	5	0	9	1	0-0	0	7.20
Kurt Krieger	R	24	2	0	0	0	4.0	6	1	5	3	0-0	0	15.75
Dan Lewandowski	R	23	2	0	0	0	1.0	3	0	1	1	0-1	0	9.00

1951 Boston Braves 4th NL 76-78 .494 20.5 GB

Billy Southworth (28-31)/Tommy Holmes (48-47)

Player	Gm by Position	B	Age	G	AB	R	H	2B	3B	HR	RBI	BB	SO	SB	Avg	OBP	Slg
Walker Cooper	C90	R	36	109	342	42	107	14	1	18	59	28	18	1	.313	.367	.518
Earl Torgeson	1B155	L	27	155	581	99	153	21	4	24	92	102	70	20	.263	.375	.437
Roy Hartsfield	2B114	R	25	120	450	63	122	11	2	6	31	41	73	7	.271	.333	.344
Bob Elliott	3B127	R	34	136	480	73	137	29	2	15	70	65	56	2	.285	.371	.448
Buddy Kerr	SS63,2B5	R	28	69	172	18	32	4	0	1	18	22	20	0	.186	.282	.227
Sam Jethroe	OF140	S	33	148	572	101	160	29	10	18	65	57	88	35	.280	.356	.460
Willard Marshall	OF136	L	30	136	469	65	132	24	7	11	62	48	18	0	.281	.351	.433
Sid Gordon	OF122,3B34	R	33	150	550	96	158	28	1	29	109	80	32	2	.287	.383	.500
Sibby Sisti	SS55,2B52,3B6*	R	30	114	362	46	101	20	2	2	38	32	50	4	.279	.341	.362
Ebba St. Claire	C62	S	29	72	220	22	62	17	2	1	25	12	24	2	.282	.322	.391
Bob Addis	OF46	L	25	85	199	23	55	7	0	1	24	9	10	3	.276	.308	.327
Johnny Logan	SS58	R	24	62	169	14	37	7	1	0	16	18	13	0	.219	.298	.272
Luis Marquez	OF43	R	25	68	122	19	24	5	1	0	11	10	20	4	.197	.274	.254
Ray Mueller	C23	R	39	28	70	8	11	2	0	1	9	7	11	0	.157	.234	.229
Luis Olmo	OF16	R	31	21	56	4	11	1	1	0	4	4	4	0	.196	.250	.250
Tommy Holmes	OF3	L	34	27	29	1	5	2	0	0	5	3	4	0	.172	.250	.241
Gene Mauch	SS10,3B3,2B2	R	25	19	20	5	2	0	0	0	1	7	4	0	.100	.333	.100
Bob Thorpe		R	24	2	2	1	1	0	1	0	1	0	0	0	.500	.500	1.500

S. Sisti, 1 G at 1B, 1 G at OF

Pitcher	T	Age	G	GS	CG	ShO	IP	H	HR	BB	SO	W-L	Sv	ERA
Warren Spahn	L	30	39	36	26	7	310.2	278	20	109	164	22-14	0	2.98
Max Surkont	R	29	37	33	11	2	237.0	230	21	89	110	12-16	1	3.99
Johnny Sain†	R	33	26	22	6	1	160.1	195	16	45	63	5-13	1	4.21
Vern Bickford	R	30	25	20	12	3	164.2	146	7	76	76	11-9	0	3.12
Chet Nichols	L	20	33	19	12	3	156.0	142	4	69	71	11-8	2	2.88
Jim Wilson	R	29	20	15	5	0	110.0	131	14	40	33	7-7	1	5.40
George Estock	R	26	37	1	0	0	60.1	56	2	37	11	0-1	3	4.33
Bob Chipman	L	32	33	0	0	0	52.0	59	5	19	17	4-3	4	4.85
Dave Cole	R	20	23	7	1	0	67.2	64	3	64	33	2-4	0	4.26
Phil Paine	R	21	21	0	0	0	35.1	36	2	20	17	2-0	0	3.06
Dick Donovan	R	23	8	2	0	0	13.2	17	0	11	4	0-0	0	5.27
Blix Donnelly	R	37	6	0	0	0	7.1	8	1	6	3	0-1	0	7.36
Sid Schacht†	R	33	5	0	0	0	4.2	6	0	2	1	0-2	0	1.93
Bobby Hogue†	R	30	3	0	0	0	5.0	4	1	3	0	0-0	0	5.40
Lew Burdette	R	24	3	0	0	0	4.1	6	0	5	1	0-0	0	6.23

1951 Philadelphia Phillies 5th NL 73-81 .474 23.5 GB

Eddie Sawyer

Player	Gm by Position	B	Age	G	AB	R	H	2B	3B	HR	RBI	BB	SO	SB	Avg	OBP	Slg
Andy Seminick	C91	R	30	101	291	42	66	8	1	11	37	63	67	1	.227	.370	.375
Eddie Waitkus	1B144	L	31	145	610	65	157	27	4	1	46	53	22	0	.257	.317	.320
Putsy Caballero	2B54,3B3,SS1	R	23	84	161	15	30	3	2	1	11	12	7	1	.186	.243	.248
Puddin' Head Jones	3B147	R	25	148	564	79	161	28	5	22	81	60	47	6	.285	.358	.470
Granny Hamner	SS150	R	24	150	589	61	150	23	7	9	72	29	32	10	.255	.290	.363
Richie Ashburn	OF154	L	24	154	643	92	221	31	5	4	63	50	37	29	.344	.393	.426
Del Ennis	OF135	R	26	144	532	76	142	20	5	15	73	68	42	4	.267	.352	.408
Dick Sisler	OF111	L	30	125	428	46	123	20	5	8	52	40	39	1	.287	.351	.414
Del Wilber	C73	R	32	84	245	30	68	7	3	8	34	17	26	0	.278	.324	.429
Eddie Pellagrini	2B53,SS8,3B6	R	33	86	197	31	46	4	5	5	30	23	25	5	.234	.326	.381
Tommy Brown†	OF32,2B14,1B12*	R	23	78	196	24	43	2	1	10	32	15	21	1	.219	.278	.393
Bill Nicholson	OF41	L	36	85	170	23	41	9	2	8	30	25	24	0	.241	.342	.459
Mike Goliat†	2B37,3B2	R	25	41	138	14	31	2	1	4	15	9	18	0	.225	.277	.341
Dick Young	2B15	L	23	15	68	7	16	5	0	0	2	3	6	0	.235	.268	.309
Jimmy Bloodworth	2B8,1B6	R	33	21	42	2	6	0	0	0	1	3	9	1	.143	.200	.143
Mel Clark	OF7	R	24	10	31	2	10	1	0	1	3	0	3	0	.323	.323	.452
Dick Whitman	OF6	L	30	19	17	0	2	0	0	0	0	0	1	0	.118	.118	.118
Ken Silvestri	C3,2B1	S	35	4	9	2	2	0	0	0	1	3	2	0	.222	.417	.222
Jackie Mayo	OF5	L	25	9	7	1	1	0	0	0	0	0	0	0	.143	.143	.143
Stan Lopata	C1	R	25	3	5	0	0	0	0	0	0	0	0	0	.000	.000	.000
Ed Sanicki	OF10	R	27	13	4	1	2	1	0	0	1	1	1	1	.500	.600	.750
Stan Hollmig		R	25	2	2	0	0	0	0	0	0	0	0	0	.000	.000	.000

T. Brown, 1 G at 3B

Pitcher	T	Age	G	GS	CG	ShO	IP	H	HR	BB	SO	W-L	Sv	ERA
Robin Roberts	R	24	44	39	22	6	315.0	284	20	64	127	21-15	2	3.03
Bubba Church	R	26	38	33	15	4	247.0	246	17	90	104	15-11	1	3.53
Russ Meyer	R	27	28	24	7	2	168.0	172	13	55	65	8-9	0	3.48
Ken Johnson	L	28	20	18	4	3	106.1	103	8	68	58	5-8	0	4.57
Niles Jordan	L	25	5	5	2	1	36.2	35	4	8	11	2-3	0	3.19
Karl Drews	R	31	5	3	1	0	23.0	29	2	7	13	1-0	0	6.26
Lou Possehl	R	25	2	1	0	0	6.0	9	0	3	6	0-1	0	6.00
Jim Konstanty	R	34	58	1	0	0	115.2	127	9	31	27	4-11	9	4.05
Ken Heintzelman	L	35	35	12	3	1	118.1	119	13	53	55	6-12	2	4.18
Jocko Thompson	L	34	29	14	3	2	119.1	102	12	59	60	4-8	1	3.85
Andy Hansen	R	26	24	0	0	0	39.0	34	4	7	11	3-1	0	2.54
Bob Miller	R	25	17	3	0	0	34.1	47	2	18	10	2-1	0	6.82
Milo Candini	R	33	15	0	0	0	30.0	33	3	18	14	1-0	0	6.00
Leo Cristante	R	24	10	1	0	0	22.0	28	3	9	6	1-1	0	4.91
Jack Brittin	R	27	3	0	0	0	4.0	5	0	6	3	0-0	0	9.00

1951 Cincinnati Reds 6th NL 68-86 .442 28.5 GB

Luke Sewell

Player	Gm by Position	B	Age	G	AB	R	H	2B	3B	HR	RBI	BB	SO	SB	Avg	OBP	Slg
Dixie Howell	C73	R	31	77	207	22	52	6	1	2	18	15	34	0	.251	.302	.319
Ted Kluszewski	1B154	L	26	154	607	74	157	35	2	13	77	35	33	6	.259	.301	.387
Connie Ryan	2B121,3B3,1B2*	R	31	136	473	75	112	17	4	16	53	79	72	11	.237	.350	.391
Grady Hatton	3B87,OF2	L	28	96	331	41	84	9	3	4	37	33	32	4	.254	.321	.335
Virgil Stallcup	SS117	R	29	121	428	33	103	17	2	8	49	6	40	2	.241	.251	.346
Johnny Wyrostek	OF139	L	31	142	537	52	167	31	3	2	61	54	54	2	.311	.376	.391
Joe Adcock	OF107	R	23	113	395	40	96	16	4	10	47	24	29	1	.243	.288	.380
Lloyd Merriman	OF102	L	26	114	359	34	87	23	2	5	36	31	34	8	.242	.303	.359
Bobby Adams	3B60,2B42,OF1	R	29	125	403	57	107	12	5	5	24	43	40	4	.266	.338	.357
Bob Usher	OF98	R	26	114	303	27	63	12	2	5	25	19	36	4	.208	.257	.310
Johnny Pramesa	C63	R	25	72	227	12	52	5	2	6	22	5	17	0	.229	.246	.348
Roy McMillan	SS54,3B12,2B1	R	20	85	199	21	42	4	0	1	8	17	26	0	.211	.273	.246
Hank Edwards†	OF34	L	32	41	127	14	40	9	1	3	20	13	17	0	.315	.379	.472
Bob Scheffing†	C41	R	37	47	122	9	31	2	0	2	14	16	9	0	.254	.345	.320
Barney McCosky†	OF11	L	34	25	50	2	16	2	1	1	11	4	2	0	.320	.370	.460
Wally Post	OF9	R	21	15	41	6	9	3	0	1	7	3	4	0	.220	.273	.366
Sammy Meeks	3B4,SS1	R	28	23	35	4	8	0	0	0	2	0	4	1	.229	.229	.229
Danny Litwhiler	OF7	R	34	12	29	3	8	1	0	2	3	2	5	0	.276	.323	.517
Hobie Landrith	C4	L	21	4	13	3	5	1	0	0	0	1	1	0	.385	.429	.462
Ted Tappe		L	20	4	3	0	1	0	0	0	0	0	0	0	.333	.333	.333
Jim Bolger		R	19	2	0	1	0	0	0	0	0	0	0	1	—	—	—

C. Ryan, 1 G at OF

Pitcher	T	Age	G	GS	CG	ShO	IP	H	HR	BB	SO	W-L	Sv	ERA
Ken Raffensberger	L	33	42	33	14	5	248.2	232	29	38	81	16-17	5	3.44
Ewell Blackwell	R	28	38	32	11	2	232.2	204	16	97	120	16-15	2	3.44
Willie Ramsdell	R	35	31	31	10	1	196.0	204	18	70	88	9-17	0	4.04
Howie Fox	R	30	40	30	9	4	228.0	239	16	69	57	9-14	2	3.83
Herm Wehmeier	R	24	39	22	10	2	184.2	167	15	89	93	7-10	2	3.70
Frank Smith	R	23	50	0	0	0	76.0	65	7	22	34	5-5	11	3.20
Bud Byerly	R	30	40	0	0	0	66.0	69	6	25	28	2-1	0	3.27
Harry Perkowski	L	28	35	7	1	0	102.0	96	2	46	56	3-6	1	2.82
Eddie Erautt	R	26	30	0	0	0	39.1	50	4	23	20	0-0	0	5.72
Kent Peterson	L	25	9	0	0	0	9.2	13	0	8	5	1-1	0	6.52
Ed Blake	R	25	3	0	0	0	4.0	10	3	1	1	0-0	0	11.25
Jim Blackburn	R	27	2	0	0	0	3.2	8	3	2	1	0-0	0	17.18

1951 Pittsburgh Pirates 7th NL 64-90 .416 32.5 GB

Billy Meyer

Player	Gm by Position	B	Age	G	AB	R	H	2B	3B	HR	RBI	BB	SO	SB	Avg	OBP	Slg
Clyde McCullough	C87	R	34	92	259	26	77	9	2	8	39	27	31	2	.297	.366	.440
Ralph Kiner	OF94,1B58	R	28	151	531	124	164	31	6	42	109	137	57	2	.309	.452	.627
Danny Murtaugh	2B65,3B3	R	33	77	151	9	30	7	0	1	11	16	19	0	.199	.284	.265
Pete Castiglione	3B99,SS28	R	30	132	482	62	126	19	4	7	42	34	28	2	.261	.311	.361
George Strickland	SS125,2B13	R	25	138	454	59	98	12	7	9	47	65	83	4	.216	.318	.333
Gus Bell	OF145	L	22	149	600	80	167	27	12	16	89	42	41	1	.278	.330	.443
Catfish Metkovich	OF69,1B37	L	30	120	423	51	124	21	3	3	40	28	23	3	.293	.338	.378
Bill Howerton†	OF53,3B4	L	29	80	219	29	60	12	2	11	37	26	44	1	.274	.351	.498
Joe Garagiola†	C61	L	25	72	212	24	54	8	2	9	35	32	20	4	.255	.358	.439
Rocky Nelson†	1B32,OF12	L	26	71	195	29	52	7	4	1	14	10	7	1	.267	.302	.359
Wally Westlake†	3B34,OF11	R	30	50	181	28	51	4	0	16	45	9	26	0	.282	.323	.569
Jack Phillips	1B53,3B4	R	29	70	156	12	37	7	3	0	12	15	17	1	.237	.304	.321
Monty Basgall	2B55	R	29	55	153	15	32	5	2	0	9	12	14	0	.209	.271	.268
Frank Thomas	OF37	R	22	39	148	21	39	9	2	2	16	9	15	0	.264	.306	.392
Pete Reiser	OF27,3B5	L	32	74	140	22	38	9	3	2	13	27	20	4	.271	.389	.421
Dick Cole†	2B34,SS8	R	25	42	106	9	25	4	0	1	11	15	9	0	.236	.331	.302
Ed Fitz Gerald	C38	R	27	55	97	8	22	6	0	0	13	7	10	1	.227	.286	.289
Tom Saffell	OF17	L	29	49	65	11	13	0	0	1	5	5	18	1	.200	.257	.246
Hank Schenz†	2B19,3B2	R	32	25	61	5	13	1	0	0	3	0	2	0	.213	.226	.230
Jack Merson	2B13	R	29	13	50	6	18	2	2	1	14	1	7	0	.360	.373	.540
Ted Beard	OF15	L	30	22	48	7	9	1	0	1	3	6	14	0	.188	.291	.271
Dick Smith	3B12	R	23	12	46	2	8	0	0	0	4	8	8	0	.174	.296	.174
Bob Dillinger†	3B10	R	32	12	43	3	10	3	0	0	0	1	0	2	.233	.250	.302
Erv Dusak†	OF12,P3,2B2*	R	30	21	39	6	12	3	0	1	7	3	11	0	.308	.357	.462
Dino Restelli	OF11	R	26	21	38	1	7	1	0	1	3	2	4	0	.184	.225	.289
Stan Rojek†	SS8	R	32	8	16	0	3	0	0	0	0	0	1	0	.188	.188	.188
Dale Long†	1B1	L	25	10	12	1	2	0	0	1	1	0	3	0	.167	.167	.417
Jack Maguire†	2B1,3B1	R	26	8	5	1	0	0	0	0	0	1	0	0	.000	.167	.000
Harry Fisher		L	25	3	3	0	0	0	0	0	0	0	0	0	.000	.000	.000

E. Dusak, 2 G at 3B

Pitcher	T	Age	G	GS	CG	ShO	IP	H	HR	BB	SO	W-L	Sv	ERA
Murry Dickson	R	34	45	35	19	3	288.2	294	32	101	112	20-16	2	4.02
Bob Friend	R	20	34	22	3	1	149.2	173	12	68	41	6-10	0	4.27
Mel Queen	R	33	39	21	4	1	168.1	149	21	99	123	7-9	0	4.44
Howie Pollet†	L	30	21	21	4	1	128.2	149	24	51	47	6-10	0	5.04
Vern Law	R	21	28	14	2	1	114.0	109	9	51	41	6-9	2	4.50
Cliff Chambers†	L	29	10	10	2	1	59.2	64	5	31	19	3-6	0	5.58
Don Carlsen	R	24	7	6	2	0	43.0	50	4	14	20	2-3	0	4.19
Len Yochim	L	22	2	2	0	0	8.2	10	0	11	5	1-1	0	8.31
Con Dempsey	R	27	3	2	0	0	7.0	11	2	4	3	0-2	0	9.00
Bill Werle	L	30	59	9	2	0	149.2	181	20	51	57	8-6	6	5.65
Ted Wilks†	R	35	48	1	1	0	82.2	69	7	24	43	3-5	12	2.83
Junior Walsh	R	32	36	1	0	0	73.1	92	9	46	32	1-4	0	6.87
Paul LaPalme	L	27	22	8	1	1	54.1	79	6	31	24	1-5	0	6.29
Bill Koski	R	19	13	1	0	0	27.0	26	2	28	6	0-1	0	6.67
Joe Muir	L	28	9	1	0	0	16.1	11	2	7	5	0-2	0	2.76
Erv Dusak†	R	30	3	1	0	0	6.2	10	2	9	2	0-1	0	12.15
Paul Pettit	L	19	2	0	0	0	2.2	2	1	1	0	0-0	0	3.38

1951 Chicago Cubs 8th NL 62-92 .403 34.5 GB

Frank Frisch (35-45)/Phil Cavarretta (27-47)

Player	Gm by Position	B	Age	G	AB	R	H	2B	3B	HR	RBI	BB	SO	SB	Avg	OBP	Slg
Smoky Burgess	C64	L	24	94	219	21	55	4	2	2	20	21	12	2	.251	.317	.315
Chuck Connors	1B57	L	30	66	201	16	48	5	1	2	18	12	25	4	.239	.282	.303
Eddie Miksis†	2B102	R	24	102	421	48	112	13	3	4	35	33	36	11	.266	.319	.340
Randy Jackson	3B143	R	25	145	557	78	153	24	6	16	76	47	44	14	.275	.332	.425
Roy Smalley	SS74	R	25	79	238	24	55	7	4	8	31	25	53	0	.231	.304	.395
Frankie Baumholtz	OF140	L	32	146	560	62	159	28	10	2	50	49	36	5	.284	.346	.380
Hank Sauer	OF132	R	34	141	525	77	138	19	4	30	89	45	77	2	.263	.325	.486
Hal Jeffcoat	OF87	R	26	113	278	44	76	20	2	4	27	16	23	8	.273	.315	.403
Gene Hermanski†	OF63	L	31	75	231	28	65	12	1	3	20	35	30	3	.281	.385	.381
Phil Cavarretta	1B53	L	34	89	206	24	64	7	1	6	28	27	28	0	.311	.393	.442
Wayne Terwilliger†	2B49	R	26	50	192	26	41	6	0	0	10	29	21	3	.214	.317	.245
Andy Pafko†	OF48	R	30	49	178	26	47	5	3	12	35	17	10	1	.264	.342	.528
Dee Fondy	1B44	L	26	49	170	23	46	7	2	3	20	11	20	5	.271	.319	.388
Jack Cusick	SS56	R	23	65	164	16	29	3	2	2	16	17	29	2	.177	.254	.256
Bob Ramazzotti	SS51,2B6,3B1	R	34	73	158	13	39	5	2	1	15	10	23	0	.247	.292	.323
Bruce Edwards†	C28,1B9	R	27	51	141	19	33	9	2	3	17	16	14	1	.234	.316	.390
Mickey Owen	C57	R	35	58	125	10	23	6	0	0	15	19	13	1	.184	.292	.232
Rube Walker†	C31	L	25	37	107	9	25	4	0	2	5	12	13	0	.234	.311	.327
Bob Borkowski	OF25	R	25	58	89	9	14	1	0	0	10	3	16	0	.157	.185	.169
Bill Serena	3B12	R	26	13	39	8	13	3	1	1	4	11	4	0	.333	.490	.538
Harry Chiti	C8	R	18	9	31	1	11	2	0	0	5	2	2	0	.355	.394	.419
Carmen Mauro	OF6	L	24	13	29	3	5	1	0	0	3	2	6	0	.172	.250	.207
Fred Richards	1B9	L	23	10	27	1	8	2	0	0	4	2	3	0	.296	.345	.370

Pitcher	T	Age	G	GS	CG	ShO	IP	H	HR	BB	SO	W-L	Sv	ERA
Bob Rush	R	25	37	29	12	2	211.1	212	16	68	129	11-12	2	3.83
Paul Minner	L	27	33	28	14	3	201.2	219	20	64	68	6-17	1	3.79
Frank Hiller	R	30	24	21	6	2	141.1	147	17	31	50	6-12	1	4.84
Turk Lown	R	27	31	18	3	1	127.0	125	14	90	39	4-9	0	5.46
Cal McLish	R	25	30	17	5	1	145.2	159	16	52	46	4-10	0	4.45
Bob Schultz	L	27	17	10	2	0	77.1	75	9	51	27	3-6	0	5.24
Dutch Leonard	R	42	41	1	0	0	81.2	69	3	28	30	10-6	3	2.64
Bob Kelly	R	23	35	11	4	0	123.2	130	8	55	48	7-4	0	4.66
Johnny Klippstein	R	23	35	11	1	1	123.2	125	10	53	56	6-6	2	4.29
Joe Hatten†	L	34	23	6	1	0	75.1	82	8	37	23	2-6	0	5.14
Monk Dubiel	R	33	22	0	0	0	54.2	46	3	22	19	2-2	1	2.30
Johnny Schmitz†	L	30	8	3	0	0	18.0	22	1	15	6	1-2	0	8.00
Andy Varga	L	20	2	0	0	0	3.0	2	0	6	1	0-0	0	3.00
Warren Hacker	R	26	2	0	0	0	1.1	3	0	0	2	0-0	0	13.50

»1952 New York Yankees 1st AL 95-59 .617 —

Casey Stengel

Player	Gm by Position	B	Age	G	AB	R	H	2B	3B	HR	RBI	BB	SO	SB	Avg	OBP	Slg
Yogi Berra	C140	L	27	142	534	97	146	17	1	30	98	66	24	2	.273	.358	.478
Joe Collins	1B119	L	29	122	428	69	120	16	8	18	59	55	47	4	.280	.364	.481
Billy Martin	2B107	R	24	109	363	32	97	13	3	3	33	22	31	3	.267	.323	.344
Gil McDougald	3B117,2B38	R	24	152	555	65	146	16	5	11	78	57	73	6	.263	.336	.369
Phil Rizzuto	SS152	R	34	152	578	89	147	24	10	2	43	67	42	17	.254	.337	.341
Mickey Mantle	OF141,3B1	S	20	142	549	94	171	37	7	23	87	75	111	4	.311	.394	.530
Hank Bauer	OF139	R	29	141	553	86	162	31	6	17	74	50	61	6	.293	.355	.463
Gene Woodling	OF118	L	29	122	408	58	126	19	6	12	63	59	31	1	.309	.397	.473
Irv Noren†	OF60,1B19	L	27	93	272	36	64	13	2	5	21	26	34	4	.235	.316	.353
Johnny Mize	1B27	L	39	78	137	9	36	9	0	4	29	11	15	0	.263	.327	.416
Bobby Brown	3B24	L	27	29	89	6	22	2	0	1	14	9	6	1	.247	.323	.303
Bob Cerv	OF27	R	26	36	87	11	21	3	2	1	8	9	22	0	.241	.313	.356
Charlie Silvera	C20	R	27	20	55	4	18	3	0	0	11	5	2	0	.327	.383	.382
Jerry Coleman	2B11	R	27	11	42	6	17	2	1	0	4	5	4	0	.405	.468	.500
Andy Carey	3B14,SS1	R	20	16	40	6	6	0	0	0	1	3	10	0	.150	.209	.150
Jim Brideweser	SS22,2B4,3B1	R	25	42	38	12	10	0	0	0	2	3	5	0	.263	.317	.263
Johnny Hopp†	1B12	L	35	15	25	4	4	0	0	0	2	2	3	2	.160	.250	.160
Kal Segrist	2B11,3B1	R	21	13	23	3	1	0	0	0	1	3	1	0	.043	.154	.043
Loren Babe	3B9	L	24	12	21	1	2	1	0	0	0	4	4	1	.095	.240	.143
Jackie Jensen†	OF5	R	25	7	19	3	2	1	1	0	2	4	4	1	.105	.261	.263
Ralph Houk	C9	R	32	9	6	0	2	0	0	0	0	1	0	0	.333	.429	.333
Archie Wilson†		R	28	3	2	0	1	0	0	0	1	0	0	0	.500	.500	.500
Charlie Keller	OF1	L	35	2	1	0	0	0	0	0	0	0	1	0	.000	.000	.000

Pitcher	T	Age	G	GS	CG	ShO	IP	H	HR	BB	SO	W-L	Sv	ERA
Vic Raschi	R	33	31	31	13	4	223.0	174	13	91	127	16-6	0	2.78
Allie Reynolds	R	37	35	29	24	6	244.1	194	10	97	160	20-8	6	2.06
Ed Lopat	L	34	20	19	10	2	149.1	127	11	53	56	10-5	0	2.53
Bill Miller	L	24	21	13	5	2	88.0	78	4	49	45	4-6	0	3.48
Tom Morgan	R	22	16	12	2	1	93.2	86	8	33	35	5-4	2	3.07
Tom Gorman	R	27	12	6	1	1	60.2	63	8	22	31	6-2	1	4.60
Johnny Sain	R	34	35	16	8	0	148.1	149	15	38	57	11-6	7	3.46
Bob Kuzava	L	29	28	12	6	1	133.0	115	7	63	67	8-8	3	3.45
Bobby Hogue†	R	31	27	0	0	0	47.1	52	6	25	12	3-5	4	5.32
Jim McDonald	R	25	26	5	1	0	69.1	71	1	40	20	3-4	0	3.50
Joe Ostrowski	L	35	20	1	0	0	40.0	56	5	14	17	2-2	2	5.63
Ray Scarborough†	R	34	9	4	1	0	34.0	27	4	15	13	5-1	0	2.91
Harry Schaeffer	L	28	5	2	0	0	17.0	18	2	18	15	0-1	0	5.29
Ewell Blackwell†	R	29	5	2	0	0	16.0	12	0	12	7	1-0	1	0.56
Johnny Schmitz†	L	31	5	2	1	0	15.0	15	0	9	3	1-1	1	3.60
Art Schallock	L	28	2	0	0	0	2.0	3	0	2	1	0-0	0	9.00

1952 Cleveland Indians 2nd AL 93-61 .604 2.0 GB

Al Lopez

Player	Gm by Position	B	Age	G	AB	R	H	2B	3B	HR	RBI	BB	SO	SB	Avg	OBP	Slg
Jim Hegan	C107	R	31	112	333	39	75	17	2	4	41	29	47	0	.225	.287	.324
Luke Easter	1B118	L	36	127	437	63	115	10	3	31	97	44	84	1	.263	.337	.513
Bobby Avila	2B149	R	28	150	597	102	179	26	11	7	45	67	36	12	.300	.371	.415
Al Rosen	3B147,1B4,SS3	R	28	148	567	101	171	32	5	28	105	75	54	8	.302	.387	.524
Ray Boone	SS96,3B2,2B1	R	28	103	316	57	83	8	2	7	45	53	33	0	.263	.372	.367
Larry Doby	OF136	L	28	140	519	104	143	26	8	32	104	90	111	5	.276	.383	.541
Dale Mitchell	OF128	L	30	134	511	61	165	26	3	5	58	52	9	6	.323	.387	.415
Harry Simpson	OF127,1B28	L	26	146	545	66	145	21	10	10	65	56	82	5	.266	.337	.396
Jim Fridley	OF54	R	27	62	175	23	44	2	0	4	16	14	40	3	.251	.311	.331
Merrill Combs	SS49,2B3	L	32	52	139	11	23	1	1	1	10	14	15	0	.165	.242	.209
Joe Tipton†	C35	R	30	43	105	15	26	2	0	6	22	21	21	1	.248	.383	.438
Birdie Tebbetts	C37	R	39	42	101	4	25	4	0	1	8	12	9	0	.248	.339	.317
Bill Glynn	1B32	L	26	44	92	15	25	5	0	2	7	5	16	1	.272	.309	.391
George Strickland†	SS30,2B1	R	26	31	88	8	19	4	0	1	8	14	15	0	.216	.324	.295
Barney McCosky	OF19	L	35	54	80	14	17	4	1	1	6	8	5	1	.213	.284	.325
Wally Westlake†	OF28	R	31	29	69	11	16	4	1	1	9	8	16	1	.232	.312	.362
Hank Majeski†	3B11,2B3	R	35	36	54	7	16	2	0	0	9	7	7	0	.296	.377	.333
Pete Reiser	OF10	L	33	34	44	7	6	1	0	3	7	4	16	1	.136	.208	.364
Bob Kennedy	OF13,3B3	R	31	22	40	6	12	3	1	0	12	9	5	1	.300	.429	.425
Dave Pope	OF10	L	31	12	34	9	10	1	1	1	4	1	7	0	.294	.314	.471
Johnny Berardino†	2B8,SS8,3B4*	R	35	35	32	5	3	0	0	0	2	10	8	0	.094	.310	.094
Quincy Trouppe	C6	S	39	6	10	1	1	0	0	0	0	1	3	0	.100	.182	.100
Snuffy Stirnweiss	3B1	R	33	1	0	0	0	0	0	0	0	0	0	0	—	—	—

J. Berardino, 2 G at 1B

Pitcher	T	Age	G	GS	CG	ShO	IP	H	HR	BB	SO	W-L	Sv	ERA
Bob Lemon	R	31	42	36	28	5	309.2	236	15	105	131	22-11	4	2.50
Mike Garcia	R	28	46	36	19	6	292.1	284	9	87	143	22-11	4	2.37
Early Wynn	R	32	42	33	19	4	285.2	239	23	132	153	23-12	3	2.90
Bob Feller	R	33	30	30	11	0	191.2	219	13	83	81	9-13	0	4.74
Lou Brissie	L	28	42	1	0	0	82.2	68	5	34	28	3-2	2	3.48
Steve Gromek	R	32	29	13	3	1	122.2	109	14	28	65	7-7	1	3.67
Mickey Harris†	L	35	29	0	0	0	46.2	42	6	21	23	3-0	1	4.63
Sam Jones	R	26	14	4	0	0	36.0	38	6	37	28	2-3	1	7.25
Dick Rozek	L	25	10	1	0	0	12.2	11	0	13	5	1-0	0	4.97
Ted Wilks†	R	36	7	0	0	0	11.2	8	0	7	6	0-0	1	3.86
Bob Chakales	R	24	5	1	0	0	12.0	19	2	8	7	1-2	0	9.75
Bill Abernathie	R	23	1	0	0	0	2.0	4	1	1	0	0-0	1	13.50
George Zuverink	R	27	1	0	0	0	1.1	1	0	0	1	0-0	0	0.00

1952 Chicago White Sox 3rd AL 81-73 .526 14.0 GB

Paul Richards

Player	Gm by Position	B	Age	G	AB	R	H	2B	3B	HR	RBI	BB	SO	SB	Avg	OBP	Slg
Sherm Lollar	C120	R	27	132	375	35	90	15	0	13	50	54	34	1	.240	.354	.384
Eddie Robinson	1B155	L	31	155	594	79	176	33	1	22	104	70	49	2	.296	.382	.466
Nellie Fox	2B151	L	24	152	648	76	192	25	10	0	39	34	14	5	.296	.334	.366
Hector Rodriguez	3B113	R	32	124	407	55	108	14	0	1	40	47	22	7	.265	.346	.307
Chico Carrasquel	SS99	R	26	100	359	36	89	7	4	1	42	33	27	2	.248	.315	.298
Minnie Minoso	OF143,3B9,SS1	R	29	147	569	96	160	24	9	13	61	71	46	22	.281	.375	.424
Sam Mele†	OF112,1B3	R	29	123	423	46	105	18	2	14	59	48	40	1	.248	.328	.400
Ray Coleman†	OF73	L	30	85	195	19	42	7	1	2	14	13	17	0	.215	.264	.292
Bud Stewart	OF60	L	36	92	225	23	60	10	0	5	30	28	17	3	.267	.350	.378
Jim Rivera†	OF53	L	29	53	201	27	50	7	3	3	18	21	27	13	.249	.320	.358
Willie Miranda†	SS54,3B5,2B2	S	26	70	150	14	33	4	1	0	7	13	14	1	.220	.287	.260
Sam Dente	SS27,3B18,2B6*	R	30	62	145	12	32	0	1	0	11	5	8	0	.221	.257	.234
Tom Wright†	OF34	L	28	60	132	15	34	10	2	1	21	16	16	1	.258	.342	.386
Al Zarilla†	OF32	L	33	39	99	14	23	4	1	2	7	14	6	1	.232	.333	.354
Rocky Krsnich	3B37	R	24	40	91	11	21	7	2	1	15	12	9	0	.231	.327	.385
Bud Sheely	C31	L	31	36	75	1	18	2	0	0	3	12	7	0	.240	.352	.267
Phil Masi	C25	R	36	30	63	9	16	1	1	0	7	10	10	0	.254	.356	.302
Jim Busby†	OF16	R	25	16	39	5	5	0	0	0	0	2	7	0	.128	.171	.128
Darrell Johnson†	C21	R	23	22	37	3	4	0	0	0	1	5	9	1	.108	.214	.108
Leo Thomas†	3B9	R	28	19	24	1	4	0	0	0	6	6	4	0	.167	.333	.167
Hank Edwards†	OF3	L	33	8	18	2	6	0	0	0	1	0	2	0	.333	.333	.333
George Wilson†	OF1	L	26	8	9	0	1	0	0	0	1	1	2	0	.111	.200	.111
Ken Landenberger	1B1	L	23	2	5	0	1	0	0	0	0	0	2	0	.200	.200	.200
Sammy Esposito	SS1	R	20	1	4	0	1	0	0	0	0	0	2	0	.250	.250	.250
Red Wilson	C2	R	23	2	3	0	0	0	0	0	0	0	1	0	.000	.000	.000
Don Nicholas		L	21	3	2	0	0	0	0	0	0	0	0	0	.000	.000	.000

S. Dente, 6 G at OF, 2 G at 1B

Pitcher	T	Age	G	GS	CG	ShO	IP	H	HR	BB	SO	W-L	Sv	ERA
Billy Pierce	L	25	33	32	14	4	255.1	214	12	79	144	15-12	1	2.57
Saul Rogovin	R	28	33	30	12	3	231.2	224	14	79	121	14-9	1	3.85
Joe Dobson	R	35	29	25	11	3	200.2	164	11	60	101	14-10	1	2.51
Marv Grissom	R	34	28	24	7	1	166.0	156	6	79	97	12-10	0	3.74
Lou Kretlow	R	31	19	11	4	2	79.0	52	5	56	63	4-4	1	2.96
Ken Holcombe†	R	33	7	7	1	0	35.0	38	3	18	12	0-5	0	6.17
Bill Kennedy	L	31	47	1	0	0	70.2	54	4	38	46	2-2	5	2.80
Harry Dorish	R	30	39	1	1	0	91.0	66	4	42	47	8-4	11	2.47
Chuck Stobbs	L	22	38	17	2	0	135.0	118	9	72	73	7-12	1	3.13
Luis Aloma	R	28	25	0	0	0	40.0	42	5	11	18	3-1	6	4.28
Hal Brown	R	27	24	8	1	0	72.1	82	8	21	31	2-3	0	4.23
Howie Judson	R	26	21	0	0	0	34.0	30	4	22	15	0-1	1	4.24
Hal Hudson†	L	25	2	0	0	0	4.0	7	0	1	4	0-0	0	2.25
Al Widmar	R	27	1	0	0	0	2.0	4	1	0	2	0-0	0	4.50

1952 Philadelphia Athletics 4th AL 79-75 .513 16.0 GB

Jimmy Dykes

Player	Gm by Position	B	Age	G	AB	R	H	2B	3B	HR	RBI	BB	SO	SB	Avg	OBP	Slg
Joe Astroth	C102	R	29	104	337	24	84	7	2	1	36	25	27	2	.249	.305	.291
Ferris Fain	1B144	L	31	145	538	82	176	43	3	2	59	105	26	3	.327	.438	.429
Skeeter Kell	2B68	R	22	75	213	24	47	8	3	0	17	14	18	5	.221	.275	.286
Billy Hitchcock	3B104,1B13	R	35	119	407	45	100	8	4	1	56	39	45	1	.246	.318	.292
Eddie Joost	SS146	R	36	146	540	94	132	26	3	20	75	122	94	5	.244	.388	.415
Dave Philley	OF149,3B2	S	32	151	586	80	154	25	4	7	71	59	35	11	.263	.334	.355
Gus Zernial	OF141	R	29	145	549	76	144	15	1	29	100	70	87	5	.262	.347	.452
Elmer Valo	OF121	L	31	129	388	69	109	26	4	5	47	101	16	12	.281	.432	.407
Pete Suder	2B43,SS17,3B16	R	36	74	228	22	55	7	2	1	20	16	17	1	.241	.291	.303
Cass Michaels†	2B55	R	26	55	200	22	50	4	5	1	18	23	11	3	.250	.330	.335
Allie Clark	OF48,1B2	R	29	71	186	23	51	12	0	7	29	10	19	0	.274	.315	.452
Ray Murray	C42	R	34	44	136	14	28	5	0	1	10	9	13	0	.206	.255	.265
Hank Majeski†	3B34	R	35	34	117	14	30	2	2	2	20	19	10	0	.256	.365	.359
Kite Thomas	OF29	R	29	75	116	24	29	6	1	6	18	20	27	0	.250	.365	.474
Joe Tipton†	C23	R	30	23	68	6	13	4	0	3	8	15	10	0	.191	.337	.382
Sherry Robertson†	2B8,OF7,3B2	L	33	43	60	8	12	3	0	0	5	21	15	1	.200	.407	.250
Hal Bevan†	3B6	R	21	8	17	1	6	0	0	0	4	0	1	2	.353	.353	.353
Tom Hamilton	1B5	L	26	9	10	1	2	1	0	0	1	1	1	0	.200	.273	.300
Jack Littrell	SS2,3B1	R	23	4	2	0	0	0	0	0	0	1	2	0	.000	.333	.000

Pitcher	T	Age	G	GS	CG	ShO	IP	H	HR	BB	SO	W-L	Sv	ERA
Bobby Shantz	L	26	33	33	27	5	279.2	230	21	63	152	24-7	0	2.48
Alex Kellner	L	27	34	33	14	2	231.1	223	21	86	105	12-14	0	4.36
Harry Byrd	R	27	37	28	15	3	228.1	244	12	98	116	15-15	2	3.31
Carl Scheib	R	25	30	19	8	1	158.0	153	21	50	42	11-7	2	4.39
Sam Zoldak	L	33	16	10	2	0	75.1	86	3	25	12	0-6	1	4.06
Charlie Bishop	R	28	6	5	1	0	30.2	29	2	24	17	2-2	0	6.46
Morrie Martin	L	29	5	5	0	0	25.1	32	1	15	13	0-2	0	6.39
Bob Hooper	R	30	43	14	4	0	144.1	158	13	68	40	8-15	6	5.18
Johnny Kucab	R	32	25	0	0	0	51.1	64	5	20	17	0-1	2	5.26
Ed Wright	R	33	24	0	0	0	41.1	55	6	20	9	2-1	1	6.53
Dick Fowler	R	31	18	3	1	0	58.2	71	4	28	14	1-2	0	6.44
Bobo Newsom†	R	44	14	5	1	0	47.2	38	2	23	22	3-3	1	3.59
Tex Hoyle	R	30	3	0	0	0	2.1	9	2	1	1	0-0	0	27.00
Marion Fricano	R	28	2	0	0	0	5.0	5	0	1	0	1-0	0	1.80
Walt Kellner	R	23	1	0	0	0	4.0	4	0	3	2	0-1	0	6.75
Len Matarazzo	R	23	1	0	0	0	1.0	1	0	1	0	0-0	0	0.00

1952 Washington Senators 5th AL 78-76 .506 17.0 GB

Bucky Harris

Player	Gm by Position	B	Age	G	AB	R	H	2B	3B	HR	RBI	BB	SO	SB	Avg	OBP	Slg
Mickey Grasso	C114	R	32	115	361	22	78	9	0	0	27	29	36	1	.216	.276	.241
Mickey Vernon	1B153	L	34	154	569	71	143	33	9	10	80	89	66	7	.251	.353	.394
Floyd Baker	2B68,SS7,3B1	L	35	79	263	27	69	8	0	0	33	30	17	1	.262	.342	.293
Eddie Yost	3B157	R	25	157	587	92	137	32	3	12	49	129	73	4	.233	.378	.359
Pete Runnels	SS147,2B1	L	24	152	555	70	158	18	3	1	64	72	55	0	.285	.368	.333
Jackie Jensen†	OF143	R	25	144	570	80	163	29	5	10	80	63	40	17	.286	.360	.407
Jim Busby†	OF128	R	25	129	512	58	125	24	4	2	47	22	48	5	.244	.281	.318
Gil Coan	OF86	L	30	107	332	50	68	11	6	5	20	32	35	9	.205	.277	.319
Ken Wood†	OF56	R	27	61	210	26	50	8	6	6	32	30	21	0	.238	.333	.419
Mel Hoderlein	2B58	S	29	72	208	16	56	8	2	0	17	18	22	2	.269	.333	.327
Clyde Kluttz	C52	R	34	58	144	7	33	5	0	1	11	12	11	0	.229	.293	.285
Frank Campos	OF23	L	28	53	112	9	29	6	1	0	8	1	13	0	.259	.278	.330
Archie Wilson†	OF24	R	28	26	96	8	20	2	3	0	14	5	11	0	.208	.255	.292
Cass Michaels†	2B22	R	26	22	86	10	20	4	1	1	7	7	15	0	.233	.290	.337
Earl Rapp†	OF10	L	31	46	67	7	19	6	0	0	9	6	13	0	.284	.351	.373
Jerry Snyder	2B19,SS4	R	22	36	57	5	9	2	0	0	2	5	8	1	.158	.226	.193
Irv Noren†	OF12	L	27	12	49	4	12	3	1	0	2	6	3	1	.245	.327	.347
Sam Mele†	OF7	R	29	9	28	2	12	3	0	2	10	1	2	0	.429	.448	.750
Fred Marsh†	2B5,OF2	R	28	9	24	1	1	0	0	0	1	1	4	0	.042	.080	.042
George Bradshaw	C9	R	27	10	23	3	5	2	0	0	6	1	2	0	.217	.280	.304
Hal Keller	C11	L	24	11	23	2	4	2	0	0	0	1	1	0	.174	.208	.261
Fred Taylor	1B5	L	27	10	19	3	5	1	0	0	4	3	2	0	.263	.364	.316
Tom Upton	SS3	R	25	5	5	1	0	0	0	0	0	1	0	0	.000	.167	.000
Buck Varner	OF1	L	21	2	4	0	0	0	0	0	0	1	1	0	.000	.200	.000
Sherry Robertson†		L	33	1	0	0	0	0	0	0	0	0	0	0	—	—	—

Pitcher	T	Age	G	GS	CG	ShO	IP	H	HR	BB	SO	W-L	Sv	ERA
Bob Porterfield	R	28	31	29	15	3	231.1	222	7	85	80	13-14	0	2.72
Connie Marrero	R	41	22	22	16	2	184.1	175	9	53	77	11-8	0	2.88
Julio Moreno	R	31	26	22	7	0	147.1	154	10	52	62	9-9	0	3.97
Spec Shea	R	31	22	21	12	2	169.0	144	6	92	65	11-7	0	2.93
Walt Masterson†	R	32	24	21	11	0	160.2	153	11	72	89	9-8	2	3.70
Randy Gumpert†	R	34	20	12	2	0	104.0	112	12	30	29	4-9	0	4.24
Lou Sleater†	L	25	14	9	3	1	57.0	56	4	30	22	4-2	0	3.63
Sid Hudson†	R	37	7	7	6	0	62.2	59	4	29	24	3-4	0	2.73
Mike Fornieles	R	20	4	2	2	1	26.1	13	1	11	12	2-2	0	1.37
Raul Sanchez	R	21	3	2	1	1	12.2	13	0	7	6	1-1	0	3.55
Sandy Consuegra	R	31	30	2	0	0	73.2	80	2	27	19	6-0	5	3.05
Don Johnson	R	25	29	6	0	0	69.0	80	4	33	37	0-5	2	4.43
Tom Ferrick	R	37	27	0	0	0	50.2	53	2	11	28	4-3	1	3.02
Joe Haynes	R	34	22	2	0	0	66.0	70	2	35	18	0-3	3	4.50
Bobo Newsom†	R	44	10	0	0	0	12.2	16	2	9	5	1-1	2	4.97
Bunky Stewart	L	21	1	0	0	0	1.0	2	0	1	1	0-0	0	18.00
Mickey Harris†	L	35	1	0	0	0	1.0	1	1	0	0	0-0	0	9.00
Harley Grossman	R	22	1	0	0	0	0.1	2	1	0	0	0-0	0	54.00

1952 Boston Red Sox 6th AL 76-78 .494 19.0 GB

Lou Boudreau

Player	Gm by Position	B	Age	G	AB	R	H	2B	3B	HR	RBI	BB	SO	SB	Avg	OBP	Slg
Sammy White	C110	R	23	115	381	35	107	20	2	10	49	16	43	2	.281	.310	.423
Dick Gernert	1B99	R	23	102	367	58	89	20	2	19	67	35	83	4	.243	.317	.463
Billy Goodman	2B103,1B23,3B5*	L	26	138	513	79	157	27	3	4	56	48	23	8	.306	.370	.394
George Kell†	3B73	R	29	75	276	41	88	15	2	6	40	31	10	0	.319	.390	.453
Johnny Lipon†	SS69,3B7	R	29	79	234	25	48	8	1	0	18	32	20	1	.205	.301	.248
Dom DiMaggio	OF123	R	35	128	486	81	143	20	1	6	33	57	61	6	.294	.371	.377
Hoot Evers†	OF105	R	31	106	401	53	105	17	4	14	59	29	55	2	.262	.318	.429
Faye Throneberry	OF86	L	21	98	310	38	80	11	3	5	23	33	67	16	.258	.331	.361
Vern Stephens	SS53,3B29	R	31	92	295	35	75	13	2	7	44	39	31	2	.254	.343	.383
Ted Lepcio	2B57,3B25,SS1	R	21	84	274	34	72	17	2	5	26	24	41	3	.263	.323	.394
Clyde Vollmer	OF70	R	30	90	250	35	66	12	4	11	50	39	47	2	.264	.370	.476
Jimmy Piersall	SS30,OF22,3B1	R	22	56	161	28	43	8	0	1	16	28	26	3	.267	.379	.335
Del Wilber†	C39	R	33	47	135	7	36	10	1	3	23	7	20	1	.267	.308	.422
Walt Dropo†	1B35	R	29	37	132	13	35	7	1	6	27	11	22	0	.265	.331	.470
Don Lenhardt†	OF27	R	29	30	105	18	31	4	0	7	24	15	18	0	.295	.383	.533
Johnny Pesky†	3B19,SS2	L	32	25	67	10	10	2	0	0	2	15	5	0	.149	.313	.179
George Schmees†	OF29,P2,1B2	L	27	42	64	8	13	3	0	0	3	10	11	0	.203	.311	.250
Al Zarilla†	OF19	L	33	21	60	9	11	0	1	2	8	7	8	2	.183	.269	.317
Gus Niarhos	C25	R	31	29	58	4	6	0	0	0	4	12	9	0	.103	.268	.103
Gene Stephens	OF13	L	19	21	53	10	12	5	0	0	5	3	8	4	.226	.268	.321
Archie Wilson†	OF13	R	28	18	38	1	10	3	0	0	2	2	3	0	.263	.300	.342
Milt Bolling	SS11	R	21	11	36	4	8	1	0	1	3	3	5	0	.222	.282	.333
Fred Hatfield†	3B17	L	27	19	25	6	8	1	1	1	3	4	2	0	.320	.452	.560
Ken Wood†	OF13	R	27	15	20	0	2	0	0	0	0	3	4	0	.100	.217	.100
Charlie Maxwell	1B3,OF3	L	25	8	15	0	1	1	0	0	0	3	11	0	.067	.222	.133
Ted Williams	OF2	L	33	6	10	2	4	0	1	1	3	2	2	0	.400	.500	.900
Paul Lehner	OF2	L	31	3	3	0	2	0	0	0	2	2	0	0	.667	.800	.667
Lou Boudreau	3B1,SS1	R	34	4	2	1	0	0	0	0	2	0	0	0	.000	.000	.000
Hal Bevan†	3B1	R	21	1	1	0	0	0	0	0	0	0	0	0	.000	.000	.000
Len Okrie	C1	R	28	1	1	0	0	0	0	0	0	0	1	0	.000	.000	.000

B. Goodman, 4 G at OF

Pitcher	T	Age	G	GS	CG	ShO	IP	H	HR	BB	SO	W-L	Sv	ERA
Mel Parnell	L	30	33	29	15	3	214.0	207	13	89	107	12-12	2	3.62
Mickey McDermott	L	24	30	21	7	2	162.0	139	14	92	117	10-9	0	3.72
Sid Hudson†	R	37	21	18	7	0	134.1	145	9	36	50	7-9	0	3.62
Dizzy Trout†	R	37	26	17	2	0	133.2	133	3	68	57	9-8	1	3.64
Willard Nixon	R	24	23	13	5	0	103.2	115	12	61	50	5-4	0	4.86
Dick Brodowski	R	19	20	12	4	0	114.2	111	12	50	42	5-5	0	4.40
Bill Henry	L	24	13	10	5	0	76.2	75	7	36	23	5-4	0	3.87
Harry Taylor	R	33	2	1	1	0	10.0	6	1	6	1	1-0	0	1.80
George Schmees	L	27	2	1	0	0	6.0	9	0	2	2	0-0	0	3.00
Ike Delock	R	22	39	7	1	1	95.0	88	9	50	46	4-9	5	4.26
Ray Scarborough†	R	34	28	8	1	1	76.2	79	8	35	29	1-5	4	4.81
Al Benton	R	41	24	0	0	0	37.2	37	1	17	20	4-3	6	2.39
Ellis Kinder	R	37	23	10	4	0	97.2	85	11	28	50	5-6	4	2.58
Ralph Brickner	R	27	14	1	0	0	33.0	32	1	11	9	3-1	1	2.18
Bill Wight†	L	30	10	2	0	0	24.1	14	3	14	5	2-1	0	2.96
Randy Gumpert†	R	34	10	1	0	0	19.2	15	1	5	6	1-0	1	4.12
Walt Masterson†	R	32	5	1	0	0	9.1	18	1	11	3	1-1	0	11.57
Hersh Freeman	R	23	4	1	1	0	13.2	13	1	5	5	1-0	0	3.29
James Atkins	R	31	3	1	0	0	10.1	11	0	7	2	0-1	0	3.48

1952 St. Louis Browns 7th AL 64-90 .416 31.0 GB

Rogers Hornsby (22-29)/Marty Marion (42-61)

Player	Gm by Position	B	Age	G	AB	R	H	2B	3B	HR	RBI	BB	SO	SB	Avg	OBP	Slg
Clint Courtney	C113	L	25	119	413	38	118	24	3	5	50	39	26	0	.286	.349	.395
Dick Kryhoski	1B86	L	27	111	342	38	83	13	1	11	42	23	42	2	.243	.296	.383
Bobby Young	2B149	L	27	149	575	59	142	15	9	4	39	56	48	3	.247	.314	.325
Jim Dyck	3B74,OF48	R	30	122	402	60	108	22	3	15	64	50	68	0	.269	.354	.450
Joe DeMaestri	SS77,2B1,3B1	R	23	81	186	13	42	9	1	1	18	8	25	0	.226	.258	.301
Bob Nieman	OF125	R	25	131	478	66	138	22	2	18	74	46	73	0	.289	.352	.456
Jim Rivera†	OF88	L	29	97	336	45	86	13	6	4	30	29	59	8	.256	.319	.366
Jim Delsing†	OF85	L	26	93	298	34	76	13	6	1	34	26	29	3	.255	.323	.349
Fred Marsh†	SS60,3B21,2B9	R	28	87	247	28	69	9	1	2	27	27	33	3	.279	.350	.348
Gordon Goldsberry	1B72,OF2	L	24	86	227	30	52	9	3	3	17	34	37	0	.229	.330	.335
Marty Marion	SS63	R	34	67	186	16	46	11	0	2	19	19	17	0	.247	.320	.339
Cass Michaels†	3B42,2B8	R	26	55	166	21	44	8	2	3	25	23	16	1	.265	.354	.392
Vic Wertz†	OF36	L	27	37	130	22	45	5	0	6	19	23	20	0	.346	.444	.523
Al Zarilla†	OF35	L	33	48	130	20	31	6	0	1	9	27	15	2	.238	.373	.308
Leo Thomas†	3B37,SS3,2B1	R	28	41	124	12	29	5	1	0	12	17	7	2	.234	.336	.290
Les Moss	C39	R	27	52	118	11	29	3	0	3	12	15	13	0	.246	.331	.347
J.W. Porter	OF29,3B2	R	19	33	104	12	26	4	1	0	7	10	10	4	.250	.316	.308
Darrell Johnson†	C22	R	23	29	78	9	22	2	1	0	9	11	4	0	.282	.371	.333
Tom Wright†	OF18	L	28	29	66	6	16	0	0	1	6	12	20	1	.242	.359	.288
George Schmees†	OF19,1B2	L	27	34	61	9	8	1	1	0	3	2	18	0	.131	.159	.180
Earl Rapp†	OF7	L	31	30	49	3	7	4	0	0	4	0	8	0	.143	.143	.224
Don Lenhardt†	OF11,1B2	R	29	18	48	5	13	4	1	1	5	4	8	0	.271	.327	.458
Ray Coleman†	OF16	L	30	20	46	5	9	3	0	0	1	5	4	0	.196	.288	.261
Roy Sievers	1B7	R	25	11	30	3	6	3	0	0	5	1	4	0	.200	.226	.300
Hank Arft	1B10	L	30	15	28	1	4	3	1	0	4	5	7	0	.143	.273	.321
Jake Crawford	OF3	R	24	7	11	1	2	1	0	0	0	1	5	1	.182	.250	.273
Willie Miranda†	SS7	S	26	7	11	2	1	0	1	0	1	3	1	0	.091	.286	.273
Stan Rojek	SS4,2B1	R	33	9	7	0	1	0	0	0	0	2	0	0	.143	.333	.143
Mike Goliat	2B3	R	26	3	4	0	0	0	0	0	0	1	1	0	.000	.200	.000

Pitcher	T	Age	G	GS	CG	ShO	IP	H	HR	BB	SO	W-L	Sv	ERA
Duane Pillette	R	29	30	30	9	1	205.1	222	14	55	62	10-13	0	3.59
Bob Cain	L	27	29	27	8	1	170.0	169	15	62	70	12-10	2	4.13
Tommy Byrne	L	32	29	24	14	0	196.0	182	16	112	91	7-14	0	4.68
Ned Garver†	R	26	21	21	7	2	148.2	130	14	55	60	7-10	0	3.69
Dick Littlefield†	L	26	7	5	3	0	46.1	35	4	17	34	2-3	0	2.72
Lou Sleater†	L	25	4	2	0	0	8.2	9	1	5	1	0-1	0	7.27
Satchel Paige	R	45	46	6	3	2	138.0	116	5	57	91	12-10	10	3.07
Earl Harrist	R	33	36	9	1	0	116.2	119	7	47	49	2-8	5	4.01
Gene Bearden	L	31	34	16	3	0	150.2	158	13	78	45	7-8	0	4.30
Dave Madison†	R	31	31	4	0	0	78.0	78	7	48	35	4-2	0	4.38
Stubby Overmire	L	33	17	4	0	0	41.0	44	3	7	10	0-3	0	3.73
Marlin Stuart†	R	33	12	2	0	0	26.0	26	3	9	13	1-2	1	4.15
Ken Holcombe†	R	33	12	1	0	0	21.0	20	1	9	7	0-2	0	3.86
Cliff Fannin	R	28	10	2	0	0	16.1	34	5	9	6	0-2	0	12.67
Bobby Hogue†	R	31	8	1	0	0	16.1	10	1	13	2	0-1	0	2.76
Johnny Hetki	R	30	3	1	0	0	9.1	15	2	2	4	0-1	0	3.86
Hal Hudson†	L	25	3	0	0	0	5.2	9	0	6	0	0-0	0	12.71
Bob Mahoney	R	24	3	0	0	0	3.0	8	0	4	1	0-0	0	18.00
Pete Taylor	R	24	1	0	0	0	2.0	4	0	3	0	0-0	0	13.50

1952 Detroit Tigers 8th AL 50-104 .325 45.0 GB

Red Rolfe (23-49)/Fred Hutchinson (27-55)

Player	Gm by Position	B	Age	G	AB	R	H	2B	3B	HR	RBI	BB	SO	SB	Avg	OBP	Slg
Joe Ginsberg	C101	L	25	113	307	29	68	13	2	6	36	51	21	1	.221	.338	.336
Walt Dropo†	1B115	R	29	115	459	56	128	17	3	23	70	26	63	2	.279	.320	.479
Jerry Priddy	2B75	R	32	75	279	37	79	23	3	4	20	42	29	1	.283	.379	.430
Fred Hatfield†	3B107,SS9	L	27	112	441	42	104	12	2	2	25	35	52	2	.236	.299	.286
Neil Berry	SS66,3B2	R	30	73	189	22	43	4	3	0	13	22	19	1	.228	.311	.280
Johnny Groth	OF139	R	25	141	524	56	149	22	2	4	51	51	39	2	.284	.348	.357
Vic Wertz†	OF79	L	27	85	285	46	70	15	3	17	51	46	44	1	.246	.352	.498
Pat Mullin	OF65	L	34	97	255	29	64	13	5	7	35	31	30	4	.251	.332	.424
Steve Souchock	OF56,3B13,1B9	R	33	92	265	40	66	16	4	13	45	21	28	1	.249	.304	.487
Al Federoff	2B70,SS7	R	27	74	231	14	56	4	2	0	14	16	13	1	.242	.294	.277
Cliff Mapes	OF62	L	30	86	193	26	38	7	0	9	23	27	42	0	.197	.295	.373
Johnny Pesky†	SS41,2B22,3B3	L	32	69	177	26	45	4	0	1	9	41	11	1	.254	.394	.294
Matt Batts	C55	R	30	56	173	11	41	4	1	3	13	14	22	1	.237	.298	.324
Don Kolloway	1B32,2B8	R	33	65	173	19	42	9	0	2	21	7	19	0	.243	.280	.329
George Kell†	3B39	R	29	39	152	11	45	8	0	1	17	15	13	0	.296	.359	.368
Don Lenhardt†	OF43	R	29	45	144	18	27	2	1	3	13	28	18	0	.188	.320	.278
Johnny Lipon†	SS39	R	29	39	136	17	30	4	2	0	12	16	6	3	.221	.303	.279
Jim Delsing†	OF32	L	26	33	113	14	31	2	1	3	15	11	8	1	.274	.344	.389
Harvey Kuenn	SS19	R	21	19	80	2	26	2	2	0	8	2	1	2	.325	.349	.400
Bob Swift	C28	R	37	28	58	3	8	1	0	0	4	7	7	0	.138	.242	.155
Russ Sullivan	OF14	L	29	15	52	7	17	2	1	3	5	3	5	1	.327	.375	.577
Johnny Hopp†	OF4,1B1	L	35	42	46	5	10	1	0	0	3	6	7	0	.217	.308	.239
George Lerchen	OF7	S	29	14	32	1	5	1	0	1	3	7	10	1	.156	.308	.281
Bill Tuttle	OF6	R	22	7	25	2	6	0	0	0	2	0	1	0	.240	.240	.240
Don Lund	OF7	R	29	8	23	1	7	0	0	0	1	3	3	0	.304	.385	.304
Ben Taylor	1B4	L	24	7	18	0	3	0	0	0	0	0	5	0	.167	.167	.167
Carl Linhart		L	22	3	2	0	0	0	0	0	0	0	0	0	.000	.000	.000
Hoot Evers†		R	31	1	1	0	1	0	0	0	0	0	0	0	1.000	1.000	1.000
Alex Garbowski		R	27	2	0	0	0	0	0	0	0	0	0	0	—	—	—

Pitcher	T	Age	G	GS	CG	ShO	IP	H	HR	BB	SO	W-L	Sv	ERA
Ted Gray	L	27	35	32	13	2	224.0	212	21	101	138	12-17	0	4.14
Virgil Trucks	R	35	35	29	8	3	197.0	190	12	82	129	5-19	1	3.97
Art Houtteman	R	24	35	28	10	2	221.0	218	19	65	109	8-20	1	4.36
Hal Newhouser	L	31	25	19	8	0	154.0	148	13	47	57	9-9	0	3.74
Bill Wight†	L	30	23	19	8	3	143.2	167	7	55	65	5-9	0	3.88
Bud Black	R	19	2	2	0	0	8.0	14	0	5	0	0-1	0	10.13
Ned Garver†	R	26	1	1	1	0	9.0	9	1	3	3	1-0	0	2.00
Hal White	R	33	41	0	0	0	63.1	53	1	39	18	1-8	5	3.69
Billy Hoeft	L	20	34	10	1	0	125.0	123	14	63	67	2-7	4	4.32
Marlin Stuart†	R	33	30	9	2	0	91.1	91	8	48	32	3-2	1	4.93
Dick Littlefield†	L	26	28	1	0	0	47.2	46	4	25	32	0-3	1	4.34
Fred Hutchinson	R	32	12	1	0	0	37.1	40	4	9	12	2-1	0	3.38
Dizzy Trout†	R	37	10	2	0	0	27.0	30	4	19	20	1-5	1	5.33
Dave Madison†	R	31	10	1	0	0	15.0	16	1	10	7	1-1	0	7.80
Ken Johnson	L	29	9	1	0	0	11.1	12	1	11	10	0-0	0	6.35
Dick Marlowe	R	23	4	1	0	0	11.0	21	1	3	3	0-2	0	7.36
Wayne McLeland	R	27	4	0	0	0	2.2	4	0	6	0	0-0	0	10.13

»1952 Brooklyn Dodgers 1st NL 96-57 .627 —

Chuck Dressen

Player	Gm by Position	B	Age	G	AB	R	H	2B	3B	HR	RBI	BB	SO	SB	Avg	OBP	Slg
Roy Campanella	C122	R	30	128	468	73	126	18	1	22	97	57	59	8	.269	.352	.453
Gil Hodges	1B153	R	28	153	508	87	129	27	1	32	102	107	90	2	.254	.386	.500
Jackie Robinson	2B146	R	33	149	510	104	157	17	3	19	75	106	40	24	.308	.440	.465
Billy Cox	3B100,SS10,2B9	R	32	116	455	56	118	12	3	6	34	25	32	10	.259	.301	.338
Pee Wee Reese	SS145	R	33	149	559	94	152	18	8	6	58	86	59	30	.272	.369	.365
Duke Snider	OF141	L	25	144	534	80	162	25	7	21	92	55	77	7	.303	.368	.494
Andy Pafko	OF139,3B13	R	31	150	551	76	158	17	5	19	85	64	48	4	.287	.366	.439
Carl Furillo	OF131	R	30	134	425	52	105	18	1	8	59	31	33	1	.247	.304	.351
George Shuba	OF67	L	27	94	256	40	78	12	1	9	40	38	29	1	.305	.395	.465
Bobby Morgan	3B60,2B5,SS4	R	26	67	191	36	45	8	0	7	16	46	35	2	.236	.392	.387
Rube Walker	C40	L	26	46	139	9	36	8	0	1	19	8	17	0	.259	.304	.338
Dick Williams	OF25,1B1,3B1	R	23	36	68	13	21	4	1	0	11	2	10	0	.309	.329	.397
Rocky Bridges	2B24,SS13,3B6	R	24	51	56	9	11	3	0	0	2	7	9	0	.196	.286	.250
Sandy Amoros	OF10	L	22	20	44	10	11	3	1	0	3	5	14	1	.250	.327	.364
Rocky Nelson	1B5	L	27	37	39	6	10	1	0	0	3	7	4	0	.256	.370	.282
Tommy Holmes	OF6	L	35	31	36	2	4	1	0	0	1	4	4	0	.111	.200	.139
Cal Abrams†	OF1	L	28	10	10	1	2	0	0	0	0	2	4	0	.200	.333	.200
Steve Lembo	C2	R	25	2	5	0	1	0	0	0	1	0	1	0	.200	.200	.200

Pitcher	T	Age	G	GS	CG	ShO	IP	H	HR	BB	SO	W-L	Sv	ERA
Carl Erskine	R	25	33	26	10	4	206.2	167	17	71	131	14-6	2	2.70
Preacher Roe	L	37	27	25	8	2	158.2	163	16	39	83	11-2	0	3.12
Ben Wade	R	29	37	24	5	1	180.0	166	19	94	118	11-9	3	3.60
Billy Loes	R	22	39	21	8	4	187.1	154	12	71	115	13-8	1	2.69
Chris Van Cuyk	L	25	23	16	4	0	97.2	104	12	40	66	5-6	1	5.16
Johnny Rutherford	R	27	22	11	4	0	97.1	97	9	29	29	7-7	2	4.25
Joe Landrum	R	23	9	5	2	0	38.0	46	3	10	17	1-3	0	5.21
Ken Lehman	L	24	4	3	0	0	15.1	19	1	6	7	1-2	0	5.28
Joe Black	R	28	56	2	1	0	142.1	102	9	41	85	15-4	15	2.15
Clem Labine	R	25	25	9	0	0	77.0	76	3	47	43	8-4	0	5.14
Clyde King	R	27	23	0	0	0	42.2	56	5	12	17	2-0	0	5.06
Ralph Branca	R	26	16	7	2	0	61.0	52	8	21	26	4-2	0	3.84
Ray Moore	R	26	14	2	0	0	28.1	29	3	26	11	1-2	0	4.76
Johnny Schmitz†	L	31	10	3	1	0	33.1	29	3	18	11	1-1	0	4.32
Jim Hughes	R	29	6	0	0	0	18.2	16	0	11	8	2-1	0	1.45
Ron Negray	R	22	4	1	0	0	13.0	15	0	5	5	0-0	0	3.46
Bud Podbielan†	R	28	3	0	0	0	2.0	4	1	3	1	0-0	0	18.00

1952 New York Giants 2nd NL 92-62 .597 4.5 GB

Leo Durocher

Player	Gm by Position	B	Age	G	AB	R	H	2B	3B	HR	RBI	BB	SO	SB	Avg	OBP	Slg
Wes Westrum	C112	R	29	114	322	47	71	11	0	14	43	76	68	1	.220	.374	.385
Whitey Lockman	1B154	L	25	154	606	99	176	17	4	13	58	67	52	2	.290	.363	.396
Davey Williams	2B138	R	24	138	540	70	137	26	3	13	55	48	63	2	.254	.324	.385
Bobby Thomson	3B91,OF63	R	28	153	608	89	164	29	14	24	108	52	74	5	.270	.331	.482
Al Dark	SS150	R	30	151	589	92	177	29	3	14	73	47	39	6	.301	.357	.431
Don Mueller	OF120	L	25	126	456	61	128	14	7	12	49	34	24	2	.281	.333	.421
Hank Thompson	OF72,3B46,2B4	L	26	128	423	67	110	13	9	17	67	50	38	4	.260	.344	.454
Bob Elliott	OF65,3B13	R	35	98	272	33	62	6	2	10	35	36	20	1	.228	.323	.375
Dusty Rhodes	OF56	L	25	67	176	34	44	8	1	10	36	23	33	1	.250	.340	.477
Sal Yvars	C59	R	28	66	151	15	37	3	0	4	18	10	16	0	.245	.296	.344
Willie Mays	OF34	R	21	34	127	17	30	2	4	4	23	16	17	4	.236	.326	.409
Monte Irvin	OF32	R	33	46	126	10	39	2	1	4	21	10	11	0	.310	.365	.437
George Wilson†	OF21,1B2	L	26	62	112	9	27	7	0	2	16	3	14	0	.241	.261	.357
Bill Rigney	3B10,2B9,SS4*	R	34	60	90	15	27	5	1	1	14	11	6	2	.300	.388	.411
Clint Hartung	OF24	R	29	28	78	6	17	2	1	3	8	9	24	0	.218	.299	.385
Bobby Hofman	2B21,3B2,1B1	R	26	32	63	11	18	2	2	2	4	8	10	0	.286	.375	.476
Ray Katt	C8	R	25	9	27	4	6	0	0	0	1	1	5	0	.222	.250	.222
Chuck Diering	OF36	R	29	41	23	2	4	1	1	0	2	4	3	0	.174	.296	.304
Daryl Spencer	3B3,SS3	R	22	7	17	0	5	0	1	0	3	1	4	0	.294	.333	.412
Bill Howerton†	OF3	L	30	11	15	2	1	1	0	0	1	3	2	0	.067	.222	.133
Ray Noble	C5	R	33	6	5	0	0	0	0	0	0	0	1	0	.000	.000	.000
Dick Wakefield		L	31	3	2	0	0	0	0	0	0	1	1	0	.000	.333	.000

B. Rigney, 1 G at 1B

Pitcher	T	Age	G	GS	CG	ShO	IP	H	HR	BB	SO	W-L	Sv	ERA
Jim Hearn	R	31	37	34	11	1	223.2	208	16	97	89	14-7	1	3.78
Sal Maglie	R	35	35	31	12	5	216.0	199	16	75	112	18-8	1	2.92
Larry Jansen	R	31	34	27	8	1	167.1	183	16	47	74	11-11	2	4.09
Jack Harshman	L	24	2	2	0	0	6.1	12	2	6	6	0-2	0	14.21
Mario Picone	R	25	2	1	0	0	9.0	11	2	5	3	0-1	0	7.00
Roger Bowman	L	24	2	1	0	0	3.0	6	0	3	3	0-0	0	12.00
Hoyt Wilhelm	R	28	71	0	0	0	159.1	127	12	57	108	15-3	11	2.43
Dave Koslo	L	32	41	17	8	2	166.1	154	10	47	67	10-7	5	3.19
Max Lanier	L	36	37	16	6	1	137.0	124	11	65	47	7-12	5	3.94
George Spencer	R	25	35	4	0	0	60.0	57	13	21	27	3-5	3	5.55
Monte Kennedy	L	30	31	6	2	1	83.1	73	6	31	48	3-4	0	3.02
Al Corwin	R	25	21	7	1	0	67.2	58	5	36	36	6-1	2	2.66
Hal Gregg	R	30	16	4	1	0	36.1	42	7	17	13	0-1	1	4.71
Bill Connelly	R	27	11	4	0	0	31.2	22	4	25	22	5-0	0	4.55
George Bamberger	R	26	5	0	0	0	4.0	6	1	6	0	0-0	0	9.00

722 Seasons: Team Rosters

1952 St. Louis Cardinals 3rd NL 88-66 .571 8.5 GB

Eddie Stanky

Player	Gm by Position	B	Age	G	AB	R	H	2B	3B	HR	RBI	BB	SO	SB	Avg	OBP	Slg
Del Rice	C147	R	29	147	495	43	128	27	2	11	65	33	38	0	.259	.313	.388
Dick Sisler†	1B114	L	31	119	418	48	109	14	5	13	60	29	35	3	.261	.312	.411
Red Schoendienst	2B142,3B11,SS3	S	29	152	620	91	188	40	7	7	67	42	30	9	.303	.347	.424
Bill Johnson	3B89	R	33	94	282	23	71	10	2	2	34	34	21	1	.252	.339	.323
Solly Hemus	SS148,3B2	L	29	151	570	105	153	28	8	15	52	96	55	1	.268	.392	.425
Enos Slaughter	OF137	L	36	140	510	73	153	17	12	11	101	70	25	6	.300	.386	.445
Stan Musial	OF129,1B25,P1	L	31	154	578	105	194	42	6	21	91	96	29	7	.336	.432	.538
Peanuts Lowrey	OF106,3B6	R	33	132	374	48	107	18	2	1	48	34	13	3	.286	.352	.353
Hal Rice	OF81	L	28	98	295	37	85	14	5	7	45	16	26	1	.288	.325	.441
Tommy Glaviano	3B52,2B1	R	28	80	162	30	39	5	1	3	19	27	26	0	.241	.366	.340
Larry Miggins	OF25,1B1	R	26	42	96	7	22	5	1	2	10	3	19	0	.229	.253	.365
Eddie Stanky	2B20	R	35	53	83	13	19	4	0	0	7	19	9	0	.229	.373	.277
Wally Westlake†	OF15	R	31	21	74	7	16	3	0	0	10	8	11	1	.216	.293	.257
Steve Bilko	1B20	R	23	20	72	7	19	6	1	1	6	4	15	0	.264	.303	.417
Les Fusselman	C32	R	31	32	63	5	10	3	0	1	3	0	9	0	.159	.159	.254
Vern Benson	3B15	L	27	20	47	6	9	2	0	2	5	5	9	0	.191	.269	.362
Virgil Stallcup†	SS12	R	30	29	31	4	4	1	0	0	1	1	5	0	.129	.156	.161
Harvey Haddix	P7,OF1	L	26	9	14	3	3	0	0	0	2	1	5	1	.214	.267	.214
Neal Hertweck	1B2	L	20	2	6	0	0	0	0	0	0	1	1	0	.000	.143	.000
Bill Sarni	C3	R	24	3	5	0	1	0	0	0	0	0	1	0	.200	.200	.200
Gene Mauch	SS2	R	26	7	3	0	0	0	0	0	0	1	2	0	.000	.250	.000
Eddie Kazak†	3B1	R	31	3	2	1	0	0	0	0	0	0	0	0	.000	.000	.000
Herb Gorman		L	27	1	1	0	0	0	0	0	0	0	0	0	.000	.000	.000

Pitcher	T	Age	G	GS	CG	ShO	IP	H	HR	BB	SO	W-L	Sv	ERA
Gerry Staley	R	31	35	33	15	0	239.2	238	21	52	93	17-14	0	3.27
Vinegar Bend Mizell	L	21	30	30	7	2	190.0	171	12	103	146	10-8	0	3.65
Joe Presko	R	23	28	18	5	1	146.2	140	15	57	63	7-10	0	4.05
Cloyd Boyer	R	24	23	14	4	2	110.1	108	11	47	44	6-6	0	4.24
Harry Brecheen	L	37	25	13	4	1	100.1	82	12	28	54	7-5	2	3.32
Cliff Chambers	L	30	26	13	2	1	98.1	110	8	33	47	4-4	1	4.12
Stu Miller	R	24	12	11	6	2	88.0	63	3	26	64	6-3	0	2.05
Harvey Haddix	L	26	7	6	3	0	42.0	31	4	10	31	2-2	0	2.79
George Munger†	R	33	1	1	0	0	4.1	7	2	1	1	0-1	0	12.46
Eddie Yuhas	R	27	54	2	0	0	99.1	90	5	35	39	12-2	6	2.72
Al Brazle	L	38	46	6	3	2	109.1	75	7	42	55	12-5	16	2.72
Bill Werle†	L	31	19	0	0	0	39.0	40	6	15	23	1-2	1	4.85
Willard Schmidt	R	24	18	3	0	0	34.2	36	6	18	30	2-3	1	5.19
Mike Clark	R	30	12	4	0	0	25.1	32	2	14	10	2-0	0	6.04
Dick Bokelmann	R	25	11	0	0	0	12.2	20	0	7	5	0-1	0	9.24
Bobby Tiefenauer	R	22	6	0	0	0	8.0	12	1	7	3	0-0	0	7.88
Jack Crimian	R	26	5	0	0	0	8.1	15	4	4	4	0-0	0	9.72
Jackie Collum	L	25	2	0	0	0	3.0	2	0	1	0	0-0	0	0.00
Fred Hahn	L	23	1	0	0	0	2.0	2	0	1	0	0-0	0	0.00
Stan Musial	L	31	1	0	0	0	0.0	0	0	0	0	0-0	0	—

1952 Philadelphia Phillies 4th NL 87-67 .565 9.5 GB

Eddie Sawyer (28-35)/Steve O'Neill (59-32)

Player	Gm by Position	B	Age	G	AB	R	H	2B	3B	HR	RBI	BB	SO	SB	Avg	OBP	Slg
Smoky Burgess	C104	L	25	110	371	49	110	27	2	6	56	49	21	3	.296	.380	.429
Eddie Waitkus	1B146	L	32	146	499	51	144	29	4	2	49	64	23	2	.289	.371	.375
Connie Ryan	2B154	R	32	154	577	81	139	24	6	12	49	69	72	13	.241	.327	.366
Puddin' Head Jones	3B147	R	26	147	541	60	135	12	3	18	72	53	36	5	.250	.323	.383
Granny Hamner	SS151	R	25	151	596	74	164	30	5	17	87	27	51	7	.275	.307	.428
Richie Ashburn	OF154	L	25	154	613	93	173	31	6	1	42	75	30	16	.282	.362	.357
Del Ennis	OF149	R	27	151	592	90	171	30	10	20	107	47	65	6	.289	.341	.475
Johnny Wyrostek†	OF88	L	32	98	321	45	88	16	3	1	37	44	26	1	.274	.363	.352
Stan Lopata	C55	R	26	57	179	25	49	9	1	4	27	36	33	1	.274	.395	.402
Mel Clark	OF38,3B1	R	25	47	155	20	52	6	4	1	15	6	13	2	.335	.364	.445
Jackie Mayo	OF27,1B6	L	26	50	119	13	29	5	0	1	4	12	17	1	.244	.313	.311
Bill Nicholson	OF19	L	37	55	88	17	24	3	0	6	19	14	26	0	.273	.390	.511
Putsy Caballero	SS8,2B7,3B7	R	24	35	42	10	10	3	0	0	6	2	3	1	.238	.273	.310
Nippy Jones	1B8	R	27	8	30	3	5	0	0	1	5	0	4	0	.167	.167	.267
Jack Lohrke	SS5,3B3,2B1	R	28	25	29	4	6	0	0	0	1	4	3	0	.207	.303	.207
Tommy Brown†	1B3,OF3	R	24	18	25	2	4	1	0	1	2	4	3	0	.160	.276	.320
Dick Young	2B2	L	24	5	9	3	2	1	0	0	0	1	3	1	.222	.300	.333
Del Wilber†		R	33	2	2	0	0	0	0	0	0	0	1	0	.000	.000	.000

Pitcher	T	Age	G	GS	CG	ShO	IP	H	HR	BB	SO	W-L	Sv	ERA
Robin Roberts	R	25	39	37	30	3	330.0	292	22	45	148	28-7	2	2.59
Russ Meyer	R	28	37	32	14	1	232.1	235	10	65	92	13-14	1	3.14
Karl Drews	R	32	33	30	15	5	228.2	213	13	52	96	14-15	0	2.72
Curt Simmons	L	23	28	28	15	6	201.1	170	11	70	141	14-8	0	2.82
Howie Fox	R	31	13	11	2	0	62.0	70	8	26	16	2-7	0	5.08
Paul Stuffel	R	25	2	1	0	0	6.0	5	0	7	3	1-0	0	3.00
Bubba Church†	R	27	2	1	0	0	5.0	11	0	1	3	0-0	0	10.80
Andy Hansen	R	27	43	0	0	0	77.1	76	6	27	18	5-6	4	3.26
Jim Konstanty	R	35	42	2	2	1	80.0	87	9	21	16	5-3	6	3.94
Steve Ridzik	R	23	24	9	2	0	92.2	74	10	37	43	4-2	0	3.01
Ken Heintzelman	L	36	23	1	0	0	42.2	41	1	12	20	1-3	1	3.16
Lou Possehl	R	26	4	1	0	0	12.2	12	3	7	4	0-1	0	4.97
Bob Miller	R	26	3	1	0	0	9.0	13	2	1	2	0-1	0	6.00
Kent Peterson	L	26	3	0	0	0	7.0	2	0	2	7	0-0	2	0.00

1952 Chicago Cubs 5th NL 77-77 .500 19.5 GB

Phil Cavarretta

Player	Gm by Position	B	Age	G	AB	R	H	2B	3B	HR	RBI	BB	SO	SB	Avg	OBP	Slg
Toby Atwell	C101	L	28	107	362	36	105	16	3	2	31	40	22	2	.290	.362	.367
Dee Fondy	1B143	L	27	145	554	69	166	21	9	10	67	28	60	13	.300	.334	.424
Eddie Miksis	2B54,SS40	R	25	93	383	44	89	20	1	2	19	20	32	4	.232	.272	.305
Randy Jackson	3B104,OF1	R	26	116	379	44	88	8	5	9	34	27	42	6	.232	.285	.351
Roy Smalley	SS82	R	26	87	261	36	58	14	1	5	30	29	58	0	.222	.305	.341
Hank Sauer	OF151	R	35	151	567	89	153	31	3	37	121	77	92	1	.270	.361	.531
Frankie Baumholtz	OF101	L	33	103	409	59	133	17	4	4	35	27	27	5	.325	.371	.416
Hal Jeffcoat	OF95	R	27	102	297	29	65	17	2	4	30	15	40	7	.219	.259	.330
Bill Serena	3B58,2B49	R	27	122	390	49	107	21	5	15	61	39	83	1	.274	.345	.469
Bob Addis	OF79	L	26	93	292	38	86	13	2	1	20	23	30	4	.295	.346	.363
Gene Hermanski	OF76	L	32	99	275	28	70	6	0	4	34	29	32	2	.255	.330	.320
Tommy Brown†	SS39,2B10,1B5	R	24	61	200	24	64	11	0	3	24	12	24	1	.320	.358	.420
Bob Ramazzotti	2B50	R	35	50	183	26	52	5	3	1	12	14	14	3	.284	.338	.361
Harry Chiti	C32	R	19	32	113	14	31	5	0	5	13	5	8	0	.274	.305	.451
Bruce Edwards	C22,2B1	R	28	50	94	7	23	2	2	1	12	8	12	0	.245	.304	.340
Phil Cavarretta	1B13	L	35	41	63	7	15	1	1	1	8	9	3	0	.238	.333	.333
Johnny Pramesa	C17	R	26	22	46	1	13	1	0	1	5	4	4	0	.283	.340	.370
Leon Brinkopf	SS6	R	25	9	22	1	4	0	0	0	2	4	5	0	.182	.308	.182
Bud Hardin	SS2,2B1	R	30	3	7	1	1	0	0	0	0	0	0	0	.143	.143	.143
Ron Northey		L	32	1	1	0	0	0	0	0	0	0	0	0	.000	.000	.000
Bob Usher		R	27	1	0	0	0	0	0	0	0	1	0	0	—	1.000	—

Pitcher	T	Age	G	GS	CG	ShO	IP	H	HR	BB	SO	W-L	Sv	ERA
Bob Rush	R	26	34	32	17	4	250.1	205	14	81	157	17-13	0	2.70
Paul Minner	L	28	28	27	12	2	180.2	180	13	54	61	14-9	0	3.74
Johnny Klippstein	R	24	41	25	7	2	202.2	208	17	89	110	9-14	3	4.44
Warren Hacker	R	27	33	20	12	5	185.0	144	17	31	84	15-9	1	2.58
Turk Lown	R	28	33	19	5	0	156.2	154	13	93	73	4-11	0	4.37
Joe Hatten	L	35	13	8	2	0	50.1	65	6	25	15	4-4	0	6.08
Dutch Leonard	R	43	45	0	0	0	66.2	56	3	24	37	2-2	11	2.16
Bob Kelly	R	24	31	15	3	2	125.1	114	7	46	50	4-9	0	3.59
Bob Schultz	L	28	29	5	1	0	74.0	63	3	51	31	6-3	0	4.01
Willie Ramsdell	R	36	19	4	0	0	67.0	41	5	24	30	2-3	0	2.42
Dick Manville	R	25	11	0	0	0	17.0	25	2	12	6	0-0	0	7.94
Vern Fear	R	27	4	0	0	0	8.0	9	1	3	4	0-0	0	7.88
Cal Howe	L	27	1	0	0	0	2.0	0	0	1	2	0-0	0	0.00
Monk Dubiel	R	34	1	0	0	0	0.2	1	0	0	1	0-0	0	0.00

1952 Cincinnati Reds 6th NL 69-85 .448 27.5 GB

Luke Sewell (39-59)/Earle Brucker (3-2)/Rogers Hornsby (27-24)

Player	Gm by Position	B	Age	G	AB	R	H	2B	3B	HR	RBI	BB	SO	SB	Avg	OBP	Slg
Andy Seminick	C99	R	31	108	336	38	86	16	1	14	50	35	65	1	.256	.330	.435
Ted Kluszewski	1B133	L	27	135	497	62	159	24	11	16	86	47	28	3	.320	.383	.509
Grady Hatton	2B120	L	29	128	433	48	92	14	1	9	57	66	60	5	.212	.319	.312
Bobby Adams	3B154	R	30	154	637	85	180	25	4	6	48	49	67	11	.283	.334	.363
Roy McMillan	SS154	R	21	154	540	60	132	32	2	7	57	45	81	4	.244	.306	.350
Willard Marshall†	OF105	L	31	107	397	52	106	23	1	8	46	37	21	0	.267	.333	.390
Bob Borkowski	OF103,1B5	R	26	126	377	42	95	11	4	4	24	26	53	1	.252	.300	.334
Joe Adcock	OF85,1B17	R	24	117	378	43	105	22	4	13	52	23	38	1	.278	.321	.460
Hank Edwards†	OF51	L	33	74	184	24	52	7	6	6	28	19	22	0	.283	.350	.484
Wally Westlake†	OF56	R	31	59	183	29	37	4	0	3	14	31	29	0	.202	.324	.273
Cal Abrams†	OF46	L	28	71	158	23	44	9	2	2	13	19	25	1	.278	.356	.399
Joe Rossi	C46	R	29	55	145	14	32	0	1	1	6	20	20	1	.221	.319	.255
Johnny Wyrostek†	OF29,1B1	L	32	30	106	12	25	1	3	1	10	18	7	1	.236	.347	.330
Eddie Pellagrini	2B22,1B8,3B1*	R	34	46	100	15	17	2	0	1	3	8	18	1	.170	.231	.220
Johnny Temple	2B22	R	24	30	97	8	19	3	0	1	5	5	1	2	.196	.235	.258
Jim Greengrass	OF17	R	24	18	68	10	21	2	1	5	24	7	12	0	.309	.373	.588
Wally Post	OF16	R	22	19	58	5	9	1	0	2	7	4	20	0	.155	.222	.276
Hobie Landrith	C14	L	22	15	50	1	13	4	0	0	4	0	4	0	.260	.260	.340
Dixie Howell	C16	R	32	17	37	4	7	1	1	2	4	3	9	0	.189	.250	.432
Dick Sisler†	OF7	L	31	11	27	3	5	1	1	0	4	3	5	0	.185	.267	.296
Eddie Kazak†	3B3,1B1	R	31	13	15	1	1	0	1	0	0	0	2	0	.067	.067	.200
Virgil Stallcup†	SS1	R	30	2	1	0	0	0	0	0	0	0	0	0	.000	.000	.000

E. Pellagrini, 1 G at SS

Pitcher	T	Age	G	GS	CG	ShO	IP	H	HR	BB	SO	W-L	Sv	ERA
Ken Raffensberger	L	34	38	33	18	6	247.0	247	18	45	93	17-13	1	2.81
Herm Wehmeier	R	25	33	26	6	1	190.1	197	23	103	83	9-11	0	5.15
Harry Perkowski	L	29	33	24	11	1	194.0	197	9	89	86	12-10	0	3.80
Bubba Church†	R	27	29	22	5	1	153.1	173	21	48	47	5-9	0	4.34
Ewell Blackwell†	R	29	23	17	3	0	102.0	107	6	60	48	3-12	0	5.38
Frank Hiller	R	31	28	15	6	1	124.1	129	7	37	50	5-8	1	4.63
Frank Smith	R	24	53	2	1	0	122.1	109	13	41	77	12-11	7	3.75
Joe Nuxhall	L	23	37	5	2	0	92.1	83	4	42	52	1-4	1	3.22
Bud Podbielan†	R	28	24	7	4	1	86.2	78	8	26	22	4-5	1	2.80
Bud Byerly	R	31	12	2	0	0	24.2	29	0	7	14	0-1	1	5.11
Phil Haugstad	R	28	9	0	0	0	12.0	8	1	13	2	0-0	0	6.75
Niles Jordan	L	26	3	1	0	0	6.1	14	1	3	2	0-1	0	9.95
Johnny Schmitz†	L	31	3	0	0	0	5.0	3	0	3	3	1-0	0	0.00
Ed Blake	R	26	2	0	0	0	3.0	3	0	0	0	0-0	0	0.00

1952 Boston Braves 7th NL 64-89 .418 32.0 GB

Tommy Holmes (13-22)/Charlie Grimm (51-67)

Player	Gm by Position	B	Age	G	AB	R	H	2B	3B	HR	RBI	BB	SO	SB	Avg	OBP	Slg
Walker Cooper	C89	R	37	102	349	33	82	12	1	10	55	22	32	1	.235	.282	.361
Earl Torgeson	1B105,OF5	L	28	122	382	49	88	17	0	5	34	81	38	11	.230	.366	.314
Jack Dittmer	2B90	L	24	93	326	26	63	7	2	7	41	26	26	1	.193	.255	.291
Eddie Mathews	3B142	L	20	145	528	80	128	23	5	25	58	59	115	6	.242	.320	.447
Johnny Logan	SS117	R	25	117	456	56	129	21	3	4	42	31	33	1	.283	.334	.368
Sam Jethroe	OF151	S	34	151	608	79	141	23	7	13	58	68	112	28	.232	.318	.357
Sid Gordon	OF142,3B2	R	34	144	522	69	151	22	2	25	75	77	49	0	.289	.384	.483
Jack Daniels	OF87	L	24	106	219	31	41	5	1	2	14	28	30	3	.187	.288	.247
Bob Thorpe	OF72	R	25	81	292	20	76	8	2	3	26	5	42	3	.260	.275	.332
Sibby Sisti	2B33,OF23,SS18*	R	31	90	245	19	52	10	1	4	24	14	43	2	.212	.255	.310
George Crowe	1B55	L	31	73	217	25	56	13	1	4	20	18	25	0	.258	.329	.382
Paul Burris	C50	R	28	55	168	14	37	4	0	2	21	7	19	0	.220	.256	.280
Ebba St. Claire	C34	S	30	39	108	5	23	2	0	2	4	8	12	0	.213	.267	.287
Roy Hartsfield	2B29	R	26	38	107	13	28	4	3	0	4	5	12	0	.262	.295	.355
Jack Cusick	SS28,3B3	R	24	49	78	5	13	1	0	0	6	6	9	0	.167	.226	.179
Willard Marshall†	OF16	L	31	21	66	5	15	4	1	2	11	4	4	0	.227	.271	.409
Pete Whisenant	OF14	R	22	24	52	3	10	2	0	0	7	4	13	1	.192	.250	.231
Billy Reed	2B14	L	29	15	52	4	13	0	0	0	0	0	5	0	.250	.264	.250
Buzz Clarkson	SS6,3B2	R	37	14	25	3	5	0	0	0	1	3	3	0	.200	.286	.200
Billy Klaus	SS4	L	23	7	4	3	0	0	0	0	0	1	1	0	.000	.200	.000

S. Sisti, 9 G at 3B

Pitcher	T	Age	G	GS	CG	ShO	IP	H	HR	BB	SO	W-L	Sv	ERA
Warren Spahn	L	31	40	35	19	5	290.0	263	19	73	183	14-19	3	2.98
Jim Wilson	R	30	33	33	14	0	234.0	234	19	90	104	12-14	0	4.23
Max Surkont	R	30	31	29	12	3	215.0	201	19	76	125	12-13	0	3.77
Vern Bickford	R	31	26	22	7	1	161.1	165	7	64	62	7-12	0	3.74
Gene Conley	R	21	4	3	0	0	12.2	23	4	9	6	0-3	0	7.82
Lew Burdette	R	25	45	9	5	0	137.0	138	8	47	47	6-11	7	3.61
Sheldon Jones	R	30	39	1	0	0	70.0	81	8	31	40	1-4	1	4.76
Ernie Johnson	R	28	29	10	2	1	92.0	100	7	31	45	6-3	1	4.11
Bob Chipman	L	33	29	0	0	0	41.2	28	5	20	16	1-1	0	2.81
Dave Cole	R	21	22	3	0	0	44.2	38	2	42	22	1-1	0	4.03
Virgil Jester	R	24	19	8	4	1	73.0	80	5	23	25	3-5	0	3.33
Dick Donovan	R	24	7	2	0	0	13.0	18	1	12	6	0-2	1	5.54
Bert Thiel	R	26	4	0	0	0	7.0	11	1	4	6	1-1	0	7.71
Dick Hoover	L	26	2	0	0	0	4.2	8	1	3	0	0-0	0	7.71

1952 Pittsburgh Pirates 8th NL 42-112 .273 54.5 GB

Billy Meyer

Player	Gm by Position	B	Age	G	AB	R	H	2B	3B	HR	RBI	BB	SO	SB	Avg	OBP	Slg
Joe Garagiola	C105	L	26	118	344	35	94	15	4	8	54	50	24	0	.273	.369	.410
Tony Bartirome	1B118	L	20	124	355	32	78	10	3	0	16	26	37	3	.220	.273	.265
Jack Merson	2B81,3B27	R	30	111	398	41	98	20	2	5	38	22	38	1	.246	.287	.344
Pete Castiglione	3B57,1B1,OF1	R	31	67	214	27	57	9	1	4	18	17	8	3	.266	.323	.374
Dick Groat	SS94	R	21	95	384	38	109	6	1	1	29	19	27	2	.284	.319	.313
Ralph Kiner	OF149	R	29	149	516	90	126	17	2	37	87	110	77	3	.244	.384	.500
Gus Bell	OF123	L	23	131	468	53	117	21	5	16	59	36	72	1	.250	.306	.419
Bobby Del Greco	OF93	R	19	99	341	34	74	14	2	1	20	38	70	6	.217	.301	.279
Catfish Metkovich	1B72,OF33	L	31	125	373	41	101	18	3	7	41	32	29	5	.271	.335	.391
Clem Koshorek	SS33,2B27,3B26	R	27	98	322	27	84	17	0	0	15	26	39	4	.261	.320	.314
George Strickland†	2B45,SS28,1B1*	R	26	76	232	17	41	6	2	5	22	21	45	4	.177	.248	.284
Clyde McCullough	C61,1B1	R	35	66	172	10	40	5	1	1	15	10	18	0	.233	.283	.291
Sonny Senerchia	3B28	R	21	29	100	5	22	5	0	3	11	4	21	0	.220	.250	.360
Brandy Davis	OF29	R	23	55	95	14	17	1	1	0	1	11	28	9	.179	.264	.211
Lee Walls	OF19	R	19	32	80	6	15	0	1	2	5	8	22	0	.188	.261	.288
Dick Hall	OF14,3B5	R	21	26	80	6	11	1	0	0	2	2	17	0	.138	.159	.150
Ed Fitz Gerald	C18,3B2	R	28	51	73	4	17	1	0	1	7	7	15	0	.233	.300	.288
Dick Smith	3B16,2B4,SS4	R	24	29	66	8	7	1	0	0	5	9	3	0	.106	.213	.121
Johnny Berardino†	2B18	R	35	19	56	2	8	4	0	0	4	4	6	0	.143	.200	.214
Ted Beard	OF13	L	31	15	44	5	8	2	1	0	3	7	9	2	.182	.294	.273
Erv Dusak	OF11	R	31	20	27	1	6	0	0	1	3	2	8	0	.222	.276	.333
Bill Howerton†	OF5,3B1	L	30	13	25	3	8	1	1	0	4	6	5	0	.320	.452	.440
Frank Thomas	OF5	R	23	6	21	1	2	0	0	0	0	1	1	0	.095	.136	.095
Jim Mangan	C4	R	22	11	13	1	2	0	0	0	2	1	3	0	.154	.214	.154
Jack Phillips	1B1	R	30	1	1	0	0	0	0	0	0	0	0	0	.000	.000	.000

G. Strickland, 1 G at 3B

Pitcher	T	Age	G	GS	CG	ShO	IP	H	HR	BB	SO	W-L	Sv	ERA
Murry Dickson	R	35	43	34	21	2	277.2	278	26	76	112	14-21	2	3.57
Howie Pollet	L	31	31	30	9	1	214.0	217	22	71	90	7-16	0	4.12
Bob Friend	R	21	35	23	6	1	185.0	186	15	84	75	7-17	0	4.18
Cal Hogue	R	24	19	12	3	0	83.2	79	7	68	34	1-8	0	4.84
Ron Necciai	R	20	12	9	0	0	54.2	63	5	32	31	1-6	0	7.08
George Munger†	R	33	5	4	0	0	26.1	30	6	10	8	0-3	0	7.18
Mel Queen	R	34	2	2	0	0	3.1	8	2	4	3	0-2	0	29.70
Woody Main	R	30	48	11	2	0	153.1	149	14	52	79	2-12	2	4.46
Ted Wilks†	R	36	44	0	0	0	72.1	65	9	31	24	5-5	4	3.61
Paul LaPalme	L	28	31	2	0	0	59.2	56	6	37	25	1-2	0	3.92
Ron Kline	R	20	27	11	0	0	78.2	74	3	66	27	0-7	0	5.49
Jim Waugh	R	18	17	7	1	0	52.1	61	4	32	18	1-6	0	6.36
Joe Muir	L	29	12	5	1	0	35.2	42	3	18	17	2-3	0	6.31
Harry Fisher	R	26	8	3	0	0	18.1	17	4	13	5	1-2	0	6.87
Jim Suchecki	R	24	5	0	0	0	10.0	14	1	4	6	0-0	0	5.40
Don Carlsen	R	25	5	1	0	0	10.0	20	1	5	2	0-1	0	10.80
Bill Werle†	L	31	5	0	0	0	4.0	9	1	1	1	0-0	0	9.00
Bill Bell	R	18	4	1	0	0	15.2	16	3	13	4	0-1	0	4.60
Jim Dunn	R	21	3	0	0	0	5.1	4	0	3	2	0-0	0	3.38
Ed Wolfe	R	23	3	0	0	0	3.2	7	1	5	1	0-0	0	7.36

»1953 New York Yankees 1st AL 99-52 .656 —

Casey Stengel

Player	Gm by Position	B	Age	G	AB	R	H	2B	3B	HR	RBI	BB	SO	SB	Avg	OBP	Slg
Yogi Berra	C133	L	28	137	503	80	149	23	5	27	108	50	32	0	.296	.363	.523
Joe Collins	1B113,OF4	L	30	127	387	72	104	11	2	17	44	59	36	2	.269	.365	.439
Billy Martin	2B146,SS18	R	25	149	587	72	151	24	6	15	75	43	56	6	.257	.314	.395
Gil McDougald	3B136,2B26	R	25	141	541	82	154	27	7	10	83	60	65	3	.285	.361	.416
Phil Rizzuto	SS133	R	35	134	413	54	112	21	3	2	54	71	39	4	.271	.383	.351
Hank Bauer	OF126	R	30	133	437	77	133	20	6	10	57	59	45	2	.304	.394	.446
Mickey Mantle	OF121,SS1	S	21	127	461	105	136	24	3	21	92	79	90	8	.295	.398	.497
Gene Woodling	OF119	L	30	125	395	64	121	26	4	10	58	82	29	2	.306	.429	.468
Irv Noren	OF96	L	28	109	345	55	92	12	6	6	46	42	39	3	.267	.350	.388
Don Bollweg	1B43	L	32	70	155	24	46	6	4	6	24	21	31	1	.297	.384	.503
Bill Renna	OF40	R	28	61	121	19	38	6	3	2	13	13	31	0	.314	.385	.463
Johnny Mize	1B15	L	40	81	104	6	26	3	0	4	27	12	17	0	.250	.339	.394
Charlie Silvera	C39,3B1	R	28	42	82	11	23	3	1	0	12	9	5	0	.280	.352	.341
Andy Carey	3B40,SS2,2B1	R	21	51	81	14	26	5	0	4	8	9	12	2	.321	.389	.531
Willie Miranda†	SS45	S	27	48	58	12	13	0	0	1	5	5	10	1	.224	.286	.276
Gus Triandos	1B12,C5	R	22	18	51	5	8	2	0	1	6	3	9	0	.157	.204	.255
Loren Babe†	3B5	L	25	5	18	2	6	1	0	2	6	0	2	0	.333	.333	.722
Jerry Coleman	2B7,SS1	R	28	8	10	1	2	0	0	0	0	0	2	0	.200	.200	.200
Ralph Houk	C8	R	33	8	9	2	2	0	0	0	1	0	1	0	.222	.222	.222
Bob Cerv		R	27	8	6	0	0	0	0	0	0	1	1	0	.000	.143	.000
Jim Brideweser	SS3	R	26	7	3	3	3	0	1	0	3	1	0	0	1.000	1.000	1.667
Art Schult		R	25	7	0	3	0	0	0	0	0	0	0	0	—	—	—
Frank Verdi	SS1	R	27	1	0	0	0	0	0	0	0	0	0	0	—	—	—

Pitcher	T	Age	G	GS	CG	ShO	IP	H	HR	BB	SO	W-L	Sv	ERA
Whitey Ford	L	24	32	30	11	3	207.0	187	13	110	110	18-6	0	3.00
Vic Raschi	R	34	28	26	7	4	181.0	150	11	55	76	13-6	1	3.33
Ed Lopat	L	35	25	24	9	3	178.1	169	13	32	50	16-4	0	2.42
Jim McDonald	R	26	27	18	6	2	129.2	128	4	39	43	9-7	0	3.82
Ewell Blackwell	R	30	8	4	0	0	19.2	17	2	13	11	2-0	1	3.66
Steve Kraly	L	24	5	3	0	0	25.0	19	2	16	8	0-2	1	3.24
Allie Reynolds	R	38	41	15	5	1	145.0	140	9	61	86	13-7	13	3.41
Johnny Sain	R	35	40	19	10	1	189.0	189	16	45	84	14-7	9	3.00
Tom Gorman	R	28	40	1	0	0	77.0	65	5	32	38	4-5	6	3.39
Bob Kuzava	L	30	33	6	2	2	92.1	92	9	34	48	6-5	4	3.31
Ray Scarborough†	R	35	25	1	0	0	54.2	52	4	26	20	2-2	2	3.29
Bill Miller	L	25	13	3	0	0	34.0	46	3	19	17	2-1	1	4.76
Art Schallock	L	29	7	1	0	0	21.1	30	2	15	13	0-0	1	2.95
Johnny Schmitz†	L	32	3	0	0	0	4.1	2	1	3	0	0-0	0	2.08

1953 Cleveland Indians 2nd AL 92-62 .597 8.5 GB

Al Lopez

Player	Gm by Position	B	Age	G	AB	R	H	2B	3B	HR	RBI	BB	SO	SB	Avg	OBP	Slg
Jim Hegan	C106	R	32	112	299	37	65	10	1	9	37	25	41	1	.217	.280	.348
Bill Glynn	1B135,OF2	L	27	147	411	60	100	14	2	3	30	44	65	1	.243	.324	.309
Bobby Avila	2B140	R	29	141	559	85	160	22	3	8	55	58	27	10	.286	.355	.379
Al Rosen	3B154,1B1,SS1	R	29	155	599	115	201	27	5	43	145	85	48	8	.336	.422	.613
George Strickland	SS122,1B1	R	27	123	419	43	119	17	4	5	47	51	52	0	.284	.362	.379
Larry Doby	OF146	L	29	149	513	92	135	18	5	29	102	96	121	3	.263	.385	.487
Dale Mitchell	OF125	L	31	134	500	76	150	26	4	13	60	42	20	3	.300	.354	.446
Bob Kennedy	OF89	R	32	100	161	22	38	5	0	3	22	19	11	0	.236	.320	.323
Harry Simpson	OF69,1B2	L	27	82	242	25	55	3	1	7	22	18	27	0	.227	.284	.335
Wally Westlake	OF72	R	32	82	218	42	72	7	1	9	46	35	29	2	.330	.427	.495
Luke Easter	1B56	L	37	68	211	26	64	9	0	7	31	15	35	0	.303	.361	.445
Al Smith	OF39,3B2	R	25	47	150	28	36	9	0	3	14	20	25	2	.240	.341	.360
Ray Boone†	SS31	R	29	34	112	21	27	1	2	4	21	24	21	1	.241	.375	.393
Joe Ginsberg†	C39	L	26	46	109	10	31	4	0	0	10	14	4	0	.284	.371	.321
Joe Tipton	C46	R	31	47	109	17	25	2	0	6	13	19	13	0	.229	.359	.413
Owen Friend†	2B19,SS8,3B1	R	26	34	68	7	16	2	0	2	13	5	16	0	.235	.288	.353
Hank Majeski	2B10,3B7,OF1	R	36	50	50	6	15	1	0	2	12	3	8	0	.300	.352	.440
Jim Lemon	OF11,1B2	R	25	16	46	5	8	1	0	1	5	3	15	0	.174	.224	.261
Barney McCosky		L	36	22	21	3	4	3	0	0	3	1	4	0	.190	.227	.333
Hank Foiles†	C7	R	24	7	7	2	1	0	0	0	0	1	1	0	.143	.250	.143
Dick Aylward	C4	R	28	4	3	0	0	0	0	0	0	0	1	0	.000	.000	.000
Dick Weik†		R	25	1	0	1	0	0	0	0	0	0	0	0	—	—	—

Pitcher	T	Age	G	GS	CG	ShO	IP	H	HR	BB	SO	W-L	Sv	ERA
Bob Lemon	R	32	41	36	23	5	286.2	283	16	110	98	21-15	1	3.36
Mike Garcia	R	29	38	35	21	3	271.2	260	18	81	134	18-9	0	3.25
Early Wynn	R	33	36	34	16	1	251.2	234	19	107	138	17-12	0	3.93
Bob Feller	R	34	25	25	10	1	175.2	163	16	60	60	10-7	0	3.59
Art Houtteman†	R	25	22	13	6	2	109.0	113	4	25	40	7-7	3	3.80
Dick Tomanek	L	22	1	1	1	0	9.0	6	1	6	6	1-0	0	2.00
Bob Hooper	R	31	43	0	0	0	69.1	50	4	38	16	5-4	7	4.02
Dave Hoskins	R	27	26	7	3	0	112.2	102	9	38	55	9-3	1	3.99
Bill Wight†	L	31	20	0	0	0	26.2	29	1	16	14	2-1	1	3.71
Lou Brissie	L	29	16	0	0	0	13.0	21	2	13	5	0-0	2	7.62
Bob Chakales	R	25	7	3	1	0	27.0	28	2	10	6	0-2	0	2.67
Al Aber†	L	25	6	0	0	0	6.0	6	0	9	4	1-1	0	7.50
Steve Gromek†	R	33	5	1	0	0	11.0	11	0	3	8	1-1	0	3.27
Ted Wilks	R	37	4	0	0	0	3.2	5	0	3	2	0-0	0	7.36

1953 Chicago White Sox 3rd AL 89-65 .578 11.5 GB

Paul Richards

Player	Gm by Position	B	Age	G	AB	R	H	2B	3B	HR	RBI	BB	SO	SB	Avg	OBP	Slg
Sherm Lollar	C107,1B1	R	28	113	334	46	96	19	0	8	54	47	29	1	.287	.388	.416
Ferris Fain	1B127	L	32	128	446	73	114	18	2	6	52	108	28	3	.256	.405	.345
Nellie Fox	2B154	L	25	154	624	92	178	31	8	3	72	49	18	4	.285	.344	.375
Bob Elliott†	3B58,OF2	R	36	67	208	24	54	11	1	4	32	31	21	1	.260	.358	.380
Chico Carrasquel	SS149	R	27	149	552	72	154	30	4	2	47	38	47	5	.279	.330	.359
Jim Rivera	OF156	L	30	156	567	79	147	26	16	11	78	53	70	22	.259	.329	.420
Minnie Minoso	OF147,3B10	R	30	151	556	104	174	24	8	15	104	74	43	25	.313	.410	.466
Sam Mele	OF138,1B2	R	30	140	481	64	132	26	8	12	82	58	47	3	.274	.353	.437
Bob Boyd	1B29,OF16	L	27	55	165	20	49	6	2	3	23	13	11	1	.297	.352	.412
Red Wilson	C63	R	24	71	164	21	41	6	1	0	10	26	12	2	.250	.353	.299
Tom Wright	OF33	L	29	77	132	14	33	5	3	2	25	12	21	0	.250	.322	.379
Rocky Krsnich	3B57	R	25	64	129	9	26	8	0	1	14	12	11	0	.202	.270	.287
Vern Stephens†	3B38,SS3	R	32	44	129	14	24	6	0	1	14	13	18	2	.186	.261	.256
Fred Marsh	3B32,SS17,1B5*	R	29	67	95	22	19	1	0	2	2	13	26	0	.200	.303	.274
Billy Pierce	P40,1B1	L	26	42	87	4	11	0	0	0	4	4	16	0	.126	.174	.126
Bud Stewart	OF16	L	37	53	59	16	16	2	0	2	13	14	3	1	.271	.411	.407
Connie Ryan†	3B16	R	33	17	54	6	12	1	0	0	6	9	12	2	.222	.333	.241
Bud Sheely	C17	L	32	31	46	4	10	1	0	0	2	9	8	0	.217	.345	.239
Bill Wilson	OF3	R	24	9	17	1	1	0	0	0	1	0	7	0	.059	.111	.059
Allie Clark†	1B1,OF1	R	30	9	15	0	1	0	0	0	0	0	5	0	.067	.067	.067
Neil Berry†	2B3	R	31	5	8	1	1	0	0	0	0	1	1	0	.125	.222	.125
Sam Dente	SS1	R	31	2	0	0	0	0	0	0	0	0	0	0	—	—	—

F. Marsh, 2 G at 2B

Pitcher	T	Age	G	GS	CG	ShO	IP	H	HR	BB	SO	W-L	Sv	ERA
Billy Pierce	L	26	40	33	19	7	271.1	216	20	102	186	18-12	3	2.72
Virgil Trucks†	R	36	24	21	13	5	176.1	151	14	67	102	15-6	1	2.86
Saul Rogovin	R	29	22	19	4	1	131.0	151	17	48	62	7-12	1	5.22
Joe Dobson	R	36	23	15	3	1	100.2	96	10	37	50	5-5	1	3.67
Bob Keegan	R	32	22	11	4	2	98.2	80	4	33	32	7-5	1	2.74
Connie Johnson	R	30	14	10	2	1	60.2	55	4	38	44	4-4	0	3.56
Tommy Byrne†	L	33	6	6	0	0	16.0	18	0	26	4	2-0	0	10.13
Harry Dorish	R	31	55	6	2	0	145.2	140	9	52	69	10-6	18	3.40
Mike Fornieles	R	21	39	16	5	0	153.0	160	8	61	72	8-7	3	3.59
Sandy Consuegra†	R	32	29	13	5	1	124.0	122	9	28	30	7-5	3	2.54
Gene Bearden	L	32	25	3	0	0	58.1	48	8	33	24	3-3	0	2.93
Luis Aloma	R	29	24	0	0	0	38.1	41	7	23	23	2-0	2	4.70
Lou Kretlow†	R	32	9	3	0	0	20.2	12	2	30	15	0-0	0	3.48
Earl Harrist†	R	34	7	0	0	0	8.1	9	1	5	1	1-0	0	7.56
Hal Hudson	L	26	1	0	0	0	0.2	0	0	0	0	0-0	0	0.00

724 Seasons: Team Rosters

1953 Boston Red Sox 4th AL 84-69 .549 16.0 GB

Lou Boudreau

Player	Gm by Position	B	Age	G	AB	R	H	2B	3B	HR	RBI	BB	SO	SB	Avg	OBP	Slg
Sammy White	C131	R	24	136	476	59	130	34	2	13	64	29	48	3	.273	.318	.435
Dick Gernert	1B136	R	24	139	494	73	125	15	1	21	71	88	82	0	.253	.371	.415
Billy Goodman	2B112,1B20	L	27	128	514	73	161	33	5	2	41	57	11	1	.313	.384	.409
George Kell	3B124,OF7	R	30	134	460	68	141	41	2	12	73	52	22	5	.307	.383	.483
Milt Bolling	SS109	R	22	109	323	30	85	12	1	5	28	23	41	1	.263	.318	.353
Jimmy Piersall	OF151	R	23	151	585	76	159	21	9	3	52	41	52	11	.272	.329	.354
Tom Umphlett	OF136	R	23	137	495	53	140	27	5	3	59	34	30	4	.283	.331	.376
Hoot Evers	OF93	R	32	99	300	39	72	10	1	11	31	23	41	2	.240	.301	.390
Gene Stephens	OF72	L	20	78	221	30	45	6	2	3	18	29	56	3	.204	.302	.290
Floyd Baker†	3B37,2B16	L	36	81	172	22	47	4	2	0	24	24	10	0	.273	.365	.320
Ted Lepcio	2B34,SS20,3B11	R	22	66	161	17	38	4	2	4	11	17	24	0	.236	.313	.360
Johnny Lipon†	SS58	R	30	60	145	18	31	7	0	0	13	14	16	1	.214	.283	.262
Del Wilber	C28,1B2	R	34	58	112	16	27	6	1	7	29	6	21	0	.241	.286	.500
Ted Williams	OF26	L	34	37	91	17	37	6	0	13	34	19	10	0	.407	.509	.901
Al Zarilla	OF18	L	34	57	67	11	13	2	0	0	4	14	13	0	.194	.333	.224
Billy Consolo	3B16,2B11	R	18	47	65	9	14	2	1	1	6	2	23	1	.215	.239	.323
Karl Olson	OF24	R	22	25	57	5	7	2	0	1	6	1	9	0	.123	.138	.211
Gus Niarhos	C16	R	32	16	35	6	7	1	1	0	2	4	4	0	.200	.300	.286
Jack Merson	2B1	R	31	1	4	0	0	0	0	0	0	0	0	0	.000	.000	.000
Dom DiMaggio		R	36	3	3	0	1	0	0	0	0	0	1	0	.333	.333	.333
Al Richter	SS1	R	26	1	0	0	0	0	0	0	0	0	0	0	—	—	—
Clyde Vollmer†		R	31	1	0	0	0	0	0	0	0	1	0	0	—	1.000	—

Pitcher	T	Age	G	GS	CG	ShO	IP	H	HR	BB	SO	W-L	Sv	ERA
Mel Parnell	L	31	38	34	12	5	241.0	217	15	116	136	21-8	0	3.06
Mickey McDermott	L	25	32	30	8	4	206.1	169	9	109	92	18-10	0	3.01
Hal Brown	R	28	30	25	6	1	166.1	177	16	57	62	11-6	0	4.65
Sid Hudson	R	38	30	17	4	0	156.0	164	13	49	60	6-9	2	3.52
Willard Nixon	R	25	23	15	5	1	116.2	114	6	59	57	4-8	0	3.93
Bill Henry	L	25	21	12	4	1	85.2	86	4	33	56	5-5	1	3.26
Marv Grissom†	R	35	13	11	1	1	59.1	61	5	30	31	2-6	0	4.70
Ellis Kinder	R	38	69	0	0	0	107.0	84	8	38	39	10-6	27	1.85
Ben Flowers	R	26	32	6	1	1	79.1	87	6	24	36	1-4	3	3.86
Ike Delock	R	23	23	1	0	0	48.2	60	2	20	22	3-1	1	4.44
Hersh Freeman	R	24	18	2	0	0	39.0	50	2	17	15	1-4	0	5.54
Bill Kennedy	L	32	16	0	0	0	24.1	24	2	17	14	0-0	2	3.70
Frank Sullivan	R	23	14	0	0	0	25.2	24	3	11	17	1-1	0	5.61
Bill Werle	L	32	5	0	0	0	11.2	7	1	1	4	0-1	0	1.54
Ken Holcombe	R	34	3	0	0	0	6.0	9	0	3	1	1-0	1	6.00

1953 Washington Senators 5th AL 76-76 .500 23.5 GB

Bucky Harris

Player	Gm by Position	B	Age	G	AB	R	H	2B	3B	HR	RBI	BB	SO	SB	Avg	OBP	Slg
Ed Fitz Gerald†	C85	R	29	88	288	23	72	13	0	3	39	19	34	2	.250	.299	.326
Mickey Vernon	1B152	L	35	152	608	101	205	43	11	15	115	63	57	4	.337	.403	.518
Wayne Terwilliger	2B133	R	28	134	464	62	117	24	4	4	46	64	65	7	.252	.343	.347
Eddie Yost	3B152	R	26	152	577	107	157	30	7	9	45	123	59	7	.272	.403	.395
Pete Runnels	SS121,2B11	L	25	137	486	64	125	15	5	2	50	64	36	3	.257	.347	.321
Jim Busby	OF150	R	26	150	586	68	183	28	7	6	82	38	45	13	.312	.358	.415
Jackie Jensen	OF146	R	26	147	552	87	147	32	8	10	84	73	51	18	.266	.357	.408
Clyde Vollmer†	OF106	R	31	118	408	54	106	15	3	11	74	48	59	0	.260	.342	.392
Mickey Grasso	C59	R	33	61	196	13	41	7	0	2	22	9	20	0	.209	.251	.276
Gil Coan	OF46	L	31	68	168	28	33	1	4	2	17	22	23	7	.196	.301	.286
Jerry Snyder	SS17,2B4	R	23	29	62	10	21	4	0	0	4	5	8	1	.339	.388	.403
Yo-Yo Davalillo	SS17	R	22	19	58	10	17	1	0	0	2	1	7	1	.293	.305	.310
Kite Thomas†	OF8,C1	R	30	38	58	10	17	3	2	1	12	11	7	0	.293	.414	.466
Mel Hoderlein	2B11,SS2	S	30	23	47	5	9	0	0	0	5	6	9	0	.191	.283	.191
Ken Wood	OF7	R	28	12	33	0	7	1	0	0	3	2	3	0	.212	.257	.242
Les Peden	C8	R	29	9	28	4	7	1	0	1	1	4	3	0	.250	.344	.393
Carmen Mauro†	OF6	L	26	17	23	1	4	0	1	0	2	1	3	0	.174	.208	.261
Gene Verble	SS8	R	25	13	21	4	4	0	0	0	2	2	1	0	.190	.261	.190
Frank Sacka	C6	R	28	7	18	2	5	0	0	0	3	3	1	0	.278	.381	.278
Bob Oldis	C7	R	25	7	16	0	4	0	0	0	3	1	2	0	.250	.294	.250
Frank Campos		L	29	10	9	0	1	0	0	0	2	1	0	0	.111	.200	.111
Tony Roig	2B2	R	25	3	8	0	1	1	0	0	0	0	1	0	.125	.125	.250
Floyd Baker†	3B1	L	36	9	7	0	0	0	0	0	0	1	0	0	.000	.222	.000
Bruce Barmes	OF1	L	23	5	5	1	1	0	0	0	0	0	0	0	.200	.200	.200

Pitcher	T	Age	G	GS	CG	ShO	IP	H	HR	BB	SO	W-L	Sv	ERA
Bob Porterfield	R	29	34	32	24	9	255.0	243	19	73	77	22-10	0	3.35
Spec Shea	R	32	23	23	11	1	164.2	151	11	75	38	12-7	0	3.94
Walt Masterson	R	33	29	20	10	4	166.1	145	16	62	95	10-12	0	3.63
Chuck Stobbs	L	23	27	20	8	0	153.0	146	11	44	67	11-8	0	3.29
Connie Marrero	R	42	22	20	10	2	145.2	130	14	48	65	8-7	2	3.03
Johnny Schmitz†	L	32	24	13	5	0	107.2	118	9	37	39	2-7	4	3.68
Tommy Byrne†	L	33	6	5	2	0	33.2	35	3	22	22	0-5	0	4.28
Bunky Stewart	L	22	2	2	1	0	15.1	17	1	11	3	0-2	0	4.70
Sonny Dixon	R	28	43	6	3	0	120.0	123	13	31	40	5-8	3	3.75
Al Sima	L	31	31	5	1	0	68.1	63	7	31	25	2-3	1	3.42
Jerry Lane	R	27	20	2	0	0	56.2	64	3	16	26	1-4	0	4.92
Julio Moreno	R	32	12	2	1	0	35.1	41	2	13	13	3-1	0	2.80
Jim Pearce	R	28	4	1	0	0	9.1	15	3	6	0	0-1	0	7.71
Sandy Consuegra†	R	32	4	0	0	0	5.0	9	0	4	0	0-0	0	10.80
Dean Stone	L	22	3	1	0	0	8.2	13	0	5	5	0-1	0	8.31

1953 Detroit Tigers 6th AL 60-94 .390 40.5 GB

Fred Hutchinson

Player	Gm by Position	B	Age	G	AB	R	H	2B	3B	HR	RBI	BB	SO	SB	Avg	OBP	Slg
Matt Batts	C103	R	31	116	374	38	104	24	3	6	42	24	36	2	.278	.322	.406
Walt Dropo	1B150	R	30	152	606	61	150	30	3	13	96	29	69	2	.248	.289	.371
Johnny Pesky	2B73	L	33	103	308	43	90	22	1	2	24	27	10	3	.292	.353	.390
Ray Boone†	3B97,SS3	R	29	101	385	73	120	16	6	22	93	48	47	2	.312	.395	.556
Harvey Kuenn	SS155	R	22	155	679	94	209	33	7	2	48	50	31	6	.308	.356	.386
Bob Nieman	OF135	R	26	142	508	72	143	32	5	15	69	57	57	0	.281	.354	.453
Jim Delsing	OF133	L	27	138	479	77	138	26	6	11	62	66	39	1	.288	.380	.436
Don Lund	OF123	R	30	131	421	51	108	21	4	9	47	39	65	3	.257	.323	.390
Fred Hatfield	3B54,2B28,SS1	L	28	109	311	41	79	11	1	3	19	40	34	3	.254	.341	.325
Steve Souchock	OF80,1B1	R	34	89	278	29	84	13	3	11	46	8	35	5	.302	.326	.489
Jerry Priddy	2B45,1B11,3B2	R	33	65	196	14	46	6	2	1	24	17	19	1	.235	.299	.301
Johnny Bucha	C56	R	28	60	158	17	35	9	0	1	14	20	14	1	.222	.309	.297
Pat Mullin	OF14	L	35	79	97	11	26	1	0	4	17	14	15	0	.268	.360	.402
Owen Friend†	2B26	R	26	31	96	10	17	4	0	3	10	6	9	0	.177	.233	.313
Russ Sullivan	OF20	L	30	23	72	7	18	5	1	1	6	13	5	0	.250	.379	.389
Joe Ginsberg†	C15	L	26	18	53	6	16	2	0	0	3	10	1	0	.302	.422	.340
Billy Hitchcock	3B12,2B1,SS1	R	36	22	38	8	8	0	0	0	0	3	3	0	.211	.268	.211
Al Kaline	OF20	R	18	30	28	9	7	0	0	1	2	1	5	1	.250	.300	.357
John Baumgartner	3B7	R	22	7	27	3	5	0	0	0	2	0	5	0	.185	.185	.185
Frank Carswell	OF3	R	33	16	15	2	4	0	0	0	2	3	1	0	.267	.389	.267
Fred Hutchinson	P3,1B1	L	33	4	6	1	1	0	0	1	1	0	0	0	.167	.167	.667
Bob Swift	C2	R	38	2	3	0	1	1	0	0	1	2	1	0	.333	.600	.667
Reno Bertoia	2B1	R	18	1	1	0	0	0	0	0	0	0	0	0	.000	.000	.000
George Freese		R	26	1	1	0	0	0	0	0	0	0	0	0	.000	.000	.000

Pitcher	T	Age	G	GS	CG	ShO	IP	H	HR	BB	SO	W-L	Sv	ERA
Ted Gray	L	28	30	28	8	0	176.0	166	25	76	115	10-15	0	4.60
Billy Hoeft	L	21	29	27	9	0	197.2	223	24	58	90	9-14	2	4.83
Ned Garver	R	27	30	26	13	0	198.1	228	16	66	69	11-11	1	4.45
Steve Gromek†	R	33	19	17	6	1	125.2	138	17	36	59	6-8	1	4.51
Ralph Branca†	R	27	17	14	7	0	102.0	98	7	31	50	4-7	1	4.15
Al Aber†	L	25	17	10	2	0	66.2	63	3	41	34	4-3	0	4.46
Art Houtteman†	R	25	16	9	3	0	68.2	87	11	29	28	2-6	1	5.90
Hal Newhouser	L	32	7	4	0	0	21.2	31	4	8	6	0-1	1	7.06
Ray Herbert	R	23	43	3	0	0	87.2	109	5	46	37	4-6	6	5.24
Dick Marlowe	R	24	42	11	2	0	119.2	152	13	42	52	6-7	0	5.26
Dave Madison	R	32	32	1	0	0	62.0	76	7	44	27	3-4	0	6.82
Hal Erickson	R	33	18	0	0	0	32.1	43	4	10	19	0-1	1	4.73
Bob Miller	L	17	13	1	0	0	36.1	43	2	21	9	1-2	0	5.94
Bill Wight†	L	31	13	4	0	0	25.1	35	4	14	10	0-3	0	8.88
Ray Scarborough†	R	35	13	0	0	0	20.2	34	3	11	12	0-2	2	8.27
Dick Weik	R	25	12	1	0	0	19.1	32	3	23	6	0-1	0	13.97
Earl Harrist†	R	34	8	1	0	0	18.2	25	2	15	7	0-2	0	8.68
Milt Jordan	R	26	8	1	0	0	17.0	26	3	5	4	0-1	0	5.82
Paul Foytack	R	22	6	0	0	0	9.2	15	1	9	7	0-0	0	11.17
Fred Hutchinson	R	33	3	0	0	0	9.2	9	0	0	4	0-0	0	2.79

1953 Philadelphia Athletics 7th AL 59-95 .383 41.5 GB

Jimmy Dykes

Player	Gm by Position	B	Age	G	AB	R	H	2B	3B	HR	RBI	BB	SO	SB	Avg	OBP	Slg
Joe Astroth	C79	R	30	82	260	28	77	15	2	3	24	27	12	1	.296	.367	.404
Eddie Robinson	1B155	L	32	156	615	64	152	28	4	22	102	63	56	1	.247	.322	.413
Cass Michaels	2B110	R	27	117	411	53	103	10	0	12	42	51	56	7	.251	.335	.363
Loren Babe†	3B93,SS1	L	25	103	343	34	77	16	2	0	20	35	22	0	.224	.300	.283
Joe DeMaestri	SS108	R	24	111	420	53	107	17	3	6	35	24	39	0	.255	.297	.352
Dave Philley	OF157,3B1	S	33	157	620	80	188	30	9	9	59	51	35	13	.303	.358	.424
Gus Zernial	OF141	R	30	147	556	85	158	21	3	42	108	57	79	4	.284	.355	.559
Ed McGhee	OF99	R	28	104	358	36	94	11	4	1	29	32	43	4	.263	.328	.324
Pete Suder	3B72,2B38,SS7	R	37	115	454	44	130	11	3	4	35	17	35	3	.286	.312	.350
Ray Murray	C78	R	35	84	268	25	76	14	3	6	41	18	25	0	.284	.331	.425
Eddie Joost	SS51	R	37	51	177	39	44	6	0	6	15	45	24	3	.249	.401	.384
Carmen Mauro†	OF49,3B1	L	26	64	165	14	44	4	4	0	17	19	21	3	.267	.342	.339
Elmer Valo	OF25	L	32	50	85	15	19	3	0	0	9	22	7	0	.224	.383	.259
Allie Clark†	OF19	R	30	20	74	6	15	4	0	3	13	3	5	0	.203	.234	.378
Tom Hamilton	1B7,OF2	L	27	58	56	8	11	2	0	0	5	7	11	0	.196	.286	.232
Kite Thomas†	OF15	R	30	24	49	1	6	0	0	0	2	3	6	0	.122	.173	.122
Neal Watlington	C9	L	30	21	44	4	7	1	0	0	3	3	8	0	.159	.213	.182
Tommy Giordano	2B11	R	27	11	40	6	7	2	0	2	5	5	6	0	.175	.267	.375
Spider Wilhelm	SS6	R	24	7	7	1	2	1	0	0	0	0	3	0	.286	.286	.429
Don Kolloway	3B1	R	34	2	1	0	0	0	0	0	0	0	1	0	.000	.000	.000

Pitcher	T	Age	G	GS	CG	ShO	IP	H	HR	BB	SO	W-L	Sv	ERA
Harry Byrd	R	28	40	37	11	2	236.2	279	23	115	122	11-20	0	5.51
Alex Kellner	L	28	25	25	14	2	201.2	210	8	51	81	11-12	0	3.93
Marion Fricano	R	29	39	23	10	0	211.0	206	21	90	67	9-12	0	3.88
Charlie Bishop	R	29	39	20	1	1	160.2	174	15	86	66	3-14	2	5.66
Bobby Shantz	L	27	16	16	6	0	105.2	107	10	26	58	5-9	0	4.09
Bob Trice	R	26	3	3	1	0	23.0	25	4	6	4	2-1	0	5.48
Morrie Martin	L	30	58	11	2	0	156.1	158	12	59	64	10-12	7	4.43
Carl Scheib	R	26	28	8	3	0	96.0	99	9	29	25	3-7	2	4.88
Frank Fanovich	L	31	26	3	0	0	61.2	62	5	37	37	0-3	0	5.55
Joe Coleman	R	30	21	9	2	1	90.0	85	8	49	18	3-4	0	4.00
Bobo Newsom	R	45	17	2	1	0	38.2	44	3	24	16	2-1	0	4.89
Rinty Monahan	R	25	4	0	0	0	10.2	11	0	7	2	0-0	0	4.22
Dick Rozek	L	26	2	0	0	0	10.2	8	3	9	2	0-0	0	5.06
Walt Kellner	R	24	2	0	0	0	3.0	1	0	4	4	0-0	0	6.00
Bill Harrington	R	25	1	0	0	0	2.0	5	0	0	0	0-0	0	13.50
Johnny Mackinson	R	29	1	0	0	0	1.1	1	0	2	0	0-0	0	0.00

1953 St. Louis Browns 8th AL 54-100 .351 46.5 GB

Marty Marion

Player	Gm by Position	B	Age	G	AB	R	H	2B	3B	HR	RBI	BB	SO	SB	Avg	OBP	Slg
Clint Courtney	C103	L	26	106	355	28	89	12	2	4	19	25	20	0	.251	.302	.330
Dick Kryhoski	1B88	L	28	104	338	35	94	18	4	16	50	26	33	0	.278	.333	.497
Bobby Young	2B148	L	28	148	537	48	137	22	2	4	25	41	40	2	.255	.309	.326
Jim Dyck	OF55,3B51	R	31	112	334	38	71	15	1	9	27	38	40	3	.213	.299	.344
Billy Hunter	SS152	R	25	154	567	50	124	18	1	1	37	24	45	3	.219	.253	.259
Johnny Groth	OF141	R	26	141	557	65	141	27	4	10	57	42	53	5	.253	.308	.370
Vic Wertz	OF121	L	28	128	440	61	118	18	6	19	70	72	44	1	.268	.376	.466
Dick Kokos	OF83	L	25	107	299	41	72	12	0	13	38	56	53	0	.241	.361	.411
Don Lenhardt	OF77,3B6	R	30	97	303	37	96	15	0	10	35	41	41	1	.317	.400	.465
Roy Sievers	1B76	R	26	92	285	37	77	15	0	8	35	32	47	0	.270	.344	.407
Les Moss	C71	R	28	78	239	21	66	14	1	2	28	18	31	0	.276	.329	.368
Vern Stephens†	3B46	R	32	46	165	16	53	8	0	4	17	18	24	0	.321	.388	.442
Bob Elliott†	3B45	R	36	48	160	19	40	7	1	5	29	30	18	0	.250	.368	.400
Hank Edwards	OF21	L	34	65	106	6	21	3	0	0	9	13	10	0	.198	.286	.226
Neil Berry†	3B18,2B15,SS6	R	31	57	99	14	28	1	2	0	11	9	10	1	.283	.343	.333
Don Larsen	P38,OF1	R	23	50	81	11	23	3	1	3	10	4	14	0	.284	.318	.457
Ed Mickelson	1B3	R	26	7	15	1	2	1	0	0	2	2	6	0	.133	.235	.200
Jim Pisoni	OF3	R	23	3	12	1	1	0	0	1	1	0	5	0	.083	.083	.333
Johnny Lipon†	3B6,2B1	R	30	7	9	0	2	0	0	0	1	0	1	0	.222	.222	.222
Dixie Upright		L	27	9	8	3	2	0	0	1	1	1	3	0	.250	.333	.625
Marty Marion	3B2	R	35	3	7	0	0	0	0	0	0	0	0	0	.000	.000	.000
Willie Miranda†	SS8,3B6	S	27	17	6	2	1	0	0	0	0	1	1	1	.167	.286	.167
Frank Kellert	1B1	R	28	2	4	0	0	0	0	0	0	0	0	0	.000	.000	.000
Babe Martin	C1	R	33	4	2	0	0	0	0	0	0	1	0	0	.000	.333	.000

Pitcher	T	Age	G	GS	CG	ShO	IP	H	HR	BB	SO	W-L	Sv	ERA
Duane Pillette	R	30	31	25	5	1	166.2	181	16	62	58	7-13	0	4.48
Don Larsen	R	23	38	22	7	2	192.2	201	11	64	96	7-12	2	4.16
Dick Littlefield	L	27	36	22	2	0	152.1	153	17	84	104	7-12	0	5.08
Harry Brecheen	L	38	26	16	3	0	117.1	122	7	31	44	5-13	1	3.07
Virgil Trucks†	R	36	16	12	4	0	88.0	83	4	32	47	5-4	2	3.07
Lou Kretlow†	R	32	22	11	0	0	81.0	93	5	52	37	1-5	0	5.11
Bob Turley	R	22	10	7	3	1	60.1	39	4	44	61	2-6	0	3.28
Marlin Stuart	R	34	60	2	0	0	114.1	136	6	44	46	8-2	7	3.94
Satchel Paige	R	46	57	4	0	0	117.1	114	12	39	51	3-9	11	3.53
Mike Blyzka	R	24	33	9	2	0	94.1	110	6	56	23	2-6	0	6.39
Bob Cain	L	28	32	13	1	0	99.2	129	8	45	36	4-10	1	6.23
Bobo Holloman	R	28	22	10	1	1	65.1	69	2	50	25	3-7	0	5.23
Max Lanier†	L	37	10	1	0	0	22.1	28	2	19	8	0-1	0	7.25
Hal White†	R	34	10	0	0	0	10.1	8	1	3	2	0-0	0	2.61
Bob Habenicht	R	27	1	0	0	0	1.2	1	0	1	1	0-0	0	5.40

»1953 Brooklyn Dodgers 1st NL 105-49 .682 —

Chuck Dressen

Player	Gm by Position	B	Age	G	AB	R	H	2B	3B	HR	RBI	BB	SO	SB	Avg	OBP	Slg
Roy Campanella	C140	R	31	144	519	103	162	26	3	41	142	67	58	4	.312	.395	.611
Gil Hodges	1B127,OF24	R	29	141	520	101	157	22	7	31	122	75	84	1	.302	.393	.550
Jim Gilliam	2B149	S	24	151	605	125	168	31	17	6	63	100	38	21	.278	.383	.415
Billy Cox	3B89,SS6,2B1	R	33	100	327	44	95	18	1	10	44	37	21	2	.291	.363	.443
Pee Wee Reese	SS135	R	34	140	524	108	142	25	7	13	61	82	61	22	.271	.374	.420
Duke Snider	OF151	L	26	153	590	132	198	38	4	42	126	82	90	16	.336	.419	.627
Carl Furillo	OF131	R	31	132	479	82	165	38	6	21	92	34	32	1	.344	.393	.580
Don Thompson	OF81	L	29	96	153	25	37	5	0	1	12	14	13	2	.242	.310	.294
Jackie Robinson	OF76,3B44,2B9*	R	34	136	484	109	159	34	7	12	95	74	30	17	.329	.425	.502
Bobby Morgan	3B36,SS21	R	27	69	196	35	51	6	2	7	33	33	47	2	.260	.370	.418
George Shuba	OF44	L	28	74	169	19	43	12	1	5	23	17	20	1	.254	.326	.426
Wayne Belardi	1B38	L	22	69	163	19	39	3	2	11	34	16	40	0	.239	.311	.485
Rube Walker	C28	L	27	43	95	5	23	6	0	3	9	7	11	0	.242	.301	.400
Dick Williams	OF24	R	24	30	55	4	12	2	0	2	5	3	10	0	.218	.271	.364
Bill Antonello	OF25	R	26	40	43	9	7	1	1	1	4	2	11	0	.163	.200	.302
Carmen Mauro†	OF1	L	26	8	9	1	0	0	0	0	0	0	4	0	.000	.000	.000
Dick Teed		S	27	1	1	0	0	0	0	0	0	0	1	0	.000	.000	.000
Dixie Howell		R	33	1	1	0	0	0	0	0	0	0	1	0	.000	.000	.000

J. Robinson, 6 G at 1B, 1 G at SS

Pitcher	T	Age	G	GS	CG	ShO	IP	H	HR	BB	SO	W-L	Sv	ERA
Carl Erskine	R	26	39	33	16	4	246.2	213	21	95	187	20-6	3	3.54
Russ Meyer	R	29	34	32	10	2	191.1	201	25	63	106	15-5	0	4.56
Billy Loes	R	23	32	25	9	1	162.2	165	21	53	75	14-8	0	4.54
Preacher Roe	L	38	25	24	9	1	157.0	171	27	40	85	11-3	0	4.36
Johnny Podres	L	20	33	18	3	1	115.0	126	12	64	82	9-4	0	4.23
Glenn Mickens	R	22	4	2	0	0	6.1	11	2	4	5	0-1	0	11.37
Ray Moore	R	27	1	1	1	0	8.0	6	1	4	4	0-1	0	3.38
Jim Hughes	R	30	48	0	0	0	85.2	80	6	41	49	4-3	9	3.47
Bob Milliken	R	26	37	10	3	0	117.2	94	13	42	65	8-4	2	3.37
Clem Labine	R	26	37	7	0	0	110.1	92	9	30	44	11-6	7	2.77
Joe Black	R	29	34	3	0	0	72.2	74	12	27	42	6-3	5	5.33
Ben Wade	R	30	32	0	0	0	90.1	79	15	33	65	7-5	3	3.79
Ralph Branca†	R	27	7	0	0	0	11.0	15	4	5	5	0-0	0	9.82
Erv Palica	R	25	4	0	0	0	6.0	10	1	8	3	0-0	0	12.00

1953 Milwaukee Braves 2nd NL 92-62 .597 13.0 GB

Charlie Grimm

Player	Gm by Position	B	Age	G	AB	R	H	2B	3B	HR	RBI	BB	SO	SB	Avg	OBP	Slg
Del Crandall	C108	R	23	116	382	55	104	13	1	15	51	33	47	2	.272	.330	.429
Joe Adcock	1B157	R	25	157	590	71	168	33	6	18	80	42	82	3	.285	.334	.453
Jack Dittmer	2B138	L	25	138	504	54	134	22	1	9	63	18	35	1	.266	.293	.367
Eddie Mathews	3B157	L	21	157	579	110	175	31	8	47	135	99	83	1	.302	.406	.627
Johnny Logan	SS150	R	26	150	611	100	167	27	8	11	73	41	33	2	.273	.326	.398
Bill Bruton	OF150	L	27	151	613	82	153	18	14	1	41	44	100	26	.250	.306	.330
Andy Pafko	OF139	R	32	140	516	70	153	23	4	17	72	37	33	2	.297	.347	.455
Sid Gordon	OF137	R	35	140	464	67	127	22	4	19	75	71	40	1	.274	.372	.461
Jim Pendleton	OF105,SS7	R	29	120	251	48	75	12	4	7	27	7	36	6	.299	.323	.462
Walker Cooper	C35	R	38	53	137	12	30	6	0	3	16	12	15	1	.219	.287	.328
Harry Hanebrink	2B21,3B1	L	25	51	80	8	19	1	1	1	8	6	8	1	.238	.291	.313
Ebba St. Claire	C27	S	31	33	80	7	16	3	0	2	5	3	9	0	.200	.229	.313
George Crowe	1B9	L	32	47	42	6	12	2	0	2	6	2	7	0	.286	.333	.476
Bob Thorpe	OF18	R	26	27	37	1	6	1	0	0	5	1	6	0	.162	.184	.189
Sibby Sisti	2B13,SS6,3B4	R	32	38	23	8	5	1	0	0	4	5	2	0	.217	.357	.261
Mel Roach	2B1	R	20	5	2	1	0	0	0	0	0	0	1	0	.000	.000	.000
Billy Klaus		L	24	2	2	1	0	0	0	0	1	0	0	0	.000	.000	.000
Paul Burris	C2	R	29	2	1	0	0	0	0	0	0	0	0	0	.000	.000	.000

Pitcher	T	Age	G	GS	CG	ShO	IP	H	HR	BB	SO	W-L	Sv	ERA
Warren Spahn	L	32	35	32	24	5	265.2	211	14	70	148	23-7	3	2.10
Johnny Antonelli	L	23	31	26	11	2	175.1	167	15	71	131	12-12	1	3.18
Max Surkont	R	31	28	24	11	2	170.0	168	22	64	83	11-5	0	4.18
Bob Buhl	R	24	30	18	8	3	154.1	133	9	73	83	13-8	0	2.97
Jim Wilson	R	31	20	18	5	0	114.0	107	16	43	71	4-9	0	4.34
Lew Burdette	R	26	46	13	6	1	175.0	177	7	56	58	15-5	8	3.24
Ernie Johnson	R	29	36	1	0	0	81.0	79	4	22	36	4-3	0	2.67
Don Liddle	L	28	31	15	4	0	128.2	119	6	55	63	7-6	2	3.08
Dave Jolly	R	28	24	0	0	0	38.1	34	4	27	23	0-1	0	3.52
Vern Bickford	R	32	20	9	2	0	58.0	60	8	35	25	2-5	1	5.28
Dave Cole	R	22	10	0	0	0	14.2	17	1	14	13	0-1	0	8.59
Joey Jay	R	17	3	1	1	1	10.0	6	0	5	4	1-0	0	0.00
Virgil Jester	R	25	2	0	0	0	2.0	4	1	4	0	0-0	0	22.50

1953 Philadelphia Phillies 3rd NL 83-71 .539 22.0 GB

Steve O'Neill

Player	Gm by Position	B	Age	G	AB	R	H	2B	3B	HR	RBI	BB	SO	SB	Avg	OBP	Slg
Smoky Burgess	C95	L	26	102	312	31	91	17	5	4	36	37	17	3	.292	.370	.417
Earl Torgeson	1B105	L	29	111	379	58	104	25	8	11	64	53	57	7	.274	.366	.470
Granny Hamner	2B93,SS71	R	26	154	609	90	168	30	8	21	92	32	28	2	.276	.313	.455
Puddin' Head Jones	3B147	R	27	149	481	61	108	16	2	19	70	85	45	1	.225	.342	.385
Ted Kazanski	SS95	R	19	95	360	39	78	17	5	2	27	26	53	1	.217	.275	.308
Richie Ashburn	OF156	L	26	156	622	110	205	25	9	2	57	61	35	14	.330	.394	.408
Del Ennis	OF150	R	28	152	578	79	165	22	3	29	125	57	53	1	.285	.355	.484
Johnny Wyrostek	OF110	L	33	125	409	42	111	14	2	6	47	38	43	0	.271	.339	.359
Connie Ryan†	2B65,1B2	R	33	90	247	47	73	14	6	5	26	30	35	5	.296	.372	.462
Eddie Waitkus	1B59	L	33	81	247	24	72	9	2	1	16	13	23	1	.291	.330	.356
Stan Lopata	C80	R	27	81	234	34	56	12	3	8	31	28	39	3	.239	.321	.419
Mel Clark	OF51	R	26	60	198	31	59	10	4	0	19	11	17	1	.298	.338	.389
Tommy Glaviano	3B14,2B12,SS1	R	29	53	74	17	15	1	2	3	5	24	20	2	.203	.410	.392
Bill Nicholson	OF12	L	38	38	62	12	13	5	1	2	16	12	20	0	.210	.338	.419
Johnny Lindell†	P5,OF2	R	36	11	18	3	7	1	0	0	2	6	2	0	.389	.542	.444
Jack Lohrke	2B2,SS2,3B1	R	29	12	13	3	2	0	0	0	0	1	2	0	.154	.214	.154
Jackie Mayo	OF1	L	27	5	4	0	0	0	0	0	0	0	1	0	.000	.000	.000
Stan Palys	OF1	R	23	2	2	0	0	0	0	0	0	1	0	0	.000	.333	.000

Pitcher	T	Age	G	GS	CG	ShO	IP	H	HR	BB	SO	W-L	Sv	ERA
Robin Roberts	R	26	44	41	33	5	346.2	324	30	61	198	23-16	2	2.75
Curt Simmons	L	24	32	30	19	4	238.0	211	17	82	138	16-13	0	3.21
Karl Drews	R	33	47	27	6	2	185.1	218	26	50	72	9-10	3	4.52
Bob Miller	R	27	35	20	8	3	157.1	169	14	42	63	8-9	2	4.00
Johnny Lindell†	R	36	5	3	2	0	23.1	22	0	23	16	1-1	0	4.24
Jim Konstanty	R	36	48	19	7	0	170.2	198	18	42	45	14-10	5	4.43
Steve Ridzik	R	24	42	12	1	0	124.0	119	15	48	53	9-6	0	3.77
Andy Hansen	R	28	30	1	0	0	51.1	60	6	24	17	0-2	3	4.03
Thornton Kipper	R	24	20	3	0	0	45.2	59	8	12	15	3-3	0	4.73
Kent Peterson	L	27	15	0	0	0	27.0	26	3	21	20	0-1	0	6.67
Paul Stuffel	R	26	2	0	0	0	0.0	0	0	4	0	0-0	0	—
Tom Qualters	R	18	1	0	0	0	0.1	4	1	1	0	0-0	0	162.00

1953 St. Louis Cardinals 3rd NL 83-71 .539 22.0 GB

Eddie Stanky

Player	Gm by Position	B	Age	G	AB	R	H	2B	3B	HR	RBI	BB	SO	SB	Avg	OBP	Slg
Del Rice	C135	R	30	135	419	32	99	22	1	6	37	48	49	0	.236	.323	.337
Steve Bilko	1B154	R	24	154	570	72	143	23	3	21	84	70	125	0	.251	.334	.412
Red Schoendienst	2B140	S	30	146	564	107	193	35	5	15	79	60	23	3	.342	.405	.502
Ray Jablonski	3B157	R	26	157	604	64	162	23	5	21	112	34	61	2	.268	.308	.427
Solly Hemus	SS150,2B3	L	30	154	585	110	163	32	11	14	61	86	40	2	.279	.382	.443
Stan Musial	OF157	L	32	157	593	127	200	53	9	30	113	105	32	3	.337	.437	.609
Rip Repulski	OF153	R	25	153	567	75	156	25	4	15	66	33	71	3	.275	.325	.413
Enos Slaughter	OF137	L	37	143	492	64	143	34	9	6	89	80	28	4	.291	.395	.433
Peanuts Lowrey	OF38,2B10,3B1	R	34	104	182	26	49	9	2	5	27	15	21	1	.269	.325	.423
Harry Elliott	OF17	R	29	24	59	6	15	6	1	1	6	3	8	0	.254	.302	.441
Sal Yvars†	C26	R	29	30	57	4	14	2	0	1	6	4	6	0	.246	.306	.333
Pete Castiglione†	3B51,2B9,SS3	R	32	67	52	9	9	2	0	0	3	2	5	0	.173	.204	.212
Dick Sisler	1B10	L	32	32	43	3	11	1	1	0	4	1	4	0	.256	.273	.326
Dick Schofield	SS15	S	18	33	39	9	7	0	0	2	4	2	11	0	.179	.220	.333
Ferrell Anderson	C12	R	35	18	35	1	10	2	0	0	1	0	4	0	.286	.286	.343
Dick Rand	C9	R	22	9	31	3	9	1	0	0	1	2	6	0	.290	.333	.323
Eddie Stanky	2B8	R	36	17	30	5	8	0	0	0	1	6	4	0	.267	.405	.267
Grant Dunlap	OF1	R	29	16	17	2	6	0	1	1	3	0	2	0	.353	.353	.647
Les Fusselman	C11	R	32	11	8	1	2	1	0	0	0	0	0	0	.250	.250	.375
Hal Rice†		L	29	8	8	0	2	0	0	0	0	0	3	0	.250	.250	.250
Bill Johnson	3B11	R	34	11	5	0	1	1	0	0	1	1	1	0	.200	.333	.400
Vern Benson		L	28	13	4	2	0	0	0	0	0	1	2	0	.000	.200	.000
Virgil Stallcup		R	31	1	1	0	0	0	0	0	0	0	0	0	.000	.000	.000
Fred Marolewski	1B1	R	24	1	0	0	0	0	0	0	0	0	0	0	—	—	—
Eddie Phillips		S	21	9	0	4	0	0	0	0	0	0	0	0	—	—	—

Pitcher	T	Age	G	GS	CG	ShO	IP	H	HR	BB	SO	W-L	Sv	ERA
Harvey Haddix	L	27	36	33	19	6	253.0	220	24	69	163	20-9	1	3.06
Vinegar Bend Mizell	L	22	33	33	10	1	224.1	193	12	114	173	13-11	0	3.49
Gerry Staley	R	32	40	32	10	1	230.0	243	31	54	88	18-9	4	3.99
Joe Presko	R	24	34	25	4	0	161.2	165	19	65	56	6-13	1	5.01
John Romonosky	R	23	2	2	0	0	7.2	9	1	4	3	0-0	0	4.70
Al Brazle	L	39	60	0	0	0	92.0	101	8	43	57	6-7	18	4.21
Hal White†	R	34	49	0	0	0	84.2	84	5	39	32	6-5	7	2.98
Stu Miller	R	25	40	18	8	2	137.2	161	19	47	79	7-8	4	5.56
Cliff Chambers	L	31	32	8	0	0	79.2	82	7	43	26	3-6	0	4.86
Mike Clark	R	31	23	2	0	0	35.2	46	2	21	17	1-0	1	4.79
Eddie Erautt†	R	28	20	1	0	0	35.2	43	6	16	15	3-1	0	6.31
Jackie Collum†	L	26	7	0	0	0	11.1	15	1	4	5	0-0	0	6.35
Willard Schmidt	R	25	6	2	0	0	17.2	21	1	13	11	0-2	0	9.17
Jack Faszholz	R	26	4	1	0	0	11.2	16	3	1	7	0-0	0	6.94
Dick Bokelmann	R	26	3	0	0	0	3.0	4	0	0	0	0-0	0	6.00
Eddie Yuhas	R	28	2	0	0	0	1.0	3	0	0	0	0-0	0	18.00

726 Seasons: Team Rosters

1953 New York Giants 5th NL 70-84 .455 35.0 GB

Leo Durocher

Player	Gm by Position	B	Age	G	AB	R	H	2B	3B	HR	RBI	BB	SO	SB	Avg	OBP	Slg
Wes Westrum	C106,3B1	R	30	107	290	40	65	5	0	12	30	56	73	2	.224	.352	.366
Whitey Lockman	1B120,OF30	L	26	150	607	85	179	22	4	9	61	52	36	3	.295	.351	.389
Davey Williams	2B95	R	25	112	340	51	101	11	2	3	34	44	19	2	.297	.382	.368
Hank Thompson	3B101,OF9,2B1	L	27	114	388	80	117	15	8	24	74	60	39	6	.302	.400	.567
Al Dark	SS110,2B26,OF17*	R	31	155	647	126	194	41	6	23	88	28	34	7	.300	.335	.488
Bobby Thomson	OF154	R	29	154	608	80	175	22	6	26	106	43	57	4	.288	.338	.472
Don Mueller	OF122	L	26	131	480	56	160	12	2	6	60	19	13	2	.333	.360	.404
Monte Irvin	OF113	R	34	124	444	72	146	21	5	21	97	55	34	2	.329	.406	.541
Daryl Spencer	SS53,3B36,2B32	R	23	118	408	55	85	18	5	20	56	42	74	0	.208	.287	.424
Bobby Hofman	3B23,2B17	R	27	74	169	21	45	7	2	12	34	12	23	1	.266	.315	.544
Dusty Rhodes	OF47	L	26	76	163	18	38	7	0	11	30	10	28	0	.233	.277	.479
Tookie Gilbert	1B44	L	24	70	160	12	27	3	0	3	16	22	21	1	.169	.269	.244
Ray Noble	C41	R	34	46	97	15	20	0	1	4	14	19	14	1	.206	.353	.351
Sal Yvars†	C20	R	29	23	47	1	13	0	0	0	1	7	1	0	.277	.370	.277
Sam Calderone	C31	R	27	35	45	4	10	2	0	0	8	1	4	0	.222	.239	.267
Ray Katt	C8	R	26	8	29	2	5	1	0	0	1	1	3	0	.172	.200	.207
Bill Rigney	3B2,2B1	R	35	19	20	2	5	0	0	0	1	0	5	0	.250	.250	.250
George Wilson		L	27	11	8	0	1	0	0	0	0	2	2	0	.125	.364	.125

A. Dark, 8 G at 3B, 1 G at P

Pitcher	T	Age	G	GS	CG	ShO	IP	H	HR	BB	SO	W-L	Sv	ERA
Jim Hearn	R	32	36	32	6	0	196.2	206	22	84	77	9-12	0	4.53
Ruben Gomez	R	25	29	26	13	3	204.0	166	17	101	113	13-11	0	3.40
Larry Jansen	R	32	36	26	6	0	184.2	185	24	55	88	11-16	1	4.14
Sal Maglie	R	36	27	24	9	3	145.1	158	19	47	80	8-9	0	4.15
Al Worthington	R	24	20	17	5	2	102.0	103	6	54	52	4-8	0	3.44
Al Dark	R	31	1	1	0	0	1.0	1	1	1	0	0-0	0	18.00
Hoyt Wilhelm	R	29	68	0	0	0	145.0	127	13	77	71	7-8	15	3.04
Al Corwin	R	26	48	7	2	1	106.2	122	17	68	49	6-4	2	4.98
Dave Koslo	L	33	37	12	2	0	111.2	135	8	36	36	6-12	2	4.76
Marv Grissom†	R	35	21	7	3	0	84.1	83	6	31	46	4-2	0	3.95
Frank Hiller	R	32	19	1	0	0	33.2	43	6	15	10	2-1	0	6.15
Monte Kennedy	L	31	18	0	0	0	22.2	30	2	19	11	0-0	0	7.15
Bill Connelly	R	28	8	2	0	0	20.1	33	4	17	11	0-1	0	11.07
Max Lanier†	L	37	3	0	0	0	5.1	8	1	3	2	0-0	0	6.75
George Spencer	R	26	1	0	0	0	2.1	3	0	2	1	0-0	0	7.71

1953 Cincinnati Reds 6th NL 68-86 .442 37.0 GB

Rogers Hornsby (64-82)/Buster Mills (4-4)

Player	Gm by Position	B	Age	G	AB	R	H	2B	3B	HR	RBI	BB	SO	SB	Avg	OBP	Slg
Andy Seminick	C112	R	32	119	387	46	91	12	0	19	64	49	82	2	.235	.323	.413
Ted Kluszewski	1B147	L	28	149	570	97	180	25	0	40	108	55	34	2	.316	.380	.570
Rocky Bridges	2B115,SS6,3B3	R	25	122	432	52	98	13	2	1	21	37	42	6	.227	.288	.273
Bobby Adams	3B150	R	31	150	607	99	167	14	6	8	49	58	67	3	.275	.338	.357
Roy McMillan	SS155	R	22	155	557	51	130	15	4	5	43	43	52	2	.233	.290	.302
Jim Greengrass	OF153	R	25	154	606	86	173	22	7	20	100	47	83	6	.285	.340	.444
Gus Bell	OF151	L	24	151	610	102	183	37	5	30	105	48	72	0	.300	.354	.525
Willard Marshall	OF95	L	32	122	357	51	95	14	6	17	62	41	28	0	.266	.342	.482
Bob Borkowski	OF67,1B2	R	27	94	249	32	67	11	1	7	29	21	41	0	.269	.328	.406
Grady Hatton	2B35,1B10,3B5	L	30	83	159	22	37	3	1	7	22	29	24	0	.233	.351	.396
Hobie Landrith	C47	L	23	52	154	15	37	3	1	3	16	12	8	2	.240	.299	.331
Johnny Temple	2B44	R	25	63	110	14	29	4	0	1	9	7	12	1	.264	.314	.327
Bob Marquis	OF10	L	28	40	44	9	12	1	1	2	3	4	11	0	.273	.333	.477
Wally Post	OF11	R	23	11	33	3	8	1	0	1	4	4	6	1	.242	.324	.364
Frank Baldwin	C6	R	24	16	20	0	2	0	0	0	0	1	9	0	.100	.143	.100
George Lerchen	OF1	S	30	22	17	2	5	1	0	0	2	5	6	0	.294	.455	.353
Joe Szekely	OF3	R	28	5	13	0	1	0	0	0	0	0	3	0	.077	.077	.077
Hank Foiles†	C3	R	24	5	13	1	2	0	0	0	0	1	2	0	.154	.214	.154
Ed Bailey	C2	L	22	2	8	1	3	1	0	0	1	1	3	0	.375	.444	.500

Pitcher	T	Age	G	GS	CG	ShO	IP	H	HR	BB	SO	W-L	Sv	ERA
Ken Raffensberger	L	35	26	26	9	1	174.0	200	23	33	47	7-14	0	3.93
Harry Perkowski	L	30	33	25	7	2	193.0	204	26	62	70	12-11	2	4.52
Bud Podbielan	R	29	36	24	8	1	186.1	214	21	67	74	6-16	1	4.73
Fred Baczewski†	L	27	24	18	10	1	138.1	125	13	52	58	11-4	1	3.45
Joe Nuxhall	L	24	30	17	5	1	141.2	136	13	69	52	9-11	2	4.32
Bubba Church†	R	28	11	7	2	0	43.2	55	9	19	12	3-3	0	5.98
Howie Judson	R	27	10	6	0	0	38.2	58	8	11	11	0-1	0	5.59
Frank Smith	R	25	50	1	0	0	83.2	89	15	25	42	8-1	2	5.49
Clyde King	R	28	35	4	0	0	76.0	78	15	32	21	3-6	2	5.21
Jackie Collum†	L	26	30	12	4	1	124.2	123	8	39	51	7-11	3	3.75
Herm Wehmeier	R	26	28	10	2	0	81.2	100	20	47	32	1-6	0	7.16
Bob Kelly†	R	25	28	5	0	0	66.1	71	7	26	29	1-2	2	4.34
Ernie Nevel	R	33	10	0	0	0	10.1	16	0	1	5	0-0	0	6.10
Eddie Erautt†	R	28	4	0	0	0	4.2	11	1	3	1	0-0	0	5.79
Barney Martin	R	30	1	0	0	0	2.0	3	0	1	1	0-0	0	9.00
Ed Blake	R	27	1	0	0	0	0.0	1	0	1	0	0-0	0	—

1953 Chicago Cubs 7th NL 65-89 .422 40.0 GB

Phil Cavarretta

Player	Gm by Position	B	Age	G	AB	R	H	2B	3B	HR	RBI	BB	SO	SB	Avg	OBP	Slg
Clyde McCullough	C73	R	36	77	229	21	59	3	2	6	23	15	23	0	.258	.303	.367
Dee Fondy	1B149	L	28	150	595	79	184	24	11	18	78	44	106	10	.309	.358	.477
Eddie Miksis	2B92,SS53	R	26	142	577	61	145	17	6	8	39	33	59	13	.251	.293	.343
Randy Jackson	3B133	R	27	139	498	61	142	22	8	19	66	42	61	8	.285	.341	.476
Roy Smalley	SS77	R	27	82	253	20	63	9	0	6	25	28	57	0	.249	.329	.356
Frankie Baumholtz	OF130	L	34	133	520	75	159	36	7	3	25	42	36	3	.306	.359	.419
Ralph Kiner†	OF116	R	30	117	414	73	117	14	2	28	87	75	67	1	.283	.394	.529
Hank Sauer	OF105	R	36	108	395	61	104	16	5	19	60	50	56	0	.263	.349	.473
Bill Serena	2B49,3B28	R	28	93	275	30	69	10	5	10	52	41	46	0	.251	.350	.433
Joe Garagiola†	C68	L	27	74	228	21	62	9	4	1	21	21	23	0	.272	.336	.360
Hal Jeffcoat	OF100	R	28	106	183	22	43	3	1	4	22	21	26	5	.235	.314	.328
Tommy Brown	SS25,OF6	R	25	65	138	19	27	7	1	2	13	13	17	1	.196	.279	.304
Catfish Metkovich†	OF38,1B7	L	32	61	124	19	29	9	0	2	12	16	10	2	.234	.326	.355
Preston Ward†	OF27,1B7	L	25	33	100	10	23	5	0	4	12	18	21	3	.230	.347	.400
Toby Atwell†	C24	L	29	24	74	10	17	2	0	1	8	13	7	0	.230	.345	.297
Carl Sawatski	C15	L	25	43	59	5	13	3	0	1	5	7	7	0	.220	.303	.322
Gene Hermanski†	OF13	L	33	18	40	1	6	1	0	0	1	4	7	1	.150	.227	.175
Bob Ramazzotti	2B18	R	36	26	39	3	6	2	0	0	4	3	4	0	.154	.214	.205
Ernie Banks	SS10	R	22	10	35	3	11	1	1	2	6	4	5	0	.314	.385	.571
Dale Talbot	OF7	R	26	8	30	5	10	0	1	0	0	0	4	1	.333	.333	.400
Gene Baker	2B6	R	28	7	22	1	5	1	0	0	0	1	4	1	.227	.261	.273
Phil Cavarretta		L	36	27	21	3	6	3	0	0	3	6	3	0	.286	.444	.429
Bob Addis†	OF3	L	27	10	12	2	2	1	0	0	1	2	0	0	.167	.286	.250
Paul Schramka	OF1	L	25	2	0	0	0	0	0	0	0	0	0	0	—	—	—

Pitcher	T	Age	G	GS	CG	ShO	IP	H	HR	BB	SO	W-L	Sv	ERA
Warren Hacker	R	28	39	32	9	0	221.2	225	35	54	106	12-19	2	4.38
Bob Rush	R	27	29	28	8	1	166.2	177	17	66	84	9-14	0	4.54
Paul Minner	L	29	31	27	9	2	201.0	227	15	40	64	12-15	1	4.21
Howie Pollet†	L	32	25	16	2	0	111.1	120	6	44	45	5-6	1	4.12
Don Elston	R	24	2	1	0	0	5.0	11	1	0	2	0-1	0	14.40
Turk Lown	R	29	49	12	2	0	148.1	166	20	84	76	8-7	3	5.16
Johnny Klippstein	R	25	48	20	5	0	167.2	169	15	107	113	10-11	6	4.83
Dutch Leonard	R	44	45	0	0	0	62.2	72	9	24	27	2-3	8	4.60
Duke Simpson	R	25	30	1	0	0	45.0	60	8	25	21	1-2	0	8.00
Bubba Church†	R	28	27	11	1	0	104.1	115	16	49	47	4-5	1	5.00
Sheldon Jones	R	31	22	2	0	0	38.1	47	3	16	9	0-2	0	5.40
Bob Kelly†	R	25	14	0	0	0	17.0	27	2	9	6	0-1	0	9.53
Jim Willis	R	26	13	3	2	0	43.1	37	1	17	15	2-1	0	3.12
Fred Baczewski†	L	27	9	0	0	0	10.0	20	1	6	3	0-0	0	6.30
Bob Schultz†	L	29	7	2	0	0	11.2	13	2	11	4	0-2	0	5.40
Bill Moisan	R	27	3	0	0	0	5.0	5	0	2	1	0-0	0	5.40

1953 Pittsburgh Pirates 8th NL 50-104 .325 55.0 GB

Fred Haney

Player	Gm by Position	B	Age	G	AB	R	H	2B	3B	HR	RBI	BB	SO	SB	Avg	OBP	Slg
Mike Sandlock	C64	S	37	64	186	10	43	5	0	0	12	12	19	0	.231	.281	.258
Preston Ward†	1B78	L	25	88	281	35	59	7	1	8	27	44	39	1	.210	.319	.327
Johnny O'Brien	2B77,SS1	R	22	89	279	28	69	13	2	2	22	21	36	1	.247	.309	.330
Danny O'Connell	3B104,2B47	R	26	149	588	88	173	26	8	7	55	57	42	3	.294	.361	.401
Eddie O'Brien	SS81	R	22	89	261	21	62	5	3	0	14	17	30	6	.238	.289	.280
Frank Thomas	OF118	R	24	128	455	68	116	22	1	30	102	50	93	1	.255	.331	.505
Cal Abrams	OF112	L	29	119	448	66	128	10	6	15	43	58	70	4	.286	.368	.435
Carlos Bernier	OF86	R	26	105	310	48	66	7	8	3	31	51	53	15	.213	.332	.316
Paul Smith	1B74,OF19	L	22	118	389	41	110	12	7	4	44	24	23	3	.283	.329	.380
Hal Rice†	OF70	L	29	78	286	39	89	16	1	4	42	17	22	0	.311	.350	.416
Dick Cole	SS77,2B7,1B1	R	27	97	235	29	64	13	1	0	23	38	26	2	.272	.374	.336
Eddie Pellagrini	2B31,3B12,SS3	R	35	78	174	16	44	3	2	4	19	14	20	1	.253	.309	.362
Pete Castiglione†	3B43	R	32	45	159	14	33	2	1	4	21	5	14	1	.208	.236	.308
Ralph Kiner†	OF41	R	30	41	148	27	40	6	1	7	29	25	21	1	.270	.383	.466
Toby Atwell†	C45	L	29	53	139	11	34	6	0	0	17	20	12	0	.245	.352	.288
Vic Janowicz	C35	R	23	42	123	10	31	3	1	2	8	5	31	0	.252	.287	.341
Johnny Lindell†	P27,1B2	R	36	58	91	11	26	6	1	4	15	16	15	0	.286	.404	.505
Joe Garagiola†	C22	L	27	27	73	9	17	5	0	2	14	10	11	1	.233	.341	.384
Gene Hermanski†	OF13	L	33	41	62	7	11	0	0	1	4	8	14	0	.177	.282	.226
Felipe Montemayor	OF12	L	23	28	55	5	6	4	0	0	2	4	13	0	.109	.210	.182
Dick Smith	SS13	R	25	13	43	4	7	0	1	0	2	6	6	0	.163	.265	.209
Catfish Metkovich†	1B5,OF4	L	32	26	41	5	6	0	1	1	7	6	3	0	.146	.255	.268
Brandy Davis	OF9	R	24	12	39	5	8	2	0	0	2	0	3	0	.205	.205	.256
Dick Hall	2B7	R	22	7	24	2	4	0	0	0	1	1	3	1	.167	.200	.167
Ed Fitz Gerald†	C5	R	29	6	17	2	2	1	0	0	1	0	2	0	.118	.118	.176
Nick Koback	C6	R	17	7	16	1	2	0	1	0	0	1	4	0	.125	.176	.250
Pete Naton	C4	R	21	6	12	2	2	0	0	0	1	2	1	0	.167	.286	.167
Jack Shepard	C2	R	22	2	4	0	1	0	0	0	0	0	2	0	.250	.250	.250
Bob Addis†		L	27	4	3	0	0	0	0	0	0	0	2	0	.000	.000	.000
Clem Koshorek		R	28	1	1	0	0	0	0	0	0	0	1	0	.000	.000	.000

Pitcher	T	Age	G	GS	CG	ShO	IP	H	HR	BB	SO	W-L	Sv	ERA
Murry Dickson	R	36	45	26	10	1	200.2	240	27	58	88	10-19	4	4.53
Paul LaPalme	L	29	35	24	7	1	176.1	191	20	64	86	8-16	2	4.59
Bob Friend	R	22	32	24	8	0	170.2	193	18	57	66	8-11	0	4.90
Johnny Lindell†	R	36	27	23	13	1	175.2	173	17	116	102	5-16	0	4.71
Paul Pettit	L	21	10	5	0	0	28.0	33	1	20	14	1-2	0	7.71
Cal Hogue	R	25	3	2	2	0	19.0	19	4	16	10	1-1	0	5.21
Johnny Hetki	R	31	54	2	0	0	118.1	120	9	33	37	3-6	3	3.95
Roy Face	R	25	41	13	2	0	119.0	145	19	30	56	6-8	0	6.58
Bob Hall	R	29	37	17	6	1	152.0	172	17	72	68	3-12	1	5.39
Roger Bowman	L	25	30	2	0	0	65.1	65	9	29	36	0-4	0	4.82
Jim Waugh	R	19	29	11	1	0	90.1	108	21	56	23	4-5	0	6.48
Bob Schultz†	L	29	11	2	0	0	18.2	26	3	10	5	0-2	0	8.20
Howie Pollet†	L	32	5	2	0	0	12.2	27	2	6	8	1-1	0	10.66
Bill MacDonald	R	24	4	1	0	0	7.1	12	0	8	4	0-1	0	12.27
Woody Main	R	31	2	0	0	0	4.0	5	1	2	4	0-0	0	11.25

»1954 Cleveland Indians 1st AL 111-43 .721 — Al Lopez

Player	Gm by Position	B	Age	G	AB	R	H	2B	3B	HR	RBI	BB	SO	SB	Avg	OBP	Slg
Jim Hegan	C137	R	33	139	423	56	99	12	7	11	40	34	48	0	.234	.289	.374
Bill Glynn	1B96,OF1	L	28	111	171	19	43	3	2	5	18	12	21	3	.251	.297	.380
Bobby Avila	2B141,SS7	R	30	143	555	112	189	27	2	15	67	59	31	9	.341	.402	.477
Al Rosen	3B87,1B46,2B1*	R	30	137	466	76	140	20	2	24	102	85	43	6	.300	.404	.506
George Strickland	SS112	R	28	112	361	42	77	12	3	6	37	55	62	2	.213	.314	.313
Larry Doby	OF153	L	30	153	577	94	157	18	4	32	126	85	94	3	.272	.364	.484
Dave Philley	OF129	S	34	133	452	48	102	13	3	12	60	57	48	2	.226	.308	.347
Al Smith	OF109,3B21,SS4	R	26	131	481	101	135	29	6	11	50	88	65	2	.281	.398	.435
Vic Wertz†	1B83,OF5	L	29	94	295	33	81	14	2	14	48	34	40	0	.275	.344	.478
Wally Westlake	OF70	R	33	85	240	36	63	9	2	11	42	26	37	0	.263	.337	.454
Rudy Regalado	3B50,2B2	R	24	65	180	21	45	5	0	2	24	19	16	0	.250	.333	.311
Sam Dente	SS60,2B7	R	32	68	169	18	45	7	1	1	19	14	4	0	.266	.319	.337
Hank Majeski	2B25,3B10	R	37	57	121	10	34	4	0	3	17	7	14	0	.281	.320	.388
Dave Pope	OF28	L	33	60	102	21	30	2	1	4	13	10	22	2	.294	.354	.451
Hal Naragon	C45	L	25	46	101	10	24	2	2	0	12	9	12	0	.238	.300	.297
Dale Mitchell	OF6,1B1	L	32	53	60	6	17	1	0	1	6	9	1	0	.283	.377	.350
Luke Easter		L	38	6	6	0	1	0	0	0	0	0	2	0	.167	.167	.167
Mickey Grasso	C4	R	34	4	6	1	2	0	0	1	1	1	1	0	.333	.500	.833
Rocky Nelson	1B2	L	29	4	4	0	0	0	0	0	0	0	1	0	.000	.000	.000
Joe Ginsberg	C1	L	27	3	2	0	1	0	1	0	1	0	0	0	.500	.667	1.500
Jim Dyck		R	32	2	1	0	1	0	0	0	1	1	0	0	1.000	1.000	1.000
Bob Kennedy†	OF1	R	33	1	0	0	0	0	0	0	0	0	0	0	—	—	—

A. Rosen, 1 G at SS

Pitcher	T	Age	G	GS	CG	ShO	IP	H	HR	BB	SO	W-L	Sv	ERA
Early Wynn	R	34	40	36	20	3	270.2	225	21	83	155	23-11	2	2.73
Mike Garcia	R	30	45	34	13	5	258.2	220	6	71	129	19-8	5	2.64
Bob Lemon	R	33	36	33	21	2	258.1	228	12	92	110	23-7	0	2.72
Art Houtteman	R	26	32	25	11	1	188.0	198	14	59	68	15-7	0	3.35
Bob Feller	R	35	19	19	9	1	140.0	127	13	39	59	13-3	0	3.09
Ray Narleski	R	25	42	2	1	0	89.0	59	8	44	52	3-3	13	2.22
Don Mossi	L	25	40	5	2	0	93.0	56	5	39	55	6-1	7	1.94
Hal Newhouser	L	33	26	1	0	0	46.2	34	3	18	25	7-2	7	2.51
Bob Hooper	R	32	17	0	0	0	34.2	39	3	16	12	0-0	2	4.93
Dave Hoskins	R	28	14	1	0	0	26.2	29	3	10	9	0-1	0	3.04
Bob Chakales†	R	26	3	0	0	0	10.1	4	0	12	3	2-0	0	0.87
Jose Santiago	R	25	1	0	0	0	1.2	0	0	2	1	0-0	0	0.00
Dick Tomanek	L	23	1	0	0	0	1.2	1	1	1	0	0-0	0	5.40

1954 New York Yankees 2nd AL 103-51 .669 8.0 GB Casey Stengel

Player	Gm by Position	B	Age	G	AB	R	H	2B	3B	HR	RBI	BB	SO	SB	Avg	OBP	Slg
Yogi Berra	C149,3B1	L	29	151	584	88	179	28	6	22	125	56	29	0	.307	.367	.488
Joe Collins	1B117	L	31	130	343	67	93	20	2	12	46	51	37	2	.271	.365	.446
Gil McDougald	2B92,3B35	R	26	126	394	66	102	22	2	12	48	62	64	3	.259	.364	.416
Andy Carey	3B120	R	22	122	411	60	124	14	6	8	65	43	38	5	.302	.373	.423
Phil Rizzuto	SS126,2B1	R	36	127	307	47	60	11	0	2	15	41	23	3	.195	.291	.251
Mickey Mantle	OF144,SS4,2B1	S	22	146	543	129	163	17	12	27	102	102	107	5	.300	.408	.525
Irv Noren	OF116,1B1	L	29	125	426	70	136	21	6	12	66	43	38	4	.319	.377	.481
Hank Bauer	OF108	R	31	114	377	73	111	16	5	12	54	40	42	4	.294	.360	.459
Gene Woodling	OF89	L	31	97	304	33	76	12	5	3	40	53	35	3	.250	.358	.352
Jerry Coleman	2B79,SS30,3B1	R	29	107	300	39	65	7	1	3	21	26	29	3	.217	.278	.277
Bill Skowron	1B61,3B5,2B2	R	23	87	215	37	73	12	9	7	41	19	18	2	.340	.392	.577
Eddie Robinson	1B29	L	33	85	142	11	37	9	0	3	27	19	21	0	.261	.344	.387
Enos Slaughter	OF30	L	38	69	125	19	31	4	2	1	19	28	8	0	.248	.386	.336
Willie Miranda	SS88,2B4,3B1	S	28	92	116	12	29	4	2	1	12	10	10	0	.250	.300	.345
Bob Cerv	OF24	R	28	56	100	14	26	6	0	5	13	11	17	0	.260	.330	.470
Bobby Brown	3B17	L	29	28	60	5	13	1	0	1	7	8	3	0	.217	.304	.283
Charlie Silvera	C18	R	29	20	37	1	10	1	0	0	4	3	2	0	.270	.341	.297
Lou Berberet	C3	L	24	5	5	1	2	0	0	0	3	1	1	0	.400	.500	.400
Frank Leja	1B6	L	18	12	5	2	1	0	0	0	0	0	1	0	.200	.200	.200
Woodie Held	SS4,3B1	R	22	4	3	2	0	0	0	0	0	2	1	0	.000	.400	.000
Gus Triandos	C1	R	23	2	1	0	0	0	0	0	0	0	1	0	.000	.000	.000
Ralph Houk		R	34	1	1	0	0	0	0	0	0	0	0	0	.000	.000	.000

Pitcher	T	Age	G	GS	CG	ShO	IP	H	HR	BB	SO	W-L	Sv	ERA
Whitey Ford	L	25	34	28	11	3	210.2	170	10	101	125	16-8	1	2.82
Ed Lopat	L	36	26	23	7	0	170.0	189	14	33	54	12-4	0	3.55
Harry Byrd	R	29	25	21	5	1	132.1	131	10	43	52	9-7	0	2.99
Bob Grim	R	24	37	20	8	1	199.0	175	9	85	108	20-6	0	3.26
Allie Reynolds	R	39	36	18	5	4	157.1	133	13	66	100	13-4	7	3.32
Tom Morgan	R	24	32	17	7	4	143.0	149	8	40	34	11-5	1	3.34
Jim McDonald	R	27	16	10	3	1	71.0	54	3	45	20	4-1	0	3.17
Tommy Byrne	L	34	5	5	4	1	40.0	36	1	19	24	3-2	0	2.70
Bob Wiesler	L	23	6	5	0	0	30.1	28	0	30	25	3-2	0	4.15
Ralph Branca†	R	28	5	3	0	0	12.2	9	0	13	7	1-0	0	2.84
Bill Miller	L	26	2	1	0	0	5.2	9	0	1	6	0-1	0	6.35
Johnny Sain	R	36	45	0	0	0	77.0	66	11	15	33	6-6	22	3.16
Tom Gorman	R	29	23	0	0	0	36.2	30	1	14	31	0-0	2	2.21
Bob Kuzava†	L	31	20	3	0	0	39.2	46	3	18	22	1-3	1	5.45
Marlin Stuart†	R	35	10	0	0	0	18.1	28	0	12	2	3-0	1	5.40
Jim Konstanty†	R	37	9	0	0	0	18.1	11	0	6	3	1-1	2	0.98
Art Schallock	L	30	6	1	1	0	17.1	20	3	11	9	0-1	0	4.15

1954 Chicago White Sox 3rd AL 94-60 .610 17.0 GB Paul Richards (91-54)/Marty Marion (3-6)

Player	Gm by Position	B	Age	G	AB	R	H	2B	3B	HR	RBI	BB	SO	SB	Avg	OBP	Slg
Sherm Lollar	C93	R	29	107	316	31	77	13	0	7	34	37	28	0	.244	.334	.351
Ferris Fain	1B64	L	33	65	235	30	71	10	1	5	51	40	14	5	.302	.399	.417
Nellie Fox	2B155	L	26	155	631	111	201	24	8	2	47	51	12	16	.319	.372	.391
Cass Michaels	3B91,2B2	R	28	101	282	35	74	13	2	7	44	56	31	10	.262	.392	.397
Chico Carrasquel	SS155	R	28	155	620	106	158	28	3	12	62	85	67	7	.255	.348	.368
Minnie Minoso	OF146,3B9	R	31	153	568	119	182	29	18	19	116	77	46	18	.320	.411	.535
Jim Rivera	OF143	L	31	145	490	62	140	16	8	13	61	49	68	18	.286	.356	.431
Johnny Groth	OF125	R	27	125	422	41	116	20	0	7	60	42	37	3	.275	.341	.372
George Kell†	1B32,3B31,OF2	R	31	71	233	25	66	10	0	5	48	18	12	1	.283	.323	.391
Matt Batts†	C42	R	32	55	158	16	36	7	1	3	19	17	15	0	.228	.299	.342
Phil Cavarretta	1B44,OF9	R	37	71	158	21	50	6	0	3	24	26	12	4	.316	.417	.411
Carl Sawatski	C33	L	26	43	109	6	20	3	3	1	12	15	20	0	.183	.276	.294
Fred Marsh	3B36,SS3,1B2*	R	30	62	98	21	30	5	2	0	4	9	16	4	.306	.364	.398
Ron Jackson	1B35	R	20	40	93	10	26	4	0	4	10	6	20	2	.280	.333	.452
Ed McGhee†	OF34	R	29	42	75	12	17	1	0	0	5	12	8	5	.227	.333	.240
Willard Marshall	OF29	L	33	47	71	7	18	2	0	1	7	11	9	0	.254	.349	.324
Bob Boyd	OF13,1B12	L	28	29	56	10	10	3	0	0	5	4	3	2	.179	.233	.232
Jack Harshman	P35,1B1	L	26	36	56	6	8	1	0	2	5	12	21	0	.143	.290	.268
Sandy Consuegra	P39,3B1	R	33	39	48	4	11	0	0	0	3	3	11	0	.229	.275	.229
Bill Wilson†	OF19	R	25	20	35	4	6	1	0	2	5	7	5	0	.171	.310	.371
Grady Hatton†	3B10,1B3	L	31	13	30	3	5	1	0	0	3	5	3	1	.167	.278	.200
Joe Kirrene	3B9	R	22	9	23	4	7	1	0	0	4	5	2	1	.304	.448	.348
Red Wilson†	C8	R	25	8	20	2	4	0	0	1	1	1	2	0	.200	.238	.350
Bud Stewart	OF2	L	38	18	13	0	1	0	0	0	0	3	2	0	.077	.250	.077
Stan Jok†	3B3	R	28	3	12	1	2	0	0	0	2	1	2	0	.167	.231	.167
Don Nicholas		L	23	7	0	3	0	0	0	0	0	1	0	0	—	1.000	—
Bob Cain		L	29	1	0	1	0	0	0	0	0	0	0	0	—	—	—

F. Marsh, 1 G at OF

Pitcher	T	Age	G	GS	CG	ShO	IP	H	HR	BB	SO	W-L	Sv	ERA
Virgil Trucks	R	37	40	33	16	5	264.2	224	13	95	152	19-12	3	2.79
Bob Keegan	R	33	31	27	14	2	209.2	211	16	82	61	16-9	2	3.09
Billy Pierce	L	27	36	26	12	4	188.2	179	15	86	148	9-10	3	3.48
Jack Harshman	L	26	35	21	9	4	177.2	157	7	96	134	14-8	1	2.95
Don Johnson	R	27	46	16	3	3	144.0	129	14	43	68	8-7	7	3.13
Sandy Consuegra	R	33	39	17	3	2	154.0	142	9	35	31	16-3	3	2.69
Harry Dorish	R	32	37	6	2	1	109.0	88	9	29	48	6-4	6	2.72
Morrie Martin†	L	31	35	2	1	0	70.0	52	5	24	31	5-4	5	2.06
Mike Fornieles	R	22	15	6	0	0	42.0	41	4	14	18	1-2	1	4.29
Dick Strahs	R	30	9	0	0	0	14.1	16	0	8	8	0-0	1	5.65
Al Sima†	L	32	5	1	0	0	7.0	11	1	2	1	0-1	1	5.14
Tom Flanigan	L	19	2	0	0	0	1.2	1	0	1	0	0-0	0	0.00
Vito Valentinetti	R	25	1	0	0	0	1.0	4	1	2	1	0-0	0	54.00

1954 Boston Red Sox 4th AL 69-85 .448 42.0 GB Lou Boudreau

Player	Gm by Position	B	Age	G	AB	R	H	2B	3B	HR	RBI	BB	SO	SB	Avg	OBP	Slg
Sammy White	C133	R	25	137	493	46	139	25	2	14	75	21	50	1	.282	.307	.426
Harry Agganis	1B119	L	25	132	434	54	109	13	8	11	57	47	57	6	.251	.321	.394
Ted Lepcio	2B80,3B24,SS14	R	23	116	398	42	102	19	4	8	45	42	62	3	.256	.328	.384
Grady Hatton†	3B93,1B1,SS1	L	31	99	302	40	85	12	3	5	33	58	25	1	.281	.399	.391
Milt Bolling	SS107,3B5	R	23	113	370	42	92	20	3	6	36	47	55	2	.249	.337	.368
Jackie Jensen	OF151	R	27	152	580	92	160	25	7	25	117	79	52	22	.276	.359	.472
Jimmy Piersall	OF126	R	24	133	474	77	135	24	2	8	38	36	42	5	.285	.338	.395
Ted Williams	OF115	L	35	117	386	93	133	23	1	29	89	136	32	0	.345	.513	.635
Billy Goodman	2B72,1B27,OF13*	L	28	127	489	71	148	25	4	1	36	51	15	3	.303	.370	.376
Billy Consolo	SS50,3B18,2B12	R	19	91	242	23	55	7	1	1	11	33	69	2	.227	.324	.277
Karl Olson	OF78	R	23	101	227	25	59	12	2	1	20	12	23	2	.260	.293	.344
Sam Mele†	1B22,OF13	R	31	42	132	22	42	6	0	7	23	12	12	0	.318	.378	.523
Charlie Maxwell	OF27	L	27	74	104	9	26	4	1	0	5	12	21	3	.250	.328	.308
George Kell†	3B25	R	31	26	93	15	24	3	0	0	10	15	3	0	.258	.361	.290
Mickey Owen	C30	R	38	32	68	6	16	3	0	1	11	9	6	0	.235	.309	.324
Don Lenhardt†	OF13,3B1	R	31	44	66	5	18	4	0	3	17	3	9	0	.273	.310	.470
Del Wilber	C18	R	35	24	61	2	8	2	1	1	7	4	6	0	.131	.179	.246
Dick Gernert	1B6	R	25	14	23	2	6	2	0	0	1	6	4	0	.261	.414	.348
Floyd Baker†	3B7,2B1	L	37	21	20	1	4	2	0	0	3	0	1	0	.200	.200	.300
Hoot Evers†	OF1	R	33	6	8	1	0	0	0	0	0	0	2	0	.000	.000	.000
Moose Morton		R	23	1	1	0	0	0	0	0	0	0	1	0	.000	.000	.000

B. Goodman, 12 G at 3B

Pitcher	T	Age	G	GS	CG	ShO	IP	H	HR	BB	SO	W-L	Sv	ERA
Willard Nixon	R	26	31	30	8	2	199.2	182	16	87	102	11-12	0	4.06
Frank Sullivan	R	24	36	26	11	3	206.1	185	18	66	124	15-12	1	3.14
Tom Brewer	R	22	33	23	7	0	162.2	152	15	95	69	10-9	0	4.65
Leo Kiely	L	24	28	19	4	1	131.0	153	12	58	59	5-8	0	3.50
Mel Parnell	L	32	19	15	4	1	92.1	104	7	35	38	3-7	0	3.70
Bill Henry	L	26	24	13	3	1	95.2	104	9	49	38	3-7	0	4.52
Ellis Kinder	R	39	48	2	0	0	107.0	106	7	36	67	8-8	15	3.62
Hal Brown	R	29	40	5	1	0	118.0	126	6	41	66	1-8	0	4.12
Sid Hudson	R	39	33	5	0	0	71.1	83	5	30	27	3-4	5	4.42
Tex Clevenger	R	21	23	8	1	0	67.2	67	9	29	43	2-4	0	4.79
Russ Kemmerer	R	22	19	9	2	1	75.1	71	4	41	37	5-3	0	3.82
Tom Hurd	R	30	16	0	0	0	29.2	21	2	12	14	2-0	1	3.03
Tom Herrin	R	24	14	1	0	0	28.1	34	3	22	8	1-2	0	7.31
Bill Werle	L	33	14	0	0	0	24.2	41	5	10	14	0-1	0	4.38
Joe Dobson	R	37	2	0	0	0	2.2	5	0	1	1	0-0	0	6.75

1954 Detroit Tigers 5th AL 68-86 .442 43.0 GB

Fred Hutchinson

Player	Gm by Position	B	Age	G	AB	R	H	2B	3B	HR	RBI	BB	SO	SB	Avg	OBP	Slg
Frank House	C107	L	24	114	352	35	88	12	1	9	38	31	34	2	.250	.307	.366
Walt Dropo	1B95	R	31	107	320	27	90	14	2	4	44	24	41	0	.281	.328	.375
Frank Bolling	2B113	R	22	117	368	46	87	15	2	6	38	36	51	3	.236	.302	.337
Ray Boone	3B148,SS1	R	30	148	543	76	160	19	7	20	85	71	53	4	.295	.376	.466
Harvey Kuenn	SS155	R	23	155	656	81	201	28	6	5	48	29	13	9	.306	.335	.390
Bill Tuttle	OF145	R	24	147	530	64	141	20	11	7	58	62	60	5	.266	.343	.385
Al Kaline	OF135	R	19	138	504	42	139	18	3	4	43	22	45	9	.276	.305	.347
Jim Delsing	OF108	L	28	122	371	39	92	24	2	6	38	49	38	4	.248	.336	.372
Bob Nieman	OF63	R	27	91	251	24	66	14	1	8	35	22	32	0	.263	.319	.422
Wayne Belardi†	1B79	L	23	88	250	27	58	7	1	11	24	33	34	1	.232	.330	.400
Fred Hatfield	2B54,3B15	L	29	81	218	31	64	12	0	2	25	28	24	4	.294	.385	.376
Red Wilson†	C53	R	25	54	170	22	48	11	1	2	22	27	12	3	.282	.379	.394
Hoot Evers†	OF24	R	33	30	60	5	11	4	0	0	5	5	8	1	.183	.258	.250
Don Lund	OF31	R	31	35	54	4	7	2	0	0	3	4	3	1	.130	.186	.167
Steve Souchock	OF9,3B2	R	35	25	39	6	7	0	1	3	8	2	10	1	.179	.220	.462
Reno Bertoia	2B15,3B8,SS3	R	19	54	37	13	6	2	0	1	2	5	9	1	.162	.262	.297
Chuck Kress†	1B7,OF1	L	32	24	37	4	7	0	1	0	3	1	4	0	.189	.211	.243
Chick King	OF7	R	23	11	28	4	6	0	1	0	3	3	8	0	.214	.290	.286
Matt Batts†	C8	R	32	12	21	1	6	1	0	0	5	2	4	0	.286	.333	.333
Johnny Pesky†		L	34	20	17	5	3	0	0	1	1	3	1	0	.176	.300	.353
Al Lakeman	C4	R	35	5	6	0	0	0	0	0	0	0	1	0	.000	.000	.000
George Bullard	SS1	R	25	4	1	0	0	0	0	0	0	0	0	0	.000	.000	.000
Walt Streuli	C1	R	18	1	0	0	0	0	0	0	0	1	0	0	—	1.000	—

Pitcher	T	Age	G	GS	CG	ShO	IP	H	HR	BB	SO	W-L	Sv	ERA
Steve Gromek	R	34	36	32	17	4	252.2	236	26	57	102	18-16	1	2.74
Ned Garver	R	28	35	32	16	3	246.1	216	20	62	93	14-11	1	2.81
George Zuverink†	R	29	35	25	9	2	203.0	201	22	62	70	9-13	4	3.59
Billy Hoeft	L	22	34	25	10	4	175.0	180	22	59	114	7-15	1	4.58
Al Aber	L	26	32	18	4	0	124.2	121	8	40	54	5-11	3	3.97
Ted Gray	L	29	19	10	2	0	72.0	70	8	56	29	3-5	0	5.38
Ray Herbert	R	24	42	4	0	0	84.1	114	6	50	44	3-6	0	5.87
Dick Marlowe	R	25	38	2	0	0	84.0	76	11	40	39	5-4	2	4.18
Bob Miller	L	18	32	1	0	0	69.2	62	1	26	27	1-1	1	2.45
Ralph Branca†	R	28	17	5	0	0	45.1	63	10	30	15	3-3	0	5.76
Dick Weik	R	26	9	1	0	0	16.1	23	3	16	9	0-1	0	7.16
Frank Lary	R	24	3	0	0	0	3.2	4	0	3	5	0-0	0	2.45
Dick Donovan	R	26	2	0	0	0	6.0	9	1	5	2	0-0	0	10.50

1954 Washington Senators 6th AL 66-88 .429 45.0 GB

Bucky Harris

Player	Gm by Position	B	Age	G	AB	R	H	2B	3B	HR	RBI	BB	SO	SB	Avg	OBP	Slg
Ed Fitz Gerald	C107	R	30	115	360	33	104	13	5	4	40	33	22	0	.289	.349	.386
Mickey Vernon	1B148	L	36	151	597	90	173	33	14	20	97	61	61	1	.290	.357	.492
Wayne Terwilliger	2B90,3B10,SS3	R	29	106	337	42	70	10	1	3	24	32	40	3	.208	.282	.270
Eddie Yost	3B155	R	27	155	539	101	138	26	4	11	47	131	71	7	.256	.405	.380
Pete Runnels	SS107,2B27,OF1	L	26	139	488	75	131	17	15	3	56	78	60	2	.268	.368	.383
Jim Busby	OF155	R	27	155	628	83	187	22	7	7	80	43	56	17	.298	.342	.389
Roy Sievers	OF133,1B8	R	27	145	514	75	119	26	6	24	102	80	77	2	.232	.331	.446
Tom Umphlett	OF101	R	24	114	342	21	75	8	3	1	33	17	42	1	.219	.255	.269
Tom Wright	OF43	L	30	76	171	13	42	4	4	1	17	18	38	0	.246	.323	.333
Johnny Pesky†	2B37,SS1	L	34	49	158	17	40	4	3	0	9	10	7	1	.253	.296	.316
Joe Tipton	C52	R	32	54	157	9	35	6	1	1	10	30	30	0	.223	.353	.293
Jerry Snyder	SS48,2B3	R	24	64	154	17	36	3	1	0	17	15	18	3	.234	.298	.266
Jim Lemon	OF33	R	26	37	128	12	30	2	3	2	13	9	34	0	.234	.283	.344
Clyde Vollmer	OF26	R	32	62	117	8	30	4	0	2	15	12	28	0	.256	.331	.342
Mel Hoderlein	SS6,2B5	S	31	14	25	0	4	1	0	0	1	1	4	0	.160	.192	.200
Carlos Paula	OF6	R	26	9	24	2	4	1	0	0	2	2	4	0	.167	.231	.208
Bob Oldis	C8,3B2	R	26	11	24	1	8	1	0	0	1	0	3	0	.333	.360	.375
Roy Dietzel	2B7,3B2	R	23	9	21	1	5	0	0	0	1	5	4	0	.238	.385	.238
Harmon Killebrew	2B3	R	18	9	13	1	4	1	0	0	3	2	3	0	.308	.400	.385
Jesse Levan	3B4,1B1	L	27	7	10	1	3	0	0	0	0	0	0	0	.300	.300	.300
Steve Korcheck	C2	R	21	2	7	0	1	0	0	0	0	0	2	0	.143	.143	.143
Vito Valentinetti†		R	25	1	0	0	0	0	0	0	0	0	0	0	—	—	—

Pitcher	T	Age	G	GS	CG	ShO	IP	H	HR	BB	SO	W-L	Sv	ERA
Bob Porterfield	R	30	32	31	21	2	244.0	249	14	77	82	13-15	0	3.32
Mickey McDermott	L	26	30	26	11	1	196.1	172	8	110	95	7-15	1	3.44
Chuck Stobbs	L	24	31	24	10	3	182.0	189	6	67	67	11-11	0	4.10
Johnny Schmitz	L	33	29	23	12	2	185.1	176	6	64	56	11-8	1	2.91
Dean Stone	L	23	31	23	10	2	178.2	161	7	69	87	12-10	0	3.22
Camilo Pascual	R	20	48	4	1	0	119.1	126	7	61	60	4-7	3	4.22
Bunky Stewart	L	23	29	2	0	0	50.2	67	3	27	27	0-2	1	7.64
Spec Shea	R	33	23	11	1	0	71.1	97	9	34	22	2-9	0	6.18
Connie Marrero	R	43	22	8	1	0	66.1	74	12	22	26	3-6	0	4.75
Gus Keriazakos	R	22	22	3	2	0	59.2	59	4	30	33	2-3	0	3.77
Sonny Dixon†	R	29	16	0	0	0	29.2	26	3	12	7	1-2	1	3.03

1954 Baltimore Orioles 7th AL 54-100 .351 57.0 GB

Jimmy Dykes

Player	Gm by Position	B	Age	G	AB	R	H	2B	3B	HR	RBI	BB	SO	SB	Avg	OBP	Slg
Clint Courtney	C111	L	27	122	397	25	107	18	3	4	37	30	7	2	.270	.323	.360
Eddie Waitkus	1B78	L	34	95	311	35	88	17	4	2	33	28	25	0	.283	.341	.383
Bobby Young	2B127	L	29	130	432	43	106	13	6	4	24	54	42	4	.245	.329	.331
Vern Stephens	3B96	R	33	101	365	31	104	17	1	8	46	17	36	0	.285	.311	.403
Billy Hunter	SS124	R	26	125	411	28	100	9	5	2	27	21	38	5	.243	.281	.304
Chuck Diering	OF119	R	31	128	418	35	108	14	1	2	29	56	57	3	.258	.349	.311
Cal Abrams†	OF115	L	30	115	423	67	124	22	7	6	25	72	67	1	.293	.400	.421
Gil Coan	OF67	L	32	94	265	29	74	11	1	2	20	16	17	9	.279	.320	.351
Bob Kennedy†	3B71,OF21	R	33	106	323	37	81	13	2	6	45	28	43	2	.251	.306	.359
Dick Kryhoski	1B69	L	29	100	300	32	78	13	2	1	34	19	24	0	.260	.305	.327
Jim Fridley	OF67	R	29	85	240	25	59	8	5	4	36	21	41	0	.246	.311	.371
Sam Mele†	OF62	R	31	72	230	17	55	9	4	5	32	18	26	1	.239	.290	.378
Jim Brideweser	SS48,2B19	R	27	73	204	18	54	7	2	0	12	15	27	1	.265	.317	.319
Les Moss	C38	R	29	50	126	7	31	3	0	0	5	14	16	0	.246	.321	.270
Vic Wertz†	OF27	L	29	29	94	5	19	1	0	1	13	11	17	0	.202	.283	.245
Chico Garcia	2B24	R	29	39	62	6	7	0	2	0	5	8	3	0	.113	.211	.177
Ray Murray	C21	R	36	22	61	4	15	4	1	0	2	2	5	0	.246	.270	.344
Joe Durham	OF10	R	22	10	40	4	9	0	0	1	3	4	7	0	.225	.295	.300
Frank Kellert	1B9	R	29	10	34	3	7	2	0	0	1	5	4	0	.206	.308	.265
Don Lenhardt†	OF7,1B2	R	31	13	33	2	5	1	0	0	1	3	9	0	.152	.222	.182
Dick Kokos	OF1	L	26	11	10	1	2	0	0	1	1	4	3	0	.200	.429	.500
Neil Berry	SS5	R	32	5	9	1	1	0	0	0	0	1	2	0	.111	.200	.111

Pitcher	T	Age	G	GS	CG	ShO	IP	H	HR	BB	SO	W-L	Sv	ERA
Bob Turley	R	23	35	35	14	0	247.1	178	7	181	185	14-15	0	3.46
Joe Coleman	R	31	33	32	15	4	221.1	184	16	96	103	13-17	0	3.50
Don Larsen	R	24	29	28	12	1	201.2	213	18	89	80	3-21	0	4.37
Duane Pillette	R	31	25	25	11	1	179.0	158	9	67	66	10-14	0	3.12
Lou Kretlow	R	33	32	20	5	0	166.2	169	12	82	82	6-11	0	4.37
Bob Kuzava†	L	31	4	4	0	0	23.2	30	0	11	15	1-3	0	4.18
Vern Bickford	R	33	1	1	0	0	4.0	5	0	1	0	0-1	0	9.00
Bob Chakales†	R	26	38	6	0	0	89.1	81	8	43	44	3-7	3	3.73
Howie Fox	R	33	38	0	0	0	73.2	80	2	34	27	1-2	2	3.67
Mike Blyzka	R	25	37	0	0	0	86.1	83	2	51	35	1-5	1	4.69
Marlin Stuart†	R	35	22	0	0	0	38.1	46	2	15	13	1-2	2	4.46
Billy O'Dell	L	21	7	2	1	0	16.1	15	0	5	6	1-1	0	2.76
Dave Koslo†	L	34	3	1	0	0	14.1	20	1	3	3	0-1	0	3.14
Dick Littlefield†	R	28	3	0	0	0	6.0	8	0	6	5	0-0	0	10.50
Jay Heard	L	34	2	0	0	0	3.1	6	1	3	2	0-0	0	13.50
Ryne Duren	R	25	1	0	0	0	2.0	3	0	1	2	0-0	0	9.00

1954 Philadelphia Athletics 8th AL 51-103 .331 60.0 GB

Eddie Joost

Player	Gm by Position	B	Age	G	AB	R	H	2B	3B	HR	RBI	BB	SO	SB	Avg	OBP	Slg
Joe Astroth	C71	R	31	77	226	22	50	8	1	1	23	21	19	0	.221	.296	.279
Lou Limmer	1B79	L	29	115	316	41	73	10	3	14	32	35	37	2	.231	.305	.415
Spook Jacobs	2B131	R	28	132	508	63	131	11	1	0	26	60	22	17	.258	.336	.283
Jim Finigan	3B136	R	25	136	487	57	147	25	6	7	51	64	66	2	.302	.381	.421
Joe DeMaestri	SS142,2B1,3B1	R	25	146	539	49	124	16	3	8	40	20	63	1	.230	.258	.315
Bill Renna	OF117	R	29	123	422	52	98	15	4	13	53	41	60	1	.232	.302	.379
Vic Power	OF101,1B21,3B1*	R	26	127	462	36	118	17	5	8	38	19	19	2	.255	.287	.366
Bill Wilson†	OF91	R	25	94	323	43	77	10	1	15	33	39	59	1	.238	.334	.415
Gus Zernial	OF90,1B2	R	31	97	336	42	84	8	2	14	62	30	60	0	.250	.316	.411
Don Bollweg	1B71	L	33	103	268	35	60	15	3	5	24	35	33	1	.224	.319	.358
Elmer Valo	OF62	L	33	95	224	28	48	11	6	1	33	51	18	2	.214	.356	.330
Pete Suder	2B35,3B20,SS2	R	38	69	205	8	41	11	1	0	16	7	16	0	.200	.225	.263
Billy Shantz	C51	R	26	51	164	13	42	9	3	1	17	17	23	0	.256	.326	.366
Jim Robertson	C50	R	26	63	147	9	27	8	0	0	8	23	25	0	.184	.298	.238
Joe Taylor	OF16	R	28	18	58	5	13	1	1	1	8	2	9	0	.224	.250	.328
Ed McGhee†	OF13	R	29	21	53	5	11	2	0	2	9	4	8	0	.208	.259	.358
Eddie Joost	SS9,3B5,2B1	R	38	19	47	7	17	3	0	1	9	10	10	0	.362	.474	.489
Jack Littrell	SS9	R	25	9	30	7	9	2	0	1	3	6	3	1	.300	.417	.467

V. Power, 1 G at SS

Pitcher	T	Age	G	GS	CG	ShO	IP	H	HR	BB	SO	W-L	Sv	ERA
Arnie Portocarrero	R	22	34	33	16	1	248.0	233	25	114	132	9-18	0	4.06
Alex Kellner	L	29	27	27	8	1	173.2	204	16	88	69	6-17	0	5.39
Marion Fricano	R	30	37	20	4	1	151.2	163	17	64	43	5-11	1	5.16
Bob Trice	R	27	19	18	8	1	119.0	146	14	48	22	7-8	0	5.60
Johnny Gray	R	26	18	16	5	0	105.0	111	10	91	51	3-12	0	6.51
Charlie Bishop	R	30	20	12	4	0	96.0	98	10	50	34	4-6	1	4.41
Bobby Shantz	L	28	2	1	0	0	8.0	12	2	3	3	1-0	0	7.88
Carl Scheib†	R	27	1	1	0	0	2.0	5	0	1	1	0-1	0	22.50
Moe Burtschy	R	32	46	0	0	0	94.2	80	7	53	54	5-4	4	3.80
Sonny Dixon†	R	29	38	6	1	1	107.1	136	8	27	42	5-7	4	4.86
Al Sima†	L	32	29	7	1	0	79.1	101	9	32	36	2-5	2	5.22
Art Ditmar	R	25	14	5	0	0	39.1	50	4	36	14	1-4	0	6.41
Morrie Martin†	L	31	13	6	2	0	52.2	57	9	19	24	2-4	0	5.47
Dutch Romberger	R	27	10	0	0	0	15.2	28	3	12	6	1-1	0	11.49
Ozzie Van Brabant	R	27	9	2	0	0	26.2	35	3	18	10	0-2	0	7.09
Lee Wheat	R	24	8	1	0	0	28.1	38	1	9	7	0-2	0	5.72
Bill Oster	L	21	8	1	0	0	15.2	19	2	12	5	0-1	0	6.32
Bill Upton	R	25	2	0	0	0	5.0	6	1	1	2	0-0	1	1.80
Dick Rozek	L	27	2	0	0	0	1.1	0	0	3	0	0-0	0	6.75
Hal Raether	R	21	1	0	0	0	2.0	1	0	4	0	0-0	0	4.50

»1954 New York Giants 1st NL 97-57 .630 —

Leo Durocher

Player	Gm by Position	B	Age	G	AB	R	H	2B	3B	HR	RBI	BB	SO	SB	Avg	OBP	Slg
Wes Westrum	C98	R	31	98	246	25	46	3	1	8	27	45	60	0	.187	.315	.305
Whitey Lockman	1B145,OF2	L	27	148	570	73	143	17	3	16	60	59	31	2	.251	.318	.375
Davey Williams	2B142	R	26	142	544	65	121	18	3	9	46	43	33	1	.222	.284	.316
Hank Thompson	3B130,2B2,OF1	L	28	136	448	76	118	18	1	26	86	90	58	3	.263	.389	.482
Al Dark	SS154	R	32	154	644	98	189	26	6	20	70	27	40	5	.293	.325	.446
Don Mueller	OF153	L	27	153	619	90	212	35	8	4	71	22	17	2	.342	.363	.444
Willie Mays	OF151	R	23	151	565	119	195	33	13	41	110	66	57	8	.345	.411	.667
Monte Irvin	OF128,1B1,3B1	R	35	135	432	62	113	13	3	19	64	70	23	7	.262	.363	.438
Ray Katt	C82	R	27	86	200	26	51	7	1	9	33	19	29	1	.255	.314	.435
Dusty Rhodes	OF37	L	27	82	164	31	56	7	3	15	50	18	25	1	.341	.410	.695
Bobby Hofman	1B21,2B10,3B8	R	28	71	125	12	28	5	0	8	30	17	15	0	.224	.317	.456
Billy Gardner	3B30,2B13,SS5	R	26	62	108	10	23	5	0	1	7	6	19	0	.213	.261	.287
Bill Taylor	OF9	L	24	55	65	4	12	1	0	2	10	3	15	0	.185	.239	.292
Ebba St. Claire	C16	S	32	20	42	5	11	1	0	2	6	12	7	0	.262	.436	.429
Foster Castleman	3B2	R	23	13	12	0	3	0	0	0	0	0	3	0	.250	.308	.250
Joe Garagiola†	C3	L	28	5	11	1	3	2	0	0	1	1	2	0	.273	.308	.455
Hoot Evers†	OF4	R	33	12	11	1	1	0	0	1	3	0	6	0	.091	.091	.364
Eric Rodin	OF3	R	24	5	6	0	0	0	0	0	0	0	0	0	.000	.000	.000
Joey Amalfitano	3B4,2B1	R	20	9	5	2	0	0	0	0	0	0	4	0	.000	.000	.000
Ron Samford	2B3	R	24	12	5	2	0	0	0	0	0	0	1	0	.000	.000	.000
Harvey Gentry		L	28	5	4	0	1	0	0	0	1	1	0	0	.250	.400	.250
Bob Lennon		L	25	3	3	0	0	0	0	0	0	0	0	0	.000	.000	.000

Pitcher	T	Age	G	GS	CG	ShO	IP	H	HR	BB	SO	W-L	Sv	ERA
Johnny Antonelli	L	24	39	37	18	6	258.2	209	22	94	152	21-7	2	2.30
Ruben Gomez	R	26	37	32	10	4	221.2	202	20	109	106	17-9	0	2.88
Sal Maglie	R	37	34	32	9	1	218.1	222	21	70	117	14-6	2	3.26
Don Liddle	L	29	28	19	4	3	126.2	100	5	55	44	9-4	0	3.06
Jim Hearn	R	33	29	18	3	2	130.0	137	10	66	45	8-8	1	4.15
Larry Jansen	R	33	13	7	0	0	40.2	57	5	15	15	2-2	0	5.98
Hoyt Wilhelm	R	30	57	0	0	0	111.1	77	5	52	64	12-4	7	2.10
Marv Grissom	R	36	56	3	1	1	122.1	100	13	50	64	10-7	19	2.35
Windy McCall	L	28	33	4	0	0	61.0	50	5	29	38	2-5	2	3.25
Al Corwin	R	27	20	0	0	0	31.1	35	4	14	14	1-3	0	4.02
Al Worthington	R	25	10	1	0	0	18.0	21	0	15	8	0-2	0	3.50
Alex Konikowski	R	26	10	0	0	0	12.0	10	1	12	6	0-0	0	7.50
George Spencer	R	27	6	0	0	0	12.1	9	1	8	4	1-0	0	3.65
Ray Monzant	R	21	6	1	0	0	7.2	8	0	11	5	0-0	0	4.70
Paul Giel	R	21	6	0	0	0	4.1	8	0	2	4	0-0	0	8.31
Mario Picone†	R	27	5	0	0	0	13.2	13	1	11	6	0-0	0	5.27

1954 Brooklyn Dodgers 2nd NL 92-62 .597 5.0 GB

Walter Alston

Player	Gm by Position	B	Age	G	AB	R	H	2B	3B	HR	RBI	BB	SO	SB	Avg	OBP	Slg
Roy Campanella	C111	R	32	111	397	43	82	14	3	19	51	42	49	1	.207	.285	.401
Gil Hodges	1B154	R	30	154	579	106	176	23	5	42	130	74	84	3	.304	.373	.579
Jim Gilliam	2B143,OF4	S	25	146	607	107	171	28	8	13	52	76	30	8	.282	.361	.418
Don Hoak	3B75	R	26	88	261	41	64	9	5	7	26	25	39	8	.245	.318	.398
Pee Wee Reese	SS140	R	35	141	554	98	171	35	8	10	69	90	62	8	.309	.404	.455
Carl Furillo	OF149	R	32	150	547	56	161	23	1	19	96	49	35	2	.294	.356	.444
Duke Snider	OF148	L	27	149	584	120	199	39	10	40	130	84	96	6	.341	.423	.647
Jackie Robinson	OF74,3B50,2B4	R	35	124	386	62	120	22	4	15	59	63	20	7	.311	.413	.505
Sandy Amoros	OF70	L	24	79	263	44	72	18	6	9	34	31	24	1	.274	.353	.490
Billy Cox	3B58,2B11,SS8	R	34	77	226	26	53	9	2	2	17	21	13	0	.235	.297	.319
Rube Walker	C47	L	28	50	155	12	28	7	0	5	23	24	17	0	.181	.291	.323
Walt Moryn	OF20	L	28	48	91	16	25	4	2	2	14	7	11	0	.275	.330	.429
George Shuba	OF13	L	29	45	65	3	10	5	0	2	10	7	10	0	.154	.240	.323
Dick Williams	OF14	R	25	16	34	5	5	0	0	1	2	2	7	0	.147	.189	.235
Don Zimmer	SS13	R	23	24	33	3	6	0	1	0	0	3	8	2	.182	.270	.242
Don Thompson	OF29	L	30	34	25	2	1	0	0	0	1	5	5	0	.040	.226	.040
Tim Thompson	C2,OF1	L	30	10	13	2	2	1	0	0	1	1	1	0	.154	.214	.231
Chuck Kress†	1B1	L	32	13	12	1	1	0	0	0	2	0	0	0	.083	.083	.083
Wayne Belardi†		L	23	11	9	0	2	0	0	0	1	2	3	0	.222	.364	.222

Pitcher	T	Age	G	GS	CG	ShO	IP	H	HR	BB	SO	W-L	Sv	ERA
Carl Erskine	R	27	38	37	12	2	260.1	239	31	92	166	18-15	1	4.15
Russ Meyer	R	30	36	28	6	2	180.1	193	17	49	70	11-6	0	3.99
Don Newcombe	R	28	29	25	6	0	144.1	158	24	49	82	9-8	0	4.55
Johnny Podres	L	21	29	21	6	2	151.2	147	13	53	79	11-7	0	4.27
Billy Loes	R	24	28	21	6	0	147.2	154	14	60	97	13-5	0	4.14
Preacher Roe	L	39	15	10	1	0	63.0	69	11	23	31	3-4	0	5.00
Karl Spooner	L	23	2	2	2	2	18.0	7	0	6	27	2-0	0	0.00
Jim Hughes	R	31	60	0	0	0	86.2	76	7	44	58	8-4	24	3.22
Clem Labine	R	27	47	2	0	0	108.1	101	7	56	43	7-6	5	4.15
Erv Palica	R	26	25	3	0	0	67.2	77	9	31	25	3-3	0	5.32
Bob Milliken	R	27	24	3	0	0	62.2	58	12	18	25	5-2	2	4.02
Ben Wade†	R	31	23	0	0	0	45.0	62	9	21	25	1-1	3	8.20
Pete Wojey	R	34	14	1	0	0	27.2	24	3	14	21	1-1	1	3.25
Bob Darnell	R	23	6	1	0	0	14.1	15	2	7	5	0-0	0	3.14
Joe Black	R	30	5	0	0	0	7.0	11	3	5	3	0-0	0	11.57
Tom Lasorda	L	26	4	0	0	0	9.0	8	2	5	5	0-0	0	5.00

1954 Milwaukee Braves 3rd NL 89-65 .578 8.0 GB

Charlie Grimm

Player	Gm by Position	B	Age	G	AB	R	H	2B	3B	HR	RBI	BB	SO	SB	Avg	OBP	Slg
Del Crandall	C136	R	24	138	463	60	112	18	2	21	64	40	56	0	.242	.305	.425
Joe Adcock	1B133	R	26	133	500	73	154	27	5	23	87	44	58	1	.308	.365	.520
Danny O'Connell	2B103,3B35,1B8*	R	27	146	541	61	151	28	4	2	37	38	46	2	.279	.326	.357
Eddie Mathews	3B127,OF10	L	22	138	476	96	138	21	4	40	103	113	61	10	.290	.423	.603
Johnny Logan	SS154	R	27	154	560	66	154	17	7	8	66	51	51	2	.275	.339	.373
Bill Bruton	OF141	L	28	142	567	89	161	20	7	4	30	40	78	34	.284	.336	.365
Andy Pafko	OF138	R	33	138	510	61	146	22	4	14	69	37	36	1	.286	.335	.427
Hank Aaron	OF116	R	20	122	468	58	131	27	6	13	69	28	39	2	.280	.322	.447
Jack Dittmer	2B55	L	26	66	192	22	47	8	0	6	20	19	17	0	.245	.319	.380
Jim Pendleton	OF50	R	30	71	173	20	38	3	1	1	16	4	21	2	.220	.236	.266
Catfish Metkovich	1B18,OF13	L	33	68	123	7	34	5	1	1	15	15	15	0	.276	.352	.358
Bobby Thomson	OF26	R	30	43	99	7	23	3	0	2	15	12	29	0	.232	.315	.323
Charlie White	C28	L	25	50	93	14	22	4	0	1	8	9	8	0	.237	.304	.312
Roy Smalley	SS9,2B7,1B2	R	28	25	36	5	8	0	0	1	7	4	9	0	.222	.310	.306
Sam Calderone	C16	R	28	22	29	3	11	2	0	0	5	4	4	0	.379	.441	.448
Mel Roach	1B1	R	21	3	4	0	0	0	0	0	0	0	1	0	.000	.000	.000
Billy Queen	OF1	R	25	3	2	0	0	0	0	0	0	0	2	0	.000	.000	.000
Sibby Sisti		R	33	9	0	2	0	0	0	0	0	0	0	0	—	—	—

D. O'Connell, 1 G at SS

Pitcher	T	Age	G	GS	CG	ShO	IP	H	HR	BB	SO	W-L	Sv	ERA
Warren Spahn	L	33	39	34	23	1	283.1	262	24	86	136	21-12	2	3.14
Lew Burdette	R	27	38	32	13	4	238.0	224	17	62	79	15-14	0	2.76
Gene Conley	R	23	28	27	12	2	194.1	171	17	79	113	14-9	0	2.96
Chet Nichols	L	23	35	20	5	1	122.1	132	5	65	55	9-11	1	4.41
Jim Wilson	R	32	27	19	6	4	127.2	129	12	36	52	8-2	0	3.52
Dave Jolly	R	29	47	1	0	0	111.1	87	6	64	62	11-6	10	2.43
Ernie Johnson	R	30	40	4	1	0	99.1	77	11	34	68	5-2	2	2.81
Bob Buhl	R	25	31	14	2	1	110.1	117	5	65	57	2-7	3	4.00
Ray Crone	R	22	19	2	1	0	49.0	44	6	19	33	1-0	1	2.02
Joey Jay	R	18	15	1	0	0	18.0	21	2	16	13	1-0	0	6.50
Dave Koslo†	L	34	12	0	0	0	17.1	13	0	9	7	1-1	1	3.12
Phil Paine	R	24	11	0	0	0	14.0	14	1	12	11	1-0	0	3.86
Charlie Gorin	L	26	5	0	0	0	9.2	5	0	6	12	0-1	0	1.86

1954 Philadelphia Phillies 4th NL 75-79 .487 22.0 GB

Steve O'Neill (40-37)/Terry Moore (35-42)

Player	Gm by Position	B	Age	G	AB	R	H	2B	3B	HR	RBI	BB	SO	SB	Avg	OBP	Slg
Smoky Burgess	C91	L	27	108	345	41	127	27	5	4	46	42	11	1	.368	.432	.510
Earl Torgeson	1B133	L	30	135	490	63	133	22	6	5	54	75	52	7	.271	.364	.371
Granny Hamner	2B152,SS1	R	27	152	596	83	178	39	11	13	89	53	44	1	.299	.351	.466
Puddin' Head Jones	3B141	R	28	142	535	64	145	28	3	12	56	61	54	4	.271	.342	.402
Bobby Morgan	SS129,3B8,2B5	R	28	135	455	58	119	25	2	14	50	70	68	3	.262	.357	.418
Richie Ashburn	OF153	L	27	153	559	111	175	16	8	1	41	125	46	11	.313	.441	.376
Del Ennis	OF142,1B1	R	29	145	556	73	145	23	2	25	119	50	60	2	.261	.318	.444
Danny Schell	OF69	R	26	92	272	25	77	14	3	7	33	17	31	0	.283	.327	.434
Stan Lopata	C75,1B1	R	28	86	259	42	75	14	5	14	42	33	37	1	.290	.369	.544
Johnny Wyrostek	OF55,1B22	L	34	92	259	28	62	12	4	3	28	29	39	0	.239	.314	.351
Mel Clark	OF63	R	27	83	233	26	56	9	7	1	24	17	21	0	.240	.291	.352
Ted Kazanski	SS38	R	20	39	104	7	14	2	0	1	8	4	14	0	.135	.164	.183
Floyd Baker†	3B7,2B2	L	37	23	22	0	5	0	0	0	0	5	4	0	.227	.370	.227
Jim Command	3B6	L	25	9	18	1	4	1	0	1	6	2	4	0	.222	.300	.444
Gus Niarhos	C3	R	33	3	5	0	1	0	0	0	0	0	1	0	.200	.200	.200
Johnny Lindell		R	37	7	5	0	1	0	0	0	2	2	3	0	.200	.429	.200
Stan Palys	OF1	R	24	2	4	0	1	0	0	0	0	1	1	0	.250	.400	.250
Mickey Micelotta	SS1	R	25	13	3	2	0	0	0	0	0	1	1	0	.000	.250	.000
Stan Jok†		R	28	3	3	0	0	0	0	0	0	0	2	0	.000	.000	.000

Pitcher	T	Age	G	GS	CG	ShO	IP	H	HR	BB	SO	W-L	Sv	ERA
Robin Roberts	R	27	45	38	29	4	336.2	289	35	56	185	23-15	4	2.97
Curt Simmons	L	25	34	33	21	3	253.0	226	14	98	125	14-15	1	2.81
Murry Dickson	R	37	40	31	12	4	226.1	256	31	73	64	10-20	3	3.78
Herm Wehmeier†	R	27	25	17	10	2	138.0	117	10	51	49	10-8	0	3.85
Bob Miller	R	28	30	16	5	0	150.0	176	14	39	42	7-9	0	4.56
Paul Penson	R	22	5	3	0	0	16.0	14	1	14	3	1-1	0	4.50
Steve Ridzik	R	25	35	6	0	0	80.2	72	7	44	45	4-5	0	4.13
Jim Konstanty†	R	37	33	1	0	0	50.1	62	7	12	11	2-3	3	3.75
Ron Mrozinski	L	23	15	4	1	0	48.0	49	10	25	26	1-1	0	4.50
Bob Greenwood	R	26	11	4	0	0	36.2	28	2	18	9	1-2	0	3.19
Thornton Kipper	R	25	11	0	0	0	13.2	22	0	12	5	0-0	1	7.90
Karl Drews†	R	34	8	0	0	0	16.0	18	2	8	6	1-0	0	5.63

1954 Cincinnati Reds 5th NL 74-80 .481 23.0 GB

Birdie Tebbetts

Player	Gm by Position	B	Age	G	AB	R	H	2B	3B	HR	RBI	BB	SO	SB	Avg	OBP	Slg
Andy Seminick	C82	R	33	86	247	25	58	9	4	7	30	48	39	0	.235	.362	.389
Ted Kluszewski	1B149	L	29	149	573	104	187	28	3	49	141	78	35	0	.326	.407	.642
Johnny Temple	2B144	R	26	146	505	60	155	14	8	0	44	62	24	21	.307	.384	.366
Bobby Adams	3B93,2B2	R	32	110	390	69	105	25	6	3	23	55	46	2	.269	.362	.387
Roy McMillan	SS154	R	23	154	588	86	147	21	2	4	42	47	54	4	.250	.308	.313
Gus Bell	OF153	L	25	153	619	104	185	38	7	17	101	48	58	5	.299	.349	.465
Jim Greengrass	OF137	R	26	139	542	79	152	27	4	27	95	41	81	0	.280	.329	.494
Wally Post	OF116	R	24	130	451	46	115	21	3	18	83	26	70	2	.255	.297	.435
Chuck Harmon	3B67,1B3	R	30	94	286	39	68	7	3	2	25	17	27	7	.238	.277	.304
Ed Bailey	C61	L	23	73	183	21	36	2	3	9	20	35	34	1	.197	.324	.388
Bob Borkowski	OF36,1B3	R	28	73	162	13	43	12	1	1	19	8	18	0	.265	.299	.370
Lloyd Merriman	OF25	L	29	73	112	12	30	8	1	0	16	23	10	3	.268	.397	.357
Hobie Landrith	C42	L	24	48	81	12	16	0	0	5	14	18	9	1	.198	.340	.383
Nino Escalera	OF14,1B8,SS1	L	24	73	69	15	11	1	1	0	3	7	11	1	.159	.234	.203
Rocky Bridges	SS20,2B19,3B13	R	26	53	52	4	12	1	0	0	2	7	7	0	.231	.322	.250
Jim Bolger	OF2	R	22	5	3	1	1	0	0	0	0	0	1	0	.333	.333	.333
Dick Murphy		L	22	6	1	1	0	0	0	0	0	0	1	0	.000	.000	.000
Grady Hatton†		L	31	1	1	0	0	0	0	0	0	0	0	0	.000	.000	.000
Johnny Lipon		R	31	1	1	0	0	0	0	0	0	0	0	0	.000	.000	.000
Connie Ryan		R	34	1	0	0	0	0	0	0	0	1	0	0	—	1.000	—

Pitcher	T	Age	G	GS	CG	ShO	IP	H	HR	BB	SO	W-L	Sv	ERA
Art Fowler	R	31	40	29	8	1	227.2	256	20	85	93	12-10	0	3.83
Corky Valentine	R	25	36	28	7	3	194.1	211	24	60	73	12-11	1	4.45
Bud Podbielan	R	30	27	24	4	0	131.0	157	20	58	42	7-10	0	5.36
Fred Baczewski	L	28	29	22	4	1	130.0	159	22	53	43	6-6	0	5.26
Jim Pearce	R	29	2	1	1	0	11.0	7	0	5	3	1-0	0	0.00
Frank Smith	R	26	50	0	0	0	81.0	60	15	29	51	5-8	20	2.67
Howie Judson	R	28	37	8	0	0	93.1	86	9	42	27	5-7	3	3.95
Jackie Collum	L	27	36	2	1	0	79.0	86	8	32	28	7-3	0	3.76
Joe Nuxhall	L	25	35	14	5	1	166.2	188	11	59	85	12-5	0	3.89
Harry Perkowski	L	31	28	12	3	1	95.2	100	16	62	32	2-8	0	6.11
Karl Drews†	R	34	22	9	1	1	60.0	79	6	19	29	4-4	0	6.00
Moe Savransky	L	25	16	0	0	0	24.0	23	6	8	7	0-2	0	4.88
Herm Wehmeier†	R	27	12	3	0	0	33.2	36	6	21	13	0-3	2	6.68
Ken Raffensberger	L	36	6	1	0	0	10.1	15	2	3	5	0-2	0	7.84
Mario Picone†	R	27	4	1	0	0	10.1	9	3	7	1	0-1	0	6.10
Cliff Ross	L	25	4	0	0	0	2.2	0	0	0	1	0-0	1	0.00
Jerry Lane	R	28	3	0	0	0	10.2	9	0	3	2	1-0	0	1.69
George Zuverink†	R	29	2	0	0	0	6.0	10	1	1	2	0-0	0	9.00

1954 St. Louis Cardinals 6th NL 72-82 .468 25.0 GB

Eddie Stanky

Player	Gm by Position	B	Age	G	AB	R	H	2B	3B	HR	RBI	BB	SO	SB	Avg	OBP	Slg
Bill Sarni	C118	R	26	123	380	40	114	18	4	9	70	25	42	3	.300	.337	.439
Joe Cunningham	1B85	L	22	85	310	40	88	11	3	11	50	43	40	1	.284	.375	.445
Red Schoendienst	2B144	S	31	148	610	98	192	38	8	5	79	54	22	4	.315	.366	.428
Ray Jablonski	3B149,1B1	R	27	152	611	80	181	33	3	12	104	49	42	9	.296	.345	.419
Alex Grammas	SS142,3B1	R	28	142	401	57	106	17	4	2	29	40	29	6	.264	.335	.342
Rip Repulski	OF152	R	26	152	619	99	175	39	5	19	79	43	75	8	.283	.329	.454
Stan Musial	OF152,1B10	L	33	153	591	120	195	41	9	35	126	103	39	1	.330	.428	.607
Wally Moon	OF148	L	24	151	635	106	193	29	9	12	76	71	73	18	.304	.371	.435
Tom Alston	1B65	L	28	66	244	28	60	14	2	4	34	24	41	3	.246	.317	.369
Solly Hemus	SS66,3B27,2B12	L	31	124	214	43	65	15	3	2	27	55	27	5	.304	.453	.430
Del Rice	C52	R	31	56	147	13	37	10	1	2	16	16	21	0	.252	.321	.374
Joe Frazier	OF11,1B1	L	31	81	88	8	26	5	2	3	18	13	17	0	.295	.388	.500
Peanuts Lowrey	OF12	R	35	74	61	6	7	1	2	0	5	9	9	0	.115	.222	.197
Sal Yvars	C21	R	30	38	57	8	14	4	0	2	8	6	5	1	.246	.328	.421
Tom Burgess	OF4	L	26	17	21	2	1	1	0	0	1	3	9	0	.048	.167	.095
Steve Bilko†	1B6	R	25	8	14	1	2	0	0	0	1	3	1	0	.143	.294	.143
Dick Schofield	SS11	S	19	43	7	17	1	0	1	0	1	0	3	1	.143	.143	.429
Pete Castiglione	3B5	R	33	5	0	1	0	0	0	0	0	0	0	0	—	—	—

Pitcher	T	Age	G	GS	CG	ShO	IP	H	HR	BB	SO	W-L	Sv	ERA
Harvey Haddix	L	28	43	35	13	3	259.2	247	26	77	184	18-13	4	3.57
Vic Raschi	R	35	30	29	6	2	179.0	182	24	71	73	8-9	0	4.73
Brooks Lawrence	R	29	35	18	8	0	158.2	141	17	72	72	15-6	1	3.74
Tom Poholsky	R	24	25	13	4	0	106.0	101	11	20	55	5-7	0	3.06
Gordon Jones	R	24	11	10	4	2	81.0	78	3	19	48	4-4	0	2.00
Ralph Beard	R	25	13	10	0	0	58.0	62	2	28	17	0-4	0	3.72
Bill Greason	R	29	3	2	0	0	4.0	8	4	4	2	0-1	0	13.50
Memo Luna	L	24	1	1	0	0	0.2	2	0	2	0	0-1	0	27.00
Al Brazle	L	40	58	0	0	0	84.1	93	10	24	30	5-4	8	4.16
Gerry Staley	R	33	48	20	3	1	155.2	198	21	47	50	7-13	2	5.26
Joe Presko	R	25	37	6	1	1	71.2	97	14	41	36	4-9	0	6.91
Cot Deal	R	31	33	0	0	0	71.2	85	14	36	25	2-3	1	6.28
Royce Lint	L	33	30	4	1	1	70.1	75	9	30	36	2-3	0	4.86
Stu Miller	R	26	19	4	0	0	46.2	55	5	29	22	2-3	2	5.79
Ben Wade†	R	31	13	0	0	0	23.0	27	3	15	19	0-0	0	5.48
Mel Wright	R	26	9	0	0	0	10.1	16	2	11	4	0-0	0	10.45
Hal White	R	35	4	0	0	0	5.0	11	2	4	2	0-0	0	19.80
Carl Scheib†	R	27	3	1	0	0	4.2	6	3	5	5	0-1	0	11.57

1954 Chicago Cubs 7th NL 64-90 .416 33.0 GB

Stan Hack

Player	Gm by Position	B	Age	G	AB	R	H	2B	3B	HR	RBI	BB	SO	SB	Avg	OBP	Slg
Joe Garagiola†	C55	L	28	63	153	16	43	5	0	5	21	28	12	0	.281	.403	.412
Dee Fondy	1B138	L	29	141	568	77	162	30	4	9	49	35	84	20	.285	.326	.400
Gene Baker	2B134	R	29	135	541	68	149	32	5	13	61	47	55	4	.275	.333	.425
Randy Jackson	3B124	R	28	126	484	77	132	17	6	19	67	44	55	2	.273	.333	.450
Ernie Banks	SS154	R	23	154	593	70	163	19	7	19	79	40	50	6	.275	.326	.427
Ralph Kiner	OF147	R	31	147	557	88	159	36	5	22	73	76	90	2	.285	.371	.487
Hank Sauer	OF141	R	37	142	520	98	150	18	1	41	103	70	68	2	.288	.375	.563
Dale Talbot	OF111	R	27	114	403	45	97	15	4	1	19	16	25	3	.241	.274	.305
Frankie Baumholtz	OF71	L	35	90	303	38	90	12	6	4	28	20	15	1	.297	.340	.416
Walker Cooper†	C48	R	39	57	158	21	49	10	2	7	32	21	23	0	.310	.398	.532
El Tappe	C46	R	27	46	119	5	22	3	0	0	4	10	9	0	.185	.246	.210
Eddie Miksis	2B21,3B2,OF1	R	27	38	99	9	20	3	0	2	3	3	9	1	.202	.225	.293
Steve Bilko†	1B22	R	25	47	92	11	22	8	1	4	12	11	24	0	.239	.320	.478
Clyde McCullough	C26,3B3	R	37	31	81	9	21	7	0	3	17	5	5	0	.259	.310	.457
Hal Rice†	OF24	L	30	51	72	5	11	0	0	0	5	8	15	0	.153	.235	.153
Vern Morgan	3B15	L	25	24	64	3	15	2	0	0	2	1	10	0	.234	.242	.266
Bill Serena	3B12,2B2	R	29	41	63	8	10	0	1	4	13	14	18	0	.159	.316	.381
Jim Fanning	C11	R	26	11	38	2	7	0	0	0	1	1	7	0	.184	.205	.184
Hal Jeffcoat	P43,OF3	R	29	56	31	13	8	2	1	1	6	1	7	2	.258	.265	.484
Luis Marquez†	OF14	R	28	17	12	2	1	0	0	0	0	2	4	3	.083	.214	.083
Don Robertson	OF6	L	23	14	6	2	0	0	0	0	0	0	2	0	.000	.000	.000
Bruce Edwards		R	30	4	3	1	0	0	0	0	1	2	2	0	.000	.400	.000
Chris Kitsos	SS1	S	26	1	0	0	0	0	0	0	0	0	0	0	—	—	—

Pitcher	T	Age	G	GS	CG	ShO	IP	H	HR	BB	SO	W-L	Sv	ERA
Bob Rush	R	28	33	32	11	0	236.1	213	12	103	124	13-15	0	3.77
Paul Minner	L	30	32	29	12	0	218.0	236	19	50	79	11-11	1	3.96
Johnny Klippstein	R	26	36	21	4	0	148.0	155	13	96	69	4-11	1	5.29
Howie Pollet	L	33	20	20	4	2	128.1	131	4	54	58	8-10	0	3.58
Dave Cole	R	23	18	14	2	1	84.0	74	7	62	37	3-8	0	5.36
Al Lary	R	25	1	1	0	0	6.0	3	0	7	4	0-0	0	3.00
Jim Davis	L	29	46	12	2	0	127.2	114	12	51	58	11-7	4	3.52
Hal Jeffcoat	R	29	43	3	1	0	104.0	110	12	58	35	5-6	7	5.19
Warren Hacker	R	29	39	18	4	1	158.2	157	28	37	80	6-13	2	4.25
Bill Tremel	R	24	33	0	0	0	51.1	45	3	28	21	1-2	4	4.21
Jim Brosnan	R	24	18	0	0	0	33.1	44	9	18	17	1-0	0	9.45
Turk Lown	R	30	15	0	0	0	22.0	23	1	15	16	0-2	0	6.14
Jim Willis	R	27	14	1	0	0	23.0	22	1	18	5	0-1	0	3.91
Bob Zick	R	27	8	0	0	0	16.1	23	1	7	9	0-0	0	8.27
Bubba Church	R	29	7	3	1	0	14.2	21	8	13	8	1-3	0	9.82
John Pyecha	R	22	1	0	0	0	2.2	4	1	2	2	0-1	0	10.13

1954 Pittsburgh Pirates 8th NL 53-101 .344 44.0 GB

Fred Haney

Player	Gm by Position	B	Age	G	AB	R	H	2B	3B	HR	RBI	BB	SO	SB	Avg	OBP	Slg
Toby Atwell	C88	L	30	96	287	36	83	8	4	3	26	43	21	2	.289	.384	.376
Bob Skinner	1B118,OF2	L	22	132	470	67	117	15	9	8	46	47	59	4	.249	.316	.370
Curt Roberts	2B131	R	24	134	496	47	115	18	7	1	36	55	49	6	.232	.309	.302
Dick Cole	SS66,3B55,2B17	R	28	138	486	40	131	22	5	1	40	41	48	0	.270	.323	.342
Gair Allie	SS95,3B19	R	22	121	418	38	83	8	6	3	30	56	84	1	.199	.294	.268
Frank Thomas	OF153	R	25	153	577	81	172	32	7	23	94	51	74	3	.298	.359	.497
Dick Hall	OF102	R	23	112	310	38	74	8	4	2	27	33	46	3	.239	.304	.310
Jerry Lynch	OF83	L	23	98	284	27	68	4	5	8	36	20	43	2	.239	.290	.373
Sid Gordon	OF73,3B40	R	36	131	363	38	111	12	0	12	49	67	24	0	.306	.405	.438
Preston Ward	1B48,OF42,3B11	L	26	117	360	37	97	16	2	7	48	39	61	0	.269	.337	.383
Jack Shepard	C67	R	23	82	227	24	69	8	2	3	22	26	33	0	.304	.370	.396
Eddie Pellagrini	3B31,2B7,SS1	R	36	73	125	12	27	6	0	0	16	9	21	0	.216	.288	.264
Hal Rice†	OF24	L	30	28	81	10	14	4	1	1	9	14	24	0	.173	.295	.284
Vic Janowicz	3B18,OF1	R	24	41	73	10	11	3	0	0	2	7	23	0	.151	.235	.192
Vern Law	P39,OF1	R	24	50	52	10	12	5	0	1	13	5	8	0	.231	.310	.385
Cal Abrams†	OF13	L	30	17	42	6	6	1	1	0	2	10	9	0	.143	.308	.214
Dick Smith	3B9	R	26	12	31	2	3	1	1	0	0	6	5	0	.097	.243	.194
Gail Henley	OF9	L	25	14	30	7	9	1	0	1	2	4	4	0	.300	.382	.433
Jim Mangan	C7	R	24	14	26	2	5	0	0	0	2	4	9	0	.192	.300	.192
Walker Cooper†	C2	R	39	14	15	0	3	2	0	0	1	2	1	0	.200	.294	.333
Nick Koback	C4	R	18	4	10	0	0	0	0	0	0	0	8	0	.000	.000	.000
Luis Marquez†	OF4	R	28	14	9	3	1	0	0	0	0	4	0	0	.111	.385	.111
Bill Hall	C1	L	25	5	7	0	0	0	0	0	0	0	0	0	.000	.000	.000
Sam Jethroe	OF1	S	36	2	1	0	0	0	0	0	0	0	0	0	.000	.000	.000

Pitcher	T	Age	G	GS	CG	ShO	IP	H	HR	BB	SO	W-L	Sv	ERA
Max Surkont	R	32	33	29	11	0	208.1	216	25	78	78	9-18	0	4.41
Dick Littlefield†	L	28	23	21	7	1	155.0	140	10	85	92	10-11	0	3.60
Bob Friend	R	23	35	20	4	2	170.1	204	16	58	73	7-12	2	5.07
Jake Thies	R	28	33	18	3	1	130.1	120	13	49	57	3-9	0	3.87
Laurin Pepper	R	23	14	8	0	0	50.2	63	4	43	17	1-5	0	7.99
Cal Hogue	R	26	3	2	0	0	11.0	11	1	12	7	0-1	0	4.91
Johnny Hetki	R	32	58	1	0	0	83.0	102	11	30	27	4-4	9	4.99
Vern Law	R	24	39	18	7	0	161.2	201	20	56	57	9-13	3	5.51
Bob Purkey	R	24	36	11	0	0	131.1	145	3	62	38	3-8	0	5.07
Paul LaPalme	L	30	33	15	2	0	120.2	147	15	54	57	4-10	0	5.52
George O'Donnell	R	25	21	10	3	0	87.1	105	4	21	8	3-9	1	4.53
Len Yochim	L	25	10	1	0	0	19.2	30	2	8	7	0-1	0	7.32
Joe Page	L	36	7	0	0	0	9.2	16	4	7	4	0-0	0	11.17
Nellie King	R	26	4	0	0	0	7.0	10	0	1	3	0-0	0	5.14

»1955 New York Yankees 1st AL 96-58 .623 —

Casey Stengel

Player	Gm by Position	B	Age	G	AB	R	H	2B	3B	HR	RBI	BB	SO	SB	Avg	OBP	Slg
Yogi Berra	C145	L	30	147	541	84	147	20	3	27	108	60	20	1	.272	.349	.470
Bill Skowron	1B74,3B3	R	24	108	288	46	92	17	3	12	61	21	32	1	.319	.369	.524
Gil McDougald	2B126,3B17	R	27	141	533	79	152	10	8	13	53	65	77	6	.285	.361	.407
Andy Carey	3B135	R	23	135	510	73	131	19	11	7	47	44	51	3	.257	.313	.378
Billy Hunter	SS98	R	27	98	255	14	58	7	1	3	20	15	18	9	.227	.269	.298
Mickey Mantle	OF145,SS2	S	23	147	517	121	158	25	11	37	99	113	97	8	.306	.431	.611
Hank Bauer	OF133,C1	R	32	139	492	97	137	20	5	20	53	56	65	8	.278	.360	.461
Irv Noren	OF126	L	30	132	371	49	94	19	1	8	59	43	33	5	.253	.331	.375
Elston Howard	OF75,C9	R	26	97	279	33	81	8	7	10	43	20	36	0	.290	.336	.477
Joe Collins	1B73,OF27	L	32	105	278	40	65	9	1	13	45	44	32	0	.234	.339	.414
Eddie Robinson	1B46	L	34	88	173	25	36	1	0	16	42	36	26	0	.208	.358	.491
Phil Rizzuto	SS79,2B1	R	37	81	143	19	37	4	1	1	9	22	18	7	.259	.369	.322
Jerry Coleman	SS29,2B13,3B1	R	30	43	96	12	22	5	0	0	8	11	11	0	.229	.321	.281
Bob Cerv	OF20	R	29	55	85	17	29	4	2	3	22	7	16	4	.341	.411	.541
Billy Martin	2B16,SS3	R	27	20	70	8	21	2	0	1	9	7	9	1	.300	.354	.371
Bobby Richardson	2B6,SS4	R	19	11	26	2	4	0	0	0	3	2	0	1	.154	.214	.154
Charlie Silvera	C11	R	30	14	26	1	5	0	0	0	1	6	4	0	.192	.344	.192
Enos Slaughter†		L	39	10	9	1	1	0	0	0	1	1	1	0	.111	.200	.111
Tom Carroll	SS4	R	18	14	6	3	2	0	0	0	0	0	2	0	.333	.333	.333
Dick Tettelbach	OF2	R	26	2	5	0	0	0	0	0	0	0	0	0	.000	.000	.000
Lou Berberet	C1	L	25	2	5	1	2	0	0	0	2	1	0	0	.400	.500	.400
Johnny Blanchard	C1	L	22	1	3	0	0	0	0	0	0	1	0	0	.000	.250	.000
Marv Throneberry	1B1	L	21	1	2	1	2	1	0	0	3	0	0	1	1.000	.667	1.500
Frank Leja	1B2	L	19	7	2	1	0	0	0	0	0	0	1	0	.000	.000	.000

Pitcher	T	Age	G	GS	CG	ShO	IP	H	HR	BB	SO	W-L	Sv	ERA
Bob Turley	R	24	36	34	13	6	246.2	168	16	177	210	17-13	1	3.06
Whitey Ford	L	26	39	33	18	5	253.2	188	20	113	137	18-7	2	2.63
Tommy Byrne	L	35	27	22	9	3	160.0	137	12	87	76	16-5	2	3.15
Don Larsen	R	25	19	13	5	1	97.0	81	8	51	44	9-2	2	3.06
Ed Lopat†	L	37	16	12	3	1	86.2	101	12	16	24	4-8	0	3.74
Rip Coleman	L	23	10	6	0	0	29.0	40	2	16	15	2-1	1	5.28
Ted Gray†	L	30	1	1	0	0	3.0	3	0	0	1	0-0	0	3.00
Jim Konstanty	R	38	45	0	0	0	73.2	68	5	24	19	7-2	11	2.32
Tom Morgan	R	25	40	1	0	0	72.0	72	3	24	17	7-3	10	3.25
Tom Sturdivant	R	25	33	1	0	0	68.1	48	6	42	48	1-3	0	3.16
Johnny Kucks	R	21	29	13	3	1	126.2	122	8	44	49	8-7	0	3.41
Bob Grim	R	25	26	11	1	1	92.1	81	9	42	63	7-5	4	4.19
Bob Wiesler	L	24	16	7	0	0	53.0	39	1	49	22	0-2	0	3.91
Johnny Sain†	R	37	3	0	0	0	5.1	6	4	1	5	0-0	0	6.75
Art Schallock†	L	31	2	0	0	0	3.0	4	1	1	2	0-0	0	6.00
Gerry Staley†	R	34	2	0	0	0	2.0	5	1	1	0	0-0	0	13.50

1955 Cleveland Indians 2nd AL 93-61 .604 3.0 GB

Al Lopez

Player	Gm by Position	B	Age	G	AB	R	H	2B	3B	HR	RBI	BB	SO	SB	Avg	OBP	Slg
Jim Hegan	C111	R	34	116	304	30	67	5	2	9	40	34	33	0	.220	.293	.339
Vic Wertz	1B63,OF9	L	30	74	257	30	65	11	2	14	55	32	33	1	.253	.332	.475
Bobby Avila	2B141	R	31	141	537	83	146	22	4	13	61	82	47	1	.272	.368	.400
Al Rosen	3B106,1B41	R	31	139	492	61	120	13	1	21	81	92	44	4	.244	.362	.402
George Strickland	SS128	R	29	130	388	34	81	9	5	2	34	49	60	1	.209	.302	.273
Larry Doby	OF129	L	31	131	491	91	143	17	5	26	75	61	100	2	.291	.369	.505
Al Smith	OF120,3B45,SS5*	R	27	154	607	123	186	27	4	22	77	93	77	11	.306	.407	.473
Ralph Kiner	OF87	R	32	113	321	56	78	13	0	18	54	65	46	0	.243	.367	.452
Gene Woodling†	OF70	L	32	79	259	33	72	15	1	5	35	36	15	2	.278	.368	.402
Hal Naragon	C52	L	26	57	127	12	41	9	2	1	14	15	8	1	.323	.394	.449
Ferris Fain†	1B51	L	34	56	118	9	30	3	0	0	8	42	13	3	.254	.451	.280
Hank Foiles	C41	R	26	62	111	13	29	9	0	1	7	17	18	0	.261	.354	.369
Sam Dente	SS53,3B13,2B4	R	33	73	105	10	27	4	0	0	10	12	8	0	.257	.331	.295
Dave Pope†	OF31	L	34	35	104	17	31	5	0	6	22	12	31	0	.298	.373	.519
Dave Philley†	OF34	S	35	43	104	15	31	4	2	2	9	12	10	0	.298	.368	.433
Joe Altobelli	1B40	L	23	42	75	8	15	3	0	2	5	5	14	0	.200	.259	.320
Hoot Evers†	OF25	R	34	39	66	10	19	7	1	2	9	3	12	0	.288	.314	.515
Dale Mitchell	1B8,OF3	L	33	61	58	4	15	2	1	0	10	4	3	0	.259	.302	.328
Hank Majeski†	3B9,2B4	R	38	36	48	3	9	2	0	2	6	8	3	0	.188	.322	.354
Bobby Young†	2B11,3B1	L	30	18	45	7	14	1	1	0	6	1	2	0	.311	.326	.378
Rudy Regalado	3B8,2B1	R	25	10	26	2	7	2	0	0	5	2	4	0	.269	.321	.346
Wally Westlake†	OF7	R	34	16	20	2	5	1	0	0	1	3	5	0	.250	.348	.300
Billy Harrell	SS11	R	26	13	19	2	8	0	0	0	1	3	3	1	.421	.500	.421
Stu Locklin	OF7	L	26	16	18	4	3	1	0	0	0	3	4	0	.167	.286	.222
Rocky Colavito	OF2	R	21	5	9	3	4	2	0	0	0	0	2	0	.444	.444	.667
Stan Pawloski	2B2	R	23	2	8	0	1	0	0	0	0	0	2	0	.125	.125	.125
Kenny Kuhn	SS4	L	18	4	6	0	2	0	0	0	0	1	0	1	.333	.429	.333
Harry Simpson†		L	29	3	1	1	0	0	0	0	0	2	0	0	.000	.667	.000

A. Smith, 1 G at 2B

Pitcher	T	Age	G	GS	CG	ShO	IP	H	HR	BB	SO	W-L	Sv	ERA
Herb Score	L	22	33	32	11	2	227.1	158	18	154	245	16-10	0	2.85
Early Wynn	R	35	32	31	16	6	230.0	207	19	80	122	17-11	0	2.82
Bob Lemon	R	34	35	31	5	0	211.1	218	17	74	100	18-10	2	3.88
Mike Garcia	R	31	38	31	6	2	210.2	230	17	56	120	11-13	3	4.02
Bud Daley	L	22	2	1	0	0	7.0	10	1	1	2	0-1	0	6.43
Ray Narleski	R	26	60	1	1	0	111.2	91	11	52	94	9-1	19	3.71
Don Mossi	L	26	57	1	0	0	81.2	81	4	18	69	4-3	9	2.42
Art Houtteman	R	27	35	12	3	1	124.1	126	15	44	53	10-6	0	3.98
Bob Feller	R	36	25	11	2	1	83.0	71	7	31	25	4-4	0	3.47
Jose Santiago	R	26	17	0	0	0	32.2	31	1	14	19	2-0	0	2.48
Bill Wight†	L	33	17	0	0	0	24.0	24	0	9	9	0-0	1	2.63
Sal Maglie†	R	38	10	2	0	0	25.2	26	0	7	11	0-2	2	3.86
Hank Aguirre	L	24	4	1	1	1	12.2	6	0	12	6	2-0	0	1.42
Hal Newhouser	L	34	2	0	0	0	2.1	1	0	4	1	0-0	0	0.00
Ted Gray†	L	30	2	0	0	0	2.0	5	1	2	1	0-0	0	18.00

1955 Chicago White Sox 3rd AL 91-63 .591 5.0 GB

Marty Marion

Player	Gm by Position	B	Age	G	AB	R	H	2B	3B	HR	RBI	BB	SO	SB	Avg	OBP	Slg
Sherm Lollar	C136	R	30	138	426	67	111	13	1	16	61	68	34	2	.261	.374	.408
Walt Dropo	1B140	R	32	141	453	55	127	15	2	19	79	42	71	0	.280	.343	.448
Nellie Fox	2B154	L	27	154	636	100	198	28	7	6	59	38	15	7	.311	.364	.406
George Kell	3B105,1B24,OF1	R	32	128	429	44	134	24	1	8	81	51	36	2	.312	.389	.429
Chico Carrasquel	SS144	R	29	145	523	83	134	11	2	11	52	61	59	1	.256	.335	.348
Jim Rivera	OF143	L	32	147	454	71	120	24	4	10	52	62	59	25	.264	.352	.401
Minnie Minoso	OF138,3B2	R	32	139	517	79	149	26	7	10	70	76	43	19	.288	.387	.424
Jim Busby†	OF99	R	28	99	337	38	82	13	4	1	27	25	37	7	.243	.294	.315
Bob Nieman	OF78	R	28	99	272	36	77	11	2	11	53	36	37	1	.283	.366	.460
Bob Kennedy†	3B55,OF20,1B3	R	34	83	214	28	65	10	2	9	43	16	16	0	.304	.352	.495
Johnny Groth†	OF26	R	28	32	77	13	26	7	0	2	11	6	13	1	.338	.376	.506
Ron Jackson	1B29	R	21	40	74	10	15	1	1	2	7	8	22	1	.203	.277	.324
Les Moss†	C32	R	30	32	59	5	15	2	0	2	7	6	10	0	.254	.333	.390
Jim Brideweser	SS26,3B3,2B2	R	28	34	58	6	12	3	2	0	4	3	7	0	.207	.246	.328
Vern Stephens†	3B18	R	34	22	56	10	14	3	0	3	7	7	11	0	.250	.328	.464
Willard Marshall	OF12	L	34	22	41	6	7	0	0	0	6	13	1	0	.171	.364	.171
Clint Courtney†	C17	L	28	19	37	7	14	3	0	1	10	7	0	0	.378	.467	.541
Buddy Peterson	SS6	R	30	6	21	7	6	1	0	0	2	3	2	0	.286	.400	.333
Bobby Adams†	3B9,2B1	R	33	28	21	8	2	0	1	0	3	4	4	0	.095	.240	.190
Gil Coan†	OF3	L	33	17	17	0	3	0	0	0	1	0	5	0	.176	.176	.176
Ron Northey	OF2	L	35	14	14	1	5	2	0	1	4	3	3	0	.357	.471	.714
Ed McGhee	OF17	R	30	26	13	6	1	0	0	0	0	6	1	2	.077	.368	.077
Earl Battey	C5	R	20	5	7	1	2	0	0	0	0	1	1	0	.286	.444	.286
Ed White	OF2	R	29	3	4	0	2	0	0	0	0	1	1	0	.500	.600	.500
Stan Jok	3B3,OF1	R	29	6	4	3	1	0	0	1	2	1	1	0	.250	.333	1.000
Sammy Esposito	3B2	R	23	3	4	3	0	0	0	0	0	1	0	0	.000	.200	.000
Phil Cavarretta	1B3	L	38	6	4	1	0	0	0	0	0	0	1	0	.000	.000	.000
Lloyd Merriman†		L	30	1	1	0	0	0	0	0	0	0	0	0	.000	.000	.000
Leroy Powell		R	21	1	0	0	0	0	0	0	0	0	0	0	—	—	—

Pitcher	T	Age	G	GS	CG	ShO	IP	H	HR	BB	SO	W-L	Sv	ERA
Billy Pierce	L	28	33	26	16	6	205.2	162	16	64	157	15-10	1	1.97
Virgil Trucks	R	38	32	26	7	3	175.0	176	19	61	91	13-8	0	3.96
Dick Donovan	R	27	29	24	11	5	187.0	186	17	48	88	15-9	0	3.32
Jack Harshman	L	27	32	23	9	0	179.1	144	16	97	116	11-7	0	3.36
Connie Johnson	R	32	17	16	5	2	99.0	95	5	52	72	7-4	0	3.45
Bob Keegan	R	34	18	11	1	0	58.2	83	4	28	29	2-5	0	5.83
Ted Gray†	L	30	2	1	0	0	3.0	9	0	2	1	0-0	0	18.00
Sandy Consuegra	R	34	44	7	3	0	126.1	120	4	18	35	6-5	7	2.64
Morrie Martin	L	32	37	0	0	0	52.0	50	4	20	22	2-3	2	3.63
Dixie Howell	R	35	35	0	0	0	73.2	70	1	25	25	8-3	9	2.93
Mike Fornieles	R	23	26	9	2	0	86.1	84	12	29	23	6-3	2	3.86
Harry Byrd†	R	30	25	12	1	1	91.0	85	10	30	44	4-6	1	4.65
Harry Dorish†	R	33	13	0	0	0	17.0	16	0	9	6	2-0	1	1.59
Bob Chakales†	R	27	7	0	0	0	12.1	11	2	6	6	0-0	0	1.46
Al Papai	R	38	7	0	0	0	11.2	10	1	8	5	0-0	0	3.86

1955 Boston Red Sox 4th AL 84-70 .545 12.0 GB

Pinky Higgins

Player	Gm by Position	B	Age	G	AB	R	H	2B	3B	HR	RBI	BB	SO	SB	Avg	OBP	Slg
Sammy White	C143	R	26	143	544	65	142	30	4	11	64	44	58	1	.261	.323	.392
Norm Zauchin	1B126	R	25	130	477	65	114	10	0	27	93	69	105	3	.239	.335	.430
Billy Goodman	2B143,1B5,OF1	L	29	149	599	100	176	31	2	0	52	99	44	5	.294	.394	.352
Grady Hatton	3B111,2B1	L	32	126	380	48	93	11	4	4	49	76	28	0	.245	.367	.326
Billy Klaus	SS126,3B8	L	26	135	541	83	153	26	2	7	60	60	44	6	.283	.351	.377
Jackie Jensen	OF150	R	28	152	574	95	158	27	6	26	116	89	63	16	.275	.369	.479
Jimmy Piersall	OF147	R	25	149	515	68	146	25	5	13	62	67	52	6	.283	.364	.427
Ted Williams	OF93	L	36	98	320	77	114	21	3	28	83	91	24	2	.356	.496	.703
Gene Stephens	OF75	L	22	109	157	25	46	9	4	3	18	20	34	0	.293	.374	.459
Faye Throneberry	OF34	L	24	60	144	20	37	7	3	6	27	14	31	0	.257	.323	.472
Ted Lepcio	3B45	R	24	51	134	19	31	9	0	6	15	13	36	1	.231	.313	.433
Eddie Joost	SS20,2B17,3B2	R	39	55	119	15	23	2	0	5	17	17	21	0	.193	.299	.336
Harry Agganis	1B20	L	26	25	83	11	26	10	1	0	10	10	10	2	.313	.383	.458
Pete Daley	C14	R	25	17	50	4	11	2	1	0	5	3	6	0	.220	.264	.300
Karl Olson	OF21	R	24	26	48	7	12	1	2	0	1	1	10	0	.250	.265	.354
Owen Friend†	SS14,2B1	R	28	14	42	3	11	3	0	0	2	4	11	0	.262	.326	.333
Sam Mele†	OF7	R	32	14	31	1	4	2	0	0	1	0	7	1	.129	.125	.194
Frank Malzone	3B4	R	25	6	20	2	7	1	0	0	1	1	3	0	.350	.381	.400
Dick Gernert	1B5	R	26	7	20	6	4	2	0	0	1	1	5	0	.200	.238	.300
Billy Consolo	2B4	R	20	8	18	4	4	0	0	0	0	5	4	0	.222	.391	.222
Haywood Sullivan	C2	R	24	2	6	1	0	0	0	0	0	0	1	0	.000	.000	.000
Milt Bolling	SS2	R	24	6	5	0	1	0	0	0	0	0	1	0	.200	.200	.200
Jim Pagliaroni	C1	R	17	1	0	0	0	0	0	0	1	0	0	0	—	.000	—

Pitcher	T	Age	G	GS	CG	ShO	IP	H	HR	BB	SO	W-L	Sv	ERA
Frank Sullivan	R	25	35	35	16	3	260.0	235	23	100	129	18-13	0	2.91
Willard Nixon	R	27	31	31	7	3	208.0	207	10	85	95	12-10	0	4.07
Tom Brewer	R	23	31	28	9	2	192.2	198	21	87	91	11-10	0	4.20
Ike Delock	R	25	29	18	6	0	143.2	136	16	61	88	9-7	3	3.76
George Susce	R	23	29	15	6	1	144.1	123	12	49	60	9-7	1	3.06
Mel Parnell	L	33	13	9	0	0	46.0	62	12	25	18	2-3	1	7.83
Frank Baumann	L	21	7	5	0	0	34.0	38	2	17	27	2-1	0	5.82
Tom Hurd	R	31	43	0	0	0	80.2	72	7	38	48	8-6	5	3.01
Ellis Kinder	R	40	43	0	0	0	66.2	57	5	15	31	5-5	18	2.84
Leo Kiely	L	25	33	4	0	0	90.0	91	5	37	36	3-3	6	2.80
Bill Henry	L	27	17	7	0	0	59.2	56	7	21	23	2-4	0	3.32
Dick Brodowski	R	22	16	0	0	0	32.0	36	5	25	10	1-0	0	5.63
Russ Kemmerer	R	23	7	2	0	0	17.1	18	3	15	13	1-1	0	7.27
Hal Brown†	R	30	2	0	0	0	4.0	2	0	2	2	1-0	0	2.25
Joe Trimble	R	24	2	0	0	0	2.0	0	0	3	1	0-0	0	0.00
Hersh Freeman†	R	26	2	0	0	0	1.2	1	0	1	1	0-0	0	0.00
Bob Smith	L	24	1	0	0	0	1.2	1	0	1	1	0-0	0	0.00

1955 Detroit Tigers 5th AL 79-75 .513 17.0 GB

Bucky Harris

Player	Gm by Position	B	Age	G	AB	R	H	2B	3B	HR	RBI	BB	SO	SB	Avg	OBP	Slg
Frank House	C93	L	25	102	328	37	85	11	1	15	53	22	25	0	.259	.308	.436
Earl Torgeson†	1B83	L	31	89	300	58	85	10	1	9	50	61	29	9	.283	.397	.413
Fred Hatfield	2B92,3B16,SS14	L	30	122	413	51	96	15	3	8	33	61	49	3	.232	.337	.341
Ray Boone	3B126	R	31	135	500	61	142	22	7	20	116	50	49	1	.284	.346	.476
Harvey Kuenn	SS141	R	24	145	620	101	190	38	5	8	62	40	27	8	.306	.347	.423
Bill Tuttle	OF154	R	25	154	603	102	168	23	4	14	78	76	54	6	.279	.358	.400
Al Kaline	OF152	R	20	152	588	121	200	24	8	27	102	82	57	6	.340	.421	.546
Jim Delsing	OF101	L	29	114	356	49	85	14	2	10	60	48	40	2	.239	.328	.374
Red Wilson	C72	R	26	78	241	26	53	9	0	2	17	26	23	1	.220	.296	.282
Harry Malmberg	2B65	R	28	67	208	25	45	5	2	0	19	29	19	0	.216	.310	.260
Bubba Phillips	OF65,3B4	R	27	95	184	18	43	4	0	3	23	14	20	2	.234	.289	.304
Ferris Fain†	1B44	L	34	58	140	23	37	8	0	2	23	52	12	2	.264	.459	.364
Jack Phillips	1B35,3B3	R	33	55	117	15	37	8	2	1	20	10	12	0	.316	.364	.444
Charlie Maxwell†	OF26,1B2	L	28	55	109	19	29	7	1	7	18	8	20	0	.266	.325	.541
Reno Bertoia	3B14,2B6,SS5	R	20	38	68	13	14	2	1	1	10	5	11	0	.206	.253	.309
J.W. Porter	1B6,C4,OF4	R	22	24	55	6	13	2	0	0	3	8	15	0	.236	.333	.273
Chick King	OF6	R	24	7	21	3	5	0	0	0	0	1	2	0	.238	.273	.238
Jim Small	OF4	L	18	12	4	2	0	0	0	0	0	1	1	0	.000	.200	.000
Walt Streuli	C2	R	19	2	4	1	1	1	0	0	1	0	0	0	.250	.200	.500
Wayne Belardi		L	24	3	3	0	0	0	0	0	0	0	1	0	.000	.000	.000
Ron Samford	SS1	R	25	1	1	0	0	0	0	0	0	0	1	0	.000	.000	.000
Steve Souchock		R	36	1	1	0	1	0	0	0	1	0	0	0	1.000	1.000	1.000

Pitcher	T	Age	G	GS	CG	ShO	IP	H	HR	BB	SO	W-L	Sv	ERA
Ned Garver	R	29	33	32	16	1	230.2	251	21	67	83	12-16	0	3.98
Frank Lary	R	25	36	31	16	2	235.0	232	10	89	98	14-15	1	3.10
Billy Hoeft	L	23	32	29	17	7	220.0	187	17	75	133	16-7	0	2.99
Steve Gromek	R	35	28	25	8	2	181.0	183	26	37	73	13-10	0	3.98
Duke Maas	R	26	18	16	5	2	86.2	91	7	50	42	5-6	0	4.88
Jim Bunning	R	23	15	8	0	0	51.0	59	8	32	37	3-5	1	6.35
Bud Black	R	22	3	2	1	1	14.0	12	0	8	7	1-1	0	1.29
Al Aber	L	27	39	1	0	0	80.0	86	9	28	37	6-3	3	3.38
Babe Birrer	R	26	36	3	1	0	80.1	77	9	29	28	4-3	3	4.15
Paul Foytack	R	24	22	1	0	0	49.2	48	4	36	38	0-1	0	5.26
Leo Cristante	R	28	20	1	0	0	36.2	37	1	14	9	0-1	0	3.19
Joe Coleman†	R	32	17	0	0	0	25.1	22	1	14	5	2-1	3	3.20
George Zuverink†	R	30	14	1	0	0	28.1	38	6	14	13	0-5	0	6.99
Van Fletcher	R	30	9	0	0	0	12.0	13	1	2	4	0-0	0	3.00
Bob Miller	L	19	7	3	1	0	25.1	26	4	12	11	2-1	0	2.49
Dick Marlowe	R	26	4	1	1	0	15.0	12	1	4	9	1-0	1	1.80
Ben Flowers†	R	28	4	0	0	0	6.0	5	1	2	2	0-0	0	6.00
Bill Froats	L	24	1	0	0	0	2.0	0	0	2	0	0-0	0	0.00
Bob Schultz	L	31	1	0	0	0	1.1	2	0	2	0	0-0	0	20.25

1955 Kansas City Athletics 6th AL 63-91 .409 33.0 GB

Lou Boudreau

Player	Gm by Position	B	Age	G	AB	R	H	2B	3B	HR	RBI	BB	SO	SB	Avg	OBP	Slg
Joe Astroth	C100	R	32	101	274	29	69	4	1	5	23	47	33	2	.252	.372	.328
Vic Power	1B144	R	27	147	596	91	190	34	10	19	76	35	27	0	.319	.354	.505
Jim Finigan	2B90,3B59	R	26	150	545	72	139	30	7	9	68	61	49	1	.255	.333	.385
Hector Lopez	3B93,2B36	R	25	128	483	50	140	15	2	15	68	33	58	1	.290	.337	.422
Joe DeMaestri	SS122	R	26	123	457	42	114	14	1	6	37	20	47	3	.249	.284	.324
Gus Zernial	OF103	R	32	120	413	62	105	9	3	30	84	30	90	1	.254	.304	.508
Harry Simpson†	OF100,1B3	L	29	112	396	42	119	16	7	5	52	34	61	3	.301	.356	.414
Bill Wilson	OF82,P1	R	26	98	273	39	61	12	0	15	38	24	63	1	.223	.288	.432
Elmer Valo	OF72	L	34	112	283	50	103	17	4	3	37	52	18	5	.364	.460	.484
Enos Slaughter†	OF77	L	39	108	267	49	86	12	4	5	34	40	17	2	.322	.408	.453
Bill Renna	OF79	R	30	100	249	33	53	7	3	7	28	31	42	0	.213	.305	.349
Billy Shantz	C78	R	27	79	217	18	56	4	1	1	12	11	14	0	.258	.293	.300
Pete Suder	2B24	R	39	26	81	3	17	4	1	0	1	2	13	0	.210	.229	.284
Clete Boyer	SS12,3B11,2B10	R	18	47	79	3	19	1	0	0	6	3	17	0	.241	.268	.253
Jack Littrell	SS22,1B6,2B4	R	26	37	70	7	14	0	1	0	1	4	12	0	.200	.243	.229
Jerry Schypinski	SS21,2B2	L	23	22	69	7	15	2	0	0	5	1	6	0	.217	.229	.246
Dick Kryhoski	1B14	L	30	28	47	2	10	2	0	0	2	6	7	0	.213	.302	.255
Tom Saffell†	OF9	L	33	9	37	5	8	0	0	0	1	4	7	1	.216	.293	.216
Spook Jacobs	2B7	R	29	13	23	7	6	0	0	0	1	3	0	1	.261	.370	.261
Bill Stewart	OF6	R	27	11	18	2	2	1	0	0	0	1	6	0	.111	.158	.167
Don Plarski	OF6	R	25	8	11	0	1	0	0	0	0	0	2	1	.091	.091	.091
Alex George	SS5	L	16	5	10	0	1	0	0	0	0	1	7	0	.100	.182	.100
Don Bollweg	1B3	L	34	12	9	1	1	0	0	0	2	3	2	0	.111	.333	.111
Jim Robertson	C4	R	27	6	8	1	2	0	0	0	0	1	2	0	.250	.333	.250
Hal Bevan	3B1	R	24	3	3	0	0	0	0	0	0	0	0	0	.000	.000	.000
Eric MacKenzie	C1	L	22	1	1	0	0	0	0	0	0	0	0	0	.000	.000	.000

Pitcher	T	Age	G	GS	CG	ShO	IP	H	HR	BB	SO	W-L	Sv	ERA
Alex Kellner	L	30	30	24	6	3	162.2	164	18	60	75	11-8	0	4.20
Art Ditmar	R	26	35	22	7	1	175.1	180	23	86	79	12-12	1	5.03
Arnie Portocarrero	R	23	24	20	4	1	111.1	109	12	67	34	5-9	0	4.77
Vic Raschi†	R	36	20	18	1	0	101.1	132	10	35	38	4-6	0	5.42
Bobby Shantz	L	29	23	17	4	1	125.0	124	8	66	58	5-10	0	4.54
Art Ceccarelli	L	25	31	16	3	1	123.2	123	20	71	68	4-7	0	5.31
Johnny Gray	R	27	8	5	0	0	26.2	28	2	24	11	0-3	0	6.41
Mike Kume	R	29	6	4	0	0	23.2	35	1	15	7	0-2	0	7.99
Walt Craddock	L	23	4	2	0	0	15.0	18	3	10	9	0-2	0	7.80
Glenn Cox	R	24	2	2	0	0	2.1	11	0	1	2	0-2	0	30.86
Tom Gorman	R	30	57	0	0	0	109.0	98	11	36	46	7-6	18	3.55
Bill Harrington	R	27	34	1	0	0	76.2	69	6	41	26	3-3	2	4.11
Cloyd Boyer	R	27	30	11	2	0	98.1	107	21	69	32	5-5	0	6.22
Johnny Sain†	R	37	25	0	0	0	44.2	54	10	10	12	2-5	1	5.44
Ray Herbert	R	25	23	11	2	0	87.2	99	10	40	30	1-8	0	6.26
Lou Sleater	L	28	16	1	0	0	25.2	33	3	21	11	1-1	0	7.71
Marion Fricano	R	31	10	0	0	0	20.0	19	2	9	5	0-0	0	3.15
Moe Burtschy	R	33	7	0	0	0	11.1	17	0	10	9	2-0	0	10.32
Gus Keriazakos	R	23	5	1	0	0	11.2	15	4	7	8	0-1	0	12.34
Bob Trice	R	28	4	0	0	0	10.0	14	4	6	2	0-0	0	9.00
Charlie Bishop	R	31	4	0	0	0	6.2	6	1	8	4	1-0	0	5.40
Lee Wheat	R	25	3	0	0	0	2.0	8	1	3	1	0-0	0	22.50
Ewell Blackwell	R	32	2	0	0	0	4.0	3	1	5	2	0-1	1	6.75
Bob Spicer	R	30	2	0	0	0	2.2	9	2	4	2	0-0	0	33.75
Ozzie Van Brabant	R	28	2	0	0	0	2.0	4	1	2	1	0-0	0	18.00
Sonny Dixon	R	30	2	0	0	0	1.2	6	1	0	0	0-0	0	16.20
Bill Wilson	R	26	1	0	0	0	1.0	1	0	1	1	0-0	0	0.00

1955 Baltimore Orioles 7th AL 57-97 .370 39.0 GB

Paul Richards

Player	Gm by Position	B	Age	G	AB	R	H	2B	3B	HR	RBI	BB	SO	SB	Avg	OBP	Slg
Hal Smith	C125	R	24	135	424	41	115	23	4	4	52	30	21	1	.271	.318	.373
Gus Triandos	1B103,C36,3B1	R	24	140	481	47	133	17	3	12	65	40	55	0	.277	.333	.399
Fred Marsh	2B76,3B18,SS16	R	31	89	303	30	66	7	1	2	19	35	33	1	.218	.300	.267
Wayne Causey	3B55,2B7,SS1	L	18	68	175	14	34	2	1	1	9	17	25	0	.194	.269	.234
Willie Miranda	SS153,2B1	S	29	153	487	42	124	12	6	1	38	42	58	4	.255	.313	.310
Chuck Diering	OF107,3B34,SS12	R	32	137	371	38	95	16	2	3	31	57	45	5	.256	.355	.334
Cal Abrams	OF96,1B4	L	31	118	309	56	75	12	3	6	32	89	69	2	.243	.413	.359
Dave Philley†	OF82,3B2	S	35	83	311	50	93	13	3	6	41	34	38	1	.299	.367	.418
Dave Pope†	OF73	L	34	86	222	21	55	8	4	1	30	16	34	5	.248	.302	.333
Jim Dyck	OF45,3B17	R	33	61	197	32	55	13	1	2	22	28	21	1	.279	.372	.386
Billy Cox	3B37,2B18,SS6	R	35	53	194	25	41	7	2	3	14	17	16	1	.211	.275	.314
Bobby Young†	2B58	L	30	59	186	5	37	3	0	1	8	11	23	1	.199	.244	.231
Hoot Evers†	OF55	R	34	60	185	21	44	10	1	6	30	19	28	2	.238	.307	.400
Bob Hale	1B44	L	21	67	182	13	65	7	1	0	29	5	19	0	.357	.376	.407
Gene Woodling†	OF44	L	32	47	145	22	32	6	2	3	18	24	18	1	.221	.329	.352
Gil Coan†	OF43	L	33	61	130	18	31	7	1	1	11	13	15	4	.238	.313	.331
Jim Pyburn	3B33,OF1	R	22	39	98	5	20	2	2	0	7	8	24	1	.204	.271	.265
Eddie Waitkus†	1B26	L	35	38	85	2	22	1	1	0	9	11	10	2	.259	.344	.294
Don Leppert	2B35	L	24	40	70	6	8	0	1	0	2	9	10	1	.114	.213	.143
Bob Kennedy†	OF14,1B6,3B1	R	34	26	70	10	10	1	0	0	5	10	10	0	.143	.250	.157
Les Moss†	C17	R	30	29	56	5	19	1	0	2	6	7	4	0	.339	.413	.464
Hank Majeski†	3B8,2B5	R	38	16	41	2	7	1	0	0	2	2	4	0	.171	.209	.195
Bill Wight†	P19,1B1	L	33	19	36	1	3	1	0	0	2	1	16	0	.083	.108	.111
Tex Nelson	OF6,1B2	L	18	25	31	4	6	0	0	0	1	7	13	0	.194	.342	.194
Tom Gastall	C15	R	23	20	27	4	4	1	0	0	0	3	5	0	.148	.233	.185
Wally Westlake†	OF7	R	34	8	24	0	3	1	0	0	0	6	5	0	.125	.300	.167
Brooks Robinson	3B6	R	18	6	22	0	2	0	0	0	1	0	10	0	.091	.091	.091
Angelo Dagres	OF5	L	20	8	15	5	4	0	0	0	3	1	2	0	.267	.278	.267
Kal Segrist	3B3,1B1,2B1	R	24	7	9	1	3	0	0	0	0	2	0	0	.333	.455	.333
Vern Stephens†	3B2	R	34	3	6	0	1	0	0	0	0	0	0	0	.167	.286	.167
Charlie Maxwell†		L	28	4	4	0	0	0	0	0	0	0	1	0	.000	.000	.000
Roger Marquis	OF1	L	18	1	1	0	0	0	0	0	0	0	0	0	.000	.000	.000

Pitcher	T	Age	G	GS	CG	ShO	IP	H	HR	BB	SO	W-L	Sv	ERA
Jim Wilson	R	33	34	31	14	4	235.1	200	17	87	96	12-18	0	3.44
Erv Palica	R	27	33	25	5	1	169.2	165	10	83	68	5-11	2	4.14
Bill Wight†	L	33	19	14	8	2	117.1	111	6	39	54	6-8	2	2.45
Saul Rogovin†	R	31	14	12	1	0	71.0	79	5	27	35	1-8	0	4.56
Harry Byrd†	R	30	14	8	1	1	65.1	64	7	28	25	3-2	1	4.55
Ed Lopat†	L	37	10	7	1	0	49.0	57	8	9	10	3-4	0	4.22
Duane Pillette	R	32	7	5	0	0	20.2	31	0	14	13	0-3	0	6.53
Ray Moore	R	29	46	14	3	1	151.2	128	14	80	80	10-10	6	3.92
Harry Dorish†	R	33	35	1	0	0	65.2	58	4	28	22	3-3	6	3.15
Don Johnson	R	28	31	5	0	0	68.0	89	4	35	27	2-4	1	5.82
Art Schallock†	L	31	30	6	1	0	80.1	92	2	42	33	3-5	0	4.15
George Zuverink†	R	30	28	5	0	0	86.1	80	5	17	31	4-3	4	2.19
Jim McDonald	R	28	21	8	0	0	51.2	76	5	30	20	3-5	0	7.14
Hal Brown†	R	30	15	5	1	0	57.0	51	5	26	26	0-4	0	4.11
Lou Kretlow	R	34	15	5	0	0	38.1	50	3	27	26	0-4	0	8.22
Ted Gray†	L	30	9	1	0	0	15.1	21	3	11	8	1-2	0	8.22
Bob Kuzava†	L	32	6	1	0	0	12.1	10	0	4	5	0-1	0	3.65
Joe Coleman†	R	32	6	2	0	0	11.2	19	5	10	4	0-1	0	10.80
Don Ferrarese	L	26	6	0	0	0	9.0	8	0	11	5	0-0	0	3.00
Bill Miller	L	27	5	1	0	0	4.0	3	0	10	4	0-1	0	13.50
Bob Alexander	R	32	4	0	0	0	4.0	8	0	2	1	1-0	0	13.50
Chuck Locke	R	23	2	0	0	0	3.0	0	0	1	1	0-0	0	0.00
Rob Harrison	R	24	1	0	0	0	2.0	3	0	4	0	0-0	0	9.00

1955 Washington Senators 8th AL 53-101 .344 43.0 GB

Chuck Dressen

Player	Gm by Position	B	Age	G	AB	R	H	2B	3B	HR	RBI	BB	SO	SB	Avg	OBP	Slg
Ed Fitz Gerald	C72	R	31	74	236	28	56	3	1	4	19	25	23	0	.237	.317	.309
Mickey Vernon	1B144	L	37	150	538	74	162	23	8	14	85	74	50	0	.301	.384	.452
Pete Runnels	2B132,SS2	L	27	134	503	66	143	16	4	2	49	55	51	3	.284	.353	.344
Eddie Yost	3B107	R	28	122	375	64	91	17	5	7	48	95	54	4	.243	.407	.371
Jose Valdivielso	SS94	R	21	94	294	32	65	12	5	2	28	21	38	1	.221	.277	.316
Roy Sievers	OF129,1B17,3B2	R	28	144	509	74	138	20	8	25	106	73	66	1	.271	.364	.489
Tom Umphlett	OF103	R	25	110	323	34	70	10	0	2	19	24	35	2	.217	.271	.266
Carlos Paula	OF86	R	27	115	351	34	105	20	7	6	45	17	43	2	.299	.332	.447
Ernie Oravetz	OF57	S	23	100	263	24	71	5	1	0	25	26	19	1	.270	.336	.297
Clint Courtney†	C67	L	28	75	238	26	71	8	4	2	30	19	9	0	.298	.349	.391
Jim Busby†	OF47	R	28	47	191	23	44	6	2	6	14	13	22	5	.230	.279	.377
Johnny Groth†	OF48	R	28	63	183	22	40	4	5	2	17	18	18	2	.219	.286	.328
Bobby Kline	SS69,2B4,3B3*	R	26	77	140	12	31	5	0	0	9	11	27	0	.221	.288	.257
Juan Delis	3B24,OF8,2B1	R	27	54	132	12	25	3	1	0	11	3	15	1	.189	.219	.227
Jerry Snyder	2B22,SS20	R	25	46	107	7	24	5	0	0	5	6	6	1	.224	.265	.271
Harmon Killebrew	3B23,2B3	R	19	38	80	12	16	1	0	4	7	9	31	0	.200	.281	.363
Tony Roig	SS21,3B8,2B1	R	27	29	57	3	13	1	1	0	4	2	15	0	.228	.254	.281
Bruce Edwards	C22,3B5	R	31	30	57	5	10	2	0	0	3	16	6	0	.175	.356	.211
Jerry Schoonmaker	OF15	R	21	20	46	5	7	0	1	1	4	5	11	1	.152	.235	.261
Steve Korcheck	C12	R	22	13	36	3	10	2	0	0	2	0	5	0	.278	.297	.333
Jim Lemon	OF6	R	27	10	25	3	5	2	0	1	3	3	4	0	.200	.286	.400
Jesse Levan		L	28	16	16	1	3	0	0	1	4	0	2	0	.188	.188	.375
Julio Becquer	1B2	L	23	10	14	1	3	0	0	0	1	0	1	0	.214	.214	.214
Tom Wright		L	31	7	7	0	0	0	0	0	0	0	1	0	.000	.000	.000
Bob Oldis	C6	R	27	6	6	1	0	0	0	0	0	1	0	0	.000	.143	.000

B. Kline, 1 G at P

Pitcher	T	Age	G	GS	CG	ShO	IP	H	HR	BB	SO	W-L	Sv	ERA
Bob Porterfield	R	31	30	27	8	2	178.0	197	14	54	74	10-17	0	4.45
Dean Stone	L	24	43	24	5	1	180.0	180	14	114	84	6-13	1	4.15
Johnny Schmitz	L	34	32	21	6	1	165.0	187	8	54	49	7-10	1	3.71
Mickey McDermott	L	27	31	20	8	1	156.0	140	9	100	78	10-10	1	3.75
Pedro Ramos	R	20	45	9	3	1	130.0	121	13	39	34	5-11	5	3.88
Camilo Pascual	R	21	43	16	1	0	129.0	158	5	70	82	2-12	3	6.14
Chuck Stobbs	L	25	41	16	2	0	140.1	169	13	57	60	4-14	3	5.00
Ted Abernathy	R	22	40	14	3	2	119.1	136	9	67	79	5-9	0	5.96
Bob Chakales†	R	27	29	0	0	0	54.2	55	4	25	28	2-3	0	5.27
Spec Shea	R	34	27	4	1	1	56.1	53	4	27	16	2-2	2	3.99
Webbo Clarke	L	27	7	2	0	0	21.1	17	2	14	9	0-0	0	4.64
Bunky Stewart	L	24	7	1	0	0	15.1	18	0	6	10	0-0	0	4.11
Bill Currie	R	26	3	0	0	0	4.1	7	3	2	2	0-0	0	12.46
Dick Hyde	R	26	3	0	0	0	2.0	2	0	1	1	0-0	0	4.50
Vince Gonzales	L	29	1	0	0	0	2.0	6	0	3	1	0-0	0	27.00
Bobby Kline	R	26	1	0	0	0	1.0	4	1	1	0	0-0	0	27.00

»1955 Brooklyn Dodgers 1st NL 98-55 .641 —

Walter Alston

Player	Gm by Position	B	Age	G	AB	R	H	2B	3B	HR	RBI	BB	SO	SB	Avg	OBP	Slg
Roy Campanella	C121	R	33	123	446	81	142	20	1	32	107	56	41	2	.318	.395	.583
Gil Hodges	1B139,OF16	R	31	150	546	75	158	24	5	27	102	80	91	2	.289	.377	.500
Jim Gilliam	2B99,OF46	S	26	147	538	110	134	20	8	7	40	70	37	15	.249	.341	.355
Jackie Robinson	3B84,OF10,1B1*	R	36	105	317	51	81	6	2	8	36	61	18	12	.256	.378	.363
Pee Wee Reese	SS142	R	36	145	553	99	156	29	4	10	61	78	60	8	.282	.371	.403
Duke Snider	OF146	L	28	148	538	126	166	34	6	42	136	104	87	9	.309	.418	.628
Carl Furillo	OF140	R	33	140	523	83	164	24	3	26	95	43	43	4	.314	.371	.520
Sandy Amoros	OF109	L	25	119	388	59	96	16	7	10	51	55	45	10	.247	.347	.402
Don Zimmer	2B62,SS21,3B8	R	24	88	280	38	67	10	1	15	50	19	66	5	.239	.289	.443
Don Hoak	3B78	R	27	94	279	50	67	13	3	5	19	46	50	9	.240	.350	.362
Rube Walker	C35	L	29	48	103	6	26	5	0	2	13	15	11	1	.252	.342	.359
Frank Kellert	1B22	R	30	39	80	12	26	4	2	4	19	9	10	0	.325	.385	.575
George Shuba	OF9	L	30	44	51	8	14	2	0	1	8	11	10	0	.275	.422	.373
Dixie Howell	C13	R	35	16	42	2	11	4	0	0	5	1	7	0	.262	.273	.357
Walt Moryn	OF7	L	29	11	19	3	5	1	0	1	3	5	4	0	.263	.417	.474
Bob Borkowski†	OF9	R	29	9	19	2	2	0	0	0	0	1	6	0	.105	.150	.105
Bert Hamric		L	27	2	1	0	0	0	0	0	0	0	1	0	.000	.000	.000

J. Robinson, 1 G at 2B

Pitcher	T	Age	G	GS	CG	ShO	IP	H	HR	BB	SO	W-L	Sv	ERA
Don Newcombe	R	29	34	31	17	1	233.2	222	35	38	143	20-5	0	3.20
Carl Erskine	R	28	31	29	7	2	194.2	185	29	64	84	11-8	1	3.79
Johnny Podres	L	22	27	24	5	2	159.1	160	15	57	114	9-10	0	3.95
Billy Loes	R	25	22	19	6	0	128.0	116	16	46	85	10-4	0	3.59
Russ Meyer	R	31	18	11	2	1	73.0	86	8	31	26	6-2	0	5.42
Clem Labine	R	28	60	8	1	0	144.1	121	12	55	67	13-5	11	3.24
Ed Roebuck	R	23	47	0	0	0	84.0	96	14	24	33	5-6	12	4.71
Karl Spooner	L	24	29	14	2	1	98.2	79	8	41	78	8-6	2	3.65
Don Bessent	R	24	24	2	1	0	63.1	51	7	21	29	8-1	3	2.70
Jim Hughes	R	32	24	0	0	0	42.2	41	10	19	20	0-2	6	4.22
Roger Craig	R	25	21	10	3	0	90.2	81	8	43	48	5-3	2	2.78
Sandy Koufax	L	19	12	5	2	2	41.2	33	2	28	30	2-2	0	3.02
Joe Black†	R	31	6	0	0	0	15.1	15	1	5	9	1-0	0	2.93
Chuck Templeton	L	23	4	0	0	0	4.2	5	2	5	3	0-1	0	11.57
Tom Lasorda	L	27	4	1	0	0	4.0	5	1	6	4	0-0	0	13.50

1955 Milwaukee Braves 2nd NL 85-69 .552 13.5 GB

Charlie Grimm

Player	Gm by Position	B	Age	G	AB	R	H	2B	3B	HR	RBI	BB	SO	SB	Avg	OBP	Slg
Del Crandall	C131	R	25	133	440	61	104	15	2	26	62	40	56	2	.236	.299	.457
George Crowe	1B79	L	34	104	303	41	85	12	4	15	55	45	44	1	.281	.374	.495
Danny O'Connell	2B114,3B7,SS1	R	28	124	453	47	102	15	4	6	40	28	43	2	.225	.276	.316
Eddie Mathews	3B137	L	23	141	499	108	144	23	5	41	101	109	98	3	.289	.413	.601
Johnny Logan	SS154	R	28	154	595	95	177	37	5	13	83	58	58	3	.297	.360	.442
Bill Bruton	OF149	L	29	149	636	106	175	30	12	9	47	43	72	25	.275	.325	.403
Hank Aaron	OF126,2B27	R	21	153	602	105	189	37	9	27	106	49	61	3	.314	.366	.540
Bobby Thomson	OF91	R	31	101	343	40	88	12	3	12	56	34	52	2	.257	.319	.414
Joe Adcock	1B78	R	27	84	288	40	76	14	0	15	45	31	44	0	.264	.339	.469
Andy Pafko	OF58,3B12	R	34	86	252	29	67	3	5	5	34	7	23	1	.266	.293	.377
Chuck Tanner	OF62	L	25	97	243	27	60	9	3	6	27	27	32	0	.247	.319	.383
Jack Dittmer	2B28	L	27	38	72	4	9	1	1	1	4	4	15	0	.125	.171	.208
Del Rice†	C22	R	32	27	71	5	14	0	1	2	7	6	12	0	.197	.260	.310
Charlie White	C10	L	26	12	30	3	7	1	0	0	4	5	7	0	.233	.361	.267
Jim Pendleton	3B1,SS1,OF1	R	31	8	10	0	0	0	0	0	0	0	2	0	.000	.000	.000
Ben Taylor	1B1	L	27	12	10	2	1	0	0	0	0	2	4	0	.100	.250	.100
Bob Roselli	C2	R	23	6	9	1	2	1	0	0	0	1	4	0	.222	.364	.333

Pitcher	T	Age	G	GS	CG	ShO	IP	H	HR	BB	SO	W-L	Sv	ERA
Lew Burdette	R	28	42	33	11	2	230.0	253	25	73	70	13-8	0	4.03
Warren Spahn	L	34	39	32	16	1	245.2	249	25	65	110	17-14	1	3.26
Bob Buhl	R	26	38	27	11	1	201.2	168	13	109	117	13-11	1	3.21
Gene Conley	R	24	22	21	10	0	158.0	152	23	52	107	11-7	0	4.16
Chet Nichols	L	24	34	21	6	0	144.0	139	20	67	44	9-8	1	4.00
Ernie Johnson	R	31	40	2	0	0	92.0	81	5	55	43	5-7	4	3.42
Dave Jolly	R	30	36	0	0	0	58.1	58	6	51	23	2-3	1	5.71
Ray Crone	R	23	33	15	6	1	140.1	117	11	42	76	10-9	0	3.46
Roberto Vargas	L	26	25	0	0	0	24.2	39	4	14	13	0-0	2	8.76
Phil Paine	R	25	15	0	0	0	25.1	20	2	14	26	2-0	0	2.49
Humberto Robinson	R	25	13	2	1	0	38.0	31	1	25	19	3-1	2	3.08
Joey Jay	R	19	12	1	0	0	19.0	23	2	13	3	0-0	0	4.74
John Edelman	R	19	5	0	0	0	5.2	7	0	8	3	0-0	0	11.12
Charlie Gorin	L	27	2	0	0	0	0.1	1	0	3	0	0-0	0	54.00
Dave Koslo	L	35	1	0	0	0	0.0	1	1	0	0	0-1	0	—

1955 New York Giants 3rd NL 80-74 .519 18.5 GB

Leo Durocher

Player	Gm by Position	B	Age	G	AB	R	H	2B	3B	HR	RBI	BB	SO	SB	Avg	OBP	Slg
Ray Katt	C122	R	28	124	326	27	70	7	2	7	28	22	38	0	.215	.268	.313
Gail Harris	1B75	L	23	79	263	27	61	9	0	12	36	20	46	0	.232	.289	.403
Wayne Terwilliger	2B78,3B1,SS1	R	30	80	257	29	66	16	1	1	18	36	42	2	.257	.348	.339
Hank Thompson	3B124,2B7,SS1	L	29	135	432	65	106	13	1	17	63	84	56	2	.245	.367	.398
Al Dark	SS115	R	33	115	475	77	134	20	3	9	45	22	32	2	.282	.319	.394
Willie Mays	OF152	R	24	152	580	123	185	18	13	51	127	79	60	24	.319	.400	.659
Don Mueller	OF146	L	28	147	605	67	185	21	4	8	83	19	12	1	.306	.326	.393
Whitey Lockman	OF81,1B68	L	28	147	576	76	157	19	0	15	49	39	34	3	.273	.320	.384
Davey Williams	2B71	R	27	82	247	25	62	4	1	4	15	17	17	0	.251	.303	.324
Bobby Hofman	1B24,C19,2B19*	R	29	96	207	32	55	7	2	10	28	22	31	0	.266	.336	.464
Billy Gardner	SS38,3B10,2B4	R	27	59	187	26	38	10	1	3	17	13	19	0	.203	.261	.316
Dusty Rhodes	OF45	L	28	94	187	22	57	5	2	6	32	27	26	1	.305	.389	.449
Monte Irvin	OF45	R	36	51	150	16	38	7	1	1	17	17	15	3	.253	.337	.333
Sid Gordon†	3B31,OF17	R	37	66	144	19	35	6	1	7	25	25	15	0	.243	.349	.444
Wes Westrum	C68	R	32	69	137	11	29	1	0	4	18	24	18	0	.212	.327	.307
Bill Taylor	OF2	L	25	65	64	9	17	4	0	4	12	1	16	0	.266	.273	.516
Foster Castleman	2B6,3B1	R	24	15	28	3	6	1	0	2	4	2	4	0	.214	.267	.464
Joey Amalfitano	SS5,3B2	R	21	36	22	8	5	1	1	0	1	2	2	0	.227	.292	.364
Gil Coan†	OF6	L	33	9	13	0	2	0	0	0	0	0	1	0	.154	.154	.154
Mickey Grasso	C8	R	35	8	2	0	0	0	0	0	0	3	0	0	.000	.600	.000

B. Hofman, 5 G at 3B

Pitcher	T	Age	G	GS	CG	ShO	IP	H	HR	BB	SO	W-L	Sv	ERA
Johnny Antonelli	L	25	38	34	14	2	235.1	206	24	82	143	14-16	1	3.33
Jim Hearn	R	34	39	33	11	1	226.2	225	27	66	86	14-16	0	3.73
Ruben Gomez	R	27	33	31	9	3	185.1	207	20	63	79	9-10	1	4.56
Sal Maglie†	R	38	23	21	6	0	129.2	142	18	48	71	9-5	0	3.75
Pete Burnside	L	24	2	2	1	0	12.2	10	1	9	2	1-0	0	2.84
Hoyt Wilhelm	R	31	59	0	0	0	103.0	104	10	40	71	4-1	0	3.93
Marv Grissom	R	37	55	0	0	0	89.1	76	6	41	49	5-4	8	2.92
Windy McCall	L	29	42	6	4	0	95.0	86	8	37	50	6-5	3	3.69
Paul Giel	R	22	34	2	0	0	82.1	70	8	50	47	4-4	0	3.39
Don Liddle	L	30	33	13	4	0	106.1	97	18	61	56	10-4	1	4.23
Ray Monzant	R	22	28	12	3	0	94.2	98	11	43	54	4-8	0	3.99
Al Corwin	R	28	13	0	0	0	24.2	25	3	17	13	0-1	0	4.01
George Spencer	R	28	1	0	0	0	1.2	1	1	3	0	0-0	0	5.40

1955 Philadelphia Phillies 4th NL 77-77 .500 21.5 GB

Mayo Smith

Player	Gm by Position	B	Age	G	AB	R	H	2B	3B	HR	RBI	BB	SO	SB	Avg	OBP	Slg
Andy Seminick†	C88	R	34	93	289	32	71	12	1	11	34	32	59	1	.246	.333	.408
Marv Blaylock	1B77,OF6	L	25	113	259	30	54	7	7	3	24	31	43	6	.208	.293	.324
Bobby Morgan	2B88,SS41,3B6*	R	29	136	483	61	112	20	2	10	49	73	72	6	.232	.331	.344
Puddin' Head Jones	3B146	R	29	146	516	65	133	20	3	16	81	77	51	6	.258	.352	.401
Roy Smalley	SS87,2B1,3B1	R	29	92	260	33	51	11	1	7	39	39	58	0	.196	.304	.327
Del Ennis	OF145	R	30	146	564	82	167	24	7	29	120	46	46	4	.296	.346	.518
Richie Ashburn	OF140	L	28	140	533	91	180	32	9	3	42	105	36	12	.338	.449	.448
Jim Greengrass†	OF83,3B2	R	27	94	323	43	88	20	2	12	37	33	43	0	.272	.339	.458
Granny Hamner	2B82,SS32	R	28	104	405	57	104	12	4	5	43	41	30	0	.257	.323	.343
Stan Lopata	C66,1B24	R	29	99	303	49	82	9	3	22	58	58	62	4	.271	.388	.538
Glen Gorbous†	OF57	L	24	91	224	25	53	9	1	4	23	21	17	0	.237	.301	.339
Earl Torgeson†	1B43	L	31	47	150	29	40	5	3	1	17	32	20	2	.267	.393	.360
Eddie Waitkus†	1B31	L	35	33	107	10	30	5	0	2	14	17	7	0	.280	.379	.383
Peanuts Lowrey	OF28,2B2,1B1	R	36	54	106	9	20	4	0	0	8	7	10	2	.189	.237	.226
Stan Palys†	OF15	R	25	15	52	8	15	3	0	1	8	6	5	1	.288	.362	.404
Mel Clark	OF8	R	28	10	32	3	5	3	0	0	1	3	4	0	.156	.229	.250
Smoky Burgess†	C6	L	28	7	21	4	4	2	0	1	1	3	1	0	.190	.292	.429
Ted Kazanski	3B4,SS4	R	21	9	12	1	1	0	0	1	1	1	1	0	.083	.154	.333
Gus Niarhos	C7	R	34	7	9	1	1	0	0	0	0	0	2	0	.111	.111	.111
Floyd Baker	3B1	L	38	5	8	0	0	0	0	0	0	0	1	0	.000	.000	.000
Jim Command		L	26	5	5	0	0	0	0	0	0	0	0	0	.000	.000	.000
Mickey Micelotta	SS2	R	26	4	4	0	0	0	0	0	0	0	0	0	.000	.000	.000
Bob Bowman	OF2	R	24	3	3	0	0	0	0	0	0	0	0	0	.000	.000	.000
Danny Schell		R	27	2	2	0	0	0	0	0	0	0	1	0	.000	.000	.000
Jim Westlake		L	24	1	1	0	0	0	0	0	0	0	1	0	.000	.000	.000
Fred Van Dusen		L	17	1	0	0	0	0	0	0	0	0	0	0	—	1.000	—
John Easton		R	22	1	0	0	0	0	0	0	0	0	0	0	—	—	—

B. Morgan, 1 G at 1B

Pitcher	T	Age	G	GS	CG	ShO	IP	H	HR	BB	SO	W-L	Sv	ERA
Robin Roberts	R	28	41	38	26	1	305.0	292	41	53	160	23-14	3	3.28
Herm Wehmeier	R	28	31	29	10	1	193.2	176	21	67	85	10-12	0	4.41
Murry Dickson	R	38	36	28	12	4	216.0	190	27	82	92	12-11	0	3.50
Curt Simmons	L	26	25	22	3	0	130.0	148	15	50	58	8-8	0	4.92
Saul Rogovin†	R	31	12	11	5	2	73.0	60	3	17	27	5-3	0	3.08
Ron Negray	R	25	19	10	2	0	71.2	71	13	21	30	4-3	0	3.52
Jim Owens	R	21	3	2	0	0	8.2	13	2	7	6	0-2	0	8.31
Jack Meyer	R	23	50	5	0	0	110.1	75	14	66	97	6-11	16	3.43
Bob Miller	R	29	40	0	0	0	89.2	80	6	28	28	8-4	1	2.41
Thornton Kipper	R	26	24	0	0	0	39.2	47	4	22	15	0-1	0	4.99
Ron Mrozinski	L	24	22	1	0	0	34.1	38	2	19	18	0-2	1	6.55
Bob Kuzava†	L	32	17	4	0	0	32.1	47	5	12	13	1-0	0	7.24
Lynn Lovenguth	R	32	14	0	0	0	18.0	17	1	10	14	0-1	0	4.50
Dave Cole	R	24	7	3	0	0	18.1	21	3	14	6	0-3	0	6.38
Steve Ridzik†	R	26	3	1	0	0	11.0	7	1	8	6	0-1	0	2.45
Jack Spring	L	22	2	0	0	0	2.2	2	2	1	2	0-1	0	6.75
Bob Greenwood	R	27	1	0	0	0	2.1	7	1	0	0	0-0	0	15.43

1955 Cincinnati Reds 5th NL 75-79 .487 23.5 GB

Birdie Tebbetts

Player	Gm by Position	B	Age	G	AB	R	H	2B	3B	HR	RBI	BB	SO	SB	Avg	OBP	Slg
Smoky Burgess†	C107	L	28	116	421	67	129	15	3	20	77	47	35	1	.306	.373	.499
Ted Kluszewski	1B153	L	30	153	612	116	192	25	0	47	113	66	40	1	.314	.382	.585
Johnny Temple	2B149,SS1	R	27	150	588	94	165	20	3	0	50	80	32	19	.281	.365	.325
Rocky Bridges	3B59,SS26,2B9	R	27	95	168	20	48	4	0	1	18	15	19	1	.286	.341	.327
Roy McMillan	SS150	R	24	151	470	50	126	21	2	1	37	66	33	4	.268	.364	.328
Gus Bell	OF154	L	26	154	610	88	188	30	6	27	104	54	57	4	.308	.361	.510
Wally Post	OF154	R	25	154	601	116	186	33	3	40	109	60	102	7	.309	.372	.574
Stan Palys†	OF55,1B1	R	25	79	222	29	51	14	0	7	30	12	35	1	.230	.271	.387
Ray Jablonski	3B28,OF28	R	28	74	221	28	53	9	0	9	28	13	35	0	.240	.289	.403
Chuck Harmon	3B39,OF32,1B4	R	31	96	198	31	50	6	3	5	28	26	24	9	.253	.345	.389
Bob Thurman	OF36	L	38	82	152	19	33	2	3	7	22	17	26	0	.217	.296	.408
Bobby Adams†	3B42,2B5	R	33	64	150	23	41	11	2	2	20	20	21	2	.273	.368	.413
Milt Smith	3B28,2B5	R	26	36	102	15	20	3	1	3	8	13	24	2	.196	.293	.333
Hobie Landrith	C27	L	25	43	87	9	22	3	0	4	7	10	14	0	.253	.330	.425
Matt Batts	C21	R	33	26	71	4	18	4	1	0	13	4	11	0	.254	.286	.338
Sam Mele†	OF13,1B1	R	32	35	62	4	13	1	0	2	7	5	13	0	.210	.279	.323
Ed Bailey	C11	L	24	21	39	3	8	1	1	1	4	4	10	0	.205	.326	.359
Jim Greengrass†	OF11	R	27	13	39	1	4	2	0	0	1	9	9	0	.103	.271	.154
Joe Brovia		L	33	21	18	0	2	0	0	0	4	1	6	0	.111	.150	.111
Glen Gorbous†	OF5	L	24	8	18	2	6	3	0	0	4	3	1	0	.333	.429	.500
Hersh Freeman†	P52,3B1	R	26	53	18	3	3	1	0	1	3	1	3	0	.167	.211	.389
Bob Borkowski†	OF11,1B1	R	29	25	18	1	3	1	0	0	1	1	2	0	.167	.211	.222
Andy Seminick†	C5	R	34	6	15	1	2	0	0	1	1	0	3	0	.133	.133	.333
Bob Hazle	OF3	L	24	6	13	0	3	0	0	0	0	0	3	0	.231	.231	.231
Al Silvera	OF1	R	19	13	7	3	1	0	0	0	2	0	1	0	.143	.143	.143

Pitcher	T	Age	G	GS	CG	ShO	IP	H	HR	BB	SO	W-L	Sv	ERA
Joe Nuxhall	L	26	50	33	14	5	257.0	240	25	78	98	17-12	3	3.47
Art Fowler	R	32	46	28	8	3	207.2	198	20	63	94	11-10	2	3.90
Gerry Staley†	R	34	30	18	2	0	119.2	146	22	28	40	5-8	0	4.66
Jackie Collum	L	28	32	17	5	0	134.0	128	17	37	49	9-8	1	3.63
Don Gross	L	24	17	11	2	1	67.1	79	11	16	33	4-5	0	4.14
Corky Valentine	R	26	10	5	0	0	26.2	29	5	16	14	2-1	0	7.43
Jim Pearce	R	30	2	1	0	0	3.1	8	0	0	0	0-1	0	10.80
Hersh Freeman†	R	26	52	0	0	0	91.2	94	3	30	37	7-4	11	2.16
Rudy Minarcin	R	25	41	12	3	1	115.2	116	17	51	45	5-9	1	4.90
Johnny Klippstein	R	27	39	14	3	2	138.0	120	13	60	68	9-10	0	3.39
Joe Black†	R	31	32	11	1	0	102.1	106	13	25	54	5-2	3	4.22
Bud Podbielan	R	31	17	2	0	0	42.0	36	4	11	26	1-2	0	3.21
Steve Ridzik†	R	26	13	2	0	0	30.0	35	4	14	6	0-3	0	4.50
Bob Hooper	R	33	8	0	0	0	13.0	20	2	6	6	0-2	0	7.62
Jerry Lane	R	29	8	0	0	0	11.0	11	2	6	5	0-2	1	4.91
Maurice Fisher	R	24	1	0	0	0	2.2	5	1	2	1	0-0	0	6.75
Fred Baczewski	L	29	1	0	0	0	1.0	2	2	0	0	0-0	0	18.00

1955 Chicago Cubs 6th NL 72-81 .471 26.0 GB

Stan Hack

Player	Gm by Position	B	Age	G	AB	R	H	2B	3B	HR	RBI	BB	SO	SB	Avg	OBP	Slg
Harry Chiti	C113	R	22	113	338	24	78	6	1	11	41	25	68	0	.231	.282	.352
Dee Fondy	1B147	L	30	150	574	69	152	23	8	17	65	35	87	8	.265	.307	.422
Gene Baker	2B154	R	30	154	609	82	163	29	7	11	52	49	57	9	.268	.323	.392
Randy Jackson	3B134	R	29	138	499	73	132	13	7	21	70	58	58	0	.265	.340	.445
Ernie Banks	SS154	R	24	154	596	98	176	29	9	44	117	45	72	9	.295	.345	.596
Eddie Miksis	OF111,3B18	R	28	131	481	52	113	14	2	9	41	32	55	3	.235	.282	.328
Jim King	OF93	L	22	113	301	43	77	12	3	11	45	24	39	2	.256	.312	.425
Hank Sauer	OF68	R	38	79	261	29	55	8	1	12	28	26	47	0	.211	.286	.387
Frankie Baumholtz	OF63	L	36	105	280	23	81	12	5	1	27	16	24	0	.289	.325	.379
Bob Speake	OF55,1B8	L	24	95	261	36	57	9	5	12	43	28	71	3	.218	.300	.429
Jim Bolger	OF51	R	23	64	160	19	33	5	4	0	7	9	17	2	.206	.257	.288
Lloyd Merriman†	OF47	L	30	72	145	15	31	6	1	1	8	21	21	1	.214	.311	.290
Walker Cooper	C31	R	40	54	111	11	31	8	1	7	15	6	19	0	.279	.322	.559
Clyde McCullough	C37	R	38	44	81	7	16	0	0	0	10	8	15	0	.198	.272	.198
Ted Tappe	OF15	L	24	23	50	12	13	2	0	4	10	11	11	0	.260	.413	.540
Gale Wade	OF9	L	26	9	33	5	6	1	0	1	1	4	3	0	.182	.270	.303
Jim Fanning	C5	R	27	5	10	0	0	0	0	0	0	1	2	0	.000	.091	.000
Owen Friend†	3B2,SS1	R	28	6	10	0	1	0	0	0	0	0	3	0	.100	.100	.100
Vern Morgan	3B2	L	26	7	7	1	1	0	0	0	1	3	4	0	.143	.400	.143
Al Lary		R	26	4	0	1	0	0	0	0	0	0	0	0	—	—	—
El Tappe	C2	R	28	2	0	0	0	0	0	0	0	0	0	0	—	—	—

Pitcher	T	Age	G	GS	CG	ShO	IP	H	HR	BB	SO	W-L	Sv	ERA
Sam Jones	R	29	36	34	12	4	241.2	175	22	185	198	14-20	0	4.10
Bob Rush	R	29	33	33	14	3	234.0	204	19	73	130	13-11	0	3.50
Warren Hacker	R	30	35	30	13	0	213.0	202	38	43	80	11-15	3	4.27
Paul Minner	L	31	22	22	7	1	157.2	173	15	47	53	9-9	0	3.48
Hal Jeffcoat	R	30	50	1	0	0	100.2	107	5	53	32	8-6	6	2.95
Jim Davis	L	30	42	16	0	0	133.2	122	16	58	62	7-11	3	4.44
Dave Hillman	R	27	25	3	0	0	57.2	63	10	25	23	0-0	0	5.31
Harry Perkowski	L	32	25	4	0	0	47.2	53	3	25	28	3-4	2	5.29
Howie Pollet	L	34	24	7	1	1	61.0	62	11	27	27	4-3	5	5.61
Bill Tremel	R	25	23	0	0	0	38.2	33	2	18	13	3-0	2	3.72
John Andre	R	32	22	3	0	0	45.0	45	7	28	19	0-1	1	5.80
Don Kaiser	R	20	11	0	0	0	18.1	20	2	5	11	0-0	0	5.40
Hy Cohen	R	24	7	1	0	0	17.0	28	2	10	4	0-0	0	7.94
Vincente Amor	R	22	4	0	0	0	6.0	11	0	3	3	0-1	0	4.50
Bubba Church	R	30	2	0	0	0	3.1	4	1	1	3	0-0	1	5.40
Bob Thorpe	R	20	2	0	0	0	3.0	4	0	0	0	0-0	0	3.00

1955 St. Louis Cardinals 7th NL 68-86 .442 30.5 GB

Eddie Stanky (17-19)/Harry Walker (51-67)

Player	Gm by Position	B	Age	G	AB	R	H	2B	3B	HR	RBI	BB	SO	SB	Avg	OBP	Slg
Bill Sarni	C99	R	27	107	325	32	83	15	2	3	34	27	33	1	.255	.313	.342
Stan Musial	1B110,OF51	L	34	154	562	97	179	30	5	33	108	80	39	5	.319	.408	.566
Red Schoendienst	2B142	S	32	145	553	68	148	21	3	11	51	54	28	7	.268	.335	.376
Ken Boyer	3B139,SS18	R	24	147	530	78	140	27	2	18	62	37	67	22	.264	.311	.425
Alex Grammas	SS126	R	29	128	366	32	88	19	2	3	25	33	36	4	.240	.308	.328
Bill Virdon	OF142	L	24	144	534	58	150	18	6	17	68	36	64	2	.281	.322	.433
Rip Repulski	OF141	R	27	147	512	64	138	28	2	23	73	49	66	5	.270	.333	.467
Wally Moon	OF100,1B51	L	25	152	593	86	175	24	8	19	76	47	65	11	.295	.349	.459
Solly Hemus	3B43,2B10,SS2	L	32	96	206	36	50	10	2	5	21	27	22	1	.243	.335	.383
Nels Burbrink	C55	R	33	58	170	11	47	8	1	0	15	14	13	1	.276	.333	.335
Harry Elliott	OF28	R	31	68	117	9	30	4	0	1	12	11	9	0	.256	.321	.316
Pete Whisenant	OF40	R	25	58	115	10	22	5	1	2	9	5	29	2	.191	.223	.304
Bob Stephenson	SS48,2B7,3B1	R	26	67	111	19	27	3	0	0	6	5	18	2	.243	.274	.270
Joe Frazier	OF14	L	32	58	70	12	14	1	0	4	9	6	12	0	.200	.269	.386
Del Rice†	C18	R	32	20	59	6	12	3	0	1	7	7	6	0	.203	.284	.305
Tom Poholsky	P30,OF1	R	25	30	44	6	8	3	0	0	3	1	6	0	.182	.200	.250
Don Blasingame	2B3,SS2	L	23	5	16	4	6	1	0	0	0	6	0	1	.375	.545	.438
Harry Walker	OF1	L	38	11	14	2	5	2	0	0	1	1	0	0	.357	.400	.500
Dick Rand	C3	R	24	3	10	1	3	0	0	1	3	1	1	0	.300	.364	.600
Tom Alston	1B7	L	29	13	8	0	1	0	0	0	0	0	0	0	.125	.125	.125
Dick Schofield	SS3	S	20	12	4	3	0	0	0	0	0	0	1	0	.000	.000	.000

Pitcher	T	Age	G	GS	CG	ShO	IP	H	HR	BB	SO	W-L	Sv	ERA
Harvey Haddix	L	29	37	30	9	2	208.0	216	27	62	150	12-16	1	4.46
Larry Jackson	R	24	37	25	4	1	177.1	189	25	72	88	9-14	2	4.31
Luis Arroyo	L	28	35	24	9	1	159.0	162	22	63	68	11-8	0	4.19
Tom Poholsky	R	25	30	24	8	2	151.0	143	26	35	66	9-11	0	3.81
Willard Schmidt	R	27	20	15	8	1	129.2	89	7	57	86	7-6	0	2.78
Gordon Jones	R	25	15	9	0	0	57.0	66	10	28	46	1-4	0	5.84
Ben Flowers†	R	28	4	4	0	0	27.1	27	1	12	19	1-0	0	3.62
Lindy McDaniel	R	19	4	2	0	0	19.0	22	4	7	7	0-0	0	4.74
Vic Raschi†	R	36	1	1	0	0	1.2	5	0	1	1	0-1	0	21.60
Paul LaPalme	L	31	56	0	0	0	91.2	76	10	34	39	4-3	3	2.75
Brooks Lawrence	R	30	46	10	2	1	96.0	102	11	58	52	3-8	1	6.56
Mel Wright	R	27	29	0	0	0	36.1	44	4	9	18	2-2	1	6.19
Frank Smith	R	27	28	0	0	0	39.0	27	3	23	17	3-1	1	3.23
Barney Schultz	R	28	19	0	0	0	29.2	28	5	15	19	1-2	4	7.89
Floyd Wooldridge	R	26	18	8	2	0	57.2	64	9	27	14	2-4	0	4.84
Bobby Tiefenauer	R	25	18	0	0	0	32.2	31	6	10	16	1-4	0	4.41
Herb Moford	R	26	14	1	0	0	24.0	29	5	15	8	1-1	2	7.88
Johnny Mackinson	R	31	8	1	0	0	20.2	24	3	10	8	0-1	0	7.84
Al Gettel	R	37	8	0	0	0	17.0	26	6	10	7	1-0	0	9.00
Tony Jacobs	R	29	1	0	0	0	2.0	6	1	1	1	0-0	0	18.00

1955 Pittsburgh Pirates 8th NL 60-94 .390 38.5 GB

Fred Haney

Player	Gm by Position	B	Age	G	AB	R	H	2B	3B	HR	RBI	BB	SO	SB	Avg	OBP	Slg
Jack Shepard	C77	R	24	94	264	24	63	10	2	2	23	33	25	1	.239	.321	.314
Dale Long	1B119	L	29	131	419	59	122	19	13	16	79	48	72	0	.291	.362	.513
Johnny O'Brien	2B78	R	24	84	278	22	83	15	2	1	25	20	19	1	.299	.346	.378
Gene Freese	3B65,2B57	R	21	134	455	69	115	21	8	14	44	34	57	5	.253	.310	.426
Dick Groat	SS149	R	24	151	521	45	139	28	2	4	51	38	26	0	.267	.317	.351
Frank Thomas	OF139	R	26	142	510	72	125	16	2	25	72	60	76	2	.245	.324	.431
Roberto Clemente	OF118	R	20	124	474	48	121	23	11	5	47	18	60	2	.255	.284	.382
Jerry Lynch	OF71,C2	L	24	88	282	43	80	18	6	5	28	22	33	2	.284	.331	.443
Dick Cole	3B33,2B24,SS12	R	29	77	239	16	54	8	3	0	21	18	22	0	.226	.285	.285
Eddie O'Brien	OF56,3B7,SS4	R	24	75	236	26	55	3	1	0	8	18	13	4	.233	.290	.254
Toby Atwell	C67	L	31	71	207	21	44	8	0	1	18	40	16	0	.213	.337	.266
George Freese	3B50	R	28	51	179	17	46	8	2	3	22	17	18	1	.257	.327	.374
Preston Ward	1B48,OF1	L	27	84	179	16	38	7	4	5	25	22	28	0	.212	.296	.380
Roman Mejias	OF44	R	24	71	167	14	36	8	1	3	21	9	13	1	.216	.256	.329
Tom Saffell†	OF47	L	33	73	113	21	19	1	0	1	3	15	22	1	.168	.266	.204
Felipe Montemayor	OF28	L	25	36	95	10	20	1	3	2	8	18	24	1	.211	.342	.347
Hardy Peterson	C31	R	25	32	81	7	20	6	0	1	10	7	7	0	.247	.311	.358
Sid Gordon†	3B8,OF4	R	37	16	47	2	8	1	0	0	1	2	6	0	.170	.204	.191
Dick Hall	P15,OF3	R	24	21	40	3	7	1	0	1	3	6	5	0	.175	.283	.275
Ron Kline	P36,3B1	R	23	37	38	1	5	0	0	0	0	1	21	0	.132	.154	.132
Curt Roberts	2B6	R	25	6	17	1	2	1	0	0	0	2	1	0	.118	.211	.176
Earl Smith	OF5	R	27	5	16	1	1	0	0	0	0	4	2	0	.063	.286	.063
Nick Koback	C2	R	19	5	7	0	2	0	0	0	0	0	1	0	.286	.286	.286
John Powers	OF2	L	25	2	4	0	1	0	0	0	0	0	0	0	.250	.250	.250
Dick Smith	SS1	R	27	4	0	1	0	0	0	0	0	1	0	0	—	1.000	—

Pitcher	T	Age	G	GS	CG	ShO	IP	H	HR	BB	SO	W-L	Sv	ERA
Vern Law	R	25	43	24	8	1	200.2	221	19	61	82	10-10	1	3.81
Max Surkont	R	33	35	22	5	0	166.1	194	23	78	84	7-14	2	5.57
Ron Kline	R	23	36	19	2	1	136.2	161	13	53	48	6-13	2	4.15
Dick Hall	R	24	15	13	4	0	94.1	92	8	28	46	6-6	1	3.91
Bob Purkey	R	25	14	10	2	0	67.2	77	5	25	24	2-7	1	5.32
Jake Thies	R	29	1	1	0	0	3.2	5	0	3	0	0-1	0	4.91
Bob Friend	R	24	44	20	9	2	200.1	178	18	52	98	14-9	2	2.83
Roy Face	R	27	42	10	4	0	125.2	128	10	40	84	5-7	5	3.58
Dick Littlefield	L	29	35	17	4	1	130.0	148	15	68	70	5-12	0	5.12
Lino Donoso	L	32	25	9	3	0	95.0	106	16	35	38	4-6	1	5.31
Nellie King	R	27	17	4	0	0	54.1	60	2	14	21	1-3	0	2.98
Laurin Pepper	R	24	14	1	0	0	20.0	30	5	25	7	0-1	0	10.35
Ben Wade	R	32	11	1	0	0	28.0	26	3	14	7	0-1	1	3.21
Roger Bowman	L	27	7	2	0	0	16.2	25	2	10	8	0-3	0	8.64
Paul Martin	R	23	7	1	0	0	7.0	13	0	17	3	0-1	0	14.14
Al Grunwald	L	25	3	0	0	0	7.2	7	1	7	2	0-0	0	4.70
Fred Waters	L	28	2	0	0	0	5.0	7	1	2	0	0-0	0	3.60
Red Swanson	R	18	1	0	0	0	2.0	2	1	3	0	0-0	0	18.00
Bill Bell	R	21	1	0	0	0	1.0	0	0	1	0	0-0	0	0.00

»1956 New York Yankees 1st AL 97-57 .630 —

Casey Stengel

Player	Gm by Position	B	Age	G	AB	R	H	2B	3B	HR	RBI	BB	SO	SB	Avg	OBP	Slg
Yogi Berra	C135,OF1	L	31	140	521	93	155	29	2	30	105	65	29	3	.298	.378	.534
Bill Skowron	1B120,3B2	R	25	134	464	78	143	21	6	23	90	50	60	4	.308	.382	.528
Billy Martin	2B105,3B16	R	28	121	458	76	121	24	5	9	49	30	56	7	.264	.310	.397
Andy Carey	3B131	R	24	132	422	54	100	18	2	7	50	45	53	9	.237	.310	.339
Gil McDougald	SS92,2B31,3B5	R	28	120	438	79	136	13	3	13	56	68	59	3	.311	.405	.443
Hank Bauer	OF146	R	33	147	539	96	130	18	7	26	84	59	72	4	.241	.316	.445
Mickey Mantle	OF144	S	24	150	533	132	188	22	5	52	130	112	99	10	.353	.464	.705
Elston Howard	OF65,C26	R	27	98	290	35	76	8	3	5	34	21	30	0	.262	.312	.362
Joe Collins	OF51,1B43	L	33	100	262	38	59	5	3	7	43	34	33	3	.225	.313	.347
Jerry Coleman	2B41,SS24,3B18	R	31	80	183	15	47	5	1	0	18	12	33	1	.257	.305	.295
Norm Siebern	OF51	L	22	54	162	27	33	1	4	4	21	19	38	1	.204	.286	.333
Bob Cerv	OF44	R	30	54	115	16	35	5	6	3	25	18	13	0	.304	.396	.530
Enos Slaughter†	OF20	L	40	24	83	15	24	4	2	0	4	5	6	1	.289	.330	.386
Billy Hunter	SS32,3B4	R	28	39	75	8	21	3	4	0	11	2	4	0	.280	.299	.427
Jerry Lumpe	SS17,3B1	L	23	20	62	12	16	3	0	0	4	5	11	1	.258	.313	.306
Eddie Robinson†	1B14	L	35	26	54	7	12	1	0	5	11	5	3	0	.222	.323	.519
Phil Rizzuto	SS30	R	38	31	52	6	12	0	0	0	6	6	6	3	.231	.310	.231
Irv Noren	OF10,1B1	L	31	29	37	4	8	1	0	0	6	12	7	0	.216	.408	.243
Tom Carroll	3B11,SS1	R	19	36	17	11	6	0	0	0	0	1	3	1	.353	.389	.353
George Wilson†	OF6	L	30	11	12	1	2	0	0	0	0	3	0	0	.167	.333	.167
Charlie Silvera	C7	R	31	7	9	0	2	0	0	0	0	2	3	0	.222	.364	.222
Bobby Richardson	2B5	R	20	5	7	1	1	0	0	0	0	0	1	0	.143	.143	.143
Lou Skizas†		R	24	6	6	0	1	0	0	0	1	0	2	0	.167	.167	.167

Pitcher	T	Age	G	GS	CG	ShO	IP	H	HR	BB	SO	W-L	Sv	ERA
Johnny Kucks	R	22	34	31	12	3	224.1	223	19	72	67	18-9	0	3.85
Whitey Ford	L	27	31	30	18	2	225.2	187	13	84	141	19-6	1	2.47
Bob Turley	R	25	27	21	5	1	132.0	138	13	103	91	8-4	1	5.05
Don Larsen	R	26	38	20	6	1	179.2	133	19	96	107	11-5	1	3.26
Tom Sturdivant	R	26	32	17	6	2	158.1	134	15	52	110	16-8	5	3.30
Ralph Terry	R	20	3	3	0	0	13.1	17	2	11	8	1-2	0	9.45
Tom Morgan	R	26	41	0	0	0	71.1	74	2	27	20	6-7	11	4.16
Tommy Byrne	L	36	37	8	1	0	109.2	108	9	72	52	7-3	6	3.36
Rip Coleman	L	24	29	9	0	0	88.1	97	6	42	42	3-5	2	3.67
Bob Grim	R	26	26	6	1	0	74.2	64	3	31	48	6-1	5	2.77
Mickey McDermott	L	28	23	9	1	0	87.0	85	10	47	38	2-6	0	4.24
Jim Konstanty†	R	39	8	0	0	0	11.0	15	3	6	6	0-0	2	4.91
Sonny Dixon	R	31	3	0	0	0	4.1	5	0	5	1	0-1	0	2.08
Jim Coates	R	23	2	0	0	0	2.0	1	0	4	0	0-0	0	13.50
Gerry Staley†	R	35	1	0	0	0	0.1	4	0	0	1	0-0	0	108.00

1956 Cleveland Indians 2nd AL 88-66 .571 9.0 GB

Al Lopez

Player	Gm by Position	B	Age	G	AB	R	H	2B	3B	HR	RBI	BB	SO	SB	Avg	OBP	Slg
Jim Hegan	C118	R	35	122	315	42	70	15	2	6	34	49	54	1	.222	.327	.340
Vic Wertz	1B133	L	31	136	481	65	127	22	0	32	106	75	87	0	.264	.364	.509
Bobby Avila	2B135	R	32	138	513	74	115	14	2	10	54	70	68	17	.224	.323	.318
Al Rosen	3B116	R	32	121	416	64	111	18	2	15	61	58	44	1	.267	.351	.428
Chico Carrasquel	SS141,3B1	R	30	141	474	60	115	15	1	7	48	52	61	0	.243	.323	.323
Jim Busby	OF133	R	29	135	494	72	116	17	3	12	50	43	47	8	.235	.301	.354
Al Smith	OF122,3B28,2B1	R	28	141	526	87	144	26	5	16	71	84	72	6	.274	.378	.433
Rocky Colavito	OF98	R	22	101	322	55	89	11	4	21	65	49	46	0	.276	.372	.531
Gene Woodling	OF85	L	33	100	317	56	83	17	0	8	38	69	29	2	.262	.395	.391
George Strickland	2B28,SS28,3B26	R	30	85	171	22	36	1	2	3	17	22	27	0	.211	.299	.292
Preston Ward†	1B60,OF17	L	28	87	150	18	38	10	0	6	21	16	20	0	.253	.325	.440
Hal Naragon	C48	L	27	53	122	11	35	3	1	3	18	13	9	0	.287	.355	.402
Sam Mele	OF20,1B8	R	33	57	114	17	29	7	0	4	20	12	20	0	.254	.320	.421
Earl Averill	C34	R	24	42	93	12	22	6	0	3	14	14	25	0	.237	.343	.398
Dave Pope†	OF18	L	35	25	70	6	17	3	1	0	3	1	12	0	.243	.250	.314
Rudy Regalado	3B14,1B1	R	26	16	47	4	11	1	0	0	2	4	1	0	.234	.308	.255
Joe Caffie	OF10	L	25	12	38	7	13	0	0	0	1	4	8	3	.342	.432	.342
Dale Mitchell†	OF1	L	34	38	30	2	4	0	0	0	6	7	2	0	.133	.297	.133
Kenny Kuhn	SS17,2B5	L	19	27	22	7	6	1	0	0	2	0	4	0	.273	.273	.318
Stu Locklin	OF1	L	27	9	6	0	1	0	0	0	0	0	1	0	.167	.167	.167
Hank Foiles†	C1	R	27	1	0	0	0	0	0	0	0	0	0	0	—	—	—
Bobby Young		L	31	1	0	0	0	0	0	0	0	0	0	0	—	—	—
Hoot Evers†		R	35	3	0	1	0	0	0	0	0	1	0	0	—	1.000	—

Pitcher	T	Age	G	GS	CG	ShO	IP	H	HR	BB	SO	W-L	Sv	ERA
Early Wynn	R	36	38	35	18	4	277.2	233	19	91	158	20-9	2	2.72
Bob Lemon	R	35	39	35	21	2	255.1	230	23	89	94	20-14	3	3.03
Herb Score	L	23	35	33	16	5	249.1	162	18	129	263	20-9	0	2.53
Mike Garcia	R	32	35	30	8	4	197.2	213	18	74	119	11-12	0	3.78
Hank Aguirre	L	25	16	9	2	1	65.1	63	7	27	31	3-5	1	3.72
Don Mossi	L	27	48	3	0	0	87.2	79	6	33	59	6-5	11	3.59
Cal McLish	R	30	37	2	0	0	61.2	67	5	32	27	2-4	1	4.96
Ray Narleski	R	27	32	0	0	0	59.1	36	5	19	42	3-2	4	1.52
Art Houtteman	R	28	22	4	0	0	46.2	60	5	31	19	2-2	1	6.56
Bob Feller	R	37	19	4	2	0	58.0	63	7	23	18	0-4	1	4.97
Bud Daley	L	23	14	0	0	0	20.1	21	2	14	13	1-0	0	6.20
Sal Maglie†	R	39	2	0	0	0	5.0	6	1	2	2	0-0	0	3.60

1956 Chicago White Sox 3rd AL 85-69 .552 12.0 GB — Marty Marion

Player	Gm by Position	B	Age	G	AB	R	H	2B	3B	HR	RBI	BB	SO	SB	Avg	OBP	Slg
Sherm Lollar	C132	R	31	136	450	55	132	28	2	11	75	53	34	2	.293	.383	.438
Walt Dropo	1B117	R	33	125	361	42	96	13	1	8	52	37	51	1	.266	.334	.374
Nellie Fox	2B154	L	28	154	649	109	192	20	10	4	52	44	14	8	.296	.347	.376
Fred Hatfield†	3B100,SS3	L	31	106	321	46	84	9	1	7	33	37	36	1	.262	.349	.361
Luis Aparicio	SS152	R	22	152	533	69	142	19	6	3	56	34	63	21	.266	.311	.341
Minnie Minoso	OF148,3B8,1B1	R	33	151	545	106	172	29	11	21	88	86	40	12	.316	.425	.525
Larry Doby	OF137	L	32	140	504	89	135	22	3	24	102	102	105	0	.268	.392	.466
Jim Rivera	OF134	L	33	139	491	76	125	23	5	12	66	49	75	20	.255	.322	.395
Dave Philley†	1B51,OF30	S	36	86	279	44	74	14	2	4	47	28	27	1	.265	.328	.373
Sammy Esposito	3B61,SS19,2B3	R	24	81	184	30	42	8	2	3	25	41	19	1	.228	.371	.342
Les Moss	C49	R	31	56	127	20	31	4	0	10	22	18	15	0	.244	.338	.512
Bubba Phillips	OF35,3B2	R	28	67	99	16	27	6	0	2	11	6	12	1	.273	.321	.394
George Kell†	3B18,1B4	R	33	21	80	7	25	5	0	1	11	8	6	0	.313	.371	.413
Ron Jackson	1B19	R	22	22	56	7	12	3	0	1	4	10	13	1	.214	.333	.321
Ron Northey	OF4	L	36	53	48	4	17	2	0	3	23	8	1	0	.354	.417	.583
Jim Delsing†	OF29	L	30	55	41	11	5	3	0	0	2	10	13	1	.122	.294	.195
Bob Nieman†	OF10	R	29	14	40	3	12	1	0	2	4	4	4	0	.300	.364	.475
Bob Kennedy†	3B6	R	35	8	13	0	1	0	0	0	0	2	4	0	.077	.200	.077
Jim Brideweser†	SS10	R	29	10	11	0	2	1	0	0	1	0	3	0	.182	.250	.273
Earl Battey	C3	R	21	4	4	1	1	0	0	0	0	1	1	0	.250	.400	.250
Cal Abrams	OF2	L	32	4	3	0	1	0	0	0	0	2	1	0	.333	.600	.333

Pitcher	T	Age	G	GS	CG	ShO	IP	H	HR	BB	SO	W-L	Sv	ERA
Billy Pierce	L	29	35	33	21	1	276.1	261	24	100	192	20-9	1	3.32
Dick Donovan	R	28	34	31	14	3	234.2	212	22	59	120	12-10	0	3.64
Jack Harshman	L	28	34	30	15	4	226.2	183	14	102	143	15-11	0	3.10
Jim Wilson†	R	34	28	21	6	3	159.2	149	15	70	82	9-12	0	4.06
Bob Keegan	R	35	20	16	4	0	105.1	119	15	35	32	5-7	0	3.93
Jim Derrington	L	16	1	1	0	0	6.0	9	2	6	3	0-1	0	7.50
Dixie Howell	R	36	34	1	0	0	64.1	79	3	36	28	5-6	4	4.62
Paul LaPalme†	L	32	29	0	0	0	45.2	31	2	27	23	3-1	2	2.36
Ellis Kinder†	R	41	29	0	0	0	29.2	33	2	8	19	3-1	3	2.73
Sandy Consuegra†	R	35	28	1	0	0	38.1	45	0	11	7	1-2	3	5.17
Gerry Staley†	R	35	26	10	5	0	101.2	98	11	20	25	8-3	0	2.92
Howie Pollet†	L	35	11	4	0	0	26.1	27	2	11	14	3-1	0	4.10
Morrie Martin†	L	33	10	0	0	0	18.1	21	1	7	9	1-0	0	4.91
Jim McDonald	R	29	8	3	0	0	18.2	29	2	7	10	0-2	0	8.68
Mike Fornieles†	R	24	6	0	0	0	15.2	22	1	6	6	0-1	0	4.60
Connie Johnson†	R	33	5	2	0	0	12.1	11	1	7	6	0-1	0	3.65
Jerry Dahlke	R	26	5	0	0	0	2.1	5	0	6	1	0-0	0	19.29
Harry Byrd	R	31	3	1	0	0	4.1	9	0	4	0	0-1	0	10.38
Bill Fischer	R	25	3	0	0	0	1.2	6	0	1	2	0-0	0	21.60
Dick Marlowe†	R	27	1	0	0	0	1.0	2	1	1	0	0-0	0	9.00

1956 Boston Red Sox 4th AL 84-70 .545 13.0 GB — Pinky Higgins

Player	Gm by Position	B	Age	G	AB	R	H	2B	3B	HR	RBI	BB	SO	SB	Avg	OBP	Slg
Sammy White	C114	R	27	114	392	28	96	15	2	5	44	35	40	2	.245	.304	.332
Mickey Vernon	1B108	L	38	119	403	67	125	28	4	15	84	57	40	1	.310	.403	.511
Billy Goodman	2B95	L	30	105	399	61	117	22	8	2	38	40	22	0	.293	.356	.404
Billy Klaus	3B106,SS26	L	27	135	520	91	141	29	5	7	59	90	43	1	.271	.378	.387
Don Buddin	SS113	R	22	114	377	49	90	24	0	5	37	65	62	2	.239	.352	.342
Jimmy Piersall	OF155	R	26	155	601	91	176	40	6	14	87	58	48	7	.293	.350	.449
Jackie Jensen	OF151	R	29	151	578	80	182	23	11	20	97	89	43	11	.315	.405	.497
Ted Williams	OF110	L	37	136	400	71	138	28	2	24	82	102	39	0	.345	.479	.605
Dick Gernert	OF50,1B37	R	27	106	306	53	89	11	0	16	68	56	57	1	.291	.399	.484
Ted Lepcio	2B57,3B22	R	25	83	284	34	74	10	0	15	51	30	77	1	.261	.335	.454
Pete Daley	C57	R	26	59	187	22	50	11	3	5	29	18	30	1	.267	.338	.439
Milt Bolling	SS26,3B11,2B1	R	25	45	118	19	25	3	2	3	8	18	20	1	.212	.319	.347
Frank Malzone	3B26	R	26	27	103	15	17	3	1	2	11	9	8	1	.165	.230	.272
Norm Zauchin	1B31	R	26	44	84	12	18	2	0	2	11	14	22	0	.214	.333	.310
Gene Stephens	OF71	L	23	104	63	22	17	2	0	1	7	12	12	0	.270	.387	.349
Faye Throneberry	OF13	L	25	24	50	6	11	2	0	1	3	3	16	0	.220	.264	.320
Gene Mauch	2B6	R	30	7	25	4	8	0	0	0	1	3	3	0	.320	.393	.320
Billy Consolo	2B25	R	21	48	11	13	2	0	0	0	1	3	5	0	.182	.357	.182
Grady Hatton†		L	33	5	5	0	2	0	0	0	2	0	0	0	.400	.400	.400
Marty Keough		L	21	3	2	1	0	0	0	0	0	1	1	0	.000	.333	.000

Pitcher	T	Age	G	GS	CG	ShO	IP	H	HR	BB	SO	W-L	Sv	ERA
Frank Sullivan	R	26	34	33	12	1	242.0	253	22	82	116	14-7	0	3.42
Tom Brewer	R	24	32	32	15	4	244.1	200	14	112	127	19-9	0	3.50
Willard Nixon	R	28	23	22	9	1	145.1	142	9	57	74	9-8	0	4.21
Mel Parnell	L	34	21	20	6	1	131.1	129	13	59	41	7-6	0	3.77
Bob Porterfield	R	32	25	18	4	1	126.0	127	21	64	53	3-12	0	5.14
Ike Delock	R	26	48	8	1	0	128.1	122	12	80	105	13-7	9	4.21
Tom Hurd	R	32	40	0	0	0	76.0	84	5	47	34	3-4	5	5.33
Dave Sisler	R	24	39	14	3	0	142.1	120	13	72	93	9-8	3	4.62
Leo Kiely	L	26	23	0	0	0	31.1	47	1	14	9	2-2	3	5.17
George Susce	R	24	21	6	0	0	69.2	71	14	44	26	2-4	0	6.20
Harry Dorish†	R	34	15	0	0	0	22.2	23	1	10	11	0-2	0	3.57
Frank Baumann	L	22	7	1	0	0	24.2	22	3	14	18	2-1	0	3.28
Rudy Minarcin	R	26	3	1	0	0	9.2	9	2	8	5	1-0	0	2.79
Johnny Schmitz†	L	35	2	0	0	0	4.1	5	0	4	0	0-0	0	0.00

1956 Detroit Tigers 5th AL 82-72 .532 15.0 GB — Bucky Harris

Player	Gm by Position	B	Age	G	AB	R	H	2B	3B	HR	RBI	BB	SO	SB	Avg	OBP	Slg
Frank House	C88	L	26	94	321	44	77	6	2	10	44	21	19	1	.240	.290	.364
Earl Torgeson	1B83	L	32	117	318	61	84	9	3	12	42	78	47	6	.264	.406	.425
Frank Bolling	2B102	R	24	102	366	53	103	21	7	7	45	42	51	6	.281	.354	.434
Ray Boone	3B130	R	32	131	481	77	148	14	6	25	81	77	46	0	.308	.403	.518
Harvey Kuenn	SS141,OF1	R	25	146	591	96	196	32	7	12	88	55	34	9	.332	.387	.470
Al Kaline	OF153	R	21	153	617	96	194	32	10	27	128	70	55	7	.314	.383	.530
Bill Tuttle	OF137	R	26	140	546	61	138	22	4	9	65	38	48	5	.253	.301	.357
Charlie Maxwell	OF136	L	29	141	500	96	163	14	3	28	87	79	74	1	.326	.414	.534
Red Wilson	C78	R	27	78	228	32	66	12	2	7	38	42	18	2	.289	.393	.452
Jack Phillips	1B56,2B1,OF1	R	34	67	224	31	66	13	2	1	20	21	19	1	.295	.354	.384
Bob Kennedy†	OF29,3B27	R	35	69	177	17	41	5	0	4	22	24	19	2	.232	.328	.328
Jim Brideweser†	SS32,2B31,3B4	R	29	70	156	23	34	4	0	0	10	20	19	3	.218	.307	.244
Wayne Belardi	1B31,OF2	L	25	79	154	24	43	3	1	6	15	15	13	0	.279	.371	.429
Jim Small	OF26	L	19	58	91	13	29	4	2	0	10	6	10	0	.319	.361	.407
Reno Bertoia	2B18,3B2	R	21	22	66	7	12	2	0	1	5	6	12	0	.182	.260	.258
Buddy Hicks	SS16,2B6,3B1	S	29	26	47	5	10	2	0	0	5	3	2	0	.213	.260	.255
J.W. Porter	C2,OF2	R	23	14	21	0	2	0	0	0	3	0	8	0	.095	.091	.095
Fred Hatfield†	2B4	L	31	8	12	2	3	0	0	0	2	2	1	0	.250	.400	.250
Jim Delsing†	OF3	L	30	10	12	0	0	0	0	0	0	3	3	0	.000	.250	.000
Charlie Lau	C3	L	23	3	9	1	2	0	0	0	0	0	1	0	.222	.222	.222
Chick King	OF4	R	25	7	9	0	2	0	0	0	1	1	4	0	.222	.300	.222
Walt Streuli	C3	R	20	3	8	0	2	1	0	0	1	1	2	0	.250	.333	.375

Pitcher	T	Age	G	GS	CG	ShO	IP	H	HR	BB	SO	W-L	Sv	ERA
Frank Lary	R	26	41	38	20	3	294.0	289	20	116	165	21-13	1	3.15
Billy Hoeft	L	24	38	34	18	4	248.0	276	22	104	172	20-14	0	4.06
Paul Foytack	R	25	43	33	16	1	256.0	211	24	142	184	15-13	4	3.59
Virgil Trucks	R	39	22	16	3	1	120.0	104	15	63	43	6-5	1	3.83
Ned Garver	R	30	6	3	1	0	17.2	15	2	13	6	0-2	0	4.08
Hal Woodeshick	L	23	2	2	0	0	5.1	12	1	3	1	0-2	0	13.50
Gene Host	L	23	1	1	0	0	4.2	9	2	2	5	0-0	0	7.71
Al Aber	L	28	42	0	0	0	63.0	65	1	25	21	4-4	7	3.43
Steve Gromek	R	36	40	13	4	0	141.0	142	25	47	64	8-6	4	4.28
Walt Masterson	R	36	35	0	0	0	49.2	54	2	32	28	1-1	0	4.17
Duke Maas	R	27	26	7	0	0	63.1	81	9	32	34	0-7	0	6.54
Jim Bunning	R	24	15	3	0	0	53.1	55	6	28	34	5-1	1	3.71
Bob Miller	L	20	11	3	0	0	31.2	37	5	22	16	0-2	0	5.68
Dick Marlowe†	R	27	7	1	0	0	11.0	12	1	9	4	1-1	0	5.73
Jim Brady	L	20	6	0	0	0	6.1	15	3	11	3	0-0	0	28.42
Bud Black	R	23	5	1	0	0	10.0	10	2	5	7	1-1	0	3.60
Pete Wojey	R	36	2	0	0	0	4.0	2	0	1	1	0-0	0	2.25

1956 Baltimore Orioles 6th AL 69-85 .448 28.0 GB — Paul Richards

Player	Gm by Position	B	Age	G	AB	R	H	2B	3B	HR	RBI	BB	SO	SB	Avg	OBP	Slg
Gus Triandos	C89,1B52	R	25	131	452	47	126	18	1	21	88	48	73	0	.279	.348	.462
Bob Boyd	1B60,OF8	L	30	70	225	28	70	8	3	2	11	30	14	0	.311	.395	.400
Billy Gardner	2B132,SS25,3B6	R	28	144	515	53	119	16	2	11	50	29	53	5	.231	.281	.334
George Kell†	3B97,1B2,2B1	R	33	102	345	45	90	17	2	8	37	25	31	0	.261	.313	.391
Willie Miranda	SS147	S	30	148	461	38	100	16	4	2	34	46	73	3	.217	.287	.282
Tito Francona	OF122,1B21	L	22	139	445	62	115	16	4	9	57	51	60	11	.258	.334	.373
Bob Nieman†	OF114	R	29	114	388	60	125	20	6	12	64	86	59	1	.322	.442	.497
Dick Williams†	OF81,1B10,2B10*	R	27	87	353	45	101	18	4	11	37	30	40	5	.286	.342	.453
Hal Smith†	C72	R	25	78	229	16	60	14	0	3	18	17	22	1	.262	.315	.362
Bob Hale	1B51	L	22	85	207	18	49	10	1	1	24	11	10	0	.237	.274	.309
Jim Pyburn	OF77	R	23	84	156	23	27	3	3	2	11	17	26	4	.173	.251	.269
Dave Philley†	OF31,3B5	S	36	32	117	13	24	4	2	1	17	18	13	3	.205	.309	.299
Hoot Evers†	OF36	R	35	48	112	20	27	3	0	1	4	24	18	1	.241	.375	.295
Bobby Adams	3B24,2B18	R	34	41	111	19	25	6	1	0	7	25	15	1	.225	.362	.297
Chuck Diering	OF40,3B2	R	33	50	97	15	18	4	0	1	4	23	19	2	.186	.342	.258
Wayne Causey	3B30,2B7	L	19	53	88	7	15	0	1	1	4	8	23	0	.170	.237	.227
Joe Frazier†	OF19	L	33	45	74	7	19	6	0	1	12	11	6	0	.257	.356	.378
Tex Nelson	OF24	L	19	39	68	5	14	2	0	0	5	7	22	0	.206	.276	.235
Grady Hatton†	2B15,3B12	L	33	27	61	4	9	1	0	1	3	13	6	0	.148	.297	.213
Tom Gastall	C20	R	24	32	56	3	11	2	0	0	4	3	8	0	.196	.246	.232
Brooks Robinson	3B14,2B1	R	19	15	44	5	10	4	0	1	1	1	5	0	.227	.244	.386
Joe Ginsberg†	C8	L	29	15	28	0	2	0	0	0	2	2	4	0	.071	.129	.071
Fred Marsh	3B8,SS8,2B5	R	32	20	24	2	3	0	0	0	0	4	3	1	.125	.250	.125
Jim Dyck†	OF9	R	34	11	23	3	5	2	0	0	0	10	5	0	.217	.455	.304
Dave Pope†	OF4	L	35	12	19	1	3	0	0	0	1	0	7	0	.158	.200	.158

D. Williams, 4 G at 3B

Pitcher	T	Age	G	GS	CG	ShO	IP	H	HR	BB	SO	W-L	Sv	ERA
Ray Moore	R	30	32	27	9	1	185.0	161	12	99	105	12-7	0	4.18
Bill Wight	L	34	35	26	7	1	174.2	198	7	72	84	9-12	0	4.02
Connie Johnson†	R	33	26	25	9	2	183.2	165	12	62	130	9-10	0	3.43
Jim Wilson†	R	34	7	7	1	0	48.1	49	5	16	31	4-2	0	5.03
Charlie Beamon	R	21	2	1	1	0	13.0	9	0	8	14	2-0	0	1.38
Rob Harrison	R	25	1	1	0	0	1.2	3	0	5	0	0-0	0	16.20
George Zuverink	R	31	62	0	0	0	97.1	112	6	34	33	7-6	16	4.16
Don Ferrarese	L	27	36	14	3	1	102.0	86	8	64	81	4-10	2	5.03
Hal Brown	R	31	35	14	4	1	151.2	142	18	37	57	9-7	2	4.04
Mike Fornieles†	R	24	30	11	1	1	111.0	109	7	25	53	4-7	1	3.97
Erv Palica	R	28	29	14	2	0	116.1	117	10	50	62	4-11	0	4.49
Billy Loes†	R	26	21	6	1	0	56.2	65	4	23	22	2-7	3	4.76
Johnny Schmitz†	L	35	18	3	0	0	38.1	49	3	14	15	0-3	0	3.99
Harry Dorish†	R	34	13	0	0	0	19.2	22	3	3	4	0-0	0	4.12
Morrie Martin†	L	33	9	0	0	0	5.0	10	1	2	3	1-1	0	10.80
Fred Besana	L	25	7	2	0	0	17.2	22	0	14	7	1-0	0	5.60
Ron Moeller	L	17	4	1	0	0	8.2	10	0	3	2	0-1	0	4.15
Sandy Consuegra†	R	35	4	1	0	0	8.2	10	2	2	1	1-1	0	4.15
Billy O'Dell	L	23	4	1	0	0	8.0	6	0	6	6	0-0	0	1.13
Mel Held	R	27	4	0	0	0	7.0	7	1	3	4	0-0	0	5.14
Babe Birrer	R	27	4	0	0	0	5.1	9	0	1	1	0-0	0	6.75
George Werley	R	17	1	0	0	0	1.0	1	0	2	0	0-0	0	9.00
Gordie Sundin	R	18	1	0	0	0	0.0	0	0	2	0	0-0	0	—

1956 Washington Senators 7th AL 59-95 .383 38.0 GB — Chuck Dressen

Player	Gm by Position	B	Age	G	AB	R	H	2B	3B	HR	RBI	BB	SO	SB	Avg	OBP	Slg
Clint Courtney	C76	L	29	101	283	31	85	20	3	5	44	20	10	0	.300	.362	.445
Pete Runnels	1B81,2B69,SS3	L	28	147	578	72	179	29	9	8	76	58	64	5	.310	.372	.433
Herb Plews	2B66,SS5,3B2	L	28	91	256	24	69	10	7	1	25	26	40	1	.270	.337	.375
Eddie Yost	3B135,OF8	R	29	152	515	94	119	17	2	11	53	151	82	8	.231	.412	.336
Jose Valdivielso	SS90	R	22	90	246	18	58	8	2	4	29	29	36	3	.236	.318	.333
Jim Lemon	OF141	R	28	146	538	77	146	21	11	27	96	65	138	2	.271	.349	.502
Whitey Herzog	OF103,1B5	L	24	117	421	49	103	13	7	4	35	35	74	8	.245	.302	.337
Karl Olson	OF101	R	25	106	313	34	77	10	2	4	22	28	41	0	.246	.305	.329
Roy Sievers	OF78,1B76	R	29	152	550	92	139	27	2	29	95	100	88	0	.253	.370	.467
Lou Berberet	C59	L	26	95	207	25	54	6	3	4	27	46	33	0	.261	.402	.377
Jerry Snyder	SS35,2B7	R	26	43	148	14	40	3	1	2	14	10	9	1	.270	.321	.345
Ed Fitz Gerald	C50	R	32	64	148	15	45	8	0	2	12	20	16	0	.304	.387	.399
Ernie Oravetz	OF31	S	24	88	137	20	34	3	2	0	11	27	20	1	.248	.370	.299
Lyle Luttrell	SS37	R	26	38	122	17	23	5	3	2	9	8	19	5	.189	.254	.328
Tony Roig	2B27,SS19	R	28	44	119	11	25	5	2	0	7	20	29	2	.210	.321	.286
Harmon Killebrew	3B20,2B4	R	20	44	99	10	22	2	0	5	13	10	39	0	.222	.291	.394
Carlos Paula	OF20	R	28	33	82	8	15	2	1	3	13	8	15	0	.183	.250	.341
Dick Tettelbach	OF18	R	27	18	64	10	10	1	2	1	9	14	15	0	.156	.304	.281
Tom Wright		L	32	2	1	0	0	0	0	0	0	0	0	0	.000	.000	.000

Pitcher	T	Age	G	GS	CG	ShO	IP	H	HR	BB	SO	W-L	Sv	ERA
Chuck Stobbs	L	26	37	33	15	1	240.0	264	29	54	97	15-15	1	3.60
Camilo Pascual	R	22	39	27	6	0	188.2	194	33	89	162	6-18	2	5.87
Dean Stone	L	25	41	21	2	0	132.0	148	10	93	86	5-7	3	6.27
Bob Wiesler	L	25	37	21	3	0	123.0	141	11	112	49	3-12	0	6.44
Ted Abernathy	R	23	5	4	2	0	30.1	35	2	10	18	1-3	0	4.15
Evelio Hernandez	R	25	4	4	1	0	22.2	24	2	8	9	1-1	0	4.76
Bob Chakales	R	28	43	1	0	0	96.0	94	3	57	33	4-4	4	4.03
Pedro Ramos	R	21	37	18	4	0	152.0	178	23	76	54	12-10	0	5.27
Connie Grob	R	23	37	1	0	0	79.1	121	14	26	27	4-5	1	7.83
Hal Griggs	R	27	34	12	1	0	98.2	120	14	76	48	1-6	1	6.02
Bunky Stewart	L	25	33	9	1	0	105.0	111	15	82	36	5-7	2	5.57
Bud Byerly	R	35	25	0	0	0	51.2	45	6	14	19	2-4	4	2.96
Tex Clevenger	R	23	20	1	0	0	31.2	33	4	21	17	0-0	0	5.40
Dick Brodowski	R	23	7	3	1	0	17.2	31	5	12	8	0-3	0	9.17

1956 Kansas City Athletics 8th AL 52-102 .338 45.0 GB

Lou Boudreau

Player	Gm by Position	B	Age	G	AB	R	H	2B	3B	HR	RBI	BB	SO	SB	Avg	OBP	Slg
Tim Thompson	C68	L	32	92	268	21	73	13	2	1	27	17	23	2	.272	.319	.347
Vic Power	1B76,2B47,OF7	R	28	127	530	77	164	21	5	14	63	24	16	2	.309	.340	.447
Jim Finigan	2B52,3B32	R	27	91	250	29	54	7	2	2	21	30	28	3	.216	.298	.284
Hector Lopez	3B121,OF20,2B8*	R	26	151	561	91	153	27	3	18	69	63	73	4	.273	.347	.428
Joe DeMaestri	SS132,2B2	R	27	133	434	41	101	16	1	6	39	25	73	3	.233	.277	.316
Harry Simpson	OF111,1B32	L	30	141	543	76	159	22	11	21	105	47	82	2	.293	.347	.490
Johnny Groth	OF84	R	29	95	244	22	63	13	3	5	37	30	31	1	.258	.335	.398
Lou Skizas†	OF74	R	24	83	297	39	94	11	3	11	39	15	17	3	.316	.346	.485
Gus Zernial	OF69	R	33	109	272	36	61	12	0	16	44	33	66	2	.224	.315	.445
Al Pilarcik	OF67	L	25	69	239	28	60	10	1	4	22	30	32	9	.251	.333	.351
Enos Slaughter†	OF56	L	40	91	223	37	62	14	3	2	23	29	20	1	.278	.362	.395
Joe Ginsberg†	C57	L	29	71	195	15	48	8	1	1	12	23	17	1	.246	.323	.313
Eddie Robinson†	1B47	L	35	75	172	13	34	5	1	2	12	26	20	0	.198	.308	.273
Hal Smith†	C36	R	25	36	142	15	39	9	2	2	24	3	12	1	.275	.284	.408
Clete Boyer	2B51,3B7	R	19	67	129	15	28	3	1	1	4	11	24	1	.217	.284	.279
Mike Baxes	SS62,2B1	R	25	73	106	9	24	3	1	1	5	18	15	0	.226	.339	.302
Spook Jacobs†	2B31	R	30	32	97	13	21	3	0	0	5	15	5	4	.216	.321	.247
Rance Pless	1B15,3B5	R	30	48	85	4	23	3	1	0	9	10	13	0	.271	.354	.329
Bill Renna	OF25	R	31	33	48	12	13	3	0	2	5	3	10	1	.271	.314	.458
Jim Pisoni	OF9	R	26	10	30	4	8	0	0	2	5	2	8	0	.267	.303	.467
Joe Astroth	C8	R	33	8	13	0	1	0	0	0	0	0	1	0	.077	.077	.077
Elmer Valo†	OF1	L	35	9	9	1	2	0	0	0	2	1	1	0	.222	.273	.222
Dave Melton	OF3	R	27	3	3	0	1	0	0	0	0	0	0	0	.333	.333	.333

H. Lopez, 4 G at SS

Pitcher	T	Age	G	GS	CG	ShO	IP	H	HR	BB	SO	W-L	Sv	ERA
Art Ditmar	R	27	44	34	14	2	254.1	254	30	108	126	12-22	1	4.42
Lou Kretlow	R	35	25	20	3	0	118.2	121	17	74	61	4-9	0	5.31
Alex Kellner	L	31	20	17	5	0	91.2	103	15	33	44	7-4	0	4.32
Troy Herriage	R	25	31	16	1	0	103.0	135	16	64	59	1-13	0	6.64
Wally Burnette	R	27	18	14	4	1	121.1	115	13	39	54	6-8	0	2.89
Jose Santiago	R	27	9	5	0	0	21.2	36	8	17	9	1-2	0	8.31
Glenn Cox	R	25	3	3	1	0	23.1	15	2	22	6	0-2	0	4.24
Art Ceccarelli	L	26	3	2	0	0	10.0	13	3	4	2	0-1	0	7.20
Walt Craddock	L	24	2	2	0	0	9.1	9	1	10	8	0-2	0	6.75
Carl Duser	L	23	2	2	0	0	6.0	14	0	2	5	1-1	0	9.00
Jack Crimian	R	30	54	7	0	0	129.0	129	19	49	59	4-8	3	5.51
Tom Gorman	R	31	52	13	1	0	171.1	168	23	68	56	9-10	3	3.83
Bobby Shantz	L	30	45	2	1	0	101.1	95	12	37	67	2-7	9	4.35
Jack McMahan†	L	23	23	9	0	0	61.2	69	7	31	13	0-5	0	4.82
Bill Harrington	R	28	23	1	0	0	37.2	40	3	26	14	2-2	1	6.45
Moe Burtschy	R	34	21	0	0	0	43.1	41	6	30	18	3-1	0	3.95
Tom Lasorda	L	28	18	5	0	0	45.1	40	6	45	28	0-4	1	6.15
George Brunet	L	21	6	1	0	0	9.0	10	1	11	5	0-0	0	7.00
Arnie Portocarrero	R	24	3	1	0	0	8.0	9	2	7	2	0-1	0	10.13
Bob Spicer	R	31	2	0	0	0	2.1	6	1	1	0	0-0	0	19.29
Bill Bradford	R	34	1	0	0	0	2.0	2	2	1	0	0-0	0	9.00

»1956 Brooklyn Dodgers 1st NL 93-61 .604 —

Walter Alston

Player	Gm by Position	B	Age	G	AB	R	H	2B	3B	HR	RBI	BB	SO	SB	Avg	OBP	Slg
Roy Campanella	C121	R	34	124	388	39	85	6	1	20	73	66	61	1	.219	.333	.394
Gil Hodges	1B138,OF30,C1	R	32	153	550	86	146	29	4	32	87	76	91	3	.265	.354	.507
Jim Gilliam	2B102,OF56	S	27	153	594	102	178	23	8	6	43	95	39	21	.300	.399	.396
Randy Jackson	3B80	R	30	101	307	37	84	15	7	8	53	28	38	2	.274	.333	.446
Pee Wee Reese	SS136,3B12	R	37	147	572	85	147	19	2	9	46	56	69	13	.257	.322	.344
Duke Snider	OF150	L	29	151	542	112	158	33	2	43	101	99	101	3	.292	.399	.598
Carl Furillo	OF146	R	34	149	523	66	151	30	0	21	83	57	41	1	.289	.357	.467
Sandy Amoros	OF86	L	26	114	292	53	76	11	8	16	58	59	51	3	.260	.385	.517
Jackie Robinson	3B72,2B22,1B9*	R	37	117	357	61	98	15	2	10	43	60	32	12	.275	.382	.412
Rube Walker	C43	L	30	54	146	5	31	6	1	3	20	7	18	0	.212	.245	.329
Charlie Neal	2B51,SS1	R	25	62	136	22	39	5	1	2	14	14	19	2	.287	.353	.382
Rocky Nelson†	1B25	L	31	31	96	7	20	2	0	4	15	4	10	0	.208	.235	.354
Chico Fernandez	SS25	R	24	34	66	11	15	2	0	1	9	3	10	2	.227	.261	.303
Gino Cimoli	OF62	R	26	73	36	3	4	1	0	0	4	1	8	1	.111	.135	.139
Dale Mitchell†	OF2	L	34	19	24	3	7	1	0	0	1	0	3	0	.292	.292	.333
Don Zimmer	SS8,3B3,2B1	R	25	17	20	4	6	1	0	0	2	0	7	0	.300	.333	.350
Dixie Howell	C6	R	36	7	13	0	3	2	0	0	1	1	3	0	.231	.267	.385
Dick Williams†		R	27	7	7	0	2	0	0	0	0	0	1	0	.286	.286	.286
Don Demeter	OF1	R	21	3	3	1	1	0	0	1	1	0	1	0	.333	.333	1.333
Bob Aspromonte		R	18	1	1	0	0	0	0	0	0	0	1	0	.000	.000	.000

J. Robinson, 2 G at OF

Pitcher	T	Age	G	GS	CG	ShO	IP	H	HR	BB	SO	W-L	Sv	ERA
Don Newcombe	R	30	38	36	18	5	268.0	219	33	46	139	27-7	0	3.06
Roger Craig	R	26	35	32	8	2	199.0	169	25	87	109	12-11	1	3.71
Carl Erskine	R	29	31	28	8	1	186.1	189	25	57	95	13-11	0	4.25
Sal Maglie†	R	39	28	26	9	3	191.0	154	21	52	108	13-5	0	2.87
Sandy Koufax	L	20	16	10	0	0	58.2	66	10	29	30	2-4	0	4.91
Billy Loes†	R	26	1	1	0	0	1.1	5	1	1	2	0-1	0	40.50
Clem Labine	R	29	62	3	1	0	115.2	111	11	39	75	10-6	19	3.35
Ed Roebuck	R	24	43	0	0	0	89.1	83	15	29	60	5-4	1	3.93
Don Bessent	R	25	38	0	0	0	79.1	63	5	31	52	4-3	9	2.50
Don Drysdale	R	19	25	12	2	0	99.0	95	9	31	55	5-5	0	2.64
Ken Lehman	L	28	25	4	0	0	49.1	65	11	23	29	2-3	0	5.66
Chuck Templeton	L	24	6	2	0	0	16.1	20	2	10	8	0-1	0	6.61
Jim Hughes†	R	33	5	0	0	0	12.0	10	3	4	8	0-0	0	5.25
Ralph Branca	R	30	1	0	0	0	2.0	1	0	2	2	0-0	0	0.00
Bob Darnell	R	25	1	0	0	0	1.1	1	0	0	0	0-0	0	0.00

1956 Milwaukee Braves 2nd NL 92-62 .597 1.0 GB

Charlie Grimm (24-22)/Fred Haney (68-40)

Player	Gm by Position	B	Age	G	AB	R	H	2B	3B	HR	RBI	BB	SO	SB	Avg	OBP	Slg
Del Crandall	C109	R	26	112	311	37	74	14	2	16	48	35	30	1	.238	.313	.450
Joe Adcock	1B129	R	28	137	454	76	132	23	1	38	103	32	86	1	.291	.337	.597
Danny O'Connell	2B138,3B4,SS1	R	29	139	498	71	119	17	9	2	42	76	42	3	.239	.342	.321
Eddie Mathews	3B150	L	24	151	552	103	150	21	2	37	95	91	86	6	.272	.373	.518
Johnny Logan	SS148	R	29	148	545	69	153	27	5	15	46	46	49	3	.281	.340	.431
Hank Aaron	OF152	R	22	153	609	106	200	34	14	26	92	37	54	2	.328	.365	.558
Bill Bruton	OF145	L	30	147	525	73	143	23	15	8	56	26	63	8	.272	.304	.419
Bobby Thomson	OF136,3B3	R	32	142	451	59	106	10	4	20	74	43	75	2	.235	.302	.408
Del Rice	C65	R	33	71	188	15	40	9	1	3	17	18	34	0	.213	.282	.319
Frank Torre	1B89	L	24	111	159	17	41	6	0	0	16	11	4	1	.258	.304	.296
Wes Covington	OF35	L	24	75	138	17	39	4	0	2	16	16	20	1	.283	.361	.355
Jack Dittmer	2B42	L	28	44	102	8	25	4	0	1	6	8	8	0	.245	.300	.314
Andy Pafko	OF37	R	35	45	93	15	24	5	0	2	9	10	13	0	.258	.330	.376
Chuck Tanner	OF8	L	26	60	63	6	15	2	0	1	4	10	10	0	.238	.342	.317
Felix Mantilla	SS15,3B3	R	21	35	53	9	15	1	1	0	3	1	8	0	.283	.309	.340
Toby Atwell†	C10	L	32	15	30	2	5	1	0	2	7	4	1	0	.167	.265	.400
Earl Hersh	OF2	L	24	7	13	0	3	3	0	0	0	0	5	0	.231	.231	.462
Jim Pendleton	SS3,3B2,1B1*	R	32	14	11	0	0	0	0	0	0	1	3	0	.000	.083	.000
Bob Roselli	C3	R	24	4	2	1	1	0	0	1	1	0	1	0	.500	.500	2.000

J. Pendleton, 1 G at 2B

Pitcher	T	Age	G	GS	CG	ShO	IP	H	HR	BB	SO	W-L	Sv	ERA
Warren Spahn	L	35	39	35	20	3	281.1	249	25	52	128	20-11	3	2.78
Lew Burdette	R	29	39	35	16	6	256.1	234	22	52	110	19-10	1	2.70
Bob Buhl	R	27	38	33	13	2	216.2	190	18	105	86	18-8	0	3.32
Ray Crone	R	24	35	21	6	0	169.2	173	19	44	73	11-10	2	3.87
Gene Conley	R	25	31	19	5	1	158.1	169	13	52	68	8-9	3	3.13
Ernie Johnson	R	32	36	0	0	0	51.0	54	9	21	26	4-3	6	3.71
Dave Jolly	R	31	29	0	0	0	45.2	39	7	35	20	2-3	7	3.74
Lou Sleater	L	29	25	1	0	0	45.2	42	6	27	32	2-2	2	3.15
Taylor Phillips	L	23	23	6	3	0	87.2	69	6	33	36	5-3	2	2.26
Bob Trowbridge	R	26	19	4	1	0	50.2	38	4	34	40	3-2	0	2.66
Red Murff	R	35	14	1	0	0	24.1	25	3	7	18	0-0	1	4.44
Chet Nichols	L	25	2	0	0	0	4.0	9	1	3	2	0-1	0	6.75
Humberto Robinson	R	26	1	0	0	0	2.0	1	0	2	0	0-0	0	0.00
Phil Paine	R	26	1	0	0	0	0.0	3	0	0	0	0-0	0	—

1956 Cincinnati Reds 3rd NL 91-63 .591 2.0 GB

Birdie Tebbetts

Player	Gm by Position	B	Age	G	AB	R	H	2B	3B	HR	RBI	BB	SO	SB	Avg	OBP	Slg
Ed Bailey	C106	L	25	118	383	59	115	8	2	28	75	52	50	2	.300	.385	.551
Ted Kluszewski	1B131	L	31	138	517	91	156	14	1	35	102	49	31	1	.302	.362	.536
Johnny Temple	2B154,OF1	R	28	154	632	88	180	18	3	2	41	58	40	14	.285	.344	.332
Ray Jablonski	3B127,2B1	R	29	130	407	42	104	25	1	15	66	37	57	2	.256	.324	.432
Roy McMillan	SS150	R	25	150	479	51	126	16	7	3	62	76	54	4	.263	.366	.344
Frank Robinson	OF152	R	20	152	572	122	166	27	6	38	83	64	95	8	.290	.379	.558
Gus Bell	OF149	L	27	150	603	82	176	31	4	29	84	50	66	6	.292	.347	.501
Wally Post	OF136	R	26	143	539	94	134	25	3	36	83	37	124	6	.249	.301	.506
Smoky Burgess	C55	L	29	90	229	28	63	10	0	12	39	26	18	0	.275	.346	.476
George Crowe	1B32	L	35	77	144	22	36	2	1	10	23	11	28	0	.250	.312	.486
Alex Grammas†	3B58,SS12,2B5	R	30	77	140	17	34	11	0	0	16	16	18	0	.243	.323	.321
Bob Thurman	OF29	L	39	80	139	25	41	5	2	8	22	10	14	0	.295	.340	.532
Stan Palys	OF10	R	26	40	53	5	12	0	0	2	5	6	13	0	.226	.300	.340
Rocky Bridges	3B51,2B8,SS7*	R	28	71	19	9	4	0	0	0	1	4	3	1	.211	.348	.211
Joe Frazier†	OF4	L	33	10	17	2	4	0	0	1	2	1	7	0	.235	.278	.412
Jim Dyck†	1B1,3B1	R	34	18	11	5	1	0	0	0	0	3	5	0	.091	.286	.091
Art Schult	OF1	R	28	5	7	3	3	0	0	0	2	1	1	0	.429	.500	.429
Bruce Edwards	C2,2B1,3B1	R	32	7	5	0	1	0	0	0	0	0	2	0	.200	.200	.200
Chuck Harmon†	OF6,1B2	R	32	13	4	2	0	0	0	0	0	0	0	1	.000	.000	.000
Bobby Balcena	OF2	R	30	7	2	2	0	0	0	0	0	0	1	0	.000	.000	.000
Matt Batts		R	34	3	2	0	0	0	0	0	0	1	1	0	.000	.333	.000
Curt Flood		R	18	5	1	0	0	0	0	0	0	0	1	0	.000	.000	.000
John Oldham		R	23	1	0	0	0	0	0	0	0	0	0	0	—	—	—
Al Silvera		R	20	1	0	0	0	0	0	0	0	0	0	0	—	—	—

R. Bridges, 1 G at OF

Pitcher	T	Age	G	GS	CG	ShO	IP	H	HR	BB	SO	W-L	Sv	ERA
Joe Nuxhall	L	27	44	32	10	2	200.2	196	18	87	120	13-11	3	3.72
Brooks Lawrence	R	31	49	30	11	1	218.2	210	26	71	96	19-10	0	3.99
Johnny Klippstein	R	28	37	29	11	0	211.0	219	26	82	86	12-11	1	4.09
Art Fowler	R	33	45	23	8	0	177.2	191	15	35	86	11-11	1	4.05
Larry Jansen	R	35	8	7	2	0	34.2	39	5	9	16	2-3	1	5.19
Hersh Freeman	R	27	64	0	0	0	108.2	112	2	34	50	14-5	18	3.40
Hal Jeffcoat	R	31	38	16	2	0	171.0	189	12	55	55	8-2	2	3.84
Joe Black	R	32	32	0	0	0	61.2	61	11	25	27	3-2	2	4.52
Tom Acker	R	26	29	7	1	1	83.2	60	7	29	54	4-3	1	2.37
Don Gross	L	25	19	7	2	0	69.1	69	4	20	47	3-0	0	1.95
Paul LaPalme†	L	32	11	2	0	0	27.0	26	7	4	4	2-4	0	4.67
Pat Scantlebury	L	38	6	2	0	0	19.0	24	5	5	10	0-1	0	6.63
Frank Smith	R	28	2	0	0	0	3.0	3	2	2	1	0-0	0	12.00
Bill Kennedy	L	35	1	0	0	0	2.0	6	1	0	0	0-0	0	18.00
Russ Meyer†	R	32	1	0	0	0	1.0	1	0	0	1	0-0	0	0.00

1956 St. Louis Cardinals 4th NL 76-78 .494 17.0 GB

Fred Hutchinson

Player	Gm by Position	B	Age	G	AB	R	H	2B	3B	HR	RBI	BB	SO	SB	Avg	OBP	Slg
Hal Smith	C66	R	25	75	227	27	64	12	0	5	23	15	22	1	.282	.326	.401
Stan Musial	1B103,OF53	L	35	156	594	87	184	33	6	27	109	75	39	2	.310	.386	.522
Don Blasingame	2B98,SS49,3B2	L	24	150	587	94	153	22	7	0	27	72	52	8	.261	.344	.322
Ken Boyer	3B149	R	25	150	595	91	182	30	2	26	98	38	65	8	.306	.347	.494
Al Dark†	SS99	R	34	100	413	54	118	14	7	4	37	21	33	3	.286	.320	.383
Rip Repulski	OF100	R	28	112	376	44	104	18	3	11	55	24	46	2	.277	.330	.428
Bobby Del Greco†	OF99	R	23	102	270	29	58	16	2	5	18	32	50	1	.215	.308	.344
Wally Moon	OF97,1B52	L	26	149	540	86	161	22	11	16	68	80	50	12	.298	.390	.469
Whitey Lockman†	OF57,1B2	L	29	70	193	14	48	0	2	0	10	18	8	2	.249	.311	.269
Ray Katt†	C47	R	29	47	158	11	41	4	0	6	20	6	24	0	.259	.289	.399
Red Schoendienst†	2B36	S	33	40	153	22	48	9	0	0	15	13	5	0	.314	.365	.373
Hank Sauer	OF37	R	39	75	151	11	45	4	0	5	24	25	31	0	.298	.403	.424
Bill Sarni†	C41	R	28	43	148	12	43	7	2	5	22	8	15	1	.291	.329	.466
Bobby Morgan†	2B13,3B11,SS6	R	30	61	113	14	22	7	0	3	20	15	24	0	.195	.287	.336
Grady Hatton†	2B13,3B1	L	33	44	73	10	18	1	2	0	7	13	7	1	.247	.360	.315
Bill Virdon†	OF24	L	25	24	71	10	15	2	0	2	9	5	8	0	.211	.269	.324
Walker Cooper	C16	R	41	40	68	5	18	5	1	2	14	3	8	0	.265	.296	.456
Rocky Nelson†	1B14,OF8	L	31	38	56	6	13	5	0	3	8	6	6	0	.232	.306	.482
Charlie Peete	OF21	L	27	23	52	3	10	2	2	0	6	6	10	0	.192	.288	.308
Jackie Brandt†	OF26	R	22	27	42	9	12	3	0	1	3	4	5	0	.286	.362	.429
Dick Schofield	SS9	S	21	16	30	3	3	2	0	0	1	0	6	0	.100	.100	.167
Joe Frazier†	OF3	L	33	14	19	1	4	2	0	1	4	3	3	0	.211	.318	.474
Chuck Harmon†	OF11,1B2,3B1	R	32	20	15	2	0	0	0	0	0	2	2	0	.000	.118	.000
Alex Grammas†	SS5	R	30	6	12	1	3	0	0	0	1	1	2	0	.250	.308	.250
Solly Hemus†		L	33	8	5	1	1	0	0	0	2	1	0	0	.200	.429	.200
Joe Cunningham	1B1	L	24	4	3	1	0	0	0	0	0	1	1	0	.000	.250	.000
Tom Alston	1B3	L	30	3	2	0	0	0	0	0	0	0	0	0	.000	.000	.000

Pitcher	T	Age	G	GS	CG	ShO	IP	H	HR	BB	SO	W-L	Sv	ERA
Vinegar Bend Mizell	L	25	33	33	11	3	208.2	172	20	92	153	14-14	0	3.62
Tom Poholsky	R	26	33	29	7	2	203.0	210	27	44	95	9-14	0	3.59
Murry Dickson†	R	39	28	27	12	3	196.1	175	20	57	109	13-8	0	3.07
Willard Schmidt	R	28	33	21	2	0	147.2	131	18	78	52	6-8	1	3.84
Herm Wehmeier†	R	29	34	19	7	2	170.2	150	16	71	68	12-9	1	3.69
Harvey Haddix†	L	30	4	4	1	1	23.2	28	3	10	16	1-0	0	5.32
Ben Flowers†	R	29	3	3	0	0	11.2	15	1	5	5	1-1	0	6.94
Dick Littlefield†	L	30	3	2	0	0	9.2	9	2	4	5	0-2	0	7.45
Larry Jackson	R	25	51	1	0	0	85.1	75	5	45	50	2-2	9	4.11
Lindy McDaniel	R	20	39	7	1	0	116.1	121	7	42	59	7-6	0	3.40
Jackie Collum	L	29	38	1	0	0	60.0	63	6	27	17	6-2	7	4.20
Jim Konstanty†	R	39	27	0	0	0	39.1	46	4	6	7	1-1	5	4.58
Ellis Kinder†	R	41	22	0	0	0	25.2	23	3	9	4	2-0	6	3.51
Bob Blaylock	R	21	14	6	0	0	41.0	45	7	24	39	1-6	0	6.37
Don Liddle†	L	31	14	2	0	0	24.2	36	8	18	14	1-2	0	8.39
Gordon Jones	R	26	5	1	0	0	11.1	14	2	5	6	0-2	0	5.56
Max Surkont†	R	34	5	0	0	0	5.2	10	3	2	5	0-0	0	9.53
Stu Miller†	R	28	3	0	0	0	7.1	12	3	5	5	0-1	1	4.91
Paul LaPalme†	L	32	1	0	0	0	0.2	4	0	2	0	0-0	0	81.00

1956 Philadelphia Phillies 5th NL 71-83 .461 22.0 GB

Mayo Smith

Player	Gm by Position	B	Age	G	AB	R	H	2B	3B	HR	RBI	BB	SO	SB	Avg	OBP	Slg
Stan Lopata	C102,1B39	R	30	146	535	96	143	33	7	32	95	75	93	5	.267	.353	.535
Marv Blaylock	1B124,OF1	L	26	136	460	61	117	14	8	10	50	50	86	5	.254	.327	.385
Ted Kazanski	2B116,SS1	R	22	117	379	35	80	11	1	4	34	20	41	0	.211	.251	.277
Puddin' Head Jones	3B149	R	30	149	520	88	144	20	4	17	78	92	49	5	.277	.383	.429
Granny Hamner	SS110,2B11,P3	R	29	122	401	42	90	24	3	4	42	30	42	2	.224	.276	.329
Richie Ashburn	OF154	L	29	154	628	94	190	26	8	3	50	79	45	10	.303	.384	.384
Del Ennis	OF153	R	31	153	630	80	164	23	3	26	95	33	62	7	.260	.299	.430
Elmer Valo†	OF87	L	35	98	291	40	84	13	3	5	37	48	21	7	.289	.392	.405
Jim Greengrass	OF62	R	28	86	215	24	44	9	2	5	25	28	43	0	.205	.294	.335
Solly Hemus†	2B49,3B1	L	33	78	187	24	54	10	4	5	24	28	21	1	.289	.397	.465
Roy Smalley	SS60	R	30	65	168	14	38	9	3	0	16	23	29	0	.226	.323	.315
Andy Seminick	C54	R	35	60	161	16	32	3	1	7	23	31	38	3	.199	.332	.360
Frankie Baumholtz	OF15	L	37	76	100	13	27	0	0	0	9	6	6	0	.270	.309	.270
Glen Gorbous	OF8	L	25	15	33	1	6	0	0	0	1	0	1	0	.182	.182	.182
Bobby Morgan†	3B5,2B3	R	30	8	25	1	5	0	0	0	1	6	4	0	.200	.355	.200
Ed Bouchee	1B6	L	23	9	22	0	6	2	0	0	1	5	6	0	.273	.407	.364
Joe Lonnett	C7	R	29	16	22	2	4	0	0	0	0	2	7	0	.182	.250	.182
Bob Bowman	OF5	R	25	6	16	2	3	0	1	1	2	0	6	0	.188	.188	.500
Wally Westlake		R	35	5	4	0	0	0	0	0	0	1	3	0	.000	.200	.000
Mack Burk	C1	R	21	15	1	3	1	0	0	0	0	0	0	0	1.000	1.000	1.000

Pitcher	T	Age	G	GS	CG	ShO	IP	H	HR	BB	SO	W-L	Sv	ERA
Robin Roberts	R	29	43	37	22	1	297.1	328	46	40	157	19-18	3	4.45
Curt Simmons	L	27	33	27	14	0	198.0	186	17	65	88	15-10	0	3.36
Harvey Haddix†	L	30	31	26	11	2	206.2	196	23	55	154	12-8	2	3.48
Saul Rogovin	R	32	22	18	3	0	106.2	122	22	27	48	7-6	0	4.98
Stu Miller†	R	28	24	15	2	0	106.2	109	16	51	55	5-8	0	4.47
Jim Owens	R	22	10	5	0	0	29.2	35	3	22	22	0-4	0	7.28
Murry Dickson†	R	39	3	3	0	0	23.0	20	1	12	1	0-3	0	5.09
Herm Wehmeier†	R	29	3	3	0	0	20.0	18	2	11	8	0-2	0	4.05
Turk Farrell	R	22	1	1	0	0	4.1	6	0	3	0	0-1	0	12.46
Bob Miller	R	30	49	6	3	1	122.1	115	14	34	53	3-6	5	3.24
Jack Meyer	R	24	41	7	2	0	96.0	86	8	51	66	7-11	2	4.41
Ron Negray	R	26	39	4	0	0	66.2	72	6	24	44	2-3	3	4.19
Ben Flowers†	R	29	32	0	0	0	41.0	54	9	10	22	0-2	0	5.71
Duane Pillette	R	33	20	0	0	0	23.1	32	2	12	10	0-0	0	6.56
Angelo LiPetri	R	25	6	0	0	0	11.0	7	2	3	8	0-0	0	3.27
Jack Sanford	R	27	3	1	0	0	13.0	7	0	13	6	1-0	0	1.38
Granny Hamner	R	29	3	1	0	0	8.1	10	0	2	4	0-1	0	4.32
Bob Ross	L	27	3	0	0	0	3.1	4	1	2	4	0-0	0	8.10

1956 New York Giants 6th NL 67-87 .435 26.0 GB

Bill Rigney

Player	Gm by Position	B	Age	G	AB	R	H	2B	3B	HR	RBI	BB	SO	SB	Avg	OBP	Slg
Bill Sarni†	C78	R	28	78	238	16	55	9	3	5	23	20	31	0	.231	.290	.357
Bill White	1B138,OF2	L	22	138	508	63	130	23	7	22	59	47	72	15	.256	.321	.459
Red Schoendienst†	2B85	S	33	92	334	39	99	12	3	2	14	28	10	1	.296	.352	.368
Foster Castleman	3B107,SS2,2B1	R	25	124	385	33	87	16	3	14	45	15	50	2	.226	.256	.392
Daryl Spencer	2B70,SS66,3B12	R	26	146	489	46	108	13	2	14	42	35	65	1	.221	.275	.342
Willie Mays	OF152	R	25	152	578	101	171	27	8	36	84	68	65	40	.296	.369	.557
Don Mueller	OF117	L	29	138	453	38	122	12	1	5	41	15	7	0	.269	.290	.333
Jackie Brandt†	OF96	R	22	98	351	45	105	16	8	11	47	17	31	3	.299	.330	.484
Dusty Rhodes	OF68	L	29	111	244	20	53	10	3	8	33	30	41	0	.217	.301	.381
Al Dark†	SS48	R	34	48	206	19	52	12	0	2	17	8	13	0	.252	.279	.340
Hank Thompson	3B44,OF10,SS1	L	30	83	183	24	43	9	0	8	29	31	26	2	.235	.346	.415
Whitey Lockman†	OF39,1B7	L	29	48	169	13	46	7	1	1	10	16	17	0	.272	.333	.343
Eddie Bressoud	SS48	R	24	49	163	15	37	4	2	0	9	12	20	1	.227	.284	.276
Wes Westrum	C67	R	33	68	132	10	29	5	2	3	8	25	28	0	.220	.346	.356
Ray Katt†	C37	R	29	37	101	10	23	4	0	7	14	6	16	0	.228	.278	.475
George Wilson†	OF8	L	30	53	68	5	9	1	0	1	2	5	14	0	.132	.192	.191
Ruben Gomez	P40,OF1	R	28	52	60	9	11	1	0	0	1	2	5	1	.183	.210	.200
Bobby Hofman	C7,3B7,1B3*	R	30	47	56	1	10	1	0	0	2	6	8	0	.179	.270	.196
Bob Lennon	OF21	L	27	26	55	3	10	1	0	0	1	4	17	0	.182	.233	.200
Gail Harris	1B11	L	24	12	38	2	5	0	1	1	1	3	10	0	.132	.233	.263
Jim Mangan	C15	R	26	20	20	2	2	0	0	0	1	4	6	0	.100	.250	.100
Wayne Terwilliger	2B6	R	31	14	18	0	4	1	0	0	0	0	5	0	.222	.222	.278
Ozzie Virgil	3B3	R	23	3	12	2	5	1	1	0	2	0	0	1	.417	.417	.667
Bill Taylor	OF1	L	26	1	4	0	1	1	0	0	0	0	1	0	.250	.250	.500
Gil Coan		L	34	4	1	2	0	0	0	0	0	0	1	0	.000	.000	.000

B. Hofman, 2 G at 2B

Pitcher	T	Age	G	GS	CG	ShO	IP	H	HR	BB	SO	W-L	Sv	ERA
Johnny Antonelli	L	26	41	36	15	5	258.1	225	20	75	145	20-13	1	2.86
Ruben Gomez	R	28	40	31	4	2	196.1	191	19	77	76	7-17	0	4.58
Al Worthington	R	27	28	24	4	0	165.2	158	20	74	95	7-14	0	3.97
Jim Hearn	R	35	30	19	2	0	129.1	124	17	44	66	5-11	1	3.97
Joe Margoneri	L	26	23	13	2	1	91.2	88	12	49	49	6-6	0	3.93
Max Surkont†	R	34	8	4	1	0	32.0	24	5	9	18	2-2	1	4.78
Mike McCormick	L	17	3	2	0	0	6.2	7	1	10	4	0-1	0	9.45
Roy Wright	R	22	1	1	0	0	2.2	8	1	2	0	0-1	0	16.88
Hoyt Wilhelm	R	32	64	0	0	0	89.1	97	7	43	71	4-9	8	3.83
Windy McCall	L	30	46	4	0	0	77.1	74	7	20	41	3-4	7	3.61
Marv Grissom	R	38	43	2	0	0	80.2	71	3	16	49	1-1	7	1.56
Steve Ridzik	R	27	41	5	1	1	92.1	80	7	65	53	6-2	0	3.80
Dick Littlefield†	L	30	31	7	0	0	97.0	78	16	39	65	4-4	2	4.08
Don Liddle†	L	31	11	5	1	0	41.1	45	5	14	21	1-2	1	3.92
Ray Monzant	R	23	4	1	1	0	13.0	8	4	7	11	1-0	0	4.15
Jim Constable	L	23	3	0	0	0	4.1	9	0	7	1	0-0	0	14.54

1956 Pittsburgh Pirates 7th NL 66-88 .429 27.0 GB

Bobby Bragan

Player	Gm by Position	B	Age	G	AB	R	H	2B	3B	HR	RBI	BB	SO	SB	Avg	OBP	Slg
Jack Shepard	C86,1B2	R	25	100	256	24	62	11	2	7	30	25	37	1	.242	.309	.383
Dale Long	1B138	L	30	148	517	64	136	20	7	27	91	54	85	1	.263	.326	.485
Bill Mazeroski	2B81	R	19	81	255	30	62	8	1	3	14	18	24	0	.243	.293	.318
Frank Thomas	3B111,OF56,2B4	R	27	157	588	69	166	24	3	25	80	36	61	0	.282	.326	.461
Dick Groat	SS141,3B2	R	25	142	520	40	142	19	3	0	37	35	25	0	.273	.317	.321
Roberto Clemente	OF139,2B2,3B1	R	21	147	543	66	169	30	7	7	60	13	58	6	.311	.330	.431
Lee Walls	OF133,3B1	R	23	143	474	72	130	20	11	11	54	50	83	3	.274	.345	.432
Bill Virdon†	OF130	L	25	133	509	67	170	21	10	8	37	33	63	6	.334	.374	.462
Bob Skinner	OF36,1B23,3B1	L	24	113	233	29	47	8	3	5	29	26	50	1	.202	.282	.326
Hank Foiles†	C73	R	27	79	222	24	47	10	2	7	25	17	56	0	.212	.266	.369
Gene Freese	3B47,2B26	R	22	65	207	17	43	9	0	3	14	16	45	2	.208	.273	.295
Johnny O'Brien	2B53,P8,SS1	R	25	73	104	13	18	1	0	0	3	5	7	0	.173	.209	.183
Dick Cole	3B18,2B12,SS6	R	30	72	99	7	21	2	1	0	9	11	9	0	.212	.291	.253
Danny Kravitz	C26,3B2	L	25	32	68	6	18	2	2	2	10	5	9	1	.265	.311	.441
Curt Roberts	2B27	R	26	31	62	6	11	5	2	0	4	5	12	1	.177	.239	.323
Eddie O'Brien	SS23,OF6,3B4*	R	25	63	53	17	14	2	0	0	3	2	2	1	.264	.291	.302
Spook Jacobs†	2B11	R	30	11	37	4	6	2	0	0	1	2	5	0	.162	.225	.216
Preston Ward†	3B5,OF5	L	28	16	30	3	10	0	1	1	11	6	4	0	.333	.432	.500
Dick Hall	P19,1B1	R	25	33	29	5	10	0	0	0	1	5	7	0	.345	.441	.345
John Powers	OF5	L	26	11	21	0	1	0	0	0	0	1	4	0	.048	.091	.048
Bobby Del Greco†	OF7,3B3	R	23	14	20	4	4	0	0	2	3	3	3	0	.200	.304	.500
Jerry Lynch	OF1	L	25	19	19	1	3	0	1	0	0	1	4	0	.158	.200	.263
Toby Atwell†	C9	L	32	12	18	0	2	0	0	0	3	1	5	0	.111	.158	.111
Bill Hall	C1	L	27	1	3	0	0	0	0	0	0	0	1	0	.000	.000	.000

E. O'Brien, 2 G at 2B, 1 G at P

Pitcher	T	Age	G	GS	CG	ShO	IP	H	HR	BB	SO	W-L	Sv	ERA
Bob Friend	R	25	49	42	19	4	314.1	310	25	85	166	17-17	3	3.46
Ron Kline	R	24	44	39	9	2	264.0	263	26	81	125	14-18	2	3.38
Vern Law	R	26	39	32	6	0	195.2	218	24	49	60	8-16	2	4.32
Laurin Pepper	R	25	11	7	0	0	30.0	30	1	25	12	1-1	0	3.00
Roy Face	R	28	68	3	0	0	135.1	131	16	42	96	12-13	6	3.52
Nellie King	R	28	38	0	0	0	60.0	54	8	19	25	4-1	5	3.15
George Munger	R	37	35	13	0	0	107.0	126	8	41	45	3-4	2	4.04
Fred Waters	L	29	23	5	1	0	51.0	48	3	30	14	2-2	0	2.82
Dick Hall	R	25	19	9	1	0	62.1	64	8	21	27	0-7	1	4.76
Howie Pollet†	L	35	19	0	0	0	23.1	18	3	8	10	0-4	3	3.09
Luis Arroyo	L	29	18	2	1	0	28.2	36	5	12	17	3-3	0	4.71
Cholly Naranjo	R	21	17	3	0	0	34.1	37	7	17	26	1-2	0	4.46
Jack McMahan†	L	23	11	0	0	0	13.1	18	1	9	9	0-0	0	6.08
Red Swanson	R	19	9	0	0	0	11.2	21	1	8	5	0-0	0	10.03
Johnny O'Brien	R	25	8	0	0	0	19.0	8	2	9	9	1-0	0	2.84
Dick Littlefield†	L	30	6	2	0	0	12.2	14	2	6	10	0-0	0	4.26
Lino Donoso	L	33	3	0	0	0	1.2	2	0	1	1	0-0	0	0.00
Bob Garber	R	27	2	0	0	0	4.0	3	1	3	3	0-0	0	2.25
Bob Purkey	R	26	2	0	0	0	4.0	2	1	0	1	0-0	0	2.25
Eddie O'Brien	R	25	1	0	0	0	2.0	1	0	0	0	0-0	0	0.00
Max Surkont†	R	34	1	0	0	0	2.0	2	0	3	1	0-0	0	4.50

1956 Chicago Cubs 8th NL 60-94 .390 33.0 GB

Stan Hack

Player	Gm by Position	B	Age	G	AB	R	H	2B	3B	HR	RBI	BB	SO	SB	Avg	OBP	Slg
Hobie Landrith	C99	L	26	111	312	22	69	10	3	4	32	39	38	0	.221	.307	.311
Dee Fondy	1B133	L	31	137	543	52	146	22	9	9	46	20	74	9	.269	.290	.392
Gene Baker	2B140	R	31	140	546	65	141	23	3	12	57	39	54	4	.258	.309	.377
Don Hoak	3B110	R	28	121	424	51	91	18	4	5	37	41	46	8	.215	.283	.311
Ernie Banks	SS139	R	25	139	538	82	160	25	8	28	85	52	62	6	.297	.358	.530
Walt Moryn	OF141	L	30	147	529	69	151	27	3	23	67	50	67	4	.285	.348	.478
Monte Irvin	OF96	R	37	111	339	44	92	13	3	15	50	41	41	1	.271	.346	.460
Pete Whisenant	OF93	R	26	103	314	37	75	16	3	11	46	24	53	8	.239	.292	.414
Eddie Miksis	3B48,OF33,2B19*	R	29	114	356	54	85	10	3	9	27	32	40	4	.239	.303	.360
Jim King	OF82	L	23	118	317	32	79	13	2	15	54	30	40	1	.249	.313	.445
Solly Drake	OF53	S	25	65	215	29	55	9	1	2	15	23	35	9	.256	.331	.335
Harry Chiti	C67	R	23	72	203	17	43	6	4	4	18	19	35	0	.212	.281	.340
Frank Kellert	1B27	R	31	71	129	10	24	3	1	4	17	12	22	0	.186	.254	.318
Jerry Kindall	SS18	R	21	32	55	7	9	1	1	0	0	6	17	1	.164	.246	.218
Clyde McCullough	C7	R	39	14	19	0	4	1	0	0	1	0	5	0	.211	.200	.263
Ed Winceniak	3B4,2B1	R	27	15	17	1	2	0	0	0	0	1	3	0	.118	.167	.118
Gale Wade	OF3	L	27	10	12	0	0	0	0	0	0	1	0	0	.000	.077	.000
Jim Fanning	C1	R	28	1	4	0	1	0	0	0	0	0	0	0	.250	.250	.250
Owen Friend		R	29	2	2	0	0	0	0	0	0	0	2	0	.000	.000	.000
Richie Myers		R	26	4	1	1	0	0	0	0	0	0	0	0	.000	.000	.000
El Tappe	C3	R	29	3	1	0	0	0	0	0	0	1	0	0	.000	.500	.000

E. Miksis, 2 G at SS

Pitcher	T	Age	G	GS	CG	ShO	IP	H	HR	BB	SO	W-L	Sv	ERA
Bob Rush	R	30	32	32	13	1	239.2	210	30	59	104	13-10	0	3.19
Sam Jones	R	30	33	28	8	2	188.2	155	21	115	176	9-14	0	3.91
Warren Hacker	R	31	34	24	4	0	168.0	190	28	44	65	3-13	0	4.66
Don Kaiser	R	21	27	22	5	1	150.1	144	15	52	74	4-9	0	3.59
Paul Minner	L	32	10	9	1	0	47.0	60	9	19	14	2-5	0	6.89
Moe Drabowsky	R	20	9	7	3	0	51.0	37	1	39	36	2-4	0	2.47
Dave Hillman	R	28	2	2	0	0	12.1	11	0	5	6	0-2	0	2.19
Turk Lown	R	32	61	0	0	0	110.2	95	10	78	74	9-8	13	3.58
Jim Davis	L	31	46	11	2	1	120.1	116	11	59	66	5-7	2	3.66
Vito Valentinetti	R	27	42	2	0	0	95.1	84	10	36	26	6-4	1	3.78
Jim Brosnan	R	26	30	10	1	1	95.0	95	9	45	51	5-9	1	3.79
Jim Hughes†	R	33	25	1	0	0	45.1	43	4	30	20	1-3	0	5.16
Russ Meyer†	R	32	20	9	0	0	57.0	71	11	26	28	1-6	0	6.32
John Briggs	R	22	3	0	0	0	5.1	5	1	4	1	0-0	0	1.69
George Piktuzis	L	24	2	0	0	0	5.0	6	1	2	3	0-0	0	7.20
Bill Tremel	R	26	1	0	0	0	1.0	3	0	0	0	0-0	0	9.00

»1957 New York Yankees 1st AL 98-56 .636 —

Casey Stengel

Player	Gm by Position	B	Age	G	AB	R	H	2B	3B	HR	RBI	BB	SO	SB	Avg	OBP	Slg
Yogi Berra	C121,OF6	L	32	134	482	74	121	14	2	24	82	57	24	1	.251	.329	.438
Bill Skowron	1B115	R	26	122	457	54	139	15	5	17	88	31	60	3	.304	.347	.470
Bobby Richardson	2B93	R	21	97	305	36	78	11	1	0	19	9	26	1	.256	.274	.298
Andy Carey	3B81	R	25	85	247	30	63	6	5	6	33	15	42	2	.255	.309	.393
Gil McDougald	SS121,2B21,3B7	R	29	141	539	87	156	25	9	13	62	59	71	2	.289	.362	.442
Mickey Mantle	OF139	S	25	144	474	121	173	28	6	34	94	146	75	16	.365	.512	.665
Hank Bauer	OF135	R	34	137	479	70	124	22	9	18	65	42	64	7	.259	.321	.455
Elston Howard	OF71,C32,1B2	R	28	110	356	33	90	13	4	8	44	16	43	2	.253	.283	.379
Tony Kubek	OF50,SS41,3B38*	L	20	127	431	56	128	21	3	3	39	24	48	6	.297	.335	.381
Harry Simpson†	OF42,1B21	L	31	75	224	27	56	7	3	7	39	19	36	1	.250	.307	.402
Enos Slaughter	OF64	L	41	96	209	24	53	7	1	5	34	40	19	0	.254	.369	.368
Jerry Coleman	2B45,3B21,SS4	R	32	72	157	23	42	7	2	2	12	20	21	1	.268	.354	.376
Joe Collins	1B32,OF15	L	34	79	149	17	30	1	0	2	10	24	18	2	.201	.310	.248
Billy Martin†	2B26,3B13	R	29	43	145	12	35	5	2	1	12	3	14	2	.241	.257	.324
Jerry Lumpe	3B30,SS6	L	24	40	103	15	35	6	2	0	11	9	13	2	.340	.389	.437
Darrell Johnson	C20	R	28	21	46	4	10	1	0	1	8	3	10	0	.217	.275	.304
Zeke Bella	OF4	R	26	5	10	0	1	0	0	0	0	1	2	0	.100	.182	.100
Bobby Del Greco†	OF6	R	24	8	7	3	3	0	0	0	0	2	2	1	.429	.556	.429
Woodie Held†		R	25	1	1	0	0	0	0	0	0	0	0	0	.000	.000	.000

T. Kubek, 1 G at 2B

Pitcher	T	Age	G	GS	CG	ShO	IP	H	HR	BB	SO	W-L	Sv	ERA
Tom Sturdivant	R	27	28	28	7	2	201.2	170	14	80	118	16-6	0	2.54
Johnny Kucks	R	23	37	23	4	1	179.1	169	13	59	78	8-10	2	3.56
Bob Turley	R	26	32	23	9	4	176.1	120	17	85	152	13-6	3	2.71
Bobby Shantz	L	31	30	21	9	1	173.0	157	15	40	72	11-5	5	2.45
Don Larsen	R	27	27	20	4	1	139.2	113	12	87	81	10-4	0	3.74
Whitey Ford	L	28	24	17	5	0	129.1	114	10	53	84	11-5	0	2.57
Sal Maglie†	R	40	6	3	1	1	26.0	22	1	7	9	2-0	3	1.73
Art Ditmar	R	28	46	11	0	0	127.1	128	9	35	64	8-3	6	3.25
Bob Grim	R	27	46	0	0	0	72.0	60	5	36	52	12-8	19	2.63
Tommy Byrne	L	37	30	4	1	0	84.2	70	8	60	57	4-6	2	4.36
Al Cicotte	R	27	20	2	0	0	65.1	57	5	30	36	2-2	2	3.03
Ralph Terry†	R	21	7	2	1	1	20.2	18	1	8	7	1-1	0	3.05

1957 Chicago White Sox 2nd AL 90-64 .584 8.0 GB

Al Lopez

Player	Gm by Position	B	Age	G	AB	R	H	2B	3B	HR	RBI	BB	SO	SB	Avg	OBP	Slg
Sherm Lollar	C96	R	32	101	351	33	90	11	2	11	70	35	24	2	.256	.342	.393
Earl Torgeson†	1B70,OF1	L	33	86	251	53	74	11	2	7	46	49	44	7	.295	.406	.438
Nellie Fox	2B155	L	29	155	619	110	196	27	8	6	61	75	13	5	.317	.403	.415
Bubba Phillips	3B97,OF20	R	29	121	393	38	106	13	3	7	42	28	32	5	.270	.322	.372
Luis Aparicio	SS142	R	23	143	575	82	148	22	6	3	41	52	55	28	.257	.317	.332
Minnie Minoso	OF152,3B1	R	34	153	568	96	176	36	5	12	103	79	54	18	.310	.408	.454
Larry Doby	OF110	L	33	119	416	57	120	27	2	14	79	56	79	2	.288	.373	.464
Jim Landis	OF90	R	23	96	274	38	58	11	3	2	16	45	61	14	.212	.329	.296
Jim Rivera	OF86,1B31	L	34	125	402	51	103	21	6	14	52	40	80	18	.256	.326	.443
Walt Dropo	1B69	R	34	93	223	24	57	2	0	13	49	16	40	0	.256	.300	.439
Sammy Esposito	3B53,SS22,2B4*	R	25	94	176	26	36	3	0	2	15	38	27	5	.205	.344	.256
Earl Battey	C43	R	22	48	115	12	20	2	3	3	6	11	38	0	.174	.246	.322
Les Moss	C39	R	32	42	115	10	31	3	0	2	12	20	18	0	.270	.375	.348
Fred Hatfield	3B44	L	32	69	114	14	23	3	0	0	8	15	20	1	.202	.316	.228
Ted Beard	OF28	L	36	38	78	15	16	1	0	0	7	18	14	3	.205	.354	.218
Dave Philley†	OF17,1B2	S	37	22	71	9	23	4	0	0	9	4	10	1	.324	.360	.380
Ron Jackson	1B13	R	23	13	60	4	19	3	0	2	8	1	12	0	.317	.328	.467
Ron Northey†		L	37	40	27	0	5	1	0	0	7	11	5	0	.185	.410	.222
Bob Kennedy†		R	36	4	2	0	0	0	0	0	0	0	1	0	.000	.000	.000
Leroy Powell		R	23	1	0	1	0	0	0	0	0	0	0	0	—	—	—

S. Esposito, 1 G at OF

Pitcher	T	Age	G	GS	CG	ShO	IP	H	HR	BB	SO	W-L	Sv	ERA
Billy Pierce	L	30	37	34	16	4	257.0	228	18	71	171	20-12	2	3.26
Jim Wilson	R	35	30	29	12	5	201.2	189	22	65	100	15-8	0	3.48
Dick Donovan	R	29	28	28	16	2	220.2	203	17	45	88	16-6	0	2.77
Jack Harshman	L	29	30	26	6	0	151.1	142	16	82	83	8-8	1	4.10
Bob Keegan	R	36	30	20	6	2	142.2	131	22	37	36	10-8	2	3.53
Gerry Staley	R	36	47	0	0	0	105.0	95	7	27	44	5-1	7	2.06
Dixie Howell	R	37	37	0	0	0	68.1	64	6	30	37	6-5	6	3.29
Paul LaPalme	L	33	35	0	0	0	40.1	35	5	19	19	1-4	7	3.35
Bill Fischer	R	26	33	11	3	1	124.0	139	1	35	48	7-8	1	3.48
Jim Derrington	L	17	20	5	0	0	37.0	29	4	29	14	0-1	0	4.86
Jim McDonald	R	30	10	0	0	0	22.1	18	2	10	12	0-1	0	2.01
Barry Latman	R	21	7	2	0	0	12.1	12	2	13	9	1-2	1	8.03
Don Rudolph	L	25	5	0	0	0	12.0	6	2	2	2	1-0	0	2.25
Jim Hughes	R	34	4	0	0	0	5.0	12	0	3	2	0-0	0	10.80
Stover McIlwain	R	17	1	0	0	0	1.0	2	0	1	0	0-0	0	0.00
Ellis Kinder	R	42	1	0	0	0	1.0	0	0	1	0	0-0	0	0.00

1957 Boston Red Sox 3rd AL 82-72 .532 16.0 GB

Pinky Higgins

Player	Gm by Position	B	Age	G	AB	R	H	2B	3B	HR	RBI	BB	SO	SB	Avg	OBP	Slg
Sammy White	C111	R	28	111	340	24	73	10	1	3	31	25	38	0	.215	.267	.276
Dick Gernert	1B71,OF16	R	28	99	316	45	75	13	3	14	58	39	62	1	.237	.324	.430
Ted Lepcio	2B68	R	26	79	232	24	56	10	2	9	37	29	61	0	.241	.328	.418
Frank Malzone	3B153	R	27	153	634	82	185	31	5	15	103	31	41	2	.292	.323	.427
Billy Klaus	SS118	L	28	127	477	76	120	18	4	10	42	55	53	2	.252	.326	.369
Jimmy Piersall	OF151	R	27	151	609	103	159	27	5	19	63	62	54	14	.261	.331	.415
Jackie Jensen	OF144	R	30	145	544	82	153	29	2	23	103	75	66	8	.281	.367	.469
Ted Williams	OF125	L	38	132	420	96	163	28	1	38	87	119	43	0	.388	.526	.731
Mickey Vernon	1B70	L	39	102	270	36	65	18	1	7	38	41	35	0	.241	.350	.393
Gene Mauch	2B58	R	31	65	222	23	60	10	3	2	28	22	26	1	.270	.335	.369
Billy Consolo	SS42,2B16,3B2	R	22	68	196	26	53	6	1	4	19	23	48	1	.270	.345	.372
Pete Daley	C77	R	27	78	191	17	43	10	0	3	25	16	31	0	.225	.288	.325
Gene Stephens	OF92	L	24	120	173	25	46	6	4	3	26	26	20	0	.266	.353	.399
Norm Zauchin	1B36	R	27	52	91	11	24	3	0	3	14	9	13	0	.264	.343	.396
Ken Aspromonte	2B24	R	25	24	78	9	21	5	0	0	4	17	10	0	.269	.396	.333
Marty Keough	OF7	L	22	9	17	1	1	0	0	0	0	4	3	0	.059	.238	.059
Billy Goodman†		L	31	18	16	1	1	1	0	0	0	2	1	0	.063	.167	.125
Haywood Sullivan	C1	R	26	2	1	0	0	0	0	0	0	0	0	0	.000	.000	.000
Milt Bolling†		R	26	1	1	0	0	0	0	0	0	0	0	0	.000	.000	.000
Faye Throneberry†		L	26	1	1	0	0	0	0	0	0	0	1	0	.000	.000	.000

Pitcher	T	Age	G	GS	CG	ShO	IP	H	HR	BB	SO	W-L	Sv	ERA
Tom Brewer	R	25	32	32	15	2	238.1	225	24	93	128	16-13	0	3.85
Frank Sullivan	R	27	31	30	14	3	240.2	206	16	48	127	14-11	0	2.73
Willard Nixon	R	29	29	29	11	1	191.0	207	10	56	96	12-13	0	3.68
Dave Sisler	R	25	22	19	5	0	122.1	135	15	61	55	7-8	1	4.71
Mike Fornieles†	R	25	25	18	7	1	125.1	136	7	38	64	8-7	2	3.52
Russ Meyer	R	33	2	1	0	0	5.0	10	0	3	1	0-0	0	5.40
Ike Delock	R	27	49	2	0	0	94.0	80	11	45	62	9-8	11	3.83
George Susce	R	25	29	5	0	0	88.1	93	6	41	40	7-3	1	4.28
Bob Porterfield	R	33	28	9	3	1	102.1	107	8	30	28	4-4	1	4.05
Rudy Minarcin	R	27	26	0	0	0	44.2	44	5	30	20	0-0	2	4.43
Bob Chakales†	R	29	18	0	0	0	32.0	53	5	11	16	0-2	3	8.16
Dean Stone†	L	26	17	8	0	0	51.1	56	5	35	32	1-3	1	5.08
Murray Wall	R	30	11	0	0	0	24.1	21	3	2	13	3-0	1	3.33
Frank Baumann	L	23	4	1	0	0	12.0	13	1	3	7	1-0	0	3.75
Russ Kemmerer†	R	25	1	0	0	0	4.0	5	0	2	1	0-0	0	4.50
Jack Spring	L	24	1	0	0	0	1.0	0	0	0	2	0-0	0	0.00

1957 Detroit Tigers 4th AL 78-76 .506 20.0 GB

Jack Tighe

Player	Gm by Position	B	Age	G	AB	R	H	2B	3B	HR	RBI	BB	SO	SB	Avg	OBP	Slg
Frank House	C97	L	27	106	348	31	90	9	0	7	36	35	26	1	.259	.327	.345
Ray Boone	1B117,3B4	R	33	129	462	48	126	25	3	12	65	57	47	1	.273	.353	.418
Frank Bolling	2B146	R	25	146	576	72	149	27	6	15	40	57	64	4	.259	.327	.405
Reno Bertoia	3B83,SS7,2B2	R	22	97	295	28	81	16	2	4	28	19	43	2	.275	.326	.383
Harvey Kuenn	SS136,3B17,1B1	R	26	151	624	74	173	30	6	9	44	47	28	5	.277	.327	.388
Al Kaline	OF145	R	22	149	577	83	170	29	4	23	90	43	38	11	.295	.343	.478
Charlie Maxwell	OF137	L	30	138	492	75	136	23	3	24	82	76	84	3	.276	.377	.482
Bill Tuttle	OF128	R	27	133	451	49	113	12	4	5	47	44	41	2	.251	.316	.328
Red Wilson	C59	R	28	59	180	21	43	8	1	3	13	24	19	2	.239	.338	.344
Jim Finigan	3B59,2B3	R	28	64	174	20	47	4	2	0	17	23	18	1	.270	.357	.316
Dave Philley†	1B27,OF12,3B1	S	37	65	173	15	49	8	1	2	16	7	16	3	.283	.309	.376
J.W. Porter	OF27,C12,1B3	R	24	58	140	14	35	8	0	2	18	14	20	0	.250	.323	.350
Johnny Groth†	OF36	R	30	38	103	11	30	10	0	0	16	6	7	0	.291	.333	.388
Ron Samford	SS35,2B11,3B4	R	27	54	91	6	20	1	2	0	5	6	15	1	.220	.276	.275
Earl Torgeson†	1B17	L	33	30	50	5	12	2	1	1	5	12	10	0	.240	.387	.380
Jim Small	OF14	L	20	36	42	7	9	2	0	0	0	2	11	0	.214	.250	.262
Steve Boros	3B9,SS5	R	20	24	41	4	6	1	0	0	2	1	8	0	.146	.167	.171
Bobo Osborne	OF5,1B4	L	21	11	27	4	4	1	0	0	1	3	7	0	.148	.233	.185
Bill Taylor†	OF5	L	27	9	23	4	8	2	0	1	3	0	3	0	.348	.348	.565
Jack Dittmer	3B3,2B1	L	29	16	22	3	5	1	0	0	2	2	1	0	.227	.292	.273
Karl Olson†	OF5	R	26	8	14	1	2	0	0	0	1	0	6	0	.143	.143	.143
Eddie Robinson†	1B1	L	36	13	9	0	0	0	0	0	0	3	0	0	.000	.308	.000
Mel Clark	OF2	R	30	5	7	0	0	0	0	0	1	0	3	0	.000	.000	.000
George Thomas	3B1	R	19	1	1	0	0	0	0	0	0	0	1	0	.000	.000	.000
Tom Yewcic	C1	R	25	1	1	0	0	0	0	0	0	0	0	0	.000	.000	.000
Jack Phillips		R	35	1	1	1	0	0	0	0	0	0	0	0	.000	.000	.000

Pitcher	T	Age	G	GS	CG	ShO	IP	H	HR	BB	SO	W-L	Sv	ERA
Frank Lary	R	27	40	35	12	2	237.2	250	23	72	107	11-16	3	3.98
Jim Bunning	R	25	45	30	14	1	267.1	214	33	72	182	20-8	1	2.69
Billy Hoeft	L	25	34	28	10	1	207.0	188	15	69	111	9-11	1	3.48
Paul Foytack	R	26	38	27	8	1	212.0	175	19	104	118	14-11	1	3.14
Duke Maas	R	28	45	26	8	2	219.1	210	23	65	116	10-14	6	3.28
Don Lee	R	23	11	6	0	0	38.2	48	6	18	19	1-3	0	4.66
Lou Sleater	L	30	41	0	0	0	69.1	61	9	28	43	3-3	2	3.76
Harry Byrd	R	32	37	1	0	0	59.0	53	6	28	20	4-3	5	3.36
Al Aber†	L	29	28	0	0	0	37.0	46	6	11	15	3-3	1	6.81
Steve Gromek	R	37	15	1	0	0	23.2	32	3	13	11	0-1	1	6.08
Joe Presko	R	28	7	0	0	0	11.0	10	0	4	3	1-1	0	1.64
Bob Shaw	R	24	7	0	0	0	9.2	11	2	7	4	0-1	0	7.45
Jim Stump	R	25	6	0	0	0	13.1	11	0	8	2	1-0	0	2.03
Jack Crimian	R	31	4	0	0	0	5.2	9	1	4	1	0-1	0	12.71
John Tsitouris	R	21	2	0	0	0	3.1	8	0	2	2	1-0	0	8.10
Pete Wojey	R	37	2	0	0	0	1.1	1	0	0	0	0-0	0	0.00
Chuck Daniel	R	23	1	0	0	0	2.1	3	1	0	2	0-0	0	7.71

1957 Baltimore Orioles 5th AL 76-76 .500 21.0 GB

Paul Richards

Player	Gm by Position	B	Age	G	AB	R	H	2B	3B	HR	RBI	BB	SO	SB	Avg	OBP	Slg
Gus Triandos	C120	R	26	129	418	44	106	21	1	19	72	38	73	0	.254	.317	.445
Bob Boyd	1B132,OF1	L	31	141	485	73	154	16	8	4	34	55	31	2	.318	.388	.408
Billy Gardner	2B148,SS9	R	29	154	644	79	169	36	3	6	55	53	67	10	.262	.325	.356
George Kell	3B80,1B22	R	34	99	310	28	92	9	0	9	44	25	16	2	.297	.352	.413
Willie Miranda	SS115	S	31	115	314	29	61	3	0	0	20	24	42	2	.194	.249	.204
Al Pilarcik	OF126	L	26	142	407	52	113	16	3	9	49	53	28	14	.278	.359	.398
Bob Nieman	OF120	R	30	129	445	61	123	17	6	13	70	63	86	4	.276	.363	.429
Jim Busby†	OF85	R	30	86	288	31	72	10	1	3	19	23	36	6	.250	.304	.323
Tito Francona	OF73,1B4	L	23	97	279	35	65	8	3	7	38	29	48	7	.233	.307	.358
Billy Goodman†	3B54,OF9,1B8*	L	31	73	263	36	81	10	3	3	33	21	18	0	.308	.362	.403
Joe Ginsberg	C66	L	30	85	175	15	48	8	2	1	18	18	19	2	.274	.342	.360
Dick Williams†	OF26,3B15,1B12	R	28	47	167	16	39	10	2	1	17	14	21	0	.234	.293	.335
Joe Durham	OF59	R	25	77	157	19	29	2	0	4	17	16	42	1	.185	.259	.274
Jim Bridewester	SS74,3B3,2B1	R	30	91	142	16	38	7	1	1	18	21	16	2	.268	.362	.352
Brooks Robinson	3B47	R	20	50	117	13	28	6	1	2	14	7	10	1	.239	.286	.359
Bob Hale	1B5	L	23	42	44	2	11	0	0	0	7	2	2	0	.250	.265	.250
Carl Powis	OF13	R	29	15	41	4	8	3	1	0	2	7	9	2	.195	.314	.317
Jim Pyburn	OF28,C1	R	24	35	40	8	9	0	0	1	2	9	6	1	.225	.367	.300
Lenny Green	OF15	L	24	19	33	2	6	1	1	1	5	1	4	0	.182	.206	.364
Tex Nelson	OF8	L	20	15	23	2	5	0	2	0	5	1	5	0	.217	.280	.391
Buddy Peterson	SS7	R	32	7	17	1	3	2	0	0	0	2	2	0	.176	.263	.294
Frank Zupo	C8	L	17	10	12	2	1	0	0	0	0	1	4	0	.083	.154	.083
Wayne Causey	2B6,3B5	L	20	14	10	2	2	0	0	0	1	5	2	0	.200	.471	.200
Eddie Robinson†		L	36	4	3	0	0	0	0	0	0	1	1	0	.000	.250	.000
Tom Patton	C1	R	21	1	2	0	0	0	0	0	0	0	2	0	.000	.000	.000
Eddie Miksis†		R	30	1	1	0	0	0	0	0	0	0	0	0	.000	.000	.000

B. Goodman, 5 G at 2B, 5 G at SS

Pitcher	T	Age	G	GS	CG	ShO	IP	H	HR	BB	SO	W-L	Sv	ERA
Ray Moore	R	31	34	32	7	1	227.1	196	17	112	117	11-13	0	3.72
Connie Johnson	R	34	35	30	14	3	242.0	212	17	66	177	14-11	0	3.20
Hal Brown	R	32	25	20	7	2	150.0	132	17	37	62	7-8	1	3.90
Billy Loes	R	27	31	18	8	3	155.1	142	8	37	86	12-7	4	3.24
Bill Wight	L	35	27	17	2	0	121.0	122	4	54	50	6-6	0	3.64
George Zuverink	R	32	56	0	0	0	112.2	105	9	39	36	10-6	9	2.48
Billy O'Dell	L	24	35	15	2	1	140.1	107	12	39	97	4-10	4	2.69
Ken Lehman†	L	29	30	3	1	0	68.0	57	1	22	32	8-3	6	2.78
Art Ceccarelli	L	27	20	8	1	0	58.0	62	3	31	30	0-5	0	4.50
Mike Fornieles†	R	25	15	4	1	1	57.0	57	4	17	43	2-6	0	4.26
Jerry Walker	R	18	13	3	1	1	27.2	24	1	14	13	1-0	1	2.93
Don Ferrarese	L	28	8	2	0	0	19.0	14	1	12	13	1-1	0	4.74
Art Houtteman†	R	29	5	1	0	0	6.2	20	0	3	3	0-0	0	17.55
Sandy Consuegra†	R	36	5	0	0	0	5.0	4	0	0	0	0-0	0	1.80
Milt Pappas	R	18	4	0	0	0	9.0	6	0	3	3	0-0	0	1.00
Charlie Beamon	R	22	4	1	0	0	8.2	8	1	7	5	0-0	0	5.19
Dizzy Trout	R	42	2	0	0	0	0.1	4	0	0	0	0-0	0	81.00

1957 Cleveland Indians 6th AL 76-77 .497 21.5 GB

Kerby Farrell

Player	Gm by Position	B	Age	G	AB	R	H	2B	3B	HR	RBI	BB	SO	SB	Avg	OBP	Slg
Jim Hegan	C58	R	36	58	148	14	32	7	0	4	15	16	23	0	.216	.291	.345
Vic Wertz	1B139	L	32	144	515	84	145	21	0	28	105	78	88	2	.282	.371	.485
Bobby Avila	2B107,3B16	R	33	129	463	60	124	19	3	5	48	46	47	2	.268	.334	.354
Al Smith	3B84,OF58	R	29	135	507	78	125	23	5	11	49	79	70	12	.247	.348	.377
Chico Carrasquel	SS122	R	31	125	392	37	108	14	1	8	57	41	53	0	.276	.351	.378
Rocky Colavito	OF130	R	23	134	461	66	116	26	0	25	84	71	80	1	.252	.348	.471
Gene Woodling	OF113	L	34	133	430	74	138	25	2	19	78	64	35	0	.321	.408	.521
Roger Maris	OF112	L	22	116	358	61	84	9	5	14	51	60	79	8	.235	.344	.405
Larry Raines	3B27,SS25,2B10*	R	27	96	244	39	64	14	0	2	16	19	40	5	.262	.318	.344
Dick Williams†	OF37,3B19	R	28	67	205	33	58	7	0	6	17	12	19	3	.283	.324	.405
George Strickland	2B48,SS23,3B19	R	31	89	201	21	47	8	2	1	19	26	29	0	.234	.323	.308
Russ Nixon	C57	L	22	62	185	15	52	7	1	2	18	12	12	0	.281	.323	.362
Hal Naragon	C39	L	28	57	121	12	31	1	1	0	8	12	9	0	.256	.326	.281
Dick Brown	C33	R	22	34	114	10	30	4	0	4	22	4	23	1	.263	.281	.404
Joe Caffie	OF19	L	26	32	89	14	24	2	1	3	10	4	11	0	.270	.301	.416
Joe Altobelli	1B56,OF7	L	25	83	87	9	18	3	2	0	9	5	14	3	.207	.253	.287
Jim Busby†	OF26	R	30	30	74	9	14	2	1	2	4	1	8	0	.189	.200	.324
Billy Harrell	SS14,3B6,2B1	R	28	22	57	6	15	1	1	1	5	4	7	3	.263	.311	.368
Kenny Kuhn	2B14,3B2,SS1	L	20	40	53	5	9	0	0	0	5	4	9	0	.170	.228	.170
Eddie Robinson†	1B7	L	36	19	27	1	6	1	0	1	3	0	3	0	.222	.241	.370
Preston Ward	1B1	L	29	10	11	2	2	1	0	0	0	0	2	0	.182	.182	.273
Bob Usher†	OF4,3B1	R	32	10	8	1	1	0	0	0	0	1	3	0	.125	.222	.125

L. Raines, 8 G at OF

Pitcher	T	Age	G	GS	CG	ShO	IP	H	HR	BB	SO	W-L	Sv	ERA
Early Wynn	R	37	40	37	13	1	263.0	270	32	104	184	14-17	1	4.31
Mike Garcia	R	33	38	27	9	1	211.1	221	14	73	110	12-8	0	3.75
Don Mossi	L	28	36	22	6	1	159.0	165	16	57	97	11-10	2	4.13
Bob Lemon	R	36	21	17	2	0	117.1	129	9	64	45	6-11	0	4.60
Herb Score	L	24	5	5	3	1	36.0	18	0	26	39	2-1	0	2.00
Ray Narleski	R	28	46	15	7	1	154.1	136	14	70	93	11-5	16	3.09
Cal McLish	R	31	42	7	2	0	144.1	118	11	67	88	9-7	1	2.74
Bud Daley	L	24	34	10	1	0	87.1	99	7	40	54	2-8	2	4.43
Dick Tomanek	L	26	34	2	0	0	69.2	67	13	37	55	2-1	0	5.68
Stan Pitula	R	26	23	5	1	0	59.2	67	8	32	17	2-2	0	4.98
Vito Valentinetti†	R	28	11	2	1	0	23.2	26	3	13	9	2-2	0	4.94
Hank Aguirre	L	26	10	1	0	0	20.1	26	0	13	9	1-1	0	5.75
Johnny Gray	R	29	7	3	1	1	20.0	21	1	13	3	1-3	0	5.85
Bob Alexander	R	34	5	0	0	0	7.0	10	0	5	1	0-1	0	9.00
Art Houtteman†	R	29	3	0	0	0	4.0	6	1	3	3	0-0	0	6.75
Hoyt Wilhelm†	R	33	2	0	0	0	3.2	2	1	1	0	1-0	1	2.45

1957 Kansas City Athletics 7th AL 59-94 .386 38.5 GB

Lou Boudreau (36-67)/Harry Craft (23-27)

Player	Gm by Position	B	Age	G	AB	R	H	2B	3B	HR	RBI	BB	SO	SB	Avg	OBP	Slg
Hal Smith	C103	R	26	107	360	41	109	26	0	13	41	14	44	2	.303	.328	.483
Vic Power	1B113,OF6,2B4	R	29	129	467	48	121	15	1	14	42	19	21	3	.259	.291	.385
Billy Hunter	2B64,SS35,3B17	R	29	116	319	39	61	10	4	8	29	27	43	1	.191	.259	.323
Hector Lopez	3B111,2B4,OF3	R	27	121	391	51	115	19	4	11	35	41	66	1	.294	.357	.448
Joe DeMaestri	SS134	R	28	135	461	44	113	14	6	9	33	22	82	6	.245	.280	.360
Gus Zernial	OF113,1B1	R	34	131	437	56	103	20	1	27	69	34	84	1	.236	.290	.471
Woodie Held†	OF92	R	25	92	326	48	78	14	3	20	50	37	81	4	.239	.321	.485
Bob Cerv	OF89	R	31	124	345	35	94	14	2	11	44	20	57	1	.272	.312	.420
Lou Skizas	OF76,3B32	R	25	119	376	34	92	14	1	18	44	27	15	5	.245	.297	.431
Billy Martin†	2B52,3B20,SS2	R	29	73	265	33	68	9	3	9	27	12	20	7	.257	.295	.415
Tim Thompson	C62	L	33	81	230	25	47	10	0	7	19	18	26	0	.204	.262	.339
Harry Simpson†	1B27,OF21	L	31	50	179	24	53	9	6	6	24	12	28	0	.296	.339	.514
Irv Noren†	1B25,OF6	L	32	81	160	8	34	8	0	2	16	11	19	0	.213	.267	.300
Milt Graff	2B53	L	26	56	155	16	28	4	3	0	10	15	10	2	.181	.260	.245
Bob Martyn	OF49	L	26	58	131	10	35	2	4	1	12	11	20	1	.267	.322	.366
Jim Pisoni	OF44	R	27	44	97	14	23	2	2	3	12	10	17	0	.237	.318	.392
Johnny Groth†	OF50	R	30	55	59	10	15	0	0	0	2	7	6	0	.254	.333	.254
Mickey McDermott	P29,1B2	L	29	58	49	6	12	1	0	4	7	9	16	0	.245	.362	.510
Clete Boyer	2B1,3B1	R	20	10	0	0	0	0	0	0	0	0	0	0	—	—	—

Pitcher	T	Age	G	GS	CG	ShO	IP	H	HR	BB	SO	W-L	Sv	ERA
Ned Garver	R	31	24	23	6	1	145.1	120	13	55	61	6-13	0	3.84
Alex Kellner	L	32	28	21	3	0	132.2	141	18	41	72	6-5	0	4.27
Ralph Terry†	R	21	21	19	3	1	130.2	119	15	47	80	4-11	0	3.38
Arnie Portocarrero	R	25	33	17	1	0	114.2	103	10	34	42	4-9	0	3.92
George Brunet	L	22	4	2	0	0	11.1	13	2	4	3	0-1	0	5.56
Virgil Trucks	R	40	48	7	0	0	116.0	106	12	62	55	9-7	7	3.03
Tom Morgan	R	27	46	13	5	0	143.2	160	19	61	32	9-7	7	4.64
Tom Gorman	R	32	38	12	3	1	124.2	125	18	33	66	5-9	3	3.83
Wally Burnette	R	28	38	9	1	0	113.0	115	8	44	57	7-12	1	4.30
Jack Urban	R	28	31	13	3	0	129.1	111	7	45	55	7-4	0	3.34
Mickey McDermott	L	29	29	4	0	0	69.0	68	9	50	29	1-4	0	5.48
Rip Coleman	L	25	19	6	1	0	41.0	53	5	25	15	0-7	0	5.93
Ryne Duren	R	28	14	6	0	0	42.2	37	4	30	37	0-3	1	5.27
Gene Host	L	24	11	2	0	0	23.2	29	5	14	9	0-2	0	7.23
Glenn Cox	R	26	10	0	0	0	14.1	18	1	9	8	1-0	0	5.02
Al Abert†	L	29	3	0	0	0	3.0	6	2	2	0	0-0	0	12.00
Harry Taylor	R	21	2	0	0	0	8.2	11	0	4	4	0-0	0	3.12
Dave Hill	L	19	2	0	0	0	2.1	6	3	3	1	0-0	0	27.00
Ed Blake	R	31	2	0	0	0	1.2	1	1	2	0	0-0	0	5.40
Hal Raether	R	24	1	0	0	0	2.0	2	1	0	0	0-0	0	9.00

1957 Washington Senators 8th AL 55-99 .357 43.0 GB

Chuck Dressen (4-16)/Cookie Lavagetto (51-83)

Player	Gm by Position	B	Age	G	AB	R	H	2B	3B	HR	RBI	BB	SO	SB	Avg	OBP	Slg
Lou Berberet	C77	L	27	99	264	24	69	11	2	7	36	41	38	0	.261	.359	.398
Pete Runnels	1B72,3B32,2B23	L	29	134	473	53	109	18	4	2	35	55	51	2	.230	.310	.298
Herb Plews	2B79,3B11,SS4	L	29	104	329	51	89	19	4	1	26	28	39	0	.271	.326	.362
Eddie Yost	3B107	R	30	110	414	47	104	13	5	9	38	73	49	1	.251	.370	.372
Rocky Bridges†	SS108,2B14,3B1	R	29	120	391	40	89	17	2	3	47	26	33	1	.228	.298	.304
Jim Lemon	OF131,1B3	R	29	137	518	58	147	23	6	17	64	49	94	1	.284	.345	.450
Roy Sievers	OF130,1B21	R	30	152	572	99	172	23	5	42	114	76	55	1	.301	.388	.579
Bob Usher†	OF95	R	32	96	295	36	77	7	1	5	27	27	38	0	.261	.324	.342
Milt Bolling†	2B53,SS37,3B1	R	26	91	277	29	63	12	1	4	19	18	59	2	.227	.277	.321
Art Schult†	1B35,OF31	R	29	77	247	30	65	14	0	4	35	14	30	0	.263	.303	.368
Clint Courtney	C59	L	30	91	232	23	62	14	1	6	27	16	11	0	.267	.346	.414
Faye Throneberry†	OF58	L	26	68	195	21	36	8	2	2	12	17	37	0	.185	.252	.277
Julio Becquer	1B43	L	25	105	186	14	42	6	2	2	22	10	29	3	.226	.269	.312
Ed Fitz Gerald	C37	R	33	45	125	14	34	8	0	1	13	10	9	2	.272	.331	.360
Jerry Snyder	SS15,2B13,3B1	R	27	42	93	6	14	1	0	1	4	4	9	0	.151	.186	.194
Whitey Herzog	OF28	L	25	36	78	7	13	3	0	0	4	13	12	1	.167	.301	.205
Neil Chrisley	OF11	L	25	26	51	6	8	2	1	0	3	7	7	0	.157	.259	.235
Lyle Luttrell	SS17	R	27	19	45	4	9	4	0	0	5	3	8	0	.200	.250	.289
Harmon Killebrew	3B7,2B1	R	21	9	31	4	9	2	0	2	5	2	8	0	.290	.333	.548
Jerry Schoonmaker	OF13	R	23	30	23	5	2	1	0	0	0	2	11	0	.087	.160	.130
Karl Olson†	OF6	R	26	8	12	2	2	0	0	0	0	1	2	0	.167	.231	.167
Dick Tettelbach	OF3	R	28	9	11	2	2	0	0	0	1	4	2	0	.182	.375	.182

Pitcher	T	Age	G	GS	CG	ShO	IP	H	HR	BB	SO	W-L	Sv	ERA
Chuck Stobbs	L	27	42	31	5	2	211.2	235	28	80	114	8-20	1	5.36
Pedro Ramos	R	22	43	30	7	1	231.0	251	43	69	91	12-16	0	4.79
Camilo Pascual	R	23	29	26	8	2	175.2	168	11	76	113	8-17	0	4.10
Russ Kemmerer†	R	25	39	26	6	2	172.1	214	20	71	81	7-11	0	4.96
Ted Abernathy	R	24	26	16	2	0	85.0	100	9	65	50	2-10	0	6.78
Bob Chakales†	R	29	4	2	0	0	18.1	20	2	10	12	0-1	0	5.40
Bob Wiesler	L	26	3	2	1	0	16.1	15	2	11	9	1-1	0	4.41
Hal Griggs	R	28	2	2	0	0	13.2	11	1	7	12	0-1	0	3.29
Ralph Lumenti	L	20	3	2	0	0	9.1	9	1	5	8	0-1	0	6.75
Don Minnick	R	26	2	1	0	0	9.1	14	1	2	7	0-1	0	4.82
Tex Clevenger	R	24	52	9	2	0	139.2	139	11	47	75	7-6	8	4.19
Dick Hyde	R	28	52	2	0	0	109.1	104	4	56	46	4-3	1	4.12
Bud Byerly	R	36	47	0	0	0	95.0	94	6	22	39	6-6	6	3.13
Evelio Hernandez	R	26	14	2	0	0	36.0	38	2	20	15	0-0	0	4.25
Jim Heise	R	24	8	2	0	0	19.0	25	2	16	8	0-3	0	8.05
Joe Black	R	33	7	0	0	0	12.2	22	4	1	2	0-1	0	7.11
Dick Brodowski	R	24	6	0	0	0	11.1	12	2	10	4	0-1	0	11.12
Garland Shifflett	R	22	6	1	0	0	8.0	6	0	10	2	0-0	0	10.13
Dean Stone†	L	26	3	0	0	0	3.1	5	0	2	3	0-0	0	8.10

»1957 Milwaukee Braves 1st NL 95-59 .617 —

Player	Gm by Position	B	Age	G	AB	R	H	2B	3B	HR	RBI	BB	SO	SB	Avg	OBP	Slg
Del Crandall	C102,OF9,1B1	R	27	118	383	45	97	11	2	15	46	30	38	1	.253	.308	.410
Frank Torre	1B117	L	25	129	364	46	99	19	5	5	40	29	19	0	.272	.339	.393
Red Schoendienst†	2B92,OF2	S	34	93	394	56	122	23	4	6	32	23	7	2	.310	.348	.434
Eddie Mathews	3B147	L	25	148	572	109	167	28	9	32	94	90	79	3	.292	.387	.540
Johnny Logan	SS129	R	30	129	494	59	135	19	7	10	49	31	49	5	.273	.319	.401
Hank Aaron	OF150	R	23	151	615	118	198	27	6	44	132	57	58	1	.322	.378	.600
Wes Covington	OF89	L	25	96	328	51	93	4	8	21	65	29	44	4	.284	.339	.537
Bill Bruton	OF79	L	31	79	306	41	85	16	9	5	30	19	35	11	.278	.317	.438
Andy Pafko	OF69	R	36	83	220	31	61	6	1	8	27	10	22	1	.277	.308	.423
Joe Adcock	1B56	R	29	65	209	31	60	13	2	12	38	20	51	0	.287	.351	.541
Danny O'Connell†	2B48	R	30	48	183	29	43	9	1	1	8	19	20	1	.235	.312	.311
Felix Mantilla	SS35,2B13,3B7*	R	22	71	182	28	43	9	1	4	21	14	34	2	.236	.296	.363
Bobby Thomson†	OF38	R	33	41	148	15	35	5	3	4	23	8	27	2	.236	.285	.392
Del Rice	C48	R	34	54	144	15	33	1	1	9	20	17	37	0	.229	.309	.438
Bob Hazle	OF40	L	26	41	134	26	54	12	0	7	27	18	15	1	.403	.477	.649
Carl Sawatski	C28	L	29	58	105	13	25	4	0	6	17	10	15	0	.238	.316	.448
Nippy Jones	1B20,OF1	R	32	30	79	5	21	2	1	2	8	3	7	0	.266	.293	.392
Chuck Tanner†	OF18	L	27	22	69	5	17	3	0	2	6	5	4	0	.246	.297	.377
John DeMerit	OF13	R	21	33	34	8	5	0	0	0	1	0	8	1	.147	.147	.147
Bobby Malkmus	2B7	R	25	13	22	6	2	0	1	0	0	3	3	0	.091	.200	.182
Dick Cole	2B10,1B1,3B1	R	31	15	14	1	1	0	0	0	0	3	5	0	.071	.235	.071
Harry Hanebrink	3B2	L	29	6	7	0	2	0	0	0	0	1	2	0	.286	.375	.286
Mel Roach	2B5	R	24	7	6	1	1	0	0	0	0	0	3	0	.167	.167	.167
Ray Shearer	OF1	R	27	2	2	1	1	0	0	0	0	1	1	0	.500	.667	.500
Hawk Taylor	C1	R	18	7	1	2	0	0	0	0	0	0	0	0	.000	.000	.000

F. Mantilla, 1 G at OF

Fred Haney

Pitcher	T	Age	G	GS	CG	ShO	IP	H	HR	BB	SO	W-L	Sv	ERA
Warren Spahn	L	36	39	35	18	4	271.0	241	23	78	111	21-11	3	2.69
Lew Burdette	R	30	37	33	14	1	256.2	260	25	59	78	17-9	0	3.72
Bob Buhl	R	28	34	31	14	2	216.2	191	15	121	117	18-7	0	2.74
Gene Conley	R	26	35	18	6	1	148.0	133	9	64	61	9-9	1	3.16
Bob Trowbridge	R	27	32	16	3	1	126.0	118	9	52	75	7-5	1	3.64
Don McMahon	R	27	32	0	0	0	46.2	33	0	29	46	2-3	9	1.54
Ernie Johnson	R	33	30	0	0	0	65.0	67	9	26	44	7-3	4	3.88
Taylor Phillips	L	24	27	6	0	0	73.0	82	3	40	36	3-2	2	5.55
Juan Pizarro	L	20	24	10	3	0	99.1	99	16	51	68	5-6	0	4.62
Dave Jolly	R	32	23	0	0	0	37.2	37	4	21	27	1-1	1	5.02
Red Murff	R	36	12	1	0	0	26.0	31	3	11	13	2-2	2	4.85
Ray Crone†	R	25	11	5	2	0	42.1	54	8	15	15	3-1	0	4.46
Phil Paine	R	27	1	0	0	0	2.0	1	0	3	2	0-0	0	0.00
Joey Jay	R	21	1	0	0	0	0.2	0	0	0	0	0-0	1	0.00

1957 St. Louis Cardinals 2nd NL 87-67 .565 8.0 GB

Player	Gm by Position	B	Age	G	AB	R	H	2B	3B	HR	RBI	BB	SO	SB	Avg	OBP	Slg
Hal Smith	C97	R	26	100	333	25	93	12	3	2	37	18	18	2	.279	.314	.351
Stan Musial	1B130	L	36	134	502	82	176	38	3	29	102	66	34	1	.351	.422	.612
Don Blasingame	2B154	L	25	154	650	108	176	25	7	8	58	71	49	21	.271	.343	.368
Eddie Kasko	3B120,SS13,2B1	R	25	134	479	59	131	16	5	1	35	33	53	6	.273	.319	.334
Al Dark	SS139,3B1	R	35	140	583	80	169	25	8	4	64	29	56	3	.290	.326	.381
Wally Moon	OF133	L	27	142	516	86	152	28	5	24	73	62	57	5	.295	.367	.508
Del Ennis	OF127	R	32	136	490	61	140	24	3	24	105	37	50	1	.286	.332	.494
Ken Boyer	OF105,3B41	R	26	142	544	79	144	18	3	19	62	44	77	12	.265	.318	.414
Joe Cunningham	1B57,OF46	L	25	122	261	50	83	15	0	9	52	56	29	3	.318	.439	.479
Hobie Landrith	C67	L	27	75	214	18	52	6	0	3	26	25	27	1	.243	.318	.313
Bobby Gene Smith	OF79	R	23	93	185	24	39	7	1	3	18	13	35	1	.211	.260	.308
Walker Cooper	C13	R	42	48	78	7	21	5	1	3	10	5	10	0	.269	.310	.474
Dick Schofield	SS23	S	22	65	56	10	9	0	0	0	1	7	13	1	.161	.254	.161
Eddie Miksis†	OF31	R	30	49	38	3	8	0	0	1	2	7	7	0	.211	.333	.289
Jim King	OF8	L	24	22	35	1	11	0	0	0	2	4	2	0	.314	.385	.314
Irv Noren†	OF8	L	32	17	30	3	11	4	1	1	10	4	6	0	.367	.429	.667
Tom Alston	1B6	L	31	9	17	2	5	1	0	0	2	1	5	0	.294	.333	.353
Gene Green	OF3	R	24	6	15	0	3	1	0	0	2	0	3	0	.200	.188	.267
Don Lassetter	OF3	R	24	4	13	2	2	0	1	0	0	1	3	0	.154	.214	.308
Chuck Harmon†	OF8	R	33	9	3	2	1	0	1	0	1	0	0	1	.333	.333	1.000

Fred Hutchinson

Pitcher	T	Age	G	GS	CG	ShO	IP	H	HR	BB	SO	W-L	Sv	ERA
Sam Jones	R	31	28	27	10	2	182.2	164	17	71	154	12-9	0	3.60
Lindy McDaniel	R	21	30	26	10	1	191.0	196	13	53	75	15-9	0	3.49
Larry Jackson	R	26	41	22	6	2	210.1	196	21	57	96	15-9	1	3.47
Vinegar Bend Mizell	L	26	33	21	7	2	149.1	136	18	51	87	8-10	0	3.74
Herm Wehmeier	R	30	36	18	5	0	165.0	165	25	54	91	10-7	0	4.31
Von McDaniel	R	18	17	13	4	2	86.2	71	7	31	45	7-5	0	3.22
Murry Dickson	R	40	14	13	3	1	74.0	87	8	25	29	5-3	0	4.14
Tom Cheney	R	22	4	3	0	0	9.0	6	0	15	10	0-1	0	5.00
Lynn Lovenguth	R	34	2	1	0	0	9.0	6	0	6	6	0-1	0	2.00
Lloyd Merritt	R	24	44	0	0	0	65.1	60	7	28	35	1-2	7	3.31
Willard Schmidt	R	29	40	8	1	0	116.2	146	13	49	63	10-3	0	4.78
Hoyt Wilhelm†	R	33	40	0	0	0	55.0	52	7	21	29	1-4	11	4.25
Billy Muffett	R	26	23	0	0	0	44.0	35	1	13	21	3-2	8	2.25
Jim Davis†	L	32	10	0	0	0	13.2	18	1	6	5	0-1	1	5.27
Bob Smith†	L	26	6	0	0	0	9.2	12	0	6	11	0-0	1	4.66
Bob Miller	R	18	5	0	0	0	9.0	13	2	5	7	0-0	0	7.00
Morrie Martin	L	34	4	1	0	0	10.2	5	0	4	7	0-0	0	2.53
Frank Barnes	R	30	3	1	0	0	10.0	13	0	9	5	0-1	0	4.50
Bob Kuzava†	L	34	3	0	0	0	2.1	4	0	2	2	0-0	0	3.86

1957 Brooklyn Dodgers 3rd NL 84-70 .545 11.0 GB

Player	Gm by Position	B	Age	G	AB	R	H	2B	3B	HR	RBI	BB	SO	SB	Avg	OBP	Slg
Roy Campanella	C100	R	35	103	330	31	80	9	0	13	62	34	50	1	.242	.316	.388
Gil Hodges	1B150,3B2,2B1	R	33	150	579	94	173	28	7	27	98	63	91	5	.299	.366	.511
Jim Gilliam	2B148,OF2	S	28	149	617	89	154	26	4	2	37	64	31	26	.250	.323	.314
Pee Wee Reese	3B75,SS23	R	38	103	330	33	74	3	1	1	29	39	32	5	.224	.306	.248
Charlie Neal	SS100,3B23,2B3	R	26	128	448	62	121	13	7	12	62	53	83	11	.270	.356	.411
Gino Cimoli	OF138	R	27	142	532	88	156	22	5	10	57	39	86	3	.293	.343	.410
Duke Snider	OF136	L	30	139	508	91	139	25	7	40	92	77	104	3	.274	.368	.587
Carl Furillo	OF107	R	35	119	395	61	121	17	4	12	66	29	33	0	.306	.358	.461
Don Zimmer	3B39,SS37,2B5	R	26	84	269	23	59	9	1	6	19	16	63	1	.219	.262	.327
Sandy Amoros	OF66	L	27	106	238	40	66	7	1	7	26	46	42	3	.277	.399	.403
Rube Walker	C50	L	31	60	166	12	30	8	0	2	23	15	33	2	.181	.243	.265
Elmer Valo	OF36	L	36	81	161	14	44	10	1	4	26	25	16	0	.273	.370	.422
Randy Jackson	3B34	R	31	48	131	7	26	1	0	2	16	9	20	0	.198	.246	.252
John Roseboro	C19,1B5	L	24	35	69	6	10	2	0	2	6	10	20	0	.145	.253	.261
Bob Kennedy†	OF9,3B3	R	36	19	31	5	4	1	0	1	4	1	5	0	.129	.156	.258
Joe Pignatano	C6	R	27	8	14	0	3	1	0	0	1	0	5	0	.214	.214	.286
Jim Gentile	1B2	L	23	4	6	1	1	0	0	1	1	1	1	0	.167	.286	.667
Rod Miller		L	17	1	1	0	0	0	0	0	0	0	1	0	.000	.000	.000

Walter Alston

Pitcher	T	Age	G	GS	CG	ShO	IP	H	HR	BB	SO	W-L	Sv	ERA
Don Drysdale	R	20	34	29	9	4	221.0	197	17	61	148	17-9	0	2.69
Don Newcombe	R	31	28	28	12	4	198.2	199	28	33	90	11-12	0	3.49
Johnny Podres	L	24	31	27	10	6	196.0	168	15	44	109	12-9	3	2.66
Danny McDevitt	L	24	22	17	5	2	119.0	105	5	72	90	7-4	0	3.25
Sal Maglie†	R	40	19	17	4	1	101.1	94	12	26	50	6-6	1	2.93
Bill Harris	R	25	1	1	0	0	7.0	9	1	1	3	0-1	0	3.86
Clem Labine	R	30	58	0	0	0	104.2	104	8	27	67	5-7	17	3.44
Ed Roebuck	R	25	44	1	0	0	96.1	70	9	46	73	8-2	8	2.71
Sandy Koufax	L	21	34	13	2	0	104.1	83	14	51	122	5-4	0	3.88
Roger Craig	R	27	32	13	1	0	111.1	102	18	47	69	6-9	0	4.61
Don Bessent	R	26	27	0	0	0	44.0	58	5	19	24	1-3	0	5.73
Carl Erskine	R	30	15	7	1	0	66.0	62	8	20	26	5-3	0	3.55
Rene Valdez	R	28	5	1	0	0	13.0	13	1	7	10	1-1	0	5.54
Ken Lehman†	L	29	3	0	0	0	7.0	7	0	1	3	0-0	0	0.00
Jackie Collum†	L	30	3	0	0	0	4.1	7	1	1	3	0-0	0	8.31
Fred Kipp	L	25	1	0	0	0	4.0	6	2	0	3	0-0	0	9.00
Don Elston†	R	28	1	0	0	0	1.0	1	0	0	1	0-0	0	0.00

1957 Cincinnati Reds 4th NL 80-74 .519 15.0 GB

Player	Gm by Position	B	Age	G	AB	R	H	2B	3B	HR	RBI	BB	SO	SB	Avg	OBP	Slg
Ed Bailey	C115	L	26	122	391	54	102	15	2	20	48	73	69	5	.261	.377	.463
George Crowe	1B120	L	36	133	494	71	134	20	1	31	92	32	62	1	.271	.314	.504
Johnny Temple	2B145	R	29	145	557	85	158	24	4	0	37	94	34	19	.284	.387	.341
Don Hoak	3B149,2B1	R	29	149	529	78	155	39	2	19	89	74	54	8	.293	.381	.482
Roy McMillan	SS151	R	26	151	448	50	122	25	5	1	55	66	44	5	.272	.371	.357
Frank Robinson	OF136,1B24	R	21	150	611	97	197	29	5	29	75	44	92	10	.322	.376	.529
Wally Post	OF124	R	27	134	467	68	114	26	2	20	74	33	84	2	.244	.291	.437
Gus Bell	OF121	L	28	121	510	65	149	20	3	13	61	30	54	0	.292	.332	.420
Smoky Burgess	C45	L	30	90	205	29	58	14	1	14	39	24	16	0	.283	.353	.566
Bob Thurman	OF44	L	40	74	190	38	47	4	2	16	40	15	33	0	.247	.306	.542
Ted Kluszewski	1B23	L	32	69	127	12	34	7	0	6	21	5	5	0	.268	.301	.465
Jerry Lynch	OF24,C2	L	26	67	124	11	32	4	1	4	13	6	18	0	.258	.290	.403
Joe Taylor	OF27	R	31	33	107	14	28	7	0	4	9	6	24	0	.262	.301	.439
Alex Grammas	SS42,2B20,3B9	R	31	73	99	14	30	4	0	0	8	10	6	1	.303	.364	.343
Pete Whisenant	OF43	R	27	67	90	18	19	3	2	5	11	5	24	0	.211	.250	.456
Art Schult†	OF5	R	29	21	34	4	9	2	0	0	4	0	2	0	.265	.286	.324
Dutch Dotterer	C4	R	25	4	12	0	1	0	0	0	2	1	2	0	.083	.154	.083
Bobby Henrich	SS7,OF6,3B2*	R	18	29	10	8	2	0	0	0	1	1	4	0	.200	.250	.200
Curt Flood	3B2,2B1	R	19	3	3	2	1	0	0	1	1	0	0	0	.333	.333	1.333
Bobby Durnbaugh	SS2	R	24	2	1	0	0	0	0	0	0	0	0	0	.000	.000	.000
Don Pavletich		R	18	1	1	0	0	0	0	0	0	0	0	0	.000	.000	.000
Rocky Bridges†	2B2,3B1,SS1	R	29	5	1	1	0	0	0	0	0	1	1	0	.000	.500	.000

B. Henrich, 1 G at 2B

Birdie Tebbetts

Pitcher	T	Age	G	GS	CG	ShO	IP	H	HR	BB	SO	W-L	Sv	ERA
Brooks Lawrence	R	32	49	32	12	1	250.1	234	26	76	121	16-13	4	3.52
Hal Jeffcoat	R	32	37	31	10	1	207.0	236	29	46	63	12-13	0	4.52
Joe Nuxhall	L	28	39	28	6	2	174.1	192	24	53	99	10-10	1	4.75
Bud Podbielan	R	33	5	3	1	0	16.0	18	4	4	13	0-1	0	6.19
Jay Hook	R	20	3	2	0	0	10.0	6	0	8	6	0-1	0	4.50
Charlie Rabe	L	25	2	1	0	0	8.1	5	2	0	6	0-1	0	2.16
Hersh Freeman	R	28	52	0	0	0	83.2	90	14	14	36	7-2	8	4.52
Tom Acker	R	27	49	6	1	0	108.2	122	16	41	67	10-5	4	4.97
Johnny Klippstein	R	29	46	18	3	1	146.0	146	17	68	99	8-11	3	5.05
Don Gross	L	26	43	16	5	0	148.1	152	21	33	73	7-9	1	4.31
Raul Sanchez	R	26	38	0	0	0	62.1	61	7	25	37	3-2	5	4.76
Art Fowler	R	34	33	7	1	0	87.2	111	11	24	45	3-0	0	6.47
Warren Hacker†	R	32	15	6	0	0	43.1	50	5	13	18	3-2	0	5.19
Vincente Amor	R	24	9	4	1	0	27.1	39	2	10	9	1-2	0	5.93
Bill Kennedy	L	36	8	0	0	0	12.2	16	1	5	8	0-2	3	6.39
Claude Osteen	L	17	3	0	0	0	4.0	4	0	3	3	0-0	0	2.25
Dave Skaugstad	L	17	2	0	0	0	5.2	4	0	6	4	0-0	0	1.59

1957 Philadelphia Phillies 5th NL 77-77 .500 18.0 GB

Player	Gm by Position	B	Age	G	AB	R	H	2B	3B	HR	RBI	BB	SO	SB	Avg	OBP	Slg
Stan Lopata	C108	R	31	116	388	50	92	18	2	18	67	56	81	2	.237	.331	.433
Ed Bouchee	1B154	L	24	154	574	78	168	35	8	17	76	84	91	1	.293	.394	.470
Granny Hamner	2B125,SS5,P1	R	30	133	502	59	114	19	5	10	62	34	42	3	.227	.274	.345
Puddin' Head Jones	3B126	R	31	133	440	58	96	19	2	9	47	61	41	1	.218	.310	.332
Chico Fernandez	SS149	R	25	149	500	42	131	14	4	5	51	31	64	18	.262	.302	.336
Richie Ashburn	OF156	L	30	156	626	93	186	26	8	0	33	94	44	13	.297	.390	.364
Rip Repulski	OF130	R	29	134	516	65	134	23	4	20	68	19	74	7	.260	.290	.436
Harry Anderson	OF109	L	25	118	400	53	107	15	4	17	61	36	61	2	.268	.333	.453
Bob Bowman	OF81	R	26	99	237	31	63	8	2	6	23	27	50	0	.266	.352	.392
Ted Kazanski	3B36,2B22,SS3	R	23	62	185	15	49	7	1	3	11	17	20	1	.265	.327	.362
Joe Lonnett	C65	R	30	67	160	12	27	5	0	5	15	22	39	0	.169	.272	.294
Solly Hemus	2B24	L	34	70	108	8	20	6	1	0	5	20	8	1	.185	.323	.259
Chuck Harmon†	OF25,3B5,1B2	R	33	57	86	14	22	2	1	0	5	1	4	7	.256	.264	.302
Roy Smalley	SS20	R	31	28	31	5	5	0	1	1	1	1	9	0	.161	.212	.323
Marv Blaylock	1B12,OF1	L	27	37	26	5	4	0	0	2	4	3	8	0	.154	.313	.385
Ron Northey†		L	37	33	26	1	7	0	0	1	5	6	6	0	.269	.406	.385
Andy Seminick	C8	R	36	8	11	0	1	0	0	0	0	1	3	0	.091	.167	.091
Don Landrum	OF2	L	21	2	7	1	1	1	0	0	0	2	1	0	.143	.333	.286
John Kennedy	3B2	R	30	5	2	1	0	0	0	0	0	0	1	0	.000	.000	.000
Glen Gorbous		L	26	3	2	1	1	1	0	0	1	1	0	0	.500	.667	1.000
Frankie Baumholtz		L	38	2	2	0	0	0	0	0	0	0	0	0	.000	.000	.000
Bobby Morgan†	2B1	R	31	2	0	0	0	0	0	0	0	0	0	0	—	—	—

Mayo Smith

Pitcher	T	Age	G	GS	CG	ShO	IP	H	HR	BB	SO	W-L	Sv	ERA
Jack Sanford	R	28	33	33	15	3	236.2	194	22	94	188	19-8	0	3.08
Robin Roberts	R	30	39	32	14	2	249.2	246	40	43	128	10-22	2	4.07
Curt Simmons	L	28	32	29	9	2	212.0	214	11	50	92	12-11	0	3.44
Harvey Haddix	L	31	27	25	8	1	170.2	176	18	39	136	10-13	0	4.06
Don Cardwell	R	21	30	19	5	1	128.1	122	17	42	92	4-8	1	4.91
Warren Hacker†	R	32	20	10	1	0	74.0	72	10	18	33	4-4	0	4.50
Turk Farrell	R	23	52	0	0	0	83.1	74	2	36	54	10-2	10	2.38
Jim Hearn	R	36	36	4	1	0	74.0	79	6	18	46	5-1	3	3.65
Seth Morehead	L	22	34	1	1	0	58.2	57	1	20	36	1-1	1	3.68
Bob Miller	R	31	32	1	0	0	60.0	61	4	17	12	2-5	6	2.70
Jack Meyer	R	25	19	2	0	0	37.2	44	7	28	34	0-2	0	5.73
Tom Qualters	R	22	6	0	0	0	7.1	12	0	4	6	0-0	0	7.36
Saul Rogovin	R	33	4	0	0	0	8.0	11	1	3	0	0-0	0	9.00
Granny Hamner	R	30	1	0	0	0	1.0	1	0	0	1	0-0	0	0.00

1957 New York Giants 6th NL 69-85 .448 26.0 GB — Bill Rigney

Player	Gm by Position	B	Age	G	AB	R	H	2B	3B	HR	RBI	BB	SO	SB	Avg	OBP	Slg
Valmy Thomas	C88	R	28	88	241	30	60	10	3	6	31	16	29	0	.249	.296	.390
Whitey Lockman	1B102,OF27	L	30	133	456	51	113	9	4	7	30	39	19	5	.248	.308	.331
Danny O'Connell†	2B68,3B30	R	30	95	364	57	97	18	3	7	28	33	30	8	.266	.330	.390
Ray Jablonski	3B70,1B6,OF1	R	30	107	305	37	88	15	1	9	57	31	47	0	.289	.346	.433
Daryl Spencer	SS110,2B36,3B6	R	27	148	534	65	133	31	2	11	50	50	50	3	.249	.313	.376
Willie Mays	OF150	R	26	152	585	112	195	26	20	35	97	76	62	38	.333	.407	.626
Don Mueller	OF115	L	30	135	450	45	116	7	1	6	37	13	16	2	.258	.280	.318
Hank Sauer	OF98	R	40	127	378	46	98	14	1	26	76	49	59	1	.259	.343	.508
Red Schoendienst†	2B57	S	34	57	254	35	78	8	4	9	33	10	8	2	.307	.337	.476
Ozzie Virgil	3B62,OF24,SS1	R	24	96	226	26	53	0	2	4	24	14	27	2	.235	.278	.305
Gail Harris	1B61	L	25	90	225	28	54	7	3	9	31	16	28	1	.240	.305	.418
Bobby Thomson†	OF71,3B1	R	33	81	215	24	52	7	4	8	38	19	39	1	.242	.302	.423
Dusty Rhodes	OF44	L	30	92	190	20	39	5	1	4	19	18	34	0	.205	.276	.305
Ray Katt	C68	R	30	72	165	11	38	3	1	2	17	15	35	1	.230	.294	.297
Eddie Bressoud	SS33,3B12	R	25	49	127	11	34	2	2	5	10	4	19	0	.268	.299	.433
Wes Westrum	C63	R	34	63	91	4	15	1	0	1	2	10	24	0	.165	.255	.209
Ruben Gomez	P38,OF1	R	29	54	87	6	16	2	0	1	2	6	16	0	.184	.237	.241
Andre Rodgers	SS20,3B8	R	22	32	86	8	21	2	1	3	9	9	21	0	.244	.320	.395
Foster Castleman	3B7,2B1,SS1	R	26	18	37	7	6	2	0	1	1	2	8	0	.162	.205	.297
Bill Taylor†		L	27	11	9	0	0	0	0	0	0	1	2	0	.000	.100	.000
Bobby Hofman		R	31	2	2	0	0	0	0	0	0	0	1	0	.000	.000	.000

Pitcher	T	Age	G	GS	CG	ShO	IP	H	HR	BB	SO	W-L	Sv	ERA
Ruben Gomez	R	29	38	36	16	1	238.1	233	28	71	92	15-13	0	3.78
Johnny Antonelli	L	27	40	30	8	3	212.1	228	19	67	114	12-18	0	3.77
Curt Barclay	R	25	37	28	5	2	183.0	196	21	48	67	9-9	0	3.44
Ray Crone†	R	25	25	17	2	0	120.2	131	11	40	56	4-8	1	4.33
Pete Burnside	L	26	10	9	1	1	30.2	47	5	13	18	1-4	0	8.80
Al Worthington	R	28	55	12	1	1	157.2	140	19	56	90	8-11	4	4.22
Marv Grissom	R	39	55	0	0	0	82.2	74	6	23	51	4-4	14	2.61
Stu Miller	R	29	38	13	0	0	124.0	110	15	45	60	7-9	1	3.63
Mike McCormick	L	18	24	5	1	0	74.2	79	7	32	50	3-1	0	4.10
Ray Monzant	R	24	24	2	0	0	49.2	55	6	16	37	3-2	0	3.99
Jim Constable	L	24	16	0	0	0	28.1	27	2	7	13	1-1	0	2.86
Steve Ridzik	R	28	15	0	0	0	26.2	19	3	19	13	0-2	0	4.73
Joe Margoneri	L	27	13	2	1	0	34.1	44	1	21	18	1-1	0	5.24
Gordon Jones	R	27	10	0	0	0	11.2	16	1	3	5	0-1	0	6.17
Jim Davis†	L	32	10	0	0	0	11.0	13	2	5	6	1-0	0	6.55
Max Surkont	R	35	5	0	0	0	6.1	9	2	2	8	0-1	0	9.95
Windy McCall	L	31	5	0	0	0	3.0	8	1	2	2	0-0	0	15.00
Sandy Consuegra†	R	36	4	0	0	0	3.2	7	1	1	1	0-0	0	2.45

1957 Chicago Cubs 7th NL 62-92 .403 33.0 GB — Bob Scheffing

Player	Gm by Position	B	Age	G	AB	R	H	2B	3B	HR	RBI	BB	SO	SB	Avg	OBP	Slg
Cal Neeman	C118	R	28	122	415	37	107	17	1	10	39	22	87	0	.258	.298	.376
Dale Long†	1B104	L	31	123	397	55	121	19	0	21	62	52	63	1	.305	.383	.511
Bobby Morgan†	2B116,3B12	R	31	125	425	43	88	20	2	5	27	52	87	5	.207	.294	.299
Ernie Banks	SS100,3B58	R	26	156	594	113	169	34	6	43	102	70	85	8	.285	.360	.579
Jack Littrell	SS47,2B6,3B5	R	28	61	153	8	29	4	2	1	13	9	43	0	.190	.233	.261
Walt Moryn	OF147	L	31	149	568	76	164	33	0	19	88	50	90	0	.289	.348	.447
Lee Walls†	OF94,3B1	R	24	117	366	42	88	10	5	6	33	27	67	5	.240	.292	.344
Chuck Tanner†	OF82	L	27	95	318	42	91	16	2	7	42	23	20	0	.286	.336	.415
Bob Speake	OF60,1B39	L	26	129	418	65	97	14	5	16	50	38	68	5	.232	.299	.404
Jim Bolger	OF63,3B3	R	25	112	273	28	75	4	1	5	29	10	36	0	.275	.303	.352
Bobby Adams	3B47,2B1	R	35	60	187	21	47	10	2	1	10	17	28	0	.251	.320	.342
Jerry Kindall	2B28,3B19,SS9	R	22	72	181	18	29	3	0	6	12	8	48	1	.160	.196	.276
Bob Will	OF30	L	25	70	112	13	25	3	0	1	10	5	21	1	.223	.254	.277
Casey Wise	2B31,SS5	S	24	43	106	12	19	3	1	0	7	11	14	0	.179	.256	.226
Jim Fanning	C35	R	29	47	89	3	16	2	0	0	4	4	17	0	.180	.223	.202
Charlie Silvera	C26	R	32	26	53	1	11	3	0	0	2	4	5	0	.208	.263	.264
Dee Fondy†	1B11	L	32	11	51	3	16	3	0	1	2	0	9	1	.314	.314	.412
Ed Winceniak	SS5,3B4,2B3	R	28	17	50	5	12	3	0	1	8	2	9	0	.240	.269	.360
Gene Baker†	3B12	R	32	12	44	4	11	3	1	1	10	6	3	0	.250	.353	.432
Bobby Del Greco†	OF16	R	24	20	40	2	8	2	0	0	3	10	17	1	.200	.360	.250
Johnny Goryl	3B9	R	23	9	38	7	8	2	0	0	1	5	9	0	.211	.318	.263
Frank Ernaga	OF10	R	26	20	35	9	11	3	2	2	7	9	14	0	.314	.455	.686
Eddie Haas	OF4	L	22	14	24	1	5	1	0	0	4	1	5	0	.208	.231	.250
Bob Lennon	OF4	L	28	9	21	2	3	1	0	1	3	1	9	0	.143	.182	.333
Gordon Massa	C6	L	21	6	15	2	7	1	0	0	3	4	3	0	.467	.579	.533
Ed Mickelson	1B2	R	30	6	12	0	0	0	0	0	0	0	4	0	.000	.000	.000
Jim Woods		R	17	2	0	1	0	0	0	0	0	0	0	0	—	—	—

Pitcher	T	Age	G	GS	CG	ShO	IP	H	HR	BB	SO	W-L	Sv	ERA
Moe Drabowsky	R	21	36	33	12	2	239.2	214	22	94	170	13-15	0	3.53
Dick Drott	R	20	38	32	7	3	229.0	200	22	129	170	15-11	0	3.58
Bob Rush	R	31	31	29	5	0	205.1	211	16	66	103	6-16	0	4.38
Don Kaiser	R	22	20	13	1	0	72.0	91	4	28	23	2-6	0	5.00
Turk Lown	R	33	67	0	0	0	93.0	74	10	51	51	5-7	12	3.77
Dick Littlefield	L	31	48	2	0	0	65.2	76	12	37	51	2-3	4	5.35
Jim Brosnan	R	27	41	5	1	0	98.2	79	11	46	73	5-5	0	3.38
Don Elston†	R	28	39	14	2	0	144.0	139	15	55	102	6-7	8	3.56
Dave Hillman	R	29	32	14	1	0	103.1	115	13	37	53	6-11	1	4.35
Tom Poholsky	R	27	28	11	1	0	84.0	117	9	22	28	1-7	0	4.93
Vito Valentinetti†	R	28	9	0	0	0	12.0	12	1	7	8	0-0	0	2.25
Jackie Collum†	L	30	9	0	0	0	10.2	8	0	9	7	1-1	1	6.75
Bob Anderson	R	21	8	0	0	0	16.1	20	2	8	7	0-1	0	7.71
Elmer Singleton	R	39	5	2	0	0	13.1	20	3	2	6	0-1	0	6.75
Ed Mayer	L	25	3	1	0	0	7.2	8	2	2	3	0-0	0	5.87
John Briggs	R	23	3	0	0	0	4.1	7	2	3	1	0-1	0	12.46
Glen Hobbie	R	21	2	0	0	0	4.1	6	0	5	3	0-0	0	10.38

1957 Pittsburgh Pirates 7th NL 62-92 .403 33.0 GB — Bobby Bragan (36-67)/Danny Murtaugh (26-25)

Player	Gm by Position	B	Age	G	AB	R	H	2B	3B	HR	RBI	BB	SO	SB	Avg	OBP	Slg
Hank Foiles	C109	R	28	109	281	32	76	10	4	9	36	37	53	1	.270	.352	.431
Dee Fondy†	1B73	L	32	95	323	42	101	13	2	2	35	25	59	11	.313	.360	.384
Bill Mazeroski	2B144	R	20	148	526	59	149	27	7	8	54	27	49	3	.283	.318	.407
Gene Freese	3B74,2B10,OF10	R	23	114	346	44	98	18	2	6	31	17	42	9	.283	.319	.399
Dick Groat	SS123,3B2	R	26	125	501	58	158	30	5	7	54	27	28	0	.315	.350	.437
Bill Virdon	OF141	L	26	144	561	59	141	28	11	8	50	33	69	3	.251	.291	.383
Roberto Clemente	OF109	R	22	111	451	42	114	17	7	4	30	23	45	0	.253	.288	.348
Bob Skinner	OF93,1B9,3B1	L	25	126	387	58	118	12	6	13	45	38	50	10	.305	.370	.468
Frank Thomas	1B71,OF59,3B31	R	28	151	594	72	172	30	1	23	89	44	66	3	.290	.335	.460
Gene Baker†	3B60,SS28,2B13	R	32	111	365	36	97	19	4	2	36	29	29	3	.266	.318	.356
Paul Smith	OF33,1B1	L	26	81	150	12	38	4	0	3	11	12	17	0	.253	.313	.340
Roman Mejias	OF42	R	26	58	142	12	39	7	4	2	15	6	13	2	.275	.309	.423
Dick Rand	C57	R	26	60	105	7	23	2	1	1	9	11	24	0	.219	.288	.286
Hardy Peterson	C30	R	27	30	73	10	22	2	1	2	11	9	10	0	.301	.378	.438
Jim Pendleton	OF9,3B2,SS1	R	33	46	59	9	18	1	1	0	9	9	14	0	.305	.394	.356
Danny Kravitz	C15	L	26	19	41	2	6	1	0	0	4	2	10	0	.146	.186	.171
John Powers	OF9	L	27	20	35	7	10	3	0	2	8	5	9	0	.286	.409	.543
Johnny O'Brien	P16,SS8,2B2	R	26	34	35	7	11	2	1	0	1	1	4	0	.314	.368	.429
Lee Walls†	OF7	R	24	8	22	3	4	1	0	0	0	2	5	1	.182	.250	.227
Dale Long†	1B7	L	31	7	22	0	4	1	0	0	5	4	10	0	.182	.296	.227
Buddy Pritchard	SS10,OF3	R	21	23	11	1	1	0	0	0	0	0	4	0	.091	.091	.091
Ken Hamlin	SS1	R	22	2	1	0	0	0	0	0	0	0	0	0	.000	.000	.000

Pitcher	T	Age	G	GS	CG	ShO	IP	H	HR	BB	SO	W-L	Sv	ERA
Bob Friend	R	26	40	38	17	3	277.0	273	28	68	143	14-18	0	3.38
Ron Kline	R	25	40	31	11	2	205.0	214	28	61	88	9-16	0	4.04
Vern Law	R	27	31	25	9	3	172.2	172	18	32	55	10-8	1	2.87
Whammy Douglas	R	22	11	8	0	0	47.0	48	5	30	28	3-3	0	3.26
Joe Trimble	R	26	5	4	0	0	19.2	23	7	13	9	0-2	0	8.24
Bennie Daniels	R	25	1	1	0	0	7.0	5	0	3	2	0-1	0	1.29
George Witt	R	23	1	1	0	0	1.1	4	1	5	0	0-1	0	40.50
Roy Face	R	29	59	1	0	0	93.2	97	9	24	53	4-6	10	3.07
Luis Arroyo	L	30	54	10	0	0	130.2	151	19	31	101	3-11	1	4.68
Bob Purkey	R	27	48	21	6	1	179.2	194	10	38	51	11-14	2	3.86
Nellie King	R	29	36	0	0	0	52.0	69	7	16	23	2-1	1	4.50
Red Swanson	R	20	32	8	1	0	72.2	68	9	31	29	3-3	0	3.72
Bob Smith†	L	26	20	4	2	0	55.0	48	2	25	35	2-4	0	3.11
Johnny O'Brien	R	26	16	1	0	0	40.0	46	7	24	19	0-3	0	6.08
Dick Hall	R	26	8	0	0	0	10.0	17	4	5	7	0-0	0	10.80
Laurin Pepper	R	26	5	1	0	0	9.0	11	1	5	4	0-1	0	8.00
Chuck Churn	R	27	5	0	0	0	8.1	9	1	4	4	0-0	0	4.32
Bob Kuzava†	L	34	4	0	0	0	2.0	3	0	3	1	0-0	0	9.00
Eddie O'Brien	R	26	3	1	1	0	12.1	11	2	3	10	1-0	0	2.19

»1958 New York Yankees 1st AL 92-62 .597 — — Casey Stengel

Player	Gm by Position	B	Age	G	AB	R	H	2B	3B	HR	RBI	BB	SO	SB	Avg	OBP	Slg
Yogi Berra	C88,OF21,1B2	L	33	122	433	60	115	17	3	22	90	35	35	3	.266	.319	.471
Bill Skowron	1B118,3B2	R	27	126	465	61	127	22	3	14	73	28	69	1	.273	.317	.424
Gil McDougald	2B115,SS19	R	30	138	503	69	126	19	1	14	65	59	75	6	.250	.329	.376
Andy Carey	3B99	R	26	102	315	39	90	19	4	12	45	34	43	1	.286	.363	.486
Tony Kubek	SS134,OF3,1B1*	L	21	138	559	66	148	21	1	2	48	25	57	5	.265	.295	.317
Mickey Mantle	OF150	S	26	150	519	127	158	21	1	42	97	129	120	18	.304	.443	.592
Norm Siebern	OF133	L	24	134	460	79	138	19	5	14	55	66	87	5	.300	.388	.454
Hank Bauer	OF123	R	35	128	452	62	121	22	6	12	50	32	56	3	.268	.316	.423
Elston Howard	C67,OF24,1B5	R	29	103	376	45	118	19	5	11	66	22	60	1	.314	.348	.479
Jerry Lumpe	3B65,SS5	L	25	81	232	34	59	8	4	3	32	23	21	1	.254	.319	.362
Bobby Richardson	2B51,3B13,SS2	R	22	73	182	18	45	6	2	0	14	8	5	1	.247	.276	.302
Marv Throneberry	1B40,OF5	L	24	60	150	30	34	5	2	7	19	19	40	1	.227	.316	.427
Enos Slaughter	OF35	L	42	77	138	21	42	4	1	4	19	21	16	2	.304	.396	.435
Harry Simpson†	OF15	L	32	24	51	1	11	2	1	0	6	6	12	0	.216	.310	.294
Bobby Shantz	P33,OF1	R	32	33	35	1	8	3	0	0	1	2	12	0	.229	.289	.314
Darrell Johnson	C4	R	29	5	16	1	4	0	0	0	0	0	2	0	.250	.250	.250
Bobby Del Greco	OF12	R	25	12	5	1	1	0	0	0	0	1	1	0	.200	.333	.200
Fritz Brickell	2B2	R	23	2	0	0	0	0	0	0	0	0	0	0	—	—	—

T. Kubek, 1 G at 2B

Pitcher	T	Age	G	GS	CG	ShO	IP	H	HR	BB	SO	W-L	Sv	ERA
Bob Turley	R	27	33	31	19	6	245.1	178	24	128	168	21-7	1	2.97
Whitey Ford	L	29	30	29	15	7	219.1	174	14	62	145	14-7	1	2.01
Don Larsen	R	28	19	19	5	3	114.1	100	4	52	55	9-6	0	3.07
Duke Maas†	R	29	22	13	2	1	101.1	93	9	36	50	7-3	0	3.82
Tom Sturdivant	R	28	15	10	0	0	70.2	77	6	38	41	3-6	0	4.20
Ryne Duren	R	29	44	1	0	0	75.2	40	4	43	87	6-4	20	2.02
Art Ditmar	R	29	38	13	4	0	139.2	124	14	38	52	9-8	4	3.42
Johnny Kucks	R	24	34	15	4	1	126.0	132	14	39	46	8-8	4	3.93
Bobby Shantz	L	32	33	13	3	0	126.0	127	8	35	80	7-6	0	3.36
Virgil Trucks†	R	41	25	0	0	0	39.2	40	1	24	26	2-1	1	4.54
Zack Monroe	R	26	21	6	1	0	58.0	57	8	27	18	4-2	1	3.26
Bob Grim†	R	28	11	0	0	0	16.1	12	3	10	11	0-1	0	5.51
Sal Maglie†	R	41	7	3	0	0	23.1	27	3	9	7	1-1	0	4.63
Murry Dickson†	R	41	6	2	0	0	20.1	18	4	12	9	1-2	1	5.75
Johnny James	R	24	1	0	0	0	3.0	2	0	4	1	0-0	0	0.00

1958 Chicago White Sox 2nd AL 82-72 .532 10.0 GB

Al Lopez

Player	Gm by Position	B	Age	G	AB	R	H	2B	3B	HR	RBI	BB	SO	SB	Avg	OBP	Slg
Sherm Lollar	C116	R	33	127	421	53	115	16	0	20	84	57	37	2	.273	.367	.454
Earl Torgeson	1B73	L	34	96	188	37	50	8	0	10	30	48	29	7	.266	.415	.468
Nellie Fox	2B155	L	30	155	623	82	187	21	6	0	49	47	11	5	.300	.357	.353
Billy Goodman	3B111,1B3,2B1*	L	32	116	425	41	127	15	5	0	40	37	21	1	.299	.355	.358
Luis Aparicio	SS145	R	24	145	557	76	148	20	9	2	40	35	38	29	.266	.309	.345
Jim Landis	OF142	R	24	142	523	72	145	23	7	15	64	52	80	19	.277	.351	.434
Al Smith	OF138,3B1	R	30	139	480	61	121	23	5	12	58	48	77	3	.252	.323	.396
Jim Rivera	OF99	L	35	116	276	37	62	8	4	9	35	24	49	21	.225	.282	.380
Bubba Phillips	3B47,OF37	R	30	84	260	26	71	10	0	5	30	15	14	3	.273	.310	.369
Ray Boone†	1B63	R	34	77	246	25	60	12	1	7	41	18	33	1	.244	.295	.386
Earl Battey	C49	R	23	68	168	24	38	8	0	8	26	24	34	1	.226	.325	.417
Don Mueller	OF43	L	31	70	166	7	42	5	0	0	16	11	9	0	.253	.298	.283
Ron Jackson	1B38	R	24	61	146	19	34	4	0	7	21	18	46	2	.233	.323	.404
Tito Francona†	OF35	L	24	41	128	10	33	3	2	1	10	14	24	2	.258	.331	.336
Sammy Esposito	3B63,SS22,2B2*	R	26	98	81	16	20	3	0	0	3	12	6	1	.247	.358	.284
Johnny Callison	OF18	L	19	18	64	10	19	4	2	1	12	6	14	1	.297	.352	.469
Walt Dropo†	1B16	R	35	28	52	3	10	1	0	2	8	5	11	0	.192	.271	.327
Ted Beard	OF15	L	37	19	22	5	2	0	0	1	2	6	5	3	.091	.286	.227
Jim McAnany	OF3	R	21	5	13	0	0	0	0	0	0	0	5	0	.000	.000	.000
Norm Cash	OF4	L	23	13	8	2	2	0	0	0	0	0	1	0	.250	.250	.250
John Romano	C2	R	23	4	7	1	2	0	0	0	1	1	0	0	.286	.375	.286
Chuck Lindstrom	C1	R	21	1	1	1	1	0	1	0	1	1	0	0	1.000	1.000	3.000
Les Moss		R	33	2	1	0	0	0	0	0	0	1	0	0	.000	.500	.000

B. Goodman, 1 G at SS; S. Esposito, 1 G at OF

Pitcher	T	Age	G	GS	CG	ShO	IP	H	HR	BB	SO	W-L	Sv	ERA
Dick Donovan	R	30	34	34	16	4	248.0	240	23	53	127	15-14	0	3.01
Early Wynn	R	38	40	34	11	4	239.2	214	27	104	179	14-16	2	4.13
Billy Pierce	L	31	35	32	19	3	245.0	204	33	66	144	17-11	2	2.68
Jim Wilson	R	36	28	23	4	1	155.2	156	21	63	70	9-9	1	4.10
Ray Moore	R	32	32	20	4	2	136.2	107	10	70	73	9-7	2	3.82
Stover McIlwain	R	18	1	1	0	0	4.0	4	1	0	4	0-0	0	2.25
Gerry Staley	R	37	50	0	0	0	85.1	81	10	24	27	4-5	8	3.16
Bob Shaw†	R	25	29	3	0	0	64.0	67	8	28	18	4-2	1	4.64
Turk Lown†	R	34	27	0	0	0	40.2	49	1	28	40	3-3	8	3.98
Tom Qualters†	R	23	26	0	0	0	43.0	45	1	20	14	0-0	0	4.19
Bill Fischer†	R	27	17	3	0	0	36.1	43	6	13	16	2-3	0	6.69
Bob Keegan	R	37	14	2	0	0	29.2	44	9	18	8	0-2	0	6.07
Barry Latman	R	22	13	3	1	1	47.2	27	1	17	28	3-0	0	0.76
Don Rudolph	L	26	7	0	0	0	7.0	4	0	5	2	1-0	1	2.57
Jim McDonald	R	31	3	0	0	0	2.1	6	1	4	0	0-0	0	19.29
Hal Trosky	R	21	2	0	0	0	3.0	5	0	2	1	1-0	0	6.00
Dixie Howell	R	38	1	0	0	0	1.2	0	0	0	0	0-0	0	0.00

1958 Boston Red Sox 3rd AL 79-75 .513 13.0 GB

Pinky Higgins

Player	Gm by Position	B	Age	G	AB	R	H	2B	3B	HR	RBI	BB	SO	SB	Avg	OBP	Slg
Sammy White	C102	R	29	102	328	25	85	15	3	6	35	21	37	1	.259	.305	.378
Dick Gernert	1B114	R	29	122	431	59	102	19	1	20	69	59	78	2	.237	.330	.425
Pete Runnels	2B106,1B42	L	30	147	568	103	183	32	5	8	59	87	49	1	.322	.416	.438
Frank Malzone	3B155	R	28	155	627	76	185	30	2	15	87	33	53	1	.295	.333	.421
Don Buddin	SS136	R	24	136	497	74	118	25	2	12	43	82	106	0	.237	.349	.368
Jackie Jensen	OF153	R	31	154	548	83	157	31	0	35	122	99	65	9	.286	.396	.535
Jimmy Piersall	OF125	R	28	130	417	55	99	13	5	8	48	42	43	12	.237	.303	.350
Ted Williams	OF114	L	39	129	411	81	135	23	2	26	85	98	49	1	.328	.458	.584
Gene Stephens	OF110	L	25	134	270	38	59	10	1	9	25	22	46	1	.219	.279	.363
Lou Berberet†	C49	L	28	57	167	11	35	5	3	2	18	31	32	0	.210	.337	.311
Ted Lepcio	2B40	R	27	50	136	10	27	3	0	6	14	12	47	0	.199	.268	.353
Marty Keough	OF25,1B2	L	23	68	118	21	26	3	3	1	9	7	29	1	.220	.262	.322
Billy Klaus	SS27	L	29	61	88	5	14	4	0	1	7	5	16	0	.159	.204	.239
Billy Consolo	2B13,SS11,3B1	R	23	46	72	13	9	2	1	0	5	6	14	0	.125	.192	.181
Pete Daley	C27	R	28	27	56	10	18	2	1	2	8	7	11	0	.321	.397	.500
Bill Renna	OF11	R	33	39	56	5	15	5	0	4	18	6	14	0	.268	.339	.571
Ken Aspromonte†	2B6	R	26	6	16	0	2	0	0	0	0	3	1	0	.125	.263	.125

Pitcher	T	Age	G	GS	CG	ShO	IP	H	HR	BB	SO	W-L	Sv	ERA
Tom Brewer	R	26	33	32	10	1	227.1	227	21	93	124	12-12	0	3.72
Frank Sullivan	R	28	32	29	10	2	199.1	216	12	49	103	13-9	3	3.57
Dave Sisler	R	26	30	25	4	1	149.1	157	22	79	71	8-9	0	4.94
Ike Delock	R	28	31	19	9	1	160.0	155	13	56	82	14-8	2	3.38
Ted Bowsfield	L	23	16	10	2	0	65.2	58	3	36	38	4-2	0	3.84
Bill Monbouquette	R	21	10	8	3	0	54.1	52	4	20	30	3-4	0	3.31
Willard Nixon	R	30	10	8	2	0	43.1	48	7	11	15	1-7	0	6.02
Frank Baumann	L	24	10	7	2	0	52.1	56	4	27	31	2-2	0	4.47
Duane Wilson	L	24	2	2	0	0	6.1	10	0	7	3	0-0	0	5.68
Murray Wall	R	31	52	1	0	0	114.1	109	14	33	53	8-9	10	3.62
Leo Kiely	L	28	47	0	0	0	81.0	77	3	18	26	5-2	12	3.00
Mike Fornieles	R	26	37	7	1	0	110.2	123	10	33	49	4-6	1	4.96
Bud Byerly†	R	37	18	0	0	0	30.1	31	1	7	16	1-2	0	1.78
Riverboat Smith	L	30	17	7	1	0	66.2	61	4	45	43	4-3	0	3.78
Al Schroll	R	26	5	0	0	0	10.0	6	1	4	7	0-0	0	4.50
Bob Porterfield†	R	34	2	0	0	0	4.0	3	1	0	1	0-0	0	4.50
Jerry Casale	R	24	2	0	0	0	3.0	1	0	2	3	0-0	0	0.00
George Susce†	R	26	2	0	0	0	2.0	6	1	1	0	0-0	0	18.00

1958 Cleveland Indians 4th AL 77-76 .503 14.5 GB

Bobby Bragan (31-36)/Joe Gordon (46-40)

Player	Gm by Position	B	Age	G	AB	R	H	2B	3B	HR	RBI	BB	SO	SB	Avg	OBP	Slg
Russ Nixon	C101	L	23	113	376	42	113	17	4	9	46	13	38	0	.301	.322	.439
Mickey Vernon	1B96	L	40	119	355	49	104	22	3	8	55	44	56	0	.293	.372	.439
Bobby Avila	2B82,3B33	R	34	113	375	54	95	21	3	5	30	55	45	5	.253	.349	.365
Billy Harrell	3B46,SS45,2B7*	R	29	101	229	36	50	4	0	7	19	15	36	12	.218	.271	.328
Billy Hunter†	SS75,3B2	R	30	76	190	21	37	10	2	0	9	17	37	4	.195	.263	.268
Minnie Minoso	OF147,3B1	R	35	149	556	94	168	25	2	24	80	59	53	14	.302	.383	.484
Rocky Colavito	OF129,1B11,P1	R	24	143	489	80	148	26	3	41	113	84	89	0	.303	.405	.620
Larry Doby	OF68	L	34	89	247	41	70	10	1	13	45	26	49	0	.283	.348	.490
Vic Power†	3B42,1B41,2B27*	R	30	93	385	63	122	24	6	12	53	13	11	2	.317	.336	.504
Billy Moran	2B74,SS38	R	24	115	257	26	58	11	0	1	18	13	23	3	.226	.262	.280
Gary Geiger	OF53,3B2,P1	L	21	91	195	28	45	3	1	1	6	27	43	2	.231	.330	.272
Roger Maris†	OF47	L	23	51	182	26	41	5	1	9	27	17	33	4	.225	.287	.412
Dick Brown	C62	R	23	68	173	20	41	5	0	7	20	12	27	1	.237	.296	.387
Chico Carrasquel†	SS32,3B14	R	32	49	156	14	40	6	0	2	21	14	12	0	.256	.318	.333
Preston Ward†	3B24,1B21	L	30	48	148	22	50	3	1	4	21	10	27	0	.338	.379	.453
Woodie Held†	OF43,SS14,3B4	R	26	67	144	12	28	4	1	3	17	15	36	1	.194	.285	.299
Randy Jackson†	3B24	R	32	29	91	7	22	3	1	4	13	3	18	0	.242	.266	.429
J.W. Porter	C20,1B4,3B1	R	25	40	85	13	17	1	0	4	19	9	23	0	.200	.284	.353
Earl Averill	3B17	R	26	17	55	2	10	1	0	2	7	4	7	1	.182	.250	.309
Carroll Hardy	OF17	R	25	27	49	10	10	3	0	1	6	6	14	1	.204	.298	.327
Vic Wertz	1B8	L	33	25	43	5	12	1	0	3	12	5	7	0	.279	.354	.512
Larry Raines	2B2	R	28	7	9	1	0	0	0	0	0	0	5	0	.000	.000	.000
Hal Naragon		L	29	9	9	2	3	0	1	0	0	0	0	0	.333	.333	.556
Rod Graber	OF2	L	28	4	8	0	1	0	0	0	0	1	2	0	.125	.222	.125
Fred Hatfield†	3B2	L	33	3	8	0	1	0	0	0	1	1	1	0	.125	.222	.125

B. Harrell, 1 G at OF; V. Power, 2 G at SS, 1 G at OF

Pitcher	T	Age	G	GS	CG	ShO	IP	H	HR	BB	SO	W-L	Sv	ERA
Cal McLish	R	32	39	30	13	0	225.2	214	25	70	97	16-8	1	2.99
Mudcat Grant	R	22	44	28	11	1	204.0	173	20	104	111	10-11	4	3.84
Ray Narleski	R	29	44	24	7	0	183.1	179	21	91	102	13-10	1	4.07
Gary Bell	R	21	33	23	10	0	182.0	141	17	73	110	12-10	1	3.31
Hal Woodeshick	L	25	14	9	3	0	71.2	71	4	25	27	6-6	0	3.64
Don Mossi	L	29	43	5	0	0	101.2	106	6	30	55	7-8	3	3.90
Hoyt Wilhelm†	R	34	30	6	1	0	90.1	70	4	35	57	2-7	5	2.49
Don Ferrarese	L	29	28	10	2	0	94.2	91	5	46	62	3-4	1	3.71
Dick Tomanek†	L	27	18	6	2	0	57.2	61	8	28	42	2-3	0	5.62
Morrie Martin†	L	35	14	0	0	0	18.2	20	0	8	5	2-0	1	2.41
Bob Kelly†	R	30	13	3	0	0	27.2	29	4	13	12	0-2	0	5.20
Herb Score	L	25	12	5	2	1	41.0	29	1	34	48	2-3	3	3.95
Bob Lemon	R	37	11	1	0	0	25.1	41	3	16	8	0-1	0	5.33
Jim Constable†	L	25	6	2	0	0	9.1	17	1	4	3	0-1	0	11.57
Chuck Churn	R	28	6	0	0	0	8.2	12	1	5	4	0-0	0	6.23
Steve Ridzik	R	29	6	0	0	0	8.2	9	1	5	6	0-2	0	2.08
Mike Garcia	R	34	6	1	0	0	8.0	15	2	7	2	1-0	0	9.00
Dick Brodowski	R	25	5	0	0	0	10.0	3	0	6	12	1-0	0	0.00
Rocky Colavito	R	24	1	0	0	0	3.0	0	0	3	1	0-0	0	0.00
Gary Geiger	R	21	1	0	0	0	2.0	2	0	1	2	0-0	0	9.00

1958 Detroit Tigers 5th AL 77-77 .500 15.0 GB

Jack Tighe (21-28)/Bill Norman (56-49)

Player	Gm by Position	B	Age	G	AB	R	H	2B	3B	HR	RBI	BB	SO	SB	Avg	OBP	Slg
Red Wilson	C101	R	29	103	298	31	89	13	1	3	29	35	30	10	.299	.373	.379
Gail Harris	1B122	L	26	134	451	63	123	18	8	20	83	36	60	1	.273	.328	.481
Frank Bolling	2B154	R	26	154	610	91	164	25	4	14	75	54	54	6	.269	.328	.392
Reno Bertoia	3B68,SS5,OF1	R	23	86	240	28	56	6	0	6	27	20	35	5	.233	.290	.333
Billy Martin	SS88,3B41	R	30	131	498	56	127	19	1	7	42	16	62	5	.255	.279	.339
Al Kaline	OF145	R	23	146	543	84	170	34	7	16	85	54	47	7	.313	.374	.490
Harvey Kuenn	OF138	R	27	139	561	73	179	39	3	8	54	51	34	5	.319	.373	.442
Charlie Maxwell	OF114,1B14	L	31	131	397	56	108	14	4	13	65	64	54	6	.272	.369	.426
Coot Veal	SS58	R	25	58	207	29	53	10	2	0	16	14	21	1	.256	.304	.324
Ozzie Virgil	3B49	R	25	49	193	19	47	10	2	3	19	8	20	1	.244	.272	.363
Johnny Groth	OF80	R	31	88	146	24	41	5	2	2	11	13	19	0	.281	.340	.384
Jim Hegan†	C45	R	37	45	130	14	25	6	0	1	7	10	32	0	.192	.250	.262
Gus Zernial	OF24	R	35	66	124	8	40	7	1	5	23	6	25	0	.323	.351	.516
Ray Boone†	1B32	R	34	39	114	16	27	4	1	6	20	14	13	0	.237	.323	.447
Tito Francona†	OF18,1B1	L	24	45	69	11	17	5	0	0	10	15	16	0	.246	.381	.319
Charlie Lau	C27	L	25	30	68	8	10	1	2	0	6	12	15	0	.147	.293	.221
Bob Hazle†	OF12	L	27	43	58	5	14	2	0	2	5	5	13	0	.241	.302	.379
Lou Skizas	OF5,3B4	R	26	23	33	4	8	2	0	1	2	5	1	0	.242	.342	.394
Milt Bolling	SS13,2B1,3B1	R	27	24	31	3	6	2	0	0	0	5	7	0	.194	.306	.258
Bill Taylor	OF1	L	28	8	8	0	3	0	0	0	1	0	2	0	.375	.375	.375
Tim Thompson	C4	L	34	4	6	1	1	0	0	0	0	3	2	0	.167	.444	.167
George Alusik	OF1	R	23	2	2	0	0	0	0	0	0	0	1	0	.000	.000	.000
Bobo Osborne		L	22	2	2	0	0	0	0	0	0	0	0	0	.000	.000	.000
Steve Boros	2B1	R	21	6	2	0	0	0	0	0	0	0	0	0	.000	.000	.000
Jack Feller	C1	R	21	1	0	0	0	0	0	0	0	0	0	0	—	—	—
George Thomas	OF1	R	20	1	0	0	0	0	0	0	0	0	0	0	—	—	—

Pitcher	T	Age	G	GS	CG	ShO	IP	H	HR	BB	SO	W-L	Sv	ERA
Frank Lary	R	28	39	34	19	3	260.1	249	20	68	131	16-15	1	2.90
Jim Bunning	R	26	35	34	10	3	219.2	188	28	79	177	14-12	0	3.52
Paul Foytack	R	27	39	33	16	2	230.0	198	23	77	135	15-13	1	3.44
Billy Hoeft	L	26	36	21	6	0	143.0	148	15	49	94	10-9	3	4.15
Hank Aguirre	L	27	44	3	0	0	69.2	67	5	27	38	3-4	5	3.75
Tom Morgan	R	28	39	1	0	0	62.2	70	7	4	32	2-5	1	3.16
George Susce†	R	26	27	10	2	0	90.2	90	7	26	42	4-3	1	3.67
Herb Moford	R	29	25	11	6	0	109.2	83	10	42	58	4-9	1	3.61
Bill Fischer†	R	27	22	0	0	0	30.2	46	6	13	16	2-4	2	7.63
Vito Valentinetti†	R	29	15	0	0	0	18.2	18	4	5	10	1-0	2	3.38
Al Cicotte†	R	28	14	2	0	0	43.0	50	1	15	21	3-1	0	3.56
Bob Shaw†	R	25	11	2	0	0	26.2	32	2	13	17	1-2	0	5.06
Herm Wehmeier†	R	31	7	3	0	0	22.2	21	2	5	11	1-0	0	2.38
Joe Presko	R	29	7	0	0	0	10.2	13	0	1	6	0-0	2	3.38
George Spencer	R	31	7	0	0	0	10.0	11	0	4	5	1-0	0	2.70
Lou Sleater†	L	31	4	0	0	0	5.1	3	2	6	4	0-0	0	6.75
Mickey McDermott	L	30	2	0	0	0	2.0	6	0	2	0	0-0	0	9.00
Don Lee	R	24	1	0	0	0	2.0	1	1	1	0	0-0	0	9.00

1958 Baltimore Orioles 6th AL 74-79 .484 17.5 GB

Paul Richards

Player	Gm by Position	B	Age	G	AB	R	H	2B	3B	HR	RBI	BB	SO	SB	Avg	OBP	Slg
Gus Triandos	C132	R	27	137	474	59	116	10	0	30	79	60	65	1	.245	.327	.456
Bob Boyd	1B99	L	32	125	401	58	124	21	5	7	36	25	24	1	.309	.350	.439
Billy Gardner	2B151,SS13	R	30	151	560	32	126	28	2	3	33	34	53	2	.225	.271	.298
Brooks Robinson	3B140,2B16	R	21	145	463	31	110	16	3	3	32	31	51	1	.238	.292	.305
Willie Miranda	SS102	S	32	102	214	15	43	6	0	1	8	14	25	1	.201	.250	.243
Al Pilarcik	OF118	L	27	141	379	40	92	21	0	1	24	42	37	7	.243	.320	.306
Gene Woodling	OF116	L	35	133	413	57	114	16	1	15	65	66	49	4	.276	.378	.429
Jim Busby	OF103,3B1	R	31	113	215	32	51	7	2	3	19	24	37	6	.237	.320	.330
Dick Williams	OF70,3B45,1B26*	R	29	128	409	36	113	17	0	4	32	37	47	0	.276	.336	.347
Bob Nieman	OF100	R	31	105	366	56	119	20	2	16	60	44	57	2	.325	.395	.522
Foster Castleman	SS91,2B4,3B4*	R	27	98	200	15	34	5	0	3	14	16	34	2	.170	.242	.240
Jim Marshall†	1B52,OF8	L	27	85	191	17	41	4	3	5	19	18	30	3	.215	.280	.346
Joe Ginsberg	C39	L	31	61	109	4	23	1	0	3	16	13	14	0	.211	.302	.303
Lenny Green	OF53	L	25	69	91	10	21	4	0	0	4	9	10	0	.231	.297	.275
Jack Harshman	P34,OF1	L	30	47	82	11	16	1	0	6	14	17	22	0	.195	.330	.427
Joe Taylor†	OF21	R	32	36	77	11	21	4	0	2	9	7	19	0	.273	.333	.403
Willie Tasby	OF16	R	25	18	50	6	10	3	0	1	1	7	15	1	.200	.310	.320
Milt Pappas	P31,2B1	R	19	32	42	2	6	2	0	1	3	0	21	0	.143	.143	.262
Hal Brown	P19,3B2	R	33	21	27	4	4	1	0	0	1	1	6	0	.148	.207	.185
Bob Hale	1B2	L	24	19	20	2	7	2	0	0	3	2	1	0	.350	.409	.450
Jerry Adair	SS10,2B1	R	21	11	19	1	2	0	0	0	0	1	7	0	.105	.150	.105
Ron Hansen	SS12	R	20	12	19	1	0	0	0	0	1	0	7	0	.000	.048	.000
Chuck Oertel	OF2	L	27	14	12	4	2	0	0	1	1	1	1	0	.167	.231	.417
Leo Burke	OF3,3B1	R	24	7	11	4	5	1	0	1	4	1	2	0	.455	.500	.818
Bert Hamric		L	30	8	8	0	1	0	0	0	0	0	6	0	.125	.125	.125
Frank Zupo	C1	L	18	1	2	0	0	0	0	0	0	0	1	0	.000	.000	.000
Eddie Miksis†	SS1	R	31	3	2	0	0	0	0	0	0	0	1	0	.000	.000	.000

D. Williams, 7 G at 2B; F. Castleman, 1 G at OF

Pitcher	T	Age	G	GS	CG	ShO	IP	H	HR	BB	SO	W-L	Sv	ERA
Jack Harshman	L	30	34	29	17	3	236.1	204	20	75	161	12-15	4	2.89
Arnie Portocarrero	R	26	32	27	10	3	204.2	173	17	57	90	15-11	2	3.25
Billy O'Dell	L	25	41	25	12	3	221.1	201	13	51	137	14-11	8	2.97
Milt Pappas	R	19	31	21	3	0	135.1	135	8	48	72	10-10	0	4.06
Connie Johnson	R	35	26	17	4	0	118.1	116	13	32	68	6-9	1	3.88
Hal Brown	R	33	19	17	4	2	96.2	96	9	20	44	7-5	1	3.07
George Zuverink	R	33	45	0	0	0	69.0	74	4	17	22	2-2	7	3.39
Billy Loes	R	28	32	10	1	0	114.0	106	10	44	44	3-9	5	3.63
Ken Lehman	L	30	31	1	1	0	62.0	64	5	18	36	2-1	0	3.48
Charlie Beamon	R	23	21	3	0	0	49.2	47	3	21	26	1-3	0	4.35
Hoyt Wilhelm†	R	34	9	4	3	1	40.2	25	2	10	35	1-3	0	1.99
Jerry Walker	R	19	6	0	0	0	10.1	16	2	5	6	0-0	0	6.97
Lou Sleater†	L	31	6	0	0	0	7.0	14	0	2	5	1-0	0	12.86
Ron Moeller	L	19	4	0	0	0	4.1	6	0	3	3	0-0	0	4.15

1958 Kansas City Athletics 7th AL 73-81 .474 19.0 GB

Harry Craft

Player	Gm by Position	B	Age	G	AB	R	H	2B	3B	HR	RBI	BB	SO	SB	Avg	OBP	Slg
Harry Chiti	C83	R	25	103	295	32	79	11	3	9	44	18	48	3	.268	.311	.417
Vic Power†	1B50,2B1	R	30	52	205	35	62	13	4	4	27	7	3	1	.302	.325	.463
Hector Lopez	2B96,3B55,SS1*	R	28	151	564	84	147	28	4	17	73	49	61	2	.261	.317	.415
Hal Smith	3B43,C31,1B14	R	27	99	315	32	86	19	2	5	46	25	47	0	.273	.323	.394
Joe DeMaestri	SS137	R	29	139	442	32	97	11	1	6	38	16	84	1	.219	.247	.290
Bill Tuttle	OF145	R	28	148	511	77	118	14	9	11	51	74	58	7	.231	.327	.358
Bob Cerv	OF136	R	32	141	515	93	157	20	7	38	104	50	82	3	.305	.371	.592
Roger Maris†	OF99	L	23	99	401	61	99	14	3	19	53	28	52	0	.247	.298	.439
Preston Ward†	1B39,3B34,OF2	L	30	81	268	28	68	10	1	6	24	27	36	0	.254	.319	.366
Mike Baxes	2B61,SS4	R	27	73	231	31	49	10	1	0	8	21	24	1	.212	.286	.264
Bob Martyn	OF63	L	27	95	226	25	59	10	7	2	23	26	36	1	.261	.336	.394
Harry Simpson†	1B43,OF11	L	32	78	212	21	56	7	1	7	27	26	33	0	.264	.345	.406
Frank House	C55	L	28	76	202	16	51	6	3	4	24	12	13	1	.252	.295	.371
Chico Carrasquel†	3B32,SS22	R	32	59	160	19	34	5	1	2	13	21	15	0	.213	.304	.294
Woodie Held†	OF41,3B4,SS1	R	26	47	131	13	28	2	0	4	16	10	28	0	.214	.276	.321
Whitey Herzog†	OF37,1B22	L	26	88	96	11	23	1	2	0	9	16	21	0	.240	.345	.292
Billy Hunter†	SS12,2B8,3B1	R	30	22	58	6	9	1	1	2	11	5	7	1	.155	.222	.310
Kent Hadley	1B2	L	23	3	11	1	2	0	0	0	0	0	4	0	.182	.182	.182
Lou Klimchock	2B2	L	18	2	10	2	2	0	0	1	1	0	1	0	.200	.200	.500
Dave Melton	OF2	R	29	9	6	0	0	0	0	0	0	0	5	0	.000	.000	.000
Jim Small	OF1	L	21	2	4	0	0	0	0	0	0	1	0	0	.000	.200	.000
Milt Graff	2B1	L	27	5	1	0	0	0	0	0	0	0	0	0	.000	.000	.000

H. Lopez, 1 G at OF

Pitcher	T	Age	G	GS	CG	ShO	IP	H	HR	BB	SO	W-L	Sv	ERA
Ralph Terry	R	22	40	33	8	3	216.2	217	29	61	134	11-13	2	4.24
Ned Garver	R	32	31	28	10	3	201.0	192	24	66	72	12-11	1	4.03
Jack Urban	R	29	30	24	5	1	132.0	150	17	51	54	8-11	1	5.93
Bob Grim†	R	28	26	14	5	1	113.2	118	7	41	54	7-6	0	3.56
Duke Maas†	R	29	10	7	3	1	55.1	49	3	13	19	4-5	1	3.90
Alex Kellner†	L	33	7	6	0	0	33.2	40	5	8	22	0-2	0	5.88
Bob Davis	R	24	8	4	0	0	31.0	45	5	12	22	0-4	0	7.84
John Tsitouris	R	22	1	1	0	0	3.0	2	0	2	1	0-0	0	3.00
Tom Gorman	R	33	50	1	0	0	89.2	86	8	20	44	4-4	8	3.51
Ray Herbert	R	28	42	16	5	0	175.0	161	20	55	108	8-8	3	3.50
Dick Tomanek†	L	27	36	2	1	0	72.1	69	5	28	50	5-5	5	3.61
Murry Dickson†	R	41	27	9	3	0	99.0	99	12	31	46	9-5	1	3.27
Bud Daley	L	25	26	5	1	0	70.2	67	5	19	39	3-2	0	3.31
Walt Craddock	L	26	23	1	0	0	36.2	41	4	20	22	0-3	0	5.89
Virgil Trucks†	R	41	16	0	0	0	22.0	18	2	15	15	0-1	3	2.05
Wally Burnette	R	29	12	4	0	0	28.1	29	2	14	11	1-1	0	3.49
Howie Reed	R	21	3	1	1	0	10.1	5	0	4	5	1-0	0	0.87
Glenn Cox	R	27	2	0	0	0	3.2	6	1	3	1	0-0	0	9.82
Ken Johnson	R	25	2	0	0	0	2.1	6	1	3	1	0-0	0	27.00
Carl Duser	L	25	1	0	0	0	2.0	5	0	1	0	0-0	0	4.50

1958 Washington Senators 8th AL 61-93 .396 31.0 GB

Cookie Lavagetto

Player	Gm by Position	B	Age	G	AB	R	H	2B	3B	HR	RBI	BB	SO	SB	Avg	OBP	Slg
Clint Courtney	C128	L	31	134	450	46	113	18	0	8	62	48	23	1	.251	.332	.344
Norm Zauchin	1B91	R	28	96	303	35	69	8	2	15	37	38	68	0	.228	.310	.416
Ken Aspromonte†	2B72,3B11,SS1	R	26	92	253	15	57	9	1	5	27	25	28	1	.225	.296	.328
Eddie Yost	3B114,OF4,1B2	R	31	134	406	55	91	16	0	8	37	81	43	3	.224	.361	.323
Rocky Bridges	SS112,2B3,3B3	R	30	116	377	38	99	14	3	5	28	27	32	0	.263	.315	.355
Albie Pearson	OF141	L	23	146	530	63	146	25	5	3	33	64	31	7	.275	.354	.358
Jim Lemon	OF137	R	30	142	501	65	123	15	9	26	75	50	120	2	.246	.314	.467
Roy Sievers	OF114,1B33	R	31	148	550	85	162	18	1	39	108	53	63	3	.295	.357	.544
Herb Plews	2B64,3B36	L	30	111	380	46	98	12	6	2	29	17	45	2	.258	.291	.337
Neil Chrisley	OF69,3B1	L	26	105	233	19	50	7	4	5	26	16	18	1	.215	.265	.343
Ossie Alvarez	SS64,2B14,3B3	R	24	87	196	20	41	3	0	0	5	16	26	1	.209	.269	.224
Julio Becquer	1B42,OF1	L	26	86	164	10	39	3	0	0	12	8	21	1	.238	.270	.256
Ed Fitz Gerald	C21,1B5	R	34	58	114	7	30	3	0	0	11	8	15	0	.263	.309	.289
Faye Throneberry	OF26	L	27	44	87	12	16	1	1	4	7	4	28	0	.184	.245	.356
Bobby Malkmus	2B26,3B2,SS1	R	26	41	70	5	13	2	1	0	3	4	15	0	.186	.230	.243
Steve Korcheck	C20	R	25	21	51	6	4	2	1	0	1	1	16	0	.078	.096	.157
Bob Allison	OF11	R	23	11	35	1	7	1	0	0	0	2	5	0	.200	.243	.229
Harmon Killebrew	3B9	R	22	13	31	2	6	0	0	0	2	0	12	0	.194	.212	.194
Johnny Schaive	2B6	R	24	7	24	1	6	0	0	0	1	1	4	0	.250	.280	.250
Jerry Snyder	2B2,SS1	R	28	6	9	1	1	0	0	0	1	1	1	0	.111	.200	.111
Lou Berberet†	C2	L	28	5	6	0	1	0	0	0	0	4	1	0	.167	.500	.167
Whitey Herzog†	OF7	L	26	8	5	0	0	0	0	0	0	1	5	0	.000	.167	.000

Pitcher	T	Age	G	GS	CG	ShO	IP	H	HR	BB	SO	W-L	Sv	ERA
Pedro Ramos	R	23	43	37	10	4	259.1	277	38	77	132	14-18	3	4.23
Russ Kemmerer	R	26	40	30	6	0	224.1	234	25	74	111	6-15	0	4.61
Camilo Pascual	R	24	31	27	6	2	177.1	166	14	60	146	8-12	0	3.15
Hal Griggs	R	29	32	21	3	0	137.0	138	20	74	69	3-11	0	5.52
Al Cicotte†	R	28	8	4	0	0	28.0	36	3	14	14	0-3	0	4.82
Ralph Lumenti	L	21	8	4	0	0	21.0	21	2	36	20	1-2	0	8.57
Bill Fischer†	R	27	3	3	0	0	21.0	24	1	5	10	0-3	0	3.86
Tex Clevenger	R	25	55	4	0	0	124.0	119	12	50	70	9-9	6	4.35
Dick Hyde	R	29	53	0	0	0	103.0	82	1	35	49	10-3	18	1.75
Vito Valentinetti†	R	29	23	10	2	0	95.2	106	16	49	33	4-6	0	5.08
Chuck Stobbs†	L	28	19	8	0	0	56.2	87	7	16	23	2-6	0	6.04
John Romonosky	R	28	18	5	1	0	55.1	52	6	28	38	2-4	0	6.51
Bud Byerly†	R	37	17	0	0	0	24.0	34	4	11	13	2-0	1	6.75
Jim Constable†	L	25	15	2	0	0	27.2	29	3	15	25	0-1	0	4.88
Joe Albanese	R	25	6	0	0	0	6.0	8	1	2	3	0-0	0	4.50
Bob Wiesler	L	27	4	0	0	0	9.1	14	2	5	5	0-0	0	6.75
Jack Spring	L	25	3	1	0	0	7.0	16	1	7	1	0-0	0	14.14

»1958 Milwaukee Braves 1st NL 92-62 .597 —

Fred Haney

Player	Gm by Position	B	Age	G	AB	R	H	2B	3B	HR	RBI	BB	SO	SB	Avg	OBP	Slg
Del Crandall	C124	R	28	131	427	50	116	23	1	18	63	48	38	4	.272	.348	.457
Frank Torre	1B122	L	26	138	372	41	115	22	5	6	55	42	14	2	.309	.386	.444
Red Schoendienst	2B105	S	35	106	427	47	112	23	1	1	24	31	21	3	.262	.313	.328
Eddie Mathews	3B149	L	26	149	546	97	137	18	1	31	77	85	85	5	.251	.349	.458
Johnny Logan	SS144	R	31	145	530	54	120	20	0	11	53	40	57	1	.226	.286	.326
Hank Aaron	OF153	R	24	153	601	109	196	34	4	30	95	59	49	4	.326	.386	.546
Bill Bruton	OF96	L	32	100	325	47	91	11	3	3	28	27	37	4	.280	.336	.360
Andy Pafko	OF93	R	37	95	164	17	39	7	1	3	23	15	17	0	.238	.306	.348
Joe Adcock	1B71,OF22	R	30	105	320	40	88	15	1	19	54	21	63	0	.275	.317	.506
Wes Covington	OF82	L	26	90	294	43	97	12	1	24	74	20	35	0	.330	.380	.622
Felix Mantilla	OF43,2B21,SS5*	R	23	85	226	37	50	5	1	7	19	20	20	2	.221	.282	.345
Mel Roach	2B27,OF7,1B1	R	25	44	136	14	42	7	0	3	10	6	15	0	.309	.336	.426
Harry Hanebrink	OF33,3B7	L	30	63	133	14	25	3	0	4	10	13	9	0	.188	.270	.301
Del Rice	C38	R	35	43	121	10	27	7	0	1	8	8	30	0	.223	.271	.306
Casey Wise	2B10,SS7,3B1	S	25	31	71	8	14	1	0	0	0	4	8	1	.197	.240	.211
Bob Hazle†	OF20	L	27	20	56	6	10	0	0	0	5	9	4	0	.179	.303	.179
Eddie Haas	OF3	L	23	9	14	2	5	0	0	0	1	2	1	0	.357	.438	.357
Carl Sawatski†	C3	L	30	10	10	1	1	0	0	0	1	2	5	0	.100	.231	.100
Joe Koppe	SS3	R	27	16	9	3	4	0	0	0	0	1	1	0	.444	.500	.444
Hawk Taylor	OF4	R	19	4	8	1	1	1	0	0	0	0	3	0	.125	.125	.250
John DeMerit	OF2	R	22	3	3	1	2	0	0	0	0	0	0	0	.667	.667	.667
Bob Roselli		R	26	1	1	0	0	0	0	0	0	0	0	0	.000	.000	.000

F. Mantilla, 2 G at 3B

Pitcher	T	Age	G	GS	CG	ShO	IP	H	HR	BB	SO	W-L	Sv	ERA
Warren Spahn	L	37	38	36	23	2	290.0	257	29	76	150	22-11	1	3.07
Lew Burdette	R	31	40	36	19	3	275.1	279	18	50	113	20-10	0	2.91
Bob Rush	R	32	28	20	5	2	147.1	142	13	31	84	10-6	0	3.42
Carl Willey	R	27	23	19	9	4	140.0	110	14	53	74	9-7	0	2.70
Joey Jay	R	22	18	12	6	3	96.2	60	8	43	74	7-5	0	2.14
Juan Pizarro	L	21	16	10	7	1	96.2	75	12	47	84	6-4	1	2.70
Bob Buhl	R	29	11	10	3	0	73.0	74	5	30	27	5-2	1	3.45
Don McMahon	R	28	38	0	0	0	58.2	50	4	29	37	7-2	8	3.68
Bob Trowbridge	R	28	27	4	0	0	55.0	53	4	26	31	1-3	1	3.93
Gene Conley	R	27	26	7	0	0	72.0	89	8	17	53	0-6	2	4.88
Humberto Robinson	R	28	19	0	0	0	41.2	30	4	13	26	2-4	1	3.02
Ernie Johnson	R	34	15	0	0	0	23.1	35	4	10	13	3-1	1	8.10
Dick Littlefield	L	32	4	0	0	0	6.1	7	2	1	7	0-1	1	4.26

744 Seasons: Team Rosters

1958 Pittsburgh Pirates 2nd NL 84-70 .545 8.0 GB

Danny Murtaugh

Player	Gm by Position	B	Age	G	AB	R	H	2B	3B	HR	RBI	BB	SO	SB	Avg	OBP	Slg
Hank Foiles	C103	R	29	104	264	31	54	10	2	8	30	45	53	0	.205	.322	.348
Ted Kluszewski	1B72	L	33	100	301	29	88	13	4	4	37	26	16	0	.292	.348	.402
Bill Mazeroski	2B152	R	21	152	567	69	156	24	6	19	68	25	71	1	.275	.308	.439
Frank Thomas	3B139,OF8,1B2	R	29	149	562	89	158	26	4	35	109	42	79	0	.281	.334	.528
Dick Groat	SS149	R	27	151	584	67	175	36	9	3	66	23	32	2	.300	.328	.408
Bill Virdon	OF143	L	27	144	604	75	161	24	11	9	46	52	70	5	.267	.324	.387
Bob Skinner	OF141	L	26	144	529	93	170	33	9	13	70	58	55	12	.321	.387	.491
Roberto Clemente	OF135	R	23	140	519	69	150	24	10	6	50	31	41	8	.289	.327	.408
Dick Stuart	1B64	R	25	67	254	38	68	12	5	16	48	11	75	0	.268	.310	.543
Roman Mejias	OF57	R	27	76	157	17	42	3	2	5	19	2	27	2	.268	.280	.408
Bill Hall	C51	L	29	51	116	15	33	6	0	1	15	15	13	0	.284	.366	.362
Danny Kravitz	C37	L	27	45	100	9	24	3	2	1	5	11	10	0	.240	.313	.340
R C Stevens	1B52	R	23	59	90	16	24	3	1	7	18	5	25	0	.267	.320	.556
John Powers	OF14	L	28	57	82	6	15	1	0	2	2	8	19	0	.183	.256	.268
Gene Baker	3B11,2B3	R	33	29	56	3	14	2	1	0	7	8	6	0	.250	.338	.321
Dick Schofield†	SS5,3B2	S	23	26	27	4	4	0	1	0	2	3	6	0	.148	.226	.222
Harry Bright	3B7	R	28	15	24	4	6	1	0	1	3	1	6	0	.250	.269	.417
Gene Freese†	3B1	R	24	17	18	1	3	0	0	1	2	1	2	0	.167	.211	.333
Hardy Peterson	C2	R	28	2	6	0	2	0	0	0	0	1	0	0	.333	.429	.333
Jim Pendleton		R	34	3	3	0	1	0	0	0	0	0	0	0	.333	.333	.333
Paul Smith†		L	27	6	3	0	1	0	0	0	0	3	0	0	.333	.667	.333
Johnny O'Brien†		R	27	3	1	1	0	0	0	0	0	0	1	0	.000	.000	.000

Pitcher	T	Age	G	GS	CG	ShO	IP	H	HR	BB	SO	W-L	Sv	ERA
Bob Friend	R	27	38	38	16	1	274.0	299	25	61	135	22-14	0	3.68
Ron Kline	R	26	32	32	11	2	237.1	220	25	92	109	13-16	0	3.53
Vern Law	R	28	35	29	6	1	202.1	235	16	39	56	14-12	3	3.96
Curt Raydon	R	24	31	20	2	1	134.1	118	18	61	85	8-4	1	3.62
George Witt	R	24	18	15	5	3	106.0	78	2	59	81	9-2	0	1.61
Bennie Daniels	R	26	8	5	1	0	27.2	31	3	15	7	0-3	0	5.53
Roy Face	R	30	57	0	0	0	84.0	77	6	22	47	5-2	20	2.89
Don Gross	L	27	40	3	0	0	74.2	67	5	38	59	5-7	7	3.98
Ron Blackburn	R	23	38	2	0	0	63.2	61	7	27	31	2-1	3	3.39
Bob Porterfield†	R	34	37	6	2	1	87.2	78	7	19	39	4-6	5	3.29
Bob Smith	L	27	35	4	0	0	61.0	61	6	31	24	2-2	1	4.43
George Perez	R	20	4	0	0	0	8.1	9	1	4	2	0-1	1	5.40
Don Williams	R	26	2	0	0	0	4.0	6	1	1	3	0-0	0	6.75
Eddie O'Brien	R	27	1	0	0	0	2.0	4	1	1	1	0-0	0	13.50

1958 San Francisco Giants 3rd NL 80-74 .519 12.0 GB

Bill Rigney

Player	Gm by Position	B	Age	G	AB	R	H	2B	3B	HR	RBI	BB	SO	SB	Avg	OBP	Slg
Bob Schmidt	C123	R	25	127	393	46	96	20	2	14	54	33	59	0	.244	.306	.412
Orlando Cepeda	1B147	R	20	148	603	88	188	38	4	25	96	29	84	15	.312	.342	.512
Danny O'Connell	2B104,3B3	R	31	107	306	44	71	12	2	3	23	51	35	2	.232	.340	.314
Jim Davenport	3B130,SS5	R	24	134	434	70	111	22	3	12	41	33	64	1	.256	.317	.403
Daryl Spencer	SS134,2B17	R	28	148	539	71	138	20	5	17	74	73	60	1	.256	.343	.406
Willie Mays	OF151	R	27	152	600	121	208	33	11	29	96	78	56	31	.347	.419	.583
Willie Kirkland	OF115	L	24	122	418	48	108	25	6	14	56	43	69	3	.258	.332	.447
Felipe Alou	OF70	R	23	75	182	21	46	9	2	4	16	19	34	4	.253	.325	.390
Hank Sauer	OF67	R	41	88	236	27	59	8	0	12	46	35	37	0	.250	.354	.436
Ray Jablonski	3B57	R	31	82	230	28	53	15	1	12	46	17	50	2	.230	.287	.461
Leon Wagner	OF57	L	24	74	221	31	70	9	0	13	35	18	34	1	.317	.371	.534
Valmy Thomas	C61	R	29	63	143	14	37	5	0	3	16	13	24	1	.259	.321	.357
Eddie Bressoud	2B57,3B6,SS4	R	26	66	137	19	36	5	3	0	8	14	22	0	.263	.331	.343
Whitey Lockman	OF25,2B15,1B7	L	31	92	122	15	29	5	0	2	7	13	8	0	.238	.311	.328
Bob Speake	OF10	L	27	66	71	9	15	3	0	3	10	13	15	0	.211	.333	.380
Andre Rodgers	SS18	R	23	22	63	7	13	3	1	2	11	4	14	0	.206	.243	.381
Jim King	OF15	L	25	34	56	8	12	2	1	2	8	10	8	0	.214	.343	.393
Jackie Brandt	OF14	R	24	18	52	7	13	1	0	0	3	6	5	1	.250	.328	.269
Don Taussig	OF36	R	26	39	50	10	10	0	0	1	4	3	8	0	.200	.245	.260
Bill White	1B3,OF2	L	24	26	29	5	7	1	0	1	4	7	5	1	.241	.389	.379
Jim Finigan	2B8,3B4	R	29	23	25	3	5	2	0	0	1	3	5	0	.200	.310	.280
Nick Testa	C1	R	30	1	0	0	0	0	0	0	0	1	0	0	—	—	—

Pitcher	T	Age	G	GS	CG	ShO	IP	H	HR	BB	SO	W-L	Sv	ERA
Johnny Antonelli	L	28	41	34	13	0	241.2	216	31	87	143	16-13	3	3.28
Ruben Gomez	R	30	42	30	8	1	207.2	204	21	77	112	10-12	1	4.38
Mike McCormick	L	19	42	28	8	2	178.1	192	19	60	82	11-8	1	4.59
John Fitzgerald	L	24	1	1	0	0	3.0	1	1	1	3	0-0	0	3.00
Al Worthington	R	29	54	12	1	0	151.1	152	17	57	76	11-7	6	3.63
Marv Grissom	R	40	51	0	0	0	65.1	71	11	26	46	7-5	10	3.99
Ray Monzant	R	25	43	16	4	1	150.2	160	21	57	93	8-11	1	4.72
Stu Miller	R	30	41	20	4	1	182.0	160	16	49	119	6-9	0	2.47
Paul Giel	R	25	29	9	0	0	92.0	89	12	55	55	4-5	0	4.70
Don Johnson	R	31	17	0	0	0	23.0	31	2	8	14	0-1	1	6.26
Ray Crone	R	26	14	1	0	0	24.0	35	5	13	7	1-2	0	6.75
Gordon Jones	R	28	11	1	0	0	30.1	33	2	5	8	3-1	1	2.37
Jim Constable†	L	25	9	0	0	0	8.0	10	1	3	4	1-0	1	5.63
Curt Barclay	R	26	6	1	0	0	16.0	16	3	5	6	1-0	0	2.81
Pete Burnside	L	27	6	1	0	0	10.2	20	3	5	4	0-0	0	6.75
Dom Zanni	R	26	1	0	0	0	4.0	7	1	1	3	1-0	0	2.25
Joe Shipley	R	23	1	0	0	0	1.1	3	0	3	0	0-0	0	33.75

1958 Cincinnati Reds 4th NL 76-78 .494 16.0 GB

Birdie Tebbetts (52-61)/Jimmy Dykes (24-17)

Player	Gm by Position	B	Age	G	AB	R	H	2B	3B	HR	RBI	BB	SO	SB	Avg	OBP	Slg
Ed Bailey	C99	L	27	112	360	39	90	23	1	11	59	47	61	2	.250	.337	.411
George Crowe	1B93,2B1	L	37	111	345	31	95	12	5	7	61	41	51	1	.275	.348	.400
Johnny Temple	2B141,1B1	R	30	141	542	82	166	31	6	3	47	91	41	15	.306	.405	.402
Don Hoak	3B112,SS1	R	30	114	417	51	109	30	0	6	50	43	36	6	.261	.333	.376
Roy McMillan	SS145	R	27	145	393	48	90	18	3	1	25	47	33	5	.229	.312	.298
Frank Robinson	OF138,3B11	R	22	148	554	90	149	25	6	31	83	62	80	10	.269	.350	.504
Gus Bell	OF107	L	29	112	385	42	97	16	2	10	46	36	40	2	.252	.314	.382
Jerry Lynch	OF101	L	27	122	420	58	131	20	5	16	68	18	54	1	.312	.338	.498
Smoky Burgess	C58	L	31	99	251	28	71	12	1	6	31	22	20	0	.283	.343	.410
Alex Grammas	SS61,3B38,2B14	R	32	105	216	25	47	8	0	0	12	34	24	2	.218	.329	.255
Pete Whisenant	OF66,2B1	R	28	85	203	33	48	9	2	11	40	18	37	3	.236	.292	.463
Bob Thurman	OF41	L	41	94	178	23	41	7	4	4	20	20	38	1	.230	.320	.382
Walt Dropo†	1B43	R	35	63	162	18	47	7	2	7	31	12	31	0	.290	.335	.488
Dee Fondy	1B36,OF22	L	33	89	124	23	27	1	1	1	11	5	27	7	.218	.246	.266
Vada Pinson	OF27	L	19	27	96	20	26	7	0	1	8	11	18	2	.271	.352	.375
Steve Bilko†	1B21	R	29	31	87	12	23	4	2	4	17	10	20	0	.264	.330	.494
Eddie Miksis†	OF32,3B14,2B7*	R	31	69	50	15	7	0	0	0	4	5	5	1	.140	.218	.140
Dutch Dotterer	C8	R	26	11	28	1	7	1	0	1	2	2	4	0	.250	.300	.393
Danny Morejon	OF11	R	27	12	26	4	5	0	0	0	1	9	2	1	.192	.400	.192
Chuck Coles	OF4	L	27	5	11	0	2	1	0	0	2	2	6	0	.182	.308	.273
Jim Fridley	OF2	R	33	5	9	2	2	2	0	0	1	0	2	0	.222	.222	.444
Hal Jeffcoat	P49,OF1	R	33	50	9	2	5	0	0	0	0	1	2	0	.556	.600	.556
Bobby Henrich	SS2	R	19	5	3	2	0	0	0	0	0	1	2	0	.000	.000	.000
Fred Hatfield†	2B1,3B1	L	33	3	1	0	0	0	0	0	0	0	0	0	.000	.000	.000

E. Miksis, 5 G at SS, 1 G at 1B

Pitcher	T	Age	G	GS	CG	ShO	IP	H	HR	BB	SO	W-L	Sv	ERA
Bob Purkey	R	28	37	34	17	3	250.0	259	25	49	70	17-11	0	3.60
Harvey Haddix	L	32	29	26	8	1	184.0	191	28	43	110	8-7	0	3.52
Joe Nuxhall	L	29	36	26	5	0	175.2	169	15	63	111	12-11	0	3.79
Brooks Lawrence	R	33	46	23	6	2	181.0	194	12	55	74	8-13	5	4.13
Don Newcombe†	R	32	20	18	7	0	133.1	159	20	28	53	7-7	1	3.85
Jim O'Toole	L	21	1	1	0	0	7.0	4	0	5	4	0-1	0	1.29
Jay Hook	R	21	1	1	0	0	3.0	3	2	2	5	0-1	0	12.00
Bob Kelly†	R	30	2	1	0	0	2.0	3	0	3	1	0-0	0	4.50
Hal Jeffcoat	R	33	49	0	0	0	75.0	76	8	26	35	6-8	9	3.72
Willard Schmidt	R	30	41	2	0	0	69.1	60	8	33	41	3-5	0	2.86
Tom Acker	R	28	38	10	3	0	124.2	126	10	43	90	4-3	1	4.55
Alex Kellner†	L	33	18	7	4	0	82.0	74	8	20	42	7-3	0	2.30
Johnny Klippstein†	R	30	12	4	0	0	33.0	37	5	14	22	3-2	1	4.91
Turk Lown†	R	34	11	0	0	0	11.2	12	2	12	9	0-2	0	5.40
Charlie Rabe	L	26	9	1	0	0	18.2	25	3	9	10	0-3	0	4.34
Orlando Pena	R	24	9	0	0	0	15.0	10	0	4	11	1-0	3	0.60
Bill Wight†	L	36	7	0	0	0	6.2	7	1	4	5	0-1	0	4.05
Hersh Freeman†	R	29	3	0	0	0	7.2	4	0	5	7	0-0	0	3.52
Gene Hayden	L	23	3	0	0	0	3.2	5	0	1	3	0-0	0	4.91
Ted Wieand	R	25	1	0	0	0	2.0	4	1	0	2	0-0	0	9.00

1958 Chicago Cubs 5th NL 72-82 .468 20.0 GB

Bob Scheffing

Player	Gm by Position	B	Age	G	AB	R	H	2B	3B	HR	RBI	BB	SO	SB	Avg	OBP	Slg
Sammy Taylor	C87	L	25	96	301	30	78	12	2	6	36	27	46	2	.259	.319	.372
Dale Long	1B137,C2	L	32	142	480	68	130	26	4	20	75	66	64	2	.271	.357	.467
Tony Taylor	2B137,3B1	R	22	140	497	63	117	15	3	6	27	40	93	21	.235	.299	.314
Al Dark†	3B111	R	36	114	464	54	137	16	4	3	43	29	23	1	.295	.339	.366
Ernie Banks	SS154	R	27	154	617	119	193	23	11	47	129	52	87	4	.313	.366	.614
Bobby Thomson	OF148,3B4	R	34	152	547	67	155	27	5	21	82	56	76	0	.283	.351	.466
Walt Moryn	OF141	L	32	143	512	77	135	26	7	26	77	62	83	1	.264	.350	.494
Lee Walls	OF132	R	25	136	513	80	156	19	3	24	72	47	62	4	.304	.370	.493
Johnny Goryl	3B44,2B35	R	24	83	219	27	53	9	3	4	14	27	34	0	.242	.331	.365
Cal Neeman	C71	R	29	76	201	30	52	7	0	12	29	21	41	0	.259	.336	.473
Jim Bolger	OF37	R	26	84	120	15	27	4	1	1	11	9	20	0	.225	.285	.300
Chuck Tanner	OF15	L	28	73	103	10	27	6	0	4	17	9	10	1	.262	.321	.437
Bobby Adams	1B11,3B9,2B7	R	36	62	96	14	27	4	4	0	4	6	15	2	.281	.324	.406
Jim Marshall†	1B15,OF11	L	27	26	81	12	22	2	0	5	11	12	13	1	.272	.372	.481
Lou Jackson	OF12	L	22	24	35	5	6	2	1	1	6	1	9	0	.171	.194	.371
El Tappe	C16	R	31	17	28	2	6	0	0	0	4	3	1	0	.214	.290	.214
Moe Thacker	C9	R	24	11	24	4	6	1	0	2	3	1	7	0	.250	.269	.542
Paul Smith†	1B4	L	27	18	20	1	3	0	0	0	1	3	4	0	.150	.261	.150
Frank Ernaga		R	27	9	8	0	1	0	0	0	0	0	2	0	.125	.125	.125
Chick King	OF7	R	27	8	8	1	2	0	0	0	0	3	1	0	.250	.455	.250
Jerry Kindall	2B3	R	23	3	6	0	1	1	0	0	0	0	3	0	.167	.167	.333
Footer Johnson		L	26	8	5	1	0	0	0	0	0	0	1	0	.000	.000	.000
Bob Will	OF1	L	26	6	4	1	1	0	0	0	0	2	0	0	.250	.500	.250
Gabe Gabler		L	27	3	3	0	0	0	0	0	0	0	3	0	.000	.000	.000
Gordon Massa		L	22	2	2	0	0	0	0	0	0	0	2	0	.000	.000	.000
Bobby Morgan		R	32	1	1	0	0	0	0	0	0	0	1	0	.000	.000	.000

Pitcher	T	Age	G	GS	CG	ShO	IP	H	HR	BB	SO	W-L	Sv	ERA
Dick Drott	R	21	39	31	4	0	167.1	156	23	99	127	7-11	0	5.43
Taylor Phillips	L	25	39	27	5	1	170.1	178	22	79	102	7-10	1	4.76
Moe Drabowsky	R	22	22	20	4	1	125.2	118	19	73	77	9-11	0	4.51
John Briggs	R	24	20	17	3	1	95.2	99	12	45	46	5-5	0	4.52
Dave Hillman	R	30	31	16	3	0	125.2	132	12	31	65	4-8	1	3.15
Jim Brosnan†	R	28	8	8	2	0	51.2	41	3	29	24	3-4	0	3.14
Dick Ellsworth	L	18	1	1	0	0	2.1	4	0	3	0	0-1	0	15.43
Don Elston	R	29	69	0	0	0	97.0	75	9	39	84	9-8	10	2.88
Glen Hobbie	R	22	55	16	2	1	168.1	163	13	93	91	10-6	2	3.74
Bill Henry	L	30	44	0	0	0	81.1	63	8	17	58	5-4	6	2.88
Dolan Nichols	R	28	24	0	0	0	41.1	46	1	16	9	0-4	1	5.01
Ed Mayer	L	26	19	0	0	0	23.2	15	0	16	14	2-2	1	3.80
Bob Anderson	R	22	17	8	2	0	65.2	61	3	29	51	3-3	0	3.97
Gene Fodge	R	26	16	4	1	0	39.2	47	5	11	15	1-1	0	4.76
Marcelino Solis	L	27	15	4	0	0	52.0	74	5	20	15	3-3	0	6.06
Hersh Freeman†	R	29	9	0	0	0	13.0	23	3	3	7	0-1	0	8.31
Freddy Rodriguez	R	34	7	0	0	0	7.1	8	2	5	5	0-0	2	7.36
John Buzhardt	R	21	6	2	1	0	24.1	16	2	7	9	3-0	0	1.85
Turk Lown†	R	34	4	0	0	0	4.0	2	0	3	4	0-0	0	4.50
Elmer Singleton	R	40	2	0	0	0	4.2	1	0	1	2	1-0	0	0.00

1958 St. Louis Cardinals 5th NL 72-82 .468 20.0 GB

Fred Hutchinson (69-75)/Stan Hack (3-7)

Player	Gm by Position	B	Age	G	AB	R	H	2B	3B	HR	RBI	BB	SO	SB	Avg	OBP	Slg
Hal Smith	C71	R	27	77	220	13	50	4	1	1	24	14	14	0	.227	.272	.268
Stan Musial	1B124	L	37	135	472	64	159	35	2	17	62	72	26	0	.337	.423	.528
Don Blasingame	2B137	L	26	143	547	71	150	19	10	2	36	57	47	20	.274	.343	.356
Ken Boyer	3B144,OF6,SS1	R	27	150	570	101	175	21	9	23	90	49	53	11	.307	.360	.496
Eddie Kasko	SS77,2B12,3B1	R	26	104	259	20	57	8	1	2	22	21	25	1	.220	.277	.282
Curt Flood	OF120,3B1	R	20	121	422	50	110	17	2	10	41	31	56	2	.261	.317	.382
Del Ennis	OF84	R	33	106	329	22	86	18	1	3	47	15	35	0	.261	.290	.350
Wally Moon	OF82	L	28	108	290	36	69	10	3	7	38	47	30	2	.238	.342	.366
Gene Green	OF75,C48	R	25	137	442	47	124	18	3	13	55	37	48	2	.281	.333	.423
Joe Cunningham	1B67,OF66	L	26	131	337	61	105	20	3	12	57	82	23	4	.312	.449	.496
Gene Freese†	SS28,2B14,3B3	R	24	62	191	28	49	11	1	6	16	10	32	1	.257	.294	.419
Irv Noren	OF77	L	33	117	178	24	47	9	1	4	22	13	21	0	.264	.327	.393
Hobie Landrith	C45	L	28	70	144	9	31	4	0	3	13	26	21	0	.215	.335	.306
Dick Schofield†	SS27	S	23	39	108	16	23	4	0	1	8	23	15	0	.213	.348	.278
Bobby Gene Smith	OF27	R	24	28	88	8	25	3	0	2	5	2	18	1	.284	.304	.386
Ruben Amaro	SS36,2B1	R	22	40	76	8	17	2	1	0	0	5	8	0	.224	.272	.276
Al Dark†	3B8,SS8	R	36	18	64	7	19	0	0	1	5	2	6	0	.297	.318	.344
Ray Katt	C14	R	31	19	41	1	7	1	0	1	4	4	6	0	.171	.239	.268
Lee Tate	SS9	R	26	10	35	4	7	2	0	0	1	4	3	0	.200	.282	.257
Ellis Burton	OF7	S	21	8	30	5	7	0	1	2	4	3	8	0	.233	.324	.500
Joe Taylor†	OF5	R	32	18	23	2	7	3	0	1	3	2	4	0	.304	.346	.565
Benny Valenzuela	3B3	R	25	10	14	0	3	1	0	0	0	1	0	0	.214	.267	.286
Johnny O'Brien†	SS5,P1,2B1	R	27	12	2	3	0	0	0	0	0	1	0	0	.000	.333	.000

Pitcher	T	Age	G	GS	CG	ShO	IP	H	HR	BB	SO	W-L	Sv	ERA
Sam Jones	R	32	35	35	14	2	250.0	204	23	107	225	14-13	0	2.88
Vinegar Bend Mizell	L	27	30	29	8	2	189.2	178	17	91	80	10-14	0	3.42
Lindy McDaniel	R	22	26	17	2	1	108.2	139	17	31	47	5-7	0	5.80
Sal Maglie†	R	41	10	10	2	0	53.0	46	14	25	21	2-6	0	4.75
Herm Wehmeier†	R	31	3	3	0	0	6.0	13	2	2	4	0-1	0	13.50
Bill Smith	L	24	2	1	0	0	9.2	12	0	4	4	0-1	0	6.52
Von McDaniel	R	19	2	1	0	0	2.0	5	0	5	0	0-0	0	13.50
Larry Jackson	R	27	49	23	11	1	198.0	211	21	51	124	13-13	8	3.68
Phil Paine	R	28	46	0	0	0	73.1	70	7	31	45	5-1	1	3.56
Billy Muffett	R	27	35	6	1	0	84.0	107	11	42	41	4-6	5	4.93
Jim Brosnan†	R	28	33	12	2	0	115.0	107	10	50	65	8-4	7	3.44
Bob Mabe	R	28	31	13	4	0	111.2	113	11	41	74	3-9	0	4.51
Bill Wight†	L	36	28	1	1	0	57.1	64	7	32	18	3-0	2	5.02
Chuck Stobbs†	L	28	17	0	0	0	39.2	40	4	14	25	1-3	1	3.63
Morrie Martin†	L	35	17	0	0	0	24.2	19	3	12	16	3-1	0	4.74
Nels Chittum	R	25	13	2	0	0	29.1	31	5	7	13	0-1	0	6.44
Frank Barnes	R	31	8	1	0	0	19.0	19	3	16	17	1-1	0	7.58
Phil Clark	R	25	7	0	0	0	7.2	11	2	3	1	0-1	1	3.52
Johnny O'Brien	R	27	1	0	0	0	2.0	7	0	2	2	0-0	0	22.50
Tom Flanigan	L	23	1	0	0	0	1.0	2	1	1	0	0-0	0	9.00

1958 Los Angeles Dodgers 7th NL 71-83 .461 21.0 GB

Walter Alston

Player	Gm by Position	B	Age	G	AB	R	H	2B	3B	HR	RBI	BB	SO	SB	Avg	OBP	Slg
John Roseboro	C104,OF5	L	25	114	384	52	104	11	9	14	43	36	56	11	.271	.333	.456
Gil Hodges	1B122,3B15,OF9*	R	34	141	475	68	123	15	1	22	64	52	87	8	.259	.330	.434
Charlie Neal	2B132,SS9	R	27	140	473	87	120	9	6	22	65	61	91	7	.254	.341	.438
Dick Gray	3B55	R	26	58	197	25	49	5	6	9	30	19	30	1	.249	.327	.472
Don Zimmer	SS114,3B12,2B1*	R	27	127	455	52	119	15	2	17	60	28	92	14	.262	.305	.415
Carl Furillo	OF119	R	36	122	411	54	119	19	3	18	83	35	28	0	.290	.343	.482
Gino Cimoli	OF104	R	28	109	325	35	80	6	3	9	27	18	49	3	.246	.292	.366
Duke Snider	OF92	L	31	106	327	45	102	12	3	15	58	32	49	2	.312	.371	.505
Jim Gilliam	OF75,3B44,2B32	S	29	147	555	81	145	25	5	2	43	78	22	18	.261	.352	.335
Norm Larker	OF43,1B35	L	27	99	253	32	70	16	5	4	29	29	21	1	.277	.352	.427
Pee Wee Reese	SS22,3B21	R	39	59	147	21	33	7	2	4	17	26	15	1	.224	.337	.381
Joe Pignatano	C57	R	28	63	142	18	31	4	0	9	17	16	26	4	.218	.306	.437
Don Demeter	OF39	R	23	43	106	11	20	2	0	5	8	5	32	2	.189	.225	.349
Steve Bilko†	1B25	R	29	47	101	13	21	1	2	7	18	8	37	0	.208	.264	.465
Elmer Valo	OF26	L	37	65	101	9	25	2	1	1	14	12	11	0	.248	.322	.317
Bob Lillis	SS19	R	28	20	69	10	27	3	1	1	5	4	2	1	.391	.421	.507
Randy Jackson†	3B17	R	32	35	65	8	12	3	0	1	4	5	10	0	.185	.243	.277
Ron Fairly	OF15	L	19	15	53	6	15	1	0	2	8	6	7	0	.283	.350	.415
Rube Walker	C20	L	32	25	44	3	5	2	0	1	7	5	10	0	.114	.200	.227
Jim Gentile	1B8	L	24	12	30	0	4	1	0	0	4	4	6	0	.133	.235	.167
Frank Howard	OF8	R	21	8	29	3	7	1	0	1	2	1	11	0	.241	.267	.379
Don Miles	OF5	L	22	8	22	0	4	0	0	0	0	0	6	0	.182	.217	.182
Earl Robinson	3B6	R	21	8	15	3	3	0	0	0	0	1	4	0	.200	.250	.200
Bob Wilson	OF1	R	33	3	5	0	1	0	0	0	0	0	1	0	.200	.200	.200

G. Hodges, 1 G at C; D. Zimmer, 1 G at OF

Pitcher	T	Age	G	GS	CG	ShO	IP	H	HR	BB	SO	W-L	Sv	ERA
Johnny Podres	L	25	39	31	10	2	210.1	208	27	78	143	13-15	1	3.72
Don Drysdale	R	21	44	29	6	1	211.2	214	21	72	131	12-13	0	4.17
Sandy Koufax	L	22	40	26	5	0	158.2	132	19	105	131	11-11	1	4.48
Stan Williams	R	21	27	21	3	2	119.0	99	10	65	80	9-7	0	4.01
Danny McDevitt	L	25	13	10	2	0	48.1	71	6	31	26	2-6	0	7.45
Don Newcombe†	R	32	11	8	1	0	34.1	53	11	8	16	0-6	0	7.86
Bob Giallombardo	L	21	6	5	0	0	26.1	29	3	15	14	1-1	0	3.76
Ralph Mauriello	R	23	3	2	0	0	11.2	10	1	8	11	1-1	0	4.63
Clem Labine	R	31	52	2	0	0	104.0	112	8	33	43	6-6	14	4.15
Johnny Klippstein†	R	30	45	0	0	0	90.0	81	12	44	73	3-5	9	3.80
Fred Kipp	L	26	40	9	0	0	102.1	107	16	45	58	6-6	0	5.01
Ed Roebuck	R	26	32	0	0	0	44.0	45	9	15	26	0-1	5	3.48
Carl Erskine	R	31	31	9	2	1	98.1	115	14	35	54	4-4	0	5.13
Don Bessent	R	27	19	0	0	0	24.1	24	3	17	13	1-0	0	3.33
Babe Birrer	R	29	16	0	0	0	34.0	43	4	7	16	0-0	1	4.50
Roger Craig	R	28	9	2	1	0	32.0	30	3	12	16	2-1	0	4.50
Larry Sherry	R	22	5	0	0	0	4.1	10	0	7	2	0-0	0	12.46
Ron Negray	R	28	4	0	0	0	11.1	12	4	7	2	0-0	0	7.15
Jackie Collum	L	31	2	0	0	0	3.1	4	2	2	0	0-0	0	8.10

1958 Philadelphia Phillies 8th NL 69-85 .448 23.0 GB

Mayo Smith (39-45)/Eddie Sawyer (30-40)

Player	Gm by Position	B	Age	G	AB	R	H	2B	3B	HR	RBI	BB	SO	SB	Avg	OBP	Slg
Stan Lopata	C80	R	32	86	258	36	64	9	0	9	33	60	63	0	.248	.391	.388
Ed Bouchee	1B89	L	25	89	334	55	86	19	5	9	39	51	74	1	.257	.355	.425
Solly Hemus	2B85,3B1	L	35	105	334	53	95	14	3	8	36	51	34	3	.284	.390	.416
Puddin' Head Jones	3B110,1B1	R	32	118	398	52	108	15	1	14	60	49	45	1	.271	.351	.420
Chico Fernandez	SS148	R	26	148	522	38	120	18	5	6	51	37	48	12	.230	.280	.318
Richie Ashburn	OF152	L	31	152	615	98	215	24	13	2	33	97	48	30	.350	.440	.441
Wally Post	OF91	R	28	110	379	51	107	21	3	12	62	32	74	0	.282	.340	.449
Harry Anderson	OF87,1B49	L	26	140	515	80	155	34	6	23	97	59	95	0	.301	.373	.524
Ted Kazanski	2B59,SS22,3B16	R	24	95	289	21	66	12	2	3	35	22	34	2	.228	.291	.315
Rip Repulski	OF56	R	30	85	238	33	58	9	4	13	40	15	47	0	.244	.296	.479
Dave Philley	OF24,1B18	S	38	91	207	30	64	11	4	3	31	15	20	1	.309	.357	.444
Bob Bowman	OF57	R	27	91	184	31	53	11	2	8	24	16	30	0	.288	.343	.500
Carl Sawatski†	C53	L	30	60	183	12	42	4	1	5	12	16	42	0	.230	.300	.344
Granny Hamner	3B22,2B11,SS3	R	31	35	133	18	40	7	3	2	18	8	16	0	.301	.340	.444
Chuck Essegian	OF30	R	26	39	114	15	28	5	2	5	16	12	34	0	.246	.317	.456
Pancho Herrera	3B16,1B11	R	24	29	63	5	17	3	0	1	6	7	15	1	.270	.347	.365
Bobby Young	2B21	L	33	32	60	7	14	1	1	1	4	1	5	0	.233	.246	.333
Jim Hegan†	C25	R	37	25	59	5	13	6	0	0	6	4	16	0	.220	.270	.322
Joe Lonnett	C15	R	31	17	50	0	7	2	0	0	2	2	11	0	.140	.167	.180
Jimmie Coker	C2	R	22	2	6	0	1	0	0	0	0	0	0	0	.167	.167	.167
Roy Smalley	SS1	R	32	1	2	0	0	0	0	0	0	0	0	0	.000	.000	.000
Mack Burk		R	23	1	1	0	0	0	0	0	0	0	0	0	.000	.000	.000

Pitcher	T	Age	G	GS	CG	ShO	IP	H	HR	BB	SO	W-L	Sv	ERA
Robin Roberts	R	31	35	34	21	1	269.2	270	30	51	130	17-14	0	3.24
Ray Semproch	R	27	36	30	12	2	204.1	211	25	58	92	13-11	0	3.92
Jack Sanford	R	29	38	27	7	2	186.2	197	15	81	106	10-13	0	4.44
Curt Simmons	L	29	29	27	7	1	168.1	196	11	40	78	7-14	1	4.38
Don Cardwell	R	22	16	14	3	0	107.2	99	16	37	77	3-6	0	4.51
Bob Conley	R	24	2	2	0	0	8.1	9	0	1	0	0-0	0	7.56
Jim Owens	R	24	1	1	0	0	7.0	4	1	5	3	1-0	0	2.57
Turk Farrell	R	24	54	0	0	0	94.0	84	7	40	73	8-9	11	3.35
Jim Hearn	R	37	39	1	0	0	73.1	88	6	27	33	5-3	0	4.17
Jack Meyer	R	26	37	5	1	0	90.1	77	8	33	87	3-6	2	3.59
Seth Morehead	L	23	27	11	0	0	92.1	121	8	26	54	1-6	0	5.85
Bob Miller	R	32	17	0	0	0	22.1	36	7	9	9	1-1	0	11.69
Johnny Gray	R	30	15	0	0	0	17.1	12	3	14	10	0-0	0	4.15
Warren Hacker	R	33	9	1	0	0	17.0	24	2	8	4	0-1	0	7.41
Don Erickson	R	26	9	0	0	0	11.2	11	3	9	9	0-1	1	4.63
John Anderson	R	25	5	1	0	0	16.0	26	5	4	9	0-0	0	7.88
Angelo LiPetri	R	27	4	0	0	0	4.0	6	1	0	1	0-0	0	11.25
Hank Mason	R	27	1	0	0	0	5.0	7	0	2	3	0-0	0	10.80
Tom Qualters†	R	23	1	0	0	0	2.0	2	0	1	0	0-0	0	4.50

»1959 Chicago White Sox 1st AL 94-60 .610 —

Al Lopez

Player	Gm by Position	B	Age	G	AB	R	H	2B	3B	HR	RBI	BB	SO	SB	Avg	OBP	Slg
Sherm Lollar	C122,1B24	R	34	140	505	63	134	22	3	22	84	55	49	4	.265	.345	.451
Earl Torgeson	1B103	L	35	127	277	40	61	5	3	9	45	62	55	7	.220	.359	.357
Nellie Fox	2B156	L	31	156	624	84	191	34	6	2	70	71	13	5	.306	.380	.389
Bubba Phillips	3B100,OF23	R	31	117	379	43	100	27	1	5	40	27	28	1	.264	.319	.380
Luis Aparicio	SS152	R	25	152	612	98	157	18	5	6	51	53	40	56	.257	.316	.332
Jim Landis	OF148	R	25	149	515	78	140	26	7	5	60	78	68	20	.272	.370	.379
Al Smith	OF128,3B1	R	31	129	472	65	112	16	4	17	55	46	74	7	.237	.311	.396
Jim Rivera	OF69	L	36	80	177	18	39	9	4	4	19	11	19	5	.220	.266	.384
Billy Goodman	3B74,2B3	L	33	104	268	21	67	14	1	1	28	19	20	3	.250	.304	.321
Jim McAnany	OF67	R	22	67	210	22	58	9	3	0	27	19	26	2	.276	.339	.348
John Romano	C38	R	24	53	126	20	37	5	1	5	25	23	18	0	.294	.407	.468
Johnny Callison	OF41	L	20	49	104	12	18	3	0	3	12	13	20	0	.173	.271	.288
Norm Cash	1B31	L	24	58	104	16	25	0	1	4	16	18	9	1	.240	.372	.375
Ted Kluszewski†	1B29	L	34	31	101	11	30	2	1	2	10	9	10	0	.297	.351	.396
Del Ennis†	OF25	R	34	26	96	10	21	6	0	2	7	4	10	0	.219	.250	.344
Harry Simpson†	OF12,1B1	L	33	38	75	5	14	5	1	2	13	4	14	0	.187	.228	.360
Sammy Esposito	3B45,SS14,2B2	R	27	69	66	12	11	1	0	1	5	11	16	0	.167	.282	.227
Earl Battey	C20	R	24	26	64	9	14	1	2	2	7	8	13	0	.219	.306	.391
Larry Doby†	OF12,1B2	L	35	21	58	1	14	1	1	0	9	2	13	1	.241	.267	.293
Ray Boone†	1B6	R	35	9	21	3	5	0	0	1	5	7	5	1	.238	.400	.381
Ron Jackson	1B5	R	25	10	14	3	3	1	0	1	2	1	0	0	.214	.313	.500
Lou Skizas	OF6	R	27	8	13	3	1	0	0	0	0	3	2	0	.077	.250	.077
Joe Hicks	OF4	L	26	6	7	0	3	0	0	0	0	1	1	0	.429	.500	.429
J.C. Martin	3B2	L	22	3	4	0	1	0	0	0	1	0	1	0	.250	.250	.250
Don Mueller		L	32	4	4	0	2	0	0	0	0	0	0	0	.500	.500	.500
Cam Carreon	C1	R	21	1	1	0	0	0	0	0	0	0	0	0	.000	.000	.000

Pitcher	T	Age	G	GS	CG	ShO	IP	H	HR	BB	SO	W-L	Sv	ERA
Early Wynn	R	39	37	37	14	5	255.2	202	20	119	179	22-10	0	3.17
Billy Pierce	L	32	34	33	12	2	224.0	217	26	62	114	14-15	0	3.62
Dick Donovan	R	31	31	29	5	1	179.2	171	15	58	71	9-10	0	3.66
Bob Shaw	R	26	47	26	8	3	230.2	217	15	54	89	18-6	3	2.69
Barry Latman	R	23	37	21	5	2	156.0	138	15	72	97	8-5	0	3.75
Gerry Staley	R	38	67	0	0	0	116.1	111	5	25	54	8-5	14	2.24
Turk Lown	R	35	60	0	0	0	93.1	73	12	42	63	9-2	15	2.89
Rudy Arias	L	28	34	0	0	0	44.0	49	7	20	28	2-0	2	4.09
Ray Moore	R	33	29	8	0	0	89.2	86	10	46	49	3-6	0	4.12
Ken McBride	R	23	11	2	0	0	22.2	20	1	17	12	0-1	1	3.18
Don Rudolph†	L	27	4	0	0	0	3.0	4	0	2	0	0-0	1	0.00
Claude Raymond	R	22	3	0	0	0	4.0	5	2	2	1	0-0	0	9.00
Joe Stanka	R	27	2	0	0	0	5.1	2	1	4	3	1-0	0	3.38
Gary Peters	L	22	2	0	0	0	1.0	2	0	2	1	0-0	0	0.00

1959 Cleveland Indians 2nd AL 89-65 .578 5.0 GB

Joe Gordon

Player	Gm by Position	B	Age	G	AB	R	H	2B	3B	HR	RBI	BB	SO	SB	Avg	OBP	Slg
Russ Nixon	C74	L	24	82	258	23	62	10	3	1	29	15	28	0	.240	.277	.314
Vic Power	1B121,2B21,3B7	R	31	147	595	102	172	31	6	10	60	40	22	9	.289	.334	.412
Billy Martin	2B67,3B4	R	31	73	242	37	63	7	0	9	24	8	18	0	.260	.290	.401
George Strickland	3B80,SS50,2B4	R	33	132	441	55	105	15	2	3	48	51	64	1	.238	.313	.302
Woodie Held	SS103,3B40,OF6*	R	27	143	525	82	132	19	3	29	71	46	118	1	.251	.313	.465
Rocky Colavito	OF154	R	25	154	588	90	151	24	0	42	111	71	86	3	.257	.337	.512
Minnie Minoso	OF148	R	36	148	570	92	172	32	0	21	92	54	46	8	.302	.377	.468
Jimmy Piersall	OF91,3B1	R	29	100	317	42	78	13	2	4	30	25	31	6	.246	.303	.338
Tito Francona	OF64,1B35	L	25	122	399	68	145	17	2	20	79	35	42	2	.363	.414	.566
Jim Baxes†	2B48,3B22	R	30	77	247	35	59	11	0	15	34	21	47	0	.239	.299	.466
Dick Brown	C48	R	24	48	141	15	31	7	0	5	16	11	39	0	.220	.288	.376
Ed Fitz Gerald†	C45	R	35	49	129	12	35	6	1	1	4	12	14	0	.271	.343	.357
Ray Webster	2B24,3B4	R	21	40	74	10	15	2	1	2	10	5	7	1	.203	.253	.338
Granny Hamner†	SS10,2B7,3B5	R	32	27	67	4	11	1	1	1	3	1	8	0	.164	.174	.254
Carroll Hardy	OF15	R	26	32	53	12	11	1	0	0	2	3	7	1	.208	.250	.226
Chuck Tanner	OF10	L	29	14	48	6	12	2	0	1	5	2	9	0	.250	.280	.354
Gene Leek	3B13,SS1	R	22	13	36	7	8	3	0	1	5	2	7	0	.222	.263	.389
Hal Naragon†	C10	L	30	14	36	6	10	4	1	0	5	3	2	0	.278	.341	.444
Elmer Valo	OF2	L	38	34	24	3	7	0	0	0	5	7	0	0	.292	.424	.292
P. Head Jones†	3B4	R	33	11	18	1	4	1	0	0	1	1	3	0	.222	.263	.278
Billy Moran	2B6,SS5	R	25	11	17	1	5	0	0	0	2	0	1	0	.294	.294	.294
Gordy Coleman	1B3	L	24	6	15	5	8	0	1	0	2	1	2	0	.533	.563	.667
Don Dillard		L	22	10	10	0	4	0	0	0	1	0	2	0	.400	.400	.400
Jim Bolger†		R	27	8	7	0	0	0	0	0	0	1	1	0	.000	.125	.000
Randy Jackson†	3B2	R	33	3	7	0	1	0	0	0	0	0	1	0	.143	.143	.143

W. Held, 3 G at 2B

Pitcher	T	Age	G	GS	CG	ShO	IP	H	HR	BB	SO	W-L	Sv	ERA
Cal McLish	R	33	35	32	13	0	235.1	253	26	72	113	19-8	1	3.63
Gary Bell	R	22	44	28	12	1	234.0	208	28	105	136	16-11	5	4.04
Herb Score	L	26	30	25	9	1	160.2	123	28	115	147	9-11	0	4.71
Mudcat Grant	R	23	38	19	6	1	165.1	140	23	81	85	10-7	3	4.14
Don Ferrarese	L	30	15	10	4	0	76.0	58	6	51	45	5-3	0	3.20
Jake Striker	L	25	1	1	0	0	6.2	8	0	4	5	1-0	0	2.70
Jim Perry	R	23	44	13	8	2	153.0	122	10	55	79	12-10	4	2.65
Mike Garcia	R	35	29	8	1	0	72.0	72	4	31	49	3-6	1	4.00
Al Cicotte	R	29	26	1	0	0	44.0	46	4	25	23	3-1	1	5.32
Bobby Locke	R	25	24	7	0	0	77.2	66	6	41	40	3-2	2	3.13
Dick Brodowski	R	26	18	0	0	0	30.0	19	3	21	9	2-2	5	1.80
Jack Harshman†	L	31	13	6	5	1	66.0	46	6	13	35	5-1	1	2.59
Riverboat Smith†	L	31	12	3	0	0	29.1	31	2	12	17	0-1	0	5.22
Bud Podbielan	R	35	6	0	0	0	12.1	17	1	2	5	0-1	0	5.84
H. Robinson†	R	29	5	0	0	0	8.2	9	0	4	6	1-0	0	4.15
John Briggs	R	25	4	1	0	0	12.2	12	1	3	5	0-1	0	2.13

1959 New York Yankees 3rd AL 79-75 .513 15.0 GB

Casey Stengel

Player	Gm by Position	B	Age	G	AB	R	H	2B	3B	HR	RBI	BB	SO	SB	Avg	OBP	Slg
Yogi Berra	C116,OF7	L	34	131	472	64	134	25	1	19	69	43	38	1	.284	.347	.462
Bill Skowron	1B72	R	28	74	282	39	84	13	5	15	59	20	47	1	.298	.349	.539
Bobby Richardson	2B109,SS14,3B12	R	23	134	469	53	141	18	6	2	33	26	20	5	.301	.335	.377
Hector Lopez†	3B76,OF35	R	29	112	406	60	115	16	2	16	69	28	54	3	.283	.336	.451
Tony Kubek	SS67,OF53,3B17*	L	22	132	512	67	143	25	7	6	51	24	46	3	.279	.313	.391
Mickey Mantle	OF143	S	27	144	541	104	154	23	4	31	75	93	126	21	.285	.390	.514
Hank Bauer	OF111	R	36	114	341	44	81	20	0	9	39	33	54	4	.238	.307	.375
Norm Siebern	OF93,1B2	L	25	120	380	52	103	17	0	11	53	41	71	3	.271	.341	.403
Elston Howard	1B50,C43,OF28	R	30	125	443	59	121	24	6	18	73	20	57	0	.273	.306	.476
Gil McDougald	2B53,SS52,3B25	R	31	127	434	44	109	16	8	4	34	35	40	0	.251	.309	.353
Marv Throneberry	1B54,OF13	L	25	80	192	27	46	5	0	8	22	18	51	0	.240	.302	.391
Clete Boyer	SS26,3B16	R	22	47	114	4	20	2	0	0	3	6	23	1	.175	.215	.193
Andy Carey	3B34	R	27	41	101	11	26	1	0	3	9	7	17	1	.257	.306	.356
Enos Slaughter†	OF26	L	43	74	99	10	17	2	0	6	21	13	19	1	.172	.265	.374
Johnny Blanchard	C12,OF8,1B1	L	26	49	59	6	10	1	0	2	4	7	12	0	.169	.258	.288
Jerry Lumpe†	3B12,SS4,2B1	L	26	18	45	2	10	0	0	0	2	6	7	0	.222	.314	.222
Fritz Brickell	SS15,2B3	R	24	18	39	4	10	1	0	1	4	1	10	0	.256	.275	.359
Jim Pisoni†	OF15	R	29	17	17	2	3	0	1	0	1	1	9	0	.176	.222	.294
Ken Hunt	OF5	R	24	6	12	2	4	1	0	0	1	0	3	0	.333	.308	.417
Gordie Windhorn	OF4	R	25	7	11	0	0	0	0	0	0	0	3	0	.000	.000	.000

T. Kubek, 1 G at 2B

Pitcher	T	Age	G	GS	CG	ShO	IP	H	HR	BB	SO	W-L	Sv	ERA
Whitey Ford	L	30	35	29	9	2	204.0	194	13	89	114	16-10	1	3.04
Art Ditmar	R	30	38	25	7	1	202.0	156	17	52	96	13-9	1	2.90
Bob Turley	R	28	33	22	7	3	154.1	141	15	83	111	8-11	0	4.32
Duke Maas	R	30	38	21	3	1	138.0	149	14	53	67	14-8	4	4.43
Don Larsen	R	29	25	18	3	1	124.2	122	14	76	69	6-7	0	4.33
Ralph Terry†	R	23	24	16	5	1	127.1	130	7	30	55	3-7	0	3.39
Mark Freeman†	R	28	1	1	0	0	7.0	6	0	2	4	0-0	0	2.57
Ryne Duren	R	30	41	0	0	0	76.2	49	6	43	96	3-6	14	1.88
Jim Coates	R	26	37	4	2	0	100.1	89	10	36	64	6-1	3	2.87
Bobby Shantz	L	33	33	4	2	2	94.2	64	4	33	66	7-3	3	2.38
Eli Grba	R	24	19	6	0	0	50.1	52	6	39	23	2-5	0	6.44
Jim Bronstad	R	23	16	3	0	0	29.1	34	2	13	14	0-3	2	5.22
Gary Blaylock†	R	27	15	1	0	0	25.2	30	0	15	20	0-1	0	3.51
Johnny Kucks†	R	25	9	1	0	0	16.2	21	5	9	9	0-1	0	8.64
Tom Sturdivant†	R	29	7	3	0	0	25.1	20	4	9	16	0-2	0	4.97
John Gabler	R	28	3	1	0	0	19.1	21	1	10	11	1-1	0	2.79
Zack Monroe	R	27	3	0	0	0	3.1	3	2	2	1	0-0	0	5.40

1959 Detroit Tigers 4th AL 76-78 .494 18.0 GB

Bill Norman (2-15)/Jimmy Dykes (74-63)

Player	Gm by Position	B	Age	G	AB	R	H	2B	3B	HR	RBI	BB	SO	SB	Avg	OBP	Slg
Lou Berberet	C95	L	29	100	338	38	73	8	2	13	44	35	59	0	.216	.284	.367
Gail Harris	1B93	L	27	114	349	39	77	4	3	9	39	29	49	0	.221	.290	.327
Frank Bolling	2B126	R	27	127	459	56	122	18	3	13	55	45	37	2	.266	.339	.403
Eddie Yost	3B146,2B1	R	32	148	521	115	145	19	0	21	61	135	77	9	.278	.435	.436
Rocky Bridges	SS110,2B5	R	31	116	381	38	102	16	3	3	35	30	35	1	.268	.320	.349
Harvey Kuenn	OF137	R	28	139	561	99	198	42	7	9	71	48	37	7	.353	.402	.501
Charlie Maxwell	OF136	L	32	145	518	81	130	12	2	31	95	81	91	0	.251	.357	.461
Al Kaline	OF136	R	24	136	511	86	167	19	2	27	94	72	42	10	.327	.410	.530
Red Wilson	C64	R	30	67	228	28	60	17	2	4	35	10	23	2	.263	.295	.408
Ted Lepcio†	SS35,2B24,3B11	R	28	76	215	25	60	8	0	7	24	17	49	2	.279	.332	.414
Bobo Osborne	1B56,OF1	L	23	86	209	27	40	7	1	3	21	16	41	1	.191	.254	.278
Gus Zernial	1B32,OF1	R	36	60	132	11	30	4	0	7	26	7	27	0	.227	.262	.417
Neil Chrisley	OF21	L	27	65	106	7	14	3	0	6	11	12	10	0	.132	.225	.330
Johnny Groth	OF41	R	32	55	102	12	24	7	1	1	10	7	14	0	.235	.284	.353
Coot Veal	SS72	R	26	77	89	12	18	1	0	1	15	8	7	0	.202	.273	.247
Larry Doby†	OF16	L	35	18	55	5	12	3	1	0	4	8	9	0	.218	.313	.309
Steve Demeter	3B4	R	24	11	18	1	2	1	0	0	1	0	1	0	.111	.111	.167
Ron Shoop	C3	R	27	3	7	1	1	0	0	0	1	0	1	0	.143	.143	.143
Charlie Lau	C2	L	26	2	6	0	1	0	0	0	0	0	2	0	.167	.167	.167
Ossie Alvarez		R	25	8	2	0	1	0	0	0	0	0	1	0	.500	.500	.500

Pitcher	T	Age	G	GS	CG	ShO	IP	H	HR	BB	SO	W-L	Sv	ERA
Paul Foytack	R	28	39	37	11	2	240.1	239	34	64	110	14-14	1	4.64
Jim Bunning	R	27	40	35	14	1	249.2	220	37	75	201	17-13	1	3.89
Frank Lary	R	29	32	32	11	3	223.0	225	23	46	137	17-10	0	3.55
Don Mossi	L	30	34	30	15	3	228.0	210	20	49	125	17-9	0	3.36
Billy Hoeft†	L	27	2	2	0	0	9.0	6	0	4	2	1-1	0	5.00
Jim Proctor	R	23	2	1	0	0	2.2	8	0	3	0	0-1	0	16.88
Bob Bruce	R	26	2	1	0	0	2.0	2	1	3	1	0-1	0	9.00
Tom Morgan	R	29	46	1	0	0	92.2	94	11	18	39	1-4	9	3.98
Ray Narleski	R	30	42	10	1	0	104.1	105	21	59	71	4-12	5	5.78
Dave Sisler†	R	27	32	0	0	0	51.2	46	4	36	29	1-3	7	4.01
Pete Burnside	L	28	30	0	0	0	62.0	55	7	25	49	1-3	1	3.77
Barney Schultz	R	32	13	0	0	0	18.1	17	1	14	17	1-2	0	4.42
Jerry Davie	R	26	11	5	1	0	36.2	40	8	17	20	2-2	0	4.17
George Susce	R	27	9	0	0	0	14.2	24	4	9	9	0-0	0	12.89
Bob Smith†	L	28	9	0	0	0	11.0	20	5	3	10	0-3	0	8.18
Jim Stump	R	27	5	0	0	0	11.1	12	1	4	6	0-0	0	2.38
Hank Aguirre	L	28	3	0	0	0	2.2	4	0	3	3	0-0	0	3.38

1959 Boston Red Sox 5th AL 75-79 .487 19.0 GB

Pinky Higgins (31-42)/Rudy York (0-1)/Billy Jurges (44-36)

Player	Gm by Position	B	Age	G	AB	R	H	2B	3B	HR	RBI	BB	SO	SB	Avg	OBP	Slg
Sammy White	C119	R	30	119	377	34	107	13	4	1	42	23	39	4	.284	.324	.347
Dick Gernert	1B75,OF25	R	30	117	298	41	78	14	1	11	42	52	49	1	.262	.369	.426
Pete Runnels	2B101,1B44,SS9	L	31	147	560	95	176	33	6	6	57	95	48	6	.314	.415	.427
Frank Malzone	3B154	R	29	154	604	90	169	34	2	19	92	42	58	6	.280	.323	.437
Don Buddin	SS150	R	25	151	485	75	117	24	1	10	53	92	99	6	.241	.366	.357
Jackie Jensen	OF146	R	32	148	535	101	148	31	0	28	112	88	67	20	.277	.372	.492
Gary Geiger	OF95	L	22	120	335	45	82	10	4	11	48	21	55	9	.245	.289	.397
Gene Stephens	OF85	L	26	92	270	34	75	13	1	3	39	29	33	5	.278	.353	.367
Ted Williams	OF76	L	40	103	272	32	69	15	0	10	43	52	27	0	.254	.372	.419
Marty Keough	OF69,1B3	L	24	96	251	40	61	13	5	7	27	26	40	3	.243	.320	.418
Vic Wertz	1B64	L	34	94	247	38	68	13	0	7	49	22	32	0	.275	.337	.413
Pumpsie Green	2B45,SS1	S	25	50	172	30	40	6	3	1	10	29	22	4	.233	.350	.320
Pete Daley	C58	R	29	65	169	9	38	7	0	1	11	13	31	1	.225	.279	.284
Jim Busby	OF34	R	32	61	102	16	23	8	0	1	5	5	18	0	.225	.266	.333
Bobby Avila†	2B11	R	35	22	45	7	11	0	0	3	6	6	11	0	.244	.333	.444
Jim Mahoney	SS30	R	25	31	23	10	3	0	0	1	4	3	7	0	.130	.231	.261
Bill Renna	OF7	R	34	14	22	2	2	0	0	0	2	5	9	0	.091	.259	.091
Jerry Mallett	OF4	R	23	4	15	1	4	0	0	0	1	1	3	0	.267	.313	.267
Billy Consolo†	SS2	R	24	10	14	3	3	1	0	0	0	2	5	0	.214	.313	.286
Herb Plews†	2B2	L	31	13	12	0	1	1	0	0	0	0	4	0	.083	.083	.167
Don Gile	C3	R	24	3	10	1	2	1	0	0	1	0	2	0	.200	.250	.300
Ted Lepcio†	2B1	R	28	3	3	1	1	1	0	0	1	0	2	0	.333	.333	.667
Haywood Sullivan	C2	R	28	4	2	0	0	0	0	0	0	1	1	0	.000	.333	.000

Pitcher	T	Age	G	GS	CG	ShO	IP	H	HR	BB	SO	W-L	Sv	ERA
Tom Brewer	R	27	36	32	11	3	215.1	219	14	88	121	10-12	2	3.76
Jerry Casale	R	25	31	26	9	3	179.2	162	20	89	93	13-8	0	4.31
Frank Sullivan	R	29	30	26	5	2	177.2	172	17	67	107	9-11	1	3.95
Bill Monbouquette	R	22	34	17	4	0	151.2	165	15	33	87	7-7	0	4.15
Ike Delock	R	29	28	17	4	0	134.1	120	12	62	55	11-6	0	2.95
Ted Wills	L	25	9	8	2	0	56.1	68	9	24	24	2-6	0	5.27
Billy Hoeft†	L	27	5	3	0	0	17.2	22	1	8	8	0-3	0	5.60
Herb Moford	R	30	4	2	0	0	8.2	10	3	6	7	0-2	0	11.42
Mike Fornieles	R	27	46	0	0	0	82.0	77	6	29	54	5-3	11	3.07
Leo Kiely	L	29	41	0	0	0	55.2	67	8	18	30	3-3	7	4.20
Frank Baumann	L	25	26	10	2	0	95.2	96	11	55	48	6-4	1	4.05
Murray Wall†	R	32	26	0	0	0	49.0	57	7	26	14	2-5	3	5.51
Nels Chittum	R	26	21	0	0	0	30.1	29	0	11	12	3-0	0	1.19
Al Schroll†	R	27	14	5	1	0	46.0	47	3	22	26	1-4	0	4.70
Earl Wilson	R	24	9	4	0	0	23.2	21	2	31	17	1-1	0	6.08
Jack Harshman†	L	31	8	2	0	0	24.2	29	2	10	14	2-3	0	6.57
Ted Bowsfield	L	24	5	2	0	0	9.0	16	2	9	4	0-1	0	15.00
Dave Sisler†	R	27	3	0	0	0	6.2	9	3	1	3	0-0	0	6.75

1959 Baltimore Orioles 6th AL 74-80 .481 20.0 GB

Paul Richards

Player	Gm by Position	B	Age	G	AB	R	H	2B	3B	HR	RBI	BB	SO	SB	Avg	OBP	Slg
Gus Triandos	C125	R	28	126	393	43	85	7	1	25	73	65	56	0	.216	.330	.430
Bob Boyd	1B109	L	33	128	415	42	110	20	2	3	41	29	14	3	.265	.312	.345
Billy Gardner	2B139,3B1,SS1	R	31	140	401	34	87	13	2	6	27	38	61	2	.217	.284	.304
Brooks Robinson	3B87,2B1	R	22	88	313	29	89	15	2	4	24	17	37	2	.284	.325	.383
Chico Carrasquel	SS89,2B22,3B2*	R	33	114	346	28	77	13	0	4	28	34	41	2	.223	.292	.295
Willie Tasby	OF137	R	26	142	505	69	126	16	5	13	48	34	80	3	.250	.303	.378
Gene Woodling	OF124	L	36	140	440	63	132	22	2	14	77	78	35	1	.300	.402	.455
Al Pilarcik	OF106	L	28	130	273	37	77	12	1	3	16	30	25	9	.282	.355	.366
Bob Nieman	OF97	R	32	118	360	49	105	18	2	21	60	42	55	1	.292	.367	.528
Billy Klaus	SS59,3B49,2B1	L	30	104	321	33	80	11	0	3	25	51	38	2	.249	.350	.312
Joe Ginsberg	C62	L	32	65	166	14	30	2	0	1	14	21	13	1	.181	.268	.211
Walt Dropo†	1B54,3B2	R	36	62	151	17	42	9	0	6	21	12	20	0	.278	.329	.457
Albie Pearson†	OF50	L	24	80	138	22	32	4	2	0	6	13	5	4	.232	.296	.290
Jim Finigan	3B42,2B6,SS2	R	30	48	119	14	30	6	0	1	10	9	10	1	.252	.300	.328
Willie Miranda	SS47,3B11,2B5	S	33	65	88	8	14	5	0	0	7	7	16	0	.159	.221	.216
Barry Shetrone	OF23	L	20	33	79	8	16	1	1	0	5	5	9	3	.203	.247	.241
Whitey Lockman†	1B22,2B5,OF1	L	32	38	69	7	15	1	1	0	2	8	4	0	.217	.299	.261
Bob Hale	1B8	L	25	40	54	2	10	3	0	0	7	2	6	0	.185	.214	.241
Bobby Avila†	OF10,2B8,3B1	R	35	20	47	1	8	0	0	0	0	4	5	0	.170	.235	.170
Jerry Adair	2B11,SS1	R	22	12	35	3	11	0	1	0	2	1	5	0	.314	.333	.371
Joe Taylor	OF12	R	33	14	32	2	5	1	0	1	2	11	5	0	.156	.372	.281
Lenny Green†	OF23	L	26	27	24	3	7	0	0	1	2	1	3	0	.292	.346	.417
Fred Valentine	OF8	S	24	12	19	0	6	0	0	0	1	3	4	0	.316	.409	.316
Leo Burke	2B2,3B2	R	25	5	10	0	2	0	0	0	0	1	5	0	.200	.273	.200
Ron Hansen	SS2	R	21	2	4	0	0	0	0	0	0	1	1	0	.000	.200	.000
Bob Saverine		S	18	1	0	1	0	0	0	0	0	0	0	0	—	—	—

C. Carrasquel, 1 G at 1B

Pitcher	T	Age	G	GS	CG	ShO	IP	H	HR	BB	SO	W-L	Sv	ERA
Hoyt Wilhelm	R	35	32	27	13	3	226.0	178	13	77	139	15-11	0	2.19
Milt Pappas	R	20	33	27	15	4	209.1	175	8	75	120	15-9	3	3.27
Billy O'Dell	L	26	38	24	6	2	199.1	163	18	67	88	10-12	1	2.93
Jerry Walker	R	20	30	22	7	2	182.0	160	13	52	100	11-10	4	2.92
Hal Brown	R	34	31	21	2	0	164.0	158	16	32	81	11-9	3	3.79
Arnie Portocarrero	R	27	27	14	1	0	90.0	107	10	32	23	2-7	0	6.80
Jack Harshman†	L	31	14	8	0	0	47.1	58	6	28	24	0-6	0	6.85
Billy Loes	R	29	37	0	0	0	64.1	58	5	25	34	4-7	14	4.06
Ernie Johnson	R	35	31	1	0	0	50.1	57	6	19	29	4-1	1	4.11
Jack Fisher	R	20	27	7	1	1	88.2	76	7	38	52	1-6	2	3.05
Billy Hoeft†	L	27	16	3	0	0	41.0	50	6	19	30	1-1	0	5.71
Wes Stock	R	25	7	0	0	0	12.2	16	1	2	8	0-0	1	3.55
George Zuverink	R	34	6	0	0	0	13.0	15	1	6	1	0-1	0	4.15
George Bamberger	R	33	3	1	0	0	8.1	15	1	2	2	0-0	1	7.56
Rip Coleman†	L	27	3	0	0	0	4.0	4	0	2	4	0-0	0	0.00

1959 Kansas City Athletics 7th AL 66-88 .429 28.0 GB

Harry Craft

Player	Gm by Position	B	Age	G	AB	R	H	2B	3B	HR	RBI	BB	SO	SB	Avg	OBP	Slg
Frank House	C95	L	29	98	347	32	82	14	3	1	30	20	23	0	.236	.282	.303
Kent Hadley	1B95	L	24	113	288	40	73	11	1	10	39	24	74	1	.253	.310	.403
Wayne Terwilliger	2B63,SS2,3B1	R	34	74	180	27	48	11	0	2	18	19	31	2	.267	.335	.361
Dick Williams	3B80,1B32,OF23*	R	30	130	488	72	130	33	1	16	75	28	60	4	.266	.309	.436
Joe DeMaestri	SS115	R	30	118	352	31	86	16	5	6	34	28	65	1	.244	.305	.369
Bill Tuttle	OF121	R	29	126	463	74	139	19	6	7	43	48	38	10	.300	.369	.413
Bob Cerv	OF119	R	33	125	463	61	132	22	4	20	87	35	87	3	.285	.332	.479
Roger Maris	OF117	L	24	122	433	69	118	21	7	16	72	58	53	2	.273	.359	.464
Jerry Lumpe†	2B61,SS56,3B4	L	26	108	403	47	98	11	5	3	28	41	32	2	.243	.313	.318
Hal Smith	3B77,C22	R	28	108	292	36	84	12	0	5	31	34	39	0	.288	.367	.380
Russ Snyder	OF64	L	25	73	243	41	76	13	2	3	21	19	29	6	.313	.367	.420
Harry Chiti	C47	R	26	55	162	20	44	11	1	5	25	17	26	0	.272	.344	.444
Hector Lopez†	2B33	R	29	35	135	22	38	10	3	6	24	8	23	1	.281	.324	.533
Ray Boone†	1B38,3B3	R	35	61	132	19	36	6	0	2	12	27	17	1	.273	.396	.364
Whitey Herzog	OF34,1B1	L	27	38	123	25	36	7	1	1	9	34	23	1	.293	.446	.390
Preston Ward	1B22,OF1	L	31	58	109	8	27	4	1	2	19	7	12	0	.248	.286	.358
Zeke Bella	OF25,1B1	L	28	47	82	10	17	2	1	1	9	9	14	0	.207	.293	.293
Lou Klimchock	2B16	L	19	17	66	10	18	1	0	4	13	1	6	0	.273	.284	.470
Ray Jablonski†	3B17	R	32	25	65	4	17	1	0	2	8	3	11	0	.262	.294	.369
Joe Morgan†	3B2	L	28	20	21	2	4	0	1	0	3	3	7	0	.190	.292	.286
Harry Simpson†	1B4	L	33	8	14	1	4	0	0	1	2	2	4	0	.286	.389	.500
Tom Carroll	SS9,3B3	R	22	14	7	1	1	0	0	0	1	0	1	0	.143	.143	.143
Bob Martyn		L	28	1	1	0	0	0	0	0	0	0	0	0	.000	.000	.000

D. Williams, 3 G at 2B

Pitcher	T	Age	G	GS	CG	ShO	IP	H	HR	BB	SO	W-L	Sv	ERA
Ned Garver	R	33	32	30	9	2	201.1	214	22	42	61	10-13	1	3.71
Bud Daley	L	26	39	29	12	2	216.1	212	24	62	125	16-13	1	3.16
Ray Herbert	R	29	37	26	10	2	183.2	196	24	62	99	11-11	1	4.85
Johnny Kucks†	R	25	33	23	6	1	151.1	163	10	42	51	8-11	1	3.87
Ralph Terry†	R	23	9	7	2	0	46.1	56	9	19	35	2-4	0	5.24
Howie Reed	R	22	6	3	0	0	20.2	26	3	10	11	0-3	0	7.40
Ken Johnson	R	26	2	2	0	0	11.0	11	2	5	8	1-1	0	4.09
Bob Grim	R	29	40	9	3	1	125.1	124	10	57	65	6-10	4	4.09
Murry Dickson	R	42	38	0	0	0	71.0	85	9	27	36	2-1	0	4.94
Tom Sturdivant†	R	29	36	3	0	0	71.2	70	9	34	57	2-6	5	4.65
Rip Coleman†	L	27	29	11	2	0	81.0	85	8	34	54	2-10	2	4.56
John Tsitouris	R	23	24	10	0	0	83.1	90	3	35	50	4-3	0	4.97
Russ Meyer	R	35	18	0	0	0	24.0	24	3	11	10	1-0	1	4.50
Tom Gorman	R	34	17	0	0	0	20.1	24	3	14	9	1-0	1	7.08
Dick Tomanek	L	28	16	0	0	0	20.2	27	6	12	13	0-1	2	6.53
Al Grunwald	L	29	6	1	0	0	11.1	18	1	11	9	0-1	1	7.94
Marty Kutyna	R	26	4	0	0	0	7.1	7	0	1	1	0-0	1	0.00
Evans Killeen	R	23	4	0	0	0	5.2	4	0	4	1	0-0	0	4.76
Mark Freeman†	R	28	3	0	0	0	3.2	6	0	3	1	0-0	0	9.82
George Brunet	L	24	2	0	0	0	4.2	10	2	7	7	0-0	0	11.57

1959 Washington Senators 8th AL 63-91 .409 31.0 GB

Cookie Lavagetto

Player	Gm by Position	B	Age	G	AB	R	H	2B	3B	HR	RBI	BB	SO	SB	Avg	OBP	Slg
Hal Naragon†	C54	L	30	71	195	12	47	3	2	0	11	8	9	0	.241	.272	.277
Roy Sievers	1B93,OF13	R	32	115	385	55	93	19	0	21	49	53	62	1	.242	.333	.455
Reno Bertoia	2B71,3B5,SS1	R	24	90	308	33	73	10	0	8	29	29	48	2	.237	.302	.347
Harmon Killebrew	3B150,OF4	R	23	153	546	98	132	20	2	42	105	90	116	3	.242	.354	.516
Billy Consolo†	SS75,2B4	R	24	79	202	25	43	5	3	0	10	36	54	1	.213	.332	.267
Bob Allison	OF149	R	24	150	570	83	149	18	9	30	85	60	92	13	.261	.333	.482
Jim Lemon	OF142	R	31	147	531	73	148	18	3	33	100	46	99	5	.279	.334	.510
Faye Throneberry	OF86	L	28	117	327	36	82	11	2	10	42	33	61	6	.251	.322	.388
Ron Samford	SS64,2B23	R	29	91	237	23	53	13	0	5	22	11	29	1	.224	.262	.342
Ken Aspromonte	2B52,SS12,1B1*	R	27	70	225	31	55	12	0	2	14	26	39	2	.244	.321	.324
Julio Becquer	1B53	L	27	108	220	20	59	12	5	1	26	8	17	3	.268	.296	.382
Lenny Green†	OF58	L	26	88	190	29	46	6	1	2	15	20	15	9	.242	.314	.316
Clint Courtney	C53	L	32	72	189	19	44	4	1	2	18	20	19	0	.233	.308	.296
J.W. Porter†	C34,1B2	R	26	37	106	8	24	4	0	1	10	11	16	0	.226	.300	.292
Albie Pearson†	OF21	L	24	25	80	9	15	1	0	0	2	14	3	1	.188	.309	.200
Norm Zauchin	1B19	R	29	19	71	11	15	4	0	3	4	7	14	2	.211	.291	.394
Ed Fitz Gerald†	C16	R	35	19	62	5	12	3	0	0	5	4	8	0	.194	.242	.242
Dan Dobbek	OF16	L	24	16	60	8	15	1	2	1	5	5	13	0	.250	.308	.383
Zoilo Versalles	SS29	R	19	29	59	4	9	0	0	1	1	4	15	1	.153	.219	.203
Johnny Schaive	2B16	R	25	16	59	3	9	2	0	0	2	0	7	0	.153	.167	.186
Steve Korcheck	C22	R	26	22	51	3	8	2	0	0	4	5	13	0	.157	.228	.196
Herb Plews†	2B6	L	31	27	40	4	9	0	0	0	2	3	5	0	.225	.279	.225
Jose Valdivielso	SS21	R	25	24	14	1	4	0	0	0	0	1	3	0	.286	.333	.286
Bobby Malkmus		R	27	6	0	0	0	0	0	0	0	0	0	0	—	—	—

K. Aspromonte, 1 G at OF

Pitcher	T	Age	G	GS	CG	ShO	IP	H	HR	BB	SO	W-L	Sv	ERA
Pedro Ramos	R	24	37	35	11	0	233.2	233	29	52	95	13-19	0	4.16
Camilo Pascual	R	25	32	30	17	6	238.2	202	10	69	185	17-10	0	2.64
Bill Fischer	R	28	34	29	6	1	187.1	211	16	43	62	9-11	0	4.28
Russ Kemmerer	R	27	37	28	8	0	206.0	221	20	71	89	8-17	0	4.50
Jim Kaat	L	20	3	2	0	0	5.0	7	1	4	2	0-2	0	12.60
Tex Clevenger	R	26	50	7	2	2	117.1	114	9	51	71	8-5	8	3.91
Chuck Stobbs	L	29	41	7	0	0	90.2	82	13	24	50	1-8	7	2.98
Hal Griggs	R	30	37	10	2	1	97.2	103	8	52	43	2-8	2	5.25
Dick Hyde	R	30	37	0	0	0	54.1	56	5	27	29	2-5	4	4.97
Hal Woodeshick	L	26	31	3	0	0	61.0	58	2	36	30	2-4	0	3.69
John Romonosky	R	29	12	2	0	0	38.1	36	4	19	22	1-0	0	3.29
Vito Valentinetti	R	30	7	1	0	0	10.2	16	0	10	7	0-2	0	10.13
Jack Kralick	L	24	6	0	0	0	12.1	13	5	6	7	0-0	0	6.57
Ralph Lumenti	L	22	2	0	0	0	3.0	2	0	1	2	0-0	0	0.00
Tom McAvoy	L	22	1	0	0	0	2.2	1	0	2	0	0-0	0	0.00
Murray Wall†	R	32	1	0	0	0	1.1	3	1	0	0	0-0	0	6.75

»1959 Los Angeles Dodgers 1st NL 88-68 .564 —

Walter Alston

Player	Gm by Position	B	Age	G	AB	R	H	2B	3B	HR	RBI	BB	SO	SB	Avg	OBP	Slg
John Roseboro	C117	L	26	118	397	39	92	14	7	10	38	52	69	7	.232	.322	.378
Gil Hodges	1B113,3B4	R	35	124	413	57	114	19	2	25	80	58	92	3	.276	.367	.513
Charlie Neal	2B151,SS1	R	28	151	616	103	177	30	11	19	83	43	86	17	.287	.337	.464
Jim Gilliam	3B132,2B8,OF3	S	30	145	553	91	156	18	4	3	34	96	25	23	.282	.387	.345
Don Zimmer	SS88,3B5,2B1	R	28	97	249	21	41	7	1	4	28	37	56	3	.165	.274	.249
Wally Moon	OF143,1B1	L	29	145	543	93	164	26	11	19	74	81	64	15	.302	.394	.495
Don Demeter	OF124	R	24	139	371	55	95	11	1	18	70	16	87	5	.256	.294	.437
Duke Snider	OF107	L	32	126	370	59	114	11	2	23	88	58	71	1	.308	.400	.535
Norm Larker	1B55,OF30	L	28	108	311	37	90	14	1	8	49	26	25	0	.289	.344	.418
Ron Fairly	OF88	L	20	118	244	27	58	12	1	4	23	31	29	0	.238	.324	.344
Maury Wills	SS82	S	26	83	242	27	63	5	2	0	7	13	27	7	.260	.298	.298
Joe Pignatano	C49	R	29	52	139	17	33	4	1	1	11	21	15	1	.237	.346	.302
Rip Repulski	OF31	R	31	53	94	11	24	4	0	2	14	13	23	0	.255	.343	.362
Carl Furillo	OF25	R	37	50	93	8	27	4	0	0	13	7	11	0	.290	.333	.333
Dick Gray†	3B11	R	27	21	52	8	8	1	0	2	4	6	12	0	.154	.241	.288
Bob Lillis	SS20	R	29	30	48	7	11	2	0	0	2	3	4	0	.229	.275	.271
Chuck Essegian†	OF10	R	27	24	46	6	14	6	0	1	5	4	11	0	.304	.360	.500
Jim Baxes†	3B10	R	30	11	33	4	10	1	0	2	5	4	7	1	.303	.395	.515
Frank Howard	OF6	R	22	9	21	2	3	0	1	0	6	2	9	0	.143	.217	.381
Solly Drake†	OF4	S	28	9	8	2	2	0	0	0	0	1	3	1	.250	.333	.250
Sandy Amoros		L	29	5	5	1	1	0	0	0	1	0	1	0	.200	.200	.200
Norm Sherry	C2	R	27	2	3	0	1	0	0	0	2	0	0	0	.333	.500	.333
Tommy Davis		R	20	1	1	0	0	0	0	0	0	0	1	0	.000	.000	.000

Pitcher	T	Age	G	GS	CG	ShO	IP	H	HR	BB	SO	W-L	Sv	ERA
Don Drysdale	R	22	44	36	15	4	270.2	237	26	93	242	17-13	2	3.46
Johnny Podres	L	26	34	29	6	2	195.0	192	23	74	145	14-9	0	4.11
Sandy Koufax	L	23	35	23	6	1	153.1	136	23	92	173	8-6	2	4.05
Danny McDevitt	L	26	39	22	6	2	145.0	149	16	51	106	10-8	4	3.97
Roger Craig	R	29	29	17	7	4	152.2	122	13	45	76	11-5	0	2.06
Clem Labine	R	32	56	0	0	0	84.2	91	11	25	37	5-10	9	3.93
Art Fowler	R	36	36	0	0	0	61.0	70	8	23	47	3-4	2	5.31
Stan Williams	R	22	35	15	2	0	124.2	102	12	86	89	5-5	0	3.97
Johnny Klippstein	R	31	28	0	0	0	45.2	48	8	33	30	4-0	2	5.91
Larry Sherry	R	23	23	9	1	1	94.1	75	9	43	72	7-2	3	2.19
Chuck Churn	R	29	14	0	0	0	30.2	28	2	10	24	3-2	1	4.99
Gene Snyder	L	28	11	2	0	0	26.1	32	1	20	20	1-1	0	5.47
Carl Erskine	R	32	10	3	0	0	23.1	33	5	13	15	0-3	1	7.71
Fred Kipp	L	27	2	0	0	0	2.2	2	0	3	1	0-0	0	0.00
Bill Harris	R	27	1	0	0	0	1.2	0	0	3	0	0-0	0	0.00

1959 Milwaukee Braves 2nd NL 86-70 .551 2.0 GB

Fred Haney

Player	Gm by Position	B	Age	G	AB	R	H	2B	3B	HR	RBI	BB	SO	SB	Avg	OBP	Slg
Del Crandall	C146	R	29	150	518	65	133	19	2	21	72	46	48	5	.257	.318	.423
Joe Adcock	1B89,OF21	R	31	115	404	53	118	19	2	25	76	32	77	0	.292	.339	.535
Felix Mantilla	2B60,SS23,3B9*	R	24	103	251	26	54	5	0	3	19	16	31	6	.215	.266	.271
Eddie Mathews	3B148	L	27	148	594	118	182	16	8	46	114	80	71	2	.306	.390	.593
Johnny Logan	SS138	R	32	138	470	59	137	17	0	13	50	57	45	1	.291	.369	.411
Hank Aaron	OF152,3B5	R	25	154	629	116	223	46	7	39	123	51	54	8	.355	.401	.636
Bill Bruton	OF133	L	33	133	478	72	138	22	6	6	41	35	54	13	.289	.338	.397
Wes Covington	OF94	L	27	103	373	38	104	17	3	7	45	26	41	0	.279	.329	.397
Frank Torre	1B87	L	27	115	263	23	60	15	1	1	33	35	12	0	.228	.321	.304
Bobby Avila†	2B51	R	35	51	172	29	41	3	2	3	19	24	31	3	.238	.330	.331
Andy Pafko	OF64	R	38	71	142	17	31	8	2	1	15	14	15	0	.218	.293	.324
Lee Maye	OF44	L	24	51	140	17	42	5	1	4	16	7	26	2	.300	.338	.436
Johnny O'Brien	2B37	R	28	44	116	16	23	4	0	1	8	11	15	0	.198	.271	.259
Mickey Vernon	1B10,OF4	L	41	74	91	8	20	4	0	3	14	7	20	0	.220	.283	.363
Casey Wise	2B20,SS5	S	26	22	76	11	13	2	0	1	5	10	5	0	.171	.267	.237
Stan Lopata	C11,1B2	R	33	25	48	0	5	0	0	0	4	3	13	0	.104	.157	.104
Mel Roach	2B8,OF4,3B1	R	26	19	31	1	3	0	0	0	0	2	4	0	.097	.152	.097
Del Rice	C9	R	36	13	29	3	6	0	0	0	1	2	3	0	.207	.250	.207
Chuck Cottier	2B10	R	23	10	24	1	3	1	0	0	1	3	7	0	.125	.222	.167
Jim Pisoni†	OF9	R	29	9	24	4	4	1	0	0	0	2	6	0	.167	.231	.208
Joe Morgan†	2B7	L	28	13	23	2	5	1	0	0	1	2	4	0	.217	.280	.261
Enos Slaughter†	OF5	L	43	11	18	0	3	0	0	0	1	3	3	0	.167	.286	.167
Ray Boone†	1B3	R	35	13	15	3	3	0	0	1	2	4	2	0	.200	.368	.400
Al Spangler	OF4	L	25	6	12	3	5	0	1	0	0	1	1	1	.417	.462	.583
John DeMerit	OF4	R	23	11	5	4	1	0	0	0	0	1	2	0	.200	.333	.200
Red Schoendienst	2B4	S	36	5	3	0	0	0	0	0	0	0	0	0	.000	.000	.000

F. Mantilla, 7 G at OF

Pitcher	T	Age	G	GS	CG	ShO	IP	H	HR	BB	SO	W-L	Sv	ERA
Lew Burdette	R	32	41	39	20	4	289.2	312	38	38	105	21-15	1	4.07
Warren Spahn	L	38	40	36	21	4	292.0	282	21	70	143	21-15	0	2.96
Bob Buhl	R	30	31	25	12	4	198.0	181	19	74	105	15-9	0	2.86
Joey Jay	R	23	34	19	4	1	136.1	130	11	64	88	6-11	0	4.09
Carl Willey	R	28	26	15	5	2	117.0	126	12	31	51	5-9	0	4.15
Don McMahon	R	29	60	0	0	0	80.2	81	5	37	55	5-3	15	2.57
Bob Rush	R	33	31	9	1	1	101.1	102	5	23	64	5-6	0	2.40
Juan Pizarro	L	22	29	14	6	2	133.2	117	13	70	126	6-2	0	3.77
Bob Trowbridge	R	29	16	0	0	0	30.1	45	2	10	22	1-0	1	5.93
Bob Giggie	R	25	13	0	0	0	20.0	24	2	10	15	1-0	1	4.05
Bob Hartman	L	21	3	0	0	0	1.2	6	0	2	1	0-0	0	27.00

1959 San Francisco Giants 3rd NL 83-71 .539 4.0 GB

Bill Rigney

Player	Gm by Position	B	Age	G	AB	R	H	2B	3B	HR	RBI	BB	SO	SB	Avg	OBP	Slg
Hobie Landrith	C109	L	29	109	283	30	71	14	0	3	29	43	23	0	.251	.345	.332
Orlando Cepeda	1B122,OF44,3B4	R	21	151	605	92	192	35	4	27	105	33	100	23	.317	.355	.522
Daryl Spencer	2B151,SS4	R	29	152	555	59	147	20	1	12	62	58	67	5	.265	.332	.369
Jim Davenport	3B121,SS1	R	25	123	469	65	121	16	3	6	38	28	65	0	.258	.301	.343
Eddie Bressoud	SS92,1B1,2B1*	R	27	104	315	36	79	17	2	9	26	28	55	0	.251	.311	.403
Willie Mays	OF147	R	28	151	575	125	180	43	5	34	104	65	58	27	.313	.381	.583
Willie Kirkland	OF117	L	25	126	463	64	126	22	3	22	68	42	84	5	.272	.335	.475
Jackie Brandt	OF116,3B18,1B3*	R	25	137	429	63	116	16	5	12	57	35	69	11	.270	.324	.415
Felipe Alou	OF69	R	24	95	247	38	68	13	2	10	33	17	38	5	.275	.318	.466
Andre Rodgers	SS66	R	24	71	228	32	57	12	1	6	24	32	50	2	.250	.342	.390
Willie McCovey	1B51	L	21	52	192	32	68	9	5	13	38	22	35	2	.354	.429	.656
Bob Schmidt	C70	R	26	71	181	17	44	7	1	5	20	13	24	0	.243	.296	.376
Leon Wagner	OF28	L	25	87	129	20	29	4	3	5	22	25	24	0	.225	.361	.419
Danny O'Connell	3B26,2B8	R	32	34	58	6	11	3	0	0	0	5	15	0	.190	.254	.241
Dusty Rhodes		L	32	54	48	1	9	2	0	0	7	5	9	0	.188	.259	.229
Jose Pagan	3B18,SS5,2B3	R	24	31	46	7	8	1	0	0	1	2	8	1	.174	.208	.196
Jim Hegan†	C21	R	38	21	30	0	4	1	0	0	0	1	10	0	.133	.161	.167
Hank Sauer	OF1	R	42	13	15	1	1	0	0	1	1	0	7	0	.067	.067	.267
Bob Speake		L	28	15	11	0	1	0	0	0	1	1	4	0	.091	.167	.091
Roger McCardell	C3	R	26	4	4	0	0	0	0	0	0	0	0	0	.000	.000	.000

E. Bressoud, 1 G at 3B; J. Brandt, 1 G at 2B

Pitcher	T	Age	G	GS	CG	ShO	IP	H	HR	BB	SO	W-L	Sv	ERA
Johnny Antonelli	L	29	40	38	17	4	282.0	247	29	76	165	19-10	1	3.10
Sam Jones	R	33	50	35	16	4	270.2	232	18	109	209	21-15	4	2.83
Mike McCormick	L	20	47	31	7	3	225.2	213	24	86	151	12-16	4	3.99
Jack Sanford	R	30	36	31	10	0	222.1	198	22	70	132	15-12	1	3.16
Marshall Renfroe	L	23	1	1	0	0	2.0	3	1	3	3	0-0	0	27.00
Stu Miller	R	31	59	9	2	0	167.2	164	15	57	95	8-7	8	2.84
Al Worthington	R	30	42	3	0	0	73.1	68	8	37	45	2-3	2	3.68
Gordon Jones	R	29	31	0	0	0	43.2	45	6	19	29	3-2	2	4.33
Eddie Fisher	R	22	17	5	0	0	40.0	57	8	8	15	2-6	1	7.88
Bud Byerly	R	38	11	0	0	0	13.0	11	2	5	4	1-0	0	1.38
Joe Shipley	R	24	10	1	0	0	18.0	16	2	17	11	0-0	0	4.50
Dom Zanni	R	27	9	0	0	0	11.0	12	2	8	11	0-0	0	6.55
Billy Muffett	R	28	5	0	0	0	6.2	11	2	3	3	0-0	0	5.40
Curt Barclay	R	27	1	0	0	0	0.1	2	0	2	0	0-0	0	54.00

1959 Pittsburgh Pirates 4th NL 78-76 .506 9.0 GB

Danny Murtaugh

Player	Gm by Position	B	Age	G	AB	R	H	2B	3B	HR	RBI	BB	SO	SB	Avg	OBP	Slg
Smoky Burgess	C101	L	32	114	377	41	112	28	5	11	59	31	16	0	.297	.349	.485
Dick Stuart	1B105,OF1	R	26	118	397	64	118	15	2	27	78	42	86	1	.297	.362	.549
Bill Mazeroski	2B133	R	22	135	493	50	119	15	6	7	59	29	54	1	.241	.283	.339
Don Hoak	3B155	R	31	155	564	60	166	29	3	8	65	71	75	9	.294	.374	.399
Dick Groat	SS145	R	28	147	593	74	163	22	7	5	51	32	35	0	.275	.312	.361
Bill Virdon	OF144	L	28	144	519	67	132	24	2	8	41	55	65	7	.254	.327	.355
Bob Skinner	OF142,1B1	L	27	143	547	78	153	18	4	13	61	67	65	10	.280	.357	.399
Roberto Clemente	OF104	R	24	105	432	60	128	17	7	4	50	15	51	2	.296	.322	.396
Roman Mejias	OF85	R	28	96	276	28	65	6	1	7	28	21	48	1	.236	.298	.341
Rocky Nelson	1B56,OF2	L	34	98	175	31	51	11	0	6	32	23	19	0	.291	.379	.457
Danny Kravitz	C45	L	28	52	162	18	41	9	1	3	21	5	14	0	.253	.274	.377
Dick Schofield	2B28,SS8,OF3	S	24	81	145	21	34	10	1	1	9	16	22	1	.234	.311	.338
Ted Kluszewski†	1B20	L	34	60	122	11	32	10	1	2	17	5	14	0	.262	.291	.410
Hank Foiles	C51	R	30	53	80	10	18	3	0	3	4	7	16	0	.225	.287	.375
Harry Bright	OF4,3B3,2B1	R	29	40	48	4	12	1	0	3	8	5	10	0	.250	.321	.458
Harry Simpson†	OF3	L	33	9	15	3	4	2	0	0	2	0	2	0	.267	.267	.400
Joe Christopher	OF9	R	23	15	12	6	0	0	0	0	0	1	4	0	.000	.077	.000
Ken Hamlin	SS3	R	24	3	8	1	1	0	0	0	0	2	1	0	.125	.300	.125
R C Stevens	1B1	R	24	3	7	2	2	0	0	1	1	0	0	0	.286	.286	.714
Hardy Peterson	C2	R	29	2	1	0	0	0	0	0	0	0	0	0	.000	.000	.000

Pitcher	T	Age	G	GS	CG	ShO	IP	H	HR	BB	SO	W-L	Sv	ERA
Bob Friend	R	28	35	35	7	2	234.2	267	19	52	104	8-19	0	4.03
Vern Law	R	29	34	33	20	2	266.0	245	25	53	110	18-9	1	2.98
Harvey Haddix	L	33	31	29	14	2	224.1	189	26	49	149	12-12	0	3.13
Ron Kline	R	27	33	29	7	0	186.0	186	23	70	91	11-13	0	4.26
George Witt	R	25	15	11	0	0	50.2	58	7	32	30	0-7	0	6.93
Dick Hall	R	28	2	1	0	0	8.2	12	1	1	3	0-0	0	3.12
Jim Umbricht	R	28	1	1	0	0	7.0	7	3	4	3	0-0	0	6.43
Roy Face	R	31	57	0	0	0	93.1	91	5	25	69	18-1	10	2.70
Bob Porterfield†	R	35	36	0	0	0	41.1	51	3	19	19	1-2	1	4.35
Bennie Daniels	R	27	34	12	0	0	100.2	115	9	39	67	7-9	1	5.45
Ron Blackburn	R	24	26	0	0	0	44.1	50	5	15	19	1-1	1	3.65
Don Gross	L	28	21	0	0	0	33.0	28	3	10	15	1-1	2	3.55
Bob Smith†	L	28	20	0	0	0	28.1	32	1	17	12	0-0	0	3.49
Fred Green	L	25	17	1	0	0	37.1	37	2	15	20	1-2	1	3.13
Al Jackson	L	23	8	3	0	0	18.0	30	1	8	13	0-0	0	6.50
Don Williams	R	27	6	0	0	0	12.0	17	1	3	3	0-0	0	6.75
Paul Giel	R	26	4	0	0	0	7.2	17	0	6	3	0-0	0	14.09

1959 Chicago Cubs 5th NL 74-80 .481 13.0 GB

Bob Scheffing

Player	Gm by Position	B	Age	G	AB	R	H	2B	3B	HR	RBI	BB	SO	SB	Avg	OBP	Slg
Sammy Taylor	C109	L	26	110	353	41	95	13	2	13	43	35	47	1	.269	.336	.428
Dale Long	1B85	L	33	110	296	34	70	10	3	14	37	31	53	0	.236	.306	.432
Tony Taylor	2B149,SS2	R	23	150	624	96	175	30	8	8	38	45	86	23	.280	.331	.393
Al Dark	3B131,1B4,SS1	R	37	136	477	60	126	22	9	6	45	55	50	1	.264	.342	.386
Ernie Banks	SS154	R	28	155	589	97	179	25	6	45	143	64	72	2	.304	.374	.596
George Altman	OF121	L	26	135	420	54	103	14	4	12	47	34	80	1	.245	.312	.383
Lee Walls	OF119	R	26	120	354	43	91	18	3	8	33	42	73	0	.257	.342	.393
Bobby Thomson	OF116	R	35	122	374	55	97	15	2	11	52	35	50	1	.259	.322	.398
Walt Moryn	OF104	L	33	117	381	41	89	14	1	14	48	44	66	0	.234	.316	.386
Jim Marshall	1B72,OF8	L	28	108	294	39	74	10	1	11	40	33	39	0	.252	.324	.405
Earl Averill	C32,3B13,OF5*	R	27	74	186	22	44	10	0	10	34	15	39	0	.237	.298	.452
Irv Noren†	OF40,1B1	L	34	65	156	27	50	6	2	4	19	13	24	2	.321	.384	.462
Art Schult	1B23,OF15	R	31	42	118	17	32	7	0	2	14	7	14	0	.271	.320	.381
Cal Neeman	C38	R	30	44	105	7	17	2	0	3	9	11	23	0	.162	.241	.267
Randy Jackson†	3B22,OF1	R	33	41	74	7	18	5	1	1	10	11	10	0	.243	.341	.378
Johnny Goryl	2B11,3B4	R	25	25	48	1	9	3	1	1	6	5	3	1	.188	.264	.354
Billy Williams	OF10	L	21	18	33	0	5	0	1	0	2	1	7	0	.152	.176	.212
Lou Jackson		L	23	6	4	2	1	0	0	0	1	0	2	0	.250	.250	.250
Chick King†	OF1	R	28	7	3	3	0	0	0	0	0	0	1	0	.000	.000	.000
Bobby Adams	1B1	R	37	3	2	0	0	0	0	0	0	0	1	0	.000	.000	.000
Don Eaddy	3B1	R	25	15	1	3	0	0	0	0	0	0	1	0	.000	.000	.000

E. Averill, 2 G at 2B

Pitcher	T	Age	G	GS	CG	ShO	IP	H	HR	BB	SO	W-L	Sv	ERA
Bob Anderson	R	23	37	36	7	1	235.1	245	21	77	113	12-13	0	4.13
Glen Hobbie	R	23	46	33	10	3	234.0	204	15	106	138	16-13	0	3.69
Dave Hillman	R	31	39	24	4	1	191.0	178	17	43	88	8-11	0	3.53
Moe Drabowsky	R	23	31	23	3	1	141.2	138	21	75	70	5-10	0	4.13
Art Ceccarelli	L	29	18	15	4	2	102.0	95	19	37	56	5-5	0	4.76
Dick Drott	R	22	8	6	1	1	27.1	25	5	26	15	1-2	0	5.93
Ben Johnson	R	28	4	2	0	0	16.2	17	1	4	6	0-0	0	2.16
Bill Henry	L	31	65	0	0	0	134.1	111	19	26	115	9-8	12	2.68
Don Elston	R	30	65	0	0	0	97.2	77	11	46	82	10-8	13	3.32
John Buzhardt	R	22	31	10	1	1	101.1	107	12	29	33	4-5	0	4.97
Elmer Singleton	R	41	21	1	0	0	43.0	40	2	12	25	2-1	0	2.72
Seth Morehead†	L	24	11	2	0	0	18.2	25	1	8	9	0-1	0	4.82
Ed Donnelly	R	24	9	0	0	0	14.1	18	1	9	6	1-1	0	3.14
Taylor Phillips†	L	26	7	2	0	0	16.2	22	3	11	5	0-2	0	7.56
Joe Schaffernoth	R	21	5	1	0	0	7.2	11	1	4	3	1-0	0	8.22
Bob Porterfield†	R	35	4	0	0	0	6.1	14	1	3	0	0-0	0	11.37
Morrie Martin	L	36	3	0	0	0	2.1	5	2	1	1	0-0	0	19.29
Riverboat Smith†	L	31	1	0	0	0	0.2	5	0	2	0	0-0	0	81.00

1959 Cincinnati Reds 5th NL 74-80 .481 13.0 GB

Mayo Smith (35-45)/Fred Hutchinson (39-35)

Player	Gm by Position	B	Age	G	AB	R	H	2B	3B	HR	RBI	BB	SO	SB	Avg	OBP	Slg
Ed Bailey	C117	L	28	121	379	43	100	13	0	12	40	62	53	2	.264	.370	.393
Frank Robinson	1B125,OF40	R	23	146	540	106	168	31	4	36	125	69	93	18	.311	.391	.583
Johnny Temple	2B149	R	31	149	598	102	186	35	6	8	67	72	40	14	.311	.380	.430
P. Head Jones†	3B68	R	33	72	233	33	58	12	1	7	31	28	26	0	.249	.330	.399
Eddie Kasko	SS84,3B31,2B2	R	27	118	329	39	93	14	1	2	31	14	38	2	.283	.309	.350
Vada Pinson	OF154	L	20	154	648	131	205	47	9	20	84	55	98	21	.316	.371	.509
Gus Bell	OF145	L	30	148	580	59	170	27	2	19	115	29	44	2	.293	.325	.445
Jerry Lynch	OF98	L	28	117	379	49	102	16	3	17	58	29	50	2	.269	.320	.462
Frank Thomas	3B64,OF33,1B14	R	30	108	374	41	84	18	2	12	47	27	56	0	.225	.278	.380
Roy McMillan	SS73	R	28	79	246	38	65	14	2	9	24	27	27	0	.264	.345	.447
Dutch Dotterer	C51	R	27	52	161	21	43	7	0	2	17	16	23	0	.267	.328	.348
Jim Pendleton	OF24,3B16,SS3	R	35	65	113	13	29	2	0	3	9	8	18	3	.257	.309	.354
Whitey Lockman†	1B20,2B6,3B1*	L	32	52	84	10	22	5	1	0	7	4	6	0	.262	.292	.345
Pete Whisenant	OF21	R	29	36	71	13	17	2	0	5	11	8	18	0	.239	.316	.479
John Powers	OF5	L	29	43	43	8	11	2	1	2	4	3	13	0	.256	.319	.488
Walt Dropo†	1B23	R	36	26	39	4	4	1	0	1	2	4	7	0	.103	.205	.205
Cliff Cook	3B9	R	22	9	21	3	8	2	1	0	5	2	8	1	.381	.435	.571
Buddy Gilbert	OF6	L	23	7	20	4	3	0	0	2	2	3	4	0	.150	.261	.450
Del Ennis†	OF3	R	34	5	12	1	4	0	0	0	1	2	2	0	.333	.429	.333
Bob Thurman		L	42	4	4	1	1	0	0	0	2	0	1	0	.250	.250	.250
Bobby Henrich	SS5,3B1	R	20	14	3	3	0	0	0	0	0	0	1	0	.000	.000	.000
Don Pavletich		R	20	1	0	1	0	0	0	0	0	0	0	0	—	—	—

W. Lockman, 1 G at OF

Pitcher	T	Age	G	GS	CG	ShO	IP	H	HR	BB	SO	W-L	Sv	ERA
Bob Purkey	R	29	38	33	9	1	218.0	241	25	43	78	13-18	1	4.25
Don Newcombe	R	33	30	29	17	2	222.0	216	25	27	100	13-8	1	3.16
Joe Nuxhall	L	30	28	21	6	1	131.2	155	10	35	75	9-9	1	4.24
Jim O'Toole	L	22	28	19	3	1	129.1	144	14	73	68	5-8	0	5.15
Jay Hook	R	22	17	15	4	0	79.0	79	11	39	37	5-5	0	5.13
Orlando Pena	R	25	46	8	1	0	136.0	150	26	39	76	5-9	5	4.76
Brooks Lawrence	R	34	43	14	3	0	128.1	144	17	45	64	7-12	10	4.77
Tom Acker	R	29	37	0	0	0	63.1	57	10	37	45	1-2	2	4.12
Willard Schmidt	R	31	36	4	0	0	70.2	80	4	30	40	3-2	0	3.95
Jim Brosnan†	R	29	26	9	1	1	83.1	79	7	26	56	8-3	2	3.35
Bob Mabe	R	29	18	1	0	0	29.2	29	6	19	8	4-2	3	5.46
Hal Jeffcoat†	R	34	17	0	0	0	21.2	21	3	10	12	0-1	1	3.32
Luis Arroyo	L	32	10	0	0	0	13.2	17	0	11	8	1-0	0	3.95
Don Rudolph†	L	27	5	0	0	0	7.1	13	1	3	8	0-0	0	4.91
James Bailey	L	24	3	1	0	0	11.2	17	1	6	7	0-1	0	6.17
Claude Osteen	L	19	2	0	0	0	7.2	11	1	9	3	0-0	0	7.04
Mike Cuellar	L	22	2	0	0	0	4.0	7	1	4	5	0-0	0	15.75

1959 St. Louis Cardinals 7th NL 71-83 .461 16.0 GB

Solly Hemus

Player	Gm by Position	B	Age	G	AB	R	H	2B	3B	HR	RBI	BB	SO	SB	Avg	OBP	Slg
Hal Smith	C141	R	28	142	452	35	122	15	3	13	50	15	28	2	.270	.295	.403
Stan Musial	1B90,OF3	L	38	115	341	37	87	13	2	14	44	60	25	0	.255	.364	.428
Don Blasingame	2B150	L	27	150	615	90	178	26	7	1	24	67	42	15	.289	.361	.359
Ken Boyer	3B143,SS12	R	28	149	563	86	174	18	5	28	94	67	77	12	.309	.384	.508
Alex Grammas	SS130	R	33	131	368	43	99	14	2	3	30	38	26	3	.269	.337	.342
Gino Cimoli	OF141	R	29	143	519	61	145	40	7	8	72	37	83	7	.279	.327	.430
Joe Cunningham	OF121,1B35	L	27	144	458	65	158	28	6	7	60	88	47	2	.345	.453	.478
Curt Flood	OF106,2B1	R	21	121	208	24	53	7	3	7	26	16	35	2	.255	.305	.418
Bill White	OF92,1B71	L	25	138	517	77	156	33	9	12	72	34	61	15	.302	.344	.470
Gene Oliver	OF42,C9,1B5	R	24	68	172	14	42	9	0	6	28	7	41	3	.244	.271	.401
George Crowe	1B14	L	38	77	103	14	31	6	0	8	29	5	12	0	.301	.330	.592
Wally Shannon	SS21,2B10	L	26	47	95	5	27	5	0	0	5	0	12	0	.284	.292	.337
Ray Jablonski†	3B19,SS1	R	32	60	87	11	22	4	0	3	14	8	19	1	.253	.313	.402
Gene Green	OF19,C11	R	26	30	74	8	14	6	0	1	3	5	18	0	.189	.241	.311
Bobby Gene Smith	OF32	R	25	43	60	11	13	1	1	1	7	1	9	0	.217	.230	.317
Dick Gray†	SS13,3B6,2B2*	R	27	36	51	9	16	1	0	1	6	6	8	3	.314	.386	.392
Lee Tate	SS39,2B2,3B2	R	27	41	50	5	7	1	1	1	4	5	7	0	.140	.232	.260
Chuck Essegian†	OF9	R	27	17	39	2	7	2	1	0	5	1	13	0	.179	.200	.282
J.W. Porter†	C19,1B1	R	26	23	33	5	7	3	0	1	2	1	4	0	.212	.257	.394
Tim McCarver	C6	L	17	8	24	3	4	1	0	0	0	2	1	0	.167	.231	.208
Ray Katt	C14	R	32	15	24	0	7	2	0	0	2	0	8	0	.292	.292	.375
Duke Carmel	OF10	L	22	10	23	2	3	1	0	0	3	1	6	0	.130	.167	.174
Solly Hemus	2B1,3B1	L	36	24	17	2	4	2	0	0	1	8	2	0	.235	.500	.353
Irv Noren†	OF2,1B1	L	34	8	8	0	1	1	0	0	0	0	2	0	.125	.125	.250
Chick King†	OF4	R	28	5	7	0	3	0	0	0	1	0	2	0	.429	.375	.429
Joe Durham	OF1	R	27	6	5	2	0	0	0	0	0	0	1	0	.000	.000	.000
Charlie O'Rourke		R	22	2	2	0	0	0	0	0	0	0	0	0	.000	.000	.000

D. Gray, 1 G at OF

Pitcher	T	Age	G	GS	CG	ShO	IP	H	HR	BB	SO	W-L	Sv	ERA
Larry Jackson	R	28	40	37	12	3	256.0	271	13	64	145	14-13	0	3.30
Vinegar Bend Mizell	L	28	31	30	8	1	201.1	196	21	89	108	13-10	0	4.20
Ernie Broglio	R	23	35	25	6	3	181.1	174	20	89	133	7-12	0	4.72
Bob Miller	R	20	11	10	3	0	70.2	66	2	21	43	4-3	0	3.31
Bob Gibson	R	23	13	9	2	1	75.2	77	4	39	48	3-5	0	3.33
Dick Ricketts	R	25	12	9	0	0	55.2	68	7	30	25	1-6	0	5.82
Tom Hughes	R	24	2	2	0	0	4.0	9	2	2	2	0-2	0	15.75
Lindy McDaniel	R	23	62	7	1	0	132.0	144	11	41	86	14-12	15	3.82
Marshall Bridges	L	28	27	4	1	0	76.0	67	10	37	76	6-3	1	4.26
Gary Blaylock†	R	27	26	12	3	0	100.0	117	14	43	61	4-5	0	5.13
Jim Brosnan†	R	29	20	1	0	0	33.0	34	5	15	18	1-3	2	4.91
Dean Stone	L	28	18	1	0	0	30.0	30	4	16	17	0-1	1	4.20
Howie Nunn	R	23	16	0	0	0	21.1	23	3	15	20	2-2	0	7.59
Alex Kellner	L	34	12	4	0	0	37.0	31	9	10	19	2-1	0	3.16
Bob Duliba	R	24	11	0	0	0	22.2	19	2	12	14	0-1	1	2.78
Hal Jeffcoat†	R	34	11	0	0	0	17.2	33	4	9	7	0-1	0	9.17
Tom Cheney	R	24	11	2	0	0	11.2	17	2	11	8	0-1	0	6.94
Jack Urban	R	30	8	0	0	0	10.2	18	1	7	4	0-0	0	9.28
Phil Clark	R	26	7	0	0	0	7.0	8	0	8	5	0-1	0	12.86
Bill Smith	L	25	6	0	0	0	8.1	11	0	3	4	0-0	1	1.08
Bob Blaylock	R	24	3	1	0	0	9.0	8	1	3	3	0-1	0	4.00
Marv Grissom	R	41	3	0	0	0	2.0	6	2	0	0	0-0	0	22.50

1959 Philadelphia Phillies 8th NL 64-90 .416 23.0 GB

Eddie Sawyer

Player	Gm by Position	B	Age	G	AB	R	H	2B	3B	HR	RBI	BB	SO	SB	Avg	OBP	Slg
Carl Sawatski	C69	L	31	74	198	15	58	10	0	9	43	32	36	0	.293	.392	.480
Ed Bouchee	1B134	L	26	136	499	75	142	29	4	15	74	70	74	0	.285	.375	.449
Sparky Anderson	2B152	R	25	152	477	42	104	9	3	0	34	42	53	6	.218	.282	.249
Gene Freese	3B109,2B6	R	25	132	400	60	107	14	5	23	70	43	61	8	.268	.343	.500
Joe Koppe	SS113,2B11	R	28	126	422	68	110	18	7	7	28	41	80	7	.261	.327	.386
Richie Ashburn	OF149	L	32	153	564	86	150	16	2	1	20	79	42	9	.266	.360	.307
Harry Anderson	OF137	L	27	142	508	50	122	28	6	14	63	43	95	1	.240	.304	.402
Wally Post	OF120	R	29	132	468	62	119	17	6	22	94	36	101	0	.254	.310	.457
Dave Philley	OF34,1B24	S	39	99	254	32	74	18	2	7	37	18	27	0	.291	.339	.461
P. Head Jones†	3B46	R	33	47	160	23	43	9	1	7	24	19	14	0	.269	.343	.469
Valmy Thomas	C65,3B1	R	30	66	140	5	28	2	0	1	7	9	19	1	.200	.253	.236
Chico Fernandez	SS40,2B2	R	27	45	123	15	26	5	1	0	3	10	11	2	.211	.269	.268
Harry Hanebrink	2B15,3B9,OF1	L	31	57	97	10	25	3	1	1	7	2	12	0	.258	.273	.340
Joe Lonnett	C43	R	32	43	93	8	16	1	0	1	10	14	17	0	.172	.284	.215
Bob Bowman	OF20,P5	R	28	57	79	7	10	0	0	2	5	5	23	0	.127	.176	.203
Granny Hamner†	SS15,3B1	R	32	21	64	10	19	4	0	2	6	5	5	0	.297	.348	.453
Solly Drake†	OF37	S	28	67	62	10	9	1	0	0	3	8	15	5	.145	.243	.161
Jim Hegan†	C25	R	38	25	51	1	10	1	0	0	8	3	10	0	.196	.232	.216
Jim Bolger†	OF9	R	27	35	48	1	4	1	0	0	1	3	8	0	.083	.135	.104
John Easton		R	26	3	3	0	0	0	0	0	0	0	3	0	.000	.000	.000

Pitcher	T	Age	G	GS	CG	ShO	IP	H	HR	BB	SO	W-L	Sv	ERA
Robin Roberts	R	32	35	35	19	2	257.1	267	34	35	137	15-17	0	4.27
Jim Owens	R	25	31	30	11	1	221.1	203	14	73	135	12-12	1	3.21
Gene Conley	R	28	25	22	12	3	180.0	159	13	42	102	12-7	1	3.00
Don Cardwell	R	23	25	22	5	1	153.0	135	22	65	106	9-10	0	4.06
Ray Semproch	R	28	30	18	2	0	111.2	119	12	59	54	3-10	3	5.40
Ruben Gomez	R	31	20	12	2	1	72.1	90	12	24	37	3-8	1	6.10
Seth Morehead†	L	24	3	3	0	0	10.0	15	3	3	8	0-2	0	9.90
Ed Keegan	R	19	3	3	0	0	9.0	19	2	13	3	0-3	0	18.00
Chris Short	L	21	3	2	0	0	14.1	19	3	10	8	0-0	0	8.16
Jack Meyer	R	27	47	1	1	0	93.2	76	9	53	71	5-3	1	3.36
Turk Farrell	R	25	38	0	0	0	57.0	61	9	25	31	1-6	6	4.74
Taylor Phillips†	L	26	32	3	1	0	63.0	72	4	31	35	1-4	1	5.00
H. Robinson†	R	29	31	4	1	0	73.0	70	6	24	32	2-4	1	3.33
Curt Simmons	L	30	7	0	0	0	10.0	16	2	0	4	0-0	0	4.50
Jim Hearn	R	38	6	0	0	0	11.0	15	2	6	1	0-2	0	5.73
Bob Bowman	R	28	5	0	0	0	6.0	5	1	5	0	0-1	0	6.00
Al Schroll†	R	27	3	0	0	0	9.1	12	1	6	4	1-1	0	8.68
Freddy Rodriguez	R	35	1	0	0	0	2.0	4	1	0	1	0-0	0	13.50

>>1960 New York Yankees 1st AL 97-57 .630 —

Casey Stengel

Player	Gm by Position	B	Age	G	AB	R	H	2B	3B	HR	RBI	BB	SO	SB	Avg	OBP	Slg
Elston Howard	C91,OF1	R	31	107	323	29	79	11	3	6	39	28	43	3	.245	.298	.353
Bill Skowron	1B142	R	29	146	538	63	166	34	3	26	91	38	95	2	.309	.353	.528
Bobby Richardson	2B141,3B11	R	24	150	460	45	116	12	3	1	26	35	19	6	.252	.303	.298
Clete Boyer	3B99,SS33	R	23	124	393	54	95	20	1	14	46	23	85	2	.242	.285	.405
Tony Kubek	SS136,OF29	L	23	147	568	77	155	25	3	14	62	31	42	3	.273	.312	.401
Mickey Mantle	OF150	S	28	153	527	119	145	17	6	40	94	111	125	14	.275	.399	.558
Roger Maris	OF131	L	25	136	499	98	141	18	7	39	112	70	65	2	.283	.371	.581
Hector Lopez	OF106,2B5,3B1	R	30	131	408	66	116	14	6	9	42	46	64	1	.284	.361	.414
Yogi Berra	C63,OF36	L	35	120	359	46	99	14	1	15	62	38	23	2	.276	.347	.446
Gil McDougald	3B84,2B42	R	32	119	337	54	87	16	4	8	34	38	45	2	.258	.337	.401
Bob Cerv†	OF51,1B3	R	34	87	216	32	54	11	1	8	28	30	36	0	.250	.349	.421
Johnny Blanchard	C28	L	27	53	99	8	24	3	1	4	14	6	17	0	.242	.292	.414
Kent Hadley	1B24	L	25	55	64	8	13	2	0	4	11	6	19	0	.203	.271	.422
Dale Long†	1B11	L	34	26	41	6	15	3	1	3	10	5	6	0	.366	.435	.707
Joe DeMaestri	2B19,SS17	R	31	49	35	8	8	1	0	0	2	0	9	0	.229	.229	.257
Ken Hunt	OF24	R	25	25	22	4	6	2	0	0	1	4	4	0	.273	.407	.364
Jim Pisoni	OF18	R	30	20	9	1	1	0	0	0	1	1	2	0	.111	.200	.111
Jesse Gonder	C1	L	24	7	7	1	2	0	0	1	3	1	1	0	.286	.333	.714
Elmer Valo†	OF2	L	39	8	5	1	0	0	0	0	0	2	1	0	.000	.286	.000
Deron Johnson	3B5	R	21	6	4	0	2	1	0	0	0	0	0	0	.500	.500	.750
Andy Carey†	3B2,OF1	R	28	4	3	1	1	0	0	0	1	0	1	0	.333	.333	.333
Billy Shantz	C1	R	32	1	0	0	0	0	0	0	0	0	0	0	—	—	—

Pitcher	T	Age	G	GS	CG	ShO	IP	H	HR	BB	SO	W-L	Sv	ERA
Whitey Ford	L	31	33	29	8	4	192.2	168	15	65	85	12-9	0	3.08
Art Ditmar	R	31	34	28	8	1	200.0	195	25	56	65	15-9	0	3.06
Bob Turley	R	29	34	24	4	1	173.1	138	14	87	87	9-3	5	3.27
Ralph Terry	R	24	35	23	7	3	166.2	149	15	52	92	10-8	1	3.40
Jim Coates	R	27	35	18	6	2	149.1	139	16	66	73	13-3	1	4.28
Bill Short	L	22	10	10	2	0	47.0	49	5	30	14	3-5	0	4.79
Bill Stafford	R	20	11	8	2	1	60.0	50	3	18	36	3-1	0	2.25
Bobby Shantz	L	34	42	0	0	0	67.2	57	5	24	54	5-4	11	2.79
Ryne Duren	R	31	42	1	0	0	49.0	27	3	49	67	3-4	9	4.96
Duke Maas	R	31	35	1	0	0	70.1	70	6	35	28	5-1	4	4.09
Luis Arroyo	L	33	29	0	0	0	40.2	30	2	22	29	5-1	7	2.88
Johnny James	R	26	28	0	0	0	43.1	38	3	26	29	5-1	2	4.36
Eli Grba	R	25	24	9	1	0	80.2	65	9	46	32	6-4	1	3.68
John Gabler	R	29	21	4	0	0	52.0	46	2	32	19	3-3	1	4.15
Fred Kipp	L	28	4	0	0	0	4.1	4	0	0	2	0-1	0	6.23
Hal Stowe	L	22	1	0	0	0	1.0	0	0	1	0	0-0	0	9.00

1960 Baltimore Orioles 2nd AL 89-65 .578 8.0 GB

Paul Richards

Player	Gm by Position	B	Age	G	AB	R	H	2B	3B	HR	RBI	BB	SO	SB	Avg	OBP	Slg
Gus Triandos	C105	R	29	109	364	36	98	18	0	12	54	41	62	0	.269	.343	.418
Jim Gentile	1B124	L	26	138	384	67	112	17	0	21	98	68	72	0	.292	.403	.500
Marv Breeding	2B152	R	26	152	551	69	147	25	2	3	43	35	80	10	.267	.313	.336
Brooks Robinson	3B152,2B3	R	23	152	595	74	175	27	9	14	88	35	49	2	.294	.329	.440
Ron Hansen	SS153	R	22	153	530	72	135	22	5	22	86	69	94	3	.255	.342	.440
Jackie Brandt	OF142,3B2,1B1	R	26	145	511	73	130	24	6	15	65	47	69	5	.254	.317	.413
Gene Woodling	OF124	L	37	140	435	68	123	18	3	11	62	84	40	3	.283	.401	.414
Gene Stephens†	OF77	L	27	84	193	38	46	11	0	5	11	25	25	4	.238	.327	.373
Al Pilarcik	OF75	L	29	104	194	30	48	5	1	4	17	15	16	0	.247	.313	.345
Walt Dropo	1B67,3B1	R	37	79	179	16	48	8	0	4	21	20	19	0	.268	.343	.380
Jim Busby†	OF71	R	33	79	159	25	41	7	1	0	12	20	14	2	.258	.341	.314
Clint Courtney	C58	L	33	83	154	14	35	3	0	1	12	30	14	0	.227	.374	.266
Dave Nicholson	OF44	R	20	54	113	17	21	1	1	5	11	20	55	0	.186	.308	.345
Willie Tasby†	OF36	R	27	39	85	9	18	2	1	0	3	9	12	1	.212	.295	.259
Albie Pearson	OF32	L	25	48	82	17	20	2	0	1	6	17	3	4	.244	.370	.305
Bob Boyd	1B17	L	34	71	82	9	26	5	2	0	9	6	5	0	.317	.364	.427
Billy Klaus	2B30,SS12,3B2	L	31	46	43	8	9	2	0	1	6	9	9	0	.209	.346	.326
Dave Philley†	OF8,3B1	S	40	14	34	6	9	2	1	1	5	4	5	1	.265	.342	.471
Joe Ginsberg†	C14	L	33	14	30	3	8	1	0	0	6	6	1	0	.267	.389	.300
John Powers†	OF4	L	30	10	18	3	2	0	0	0	0	3	1	0	.111	.238	.111
Valmy Thomas	C8	R	31	8	16	0	1	0	0	0	0	1	0	0	.063	.118	.063
Ray Barker	OF1	L	24	5	6	0	0	0	0	0	0	0	3	0	.000	.000	.000
Bobby Thomson†	OF2	R	36	3	6	0	0	0	0	0	0	0	3	0	.000	.000	.000
Jerry Adair	2B3	R	23	3	5	1	1	0	0	1	1	0	0	0	.200	.200	.800
Gene Green	OF1	R	27	1	4	0	1	0	0	0	0	0	0	0	.250	.250	.250
Del Rice†	C1	R	37	1	1	0	0	0	0	0	0	0	0	0	.000	.000	.000
Barry Shetrone		L	21	1	0	1	0	0	0	0	0	0	0	0	—	—	—

Pitcher	T	Age	G	GS	CG	ShO	IP	H	HR	BB	SO	W-L	Sv	ERA
Milt Pappas	R	21	30	27	11	3	205.2	184	15	83	126	15-11	0	3.37
Steve Barber	L	21	36	27	6	1	181.2	148	10	113	112	10-7	2	3.22
Chuck Estrada	R	22	36	25	12	1	208.2	162	18	101	144	18-11	2	3.58
Jack Fisher	R	21	40	20	8	3	197.2	174	13	78	99	12-11	2	3.41
Hal Brown	R	35	30	20	6	1	159.0	155	14	22	66	12-5	0	3.06
Jerry Walker	R	21	29	18	1	0	118.0	107	15	56	48	3-4	5	3.74
Hoyt Wilhelm	R	36	41	11	3	1	147.0	125	13	39	107	11-8	7	3.31
Gordon Jones	R	30	29	0	0	0	55.0	59	9	13	30	1-1	2	4.42
Billy Hoeft	L	28	19	0	0	0	18.2	18	2	14	14	2-1	0	4.34
Wes Stock	R	26	17	0	0	0	34.1	26	2	14	23	2-2	2	2.88
Arnie Portocarrero	R	28	13	5	1	0	40.2	44	6	9	15	3-2	0	4.43
Rip Coleman	L	28	5	1	0	0	4.0	8	0	5	0	0-2	0	11.25
John Anderson	R	27	4	0	0	0	4.2	8	0	4	1	0-0	0	13.50
Bob Mabe	R	30	2	0	0	0	0.2	4	0	1	0	0-0	0	27.00

1960 Chicago White Sox 3rd AL 87-67 .565 10.0 GB

Al Lopez

Player	Gm by Position	B	Age	G	AB	R	H	2B	3B	HR	RBI	BB	SO	SB	Avg	OBP	Slg
Sherm Lollar	C123	R	35	129	421	43	106	23	0	7	46	42	39	2	.252	.326	.356
Roy Sievers	1B114,OF6	R	33	127	444	87	131	22	0	28	93	74	69	1	.295	.396	.534
Nellie Fox	2B149	L	32	150	605	85	175	24	10	2	59	50	13	2	.289	.351	.372
Gene Freese	3B122	R	26	127	455	60	124	32	6	17	79	29	65	10	.273	.312	.481
Luis Aparicio	SS153	R	26	153	600	86	166	20	7	2	61	43	39	51	.277	.323	.343
Minnie Minoso	OF154	R	37	154	591	89	184	32	4	20	105	52	63	17	.311	.374	.481
Jim Landis	OF147	R	26	148	494	89	125	25	6	10	49	80	84	23	.253	.365	.389
Al Smith	OF141	R	32	142	536	80	169	31	3	12	72	50	65	8	.315	.374	.451
Ted Kluszewski	1B39	L	35	81	181	20	53	9	0	5	39	22	10	0	.293	.364	.425
Sammy Esposito	3B37,SS11,2B5	R	28	57	77	14	14	5	0	1	11	10	20	0	.182	.273	.286
Billy Goodman	3B20,2B7	L	34	30	77	5	18	4	0	0	6	12	8	0	.234	.337	.286
Joe Ginsberg†	C25	L	33	28	75	8	19	4	0	0	9	10	8	1	.253	.345	.307
Earl Torgeson	1B10	L	36	68	57	12	15	2	0	2	9	21	8	1	.263	.462	.404
Joe Hicks	OF14	L	27	36	47	3	9	1	0	0	2	6	3	0	.191	.291	.213
Floyd Robinson	OF17	L	24	22	46	7	13	0	0	0	1	11	8	2	.283	.431	.283
Dick Brown	C14	R	25	16	43	4	7	0	0	3	5	3	11	0	.163	.217	.372
J.C. Martin	3B5,1B1	L	23	7	20	0	2	1	0	0	2	0	6	0	.100	.100	.150
Cam Carreon	C7	R	22	8	17	2	4	0	0	0	2	1	3	0	.235	.278	.235
Jim Rivera	OF24	L	37	48	17	17	5	0	0	1	1	3	3	4	.294	.400	.471
Earl Averill†	C5	R	28	10	14	2	3	0	0	0	2	4	2	0	.214	.389	.214
Stan Johnson	OF2	L	23	5	6	1	1	0	0	1	1	0	1	0	.167	.167	.667
Jim McAnany		R	23	3	2	0	0	0	0	0	0	0	2	0	.000	.000	.000

Pitcher	T	Age	G	GS	CG	ShO	IP	H	HR	BB	SO	W-L	Sv	ERA
Early Wynn	R	40	36	35	13	4	237.1	220	20	112	158	13-12	1	3.49
Bob Shaw	R	27	36	32	7	1	192.2	221	16	62	46	13-13	0	4.06
Billy Pierce	L	33	32	30	8	1	196.1	201	24	46	108	14-7	0	3.62
Herb Score	L	27	23	22	5	1	113.2	91	10	87	78	5-10	0	3.72
Gerry Staley	R	39	64	0	0	0	115.1	94	8	25	52	13-8	10	2.42
Frank Baumann	L	26	47	20	7	2	185.1	169	11	53	71	13-6	3	2.67
Turk Lown	R	36	45	0	0	0	67.1	60	6	34	39	2-3	5	3.88
Russ Kemmerer†	R	28	36	7	2	1	120.2	111	5	45	76	6-3	2	2.98
Dick Donovan	R	32	33	8	0	0	78.2	87	13	25	30	6-1	3	5.38
Mike Garcia	R	36	15	0	0	0	17.2	23	2	10	8	0-2	0	4.58
Ray Moore†	R	34	14	0	0	0	20.2	19	5	11	3	1-1	0	5.66
Bob Rush†	R	34	9	0	0	0	14.1	16	4	5	12	0-0	0	5.65
Ken McBride	R	24	5	0	0	0	4.2	6	0	3	4	0-1	0	3.86
Don Ferrarese	L	31	5	0	0	0	4.0	8	2	9	4	0-1	0	18.00
Al Worthington†	R	31	4	0	0	0	5.1	3	0	4	1	1-1	0	3.38
Jake Striker	L	26	2	0	0	0	3.2	5	1	1	1	0-0	0	4.91
Gary Peters	L	23	2	0	0	0	3.1	4	0	1	4	0-0	0	2.70

1960 Cleveland Indians 4th AL 76-78 .494 21.0 GB

Joe Gordon (49-46)/Jo-Jo White (1-0)/Jimmy Dykes (26-32)

Player	Gm by Position	B	Age	G	AB	R	H	2B	3B	HR	RBI	BB	SO	SB	Avg	OBP	Slg
John Romano	C99	R	25	108	316	40	86	12	2	16	52	37	50	0	.272	.349	.475
Vic Power	1B147,SS5,3B4	R	32	147	580	69	167	26	3	10	84	24	20	9	.288	.313	.395
Ken Aspromonte†	2B80,3B36	R	28	117	459	65	133	20	1	10	48	53	32	4	.290	.364	.403
Bubba Phillips	3B85,OF25	R	32	113	304	34	63	14	1	4	33	14	37	1	.207	.249	.299
Woodie Held	SS109	R	28	109	376	45	97	15	1	21	67	44	73	0	.258	.342	.471
Tito Francona	OF138,1B13	L	26	147	544	84	159	36	2	17	79	67	67	4	.292	.372	.460
Jimmy Piersall	OF134	R	30	138	486	70	137	12	4	18	66	24	38	18	.282	.313	.434
Harvey Kuenn	OF119,3B5	R	29	126	474	65	146	24	0	9	54	55	25	3	.308	.379	.416
Johnny Temple	2B77,3B17	R	32	98	381	50	102	13	1	2	19	32	20	11	.268	.326	.323
Mike de la Hoz	SS38,3B8	R	21	49	160	20	41	6	2	6	23	9	12	0	.256	.290	.431
Marty Keough†	OF42	L	25	65	149	19	37	5	0	3	11	9	23	2	.248	.294	.342
Walt Bond	OF36	L	22	40	131	19	29	2	1	5	18	13	14	4	.221	.302	.366
Red Wilson†	C30	R	31	32	88	5	19	3	0	1	10	6	7	0	.216	.268	.284
Russ Nixon†	C25	L	25	25	82	6	20	5	0	1	6	6	6	0	.244	.308	.341
Bob Hale	1B5	L	26	70	70	2	21	7	0	0	12	3	6	0	.300	.312	.400
Hank Foiles†	C22	R	31	24	68	9	19	1	0	1	6	7	5	0	.279	.347	.338
Joe Morgan†	3B12,OF2	L	29	22	47	6	14	2	0	2	4	6	4	0	.298	.377	.468
George Strickland	SS14,3B12,2B2	R	34	32	42	4	7	0	0	1	3	4	8	0	.167	.255	.238
Rocky Bridges†	SS7,3B3	R	32	10	27	1	9	0	0	0	3	1	2	0	.333	.357	.333
Ty Cline	OF6	L	21	7	26	2	8	1	1	0	2	0	4	0	.308	.308	.423
Chuck Tanner	OF4	L	30	21	25	2	7	1	0	0	4	4	6	1	.280	.367	.320
Carroll Hardy†	OF17	R	27	29	18	7	2	1	0	0	1	2	2	0	.111	.200	.167
John Powers†	OF5	L	30	8	12	2	2	1	1	0	0	2	2	0	.167	.286	.417
Don Dillard	OF1	L	23	6	7	0	1	0	0	0	0	1	3	0	.143	.250	.143
Pete Whisenant†	OF2	R	30	7	6	0	1	0	0	0	0	0	2	0	.167	.167	.167
Steve Demeter	3B3	R	25	4	5	0	0	0	0	0	0	0	1	0	.000	.000	.000

Pitcher	T	Age	G	GS	CG	ShO	IP	H	HR	BB	SO	W-L	Sv	ERA
Jim Perry	R	24	41	36	10	4	261.1	257	35	91	120	18-10	1	3.62
Gary Bell	R	23	28	23	6	2	154.2	139	15	82	109	9-10	1	4.13
Barry Latman	R	24	31	20	4	0	147.1	146	19	72	94	7-7	0	4.03
Mudcat Grant	R	24	33	19	5	0	159.2	147	26	78	75	9-8	0	4.40
Wynn Hawkins	R	24	15	9	1	0	66.0	68	10	39	39	4-4	0	4.23
Jack Harshman	L	32	15	8	0	0	54.1	50	7	30	25	2-4	0	3.98
Ted Bowsfield†	L	25	11	6	1	1	40.2	47	1	20	14	3-4	0	5.09
Johnny Klippstein	R	32	49	0	0	0	74.1	53	8	35	46	5-5	14	2.91
Dick Stigman	L	24	41	18	3	0	133.2	118	13	87	104	5-11	9	4.51
Bobby Locke	R	26	32	11	2	2	123.0	121	10	37	53	3-5	2	3.37
John Briggs†	R	26	21	2	0	0	36.1	32	4	15	19	4-2	1	4.46
Don Newcombe†	R	34	20	2	0	0	54.0	61	6	8	27	2-3	1	4.33
Frank Funk	R	24	9	0	0	0	31.2	27	3	9	18	4-2	1	1.99
Carl Mathias	L	24	7	0	0	0	15.1	14	2	8	13	0-1	0	3.52
Mike Lee	L	19	7	0	0	0	9.0	6	1	11	6	0-0	0	2.00
Bobby Tiefenauer	R	30	6	0	0	0	9.0	8	0	3	2	0-1	0	2.00
Carl Thomas	R	28	4	0	0	0	9.2	8	1	10	5	1-0	0	7.45
Bob Grim†	R	30	3	0	0	0	2.1	6	0	1	2	0-1	0	11.57

1960 Washington Senators 5th AL 73-81 .474 24.0 GB

Cookie Lavagetto

Player	Gm by Position	B	Age	G	AB	R	H	2B	3B	HR	RBI	BB	SO	SB	Avg	OBP	Slg
Earl Battey	C136	R	25	137	466	49	126	24	2	15	60	48	68	4	.270	.346	.427
Julio Becquer	1B77,P1	L	28	110	298	41	75	15	7	4	35	12	35	1	.252	.282	.389
Billy Gardner	2B145,SS13	R	32	145	592	71	152	26	5	9	56	43	76	0	.257	.313	.363
Reno Bertoia	3B112,2B21	R	25	121	460	44	122	17	7	4	45	26	58	3	.265	.313	.359
Jose Valdivielso	SS115,3B1	R	26	117	268	23	57	1	1	2	19	20	36	1	.213	.276	.246
Jim Lemon	OF145	R	32	148	528	81	142	10	1	38	100	67	114	2	.269	.354	.508
Bob Allison	OF140,1B4	R	25	144	501	79	126	30	3	15	69	92	94	11	.251	.367	.413
Lenny Green	OF100	L	27	127	330	62	97	16	7	5	33	43	25	21	.294	.383	.430
Harmon Killebrew	1B71,3B65	R	24	124	442	84	122	19	1	31	80	71	106	1	.276	.375	.534
Dan Dobbek	OF78	L	25	110	248	32	54	8	2	10	30	35	41	4	.218	.316	.387
Billy Consolo	SS82,2B12,3B2	R	25	100	174	23	36	4	2	3	15	25	29	1	.207	.310	.305
Faye Throneberry	OF34	L	29	85	157	18	39	7	1	1	23	18	33	1	.248	.326	.325
Pete Whisenant†	OF47	R	30	58	115	19	26	9	0	3	9	19	14	2	.226	.336	.383
Hal Naragon	C29	L	31	33	92	7	19	2	0	0	5	8	4	0	.207	.275	.228
Don Mincher	1B20	L	22	27	79	10	19	4	1	2	5	11	11	0	.241	.330	.392
Elmer Valo†	OF6	L	39	76	64	6	18	3	0	0	16	17	4	0	.281	.424	.328
Zoilo Versalles	SS15	R	20	15	45	2	6	2	2	0	4	2	5	0	.133	.170	.267
Johnny Schaive	2B4	R	26	6	12	1	3	1	0	0	0	0	3	0	.250	.250	.333
Ken Aspromonte†		R	28	4	3	0	0	0	0	0	0	0	1	0	.000	.000	.000
Jake Jacobs		R	23	6	2	0	0	0	0	0	0	0	0	0	.000	.000	.000

Pitcher	T	Age	G	GS	CG	ShO	IP	H	HR	BB	SO	W-L	Sv	ERA
Pedro Ramos	R	25	43	36	14	1	274.0	254	24	99	160	11-18	2	3.45
Camilo Pascual	R	26	26	22	8	3	151.2	139	11	53	143	12-8	2	3.03
Jack Kralick	L	25	35	18	7	2	151.0	139	12	45	71	8-6	1	3.04
Jim Kaat	L	21	13	9	0	0	50.0	48	8	31	25	1-5	0	5.58
Russ Kemmerer†	R	28	3	3	0	0	17.1	18	2	10	10	0-2	0	7.79
Tex Clevenger	R	27	53	11	1	0	128.2	150	10	49	49	5-11	7	4.20
Don Lee	R	26	44	20	1	0	165.0	160	16	64	88	8-7	3	3.44
Hal Woodeshick	L	27	41	14	1	0	115.0	131	7	60	46	4-5	4	4.70
Chuck Stobbs	L	30	40	13	1	1	119.1	115	13	38	72	12-7	2	3.32
Ray Moore†	R	34	37	0	0	0	65.2	49	5	27	29	3-2	13	2.88
Rudy Hernandez	R	28	21	0	0	0	34.2	34	2	21	22	4-1	0	4.41
Bill Fischer†	R	29	20	7	1	0	77.0	85	7	17	31	3-5	0	4.91
Tom Morgan†	R	30	14	0	0	0	24.0	36	6	5	11	1-3	0	3.75
Ted Sadowski	R	24	9	1	0	0	17.1	17	4	9	12	1-0	1	5.19
Dick Hyde	R	31	9	0	0	0	8.2	11	2	5	4	0-1	0	4.15
Ted Abernathy	R	27	2	0	0	0	3.0	4	0	4	1	0-0	0	12.00
Hector Maestri	R	25	1	0	0	0	2.0	1	0	1	1	0-0	0	0.00
Julio Becquer	L	28	1	0	0	0	1.0	1	1	0	0	0-0	0	9.00

1960 Detroit Tigers 6th AL 71-83 .461 26.0 GB

Jimmy Dykes (44-52)/Billy Hitchcock (1-0)/Joe Gordon (26-31)

Player	Gm by Position	B	Age	G	AB	R	H	2B	3B	HR	RBI	BB	SO	SB	Avg	OBP	Slg
Lou Berberet	C81	L	30	85	232	18	45	4	0	5	23	41	31	2	.194	.313	.276
Norm Cash	1B99,OF4	L	25	121	353	64	101	16	3	18	63	65	58	4	.286	.402	.501
Frank Bolling	2B138	R	28	139	536	64	136	20	4	9	59	40	48	7	.254	.308	.356
Eddie Yost	3B142	R	33	143	497	78	129	23	2	14	47	125	69	5	.260	.414	.398
Chico Fernandez	SS130	R	28	133	435	44	105	13	3	4	35	39	50	13	.241	.303	.313
Rocky Colavito	OF144	R	26	145	555	67	138	18	1	35	87	53	80	3	.249	.317	.474
Al Kaline	OF142	R	25	147	551	77	153	29	4	15	68	65	47	19	.278	.354	.426
Charlie Maxwell	OF120	L	33	134	482	70	114	16	5	24	81	58	75	5	.237	.325	.440
Steve Bilko	1B62	R	31	78	222	20	46	11	2	9	25	27	31	0	.207	.292	.396
Neil Chrisley	OF47,1B2	L	28	96	220	27	56	10	3	5	24	19	26	2	.255	.311	.395
Red Wilson†	C45	R	31	45	134	17	29	4	0	1	14	16	14	3	.216	.298	.269
Ozzie Virgil	3B42,2B8,SS5*	R	27	62	132	16	30	4	2	3	13	4	14	1	.227	.248	.356
Harry Chiti†	C36	R	27	37	104	9	17	0	0	2	5	10	12	0	.163	.235	.221
Casey Wise	2B17,SS10,3B1	S	27	30	68	6	10	0	2	2	5	4	9	1	.147	.194	.294
Sandy Amoros†	OF10	L	30	65	67	7	10	0	0	1	7	12	10	0	.149	.275	.194
Coot Veal	SS22,3B3,2B1	R	27	27	64	8	19	5	1	0	8	11	7	0	.297	.400	.406
Hank Foiles†	C22	R	31	26	56	5	14	3	0	0	3	1	8	1	.250	.263	.304
Dick Gernert†	1B13,OF6	R	31	21	50	6	15	4	0	1	5	4	5	0	.300	.352	.440
Dick McAuliffe	SS7	L	20	8	27	2	7	0	1	0	1	2	6	0	.259	.310	.333
Johnny Groth	OF8	R	33	25	19	3	7	1	0	0	2	3	1	0	.368	.455	.421
Gail Harris	1B5	L	28	8	5	0	0	0	0	0	0	2	1	0	.000	.286	.000
Rocky Bridges†	3B7,SS3	R	32	10	5	0	1	0	0	0	0	0	0	0	.200	.200	.200
Em Lindbeck		L	24	2	1	0	0	0	0	0	0	1	0	0	.000	.500	.000

O. Virgil, 1 G at C

Pitcher	T	Age	G	GS	CG	ShO	IP	H	HR	BB	SO	W-L	Sv	ERA
Frank Lary	R	30	38	36	15	2	274.1	262	25	62	149	15-15	1	3.51
Jim Bunning	R	28	36	34	10	3	252.0	217	20	64	201	11-14	0	2.79
Don Mossi	L	31	23	22	9	2	158.1	158	17	32	69	9-8	0	3.47
Dave Sisler	R	28	41	0	0	0	80.0	56	3	45	47	7-5	6	2.48
Hank Aguirre	L	29	37	6	1	0	94.2	75	7	30	80	5-3	10	2.85
Bob Bruce	R	27	34	15	1	0	130.0	127	16	56	76	4-7	0	3.74
Pete Burnside	L	29	31	15	2	0	113.2	122	14	50	71	7-7	2	4.28
Paul Foytack	R	29	28	13	1	0	96.2	108	11	49	38	2-11	2	6.14
Tom Morgan†	R	30	22	0	0	0	29.0	33	6	10	12	3-2	1	4.66
Bill Fischer†	R	29	20	6	1	0	55.0	50	6	18	24	5-3	0	3.44
Phil Regan	R	23	17	7	0	0	68.0	70	11	25	38	0-4	1	4.50
Ray Semproch	R	29	17	0	0	0	27.0	29	2	16	9	3-0	0	4.00
Clem Labine†	R	33	14	0	0	0	19.1	19	2	12	6	0-3	2	5.12
George Spencer	R	33	5	0	0	0	7.2	10	1	5	4	0-1	0	3.52

1960 Boston Red Sox 7th AL 65-89 .422 32.0 GB

Billy Jurges (15-27)/Del Baker (2-5)/Pinky Higgins (48-57)

Player	Gm by Position	B	Age	G	AB	R	H	2B	3B	HR	RBI	BB	SO	SB	Avg	OBP	Slg
Russ Nixon†	C74	L	25	80	272	24	81	17	3	5	33	13	23	0	.298	.329	.438
Vic Wertz	1B117	L	35	131	443	45	125	22	0	19	103	37	54	0	.282	.335	.460
Pete Runnels	2B129,1B57,3B3	L	32	143	528	80	169	29	2	2	35	71	51	5	.320	.401	.394
Frank Malzone	3B151	R	30	152	595	60	161	30	2	14	79	36	42	2	.271	.313	.398
Don Buddin	SS124	R	26	124	428	62	105	21	5	6	36	62	59	4	.245	.338	.360
Willie Tasby†	OF102	R	27	105	385	68	108	17	1	7	37	51	54	3	.281	.371	.384
Lu Clinton	OF89	R	22	96	298	37	68	17	5	6	37	20	66	4	.228	.278	.379
Ted Williams	OF87	L	41	113	310	56	98	15	0	29	72	75	41	1	.316	.451	.645
Pumpsie Green	2B69,SS41	S	26	133	260	36	63	10	3	3	21	44	47	3	.242	.350	.338
Gary Geiger	OF66	L	23	77	245	32	74	13	3	9	33	23	38	2	.302	.369	.490
Carroll Hardy†	OF59	R	27	73	145	26	34	5	2	2	15	17	40	3	.234	.313	.338
Rip Repulski†	OF33	R	32	73	136	14	33	6	1	3	20	10	25	0	.243	.289	.368
Haywood Sullivan	C50	R	29	52	124	9	20	1	0	3	10	16	24	0	.161	.255	.242
Bobby Thomson†	OF27,1B1	R	36	40	114	12	30	3	1	5	20	11	15	0	.263	.323	.439
Gene Stephens†	OF31	L	27	35	109	9	25	4	0	2	11	14	22	5	.229	.312	.321
Marty Keough†	OF29	L	25	38	105	15	26	6	1	1	9	8	8	2	.248	.296	.352
Ed Sadowski	C36	R	28	38	93	10	20	2	0	3	8	8	13	0	.215	.284	.333
Ray Boone†	1B22	R	36	34	78	6	16	1	0	1	11	11	15	0	.205	.300	.256
Jim Pagliaroni	C18	R	22	28	62	7	19	5	2	2	9	13	11	0	.306	.434	.548
Don Gile	C15,1B11	R	25	29	51	6	9	1	1	1	4	1	13	0	.176	.189	.294
Ron Jackson	1B9	R	26	10	31	1	7	2	0	0	0	1	6	0	.226	.250	.290
Marlan Coughtry	2B13,3B1	L	25	15	19	3	3	0	0	0	0	5	8	0	.158	.333	.158
Ray Webster	2B1	R	22	7	3	1	0	0	0	0	1	1	0	0	.000	.200	.000
Jim Busby†	OF1	R	33	1	0	0	0	0	0	0	0	0	0	0	—	—	—

Pitcher	T	Age	G	GS	CG	ShO	IP	H	HR	BB	SO	W-L	Sv	ERA
Bill Monbouquette	R	23	35	30	12	3	215.0	217	18	68	134	14-11	0	3.64
Tom Brewer	R	28	34	29	8	1	186.2	220	13	72	60	10-15	1	4.82
Ike Delock	R	30	24	23	3	1	129.1	145	21	52	49	9-10	0	4.73
Frank Sullivan	R	30	40	22	4	0	153.2	164	12	52	98	6-16	1	5.10
Billy Muffett	R	29	23	14	4	1	125.0	116	6	36	75	6-4	0	3.24
Earl Wilson	R	25	13	9	2	0	65.0	61	4	48	40	3-2	0	4.71
Mike Fornieles	R	28	70	0	0	0	109.0	86	6	49	64	10-5	14	2.64
Tom Sturdivant	R	30	40	3	0	0	101.1	106	16	45	67	3-3	1	4.97
Jerry Casale	R	26	29	14	1	0	96.1	113	14	67	54	2-9	0	6.17
Tom Borland	L	27	26	4	0	0	51.0	67	4	23	32	0-4	3	6.53
Ted Bowsfield†	L	25	17	2	0	0	21.0	20	1	13	18	1-2	2	5.14
Dave Hillman	R	32	16	3	0	0	36.2	41	6	12	14	0-3	0	5.65
Ted Wills	L	26	15	0	0	0	30.1	38	4	16	28	1-1	1	7.42
Chet Nichols	L	29	6	1	0	0	12.2	12	0	4	11	0-2	0	4.26
Al Worthington†	R	31	6	0	0	0	11.2	17	1	11	7	0-1	0	7.71
Nels Chittum	R	27	6	0	0	0	8.1	8	0	6	5	0-0	0	4.32
Tracy Stallard	R	22	4	0	0	0	4.0	0	0	2	6	0-0	0	0.00
Arnold Earley	L	27	2	0	0	0	4.0	9	1	4	5	0-1	0	15.75

1960 Kansas City Athletics 8th AL 58-96 .377 39.0 GB

Bob Elliott

Player	Gm by Position	B	Age	G	AB	R	H	2B	3B	HR	RBI	BB	SO	SB	Avg	OBP	Slg
Pete Daley	C61,OF1	R	30	73	228	19	60	10	2	5	25	16	41	0	.263	.311	.390
Marv Throneberry	1B71	L	26	104	236	29	59	9	2	11	41	23	60	0	.250	.315	.445
Jerry Lumpe	2B134,SS15	L	27	146	574	69	156	19	3	8	53	48	49	1	.272	.326	.357
Andy Carey†	3B91	R	28	102	343	30	80	14	4	12	53	26	52	0	.233	.287	.402
Ken Hamlin	SS139	R	25	140	428	51	96	10	2	2	24	44	48	1	.224	.297	.271
Bill Tuttle	OF148	R	30	151	559	75	143	21	3	8	40	66	52	1	.256	.336	.347
Russ Snyder	OF91	L	26	125	304	45	79	10	5	4	26	20	28	7	.260	.306	.365
Norm Siebern	OF75,1B69	L	26	144	520	69	145	31	6	19	69	72	68	0	.279	.366	.471
Dick Williams	3B57,1B34,OF25	R	31	127	420	47	121	31	0	12	65	39	68	0	.288	.346	.448
Hank Bauer	OF67	R	37	95	255	30	70	15	0	3	31	21	36	1	.275	.326	.369
Whitey Herzog	OF69,1B2	L	28	83	252	43	67	10	2	8	38	40	32	0	.266	.364	.417
Harry Chiti†	C52	R	27	58	190	16	42	7	0	5	28	17	33	1	.221	.288	.337
Danny Kravitz†	C47	L	29	59	175	17	41	7	2	4	14	11	19	0	.234	.280	.366
Bob Johnson	SS30,2B27,3B11	R	24	76	146	12	30	4	0	1	9	19	23	2	.205	.301	.253
Bob Cerv†	OF21	R	34	23	78	14	20	1	1	6	12	10	17	0	.256	.337	.526
Jim Delsing	OF10	L	34	16	40	2	10	3	0	0	5	3	5	0	.250	.302	.325
Leo Posada	OF9	R	24	10	36	8	13	0	2	1	2	3	7	1	.361	.410	.556
Ray Jablonski	3B6	R	33	21	32	3	7	1	0	0	3	4	8	0	.219	.297	.250
Jim McManus	1B3	L	23	5	13	3	4	0	0	1	2	1	2	0	.308	.357	.538
Chet Boak	2B5	R	25	5	13	1	2	0	0	0	1	0	2	0	.154	.200	.154
Lou Klimchock	2B1	L	20	10	10	0	3	0	0	0	0	0	0	0	.300	.300	.300
Hank Foiles†	C2	R	31	6	7	1	4	0	0	0	1	3	2	0	.571	.700	.571
Wayne Terwilliger	2B2	R	35	2	1	0	0	0	0	0	0	0	0	0	.000	.000	.000

Pitcher	T	Age	G	GS	CG	ShO	IP	H	HR	BB	SO	W-L	Sv	ERA
Bud Daley	L	27	37	35	13	1	231.0	234	27	96	126	16-16	0	4.56
Ray Herbert	R	30	37	33	14	0	252.2	256	17	72	122	14-15	1	3.28
Dick Hall	R	29	29	28	9	1	182.1	183	28	38	79	8-13	0	4.05
Johnny Kucks	R	26	31	17	1	0	114.0	140	22	43	38	4-10	0	6.00
Ned Garver	R	34	28	15	5	2	122.1	110	15	35	50	4-9	0	3.83
Don Larsen	R	30	22	15	0	0	83.2	97	11	42	43	1-10	0	5.38
George Brunet†	L	25	3	2	0	0	10.1	12	0	10	4	0-2	0	4.35
Marty Kutyna	R	27	51	0	0	0	61.2	64	7	32	20	3-2	4	3.94
Ken Johnson	R	27	42	6	2	0	120.1	120	16	45	83	5-10	3	4.26
Bob Trowbridge	R	30	22	1	0	0	68.1	70	6	34	33	1-3	2	4.61
Bob Davis	R	26	21	0	0	0	32.0	31	1	22	28	0-0	1	3.66
Leo Kiely	L	30	20	0	0	0	20.2	21	1	5	6	1-2	1	1.74
John Tsitouris	R	24	14	2	0	0	33.0	38	3	21	12	0-2	0	6.55
Bob Giggie†	R	26	10	0	0	0	18.2	24	1	15	8	1-0	0	5.79
John Briggs†	R	26	8	1	0	0	11.1	19	3	12	8	0-2	0	12.71
Dave Wickersham	R	24	5	0	0	0	8.1	4	0	1	3	0-0	2	1.08
Ray Blemker	L	22	1	0	0	0	1.2	3	1	2	0	0-0	0	27.00
Howie Reed	R	23	1	0	0	0	1.2	2	1	0	1	0-0	0	0.00

»1960 Pittsburgh Pirates 1st NL 95-59 .617 —

Danny Murtaugh

Player	Gm by Position	B	Age	G	AB	R	H	2B	3B	HR	RBI	BB	SO	SB	Avg	OBP	Slg
Smoky Burgess	C89	L	33	110	337	33	99	15	2	7	39	35	13	0	.294	.356	.412
Dick Stuart	1B108	R	27	122	438	48	114	17	5	23	83	39	107	0	.260	.317	.479
Bill Mazeroski	2B151	R	23	151	538	58	147	21	5	11	64	40	50	4	.273	.320	.392
Don Hoak	3B155	R	32	155	553	97	156	24	9	16	79	74	74	3	.282	.366	.445
Dick Groat	SS136	R	29	138	573	85	186	26	4	2	50	39	35	0	.325	.371	.394
Roberto Clemente	OF142	R	25	144	570	89	179	22	6	16	94	39	72	4	.314	.357	.458
Bob Skinner	OF141	L	28	145	571	83	156	33	6	15	86	59	86	11	.273	.340	.431
Bill Virdon	OF109	L	29	120	409	60	108	16	9	8	40	40	44	8	.264	.326	.406
Gino Cimoli	OF91	R	30	101	307	36	82	14	4	0	28	32	43	1	.267	.336	.339
Hal Smith	C71	R	29	77	258	37	76	18	2	11	45	22	48	1	.295	.351	.508
Rocky Nelson	1B73	L	35	93	200	34	60	11	1	7	35	24	15	1	.300	.382	.470
Dick Schofield	SS23,2B10,3B1	S	25	65	102	9	34	4	1	0	10	16	20	0	.333	.429	.392
Joe Christopher	OF17	R	24	50	56	21	13	2	0	1	3	5	8	1	.232	.295	.321
Gene Baker	3B7,2B1	R	35	33	37	5	9	0	0	0	4	2	9	0	.243	.275	.243
Bob Oldis	C22	R	32	22	20	1	4	1	0	0	1	1	2	0	.200	.238	.250
Mickey Vernon		L	42	9	8	0	1	0	0	0	1	1	0	0	.125	.222	.125
Dick Barone	SS2	R	27	3	6	0	0	0	0	0	0	0	1	0	.000	.000	.000
Danny Kravitz†	C1	L	29	8	6	0	0	0	0	0	0	1	2	0	.000	.143	.000
Harry Bright		R	30	4	4	0	0	0	0	0	0	0	2	0	.000	.000	.000
R C Stevens	1B7	R	25	9	3	1	0	0	0	0	0	0	1	0	.000	.000	.000
Roman Mejias		R	29	3	1	1	0	0	0	0	0	0	1	0	.000	.000	.000

Pitcher	T	Age	G	GS	CG	ShO	IP	H	HR	BB	SO	W-L	Sv	ERA
Bob Friend	R	29	38	37	16	4	275.2	266	18	45	183	18-12	1	3.00
Vern Law	R	30	35	35	18	3	271.2	266	25	40	120	20-9	0	3.08
Harvey Haddix	L	34	29	28	4	0	172.1	189	13	38	101	11-10	1	3.97
V. Bend Mizell†	L	29	23	23	8	3	155.2	141	7	46	71	13-5	0	3.12
Tom Cheney	R	25	11	8	1	1	52.0	44	5	33	35	2-2	0	3.98
Bennie Daniels	R	28	10	6	0	0	40.1	52	4	17	16	1-3	0	7.81
George Witt	R	26	10	6	0	0	30.0	33	3	12	15	1-2	0	4.20
Roy Face	R	32	68	0	0	0	114.2	93	11	29	72	10-8	24	2.90
Fred Green	L	26	45	0	0	0	70.0	61	4	33	49	8-4	3	3.21
Joe Gibbon	L	25	27	9	0	0	80.1	87	5	31	60	4-2	0	4.03
Jim Umbricht	R	29	17	3	0	0	40.2	40	5	27	26	1-2	1	5.09
Paul Giel	R	27	16	0	0	0	33.0	35	3	15	21	2-0	0	5.73
Clem Labine†	R	33	15	0	0	0	30.1	29	0	11	21	3-0	3	1.48
Earl Francis	R	24	7	0	0	0	18.0	14	0	4	8	1-0	0	2.00
Don Gross	L	29	5	0	0	0	5.1	5	1	0	3	0-0	0	3.38
Diomedes Olivo	L	41	4	0	0	0	9.2	8	1	5	10	0-0	0	2.79

1960 Milwaukee Braves 2nd NL 88-66 .571 7.0 GB

Chuck Dressen

Player	Gm by Position	B	Age	G	AB	R	H	2B	3B	HR	RBI	BB	SO	SB	Avg	OBP	Slg
Del Crandall	C141	R	30	142	537	81	158	14	1	19	77	34	36	4	.294	.334	.430
Joe Adcock	1B136	R	32	138	514	55	153	21	4	25	91	46	86	2	.298	.354	.500
Chuck Cottier	2B92	R	24	95	229	29	52	8	0	3	19	14	21	1	.227	.273	.301
Eddie Mathews	3B153	L	28	153	548	108	152	19	7	39	124	111	113	7	.277	.397	.551
Johnny Logan	SS136	R	33	136	482	52	118	14	4	7	42	43	40	1	.245	.309	.334
Hank Aaron	OF153,2B2	R	26	153	590	102	172	20	11	40	126	60	63	16	.292	.352	.566
Bill Bruton	OF149	L	34	151	629	112	180	27	13	12	54	41	97	22	.286	.330	.428
Al Spangler	OF92	L	26	101	105	26	28	5	2	0	6	14	17	6	.267	.355	.352
Wes Covington	OF72	L	28	95	281	25	70	16	1	10	35	15	37	1	.249	.288	.420
Red Schoendienst	2B62	S	37	68	226	21	58	9	1	1	19	17	13	1	.257	.311	.319
Felix Mantilla	2B26,SS25,OF8	R	25	63	148	21	38	7	0	3	11	7	16	3	.257	.291	.365
Al Dark†	OF25,1B10,3B4*	R	38	50	141	16	42	6	2	1	18	7	13	0	.298	.329	.390
Mel Roach	OF21,2B20,1B1*	R	27	48	140	12	42	12	0	3	18	6	19	0	.300	.329	.450
Lee Maye	OF19	L	25	41	83	14	25	6	0	0	2	7	21	5	.301	.359	.373
Charlie Lau	C16	L	27	21	53	4	10	2	0	0	2	6	10	0	.189	.271	.226
Frank Torre	1B17	L	28	21	44	2	9	1	0	0	5	3	2	0	.205	.245	.227
Eddie Haas	OF2	L	25	32	32	4	7	2	0	1	5	5	14	0	.219	.324	.375
Ray Boone†	1B4	R	36	7	12	3	3	1	0	0	4	5	1	0	.250	.471	.333
Mike Krsnich	OF3	R	28	4	9	0	3	1	0	0	2	0	0	0	.333	.333	.444
Stan Lopata	C4	R	34	7	8	0	1	0	0	0	0	1	3	0	.125	.222	.125
Len Gabrielson	OF1	L	20	4	3	1	0	0	0	0	0	1	0	0	.000	.250	.000
Joe Torre		R	19	2	2	0	1	0	0	0	0	0	1	0	.500	.500	.500

A. Dark, 3 G at 2B; M. Roach, 1 G at 3B

Pitcher	T	Age	G	GS	CG	ShO	IP	H	HR	BB	SO	W-L	Sv	ERA
Warren Spahn	L	39	40	33	18	4	267.2	254	24	74	154	21-10	2	3.50
Bob Buhl	R	31	36	33	11	2	238.2	202	23	103	121	16-9	0	3.09
Lew Burdette	R	33	45	32	18	4	275.2	277	19	35	83	19-13	4	3.36
Carl Willey	R	29	28	21	2	1	144.2	136	19	65	109	6-7	0	4.35
Juan Pizarro	L	23	21	17	3	0	114.2	105	13	72	88	6-7	0	4.55
Don McMahon	R	30	48	0	0	0	63.2	66	9	32	50	3-6	10	5.94
Ron Piche	R	25	37	0	0	0	48.0	48	3	23	38	3-5	9	3.56
Joey Jay	R	24	32	11	3	0	133.1	128	10	59	90	9-8	1	3.24
George Brunet†	L	25	17	6	0	0	49.2	53	6	22	39	2-0	0	5.07
Bob Rush†	R	34	10	0	0	0	15.0	24	2	5	8	2-0	1	4.20
Ken MacKenzie	L	26	9	0	0	0	8.1	9	2	3	9	0-1	0	6.48
Don Nottebart	R	24	5	1	0	0	15.1	14	0	15	8	1-0	1	4.11
Terry Fox	R	24	5	0	0	0	8.1	6	0	6	5	0-0	0	4.32
Bob Giggie†	R	26	3	0	0	0	4.1	5	0	4	5	0-0	0	4.15

1960 St. Louis Cardinals 3rd NL 86-68 .558 9.0 GB

Solly Hemus

Player	Gm by Position	B	Age	G	AB	R	H	2B	3B	HR	RBI	BB	SO	SB	Avg	OBP	Slg
Hal Smith	C124	R	29	127	337	20	77	16	0	2	28	29	33	1	.228	.291	.294
Bill White	1B123,OF29	L	26	144	554	81	157	27	10	16	79	42	83	12	.283	.334	.455
Julian Javier	2B119	R	23	119	451	55	107	19	8	4	21	21	72	19	.237	.273	.341
Ken Boyer	3B146	R	29	151	552	95	168	26	10	32	97	56	77	8	.304	.370	.562
Daryl Spencer	SS138,2B16	R	30	148	507	70	131	20	3	16	58	81	74	1	.258	.365	.404
Curt Flood	OF134,3B1	R	22	140	396	37	94	20	1	8	38	35	54	0	.237	.303	.354
Joe Cunningham	OF116,1B15	L	28	139	492	68	138	28	3	6	39	59	59	1	.280	.363	.386
Walt Moryn†	OF62	L	34	75	200	24	49	4	3	11	35	17	38	0	.245	.299	.460
Stan Musial	OF59,1B29	L	39	116	331	49	91	17	1	17	63	41	34	1	.275	.354	.486
Alex Grammas	SS46,2B38,3B13	R	34	102	196	20	48	4	1	4	17	12	15	0	.245	.290	.337
Bob Nieman	OF55	R	33	81	188	19	54	13	5	4	31	24	31	0	.287	.372	.473
Carl Sawatski	C67	L	32	78	179	16	41	4	0	6	27	22	24	0	.229	.310	.352
Leon Wagner	OF32	L	26	39	98	12	21	2	0	4	11	17	17	0	.214	.333	.357
George Crowe	1B5	L	39	73	72	5	17	3	0	4	13	5	16	0	.236	.278	.444
Charlie James	OF37	R	22	43	50	5	9	1	0	2	5	1	12	0	.180	.196	.320
Don Landrum	OF13	L	24	13	49	7	12	0	1	2	3	4	6	3	.245	.315	.408
John Glenn	OF28	R	31	32	31	4	8	0	1	0	5	0	9	0	.258	.250	.323
Ellis Burton	OF23	S	23	29	28	5	6	1	0	0	2	4	14	0	.214	.313	.250
Wally Shannon	2B15,SS1	L	27	18	23	2	4	0	0	0	1	3	6	0	.174	.296	.174
Tim McCarver	C5	L	18	10	10	3	2	0	0	0	0	0	2	0	.200	.200	.200
Chris Cannizzaro	C6	R	22	7	9	0	2	0	0	0	1	1	3	0	.222	.273	.222
Julio Gotay	SS2,3B1	R	21	3	8	1	3	0	0	0	0	0	2	1	.375	.375	.375
Ed Olivares	3B1	R	21	3	5	0	0	0	0	0	0	0	3	0	.000	.000	.000
Dick Gray	2B4,3B1	R	28	9	5	1	0	0	0	0	1	2	2	0	.000	.250	.000
Gary Kolb	OF2	L	20	9	3	1	0	0	0	0	0	0	0	0	.000	.000	.000
Duke Carmel	1B2,OF1	L	23	4	3	0	0	0	0	0	0	1	1	1	.000	.250	.000
Darrell Johnson	C8	R	31	8	2	0	0	0	0	0	0	1	0	0	.000	.333	.000
Del Rice†	C1	R	37	1	2	0	0	0	0	0	0	1	0	0	.000	.333	.000
Bob Sadowski	2B1	L	23	1	1	0	0	0	0	0	0	1	0	0	.000	.500	.000
Doug Clemens	OF1	L	21	1	0	0	0	0	0	0	0	0	0	0	—	—	—
Rocky Bridges†	2B3	R	32	3	0	0	0	0	0	0	0	0	0	0	—	—	—

Pitcher	T	Age	G	GS	CG	ShO	IP	H	HR	BB	SO	W-L	Sv	ERA
Larry Jackson	R	29	43	38	14	3	282.0	277	22	70	171	18-13	0	3.48
Ray Sadecki	L	19	26	26	7	1	157.1	148	15	86	95	9-9	0	3.78
Curt Simmons†	L	31	23	17	3	1	152.0	149	11	31	63	7-4	0	2.66
Ron Kline	R	28	34	17	1	0	117.2	133	21	43	54	4-9	1	6.04
V. Bend Mizell†	L	29	9	9	0	0	55.1	64	7	28	42	1-3	0	4.55
Mel Nelson	L	24	2	1	0	0	8.0	7	1	2	7	0-1	0	3.38
Lindy McDaniel	R	24	65	2	1	0	116.1	85	8	24	105	12-4	26	2.09
Ernie Broglio	R	24	52	24	9	3	226.1	172	18	100	188	21-9	0	2.74
Bob Gibson	R	24	27	12	2	0	86.2	97	7	48	69	3-6	0	5.61
Bob Duliba	R	25	27	0	0	0	40.2	49	6	16	23	4-4	0	4.20
Marshall Bridges†	L	29	20	1	0	0	31.1	33	2	16	27	2-2	1	3.45
Bob Miller	R	21	15	7	0	0	52.2	53	2	17	33	4-3	0	3.42
Bob Grim†	R	30	15	0	0	0	20.2	22	1	9	15	1-0	0	3.05
Ed Bauta	R	25	9	0	0	0	15.2	14	4	11	6	0-0	1	6.32
Frank Barnes	R	33	4	1	0	0	7.2	8	1	9	8	0-1	1	3.52
Cal Browning	L	22	1	0	0	0	0.2	5	1	1	0	0-0	0	40.50

1960 Los Angeles Dodgers 4th NL 82-72 .532 13.0 GB

Walter Alston

Player	Gm by Position	B	Age	G	AB	R	H	2B	3B	HR	RBI	BB	SO	SB	Avg	OBP	Slg
John Roseboro	C87,1B1,3B1	L	27	103	287	22	61	15	3	8	42	44	53	7	.213	.323	.369
Norm Larker	1B119,OF2	L	29	133	440	56	142	26	3	5	78	36	24	1	.323	.368	.430
Charlie Neal	2B136,SS3	R	29	139	477	60	122	23	2	8	40	48	75	5	.256	.321	.363
Jim Gilliam	3B130,2B30	S	31	151	557	96	138	20	2	5	40	96	28	12	.248	.359	.318
Maury Wills	SS145	S	27	148	516	75	152	15	2	0	27	35	47	50	.295	.342	.331
Wally Moon	OF127	L	30	138	469	74	140	21	6	13	69	67	53	6	.299	.383	.452
Frank Howard	OF115,1B4	R	23	117	448	54	120	15	2	23	77	32	108	0	.268	.320	.464
Tommy Davis	OF87,3B5	R	21	110	352	43	97	18	1	11	44	13	35	6	.276	.302	.426
Duke Snider	OF75	L	33	101	235	38	57	13	5	14	36	46	54	1	.243	.366	.519
Gil Hodges	1B92,3B10	R	36	101	197	22	39	8	1	8	30	26	37	0	.198	.291	.371
Don Demeter	OF62	R	25	64	168	23	46	7	1	9	29	8	34	0	.274	.306	.488
Norm Sherry	C44	R	28	47	138	22	39	4	1	8	19	12	29	0	.283	.353	.500
Joe Pignatano	C40	R	30	58	90	11	21	4	0	2	9	15	17	1	.233	.343	.344
Willie Davis	OF22	L	20	22	88	12	28	6	1	2	10	4	12	3	.318	.348	.477
Chuck Essegian	OF18	R	28	52	79	8	17	3	0	3	11	8	24	0	.215	.284	.367
Charley Smith	3B18	R	22	18	60	2	10	1	1	0	5	1	15	0	.167	.172	.217
Bob Lillis	SS23,3B14,2B1	R	30	48	60	6	16	4	0	0	6	2	6	2	.267	.290	.333
Bob Aspromonte	SS15,3B4	R	22	21	55	1	10	1	0	1	6	0	6	1	.182	.196	.255
Ron Fairly	OF13	L	21	14	37	6	4	0	3	1	3	7	12	0	.108	.250	.351
Irv Noren†		L	35	26	25	1	5	0	0	1	1	1	8	0	.200	.259	.320
Doug Camilli	C6	R	23	6	24	4	8	2	0	1	3	1	4	0	.333	.360	.542
Sandy Amoros†	OF3	L	30	9	14	1	2	0	0	0	0	3	2	0	.143	.294	.143
Carl Furillo	OF2	R	38	8	10	1	2	0	1	0	1	0	2	0	.200	.200	.400
Rip Repulski†	OF2	R	32	4	5	0	1	0	0	0	0	0	1	0	.200	.200	.200

Pitcher	T	Age	G	GS	CG	ShO	IP	H	HR	BB	SO	W-L	Sv	ERA
Don Drysdale	R	23	41	36	15	5	269.0	214	27	72	246	15-14	2	2.84
Johnny Podres	L	27	34	33	8	1	227.2	217	25	71	159	14-12	0	3.08
Stan Williams	R	23	38	30	9	2	207.1	162	26	72	175	14-10	1	3.00
Sandy Koufax	L	24	37	26	7	2	175.0	133	20	100	197	8-13	1	3.91
Roger Craig	R	30	21	15	6	1	115.2	99	0	43	69	8-3	0	3.27
Jim Golden	R	24	1	1	0	0	7.0	6	1	4	4	1-0	0	6.43
Ed Roebuck	R	28	58	0	0	0	116.2	109	13	38	77	8-3	8	2.78
Larry Sherry	R	24	57	3	1	0	142.1	125	14	82	114	14-10	7	3.79
Danny McDevitt	L	27	24	7	0	0	53.0	51	7	42	30	0-4	0	4.25
Ed Palmquist	R	27	22	0	0	0	39.0	34	6	16	23	0-1	0	2.54
Clem Labine†	R	33	13	0	0	0	17.0	26	1	8	15	0-1	1	5.82
Ed Rakow	R	24	9	2	0	0	22.0	30	5	11	9	0-1	0	7.36
Phil Ortega	R	20	3	1	0	0	6.1	12	1	5	4	0-0	0	17.05

1960 San Francisco Giants 5th NL 79-75 .513 16.0 GB

Bill Rigney (33-25)/Tom Sheehan (46-50)

Player	Gm by Position	B	Age	G	AB	R	H	2B	3B	HR	RBI	BB	SO	SB	Avg	OBP	Slg
Bob Schmidt	C108	R	27	110	344	31	92	12	1	8	37	26	51	0	.267	.317	.378
Willie McCovey	1B71	L	22	101	260	37	62	15	3	13	51	45	53	1	.238	.349	.469
on Blasingame	2B133	L	28	136	523	72	123	12	8	2	31	49	53	14	.235	.302	.300
Jim Davenport	3B103,SS7	R	26	112	363	43	91	15	3	6	38	26	58	0	.251	.306	.358
Eddie Bressoud	SS115	R	28	116	386	37	87	19	6	9	43	35	72	1	.225	.290	.376
Willie Mays	OF152	R	29	153	595	107	190	29	12	29	103	61	70	25	.319	.381	.555
Willie Kirkland	OF143	L	26	146	515	59	130	21	10	21	65	44	86	12	.252	.315	.454
Felipe Alou	OF95	R	25	106	322	48	85	17	3	8	44	16	42	10	.264	.299	.410
Orlando Cepeda	OF91,1B63	R	22	151	569	81	169	36	3	24	96	34	91	15	.297	.343	.497
Joey Amalfitano	3B63,2B33,SS3*	R	26	106	328	47	91	15	3	1	27	26	31	2	.277	.335	.351
Andre Rodgers	SS41,3B21,1B6*	R	25	81	217	22	53	8	5	2	22	24	44	1	.244	.325	.355
Hobie Landrith	C70	L	30	71	190	18	46	10	0	1	20	23	11	1	.242	.321	.311
Jim Marshall	1B28,OF6	L	29	75	118	19	28	2	2	2	13	17	24	0	.237	.331	.339
Dave Philley†	OF10,3B3	S	40	39	61	5	10	0	0	1	7	6	14	0	.164	.239	.213
Dale Long†	1B10	L	34	37	54	4	9	0	0	3	6	7	7	0	.167	.262	.333
Jose Pagan	SS11,3B1	R	25	18	49	8	14	2	2	0	2	1	6	2	.286	.300	.408
Neil Wilson	C6	L	25	6	10	0	0	0	0	0	0	1	2	0	.000	.091	.000
Matty Alou	OF1	L	21	4	3	1	1	0	0	0	0	0	0	0	.333	.333	.333

J. Amalfitano, 1 G at OF; A. Rodgers, 2 G at OF

Pitcher	T	Age	G	GS	CG	ShO	IP	H	HR	BB	SO	W-L	Sv	ERA
Sam Jones	R	34	39	35	13	3	234.0	200	18	91	190	18-14	0	3.19
Mike McCormick	L	21	40	34	15	4	253.0	228	15	65	154	15-12	3	2.70
Jack Sanford	R	31	37	34	11	6	219.0	199	11	99	125	12-14	0	3.82
Billy O'Dell	L	27	43	24	6	1	202.2	198	16	72	145	8-13	2	3.20
Juan Marichal	R	22	11	11	6	1	81.1	59	5	28	58	6-2	0	2.66
Stu Miller	R	32	47	3	2	0	101.2	100	9	31	65	7-6	2	3.90
Johnny Antonelli	L	30	41	10	1	1	112.1	106	7	47	57	6-7	11	3.77
Billy Loes	R	30	37	0	0	0	45.2	40	9	17	28	3-2	5	4.93
Bud Byerly	R	39	19	0	0	0	22.0	32	3	6	13	1-0	2	5.32
Georges Maranda	R	28	17	4	0	0	50.2	50	6	30	28	1-4	0	4.62
Sherman Jones	R	25	16	0	0	0	32.0	37	3	11	10	1-1	1	3.09
Joe Shipley	R	25	15	0	0	0	20.0	20	2	9	9	0-0	0	5.40
Don Choate	R	21	4	0	0	0	8.0	7	0	4	7	0-0	0	2.25
Eddie Fisher	R	23	3	1	1	0	12.2	11	2	2	7	1-0	0	3.55
Ray Monzant	R	27	1	0	0	0	1.0	1	1	0	1	0-0	0	9.00

1960 Cincinnati Reds 6th NL 67-87 .435 28.0 GB

Fred Hutchinson

Player	Gm by Position	B	Age	G	AB	R	H	2B	3B	HR	RBI	BB	SO	SB	Avg	OBP	Slg
Ed Bailey	C129	L	29	133	441	52	115	19	3	13	67	59	70	1	.261	.346	.406
Frank Robinson	1B78,OF51,3B1	R	24	139	464	86	138	33	6	31	83	82	67	13	.297	.407	.595
Billy Martin	2B97	R	32	103	317	34	78	17	1	3	16	27	34	0	.246	.304	.334
Eddie Kasko	3B86,2B33,SS15	R	28	126	479	56	140	21	1	6	51	46	37	9	.292	.359	.378
Roy McMillan	SS116,2B10	R	29	124	399	42	94	12	2	10	42	35	40	2	.236	.301	.351
Vada Pinson	OF154	L	21	154	652	107	187	37	12	20	61	47	96	32	.287	.339	.472
Gus Bell	OF131	L	31	143	515	65	135	19	5	12	62	29	40	4	.262	.300	.388
Wally Post†	OF67	R	30	77	249	36	70	14	0	17	38	28	51	0	.281	.350	.542
Gordy Coleman	1B66	L	25	66	251	26	68	10	1	6	32	12	32	1	.271	.308	.390
Jerry Lynch	OF32	L	29	102	159	23	46	8	2	6	27	16	25	0	.289	.356	.478
Cliff Cook	3B47,OF4	R	23	54	149	9	31	7	0	3	13	8	51	0	.208	.247	.315
Puddin' Head Jones	3B46,2B1	R	34	79	149	16	40	7	0	3	27	31	16	1	.268	.388	.376
Leo Cardenas	SS47	R	21	48	142	13	33	2	4	1	12	6	32	0	.232	.264	.324
Elio Chacon	2B43,OF2	R	23	49	116	14	21	1	0	0	7	14	23	7	.181	.271	.190
Tony Gonzalez†	OF31	L	23	39	99	10	21	5	1	3	14	4	27	1	.212	.248	.374
Lee Walls†	OF24,1B2	R	27	29	84	12	23	3	2	1	7	17	20	2	.274	.392	.393
Dutch Dotterer	C31	R	28	33	79	4	18	5	0	2	11	13	10	0	.228	.337	.367
Harry Anderson†	1B15,OF4	L	28	42	66	6	11	3	0	1	9	11	20	0	.167	.282	.258
Joe Azcue	C14	R	20	14	31	1	3	0	0	0	3	2	6	0	.097	.152	.097
Frank House	C8	L	30	23	28	0	5	2	0	0	3	0	2	0	.179	.179	.250
Joe Gaines	OF3	R	23	11	15	2	3	0	0	0	1	0	1	0	.200	.200	.200
Whitey Lockman	1B5	L	33	21	10	6	2	0	0	1	1	2	3	0	.200	.385	.500
Rogelio Alvarez	1B2	R	22	3	9	1	1	0	0	0	0	0	3	0	.111	.111	.111
Pete Whisenant†		R	30	1	1	0	0	0	0	0	0	0	0	0	.000	.000	.000

Pitcher	T	Age	G	GS	CG	ShO	IP	H	HR	BB	SO	W-L	Sv	ERA
Bob Purkey	R	30	41	33	11	1	252.2	259	23	59	97	17-11	0	3.60
Jay Hook	R	23	36	33	10	2	222.0	222	31	73	103	11-18	0	4.50
Jim O'Toole	L	23	34	31	7	2	196.1	198	14	66	124	12-12	1	3.80
Cal McLish	R	34	37	21	2	1	151.1	170	16	48	56	4-14	0	4.16
Don Newcombe†	R	34	16	15	1	0	82.2	99	12	14	36	4-6	0	4.57
Jim Maloney	R	20	11	10	2	1	63.2	61	5	37	48	2-6	0	4.66
Jim Brosnan	R	30	57	2	0	0	99.0	79	4	22	62	7-2	12	2.36
Bill Henry	L	32	51	0	0	0	67.2	62	8	20	58	1-5	17	3.19
Joe Nuxhall	L	31	38	6	0	0	112.0	130	8	27	72	1-8	0	4.42
Bob Grim†	R	30	26	0	0	0	30.1	32	3	10	22	2-2	2	4.45
Claude Osteen	L	20	20	3	0	0	48.1	53	5	30	15	0-1	0	5.03
Marshall Bridges†	L	29	14	0	0	0	25.1	14	1	7	26	4-0	2	1.07
Raul Sanchez	R	29	8	0	0	0	14.2	12	1	11	5	1-0	0	4.91
Brooks Lawrence	R	35	7	0	0	0	7.2	9	1	8	2	1-0	1	10.57
Ted Wieand	R	27	5	0	0	0	4.1	4	2	5	3	0-1	0	10.38
Orlando Pena	R	26	4	0	0	0	9.1	8	0	3	9	0-1	0	2.89
Duane Richards	R	23	2	0	0	0	3.0	5	0	2	2	0-0	0	9.00

1960 Chicago Cubs 7th NL 60-94 .390 35.0 GB

Charlie Grimm (6-11)/Lou Boudreau (54-83)

Player	Gm by Position	B	Age	G	AB	R	H	2B	3B	HR	RBI	BB	SO	SB	Avg	OBP	Slg
Moe Thacker	C50	R	26	54	90	5	14	1	0	0	6	14	20	1	.156	.269	.167
Ed Bouchee†	1B80	L	27	98	299	33	71	11	1	5	44	45	51	2	.237	.335	.331
Jerry Kindall	2B82,SS2	R	25	89	246	17	59	16	2	2	23	5	52	4	.240	.253	.346
Ron Santo	3B94	R	20	95	347	44	87	24	2	9	44	31	44	0	.251	.311	.409
Ernie Banks	SS156	R	29	156	597	94	162	32	7	41	117	71	69	1	.271	.350	.554
Richie Ashburn	OF146	L	33	151	547	99	159	16	5	0	40	116	50	16	.291	.415	.338
Bob Will	OF121	L	28	138	475	58	121	20	9	6	53	47	54	1	.255	.321	.373
George Altman	OF79,1B21	L	27	119	334	50	89	16	4	13	51	32	67	4	.266	.330	.455
Frank Thomas	1B50,OF49,3B33	R	31	135	479	54	114	12	1	21	64	28	74	1	.238	.280	.399
Don Zimmer	2B75,3B45,SS5*	R	29	132	368	37	95	16	7	6	35	27	56	8	.258	.307	.389
Sammy Taylor	C43	L	27	74	150	14	31	9	0	3	17	6	18	0	.207	.241	.327
Walt Moryn†	OF30	L	34	38	109	12	32	4	0	2	11	13	19	2	.294	.366	.385
El Tappe	C49	R	33	51	103	11	24	7	0	0	3	11	12	0	.233	.313	.301
Al Heist	OF33	R	32	41	102	11	28	5	3	1	6	10	12	3	.275	.339	.412
Earl Averill†	C34,3B1,OF1	R	28	52	102	14	24	4	0	1	13	11	16	1	.235	.310	.304
Dick Gernert†	1B18,OF5	R	31	52	96	8	24	3	0	0	11	10	19	1	.250	.321	.281
Tony Taylor†	2B19	R	24	19	76	14	20	3	3	1	9	8	12	2	.263	.337	.421
Danny Murphy	OF21	L	17	31	75	7	9	2	0	1	6	4	13	0	.120	.175	.187
Lou Johnson	OF25	R	25	34	68	6	14	2	1	0	1	5	19	3	.206	.270	.265
Del Rice†	C18	R	37	18	52	2	12	3	0	0	4	2	7	0	.231	.255	.288
Billy Williams	OF12	L	22	12	47	4	13	0	2	2	7	5	12	0	.277	.346	.489
Jim Hegan	C22	R	39	24	43	4	9	2	1	1	5	1	10	0	.209	.244	.372
Grady Hatton	2B8	L	37	28	38	3	13	0	0	0	7	2	5	0	.342	.381	.342
Dick Bertell	C5	R	24	5	15	0	2	0	0	0	2	3	1	0	.133	.263	.133
Sammy Drake	3B6,2B2	S	25	15	15	5	1	0	0	0	0	1	4	0	.067	.125	.067
Art Schult	OF4,1B1	R	32	12	15	1	2	1	0	0	1	1	3	0	.133	.188	.200
Cal Neeman†	C9	R	31	9	13	0	2	1	0	0	0	0	5	0	.154	.154	.231
Irv Noren†	1B1,OF1	L	35	12	11	0	1	0	0	0	1	3	4	0	.091	.286	.091
Nelson Mathews	OF2	R	18	3	8	1	2	0	0	0	0	0	2	0	.250	.250	.250
Jim McKnight	2B1,OF1	R	24	3	6	0	2	0	0	0	0	0	1	0	.333	.333	.333

D. Zimmer, 2 G at OF

Pitcher	T	Age	G	GS	CG	ShO	IP	H	HR	BB	SO	W-L	Sv	ERA
Glen Hobbie	R	24	46	36	16	4	258.2	253	27	101	134	16-20	1	3.97
Bob Anderson	R	24	38	30	5	0	203.2	201	26	68	115	9-11	1	4.11
Dick Ellsworth	L	20	31	27	6	0	176.2	170	12	72	94	7-13	0	3.72
Don Cardwell†	R	24	31	26	6	1	177.0	166	19	68	129	8-14	0	4.37
Jim Brewer	L	22	5	4	0	0	21.2	25	2	6	7	0-3	0	5.82
Don Elston	R	31	60	0	0	0	127.0	109	17	55	85	8-9	11	3.40
Seth Morehead	L	25	45	7	2	0	123.1	123	17	46	64	2-9	4	3.94
Joe Schaffernoth	R	22	33	0	0	0	55.0	46	2	17	33	2-3	3	2.78
Moe Drabowsky	R	24	32	7	0	0	50.1	71	3	23	26	3-1	1	6.44
Mark Freeman	R	29	30	8	1	0	76.2	70	10	33	50	3-3	1	5.63
Dick Drott	R	23	23	9	0	0	55.1	63	7	42	32	0-6	0	7.16
Ben Johnson	R	29	17	0	0	0	29.1	39	3	11	9	2-1	1	4.91
Mel Wright	R	32	9	0	0	0	16.1	17	1	3	8	0-1	2	4.96
Art Ceccarelli	L	30	7	1	0	0	13.0	16	1	4	10	0-0	0	5.54
John Goetz	R	22	4	0	0	0	6.1	10	2	4	6	0-0	0	12.79
Dick Burwell	R	20	3	1	0	0	9.2	11	2	7	1	0-0	0	5.59
Al Schroll	R	28	2	0	0	0	2.2	3	1	5	2	0-0	0	10.13

1960 Philadelphia Phillies 8th NL 59-95 .383 36.0 GB

Eddie Sawyer (0-1)/Andy Cohen (1-0)/Gene Mauch (58-94)

Player	Gm by Position	B	Age	G	AB	R	H	2B	3B	HR	RBI	BB	SO	SB	Avg	OBP	Slg
Jimmie Coker	C76	R	24	81	252	18	54	5	3	6	34	23	45	0	.214	.289	.329
Pancho Herrera	1B134,2B17	R	26	145	512	61	144	26	6	17	71	51	136	2	.281	.348	.455
Tony Taylor†	2B123,3B4	R	24	127	505	66	145	22	4	4	35	33	86	24	.287	.330	.370
Al Dark†	3B53,1B1	R	38	55	198	29	48	5	1	3	14	19	14	1	.242	.315	.323
Ruben Amaro	SS92	R	24	92	264	25	61	9	1	0	16	21	32	0	.231	.292	.273
Ken Walters	OF119	R	26	124	426	42	102	10	0	8	37	16	50	4	.239	.266	.319
Bobby Del Greco	OF89	R	27	100	300	48	71	16	4	10	26	54	64	1	.237	.355	.417
Johnny Callison	OF86	L	21	99	288	36	75	11	5	9	30	45	70	0	.260	.360	.427
Tony Curry	OF64	L	21	95	245	26	64	14	2	6	34	16	53	0	.261	.308	.408
Tony Gonzalez†	OF67	L	23	78	241	27	72	17	5	6	33	11	47	2	.299	.337	.485
Bobby Gene Smith	OF70,3B1	R	26	98	217	24	62	5	2	4	27	10	28	2	.286	.317	.382
Lee Walls†	3B34,OF13,1B7	R	27	65	181	19	36	6	1	3	19	14	32	3	.199	.253	.293
Joe Koppe	SS55,3B2	R	29	58	170	13	29	6	1	1	13	23	47	3	.171	.272	.235
Cal Neeman†	C52	R	31	59	160	13	29	6	2	4	13	16	42	0	.181	.264	.319
Clay Dalrymple	C48	L	23	82	158	11	43	6	2	4	21	15	21	0	.272	.343	.411
Ted Lepcio	3B50,SS14,2B5	R	29	69	141	16	32	7	0	2	8	17	41	0	.227	.315	.319
Bobby Malkmus	SS29,2B23,3B12	R	28	79	133	16	28	4	1	1	12	11	28	2	.211	.267	.278
Harry Anderson†	OF16,1B12	L	28	38	93	10	23	2	0	5	12	10	19	0	.247	.333	.430
Wally Post†	OF22	R	30	34	84	11	24	6	1	2	12	9	24	0	.286	.351	.452
Joe Morgan†	3B24	L	29	26	83	5	11	2	2	0	2	6	11	0	.133	.191	.205
Ed Bouchee†	1B22	L	27	22	65	1	17	4	0	0	8	9	11	0	.262	.355	.323
Jim Woods	3B11	R	20	11	34	4	6	0	0	1	3	3	13	0	.176	.243	.265
Dave Philley†	OF3,1B2	S	40	14	15	2	5	2	0	0	4	3	2	0	.333	.444	.467
Bobby Wine	SS4	R	21	4	14	1	2	0	0	0	0	0	2	0	.143	.143	.143

Pitcher	T	Age	G	GS	CG	ShO	IP	H	HR	BB	SO	W-L	Sv	ERA
Robin Roberts	R	33	35	33	13	2	237.1	256	31	34	122	12-16	1	4.02
John Buzhardt	R	23	30	29	5	0	200.1	198	14	68	73	5-16	0	3.86
Gene Conley	R	29	29	25	9	2	183.1	192	10	42	117	8-14	0	3.68
Jim Owens	R	26	31	22	6	0	150.0	182	21	64	83	4-14	0	5.04
Art Mahaffey	R	22	14	12	5	1	93.1	78	9	34	56	7-3	0	2.31
Don Cardwell†	R	24	5	4	0	0	28.1	28	4	11	21	1-2	0	4.45
Jack Meyer	R	28	7	4	0	0	25.0	25	2	11	18	3-1	0	4.32
Curt Simmons†	L	31	4	2	0	0	4.0	13	3	6	4	0-0	0	18.00
Turk Farrell	R	26	59	0	0	0	103.1	88	3	29	70	10-6	11	2.70
Chris Short	L	22	42	10	2	0	107.1	101	8	52	54	6-9	3	3.94
Humberto Robinson	R	30	33	1	0	0	49.2	48	6	22	31	0-4	0	3.44
Dallas Green	R	25	23	10	5	1	108.2	100	10	44	51	3-6	0	4.06
Ruben Gomez	R	32	22	1	0	0	52.1	68	7	9	24	0-3	1	5.33
Taylor Phillips	L	27	10	1	0	0	14.0	21	2	4	6	0-1	0	8.36
Al Neiger	L	21	6	0	0	0	12.2	16	2	4	3	0-0	0	5.68
Hank Mason	R	29	3	0	0	0	5.2	9	1	5	3	0-0	0	9.53

»1961 New York Yankees 1st AL 109-53 .673 —

Ralph Houk

Player	Gm by Position	B	Age	G	AB	R	H	2B	3B	HR	RBI	BB	SO	SB	Avg	OBP	Slg
Elston Howard	C111,1B9	R	32	129	446	64	155	17	5	21	77	28	65	0	.348	.387	.549
Bill Skowron	1B149	R	30	150	561	76	150	23	4	28	89	35	108	0	.267	.318	.472
Bobby Richardson	2B161	R	25	162	662	80	173	17	5	3	49	30	23	9	.261	.295	.316
Clete Boyer	3B141,SS12,OF1	R	24	148	504	61	113	19	5	11	55	63	83	1	.224	.308	.347
Tony Kubek	SS145	L	24	153	617	84	170	38	6	8	46	27	60	1	.276	.306	.395
Roger Maris	OF160	L	26	161	590	132	159	16	4	61	142	94	67	0	.269	.372	.620
Mickey Mantle	OF150	S	29	153	514	132	163	16	6	54	128	126	112	12	.317	.448	.687
Yogi Berra	OF87,C15	L	36	119	395	62	107	11	0	22	61	35	28	2	.271	.330	.466
Johnny Blanchard	C48,OF15	L	28	93	243	38	74	10	1	21	54	27	28	1	.305	.382	.613
Hector Lopez	OF72	R	31	93	243	27	54	7	2	3	22	24	38	1	.222	.292	.305
Bob Cerv†	OF30,1B3	R	35	57	118	17	32	5	1	6	20	12	17	1	.271	.344	.483
Billy Gardner†	3B33,2B6	R	33	41	99	11	21	5	0	1	2	6	18	0	.212	.278	.293
Joe DeMaestri	SS18,2B5,3B4	R	32	30	41	1	6	0	0	0	2	0	13	0	.146	.146	.146
Deron Johnson†	3B8	R	22	13	19	1	2	0	0	0	2	2	5	0	.105	.182	.105
Earl Torgeson†	1B8	L	37	22	18	3	2	0	0	0	0	8	3	0	.111	.385	.111
Jack Reed	OF27	R	28	28	13	4	2	0	0	0	1	1	1	0	.154	.214	.154
Bob Hale†	1B5	L	27	11	13	2	2	0	0	1	1	0	0	0	.154	.154	.385
Jesse Gonder		L	25	15	12	2	4	1	0	0	3	3	1	0	.333	.467	.417
Tom Tresh	SS3	S	23	9	8	1	2	0	0	0	0	0	1	0	.250	.250	.250
Lee Thomas†		L	25	2	2	0	1	0	0	0	0	0	0	0	.500	.500	.500

Pitcher	T	Age	G	GS	CG	ShO	IP	H	HR	BB	SO	W-L	Sv	ERA
Whitey Ford	L	32	39	39	11	3	283.0	242	23	92	209	25-4	0	3.21
Ralph Terry	R	25	31	27	9	2	188.1	162	19	42	86	16-3	0	3.15
Bill Stafford	R	21	36	25	8	3	195.0	168	13	59	101	14-9	2	2.68
Rollie Sheldon	R	24	35	21	6	2	162.2	149	17	55	84	11-5	0	3.60
Bud Daley†	L	28	23	17	7	0	129.2	127	17	51	83	8-9	0	3.96
Bob Turley	R	30	15	12	1	0	72.0	74	11	51	48	3-5	0	5.75
Art Ditmar†	R	32	12	8	1	0	54.1	59	9	14	24	2-3	0	4.64
Luis Arroyo	L	34	65	0	0	0	119.0	83	5	49	87	15-5	29	2.19
Jim Coates	R	28	43	11	4	1	141.1	128	15	53	80	11-5	5	3.44
Hal Reniff	R	22	25	0	0	0	45.1	31	1	31	21	2-0	2	2.58
Tex Clevenger†	R	28	21	0	0	0	31.2	35	3	21	14	1-1	0	4.83
Danny McDevitt†	L	28	8	2	0	0	13.0	18	2	8	8	1-2	1	7.62
Al Downing	L	20	5	1	0	0	9.0	7	0	12	12	0-1	0	8.00
Ryne Duren†	R	32	4	0	0	0	5.0	2	2	4	7	0-1	0	5.40
Johnny James†	R	27	1	0	0	0	1.1	1	0	0	2	0-0	0	0.00
Duke Maas	R	32	1	0	0	0	0.1	2	0	0	0	0-0	0	54.00

754 Seasons: Team Rosters

1961 Detroit Tigers 2nd AL 101-61 .623 8.0 GB

Bob Scheffing

Player	Gm by Position	B	Age	G	AB	R	H	2B	3B	HR	RBI	BB	SO	SB	Avg	OBP	Slg
Dick Brown	C91	R	26	93	308	32	82	12	2	16	45	22	57	0	.266	.312	.474
Norm Cash	1B157	L	26	159	535	119	193	22	8	41	132	124	85	11	.361	.487	.662
Jake Wood	2B162	R	24	162	663	96	171	17	14	11	69	58	141	30	.258	.320	.376
Steve Boros	3B116	R	24	116	396	51	107	18	2	5	62	68	42	4	.270	.382	.364
Chico Fernandez	SS121,3B8	R	29	133	435	41	108	15	4	3	40	36	45	8	.248	.305	.322
Rocky Colavito	OF161	R	27	163	583	129	169	30	2	45	140	113	75	1	.290	.402	.580
Bill Bruton	OF155	L	35	160	596	99	153	15	5	17	63	61	66	22	.257	.327	.384
Al Kaline	OF147,3B1	R	26	153	586	116	190	41	7	19	82	66	42	14	.324	.393	.515
Dick McAuliffe	SS55,3B22	L	21	80	285	36	73	12	4	6	33	24	39	2	.256	.322	.389
Mike Roarke	C85	R	30	86	229	21	51	6	1	2	22	20	31	0	.223	.283	.284
Charlie Maxwell	OF25	L	34	79	131	11	30	4	2	5	18	20	24	0	.229	.333	.405
Bubba Morton	OF30	R	29	77	108	26	31	5	1	2	19	9	25	3	.287	.342	.407
Bobo Osborne	1B11,3B8	L	25	71	93	8	20	7	0	2	13	20	15	1	.215	.354	.355
Reno Bertoia†	3B13,2B7,SS1	R	26	24	46	6	10	1	0	1	4	3	8	2	.217	.265	.304
Ozzie Virgil†	3B9,C3,2B1*	R	28	20	30	1	4	0	0	1	1	1	5	0	.133	.161	.233
Frank House	C14	L	31	17	22	3	5	1	1	0	3	4	2	0	.227	.333	.364
George Alusik	OF1	R	26	15	14	0	2	0	0	0	2	1	4	0	.143	.188	.143
Harry Chiti	C5	R	28	5	12	0	1	0	0	0	0	1	2	0	.083	.154	.083
Bill Freehan	C3	R	19	4	10	1	4	0	0	0	4	1	0	0	.400	.455	.400
Chuck Cottier†	SS8,2B2	R	25	10	7	2	2	0	0	0	1	1	1	0	.286	.375	.286
George Thomas†	OF2,SS1	R	23	17	6	2	0	0	0	0	0	0	4	0	.000	.000	.000
Vic Wertz†		L	36	8	6	0	1	0	0	0	1	0	1	0	.167	.167	.167
Dick Gernert†		R	32	6	5	1	1	0	0	1	1	1	2	0	.200	.333	.800

O. Virgil, 1 G at SS

Pitcher	T	Age	G	GS	CG	ShO	IP	H	HR	BB	SO	W-L	Sv	ERA
Jim Bunning	R	29	38	37	12	4	268.0	232	25	71	194	17-11	1	3.19
Frank Lary	R	31	36	36	22	4	275.1	252	24	66	146	23-9	0	3.24
Don Mossi	L	32	35	34	12	1	240.1	237	29	47	137	15-7	1	2.96
Paul Foytack	R	30	32	20	6	0	169.2	152	27	56	89	11-10	0	3.93
Phil Regan	R	24	32	16	6	0	120.0	134	19	41	46	10-7	2	5.25
Ron Kline†	R	29	10	8	3	1	56.1	53	3	17	27	5-3	0	2.72
Hank Aguirre	L	30	45	0	0	0	55.1	44	5	38	32	4-4	8	3.25
Terry Fox	R	25	39	0	0	0	57.1	42	6	16	32	5-2	12	1.41
Bill Fischer†	R	30	26	1	0	0	46.2	54	10	17	18	3-2	3	5.01
Bob Bruce	R	28	14	6	0	0	44.2	57	6	24	25	1-2	0	4.43
Jim Donohue†	R	22	14	0	0	0	20.1	23	2	15	20	1-1	1	3.54
Gerry Staley†	R	40	13	0	0	0	13.1	15	1	6	8	1-1	2	3.38
Hal Woodeshick†	L	28	12	2	0	0	18.1	25	3	17	13	1-1	0	7.85
Manny Montejo	R	25	12	0	0	0	16.1	13	2	6	15	0-0	0	3.86
Fred Gladding	R	25	8	0	0	0	16.1	18	1	11	11	1-0	0	3.31
Ron Nischwitz	L	23	6	1	0	0	11.1	13	2	8	8	0-1	0	5.56
Howie Koplitz	R	23	4	1	1	0	12.0	16	0	8	9	2-0	0	2.25
Joe Grzenda	L	24	4	0	0	0	5.2	9	2	2	0	1-0	0	7.94
Jerry Casale†	R	27	3	1	0	0	12.0	15	3	3	6	0-0	0	5.25

1961 Baltimore Orioles 3rd AL 95-67 .586 14.0 GB

Paul Richards (78-57)/Lum Harris (17-10)

Player	Gm by Position	B	Age	G	AB	R	H	2B	3B	HR	RBI	BB	SO	SB	Avg	OBP	Slg
Gus Triandos	C114	R	30	115	397	35	97	21	0	17	63	44	60	0	.244	.320	.426
Jim Gentile	1B144	L	27	148	486	96	147	25	2	46	141	96	106	1	.302	.423	.646
Jerry Adair	2B107,SS27,3B2	R	24	133	386	41	102	21	1	9	37	35	51	5	.264	.326	.394
Brooks Robinson	3B163,2B2,SS1	R	24	163	668	89	192	38	7	7	61	47	57	1	.287	.334	.397
Ron Hansen	SS149,2B7	R	23	155	533	51	132	13	2	12	51	66	96	1	.248	.329	.347
Jackie Brandt	OF136,3B1	R	27	139	516	93	153	18	5	16	72	62	51	10	.297	.371	.444
Russ Snyder	OF108	L	27	115	312	46	91	13	5	1	13	20	32	5	.292	.333	.375
Whitey Herzog	OF98	L	29	113	323	39	94	11	6	5	35	50	41	1	.291	.387	.409
Dick Williams	OF75,1B20,3B2	R	32	103	310	37	64	15	2	8	24	20	38	0	.206	.251	.345
Marv Breeding	2B80	R	27	90	244	32	51	8	0	1	16	14	33	5	.209	.250	.254
Earl Robinson	OF82	R	24	96	222	37	59	12	3	8	30	31	54	4	.266	.354	.455
Dave Philley	OF25,1B1	S	41	99	144	13	36	9	2	1	23	10	20	2	.250	.293	.361
Hank Foiles	C38	R	32	43	124	18	34	6	0	6	19	12	27	0	.274	.336	.468
Marv Throneberry†	OF15,1B11	L	27	56	96	9	20	3	0	5	11	12	20	0	.208	.296	.396
Jim Busby	OF71	R	34	75	89	15	23	3	1	0	6	8	10	2	.258	.316	.315
Gene Stephens†	OF30	L	28	32	58	4	11	2	0	0	2	14	7	1	.190	.347	.224
Charlie Lau†	C17	L	28	17	47	3	8	0	0	1	4	1	3	0	.170	.188	.234
Clint Courtney†	C16	L	34	22	45	3	12	2	0	0	4	10	3	0	.267	.400	.311
Walt Dropo	1B12	R	38	14	27	1	7	0	0	1	2	4	3	0	.259	.355	.370
Boog Powell	OF3	L	19	4	13	0	1	0	0	0	0	0	2	0	.077	.077	.077
Barry Shetrone	OF2	L	22	3	7	0	1	0	0	0	0	0	2	0	.143	.143	.143
Frank Zupo	C4	L	21	5	4	1	2	1	0	0	1	1	1	0	.500	.600	.750
Chuck Essegian†		R	29	1	1	0	0	0	0	0	0	0	0	0	.000	.000	.000

Pitcher	T	Age	G	GS	CG	ShO	IP	H	HR	BB	SO	W-L	Sv	ERA
Steve Barber	L	22	37	34	14	8	248.1	194	13	130	150	18-12	1	3.33
Chuck Estrada	R	23	33	31	6	1	212.0	159	19	132	160	15-9	0	3.69
Jack Fisher	R	22	36	25	10	1	196.0	205	17	75	118	10-13	1	3.90
Milt Pappas	R	22	26	23	11	4	177.2	134	16	78	89	13-9	1	3.04
Hal Brown	R	36	27	23	6	3	166.2	153	14	33	61	10-6	1	3.19
Hoyt Wilhelm	R	37	51	1	0	0	109.2	89	5	41	87	9-7	18	2.30
Billy Hoeft	L	29	35	12	3	1	138.0	106	7	55	100	7-4	3	2.02
Wes Stock	R	27	35	1	0	0	71.2	58	3	27	47	5-0	3	3.01
Dick Hall	R	30	29	13	4	2	122.1	102	10	30	92	7-5	4	3.09
Dick Hyde	R	32	15	0	0	0	21.0	18	1	13	15	1-2	0	5.57
Gordon Jones	R	31	3	0	0	0	5.0	5	3	0	4	0-1	1	5.40
Jim Lehew	R	23	2	0	0	0	2.0	1	0	0	0	0-0	0	0.00
John Papa	R	20	2	0	0	0	1.0	2	1	3	3	0-0	0	18.00

1961 Chicago White Sox 4th AL 86-76 .531 23.0 GB

Al Lopez

Player	Gm by Position	B	Age	G	AB	R	H	2B	3B	HR	RBI	BB	SO	SB	Avg	OBP	Slg
Sherm Lollar	C107	R	36	116	337	38	95	10	1	7	41	37	22	0	.282	.360	.380
Roy Sievers	1B132	R	34	141	492	76	145	26	6	27	92	61	62	1	.295	.377	.537
Nellie Fox	2B159	L	33	159	606	67	152	11	5	2	51	59	12	2	.251	.323	.295
Al Smith	3B80,OF71	R	33	147	532	88	148	29	4	28	93	56	67	4	.278	.348	.506
Luis Aparicio	SS156	R	27	156	625	90	170	24	4	6	45	38	33	53	.272	.313	.352
Minnie Minoso	OF147	R	38	152	540	91	151	28	3	14	82	67	46	9	.280	.369	.420
Jim Landis	OF139	R	27	140	534	87	151	18	8	22	85	65	71	19	.283	.362	.470
Floyd Robinson	OF106	L	25	132	432	69	134	20	7	11	59	52	32	7	.310	.389	.465
J.C. Martin	1B60,3B36	L	24	110	274	26	63	8	3	5	32	21	31	1	.230	.290	.336
Cam Carreon	C71	R	23	78	229	32	62	5	1	4	27	21	24	0	.271	.331	.354
Andy Carey†	3B54	R	29	56	143	21	38	12	3	0	14	11	24	0	.266	.323	.392
Sammy Esposito	3B28,SS20,2B11	R	29	63	94	12	16	5	0	1	8	12	21	0	.170	.259	.255
Al Pilarcik†	OF17	L	30	47	62	9	11	1	0	1	6	9	5	1	.177	.282	.242
Wes Covington†	OF14	L	29	22	59	5	17	1	0	4	15	4	5	0	.288	.333	.508
Mike Hershberger	OF13	R	21	15	55	9	17	3	0	0	5	2	2	1	.309	.333	.364
Billy Goodman	3B7,1B2,2B1	L	35	41	51	4	13	4	0	1	10	7	6	0	.255	.339	.392
Bob Roselli	C10	R	29	22	38	2	10	3	0	0	4	0	11	0	.263	.263	.342
Earl Torgeson†	1B1	L	37	20	15	1	1	0	0	0	1	3	5	0	.067	.211	.067
Dean Look	OF1	R	23	3	6	0	0	0	0	0	0	0	1	0	.000	.000	.000
Joe Ginsberg†	C2	L	34	6	3	0	0	0	0	0	0	1	2	0	.000	.250	.000
Ted Lepcio†	3B1	R	30	5	2	0	0	0	0	0	0	1	0	0	.000	.333	.000
Jim Rivera†		L	38	1	0	0	0	0	0	0	0	0	0	0	—	—	—

Pitcher	T	Age	G	GS	CG	ShO	IP	H	HR	BB	SO	W-L	Sv	ERA
Billy Pierce	L	34	39	28	5	1	180.0	190	17	54	106	10-9	3	3.80
Cal McLish	R	35	31	27	4	0	162.1	178	21	47	80	10-13	1	4.38
Juan Pizarro	L	24	39	25	12	1	194.2	164	17	89	188	14-7	2	3.05
Ray Herbert†	R	31	21	20	4	0	137.2	142	15	36	50	9-6	0	4.05
Early Wynn	R	41	17	16	5	0	110.1	88	11	47	64	8-2	0	3.51
Bob Shaw†	R	28	14	10	3	0	71.1	85	11	20	31	3-4	0	3.79
Herb Score	L	28	8	5	1	0	24.1	22	3	24	14	1-2	0	6.66
Joe Horlen	R	23	5	4	0	0	17.2	25	2	13	11	1-3	0	6.62
Turk Lown	R	37	59	0	0	0	101.0	87	13	35	50	7-5	11	2.76
Frank Baumann	L	27	53	23	5	1	187.2	249	22	59	75	10-13	3	5.61
Russ Kemmerer	R	29	47	2	0	0	96.2	102	10	26	35	3-3	2	4.38
Warren Hacker	R	36	42	0	0	0	57.1	62	8	8	40	3-3	8	3.77
Don Larsen†	R	31	25	3	0	0	74.1	64	5	29	53	7-2	2	4.12
Gerry Staley†	R	40	16	0	0	0	18.0	17	3	5	8	0-3	0	5.00
Gary Peters	L	24	3	0	0	0	10.1	10	0	2	6	0-0	1	1.74
Alan Brice	R	23	3	0	0	0	3.1	4	0	3	3	0-1	0	0.00
Mike DeGerick	R	18	1	0	0	0	1.2	2	0	1	0	0-0	0	5.40

1961 Cleveland Indians 5th AL 78-83 .484 30.5 GB

Jimmy Dykes (77-83)/Mel Harder (1-0)

Player	Gm by Position	B	Age	G	AB	R	H	2B	3B	HR	RBI	BB	SO	SB	Avg	OBP	Slg
John Romano	C141	R	26	142	509	76	152	29	1	21	80	61	60	0	.299	.377	.483
Vic Power	1B141,2B7	R	33	147	563	64	151	34	4	5	63	38	16	4	.268	.309	.369
Johnny Temple	2B129	R	33	129	518	73	143	22	3	3	30	61	36	9	.276	.351	.347
Bubba Phillips	3B143	R	33	143	546	64	144	23	1	18	72	29	61	1	.264	.305	.408
Woodie Held	SS144	R	29	146	509	67	136	23	5	23	78	69	111	0	.267	.354	.468
Tito Francona	OF138,1B14	L	27	155	592	87	178	30	8	16	85	56	52	2	.301	.363	.459
Willie Kirkland	OF138	L	27	146	525	84	136	22	5	27	95	48	77	7	.259	.318	.474
Jimmy Piersall	OF120	R	31	121	484	81	156	26	7	6	40	43	46	8	.322	.378	.442
Mike de la Hoz	2B17,SS17,3B16	R	22	61	173	20	45	10	0	3	23	7	10	0	.260	.295	.370
Chuck Essegian†	OF49	R	29	60	166	25	48	7	1	12	35	10	33	0	.289	.328	.560
Don Dillard	OF39	L	24	74	147	27	40	5	0	7	17	15	28	0	.272	.340	.449
Valmy Thomas	C27	R	32	27	86	7	18	3	0	2	6	6	7	0	.209	.261	.314
Ken Aspromonte†	2B21	R	29	22	70	5	16	6	1	0	5	6	3	0	.229	.286	.343
Bob Nieman†	OF12	R	34	39	65	2	23	6	0	2	10	7	4	1	.354	.417	.538
Walt Bond	OF12	L	23	38	52	7	9	1	1	2	7	6	10	1	.173	.267	.346
Ty Cline	OF12	L	22	12	43	9	9	2	1	0	1	6	1	1	.209	.333	.302
Jack Kubiszyn	3B8,SS7,2B2	R	24	25	42	4	9	0	0	0	0	2	5	0	.214	.250	.214
Bob Hale†		L	27	42	36	0	6	0	0	0	6	1	7	0	.167	.200	.167
Hal Jones	1B10	R	25	12	35	2	6	0	0	2	4	2	12	0	.171	.216	.343
Al Luplow	OF5	L	22	5	18	0	1	0	0	0	0	2	6	0	.056	.150	.056
Joe Morgan	OF2	L	30	4	10	0	2	0	0	0	0	1	3	0	.200	.273	.200

Pitcher	T	Age	G	GS	CG	ShO	IP	H	HR	BB	SO	W-L	Sv	ERA
Mudcat Grant	R	25	35	35	11	3	244.2	207	32	109	146	15-9	0	3.86
Jim Perry	R	25	35	35	6	1	223.2	238	28	87	90	10-17	0	4.71
Gary Bell	R	24	34	34	11	2	228.1	214	32	100	163	12-16	0	4.10
Wynn Hawkins	R	25	30	21	3	1	133.0	139	16	59	51	7-9	1	4.06
Johnny Antonelli†	L	31	11	7	0	0	48.0	68	8	18	23	0-4	0	6.56
Sam McDowell	L	18	1	1	0	0	6.1	3	0	5	5	0-0	0	0.00
Frank Funk	R	25	56	0	0	0	92.1	79	9	31	64	11-11	11	3.31
Bob Allen	L	23	48	0	0	0	81.2	96	7	40	42	3-2	3	3.75
Barry Latman	R	25	45	18	4	2	176.2	163	23	54	108	13-5	5	4.02
Bobby Locke	R	27	37	4	0	0	95.1	112	12	40	37	4-4	2	4.53
Dick Stigman	L	25	22	6	0	0	64.1	65	9	25	48	2-5	0	4.62
Joe Schaffernoth†	R	23	15	0	0	0	17.0	16	2	14	9	0-1	0	4.76
Bill Dailey	R	26	12	0	0	0	19.0	16	0	6	7	1-0	0	0.95
Russ Heman†	R	28	6	0	0	0	10.0	8	0	8	4	0-0	1	3.60
Steve Hamilton	L	25	2	0	0	0	3.0	2	0	3	4	0-0	0	3.00

1961 Boston Red Sox 6th AL 76-86 .469 33.0 GB

Pinky Higgins

Player	Gm by Position	B	Age	G	AB	R	H	2B	3B	HR	RBI	BB	SO	SB	Avg	OBP	Slg
Jim Pagliaroni	C108	R	23	120	376	50	91	17	0	16	58	55	74	1	.242	.342	.415
Pete Runnels	1B113,3B11,2B7*	L	33	143	360	49	114	20	3	3	38	46	32	5	.317	.396	.414
Chuck Schilling	2B158	R	23	158	646	87	167	25	2	5	62	78	77	7	.259	.340	.327
Frank Malzone	3B149	R	31	151	590	74	157	21	4	14	87	44	49	1	.266	.314	.386
Don Buddin	SS109	R	27	115	339	58	89	22	3	6	42	72	45	2	.263	.394	.398
Carl Yastrzemski	OF147	L	21	148	583	71	155	31	6	11	80	50	96	6	.266	.324	.396
Gary Geiger	OF137	L	24	140	499	82	116	21	6	18	64	87	91	16	.232	.349	.407
Jackie Jensen	OF131	R	34	137	498	64	131	21	2	13	66	66	69	9	.263	.350	.392
Vic Wertz†	1B86	L	36	99	317	33	83	16	2	11	60	38	43	0	.262	.333	.429
Carroll Hardy	OF76	R	28	85	281	46	74	20	2	3	36	26	53	4	.263	.330	.381
Russ Nixon	C66	L	26	87	242	24	70	12	2	1	19	13	19	0	.289	.327	.368
Pumpsie Green	SS57,2B7	S	27	88	219	33	57	12	3	6	27	42	32	4	.260	.376	.425
Lu Clinton	OF13	R	23	17	51	4	13	2	1	0	3	2	10	0	.255	.283	.333
Billy Harrell	3B10,SS7,1B3	R	32	37	37	10	6	2	0	0	1	1	8	1	.162	.184	.216
Rip Repulski	OF4	R	33	15	25	2	7	1	0	0	1	1	5	0	.280	.308	.320
Joe Ginsberg†	C6	L	34	19	24	1	6	0	0	0	5	0	2	0	.250	.250	.250
Don Gile	1B6,C1	R	26	8	18	2	5	0	0	1	1	1	5	0	.278	.316	.444

P. Runnels, 1 G at SS

Pitcher	T	Age	G	GS	CG	ShO	IP	H	HR	BB	SO	W-L	Sv	ERA
Bill Monbouquette	R	24	32	32	12	1	236.1	233	24	100	161	14-14	0	3.39
Gene Conley	R	30	33	30	6	2	199.2	229	33	65	113	11-14	1	4.91
Ike Delock	R	31	28	28	3	1	156.0	185	24	52	80	6-9	0	4.90
Don Schwall	R	25	25	25	10	2	178.2	167	8	110	91	15-7	0	3.22
Tom Brewer	R	29	10	9	0	0	42.0	37	4	29	13	3-2	0	3.43
Mike Fornieles	R	29	57	2	1	0	119.1	121	18	54	70	9-8	15	4.68
Tracy Stallard	R	23	43	14	1	0	132.2	110	15	96	109	2-7	2	4.88
Billy Muffett	R	30	38	11	2	0	112.2	130	18	36	47	3-11	2	5.67
Arnold Earley	L	28	33	0	0	0	49.2	42	3	34	44	2-4	7	3.99
Dave Hillman	R	33	28	1	0	0	78.0	70	8	23	39	3-2	0	2.77
Chet Nichols	L	30	26	2	0	0	51.2	40	3	26	20	3-2	3	2.09
Galen Cisco	R	25	17	8	0	0	52.1	67	5	28	26	2-4	0	6.71
Ted Wills	L	27	17	0	0	0	19.2	24	2	19	11	3-2	0	5.95
Wilbur Wood	L	19	6	1	0	0	13.0	14	2	7	7	0-0	0	5.54
Tom Borland	L	28	1	0	0	0	1.0	3	0	0	0	0-0	0	18.00

Seasons: Team Rosters 755

1961 Minnesota Twins 7th AL 70-90 .438 38.0 GB

Cookie Lavagetto (19-30)/Sam Mele (2-5)/Cookie Lavagetto (4-6)/Sam Mele (45-49)

Player	Gm by Position	B	Age	G	AB	R	H	2B	3B	HR	RBI	BB	SO	SB	Avg	OBP	Slg
Earl Battey	C131	R	26	133	460	70	139	24	1	17	55	53	66	3	.302	.377	.470
Harmon Killebrew	1B119,3B45,OF2	R	25	150	541	94	156	20	7	46	122	107	109	1	.288	.405	.606
Billy Martin†	2B105,SS1	R	33	108	374	44	92	15	5	6	36	13	42	3	.246	.275	.361
Bill Tuttle†	3B85,OF64,2B2	R	31	113	370	38	91	12	3	5	38	43	41	1	.246	.321	.335
Zoilo Versalles	SS129	R	21	129	510	65	143	25	5	7	53	25	61	16	.280	.314	.390
Lenny Green	OF153	L	28	156	600	92	171	28	7	9	50	81	50	17	.285	.374	.400
Bob Allison	OF150,1B18	R	26	159	556	83	136	21	3	29	105	103	100	2	.245	.363	.450
Jim Lemon	OF120	R	33	129	423	57	109	26	1	14	52	44	98	1	.258	.329	.423
Billy Gardner†	2B41,3B2	R	33	45	154	13	36	9	0	1	11	10	14	0	.234	.280	.312
Jose Valdivielso	SS43,2B15,3B14	R	27	76	149	15	29	5	0	1	9	8	19	1	.195	.234	.248
Hal Naragon	C36	L	32	57	139	10	42	2	1	2	11	4	8	0	.302	.326	.374
Dan Dobbek	OF48	L	26	72	125	12	21	3	1	4	14	13	18	1	.168	.255	.304
Ted Lepcio†	3B35,2B22,SS6	R	30	47	112	11	19	3	1	7	19	8	31	1	.170	.230	.402
Reno Bertoia†	3B32	R	26	35	104	17	22	2	0	1	8	20	12	0	.212	.333	.260
Don Mincher	1B29	L	23	35	101	18	19	5	1	5	11	22	11	0	.188	.333	.406
Joe Altobelli	OF25,1B2	L	29	41	95	10	21	2	1	3	14	13	14	0	.221	.312	.358
Julio Becquer†	1B18,OF5,P1	L	29	57	84	13	20	2	1	5	18	2	12	0	.238	.253	.476
Elmer Valo†	OF1	L	40	33	32	0	5	2	0	0	4	3	3	0	.156	.250	.219
Ron Henry	C5,1B1	R	24	20	28	1	4	0	0	0	3	2	7	0	.143	.194	.143
Rich Rollins	2B5,3B4	R	23	13	17	3	5	1	0	0	3	2	2	0	.294	.400	.353
Jake Jacobs	OF3	R	24	4	8	0	2	0	0	0	0	0	2	0	.250	.250	.250
Pete Whisenant†	OF5	R	31	10	6	1	0	0	0	0	0	1	2	0	.000	.143	.000
Jim Snyder	2B3	R	28	3	5	0	0	0	0	0	0	0	1	0	.000	.000	.000
Billy Consolo	2B3,SS3,3B1	R	26	11	5	1	0	0	0	0	0	0	1	0	.000	.000	.000

Pitcher	T	Age	G	GS	CG	ShO	IP	H	HR	BB	SO	W-L	Sv	ERA
Pedro Ramos	R	26	42	34	9	3	264.1	265	39	79	174	11-20	2	3.95
Camilo Pascual	R	27	35	33	15	8	252.1	205	26	100	221	15-16	0	3.46
Jack Kralick	L	26	33	33	11	2	242.0	257	21	64	137	13-11	0	3.61
Jim Kaat	L	22	36	29	8	1	200.2	188	12	82	122	9-17	0	3.90
Al Schroll	R	29	11	8	2	0	50.0	53	5	27	24	4-4	0	5.22
Bert Cueto	R	23	7	5	0	0	21.1	27	7	10	5	1-3	0	7.17
Ray Moore	R	35	46	0	0	0	56.1	49	8	38	45	4-4	14	3.67
Don Lee	R	27	37	10	4	0	115.0	93	12	35	65	3-6	3	3.52
Bill Pleis	L	23	37	0	0	0	56.1	59	4	34	32	4-2	2	4.95
Chuck Stobbs	L	31	24	3	0	0	44.2	56	8	15	17	2-3	2	7.46
Danny McDevitt†	L	28	16	1	0	0	26.2	20	1	19	15	1-0	0	2.36
Ted Sadowski	R	25	15	1	0	0	33.0	49	6	11	12	0-2	0	6.82
Paul Giel†	R	28	12	0	0	0	19.1	24	6	17	14	1-0	0	9.78
Ed Palmquist†	R	28	9	2	0	0	21.0	33	7	13	13	1-1	0	9.43
Lee Stange	R	24	7	0	0	0	12.1	15	1	10	10	1-0	0	2.92
Gerry Arrigo	L	20	7	2	0	0	9.2	9	0	10	6	0-1	0	10.24
Gary Dotter	L	18	2	0	0	0	6.0	6	0	4	2	0-0	0	9.00
Julio Becquer	L	29	1	0	0	0	1.1	4	0	1	0	0-0	0	20.25
Fred Bruckbauer	R	23	1	0	0	0	0.0	3	0	1	0	0-0	0	—

1961 Los Angeles Angels 8th AL 70-91 .435 38.5 GB

Bill Rigney

Player	Gm by Position	B	Age	G	AB	R	H	2B	3B	HR	RBI	BB	SO	SB	Avg	OBP	Slg
Earl Averill	C88,OF9,2B1	R	29	115	323	56	86	9	0	21	59	62	70	1	.266	.384	.489
Steve Bilko	1B86,OF3	R	32	114	294	49	82	16	1	20	59	58	81	1	.279	.395	.544
Ken Aspromonte†	2B62	R	29	66	238	29	53	10	0	2	14	33	21	0	.223	.322	.290
Eddie Yost	3B67	R	34	76	213	29	43	4	0	3	15	50	48	0	.202	.358	.263
Joe Koppe†	SS88,2B3,3B1	R	30	91	338	46	85	12	2	5	40	45	77	3	.251	.339	.343
Ken Hunt	OF134,2B1	R	26	149	479	70	122	29	3	25	84	49	120	8	.255	.325	.484
Leon Wagner	OF116	L	27	133	453	74	127	19	2	28	79	48	65	5	.280	.348	.517
Albie Pearson	OF113	L	26	144	427	92	123	21	3	7	41	96	40	11	.288	.420	.400
Lee Thomas†	OF86,1B34	L	25	130	450	77	128	11	5	24	70	47	74	0	.284	.353	.491
George Thomas†	OF45,3B38	R	23	79	282	39	79	12	1	13	59	21	66	3	.280	.334	.468
Ted Kluszewski	1B66	L	36	107	263	32	64	12	0	15	39	24	23	0	.243	.303	.460
Rocky Bridges	2B58,SS25,3B4	R	33	84	229	20	55	5	1	2	15	26	37	1	.240	.320	.297
Gene Leek	3B49,SS7,OF1	R	24	57	199	16	45	9	1	5	20	7	54	0	.226	.260	.357
Billy Moran	2B51,SS2	R	27	54	173	17	45	7	1	2	22	17	16	0	.260	.328	.347
Ed Sadowski	C56	R	29	69	164	16	38	13	0	4	12	11	33	2	.232	.278	.384
Tom Satriano	3B23,2B10,SS1	L	20	35	96	15	19	5	1	1	8	12	16	2	.198	.294	.302
Ken Hamlin	SS39	R	26	42	91	4	19	3	0	1	5	11	9	0	.209	.298	.275
Del Rice	C30	R	38	44	83	11	20	4	0	4	11	20	19	0	.241	.385	.434
Bob Cerv†	OF15	R	35	18	57	3	9	3	0	2	6	1	8	0	.158	.169	.316
Bob Rodgers	C14	S	22	16	56	8	18	2	0	2	13	1	6	0	.321	.333	.464
Fritz Brickell	SS17	R	26	21	49	3	6	0	0	0	3	6	9	0	.122	.218	.122
Faye Throneberry	OF5	L	30	24	31	1	6	1	0	0	0	5	10	0	.194	.306	.226
Jim Fregosi	SS11	R	19	11	27	7	6	0	0	0	3	1	4	0	.222	.250	.222
Julio Becquer†	1B5	L	29	11	8	0	0	0	0	0	0	1	5	0	.000	.111	.000
Chuck Tanner	OF1	L	31	7	8	0	1	0	0	0	0	2	2	0	.125	.300	.125
Leo Burke		R	27	6	5	0	0	0	0	0	0	0	1	0	.000	.000	.000
Dan Ardell	1B1	L	20	7	4	1	1	0	0	0	0	1	2	0	.250	.400	.250
Lou Johnson	OF1	R	26	1	0	0	0	0	0	0	0	0	0	0	—	—	—

Pitcher	T	Age	G	GS	CG	ShO	IP	H	HR	BB	SO	W-L	Sv	ERA
Ken McBride	R	25	38	36	11	1	241.2	229	28	102	180	12-15	1	3.65
Eli Grba	R	26	40	30	8	0	211.2	197	26	114	105	11-13	2	4.25
Ted Bowsfield	L	26	41	21	4	1	157.0	154	18	63	88	11-8	0	3.73
Ron Moeller	L	22	33	18	1	1	112.2	122	15	83	87	4-8	0	5.83
Jerry Casale†	R	27	13	7	0	0	42.2	52	9	25	35	1-5	1	6.54
Dean Chance	R	20	5	4	0	0	18.1	33	0	5	11	0-2	0	6.87
Bob Sprout	L	19	1	1	0	0	4.0	4	0	3	2	0-0	0	4.50
Tom Morgan	R	31	59	0	0	0	91.2	74	7	17	39	8-2	10	2.36
Art Fowler	R	38	53	3	0	0	89.0	68	12	29	78	5-8	11	3.64
Ryne Duren†	R	32	40	14	1	1	99.0	87	13	75	108	6-12	2	5.18
Jim Donohue†	R	22	38	7	0	0	100.1	93	16	50	79	4-6	5	4.31
Johnny James†	R	27	36	3	0	0	71.1	66	12	54	41	0-2	0	5.30
Ron Kline†	R	29	26	12	0	0	104.2	119	16	44	70	3-6	1	4.90
Jack Spring	L	28	18	4	0	0	38.0	35	4	15	27	3-0	0	4.26
Ned Garver	R	35	12	2	0	0	29.0	40	2	16	9	0-3	0	5.59
Tex Clevenger†	R	28	12	0	0	0	16.0	13	1	13	11	2-1	1	1.69
Russ Heman†	R	28	6	0	0	0	10.0	4	1	2	2	0-0	0	1.80
Ray Semproch	R	30	2	0	0	0	1.0	1	0	3	1	0-0	0	9.00

1961 Washington Senators 9th AL 61-100 .379 47.5 GB

Mickey Vernon

Player	Gm by Position	B	Age	G	AB	R	H	2B	3B	HR	RBI	BB	SO	SB	Avg	OBP	Slg
Gene Green	C79,OF21	R	28	110	364	52	102	16	3	18	62	35	65	0	.280	.341	.489
Dale Long	1B95	L	35	123	377	52	94	20	4	17	49	39	41	0	.249	.317	.459
Chuck Cottier†	2B100	R	25	101	337	37	79	14	4	2	34	30	51	9	.234	.296	.318
Danny O'Connell	3B73,2B61	R	34	138	493	61	128	30	1	1	37	77	62	15	.260	.361	.331
Coot Veal	SS63	R	28	69	218	21	44	10	0	0	8	19	29	1	.202	.273	.248
Willie Tasby	OF139	R	28	141	494	54	124	13	2	17	63	58	94	4	.251	.330	.389
Marty Keough	OF100,1B10	L	26	135	390	57	97	18	9	9	34	32	60	12	.249	.307	.410
Chuck Hinton	OF92	R	27	106	339	51	88	13	5	6	34	40	81	22	.260	.337	.381
Gene Woodling	OF90	L	38	110	342	39	107	16	4	10	57	50	24	1	.313	.403	.471
Jim King	OF91,C1	L	28	110	263	43	71	12	1	11	46	38	45	4	.270	.363	.449
Billy Klaus	3B51,SS18,2B1*	L	32	91	251	26	57	8	2	7	30	30	34	2	.227	.311	.359
ob Johnson	SS57,2B2,3B2	R	25	61	224	27	66	13	1	6	28	19	26	4	.295	.350	.442
Pete Daley	C72	R	31	72	203	12	39	7	1	2	17	14	37	0	.192	.244	.266
Harry Bright	3B40,C8,2B1	R	31	72	183	20	44	6	0	4	21	19	23	0	.240	.310	.339
Bud Zipfel	1B44	L	22	50	170	17	34	7	5	4	18	15	49	1	.200	.262	.371
Jim Mahoney	SS31,2B2	R	27	43	108	10	26	0	1	0	6	5	23	1	.241	.274	.259
R C Stevens	1B25	R	26	33	62	2	8	1	0	0	2	7	15	1	.129	.217	.145
Ken Retzer	C16	L	27	16	53	7	18	4	0	1	3	4	5	0	.340	.386	.472
Joe Hicks	OF7	L	28	12	29	2	5	0	0	1	1	0	4	0	.172	.172	.276
Dutch Dotterer	C7	R	29	7	19	1	5	2	0	0	1	3	5	0	.263	.364	.368
Ron Stillwell	SS5	R	21	8	16	3	2	1	0	0	1	1	4	0	.125	.176	.188
Ed Brinkman	3B3	R	19	4	11	0	1	0	0	0	0	1	1	0	.091	.167	.091
Chet Boak	2B1	R	26	5	7	0	0	0	0	0	0	1	1	1	.000	.125	.000

B. Klaus, 1 G at OF

Pitcher	T	Age	G	GS	CG	ShO	IP	H	HR	BB	SO	W-L	Sv	ERA
Joe McClain	R	28	33	29	7	2	212.0	221	22	48	76	8-18	1	3.86
Bennie Daniels	R	29	32	28	12	1	212.0	184	14	80	110	12-11	0	3.44
Dick Donovan	R	33	23	22	11	2	168.2	138	10	35	62	10-10	0	2.40
Ed Hobaugh	R	27	26	18	3	0	126.1	142	12	64	67	7-9	0	4.42
Tom Sturdivant†	R	31	15	10	1	1	80.0	67	6	40	39	2-6	0	4.61
Tom Cheney†	R	26	10	7	0	0	29.2	32	8	26	20	1-3	0	8.80
Hal Woodeshick†	L	28	7	6	1	0	40.1	38	3	24	24	3-2	0	4.02
Claude Osteen†	L	21	3	3	0	0	18.1	14	3	9	14	1-1	0	4.91
Carl Mathias	L	25	4	3	0	0	13.2	22	3	4	7	0-1	0	11.20
Hector Maestri	R	26	1	1	0	0	6.0	6	1	2	2	0-1	0	1.50
Carl Bouldin	R	21	2	1	0	0	3.1	9	0	2	2	0-1	0	16.20
Marty Kutyna	R	28	50	6	0	0	143.0	147	12	48	64	6-8	3	3.97
Dave Sisler	R	29	45	1	0	0	60.1	55	6	48	30	2-8	11	4.18
Johnny Klippstein	R	33	42	1	0	0	71.2	83	13	43	41	2-2	0	6.78
Pete Burnside	L	30	33	16	4	2	113.1	106	11	51	56	4-9	2	4.53
John Gabler	R	30	29	9	0	0	92.2	104	5	37	33	3-8	4	4.86
Mike Garcia	R	37	16	0	0	0	19.0	23	1	13	14	0-1	0	4.74
Rudy Hernandez	R	29	7	0	0	0	9.0	8	0	3	4	0-1	0	3.00
Roy Heiser	R	19	3	0	0	0	5.2	6	1	9	1	0-0	0	6.35

1961 Kansas City Athletics 9th AL 61-100 .379 47.5 GB

Joe Gordon (26-33)/Hank Bauer (35-67)

Player	Gm by Position	B	Age	G	AB	R	H	2B	3B	HR	RBI	BB	SO	SB	Avg	OBP	Slg
Haywood Sullivan	C88,1B16,OF5	R	30	117	331	42	80	16	2	6	40	46	45	1	.242	.333	.356
Norm Siebern	1B109,OF47	L	27	153	560	68	166	36	5	18	98	82	91	2	.296	.384	.475
Jerry Lumpe	2B147	L	28	148	569	81	167	29	9	3	54	48	39	1	.293	.348	.392
Wayne Causey	3B88,SS11,2B9	L	24	104	312	37	86	14	1	8	49	37	28	0	.276	.348	.404
Dick Howser	SS157	R	25	158	611	108	171	29	6	3	45	92	38	37	.280	.377	.362
Leo Posada	OF102	R	25	116	344	37	87	10	4	7	53	36	84	0	.253	.321	.366
Bobby Del Greco†	OF73	R	28	74	239	34	55	14	1	5	21	30	31	1	.230	.317	.360
Jay Hankins	OF65	L	25	76	173	23	32	0	3	3	6	8	17	2	.185	.225	.272
Deron Johnson†	OF59,3B19,1B3	R	22	83	283	31	61	11	3	8	42	14	44	0	.216	.252	.360
Joe Pignatano	C83,3B2	R	31	92	243	31	59	10	3	4	22	36	42	2	.243	.347	.358
Gene Stephens†	OF54	L	28	62	183	22	38	6	1	4	26	16	27	3	.208	.279	.317
Jim Rivera†	OF43	L	38	64	141	20	34	8	0	2	10	24	14	6	.241	.352	.340
Marv Throneberry†	1B30,OF10	L	27	40	130	17	31	2	1	6	24	19	30	0	.238	.336	.408
Andy Carey†	3B39	R	29	39	123	20	30	6	2	3	11	15	23	0	.244	.336	.398
Lou Klimchock	1B11,OF7,3B6*	L	21	57	121	8	26	4	1	1	16	5	13	0	.215	.244	.289
Reno Bertoia†	3B29,2B6	R	26	39	120	12	29	2	0	0	13	9	15	1	.242	.286	.258
Hank Bauer	OF35	R	38	43	106	11	28	3	1	3	18	9	8	1	.264	.319	.396
Bill Tuttle†	OF25	R	31	25	84	15	22	2	2	0	8	9	9	0	.262	.333	.333
Al Pilarcik†	OF21	L	30	35	60	9	12	1	1	0	6	9	7	1	.200	.269	.250
Bob Boyd†	1B8	L	35	26	48	7	11	2	0	0	9	1	2	0	.229	.240	.271
Wes Covington†	OF12	L	29	17	44	3	7	0	0	1	6	4	7	0	.159	.260	.227
Frank Cipriani	OF11	R	20	13	36	2	9	0	0	0	2	2	4	0	.250	.289	.250
Charlie Shoemaker	2B6	L	21	7	26	5	10	2	0	0	1	2	2	0	.385	.429	.462
Gordon MacKenzie	C7	R	23	11	24	1	3	0	0	0	1	1	6	0	.125	.160	.125
Ozzie Virgil†	3B4,C3	R	28	11	21	1	3	0	0	0	0	0	3	0	.143	.143	.143
Don Larsen†	P8,OF1	R	31	18	20	2	6	0	0	1	4	1	5	0	.300	.333	.450
Billy Bryan	C4	L	22	9	19	2	3	0	0	1	2	2	7	0	.158	.238	.316
Bobby Prescott	OF2	R	30	10	12	0	1	0	0	0	0	2	5	0	.083	.214	.083
Chuck Essegian†	OF1	R	29	4	6	1	2	1	0	0	1	1	2	0	.333	.429	.500
Stan Johnson	OF2	L	24	3	3	1	0	0	0	0	0	2	1	0	.000	.400	.000
Clint Courtney†		L	34	1	1	0	0	0	0	0	0	0	0	0	.000	.000	.000

L. Klimchock, 1 G at 2B

Pitcher	T	Age	G	GS	CG	ShO	IP	H	HR	BB	SO	W-L	Sv	ERA
Jim Archer	L	29	39	27	9	2	205.1	204	11	60	110	9-15	5	3.20
Jerry Walker	R	22	36	24	4	0	168.0	161	23	96	56	8-14	2	4.82
Bob Shaw†	R	28	26	24	6	0	150.1	165	13	58	60	9-10	0	4.31
Norm Bass	R	22	40	23	6	2	170.2	164	17	82	74	11-11	0	4.69
Ray Herbert†	R	31	13	12	1	0	83.2	103	10	30	34	3-6	0	5.38
Bud Daley†	L	28	16	10	2	0	63.2	84	6	22	36	4-8	1	4.95
Lew Krausse	R	18	12	8	2	1	55.2	49	3	46	32	2-5	0	4.85
Bill Kirk	L	25	1	1	0	0	3.0	6	2	1	3	0-0	0	12.00
Bill Kunkel	R	24	58	2	0	0	88.2	103	11	32	46	3-4	4	5.18
Ed Rakow	R	25	45	11	1	0	124.2	131	14	49	81	2-8	1	4.76
Joe Nuxhall	L	32	37	13	1	0	128.0	135	12	65	81	5-8	1	5.34
Gerry Staley†	R	40	23	0	0	0	30.0	32	4	10	16	1-1	2	3.60
Art Ditmar†	R	32	20	5	0	0	54.0	60	6	23	19	0-5	1	5.67
Dave Wickersham	R	25	17	0	0	0	21.0	25	0	5	10	2-1	2	5.14
Bill Fischer†	R	30	15	0	0	0	21.0	26	2	6	12	1-0	2	3.86
Don Larsen†	R	31	8	1	0	0	15.0	21	2	11	13	1-0	0	4.20
Ken Johnson†	R	28	6	1	0	0	9.1	11	2	7	4	0-4	0	10.61
Ed Keegan	R	21	6	0	0	0	6.0	6	0	5	3	0-0	1	4.50
John Wyatt	R	26	5	0	0	0	7.1	8	0	4	6	0-0	1	2.45
Mickey McDermott†	L	33	4	0	0	0	5.2	14	0	10	3	0-0	0	14.29
Dan Pfister	R	24	2	0	0	0	2.1	5	2	4	3	0-0	0	15.43
Paul Giel†	R	28	1	0	0	0	1.2	6	1	3	1	0-0	0	37.80

»1961 Cincinnati Reds 1st NL 93-61 .604 —

Fred Hutchinson

Player	Gm by Position	B	Age	G	AB	R	H	2B	3B	HR	RBI	BB	SO	SB	Avg	OBP	Slg
Jerry Zimmerman	C76	R	26	76	204	8	42	5	0	0	10	11	21	1	.206	.252	.230
Gordy Coleman	1B150	L	26	150	520	63	149	27	4	26	87	45	67	1	.287	.341	.504
Don Blasingame†	2B116	L	29	123	450	59	100	18	4	1	21	39	38	4	.222	.286	.287
Gene Freese	3B151,2B1	R	27	152	575	78	159	27	2	26	87	27	78	8	.277	.307	.466
Eddie Kasko	SS112,3B12,2B6	R	29	126	469	64	127	22	1	2	27	32	36	4	.271	.320	.335
Vada Pinson	OF153	L	22	154	607	101	208	34	8	16	87	39	63	23	.343	.379	.504
Frank Robinson	OF150,3B1	R	25	153	545	117	176	32	7	37	124	71	64	22	.323	.404	.611
Wally Post	OF81	R	31	99	282	44	83	16	3	20	57	22	61	0	.294	.346	.585
Gus Bell	OF75	L	32	103	235	27	60	10	1	3	33	18	21	1	.255	.298	.345
Leo Cardenas	SS63	R	22	74	198	23	61	18	1	5	24	15	39	1	.308	.353	.485
Jerry Lynch	OF44	L	30	96	181	33	57	13	2	13	50	27	25	2	.315	.407	.624
Johnny Edwards	C52	L	23	52	145	14	27	5	0	2	14	18	28	1	.186	.279	.262
Elio Chacon	2B42,OF7	R	24	61	132	26	35	4	2	2	5	21	22	1	.265	.374	.371
Bob Schmidt†	C27	R	28	27	70	4	9	0	0	1	4	8	14	0	.129	.218	.171
Dick Gernert†	1B21	R	32	40	63	4	19	1	0	0	7	7	9	0	.302	.361	.317
Darrell Johnson†	C20	R	32	20	54	3	17	2	0	1	6	1	2	0	.315	.321	.407
Ed Bailey†	C12	L	30	12	43	4	13	4	0	0	2	3	5	0	.302	.348	.395
Jim Maloney	P27,OF1	L	21	30	29	6	11	0	0	1	4	2	4	0	.379	.438	.483
Jim Baumer	2B9	R	30	10	24	0	3	0	0	0	0	0	9	0	.125	.125	.125
Pete Whisenant†	OF12,C1,3B1	R	31	26	15	6	3	0	0	0	1	2	4	1	.200	.294	.200
Puddin' Head Jones	3B1	R	35	9	7	1	0	0	0	0	0	2	3	0	.000	.222	.000
Cliff Cook	3B1	R	24	4	5	0	0	0	0	0	0	0	4	0	.000	.000	.000
Harry Anderson		L	29	4	4	0	1	0	0	0	0	0	1	0	.250	.250	.250
Joe Gaines	OF3	R	24	5	3	2	0	0	0	0	0	2	1	0	.000	.400	.000
Hal Bevan		R	30	3	3	1	1	0	0	1	1	0	2	0	.333	.333	1.333
Claude Osteen†	P1,OF1	L	21	6	0	2	0	0	0	0	0	0	0	0	—	—	—

Pitcher	T	Age	G	GS	CG	ShO	IP	H	HR	BB	SO	W-L	Sv	ERA
Jim O'Toole	L	24	39	35	11	3	252.2	229	16	93	178	19-9	2	3.10
Joey Jay	R	25	34	34	14	4	247.1	217	25	92	157	21-10	0	3.53
Bob Purkey	R	31	36	34	13	1	246.1	245	27	51	116	16-12	1	3.73
Ken Hunt	R	22	29	22	4	0	136.1	130	13	66	75	9-10	0	3.96
Ken Johnson†	R	28	15	11	3	1	83.0	71	11	22	42	6-2	1	3.25
Jim Brosnan	R	31	53	0	0	0	80.0	77	7	18	40	10-4	16	3.04
Bill Henry	L	33	47	0	0	0	53.1	50	8	15	53	2-1	16	2.19
Jim Maloney	R	21	27	11	1	0	94.2	86	16	59	57	6-7	2	4.37
Sherman Jones	R	26	24	2	0	0	55.0	51	6	27	32	1-1	2	4.42
Howie Nunn	R	25	24	0	0	0	37.2	35	0	24	26	2-1	0	3.58
Jay Hook	R	24	22	5	0	0	62.2	83	14	22	36	1-3	0	7.76
Marshall Bridges	L	30	13	0	0	0	20.2	26	4	11	17	0-1	0	7.84
Claude Osteen†	L	21	1	0	0	0	0.1	0	0	0	0	0-0	0	0.00

1961 Los Angeles Dodgers 2nd NL 89-65 .578 4.0 GB

Walter Alston

Player	Gm by Position	B	Age	G	AB	R	H	2B	3B	HR	RBI	BB	SO	SB	Avg	OBP	Slg
John Roseboro	C125	L	28	128	394	59	99	16	6	18	59	56	62	6	.251	.346	.459
Gil Hodges	1B100	R	37	109	215	25	52	4	0	8	31	24	43	3	.242	.313	.372
Charlie Neal	2B104	R	30	108	341	40	80	6	1	10	48	30	49	3	.235	.297	.346
Jim Gilliam	3B74,2B71,OF11	S	32	144	439	74	107	26	3	4	32	79	34	8	.244	.358	.344
Maury Wills	SS148	S	28	148	613	105	173	12	10	1	31	59	50	35	.282	.346	.339
Wally Moon	OF133	L	31	134	463	79	152	25	3	17	88	89	79	7	.328	.434	.505
Willie Davis	OF114	L	21	128	339	56	86	19	6	12	45	27	46	12	.254	.316	.451
Tommy Davis	OF86,3B59	R	22	132	460	60	128	13	2	15	58	32	53	10	.278	.325	.413
Norm Larker	1B86,OF1	L	30	97	282	29	76	16	1	5	38	24	22	0	.270	.326	.387
Frank Howard	OF65,1B7	R	24	92	267	36	79	10	2	15	45	21	50	0	.296	.347	.517
Ron Fairly	OF71,1B23	L	22	111	245	42	79	15	2	10	48	48	22	0	.322	.434	.522
Duke Snider	OF66	L	34	85	233	35	69	8	3	16	56	29	43	1	.296	.375	.562
Daryl Spencer†	3B57,SS3	R	31	60	189	27	46	7	0	8	27	20	35	0	.243	.327	.407
Norm Sherry	C45	R	29	47	121	10	31	2	0	5	21	9	30	0	.256	.308	.397
Bob Aspromonte	3B9,SS4,2B2	R	23	47	58	7	14	3	0	0	2	4	12	0	.241	.290	.293
Gordie Windhorn	OF17	R	27	34	33	10	8	2	1	2	6	4	3	0	.242	.324	.545
Doug Camilli	C12	R	24	13	30	3	4	0	0	3	4	1	9	0	.133	.161	.433
Don Demeter†	OF14	R	26	15	29	3	5	0	0	1	2	3	6	0	.172	.250	.276
Charley Smith†	3B4,SS3	R	23	9	24	4	6	1	0	2	3	1	6	0	.250	.280	.542
Carl Warwick†	OF12	R	24	19	11	2	1	0	0	0	1	2	3	0	.091	.231	.091
Bob Lillis†	3B12,2B1,SS1	R	31	19	9	0	1	0	0	0	1	1	1	0	.111	.200	.111
Tim Harkness	1B2	L	23	5	8	4	4	2	0	0	0	3	1	1	.500	.636	.750

Pitcher	T	Age	G	GS	CG	ShO	IP	H	HR	BB	SO	W-L	Sv	ERA
Don Drysdale	R	24	40	37	10	3	244.0	236	29	83	182	13-10	0	3.69
Sandy Koufax	L	25	42	35	15	2	255.2	212	27	96	269	18-13	1	3.52
Stan Williams	R	24	41	35	6	2	235.1	213	21	108	205	15-12	0	3.90
Johnny Podres	L	28	32	29	6	1	182.2	192	27	51	124	18-5	0	3.74
Phil Ortega	R	21	4	2	1	0	13.0	10	6	2	15	0-2	0	5.54
Larry Sherry	R	25	53	1	0	0	94.2	90	10	39	79	4-4	15	3.90
Ron Perranoski	L	25	53	1	0	0	91.2	82	5	41	56	7-5	6	2.65
Turk Farrell†	R	27	50	0	0	0	89.0	107	12	43	80	6-6	10	5.06
Roger Craig	R	31	40	14	2	0	112.2	130	22	52	63	5-6	2	6.15
Jim Golden	R	25	28	0	0	0	42.0	52	7	20	18	1-1	0	5.79
Ed Roebuck	R	29	5	0	0	0	9.0	12	1	2	9	2-0	0	5.00
Ed Palmquist†	R	28	5	0	0	0	8.2	10	0	7	5	0-1	1	6.23

1961 San Francisco Giants 3rd NL 85-69 .552 8.0 GB

Alvin Dark

Player	Gm by Position	B	Age	G	AB	R	H	2B	3B	HR	RBI	BB	SO	SB	Avg	OBP	Slg
Ed Bailey†	C103,OF1	L	30	107	340	39	81	9	1	13	51	42	41	1	.238	.324	.385
Willie McCovey	1B84	L	23	106	328	59	89	12	3	18	50	37	60	1	.271	.350	.491
Joey Amalfitano	2B95,3B6	R	27	109	384	64	98	11	4	2	23	44	59	7	.255	.331	.320
Jim Davenport	3B132	R	27	137	436	64	121	28	4	12	65	45	65	4	.278	.342	.443
Jose Pagan	SS132,OF4	R	26	134	434	38	110	15	2	5	46	31	45	8	.253	.306	.332
Willie Mays	OF153	R	30	154	572	129	176	32	3	40	123	81	77	18	.308	.393	.584
Felipe Alou	OF122	R	26	132	415	59	120	19	0	18	52	26	41	11	.289	.333	.465
Harvey Kuenn	OF93,3B32,SS1	R	30	131	471	60	125	22	4	5	46	47	34	5	.265	.329	.361
Orlando Cepeda	1B81,OF80	R	23	152	585	105	182	28	4	46	142	39	91	12	.311	.362	.609
Chuck Hiller	2B67	L	26	70	240	38	57	12	1	2	12	32	30	4	.238	.328	.321
Matty Alou	OF58	L	22	81	200	38	62	7	2	6	24	15	18	3	.310	.356	.455
Eddie Bressoud	SS34,3B3,2B1	R	29	59	114	14	24	6	0	3	11	11	23	1	.211	.276	.342
John Orsino	C25	R	23	25	83	5	23	3	2	4	12	3	13	0	.277	.310	.506
Hobie Landrith	C30	L	31	43	71	11	17	4	0	2	10	12	7	0	.239	.337	.380
Tom Haller	C25	L	24	30	62	5	9	1	0	2	8	9	23	0	.145	.260	.258
Ernie Bowman	2B13,SS12,3B7	R	25	38	38	10	8	0	2	0	2	1	8	2	.211	.231	.316
Jim Marshall	1B4,OF2	L	30	44	36	5	8	0	0	1	7	3	8	0	.222	.275	.306
Bob Farley	OF3,1B1	L	23	13	20	3	2	0	0	0	1	3	5	0	.100	.217	.100
Bob Schmidt†	C2	R	28	2	6	0	1	0	0	0	1	0	1	0	.167	.143	.167
Don Blasingame†		L	29	3	1	1	0	0	0	0	0	2	1	0	.000	.667	.000

Pitcher	T	Age	G	GS	CG	ShO	IP	H	HR	BB	SO	W-L	Sv	ERA
Mike McCormick	L	22	40	35	13	3	250.0	235	33	75	163	13-16	0	3.20
Jack Sanford	R	32	38	33	6	0	217.1	203	22	87	112	13-9	0	4.22
Juan Marichal	R	23	29	27	9	3	185.0	183	24	48	124	13-10	0	3.89
Billy Loes	R	31	26	18	3	1	114.2	114	13	39	55	6-5	0	4.24
Stu Miller	R	33	63	0	0	0	122.0	95	4	37	89	14-5	17	2.66
Billy O'Dell	L	28	46	14	4	1	130.1	132	10	33	110	7-5	2	3.59
Sam Jones	R	35	37	17	2	0	128.1	134	12	57	105	8-8	1	4.49
Bobby Bolin	R	22	37	1	0	0	48.0	37	6	37	48	2-2	5	3.19
Dick LeMay	L	22	27	5	1	0	83.1	65	11	36	54	3-6	3	3.56
Jim Duffalo	R	25	24	4	1	0	61.2	59	9	32	37	5-1	1	4.23
Eddie Fisher	R	24	15	1	0	0	33.2	36	7	9	16	0-2	1	5.35
Dom Zanni	R	29	8	0	0	0	13.2	13	1	12	11	1-0	0	3.95

1961 Milwaukee Braves 4th NL 83-71 .539 10.0 GB

Chuck Dressen (71-58)/Birdie Tebbetts (12-13)

Player	Gm by Position	B	Age	G	AB	R	H	2B	3B	HR	RBI	BB	SO	SB	Avg	OBP	Slg
Joe Torre	C112	R	20	113	406	40	113	21	4	10	42	28	60	3	.278	.330	.424
Joe Adcock	1B148	R	33	152	562	77	160	20	0	35	108	59	94	2	.285	.354	.507
Frank Bolling	2B148	R	29	148	585	86	153	16	4	15	56	57	62	7	.262	.329	.379
Eddie Mathews	3B151	L	29	152	572	103	175	23	6	32	91	93	95	12	.306	.402	.535
Roy McMillan	SS154	R	30	154	505	42	111	16	0	7	48	61	86	2	.220	.305	.293
Hank Aaron	OF154,3B2	R	27	155	603	115	197	39	10	34	120	56	64	21	.327	.381	.594
Frank Thomas†	OF109,1B11	R	32	124	423	58	120	13	3	25	67	29	70	2	.284	.335	.506
Lee Maye	OF96	L	26	110	373	68	101	11	5	14	41	36	50	10	.271	.337	.440
Gino Cimoli†	OF31	R	31	37	117	12	23	5	0	3	4	11	15	1	.197	.266	.316
Mack Jones	OF26	L	22	28	104	13	24	3	2	0	12	12	28	4	.231	.322	.298
Al Spangler	OF44	L	27	68	97	23	26	2	0	0	6	28	9	4	.268	.432	.289
Felix Mantilla	SS19,2B10,OF10*	R	26	45	93	13	20	3	0	1	5	10	16	1	.215	.298	.280
Charlie Lau†	C25	L	28	28	82	3	17	5	0	0	5	14	11	1	.207	.323	.268
John DeMerit	OF21	R	25	32	74	5	12	3	0	2	5	5	19	0	.162	.225	.284
Sammy White	C20	R	32	21	63	1	14	1	0	1	5	2	9	0	.222	.242	.286
Bob Boyd†	1B3	L	35	36	41	3	10	0	0	0	3	1	7	0	.244	.256	.244
Mel Roach†	OF9,1B2	R	28	13	36	3	6	0	0	1	6	2	4	0	.167	.244	.250
Del Crandall	C5	R	31	15	30	3	6	3	0	0	1	1	0	0	.200	.226	.300
Hawk Taylor	OF5,C1	R	22	20	26	1	5	0	0	1	1	3	11	0	.192	.276	.308
Wes Covington†	OF5	L	29	9	21	3	4	1	0	0	0	2	4	0	.190	.261	.238
Johnny Logan†	SS2	R	34	18	19	0	2	1	0	0	1	1	3	0	.105	.150	.158
Neil Chrisley		L	29	10	9	1	2	0	0	0	0	1	1	0	.222	.300	.222
Billy Martin†		R	33	6	6	1	0	0	0	0	0	0	1	0	.000	.000	.000
Phil Roof	C1	R	20	1	0	0	0	0	0	0	0	0	0	0	—	—	—

F. Mantilla, 6 G at 3B

Pitcher	T	Age	G	GS	CG	ShO	IP	H	HR	BB	SO	W-L	Sv	ERA
Lew Burdette	R	34	40	36	14	3	272.1	295	31	33	92	18-11	0	4.00
Warren Spahn	L	40	38	34	21	4	262.2	236	24	64	115	21-13	0	3.02
Bob Buhl	R	32	32	28	9	1	188.1	180	23	98	77	9-10	0	4.11
Carl Willey	R	30	35	22	4	0	159.2	147	20	65	91	6-12	0	3.83
Bob Hendley	L	22	19	13	3	0	97.0	96	8	39	44	5-7	0	3.90
Tony Cloninger	R	20	19	10	3	0	84.0	84	16	33	51	7-2	0	5.25
Don McMahon	R	31	53	0	0	0	92.0	84	4	51	55	6-4	8	2.84
Don Nottebart	R	25	38	11	2	0	126.1	117	11	48	66	6-7	3	4.06
Moe Drabowsky	R	25	16	0	0	0	25.1	26	4	18	5	0-2	2	4.62
Claude Raymond	R	24	13	0	0	0	20.1	22	2	9	13	1-0	2	3.98
Ron Piche	R	26	12	1	1	0	23.1	20	1	16	16	2-2	1	3.47
Seth Morehead	L	26	12	0	0	0	15.1	16	4	7	13	1-0	0	6.46
Johnny Antonelli†	L	31	9	0	0	0	10.2	16	2	3	8	1-0	0	7.59
Ken MacKenzie	L	27	5	0	0	0	7.0	8	1	2	5	0-1	0	5.14
George Brunet	L	26	5	0	0	0	5.0	7	1	2	0	0-0	0	5.40
Chi Chi Olivo	R	33	3	0	0	0	2.0	3	1	5	1	0-0	0	18.00

1961 St. Louis Cardinals 5th NL 80-74 .519 13.0 GB

Solly Hemus (33-41)/Johnny Keane (47-33)

Player	Gm by Position	B	Age	G	AB	R	H	2B	3B	HR	RBI	BB	SO	SB	Avg	OBP	Slg
Jimmie Schaffer	C68	R	25	68	153	15	39	7	0	1	16	9	29	0	.255	.301	.320
Bill White	1B151	L	27	153	591	89	169	28	11	20	90	64	84	8	.286	.354	.472
Julian Javier	2B113	R	24	113	445	58	124	14	3	2	41	30	51	11	.279	.326	.337
Ken Boyer	3B153	R	30	153	589	109	194	26	11	24	95	68	91	6	.329	.397	.533
Alex Grammas	SS65,2B18,3B3	R	35	89	170	23	36	10	1	0	21	19	21	0	.212	.293	.282
Curt Flood	OF119	R	23	132	335	53	108	15	5	2	21	35	33	6	.322	.391	.415
Stan Musial	OF103	L	40	123	372	46	107	22	4	15	70	52	35	0	.288	.371	.489
Charlie James	OF90	R	23	108	349	43	89	19	2	4	44	15	59	2	.255	.288	.355
Joe Cunningham	OF86,1B10	L	29	113	322	60	92	11	2	7	40	53	32	1	.286	.403	.398
Bob Lillis†	SS56,2B24	R	31	86	230	24	50	4	0	0	21	7	13	3	.217	.245	.235
Don Taussig	OF87	R	29	98	188	27	54	14	5	2	25	16	34	2	.287	.338	.447
Carl Sawatski	C60,OF1	L	33	86	174	23	52	8	0	10	33	25	17	0	.299	.385	.517
Carl Warwick†	OF48	R	24	55	152	27	38	6	2	4	16	18	33	3	.250	.324	.395
Daryl Spencer†	SS37	R	31	37	130	19	33	4	0	4	21	23	17	1	.254	.366	.377
Hal Smith	C45	R	30	45	125	6	31	4	1	0	10	11	12	0	.248	.309	.296
Red Schoendienst	2B32	S	38	72	120	9	36	9	0	1	12	12	6	1	.300	.364	.400
Jerry Buchek	SS31	R	19	31	90	6	12	2	0	0	9	0	28	0	.133	.151	.156
Tim McCarver	C20	L	19	22	67	5	16	2	1	1	6	0	5	0	.239	.239	.343
Don Landrum	OF25,2B1	L	25	28	66	5	11	2	0	1	3	5	14	1	.167	.225	.242
Gene Oliver	C15,OF1	R	26	22	52	8	14	2	0	4	9	6	10	0	.269	.367	.538
Julio Gotay	SS10	R	22	10	45	5	11	4	0	0	5	3	5	0	.244	.292	.333
Walt Moryn†	OF7	L	35	17	32	0	4	2	0	0	2	1	5	0	.125	.152	.188
Ed Olivares	OF10	R	22	21	30	2	5	0	0	0	1	0	4	1	.167	.161	.167
Bob Nieman†	OF4	R	34	6	17	0	8	1	0	0	2	0	2	0	.471	.471	.529
Doug Clemens	OF3	L	22	6	12	1	2	1	0	0	0	3	1	0	.167	.333	.250
George Crowe		L	40	7	7	0	1	0	0	0	0	0	1	0	.143	.143	.143
Chris Cannizzaro	C5	R	23	6	2	0	1	0	0	0	0	0	0	0	.500	.500	.500

Pitcher	T	Age	G	GS	CG	ShO	IP	H	HR	BB	SO	W-L	Sv	ERA
Ray Sadecki	L	20	31	31	13	0	222.2	196	28	102	114	14-10	0	3.72
Curt Simmons	L	32	30	29	6	2	195.2	203	14	64	99	9-10	0	3.13
Larry Jackson	R	30	33	28	12	3	211.0	203	20	56	113	14-11	0	3.75
Bob Gibson	R	25	35	27	10	2	211.1	186	13	119	166	13-12	1	3.24
Ernie Broglio	R	25	29	26	7	2	174.2	166	19	75	113	9-12	0	4.12
Ray Washburn	R	23	3	2	1	0	20.1	10	1	7	12	1-1	0	1.77
Lindy McDaniel	R	25	55	0	0	0	94.1	117	11	31	65	10-6	9	4.87
Bob Miller	R	22	34	5	0	0	74.1	82	6	46	39	1-3	3	4.24
Al Cicotte	R	31	29	7	0	0	75.0	83	16	34	51	2-6	1	5.28
Craig Anderson	R	22	25	0	0	0	38.2	38	3	12	21	4-3	1	3.26
Mickey McDermott†	L	33	19	0	0	0	27.0	29	3	15	15	1-0	4	3.67
Ed Bauta	R	26	13	0	0	0	19.1	12	2	5	12	2-0	5	1.40
Bobby Tiefenauer	R	31	3	0	0	0	4.1	9	0	4	3	0-0	0	6.23

1961 Pittsburgh Pirates 6th NL 75-79 .487 18.0 GB

Danny Murtaugh

Player	Gm by Position	B	Age	G	AB	R	H	2B	3B	HR	RBI	BB	SO	SB	Avg	OBP	Slg
Smoky Burgess	C92	L	34	100	323	37	98	17	3	12	52	30	16	1	.303	.365	.486
Dick Stuart	1B132,OF1	R	28	138	532	83	160	28	8	35	117	34	121	0	.301	.344	.581
Bill Mazeroski	2B152	R	24	152	558	71	148	21	2	13	59	26	55	2	.265	.298	.380
Don Hoak	3B143	R	33	145	503	72	150	27	7	12	61	73	53	4	.298	.388	.451
Dick Groat	SS144,3B1	R	30	148	596	71	164	25	6	6	55	40	44	0	.275	.320	.367
Bill Virdon	OF145	L	30	146	599	81	156	22	8	9	58	49	45	5	.260	.313	.369
Roberto Clemente	OF144	R	26	146	572	100	201	30	10	23	89	35	59	4	.351	.390	.559
Bob Skinner	OF97	L	29	119	381	61	102	20	3	3	42	51	49	3	.268	.358	.360
Hal Smith	C65	R	30	67	193	12	43	10	0	3	26	11	38	0	.223	.267	.321
Joe Christopher	OF55	R	25	76	186	25	49	7	3	0	14	18	24	6	.263	.327	.333
Rocky Nelson	1B35	L	36	75	127	15	25	5	1	5	13	17	11	0	.197	.301	.370
Dick Schofield	3B11,SS9,2B5*	S	26	60	78	16	15	2	1	0	2	10	19	0	.192	.284	.244
Gino Cimoli†	OF19	R	31	21	67	4	20	3	1	0	6	2	13	0	.299	.319	.373
Walt Moryn†	OF11	L	35	40	65	6	13	1	0	3	9	2	10	0	.200	.235	.354
Don Leppert	C21	L	29	22	60	6	16	2	1	3	5	1	11	0	.267	.279	.483
Johnny Logan†	3B7,SS6	R	34	27	52	5	12	4	0	0	5	4	8	0	.231	.286	.308
Donn Clendenon	OF8	R	25	9	35	7	11	1	1	0	2	5	10	0	.314	.400	.400
Gene Baker	3B3	R	36	9	10	1	1	0	0	0	0	3	2	0	.100	.308	.100
Bob Oldis	C4	R	33	4	5	0	0	0	0	0	0	0	0	0	.000	.000	.000
Roman Mejias	OF2	R	30	4	1	1	0	0	0	0	0	0	1	0	.000	.000	.000

D. Schofield, 3 G at OF

Pitcher	T	Age	G	GS	CG	ShO	IP	H	HR	BB	SO	W-L	Sv	ERA
Bob Friend	R	30	41	35	10	1	236.0	271	16	45	108	14-19	1	3.85
Joe Gibbon	L	26	30	29	7	3	195.1	185	16	57	145	13-10	0	3.32
Harvey Haddix	L	35	29	22	5	2	156.0	159	15	41	99	10-6	0	4.10
Vinegar Bend Mizell	L	30	25	17	2	1	100.0	120	16	31	37	7-10	0	5.04
Earl Francis	R	25	23	15	0	0	102.2	110	4	47	53	2-8	0	4.21
Tom Sturdivant†	R	31	13	11	6	1	85.2	81	6	17	45	5-2	1	2.84
Vern Law	R	31	11	10	1	0	59.1	72	10	18	20	3-4	0	4.70
Larry Foss	R	25	3	3	0	0	15.1	15	3	11	9	1-1	0	5.87
Al Jackson	L	25	3	2	1	0	23.2	20	2	4	15	1-0	0	3.42
Roy Face	R	33	62	0	0	0	92.0	94	12	10	55	6-12	17	3.82
Clem Labine	R	34	56	1	0	0	92.2	102	4	31	49	4-1	8	3.69
Bobby Shantz	L	35	43	6	2	1	89.1	91	5	26	61	6-3	2	3.32
Al McBean	R	23	27	2	0	0	74.1	72	4	42	49	3-2	0	3.75
Fred Green	L	27	13	0	0	0	20.2	27	2	9	4	0-0	0	4.79
George Witt	R	27	9	1	0	0	15.2	17	5	5	9	0-1	0	6.32
Jim Umbricht	R	30	1	0	0	0	3.1	5	0	2	1	0-0	0	2.70
Tom Cheney†	R	26	1	0	0	0	0.0	1	1	4	0	0-0	0	—

1961 Chicago Cubs 7th NL 64-90 .416 29.0 GB

V. Himsl (5-6)/H. Craft (4-8)/V. Himsl (5-12)/E. Tappe (2-0)/H. Craft (3-1)/V. Himsl (0-3)/E. Tappe (35-43)/L. Klein (5-6)/E. Tappe (5-11)

Player	Gm by Position	B	Age	G	AB	R	H	2B	3B	HR	RBI	BB	SO	SB	Avg	OBP	Slg
Dick Bertell	C90	R	25	92	267	20	73	7	1	2	33	15	33	0	.273	.308	.330
Ed Bouchee	1B107	L	28	112	319	49	79	12	3	12	38	58	77	1	.248	.371	.417
Don Zimmer	2B116,3B5,OF1	R	30	128	477	57	120	25	4	13	40	25	70	5	.252	.291	.403
Ron Santo	3B153	R	21	154	578	84	164	32	6	23	83	73	77	2	.284	.362	.479
Ernie Banks	SS104,OF23,1B7	R	30	138	511	75	142	22	4	29	80	54	75	1	.278	.346	.507
Billy Williams	OF135	L	23	146	529	75	147	20	7	25	86	45	70	6	.278	.338	.484
George Altman	OF130,1B3	L	28	138	518	77	157	28	12	27	96	40	92	6	.303	.353	.560
Al Heist	OF99	R	33	109	321	48	82	14	3	7	37	39	51	3	.255	.337	.383
Jerry Kindall	2B50,SS47	R	26	96	310	37	75	22	3	9	44	18	89	2	.242	.288	.419
Richie Ashburn	OF76	L	34	109	307	49	79	7	4	0	19	55	27	7	.257	.373	.306
Sammy Taylor	C75	L	28	89	235	26	56	8	2	8	23	23	39	0	.238	.316	.391
Andre Rodgers	1B42,SS24,OF2*	R	26	73	214	27	57	17	0	6	23	25	54	1	.266	.343	.430
Bob Will	OF30,1B1	L	29	86	113	9	29	9	0	0	8	15	19	0	.257	.341	.336
Frank Thomas†	OF10,1B6	R	32	15	50	7	13	2	0	2	6	2	8	0	.260	.288	.420
Mel Roach†	1B7,2B7	R	28	23	39	1	5	2	0	0	1	3	9	1	.128	.190	.179
Moe Thacker	C25	R	27	25	35	3	6	0	0	0	2	11	11	0	.171	.383	.171
Ken Hubbs	2B8	R	19	10	28	4	5	1	1	1	2	0	8	0	.179	.179	.393
Cuno Barragan	C10	R	29	10	28	3	6	0	0	1	2	2	7	0	.214	.267	.321
Moe Morhardt	1B7	L	24	7	18	3	5	0	0	0	1	3	5	0	.278	.381	.278
Danny Murphy	OF4	L	18	4	13	3	5	0	0	2	3	1	5	0	.385	.429	.846
Lou Brock	OF3	L	22	4	11	1	1	0	0	0	0	1	3	0	.091	.167	.091
Jim McAnany	OF1	R	24	11	10	1	3	1	0	0	0	1	3	0	.300	.364	.400
Nelson Mathews	OF2	R	19	3	9	0	1	0	0	0	0	0	2	0	.111	.111	.111
George Freese		R	34	9	7	0	2	0	0	0	1	1	4	0	.286	.375	.286
Sammy Drake	OF1	S	26	13	5	1	0	0	0	0	0	1	1	0	.000	.167	.000

A. Rodgers, 1 G at 2B

Pitcher	T	Age	G	GS	CG	ShO	IP	H	HR	BB	SO	W-L	Sv	ERA
Don Cardwell	R	25	39	38	13	3	259.1	243	22	88	156	15-14	0	3.82
Dick Ellsworth	L	21	37	31	7	1	186.2	213	23	48	91	10-11	0	3.86
Glen Hobbie	R	25	36	29	7	2	198.2	207	26	54	103	7-13	2	4.26
Jack Curtis	L	24	31	27	6	0	180.1	220	23	51	57	10-13	0	4.89
Don Elston	R	32	58	0	0	0	93.1	108	11	45	59	6-7	8	5.59
Bob Anderson	R	25	57	12	1	0	152.0	162	14	56	96	7-10	8	4.26
Barney Schultz	R	34	41	0	0	0	66.2	57	6	25	59	7-6	7	2.70
Jim Brewer	L	23	36	11	0	0	86.2	116	17	21	57	1-7	0	5.82
Dick Drott	R	24	35	8	0	0	98.0	75	13	51	48	1-4	0	4.22
Joe Schaffernoth†	R	23	21	0	0	0	38.1	43	7	18	23	0-4	0	6.34
Mel Wright	R	33	11	0	0	0	21.0	42	3	4	6	0-1	0	10.71
Dick Burwell	R	21	2	0	0	0	4.0	6	0	4	0	0-0	0	9.00

1961 Philadelphia Phillies 8th NL 47-107 .305 46.0 GB

Gene Mauch

Player	Gm by Position	B	Age	G	AB	R	H	2B	3B	HR	RBI	BB	SO	SB	Avg	OBP	Slg
Clay Dalrymple	C122	L	24	129	378	23	83	11	1	5	42	30	30	0	.220	.281	.294
Pancho Herrera	1B115	R	27	126	400	56	103	17	2	13	51	55	120	5	.258	.351	.408
Tony Taylor	2B91,3B3	R	25	106	400	47	100	17	3	2	26	29	59	11	.250	.304	.323
Charley Smith†	3B94,SS14	R	23	112	411	43	102	13	4	9	47	23	76	3	.248	.294	.365
Ruben Amaro	SS132,1B3,2B1	R	25	135	381	34	98	14	9	1	32	53	59	1	.257	.351	.349
Johnny Callison	OF124	L	22	138	455	74	121	20	11	9	47	69	76	10	.266	.363	.418
Tony Gonzalez	OF118	L	24	126	426	58	118	16	8	12	58	49	66	15	.277	.358	.437
Don Demeter†	OF79,1B22	R	26	106	382	54	98	18	4	20	68	19	74	2	.257	.300	.482
Bobby Malkmus	2B58,SS34,3B25	R	29	121	342	39	79	8	2	7	31	20	43	1	.231	.276	.327
Lee Walls	1B28,3B26,OF17	R	28	91	261	32	73	6	4	8	30	19	48	2	.280	.329	.425
Ken Walters	OF56,1B5,3B1	R	27	86	180	23	41	8	2	2	14	5	25	2	.228	.251	.328
Bobby Gene Smith	OF47	R	27	79	174	16	44	7	0	2	18	15	32	0	.253	.313	.328
Wes Covington†	OF45	L	29	57	165	23	50	9	0	7	26	15	17	0	.303	.355	.485
Bobby Del Greco†	OF32,2B1,3B1	R	28	41	112	14	29	5	0	2	11	12	17	0	.259	.344	.357
Darrell Johnson†	C21	R	32	21	61	4	14	1	0	0	3	3	8	0	.230	.277	.246
Bob Sadowski	3B14	L	24	16	54	4	7	0	0	0	0	4	7	1	.130	.203	.130
Jim Woods	3B15	R	21	23	48	6	11	3	0	2	9	4	15	0	.229	.296	.417
C. Choo Coleman	C14	L	23	34	47	3	6	1	0	0	4	2	8	0	.128	.180	.149
Elmer Valo†	OF1	L	40	50	43	4	8	2	0	1	8	8	6	0	.186	.327	.302
Chris Short	P39,C1	R	23	40	37	1	6	0	0	0	2	1	10	1	.162	.184	.162
George Williams	2B15	R	21	17	36	4	9	0	0	0	1	4	4	0	.250	.325	.250
Tony Curry	OF8	L	22	15	36	3	7	2	0	0	3	1	8	0	.194	.216	.250
Don Ferrarese	P42,OF1	R	32	43	35	1	6	0	0	0	1	1	4	0	.171	.194	.171
Cal Neeman	C19	R	32	19	31	0	7	1	0	0	2	4	8	1	.226	.306	.258
Jim Owens	P20,OF1	R	27	21	27	0	2	0	0	0	1	4	12	0	.074	.194	.074
Jimmie Coker	C11	R	25	11	25	3	10	1	0	1	4	7	4	1	.400	.531	.560
Al Kenders	C10	R	24	10	23	0	4	1	0	0	1	1	0	0	.174	.208	.217
Joe Koppe†	SS5	R	30	6	3	1	0	0	0	0	0	0	0	0	.000	.000	.000

Pitcher	T	Age	G	GS	CG	ShO	IP	H	HR	BB	SO	W-L	Sv	ERA
Art Mahaffey	R	23	36	32	12	3	219.1	205	27	70	158	11-19	0	4.10
John Buzhardt	R	24	41	27	6	1	202.1	200	28	65	92	6-18	0	4.49
Robin Roberts	R	34	26	18	2	0	117.0	154	19	23	54	1-10	0	5.85
Jim Owens	R	27	20	17	3	0	106.2	119	8	32	38	5-10	0	4.47
Jack Baldschun	R	24	65	0	0	0	99.2	90	7	49	59	5-3	3	3.88
Frank Sullivan	R	31	49	18	1	1	159.1	161	19	55	114	3-16	6	4.29
Don Ferrarese	L	32	42	14	3	1	138.2	120	14	68	89	5-12	1	3.76
Dallas Green	R	26	42	10	1	1	128.0	160	8	47	51	2-4	1	4.85
Ken Lehman	L	33	41	2	0	0	63.1	61	6	25	27	1-1	1	4.26
Chris Short	L	23	39	16	1	0	127.1	157	12	71	80	6-12	1	5.94
Paul Brown	R	20	5	1	0	0	10.0	13	3	8	1	0-1	0	8.10
Turk Farrell†	R	27	5	0	0	0	9.2	10	3	6	10	2-1	0	6.52
Jack Meyer	R	29	1	0	0	0	2.0	2	1	2	2	0-0	0	9.00

»1962 New York Yankees 1st AL 96-66 .593 —

Ralph Houk

Player	Gm by Position	B	Age	G	AB	R	H	2B	3B	HR	RBI	BB	SO	SB	Avg	OBP	Slg
Elston Howard	C129	R	33	136	494	63	138	23	5	21	91	31	76	1	.279	.318	.474
Bill Skowron	1B135	R	31	140	478	63	129	16	6	23	80	36	99	0	.270	.325	.473
Bobby Richardson	2B161	R	26	161	692	99	209	38	5	8	59	37	24	11	.302	.337	.406
Clete Boyer	3B157	R	25	158	566	85	154	24	1	18	68	51	106	3	.272	.331	.413
Tom Tresh	SS111,OF43	S	24	157	622	94	178	26	5	20	93	67	74	4	.286	.359	.441
Roger Maris	OF154	L	27	157	590	92	151	34	1	33	100	87	78	1	.256	.356	.485
Mickey Mantle	OF117	S	30	123	377	96	121	15	1	30	89	122	78	9	.321	.486	.605
Hector Lopez	OF84,2B1,3B1	R	32	106	335	45	92	19	1	6	48	33	53	0	.275	.338	.391
Johnny Blanchard	OF47,C15,1B2	L	29	93	246	33	57	7	0	13	39	28	32	0	.232	.309	.419
Yogi Berra	C31,OF28	L	37	86	232	25	52	8	0	10	35	24	18	0	.224	.297	.388
Tony Kubek	SS35,OF6	L	25	45	169	28	53	6	1	4	17	12	17	2	.314	.357	.432
Joe Pepitone	OF32,1B16	L	21	63	138	14	33	3	2	7	17	3	21	1	.239	.255	.442
Phil Linz	SS21,3B8,2B5*	R	23	71	129	28	37	8	0	1	14	6	17	6	.287	.316	.372
Dale Long†	1B31	L	36	41	94	12	28	4	0	4	17	18	9	1	.298	.404	.468
Jack Reed	OF75	R	29	88	43	17	13	2	1	1	4	4	7	2	.302	.362	.465
Bob Cerv†	OF3	R	36	14	17	1	2	1	0	0	0	2	3	0	.118	.250	.176
Billy Gardner†	2B1,3B1	R	34	4	1	1	0	0	0	0	0	0	1	0	.000	.000	.000
Jake Gibbs	3B1	L	23	2	0	2	0	0	0	0	0	0	0	0	—	—	—

P. Linz, 2 G at OF

Pitcher	T	Age	G	GS	CG	ShO	IP	H	HR	BB	SO	W-L	Sv	ERA
Ralph Terry	R	26	43	39	14	3	298.2	257	40	57	176	23-12	2	3.19
Whitey Ford	L	33	38	37	7	0	257.2	243	22	69	160	17-8	0	2.90
Bill Stafford	R	22	35	33	7	2	213.1	188	23	77	109	14-9	0	3.67
Hal Brown†	R	37	2	1	0	0	6.2	9	3	2	2	0-1	0	6.75
Marshall Bridges	L	31	52	0	0	0	71.2	49	4	48	66	8-4	18	3.14
Jim Coates	R	29	50	6	0	0	117.2	119	9	50	67	7-6	6	4.44
Bud Daley	L	29	43	6	0	0	105.1	105	8	21	55	7-5	4	3.59
Jim Bouton	R	23	36	16	3	1	133.0	124	9	59	71	7-7	2	3.99
Rollie Sheldon	R	25	34	16	2	0	118.0	136	12	28	54	7-8	1	5.49
Luis Arroyo	L	35	27	0	0	0	33.2	33	5	17	21	1-3	7	4.81
Bob Turley	R	31	24	8	0	0	69.0	68	8	47	42	3-3	1	4.57
Tex Clevenger	R	29	21	0	0	0	38.0	36	3	17	11	2-0	0	2.84
Hal Reniff	R	23	2	0	0	0	3.2	6	0	5	1	0-0	0	7.36
Jack Cullen	R	22	2	0	0	0	3.0	2	0	2	2	0-0	1	0.00
Al Downing	L	21	1	0	0	0	1.0	0	0	0	1	0-0	0	0.00

1962 Minnesota Twins 2nd AL 91-71 .562 5.0 GB

Sam Mele

Player	Gm by Position	B	Age	G	AB	R	H	2B	3B	HR	RBI	BB	SO	SB	Avg	OBP	Slg
Earl Battey	C147	R	27	148	522	58	146	20	3	11	57	57	48	0	.280	.348	.393
Vic Power	1B142,2B2	R	34	144	611	80	177	28	2	16	63	22	35	7	.290	.316	.421
Bernie Allen	2B158	L	23	159	573	79	154	27	7	12	64	62	82	0	.269	.338	.403
Rich Rollins	3B159,SS1	R	24	159	624	96	186	23	5	16	96	75	62	3	.298	.374	.428
Zoilo Versalles	SS160	R	22	160	568	69	137	18	3	17	67	37	71	5	.241	.287	.373
Lenny Green	OF156	L	29	158	619	97	168	33	3	14	63	88	36	8	.271	.367	.402
Harmon Killebrew	OF151,1B4	R	26	155	552	85	134	21	1	48	126	106	142	1	.243	.366	.545
Bob Allison	OF147	R	27	149	519	102	138	24	8	29	102	84	115	8	.266	.370	.511
Bill Tuttle	OF104	R	32	110	123	21	26	4	1	1	13	19	14	1	.211	.317	.285
Don Mincher	1B25	L	24	86	121	20	29	1	1	9	29	34	24	0	.240	.406	.488
George Banks	OF17,3B6	R	23	63	103	22	26	0	2	4	15	21	27	0	.252	.372	.408
Jerry Zimmerman	C34	R	27	34	62	8	17	4	0	0	7	3	5	0	.274	.318	.339
Hal Naragon	C9	L	33	24	35	1	8	1	0	0	3	3	1	0	.229	.282	.257
Johnny Goryl	2B4,SS1	R	28	37	26	6	5	0	1	2	2	2	6	0	.192	.250	.500
Marty Martinez	SS11,3B1	S	20	37	18	13	3	0	1	0	3	3	4	0	.167	.286	.278
Jim Lemon	OF3	R	34	12	17	1	3	0	0	1	5	3	4	0	.176	.286	.353
Jim Snyder	2B5,1B1	R	29	12	10	1	1	0	0	0	1	0	0	0	.100	.100	.100
Tony Oliva	OF2	L	21	9	9	3	4	1	0	0	3	3	2	0	.444	.583	.556

Pitcher	T	Age	G	GS	CG	ShO	IP	H	HR	BB	SO	W-L	Sv	ERA
Jack Kralick	L	27	39	37	7	1	242.2	239	30	61	139	12-11	0	3.86
Jim Kaat	L	23	39	35	16	5	269.0	243	23	75	173	18-14	1	3.14
Camilo Pascual	R	28	34	33	18	5	257.2	236	25	59	206	20-11	0	3.32
Don Lee†	R	28	9	9	1	0	52.0	51	8	24	28	3-3	0	4.50
Ray Moore	R	36	49	0	0	0	64.2	55	8	30	58	8-3	9	4.73
Lee Stange	R	25	44	6	1	0	95.0	98	14	39	70	4-3	3	4.45
Dick Stigman	L	26	40	15	6	0	142.2	122	19	64	116	12-5	3	3.66
Georges Maranda	R	30	32	4	0	0	72.2	69	11	35	36	1-3	0	4.46
Joe Bonikowski	R	21	30	13	3	0	99.2	95	6	38	45	5-7	2	3.88
Bill Pleis	L	24	21	4	0	0	45.0	46	7	14	31	2-5	3	4.40
Frank Sullivan†	R	32	21	0	0	0	33.1	33	3	13	10	4-1	5	3.24
Ted Sadowski	R	26	19	0	0	0	34.0	37	6	11	15	1-1	0	5.03
Jackie Collum†	L	35	8	3	0	0	15.1	29	1	11	5	0-2	0	11.15
Ruben Gomez†	R	34	6	2	1	0	19.1	17	3	11	8	1-1	0	4.66
Jim Donohue†	R	23	6	1	0	0	10.1	12	2	6	3	0-1	1	6.97
Jim Manning	R	18	5	1	0	0	7.0	14	0	1	3	0-0	0	5.14
Jim Roland	L	19	1	0	0	0	2.0	1	0	0	1	0-0	0	0.00
Gerry Arrigo	L	21	1	0	0	0	1.0	3	0	1	1	0-0	0	18.00

1962 Los Angeles Angels 3rd AL 86-76 .531 10.0 GB

Bill Rigney

Player	Gm by Position	B	Age	G	AB	R	H	2B	3B	HR	RBI	BB	SO	SB	Avg	OBP	Slg
Bob Rodgers	C150	S	23	155	565	65	146	34	6	6	61	45	68	1	.258	.309	.372
Lee Thomas	1B90,OF74	L	26	160	583	88	169	21	2	26	104	55	74	6	.290	.355	.467
Billy Moran	2B160	R	28	160	659	90	186	25	3	17	74	39	80	5	.282	.324	.407
Felix Torres	3B123	R	30	127	451	44	117	19	4	11	74	28	73	0	.259	.306	.392
Joe Koppe	SS118,2B5,3B4	R	31	128	375	47	85	16	0	4	40	73	84	2	.227	.352	.301
Albie Pearson	OF160	L	27	160	614	115	160	29	6	5	42	95	36	15	.261	.360	.352
Leon Wagner	OF156	L	28	160	612	96	164	21	5	37	107	50	87	7	.268	.326	.500
George Thomas	OF51	R	24	56	181	13	43	10	2	4	12	21	37	0	.238	.320	.381
Earl Averill	OF49,C6	R	30	92	187	21	41	9	0	4	22	43	47	0	.219	.366	.332
Jim Fregosi	SS52	R	20	58	175	15	51	3	4	3	23	18	27	2	.291	.356	.406
Steve Bilko	1B50	R	33	64	164	26	47	9	1	8	38	25	35	1	.287	.374	.500
Tom Burgess	1B35,OF2	L	34	87	143	17	28	7	1	2	13	36	20	2	.196	.354	.301
Eddie Yost	3B28,1B7	R	35	52	104	22	25	9	1	0	10	30	21	0	.240	.412	.346
Leo Burke	OF12,3B4,SS1	R	28	19	64	8	17	1	0	4	14	5	11	0	.266	.329	.469
Ed Sadowski	C18	R	30	27	55	4	11	4	0	1	3	2	14	1	.200	.228	.327
Gordie Windhorn†	OF27	R	28	40	45	9	8	6	0	0	1	7	10	1	.178	.288	.311
Marlan Coughtry†	3B5,2B2	L	27	11	22	0	4	0	0	0	2	0	6	0	.182	.182	.182
Billy Consolo†	3B20,SS4,2B1	R	27	28	20	4	2	0	0	0	0	3	11	2	.100	.217	.100
Tom Satriano	3B5	L	21	10	19	4	8	2	0	2	6	0	1	0	.421	.421	.842
Frank Leja	1B4	L	26	7	16	0	0	0	0	0	0	1	6	0	.000	.059	.000
Gene Leek	3B4	R	25	7	14	0	2	0	0	0	0	0	6	0	.143	.143	.143
Ken Hunt	1B3	R	27	13	11	4	2	0	0	1	1	1	5	1	.182	.250	.455
Dick Simpson	OF4	R	18	6	8	1	2	1	0	0	1	2	3	0	.250	.400	.375
Chuck Tanner	OF2	L	32	7	8	0	1	0	0	0	0	0	0	0	.125	.125	.125
Ed Kirkpatrick	C1	L	17	3	6	0	0	0	0	0	0	0	2	0	.000	.000	.000

Pitcher	T	Age	G	GS	CG	ShO	IP	H	HR	BB	SO	W-L	Sv	ERA
Bo Belinsky	L	25	33	31	5	3	187.1	149	12	122	145	10-11	1	3.56
Eli Grba	R	27	40	29	1	0	176.1	185	19	75	90	8-9	1	4.54
Ted Bowsfield	L	27	34	25	1	0	139.0	154	12	40	52	9-8	1	4.40
Ken McBride	R	26	24	23	6	4	149.1	136	9	70	83	11-5	0	3.50
Don Lee†	R	28	27	22	4	2	153.1	153	12	39	74	8-8	2	3.11
Bobby Darwin	R	19	1	1	0	0	3.1	8	0	4	6	0-1	0	10.80
Jack Spring	L	29	57	0	0	0	65.0	66	7	30	31	4-2	6	4.02
Dean Chance	R	21	50	24	6	2	206.2	195	14	66	127	14-10	8	2.96
Art Fowler	R	39	48	0	0	0	77.0	67	6	25	38	4-3	5	2.81
Tom Morgan	R	32	48	0	0	0	58.2	53	6	19	29	5-2	9	2.91
Ryne Duren	R	33	42	3	0	0	71.1	53	1	57	74	2-9	8	4.42
Bob Botz	R	27	35	0	0	0	63.0	71	7	11	24	2-1	2	3.43
Dan Osinski†	R	28	33	0	0	0	54.1	45	3	30	44	6-4	4	2.82
Jim Donohue†	R	23	12	1	0	0	24.1	24	4	11	14	1-0	0	3.70
Julio Navarro	R	26	9	0	0	0	15.1	20	2	4	11	1-1	0	4.70
George Witt†	R	28	5	2	0	0	10.0	15	4	5	10	1-1	0	8.10
Joe Nuxhall†	L	33	5	0	0	0	5.1	7	0	5	2	0-0	0	10.13
Fred Newman	R	20	4	1	0	0	6.1	11	0	3	4	0-1	0	9.95

1962 Detroit Tigers 4th AL 85-76 .528 10.5 GB

Bob Scheffing

Player	Gm by Position	B	Age	G	AB	R	H	2B	3B	HR	RBI	BB	SO	SB	Avg	OBP	Slg
Dick Brown	C132	R	27	134	431	40	104	12	0	12	40	21	66	0	.241	.279	.353
Norm Cash	1B146,OF3	L	27	148	507	94	123	16	2	39	89	104	82	6	.243	.382	.513
Jake Wood	2B90	R	25	111	367	68	83	10	5	8	30	33	59	24	.226	.291	.346
Steve Boros	3B105,2B6	R	25	116	356	46	81	14	1	16	47	53	62	3	.228	.331	.407
Chico Fernandez	SS138,3B2,1B1	R	30	141	503	64	125	17	2	20	59	42	69	10	.249	.305	.410
Rocky Colavito	OF161	R	28	161	601	90	164	30	2	37	112	96	68	2	.273	.371	.514
Bill Bruton	OF145	L	36	147	561	90	156	27	5	16	74	55	67	14	.278	.346	.430
Al Kaline	OF100	R	27	100	398	78	121	16	6	29	94	47	39	4	.304	.376	.593
Dick McAuliffe	2B70,3B49,SS16	L	22	139	471	50	124	20	5	12	63	64	76	4	.263	.349	.403
Bubba Morton	OF62,1B3	R	30	90	195	30	51	6	3	4	17	32	32	1	.262	.366	.385
Mike Roarke	C53	R	31	56	136	11	29	4	1	4	14	13	17	0	.213	.287	.346
Vic Wertz	1B16	L	37	74	105	7	34	2	0	5	18	5	13	0	.324	.357	.486
Don Buddin†	SS19,2B5,3B2	R	28	31	83	14	19	3	0	0	4	20	16	1	.229	.385	.265
Bobo Osborne	3B13,1B7,C1	L	26	64	74	12	17	1	0	0	7	16	25	0	.230	.374	.243
Purnal Goldy	OF15	R	24	20	70	8	16	1	1	3	12	0	12	0	.229	.236	.400
Charlie Maxwell†	OF15,1B1	L	35	30	67	5	13	2	0	1	9	8	10	0	.194	.273	.269
Bob Farley†	OF11,1B6	L	24	36	50	9	8	2	0	1	4	14	10	0	.160	.338	.260
Frank Kostro	3B11	R	24	16	41	5	11	3	0	0	3	1	6	0	.268	.279	.341
George Alusik†		R	27	2	2	0	0	0	0	0	0	0	0	0	.000	.000	.000
Reno Bertoia	2B1,3B1,SS1	R	27	5	0	3	0	0	0	0	0	0	0	0	—	—	—

Pitcher	T	Age	G	GS	CG	ShO	IP	H	HR	BB	SO	W-L	Sv	ERA
Jim Bunning	R	30	41	35	12	2	258.0	262	28	74	184	19-10	6	3.59
Don Mossi	L	33	35	27	8	1	180.1	195	24	36	121	11-13	1	4.19
Phil Regan	R	25	35	23	6	0	171.1	169	23	64	87	11-9	0	4.04
Hank Aguirre	L	31	42	22	11	2	216.0	162	14	65	156	16-8	3	2.21
Paul Foytack	R	31	29	21	5	1	143.2	145	18	86	63	10-7	0	4.39
Frank Lary	R	32	17	14	2	1	80.0	98	17	21	41	2-6	0	5.74
Howie Koplitz	R	24	10	6	1	0	37.2	54	5	10	10	3-0	0	5.26
Ron Nischwitz	L	24	48	0	0	0	64.2	73	5	26	28	4-5	4	3.90
Terry Fox	R	26	44	0	0	0	58.0	48	2	16	23	3-1	16	1.71
Ron Kline	R	30	36	4	0	0	77.1	88	9	28	47	3-6	2	4.31
Sam Jones	R	36	30	6	1	0	81.1	77	13	35	73	2-4	1	3.65
Jerry Casale	R	28	18	1	0	0	36.2	33	5	18	16	1-2	0	4.66
Doug Gallagher	L	22	9	2	0	0	25.0	31	2	15	14	0-4	1	4.68
Fred Gladding	R	26	6	0	0	0	5.0	3	0	2	4	0-0	0	0.00
Bob Humphreys	R	26	4	0	0	0	5.0	8	3	2	3	0-1	1	7.20
Tom Fletcher	L	20	1	0	0	0	2.0	2	0	2	1	0-0	0	0.00
Bill Faul	R	22	1	0	0	0	1.2	4	1	3	2	0-0	0	32.40

1962 Chicago White Sox 5th AL 85-77 .525 11.0 GB

Al Lopez

Player	Gm by Position	B	Age	G	AB	R	H	2B	3B	HR	RBI	BB	SO	SB	Avg	OBP	Slg
Cam Carreon	C93	R	24	106	313	31	80	19	1	4	37	33	37	1	.256	.328	.361
Joe Cunningham	1B143,OF5	L	30	149	526	91	155	32	7	8	70	101	59	3	.295	.410	.428
Nellie Fox	2B154	L	34	157	621	79	166	27	7	2	54	38	12	1	.267	.314	.343
Al Smith	3B105,OF39	R	34	142	511	62	149	23	8	16	82	57	60	3	.292	.363	.462
Luis Aparicio	SS152	R	28	153	581	72	140	23	5	7	40	32	36	31	.241	.280	.334
Floyd Robinson	OF155	L	26	156	600	89	187	45	10	11	109	72	47	4	.312	.384	.475
Jim Landis	OF144	R	28	149	534	82	122	21	6	15	61	80	105	19	.228	.337	.375
Mike Hershberger	OF135	R	22	148	427	54	112	14	2	4	46	37	36	10	.262	.324	.333
Sherm Lollar	C66	R	37	84	220	17	59	12	0	2	26	32	23	1	.268	.369	.350
Charlie Maxwell†	OF56,1B6	L	35	69	206	30	61	8	3	9	43	34	32	0	.296	.394	.495
Charley Smith	3B54	R	24	65	145	11	30	4	0	2	17	9	32	0	.207	.256	.276
Bob Sadowski	3B16,2B12	L	25	79	130	22	30	3	3	6	24	13	22	0	.231	.299	.438
Sammy Esposito	3B41,SS20,2B7	R	30	75	81	14	19	1	0	0	4	17	13	0	.235	.367	.247
Bob Roselli	C20	R	30	35	64	4	12	3	1	1	5	11	15	1	.188	.316	.313
Bob Farley†	1B14	L	24	35	53	7	10	1	1	1	4	13	13	0	.189	.348	.302
Deacon Jones	1B6	L	28	18	28	3	9	2	0	0	8	4	6	0	.321	.394	.393
J.C. Martin	C6,1B1,3B1	L	25	18	26	0	2	0	0	0	2	0	3	0	.077	.077	.077
Ramon Conde	3B7	R	27	14	16	0	0	0	0	0	1	3	3	0	.000	.158	.000
Al Weis	SS4,2B1,3B1	S	24	7	12	2	1	0	0	0	1	0	3	0	.083	.267	.083
Brian McCall	OF1	L	19	4	8	2	3	0	0	2	3	0	2	0	.375	.375	1.125
Ken Berry	OF2	R	21	3	6	2	2	0	0	0	0	0	0	0	.333	.333	.333
Dick Kenworthy	2B2	R	21	3	4	0	0	0	0	0	0	0	3	0	.000	.000	.000

Pitcher	T	Age	G	GS	CG	ShO	IP	H	HR	BB	SO	W-L	Sv	ERA
Ray Herbert	R	32	35	35	12	2	236.2	228	13	74	115	20-9	0	3.27
Juan Pizarro	L	25	36	32	9	1	203.1	182	16	97	173	12-14	1	3.81
Early Wynn	R	42	27	26	11	3	167.2	171	15	56	91	7-15	0	4.46
John Buzhardt	R	25	28	25	8	2	152.1	156	16	59	64	8-12	0	4.19
Joe Horlen	R	24	20	19	5	1	108.2	108	10	43	63	7-6	0	4.89
Eddie Fisher	R	25	57	12	2	1	182.2	169	17	45	88	9-5	5	3.10
Dom Zanni	R	30	44	2	0	0	86.1	67	12	31	66	6-5	5	3.75
Turk Lown	R	38	42	0	0	0	56.1	58	3	25	40	4-2	6	3.04
Frank Baumann	L	28	40	10	3	1	119.2	117	10	36	55	7-6	4	3.38
Dean Stone†	L	31	27	0	0	0	30.1	28	3	9	23	1-0	5	3.26
Mike Joyce	R	21	25	1	0	0	43.1	40	2	14	9	2-1	2	3.32
Russ Kemmerer†	R	30	20	0	0	0	28.0	30	3	11	17	2-1	0	3.86
Dave DeBusschere	R	21	12	0	0	0	18.0	5	1	23	8	0-0	0	2.00
Gary Peters	L	25	5	0	0	0	6.1	8	0	1	4	0-1	0	5.68
Herb Score	L	29	4	0	0	0	6.0	6	1	4	3	0-0	0	4.50
Verle Tiefenthaler	R	24	3	0	0	0	3.2	6	1	7	1	0-0	0	9.82
Frank Kreutzer	L	23	1	0	0	0	1.1	0	0	1	1	0-0	0	0.00
Mike DeGerick	R	19	1	0	0	0	1.0	1	0	0	0	0-0	0	0.00

Seasons: Team Rosters 759

1962 Cleveland Indians 6th AL 80-82 .494 16.0 GB

Mel McGaha (78-82)/Mel Harder (2-0)

Player	Gm by Position	B	Age	G	AB	R	H	2B	3B	HR	RBI	BB	SO	SB	Avg	OBP	Slg
John Romano	C130	R	27	135	459	71	120	19	3	25	81	73	64	0	.261	.363	.479
Tito Francona	1B158	L	28	158	621	82	169	28	5	14	70	47	74	3	.272	.327	.401
Jerry Kindall	2B154	R	27	154	530	51	123	21	1	13	55	45	107	4	.232	.290	.349
Bubba Phillips	3B145,OF3,2B1	R	34	148	562	53	145	26	0	10	54	20	55	4	.258	.289	.358
Woodie Held	SS133,3B5,OF1	R	30	139	466	55	116	12	2	19	58	73	107	5	.249	.362	.406
Willie Kirkland	OF125	L	28	137	419	56	84	9	1	21	72	43	62	9	.200	.272	.377
Ty Cline	OF107	L	23	118	375	53	93	15	5	2	28	28	50	5	.248	.308	.331
Chuck Essegian	OF90	R	30	106	336	59	92	12	0	21	50	42	68	0	.274	.363	.497
Al Luplow	OF86	L	23	97	318	54	88	15	3	14	45	36	44	1	.277	.359	.475
Willie Tasby†	OF66,3B1	R	29	75	199	25	48	7	0	4	17	25	41	0	.241	.326	.337
Don Dillard	OF50	L	25	95	174	22	40	5	1	5	14	11	25	0	.230	.276	.356
Doc Edwards	C39	R	25	53	143	13	39	6	0	3	9	9	14	0	.273	.325	.378
Gene Green	OF33,1B2	R	29	66	143	16	40	4	1	11	28	8	21	0	.280	.316	.552
Jim Mahoney	SS23,2B8,3B1	R	28	41	74	12	18	4	0	3	5	3	14	0	.243	.269	.419
Jack Kubiszyn	SS18,3B1	R	25	25	59	3	10	2	0	1	2	5	7	0	.169	.231	.254
Max Alvis	3B12	R	24	12	51	1	11	2	0	0	3	2	13	3	.216	.245	.255
Walt Bond	OF12	L	24	12	50	10	19	3	0	6	17	4	9	1	.380	.426	.800
Ken Aspromonte†	2B6,3B3	R	30	20	28	4	4	2	0	0	1	6	5	0	.143	.286	.214
Hal Jones	1B4	R	26	5	16	2	5	1	0	0	1	0	4	0	.313	.353	.375
Tommie Agee	OF3	R	19	5	14	0	3	0	0	0	2	0	4	0	.214	.214	.214
Mike de la Hoz	2B2	R	23	12	12	0	1	0	0	0	0	0	3	0	.083	.083	.083
Marlan Coughtry†		L	27	3	2	1	1	0	0	0	1	1	1	0	.500	.667	.500
Bob Nieman†		R	35	2	1	0	0	0	0	0	0	1	0	0	.000	.000	.000

Pitcher	T	Age	G	GS	CG	ShO	IP	H	HR	BB	SO	W-L	Sv	ERA
Dick Donovan	R	34	34	34	16	5	250.2	255	23	47	94	20-10	0	3.59
Pedro Ramos	R	27	37	27	7	2	201.1	189	28	85	96	10-12	1	3.71
Jim Perry	R	26	35	27	7	3	193.2	213	21	59	74	12-12	0	4.14
Mudcat Grant	R	26	26	23	6	1	149.2	128	24	81	90	7-10	0	4.27
Sam McDowell	L	19	25	13	0	0	87.2	81	9	70	70	3-7	1	6.06
Ron Taylor	R	24	8	4	1	0	33.1	36	6	13	15	2-2	0	5.94
Floyd Weaver	R	21	1	1	0	0	5.0	3	1	0	8	1-0	0	1.80
Gary Bell	R	25	57	6	1	0	107.2	104	14	52	80	10-9	12	4.26
Frank Funk	R	26	47	0	0	0	80.2	62	11	32	49	2-1	6	3.24
Barry Latman	R	26	45	21	7	1	179.1	179	23	72	117	8-13	5	4.17
Bob Allen	L	24	30	0	0	0	30.2	29	5	25	23	1-1	4	5.87
Bill Dailey	R	27	27	0	0	0	42.2	43	0	17	24	2-2	1	3.59
Ruben Gomez†	R	34	15	4	0	0	45.1	50	5	25	21	1-2	1	4.37
Bob Hartman	L	24	8	2	0	0	17.1	14	1	8	11	0-1	0	3.12
Dave Tyriver	R	24	4	0	0	0	10.2	10	2	7	7	0-0	0	4.22
Wynn Hawkins	R	26	3	0	0	0	3.2	9	1	1	0	1-0	0	7.36
Jackie Collum†	L	35	1	0	0	0	1.1	4	0	0	1	0-0	0	13.50
Don Rudolph†	L	30	1	0	0	0	0.1	1	0	0	0	0-0	0	0.00

1962 Baltimore Orioles 7th AL 77-85 .475 19.0 GB

Billy Hitchcock

Player	Gm by Position	B	Age	G	AB	R	H	2B	3B	HR	RBI	BB	SO	SB	Avg	OBP	Slg
Gus Triandos	C63	R	31	66	207	20	33	7	0	6	23	29	43	0	.159	.262	.280
Jim Gentile	1B150	L	28	152	545	80	137	21	1	33	87	77	100	1	.251	.346	.475
Marv Breeding	2B73,3B1,SS1	R	28	95	240	27	59	10	1	2	18	8	41	2	.246	.273	.321
Brooks Robinson	3B162,SS3,2B2	R	25	162	634	77	192	29	9	23	86	42	70	3	.303	.342	.486
Jerry Adair	SS113,2B34,3B1	R	25	139	538	67	153	29	4	11	48	27	77	7	.284	.319	.414
Jackie Brandt	OF138,3B2	R	28	143	505	76	129	29	5	19	75	55	64	9	.255	.330	.446
Russ Snyder	OF121	L	28	139	416	47	127	19	4	9	40	17	46	7	.305	.335	.435
Boog Powell	OF112,1B1	L	20	124	400	44	97	13	2	15	53	38	79	1	.243	.311	.398
Johnny Temple†	2B71	R	34	78	270	28	71	8	1	1	17	36	22	7	.263	.352	.311
Whitey Herzog	OF70	L	30	99	263	34	70	13	1	7	35	41	36	2	.266	.369	.403
Charlie Lau	C56	L	29	81	197	21	58	11	2	6	37	7	11	1	.294	.319	.462
Ron Hansen	SS64	R	24	71	196	12	34	7	0	3	17	30	36	0	.173	.289	.255
Dick Williams	OF29,1B21,3B4	R	33	82	178	20	44	7	1	1	18	14	26	0	.247	.303	.315
Dave Nicholson	OF80	R	22	97	173	25	30	4	1	9	15	27	76	3	.173	.289	.364
Hobie Landrith†	C60	L	32	60	167	18	37	4	1	4	17	19	9	0	.222	.302	.329
Earl Robinson	OF17	R	25	29	63	12	18	3	1	1	4	8	10	2	.286	.361	.413
Barry Shetrone	OF6	L	23	21	24	3	6	1	0	1	1	0	5	0	.250	.250	.417
Darrell Johnson†	C6	R	33	6	22	0	4	0	0	0	1	0	4	0	.182	.182	.182
Pete Ward	OF6	L	22	8	21	1	3	2	0	0	2	4	5	0	.143	.280	.238
Bob Saverine	2B7	S	21	8	21	2	5	2	0	0	1	1	3	0	.238	.273	.333
Nate Smith	C3	R	27	5	9	3	2	1	0	0	0	1	4	0	.222	.364	.333
Marv Throneberry†	OF2	L	28	9	9	1	0	0	0	0	0	4	6	0	.000	.308	.000
Andy Etchebarren	C2	R	19	2	6	0	2	0	0	0	1	0	2	0	.333	.333	.333
Mickey McGuire	SS5	R	21	6	4	0	0	0	0	0	0	0	0	0	.000	.000	.000
Ozzie Virgil		R	29	1	0	0	0	0	0	0	0	1	0	0	—	1.000	—

Pitcher	T	Age	G	GS	CG	ShO	IP	H	HR	BB	SO	W-L	Sv	ERA
Chuck Estrada	R	24	34	33	6	0	223.1	199	24	121	165	9-17	0	3.83
Milt Pappas	R	23	35	32	9	1	205.1	200	31	75	130	12-10	0	4.03
Robin Roberts	R	35	27	25	6	0	191.1	176	17	41	102	10-9	0	2.78
Jack Fisher	R	23	32	25	4	0	152.0	173	23	56	81	7-9	1	5.09
Steve Barber	L	23	28	19	5	2	140.1	145	9	61	89	9-6	0	3.46
Hal Brown†	R	37	22	11	0	0	85.2	88	12	21	25	6-4	1	4.10
Art Quirk	L	24	7	5	0	0	27.1	36	3	18	18	2-2	0	5.93
John Miller	R	21	2	1	0	0	10.0	2	0	5	4	1-1	0	0.90
Dave McNally	L	19	1	1	1	1	9.0	2	0	3	4	1-0	0	0.00
Billy Hoeft	L	30	57	4	0	0	113.2	103	7	43	73	4-8	7	4.59
Wes Stock	R	28	53	0	0	0	65.0	50	7	36	34	3-2	3	4.43
Hoyt Wilhelm	R	38	52	0	0	0	93.0	64	5	34	90	7-10	15	1.94
Dick Hall	R	31	43	6	1	0	118.1	102	9	19	71	6-6	6	2.28
Dick Luebke	L	27	10	0	0	0	13.1	12	0	6	7	0-1	0	2.70
Jim Lehew	R	24	6	0	0	0	9.2	10	0	3	2	0-0	0	1.86
Bill Short	L	24	5	0	0	0	4.0	8	0	6	3	0-0	0	15.75
John Papa	R	21	1	0	0	0	1.0	3	0	1	0	0-0	0	27.00

1962 Boston Red Sox 8th AL 76-84 .475 19.0 GB

Pinky Higgins

Player	Gm by Position	B	Age	G	AB	R	H	2B	3B	HR	RBI	BB	SO	SB	Avg	OBP	Slg
Jim Pagliaroni	C73	R	24	90	260	39	67	14	0	11	37	36	55	2	.258	.359	.438
Pete Runnels	1B151	L	34	152	562	80	183	33	5	10	60	79	57	3	.326	.408	.456
Chuck Schilling	2B118	R	24	119	413	48	95	17	1	7	35	29	48	1	.230	.286	.327
Frank Malzone	3B156	R	32	156	619	74	175	20	3	21	95	35	43	0	.283	.319	.426
Eddie Bressoud	SS153	R	30	153	599	79	166	40	9	14	68	46	118	2	.277	.329	.444
Carl Yastrzemski	OF160	L	22	160	646	99	191	43	6	19	94	66	82	7	.296	.363	.469
Gary Geiger	OF129	L	25	131	466	67	116	18	4	16	54	67	66	18	.249	.344	.408
Carroll Hardy	OF105	R	29	115	362	52	78	13	5	8	36	54	68	3	.215	.318	.345
Lu Clinton	OF103	R	24	114	398	63	117	24	10	18	75	34	79	2	.294	.349	.540
Bob Tillman	C66	R	25	81	249	28	57	6	4	14	38	19	65	0	.229	.283	.454
Billy Gardner†	2B38,3B7,SS4	R	34	53	199	22	54	9	2	0	12	10	39	0	.271	.310	.337
Russ Nixon	C38	L	27	65	151	11	42	7	2	1	19	8	14	0	.278	.313	.371
Pumpsie Green	2B18,SS5	S	28	56	91	12	21	2	1	2	11	11	18	1	.231	.308	.341
Dave Philley	OF4	S	42	38	42	3	6	2	0	0	4	5	3	0	.143	.250	.190
Don Gile	1B14	R	27	18	41	3	2	0	0	1	3	3	15	0	.049	.133	.122

Pitcher	T	Age	G	GS	CG	ShO	IP	H	HR	BB	SO	W-L	Sv	ERA
Bill Monbouquette	R	25	35	35	11	4	235.1	227	22	65	153	15-13	0	3.33
Gene Conley	R	31	34	33	9	2	241.2	238	28	68	134	15-14	1	3.95
Don Schwall	R	26	33	32	5	1	182.1	180	18	121	89	9-15	0	4.94
Earl Wilson	R	27	31	28	4	1	191.1	163	21	111	137	12-8	0	3.90
Ike Delock	R	32	17	13	4	2	86.1	89	10	24	49	4-5	0	3.75
Wilbur Wood	L	20	1	1	0	0	7.2	6	0	3	3	0-0	0	3.52
Billy Muffett	R	31	1	1	0	0	4.0	8	0	2	1	0-0	0	9.00
Pete Smith	R	22	1	1	0	0	3.2	7	3	2	1	0-1	0	19.64
Dick Radatz	R	25	62	0	0	0	124.2	95	9	40	144	9-6	24	2.24
Mike Fornieles	R	30	42	1	0	0	82.1	96	14	37	36	3-6	5	5.36
Arnold Earley	L	29	38	3	0	0	68.1	76	8	46	59	4-5	5	5.80
Chet Nichols	L	31	29	1	0	0	57.0	61	3	22	33	1-1	3	3.00
Hal Kolstad	R	27	27	2	0	0	61.1	65	11	35	36	0-2	2	5.43
Galen Cisco†	R	26	23	9	1	0	83.0	95	11	50	43	4-7	0	6.72
Merlin Nippert	R	23	4	0	0	0	6.0	4	1	4	3	0-0	0	4.50
Bill MacLeod	L	20	2	0	0	0	1.2	4	0	1	2	0-1	0	5.40
Tracy Stallard	R	24	1	0	0	0	1.0	0	0	0	0	0-0	0	0.00
Ted Wills†	L	28	1	0	0	0	0.0	2	0	1	0	0-0	0	—

1962 Kansas City Athletics 9th AL 72-90 .444 24.0 GB

Hank Bauer

Player	Gm by Position	B	Age	G	AB	R	H	2B	3B	HR	RBI	BB	SO	SB	Avg	OBP	Slg
Haywood Sullivan	C94,1B1	R	31	95	274	33	68	7	2	4	29	31	54	1	.248	.325	.332
Norm Siebern	1B162	L	28	162	600	114	185	25	6	25	117	110	88	3	.308	.412	.495
Jerry Lumpe	2B156,SS2	L	29	156	641	89	193	34	10	10	83	44	38	0	.301	.341	.432
Ed Charles	3B140,2B2	R	29	147	535	81	154	24	7	17	74	54	70	20	.288	.356	.454
Dick Howser	SS72	R	26	83	286	53	68	8	3	6	34	38	8	19	.238	.326	.350
Gino Cimoli	OF147	R	32	152	550	67	151	20	15	10	71	40	89	2	.275	.323	.420
Bobby Del Greco	OF124	R	29	132	338	61	86	21	1	9	38	49	62	4	.254	.370	.402
Manny Jimenez	OF122	L	23	139	479	48	144	24	2	11	69	31	34	0	.301	.354	.428
Jose Tartabull	OF85	L	23	107	310	49	86	6	5	0	22	20	19	19	.277	.321	.329
Wayne Causey	SS51,3B26,2B9	L	25	117	305	40	77	14	1	4	38	41	30	2	.252	.340	.344
Joe Azcue	C70	R	22	72	223	18	51	9	1	2	25	17	27	1	.229	.287	.305
George Alusik†	OF50,1B1	R	27	90	209	29	57	10	1	11	35	16	29	1	.273	.326	.488
Billy Consolo†	SS48	R	27	54	154	11	37	4	2	0	16	23	33	1	.240	.337	.292
Billy Bryan	C22	L	23	25	74	5	11	2	1	2	7	5	32	0	.149	.203	.284
Leo Posada	OF11	R	26	29	46	6	9	1	1	0	3	7	14	0	.196	.302	.261
John Wojcik	OF12	L	20	16	43	8	13	4	0	0	9	13	4	3	.302	.474	.395
Deron Johnson	1B2,3B2,OF2	R	23	17	19	1	2	1	0	0	0	3	8	0	.105	.227	.158
Gordie Windhorn†	OF7	R	28	14	19	1	3	1	0	0	1	0	3	0	.158	.158	.211
Bill Kern	OF3	R	29	8	16	1	4	0	0	1	1	0	3	0	.250	.250	.438
Charlie Shoemaker	2B4	L	22	5	11	1	2	0	0	0	0	0	2	0	.182	.182	.182
Marlan Coughtry†	3B3	L	27	6	11	1	2	0	0	0	1	4	3	0	.182	.400	.182
Gene Stephens		L	29	5	4	0	0	0	0	0	0	1	1	0	.000	.200	.000
Hector Martinez		R	23	1	1	0	0	0	0	0	0	0	1	0	.000	.000	.000

Pitcher	T	Age	G	GS	CG	ShO	IP	H	HR	BB	SO	W-L	Sv	ERA
Ed Rakow	R	26	42	35	11	2	235.1	232	31	98	159	14-17	1	4.25
Dan Pfister	R	25	41	25	2	1	196.1	175	27	106	123	4-14	1	4.54
Jerry Walker	R	23	31	21	3	1	143.1	165	27	78	57	8-9	0	5.90
Orlando Pena	R	28	13	12	6	1	89.2	71	9	27	56	6-4	0	3.01
Art Ditmar	R	33	6	5	0	0	21.2	31	1	13	13	0-2	0	6.65
Bob Giggie	R	28	4	2	0	0	14.1	17	5	3	4	1-1	0	6.28
John Wyatt	R	27	59	9	0	0	125.0	121	12	80	106	10-7	11	4.46
Diego Segui	R	24	37	13	2	0	116.2	89	16	46	71	8-5	6	3.86
Bill Fischer	R	31	34	16	5	0	127.2	150	16	8	38	4-12	2	3.95
Danny McDevitt	L	29	33	1	0	0	51.0	47	5	41	28	0-3	2	5.82
Dave Wickersham	R	26	30	9	3	0	110.0	105	13	43	61	11-4	1	4.17
Norm Bass	R	23	22	10	0	0	75.1	96	7	46	33	2-6	0	6.09
Gordon Jones	R	32	21	0	0	0	32.2	31	10	14	28	3-2	6	6.34
Jim Archer	L	30	18	1	0	0	27.2	40	8	10	12	0-1	0	9.43
Bob Grim	R	32	12	0	0	0	13.0	14	0	8	3	0-1	3	6.23
Moe Drabowsky†	R	26	10	3	0	0	28.0	29	8	10	19	1-1	0	5.14
Bill Kunkel	R	25	9	0	0	0	7.2	8	3	4	6	0-0	0	3.52
Dan Osinski†	R	28	4	0	0	0	4.2	8	1	8	4	0-0	0	17.36
Don Williams	R	30	3	0	0	0	4.0	6	0	0	1	0-0	0	9.00
Granny Hamner	R	35	3	0	0	0	4.0	10	0	6	0	0-1	0	9.00
Fred Norman	L	19	2	0	0	0	4.0	4	0	1	2	0-0	0	2.25
Rupe Toppin	R	20	2	0	0	0	2.0	1	0	5	1	0-0	0	13.50

1962 Washington Senators 10th AL 60-101 .373 35.5 GB

Mickey Vernon

Player	Gm by Position	B	Age	G	AB	R	H	2B	3B	HR	RBI	BB	SO	SB	Avg	OBP	Slg
Ken Retzer	C99	L	28	109	340	36	97	11	2	8	37	26	21	2	.285	.334	.400
Harry Bright	1B99,C3,3B1	R	32	113	392	55	107	15	4	17	67	26	51	2	.273	.319	.462
Chuck Cottier	2B134	R	26	136	443	50	107	14	6	6	40	44	57	14	.242	.310	.341
Bob Johnson	3B72,SS50,2B3*	R	26	135	466	58	134	20	2	12	43	32	50	9	.288	.334	.416
Ken Hamlin	SS87,2B2	R	27	98	292	29	74	12	0	3	22	22	27	2	.253	.303	.325
Chuck Hinton	OF136,2B12,SS1	R	28	151	542	73	168	25	6	17	75	47	66	28	.310	.361	.472
Jimmy Piersall	OF132	R	32	135	471	38	115	20	4	4	31	39	53	12	.244	.301	.329
Jim King	OF101	L	29	132	333	39	81	15	0	11	35	55	37	4	.243	.353	.387
Bob Schmidt	C88	R	29	88	256	28	62	14	0	10	31	14	37	0	.242	.281	.414
Danny O'Connell	3B41,2B22	R	35	84	236	24	62	7	2	2	18	23	28	5	.263	.327	.335
Don Lock	OF67	R	25	71	225	30	57	6	2	12	37	30	63	4	.253	.336	.458
Johnny Schaive	3B49,2B6	R	28	82	225	20	57	15	1	6	29	6	25	0	.253	.270	.409
Dale Long†	1B51	L	36	67	191	17	46	8	0	4	24	18	22	5	.241	.307	.346
Bud Zipfel	1B26,OF23	L	23	68	184	21	44	4	1	6	21	17	43	1	.239	.307	.370
Joe Hicks	OF42	L	29	102	174	20	39	4	2	6	14	15	34	3	.224	.286	.374
Ed Brinkman	SS38,3B10	R	20	54	133	8	22	7	1	0	4	11	28	1	.165	.228	.233
Gene Woodling†	OF30	L	39	44	107	19	30	4	0	5	16	24	5	1	.280	.421	.458
John Kennedy	SS9,3B2	R	21	14	42	6	11	0	1	1	2	2	7	0	.262	.295	.381
Willie Tasby†	OF10	R	29	11	34	4	7	0	0	0	1	4	8	0	.206	.250	.206
Ron Stillwell	2B6,SS1	R	22	6	22	5	6	0	0	0	2	2	2	0	.273	.333	.273

B. Johnson, 1 G at OF

Pitcher	T	Age	G	GS	CG	ShO	IP	H	HR	BB	SO	W-L	Sv	ERA
Dave Stenhouse	R	28	34	26	9	2	197.0	169	24	90	123	11-12	0	3.65
Don Rudolph†	L	30	37	23	6	2	176.1	187	13	42	68	8-10	0	3.62
Tom Cheney	R	27	37	23	4	3	173.1	134	12	97	147	7-9	1	3.17
Claude Osteen	L	22	28	22	7	2	150.1	140	12	47	59	8-13	1	3.65
Pete Burnside	L	31	40	20	6	2	149.2	152	20	51	74	5-11	2	4.45
Carl Bouldin	R	22	6	3	1	0	20.0	26	0	9	12	1-2	0	5.85
Bob Baird	L	22	3	3	0	0	10.2	13	0	8	3	0-1	0	6.75
Marty Kutyna	R	29	54	0	0	0	78.0	83	9	27	25	5-6	0	4.04
Bennie Daniels	R	30	44	21	3	1	161.1	172	14	68	66	7-16	2	4.85
Jim Hannan	R	22	42	3	0	0	68.0	56	6	49	39	2-4	4	3.31
Steve Hamilton	L	26	41	10	1	0	107.1	103	10	39	83	3-8	2	3.77
Ed Hobaugh	R	28	26	2	0	0	69.1	66	9	25	37	2-1	1	3.76
Ray Rippelmeyer	R	28	18	1	0	0	39.1	47	7	17	17	1-2	0	5.49
Joe McClain	R	29	10	4	0	0	24.0	33	8	11	6	0-4	0	9.38
Fred Green	L	28	5	0	0	0	7.0	7	3	6	3	0-0	0	6.43
Jack Jenkins	R	19	3	1	1	0	13.1	12	4	7	10	0-1	0	4.05

»1962 San Francisco Giants 1st NL 103-62 .624 — Alvin Dark

Player	Gm by Position	B	Age	G	AB	R	H	2B	3B	HR	RBI	BB	SO	SB	Avg	OBP	Slg
Tom Haller	C91	L	25	99	272	53	71	13	1	18	55	51	59	1	.261	.384	.515
Orlando Cepeda	1B160,OF2	R	24	162	625	105	191	26	1	35	114	37	97	10	.306	.347	.518
Chuck Hiller	2B161	L	27	161	602	94	166	22	2	3	48	55	49	5	.276	.341	.334
Jim Davenport	3B141	R	28	144	485	83	144	25	5	14	58	45	76	2	.297	.357	.456
Jose Pagan	SS164	R	27	164	580	73	150	25	6	7	57	47	77	13	.259	.312	.359
Willie Mays	OF161	R	31	162	621	130	189	36	5	49	141	78	85	18	.304	.384	.615
Felipe Alou	OF150	R	27	154	561	96	177	30	3	25	98	33	66	10	.316	.356	.513
Harvey Kuenn	OF105,3B30	R	31	130	487	73	148	23	5	10	68	49	37	3	.304	.365	.433
Ed Bailey	C75	L	31	96	254	32	59	9	1	17	45	42	42	1	.232	.351	.476
Willie McCovey	OF57,1B17	L	24	91	229	41	67	6	1	20	54	29	35	3	.293	.368	.590
Matty Alou	OF57	L	23	78	195	28	57	8	1	3	14	14	17	3	.292	.349	.390
Manny Mota	OF27,3B7,2B3	R	24	47	74	9	13	1	0	0	9	7	8	3	.176	.253	.189
John Orsino	C16	R	24	18	48	4	13	2	0	0	4	5	11	0	.271	.333	.313
Ernie Bowman	2B17,3B11,SS10	R	26	46	42	9	8	1	0	1	4	1	10	0	.190	.227	.286
Bob Nieman†	OF3	R	35	30	30	1	9	2	0	1	3	1	9	0	.300	.323	.467
Carl Boles	OF7	R	27	19	24	4	9	0	0	0	1	0	6	0	.375	.375	.375
Cap Peterson	SS2	R	19	4	6	1	1	0	0	0	0	1	4	0	.167	.286	.167
Joe Pignatano†	C7	R	32	7	5	2	1	0	0	0	0	4	0	0	.200	.556	.200
Dick Phillips	1B1	L	30	5	3	1	0	0	0	0	1	1	1	0	.000	.250	.000

Pitcher	T	Age	G	GS	CG	ShO	IP	H	HR	BB	SO	W-L	Sv	ERA
Billy O'Dell	L	29	43	39	20	2	280.2	282	18	66	195	19-14	0	3.53
Jack Sanford	R	33	39	38	13	2	265.1	233	23	92	147	24-7	0	3.43
Juan Marichal	R	24	37	36	18	3	262.2	233	34	90	153	18-11	1	3.36
Billy Pierce	L	35	30	23	7	2	162.1	147	19	35	76	16-6	1	3.49
Mike McCormick	L	23	28	15	1	0	98.2	112	18	45	42	5-5	0	5.38
Gaylord Perry	R	23	13	7	1	0	43.0	54	3	14	20	3-1	0	5.23
Stu Miller	R	34	59	0	0	0	107.0	107	8	42	78	5-8	19	4.12
Don Larsen	R	32	49	0	0	0	86.1	83	9	47	58	5-4	11	4.38
Bobby Bolin	R	23	41	5	2	0	92.0	84	10	35	74	7-3	5	3.62
Jim Duffalo	R	26	24	2	0	0	42.0	42	3	23	29	1-2	0	3.64
Bob Garibaldi	R	20	9	0	0	0	12.1	13	1	5	9	0-0	1	5.11
Dick LeMay	L	23	9	0	0	0	9.1	9	2	9	5	0-1	1	7.71

1962 Los Angeles Dodgers 2nd NL 102-63 .618 1.0 GB Walter Alston

Player	Gm by Position	B	Age	G	AB	R	H	2B	3B	HR	RBI	BB	SO	SB	Avg	OBP	Slg
John Roseboro	C128	L	29	128	389	45	97	16	7	7	55	50	60	12	.249	.341	.380
Ron Fairly	1B120,OF48	L	23	147	460	80	128	15	7	14	71	75	59	1	.278	.379	.433
Jim Gilliam	2B113,3B90,OF1	S	33	160	588	83	159	24	1	4	43	93	35	17	.270	.370	.335
Daryl Spencer	3B57,SS10	R	32	77	157	24	37	5	1	2	12	32	31	0	.236	.365	.318
Maury Wills	SS165	S	29	165	695	130	208	13	10	6	48	51	57	104	.299	.347	.373
Willie Davis	OF156	L	22	157	600	103	171	18	10	21	85	42	72	32	.285	.334	.453
Tommy Davis	OF146,3B39	R	23	163	665	120	230	27	9	27	153	33	65	18	.346	.374	.535
Frank Howard	OF131	R	25	141	493	80	146	25	6	31	119	39	108	1	.296	.346	.560
Larry Burright	2B109,SS1	R	24	115	249	35	51	6	5	4	30	21	67	4	.205	.264	.317
Wally Moon	OF36,1B32	L	32	95	244	36	59	9	1	4	31	30	33	5	.242	.326	.336
Duke Snider	OF39	L	35	80	158	28	44	11	3	5	30	36	32	2	.278	.418	.481
Andy Carey	3B42	R	30	53	111	12	26	5	1	2	13	16	23	0	.234	.333	.351
Lee Walls	OF17,1B11,3B4	R	29	60	109	9	29	3	1	0	17	10	21	1	.266	.325	.312
Doug Camilli	C39	R	25	45	88	16	25	5	2	4	22	12	21	0	.284	.366	.523
Norm Sherry	C34	R	30	35	88	7	16	2	0	3	16	6	17	0	.182	.240	.307
Tim Harkness	1B59	L	24	92	62	9	16	2	0	2	7	10	20	1	.258	.370	.387
Ken McMullen	OF2	R	20	6	11	0	3	0	0	0	0	0	3	0	.273	.273	.273
Dick Tracewski	SS4	R	27	15	2	3	0	0	0	0	0	2	0	0	.000	.500	.000

Pitcher	T	Age	G	GS	CG	ShO	IP	H	HR	BB	SO	W-L	Sv	ERA
Don Drysdale	R	25	43	41	19	2	314.1	272	21	78	232	25-9	1	2.83
Johnny Podres	L	29	40	40	8	0	255.0	270	20	71	178	15-13	0	3.81
Stan Williams	R	25	40	28	4	1	185.2	184	16	98	108	14-12	1	4.46
Sandy Koufax	L	26	28	26	11	2	184.1	134	13	57	216	14-7	1	2.54
Joe Moeller	R	19	19	15	1	0	85.2	87	10	58	46	6-5	1	5.25
Pete Richert	L	22	19	12	1	0	81.1	77	6	45	75	5-4	0	3.87
Ron Perranoski	L	26	70	0	0	0	107.1	103	1	36	68	6-6	20	2.85
Ed Roebuck	R	30	64	0	0	0	119.1	102	11	54	72	10-2	9	3.09
Larry Sherry	R	26	58	0	0	0	90.0	81	8	44	71	7-3	11	3.20
Phil Ortega	R	22	24	3	0	0	53.2	60	8	39	30	0-2	1	6.88
Jack Smith	R	26	8	0	0	0	10.0	10	0	4	7	0-0	1	4.50
Willard Hunter†	L	28	1	0	0	0	2.0	6	1	4	1	0-0	0	40.50

1962 Cincinnati Reds 3rd NL 98-64 .605 3.5 GB Fred Hutchinson

Player	Gm by Position	B	Age	G	AB	R	H	2B	3B	HR	RBI	BB	SO	SB	Avg	OBP	Slg
Johnny Edwards	C130	L	24	133	452	47	115	28	5	8	50	45	70	1	.254	.322	.392
Gordy Coleman	1B128	L	27	136	476	73	132	13	1	28	86	36	68	2	.277	.331	.485
Don Blasingame	2B137	L	30	141	494	77	139	9	7	2	35	63	44	4	.281	.364	.340
Eddie Kasko	3B114,SS21	R	30	134	533	74	148	26	2	4	41	35	44	3	.278	.326	.356
Leo Cardenas	SS149	R	23	153	589	77	173	31	4	10	60	39	99	2	.294	.341	.411
Frank Robinson	OF161	R	26	162	609	134	208	51	2	39	136	76	62	18	.342	.421	.624
Vada Pinson	OF152	L	23	155	619	107	181	31	7	23	100	45	68	26	.292	.341	.477
Wally Post	OF90	R	32	109	285	43	75	10	3	17	62	32	67	1	.263	.341	.498
Jerry Lynch	OF73	L	31	114	288	41	81	15	4	12	57	24	38	3	.281	.335	.486
Marty Keough	OF71,1B29	L	27	111	230	34	64	8	2	7	27	21	31	3	.278	.346	.422
Don Zimmer†	3B43,2B17,SS1	R	31	63	192	16	48	11	2	2	16	14	30	1	.250	.304	.359
Hank Foiles	C41	R	33	43	131	17	36	6	1	7	25	13	39	0	.275	.340	.496
Cookie Rojas	2B30,3B1	R	23	39	86	9	19	2	0	0	6	9	4	1	.221	.302	.244
Don Pavletich	1B25,C2	R	23	34	63	7	14	3	0	1	7	8	18	0	.222	.310	.317
Joe Gaines	OF13	R	25	64	52	12	12	3	0	1	7	8	16	0	.231	.333	.346
Gene Freese	3B10	R	28	18	42	2	6	1	0	0	1	6	8	0	.143	.250	.167
Rogelio Alvarez	1B13	R	24	14	28	1	6	0	0	0	2	1	10	0	.214	.241	.214
Tommy Harper	3B6	R	21	6	23	1	4	0	0	0	1	2	6	1	.174	.240	.174
Cliff Cook†	3B4	R	25	6	5	0	0	0	0	0	0	0	2	0	.000	.000	.000
Jesse Gonder		L	26	4	4	0	0	0	0	0	0	0	3	0	.000	.000	.000
Darrell Johnson†	C2	R	33	2	4	0	0	0	0	0	0	2	0	0	.000	.333	.000

Pitcher	T	Age	G	GS	CG	ShO	IP	H	HR	BB	SO	W-L	Sv	ERA
Bob Purkey	R	32	37	37	18	2	288.1	260	28	64	141	23-5	0	2.81
Joey Jay	R	26	39	37	16	4	273.0	269	26	100	155	21-14	0	3.76
Jim O'Toole	L	25	36	34	11	3	251.2	222	20	87	170	16-13	0	3.50
Jim Maloney	R	22	22	17	3	0	115.1	90	11	66	105	9-7	1	3.51
Joe Nuxhall†	L	33	12	9	1	0	66.0	59	4	25	57	5-0	1	2.45
Sammy Ellis	R	21	8	4	0	0	28.0	29	6	29	27	2-2	0	6.75
John Tsitouris	R	26	4	2	1	1	21.1	13	0	7	7	1-0	0	0.84
Jim Brosnan	R	32	48	0	0	0	64.2	76	6	18	51	4-4	13	3.34
Johnny Klippstein	R	34	40	7	0	0	108.2	113	13	64	67	7-6	4	4.47
Bill Henry	L	34	40	0	0	0	37.1	40	5	20	35	4-2	11	4.58
Dave Sisler	R	30	35	0	0	0	43.2	44	4	26	27	4-3	1	3.92
Ted Wills†	L	28	26	5	0	0	61.0	61	12	23	58	0-2	3	5.31
Moe Drabowsky†	R	26	23	10	1	0	83.0	84	13	31	56	2-6	1	4.99
Howie Nunn	R	26	6	0	0	0	9.2	15	0	3	4	0-0	0	5.59
Bob Miller†	L	26	6	0	0	0	5.1	14	1	3	4	0-0	0	21.94
Dave Hillman†	R	34	2	0	0	0	3.2	8	0	1	0	0-0	0	9.82

1962 Pittsburgh Pirates 4th NL 93-68 .578 8.0 GB Danny Murtaugh

Player	Gm by Position	B	Age	G	AB	R	H	2B	3B	HR	RBI	BB	SO	SB	Avg	OBP	Slg
Smoky Burgess	C101	L	35	103	360	38	118	19	2	13	61	31	19	0	.328	.375	.500
Dick Stuart	1B101	R	29	114	394	52	90	11	4	16	64	32	94	0	.228	.286	.398
Bill Mazeroski	2B159	R	25	159	572	55	155	24	9	14	81	37	47	0	.271	.315	.418
Don Hoak	3B116	R	34	121	411	63	99	14	8	5	48	49	49	4	.241	.320	.350
Dick Groat	SS161	R	31	161	678	76	199	34	3	2	61	31	61	2	.294	.325	.361
Bill Virdon	OF156	L	31	156	663	82	164	27	10	6	47	36	65	5	.247	.286	.345
Roberto Clemente	OF142	R	27	144	538	95	168	28	9	10	74	35	73	6	.312	.352	.454
Bob Skinner	OF139	L	30	144	510	87	154	29	7	20	75	76	89	10	.302	.395	.504
Donn Clendenon	1B52,OF19	R	26	80	222	39	67	8	5	7	28	26	58	16	.302	.376	.477
Don Leppert	C44	L	30	45	139	14	37	6	1	3	18	12	21	0	.266	.327	.388
Howie Goss	OF66	R	27	89	111	19	27	6	0	2	10	9	36	5	.243	.306	.351
Dick Schofield	3B20,2B2,SS1	S	27	54	104	19	30	3	0	2	10	17	22	0	.288	.382	.375
Jim Marshall†	1B26	L	31	55	100	13	22	5	1	2	12	15	19	1	.220	.319	.350
Johnny Logan	3B19	R	35	44	80	7	24	3	0	1	12	7	6	0	.300	.348	.375
Cal Neeman	C24	R	33	24	50	5	9	1	1	1	5	3	10	0	.180	.226	.300
Bob Bailey	3B12	R	19	14	42	6	7	2	1	0	6	6	10	1	.167	.271	.262
Willie Stargell	OF9	L	22	10	31	1	9	3	1	0	4	3	10	0	.290	.353	.452
Orlando McFarlane	C8	R	24	8	23	0	2	0	0	0	1	1	4	0	.087	.125	.087
Elmo Plaskett	C4	R	24	7	14	2	4	0	0	1	3	1	3	0	.286	.333	.500
Larry Elliot	OF3	L	24	8	10	2	3	0	0	1	2	0	1	0	.300	.300	.600
Coot Veal		R	29	1	1	0	0	0	0	0	0	0	1	0	.000	.000	.000

Pitcher	T	Age	G	GS	CG	ShO	IP	H	HR	BB	SO	W-L	Sv	ERA
Bob Friend	R	31	39	36	13	5	261.2	280	23	53	144	18-14	1	3.06
Al McBean	R	24	33	29	6	2	189.2	212	11	65	119	15-10	0	3.70
Earl Francis	R	26	36	23	5	1	176.0	153	8	83	121	9-8	0	3.07
Harvey Haddix	L	36	28	20	4	0	141.1	146	17	42	101	9-6	0	4.20
Vern Law	R	32	23	20	7	2	139.1	156	21	27	78	10-7	0	3.94
Bob Veale	L	26	11	6	2	0	45.2	39	2	25	42	2-2	1	3.74
Tommie Sisk	R	20	5	3	1	0	17.2	18	1	8	6	0-2	0	4.08
V. Bend Mizell†	L	31	4	3	0	0	16.1	15	3	10	6	1-1	0	4.96
Roy Face	R	34	63	0	0	0	91.0	74	7	18	45	8-7	28	1.88
Diomedes Olivo	L	43	62	1	0	0	84.1	88	5	25	66	5-1	7	2.77
Tom Sturdivant	R	32	49	12	2	1	125.1	120	12	39	76	9-5	2	3.73
Jack Lamabe	R	25	46	0	0	0	78.0	70	4	40	56	3-1	2	2.88
Joe Gibbon	L	27	19	8	0	0	57.0	53	4	24	26	3-4	0	3.63
Tom Butters	R	24	4	0	0	0	6.0	5	0	6	10	0-0	0	1.50
Bob Priddy	R	22	2	0	0	0	3.0	4	0	1	1	1-0	0	3.00

1962 Milwaukee Braves 5th NL 86-76 .531 15.5 GB Birdie Tebbetts

Player	Gm by Position	B	Age	G	AB	R	H	2B	3B	HR	RBI	BB	SO	SB	Avg	OBP	Slg
Del Crandall	C90,1B5	R	32	107	350	35	104	12	3	8	45	27	24	3	.297	.348	.417
Joe Adcock	1B112	R	34	121	391	48	97	12	1	29	78	50	91	2	.248	.333	.506
Frank Bolling	2B119	R	30	122	406	45	110	17	4	9	43	35	45	2	.271	.333	.399
Eddie Mathews	3B140,1B7	L	30	152	536	106	142	25	6	29	90	101	90	4	.265	.381	.496
Roy McMillan	SS135	R	31	137	468	66	115	13	0	12	41	60	53	2	.246	.336	.350
Hank Aaron	OF153,1B1	R	28	156	592	127	191	28	6	45	128	66	73	15	.323	.390	.618
Lee Maye	OF94	L	27	99	349	40	85	10	0	10	41	25	58	9	.244	.294	.358
Mack Jones	OF91	L	23	91	333	51	85	17	4	10	36	44	100	5	.255	.354	.420
Tommie Aaron	1B110,OF42,2B1*	R	22	141	334	54	77	20	2	8	38	41	58	6	.231	.312	.374
Joe Torre	C63	R	21	80	220	23	62	8	1	5	26	24	24	1	.282	.355	.395
Gus Bell†	OF58	L	33	79	214	28	61	11	3	5	24	12	17	0	.285	.322	.435
Amado Samuel	SS36,2B28,3B3	R	23	76	209	16	43	10	0	3	20	12	54	0	.206	.248	.297
Denis Menke	2B20,3B15,SS9*	R	21	50	146	12	28	3	1	2	16	16	38	0	.192	.277	.267
Howie Bedell	OF45	L	26	58	138	15	27	1	2	0	2	11	22	1	.196	.255	.232
Lou Johnson	OF55	R	27	61	117	22	33	4	5	2	13	11	27	6	.282	.349	.453
Ken Aspromonte†	2B12,3B6	R	30	34	79	11	23	2	0	0	7	6	5	0	.291	.341	.316
Bob Uecker	C24	R	27	33	64	5	16	2	0	1	8	7	15	0	.250	.324	.328
Hawk Taylor	OF11	R	23	20	47	3	12	0	0	0	2	2	10	0	.255	.286	.255
Ethan Blackaby	OF3	L	21	6	13	0	2	1	0	0	0	1	8	0	.154	.214	.231
Mike Krsnich	OF3,1B1,3B1	R	30	11	12	0	1	1	0	0	2	0	4	0	.083	.083	.167
Lou Klimchock		L	22	8	8	0	0	0	0	0	0	0	2	0	.000	.000	.000

T. Aaron, 1 G at 3B; D. Menke, 2 G at 1B, 1 G at OF

Pitcher	T	Age	G	GS	CG	ShO	IP	H	HR	BB	SO	W-L	Sv	ERA
Warren Spahn	L	41	34	34	22	0	269.1	248	25	55	118	18-14	0	3.04
Bob Shaw	R	29	38	29	12	3	225.0	223	20	44	124	15-9	2	2.80
Bob Hendley	L	23	35	29	7	2	200.0	188	17	59	112	11-13	1	3.60
Lew Burdette	R	35	37	19	6	1	143.2	172	26	23	59	10-9	2	4.89
Tony Cloninger	R	21	24	15	4	1	111.0	113	10	46	69	8-3	0	4.30
Denny Lemaster	L	23	17	12	4	1	86.2	75	11	32	69	3-4	0	3.01
Ron Piche	R	27	14	8	2	0	52.0	54	6	29	28	3-2	0	4.85
Jim Constable	L	29	3	2	1	1	18.0	14	1	4	12	1-1	1	2.00
Bob Buhl†	R	33	1	1	0	0	2.0	6	0	4	1	0-1	0	22.50
Don Nottebart	R	26	39	0	0	0	64.0	64	4	20	36	2-2	2	3.23
Jack Curtis†	L	25	30	5	0	0	75.2	82	8	27	40	4-4	1	4.16
Carl Willey	R	31	30	6	0	0	73.1	95	9	20	40	2-5	1	5.40
Hank Fischer	R	22	29	0	0	0	37.1	43	4	20	29	2-3	4	5.30
Claude Raymond	R	25	26	0	0	0	42.2	37	5	15	40	5-5	10	2.74
Cecil Butler	R	24	9	2	1	0	31.0	26	4	9	22	2-0	0	2.61
Don McMahon†	R	32	2	0	0	0	3.0	3	1	0	3	0-1	0	6.00

Seasons: Team Rosters 761

1962 St. Louis Cardinals 6th NL 84-78 .519 17.5 GB — Johnny Keane

Player	Gm by Position	B	Age	G	AB	R	H	2B	3B	HR	RBI	BB	SO	SB	Avg	OBP	Slg
Gene Oliver	C98,OF8,1B3	R	27	122	345	42	89	19	1	14	45	50	59	5	.258	.352	.441
Bill White	1B146,OF27	L	28	159	614	93	199	31	3	20	102	58	69	9	.324	.386	.482
Julian Javier	2B151,SS4	R	25	155	598	97	157	25	5	7	39	47	73	26	.263	.316	.356
Ken Boyer	3B160	R	31	160	611	92	178	27	5	24	98	75	104	12	.291	.369	.470
Julio Gotay	SS120,2B8,OF2*	R	23	127	369	47	94	12	1	2	27	27	47	7	.255	.316	.309
Curt Flood	OF151	R	24	151	635	99	188	30	5	12	70	42	57	8	.296	.346	.416
Stan Musial	OF119	L	41	135	433	57	143	18	1	19	82	64	46	3	.330	.416	.508
Charlie James	OF116	R	24	129	388	50	107	13	4	8	59	10	58	3	.276	.301	.392
Carl Sawatski	C70	L	34	85	222	26	56	9	1	13	42	36	38	0	.252	.351	.477
Dal Maxvill	SS76,3B1	R	23	79	189	20	42	3	1	1	18	17	39	1	.222	.287	.265
Fred Whitfield	1B38	L	24	73	158	20	42	7	1	8	34	7	30	1	.266	.299	.475
Red Schoendienst	2B21,3B4	S	39	98	143	21	43	4	0	2	12	9	12	0	.301	.346	.371
Bobby Gene Smith†	OF80	R	28	91	130	13	30	9	0	0	12	7	14	1	.231	.270	.300
Minnie Minoso	OF27	R	39	39	97	14	19	5	0	1	10	7	17	4	.196	.271	.278
Doug Clemens	OF34	L	23	48	93	12	22	1	1	1	12	17	19	0	.237	.355	.301
Jimmie Schaffer	C69	R	26	70	66	7	16	2	1	0	6	6	16	1	.242	.301	.303
Don Landrum†	OF26	L	26	32	35	11	11	0	0	0	3	4	2	2	.314	.375	.314
Carl Warwick†	OF10	R	25	13	23	4	8	0	0	1	4	2	2	2	.348	.385	.478
Alex Grammas†	SS16,2B2	R	36	21	18	0	2	0	0	0	1	1	6	0	.111	.158	.111
Mike Shannon	OF7	R	22	10	15	3	2	0	0	0	0	1	3	0	.133	.188	.133
Bob Burda	OF6	L	23	7	14	0	1	0	0	0	0	3	1	1	.071	.235	.071
Gary Kolb	OF6	L	22	6	14	1	5	0	0	0	0	1	3	0	.357	.400	.357

J. Gotay, 1 G at 3B

Pitcher	T	Age	G	GS	CG	ShO	IP	H	HR	BB	SO	W-L	Sv	ERA
Larry Jackson	R	31	36	35	11	2	252.1	267	25	64	112	16-11	0	3.75
Bob Gibson	R	26	32	30	15	5	233.2	174	15	95	208	15-13	1	2.85
Ernie Broglio	R	26	34	30	11	4	222.1	193	22	93	132	12-9	0	3.00
Ray Washburn	R	24	34	25	2	1	175.2	187	25	58	109	12-9	0	4.10
Curt Simmons	L	33	31	22	9	4	154.0	167	18	32	74	10-10	0	3.51
Ray Sadecki	L	21	22	17	4	1	102.1	121	13	43	50	6-8	1	5.54
Harvey Branch	L	23	1	1	0	0	5.0	5	1	5	2	0-1	0	5.40
Lindy McDaniel	R	26	55	2	0	0	107.0	96	12	29	79	3-10	14	4.12
Don Ferrarese†	L	33	38	0	0	0	56.2	55	2	31	45	1-4	1	2.70
Bobby Shantz†	L	36	28	0	0	0	57.2	45	7	20	47	5-3	4	2.18
Bob Duliba	R	27	28	0	0	0	39.1	33	3	17	22	2-0	2	2.06
Ed Bauta	R	27	20	0	0	0	32.1	28	5	21	25	1-0	1	5.01
Paul Toth†	R	27	6	1	1	0	16.2	18	1	4	5	1-0	0	5.40
John Anderson†	R	29	5	0	0	0	6.1	4	0	3	3	0-0	1	1.42
Bobby Locke†	R	28	1	0	0	0	2.0	1	0	2	1	0-0	0	0.00

1962 Philadelphia Phillies 7th NL 81-80 .503 20.0 GB — Gene Mauch

Player	Gm by Position	B	Age	G	AB	R	H	2B	3B	HR	RBI	BB	SO	SB	Avg	OBP	Slg
Clay Dalrymple	C119	L	25	123	370	40	102	13	3	11	54	70	32	1	.276	.393	.446
Roy Sievers	1B130,OF7	R	35	144	477	61	125	19	5	21	80	56	80	2	.262	.346	.455
Tony Taylor	2B150,SS2	R	26	152	625	87	162	21	5	7	43	68	82	20	.259	.336	.342
Don Demeter	3B105,OF63,1B1	R	27	153	550	85	169	24	3	29	107	41	93	2	.307	.359	.520
Bobby Wine	SS89,3B20	R	23	112	311	30	76	15	0	4	25	11	49	2	.244	.268	.331
Johnny Callison	OF152	L	23	157	603	107	181	26	10	23	83	54	96	10	.300	.363	.491
Tony Gonzalez	OF114	L	25	118	437	76	132	16	4	20	63	40	82	17	.302	.371	.494
Ted Savage	OF109	R	25	127	335	54	89	11	2	7	39	40	66	16	.266	.345	.373
Wes Covington	OF88	L	30	116	304	36	86	12	1	9	44	19	44	0	.283	.324	.418
Billy Klaus	3B53,SS30,2B11	L	33	102	248	30	51	8	2	4	20	29	43	1	.206	.290	.302
Ruben Amaro	SS78,1B1	R	26	79	226	24	55	10	0	0	19	30	28	5	.243	.330	.288
Frank Torre	1B76	L	30	108	168	13	52	8	2	0	20	24	6	1	.310	.404	.381
Mel Roach	3B26,2B9,1B4*	R	29	65	105	9	20	4	0	0	8	5	19	0	.190	.225	.229
Sammy White	C40	R	33	41	97	7	21	4	0	2	12	2	16	0	.216	.238	.320
Bob Oldis	C30	R	34	38	80	9	21	1	0	1	10	13	10	0	.263	.366	.313
Jacke Davis	OF26	R	26	48	75	9	16	0	1	1	6	4	20	1	.213	.253	.280
John Herrnstein	OF1	L	24	6	5	0	1	0	0	0	1	1	3	0	.200	.333	.200
Bobby Malkmus	SS1	R	30	8	5	3	1	1	0	0	0	0	0	0	.200	.200	.400
Billy Consolo†	3B1	R	27	13	5	3	2	0	0	0	0	0	1	0	.400	.400	.400
Jimmie Coker		R	26	5	3	0	0	0	0	0	1	1	2	0	.000	.200	.000

M. Roach, 3 G at OF

Pitcher	T	Age	G	GS	CG	ShO	IP	H	HR	BB	SO	W-L	Sv	ERA
Art Mahaffey	R	24	41	39	20	2	274.0	253	36	81	177	19-14	0	3.94
Jack Hamilton	R	23	41	26	4	1	182.0	185	18	107	101	9-12	2	5.09
Dennis Bennett	L	22	31	24	7	2	174.2	144	17	68	149	9-9	3	3.81
Cal McLish	R	36	32	24	5	1	154.2	184	15	45	71	11-5	1	4.25
Jim Owens	R	28	23	12	1	0	69.2	90	12	33	21	2-4	0	6.33
Jack Baldschun	R	25	67	0	0	0	112.2	95	6	58	95	12-7	13	2.96
Chris Short	L	24	47	12	4	0	142.0	149	13	56	91	11-9	3	3.42
Dallas Green	R	27	37	10	2	0	129.1	145	10	43	58	6-6	1	3.83
Bill Smith	L	28	24	5	0	0	50.1	59	8	10	26	1-5	0	4.29
Paul Brown	R	21	23	9	0	0	63.2	74	9	33	29	0-6	1	5.94
Frank Sullivan†	R	32	19	0	0	0	23.0	38	2	12	12	0-2	0	6.26
John Boozer	R	23	9	0	0	0	20.1	22	3	10	13	0-0	0	5.75
Bobby Locke†	R	28	5	0	0	0	15.2	16	4	10	9	1-0	0	5.74
Don Ferrarese†	L	33	5	0	0	0	6.2	9	1	3	6	0-1	0	8.10
Ed Keegan	R	22	4	0	0	0	8.0	6	1	5	5	0-0	0	2.25

1962 Houston Colt .45s 8th NL 64-96 .400 36.5 GB — Harry Craft

Player	Gm by Position	B	Age	G	AB	R	H	2B	3B	HR	RBI	BB	SO	SB	Avg	OBP	Slg
Hal Smith	C92,3B6,1B2	R	31	109	345	32	81	14	0	12	35	24	55	0	.235	.286	.380
Norm Larker	1B135,OF6	L	31	147	506	58	133	19	5	9	63	70	47	1	.263	.358	.374
Joey Amalfitano	2B110,3B5	R	28	117	380	44	90	12	5	1	27	45	43	4	.237	.317	.303
Bob Aspromonte	3B142,SS11,2B1	R	24	149	534	59	142	18	4	11	59	46	54	4	.266	.332	.376
Bob Lillis	SS99,2B33,3B9	R	32	129	457	38	114	12	4	1	30	28	23	7	.249	.292	.300
Roman Mejias	OF142	R	31	146	566	82	162	12	3	24	76	30	83	12	.286	.326	.445
Carl Warwick†	OF128	R	25	130	477	63	124	17	1	16	60	38	77	2	.260	.312	.400
Al Spangler	OF121	L	28	129	418	51	119	10	9	5	35	70	46	7	.285	.389	.388
Jim Pendleton	OF90,1B8,3B3*	R	38	117	321	30	79	12	2	8	36	14	57	0	.246	.279	.371
Merritt Ranew	C58	L	24	71	218	26	51	6	8	4	24	14	43	2	.234	.287	.390
Billy Goodman	2B31,3B17,1B1	L	36	82	161	12	41	4	1	0	10	12	11	0	.255	.306	.292
J.C. Hartman	SS48	R	28	51	148	11	33	5	0	0	5	4	16	1	.223	.248	.257
Pidge Browne	1B26	L	33	65	100	8	21	4	2	1	10	13	9	0	.210	.298	.320
Johnny Temple†	2B26,3B1	R	34	31	95	14	25	4	0	0	12	7	11	1	.263	.311	.305
Jim Campbell	C25	R	25	27	86	6	19	4	0	3	6	6	23	0	.221	.272	.372
Don Buddin†	SS27,3B9	R	28	40	80	10	13	4	1	2	10	17	17	0	.163	.316	.313
Al Heist	OF23	R	34	27	72	4	16	1	0	0	3	3	9	0	.222	.263	.236
Dave Roberts	OF12,1B6	L	29	16	53	3	13	3	0	1	10	8	8	0	.245	.349	.358
Bob Cerv†	OF6	R	36	19	31	2	7	0	0	2	3	2	10	0	.226	.273	.419
Johnny Weekly	OF7	R	25	13	26	3	5	1	0	2	2	7	4	0	.192	.364	.462
Don Taussig	OF4	R	30	16	25	1	5	0	0	1	1	2	11	0	.200	.259	.320
Dick Gernert	1B9	R	33	10	24	1	5	0	0	0	1	5	7	0	.208	.345	.208
Ron Davis	OF5	R	20	6	14	1	3	0	0	0	1	1	7	1	.214	.267	.214
Ernie Fazio	SS10	R	20	12	12	3	1	0	0	0	1	2	5	0	.083	.214	.083
Jim Busby	OF10,C1	R	35	15	11	2	2	0	0	0	1	2	3	0	.182	.308	.182
George Williams	2B3	R	22	5	8	1	3	1	0	0	2	0	1	0	.375	.375	.500

J. Pendleton, 2 G at SS

Pitcher	T	Age	G	GS	CG	ShO	IP	H	HR	BB	SO	W-L	Sv	ERA
Ken Johnson	R	29	33	31	5	1	197.0	195	18	46	178	7-16	0	3.84
Turk Farrell	R	28	43	29	11	2	241.2	210	21	55	203	10-20	4	3.02
Bob Bruce	R	29	32	27	6	0	175.0	164	16	82	135	10-9	0	4.06
Hal Woodeshick	L	29	31	26	2	1	139.1	161	3	54	82	5-16	0	4.39
George Brunet	L	27	17	11	2	0	54.0	62	2	21	36	2-4	0	4.50
Bobby Shantz†	L	36	3	3	1	0	20.2	15	1	5	14	1-1	0	1.31
Don McMahon†	R	32	51	0	0	0	76.2	53	4	33	69	5-5	8	1.53
Bobby Tiefenauer	R	32	43	0	0	0	85.0	91	6	21	60	2-4	1	4.34
Jim Golden	R	26	37	18	5	2	152.2	163	13	50	88	7-11	1	4.07
Russ Kemmerer†	R	30	36	2	0	0	68.0	72	10	15	23	5-3	3	4.10
Jim Umbricht	R	31	34	0	0	0	67.0	51	3	17	55	4-0	2	2.01
Dave Giusti	R	22	22	5	0	0	73.2	82	7	30	43	2-3	0	5.62
Dean Stone†	L	31	15	7	2	2	52.1	61	4	20	31	3-2	0	4.47
John Anderson†	R	29	10	0	0	0	17.2	26	1	3	6	0-0	0	5.09
George Witt†	R	28	8	2	0	0	15.1	20	2	9	10	0-2	0	7.04
Dick Drott	R	25	6	1	0	0	13.0	12	1	9	10	1-0	0	7.62
Al Cicotte	R	32	5	0	0	0	4.2	8	1	1	4	0-0	0	3.86

1962 Chicago Cubs 9th NL 59-103 .364 42.5 GB — El Tappe (4-16)/Lou Klein (12-18)/Charlie Metro (43-69)

Player	Gm by Position	B	Age	G	AB	R	H	2B	3B	HR	RBI	BB	SO	SB	Avg	OBP	Slg
Dick Bertell	C76	R	26	77	215	19	65	6	2	2	18	13	30	0	.302	.343	.377
Ernie Banks	1B149,3B3	R	31	154	610	87	164	20	6	37	104	30	71	5	.269	.306	.503
Ken Hubbs	2B159	R	20	160	661	90	172	24	9	5	49	35	129	3	.260	.299	.346
Ron Santo	3B157,SS8	R	22	162	604	44	137	20	4	17	83	65	94	4	.227	.302	.358
Andre Rodgers	SS133,1B1	R	27	138	461	40	128	20	8	5	44	44	93	5	.278	.343	.388
Billy Williams	OF159	L	24	159	618	94	184	22	8	22	91	70	72	9	.298	.369	.466
George Altman	OF129,1B16	L	29	147	534	74	170	27	5	22	74	62	89	19	.318	.393	.511
Lou Brock	OF106	L	23	123	434	73	114	24	7	9	35	35	96	16	.263	.319	.412
Don Landrum†	OF59	L	26	83	238	29	67	5	2	1	15	30	31	9	.282	.369	.332
Cuno Barragan	C55	R	30	58	134	11	27	6	1	0	12	21	28	0	.201	.306	.261
Moe Thacker	C65	R	28	65	107	8	20	5	0	0	9	14	40	0	.187	.287	.234
Bob Will	OF9	L	30	87	92	6	22	3	0	2	15	13	22	0	.239	.327	.337
Jim McKnight	3B9,OF5,2B2	R	26	60	85	6	19	0	1	0	5	2	13	0	.224	.241	.247
Alex Grammas†	SS13,2B3,3B1	R	36	23	60	3	14	3	0	0	3	2	7	1	.233	.270	.283
Elder White	SS15,3B1	R	27	23	53	4	8	2	0	0	1	8	11	3	.151	.274	.189
El Tappe	C26	R	35	26	53	3	11	0	0	0	6	4	3	0	.208	.288	.208
Nelson Mathews	OF14	R	20	15	49	5	15	2	0	2	13	5	4	3	.306	.393	.469
Danny Murphy	OF5	L	19	14	35	5	7	3	1	0	3	2	9	0	.200	.243	.343
Bobby Gene Smith†	OF7	R	28	13	29	3	5	0	0	1	2	2	6	0	.172	.219	.276
Billy Ott	OF7	S	21	12	28	3	4	0	0	0	2	2	10	0	.143	.200	.250
Daryl Robertson	SS6,3B1	R	26	9	19	0	2	0	0	0	2	2	10	0	.105	.182	.105
Moe Morhardt		L	25	18	16	1	2	0	0	0	2	2	8	0	.125	.222	.125
Sammy Taylor†	C6	L	29	7	15	0	2	1	0	0	1	3	3	0	.133	.278	.200
Jim McAnany		R	25	7	6	0	0	0	0	0	0	1	2	0	.000	.143	.000

Pitcher	T	Age	G	GS	CG	ShO	IP	H	HR	BB	SO	W-L	Sv	ERA
Dick Ellsworth	L	22	37	33	6	0	208.2	241	23	77	113	9-20	1	5.09
Bob Buhl†	R	33	34	30	8	1	212.0	204	23	94	109	12-13	0	3.69
Cal Koonce	R	21	35	30	3	1	190.2	200	17	86	84	10-10	0	3.97
Don Cardwell	R	26	41	29	6	1	195.2	205	27	60	104	7-16	4	4.92
Glen Hobbie	R	26	42	23	5	0	162.0	198	19	62	87	5-14	0	5.22
Paul Toth†	R	27	6	4	1	0	34.0	29	2	10	11	3-1	0	4.24
Jack Curtis†	L	25	4	3	0	0	18.0	18	2	6	8	0-2	0	3.50
George Gerberman	R	20	1	1	0	0	5.1	3	1	5	1	0-0	0	1.69
Bob Anderson	R	26	57	4	0	0	107.2	111	9	60	82	2-7	4	5.02
Don Elston	R	33	57	0	0	0	66.1	57	6	32	37	4-8	8	2.44
Barney Schultz	R	35	51	0	0	0	77.2	66	7	23	58	5-5	5	3.82
Dave Gerard	R	25	39	0	0	0	58.2	67	10	28	30	2-3	3	4.91
Tony Balsamo	R	24	18	0	0	0	29.1	34	1	20	27	0-1	0	6.44
Al Lary	R	33	15	3	0	0	34.0	42	5	15	18	0-1	0	7.15
Morrie Steevens	L	21	12	1	0	0	15.0	10	0	11	5	0-1	0	2.40
Freddie Burdette	R	25	8	0	0	0	9.2	5	2	8	5	0-0	1	3.72
Jack Warner	R	21	7	0	0	0	7.0	9	3	0	3	0-0	0	7.71
Jim Brewer	L	24	6	1	0	0	5.2	10	2	3	1	0-1	0	9.53
Don Prince	R	24	1	0	0	0	1.0	0	0	1	0	0-0	0	0.00

762 Seasons: Team Rosters

1962 New York Mets 10th NL 40-120 .250 60.5 GB — Casey Stengel

Player	Gm by Position	B	Age	G	AB	R	H	2B	3B	HR	RBI	BB	SO	SB	Avg	OBP	Slg
Chris Cannizzaro	C56,OF1	R	24	59	133	9	32	2	1	0	9	19	26	1	.241	.335	.271
Marv Throneberry†	1B97	L	28	116	357	29	87	11	3	16	49	34	83	1	.244	.306	.426
Charlie Neal	2B85,SS39,3B12	R	31	136	508	59	132	14	9	11	58	56	90	2	.260	.330	.388
Felix Mantilla	3B95,SS25,2B14	R	27	141	466	54	128	17	4	11	59	37	51	3	.275	.330	.399
Elio Chacon	SS110,2B2,3B1	R	25	118	368	49	87	10	3	2	27	76	64	12	.236	.368	.296
Frank Thomas	OF126,1B11,3B10	R	33	156	571	69	152	23	3	34	94	48	95	2	.266	.329	.496
Jim Hickman	OF124	R	25	140	392	54	96	18	2	13	46	47	96	4	.245	.328	.401
Richie Ashburn	OF97,2B2	L	35	135	389	60	119	7	3	7	28	81	39	12	.306	.424	.393
Rod Kanehl	2B62,3B30,OF20*	R	28	133	351	52	87	10	2	4	27	23	36	8	.248	.296	.322
Joe Christopher	OF94	R	26	119	271	36	66	10	2	6	32	35	42	11	.244	.338	.362
Gene Woodling†	OF48	L	39	81	190	18	52	8	1	5	24	24	22	0	.274	.353	.405
Sammy Taylor†	C50	L	29	68	158	12	35	4	2	3	20	23	17	0	.222	.323	.329
C. Choo Coleman	C44	L	24	55	152	24	38	7	2	6	17	11	24	2	.250	.303	.441
Gil Hodges	1B47	R	38	54	127	15	32	1	0	9	17	15	27	0	.252	.331	.472
Cliff Cook†	3B16,OF10	R	25	40	112	12	26	6	1	2	9	4	34	1	.232	.275	.357
Gus Bell†	OF26	L	33	30	101	8	15	2	0	1	6	10	7	0	.149	.221	.198
Ed Bouchee	1B19	L	29	50	87	7	14	2	0	3	10	18	17	0	.161	.302	.287
Joe Pignatano†	C25	R	32	27	56	2	13	2	0	0	2	2	11	0	.232	.259	.268
Sammy Drake	2B10,3B6	S	27	25	52	2	10	0	0	0	7	6	12	0	.192	.276	.192
Don Zimmer†	3B14	R	31	14	52	3	4	1	0	0	1	3	10	0	.077	.127	.096
Rick Herrscher	1B10,3B6,OF4*	R	25	35	50	5	11	3	0	1	6	5	11	0	.220	.291	.340
Hobie Landrith†	C21	L	32	23	45	6	13	3	0	1	7	8	3	0	.289	.389	.422
Harry Chiti	C14	R	29	15	41	2	8	1	0	0	0	1	8	0	.195	.233	.220
Jim Marshall†	1B5,OF1	L	31	17	32	6	11	1	0	3	4	3	6	0	.344	.400	.656
Bobby Gene Smith†	OF6	R	28	8	22	1	3	0	1	0	2	3	2	0	.136	.240	.227
John DeMerit	OF9	R	26	14	16	3	3	0	0	1	1	2	4	0	.188	.278	.375
Ed Kranepool	1B3	L	17	3	6	0	1	1	0	0	0	0	1	0	.167	.167	.333
Joe Ginsberg	C2	L	35	2	5	0	0	0	0	0	0	0	1	0	.000	.000	.000

R. Kanehl, 3 G at 1B, 2 G at SS; R. Herrscher, 3 G at SS

Pitcher	T	Age	G	GS	CG	ShO	IP	H	HR	BB	SO	W-L	Sv	ERA
Jay Hook	R	25	37	34	13	0	213.2	230	31	71	113	8-19	0	4.84
Roger Craig	R	32	42	33	13	0	233.1	261	35	70	118	10-24	3	4.51
Al Jackson	L	26	36	33	12	4	231.1	244	16	78	118	8-20	0	4.40
Bob Miller	R	23	33	21	1	0	143.2	146	20	62	91	1-12	0	4.89
Galen Cisco†	R	26	4	2	1	0	19.1	15	0	11	13	1-1	0	3.26
Craig Anderson	R	23	50	14	2	0	131.1	150	18	63	62	3-17	4	5.35
Ken MacKenzie	L	28	42	1	0	0	80.0	87	10	34	51	5-4	1	4.95
Bob Moorhead	R	24	38	7	0	0	105.1	118	13	42	63	0-2	0	4.53
Ray Daviault	R	28	36	3	0	0	81.0	92	14	48	51	1-5	0	6.22
Willard Hunter†	L	28	27	6	1	0	63.0	67	9	34	40	1-6	0	5.57
V. Bend Mizell†	L	31	17	2	0	0	38.0	48	10	25	15	0-2	0	7.34
Bob Miller†	L	26	17	0	0	0	20.1	24	2	8	8	2-2	1	7.08
Dave Hillman†	R	34	13	1	0	0	15.2	21	5	8	8	0-0	1	6.32
Sherman Jones	R	27	8	3	0	0	23.1	31	3	8	11	0-4	0	7.71
Herb Moford	R	33	7	0	0	0	15.0	21	3	1	5	0-1	0	7.20
Larry Foss	R	26	5	1	0	0	11.2	17	2	7	3	0-1	0	4.63
Clem Labine	R	35	3	0	0	0	4.0	5	1	1	2	0-0	0	11.25

»1963 New York Yankees 1st AL 104-57 .646 — — Ralph Houk

Player	Gm by Position	B	Age	G	AB	R	H	2B	3B	HR	RBI	BB	SO	SB	Avg	OBP	Slg
Elston Howard	C132	R	34	135	487	75	140	21	6	28	85	35	68	0	.287	.342	.528
Joe Pepitone	1B143,OF16	L	22	157	580	79	157	16	3	27	89	23	63	3	.271	.304	.448
Bobby Richardson	2B150	R	27	151	630	72	167	20	6	3	48	25	22	15	.265	.294	.330
Clete Boyer	3B141,SS9,2B1	R	26	152	557	59	140	20	3	12	54	33	91	4	.251	.295	.363
Tony Kubek	SS132,OF1	L	26	135	557	72	143	21	3	7	44	28	68	4	.257	.294	.343
Tom Tresh	OF144	S	25	145	520	91	140	28	5	25	71	83	79	3	.269	.371	.487
Hector Lopez	OF124,2B1	R	33	130	433	54	108	13	4	14	52	35	71	1	.249	.304	.395
Jack Reed	OF89	R	30	106	73	18	15	3	1	0	1	9	14	5	.205	.293	.274
Roger Maris	OF86	L	28	90	312	53	84	14	1	23	53	35	40	1	.269	.346	.542
Johnny Blanchard	OF64	L	30	76	218	22	49	4	0	16	45	26	30	0	.225	.305	.463
Phil Linz	SS22,3B13,OF12*	R	24	72	186	22	50	9	0	2	12	15	18	1	.269	.328	.349
Mickey Mantle	OF52	S	31	65	172	40	54	8	0	15	35	40	32	2	.314	.441	.622
Harry Bright†	1B35,3B12	R	33	60	157	15	37	7	0	7	23	13	31	0	.236	.297	.414
Yogi Berra	C35	L	38	64	147	20	43	6	0	8	28	15	17	1	.293	.360	.497
Pedro Gonzalez	2B7	R	25	14	26	3	5	1	0	0	1	0	5	0	.192	.192	.231
Dale Long	1B2	L	37	14	15	1	3	0	0	0	0	1	3	0	.200	.250	.200
Jake Gibbs	C1	L	24	4	8	1	2	0	0	0	0	0	1	0	.250	.250	.250

P. Linz, 6 G at 2B

Pitcher	T	Age	G	GS	CG	ShO	IP	H	HR	BB	SO	W-L	Sv	ERA
Whitey Ford	L	34	38	37	13	3	269.1	240	26	56	189	24-7	1	2.74
Ralph Terry	R	27	40	37	18	3	268.0	246	29	39	114	17-15	1	3.22
Jim Bouton	R	24	40	30	12	6	249.1	191	18	87	148	21-7	1	2.53
Al Downing	L	22	24	22	10	4	175.2	114	7	80	171	13-5	0	2.56
Stan Williams	R	26	29	21	6	1	146.0	137	7	57	98	9-8	0	3.21
Bill Stafford	R	23	28	14	0	0	89.2	104	16	42	52	4-8	3	6.02
Hal Reniff	R	24	48	0	0	0	89.1	63	3	42	56	4-3	18	2.62
Steve Hamilton†	L	27	34	0	0	0	62.1	49	3	24	63	5-1	5	2.60
Marshall Bridges	L	32	23	0	0	0	33.0	27	2	30	35	2-0	1	3.82
Bill Kunkel	R	26	22	0	0	0	46.1	42	3	13	31	3-2	0	2.72
Tom Metcalf	R	22	8	0	0	0	13.0	12	1	3	3	1-0	0	2.77
Luis Arroyo	L	36	6	0	0	0	6.0	12	0	3	5	1-1	0	13.50
Bud Daley	L	30	1	0	0	0	1.0	2	0	0	0	0-0	1	0.00

1963 Chicago White Sox 2nd AL 94-68 .580 10.5 GB — Al Lopez

Player	Gm by Position	B	Age	G	AB	R	H	2B	3B	HR	RBI	BB	SO	SB	Avg	OBP	Slg
J.C. Martin	C98,1B3,3B1	L	26	105	259	25	53	11	1	5	28	26	35	0	.205	.278	.313
Tom McCraw	1B97	L	22	102	280	38	71	11	3	6	33	21	46	15	.254	.309	.379
Nellie Fox	2B134	L	35	137	539	54	140	19	0	2	42	24	17	0	.260	.299	.306
Pete Ward	3B154,2B1,SS1	L	23	157	600	80	177	34	6	22	84	52	77	7	.295	.353	.482
Ron Hansen	SS144	R	25	144	482	55	109	17	2	13	67	78	74	1	.226	.330	.351
Floyd Robinson	OF137	L	27	146	527	71	149	21	6	13	71	62	43	4	.283	.361	.419
Jim Landis	OF124	R	29	133	396	56	89	6	6	13	45	47	75	8	.225	.316	.369
Dave Nicholson	OF123	R	23	126	449	53	103	11	4	22	70	63	175	2	.229	.319	.419
Mike Hershberger	OF119	R	23	135	476	64	133	26	2	3	45	39	39	9	.279	.338	.361
Cam Carreon	C92	R	25	101	270	28	74	10	1	2	35	23	32	1	.274	.332	.341
Al Weis	2B48,SS27,3B1	S	25	99	210	41	57	9	0	0	18	18	37	15	.271	.333	.314
Joe Cunningham	1B58	L	31	67	210	32	60	12	1	1	31	33	23	1	.286	.388	.367
Charlie Maxwell	OF24,1B17	L	36	71	130	17	30	4	2	3	17	31	27	0	.231	.370	.362
Jim Lemon†	1B25	R	35	36	80	4	16	0	1	1	8	12	32	0	.200	.304	.263
Sherm Lollar	C23,1B2	R	38	35	73	4	17	4	0	0	6	8	7	0	.233	.317	.288
Don Buford	3B9,2B2	S	26	12	42	9	12	1	2	0	5	5	7	1	.286	.354	.405
Gene Stephens	OF5	L	30	6	18	5	7	0	0	1	2	1	3	0	.389	.421	.556
Deacon Jones	1B1	L	29	17	16	4	3	0	1	1	2	2	2	0	.188	.316	.500
Brian McCall	OF2	L	20	3	7	1	0	0	0	0	0	1	2	0	.000	.125	.000
Charley Smith	SS1	R	25	4	7	0	2	0	1	0	1	0	2	0	.286	.286	.571
Ken Berry	OF2,2B1	R	22	4	5	2	1	0	0	0	0	1	1	0	.200	.333	.200
Sammy Esposito†		R	31	1	0	0	0	0	0	0	0	0	0	0	—	—	—

Pitcher	T	Age	G	GS	CG	ShO	IP	H	HR	BB	SO	W-L	Sv	ERA
Ray Herbert	R	33	33	33	14	7	224.2	230	12	35	105	13-10	0	3.24
Gary Peters	L	26	41	30	13	4	243.0	192	9	68	189	19-8	1	2.33
Juan Pizarro	L	26	32	28	10	3	214.2	177	14	63	163	16-8	1	2.39
Joe Horlen	R	25	33	21	3	0	124.0	122	10	55	61	11-7	0	3.27
John Buzhardt	R	26	19	18	6	3	126.1	100	8	31	59	9-4	0	2.42
Fritz Ackley	R	26	2	2	0	0	13.0	7	2	7	11	1-0	0	2.08
Frank Kreutzer	L	24	1	1	0	0	5.0	3	1	1	0	1-0	0	1.80
Hoyt Wilhelm	R	39	55	3	0	0	136.1	106	8	30	111	5-8	21	2.64
Jim Brosnan†	R	33	45	0	0	0	73.0	71	7	22	46	3-8	14	2.84
Eddie Fisher	R	26	33	15	2	1	120.2	114	14	28	67	9-8	0	3.95
Dave DeBusschere	R	22	24	10	1	0	84.1	80	9	34	53	3-4	0	3.09
Frank Baumann	L	29	24	1	0	0	50.1	52	2	17	31	2-1	1	3.04
Taylor Phillips	L	30	9	0	0	0	14.0	16	2	13	13	0-0	0	10.29
Bruce Howard	R	20	7	0	0	0	17.0	12	0	14	9	2-1	1	2.65
Mike Joyce	R	22	6	0	0	0	10.2	13	1	8	7	0-0	0	8.44
Dom Zanni†	R	31	5	0	0	0	4.1	5	1	4	2	0-0	0	8.31
Joe Shipley	R	28	3	0	0	0	4.2	9	0	6	3	0-1	0	5.79
Fred Talbot	R	22	1	0	0	0	3.0	2	0	4	2	0-0	0	3.00

1963 Minnesota Twins 3rd AL 91-70 .565 13.0 GB — Sam Mele

Player	Gm by Position	B	Age	G	AB	R	H	2B	3B	HR	RBI	BB	SO	SB	Avg	OBP	Slg
Earl Battey	C146	R	28	147	508	64	145	17	1	26	84	61	75	0	.285	.369	.476
Vic Power	1B124,2B18,3B5	R	35	138	541	65	146	28	2	10	52	22	24	3	.270	.297	.384
Bernie Allen	2B128	L	24	139	421	52	101	20	1	9	43	38	52	0	.240	.302	.356
Rich Rollins	3B132,2B1	R	25	136	531	75	163	23	1	16	61	36	59	2	.307	.359	.444
Zoilo Versalles	SS159	R	23	159	621	74	162	31	13	10	54	33	66	7	.261	.303	.401
Bob Allison	OF147	R	28	148	527	99	143	25	4	35	91	90	109	6	.271	.378	.533
Jimmie Hall	OF143	L	25	156	497	88	129	21	5	33	80	63	101	3	.260	.342	.521
Harmon Killebrew	OF137	R	27	142	515	88	133	18	0	45	96	72	105	0	.258	.349	.555
Lenny Green	OF119	L	30	145	280	41	67	10	1	4	27	31	21	11	.239	.315	.325
Don Mincher	1B60	L	25	82	225	41	58	8	0	17	42	30	51	0	.258	.351	.520
Johnny Goryl	2B34,3B11,SS7	R	29	64	150	29	43	5	3	9	24	15	29	0	.287	.353	.540
George Banks	3B21	R	24	25	71	5	11	4	0	3	8	9	21	0	.155	.259	.338
Jerry Zimmerman	C39	R	28	39	56	3	13	1	0	0	3	2	8	0	.232	.259	.250
Wally Post†	OF12	R	33	21	47	6	9	0	1	2	6	2	17	0	.191	.224	.362
Vic Wertz†	1B6	L	38	35	44	3	6	0	0	3	7	6	5	0	.136	.240	.341
Paul Ratliff	C7	L	19	10	21	2	4	1	0	1	3	2	7	0	.190	.292	.381
Jim Lemon†	OF4	R	35	7	17	0	2	0	0	0	1	1	5	0	.118	.167	.118
Jay Ward	3B4,OF1	R	24	9	15	0	1	1	0	0	2	1	5	0	.067	.125	.133
Tony Oliva		L	22	7	7	0	3	0	0	0	1	0	2	0	.429	.429	.429
Bill Tuttle	OF14	R	33	16	3	0	0	0	0	0	0	1	0	0	.000	.250	.000
Julio Becquer		L	31	1	0	1	0	0	0	0	0	0	0	0	—	—	—

Pitcher	T	Age	G	GS	CG	ShO	IP	H	HR	BB	SO	W-L	Sv	ERA
Dick Stigman	L	27	33	33	15	3	241.0	210	32	81	193	15-15	0	3.25
Camilo Pascual	R	29	31	31	18	3	248.1	205	21	81	202	21-9	0	2.46
Jim Kaat	L	24	31	27	7	1	178.1	195	24	38	105	10-10	1	4.19
Jim Perry†	R	27	35	25	5	0	168.1	167	17	57	65	9-9	1	3.74
Lee Stange	R	26	32	20	7	2	164.2	145	21	43	100	12-5	0	2.62
Jim Roland	L	20	10	7	2	1	49.0	32	4	27	34	4-1	0	2.57
Dwight Siebler	R	25	7	5	2	0	38.2	25	6	12	22	2-1	0	2.79
Jack Kralick†	L	28	5	5	1	1	25.2	28	2	8	13	1-4	0	3.86
Bill Dailey	R	28	66	0	0	0	108.2	80	9	19	72	6-3	21	1.99
Bill Pleis	L	25	36	4	1	0	68.0	67	10	16	37	6-2	0	4.37
Garry Roggenburk	L	23	36	2	0	0	50.0	47	3	22	24	2-4	4	2.16
Ray Moore	R	37	31	1	0	0	38.2	50	8	17	38	1-3	2	6.98
Mike Fornieles†	R	31	11	0	0	0	22.2	24	0	13	7	1-1	0	4.76
Fred Lasher	R	21	11	0	0	0	11.1	12	1	11	10	0-0	0	4.76
Frank Sullivan	R	33	10	0	0	0	11.0	15	1	4	2	0-1	1	5.73
Gerry Arrigo	L	22	5	1	0	0	15.2	12	2	4	13	1-2	0	2.87
Don Williams	R	27	3	0	0	0	4.1	8	1	6	2	0-0	0	10.38
Gary Dotter	L	20	2	0	0	0	2.0	0	0	0	2	0-0	0	0.00

1963 Baltimore Orioles 4th AL 86-76 .531 18.5 GB — Billy Hitchcock

Player	Gm by Position	B	Age	G	AB	R	H	2B	3B	HR	RBI	BB	SO	SB	Avg	OBP	Slg
John Orsino	C109,1B3	R	25	116	379	53	103	18	1	19	56	38	53	2	.272	.349	.475
Jim Gentile	1B143	L	29	145	496	65	123	16	1	24	72	76	101	1	.248	.353	.429
Jerry Adair	2B103	R	26	109	382	34	87	21	3	6	30	9	51	3	.228	.246	.346
Brooks Robinson	3B160,SS1	R	26	161	589	67	148	26	4	11	67	46	84	2	.251	.305	.365
Luis Aparicio	SS145	R	29	146	601	73	150	18	8	5	45	36	35	40	.250	.291	.331
Jackie Brandt	OF134,3B1	R	29	142	451	49	112	15	5	15	61	34	85	4	.248	.298	.404
Russ Snyder	OF130	L	29	148	429	51	110	21	2	7	36	40	48	18	.256	.321	.364
Boog Powell	OF121,1B23	L	21	140	491	67	130	22	2	25	82	49	87	1	.265	.328	.470
Al Smith	OF97	R	35	120	368	45	100	17	1	10	39	32	74	9	.272	.335	.405
Bob Johnson	2B50,1B8,SS7*	R	27	82	254	34	75	10	0	8	32	18	35	5	.295	.347	.429
Dick Brown	C58	R	28	59	171	13	42	7	0	2	13	15	35	1	.246	.310	.322
Bob Saverine	OF59,2B19,SS13	S	22	115	167	21	39	1	2	1	12	25	44	8	.234	.332	.281
Joe Gaines	OF39	R	26	66	126	24	36	4	1	6	20	20	39	2	.286	.381	.476
Sam Bowens	OF13	R	24	15	48	8	16	3	1	1	9	4	5	1	.333	.385	.500
Charlie Lau†	C8	L	30	29	48	4	9	2	0	0	6	1	5	0	.188	.204	.229
Fred Valentine	OF10	S	28	26	41	5	11	1	0	0	1	8	5	0	.268	.388	.293
Hobie Landrith†	C1	L	33	2	1	0	0	0	0	0	0	0	0	0	.000	.000	.000

B. Johnson, 5 G at 3B

Pitcher	T	Age	G	GS	CG	ShO	IP	H	HR	BB	SO	W-L	Sv	ERA
Steve Barber	L	24	39	36	11	2	258.2	253	12	92	180	20-13	0	2.75
Robin Roberts	R	36	35	35	9	2	251.1	230	35	40	124	14-13	0	3.33
Milt Pappas	R	24	34	32	11	4	216.2	186	21	69	120	16-9	0	3.03
Mike McCormick	L	24	25	21	2	0	136.0	132	18	66	75	6-8	0	4.30
Dave McNally	L	20	29	20	2	0	125.2	133	9	55	78	7-8	1	4.58
Chuck Estrada	R	25	8	7	0	0	31.1	26	2	19	16	3-2	0	4.60
Ike Delock†	R	33	7	5	0	0	30.1	25	7	16	11	1-3	0	5.04
John Miller	R	22	3	2	0	0	17.0	12	0	14	16	1-1	0	3.18
Wally Bunker	R	18	1	1	0	0	4.0	10	1	3	1	0-1	0	13.50
Stu Miller	R	35	71	0	0	0	112.1	93	5	53	114	5-8	27	2.24
Dick Hall	R	32	47	3	0	0	111.2	91	12	16	74	5-5	12	2.98
Wes Stock	R	29	47	0	0	0	75.1	69	11	31	55	7-0	1	3.94
Herm Starrette	R	24	18	0	0	0	26.0	26	1	7	13	0-1	0	3.46
Dean Stone	L	32	17	0	0	0	19.1	23	0	10	12	1-2	1	5.12
George Brunet†	L	28	16	0	0	0	20.0	25	3	9	13	0-1	1	5.40
Buster Narum	R	22	7	0	0	0	9.0	8	0	5	5	0-0	0	3.00
Pete Burnside†	L	32	6	0	0	0	7.1	11	0	2	6	0-1	0	4.91

1963 Cleveland Indians 5th AL 79-83 .488 25.5 GB

Birdie Tebbetts

Player	Gm by Position	B	Age	G	AB	R	H	2B	3B	HR	RBI	BB	SO	SB	Avg	OBP	Slg
Joe Azcue	C91	R	23	94	320	26	91	16	0	14	46	15	46	1	.284	.314	.466
Fred Whitfield	1B92	L	25	109	346	44	87	17	3	21	54	24	61	0	.251	.302	.500
Woodie Held	2B96,OF35,SS5*	R	31	133	416	61	103	19	4	17	61	61	96	2	.248	.352	.435
Max Alvis	3B158	R	25	158	602	81	165	32	7	22	67	36	109	9	.274	.324	.460
Larry Brown	SS46,2B27	R	23	74	247	28	63	6	0	5	18	22	27	4	.255	.316	.340
Tito Francona	OF122,1B11	L	29	142	500	57	114	29	0	10	41	47	77	9	.228	.296	.346
Willie Kirkland	OF112	L	29	127	427	51	98	13	2	15	47	45	99	8	.230	.303	.375
Vic Davalillo	OF89	L	26	90	370	44	108	18	5	7	36	16	41	3	.292	.321	.424
Al Luplow	OF85	L	24	100	295	34	69	6	2	7	27	33	62	4	.234	.316	.339
Joe Adcock	1B78	R	35	97	283	28	71	7	1	13	49	30	53	1	.251	.320	.420
John Romano	C71,OF4	R	28	89	255	28	55	5	2	10	34	38	49	4	.216	.317	.369
Jerry Kindall	SS46,2B37,1B4	R	28	86	234	27	48	4	1	5	20	18	71	3	.205	.266	.295
Dick Howser†	SS44	R	27	49	162	25	40	5	0	1	10	22	18	9	.247	.333	.296
Mike de la Hoz	2B34,3B6,SS2*	R	24	67	150	15	40	10	0	5	25	9	29	0	.267	.313	.433
Tony Martinez	SS41	R	23	43	141	10	22	4	0	0	8	5	18	1	.156	.184	.184
Willie Tasby	OF37,2B1	R	30	52	116	11	26	3	1	4	5	15	25	0	.224	.318	.371
Gene Green†	OF18	R	30	43	78	4	16	3	0	2	7	4	22	0	.205	.259	.321
Bob Chance	OF14	L	22	16	52	5	15	4	0	2	7	1	10	0	.288	.302	.481
Doc Edwards†	C10	R	26	10	31	6	8	2	0	0	0	2	6	0	.258	.303	.323
Ellis Burton†	OF16	S	26	26	31	6	6	3	0	1	1	4	4	0	.194	.286	.387
Tommie Agee	OF13	R	20	13	27	3	4	1	0	1	3	2	9	0	.148	.207	.296
Sammy Taylor†	C2	L	30	4	10	1	3	0	0	0	1	0	2	0	.300	.300	.300
Cal Neeman†	C9	R	34	9	9	0	0	0	0	0	1	1	5	0	.000	.100	.000
Bob Lipski	C2	L	24	2	1	0	0	0	0	0	0	0	1	0	.000	.000	.000
Jim Lawrence	C2	L	24	2	0	0	0	0	0	0	0	0	0	0	—	—	—

W. Held, 3 G at 3B; M. de la Hoz, 2 G at OF

Pitcher	T	Age	G	GS	CG	ShO	IP	H	HR	BB	SO	W-L	Sv	ERA
Mudcat Grant	R	27	38	32	10	2	229.1	213	30	87	157	13-14	1	3.69
Dick Donovan	R	35	30	30	7	3	206.0	211	27	28	84	11-13	0	4.24
Jack Kralick†	L	28	28	27	10	3	197.1	187	19	41	116	13-9	0	2.92
Pedro Ramos	R	28	36	22	5	0	184.2	156	29	41	169	9-8	0	3.12
Barry Latman	R	27	38	21	4	2	149.1	146	23	52	133	7-12	2	4.94
Sam McDowell	L	20	14	12	3	1	65.0	63	6	44	63	3-5	0	4.85
Tommy John	L	20	6	3	0	0	20.1	23	1	6	9	0-2	0	2.21
Gary Bell	R	26	58	7	0	0	119.0	91	13	52	98	8-5	5	2.95
Ted Abernathy	R	30	43	0	0	0	59.1	54	3	29	47	7-2	12	2.88
Bob Allen	L	25	43	0	0	0	56.0	58	5	29	51	1-2	2	4.66
Jerry Walker	R	24	39	2	0	0	88.0	92	15	36	41	6-6	1	4.91
Early Wynn	R	43	20	5	1	0	55.1	50	2	15	29	1-2	1	2.28
Ron Nischwitz	L	25	14	0	0	0	16.2	17	3	8	10	0-2	1	6.48
Jim Perry†	R	27	5	0	0	0	10.1	12	0	2	7	0-0	0	5.23
Jack Curtis	L	26	4	0	0	0	5.0	8	0	5	3	0-0	0	18.00
Gordon Seyfried	R	25	3	1	0	0	7.1	9	0	3	1	0-1	0	1.23

1963 Detroit Tigers 5th AL 79-83 .488 25.5 GB

Bob Scheffing (24-36)/Chuck Dressen (55-47)

Player	Gm by Position	B	Age	G	AB	R	H	2B	3B	HR	RBI	BB	SO	SB	Avg	OBP	Slg
Gus Triandos	C90	R	32	106	327	28	78	13	0	14	41	32	67	0	.239	.315	.407
Norm Cash	1B142	L	28	147	493	67	133	19	1	26	79	89	76	2	.270	.386	.471
Jake Wood	2B81,3B1	R	26	85	351	50	95	11	2	11	27	24	61	18	.271	.330	.407
Bubba Phillips	3B117,OF5	R	35	128	464	42	114	11	2	5	45	19	42	6	.246	.276	.310
Dick McAuliffe	SS133,2B15	L	23	150	568	77	149	18	6	13	61	64	75	11	.262	.334	.384
Rocky Colavito	OF159	R	29	160	597	91	162	29	2	22	91	84	78	0	.271	.358	.437
Al Kaline	OF140	R	28	145	551	89	172	24	3	27	101	54	48	6	.312	.375	.514
Bill Bruton	OF138	L	37	145	524	84	134	21	8	8	48	59	70	14	.256	.330	.372
Bill Freehan	C73,1B19	R	21	100	300	37	73	12	2	9	36	39	56	2	.243	.331	.387
Don Wert	3B47,2B21,SS8	R	24	78	251	31	65	6	2	7	25	24	51	3	.259	.326	.382
George Smith	2B52	R	25	52	171	16	37	8	2	0	17	18	34	4	.216	.298	.287
George Thomas†	OF40,2B1	R	25	49	109	13	26	4	1	1	11	11	22	2	.239	.306	.321
Gates Brown	OF16	L	24	55	82	16	22	3	1	2	14	8	13	2	.268	.333	.402
Whitey Herzog	1B7,OF4	L	31	52	53	5	8	2	1	0	7	11	17	0	.151	.303	.226
Frank Kostro†	3B6,1B3,OF3	R	25	31	52	4	12	1	0	0	2	9	13	0	.231	.344	.250
Chico Fernandez†	SS14	R	31	15	49	3	7	1	0	0	2	6	11	0	.143	.236	.163
Mike Roarke	C16	R	32	23	44	5	14	0	0	0	1	2	3	0	.318	.362	.318
Willie Horton	OF9	R	20	15	43	6	14	2	1	1	4	0	8	2	.326	.326	.488
Coot Veal	SS12	R	30	15	32	5	7	0	0	0	4	4	4	0	.219	.297	.219
Bubba Morton†	OF3	R	31	6	11	2	1	0	0	0	2	2	1	0	.091	.231	.091
Purnal Goldy		R	25	9	8	1	2	0	0	0	0	0	4	0	.250	.250	.250
John Sullivan	C2	L	22	3	5	0	0	0	0	0	0	2	1	0	.000	.286	.000
Vic Wertz†		L	38	6	5	0	0	0	0	0	0	0	1	0	.000	.000	.000

Pitcher	T	Age	G	GS	CG	ShO	IP	H	HR	BB	SO	W-L	Sv	ERA
Jim Bunning	R	31	39	35	6	2	248.1	245	38	69	196	12-13	1	3.88
Hank Aguirre	L	32	38	33	14	3	225.2	222	25	68	134	14-15	0	3.67
Phil Regan	R	26	38	27	5	1	189.0	179	33	59	115	15-9	1	3.86
Mickey Lolich	L	22	33	18	4	0	144.1	145	13	56	103	5-9	0	3.55
Don Mossi	L	34	24	16	3	0	122.2	110	20	17	68	7-7	2	3.74
Frank Lary	R	33	16	14	6	0	107.1	90	15	26	46	4-9	0	3.27
Denny McLain	R	19	3	3	2	0	21.0	20	2	16	22	2-1	0	4.29
Terry Fox	R	27	46	0	0	0	80.1	81	9	20	35	8-6	11	3.59
Bob Anderson	R	27	32	3	0	0	60.0	58	5	21	38	3-1	0	3.30
Bill Faul	R	23	28	10	2	0	97.0	93	14	48	64	5-6	1	4.64
Tom Sturdivant†	R	33	28	0	0	0	55.0	43	7	24	36	1-2	2	3.76
Fred Gladding	R	27	22	0	0	0	27.1	19	1	14	24	1-1	7	1.98
Dick Egan	L	26	20	0	0	0	21.0	25	4	3	16	0-1	0	5.14
Willie Smith	L	24	11	2	0	0	21.2	24	2	13	16	1-0	2	4.57
Paul Foytack†	R	32	9	0	0	0	17.2	18	4	8	7	0-1	1	8.66
Alan Koch	R	25	7	1	0	0	10.0	21	3	9	5	1-1	0	10.80
Bob Dustal	R	27	7	0	0	0	6.0	10	0	5	4	0-1	0	9.00
Larry Foster	R	25	1	0	0	0	2.0	4	0	1	1	0-0	0	13.50

1963 Boston Red Sox 7th AL 76-85 .472 28.0 GB

Johnny Pesky

Player	Gm by Position	B	Age	G	AB	R	H	2B	3B	HR	RBI	BB	SO	SB	Avg	OBP	Slg
Bob Tillman	C95	R	26	96	307	24	69	10	2	8	32	34	64	0	.225	.304	.349
Dick Stuart	1B155	R	30	157	612	81	160	25	4	42	118	44	144	0	.261	.312	.521
Chuck Schilling	2B143	R	25	146	576	63	135	25	0	8	33	41	72	3	.234	.291	.319
Frank Malzone	3B148	R	33	151	580	66	169	25	2	15	71	31	45	0	.291	.327	.419
Eddie Bressoud	SS137	R	31	140	497	61	129	23	6	20	60	52	93	1	.260	.329	.451
Carl Yastrzemski	OF151	L	23	151	570	91	183	40	3	14	68	95	72	8	.321	.418	.475
Lu Clinton	OF146	R	25	148	560	71	130	23	7	22	77	49	118	0	.232	.294	.416
Gary Geiger	OF95,1B6	L	26	121	399	67	105	13	5	16	44	36	63	9	.263	.327	.441
Roman Mejias	OF86	R	32	111	357	43	81	18	0	11	39	14	36	4	.227	.260	.370
Russ Nixon	C76	L	28	98	287	27	77	18	1	5	30	22	32	0	.268	.327	.390
Felix Mantilla	SS27,OF11,2B5	R	28	66	178	27	56	8	0	6	15	20	14	2	.315	.384	.461
Dick Williams	3B17,1B11,OF7	R	34	79	136	15	35	8	0	2	12	15	25	0	.257	.329	.360
Billy Gardner	2B21,3B2	R	35	36	84	4	16	2	1	0	1	4	19	0	.190	.236	.238
Jim Gosger	OF4	L	20	19	16	3	1	1	0	0	0	3	5	0	.063	.211	.063
Rico Petrocelli	SS1	R	20	1	4	0	1	1	0	0	1	0	1	0	.250	.250	.500

Pitcher	T	Age	G	GS	CG	ShO	IP	H	HR	BB	SO	W-L	Sv	ERA
Bill Monbouquette	R	26	37	36	13	1	266.2	258	31	42	174	20-10	0	3.81
Earl Wilson	R	28	37	34	6	3	210.2	184	18	105	123	11-16	0	3.76
Dave Morehead	R	20	29	29	6	1	174.2	137	20	99	136	10-13	0	3.81
Bob Heffner	R	24	20	19	3	1	124.2	131	15	36	77	4-9	0	4.26
Gene Conley	R	32	9	9	0	0	40.2	51	4	21	14	3-4	0	6.64
Bob Turley†	R	32	11	7	0	0	41.1	42	6	28	35	1-4	0	6.10
Ike Delock†	R	33	6	6	1	0	32.0	31	4	12	23	1-2	0	4.50
Jerry Stephenson	R	19	1	1	0	0	2.1	5	0	2	3	0-0	0	7.71
Dick Radatz	R	26	66	0	0	0	132.1	94	9	51	162	15-6	25	1.97
Jack Lamabe	R	26	65	2	0	0	151.1	139	8	46	93	7-4	6	3.15
Arnold Earley	L	30	53	4	0	0	115.2	124	13	43	97	3-7	1	4.75
Wilbur Wood	L	21	25	6	0	0	64.1	67	10	13	28	0-5	0	3.78
Chet Nichols	L	32	21	7	0	0	52.2	61	8	24	27	1-3	0	4.78
Mike Fornieles†	R	31	9	0	0	0	14.0	16	0	5	5	0-0	0	6.43
Hal Kolstad	R	28	7	0	0	0	11.0	16	4	6	6	0-2	0	13.09
Pete Smith	R	23	6	1	0	0	15.0	11	2	6	6	0-0	0	3.60

1963 Kansas City Athletics 8th AL 73-89 .451 31.5 GB

Ed Lopat

Player	Gm by Position	B	Age	G	AB	R	H	2B	3B	HR	RBI	BB	SO	SB	Avg	OBP	Slg
Doc Edwards†	C63	R	26	71	240	16	60	12	0	6	35	11	23	0	.250	.287	.375
Norm Siebern	1B131,OF16	L	29	152	556	80	151	25	2	16	83	79	82	1	.272	.358	.410
Jerry Lumpe	2B155	L	30	157	595	75	161	26	7	5	59	58	44	3	.271	.333	.363
Ed Charles	3B158	R	30	158	603	82	161	28	2	15	79	58	79	15	.267	.332	.395
Wayne Causey	SS135,3B2	L	26	139	554	72	155	32	4	8	44	56	54	4	.280	.345	.395
Gino Cimoli	OF136	R	33	145	529	56	139	19	11	4	48	39	72	3	.263	.313	.363
Bobby Del Greco	OF110,3B2	R	30	121	306	40	65	7	1	8	29	40	52	1	.212	.311	.320
Jose Tartabull	OF71	L	24	79	242	27	58	8	5	1	19	17	17	16	.240	.290	.326
Chuck Essegian	OF53	R	31	101	231	23	52	9	0	5	27	19	48	0	.225	.285	.329
Ken Harrelson	1B34,OF28	R	21	79	226	16	52	10	1	6	23	23	58	1	.230	.299	.363
George Alusik	OF63	R	28	87	221	28	59	11	0	9	37	26	33	0	.267	.345	.439
Charlie Lau†	C50	L	30	62	187	15	55	11	0	3	26	14	17	1	.294	.340	.401
Manny Jimenez	OF40	L	24	60	157	12	44	9	0	0	15	16	14	0	.280	.361	.338
Haywood Sullivan	C37	R	32	40	113	9	24	6	1	0	8	15	15	0	.212	.300	.283
Billy Bryan	C24	L	24	24	65	11	11	1	1	3	7	9	22	0	.169	.270	.354
John Wojcik	OF17	L	21	19	59	7	11	0	0	0	2	8	8	2	.186	.284	.186
Tony La Russa	SS14,2B3	R	18	34	44	4	11	1	0	1	1	7	12	0	.250	.346	.318
Dick Howser†	SS10	R	27	15	41	4	8	0	0	0	1	7	3	0	.195	.313	.195
Dick Green	SS6,2B4	R	22	13	37	5	10	2	0	1	4	2	10	0	.270	.317	.405
Jay Hankins	OF9	L	27	10	34	2	6	0	1	1	4	0	3	0	.176	.176	.324
Sammy Esposito†	2B7,SS4,3B3	R	31	18	25	3	5	1	0	0	2	3	3	0	.200	.276	.240
Tommie Reynolds	OF5	S	21	8	19	1	1	1	0	0	0	1	7	0	.053	.143	.105
Hector Martinez	OF3	R	24	6	14	2	4	0	0	1	3	1	3	0	.286	.375	.500
Joe Azcue†	C1	R	23	2	4	0	0	0	0	0	0	0	1	0	.000	.000	.000

Pitcher	T	Age	G	GS	CG	ShO	IP	H	HR	BB	SO	W-L	Sv	ERA
Dave Wickersham	R	27	38	34	4	1	237.2	244	21	79	118	12-15	1	4.09
Orlando Pena	R	29	35	33	9	3	217.0	218	24	53	128	12-20	0	3.69
Ed Rakow	R	27	34	26	7	1	174.1	173	18	61	104	9-10	0	3.92
Diego Segui	R	25	38	23	4	1	167.0	173	17	73	116	9-6	0	3.77
Moe Drabowsky	R	27	26	22	9	2	174.1	135	16	64	109	7-13	0	3.05
Fred Norman	L	20	2	2	0	0	6.1	9	1	7	6	0-1	0	11.37
John O'Donoghue	L	23	1	1	0	0	6.0	6	0	2	1	0-1	0	1.50
John Wyatt	R	28	63	0	0	0	92.0	83	12	43	81	6-4	21	3.13
Bill Fischer	R	32	45	2	0	0	95.2	86	13	29	34	9-6	3	3.57
Ted Bowsfield	L	28	41	11	2	1	111.1	115	14	47	67	5-7	3	4.45
Dale Willis	R	25	25	0	0	0	44.2	46	3	25	47	0-2	1	5.04
Pete Lovrich	R	20	20	1	0	0	20.2	25	5	10	16	1-1	0	7.84
Tom Sturdivant†	R	33	17	3	0	0	53.0	47	3	17	26	1-2	0	3.74
Dave Thies	R	26	9	2	0	0	25.1	26	2	12	9	0-1	0	4.62
Jose Santiago	R	22	4	0	0	0	7.0	8	4	2	6	1-0	0	9.00
Aurelio Monteagudo	R	19	4	0	0	0	7.0	4	0	3	3	0-0	0	2.57
Dan Pfister	R	26	3	1	0	0	9.1	8	1	3	9	1-0	0	1.93
Norm Bass	R	24	3	1	0	0	7.2	11	2	9	4	0-0	0	11.74
Bill Landis	L	20	1	0	0	0	1.2	0	0	1	3	0-0	0	0.00

1963 Los Angeles Angels 9th AL 70-91 .435 34.0 GB

Bill Rigney

Player	Gm by Position	B	Age	G	AB	R	H	2B	3B	HR	RBI	BB	SO	SB	Avg	OBP	Slg
Bob Rodgers	C85	S	24	100	300	24	70	6	0	4	23	29	35	2	.233	.303	.293
Lee Thomas	1B104,OF43	L	27	149	528	52	116	12	6	9	55	53	82	6	.220	.301	.316
Billy Moran	2B151	R	29	153	597	67	164	29	5	7	65	31	57	1	.275	.310	.375
Felix Torres	3B122,1B2	R	31	138	463	40	121	32	1	4	51	30	73	1	.261	.307	.361
Jim Fregosi	SS151	R	21	154	592	83	170	29	12	9	50	36	104	2	.287	.325	.422
Albie Pearson	OF148	L	28	154	578	92	176	26	5	6	47	92	37	17	.304	.402	.398
Leon Wagner	OF141	L	29	149	550	73	160	11	1	26	90	49	73	5	.291	.352	.456
Bob Perry	OF55	R	28	61	166	16	42	9	0	3	14	9	31	1	.253	.300	.361
Charlie Dees	1B56	L	28	60	202	23	62	11	1	3	27	11	31	3	.307	.362	.416
Ed Sadowski	C68	R	31	80	174	24	30	1	1	4	15	17	33	2	.172	.245	.259
George Thomas†	OF39,3B10,1B4	R	25	53	167	14	35	7	1	4	15	9	32	0	.210	.254	.335
Bob Sadowski	OF25,3B6,2B4	L	26	88	144	12	36	6	0	1	22	15	34	2	.250	.317	.313
Joe Koppe	SS19,3B18,2B14*	R	32	76	143	11	30	4	1	1	12	9	30	0	.210	.258	.273
Ken Hunt†	OF50	R	28	59	142	17	26	6	1	5	16	15	49	0	.183	.261	.345
Frank Kostro†	3B19,1B5,OF3	R	25	43	99	6	22	2	1	2	10	6	17	0	.222	.264	.323
Hank Foiles†	C30	R	34	41	84	8	18	1	0	2	10	8	13	0	.214	.290	.393
Ed Kirkpatrick	C14,OF10	L	18	34	77	4	15	5	0	2	7	6	19	1	.195	.259	.338
Jimmy Piersall†	OF18	R	33	20	52	4	16	1	0	0	4	5	5	0	.308	.368	.327
Tom Satriano	3B13,C2,1B1	L	22	23	50	1	9	1	0	0	2	9	10	0	.180	.305	.200

J. Koppe, 3 G at OF

Pitcher	T	Age	G	GS	CG	ShO	IP	H	HR	BB	SO	W-L	Sv	ERA
Ken McBride	R	27	36	36	11	2	251.0	198	22	82	147	13-12	0	3.26
Dean Chance	R	22	45	35	6	2	248.0	229	10	90	168	13-18	3	3.19
Don Lee	R	29	40	22	3	2	154.0	148	12	51	89	8-11	1	3.68
Bo Belinsky	L	26	13	13	2	0	76.2	78	12	35	60	2-9	0	5.75
Bob Turley†	R	32	19	12	3	2	87.1	71	5	51	70	2-7	0	3.30
Fred Newman	R	21	12	8	0	0	44.0	56	6	15	16	1-5	0	5.32
Mike Lee	L	22	6	4	0	0	26.0	30	3	14	11	1-1	0	3.81
Aubrey Gatewood	R	24	4	3	1	0	24.0	12	0	16	13	1-1	0	1.50
Julio Navarro	R	27	57	0	0	0	90.1	75	7	32	53	4-5	12	2.89
Art Fowler	R	40	57	0	0	0	89.1	70	5	19	53	5-3	10	2.42
Dan Osinski	R	29	47	16	4	1	159.1	145	15	80	100	8-8	0	3.28
Jack Spring	L	30	45	0	0	0	38.1	40	3	9	13	3-0	2	3.05
Mel Nelson	L	27	36	3	0	0	52.2	55	7	32	41	2-3	1	5.30
Paul Foytack†	R	32	25	8	0	0	70.1	68	9	29	37	5-5	0	3.71
Tom Morgan	R	33	13	0	0	0	16.1	20	1	6	7	0-0	1	5.51
Eli Grba	R	28	12	1	0	0	17.1	14	2	10	5	1-2	0	4.67
Bob Duliba	R	28	6	0	0	0	7.2	3	0	6	4	1-1	1	1.17
Ron Moeller†	L	24	3	0	0	0	2.2	5	1	1	2	0-0	0	6.75

1963 Washington Senators 10th AL 56-106 .346 48.5 GB

Mickey Vernon (14-26)/Eddie Yost (0-1)/Gil Hodges (42-79)

Player	Gm by Position	B	Age	G	AB	R	H	2B	3B	HR	RBI	BB	SO	SB	Avg	OBP	Slg
Ken Retzer	C81	L	29	95	265	21	64	10	0	5	31	17	20	2	.242	.290	.336
Bobo Osborne	1B81,3B16	L	27	125	358	42	76	14	1	12	44	49	83	0	.212	.308	.358
Chuck Cottier	2B85,SS24,3B1	R	27	113	337	30	69	16	4	5	21	24	63	2	.205	.257	.320
Don Zimmer†	3B78,2B2	R	32	83	298	37	74	12	1	13	44	18	57	3	.248	.296	.426
Ed Brinkman	SS143	R	21	145	514	44	117	20	3	7	45	31	86	5	.228	.276	.319
Don Lock	OF146	R	26	149	531	71	134	20	1	27	82	70	151	7	.252	.338	.446
Chuck Hinton	OF125,3B19,1B6*	R	29	150	566	80	152	20	12	15	55	64	79	25	.269	.340	.426
Jim King	OF123	L	30	136	459	61	106	16	5	24	62	45	43	3	.231	.300	.444
Dick Phillips	1B68,2B5,3B4	L	31	124	321	33	76	8	0	10	32	29	35	1	.237	.300	.355
Minnie Minoso	OF74,3B8	R	40	109	315	38	72	12	2	4	30	33	38	8	.229	.315	.317
Don Blasingame†	2B64	L	31	69	254	29	65	10	2	2	12	24	18	3	.256	.320	.335
Don Leppert	C60	L	31	73	211	20	50	11	0	6	24	20	29	0	.237	.305	.374
Marv Breeding†	3B29,2B22,SS2	R	29	58	197	20	54	7	2	1	14	7	21	1	.274	.299	.345
Tom Brown	OF16,1B14	S	22	61	116	8	17	4	0	1	4	11	45	2	.147	.227	.207
Hobie Landrith†	C37	L	33	42	103	6	18	3	0	1	7	15	12	0	.175	.280	.233
Jimmy Piersall†	OF25	R	33	29	94	9	23	1	0	1	5	6	11	4	.245	.284	.287
John Kennedy	3B26,SS2	R	22	36	62	3	11	1	1	0	4	6	22	2	.177	.261	.226
Bennie Daniels	P35,OF1	L	31	36	46	5	7	1	0	0	3	7	20	0	.152	.278	.174
Ken Hunt†	OF5	R	28	7	20	1	4	0	0	1	4	2	6	0	.200	.273	.350
Cal Neeman†	C12	R	34	14	18	1	1	0	0	0	0	1	0	0	.056	.105	.056
Bob Schmidt	C6	R	30	9	15	3	3	1	0	0	0	3	5	0	.200	.333	.267
Lou Klimchock†	2B3	L	23	9	14	1	2	0	0	0	2	0	1	0	.143	.143	.143
Johnny Schaive		R	29	3	3	0	0	0	0	0	0	0	1	0	.000	.000	.000
Barry Shetrone		L	24	2	2	0	0	0	0	0	0	0	0	0	.000	.000	.000

C. Hinton, 2 G at SS

Pitcher	T	Age	G	GS	CG	ShO	IP	H	HR	BB	SO	W-L	Sv	ERA
Claude Osteen	L	23	40	29	8	2	212.1	222	23	60	109	9-14	0	3.35
Don Rudolph	L	31	37	26	4	0	174.0	189	28	36	70	7-19	1	4.55
Bennie Daniels	R	31	35	24	6	1	168.2	163	19	58	88	5-10	1	4.38
Tom Cheney	R	28	23	21	7	4	136.1	99	14	40	97	8-9	0	2.71
Dave Stenhouse	R	29	16	16	2	1	87.0	90	12	45	47	3-9	0	4.55
Steve Ridzik	R	34	20	10	0	0	89.2	82	16	35	47	5-6	1	4.82
Bob Baird	L	23	5	3	0	0	11.2	12	1	7	7	0-3	0	7.71
Jack Jenkins	R	20	4	2	0	0	12.1	16	2	12	5	0-2	0	5.84
Ron Kline	R	31	62	1	0	0	93.2	85	3	30	49	3-8	17	2.79
Pete Burnside†	L	32	38	1	0	0	67.1	84	12	24	23	0-1	0	6.15
Jim Duckworth	R	24	37	15	2	0	120.2	131	13	67	66	4-12	0	6.04
Ed Roebuck†	R	31	26	0	0	0	57.1	63	5	29	25	2-1	4	3.30
Jim Bronstad	R	27	25	0	0	0	57.1	66	9	22	22	1-3	1	5.65
Jim Coates†	R	30	20	2	0	0	44.1	51	4	21	31	2-4	0	5.28
Jim Hannan	R	23	13	2	0	0	27.2	23	2	17	14	2-2	0	4.88
Carl Bouldin	R	23	10	3	0	0	23.1	31	3	8	10	2-2	0	5.79
Ed Hobaugh	R	29	9	1	0	0	16.0	20	3	6	11	0-0	0	6.19
Ron Moeller†	L	24	8	3	0	0	24.1	31	4	10	10	2-0	0	6.29
Art Quirk	L	25	7	3	0	0	21.0	23	3	8	12	1-0	0	4.29
Steve Hamilton†	L	27	3	0	0	0	2.0	5	0	2	1	0-1	0	13.50

»1963 Los Angeles Dodgers 1st NL 99-63 .611 —

Walter Alston

Player	Gm by Position	B	Age	G	AB	R	H	2B	3B	HR	RBI	BB	SO	SB	Avg	OBP	Slg
John Roseboro	C134	L	30	135	470	50	111	13	7	9	49	36	50	7	.236	.291	.351
Ron Fairly	1B119,OF45	L	24	152	490	62	133	21	0	12	77	58	69	5	.271	.347	.388
Jim Gilliam	2B119,3B55	S	34	148	525	77	148	27	4	6	49	60	28	19	.282	.354	.383
Ken McMullen	3B71,2B1,OF1	R	21	79	233	16	55	9	0	5	28	20	46	1	.236	.297	.339
Maury Wills	SS109,3B33	S	30	134	527	83	159	19	3	0	34	44	48	40	.302	.355	.349
Willie Davis	OF153	L	23	156	515	60	126	19	8	9	60	25	61	25	.245	.281	.365
Tommy Davis	OF129,3B40	R	24	146	556	69	181	19	3	16	88	29	59	15	.326	.359	.457
Frank Howard	OF111	R	26	123	417	58	114	16	1	28	64	33	116	1	.273	.330	.518
Wally Moon	OF96	L	33	122	343	41	90	13	2	8	48	45	43	5	.262	.345	.382
Bill Skowron	1B66,3B1	R	32	89	237	19	48	8	0	4	19	13	49	0	.203	.252	.287
Dick Tracewski	SS81,2B23	R	28	104	217	23	49	2	1	1	10	19	39	2	.226	.287	.258
Nate Oliver	2B57,SS2	R	22	65	163	23	39	2	3	1	9	13	25	3	.239	.298	.307
Doug Camilli	C47	R	26	49	117	9	19	1	1	3	10	11	22	0	.162	.234	.265
Lee Walls	OF18,1B5,3B2	R	30	64	86	12	20	1	0	3	11	7	25	0	.233	.290	.349
Al Ferrara	OF11	R	23	21	44	2	7	0	0	1	1	6	9	0	.159	.275	.227
Marv Breeding†	2B17,3B1,SS1	R	29	20	36	6	6	0	0	0	1	2	5	1	.167	.211	.167
Don Zimmer†	3B10,2B1,SS1	R	32	22	23	4	5	1	0	1	2	3	10	0	.217	.308	.391
Daryl Spencer†	3B3	R	33	7	9	0	1	0	0	0	0	3	2	0	.111	.333	.111
Dick Nen	1B5	L	23	7	8	2	1	0	0	1	1	3	3	0	.125	.364	.500
Derrell Griffith	2B1	L	19	1	2	0	0	0	0	0	0	0	0	0	.000	.000	.000
Roy Gleason		S	20	8	1	3	1	1	0	0	0	0	0	0	1.000	1.000	2.000

Pitcher	T	Age	G	GS	CG	ShO	IP	H	HR	BB	SO	W-L	Sv	ERA
Don Drysdale	R	26	42	42	17	3	315.1	287	25	57	251	19-17	0	2.63
Sandy Koufax	L	27	40	40	20	11	311.0	214	18	58	306	25-5	0	1.88
Johnny Podres	L	30	37	34	10	5	198.1	196	16	64	134	14-12	1	3.54
Bob Miller	R	24	42	23	2	0	187.0	171	7	65	125	10-8	1	2.89
Pete Richert	L	23	20	12	1	0	78.0	80	7	28	54	5-3	0	4.50
Nick Willhite	L	22	8	8	1	1	38.0	44	5	10	28	2-3	0	3.79
Ron Perranoski	L	27	69	0	0	0	129.0	112	7	43	75	16-3	21	1.67
Larry Sherry	R	27	36	3	0	0	79.2	82	8	24	47	2-6	3	3.73
Ed Roebuck†	R	31	29	0	0	0	40.1	54	4	21	26	2-4	0	4.24
Dick Calmus	R	19	21	1	0	0	44.0	32	3	16	25	3-1	0	2.66
Ken Rowe	R	29	14	0	0	0	28.0	28	2	11	12	1-1	1	2.89
Dick Scott	L	30	9	0	0	0	12.0	17	6	3	6	0-0	2	6.75
Jack Smith	R	27	4	0	0	0	8.1	10	2	2	5	0-0	0	7.56
Phil Ortega	R	23	1	0	0	0	1.0	2	1	0	1	0-0	0	18.00

1963 St. Louis Cardinals 2nd NL 93-69 .574 6.0 GB

Johnny Keane

Player	Gm by Position	B	Age	G	AB	R	H	2B	3B	HR	RBI	BB	SO	SB	Avg	OBP	Slg
Tim McCarver	C126	L	21	127	405	39	117	12	7	4	51	27	43	5	.289	.333	.383
Bill White	1B162	L	29	162	658	106	200	26	8	27	109	59	100	10	.304	.360	.491
Julian Javier	2B161	R	26	161	609	82	160	27	9	9	46	24	86	18	.263	.296	.381
Ken Boyer	3B159	R	32	159	617	86	176	28	2	24	111	70	90	1	.285	.358	.454
Dick Groat	SS158	R	32	158	631	85	201	43	11	6	73	56	58	3	.319	.377	.450
Curt Flood	OF158	R	25	158	662	112	200	34	9	5	63	42	57	17	.302	.345	.403
George Altman	OF124	L	30	135	464	62	127	18	7	9	47	47	93	13	.274	.339	.401
Charlie James	OF101	R	25	116	347	34	93	14	2	10	45	10	64	2	.268	.291	.406
Stan Musial	OF96	L	42	124	337	34	86	10	2	12	58	35	43	2	.255	.325	.404
Carl Sawatski	C27	L	35	56	105	12	25	0	0	6	14	15	28	2	.238	.333	.410
Gene Oliver†	C35	R	28	39	102	10	23	4	0	6	18	13	19	0	.225	.308	.441
Gary Kolb	OF58,C1,3B1	L	23	75	96	23	26	1	5	3	10	22	26	2	.271	.403	.479
Dal Maxvill	SS24,2B9,3B3	R	24	53	51	12	12	2	0	0	3	6	11	0	.235	.316	.275
Leo Burke†	OF11,3B5	R	29	30	49	6	10	2	1	1	5	4	12	0	.204	.264	.347
Duke Carmel†	OF38,1B1	L	26	57	44	9	10	1	0	1	2	9	11	0	.227	.358	.318
Mike Shannon	OF26	R	23	32	26	3	8	0	0	1	2	0	6	0	.308	.333	.423
Corky Withrow	OF2	R	25	6	9	0	0	0	0	0	1	0	2	0	.000	.000	.000
Dave Ricketts	C3	S	27	3	8	0	2	0	0	0	0	0	2	0	.250	.250	.250
Doug Clemens	OF3	L	24	5	6	1	1	0	0	1	2	1	2	0	.167	.286	.667
Jeoff Long		R	21	5	5	0	1	0	0	0	0	0	1	0	.200	.200	.200
Jack Damaska	2B1,OF1	R	25	5	5	1	1	0	0	0	1	0	4	0	.200	.200	.200
Phil Gagliano	2B3,3B1	R	21	10	5	1	2	0	0	0	1	1	1	0	.400	.500	.400
Red Schoendienst		S	40	6	5	0	0	0	0	0	0	0	1	0	.000	.000	.000
Jerry Buchek	SS1	R	21	3	4	0	1	0	0	0	0	0	2	0	.250	.250	.250
Moe Thacker	C3	R	29	3	4	0	0	0	0	0	0	0	3	0	.000	.000	.000
Jim Beauchamp		R	23	4	3	0	0	0	0	0	0	0	2	0	.000	.000	.000
Clyde Bloomfield	3B1	R	27	1	0	0	0	0	0	0	0	0	0	0	—	—	—

Pitcher	T	Age	G	GS	CG	ShO	IP	H	HR	BB	SO	W-L	Sv	ERA
Ernie Broglio	R	27	39	35	11	5	250.0	202	24	90	145	18-8	0	2.99
Bob Gibson	R	27	36	33	14	2	254.2	224	19	96	204	18-9	0	3.39
Curt Simmons	L	34	32	32	11	6	232.2	209	13	48	127	15-9	0	2.48
Ray Sadecki	L	22	36	28	4	1	193.1	198	25	78	136	10-10	1	4.10
Lew Burdette†	R	36	21	14	3	0	98.1	106	6	16	45	3-8	2	3.75
Ray Washburn	R	25	11	11	4	2	64.1	50	5	14	47	5-3	0	3.08
Bobby Shantz	L	37	55	0	0	0	79.1	55	6	17	70	6-4	11	2.61
Ron Taylor	R	25	54	9	2	0	133.1	119	10	30	91	9-7	11	2.84
Ed Bauta†	R	28	38	0	0	0	52.2	55	2	21	30	3-4	3	3.93
Barney Schultz†	R	36	24	0	0	0	35.1	36	5	8	26	2-0	1	3.57
Diomedes Olivo	L	44	19	0	0	0	13.1	16	1	9	9	0-5	0	5.40
Harry Fanok	R	23	12	0	0	0	25.2	24	3	21	25	2-1	1	5.26
Sam Jones	R	37	11	0	0	0	11.0	15	0	5	8	2-0	2	9.00
Bob Humphreys	R	27	9	0	0	0	10.2	11	4	7	8	0-1	0	5.06
Ken MacKenzie†	L	29	8	0	0	0	8.2	9	1	3	7	0-0	0	4.15

1963 San Francisco Giants 3rd NL 88-74 .543 11.0 GB

Alvin Dark

Player	Gm by Position	B	Age	G	AB	R	H	2B	3B	HR	RBI	BB	SO	SB	Avg	OBP	Slg
Ed Bailey	C88	L	32	105	308	41	81	8	0	21	68	50	64	0	.263	.366	.494
Orlando Cepeda	1B150,OF3	R	25	156	579	100	183	33	4	34	97	37	70	8	.316	.366	.563
Chuck Hiller	2B109	L	28	111	417	44	93	10	2	6	33	20	23	3	.223	.261	.300
Jim Davenport	3B127,2B22,SS1	R	29	147	460	40	116	19	3	4	36	32	87	5	.252	.297	.333
Jose Pagan	SS143,2B1,OF1	R	28	148	483	46	113	12	1	6	39	26	67	10	.234	.277	.300
Willie Mays	OF157,SS1	R	32	157	596	115	187	32	7	38	103	66	83	8	.314	.380	.582
Felipe Alou	OF153	R	28	157	565	75	159	31	9	20	82	27	87	11	.281	.319	.474
Willie McCovey	OF135,1B23	L	25	152	564	103	158	19	5	44	102	50	119	1	.280	.350	.566
Harvey Kuenn	OF64,3B53	R	32	120	417	61	121	13	2	6	31	44	38	2	.290	.358	.374
Tom Haller	C85,OF7	L	26	98	298	32	76	8	1	14	44	34	45	4	.255	.332	.430
Joey Amalfitano	2B37,3B7	R	29	54	137	11	24	3	0	1	7	12	18	2	.175	.245	.219
Ernie Bowman	SS40,2B26,3B12	R	27	81	125	10	23	3	0	0	4	0	15	1	.184	.181	.208
Matty Alou	OF20	L	24	63	76	4	11	1	0	0	2	2	13	0	.145	.177	.158
Cap Peterson	2B8,3B5,OF3*	R	20	22	54	7	14	2	0	1	2	2	13	0	.259	.286	.352
Jesus Alou	OF12	R	21	16	24	3	6	1	0	0	5	0	3	0	.250	.280	.292
Jim Ray Hart	3B7	R	21	7	20	1	4	1	0	0	2	3	6	0	.200	.360	.250
Norm Larker†	1B11	L	32	19	14	0	1	0	0	0	0	2	2	0	.071	.188	.071
Jose Cardenal	OF2	R	19	9	5	1	1	0	0	0	2	1	1	0	.200	.333	.200
Jimmie Coker	C2	R	27	4	5	0	1	0	0	0	0	1	2	0	.200	.333	.200

C. Peterson, 1 G at SS

Pitcher	T	Age	G	GS	CG	ShO	IP	H	HR	BB	SO	W-L	Sv	ERA
Jack Sanford	R	34	42	42	11	1	284.1	273	21	76	158	16-13	0	3.51
Juan Marichal	R	25	41	40	18	5	321.1	259	27	61	248	25-8	0	2.41
Billy O'Dell	L	30	36	33	10	3	222.1	218	14	70	116	14-10	1	3.16
Bobby Bolin	R	24	47	12	2	0	137.1	128	13	57	134	10-6	7	3.28
Don Larsen	R	33	46	0	0	0	62.0	46	8	30	44	7-7	3	3.05
Billy Pierce	L	36	38	13	3	1	99.0	106	12	20	52	3-11	8	4.27
Jack Fisher	R	24	36	12	2	0	116.0	132	12	38	57	6-10	1	4.58
Jim Duffalo	R	27	34	5	0	0	75.1	56	3	37	55	4-2	2	2.87
Gaylord Perry	R	24	31	4	0	0	76.0	84	10	29	52	1-6	2	4.03
Billy Hoeft	L	31	23	0	0	0	24.1	26	5	10	8	2-0	4	4.44
Al Stanek	L	19	11	0	0	0	13.1	10	1	12	5	0-0	0	4.73
Frank Linzy	R	22	8	1	0	0	16.2	22	0	10	14	0-0	0	4.86
John Pregenzer	R	27	6	0	0	0	9.1	8	0	8	5	0-0	1	4.82
Bob Garibaldi	R	21	4	0	0	0	8.0	8	0	4	4	0-1	1	1.13
Jim Constable	L	30	4	0	0	0	2.1	3	0	1	1	0-0	0	3.86
Ron Herbel	R	25	2	0	0	0	1.1	1	0	1	1	0-0	0	6.75

1963 Philadelphia Phillies 4th NL 87-75 .537 12.0 GB

Gene Mauch

Player	Gm by Position	B	Age	G	AB	R	H	2B	3B	HR	RBI	BB	SO	SB	Avg	OBP	Slg
Clay Dalrymple	C142	L	26	142	452	40	114	15	3	10	40	45	55	0	.252	.327	.365
Roy Sievers	1B126	R	36	138	450	46	108	19	2	19	82	43	72	0	.240	.308	.418
Tony Taylor	2B149,3B13	R	27	157	640	102	180	20	10	5	49	42	99	23	.281	.330	.367
Don Hoak	3B106	R	35	115	377	35	87	11	3	6	24	27	52	5	.231	.282	.324
Bobby Wine	SS132,3B8	R	24	142	418	29	90	14	3	6	44	14	83	1	.215	.241	.306
Johnny Callison	OF157	L	24	157	626	96	178	36	11	26	78	50	111	8	.284	.339	.502
Tony Gonzalez	OF151	L	26	155	555	78	170	36	12	4	66	53	68	13	.306	.372	.436
Don Demeter	OF119,3B43,1B26	R	28	154	515	63	133	20	2	22	83	31	93	1	.258	.306	.433
Wes Covington	OF101	L	31	119	353	46	107	24	1	17	64	26	56	1	.303	.354	.521
Ruben Amaro	SS63,3B45,1B5	R	27	115	217	25	47	9	2	2	19	19	31	0	.217	.276	.304
Frank Torre	1B56	L	31	92	112	8	28	7	2	1	10	11	7	0	.250	.333	.375
Bob Oldis	C43	R	35	47	85	8	19	3	0	0	8	3	5	0	.224	.250	.259
Cookie Rojas	2B25,OF1	R	24	64	77	18	17	0	1	1	2	3	8	4	.221	.259	.286
Earl Averill	C20,OF8,1B1*	R	31	47	71	8	19	2	0	3	8	9	14	0	.268	.341	.423
Jim Lemon†	OF18	R	35	31	59	6	16	2	0	2	6	8	18	0	.271	.353	.407
Dick Allen	OF7,3B1	R	21	10	24	6	7	2	1	0	2	0	5	0	.292	.280	.458
Wayne Graham	OF6	R	26	10	22	1	4	0	0	0	0	3	1	0	.182	.280	.182
Cal Emery	1B2	L	26	16	19	0	3	1	0	0	0	0	2	0	.158	.158	.211
Billy Klaus	SS5,3B3	L	34	11	18	1	1	0	0	0	0	1	4	0	.056	.105	.056
John Herrnstein	OF2,1B1	L	25	15	12	1	2	0	0	1	1	1	5	0	.167	.231	.417
Mickey Harrington		R	28	1	0	0	0	0	0	0	0	0	0	0	—	—	—

E. Averill, 1 G at 3B

Pitcher	T	Age	G	GS	CG	ShO	IP	H	HR	BB	SO	W-L	Sv	ERA
Cal McLish	R	37	32	32	10	2	209.2	184	14	56	98	13-11	0	3.26
Ray Culp	R	21	34	30	10	5	203.1	148	15	102	176	14-11	0	2.97
Chris Short	L	25	38	27	6	3	198.0	185	12	69	160	9-12	0	2.95
Art Mahaffey	R	25	26	22	6	1	149.0	143	18	48	97	7-10	0	3.99
Dennis Bennett	L	23	23	16	6	1	119.1	102	12	33	82	9-5	1	2.64
Marcelino Lopez	L	19	4	2	0	0	6.0	8	0	7	2	1-0	0	6.00
Jack Baldschun	R	26	65	0	0	0	113.2	99	7	42	89	11-7	16	2.30
Johnny Klippstein	R	35	49	1	0	0	112.0	80	3	46	86	5-6	8	1.93
Dallas Green	R	28	40	14	4	0	120.0	134	10	38	68	7-5	2	3.23
Ryne Duren	R	34	33	7	1	0	87.1	65	6	52	84	6-2	2	3.30
John Boozer	R	24	26	8	2	0	83.0	67	11	33	69	3-4	1	2.93
Jack Hamilton	R	24	19	1	0	0	30.0	22	3	17	23	2-1	1	5.40
Bobby Locke	R	29	9	0	0	0	10.2	10	0	5	7	0-0	0	5.91
Paul Brown	R	22	6	2	0	0	15.1	15	2	5	11	0-1	0	4.11

1963 Cincinnati Reds 5th NL 86-76 .531 13.0 GB

Fred Hutchinson

Player	Gm by Position	B	Age	G	AB	R	H	2B	3B	HR	RBI	BB	SO	SB	Avg	OBP	Slg
Johnny Edwards	C148	L	25	148	495	46	128	19	4	11	67	45	93	1	.259	.322	.380
Gordy Coleman	1B107	L	28	123	365	38	90	20	2	14	59	29	51	1	.247	.303	.427
Pete Rose	2B157,OF1	S	22	157	623	101	170	25	9	6	41	55	72	13	.273	.334	.371
Gene Freese	3B62,OF1	R	29	66	217	20	53	9	1	6	26	17	42	4	.244	.303	.378
Leo Cardenas	SS157	R	24	158	565	42	133	22	4	7	48	23	101	3	.235	.270	.326
Vada Pinson	OF162	L	24	162	652	96	204	37	14	22	106	36	80	27	.313	.347	.514
Frank Robinson	OF139,1B1	R	27	140	482	79	125	19	3	21	91	81	69	26	.259	.379	.442
Tommy Harper	OF118,3B1	R	22	129	408	67	106	12	3	10	37	44	72	12	.260	.335	.377
Eddie Kasko	3B48,SS15,2B1	R	31	76	199	25	48	9	0	3	10	21	29	0	.241	.311	.332
Bob Skinner†	OF51	L	31	72	194	25	49	10	2	3	17	21	42	1	.253	.332	.371
Don Pavletich	1B57,C13	R	24	71	183	18	38	11	0	5	18	17	12	0	.208	.274	.350
Marty Keough	1B46,OF28	L	28	95	172	21	39	8	2	6	21	25	37	1	.227	.337	.401
Daryl Spencer†	3B48	R	33	50	155	21	37	7	0	1	23	31	37	1	.239	.359	.303
Ken Walters	OF21,1B1	R	29	49	75	6	14	2	0	1	7	4	14	0	.187	.238	.253
Charlie Neal†	3B19,2B1,SS1	R	32	34	64	2	10	1	0	0	3	5	15	0	.156	.217	.172
Jesse Gonder†	C7	L	27	31	32	5	10	2	0	3	5	1	12	0	.313	.333	.656
Jerry Lynch†	OF7	L	32	22	32	5	8	3	0	2	9	1	5	0	.250	.294	.531
Gene Green†	C8	R	30	15	31	3	7	1	0	1	3	0	8	0	.226	.250	.355
Don Blasingame†	2B11,3B2	L	31	18	31	4	5	2	0	0	0	7	5	0	.161	.316	.226
Wally Post†	OF1	R	33	5	7	1	0	0	0	0	0	0	1	0	.000	.125	.000
Sammy Taylor†	C2	L	30	3	6	0	0	0	0	0	0	0	2	0	.000	.000	.000
Hank Foiles†	C1	R	34	1	3	0	0	0	0	0	0	1	0	1	.000	.250	.000
Harry Bright†	1B1	R	33	1	1	0	0	0	0	0	0	0	1	0	.000	.000	.000

Pitcher	T	Age	G	GS	CG	ShO	IP	H	HR	BB	SO	W-L	Sv	ERA
Jim Maloney	R	23	33	33	13	6	250.1	183	17	88	265	23-7	0	2.77
Jim O'Toole	L	26	33	32	12	5	234.1	208	13	57	146	17-14	0	2.88
Joe Nuxhall	L	34	35	29	14	2	217.1	194	14	39	169	15-8	2	2.61
Joey Jay	R	27	30	22	4	1	170.0	172	19	73	116	7-18	1	4.29
John Tsitouris	R	27	30	21	8	3	191.0	167	20	38	113	12-8	0	3.16
Bob Purkey	R	33	21	21	4	1	137.0	143	12	33	55	6-10	0	3.55
Al Worthington	R	34	50	0	0	0	81.1	75	6	31	55	4-4	10	2.99
Bill Henry	L	35	47	0	0	0	52.0	55	4	11	45	1-3	14	4.15
Dom Zanni†	R	31	31	1	0	0	43.0	39	2	21	40	1-1	5	4.19
Jim Owens	R	29	19	3	0	0	42.1	42	6	24	29	0-2	4	5.31
Jim Coates†	R	30	9	0	0	0	16.1	21	2	7	11	0-0	0	5.51
Jim Brosnan†	R	33	6	0	0	0	4.2	8	2	3	4	0-1	0	7.71

1963 Milwaukee Braves 6th NL 84-78 .519 15.0 GB

Bobby Bragan

Player	Gm by Position	B	Age	G	AB	R	H	2B	3B	HR	RBI	BB	SO	SB	Avg	OBP	Slg
Joe Torre	C105,1B37,OF2	R	22	142	501	57	147	19	4	14	71	42	79	1	.293	.350	.431
Gene Oliver†	1B55,OF35,C2	R	28	95	296	34	74	12	2	11	47	27	59	4	.250	.320	.416
Frank Bolling	2B141	R	31	142	542	73	132	18	2	5	43	41	47	2	.244	.299	.312
Eddie Mathews	3B121,OF42	L	31	158	547	82	144	27	4	23	84	124	119	3	.263	.399	.453
Roy McMillan	SS94	R	32	100	320	35	80	10	1	4	29	17	25	1	.250	.291	.325
Hank Aaron	OF161	R	29	161	631	121	201	29	4	44	130	78	94	31	.319	.391	.586
Lee Maye	OF111	L	28	124	442	67	120	22	7	11	34	36	52	14	.271	.329	.428
Mack Jones	OF80	L	24	93	228	36	50	11	4	3	22	26	59	8	.219	.317	.342
Denis Menke	SS82,3B51,2B22*	R	22	146	518	58	121	16	4	11	50	37	106	6	.234	.289	.344
Del Crandall	C75,1B7	R	33	86	259	18	52	4	0	3	28	18	22	1	.201	.251	.251
Ty Cline	OF62	L	24	72	174	17	41	2	1	0	10	10	31	2	.236	.283	.259
Norm Larker†	1B42	L	32	64	147	15	26	6	0	1	14	24	24	0	.177	.297	.238
Tommie Aaron	1B45,OF14,2B6*	R	23	72	135	6	27	6	1	1	15	11	27	0	.200	.257	.281
Len Gabrielson	OF22,1B16,3B3	L	23	46	120	14	26	5	0	3	15	8	23	1	.217	.264	.333
Don Dillard	OF30	L	26	67	119	9	28	6	4	1	12	5	21	0	.235	.270	.378
Lou Klimchock†	1B12	L	23	24	46	6	9	1	0	0	1	0	12	0	.196	.196	.217
Hawk Taylor	OF8	R	24	16	29	1	2	0	0	0	0	1	12	0	.069	.100	.069
Bubba Morton†	OF9	R	31	15	28	1	5	0	0	0	4	2	3	0	.179	.258	.179
Amado Samuel	SS7,2B4	R	24	15	17	0	3	1	0	0	0	0	4	0	.176	.176	.235
Bob Uecker	C6	R	28	13	16	3	4	2	0	0	0	2	5	0	.250	.333	.375
Gus Bell		L	34	3	3	0	1	0	0	0	0	0	0	0	.333	.333	.333
Rico Carty		R	23	2	2	0	0	0	0	0	0	0	2	0	.000	.000	.000
Woody Woodward	SS5	R	20	10	2	1	0	0	0	0	0	0	0	0	.000	.000	.000

D. Menke, 1 G at 1B, 1 G at OF; T. Aaron, 1 G at 3B

Pitcher	T	Age	G	GS	CG	ShO	IP	H	HR	BB	SO	W-L	Sv	ERA
Warren Spahn	L	42	33	33	22	7	259.2	241	23	49	102	23-7	0	2.60
Denny Lemaster	L	24	46	31	10	1	237.0	199	30	85	190	11-14	1	3.04
Bob Hendley	L	24	41	24	7	3	169.1	153	16	64	105	9-9	3	3.93
Bob Sadowski	R	25	19	18	5	1	116.2	99	8	30	72	5-7	0	2.62
Lew Burdette†	R	36	15	13	4	1	84.1	71	15	24	28	6-5	0	3.63
Bob Shaw	R	30	48	16	3	3	159.0	144	10	55	105	7-11	13	2.66
Claude Raymond	R	26	45	0	0	0	53.1	57	12	27	44	4-6	5	5.40
Tony Cloninger	R	22	41	18	4	2	145.1	131	17	63	100	9-11	1	3.78
Ron Piche	R	28	37	1	0	0	53.0	53	4	25	40	1-1	0	3.40
Hank Fischer	R	23	31	6	1	0	74.1	74	8	28	72	4-3	0	4.96
Dan Schneider	L	20	30	3	0	0	43.2	36	2	20	19	1-0	0	3.09
Frank Funk	R	27	25	0	0	0	43.2	42	3	13	19	3-3	0	2.68
Bobby Tiefenauer	R	33	12	0	0	0	29.2	20	1	4	22	1-1	2	1.21
Wade Blasingame	L	19	2	0	0	0	3.0	7	0	2	6	0-0	0	12.00

1963 Chicago Cubs 7th NL 82-80 .506 17.0 GB

Bob Kennedy

Player	Gm by Position	B	Age	G	AB	R	H	2B	3B	HR	RBI	BB	SO	SB	Avg	OBP	Slg
Dick Bertell	C99	R	27	100	322	15	75	7	2	2	14	24	41	0	.233	.284	.286
Ernie Banks	1B125	R	32	130	432	41	98	20	1	18	64	39	73	0	.227	.292	.403
Ken Hubbs	2B152	R	21	154	566	54	133	19	3	8	47	39	93	8	.235	.285	.322
Ron Santo	3B162	R	23	162	630	79	187	29	6	25	99	42	92	6	.297	.339	.481
Andre Rodgers	SS150	R	28	150	516	51	118	17	4	5	33	65	90	5	.229	.324	.306
Billy Williams	OF160	L	25	161	612	87	175	36	9	25	95	68	78	7	.286	.358	.497
Lou Brock	OF140	L	24	148	547	79	141	19	11	9	37	31	122	24	.258	.300	.382
Ellis Burton†	OF90	S	26	93	322	45	74	16	1	12	41	36	59	6	.230	.311	.398
Don Landrum	OF57	L	27	84	227	27	55	4	1	1	10	13	42	6	.242	.294	.282
Nelson Mathews	OF46	R	21	61	155	12	24	3	2	4	10	16	48	3	.155	.234	.277
Merritt Ranew	C37,1B9	L	25	78	154	18	52	8	1	3	15	9	32	1	.338	.380	.461
Jimmie Schaffer	C54	R	27	57	142	17	34	7	0	7	19	11	35	0	.239	.294	.437
Steve Boros	1B14,OF11	R	26	41	90	9	19	5	1	3	7	12	19	0	.211	.304	.389
John Boccabella	1B24	R	22	24	74	7	14	4	1	1	5	6	21	0	.189	.247	.311
Leo Burke†	2B10,1B4	R	29	27	49	4	9	0	0	2	7	4	13	0	.184	.241	.306
Jimmy Stewart	SS9,2B1	S	24	13	37	1	11	2	0	0	1	1	7	1	.297	.316	.351
Billy Cowan	OF10	R	24	14	36	1	9	1	1	1	2	0	11	0	.250	.250	.417
Ken Aspromonte	2B7,1B2	R	31	20	34	2	5	3	0	0	4	4	4	0	.147	.237	.235
Alex Grammas	SS13	R	37	16	27	1	5	0	0	0	0	0	3	0	.185	.185	.185
Bob Will	1B1	L	31	23	23	0	4	0	0	0	1	1	3	0	.174	.208	.174
Cuno Barragan	C1	R	31	1	1	0	0	0	0	0	0	0	1	0	.000	.000	.000

Pitcher	T	Age	G	GS	CG	ShO	IP	H	HR	BB	SO	W-L	Sv	ERA
Dick Ellsworth	L	23	37	37	19	4	290.2	223	14	75	185	22-10	0	2.11
Larry Jackson	R	32	37	37	13	4	275.0	256	11	54	153	14-18	0	2.55
Bob Buhl	R	34	37	34	6	0	226.0	219	24	62	108	11-14	0	3.38
Glen Hobbie	R	27	36	24	4	1	165.1	172	17	49	94	7-10	0	3.92
Paul Toth	R	28	27	14	3	2	130.2	115	9	35	66	5-9	0	3.10
Cal Koonce	R	22	21	13	0	0	72.2	75	9	32	44	2-6	0	4.58
Lindy McDaniel	R	27	57	0	0	0	88.0	82	9	27	75	13-7	22	2.86
Don Elston	R	34	51	0	0	0	70.0	57	6	21	41	4-1	4	2.83
Jim Brewer	L	25	29	1	0	0	49.2	59	10	15	35	3-2	0	4.89
Barney Schultz†	R	36	15	0	0	0	27.1	25	5	9	18	1-0	2	3.62
Tom Baker	L	29	10	1	0	0	18.0	20	2	7	14	0-1	0	3.00
Dick LeMay	L	24	9	1	0	0	15.1	26	1	4	10	0-1	0	5.28
Jack Warner	R	22	8	0	0	0	22.2	21	1	8	7	0-1	0	2.78
Freddie Burdette	R	26	4	0	0	0	4.2	5	1	2	1	0-0	0	3.86
Phil Mudrock	R	26	1	0	0	0	1.0	2	0	0	0	0-0	0	9.00

1963 Pittsburgh Pirates 8th NL 74-88 .457 25.0 GB

Danny Murtaugh

Player	Gm by Position	B	Age	G	AB	R	H	2B	3B	HR	RBI	BB	SO	SB	Avg	OBP	Slg
Jim Pagliaroni	C85	R	25	92	252	27	58	5	0	11	26	36	57	0	.230	.330	.381
Donn Clendenon	1B151	R	27	154	563	65	155	28	7	15	57	39	136	22	.275	.326	.430
Bill Mazeroski	2B138	R	26	142	534	43	131	22	3	8	52	32	46	2	.245	.286	.343
Bob Bailey	3B153,SS3	R	20	154	570	60	130	15	3	12	45	58	98	10	.228	.303	.328
Dick Schofield	SS117,2B20,3B1	S	28	138	541	54	133	18	2	3	32	69	83	2	.246	.333	.303
Roberto Clemente	OF151	R	28	152	600	77	192	23	8	17	76	31	64	12	.320	.356	.470
Bill Virdon	OF142	L	32	142	554	58	149	22	6	8	53	43	55	1	.269	.321	.374
Willie Stargell	OF65,1B16	L	23	108	304	34	74	11	6	11	47	19	85	0	.243	.290	.428
Smoky Burgess	C72	L	36	91	264	20	74	10	1	6	37	24	14	0	.280	.338	.394
Jerry Lynch†	OF64	L	32	88	237	26	63	6	3	10	36	22	28	0	.266	.328	.443
Johnny Logan	SS44,3B4	R	36	81	181	15	42	2	1	0	9	23	27	0	.232	.325	.254
Ted Savage	OF47	R	26	85	149	22	29	2	1	5	14	14	31	4	.195	.268	.322
Manny Mota	OF37,2B1	R	25	59	126	20	34	2	3	0	7	7	18	0	.270	.313	.333
Bob Skinner†	OF32	L	31	34	122	18	33	5	5	0	8	13	22	4	.270	.341	.393
Ron Brand	C33,2B2,3B2	R	23	46	66	8	19	2	0	1	7	10	11	0	.288	.390	.364
Gene Alley	3B7,2B4,SS4	R	22	17	51	3	11	1	0	0	0	2	12	0	.216	.245	.235
Elmo Plaskett	C5,3B1	R	25	10	21	1	3	0	0	0	2	0	5	0	.143	.143	.143
Larry Elliot		L	25	4	4	0	0	0	0	0	0	0	3	0	.000	.000	.000
Julio Gotay	2B1	R	24	4	2	0	1	0	0	0	0	0	0	0	.500	.500	.500

Pitcher	T	Age	G	GS	CG	ShO	IP	H	HR	BB	SO	W-L	Sv	ERA
Bob Friend	R	32	39	38	12	4	268.2	236	13	44	144	17-16	0	2.34
Don Cardwell	R	27	33	32	7	2	213.2	195	21	52	112	13-15	0	3.07
Don Schwall	R	27	33	24	3	2	167.2	158	13	74	86	6-12	0	3.33
Joe Gibbon	L	28	37	22	5	0	147.1	147	7	54	110	5-12	1	3.30
Vern Law	R	33	18	12	1	1	76.2	91	11	13	31	4-5	0	4.93
Tom Parsons	R	23	1	1	0	0	4.1	7	1	2	2	0-1	0	8.31
Tommie Sisk	R	21	57	4	1	0	108.0	85	6	45	73	1-3	1	2.92
Roy Face	R	35	56	0	0	0	69.2	75	6	19	41	3-9	16	3.23
Al McBean	R	25	55	7	2	1	122.1	100	5	39	74	13-3	11	2.57
Harvey Haddix	L	37	49	1	0	0	70.0	67	7	20	70	3-4	1	3.34
Bob Veale	L	27	34	7	3	2	77.2	59	1	40	68	5-2	3	1.04
Earl Francis	R	27	33	13	0	0	97.1	107	6	43	72	4-6	0	4.53
Tom Butters	R	25	6	1	0	0	16.1	15	1	8	11	0-0	0	4.41
Tom Sturdivant†	R	33	3	0	0	0	8.1	8	1	4	6	0-0	0	6.48

1963 Houston Colt .45s 9th NL 66-96 .407 33.0 GB

Harry Craft

Player	Gm by Position	B	Age	G	AB	R	H	2B	3B	HR	RBI	BB	SO	SB	Avg	OBP	Slg
John Bateman	C115	R	22	128	404	23	85	8	6	10	59	13	103	0	.210	.249	.334
Rusty Staub	1B109,OF49	L	19	150	513	43	115	17	4	6	45	59	58	0	.224	.309	.308
Ernie Fazio	2B84,3B1,SS1	R	21	102	228	31	42	10	3	2	5	27	70	4	.184	.273	.281
Bob Aspromonte	3B131,1B1	R	25	136	468	42	100	9	5	8	49	40	57	3	.214	.276	.306
Bob Lillis	SS124,2B19,3B6	R	33	147	469	31	93	13	1	1	19	15	35	3	.198	.229	.237
Carl Warwick	OF141,1B2	R	26	150	528	49	134	19	5	7	47	49	70	3	.254	.319	.348
Howie Goss	OF123	R	28	133	411	37	86	18	2	9	44	31	128	4	.209	.264	.328
Al Spangler	OF113	L	29	120	430	52	121	25	4	4	27	50	38	5	.281	.355	.386
Pete Runnels	1B70,2B36,3B3	L	35	124	388	35	98	9	1	2	23	45	42	2	.253	.332	.296
Johnny Temple	2B61,3B29	R	35	100	322	22	85	12	1	1	17	41	24	7	.264	.347	.317
Jimmy Wynn	OF53,SS21,3B2	R	21	70	250	31	61	10	5	4	27	30	53	4	.244	.319	.372
Jim Campbell	C42	R	26	55	158	9	35	3	0	4	19	10	40	0	.222	.268	.316
J.C. Hartman	SS32	R	29	39	90	2	11	1	0	0	3	2	13	1	.122	.151	.133
Johnny Weekly	OF23	R	26	34	80	4	18	3	0	3	14	7	14	0	.225	.292	.375
Hal Smith	C11	R	32	31	58	1	14	2	0	0	2	4	15	0	.241	.290	.276
Brock Davis	OF14	L	19	34	55	7	11	2	0	1	2	4	10	0	.200	.254	.291
Carroll Hardy	OF10	R	30	15	44	5	10	3	0	0	3	3	7	1	.227	.277	.295
Glenn Vaughan	SS9,3B1	S	19	9	30	1	5	0	0	0	0	2	5	1	.167	.219	.167
Joe Morgan	2B7	L	19	8	25	5	6	0	1	0	3	5	5	1	.240	.367	.320
Dave Adlesh	C6	R	19	6	8	0	0	0	0	0	0	0	4	0	.000	.000	.000
Mike White	2B2	R	24	3	7	0	2	0	0	0	0	0	0	0	.286	.286	.286
Jerry Grote	C3	R	20	3	5	0	1	0	0	0	1	1	3	0	.200	.286	.200
Ivan Murrell	OF2	R	18	2	5	1	1	0	0	0	0	0	2	0	.200	.200	.200
Aaron Pointer	OF1	R	21	2	5	0	1	0	0	0	0	0	1	0	.200	.200	.200
John Paciorek	OF1	R	18	1	3	4	3	0	0	0	3	2	0	0	1.000	1.000	1.000
Sonny Jackson	SS1	L	18	1	3	0	0	0	0	0	0	0	1	0	.000	.000	.000

Pitcher	T	Age	G	GS	CG	ShO	IP	H	HR	BB	SO	W-L	Sv	ERA
Ken Johnson	R	30	37	32	6	1	224.0	204	12	50	148	11-17	1	2.65
Don Nottebart	R	27	31	27	9	2	193.0	170	10	39	118	11-8	0	3.17
Turk Farrell	R	29	34	26	12	0	202.1	161	12	35	141	14-13	1	3.02
Bob Bruce	R	30	30	25	1	1	170.1	162	7	60	123	5-9	0	3.59
Hal Brown	R	38	26	20	6	3	141.1	137	14	8	68	5-11	0	3.31
Dick Drott	R	26	27	14	2	1	97.2	95	13	49	58	2-12	0	4.98
Larry Yellen	R	20	1	1	0	0	5.0	7	0	1	3	0-0	0	3.60
Jay Dahl	L	17	1	1	0	0	2.2	7	0	0	0	0-1	0	16.88
Hal Woodeshick	L	30	55	0	0	0	114.0	75	3	42	94	11-9	10	1.97
Don McMahon	R	33	49	2	0	0	79.2	83	10	26	51	1-5	5	4.07
Jim Umbricht	R	32	35	3	0	0	76.0	52	6	21	48	4-3	0	2.61
Chris Zachary	R	19	22	7	0	0	57.0	62	5	22	42	2-2	0	4.89
Russ Kemmerer	R	31	17	0	0	0	36.2	48	1	8	12	0-0	1	5.65
Jim Dickson	R	25	13	0	0	0	14.2	22	0	2	6	0-1	2	6.14
Conrad Cardinal	R	21	6	1	0	0	13.1	15	0	7	7	0-1	0	6.08
George Brunet†	L	28	5	2	0	0	12.2	24	2	6	11	0-3	0	7.11
Jim Golden	R	27	3	1	0	0	6.1	12	0	2	5	0-1	0	5.68
Joe Hoerner	L	26	1	0	0	0	3.0	2	0	0	2	0-0	0	0.00
Danny Coombs	L	21	1	0	0	0	0.1	3	0	0	0	0-0	0	27.00

1963 New York Mets 10th NL 51-111 .315 48.0 GB

Casey Stengel

Player	Gm by Position	B	Age	G	AB	R	H	2B	3B	HR	RBI	BB	SO	SB	Avg	OBP	Slg
C. Choo Coleman	C91,OF1	L	25	106	247	22	44	0	0	3	9	24	49	5	.178	.264	.215
Tim Harkness	1B106	L	25	123	375	35	79	12	3	10	41	36	79	4	.211	.290	.339
Ron Hunt	2B142,3B1	R	22	143	533	64	145	28	4	10	42	40	50	5	.272	.334	.396
Charlie Neal†	3B66,SS8	R	32	72	253	26	57	12	1	3	18	27	49	1	.225	.302	.316
Al Moran	SS116,3B1	R	24	119	331	26	64	5	2	1	23	36	60	3	.193	.274	.230
Duke Snider	OF106	L	36	129	354	44	86	8	3	14	45	56	74	0	.243	.345	.401
Frank Thomas	OF96,1B15,3B1	R	34	126	420	34	109	9	1	15	60	33	48	0	.260	.317	.393
Jim Hickman	OF82,3B59	R	26	146	494	53	113	21	6	17	51	44	120	0	.229	.291	.399
Ed Kranepool	OF55,1B20	L	18	86	273	22	57	12	2	2	14	18	50	4	.209	.256	.289
Rod Kanehl	OF58,3B13,2B12*	R	29	109	191	26	46	6	0	1	9	5	26	6	.241	.268	.288
Joe Hicks	OF41	L	30	56	159	16	36	6	1	5	22	7	31	0	.226	.272	.371
Duke Carmel†	OF21,1B18	L	26	47	149	11	35	5	3	3	18	16	37	2	.235	.307	.369
Joe Christopher	OF45	R	27	64	149	11	33	5	1	1	8	13	21	1	.221	.295	.289
Norm Sherry	C61	R	31	63	147	6	20	1	0	2	11	10	26	1	.136	.205	.184
Chico Fernandez†	SS45,3B5,2B3	R	31	58	145	12	29	6	0	1	9	9	30	3	.200	.244	.262
Jesse Gonder†	C31	L	27	42	126	12	38	4	0	3	15	6	25	1	.302	.328	.405
Jimmy Piersall†	OF38	R	33	40	124	13	24	4	1	1	10	10	14	1	.194	.250	.266
Cliff Cook	OF21,3B9,1B5	R	26	50	106	9	15	2	1	2	8	12	37	0	.142	.229	.236
Larry Burright	SS19,2B15,3B1	R	25	41	100	9	22	2	1	0	3	8	25	1	.220	.291	.260
Pumpsie Green	3B16	S	29	17	54	8	15	1	2	1	5	12	13	0	.278	.409	.426
Ted Schreiber	3B17,SS9,2B3	R	24	39	50	1	8	0	0	0	2	4	14	0	.160	.236	.160
Dick Smith	OF10,1B2	R	24	20	42	4	10	0	1	0	3	5	10	3	.238	.319	.286
Sammy Taylor†	C13	L	30	22	35	3	9	0	1	0	6	5	7	0	.257	.341	.314
Chris Cannizzaro	C15	R	25	16	33	4	8	1	0	0	4	1	8	0	.242	.257	.273
Gil Hodges	1B10	R	39	11	22	2	5	0	0	0	3	3	2	0	.227	.320	.227
Cleon Jones	OF5	R	20	6	15	1	2	0	0	0	1	0	4	0	.133	.133	.133
Marv Throneberry	1B3	L	29	14	14	0	2	1	0	0	1	1	5	0	.143	.200	.214

R. Kanehl, 3 G at 1B

Pitcher	T	Age	G	GS	CG	ShO	IP	H	HR	BB	SO	W-L	Sv	ERA
Al Jackson	L	27	37	34	11	0	227.0	237	25	84	142	13-17	1	3.96
Roger Craig	R	33	46	31	14	0	236.0	249	28	58	108	5-22	2	3.78
Carl Willey	R	32	30	28	7	4	183.0	149	24	69	101	9-14	0	3.10
Tracy Stallard	R	25	39	23	5	0	154.2	156	23	77	110	6-17	1	4.71
Craig Anderson	R	24	3	2	0	0	9.1	17	0	3	6	0-2	0	8.68
Larry Bearnarth	R	21	58	2	0	0	126.1	127	7	47	48	3-8	4	3.42
Galen Cisco	R	27	51	17	1	0	155.2	165	15	64	81	7-15	0	4.34
Jay Hook	R	26	41	20	3	0	152.2	168	21	53	89	4-14	1	5.48
Ken MacKenzie†	L	29	34	0	0	0	57.2	63	11	12	41	3-1	3	4.99
Don Rowe	L	27	26	1	0	0	54.2	59	6	21	27	0-0	0	4.28
Grover Powell	L	22	20	4	1	1	49.2	37	2	32	39	1-1	0	2.72
Ed Bauta†	R	28	9	0	0	0	19.0	22	0	9	13	0-0	0	5.21
Steve Dillon	L	20	1	0	0	0	1.2	3	0	0	1	0-0	0	10.80

»1964 New York Yankees 1st AL 99-63 .611 —

Yogi Berra

Player	Gm by Position	B	Age	G	AB	R	H	2B	3B	HR	RBI	BB	SO	SB	Avg	OBP	Slg
Elston Howard	C146	R	35	150	550	63	172	27	3	15	84	48	73	1	.313	.371	.455
Joe Pepitone	1B155,OF30	L	23	160	613	71	154	12	3	28	100	24	63	2	.251	.281	.418
Bobby Richardson	2B157,SS1	R	28	159	679	90	181	25	4	4	50	28	36	11	.267	.294	.333
Clete Boyer	3B123,SS21	R	27	147	510	43	111	10	5	8	52	36	93	6	.218	.269	.304
Tony Kubek	SS99	L	27	106	415	46	95	16	3	8	31	26	55	4	.229	.275	.340
Tom Tresh	OF146	S	26	153	533	75	131	25	5	16	73	73	110	13	.246	.342	.402
Roger Maris	OF137	L	29	141	513	86	144	12	2	26	71	62	78	3	.281	.364	.464
Mickey Mantle	OF132	S	32	143	465	92	141	25	2	35	111	99	102	6	.303	.423	.591
Phil Linz	SS55,3B41,2B5*	S	25	112	368	63	92	21	3	5	25	43	61	3	.250	.332	.364
Hector Lopez	OF103,3B1	R	34	127	285	34	74	9	3	10	34	24	54	1	.260	.317	.418
Johnny Blanchard	C25,OF14,1B3	L	31	77	161	18	41	8	0	7	28	24	24	1	.255	.344	.435
Pedro Gonzalez	1B31,OF20,3B9*	R	26	80	112	18	31	8	1	0	5	7	22	3	.277	.331	.366
Archie Moore	OF8,1B7	L	22	31	23	4	4	2	0	0	1	2	9	0	.174	.240	.261
Elvio Jimenez	OF1	R	24	1	6	0	2	0	0	0	0	0	0	0	.333	.333	.333
Jake Gibbs	C2	L	25	3	6	1	1	0	0	0	0	0	2	0	.167	.167	.167
Mike Hegan	1B2	L	21	5	5	0	0	0	0	0	0	1	2	0	.000	.167	.000
Harry Bright	1B2	R	34	4	5	0	1	0	0	0	0	1	1	0	.200	.333	.200
Roger Repoz	OF9	L	23	11	1	1	0	0	0	0	0	1	1	0	.000	.500	.000

P. Linz, 3 G at OF; P. Gonzalez, 6 G at 2B

Pitcher	T	Age	G	GS	CG	ShO	IP	H	HR	BB	SO	W-L	Sv	ERA
Jim Bouton	R	25	38	37	11	4	271.1	227	32	60	125	18-13	0	3.02
Whitey Ford	L	35	39	36	12	8	244.2	212	10	57	172	17-6	1	2.13
Al Downing	L	23	37	35	11	1	244.0	201	18	120	217	13-8	2	3.47
Ralph Terry	R	28	27	14	2	1	115.0	130	20	31	77	7-11	4	4.54
Rollie Sheldon	R	27	19	12	3	0	102.1	92	18	18	57	5-2	1	3.61
Mel Stottlemyre	R	22	13	12	5	2	96.0	77	3	35	49	9-3	0	2.06
Pete Mikkelsen	R	24	50	0	0	0	86.0	79	3	41	63	7-4	12	3.56
Hal Reniff	R	25	41	0	0	0	69.1	47	3	30	38	6-4	9	3.12
Bill Stafford	R	24	31	1	0	0	60.2	50	4	22	39	5-0	4	2.67
Steve Hamilton	L	28	30	3	1	0	60.1	55	6	15	49	7-2	3	3.28
Stan Williams	R	27	21	10	1	0	82.0	76	7	38	54	1-5	0	3.84
Bud Daley	L	31	13	3	0	0	35.0	37	3	25	16	3-2	1	4.63
Pedro Ramos†	R	29	13	0	0	0	21.2	13	1	0	21	1-0	8	1.25
Bob Meyer†	L	24	7	1	0	0	18.1	16	1	12	12	0-3	0	4.91

1964 Chicago White Sox 2nd AL 98-64 .605 1.0 GB

Al Lopez

Player	Gm by Position	B	Age	G	AB	R	H	2B	3B	HR	RBI	BB	SO	SB	Avg	OBP	Slg
J.C. Martin	C120	L	27	122	294	23	58	10	1	4	22	16	30	0	.197	.241	.279
Tom McCraw	1B84,OF36	L	23	125	368	47	96	11	5	6	36	32	65	15	.261	.325	.367
Al Weis	2B116,SS9,OF2	S	26	133	328	36	81	4	4	2	23	22	41	22	.247	.299	.302
Pete Ward	3B138	L	24	144	539	61	152	28	3	23	94	56	76	1	.282	.348	.473
Ron Hansen	SS158	R	26	158	575	85	150	25	3	20	68	73	73	1	.261	.347	.419
Floyd Robinson	OF138	L	28	141	525	83	158	17	3	11	59	70	41	9	.301	.388	.408
Mike Hershberger	OF134	R	24	141	452	55	104	15	3	2	31	48	47	8	.230	.308	.290
Jim Landis	OF101	R	30	106	298	30	62	8	4	1	18	36	64	5	.208	.305	.272
Don Buford	2B92,3B37	S	27	135	442	62	116	14	6	4	30	46	62	12	.262	.337	.348
Dave Nicholson	OF92	R	24	97	294	40	60	6	1	13	39	52	126	0	.204	.329	.364
Bill Skowron†	1B70	R	33	73	273	19	80	11	3	4	38	19	36	0	.293	.337	.399
Jerry McNertney	C69	R	27	73	186	16	40	5	0	3	23	19	24	0	.215	.290	.290
Gene Stephens	OF59	L	31	82	141	21	33	4	2	3	17	21	28	1	.234	.335	.355
Joe Cunningham†	1B33	L	32	40	108	13	27	7	0	0	10	14	14	0	.250	.352	.315
Cam Carreon	C34	R	26	37	95	12	26	5	0	0	4	7	13	0	.274	.330	.326
Jeoff Long†	1B5,OF5	R	22	23	35	0	5	0	0	0	5	4	15	0	.143	.225	.143
Ken Berry	OF12	R	23	12	32	4	12	1	0	1	4	5	3	0	.375	.459	.500
Minnie Minoso	OF5	R	41	30	31	4	7	0	0	1	5	5	3	0	.226	.351	.323
Charley Smith†	3B2	R	26	2	7	1	1	0	1	0	0	1	1	0	.143	.250	.429
Marv Staehle		L	22	6	5	0	2	0	0	0	2	0	0	1	.400	.400	.400
Smoky Burgess†		L	37	7	5	1	1	0	0	0	1	2	0	0	.200	.429	.800
Dick Kenworthy		R	23	2	2	0	0	0	0	0	0	0	1	0	.000	.000	.000
Charlie Maxwell		L	37	2	2	0	0	0	0	0	0	0	0	0	.000	.000	.000
Jim Hicks		R	24	2	0	0	0	0	0	0	0	0	0	0	—	—	—

Pitcher	T	Age	G	GS	CG	ShO	IP	H	HR	BB	SO	W-L	Sv	ERA
Gary Peters	L	27	37	36	11	3	273.2	217	20	104	205	20-8	0	2.50
Juan Pizarro	L	27	33	33	11	4	239.0	193	23	55	162	19-9	0	2.56
Joe Horlen	R	26	32	28	9	2	210.2	142	11	55	138	13-9	0	1.88
John Buzhardt	R	27	31	25	8	3	160.0	150	13	35	97	10-8	0	2.98
Ray Herbert	R	34	20	19	1	1	111.2	117	14	17	40	6-7	0	3.47
Fred Talbot	R	23	17	12	3	2	75.1	83	7	20	34	4-5	0	3.70
Bruce Howard	R	21	3	3	1	1	22.1	10	0	8	17	2-1	0	0.81
Fritz Ackley	R	27	3	2	0	0	6.1	10	2	4	6	0-0	0	8.53
Hoyt Wilhelm	R	40	73	0	0	0	131.1	94	7	30	95	12-9	27	1.99
Eddie Fisher	R	27	59	2	0	0	125.0	86	13	32	74	6-3	9	3.02
Don Mossi	L	35	34	0	0	0	40.0	37	9	7	36	3-1	7	2.93
Frank Baumann	L	30	22	0	0	0	32.0	40	4	16	19	0-3	1	6.19
Frank Kreutzer†	L	25	17	2	0	0	40.1	37	1	18	32	3-1	1	3.35

1964 Baltimore Orioles 3rd AL 97-65 .599 2.0 GB

Hank Bauer

Player	Gm by Position	B	Age	G	AB	R	H	2B	3B	HR	RBI	BB	SO	SB	Avg	OBP	Slg
Dick Brown	C84	R	29	88	230	24	59	6	0	8	32	12	45	2	.257	.294	.387
Norm Siebern	1B149	L	30	150	478	92	117	24	2	12	56	106	87	2	.245	.379	.379
Jerry Adair	2B153	R	27	155	569	56	141	20	3	9	47	28	72	3	.248	.283	.341
Brooks Robinson	3B163	R	27	163	612	82	194	35	3	28	118	51	64	1	.317	.368	.521
Luis Aparicio	SS145	R	30	146	578	93	154	20	3	10	37	49	51	57	.266	.324	.363
Sam Bowens	OF135	R	25	139	501	58	132	25	2	22	71	42	99	4	.263	.323	.453
Jackie Brandt	OF134	R	30	137	523	66	127	25	1	13	47	45	104	1	.243	.305	.369
Boog Powell	OF124,1B5	L	22	134	424	74	123	17	0	39	99	76	91	0	.290	.399	.606
John Orsino	C66,1B5	R	26	81	248	21	55	10	0	8	23	23	55	0	.222	.290	.359
Bob Johnson	SS18,1B15,2B15*	R	28	93	210	18	52	8	2	3	29	9	37	0	.248	.281	.348
Charlie Lau†	C47	L	31	62	158	16	41	15	1	1	14	17	27	0	.259	.333	.386
Willie Kirkland†	OF58	L	30	66	150	14	30	5	0	3	22	17	26	3	.200	.281	.293
Earl Robinson	OF34	R	27	37	121	11	33	5	1	3	10	7	24	1	.273	.310	.405
Russ Snyder	OF40	L	30	56	93	11	27	3	0	1	7	11	22	0	.290	.362	.355
Gino Cimoli†	OF35	R	34	38	58	6	8	3	2	0	3	2	13	0	.138	.164	.259
Bob Saverine	SS15,OF2	S	23	46	34	14	5	1	0	0	0	3	6	3	.147	.216	.176
Joe Gaines†	OF5	R	27	16	26	2	4	0	0	1	2	3	7	0	.154	.241	.269
Lenny Green†	OF8	L	31	14	21	0	4	0	0	0	1	7	3	1	.190	.393	.190
Lou Jackson	OF1	L	28	4	8	0	3	0	0	0	0	0	2	0	.375	.375	.375
Paul Blair	OF6	R	20	8	1	0	0	0	0	0	0	0	1	0	.000	.000	.000
Lou Piniella		R	20	4	1	0	0	0	0	0	0	0	0	0	.000	.000	.000

B. Johnson, 1 G at 3B, 1 G at OF

Pitcher	T	Age	G	GS	CG	ShO	IP	H	HR	BB	SO	W-L	Sv	ERA
Milt Pappas	R	25	37	36	13	7	251.2	225	21	48	157	16-7	0	2.97
Robin Roberts	R	37	31	31	8	4	204.0	203	18	52	109	13-7	0	2.91
Wally Bunker	R	19	29	29	12	1	214.0	161	17	62	96	19-5	0	2.69
Steve Barber	L	25	36	26	4	0	157.0	144	15	81	118	9-13	1	3.84
Dave McNally	L	21	30	23	5	3	159.1	157	15	51	88	9-11	0	3.67
Frank Bertaina	L	20	6	4	1	1	26.0	18	3	13	18	1-0	0	2.77
Mike McCormick	L	25	4	2	0	0	17.1	21	1	8	13	0-2	0	5.19
Stu Miller	R	36	66	0	0	0	97.0	77	7	34	87	7-7	23	3.06
Harvey Haddix	L	38	49	0	0	0	89.2	68	4	23	90	5-5	10	2.31
Dick Hall	R	33	45	0	0	0	87.2	58	8	16	52	9-1	7	1.85
Dave Vineyard	R	23	19	6	1	0	54.0	57	5	27	50	2-5	0	4.17
Chuck Estrada	R	26	17	6	0	0	54.2	62	8	21	32	3-2	0	5.27
Wes Stock†	R	30	14	0	0	0	20.2	17	5	8	14	2-0	0	3.92
Sam Jones	R	38	7	0	0	0	10.1	5	1	5	6	0-0	0	2.61
Ken Rowe	R	30	6	0	0	0	4.0	10	1	1	4	1-0	0	9.00
Herm Starrette	R	25	5	0	0	0	11.0	9	0	6	5	1-0	0	1.64

1964 Detroit Tigers 4th AL 85-77 .525 14.0 GB

Chuck Dressen

Player	Gm by Position	B	Age	G	AB	R	H	2B	3B	HR	RBI	BB	SO	SB	Avg	OBP	Slg
Bill Freehan	C141,1B1	R	22	144	520	69	156	14	8	18	80	36	68	5	.300	.350	.462
Norm Cash	1B137	L	29	144	479	63	123	15	5	23	83	70	66	2	.257	.351	.453
Jerry Lumpe	2B158	L	31	158	624	75	160	21	6	6	46	50	61	2	.256	.312	.338
Don Wert	3B142,SS4	R	25	148	525	63	135	18	5	9	55	50	74	3	.257	.325	.362
Dick McAuliffe	SS160	L	24	162	557	85	134	18	7	24	66	77	96	8	.241	.334	.427
Al Kaline	OF136	R	29	146	525	77	154	31	5	17	68	75	51	4	.293	.383	.469
Gates Brown	OF106	L	25	123	426	65	116	22	6	15	54	31	53	11	.272	.326	.458
George Thomas	OF90,3B1	R	26	105	308	39	88	15	2	12	44	18	53	4	.286	.329	.464
Don Demeter	OF88,1B23	R	29	134	441	57	113	22	1	22	80	17	85	4	.256	.290	.460
Bill Bruton	OF81	L	38	106	296	42	82	11	5	5	33	32	54	14	.277	.347	.399
Jake Wood	1B11,2B10,3B6*	R	27	64	125	11	29	2	2	1	7	4	24	0	.232	.254	.304
Bubba Phillips	3B22,OF1	R	36	46	87	14	22	1	0	3	6	10	13	1	.253	.327	.368
Mike Roarke	C27	R	33	29	82	4	19	1	0	0	7	10	10	0	.232	.315	.244
Willie Horton	OF23	R	21	25	80	6	13	1	3	1	10	11	20	0	.163	.272	.288
Jim Northrup	OF2	L	24	5	12	1	1	1	0	0	0	0	3	1	.083	.083	.167
Mickey Stanley	OF4	R	21	4	11	3	3	0	0	0	1	0	1	0	.273	.273	.273
Bill Roman	1B2	L	25	3	8	2	3	0	0	1	1	0	2	0	.375	.375	.750
George Smith	2B3	R	26	5	7	1	2	0	0	0	2	1	4	1	.286	.375	.286
John Sullivan	C2	L	23	2	3	0	0	0	0	0	0	0	1	0	.000	.000	.000

J. Wood, 1 G at OF

Pitcher	T	Age	G	GS	CG	ShO	IP	H	HR	BB	SO	W-L	Sv	ERA
Dave Wickersham	R	28	40	36	11	1	254.0	224	28	81	164	19-12	1	3.44
Mickey Lolich	L	23	44	33	12	6	232.0	196	26	64	192	18-9	2	3.26
Hank Aguirre	L	33	32	27	3	0	161.2	134	15	59	88	5-10	1	3.79
Phil Regan	R	27	32	21	2	0	146.2	162	21	49	91	5-10	1	5.03
Denny McLain	R	20	19	16	3	0	100.0	84	16	37	70	4-5	0	4.05
Joe Sparma	R	22	21	11	3	2	84.0	62	4	45	71	5-6	0	3.00
Frank Lary†	R	34	6	4	0	0	18.0	24	3	10	6	0-2	0	7.00
Bill Faul	R	24	1	1	0	0	5.0	5	2	2	1	0-0	0	10.80
Ed Rakow	R	28	42	13	1	0	152.1	155	14	59	96	8-9	3	3.72
Fred Gladding	R	28	42	0	0	0	67.1	57	7	27	59	7-4	7	3.07
Larry Sherry	R	28	38	0	0	0	66.1	52	7	37	58	7-5	11	3.66
Terry Fox	R	28	32	0	0	0	61.0	77	4	16	28	4-3	5	3.39
Julio Navarro†	R	28	26	0	0	0	41.0	40	9	16	36	2-1	2	3.95
Dick Egan	L	27	23	0	0	0	34.1	33	4	17	21	0-0	2	4.46
Jack Hamilton	R	25	5	1	0	0	15.0	24	2	8	5	0-1	0	8.40
Johnny Seale	L	25	4	0	0	0	10.0	6	1	4	5	1-0	0	3.60
Alan Koch†	R	26	3	0	0	0	4.0	6	1	3	1	0-0	0	6.75
Fritz Fisher	L	22	1	0	0	0	0.1	2	0	2	1	0-0	0	108.00

1964 Los Angeles Angels 5th AL 82-80 .506 17.0 GB

Bill Rigney

Player	Gm by Position	B	Age	G	AB	R	H	2B	3B	HR	RBI	BB	SO	SB	Avg	OBP	Slg
Bob Rodgers	C146	S	25	148	514	38	125	18	3	4	54	40	71	4	.243	.299	.313
Joe Adcock	1B105	R	36	118	366	39	98	13	0	21	64	48	61	0	.268	.352	.475
Bobby Knoop	2B161	R	25	162	486	42	105	8	1	7	38	46	109	3	.216	.289	.280
Felix Torres	3B72,1B3	R	32	100	277	25	64	10	0	12	28	13	56	1	.231	.266	.397
Jim Fregosi	SS137	R	22	147	505	86	140	22	9	18	72	72	87	8	.277	.369	.463
Willie Smith	OF87,P15	L	25	118	359	46	108	14	6	11	51	8	39	7	.301	.317	.465
Lu Clinton†	OF86	R	26	91	306	30	76	18	0	9	38	31	40	3	.248	.317	.395
Jimmy Piersall	OF72	R	34	87	255	28	80	11	0	2	13	16	32	5	.314	.353	.380
Albie Pearson	OF66	L	29	107	265	34	59	5	1	2	16	35	22	6	.223	.316	.272
Tom Satriano	3B38,1B32,C25*	L	23	108	255	18	51	9	0	1	17	30	37	0	.200	.282	.247
Bob Perry	OF62	R	29	70	221	19	61	8	1	3	16	14	52	1	.276	.318	.362
Vic Power†	1B48,3B28,2B5	R	36	68	221	17	55	6	0	3	13	8	14	1	.249	.275	.317
Ed Kirkpatrick	OF63	L	19	75	219	20	53	13	3	2	22	23	30	2	.242	.315	.356
Billy Moran†	3B47,2B3,SS1	R	30	50	198	26	53	10	1	0	11	13	20	1	.268	.315	.328
Lee Thomas†	OF47,1B1	L	28	47	172	14	47	8	1	2	24	18	22	1	.273	.340	.366
Joe Koppe	SS31,2B13,3B3	R	33	54	113	10	29	4	1	0	6	14	16	0	.257	.339	.310
Lenny Green†	OF23	L	31	39	92	13	23	2	0	2	4	10	8	2	.250	.327	.337
Dick Simpson	OF16	R	20	21	50	11	7	1	0	2	4	8	15	2	.140	.259	.280
Rick Reichardt	OF11	R	21	11	37	0	6	0	0	0	0	1	12	1	.162	.184	.162
Paul Schaal	2B9,3B9	R	21	17	32	3	4	0	0	0	0	2	5	0	.125	.176	.125
Charlie Dees	1B12	L	29	26	26	3	2	1	0	0	1	1	4	1	.077	.143	.115
Jack Hiatt	C3,1B2	R	21	9	16	2	6	0	0	0	2	2	3	0	.375	.444	.375
Hank Foiles		R	35	4	4	0	1	0	0	0	0	0	2	0	.250	.250	.250

T. Satriano, 2 G at SS, 1 G at 2B

Pitcher	T	Age	G	GS	CG	ShO	IP	H	HR	BB	SO	W-L	Sv	ERA
Dean Chance	R	23	46	35	15	11	278.1	194	7	86	207	20-9	4	1.65
Fred Newman	R	22	32	28	7	2	190.0	177	9	39	83	13-10	0	2.75
Bo Belinsky	L	27	23	22	4	1	135.1	120	8	49	91	9-8	0	2.86
Ken McBride	R	28	29	21	0	0	116.1	104	14	75	66	4-13	1	5.26
George Brunet	L	29	10	7	0	0	42.1	38	2	25	36	2-2	0	3.61
Bob Meyer†	L	24	6	5	0	0	18.0	25	2	13	13	1-1	0	5.00
Bob Lee	R	26	64	5	0	0	137.0	87	6	58	111	6-5	19	1.51
Bob Duliba	R	29	58	0	0	0	72.2	80	5	22	33	6-4	9	3.59
Dan Osinski	R	30	47	4	1	1	93.0	87	8	39	88	3-3	2	3.48
Barry Latman	R	28	40	18	2	1	138.0	128	15	52	81	6-10	2	3.85
Don Lee	R	30	33	8	0	0	89.1	99	6	25	73	5-4	2	2.72
Aubrey Gatewood	R	25	15	7	0	0	60.1	59	4	12	25	3-3	0	2.24
Willie Smith	L	25	15	1	0	0	31.2	34	5	10	20	1-4	0	2.84
Bill Kelso	R	24	10	1	1	1	23.2	19	3	9	21	2-0	0	2.28
Jack Spring†	L	31	6	0	0	0	3.1	3	1	3	0	1-0	0	2.70
Julio Navarro†	R	28	5	0	0	0	9.1	5	0	5	8	0-0	1	1.93
Art Fowler	R	41	4	0	0	0	7.0	8	2	5	5	0-2	1	10.29
Ed Sukla	R	21	2	0	0	0	2.2	2	1	1	3	0-1	0	6.75
Paul Foytack	R	33	2	0	0	0	2.1	4	2	2	1	0-1	0	15.43

1964 Cleveland Indians 6th AL 79-83 .488 20.0 GB

George Strickland (33-39)/Birdie Tebbetts (46-44)

Player	Gm by Position	B	Age	G	AB	R	H	2B	3B	HR	RBI	BB	SO	SB	Avg	OBP	Slg
John Romano	C96,1B1	R	29	106	352	46	85	18	1	19	47	51	83	2	.241	.346	.460
Bob Chance	1B81,OF31	L	23	120	390	45	109	16	1	14	75	40	101	3	.279	.346	.433
Larry Brown	2B103,SS4	R	24	115	335	33	77	12	1	12	40	24	55	1	.230	.283	.379
Max Alvis	3B105	R	26	107	381	51	96	14	3	18	53	29	77	5	.252	.313	.446
Dick Howser	SS162	R	28	162	637	101	163	23	4	3	52	76	39	20	.256	.335	.319
Leon Wagner	OF163	L	30	163	641	94	162	19	2	31	100	56	121	14	.253	.316	.434
Vic Davalillo	OF143	L	27	150	577	64	156	26	2	6	51	34	77	21	.270	.309	.354
Tito Francona	OF69,1B17	L	30	111	270	35	67	13	2	8	24	44	46	1	.248	.361	.400
Woodie Held	2B52,OF41,3B30	R	32	118	364	50	86	13	0	18	49	43	88	1	.236	.328	.420
Fred Whitfield	1B79	L	26	101	293	29	79	13	1	10	29	12	58	0	.270	.301	.423
Chico Salmon	OF53,2B32,1B13	R	23	86	283	43	87	17	2	4	25	13	37	10	.307	.340	.424
Joe Azcue	C76	R	24	83	271	20	74	9	1	4	34	16	38	0	.273	.314	.358
Billy Moran†	3B42,2B15,1B2	R	30	69	151	14	31	6	0	1	10	18	16	0	.205	.291	.265
Al Smith†	OF48,3B1	R	36	61	136	15	22	1	1	4	9	8	32	0	.162	.214	.272
Jerry Kindall†	1B23	R	29	23	25	5	9	1	0	2	2	2	7	0	.360	.407	.640
Al Luplow	OF5	L	25	19	18	1	2	0	0	0	1	1	8	0	.111	.158	.111
George Banks†	OF3,2B1,3B1	R	25	9	17	6	5	1	0	2	3	6	6	0	.294	.478	.706
Tony Martinez	2B4,SS1	R	24	9	14	1	3	1	0	0	2	0	2	0	.214	.214	.286
Tommie Agee	OF12	R	21	13	12	0	2	0	0	0	0	0	3	0	.167	.167	.167
Paul Dicken		R	20	11	11	0	0	0	0	0	0	0	5	0	.000	.000	.000
Wally Post	OF2	R	34	5	8	1	0	0	0	0	0	3	4	0	.000	.273	.000
Duke Sims	C1	L	23	2	6	0	0	0	0	0	0	0	2	0	.000	.000	.000
Vern Fuller		R	20	2	1	0	0	0	0	0	0	0	0	0	.000	.000	.000

Pitcher	T	Age	G	GS	CG	ShO	IP	H	HR	BB	SO	W-L	Sv	ERA
Jack Kralick	L	29	30	29	8	3	190.2	196	17	51	119	12-7	0	3.21
Sam McDowell	L	21	31	24	6	2	173.1	148	8	100	177	11-6	1	2.70
Dick Donovan	R	36	30	23	5	0	158.1	181	19	29	83	7-9	1	4.55
Pedro Ramos†	R	29	36	19	3	1	133.0	144	18	26	98	7-10	0	5.14
Luis Tiant	R	23	19	16	9	3	127.0	94	13	47	105	10-4	1	2.83
Tommy John	L	21	25	14	2	1	94.1	97	10	35	65	2-9	0	3.91
Lee Stange†	R	27	23	14	0	0	91.2	98	14	31	78	4-8	0	4.12
Mudcat Grant†	R	28	13	9	1	0	62.0	82	11	25	43	3-4	0	5.95
Don McMahon	R	34	70	0	0	0	101.0	67	7	52	92	6-4	16	2.41
Gary Bell	R	27	56	2	0	0	106.0	106	15	53	89	8-6	4	4.33
Ted Abernathy	R	31	53	0	0	0	72.2	66	5	46	57	2-6	11	4.33
Sonny Siebert	R	27	41	14	3	1	156.0	142	15	57	144	7-9	3	3.23
Tom Kelley	R	20	6	0	0	0	9.2	9	1	9	7	0-0	0	5.59
Jerry Walker	R	25	6	0	0	0	9.2	9	1	4	5	0-1	0	4.66
Gordon Seyfried	R	26	2	0	0	0	2.1	4	0	0	0	0-0	0	0.00

1964 Minnesota Twins 6th AL 79-83 .488 20.0 GB

Sam Mele

Player	Gm by Position	B	Age	G	AB	R	H	2B	3B	HR	RBI	BB	SO	SB	Avg	OBP	Slg
Earl Battey	C125	R	29	131	405	33	110	17	1	12	52	51	49	1	.272	.348	.407
Bob Allison	1B93,OF61	R	29	149	492	90	141	27	4	32	86	92	99	10	.287	.404	.553
Bernie Allen	2B71	L	25	74	243	28	52	8	1	6	20	33	30	1	.214	.309	.329
Rich Rollins	3B146	R	26	148	596	87	161	25	10	12	68	53	80	2	.270	.334	.406
Zoilo Versalles	SS160	R	24	160	659	94	171	33	10	20	64	42	88	14	.259	.311	.431
Tony Oliva	OF159	L	23	161	672	109	217	43	9	32	94	34	68	12	.323	.359	.557
Harmon Killebrew	OF157	R	28	158	577	95	156	11	1	49	111	93	135	0	.270	.377	.548
Jimmie Hall	OF137	L	26	149	510	61	144	20	3	25	75	44	112	5	.282	.338	.480
Don Mincher	1B76	L	26	120	287	45	68	12	4	23	56	27	51	0	.237	.300	.547
Jerry Kindall†	2B51,SS7,1B1	R	29	62	128	8	19	2	0	1	6	7	44	0	.148	.199	.188
Jerry Zimmerman	C63	R	29	63	120	6	24	3	0	0	12	10	15	0	.200	.278	.225
Johnny Goryl	2B28,3B13	R	30	58	114	9	16	0	2	0	1	10	25	1	.140	.216	.175
Frank Kostro	3B12,2B7,OF2*	R	26	59	103	10	28	5	0	3	12	4	21	0	.272	.303	.408
Jim Snyder	2B25	R	31	26	71	3	11	2	0	1	9	4	11	0	.155	.208	.225
Vic Power†	1B12,2B1	R	36	19	45	6	10	2	0	0	1	1	3	0	.222	.239	.267
Ron Henry	C13	R	27	22	41	4	5	1	1	2	5	2	17	0	.122	.163	.341
Jay Ward	2B9,OF3	R	25	12	31	4	7	2	0	0	2	6	13	0	.226	.351	.290
Bill Bethea	2B7,SS3	R	22	10	30	4	5	1	0	0	2	4	4	0	.167	.265	.200
Joe McCabe	C12	R	25	14	19	1	3	0	0	0	2	0	8	0	.158	.150	.158
Lenny Green†	OF7	L	31	26	15	3	0	0	0	0	0	4	6	0	.000	.211	.000
Rich Reese	1B1	L	22	10	7	0	0	0	0	0	0	0	1	0	.000	.000	.000
Clyde Bloomfield	2B3,SS2	R	28	7	7	1	1	0	0	0	0	0	0	0	.143	.143	.143
Joe Nossek	OF2	R	23	7	1	1	0	0	0	0	0	0	0	0	.000	.000	.000
George Banks†		R	25	1	1	0	0	0	0	0	0	0	1	0	.000	.000	.000

F. Kostro, 1 G at 1B

Pitcher	T	Age	G	GS	CG	ShO	IP	H	HR	BB	SO	W-L	Sv	ERA
Camilo Pascual	R	30	36	36	14	1	267.1	245	30	98	213	15-12	0	3.30
Jim Kaat	L	25	36	34	13	0	243.0	231	23	60	171	17-11	1	3.22
Dick Stigman	L	28	32	29	5	1	190.0	160	31	70	159	6-15	0	4.03
Mudcat Grant†	R	28	26	23	10	1	166.0	162	21	36	75	11-9	1	2.82
Lee Stange†	R	27	14	11	2	0	79.2	78	13	19	54	3-6	0	4.74
Dave Boswell	R	19	4	4	0	0	23.1	21	4	12	25	2-0	0	4.24
Bill Pleis	L	26	47	0	0	0	50.2	43	6	31	42	4-1	4	3.91
Jim Perry	R	28	42	1	0	0	65.1	61	7	23	55	6-3	2	3.44
Gerry Arrigo	L	23	41	12	2	1	105.1	97	11	45	96	7-4	1	3.84
Al Worthington†	R	35	41	0	0	0	72.1	47	4	28	59	5-6	14	1.37
Johnny Klippstein†	R	36	33	0	0	0	45.2	44	4	20	39	0-4	2	1.97
Jim Roland	L	21	30	13	1	0	94.1	76	12	55	63	2-6	3	4.10
Bill Dailey	R	29	14	0	0	0	15.1	23	3	17	6	1-2	0	8.22
Garland Shifflett	R	29	10	0	0	0	17.2	22	1	7	8	0-2	1	4.58
Dwight Siebler	R	26	9	0	0	0	11.0	10	1	6	10	0-0	0	4.91
Bill Fischer	R	33	9	0	0	0	7.1	16	2	5	2	0-1	0	7.36
Jerry Fosnow	L	23	7	0	0	0	10.2	13	3	8	9	0-1	0	10.97
Bill Whitby	R	20	4	0	0	0	6.1	8	3	1	2	0-0	0	8.53
Gary Dotter	L	21	3	0	0	0	4.1	3	1	3	6	0-0	0	2.08
Chuck Nieson	R	21	2	0	0	0	2.0	1	1	1	5	0-0	0	4.50

1964 Boston Red Sox 8th AL 72-90 .444 27.0 GB

Johnny Pesky (70-90)/Billy Herman (2-0)

Player	Gm by Position	B	Age	G	AB	R	H	2B	3B	HR	RBI	BB	SO	SB	Avg	OBP	Slg
Bob Tillman	C131	R	27	131	425	43	118	18	1	17	61	49	74	0	.278	.352	.445
Dick Stuart	1B155	R	31	156	603	73	168	27	1	33	114	37	130	0	.279	.320	.491
Dalton Jones	2B85,3B1,SS1	L	20	118	374	37	86	16	4	6	39	22	38	6	.230	.274	.342
Frank Malzone	3B143	R	34	148	537	62	142	19	0	13	56	37	43	0	.264	.312	.372
Eddie Bressoud	SS158	R	32	158	566	86	166	41	3	15	55	72	99	1	.293	.372	.456
Carl Yastrzemski	OF148,3B2	L	24	151	567	77	164	29	9	15	67	75	90	6	.289	.374	.451
Lee Thomas†	OF107,1B1	L	28	107	401	44	103	19	2	13	42	34	29	2	.257	.319	.411
Tony Conigliaro	OF106	R	19	111	404	69	117	21	2	24	52	35	78	2	.290	.354	.530
Felix Mantilla	OF48,2B45,3B7*	R	29	133	425	69	123	20	1	30	64	41	46	0	.289	.357	.553
Chuck Schilling	2B42	R	26	47	163	18	32	6	0	0	7	15	22	0	.196	.263	.233
Russ Nixon	C45	L	29	81	163	10	38	7	0	1	20	14	29	0	.233	.297	.294
Tony Horton	OF24,1B8	R	19	36	126	9	28	5	0	1	8	3	20	0	.222	.238	.286
Lu Clinton†	OF35	R	26	37	120	15	31	4	3	3	6	9	33	1	.258	.310	.417
Roman Mejias	OF37	R	33	62	101	14	24	3	1	2	4	7	16	0	.238	.294	.347
Dick Williams	1B21,3B13,OF5	R	35	61	69	10	11	2	0	5	11	7	10	0	.159	.247	.406
Al Smith†	3B10,OF8	R	36	29	51	10	11	4	0	2	7	13	10	0	.216	.385	.412
Gary Geiger	OF4	L	27	5	13	3	5	0	1	0	1	2	2	0	.385	.467	.538
Bobby Guindon	1B1,OF1	L	20	5	8	0	1	1	0	0	0	1	4	0	.125	.222	.250
Mike Ryan	C1	R	22	1	3	0	1	0	0	0	2	1	0	0	.333	.500	.333

F. Mantilla, 6 G at SS

Pitcher	T	Age	G	GS	CG	ShO	IP	H	HR	BB	SO	W-L	Sv	ERA
Bill Monbouquette	R	27	36	35	7	5	234.0	258	34	40	120	13-14	1	4.04
Earl Wilson	R	29	33	31	5	0	202.1	213	37	73	166	11-12	0	4.49
Dave Morehead	R	21	32	30	3	1	166.2	156	14	112	139	8-15	0	4.97
Jack Lamabe	R	27	39	25	3	0	177.1	235	25	57	109	9-13	1	5.89
Ed Connolly	L	24	27	15	1	1	80.2	80	3	64	73	4-11	0	4.91
Dick Radatz	R	27	79	0	0	0	157.0	103	13	58	181	16-9	29	2.29
Bob Heffner	R	25	55	10	1	1	158.2	152	20	44	112	7-9	6	4.08
Bill Spanswick	L	25	29	7	0	0	65.1	75	9	44	55	2-3	0	6.89
Pete Charton	R	21	25	5	0	0	65.0	67	12	24	37	0-2	0	5.26
Arnold Earley	L	31	25	3	1	0	50.1	51	3	18	45	1-1	1	2.68
Jay Ritchie	R	27	21	0	0	0	46.0	43	4	14	35	1-1	0	2.74
Dave Gray	R	21	9	1	0	0	13.0	18	3	20	17	0-0	0	9.00
Wilbur Wood†	L	22	4	0	0	0	5.2	13	1	3	5	0-0	0	17.47

1964 Washington Senators 9th AL 62-100 .383 37.0 GB

Gil Hodges

Player	Gm by Position	B	Age	G	AB	R	H	2B	3B	HR	RBI	BB	SO	SB	Avg	OBP	Slg
Mike Brumley	C132	L	25	136	426	36	104	19	2	2	35	40	54	1	.244	.309	.312
Bill Skowron†	1B66	R	33	73	262	28	71	10	0	13	41	11	56	0	.271	.306	.458
Don Blasingame	2B135	L	32	143	506	56	135	17	2	1	34	40	44	8	.267	.320	.314
John Kennedy	3B106,SS49,2B2	R	23	148	482	55	111	16	4	7	35	29	119	3	.230	.280	.324
Ed Brinkman	SS125	R	22	132	447	54	100	20	3	8	34	26	99	2	.224	.271	.336
Don Lock	OF149	R	27	152	512	73	127	17	4	28	80	79	137	4	.248	.346	.461
Chuck Hinton	OF131,3B2	R	30	138	514	71	141	25	7	11	53	57	77	17	.274	.346	.414
Jim King	OF121	L	31	134	415	46	100	15	1	18	56	55	65	3	.241	.335	.412
Don Zimmer	3B87,OF4,C2*	R	33	121	341	38	84	16	2	12	38	27	94	1	.246	.302	.411
Dick Phillips	1B61,3B4	L	32	109	234	17	54	6	1	2	23	27	22	1	.231	.307	.291
Fred Valentine	OF57	S	29	102	212	20	48	5	0	4	20	21	44	4	.226	.304	.307
Chuck Cottier	2B53,3B3,SS2	R	28	73	137	16	23	6	2	3	10	19	33	2	.168	.268	.307
Joe Cunningham†	1B41	L	32	49	126	15	27	4	0	0	7	23	13	0	.214	.344	.246
Don Leppert	C43	L	32	50	122	6	19	3	0	3	12	11	32	0	.156	.224	.254
Willie Kirkland†	OF27	L	30	32	102	8	22	6	0	5	13	6	30	0	.216	.259	.422
Ken Hunt	OF37	R	29	51	96	9	13	4	0	1	4	14	35	0	.135	.243	.208
Roy Sievers†	1B15	R	37	33	58	5	10	1	0	4	11	9	14	0	.172	.284	.397
Ken Retzer	C13	L	30	17	32	1	3	0	0	0	1	5	4	0	.094	.237	.094

D. Zimmer, 1 G at 2B

Pitcher	T	Age	G	GS	CG	ShO	IP	H	HR	BB	SO	W-L	Sv	ERA
Claude Osteen	L	24	37	36	13	0	257.0	256	20	64	133	15-13	0	3.33
Buster Narum	R	23	38	32	7	2	199.0	195	31	73	121	9-15	0	4.30
Bennie Daniels	R	32	33	24	3	2	163.0	147	20	64	73	8-10	0	3.70
Dave Stenhouse	R	30	26	14	1	0	88.0	80	12	39	44	2-7	1	4.81
Frank Kreutzer†	L	25	13	9	0	0	45.1	48	6	23	27	2-6	0	4.76
Don Loun	L	23	2	2	1	1	13.0	13	0	3	3	1-1	0	2.08
Pete Craig	R	23	2	1	0	0	1.2	8	1	4	0	0-0	0	48.60
Ron Kline	R	32	61	0	0	0	81.1	81	4	21	40	10-7	14	2.32
Steve Ridzik	R	35	49	3	0	0	112.0	96	10	31	60	5-5	2	2.89
Jim Hannan	R	24	49	7	0	0	106.0	108	13	45	67	4-7	3	4.16
Alan Koch†	R	26	32	14	1	0	114.0	110	18	43	67	3-10	0	4.89
Jim Duckworth	R	25	30	2	0	0	56.0	52	9	25	56	1-6	3	4.34
Don Rudolph	L	32	28	8	0	0	70.1	81	10	12	32	1-3	0	4.09
Marshall Bridges	L	33	17	0	0	0	30.0	37	3	17	16	0-3	2	5.70
Tom Cheney	R	29	15	6	1	0	48.2	45	10	13	25	1-3	1	3.70
Carl Bouldin	R	24	9	3	0	0	25.0	30	2	11	12	0-3	0	5.40
Howie Koplitz	R	26	6	1	0	0	17.0	20	3	13	9	0-0	0	4.76
Jim Bronstad	R	28	4	0	0	0	7.0	10	0	2	9	0-1	0	5.14
Ed Roebuck†	R	32	2	0	0	0	1.0	0	0	2	0	0-0	0	9.00

1964 Kansas City Athletics 10th AL 57-105 .352 42.0 GB

Ed Lopat (17-35)/Mel McGaha (40-70)

Player	Gm by Position	B	Age	G	AB	R	H	2B	3B	HR	RBI	BB	SO	SB	Avg	OBP	Slg
Doc Edwards	C79,1B7	R	27	97	294	25	66	10	0	5	28	13	40	0	.224	.265	.310
Jim Gentile	1B128	L	30	136	439	71	110	10	0	28	71	84	122	0	.251	.372	.465
Dick Green	2B120	R	23	130	435	48	115	14	5	11	37	27	87	3	.264	.311	.395
Ed Charles	3B147	R	31	150	557	69	134	25	2	16	63	64	92	12	.241	.321	.379
Wayne Causey	SS131,2B17,3B9	L	27	157	604	82	170	31	4	8	49	88	65	0	.281	.377	.386
Rocky Colavito	OF159	R	30	160	588	89	161	31	2	34	102	83	56	3	.274	.366	.507
Nelson Mathews	OF154	R	22	157	573	58	137	27	5	14	60	43	143	2	.239	.293	.377
Jose Tartabull	OF59	L	25	104	100	9	20	2	0	0	3	5	6	3	.200	.238	.220
Bert Campaneris	SS38,OF27,3B6	R	22	67	269	27	69	14	3	4	22	15	41	10	.257	.306	.375
Billy Bryan	C65	L	25	93	220	19	53	9	2	13	36	16	69	0	.241	.290	.477
Manny Jimenez	OF49	L	25	95	204	19	46	7	0	12	38	15	24	0	.225	.293	.436
George Alusik	OF44,1B12	R	29	102	204	18	49	10	1	3	19	30	36	0	.240	.342	.343
Ken Harrelson	OF24,1B15	R	22	49	139	15	27	5	0	7	12	13	34	0	.194	.263	.381
Charlie Lau†	C35	L	31	43	118	11	32	7	1	2	9	10	18	0	.271	.326	.398
Tommie Reynolds	OF25,3B3	S	22	31	94	11	19	1	0	2	9	10	22	0	.202	.292	.277
George Williams	2B20,3B2,SS2*	R	24	37	91	10	19	6	0	0	2	6	12	0	.209	.265	.275
Rick Joseph	1B12,3B3	R	24	17	54	3	12	2	0	0	1	3	11	0	.222	.263	.259
Dave Duncan	C22	R	18	25	53	2	9	0	1	1	5	2	20	0	.170	.200	.264
Charlie Shoemaker	2B14	L	24	16	52	6	11	2	2	0	3	0	9	0	.212	.212	.327
Larry Stahl	OF10	L	23	15	46	7	12	1	0	3	6	1	10	0	.261	.277	.478
John Wojcik	OF6	L	22	6	22	1	3	0	0	0	0	2	8	0	.136	.208	.136
Gino Cimoli†	OF4	R	34	4	9	1	0	0	0	0	0	0	1	0	.000	.000	.000

G. Williams, 2 G at OF

Pitcher	T	Age	G	GS	CG	ShO	IP	H	HR	BB	SO	W-L	Sv	ERA
Diego Segui	R	26	40	35	5	2	217.0	219	30	94	155	8-17	0	4.56
Orlando Pena	R	30	40	32	5	0	219.1	231	40	73	184	12-14	0	4.43
John O'Donoghue	L	24	39	32	2	1	173.2	202	24	65	79	10-14	0	4.92
Bob Meyer†	L	24	9	7	2	0	42.0	37	2	33	30	1-4	0	3.86
Aurelio Monteagudo	R	20	11	6	0	0	31.1	40	11	10	14	0-4	0	8.90
Blue Moon Odom	R	19	5	5	1	1	17.0	29	5	11	10	1-2	0	10.06
Lew Krausse	R	21	5	4	0	0	14.2	22	1	9	9	0-2	0	7.36
John Wyatt	R	29	81	0	0	0	128.0	111	23	52	74	9-8	20	3.59
Moe Drabowsky	R	28	53	21	1	0	168.1	176	24	72	119	5-13	1	5.29
Ted Bowsfield	L	29	50	9	2	1	118.2	135	12	31	45	4-7	0	4.10
Wes Stock†	R	30	50	0	0	0	93.0	69	10	34	101	6-3	5	1.94
Jose Santiago	R	23	34	8	0	0	83.2	84	9	35	64	0-6	0	4.73
Ken Sanders	R	22	21	0	0	0	27.0	23	2	17	18	0-2	1	3.67
Joe Grzenda	L	27	20	0	0	0	25.0	34	2	13	17	0-2	0	5.40
Dan Pfister	R	27	19	3	0	0	41.1	50	10	29	21	1-5	0	6.53
Vern Handrahan	R	25	18	1	0	0	35.2	33	9	25	18	0-1	0	6.06
Jack Aker	R	23	9	0	0	0	16.1	17	6	10	7	0-1	0	8.82
Tom Sturdivant†	R	34	3	0	0	0	3.2	4	0	1	1	0-0	0	9.82

»1964 St. Louis Cardinals 1st NL 93-69 .574 —

Johnny Keane

Player	Gm by Position	B	Age	G	AB	R	H	2B	3B	HR	RBI	BB	SO	SB	Avg	OBP	Slg
Tim McCarver	C137	L	22	143	465	53	134	19	3	9	52	40	44	2	.288	.343	.400
Bill White	1B160	L	30	160	631	92	191	37	4	21	102	52	103	7	.303	.355	.474
Julian Javier	2B154	R	27	155	535	66	129	19	5	12	65	30	82	9	.241	.282	.363
Ken Boyer	3B162	R	33	162	628	100	185	30	10	24	119	70	85	3	.295	.365	.489
Dick Groat	SS160	R	33	161	636	70	186	35	6	1	70	44	42	2	.292	.335	.371
Curt Flood	OF162	R	26	162	679	97	211	25	3	5	46	43	53	8	.311	.356	.378
Lou Brock†	OF102	L	25	103	419	81	146	21	9	12	44	27	87	33	.348	.387	.527
Mike Shannon	OF88	R	24	88	253	30	66	8	2	9	43	19	54	4	.261	.310	.415
Charlie James	OF60	R	26	88	233	24	52	9	1	5	17	11	58	0	.223	.261	.335
Carl Warwick	OF49	R	27	88	158	14	41	7	1	3	15	11	30	2	.259	.306	.373
Bob Skinner†	OF31	L	32	55	118	10	32	5	0	1	16	11	20	0	.271	.333	.339
Bob Uecker	C40	R	29	40	106	8	21	1	0	1	6	17	24	0	.198	.315	.236
Johnny Lewis	OF36	L	24	40	94	10	22	2	2	2	7	13	23	0	.234	.324	.362
Doug Clemens†	OF22	L	25	33	78	8	16	4	3	1	9	6	16	0	.205	.271	.372
Phil Gagliano	2B12,OF2,1B1*	R	22	40	58	5	15	4	0	1	9	3	10	0	.259	.290	.379
Jeoff Long†	OF4,1B3	R	22	28	43	5	10	1	0	1	4	6	18	0	.233	.340	.326
Jerry Buchek	SS20,2B9,3B1	R	22	35	30	7	6	0	2	0	1	3	11	0	.200	.273	.333
Dal Maxvill	2B15,SS13,3B1*	R	25	37	26	4	6	0	0	0	4	0	7	1	.231	.231	.231
Ed Spiezio		R	22	12	12	0	4	0	0	0	0	0	1	0	.333	.333	.333
Joe Morgan		L	33	3	3	0	0	0	0	0	0	0	2	0	.000	.000	.000

P. Gagliano, 1 G at 3B; D. Maxvill, 1 G at OF

Pitcher	T	Age	G	GS	CG	ShO	IP	H	HR	BB	SO	W-L	Sv	ERA
Bob Gibson	R	28	40	36	17	2	287.1	250	25	86	245	19-12	1	3.01
Curt Simmons	L	35	34	34	12	3	244.0	233	24	49	104	18-9	0	3.43
Ray Sadecki	L	23	37	32	9	2	220.0	232	16	60	119	20-11	1	3.68
Ernie Broglio†	R	28	11	11	3	1	69.1	65	7	26	36	3-5	0	3.50
Ray Washburn	R	26	15	10	0	0	60.0	60	7	17	28	3-4	2	4.05
Ron Taylor	R	26	63	2	0	0	101.1	109	15	33	69	8-4	7	4.62
Roger Craig	R	34	39	19	3	0	166.0	180	16	35	84	7-9	5	3.25
Mike Cuellar	L	27	32	7	1	0	72.0	80	8	33	56	5-5	4	4.50
Barney Schultz	R	37	30	0	0	0	49.1	35	5	11	29	1-3	14	1.64
Bob Humphreys	R	28	28	0	0	0	42.2	32	3	15	36	2-0	2	2.53
Gordie Richardson	L	25	19	6	1	0	47.0	40	2	15	28	4-2	1	2.30
Bobby Shantz†	L	38	16	0	0	0	17.1	14	2	7	12	1-3	0	3.12
Glen Hobbie†	R	28	13	5	1	0	44.1	41	4	15	18	1-2	1	4.26
Lew Burdette†	R	37	8	0	0	0	10.0	10	1	3	3	1-0	0	1.80
Harry Fanok	R	24	4	0	0	0	7.2	5	0	3	10	0-0	0	5.87
Dave Bakenhaster	R	19	2	0	0	0	3.0	9	1	1	0	0-0	0	6.00
Jack Spring	L	31	2	0	0	0	3.0	8	1	1	0	0-0	0	3.00
Dave Dowling	L	21	1	0	0	0	1.0	2	0	0	0	0-0	0	0.00

1964 Cincinnati Reds 2nd NL 92-70 .568 1.0 GB

Fred Hutchinson (54-45)/Dick Sisler (3-3)/Fred Hutchinson (6-4)/Dick Sisler (29-18)

Player	Gm by Position	B	Age	G	AB	R	H	2B	3B	HR	RBI	BB	SO	SB	Avg	OBP	Slg
Johnny Edwards	C120	L	26	126	423	47	119	23	1	7	55	34	65	1	.281	.331	.390
Deron Johnson	1B131,OF10,3B1	R	25	140	477	63	130	24	4	21	79	37	98	4	.273	.326	.472
Pete Rose	2B128	S	23	136	516	64	139	13	2	4	34	36	51	4	.269	.319	.326
Steve Boros	3B114	R	27	117	370	31	95	12	3	2	31	47	43	4	.257	.342	.322
Leo Cardenas	SS163	R	25	163	597	61	150	32	2	9	69	41	110	4	.251	.299	.357
Vada Pinson	OF156	L	25	156	625	99	166	23	11	23	84	42	99	8	.266	.316	.448
Frank Robinson	OF156	R	28	156	568	103	174	38	6	29	96	79	67	23	.306	.396	.548
Tommy Harper	OF92,3B2	R	23	102	317	42	77	5	2	4	22	39	56	24	.243	.326	.309
Chico Ruiz	3B49,2B30	S	25	77	311	33	76	13	2	2	16	7	41	11	.244	.269	.318
Marty Keough	OF81,1B4	L	29	109	276	29	71	9	1	9	28	22	58	1	.257	.314	.395
Gordy Coleman	1B49	L	29	89	198	18	48	6	2	5	27	13	30	2	.242	.291	.369
Mel Queen	OF20	L	22	48	95	7	19	2	0	2	12	4	19	0	.200	.232	.284
Bobby Klaus†	2B18,3B11,SS3	R	26	40	93	10	17	5	1	2	6	4	13	1	.183	.212	.323
Don Pavletich	C27,1B1	R	25	34	91	12	22	4	0	5	11	10	17	0	.242	.314	.451
Hal Smith	C20	R	33	32	66	6	8	1	0	0	3	12	20	1	.121	.256	.136
Bob Skinner†	OF12	L	32	25	59	6	13	3	0	3	5	4	12	0	.220	.270	.424
Jimmie Coker	C11	R	28	11	32	3	10	2	0	1	4	3	5	0	.313	.371	.469
Tony Perez	1B6	R	22	12	25	1	2	1	0	0	1	3	9	0	.080	.179	.120
Johnny Temple		R	36	6	3	0	0	0	0	0	0	2	1	0	.000	.400	.000
Tommy Helms		R	23	2	1	0	0	0	0	0	0	0	1	0	.000	.000	.000

Pitcher	T	Age	G	GS	CG	ShO	IP	H	HR	BB	SO	W-L	Sv	ERA
Jim Maloney	R	24	31	31	11	2	216.0	175	16	83	214	15-10	0	2.71
Jim O'Toole	L	27	30	30	9	3	220.0	194	8	51	145	17-7	0	2.66
Bob Purkey	R	34	34	25	9	2	195.2	181	16	49	78	11-9	1	3.04
John Tsitouris	R	28	37	24	6	1	175.1	178	20	75	146	9-13	2	3.80
Joey Jay	R	28	34	23	10	0	183.0	167	17	36	134	11-11	2	3.39
Joe Nuxhall	L	35	32	22	7	4	154.2	146	19	51	111	9-8	2	4.07
Sammy Ellis	R	23	52	5	2	0	122.1	101	9	28	125	10-3	14	2.57
Billy McCool	L	19	40	3	0	0	89.1	66	3	29	87	6-5	7	2.42
Bill Henry	L	36	37	0	0	0	52.0	31	2	12	28	2-2	6	0.87
Ryne Duren†	R	35	26	0	0	0	43.2	41	1	15	39	0-2	1	2.89
Al Worthington†	R	35	6	0	0	0	7.0	14	0	2	6	1-0	0	10.29
Jim Dickson	R	26	4	0	0	0	5.0	8	0	5	6	1-0	0	7.20
Chet Nichols	L	33	3	0	0	0	3.0	4	1	0	3	0-0	0	6.00

1964 Philadelphia Phillies 2nd NL 92-70 .568 1.0 GB

Gene Mauch

Player	Gm by Position	B	Age	G	AB	R	H	2B	3B	HR	RBI	BB	SO	SB	Avg	OBP	Slg
Clay Dalrymple	C124	L	27	127	382	36	91	16	3	6	46	39	40	0	.238	.303	.343
John Herrnstein	OF69,1B68	L	26	125	303	38	71	12	4	6	25	22	67	1	.234	.288	.360
Tony Taylor	2B150	R	28	154	570	62	143	13	6	4	46	46	74	13	.251	.320	.316
Dick Allen	3B162	R	22	162	632	125	201	38	13	29	91	67	138	3	.318	.382	.557
Bobby Wine	SS108,3B16	R	25	126	283	28	60	8	3	4	34	25	37	1	.212	.274	.304
Johnny Callison	OF162	L	25	162	654	101	179	30	10	31	104	36	95	6	.274	.316	.492
Tony Gonzalez	OF119	L	27	131	421	55	117	25	3	4	40	44	74	0	.278	.352	.380
Wes Covington	OF108	L	32	129	339	37	95	18	0	13	58	38	50	0	.280	.355	.448
Cookie Rojas	OF70,2B20,SS18*	R	25	109	340	58	99	19	5	2	31	22	17	1	.291	.334	.394
Ruben Amaro	SS79,1B58,2B3*	R	28	129	299	31	79	11	0	4	34	16	37	1	.264	.307	.341
Gus Triandos	C64,1B1	R	33	73	188	17	47	9	0	8	33	26	41	0	.250	.339	.426
Danny Cater	OF39,1B7,3B1	R	24	60	152	13	45	9	1	1	13	7	15	1	.296	.325	.388
Frank Thomas†	1B36	R	35	39	143	20	42	11	0	7	26	5	12	0	.294	.311	.517
Roy Sievers†	1B33	R	37	49	120	7	22	3	1	4	16	13	20	0	.183	.265	.325
Alex Johnson	OF35	R	21	43	109	18	33	7	1	4	18	6	26	1	.303	.345	.495
John Briggs	OF19,1B1	L	20	61	66	16	17	2	0	1	6	9	12	1	.258	.347	.333
Vic Power†	1B17	R	36	18	48	1	10	4	0	0	3	2	3	0	.208	.240	.292
Costen Shockley	1B9	L	22	11	35	4	8	0	0	1	2	2	8	0	.229	.263	.314
Adolfo Phillips	OF4	R	22	13	13	4	3	0	0	0	0	3	3	0	.231	.375	.231
Don Hoak		R	36	6	4	0	0	0	0	0	0	0	2	0	.000	.000	.000
Pat Corrales		R	23	2	1	1	0	0	0	0	0	1	0	0	.000	.500	.000

C. Rojas, 1 G at C, 1 G at 3B; R. Amaro, 3 G at 3B, 1 G at OF

Pitcher	T	Age	G	GS	CG	ShO	IP	H	HR	BB	SO	W-L	Sv	ERA
Jim Bunning	R	32	41	39	13	5	284.1	248	23	46	219	19-8	2	2.63
Dennis Bennett	L	24	41	32	7	2	208.0	222	23	58	125	12-14	1	3.68
Chris Short	L	26	42	31	12	4	220.2	174	10	51	181	17-9	2	2.20
Art Mahaffey	R	26	34	29	2	2	157.1	161	17	82	80	12-9	0	4.52
Ray Culp	R	22	30	19	3	1	135.0	139	15	56	96	8-7	0	4.13
Cal McLish	R	38	2	1	0	0	5.1	6	0	1	6	0-1	0	3.38
Jack Baldschun	R	27	71	0	0	0	118.1	111	8	40	96	6-9	21	3.12
Ed Roebuck†	R	32	60	0	0	0	77.1	55	7	25	42	5-3	12	2.21
Rick Wise	R	18	25	8	0	0	69.0	78	7	25	39	5-3	0	4.04
Dallas Green	R	29	25	0	0	0	42.0	63	4	14	21	2-1	0	5.79
John Boozer	R	25	22	3	0	0	60.1	64	6	18	51	3-4	2	5.07
Bobby Shantz†	L	38	14	0	0	0	32.0	23	1	6	18	1-1	0	2.25
Johnny Klippstein†	R	36	11	0	0	0	22.1	22	6	8	13	2-1	1	4.03
Bobby Locke	R	30	8	0	0	0	19.1	21	2	6	11	0-0	0	2.79
Morrie Steevens	L	23	4	0	0	0	2.2	5	0	1	3	0-0	0	3.38
Gary Kroll†	R	22	2	0	0	0	3.0	3	0	2	2	0-0	0	3.00
Ryne Duren†	R	35	2	0	0	0	3.0	5	0	1	5	0-0	0	6.00
Dave Bennett	R	18	1	0	0	0	1.0	2	0	0	1	0-0	0	9.00

1964 San Francisco Giants 4th NL 90-72 .556 3.0 GB

Alvin Dark

Player	Gm by Position	B	Age	G	AB	R	H	2B	3B	HR	RBI	BB	SO	SB	Avg	OBP	Slg
Tom Haller	C113,OF3	L	27	117	388	43	98	14	3	16	48	55	51	4	.253	.345	.428
Orlando Cepeda	1B139,OF1	R	26	142	529	75	161	27	2	31	97	43	83	9	.304	.361	.539
Hal Lanier	2B98,SS3	R	21	98	383	40	105	16	3	2	28	5	44	2	.274	.283	.347
Jim Ray Hart	3B149,OF6	R	22	153	566	71	162	15	6	31	81	47	94	5	.286	.342	.498
Jose Pagan	SS132,OF8	R	29	134	367	33	82	10	1	1	28	35	66	5	.223	.289	.264
Willie Mays	OF155,1B1,3B1*	R	33	157	578	121	171	21	9	47	111	82	72	19	.296	.383	.607
Jesus Alou	OF108	R	22	115	376	42	103	11	0	3	28	13	35	6	.274	.305	.327
Harvey Kuenn	OF88,1B11,3B2	R	33	111	351	42	92	16	2	4	22	35	32	0	.262	.329	.353
Willie McCovey	OF83,1B26	L	26	130	364	55	80	14	1	18	54	61	73	2	.220	.336	.412
Jim Davenport	SS64,3B41,2B30	R	30	116	297	24	70	10	6	2	26	29	46	2	.236	.299	.330
Matty Alou	OF80	L	25	110	250	28	66	4	2	1	14	11	25	5	.264	.302	.308
Chuck Hiller	2B60,3B1	L	29	80	205	21	37	8	1	1	17	17	23	1	.180	.243	.244
Del Crandall	C65	R	34	69	195	12	45	8	1	3	11	22	21	0	.231	.309	.328
Duke Snider	OF43	L	37	91	167	16	35	7	0	4	17	22	40	0	.210	.302	.323
Cap Peterson	OF10,1B2,2B1*	R	21	66	74	8	15	1	1	1	8	3	20	0	.203	.234	.284
Gil Garrido	SS14	R	23	14	25	1	2	0	0	0	1	2	7	1	.080	.148	.080
Jose Cardenal	OF16	R	20	20	15	3	0	0	0	0	0	2	3	2	.000	.118	.000
Randy Hundley	C2	R	22	2	1	1	0	0	0	0	0	0	1	0	.000	.000	.000

W. Mays, 1 G at SS; C. Peterson, 1 G at 3B

Pitcher	T	Age	G	GS	CG	ShO	IP	H	HR	BB	SO	W-L	Sv	ERA
Juan Marichal	R	26	33	33	22	4	269.0	241	18	52	206	21-8	0	2.48
Bob Hendley	L	25	30	29	4	1	163.1	161	18	59	104	10-11	0	3.64
Bobby Bolin	R	25	38	23	5	3	174.2	143	16	77	146	6-9	1	3.25
Ron Herbel	R	26	40	22	7	2	161.0	162	7	61	98	9-9	1	3.07
Jack Sanford	R	35	18	17	3	1	106.1	91	7	37	64	5-7	1	3.30
Dick Estelle	L	22	6	6	0	0	41.2	39	3	23	23	1-2	0	3.02
Bob Shaw	R	31	61	1	0	0	93.1	105	5	31	57	7-6	11	3.76
Gaylord Perry	R	25	44	19	5	2	206.1	179	16	43	155	12-11	5	2.75
Billy O'Dell	L	31	36	8	1	0	85.0	82	10	35	54	8-7	2	5.40
Jim Duffalo	R	28	35	3	1	0	74.0	57	9	31	55	5-1	3	2.92
Billy Pierce	L	37	34	1	0	0	49.0	40	6	10	29	3-0	4	2.20
John Pregenzer	R	28	13	0	0	0	18.1	21	1	11	8	2-0	0	4.91
Ken MacKenzie	L	30	10	0	0	0	9.0	9	1	3	3	0-0	1	5.00
Masanori Murakami	L	20	9	0	0	0	15.0	8	1	1	15	1-0	1	1.80
Don Larsen†	R	34	6	0	0	0	10.1	10	0	6	6	0-1	0	4.35

1964 Milwaukee Braves 5th NL 88-74 .543 5.0 GB

Bobby Bragan

Player	Gm by Position	B	Age	G	AB	R	H	2B	3B	HR	RBI	BB	SO	SB	Avg	OBP	Slg
Joe Torre	C96,1B70	R	23	154	601	87	193	36	5	20	109	36	67	2	.321	.365	.498
Gene Oliver	1B76,C1	R	29	93	279	45	77	15	1	13	49	17	41	3	.276	.319	.477
Frank Bolling	2B117	R	32	120	352	35	70	11	1	5	34	21	44	0	.199	.245	.278
Eddie Mathews	3B128,1B7	L	32	141	502	83	117	19	1	23	74	85	100	2	.233	.344	.412
Denis Menke	SS141,2B15,3B6	R	23	151	505	79	143	29	5	20	65	68	77	4	.283	.368	.479
Hank Aaron	OF139,2B11	R	30	145	570	103	187	30	2	24	95	62	46	22	.328	.393	.514
Lee Maye	OF135,3B5	L	29	153	588	96	179	44	5	10	74	34	54	5	.304	.346	.447
Rico Carty	OF121	R	24	133	455	72	150	28	4	22	88	43	78	1	.330	.388	.554
Felipe Alou	OF92,1B18	R	29	121	415	60	105	26	3	9	51	30	41	5	.253	.306	.395
Ed Bailey	C80	L	33	95	271	30	71	10	1	5	34	34	39	2	.262	.343	.362
Mike de la Hoz	2B25,3B25,SS8	R	25	78	189	25	55	7	1	4	12	14	22	1	.291	.346	.402
Ty Cline	OF54,1B6	L	25	101	116	22	35	4	2	1	13	8	22	0	.302	.359	.397
Woody Woodward	2B40,SS18,3B7*	R	21	77	115	18	24	2	1	0	11	6	28	0	.209	.260	.243
Gary Kolb	OF14,3B7,2B6*	L	24	36	64	7	12	1	0	0	2	6	10	3	.188	.257	.203
Sandy Alomar	SS19	S	20	19	53	3	13	1	0	0	6	0	11	1	.245	.245	.264
Len Gabrielson†	1B12,OF2	L	24	24	38	0	7	2	0	0	1	1	8	1	.184	.205	.237
Lou Klimchock	3B4,2B2	L	24	10	21	3	7	2	0	0	2	1	2	0	.333	.364	.429
Merritt Ranew†	C3	L	26	9	17	1	2	0	0	0	0	0	3	0	.118	.118	.118
Roy McMillan†	SS8	R	33	8	13	1	4	0	0	0	2	0	2	0	.308	.308	.308
Ethan Blackaby	OF5	L	23	9	12	0	1	0	0	0	1	1	2	0	.083	.154	.083
Bill Southworth	3B2	R	18	3	7	2	2	0	0	1	2	0	3	0	.286	.444	.714
Gus Bell		L	35	3	3	0	0	0	0	0	0	0	1	0	.000	.000	.000
Phil Roof	C1	R	23	1	2	0	0	0	0	0	0	0	1	0	.000	.000	.000

W. Woodward, 1 G at 1B; G. Kolb, 2 G at C

Pitcher	T	Age	G	GS	CG	ShO	IP	H	HR	BB	SO	W-L	Sv	ERA
Denny Lemaster	L	25	39	35	9	3	221.0	216	27	75	185	17-11	1	4.15
Tony Cloninger	R	23	38	34	15	3	242.2	206	20	82	163	19-14	2	3.56
Hank Fischer	R	24	37	28	9	5	168.1	177	17	39	99	11-10	2	4.01
Warren Spahn	L	43	38	25	4	1	173.2	204	23	52	78	6-13	4	5.29
Arnie Umbach	R	21	1	1	0	0	8.1	11	0	4	7	1-0	0	3.24
Bob Sadowski	R	26	51	18	5	0	166.2	159	18	56	96	9-10	5	4.10
Bobby Tiefenauer	R	34	46	0	0	0	73.0	61	6	15	48	4-6	13	3.21
Billy Hoeft	L	32	42	0	0	0	73.1	76	9	18	47	4-0	4	3.80
Chi Chi Olivo	R	36	38	0	0	0	60.0	55	7	21	45	2-1	5	3.75
Wade Blasingame	L	20	28	13	3	1	116.2	113	15	51	70	9-5	2	4.24
Jack Smith	R	28	22	0	0	0	31.0	28	3	11	19	2-2	0	3.77
Dan Schneider	L	21	13	5	0	0	36.1	38	6	13	14	1-2	0	5.45
Clay Carroll	R	23	11	1	0	0	20.1	15	1	3	17	2-0	1	1.77
Phil Niekro	R	25	10	0	0	0	15.0	15	1	7	8	0-0	0	4.80
Dave Eilers	R	27	6	0	0	0	7.2	11	1	1	1	0-0	0	4.70
Frank Lary†	R	34	5	2	0	0	12.1	15	4	0	4	1-0	0	4.38
Cecil Butler	R	26	2	0	0	0	4.1	7	2	0	2	0-0	0	8.31
Dick Kelley	L	24	2	0	0	0	2.0	2	0	3	2	0-0	0	18.00
John Braun	R	24	1	0	0	0	2.0	2	0	1	1	0-0	0	0.00

1964 Los Angeles Dodgers 6th NL 80-82 .494 13.0 GB

Walter Alston

Player	Gm by Position	B	Age	G	AB	R	H	2B	3B	HR	RBI	BB	SO	SB	Avg	OBP	Slg
John Roseboro	C128	L	31	134	414	42	119	24	1	3	45	44	61	3	.287	.357	.372
Ron Fairly	1B141	L	25	150	454	62	116	19	5	10	74	65	59	4	.256	.349	.385
Nate Oliver	2B98,SS1	R	23	99	321	28	78	9	0	0	21	31	57	7	.243	.309	.271
Jim Gilliam	3B86,2B25,OF2	S	35	116	334	44	76	8	3	2	27	42	21	4	.228	.318	.287
Maury Wills	SS149,3B6	S	31	158	630	81	173	15	5	2	34	41	73	53	.275	.318	.324
Willie Davis	OF155	L	24	157	613	91	180	23	7	12	77	22	59	42	.294	.316	.413
Tommy Davis	OF148	R	25	152	592	70	163	20	5	14	86	29	68	11	.275	.311	.397
Frank Howard	OF122	R	27	134	433	60	98	13	2	24	69	51	113	1	.226	.303	.432
Dick Tracewski	2B56,3B30,SS19	R	29	106	304	31	75	13	4	1	26	31	61	3	.247	.315	.326
Derrell Griffith	3B35,OF29	L	20	78	238	27	69	16	2	4	23	5	21	5	.290	.307	.424
Wes Parker	OF69,1B31	S	24	124	214	29	55	7	1	3	10	14	45	5	.257	.303	.341
Doug Camilli	C46	R	27	50	123	1	22	3	0	0	10	8	19	0	.179	.226	.203
Wally Moon	OF23	L	34	68	118	8	26	2	1	2	9	12	22	1	.220	.292	.305
Johnny Werhas	3B28	R	26	29	83	6	16	2	1	0	8	13	12	0	.193	.296	.241
Ken McMullen	1B13,3B4,OF3	R	22	24	67	3	14	0	0	1	2	3	7	0	.209	.243	.254
Bart Shirley	3B10,SS8	R	24	18	62	6	17	1	1	0	7	4	8	0	.274	.318	.323
Jeff Torborg	C27	R	22	28	43	4	10	1	1	0	4	3	8	0	.233	.292	.302
Lee Walls	OF6,C1	R	31	37	28	1	5	1	0	0	3	2	12	0	.179	.233	.214
Willie Crawford	OF4	L	17	10	16	3	5	1	0	0	0	1	7	1	.313	.353	.375

Pitcher	T	Age	G	GS	CG	ShO	IP	H	HR	BB	SO	W-L	Sv	ERA
Don Drysdale	R	27	40	40	21	5	321.1	242	15	68	237	18-16	0	2.18
Sandy Koufax	L	28	29	28	15	7	223.0	154	13	53	223	19-5	1	1.74
Phil Ortega	R	24	34	25	4	3	157.1	149	22	56	107	7-9	1	4.00
Joe Moeller	R	21	27	24	1	0	145.1	153	14	31	97	7-13	0	4.21
Larry Miller	L	27	16	14	1	0	79.2	87	1	28	50	4-8	0	4.18
Nick Willhite	L	23	10	7	2	0	43.2	43	4	13	24	2-4	0	3.71
Pete Richert	L	24	8	6	1	1	34.2	38	2	18	25	2-3	0	4.15
John Purdin	R	21	3	2	1	1	16.0	6	1	6	8	2-0	0	0.56
Bill Singer	R	20	2	2	0	0	14.0	11	0	12	3	0-1	0	3.21
Johnny Podres	L	31	2	2	0	0	2.2	5	1	3	0	0-2	0	16.88
Bob Miller	R	25	74	2	0	0	137.2	115	1	63	94	7-7	9	2.62
Ron Perranoski	L	28	72	0	0	0	125.1	128	5	46	79	5-7	14	3.09
Jim Brewer	L	26	34	5	1	1	93.0	79	5	25	63	4-3	1	3.00
Howie Reed	R	27	26	7	0	0	90.0	79	4	36	52	3-4	1	3.20

1964 Pittsburgh Pirates 6th NL 80-82 .494 13.0 GB

Danny Murtaugh

Player	Gm by Position	B	Age	G	AB	R	H	2B	3B	HR	RBI	BB	SO	SB	Avg	OBP	Slg
Jim Pagliaroni	C96	R	26	97	302	33	89	12	3	10	36	41	56	1	.295	.383	.454
Donn Clendenon	1B119	R	28	133	457	53	129	23	8	12	64	26	96	12	.282	.321	.446
Bill Mazeroski	2B162	R	27	162	601	66	161	22	8	10	64	29	52	1	.268	.300	.381
Bob Bailey	3B105,OF35,SS2	R	21	143	530	73	149	26	3	11	51	44	78	10	.281	.336	.404
Dick Schofield	SS111	S	29	121	398	50	98	22	5	3	36	54	60	1	.246	.345	.349
Roberto Clemente	OF154	R	29	155	622	95	211	40	7	12	87	51	87	5	.339	.388	.484
Bill Virdon	OF134	L	33	145	473	59	115	11	3	3	27	30	48	1	.243	.287	.298
Manny Mota	OF93,C1,2B1	R	26	115	271	43	75	8	3	5	32	10	31	4	.277	.309	.384
Willie Stargell	OF59,1B50	L	24	117	421	53	115	19	7	21	78	17	92	1	.273	.304	.501
Jerry Lynch	OF78	L	33	114	297	35	81	14	2	16	66	26	57	0	.273	.328	.495
Gene Freese	3B72	R	30	99	289	33	65	13	2	9	40	19	45	1	.225	.269	.377
Gene Alley	SS61,3B3,2B1	R	23	81	209	30	44	3	1	6	13	21	56	0	.211	.286	.321
Smoky Burgess†	C44	L	37	68	171	9	42	3	1	2	17	13	14	2	.246	.303	.310
Orlando McFarlane	C35,OF1	R	26	37	78	5	19	5	0	0	1	4	27	0	.244	.280	.308
Jerry May	C11	R	20	11	31	1	8	0	0	0	3	3	9	0	.258	.314	.258
Dave Wissman	OF10	L	23	16	27	2	4	0	0	0	0	1	9	0	.148	.179	.148
Rex Johnston	OF8	S	26	14	7	1	0	0	0	0	0	3	0	0	.000	.300	.000
Julio Gotay		R	25	3	2	1	1	0	0	0	0	1	0	0	.500	.667	.500

Pitcher	T	Age	G	GS	CG	ShO	IP	H	HR	BB	SO	W-L	Sv	ERA
Bob Veale	L	28	40	38	14	1	279.2	222	8	124	250	18-12	0	2.74
Bob Friend	R	33	35	35	13	3	240.1	253	10	50	128	13-18	0	3.33
Vern Law	R	34	35	29	7	5	192.0	203	18	32	93	12-13	0	3.61
Joe Gibbon	L	29	28	24	3	0	146.2	145	10	54	97	10-7	0	3.68
Steve Blass	R	22	24	13	3	1	104.2	107	9	45	67	5-8	0	4.04
Don Schwall	R	28	15	9	0	0	49.2	53	1	15	36	4-3	0	4.35
Don Cardwell	R	28	4	4	1	1	19.1	15	1	7	10	1-2	0	2.79
Wilbur Wood†	L	22	3	2	1	0	17.1	16	0	11	7	0-2	0	3.63
Earl Francis	R	28	2	1	0	0	6.1	7	2	1	6	0-1	0	8.53
Al McBean	R	26	58	0	0	0	89.2	76	4	17	41	8-3	22	1.91
Roy Face	R	36	55	0	0	0	79.2	82	11	27	63	3-3	4	5.20
Tommie Sisk	R	22	42	1	0	0	61.1	91	4	29	35	1-4	0	6.16
Frank Bork	L	23	33	2	0	0	42.0	51	6	11	31	2-2	2	4.07
Tom Butters	R	26	28	4	0	0	64.1	52	3	37	58	2-2	0	2.38
Bob Priddy	R	24	19	0	0	0	34.1	35	2	15	23	1-2	1	3.93
Fred Green	L	30	8	0	0	0	7.1	10	1	0	2	0-0	0	1.23
John Gelnar	R	21	7	0	0	0	9.0	11	2	1	4	0-0	0	5.00

1964 Chicago Cubs 8th NL 76-86 .469 17.0 GB

Bob Kennedy

Player	Gm by Position	B	Age	G	AB	R	H	2B	3B	HR	RBI	BB	SO	SB	Avg	OBP	Slg
Dick Bertell	C110	R	28	112	353	29	84	11	3	4	35	33	67	2	.238	.305	.320
Ernie Banks	1B157	R	33	157	591	67	156	29	6	23	95	36	84	1	.264	.307	.450
Joey Amalfitano	2B86,1B1,SS1	R	30	100	324	51	78	19	6	4	27	40	42	2	.241	.333	.373
Ron Santo	3B161	R	24	161	592	94	185	33	13	30	114	86	96	3	.313	.398	.564
Andre Rodgers	SS126	R	29	129	448	50	107	17	3	12	46	53	88	5	.239	.317	.371
Billy Williams	OF162	L	26	162	645	100	201	39	2	33	98	59	84	10	.312	.370	.532
Billy Cowan	OF134	R	25	139	497	52	120	16	4	19	50	18	128	12	.241	.268	.404
Len Gabrielson†	OF68,1B8	L	24	89	272	22	67	11	2	5	23	19	37	9	.246	.298	.357
Jimmy Stewart	2B61,SS45,OF4*	S	25	132	415	59	105	17	0	3	33	49	61	10	.253	.331	.316
Lou Brock†	OF52	L	25	52	215	30	54	9	2	2	14	13	40	10	.251	.300	.340
Doug Clemens†	OF40	L	25	54	140	23	39	10	2	2	12	18	22	0	.279	.363	.421
Jimmie Schaffer	C43	R	28	54	122	9	25	6	1	2	9	17	17	2	.205	.307	.320
Ellis Burton	OF29	S	27	42	105	12	20	3	2	2	7	17	22	4	.190	.303	.314
Leo Burke	OF18,2B5,3B4*	R	30	59	103	11	27	3	1	1	14	7	31	0	.262	.315	.340
Ron Campbell	2B26	R	24	26	92	7	25	6	1	1	10	1	21	0	.272	.277	.391
Vic Roznovsky	C26	L	25	35	76	2	15	1	0	0	2	5	18	0	.197	.244	.211
Billy Ott	OF10	S	23	20	39	4	7	3	0	0	1	3	10	0	.179	.238	.256
Merritt Ranew†	C9	L	26	16	33	0	3	0	0	0	1	2	6	0	.091	.167	.091
John Boccabella	1B5,OF2	R	23	9	23	4	9	2	1	0	6	0	3	0	.391	.391	.565
Don Kessinger	SS4	S	21	4	12	1	2	0	0	0	0	0	1	0	.167	.167	.167
Don Landrum	OF1	L	28	11	11	2	0	0	0	0	0	1	2	0	.000	.083	.000
Paul Popovich		S	23	1	1	0	1	0	0	0	0	0	0	0	1.000	1.000	1.000

J. Stewart, 1 G at 3B; L. Burke, 2 G at 1B, 1 G at C

Pitcher	T	Age	G	GS	CG	ShO	IP	H	HR	BB	SO	W-L	Sv	ERA
Larry Jackson	R	33	40	38	19	3	297.2	265	17	58	148	24-11	0	3.14
Dick Ellsworth	L	24	37	36	16	1	256.2	267	34	71	148	14-18	0	3.75
Bob Buhl	R	35	36	35	11	3	227.2	208	22	68	107	15-14	0	3.83
Lew Burdette†	R	37	28	17	8	2	131.0	152	15	19	40	9-9	0	4.88
Ernie Broglio†	R	28	18	16	3	0	100.1	111	12	30	46	4-7	1	4.04
Fred Norman	L	21	8	5	0	0	31.2	34	9	21	20	0-4	0	6.54
Glen Hobbie†	R	28	8	4	0	0	27.1	39	4	10	14	0-3	0	7.90
Paul Toth	R	29	4	2	0	0	10.2	15	2	5	0	0-2	0	8.44
Lindy McDaniel	R	28	63	0	0	0	95.0	104	4	23	71	1-7	15	3.88
Don Elston	R	35	48	0	0	0	54.1	68	4	34	26	2-5	1	5.30
Wayne Schurr	R	26	26	0	0	0	48.1	57	3	11	29	0-0	0	3.72
Sterling Slaughter	R	22	20	6	1	0	51.2	64	8	32	32	2-4	0	5.75
Bobby Shantz†	L	38	20	0	0	0	11.1	15	2	6	12	0-1	1	5.56
Freddie Burdette	R	27	18	0	0	0	20.0	17	2	10	4	1-0	0	3.15
Lee Gregory	L	26	11	0	0	0	18.0	23	3	5	8	0-0	0	3.50
Jack Warner	R	23	7	0	0	0	9.1	12	0	4	6	0-0	0	2.89
Jack Spring†	L	31	7	0	0	0	6.0	4	0	2	1	0-0	0	6.00
Cal Koonce	R	23	6	2	0	0	31.0	30	1	7	17	3-0	0	2.03
John Flavin	L	22	5	1	0	0	4.2	11	0	3	5	0-1	0	13.50
Paul Jaeckel	R	22	4	0	0	0	8.0	4	0	3	2	1-0	1	0.00
Dick Scott	L	31	3	0	0	0	4.1	10	2	1	1	0-0	0	12.46

1964 Houston Colt .45s 9th NL 66-96 .407 27.0 GB

Harry Craft (61-88)/Lum Harris (5-8)

Player	Gm by Position	B	Age	G	AB	R	H	2B	3B	HR	RBI	BB	SO	SB	Avg	OBP	Slg
Jerry Grote	C98	R	21	100	298	26	54	9	3	3	24	20	75	0	.181	.240	.262
Walt Bond	1B76,OF71	L	26	148	543	63	138	16	7	20	85	38	90	2	.254	.310	.420
Nellie Fox	2B115	L	36	133	442	45	117	12	6	0	28	27	13	0	.265	.320	.319
Bob Aspromonte	3B155	R	26	157	553	51	155	20	3	12	69	35	54	6	.280	.329	.392
Eddie Kasko	SS128,3B2	R	32	133	448	45	109	16	1	0	22	37	52	4	.243	.302	.283
Al Spangler	OF127	L	30	135	449	51	110	18	5	4	38	41	43	7	.245	.311	.334
Joe Gaines†	OF81	R	27	89	307	37	78	9	7	7	34	27	69	8	.254	.318	.397
Mike White	OF72,2B10,3B3	R	25	89	280	30	76	11	3	0	27	20	47	1	.271	.319	.332
Bob Lillis	2B52,SS43,3B12	R	34	109	332	31	89	11	2	0	17	11	10	4	.268	.291	.313
Rusty Staub	1B49,OF38	L	20	89	292	26	63	10	2	8	35	21	31	1	.216	.272	.346
John Bateman	C72	R	23	74	221	18	42	8	0	5	19	17	48	0	.190	.249	.294
Jimmy Wynn	OF64	R	22	67	219	19	49	7	0	5	18	24	58	5	.224	.301	.324
Carroll Hardy	OF41	R	31	46	157	13	29	1	1	2	12	8	30	0	.185	.232	.242
Dave Roberts	1B34,OF4	L	31	61	125	9	23	4	1	1	7	14	28	0	.184	.270	.256
Jim Beauchamp	OF15,1B2	R	24	23	55	6	9	2	0	2	4	5	16	0	.164	.246	.309
Pete Runnels	1B14	L	36	22	51	3	10	1	0	0	3	8	7	0	.196	.305	.216
Joe Morgan	2B10	L	20	10	37	4	7	0	0	0	0	6	7	0	.189	.302	.189
Sonny Jackson	SS7	L	19	9	23	3	8	1	0	0	1	2	3	1	.348	.400	.391
John Hoffman	C5	L	20	6	15	1	1	0	0	0	0	1	7	0	.067	.125	.067
Johnny Weekly	OF5	R	27	6	15	0	2	0	0	0	3	1	3	0	.133	.167	.133
Ivan Murrell	OF5	R	19	10	14	1	2	1	0	0	1	0	6	0	.143	.133	.214
Dave Adlesh	C3	R	20	3	10	0	2	0	0	0	0	0	5	0	.200	.200	.200
Walt Williams	OF5	R	20	10	9	1	0	0	0	0	0	0	2	1	.000	.000	.000
Steve Hertz	3B2	R	19	5	4	2	0	0	0	0	0	0	3	0	.000	.000	.000
Brock Davis	OF1	L	20	1	3	0	0	0	0	0	0	1	1	0	.000	.250	.000

Pitcher	T	Age	G	GS	CG	ShO	IP	H	HR	BB	SO	W-L	Sv	ERA
Ken Johnson	R	31	35	35	7	1	218.0	209	15	44	117	11-16	0	3.63
Bob Bruce	R	31	35	29	9	4	202.1	191	8	33	135	15-9	0	2.76
Turk Farrell	R	30	32	27	7	0	198.1	196	21	52	117	11-10	0	3.27
Don Nottebart	R	28	28	24	2	0	157.0	165	12	37	90	6-11	0	3.90
Hal Brown	R	39	27	21	3	0	132.0	154	18	26	53	3-15	1	3.95
Chris Zachary	R	20	1	1	0	0	4.0	6	1	1	2	0-1	0	9.00
Hal Woodeshick	L	31	61	0	0	0	78.1	73	3	32	58	2-9	23	2.76
Jim Owens	R	30	48	11	0	0	118.0	115	7	32	88	8-7	6	3.28
Claude Raymond	R	27	38	0	0	0	79.2	64	3	22	56	5-5	0	2.82
Gordon Jones	R	34	34	0	0	0	50.0	58	3	14	28	0-1	0	4.14
Don Larsen†	R	34	30	10	2	1	103.1	92	4	20	58	4-8	1	2.26
Larry Yellen	R	21	13	1	0	0	21.0	27	4	10	9	0-0	0	6.86
Dave Giusti	R	24	8	0	0	0	25.2	24	1	8	16	0-0	0	3.16
Danny Coombs	L	22	7	1	0	0	18.0	21	1	10	14	1-1	0	5.00
Joe Hoerner	L	27	7	0	0	0	11.0	13	3	6	4	0-0	0	4.91
Larry Dierker	R	17	3	1	0	0	9.0	7	1	3	5	0-1	0	2.00
Don Bradey	R	29	3	1	0	0	2.1	6	0	3	2	0-2	0	19.29

1964 New York Mets 10th NL 53-109 .327 40.0 GB

Casey Stengel

Player	Gm by Position	B	Age	G	AB	R	H	2B	3B	HR	RBI	BB	SO	SB	Avg	OBP	Slg
Jesse Gonder	C97	L	28	131	341	28	92	11	1	7	35	29	65	0	.270	.329	.370
Ed Kranepool	1B104,OF6	L	19	119	420	47	108	19	4	10	45	32	50	0	.257	.310	.393
Ron Hunt	2B109,3B12	R	23	127	475	59	144	19	6	6	42	29	30	6	.303	.357	.406
Charley Smith†	3B85,SS36,OF13	R	26	127	443	44	106	12	0	20	58	19	101	2	.239	.275	.402
Roy McMillan†	SS111	R	33	113	379	30	80	8	2	1	25	14	16	3	.211	.246	.251
Joe Christopher	OF145	R	28	154	543	78	163	26	8	16	76	48	92	6	.300	.360	.466
Jim Hickman	OF113,3B1	R	27	139	409	48	105	14	1	11	57	36	90	0	.257	.319	.377
George Altman	OF109	L	31	124	422	48	97	14	1	9	47	18	70	4	.230	.262	.332
Rod Kanehl	2B34,OF25,3B19*	R	30	98	254	25	59	7	1	1	11	7	18	3	.232	.256	.280
Hawk Taylor	C45,OF16	R	25	92	225	20	54	8	0	4	23	8	33	0	.240	.272	.329
Larry Elliot	OF63	L	26	80	224	27	51	8	0	9	22	28	55	1	.228	.320	.384
Bobby Klaus†	3B28,2B25,SS5	R	26	56	209	25	51	8	3	2	11	25	30	3	.244	.325	.340
Frank Thomas†	OF31,1B19,3B2	R	35	60	197	19	50	6	1	3	19	10	29	1	.254	.295	.340
Chris Cannizzaro	C53	R	26	60	164	11	51	10	0	0	10	14	28	0	.311	.367	.372
Amado Samuel	SS34,3B17,2B3	R	25	53	142	7	33	7	0	0	5	4	24	0	.232	.264	.282
Tim Harkness	1B32	L	26	39	117	11	33	2	1	2	13	9	18	1	.282	.336	.368
Dick Smith	1B18,OF13	R	25	46	94	14	21	6	1	0	3	1	29	6	.223	.247	.309
John Stephenson	3B14,OF8	L	23	37	57	2	9	0	0	1	2	4	18	0	.158	.226	.211
Wayne Graham	3B11	R	27	20	33	1	3	1	0	0	0	0	5	0	.091	.091	.121
Al Moran	SS15,3B1	R	25	16	22	2	5	0	0	0	4	2	2	0	.227	.280	.227
Larry Burright	2B3	R	26	3	7	0	0	0	0	0	0	0	0	0	.000	.000	.000

R. Kanehl, 2 G at 1B

Pitcher	T	Age	G	GS	CG	ShO	IP	H	HR	BB	SO	W-L	Sv	ERA
Jack Fisher	R	25	40	34	8	1	227.2	256	23	56	115	10-17	0	4.23
Tracy Stallard	R	26	36	34	11	2	225.2	213	20	73	118	10-20	0	3.79
Al Jackson	L	28	40	31	11	3	213.1	229	18	60	112	11-16	1	4.26
Galen Cisco	R	28	36	25	5	2	191.2	182	17	54	78	6-19	0	3.62
Frank Lary†	R	34	13	8	3	1	57.1	62	7	14	27	2-3	1	4.55
Dennis Ribant	R	22	14	7	1	1	57.2	65	8	9	35	1-5	1	5.15
Tom Parsons	R	24	4	2	1	0	19.1	20	1	6	10	1-2	0	4.19
Jay Hook	R	27	3	2	0	0	9.2	17	2	7	5	0-1	0	9.31
Bill Wakefield	R	23	62	4	0	0	119.2	103	10	61	61	3-5	2	3.61
Larry Bearnarth	R	22	44	1	0	0	78.0	79	6	38	31	5-5	3	4.15
Willard Hunter	L	30	41	0	0	0	49.0	54	4	9	22	3-3	5	4.41
Ron Locke	L	22	25	3	0	0	41.1	46	3	22	17	1-2	0	3.48
Tom Sturdivant†	R	34	16	0	0	0	28.2	34	2	7	18	0-0	1	5.97
Carl Willey	R	33	14	3	0	0	30.0	37	5	8	14	0-2	0	3.60
Darrell Sutherland	R	22	10	4	0	0	26.2	32	1	12	9	0-3	0	7.76
Jerry Hinsley	R	20	9	2	0	0	15.1	21	0	7	11	0-2	0	8.22
Gary Kroll†	R	22	8	2	0	0	21.2	19	1	15	24	0-1	0	4.15
Ed Bauta	R	29	8	0	0	0	10.0	17	1	3	3	0-2	1	5.40
Craig Anderson	R	25	4	1	0	0	13.0	21	0	3	5	0-1	0	5.54
Steve Dillon	L	21	2	0	0	0	3.0	4	1	2	2	0-0	0	9.00

»1965 Minnesota Twins 1st AL 102-60 .630 —

Sam Mele

Player	Gm by Position	B	Age	G	AB	R	H	2B	3B	HR	RBI	BB	SO	SB	Avg	OBP	Slg
Earl Battey	C128	R	30	131	394	36	117	22	2	6	60	50	23	0	.297	.375	.409
Don Mincher	1B99,OF1	L	27	128	346	43	87	17	3	22	65	49	73	1	.251	.344	.509
Jerry Kindall	2B106,3B10,SS7	R	30	125	342	41	67	12	1	6	36	36	97	2	.196	.274	.289
Rich Rollins	3B112,2B16	R	27	140	469	59	117	22	1	5	32	37	54	4	.249	.309	.333
Zoilo Versalles	SS160	R	25	160	666	126	182	45	12	19	77	41	122	27	.273	.319	.462
Tony Oliva	OF147	L	24	149	576	107	185	40	5	16	98	55	64	19	.321	.378	.491
Jimmie Hall	OF141	L	27	148	522	81	149	25	4	20	86	51	79	14	.285	.347	.464
Bob Allison	OF122,1B3	R	30	135	438	71	102	14	5	23	78	73	114	10	.233	.342	.445
Harmon Killebrew	1B72,3B44,OF1	R	29	113	401	78	108	16	1	25	75	72	69	0	.269	.384	.501
Sandy Valdespino	OF57	L	26	108	245	38	64	8	2	1	22	20	28	7	.261	.319	.322
Joe Nossek	OF48,3B9	R	24	87	170	19	37	9	0	2	16	7	22	2	.218	.250	.306
Jerry Zimmerman	C82	R	30	83	154	8	33	1	1	1	11	12	23	0	.214	.275	.253
Frank Quilici	2B52,SS4	R	26	56	149	16	31	5	1	0	7	15	33	1	.208	.280	.255
Andy Kosco	OF14,1B2	R	23	23	55	3	13	4	0	1	6	1	15	0	.236	.241	.364
Bernie Allen	2B10,3B1	L	26	19	39	2	9	2	0	0	6	6	8	0	.231	.326	.282
Frank Kostro	2B7,3B6,OF2	R	27	20	31	2	5	2	0	0	1	4	5	0	.161	.250	.226
Cesar Tovar	2B4,3B2,OF2*	R	24	18	25	3	5	1	0	0	2	2	3	2	.200	.259	.240
Ted Uhlaender	OF4	L	24	13	22	1	4	0	0	0	1	0	2	1	.182	.182	.182
John Sevcik	C11	R	22	12	16	1	1	1	0	0	0	1	5	0	.063	.118	.125
Rich Reese	1B6,OF1	L	23	14	7	0	2	1	0	0	0	2	2	0	.286	.444	.429

C. Tovar, 1 G at SS

Pitcher	T	Age	G	GS	CG	ShO	IP	H	HR	BB	SO	W-L	Sv	ERA
Jim Kaat	L	26	45	42	7	2	264.1	267	25	63	154	18-11	2	2.83
Mudcat Grant	R	29	41	39	14	6	270.1	252	34	61	142	21-7	0	3.30
Camilo Pascual	R	31	27	27	5	1	156.0	126	12	63	96	9-3	0	3.35
Jim Perry	R	29	36	19	4	2	167.2	142	18	47	88	12-7	0	2.63
Jim Merritt	L	21	16	9	1	0	76.2	68	11	20	61	5-4	2	3.17
Al Worthington	R	36	62	0	0	0	80.1	57	4	41	59	10-7	21	2.13
Johnny Klippstein	R	37	56	0	0	0	76.1	59	8	31	59	9-3	5	2.24
Bill Pleis	L	27	41	2	0	0	51.1	49	3	27	33	4-4	4	2.98
Dick Stigman	L	29	33	8	0	0	70.0	59	14	33	70	4-2	4	4.37
Jerry Fosnow	L	24	29	0	0	0	46.2	33	7	25	35	3-3	2	4.44
Mel Nelson	L	29	28	3	0	0	54.2	57	7	23	31	0-4	3	4.12
Dave Boswell	R	20	27	12	1	0	106.0	77	20	46	85	6-5	0	3.40
Garry Roggenburk	L	25	12	0	0	0	21.0	21	1	12	6	1-0	2	3.43
Dwight Siebler	R	27	7	1	0	0	15.0	11	2	11	15	0-0	0	4.20
Pete Cimino	R	22	1	0	0	0	1.0	0	0	0	0	0-0	0	0.00

1965 Chicago White Sox 2nd AL 95-67 .586 7.0 GB — Al Lopez

Player	Gm by Position	B	Age	G	AB	R	H	2B	3B	HR	RBI	BB	SO	SB	Avg	OBP	Slg
J.C. Martin	C112,1B4,3B2	L	28	119	230	21	60	12	0	2	21	24	29	2	.261	.333	.339
Bill Skowron	1B145	R	34	146	559	63	153	24	3	18	78	32	77	1	.274	.316	.424
Don Buford	2B139,3B41	S	28	155	586	93	166	22	5	10	47	67	76	17	.283	.358	.389
Pete Ward	3B134,2B1	L	25	138	507	62	125	25	3	10	57	56	83	2	.247	.327	.367
Ron Hansen	SS161,2B1	R	27	162	587	61	138	23	4	11	66	60	73	1	.235	.304	.344
Ken Berry	OF156	R	24	157	472	51	103	17	4	12	42	28	96	4	.218	.268	.347
Floyd Robinson	OF153	L	29	156	577	70	153	15	6	14	66	76	51	4	.265	.352	.385
Danny Cater	OF127,3B11,1B3	R	25	142	514	74	139	18	4	14	55	33	65	3	.270	.316	.403
John Romano	C111,OF4,1B2	R	30	122	356	39	86	11	0	18	48	59	74	0	.242	.355	.424
Tom McCraw	1B72,OF64	L	24	133	273	38	66	12	1	5	21	25	48	12	.238	.309	.344
Al Weis	2B74,SS7,3B2*	S	27	103	135	29	40	4	3	1	12	12	22	4	.296	.360	.393
Dave Nicholson	OF36	R	25	54	85	11	13	2	1	2	12	9	40	0	.153	.234	.271
Smoky Burgess	C5	L	38	80	77	2	22	4	0	2	24	11	7	0	.286	.371	.416
Bill Voss	OF10	L	21	11	33	4	6	0	1	1	3	3	5	0	.182	.250	.333
Gene Freese†	3B8	R	31	17	32	2	9	0	1	1	4	5	9	0	.281	.368	.438
Jimmie Schaffer†	C14	R	29	17	31	2	6	3	1	0	1	3	4	0	.194	.265	.355
Jim Hicks	OF5	R	25	13	19	2	5	1	0	1	2	0	9	0	.263	.263	.474
Tommie Agee	OF9	R	22	10	19	2	3	1	0	0	3	2	6	0	.158	.238	.211
Duane Josephson	C4	R	23	4	9	2	1	0	0	0	0	2	4	0	.111	.273	.111
Marv Staehle		L	23	7	7	0	3	0	0	0	2	0	0	0	.429	.429	.429
Bill Heath		L	26	1	1	0	0	0	0	0	0	0	0	0	.000	.000	.000
Dick Kenworthy		R	24	3	1	0	0	0	0	0	0	1	0	0	.000	.667	.000

A. Weis, 2 G at OF

Pitcher	T	Age	G	GS	CG	ShO	IP	H	HR	BB	SO	W-L	Sv	ERA
Joe Horlen	R	27	34	34	7	4	219.0	203	16	39	125	13-13	0	2.88
John Buzhardt	R	28	32	30	4	1	188.2	167	12	56	108	13-8	1	3.01
Gary Peters	L	28	33	30	1	0	176.1	181	19	63	95	10-12	0	3.62
Tommy John	L	22	39	27	6	1	183.2	162	12	58	126	14-7	3	3.09
Bruce Howard	R	22	30	22	1	1	148.0	123	13	72	120	9-8	0	3.47
Juan Pizarro	L	28	18	18	2	1	97.0	96	9	37	65	6-3	0	3.43
Eddie Fisher	R	28	82	0	0	0	165.1	118	13	43	90	15-7	24	2.40
Hoyt Wilhelm	R	41	66	0	0	0	144.0	88	11	32	106	7-7	20	1.81
Bob Locker	R	27	51	0	0	0	91.1	71	6	30	69	5-2	2	3.15
Greg Bollo	R	21	15	0	0	0	22.2	12	5	9	16	0-0	0	3.57
Ted Wills	L	31	15	0	0	0	19.0	17	2	14	12	2-0	1	2.84
Frank Lary†	R	35	14	1	0	0	26.2	23	4	7	14	1-0	2	4.05

1965 Baltimore Orioles 3rd AL 94-68 .580 8.0 GB — Hank Bauer

Player	Gm by Position	B	Age	G	AB	R	H	2B	3B	HR	RBI	BB	SO	SB	Avg	OBP	Slg
Dick Brown	C92	R	30	96	255	17	59	9	1	5	30	17	53	2	.231	.278	.333
Boog Powell	1B78,OF71	L	23	144	472	54	117	20	2	17	72	71	93	1	.248	.347	.407
Jerry Adair	2B157	R	28	157	582	51	151	26	3	7	66	35	65	6	.259	.303	.351
Brooks Robinson	3B143	R	28	144	559	81	166	25	2	18	80	47	47	3	.297	.351	.445
Luis Aparicio	SS141	R	31	144	564	67	127	20	10	8	40	46	56	26	.225	.286	.339
Curt Blefary	OF136	L	21	144	462	72	120	23	4	22	70	88	73	4	.260	.381	.470
Paul Blair	OF116	R	21	119	364	49	85	19	2	5	25	32	52	8	.234	.302	.338
Russ Snyder	OF106	L	31	132	345	49	93	11	2	1	29	27	38	3	.270	.323	.322
Norm Siebern	1B76	L	31	106	297	44	76	13	4	8	32	50	49	1	.256	.362	.407
Bob Johnson	1B34,SS23,3B13*	R	29	87	273	36	66	13	2	5	27	15	34	1	.242	.282	.359
Jackie Brandt	OF84	R	31	96	243	35	59	17	0	8	24	21	40	1	.243	.303	.412
John Orsino	C62,1B5	R	27	77	232	30	54	10	2	9	28	23	51	1	.233	.313	.409
Sam Bowens	OF68	R	26	84	203	16	33	4	1	7	20	10	41	7	.163	.199	.296
Charlie Lau	C35	L	32	68	132	15	39	5	2	2	18	17	18	0	.295	.371	.409
Dave Johnson	3B9,2B3,SS2	R	22	20	47	5	8	3	0	0	1	5	6	3	.170	.245	.234
Carl Warwick†	OF3	R	28	9	14	3	0	0	0	0	0	3	2	0	.000	.176	.000
Andy Etchebarren	C5	R	22	5	6	1	1	0	0	1	4	0	2	0	.167	.167	.667
Mark Belanger	SS4	R	21	11	3	1	1	0	0	0	0	0	0	0	.333	.333	.333

B. Johnson, 5 G at 2B

Pitcher	T	Age	G	GS	CG	ShO	IP	H	HR	BB	SO	W-L	Sv	ERA
Milt Pappas	R	26	34	34	9	3	221.1	192	22	52	127	13-9	0	2.60
Steve Barber	L	26	37	32	7	2	220.2	177	16	81	130	15-10	0	2.69
Dave McNally	L	22	35	29	6	2	198.2	163	15	73	116	11-6	0	2.85
Wally Bunker	R	20	34	27	4	1	189.0	170	16	58	84	10-8	2	3.38
John Miller	R	24	16	16	1	0	93.1	75	4	58	71	6-4	0	3.18
Robin Roberts†	R	38	20	15	5	1	114.2	110	17	20	63	5-7	0	3.38
Frank Bertaina	L	21	2	1	0	0	6.0	9	0	4	5	0-0	0	6.00
Stu Miller	R	37	67	0	0	0	119.1	87	5	32	104	14-7	24	1.89
Dick Hall	R	34	48	0	0	0	93.2	84	8	11	79	11-8	12	3.07
Jim Palmer	R	19	27	6	0	0	92.0	75	6	56	75	5-4	1	3.72
Don Larsen†	R	35	27	1	0	0	54.0	53	4	20	40	1-2	1	2.67
Harvey Haddix	L	39	24	0	0	0	33.2	31	5	23	21	3-2	1	3.48
Ken Rowe	R	31	6	0	0	0	13.0	17	0	2	3	0-0	0	3.46
Darold Knowles	L	23	5	1	0	0	14.2	14	2	10	12	0-1	0	9.20
Herm Starrette	R	26	4	0	0	0	9.0	8	0	3	3	0-0	0	1.00
Ed Barnowski	R	21	4	0	0	0	4.1	3	0	7	6	0-0	0	2.08

1965 Detroit Tigers 4th AL 89-73 .549 13.0 GB — Bob Swift (24-18)/Chuck Dressen (65-55)

Player	Gm by Position	B	Age	G	AB	R	H	2B	3B	HR	RBI	BB	SO	SB	Avg	OBP	Slg
Bill Freehan	C129	R	23	130	431	45	101	15	0	10	43	39	63	4	.234	.306	.339
Norm Cash	1B139	L	30	142	467	79	124	23	1	30	82	77	62	6	.266	.371	.512
Jerry Lumpe	2B139	L	32	145	502	72	129	15	3	4	39	56	34	7	.257	.333	.323
Don Wert	3B161,SS3,2B1	R	26	162	609	81	159	22	2	12	54	73	71	5	.261	.341	.363
Dick McAuliffe	SS112	L	25	113	404	61	105	13	6	15	54	49	62	6	.260	.342	.433
Willie Horton	OF141,3B1	R	22	143	512	69	140	20	2	29	104	48	101	5	.273	.340	.490
Al Kaline	OF112,3B1	R	30	125	399	72	112	18	2	18	72	72	49	6	.281	.388	.471
Don Demeter	OF81,1B34	R	30	122	389	50	108	16	4	16	58	23	65	4	.278	.325	.463
Gates Brown	OF56	L	26	96	227	33	58	14	2	10	43	17	33	6	.256	.305	.467
Jim Northrup	OF54	L	25	80	219	20	45	12	3	2	16	12	50	1	.205	.253	.315
Ray Oyler	SS57,2B11,1B1*	R	26	82	194	22	36	6	0	5	13	21	61	1	.186	.265	.294
George Thomas	OF59,2B1	R	27	79	169	19	36	5	1	3	10	12	39	2	.213	.269	.308
Mickey Stanley	OF29	R	22	30	117	14	28	6	0	3	13	3	12	1	.239	.256	.368
Jake Wood	2B20,1B1,3B1*	R	28	58	104	12	30	3	0	2	7	10	19	3	.288	.357	.375
John Sullivan	C29	L	24	34	86	5	23	0	0	2	11	9	13	0	.267	.340	.337
Jackie Moore	C20	R	26	21	53	2	5	0	0	0	2	6	12	0	.094	.183	.094
George Smith	2B22,3B3,SS3	R	27	32	53	6	5	0	0	1	1	3	18	0	.094	.143	.151
Bill Roman	1B6	L	26	21	27	0	2	0	0	0	0	2	7	0	.074	.138	.074
Wayne Redmond	OF2	R	19	4	4	1	0	0	0	0	0	1	1	0	.000	.200	.000

R. Oyler, 1 G at 3B; J. Wood, 1 G at SS

Pitcher	T	Age	G	GS	CG	ShO	IP	H	HR	BB	SO	W-L	Sv	ERA
Mickey Lolich	L	24	43	37	7	3	243.2	216	23	72	226	15-9	3	3.44
Hank Aguirre	L	34	32	32	10	2	208.1	185	24	60	141	14-10	0	3.59
Denny McLain	R	21	33	29	13	4	220.1	174	25	62	192	16-6	1	2.61
Joe Sparma	R	23	30	28	6	0	167.0	142	13	75	127	13-8	0	3.18
Dave Wickersham	R	29	34	27	8	3	195.1	179	12	61	109	9-14	0	3.78
Fred Gladding	R	29	46	0	0	0	70.0	63	6	29	43	6-2	5	2.83
Terry Fox	R	29	42	0	0	0	77.2	59	7	31	34	6-4	10	2.78
Larry Sherry	R	29	39	0	0	0	78.1	71	5	40	46	3-6	5	3.10
Orlando Pena†	R	31	30	0	0	0	57.1	54	5	20	55	4-6	4	2.51
Ron Nischwitz	L	27	20	0	0	0	22.2	21	2	6	12	1-0	1	2.78
Phil Regan	R	28	16	7	1	0	51.2	57	6	20	37	1-5	0	5.05
Julio Navarro	R	29	15	1	0	0	30.0	25	5	12	22	0-2	1	4.20
Ed Rakow	R	29	6	0	0	0	13.1	14	2	11	10	0-0	0	6.08
John Hiller	L	22	5	0	0	0	6.0	5	0	1	4	0-0	1	0.00
Jack Hamilton	R	26	4	1	0	0	4.1	6	1	4	3	1-1	0	14.54
Johnny Seale	L	26	4	0	0	0	3.0	7	1	2	3	0-0	0	12.00
Leo Marentette	R	24	2	0	0	0	3.0	1	0	1	3	0-0	0	0.00
Vern Holtgrave	R	22	1	0	0	0	3.0	4	0	2	2	0-0	0	6.00

1965 Cleveland Indians 5th AL 87-75 .537 15.0 GB — Birdie Tebbetts

Player	Gm by Position	B	Age	G	AB	R	H	2B	3B	HR	RBI	BB	SO	SB	Avg	OBP	Slg
Joe Azcue	C108	R	25	111	335	16	77	7	0	2	35	27	54	2	.230	.290	.269
Fred Whitfield	1B122	L	27	132	468	49	137	23	1	26	90	16	42	2	.293	.316	.513
Pedro Gonzalez†	2B112,OF3,3B2	R	27	116	400	38	101	14	3	5	39	18	57	7	.253	.288	.340
Max Alvis	3B156	R	27	159	604	88	149	24	2	21	61	47	121	12	.247	.308	.397
Larry Brown	SS95,2B26	R	25	124	438	52	111	22	2	8	40	38	62	5	.253	.315	.368
Rocky Colavito	OF162	R	31	162	592	92	170	25	2	26	108	93	63	1	.287	.383	.468
Leon Wagner	OF134	L	31	144	517	91	152	18	1	28	79	60	52	12	.294	.369	.495
Vic Davalillo	OF134	L	28	142	505	67	152	19	1	5	40	35	50	26	.301	.344	.372
Chuck Hinton	OF72,1B40,2B23*	R	31	133	431	59	110	17	6	18	54	53	65	17	.255	.336	.448
Dick Howser	SS73,2B17	R	29	107	307	47	72	8	2	1	6	57	25	17	.235	.354	.283
Chico Salmon	1B28,OF17,2B5*	R	24	79	120	20	29	8	0	3	12	5	19	7	.242	.281	.383
Duke Sims	C40	L	24	48	118	9	21	0	0	6	15	15	33	0	.178	.271	.331
Phil Roof†	C41	R	24	43	52	3	9	1	0	0	3	5	13	0	.173	.259	.192
Cam Carreon	C19	R	27	19	52	6	12	2	1	1	7	9	6	1	.231	.344	.365
Al Luplow	OF6	L	26	53	45	3	6	2	0	1	4	3	14	0	.133	.188	.244
Lu Clinton†	OF9	R	27	12	34	2	6	1	0	1	2	3	7	0	.176	.243	.294
Billy Moran	2B7,SS1	R	31	22	24	1	3	0	0	0	0	2	5	0	.125	.222	.125
Bill Davis		L	23	10	10	0	3	1	0	0	0	0	1	0	.300	.300	.400
Ray Barker†	1B3	L	29	11	6	0	0	0	0	0	0	2	2	0	.000	.250	.000
George Banks	3B1	R	26	4	5	0	1	1	0	0	0	1	3	0	.200	.333	.400
Tony Martinez		R	25	4	3	0	0	0	0	0	0	0	0	0	.000	.000	.000
Richie Scheinblum		S	22	4	1	1	0	0	0	0	0	0	0	0	.000	.000	.000
Ralph Gagliano		L	18	1	0	0	0	0	0	0	0	0	0	0	—	—	—

C. Hinton, 1 G at 3B; C. Salmon, 5 G at 3B

Pitcher	T	Age	G	GS	CG	ShO	IP	H	HR	BB	SO	W-L	Sv	ERA
Sam McDowell	L	22	42	35	14	3	273.0	178	9	132	325	17-11	4	2.18
Luis Tiant	R	24	41	30	10	2	196.1	166	20	66	152	11-11	1	3.53
Sonny Siebert	R	28	39	27	4	1	188.2	139	14	46	191	16-8	1	2.43
Ralph Terry	R	29	30	26	6	2	165.2	154	22	23	84	11-6	0	3.69
Jack Kralick	L	30	30	16	1	0	86.0	106	9	21	34	5-11	0	4.92
Tom Kelley	R	21	4	4	1	0	30.0	19	3	13	31	2-1	0	2.40
Gary Bell	R	28	60	0	0	0	103.2	86	7	50	86	6-5	17	3.04
Don McMahon	R	35	58	0	0	0	85.0	79	8	37	60	3-3	11	3.28
Lee Stange	R	28	41	12	4	2	132.0	122	13	26	80	8-4	0	3.34
Floyd Weaver	R	24	32	1	0	0	61.1	61	10	24	37	2-2	1	5.43
Steve Hargan	R	22	17	8	1	0	60.1	55	2	28	37	4-3	2	3.43
Bobby Tiefenauer†	R	35	15	0	0	0	22.1	24	3	10	13	0-5	4	4.84
Jack Spring	L	32	14	0	0	0	21.2	21	2	10	9	1-2	0	3.74
Dick Donovan	R	37	12	3	0	0	22.2	32	6	6	12	1-3	0	5.96
Mike Hedlund	R	18	6	0	0	0	5.1	6	0	5	4	0-0	0	5.06
Stan Williams	R	28	3	0	0	0	4.1	6	1	3	1	0-0	0	6.23

1965 New York Yankees 6th AL 77-85 .475 25.0 GB — Johnny Keane

Player	Gm by Position	B	Age	G	AB	R	H	2B	3B	HR	RBI	BB	SO	SB	Avg	OBP	Slg
Elston Howard	C95,1B5,OF1	R	36	110	391	38	91	15	1	9	45	24	65	0	.233	.278	.345
Joe Pepitone	1B115,OF41	L	24	143	531	51	131	18	3	18	62	43	59	4	.247	.305	.394
Bobby Richardson	2B158	R	29	160	664	76	164	28	2	6	47	37	39	7	.247	.287	.322
Clete Boyer	3B147,SS2	R	28	148	514	69	129	23	6	18	58	39	79	4	.251	.304	.424
Tony Kubek	SS93,OF3,1B1	L	28	109	339	26	74	5	3	5	35	20	48	1	.218	.258	.295
Tom Tresh	OF154	S	27	156	602	94	168	29	6	26	74	59	92	5	.279	.348	.477
Mickey Mantle	OF108	S	33	122	361	44	92	12	1	19	46	73	76	4	.255	.379	.452
Ross Moschitto	OF89	R	20	96	27	12	5	0	0	1	3	0	12	0	.185	.179	.296
Phil Linz	SS71,3B4,OF4*	R	26	99	285	37	59	12	1	2	16	30	33	2	.207	.281	.277
Hector Lopez	OF75,1B2	R	35	111	283	25	74	12	2	7	39	26	61	0	.261	.322	.392
Roger Repoz	OF69	L	24	79	218	34	48	7	4	12	28	25	57	1	.220	.298	.454
Ray Barker†	1B61,3B3	L	29	98	205	21	52	11	0	7	31	20	46	1	.254	.326	.410
Roger Maris	OF43	L	30	46	155	22	37	7	0	8	27	29	29	0	.239	.357	.439
Horace Clarke	3B17,2B7,SS1	S	25	51	108	13	28	1	0	1	9	6	6	2	.259	.296	.296
Doc Edwards†	C43	R	28	45	100	3	19	3	0	1	9	13	14	1	.190	.289	.250
Jake Gibbs	C21	L	26	37	68	6	15	1	0	2	7	4	20	0	.221	.267	.324
Art Lopez	OF16	L	28	38	49	5	7	0	0	0	0	1	6	0	.143	.160	.143
Roy White	OF10,2B1	S	21	14	42	7	14	2	0	0	3	4	7	2	.333	.404	.381
Bob Schmidt	C20	R	32	20	40	4	10	1	0	1	3	3	8	0	.250	.302	.350
Bobby Murcer	SS11	L	19	11	37	2	9	0	1	1	4	5	12	0	.243	.333	.378
Johnny Blanchard†	C12	L	32	12	34	1	5	1	0	1	3	7	3	0	.147	.286	.265
Archie Moore	OF5	L	23	9	17	1	7	2	0	1	4	4	4	0	.412	.524	.706
Duke Carmel	1B2	L	28	6	8	0	0	0	0	0	0	0	5	0	.000	.000	.000
Pedro Gonzalez†		R	27	7	5	0	2	1	0	0	0	0	2	0	.400	.400	.600

P. Linz, 1 G at 2B

Pitcher	T	Age	G	GS	CG	ShO	IP	H	HR	BB	SO	W-L	Sv	ERA
Mel Stottlemyre	R	23	37	37	18	4	291.0	250	18	88	155	20-9	0	2.63
Whitey Ford	L	36	37	36	9	2	244.1	241	22	50	162	16-13	1	3.24
Al Downing	L	24	35	32	8	2	212.0	185	16	105	179	12-14	0	3.40
Jim Bouton	R	26	30	25	2	0	151.1	158	23	60	97	4-15	0	4.82
Bill Stafford	R	25	22	15	1	0	111.1	93	16	31	71	3-8	0	3.56
Jack Cullen	R	25	12	9	2	1	59.0	59	2	21	25	3-4	0	3.05
Rich Beck	R	24	3	3	1	1	21.0	22	1	7	10	2-1	0	2.14
Pedro Ramos	R	30	65	0	0	0	92.1	80	7	27	68	5-5	19	2.92
Hal Reniff	R	26	51	0	0	0	85.1	74	4	48	74	3-4	3	3.80
Steve Hamilton	L	29	46	1	0	0	58.1	47	2	16	51	3-1	5	1.39
Pete Mikkelsen	R	25	41	3	0	0	82.1	78	10	36	69	4-9	1	3.28
Gil Blanco	L	19	17	1	0	0	20.1	16	1	12	14	1-1	0	3.98
Bobby Tiefenauer†	R	35	10	0	0	0	20.1	19	3	5	15	1-1	2	3.54
Rollie Sheldon†	R	28	3	0	0	0	6.1	5	0	1	7	0-0	0	1.42
Jim Brenneman	R	24	3	0	0	0	2.0	5	1	3	2	0-0	0	18.00
Mike Jurewicz	L	19	2	0	0	0	2.1	5	0	1	2	0-0	0	7.71

1965 California Angels 7th AL 75-87 .463 27.0 GB — Bill Rigney

Player	Gm by Position	B	Age	G	AB	R	H	2B	3B	HR	RBI	BB	SO	SB	Avg	OBP	Slg
Bob Rodgers	C128	S	26	132	411	33	86	14	3	1	32	35	61	4	.209	.271	.265
Vic Power	1B107,2B6,3B2	R	37	124	197	11	51	7	1	1	20	5	13	2	.259	.281	.320
Bobby Knoop	2B142	R	26	142	465	47	125	24	4	7	43	31	101	3	.269	.313	.383
Paul Schaal	3B153,2B1	R	22	155	483	48	108	12	2	9	45	61	88	6	.224	.310	.313
Jim Fregosi	SS160	R	23	161	602	66	167	19	7	15	64	54	107	13	.277	.337	.407
Jose Cardenal	OF129,3B2,2B1	R	21	134	512	58	128	23	2	11	57	27	72	37	.250	.287	.367
Willie Smith	OF123,1B2	L	26	136	459	52	120	14	9	14	57	32	60	9	.261	.308	.423
Albie Pearson	OF101	L	30	122	360	41	100	17	2	4	21	51	17	12	.278	.370	.369
Joe Adcock	1B97	R	37	122	349	30	84	14	0	14	47	37	74	2	.241	.315	.401
Lu Clinton†	OF73	R	27	89	222	29	54	12	3	1	8	23	37	2	.243	.316	.338
Jimmy Piersall	OF41	R	35	53	112	10	30	5	2	2	12	5	15	2	.268	.305	.402
Costen Shockley	1B31,OF1	L	23	40	107	5	20	2	0	2	17	9	16	0	.187	.252	.262
Al Spangler†	OF24	L	31	51	96	17	25	1	0	0	1	8	9	4	.260	.317	.271
Merritt Ranew	C24	L	27	41	91	12	19	4	0	1	10	7	22	0	.209	.260	.286
Tom Satriano	3B15,C12,2B12*	L	24	47	79	8	13	2	0	1	4	10	10	1	.165	.258	.228
Julio Gotay	2B23,3B9,SS1	R	26	40	77	6	19	4	0	1	3	4	9	0	.247	.284	.338
Rick Reichardt	OF20	R	22	20	75	8	20	4	0	1	6	5	12	4	.267	.321	.360
Ed Kirkpatrick	OF19	L	20	19	73	8	19	5	0	3	8	3	9	1	.260	.289	.452
Bobby Gene Smith	OF15	R	31	23	57	1	13	3	0	0	5	2	10	0	.228	.262	.281
Tom Egan	C16	R	19	18	38	3	10	0	1	0	1	3	12	0	.263	.317	.316
Joe Koppe	2B10,3B4,SS4	R	34	23	33	3	7	1	0	1	2	3	10	1	.212	.278	.333
Charlie Dees	1B8	L	30	12	32	1	5	0	0	0	1	1	8	1	.156	.182	.156
Dick Simpson	OF8	R	21	8	27	2	6	1	0	0	3	2	8	1	.222	.267	.259
Phil Roof†	C9	R	24	9	22	1	3	0	0	0	0	0	6	0	.136	.136	.136
Jackie Hernandez	SS2,3B1	R	24	6	6	2	2	1	0	0	1	0	1	1	.333	.333	.500
Gino Cimoli	OF1	R	35	4	5	1	0	0	0	0	1	0	2	0	.000	.000	.000

T. Satriano, 3 G at 1B

Pitcher	T	Age	G	GS	CG	ShO	IP	H	HR	BB	SO	W-L	Sv	ERA
Fred Newman	R	23	36	36	10	2	260.2	225	15	64	109	14-16	0	2.93
Dean Chance	R	24	36	33	10	4	225.2	197	12	101	164	15-10	0	3.15
Marcelino Lopez	L	21	35	32	8	1	215.1	185	12	82	122	14-13	1	2.93
George Brunet	L	30	41	26	8	3	197.0	149	9	69	141	9-11	2	2.56
Rudy May	L	20	30	19	2	1	124.0	111	7	78	76	4-9	0	3.92
Jack Sanford†	R	36	9	5	0	0	29.1	35	2	10	13	1-2	1	4.60
Ken McBride	R	29	8	4	0	0	22.0	24	1	14	11	0-3	0	6.14
Jim McGlothlin	R	21	3	3	1	0	18.0	18	1	7	9	0-3	0	3.50
Bob Lee	R	27	69	0	0	0	131.1	95	11	42	89	9-7	23	1.92
Aubrey Gatewood	R	26	46	3	0	0	92.0	91	5	37	37	4-5	0	3.42
Ed Sukla	R	22	25	0	0	0	32.0	32	3	10	15	2-3	3	4.50
Barry Latman	R	29	18	0	0	0	31.2	30	3	16	18	1-1	0	2.84
Jim Coates	R	32	17	0	0	0	28.0	23	1	16	15	2-0	3	3.54
Ron Piche	R	30	14	1	0	0	19.2	20	5	12	14	0-3	0	6.86
Don Lee†	R	31	10	0	0	0	14.0	21	4	5	12	0-1	0	6.43
Dick Wantz	R	25	1	0	0	0	1.0	3	0	0	2	0-0	0	18.00

1965 Washington Senators 8th AL 70-92 .432 32.0 GB — Gil Hodges

Player	Gm by Position	B	Age	G	AB	R	H	2B	3B	HR	RBI	BB	SO	SB	Avg	OBP	Slg
Mike Brumley	C66	L	26	79	216	15	45	4	0	3	15	20	33	1	.208	.280	.269
Dick Nen	1B65	L	25	69	246	18	64	7	1	6	31	19	47	1	.260	.312	.370
Don Blasingame	2B110	L	33	129	403	47	90	8	8	1	18	35	45	5	.223	.287	.290
Ken McMullen	3B142,OF8,1B1	R	23	150	555	75	146	18	6	18	54	47	90	2	.263	.323	.414
Ed Brinkman	SS150	R	23	154	444	35	82	13	2	5	35	38	82	1	.185	.251	.257
Frank Howard	OF138	R	28	149	516	53	149	22	6	21	84	55	112	0	.289	.358	.477
Don Lock	OF136	R	28	143	418	52	90	15	1	16	39	57	115	1	.215	.315	.371
Woodie Held	OF106,3B5,2B4*	R	33	122	332	46	82	16	2	16	54	49	74	1	.247	.345	.452
Ken Hamlin	2B77,SS47,3B1	R	30	117	362	45	99	21	1	4	22	33	45	8	.273	.333	.370
Willie Kirkland	OF92	L	31	123	312	38	72	9	1	14	54	19	65	3	.231	.270	.401
Jim King	OF88	L	32	120	258	46	55	10	2	14	49	44	50	1	.213	.337	.430
Don Zimmer	C33,3B26,2B12	R	34	95	226	20	45	6	0	2	17	26	59	2	.199	.284	.252
Joe Cunningham	1B59	L	33	95	201	29	46	9	1	3	20	46	27	0	.229	.375	.328
Bob Chance	1B48,OF3	L	24	72	199	20	51	9	0	4	14	18	44	0	.256	.317	.362
Doug Camilli	C59	R	28	75	193	13	37	6	1	3	18	16	34	0	.192	.257	.280
Jim French	C13	L	23	13	37	4	11	0	0	1	7	9	5	1	.297	.435	.378
Fred Valentine	OF11	S	30	12	29	6	7	0	0	0	1	4	5	3	.241	.353	.241
Joe McCabe	C11	R	26	14	27	1	5	0	0	1	5	4	13	1	.185	.281	.296
Roy Sievers	1B7	R	38	12	21	3	4	1	0	0	0	4	3	0	.190	.320	.238
Paul Casanova	C4	R	23	5	13	2	4	1	0	0	1	1	3	0	.308	.357	.385
Brant Alyea	1B3,OF1	R	24	8	13	3	3	0	0	2	6	1	4	0	.231	.286	.692
Chuck Cottier		R	29	7	1	1	0	0	0	0	0	0	0	0	.000	.000	.000

W. Held, 2 G at SS

Pitcher	T	Age	G	GS	CG	ShO	IP	H	HR	BB	SO	W-L	Sv	ERA
Pete Richert	L	25	34	29	6	0	194.0	146	18	84	161	15-12	0	2.60
Phil Ortega	R	25	35	29	4	2	179.2	176	33	97	88	12-15	0	5.11
Buster Narum	R	24	46	24	2	0	173.2	176	16	91	86	4-12	0	4.46
Bennie Daniels	R	33	33	18	1	0	116.1	135	16	39	42	5-13	1	4.72
Pete Craig	R	24	3	3	0	0	14.1	18	1	8	2	0-3	0	8.16
Joe Coleman	R	18	2	2	2	0	18.0	9	0	8	7	2-0	0	1.50
Ron Kline	R	33	74	0	0	0	99.1	106	7	32	52	7-6	29	2.63
Steve Ridzik	R	36	63	0	0	0	109.2	108	18	43	72	6-4	8	4.02
Mike McCormick	L	26	44	21	3	1	158.0	158	17	36	88	8-8	1	3.36
Marshall Bridges	L	34	40	0	0	0	57.1	62	3	25	39	1-2	0	2.67
Howie Koplitz	R	27	33	11	0	0	106.2	97	11	48	59	4-7	1	4.05
Frank Kreutzer	L	26	33	14	2	1	85.1	73	7	54	65	2-6	0	4.32
Jim Duckworth	R	26	17	8	0	0	64.0	45	11	36	74	2-2	0	3.94
Ryne Duren†	R	36	16	0	0	0	23.0	24	0	18	18	1-1	0	6.65
Dallas Green	R	30	6	2	0	0	14.1	14	0	3	6	0-0	0	3.14
Nick Willhite†	L	24	5	0	0	0	6.1	10	2	4	3	0-0	0	7.11
Jim Hannan	R	25	4	1	1	1	14.2	18	0	6	5	1-1	0	4.91
Barry Moore	L	22	1	0	0	0	1.0	1	0	1	0	0-0	0	0.00

1965 Boston Red Sox 9th AL 62-100 .383 40.0 GB — Billy Herman

Player	Gm by Position	B	Age	G	AB	R	H	2B	3B	HR	RBI	BB	SO	SB	Avg	OBP	Slg
Bob Tillman	C106	R	28	111	368	20	79	10	3	6	35	40	69	0	.215	.288	.307
Lee Thomas	1B127,OF20	L	29	151	521	74	141	27	4	22	75	72	42	6	.271	.361	.464
Felix Mantilla	2B123,OF27,1B2	R	30	150	534	60	147	17	2	18	92	79	84	7	.275	.374	.416
Frank Malzone	3B96	R	35	106	364	40	87	20	0	3	34	28	38	1	.239	.293	.319
Rico Petrocelli	SS93	R	22	103	323	38	75	15	2	13	33	36	71	0	.232	.309	.412
Tony Conigliaro	OF137	R	20	138	521	82	140	21	5	32	82	51	116	4	.269	.338	.512
Carl Yastrzemski	OF130	L	25	133	494	78	154	45	3	20	72	70	58	7	.312	.395	.536
Lenny Green	OF95	L	32	119	373	69	103	24	6	7	24	48	43	8	.276	.361	.429
Dalton Jones	3B81,2B8	L	21	112	367	41	99	13	5	5	37	28	45	8	.270	.325	.373
Jim Gosger	OF81	L	22	81	324	45	83	15	4	9	35	29	61	3	.256	.318	.410
Eddie Bressoud	SS86,3B2,OF1	R	33	107	296	29	67	11	1	8	25	29	77	0	.226	.297	.351
Chuck Schilling	2B41	R	27	71	171	14	41	3	2	3	9	13	17	0	.240	.292	.333
Tony Horton	1B44	R	20	60	163	23	48	8	1	7	23	18	36	0	.294	.361	.485
Russ Nixon	C38	L	30	59	137	11	37	5	1	0	11	6	23	0	.270	.295	.321
Mike Ryan	C33	R	23	33	107	7	17	0	1	3	9	5	19	0	.159	.193	.262
Gary Geiger	OF16	L	28	24	45	5	9	3	0	1	2	13	10	3	.200	.379	.333
Jerry Moses		R	18	4	4	1	1	0	0	1	1	0	2	0	.250	.250	1.000
Rudy Schlesinger		R	23	1	1	0	0	0	0	0	0	0	0	0	.000	.000	.000

Pitcher	T	Age	G	GS	CG	ShO	IP	H	HR	BB	SO	W-L	Sv	ERA
Earl Wilson	R	30	36	36	8	1	230.2	221	27	77	164	13-14	0	3.98
Bill Monbouquette	R	28	35	35	10	2	228.2	239	32	40	110	10-18	0	3.70
Dave Morehead	R	22	34	33	5	2	192.2	157	18	113	163	10-18	0	4.06
Jim Lonborg	R	23	32	31	7	1	185.1	193	20	65	113	9-17	0	4.47
Dennis Bennett	L	25	34	18	3	0	141.2	152	15	53	85	5-7	0	4.38
Jerry Stephenson	R	21	15	8	0	0	52.0	62	7	33	49	1-5	0	6.23
Dick Radatz	R	28	63	0	0	0	124.1	104	11	53	121	9-11	22	3.91
Arnold Earley	L	32	57	0	0	0	74.1	79	5	29	47	0-1	0	3.63
Jay Ritchie	R	28	44	0	0	0	71.0	83	3	26	55	1-2	2	3.17
Bob Duliba	R	30	39	0	0	0	64.1	60	6	22	27	4-2	1	3.78
Bob Heffner	R	26	27	1	0	0	49.0	59	9	18	42	0-2	0	7.16
Jack Lamabe†	R	28	14	0	0	0	25.1	34	5	14	17	0-3	0	8.17

1965 Kansas City Athletics 10th AL 59-103 .364 43.0 GB

Mel McGaha (5-21)/Haywood Sullivan (54-82)

Player	Gm by Position	B	Age	G	AB	R	H	2B	3B	HR	RBI	BB	SO	SB	Avg	OBP	Slg
Billy Bryan	C95	L	26	108	325	36	82	11	5	14	51	29	87	0	.252	.315	.446
Ken Harrelson	1B125,OF4	R	23	150	483	61	115	17	3	23	66	66	112	9	.238	.329	.429
Dick Green	2B126	R	24	133	474	64	110	15	1	15	55	50	110	0	.232	.308	.363
Ed Charles	3B128,2B1,SS1	R	32	134	480	55	129	19	7	8	56	44	72	13	.269	.332	.388
Bert Campaneris	SS109,OF39,P1*	R	23	144	578	67	156	23	12	6	42	41	71	51	.270	.326	.382
Mike Hershberger	OF144	R	25	150	494	43	114	15	5	5	48	37	42	7	.231	.289	.312
Jim Landis	OF108	R	31	118	364	46	87	15	1	3	36	57	84	8	.239	.346	.310
Tommie Reynolds	OF83,3B1	S	23	90	270	34	64	11	3	1	22	36	41	9	.237	.327	.311
Wayne Causey	SS62,2B45,3B35	L	28	144	513	48	134	17	8	3	34	61	48	1	.261	.341	.343
Jose Tartabull	OF54	L	26	68	218	28	68	11	4	1	19	18	20	11	.312	.361	.413
Rene Lachemann	C75	R	20	92	216	20	49	7	1	9	29	12	57	0	.227	.264	.394
Nelson Mathews	OF57	R	23	67	184	17	39	7	7	2	15	24	49	0	.212	.300	.359
Johnny Blanchard†	OF20,C14	L	32	52	120	10	24	2	0	2	11	8	16	0	.200	.250	.267
Jim Gentile†	1B35	L	31	38	118	14	29	5	0	10	22	9	26	0	.246	.305	.542
Santiago Rosario	1B31,OF3	L	25	81	85	8	20	3	0	2	8	6	16	0	.235	.287	.341
Larry Stahl	OF21	L	24	28	81	9	16	2	1	4	14	5	16	1	.198	.250	.395
Skip Lockwood	3B7	R	18	42	33	4	4	0	0	0	0	7	11	0	.121	.293	.121
Doc Edwards†	C6	R	28	6	20	1	3	0	0	0	0	1	2	0	.150	.190	.150
Randy Schwartz	1B2	L	21	3	7	0	2	0	0	0	1	0	4	0	.286	.286	.286
Lu Clinton†	OF1	R	27	1	1	0	0	0	0	0	0	0	0	0	.000	.000	.000
John Sanders		R	19	1	0	0	0	0	0	0	0	0	0	0	—	—	—

B. Campaneris, 1 G at C, 1 G at 1B, 1 G at 2B, 1 G at 3B

Pitcher	T	Age	G	GS	CG	ShO	IP	H	HR	BB	SO	W-L	Sv	ERA
Fred Talbot	R	24	39	33	2	1	198.0	188	25	86	117	10-12	0	4.14
John O'Donoghue	L	25	34	30	4	1	177.2	183	15	66	82	9-18	0	3.95
Rollie Sheldon†	R	28	32	29	4	1	186.2	180	22	56	105	10-8	0	3.95
Diego Segui	R	27	40	25	5	1	163.0	166	18	67	119	5-15	0	4.64
Catfish Hunter	R	19	32	20	3	2	133.0	124	21	46	82	8-8	0	4.26
Lew Krausse	R	22	7	5	0	0	25.0	29	1	8	22	2-4	0	5.04
Dick Joyce	L	21	5	3	0	0	13.0	12	0	4	7	0-1	0	2.77
Satchel Paige	R	58	1	1	0	0	3.0	1	0	0	1	0-0	0	0.00
Jim Dickson	R	27	68	0	0	0	85.2	68	6	47	54	3-2	0	3.47
John Wyatt	R	30	65	0	0	0	88.2	78	8	53	70	2-6	18	3.25
Wes Stock	R	31	62	2	0	0	99.2	96	18	40	52	0-4	4	5.24
Don Mossi	L	36	51	0	0	0	55.1	59	0	20	41	5-8	7	3.74
Jack Aker	R	24	34	0	0	0	51.1	45	3	18	26	4-3	3	3.16
Moe Drabowsky	R	29	14	5	0	0	38.2	44	5	18	25	1-5	0	4.42
Orlando Pena†	R	31	12	5	0	0	35.1	42	4	13	24	0-6	0	6.88
Don Buschhorn	R	19	12	3	0	0	31.0	36	7	8	9	0-1	0	4.35
Jesse Hickman	R	26	12	0	0	0	15.1	9	3	8	16	0-1	0	5.87
Ron Tompkins	R	20	5	1	0	0	10.1	9	0	3	4	0-0	0	3.48
Paul Lindblad	L	23	4	0	0	0	7.1	12	3	0	12	0-1	0	11.05
Aurelio Monteagudo	R	21	4	0	0	0	7.0	5	1	4	5	0-0	0	3.86
Jose Santiago	R	24	4	0	0	0	5.0	8	1	4	8	0-0	0	9.00
Bert Campaneris	R	23	1	0	0	0	1.0	1	0	2	1	0-0	0	9.00
Blue Moon Odom	R	20	1	0	0	0	1.0	2	0	2	0	0-0	0	9.00
Tom Harrison	R	20	1	0	0	0	0.2	2	0	1	0	0-0	0	13.50

»1965 Los Angeles Dodgers 1st NL 97-65 .599 —

Walter Alston

Player	Gm by Position	B	Age	G	AB	R	H	2B	3B	HR	RBI	BB	SO	SB	Avg	OBP	Slg
John Roseboro	C131,3B1	L	32	136	437	42	102	10	0	8	57	34	51	1	.233	.289	.311
Wes Parker	1B154,OF1	S	25	154	542	80	129	24	7	8	51	75	95	13	.238	.334	.352
Jim Lefebvre	2B156	S	23	157	544	57	136	21	4	12	69	71	92	3	.250	.337	.369
John Kennedy	3B95,SS5	R	24	104	105	12	18	3	0	1	5	8	33	1	.171	.243	.229
Maury Wills	SS155	S	32	158	650	92	186	14	7	0	33	40	64	94	.286	.330	.329
Ron Fairly	OF148,1B13	L	26	158	555	73	152	28	1	9	70	76	72	2	.274	.361	.377
Willie Davis	OF141	L	25	142	558	52	133	24	3	10	57	14	81	25	.238	.263	.346
Lou Johnson	OF128	R	30	131	468	57	121	24	1	12	58	24	81	15	.259	.315	.391
Jim Gilliam	3B80,OF22,2B5	S	36	111	372	54	104	19	4	4	39	53	31	9	.280	.374	.384
Dick Tracewski	3B53,2B14,SS7	R	30	78	186	17	40	6	0	1	20	25	30	2	.215	.313	.263
Jeff Torborg	C53	R	23	56	150	8	36	5	1	3	13	10	26	0	.240	.290	.347
Wally Moon	OF23	L	35	53	89	6	18	3	0	1	11	13	22	2	.202	.304	.270
Al Ferrara	OF27	R	25	41	81	5	17	2	1	1	10	9	20	0	.210	.297	.296
Don LeJohn	3B26	R	31	34	78	2	20	2	0	0	7	5	13	0	.256	.301	.282
Tommy Davis	OF16	R	26	17	60	3	15	1	1	0	9	2	4	2	.250	.270	.300
Derrell Griffith	OF11	L	21	22	41	3	7	0	0	1	2	0	9	0	.171	.171	.244
Willie Crawford	OF8	L	18	52	27	10	4	0	0	0	0	2	8	2	.148	.207	.148
Hector Valle	C6	R	24	9	13	1	4	0	0	0	2	2	3	0	.308	.400	.308
Dick Smith	OF9	R	26	10	6	0	0	0	0	0	1	0	3	0	.000	.000	.000
Johnny Werhas	1B1	R	27	4	3	1	0	0	0	0	0	1	2	0	.000	.250	.000
Nate Oliver	2B2	R	24	8	1	3	1	0	0	0	0	0	0	1	1.000	1.000	1.000

Pitcher	T	Age	G	GS	CG	ShO	IP	H	HR	BB	SO	W-L	Sv	ERA
Don Drysdale	R	28	44	42	20	7	308.1	270	30	66	210	23-12	1	2.77
Sandy Koufax	L	29	43	41	27	8	335.2	216	26	71	382	26-8	2	2.04
Claude Osteen	L	25	40	40	9	1	287.0	253	19	78	162	15-15	0	2.79
Johnny Podres	L	32	27	22	2	1	134.0	126	17	39	63	7-6	1	3.43
Bob Miller	R	26	61	1	0	0	103.0	82	9	26	77	6-7	9	2.97
Ron Perranoski	L	29	59	0	0	0	104.2	85	2	40	53	6-6	17	2.24
Howie Reed	R	28	38	5	0	0	78.0	73	6	27	47	7-5	1	3.12
Jim Brewer	L	27	19	2	0	0	49.1	33	1	28	31	3-2	2	1.82
Nick Willhite†	L	24	15	6	0	0	42.0	47	7	22	28	2-2	1	5.36
John Purdin	R	22	11	2	0	0	22.2	26	8	13	16	2-1	0	6.75
Mike Kekich	L	20	5	1	0	0	10.1	10	2	13	9	0-1	0	9.58
Bill Singer	R	21	2	0	0	0	1.0	2	0	2	1	0-0	0	0.00

1965 San Francisco Giants 2nd NL 95-67 .586 2.0 GB

Herman Franks

Player	Gm by Position	B	Age	G	AB	R	H	2B	3B	HR	RBI	BB	SO	SB	Avg	OBP	Slg
Tom Haller	C133	L	28	134	422	40	106	4	3	16	49	47	67	0	.251	.335	.389
Willie McCovey	1B156	L	27	160	540	93	149	17	4	39	92	88	118	0	.276	.381	.539
Hal Lanier	2B158,SS1	R	22	159	522	41	118	15	9	0	39	21	67	2	.226	.256	.289
Jim Ray Hart	3B144,OF15	R	23	160	591	91	177	30	6	23	96	47	75	6	.299	.349	.487
Dick Schofield†	SS93	S	30	101	379	39	77	10	1	2	19	33	50	2	.203	.272	.251
Willie Mays	OF151	R	34	157	558	118	177	21	3	52	112	76	71	9	.317	.398	.645
Jesus Alou	OF136	R	23	143	543	76	162	19	4	9	52	13	40	8	.298	.317	.398
Matty Alou	OF103,P1	L	26	117	324	37	75	12	2	2	18	17	28	10	.231	.274	.299
Jim Davenport	3B39,SS37,2B26	R	31	106	271	29	68	14	3	4	31	21	47	0	.251	.304	.369
Len Gabrielson†	OF77,1B5	L	25	88	269	36	81	6	5	4	26	26	48	4	.301	.365	.405
Cap Peterson	OF27	R	22	63	105	14	26	7	0	3	15	10	16	0	.248	.310	.400
Jose Pagan†	SS26	R	30	26	83	10	17	4	0	0	5	8	9	1	.205	.272	.253
Ken Henderson	OF48	S	19	63	73	10	14	1	1	0	7	9	19	1	.192	.277	.233
Tito Fuentes	SS18,2B7,3B1	S	21	26	72	12	15	1	0	0	1	5	14	0	.208	.269	.222
Jack Hiatt	C21,1B7	R	22	40	67	5	19	4	0	1	7	12	14	0	.284	.392	.388
Harvey Kuenn†	OF14,1B7	R	34	23	59	4	14	0	0	0	6	10	3	3	.237	.352	.237
Dick Bertell†	C22	R	29	22	48	1	9	1	0	0	3	7	5	0	.188	.291	.208
Orlando Cepeda	1B4,OF2	R	27	33	34	1	6	1	0	1	5	3	9	0	.176	.225	.294
Ed Bailey†	C12,1B2	L	34	24	28	1	3	0	0	0	3	6	7	0	.107	.250	.107
Bob Burda	1B11,OF1	L	26	31	27	0	3	0	0	0	5	5	6	0	.111	.235	.111
Randy Hundley	C6	R	23	6	15	0	1	0	0	0	0	0	4	0	.067	.067	.067
Ollie Brown	OF4	R	21	6	10	0	2	1	0	0	0	0	2	0	.200	.200	.300
Bob Schroder	2B4,3B1	L	20	31	9	4	2	0	0	0	1	1	1	0	.222	.300	.222
Bob Barton	C2	R	23	4	7	1	4	0	0	0	1	0	0	0	.571	.571	.571
Chuck Hiller†	2B2	L	30	7	7	1	1	0	0	1	1	0	1	0	.143	.143	.571

Pitcher	T	Age	G	GS	CG	ShO	IP	H	HR	BB	SO	W-L	Sv	ERA
Juan Marichal	R	27	39	37	24	10	295.1	224	27	46	240	22-13	1	2.13
Bob Shaw	R	32	42	33	6	1	235.0	213	17	53	148	16-9	2	2.64
Gaylord Perry	R	26	47	26	6	0	195.2	194	21	70	170	8-12	1	4.19
Jack Sanford†	R	36	23	16	0	0	91.0	92	11	30	43	4-5	2	3.96
Warren Spahn†	L	44	16	11	3	0	71.2	70	8	21	34	3-4	0	3.39
Bill Hands	R	25	4	2	0	0	6.0	13	0	6	5	0-2	0	16.50
Frank Linzy	R	24	57	0	0	0	81.2	76	2	23	35	9-3	21	1.43
Ron Herbel	R	27	47	21	1	0	170.2	172	16	47	106	12-9	1	3.85
Bobby Bolin	R	26	45	13	2	0	163.0	125	17	56	135	14-6	2	2.76
Masanori Murakami	L	21	45	1	0	0	74.1	57	9	22	85	4-1	8	3.75
Bill Henry†	L	37	35	0	0	0	42.0	40	2	8	35	2-2	4	3.64
Bob Hendley†	L	26	8	2	0	0	15.0	27	6	13	8	0-0	0	12.60
Bob Priddy	R	25	8	0	0	0	10.1	6	1	2	7	1-0	0	1.74
Dick Estelle	L	23	6	1	0	0	11.1	12	0	8	6	0-0	0	3.97
Jim Duffalo†	R	29	2	0	0	0	0.1	1	0	2	0	0-1	0	27.00
Matty Alou	L	26	1	0	0	0	2.0	3	0	1	3	0-0	0	0.00

1965 Pittsburgh Pirates 3rd NL 90-72 .556 7.0 GB

Harry Walker

Player	Gm by Position	B	Age	G	AB	R	H	2B	3B	HR	RBI	BB	SO	SB	Avg	OBP	Slg
Jim Pagliaroni	C131	R	27	134	403	42	108	15	0	17	65	41	84	0	.268	.337	.432
Donn Clendenon	1B158,3B1	R	29	162	612	89	184	32	14	14	96	48	128	9	.301	.351	.467
Bill Mazeroski	2B127	R	28	130	494	52	134	17	1	6	54	18	34	2	.271	.294	.346
Bob Bailey	3B142,OF28	R	22	159	626	87	160	28	3	11	49	70	93	10	.256	.330	.363
Gene Alley	SS110,2B40,3B1	R	24	153	500	47	126	21	6	5	47	32	82	7	.252	.302	.348
Roberto Clemente	OF145	R	30	152	589	91	194	21	14	10	65	43	78	8	.329	.378	.463
Willie Stargell	OF137,1B7	L	25	144	533	68	145	25	8	27	107	39	127	1	.272	.328	.501
Bill Virdon	OF128	L	34	135	481	58	134	22	5	4	24	30	49	4	.279	.322	.370
Manny Mota	OF95	R	27	121	294	47	82	7	6	4	29	22	32	2	.279	.330	.384
Andre Rodgers	SS33,3B15,1B6*	R	30	75	178	17	51	12	0	2	25	18	28	2	.287	.350	.388
Del Crandall	C60	R	35	60	140	11	30	2	0	2	10	14	10	1	.214	.288	.271
Jerry Lynch	OF26	L	34	73	121	7	34	1	0	5	16	8	26	0	.281	.328	.413
Dick Schofield†	SS28	S	30	31	109	13	25	5	0	0	6	15	19	1	.229	.317	.275
Gene Freese†	3B19	R	31	43	80	6	21	4	0	0	8	6	18	0	.263	.326	.313
Ozzie Virgil	C15,3B7,2B5	R	32	39	49	3	13	2	0	1	5	2	10	0	.265	.294	.367
Jose Pagan†	3B15,SS7	R	30	42	38	6	9	1	0	0	1	1	7	1	.237	.275	.263
Al McBean	P62,OF1	R	27	62	27	2	6	1	0	0	2	1	12	0	.222	.250	.259
Hal Smith	C4	R	34	4	3	0	0	0	0	0	0	0	1	0	.000	.000	.000
George Spriggs	OF1	L	24	9	2	5	1	0	0	0	0	0	0	2	.500	.500	.500
Bob Oliver	OF3	R	22	3	2	1	0	0	0	0	0	0	0	0	.000	.000	.000
Jerry May	C4	R	21	4	2	0	1	0	0	0	1	0	0	0	.500	.500	.500

A. Rodgers, 1 G at 2B

Pitcher	T	Age	G	GS	CG	ShO	IP	H	HR	BB	SO	W-L	Sv	ERA
Bob Veale	L	29	39	37	14	7	266.0	221	5	119	276	17-12	0	2.84
Don Cardwell	R	29	37	34	12	2	240.1	214	21	59	107	13-10	0	3.18
Bob Friend	R	34	34	34	8	2	222.0	221	17	47	74	8-12	0	3.24
Vern Law	R	35	29	28	13	4	217.1	182	17	35	101	17-9	0	2.15
Al McBean	R	27	62	1	0	0	114.0	111	5	42	54	6-6	18	2.29
Don Schwall	R	29	43	1	0	0	77.0	77	5	30	55	9-6	4	2.92
Frank Carpin	L	26	39	0	0	0	39.2	35	0	24	27	3-1	4	3.18
Tommie Sisk	R	23	38	12	1	1	111.1	103	6	50	66	7-3	0	3.40
Wilbur Wood	L	23	34	1	0	0	51.1	44	3	16	29	1-1	0	3.16
Joe Gibbon	L	30	31	15	1	0	105.2	85	7	34	63	4-9	1	4.51
Roy Face	R	37	16	0	0	0	20.1	20	1	7	19	5-2	0	2.66
Tom Butters	R	27	5	0	0	0	9.0	9	2	5	6	0-1	0	7.00
Luke Walker	L	21	2	0	0	0	5.0	2	0	1	5	0-0	0	0.00

1965 Cincinnati Reds 4th NL 89-73 .549 8.0 GB

Dick Sisler

Player	Gm by Position	B	Age	G	AB	R	H	2B	3B	HR	RBI	BB	SO	SB	Avg	OBP	Slg
Johnny Edwards	C110	L	27	114	371	47	99	22	2	17	51	50	45	0	.267	.353	.474
Tony Perez	1B93	R	23	104	281	40	73	14	4	12	47	21	67	0	.260	.315	.466
Pete Rose	2B162	S	24	162	670	117	209	35	11	11	81	69	76	8	.312	.382	.446
Deron Johnson	3B159	R	26	159	616	92	177	30	7	32	130	52	97	0	.287	.340	.515
Leo Cardenas	SS155	R	26	156	557	65	160	25	11	11	57	60	100	1	.287	.355	.431
Vada Pinson	OF159	L	26	159	669	97	204	34	10	22	94	43	81	21	.305	.352	.484
Tommy Harper	OF159,3B2,2B1	R	24	159	646	126	166	28	3	18	64	78	127	35	.257	.340	.393
Frank Robinson	OF155	R	29	156	582	109	172	33	5	33	113	70	100	13	.296	.386	.540
Gordy Coleman	1B89	L	30	108	325	39	98	19	0	14	57	24	38	0	.302	.348	.489
Don Pavletich	C54,1B9	R	26	68	191	25	61	11	1	8	32	23	27	1	.319	.394	.513
Art Shamsky	OF18,1B1	L	23	64	96	13	25	4	3	2	10	10	29	1	.260	.333	.427
Jimmie Coker	C19	R	29	24	61	3	15	2	0	2	9	8	16	0	.246	.329	.377
Marty Keough	1B32,OF4	L	30	62	43	14	5	0	0	0	3	3	14	0	.116	.191	.116
Tommy Helms	SS8,3B2,2B1	R	24	21	42	4	16	2	2	0	6	3	7	1	.381	.435	.524
Charlie James	OF7	R	27	26	39	2	8	0	0	0	2	1	9	0	.205	.225	.205
Chico Ruiz	3B4,SS3	S	26	29	18	7	2	1	0	0	1	0	5	1	.111	.111	.167
Lee May		R	22	5	4	1	0	0	0	0	0	0	1	0	.000	.000	.000
Mel Queen	OF1	L	23	5	3	0	0	0	0	0	0	0	1	0	.000	.000	.000
Steve Boros	3B2	R	28	2	0	0	0	0	0	0	0	0	0	0	—	—	—

Pitcher	T	Age	G	GS	CG	ShO	IP	H	HR	BB	SO	W-L	Sv	ERA
Sammy Ellis	R	24	44	39	15	2	263.2	222	22	104	183	22-10	2	3.79
Jim Maloney	R	25	33	33	14	5	255.1	189	13	110	244	20-9	0	2.54
Joey Jay	R	29	37	24	4	1	155.2	150	21	63	102	9-8	1	4.22
Jim O'Toole	L	28	29	22	2	0	127.2	154	14	47	71	3-10	1	5.92
John Tsitouris	R	29	31	20	3	0	131.0	134	18	65	91	6-9	1	4.95
Joe Nuxhall	L	36	32	16	5	1	148.2	142	18	31	117	11-4	2	3.45
Billy McCool	L	20	62	2	0	0	105.1	93	9	47	120	9-10	21	4.27
Roger Craig	R	35	40	0	0	0	64.1	74	6	25	30	1-4	3	3.64
Gerry Arrigo	L	24	27	5	0	0	54.0	75	4	30	43	2-4	2	6.17
Ted Davidson	L	25	24	1	0	0	68.2	57	5	17	54	4-3	1	2.23
Jim Duffalo†	R	29	22	0	0	0	44.1	33	3	30	34	0-1	0	3.45
Bobby Locke	R	31	11	0	0	0	17.1	20	2	8	8	0-1	0	5.71
Dom Zanni	R	33	8	0	0	0	13.1	7	1	5	10	0-0	0	1.35
Bill Henry†	L	37	3	0	0	0	5.0	3	0	1	5	2-0	0	0.00
Darrell Osteen	R	22	3	0	0	0	3.0	2	0	4	1	0-0	0	0.00

1965 Milwaukee Braves 5th NL 86-76 .531 11.0 GB

Bobby Bragan

Player	Gm by Position	B	Age	G	AB	R	H	2B	3B	HR	RBI	BB	SO	SB	Avg	OBP	Slg
Joe Torre	C100,1B49	R	24	148	523	68	152	21	1	27	80	61	79	0	.291	.372	.489
Felipe Alou	OF91,1B69,3B2*	R	30	143	555	80	165	29	2	23	78	31	63	8	.297	.338	.481
Frank Bolling	2B147	R	33	148	535	55	141	26	3	7	50	24	41	0	.264	.295	.363
Eddie Mathews	3B153	L	33	156	546	77	137	23	0	32	95	73	110	1	.251	.341	.469
Woody Woodward	SS107,2B8	R	22	112	265	17	55	7	4	0	11	10	50	2	.208	.235	.264
Hank Aaron	OF148	R	31	150	570	109	181	40	1	32	89	60	81	24	.318	.379	.560
Mack Jones	OF133	L	26	143	504	78	132	18	7	31	75	29	122	8	.262	.313	.510
Ty Cline	OF86,1B5	L	26	123	220	27	42	5	3	0	10	16	50	2	.191	.246	.241
Gene Oliver	C64,1B52,OF1	R	30	122	392	56	106	20	0	21	58	36	61	5	.270	.336	.482
Rico Carty	OF73	R	25	83	271	37	84	18	1	10	35	17	44	1	.310	.355	.494
Denis Menke	SS54,1B8,3B4	R	24	71	181	16	44	13	1	4	18	18	28	1	.243	.313	.392
Mike de la Hoz	SS41,3B22,2B10*	R	26	81	176	15	45	3	2	2	11	8	21	0	.256	.293	.330
Sandy Alomar	SS39,2B19	S	21	67	108	16	26	1	1	0	8	4	12	12	.241	.268	.269
Jesse Gonder†	C13	L	29	31	53	2	8	2	0	1	5	4	9	0	.151	.211	.245
Lee Maye†	OF13	L	30	15	53	8	16	2	0	2	7	2	6	0	.302	.339	.453
Lou Klimchock	1B4	L	25	34	39	3	3	0	0	0	3	2	8	0	.077	.119	.077
Frank Thomas†	1B6,OF3	R	36	15	33	3	7	3	0	0	1	2	11	0	.212	.250	.303
Billy Cowan†	OF10	R	26	19	27	4	5	1	0	0	0	0	9	0	.185	.185	.222
Gary Kolb†	OF13	L	25	24	27	3	7	0	0	0	1	1	6	0	.259	.286	.259
Billy O'Dell	P62,1B1	S	32	62	23	1	4	1	0	0	2	1	11	0	.174	.208	.217
Don Dillard	OF1	L	28	20	19	1	3	0	0	1	3	0	6	0	.158	.158	.316
Tommie Aaron	1B6	R	25	8	16	1	3	0	0	0	1	1	2	0	.188	.235	.188
Johnny Blanchard†	OF1	L	32	10	10	1	1	0	0	1	2	2	1	0	.100	.250	.400
Jim Beauchamp†	1B2	R	25	4	3	0	0	0	0	0	0	1	1	0	.000	.250	.000

F. Alou, 1 G at SS; M. de la Hoz, 1 G at 1B

Pitcher	T	Age	G	GS	CG	ShO	IP	H	HR	BB	SO	W-L	Sv	ERA
Tony Cloninger	R	24	40	38	16	1	279.0	247	20	119	211	24-11	1	3.29
Wade Blasingame	L	21	38	36	10	1	224.2	200	17	116	117	16-10	1	3.77
Ken Johnson†	R	32	29	26	8	1	179.2	165	15	37	123	13-8	2	3.21
Denny Lemaster	L	26	32	23	4	1	146.1	140	12	58	111	7-13	0	4.43
Hank Fischer	R	25	31	19	2	0	122.2	126	18	39	79	8-9	0	3.89
Billy O'Dell	L	32	62	1	0	0	111.1	87	10	30	78	10-6	18	2.18
Dan Osinski	R	31	61	0	0	0	83.0	81	4	40	54	0-3	6	2.82
Phil Niekro	R	26	41	1	0	0	74.2	73	5	26	49	2-3	6	2.89
Bob Sadowski	R	27	34	13	3	0	123.0	117	11	35	78	5-9	3	4.32
Dick Kelley	L	25	21	4	0	0	45.0	37	5	20	31	1-1	0	3.00
Clay Carroll	R	24	19	1	0	0	34.2	35	3	13	16	0-1	1	4.41
Chi Chi Olivo	R	37	8	0	0	0	13.0	12	1	5	11	0-1	0	1.38
Bobby Tiefenauer†	R	35	6	0	0	0	7.0	8	1	3	7	0-1	0	7.71
Dave Eilers†	R	28	6	0	0	0	3.2	8	1	0	1	0-0	0	12.27

1965 Philadelphia Phillies 6th NL 85-76 .528 11.5 GB

Gene Mauch

Player	Gm by Position	B	Age	G	AB	R	H	2B	3B	HR	RBI	BB	SO	SB	Avg	OBP	Slg
Clay Dalrymple	C102	L	28	103	301	14	64	5	5	4	23	34	37	0	.213	.292	.302
Dick Stuart	1B143,3B1	R	32	149	538	53	126	19	1	28	95	39	136	1	.234	.287	.429
Tony Taylor	2B86,3B5	R	29	106	323	41	74	14	3	3	27	22	58	5	.229	.302	.319
Dick Allen	3B160,SS2	R	23	161	619	93	187	31	14	20	85	74	150	15	.302	.375	.494
Bobby Wine	SS135,1B4	R	26	139	394	31	90	8	1	5	33	31	69	0	.228	.284	.292
Johnny Callison	OF159	L	26	160	619	93	162	25	16	32	101	57	117	6	.262	.328	.509
Tony Gonzalez	OF104	L	28	108	370	48	109	19	1	13	41	31	52	3	.295	.351	.457
Alex Johnson	OF82	R	22	97	262	27	77	9	3	8	28	15	60	4	.294	.337	.443
Cookie Rojas	2B84,OF55,SS11*	R	26	142	521	78	158	25	3	3	42	42	33	5	.303	.356	.380
Wes Covington	OF64	L	33	101	235	27	58	10	1	15	45	26	47	0	.247	.322	.489
John Briggs	OF66	L	21	93	229	47	54	9	4	4	23	42	44	3	.236	.349	.362
Ruben Amaro	1B60,SS60,2B6	R	29	118	184	26	39	7	0	0	15	27	22	1	.212	.312	.250
Pat Corrales	C62	R	24	63	174	16	39	8	1	2	15	25	42	0	.224	.323	.316
Adolfo Phillips	OF32	R	23	41	87	14	20	4	0	3	5	5	34	3	.230	.272	.379
John Herrnstein	1B18,OF14	L	27	63	85	8	17	2	0	1	5	2	18	0	.200	.227	.259
Gus Triandos†	C28	R	34	30	82	3	14	2	0	0	4	9	17	0	.171	.253	.195
Frank Thomas†	OF12,1B11,3B1	R	36	35	77	7	20	4	0	1	7	4	10	0	.260	.289	.351
Bill Sorrell	3B1	L	24	10	13	2	5	0	0	1	2	2	1	0	.385	.467	.615
Bobby Del Greco	OF4	R	32	8	4	1	0	0	0	0	0	0	3	0	.000	.000	.000

C. Rojas, 2 G at C, 1 G at 1B

Pitcher	T	Age	G	GS	CG	ShO	IP	H	HR	BB	SO	W-L	Sv	ERA
Chris Short	L	27	47	40	15	5	297.1	260	18	89	237	18-11	2	2.82
Jim Bunning	R	33	39	39	15	7	291.0	253	23	62	268	19-9	0	2.60
Ray Culp	R	23	33	30	11	2	204.1	188	14	78	134	14-10	0	3.22
Ray Herbert	R	35	25	19	4	1	130.2	162	13	19	51	5-8	1	3.86
Jack Baldschun	R	28	65	0	0	0	99.0	102	4	42	81	5-8	6	3.82
Gary Wagner	R	25	59	0	0	0	105.0	87	6	49	91	7-7	7	3.00
Ed Roebuck	R	33	44	0	0	0	50.1	55	2	15	29	5-3	3	3.40
Bo Belinsky	L	28	30	14	3	0	109.2	103	13	48	71	4-9	1	4.84
Art Mahaffey	R	27	22	9	1	0	71.0	82	11	32	52	2-5	0	6.21
Lew Burdette†	R	38	19	9	1	1	70.2	95	5	17	23	3-3	0	5.48
Fergie Jenkins	R	21	7	0	0	0	12.1	7	2	2	10	2-1	1	2.19
Grant Jackson	L	22	6	2	0	0	13.2	17	4	5	15	1-1	0	7.24
Ryne Duren†	R	36	6	0	0	0	11.0	10	0	4	6	0-0	0	3.27
Morrie Steevens	L	24	6	0	0	0	2.2	5	1	4	3	0-1	0	16.88

1965 St. Louis Cardinals 7th NL 80-81 .497 16.5 GB

Red Schoendienst

Player	Gm by Position	B	Age	G	AB	R	H	2B	3B	HR	RBI	BB	SO	SB	Avg	OBP	Slg
Tim McCarver	C111	L	23	113	409	48	113	17	2	11	48	31	26	5	.276	.327	.408
Bill White	1B144	L	31	148	543	82	157	26	3	24	73	63	86	3	.289	.364	.481
Julian Javier	2B69	R	28	77	229	34	52	6	4	2	23	8	44	5	.227	.260	.314
Ken Boyer	3B143	R	34	144	535	71	139	18	2	13	75	57	73	2	.260	.328	.374
Dick Groat	SS148,3B2	R	34	153	587	55	149	26	5	0	52	56	50	1	.254	.316	.315
Lou Brock	OF153	L	26	155	631	107	182	35	8	16	69	45	116	63	.288	.345	.445
Curt Flood	OF151	R	27	156	617	90	191	30	3	11	83	51	50	9	.310	.366	.421
Mike Shannon	OF101,C4	R	25	124	244	32	54	17	3	3	25	28	46	2	.221	.305	.352
Phil Gagliano	2B57,OF25,3B19	R	23	122	363	46	87	14	2	8	53	40	45	2	.240	.312	.355
Tito Francona	OF34,1B13	L	31	81	174	15	45	6	2	5	19	17	30	0	.259	.323	.402
Jerry Buchek	2B33,SS18,3B1	R	23	55	166	17	41	8	3	3	21	13	46	1	.247	.300	.386
Bob Skinner	OF33	L	33	80	152	25	47	5	4	5	26	12	30	1	.309	.360	.493
Bob Uecker	C49	R	30	53	145	17	33	7	0	2	10	24	27	0	.228	.345	.317
Dal Maxvill	2B49,SS12	R	26	68	89	10	12	2	2	0	10	7	15	0	.135	.206	.202
Carl Warwick†	OF21,1B4	R	28	50	77	3	12	2	1	0	6	4	18	1	.156	.198	.208
Bobby Tolan	OF17	L	19	17	69	8	13	2	0	0	6	0	4	2	.188	.197	.217
Ted Savage	OF20	R	28	30	63	7	10	3	0	1	4	6	9	1	.159	.232	.254
George Kernek	1B7	L	25	10	31	6	9	3	1	0	3	2	4	0	.290	.333	.452
Dave Ricketts	C11	S	29	11	29	1	7	0	0	0	0	1	3	0	.241	.267	.241
Ed Spiezio	3B3	R	23	10	18	0	3	0	0	0	5	1	4	0	.167	.250	.167

Pitcher	T	Age	G	GS	CG	ShO	IP	H	HR	BB	SO	W-L	Sv	ERA
Bob Gibson	R	29	38	36	20	6	299.0	243	34	103	270	20-12	1	3.07
Curt Simmons	L	36	34	32	5	0	203.0	229	19	54	96	9-15	0	4.08
Ray Sadecki	L	24	36	28	4	0	172.2	192	26	64	122	6-15	1	5.21
Tracy Stallard	R	27	40	26	4	1	194.1	172	25	70	99	11-8	0	3.38
Bob Purkey	R	35	32	17	3	1	124.1	148	20	33	39	10-9	2	5.79
Ray Washburn	R	27	28	16	1	1	119.1	114	15	28	67	9-11	2	3.62
Larry Jaster	L	21	4	3	3	0	28.0	21	1	7	10	3-0	0	1.61
Hal Woodeshick†	L	32	51	0	0	0	59.2	47	1	27	37	3-2	15	1.81
Don Dennis	R	23	41	0	0	0	55.0	47	3	16	29	2-3	6	2.29
Nelson Briles	R	21	37	2	0	0	82.1	79	4	26	52	3-3	4	3.50
Barney Schultz	R	38	34	0	0	0	42.1	39	8	11	38	2-2	2	3.83
Ron Taylor†	R	27	25	0	0	0	43.2	43	6	15	26	2-1	1	4.53
Steve Carlton	L	20	15	2	0	0	25.0	27	3	8	21	0-0	0	2.52
Dennis Aust	R	24	6	0	0	0	7.1	6	0	2	7	0-0	1	4.91
Earl Francis	R	29	2	0	0	0	5.1	7	1	3	3	0-0	0	5.06

1965 Chicago Cubs 8th NL 72-90 .444 25.0 GB

Bob Kennedy (24-32)/Lou Klein (48-58)

Player	Gm by Position	B	Age	G	AB	R	H	2B	3B	HR	RBI	BB	SO	SB	Avg	OBP	Slg
Vic Roznovsky	C63	L	26	71	172	9	38	4	1	3	15	16	30	1	.221	.295	.308
Ernie Banks	1B162	R	34	163	612	79	162	25	3	28	106	55	64	3	.265	.328	.453
Glenn Beckert	2B153	R	24	154	614	73	147	21	3	3	30	28	52	6	.239	.275	.298
Ron Santo	3B164	R	25	164	608	88	173	30	4	33	101	88	109	3	.285	.378	.510
Don Kessinger	SS105	S	22	106	309	19	62	4	3	0	14	20	44	1	.201	.252	.233
Billy Williams	OF164	L	27	164	645	115	203	39	6	34	108	65	76	10	.315	.377	.552
Don Landrum	OF115	L	29	131	425	60	96	20	4	6	34	36	84	14	.226	.300	.334
Doug Clemens	OF105	L	26	128	340	36	75	11	0	4	26	38	53	5	.221	.300	.288
Jimmy Stewart	OF55,SS48	S	26	116	282	26	63	9	4	0	19	30	53	13	.223	.301	.284
George Altman	OF45,1B2	L	32	90	196	24	46	7	1	4	23	19	36	3	.235	.302	.342
Roberto Pena	SS50	R	28	51	170	17	37	5	1	2	12	16	19	1	.218	.291	.294
Chris Krug	C58	R	25	60	169	16	34	5	0	5	24	13	52	0	.201	.258	.320
Ed Bailey†	C54,1B3	L	34	66	150	13	38	6	0	5	23	34	28	0	.253	.385	.393
Harvey Kuenn†	OF35,1B1	R	34	54	120	11	26	5	0	0	6	22	13	1	.217	.336	.258
Joey Amalfitano	2B24,SS4	R	31	67	96	13	26	4	0	0	8	12	14	2	.271	.364	.313
Dick Bertell†	C34	R	29	34	84	6	18	2	0	0	7	11	10	0	.214	.302	.238
Len Gabrielson†	OF14,1B1	L	25	28	48	4	12	0	0	3	5	7	16	0	.250	.345	.438
Ellis Burton	OF12	S	28	17	40	6	7	1	0	0	4	1	10	1	.175	.186	.200
Don Young	OF11	R	19	11	35	1	2	0	0	1	2	0	11	0	.057	.056	.143
Harry Bright		R	35	27	25	1	7	1	0	0	4	0	8	0	.280	.269	.320
John Boccabella	1B2,OF1	R	24	6	12	2	4	0	0	2	4	1	2	0	.333	.385	.833
Leo Burke	C2,OF1	R	31	12	10	2	2	0	0	0	0	0	4	0	.200	.200	.200
Byron Browne	OF4	R	22	4	6	0	0	0	0	0	0	0	2	0	.000	.000	.000
Ron Campbell		R	25	2	2	0	0	0	0	0	0	0	1	0	.000	.000	.000
Chuck Hartenstein		R	23	1	0	0	0	0	0	0	0	0	0	0	—	—	—

Pitcher	T	Age	G	GS	CG	ShO	IP	H	HR	BB	SO	W-L	Sv	ERA
Larry Jackson	R	34	39	39	12	4	257.1	268	28	57	131	14-21	0	3.85
Dick Ellsworth	L	25	36	34	8	0	222.1	227	22	57	130	14-15	1	3.81
Bob Buhl	R	36	32	31	2	0	184.1	207	26	57	92	13-11	0	4.39
Cal Koonce	R	24	38	23	4	1	173.0	181	17	52	88	7-9	0	3.69
Bill Faul	R	25	17	16	5	3	96.2	83	12	18	59	6-6	0	3.54
Bob Hendley†	L	26	18	10	2	0	62.0	59	9	25	38	4-4	0	4.35
Ted Abernathy	R	32	84	0	0	0	136.1	113	7	56	104	4-6	31	2.57
Lindy McDaniel	R	29	71	0	0	0	128.2	115	12	47	92	5-6	2	2.59
Bob Humphreys	R	29	41	0	0	0	65.2	59	6	27	38	2-0	0	3.15
Billy Hoeft	L	33	29	2	1	0	51.1	41	3	20	44	2-2	1	2.81
Ernie Broglio	R	29	26	6	0	0	50.2	63	7	46	22	1-6	0	6.93
Jack Warner	R	24	11	0	0	0	15.2	22	1	9	7	0-1	0	8.62
Lew Burdette†	R	38	7	3	0	0	20.1	26	3	4	5	0-2	0	5.31
Frank Baumann	L	31	4	0	0	0	3.2	4	0	3	2	0-1	0	7.36
Ken Holtzman	L	19	3	0	0	0	4.0	2	1	3	3	0-0	0	2.25

1965 Houston Colt .45s 9th NL 65-97 .401 32.0 GB — Lum Harris

Player	Gm by Position	B	Age	G	AB	R	H	2B	3B	HR	RBI	BB	SO	SB	Avg	OBP	Slg
Ron Brand	C102,3B6,OF5	R	25	117	391	27	92	6	3	2	37	19	34	10	.235	.281	.281
Walt Bond	1B74,OF38	L	27	117	407	46	107	17	2	7	47	42	51	2	.263	.337	.366
Joe Morgan	2B157	L	21	157	601	100	163	22	12	14	40	97	77	20	.271	.373	.418
Bob Aspromonte	3B146,1B6,SS4	R	27	152	578	53	152	15	2	5	52	38	54	2	.263	.310	.322
Bob Lillis	SS104,3B9,2B6	R	35	124	408	34	90	12	1	0	20	20	10	2	.221	.267	.255
Jimmy Wynn	OF155	R	23	157	564	90	155	30	7	22	73	84	126	43	.275	.371	.470
Rusty Staub	OF112,1B1	L	21	131	410	43	105	20	1	14	63	52	57	3	.256	.339	.412
Lee Maye†	OF103	L	30	108	415	38	104	17	7	3	36	20	37	1	.251	.285	.347
Joe Gaines	OF65	R	28	100	229	21	52	8	1	6	31	18	59	4	.227	.290	.349
Jim Gentile†	1B68	L	31	81	227	22	55	11	1	7	31	34	72	0	.242	.352	.392
Eddie Kasko	SS59,3B2	R	33	68	215	18	53	7	1	1	10	11	20	1	.247	.296	.302
John Bateman	C39	R	24	45	142	15	28	3	1	7	14	12	37	0	.197	.256	.380
Al Spangler†	OF33	L	31	38	112	18	24	1	1	1	7	14	8	1	.214	.299	.268
Gus Triandos†	C20	R	34	24	72	5	13	2	0	2	7	5	14	0	.181	.244	.292
Frank Thomas†	1B16,3B2,OF1	R	36	23	58	7	10	2	0	3	9	3	15	0	.172	.210	.362
Jim Beauchamp†	OF9,1B3	R	25	24	53	5	10	1	0	0	4	5	11	0	.189	.259	.208
Chuck Harrison	1B12	R	24	15	45	2	9	4	0	1	9	8	9	0	.200	.321	.356
Nellie Fox	3B6,1B2,2B1	L	37	21	41	3	11	2	0	0	1	0	2	0	.268	.286	.317
Dave Adlesh	C13	R	21	15	34	2	5	1	0	0	3	2	12	0	.147	.216	.176
Sonny Jackson	SS8,3B1	L	20	10	23	1	3	0	0	0	0	1	1	1	.130	.167	.130
Norm Miller	OF2	L	19	11	15	2	3	0	1	0	1	1	7	0	.200	.250	.333
Mike White	3B1	R	26	8	9	0	0	0	0	0	0	1	2	0	.000	.100	.000
John Hoffman	C2	L	21	2	6	1	2	0	0	0	1	0	3	0	.333	.333	.333
Jim Mahoney	SS5	R	31	5	5	0	1	0	0	0	0	0	3	0	.200	.200	.200
Gene Ratliff		R	19	4	4	0	0	0	0	0	0	0	4	0	.000	.000	.000

Pitcher	T	Age	G	GS	CG	ShO	IP	H	HR	BB	SO	W-L	Sv	ERA
Bob Bruce	R	32	35	34	7	1	229.2	241	22	38	145	9-18	0	3.72
Turk Farrell	R	31	33	29	8	3	208.1	202	18	35	122	11-11	1	3.50
Don Nottebart	R	29	29	25	3	0	158.0	166	14	55	77	4-15	0	4.67
Larry Dierker	R	18	26	19	1	0	146.2	135	16	37	109	7-8	0	3.50
Robin Roberts†	R	38	10	10	3	2	76.0	61	1	10	34	5-2	0	1.89
Ken Johnson†	R	32	8	8	1	0	51.2	52	4	11	28	3-2	0	4.18
Jack Lamabe†	R	28	3	2	0	0	12.2	17	3	3	6	0-2	0	4.26
Chris Zachary	R	21	4	2	0	0	10.2	12	0	6	4	0-2	0	4.22
Jim Ray	R	20	3	2	0	0	7.2	11	1	6	7	0-2	0	10.57
Carroll Sembera	R	23	2	1	0	0	7.1	5	0	3	4	0-1	0	3.68
Don Arlich	L	22	1	1	0	0	6.0	5	0	1	0	0-0	0	3.00
Don Larsen†	R	35	1	1	0	0	5.1	8	0	3	1	0-1	0	5.06
Jim Owens	R	31	50	0	0	0	71.1	64	4	29	53	6-5	8	3.28
Dave Giusti	R	25	38	13	4	1	131.1	132	13	46	92	8-7	3	4.32
Claude Raymond	R	28	33	7	2	0	96.1	87	6	16	79	7-4	5	2.90
Ron Taylor†	R	27	32	1	0	0	57.2	68	5	16	37	1-5	4	6.40
Hal Woodeshick†	L	32	27	0	0	0	32.1	27	3	18	22	3-4	3	3.06
Danny Coombs	L	23	26	3	0	0	47.0	54	3	23	35	0-2	0	4.79
Mike Cuellar	L	28	25	4	0	0	56.0	55	3	21	46	1-4	2	3.54
Ken MacKenzie	L	31	21	0	0	0	37.0	46	7	6	26	0-3	0	3.89
Don Lee†	R	31	7	0	0	0	8.0	8	0	3	3	0-0	0	3.38
Bruce Von Hoff	R	21	3	0	0	0	3.0	3	0	2	1	0-0	0	9.00
Gordon Jones	R	35	1	0	0	0	1.0	0	0	0	0	0-0	0	0.00

1965 New York Mets 10th NL 50-112 .309 47.0 GB — Casey Stengel (31-64)/Wes Westrum (19-48)

Player	Gm by Position	B	Age	G	AB	R	H	2B	3B	HR	RBI	BB	SO	SB	Avg	OBP	Slg
Chris Cannizzaro	C112	R	27	114	251	17	46	8	2	0	7	28	60	0	.183	.270	.231
Ed Kranepool	1B147	L	20	153	525	44	133	24	4	10	53	39	71	1	.253	.303	.371
Chuck Hiller†	2B80,OF4,3B2	L	30	100	286	24	68	11	1	5	21	14	24	1	.238	.275	.336
Charley Smith	3B131,SS6,2B1	R	27	135	499	49	122	20	3	16	62	17	123	2	.244	.273	.393
Roy McMillan	SS153	R	34	157	528	44	128	19	2	1	42	24	60	1	.242	.280	.292
Johnny Lewis	OF142	L	25	148	477	64	117	15	3	15	45	59	117	4	.245	.331	.384
Joe Christopher	OF112	R	29	148	437	38	109	18	3	5	40	35	82	4	.249	.311	.339
Ron Swoboda	OF112	R	21	135	399	52	91	15	3	19	50	33	102	2	.228	.291	.424
Jim Hickman	OF91,1B30,3B14	R	28	141	369	32	87	18	0	15	40	27	76	3	.236	.291	.407
Bobby Klaus	2B72,SS28,3B25	R	27	119	288	30	55	12	0	2	12	45	49	1	.191	.302	.253
Ron Hunt	2B46,3B6	R	24	57	196	21	47	12	1	1	10	14	19	2	.240	.309	.327
Billy Cowan†	OF61,2B2,SS1	R	26	82	156	16	28	8	2	3	9	4	45	3	.179	.205	.314
John Stephenson	C47,OF2	L	24	62	121	9	26	5	0	4	15	8	19	0	.215	.264	.355
Jesse Gonder†	C31	L	29	53	105	6	25	4	0	4	9	11	20	0	.238	.308	.390
Danny Napoleon	OF15,3B7	R	23	68	97	5	14	1	1	0	7	8	23	0	.144	.222	.175
Gary Kolb†	OF29,1B1,3B1	L	25	40	90	8	15	2	0	1	7	3	28	3	.167	.191	.222
Cleon Jones	OF23	R	22	30	74	2	11	1	0	1	9	2	23	1	.149	.171	.203
Hawk Taylor	C15,1B1	R	26	25	46	5	7	0	0	4	10	1	8	0	.152	.167	.413
Bud Harrelson	SS18	S	21	19	37	3	4	1	1	0	0	2	11	0	.108	.154	.189
Jimmie Schaffer†	C21	R	29	24	37	0	5	2	0	0	0	1	15	0	.135	.158	.189
Greg Goossen	C8	R	19	11	31	2	9	0	0	1	2	1	5	0	.290	.313	.387
Kevin Collins	3B7,SS3	L	18	11	23	3	4	1	0	0	0	1	9	0	.174	.208	.217
Yogi Berra	C2	L	40	4	9	1	2	0	0	0	0	0	3	0	.222	.222	.222

Pitcher	T	Age	G	GS	CG	ShO	IP	H	HR	BB	SO	W-L	Sv	ERA
Jack Fisher	R	26	43	36	10	0	253.2	252	22	68	116	8-24	1	3.94
Al Jackson	L	29	37	31	7	3	205.1	217	17	61	120	8-20	1	4.34
Warren Spahn†	L	44	20	19	5	0	126.0	140	18	35	56	4-12	0	4.36
Frank Lary†	R	35	14	7	0	0	57.1	48	2	16	23	1-3	1	2.98
Rob Gardner	L	20	5	4	0	0	28.0	23	4	7	19	0-2	0	3.21
Dick Selma	R	21	4	4	1	1	26.2	22	2	9	26	2-1	0	3.71
Larry Bearnarth	R	23	40	3	0	0	60.2	75	6	28	16	3-5	1	4.60
Tug McGraw	L	20	37	9	2	0	97.2	88	8	48	57	2-7	1	3.32
Galen Cisco	R	29	35	17	1	1	112.1	119	12	51	58	4-8	0	4.49
Tom Parsons	R	25	35	11	1	1	90.2	108	17	17	58	1-10	1	4.67
Gordie Richardson	L	26	35	0	0	0	52.1	41	5	16	43	2-2	2	3.78
Gary Kroll	R	23	32	11	1	0	87.0	83	12	41	62	6-6	1	4.45
Larry Miller	L	28	28	5	0	0	57.1	66	6	25	36	1-4	0	5.02
Jim Bethke	R	18	25	0	0	0	40.0	41	3	22	19	2-0	0	4.28
Dennis Ribant	R	23	19	1	0	0	35.1	29	5	6	13	1-3	3	3.82
Darrell Sutherland	R	23	18	2	0	0	48.0	33	4	17	16	3-1	0	2.81
Carl Willey	R	34	13	3	1	0	28.0	30	2	15	13	1-2	0	4.18
Dave Eilers†	R	28	11	0	0	0	18.0	20	2	4	9	1-1	2	4.00
Bob Moorhead	R	27	9	0	0	0	14.1	16	0	5	5	0-1	0	4.40
Dennis Musgraves	R	21	5	1	0	0	16.0	11	0	7	11	0-0	0	0.56

»1966 Baltimore Orioles 1st AL 97-63 .606 — — Hank Bauer

Player	Gm by Position	B	Age	G	AB	R	H	2B	3B	HR	RBI	BB	SO	SB	Avg	OBP	Slg
Andy Etchebarren	C121	R	23	121	412	49	91	14	6	11	50	38	106	0	.221	.293	.364
Boog Powell	1B136	L	24	140	491	78	141	18	0	34	109	67	125	0	.287	.372	.532
Dave Johnson	2B126,SS3	R	23	131	501	47	129	20	3	7	56	31	64	3	.257	.298	.351
Brooks Robinson	3B157	R	29	157	620	91	167	35	2	23	100	56	36	2	.269	.333	.444
Luis Aparicio	SS151	R	32	151	659	97	182	25	8	6	41	33	42	25	.276	.311	.366
Frank Robinson	OF151,1B3	R	30	155	576	122	182	34	2	49	122	87	90	8	.316	.410	.637
Paul Blair	OF127	R	22	133	303	35	84	20	2	6	33	15	36	5	.277	.309	.416
Curt Blefary	OF109,1B20	L	22	131	419	73	107	14	3	23	64	73	56	1	.255	.371	.468
Russ Snyder	OF104	L	32	117	373	66	114	21	5	3	41	38	37	2	.306	.368	.413
Sam Bowens	OF68	R	27	80	243	26	51	9	1	6	20	17	52	9	.210	.275	.329
Bob Johnson	2B20,1B17,3B3	R	30	71	157	13	34	5	0	1	10	12	24	0	.217	.276	.268
Vic Roznovsky	C34	L	27	41	97	4	23	5	0	1	10	9	11	0	.237	.308	.320
Woodie Held	OF10,2B5,3B3*	R	34	56	82	6	17	3	1	1	7	12	30	0	.207	.309	.305
Larry Haney	C20	R	23	20	56	3	9	1	0	1	3	1	15	0	.161	.190	.232
Jerry Adair†	2B13	R	29	17	52	3	15	1	0	0	3	4	8	0	.288	.333	.308
Mark Belanger	SS6	R	22	8	19	2	3	1	0	0	0	0	3	0	.158	.158	.211
Charlie Lau		L	33	18	12	1	6	2	1	0	5	4	1	0	.500	.588	.833
Mike Epstein	1B4	L	23	6	11	1	2	0	1	0	3	1	3	0	.182	.250	.364
Cam Carreon	C3	R	28	4	9	2	2	2	0	0	2	3	2	0	.222	.417	.444

W. Held, 3 G at SS

Pitcher	T	Age	G	GS	CG	ShO	IP	H	HR	BB	SO	W-L	Sv	ERA
Dave McNally	L	23	34	33	5	1	213.0	212	22	64	158	13-6	0	3.17
Jim Palmer	R	20	30	30	6	0	208.1	176	21	91	147	15-10	0	3.46
Wally Bunker	R	21	29	24	3	0	142.2	151	16	48	89	10-6	0	4.29
Steve Barber	L	27	25	25	5	3	133.1	104	6	49	91	10-5	0	2.30
John Miller	R	25	23	16	0	0	100.2	92	15	58	81	4-8	0	4.74
Frank Bertaina	L	22	16	9	0	0	63.1	52	3	36	46	2-5	0	3.13
Bill Short†	L	28	6	6	1	1	37.2	34	2	10	27	2-3	0	2.87
Tom Phoebus	R	24	3	3	2	2	22.0	16	0	6	17	2-1	0	1.23
Stu Miller	R	38	51	0	0	0	92.0	65	5	22	67	9-4	18	2.25
Moe Drabowsky	R	30	44	3	0	0	96.0	62	10	29	98	6-0	7	2.81
Eddie Fisher†	R	29	44	0	0	0	71.2	60	4	19	39	5-3	13	2.64
Eddie Watt	R	25	43	13	1	0	145.2	123	11	44	102	9-7	4	3.83
Dick Hall	R	35	32	0	0	0	66.0	59	8	8	44	6-2	7	3.95
Gene Brabender	R	24	31	1	0	0	71.0	57	4	29	62	4-3	2	3.55
Ed Barnowski	R	22	2	0	0	0	3.0	4	0	1	2	0-0	0	3.00

1966 Minnesota Twins 2nd AL 89-73 .549 9.0 GB — Sam Mele

Player	Gm by Position	B	Age	G	AB	R	H	2B	3B	HR	RBI	BB	SO	SB	Avg	OBP	Slg
Earl Battey	C113	R	31	115	364	30	93	12	1	4	34	43	30	4	.255	.337	.327
Don Mincher	1B130	L	28	139	431	53	108	30	0	14	62	58	68	3	.251	.340	.418
Bernie Allen	2B89,3B2	L	27	101	319	34	76	18	1	5	30	26	40	2	.238	.299	.348
Harmon Killebrew	3B107,1B42,OF18	R	30	162	569	89	160	27	1	39	110	103	98	0	.281	.391	.538
Zoilo Versalles	SS135	R	26	137	543	73	135	20	6	7	36	40	85	10	.249	.307	.346
Tony Oliva	OF159	L	25	159	622	99	191	32	7	25	87	42	72	13	.307	.353	.502
Jimmie Hall	OF103	L	28	120	356	52	85	7	4	20	47	33	66	1	.239	.302	.449
Ted Uhlaender	OF100	L	25	105	367	39	83	12	2	2	22	27	33	10	.226	.280	.286
Cesar Tovar	2B76,SS31,OF24	R	25	134	465	57	121	19	5	2	41	44	50	16	.260	.325	.335
Rich Rollins	3B65,2B2,OF1	R	28	90	269	30	66	7	1	10	40	13	34	0	.245	.286	.390
Bob Allison	OF56	R	31	70	168	34	37	6	1	8	19	30	34	6	.220	.345	.411
Andy Kosco	OF40,1B5	R	24	57	158	11	35	5	0	2	13	7	31	0	.222	.251	.291
Jerry Zimmerman	C59	R	31	60	119	11	30	4	0	1	15	15	23	0	.252	.338	.328
Sandy Valdespino	OF23	L	27	52	108	11	19	1	1	2	9	4	24	2	.176	.211	.259
Russ Nixon	C32	L	31	51	96	5	25	2	1	0	7	7	13	0	.260	.314	.302
George Mitterwald	C3	R	21	3	5	1	1	0	0	0	0	0	0	0	.200	.200	.200
Rich Reese		L	24	3	2	0	0	0	0	0	0	1	2	0	.000	.333	.000
Ron Clark	3B1	R	23	5	1	1	1	0	0	0	1	0	0	0	1.000	.500	1.000
Joe Nossek†	OF2	R	25	4	0	0	0	0	0	0	0	0	0	0	—	—	—

Pitcher	T	Age	G	GS	CG	ShO	IP	H	HR	BB	SO	W-L	Sv	ERA
Jim Kaat	L	27	41	41	19	3	304.2	271	29	55	205	25-13	0	2.75
Mudcat Grant	R	30	35	35	10	3	249.0	248	23	49	110	13-13	0	3.25
Jim Perry	R	30	33	25	8	1	184.1	149	17	53	122	11-7	0	2.54
Dave Boswell	R	21	28	21	8	1	169.1	120	19	65	173	12-5	0	3.14
Camilo Pascual	R	32	21	19	2	0	103.0	113	9	30	56	8-6	0	4.89
Jim Merritt	L	22	31	18	5	1	144.0	112	17	33	124	7-14	3	3.38
Al Worthington	R	37	65	0	0	0	91.1	66	6	27	93	6-3	16	2.46
Pete Cimino	R	23	35	0	0	0	64.2	53	4	30	57	2-5	4	2.92
Johnny Klippstein	R	38	26	0	0	0	39.2	35	2	20	26	1-1	3	3.40
Dwight Siebler	R	28	23	2	0	0	49.2	47	6	14	24	2-2	1	3.44
Garry Roggenburk†	L	26	12	0	0	0	12.1	14	4	10	3	1-2	1	5.84
Bill Pleis	L	28	8	0	0	0	9.1	5	1	4	9	1-2	0	1.93
Jim Ollom	L	20	3	1	0	0	10.0	6	1	1	11	0-0	0	3.60
Ron Keller	R	23	2	0	0	0	5.1	7	1	1	1	0-0	0	5.06
Jim Roland	L	23	1	0	0	0	2.0	0	0	0	1	0-0	0	0.00

1966 Detroit Tigers 3rd AL 88-74 .543 10.0 GB — Chuck Dressen (16-10)/Bob Swift (32-25)/Frank Skaff (40-39)

Player	Gm by Position	B	Age	G	AB	R	H	2B	3B	HR	RBI	BB	SO	SB	Avg	OBP	Slg
Bill Freehan	C132,1B5	R	24	136	492	47	115	22	0	12	46	40	72	5	.234	.294	.352
Norm Cash	1B158	L	31	160	603	98	168	18	3	32	93	66	91	2	.279	.351	.478
Jerry Lumpe	2B95	L	33	113	385	30	89	14	3	1	26	24	44	0	.231	.275	.291
Don Wert	3B150	R	27	150	559	56	150	20	2	11	70	64	69	6	.268	.342	.370
Dick McAuliffe	SS105,3B15	L	26	124	430	83	118	16	8	23	56	66	80	5	.274	.373	.509
Willie Horton	OF137	R	23	146	526	72	138	22	6	27	100	44	103	1	.262	.321	.481
Al Kaline	OF136	R	31	142	479	85	138	29	1	29	88	81	66	5	.288	.392	.534
Jim Northrup	OF113	L	26	123	419	53	111	24	6	16	58	33	52	4	.265	.322	.465
Mickey Stanley	OF82	R	23	92	235	28	68	15	4	3	19	17	20	2	.289	.336	.426
Jake Wood	2B52,3B4,1B2	R	29	98	230	39	58	9	3	2	27	28	48	4	.252	.336	.343
Ray Oyler	SS69	R	27	71	210	16	36	8	3	1	9	23	62	0	.171	.263	.252
Gates Brown	OF43	L	27	88	169	27	45	5	1	7	27	18	19	3	.266	.337	.432
Orlando McFarlane	C33	R	28	49	138	16	35	7	0	5	13	9	46	0	.254	.304	.413
Dick Tracewski	2B70,SS3	R	31	81	124	15	24	1	1	0	7	10	32	1	.194	.252	.218
Don Demeter†	OF27,1B4	R	31	32	99	12	21	5	0	5	12	3	19	1	.212	.235	.414
Arlo Brunsberg	C2	L	25	2	3	1	1	1	0	0	0	0	0	0	.333	.500	.667
Don Pepper	1B1	L	22	4	3	0	0	0	0	0	0	0	1	0	.000	.000	.000

Pitcher	T	Age	G	GS	CG	ShO	IP	H	HR	BB	SO	W-L	Sv	ERA
Denny McLain	R	22	38	38	14	4	264.1	205	42	104	192	20-14	0	3.92
Mickey Lolich	L	25	40	33	5	1	203.2	204	24	83	173	14-14	3	4.77
Earl Wilson†	R	31	23	23	8	2	163.1	126	16	38	133	13-6	0	2.59
Larry Sherry	R	30	55	0	0	0	77.2	66	8	36	63	8-5	20	3.82
Orlando Pena	R	32	54	0	0	0	108.0	105	16	35	79	4-2	7	3.08
Fred Gladding	R	30	51	0	0	0	74.0	62	6	29	57	5-0	2	3.28
Dave Wickersham	R	30	38	14	3	0	140.2	139	14	54	93	8-3	1	3.20
Johnny Podres†	L	33	36	13	2	1	107.2	106	12	34	53	4-5	4	3.43
Hank Aguirre	L	35	30	14	2	0	103.2	104	14	26	50	3-9	0	3.82
Bill Monbouquette	R	29	30	14	2	1	102.2	120	14	22	61	7-8	0	4.73
Joe Sparma	R	24	29	13	0	1	91.2	103	14	52	61	2-7	0	5.30
Terry Fox†	R	30	4	0	0	0	10.0	9	3	2	6	0-1	1	6.30
George Korince	R	20	2	0	0	0	3.0	1	0	3	2	0-0	0	0.00
John Hiller	L	23	1	0	0	0	2.0	2	0	2	1	0-0	0	9.00
Bill Graham	R	29	1	0	0	0	2.0	2	0	0	2	0-0	0	0.00
Julio Navarro	R	30	1	0	0	0	0.0	2	2	0	0	0-0	0	—

776 Seasons: Team Rosters

1966 Chicago White Sox 4th AL 83-79 .512 15.0 GB

Eddie Stanky

Player	Gm by Position	B	Age	G	AB	R	H	2B	3B	HR	RBI	BB	SO	SB	Avg	OBP	Slg
John Romano	C102	R	31	122	329	33	76	12	0	15	47	58	72	0	.231	.344	.404
Tom McCraw	1B121,OF41	L	25	151	389	49	89	16	4	5	48	29	40	20	.229	.288	.329
Al Weis	2B96,SS18	S	28	129	187	20	29	4	1	0	9	17	50	3	.155	.233	.187
Don Buford	3B133,2B37,OF11	S	29	163	607	85	148	26	7	8	52	69	71	51	.244	.323	.349
Jerry Adair†	SS75,2B50	R	29	105	370	27	90	18	2	4	36	17	44	3	.243	.275	.335
Tommie Agee	OF159	R	23	160	629	98	172	27	8	22	86	41	127	44	.273	.326	.447
Ken Berry	OF141	R	25	147	443	50	120	20	2	8	34	28	63	7	.271	.316	.379
Floyd Robinson	OF113	L	30	127	342	44	81	11	2	5	35	44	32	8	.237	.330	.325
Bill Skowron	1B98	R	35	120	337	27	84	15	2	6	29	26	45	1	.249	.308	.359
Pete Ward	OF59,3B16,1B5	L	26	84	251	22	55	7	1	3	28	24	49	3	.219	.290	.291
Lee Elia	SS75	R	28	80	195	16	40	5	2	3	22	15	39	0	.205	.265	.297
Wayne Causey†	2B60,3B1,SS1	L	29	78	164	23	40	8	2	0	13	24	13	2	.244	.333	.317
J.C. Martin	C63	L	29	67	157	13	40	5	3	2	20	14	24	0	.255	.316	.363
Gene Freese†	3B34	R	32	48	106	8	22	2	0	3	10	8	20	2	.208	.270	.311
Ron Hansen	SS23	R	28	23	74	3	13	1	0	0	4	15	10	0	.176	.322	.189
Smoky Burgess	C2	L	39	79	67	0	21	5	0	0	15	11	8	0	.313	.413	.388
Danny Cater†	OF18	R	26	21	60	3	11	1	1	0	4	0	10	3	.183	.194	.233
Jerry McNertney	C37	R	29	44	59	3	13	0	0	0	1	7	6	1	.220	.303	.220
Duane Josephson	C11	R	24	11	38	3	9	1	0	0	3	3	3	0	.237	.293	.263
Ed Stroud	OF11	L	26	12	36	3	6	2	0	0	1	2	8	3	.167	.231	.222
Buddy Bradford	OF9	R	21	14	28	3	4	0	0	0	0	2	6	0	.143	.200	.143
Jim Hicks	OF10,1B2	R	26	18	26	3	5	0	1	0	1	1	5	0	.192	.222	.269
Dick Kenworthy	3B6	R	25	9	25	1	5	0	0	0	0	0	0	0	.200	.200	.200
Marv Staehle	2B6	L	24	8	15	2	2	0	0	0	0	4	2	1	.133	.316	.133
Deacon Jones		L	32	5	5	0	2	0	0	0	0	0	0	0	.400	.400	.400
Bill Voss	OF1	L	22	2	2	0	0	0	0	0	0	0	2	0	.000	.000	.000

Pitcher	T	Age	G	GS	CG	ShO	IP	H	HR	BB	SO	W-L	Sv	ERA
Tommy John	L	23	34	33	10	5	223.0	195	13	57	138	14-11	0	2.62
Joe Horlen	R	28	37	29	4	2	211.0	185	14	53	124	10-13	1	2.43
Gary Peters	L	29	30	27	11	4	204.2	156	11	45	129	12-10	0	1.98
John Buzhardt	R	29	33	22	5	4	150.1	144	13	30	66	6-11	1	3.83
Bruce Howard	R	23	27	21	4	2	149.0	110	14	44	85	9-5	0	2.30
Jack Lamabe	R	29	34	17	3	2	121.1	116	9	35	67	7-9	0	3.93
Fred Klages	R	22	3	3	0	0	15.2	9	0	7	6	1-0	0	1.72
Bob Locker	R	28	56	0	0	0	95.0	73	2	23	70	9-8	12	2.46
Hoyt Wilhelm	R	42	46	0	0	0	81.1	50	6	17	61	5-2	6	1.66
Dennis Higgins	R	26	42	1	0	0	93.0	66	9	33	86	1-0	5	2.52
Juan Pizarro	L	29	34	9	1	0	88.2	91	9	39	42	8-6	3	3.76
Eddie Fisher†	R	29	23	0	0	0	35.1	27	1	17	18	1-3	6	2.29
Greg Bollo	R	22	3	1	0	0	7.0	7	0	3	4	0-1	0	2.57

1966 Cleveland Indians 5th AL 81-81 .500 17.0 GB

Birdie Tebbetts (66-57)/George Strickland (15-24)

Player	Gm by Position	B	Age	G	AB	R	H	2B	3B	HR	RBI	BB	SO	SB	Avg	OBP	Slg
Joe Azcue	C97	R	26	98	302	22	83	10	1	9	37	20	22	0	.275	.319	.404
Fred Whitfield	1B132	L	28	137	502	59	121	15	2	27	78	27	76	1	.241	.283	.440
Pedro Gonzalez	2B104,3B1,OF1	R	28	110	352	21	82	9	2	2	17	15	54	8	.233	.268	.287
Max Alvis	3B157	R	28	157	596	67	146	22	3	17	55	50	98	4	.245	.304	.378
Larry Brown	SS90,2B10	R	26	105	340	29	78	12	0	3	17	36	58	0	.229	.309	.291
Rocky Colavito	OF146	R	32	151	533	68	127	13	0	30	72	76	81	2	.238	.336	.432
Leon Wagner	OF139	L	32	150	549	70	153	20	0	23	66	46	69	5	.279	.334	.441
Vic Davalillo	OF108	L	29	121	344	42	86	6	4	3	19	24	37	8	.250	.297	.317
Chico Salmon	SS61,2B28,1B24*	R	25	126	422	46	108	13	2	7	40	21	41	10	.256	.289	.346
Chuck Hinton	OF104,1B6,2B2	R	32	123	348	46	89	9	3	12	50	35	66	10	.256	.323	.402
Jim Landis	OF61	R	32	85	158	23	35	5	1	3	14	20	25	2	.222	.317	.323
Dick Howser	2B26,SS26	R	30	67	140	18	32	9	1	2	4	15	23	2	.229	.299	.350
Duke Sims	C48	L	25	52	133	12	35	2	2	6	19	11	31	0	.263	.338	.444
Del Crandall	C49	R	36	50	108	10	25	2	0	4	8	14	9	0	.231	.320	.361
Vern Fuller	2B16	R	22	16	47	7	11	2	1	2	2	7	6	0	.234	.357	.447
Jim Gentile†	1B9	L	32	33	47	2	6	1	0	2	4	5	18	0	.128	.212	.277
Bill Davis	1B9	L	24	23	38	2	6	1	0	1	4	6	9	0	.158	.267	.263
Jose Vidal	OF11	R	26	17	32	4	6	1	1	0	3	5	11	0	.188	.297	.281
Buddy Booker	C12	L	24	18	28	6	6	1	0	2	5	2	6	0	.214	.267	.464
Tony Martinez	SS5,2B4	R	26	17	17	2	5	0	0	0	0	1	6	1	.294	.333	.294
Tony Curry		L	27	19	16	4	2	0	0	0	3	3	8	0	.125	.263	.125
George Banks		R	27	4	4	0	1	0	0	0	1	0	1	0	.250	.250	.250
Paul Dicken		R	22	2	2	0	0	0	0	0	0	0	1	0	.000	.000	.000

C. Salmon, 10 G at OF, 6 G at 3B

Pitcher	T	Age	G	GS	CG	ShO	IP	H	HR	BB	SO	W-L	Sv	ERA
Gary Bell	R	29	40	37	12	0	254.1	211	19	79	194	14-15	0	3.22
Sonny Siebert	R	29	34	32	11	1	241.0	193	25	62	163	16-8	1	2.80
Sam McDowell	L	23	35	28	8	5	194.1	130	12	102	225	9-8	3	2.87
Steve Hargan	R	23	38	21	7	3	192.0	173	9	45	132	13-10	0	2.48
Luis Tiant	R	25	46	16	7	5	155.0	121	16	50	145	12-11	8	2.79
Dick Radatz†	R	29	39	0	0	0	56.2	49	6	34	49	0-3	10	4.61
Bob Allen	L	28	36	0	0	0	51.1	56	2	13	33	2-2	5	4.21
John O'Donoghue	L	26	32	13	2	0	108.0	109	13	23	49	6-8	0	3.83
Tom Kelley	R	22	31	7	1	0	95.1	97	14	42	64	4-8	0	4.34
Jack Kralick	L	31	27	4	0	0	68.1	69	9	20	31	3-4	0	3.82
Don McMahon†	R	36	12	0	0	0	12.1	8	1	6	5	1-1	1	2.92
Lee Stange†	R	29	8	2	1	0	16.0	17	1	3	8	1-0	0	2.81
Bob Heffner	R	27	5	1	0	0	13.0	12	1	3	7	0-1	0	3.46
George Culver	R	22	5	1	0	0	9.2	15	1	7	6	0-2	0	8.38

1966 California Angels 6th AL 80-82 .494 18.0 GB

Bill Rigney

Player	Gm by Position	B	Age	G	AB	R	H	2B	3B	HR	RBI	BB	SO	SB	Avg	OBP	Slg
Bob Rodgers	C133	S	27	133	454	45	107	20	3	7	48	29	57	3	.236	.281	.339
Norm Siebern	1B99	L	32	125	336	29	83	14	1	5	41	63	61	0	.247	.361	.339
Bobby Knoop	2B161	R	27	161	590	54	137	18	11	17	72	43	144	1	.232	.282	.386
Paul Schaal	3B131	R	23	138	386	59	94	15	7	6	24	68	56	6	.244	.362	.365
Jim Fregosi	SS162,1B1	R	24	162	611	78	154	32	7	13	67	67	89	17	.252	.325	.391
Jose Cardenal	OF146	R	22	154	561	67	155	15	3	16	48	34	69	24	.276	.320	.399
Ed Kirkpatrick	OF102,1B3	L	21	117	312	31	60	7	4	9	44	51	67	7	.192	.313	.327
Rick Reichardt	OF87	R	23	89	319	48	92	5	4	16	44	27	61	8	.288	.367	.480
Jay Johnstone	OF61	L	20	61	254	35	67	12	4	3	17	11	36	3	.264	.297	.378
Joe Adcock	1B71	R	38	83	231	33	63	10	3	18	48	31	48	2	.273	.355	.576
Tom Satriano	C43,1B36,3B25*	L	25	103	226	16	54	5	3	0	24	27	32	3	.239	.320	.288
Willie Smith	OF52	L	27	90	195	18	36	3	2	1	20	12	37	1	.185	.239	.236
Frank Malzone	3B35	R	36	82	155	6	32	5	0	2	12	10	11	0	.206	.253	.277
Jackie Warner	OF37	R	22	45	123	22	26	4	1	7	16	9	55	0	.211	.263	.431
Jimmy Piersall	OF63	R	36	75	123	14	26	5	0	0	14	13	19	1	.211	.283	.252
Bubba Morton	OF14	R	34	15	50	4	11	1	0	0	4	2	6	1	.220	.250	.240
Jackie Hernandez	3B11,2B8,SS8*	R	25	58	23	19	1	0	0	0	2	1	4	1	.043	.080	.043
Charlie Vinson	1B11	L	22	13	22	3	4	2	0	1	6	5	9	0	.182	.357	.409
Tom Egan	C6	R	20	7	11	0	0	0	0	0	0	1	5	0	.000	.083	.000
Al Spangler	OF3	L	32	6	9	2	6	0	0	0	0	2	2	0	.667	.727	.667
Albie Pearson	OF1	L	31	2	3	0	0	0	0	0	0	0	1	0	.000	.000	.000
Ed Bailey		L	35	5	3	0	0	0	0	0	0	1	1	0	.000	.250	.000
Willie Montanez	1B2	L	18	8	2	2	0	0	0	0	0	0	2	1	.000	.000	.000

T. Satriano, 4 G at 2B; J. Hernandez, 3 G at OF

Pitcher	T	Age	G	GS	CG	ShO	IP	H	HR	BB	SO	W-L	Sv	ERA
Dean Chance	R	25	41	37	11	2	259.2	206	18	114	180	12-17	1	3.08
George Brunet	L	31	41	32	8	2	212.0	183	21	106	148	13-13	0	3.31
Marcelino Lopez	L	22	37	32	6	2	199.0	188	20	68	132	7-14	1	3.93
Fred Newman	R	24	21	19	1	0	102.2	112	7	31	42	4-7	0	4.73
Clyde Wright	L	25	20	13	3	1	91.1	92	11	25	37	4-7	0	3.74
Jim McGlothlin	R	22	19	11	0	0	67.2	79	9	19	41	3-1	0	4.52
Jorge Rubio	R	21	7	4	1	1	27.1	22	2	16	27	2-1	0	2.96
Bob Lee	R	28	61	0	0	0	101.2	90	8	31	46	5-4	16	2.74
Lew Burdette	R	39	54	0	0	0	79.2	80	4	12	27	7-2	5	3.39
Jack Sanford	R	37	50	6	0	0	108.0	108	11	27	54	13-7	5	3.83
Minnie Rojas	R	27	47	2	0	0	84.1	83	9	15	37	7-4	10	2.88
Howie Reed†	R	29	19	1	0	0	43.0	39	5	15	17	0-1	1	2.93
Ed Sukla	R	23	12	0	0	0	16.2	18	4	6	8	1-1	1	6.48
Dick Egan	L	29	11	0	0	0	14.1	17	2	6	11	0-0	0	4.40
Jim Coates	R	33	9	4	1	1	31.2	32	3	10	16	1-1	0	3.98
Bill Kelso	R	26	5	0	0	0	11.1	11	1	6	11	1-1	0	2.38
Ramon Lopez	R	33	4	1	0	0	7.0	4	1	4	2	0-1	0	5.14

1966 Kansas City Athletics 7th AL 74-86 .463 23.0 GB

Alvin Dark

Player	Gm by Position	B	Age	G	AB	R	H	2B	3B	HR	RBI	BB	SO	SB	Avg	OBP	Slg
Phil Roof	C123,1B2	R	25	127	369	33	77	14	3	7	44	37	95	2	.209	.285	.320
Ken Harrelson†	1B58,OF3	R	24	63	210	24	47	5	0	5	22	27	59	9	.224	.312	.319
Dick Green	2B137,3B2	R	25	140	507	58	127	24	3	9	62	27	101	6	.250	.297	.363
Ed Charles	3B104,1B1,OF1	R	33	118	385	52	110	18	8	9	42	30	53	12	.286	.337	.444
Bert Campaneris	SS138	R	24	142	573	82	153	29	10	5	42	25	72	52	.267	.302	.379
Mike Hershberger	OF143	R	26	146	538	55	136	27	7	2	57	47	37	13	.253	.313	.340
Larry Stahl	OF94	L	25	119	312	37	78	11	5	5	34	17	63	5	.250	.289	.365
Joe Nossek†	OF78,3B1	R	25	87	230	13	60	10	3	1	27	8	21	4	.261	.285	.343
Danny Cater†	1B53,3B42,OF22	R	26	116	425	47	124	16	3	7	52	28	37	1	.292	.334	.393
Roger Repoz†	OF52,1B45	L	25	101	319	40	69	10	3	11	34	44	80	3	.216	.314	.370
Jim Gosger†	OF77	L	23	88	272	34	61	14	1	5	27	37	53	5	.224	.321	.338
Ossie Chavarria	OF26,SS23,2B14*	R	25	86	191	26	46	10	0	2	10	18	43	3	.241	.306	.325
Jose Tartabull†	OF33	L	27	37	127	13	30	2	3	0	4	11	13	8	.236	.297	.299
Wayne Causey†	3B15,SS10	L	29	28	79	1	18	0	0	0	5	7	6	1	.228	.284	.228
Billy Bryan†	C21,1B3	L	27	32	76	0	10	4	0	0	7	6	17	0	.132	.193	.184
Ken Suarez	C34	R	23	35	69	5	10	0	1	0	2	15	26	2	.145	.298	.174
Tim Talton	C14,1B9	L	27	37	53	8	18	3	1	2	6	1	5	0	.340	.364	.547
Rick Monday	OF15	L	20	17	41	4	4	1	1	0	2	6	16	1	.098	.213	.171
Manny Jimenez	OF12	L	27	13	35	1	4	0	1	0	1	6	4	0	.114	.244	.171
Ernie Fazio	2B10,SS4	R	24	27	34	3	7	0	1	0	2	4	10	1	.206	.289	.265
John Donaldson	2B9	L	23	15	30	4	4	0	0	0	1	3	4	1	.133	.212	.133
Sal Bando	3B7	R	22	11	24	1	7	1	1	0	1	1	3	0	.292	.320	.417
Ron Stone	OF4,1B3	L	23	26	22	2	6	1	0	0	0	0	2	1	.273	.273	.318
Don Blasingame†	2B4	L	34	12	19	1	3	0	0	0	1	2	3	0	.158	.238	.158
Randy Schwartz	1B2	L	22	10	11	0	1	0	0	0	1	1	3	0	.091	.167	.091
Rene Lachemann	C6	R	21	7	5	0	1	1	0	0	0	0	1	0	.200	.200	.400

O. Chavarria, 8 G at 1B, 5 G at 3B

Pitcher	T	Age	G	GS	CG	ShO	IP	H	HR	BB	SO	W-L	Sv	ERA
Catfish Hunter	R	20	30	25	4	0	176.2	158	17	64	103	9-11	0	4.02
Lew Krausse	R	23	36	22	4	1	177.2	144	8	63	87	14-9	3	2.99
Jim Nash	R	21	18	17	5	0	127.0	95	6	47	98	12-1	1	2.06
Blue Moon Odom	R	21	14	14	4	2	90.1	70	1	53	47	5-5	0	2.49
Chuck Dobson	R	22	14	14	1	0	83.2	71	7	50	61	4-6	0	4.09
Rollie Sheldon†	R	29	14	13	1	1	69.0	73	3	26	26	4-7	0	3.13
Fred Talbot†	R	25	11	11	0	0	67.2	65	6	28	37	4-4	0	4.79
Ralph Terry†	R	30	15	10	0	0	64.0	65	7	15	33	1-5	0	3.80
Bill Stafford	R	26	9	8	0	0	39.2	42	2	12	31	0-4	0	4.99
Gil Blanco	L	20	11	8	0	0	38.1	31	3	36	21	2-4	0	4.70
Jack Aker	R	25	66	0	0	0	113.0	81	7	28	68	8-4	32	1.99
Paul Lindblad	L	24	38	14	0	0	121.0	138	14	37	69	5-10	1	4.17
Ken Sanders†	R	24	38	1	0	0	65.1	59	7	48	41	3-4	1	3.72
Wes Stock	R	32	35	0	0	0	44.0	30	3	21	31	2-2	3	2.66
Jim Dickson	R	28	24	1	0	0	37.0	37	4	23	20	1-0	1	5.35
Joe Grzenda	L	29	21	0	0	0	22.0	28	1	12	14	0-2	0	3.27
John Wyatt†	R	31	19	0	0	0	23.2	19	3	16	25	0-3	2	5.32
Vern Handrahan	R	27	16	1	0	0	25.1	20	5	15	18	0-1	1	4.26
Guido Grilli†	L	27	16	0	0	0	15.2	19	0	11	8	0-1	1	6.89
Jim Duckworth†	R	27	8	0	0	0	12.0	14	2	10	10	0-2	1	9.00
A. Monteagudo†	R	22	6	0	0	0	12.2	12	0	7	3	0-0	0	2.84
Bill Edgerton	L	24	6	1	0	0	8.1	10	0	7	3	0-1	0	3.24
Jesse Hickman	R	27	1	0	0	0	1.0	0	0	1	0	0-0	0	0.00

1966 Washington Senators 8th AL 71-88 .447 25.5 GB

Gil Hodges

Player	Gm by Position	B	Age	G	AB	R	H	2B	3B	HR	RBI	BB	SO	SB	Avg	OBP	Slg
Paul Casanova	C119	R	24	122	429	45	109	16	5	13	44	14	78	1	.254	.278	.406
Dick Nen	1B76	L	26	94	235	20	50	8	0	6	30	28	46	0	.213	.294	.323
Bob Saverine	2B70,3B26,SS11*	S	25	120	406	54	102	10	4	5	24	27	62	4	.251	.300	.333
Ken McMullen	3B141,1B8,OF1	R	24	147	524	48	122	19	4	13	54	44	89	3	.233	.289	.359
Ed Brinkman	SS158	R	24	158	582	42	133	18	9	7	48	29	105	7	.229	.263	.326
Fred Valentine	OF138,1B2	S	31	146	508	77	140	29	7	16	59	51	63	22	.276	.351	.455
Frank Howard	OF135	R	29	146	493	52	137	19	4	18	71	53	104	1	.278	.348	.442
Don Lock	OF129	R	29	138	386	52	90	13	1	16	48	57	126	2	.233	.333	.396
Jim King	OF85	L	33	117	310	41	77	14	2	10	30	38	41	4	.248	.330	.403
Ken Harrelson†	1B70	R	24	71	250	25	62	8	1	7	28	26	53	4	.248	.321	.372
Don Blasingame†	2B58,SS1	L	34	68	200	18	43	9	0	1	11	18	21	2	.215	.280	.275
Willie Kirkland	OF68	L	32	124	163	21	31	2	1	6	17	16	50	2	.190	.261	.325
Ken Hamlin	2B50,3B1	R	31	66	158	13	34	7	1	1	16	13	21	1	.215	.267	.291
Doug Camilli	C39	R	29	44	107	5	22	4	0	2	8	3	19	0	.206	.234	.299
Bob Chance	1B13	L	25	37	57	1	10	3	0	1	8	2	23	0	.175	.200	.281
Dick Phillips	1B5	L	34	25	37	3	6	0	0	0	4	2	5	0	.162	.225	.162
Tim Cullen	3B8,2B5	R	24	18	34	8	8	1	0	0	0	2	8	0	.235	.278	.265
Hank Allen	OF9	R	25	9	31	2	12	0	0	1	6	3	6	0	.387	.441	.484
Jim French	C10	L	24	10	24	0	5	1	0	0	3	4	5	0	.208	.321	.250
John Orsino	1B5,C2	R	28	14	23	1	4	1	0	0	0	0	7	0	.174	.174	.217
Mike Brumley	C7	L	27	9	18	1	2	1	0	0	0	0	2	0	.111	.111	.167
Joe Cunningham	1B3	L	34	3	8	0	1	0	0	0	0	0	1	0	.125	.125	.125

B. Saverine, 9 G at OF

Pitcher	T	Age	G	GS	CG	ShO	IP	H	HR	BB	SO	W-L	Sv	ERA
Pete Richert	L	26	36	34	7	0	245.2	196	36	69	195	14-14	0	3.37
Mike McCormick	L	27	41	32	8	3	216.0	193	23	51	101	11-14	0	3.46
Phil Ortega	R	26	33	31	5	1	197.1	158	29	53	121	12-12	0	3.92
Jim Hannan	R	26	30	18	2	0	114.0	125	9	59	68	3-9	0	4.26
Diego Segui	R	28	21	13	1	1	72.0	82	8	24	54	3-7	0	5.00
Barry Moore	L	23	12	11	1	0	62.1	55	3	39	28	3-3	0	3.75
Dick Bosman	R	22	13	7	0	0	39.0	60	4	12	20	2-6	0	7.62
Frank Kreutzer	L	27	9	6	0	0	31.1	30	9	10	24	0-5	0	6.03
Jim Duckworth†	R	27	5	4	0	0	14.1	14	2	10	14	0-3	0	5.02
Joe Coleman	R	19	1	1	1	0	9.0	6	0	2	4	1-0	0	2.00
Casey Cox	R	24	66	0	0	0	113.0	104	6	35	46	4-5	7	3.50
Ron Kline	R	34	63	0	0	0	90.1	79	12	17	46	6-4	23	2.39
Bob Humphreys	R	30	58	1	0	0	111.2	91	6	28	88	7-3	3	2.82
Dick Lines	L	27	53	0	0	0	83.0	63	4	24	49	5-2	2	2.28
Dave Baldwin	R	28	4	0	0	0	7.0	8	0	1	4	0-0	0	3.86
Tom Cheney	R	31	3	1	0	0	5.1	4	1	6	3	0-1	0	5.06
Buster Narum	R	25	3	0	0	0	3.1	11	2	4	0	0-0	0	21.60
Pete Craig	R	25	1	0	0	0	2.0	2	0	1	1	0-0	0	4.50
Howie Koplitz	R	28	1	0	0	0	2.0	0	0	1	0	0-0	0	0.00
Al Closter	L	23	1	0	0	0	0.1	1	0	2	0	0-0	0	0.00

1966 Boston Red Sox 9th AL 72-90 .444 26.0 GB

Billy Herman (64-82)/Pete Runnels (8-8)

Player	Gm by Position	B	Age	G	AB	R	H	2B	3B	HR	RBI	BB	SO	SB	Avg	OBP	Slg
Mike Ryan	C114	R	24	116	369	27	79	15	3	2	32	29	68	1	.214	.271	.287
George Scott	1B158,3B5	R	22	162	601	73	147	18	7	27	90	65	152	4	.245	.324	.433
George Smith	2B109,SS19	R	28	128	403	41	86	19	4	8	37	37	86	4	.213	.283	.340
Joe Foy	3B139,SS13	R	23	151	554	97	145	23	8	15	63	91	80	2	.262	.364	.413
Rico Petrocelli	SS127,3B5	R	23	139	522	58	124	20	1	18	59	41	99	1	.238	.295	.383
Carl Yastrzemski	OF158	L	26	160	594	81	165	39	2	16	80	84	60	8	.278	.368	.431
Tony Conigliaro	OF146	R	21	150	558	77	148	26	7	28	93	52	112	0	.265	.330	.487
Don Demeter†	OF57,1B2	R	31	73	226	31	66	13	1	9	29	5	42	1	.292	.305	.478
Dalton Jones	2B70,3B3	L	22	115	252	26	59	11	5	4	23	22	27	1	.234	.303	.365
Bob Tillman	C72	R	29	78	204	12	47	8	0	3	24	22	35	0	.230	.303	.314
Jose Tartabull†	OF46	L	27	68	195	28	54	7	4	0	11	6	11	11	.277	.297	.354
George Thomas	OF48,3B6,C2*	R	28	69	173	25	41	4	0	5	20	23	33	1	.237	.332	.347
Eddie Kasko	SS20,3B10,2B8	R	34	58	136	11	29	7	0	1	12	15	19	1	.213	.291	.287
Lenny Green	OF27	L	33	85	133	18	32	6	0	1	12	15	19	0	.241	.325	.308
Jim Gosger†	OF32	L	23	40	126	16	32	4	0	5	17	15	20	0	.254	.333	.405
Reggie Smith	OF6	S	21	6	26	1	4	1	0	0	0	0	5	0	.154	.154	.192
Tony Horton	1B6	R	21	6	22	0	3	0	0	0	2	0	5	0	.136	.136	.136
Mike Andrews	2B5	R	22	5	18	1	3	0	0	0	0	0	2	0	.167	.167	.167
Joe Christopher	OF2	R	30	12	13	1	1	0	0	0	0	2	4	0	.077	.200	.077

G. Thomas, 2 G at 1B

Pitcher	T	Age	G	GS	CG	ShO	IP	H	HR	BB	SO	W-L	Sv	ERA
Jose Santiago	R	25	35	28	7	1	172.0	155	17	58	119	12-13	2	3.66
Jim Lonborg	R	24	45	23	3	1	181.2	173	18	55	131	10-10	2	3.86
Lee Stange†	R	29	28	19	8	2	153.1	140	17	43	77	7-9	0	3.35
Earl Wilson†	R	31	15	14	5	1	100.2	88	14	36	67	5-5	0	3.84
Dennis Bennett	L	26	16	13	0	0	75.0	75	9	23	47	3-3	0	3.24
Jerry Stephenson	R	22	15	11	1	0	66.1	68	6	44	50	2-5	0	5.83
Hank Fischer†	R	26	6	5	1	0	31.0	35	4	11	26	2-3	0	2.90
Don McMahon†	R	36	49	0	0	0	78.0	65	7	38	57	8-7	9	2.65
Dan Osinski	R	32	44	1	0	0	67.1	68	8	28	44	4-3	2	3.61
John Wyatt†	R	31	42	0	0	0	71.2	59	3	27	63	3-4	8	3.14
Bucky Brandon	R	25	40	17	5	2	157.2	129	13	70	101	8-8	2	3.31
Dick Stigman	L	30	34	10	1	1	81.0	85	15	46	65	2-1	0	5.44
Ken Sanders†	R	24	24	0	0	0	47.1	36	2	28	33	3-6	2	3.80
Rollie Sheldon†	R	29	23	10	1	0	79.2	106	15	23	38	1-6	0	4.97
Dick Radatz†	R	29	16	0	0	0	19.0	24	3	11	19	0-2	4	4.74
Dave Morehead	R	23	12	5	0	0	28.0	31	7	7	20	1-2	0	5.46
Bob Sadowski	R	28	11	5	0	0	33.1	41	4	9	11	1-1	0	5.40
Bill Short†	L	28	8	0	0	0	8.1	10	1	2	2	0-0	0	4.32
Guido Grilli†	L	27	6	0	0	0	4.2	5	1	9	4	0-1	0	7.71
Pete Magrini	R	24	3	1	0	0	7.1	8	0	8	3	0-1	0	9.82
Garry Roggenburk†	L	26	1	0	0	0	0.1	1	0	1	0	0-0	0	0.00

1966 New York Yankees 10th AL 70-89 .440 26.5 GB

Johnny Keane (4-16)/Ralph Houk (66-73)

Player	Gm by Position	B	Age	G	AB	R	H	2B	3B	HR	RBI	BB	SO	SB	Avg	OBP	Slg
Elston Howard	C100,1B13	R	37	126	410	38	105	19	2	6	35	37	65	0	.256	.317	.356
Joe Pepitone	1B119,OF55	L	25	152	585	85	149	21	4	31	83	29	58	4	.255	.290	.463
Bobby Richardson	2B147,3B2	R	30	149	610	71	153	21	3	7	42	25	28	6	.251	.280	.330
Clete Boyer	3B85,SS59	R	29	144	500	59	120	22	4	14	57	46	48	6	.240	.303	.384
Horace Clarke	SS63,2B16,3B4	S	26	96	312	37	83	10	4	6	28	27	24	5	.266	.324	.381
Mickey Mantle	OF97	S	34	108	333	40	96	12	1	23	56	57	76	1	.288	.389	.538
Roger Maris	OF95	L	31	119	348	37	81	9	2	13	43	36	60	0	.233	.307	.382
Tom Tresh	OF84,3B64	S	28	151	537	76	125	12	4	27	68	86	89	5	.233	.341	.421
Roy White	OF82,2B2	S	22	115	316	39	71	13	2	7	20	37	43	14	.225	.308	.345
Jake Gibbs	C54	L	27	62	182	19	47	6	0	3	20	19	16	5	.258	.327	.341
Lu Clinton	OF63	R	28	80	159	18	35	10	2	5	21	16	27	0	.220	.288	.403
Hector Lopez	OF29	R	36	54	117	14	25	4	1	4	16	8	20	0	.214	.268	.368
Steve Whitaker	OF31	L	23	31	114	15	28	3	2	7	15	9	24	0	.246	.306	.491
Ray Barker	1B47	L	30	61	75	11	14	5	0	3	13	4	20	0	.187	.225	.373
Bobby Murcer	SS18	L	20	21	69	3	12	1	1	0	5	4	5	2	.174	.219	.217
Billy Bryan†	C14,1B3	L	27	27	69	5	15	2	0	4	5	5	19	0	.217	.270	.420
Dick Schofield†	SS19	S	31	25	58	5	9	2	0	0	2	9	8	0	.155	.265	.190
Roger Repoz†	OF30	L	25	37	43	4	15	4	1	0	9	4	8	0	.349	.396	.488
Mike Hegan	1B13	L	23	13	39	7	8	0	1	0	2	7	11	1	.205	.326	.256
Mike Ferraro	3B10	R	21	10	28	4	5	0	0	0	0	3	3	0	.179	.281	.179
John Miller	1B3,OF3	R	22	6	23	1	2	0	0	1	2	0	9	0	.087	.087	.217
Ruben Amaro	SS14	R	30	14	23	0	5	0	0	0	3	0	2	0	.217	.217	.217

Pitcher	T	Age	G	GS	CG	ShO	IP	H	HR	BB	SO	W-L	Sv	ERA
Mel Stottlemyre	R	24	37	35	9	3	251.0	239	18	82	146	12-20	1	3.80
Fritz Peterson	L	24	34	32	11	2	215.0	196	15	40	96	12-11	0	3.31
Al Downing	L	25	30	30	1	0	200.0	178	23	79	152	10-11	0	3.56
Fred Talbot†	R	25	23	19	3	0	124.1	123	16	45	48	7-7	0	4.13
Jim Bouton	R	27	24	19	3	0	120.1	117	13	38	65	3-8	1	2.69
Bob Friend†	R	35	12	8	0	0	44.2	61	2	9	22	1-4	0	4.84
Stan Bahnsen	R	21	4	3	1	0	23.0	15	3	7	16	1-1	1	3.52
Hal Reniff	R	27	56	0	0	0	95.1	80	2	49	79	3-7	9	3.21
Pedro Ramos	R	31	52	1	0	0	89.2	98	10	18	58	3-9	13	3.61
Steve Hamilton	L	30	44	3	1	1	90.0	69	8	22	57	8-3	3	3.00
Dooley Womack	R	26	42	1	0	0	75.0	52	6	23	50	7-3	4	2.64
Whitey Ford	L	37	22	9	0	0	73.0	79	8	24	43	2-5	0	2.47
Jack Cullen	R	26	5	0	0	0	11.1	11	0	5	7	1-0	0	3.97
Bill Henry	L	24	2	0	0	0	3.0	0	0	2	3	0-0	0	0.00

»1966 Los Angeles Dodgers 1st NL 95-67 .586 —

Walter Alston

Player	Gm by Position	B	Age	G	AB	R	H	2B	3B	HR	RBI	BB	SO	SB	Avg	OBP	Slg
John Roseboro	C138	L	33	142	445	47	123	23	2	9	53	44	51	3	.276	.343	.398
Wes Parker	1B140,OF14	S	26	156	475	67	120	17	5	12	51	69	83	7	.253	.351	.385
Jim Lefebvre	2B119,3B40	S	24	152	544	69	149	23	3	24	74	48	72	1	.274	.333	.460
John Kennedy	3B87,SS28,2B15	R	25	125	274	15	55	9	2	3	24	10	64	1	.201	.241	.281
Maury Wills	SS139,3B4	S	33	143	594	60	162	14	2	1	39	34	60	38	.273	.314	.308
Willie Davis	OF152	L	26	153	624	74	177	31	6	11	61	15	68	21	.284	.302	.405
Lou Johnson	OF148	R	31	152	526	71	143	20	2	17	73	21	75	8	.272	.316	.414
Ron Fairly	OF98,1B25	L	27	117	351	53	101	20	0	14	61	52	38	3	.288	.380	.464
Tommy Davis	OF79,3B2	R	27	100	313	27	98	11	1	3	27	16	36	3	.313	.345	.383
Jim Gilliam	3B70,1B2,2B2	S	37	88	235	30	51	9	0	1	16	34	17	2	.217	.315	.268
Jeff Torborg	C45	R	24	46	120	4	27	3	0	1	13	10	23	0	.225	.278	.275
Nate Oliver	2B68,SS2,3B1	R	25	80	119	17	23	2	0	0	3	13	17	3	.193	.276	.210
Al Ferrara	OF32	R	26	63	115	15	31	4	0	5	23	9	35	0	.270	.333	.435
Dick Stuart†	1B25	R	33	38	91	4	24	1	0	3	9	11	17	0	.264	.356	.374
Jim Barbieri	OF20	L	24	39	82	9	23	5	0	0	3	9	7	2	.280	.352	.341
Dick Schofield†	3B19,SS3	S	31	20	70	10	18	0	0	0	4	8	8	1	.257	.350	.257
Wes Covington†	OF2	L	34	37	33	1	4	0	1	1	6	6	5	0	.121	.293	.273
Derrell Griffith	OF7	L	22	23	15	3	1	0	0	0	2	2	3	0	.067	.176	.067
Bart Shirley	SS5	R	26	12	5	2	1	0	0	0	0	0	2	0	.200	.200	.200
Tom Hutton	1B3	L	20	3	2	0	0	0	0	0	0	0	0	0	.000	.000	.000
Jim Campanis	C1	R	22	1	1	0	0	0	0	0	0	0	0	0	.000	.000	.000
Willie Crawford		L	19	6	0	1	0	0	0	0	0	0	0	0	—	—	—

Pitcher	T	Age	G	GS	CG	ShO	IP	H	HR	BB	SO	W-L	Sv	ERA
Sandy Koufax	L	30	41	41	27	5	323.0	241	19	77	317	27-9	0	1.73
Don Drysdale	R	29	40	40	11	3	273.2	279	21	45	177	13-16	0	3.42
Claude Osteen	L	26	39	38	8	3	240.1	238	6	65	137	17-14	0	2.85
Don Sutton	R	21	37	35	6	2	225.2	192	19	52	209	12-12	0	2.99
Phil Regan	R	29	65	0	0	0	116.2	85	6	24	88	14-1	21	1.62
Ron Perranoski	L	30	55	0	0	0	82.0	82	4	31	50	6-7	7	3.18
Bob Miller	R	27	46	0	0	0	84.1	70	5	29	58	4-2	5	2.77
Joe Moeller	R	23	29	8	0	0	78.2	73	4	14	31	2-4	0	2.52
Jim Brewer	L	28	13	0	0	0	22.0	17	0	11	8	0-2	2	3.68
Nick Willhite	L	25	6	0	0	0	4.1	3	0	5	4	0-0	0	2.08
Bill Singer	R	22	3	0	0	0	4.0	4	0	2	4	0-0	0	0.00
Howie Reed†	R	29	1	0	0	0	1.2	1	0	0	0	0-0	0	0.00
Johnny Podres†	L	33	1	0	0	0	1.2	2	0	1	1	0-0	0	0.00

778 Seasons: Team Rosters

1966 San Francisco Giants 2nd NL 93-68 .578 1.5 GB — Herman Franks

Player	Gm by Position	B	Age	G	AB	R	H	2B	3B	HR	RBI	BB	SO	SB	Avg	OBP	Slg
Tom Haller	C136,1B4	L	29	142	471	74	113	19	2	27	67	53	74	1	.240	.323	.461
Willie McCovey	1B145	L	28	150	502	85	148	26	6	36	96	76	100	2	.295	.391	.586
Hal Lanier	2B112,SS41	R	23	149	459	37	106	14	2	3	37	16	49	1	.231	.256	.290
Jim Ray Hart	3B139,OF17	R	24	156	578	88	165	23	4	33	93	48	75	2	.285	.342	.510
Tito Fuentes	SS76,2B60	S	22	133	541	63	141	21	3	9	40	9	57	6	.261	.276	.360
Willie Mays	OF150	R	35	152	552	99	159	29	4	37	103	70	81	5	.288	.368	.556
Ollie Brown	OF114	R	22	115	348	32	81	7	1	7	33	33	66	2	.233	.303	.319
Jesus Alou	OF100	R	24	110	370	41	96	13	1	1	20	9	22	5	.259	.279	.308
Jim Davenport	SS58,3B36,2B21*	R	32	111	305	42	76	6	2	9	30	22	40	1	.249	.300	.370
Len Gabrielson	OF67,1B6	L	26	94	240	27	52	7	0	4	16	21	51	0	.217	.278	.296
Cap Peterson	OF51,1B2	R	23	89	190	13	45	6	1	2	19	11	32	2	.237	.279	.311
Don Landrum	OF54	L	30	72	102	9	19	4	0	1	7	9	18	1	.186	.259	.255
Bob Barton	C39	R	24	43	91	1	16	2	1	0	3	5	5	0	.176	.216	.220
Ozzie Virgil	C13,3B13,1B5*	R	33	42	89	7	19	2	0	2	9	4	12	1	.213	.245	.303
Orlando Cepeda†	OF8,1B6	R	28	19	49	5	14	2	0	3	15	4	11	0	.286	.352	.510
Bob Burda	1B7,OF4	L	27	37	43	3	7	3	0	0	2	2	5	0	.163	.196	.233
Bob Schroder	SS9	L	21	10	33	0	8	0	0	0	2	0	2	0	.242	.242	.242
Frank Johnson	OF13	R	23	15	32	2	7	0	0	0	2	2	7	0	.219	.265	.219
Ken Henderson	OF10	S	20	11	29	4	9	1	1	1	1	2	3	0	.310	.375	.517
Don Mason	2B9	L	21	42	25	8	3	0	0	1	1	0	2	0	.120	.120	.240
Dick Dietz	C6	R	24	13	23	1	1	0	0	0	0	0	9	0	.043	.083	.043
Jack Hiatt	1B7	R	23	18	23	2	7	2	0	0	1	4	5	0	.304	.407	.391
Dick Schofield†	SS8	S	31	11	16	4	1	0	0	0	0	2	2	0	.063	.167	.063

J. Davenport, 2 G at 1B; O. Virgil, 2 G at 2B, 2 G at OF

Pitcher	T	Age	G	GS	CG	ShO	IP	H	HR	BB	SO	W-L	Sv	ERA
Juan Marichal	R	28	37	36	25	4	307.1	228	32	36	222	25-6	0	2.23
Gaylord Perry	R	27	36	35	13	3	255.2	242	15	40	201	21-8	0	2.99
Bobby Bolin	R	27	36	34	10	4	224.1	174	25	70	143	11-10	1	2.89
Ray Sadecki†	L	25	26	19	3	1	105.0	125	20	39	62	3-7	0	5.40
Ron Herbel	R	28	32	18	0	0	129.2	149	15	39	55	4-5	1	4.16
Lindy McDaniel	R	30	64	0	0	0	121.2	103	5	35	93	10-5	6	2.66
Frank Linzy	R	25	51	0	0	0	100.1	107	4	34	57	7-11	16	2.96
Bob Priddy	R	26	38	3	0	0	91.0	88	8	28	51	6-3	1	3.96
Joe Gibbon	L	31	37	10	1	0	81.0	86	4	16	48	4-6	1	3.67
Bill Henry	L	38	35	0	0	0	22.0	15	3	10	15	1-1	1	2.45
Bob Shaw†	R	33	13	6	0	0	31.2	45	9	7	21	1-4	0	6.25
Billy Hoeft†	L	34	4	0	0	0	3.2	4	0	3	3	0-2	0	7.36
Rich Robertson	R	21	1	0	0	0	2.1	3	0	2	2	0-0	0	7.71
Bob Garibaldi	R	24	1	0	0	0	1.0	1	0	0	0	0-0	0	0.00

1966 Pittsburgh Pirates 3rd NL 92-70 .568 3.0 GB — Harry Walker

Player	Gm by Position	B	Age	G	AB	R	H	2B	3B	HR	RBI	BB	SO	SB	Avg	OBP	Slg
Jim Pagliaroni	C118	R	28	123	374	37	88	20	0	11	49	50	71	0	.235	.329	.377
Donn Clendenon	1B152	R	30	155	571	80	171	22	10	28	98	52	142	8	.299	.358	.520
Bill Mazeroski	2B162	R	29	162	621	56	163	22	7	16	82	31	62	4	.262	.296	.398
Bob Bailey	3B96,OF20	R	23	126	380	51	106	19	3	13	46	47	65	5	.279	.360	.447
Gene Alley	SS143	R	25	147	579	88	173	28	10	7	43	27	83	8	.299	.334	.418
Roberto Clemente	OF154	R	31	154	638	105	202	31	11	29	119	46	109	7	.317	.360	.536
Matty Alou	OF136	L	27	141	535	86	183	18	9	2	27	24	44	23	.342	.373	.421
Willie Stargell	OF127,1B15	L	26	140	485	84	153	30	0	33	102	48	109	2	.315	.381	.581
Jose Pagan	3B83,SS18,2B3*	R	31	109	368	44	97	15	6	4	54	13	38	0	.264	.292	.370
Manny Mota	OF96,3B4	R	28	116	322	54	107	16	7	5	46	25	28	7	.332	.383	.472
Jesse Gonder	C52	L	30	59	160	13	36	3	1	7	16	12	39	0	.225	.287	.388
Jerry Lynch	OF4	L	35	64	56	5	12	1	0	1	6	4	10	0	.214	.267	.286
Jerry May	C41	R	22	42	52	6	13	4	0	1	2	2	15	0	.250	.291	.385
Andre Rodgers	SS5,3B3,OF3*	R	31	36	49	6	9	1	0	0	4	8	7	0	.184	.293	.204
Gene Michael	SS8,2B2,3B1	S	28	30	33	9	5	2	1	0	2	0	7	0	.152	.152	.273
Dave Roberts	1B2	L	33	14	16	3	2	1	0	0	0	0	7	0	.125	.125	.188
George Spriggs		L	25	9	7	0	1	0	0	0	0	0	3	0	.143	.143	.143
Don Bosch	OF1	S	23	3	2	0	0	0	0	0	0	0	0	0	.000	.000	.000

J. Pagan, 3 G at OF; A. Rodgers, 2 G at 1B

Pitcher	T	Age	G	GS	CG	ShO	IP	H	HR	BB	SO	W-L	Sv	ERA
Bob Veale	L	30	38	37	12	3	268.1	228	18	102	229	16-12	0	3.02
Woodie Fryman	L	26	36	28	9	3	181.2	182	13	47	105	12-9	1	3.81
Vern Law	R	36	31	28	8	4	177.2	203	19	24	88	12-8	0	4.05
Steve Blass	R	24	34	25	1	0	155.2	173	12	46	76	11-7	0	3.87
Tommie Sisk	R	24	34	23	4	1	150.0	146	14	52	60	10-5	1	4.14
Pete Mikkelsen	R	26	71	0	0	0	126.0	106	8	51	76	9-8	14	3.07
Roy Face	R	38	54	0	0	0	70.0	68	9	24	67	6-6	18	2.70
Al McBean	R	28	47	0	0	0	86.2	95	9	24	54	4-3	3	3.22
Billy O'Dell†	L	33	37	2	0	0	71.1	74	3	23	47	3-2	4	2.78
Don Cardwell	R	30	32	14	1	0	101.2	112	15	27	60	6-6	1	4.60
Don Schwall†	R	30	11	4	0	0	41.2	31	3	21	24	3-2	0	2.16
Bob Purkey	R	36	10	0	0	0	19.2	16	0	4	5	0-1	1	1.37
Luke Walker	L	22	10	1	0	0	10.0	8	0	15	7	0-1	0	4.50
Jim Shellenback	L	22	2	0	0	0	3.0	3	2	3	0	0-0	0	9.00

1966 Philadelphia Phillies 4th NL 87-75 .537 8.0 GB — Gene Mauch

Player	Gm by Position	B	Age	G	AB	R	H	2B	3B	HR	RBI	BB	SO	SB	Avg	OBP	Slg
Clay Dalrymple	C110	L	29	114	331	30	81	13	3	4	39	60	57	0	.245	.365	.338
Bill White	1B158	L	32	159	577	85	159	23	6	22	103	68	109	16	.276	.352	.451
Cookie Rojas	2B106,OF56,SS2	R	27	156	626	77	168	18	1	6	55	35	46	4	.268	.310	.329
Dick Allen	3B91,OF47	R	24	141	524	112	166	25	10	40	110	68	136	10	.317	.396	.632
Dick Groat	SS139,3B20,1B1	R	35	155	584	58	152	21	4	2	53	40	38	2	.260	.311	.320
Johnny Callison	OF154	L	27	155	612	93	169	40	7	11	55	56	83	8	.276	.338	.418
Tony Gonzalez	OF121	L	29	132	384	53	110	20	4	6	40	26	60	2	.286	.335	.406
Jackie Brandt	OF71	R	32	82	164	16	41	6	1	1	15	17	36	0	.250	.317	.317
Tony Taylor	2B68,3B52	R	30	125	434	47	105	14	8	5	40	31	56	8	.242	.294	.346
John Briggs	OF69	L	22	81	255	43	72	13	5	10	23	41	55	3	.282	.380	.490
Bob Uecker	C76	R	31	78	207	15	43	6	0	7	30	22	36	0	.208	.279	.338
Harvey Kuenn†	OF31,1B13,3B1	R	35	86	159	15	47	9	0	0	15	10	16	0	.296	.333	.352
Doug Clemens	OF28,1B1	L	27	79	121	10	31	1	0	1	15	16	25	1	.256	.353	.289
Bobby Wine	SS40,OF2	R	27	46	89	8	21	5	0	0	5	6	13	0	.236	.292	.292
Phil Linz	3B14,SS6,2B3	R	27	40	70	4	14	3	0	0	6	2	14	0	.200	.222	.243
Jimmie Schaffer	C6	R	30	8	15	2	2	1	0	1	4	1	7	0	.133	.188	.400
John Herrnstein†	OF2	L	28	4	10	0	1	0	0	0	1	0	7	0	.100	.100	.100
Gary Sutherland	SS1	R	21	3	3	0	0	0	0	0	0	0	0	0	.000	.000	.000
Adolfo Phillips†	OF1	R	24	2	3	1	0	0	0	0	0	0	0	0	.000	.000	.000

Pitcher	T	Age	G	GS	CG	ShO	IP	H	HR	BB	SO	W-L	Sv	ERA
Jim Bunning	R	34	43	41	16	5	314.0	260	26	55	252	19-14	1	2.41
Chris Short	L	28	42	39	19	4	272.0	257	28	68	177	20-10	0	3.54
Larry Jackson†	R	35	35	33	12	5	247.0	243	22	58	107	15-13	0	2.99
Bob Buhl†	R	37	32	18	1	0	132.0	156	10	39	59	6-8	1	4.77
Rick Wise	R	20	22	13	3	0	99.1	100	5	24	58	5-6	0	3.71
John Boozer	R	27	2	2	0	0	5.1	8	1	3	5	0-0	0	6.75
Darold Knowles	L	24	69	0	0	0	100.1	98	4	46	88	6-5	13	3.05
Terry Fox†	R	30	36	0	0	0	44.1	57	3	17	22	3-2	4	4.47
Ray Culp	R	24	34	12	1	0	110.2	106	19	53	100	7-4	1	5.04
Ray Herbert	R	36	23	2	0	0	50.1	55	7	14	15	2-5	2	4.29
Joe Verbanic	R	23	17	0	0	0	14.0	12	2	10	7	1-1	0	5.14
Roger Craig	R	36	14	0	0	0	22.2	31	4	5	13	2-1	1	5.56
John Morris	L	24	13	0	0	0	13.2	15	2	3	8	1-1	0	5.27
Bo Belinsky	L	29	9	1	0	0	15.1	14	3	5	8	0-2	0	2.93
Ed Roebuck	R	34	6	0	0	0	6.0	9	0	2	5	0-2	0	6.00
Gary Wagner	R	26	5	1	0	0	6.1	8	1	5	2	0-1	0	8.53
Steve Ridzik	R	37	2	0	0	0	2.1	5	0	1	0	0-0	0	7.71
Grant Jackson	L	23	2	0	0	0	1.2	2	0	3	0	0-0	0	5.40
Fergie Jenkins†	R	22	1	0	0	0	2.1	3	0	1	2	0-0	0	3.86

1966 Atlanta Braves 5th NL 85-77 .525 10.0 GB — Bobby Bragan (52-59)/Billy Hitchcock (33-18)

Player	Gm by Position	B	Age	G	AB	R	H	2B	3B	HR	RBI	BB	SO	SB	Avg	OBP	Slg
Joe Torre	C114,1B36	R	25	148	546	83	172	20	3	36	101	60	61	0	.315	.382	.560
Felipe Alou	1B90,OF79,3B3*	R	31	154	666	122	218	32	6	31	74	24	51	5	.327	.361	.533
Woody Woodward	2B79,SS73	R	23	144	455	46	120	23	3	0	43	37	54	2	.264	.323	.327
Eddie Mathews	3B127	L	34	134	452	72	113	21	4	16	53	63	82	1	.250	.341	.420
Denis Menke	SS106,3B39,1B7	R	25	138	454	55	114	20	4	15	60	71	87	0	.251	.355	.412
Hank Aaron	OF158,2B2	R	32	158	603	117	168	23	1	44	127	76	96	21	.279	.356	.539
Rico Carty	OF126,C17,1B2*	R	26	151	521	73	170	25	2	15	76	60	74	4	.326	.391	.468
Mack Jones	OF112,1B1	L	27	118	417	60	110	14	1	23	66	39	85	16	.264	.335	.468
Frank Bolling	2B67	R	34	75	227	16	48	7	0	1	18	10	14	1	.211	.244	.256
Gene Oliver	C48,1B5,OF2	R	31	76	191	19	37	9	1	8	24	16	43	2	.194	.255	.377
Lee Thomas†	1B36	L	30	39	126	11	25	1	1	6	15	10	15	1	.198	.261	.365
Gary Geiger	OF49	L	29	78	126	23	33	5	3	4	10	21	29	0	.262	.367	.444
Mike de la Hoz	3B30,2B8,SS1	R	27	71	110	11	24	3	0	2	7	5	18	0	.218	.250	.300
Felix Millan	2B25,3B1,SS1	R	22	37	91	20	25	6	0	0	5	2	6	3	.275	.290	.341
Ty Cline†	OF19,1B6	L	27	42	71	12	18	0	0	0	6	3	11	2	.254	.303	.254
Sandy Alomar	2B21,SS5	S	22	31	44	4	4	1	0	0	2	1	10	0	.091	.111	.114
John Herrnstein†	OF5	L	28	17	18	2	4	0	0	0	0	1	7	0	.222	.222	.222
Marty Keough†	1B4,OF3	L	31	17	17	1	1	0	0	0	1	1	6	0	.059	.111	.059
Lee Bales	2B7,3B3	S	21	12	16	4	1	0	0	0	0	0	5	0	.063	.063	.063
Bill Robinson	OF5	R	23	6	11	1	3	0	1	0	3	0	1	0	.273	.273	.455
George Kopacz	1B2	L	25	6	9	1	0	0	0	0	0	1	5	0	.000	.100	.000
Ed Sadowski	C3	R	34	3	9	1	1	0	0	0	1	1	1	0	.111	.200	.111
Adrian Garrett	OF1	L	23	4	3	0	0	0	0	0	0	0	2	0	.000	.000	.000

F. Alou, 1 G at SS; R. Carty, 1 G at 3B

Pitcher	T	Age	G	GS	CG	ShO	IP	H	HR	BB	SO	W-L	Sv	ERA
Tony Cloninger	R	25	39	38	11	1	257.2	253	29	116	178	14-11	1	4.12
Ken Johnson	R	33	32	31	11	2	215.2	213	24	46	105	14-8	0	3.30
Denny Lemaster	L	27	27	27	10	3	171.0	170	25	41	139	11-8	0	3.74
Dick Kelley	L	26	20	13	2	2	81.0	75	6	21	50	7-5	0	3.22
Wade Blasingame	L	22	16	12	0	0	67.2	71	5	25	34	3-7	0	5.32
Pat Jarvis	R	25	10	9	3	1	62.1	46	1	12	41	6-2	0	2.31
Hank Fischer†	R	26	14	8	0	0	48.1	55	3	14	22	2-3	0	3.91
Don Schwall†	R	30	11	8	0	0	45.1	44	2	19	27	3-3	0	4.37
Joey Jay†	R	30	9	8	0	0	29.2	39	4	20	19	0-4	1	7.89
Ron Reed	R	23	2	2	0	0	8.1	7	1	4	6	1-1	0	2.16
Charlie Vaughan	L	18	1	1	0	0	7.0	8	0	3	6	1-0	0	2.57
Clay Carroll	R	25	73	3	0	0	144.1	127	8	29	67	8-7	11	2.37
Chi Chi Olivo	R	38	47	0	0	0	66.0	59	4	19	41	5-4	7	4.23
Ted Abernathy†	R	33	38	0	0	0	65.1	58	5	36	42	4-4	4	3.86
Phil Niekro	R	27	28	0	0	0	50.1	48	4	23	17	4-3	2	4.11
Billy O'Dell†	L	33	24	0	0	0	41.1	44	3	18	20	2-3	6	2.40
Arnie Umbach	R	23	22	3	0	0	40.2	40	1	18	23	0-2	0	3.10
Jay Ritchie	R	29	22	0	0	0	35.1	32	3	12	33	0-1	4	4.08
Dan Schneider	L	23	14	0	0	0	26.1	35	1	5	11	0-0	0	3.42
Herb Hippauf	L	27	3	0	0	0	2.2	6	0	1	1	0-1	0	13.50
Cecil Upshaw	R	23	1	0	0	0	3.0	0	0	3	2	0-0	0	0.00

1966 St. Louis Cardinals 6th NL 83-79 .512 12.0 GB — Red Schoendienst

Player	Gm by Position	B	Age	G	AB	R	H	2B	3B	HR	RBI	BB	SO	SB	Avg	OBP	Slg
Tim McCarver	C148	L	24	150	543	50	149	19	13	12	68	36	38	9	.274	.319	.424
Orlando Cepeda†	1B120	R	28	123	452	65	137	24	0	17	58	34	68	9	.303	.362	.469
Julian Javier	2B145	R	29	147	460	52	105	13	5	7	31	26	63	11	.228	.269	.324
Charley Smith	3B107,SS1	R	28	116	391	34	104	13	4	10	43	22	81	0	.266	.301	.396
Dal Maxvill	SS128,2B5,OF1	R	27	134	394	25	96	14	3	0	24	37	61	3	.244	.312	.294
Curt Flood	OF159	R	28	160	626	64	167	21	5	10	78	26	50	14	.267	.298	.364
Lou Brock	OF154	L	27	156	643	94	183	24	12	15	46	31	134	74	.285	.320	.429
Mike Shannon	OF129,C1	R	26	137	459	61	132	20	6	16	64	37	106	8	.288	.339	.462
Jerry Buchek	2B49,SS48,3B4	R	24	100	284	23	67	10	4	4	25	23	71	0	.236	.288	.342
Phil Gagliano	3B41,1B8,OF5*	R	24	90	213	23	54	8	2	2	15	24	29	2	.254	.329	.338
Tito Francona	1B30,OF9	L	32	83	156	14	33	4	1	4	17	7	27	0	.212	.250	.327
Bobby Tolan	OF26,1B1	L	20	43	93	10	16	5	1	1	6	6	15	1	.172	.233	.280
Alex Johnson	OF22	R	23	25	86	7	16	0	1	2	6	5	18	1	.186	.231	.279
Ed Spiezio	3B19	R	24	26	73	4	16	5	1	2	10	5	11	1	.219	.269	.397
Pat Corrales	C27	R	25	28	72	5	13	2	0	0	3	2	17	1	.181	.221	.208
George Kernek	1B16	L	26	20	50	5	12	0	1	0	3	4	9	1	.240	.309	.280
Bob Skinner		L	34	49	45	2	7	1	0	1	5	2	17	0	.156	.208	.244
Ted Savage	OF7	R	29	16	29	4	5	2	1	0	3	4	7	4	.172	.273	.310
Jimy Williams	SS7,2B3	R	22	13	11	1	3	0	0	0	1	1	5	0	.273	.333	.273

P. Gagliano, 1 G at 2B

Pitcher	T	Age	G	GS	CG	ShO	IP	H	HR	BB	SO	W-L	Sv	ERA
Bob Gibson	R	30	35	35	20	5	280.1	210	20	78	225	21-12	0	2.44
Al Jackson	L	30	36	30	11	3	232.2	222	18	45	90	13-15	0	2.51
Ray Washburn	R	28	27	26	4	1	170.0	183	15	44	98	11-9	0	3.76
Larry Jaster	L	22	26	21	6	5	151.2	124	17	45	92	11-5	0	3.26
Steve Carlton	L	21	9	9	2	1	52.0	56	2	18	25	3-3	0	3.12
Curt Simmons†	L	37	10	5	1	0	33.1	35	3	14	14	1-1	0	4.59
Ray Sadecki†	L	25	5	3	1	0	24.1	16	2	9	21	2-1	0	2.22
Jim Cosman	R	23	1	1	1	1	9.0	2	0	2	5	1-0	0	0.00
Hal Woodeshick	L	33	59	0	0	0	70.1	57	5	23	30	2-1	4	1.92
Joe Hoerner	L	29	57	0	0	0	76.0	57	5	21	63	5-1	13	1.54
Nelson Briles	R	22	49	17	0	0	154.0	162	14	54	100	4-15	6	3.21
Don Dennis	R	24	38	1	0	0	59.2	73	8	17	25	4-2	2	4.98
Tracy Stallard	R	28	20	7	0	0	52.1	65	9	25	35	1-5	1	5.68
Ron Piche	R	31	20	0	0	0	25.1	21	4	18	21	1-3	2	4.26
Art Mahaffey	R	28	12	5	0	0	35.0	37	7	21	19	1-4	1	6.43
Dennis Aust	R	25	9	0	0	0	9.2	12	1	6	7	1-1	1	6.52
Dick Hughes	R	28	6	2	1	0	21.0	12	0	7	20	2-1	1	1.71
Ron Willis	R	22	4	0	0	0	3.0	1	0	1	2	0-0	1	0.00

1966 Cincinnati Reds 7th NL 76-84 .475 18.0 GB

Don Heffner (37-46)/Dave Bristol (39-38)

Player	Gm by Position	B	Age	G	AB	R	H	2B	3B	HR	RBI	BB	SO	SB	Avg	OBP	Slg
Johnny Edwards	C98	L	28	98	282	24	54	8	0	6	39	31	42	1	.191	.269	.284
Tony Perez	1B75	R	24	99	257	25	68	10	4	4	39	14	44	1	.265	.304	.381
Pete Rose	2B140,3B16	S	25	156	654	97	205	38	5	16	70	37	61	4	.313	.351	.460
Tommy Helms	3B113,2B20	R	25	138	542	72	154	23	1	9	49	24	31	3	.284	.315	.380
Leo Cardenas	SS160	R	27	160	568	59	145	25	4	20	81	45	87	9	.255	.309	.419
Vada Pinson	OF154	L	27	156	618	70	178	35	6	16	76	33	83	18	.288	.326	.442
Tommy Harper	OF147	R	25	149	553	85	154	22	5	5	31	57	85	29	.278	.348	.363
Deron Johnson	OF106,1B71,3B18	R	27	142	505	75	130	25	3	24	81	39	87	1	.257	.309	.461
Don Pavletich	C55,1B10	R	27	83	235	29	69	13	2	12	38	18	37	1	.294	.344	.519
Art Shamsky	OF74	L	24	96	234	41	54	5	0	21	47	32	45	0	.231	.321	.521
Gordy Coleman	1B65	L	31	91	227	20	57	7	0	5	37	16	45	2	.251	.299	.348
Jimmie Coker	C39,OF2	R	30	50	111	9	28	3	0	4	14	8	5	0	.252	.300	.387
Chico Ruiz	3B27,OF8,SS6	S	27	82	110	13	28	2	1	0	5	5	14	1	.255	.287	.291
Dick Simpson	OF64	R	22	92	84	26	20	2	0	4	14	10	32	0	.238	.333	.405
Lee May	1B16	R	23	25	75	14	25	5	1	2	10	0	14	0	.333	.333	.507
Mel Queen	OF32,P7	L	24	56	55	4	7	1	0	0	5	10	12	0	.127	.250	.145

Pitcher	T	Age	G	GS	CG	ShO	IP	H	HR	BB	SO	W-L	Sv	ERA
Sammy Ellis	R	25	41	36	7	0	221.0	226	35	78	154	12-19	0	5.29
Jim Maloney	R	26	32	32	10	5	224.2	174	18	90	216	16-8	0	2.80
Milt Pappas	R	27	33	32	6	2	209.2	224	23	39	133	12-11	0	4.29
Jim O'Toole	L	29	25	24	2	0	142.0	139	16	49	96	5-7	0	3.55
Joey Jay†	R	30	12	10	1	1	73.2	78	8	23	44	6-2	0	3.91
Hank Fischer†	R	26	11	9	0	0	38.0	53	3	15	24	0-6	0	6.63
Don Nottebart	R	30	59	1	0	0	111.1	97	11	43	69	5-4	11	3.07
Billy McCool	L	21	57	0	0	0	105.1	76	5	41	104	8-8	18	2.48
Ted Davidson	L	26	54	0	0	0	85.1	82	11	23	54	5-4	4	3.90
Jack Baldschun	R	29	42	0	0	0	57.1	71	4	25	44	1-5	0	5.49
Joe Nuxhall	L	37	35	16	2	1	130.0	136	14	42	71	6-8	0	4.50
Darrell Osteen	R	23	13	0	0	0	15.0	26	3	9	17	0-2	1	12.00
Mel Queen	R	24	7	0	0	0	7.0	11	0	6	9	0-0	1	6.43
Dom Zanni	R	34	5	0	0	0	7.1	5	0	3	5	0-0	0	0.00
Gerry Arrigo†	L	25	3	0	0	0	7.1	7	2	3	3	0-0	0	4.91
John Tsitouris	R	30	1	0	0	0	1.0	3	0	1	0	0-0	0	18.00

1966 Houston Astros 8th NL 72-90 .444 23.0 GB

Grady Hatton

Player	Gm by Position	B	Age	G	AB	R	H	2B	3B	HR	RBI	BB	SO	SB	Avg	OBP	Slg
John Bateman	C121	R	25	131	433	39	121	24	3	17	70	20	74	0	.279	.315	.467
Chuck Harrison	1B114	R	25	119	434	52	111	23	2	9	52	37	69	2	.256	.316	.380
Joe Morgan	2B117	L	22	122	425	60	121	14	8	5	42	89	43	11	.285	.410	.391
Bob Aspromonte	3B149,1B2,SS2	R	28	152	560	55	141	16	3	8	52	35	63	0	.252	.297	.334
Sonny Jackson	SS150	L	21	150	596	80	174	6	5	3	25	42	53	49	.292	.341	.334
Rusty Staub	OF148,1B1	L	22	153	554	60	155	28	3	13	81	58	61	2	.280	.345	.412
Jimmy Wynn	OF104	R	24	105	418	62	107	21	1	18	62	41	81	13	.256	.321	.440
Lee Maye	OF97	L	31	115	358	38	103	12	4	9	36	20	26	4	.288	.323	.419
Dave Nicholson	OF90	R	26	100	280	36	69	8	4	10	31	46	92	1	.246	.356	.411
Ron Davis	OF48	R	24	48	194	21	48	10	1	2	19	13	26	2	.247	.308	.340
Bob Lillis	2B35,SS18,3B6	R	36	68	164	14	38	6	0	0	11	7	4	1	.232	.260	.268
Felix Mantilla	1B14,3B14,2B9*	R	31	77	151	16	33	5	0	6	22	11	32	1	.219	.279	.371
Jim Gentile†	1B43	L	32	49	144	16	35	6	1	7	18	21	39	0	.243	.355	.444
Bill Heath	C37	L	27	55	123	12	37	6	0	0	8	9	11	1	.301	.353	.350
Ron Brand	C25,2B9,OF3*	R	26	56	123	12	30	2	0	0	10	9	13	0	.244	.301	.260
Norm Miller	OF8,3B2	L	20	11	34	1	5	0	0	1	3	2	8	0	.147	.194	.235
Gene Freese†	3B4,2B3,OF1	R	32	21	33	1	3	0	0	0	0	5	11	1	.091	.211	.091
Brock Davis	OF7	L	22	10	27	2	4	1	0	0	1	5	4	1	.148	.281	.185
Aaron Pointer	OF11	R	24	11	26	5	9	1	0	1	5	5	6	1	.346	.469	.500
Joe Gaines	OF3	R	29	11	13	4	1	1	0	0	0	3	5	0	.077	.250	.154
Nate Colbert		R	20	19	7	3	0	0	0	0	0	0	4	0	.000	.000	.000
Greg Sims	OF1	S	20	7	6	1	1	0	0	0	0	1	3	0	.167	.286	.167
Dave Adlesh	C1	R	22	3	6	0	0	0	0	0	0	0	4	0	.000	.000	.000
Julio Gotay	3B1	R	27	4	5	0	0	0	0	0	0	0	0	0	.000	.000	.000
Bob Watson		R	20	1	1	0	0	0	0	0	0	0	0	0	.000	.000	.000

F. Mantilla, 1 G at OF; R. Brand, 1 G at 3B

Pitcher	T	Age	G	GS	CG	ShO	IP	H	HR	BB	SO	W-L	Sv	ERA
Dave Giusti	R	26	34	33	9	4	210.0	215	23	54	131	15-14	0	4.20
Mike Cuellar	L	29	38	28	11	1	227.1	193	10	52	175	12-10	2	2.22
Larry Dierker	R	19	29	28	8	2	187.0	173	17	45	108	10-8	0	3.18
Bob Bruce	R	33	25	23	1	0	129.2	160	16	29	71	3-13	0	5.34
Turk Farrell	R	32	32	21	3	0	152.2	167	23	28	101	6-10	2	4.60
Robin Roberts†	R	39	13	12	1	1	63.2	79	7	10	26	3-5	1	3.82
Chris Zachary	R	22	10	8	0	0	55.0	44	1	32	37	3-5	0	3.44
Claude Raymond	R	29	62	0	0	0	92.0	85	10	25	73	7-5	16	3.13
Jim Owens	R	32	40	0	0	0	50.0	53	5	17	32	4-7	2	4.68
Ron Taylor	R	28	36	1	0	0	64.2	89	5	10	29	2-3	0	5.71
Barry Latman	R	30	31	9	1	1	103.0	88	5	35	74	2-7	1	2.71
Carroll Sembera	R	24	24	0	0	0	33.0	36	3	16	21	1-2	1	3.00
Gary Kroll	R	24	10	0	0	0	23.2	26	2	11	22	0-0	0	3.80
A. Monteagudo†	R	22	10	0	0	0	15.1	14	1	11	7	0-0	1	4.70
Frank Carpin	L	27	10	0	0	0	6.0	9	0	6	2	1-0	0	7.50
Don Lee†	R	32	9	0	0	0	18.0	17	1	4	9	2-0	0	2.50
Don Arlich	L	23	7	0	0	0	4.0	11	0	4	1	0-1	0	15.75
Danny Coombs	L	24	2	0	0	0	2.2	4	0	0	3	0-0	0	3.38
Don Wilson	R	21	1	0	0	0	6.0	5	1	1	7	1-0	0	3.00
Jim Ray	R	21	1	0	0	0	0.0	0	0	1	0	0-0	0	—

1966 New York Mets 9th NL 66-95 .410 28.5 GB

Wes Westrum

Player	Gm by Position	B	Age	G	AB	R	H	2B	3B	HR	RBI	BB	SO	SB	Avg	OBP	Slg
Jerry Grote	C115,3B2	R	23	120	317	26	75	12	2	3	31	40	81	4	.237	.327	.315
Ed Kranepool	1B132,OF11	L	21	146	464	51	118	15	2	16	57	41	66	1	.254	.316	.399
Ron Hunt	2B123,3B1,SS1	R	25	132	479	63	138	19	2	3	33	41	34	8	.288	.356	.355
Ken Boyer	3B130,1B2	R	35	136	496	62	132	28	2	14	61	30	64	4	.266	.304	.415
Eddie Bressoud	SS94,3B32,1B9*	R	34	133	405	48	91	15	5	10	49	47	107	2	.225	.304	.360
Cleon Jones	OF129	R	23	139	495	74	136	16	4	8	57	30	62	16	.275	.318	.372
Al Luplow	OF101	L	27	111	334	31	84	9	1	7	31	38	46	2	.251	.331	.347
Ron Swoboda	OF97	R	22	112	342	34	76	9	4	8	50	31	76	4	.222	.296	.342
Chuck Hiller	2B45,3B14,OF9	L	31	108	254	25	71	8	2	2	14	15	22	0	.280	.332	.350
Roy McMillan	SS71	R	35	76	220	24	47	9	1	1	12	20	25	1	.214	.284	.277
Larry Elliot	OF54	L	28	65	199	24	49	14	2	5	32	17	46	0	.246	.306	.412
Johnny Lewis	OF49	L	26	65	166	21	32	6	1	5	20	21	43	2	.193	.282	.331
Jim Hickman	OF45,1B17	R	29	58	160	15	38	7	0	4	16	13	34	2	.238	.299	.356
John Stephenson	C52,OF1	L	25	63	143	17	28	1	1	1	11	8	28	0	.196	.248	.238
Billy Murphy	OF57	R	22	84	135	15	31	4	1	3	13	7	34	1	.230	.271	.341
Hawk Taylor	C29,1B13	R	27	53	109	5	19	2	0	3	12	3	19	0	.174	.204	.275
Bud Harrelson	SS29	S	22	33	99	20	22	2	4	0	4	13	23	7	.222	.313	.323
Dick Stuart†	1B23	R	33	31	87	7	19	0	0	4	13	9	26	0	.218	.292	.356
Danny Napoleon	OF10	R	24	12	33	2	7	2	0	0	0	1	10	0	.212	.235	.273
Greg Goossen	C11	R	20	13	32	1	6	2	0	1	5	1	11	0	.188	.235	.344
C. Choo Coleman	C5	L	28	6	16	2	3	0	0	0	0	0	4	0	.188	.188	.188
Shaun Fitzmaurice	OF5	R	23	9	13	2	2	0	0	0	0	2	6	1	.154	.267	.154
Lou Klimchock		L	26	5	5	0	0	0	0	0	0	0	3	0	.000	.000	.000

E. Bressoud, 7 G at 2B

Pitcher	T	Age	G	GS	CG	ShO	IP	H	HR	BB	SO	W-L	Sv	ERA
Jack Fisher	R	27	38	33	10	2	230.0	229	26	54	127	11-14	0	3.68
Dennis Ribant	R	24	39	26	10	1	188.1	184	20	40	84	11-9	3	3.20
Bob Shaw†	R	33	26	25	7	2	167.2	171	12	42	104	11-10	0	3.92
Bob Friend†	R	35	22	12	2	1	86.0	101	11	16	30	5-8	1	4.40
Tug McGraw	L	21	15	12	1	0	62.1	72	11	25	34	2-9	0	5.34
Nolan Ryan	R	19	2	1	0	0	3.0	5	1	3	6	0-1	0	15.00
Jack Hamilton	R	27	57	13	3	1	148.2	138	13	88	93	6-13	13	3.93
Rob Gardner	L	21	41	17	3	0	133.2	147	15	64	74	4-8	1	5.12
Bill Hepler	L	20	37	3	0	0	69.0	71	3	51	25	3-3	0	3.52
Darrell Sutherland	R	24	31	0	0	0	44.1	60	6	25	23	2-0	1	4.87
Dick Selma	R	22	30	7	0	0	80.2	84	11	39	58	4-6	1	4.24
Larry Bearnarth	R	24	29	1	0	0	54.2	59	11	20	27	2-3	0	4.45
Dave Eilers	R	29	23	0	0	0	34.2	39	7	7	14	1-1	0	4.67
Gerry Arrigo†	L	25	17	5	0	0	43.1	47	5	16	28	3-3	0	3.74
Gordie Richardson	L	27	15	1	0	0	18.2	24	7	6	15	0-2	1	9.16
Ralph Terry†	R	30	11	1	0	0	24.2	27	1	11	14	0-1	1	4.74
Dick Rusteck	L	24	8	3	1	1	24.0	24	1	8	9	1-2	0	3.00
Larry Miller	L	29	4	1	0	0	8.1	9	3	4	7	0-2	0	7.56
Dallas Green	R	31	4	0	0	0	5.0	6	2	2	1	0-0	0	5.40

1966 Chicago Cubs 10th NL 59-103 .364 36.0 GB

Leo Durocher

Player	Gm by Position	B	Age	G	AB	R	H	2B	3B	HR	RBI	BB	SO	SB	Avg	OBP	Slg
Randy Hundley	C149	R	24	149	526	50	124	22	3	19	63	35	113	1	.236	.285	.397
Ernie Banks	1B130,3B8	R	35	141	511	52	139	23	7	15	75	29	59	0	.272	.315	.432
Glenn Beckert	2B152,SS1	R	25	153	656	73	188	23	7	1	59	26	36	10	.287	.317	.348
Ron Santo	3B152,SS8	R	26	155	561	93	175	21	8	30	94	95	78	4	.312	.412	.538
Don Kessinger	SS148	S	23	150	533	50	146	8	2	1	43	26	46	13	.274	.306	.302
Billy Williams	OF162	L	28	162	648	100	179	23	5	29	91	69	61	6	.276	.347	.461
Byron Browne	OF114	R	23	120	419	46	102	15	7	16	51	40	143	3	.243	.316	.427
Adolfo Phillips†	OF111	R	24	116	416	68	109	29	1	16	36	43	135	32	.262	.348	.452
John Boccabella	OF33,1B30,C5	R	25	75	206	22	47	9	0	6	25	14	39	0	.228	.274	.359
George Altman	OF42,1B4	L	33	88	185	19	41	6	0	5	17	14	37	2	.222	.276	.335
Lee Thomas†	1B20,OF17	L	30	75	149	15	36	4	0	1	9	14	15	0	.242	.319	.289
Jimmy Stewart	OF15,2B4,3B2*	S	27	57	90	4	16	4	1	0	4	7	12	1	.178	.253	.244
Ron Campbell	SS11,3B7	R	26	24	60	4	13	1	0	0	4	6	5	1	.217	.284	.233
Joey Amalfitano	2B12,3B3,SS2	R	32	41	38	8	6	2	0	0	3	4	10	0	.158	.227	.211
Bob Raudman	OF8	L	24	8	29	1	7	2	0	0	2	1	4	0	.241	.267	.310
Chris Krug	C10	R	26	11	28	1	6	1	0	0	1	1	8	0	.214	.241	.250
Don Bryant	C10	R	24	13	26	2	8	2	0	0	4	1	4	1	.308	.357	.385
Marty Keough†	OF5	L	31	33	26	3	6	1	0	0	5	5	9	1	.231	.375	.269
Carl Warwick	OF10	R	29	16	22	3	5	0	0	0	0	0	6	0	.227	.227	.227
Roberto Pena	SS5	R	29	6	17	0	3	2	0	0	1	0	4	0	.176	.176	.294
John Herrnstein†	1B4,OF1	L	28	9	17	3	3	0	0	0	0	3	8	0	.176	.300	.176
Ty Cline†	OF5	L	27	7	17	3	6	0	0	0	2	0	2	1	.353	.353	.353
Wes Covington†	OF1	L	34	9	11	0	1	0	0	0	0	1	2	0	.091	.167	.091
Paul Popovich	2B2	S	25	2	6	0	0	0	0	0	0	0	2	0	.000	.000	.000
Frank Thomas		R	37	5	5	0	0	0	0	0	0	0	1	0	.000	.000	.000
Harvey Kuenn†	OF1	R	35	3	3	0	1	0	0	0	0	0	1	0	.333	.333	.333

J. Stewart, 2 G at SS

Pitcher	T	Age	G	GS	CG	ShO	IP	H	HR	BB	SO	W-L	Sv	ERA
Dick Ellsworth	L	26	38	37	9	0	269.1	321	28	51	144	8-22	0	3.98
Ken Holtzman	L	20	34	33	9	0	220.2	194	27	68	171	11-16	0	3.79
Bill Hands	R	26	41	26	0	0	159.0	168	17	59	93	8-13	2	4.58
Ernie Broglio	R	30	15	11	2	0	62.1	70	14	38	34	2-6	1	6.35
Curt Simmons†	L	37	19	10	3	1	77.1	79	7	21	24	4-7	0	4.07
Robin Roberts†	R	39	11	9	1	0	48.1	62	8	11	28	2-3	0	6.14
Rich Nye	L	21	3	2	0	0	17.0	16	1	7	9	0-2	0	2.12
Larry Jackson†	R	35	3	2	0	0	8.0	14	3	4	5	0-2	0	13.50
Dave Dowling	L	23	1	1	1	0	9.0	10	0	0	3	1-0	0	2.00
Bob Buhl†	R	37	1	1	0	0	2.1	4	1	1	1	0-0	0	15.43
Fergie Jenkins†	R	22	60	12	2	1	182.0	147	24	51	148	6-8	5	3.31
Cal Koonce	R	25	45	5	0	0	108.2	113	13	35	65	5-5	2	3.81
Bob Hendley	L	27	43	6	0	0	89.2	98	10	39	65	4-5	7	3.91
Billy Hoeft†	L	34	36	0	0	0	41.0	43	4	14	30	1-2	3	4.61
Ted Abernathy†	R	33	20	0	0	0	27.2	26	4	17	18	1-3	4	6.18
Bill Faul	R	26	17	6	1	0	51.1	47	12	18	32	1-4	0	5.08
Don Lee†	R	32	16	0	0	0	19.0	28	3	12	7	2-1	0	7.11
Arnold Earley	L	33	13	0	0	0	17.2	14	1	9	12	2-1	0	3.57
Billy Connors	R	24	11	0	0	0	16.0	20	4	7	3	0-1	0	7.31
Chuck Estrada	R	28	9	1	0	0	12.1	16	2	5	3	1-1	0	7.30
Chuck Hartenstein	R	24	5	0	0	0	9.1	8	0	3	4	0-0	0	1.93
Len Church	R	24	4	0	0	0	6.0	10	1	7	3	0-1	0	7.50
Fred Norman	L	23	2	0	0	0	4.0	5	0	2	6	0-0	0	4.50

»1967 Boston Red Sox 1st AL 92-70 .568 —

Dick Williams

Player	Gm by Position	B	Age	G	AB	R	H	2B	3B	HR	RBI	BB	SO	SB	Avg	OBP	Slg
Mike Ryan	C79	R	25	79	226	21	45	4	2	2	27	26	42	2	.199	.282	.261
George Scott	1B152,3B2	R	23	159	565	74	171	21	7	19	82	63	119	10	.303	.373	.465
Mike Andrews	2B139,SS6	R	23	142	494	79	130	20	0	8	40	62	72	7	.263	.346	.352
Joe Foy	3B118,OF1	R	24	130	446	70	112	22	4	16	49	46	87	8	.251	.325	.426
Rico Petrocelli	SS141	R	24	142	491	53	127	24	2	17	66	49	93	2	.259	.330	.420
Carl Yastrzemski	OF161	L	27	161	579	112	189	31	4	44	121	91	69	10	.326	.418	.622
Reggie Smith	OF144,2B6	S	22	158	565	78	139	24	6	15	61	57	95	16	.246	.315	.389
Tony Conigliaro	OF95	R	22	95	349	59	100	11	5	20	67	27	58	4	.287	.341	.519
Jerry Adair†	3B35,SS30,2B23	R	30	89	316	41	92	13	1	3	26	13	35	1	.291	.321	.367
Jose Tartabull	OF83	L	28	115	247	36	55	1	2	0	10	23	26	6	.223	.287	.243
Dalton Jones	3B30,2B19,1B1	L	23	89	159	18	46	6	2	3	25	11	23	0	.289	.333	.409
Russ Gibson	C48	R	28	49	138	8	28	7	0	1	15	12	31	0	.203	.263	.275
Elston Howard†	C41	R	38	42	116	9	17	3	0	1	11	9	24	0	.147	.211	.198
George Thomas	OF43,1B3,C1	R	29	65	89	10	19	2	0	1	6	3	23	0	.213	.255	.270
Ken Harrelson†	OF23,1B1	R	25	23	80	9	16	4	1	3	14	5	12	1	.200	.247	.388
Bob Tillman†	C26	R	30	30	64	4	12	1	0	1	4	3	18	0	.188	.224	.250
Norm Siebern†	1B13,OF1	L	33	33	44	2	9	0	2	0	7	6	8	0	.205	.300	.295
Don Demeter†	OF12,3B1	R	32	20	43	7	12	5	0	1	4	3	11	0	.279	.326	.465
Tony Horton†	1B6	R	22	21	39	2	12	3	0	0	9	0	5	0	.308	.300	.385
Jim Landis†	OF5	R	33	5	7	1	1	0	0	1	1	1	3	0	.143	.250	.571
Ken Poulsen	3B2,SS1	L	19	5	5	0	1	1	0	0	0	0	2	0	.200	.200	.400

Pitcher	T	Age	G	GS	CG	ShO	IP	H	HR	BB	SO	W-L	Sv	ERA
Jim Lonborg	R	25	39	39	15	2	273.1	228	23	83	246	22-9	0	3.16
Lee Stange	R	30	35	24	6	2	181.2	171	14	32	101	8-10	1	2.77
Gary Bell†	R	30	29	24	8	0	165.1	143	16	47	115	12-8	3	3.16
Dennis Bennett†	L	27	13	11	4	1	69.2	72	12	22	34	4-3	0	3.88
Dave Morehead	R	24	10	9	1	1	47.2	48	0	22	40	5-4	0	4.34
Billy Rohr	L	21	10	8	2	1	42.1	43	4	22	16	2-3	0	5.10
Gary Waslewski	R	25	12	8	0	0	42.0	34	3	20	20	2-2	0	3.21
Jerry Stephenson	R	23	8	6	0	0	39.2	32	4	16	24	3-1	1	3.86
John Wyatt	R	32	60	0	0	0	93.1	71	6	39	68	10-7	20	2.60
Jose Santiago	R	26	50	11	2	0	145.1	138	14	47	109	12-4	5	3.59
Bucky Brandon	R	26	39	19	2	0	157.2	147	21	59	96	5-11	3	4.17
Dan Osinski	R	33	34	0	0	0	63.2	61	5	14	38	3-1	2	2.54
Sparky Lyle	L	22	27	0	0	0	43.1	33	3	14	42	1-2	5	2.28
Bill Landis	L	24	18	1	0	0	25.2	24	6	11	23	1-0	0	5.26
Galen Cisco	R	31	11	0	0	0	22.1	21	4	8	8	0-1	1	3.63
Don McMahon†	R	37	11	0	0	0	17.2	14	4	13	10	1-2	2	3.57
Hank Fischer	R	27	9	2	1	0	26.2	24	3	8	18	1-2	1	2.36
Ken Brett	L	18	1	0	0	0	2.0	3	0	0	2	0-0	0	4.50

1967 Detroit Tigers 2nd AL 91-71 .562 1.0 GB

Mayo Smith

Player	Gm by Position	B	Age	G	AB	R	H	2B	3B	HR	RBI	BB	SO	SB	Avg	OBP	Slg
Bill Freehan	C147,1B11	R	25	155	517	66	146	23	1	20	74	73	71	1	.282	.389	.447
Norm Cash	1B146	L	32	152	488	64	118	16	5	22	72	81	100	3	.242	.352	.430
Dick McAuliffe	2B145,SS43	L	27	153	557	92	133	16	7	22	65	105	118	6	.239	.364	.411
Don Wert	3B140,SS1	R	28	142	534	60	137	23	2	6	40	44	59	1	.257	.320	.341
Ray Oyler	SS146	R	28	148	367	33	76	14	2	1	29	37	91	0	.207	.281	.264
Jim Northrup	OF143	L	27	144	495	63	134	18	6	10	61	43	83	7	.271	.332	.392
Al Kaline	OF130	R	32	131	458	94	141	28	2	25	78	83	47	8	.308	.411	.541
Mickey Stanley	OF128,1B8	R	24	145	333	38	70	7	3	7	24	29	46	9	.210	.273	.312
Willie Horton	OF110	R	24	122	401	47	110	20	3	19	67	36	80	0	.274	.338	.481
Jerry Lumpe	2B54,3B6	L	34	81	177	19	41	4	0	4	17	16	18	0	.232	.295	.322
Lenny Green	OF44	L	34	58	151	22	42	8	1	1	13	9	17	1	.278	.317	.364
Eddie Mathews†	3B21,1B13	L	35	36	108	14	25	3	0	6	19	15	23	0	.231	.331	.426
Dick Tracewski	SS44,2B12,3B10	R	32	74	107	19	30	4	2	1	9	8	20	1	.280	.325	.383
Jim Price	C24	R	25	44	92	9	24	4	0	0	8	4	10	0	.261	.292	.304
Gates Brown	OF20	L	28	51	91	17	17	1	1	2	9	13	15	0	.187	.286	.286
Jim Landis†	OF12	R	33	25	48	4	10	0	0	2	4	7	12	0	.208	.304	.333
Bill Heath†	C7	L	28	20	32	0	4	0	0	0	4	1	4	0	.125	.152	.125
Jake Wood†	1B2,2B2	R	30	14	20	2	1	1	0	0	0	1	7	0	.050	.095	.100
Tommy Matchick	SS1	L	23	8	6	1	1	0	0	0	0	0	2	0	.167	.167	.167
Wayne Comer	OF1	R	23	4	3	0	1	0	0	0	0	0	0	0	.333	.333	.333
Dave Campbell	1B1	R	25	2	2	0	0	0	0	0	0	0	1	0	.000	.000	.000

Pitcher	T	Age	G	GS	CG	ShO	IP	H	HR	BB	SO	W-L	Sv	ERA
Earl Wilson	R	32	39	38	12	0	264.0	216	34	92	184	22-11	0	3.27
Denny McLain	R	23	37	37	10	3	235.0	209	35	73	161	17-16	0	3.79
Joe Sparma	R	25	37	37	11	5	217.2	186	20	85	153	16-9	0	3.76
Mickey Lolich	L	26	31	30	11	6	204.0	165	14	56	174	14-13	0	3.04
Fred Gladding	R	31	42	1	0	0	77.0	62	6	19	64	6-4	12	1.99
Mike Marshall	R	24	37	0	0	0	59.0	51	6	20	41	1-3	10	1.98
Dave Wickersham	R	31	36	4	0	0	85.1	72	6	33	44	4-5	4	2.74
Hank Aguirre	L	36	31	1	0	0	41.1	34	2	17	33	0-1	0	2.40
Pat Dobson	R	25	28	1	0	0	49.1	38	6	27	34	1-2	0	2.92
John Hiller	L	24	23	6	2	2	65.0	57	4	9	49	4-3	3	2.63
Johnny Podres	L	34	21	8	0	0	63.1	58	12	11	34	3-1	1	3.84
Larry Sherry†	R	31	20	0	0	0	28.0	35	3	7	20	0-1	1	6.43
Fred Lasher	R	25	17	0	0	0	30.0	25	1	11	28	2-1	9	3.90
George Korince	R	21	9	0	0	0	14.0	10	1	11	11	1-0	0	5.14
Johnny Klippstein	R	39	5	0	0	0	6.2	6	1	1	4	0-0	0	5.40
Orlando Pena†	R	33	2	0	0	0	2.0	5	0	0	2	0-1	0	13.50
Bill Monbouquette†	R	30	2	0	0	0	2.0	1	0	0	2	0-0	0	0.00

1967 Minnesota Twins 2nd AL 91-71 .562 1.0 GB

Sam Mele (25-25)/Cal Ermer (66-46)

Player	Gm by Position	B	Age	G	AB	R	H	2B	3B	HR	RBI	BB	SO	SB	Avg	OBP	Slg
Jerry Zimmerman	C104	R	32	104	234	13	39	3	0	1	12	22	49	0	.167	.243	.192
Harmon Killebrew	1B160,3B3	R	31	163	547	105	147	24	1	44	113	131	111	1	.269	.408	.558
Rod Carew	2B134	L	21	137	514	66	150	22	7	8	51	37	91	5	.292	.341	.409
Rich Rollins	3B97	R	29	109	339	31	83	11	2	6	39	27	58	1	.245	.305	.342
Zoilo Versalles	SS159	R	27	160	581	63	116	16	7	6	50	33	113	5	.200	.249	.282
Tony Oliva	OF146	L	26	146	557	76	161	34	6	17	83	44	61	11	.289	.347	.463
Bob Allison	OF145	R	32	153	496	73	128	21	6	24	75	74	114	6	.258	.356	.470
Ted Uhlaender	OF118	L	26	133	415	41	107	19	7	6	49	13	45	4	.258	.285	.381
Cesar Tovar	OF74,3B70,2B36*	R	26	164	649	98	173	32	7	6	47	46	51	19	.267	.325	.365
Russ Nixon	C69	L	32	74	170	16	40	6	1	1	22	18	29	0	.235	.304	.300
Earl Battey	C41	R	32	48	109	6	18	3	1	0	8	13	24	0	.165	.254	.211
Rich Reese	1B36,OF10	L	25	95	101	13	25	5	0	4	20	8	17	0	.248	.300	.416
Sandy Valdespino	OF65	L	28	99	97	9	16	2	0	1	3	5	22	3	.165	.204	.216
Ron Clark	3B16	R	24	20	60	7	10	3	1	2	11	4	9	0	.167	.215	.350
Frank Kostro	OF3,3B1	R	29	32	31	4	10	0	0	0	2	3	2	0	.323	.382	.323
Jackie Hernandez	SS15,3B13	R	26	29	28	1	4	0	0	0	3	0	6	0	.143	.143	.143
Andy Kosco	OF7	R	25	9	28	4	4	1	0	0	4	2	4	0	.143	.200	.179
Hank Izquierdo	C16	R	36	16	26	4	7	2	0	0	2	1	2	0	.269	.296	.346
Frank Quilici	2B13,3B8,SS1	R	28	23	19	2	2	1	0	0	0	3	4	0	.105	.227	.158
Walt Bond	OF3	L	29	10	16	4	5	1	0	1	5	3	1	0	.313	.400	.563
Carroll Hardy	OF4	R	34	11	8	1	3	0	0	1	2	1	1	0	.375	.444	.750
Graig Nettles		L	22	3	3	0	1	1	0	0	0	0	0	0	.333	.333	.667
Pat Kelly		L	22	8	1	1	0	0	0	0	0	0	1	0	.000	.000	.000

C. Tovar, 9 G at SS

Pitcher	T	Age	G	GS	CG	ShO	IP	H	HR	BB	SO	W-L	Sv	ERA
Dean Chance	R	26	41	39	18	5	283.2	244	17	68	220	20-14	1	2.73
Jim Kaat	L	28	42	38	13	2	263.1	269	21	42	211	16-13	0	3.04
Dave Boswell	R	22	37	32	11	3	222.2	162	14	107	204	14-12	0	3.27
Jim Merritt	L	23	37	28	11	4	227.2	196	21	30	161	13-7	0	2.53
Mudcat Grant	R	31	27	14	2	0	95.1	121	10	17	50	5-6	0	4.72
Al Worthington	R	38	59	0	0	0	92.0	77	6	38	80	8-9	16	2.84
Ron Kline	R	35	54	0	0	0	71.2	71	10	15	36	7-1	5	3.77
Jim Perry	R	31	37	11	3	2	130.2	123	8	50	94	8-7	0	3.03
Jim Roland	L	24	25	0	0	0	35.2	33	3	17	16	0-1	2	3.03
Jim Ollom	L	21	21	2	0	0	35.0	33	4	11	17	0-1	0	5.40
Dwight Siebler	R	29	2	0	0	0	3.0	4	0	1	0	0-0	0	3.00
Mel Nelson	L	31	1	0	0	0	0.1	3	1	0	0	0-0	0	54.00

1967 Chicago White Sox 4th AL 89-73 .549 3.0 GB

Eddie Stanky

Player	Gm by Position	B	Age	G	AB	R	H	2B	3B	HR	RBI	BB	SO	SB	Avg	OBP	Slg
J.C. Martin	C96,1B1	L	30	101	252	22	59	12	1	4	22	30	41	4	.234	.317	.337
Tom McCraw	1B123,OF6	L	26	125	453	55	107	18	3	11	45	33	55	24	.236	.288	.362
Wayne Causey	2B96,SS2	L	30	124	292	21	66	10	3	1	28	32	35	2	.226	.302	.291
Don Buford	3B121,2B51,OF1	S	30	156	535	61	129	10	9	4	32	65	51	34	.241	.322	.316
Ron Hansen	SS157	R	29	157	498	35	116	20	0	8	51	64	51	0	.233	.317	.321
Tommie Agee	OF152	R	24	158	529	73	124	26	2	14	52	44	129	28	.234	.302	.371
Ken Berry	OF143	R	26	147	485	49	117	14	4	7	41	46	68	9	.241	.310	.330
Pete Ward	OF89,1B39,3B22	L	27	146	467	49	109	16	2	18	62	61	109	3	.233	.334	.392
Walt Williams	OF73	R	23	104	275	35	66	16	3	3	15	17	20	3	.240	.289	.353
Rocky Colavito†	OF58	R	33	60	190	20	42	4	1	3	29	25	10	1	.221	.306	.300
Duane Josephson	C59	R	25	62	189	11	45	5	1	1	9	6	24	0	.238	.262	.291
Ken Boyer†	3B33,1B18	R	36	57	180	17	47	5	1	4	21	7	25	0	.261	.287	.367
Jerry McNertney	C52	R	30	56	123	8	28	6	0	3	13	6	14	0	.228	.275	.350
Jerry Adair†	2B27	R	30	28	98	6	20	4	0	0	9	4	17	0	.204	.240	.245
Dick Kenworthy	3B35	R	26	50	97	9	22	4	1	4	11	4	17	0	.227	.262	.412
Smoky Burgess		L	40	77	60	2	8	1	0	2	11	14	8	0	.133	.303	.250
Marv Staehle	2B17,SS5	L	25	32	54	1	6	1	0	0	1	4	8	1	.111	.172	.130
Al Weis	2B32,SS13	S	29	50	53	9	13	2	0	0	4	1	7	3	.245	.273	.283
Jim King†	OF12	L	34	23	50	2	6	1	0	0	2	4	16	0	.120	.185	.140
Ed Stroud†	OF12	L	27	20	27	6	8	0	1	0	3	1	5	7	.296	.345	.370
Bill Voss	OF11	L	23	13	22	4	2	0	0	0	0	0	1	1	.091	.091	.091
Buddy Bradford	OF14	R	22	24	20	6	2	1	0	0	1	1	7	1	.100	.143	.150
Jimmy Stewart†	OF6,2B5,SS2	S	28	24	18	5	3	0	0	0	1	1	6	1	.167	.211	.167
Sandy Alomar†	SS8,2B2	S	23	12	15	4	3	0	0	0	0	2	0	2	.200	.294	.200
Rich Morales	SS7	R	23	8	10	0	0	0	0	0	0	0	2	0	.000	.000	.000
Bill Skowron†		R	36	8	8	0	0	0	0	0	1	0	1	0	.000	.000	.000
Cotton Nash	1B3	R	24	3	3	1	0	0	0	0	0	1	0	0	.000	.250	.000
Ed Herrmann	C2	L	20	2	3	1	2	1	0	0	1	1	0	0	.667	.750	1.000

Pitcher	T	Age	G	GS	CG	ShO	IP	H	HR	BB	SO	W-L	Sv	ERA
Gary Peters	L	30	38	36	11	3	260.0	187	15	91	215	16-11	0	2.28
Joe Horlen	R	29	35	35	13	6	258.0	188	13	58	103	19-7	0	2.06
Tommy John	L	24	31	29	9	6	178.1	143	12	47	110	10-13	0	2.47
Bruce Howard	R	24	30	17	1	0	112.2	102	9	52	76	3-10	0	3.43
Jim O'Toole	L	30	15	10	1	1	54.1	53	4	18	37	4-3	0	2.82
Fred Klages	R	23	11	9	0	0	44.2	43	6	16	17	4-4	0	3.83
Cisco Carlos	R	26	8	7	1	1	41.2	23	0	9	27	2-0	0	0.86
Aurelio Monteagudo	R	23	1	1	0	0	1.1	4	1	2	0	0-1	0	20.25
Bob Locker	R	29	77	0	0	0	124.2	102	5	23	80	7-5	20	2.09
Don McMahon†	R	37	52	0	0	0	91.2	54	5	27	74	5-0	3	1.67
Wilbur Wood	L	25	51	8	0	0	95.1	95	2	28	47	4-2	4	2.45
Hoyt Wilhelm	R	43	49	0	0	0	89.0	58	2	34	76	8-3	12	1.31
John Buzhardt†	R	30	28	7	0	0	88.2	100	11	37	33	3-9	0	3.96
Steve Jones	L	26	11	3	0	0	25.2	21	1	12	17	2-2	0	4.21
Dennis Higgins	R	27	9	0	0	0	12.1	13	0	10	8	1-2	0	5.84
Roger Nelson	R	23	5	0	0	0	7.0	4	1	0	4	0-1	0	1.29
Jack Lamabe†	R	30	3	0	0	0	5.0	7	0	1	3	1-0	0	1.80

1967 California Angels 5th AL 84-77 .522 7.5 GB

Bill Rigney

Player	Gm by Position	B	Age	G	AB	R	H	2B	3B	HR	RBI	BB	SO	SB	Avg	OBP	Slg
Bob Rodgers	C134,OF1	S	28	139	429	29	94	13	3	6	41	34	55	1	.219	.277	.305
Don Mincher	1B142,OF1	L	29	147	487	81	133	23	3	25	76	69	69	0	.273	.367	.487
Bobby Knoop	2B159	R	28	159	511	51	125	18	5	9	38	44	136	2	.245	.305	.352
Paul Schaal	3B88,SS2,2B1	R	24	99	272	31	51	9	1	6	20	38	39	2	.188	.286	.294
Jim Fregosi	SS151	R	25	151	590	75	171	23	6	9	56	49	77	9	.290	.349	.395
Rick Reichardt	OF138	R	24	146	498	56	132	14	2	17	69	35	90	5	.265	.320	.404
Jimmie Hall	OF120	L	29	129	401	54	100	8	3	16	55	42	65	4	.249	.318	.404
Jose Cardenal	OF101	R	23	108	381	40	90	13	5	6	27	15	63	10	.236	.268	.344
Jay Johnstone	OF63	L	21	79	230	18	48	7	1	2	10	5	37	3	.209	.226	.274
Tom Satriano	3B38,C23,2B15*	L	26	90	201	13	45	7	0	4	21	28	25	1	.224	.319	.318
Bubba Morton	OF61	R	35	80	201	23	63	9	3	0	32	22	29	0	.313	.387	.388
Roger Repoz†	OF63	L	26	74	176	25	44	9	1	5	20	19	37	2	.250	.318	.398
Woodie Held†	3B19,OF17,SS13*	R	35	58	141	15	31	3	0	4	17	18	41	0	.220	.317	.326
Aurelio Rodriguez	3B29	R	19	29	130	14	31	3	1	1	8	2	21	1	.238	.250	.300
Bill Skowron†	1B32	R	36	62	123	8	27	2	1	1	10	4	18	0	.220	.267	.276
Johnny Werhas†	3B30,1B4,OF1	R	29	49	75	8	12	1	1	2	6	10	22	0	.160	.264	.280
Hawk Taylor†	C19	R	28	23	52	5	16	3	0	1	3	4	8	0	.308	.357	.423
Orlando McFarlane	C6	R	29	12	22	0	5	0	0	0	3	1	7	0	.227	.250	.227
Len Gabrielson†	OF1	L	27	11	12	2	1	0	0	0	2	2	4	0	.083	.214	.083
Ed Kirkpatrick	C2,OF1	L	22	3	8	0	0	0	0	0	0	0	2	0	.000	.000	.000
Don Wallace	2B4,1B1,3B1	L	26	23	6	2	0	0	0	0	0	3	2	0	.000	.333	.000
Moose Stubing		L	29	5	5	0	0	0	0	0	0	0	4	0	.000	.000	.000
Jim Hibbs		R	22	3	3	0	0	0	0	0	0	0	2	0	.000	.000	.000
Jimmy Piersall	OF1	R	37	5	3	0	0	0	0	0	0	0	2	0	.000	.000	.000
Tom Egan	C1	R	21	1	1	0	0	0	0	0	0	0	0	0	.000	.000	.000

T. Satriano, 5 G at 1B; W. Held, 3 G at 2B

Pitcher	T	Age	G	GS	CG	ShO	IP	H	HR	BB	SO	W-L	Sv	ERA
George Brunet	L	32	40	37	7	2	250.0	203	19	90	165	11-19	1	3.31
Rickey Clark	R	21	32	30	1	1	174.0	144	15	69	81	12-11	0	2.59
Jim McGlothlin	R	23	32	29	9	6	197.1	163	13	56	137	12-8	0	2.96
Jack Hamilton†	R	28	26	20	0	0	119.1	104	6	63	74	9-6	0	3.24
Clyde Wright	L	26	20	11	1	0	77.1	76	5	24	35	5-5	0	3.26
Jack Sanford†	R	38	12	9	0	0	48.1	53	6	7	21	3-2	1	4.47
Nick Willhite†	L	26	10	7	0	0	39.1	39	8	16	22	0-2	0	4.35
Jorge Rubio	R	22	3	3	0	0	15.0	18	2	9	4	0-2	0	3.60
Marcelino Lopez†	L	23	4	3	0	0	9.0	11	1	9	6	0-2	0	9.00
Minnie Rojas	R	28	72	0	0	0	121.2	106	7	38	83	12-9	27	2.52
Bill Kelso	R	27	69	1	0	0	112.0	85	6	63	91	5-3	11	2.97
Pete Cimino	R	24	46	1	0	0	88.1	73	12	31	80	3-3	1	3.26
Jim Coates	R	34	25	1	0	0	52.1	47	5	23	39	1-2	0	4.30
Lew Burdette	R	40	19	0	0	0	18.1	16	4	0	8	1-0	1	4.91
Curt Simmons†	L	38	14	4	1	1	34.2	44	1	9	13	2-1	1	2.60
Jim Weaver	L	28	13	2	0	0	30.1	26	2	9	20	3-0	1	2.67
Ken Turner	L	23	13	1	0	0	17.1	16	4	4	6	1-2	0	4.15
Bobby Locke	R	33	9	1	0	0	19.1	14	1	3	7	3-0	2	2.33
Fred Newman	R	25	3	1	0	0	6.1	8	1	2	0	1-0	0	1.42

1967 Baltimore Orioles 6th AL 76-85 .472 15.5 GB

Hank Bauer

Player	Gm by Position	B	Age	G	AB	R	H	2B	3B	HR	RBI	BB	SO	SB	Avg	OBP	Slg
Andy Etchebarren	C110	R	24	112	330	29	71	13	0	7	35	38	80	1	.215	.298	.318
Boog Powell	1B114	L	25	125	415	53	97	14	1	13	55	55	94	1	.234	.324	.366
Dave Johnson	2B144,3B3	R	24	148	510	62	126	30	3	10	64	59	82	4	.247	.325	.376
Brooks Robinson	3B158	R	30	158	610	88	164	25	5	22	77	54	54	1	.269	.328	.434
Luis Aparicio	SS131	R	33	134	546	55	127	22	5	4	31	29	44	18	.233	.270	.313
Paul Blair	OF146	R	23	151	552	72	162	27	12	11	64	50	68	8	.293	.353	.446
Frank Robinson	OF126,1B2	R	31	129	479	83	149	23	7	30	94	71	84	2	.311	.403	.576
Curt Blefary	OF103,1B52	L	23	155	554	69	134	19	5	22	81	73	94	4	.242	.337	.413
Russ Snyder	OF69	L	33	108	275	40	65	8	2	4	23	32	48	5	.236	.314	.324
Mark Belanger	SS38,2B26,3B2	R	23	69	184	19	32	5	0	1	10	12	46	6	.174	.224	.217
Larry Haney	C57	R	24	58	164	13	44	11	0	3	20	6	28	1	.268	.294	.390
Sam Bowens	OF32	R	28	62	120	13	22	2	1	5	12	11	43	3	.183	.258	.342
Vic Roznovsky	C23	L	28	45	97	7	20	5	0	0	10	1	20	0	.206	.212	.258
Dave May	OF19	L	23	36	85	12	20	1	1	1	7	6	13	0	.235	.286	.306
Curt Motton	OF18	R	26	27	65	5	13	2	0	2	9	5	14	0	.200	.267	.323
Woodie Held†	2B9,3B5,OF2	R	35	26	41	4	6	3	0	1	6	6	12	0	.146	.286	.293
Mickey McGuire	2B4	R	26	10	17	2	4	0	0	0	2	0	2	0	.235	.235	.235
Mike Epstein†	1B3	L	24	9	13	0	2	0	0	0	0	3	5	0	.154	.313	.154
Charlie Lau†		L	34	11	8	0	1	1	0	0	3	2	2	0	.125	.273	.250
Bob Johnson†		R	31	4	3	1	1	0	0	0	0	1	1	0	.333	.500	.333

Pitcher	T	Age	G	GS	CG	ShO	IP	H	HR	BB	SO	W-L	Sv	ERA
Tom Phoebus	R	25	33	33	7	4	208.0	177	16	114	179	14-9	0	3.33
Dave McNally	L	24	24	22	3	1	119.0	134	13	39	70	7-7	0	4.54
Pete Richert†	L	27	26	19	5	1	132.1	107	11	41	90	7-10	2	2.99
Steve Barber†	L	28	15	15	1	1	74.2	47	5	61	48	4-9	0	4.10
Jim Hardin	R	23	19	14	5	2	111.0	85	5	27	64	8-3	0	2.27
Gene Brabender	R	25	14	14	3	1	94.0	77	6	23	71	6-4	0	3.35
Jim Palmer	R	21	9	9	2	1	49.0	34	6	20	23	3-1	0	2.94
Marcelino Lopez†	L	23	4	4	0	0	17.2	15	1	10	15	1-0	0	2.55
Dave Leonhard	R	26	3	2	0	0	14.1	11	1	6	9	0-0	1	3.14
Mike Adamson	R	19	3	2	0	0	9.2	9	1	12	8	0-1	0	8.38
Eddie Watt	R	26	49	0	0	0	103.2	67	5	37	93	3-5	8	2.26
Eddie Fisher	R	30	46	0	0	0	89.2	82	7	26	53	4-3	1	3.61
Moe Drabowsky	R	31	43	0	0	0	95.1	66	7	25	96	7-5	12	1.60
Stu Miller	R	39	42	0	0	0	81.1	63	5	36	60	3-10	8	2.55
Bill Dillman	R	22	32	15	2	1	124.0	115	13	33	69	5-9	3	4.35
Wally Bunker	R	22	29	9	1	0	88.0	83	7	31	51	3-7	1	4.09
John Buzhardt†	R	30	7	1	0	0	11.2	14	1	5	7	0-1	0	4.63
Frank Bertaina†	L	23	5	2	0	0	21.2	17	4	14	19	1-1	0	3.32
John Miller	R	26	2	0	0	0	6.0	7	1	3	6	0-0	0	7.50
Tom Fisher	R	25	2	0	0	0	3.1	2	0	2	1	0-0	0	0.00
Paul Gilliford	L	22	2	0	0	0	3.0	6	1	1	2	0-0	0	12.00

1967 Washington Senators 6th AL 76-85 .472 15.5 GB

Gil Hodges

Player	Gm by Position	B	Age	G	AB	R	H	2B	3B	HR	RBI	BB	SO	SB	Avg	OBP	Slg
Paul Casanova	C137	R	25	141	528	47	131	19	1	9	53	17	65	1	.248	.273	.339
Mike Epstein†	1B80	L	24	96	284	32	65	7	4	9	29	38	74	1	.229	.331	.377
Bernie Allen	2B75	L	28	87	254	13	49	5	1	3	18	18	43	1	.193	.244	.256
Ken McMullen	3B145	R	25	146	563	73	138	22	2	16	67	46	84	5	.245	.301	.377
Ed Brinkman	SS109	R	25	109	320	21	60	9	2	1	18	24	58	1	.188	.252	.238
Frank Howard	OF141,1B4	R	30	149	519	71	133	20	2	36	89	60	155	0	.256	.338	.511
Fred Valentine	OF136	S	32	151	457	52	107	16	1	11	44	56	76	17	.234	.330	.346
Cap Peterson	OF101	R	24	122	405	35	97	17	2	8	46	32	61	0	.240	.299	.351
Tim Cullen	SS69,2B46,3B15*	R	25	124	402	35	95	7	0	2	31	40	47	4	.236	.306	.269
Hank Allen	OF99	R	26	116	292	34	68	8	4	3	17	13	53	3	.233	.264	.318
Dick Nen	1B65,OF1	L	27	110	238	21	52	7	1	6	29	21	39	0	.218	.280	.332
Bob Saverine	2B48,SS10,3B8*	S	26	89	233	22	55	13	0	0	8	17	34	8	.236	.287	.292
Ed Stroud†	OF79	L	27	87	204	36	41	5	3	1	10	25	29	8	.201	.289	.270
Jim King†	OF31,C1	L	34	47	100	10	21	2	2	1	12	15	13	1	.210	.328	.300
Doug Camilli	C24	R	30	30	82	5	15	1	0	2	5	4	16	0	.183	.221	.268
Ken Harrelson†	1B23	R	25	26	79	10	16	0	0	3	10	7	15	1	.203	.261	.316
Frank Coggins	2B19	S	23	19	75	9	23	3	0	1	8	2	17	1	.307	.321	.387
Bob Chance	1B10	L	26	27	42	5	9	2	0	3	7	7	13	0	.214	.340	.476
Jim French	C6	L	25	6	16	0	1	0	0	0	1	3	4	0	.063	.211	.063
John Orsino		R	29	1	1	0	0	0	0	0	0	0	1	0	.000	.000	.000

T. Cullen, 1 G at OF; B. Saverine, 2 G at OF

Pitcher	T	Age	G	GS	CG	ShO	IP	H	HR	BB	SO	W-L	Sv	ERA
Phil Ortega	R	27	34	34	5	2	219.2	189	16	57	122	10-10	0	3.03
Camilo Pascual	R	33	28	27	5	1	164.2	147	15	43	106	12-10	0	3.28
Barry Moore	L	24	27	26	3	1	143.2	127	15	71	74	7-11	0	3.76
Joe Coleman	R	20	28	22	3	0	134.0	154	6	47	77	8-9	0	4.63
Frank Bertaina†	L	23	18	17	4	4	95.2	90	8	37	67	6-5	0	2.92
Pete Richert†	L	27	11	10	1	1	54.1	49	5	15	41	2-6	0	4.64
Dick Bosman	R	23	7	7	2	1	51.1	38	3	10	25	3-1	0	1.75
Buster Narum	R	26	2	2	0	0	11.2	8	1	4	8	1-0	0	3.09
Darold Knowles	L	25	61	1	0	0	113.1	91	5	52	85	6-8	14	2.70
Dave Baldwin	R	29	58	0	0	0	68.2	53	2	20	52	2-4	12	1.70
Dick Lines	L	28	54	0	0	0	85.2	83	6	24	54	2-5	4	3.36
Casey Cox	R	25	54	0	0	0	73.0	67	2	21	32	7-4	1	2.96
Bob Humphreys	R	31	48	2	0	0	105.2	93	13	41	54	6-2	4	4.17
Bob Priddy	R	27	46	8	1	0	110.0	98	12	33	57	3-7	4	3.44
Jim Hannan	R	27	8	2	0	0	21.2	28	3	7	14	1-1	0	5.40
Dick Nold	R	24	7	3	0	0	20.1	19	1	13	10	0-2	0	4.87

1967 Cleveland Indians 8th AL 75-87 .463 17.0 GB

Joe Adcock

Player	Gm by Position	B	Age	G	AB	R	H	2B	3B	HR	RBI	BB	SO	SB	Avg	OBP	Slg
Joe Azcue	C86	R	27	86	295	33	74	12	5	11	34	22	35	0	.251	.307	.437
Tony Horton†	1B94	R	22	106	363	35	102	13	4	10	44	18	52	3	.281	.321	.421
Vern Fuller	2B64,SS2	R	23	73	206	18	46	10	0	7	21	19	55	2	.223	.300	.374
Max Alvis	3B161	R	29	161	637	66	163	23	4	21	70	38	107	3	.256	.301	.403
Larry Brown	SS150	R	27	152	485	38	110	16	2	7	37	53	62	4	.227	.308	.311
Chuck Hinton	OF136,2B5	R	33	147	498	55	122	19	3	10	37	43	100	6	.245	.304	.355
Vic Davalillo	OF125	L	30	139	359	47	103	17	5	2	22	10	30	6	.287	.307	.379
Leon Wagner	OF117	L	33	135	433	56	105	15	1	15	54	37	76	3	.242	.317	.386
Lee Maye	OF77,2B1	L	32	115	297	43	77	20	4	9	27	26	47	3	.259	.321	.444
Duke Sims	C85	L	26	88	272	25	55	8	2	12	37	30	64	3	.202	.294	.379
Fred Whitfield	1B66	L	29	100	257	24	56	10	0	9	31	25	45	3	.218	.290	.362
Chico Salmon	OF28,1B24,2B24*	R	26	90	203	19	46	13	1	2	19	17	29	10	.227	.288	.330
Rocky Colavito†	OF50	R	33	63	191	10	46	9	0	5	21	24	31	2	.241	.329	.366
Pedro Gonzalez	2B64,1B4,3B4*	R	29	80	189	19	43	6	0	1	8	12	36	4	.228	.275	.275
Don Demeter†	OF35,3B1	R	32	51	121	15	25	4	0	5	12	6	16	0	.207	.256	.364
Gus Gil	2B49,1B1	R	28	51	96	11	11	4	0	0	5	9	18	0	.115	.198	.156
Richie Scheinblum	OF18	S	24	18	66	8	21	4	2	0	6	5	10	0	.318	.361	.439
Jose Vidal	OF10	R	27	16	34	4	4	0	0	0	0	7	12	0	.118	.268	.118
Willie Smith	OF4,1B3	L	28	21	32	0	7	2	0	0	2	1	10	0	.219	.242	.281
Jim King†	OF1	L	34	19	21	2	3	0	0	0	0	1	2	0	.143	.182	.143
Ray Fosse	C7	R	20	7	16	0	1	0	0	0	0	0	5	0	.063	.063	.063
Gordy Lund	SS2	R	26	3	8	1	2	1	0	0	0	0	2	0	.250	.250	.375

C. Salmon, 14 G at SS, 4 G at 3B; P. Gonzalez, 3 G at SS

Pitcher	T	Age	G	GS	CG	ShO	IP	H	HR	BB	SO	W-L	Sv	ERA
Sam McDowell	L	24	37	37	10	1	236.1	201	21	123	236	13-15	0	3.85
Steve Hargan	R	24	30	29	15	6	223.0	180	9	72	141	14-13	0	2.62
Luis Tiant	R	26	33	29	9	1	213.2	177	24	67	219	12-9	2	2.74
Sonny Siebert	R	30	34	26	7	1	185.1	136	17	54	136	10-12	4	2.38
John O'Donoghue	L	27	33	17	5	2	130.2	120	10	33	81	8-9	2	3.24
Gary Bell†	R	30	9	9	1	0	60.2	50	7	24	39	1-5	0	3.71
Stan Williams	R	30	16	8	2	1	79.0	64	6	24	75	6-4	1	2.62
George Culver	R	23	53	1	0	0	75.0	71	2	31	41	7-3	3	3.96
Orlando Pena†	R	33	48	1	0	0	88.1	67	8	22	72	0-3	8	3.36
Bob Allen	L	29	47	0	0	0	54.1	49	4	25	50	0-5	5	2.98
Steve Bailey	R	25	32	1	0	0	64.2	62	5	42	46	2-5	2	3.90
Ed Connolly	L	27	15	4	0	0	49.1	63	6	34	45	2-1	0	7.48
Bobby Tiefenauer	R	37	5	0	0	0	11.1	9	0	3	6	0-1	0	0.79
Dick Radatz†	R	30	3	0	0	0	3.0	5	1	2	1	0-0	0	6.00
Jack Kralick	L	32	2	0	0	0	2.0	4	0	1	1	0-2	0	9.00
Tom Kelley	R	23	1	0	0	0	1.0	0	0	2	0	0-0	0	0.00

1967 New York Yankees 9th AL 72-90 .444 20.0 GB

Ralph Houk

Player	Gm by Position	B	Age	G	AB	R	H	2B	3B	HR	RBI	BB	SO	SB	Avg	OBP	Slg
Jake Gibbs	C99	L	28	116	374	33	87	7	1	4	25	28	57	7	.233	.291	.289
Mickey Mantle	1B131	S	35	144	440	63	108	17	0	22	55	107	113	1	.245	.391	.434
Horace Clarke	2B140	S	27	143	588	74	160	17	0	3	29	42	64	21	.272	.321	.316
Charley Smith	3B115	R	29	135	425	38	95	15	3	9	38	32	110	0	.224	.278	.336
Ruben Amaro	SS123,3B3,1B2	R	31	130	417	31	93	12	0	1	17	43	49	3	.223	.297	.259
Joe Pepitone	OF123,1B6	L	26	133	501	45	126	18	3	13	64	34	62	1	.251	.301	.377
Tom Tresh	OF118	S	29	130	448	45	98	23	3	14	53	50	86	1	.219	.301	.377
Steve Whitaker	OF114	L	24	122	441	37	107	12	3	11	50	23	89	2	.243	.283	.358
Bill Robinson	OF102	R	24	116	342	31	67	6	1	7	29	28	56	2	.196	.259	.281
Roy White	OF36,3B17	S	23	70	214	22	48	8	0	2	18	19	25	10	.224	.287	.290
Elston Howard†	C48,1B1	R	38	66	199	13	39	6	0	3	17	12	36	0	.196	.247	.271
John Kennedy	SS36,3B34,2B2	R	26	78	179	22	35	4	0	1	17	17	35	2	.196	.265	.235
Dick Howser	2B22,3B12,SS3	R	31	63	149	18	40	6	0	0	10	25	15	1	.268	.381	.309
Mike Hegan	1B54,OF10	L	24	68	118	12	16	4	1	1	3	20	40	7	.136	.266	.212
Bob Tillman†	C15	R	30	22	63	5	16	1	0	2	9	7	17	0	.254	.324	.365
Jerry Kenney	SS18	L	22	20	58	4	18	2	0	1	5	10	8	2	.310	.412	.397
Frank Fernandez	C7,OF2	R	24	9	28	1	6	2	0	1	4	2	7	1	.214	.281	.393
Tom Shopay	OF7	L	22	8	27	2	8	1	0	2	6	1	5	2	.296	.310	.556
Ray Barker	1B13	L	31	17	26	2	2	0	0	0	0	3	5	0	.077	.172	.077
Billy Bryan	C1	L	28	16	12	1	2	0	0	1	2	5	3	0	.167	.412	.417
Ross Moschitto	OF8	R	22	14	9	1	1	0	0	0	0	1	2	0	.111	.200	.111
Frank Tepedino	1B1	L	19	9	5	0	2	0	0	0	0	1	1	0	.400	.500	.400
Lu Clinton	OF1	R	29	6	4	1	2	1	0	0	2	1	1	0	.500	.600	.750
Charlie Sands		L	19	1	1	0	0	0	0	0	0	0	1	0	.000	.000	.000

Pitcher	T	Age	G	GS	CG	ShO	IP	H	HR	BB	SO	W-L	Sv	ERA
Mel Stottlemyre	R	25	36	36	10	4	255.0	235	20	88	151	15-15	0	2.96
Fritz Peterson	L	25	36	30	6	1	181.1	179	11	43	102	8-14	0	3.47
Al Downing	L	26	31	28	10	4	201.2	158	13	61	171	14-10	0	2.63
Fred Talbot	R	26	29	22	2	0	138.2	132	20	54	61	6-8	0	4.22
Steve Barber†	L	28	17	17	3	1	97.2	103	4	54	70	6-9	0	4.05
Whitey Ford	L	38	7	7	2	1	44.0	40	2	9	21	2-4	0	1.64
Cecil Perkins	R	26	2	1	0	0	5.0	6	1	2	1	0-1	0	9.00
Dooley Womack	R	27	65	0	0	0	97.0	80	6	35	57	5-6	18	2.41
Steve Hamilton	L	31	44	0	0	0	62.0	57	7	23	55	2-4	4	3.48
Thad Tillotson	R	26	43	5	1	0	98.1	99	9	39	62	3-9	2	4.03
Bill Monbouquette†	R	30	33	10	2	1	133.1	122	6	17	53	6-5	1	2.36
Joe Verbanic	R	24	28	6	1	1	80.1	74	6	21	39	4-3	2	2.80
Hal Reniff†	R	28	24	0	0	0	40.0	40	0	14	24	0-2	0	4.28
Jim Bouton	R	28	17	1	0	0	44.1	47	5	18	31	1-0	0	4.67
Dale Roberts	L	25	2	0	0	0	2.0	3	0	2	0	0-0	0	9.00

1967 Kansas City Athletics 10th AL 62-99 .385 29.5 GB

Alvin Dark (52-69)/Luke Appling (10-30)

Player	Gm by Position	B	Age	G	AB	R	H	2B	3B	HR	RBI	BB	SO	SB	Avg	OBP	Slg
Phil Roof	C113	R	26	114	327	23	67	14	5	6	24	23	85	4	.205	.266	.333
Ray Webster	1B83,OF15	L	24	122	360	41	92	15	4	11	51	32	44	5	.256	.320	.411
John Donaldson	2B101,SS1	L	24	105	377	27	104	16	5	0	28	37	39	6	.276	.343	.345
Dick Green	3B59,2B50,1B1*	R	26	122	349	26	69	12	4	5	37	30	68	6	.198	.260	.298
Bert Campaneris	SS145	R	25	147	601	85	149	29	6	3	32	36	82	55	.248	.297	.331
Mike Hershberger	OF130	R	27	142	480	55	122	25	1	1	49	38	40	10	.254	.314	.317
Rick Monday	OF113	L	21	124	406	52	102	14	6	14	58	42	107	3	.251	.322	.419
Jim Gosger	OF113	L	24	134	356	31	86	14	5	5	36	53	69	5	.242	.337	.351
Danny Cater	3B56,OF55,1B44	R	27	142	529	55	143	17	4	4	46	34	56	4	.270	.317	.340
Ken Harrelson†	1B45	R	25	61	174	23	53	11	0	6	30	17	17	8	.305	.361	.471
Joe Nossek	OF63	R	26	87	166	12	34	6	1	0	10	4	26	2	.205	.221	.253
Sal Bando	3B44	R	23	47	130	11	25	3	2	0	6	10	24	1	.192	.295	.246
Reggie Jackson	OF34	L	21	35	118	13	21	4	4	1	6	10	46	1	.178	.269	.305
Ted Kubiak	SS20,2B10,3B5	S	25	53	102	6	16	2	1	0	5	12	20	0	.157	.243	.196
Dave Duncan	C32	R	21	34	101	9	19	4	0	5	11	4	50	0	.188	.219	.376
Catfish Hunter	P35,1B1	R	21	37	92	9	18	4	0	2	6	0	32	0	.196	.196	.304
Roger Repoz†	OF31	L	26	40	87	9	21	6	1	2	8	12	20	4	.241	.340	.402
Ken Suarez	C36	R	24	39	63	7	15	5	0	2	9	16	21	1	.238	.388	.413
Ed Charles†	3B18	R	34	19	61	5	15	1	0	0	5	12	13	1	.246	.378	.262
Tim Talton	C22,1B1	L	28	46	59	7	15	3	1	0	5	7	13	0	.254	.328	.339
Ossie Chavarria	2B17,3B7,OF3*	R	26	38	59	2	6	2	0	0	4	7	16	1	.102	.209	.136
Joe Rudi	1B9,OF6	R	20	19	43	4	8	2	0	0	1	3	7	0	.186	.239	.233
Allan Lewis		S	25	34	6	7	1	0	0	0	0	0	3	14	.167	.167	.167
Hoss Bowlin	3B2	R	26	2	5	0	1	0	0	0	0	0	0	0	.200	.200	.200

D. Green, 1 G at SS; O. Chavarria, 2 G at SS

Pitcher	T	Age	G	GS	CG	ShO	IP	H	HR	BB	SO	W-L	Sv	ERA
Catfish Hunter	R	21	35	35	13	5	259.2	209	16	84	196	13-17	0	2.81
Jim Nash	R	22	37	34	8	2	222.1	200	21	87	186	12-17	0	3.76
Chuck Dobson	R	23	32	29	4	1	197.2	172	17	75	110	10-10	0	3.69
Blue Moon Odom	R	22	29	17	0	0	103.2	94	9	68	67	3-8	0	5.04
George Lauzerique	R	19	3	2	0	0	16.0	11	2	6	10	0-2	0	2.25
Jack Aker	R	26	57	0	0	0	88.0	87	9	32	65	3-8	12	4.30
Tony Pierce	L	21	49	6	0	0	97.2	79	6	30	61	3-4	7	3.04
Lew Krausse	R	24	48	19	0	0	160.0	140	17	67	96	7-17	6	4.28
Paul Lindblad	L	25	46	10	1	1	115.2	106	15	35	83	5-8	6	3.58
Diego Segui	R	29	36	3	0	0	70.0	62	4	31	52	3-4	1	3.09
Roberto Rodriguez	R	25	15	5	0	0	40.1	42	4	14	29	1-1	2	3.57
Bill Stafford	R	27	14	0	0	0	16.0	12	0	8	10	0-1	0	1.69
Jack Sanford†	R	38	10	1	0	0	22.0	24	1	14	13	1-2	0	6.55
Bob Duliba	R	32	7	0	0	0	9.2	13	3	1	6	0-0	0	6.52
Bill Edgerton	L	25	7	0	0	0	8.1	11	1	3	6	1-0	0	2.16
Wes Stock	R	33	1	0	0	0	1.0	3	0	2	0	0-0	0	18.00

»1967 St. Louis Cardinals 1st NL 101-60 .627 —

Red Schoendienst

Player	Gm by Position	B	Age	G	AB	R	H	2B	3B	HR	RBI	BB	SO	SB	Avg	OBP	Slg
Tim McCarver	C130	L	25	138	471	68	139	26	3	14	69	54	32	8	.295	.369	.452
Orlando Cepeda	1B151	R	29	151	563	91	183	37	0	25	111	62	75	11	.325	.399	.524
Julian Javier	2B138	R	30	140	520	68	146	16	3	14	64	25	92	6	.281	.314	.404
Mike Shannon	3B122,OF6	R	27	130	482	53	118	18	3	12	77	37	89	2	.245	.302	.369
Dal Maxvill	SS148,2B7	R	28	152	476	37	108	14	4	1	41	48	66	0	.227	.297	.279
Lou Brock	OF157	L	28	159	689	113	206	32	12	21	76	24	109	52	.299	.327	.472
Curt Flood	OF126	R	29	134	514	68	172	24	1	5	50	37	46	2	.335	.378	.414
Roger Maris	OF118	L	32	125	410	64	107	18	7	9	55	52	61	0	.261	.346	.405
Bobby Tolan	OF80,1B13	L	21	110	265	35	67	7	3	6	32	19	43	12	.253	.309	.370
Phil Gagliano	2B27,3B25,1B4*	R	25	73	217	20	48	7	0	2	21	19	26	0	.221	.283	.281
Alex Johnson	OF57	R	24	81	175	20	39	9	2	1	12	9	26	6	.223	.271	.314
Ed Spiezio	3B19,OF7	R	25	55	105	9	22	2	0	3	10	7	18	2	.210	.265	.314
Dave Ricketts	C21	S	31	52	99	11	27	8	0	1	14	4	7	0	.273	.295	.384
Eddie Bressoud	SS48,3B1	R	35	52	67	8	9	1	1	1	1	9	18	0	.134	.237	.224
John Romano	C20	R	32	24	58	1	7	1	0	0	2	13	15	1	.121	.282	.138
Ted Savage†		R	30	9	8	1	1	0	0	0	0	1	3	0	.125	.222	.125
Steve Huntz	2B2	S	21	3	6	1	1	0	0	0	0	1	2	0	.167	.286	.167
Jimy Williams	SS1	R	23	1	2	0	0	0	0	0	0	0	1	0	.000	.000	.000

P. Gagliano, 2 G at SS

Pitcher	T	Age	G	GS	CG	ShO	IP	H	HR	BB	SO	W-L	Sv	ERA
Steve Carlton	L	22	30	28	11	2	193.0	173	10	62	168	14-9	1	2.98
Dick Hughes	R	29	37	27	12	3	222.1	164	22	48	161	16-6	3	2.67
Ray Washburn	R	29	27	27	3	1	186.1	190	14	42	98	10-7	0	3.53
Bob Gibson	R	31	24	24	10	2	175.1	151	10	40	147	13-7	0	2.98
Larry Jaster	L	23	34	23	2	1	152.1	141	12	44	87	9-7	3	3.01
Jim Cosman	R	24	10	5	0	0	31.1	21	2	24	11	1-0	0	3.16
Ron Willis	R	23	65	0	0	0	81.0	76	3	43	42	6-5	10	2.67
Joe Hoerner	L	30	57	0	0	0	66.0	52	5	20	50	4-4	15	2.59
Nelson Briles	R	23	49	14	4	2	155.1	139	8	40	94	14-5	6	2.43
Al Jackson	L	31	38	11	1	1	107.0	117	7	29	43	9-4	1	3.95
Hal Woodeshick	L	34	36	0	0	0	41.2	41	2	28	20	2-1	2	5.18
Jack Lamabe†	R	30	23	1	1	1	47.2	43	2	10	30	3-4	4	2.83
Mike Torrez	R	20	3	1	0	0	5.2	5	0	1	5	0-1	0	3.18

1967 San Francisco Giants 2nd NL 91-71 .562 10.5 GB

Herman Franks

Player	Gm by Position	B	Age	G	AB	R	H	2B	3B	HR	RBI	BB	SO	SB	Avg	OBP	Slg
Tom Haller	C136,OF1	L	30	141	455	54	114	23	5	14	49	62	61	0	.251	.344	.415
Willie McCovey	1B127	L	29	135	456	73	126	17	4	31	91	71	110	3	.276	.378	.535
Tito Fuentes	2B130,SS5	S	23	133	344	27	72	12	1	5	29	27	61	4	.209	.266	.294
Jim Ray Hart	3B89,OF72	R	25	158	578	98	167	26	7	29	99	77	100	1	.289	.373	.509
Hal Lanier	SS137,2B34	R	24	151	525	37	112	16	3	0	42	16	61	2	.213	.239	.255
Willie Mays	OF134	R	36	141	486	83	128	22	2	22	70	51	92	6	.263	.334	.453
Jesus Alou	OF123	R	25	129	510	55	149	15	4	5	30	14	39	1	.292	.316	.367
Ollie Brown	OF115	R	23	120	412	44	110	12	1	13	53	25	65	0	.267	.312	.396
Jim Davenport	3B64,SS28,2B12	R	33	124	295	42	81	10	3	5	30	39	50	1	.275	.366	.380
Ken Henderson	OF52	S	21	65	179	15	34	3	0	4	14	19	52	0	.190	.274	.274
Jack Hiatt	1B36,C3,OF2	R	24	73	153	24	42	6	0	6	26	27	37	0	.275	.387	.431
Bob Schroder	2B45,3B4	L	22	62	135	20	31	4	0	0	7	15	15	1	.230	.307	.259
Ty Cline†	OF37	L	28	64	122	18	33	5	5	0	4	9	13	2	.270	.326	.393
Dick Dietz	C43	R	25	56	120	10	27	3	0	4	19	25	44	0	.225	.358	.350
Bobby Etheridge	3B37	R	24	40	115	13	26	7	2	1	15	7	12	0	.226	.297	.348
Dick Groat†	SS24,2B1	R	36	34	70	4	12	1	1	0	4	6	7	0	.171	.237	.214
Norm Siebern†	1B15,OF2	L	33	46	58	6	9	1	1	0	4	14	13	0	.155	.319	.207
Cesar Gutierrez	SS15,2B1	R	24	18	21	4	3	0	0	0	0	1	4	1	.143	.217	.143
Bob Barton	C7	R	25	7	19	0	4	0	0	0	1	0	2	0	.211	.250	.211
Bill Sorrell	OF5	L	26	18	17	1	3	1	0	0	1	3	2	0	.176	.300	.235
Frank Johnson	OF3	R	24	8	10	3	3	0	0	0	0	1	2	0	.300	.364	.300
Don Mason	2B2	L	22	4	3	0	0	0	0	0	0	0	0	0	.000	.000	.000
Dave Marshall		L	24	1	0	0	0	0	0	0	0	0	0	0	—	—	—

Pitcher	T	Age	G	GS	CG	ShO	IP	H	HR	BB	SO	W-L	Sv	ERA
Gaylord Perry	R	28	39	37	18	3	293.0	231	20	84	230	15-17	1	2.61
Mike McCormick	L	28	40	35	14	5	262.1	220	25	81	150	22-10	0	2.85
Juan Marichal	R	29	26	26	18	2	202.1	195	20	42	166	14-10	0	2.76
Ray Sadecki	L	26	35	24	10	2	188.0	165	8	58	145	12-6	0	2.78
Frank Linzy	R	26	57	0	0	0	95.2	67	4	34	38	7-7	17	1.51
Ron Herbel	R	29	42	11	1	1	125.2	125	10	35	52	4-5	1	3.08
Lindy McDaniel	R	31	41	3	0	0	72.2	69	5	24	48	2-6	3	3.72
Bobby Bolin	R	28	37	15	0	0	120.0	120	16	50	69	6-8	0	4.88
Joe Gibbon	L	32	28	10	3	1	82.0	65	4	33	63	6-2	1	3.07
Bill Henry	L	39	28	1	0	0	21.2	16	1	9	23	2-0	2	2.08
Nestor Chavez	R	19	2	0	0	0	5.0	4	0	3	3	1-0	0	0.00
Ron Bryant	L	19	1	0	0	0	4.0	3	0	0	2	0-0	0	4.50
Rich Robertson	R	22	1	0	0	0	2.0	3	0	0	1	0-0	0	4.50

1967 Chicago Cubs 3rd NL 87-74 .540 14.0 GB

Leo Durocher

Player	Gm by Position	B	Age	G	AB	R	H	2B	3B	HR	RBI	BB	SO	SB	Avg	OBP	Slg
Randy Hundley	C152	R	25	152	539	68	144	25	3	14	60	44	75	2	.267	.322	.403
Ernie Banks	1B147	R	36	151	573	68	158	26	4	23	95	27	93	2	.276	.310	.455
Glenn Beckert	2B144	R	26	146	597	91	167	32	3	5	40	30	25	10	.280	.314	.369
Ron Santo	3B161	R	27	161	586	107	176	23	4	31	98	96	103	1	.300	.395	.512
Don Kessinger	SS143	S	24	145	580	61	134	10	7	0	42	33	80	6	.231	.275	.272
Billy Williams	OF162	L	29	162	634	92	176	21	12	28	84	68	67	6	.278	.346	.481
Adolfo Phillips	OF141	R	25	144	448	66	120	20	7	17	70	80	93	24	.268	.384	.458
Ted Savage†	OF86,3B1	R	30	96	225	40	49	10	1	5	33	40	54	7	.218	.346	.338
Lee Thomas	OF43,1B10	L	31	77	191	16	42	4	1	2	23	15	22	1	.220	.284	.283
Paul Popovich	SS31,2B17,3B2	S	26	49	159	18	34	4	0	0	2	9	12	0	.214	.265	.239
Clarence Jones	OF31,1B13	L	25	53	135	13	34	7	0	2	16	14	33	0	.252	.314	.348
Al Spangler	OF41	L	33	62	130	18	33	7	0	0	13	23	17	2	.254	.361	.308
Norm Gigon	2B12,OF4,3B1	R	29	34	70	8	12	3	1	1	6	4	14	0	.171	.234	.286
John Stephenson	C13	L	26	18	49	3	11	3	1	0	5	1	6	0	.224	.255	.327
John Boccabella	OF9,1B3,C1	R	26	25	35	0	6	1	1	0	8	3	7	0	.171	.250	.257
Bob Raudman	OF8	L	25	8	26	0	4	0	0	0	1	1	4	0	.154	.185	.154
Byron Browne	OF8	R	24	10	19	3	3	2	0	0	2	4	5	1	.158	.304	.263
George Altman	OF4,1B1	L	34	15	18	1	2	2	0	0	1	2	8	0	.111	.200	.222
Jimmy Stewart†		S	28	6	6	1	1	0	0	0	1	0	0	0	.167	.167	.167
Dick Bertell	C2	R	31	2	6	1	1	0	1	0	0	0	1	0	.167	.167	.500
Joe Campbell	OF1	R	23	1	3	0	0	0	0	0	0	0	3	0	.000	.000	.000
Joey Amalfitano		R	33	4	1	0	0	0	0	0	0	0	1	0	.000	.000	.000

Pitcher	T	Age	G	GS	CG	ShO	IP	H	HR	BB	SO	W-L	Sv	ERA
Fergie Jenkins	R	23	38	38	20	3	289.1	230	30	83	236	20-13	0	2.80
Rich Nye	L	22	35	30	7	0	205.0	179	15	52	119	13-10	0	3.20
Joe Niekro	R	22	36	22	7	2	169.2	171	15	32	77	10-7	0	3.34
Ray Culp	R	25	30	22	4	1	152.2	138	22	59	111	8-11	0	3.89
Curt Simmons†	L	38	17	14	3	0	82.0	100	10	23	31	3-7	0	4.94
Ken Holtzman	L	21	12	12	3	0	92.2	76	11	44	62	9-0	0	2.53
Dick Calmus	R	23	1	1	0	0	4.1	5	2	0	1	0-0	0	8.31
Bill Hands	R	27	49	11	3	1	150.0	134	9	48	84	7-8	6	2.46
Chuck Hartenstein	R	25	45	0	0	0	73.0	74	4	17	20	9-5	10	3.08
Cal Koonce†	R	26	34	0	0	0	51.0	52	2	21	28	2-2	2	4.59
Bill Stoneman	R	23	28	2	0	0	63.0	51	7	22	52	2-4	4	3.29
Dick Radatz†	R	30	20	0	0	0	23.1	12	4	24	18	1-0	5	6.56
Rob Gardner	L	22	18	5	0	0	31.2	33	2	6	16	0-2	0	3.98
Bob Shaw†	R	34	9	3	0	0	22.1	33	0	9	7	0-2	0	6.04
Jim Ellis	L	22	8	1	0	0	16.2	20	1	9	8	1-1	0	3.24
Bob Hendley†	L	28	7	0	0	0	12.1	17	4	3	10	2-0	1	6.57
Pete Mikkelsen†	R	27	7	0	0	0	7.0	9	1	5	0	0-0	0	6.43
John Upham	L	25	5	0	0	0	1.1	4	1	2	2	0-1	0	33.75
Rick James	R	19	3	1	0	0	4.2	9	1	2	2	0-1	0	13.50
Don Larsen	R	37	3	0	0	0	4.0	5	1	2	1	0-0	0	9.00
Fred Norman	L	24	1	0	0	0	1.0	0	0	0	3	0-0	0	0.00

1967 Cincinnati Reds 4th NL 87-75 .537 14.5 GB

Dave Bristol

Player	Gm by Position	B	Age	G	AB	R	H	2B	3B	HR	RBI	BB	SO	SB	Avg	OBP	Slg
Johnny Edwards	C73	L	29	80	209	10	43	6	0	2	20	16	28	1	.206	.261	.263
Lee May	1B81,OF48	R	24	127	438	54	116	29	2	12	57	19	80	4	.265	.308	.422
Tommy Helms	2B88,SS46	R	26	137	497	40	136	27	4	2	35	24	41	5	.274	.305	.356
Tony Perez	3B139,1B18,2B1	R	25	156	600	78	174	28	7	26	102	33	102	0	.290	.328	.490
Leo Cardenas	SS108	R	28	108	379	30	97	14	3	2	21	34	77	4	.256	.320	.325
Vada Pinson	OF157	L	28	158	650	90	187	28	13	18	66	26	86	26	.288	.318	.454
Pete Rose	OF123,2B35	S	26	148	585	86	176	32	8	12	76	56	66	11	.301	.364	.444
Tommy Harper	OF100	R	26	103	365	55	82	17	3	7	22	43	51	23	.225	.306	.345
Deron Johnson	1B81,3B24	R	28	108	361	39	81	18	1	13	53	22	104	0	.224	.270	.388
Chico Ruiz	2B56,3B13,SS11*	S	28	105	250	32	55	12	4	0	13	11	35	9	.220	.258	.300
Don Pavletich	C66,1B6,3B1	R	28	74	231	25	55	14	3	6	34	21	38	2	.238	.310	.403
Art Shamsky	OF40	L	25	76	147	6	29	3	1	3	13	15	34	0	.197	.274	.293
Floyd Robinson	OF39	L	31	55	130	19	31	6	2	1	10	14	14	3	.238	.310	.338
Jimmie Coker	C34	R	31	45	97	8	18	2	1	2	4	4	20	0	.186	.218	.289
Johnny Bench	C26	R	19	26	86	7	14	3	1	1	6	5	19	0	.163	.207	.256
Dick Simpson	OF26	R	23	44	54	8	14	3	0	1	6	7	11	0	.259	.339	.370
Jake Wood†	OF2	R	30	16	17	1	2	0	0	0	1	1	3	0	.118	.167	.118
Gordy Coleman	1B2	L	32	4	7	0	0	0	0	0	0	1	0	0	.000	.125	.000
Len Boehmer	2B1	R	26	2	3	0	0	0	0	0	0	0	0	0	.000	.000	.000

C. Ruiz, 5 G at OF

Pitcher	T	Age	G	GS	CG	ShO	IP	H	HR	BB	SO	W-L	Sv	ERA
Gary Nolan	R	19	33	32	8	5	226.2	193	18	62	206	14-8	0	2.58
Milt Pappas	R	28	34	32	5	3	217.2	218	19	38	129	16-13	0	3.35
Jim Maloney	R	27	30	29	6	3	196.1	181	8	72	153	15-11	0	3.25
Sammy Ellis	R	26	32	27	8	1	175.2	197	18	67	80	8-11	0	3.84
Mel Queen	R	25	31	24	6	2	195.2	155	17	52	154	14-8	0	2.76
John Tsitouris	R	31	2	1	0	0	8.0	4	1	6	4	1-0	0	3.38
Ted Abernathy	R	34	70	0	0	0	106.1	63	1	41	88	6-3	28	1.27
Don Nottebart	R	31	47	0	0	0	79.1	75	4	19	48	0-3	4	1.93
Gerry Arrigo	L	26	32	5	1	1	74.0	61	6	35	56	6-6	1	3.16
Billy McCool	L	22	31	11	0	0	97.1	92	8	56	83	3-7	2	3.42
Bob Lee†	R	29	27	1	0	0	50.2	51	0	25	33	3-3	2	4.44
Darrell Osteen	R	24	10	0	0	0	14.1	10	1	13	13	0-2	2	6.28
Ted Davidson	L	27	9	0	0	0	13.0	13	0	3	6	1-0	0	4.15
Jack Baldschun	R	30	9	0	0	0	13.0	15	0	9	12	0-0	0	4.15

1967 Philadelphia Phillies 5th NL 82-80 .506 19.5 GB

Gene Mauch

Player	Gm by Position	B	Age	G	AB	R	H	2B	3B	HR	RBI	BB	SO	SB	Avg	OBP	Slg
Clay Dalrymple	C97	L	30	101	268	12	46	7	1	3	21	36	49	1	.172	.271	.239
Bill White	1B95	L	33	110	308	29	77	6	2	8	33	52	61	6	.250	.359	.360
Cookie Rojas	2B137,OF9,C3*	R	28	147	528	60	137	21	2	4	45	30	58	8	.259	.297	.330
Dick Allen	3B121,2B1,SS1	R	25	122	463	89	142	31	10	23	77	75	117	20	.307	.404	.566
Bobby Wine	SS134,1B2	R	28	135	363	27	69	12	5	2	28	29	77	3	.190	.249	.267
Johnny Callison	OF147	L	28	149	556	62	145	30	5	14	64	55	63	6	.261	.329	.408
Tony Gonzalez	OF143	L	30	149	508	74	172	23	9	9	59	47	58	10	.339	.396	.472
Don Lock	OF97	R	30	112	313	46	79	13	1	14	51	43	98	9	.252	.349	.435
Tony Taylor	1B58,3B44,2B42*	R	31	132	462	55	110	16	6	2	34	42	74	10	.238	.308	.312
John Briggs	OF94	L	23	106	332	47	77	12	4	9	30	41	72	3	.232	.315	.373
Gene Oliver†	C79,1B2	R	32	85	263	29	59	16	0	7	34	29	56	2	.224	.300	.365
Gary Sutherland	SS66,OF25	R	22	103	231	23	57	12	1	1	19	17	22	0	.247	.298	.320
Doug Clemens	OF10	L	28	69	73	2	13	5	0	0	4	8	15	0	.178	.262	.247
Tito Francona†	1B24,OF1	L	33	27	73	7	15	1	0	0	3	7	10	0	.205	.272	.219
Billy Cowan	OF20,2B1,3B1	R	28	34	59	11	9	0	0	3	6	4	14	1	.153	.203	.305
Chuck Hiller†	2B6	L	32	31	43	4	13	1	0	0	2	2	4	0	.302	.333	.326
Rick Joseph	1B13	R	27	17	41	4	9	2	0	1	5	4	10	0	.220	.289	.341
Bob Uecker†	C17	R	32	18	35	3	6	2	0	0	7	5	9	0	.171	.275	.229
Dick Groat†	SS6	R	36	10	26	3	3	0	0	0	1	4	4	0	.115	.233	.115
Jackie Brandt†	OF3	R	33	16	19	1	2	1	0	0	1	0	6	0	.105	.105	.158
Phil Linz†	SS7,3B1	R	28	23	18	4	4	2	0	1	5	2	1	0	.222	.300	.500
Jimmie Schaffer	C1	R	31	2	2	1	0	0	0	0	0	1	1	0	.000	.333	.000
Terry Harmon		R	23	2	0	0	0	0	0	0	0	0	0	0	—	—	—

C. Rojas, 2 G at SS, 1 G at P, 1 G at 3B; T. Taylor, 3 G at SS

Pitcher	T	Age	G	GS	CG	ShO	IP	H	HR	BB	SO	W-L	Sv	ERA
Jim Bunning	R	35	40	40	16	6	302.1	241	18	73	253	17-15	0	2.29
Larry Jackson	R	36	40	37	11	4	261.2	242	17	54	139	13-15	0	3.10
Chris Short	L	29	29	26	8	2	199.1	163	9	74	142	9-11	1	2.39
Rick Wise	R	21	36	25	6	3	181.1	177	8	45	111	11-11	0	3.28
Dick Ellsworth	L	27	32	21	3	1	125.1	152	6	36	45	6-7	0	4.38
Turk Farrell†	R	33	50	1	0	0	92.0	76	6	15	68	9-6	12	2.05
Dick Hall	R	36	48	1	1	0	86.0	83	5	12	49	10-8	8	2.20
Grant Jackson	L	24	43	4	0	0	84.1	86	3	43	83	2-3	1	3.84
John Boozer	R	28	28	7	1	0	74.2	86	6	24	48	5-4	1	4.10
Dallas Green	R	32	8	0	0	0	15.0	25	2	6	12	0-0	0	9.00
Ruben Gomez	R	39	7	0	0	0	11.1	8	2	7	9	0-0	0	3.97
Pedro Ramos	R	32	6	0	0	0	8.0	14	1	8	1	0-0	0	9.00
Larry Loughlin	L	25	3	0	0	0	5.1	9	1	4	5	0-0	0	15.19
Bob Buhl	R	38	3	0	0	0	3.0	6	2	2	1	0-0	0	12.00
Gary Wagner	R	27	1	0	0	0	2.0	1	0	1	0	0-0	0	0.00
Dick Thoenen	R	23	1	0	0	0	1.0	2	0	0	0	0-0	0	9.00
Cookie Rojas	R	28	1	0	0	0	1.0	1	0	0	0	0-0	0	0.00

1967 Pittsburgh Pirates 6th NL 81-81 .500 20.5 GB

Harry Walker (42-42)/Danny Murtaugh (39-39)

Player	Gm by Position	B	Age	G	AB	R	H	2B	3B	HR	RBI	BB	SO	SB	Avg	OBP	Slg
Jerry May	C110	R	23	110	325	23	88	13	2	3	22	36	55	0	.271	.348	.351
Donn Clendenon	1B123	R	31	131	478	46	119	15	2	13	56	34	107	4	.249	.298	.370
Bill Mazeroski	2B163	R	30	163	639	62	167	25	3	9	77	30	55	1	.261	.292	.352
Maury Wills	3B144,SS2	S	34	149	616	92	186	12	9	3	45	31	44	29	.302	.334	.365
Gene Alley	SS146	R	26	152	550	59	158	25	7	6	55	36	70	10	.287	.337	.391
Roberto Clemente	OF145	R	32	147	585	103	209	26	10	23	110	41	103	9	.357	.400	.554
Matty Alou	OF134,1B1	L	28	139	550	87	186	21	7	2	28	24	42	16	.338	.372	.413
Manny Mota	OF99,3B2	R	29	120	349	53	112	14	8	4	56	14	46	3	.321	.343	.441
Willie Stargell	OF98,1B37	L	27	134	462	54	125	18	6	20	73	67	103	1	.271	.365	.465
Jose Pagan	3B25,OF23,SS16*	R	32	81	211	17	61	6	2	1	19	10	28	1	.289	.323	.351
Al Luplow†	OF25	L	28	55	103	13	19	1	0	1	8	6	14	1	.184	.232	.223
Jim Pagliaroni	C38	R	29	44	100	4	20	1	1	0	9	16	26	0	.200	.314	.230
Manny Sanguillen	C28	R	23	30	96	6	26	4	0	0	8	4	12	0	.271	.300	.313
Andre Rodgers	1B9,3B5,SS3*	R	32	47	61	8	14	3	0	2	4	8	18	1	.230	.314	.377
George Spriggs	OF13	L	26	38	57	14	10	1	1	0	5	6	20	3	.175	.246	.228
Manny Jimenez	OF6	L	28	50	56	3	14	2	0	2	10	1	4	0	.250	.276	.393
Jesse Gonder	C18	L	31	22	36	4	5	1	0	0	3	5	9	0	.139	.279	.167
Bob Robertson	1B9	R	20	9	35	4	6	0	0	2	4	3	12	0	.171	.237	.343

J. Pagan, 2 G at 2B, 1 G at C; A. Rodgers, 2 G at 2B

Pitcher	T	Age	G	GS	CG	ShO	IP	H	HR	BB	SO	W-L	Sv	ERA
Tommie Sisk	R	25	37	31	11	2	207.2	196	6	78	85	13-13	1	3.34
Bob Veale	L	31	33	31	6	1	203.0	184	12	119	179	16-8	0	3.64
Dennis Ribant	R	25	38	22	2	0	172.0	186	16	40	75	9-8	0	4.08
Woodie Fryman	L	27	28	18	3	1	113.1	121	12	44	74	3-8	1	4.05
Steve Blass	R	25	32	16	2	0	126.2	126	12	47	72	6-8	0	3.55
Bob Moose	R	19	2	2	1	0	14.2	14	1	4	7	1-0	0	3.68
Roy Face	R	39	61	0	0	0	74.1	62	5	22	41	7-5	17	2.42
Al McBean	R	29	51	8	5	0	131.0	118	6	43	54	7-4	4	2.54
Juan Pizarro	L	30	50	9	1	1	107.0	99	10	52	96	8-10	9	3.95
Pete Mikkelsen†	R	27	32	0	0	0	56.1	50	7	19	30	1-2	2	4.31
Billy O'Dell	L	34	27	11	1	0	86.2	88	10	41	34	5-6	0	5.82
Vern Law	R	37	25	10	1	0	97.0	122	5	18	43	2-6	0	4.18
John Gelnar	R	24	10	1	0	0	19.0	30	4	11	5	0-1	0	8.05
Bruce Dal Canton	R	25	8	2	1	0	24.0	19	1	10	13	2-1	0	1.88
Jim Shellenback	L	23	6	2	1	0	23.1	23	1	12	11	1-1	0	2.70
Bill Short	L	29	6	0	0	0	2.1	1	0	1	1	0-0	1	3.86

1967 Atlanta Braves 7th NL 77-85 .475 24.5 GB

Billy Hitchcock (77-82)/Ken Silvestri (0-3)

Player	Gm by Position	B	Age	G	AB	R	H	2B	3B	HR	RBI	BB	SO	SB	Avg	OBP	Slg
Joe Torre	C114,1B23	R	26	135	477	67	132	18	1	20	68	49	75	2	.277	.345	.444
Felipe Alou	1B85,OF56	R	32	140	574	76	157	26	3	15	43	32	50	6	.274	.318	.408
Woody Woodward	2B120,SS16	R	24	136	429	30	97	15	2	0	25	37	51	0	.226	.287	.270
Clete Boyer	3B150,SS6	R	30	154	572	63	140	18	3	26	96	39	81	6	.245	.292	.423
Denis Menke	SS124,3B3	R	26	129	418	37	95	14	3	7	39	65	80	5	.227	.333	.325
Hank Aaron	OF152,2B1	R	33	155	600	113	184	37	3	39	109	63	97	17	.307	.369	.573
Mack Jones	OF126	L	28	140	454	72	115	23	4	17	50	64	108	10	.253	.355	.434
Rico Carty	OF112,1B9	R	27	134	444	41	113	16	2	15	64	49	70	4	.255	.329	.401
Tito Francona†	1B56,OF6	L	33	82	254	28	63	5	1	6	25	20	34	1	.248	.304	.346
Bob Uecker†	C59	R	32	62	158	14	23	2	0	3	13	19	51	0	.146	.236	.215
Mike de la Hoz	2B23,3B22,SS1	R	28	74	143	10	29	3	0	3	14	4	14	1	.203	.224	.287
Felix Millan	2B41	R	23	41	136	13	32	3	3	2	6	4	10	1	.235	.266	.346
Gary Geiger	OF38	L	30	69	117	17	19	1	1	1	5	20	35	1	.162	.285	.214
Marty Martinez	SS25,2B9,C3*	S	25	44	73	14	21	2	1	0	5	11	11	0	.288	.384	.342
Gene Oliver†	C14	R	32	17	51	8	10	2	0	3	6	6	8	0	.196	.281	.412
Charlie Lau†		L	34	52	45	3	9	1	0	1	5	4	9	0	.200	.265	.289
Mike Lum	OF6	L	21	9	26	1	6	0	0	0	1	1	4	0	.231	.259	.231
Remy Hermoso	SS9,2B2	R	19	11	26	3	8	0	0	0	0	2	4	1	.308	.357	.308
Cito Gaston	OF7	R	23	9	25	1	3	0	0	0	1	0	5	1	.120	.120	.200
Dave Nicholson	OF7	R	27	10	25	2	5	0	0	0	1	2	9	0	.200	.250	.200
Ty Cline†	OF1	L	28	10	8	0	0	0	0	0	0	0	3	0	.000	.111	.000
Glen Clark		S	26	4	4	0	0	0	0	0	0	0	1	0	.000	.000	.000
Jim Beauchamp		R	27	4	3	0	0	0	0	0	1	0	0	0	.000	.000	.000

M. Martinez, 2 G at 3B, 1 G at 1B

Pitcher	T	Age	G	GS	CG	ShO	IP	H	HR	BB	SO	W-L	Sv	ERA
Denny Lemaster	L	28	31	31	8	2	215.1	184	20	72	148	9-9	0	3.34
Pat Jarvis	R	26	32	30	7	1	194.0	195	15	62	118	15-10	0	3.66
Ken Johnson	R	34	29	29	6	0	210.1	191	19	38	85	13-9	0	2.74
Tony Cloninger	R	26	16	16	1	0	76.2	85	13	31	55	4-7	0	5.17
Bob Bruce	R	34	12	7	1	0	38.2	42	3	15	22	2-3	1	4.89
Ron Reed	R	24	3	3	0	0	21.1	21	1	3	11	1-1	0	2.95
Jim Britton	R	23	2	2	0	0	13.1	15	2	2	4	0-2	0	6.08
George Stone	L	20	2	1	0	0	7.1	8	0	1	5	0-0	0	4.91
Jay Ritchie	R	30	52	0	0	0	82.1	75	6	29	57	4-6	2	3.17
Phil Niekro	R	28	46	20	10	1	207.0	164	9	55	129	11-9	9	1.87
Ramon Hernandez	L	26	46	0	0	0	51.2	60	5	14	28	0-2	5	4.18
Clay Carroll	R	26	42	7	1	0	93.0	111	6	29	35	6-12	0	5.52
Dick Kelley	L	27	39	9	1	1	98.0	88	8	42	75	2-9	2	3.77
Cecil Upshaw	R	24	30	0	0	0	45.1	42	4	8	31	2-3	8	2.58
Claude Raymond†	R	30	28	0	0	0	34.1	33	2	11	14	4-1	5	2.62
Ed Rakow	R	31	17	3	0	0	39.1	36	4	15	25	3-2	4	5.26
Wade Blasingame†	L	23	10	4	0	0	25.1	27	1	21	20	1-0	0	4.62
Don Schwall	R	31	1	0	0	0	0.2	0	0	1	0	0-0	0	0.00

1967 Los Angeles Dodgers 8th NL 73-89 .451 28.5 GB

Walter Alston

Player	Gm by Position	B	Age	G	AB	R	H	2B	3B	HR	RBI	BB	SO	SB	Avg	OBP	Slg
John Roseboro	C107	L	34	116	334	37	91	18	2	4	24	38	33	2	.272	.348	.374
Wes Parker	1B112,OF18	S	27	139	413	56	102	16	5	5	31	65	83	10	.247	.358	.346
Ron Hunt	2B90,3B8	R	26	110	388	44	102	17	3	3	33	39	24	2	.263	.344	.345
Jim Lefebvre	3B92,2B34,1B5	S	25	136	494	51	129	18	5	8	50	44	64	1	.261	.322	.366
Gene Michael	SS83	S	29	98	223	20	45	3	1	0	7	11	30	1	.202	.246	.224
Willie Davis	OF138	L	27	143	569	65	146	27	9	6	41	29	65	20	.257	.295	.367
Ron Fairly	OF97,1B68	L	28	153	486	45	107	19	0	10	55	54	51	1	.220	.295	.321
Al Ferrara	OF94	R	27	122	347	41	96	16	1	16	50	33	73	0	.277	.345	.467
Lou Johnson	OF91	R	32	104	330	39	89	14	1	11	41	24	52	4	.270	.330	.418
Bob Bailey	3B65,OF27,1B4*	R	24	116	322	21	73	8	2	4	28	40	50	5	.227	.310	.301
Len Gabrielson†	OF68	L	27	90	238	20	62	10	3	7	29	15	41	3	.261	.307	.416
Nate Oliver	2B39,SS32,OF1	R	26	77	232	18	55	6	2	0	7	13	50	3	.237	.283	.280
Dick Schofield	SS69,2B4,3B2	S	32	84	232	23	50	10	1	2	15	31	40	1	.216	.307	.293
Jeff Torborg	C75	R	25	76	196	11	42	4	1	2	12	13	31	1	.214	.265	.276
Jim Hickman	OF37,1B2,3B2*	R	30	65	98	7	16	6	1	0	10	14	28	1	.163	.268	.245
Jim Campanis	C23	R	23	41	62	3	10	1	0	2	2	9	14	0	.161	.268	.274
Luis Alcaraz	2B17	R	26	17	60	1	14	1	0	0	3	1	13	1	.233	.242	.250
Tommy Dean	SS12	R	21	12	28	1	4	1	0	0	2	0	9	0	.143	.143	.179
Johnny Werhas†		R	29	7	7	0	1	0	0	0	0	0	3	0	.143	.143	.143
Willie Crawford	OF1	L	20	4	4	0	1	0	0	0	0	1	3	0	.250	.400	.250

B. Bailey, 1 G at SS; J. Hickman, 1 G at P

Pitcher	T	Age	G	GS	CG	ShO	IP	H	HR	BB	SO	W-L	Sv	ERA
Claude Osteen	L	27	39	39	14	5	288.1	298	19	52	152	17-17	0	3.22
Don Drysdale	R	30	38	38	9	3	282.0	269	19	60	196	13-16	0	2.74
Don Sutton	R	22	37	34	11	3	232.2	223	18	57	169	11-15	1	3.95
Bill Singer	R	23	32	29	7	3	204.1	185	5	61	169	12-8	0	2.64
Alan Foster	R	20	4	2	0	0	16.2	10	0	3	15	0-1	0	2.16
John Duffie	R	21	2	2	0	0	9.2	11	1	4	6	0-2	0	2.79
Ron Perranoski	L	31	70	0	0	0	110.0	97	4	45	75	6-7	16	2.45
Phil Regan	R	30	55	3	0	0	96.1	108	2	32	53	6-9	6	2.99
Bob Miller	R	28	52	4	0	0	85.2	88	9	27	32	2-9	0	4.31
Jim Brewer	L	29	30	11	0	0	100.2	78	8	31	74	5-4	1	2.68
Dick Egan	L	30	20	0	0	0	31.2	34	3	15	20	1-1	0	6.25
Joe Moeller	R	24	6	0	0	0	5.0	9	1	3	2	0-0	0	9.00
Bob Lee†	R	29	4	0	0	0	6.2	6	2	3	2	0-0	0	5.40
Jim Hickman	R	30	1	0	0	0	2.0	2	1	0	0	0-0	0	4.50
Bruce Brubaker	R	25	1	0	0	0	1.1	3	1	0	2	0-0	0	20.25

1967 Houston Astros 9th NL 69-93 .426 32.5 GB

Grady Hatton

Player	Gm by Position	B	Age	G	AB	R	H	2B	3B	HR	RBI	BB	SO	SB	Avg	OBP	Slg
John Bateman	C71	R	26	76	252	16	48	9	0	2	17	17	53	0	.190	.245	.250
Eddie Mathews†	1B79,3B24	L	35	101	328	39	78	13	2	10	38	48	65	2	.238	.333	.381
Joe Morgan	2B130,OF1	L	23	133	494	73	136	27	11	6	42	81	51	29	.275	.378	.411
Bob Aspromonte	3B133	R	29	137	486	51	143	24	5	6	58	45	44	2	.294	.354	.401
Sonny Jackson	SS128	L	22	129	520	67	123	18	3	0	25	36	45	22	.237	.285	.283
Jimmy Wynn	OF157	R	25	158	594	102	148	29	3	37	107	74	137	16	.249	.331	.495
Rusty Staub	OF144	L	23	149	546	71	182	44	1	10	74	60	47	0	.333	.398	.473
Ron Davis	OF80	R	25	94	285	31	73	19	1	7	38	17	48	5	.256	.303	.404
Julio Gotay	2B30,SS20,3B3	R	28	77	234	30	66	10	2	2	15	15	30	1	.282	.329	.368
Ron Brand	C67,2B1,OF1	R	27	84	215	22	52	8	1	0	18	23	17	4	.242	.321	.288
Norm Miller	OF53	L	21	64	190	15	39	9	3	1	14	19	42	2	.205	.278	.300
Chuck Harrison	1B59	R	26	70	177	13	43	7	3	2	26	13	30	0	.243	.292	.350
Doug Rader	1B36,3B7	R	22	47	162	24	54	10	4	2	26	7	31	0	.333	.360	.481
Jim Landis†	OF44	R	33	50	143	19	36	11	1	1	14	20	35	2	.252	.341	.364
Dave Adlesh	C31	R	23	39	94	4	17	1	0	1	4	11	28	0	.181	.264	.223
Jackie Brandt†	1B14,OF6,3B1	R	33	41	89	7	21	4	1	1	15	8	9	0	.236	.296	.337
Bob Lillis	SS23,2B3,3B2	R	37	37	82	3	20	1	0	0	5	1	8	0	.244	.253	.256
Aaron Pointer	OF22	R	25	27	70	6	11	4	0	1	10	13	26	1	.157	.291	.257
Hal King	C11	L	23	15	44	2	11	1	2	0	6	2	9	0	.250	.283	.364
Ivan Murrell	OF6	R	22	10	29	2	9	0	0	0	1	1	9	1	.310	.333	.310
Lee Bales	2B6,SS1	S	22	19	27	4	3	0	0	0	2	8	7	1	.111	.306	.111
Bob Watson	1B3	R	21	6	14	1	3	0	0	1	2	0	3	0	.214	.214	.429
Bill Heath†	C5	L	28	9	11	0	1	0	0	0	0	4	3	0	.091	.333	.091
Jose Herrera		R	25	5	4	0	1	0	0	0	1	0	1	0	.250	.250	.250
Candy Harris		S	19	6	1	0	0	0	0	0	0	0	1	0	.000	.000	.000

Pitcher	T	Age	G	GS	CG	ShO	IP	H	HR	BB	SO	W-L	Sv	ERA
Dave Giusti	R	27	37	33	8	1	221.2	231	20	58	157	11-15	1	4.18
Mike Cuellar	L	30	36	32	16	3	246.1	233	16	63	203	16-11	1	3.03
Don Wilson	R	22	31	28	7	3	184.0	141	10	69	159	10-9	0	2.79
Bo Belinsky	L	30	27	18	0	0	115.1	112	12	54	80	3-9	0	4.68
Larry Dierker	R	20	15	15	4	0	99.0	95	4	25	68	6-5	0	3.36
Wade Blasingame†	L	23	15	14	0	0	77.0	91	9	27	46	4-7	0	5.96
Bruce Von Hoff	R	23	10	10	0	0	50.1	52	3	28	22	0-3	0	4.83
Chris Zachary	R	23	9	7	0	0	36.1	42	5	12	18	1-6	0	5.70
Howie Reed	R	30	4	2	0	0	18.1	19	0	2	9	1-1	0	3.44
Dan Schneider	L	24	54	0	0	0	52.2	60	5	27	39	0-2	2	4.96
Carroll Sembera	R	25	45	0	0	0	59.2	66	7	19	48	2-6	3	4.83
Barry Latman	R	31	39	1	0	0	77.2	73	13	34	70	3-6	0	4.52
Dave Eilers	R	30	35	0	0	0	59.1	68	3	17	27	6-4	1	3.94
Larry Sherry†	R	31	29	0	0	0	40.2	53	4	13	32	1-2	6	4.87
Claude Raymond†	R	30	21	0	0	0	31.0	31	5	7	17	0-4	5	3.19
Tom Dukes	R	24	17	0	0	0	23.2	25	2	11	23	0-2	1	5.32
Jim Owens	R	33	10	0	0	0	10.2	12	1	2	6	0-1	0	4.22
Turk Farrell†	R	33	7	0	0	0	11.2	11	0	7	10	1-0	0	4.63
Danny Coombs	L	25	6	2	0	0	24.1	21	0	9	23	3-0	0	3.33
Pat House	L	26	6	0	0	0	4.0	3	0	0	2	1-0	1	4.50
Arnold Earley	L	34	2	0	0	0	1.1	5	1	1	1	0-0	0	27.00
John Buzhardt†	R	30	1	0	0	0	0.2	0	0	0	0	0-0	0	0.00

1967 New York Mets 10th NL 61-101 .377 40.5 GB

Wes Westrum (57-94)/Salty Parker (4-7)

Player	Gm by Position	B	Age	G	AB	R	H	2B	3B	HR	RBI	BB	SO	SB	Avg	OBP	Slg
Jerry Grote	C119	R	24	120	344	25	67	8	0	4	23	14	65	2	.195	.226	.253
Ed Kranepool	1B139	L	22	141	469	37	126	17	1	10	54	37	51	0	.269	.321	.373
Jerry Buchek	2B95,3B17,SS9	R	25	124	411	35	97	11	2	14	41	26	101	3	.236	.283	.375
Ed Charles†	3B89	R	34	101	323	32	77	13	2	3	31	24	58	4	.238	.300	.319
Bud Harrelson	SS149	S	23	151	540	59	137	16	4	1	28	48	64	12	.254	.317	.304
Tommy Davis	OF149,1B1	R	28	154	577	72	174	32	0	16	73	31	71	9	.302	.342	.440
Cleon Jones	OF115	R	24	129	411	46	101	10	5	5	30	19	57	12	.246	.282	.331
Ron Swoboda	OF108,1B20	R	23	134	449	47	126	17	3	13	53	41	96	3	.281	.340	.419
Bob Johnson†	2B39,1B23,SS14*	R	31	90	230	26	80	8	3	5	27	12	29	1	.348	.377	.474
Ken Boyer†	3B44,1B8	R	36	56	166	17	39	7	2	3	13	26	22	2	.235	.335	.355
Larry Stahl	OF43	L	26	71	155	9	37	5	0	1	18	8	25	2	.239	.283	.290
John Sullivan	C57	L	26	65	147	4	32	5	0	0	6	6	26	0	.218	.248	.252
Tommie Reynolds	OF72,3B5,C1	S	25	101	136	16	28	1	0	2	9	11	26	1	.206	.278	.257
Al Luplow†	OF33	L	28	41	112	11	23	1	0	3	9	8	19	0	.205	.260	.295
Don Bosch	OF39	S	24	44	93	7	13	0	1	0	2	5	24	3	.140	.184	.161
Greg Goossen	C23	R	21	37	69	2	11	1	0	0	3	4	26	0	.159	.216	.174
Bob Heise	2B12,SS3,3B2	R	20	16	62	7	20	4	0	0	3	3	1	0	.323	.354	.387
Amos Otis	OF16,3B1	R	20	19	59	6	13	2	0	0	1	5	13	0	.220	.292	.254
Phil Linz†	2B11,SS8,3B1*	R	28	24	58	8	12	2	0	0	1	4	10	0	.207	.270	.241
Chuck Hiller†	2B14	L	32	25	54	0	5	3	0	0	3	2	11	0	.093	.125	.148
Ken Boswell	2B6,3B4	L	21	11	40	2	9	3	0	1	4	1	5	0	.225	.233	.375
Joe Moock	3B12	L	23	13	40	2	9	2	0	0	5	0	7	0	.225	.225	.275
Hawk Taylor†	C12	R	28	13	37	3	9	3	0	0	4	2	8	0	.243	.282	.324
Johnny Lewis	OF10	L	27	13	34	2	4	1	0	0	2	2	11	0	.118	.167	.147
Sandy Alomar†	SS10,3B3,2B2	S	23	15	22	1	0	0	0	0	0	0	6	0	.000	.000	.000
Bart Shirley	2B3	R	27	6	12	1	0	0	0	0	0	0	5	0	.000	.000	.000
Kevin Collins	2B2	L	20	4	10	1	1	0	0	0	0	0	3	1	.100	.100	.100

B. Johnson, 1 G at 3B; P. Linz, 1 G at OF

Pitcher	T	Age	G	GS	CG	ShO	IP	H	HR	BB	SO	W-L	Sv	ERA
Tom Seaver	R	22	35	34	18	2	251.0	224	19	78	170	16-13	0	2.76
Jack Fisher	R	28	39	30	7	1	220.1	251	21	64	117	9-18	0	4.70
Don Cardwell	R	31	26	16	3	3	118.1	112	8	39	71	5-9	0	3.57
Bob Shaw†	R	34	23	13	3	1	98.2	105	9	28	49	3-9	0	4.29
Bob Hendley†	L	28	15	13	2	0	70.2	65	11	28	36	3-3	0	3.44
Danny Frisella	R	21	14	11	0	0	74.0	68	6	33	51	1-6	0	3.41
Bill Denehy	R	21	15	8	0	0	53.2	51	8	29	35	1-7	0	4.70
Cal Koonce†	R	26	11	6	2	1	45.0	45	2	7	24	3-3	0	2.80
Dennis Bennett†	L	27	8	6	0	0	26.1	37	4	7	14	1-1	0	5.13
Tug McGraw	L	22	4	4	0	0	17.1	13	3	13	18	0-3	0	7.79
Bill Graham	R	30	5	3	1	0	27.1	20	3	11	14	1-2	0	2.63
Les Rohr	L	21	3	3	0	0	17.0	13	1	9	15	2-1	0	2.12
Ron Taylor	R	29	50	0	0	0	73.0	60	1	23	46	4-6	8	2.34
Don Shaw	L	23	40	0	0	0	51.1	40	5	23	44	4-5	3	2.98
Dick Selma	R	23	38	4	0	0	81.1	71	3	36	52	2-4	2	2.77
Hal Reniff†	R	28	29	0	0	0	43.0	42	1	23	21	3-3	4	3.35
Jack Hamilton†	R	28	17	1	0	0	31.1	24	2	16	22	2-0	1	3.73
Jack Lamabe†	R	30	16	2	0	0	31.2	24	4	8	23	0-3	1	3.98
Joe Grzenda	L	30	11	0	0	0	16.2	14	0	8	9	0-0	0	2.16
Jerry Koosman	L	24	9	3	0	0	22.1	22	3	19	11	0-2	0	6.04
Chuck Estrada	R	29	9	2	0	0	22.0	28	5	17	15	1-2	0	9.41
Billy Connors	R	25	6	1	0	0	13.0	8	3	5	13	0-0	0	6.23
Billy Wynne	R	23	6	1	0	0	8.2	12	0	2	4	0-0	0	3.12
Nick Willhite†	L	26	4	1	0	0	8.1	9	1	5	9	0-1	0	8.64
Jerry Hinsley	R	23	2	0	0	0	5.0	6	0	4	3	0-0	0	3.60
Ralph Terry	R	31	2	0	0	0	3.1	1	0	0	5	0-0	0	0.00
Al Schmelz	R	23	2	0	0	0	3.0	4	1	1	2	0-0	0	3.00

»1968 Detroit Tigers 1st AL 103-59 .636 —

Mayo Smith

Player	Gm by Position	B	Age	G	AB	R	H	2B	3B	HR	RBI	BB	SO	SB	Avg	OBP	Slg
Bill Freehan	C138,1B21,OF1	R	26	155	540	73	142	24	2	25	84	65	64	0	.263	.366	.454
Norm Cash	1B117	L	33	127	411	50	108	15	1	25	63	39	70	1	.263	.329	.487
Dick McAuliffe	2B148,SS5	L	28	151	570	95	142	24	10	16	56	82	99	8	.249	.344	.411
Don Wert	3B150,SS2	R	29	150	536	44	107	15	1	12	37	37	79	0	.200	.258	.299
Ray Oyler	SS111	R	29	111	215	13	29	6	1	1	12	20	59	0	.135	.213	.186
Jim Northrup	OF151	L	28	154	580	76	153	29	7	21	90	50	87	4	.264	.324	.447
Willie Horton	OF139	R	25	143	512	68	146	20	2	36	85	49	110	0	.285	.352	.543
Mickey Stanley	OF130,1B15,SS9*	R	25	153	583	88	151	16	6	11	60	42	57	4	.259	.311	.364
Al Kaline	OF74,1B22	R	33	102	327	49	94	14	1	10	53	55	39	6	.287	.392	.428
Tommy Matchick	SS59,2B13,1B6	L	24	80	227	18	46	6	2	3	14	10	46	0	.203	.248	.286
Dick Tracewski	SS51,3B16,2B14	R	33	90	212	30	33	3	1	4	15	24	51	3	.156	.239	.236
Jim Price	C42	R	26	64	132	12	23	4	0	3	13	13	14	0	.174	.253	.273
Gates Brown	OF17,1B1	L	29	67	92	15	34	7	2	6	15	12	4	0	.370	.442	.685
Eddie Mathews	1B6,3B6	L	36	31	52	4	11	0	0	3	8	5	12	0	.212	.281	.385
Wayne Comer	OF27,C1	R	24	48	48	8	6	0	1	1	3	2	7	0	.125	.160	.229
Dave Campbell	2B5	R	26	9	8	1	1	0	0	1	2	1	3	0	.125	.222	.500
Lenny Green	OF2	L	35	6	4	0	1	0	0	0	0	1	0	0	.250	.400	.250
Bob Christian	1B1,OF1	R	22	3	3	0	1	1	0	0	0	0	0	0	.333	.333	.667

M. Stanley, 1 G at 2B

Pitcher	T	Age	G	GS	CG	ShO	IP	H	HR	BB	SO	W-L	Sv	ERA
Denny McLain	R	24	41	41	28	6	336.0	241	31	63	280	31-6	0	1.96
Earl Wilson	R	33	34	33	10	3	224.1	192	20	65	168	13-12	0	2.85
Mickey Lolich	L	27	39	32	8	4	220.0	178	23	65	197	17-9	1	3.19
Joe Sparma	R	26	34	31	7	1	182.1	169	14	77	110	10-10	0	3.70
Les Cain	L	20	8	4	0	0	24.0	25	1	20	13	1-0	0	3.00
Pat Dobson	R	26	47	10	2	1	125.0	89	13	48	93	5-8	7	2.66
John Hiller	L	25	39	12	4	1	128.0	92	9	51	78	9-6	2	2.39
Daryl Patterson	R	24	38	1	0	0	68.0	53	3	27	49	2-3	7	2.12
Fred Lasher	R	26	34	0	0	0	48.2	37	5	22	32	5-1	5	3.33
John Warden	L	21	28	0	0	0	37.1	30	5	15	25	4-1	3	3.62
John Wyatt†	R	33	22	0	0	0	30.1	26	2	11	25	1-0	2	2.37
Don McMahon†	R	38	20	0	0	0	35.2	22	2	10	33	3-1	1	2.02
Dennis Ribant†	R	26	14	0	0	0	24.1	20	1	10	7	2-2	1	2.22
Jim Rooker	L	25	2	0	0	0	4.2	4	0	1	4	0-0	0	3.86
Roy Face†	R	40	2	0	0	0	1.0	2	0	1	1	0-0	0	0.00

1968 Baltimore Orioles 2nd AL 91-71 .562 12.0 GB

Hank Bauer (43-37)/Earl Weaver (48-34)

Player	Gm by Position	B	Age	G	AB	R	H	2B	3B	HR	RBI	BB	SO	SB	Avg	OBP	Slg
Andy Etchebarren	C70	R	25	74	189	20	44	11	2	5	20	19	46	0	.233	.311	.392
Boog Powell	1B149	L	26	154	550	60	137	21	1	22	85	73	97	7	.249	.338	.411
Dave Johnson	2B127,SS34	R	25	145	504	50	122	24	4	9	56	44	80	7	.242	.308	.359
Brooks Robinson	3B162	R	31	162	608	65	154	36	6	17	75	44	55	1	.253	.304	.416
Mark Belanger	SS145	R	24	145	472	40	98	13	0	2	21	40	114	10	.208	.272	.248
Paul Blair	OF132,3B1	R	24	141	421	48	89	22	1	7	38	37	60	4	.211	.277	.318
Frank Robinson	OF117,1B3	R	32	130	421	69	113	27	1	15	52	73	84	11	.268	.390	.444
Curt Blefary	OF92,C40,1B12	L	24	137	451	50	90	8	1	15	39	65	66	6	.200	.301	.322
Don Buford	OF65,2B58,3B2	S	31	130	426	65	120	13	4	15	46	57	46	27	.282	.367	.437
Curt Motton	OF54	R	27	83	217	27	43	7	0	8	25	31	43	1	.198	.298	.341
Ellie Hendricks	C53	L	27	79	183	19	37	8	1	7	23	19	51	0	.202	.279	.372
Dave May	OF61	L	24	84	152	15	29	6	3	0	7	19	27	3	.191	.285	.270
Fred Valentine†	OF26	S	33	47	91	9	17	3	2	2	5	7	20	0	.187	.253	.330
Larry Haney	C32	R	25	38	89	5	21	3	1	1	5	0	19	0	.236	.236	.326
Merv Rettenmund	OF23	R	25	31	64	10	19	5	0	2	7	18	20	1	.297	.452	.469
Chico Fernandez	SS7,2B4	R	29	24	18	0	2	0	0	0	0	1	2	0	.111	.158	.111
Mike Fiore	1B5,OF1	L	23	6	17	2	1	0	0	0	0	4	4	0	.059	.273	.059
Bobby Floyd	SS4	R	24	5	9	0	1	1	0	0	0	0	3	0	.111	.100	.222

Pitcher	T	Age	G	GS	CG	ShO	IP	H	HR	BB	SO	W-L	Sv	ERA
Tom Phoebus	R	26	36	36	9	3	240.2	186	10	105	193	15-15	0	2.62
Dave McNally	L	25	35	35	18	5	273.0	175	24	55	202	22-10	0	1.95
Jim Hardin	R	24	35	35	16	2	244.0	188	20	70	160	18-13	0	2.51
Dave Leonhard	R	27	28	18	5	2	126.1	95	10	57	61	7-7	1	3.13
Wally Bunker	R	23	18	10	2	1	71.0	59	4	14	44	2-0	0	2.41
Bruce Howard†	R	25	10	5	0	0	31.0	30	2	26	19	0-2	0	3.77
Mike Adamson	R	20	2	2	0	0	7.2	9	2	4	4	0-2	0	9.39
Eddie Watt	R	27	59	0	0	0	83.1	63	1	35	72	5-5	11	2.27
Moe Drabowsky	R	32	45	0	0	0	61.1	35	3	25	46	4-4	7	1.91
Gene Brabender	R	26	37	15	3	2	125.0	116	9	48	92	6-7	3	3.31
Pete Richert	L	28	36	0	0	0	62.1	51	7	12	47	6-3	6	3.47
Roger Nelson	R	24	19	6	0	0	71.0	49	3	26	70	4-3	1	2.41
John Morris	L	26	19	0	0	0	31.2	19	4	17	22	2-0	0	2.56
John O'Donoghue	L	28	16	0	0	0	22.0	34	2	7	11	0-0	2	6.14
Fred Beene	R	25	1	0	0	0	1.0	2	0	1	1	0-0	0	9.00

1968 Cleveland Indians 3rd AL 86-75 .534 16.5 GB

Alvin Dark

Player	Gm by Position	B	Age	G	AB	R	H	2B	3B	HR	RBI	BB	SO	SB	Avg	OBP	Slg
Joe Azcue	C97	R	28	115	357	23	100	10	0	4	42	28	33	1	.280	.331	.342
Tony Horton	1B128	R	23	133	477	57	119	29	3	14	59	34	56	3	.249	.302	.411
Vern Fuller	2B73,3B23,SS4	R	24	97	244	14	59	8	2	0	18	24	49	2	.242	.316	.291
Max Alvis	3B128	R	30	131	452	38	101	17	3	8	37	41	91	5	.223	.292	.327
Larry Brown	SS154	R	28	154	495	43	116	18	3	6	35	43	46	1	.234	.300	.319
Jose Cardenal	OF153	R	24	157	583	78	150	21	7	7	44	39	74	40	.257	.305	.353
Tommy Harper	OF115,2B2	R	27	130	235	26	51	15	2	6	26	26	56	11	.217	.295	.374
Lee Maye	OF80,1B1	L	33	109	299	20	84	13	2	4	26	15	24	0	.281	.316	.378
Duke Sims	C84,1B31,OF4	L	27	122	361	48	90	21	0	11	44	62	68	1	.249	.366	.399
Chico Salmon	2B45,3B18,SS15*	R	27	103	276	24	59	8	1	3	12	12	30	7	.214	.253	.283
Russ Snyder†	OF54,1B1	L	34	68	217	30	61	8	2	2	23	25	21	1	.281	.354	.364
Lou Johnson†	OF57	R	33	65	202	25	52	11	1	5	23	9	24	6	.257	.298	.396
Dave Nelson	2B59,SS14	R	24	88	189	26	44	4	5	0	19	17	35	23	.233	.295	.307
Vic Davalillo†	OF49	L	31	51	180	15	43	2	3	2	13	3	19	8	.239	.254	.317
Jimmie Hall†	OF29	L	30	53	111	4	22	4	0	1	8	10	19	1	.198	.264	.261
Billy Harris	2B27,3B10,SS1	L	24	38	94	10	20	5	1	0	3	8	22	2	.213	.275	.287
Richie Scheinblum	OF16	S	25	19	55	3	12	5	0	0	5	5	8	0	.218	.281	.309
Jose Vidal	OF26,1B1	R	28	37	54	5	9	0	0	2	5	2	15	3	.167	.196	.278
Leon Wagner†	OF10	L	34	38	49	5	9	4	0	0	6	6	6	0	.184	.273	.265
Willie Smith†	1B7,P2,OF1	L	29	33	42	1	6	2	0	0	3	3	14	0	.143	.213	.190
Mike Paul	P36,1B1	L	23	36	24	2	4	0	0	0	0	1	13	0	.167	.200	.167
Lou Klimchock	3B4,1B1,2B1	L	28	11	15	0	2	0	0	0	3	1	0	0	.133	.176	.133
Ken Suarez	C12,2B1,3B1*	R	25	17	10	1	1	0	0	0	0	1	3	0	.100	.182	.100
Lou Piniella	OF2	R	24	6	5	1	0	0	0	0	1	0	0	0	.000	.000	.000
Russ Nagelson		L	23	5	3	0	1	0	0	0	0	2	2	0	.333	.600	.333
Eddie Leon	SS6	R	21	6	1	0	0	0	0	0	0	0	1	0	.000	.000	.000
Ray Fosse	C1	R	21	1	0	0	0	0	0	0	0	0	0	0	—	—	—

C. Salmon, 13 G at OF, 11 G at 1B; K. Suarez, 1 G at OF

Pitcher	T	Age	G	GS	CG	ShO	IP	H	HR	BB	SO	W-L	Sv	ERA
Sam McDowell	L	25	38	37	11	3	269.0	181	13	110	283	15-14	0	1.81
Luis Tiant	R	27	34	32	19	9	258.1	152	16	73	264	21-9	0	1.60
Sonny Siebert	R	31	31	30	8	4	206.0	145	12	88	146	12-10	0	2.97
Steve Hargan	R	25	32	27	4	2	158.1	139	11	81	78	8-15	0	4.15
Stan Williams	R	31	44	24	6	2	194.1	163	14	51	147	13-11	9	2.50
Steve Bailey	R	26	2	1	0	0	5.0	4	1	2	1	0-1	0	3.60
Eddie Fisher	R	31	54	0	0	0	94.2	87	8	17	42	4-2	4	2.85
Vicente Romo†	R	25	40	1	0	0	83.1	43	5	32	54	5-3	12	1.62
Mike Paul	L	23	36	7	0	0	91.2	72	11	35	87	5-8	3	3.93
Hal Kurtz	R	24	28	0	0	0	38.0	37	2	15	16	1-0	1	5.21
Billy Rohr	L	22	17	0	0	0	18.1	18	5	10	5	1-0	1	6.87
Horacio Pina	R	23	12	3	0	0	31.1	24	0	15	24	1-1	2	1.72
Rob Gardner	L	23	5	0	0	0	2.2	5	0	2	6	0-0	0	6.75
Tommy Gramly	R	23	3	0	0	0	3.1	3	0	2	1	0-1	0	2.70
Darrell Sutherland	R	26	3	0	0	0	3.1	6	0	4	2	0-0	0	8.10
Mike Hedlund	R	21	3	0	0	0	1.2	6	0	2	0	0-0	0	10.80
Willie Smith†	L	29	2	0	0	0	5.0	2	0	1	1	0-0	0	0.00

1968 Boston Red Sox 4th AL 86-76 .531 17.0 GB

Dick Williams

Player	Gm by Position	B	Age	G	AB	R	H	2B	3B	HR	RBI	BB	SO	SB	Avg	OBP	Slg
Russ Gibson	C74,1B1	R	29	76	231	15	52	11	1	3	20	8	38	1	.225	.247	.320
George Scott	1B112,3B6	R	24	124	350	23	60	14	0	3	25	26	88	3	.171	.236	.237
Mike Andrews	2B139,SS4,3B1	R	24	147	536	77	145	22	1	7	45	81	57	3	.271	.368	.354
Joe Foy	3B147,OF3	R	25	150	515	65	116	18	2	10	60	84	91	26	.225	.336	.326
Rico Petrocelli	SS117,1B1	R	25	123	406	41	95	17	2	12	46	31	73	0	.234	.292	.374
Reggie Smith	OF155	S	23	155	558	78	148	37	5	15	69	64	77	22	.265	.342	.430
Carl Yastrzemski	OF155,1B3	L	28	157	539	90	162	32	2	23	74	119	90	13	.301	.426	.495
Ken Harrelson	OF132,1B19	R	26	150	535	79	147	17	4	35	109	69	90	2	.275	.356	.518
Dalton Jones	1B56,2B26,3B8	L	24	111	354	38	83	13	0	5	29	17	53	1	.234	.271	.314
Jerry Adair	SS46,2B12,3B7*	R	31	74	208	18	45	1	0	2	12	9	28	0	.216	.252	.250
Elston Howard	C68	R	39	71	203	22	49	4	0	5	18	22	45	1	.241	.317	.335
Jose Tartabull	OF43	L	29	72	139	24	39	6	0	0	6	6	5	2	.281	.306	.324
Russ Nixon	C27	L	33	29	85	1	13	2	0	0	6	7	13	0	.153	.217	.176
Joe Lahoud	OF25	L	21	29	78	5	15	1	0	1	6	16	16	0	.192	.330	.244
Luis Alvarado	SS11	R	19	11	46	3	6	2	0	0	1	1	11	0	.130	.167	.174
Gene Oliver†	C10,OF1	R	33	16	35	2	5	0	0	0	1	4	12	0	.143	.250	.143
Norm Siebern	1B2,OF2	L	34	27	30	0	2	0	0	0	0	0	5	0	.067	.067	.067
Floyd Robinson†	OF11	L	32	24	24	1	3	0	0	0	2	3	4	1	.125	.250	.125
Jerry Moses	C6	R	21	6	18	2	6	0	0	2	4	1	4	0	.333	.368	.667
George Thomas	OF9	R	30	12	10	3	2	0	0	1	1	1	3	1	.200	.273	.500

J. Adair, 1 G at 1B

Pitcher	T	Age	G	GS	CG	ShO	IP	H	HR	BB	SO	W-L	Sv	ERA
Ray Culp	R	26	35	30	11	6	216.1	166	18	82	190	16-6	0	2.91
Dick Ellsworth	L	28	31	28	10	1	196.0	196	16	37	106	16-7	0	3.03
Gary Bell	R	31	35	27	9	3	199.1	177	7	68	103	11-11	1	3.12
Jose Santiago	R	27	18	18	7	2	124.0	96	9	42	86	9-4	0	2.25
Jim Lonborg	R	26	23	17	4	1	113.1	89	11	59	73	6-10	0	4.29
Juan Pizarro†	L	31	19	12	6	0	107.2	97	15	44	84	6-8	2	3.59
Dave Morehead	R	25	11	9	3	1	55.0	52	3	20	28	1-4	0	2.45
Lee Stange	R	31	50	2	1	0	103.0	89	10	25	53	5-5	12	3.93
Sparky Lyle	L	23	49	0	0	0	65.2	67	6	14	52	6-1	11	2.74
Bill Landis	L	25	38	1	0	0	60.0	48	4	30	59	3-3	3	3.15
Gary Waslewski	R	26	34	11	2	0	105.1	108	9	40	59	4-7	2	3.67
Jerry Stephenson	R	24	23	7	2	0	68.2	81	4	42	51	2-8	0	5.64
Bucky Brandon	R	27	8	0	0	0	12.2	19	1	9	10	0-0	0	6.39
John Wyatt†	R	33	8	0	0	0	10.2	9	2	6	11	1-2	0	4.22
Garry Roggenburk	L	28	4	0	0	0	8.1	9	0	3	4	0-0	0	2.16
Fred Wenz	R	26	1	0	0	0	1.0	0	0	2	3	0-0	0	0.00

1968 New York Yankees 5th AL 83-79 .512 20.0 GB

Ralph Houk

Player	Gm by Position	B	Age	G	AB	R	H	2B	3B	HR	RBI	BB	SO	SB	Avg	OBP	Slg
Jake Gibbs	C121	L	29	124	423	31	90	12	3	3	29	27	68	9	.213	.270	.277
Mickey Mantle	1B131	S	36	144	435	57	103	14	1	18	54	106	97	6	.237	.385	.398
Horace Clarke	2B139	S	28	148	579	52	133	6	1	2	26	23	46	20	.230	.258	.254
Bobby Cox	3B132	R	27	135	437	33	100	15	1	7	41	41	85	3	.229	.300	.316
Tom Tresh	SS119,OF27	S	30	152	507	60	99	18	3	11	52	76	97	10	.195	.304	.308
Roy White	OF154	S	24	159	577	89	154	20	7	17	62	73	50	20	.267	.350	.414
Bill Robinson	OF98	R	25	107	342	34	82	16	7	6	40	26	54	7	.240	.294	.380
Andy Kosco	OF95,1B28	R	26	131	466	47	112	19	1	15	59	16	71	2	.240	.268	.382
Joe Pepitone	OF92,1B12	L	27	108	380	41	93	9	3	15	56	37	45	8	.245	.311	.403
Dick Howser	2B29,3B2,SS1	R	32	85	150	24	23	2	1	0	3	35	17	0	.153	.321	.180
Frank Fernandez	C45,OF4	R	25	51	135	15	23	6	1	7	30	35	50	1	.170	.341	.385
Gene Michael	SS43,P1	S	30	61	116	8	23	3	0	1	8	2	23	3	.198	.218	.250
Rocky Colavito†	OF28,P1	R	34	39	91	13	20	2	2	5	13	14	17	0	.220	.330	.451
Mike Ferraro	3B22	R	23	23	87	5	14	0	1	0	1	2	17	0	.161	.180	.184
Charley Smith	3B13	R	30	46	70	2	16	4	1	1	7	5	18	0	.229	.280	.357
Steve Whitaker	OF14	L	25	28	60	3	7	2	0	0	3	8	18	0	.117	.221	.150
Ruben Amaro	SS23,1B22	R	32	47	41	3	5	1	0	0	0	9	6	0	.122	.280	.146
Ellie Rodriguez	C9	R	22	9	24	1	5	0	0	0	1	3	3	0	.208	.296	.208
Tony Solaita	1B1	R	21	1	1	0	0	0	0	0	0	0	1	0	.000	.000	.000

Pitcher	T	Age	G	GS	CG	ShO	IP	H	HR	BB	SO	W-L	Sv	ERA
Mel Stottlemyre	R	26	36	36	19	6	278.2	243	21	65	140	21-12	0	2.45
Stan Bahnsen	R	23	37	34	10	1	267.1	216	14	68	162	17-12	0	2.05
Fritz Peterson	L	26	36	27	6	2	212.1	187	13	29	115	12-11	0	2.63
Steve Barber	L	29	20	19	3	1	128.1	127	7	64	87	6-5	0	3.23
Al Downing	L	27	15	12	1	0	61.1	54	7	20	40	3-3	0	3.52
Bill Monbouquette†	R	31	17	11	2	0	89.1	92	7	13	32	5-7	0	4.43
Dooley Womack	R	28	45	0	0	0	61.2	53	6	29	27	3-7	2	3.21
Joe Verbanic	R	25	40	11	2	1	97.0	104	6	41	40	6-7	4	3.15
Steve Hamilton	L	32	40	0	0	0	50.2	37	0	13	42	2-2	11	2.13
Fred Talbot	R	27	29	11	1	0	99.0	89	6	42	67	1-9	0	3.36
Lindy McDaniel†	R	32	24	0	0	0	51.1	30	5	12	43	4-1	10	1.75
Jim Bouton	R	29	12	3	1	0	44.0	49	5	9	24	1-1	0	3.68
Thad Tillotson	R	27	7	0	0	0	10.1	11	0	7	1	1-0	0	4.35
John Wyatt†	R	33	7	0	0	0	8.1	7	1	9	6	0-2	0	2.16
Gene Michael	R	30	1	0	0	0	3.0	5	0	0	3	0-0	0	0.00
Rocky Colavito	R	34	1	0	0	0	2.2	1	0	2	1	1-0	0	0.00
John Cumberland	L	21	1	0	0	0	2.0	3	1	1	1	0-0	0	9.00

1968 Oakland Athletics 6th AL 82-80 .506 21.0 GB

Bob Kennedy

Player	Gm by Position	B	Age	G	AB	R	H	2B	3B	HR	RBI	BB	SO	SB	Avg	OBP	Slg
Dave Duncan	C79	R	22	82	246	15	47	4	0	7	28	25	68	1	.191	.266	.293
Danny Cater	1B121,OF20,2B1	R	28	147	504	53	146	28	3	6	62	35	43	8	.290	.336	.393
John Donaldson	2B98,3B5,SS1	L	25	127	363	37	80	9	2	2	27	45	44	5	.220	.307	.273
Sal Bando	3B162,OF1	R	24	162	605	67	152	25	5	9	67	51	78	13	.251	.314	.354
Bert Campaneris	SS155,OF3	R	26	159	642	87	177	25	9	4	38	50	69	62	.276	.330	.361
Reggie Jackson	OF151	L	22	154	553	82	138	13	6	29	74	50	171	14	.250	.316	.452
Rick Monday	OF144	L	22	148	482	56	132	24	7	8	49	72	143	14	.274	.371	.402
Mike Hershberger	OF90	R	28	99	246	23	67	9	2	5	32	21	22	8	.272	.327	.386
Dick Green	2B61,C1,3B1	R	27	76	202	19	47	6	0	6	18	21	41	3	.233	.307	.351
Jim Pagliaroni	C63	R	30	66	199	19	49	4	0	6	20	24	42	0	.246	.330	.357
Ray Webster	1B55	L	25	66	196	17	42	11	1	3	23	12	24	3	.214	.258	.327
Joe Rudi	OF56	R	21	68	181	10	32	5	1	1	12	12	32	1	.177	.236	.232
Jim Gosger	OF64	L	25	88	150	7	27	1	1	0	5	17	21	4	.180	.262	.200
Ted Kubiak	2B24,SS12	S	26	48	120	10	30	5	2	0	8	8	18	1	.250	.305	.325
Joe Keough	OF29,1B1	L	22	34	98	7	21	2	1	2	18	8	11	1	.214	.274	.316
Floyd Robinson†	OF18	L	32	53	81	5	20	5	0	1	14	4	10	0	.247	.276	.346
Phil Roof	C32	R	27	34	64	5	12	0	0	0	2	2	15	1	.188	.212	.234
Rene Lachemann	C16	R	23	19	60	3	9	1	0	0	4	1	11	0	.150	.177	.167
Allan Lewis	OF1	S	26	26	4	9	1	0	0	0	0	1	0	8	.250	.400	.250
Tony La Russa		R	23	5	3	0	1	0	0	0	0	0	0	0	.333	.333	.333

Pitcher	T	Age	G	GS	CG	ShO	IP	H	HR	BB	SO	W-L	Sv	ERA
Catfish Hunter	R	22	36	34	11	2	234.0	210	29	69	172	13-13	1	3.35
Chuck Dobson	R	24	35	34	11	3	225.1	197	20	80	168	12-14	0	3.00
Jim Nash	R	23	34	33	12	6	228.2	185	18	55	169	13-13	0	2.28
Blue Moon Odom	R	23	32	31	9	4	231.1	179	9	98	143	16-10	0	2.45
Lew Krausse	R	25	36	25	2	1	185.0	147	16	62	105	10-11	4	3.11
Jack Aker	R	27	54	0	0	0	74.2	72	6	33	44	4-4	11	4.10
Diego Segui	R	30	52	0	0	0	83.0	51	7	32	72	6-5	6	2.39
Ed Sprague	R	22	47	1	0	0	68.2	51	5	34	34	3-4	4	3.28
Paul Lindblad	L	26	47	1	0	0	56.1	51	6	14	42	4-3	2	2.40
Tony Pierce	L	22	17	3	0	0	32.2	39	3	10	16	1-2	1	3.86
Warren Bogle	L	21	16	1	0	0	23.0	26	3	8	26	0-0	0	4.30
Ken Sanders	R	26	7	0	0	0	10.2	8	1	8	6	0-1	0	3.38
Rollie Fingers	R	21	1	0	0	0	1.1	4	1	1	0	0-0	0	27.00
George Lauzerique	R	20	1	0	0	0	1.0	0	0	0	0	0-0	0	0.00

1968 Minnesota Twins 7th AL 79-83 .488 24.0 GB

Cal Ermer

Player	Gm by Position	B	Age	G	AB	R	H	2B	3B	HR	RBI	BB	SO	SB	Avg	OBP	Slg
John Roseboro	C117	L	35	135	380	31	82	12	0	8	39	46	57	2	.216	.300	.311
Rich Reese	1B87,OF15	L	26	126	332	40	86	15	2	4	28	18	36	3	.259	.301	.352
Rod Carew	2B117,SS4	L	22	127	461	46	126	27	2	1	42	26	71	12	.273	.312	.347
Cesar Tovar	OF78,3B75,SS35*	R	27	157	613	89	167	31	6	6	47	34	41	35	.272	.326	.372
Jackie Hernandez	SS79,1B1	R	27	83	199	13	35	3	0	2	17	9	52	5	.176	.218	.221
Ted Uhlaender	OF129	L	27	140	488	52	138	21	5	7	52	28	46	16	.283	.324	.389
Tony Oliva	OF126	L	27	128	470	54	136	24	5	18	68	45	61	10	.289	.357	.477
Bob Allison	OF117,1B17	L	33	145	469	63	116	16	8	22	52	52	98	9	.247	.324	.456
Harmon Killebrew	1B77,3B11	R	32	100	295	40	62	7	2	17	40	70	70	0	.210	.361	.420
Frank Quilici	2B48,3B40,SS6*	R	29	97	229	22	56	11	4	1	22	21	45	0	.245	.305	.341
Ron Clark	3B52,SS43,2B10	R	25	104	227	14	42	5	1	1	13	16	44	3	.185	.245	.229
Rich Rollins	3B56	R	30	93	203	14	49	5	0	6	30	10	34	3	.241	.287	.355
Bruce Look	C41	L	25	59	118	7	29	4	0	0	9	20	24	0	.246	.353	.280
Frank Kostro	OF24,1B5	R	30	63	108	9	26	4	1	0	9	6	20	0	.241	.274	.296
Jim Holt	OF38,1B1	L	24	70	106	9	22	2	1	0	8	4	20	0	.208	.236	.245
Rick Renick	SS40	R	24	42	97	16	21	5	2	3	13	9	42	0	.216	.283	.402
Graig Nettles	OF16,3B5,1B3	L	23	22	76	13	17	2	1	5	8	7	20	0	.224	.298	.474
Jerry Zimmerman	C24	R	33	24	45	3	5	1	0	0	2	3	10	0	.111	.180	.133
Pat Kelly	OF10	L	23	12	35	2	4	2	0	1	2	3	10	0	.114	.205	.257
George Mitterwald	C10	R	23	11	34	1	7	1	0	0	1	3	8	0	.206	.270	.235

C. Tovar, 18 G at 2B, 1 G at P, 1 G at C, 1 G at 1B; F. Quilici, 1 G at 1B

Pitcher	T	Age	G	GS	CG	ShO	IP	H	HR	BB	SO	W-L	Sv	ERA
Dean Chance	R	27	43	39	15	6	292.0	224	15	63	234	16-16	1	2.53
Jim Merritt	L	24	38	34	11	1	238.1	207	21	52	181	12-16	1	3.25
Jim Kaat	L	29	30	29	9	2	208.0	192	16	40	130	14-12	0	2.94
Dave Boswell	R	23	34	28	7	2	190.0	148	19	87	143	10-13	0	3.32
Jim Perry	R	32	32	18	3	2	139.0	113	8	26	69	8-6	1	2.27
Tom Hall	L	20	8	4	0	0	29.2	27	1	12	18	2-1	0	2.43
Buzz Stephen	R	23	2	2	0	0	11.1	11	0	7	4	1-1	0	4.76
Danny Morris	R	22	3	2	0	0	10.2	11	0	4	6	0-1	0	1.69
Cesar Tovar	R	27	1	1	0	0	1.0	0	0	1	1	0-0	0	0.00
Ron Perranoski	L	32	66	0	0	0	87.0	86	5	38	65	8-7	6	3.10
Al Worthington	R	39	54	0	0	0	76.1	67	1	32	57	4-5	18	2.71
Bob Miller	R	29	45	0	0	0	72.1	65	1	24	41	0-3	2	2.74
Jim Roland	L	25	28	4	1	0	61.2	55	3	24	36	4-1	0	3.50
Ron Keller	R	25	7	1	0	0	16.0	18	2	4	11	0-1	0	2.81

1968 California Angels 8th AL 67-95 .414 36.0 GB

Bill Rigney

Player	Gm by Position	B	Age	G	AB	R	H	2B	3B	HR	RBI	BB	SO	SB	Avg	OBP	Slg
Bob Rodgers	C87	S	29	91	258	13	49	6	0	1	14	16	48	2	.190	.244	.225
Don Mincher	1B113	L	30	120	399	35	94	12	1	13	48	43	65	0	.236	.312	.368
Bobby Knoop	2B151	R	29	152	494	48	123	20	4	3	39	35	128	3	.249	.301	.324
Aurelio Rodriguez	3B70,2B2	R	20	76	223	14	54	10	1	1	16	17	36	0	.242	.299	.309
Jim Fregosi	SS159	R	26	159	614	77	150	21	13	9	49	60	101	9	.244	.315	.365
Rick Reichardt	OF148	R	25	151	534	62	136	20	3	21	73	42	118	8	.255	.328	.421
Roger Repoz	OF114	L	27	133	375	30	90	8	1	13	54	38	83	8	.240	.309	.371
Vic Davalillo†	OF86	L	31	93	339	34	101	15	4	1	18	15	34	17	.298	.326	.375
Tom Satriano	C85,2B14,3B11*	L	27	111	297	20	75	9	0	8	35	37	44	0	.253	.337	.364
Chuck Hinton	1B48,OF37,3B13*	R	34	116	267	28	52	10	3	7	23	24	61	3	.195	.259	.333
Paul Schaal	3B58	R	25	60	219	22	46	7	1	2	16	29	25	5	.210	.307	.279
Bubba Morton	OF50,3B1	R	36	81	163	13	44	6	0	1	18	14	18	2	.270	.341	.325
Ed Kirkpatrick	OF45,C4,1B2	L	23	89	161	23	37	4	0	1	15	25	32	1	.230	.332	.273
Jimmie Hall†	OF39	L	30	46	126	15	27	3	0	1	8	16	19	1	.214	.303	.262
Jay Johnstone	OF29	L	22	41	115	11	30	4	1	0	3	7	15	2	.261	.303	.313
Jim Spencer	1B19	L	21	19	68	2	13	1	0	0	5	3	10	0	.191	.233	.206
Chuck Cottier	3B27,2B4	R	32	33	67	2	13	4	1	0	1	2	15	0	.194	.217	.284
Jarvis Tatum	OF11	R	21	17	51	7	9	1	0	0	2	0	9	0	.176	.176	.196
Woodie Held†	2B5,3B5,SS5*	R	36	33	45	4	5	1	0	0	0	5	15	0	.111	.231	.133
Tom Egan	C14	R	22	16	43	2	5	1	0	1	4	2	15	0	.116	.156	.209
Bobby Trevino	OF11	R	24	17	40	1	9	1	0	0	1	2	9	0	.225	.262	.250
Winston Llenas	3B9	R	24	16	39	5	5	1	0	0	1	2	5	0	.128	.190	.154
Orlando McFarlane	C9	R	30	18	31	1	9	0	0	0	2	5	9	0	.290	.389	.290
Wayne Causey†	2B4	L	31	4	11	0	0	0	0	0	0	0	1	0	.000	.000	.000
Tom Burgmeier	P56,OF1	L	24	71	2	7	0	0	0	0	0	1	0	1	.000	.333	.000

T. Satriano, 1 G at 1B; C. Hinton, 9 G at 2B; W. Held, 3 G at OF

Pitcher	T	Age	G	GS	CG	ShO	IP	H	HR	BB	SO	W-L	Sv	ERA
George Brunet	L	33	39	36	8	5	245.1	191	23	68	132	13-17	0	2.86
Jim McGlothlin	R	24	40	32	8	0	208.1	187	19	60	135	10-15	3	3.54
Sammy Ellis	R	27	42	24	3	0	164.0	150	22	56	93	9-10	2	3.95
Rickey Clark	R	22	21	17	0	0	94.1	74	4	54	60	1-11	0	3.53
Tom Murphy	R	22	15	15	3	0	99.1	67	5	28	56	5-6	0	2.17
Bill Harrelson	R	22	10	5	1	0	33.2	28	4	26	22	1-6	0	5.08
Tom Burgmeier	L	24	56	2	0	0	72.2	65	5	24	33	1-4	5	4.33
Marty Pattin	R	25	52	4	0	0	84.0	67	7	37	66	4-4	3	2.79
Clyde Wright	L	27	41	13	2	1	125.2	123	13	44	71	10-6	3	3.94
Minnie Rojas	R	29	38	0	0	0	55.0	55	11	15	33	4-3	6	4.25
Bobby Locke	R	34	29	0	0	0	36.1	51	3	13	21	2-3	2	6.44
Andy Messersmith	R	22	28	5	2	1	81.1	44	3	35	74	4-2	4	2.21
Jack Hamilton	R	29	21	2	1	0	38.0	34	0	15	18	3-1	2	3.32
Dennis Bennett	L	28	16	7	1	0	48.1	46	6	17	36	0-5	1	3.54
Jim Weaver	L	29	14	0	0	0	22.2	22	4	10	8	0-1	0	2.38
Bob Heffner	R	29	7	0	0	0	8.0	6	0	6	3	0-0	0	2.25
Steve Kealey	R	21	6	0	0	0	10.0	10	0	5	4	0-1	0	2.70
Pete Cimino	R	25	4	0	0	0	7.0	7	0	4	2	0-0	0	2.57
Larry Sherry	R	32	3	0	0	0	3.0	7	2	2	2	0-0	0	6.00

1968 Chicago White Sox 8th AL 67-95 .414 36.0 GB

Eddie Stanky (34-45)/Les Moss (0-2)/Al Lopez (6-5)/Les Moss (12-22)/Al Lopez (15-21)

Player	Gm by Position	B	Age	G	AB	R	H	2B	3B	HR	RBI	BB	SO	SB	Avg	OBP	Slg
Duane Josephson	C122	R	26	128	434	35	107	16	6	6	45	18	52	2	.247	.284	.353
Tom McCraw	1B135	L	27	136	477	51	112	16	12	9	44	36	58	20	.235	.293	.375
Sandy Alomar	2B99,3B27,SS9*	S	24	133	363	41	92	8	2	0	12	20	42	21	.253	.292	.287
Pete Ward	3B77,1B31,OF22	L	28	125	399	43	86	15	0	15	50	76	85	4	.216	.354	.366
Luis Aparicio	SS154	R	34	155	622	55	164	24	4	4	36	33	43	17	.264	.302	.334
Ken Berry	OF151	R	27	153	504	49	127	21	2	7	32	25	64	6	.252	.288	.343
Tommy Davis	OF116,1B6	R	29	132	456	30	122	5	3	8	50	16	48	8	.268	.289	.344
Buddy Bradford	OF99	R	23	103	281	32	61	11	0	5	24	23	67	8	.217	.277	.310
Jerry McNertney	C64,1B1	R	31	74	169	18	37	4	1	3	18	18	29	0	.219	.300	.308
Bill Voss	OF55	L	24	61	167	14	26	2	1	2	15	16	34	5	.156	.238	.216
Leon Wagner†	OF46	L	34	69	162	14	46	8	0	1	18	21	31	2	.284	.366	.352
Tim Cullen†	2B71	R	26	72	155	16	31	7	0	2	13	15	23	0	.200	.275	.284
Walt Williams	OF34	R	24	63	133	6	32	6	0	1	8	4	17	0	.241	.271	.308
Dick Kenworthy	3B38	R	27	58	122	2	27	2	0	0	2	5	21	0	.221	.252	.238
Bill Melton	3B33	R	22	34	109	5	29	8	0	2	16	10	32	1	.266	.322	.394
Wayne Causey†	2B41	L	31	59	100	8	18	2	0	0	7	14	7	0	.180	.284	.200
Ron Hansen†	3B29,SS7,2B2	R	30	40	87	7	20	3	0	1	4	11	12	0	.230	.316	.299
Russ Snyder†	OF22	L	34	38	82	2	11	2	0	1	5	4	16	0	.134	.172	.195
Carlos May	OF17	L	20	17	67	4	12	1	0	0	1	3	15	0	.179	.214	.194
Woodie Held†	OF33,3B5,2B1	R	36	40	54	5	9	1	0	0	2	5	14	0	.167	.246	.185
Gail Hopkins	1B7	L	25	29	37	4	8	2	0	0	2	6	3	0	.216	.326	.270
Rich Morales	SS7,2B5	R	24	10	29	2	5	0	0	0	0	2	5	0	.172	.226	.172
Ken Boyer†	3B5,1B1	R	37	10	24	0	3	0	0	0	0	1	6	0	.125	.160	.125
Buddy Booker	C3	L	26	5	5	0	0	0	0	0	0	1	2	0	.000	.167	.000

S. Alomar, 1 G at OF

Pitcher	T	Age	G	GS	CG	ShO	IP	H	HR	BB	SO	W-L	Sv	ERA
Joe Horlen	R	30	35	35	4	1	223.2	197	16	70	102	12-14	0	2.37
Jack Fisher	R	29	35	28	2	0	180.2	176	14	48	80	8-13	0	2.99
Tommy John	L	25	25	25	5	1	177.1	135	10	49	117	10-5	0	1.98
Gary Peters	L	31	31	25	6	1	162.2	146	7	60	110	4-13	1	3.76
Cisco Carlos	R	27	29	21	0	0	122.1	121	13	37	57	4-14	0	3.90
Bob Priddy	R	28	35	18	2	0	114.0	106	14	41	66	3-11	0	3.63
Jerry Nyman	L	25	8	7	1	1	40.1	38	1	16	27	2-1	0	2.01
Wilbur Wood	L	26	88	2	0	0	159.0	127	8	33	74	13-12	16	1.87
Hoyt Wilhelm	R	44	72	0	0	0	93.2	69	4	24	72	4-4	12	1.73
Bob Locker	R	30	70	0	0	0	90.1	78	4	27	62	5-4	10	2.29
Don McMahon†	R	38	25	0	0	0	46.0	31	2	20	32	2-1	0	1.96
Dennis Ribant†	R	26	17	0	0	0	31.1	42	3	17	20	0-2	1	6.03
Danny Lazar	L	24	8	1	0	0	13.1	14	1	4	11	0-1	0	4.05
Fred Rath	R	24	5	0	0	0	11.1	8	0	3	3	0-0	0	1.59
Billy Wynne	R	24	1	0	0	0	2.0	2	0	2	1	0-0	0	4.50

1968 Washington Senators 10th AL 65-96 .404 37.5 GB

Jim Lemon

Player	Gm by Position	B	Age	G	AB	R	H	2B	3B	HR	RBI	BB	SO	SB	Avg	OBP	Slg
Paul Casanova	C92	R	26	96	322	19	63	6	0	4	25	7	52	0	.196	.210	.252
Mike Epstein	1B110	L	25	123	385	40	90	8	2	13	33	48	91	1	.234	.338	.366
Bernie Allen	2B110,3B2	L	29	120	373	31	90	12	4	6	40	28	35	2	.241	.301	.343
Ken McMullen	3B145,SS11	R	26	151	557	66	138	11	2	20	62	63	66	1	.248	.326	.382
Ron Hansen†	SS81,3B5	R	30	86	275	28	51	12	0	8	28	35	49	0	.185	.281	.316
Del Unser	OF156,1B1	L	23	156	635	66	146	13	7	1	30	46	66	11	.230	.282	.277
Frank Howard	OF107,1B55	R	31	158	598	79	164	28	3	44	106	54	141	0	.274	.338	.552
Ed Stroud	OF84	L	28	105	306	41	73	10	10	4	23	20	50	9	.239	.284	.376
Cap Peterson	OF52	R	25	94	226	20	46	8	1	3	18	18	31	2	.204	.262	.288
Ed Brinkman	SS74,2B2,OF1	R	26	77	193	12	36	3	0	0	6	19	31	0	.187	.259	.202
Frank Coggins	2B52	S	24	62	171	15	30	6	1	0	7	9	33	1	.175	.215	.222
Jim French	C53	L	26	59	165	9	32	5	0	1	10	19	19	1	.194	.277	.242
Brant Alyea	OF39	R	27	53	150	18	40	11	1	6	23	10	39	0	.267	.317	.473
Hank Allen	OF25,3B16,2B11	R	27	68	128	16	28	2	2	1	9	7	16	0	.219	.265	.289
Sam Bowens	OF27	R	29	57	115	14	22	4	0	4	7	11	39	0	.191	.262	.330
Tim Cullen†	SS33,2B16,3B3	R	26	47	114	8	31	4	2	1	16	7	12	0	.272	.323	.368
Billy Bryan	C28	L	29	40	108	7	22	3	0	3	8	14	27	0	.204	.301	.315
Fred Valentine†	OF27	S	33	37	101	11	24	2	0	3	7	6	11	1	.238	.291	.347
Gary Holman	1B33,OF10	L	24	75	85	10	25	5	1	0	7	13	15	0	.294	.388	.376
Dick Billings	OF8,3B4	R	25	12	33	3	6	1	0	1	3	5	13	0	.182	.282	.303
Gene Martin	OF2	L	21	9	11	1	4	1	0	1	1	0	1	0	.364	.364	.727

Pitcher	T	Age	G	GS	CG	ShO	IP	H	HR	BB	SO	W-L	Sv	ERA
Joe Coleman	R	21	33	33	12	2	223.0	212	19	51	139	12-16	0	3.27
Camilo Pascual	R	34	31	31	8	4	201.0	181	11	59	111	13-12	0	2.69
Frank Bertaina	L	24	27	23	1	0	127.1	133	15	69	81	7-13	0	4.66
Jim Hannan	R	28	25	22	4	1	140.1	147	4	50	75	10-6	0	3.01
Barry Moore	L	25	32	18	0	0	117.2	116	8	42	56	4-6	3	3.37
Phil Ortega	R	28	31	16	1	1	115.2	115	12	62	57	5-12	0	4.98
Bruce Howard†	R	25	13	7	0	0	48.2	62	7	23	23	1-4	0	5.36
Gerry Schoen	R	21	1	1	0	0	3.2	6	1	1	1	0-1	0	7.36
Dennis Higgins	R	28	59	0	0	0	99.2	81	8	46	66	4-4	13	3.25
Bob Humphreys	R	32	56	0	0	0	92.2	78	13	30	56	5-7	2	3.69
Dick Bosman	R	24	46	10	0	0	139.0	139	9	35	63	2-9	1	3.69
Dave Baldwin	R	30	40	0	0	0	42.0	40	7	12	30	0-2	5	4.07
Darold Knowles	L	26	32	0	0	0	41.1	38	0	12	37	1-1	4	2.18
Bill Haywood	R	31	14	0	0	0	23.0	27	1	12	10	0-0	0	4.70
Steve Jones	L	27	7	0	0	0	10.2	8	3	7	11	1-2	0	5.91
Casey Cox	R	26	4	0	0	0	7.2	7	0	0	4	0-1	0	2.35
Jim Miles	R	24	3	0	0	0	4.1	8	0	2	5	0-0	0	12.46
Bill Denehy	R	22	3	0	0	0	2.0	4	0	4	1	0-0	0	9.00

»1968 St. Louis Cardinals 1st NL 97-65 .599 —

Red Schoendienst

Player	Gm by Position	B	Age	G	AB	R	H	2B	3B	HR	RBI	BB	SO	SB	Avg	OBP	Slg
Tim McCarver	C109	L	26	128	434	35	110	15	6	5	48	26	31	4	.253	.295	.350
Orlando Cepeda	1B154	R	30	157	600	71	149	26	2	16	73	43	96	8	.248	.306	.378
Julian Javier	2B139	R	31	139	519	54	135	25	4	4	52	24	61	10	.260	.291	.347
Mike Shannon	3B156	R	28	156	576	62	153	29	2	15	79	37	114	1	.266	.309	.401
Dal Maxvill	SS151	R	29	151	459	51	116	8	5	1	24	52	71	0	.253	.329	.298
Lou Brock	OF156	L	29	159	660	92	184	46	14	6	51	46	124	62	.279	.328	.418
Curt Flood	OF149	R	30	150	618	71	186	17	4	5	60	33	58	11	.301	.339	.366
Roger Maris	OF84	L	33	100	310	25	79	18	2	5	45	24	38	0	.255	.307	.374
Bobby Tolan	OF67,1B9	L	22	92	278	28	64	12	1	5	17	13	42	9	.230	.272	.335
Johnny Edwards	C54	L	30	85	230	14	55	9	1	3	29	16	20	1	.239	.287	.326
Dick Schofield	SS43,2B23	S	33	69	127	14	28	7	1	1	8	13	31	1	.220	.303	.315
Phil Gagliano	2B17,3B10,OF5	R	26	53	105	13	24	4	2	0	13	7	12	0	.229	.281	.305
Ron Davis†	OF25	R	26	33	79	11	14	4	2	0	5	5	17	1	.177	.221	.278
Dick Simpson†	OF22	R	24	26	56	11	13	0	0	3	8	8	21	0	.232	.323	.393
Ed Spiezio	OF11,3B2	R	26	29	51	1	8	0	0	0	2	5	6	1	.157	.228	.157
Dave Ricketts	C1	S	32	20	22	1	3	0	0	0	1	0	3	0	.136	.136	.136
Joe Hague	OF3,1B2	L	24	7	17	2	4	0	0	1	1	2	2	0	.235	.316	.412
Floyd Wicker		L	24	5	4	2	2	0	0	0	0	0	0	0	.500	.500	.500
Ted Simmons	C2	S	18	2	3	0	1	0	0	0	1	1	1	0	.333	.500	.333

Pitcher	T	Age	G	GS	CG	ShO	IP	H	HR	BB	SO	W-L	Sv	ERA
Bob Gibson	R	32	34	34	28	13	304.2	198	11	62	268	22-9	0	1.12
Nelson Briles	R	24	33	33	13	4	243.2	251	18	55	141	19-11	0	2.81
Steve Carlton	L	23	34	33	10	5	231.2	214	11	61	162	13-11	0	2.99
Ray Washburn	R	30	31	30	8	4	215.0	191	9	47	124	14-8	0	2.26
Larry Jaster	L	24	31	21	3	1	154.1	153	13	38	70	9-13	0	3.50
Ron Willis	R	24	48	0	0	0	63.2	50	4	28	39	2-3	4	3.39
Joe Hoerner	L	31	47	0	0	0	48.2	34	2	12	42	8-2	17	1.48
Wayne Granger	R	24	34	0	0	0	44.0	40	2	12	27	4-2	4	2.25
Dick Hughes	R	30	25	5	0	0	64.0	45	7	21	49	2-2	4	3.52
Mel Nelson	L	32	18	4	1	0	52.2	49	3	9	16	2-1	1	2.91
Hal Gilson†	L	26	13	0	0	0	21.2	27	1	11	19	0-2	2	4.57
Mike Torrez	R	21	5	2	0	0	19.1	20	1	12	6	2-1	0	2.79
Pete Mikkelsen†	R	28	5	0	0	0	16.0	10	0	7	8	0-0	0	1.13

1968 San Francisco Giants 2nd NL 88-74 .543 9.0 GB

Herman Franks

Player	Gm by Position	B	Age	G	AB	R	H	2B	3B	HR	RBI	BB	SO	SB	Avg	OBP	Slg
Dick Dietz	C90	R	26	98	301	21	82	14	2	6	38	34	68	1	.272	.347	.392
Willie McCovey	1B146	L	30	148	523	81	153	16	4	36	105	72	71	4	.293	.378	.545
Ron Hunt	2B147	R	27	148	529	79	132	19	0	2	28	78	41	6	.250	.371	.297
Jim Davenport	3B82,SS17,2B1	R	34	113	272	27	61	1	1	1	17	26	32	0	.224	.292	.246
Hal Lanier	SS150	R	25	151	486	37	100	14	1	0	27	12	57	2	.206	.222	.239
Willie Mays	OF142,1B1	R	37	148	498	84	144	20	5	23	79	67	81	12	.289	.372	.488
Jesus Alou	OF105	R	26	120	419	26	110	15	4	0	39	9	23	1	.263	.278	.317
Bobby Bonds	OF80	R	22	81	307	55	78	10	5	9	35	38	84	16	.254	.336	.407
Jim Ray Hart	3B72,OF65	R	26	136	480	67	124	14	3	23	78	46	74	3	.258	.323	.444
Ty Cline	OF70,1B24	L	29	116	291	37	65	6	3	1	28	11	26	0	.223	.253	.275
Jack Hiatt	C58,1B10	R	25	90	224	14	52	10	2	4	34	41	61	0	.232	.351	.348
Dave Marshall	OF50	L	25	76	174	17	46	5	1	1	16	20	37	2	.264	.338	.322
Frank Johnson	3B36,OF8,SS5*	R	25	67	174	11	33	2	0	1	7	12	23	1	.190	.246	.218
Ollie Brown	OF35	R	24	40	95	7	22	4	0	0	11	3	23	1	.232	.270	.274
Bob Barton	C45	R	26	46	92	4	24	2	0	0	5	7	18	0	.261	.310	.283
Nate Oliver	2B14,SS13,3B1	R	27	36	73	3	13	2	0	0	1	1	13	0	.178	.189	.205
Bob Schroder	2B12,SS4,3B2	L	23	35	44	5	7	1	1	0	2	7	3	0	.159	.283	.227
Don Mason	2B5,SS4,3B2	L	23	10	19	3	3	0	0	0	1	1	4	1	.158	.200	.158
Ken Henderson	OF2	S	22	3	3	1	1	0	0	0	0	2	1	0	.333	.600	.333

F. Johnson, 3 G at 2B

Pitcher	T	Age	G	GS	CG	ShO	IP	H	HR	BB	SO	W-L	Sv	ERA
Juan Marichal	R	30	38	38	30	5	326.0	295	21	46	218	26-9	0	2.43
Gaylord Perry	R	29	39	38	19	3	291.0	240	10	59	173	16-15	1	2.44
Ray Sadecki	L	27	38	36	13	6	254.0	225	14	70	206	12-18	0	2.91
Mike McCormick	L	29	38	28	9	2	198.1	196	17	49	121	12-14	1	3.58
Bobby Bolin	R	29	34	19	6	3	176.2	128	9	46	126	10-5	0	1.99
Frank Linzy	R	27	57	0	0	0	94.2	76	1	27	36	9-8	12	2.09
Joe Gibbon	L	33	29	0	0	0	40.0	33	3	19	22	1-2	1	1.58
Ron Herbel	R	30	28	2	0	0	42.2	55	5	15	18	0-0	0	3.38
Lindy McDaniel†	R	32	12	0	0	0	19.1	30	2	5	9	0-0	0	7.45
Bill Monbouquette†	R	31	7	0	0	0	12.1	11	4	2	5	0-1	1	3.65
Bill Henry†	L	40	7	1	0	0	5.0	4	0	3	0	0-2	0	5.40
Rich Robertson	R	23	3	1	0	0	9.0	9	0	3	8	2-0	0	6.00

1968 Chicago Cubs 3rd NL 84-78 .519 13.0 GB

Leo Durocher

Player	Gm by Position	B	Age	G	AB	R	H	2B	3B	HR	RBI	BB	SO	SB	Avg	OBP	Slg
Randy Hundley	C160	R	26	160	553	41	125	18	4	7	65	39	69	1	.226	.280	.311
Ernie Banks	1B147	R	37	150	552	71	136	27	0	32	83	27	67	2	.246	.287	.469
Glenn Beckert	2B155	R	27	155	643	98	189	28	4	4	37	31	20	8	.294	.326	.369
Ron Santo	3B162	R	28	162	577	86	142	17	3	26	98	96	106	3	.246	.354	.421
Don Kessinger	SS159	S	25	160	655	63	157	14	7	1	32	38	86	9	.240	.283	.287
Billy Williams	OF163	L	30	163	642	91	185	30	8	30	98	48	53	4	.288	.336	.500
Adolfo Phillips	OF141	R	26	143	439	49	106	20	5	13	33	47	90	9	.241	.320	.399
Jim Hickman	OF66	R	31	75	188	22	42	6	3	5	23	18	38	1	.223	.290	.367
Lou Johnson†	OF57	R	33	62	205	14	50	14	3	1	14	6	23	3	.244	.289	.356
Al Spangler	OF48	L	34	88	177	21	48	9	3	2	18	20	24	0	.271	.343	.390
Willie Smith†	OF38,1B4,P1	L	29	55	142	13	39	8	2	5	25	12	33	0	.275	.333	.465
Dick Nen	1B52	L	28	81	94	8	17	1	1	2	16	6	17	0	.181	.225	.277
Jose Arcia	OF17,2B10,SS7*	R	24	59	84	15	16	4	0	1	8	3	24	0	.190	.218	.274
Lee Elia	SS2,2B1,3B1	R	30	15	17	1	3	0	0	0	3	0	6	0	.176	.222	.176
Jimmy McMath	OF3	L	18	6	14	0	2	0	0	0	2	0	6	0	.143	.143	.143
John Boccabella	C4,OF1	R	27	7	14	0	1	0	0	0	1	2	2	0	.071	.176	.071
Gene Oliver†	1B2,C1,OF1	R	33	8	11	1	4	0	0	0	1	3	2	0	.364	.500	.364
John Upham	P2,OF2	L	26	13	10	0	2	0	0	0	0	0	3	0	.200	.200	.200
Randy Bobb	C7	R	20	7	8	0	1	0	0	0	0	1	2	0	.125	.222	.125
Ted Savage†	OF2	R	31	3	8	0	2	0	0	0	0	0	1	0	.250	.250	.250
Vic LaRose	2B2,SS2	R	23	4	2	0	0	0	0	0	0	0	1	0	.000	.333	.000
John Felske	C3	R	26	4	2	0	0	0	0	0	0	0	1	0	.000	.000	.000
Bill Plummer	C1	R	21	2	2	0	0	0	0	0	0	0	1	0	.000	.000	.000
Clarence Jones	1B1	L	26	5	2	0	0	0	0	0	0	2	1	0	.000	.500	.000
John Stephenson		L	27	2	2	0	0	0	0	0	0	0	0	0	.000	.000	.000

J. Arcia, 1 G at 3B

Pitcher	T	Age	G	GS	CG	ShO	IP	H	HR	BB	SO	W-L	Sv	ERA
Fergie Jenkins	R	24	40	40	20	3	308.0	255	26	65	260	20-15	0	2.63
Bill Hands	R	28	38	34	11	4	258.2	221	26	36	148	16-10	0	2.89
Ken Holtzman	L	22	34	32	6	3	215.0	201	17	76	151	11-14	1	3.35
Joe Niekro	R	23	34	29	2	1	177.0	204	18	59	65	14-10	2	4.32
Rich Nye	L	23	27	20	6	1	132.2	145	16	34	74	7-12	1	3.80
Phil Regan†	R	31	68	0	0	0	127.0	109	9	24	60	10-5	25	2.20
Jack Lamabe	R	31	42	0	0	0	61.1	68	7	24	30	3-2	1	4.26
Chuck Hartenstein	R	26	28	0	0	0	35.2	41	3	11	17	2-4	1	4.54
Bill Stoneman	R	24	18	0	0	0	29.1	35	6	14	18	0-1	0	5.52
Gary Ross	R	20	13	5	1	0	41.0	44	1	25	31	1-1	0	4.17
Bobby Tiefenauer	R	38	9	0	0	0	13.1	20	2	2	9	0-1	1	6.08
Darcy Fast	L	21	8	1	0	0	10.0	8	1	8	10	0-1	0	5.40
Ramon Hernandez	L	27	8	0	0	0	9.0	14	1	0	3	0-1	0	9.00
Archie Reynolds	R	22	7	1	0	0	13.1	14	1	7	6	0-1	0	6.75
Frank Reberger	R	24	3	1	0	0	6.0	9	1	2	3	0-1	0	4.50
Pete Mikkelsen†	R	28	3	0	0	0	4.2	7	3	1	5	0-0	0	7.71
John Upham	L	26	2	0	0	0	7.0	2	0	3	2	0-0	0	0.00
Willie Smith†	L	29	1	0	0	0	2.2	0	0	2	0	0-0	0	0.00
Jophrey Brown	R	23	1	0	0	0	2.0	2	0	1	0	0-0	0	4.50

1968 Cincinnati Reds 4th NL 83-79 .512 14.0 GB

Dave Bristol

Player	Gm by Position	B	Age	G	AB	R	H	2B	3B	HR	RBI	BB	SO	SB	Avg	OBP	Slg
Johnny Bench	C154	R	20	154	564	67	155	40	2	15	82	31	96	1	.275	.311	.433
Lee May	1B122,OF33	R	25	146	559	78	162	32	1	22	80	34	100	4	.290	.337	.469
Tommy Helms	2B127,SS2,3B1	R	27	127	507	35	146	28	2	2	47	12	27	5	.288	.305	.363
Tony Perez	3B160	R	26	160	625	93	176	25	7	18	92	51	92	3	.282	.338	.430
Leo Cardenas	SS136	R	29	137	452	45	106	13	2	7	41	36	83	2	.235	.292	.319
Pete Rose	OF148,2B3,1B1	S	27	149	626	94	210	42	6	10	49	56	76	3	.335	.391	.470
Alex Johnson	OF140	R	25	149	603	79	188	32	6	2	58	26	71	16	.312	.342	.395
Vada Pinson	OF123	L	29	130	499	60	135	29	6	5	48	32	59	17	.271	.311	.383
Mack Jones	OF60	L	29	103	234	40	59	9	1	10	34	28	46	2	.252	.341	.427
Fred Whitfield	1B41	L	30	87	171	15	44	8	0	6	32	9	29	0	.257	.302	.409
Chico Ruiz	2B34,1B16,3B5*	S	29	85	139	15	36	2	1	0	9	12	18	4	.259	.316	.288
Woody Woodward†	SS41,2B9,1B1	R	25	56	119	13	29	2	0	0	10	7	23	1	.244	.297	.261
Don Pavletich	1B22,C5	R	29	46	98	11	28	3	1	2	11	8	23	0	.286	.352	.398
Jim Beauchamp	OF13,1B1	R	28	31	57	10	15	2	0	2	14	4	19	0	.263	.306	.404
Pat Corrales	C20	R	27	20	56	3	15	4	0	0	6	6	16	0	.268	.349	.339
Hal McRae	2B16	R	22	17	51	1	10	1	0	0	2	4	14	1	.196	.255	.216
Bob Johnson†	SS2,1B1	R	32	16	15	2	4	0	0	0	1	1	2	0	.267	.313	.267
Jimmie Schaffer	C2	R	32	4	6	0	1	0	0	0	1	0	3	0	.167	.167	.167

C. Ruiz, 3 G at SS

Pitcher	T	Age	G	GS	CG	ShO	IP	H	HR	BB	SO	W-L	Sv	ERA
George Culver	R	24	42	35	5	2	226.1	229	8	84	114	11-16	2	3.22
Jim Maloney	R	28	33	32	8	5	207.0	183	17	80	181	16-10	0	3.61
Gerry Arrigo	L	27	36	31	5	1	205.1	181	13	77	140	12-10	0	3.33
Gary Nolan	R	20	23	22	4	2	150.0	105	10	49	111	9-4	0	2.40
Tony Cloninger†	R	27	17	17	2	2	91.1	81	7	48	65	4-3	0	4.04
Milt Pappas†	R	29	15	11	0	0	62.2	70	9	10	43	2-5	0	5.60
Mel Queen	R	26	5	4	0	0	18.1	25	7	6	20	0-1	0	5.89
John Tsitouris	R	32	3	3	0	0	12.2	16	6	8	6	0-3	0	7.11
Ted Abernathy	R	35	78	0	0	0	134.2	111	9	55	64	10-7	13	2.47
Clay Carroll†	R	27	58	1	0	0	121.1	102	3	32	61	7-7	17	2.29
Bob Lee	R	30	44	1	0	0	65.1	73	4	37	34	2-4	3	5.10
Bill Kelso	R	28	35	0	0	0	54.0	56	6	15	39	4-1	1	4.00
Billy McCool	L	23	30	4	0	0	50.2	59	4	41	30	3-4	2	4.97
Jay Ritchie	R	31	28	2	0	0	56.2	68	7	13	32	2-3	0	4.61
Ted Davidson†	L	28	23	0	0	0	21.2	27	3	7	7	1-0	0	6.23
Dan McGinn	L	24	14	0	0	0	12.0	13	1	11	16	0-1	0	5.25

1968 Atlanta Braves 5th NL 81-81 .500 16.0 GB

Lum Harris

Player	Gm by Position	B	Age	G	AB	R	H	2B	3B	HR	RBI	BB	SO	SB	Avg	OBP	Slg
Joe Torre	C92,1B29	R	27	115	424	45	115	11	2	10	55	34	72	1	.271	.332	.377
Deron Johnson	1B97,3B21	R	29	127	342	29	71	11	1	8	33	35	79	0	.208	.285	.316
Felix Millan	2B145	R	24	149	570	49	165	22	2	1	33	22	26	6	.289	.321	.340
Clete Boyer	3B69	R	31	71	273	19	62	7	2	4	17	16	32	2	.227	.275	.311
Sonny Jackson	SS99	L	23	105	358	37	81	8	2	1	19	25	35	16	.226	.282	.268
Felipe Alou	OF158	R	33	160	662	72	210	37	5	11	57	48	56	12	.317	.365	.438
Hank Aaron	OF151,1B14	R	34	160	606	84	174	33	4	29	86	64	62	28	.287	.354	.498
Mike Lum	OF95	L	22	122	232	22	52	7	3	3	21	14	35	3	.224	.277	.319
Marty Martinez	SS54,3B37,2B16*	S	26	113	356	34	82	5	3	0	12	29	28	6	.230	.291	.261
Tito Francona	OF65,1B33	L	34	122	346	32	99	13	1	2	47	51	45	3	.286	.376	.347
Tommie Aaron	OF62,1B28,3B1	R	28	98	283	21	69	10	3	1	25	21	37	3	.244	.295	.311
Bob Tillman	C75	R	31	86	236	16	52	4	0	5	20	16	55	1	.220	.278	.301
Bob Johnson†	3B48,2B4	R	32	59	187	15	49	5	1	0	11	10	20	0	.262	.298	.299
Sandy Valdespino	OF20	L	29	36	86	8	20	1	0	1	4	10	20	0	.233	.320	.279
Gil Garrido	SS17	R	27	18	53	5	11	0	0	0	2	2	2	0	.208	.228	.208
Wayne Causey†	2B6,3B2,SS2	L	31	16	37	2	4	0	0	1	4	0	4	0	.108	.103	.243
Mike Page	OF6	L	27	20	28	1	5	0	0	0	0	1	9	0	.179	.207	.179
Walt Hriniak	C9	L	25	9	26	0	9	0	0	0	3	0	3	0	.346	.346	.346
Woody Woodward†	SS6,3B2,2B1	R	25	12	24	2	4	1	0	0	1	1	6	1	.167	.200	.208
Ralph Garr		L	22	11	7	3	2	0	0	0	0	1	0	1	.286	.375	.286
Dusty Baker	OF3	R	19	6	5	0	2	0	0	0	0	0	1	0	.400	.400	.400

M. Martinez, 14 G at C

Pitcher	T	Age	G	GS	CG	ShO	IP	H	HR	BB	SO	W-L	Sv	ERA
Phil Niekro	R	29	37	34	15	5	257.0	228	16	45	140	14-12	2	2.59
Pat Jarvis	R	27	34	34	14	1	256.0	202	15	50	157	16-12	0	2.60
Ron Reed	R	25	35	28	6	1	201.2	189	10	49	111	11-10	0	3.35
Milt Pappas†	R	29	22	19	3	1	121.1	111	8	22	75	10-8	0	2.37
Ken Johnson	R	35	31	16	1	0	135.0	145	10	25	57	5-8	0	3.47
George Stone	L	21	17	10	2	0	75.0	63	9	19	52	7-4	0	2.76
Al Santorini	R	20	1	1	0	0	3.0	4	1	0	0	0-1	0	0.00
Cecil Upshaw	R	25	52	0	0	0	116.2	98	6	24	74	8-7	13	2.47
Claude Raymond	R	31	36	0	0	0	60.1	56	4	18	37	3-5	10	2.83
Jim Britton	R	24	34	9	2	2	90.0	81	1	34	61	4-6	3	3.10
Dick Kelley	L	28	31	11	1	1	98.0	86	4	45	73	2-4	1	2.76
Clay Carroll†	R	27	10	0	0	0	22.1	26	1	6	10	0-1	0	4.84
Tony Cloninger†	R	27	8	1	0	0	19.0	15	0	11	7	1-3	0	4.26
Rick Kester	R	21	5	0	0	0	6.1	8	0	3	9	0-0	0	5.68
Ted Davidson†	L	28	4	0	0	0	6.2	10	2	4	3	0-0	0	6.75
Skip Guinn	L	23	3	0	0	0	5.0	3	0	3	4	0-0	0	3.60
Stu Miller	R	40	2	0	0	0	1.1	1	0	4	1	0-0	0	27.00

1968 Pittsburgh Pirates 6th NL 80-82 .494 17.0 GB

Larry Shepard

Player	Gm by Position	B	Age	G	AB	R	H	2B	3B	HR	RBI	BB	SO	SB	Avg	OBP	Slg
Jerry May	C135	R	24	137	416	26	91	15	2	1	33	41	80	0	.219	.293	.272
Donn Clendenon	1B155	R	32	158	584	63	150	20	6	17	87	47	163	10	.257	.309	.399
Bill Mazeroski	2B142	R	31	143	506	36	127	18	2	3	42	38	38	3	.251	.304	.312
Maury Wills	3B141,SS10	S	35	153	627	76	174	12	6	0	31	45	57	52	.278	.326	.316
Gene Alley	SS109,2B24	R	27	133	474	48	116	20	2	4	39	39	78	13	.245	.307	.321
Matty Alou	OF144	L	29	146	558	59	185	28	4	0	52	27	26	18	.332	.362	.396
Roberto Clemente	OF131	R	33	132	502	74	146	18	12	18	57	51	77	2	.291	.355	.482
Willie Stargell	OF113,1B13	L	28	128	435	57	103	15	1	24	67	47	105	5	.237	.315	.441
Manny Mota	OF92,2B1,3B1	R	30	111	331	35	93	10	2	1	33	20	19	4	.281	.320	.332
Freddie Patek	SS52,OF5,3B1	R	23	61	208	31	53	4	2	2	18	12	37	18	.255	.298	.322
Jose Pagan	3B30,OF19,SS8*	R	33	80	163	24	36	7	1	4	21	11	32	2	.221	.278	.350
Gary Kolb	OF25,C10,3B4*	L	28	74	119	16	26	4	1	2	6	11	17	2	.218	.285	.319
Steve Blass	P33,OF1	R	26	35	80	7	11	1	0	0	8	2	30	0	.138	.155	.150
Carl Taylor	C29,OF2	R	24	44	71	5	15	1	0	0	7	10	10	1	.211	.309	.225
Manny Jimenez	OF5	L	29	66	66	7	20	1	1	1	11	6	15	0	.303	.403	.394
Chris Cannizzaro	C25	R	30	25	58	5	14	2	2	1	7	9	13	0	.241	.343	.397
Chuck Hiller	2B2	L	33	11	13	2	5	1	0	0	1	0	0	0	.385	.385	.462
Al Oliver	OF1	L	21	4	8	1	1	0	0	0	0	0	4	0	.125	.125	.125
Bill Virdon	OF4	L	37	6	3	1	1	0	0	1	2	0	2	0	.333	.333	1.333
Richie Hebner		L	20	2	1	0	0	0	0	0	1	0	0	0	.000	.000	.000

J. Pagan, 2 G at 2B, 1 G at 1B; G. Kolb, 1 G at 2B

Pitcher	T	Age	G	GS	CG	ShO	IP	H	HR	BB	SO	W-L	Sv	ERA
Bob Veale	L	32	36	33	13	4	245.1	187	13	94	171	13-14	0	2.05
Steve Blass	R	26	33	31	12	7	220.1	191	13	57	132	18-6	0	2.12
Al McBean	R	30	36	28	9	2	198.1	204	10	63	100	9-12	0	3.58
Jim Bunning	R	36	27	26	3	1	160.0	168	14	48	95	4-14	0	3.88
Bob Moose	R	20	38	22	3	3	171.1	136	5	41	126	8-12	3	2.73
Ron Kline	R	36	56	0	0	0	112.2	94	3	31	48	12-5	7	1.68
Roy Face†	R	40	43	0	0	0	52.0	46	3	7	34	2-4	13	2.60
Luke Walker	L	24	39	2	0	0	61.2	42	1	39	66	0-3	3	2.04
Tommie Sisk	R	26	33	11	0	0	96.0	101	3	35	41	5-5	1	3.28
Dock Ellis	R	23	26	10	2	0	104.0	82	4	38	52	6-5	0	2.51
Juan Pizarro†	L	31	12	0	0	0	11.0	14	2	10	6	1-1	0	3.27
Dave Wickersham	R	32	11	0	0	0	20.2	21	0	13	9	1-0	1	3.48
Bill Henry†	L	40	10	0	0	0	16.2	29	2	3	9	0-0	0	8.10
Bruce Dal Canton	R	26	7	0	0	0	17.0	7	0	6	8	1-1	2	2.12

1968 Los Angeles Dodgers 7th NL 76-86 .469 21.0 GB

Walter Alston

Player	Gm by Position	B	Age	G	AB	R	H	2B	3B	HR	RBI	BB	SO	SB	Avg	OBP	Slg
Tom Haller	C139	L	31	144	474	37	135	27	5	4	53	46	76	1	.285	.345	.388
Wes Parker	1B114,OF28	S	28	135	468	42	112	22	2	3	27	49	87	4	.239	.312	.314
Paul Popovich	2B89,SS45,3B7	S	27	134	418	35	97	8	1	2	25	29	37	1	.232	.280	.270
Bob Bailey	3B90,SS1,OF1	R	25	105	322	24	73	9	3	8	39	38	69	1	.227	.308	.348
Zoilo Versalles	SS119	R	28	122	403	29	79	16	3	2	24	26	84	6	.196	.244	.266
Willie Davis	OF158	L	28	160	643	86	161	24	10	7	31	31	88	36	.250	.284	.351
Ron Fairly	OF105,1B36	L	29	141	441	32	103	15	1	4	43	41	61	0	.234	.301	.299
Len Gabrielson	OF86	L	28	108	304	38	82	16	1	10	35	32	47	1	.270	.337	.428
Jim Lefebvre	2B62,3B16,OF5*	S	26	84	286	23	69	12	1	5	31	26	55	0	.241	.304	.343
Ken Boyer†	3B34,1B32	R	37	83	221	20	60	7	2	6	41	16	34	2	.271	.317	.403
Willie Crawford	OF48	L	21	61	175	25	44	12	1	4	14	20	64	1	.251	.335	.400
Jim Fairey	OF63	L	23	99	156	17	31	3	3	1	10	9	32	1	.199	.241	.276
Ted Savage†	OF39	R	31	61	126	7	26	6	1	2	7	10	20	1	.206	.270	.317
Rocky Colavito†	OF33	R	34	40	113	8	23	3	0	3	11	15	18	0	.204	.295	.310
Luis Alcaraz	2B20,3B13,SS1	R	27	41	106	4	16	1	0	2	5	9	23	1	.151	.217	.217
Jeff Torborg	C37	R	26	37	93	2	15	2	0	0	4	6	10	0	.161	.212	.183
Bill Sudakis	3B24	S	22	24	87	11	24	4	2	3	12	15	14	1	.276	.382	.471
Bart Shirley	SS21,2B18	R	28	39	83	6	15	3	0	0	4	10	13	0	.181	.269	.217
Jim Campanis	C4	R	24	4	11	0	1	0	0	0	0	1	2	0	.091	.167	.091
Cleo James	OF2	R	27	10	10	2	2	1	0	0	0	0	6	0	.200	.200	.300
Al Ferrara	OF2	R	28	2	7	0	1	0	0	0	0	0	2	0	.143	.143	.143

J. Lefebvre, 3 G at 1B

Pitcher	T	Age	G	GS	CG	ShO	IP	H	HR	BB	SO	W-L	Sv	ERA
Bill Singer	R	24	37	36	12	6	256.1	227	14	78	227	13-17	0	2.88
Claude Osteen	L	28	39	36	5	3	253.2	267	14	54	119	12-18	0	3.09
Don Drysdale	R	31	31	31	12	8	239.0	201	11	56	155	14-12	0	2.15
Don Sutton	R	23	35	27	7	2	207.2	179	6	59	162	11-15	1	2.60
Mike Kekich	L	23	25	20	1	1	115.0	116	9	46	84	2-10	0	3.91
Joe Moeller	R	25	3	3	0	0	16.0	17	1	2	11	1-1	0	5.06
Alan Foster	R	21	3	3	0	0	15.2	11	1	2	10	1-1	0	1.72
Jim Brewer	L	30	54	0	0	0	76.1	59	5	33	75	8-3	14	2.48
Jack Billingham	R	25	50	1	0	0	70.2	54	0	30	46	3-0	8	2.17
Mudcat Grant	R	32	37	4	1	0	94.2	77	1	19	35	6-4	3	2.09
John Purdin	R	25	35	1	0	0	55.2	42	2	21	38	2-3	2	3.07
Hank Aguirre	L	37	25	0	0	0	39.1	32	0	13	25	1-2	3	0.69
Phil Regan†	R	31	5	0	0	0	7.2	10	1	1	7	2-0	0	3.52
Vicente Romo†	R	25	1	0	0	0	1.0	1	0	0	0	0-0	0	0.00

1968 Philadelphia Phillies 7th NL 76-86 .469 21.0 GB

Gene Mauch (27-27)/George Myatt (1-0)/Bob Skinner (48-59)

Player	Gm by Position	B	Age	G	AB	R	H	2B	3B	HR	RBI	BB	SO	SB	Avg	OBP	Slg
Mike Ryan	C96	R	26	96	296	12	53	6	1	1	15	15	59	0	.179	.218	.216
Bill White	1B111	L	34	127	385	34	92	16	2	9	40	39	79	0	.239	.309	.361
Cookie Rojas	2B150,C1	R	29	152	621	53	144	19	0	9	48	16	55	4	.232	.248	.306
Tony Taylor	3B138,2B5,1B1	R	32	145	547	59	137	20	2	3	38	39	60	22	.250	.302	.311
Roberto Pena	SS133	R	31	138	500	56	130	13	2	1	38	34	63	3	.260	.307	.300
Dick Allen	OF139,3B10	R	26	152	521	87	137	17	9	33	90	74	161	7	.263	.352	.520
Tony Gonzalez	OF117	L	31	121	416	45	110	13	4	3	38	40	42	6	.264	.335	.337
Johnny Callison	OF109	L	29	121	398	46	97	18	4	14	40	42	70	4	.244	.319	.415
John Briggs	OF65,1B36	L	24	110	338	36	86	13	1	7	31	58	72	8	.254	.364	.361
Don Lock	OF78	R	31	99	248	27	52	7	2	8	34	26	64	3	.210	.283	.351
Clay Dalrymple	C80	L	31	85	241	19	50	9	1	3	26	22	57	1	.207	.272	.290
Rick Joseph	1B30,3B14,OF1	R	28	66	155	20	34	5	0	3	12	16	35	0	.219	.295	.310
Gary Sutherland	2B17,3B10,SS10*	R	23	67	138	16	38	7	0	0	15	8	15	0	.275	.313	.326
Bobby Wine	SS25,3B1	R	29	27	71	5	12	3	0	2	7	6	17	0	.169	.234	.296
Doug Clemens	OF17	L	29	29	57	6	12	1	1	2	8	7	13	0	.211	.292	.368
John Sullivan	C8	L	27	12	18	0	4	0	0	0	1	2	4	0	.222	.300	.222
Don Money	SS4	R	21	4	13	1	3	2	0	0	2	2	4	0	.231	.333	.385
Larry Hisle	OF6	R	21	7	11	1	4	1	0	0	1	1	4	0	.364	.417	.455
Howie Bedell		L	32	9	7	0	1	0	0	0	1	1	0	0	.143	.222	.143

G. Sutherland, 7 G at OF

Pitcher	T	Age	G	GS	CG	ShO	IP	H	HR	BB	SO	W-L	Sv	ERA
Chris Short	L	30	42	36	9	2	269.2	236	25	81	202	19-13	1	2.94
Larry Jackson	R	37	34	34	12	2	243.2	229	9	60	127	13-17	0	2.77
Woodie Fryman	L	28	34	32	10	5	213.2	198	12	64	151	12-14	0	2.78
Rick Wise	R	22	30	30	7	1	182.0	210	12	37	97	9-15	0	4.55
Jerry Johnson	R	24	16	11	2	0	80.2	82	5	29	40	4-4	0	3.24
Turk Farrell	R	34	54	0	0	0	83.0	83	7	32	57	4-6	12	3.47
Gary Wagner	R	28	44	0	0	0	78.0	69	0	31	43	4-4	8	3.00
John Boozer	R	29	38	0	0	0	68.2	76	3	15	49	2-2	5	3.67
Grant Jackson	L	25	33	6	1	0	61.0	59	4	20	49	1-6	1	2.95
Dick Hall	R	37	32	0	0	0	46.0	53	6	5	31	4-1	0	4.89
Jeff James	R	26	29	13	1	1	116.0	112	8	46	83	4-4	0	4.27
Paul Brown	R	27	2	0	0	0	4.0	6	0	1	4	0-0	0	9.00
Larry Colton	R	26	1	0	0	0	2.0	3	0	0	2	0-0	0	4.50

1968 New York Mets 9th NL 73-89 .451 24.0 GB

Gil Hodges

Player	Gm by Position	B	Age	G	AB	R	H	2B	3B	HR	RBI	BB	SO	SB	Avg	OBP	Slg
Jerry Grote	C115	R	25	124	404	29	114	18	0	3	31	44	81	1	.282	.357	.349
Ed Kranepool	1B113,OF2	L	23	127	373	29	86	13	1	3	20	19	39	0	.231	.271	.295
Phil Linz	2B71	R	29	78	258	19	54	7	0	0	17	10	41	1	.209	.243	.236
Ed Charles	3B106,1B2	R	35	117	369	41	102	11	1	15	53	28	57	5	.276	.328	.434
Bud Harrelson	SS106	S	24	111	402	38	88	7	3	0	14	29	68	4	.219	.273	.251
Cleon Jones	OF139	R	25	147	509	63	151	29	4	14	55	31	98	23	.297	.341	.452
Tommie Agee	OF127	R	25	132	368	30	80	12	3	5	17	15	103	13	.217	.255	.307
Ron Swoboda	OF125	R	24	132	450	46	109	14	6	11	59	52	113	8	.242	.325	.373
Art Shamsky	OF82,1B17	L	26	116	345	30	82	14	4	12	48	21	58	1	.238	.292	.406
Ken Boswell	2B69	L	22	75	284	37	74	7	2	4	11	16	27	7	.261	.300	.342
Al Weis	SS59,2B29,3B2	S	30	90	274	15	47	6	0	1	14	21	63	3	.172	.234	.204
J.C. Martin	C53,1B14	L	31	78	244	20	55	9	2	3	31	21	31	0	.225	.298	.316
Jerry Buchek	3B37,2B12,OF9	R	26	73	192	8	35	4	0	1	11	10	53	1	.182	.234	.219
Larry Stahl	OF47,1B9	L	27	53	183	15	43	7	2	3	10	21	38	3	.235	.314	.344
Kevin Collins	3B40,2B6,SS1	L	21	58	154	12	31	5	2	1	13	7	37	0	.201	.233	.279
Don Bosch	OF33	S	25	50	111	14	19	1	0	3	7	9	33	0	.171	.231	.261
Greg Goossen	1B31,C1	R	22	38	106	4	22	7	0	0	6	10	21	0	.208	.288	.274
Bob Heise	SS6,2B1	R	21	6	23	3	5	0	0	0	1	1	1	0	.217	.250	.217
Mike Jorgensen	1B4	L	19	8	14	0	2	1	0	0	0	0	4	0	.143	.143	.214
Duffy Dyer	C1	R	22	1	3	0	1	0	0	0	0	1	1	0	.333	.500	.333

Pitcher	T	Age	G	GS	CG	ShO	IP	H	HR	BB	SO	W-L	Sv	ERA
Tom Seaver	R	23	36	35	14	5	277.2	224	15	48	205	16-12	1	2.20
Jerry Koosman	L	25	35	34	17	7	263.2	221	16	69	178	19-12	0	2.08
Don Cardwell	R	32	29	25	5	1	179.2	156	9	50	82	7-13	1	2.96
Dick Selma	R	24	33	23	4	3	169.2	148	11	54	117	9-10	0	2.76
Nolan Ryan	R	21	21	18	3	0	134.0	93	12	75	133	6-9	0	3.09
Jim McAndrew	R	24	12	12	2	1	79.0	66	5	17	46	4-7	0	2.28
Les Rohr	L	22	2	1	0	0	6.0	9	0	7	5	0-2	0	4.50
Ron Taylor	R	30	58	0	0	0	76.2	64	4	18	49	1-5	13	2.70
Cal Koonce	R	27	55	2	0	0	97.0	80	4	32	50	6-4	11	2.41
Bill Short	L	30	34	0	0	0	30.1	24	0	14	24	0-3	1	4.75
Al Jackson	L	32	25	9	0	0	92.2	88	5	17	59	3-7	3	3.69
Danny Frisella	R	22	19	4	0	0	50.2	53	5	17	47	2-4	2	3.91
Billy Connors	R	26	9	0	0	0	14.0	21	0	7	8	0-1	0	9.00
Don Shaw	L	24	7	0	0	0	12.1	3	1	5	11	0-0	0	0.73

1968 Houston Astros 10th NL 72-90 .444 25.0 GB

Grady Hatton (23-38)/Harry Walker (49-52)

Player	Gm by Position	B	Age	G	AB	R	H	2B	3B	HR	RBI	BB	SO	SB	Avg	OBP	Slg
John Bateman	C108	R	27	111	350	28	87	19	0	4	33	23	46	1	.249	.297	.337
Rusty Staub	1B147,OF15	L	24	161	591	54	172	37	1	6	72	73	57	2	.291	.373	.387
Denis Menke	2B119,SS35,1B5*	R	27	150	542	56	135	23	6	6	56	64	81	5	.249	.334	.347
Doug Rader	3B86,1B5	R	23	98	333	42	89	16	4	6	43	31	51	2	.267	.328	.393
Hector Torres	SS127,2B1	R	22	128	466	44	104	11	1	1	24	18	64	2	.223	.252	.258
Jimmy Wynn	OF153	R	26	156	542	85	146	23	5	26	67	90	131	11	.269	.376	.474
Norm Miller	OF74	L	22	79	257	35	61	18	2	6	28	22	48	6	.237	.304	.393
Ron Davis†	OF52	R	26	52	217	22	46	10	1	1	12	13	48	0	.212	.268	.281
Bob Aspromonte	3B75,OF36,1B1*	R	30	124	409	25	92	9	2	1	46	35	57	1	.225	.285	.264
Lee Thomas	OF48,1B2	L	32	90	201	14	39	4	0	1	11	14	22	1	.194	.249	.229
Dick Simpson†	OF49	R	24	59	177	25	33	7	2	3	11	20	61	4	.186	.282	.299
Julio Gotay	2B48,3B1	R	29	75	165	9	41	3	0	1	11	4	4	1	.248	.271	.285
Bob Watson	OF40	R	22	45	140	13	32	7	0	2	8	13	32	1	.229	.297	.321
Dave Adlesh	C36	R	24	40	104	3	19	1	1	0	4	5	27	0	.183	.227	.212
Jose Herrera	OF17,2B7	R	26	27	100	9	24	5	0	0	7	4	12	0	.240	.269	.290
Ron Brand	C29,3B1,OF1	R	28	43	81	7	13	2	0	0	4	9	11	1	.160	.261	.185
Ivan Murrell	OF15	R	23	32	59	3	6	1	1	0	3	1	17	0	.102	.117	.153
Hal King	C19	L	24	27	55	4	8	2	1	0	2	7	16	0	.145	.242	.218
Nate Colbert	OF11,1B5	R	22	20	53	5	8	1	0	0	4	1	23	1	.151	.164	.170
Leon McFadden	SS16	R	24	16	47	2	13	1	0	0	1	6	10	1	.277	.358	.298
Joe Morgan	2B5,OF1	L	24	10	20	6	5	0	1	0	0	7	4	3	.250	.444	.350
Byron Browne	OF2	R	25	10	13	0	3	0	0	0	1	4	6	0	.231	.412	.231
John Mayberry	1B2	L	19	4	9	0	0	0	0	0	0	0	2	0	.000	.100	.000
Danny Walton		R	20	2	2	0	0	0	0	0	0	0	1	0	.000	.000	.000

D. Menke, 4 G at 3B; B. Aspromonte, 1 G at SS

Pitcher	T	Age	G	GS	CG	ShO	IP	H	HR	BB	SO	W-L	Sv	ERA
Dave Giusti	R	28	37	34	12	2	251.0	226	15	67	186	11-14	1	3.19
Larry Dierker	R	21	32	32	10	1	233.2	206	14	89	161	12-15	0	3.31
Denny Lemaster	L	29	33	32	7	2	224.0	231	11	72	146	10-15	0	2.81
Don Wilson	R	23	33	30	9	3	208.2	187	9	70	175	13-16	0	3.28
Mike Cuellar	L	31	28	24	11	2	170.2	152	8	45	133	8-11	1	2.74
Tom Dukes	R	25	43	0	0	0	52.2	62	3	28	37	2-2	4	4.27
Jim Ray	R	23	41	2	1	0	80.2	65	5	25	71	2-3	1	2.68
Danny Coombs	L	26	40	2	0	0	46.2	52	0	17	29	4-3	2	3.28
John Buzhardt	R	31	39	4	0	0	83.2	73	0	35	37	4-4	5	3.12
Steve Shea	R	25	30	0	0	0	34.2	27	0	11	15	4-4	6	3.38
Wade Blasingame	L	24	22	2	0	0	36.0	45	3	10	22	1-2	1	4.75
Pat House	L	27	18	0	0	0	16.1	21	0	6	6	1-1	0	7.71
Fred Gladding	R	32	7	0	0	0	4.1	8	0	3	2	0-0	2	14.54
Hal Gilson†	L	26	2	0	0	0	3.2	7	0	1	1	0-0	0	7.36

Seasons: Team Rosters

789

»1969 Baltimore Orioles 1st AL East 109-53 .673 —

Earl Weaver

Player	Gm by Position	B	Age	G	AB	R	H	2B	3B	HR	RBI	BB	SO	SB	Avg	OBP	Slg
Ellie Hendricks	C87,1B4	L	28	105	295	36	72	5	0	12	38	39	44	0	.244	.333	.383
Boog Powell	1B144	L	27	152	533	83	162	25	0	37	121	72	76	1	.304	.383	.559
Dave Johnson	2B142,SS2	R	26	142	511	52	143	34	1	7	57	57	52	3	.280	.351	.391
Brooks Robinson	3B156	R	32	156	598	73	140	21	3	23	84	56	55	2	.234	.298	.395
Mark Belanger	SS148	R	25	150	530	76	152	17	4	2	50	53	54	14	.287	.351	.345
Paul Blair	OF150	R	25	150	625	102	178	32	5	26	76	40	72	20	.285	.327	.477
Frank Robinson	OF134,1B19	R	33	148	539	111	166	19	5	32	100	88	62	9	.308	.415	.540
Don Buford	OF128,2B10,3B6	S	32	144	554	99	161	31	3	11	64	96	62	19	.291	.397	.417
Andy Etchebarren	C72	R	26	73	217	29	54	9	2	3	26	28	42	1	.249	.350	.350
Merv Rettenmund	OF78	R	26	95	190	27	47	10	3	4	25	28	28	6	.247	.338	.395
Dave May	OF40	L	25	78	120	8	29	6	0	3	10	9	23	2	.242	.305	.367
Chico Salmon	1B17,2B9,SS9*	R	28	52	91	18	27	5	0	3	12	10	22	0	.297	.375	.451
Curt Motton	OF20	R	28	56	89	15	27	6	0	6	21	13	10	3	.303	.398	.573
Bobby Floyd	2B15,SS15,3B9	R	25	39	84	7	17	4	0	0	1	6	17	0	.202	.253	.250
Clay Dalrymple	C30	L	32	37	80	8	19	1	1	3	6	13	8	0	.238	.340	.388
Terry Crowley	1B3,OF2	L	22	7	18	2	6	0	0	0	3	1	4	0	.333	.350	.333

C. Salmon, 3 G at 3B, 1 G at OF

Pitcher	T	Age	G	GS	CG	ShO	IP	H	HR	BB	SO	W-L	Sv	ERA
Dave McNally	L	26	41	40	11	4	268.2	232	21	84	166	20-7	0	3.22
Mike Cuellar	L	32	39	39	18	5	290.2	213	18	79	182	23-11	0	2.38
Tom Phoebus	R	27	35	33	6	2	202.0	180	23	87	117	14-7	0	3.52
Jim Palmer	R	23	26	23	11	6	181.0	131	11	64	123	16-4	0	2.34
Jim Hardin	R	25	30	20	3	1	137.2	128	18	43	64	6-7	1	3.60
Eddie Watt	R	28	56	0	0	0	71.0	49	3	26	46	5-2	16	1.65
Pete Richert	L	29	44	0	0	0	57.1	42	7	14	54	7-4	12	2.20
Dick Hall	R	38	39	0	0	0	65.2	49	3	9	31	5-2	6	1.92
Dave Leonhard	R	28	37	3	1	1	94.0	78	8	38	37	7-4	1	2.49
Marcelino Lopez	L	25	27	4	0	0	69.1	65	3	34	57	5-3	0	4.41
Al Severinsen	R	24	12	0	0	0	19.2	14	2	10	13	1-1	0	2.29
Mike Adamson	R	21	6	0	0	0	8.0	10	0	6	2	0-1	0	4.50
Frank Bertaina†	L	25	3	0	0	0	6.0	1	0	3	5	0-0	0	0.00
Fred Beene	R	26	2	0	0	0	2.2	2	0	1	0	0-0	0	0.00

1969 Detroit Tigers 2nd AL East 90-72 .556 19.0 GB

Mayo Smith

Player	Gm by Position	B	Age	G	AB	R	H	2B	3B	HR	RBI	BB	SO	SB	Avg	OBP	Slg
Bill Freehan	C120,1B20	R	27	143	489	61	128	16	3	16	49	53	55	1	.262	.342	.405
Norm Cash	1B134	L	34	142	483	81	135	15	4	22	74	63	80	2	.280	.368	.464
Dick McAuliffe	2B72	L	29	74	271	49	71	10	5	11	33	47	41	2	.262	.369	.458
Don Wert	3B129	R	30	132	423	46	95	11	1	14	50	49	60	3	.225	.303	.355
Tom Tresh†	SS77,OF11,3B1	S	31	94	331	46	74	13	1	13	37	39	47	2	.224	.305	.387
Jim Northrup	OF143	L	29	148	543	79	160	31	5	25	66	52	83	4	.295	.358	.508
Willie Horton	OF136	R	26	141	508	66	133	17	1	28	91	52	93	3	.262	.332	.465
Al Kaline	OF118,1B9	R	34	131	456	74	124	17	0	21	69	54	61	1	.272	.346	.447
Mickey Stanley	OF101,SS59,1B4	R	26	149	592	73	139	28	1	16	70	52	56	8	.235	.299	.367
Tommy Matchick	2B47,3B27,SS6*	L	25	94	298	25	72	11	2	0	32	15	51	3	.242	.276	.292
Jim Price	C51	R	27	72	192	21	45	8	0	9	28	18	20	0	.234	.294	.417
Ike Brown	2B45,3B12,OF3*	R	27	70	170	24	39	4	3	5	12	26	43	2	.229	.338	.376
Gates Brown	OF14	L	30	60	93	13	19	1	2	1	6	5	17	0	.204	.250	.290
Dick Tracewski	SS41,2B13,3B6	R	34	66	79	10	11	2	0	0	4	15	20	3	.139	.277	.165
Cesar Gutierrez†	SS16	R	26	17	49	5	12	1	0	0	0	5	3	1	.245	.315	.265
Dave Campbell	1B13,2B5,3B1	R	27	32	39	4	4	1	0	0	2	4	15	0	.103	.205	.128
Ron Woods†	OF7	R	26	17	15	3	4	0	0	1	3	2	3	0	.267	.353	.467
Wayne Redmond		R	23	5	3	0	0	0	0	0	0	0	2	0	.000	.000	.000

T. Matchick, 2 G at 1B; I. Brown, 1 G at SS

Pitcher	T	Age	G	GS	CG	ShO	IP	H	HR	BB	SO	W-L	Sv	ERA
Denny McLain	R	25	42	41	23	9	325.0	288	25	67	181	24-9	0	2.80
Mickey Lolich	L	28	37	36	15	1	280.2	214	22	122	271	19-11	1	3.14
Earl Wilson	R	34	35	35	5	1	214.2	209	23	69	150	12-10	0	3.31
Joe Sparma	R	27	23	16	3	2	92.2	78	5	77	41	6-8	0	4.76
Pat Dobson	R	27	49	9	1	0	105.0	100	10	39	64	5-10	9	3.60
John Hiller	L	26	40	8	1	1	99.1	97	13	44	74	4-4	4	3.99
Mike Kilkenny	L	24	39	15	6	4	128.1	99	13	63	97	8-6	2	3.37
Don McMahon†	R	39	34	0	0	0	37.0	25	2	18	38	3-5	11	3.89
Fred Lasher	R	27	32	0	0	0	44.0	34	5	22	26	2-1	0	3.07
Tom Timmermann	R	29	31	1	1	0	55.2	50	1	26	42	4-3	1	2.75
Daryl Patterson	R	25	18	0	0	0	22.1	15	2	19	12	0-2	0	2.82
Dick Radatz†	R	32	11	0	0	0	18.2	14	3	5	18	2-2	0	3.38
Bob Reed	R	24	8	1	0	0	14.2	9	0	8	9	0-0	0	1.84
Gary Taylor	R	23	7	0	0	0	10.1	10	2	6	3	0-1	0	5.23
Fred Scherman	L	24	4	0	0	0	4.0	6	2	0	3	1-0	0	6.75
Norm McRae	R	21	3	0	0	0	3.0	2	0	1	3	0-0	0	6.00

1969 Boston Red Sox 3rd AL East 87-75 .537 22.0 GB

Dick Williams (82-71)/Eddie Popowski (5-4)

Player	Gm by Position	B	Age	G	AB	R	H	2B	3B	HR	RBI	BB	SO	SB	Avg	OBP	Slg
Russ Gibson	C83	R	30	85	287	21	72	9	1	3	27	15	25	1	.251	.289	.321
Dalton Jones	1B81,3B9,2B1	L	25	111	336	50	74	18	3	3	33	39	36	1	.220	.303	.318
Mike Andrews	2B120	R	25	121	464	79	136	26	2	15	59	71	53	1	.293	.390	.455
George Scott	3B109,1B53	R	25	152	549	63	139	14	5	16	52	61	74	4	.253	.331	.384
Rico Petrocelli	SS153,3B1	R	26	154	535	92	159	32	2	40	97	98	68	3	.297	.403	.589
Carl Yastrzemski	OF143,1B22	L	29	162	603	96	154	28	2	40	111	101	91	15	.255	.362	.507
Reggie Smith	OF139	S	24	143	543	87	168	29	7	25	93	54	67	7	.309	.368	.527
Tony Conigliaro	OF137	R	24	141	506	57	129	21	3	20	82	48	111	2	.255	.321	.427
Syd O'Brien	3B53,SS15,2B12	R	24	100	263	47	64	10	5	9	29	15	37	2	.243	.287	.422
Dick Schofield	2B37,SS11,3B9*	S	34	94	226	30	58	9	3	2	20	29	44	0	.257	.349	.350
Joe Lahoud	OF66,1B1	L	22	101	218	32	41	5	0	9	21	40	43	2	.188	.317	.335
Jerry Moses	C36	R	22	53	135	13	41	9	1	4	17	5	23	0	.304	.326	.474
Tom Satriano†	C44	L	28	47	127	9	24	2	0	0	11	22	12	0	.189	.310	.205
Billy Conigliaro	OF24	R	21	32	80	14	23	6	2	4	7	9	23	1	.288	.367	.563
Don Lock†	OF28,1B4	R	32	53	58	8	13	1	0	1	2	11	21	0	.224	.348	.293
Joe Azcue†	C19	R	29	19	51	7	11	2	0	0	3	4	5	0	.216	.273	.255
George Thomas	OF12,1B10,C1*	R	31	29	51	9	18	3	1	0	8	3	11	0	.353	.400	.451
Ken Harrelson†	1B10	R	27	10	46	6	10	1	0	3	8	4	6	0	.217	.275	.435
Tony Muser	1B2	L	21	2	9	0	1	0	0	0	1	1	1	0	.111	.200	.111
Carlton Fisk	C1	R	21	2	5	0	0	0	0	0	0	0	2	0	.000	.000	.000
Luis Alvarado	SS5	R	20	6	5	0	0	0	0	0	0	0	2	0	.000	.000	.000

D. Schofield, 5 G at OF; G. Thomas, 1 G at 3B

Pitcher	T	Age	G	GS	CG	ShO	IP	H	HR	BB	SO	W-L	Sv	ERA
Ray Culp	R	27	32	32	9	2	227.0	195	25	79	172	17-8	0	3.81
Mike Nagy	R	21	33	28	7	1	196.2	183	10	106	84	12-2	0	3.11
Jim Lonborg	R	27	29	23	4	0	143.2	148	15	65	100	7-11	0	4.51
Sonny Siebert†	R	32	43	22	2	0	163.1	151	21	68	127	14-10	5	3.80
Ken Brett	L	20	8	8	0	0	39.1	41	6	22	23	2-3	0	5.26
Mike Garman	R	19	2	2	0	0	12.1	13	0	10	10	1-0	0	4.38
Dick Ellsworth†	L	29	2	2	0	0	12.0	16	1	4	4	0-0	0	3.75
Sparky Lyle	L	24	71	0	0	0	102.2	91	8	48	93	8-3	17	2.54
Vicente Romo†	R	26	52	11	4	1	127.1	116	14	50	89	7-9	11	3.18
Bill Landis	L	26	45	5	0	0	82.1	82	7	49	50	5-5	1	5.25
Lee Stange	R	32	41	15	2	0	137.0	137	14	56	59	6-9	3	3.68
Ray Jarvis	R	23	29	12	2	0	100.1	105	8	43	36	5-6	1	4.75
Bill Lee	L	22	20	1	0	0	52.0	56	9	28	45	1-3	0	4.50
Ron Kline†	R	37	16	0	0	0	17.0	24	4	17	7	0-1	1	4.76
Jose Santiago	R	28	10	0	0	0	7.2	11	2	4	4	0-0	0	3.52
Fred Wenz	R	27	8	0	0	0	11.0	9	7	10	11	1-0	0	5.73
Garry Roggenburk†	L	29	7	0	0	0	9.2	13	1	5	8	0-1	0	8.38
Gary Wagner†	R	29	6	1	0	0	16.1	18	1	15	9	1-3	0	6.06
Juan Pizarro†	L	32	6	0	0	0	9.0	14	2	6	4	0-1	2	6.00

1969 Washington Senators 4th AL East 86-76 .531 23.0 GB

Ted Williams

Player	Gm by Position	B	Age	G	AB	R	H	2B	3B	HR	RBI	BB	SO	SB	Avg	OBP	Slg
Paul Casanova	C122	R	27	124	379	26	82	9	2	4	37	18	52	0	.216	.254	.282
Mike Epstein	1B118	L	26	131	403	73	112	18	1	30	85	85	99	2	.278	.414	.551
Bernie Allen	2B110,3B6	L	30	122	365	33	90	17	4	9	45	50	35	5	.247	.337	.389
Ken McMullen	3B154	R	27	158	562	83	153	25	2	19	87	70	103	4	.272	.349	.425
Ed Brinkman	SS150	R	27	151	576	71	153	18	5	2	43	50	42	2	.266	.328	.325
Del Unser	OF149	L	24	153	581	69	166	19	8	7	57	58	54	8	.286	.349	.382
Frank Howard	OF114,1B70	R	32	161	592	111	175	17	2	48	111	102	96	1	.296	.402	.574
Hank Allen	OF91,3B6,2B3	R	28	109	271	42	75	9	3	1	17	13	28	12	.277	.311	.343
Tim Cullen	2B105,SS9,3B1	R	27	119	249	22	52	7	0	1	15	14	27	1	.209	.253	.249
Lee Maye†	OF65	L	34	71	238	41	69	9	3	9	26	20	25	1	.290	.345	.466
Brant Alyea	OF69,1B3	R	28	104	237	29	59	4	0	11	40	34	67	1	.249	.341	.405
Ed Stroud	OF85	L	29	123	206	35	52	5	6	4	29	30	33	12	.252	.353	.393
Jim French	C63	L	27	63	158	14	29	6	3	2	13	41	15	1	.184	.348	.297
Zoilo Versalles†	SS13,2B6,3B5	R	29	31	75	9	20	2	1	0	6	3	13	1	.267	.304	.320
Sam Bowens	OF30	R	30	33	57	6	11	1	0	0	4	5	14	1	.193	.258	.211
Dick Billings	OF6,3B1	R	26	27	37	3	5	0	0	0	0	6	8	0	.135	.256	.135
Gary Holman	1B11,OF3	L	25	41	31	1	5	1	0	0	2	4	7	0	.161	.257	.194
Dick Smith	OF9	R	24	21	28	2	3	0	0	0	0	4	7	0	.107	.242	.107
Doug Camilli	C1	R	32	1	3	0	1	0	0	0	0	0	2	0	.333	.333	.333
Toby Harrah	SS1	R	20	8	1	4	0	0	0	0	0	0	0	0	.000	.000	.000

Pitcher	T	Age	G	GS	CG	ShO	IP	H	HR	BB	SO	W-L	Sv	ERA
Joe Coleman	R	22	40	36	12	4	247.2	222	26	100	182	12-13	1	3.27
Jim Hannan	R	29	35	28	1	1	158.1	138	17	91	72	7-6	0	3.64
Dick Bosman	R	25	31	26	5	2	193.0	156	11	39	99	14-5	1	2.19
Barry Moore	L	26	31	25	4	0	134.0	123	12	67	51	9-8	0	4.30
Camilo Pascual†	R	35	14	13	0	0	55.1	49	12	38	34	2-5	0	6.83
Cisco Carlos†	R	28	6	4	0	0	17.2	23	2	6	5	1-1	0	4.58
Dennis Higgins	R	29	55	0	0	0	85.1	79	7	56	71	10-9	16	3.48
Darold Knowles	L	27	53	0	0	0	84.1	73	8	31	59	9-2	13	2.24
Casey Cox	R	27	52	13	4	0	171.2	161	15	64	73	12-7	0	2.78
Bob Humphreys	R	33	47	0	0	0	79.2	69	3	38	43	3-3	5	3.05
Dave Baldwin	R	31	43	0	0	0	66.2	57	4	34	51	2-4	4	4.05
Jim Shellenback†	L	25	30	11	2	0	84.2	87	8	48	50	4-7	1	4.04
Frank Bertaina†	L	25	14	5	0	0	35.2	43	8	23	25	1-3	0	6.56
Jim Miles	R	25	10	1	0	0	20.1	19	2	15	15	0-1	0	6.20
Jan Dukes	L	23	8	0	0	0	11.0	8	0	4	3	0-2	0	2.45
Frank Kreutzer	L	30	4	0	0	0	2.0	3	0	2	2	0-0	0	4.50

1969 New York Yankees 5th AL East 80-81 .497 28.5 GB

Ralph Houk

Player	Gm by Position	B	Age	G	AB	R	H	2B	3B	HR	RBI	BB	SO	SB	Avg	OBP	Slg
Jake Gibbs	C66	L	30	71	219	18	49	9	2	0	18	23	30	3	.224	.294	.283
Joe Pepitone	1B132	L	28	135	513	49	124	16	3	27	70	30	42	8	.242	.284	.442
Horace Clarke	2B156	S	29	156	641	82	183	26	7	4	48	53	41	33	.285	.339	.367
Jerry Kenney	3B83,OF31,SS10	L	24	130	447	49	115	14	2	2	34	48	36	25	.257	.328	.311
Gene Michael	SS118	S	31	119	412	41	112	24	4	2	31	43	56	7	.272	.341	.364
Roy White	OF126	S	25	130	448	55	130	30	5	7	74	81	51	18	.290	.392	.426
Bobby Murcer	OF118,3B31	L	23	152	564	82	146	24	4	26	82	50	103	7	.259	.319	.454
Ron Woods†	OF67	R	26	72	171	18	30	5	2	1	7	22	29	2	.175	.273	.246
Frank Fernandez	C65,OF14	R	26	89	229	34	51	6	1	12	29	65	68	1	.223	.399	.415
Bill Robinson	OF62,1B1	R	26	87	222	23	38	11	2	3	21	16	39	3	.171	.226	.279
Jimmie Hall†	OF50,1B7	L	31	80	212	21	50	8	5	3	26	19	34	8	.236	.296	.363
Bobby Cox	3B56,2B6	R	28	85	191	17	41	7	1	2	17	34	41	0	.215	.332	.293
Tom Tresh†	SS41	S	31	45	143	13	26	5	2	1	9	17	23	2	.182	.269	.266
Len Boehmer	1B21,3B8,2B1*	R	28	45	108	5	19	4	0	0	7	8	10	0	.176	.233	.213
Thurman Munson	C25	R	22	26	86	6	22	1	2	1	9	10	10	0	.256	.330	.349
Jim Lyttle	OF28	L	23	28	83	7	15	4	0	0	4	4	19	1	.181	.218	.229
John Ellis	C15	R	20	22	62	2	18	4	0	0	8	1	11	0	.290	.308	.403
Tom Shopay	OF11	L	24	28	48	2	4	0	1	0	0	2	10	0	.083	.120	.125
Billy Cowan†	OF14,1B6	R	30	32	48	5	8	0	0	1	3	3	9	0	.167	.216	.229
Frank Tepedino	OF13	L	21	13	39	6	9	0	0	0	4	4	4	1	.231	.302	.231
Dave McDonald	1B7	L	26	9	23	0	5	1	0	0	2	5	3	1	.217	.280	.261
Dick Simpson†	OF5	R	25	6	11	2	3	2	0	0	4	3	6	0	.273	.429	.455
Ron Blomberg	OF2	L	20	4	6	0	3	0	0	0	0	1	0	0	.500	.571	.500
Nate Oliver†		R	28	1	1	0	0	0	0	0	0	0	0	0	.000	.000	.000

L. Boehmer, 1 G at SS

Pitcher	T	Age	G	GS	CG	ShO	IP	H	HR	BB	SO	W-L	Sv	ERA
Mel Stottlemyre	R	27	39	39	24	3	303.0	267	19	97	113	20-14	0	2.82
Fritz Peterson	L	27	37	37	16	4	272.0	228	15	43	150	17-16	0	2.55
Stan Bahnsen	R	24	40	33	5	1	220.2	222	28	90	130	9-16	1	3.83
Bill Burbach	R	21	31	24	2	1	140.2	112	15	102	82	6-8	0	3.65
Al Downing	L	28	30	15	5	1	130.2	117	12	49	85	7-5	0	3.38
Lindy McDaniel	R	33	51	0	0	0	83.2	84	4	23	60	5-6	5	3.55
Jack Aker†	R	28	38	0	0	0	65.2	51	4	22	40	8-4	11	2.06
Steve Hamilton	L	33	38	0	0	0	57.0	39	7	21	39	3-4	2	3.32
Mike Kekich	L	24	28	13	1	0	105.0	91	11	49	66	4-6	1	4.54
Ken Johnson†	R	36	12	0	0	0	26.0	19	1	11	21	1-2	0	3.46
Fred Talbot†	R	28	8	0	0	0	12.1	13	1	6	7	0-0	0	5.11
Don Nottebart†	R	33	4	0	0	0	6.0	6	1	0	5	0-0	0	4.50
Ron Klimkowski	R	25	3	1	0	0	14.0	6	0	5	3	0-0	0	0.64
John Cumberland	L	22	2	0	0	0	4.0	3	0	4	0	0-0	0	4.50

1969 Cleveland Indians 6th AL East 62-99 .385 46.5 GB

Alvin Dark

Player	Gm by Position	B	Age	G	AB	R	H	2B	3B	HR	RBI	BB	SO	SB	Avg	OBP	Slg
Duke Sims	C102,OF3,1B1	L	28	114	326	40	77	8	0	18	45	66	80	1	.236	.374	.426
Tony Horton	1B157	R	24	159	625	77	174	25	4	27	93	37	91	3	.278	.319	.461
Vern Fuller	2B102,3B7	R	25	108	254	25	60	11	1	4	22	20	53	2	.236	.295	.335
Max Alvis	3B58,SS1	R	31	66	191	13	43	6	0	1	15	14	26	1	.225	.275	.272
Larry Brown	SS101,3B29,2B5	R	29	132	469	48	112	10	2	4	24	44	43	5	.239	.304	.294
Ken Harrelson†	OF144,1B16	R	27	149	519	83	115	13	4	27	84	95	96	17	.222	.341	.418
Jose Cardenal	OF142,3B5	R	25	146	557	75	143	26	3	11	45	49	58	36	.257	.314	.373
Russ Snyder	OF84	L	35	122	266	26	66	10	0	2	24	25	33	3	.248	.312	.308
Lou Klimchock	3B56,2B21,C1	L	29	90	258	26	74	13	2	6	26	18	14	0	.287	.331	.422
Zoilo Versalles†	2B46,3B30,SS3	R	29	72	217	21	49	11	1	1	13	21	47	3	.226	.298	.300
Eddie Leon	SS64	R	22	64	213	20	51	6	0	3	19	19	37	2	.239	.306	.310
Richie Scheinblum	OF50	S	26	102	199	13	37	5	1	1	13	19	30	0	.186	.253	.236
Frank Baker	OF46	L	25	52	172	21	44	5	3	3	15	14	34	2	.256	.312	.372
Dave Nelson	2B33,OF2	R	25	52	123	11	25	0	0	0	6	9	26	4	.203	.259	.203
Chuck Hinton	OF40,3B14	R	35	94	121	18	31	3	2	3	19	8	22	2	.256	.303	.388
Ray Fosse	C37	R	22	37	116	11	20	3	0	2	9	8	29	1	.172	.230	.250
Cap Peterson	OF30,3B4	R	26	76	110	8	25	3	0	1	14	24	18	0	.227	.365	.282
Lee Maye†	OF28	L	34	43	108	9	27	5	0	1	15	8	15	1	.250	.305	.324
Ken Suarez	C36	R	26	36	85	7	25	5	0	1	9	15	12	1	.294	.400	.388
Joe Azcue†	C6	R	29	7	24	1	7	0	0	1	1	4	3	0	.292	.393	.417
Russ Nagelson	OF3,1B1	L	24	12	17	1	6	0	0	0	0	3	3	0	.353	.450	.353
Lou Camilli	3B13	S	22	13	14	0	0	0	0	0	0	0	3	0	.000	.000	.000
Jimmie Hall†	OF3	L	31	4	10	1	0	0	0	0	0	2	3	1	.000	.167	.000
Jack Heidemann	SS3	R	19	3	3	0	0	0	0	0	0	0	2	0	.000	.250	.000

Pitcher	T	Age	G	GS	CG	ShO	IP	H	HR	BB	SO	W-L	Sv	ERA
Sam McDowell	L	26	39	38	18	4	285.0	222	13	102	279	18-14	1	2.94
Luis Tiant	R	28	38	37	9	1	249.2	229	37	129	156	9-20	0	3.71
Steve Hargan	R	26	32	23	1	1	143.2	145	14	81	76	5-14	0	5.70
Dick Ellsworth†	L	29	34	22	3	1	135.0	162	10	40	48	6-9	0	4.13
Sonny Siebert†	R	32	2	2	0	0	14.0	10	1	8	6	0-1	0	3.21
Stan Williams	R	32	61	15	3	0	178.1	155	25	67	139	6-14	12	3.94
Juan Pizarro†	L	32	48	4	1	0	82.2	67	6	49	44	3-3	4	3.16
Mike Paul	L	24	47	12	0	0	117.1	104	12	54	98	5-10	2	3.61
Ron Law	R	23	35	1	0	0	52.1	68	2	34	29	3-4	1	4.99
Horacio Pina	R	24	31	4	0	0	46.2	44	6	27	32	4-2	1	5.21
Larry Burchart	R	23	29	0	0	0	42.1	42	2	24	26	0-2	0	4.25
Jack Hamilton†	R	30	20	0	0	0	30.2	37	2	23	13	0-2	1	4.40
Gary Kroll	R	27	19	0	0	0	24.0	16	3	22	28	0-0	0	4.13
Phil Hennigan	R	23	9	0	0	0	16.1	14	0	4	10	2-1	0	3.31
Gary Boyd	R	22	8	3	0	0	11.0	8	1	14	9	0-2	0	9.00
Vicente Romo†	R	26	3	0	0	0	8.0	7	0	3	7	1-1	0	2.25

1969 Minnesota Twins 1st AL West 97-65 .599 —

Billy Martin

Player	Gm by Position	B	Age	G	AB	R	H	2B	3B	HR	RBI	BB	SO	SB	Avg	OBP	Slg
John Roseboro	C111	L	36	115	361	33	95	12	0	3	32	39	44	5	.263	.333	.321
Rich Reese	1B117,OF5	L	27	132	419	52	135	24	4	16	69	23	57	1	.322	.362	.513
Rod Carew	2B118	L	23	123	458	79	152	30	4	8	56	37	72	19	.332	.386	.467
Harmon Killebrew	3B105,1B80	R	33	162	555	106	153	20	2	49	140	145	84	8	.276	.427	.584
Leo Cardenas	SS160	R	30	160	578	67	162	24	4	10	70	66	96	5	.280	.353	.388
Tony Oliva	OF152	L	28	153	637	97	197	39	4	24	101	45	66	10	.309	.355	.496
Ted Uhlaender	OF150	L	28	152	554	93	151	18	2	8	62	44	52	15	.273	.328	.356
Cesar Tovar	OF113,2B41,3B20	R	28	158	535	99	154	25	5	11	52	37	37	45	.288	.342	.415
Graig Nettles	OF54,3B21	L	24	96	225	27	50	9	2	7	26	32	47	1	.222	.319	.373
Bob Allison	OF58,1B3	R	34	81	189	18	43	8	2	8	27	29	39	2	.228	.333	.418
George Mitterwald	C63,OF1	R	24	69	187	18	48	8	0	5	13	17	47	0	.257	.327	.380
Charlie Manuel	OF46	L	25	83	164	14	34	6	0	2	24	28	33	1	.207	.320	.280
Frank Quilici	3B84,2B36,SS1	R	30	118	144	19	25	3	1	2	12	12	22	2	.174	.236	.250
Rick Renick	3B30,OF10,SS6	R	25	71	139	21	34	3	0	5	17	12	32	0	.245	.307	.374
Tom Tischinski	C32	R	24	37	47	2	9	0	0	0	2	8	8	0	.191	.309	.191
Jim Holt	OF5,1B1	L	25	12	14	3	5	0	0	1	2	0	4	0	.357	.357	.571
Cotton Nash	1B6,OF1	R	26	6	9	0	2	0	0	0	0	1	2	0	.222	.300	.222
Ron Clark†	3B2	R	26	5	8	0	1	0	0	0	0	0	0	0	.125	.125	.125
Rick Dempsey	C3	R	19	5	6	1	3	1	0	0	0	1	0	0	.500	.571	.667
Herman Hill	OF2	L	23	16	2	4	0	0	0	0	0	0	1	1	.000	.000	.000
Frank Kostro		R	31	2	2	0	0	0	0	0	0	0	1	0	.000	.000	.000

Pitcher	T	Age	G	GS	CG	ShO	IP	H	HR	BB	SO	W-L	Sv	ERA
Dave Boswell	R	24	39	38	10	0	256.1	215	18	99	190	20-12	0	3.23
Jim Perry	R	33	46	36	12	3	261.2	244	18	66	153	20-6	0	2.82
Jim Kaat	L	30	40	32	10	0	242.1	252	23	75	139	14-13	1	3.49
Tom Hall	L	21	31	18	5	2	140.2	129	12	50	92	8-7	0	3.33
Dean Chance	R	28	20	15	1	0	88.1	76	6	35	50	5-4	0	2.95
Ron Perranoski	L	33	75	0	0	0	119.2	85	4	52	62	9-10	31	2.11
Bob Miller	R	30	48	11	1	0	119.1	118	9	32	57	5-5	3	3.02
Al Worthington	R	40	46	0	0	0	61.0	65	7	20	51	4-1	3	4.57
Dick Woodson	R	24	44	10	2	0	110.1	99	11	49	66	7-5	1	3.67
Joe Grzenda	L	32	38	0	0	0	48.2	52	4	17	24	4-1	3	3.88
Jerry Crider	R	27	21	1	0	0	28.2	31	3	15	16	1-0	1	4.71
Charley Walters	R	22	6	0	0	0	6.2	6	1	3	2	0-0	0	5.40
Bill Zepp	R	22	4	0	0	0	5.1	6	1	4	2	0-0	0	6.75
Danny Morris	R	23	3	1	0	0	5.1	5	1	4	1	0-1	0	5.06
Bucky Brandon†	R	28	3	0	0	0	3.1	5	1	3	1	0-0	0	2.70

1969 Oakland Athletics 2nd AL West 88-74 .543 9.0 GB

Hank Bauer (80-69)/John McNamara (8-5)

Player	Gm by Position	B	Age	G	AB	R	H	2B	3B	HR	RBI	BB	SO	SB	Avg	OBP	Slg
Phil Roof	C106	R	28	106	247	19	58	6	1	2	19	33	55	1	.235	.337	.291
Danny Cater	1B132,OF20,2B4	R	29	152	584	64	153	24	2	10	76	28	40	1	.262	.296	.361
Dick Green	2B131	R	28	136	483	61	133	25	6	12	64	53	94	2	.275	.353	.427
Sal Bando	3B162	R	25	162	609	106	171	25	3	31	113	111	82	1	.281	.400	.484
Bert Campaneris	SS125	R	27	135	547	71	142	15	2	2	25	30	62	62	.260	.302	.305
Reggie Jackson	OF150	L	23	152	549	123	151	36	3	47	118	114	142	13	.275	.410	.608
Rick Monday	OF119	L	23	122	399	57	108	17	4	12	54	72	100	12	.271	.388	.424
Tommie Reynolds	OF89	S	27	107	315	51	81	10	0	2	20	34	29	1	.257	.343	.308
Ted Kubiak	SS42,2B33	S	27	92	305	38	76	9	1	2	27	25	35	2	.249	.304	.305
Jose Tartabull	OF63	L	30	75	266	28	71	11	1	0	11	9	11	3	.267	.290	.316
Mike Hershberger	OF35	R	29	51	129	11	26	2	0	1	10	10	15	1	.202	.259	.240
Dave Duncan	C56	R	23	58	127	11	16	3	0	3	22	19	41	0	.126	.236	.220
Joe Rudi	OF18,1B11	R	22	35	122	10	23	3	1	2	6	5	16	1	.189	.220	.279
Larry Haney†	C53	R	26	53	86	8	13	4	0	2	12	7	19	0	.151	.221	.267
Tito Francona†	1B19,OF1	L	35	32	85	12	29	6	1	3	20	12	11	0	.341	.418	.541
Bobby Brooks	OF21	R	23	29	79	13	19	5	0	3	10	20	24	0	.241	.396	.418
Ray Webster	1B13	L	26	64	77	5	20	0	1	1	13	12	8	0	.260	.359	.325
Bob Johnson†	1B7,2B2	R	33	51	67	5	23	1	0	1	9	3	4	0	.343	.375	.403
Gene Tenace	C13	R	22	16	38	1	6	0	0	1	2	1	15	0	.158	.200	.237
Jim Pagliaroni†	C7	R	31	14	27	1	4	1	0	1	2	5	2	0	.148	.303	.296
Bill McNulty	OF5	R	22	5	17	0	0	0	0	0	0	0	10	0	.000	.000	.000
John Donaldson†	2B1	L	26	12	13	1	1	0	0	0	0	2	4	0	.077	.200	.077
Tony La Russa		R	24	8	8	0	0	0	0	0	0	0	1	0	.000	.000	.000
Joe Nossek†	OF12	R	28	13	6	0	0	0	0	0	0	0	0	0	.000	.000	.000
Allan Lewis		S	27	12	1	2	0	0	0	0	0	0	0	0	.000	.000	.000

Pitcher	T	Age	G	GS	CG	ShO	IP	H	HR	BB	SO	W-L	Sv	ERA
Catfish Hunter	R	23	38	35	10	3	247.0	210	34	85	150	12-15	0	3.35
Chuck Dobson	R	25	35	35	11	1	235.1	244	16	80	137	15-13	0	3.86
Blue Moon Odom	R	24	32	32	10	3	231.1	179	15	112	150	15-6	0	2.92
Jim Nash	R	24	26	19	3	1	115.1	112	17	30	75	8-8	0	3.67
Rollie Fingers	R	22	60	8	1	1	119.0	116	13	41	61	6-7	12	3.71
Paul Lindblad	L	27	60	0	0	0	78.1	72	8	33	64	9-6	9	4.14
Lew Krausse	R	26	43	16	4	2	140.0	134	23	48	85	7-7	7	4.44
Jim Roland	L	26	39	3	2	0	86.1	59	2	46	48	5-1	1	2.19
Marcel Lachemann	R	28	28	0	0	0	43.1	43	1	19	16	4-1	2	3.95
Ed Sprague	R	23	27	0	0	0	46.1	47	4	31	20	1-1	2	4.47
George Lauzerique	R	21	19	8	1	0	61.1	58	14	27	39	3-4	0	4.70
Vida Blue	L	19	12	4	0	0	42.0	49	13	18	24	1-1	1	6.21
Fred Talbot†	R	28	12	2	0	0	19.0	22	2	7	9	1-2	1	5.21
John Wyatt	R	34	4	0	0	0	8.1	8	0	6	5	0-1	0	5.40
Juan Pizarro†	L	32	3	0	0	0	7.2	3	1	3	4	1-1	1	2.35

1969 California Angels 3rd AL West 71-91 .438 26.0 GB

Bill Rigney (11-28)/Lefty Phillips (60-63)

Player	Gm by Position	B	Age	G	AB	R	H	2B	3B	HR	RBI	BB	SO	SB	Avg	OBP	Slg
Joe Azcue†	C80	R	29	80	248	15	54	6	0	1	19	27	28	0	.218	.295	.254
Jim Spencer	1B107	L	22	113	386	39	98	14	3	10	31	26	53	1	.254	.304	.383
Sandy Alomar†	2B134	S	25	134	559	60	140	10	2	1	30	36	48	18	.250	.296	.281
Aurelio Rodriguez	3B159	R	21	159	561	47	130	17	2	7	49	32	88	5	.232	.272	.307
Jim Fregosi	SS160	R	27	161	580	78	151	22	6	12	47	93	86	9	.260	.361	.381
Jay Johnstone	OF144	L	23	148	540	64	146	20	5	10	59	38	75	3	.270	.321	.381
Rick Reichardt	OF136,1B3	R	26	137	493	60	125	11	4	13	68	43	100	3	.254	.319	.371
Bill Voss	OF111,1B2	L	25	133	349	33	91	11	4	2	40	35	40	5	.261	.327	.332
Roger Repoz	OF48,1B31	L	28	103	219	25	36	1	1	8	19	32	52	1	.164	.270	.288
Bubba Morton	OF49,1B1	R	37	87	172	18	42	10	1	7	32	28	29	0	.244	.356	.436
Lou Johnson	OF44	R	34	67	133	10	27	8	0	0	9	10	19	5	.203	.272	.263
Tom Egan	C46	R	23	46	120	7	17	1	0	5	16	17	41	0	.142	.248	.275
Tom Satriano†	C36,1B5,2B2	L	28	41	108	5	28	2	0	1	16	18	15	0	.259	.364	.306
Vic Davalillo†	OF22,1B3	L	32	33	71	10	11	1	1	0	1	6	5	3	.155	.231	.197
Bobby Knoop†	2B27	R	30	27	71	5	14	1	0	1	6	13	16	1	.197	.318	.254
Billy Cowan†	OF13	R	30	28	56	10	17	1	0	4	10	3	9	0	.304	.350	.536
Dick Stuart	1B13	R	36	22	51	3	8	2	0	1	4	3	21	0	.157	.204	.255
Jim Hicks†	OF10,1B8	R	29	37	48	6	4	0	0	3	8	13	18	0	.083	.274	.271
Winston Llenas	3B9	R	25	34	47	4	8	2	0	0	0	2	10	0	.170	.204	.213
Bob Rodgers	C18	S	30	18	46	4	9	1	0	0	2	5	8	0	.196	.288	.217
Ruben Amaro	1B18,2B9,SS5*	R	33	41	27	4	6	0	0	0	1	4	6	0	.222	.323	.222
Randy Brown	C10,OF1	L	24	13	25	3	4	1	0	0	0	6	1	0	.160	.323	.200
Jarvis Tatum	OF5	R	22	10	22	2	7	0	0	0	0	0	6	0	.318	.318	.318
Marty Perez	SS7,2B2,3B2	R	22	13	13	3	3	0	0	0	0	2	1	0	.231	.333	.231
Bob Chance	1B1	L	28	5	7	0	1	0	0	0	1	0	4	0	.143	.143	.143
Chuck Cottier	2B2	R	33	2	2	0	0	0	0	0	0	0	0	0	.000	.000	.000

R. Amaro, 2 G at 3B

Pitcher	T	Age	G	GS	CG	ShO	IP	H	HR	BB	SO	W-L	Sv	ERA
Tom Murphy	R	23	36	35	4	0	215.2	213	12	69	100	10-16	0	4.21
Jim McGlothlin	R	25	37	35	4	1	201.0	188	19	58	96	8-16	0	3.18
Andy Messersmith	R	23	40	33	10	2	250.0	169	17	100	211	16-11	2	2.52
Rudy May	L	24	43	25	4	0	180.1	142	20	66	133	10-13	2	3.44
George Brunet†	L	34	23	19	2	2	100.2	98	15	39	56	6-7	0	3.84
Eddie Fisher	R	32	52	1	0	0	96.2	100	9	28	47	3-2	2	3.63
Ken Tatum	R	25	45	0	0	0	86.1	51	1	39	65	7-2	22	1.36
Hoyt Wilhelm†	R	45	44	0	0	0	65.2	45	4	18	53	5-7	10	2.47
Clyde Wright	L	28	37	5	0	0	63.2	66	4	30	31	1-8	0	4.10
Pedro Borbon	R	22	22	0	0	0	41.0	55	5	11	20	2-3	0	6.15
Steve Kealey	R	22	15	3	1	1	36.2	48	4	13	17	2-0	0	3.93
Bob Priddy†	R	29	15	0	0	0	26.1	24	4	7	15	0-1	0	4.78
Vern Geishert	R	23	11	3	0	0	31.0	32	4	7	18	1-1	1	4.65
Greg Washburn	R	22	8	2	0	0	11.1	21	0	5	4	0-2	0	7.94
Rickey Clark	R	23	6	1	0	0	9.2	12	2	7	6	0-0	0	5.59
Phil Ortega	R	29	5	0	0	0	8.0	13	3	7	4	0-0	0	10.13
Lloyd Allen	R	19	4	1	0	0	10.0	5	1	10	5	0-1	0	5.40
Tom Bradley	R	22	3	0	0	0	2.0	9	1	0	2	0-1	0	27.00
Wally Wolf	R	27	2	0	0	0	2.1	3	1	3	2	0-0	0	11.57

1969 Kansas City Royals 4th AL West 69-93 .426 28.0 GB — Joe Gordon

Player	Gm by Position	B	Age	G	AB	R	H	2B	3B	HR	RBI	BB	SO	SB	Avg	OBP	Slg
Ellie Rodriguez	C90	R	23	95	267	27	63	10	0	2	20	31	26	3	.236	.333	.296
Mike Fiore	1B91,OF13	L	24	107	339	53	93	14	1	12	35	84	63	4	.274	.420	.428
Jerry Adair	2B109,SS8,3B1	R	32	126	432	29	108	9	1	5	48	20	36	1	.250	.285	.310
Joe Foy	3B113,1B16,OF16*	R	26	145	519	72	136	19	2	11	71	74	75	37	.262	.354	.370
Jackie Hernandez	SS144	R	28	145	504	54	112	14	2	4	40	38	111	17	.222	.278	.282
Lou Piniella	OF129	R	25	135	493	43	139	21	6	11	68	33	56	2	.282	.325	.416
Pat Kelly	OF107	L	24	112	417	61	110	20	4	8	32	49	70	40	.264	.348	.388
Bob Oliver	OF98,1B12,3B8	R	26	118	394	43	100	8	4	13	43	21	74	5	.254	.294	.393
Ed Kirkpatrick	OF82,C8,1B2*	L	24	120	315	40	81	11	4	14	49	43	42	3	.257	.348	.451
Chuck Harrison	1B55	R	28	75	213	18	47	5	1	3	18	16	20	1	.221	.276	.296
Buck Martinez	C55,OF1	R	20	72	205	14	47	6	1	4	23	8	25	0	.229	.258	.327
Paul Schaal	3B49,2B6,SS6	R	26	61	205	22	54	6	0	1	13	25	27	2	.263	.346	.307
Juan Rios	2B46,SS32,3B4	R	26	87	196	20	44	5	1	1	5	7	19	1	.224	.262	.276
Joe Keough	OF49,1B1	L	23	70	166	17	31	2	0	0	7	13	13	5	.187	.254	.199
Hawk Taylor	OF18,C6	R	30	64	89	7	24	5	0	3	21	6	18	0	.270	.313	.427
Jim Campanis	C26	R	25	30	83	4	13	5	0	0	5	5	19	0	.157	.202	.217
Luis Alcaraz	2B19,3B2,SS1	R	28	22	79	15	20	2	1	1	7	7	9	0	.253	.314	.342
Scott Northey	OF18	R	22	20	61	11	16	2	2	1	7	7	19	6	.262	.338	.410
George Spriggs	OF6	L	28	23	29	4	4	2	1	0	0	3	8	0	.138	.242	.276
Dennis Paepke	C8	R	24	12	27	2	3	1	0	0	0	2	3	0	.111	.172	.148
Fred Rico	OF9,3B1	R	24	12	26	2	6	2	0	0	2	9	10	0	.231	.429	.308
Tom Burgmeier	P31,OF1	L	25	47	18	7	3	0	0	0	0	0	4	0	.167	.167	.167
Fran Healy	C5	R	22	6	10	0	4	1	0	0	0	0	5	0	.400	.400	.500
Billy Harris	2B1	L	25	5	7	1	2	1	0	0	0	0	1	0	.286	.286	.429

J. Foy, 5 G at SS, 3 G at 2B; E. Kirkpatrick, 2 G at 3B, 1 G at 2B

Pitcher	T	Age	G	GS	CG	ShO	IP	H	HR	BB	SO	W-L	Sv	ERA
Wally Bunker	R	24	35	31	10	1	222.2	198	29	62	130	12-11	2	3.23
Bill Butler	L	22	34	29	5	4	193.2	174	15	91	156	9-10	0	3.90
Roger Nelson	R	25	29	29	8	1	193.1	170	12	65	82	7-13	0	3.31
Dick Drago	R	24	41	26	10	2	200.2	190	19	65	108	11-13	1	3.77
Jim Rooker	L	26	28	22	8	1	158.1	136	13	73	108	4-16	0	3.75
Moe Drabowsky	R	33	52	0	0	0	98.0	68	10	30	76	11-9	11	2.94
Mike Hedlund	R	22	34	16	1	0	125.0	123	8	40	74	3-6	2	3.24
Dave Wickersham	R	33	34	0	0	0	50.0	58	6	14	27	2-3	5	3.96
Tom Burgmeier	L	25	31	0	0	0	54.0	67	5	21	23	3-1	0	4.17
Dave Morehead	R	26	21	2	0	0	33.0	28	7	28	32	2-3	0	5.73
Steve Jones	L	28	20	4	0	0	44.2	45	3	24	31	2-3	0	4.23
Don O'Riley	R	24	18	0	0	0	23.1	32	0	15	10	1-1	1	6.94
Galen Cisco	R	33	15	0	0	0	22.1	17	4	15	18	1-1	1	3.63
Chris Zachary	R	25	8	2	0	0	18.1	27	4	7	6	0-1	0	7.85
Al Fitzmorris	R	23	7	0	0	0	10.2	9	1	4	3	1-1	2	4.22
Gerald Cram	R	21	5	2	0	0	16.2	15	0	6	10	0-1	0	3.24

1969 Chicago White Sox 5th AL West 68-94 .420 29.0 GB — Al Lopez (8-9)/Don Gutteridge (60-85)

Player	Gm by Position	B	Age	G	AB	R	H	2B	3B	HR	RBI	BB	SO	SB	Avg	OBP	Slg
Ed Herrmann	C92	L	22	102	290	31	67	8	0	8	31	30	35	0	.231	.319	.341
Gail Hopkins	1B101	L	26	124	373	52	99	13	3	8	46	50	28	2	.265	.351	.381
Bobby Knoop†	2B104	R	30	104	345	34	79	14	1	6	41	35	68	2	.229	.301	.328
Bill Melton	3B148,OF11	R	23	157	556	67	142	26	2	23	87	56	106	1	.255	.326	.433
Luis Aparicio	SS154	R	35	156	599	77	168	24	5	5	51	66	29	24	.280	.352	.362
Ken Berry	OF120	R	28	130	297	25	69	12	2	4	18	24	50	1	.232	.296	.327
Walt Williams	OF111	R	25	135	471	59	143	22	1	3	32	26	33	6	.304	.343	.374
Carlos May	OF100	L	21	100	367	62	103	18	2	18	62	58	66	1	.281	.385	.488
Buddy Bradford	OF88	R	24	93	273	36	70	8	2	11	27	34	75	5	.256	.347	.421
Tom McCraw	1B44,OF41	L	28	93	240	21	62	12	2	2	25	21	24	1	.258	.326	.350
Pete Ward	1B25,3B21,OF9	L	29	105	199	22	49	7	0	6	32	33	38	0	.246	.359	.372
Don Pavletich	C51,1B13	R	30	78	188	26	46	12	0	6	33	28	45	0	.245	.338	.404
Ron Hansen	2B26,1B21,SS8*	R	31	85	185	15	48	6	1	2	22	18	25	2	.259	.327	.335
Duane Josephson	C47	R	27	52	162	19	39	6	2	1	20	13	17	0	.241	.296	.321
Bob Christian	OF38	R	23	39	129	11	28	4	0	3	16	10	19	3	.217	.273	.318
Rich Morales	2B38,SS13,3B1	R	25	55	121	12	26	0	1	0	6	7	18	1	.215	.269	.231
Angel Bravo	OF25	L	26	27	90	10	26	4	2	1	3	3	5	2	.289	.319	.411
Woodie Held	OF18,3B3,SS3*	R	37	56	63	9	9	2	0	3	6	13	19	0	.143	.299	.317
Sandy Alomar†	2B22	S	25	22	58	8	13	2	0	0	4	4	6	2	.224	.274	.259
Bob Spence	1B6	L	23	12	26	0	4	1	0	0	3	0	9	0	.154	.148	.192
Chuck Brinkman	C14	R	24	14	15	2	1	1	0	0	0	1	5	0	.067	.125	.067
Doug Adams	C4	L	26	8	14	1	3	0	0	0	1	1	3	0	.214	.267	.214
Jose Ortiz	OF8	R	22	16	11	0	3	1	0	0	2	1	0	0	.273	.333	.364

R. Hansen, 7 G at 3B; W. Held, 1 G at 2B

Pitcher	T	Age	G	GS	CG	ShO	IP	H	HR	BB	SO	W-L	Sv	ERA
Joe Horlen	R	31	36	35	7	2	235.2	237	20	77	121	13-16	0	3.78
Tommy John	L	26	33	33	6	2	232.1	230	16	90	128	9-11	0	3.25
Gary Peters	L	32	36	32	7	3	218.2	238	21	78	140	10-15	0	4.53
Billy Wynne	R	25	20	20	6	1	128.2	143	14	50	67	7-7	0	4.06
Paul Edmondson	R	26	14	13	1	0	87.2	72	5	39	46	1-6	0	3.70
Jerry Nyman	L	26	20	10	2	1	64.2	58	7	39	40	4-4	0	5.29
Sammy Ellis	R	28	10	5	0	0	29.1	42	6	16	15	0-3	0	5.83
Bart Johnson	R	19	4	3	0	0	22.1	22	2	6	18	1-3	0	3.22
Fred Rath	R	25	3	2	0	0	11.2	11	4	8	4	0-2	0	7.71
Wilbur Wood	L	27	76	0	0	0	119.2	113	13	40	73	10-11	15	3.01
Dan Osinski	R	35	51	0	0	0	60.2	56	3	23	27	5-5	2	3.56
Cisco Carlos†	R	28	25	4	0	0	49.1	52	4	23	28	4-3	0	5.66
Gary Bell†	R	32	23	2	0	0	38.2	48	8	23	26	0-0	0	6.28
Don Secrist	L	25	19	0	0	0	40.0	35	7	14	23	0-1	0	6.08
Danny Murphy	R	26	17	0	0	0	31.1	28	2	10	16	2-1	4	2.01
Bob Locker†	R	31	17	0	0	0	22.0	26	6	6	15	2-3	4	6.55
Danny Lazar	L	25	9	3	0	0	20.2	21	5	11	9	0-0	0	6.53
Jack Hamilton†	R	30	8	0	0	0	12.1	23	1	7	5	0-3	0	11.68
Bob Priddy†	R	29	4	0	0	0	8.0	10	2	2	5	0-0	0	4.50
Denny O'Toole	R	20	2	0	0	0	4.0	5	0	2	4	0-0	0	6.75

1969 Seattle Pilots 6th AL West 64-98 .395 33.0 GB — Joe Schultz

Player	Gm by Position	B	Age	G	AB	R	H	2B	3B	HR	RBI	BB	SO	SB	Avg	OBP	Slg
Jerry McNertney	C122	R	32	128	410	39	99	18	1	8	55	29	63	1	.241	.291	.349
Don Mincher	1B122	L	31	140	427	53	105	14	0	25	78	78	69	10	.246	.366	.454
John Donaldson†	2B90,3B2,SS1	L	26	95	338	22	79	8	3	1	19	36	36	6	.234	.307	.284
Tommy Harper	2B59,3B59,OF26	R	28	148	537	78	126	10	2	9	41	95	90	73	.235	.349	.311
Ray Oyler	SS106	R	30	106	255	24	42	5	0	7	22	31	80	1	.165	.260	.267
Wayne Comer	OF139,C1,3B1	R	25	147	481	88	118	18	1	15	54	82	79	18	.245	.354	.380
Tommy Davis†	OF112,1B1	R	30	123	454	52	123	29	1	6	80	30	46	19	.271	.318	.379
Steve Hovley	OF84	L	24	91	329	41	91	14	3	3	20	30	34	10	.277	.338	.365
Mike Hegan	OF64,1B19	L	26	95	267	54	78	9	6	8	37	62	61	6	.292	.427	.461
Gus Gil	3B38,2B18,SS12	R	30	92	221	20	49	7	0	0	17	16	28	2	.222	.272	.253
Rich Rollins	3B47,SS1	R	31	58	187	15	42	7	0	4	21	7	19	2	.225	.270	.326
Ron Clark†	SS38,3B15,2B5*	R	26	57	163	9	32	5	0	0	12	13	29	1	.196	.258	.227
Greg Goossen	1B31,OF2	R	23	52	139	19	43	8	1	10	24	14	29	1	.309	.385	.597
John Kennedy	SS33,3B23	R	28	61	128	18	30	3	1	4	14	14	25	4	.234	.315	.367
Steve Whitaker	OF39	L	26	69	116	15	29	2	1	6	13	12	29	2	.250	.323	.440
Jim Pagliaroni†	C29,1B2,OF1	R	31	40	110	10	29	4	1	5	14	13	16	0	.264	.333	.455
Danny Walton	OF23	R	21	23	92	12	20	1	2	3	10	5	26	2	.217	.275	.370
Merritt Ranew	C13,OF3,3B1	L	31	54	81	11	20	2	0	0	4	10	14	0	.247	.330	.272
Larry Haney†	C20	R	26	22	59	3	15	3	0	2	7	6	12	1	.254	.323	.407
Jim Gosger†	OF26	L	26	39	55	4	6	2	1	1	1	6	11	2	.109	.197	.236
Dick Simpson†	OF17	R	25	26	51	8	9	2	0	2	5	4	17	3	.176	.236	.333
Fred Stanley	SS15,2B1	R	21	17	43	2	12	2	1	0	4	3	8	1	.279	.333	.372
Gordy Lund	SS17,2B1,3B1	R	28	20	38	4	10	0	0	0	1	5	7	1	.263	.349	.263
Sandy Valdespino†	OF7	L	30	20	38	3	8	1	0	0	2	1	7	0	.211	.250	.237
Jose Vidal	OF6	R	29	18	26	7	5	0	1	1	2	4	8	1	.192	.323	.385
Freddie Velazquez	C5	R	31	6	16	1	2	2	0	0	2	1	3	0	.125	.176	.250
Billy Williams	OF3	L	36	4	10	1	0	0	0	0	0	1	3	0	.000	.167	.000
Mike Ferraro		R	24	5	4	0	0	0	0	0	0	1	0	0	.000	.200	.000

R. Clark, 1 G at 1B

Pitcher	T	Age	G	GS	CG	ShO	IP	H	HR	BB	SO	W-L	Sv	ERA
Gene Brabender	R	27	40	29	7	1	202.1	193	26	103	139	13-14	0	4.36
Marty Pattin	R	26	34	27	2	1	158.2	166	29	71	126	7-12	0	5.62
Fred Talbot†	R	28	25	16	1	1	114.2	125	12	41	67	5-8	0	4.16
Steve Barber	L	30	25	16	0	0	86.1	99	9	48	69	4-7	0	4.80
Mike Marshall	R	26	20	14	3	1	87.2	99	8	35	47	3-10	0	5.13
George Brunet†	L	34	12	11	2	0	63.2	70	11	28	37	2-5	0	5.37
Gary Bell†	R	32	13	11	1	1	61.1	76	8	34	30	2-6	2	4.70
Bob Meyer	L	29	6	5	1	0	32.2	30	4	10	17	0-3	0	3.31
Miguel Fuentes	R	23	8	4	1	0	26.0	29	1	16	14	1-3	0	5.19
Garry Roggenburk†	L	29	7	4	1	0	24.1	27	6	11	11	2-2	0	4.44
Skip Lockwood	R	22	6	3	0	0	23.0	24	3	6	10	0-1	0	3.52
Gary Timberlake	L	20	2	2	0	0	6.0	7	0	9	4	0-0	0	7.50
Diego Segui	R	31	66	8	2	0	142.1	127	14	61	113	12-6	12	3.35
Jim Bouton†	R	30	57	1	0	0	92.0	77	12	38	68	2-1	1	3.91
John O'Donoghue	L	29	55	0	0	0	70.0	58	5	37	48	2-2	6	2.96
Bob Locker†	R	31	51	0	0	0	78.1	69	3	26	46	3-3	6	2.18
John Gelnar	R	26	39	10	0	0	108.2	103	7	26	69	3-10	3	3.31
Jack Aker†	R	28	15	0	0	0	16.2	25	4	13	7	0-2	3	7.56
Dick Baney	R	22	9	1	0	0	18.2	21	2	7	9	1-0	0	3.86
Dooley Womack†	R	29	9	0	0	0	14.1	15	0	3	8	2-1	0	2.51
Bucky Brandon†	R	28	8	1	0	0	15.0	15	4	16	10	0-1	0	8.40
John Morris	L	27	6	0	0	0	12.2	16	2	8	8	0-0	0	6.39
Bill Edgerton	L	27	4	0	0	0	4.0	10	1	0	2	0-1	0	13.50
Jerry Stephenson	R	25	2	0	0	0	2.2	6	0	3	1	0-0	0	10.13
Dick Bates	R	23	1	0	0	0	1.2	3	1	3	3	0-0	0	27.00

>>1969 New York Mets 1st NL East 100-62 .617 — — Gil Hodges

Player	Gm by Position	B	Age	G	AB	R	H	2B	3B	HR	RBI	BB	SO	SB	Avg	OBP	Slg
Jerry Grote	C112	R	26	113	365	38	92	12	3	6	40	32	59	2	.252	.313	.351
Ed Kranepool	1B106,OF2	L	24	112	353	36	84	9	2	11	49	37	32	3	.238	.307	.368
Ken Boswell	2B96	L	23	102	362	48	101	14	7	3	32	36	47	7	.279	.347	.381
Wayne Garrett	3B72,2B47,SS9	L	21	124	400	38	87	11	3	1	39	40	75	4	.218	.290	.268
Bud Harrelson	SS119	S	25	123	395	42	98	11	6	0	24	54	54	1	.248	.341	.306
Tommie Agee	OF146	R	26	149	565	97	153	23	4	26	76	59	137	12	.271	.342	.464
Cleon Jones	OF122,1B15	R	26	137	483	92	164	25	4	12	75	64	60	16	.340	.422	.482
Ron Swoboda	OF97	R	25	109	327	38	77	10	2	9	52	43	90	1	.235	.326	.361
Art Shamsky	OF78,1B9	L	27	100	303	42	91	9	3	14	47	36	32	1	.300	.375	.488
Al Weis	SS52,2B43,3B1	S	31	103	247	20	53	9	2	2	23	15	51	3	.215	.259	.291
Rod Gaspar	OF91	S	23	118	215	26	49	6	1	1	14	25	19	7	.228	.313	.279
Bobby Pfeil	3B49,2B11,OF2	R	25	62	211	20	49	9	0	0	10	7	27	0	.232	.260	.275
Donn Clendenon†	1B58,OF1	R	33	72	202	31	51	5	0	12	37	19	62	3	.252	.321	.455
J.C. Martin	C48,1B2	L	32	66	177	12	37	5	1	4	21	12	32	0	.209	.257	.316
Ed Charles	3B52	R	36	61	169	21	35	8	1	3	18	18	31	4	.207	.286	.320
Amos Otis	OF35,3B3	R	22	48	93	6	14	3	1	0	4	6	27	1	.151	.202	.204
Duffy Dyer	C19	R	23	29	74	5	19	3	1	3	12	4	22	0	.257	.295	.446
Kevin Collins†	3B14	L	22	16	40	1	6	3	0	1	2	3	10	0	.150	.209	.300
Jim Gosger†	OF5	L	26	10	15	0	2	2	0	0	1	1	6	0	.133	.188	.267
Bob Heise	SS3	R	22	4	10	1	3	1	0	0	0	3	2	0	.300	.462	.400

Pitcher	T	Age	G	GS	CG	ShO	IP	H	HR	BB	SO	W-L	Sv	ERA
Tom Seaver	R	24	36	35	18	5	273.1	202	24	82	208	25-7	0	2.21
Gary Gentry	R	22	35	35	6	3	233.2	192	24	81	154	13-12	0	3.43
Jerry Koosman	L	26	32	32	16	6	241.0	187	14	68	180	17-9	0	2.28
Don Cardwell	R	33	30	21	4	0	152.1	145	15	47	60	8-10	0	3.01
Jim McAndrew	R	25	27	21	4	2	135.0	112	12	44	90	6-7	0	3.47
Ron Taylor	R	31	59	0	0	0	76.0	61	7	24	42	9-4	13	2.72
Tug McGraw	L	24	42	4	1	0	100.1	89	6	47	92	9-3	12	2.24
Cal Koonce	R	28	40	0	0	0	83.0	85	8	42	48	6-3	7	4.99
Nolan Ryan	R	22	25	10	2	0	89.1	60	3	53	92	6-3	1	3.53
Jack DiLauro	L	26	23	4	0	0	63.2	50	4	18	27	1-4	1	2.40
Al Jackson†	L	33	9	0	0	0	11.0	18	1	4	10	0-0	0	10.64
Danny Frisella	R	23	3	0	0	0	4.2	8	1	3	5	0-0	0	7.71
Bob Johnson	R	26	2	0	0	0	1.2	1	0	1	1	0-0	0	0.00
Jesse Hudson	L	20	1	0	0	0	2.0	2	0	2	3	0-0	0	4.50
Les Rohr	L	23	1	0	0	0	1.1	5	0	1	0	0-0	0	20.25

1969 Chicago Cubs 2nd NL East 92-70 .568 8.0 GB

Leo Durocher

Player	Gm by Position	B	Age	G	AB	R	H	2B	3B	HR	RBI	BB	SO	SB	Avg	OBP	Slg
Randy Hundley	C151	R	27	151	522	67	133	15	1	18	64	61	90	2	.255	.334	.391
Ernie Banks	1B153	R	38	155	565	60	143	19	2	23	106	42	101	0	.253	.309	.416
Glenn Beckert	2B129	R	28	131	543	69	158	22	1	1	37	24	24	6	.291	.325	.341
Ron Santo	3B160	R	29	160	575	97	166	18	4	29	123	96	97	1	.289	.384	.485
Don Kessinger	SS157	S	26	158	664	109	181	38	6	4	53	61	70	11	.273	.332	.366
Billy Williams	OF159	L	31	163	642	103	188	33	10	21	95	59	70	3	.293	.355	.474
Jim Hickman	OF125	R	32	134	338	38	80	11	2	21	54	47	74	2	.237	.326	.467
Don Young	OF100	R	23	101	272	36	65	12	3	6	27	38	74	1	.239	.343	.371
Al Spangler	OF58	L	35	82	213	23	45	8	1	4	23	21	16	0	.211	.284	.315
Willie Smith	OF33,1B24	L	30	103	195	21	48	9	1	9	25	25	49	1	.246	.330	.441
Paul Popovich†	2B25,SS7,3B6*	S	28	60	154	26	48	6	0	1	14	18	14	0	.312	.387	.370
Jim Qualls	OF35,2B4	S	22	43	120	12	30	5	3	0	9	2	14	2	.250	.266	.342
Oscar Gamble	OF24	L	19	24	71	6	16	1	1	1	5	10	12	0	.225	.321	.310
Adolfo Phillips†	OF25	R	27	28	49	5	11	3	1	0	1	16	15	1	.224	.424	.327
Nate Oliver†	2B13	R	28	44	44	15	7	3	0	1	4	1	10	0	.159	.196	.295
Ken Rudolph	C11,OF3	R	22	27	34	7	7	1	0	1	6	6	11	0	.206	.325	.324
Bill Heath	C9	L	30	27	32	1	5	0	1	0	1	12	4	0	.156	.378	.219
Gene Oliver	C6	R	34	23	27	0	6	3	0	0	0	1	9	0	.222	.276	.333
Jimmie Hall†	OF5	L	31	11	24	1	5	1	0	0	1	1	5	0	.208	.240	.250
Rick Bladt	OF7	R	22	10	13	1	2	0	0	0	1	0	5	0	.154	.154	.154
Manny Jimenez		L	30	6	6	0	1	0	0	0	0	0	2	0	.167	.167	.167
Johnny Hairston	C1,OF1	R	24	3	4	0	1	0	0	0	0	0	2	0	.250	.250	.250
Randy Bobb	C2	R	21	3	2	0	0	0	0	0	0	0	1	0	.000	.000	.000
Charley Smith		R	31	2	2	0	0	0	0	0	0	0	0	0	.000	.000	.000

P. Popovich, 1 G at OF

Pitcher	T	Age	G	GS	CG	ShO	IP	H	HR	BB	SO	W-L	Sv	ERA
Fergie Jenkins	R	25	43	42	23	7	311.1	284	27	71	273	21-15	1	3.21
Bill Hands	R	29	41	41	18	3	300.0	268	21	73	181	20-14	0	2.49
Ken Holtzman	L	23	39	39	12	6	261.1	248	18	93	176	17-13	0	3.58
Dick Selma†	R	25	36	25	4	2	168.2	137	13	72	161	10-8	1	3.63
Joe Niekro†	R	24	4	3	0	0	19.1	24	3	6	7	0-1	0	3.72
Archie Reynolds	R	23	2	2	0	0	7.1	11	1	7	4	0-1	0	2.45
Dave Lemonds	L	20	2	1	0	0	4.2	5	0	5	0	0-1	0	3.86
Gary Ross†	R	21	2	1	0	0	2.0	1	0	2	2	0-0	0	13.50
Phil Regan	R	32	71	0	0	0	112.0	120	6	35	56	12-6	17	3.70
Ted Abernathy	R	36	56	0	0	0	85.1	75	8	42	55	4-3	3	3.16
Hank Aguirre	L	38	41	0	0	0	45.0	45	2	12	19	1-0	1	2.60
Rich Nye	L	24	34	5	1	0	68.2	72	13	21	39	3-5	3	5.11
Don Nottebart†	R	33	16	0	0	0	18.0	28	2	7	8	1-1	0	7.00
Ken Johnson†	R	36	9	1	0	0	19.0	17	2	13	18	1-2	1	2.84
Jim Colborn	R	23	6	2	0	0	14.2	15	2	9	4	1-0	0	3.07
Joe Decker	R	22	4	1	0	0	12.1	10	0	6	13	1-0	0	2.92
Alec Distaso	R	20	2	0	0	0	4.2	6	0	1	1	0-0	0	3.86

1969 Pittsburgh Pirates 3rd NL East 88-74 .543 12.0 GB

Larry Shepard (84-73)/Alex Grammas (4-1)

Player	Gm by Position	B	Age	G	AB	R	H	2B	3B	HR	RBI	BB	SO	SB	Avg	OBP	Slg
Manny Sanguillen	C113	R	25	129	459	62	139	21	6	5	57	12	48	8	.303	.324	.407
Al Oliver	1B106,OF21	L	22	129	463	55	132	19	2	17	70	21	38	8	.285	.333	.445
Bill Mazeroski	2B65	R	32	67	227	13	52	7	1	3	25	22	16	1	.229	.298	.308
Richie Hebner	3B124,1B1	L	21	129	459	72	138	23	4	8	47	53	53	4	.301	.380	.420
Freddie Patek	SS146	R	24	147	460	48	110	9	1	5	32	53	86	15	.239	.318	.296
Matty Alou	OF162	L	30	162	698	105	231	41	6	1	48	42	35	22	.331	.369	.411
Roberto Clemente	OF135	R	34	138	507	87	175	20	12	19	91	56	73	4	.345	.411	.544
Willie Stargell	OF116,1B23	L	29	145	522	89	160	31	6	29	92	61	120	1	.307	.382	.556
Gene Alley	2B53,SS25,3B5	R	28	82	285	28	70	3	2	8	32	19	48	4	.246	.293	.354
Jose Pagan	3B44,OF23,2B1	R	34	108	274	29	78	11	4	9	42	17	46	1	.285	.325	.453
Carl Taylor	OF36,1B24	R	25	104	221	30	77	10	1	4	33	31	36	0	.348	.432	.457
Jerry May	C52	R	25	62	190	21	44	8	0	7	23	9	53	1	.232	.268	.384
Jose Martinez	2B42,SS20,3B5*	R	26	77	168	20	45	6	0	1	16	9	32	1	.268	.309	.321
Bob Robertson	1B26	R	22	32	96	7	20	4	1	1	9	8	30	1	.208	.267	.302
Ron Davis	OF51	R	27	62	64	10	15	1	1	0	4	7	14	0	.234	.310	.281
Dave Cash	2B17	R	21	18	61	8	17	3	1	0	4	9	9	2	.279	.371	.361
Gary Kolb	C7	L	29	29	37	4	3	1	0	0	3	2	14	0	.081	.128	.108
Johnny Jeter	OF20	R	24	28	29	7	9	1	1	1	6	3	15	1	.310	.375	.517
Angel Mangual	OF3	R	22	6	4	1	1	1	0	0	0	0	0	0	.250	.250	.500

J. Martinez, 2 G at OF

Pitcher	T	Age	G	GS	CG	ShO	IP	H	HR	BB	SO	W-L	Sv	ERA
Bob Veale	L	33	34	34	9	1	225.2	232	8	91	213	13-14	0	3.23
Dock Ellis	R	24	35	33	8	2	218.2	206	14	76	173	11-17	0	3.58
Steve Blass	R	27	38	32	9	0	210.0	207	21	86	147	16-10	2	4.46
Jim Bunning†	R	37	25	25	4	0	156.0	147	10	49	124	10-9	0	3.81
Gene Garber	R	21	2	1	0	0	5.0	6	3	1	3	0-0	0	5.40
Bruce Dal Canton	R	27	57	0	0	0	86.1	79	3	49	56	8-2	5	3.34
Chuck Hartenstein	R	27	56	0	0	0	95.2	84	9	27	44	5-4	10	3.95
Bob Moose	R	21	44	19	6	1	170.0	149	9	62	165	14-3	4	2.91
Joe Gibbon†	L	34	35	0	0	0	51.1	38	5	17	35	5-1	9	1.93
Luke Walker	L	25	31	15	3	1	118.2	98	5	57	96	4-6	0	3.64
Lou Marone	L	23	29	0	0	0	35.1	24	2	13	25	1-1	0	2.55
Ron Kline†	R	37	20	0	0	0	31.0	37	3	5	15	1-3	3	5.81
Bo Belinsky	L	32	8	3	0	0	17.2	17	1	14	15	0-3	0	4.58
Jim Shellenback†	L	25	8	0	0	0	16.2	14	1	4	7	0-0	0	3.24
Pedro Ramos†	R	34	5	0	0	0	6.0	8	2	0	4	0-1	0	6.00
Frank Brosseau	R	24	2	0	0	0	1.2	2	0	2	2	0-0	0	10.80

1969 St. Louis Cardinals 4th NL East 87-75 .537 13.0 GB

Red Schoendienst

Player	Gm by Position	B	Age	G	AB	R	H	2B	3B	HR	RBI	BB	SO	SB	Avg	OBP	Slg
Tim McCarver	C136	L	27	138	515	46	134	27	3	7	51	49	26	4	.260	.323	.365
Joe Torre	1B144,C17	R	28	159	602	72	174	29	6	18	101	66	85	0	.289	.361	.447
Julian Javier	2B141	R	32	143	493	59	139	28	2	10	42	40	74	8	.282	.336	.408
Mike Shannon	3B149	R	29	150	551	51	140	15	5	12	55	49	87	1	.254	.315	.365
Dal Maxvill	SS131	R	30	132	372	27	65	10	2	2	32	44	52	1	.175	.263	.228
Lou Brock	OF157	L	30	157	655	97	195	33	10	12	47	50	115	53	.298	.349	.434
Curt Flood	OF152	R	31	153	606	80	173	31	3	4	57	48	57	9	.285	.344	.366
Vada Pinson	OF124	L	30	132	495	58	126	22	6	10	70	35	63	4	.255	.303	.384
Steve Huntz	SS52,2B12,3B6	S	23	71	139	13	27	4	0	3	13	27	34	0	.194	.325	.288
Phil Gagliano	2B20,1B9,3B9*	R	27	62	128	7	29	2	0	1	10	14	12	0	.227	.303	.266
Joe Hague	OF17,1B9	L	25	40	100	8	17	2	1	2	8	12	23	0	.170	.259	.270
Vic Davalillo†	OF23,P2	L	32	63	98	15	26	3	0	2	10	7	8	1	.265	.314	.357
Bill White	1B15	L	35	49	57	7	12	1	0	0	4	11	15	1	.211	.338	.228
Byron Browne	OF16	R	26	22	53	9	12	0	1	1	7	11	14	0	.226	.359	.321
Jim Hicks†	OF15	R	29	19	44	5	8	0	2	1	3	4	14	0	.182	.250	.341
Dave Ricketts	C8	S	33	30	44	2	12	1	0	0	5	4	5	0	.273	.320	.295
Jerry Davanon†	SS16	R	23	16	40	7	12	3	0	1	7	6	8	0	.300	.391	.450
Bob Johnson†	3B4,1B1	R	33	19	29	1	6	0	0	1	2	2	4	0	.207	.258	.310
Leron Lee	OF7	L	21	7	23	3	5	1	0	0	0	3	8	0	.217	.308	.261
Chip Coulter	2B6	S	24	6	19	3	6	1	1	0	4	2	6	0	.316	.381	.474
Ted Simmons	C4	S	19	5	14	0	3	0	1	0	3	1	1	0	.214	.250	.357
Boots Day	OF1	L	21	11	6	1	0	0	0	0	0	1	1	0	.000	.143	.000
Joe Nossek†	OF1	R	28	9	5	2	1	0	0	0	0	0	3	0	.200	.200	.200

P. Gagliano, 2 G at OF

Pitcher	T	Age	G	GS	CG	ShO	IP	H	HR	BB	SO	W-L	Sv	ERA
Bob Gibson	R	33	35	35	28	4	314.0	251	12	95	269	20-13	0	2.18
Nelson Briles	R	25	36	33	10	3	227.2	218	17	63	126	15-13	0	3.52
Steve Carlton	L	24	31	31	12	2	236.1	185	15	93	210	17-11	0	2.17
Ray Washburn	R	31	28	16	2	0	132.1	133	9	49	80	3-8	1	3.06
Mike Torrez	R	22	24	15	3	0	107.2	96	7	62	61	10-4	0	3.59
Dave Giusti	R	29	22	12	2	1	99.2	96	7	37	62	3-7	0	3.61
Santiago Guzman	R	19	1	1	0	0	7.1	9	2	3	7	0-1	0	4.91
Jerry Reuss	L	20	1	1	0	0	7.0	2	0	3	3	1-0	0	0.00
Jim Ellis	L	24	2	1	0	0	5.1	7	0	3	0	0-0	0	1.69
Reggie Cleveland	R	21	1	1	0	0	4.0	7	0	1	3	0-0	0	9.00
Joe Hoerner	L	32	45	0	0	0	53.1	44	5	9	35	2-3	15	2.87
Mudcat Grant†	R	33	30	3	1	0	63.1	62	9	22	35	7-5	7	4.12
Chuck Taylor	R	27	27	13	5	1	126.2	108	8	30	62	7-5	0	2.56
Ron Willis†	R	25	26	0	0	0	32.1	26	4	19	23	1-2	0	4.18
Gary Waslewski†	R	27	12	0	0	0	20.2	19	3	8	16	0-2	1	3.92
Mel Nelson	L	33	8	0	0	0	5.1	13	0	3	3	0-1	0	11.81
Sal Campisi	R	26	7	0	0	0	9.2	4	0	6	7	1-0	0	0.93
Tom Hilgendorf	L	27	6	0	0	0	6.1	3	0	2	2	0-0	2	1.42
Vic Davalillo	L	32	2	0	0	0	0.0	2	0	2	0	0-0	0	—
Dennis Ribant†	R	27	1	0	0	0	1.1	4	1	1	0	0-0	0	13.50

1969 Philadelphia Phillies 5th NL East 63-99 .389 37.0 GB

Bob Skinner (44-64)/George Myatt (19-35)

Player	Gm by Position	B	Age	G	AB	R	H	2B	3B	HR	RBI	BB	SO	SB	Avg	OBP	Slg
Mike Ryan	C132	R	27	133	446	41	91	17	2	12	44	30	66	1	.204	.256	.332
Dick Allen	1B117	R	27	118	438	79	126	23	3	32	89	64	144	9	.288	.375	.573
Cookie Rojas	2B95,OF2	R	30	110	391	35	89	11	1	4	30	23	28	1	.228	.269	.292
Tony Taylor	3B71,2B57,1B10	R	33	138	557	68	146	24	5	3	30	42	62	19	.262	.317	.339
Don Money	SS126	R	22	127	450	41	103	22	2	6	42	43	83	1	.229	.296	.327
Larry Hisle	OF140	R	22	145	482	75	128	23	5	20	56	48	152	18	.266	.338	.459
Johnny Callison	OF129	L	30	134	495	66	131	29	5	16	64	49	73	2	.265	.332	.440
John Briggs	OF108,1B2	L	25	124	361	51	86	20	3	12	46	64	78	9	.238	.351	.410
Deron Johnson	OF72,3B50,1B18	R	30	138	475	51	121	19	4	17	80	60	111	4	.255	.333	.419
Rick Joseph	3B58,1B17,2B1	R	29	99	264	35	72	15	0	6	37	22	57	2	.273	.329	.398
Ron Stone	OF69	L	26	103	222	22	53	7	1	1	24	29	28	3	.239	.332	.293
Terry Harmon	SS38,2B19,3B2	R	25	87	201	25	48	8	1	0	16	22	31	1	.239	.323	.289
ave Watkins	C54,OF5,3B1	R	25	69	148	17	26	2	1	4	12	22	53	2	.176	.291	.284
Rich Barry	OF9	R	28	20	32	4	6	1	0	0	0	5	6	0	.188	.316	.219
Gene Stone	1B5	L	25	18	28	4	6	0	1	0	0	4	9	0	.214	.313	.286
Scott Reid	OF5	L	22	13	19	5	4	0	0	0	0	7	5	0	.211	.423	.211
Vic Roznovsky	C2	L	30	13	13	0	3	0	0	0	1	1	4	0	.231	.286	.231
Don Lock†	OF1	R	32	4	4	0	0	0	0	0	0	0	1	0	.000	.000	.000
Leroy Reams		L	25	1	1	0	0	0	0	0	0	0	1	0	.000	.000	.000

Pitcher	T	Age	G	GS	CG	ShO	IP	H	HR	BB	SO	W-L	Sv	ERA
Grant Jackson	L	26	38	35	13	4	253.0	237	16	92	180	14-18	1	3.34
Woodie Fryman	L	29	36	35	10	1	228.1	243	15	89	150	12-15	0	4.41
Rick Wise	R	23	33	31	14	4	220.0	215	17	61	144	15-13	0	3.23
Jerry Johnson	R	25	33	21	4	2	147.1	151	18	57	82	6-13	1	4.28
Billy Champion	R	21	23	20	4	2	116.2	130	7	63	70	5-10	1	5.01
Jeff James	R	27	6	5	1	0	31.2	36	5	14	21	2-2	0	5.40
Chris Short	L	31	2	2	0	0	10.0	11	2	4	5	0-0	0	7.20
John Boozer	R	30	46	2	0	0	82.0	91	12	36	47	1-2	6	4.28
Turk Farrell	R	35	46	0	0	0	74.1	92	8	27	40	3-4	3	4.00
Al Raffo	R	27	45	0	0	0	72.1	81	6	25	38	1-3	1	4.11
Billy Wilson	R	26	37	0	0	0	62.1	53	6	36	48	2-5	6	3.32
Lowell Palmer	R	21	26	9	1	1	90.0	91	12	47	68	2-8	0	5.20
Barry Lersch	R	24	10	0	0	0	17.2	20	6	10	13	0-3	2	7.13
Gary Wagner†	R	29	9	2	0	0	19.1	31	3	7	8	0-3	0	7.91
Luis Peraza	R	27	8	0	0	0	9.0	12	1	2	7	0-0	0	6.00

1969 Montreal Expos 6th NL East 52-110 .321 48.0 GB

Gene Mauch

Player	Gm by Position	B	Age	G	AB	R	H	2B	3B	HR	RBI	BB	SO	SB	Avg	OBP	Slg
Ron Brand	C84,OF2	R	29	103	287	19	74	12	0	0	20	30	19	2	.258	.327	.300
Bob Bailey	1B85,OF12,3B1	R	26	111	358	46	95	16	6	9	53	40	76	3	.265	.337	.419
Gary Sutherland	2B139,SS15,OF1	R	24	141	544	63	130	26	1	3	35	37	31	5	.239	.289	.307
Coco Laboy	3B156	R	28	157	562	53	145	29	1	18	83	40	96	0	.258	.308	.409
Bobby Wine	SS118,1B1,3B1	R	30	121	370	23	74	8	1	3	25	28	49	0	.200	.256	.251
Rusty Staub	OF156	L	25	158	549	89	166	26	5	29	79	110	61	3	.302	.426	.526
Mack Jones	OF129	L	30	135	455	73	123	23	5	22	79	67	110	6	.270	.379	.488
Adolfo Phillips†	OF53	R	27	58	199	25	43	4	4	4	7	19	62	6	.216	.286	.337
Ron Fairly†	1B52,OF21	L	30	70	253	35	73	13	4	12	39	28	22	1	.289	.358	.514
John Bateman	C66	R	28	74	235	16	49	4	0	8	19	12	44	0	.209	.250	.328
Ty Cline	OF41,1B17	L	30	101	209	26	50	5	3	2	12	32	22	4	.239	.346	.321
Maury Wills†	SS46,2B1	S	36	47	189	23	42	3	0	0	8	20	21	15	.222	.295	.238
Donn Clendenon†	1B24,OF11	R	33	38	129	14	31	6	1	4	14	6	32	0	.240	.272	.395
Jose Herrera	OF31,2B2,3B1	R	27	47	126	7	36	5	0	2	12	3	14	1	.286	.302	.373
Don Bosch	OF32	S	26	49	112	13	20	5	0	1	4	8	20	1	.179	.233	.250
Kevin Collins†	2B20,3B16	L	22	52	96	5	23	5	1	2	12	8	16	0	.240	.292	.375
Manny Mota†	OF22	R	31	31	89	6	28	1	1	0	0	6	11	1	.315	.358	.348
John Boccabella	C32	R	28	40	86	4	9	2	0	1	6	6	30	1	.105	.170	.163
Remy Hermoso	2B18,SS6	R	21	28	74	6	12	0	0	0	3	5	10	3	.162	.225	.162
Jim Fairey	OF13	L	24	20	49	6	14	1	0	1	6	1	7	0	.286	.300	.367
Floyd Wicker	OF11	L	25	41	39	2	4	0	0	0	2	2	20	0	.103	.146	.103
Marv Staehle	2B4	L	27	6	17	4	7	2	0	1	1	2	0	0	.412	.474	.706
Don Hahn	OF3	R	20	4	9	0	1	0	0	0	2	0	5	0	.111	.111	.111
Garry Jestadt	SS1	R	22	6	6	1	0	0	0	0	1	0	0	0	.000	.000	.000

Pitcher	T	Age	G	GS	CG	ShO	IP	H	HR	BB	SO	W-L	Sv	ERA
Bill Stoneman	R	25	42	36	8	5	235.2	233	26	123	185	11-19	0	4.39
Jerry Robertson	R	25	38	27	3	0	179.2	186	17	81	133	5-16	1	3.96
Mike Wegener	R	22	32	26	4	1	165.2	150	10	96	124	5-14	0	4.40
Steve Renko	R	24	18	15	4	0	103.1	94	14	50	68	6-7	0	4.01
Mudcat Grant†	R	33	11	10	1	0	50.2	64	7	14	20	1-6	0	4.80
Carl Morton	R	25	8	5	0	0	29.1	29	2	18	16	0-3	0	4.60
Bob Reynolds	R	22	1	1	0	0	1.1	3	0	3	2	0-0	0	20.25
Dan McGinn	L	25	74	1	0	0	132.1	123	8	65	112	7-10	6	3.94
Roy Face	R	41	44	0	0	0	59.1	62	11	15	34	4-2	5	3.94
Don Shaw	L	25	35	1	0	0	65.2	61	9	37	45	2-5	1	5.21
Howie Reed	R	32	31	15	2	1	106.0	119	7	50	59	6-7	1	4.84
Gary Waslewski†	R	27	30	14	3	1	109.1	102	5	63	63	3-7	1	3.29
Larry Jaster	L	25	24	11	1	0	77.0	95	17	28	39	1-6	0	5.49
Carroll Sembera	R	27	23	0	0	0	33.0	28	1	24	15	0-2	2	3.55
Dick Radatz†	R	32	22	0	0	0	34.2	32	6	18	32	0-4	3	5.71
Claude Raymond†	R	32	15	0	0	0	22.0	21	2	8	11	1-2	1	4.09
Steve Shea	R	26	10	0	0	0	15.2	18	2	8	11	0-0	0	2.87
Leo Marentette	R	28	3	0	0	0	5.1	9	1	1	4	0-0	0	6.75

1969 Atlanta Braves 1st NL West 93-69 .574 —

Lum Harris

Player	Gm by Position	B	Age	G	AB	R	H	2B	3B	HR	RBI	BB	SO	SB	Avg	OBP	Slg
Bob Didier	C114	S	20	114	352	30	90	16	1	0	32	34	39	1	.256	.321	.307
Orlando Cepeda	1B153	R	31	154	573	74	147	28	2	22	88	55	76	12	.257	.325	.428
Felix Millan	2B162	R	25	162	652	98	174	23	5	6	57	34	35	14	.267	.310	.345
Clete Boyer	3B141	R	32	144	496	57	124	16	1	14	57	55	87	3	.250	.328	.371
Sonny Jackson	SS97	L	24	98	318	41	76	3	5	1	27	35	33	12	.239	.317	.289
Hank Aaron	OF144,1B4	R	35	147	547	100	164	30	3	44	97	87	47	9	.300	.396	.607
Felipe Alou	OF116	R	34	123	476	54	134	13	1	5	32	23	23	4	.282	.319	.345
Mike Lum	OF89	L	23	121	168	20	45	8	0	1	22	16	18	0	.268	.326	.333
Tony Gonzalez†	OF82	L	32	89	320	51	94	15	2	10	50	27	22	3	.294	.354	.447
Rico Carty	OF79	R	29	104	304	47	104	15	0	16	58	32	28	0	.342	.401	.549
Gil Garrido	SS81	R	28	82	227	18	50	5	1	0	10	16	11	0	.220	.272	.251
Bob Aspromonte	OF24,3B23,SS18*	R	31	82	198	16	50	8	1	3	24	13	19	0	.253	.304	.348
Bob Tillman	C69	R	32	69	190	18	37	5	0	12	29	18	47	0	.195	.263	.411
Tito Francona†	OF15,1B7	L	35	51	88	5	26	1	0	2	22	13	10	0	.295	.371	.375
Tommie Aaron	1B16,OF8	R	29	49	60	13	15	2	0	1	5	6	6	0	.250	.318	.333
Ralph Garr	OF7	L	23	22	27	6	6	1	0	0	2	2	4	1	.222	.276	.259
Darrell Evans	3B6	L	22	12	26	3	6	0	0	0	1	1	8	0	.231	.250	.231
Dusty Baker	OF3	R	20	3	7	0	0	0	0	0	0	0	3	0	.000	.000	.000
Walt Hriniak†	C6	L	26	7	7	0	1	0	0	0	0	2	1	0	.143	.333	.143
Oscar Brown	OF3	R	23	7	4	2	1	0	0	0	0	0	1	0	.250	.250	.250
Jim Breazeale	1B1	L	19	2	1	1	0	0	0	0	0	2	0	0	.000	.667	.000

B. Aspromonte, 2 G at 2B

Pitcher	T	Age	G	GS	CG	ShO	IP	H	HR	BB	SO	W-L	Sv	ERA
Phil Niekro	R	30	40	35	21	4	284.1	235	21	57	193	23-13	1	2.56
Ron Reed	R	26	36	33	7	1	241.1	227	24	56	160	18-10	0	3.47
Pat Jarvis	R	28	37	33	4	1	217.1	204	25	73	123	13-11	0	4.43
Milt Pappas	R	30	26	24	1	0	144.0	149	14	44	72	6-10	0	3.63
George Stone	L	22	36	20	3	0	165.1	166	20	48	102	13-10	3	3.65
Jim Britton	R	25	24	13	2	1	88.0	69	10	49	60	7-5	1	3.78
Mike McQueen	L	18	1	1	0	0	3.0	2	0	3	3	0-0	0	3.00
Garry Hill	R	22	1	1	0	0	2.0	6	1	1	2	0-1	0	18.00
Cecil Upshaw	R	26	62	0	0	0	105.1	102	7	29	57	6-4	27	2.91
Paul Doyle	L	29	36	0	0	0	39.0	31	4	16	25	2-0	4	2.08
Claude Raymond†	R	32	33	0	0	0	48.0	56	4	13	15	2-2	1	5.25
Gary Neibauer	R	24	29	0	0	0	57.2	42	9	31	42	1-2	0	3.90
Ken Johnson†	R	36	9	2	0	0	29.0	32	4	9	20	0-1	1	4.97
Hoyt Wilhelm†	R	45	8	0	0	0	12.1	5	0	4	14	2-0	4	0.73
Larry Maxie	R	28	2	0	0	0	3.0	1	0	1	1	0-0	0	3.00
Rick Kester	R	22	1	0	0	0	2.0	5	1	0	2	0-0	0	13.50
Bob Priddy†	R	29	1	0	0	0	2.0	1	0	1	1	0-0	0	0.00
Charlie Vaughan	L	21	1	0	0	0	1.0	1	0	3	1	0-0	0	18.00

1969 San Francisco Giants 2nd NL West 90-72 .556 3.0 GB

Clyde King

Player	Gm by Position	B	Age	G	AB	R	H	2B	3B	HR	RBI	BB	SO	SB	Avg	OBP	Slg
Dick Dietz	C73	R	27	79	244	28	56	8	1	11	35	53	53	0	.230	.372	.406
Willie McCovey	1B148	L	31	149	491	101	157	26	2	45	126	121	66	0	.320	.453	.656
Ron Hunt	2B125,3B1	R	28	128	478	72	125	23	3	3	41	51	47	9	.262	.361	.341
Jim Davenport	3B104,1B1,SS1*	R	35	112	303	20	73	10	1	2	42	29	37	0	.241	.304	.300
Hal Lanier	SS150	R	26	150	495	37	113	9	1	0	35	25	68	0	.228	.263	.251
Bobby Bonds	OF155	R	23	158	622	120	161	25	6	32	90	81	187	45	.259	.351	.473
Ken Henderson	OF111,3B3	S	23	113	374	42	84	14	4	6	44	42	64	6	.225	.308	.332
Willie Mays	OF109,1B1	R	38	117	403	64	114	17	3	13	58	49	71	6	.283	.362	.437
Dave Marshall	OF87	L	26	110	267	32	62	7	1	2	33	40	68	1	.232	.340	.288
Don Mason	2B51,3B21,SS7	L	24	104	250	43	57	4	2	0	13	36	29	1	.228	.324	.260
Jim Ray Hart	OF68,3B3	R	27	95	236	27	60	9	0	3	26	28	49	0	.254	.343	.331
Jack Hiatt	C60,1B3	R	26	69	194	18	38	4	0	7	34	48	58	0	.196	.352	.325
Tito Fuentes	3B36,SS30	S	25	67	183	28	54	4	3	1	14	15	25	2	.295	.350	.366
Bob Burda	1B45,OF19	L	30	97	161	20	37	8	0	6	27	21	12	0	.230	.317	.391
Bobby Etheridge	3B39,SS1	R	26	56	131	13	34	9	0	1	10	19	26	0	.260	.358	.351
Bob Barton	C49	R	27	49	106	5	18	2	0	0	1	9	19	0	.170	.241	.189
John Stephenson	C9,3B1	L	28	22	27	2	6	2	0	0	3	0	4	0	.222	.214	.296
Cesar Gutierrez†	3B7,SS4	R	26	15	23	4	5	1	0	0	0	6	2	1	.217	.379	.261
Leon Wagner	OF1	L	35	11	12	0	4	0	0	0	2	2	1	0	.333	.467	.333
Frank Johnson	OF7	R	26	7	10	2	1	0	0	0	0	0	1	0	.100	.100	.100
John Harrell	C2	R	21	2	6	0	3	0	0	0	2	2	1	0	.500	.625	.500
George Foster	OF8	R	20	9	5	1	2	0	0	0	1	0	1	0	.400	.400	.400
Ozzie Virgil		R	36	1	1	0	0	0	0	0	0	0	0	0	.000	.000	.000

J. Davenport, 1 G at OF

Pitcher	T	Age	G	GS	CG	ShO	IP	H	HR	BB	SO	W-L	Sv	ERA
Gaylord Perry	R	30	40	39	26	3	325.1	290	23	91	233	19-14	0	2.49
Juan Marichal	R	31	37	36	27	8	299.2	244	15	54	205	21-11	0	2.10
Mike McCormick	L	30	32	28	9	0	196.2	175	20	77	76	11-9	0	3.34
Bobby Bolin	R	30	30	22	2	0	146.1	149	17	49	102	7-7	0	4.43
Ray Sadecki	L	28	29	17	4	3	138.1	137	18	53	104	5-8	0	4.23
Ron Bryant	L	21	16	8	0	0	57.2	60	8	25	30	4-3	1	4.37
Bob Garibaldi	R	27	1	1	0	0	5.0	6	0	2	1	0-1	0	1.80
Frank Linzy	R	28	58	0	0	0	116.1	129	5	38	62	14-9	11	3.64
Ron Herbel	R	31	39	4	2	0	87.1	92	7	23	34	4-1	1	4.02
Rich Robertson	R	24	17	7	1	1	44.1	53	4	21	20	1-3	0	5.48
Joe Gibbon†	L	34	16	0	0	0	20.0	15	1	13	9	1-3	2	3.60
Don McMahon†	R	39	13	0	0	0	23.2	13	1	9	21	3-1	2	3.04
Ron Kline†	R	37	7	0	0	0	11.0	16	1	6	7	0-2	0	4.09
Mike Davison	L	23	1	0	0	0	2.0	2	0	0	2	0-0	0	4.50

1969 Cincinnati Reds 3rd NL West 89-73 .549 4.0 GB

Dave Bristol

Player	Gm by Position	B	Age	G	AB	R	H	2B	3B	HR	RBI	BB	SO	SB	Avg	OBP	Slg
Johnny Bench	C147	R	21	148	532	83	156	23	1	26	90	49	86	6	.293	.353	.487
Lee May	1B156,OF7	R	26	158	607	85	169	32	3	38	110	45	142	5	.278	.331	.529
Tommy Helms	2B125,SS4	R	28	126	480	38	129	18	1	1	40	18	33	4	.269	.296	.317
Tony Perez	3B160	R	27	160	629	103	185	31	2	37	122	63	131	4	.294	.357	.526
Woody Woodward	SS93,2B2	R	26	97	241	36	63	12	0	0	15	24	40	3	.261	.333	.311
Pete Rose	OF156,2B2	S	28	156	627	120	218	33	11	16	82	88	65	7	.348	.428	.512
Bobby Tolan	OF150	L	23	152	637	104	194	25	10	21	93	27	92	26	.305	.347	.474
Alex Johnson	OF132	R	26	139	523	86	165	18	4	17	88	25	69	11	.315	.350	.463
Jimmy Stewart	OF66,2B18,3B6*	S	30	119	221	26	56	3	4	4	24	19	33	4	.253	.311	.357
Darrel Chaney	SS91	S	21	93	209	21	40	5	2	0	15	24	75	1	.191	.278	.234
Chico Ruiz	2B39,SS29,3B7*	S	30	88	196	19	48	4	1	0	13	14	28	4	.245	.292	.276
Ted Savage	OF17,2B1	R	32	68	110	20	25	7	0	2	11	20	27	3	.227	.344	.345
Fred Whitfield	1B14	L	31	74	74	2	11	0	0	1	8	18	27	0	.149	.315	.189
Pat Corrales	C29	R	28	29	72	10	19	5	0	1	5	8	17	0	.264	.346	.375
Jim Beauchamp	OF9,1B3	R	29	43	60	8	15	1	0	1	8	5	13	0	.250	.308	.317
Danny Breeden	C3	R	27	3	8	0	1	0	0	0	1	0	3	0	.125	.125	.125
Bernie Carbo		L	21	4	3	0	0	0	0	0	0	0	2	0	.000	.000	.000
Clyde Mashore		R	24	2	1	1	0	0	0	0	0	0	0	0	.000	.000	.000
Mike de la Hoz		R	30	1	1	0	0	0	0	0	0	0	1	0	.000	.000	.000

J. Stewart, 1 G at SS; C. Ruiz, 2 G at 1B, 1 G at OF

Pitcher	T	Age	G	GS	CG	ShO	IP	H	HR	BB	SO	W-L	Sv	ERA
Jim Merritt	L	25	42	36	8	1	251.0	269	33	61	144	17-9	0	4.37
Tony Cloninger	R	28	35	34	6	2	189.2	184	24	103	103	11-17	0	5.03
Jim Maloney	R	29	30	27	6	3	178.2	135	11	86	102	12-5	0	2.77
Gerry Arrigo	L	28	20	16	1	0	91.0	89	9	61	35	4-7	0	4.15
Gary Nolan	R	21	16	15	2	1	108.2	102	11	40	83	8-8	0	3.56
Mel Queen	R	27	2	2	0	0	12.0	7	2	3	7	1-0	0	2.25
Wayne Granger	R	25	90	0	0	0	144.2	143	10	40	68	9-6	27	2.80
Clay Carroll	R	28	71	4	0	0	150.2	149	9	78	90	12-6	7	3.52
Pedro Ramos†	R	34	38	0	0	0	66.1	73	8	24	40	4-3	2	5.16
Jack Fisher	R	30	34	15	0	0	113.0	137	15	30	55	4-4	1	5.50
Al Jackson†	L	33	33	0	0	0	27.1	27	5	17	16	1-0	3	5.27
George Culver	R	25	32	13	0	0	101.1	117	8	52	58	5-7	4	4.26
Dennis Ribant†	R	27	7	0	0	0	8.1	6	1	3	7	0-0	0	1.08
Jose Pena	R	26	6	0	0	0	5.0	10	0	5	3	1-1	0	18.00
John Noriega	R	25	5	0	0	0	7.2	12	1	3	4	0-0	0	5.87
Camilo Pascual†	R	35	5	1	0	0	7.1	14	2	4	3	0-0	0	8.59
Bill Short	L	31	4	0	0	0	2.1	4	0	1	0	0-0	0	15.43

1969 Los Angeles Dodgers 4th NL West 85-77 .525 8.0 GB

Walter Alston

Player	Gm by Position	B	Age	G	AB	R	H	2B	3B	HR	RBI	BB	SO	SB	Avg	OBP	Slg
Tom Haller	C132	L	32	134	445	46	117	18	3	6	39	48	58	0	.263	.337	.357
Wes Parker	1B128,OF2	S	29	132	471	76	131	23	4	13	68	56	46	4	.278	.353	.427
Ted Sizemore	2B118,SS46,OF1	R	24	159	590	69	160	20	5	4	46	45	40	5	.271	.328	.342
Bill Sudakis	3B121	S	23	132	462	50	108	17	5	14	53	40	94	3	.234	.294	.383
Maury Wills†	SS104	S	36	104	434	57	129	7	8	4	39	39	40	25	.297	.356	.378
Willie Davis	OF125	L	29	129	498	66	155	23	8	11	59	33	39	24	.311	.356	.456
Willie Crawford	OF113	L	22	129	389	64	96	17	5	11	41	49	85	4	.247	.331	.401
Andy Kosco	OF109,1B3	R	27	120	424	51	105	13	2	19	74	21	66	0	.248	.282	.422
Manny Mota†	OF80	R	31	85	294	35	95	6	4	3	30	26	25	5	.323	.377	.401
Jim Lefebvre	3B44,2B37,1B6	S	27	95	275	29	65	15	2	4	44	48	37	2	.236	.349	.349
Bill Russell	OF86	R	20	98	212	35	48	6	2	5	15	22	45	4	.226	.301	.344
Len Gabrielson	OF47,1B2	L	29	83	178	13	48	5	1	1	18	12	25	1	.270	.313	.326
Jeff Torborg	C50	R	27	51	124	7	23	4	0	0	7	9	17	1	.185	.241	.218
Billy Grabarkewitz	SS18,3B6,2B3	R	23	34	65	4	6	1	1	0	5	4	19	1	.092	.145	.138
Ron Fairly†	1B12,OF10	L	30	30	64	3	14	3	2	0	8	9	6	0	.219	.315	.328
Paul Popovich†	2B23,SS3	S	28	28	50	5	10	0	0	0	4	1	4	0	.200	.212	.200
Tom Hutton	1B16	L	23	16	48	2	13	0	0	0	4	5	7	0	.271	.340	.271
John Miller	OF6,1B5,3B2*	R	25	26	38	3	8	1	0	1	1	2	9	0	.211	.250	.316
Ken Boyer	1B4	R	38	25	34	0	7	2	0	0	4	2	7	0	.206	.250	.265
Von Joshua	OF8	L	21	14	8	2	2	0	0	0	0	0	2	1	.250	.250	.250
Bob Stinson	C4	S	23	4	8	1	3	0	0	0	2	0	2	0	.375	.375	.375
Steve Garvey		R	20	3	3	0	1	0	0	0	0	0	1	0	.333	.333	.333
Bill Buckner		L	19	1	1	0	0	0	0	0	0	0	0	0	.000	.000	.000
Bobby Valentine		R	19	5	0	3	0	0	0	0	0	0	0	0	—	—	—

J. Miller, 1 G at 2B

Pitcher	T	Age	G	GS	CG	ShO	IP	H	HR	BB	SO	W-L	Sv	ERA
Claude Osteen	L	29	41	41	16	7	321.0	293	17	74	183	20-15	0	2.66
Don Sutton	R	24	41	41	11	4	293.1	269	25	91	217	17-18	0	3.47
Bill Singer	R	25	41	40	16	2	315.2	244	22	74	247	20-12	1	2.34
Alan Foster	R	22	24	15	2	2	102.2	119	11	29	59	3-9	0	4.38
Don Drysdale	R	32	12	12	1	1	62.2	71	9	13	24	5-4	0	4.45
Jim Bunning†	R	37	9	9	1	0	56.1	65	5	10	33	3-1	0	3.36
Jim Brewer	L	31	59	0	0	0	88.1	71	5	41	92	7-6	20	2.55
Pete Mikkelsen	R	29	48	0	0	0	81.1	57	9	30	51	7-5	4	2.77
Al McBean†	R	31	31	0	0	0	48.1	46	6	21	26	2-6	4	3.91
Joe Moeller	R	26	23	4	0	0	51.1	54	4	13	25	1-0	1	3.33
Ray Lamb	R	24	10	0	0	0	15.0	12	2	7	11	0-1	1	1.80
John Purdin	R	26	9	0	0	0	16.1	19	7	12	6	0-0	0	6.06
Bobby Darwin	R	26	3	0	0	0	3.2	4	0	5	0	0-0	0	9.82
Jack Jenkins	R	26	1	0	0	0	1.0	0	0	0	1	0-0	0	0.00

1969 Houston Astros 5th NL West 81-81 .500 12.0 GB

Harry Walker

Player	Gm by Position	B	Age	G	AB	R	H	2B	3B	HR	RBI	BB	SO	SB	Avg	OBP	Slg
Johnny Edwards	C151	L	31	151	496	52	115	20	6	6	50	53	69	2	.232	.306	.333
Curt Blefary	1B152,OF1	L	25	155	542	66	137	26	7	12	67	77	79	8	.253	.347	.393
Joe Morgan	2B132,OF14	L	25	147	535	94	126	18	5	15	43	110	74	49	.236	.365	.372
Doug Rader	3B154,1B4	R	24	155	569	62	140	25	3	11	83	62	103	1	.246	.325	.359
Denis Menke	SS131,2B23,1B9*	R	28	154	553	72	149	25	5	10	90	87	87	2	.269	.369	.387
Jimmy Wynn	OF149	R	27	149	495	113	133	17	1	33	87	148	142	23	.269	.436	.507
Norm Miller	OF114	L	23	119	409	58	108	21	4	4	50	47	77	4	.264	.348	.364
Jesus Alou	OF112	R	27	115	452	49	112	19	4	5	34	15	30	4	.248	.276	.341
Marty Martinez	OF21,SS17,3B15*	S	27	78	198	14	61	5	4	0	15	10	21	0	.308	.340	.374
Gary Geiger	OF65	L	32	93	125	19	28	4	1	0	16	24	34	2	.224	.351	.272
Sandy Valdespino†	OF29	L	30	41	119	17	29	4	0	0	12	15	19	2	.244	.326	.277
Julio Gotay	2B16,3B1	R	30	46	81	7	21	5	0	0	9	7	13	2	.259	.318	.321
Tommy Davis†	OF21	R	30	24	79	2	19	3	0	1	9	8	9	1	.241	.318	.316
Leon McFadden	OF17,SS8	R	25	44	74	3	13	2	0	0	3	4	9	1	.176	.218	.203
Hector Torres	SS22	R	23	34	69	5	11	1	0	1	8	2	12	0	.159	.183	.217
Don Bryant	C28	R	27	31	59	2	11	1	0	1	6	4	13	0	.186	.250	.254
Bob Watson	OF6,1B5,C1	R	23	20	40	3	11	3	0	0	3	6	5	0	.275	.396	.350
Keith Lampard	OF1	L	23	9	12	2	3	0	0	1	2	0	3	0	.250	.250	.500
Cesar Geronimo	OF9	L	21	28	8	8	2	1	0	0	0	0	3	0	.250	.250	.375
John Mayberry		L	20	5	4	0	0	0	0	0	0	1	1	0	.000	.200	.000

D. Menke, 1 G at 3B; M. Martinez, 7 G at C, 1 G at P, 1 G at 2B

Pitcher	T	Age	G	GS	CG	ShO	IP	H	HR	BB	SO	W-L	Sv	ERA
Larry Dierker	R	22	39	37	20	4	305.1	240	18	72	232	20-13	0	2.33
Denny Lemaster	L	30	38	37	11	1	244.2	232	20	72	173	13-17	1	3.16
Don Wilson	R	24	34	34	13	1	225.0	210	16	97	235	16-12	0	4.00
Tom Griffin	R	21	31	31	6	3	188.1	156	19	93	200	11-10	0	3.54
Fred Gladding	R	33	57	0	0	0	72.2	83	2	27	40	4-8	29	4.21
Jack Billingham	R	26	52	4	1	0	82.2	92	12	29	71	6-7	2	4.25
Jim Ray	R	24	40	13	0	0	115.0	105	11	48	115	8-2	0	3.91
Dooley Womack†	R	29	30	0	0	0	51.1	49	1	20	32	2-1	0	3.51
Skip Guinn	L	24	28	0	0	0	27.0	34	3	21	33	1-2	0	6.67
Wade Blasingame	L	25	26	5	0	0	52.0	66	4	33	33	0-5	1	5.37
Jim Bouton†	R	30	16	1	1	0	30.2	32	1	12	32	0-2	1	4.11
Danny Coombs	L	27	8	0	0	0	8.0	12	0	2	3	0-1	0	6.75
Dan Schneider	L	26	6	0	0	0	7.1	16	2	5	3	0-1	0	13.50
Bob Watkins	R	21	5	0	0	0	15.2	13	1	13	11	0-0	0	5.17
Bill Henry	L	41	3	0	0	0	5.0	2	0	2	2	0-0	0	0.00
Ron Willis†	R	25	3	0	0	0	2.1	3	0	2	0	0-0	0	0.00
Scipio Spinks	R	21	1	0	0	0	2.0	1	0	1	4	0-0	0	0.00
Marty Martinez	R	27	1	0	0	0	0.2	1	1	0	0	0-0	0	13.50

1969 San Diego Padres 6th NL West 52-110 .321 41.0 GB

Preston Gomez

Player	Gm by Position	B	Age	G	AB	R	H	2B	3B	HR	RBI	BB	SO	SB	Avg	OBP	Slg
Chris Cannizzaro	C132	R	31	134	418	23	92	14	3	4	33	42	81	0	.220	.290	.297
Nate Colbert	1B134	R	23	139	483	64	123	20	9	24	66	45	123	6	.255	.322	.482
Jose Arcia	2B68,SS37,3B8*	R	25	120	302	35	65	11	3	0	10	14	47	14	.215	.255	.272
Ed Spiezio	3B98,OF1	R	27	121	355	29	83	9	0	13	43	38	64	1	.234	.313	.369
Tommy Dean	SS97,2B2	R	23	101	273	14	48	9	2	2	9	27	54	0	.176	.251	.245
Ollie Brown	OF148	R	25	151	568	76	150	18	3	20	61	44	97	10	.264	.319	.412
Cito Gaston	OF113	R	25	129	391	20	90	11	7	2	28	24	117	4	.230	.275	.309
Al Ferrara	OF96	R	29	138	366	39	95	22	1	14	56	45	69	0	.260	.349	.440
Roberto Pena	SS65,2B33,3B27*	R	32	139	472	44	118	16	3	4	30	21	63	0	.250	.286	.322
Ivan Murrell	OF72,1B2	R	24	111	247	19	63	10	6	3	25	11	65	3	.255	.291	.381
John Sipin	2B60	R	22	68	229	22	51	12	2	2	9	8	44	2	.223	.251	.319
Van Kelly	3B49,2B10	L	23	73	209	16	51	7	1	3	15	12	24	0	.244	.285	.330
Tony Gonzalez†	OF49	L	32	53	182	17	41	4	0	2	8	19	24	1	.225	.309	.280
Larry Stahl	OF37,1B13	L	28	95	162	10	32	6	2	3	10	17	31	3	.198	.278	.315
Walt Hriniak†	C19	L	26	31	66	4	15	0	0	0	1	8	11	0	.227	.329	.227
Jerry Davanon†	2B15,SS7	R	23	24	59	4	8	1	0	0	3	3	12	0	.136	.177	.153
Bill Davis	1B14	L	27	31	57	1	10	1	0	0	1	8	18	0	.175	.288	.193
Jerry Morales	OF19	R	20	19	41	5	8	2	0	1	6	5	7	0	.195	.283	.317
Fred Kendall	C9	R	20	10	26	2	4	0	0	0	0	2	5	0	.154	.214	.154
Jim Williams	OF6	R	22	13	25	4	7	1	0	0	2	3	11	0	.280	.345	.320
Ron Slocum	2B4,3B4,SS1	R	23	13	24	6	7	1	0	1	5	0	5	0	.292	.280	.458
Sonny Ruberto	C15	R	23	19	21	3	3	0	0	0	0	1	7	0	.143	.182	.143
Rafael Robles	SS6	R	21	6	20	1	2	0	0	0	0	1	3	1	.100	.143	.100
Chris Krug	C7	R	29	8	17	0	1	0	0	0	0	1	6	0	.059	.111	.059
Frankie Libran	SS9	R	21	10	10	1	1	1	0	0	1	1	2	0	.100	.182	.200

J. Arcia, 4 G at OF, 1 G at 1B; R. Pena, 12 G at 1B

Pitcher	T	Age	G	GS	CG	ShO	IP	H	HR	BB	SO	W-L	Sv	ERA
Clay Kirby	R	21	35	35	2	0	215.2	204	18	100	113	7-20	0	3.80
Joe Niekro†	R	24	37	31	8	3	202.0	213	15	45	55	8-17	0	3.70
Al Santorini	R	21	32	30	2	1	184.2	194	11	73	111	8-14	0	3.95
Dick Kelley	L	29	27	23	1	1	136.0	113	11	61	96	4-8	0	3.57
Johnny Podres	L	36	17	9	1	0	64.2	66	7	28	17	5-6	0	4.31
Mike Corkins	R	23	6	4	0	0	17.0	27	3	8	13	1-3	0	8.47
Dick Selma†	R	25	4	3	1	0	22.0	19	3	9	20	2-2	0	4.09
Al McBean†	R	31	1	1	0	0	7.0	10	1	2	1	0-1	0	5.14
Frank Reberger	R	25	67	0	0	0	87.2	83	6	41	65	1-2	6	3.59
Jack Baldschun	R	32	61	0	0	0	77.0	80	7	29	67	7-2	1	4.79
Billy McCool	L	24	54	0	0	0	58.2	59	2	42	35	3-5	7	4.30
Tommie Sisk	R	27	53	13	1	0	143.0	160	11	48	59	2-13	6	4.78
Gary Ross†	R	21	46	7	0	0	109.2	104	5	56	58	3-12	3	4.19
Dave Roberts	L	24	22	5	0	0	48.2	65	5	19	19	0-3	1	4.81
Tom Dukes	R	26	13	0	0	0	22.1	26	2	10	15	1-0	1	7.25
Leon Everitt	R	22	5	0	0	0	15.2	18	4	12	11	0-1	0	8.04
Steve Arlin	R	23	4	1	0	0	10.2	13	2	9	9	0-1	0	9.28

»1970 Baltimore Orioles 1st AL East 108-54 .667 —

Earl Weaver

Player	Gm by Position	B	Age	G	AB	R	H	2B	3B	HR	RBI	BB	SO	SB	Avg	OBP	Slg
Ellie Hendricks	C95	L	29	106	322	32	78	9	0	12	41	33	44	1	.242	.312	.382
Boog Powell	1B145	L	28	154	526	82	156	28	0	35	114	104	80	1	.297	.412	.549
Dave Johnson	2B149,SS2	R	27	149	530	68	149	27	1	10	53	66	68	2	.281	.360	.392
Brooks Robinson	3B156	R	33	158	608	84	168	31	4	18	94	53	53	1	.276	.335	.429
Mark Belanger	SS143	R	26	145	459	53	100	6	5	1	36	52	65	13	.218	.303	.259
Don Buford	OF130,2B3,3B3	S	33	144	504	99	137	15	2	17	66	109	55	16	.272	.406	.411
Paul Blair	OF128,3B1	R	26	133	480	79	128	24	2	18	65	56	93	24	.267	.344	.438
Frank Robinson	OF120,1B7	R	34	132	471	88	144	24	1	25	78	69	70	2	.306	.398	.520
Merv Rettenmund	OF93	R	27	106	338	60	109	17	2	18	58	38	59	13	.322	.394	.544
Andy Etchebarren	C76	R	27	78	230	19	56	10	1	4	28	21	41	4	.243	.313	.348
Chico Salmon	SS33,2B12,3B11*	R	29	63	172	19	43	4	0	7	22	8	30	2	.250	.287	.395
Terry Crowley	OF27,1B23	L	23	83	152	25	39	5	0	5	20	35	26	2	.257	.394	.388
Bobby Grich	SS20,2B9,3B1	R	21	30	95	11	20	1	3	0	8	9	21	1	.211	.279	.284
Curt Motton	OF21	R	29	52	84	16	19	3	1	3	19	18	20	1	.226	.369	.393
Clay Dalrymple	C11	L	33	13	32	4	7	1	0	1	3	7	4	0	.219	.350	.344
Dave May†	OF9	L	26	25	31	6	6	0	1	1	6	4	4	0	.194	.286	.355
Johnny Oates	C4	L	24	5	18	2	5	0	1	0	2	2	0	0	.278	.333	.389
Don Baylor	OF6	R	21	8	17	4	4	0	0	0	4	2	3	1	.235	.300	.235
Roger Freed	1B3,OF1	R	24	4	13	0	2	0	0	0	1	3	4	0	.154	.294	.154
Bobby Floyd†	SS2,2B1	R	26	3	2	0	0	0	0	0	0	0	2	0	.000	.000	.000

C. Salmon, 2 G at 1B

Pitcher	T	Age	G	GS	CG	ShO	IP	H	HR	BB	SO	W-L	Sv	ERA
Mike Cuellar	L	33	40	40	21	4	297.2	273	34	69	190	24-8	0	3.48
Dave McNally	L	27	40	40	16	1	296.0	277	29	78	185	24-9	0	3.22
Jim Palmer	R	24	39	39	17	5	305.0	263	21	100	199	20-10	0	2.71
Tom Phoebus	R	28	27	21	3	0	135.0	106	11	62	72	5-5	0	3.07
Jim Hardin	R	26	36	19	3	2	145.1	150	13	26	78	6-5	1	3.53
Eddie Watt	R	29	53	0	0	0	55.1	44	3	29	33	7-7	12	3.25
Pete Richert	L	30	50	0	0	0	54.2	36	5	24	66	7-2	13	1.98
Dick Hall	R	39	32	0	0	0	61.1	51	8	6	30	10-5	3	3.08
Marcelino Lopez	L	26	25	3	0	0	60.2	47	2	37	49	1-1	0	2.08
Dave Leonhard	R	29	23	0	0	0	28.1	32	5	18	14	0-0	1	5.08
Moe Drabowsky†	R	34	21	0	0	0	33.1	30	7	15	21	4-2	1	3.78
Fred Beene	R	27	4	0	0	0	6.0	8	1	5	4	0-0	0	6.00

1970 New York Yankees 2nd AL East 93-69 .574 15.0 GB

Ralph Houk

Player	Gm by Position	B	Age	G	AB	R	H	2B	3B	HR	RBI	BB	SO	SB	Avg	OBP	Slg
Thurman Munson	C125	R	23	132	453	59	137	25	4	6	53	57	56	5	.302	.386	.415
Danny Cater	1B131,3B42,OF7	R	30	155	582	64	175	26	5	6	76	34	44	4	.301	.340	.393
Horace Clarke	2B157	S	30	158	686	81	172	24	2	4	46	35	35	23	.251	.286	.309
Jerry Kenney	3B135,2B2	L	25	140	404	46	78	10	7	4	35	52	44	20	.193	.284	.282
Gene Michael	SS123,3B4,2B3	S	32	134	435	42	93	10	1	2	38	50	93	3	.214	.292	.255
Roy White	OF161	S	26	162	609	109	180	30	6	22	94	95	66	24	.296	.387	.473
Bobby Murcer	OF155	L	24	159	581	95	146	23	3	23	78	87	100	15	.251	.348	.420
Curt Blefary	OF79,1B6	L	26	99	269	34	57	6	0	9	37	43	37	1	.212	.324	.335
John Ellis	1B53,3B5,C2	R	21	78	226	24	56	12	1	7	29	18	47	0	.248	.305	.403
Ron Woods	OF78	R	27	95	225	30	51	5	3	8	27	33	35	4	.227	.324	.382
Jake Gibbs	C44	L	31	49	153	23	46	9	2	8	26	7	14	2	.301	.331	.542
Jim Lyttle	OF70	L	24	87	126	20	39	7	1	3	14	10	26	3	.310	.355	.452
Frank Baker	SS35	L	23	35	117	6	27	4	1	0	11	14	26	1	.231	.323	.282
Ron Hansen	SS15,3B11,2B1	R	32	59	91	13	27	4	0	4	14	19	9	0	.297	.420	.473
Pete Ward	1B13	L	30	66	77	5	20	2	2	1	18	9	17	0	.260	.333	.377
Bobby Mitchell	OF7	R	26	10	22	1	5	2	0	0	4	2	3	0	.227	.320	.318
Frank Tepedino	1B1,OF1	L	22	16	19	2	6	2	0	0	2	1	2	0	.316	.350	.421

Pitcher	T	Age	G	GS	CG	ShO	IP	H	HR	BB	SO	W-L	Sv	ERA
Mel Stottlemyre	R	28	37	37	14	0	271.0	262	23	84	126	15-13	0	3.09
Fritz Peterson	L	28	39	37	8	2	260.1	247	24	40	127	20-11	0	2.90
Stan Bahnsen	R	25	36	35	6	2	232.2	227	23	75	116	14-11	0	3.33
Steve Kline	R	22	16	15	5	0	100.1	99	8	24	49	6-6	0	3.41
Mike Kekich	L	25	26	14	1	0	98.2	103	12	55	63	6-3	0	4.83
John Cumberland†	L	23	15	8	1	0	64.0	62	9	15	38	3-4	0	3.94
Bill Burbach	R	22	4	4	0	0	16.2	23	2	9	10	0-2	0	10.26
Rob Gardner	L	25	1	1	0	0	7.1	8	2	4	6	1-0	0	4.91
Lindy McDaniel	R	34	62	0	0	0	111.2	88	7	23	81	9-5	29	2.01
Ron Klimkowski	R	26	45	3	1	1	98.1	80	7	33	40	6-7	1	2.65
Jack Aker	R	29	41	0	0	0	70.0	57	3	20	36	4-2	16	2.06
Steve Hamilton†	L	34	35	0	0	0	45.1	36	3	16	33	4-3	3	2.78
Gary Waslewski†	R	28	26	5	0	0	55.0	42	4	27	27	2-2	0	3.11
Mike McCormick†	L	31	9	4	0	0	20.2	26	2	13	12	2-0	0	6.10
Joe Verbanic	R	27	7	0	0	0	15.2	20	1	12	8	1-0	0	4.60
Gary Jones	L	25	2	0	0	0	2.0	3	0	1	2	0-0	0	0.00
Loyd Colson	R	22	1	0	0	0	2.0	3	0	0	3	0-0	0	4.50

Seasons: Team Rosters 795

1970 Boston Red Sox 3rd AL East 87-75 .537 21.0 GB

Eddie Kasko

Player	Gm by Position	B	Age	G	AB	R	H	2B	3B	HR	RBI	BB	SO	SB	Avg	OBP	Slg
Jerry Moses	C88,OF1	R	23	92	315	26	83	18	1	6	35	21	45	1	.263	.313	.384
Carl Yastrzemski	1B94,OF69	L	30	161	566	125	186	29	0	40	102	128	66	23	.329	.452	.592
Mike Andrews	2B148	R	26	151	589	91	149	28	1	17	65	81	63	2	.253	.344	.390
George Scott	3B68,1B59	R	26	127	480	50	142	24	5	16	63	44	95	4	.296	.355	.467
Rico Petrocelli	SS141,3B18	R	27	157	583	82	152	31	3	29	103	67	82	1	.261	.334	.473
Tony Conigliaro	OF146	R	25	146	560	89	149	20	1	36	116	43	93	4	.266	.324	.498
Reggie Smith	OF145	S	25	147	580	109	176	32	7	22	74	51	60	10	.303	.361	.497
Billy Conigliaro	OF108	R	22	114	398	59	108	16	3	18	58	35	73	3	.271	.339	.462
Luis Alvarado	3B29,SS27	R	21	59	183	19	41	11	0	1	10	9	30	1	.224	.258	.301
Tom Satriano	C51	L	29	59	165	21	39	9	1	3	13	21	23	0	.236	.326	.358
Dick Schofield	2B15,3B15,SS3	S	35	76	139	16	26	1	2	1	14	21	26	0	.187	.294	.245
John Kennedy†	3B33,2B2	R	29	43	129	15	33	7	1	4	17	6	14	0	.256	.292	.419
George Thomas	OF26,3B6	R	32	38	99	13	34	8	0	2	13	11	12	0	.343	.420	.485
Bob Montgomery	C22	R	26	22	78	8	14	2	0	1	4	6	20	0	.179	.244	.244
Don Pavletich	1B16,C10	R	31	32	65	4	9	1	1	0	6	10	15	1	.138	.250	.185
Mike Fiore†	1B17,OF2	L	25	41	50	5	7	0	0	0	4	8	4	0	.140	.254	.140
Joe Lahoud	OF13	L	23	17	49	6	12	1	0	2	5	7	6	0	.245	.339	.388
Mike Derrick	OF2,1B1	L	26	24	33	3	7	1	0	0	5	0	11	0	.212	.206	.242
Carmen Fanzone	3B5	R	26	10	15	0	3	1	0	0	3	2	2	0	.200	.316	.267
Tommy Matchick†	3B2,2B1,SS1	L	26	10	14	2	1	0	0	0	0	2	2	0	.071	.188	.071

Pitcher	T	Age	G	GS	CG	ShO	IP	H	HR	BB	SO	W-L	Sv	ERA
Gary Peters	L	33	34	34	10	4	221.2	221	20	83	155	16-11	0	4.06
Ray Culp	R	28	33	33	15	1	251.1	211	22	91	197	17-14	0	3.04
Sonny Siebert	R	33	33	33	7	2	222.2	207	29	60	142	15-8	0	3.44
Mike Nagy	R	22	23	20	4	0	128.2	138	16	64	56	6-5	0	4.48
Sparky Lyle	L	25	63	0	0	0	67.1	62	5	34	51	1-7	20	3.88
Vicente Romo	R	27	48	10	0	0	108.0	115	14	43	71	7-3	6	4.08
Ken Brett	L	21	41	14	1	0	139.1	118	17	79	155	8-9	2	4.07
Gary Wagner	R	30	38	0	0	0	40.1	36	3	19	20	3-1	7	3.35
Cal Koonce†	R	29	23	8	1	0	76.1	64	7	29	37	3-4	2	3.54
Lee Stange†	R	33	20	0	0	0	27.1	34	5	12	14	2-2	2	5.60
Ed Phillips	R	25	18	0	0	0	23.2	29	4	10	23	0-2	0	5.32
Chuck Hartenstein†	R	28	17	0	0	0	19.0	21	6	12	12	0-3	1	8.05
Ray Jarvis	R	24	15	0	0	0	16.0	17	1	14	8	0-1	0	3.94
Bill Lee	L	23	11	5	0	0	37.0	48	3	14	19	2-2	1	4.62
Jim Lonborg	R	28	9	4	0	0	34.0	33	3	9	21	4-1	0	3.18
Jose Santiago	R	29	8	0	0	0	11.1	18	0	8	8	0-2	1	10.32
Bobby Bolin†	R	31	6	0	0	0	8.0	2	0	5	8	2-0	2	0.00
Roger Moret	L	20	3	1	0	0	8.1	7	0	4	2	1-0	0	3.24
Dick Mills	R	25	2	0	0	0	4.0	6	0	3	3	0-0	0	2.25
John Curtis	L	22	1	0	0	0	2.1	4	1	1	1	0-0	0	11.57

1970 Detroit Tigers 4th AL East 79-83 .488 29.0 GB

Mayo Smith

Player	Gm by Position	B	Age	G	AB	R	H	2B	3B	HR	RBI	BB	SO	SB	Avg	OBP	Slg
Bill Freehan	C114	R	28	117	395	44	95	17	3	16	52	52	48	0	.241	.332	.420
Norm Cash	1B114	L	35	130	370	58	96	18	2	15	53	72	58	0	.259	.383	.441
Dick McAuliffe	2B127,SS15,3B12	L	30	146	530	73	124	21	1	12	50	101	62	5	.234	.358	.345
Don Wert	3B117,2B2	R	31	128	363	34	79	13	0	6	33	44	56	1	.218	.307	.303
Cesar Gutierrez	SS135	R	27	135	415	40	101	11	6	0	22	18	39	4	.243	.275	.299
Jim Northrup	OF136	L	30	139	504	71	132	21	3	24	80	58	68	3	.262	.343	.458
Mickey Stanley	OF132,1B9	R	27	142	568	83	143	21	11	13	47	45	56	10	.252	.305	.396
Willie Horton	OF96	R	27	96	371	53	113	18	2	17	69	28	43	0	.305	.354	.501
Al Kaline	OF91,1B52	R	35	131	467	64	130	24	4	16	71	77	49	2	.278	.377	.450
Elliott Maddox	3B40,OF37,SS19*	R	22	109	258	30	64	13	4	3	24	30	42	2	.248	.332	.364
Dalton Jones	2B35,3B18,1B10	L	26	89	191	29	42	7	0	6	21	33	33	1	.220	.333	.351
Jim Price	C38	R	28	52	132	12	24	4	0	5	15	21	23	0	.182	.290	.326
Gates Brown	OF26	L	31	81	124	18	28	3	0	3	24	20	14	0	.226	.331	.323
Ike Brown	2B23,OF4,3B1	R	28	56	94	17	27	5	0	4	15	13	26	0	.287	.376	.468
Ken Szotkiewicz	SS44	L	23	47	84	9	9	1	0	3	9	12	29	0	.107	.216	.226
Gene Lamont	C15	L	23	15	44	3	13	3	1	1	4	2	9	0	.295	.340	.477
Russ Nagelson†	OF4,1B1	L	25	28	32	5	6	0	0	0	2	5	6	0	.188	.297	.188
Kevin Collins	1B1	L	23	25	24	2	5	1	0	1	3	1	10	0	.208	.240	.375
Tim Hosley	C4	R	23	7	12	1	2	0	0	1	2	0	6	0	.167	.154	.417

E. Maddox, 1 G at 2B

Pitcher	T	Age	G	GS	CG	ShO	IP	H	HR	BB	SO	W-L	Sv	ERA
Mickey Lolich	L	29	40	39	13	3	272.2	272	27	109	230	14-19	0	3.80
Joe Niekro	R	25	38	34	6	2	213.0	221	28	72	101	12-13	0	4.06
Les Cain	L	22	29	29	5	0	180.2	167	15	98	156	12-7	0	3.84
Mike Kilkenny	L	25	36	21	3	0	129.0	141	10	70	105	7-6	0	5.16
Earl Wilson†	R	35	18	16	4	1	96.0	87	15	32	74	4-6	0	4.41
Denny McLain	R	26	14	14	1	0	91.1	100	19	28	52	3-5	0	4.63
Tom Timmermann	R	30	61	0	0	0	85.1	90	3	34	49	6-7	27	4.11
Fred Scherman	L	25	48	0	0	0	69.2	61	5	28	58	4-4	1	3.23
John Hiller	L	27	47	5	1	1	104.0	82	12	46	89	6-6	3	3.03
Daryl Patterson	R	26	43	0	0	0	78.0	81	9	39	55	7-1	2	4.85
Norm McRae	R	22	19	0	0	0	31.1	26	1	25	16	0-0	0	2.87
Bob Reed	R	25	16	4	0	0	46.1	54	5	14	26	2-4	2	4.86
Fred Lasher†	R	28	12	0	0	0	9.0	10	0	12	8	1-3	3	5.00
Jerry Robertson	R	26	11	0	0	0	14.2	19	1	5	11	0-0	0	3.68
Lerrin LaGrow	R	21	10	0	0	0	12.1	16	2	6	7	0-1	0	7.30
Dennis Saunders	R	21	8	0	0	0	14.0	16	1	5	8	1-1	1	3.21

1970 Cleveland Indians 5th AL East 76-86 .469 32.0 GB

Alvin Dark

Player	Gm by Position	B	Age	G	AB	R	H	2B	3B	HR	RBI	BB	SO	SB	Avg	OBP	Slg
Ray Fosse	C120	R	23	120	450	62	138	17	1	18	61	39	55	1	.307	.361	.469
Tony Horton	1B112	R	25	115	413	48	111	19	3	17	59	30	54	3	.269	.321	.453
Eddie Leon	2B141,SS23,3B1	R	23	152	549	58	136	20	4	10	56	47	89	1	.248	.308	.353
Graig Nettles	3B154,OF3	L	25	157	549	81	129	13	1	26	62	81	77	3	.235	.336	.404
Jack Heidemann	SS132	R	20	133	445	44	94	14	2	6	37	34	88	2	.211	.265	.292
Vada Pinson	OF141,1B7	L	31	148	574	74	164	28	6	24	82	28	69	7	.286	.319	.481
Ted Uhlaender	OF134	L	29	141	473	56	127	21	2	11	46	39	44	3	.268	.321	.391
Roy Foster	OF131	R	24	139	477	66	128	26	0	23	60	54	75	3	.268	.357	.468
Duke Sims	C39,OF36,1B29	L	29	110	345	46	91	12	0	23	56	46	59	0	.264	.360	.499
Chuck Hinton	1B40,OF35,C4*	R	36	107	195	24	62	4	0	9	29	25	34	0	.318	.392	.477
Buddy Bradford†	OF64,3B1	R	25	75	163	25	32	6	1	7	23	21	43	0	.196	.290	.374
Larry Brown	SS27,3B17,2B16	R	30	72	155	17	40	5	2	0	15	20	14	1	.258	.339	.316
Sam McDowell	P39,1B1,2B1	L	27	40	105	5	13	0	0	1	2	2	42	0	.124	.140	.152
Lou Klimchock	1B5,2B5	L	30	41	56	5	9	0	0	1	2	3	9	0	.161	.213	.214
Ted Ford	OF12	R	23	26	46	5	8	1	0	1	1	3	13	0	.174	.224	.261
John Lowenstein	2B10,3B2,OF2*	L	23	17	43	5	11	3	1	1	6	1	9	1	.256	.273	.442
Rich Rollins†	3B5	R	32	42	43	6	10	0	0	2	4	3	5	0	.233	.283	.372
Ken Harrelson	1B13	R	28	17	39	3	11	1	0	1	1	6	4	0	.282	.378	.385
Vern Fuller	2B16,3B4,1B1	R	26	29	33	3	6	2	0	1	2	3	9	0	.182	.250	.333
Russ Nagelson†	OF4	L	25	17	24	3	3	1	0	1	2	3	9	0	.125	.222	.292
Lou Camilli	SS3,2B2,3B1	S	23	16	15	0	0	0	0	0	0	2	2	0	.000	.118	.000
Jim Rittwage	P8,3B1	R	25	8	8	1	3	1	0	0	0	0	0	0	.375	.375	.500

C. Hinton, 3 G at 2B, 2 G at 3B; J. Lowenstein, 1 G at SS

Pitcher	T	Age	G	GS	CG	ShO	IP	H	HR	BB	SO	W-L	Sv	ERA
Sam McDowell	L	27	39	39	19	1	305.0	236	25	131	304	20-12	0	2.92
Rich Hand	R	21	35	25	3	1	159.2	132	27	69	110	6-13	3	3.83
Steve Hargan	R	27	23	19	8	1	142.2	101	14	53	72	11-3	0	2.90
Steve Dunning	R	21	19	17	0	0	94.1	93	16	54	77	4-9	0	4.96
Mike Paul	L	25	30	15	1	0	88.0	91	13	45	70	2-8	0	4.81
Barry Moore†	L	27	13	12	0	0	70.1	70	8	46	35	3-5	0	4.22
Dennis Higgins	R	30	58	0	0	0	90.1	82	8	54	82	4-6	11	3.99
Dean Chance†	R	29	45	19	1	1	155.0	172	18	59	109	9-8	4	4.24
Fred Lasher†	R	28	43	1	0	0	57.2	57	6	30	44	1-7	5	4.06
Phil Hennigan	R	24	42	1	0	0	71.2	69	7	44	43	6-3	3	4.02
Rick Austin	L	23	31	8	1	1	67.2	74	10	26	53	2-5	3	4.79
Dick Ellsworth†	L	30	29	1	0	0	43.2	49	4	14	13	3-3	2	4.53
Vince Colbert	R	24	23	0	0	0	31.0	37	4	16	17	1-1	2	7.26
Steve Mingori	L	26	21	0	0	0	20.1	17	2	12	16	1-0	1	2.66
Bob Miller†	R	31	15	2	0	0	28.0	35	1	15	15	2-2	1	4.18
Jim Rittwage	R	25	8	3	1	0	26.0	18	0	21	16	1-1	0	4.15

1970 Washington Senators 6th AL East 70-92 .432 38.0 GB

Ted Williams

Player	Gm by Position	B	Age	G	AB	R	H	2B	3B	HR	RBI	BB	SO	SB	Avg	OBP	Slg
Paul Casanova	C100	R	28	104	328	25	75	17	3	6	30	10	47	0	.229	.251	.354
Mike Epstein	1B122	L	27	140	430	55	110	15	3	20	56	73	117	2	.256	.371	.444
Tim Cullen	2B112,SS6	R	28	123	262	22	56	10	2	1	18	31	38	3	.214	.301	.279
Aurelio Rodriguez†	3B136,SS7	R	22	142	547	64	135	31	5	19	76	37	81	15	.247	.300	.426
Ed Brinkman	SS157	R	28	158	625	63	164	17	2	1	40	60	41	8	.262	.330	.301
Frank Howard	OF120,1B48	R	33	161	566	90	160	15	1	44	126	132	125	1	.283	.416	.546
Ed Stroud	OF118	L	30	129	433	69	115	11	5	5	32	40	79	29	.266	.331	.349
Del Unser	OF103	L	25	119	322	37	83	5	1	5	30	30	29	1	.258	.319	.326
Rick Reichardt†	OF79,3B1	R	27	107	277	42	70	14	2	15	46	23	69	2	.253	.328	.480
Bernie Allen	2B80,3B12	L	31	104	261	31	61	7	1	8	29	43	21	0	.234	.342	.360
Lee Maye†	OF68,3B1	L	35	96	255	28	67	12	1	7	30	21	32	4	.263	.321	.400
Jim French	C62,OF1	L	28	69	166	20	35	3	1	1	13	38	23	0	.211	.358	.259
Wayne Comer†	OF58,3B1	R	26	77	129	21	30	4	0	0	8	22	16	4	.233	.346	.264
Tom Grieve	OF39	R	22	47	116	12	23	5	1	3	10	14	38	0	.198	.290	.336
Dave Nelson	2B33	R	26	47	107	5	17	1	0	0	4	7	24	2	.159	.207	.168
John Roseboro	C30	L	37	46	86	7	20	4	0	1	6	18	10	1	.233	.365	.314
Ken McMullen†	3B15	R	28	15	59	5	12	2	0	0	3	5	10	0	.203	.266	.237
Hank Allen†	OF17	R	29	22	38	3	8	2	0	0	4	5	9	0	.211	.295	.263
Greg Goossen†	OF5,1B2	R	24	21	36	2	8	3	0	0	1	2	8	0	.222	.256	.306
Dick Billings	C8	R	27	11	24	3	6	2	0	0	1	2	3	0	.250	.308	.458
Jeff Burroughs	OF3	R	19	6	12	1	2	0	0	0	1	2	5	0	.167	.286	.167
Dick Nen	1B1	L	30	6	5	1	1	0	0	0	0	1	1	0	.200	.200	.200
Larry Biittner		L	24	2	2	0	0	0	0	0	0	0	0	0	.000	.000	.000

Pitcher	T	Age	G	GS	CG	ShO	IP	H	HR	BB	SO	W-L	Sv	ERA
Dick Bosman	R	26	36	34	7	3	230.2	212	16	71	134	16-12	0	3.00
Casey Cox	R	28	37	30	1	0	192.1	211	27	44	68	8-12	1	4.45
Joe Coleman	R	23	39	29	6	1	218.2	190	25	89	152	8-12	0	3.58
George Brunet†	L	35	24	20	2	1	118.0	124	10	48	67	8-6	0	4.42
Bill Gogolewski	R	22	8	5	0	0	33.2	33	2	25	19	2-2	0	4.81
Darold Knowles	L	28	71	0	0	0	119.1	100	4	58	71	2-14	27	2.04
Horacio Pina	R	25	61	0	0	0	71.0	66	4	35	41	5-3	6	2.79
Joe Grzenda	L	33	49	3	0	0	84.2	86	8	34	38	3-6	6	5.00
Jim Hannan	R	30	42	17	1	1	128.0	119	17	54	61	9-11	0	4.01
Jim Shellenback	L	26	39	14	2	1	117.1	107	6	51	57	6-7	0	3.68
Jackie Brown	R	27	24	5	1	0	57.0	49	8	37	47	2-2	0	3.95
Dick Such	R	25	21	5	0	0	50.0	48	8	45	41	1-5	0	7.56
Denny Riddleberger	L	24	8	0	0	0	9.1	7	1	2	5	0-0	0	0.96
Jan Dukes	L	24	5	0	0	0	6.2	6	0	1	4	0-0	0	2.70
Bob Humphreys†	R	34	5	0	0	0	6.2	4	1	9	6	0-0	0	1.35
Cisco Carlos	R	29	5	0	0	0	6.0	3	0	4	2	0-0	0	1.50
Pedro Ramos	R	35	4	0	0	0	8.1	10	2	4	10	0-0	0	7.56

1970 Minnesota Twins 1st AL West 98-64 .605 —

Bill Rigney

Player	Gm by Position	B	Age	G	AB	R	H	2B	3B	HR	RBI	BB	SO	SB	Avg	OBP	Slg
George Mitterwald	C117	R	25	117	369	36	82	12	2	15	46	34	84	3	.222	.291	.388
Rich Reese	1B146	L	28	153	501	63	131	15	5	10	56	48	70	5	.261	.332	.371
Danny Thompson	2B81,3B37,SS6	R	23	96	302	25	66	9	0	0	22	7	39	0	.219	.234	.248
Harmon Killebrew	3B138,1B28	R	34	157	527	96	143	20	1	41	113	128	84	0	.271	.411	.546
Leo Cardenas	SS160	R	31	160	588	67	145	34	4	11	65	42	101	2	.247	.300	.374
Tony Oliva	OF157	L	29	157	628	96	204	36	7	23	107	38	67	5	.325	.364	.514
Cesar Tovar	OF151,2B8,3B4	R	29	161	650	120	195	36	13	10	54	52	47	30	.300	.356	.442
Jim Holt	OF130,1B2	L	26	142	319	37	85	9	3	3	40	17	32	3	.266	.300	.342
Brant Alyea	OF75	R	29	94	258	34	75	12	1	16	61	28	51	3	.291	.366	.531
Rod Carew	2B45,1B1	L	24	51	191	27	70	12	3	4	28	11	28	4	.366	.407	.524
Rick Renick	3B30,OF25,SS1	R	26	81	179	20	41	8	0	7	25	22	29	0	.229	.317	.391
Paul Ratliff	C53	L	26	69	149	19	40	7	2	5	22	15	51	0	.268	.363	.443
Frank Quilici	2B73,3B27,SS1	R	31	111	141	19	32	3	0	2	12	15	16	0	.227	.297	.291
Jim Perry	P40,OF1	S	34	41	97	9	24	4	0	1	6	1	14	0	.247	.253	.320
Bob Allison	OF17,1B7	R	35	47	72	15	15	5	0	1	7	14	20	1	.208	.345	.319
Charlie Manuel	OF11	L	26	59	64	4	12	0	0	1	7	6	17	0	.188	.260	.234
Tom Tischinski	C22	R	25	24	46	6	9	0	0	1	2	9	6	0	.196	.327	.261
Herman Hill	OF14	L	24	27	22	8	2	0	0	0	0	0	6	0	.091	.091	.091
Jim Nettles	OF11	L	23	13	20	3	5	0	0	0	1	0	5	0	.250	.286	.250
Minnie Mendoza	3B5,2B4	R	36	16	16	2	3	0	0	0	0	0	1	0	.188	.188	.188
Steve Brye	OF6	R	21	9	11	1	2	1	0	0	2	2	4	0	.182	.308	.273
Rick Dempsey	C3	R	20	5	7	1	0	0	0	0	0	1	1	0	.000	.125	.000
Cotton Nash	1B2	R	27	4	4	1	1	0	0	0	2	1	1	0	.250	.400	.250

Pitcher	T	Age	G	GS	CG	ShO	IP	H	HR	BB	SO	W-L	Sv	ERA
Jim Perry	R	34	40	40	13	4	278.2	258	20	57	168	24-12	0	3.04
Jim Kaat	L	31	45	34	4	1	230.1	244	26	58	120	14-10	0	3.56
Bert Blyleven	R	19	27	25	5	1	164.0	143	17	47	135	10-9	0	3.18
Luis Tiant	R	29	18	17	2	1	92.2	84	12	41	50	7-3	0	3.40
Dave Boswell	R	25	18	15	0	0	68.2	80	12	44	45	3-7	0	6.42
Stan Williams	R	33	68	0	0	0	113.1	85	8	32	76	10-1	15	1.99
Ron Perranoski	L	34	67	0	0	0	111.0	108	7	42	55	7-8	34	2.43
Tom Hall	L	22	52	11	1	0	155.1	94	11	66	184	11-6	4	2.55
Bill Zepp	R	23	43	20	1	1	151.0	154	9	51	64	9-4	2	3.22
Dick Woodson	R	25	21	0	0	0	30.2	29	2	19	22	1-2	1	3.82
Steve Barber	R	22	18	0	0	0	27.1	26	1	18	14	0-0	2	4.61
Pete Hamm	R	22	10	0	0	0	16.1	17	3	7	3	0-2	0	5.51
Hal Haydel	R	25	4	0	0	0	9.0	7	2	4	4	2-0	0	3.00

1970 Oakland Athletics 2nd AL West 89-73 .549 9.0 GB

John McNamara

Player	Gm by Position	B	Age	G	AB	R	H	2B	3B	HR	RBI	BB	SO	SB	Avg	OBP	Slg
Frank Fernandez	C76,OF1	R	27	94	252	30	54	5	0	15	44	40	76	1	.214	.327	.413
Don Mincher	1B137	L	32	140	463	62	114	18	0	27	74	56	71	5	.246	.327	.460
Dick Green	2B127,3B5,C1	R	29	135	384	34	73	7	0	4	29	38	73	3	.190	.267	.240
Sal Bando	3B152	R	26	155	502	93	132	20	2	20	75	118	88	6	.263	.407	.430
Bert Campaneris	SS143	R	28	147	603	97	168	28	4	22	64	36	73	42	.279	.321	.448
Felipe Alou	OF145,1B1	R	35	154	575	70	156	25	3	8	55	32	31	10	.271	.308	.367
Reggie Jackson	OF142	L	24	149	426	57	101	21	2	23	66	75	135	26	.237	.359	.458
Rick Monday	OF109	L	24	112	376	63	109	19	7	10	37	58	99	17	.290	.387	.457
Joe Rudi	OF63,1B28	R	23	106	350	40	108	23	2	11	42	16	61	3	.309	.341	.480
Dave Duncan	C73	R	24	86	232	21	60	7	0	10	29	22	38	0	.259	.320	.418
Tommy Davis†	OF45,1B8	R	31	66	200	17	58	9	1	1	27	8	18	2	.290	.318	.360
Tony La Russa	2B44	R	25	52	106	6	21	4	1	0	6	15	19	0	.198	.301	.255
Gene Tenace	C30	R	23	38	105	19	32	6	0	7	20	23	30	0	.305	.430	.562
Steve Hovley†	OF42	L	25	72	100	8	19	1	0	0	1	5	11	3	.190	.229	.200
John Donaldson	2B21,SS6,3B1	L	27	41	89	4	22	2	1	1	11	9	6	1	.247	.316	.326
Roberto Pena†	SS12,3B5	R	33	19	58	4	15	1	0	0	3	3	4	1	.259	.295	.276
Jim Driscoll	2B7,SS7	L	26	21	52	2	10	0	0	1	2	2	15	0	.192	.236	.250
Bob Johnson	3B6,1B1	R	34	30	46	6	8	1	0	1	2	3	2	2	.174	.235	.261
Tito Francona†	1B6,OF1	L	36	32	33	2	8	0	0	1	6	6	6	0	.242	.375	.333
Bobby Brooks	OF5	R	24	7	18	2	6	1	0	2	5	1	7	0	.333	.368	.722
Jose Tartabull	OF6	L	31	24	13	5	3	2	0	0	2	0	2	1	.231	.231	.385
Allan Lewis	OF2	S	28	25	8	8	2	0	0	1	1	0	0	7	.250	.250	.625
Larry Haney	C1	R	27	2	2	2	0	0	0	0	0	2	1	0	.000	.500	.000

Pitcher	T	Age	G	GS	CG	ShO	IP	H	HR	BB	SO	W-L	Sv	ERA
Chuck Dobson	R	26	41	40	13	5	267.0	230	32	92	149	16-15	0	3.74
Catfish Hunter	R	24	40	40	9	1	262.1	253	32	74	178	18-14	0	3.81
Blue Moon Odom	R	25	29	29	4	1	156.1	128	14	100	88	9-8	0	3.80
Al Downing†	L	29	10	6	1	0	41.0	39	5	22	26	3-3	0	3.95
Vida Blue	L	20	6	6	2	2	38.2	20	0	12	35	2-0	0	2.09
Mudcat Grant†	R	34	72	0	0	0	123.1	104	8	30	54	6-2	24	1.82
Paul Lindblad	L	28	62	0	0	0	63.1	52	7	28	42	8-2	3	2.70
Diego Segui	R	32	47	19	3	2	162.0	130	9	68	95	10-10	2	2.56
Rollie Fingers	R	23	45	19	1	0	148.0	137	13	48	79	7-9	2	3.65
Marcel Lachemann	R	29	41	0	0	0	58.1	58	6	18	39	3-3	3	2.78
Bob Locker†	R	32	38	0	0	0	56.1	49	1	19	33	3-3	4	2.88
Jim Roland	L	27	28	2	0	0	43.1	28	2	23	26	3-3	2	2.70
Roberto Rodriguez†	R	28	6	0	0	0	12.1	10	2	3	8	0-0	0	2.92
Darrell Osteen	R	27	3	1	0	0	5.2	9	0	3	3	1-0	0	6.35
Dooley Womack	R	30	2	0	0	0	3.0	4	2	1	3	0-0	0	15.00
Fred Talbot	R	29	1	0	0	0	1.2	2	1	1	0	0-1	0	10.80

1970 California Angels 3rd AL West 86-76 .531 12.0 GB

Lefty Phillips

Player	Gm by Position	B	Age	G	AB	R	H	2B	3B	HR	RBI	BB	SO	SB	Avg	OBP	Slg
Joe Azcue	C112	R	30	114	351	19	85	13	1	2	25	24	40	0	.242	.292	.302
Jim Spencer	1B142	L	23	146	511	61	140	20	4	12	68	28	61	0	.274	.309	.399
Sandy Alomar	2B153,SS10,3B1	S	26	162	672	82	169	18	2	2	36	49	65	35	.251	.302	.293
Ken McMullen†	3B122	R	28	124	422	50	98	9	3	14	61	59	81	1	.232	.329	.367
Jim Fregosi	SS150,1B6	R	28	158	601	95	167	33	5	22	82	69	92	0	.278	.353	.459
Alex Johnson	OF156	R	27	156	614	85	202	26	6	14	86	35	68	17	.329	.370	.459
Roger Repoz	OF110,1B18	L	29	137	407	50	97	17	6	18	47	45	90	4	.238	.317	.442
Jay Johnstone	OF100	L	24	119	320	34	76	10	5	11	39	24	53	1	.238	.290	.403
Tom Egan	C79	R	24	79	210	14	50	6	0	4	20	14	67	0	.238	.286	.324
Jarvis Tatum	OF58	R	23	75	181	28	43	7	0	0	6	17	35	1	.238	.302	.276
Bill Voss	OF55	L	26	80	181	21	44	4	3	3	30	23	18	2	.243	.327	.348
Billy Cowan	OF27,1B14,3B2	R	31	68	134	20	37	9	1	5	25	11	29	0	.276	.336	.470
Tommie Reynolds	OF32,3B1	S	28	59	120	11	30	3	1	1	6	6	10	1	.250	.291	.317
Chico Ruiz	3B27,2B3,SS3*	S	31	68	107	10	26	3	1	0	12	7	16	3	.243	.293	.290
Tony Gonzalez†	OF24	L	33	26	92	9	28	2	0	1	12	2	11	3	.304	.326	.359
Aurelio Rodriguez†	3B17	R	22	17	63	6	17	2	2	0	7	3	6	0	.270	.313	.365
Doug Griffin	2B11,3B8	R	23	18	55	2	7	1	0	0	4	6	5	0	.127	.213	.145
Mickey Rivers	OF5	L	21	17	25	6	8	2	0	0	3	3	5	1	.320	.414	.400
Ray Oyler	SS13,3B2	R	31	24	24	2	2	0	0	0	1	3	6	0	.083	.185	.083
Tom Silverio	OF5,1B1	L	24	15	15	1	0	0	0	0	0	2	4	0	.000	.118	.000
Rick Reichardt†	OF1	R	27	9	6	1	1	0	0	0	1	3	0	0	.167	.400	.167
Randy Brown	C5	L	25	5	4	0	0	0	0	0	0	0	0	0	.000	.000	.000
Jim Hicks		R	30	4	4	0	1	0	0	0	0	0	2	0	.250	.250	.250
Marty Perez	SS2	R	23	3	3	0	0	0	0	0	1	0	0	0	.000	.000	.000

C. Ruiz, 2 G at 1B, 1 G at C

Pitcher	T	Age	G	GS	CG	ShO	IP	H	HR	BB	SO	W-L	Sv	ERA
Clyde Wright	L	29	39	39	7	2	260.2	226	24	88	110	22-12	0	2.83
Tom Murphy	R	24	39	38	5	2	227.0	223	32	81	99	16-13	0	4.24
Rudy May	L	25	38	34	2	2	208.2	190	20	81	164	7-13	0	4.01
Andy Messersmith	R	24	37	26	6	1	194.2	144	21	78	162	11-10	5	3.01
Tom Bradley	R	23	17	11	1	1	69.2	71	3	33	53	2-5	0	4.13
Eddie Fisher	R	33	67	2	0	0	130.1	117	15	35	74	4-4	8	3.04
Ken Tatum	R	26	62	0	0	0	88.2	68	12	26	50	7-4	17	2.94
Paul Doyle†	L	30	40	0	0	0	42.0	43	7	21	34	3-1	5	5.14
Dave LaRoche	L	22	38	0	0	0	49.2	41	6	21	44	4-1	4	3.44
Mel Queen	R	28	34	3	0	0	60.0	58	5	28	44	3-6	9	4.20
Greg Garrett	L	22	32	7	0	0	74.2	48	6	44	53	5-6	0	2.65
Steve Kealey	R	23	17	0	0	0	21.2	19	2	6	14	1-0	1	4.15
Lloyd Allen	R	20	8	2	0	0	24.0	23	0	11	12	1-1	0	2.63
Wally Wolf	R	28	4	0	0	0	5.1	3	1	4	5	0-0	0	5.06
Terry Cox	R	21	3	0	0	0	2.1	4	0	0	3	0-0	0	3.86
Harvey Shank	R	23	1	0	0	0	3.0	2	0	2	1	0-0	0	0.00

1970 Kansas City Royals 4th AL West 65-97 .401 33.0 GB

Charlie Metro (19-33)/Bob Lemon (46-64)

Player	Gm by Position	B	Age	G	AB	R	H	2B	3B	HR	RBI	BB	SO	SB	Avg	OBP	Slg
Ed Kirkpatrick	C89,OF19,1B16	L	25	134	424	59	97	17	2	18	62	55	65	4	.229	.319	.406
Bob Oliver	1B115,3B46	R	27	160	612	83	159	24	6	27	99	42	126	3	.260	.309	.451
Cookie Rojas†	2B97	R	31	98	384	36	100	13	3	2	28	20	29	3	.260	.296	.326
Paul Schaal	3B97,SS10,2B6	R	27	124	380	50	102	12	3	5	35	43	39	7	.268	.343	.355
Jackie Hernandez	SS77	R	29	83	238	14	55	4	1	2	10	15	50	1	.231	.281	.282
Amos Otis	OF159	R	23	159	620	91	176	36	9	11	58	68	67	33	.284	.353	.424
Lou Piniella	OF139,1B1	R	26	144	542	54	163	24	5	11	88	35	42	3	.301	.342	.424
Pat Kelly	OF118	L	25	136	452	56	106	16	1	6	38	76	105	34	.235	.347	.314
Rich Severson	SS50,2B25	R	25	77	240	22	60	11	1	1	22	16	33	0	.250	.300	.317
Ellie Rodriguez	C75	R	24	80	231	25	52	8	2	1	15	27	35	2	.225	.312	.290
Joe Keough	OF34,1B18	L	24	57	183	28	59	6	2	4	21	23	18	1	.322	.396	.443
Tommy Matchick†	SS43,2B10,3B1	L	26	55	158	11	31	3	2	0	11	5	23	0	.196	.226	.241
Bill Sorrell	3B29,OF4,1B3	L	29	57	135	12	36	2	0	4	14	10	13	1	.267	.317	.370
George Spriggs	OF36	L	29	51	130	12	27	2	3	1	7	14	32	4	.208	.283	.292
Luis Alcaraz	2B31	R	29	35	120	10	20	5	1	1	14	4	13	0	.167	.192	.250
Mike Fiore†	1B20	L	25	25	72	6	13	2	0	0	4	13	24	1	.181	.306	.208
Jim Rooker	P38,OF1	R	27	41	70	12	14	4	0	1	13	2	35	0	.200	.230	.300
Hawk Taylor	C3,1B1	R	31	57	55	3	9	3	0	0	6	6	16	0	.164	.258	.218
Jim Campanis	C13,OF1	R	26	31	54	6	7	0	0	2	2	4	14	0	.130	.203	.241
Bobby Floyd†	SS8,3B6	R	26	14	43	5	14	4	0	0	9	4	9	0	.326	.375	.419
Jerry Adair	2B7	R	33	7	27	0	4	0	0	0	1	5	3	0	.148	.281	.148
Buck Martinez	C5	R	21	6	9	1	1	0	0	0	0	2	1	0	.111	.273	.111

Pitcher	T	Age	G	GS	CG	ShO	IP	H	HR	BB	SO	W-L	Sv	ERA
Dick Drago	R	25	35	34	7	1	240.0	239	20	72	127	9-15	0	3.75
Jim Rooker	L	27	38	29	6	3	203.2	190	11	102	117	10-15	1	3.54
Bob Johnson	R	27	40	26	10	1	214.0	178	18	82	206	8-13	4	3.07
Bill Butler	L	23	25	25	2	1	140.2	117	17	87	75	4-12	0	3.77
Dave Morehead	R	27	28	17	1	0	121.2	121	9	62	69	3-5	1	3.62
Wally Bunker	R	25	24	15	2	1	121.2	109	16	50	59	2-11	0	4.22
Roger Nelson	R	26	4	2	0	0	9.0	18	3	0	3	0-2	0	10.00
Paul Splittorff	L	23	2	1	0	0	8.2	16	1	5	10	0-1	0	7.27
Ken Wright	R	23	47	0	0	0	53.1	49	2	29	30	1-2	3	5.23
Al Fitzmorris	R	24	43	11	2	0	117.2	112	14	52	47	8-5	1	4.44
Tom Burgmeier	L	26	41	0	0	0	68.1	59	6	23	43	6-6	1	3.16
Ted Abernathy†	R	37	36	0	0	0	55.2	41	3	38	49	9-3	12	2.59
Moe Drabowsky†	R	34	24	0	0	0	35.2	28	3	12	38	1-2	2	3.28
Aurelio Monteagudo	R	26	21	0	0	0	27.1	20	2	9	18	1-1	0	2.96
Don O'Riley	R	25	9	2	0	0	23.1	26	5	9	13	0-0	0	5.40
Mike Hedlund	R	23	9	0	0	0	15.0	18	6	7	5	2-3	0	7.20
Jim York	R	22	4	0	0	0	8.0	5	2	2	6	1-1	0	3.38

1970 Milwaukee Brewers 4th AL West 65-97 .401 33.0 GB

Dave Bristol

Player	Gm by Position	B	Age	G	AB	R	H	2B	3B	HR	RBI	BB	SO	SB	Avg	OBP	Slg
Phil Roof	C107,1B1	R	29	110	321	39	73	7	1	13	37	32	72	3	.227	.306	.377
Mike Hegan	1B139,OF8	L	27	148	476	70	116	21	2	11	52	67	116	9	.244	.336	.366
Ted Kubiak	2B91,SS73	S	28	158	540	63	136	9	6	4	41	72	51	4	.252	.340	.313
Tommy Harper	3B128,2B22,OF13	R	29	154	604	104	179	35	4	31	82	77	107	38	.296	.377	.522
Roberto Pena†	SS99,2B15,1B7	R	33	121	416	36	99	19	1	3	42	25	45	3	.238	.282	.310
Danny Walton	OF114	R	22	117	397	32	102	20	1	17	66	51	126	2	.257	.349	.441
Russ Snyder	OF106	L	36	124	276	34	64	11	0	4	31	16	40	1	.232	.270	.315
Dave May†	OF99	L	26	101	342	36	82	8	1	7	31	44	56	8	.240	.329	.330
Jerry McNertney	C94,1B13	R	33	111	296	27	72	11	1	6	22	22	33	1	.243	.302	.348
Ted Savage	OF82,1B1	R	33	114	276	43	77	10	5	12	50	57	44	10	.279	.402	.482
Bob Burda†	OF64,1B7	L	31	78	222	19	55	9	0	4	20	16	17	0	.248	.303	.342
Steve Hovley†	OF38	L	25	40	135	17	38	9	0	0	16	17	11	5	.281	.366	.348
Gus Gil	2B38,3B14	R	31	64	119	12	22	4	0	1	12	21	12	2	.185	.303	.244
Max Alvis	3B36	R	32	62	115	16	21	2	0	3	12	5	20	1	.183	.217	.278
Mike Hershberger	OF35	R	30	49	98	7	23	5	0	1	6	10	8	1	.235	.306	.316
Bernie Smith	OF39	R	28	44	76	8	21	3	1	1	6	11	12	1	.276	.382	.382
Tito Francona†	1B13	L	36	52	65	4	15	3	0	0	4	6	15	1	.231	.296	.277
Hank Allen†	OF14,2B5,1B4	R	29	28	61	4	14	4	0	0	4	7	5	0	.230	.309	.295
John Kennedy†	2B16,3B5,SS4*	R	29	25	55	8	14	2	0	2	6	5	9	0	.255	.317	.400
Greg Goossen†	1B15	R	24	21	47	3	12	3	0	1	3	10	12	0	.255	.407	.383
Floyd Wicker	OF12	L	26	15	41	3	8	1	0	1	3	1	8	0	.195	.214	.293
Rich Rollins†	3B7	R	32	14	25	3	5	1	0	0	5	3	4	0	.200	.276	.240
Wayne Comer†	OF5	R	26	13	17	1	1	0	0	0	1	0	3	0	.059	.059	.059
Sandy Valdespino	OF1	L	31	8	9	0	0	0	0	0	0	0	4	0	.000	.000	.000
Pete Koegel	OF1	R	22	7	8	2	2	0	0	1	1	1	3	0	.250	.333	.625
Fred Stanley	2B2	R	22	6	0	1	0	0	0	0	0	0	0	0	—	—	—

J. Kennedy, 1 G at 1B

Pitcher	T	Age	G	GS	CG	ShO	IP	H	HR	BB	SO	W-L	Sv	ERA
Lew Krausse	R	27	37	35	8	1	216.0	235	33	67	130	13-18	0	4.75
Marty Pattin	R	27	37	29	11	0	233.1	204	20	71	161	14-12	0	3.39
Skip Lockwood	R	23	27	26	3	1	173.2	173	22	79	93	5-12	0	4.30
Gene Brabender	R	28	29	21	2	0	128.2	127	8	79	76	6-15	1	6.02
Bobby Bolin†	R	31	32	20	3	0	132.0	131	20	67	81	5-11	1	4.91
Al Downing†	L	29	17	16	1	0	94.1	79	8	59	53	2-10	0	3.34
Ray Peters	R	23	2	2	0	0	2.0	7	0	5	1	0-2	0	31.50
John Gelnar	R	27	53	0	0	0	92.1	98	7	23	48	4-3	4	4.19
Ken Sanders	R	28	50	0	0	0	92.1	64	1	25	64	5-2	13	1.75
Dave Baldwin	R	32	28	0	0	0	35.1	25	4	18	26	2-1	1	2.55
Bob Locker†	R	32	28	0	0	0	31.2	37	1	10	19	0-1	3	3.41
John O'Donoghue†	L	30	25	0	0	0	23.1	29	4	9	13	2-0	0	5.01
Bob Humphreys†	R	34	23	1	0	0	45.2	37	3	22	32	2-4	3	3.15
John Morris	L	28	20	9	2	0	73.1	70	4	22	40	4-3	0	3.93
Dick Ellsworth†	L	30	14	0	0	0	15.2	11	0	3	9	0-0	1	1.72
George Lauzerique	R	22	11	4	1	0	35.0	41	7	14	24	1-2	0	6.94
Bob Meyer	L	30	10	0	0	0	18.1	24	3	12	20	0-1	0	6.38
Wayne Twitchell	R	22	2	0	0	0	1.2	3	0	1	5	0-0	0	10.80
Bruce Brubaker	R	28	1	0	0	0	2.0	2	1	1	0	0-0	0	9.00

1970 Chicago White Sox 6th AL West 56-106 .346 42.0 GB

Don Gutteridge (49-87)/Bill Adair (4-6)/Chuck Tanner (3-13)

Player	Gm by Position	B	Age	G	AB	R	H	2B	3B	HR	RBI	BB	SO	SB	Avg	OBP	Slg
Ed Herrmann	C88	L	23	96	297	42	84	9	0	19	52	31	41	0	.283	.356	.505
Gail Hopkins	1B77,C8	L	27	116	287	32	82	8	1	6	29	28	19	0	.286	.346	.383
Bobby Knoop	2B126	R	31	130	402	34	92	13	2	5	36	34	79	0	.229	.290	.308
Bill Melton	OF71,3B70	R	24	141	514	74	135	15	1	33	96	56	107	2	.263	.340	.488
Luis Aparicio	SS146	R	36	146	552	86	173	29	3	5	43	53	34	8	.313	.372	.404
Carlos May	OF141,1B7	L	22	150	555	83	158	28	4	12	68	79	96	12	.285	.373	.414
Ken Berry	OF138	R	29	141	463	45	128	12	2	7	50	43	61	6	.276	.344	.356
Walt Williams	OF79	R	26	110	315	43	79	18	1	3	15	19	30	3	.251	.296	.343
Syd O'Brien	3B68,2B43,SS5	R	25	121	441	48	109	13	2	8	44	22	62	3	.247	.285	.340
Tom McCraw	1B59,OF49	L	29	129	332	39	73	11	2	6	31	21	50	12	.220	.273	.319
Duane Josephson	C84	R	28	96	285	28	90	12	1	4	41	24	28	0	.316	.370	.407
Bob Spence	1B37	L	24	46	130	11	29	4	1	4	15	11	32	0	.223	.285	.362
Rich McKinney	3B23,SS11	R	23	43	119	12	20	5	0	4	17	11	25	3	.168	.242	.311
John Matias	OF22,1B18	L	25	58	117	7	22	2	0	2	6	3	22	1	.188	.215	.256
Rich Morales	SS24,3B20,2B12	R	26	62	112	6	18	2	0	1	2	9	16	1	.161	.228	.205
Buddy Bradford†	OF27	R	25	32	91	8	17	3	0	2	8	10	30	1	.187	.265	.286
Ossie Blanco	1B22,OF1	R	24	34	66	4	13	0	0	0	8	3	14	0	.197	.225	.197
Jose Ortiz	OF8	R	23	15	24	4	8	1	0	0	1	2	2	1	.333	.407	.375
Chuck Brinkman	C9	R	25	9	20	4	5	1	0	0	0	3	3	0	.250	.348	.300
Bob Christian	OF4	R	24	12	15	3	4	0	0	1	3	1	4	0	.267	.313	.467
Art Kusnyer	C3	R	24	4	10	0	1	0	0	0	0	0	4	0	.100	.100	.100
Lee Maye†		L	35	6	6	0	1	0	0	0	1	0	1	0	.167	.167	.167

Pitcher	T	Age	G	GS	CG	ShO	IP	H	HR	BB	SO	W-L	Sv	ERA
Tommy John	L	27	37	37	10	3	269.1	253	19	101	138	12-17	0	3.27
Jerry Janeski	R	24	35	35	4	1	205.2	247	22	63	79	10-17	0	4.77
Joe Horlen	R	32	28	26	4	0	172.1	198	18	41	77	6-16	0	4.86
Bart Johnson	R	20	18	15	2	1	89.2	92	11	46	71	4-7	0	4.82
Bob Miller†	R	31	15	12	0	0	70.0	88	11	33	36	4-6	0	5.01
Billy Wynne	R	26	12	9	0	0	44.0	54	8	22	19	1-4	0	5.32
Gerry Arrigo	L	29	5	3	0	0	13.1	24	4	9	12	0-3	0	12.83
Wilbur Wood	L	28	77	0	0	0	121.2	118	7	36	85	9-13	21	2.81
Danny Murphy	R	27	51	0	0	0	80.2	82	11	49	42	2-3	5	5.69
Jerry Crider	R	28	32	8	0	0	91.0	101	13	34	40	4-7	4	4.45
Floyd Weaver	R	29	31	3	0	0	61.2	52	7	31	51	1-2	0	4.38
Barry Moore†	L	27	24	7	0	0	70.2	85	12	34	34	0-4	0	6.37
Tommie Sisk	R	28	17	1	0	0	33.1	37	6	13	16	1-1	0	5.40
Lee Stange†	R	33	16	0	0	0	22.1	28	5	5	14	1-0	0	5.24
Jim Magnuson	L	23	13	6	0	0	44.2	45	7	16	20	1-5	0	4.84
Don Secrist	L	26	9	0	0	0	14.2	19	2	12	9	0-0	0	5.52
Virle Rounsaville	R	25	8	0	0	0	6.1	10	1	2	3	0-1	0	9.95
Don Eddy	L	23	7	0	0	0	11.2	10	0	6	9	0-0	0	2.31
Denny O'Toole	R	21	3	0	0	0	3.1	5	0	2	3	0-0	0	2.70
Steve Hamilton†	L	34	3	0	0	0	3.0	4	0	1	3	0-0	0	6.00
Rich Moloney	R	20	1	0	0	0	1.0	2	0	0	1	0-0	0	0.00

»1970 Pittsburgh Pirates 1st NL East 89-73 .549 —

Danny Murtaugh

Player	Gm by Position	B	Age	G	AB	R	H	2B	3B	HR	RBI	BB	SO	SB	Avg	OBP	Slg
Manny Sanguillen	C125	R	26	128	486	63	158	19	9	7	61	17	45	2	.325	.344	.444
Bob Robertson	1B99,3B5,OF3	R	23	117	390	69	112	19	4	27	82	51	98	4	.287	.367	.564
Bill Mazeroski	2B102	R	33	112	367	29	84	14	0	7	39	27	40	2	.229	.283	.324
Richie Hebner	3B117	L	22	120	420	60	122	24	8	11	46	42	48	2	.290	.362	.464
Gene Alley	SS108,2B8,3B2	R	29	121	426	46	104	16	5	8	41	31	70	7	.244	.297	.362
Matty Alou	OF153	L	31	155	677	97	201	21	8	1	47	30	18	19	.297	.329	.356
Willie Stargell	OF125,1B1	L	30	136	474	70	125	18	3	31	85	44	119	0	.264	.329	.511
Roberto Clemente	OF104	R	35	108	412	65	145	22	10	14	60	38	66	3	.352	.407	.556
Al Oliver	OF80,1B77	L	23	151	551	63	149	33	5	12	83	35	35	1	.270	.326	.414
Freddie Patek	SS65	R	25	84	237	42	58	10	5	1	19	29	46	8	.245	.322	.342
Jose Pagan	3B53,OF4,1B1*	R	35	95	230	21	61	14	1	7	29	20	24	1	.265	.321	.426
Dave Cash	2B55	R	22	64	210	30	66	7	6	1	28	17	25	5	.314	.365	.419
Jerry May	C45	R	26	51	139	13	29	4	2	1	16	21	25	0	.209	.313	.288
Johnny Jeter	OF56	R	25	85	126	27	30	3	2	2	12	13	34	9	.238	.314	.341
Gene Clines	OF7	R	23	31	37	4	15	2	0	0	3	2	5	2	.405	.436	.459
Jose Martinez	3B7,2B4,SS1	R	27	19	20	1	1	0	0	0	0	1	5	0	.050	.095	.050
George Kopacz	1B3	L	29	10	16	1	3	0	0	0	0	0	5	0	.188	.188	.188
Dave Ricketts	C7	S	34	14	11	0	2	0	0	0	0	1	3	0	.182	.250	.182
Milt May		L	19	5	4	1	2	1	0	0	2	0	0	0	.500	.600	.750

J. Pagan, 1 G at 2B

Pitcher	T	Age	G	GS	CG	ShO	IP	H	HR	BB	SO	W-L	Sv	ERA
Bob Veale	L	34	34	32	5	1	202.0	189	15	94	178	10-15	0	3.92
Steve Blass	R	28	31	31	6	1	196.2	187	14	73	120	10-12	0	3.52
Dock Ellis	R	25	30	30	9	4	201.2	194	9	87	128	13-10	0	3.21
Bob Moose	R	22	28	27	9	2	189.2	186	14	64	119	11-10	0	3.99
Jim Nelson	R	22	15	10	1	1	68.1	64	5	38	42	4-2	0	3.42
Fred Cambria	R	22	6	5	0	0	33.1	37	2	12	14	1-2	0	3.51
Dave Giusti	R	30	66	1	0	0	103.0	98	7	39	85	9-3	26	3.06
Luke Walker	L	26	42	19	5	3	163.0	129	6	89	124	15-6	3	3.04
Bruce Dal Canton	R	28	41	6	1	0	84.2	94	7	39	53	9-4	1	4.57
Joe Gibbon	L	35	41	0	0	0	41.0	44	2	24	26	0-1	5	4.83
Orlando Pena	R	36	23	0	0	0	37.2	38	6	7	25	2-1	2	4.78
John Lamb	R	23	23	0	0	0	32.1	23	2	13	24	0-1	3	2.78
Chuck Hartenstein†	R	28	17	0	0	0	23.2	25	3	8	14	1-1	1	4.56
Gene Garber	R	22	14	0	0	0	22.1	22	4	10	7	0-3	0	5.24
George Brunet†	L	35	12	1	0	0	16.2	19	1	9	17	1-1	0	2.70
Mudcat Grant†	R	34	8	0	0	0	12.0	8	2	2	4	2-1	0	2.25
Dick Colpaert	R	26	8	0	0	0	10.2	9	3	8	6	1-0	0	5.91
Al McBean†	R	32	7	0	0	0	10.0	13	2	7	3	0-0	1	8.10
Ed Acosta	R	26	3	0	0	0	2.2	5	1	2	1	0-0	1	13.50
Lou Marone	L	24	1	0	0	0	2.1	2	1	0	0	0-0	0	3.86

1970 Chicago Cubs 2nd NL East 84-78 .519 5.0 GB

Leo Durocher

Player	Gm by Position	B	Age	G	AB	R	H	2B	3B	HR	RBI	BB	SO	SB	Avg	OBP	Slg
Randy Hundley	C73	R	28	73	250	13	61	5	0	7	36	16	52	0	.244	.288	.348
Jim Hickman	OF79,1B74	R	33	149	514	102	162	33	4	32	115	93	99	0	.315	.419	.582
Glenn Beckert	2B138,OF1	R	29	143	591	99	170	15	6	3	36	32	22	4	.288	.323	.349
Ron Santo	3B152,OF1	R	30	154	555	83	148	30	4	26	114	92	108	2	.267	.369	.476
Don Kessinger	SS154	S	27	154	631	100	168	21	14	1	39	66	59	12	.266	.337	.349
Billy Williams	OF160	L	32	161	636	137	205	34	4	42	129	72	65	7	.322	.391	.586
Johnny Callison	OF144	L	31	147	477	65	126	23	2	19	68	60	63	7	.264	.348	.440
Cleo James	OF90	R	29	100	176	33	37	7	2	3	14	17	24	5	.210	.298	.324
Ernie Banks	1B62	R	39	72	222	25	56	6	2	12	44	20	33	0	.252	.313	.459
Joe Pepitone†	OF56,1B13	L	29	56	213	38	57	9	2	12	44	15	15	0	.268	.313	.498
Paul Popovich	2B22,SS17,3B16	S	29	78	186	22	47	5	1	4	20	18	18	0	.253	.324	.355
Jack Hiatt†	C63,1B2	R	27	66	178	19	43	12	1	2	22	31	48	0	.242	.352	.354
Willie Smith	1B43,OF1	L	31	87	167	15	36	9	1	5	24	11	32	2	.216	.267	.371
J.C. Martin	C36,1B3	L	33	40	77	11	12	1	0	1	4	20	11	0	.156	.333	.208
Tommy Davis†	OF10	R	31	11	42	4	11	2	0	2	8	1	1	0	.262	.279	.452
Ken Rudolph	C16	R	23	20	40	1	4	1	0	0	2	1	12	0	.100	.122	.125
Phil Gagliano†	2B16,1B1,3B1	R	28	26	40	5	6	0	0	0	5	5	5	0	.150	.244	.150
Jimmie Hall†	OF8	L	32	28	32	2	3	1	0	0	1	4	12	0	.094	.194	.125
Al Spangler	OF6	L	36	21	14	2	2	1	0	1	1	3	3	0	.143	.294	.429
Boots Day†	OF7	L	22	11	8	2	2	0	0	0	0	0	3	0	.250	.250	.250
Terry Hughes	3B1,OF1	R	21	2	3	0	1	0	0	0	0	0	0	0	.333	.333	.333
Adrian Garrett		L	27	3	3	0	0	0	0	0	0	0	3	0	.000	.000	.000
Brock Davis	OF1	L	26	6	3	0	0	0	0	0	0	0	1	0	.000	.000	.000
Roger Metzger	SS1	S	22	1	2	0	0	0	0	0	0	0	0	0	.000	.000	.000
Roe Skidmore		R	24	1	1	0	1	0	0	0	0	0	0	0	1.000	1.000	1.000

Pitcher	T	Age	G	GS	CG	ShO	IP	H	HR	BB	SO	W-L	Sv	ERA
Fergie Jenkins	R	26	40	39	24	3	313.0	265	30	60	274	22-16	0	3.39
Ken Holtzman	L	24	39	38	15	1	287.2	271	30	94	202	17-11	0	3.38
Bill Hands	R	30	39	38	12	2	265.0	278	20	76	170	18-15	1	3.70
Milt Pappas†	R	31	21	20	6	2	144.2	135	14	36	80	10-8	0	2.68
Joe Decker	R	23	24	17	1	0	108.2	108	12	56	79	2-7	0	4.64
Phil Regan	R	33	54	0	0	0	75.2	81	8	32	31	5-9	12	4.76
Jim Colborn	R	24	34	5	0	0	72.2	88	3	23	50	3-1	4	3.59
Roberto Rodriguez†	R	28	26	0	0	0	43.1	50	6	15	46	3-2	2	5.82
Larry Gura	L	22	20	3	1	0	38.0	35	6	23	21	1-3	1	3.79
Hank Aguirre	L	39	17	0	0	0	14.0	13	3	9	11	3-0	1	4.50
Juan Pizarro	L	33	12	0	0	0	15.2	16	2	9	14	0-0	1	4.60
Ted Abernathy†	R	37	11	0	0	0	9.0	9	0	5	2	0-0	1	2.00
Archie Reynolds	R	24	7	1	0	0	15.0	17	2	9	9	0-2	0	6.60
Jim Dunegan	R	22	7	0	0	0	13.1	13	2	12	3	0-2	0	4.73
Bob Miller†	R	31	7	1	0	0	9.0	6	3	6	4	0-0	2	5.00
Steve Barber†	L	31	5	0	0	0	5.2	10	0	6	3	0-1	0	9.53
Hoyt Wilhelm†	R	46	3	0	0	0	3.2	4	1	3	1	0-1	0	9.82
Jim Cosman	R	27	1	0	0	0	1.0	3	1	1	0	0-0	0	27.00

1970 New York Mets 3rd NL East 83-79 .512 6.0 GB

Gil Hodges

Player	Gm by Position	B	Age	G	AB	R	H	2B	3B	HR	RBI	BB	SO	SB	Avg	OBP	Slg
Jerry Grote	C125	R	27	126	415	38	106	14	1	2	34	36	39	2	.255	.313	.308
Donn Clendenon	1B100	R	34	121	396	65	114	18	3	22	97	39	91	4	.288	.348	.515
Ken Boswell	2B101	L	24	105	351	32	89	13	2	5	44	41	32	5	.254	.331	.345
Joe Foy	3B97	R	27	99	322	39	76	12	0	6	37	68	58	22	.236	.373	.329
Bud Harrelson	SS156	S	26	157	564	72	137	18	8	1	42	95	74	23	.243	.351	.309
Tommie Agee	OF150	R	27	153	636	107	182	30	7	24	75	55	156	31	.286	.344	.469
Cleon Jones	OF130	R	27	134	506	71	140	25	8	10	63	57	87	12	.277	.352	.417
Ron Swoboda	OF100	R	26	115	245	29	57	8	2	9	40	40	72	2	.233	.340	.392
Art Shamsky	OF58,1B56	L	28	122	403	48	118	19	2	11	49	49	33	1	.293	.371	.432
Wayne Garrett	3B70,2B45,SS1	L	22	114	366	74	93	17	4	12	45	81	60	5	.254	.390	.421
Ken Singleton	OF51	S	23	69	198	22	52	8	0	5	26	30	48	1	.263	.361	.379
Dave Marshall	OF43	L	27	92	189	21	46	10	1	6	29	17	43	4	.243	.304	.402
Duffy Dyer	C57	R	24	59	148	8	31	1	0	2	12	21	32	1	.209	.308	.257
Al Weis	2B44,SS15	S	32	75	121	20	25	7	1	1	11	7	21	1	.207	.254	.306
Mike Jorgensen	1B50,OF10	L	21	76	87	15	17	3	1	3	4	10	23	2	.195	.278	.356
Ed Kranepool	1B8	L	25	43	47	2	8	0	0	0	3	5	2	0	.170	.250	.170
Ted Martinez	2B4,SS1	R	22	4	16	0	1	0	0	0	0	0	3	0	.063	.063	.063
Rod Gaspar	OF8	S	24	11	14	4	0	0	0	0	0	1	4	1	.000	.067	.000
Tim Foli	3B2,SS2	R	19	5	11	0	4	0	0	0	1	0	2	0	.364	.364	.364
Lee Stanton	OF1	R	24	4	4	0	1	0	1	0	0	0	0	0	.250	.250	.750

Pitcher	T	Age	G	GS	CG	ShO	IP	H	HR	BB	SO	W-L	Sv	ERA
Tom Seaver	R	25	37	36	19	2	290.2	230	21	83	283	18-12	0	2.82
Jerry Koosman	L	27	30	29	5	1	212.0	189	22	71	118	12-7	0	3.14
Gary Gentry	R	23	32	29	5	2	188.1	155	19	86	134	9-9	1	3.68
Jim McAndrew	R	26	32	27	9	3	184.1	166	18	38	111	10-14	2	3.56
Ray Sadecki	L	29	28	19	4	0	138.2	134	18	52	89	8-4	0	3.89
Nolan Ryan	R	23	27	19	5	2	131.2	86	10	97	125	7-11	1	3.42
Tug McGraw	L	25	57	0	0	0	90.2	77	6	49	81	4-6	10	3.28
Ron Taylor	R	32	57	0	0	0	66.1	65	5	16	28	5-4	13	3.93
Danny Frisella	R	24	30	1	0	0	65.2	49	4	34	54	8-3	1	3.02
Rich Folkers	L	23	16	1	0	0	29.1	36	6	25	15	0-2	2	6.44
Don Cardwell†	R	34	16	1	0	0	25.0	31	3	6	8	0-2	0	6.48
Cal Koonce†	R	29	13	0	0	0	22.0	25	2	14	10	0-2	0	3.27
Ron Herbel†	R	32	12	0	0	0	13.0	14	1	2	8	2-2	1	1.38
Dean Chance†	R	29	3	0	0	0	2.0	3	0	2	0	0-1	1	13.50

1970 St. Louis Cardinals 4th NL East 76-86 .469 13.0 GB

Red Schoendienst

Player	Gm by Position	B	Age	G	AB	R	H	2B	3B	HR	RBI	BB	SO	SB	Avg	OBP	Slg
Joe Torre	C90,3B73,1B1	R	29	161	624	89	203	27	9	21	100	70	91	2	.325	.398	.498
Joe Hague	1B82,OF52	L	26	139	451	58	122	16	4	14	68	63	87	2	.271	.358	.417
Julian Javier	2B137	R	33	139	513	62	129	16	3	2	42	24	70	6	.251	.284	.306
Mike Shannon	3B51	R	30	55	174	18	37	9	2	0	22	16	20	1	.213	.275	.287
Dal Maxvill	SS136,2B22	R	31	152	399	35	80	5	2	0	28	51	56	0	.201	.287	.223
Lou Brock	OF152	L	31	155	664	114	202	29	5	13	57	60	99	51	.304	.361	.422
Jose Cardenal	OF134	R	26	148	552	73	162	32	6	10	74	45	70	26	.293	.348	.428
Leron Lee	OF77	L	22	121	264	28	60	13	1	6	23	24	66	5	.227	.290	.352
Dick Allen	1B79,3B38,OF3	R	28	122	459	88	128	17	5	34	101	71	118	5	.279	.377	.560
Ted Simmons	C79	S	20	82	284	29	69	8	2	3	24	37	37	2	.243	.333	.317
Carl Taylor	OF46,1B15,3B1	R	26	104	245	39	61	12	2	6	45	41	30	5	.249	.358	.388
Vic Davalillo	OF54	L	33	111	183	29	57	14	3	1	33	13	19	4	.311	.355	.437
Ed Crosby	SS35,3B3,2B2	L	21	38	95	9	24	4	1	0	6	7	5	0	.253	.308	.316
Milt Ramirez	SS59,3B1	R	20	62	79	8	15	2	1	0	3	8	9	0	.190	.264	.241
Luis Melendez	OF18	R	20	21	70	11	21	1	0	0	8	2	12	3	.300	.315	.314
Jim Beauchamp†	OF10,1B5	R	30	44	58	8	15	2	0	1	6	8	11	2	.259	.338	.345
Cookie Rojas†	2B10,OF3,SS2	R	31	23	47	2	5	0	0	0	2	3	4	0	.106	.176	.106
Phil Gagliano†	3B6,1B3,2B2	R	28	18	32	0	6	0	0	0	2	1	3	0	.188	.212	.188
Jim Kennedy	SS7,2B5	L	23	12	24	1	3	0	0	0	0	0	0	0	.125	.125	.125
Jerry Davanon	3B5,2B3	R	24	11	18	2	2	1	0	0	0	2	5	0	.111	.200	.167
Jose Cruz	OF4	L	22	6	17	2	6	1	0	0	1	4	0	0	.353	.500	.412
Jim Campbell		L	27	13	13	0	3	0	0	0	1	0	3	0	.231	.231	.231
Jorge Roque	OF1	R	20	5	1	2	0	0	0	0	0	0	1	0	.000	.500	.000
Joe Nossek		R	29	1	1	0	0	0	0	0	0	0	0	0	.000	.000	.000
Bart Zeller	C1	R	28	1	0	0	0	0	0	0	0	0	0	0	—	—	—

Pitcher	T	Age	G	GS	CG	ShO	IP	H	HR	BB	SO	W-L	Sv	ERA
Bob Gibson	R	34	34	34	23	3	294.0	262	13	88	274	23-7	0	3.12
Steve Carlton	L	25	34	33	13	2	253.2	239	25	109	193	10-19	0	3.73
Mike Torrez	R	23	30	28	5	1	179.1	168	12	103	100	8-10	0	4.22
Jerry Reuss	L	21	20	20	5	2	127.1	132	9	49	74	7-8	0	4.10
Nelson Briles	R	26	30	19	1	1	106.2	129	14	36	59	6-7	0	6.24
George Culver†	R	26	11	7	2	0	56.2	64	6	24	23	3-3	0	4.61
Frank Bertaina	L	26	8	5	0	0	31.1	36	1	15	14	1-2	0	3.16
Harry Parker	R	22	7	4	0	0	22.1	24	0	15	9	1-1	0	3.22
Chuck Taylor	R	28	56	7	1	1	124.1	116	5	31	64	6-7	8	3.11
Frank Linzy†	R	29	47	0	0	0	61.1	66	3	23	19	3-5	2	3.67
Sal Campisi	R	27	37	0	0	0	49.1	53	2	37	26	2-2	4	2.92
Tom Hilgendorf	L	28	23	0	0	0	20.2	22	0	13	13	0-4	3	3.92
Billy McCool	L	25	18	0	0	0	21.2	20	0	16	12	0-3	1	6.23
Reggie Cleveland	R	22	16	1	0	0	26.0	31	3	18	22	0-4	0	7.62
Al Hrabosky	L	20	16	1	0	0	19.0	22	2	7	12	2-1	0	4.74
Bob Chlupsa	R	24	14	0	0	0	16.1	26	2	9	10	0-2	0	8.82
Ted Abernathy†	R	37	11	0	0	0	18.1	15	0	12	8	1-0	1	2.95
Santiago Guzman	R	20	8	3	1	0	13.2	14	1	13	9	1-1	0	7.24
Jerry Johnson†	R	26	7	0	0	0	11.1	6	1	3	5	2-0	1	3.18
Chuck Hartenstein†	R	28	6	0	0	0	13.1	24	1	5	9	0-0	0	8.78
Rich Nye†	L	25	6	0	0	0	8.0	13	2	6	5	0-0	0	4.50
Fred Norman†	L	27	1	0	0	0	1.0	1	0	0	0	0-0	0	0.00

1970 Philadelphia Phillies 5th NL East 73-88 .453 15.5 GB

Frank Lucchesi

Player	Gm by Position	B	Age	G	AB	R	H	2B	3B	HR	RBI	BB	SO	SB	Avg	OBP	Slg
Mike Ryan	C46	R	28	46	134	14	24	8	0	2	11	16	24	0	.179	.265	.284
Deron Johnson	1B154,3B3	R	31	159	574	66	147	28	3	27	93	72	132	0	.256	.338	.456
Denny Doyle	2B103	L	26	112	413	43	86	10	7	2	16	33	64	6	.208	.266	.281
Don Money	3B119,SS2	R	23	120	447	66	132	25	4	14	66	43	68	4	.295	.361	.463
Larry Bowa	SS143,2B1	S	24	145	547	50	137	17	6	0	34	21	48	24	.250	.277	.303
Larry Hisle	OF121	R	23	126	405	52	83	22	4	10	44	53	139	5	.205	.299	.353
Ron Stone	OF99,1B6	L	27	123	321	30	84	12	5	3	39	38	45	5	.262	.338	.358
John Briggs	OF95	L	26	110	341	43	92	15	7	9	47	39	65	5	.270	.342	.434
Tony Taylor	2B59,3B38,OF18*	R	34	124	439	74	132	26	9	9	55	50	67	9	.301	.374	.462
Oscar Gamble	OF74	L	20	88	275	31	72	12	4	1	19	27	37	5	.262	.330	.345
Byron Browne	OF88	R	27	104	270	29	67	17	2	10	36	33	72	1	.248	.327	.437
Tim McCarver	C44	L	28	44	164	16	47	11	1	4	14	14	10	2	.287	.346	.439
Terry Harmon	SS35,2B14,3B2	R	26	71	129	16	32	2	4	0	7	12	22	6	.248	.315	.326
Rick Joseph	OF12,1B10,3B9	R	30	71	119	7	27	2	1	3	10	6	28	0	.227	.264	.336
Mike Compton	C40	R	25	47	110	8	18	0	1	1	7	9	22	0	.164	.240	.209
Jim Hutto	OF22,1B12,C5*	R	22	57	92	7	17	2	0	3	12	5	20	0	.185	.222	.304
Doc Edwards	C34	R	33	35	78	5	21	0	0	0	6	4	10	0	.269	.313	.269
Del Bates	C20	L	30	22	60	1	8	2	0	0	1	6	15	0	.133	.257	.167
Scott Reid	OF18	L	23	25	49	5	6	1	0	0	1	11	22	0	.122	.283	.143
Joe Lis	OF9	R	23	13	37	1	7	2	0	1	4	5	11	0	.189	.286	.324
Willie Montanez	OF10,1B5	L	22	18	25	3	6	0	0	0	3	1	4	0	.240	.269	.240
Dick Selma	P73,3B2,1B1	R	26	73	20	1	3	1	0	0	2	1	8	0	.150	.190	.200
Sam Parrilla	OF3	R	27	11	16	0	2	1	0	0	0	1	4	0	.125	.176	.188
Greg Luzinski	1B3	R	19	8	12	0	2	0	0	0	0	3	5	0	.167	.333	.167
John Vukovich	SS2,3B1	R	22	3	8	1	1	0	0	0	0	1	0	0	.125	.222	.125

T. Taylor, 1 G at SS; J. Hutto, 1 G at 3B

Pitcher	T	Age	G	GS	CG	ShO	IP	H	HR	BB	SO	W-L	Sv	ERA
Rick Wise	R	24	35	34	5	1	220.1	253	15	65	113	13-14	0	4.17
Chris Short	L	32	36	34	7	2	199.0	211	13	66	133	9-16	1	4.30
Jim Bunning	R	38	34	33	4	0	219.0	233	19	56	147	10-15	0	4.11
Grant Jackson	L	27	32	23	1	0	149.2	170	17	61	104	5-15	0	5.29
Woodie Fryman	L	30	27	20	4	3	127.2	122	11	43	97	8-6	0	4.09
Dick Selma	R	26	73	0	0	0	134.1	108	8	59	153	8-9	22	2.75
Joe Hoerner	L	33	44	0	0	0	57.2	53	5	20	39	9-5	9	2.65
Barry Lersch	R	25	42	11	3	0	138.0	119	17	47	92	6-3	3	3.26
Lowell Palmer	R	22	38	5	0	0	102.0	98	15	55	85	1-2	0	5.47
Billy Wilson	R	27	37	0	0	0	58.1	57	5	33	41	1-0	0	4.78
Fred Wenz	R	28	22	0	0	0	30.1	27	2	13	24	2-0	1	4.15
Billy Champion	R	22	7	1	0	0	14.0	21	3	10	12	0-2	0	9.00
Mike Jackson	L	24	5	0	0	0	6.1	6	0	4	4	1-1	0	1.42
Ken Reynolds	L	23	4	0	0	0	2.1	3	0	4	1	0-0	0	0.00
Bill Laxton	L	22	2	0	0	0	2.0	2	2	2	2	0-0	0	13.50

1970 Montreal Expos 6th NL East 73-89 .451 16.0 GB

Gene Mauch

Player	Gm by Position	B	Age	G	AB	R	H	2B	3B	HR	RBI	BB	SO	SB	Avg	OBP	Slg
John Bateman	C137	R	29	139	520	51	123	21	5	15	68	28	75	8	.237	.275	.383
Ron Fairly	1B118,OF4	L	31	119	385	54	111	19	0	15	61	72	64	10	.288	.402	.455
Gary Sutherland	2B97,SS15,3B1	R	25	116	359	37	74	10	0	3	26	31	22	2	.206	.271	.259
Coco Laboy	3B132,2B3	R	29	137	432	37	86	26	1	5	53	31	81	0	.199	.254	.299
Bobby Wine	SS159	R	31	159	501	40	116	21	3	3	51	39	94	0	.232	.287	.303
Rusty Staub	OF160	L	26	160	569	98	156	23	7	30	94	112	93	12	.274	.394	.497
Mack Jones	OF87	L	31	108	271	51	65	11	3	14	32	59	74	5	.240	.398	.458
Adolfo Phillips	OF75	R	28	92	214	36	51	6	3	6	21	36	51	7	.238	.352	.379
Bob Bailey	3B48,OF44,1B18	R	27	131	352	77	101	19	3	28	84	72	70	5	.287	.407	.597
Marv Staehle	2B91,SS1	L	28	104	321	41	70	9	1	0	26	39	21	1	.218	.306	.252
Jim Gosger	OF71,1B19	L	27	91	274	38	72	11	2	5	37	35	35	5	.263	.348	.372
Jim Fairey	OF59	L	25	92	211	35	51	9	3	3	25	14	38	1	.242	.293	.355
Don Hahn	OF61	R	21	82	149	22	38	8	0	0	8	27	27	4	.255	.374	.309
John Boccabella	1B33,C24,3B1	R	29	61	145	18	39	3	1	5	17	11	24	0	.269	.321	.407
Ron Brand	SS19,3B12,C9*	R	30	72	126	10	30	2	3	0	9	9	16	2	.238	.287	.302
Boots Day†	OF35	L	22	41	108	14	29	4	0	0	5	6	18	3	.269	.307	.306
Jack Hiatt†	C12,1B2	R	27	17	43	4	14	2	0	0	7	14	14	0	.326	.491	.372
Clyde Mashore	OF10	R	25	13	25	2	4	0	0	1	3	4	11	0	.160	.276	.280
Fred Whitfield	1B4	L	32	4	15	0	1	0	0	0	0	1	3	0	.067	.125	.067
Jim Qualls	2B2,OF2	S	23	9	9	1	1	0	0	0	1	0	0	0	.111	.111	.111
Ty Cline†		L	31	2	2	0	1	0	0	0	0	0	0	0	.500	.500	.500
Remy Hermoso	2B1,3B1	R	22	4	1	1	0	0	0	0	0	0	0	0	.000	.000	.000
Jose Herrera		R	28	1	1	0	0	0	0	0	0	0	1	0	.000	.000	.000

R. Brand, 5 G at OF, 3 G at 2B

Pitcher	T	Age	G	GS	CG	ShO	IP	H	HR	BB	SO	W-L	Sv	ERA
Carl Morton	R	26	43	37	10	4	284.2	281	27	125	154	18-11	0	3.60
Steve Renko	R	25	41	33	7	1	222.2	203	27	104	142	13-11	1	4.32
Bill Stoneman	R	26	40	30	5	3	207.2	209	26	109	176	7-15	0	4.59
Mike Wegener	R	23	25	16	1	0	104.1	100	16	56	35	3-6	0	5.26
Rich Nye†	L	25	8	6	2	0	46.1	47	3	20	21	3-2	0	4.08
Joe Sparma	R	28	9	6	1	0	29.1	34	7	25	23	0-4	0	7.06
Gary Waslewski†	R	28	6	4	0	0	24.2	23	3	15	19	0-2	0	5.11
Claude Raymond	R	33	59	0	0	0	83.1	76	13	27	68	6-7	23	4.43
Howie Reed	R	33	57	1	0	0	89.0	81	7	40	42	6-5	5	3.13
Dan McGinn	L	26	52	19	3	2	130.2	154	13	78	83	7-10	0	5.44
John Strohmayer	R	23	42	0	0	0	76.0	85	7	39	74	3-1	0	4.86
Mike Marshall†	R	27	24	5	0	0	64.2	56	4	29	38	3-7	3	3.48
Bill Dillman	R	25	18	0	0	0	30.2	28	4	18	17	2-3	0	5.28
John O'Donoghue†	L	30	9	3	0	0	22.1	20	2	11	6	2-3	0	5.24
Balor Moore	L	19	6	2	0	0	9.2	14	0	8	6	0-2	0	7.45
Carroll Sembera	R	28	5	0	0	0	6.2	14	2	11	6	0-0	0	18.90
Ken Johnson	R	37	3	0	0	0	6.0	9	1	1	4	0-0	0	7.50

1970 Cincinnati Reds 1st NL West 102-60 .630 —

Sparky Anderson

Player	Gm by Position	B	Age	G	AB	R	H	2B	3B	HR	RBI	BB	SO	SB	Avg	OBP	Slg
Johnny Bench	C139,OF24,1B12*	R	22	158	605	97	177	35	4	45	148	54	102	5	.293	.345	.587
Lee May	1B153	R	27	153	605	78	153	34	2	34	94	38	125	1	.253	.297	.484
Tommy Helms	2B148,SS12	R	29	150	575	42	136	21	1	1	45	21	33	2	.237	.262	.282
Tony Perez	3B153,1B8	R	28	158	587	107	186	28	6	40	129	83	134	8	.317	.401	.589
Dave Concepcion	SS93,2B3	R	22	101	265	38	69	6	3	1	19	23	45	10	.260	.324	.317
Pete Rose	OF159	S	29	159	649	120	205	37	9	15	52	73	64	12	.316	.385	.470
Bobby Tolan	OF150	L	24	152	589	112	186	34	6	16	80	62	94	57	.316	.384	.475
Bernie Carbo	OF119	L	22	125	365	54	113	19	3	21	63	94	77	10	.310	.454	.551
Woody Woodward	SS77,3B20,2B10*	R	27	100	264	23	59	8	3	1	14	20	21	1	.223	.280	.288
Hal McRae	OF46,3B6,2B1	R	24	70	165	18	41	6	1	8	23	15	23	0	.248	.313	.442
Pat Corrales	C42	R	29	43	106	9	25	5	1	1	10	8	22	0	.236	.289	.330
Jimmy Stewart	OF48,2B18,3B9*	S	31	101	105	15	28	3	1	1	8	8	13	5	.267	.322	.343
Darrel Chaney	SS30,2B18,3B3	S	22	57	95	7	22	3	0	1	4	3	26	1	.232	.263	.295
Angel Bravo	OF22	L	27	65	65	10	18	1	1	0	3	9	13	0	.277	.365	.323
Ty Cline†	OF20,1B2	L	31	48	63	13	17	7	1	0	8	12	11	1	.270	.387	.413
Frank Duffy	SS5	R	23	6	11	1	2	2	0	0	0	1	2	1	.182	.250	.364
Wayne Granger	P67,OF1	R	26	67	10	0	1	0	0	0	0	0	4	0	.100	.100	.100
Bill Plummer	C4	R	23	4	8	0	1	0	0	0	0	0	2	0	.125	.222	.125
Jay Ward	3B2,1B1,2B1	R	31	6	3	0	0	0	0	0	0	2	1	0	.000	.400	.000

J. Bench, 1 G at 3B; W. Woodward, 2 G at 1B; J. Stewart, 1 G at C, 1 G at 1B

Pitcher	T	Age	G	GS	CG	ShO	IP	H	HR	BB	SO	W-L	Sv	ERA
Gary Nolan	R	22	37	37	4	2	250.2	226	25	96	181	18-7	0	3.27
Jim Merritt	L	26	35	35	12	1	234.0	248	21	53	136	20-12	0	4.08
Jim McGlothlin	R	26	35	34	5	3	210.2	192	19	86	97	14-10	0	3.59
Wayne Simpson	R	21	26	26	10	2	176.0	125	15	81	119	14-3	0	3.02
Tony Cloninger	R	29	30	18	0	0	148.0	136	10	78	56	9-7	1	3.83
Wayne Granger	R	26	67	0	0	0	84.2	79	5	27	38	6-5	35	2.66
Clay Carroll	R	29	65	0	0	0	104.1	104	4	27	63	9-4	16	2.59
Don Gullett	L	19	44	2	0	0	77.2	54	4	44	76	5-2	6	2.43
Ray Washburn	R	32	35	3	0	0	66.1	90	7	48	37	4-4	0	6.92
Pedro Borbon	R	23	12	1	0	0	17.1	21	2	6	6	0-2	0	6.75
John Noriega	R	26	8	0	0	0	18.0	25	0	10	6	0-0	0	8.00
Jim Maloney	R	30	7	3	0	0	16.2	26	3	15	7	0-1	1	11.34
Milt Wilcox	R	20	5	2	1	1	22.1	19	2	7	13	3-1	1	2.42
Mel Behney	L	22	5	1	0	0	10.0	15	1	8	2	0-2	0	4.50
Bo Belinsky	L	33	3	0	0	0	8.0	10	0	6	6	0-0	0	4.50

1970 Los Angeles Dodgers 2nd NL West 87-74 .540 14.5 GB

Walter Alston

Player	Gm by Position	B	Age	G	AB	R	H	2B	3B	HR	RBI	BB	SO	SB	Avg	OBP	Slg
Tom Haller	C106	L	33	112	325	47	93	16	6	10	47	32	35	3	.286	.351	.465
Wes Parker	1B161	S	30	161	614	84	196	47	4	10	111	79	70	8	.319	.392	.458
Ted Sizemore	2B86,OF9,SS2	R	25	96	340	40	104	10	1	1	34	34	19	5	.306	.367	.350
Billy Grabarkewitz	3B97,SS50,2B20	R	24	156	529	92	153	20	8	17	84	95	149	19	.289	.399	.454
Maury Wills	SS126,3B4	S	37	132	522	77	141	19	3	0	34	50	34	28	.270	.333	.318
Willie Davis	OF143	L	30	146	593	92	181	23	16	8	93	29	54	38	.305	.335	.438
Manny Mota	OF111,3B1	R	32	124	417	63	127	12	6	3	37	47	37	11	.305	.377	.384
Willie Crawford	OF94	L	23	109	299	48	70	8	6	8	40	33	88	4	.234	.313	.381
Jim Lefebvre	2B70,3B21,1B1	S	28	109	314	33	79	15	1	4	44	29	42	1	.252	.314	.344
Bill Russell	OF79,SS1	R	21	81	278	30	72	11	9	0	28	16	28	9	.259	.303	.363
Bill Sudakis	C38,3B37,OF3*	S	24	94	269	37	71	11	0	14	44	35	46	4	.264	.352	.461
Andy Kosco	OF58,1B1	R	28	74	224	21	51	12	0	8	27	1	40	1	.228	.230	.388
Jeff Torborg	C63	R	28	64	134	11	31	8	0	1	17	14	15	1	.231	.300	.313
Von Joshua	OF41	L	22	72	109	23	29	1	3	1	8	6	24	2	.266	.302	.358
Steve Garvey	3B27,2B1	R	21	34	93	8	25	5	0	1	6	6	17	1	.269	.310	.355
Bill Buckner	OF20,1B1	L	20	28	68	6	13	3	1	0	4	3	7	0	.191	.225	.265
Len Gabrielson	OF2,1B1	L	30	43	42	1	8	2	0	0	6	1	15	0	.190	.205	.238
Gary Moore	OF5,1B1	R	25	7	16	2	3	0	2	0	0	0	1	1	.188	.188	.438
Tom Paciorek	OF3	R	23	8	9	2	2	1	0	0	0	0	3	0	.222	.300	.333
Joe Ferguson	C3	R	23	5	4	0	1	0	0	0	1	2	2	0	.250	.429	.250
Bob Stinson	C3	S	24	4	3	1	0	0	0	0	0	0	1	0	.000	.000	.000

B. Sudakis, 1 G at 1B

Pitcher	T	Age	G	GS	CG	ShO	IP	H	HR	BB	SO	W-L	Sv	ERA
Don Sutton	R	25	38	38	10	4	260.1	251	38	78	201	15-13	0	4.08
Claude Osteen	L	30	37	37	11	4	258.2	280	24	52	114	16-14	0	3.83
Alan Foster	R	23	33	33	7	1	198.2	200	22	81	83	10-13	0	4.26
Joe Moeller	R	27	31	19	2	1	135.1	131	16	43	63	7-9	4	3.92
Sandy Vance	R	23	20	18	2	0	115.0	109	9	37	45	7-7	0	3.13
Bill Singer	R	26	16	16	5	3	106.1	79	10	32	93	8-5	0	3.13
Jim Brewer	L	32	58	0	0	0	89.0	66	10	33	91	7-6	24	3.13
Ray Lamb	R	25	35	0	0	0	57.0	59	4	27	32	6-1	0	3.79
Pete Mikkelsen	R	30	33	0	0	0	62.0	48	5	20	47	4-2	6	2.76
Fred Norman†	L	27	30	0	0	0	62.0	65	8	33	47	2-0	1	5.23
Jose Pena	R	27	29	0	0	0	57.0	51	8	29	31	4-3	4	4.42
Camilo Pascual	R	36	10	0	0	0	14.0	12	2	5	8	0-0	0	2.57
Charlie Hough	R	22	8	0	0	0	17.0	18	7	11	8	0-0	2	5.29
Mike Strahler	R	23	6	0	0	0	18.2	13	1	10	11	1-1	1	1.45
Jerry Stephenson	R	26	3	0	0	0	6.2	11	0	5	6	0-0	0	9.45
Al McBean†	R	32	1	0	0	0	1.0	1	0	0	0	0-0	0	0.00

1970 San Francisco Giants 3rd NL West 86-76 .531 16.0 GB

Clyde King (19-23)/Charlie Fox (67-53)

Player	Gm by Position	B	Age	G	AB	R	H	2B	3B	HR	RBI	BB	SO	SB	Avg	OBP	Slg
Dick Dietz	C139	R	28	148	493	82	148	36	2	22	107	109	106	0	.300	.426	.515
Willie McCovey	1B146	L	32	152	495	98	143	39	2	39	126	137	75	0	.289	.444	.612
Ron Hunt	2B85,3B16	R	29	117	367	70	103	17	1	6	41	44	29	1	.281	.394	.381
Al Gallagher	3B91	R	24	109	282	31	75	15	2	4	28	30	37	2	.266	.335	.376
Hal Lanier	SS130,2B4,1B2	R	27	134	438	33	101	13	1	2	41	21	41	1	.231	.265	.279
Bobby Bonds	OF157	R	24	157	663	134	200	36	10	26	78	77	189	48	.302	.375	.504
Ken Henderson	OF146	S	24	148	554	104	163	35	3	17	88	87	78	20	.294	.394	.460
Willie Mays	OF129,1B5	R	39	139	478	94	139	15	2	28	83	79	90	5	.291	.390	.506
Tito Fuentes	2B78,SS36,3B24	S	26	123	435	49	116	13	7	2	32	36	52	4	.267	.323	.343
Jim Ray Hart	3B56,OF18	R	28	76	255	30	72	12	1	8	37	30	29	0	.282	.360	.431
Frank Johnson	OF33,1B27	R	27	67	161	25	44	1	2	3	31	19	18	1	.273	.357	.360
Bob Heise	SS33,2B28,3B2	R	23	67	154	15	36	5	1	1	22	5	13	0	.234	.256	.299
Bob Taylor	OF26,C1	L	26	63	84	12	16	0	0	2	10	12	13	0	.190	.320	.262
Russ Gibson	C23	R	31	24	69	3	16	6	0	0	6	7	12	0	.232	.303	.319
John Stephenson	C9,OF1	L	29	23	43	3	3	1	0	0	6	2	7	0	.070	.109	.093
Jim Davenport	3B10	R	36	22	37	3	9	1	0	0	4	7	6	0	.243	.356	.270
Don Mason	2B14	L	25	46	36	4	5	0	0	0	1	5	7	0	.139	.244	.139
Steve Whitaker	OF9	L	27	16	27	3	3	1	0	0	4	2	14	0	.111	.167	.148
Bob Burda†	1B8,OF1	L	31	28	23	1	6	0	0	0	3	5	2	0	.261	.414	.261
George Foster	OF7	R	21	9	19	2	6	1	1	1	4	2	5	0	.316	.381	.632
Bernie Williams	OF6	R	21	7	16	2	5	2	0	0	1	2	1	1	.313	.389	.438
Ed Goodson	1B2	L	22	7	11	1	3	0	0	0	0	0	2	0	.273	.273	.273

Pitcher	T	Age	G	GS	CG	ShO	IP	H	HR	BB	SO	W-L	Sv	ERA
Gaylord Perry	R	31	41	41	23	5	328.2	292	27	84	214	23-13	0	3.20
Juan Marichal	R	32	34	33	14	1	242.2	269	28	48	123	12-10	0	4.12
Rich Robertson	R	25	41	26	6	0	183.2	199	22	96	121	8-9	1	4.85
Skip Pitlock	L	22	18	15	1	0	87.0	92	13	48	56	5-5	0	4.66
Miguel Puente	R	22	6	4	1	0	18.2	25	5	11	14	1-3	0	8.20
Don McMahon	R	40	61	0	0	0	94.1	70	9	45	74	9-5	19	2.96
Frank Reberger	R	26	45	18	3	0	152.0	178	13	98	117	7-8	2	5.57
Ron Bryant	L	22	34	11	1	0	96.0	103	7	38	66	5-8	0	4.78
Jerry Johnson†	R	26	33	1	0	0	65.1	67	5	38	44	3-4	3	4.27
Mike Davison	L	24	31	0	0	0	36.0	46	4	22	21	3-5	1	6.50
Mike McCormick†	L	31	23	11	1	0	78.1	80	15	36	37	3-4	2	6.20
Frank Linzy†	R	29	20	0	0	0	25.2	33	2	11	16	2-1	1	7.01
Don Carrithers	R	20	11	2	0	0	22.0	31	5	14	14	2-1	0	7.36
John Cumberland†	L	23	7	0	0	0	11.0	6	0	4	6	2-0	0	0.82
Bill Faul	R	30	7	0	0	0	9.2	15	1	6	6	0-0	1	7.45
Jim Johnson	L	24	3	0	0	0	6.2	8	0	5	2	1-0	0	8.10

1970 Houston Astros 4th NL West 79-83 .488 23.0 GB

Harry Walker

Player	Gm by Position	B	Age	G	AB	R	H	2B	3B	HR	RBI	BB	SO	SB	Avg	OBP	Slg
Johnny Edwards	C139	L	32	140	458	46	101	16	4	7	49	51	63	1	.221	.299	.319
Bob Watson	1B83,C6,OF1	R	24	97	327	48	89	19	2	11	61	24	59	1	.272	.324	.443
Joe Morgan	2B142	L	26	144	548	102	147	28	9	8	52	102	55	42	.268	.383	.396
Doug Rader	3B154,1B1	R	25	156	576	90	145	25	3	25	87	57	102	3	.252	.322	.436
Denis Menke	SS133,2B21,1B5*	R	29	154	562	82	171	26	6	13	92	82	80	6	.304	.392	.441
Jimmy Wynn	OF151	R	28	157	554	82	156	32	2	27	88	106	96	24	.282	.394	.493
Jesus Alou	OF108	R	28	117	458	59	140	27	3	1	44	21	15	3	.306	.335	.384
Cesar Cedeno	OF90	R	19	90	355	46	110	21	4	7	42	15	57	17	.310	.340	.451
Joe Pepitone†	1B50,OF28	L	29	75	279	44	70	9	5	14	35	18	28	5	.251	.298	.470
Norm Miller	OF72,C1	L	24	90	226	29	54	9	0	4	29	41	33	3	.239	.357	.332
Tommy Davis†	OF53	R	31	57	213	24	60	12	2	3	30	7	25	8	.282	.305	.399
Marty Martinez	SS29,3B10,C6*	S	28	75	150	12	33	3	0	0	12	9	22	0	.220	.264	.240
John Mayberry	1B45	L	21	50	148	23	32	3	2	5	14	21	33	1	.216	.318	.365
Larry Howard	C26,1B2,OF1	R	25	31	88	11	27	6	0	2	16	10	23	0	.307	.378	.443
Keith Lampard	OF16,1B2	L	24	53	72	8	17	8	1	0	5	5	24	0	.236	.295	.375
Hector Torres	SS22,2B6	R	24	31	65	6	16	1	2	0	5	6	8	0	.246	.310	.323
Cesar Geronimo	OF26	L	22	47	37	5	9	0	0	0	2	2	5	0	.243	.293	.243
Jim Beauchamp†	OF16	R	30	31	26	3	5	0	0	1	4	3	7	0	.192	.276	.308
Don Bryant	C13	R	28	15	24	2	5	0	0	0	3	1	8	0	.208	.231	.208
Gary Geiger	OF2	L	33	5	4	0	1	0	0	0	0	0	0	0	.250	.250	.250
Leon McFadden		R	26	2	0	0	0	0	0	0	0	0	0	0	—	—	—

D. Menke, 5 G at 3B, 3 G at OF; M. Martinez, 4 G at 2B

Pitcher	T	Age	G	GS	CG	ShO	IP	H	HR	BB	SO	W-L	Sv	ERA
Larry Dierker	R	23	37	36	17	2	269.2	263	31	82	191	16-12	1	3.87
Don Wilson	R	25	29	27	3	0	184.1	188	15	66	94	11-6	0	3.91
Jack Billingham	R	27	46	24	8	2	187.2	190	10	63	134	13-9	0	3.98
Denny Lemaster	L	31	39	21	3	0	162.0	169	22	65	103	7-12	3	4.56
Tom Griffin	R	22	23	20	2	1	111.1	118	9	72	72	3-13	0	5.74
Wade Blasingame	L	26	13	13	1	0	77.2	76	4	23	55	3-3	0	3.48
Ken Forsch	R	23	4	4	1	0	24.0	28	1	5	13	1-2	0	5.63
Fred Gladding	R	34	63	0	0	0	71.0	84	4	24	46	7-4	18	4.06
Jim Ray	R	25	52	2	0	0	105.0	97	13	49	67	6-3	5	3.26
Jack DiLauro	L	27	42	0	0	0	33.2	34	4	17	23	1-3	3	4.28
Ron Cook	L	22	41	7	0	0	82.1	80	4	42	50	4-4	2	3.72
George Culver†	R	26	32	0	0	0	45.0	44	1	21	31	3-3	3	3.20
Jim Bouton	R	31	29	6	1	0	73.1	84	5	33	49	4-6	0	5.40
Scipio Spinks	R	22	5	2	0	0	13.2	17	5	9	6	0-1	0	9.88
Mike Marshall†	R	27	4	0	0	0	5.1	8	0	4	5	0-1	0	8.44
Dan Osinski	R	36	3	0	0	0	3.2	5	0	2	1	0-1	0	9.82
Buddy Harris	R	21	2	0	0	0	6.1	6	3	0	2	0-0	0	5.68

1970 Atlanta Braves 5th NL West 76-86 .469 26.0 GB

Lum Harris

Player	Gm by Position	B	Age	G	AB	R	H	2B	3B	HR	RBI	BB	SO	SB	Avg	OBP	Slg
Bob Tillman	C70	R	33	71	223	19	53	5	0	11	30	20	66	0	.238	.299	.408
Orlando Cepeda	1B148	R	32	148	567	87	173	33	0	34	111	47	75	6	.305	.365	.543
Felix Millan	2B142	R	26	142	590	100	183	25	5	2	37	35	23	16	.310	.352	.380
Clete Boyer	3B126,SS5	R	33	134	475	44	117	14	1	16	62	41	71	2	.246	.305	.381
Sonny Jackson	SS87	L	25	103	328	60	85	14	3	0	20	45	27	11	.259	.347	.320
Rico Carty	OF133	R	30	136	478	84	175	23	3	25	101	77	46	1	.366	.454	.584
Hank Aaron	OF125,1B11	R	36	150	516	103	154	26	1	38	118	74	63	9	.298	.385	.574
Tony Gonzalez†	OF119	L	33	123	430	57	114	18	2	7	55	46	45	3	.265	.345	.365
Gil Garrido	SS80,2B26	R	29	101	367	38	97	5	4	1	19	15	16	0	.264	.290	.308
Mike Lum	OF98	L	24	123	291	25	74	17	2	7	28	17	43	3	.254	.306	.399
Hal King	C62	L	26	89	204	29	53	8	0	11	30	32	41	1	.260	.364	.461
Bob Didier	C57	S	21	57	168	9	25	2	1	0	7	12	11	1	.149	.210	.173
Bob Aspromonte	3B30,SS4,1B1*	R	32	62	127	5	27	3	0	0	7	13	13	0	.213	.282	.236
Ralph Garr	OF21	L	24	37	96	18	27	3	0	0	8	5	12	5	.281	.314	.313
Tommie Aaron	1B16,OF12	R	30	44	63	3	13	2	0	2	7	3	10	0	.206	.242	.333
Oscar Brown	OF25	R	24	28	47	6	18	2	1	1	7	7	7	0	.383	.464	.532
Jimmie Hall†	OF28	L	32	39	47	7	10	2	0	2	4	2	14	0	.213	.245	.383
Darrell Evans	3B12	L	23	12	44	4	14	1	1	0	9	7	5	0	.318	.423	.386
Dusty Baker	OF11	R	21	13	24	3	7	0	0	0	4	2	4	0	.292	.333	.292
Earl Williams	1B4,3B3	R	21	10	19	4	7	4	0	0	5	3	4	0	.368	.417	.579

B. Aspromonte, 1 G at OF

Pitcher	T	Age	G	GS	CG	ShO	IP	H	HR	BB	SO	W-L	Sv	ERA
Pat Jarvis	R	29	36	34	11	1	254.0	240	21	72	173	16-16	0	3.61
Jim Nash	R	25	34	33	6	2	212.1	211	22	90	153	13-9	0	4.07
Phil Niekro	R	31	34	32	10	3	229.2	222	40	68	168	12-18	0	4.27
George Stone	L	23	35	30	9	2	207.1	218	27	50	131	11-11	0	3.86
Ron Reed	R	27	21	18	6	0	134.2	140	16	39	68	7-10	0	4.41
Hoyt Wilhelm†	R	46	50	0	0	0	78.1	69	7	39	67	6-4	13	3.10
Bob Priddy	R	30	41	0	0	0	73.0	75	9	24	32	5-5	8	5.42
Mike McQueen	L	19	22	8	1	0	66.0	67	10	31	54	1-5	1	5.59
Julio Navarro	R	34	17	0	0	0	26.1	24	7	1	21	0-0	1	4.10
Don Cardwell†	R	34	16	2	1	1	23.0	31	5	13	16	2-1	0	9.00
Rick Kester	R	23	15	0	0	0	32.1	36	3	19	20	0-0	0	5.57
Larry Jaster	L	26	14	0	0	0	22.1	33	5	8	9	1-1	0	6.85
Milt Pappas†	R	31	11	3	1	0	35.2	44	6	7	25	2-2	0	6.06
Gary Neibauer	R	25	7	0	0	0	12.2	11	0	8	9	0-3	0	4.97
Steve Barber†	L	31	5	2	0	0	14.2	17	3	5	11	0-1	0	4.91
Ron Kline	R	38	5	0	0	0	6.1	9	4	2	3	0-0	1	7.11
Aubrey Gatewood	R	31	3	0	0	0	2.0	4	0	2	0	0-0	0	4.50

1970 San Diego Padres 6th NL West 63-99 .389 39.0 GB

Preston Gomez

Player	Gm by Position	B	Age	G	AB	R	H	2B	3B	HR	RBI	BB	SO	SB	Avg	OBP	Slg
Chris Cannizzaro	C110	R	32	111	341	27	95	13	3	5	42	48	49	2	.279	.366	.378
Nate Colbert	1B153,3B1	R	24	156	572	84	148	17	6	38	86	56	150	3	.259	.328	.509
Dave Campbell	2B153	R	28	154	581	71	127	28	2	12	40	40	115	18	.219	.268	.336
Ed Spiezio	3B93	R	28	110	316	45	90	18	1	12	42	43	42	4	.285	.373	.462
Jose Arcia	SS67,2B20,3B9*	R	26	114	229	28	51	9	3	0	17	12	36	3	.223	.282	.288
Cito Gaston	OF142	R	26	146	584	92	186	26	9	29	93	41	142	4	.318	.364	.543
Ollie Brown	OF137	R	26	139	534	79	156	34	1	23	89	34	78	5	.292	.331	.489
Ivan Murrell	OF101,1B1	R	25	125	347	43	85	9	3	12	35	17	93	9	.245	.287	.392
Al Ferrara	OF96	R	30	138	372	44	103	15	4	13	51	46	63	0	.277	.372	.444
Steve Huntz	SS57,3B51	S	24	106	352	54	77	8	0	11	37	66	69	0	.219	.341	.335
Bob Barton	C59	R	28	61	188	15	41	6	0	4	16	15	37	1	.218	.278	.314
Tommy Dean	SS55	R	24	61	158	18	35	5	1	2	13	11	29	2	.222	.271	.304
Ray Webster	1B15,OF1	L	27	95	116	12	30	3	0	2	11	11	12	1	.259	.323	.336
Van Kelly	3B27,2B1	L	24	38	89	9	15	3	0	1	9	15	21	0	.169	.288	.236
Rafael Robles	SS23	R	22	23	89	5	19	1	0	0	3	5	11	3	.213	.263	.225
Ron Slocum	C19,SS17,3B11*	R	24	60	71	8	10	2	2	1	11	8	24	0	.141	.238	.268
Larry Stahl	OF20	L	29	52	66	5	12	2	0	0	3	2	14	2	.182	.206	.212
Jerry Morales	OF26	R	21	28	58	6	9	0	1	1	4	3	11	0	.155	.197	.241
Dave Robinson	OF13	S	24	15	38	5	12	2	0	2	6	5	4	2	.316	.395	.526
Jim Williams	OF6	R	23	11	14	4	4	0	0	0	0	1	3	1	.286	.333	.286
Fred Kendall	C2,1B1,OF1	R	21	4	9	0	0	0	0	0	1	0	0	0	.000	.000	.000

J. Arcia, 7 G at OF; R. Slocum, 9 G at 2B

Pitcher	T	Age	G	GS	CG	ShO	IP	H	HR	BB	SO	W-L	Sv	ERA
Pat Dobson	R	28	40	34	8	1	251.0	257	28	78	185	14-15	1	3.76
Clay Kirby	R	22	36	34	6	1	214.2	198	29	120	154	10-16	0	4.53
Danny Coombs	L	28	35	27	5	1	188.1	185	12	76	105	10-14	0	3.30
Mike Corkins	R	24	24	18	1	0	111.0	109	11	79	75	5-6	0	4.62
Al Santorini	R	22	21	12	0	0	75.2	91	11	43	41	1-8	1	6.07
Earl Wilson†	R	35	15	9	0	0	65.0	82	5	19	29	1-6	0	4.85
Steve Arlin	R	24	2	2	1	1	12.2	11	0	8	3	1-0	0	2.84
Jerry Nyman	L	27	2	2	0	0	5.1	8	1	2	2	0-2	0	15.19
Ron Herbel†	R	32	64	1	0	0	111.0	114	14	39	53	7-5	9	4.95
Tom Dukes	R	27	53	0	0	0	69.0	62	7	25	56	1-6	10	4.04
Dave Roberts	L	25	43	21	3	2	181.2	182	16	43	102	8-14	1	3.81
Ron Willis	R	26	42	0	0	0	56.0	53	4	28	20	2-2	4	4.02
Gary Ross	R	22	33	2	0	0	62.1	72	8	36	39	2-3	1	5.20
Jack Baldschun	R	33	12	0	0	0	13.1	24	2	4	12	1-0	0	10.13
Roberto Rodriguez†	R	28	10	0	0	0	16.1	26	1	5	8	0-0	3	6.61
Paul Doyle†	L	30	9	0	0	0	7.0	9	0	6	2	0-2	2	6.43

»1971 Baltimore Orioles 1st AL East 101-57 .639 — Earl Weaver

Player	Gm by Position	B	Age	G	AB	R	H	2B	3B	HR	RBI	BB	SO	SB	Avg	OBP	Slg
Ellie Hendricks	C90,1B3	L	30	101	316	33	79	14	1	9	42	39	38	0	.250	.334	.386
Boog Powell	1B124	L	29	128	418	59	107	19	0	22	92	82	64	1	.256	.379	.459
Dave Johnson	2B140	R	28	142	510	67	144	26	1	18	72	51	55	3	.282	.351	.443
Brooks Robinson	3B156	R	34	156	589	67	160	21	1	20	92	63	50	0	.272	.341	.413
Mark Belanger	SS149	R	27	150	500	67	133	19	4	0	35	73	48	10	.266	.365	.320
Paul Blair	OF138	R	27	141	516	75	135	24	8	10	44	32	94	14	.262	.306	.397
Merv Rettenmund	OF134	R	28	141	491	81	156	23	4	11	75	87	60	15	.318	.422	.448
Don Buford	OF115	S	34	122	449	99	130	19	4	19	54	89	62	15	.290	.413	.477
Frank Robinson	OF92,1B37	R	35	133	455	82	128	16	2	28	99	72	62	3	.281	.384	.510
Andy Etchebarren	C70	R	28	70	222	21	60	8	0	9	29	16	40	1	.270	.321	.428
Chico Salmon	1B9,2B9,3B6*	R	30	42	84	11	15	1	0	2	7	3	21	0	.179	.205	.262
Jerry Davanon	2B20,SS11,3B3*	R	25	38	81	14	19	5	0	0	4	12	20	0	.235	.340	.296
Tom Shopay	OF13	L	26	47	74	10	19	2	0	0	5	3	7	2	.257	.286	.284
Curt Motton	OF16	R	30	38	53	13	10	1	0	4	8	10	12	0	.189	.317	.434
Clay Dalrymple	C18	L	34	23	49	6	10	1	0	1	6	16	13	0	.204	.409	.286
Bobby Grich	SS5,2B2	R	22	7	30	7	9	0	0	1	6	5	8	1	.300	.400	.400
Terry Crowley	OF6,1B2	L	24	18	23	2	4	0	0	0	1	3	4	0	.174	.269	.174
Don Baylor	OF1	R	22	1	2	0	0	0	0	0	1	2	1	0	.000	.600	.000

C. Salmon, 5 G at SS; J. Davanon, 1 G at 1B

Pitcher	T	Age	G	GS	CG	ShO	IP	H	HR	BB	SO	W-L	Sv	ERA
Mike Cuellar	L	34	38	38	21	4	292.1	250	30	78	124	20-9	0	3.08
Pat Dobson	R	29	38	37	18	4	282.1	248	24	63	187	20-8	1	2.90
Jim Palmer	R	25	37	37	20	3	282.0	231	19	106	184	20-9	0	2.68
Dave McNally	L	28	30	30	11	1	224.1	188	24	58	91	21-5	0	2.89
Dave Leonhard	R	30	12	6	1	1	54.0	51	5	19	18	2-3	1	2.83
Eddie Watt	R	30	35	0	0	0	39.2	39	1	8	26	3-1	11	1.82
Pete Richert	L	31	35	0	0	0	36.1	26	3	22	35	3-5	4	3.47
Grant Jackson	L	28	29	9	0	0	77.2	72	7	20	51	4-3	0	3.13
Tom Dukes	R	28	28	0	0	0	38.1	40	4	8	30	1-5	4	3.52
Dick Hall	R	40	27	0	0	0	43.1	52	4	11	26	6-6	1	4.98
Dave Boswell†	R	26	15	1	0	0	24.2	32	4	15	14	1-2	0	4.38
Jim Hardin†	R	27	6	0	0	0	5.2	12	0	3	3	0-0	0	4.76
Orlando Pena	R	37	5	0	0	0	14.2	16	0	5	4	0-1	0	3.07

1971 Detroit Tigers 2nd AL East 91-71 .562 12.0 GB Billy Martin

Player	Gm by Position	B	Age	G	AB	R	H	2B	3B	HR	RBI	BB	SO	SB	Avg	OBP	Slg
Bill Freehan	C144,OF1	R	29	148	516	57	143	26	4	21	71	54	48	2	.277	.353	.465
Norm Cash	1B131	L	36	135	452	72	128	10	3	32	91	59	86	1	.283	.372	.531
Dick McAuliffe	2B123,SS7	L	31	128	477	67	99	16	6	18	57	53	67	4	.208	.293	.379
Aurelio Rodriguez	3B153,SS1	R	23	154	604	68	153	30	7	15	39	27	93	4	.253	.288	.401
Ed Brinkman	SS159	R	29	159	527	40	120	18	2	1	37	44	54	1	.228	.293	.275
Mickey Stanley	OF139	R	28	139	401	43	117	14	5	7	41	24	44	1	.292	.329	.404
Al Kaline	OF129,1B5	R	36	133	405	69	119	19	2	15	54	82	57	4	.294	.416	.462
Willie Horton	OF118	R	28	119	450	64	130	25	1	22	72	37	75	1	.289	.349	.496
Jim Northrup	OF108,1B32	L	31	136	459	72	124	27	2	16	71	60	43	7	.270	.355	.442
Gates Brown	OF56	L	32	82	195	37	66	2	3	11	29	21	17	4	.338	.408	.549
Tony Taylor†	2B51,3B3	R	35	55	181	27	52	10	2	3	19	12	11	5	.287	.335	.414
Dalton Jones	OF16,3B13,1B3*	L	27	83	138	15	35	5	0	5	11	9	21	1	.254	.304	.399
Ike Brown	1B17,OF9,2B8*	R	29	59	110	20	28	1	0	8	19	19	25	0	.255	.359	.482
Jim Price	C25	R	29	29	54	4	13	2	0	1	7	6	3	0	.241	.323	.333
Kevin Collins	3B4,OF2,2B1	L	24	35	41	6	11	2	1	1	4	0	12	0	.268	.268	.439
Cesar Gutierrez	SS14,3B5,2B2	R	28	38	37	8	7	0	0	0	4	0	3	0	.189	.211	.189
Tim Hosley	C4,1B1	R	24	7	16	2	3	0	0	2	6	0	1	0	.188	.188	.563
Gene Lamont	C7	L	24	7	15	2	1	0	0	0	1	0	5	0	.067	.067	.067
Marvin Lane	OF6	R	21	8	14	0	2	0	0	0	1	1	3	0	.143	.200	.143
John Young	1B1	L	22	2	4	1	2	1	0	0	1	0	0	0	.500	.500	.750

D. Jones, 1 G at 2B; I. Brown, 4 G at 3B, 1 G at SS

Pitcher	T	Age	G	GS	CG	ShO	IP	H	HR	BB	SO	W-L	Sv	ERA
Mickey Lolich	L	30	45	45	29	4	376.0	336	36	92	308	25-14	0	2.92
Joe Coleman	R	24	39	38	16	3	286.0	241	17	96	236	20-9	0	3.15
Les Cain	L	23	26	26	3	1	144.2	121	14	91	118	10-9	0	4.35
Bill Gilbreth	L	23	9	5	2	0	30.0	28	4	21	14	2-1	0	4.80
Fred Scherman	L	26	69	1	1	0	113.0	91	11	49	46	11-6	20	2.71
Tom Timmermann	R	31	52	2	0	0	84.0	82	6	37	51	7-6	4	3.86
Joe Niekro	R	26	31	15	0	0	122.1	136	13	49	43	6-7	1	4.49
Dean Chance	R	30	31	14	0	0	89.2	91	5	50	64	4-6	0	3.51
Bill Denehy	R	25	31	1	0	0	49.0	47	4	28	27	0-3	1	4.22
Mike Kilkenny	L	26	30	11	2	0	86.1	83	8	44	47	4-5	1	5.00
Bill Zepp	R	24	16	4	0	0	31.2	41	2	17	15	1-1	2	5.12
Daryl Patterson†	R	27	12	0	0	0	9.1	14	1	6	5	0-1	0	4.82
Ron Perranoski†	L	35	11	0	0	0	18.0	16	2	3	8	0-1	2	2.50
Jim Hannan†	R	31	7	0	0	0	11.0	7	1	7	6	1-0	0	3.27
Jack Whillock	R	28	7	0	0	0	8.0	10	0	2	6	0-2	1	5.63
Chuck Seelbach	R	23	5	0	0	0	4.0	6	2	7	1	0-0	0	13.50
Dave Boswell†	R	26	3	0	0	0	4.1	3	0	6	3	0-0	0	6.23
Jim Foor	L	22	3	0	0	0	1.0	2	0	4	2	0-0	0	18.00

1971 Boston Red Sox 3rd AL East 85-77 .525 18.0 GB Eddie Kasko

Player	Gm by Position	B	Age	G	AB	R	H	2B	3B	HR	RBI	BB	SO	SB	Avg	OBP	Slg
Duane Josephson	C87	R	29	91	306	38	75	14	1	10	39	22	35	2	.245	.294	.395
George Scott	1B143	R	27	146	537	72	141	16	4	24	78	41	102	0	.263	.317	.441
Doug Griffin	2B124	R	24	125	483	51	118	23	2	3	27	31	45	11	.244	.291	.319
Rico Petrocelli	3B156	R	28	158	553	82	139	24	4	28	89	91	108	2	.251	.354	.461
Luis Aparicio	SS121	R	37	125	491	56	114	23	0	4	45	35	43	6	.232	.284	.303
Reggie Smith	OF159	S	26	159	618	85	175	33	2	30	96	63	82	11	.283	.352	.489
Carl Yastrzemski	OF146	L	31	148	508	75	129	21	2	15	70	106	60	8	.254	.381	.392
Billy Conigliaro	OF100	R	23	101	351	42	92	26	1	11	33	25	68	3	.262	.310	.436
John Kennedy	2B37,SS33,3B5	R	30	74	272	41	75	12	5	5	22	14	42	1	.276	.320	.412
Joe Lahoud	OF69	L	24	107	256	39	55	9	3	14	32	40	45	2	.215	.330	.438
Bob Montgomery	C66	R	27	67	205	19	49	11	2	2	24	16	43	1	.239	.300	.341
Phil Gagliano	OF11,2B7,3B4	R	29	47	68	11	22	5	0	0	13	11	5	0	.324	.413	.397
Mike Fiore	1B12	L	26	51	62	9	11	2	0	1	6	12	14	0	.177	.311	.258
Juan Beniquez	SS15	R	21	16	57	8	17	2	0	0	4	3	4	3	.298	.333	.333
Carlton Fisk	C14	R	23	14	48	7	15	2	1	2	6	1	10	0	.313	.327	.521
Cecil Cooper	1B11	L	21	14	42	9	13	4	1	0	3	5	4	1	.310	.388	.452
Ben Oglivie	OF11	L	22	14	38	2	10	3	0	0	4	0	5	0	.263	.263	.342
Rick Miller	OF14	L	23	15	33	9	11	5	0	1	7	8	8	0	.333	.452	.576
Don Pavletich	C8	R	32	14	27	5	7	1	0	1	3	5	5	0	.259	.375	.407
George Thomas†	OF5	R	33	9	13	0	1	0	0	0	1	1	4	0	.077	.143	.077
Buddy Hunter	2B6	R	23	8	9	2	2	1	0	0	0	2	1	0	.222	.364	.333

Pitcher	T	Age	G	GS	CG	ShO	IP	H	HR	BB	SO	W-L	Sv	ERA
Ray Culp	R	29	35	35	12	3	242.1	236	21	67	151	14-16	0	3.60
Sonny Siebert	R	34	32	32	12	4	235.1	220	20	60	131	16-10	0	2.91
Gary Peters	L	34	34	32	9	1	214.0	241	25	70	100	14-11	1	4.37
Jim Lonborg	R	29	27	26	5	1	167.2	167	15	67	100	10-7	0	4.13
Roger Moret	L	21	13	7	4	1	71.0	50	5	40	47	4-3	0	2.92
Mike Nagy	R	23	12	7	0	0	38.0	46	4	20	9	1-3	0	6.63
John Curtis	L	23	5	3	1	0	26.0	30	3	6	19	2-2	0	3.12
Mike Garman	R	21	3	3	0	0	18.2	15	3	9	6	1-1	0	3.86
Bobby Bolin	R	32	52	0	0	0	69.2	74	7	24	51	5-3	6	4.26
Sparky Lyle	L	26	50	0	0	0	52.1	41	5	23	37	6-4	16	2.75
Bill Lee	L	24	47	3	0	0	102.0	102	7	46	74	9-2	2	2.74
Ken Tatum	R	27	36	1	0	0	53.2	50	3	25	21	2-4	9	4.19
Ken Brett	L	22	29	2	0	0	59.0	57	7	35	57	0-3	1	5.34
Luis Tiant	R	30	21	10	1	0	72.1	73	8	32	59	1-7	0	4.85
Cal Koonce	R	30	13	1	0	0	21.0	22	3	11	9	0-1	0	5.57

1971 New York Yankees 4th AL East 82-80 .506 21.0 GB Ralph Houk

Player	Gm by Position	B	Age	G	AB	R	H	2B	3B	HR	RBI	BB	SO	SB	Avg	OBP	Slg
Thurman Munson	C117,OF1	R	24	125	451	71	113	15	4	10	42	52	65	6	.251	.335	.368
Danny Cater	1B78,3B52	R	31	121	428	39	118	16	5	4	50	19	25	0	.276	.308	.364
Horace Clarke	2B156	S	31	159	625	76	156	23	7	2	41	64	43	17	.250	.321	.318
Jerry Kenney	3B109,SS5,1B1	L	26	120	325	50	85	10	3	0	20	56	38	9	.262	.368	.311
Gene Michael	SS136	S	33	139	456	36	102	15	0	3	35	48	64	3	.224	.299	.276
Roy White	OF145	S	27	147	524	86	153	22	7	19	84	86	66	14	.292	.388	.469
Bobby Murcer	OF143	L	25	146	529	94	175	25	6	25	94	91	60	14	.331	.427	.543
Felipe Alou†	OF80,1B42	R	36	131	461	52	133	20	6	8	69	32	24	5	.289	.334	.410
John Ellis	1B65,C2	R	22	83	238	16	58	12	1	3	34	23	42	0	.244	.322	.340
Jake Gibbs	C51	L	32	70	206	23	45	9	0	5	21	12	23	2	.218	.270	.335
Ron Blomberg	OF57	L	22	64	199	30	64	6	2	7	31	14	23	2	.322	.363	.477
Ron Hansen	3B30,2B9,SS3	R	33	61	145	6	30	3	0	2	20	9	27	0	.207	.245	.269
Ron Swoboda†	OF47	R	27	54	138	17	36	2	1	2	20	27	35	0	.261	.391	.333
Jim Lyttle	OF29	L	25	49	86	7	17	5	0	1	7	8	18	0	.198	.271	.291
Frank Baker	SS38	L	24	43	79	9	11	2	0	0	2	16	22	3	.139	.281	.165
Curt Blefary†	OF6,1B4	L	27	21	36	4	7	1	0	1	2	3	5	0	.194	.256	.306
Ron Woods†	OF9	R	28	25	32	4	8	1	0	1	2	4	2	0	.250	.333	.375
Rusty Torres	OF5	S	22	9	26	5	10	3	0	2	3	0	8	0	.385	.385	.731
Danny Walton†	OF4	R	23	5	14	1	2	0	0	1	2	0	7	0	.143	.143	.357
Frank Tepedino†	OF1	L	23	6	6	0	0	0	0	0	0	0	0	0	.000	.000	.000
Len Boehmer	3B1	R	30	3	5	0	0	0	0	0	0	0	0	0	.000	.000	.000

Pitcher	T	Age	G	GS	CG	ShO	IP	H	HR	BB	SO	W-L	Sv	ERA
Fritz Peterson	L	29	37	35	16	4	274.0	269	25	42	139	15-13	1	3.05
Mel Stottlemyre	R	29	35	35	19	7	269.2	234	16	69	132	16-12	0	2.87
Stan Bahnsen	R	26	36	34	14	3	242.0	221	20	72	110	14-12	0	3.35
Steve Kline	R	23	31	30	15	1	222.1	206	21	37	81	12-13	0	2.96
Mike Kekich	L	26	37	24	3	0	170.1	167	13	82	93	10-9	0	4.07
Lindy McDaniel	R	35	44	0	0	0	69.2	82	12	24	39	5-10	4	5.04
Jack Aker	R	30	41	0	0	0	55.2	48	3	26	24	4-4	4	2.59
Gary Waslewski	R	29	24	0	0	0	35.2	28	2	16	17	0-1	1	3.28
Roger Hambright	R	22	18	0	0	0	26.2	22	5	10	14	3-1	2	4.39
Al Closter	L	28	14	1	0	0	28.1	33	4	13	22	2-2	0	5.08
Jim Hardin†	R	27	12	3	0	0	28.1	35	3	9	14	0-2	0	5.08
Gary Jones	L	26	12	0	0	0	14.0	19	1	7	10	0-0	0	9.00
Terry Ley	L	24	6	0	0	0	9.0	9	1	9	7	0-0	0	5.00
Bill Burbach	R	23	2	0	0	0	3.1	6	0	5	3	0-1	0	10.80
Rob Gardner†	L	26	2	0	0	0	3.0	3	0	2	2	0-0	0	3.00

1971 Washington Senators 5th AL East 63-96 .396 38.5 GB Ted Williams

Player	Gm by Position	B	Age	G	AB	R	H	2B	3B	HR	RBI	BB	SO	SB	Avg	OBP	Slg
Paul Casanova	C83	R	29	94	311	19	63	9	1	5	26	14	52	0	.203	.238	.286
Don Mincher†	1B88	L	33	100	323	35	94	15	1	10	45	53	52	2	.291	.389	.437
Tim Cullen	2B78,SS62	R	29	125	403	34	77	13	4	2	26	33	47	2	.191	.252	.258
Dave Nelson	3B84,2B1	R	27	85	329	47	92	11	3	5	33	23	29	17	.280	.328	.377
Toby Harrah	SS116,3B7	R	22	127	383	45	88	11	3	2	22	40	48	10	.230	.300	.290
Del Unser	OF151	L	26	153	581	63	148	19	6	9	41	59	68	11	.255	.325	.355
Elliott Maddox	OF103,3B12	R	23	128	258	38	56	8	2	1	18	51	42	10	.217	.344	.275
Frank Howard	OF100,1B68	R	34	153	549	60	153	25	2	26	83	77	121	1	.279	.367	.474
Dick Billings	C62,OF32,3B2	R	28	116	349	32	86	14	0	6	48	21	54	2	.246	.296	.338
Bernie Allen	2B41,3B34	L	32	97	229	18	61	11	1	4	22	33	27	2	.266	.359	.376
Lenny Randle	2B66	S	22	75	215	27	47	11	0	2	13	24	56	1	.219	.298	.298
Tom McCraw	OF60,1B30	L	30	122	207	33	44	6	4	7	25	19	38	3	.213	.291	.382
Jeff Burroughs	OF50	R	20	59	181	20	42	9	0	5	25	22	55	1	.232	.319	.365
Larry Biittner	OF41,1B3	L	25	66	171	12	44	4	1	0	16	16	20	1	.257	.323	.292
Joe Foy	3B37,2B3,SS1	R	28	41	128	12	30	8	0	0	11	27	14	4	.234	.363	.297
Mike Epstein†	1B24	L	28	24	85	6	21	1	1	1	9	12	31	1	.247	.366	.318
Richie Scheinblum	OF13	S	28	27	49	5	7	3	0	0	4	8	5	0	.143	.263	.204
Jim French	C14	L	29	14	41	6	6	2	0	0	4	7	7	0	.146	.271	.195
Don Wert	3B7,SS7,2B1	R	32	20	40	2	2	1	0	0	2	4	10	0	.050	.156	.075
Curt Flood	OF10	R	33	13	35	4	7	0	0	0	2	5	2	0	.200	.300	.200
Frank Fernandez†	OF6,C1	R	28	18	30	0	3	0	0	0	4	4	10	0	.100	.194	.100
Tom Ragland	2B10	R	25	10	23	1	4	0	0	0	0	1	5	0	.174	.208	.174
Jim Mason	SS3	L	20	3	9	0	3	0	0	0	0	1	3	0	.333	.400	.333
Rick Stelmaszek	C3	L	22	6	9	0	0	0	0	0	0	0	3	0	.000	.000	.000
Bill Fahey	C2	L	21	2	8	0	0	0	0	0	0	0	0	0	.000	.000	.000

Pitcher	T	Age	G	GS	CG	ShO	IP	H	HR	BB	SO	W-L	Sv	ERA
Dick Bosman	R	27	35	35	7	1	236.2	245	29	71	113	12-16	0	3.73
Denny McLain	R	27	33	32	9	3	216.2	233	31	72	103	10-22	0	4.28
Pete Broberg	R	21	18	18	7	1	124.2	104	10	53	89	5-9	0	3.47
Bill Gogolewski	R	23	27	17	4	1	124.1	112	5	39	70	6-5	0	2.75
Mike Thompson	R	21	16	12	0	0	66.2	53	3	54	41	1-6	0	4.86
Jackie Brown	R	28	14	9	0	0	47.0	60	9	27	21	3-4	0	5.94
Denny Riddleberger	L	25	57	0	0	0	69.2	67	9	32	56	3-1	1	3.23
Horacio Pina	R	26	56	0	0	0	57.2	47	2	31	38	1-1	2	3.59
Casey Cox	R	29	54	11	0	0	124.1	131	9	40	43	5-7	7	3.98
Joe Grzenda	L	34	46	0	0	0	70.1	54	2	17	56	5-2	5	1.92
Paul Lindblad†	L	29	43	0	0	0	83.2	58	6	29	50	6-4	8	2.58
Jim Shellenback	L	27	40	15	3	1	120.0	123	10	49	47	3-11	0	3.53
Jerry Janeski	R	25	23	10	0	0	61.2	72	5	34	19	1-5	1	4.96
Darold Knowles†	L	29	12	0	0	0	15.1	17	2	6	16	2-2	2	3.52

1971 Cleveland Indians 6th AL East 60-102 .370 43.0 GB

Alvin Dark (42-61)/Johnny Lipon (18-41)

Player	Gm by Position	B	Age	G	AB	R	H	2B	3B	HR	RBI	BB	SO	SB	Avg	OBP	Slg
Ray Fosse	C126,1B4	R	24	133	486	53	134	21	1	12	62	36	62	4	.276	.329	.397
Chris Chambliss	1B108	L	22	111	415	49	114	20	4	9	48	40	83	2	.275	.341	.407
Eddie Leon	2B107,SS24	R	24	131	429	35	112	12	2	4	35	34	69	3	.261	.317	.326
Graig Nettles	3B158	L	26	158	598	78	156	18	1	28	86	82	56	7	.261	.350	.435
Jack Heidemann	SS81	R	21	81	240	16	50	7	0	0	9	12	46	1	.208	.251	.238
Vada Pinson	OF141,1B3	L	32	146	566	60	149	23	4	11	35	21	58	25	.263	.295	.376
Ted Uhlaender	OF131	L	30	141	500	52	144	20	3	2	47	38	44	3	.288	.336	.352
Roy Foster	OF107	R	25	125	396	51	97	21	1	18	45	35	48	6	.245	.314	.439
Ted Ford	OF55	R	24	74	196	15	38	6	0	2	14	9	34	2	.194	.229	.255
Frank Baker	OF51	L	27	73	181	18	38	12	1	1	23	12	34	1	.210	.262	.304
Ken Harrelson	1B40,OF7	R	29	52	161	20	32	2	0	5	14	24	21	1	.199	.301	.304
Chuck Hinton	1B20,OF20,C5	R	37	88	147	13	33	7	0	5	14	20	34	0	.224	.317	.374
John Lowenstein	2B29,OF18,SS3	L	24	58	140	15	26	5	0	4	9	16	28	1	.186	.269	.307
Kurt Bevacqua	2B36,OF5,3B3*	R	24	55	137	9	28	3	1	3	13	4	28	0	.204	.222	.307
Fred Stanley	SS55,2B3	R	23	60	129	14	29	4	0	2	12	27	25	1	.225	.361	.302
Ken Suarez	C48	R	28	50	123	10	25	7	0	1	9	18	15	0	.203	.310	.285
Gomer Hodge	1B3,3B3,2B2	S	27	80	83	3	17	3	0	1	9	4	19	0	.205	.256	.277
Lou Camilli	SS23,2B16	S	24	39	81	5	16	2	0	0	0	8	10	0	.198	.270	.222
Larry Brown†	SS13	R	31	13	50	4	11	1	0	0	5	3	3	0	.220	.278	.240
Buddy Bradford†	OF18	R	26	20	38	4	6	2	1	0	3	6	10	0	.158	.273	.263
Jim Clark	OF3,1B1	R	24	13	18	2	3	0	1	0	0	2	7	0	.167	.250	.278

K. Bevacqua, 2 G at SS

Pitcher	T	Age	G	GS	CG	ShO	IP	H	HR	BB	SO	W-L	Sv	ERA
Sam McDowell	L	28	35	31	8	2	214.2	160	22	153	192	13-17	1	3.40
Steve Dunning	R	22	31	29	3	1	184.0	173	25	109	132	8-14	1	4.50
Alan Foster	R	24	36	26	3	0	181.2	158	19	82	97	8-12	0	4.16
Mike Paul	L	26	17	12	1	0	62.0	78	8	14	33	2-7	0	5.95
Rich Hand	R	22	15	12	0	0	60.2	74	6	38	26	2-6	0	5.79
Phil Hennigan	R	25	57	0	0	0	82.0	80	13	51	69	4-3	14	4.94
Steve Mingori	L	27	54	0	0	0	56.2	31	2	24	45	1-2	4	1.43
Vince Colbert	R	25	50	10	2	0	142.2	140	11	71	74	7-6	2	3.97
Ray Lamb	R	26	43	21	3	1	158.1	147	11	69	91	6-12	1	3.35
Ed Farmer	R	21	43	4	0	0	78.2	77	9	41	48	5-4	4	4.35
Steve Hargan	R	28	37	16	1	0	113.1	138	18	56	52	1-13	1	6.19
Rick Austin	L	24	23	0	0	0	23.0	25	3	20	20	0-0	1	5.09
Mark Ballinger	R	22	18	0	0	0	34.2	30	3	13	25	1-2	0	4.67
Chuck Machemehl	R	24	14	0	0	0	18.1	16	2	15	9	0-2	3	6.38
Camilo Pascual	R	37	9	1	0	0	23.1	17	0	11	20	2-2	0	3.09
Bob Kaiser	L	21	5	0	0	0	6.0	8	2	3	4	0-0	0	4.50

1971 Oakland Athletics 1st AL West 101-60 .627 —

Dick Williams

Player	Gm by Position	B	Age	G	AB	R	H	2B	3B	HR	RBI	BB	SO	SB	Avg	OBP	Slg
Dave Duncan	C102	R	25	103	363	39	92	13	1	15	40	28	77	1	.253	.307	.419
Mike Epstein†	1B96	L	28	104	329	43	77	13	0	18	51	62	71	0	.234	.368	.438
Dick Green	2B143,SS1	R	30	144	475	58	116	14	1	12	49	51	83	1	.244	.320	.354
Sal Bando	3B153	R	27	153	538	75	146	23	1	24	94	86	55	3	.271	.377	.452
Bert Campaneris	SS133	R	29	134	569	80	143	18	4	5	47	29	64	34	.251	.287	.323
Reggie Jackson	OF145	L	25	150	567	87	157	29	3	32	80	63	161	16	.277	.352	.508
Joe Rudi	OF121,1B5	R	24	127	513	62	137	23	4	10	52	28	62	3	.267	.304	.386
Rick Monday	OF111	L	25	116	355	53	87	9	3	18	56	49	93	6	.245	.335	.439
Angel Mangual	OF81	R	24	94	287	32	82	8	1	4	30	17	27	1	.286	.324	.362
Tommy Davis	1B35,OF16,2B3*	R	32	79	219	26	71	8	1	3	42	15	19	7	.324	.363	.411
Larry Brown†	SS31,2B23,3B10	R	31	70	189	14	37	2	1	1	9	7	19	1	.196	.228	.233
Gene Tenace	C52,OF1	R	24	65	179	26	49	7	0	7	25	29	34	2	.274	.381	.430
George Hendrick	OF36	R	21	42	114	8	27	4	1	0	8	3	20	0	.237	.254	.289
Curt Blefary†	C14,OF14,3B5*	L	27	50	101	15	22	2	0	5	12	15	15	0	.218	.325	.386
Don Mincher†	1B27	L	33	28	92	9	22	6	1	2	8	20	14	1	.239	.375	.391
Mike Hegan†	1B47,OF2	L	28	65	55	5	13	3	0	0	3	5	13	1	.236	.300	.291
Dwain Anderson	SS10,2B5,3B1	R	23	16	37	3	10	2	1	0	3	5	9	0	.270	.372	.378
Steve Hovley	OF11	L	26	24	27	3	3	2	0	0	3	7	9	2	.111	.306	.185
Adrian Garrett	OF5	L	28	14	21	1	3	0	0	1	2	5	7	0	.143	.308	.286
Frank Fernandez†	C3	R	28	4	9	1	1	1	0	0	1	1	3	0	.111	.200	.222
Tony La Russa†	2B7,SS4,3B2	R	26	23	8	3	0	0	0	0	0	0	4	0	.000	.000	.000
Felipe Alou†	OF2	R	36	2	8	0	2	1	0	0	0	0	1	0	.250	.250	.375
Ray Webster†	1B1	L	28	7	5	0	0	0	0	0	0	0	2	0	.000	.000	.000
Ron Clark		R	28	2	1	0	0	0	0	0	0	1	0	0	.000	.500	.000

T. Davis, 2 G at 3B; C. Blefary, 2 G at 2B

Pitcher	T	Age	G	GS	CG	ShO	IP	H	HR	BB	SO	W-L	Sv	ERA
Vida Blue	L	21	39	39	24	8	312.0	209	19	88	301	24-8	0	1.82
Catfish Hunter	R	25	37	37	16	4	273.2	225	27	80	181	21-11	0	2.96
Chuck Dobson	R	27	30	30	7	1	189.0	185	24	71	100	15-5	0	3.81
Blue Moon Odom	R	26	25	25	3	1	140.2	147	13	71	69	10-12	0	4.29
Diego Segui	R	33	26	21	5	0	146.1	122	13	63	81	10-8	0	3.14
Rollie Fingers	R	24	48	8	2	1	129.1	94	14	30	98	4-6	17	2.99
Bob Locker	R	33	47	0	0	0	72.1	68	3	19	46	7-2	6	2.86
Darold Knowles†	L	29	43	0	0	0	52.2	40	3	16	40	5-2	7	3.59
Jim Roland	L	28	31	0	0	0	45.1	34	4	19	30	1-3	1	3.18
Ron Klimkowski	R	27	26	0	0	0	45.1	37	3	23	25	2-2	2	3.38
Mudcat Grant†	R	35	15	0	0	0	27.1	25	3	6	13	1-0	3	1.98
Paul Lindblad†	L	29	8	0	0	0	16.0	18	1	2	4	1-0	0	3.94
Rob Gardner†	L	26	4	1	0	0	7.2	8	1	3	5	0-0	0	2.35
Jim Panther	R	26	4	0	0	0	5.2	10	1	5	4	0-1	0	11.12
Daryl Patterson†	R	27	4	0	0	0	5.2	5	2	4	2	0-0	0	7.94
Marcel Lachemann	R	30	1	0	0	0	0.1	2	0	1	0	0-0	0	54.00

1971 Kansas City Royals 2nd AL West 85-76 .528 16.0 GB

Bob Lemon

Player	Gm by Position	B	Age	G	AB	R	H	2B	3B	HR	RBI	BB	SO	SB	Avg	OBP	Slg
Jerry May	C71	R	27	71	218	16	55	13	2	1	24	27	37	0	.252	.329	.344
Gail Hopkins	1B83	L	28	103	295	35	82	16	1	9	47	37	13	3	.278	.364	.431
Cookie Rojas	2B111,SS2,OF1	R	32	115	414	56	124	22	2	6	59	39	35	8	.300	.357	.406
Paul Schaal	3B161	R	28	161	548	80	150	31	6	11	63	103	51	7	.274	.387	.412
Freddie Patek	SS147	R	26	147	591	86	158	21	11	6	36	44	80	49	.267	.323	.371
Amos Otis	OF144	R	24	147	555	80	167	26	4	15	79	40	74	52	.301	.345	.443
Lou Piniella	OF115	R	27	126	448	43	125	21	5	3	51	21	43	5	.279	.311	.368
Joe Keough	OF100	L	25	110	351	34	87	14	2	3	30	35	26	0	.248	.316	.325
Bob Oliver	1B68,OF48,3B2	R	28	128	373	35	91	12	2	8	52	14	88	0	.244	.277	.351
Ed Kirkpatrick	OF61,C59	L	26	120	365	46	80	12	1	9	46	48	60	3	.219	.308	.332
Bobby Knoop	2B52,3B1	R	32	72	161	14	33	8	1	1	11	15	36	1	.205	.270	.286
Dennis Paepke	C32,OF17	R	26	60	152	11	31	6	0	2	14	8	29	0	.204	.242	.283
Chuck Harrison	1B39	R	30	49	143	9	31	4	0	2	21	11	19	0	.217	.266	.287
Bobby Floyd	SS15,2B8,3B1	R	27	31	66	8	10	3	0	0	2	7	21	0	.152	.233	.197
Sandy Valdespino	OF15	L	32	18	63	10	20	6	0	2	15	2	5	0	.317	.338	.508
Buck Martinez	C21	R	22	22	46	3	7	2	0	0	1	5	9	0	.152	.231	.196
Carl Taylor†	OF12	R	27	20	39	3	7	0	0	0	3	5	13	0	.179	.261	.179
Rich Severson	2B6,SS6,3B1	R	26	16	30	4	9	0	2	0	1	3	5	0	.300	.364	.433
Ted Savage†	OF9	R	34	19	29	2	5	0	0	0	1	3	6	2	.172	.250	.172

Pitcher	T	Age	G	GS	CG	ShO	IP	H	HR	BB	SO	W-L	Sv	ERA
Dick Drago	R	26	35	34	15	4	241.1	251	14	46	109	17-11	0	2.98
Mike Hedlund	R	24	32	30	7	1	205.2	168	15	72	76	15-8	0	2.71
Paul Splittorff	L	24	22	22	6	3	144.1	129	4	35	80	8-9	0	2.68
Bruce Dal Canton	R	29	25	22	2	0	141.1	144	8	44	58	8-6	0	3.44
Ken Wright	R	24	21	12	1	1	78.0	66	6	47	56	3-6	1	3.69
Wally Bunker	R	26	7	6	0	0	32.1	35	7	6	15	2-3	0	5.01
Monty Montgomery	R	24	3	2	0	0	21.1	16	0	3	12	3-0	0	2.11
Tom Burgmeier	L	27	67	0	0	0	88.1	71	3	30	44	9-7	17	1.73
Ted Abernathy	R	38	63	0	0	0	1.0	60	3	50	55	4-6	23	2.56
Jim York	R	23	53	0	0	0	93.1	70	7	44	103	5-5	3	2.89
Al Fitzmorris	R	25	36	15	2	1	127.1	112	6	55	53	7-5	0	4.17
Jim Rooker	L	28	20	7	1	1	54.0	59	2	24	31	2-7	0	5.33
Bill Butler	L	24	14	6	0	0	44.1	45	6	18	32	1-2	0	3.45
Roger Nelson	R	27	13	1	0	0	34.0	35	1	5	29	0-1	0	5.29
Lance Clemons	L	23	10	3	0	0	24.0	26	2	12	20	1-0	0	4.13
Mike McCormick	L	32	4	1	0	0	9.2	14	0	5	2	0-0	0	9.31

1971 Chicago White Sox 3rd AL West 79-83 .488 22.5 GB

Chuck Tanner

Player	Gm by Position	B	Age	G	AB	R	H	2B	3B	HR	RBI	BB	SO	SB	Avg	OBP	Slg
Ed Herrmann	C97	L	24	101	294	32	63	6	0	11	35	44	48	2	.214	.317	.347
Carlos May	1B130,OF9	L	23	141	500	64	147	21	7	7	70	62	61	16	.294	.375	.406
Mike Andrews	2B76,1B25	R	27	109	330	45	93	16	0	12	47	67	36	3	.282	.400	.439
Bill Melton	3B148	R	25	150	543	72	146	18	2	33	86	61	87	3	.269	.352	.492
Luis Alvarado	SS71,2B16	R	22	99	264	22	57	14	1	0	8	11	34	1	.216	.246	.277
Rick Reichardt	OF128,1B9	R	28	138	496	53	138	14	2	19	62	37	90	5	.278	.335	.429
Jay Johnstone	OF119	L	25	124	388	53	101	14	1	16	40	38	50	10	.260	.329	.425
Walt Williams	OF90,3B1	R	27	114	361	43	106	17	3	8	35	24	27	5	.294	.344	.424
Rich McKinney	2B67,OF25,3B5	R	24	114	369	35	100	11	2	8	46	35	37	0	.271	.334	.377
Lee Richard	SS68,OF16	R	22	87	260	38	60	7	3	2	17	20	46	8	.231	.286	.304
Tom Egan	C77,1B1	R	25	85	251	29	60	11	1	10	34	26	94	1	.239	.320	.410
Pat Kelly	OF61	L	26	67	213	32	62	6	3	3	22	36	29	14	.291	.394	.390
Rich Morales	SS57,3B18,2B3*	R	27	84	185	19	45	8	0	2	14	22	26	2	.243	.336	.319
Mike Hershberger	OF59	R	31	74	177	22	46	9	0	2	15	30	23	6	.260	.377	.345
Ed Stroud	OF44	L	31	53	141	19	25	4	3	0	2	11	20	4	.177	.237	.248
Steve Huntz	2B14,SS7,3B6	S	25	35	86	10	18	3	1	2	6	7	9	1	.209	.266	.337
Lee Maye	OF10	L	36	32	44	6	9	2	0	1	7	5	7	0	.205	.280	.318
Bob Spence	1B7	L	25	14	27	2	4	0	0	0	1	5	6	0	.148	.273	.148
Chuck Brinkman	C14	R	26	15	20	0	4	0	0	0	1	3	5	0	.200	.304	.200
Ken Hottman	OF5	R	23	6	16	1	2	0	0	0	0	1	2	0	.125	.176	.125
Tony Muser	1B4	L	23	11	16	2	5	0	1	0	0	1	1	0	.313	.353	.438
Ron Lolich	OF2	R	24	2	8	0	1	1	0	0	0	0	2	0	.125	.125	.250

R. Morales, 1 G at OF

Pitcher	T	Age	G	GS	CG	ShO	IP	H	HR	BB	SO	W-L	Sv	ERA
Wilbur Wood	L	29	44	42	22	7	334.0	272	21	62	210	22-13	1	1.91
Tom Bradley	R	24	45	39	7	6	285.2	273	16	74	206	15-15	2	2.96
Tommy John	L	28	38	35	10	3	229.1	244	17	58	131	13-16	0	3.61
Joe Horlen	R	33	34	18	3	0	137.1	150	12	30	82	8-9	2	4.26
Steve Kealey	R	24	54	1	0	0	77.1	69	10	26	50	2-2	6	3.84
Bart Johnson	R	21	53	16	4	0	178.0	148	9	111	153	12-10	14	2.93
Vicente Romo	R	28	45	2	0	0	72.0	52	5	37	48	1-7	5	3.38
Terry Forster	L	19	45	3	0	0	49.2	46	5	23	48	2-3	1	3.99
Don Eddy	L	24	22	0	0	0	22.2	19	3	19	14	0-2	0	2.38
Rich Hinton	L	24	18	2	0	0	24.1	27	1	6	15	3-4	0	4.44
Jim Magnuson	L	24	15	4	0	0	30.0	30	0	16	11	1-1	0	4.50
Stan Perzanowski	R	20	5	0	0	0	6.0	14	1	3	5	0-1	1	12.00
Pat Jacquez	R	24	2	0	0	0	2.0	4	0	2	1	0-0	0	4.50
Denny O'Toole	R	22	1	0	0	0	2.0	0	0	1	2	0-0	0	0.00

1971 California Angels 4th AL West 76-86 .469 25.5 GB

Lefty Phillips

Player	Gm by Position	B	Age	G	AB	R	H	2B	3B	HR	RBI	BB	SO	SB	Avg	OBP	Slg
John Stephenson	C88	L	30	98	279	24	61	17	0	3	25	22	21	0	.219	.281	.312
Jim Spencer	1B145	L	24	148	510	50	121	21	2	18	59	48	63	0	.237	.304	.392
Sandy Alomar	2B137,SS28	S	27	162	689	77	179	24	3	4	42	41	60	39	.260	.301	.321
Ken McMullen	3B158	R	29	160	593	63	148	19	2	21	68	53	74	1	.250	.312	.395
Jim Fregosi	SS74,1B18,OF7	R	29	107	347	31	81	15	1	5	33	39	61	2	.233	.317	.326
Ken Berry	OF101	R	30	111	298	29	66	17	0	3	22	18	33	3	.221	.269	.309
Roger Repoz	OF97,1B13	L	30	113	297	39	59	11	1	13	41	60	69	3	.199	.333	.374
Tony Gonzalez	OF88	L	34	111	314	32	77	9	2	3	38	28	28	0	.245	.310	.315
Mickey Rivers	OF75	L	22	78	268	31	71	12	2	1	12	19	38	13	.265	.316	.336
Tony Conigliaro	OF72	R	26	74	266	23	59	18	0	4	15	23	52	3	.222	.285	.335
Syd O'Brien	SS52,2B7,3B6*	R	26	90	251	25	50	8	1	5	21	15	33	0	.199	.247	.299
Alex Johnson	OF61	R	28	65	242	19	63	8	0	2	21	15	34	5	.260	.308	.318
Jerry Moses	C63,OF1	R	24	69	181	12	41	8	2	4	15	10	34	0	.227	.266	.359
Billy Cowan	OF40,1B5	R	32	74	174	12	48	8	0	4	20	7	41	1	.276	.304	.391
Jeff Torborg	C49	R	29	55	123	6	25	5	0	0	5	3	6	0	.203	.220	.244
Tommie Reynolds	OF26,3B1	S	29	45	86	4	16	3	0	2	8	9	6	0	.186	.286	.291
Billy Parker	2B20	R	24	20	70	4	16	0	1	1	6	2	20	1	.229	.250	.300
Bruce Christensen	SS24	L	23	29	63	4	17	1	0	0	3	6	5	0	.270	.333	.286
Chico Ruiz	3B3,2B2	S	32	31	19	4	5	0	0	0	0	2	7	1	.263	.333	.263
Art Kusnyer	C6	R	25	6	13	0	2	0	0	0	0	0	3	0	.154	.154	.154
Rudy Meoli		L	20	7	3	0	0	0	0	0	0	0	1	0	.000	.000	.000
Tom Silverio	OF1	L	25	3	3	0	1	0	0	0	0	0	0	0	.333	.333	.333

S. O'Brien, 1 G at 1B, 1 G at OF

Pitcher	T	Age	G	GS	CG	ShO	IP	H	HR	BB	SO	W-L	Sv	ERA
Andy Messersmith	R	25	38	38	14	4	276.2	224	16	121	179	20-13	0	2.99
Clyde Wright	L	30	37	37	10	2	276.2	225	17	82	135	16-17	0	2.99
Tom Murphy	R	25	37	36	7	0	243.1	228	24	82	89	6-17	0	3.77
Rudy May	L	26	32	31	7	2	208.1	160	12	87	156	11-12	0	3.02
Rickey Clark	R	25	11	7	1	1	44.0	36	6	28	28	2-1	1	2.86
Andy Hassler	L	19	6	4	0	0	18.2	25	0	15	13	0-3	0	3.86
Eddie Fisher	R	34	57	3	0	0	119.0	92	11	50	82	10-8	3	2.72
Dave LaRoche	L	23	56	0	0	0	72.0	55	3	27	63	5-1	9	2.50
Lloyd Allen	R	21	54	1	0	0	94.0	75	4	40	72	4-6	15	2.49
Mel Queen	R	29	44	0	0	0	65.2	49	3	29	53	2-2	4	1.78
Archie Reynolds	R	25	15	1	0	0	27.1	32	2	18	15	0-3	0	4.61
Jim Maloney	R	31	13	4	0	0	30.1	35	3	24	13	0-3	0	5.04
Billy Wynne	R	27	3	0	0	0	3.2	6	0	2	6	0-0	0	4.91
Fred Lasher	R	29	2	0	0	0	1.1	4	0	2	0	0-0	0	27.00

1971 Minnesota Twins 5th AL West 74-86 .463 26.5 GB

Bill Rigney

Player	Gm by Position	B	Age	G	AB	R	H	2B	3B	HR	RBI	BB	SO	SB	Avg	OBP	Slg
George Mitterwald	C120	R	26	125	388	38	97	13	1	13	44	39	104	3	.250	.316	.389
Rich Reese	1B95,OF9	L	29	120	329	40	72	8	3	10	39	20	35	7	.219	.270	.353
Rod Carew	2B142,3B2	L	25	147	577	88	177	16	10	2	48	45	81	6	.307	.356	.380
Steve Braun	3B73,2B28,SS10*	L	23	128	343	51	87	12	2	5	35	48	50	8	.254	.350	.344
Leo Cardenas	SS153	R	32	153	554	59	146	25	4	18	75	51	69	3	.264	.321	.421
Cesar Tovar	OF154,3B7,2B2	R	30	157	657	94	204	29	3	1	45	45	39	18	.311	.356	.368
Tony Oliva	OF121	L	30	126	487	73	164	30	3	22	81	25	44	4	.337	.369	.546
Jim Holt	OF106,1B3	L	27	126	340	35	88	11	3	1	29	16	28	5	.259	.292	.318
Harmon Killebrew	1B90,3B64	R	35	147	500	61	127	19	1	28	119	114	96	3	.254	.386	.464
Jim Nettles	OF62	L	24	70	168	17	42	5	1	6	24	19	24	3	.250	.321	.399
Brant Alyea	OF48	R	30	79	158	13	28	4	0	2	15	24	38	1	.177	.282	.241
Steve Brye	OF28	R	22	28	107	10	24	1	0	3	11	7	15	3	.224	.270	.318
Phil Roof†	C29	R	30	31	87	6	21	4	0	0	6	8	18	0	.241	.305	.287
Eric Soderholm	3B20	R	22	21	64	9	10	4	0	1	4	10	17	0	.156	.299	.266
Danny Thompson	3B17,2B3,SS1	R	24	48	57	10	15	2	0	0	7	7	12	0	.263	.338	.298
Rick Renick	3B7,OF7	R	27	27	45	4	10	2	0	1	8	5	14	0	.222	.308	.333
Paul Ratliff†	C15	L	27	21	44	3	7	1	0	2	6	4	17	0	.159	.224	.318
Paul Powell	OF15	R	23	20	31	7	5	0	0	1	2	3	12	0	.161	.235	.258
George Thomas†	OF11,1B1,3B1	R	33	23	30	4	8	1	0	0	2	4	3	0	.267	.353	.300
Tom Tischinski	C21	R	26	21	23	0	3	2	0	0	2	1	4	0	.130	.200	.217
Charlie Manuel	OF1	L	27	18	16	1	2	1	0	0	1	1	8	0	.125	.176	.188
Rick Dempsey	C6	R	21	6	13	2	4	1	0	0	0	1	1	0	.308	.357	.385

S. Braun, 2 G at OF

Pitcher	T	Age	G	GS	CG	ShO	IP	H	HR	BB	SO	W-L	Sv	ERA
Jim Perry	R	35	40	39	8	0	270.0	263	39	102	126	17-17	1	4.23
Bert Blyleven	R	20	38	38	17	5	278.1	267	21	59	224	16-15	0	2.81
Jim Kaat	L	32	39	38	15	4	260.1	275	16	47	137	13-14	0	3.32
Steve Luebber	R	21	18	12	0	0	68.0	73	7	37	35	2-5	1	5.03
Pete Hamm	R	23	13	8	1	0	44.0	55	7	18	16	2-4	0	6.75
Steve Barber	R	23	4	2	0	0	11.2	8	2	13	4	1-0	0	6.17
Ray Corbin	R	22	52	11	2	0	140.1	141	19	70	83	8-11	3	4.10
Tom Hall	L	23	48	11	0	0	129.2	104	13	58	137	4-7	9	3.33
Stan Williams†	R	34	46	1	0	0	78.0	63	7	44	47	4-5	4	4.15
Ron Perranoski†	L	35	36	0	0	0	42.2	60	2	28	21	1-4	5	6.75
Hal Haydel	R	26	31	0	0	0	40.0	33	3	20	29	4-2	1	4.28
Jim Strickland	L	25	24	0	0	0	31.1	20	2	18	21	1-0	1	1.44
Bob Gebhard	R	28	17	0	0	0	18.0	17	0	11	13	1-2	0	3.00
Sal Campisi	R	28	6	0	0	0	4.1	5	1	4	2	0-0	0	4.15

1971 Milwaukee Brewers 6th AL West 69-92 .429 32.0 GB

Dave Bristol

Player	Gm by Position	B	Age	G	AB	R	H	2B	3B	HR	RBI	BB	SO	SB	Avg	OBP	Slg
Ellie Rodriguez	C114	R	25	115	319	28	67	10	1	1	30	41	51	1	.210	.311	.257
John Briggs†	OF65,1B60	L	27	125	375	51	99	11	1	21	59	71	79	1	.264	.378	.467
Ron Theobald	2B111,3B1,SS1	R	27	126	388	50	107	12	2	1	23	38	39	11	.276	.342	.325
Tommy Harper	OF90,3B70,2B1	R	30	152	585	79	151	26	3	14	52	65	92	25	.258	.333	.385
Rick Auerbach	SS78	R	21	79	236	22	48	10	0	1	9	20	40	3	.203	.271	.258
Dave May	OF142	L	27	144	501	74	139	20	3	16	65	50	59	15	.277	.343	.425
Bill Voss	OF79	L	27	97	275	31	69	4	0	10	30	24	45	2	.251	.312	.375
Jose Cardenal†	OF52	R	27	53	198	20	51	10	0	3	32	13	20	9	.258	.297	.354
Roberto Pena	1B50,3B37,SS23*	R	34	113	274	17	65	9	3	3	28	15	37	2	.237	.279	.325
Andy Kosco	OF45,1B29,3B12	R	29	98	264	27	60	6	2	10	39	24	57	1	.227	.291	.379
Ted Kubiak†	2B48,SS39	S	29	89	260	26	59	6	5	3	17	41	31	0	.227	.330	.323
Bob Heise†	SS51,3B11,2B3*	R	24	68	189	10	48	7	0	0	7	7	15	1	.254	.279	.291
Mike Hegan†	1B45	L	28	46	122	19	27	4	1	4	11	26	19	1	.221	.356	.369
Tommy Matchick	3B41,2B1	L	27	42	114	6	25	1	0	1	7	7	23	3	.219	.264	.254
Phil Roof†	C39	R	30	41	114	6	22	2	1	1	10	8	28	0	.193	.252	.254
Rob Ellis	3B19,OF15	R	20	36	111	9	22	2	0	0	6	12	24	0	.198	.278	.216
Frank Tepedino†	1B28	L	23	53	106	11	21	1	0	2	7	4	17	2	.198	.234	.264
Darrell Porter	C22	L	19	22	70	4	15	2	0	2	9	9	20	2	.214	.300	.329
Danny Walton†	OF19,3B1	R	23	30	69	5	14	3	0	2	9	7	22	0	.203	.286	.333
Bobby Mitchell	OF19	R	27	35	55	7	10	1	1	2	6	6	18	0	.182	.262	.345
Al Yates	OF12	R	26	24	47	5	13	2	0	1	4	3	7	1	.277	.308	.383
Paul Ratliff†	C13	L	27	23	41	3	7	1	0	3	7	5	21	0	.171	.277	.415
Bernie Smith	OF12	R	29	15	36	1	5	1	0	1	3	0	5	0	.139	.162	.250
Gus Gil	2B8,3B6	R	32	14	32	3	5	1	0	0	3	10	5	1	.156	.357	.188
Dick Schofield†	3B12,SS4,2B2	S	36	23	28	2	3	2	0	0	1	2	8	0	.107	.194	.179
Ted Savage†	OF6	R	34	14	17	2	3	0	0	0	1	5	4	1	.176	.364	.176
Floyd Wicker†		L	27	11	8	0	1	0	0	0	0	2	3	0	.125	.300	.125
Pete Koegel†	1B1	R	23	2	3	0	0	0	0	0	0	2	2	0	.000	.400	.000

R. Pena, 1 G at 2B; B. Heise, 1 G at OF

Pitcher	T	Age	G	GS	CG	ShO	IP	H	HR	BB	SO	W-L	Sv	ERA
Marty Pattin	R	28	36	36	9	5	264.2	225	29	73	169	14-14	0	3.13
Bill Parsons	R	22	36	35	12	4	244.2	219	19	93	139	13-17	0	3.20
Skip Lockwood	R	24	33	32	5	1	208.0	191	13	91	115	10-15	0	3.33
Jim Slaton	R	21	26	23	5	4	147.2	140	16	71	63	10-8	0	3.78
Lew Krausse	R	28	43	22	1	0	180.1	164	23	62	92	8-12	0	2.94
Ken Sanders	R	29	83	0	0	0	136.1	111	9	34	80	7-12	31	1.91
John Morris	L	29	43	1	0	0	67.2	69	4	27	42	2-2	1	3.72
Marcelino Lopez	L	27	31	11	0	0	67.2	64	5	60	42	2-7	0	4.66
Jim Hannan†	R	31	21	1	0	0	32.1	38	7	21	17	1-1	0	5.01
Floyd Weaver	R	30	21	0	0	0	27.1	33	3	18	12	0-1	0	7.24
Dick Ellsworth	L	31	11	0	0	0	14.2	22	1	7	10	0-1	0	4.91
Jerry Bell	R	23	8	0	0	0	14.2	10	0	6	8	2-1	0	3.07
Bob Reynolds†	R	24	3	0	0	0	6.0	4	0	3	4	0-1	0	3.00
Larry Bearnarth	R	29	2	0	0	0	3.0	10	1	2	2	0-0	0	18.00
John Gelnar	R	28	2	0	0	0	1.1	3	0	1	0	0-0	0	13.50

»1971 Pittsburgh Pirates 1st NL East 97-65 .599 —

Danny Murtaugh

Player	Gm by Position	B	Age	G	AB	R	H	2B	3B	HR	RBI	BB	SO	SB	Avg	OBP	Slg
Manny Sanguillen	C135	R	27	138	533	60	170	26	5	7	81	19	32	6	.319	.345	.426
Bob Robertson	1B126	R	24	131	469	65	127	18	2	26	72	60	101	1	.271	.356	.484
Dave Cash	2B105,3B24,SS3	R	23	123	478	79	138	17	4	2	34	46	33	13	.289	.349	.354
Richie Hebner	3B108	L	23	112	388	50	105	17	8	17	67	32	68	2	.271	.326	.487
Gene Alley	SS108,3B1	R	30	114	348	38	79	8	7	6	28	35	43	9	.227	.296	.342
Willie Stargell	OF135	L	31	141	511	104	151	26	0	48	125	83	154	0	.295	.398	.628
Roberto Clemente	OF124	R	36	132	522	82	178	29	8	13	86	26	65	1	.341	.370	.502
Al Oliver	OF116,1B25	L	24	143	529	69	149	31	7	14	64	27	72	4	.282	.317	.446
Vic Davalillo	OF61,1B16	L	34	99	295	48	84	14	6	1	33	11	31	10	.285	.312	.383
Gene Clines	OF74	R	24	97	273	52	84	12	4	1	24	22	36	15	.308	.366	.392
Jackie Hernandez	SS75,3B9	R	30	88	233	30	48	7	3	3	26	17	45	0	.206	.257	.300
Bill Mazeroski	2B46,3B7	R	34	70	193	17	49	3	1	1	16	15	8	0	.254	.303	.295
Jose Pagan	3B41,OF3,1B2	R	36	57	158	16	38	1	0	5	15	16	25	0	.241	.311	.342
Rennie Stennett	2B36	R	20	50	153	24	54	5	4	1	15	7	9	1	.353	.377	.458
Milt May	C31	L	20	49	126	15	35	1	0	6	25	9	16	0	.278	.321	.429
Charlie Sands	C3	L	23	28	25	4	5	2	0	1	5	7	6	0	.200	.375	.400
Richie Zisk	OF6	R	22	7	15	2	3	1	0	1	2	4	7	0	.200	.368	.467
Carl Taylor†	OF6	R	27	7	12	1	2	0	1	0	0	0	5	0	.167	.167	.333
Rimp Lanier		L	22	6	4	0	0	0	0	0	0	0	1	0	.000	.200	.000
Frank Taveras		R	21	1	0	0	0	0	0	0	0	0	0	0	—	—	—

Pitcher	T	Age	G	GS	CG	ShO	IP	H	HR	BB	SO	W-L	Sv	ERA
Steve Blass	R	29	33	33	12	5	240.0	226	16	68	136	15-8	0	2.85
Dock Ellis	R	26	31	31	11	2	226.2	207	15	63	137	19-9	0	3.06
Bob Johnson	R	28	31	27	7	1	174.2	170	19	55	101	9-10	0	3.45
Luke Walker	L	27	28	24	4	2	159.2	157	9	53	86	10-8	0	3.55
Bob Moose	R	23	30	18	3	1	140.0	169	12	35	68	11-7	1	4.11
Bruce Kison	R	21	18	13	2	1	95.1	93	6	36	60	6-5	0	3.40
Dave Giusti	R	31	58	0	0	0	86.0	79	5	31	55	5-6	30	2.93
Mudcat Grant†	R	35	42	0	0	0	75.0	79	8	28	22	5-3	7	3.60
Nelson Briles	R	27	37	14	4	2	136.0	131	12	35	76	8-4	1	3.04
Bob Veale	L	35	37	0	0	0	46.1	59	5	24	40	6-0	2	6.99
Jim Nelson	R	23	17	2	0	0	34.2	27	0	26	11	2-2	0	2.34
Bob Miller†	R	32	16	0	0	0	28.0	20	1	13	13	1-2	3	1.29
Ramon Hernandez	L	30	10	0	0	0	12.1	5	0	2	7	0-1	4	0.73
John Lamb	R	24	2	0	0	0	4.1	3	0	1	1	0-0	0	0.00
Frank Brosseau	R	26	1	0	0	0	2.0	1	0	0	0	0-0	0	0.00

1971 St. Louis Cardinals 2nd NL East 90-72 .556 7.0 GB

Red Schoendienst

Player	Gm by Position	B	Age	G	AB	R	H	2B	3B	HR	RBI	BB	SO	SB	Avg	OBP	Slg
Ted Simmons	C130	S	21	133	510	64	155	32	4	7	77	36	50	1	.304	.347	.424
Joe Hague	1B91,OF36	L	27	129	380	46	86	9	3	16	54	58	69	0	.226	.330	.392
Ted Sizemore	2B93,SS39,OF15*	R	26	135	478	53	126	14	5	3	42	42	26	4	.264	.322	.333
Joe Torre	3B161	R	30	161	634	97	230	34	8	24	137	63	70	4	.363	.421	.555
Dal Maxvill	SS140	R	32	142	356	31	80	10	1	0	24	43	45	1	.225	.307	.258
Lou Brock	OF157	L	32	157	640	126	200	37	7	7	61	76	107	64	.313	.385	.425
Matty Alou	OF94,1B57	L	32	149	609	85	192	28	6	7	74	34	27	19	.315	.352	.415
Jose Cardenal†	OF83	R	27	89	301	37	73	12	4	7	48	29	35	12	.243	.303	.379
Jose Cruz	OF83	L	23	83	292	46	80	13	2	9	27	49	35	6	.274	.377	.425
Julian Javier	2B80,3B1	R	34	90	259	32	67	6	4	3	28	9	33	5	.259	.286	.347
Luis Melendez	OF66	R	21	88	173	25	39	3	1	0	11	24	29	2	.225	.320	.254
Jim Beauchamp	1B44,OF1	R	31	77	162	24	38	8	3	2	16	9	26	3	.235	.274	.358
Jerry McNertney	C36	R	34	56	128	15	37	4	2	4	22	12	14	0	.289	.343	.445
Ted Kubiak†	SS17,2B14	S	29	32	72	8	18	3	2	1	10	11	12	1	.250	.345	.389
Bob Burda	1B13,OF1	L	32	65	71	6	21	0	0	1	12	10	11	0	.296	.386	.338
Dick Schofield†	SS17,2B13,3B3	S	36	34	60	7	13	2	0	1	6	10	9	0	.217	.347	.300
Leron Lee†	OF8	L	23	25	28	3	5	1	0	1	2	4	12	0	.179	.281	.321
Bob Stinson	C6,OF3	S	25	17	19	3	4	1	0	0	1	1	7	0	.211	.250	.263
Milt Ramirez	SS4	R	21	4	11	2	3	0	0	0	0	2	1	0	.273	.385	.273
Jorge Roque	OF3	R	21	3	10	2	3	0	0	0	1	0	3	1	.300	.300	.300

T. Sizemore, 1 G at 3B

Pitcher	T	Age	G	GS	CG	ShO	IP	H	HR	BB	SO	W-L	Sv	ERA
Steve Carlton	L	26	37	36	18	4	273.1	275	23	98	172	20-9	0	3.56
Jerry Reuss	L	22	36	35	7	2	211.0	228	15	109	131	14-14	0	4.78
Reggie Cleveland	R	23	34	34	10	2	222.0	238	20	53	148	12-12	0	4.01
Bob Gibson	R	35	31	31	20	5	245.2	215	14	76	185	16-13	0	3.04
Chris Zachary	R	27	23	12	1	1	89.2	114	3	26	48	3-10	0	5.32
Mike Torrez†	R	24	9	6	0	0	36.0	41	2	30	8	1-2	0	6.00
Santiago Guzman	R	21	2	1	0	0	10.0	6	0	2	13	0-0	0	0.00
Moe Drabowsky	R	35	51	0	0	0	60.1	45	2	33	49	6-1	8	3.43
Frank Linzy	R	30	50	0	0	0	59.1	49	2	27	24	4-3	6	2.12
Don Shaw	L	27	45	0	0	0	51.0	45	1	31	19	7-2	2	2.65
Chuck Taylor	R	29	43	1	0	0	71.1	72	7	25	46	3-1	3	3.53
Al Santorini†	R	23	19	5	0	0	49.2	51	2	19	21	0-2	2	3.81
Daryl Patterson†	R	27	13	2	0	0	26.2	20	3	15	11	0-1	1	4.39
Stan Williams†	R	34	10	0	0	0	12.2	13	0	2	8	3-0	0	1.42
Rudy Arroyo	L	21	9	0	0	0	11.2	18	2	5	5	0-1	0	5.40
George Brunet	L	36	7	0	0	0	9.1	12	3	7	4	0-1	0	5.79
Bob Reynolds†	R	24	4	0	0	0	7.0	15	2	6	4	0-0	0	10.29
Harry Parker	R	23	4	0	0	0	5.0	6	2	2	2	0-0	0	7.20
Fred Norman†	L	28	4	0	0	0	3.2	7	1	7	4	0-0	0	12.27
Dennis Higgins	R	31	3	0	0	0	7.0	6	0	2	6	1-0	0	3.86
Al Hrabosky	L	21	1	0	0	0	2.0	2	0	0	2	0-0	0	0.00
Bob Chlupsa	R	25	1	0	0	0	2.0	3	0	0	1	0-0	0	9.00
Mike Jackson	L	25	1	0	0	0	0.2	1	0	1	0	0-0	0	0.00

1971 Chicago Cubs 3rd NL East 83-79 .512 14.0 GB

Leo Durocher

Player	Gm by Position	B	Age	G	AB	R	H	2B	3B	HR	RBI	BB	SO	SB	Avg	OBP	Slg
Chris Cannizzaro†	C70	R	33	71	197	18	42	8	1	5	23	28	24	0	.213	.311	.340
Joe Pepitone	1B95,OF23	L	30	115	427	50	131	19	4	16	61	24	41	1	.307	.347	.482
Glenn Beckert	2B129	R	30	131	530	80	181	18	5	2	42	24	24	3	.342	.367	.406
Ron Santo	3B149,OF6	R	31	154	555	77	148	22	1	21	88	79	95	4	.267	.354	.423
Don Kessinger	SS154	S	28	155	617	77	159	18	6	2	38	52	54	15	.258	.318	.316
Billy Williams	OF154	L	33	157	594	86	179	27	5	28	93	77	44	7	.301	.383	.505
Brock Davis	OF93	L	27	106	301	22	77	7	5	0	28	35	34	0	.256	.335	.312
Johnny Callison	OF89	L	32	103	290	27	61	12	1	8	38	36	55	2	.210	.298	.341
Jim Hickman	OF69,1B44	R	34	117	383	50	98	13	2	19	60	50	61	0	.256	.342	.449
Paul Popovich	2B40,3B16,SS1	S	30	89	226	24	49	7	1	4	28	14	17	0	.217	.260	.310
Cleo James	OF48,3B2	R	30	54	150	25	43	7	0	2	13	10	16	6	.287	.353	.373
J.C. Martin	C43,OF1	L	34	47	125	13	33	5	0	2	17	12	16	1	.264	.336	.352
Jose Ortiz	OF30	R	24	36	88	10	26	7	1	0	3	4	10	2	.295	.347	.398
Ernie Banks	1B20	R	40	39	83	4	16	2	0	3	6	6	14	0	.193	.247	.325
Ken Rudolph	C25	R	24	25	76	5	15	3	0	0	7	6	20	0	.197	.265	.237
Danny Breeden	C25	R	29	25	65	3	10	1	0	0	4	9	18	0	.154	.263	.169
Hector Torres	SS18,2B4	R	25	31	58	4	13	3	0	0	2	4	10	0	.224	.274	.276
Carmen Fanzone	OF6,3B3,1B2	R	27	12	43	5	8	2	0	2	5	2	7	0	.186	.222	.372
Frank Fernandez†	C16	R	28	17	41	11	7	1	0	4	4	17	15	0	.171	.414	.488
Pat Bourque	1B11	L	24	14	37	3	7	0	1	1	3	3	9	0	.189	.250	.324
Hal Breeden	1B8	R	27	23	36	1	5	1	0	1	2	2	7	0	.139	.184	.250
Gene Hiser	OF9	L	22	17	29	4	6	0	0	0	1	4	8	1	.207	.303	.207
Randy Hundley	C8	R	29	9	21	1	7	1	0	0	2	0	2	0	.333	.333	.381
Bill North	OF6	S	23	8	16	3	6	0	0	0	0	4	6	1	.375	.524	.375
Ray Webster†	1B1	L	28	16	16	1	5	2	0	0	0	1	3	0	.313	.353	.438
Al Spangler		L	37	5	5	0	2	0	0	0	0	0	1	0	.400	.400	.400
Garry Jestadt†	3B1	R	24	3	3	0	0	0	0	0	0	0	0	0	.000	.000	.000

Pitcher	T	Age	G	GS	CG	ShO	IP	H	HR	BB	SO	W-L	Sv	ERA
Fergie Jenkins	R	27	39	39	30	3	325.0	304	29	37	263	24-13	0	2.77
Milt Pappas	R	32	35	35	14	5	261.1	279	25	62	99	17-14	0	3.51
Bill Hands	R	31	36	35	14	1	242.1	248	27	50	128	12-18	0	3.42
Ken Holtzman	L	25	30	29	9	3	195.0	213	18	64	143	9-15	0	4.48
Juan Pizarro	L	34	16	14	6	3	101.1	78	10	40	67	7-6	0	3.46
Burt Hooton	R	21	3	3	2	1	21.1	8	2	10	22	2-0	0	2.11
Phil Regan	R	34	48	1	0	0	73.1	84	4	33	28	5-5	6	3.93
Ron Tompkins	R	26	35	0	0	0	39.2	31	3	21	20	0-2	3	4.08
Bill Bonham	R	22	33	2	0	0	60.0	63	6	36	41	2-1	0	4.65
Ray Newman	L	26	30	0	0	0	38.1	30	4	17	35	1-2	2	3.52
Joe Decker	R	24	21	4	0	0	45.2	62	2	25	37	3-2	0	4.73
Earl Stephenson	L	23	16	0	0	0	20.1	24	1	11	11	1-0	1	4.43
Jim Colborn	R	25	14	0	0	0	10.1	18	1	3	2	0-1	0	6.97
Larry Gura	L	23	6	0	0	0	3.0	6	0	1	2	0-0	1	6.00
Bob Miller†	R	32	2	0	0	0	7.0	10	0	1	2	0-0	0	5.14

1971 New York Mets 3rd NL East 83-79 .512 14.0 GB

Gil Hodges

Player	Gm by Position	B	Age	G	AB	R	H	2B	3B	HR	RBI	BB	SO	SB	Avg	OBP	Slg
Jerry Grote	C122	R	28	125	403	35	109	25	0	2	35	40	47	1	.270	.339	.347
Ed Kranepool	1B108,OF11	L	26	122	421	61	118	20	4	14	58	38	33	0	.280	.340	.447
Ken Boswell	2B109	L	25	116	392	46	107	20	1	5	40	36	31	5	.273	.334	.367
Bob Aspromonte	3B97	R	33	104	342	21	77	9	1	5	33	29	25	0	.225	.285	.301
Bud Harrelson	SS140	S	27	142	547	55	138	16	6	0	32	53	59	28	.252	.319	.303
Cleon Jones	OF132	R	28	136	505	63	161	24	6	14	69	53	87	6	.319	.382	.473
Tommie Agee	OF107	R	28	113	425	58	121	19	0	14	50	50	84	28	.285	.362	.428
Ken Singleton	OF96	S	24	115	298	34	73	5	0	13	46	61	64	0	.245	.374	.393
Tim Foli	2B58,3B36,SS12*	R	20	97	288	32	65	12	2	0	24	18	50	5	.226	.272	.281
Donn Clendenon	1B72	R	35	88	263	29	65	10	0	11	37	21	78	1	.247	.302	.411
Dave Marshall	OF64	L	28	100	214	28	51	9	1	3	21	26	54	3	.238	.322	.332
Wayne Garrett	3B53,2B9	L	23	56	202	20	43	2	0	1	11	28	31	1	.213	.310	.238
Don Hahn	OF80	R	22	98	178	16	42	5	1	1	11	21	32	2	.236	.317	.292
Duffy Dyer	C53	R	25	59	169	13	39	7	1	2	18	14	45	1	.231	.292	.320
Art Shamsky	OF38,1B1	L	29	68	135	13	25	6	2	5	18	21	18	1	.185	.299	.370
Ted Martinez	SS23,2B13,3B3*	R	23	38	125	16	36	5	2	1	10	4	22	6	.288	.323	.384
Mike Jorgensen	OF31,1B1	L	22	45	118	16	26	1	1	5	11	11	24	1	.220	.303	.373
Lee Stanton	OF5	R	25	5	21	2	4	1	0	0	2	2	4	0	.190	.261	.238
John Milner	OF3	L	21	9	18	1	3	1	0	0	1	0	3	0	.167	.167	.222
Al Weis	2B5,3B2	S	33	11	11	3	0	0	0	0	1	2	4	0	.000	.143	.000
Frank Estrada	C1	R	23	1	2	0	1	0	0	0	0	0	0	0	.500	.500	.500

T. Foli, 1 G at OF; T. Martinez, 1 G at OF

Pitcher	T	Age	G	GS	CG	ShO	IP	H	HR	BB	SO	W-L	Sv	ERA
Tom Seaver	R	26	36	35	21	4	286.1	210	18	61	289	20-10	0	1.76
Gary Gentry	R	24	32	31	8	3	203.2	167	16	82	155	12-11	0	3.23
Nolan Ryan	R	24	30	26	3	0	152.0	125	8	116	137	10-14	0	3.97
Jerry Koosman	L	28	26	24	4	0	165.2	160	12	51	96	6-11	0	3.04
Ray Sadecki	L	30	34	20	5	2	163.1	139	10	44	120	7-7	0	2.92
Jon Matlack	L	21	7	6	0	0	37.0	31	2	15	24	0-3	0	4.14
Danny Frisella	R	25	53	0	0	0	90.2	76	6	30	93	8-5	12	1.99
Tug McGraw	L	26	51	1	0	0	111.0	73	4	41	109	11-4	8	1.70
Ron Taylor	R	33	45	0	0	0	69.0	71	7	11	32	2-2	2	3.65
Charlie Williams	R	23	31	9	1	0	90.1	92	7	41	53	5-6	0	4.78
Jim McAndrew	R	27	24	10	0	0	90.1	78	10	32	42	2-5	0	4.38
Buzz Capra	R	23	3	0	0	0	5.1	3	0	5	6	0-1	0	8.44
Don Rose	R	24	1	0	0	0	2.0	2	0	0	1	0-0	0	0.00

1971 Montreal Expos 5th NL East 71-90 .441 25.5 GB

Gene Mauch

Player	Gm by Position	B	Age	G	AB	R	H	2B	3B	HR	RBI	BB	SO	SB	Avg	OBP	Slg
John Bateman	C137	R	30	139	492	34	119	17	3	10	56	19	87	1	.242	.273	.350
Ron Fairly	1B135,OF10	L	32	146	447	58	115	23	0	13	71	81	65	1	.257	.373	.396
Ron Hunt	2B133,3B19	R	30	152	520	89	145	20	3	5	38	58	41	5	.279	.402	.358
Bob Bailey	3B120,OF51,1B9	R	28	157	545	65	137	21	4	14	83	97	105	13	.251	.359	.382
Bobby Wine	SS119	R	32	119	340	25	68	9	0	1	16	25	46	0	.200	.253	.235
Rusty Staub	OF162	L	27	162	599	94	186	34	6	19	97	74	42	9	.311	.392	.482
Boots Day	OF120	L	23	127	371	53	105	10	2	4	33	33	39	9	.283	.342	.353
Jim Fairey	OF58	L	26	92	200	19	49	8	1	1	19	12	23	3	.245	.285	.310
Gary Sutherland	2B56,SS46,OF4*	R	26	111	304	25	78	7	2	4	26	18	12	3	.257	.302	.332
John Boccabella	C37,1B37,3B2	R	30	74	177	15	39	11	0	3	15	14	26	0	.220	.278	.333
Coco Laboy	3B65,2B2	R	30	76	151	10	38	4	0	1	14	11	19	0	.252	.302	.298
Ron Woods†	OF45	R	28	51	138	26	41	7	3	1	17	19	18	0	.297	.382	.413
Clyde Mashore	OF47,3B1	R	26	66	114	20	22	5	0	1	7	10	22	1	.193	.258	.263
Stan Swanson	OF38	R	27	49	106	14	26	3	0	2	11	10	13	1	.245	.310	.330
Jim Gosger	OF23,1B6	L	28	51	102	7	16	2	2	0	8	9	17	1	.157	.230	.216
Mack Jones	OF27	L	32	43	91	11	15	3	0	3	9	15	24	1	.165	.296	.297
Ron Swoboda†	OF26	R	27	39	75	7	19	4	3	0	6	11	16	0	.253	.364	.387
Ron Brand	SS22,3B4,OF4*	R	31	47	56	3	12	0	0	0	1	3	5	1	.214	.254	.214
Dave McDonald	1B8,OF1	L	28	24	39	3	4	2	0	1	4	4	14	0	.103	.178	.231
Rich Hacker	SS16	S	23	16	33	2	4	1	0	0	2	3	12	0	.121	.194	.152
Terry Humphrey	C9	R	21	9	26	1	5	1	0	0	1	0	4	0	.192	.192	.231

G. Sutherland, 2 G at 3B; R. Brand, 1 G at C, 1 G at 2B

Pitcher	T	Age	G	GS	CG	ShO	IP	H	HR	BB	SO	W-L	Sv	ERA
Bill Stoneman	R	27	39	39	20	3	294.2	243	20	146	251	17-16	0	3.15
Steve Renko	R	26	40	37	9	3	275.2	256	24	135	129	15-14	0	3.75
Carl Morton	R	27	36	35	9	0	213.2	252	22	83	84	10-18	1	4.80
Ernie McAnally	R	24	31	25	8	2	177.2	150	9	87	98	11-12	0	3.90
John Strohmayer	R	24	27	14	2	0	114.0	124	16	31	56	7-5	1	4.34
Mike Marshall	R	28	66	0	0	0	111.1	100	9	50	85	5-8	23	4.28
Howie Reed	R	34	43	0	0	0	56.2	66	8	24	25	2-3	0	4.29
Claude Raymond	R	34	37	0	0	0	53.2	81	5	25	29	1-7	0	4.70
Dan McGinn	L	27	28	6	1	0	71.0	74	7	42	40	1-4	0	5.96
Jim Britton	R	27	16	6	0	0	45.2	49	10	27	23	2-3	0	5.72
John O'Donoghue	L	31	13	0	0	0	17.1	19	3	7	7	0-0	0	4.67
Mike Torrez†	R	24	1	0	0	0	3.0	4	0	1	2	0-0	0	0.00

1971 Philadelphia Phillies 6th NL East 67-95 .414 30.0 GB

Frank Lucchesi

Player	Gm by Position	B	Age	G	AB	R	H	2B	3B	HR	RBI	BB	SO	SB	Avg	OBP	Slg
Tim McCarver	C125	L	29	134	474	51	132	20	5	8	46	43	26	5	.278	.337	.392
Deron Johnson	1B136,3B22	R	32	158	582	74	154	29	0	34	95	72	146	0	.265	.347	.490
Denny Doyle	2B91	L	27	95	342	34	79	12	1	3	24	19	31	4	.231	.280	.298
John Vukovich	3B74	R	23	74	217	11	36	5	0	0	14	12	34	2	.166	.211	.189
Larry Bowa	SS157	S	25	159	650	74	162	18	5	0	25	36	61	28	.249	.293	.292
Willie Montanez	OF158,1B9	L	23	158	599	78	153	27	6	30	99	67	105	4	.255	.327	.471
Roger Freed	OF106,C1	R	25	118	348	23	77	12	1	6	37	44	86	0	.221	.312	.313
Oscar Gamble	OF80	L	21	92	280	24	62	11	1	6	23	21	35	5	.221	.275	.332
Don Money	3B68,OF40,2B20	R	24	121	439	40	98	22	8	7	38	31	80	4	.223	.276	.358
Terry Harmon	2B58,SS9,3B3*	R	27	79	221	27	45	4	2	0	12	20	45	3	.204	.279	.240
Ron Stone	OF51,1B3	L	28	95	185	16	42	8	1	2	23	25	36	2	.227	.315	.314
Mike Ryan	C43	R	29	43	134	9	22	5	1	3	6	10	32	0	.164	.222	.284
Joe Lis	OF35	R	24	59	123	16	26	6	0	6	10	16	43	0	.211	.308	.407
Tony Taylor†	2B14,3B11,1B2	R	35	36	107	9	25	2	1	1	5	9	10	2	.234	.291	.299
Greg Luzinski	1B28	R	20	28	100	13	30	8	0	3	15	12	32	2	.300	.386	.470
Mike Anderson	OF26	R	20	26	89	11	22	5	1	2	5	13	28	0	.247	.343	.393
Larry Hisle	OF27	R	24	36	76	7	15	3	0	0	3	6	22	1	.197	.256	.237
Bobby Pfeil	3B15,C4,OF3*	R	27	44	70	5	19	3	0	2	9	6	9	1	.271	.329	.400
Byron Browne	OF30	R	28	58	68	5	14	3	0	3	5	8	23	0	.206	.289	.382
Pete Koegel†	C7,OF1	R	23	12	26	1	6	1	0	0	3	2	7	0	.231	.286	.269
John Briggs†	OF8	L	27	10	22	3	4	1	0	0	3	6	2	0	.182	.357	.227
Billy Wilson	P38,3B1	R	28	38	10	0	1	0	0	0	0	0	2	0	.100	.100	.100

T. Harmon, 2 G at 1B; B. Pfeil, 1 G at 1B, 1 G at 2B, 1 G at SS

Pitcher	T	Age	G	GS	CG	ShO	IP	H	HR	BB	SO	W-L	Sv	ERA
Rick Wise	R	25	38	37	17	4	272.1	261	20	70	155	17-14	0	2.88
Barry Lersch	R	26	38	30	3	0	214.1	203	28	50	113	5-14	0	3.78
Chris Short	L	33	31	26	5	2	173.0	182	22	63	95	7-14	1	3.85
Ken Reynolds	L	24	35	25	2	1	162.1	163	11	82	81	5-9	0	4.49
Jim Bunning	R	39	29	16	1	0	110.0	126	11	37	58	5-12	1	5.48
Bucky Brandon	R	30	52	0	0	0	83.0	81	5	47	44	6-6	4	3.90
Joe Hoerner	L	34	49	0	0	0	73.0	57	6	21	57	4-5	9	1.97
Billy Wilson	R	28	38	0	0	0	58.2	39	4	22	40	4-6	7	3.07
Woodie Fryman	L	31	37	17	3	2	149.1	133	7	46	104	10-7	2	3.38
Billy Champion	R	23	37	9	0	0	108.2	100	10	48	49	3-5	0	4.39
Dick Selma	R	27	17	0	0	0	24.2	21	2	8	15	0-2	1	3.28
Wayne Twitchell	R	23	6	1	0	0	16.0	8	1	10	15	1-0	0	0.00
Manny Muniz	R	23	5	0	0	0	10.1	9	2	8	6	0-1	0	6.97
Lowell Palmer	R	23	3	1	0	0	15.0	13	3	13	6	0-0	0	6.00

1971 San Francisco Giants 1st NL West 90-72 .556 —

Charlie Fox

Player	Gm by Position	B	Age	G	AB	R	H	2B	3B	HR	RBI	BB	SO	SB	Avg	OBP	Slg
Dick Dietz	C135	R	29	142	453	58	114	19	0	19	72	97	86	1	.252	.387	.419
Willie McCovey	1B95	L	33	105	329	45	91	13	0	18	70	64	57	0	.277	.396	.480
Tito Fuentes	2B152	S	27	152	630	63	172	28	6	4	52	18	46	12	.273	.299	.356
Al Gallagher	3B128	R	25	136	429	47	119	18	5	5	57	40	57	2	.277	.340	.378
Chris Speier	SS156	R	21	157	601	74	141	17	6	8	46	56	90	4	.235	.307	.323
Bobby Bonds	OF154	R	25	155	619	110	178	32	4	33	102	62	137	26	.288	.355	.512
Ken Henderson	OF138,1B1	S	25	141	504	80	133	26	6	15	65	84	76	18	.264	.370	.429
Willie Mays	OF84,1B48	R	40	136	417	82	113	24	5	18	61	112	123	23	.271	.425	.482
Hal Lanier	3B83,2B13,SS8*	R	28	109	206	21	48	8	0	1	13	15	26	0	.233	.283	.286
Jimmy Rosario	OF67	S	26	92	192	26	43	6	1	0	13	33	35	7	.224	.338	.266
Dave Kingman	1B20,OF14	R	22	41	115	17	32	10	2	6	24	9	35	5	.278	.328	.557
George Foster†	OF30	R	22	36	105	11	28	5	0	3	8	6	27	0	.267	.304	.400
Fran Healy	C22	R	24	47	93	10	26	3	0	2	11	15	24	1	.280	.380	.376
Bernie Williams	OF27	R	22	35	73	8	13	1	0	1	5	12	24	1	.178	.294	.233
Russ Gibson	C22	R	32	25	57	2	11	1	1	1	7	2	13	0	.193	.220	.298
Frank Johnson	1B9,OF4	R	28	32	49	4	4	1	0	0	5	3	9	0	.082	.132	.102
Ed Goodson	1B14	L	23	20	42	4	8	1	0	0	1	2	4	0	.190	.227	.214
Jim Ray Hart	3B3,OF3	R	29	31	39	5	10	0	0	2	5	6	8	0	.256	.356	.410
Frank Duffy†	SS6,2B1,3B1	R	24	21	28	4	5	0	0	0	2	0	10	0	.179	.179	.179
Floyd Wicker†	OF7	L	27	9	21	3	3	0	0	0	1	2	5	0	.143	.250	.143
Chris Arnold	2B3	R	23	6	13	2	3	0	0	1	3	1	2	0	.231	.286	.462
Jim Howarth	OF6	L	24	7	13	3	3	1	0	0	2	3	3	0	.231	.375	.308
Bob Heise†	SS3,3B2,2B1	R	24	13	11	2	0	0	0	0	0	0	1	0	.000	.000	.000
Dave Rader	C1	L	22	3	4	0	0	0	0	0	0	0	0	0	.000	.000	.000

H. Lanier, 3 G at 1B

Pitcher	T	Age	G	GS	CG	ShO	IP	H	HR	BB	SO	W-L	Sv	ERA
Gaylord Perry	R	32	37	37	14	2	280.0	255	20	67	158	16-12	0	2.76
Juan Marichal	R	33	37	37	18	4	279.0	244	27	56	159	18-11	0	2.94
Ron Bryant	L	23	27	22	3	2	140.0	146	9	49	79	7-10	0	3.79
Steve Stone	R	23	24	19	2	2	110.2	110	9	55	63	5-9	0	4.15
Don Carrithers	R	21	22	12	2	1	80.1	77	6	37	41	5-3	1	4.03
Frank Reberger	R	27	13	7	0	0	43.2	37	5	19	21	3-0	0	3.92
Jim Willoughby	R	22	2	1	0	0	4.0	8	0	1	3	0-1	0	9.00
Jerry Johnson	R	27	67	0	0	0	109.0	93	9	48	85	12-9	18	2.97
Don McMahon	R	41	61	0	0	0	82.0	73	9	37	71	10-6	4	4.06
John Cumberland	L	24	45	21	5	2	185.0	153	22	55	65	9-6	2	2.92
Steve Hamilton	L	35	39	0	0	0	44.2	29	4	11	38	2-2	4	3.02
Rich Robertson	R	26	23	6	1	0	61.0	66	5	31	32	2-2	1	4.57
Jim Barr	R	23	17	0	0	0	35.1	33	3	5	16	1-1	0	3.57

1971 Los Angeles Dodgers 2nd NL West 89-73 .549 1.0 GB

Walter Alston

Player	Gm by Position	B	Age	G	AB	R	H	2B	3B	HR	RBI	BB	SO	SB	Avg	OBP	Slg
Duke Sims	C74	L	30	90	230	23	63	7	2	6	25	30	39	0	.274	.357	.400
Wes Parker	1B148,OF18	S	31	157	533	69	146	24	1	6	62	63	63	6	.274	.347	.356
Jim Lefebvre	2B102,3B7	S	29	119	388	40	95	14	2	12	68	39	55	0	.245	.314	.384
Steve Garvey	3B79	R	22	81	225	27	51	12	1	7	26	21	33	1	.227	.290	.382
Maury Wills	SS144,3B4	S	38	149	601	73	169	14	3	3	44	40	44	15	.281	.323	.329
Willie Davis	OF157	L	31	158	641	84	198	33	10	10	74	23	47	20	.309	.330	.438
Willie Crawford	OF97	L	24	114	342	64	96	16	6	9	40	28	49	5	.281	.334	.442
Bill Buckner	OF86,1B11	L	21	108	358	37	99	15	1	5	41	11	18	4	.277	.306	.366
Dick Allen	3B67,OF60,1B28	R	29	155	549	82	162	24	1	23	90	93	113	8	.295	.395	.468
Bobby Valentine	SS37,3B23,2B21*	R	21	101	281	32	70	10	2	1	25	15	20	5	.249	.287	.310
Manny Mota	OF80	R	33	91	269	24	84	13	5	0	34	20	20	4	.312	.361	.398
Bill Russell	2B41,OF40,SS6	R	22	91	211	29	48	7	4	2	15	11	39	6	.227	.265	.327
Tom Haller	C67	L	34	84	202	23	54	5	0	5	32	25	30	0	.267	.346	.366
Joe Ferguson	C35	R	24	36	102	13	22	3	0	2	7	12	15	1	.216	.304	.304
Bill Sudakis	C19,3B3,1B1*	S	25	41	83	10	16	3	0	3	7	12	22	0	.193	.302	.337
Billy Grabarkewitz	2B13,3B10,SS1	R	25	44	71	9	16	5	0	0	6	19	16	1	.225	.389	.296
Bobby Darwin	OF4	R	28	11	20	2	5	1	0	1	4	2	9	0	.250	.318	.450
Von Joshua	OF5	L	23	11	7	2	0	0	0	0	0	0	1	0	.000	.000	.000
Ron Cey		R	23	2	2	0	0	0	0	0	0	0	2	0	.000	.000	.000
Tom Paciorek	OF1	R	24	2	2	0	1	0	0	0	1	0	0	0	.500	.500	.500

B. Valentine, 11 G at OF; B. Sudakis, 1 G at OF

Pitcher	T	Age	G	GS	CG	ShO	IP	H	HR	BB	SO	W-L	Sv	ERA
Claude Osteen	L	31	38	38	11	4	259.0	262	25	63	109	14-11	0	3.51
Don Sutton	R	26	38	37	12	4	265.1	231	10	55	194	17-12	1	2.54
Al Downing	L	30	37	36	12	5	262.1	245	16	84	136	20-9	0	2.68
Bill Singer	R	27	31	31	8	1	203.1	195	19	71	144	10-17	0	4.16
Doyle Alexander	R	20	17	12	4	0	92.1	105	6	18	30	6-6	0	3.80
Jim Brewer	L	33	55	0	0	0	81.1	55	4	24	66	6-5	22	1.88
Pete Mikkelsen	R	31	41	0	0	0	74.0	67	10	17	46	8-5	5	3.65
Joe Moeller	R	28	28	1	0	0	66.1	72	5	12	32	2-4	1	3.80
Jose Pena	R	28	21	0	0	0	43.0	32	7	18	44	2-0	1	3.56
Bob O'Brien	L	22	14	4	1	1	42.0	42	4	13	15	2-2	0	3.00
Sandy Vance	R	24	10	3	0	0	26.0	38	1	9	11	2-1	0	6.92
Hoyt Wilhelm†	R	47	9	0	0	0	17.2	6	1	4	15	0-1	3	1.02
Mike Strahler	R	24	6	0	0	0	12.2	10	1	8	7	0-0	0	2.84
Charlie Hough	R	23	4	0	0	0	4.1	3	1	3	4	0-0	0	4.15

1971 Atlanta Braves 3rd NL West 82-80 .506 8.0 GB

Lum Harris

Player	Gm by Position	B	Age	G	AB	R	H	2B	3B	HR	RBI	BB	SO	SB	Avg	OBP	Slg
Earl Williams	C72,3B42,1B31	R	22	145	497	64	129	14	1	33	87	42	80	0	.260	.324	.491
Hank Aaron	1B71,OF60	R	37	139	495	95	162	22	3	47	118	71	58	1	.327	.410	.669
Felix Millan	2B141	R	27	143	577	65	167	20	8	2	45	37	22	11	.289	.332	.362
Darrell Evans	3B72,OF3	L	24	89	260	42	63	11	1	12	38	39	54	2	.242	.338	.431
Marty Perez	SS126,2B1	R	24	130	410	28	93	15	3	4	32	25	44	1	.227	.272	.307
Ralph Garr	OF153	L	25	154	639	101	219	24	6	9	44	30	68	30	.343	.372	.441
Sonny Jackson	OF145	L	26	149	547	58	141	20	5	2	25	35	45	7	.258	.302	.324
Mike Lum	OF125,1B1	L	25	145	454	56	122	14	1	13	55	47	43	0	.269	.340	.390
Orlando Cepeda	1B63	R	33	71	250	31	69	10	1	14	44	22	29	3	.276	.330	.492
Hal King	C60	L	27	86	198	14	41	9	0	5	19	29	43	0	.207	.320	.328
Zoilo Versalles	3B30,SS24,2B1	R	31	66	194	21	37	11	0	5	22	11	40	2	.191	.233	.325
Bob Didier	C50	S	22	51	155	9	34	4	1	0	5	6	17	0	.219	.248	.258
Gil Garrido	SS32,3B28,2B18	R	30	79	125	8	27	3	0	0	12	15	12	0	.216	.300	.240
Clete Boyer	3B25,SS1	R	34	30	98	10	24	1	0	6	19	8	11	0	.245	.299	.439
Dusty Baker	OF18	R	22	29	62	2	14	2	0	0	4	1	14	0	.226	.238	.258
Tommie Aaron	1B11,3B7	R	31	25	53	4	12	2	0	0	3	3	5	0	.226	.268	.264
Oscar Brown	OF15	R	25	27	43	4	9	4	0	0	5	3	8	0	.209	.261	.302
Marv Staehle	2B7,3B1	L	29	22	36	5	4	0	0	0	1	5	4	0	.111	.238	.111
Jim Breazeale	1B4	L	21	10	21	1	4	0	0	1	3	0	3	0	.190	.182	.333
Leo Foster	SS3	R	20	9	10	1	0	0	0	0	0	0	1	0	.000	.000	.000
Tony La Russa†	2B9	R	26	9	7	1	2	0	0	0	0	1	1	0	.286	.375	.286

Pitcher	T	Age	G	GS	CG	ShO	IP	H	HR	BB	SO	W-L	Sv	ERA
Phil Niekro	R	32	42	36	18	4	268.2	248	27	70	173	15-14	2	2.98
Ron Reed	R	28	32	32	8	1	222.1	221	26	54	129	13-14	0	3.72
George Stone	L	24	27	24	4	2	172.2	186	19	35	110	6-8	0	3.60
Pat Jarvis	R	30	35	23	3	3	162.1	162	16	51	68	6-14	1	4.10
Tom Kelley	R	27	28	20	5	0	143.0	140	8	69	68	9-5	0	2.96
Jim Nash	R	26	32	19	2	0	133.0	166	17	50	65	9-7	2	4.94
Cecil Upshaw	R	28	49	0	0	0	82.0	95	5	28	56	11-6	17	3.51
Bob Priddy	R	31	40	0	0	0	64.0	71	8	44	36	4-9	4	4.22
Steve Barber	L	32	39	3	0	0	75.0	92	6	25	40	3-1	2	4.80
Ron Herbel	R	33	25	0	0	0	51.2	61	6	23	22	0-1	1	5.23
Mike McQueen	L	20	17	3	0	0	56.0	47	7	23	38	4-1	1	3.54
Tom House	L	24	11	1	0	0	20.2	20	2	3	11	1-0	0	3.05
Gary Neibauer	R	26	6	1	0	0	21.0	14	3	9	6	1-0	1	2.14
Hoyt Wilhelm†	R	47	3	0	0	0	2.1	6	2	1	1	0-0	0	15.43

Seasons: Team Rosters 805

1971 Cincinnati Reds 4th NL West 79-83 .488 11.0 GB

Sparky Anderson

Player	Gm by Position	B	Age	G	AB	R	H	2B	3B	HR	RBI	BB	SO	SB	Avg	OBP	Slg
Johnny Bench	C141,1B12,OF12*	R	23	149	562	80	134	19	2	27	61	49	83	2	.238	.299	.423
Lee May	1B143	R	28	147	553	85	154	17	3	39	98	42	135	3	.278	.332	.532
Tommy Helms	2B149	R	30	150	547	40	141	26	1	3	52	26	33	3	.258	.289	.325
Tony Perez	3B148,1B44	R	29	158	609	72	164	22	3	25	91	51	120	4	.269	.325	.438
Dave Concepcion	SS112,2B10,3B7*	R	23	130	327	24	67	4	4	1	20	18	51	9	.205	.246	.251
Pete Rose	OF158	S	30	160	632	86	192	27	4	13	44	68	50	13	.304	.373	.421
George Foster†	OF102	R	22	104	368	39	86	18	4	10	50	23	93	7	.234	.289	.386
Hal McRae	OF91	R	25	99	337	39	89	24	2	9	34	11	35	3	.264	.291	.427
Bernie Carbo	OF90	L	23	106	310	33	68	20	1	5	20	54	56	2	.219	.338	.339
Woody Woodward	SS85,3B63,2B9	R	28	136	273	22	66	9	1	0	18	27	28	4	.242	.309	.282
Buddy Bradford†	OF66	R	26	79	100	17	20	3	0	2	12	14	23	4	.200	.316	.290
Ty Cline	OF28,1B2	L	32	69	97	12	19	1	0	0	1	18	16	2	.196	.333	.206
Pat Corrales	C39	R	30	40	94	6	17	2	0	0	6	6	17	0	.181	.230	.202
Jimmy Stewart	OF19,3B9,2B6	S	32	80	82	7	19	2	2	0	9	9	12	3	.232	.308	.305
Willie Smith	1B10	L	32	31	55	3	9	2	0	1	4	3	9	0	.164	.207	.255
Al Ferrara†	OF5	R	31	32	33	2	6	0	0	1	5	3	10	0	.182	.270	.273
Darrel Chaney	SS7,2B1,3B1	S	23	10	24	2	3	0	0	0	1	1	3	0	.125	.160	.125
Bill Plummer	C4,3B2	R	24	10	19	0	0	0	0	0	0	0	4	0	.000	.000	.000
Frank Duffy†	SS10	R	24	13	16	0	3	1	0	0	1	1	2	0	.188	.235	.250
Angel Bravo†		L	28	5	5	0	1	0	0	0	0	0	1	0	.200	.200	.200

J. Bench, 3 G at 3B; D. Concepcion, 5 G at OF

Pitcher	T	Age	G	GS	CG	ShO	IP	H	HR	BB	SO	W-L	Sv	ERA
Gary Nolan	R	23	35	35	9	0	244.2	208	12	59	146	12-15	0	3.16
Don Gullett	L	20	35	31	4	3	217.2	196	14	64	107	16-6	0	2.65
Jim McGlothlin	R	27	30	26	6	0	170.2	151	15	47	93	8-12	0	3.22
Ross Grimsley	L	21	26	26	6	3	161.1	151	15	43	67	10-7	0	3.57
Wayne Simpson	R	22	22	21	1	0	117.1	106	9	77	61	4-7	0	4.76
Greg Garrett	L	23	2	1	0	0	8.2	7	0	10	2	0-1	0	1.04
Wayne Granger	R	27	70	0	0	0	100.0	94	8	28	51	7-6	11	3.33
Clay Carroll	R	30	61	0	0	0	93.2	78	5	42	64	10-4	15	2.50
Joe Gibbon	L	36	50	0	0	0	64.1	54	3	32	34	5-6	11	2.94
Jim Merritt	L	27	28	11	0	0	107.0	115	14	31	38	1-11	0	4.37
Tony Cloninger	R	30	28	8	1	1	97.1	79	12	49	51	3-6	0	3.88
Milt Wilcox	R	21	18	3	0	0	43.1	43	2	17	21	2-2	1	3.32
Ed Sprague	R	25	7	0	0	0	11.0	8	0	1	7	1-0	0	0.00
Pedro Borbon	R	24	3	0	0	0	4.1	3	1	1	4	0-0	0	4.15
Steve Blateric	R	27	2	0	0	0	2.2	5	2	0	4	0-0	0	13.50

1971 Houston Astros 4th NL West 79-83 .488 11.0 GB

Harry Walker

Player	Gm by Position	B	Age	G	AB	R	H	2B	3B	HR	RBI	BB	SO	SB	Avg	OBP	Slg
Johnny Edwards	C104	L	33	106	317	18	74	13	4	1	23	26	38	1	.233	.291	.309
Denis Menke	1B101,3B32,SS17*	R	30	146	475	57	117	26	3	1	43	59	68	4	.246	.328	.320
Joe Morgan	2B157	L	27	160	583	87	149	27	11	13	56	88	52	40	.256	.351	.407
Doug Rader	3B135	R	26	135	484	51	118	21	4	12	56	40	112	5	.244	.303	.378
Roger Metzger	SS148	S	23	150	562	64	132	14	11	0	26	44	50	15	.235	.294	.299
Cesar Cedeno	OF157,1B2	R	20	161	611	85	161	40	6	10	81	25	102	20	.264	.293	.398
Jimmy Wynn	OF116	R	29	123	404	38	82	16	0	7	45	56	63	10	.203	.302	.295
Jesus Alou	OF109	R	29	122	433	41	121	21	4	2	40	13	17	3	.279	.305	.360
Bob Watson	OF87,1B45	R	25	129	468	49	135	17	3	9	67	41	56	0	.288	.347	.395
Jack Hiatt	C65,1B1	R	28	69	174	16	48	8	1	1	16	35	39	0	.276	.401	.351
John Mayberry	1B37	L	22	46	137	16	25	0	1	7	14	13	32	0	.182	.260	.350
Rich Chiles	OF27	L	21	67	119	12	27	5	1	2	15	6	20	0	.227	.268	.336
Cesar Geronimo	OF64	L	23	94	82	13	18	2	2	1	6	5	31	2	.220	.264	.329
Norm Miller	OF20,C1	L	25	45	74	5	19	5	0	2	10	5	13	0	.257	.313	.405
Larry Howard	C22	R	26	24	64	6	15	3	0	2	14	3	17	0	.234	.265	.375
Marty Martinez	2B9,SS7,1B4*	S	29	32	62	4	16	3	1	0	4	3	6	1	.258	.292	.339
Ray Busse	SS5,3B3	R	22	10	34	2	5	3	0	0	4	2	9	0	.147	.194	.235
Derrel Thomas	2B1	R	20	5	5	0	0	0	0	0	0	0	2	0	.000	.000	.000
Jay Schlueter	OF2	R	21	7	3	1	1	0	0	0	0	0	1	0	.333	.333	.333

D. Menke, 5 G at 2B; M. Martinez, 3 G at 3B

Pitcher	T	Age	G	GS	CG	ShO	IP	H	HR	BB	SO	W-L	Sv	ERA
Don Wilson	R	26	35	34	18	3	268.0	195	15	79	180	16-10	0	2.45
Jack Billingham	R	28	33	33	8	3	228.1	205	9	68	139	10-16	0	3.39
Wade Blasingame	L	27	30	28	2	0	158.1	177	11	45	93	9-11	0	4.60
Ken Forsch	R	24	33	23	7	2	188.1	162	8	53	131	8-8	0	2.53
Larry Dierker	R	24	24	23	6	2	159.0	150	8	33	91	12-6	0	2.72
Tom Griffin	R	23	10	6	0	0	37.2	44	4	20	29	0-6	0	4.78
Ron Cook	L	23	5	4	0	0	25.2	23	2	8	10	0-4	0	4.91
J.R. Richard	R	21	4	4	1	0	21.0	17	1	16	29	2-1	0	3.43
Scipio Spinks	R	23	5	3	1	0	29.1	22	2	13	26	1-0	0	3.68
George Culver	R	27	59	0	0	0	95.1	89	4	38	57	5-8	7	2.64
Fred Gladding	R	35	48	0	0	0	51.1	51	0	22	17	4-5	12	2.10
Jim Ray	R	26	47	1	0	0	97.2	72	3	31	46	10-4	3	2.12
Denny Lemaster	L	32	42	0	0	0	60.0	59	4	22	28	0-2	2	3.45
Buddy Harris	R	22	20	0	0	0	30.2	33	3	16	21	1-1	0	6.46
Bill Greif	R	21	7	3	0	0	16.0	18	1	8	14	1-1	0	5.06
Skip Guinn	L	26	4	0	0	0	4.2	1	0	3	3	0-0	1	0.00
Larry Yount	R	21	1	0	0	0	0.0	0	0	0	0	0-0	0	—

1971 San Diego Padres 6th NL West 61-100 .379 28.5 GB

Preston Gomez

Player	Gm by Position	B	Age	G	AB	R	H	2B	3B	HR	RBI	BB	SO	SB	Avg	OBP	Slg
Bob Barton	C119	R	29	121	376	23	94	17	2	5	23	35	49	0	.250	.317	.346
Nate Colbert	1B153	R	25	156	565	81	149	25	3	27	84	63	119	5	.264	.339	.462
Don Mason	2B90,3B3	L	26	113	344	43	73	12	1	2	11	27	35	6	.212	.270	.270
Ed Spiezio	3B91,OF1	R	29	97	308	16	71	10	1	7	36	22	50	6	.231	.286	.338
Enzo Hernandez	SS143	R	22	143	549	58	122	9	3	0	12	54	34	21	.222	.295	.250
Ollie Brown	OF134	R	27	145	484	36	132	16	0	9	55	52	74	3	.273	.346	.362
Cito Gaston	OF133	R	27	141	518	57	118	13	9	17	61	24	121	1	.228	.264	.386
Larry Stahl	OF75,1B7	L	30	114	308	27	78	13	4	8	36	26	59	4	.253	.310	.399
Dave Campbell	2B69,3B40,SS4*	R	29	108	365	38	83	14	2	7	29	37	75	9	.227	.299	.334
Leron Lee†	OF68	L	23	79	256	29	70	20	2	4	21	18	45	4	.273	.321	.414
Ivan Murrell	OF72	R	26	103	255	23	60	6	3	7	24	7	60	5	.235	.263	.365
Garry Jestadt†	3B49,2B23,SS1	R	24	75	189	17	55	13	0	0	13	11	24	1	.291	.328	.360
Fred Kendall	C39,1B1,3B1	R	22	49	111	2	19	1	0	1	7	7	16	1	.171	.220	.207
Johnny Jeter	OF17	R	26	18	75	8	24	4	0	1	3	2	16	2	.320	.338	.413
Tommy Dean	SS28,3B11,2B1	R	25	41	70	2	8	0	0	0	1	4	13	1	.114	.162	.114
Chris Cannizzaro†	C19	R	33	21	63	2	12	1	0	1	8	11	10	0	.190	.320	.254
Angel Bravo†	OF9	L	28	52	58	6	9	2	0	0	6	8	12	0	.155	.265	.190
Ron Slocum	3B6	R	25	7	18	1	0	0	0	0	0	0	8	0	.000	.053	.000
Mike Ivie	C6	R	18	6	17	0	8	0	0	0	3	1	1	0	.471	.526	.471
Jerry Morales	OF7	R	22	12	17	1	2	0	0	0	1	2	2	1	.118	.211	.118
Rod Gaspar	OF2	S	25	16	17	1	2	0	0	0	2	3	3	0	.118	.250	.118
Al Ferrara†	OF2	R	31	17	17	0	2	1	0	0	2	5	5	0	.118	.318	.176
Ray Webster†		L	28	10	8	0	1	0	0	0	0	2	1	0	.125	.300	.125
Dave Robinson		S	25	7	6	0	0	0	0	0	0	1	3	0	.000	.143	.000

D. Campbell, 2 G at 1B, 2 G at OF

Pitcher	T	Age	G	GS	CG	ShO	IP	H	HR	BB	SO	W-L	Sv	ERA
Clay Kirby	R	23	38	36	13	2	267.1	213	20	103	231	15-13	0	2.83
Dave Roberts	L	26	37	34	14	2	269.2	238	9	61	135	14-17	0	2.10
Steve Arlin	R	25	36	34	10	4	227.2	211	8	103	156	9-19	0	3.48
Tom Phoebus	R	29	29	21	2	0	133.1	144	14	64	80	3-11	0	4.46
Fred Norman†	L	28	20	18	5	0	127.1	114	7	56	77	3-12	0	3.32
Ed Acosta	R	27	8	6	3	1	46.0	43	4	7	16	3-3	0	2.74
Al Severinsen	R	26	59	0	0	0	70.0	77	4	30	31	2-5	8	3.47
Dick Kelley	L	31	48	1	0	0	59.2	52	5	23	42	2-3	2	3.47
Bob Miller†	R	32	38	0	0	0	63.2	53	0	26	36	7-3	7	1.41
Danny Coombs	L	29	19	7	0	0	57.2	81	10	25	37	1-6	0	6.24
Al Santorini†	R	23	18	3	0	0	38.1	43	4	11	21	0-2	0	3.76
Bill Laxton	L	23	18	0	0	0	27.2	32	4	26	23	0-2	0	6.83
Gary Ross	R	23	13	0	0	0	24.1	27	0	11	13	1-3	0	2.96
Mike Corkins	R	25	8	0	0	0	13.0	14	1	6	16	0-0	0	3.46
Mike Caldwell	L	22	6	0	0	0	6.2	4	0	3	5	1-0	0	0.00
Jay Franklin	R	18	3	1	0	0	5.2	5	3	4	4	0-1	0	6.35

»1972 Detroit Tigers 1st AL East 86-70 .551 —

Billy Martin

Player	Gm by Position	B	Age	G	AB	R	H	2B	3B	HR	RBI	BB	SO	SB	Avg	OBP	Slg
Bill Freehan	C105,1B1	R	30	111	374	51	98	18	2	10	56	48	51	0	.262	.354	.401
Norm Cash	1B134	L	37	137	440	51	114	16	0	22	61	50	64	0	.259	.338	.445
Dick McAuliffe	2B116,SS3,3B1	L	32	122	408	47	98	16	3	8	30	59	59	0	.240	.339	.353
Aurelio Rodriguez	3B153,SS2	R	24	153	601	65	142	23	5	13	56	28	104	2	.236	.272	.356
Ed Brinkman	SS156	R	30	156	516	42	105	19	1	6	49	38	51	0	.203	.259	.279
Mickey Stanley	OF139	R	29	142	435	45	102	16	6	14	55	29	49	1	.234	.278	.395
Jim Northrup	OF127,1B2	L	32	134	426	40	111	15	2	8	42	38	47	4	.261	.324	.362
Willie Horton	OF98	R	29	108	333	44	77	9	5	11	36	27	47	0	.231	.293	.387
Al Kaline	OF84,1B11	R	37	106	278	46	87	11	2	10	32	28	33	1	.313	.374	.475
Gates Brown	OF72	L	33	103	252	33	58	5	0	10	31	26	28	3	.230	.304	.369
Tony Taylor	2B67,3B8,1B1	R	36	78	228	33	69	12	4	1	20	14	34	5	.303	.346	.404
Tom Haller	C36	L	35	59	121	7	25	5	2	2	13	15	14	0	.207	.292	.331
Duke Sims†	C25,OF4	L	31	38	98	11	31	4	0	4	19	19	18	0	.316	.432	.480
Ike Brown	OF22,1B13,2B3*	R	30	51	84	12	21	3	0	2	10	17	23	1	.250	.376	.357
Paul Jata	1B12,OF10,C1	R	22	32	74	8	17	2	0	0	3	7	14	0	.230	.296	.257
Frank Howard†	1B10,OF1	R	35	14	33	1	8	1	0	1	7	4	8	0	.242	.324	.364
John Knox	2B4	L	23	14	13	1	1	1	0	0	0	1	2	0	.077	.143	.154
Wayne Comer	OF17	R	28	27	9	1	1	0	0	0	1	0	1	0	.111	.100	.111
Dalton Jones†		L	28	7	7	0	0	0	0	0	0	0	2	0	.000	.000	.000
Marvin Lane	OF3	R	22	8	6	2	0	0	0	0	0	0	2	0	.000	.000	.000
Ike Blessitt	OF1	R	22	4	5	0	0	0	0	0	0	0	2	0	.000	.000	.000
John Gamble	SS1	R	24	6	3	0	0	0	0	0	0	0	0	0	.000	.000	.000
Joe Staton	1B2	L	24	6	2	1	0	0	0	0	0	0	1	0	.000	.000	.000
Gene Lamont	C1	L	25	1	0	0	0	0	0	0	0	0	0	0	—	—	—

I. Brown, 1 G at 3B, 1 G at SS

Pitcher	T	Age	G	GS	CG	ShO	IP	H	HR	BB	SO	W-L	Sv	ERA
Mickey Lolich	L	31	41	41	23	4	327.1	282	29	74	250	22-14	0	2.50
Joe Coleman	R	25	40	39	9	3	280.0	216	23	110	222	19-14	0	2.80
Tom Timmermann	R	32	34	25	3	2	149.2	121	12	41	88	8-10	0	2.89
Woodie Fryman†	L	32	16	14	6	1	113.2	93	6	31	72	10-3	0	2.06
Bill Slayback	R	24	23	13	3	1	81.2	74	4	25	65	5-6	0	3.20
Les Cain	L	24	5	5	0	0	23.2	18	2	16	16	0-3	0	3.80
Fred Holdsworth	R	20	2	2	0	0	7.0	13	0	2	5	0-1	0	12.86
Chuck Seelbach	R	24	61	3	0	0	112.0	96	6	39	76	9-8	14	2.89
Fred Scherman	L	27	57	3	0	0	94.0	91	5	53	53	7-3	12	3.64
Chris Zachary	R	28	25	1	0	0	38.1	27	2	15	21	1-1	1	1.41
John Hiller	L	29	24	3	1	0	44.1	39	4	13	26	1-2	3	2.03
Joe Niekro	R	27	18	7	1	0	47.0	62	3	8	24	3-2	1	3.83
Ron Perranoski†	L	36	17	0	0	0	18.2	23	2	8	10	0-1	0	7.71
Lerrin LaGrow	R	23	16	0	0	0	27.1	22	0	6	9	0-1	2	1.32
Phil Meeler	R	23	7	0	0	0	8.1	10	0	7	5	0-1	0	4.32
Bob Strampe	R	22	7	0	0	0	4.2	6	0	7	4	0-0	0	11.57
Jim Foor	L	23	7	0	0	0	3.2	6	1	6	2	1-0	0	14.73
Bill Gilbreth	L	24	2	0	0	0	5.0	10	1	4	2	0-0	0	16.20
Don Leshnock	L	25	1	0	0	0	1.0	2	0	0	2	0-0	0	0.00
Mike Kilkenny†	L	27	1	0	0	0	1.0	1	1	0	0	0-0	0	9.00

806 Seasons: Team Rosters

1972 Boston Red Sox 2nd AL East 85-70 .548 0.5 GB

Eddie Kasko

Player	Gm by Position	B	Age	G	AB	R	H	2B	3B	HR	RBI	BB	SO	SB	Avg	OBP	Slg
Carlton Fisk	C131	R	24	131	457	74	134	28	9	22	61	52	83	5	.293	.370	.538
Danny Cater	1B90	R	32	92	317	32	75	17	1	8	39	15	33	0	.237	.270	.372
Doug Griffin	2B129	R	25	129	470	43	122	12	1	2	35	45	48	9	.260	.325	.302
Rico Petrocelli	3B146	R	29	147	521	62	125	15	2	15	75	78	91	0	.240	.339	.363
Luis Aparicio	SS109	R	38	110	436	47	112	26	3	3	39	26	28	3	.257	.299	.351
Tommy Harper	OF144	R	31	144	556	92	141	29	2	14	49	67	104	25	.254	.341	.388
Reggie Smith	OF129	S	27	131	467	75	126	25	4	21	74	68	63	15	.270	.365	.475
Carl Yastrzemski	OF83,1B42	L	32	125	455	70	120	18	2	12	68	67	44	5	.264	.357	.391
Ben Oglivie	OF65	L	23	94	253	27	61	10	2	8	30	18	61	1	.241	.293	.391
John Kennedy	2B32,SS27,3B11	R	31	71	212	22	52	11	1	2	22	18	40	0	.245	.311	.335
Juan Beniquez	SS27	R	22	33	99	10	24	4	1	1	8	7	11	2	.242	.287	.333
Rick Miller	OF75	L	24	89	98	13	21	4	1	3	15	11	27	0	.214	.291	.367
Duane Josephson	1B16,C6	R	30	26	82	11	22	4	1	1	7	4	11	0	.268	.310	.378
Phil Gagliano	OF12,3B5,2B4*	R	30	52	82	9	21	4	1	0	10	10	13	1	.256	.333	.329
Bob Montgomery	C22	R	28	24	77	7	22	1	0	2	7	3	17	0	.286	.309	.377
Bob Burda	1B15,OF1	L	33	45	73	4	12	1	0	2	9	8	11	0	.164	.241	.260
Dwight Evans	OF17	R	20	18	57	2	15	3	1	1	6	7	13	0	.263	.344	.404
Andy Kosco†	OF12	R	30	17	47	5	10	2	1	3	6	2	9	0	.213	.260	.489
Cecil Cooper	1B3	L	22	12	17	0	4	1	0	0	2	2	5	0	.235	.316	.294
Bob Gallagher		L	23	7	5	0	0	0	0	0	0	0	3	0	.000	.000	.000
Vic Correll	C1	R	26	1	4	1	2	0	0	0	1	0	1	0	.500	.500	.500

P. Gagliano, 2 G at 1B

Pitcher	T	Age	G	GS	CG	ShO	IP	H	HR	BB	SO	W-L	Sv	ERA
Marty Pattin	R	29	38	35	13	4	253.0	232	19	65	168	17-13	0	3.24
Sonny Siebert	R	35	32	30	7	3	196.1	204	17	59	123	12-12	0	3.80
Lynn McGlothen	R	22	22	22	4	1	145.0	135	9	59	112	8-7	0	3.41
John Curtis	L	24	26	21	8	3	154.1	161	8	50	106	11-8	0	3.73
Ray Culp	R	30	16	16	4	1	105.0	104	8	53	52	5-8	0	4.46
Bill Lee	L	25	47	0	0	0	84.1	75	5	32	43	7-4	5	3.20
Luis Tiant	R	31	43	19	12	6	179.0	128	7	65	123	15-6	3	1.91
Gary Peters	L	35	33	4	0	0	85.1	91	10	38	67	3-3	1	4.32
Don Newhauser	R	24	31	0	0	0	37.0	30	2	25	27	4-2	4	2.43
Lew Krausse	R	29	24	7	0	0	60.2	74	9	28	35	1-3	1	6.38
Ken Tatum	R	28	22	0	0	0	29.1	32	3	15	15	0-2	4	3.07
Bobby Bolin	R	33	21	0	0	0	30.2	24	3	11	27	0-1	5	2.93
Bob Veale†	L	36	6	0	0	0	8.0	2	0	3	10	2-0	2	0.00
Roger Moret	L	22	3	0	0	0	5.0	5	0	6	4	0-0	0	3.60
Stan Williams	R	35	3	0	0	0	4.1	5	0	1	3	0-0	0	6.23
Mike Garman	R	22	3	1	0	0	3.1	4	1	2	1	0-1	0	10.80
Mike Nagy	R	24	1	0	0	0	2.0	3	0	0	2	0-0	0	9.00

1972 Baltimore Orioles 3rd AL East 80-74 .519 5.0 GB

Earl Weaver

Player	Gm by Position	B	Age	G	AB	R	H	2B	3B	HR	RBI	BB	SO	SB	Avg	OBP	Slg
Johnny Oates	C82	L	26	85	253	20	66	12	1	4	21	28	31	5	.261	.332	.364
Boog Powell	1B133	L	30	140	465	53	117	20	1	21	81	65	92	4	.252	.346	.434
Dave Johnson	2B116	R	29	118	376	31	83	22	3	5	32	52	68	1	.221	.320	.335
Brooks Robinson	3B152	R	35	153	556	48	139	23	2	8	64	43	45	1	.250	.303	.342
Mark Belanger	SS105	R	28	113	285	36	53	9	1	2	16	18	53	6	.186	.236	.246
Paul Blair	OF139	R	28	142	477	47	111	20	8	8	49	25	78	7	.233	.267	.358
Don Buford	OF105	S	35	125	408	46	84	6	2	5	22	69	83	8	.206	.326	.267
Merv Rettenmund	OF98	R	29	102	301	40	70	10	2	6	21	41	37	6	.233	.325	.339
Bobby Grich	SS81,2B45,1B16*	R	23	133	460	66	128	21	3	12	50	53	96	13	.278	.358	.415
Don Baylor	OF84,1B9	R	23	102	320	33	81	13	3	11	38	29	50	24	.253	.330	.416
Terry Crowley	OF68,1B15	L	25	97	247	30	57	10	0	11	29	32	26	0	.231	.319	.405
Andy Etchebarren	C70	R	29	71	188	11	38	6	1	2	21	17	43	0	.202	.276	.277
Ellie Hendricks†	C28	L	31	33	84	6	13	4	0	0	4	12	19	0	.155	.258	.202
Tommy Davis†	OF18,1B3	R	33	26	82	9	21	3	0	0	6	6	18	2	.256	.307	.293
Tom Shopay	OF3	L	27	49	40	3	9	0	0	0	2	5	12	0	.225	.311	.225
Rich Coggins	OF13	L	21	16	39	5	13	4	0	0	1	1	6	0	.333	.350	.436
Chico Salmon	1B2,3B1	R	31	17	16	2	1	1	0	0	0	0	4	0	.063	.063	.125
Al Bumbry	OF2	L	25	9	11	5	4	0	1	0	0	0	0	1	.364	.364	.545
Tommy Matchick	3B3	L	28	3	9	0	2	0	0	0	0	0	1	0	.222	.222	.222
Enos Cabell	1B1	R	22	3	5	0	0	0	0	0	1	0	0	0	.000	.000	.000
Sergio Robles	C1	R	26	2	5	0	1	0	0	0	0	0	0	0	.200	.200	.200

B. Grich, 8 G at 3B

Pitcher	T	Age	G	GS	CG	ShO	IP	H	HR	BB	SO	W-L	Sv	ERA
Jim Palmer	R	26	36	36	18	3	274.1	219	21	70	184	21-10	0	2.07
Pat Dobson	R	30	38	36	13	3	268.1	220	13	69	161	16-18	0	2.65
Dave McNally	L	29	36	36	12	6	241.0	220	15	68	120	13-17	0	2.95
Mike Cuellar	L	35	35	35	17	4	248.1	197	21	71	132	18-12	0	2.57
Roric Harrison	R	25	39	2	0	0	94.0	68	2	34	62	3-4	4	2.30
Eddie Watt	R	31	38	0	0	0	45.2	30	2	20	23	2-3	7	2.17
Doyle Alexander	R	21	35	9	2	2	106.1	78	5	30	49	6-8	2	2.45
Grant Jackson	L	29	32	0	0	0	41.0	33	1	9	34	1-1	8	2.63
Mickey Scott	L	24	15	0	0	0	23.0	23	2	5	11	0-1	0	2.74
Dave Leonhard	R	31	14	0	0	0	20.0	20	3	12	7	0-0	0	4.50
Bob Reynolds	R	25	3	0	0	0	9.2	8	0	7	5	0-0	0	1.86

1972 New York Yankees 4th AL East 79-76 .510 6.5 GB

Ralph Houk

Player	Gm by Position	B	Age	G	AB	R	H	2B	3B	HR	RBI	BB	SO	SB	Avg	OBP	Slg
Thurman Munson	C132	R	25	140	511	54	143	16	3	7	46	47	58	6	.280	.343	.364
Felipe Alou	1B95,OF15	R	37	120	324	33	90	18	1	6	37	22	27	1	.278	.326	.395
Horace Clarke	2B143	S	32	147	547	65	132	20	2	3	37	56	44	18	.241	.315	.302
Celerino Sanchez	3B68	R	28	71	250	18	62	8	3	0	22	12	30	0	.248	.292	.304
Gene Michael	SS121	S	34	126	391	29	91	7	4	1	32	32	45	4	.233	.290	.279
Roy White	OF155	S	28	155	556	76	150	29	0	10	54	99	59	23	.270	.384	.376
Bobby Murcer	OF151	L	26	153	585	102	171	30	7	33	96	63	67	11	.292	.361	.537
Johnny Callison	OF74	L	33	92	275	28	71	10	0	9	34	18	34	3	.258	.299	.393
Ron Blomberg	1B95	L	23	107	299	36	80	22	1	14	49	38	26	0	.268	.355	.488
Bernie Allen	3B44,2B20	L	33	84	220	26	50	9	0	9	21	23	42	0	.227	.296	.391
Rusty Torres	OF62	S	23	80	199	15	42	7	0	3	13	18	44	0	.211	.280	.291
John Ellis	C25,1B8	R	23	52	136	13	40	5	1	5	25	8	22	0	.294	.333	.456
Rich McKinney	3B33	R	25	37	121	10	26	2	0	1	7	7	13	1	.215	.258	.256
Jerry Kenney	SS45,3B1	L	27	50	119	16	25	2	0	0	7	16	13	3	.210	.304	.227
Ron Swoboda	OF35,1B2	R	28	63	113	9	28	8	0	1	12	17	29	0	.248	.341	.345
Hal Lanier	3B47,SS9,2B3	R	29	60	103	5	22	3	0	0	6	2	13	1	.214	.234	.243
Charlie Spikes	OF9	R	21	14	34	2	5	1	0	0	3	1	13	0	.147	.171	.176
Frank Tepedino		L	24	8	8	0	0	0	0	0	0	0	1	0	.000	.000	.000

Pitcher	T	Age	G	GS	CG	ShO	IP	H	HR	BB	SO	W-L	Sv	ERA
Mel Stottlemyre	R	30	36	36	9	7	260.0	250	13	85	110	14-18	0	3.22
Fritz Peterson	L	30	35	35	12	3	250.1	270	17	44	100	17-15	0	3.24
Steve Kline	R	24	32	32	11	4	236.1	210	11	44	58	16-9	0	2.40
Mike Kekich	L	27	29	28	2	0	175.1	172	13	76	78	10-13	0	3.70
Rob Gardner	L	27	20	14	1	0	97.0	91	9	28	58	8-5	0	3.06
Larry Gowell	R	24	2	1	0	0	7.0	3	0	2	7	0-1	0	1.29
Doc Medich	R	23	1	1	0	0	0.0	2	0	2	0	0-0	0	—
Sparky Lyle	L	27	59	0	0	0	107.2	84	3	29	75	9-5	35	1.92
Lindy McDaniel	R	36	37	0	0	0	68.0	54	4	25	47	3-1	0	2.25
Fred Beene	R	29	29	1	0	0	57.2	55	3	24	37	1-3	3	2.34
Ron Klimkowski	R	28	16	2	0	0	31.1	32	3	15	11	0-3	1	4.02
Jim Roland†	L	29	16	0	0	0	25.0	27	3	16	13	0-1	0	5.04
Wade Blasingame†	L	28	12	1	0	0	17.0	14	5	11	7	0-1	0	4.24
Rich Hinton†	L	25	7	3	0	0	16.2	20	2	8	13	1-0	0	4.86
Casey Cox†	R	30	5	1	0	0	11.2	13	0	3	4	0-1	0	4.63
Jack Aker†	R	31	4	0	0	0	6.0	5	0	3	1	0-0	0	3.00
Al Closter	L	29	2	0	0	0	2.1	2	1	4	2	0-0	0	11.57
Steve Blateric	R	28	1	0	0	0	4.0	2	0	0	4	0-0	0	0.00

1972 Cleveland Indians 5th AL East 72-84 .462 14.0 GB

Ken Aspromonte

Player	Gm by Position	B	Age	G	AB	R	H	2B	3B	HR	RBI	BB	SO	SB	Avg	OBP	Slg
Ray Fosse	C124,1B3	R	25	134	457	42	110	20	1	10	41	45	46	5	.241	.312	.354
Chris Chambliss	1B119	L	23	121	466	51	136	27	2	6	44	26	63	3	.292	.327	.397
Jack Brohamer	2B132,3B1	L	22	136	527	49	123	13	2	5	35	27	46	3	.233	.271	.294
Graig Nettles	3B150	L	27	150	557	65	141	28	0	17	70	57	50	2	.253	.325	.395
Frank Duffy	SS126	R	25	130	385	23	92	16	4	3	27	31	54	6	.239	.297	.325
Buddy Bell	OF123,3B6	R	20	132	466	49	119	21	1	9	36	34	29	5	.255	.310	.363
Del Unser	OF119	L	27	132	383	29	91	12	0	1	17	28	46	5	.238	.288	.277
Alex Johnson	OF95	R	29	108	356	31	85	10	1	8	37	22	40	6	.239	.283	.340
Tom McCraw	OF84,1B38	L	31	129	391	43	101	13	5	7	33	41	47	12	.258	.333	.371
Eddie Leon	2B36,SS35	R	25	89	225	14	45	2	1	4	16	20	47	0	.200	.265	.271
John Lowenstein	OF58,1B2	L	25	68	151	16	32	8	1	6	21	20	43	2	.212	.304	.397
Roy Foster	OF45	R	26	73	143	19	32	4	0	4	13	21	23	0	.224	.325	.336
Jerry Moses	C39,1B3	R	25	52	141	9	31	3	0	4	14	11	29	0	.220	.290	.326
Ron Lolich	OF22	R	25	24	80	4	15	1	0	2	8	4	20	0	.188	.224	.275
Lou Camilli	SS8,2B2	S	25	39	41	2	6	2	0	0	3	3	8	0	.146	.205	.195
Kurt Bevacqua	OF11,3B1	R	25	19	35	2	4	0	0	1	1	3	10	0	.114	.184	.200
Jack Heidemann	SS10	R	22	10	20	0	3	0	0	0	0	2	6	0	.150	.261	.150
Fred Stanley†	SS5,2B1	R	24	6	12	1	2	1	0	0	0	2	3	0	.167	.286	.250
Steve Mingori	P41,OF1	L	28	42	8	0	1	0	0	0	0	0	2	0	.125	.125	.125
Adolfo Phillips	OF10	R	30	12	7	2	0	0	0	0	0	2	2	0	.000	.222	.000
Larry Johnson	C1	R	21	1	2	0	1	0	0	0	0	0	1	0	.500	.500	.500

Pitcher	T	Age	G	GS	CG	ShO	IP	H	HR	BB	SO	W-L	Sv	ERA
Gaylord Perry	R	33	41	40	29	5	342.2	253	17	82	234	24-16	1	1.92
Dick Tidrow	R	25	39	34	10	3	237.1	200	21	70	123	14-15	0	2.77
Milt Wilcox	R	22	32	27	4	2	156.0	145	18	72	90	7-14	0	3.40
Steve Dunning	R	23	16	16	1	0	105.0	98	16	43	52	6-4	0	3.26
Vince Colbert	R	26	22	11	1	1	74.2	74	8	38	36	1-7	0	4.58
Marcelino Lopez	L	28	4	2	0	0	8.1	8	0	10	1	0-0	0	5.40
Ed Farmer	R	22	46	1	0	0	61.1	51	10	27	33	2-5	7	4.40
Steve Mingori	L	28	41	0	0	0	57.0	67	4	36	47	0-6	10	3.95
Phil Hennigan	R	26	38	1	0	0	67.1	54	8	18	44	5-3	5	2.67
Denny Riddleberger	L	26	38	0	0	0	54.0	45	5	22	34	1-3	0	2.50
Ray Lamb	R	27	34	9	0	0	107.2	101	5	29	64	5-6	0	3.09
Mike Kilkenny†	L	27	22	7	1	0	58.0	51	5	39	44	4-1	1	3.41
Tom Hilgendorf	L	30	19	5	1	0	47.0	51	4	21	25	3-1	0	2.68
Steve Hargan	R	29	12	1	0	0	20.0	23	1	15	10	0-3	0	5.85
Bill Butler	L	25	6	2	0	0	11.2	9	1	10	6	0-0	0	1.54
Lowell Palmer†	R	24	1	0	0	0	2.0	2	0	2	3	0-0	0	4.50

1972 Milwaukee Brewers 6th AL East 65-91 .417 21.0 GB

Dave Bristol (10-20)/Roy McMillan (1-1)/Del Crandall (54-70)

Player	Gm by Position	B	Age	G	AB	R	H	2B	3B	HR	RBI	BB	SO	SB	Avg	OBP	Slg
Ellie Rodriguez	C114	R	26	116	355	31	101	14	2	2	35	52	43	1	.285	.382	.352
George Scott	1B139,3B23	R	28	152	578	71	154	24	4	20	88	43	130	16	.266	.321	.426
Ron Theobald	2B113	R	28	125	391	45	86	11	0	1	19	68	38	0	.220	.342	.256
Mike Ferraro	3B115,SS1	R	27	124	381	19	97	18	1	2	29	17	41	0	.255	.284	.323
Rick Auerbach	SS153	R	22	153	554	50	121	16	3	2	30	43	62	24	.218	.277	.269
Dave May	OF138	L	28	143	500	49	119	20	2	9	45	47	56	11	.238	.306	.340
John Briggs	OF106,1B28	L	28	135	418	58	111	14	1	21	65	84	67	1	.266	.347	.455
Joe Lahoud	OF97	L	25	111	316	35	75	9	3	12	34	45	54	3	.237	.331	.399
Bob Heise	2B49,3B24,SS9	R	25	95	271	23	72	10	1	0	12	12	14	1	.266	.301	.310
Billy Conigliaro	OF50	R	24	52	191	22	44	6	2	7	16	8	54	1	.230	.261	.393
Ollie Brown†	OF56,3B1	R	28	66	179	21	50	8	0	3	25	17	24	0	.279	.342	.374
Brock Davis	OF43	L	28	85	154	17	49	2	0	0	12	12	23	6	.318	.365	.331
Tommie Reynolds	OF41,1B1,3B1	S	30	72	130	13	26	5	1	2	13	10	25	0	.200	.262	.300
John Felske	C23,1B8	R	30	37	80	6	11	3	0	1	5	8	23	0	.138	.216	.213
Syd O'Brien†	3B9,2B7	R	27	31	58	5	12	2	0	1	5	2	13	0	.207	.230	.293
Darrell Porter	C18	L	20	18	56	2	7	1	0	1	2	5	21	0	.125	.210	.196
Ron Clark†	2B11,3B9	R	29	22	54	8	10	1	1	2	5	5	11	0	.185	.250	.352
Paul Ratliff	C13	L	28	22	42	1	3	0	0	1	4	2	23	0	.071	.114	.143
Bill Voss†	OF11	L	28	27	36	1	3	1	0	0	1	5	4	0	.083	.195	.111
Joe Azcue†	C9	R	32	11	14	0	2	0	0	0	0	1	5	0	.143	.200	.143
Curt Motton†	OF3	R	31	6	6	1	1	0	0	1	2	1	2	0	.167	.286	.667

Pitcher	T	Age	G	GS	CG	ShO	IP	H	HR	BB	SO	W-L	Sv	ERA
Jim Lonborg	R	30	33	30	11	2	223.0	197	17	76	143	14-12	1	2.83
Bill Parsons	R	23	33	30	10	2	214.0	194	27	68	111	13-13	0	3.91
Skip Lockwood	R	25	29	27	5	3	170.0	148	11	71	106	8-15	0	3.60
Ken Brett	L	23	26	22	2	1	133.0	121	13	49	74	7-12	0	4.53
Gary Ryerson	L	24	20	14	4	1	102.0	119	9	21	45	3-8	0	3.62
Jim Slaton	R	22	9	8	0	0	44.0	50	3	21	17	1-6	0	5.52
Ken Sanders	R	30	62	0	0	0	92.1	88	10	31	51	2-9	17	3.12
Frank Linzy	R	31	47	0	0	0	77.1	70	4	27	24	2-2	12	3.03
Jim Colborn	R	26	39	12	4	1	147.2	135	14	43	97	7-7	0	3.11
Earl Stephenson	L	24	35	8	1	0	80.1	79	5	33	33	3-5	0	3.25
Jerry Bell	R	24	25	3	0	0	70.2	50	1	33	20	5-1	0	1.66
Archie Reynolds	R	26	5	2	0	0	18.2	26	2	8	13	0-1	0	7.23
Chuck Taylor†	R	30	5	0	0	0	11.2	8	0	3	5	0-0	1	1.54
Ray Newman	L	27	4	0	0	0	7.0	4	0	2	1	0-0	1	0.00

1972 Oakland Athletics 1st AL West 93-62 .600 —

Dick Williams

Player	Gm by Position	B	Age	G	AB	R	H	2B	3B	HR	RBI	BB	SO	SB	Avg	OBP	Slg
Dave Duncan	C113	R	26	121	403	39	88	13	0	19	59	34	68	0	.218	.283	.392
Mike Epstein	1B137	L	29	138	455	63	123	18	2	26	70	68	68	0	.270	.376	.490
Tim Cullen	2B65,3B4,SS1	R	30	72	142	10	37	8	1	0	15	5	17	0	.261	.286	.331
Sal Bando	3B151,2B1	R	28	152	535	64	126	20	3	15	77	78	55	3	.236	.341	.368
Bert Campaneris	SS148	R	30	149	625	85	150	25	2	8	32	32	88	52	.240	.278	.325
Joe Rudi	OF147,3B1	R	25	147	593	94	181	32	9	19	75	37	62	3	.305	.345	.486
Reggie Jackson	OF135	L	26	135	499	72	132	25	2	25	75	59	125	9	.265	.350	.473
Angel Mangual	OF74	R	25	91	272	19	67	13	2	5	32	14	48	0	.246	.285	.364
Gene Tenace	C49,OF9,1B7*	R	25	82	227	22	51	5	3	5	32	24	42	0	.225	.307	.339
Larry Brown	2B46,3B1	R	32	47	142	11	26	2	0	0	4	13	8	0	.183	.250	.197
George Hendrick	OF41	R	22	58	121	10	22	1	1	4	15	3	22	3	.182	.205	.306
Matty Alou†	OF32,1B1	L	33	32	121	11	34	5	0	1	16	11	12	2	.281	.341	.347
Bill Voss†	OF34	L	28	40	97	10	22	5	1	1	5	9	16	0	.227	.296	.330
Ted Kubiak†	2B49,3B1	S	30	51	94	14	17	4	1	0	8	9	11	0	.181	.250	.245
Mike Hegan	1B64,OF3	L	29	98	79	13	26	3	1	1	5	7	20	1	.329	.375	.430
Ollie Brown†	OF16	R	28	20	54	5	13	1	0	1	4	6	14	1	.241	.317	.315
Don Mincher†	1B11	L	34	47	54	2	8	1	0	0	5	10	16	0	.148	.281	.167
Dick Green	2B26	R	31	26	42	1	12	1	1	0	3	3	5	0	.286	.348	.357
Marty Martinez†	2B17,SS6,3B1	S	30	22	40	3	5	0	0	0	1	3	6	0	.125	.186	.125
Bobby Brooks	OF11	R	26	15	39	4	7	0	0	0	5	8	8	0	.179	.319	.179
Dal Maxvill†	2B24,SS4	R	33	27	36	2	9	1	0	0	1	1	11	0	.250	.270	.278
Brant Alyea†	OF8	R	31	20	31	3	6	1	0	1	2	3	5	0	.194	.265	.323
Gonzalo Marquez	1B2	L	26	23	21	2	8	0	0	0	4	3	4	1	.381	.462	.381
Ron Clark†	2B11,3B3	R	29	14	15	1	4	2	0	0	1	2	4	0	.267	.353	.400
Adrian Garrett	OF2	L	29	14	11	0	0	0	0	0	0	1	4	0	.000	.083	.000
Curt Blefary†	1B1,2B1,OF1	L	28	8	11	1	5	2	0	0	1	0	1	0	.455	.417	.636
Bill McNulty	3B3	R	25	4	10	0	1	0	0	0	0	2	1	0	.100	.250	.100
Allan Lewis	OF6	S	30	24	10	5	2	1	0	0	2	0	1	8	.200	.200	.300
Dwain Anderson†	3B1,SS1	R	24	3	7	2	0	0	0	0	0	1	4	0	.000	.125	.000
Art Shamsky†		L	30	8	7	0	0	0	0	0	0	1	2	0	.000	.125	.000
Larry Haney	C4,2B1	R	29	5	4	0	0	0	0	0	0	0	1	0	.000	.000	.000
Orlando Cepeda†		R	34	3	3	0	0	0	0	0	0	0	0	0	.000	.000	.000

G. Tenace, 2 G at 2B, 2 G at 3B

Pitcher	T	Age	G	GS	CG	ShO	IP	H	HR	BB	SO	W-L	Sv	ERA
Catfish Hunter	R	26	38	37	16	5	295.1	200	21	70	191	21-7	0	2.04
Ken Holtzman	L	26	39	37	16	4	265.1	232	23	52	134	19-11	0	2.51
Blue Moon Odom	R	27	31	30	4	2	194.1	164	10	87	86	15-6	0	2.50
Vida Blue	L	22	25	23	5	4	151.0	117	11	48	111	6-10	0	2.80
Dave Hamilton	L	24	25	14	1	0	101.1	94	7	31	55	6-6	0	2.93
Denny McLain†	R	28	5	5	0	0	22.1	32	4	8	8	1-2	0	6.04
Rollie Fingers	R	25	65	0	0	0	111.1	85	8	32	113	11-9	21	2.51
Bob Locker	R	34	56	0	0	0	78.0	69	1	16	47	6-1	10	2.65
Darold Knowles	L	30	54	0	0	0	65.2	49	1	37	36	5-1	11	1.37
Joe Horlen	R	34	32	6	0	0	84.0	74	3	20	58	3-4	1	3.00
Gary Waslewski	R	30	8	0	0	0	17.2	12	3	8	8	0-3	0	2.04
Diego Segui†	R	34	7	3	0	0	22.2	25	2	7	11	0-1	0	3.57
Don Shaw†	L	28	3	0	0	0	5.1	12	2	2	4	0-1	0	16.88
Jim Roland†	L	29	2	0	0	0	2.1	5	0	0	0	0-0	0	3.86
Mike Kilkenny†	L	27	1	0	0	0	1.0	0	0	0	0	0-0	0	0.00

1972 Chicago White Sox 2nd AL West 87-67 .565 5.5 GB

Chuck Tanner

Player	Gm by Position	B	Age	G	AB	R	H	2B	3B	HR	RBI	BB	SO	SB	Avg	OBP	Slg
Ed Herrmann	C112	L	25	116	354	23	88	9	0	10	40	43	37	0	.249	.333	.359
Dick Allen	1B143,3B2	R	30	148	506	90	156	28	5	37	113	99	126	19	.308	.420	.603
Mike Andrews	2B145,1B5	R	28	148	505	58	111	18	0	7	50	70	78	2	.220	.313	.297
Ed Spiezio†	3B74	R	30	74	277	20	66	10	1	2	22	13	43	0	.238	.276	.303
Rich Morales	SS86,2B16,3B14	R	28	110	287	24	59	7	1	2	20	19	49	2	.206	.261	.258
Carlos May	OF145,1B5	L	24	148	523	83	161	26	3	12	68	79	70	23	.308	.405	.438
Pat Kelly	OF109	L	27	119	402	57	105	14	7	5	24	55	69	32	.261	.355	.368
Jay Johnstone	OF97	L	26	113	261	27	49	9	0	4	17	25	42	2	.188	.259	.268
Rick Reichardt	OF90	R	29	101	291	31	73	14	4	8	43	28	63	2	.251	.321	.409
Luis Alvarado	SS81,2B16,3B2	R	23	103	254	30	54	4	1	4	29	13	36	2	.213	.254	.283
Walt Williams	OF57,3B1	R	28	77	221	22	55	7	1	2	11	13	20	6	.249	.289	.317
Bill Melton	3B56	R	26	57	208	22	51	5	0	7	30	23	31	1	.245	.319	.370
Tom Egan	C46	R	26	50	141	8	27	3	0	2	9	4	48	0	.191	.224	.255
Jorge Orta	SS18,2B14,3B9	L	21	51	124	20	25	3	1	3	11	6	37	3	.202	.244	.315
Jim Lyttle	OF21	L	26	44	82	8	19	5	2	0	5	1	28	0	.232	.241	.341
Tony Muser	1B29,OF1	L	24	44	61	6	17	2	2	1	9	2	6	1	.279	.302	.426
Chuck Brinkman	C33	R	27	35	52	1	7	0	0	0	0	4	7	0	.135	.196	.135
Buddy Bradford	OF28	R	27	35	48	13	13	2	0	2	8	4	13	3	.271	.340	.438
Lee Richard	OF6,SS1	R	23	11	29	5	7	0	0	0	1	0	7	1	.241	.241	.241
Rudy Hernandez	SS6	R	20	8	21	0	4	0	0	0	1	0	3	0	.190	.190	.190
Hank Allen	3B6	R	31	9	21	1	3	0	0	0	0	0	2	0	.143	.143	.143
Jim Qualls	OF1	S	25	11	10	0	0	0	0	0	0	0	2	0	.000	.000	.000
Hugh Yancy	3B3	R	21	3	9	0	1	0	0	0	0	0	0	0	.111	.111	.111

Pitcher	T	Age	G	GS	CG	ShO	IP	H	HR	BB	SO	W-L	Sv	ERA
Wilbur Wood	L	30	49	49	20	8	376.2	325	28	74	193	24-17	0	2.51
Stan Bahnsen	R	27	43	41	5	1	252.1	263	22	73	157	21-16	0	3.60
Tom Bradley	R	25	40	40	11	2	260.0	225	19	65	209	15-14	0	2.98
Dave Lemonds	L	23	31	18	0	0	94.2	87	6	38	69	4-7	0	2.95
Eddie Fisher†	R	35	6	4	0	0	22.1	31	1	9	10	0-1	0	4.43
Terry Forster	L	20	62	0	0	0	100.0	75	0	44	104	6-5	29	2.25
Steve Kealey	R	25	40	0	0	0	57.1	50	4	12	37	3-2	4	3.30
Goose Gossage	R	20	36	1	0	0	80.0	72	2	44	57	7-1	2	4.28
Vicente Romo	R	29	28	0	0	0	51.2	47	5	18	46	3-0	1	3.31
Cy Acosta	R	25	26	0	0	0	34.2	25	2	17	28	3-0	5	1.56
Phil Regan†	R	35	10	0	0	0	13.1	18	1	6	4	0-1	0	4.05
Bart Johnson	R	22	9	0	0	0	13.2	18	2	13	9	0-3	1	9.22
Moe Drabowsky†	R	36	7	0	0	0	7.1	6	0	2	4	0-0	0	2.45
Jim Geddes	R	23	5	1	0	0	10.1	12	1	10	3	0-0	0	6.97
Ken Frailing	L	24	4	0	0	0	3.0	3	1	1	1	1-0	0	3.00
Denny O'Toole	R	23	3	0	0	0	5.0	10	0	2	5	0-0	0	5.40
Dan Neumeier	R	24	3	0	0	0	3.0	2	0	3	0	0-0	0	9.00

1972 Minnesota Twins 3rd AL West 77-77 .500 15.5 GB

Bill Rigney (36-34)/Frank Quilici (41-43)

Player	Gm by Position	B	Age	G	AB	R	H	2B	3B	HR	RBI	BB	SO	SB	Avg	OBP	Slg
George Mitterwald	C61	R	27	64	163	12	30	4	1	1	8	9	37	0	.184	.225	.239
Harmon Killebrew	1B130	R	36	139	433	53	100	13	2	26	74	94	91	0	.231	.367	.450
Rod Carew	2B139	L	26	142	535	61	170	21	6	0	51	43	60	12	.318	.369	.379
Eric Soderholm	3B79	R	23	93	287	28	54	10	0	13	39	19	48	3	.188	.245	.359
Danny Thompson	SS144	R	25	144	573	54	158	22	6	4	48	34	57	3	.276	.318	.356
Bobby Darwin	OF142	R	29	145	513	48	137	20	2	22	80	38	145	2	.267	.326	.442
Cesar Tovar	OF139	R	31	141	548	86	145	20	6	2	31	39	39	21	.265	.329	.334
Steve Brye	OF93	R	23	100	253	18	61	9	3	0	12	17	38	3	.241	.292	.300
Steve Braun	3B74,2B20,SS11*	L	24	121	402	40	116	21	0	2	50	45	38	4	.289	.360	.356
Jim Nettles	OF78,1B1	L	25	102	235	28	48	5	2	4	15	32	52	4	.204	.302	.294
Rich Reese	1B98,OF13	L	30	132	197	23	43	3	2	5	26	25	27	0	.218	.305	.330
Glenn Borgmann	C56	R	22	56	175	11	41	4	0	3	14	25	25	0	.234	.325	.309
Phil Roof	C61	R	31	61	146	16	30	11	1	3	12	6	27	0	.205	.235	.356
Charlie Manuel	OF28	L	28	63	122	6	25	5	0	1	8	4	16	0	.205	.233	.270
Rick Renick	OF21,1B6,3B4*	R	28	55	93	10	16	2	0	4	8	15	25	0	.172	.282	.323
Dan Monzon	2B13,3B5,SS3*	R	26	55	55	13	15	1	0	0	5	8	12	1	.273	.365	.291
Rick Dempsey	C23	R	22	25	40	0	8	1	0	0	0	6	8	0	.200	.304	.225
Tony Oliva	OF9	L	31	10	28	1	9	1	0	0	1	2	5	0	.321	.367	.357
Jim Holt	OF7,1B1	L	28	10	27	6	12	1	0	1	6	0	1	0	.444	.429	.593
Mike Adams	OF1	R	23	3	6	0	2	0	0	0	0	0	1	0	.333	.333	.333
Bucky Guth	SS1	R	24	3	3	1	0	0	0	0	0	0	0	0	.000	.000	.000

S. Braun, 9 G at OF; R. Renick, 1 G at SS; D. Monzon, 1 G at OF

Pitcher	T	Age	G	GS	CG	ShO	IP	H	HR	BB	SO	W-L	Sv	ERA
Bert Blyleven	R	21	39	38	11	3	287.1	247	22	69	228	17-17	0	2.73
Dick Woodson	R	27	36	36	9	3	251.2	193	19	101	150	14-14	0	2.72
Jim Perry	R	36	35	35	5	2	217.2	191	14	60	85	13-16	0	3.35
Ray Corbin	R	23	31	19	5	3	161.2	135	12	53	83	8-9	0	2.62
Jim Kaat	L	33	15	15	5	0	113.1	94	6	20	64	10-2	0	2.06
Dave Goltz	R	23	15	11	2	0	91.0	75	5	26	38	3-3	1	2.67
Wayne Granger	R	28	63	0	0	0	89.2	83	7	28	45	4-6	19	3.01
Dave LaRoche	L	24	62	0	0	0	95.1	72	9	39	79	5-7	10	2.83
Jim Strickland	L	26	25	0	0	0	36.0	28	7	19	30	3-1	3	2.50
Tom Norton	R	22	21	0	0	0	32.1	31	1	14	22	0-1	0	2.78
Bob Gebhard	R	29	13	0	0	0	21.0	36	3	13	13	0-1	1	8.57
Steve Luebber	R	22	2	0	0	0	2.1	3	0	2	1	0-0	0	0.00

1972 Kansas City Royals 4th AL West 76-78 .494 16.5 GB

Bob Lemon

Player	Gm by Position	B	Age	G	AB	R	H	2B	3B	HR	RBI	BB	SO	SB	Avg	OBP	Slg
Ed Kirkpatrick	C108,1B1	L	27	113	364	43	100	15	1	9	43	51	50	3	.275	.365	.396
John Mayberry	1B146	L	23	149	503	65	150	24	3	25	100	78	74	0	.298	.394	.507
Cookie Rojas	2B131,3B6,SS2	R	33	137	487	49	127	25	0	3	53	41	35	2	.261	.315	.331
Paul Schaal	3B123,SS1	R	29	127	435	47	99	19	3	6	41	61	59	1	.228	.323	.326
Freddie Patek	SS136	R	27	136	518	59	110	25	4	0	32	47	64	33	.212	.280	.276
Lou Piniella	OF150	R	28	151	574	65	179	33	4	11	72	34	59	7	.312	.356	.441
Amos Otis	OF137	R	25	143	540	75	158	28	2	11	54	50	59	28	.293	.352	.413
Richie Scheinblum	OF119	S	29	134	450	60	135	21	4	8	66	58	40	0	.300	.383	.418
Steve Hovley	OF68	L	27	105	196	24	53	5	1	3	24	24	29	3	.270	.351	.352
Bobby Floyd	3B30,SS29,2B2	R	28	61	134	9	24	3	0	0	5	5	29	1	.179	.209	.201
Jerry May	C41	R	28	53	116	10	22	5	1	1	4	14	13	0	.190	.277	.276
Carl Taylor	C21,OF7,1B6*	R	28	63	113	17	30	2	1	0	11	17	16	4	.265	.361	.301
Bobby Knoop	2B33,3B4	R	33	44	97	8	23	5	0	0	7	9	16	0	.237	.299	.289
Gail Hopkins	1B13,3B1	L	29	53	71	1	15	2	0	0	5	7	4	0	.211	.282	.239
Joe Keough	OF16	L	26	56	64	8	14	2	0	0	5	8	7	2	.219	.324	.250
Bob Oliver†	OF16	R	29	16	63	7	17	2	1	1	6	2	12	1	.270	.292	.381
Ron Hansen	SS6,3B4,2B1	R	34	16	30	2	4	0	0	0	2	3	6	0	.133	.212	.133
Jim Wohlford	2B8	R	21	15	25	3	6	1	0	0	0	2	6	0	.240	.321	.280
Dennis Paepke	C2	R	27	2	6	0	0	0	0	0	0	1	2	0	.000	.143	.000

C. Taylor, 5 G at 3B

Pitcher	T	Age	G	GS	CG	ShO	IP	H	HR	BB	SO	W-L	Sv	ERA
Dick Drago	R	27	34	33	11	2	239.1	230	22	51	135	12-17	0	3.01
Paul Splittorff	L	25	35	33	12	2	216.0	189	11	67	140	12-12	0	3.13
Roger Nelson	R	28	34	19	10	6	173.1	120	13	31	120	11-6	2	2.08
Mike Hedlund	R	25	29	16	1	0	113.0	119	10	41	52	5-7	0	4.78
Jim Rooker	L	29	18	10	4	2	72.0	78	3	24	44	5-6	0	4.38
Tom Murphy†	R	26	18	9	1	1	70.1	77	3	16	34	4-4	1	3.07
Monty Montgomery	R	25	9	8	1	1	56.1	55	2	17	24	3-3	0	3.04
Steve Busby	R	22	5	5	3	0	40.0	28	1	8	31	3-1	0	1.58
Tom Burgmeier	L	28	51	0	0	0	55.1	67	0	33	18	6-2	9	4.23
Ted Abernathy	R	39	45	0	0	0	58.1	44	2	19	28	3-4	5	1.70
Al Fitzmorris	R	26	38	2	0	0	101.0	99	10	28	51	2-5	3	3.74
Bruce Dal Canton	R	30	35	16	1	0	132.1	135	7	29	75	6-6	2	3.40
Norm Angelini	L	24	21	0	0	0	16.0	13	1	12	16	2-1	2	2.25
Ken Wright	R	25	17	0	0	0	18.1	15	0	15	18	1-2	4	4.91
Mike Jackson	L	26	7	3	0	0	19.2	24	0	14	15	1-2	0	6.41

1972 California Angels 5th AL West 75-80 .484 18.0 GB

Del Rice

Player	Gm by Position	B	Age	G	AB	R	H	2B	3B	HR	RBI	BB	SO	SB	Avg	OBP	Slg
Art Kusnyer	C63	R	26	64	179	13	37	2	1	2	13	16	33	0	.207	.276	.263
Bob Oliver†	1B127,OF8	R	29	134	509	47	137	20	4	19	70	27	97	4	.269	.307	.436
Sandy Alomar	2B154,SS4	S	28	155	610	65	146	20	3	1	25	47	55	20	.239	.292	.287
Ken McMullen	3B137	R	30	137	472	36	127	18	1	9	34	48	59	1	.269	.335	.369
Leo Cardenas	SS150	R	33	150	551	25	123	11	2	6	42	35	73	1	.223	.272	.283
Vada Pinson	OF134,1B1	L	33	136	484	56	133	24	2	7	49	30	54	17	.275	.321	.376
Lee Stanton	OF124	R	26	127	402	44	101	15	3	12	39	22	100	2	.251	.295	.393
Ken Berry	OF116	R	31	119	409	41	118	15	3	5	39	35	47	5	.289	.347	.377
Jim Spencer	1B35,OF24	L	25	82	212	13	47	5	0	1	14	12	25	0	.222	.262	.259
Mickey Rivers	OF48	L	23	58	159	18	34	6	2	0	7	8	26	4	.214	.256	.277
Jeff Torborg	C58	R	30	59	153	5	32	3	0	0	8	14	21	0	.209	.280	.229
John Stephenson	C56	L	31	66	146	14	40	3	1	2	17	11	8	0	.274	.342	.349
Andy Kosco†	OF36	R	30	49	142	15	34	4	2	6	13	5	23	1	.239	.267	.423
Billy Parker	3B21,2B9,OF5*	R	25	36	80	11	17	2	0	2	8	9	17	0	.213	.286	.313
Winston Llenas	3B10,2B2,OF2	R	28	44	64	3	17	3	0	0	7	3	8	0	.266	.290	.313
Jack Hiatt†	C17	R	29	22	45	4	13	0	1	1	5	5	11	0	.289	.360	.400
Syd O'Brien†	3B8,SS4,2B3*	R	27	36	39	10	7	2	0	1	1	6	10	0	.179	.289	.308
Curt Motton†	OF9	R	31	42	39	6	6	1	0	0	1	5	12	0	.154	.250	.179
Doug Howard	OF8,1B1,3B1	R	24	11	38	4	10	1	0	0	2	1	3	0	.263	.300	.289
Chris Coletta	OF7	L	27	14	30	5	9	1	0	1	7	1	4	0	.300	.323	.433
Tom Silverio	OF4	L	26	13	12	1	2	0	0	0	0	0	5	0	.167	.167	.167
Roger Repoz		L	31	3	3	0	1	0	0	0	0	0	2	0	.333	.333	.333
Billy Cowan		R	33	3	3	0	0	0	0	0	0	0	2	0	.000	.000	.000
Joe Azcue†	C2	R	32	3	2	0	0	0	0	0	0	0	1	0	.000	.000	.000

B. Parker, 1 G at SS; S. O'Brien, 1 G at 1B

Pitcher	T	Age	G	GS	CG	ShO	IP	H	HR	BB	SO	W-L	Sv	ERA
Nolan Ryan	R	25	39	39	20	9	284.0	166	14	157	329	19-16	0	2.28
Clyde Wright	L	31	35	35	15	2	251.0	229	14	80	87	18-11	0	2.98
Rudy May	L	27	35	30	10	3	205.1	162	15	82	169	12-11	1	2.94
Andy Messersmith	R	26	25	21	10	3	169.2	125	5	68	142	8-11	2	2.81
Rickey Clark	R	26	26	15	2	0	109.2	105	10	55	61	4-9	1	4.51
Dick Lange	R	23	2	1	0	0	7.2	7	0	2	8	0-0	0	4.70
Eddie Fisher†	R	35	43	1	0	0	81.1	73	6	31	32	4-5	4	3.76
Lloyd Allen	R	22	42	6	0	0	85.1	76	7	55	53	3-7	5	3.48
Steve Barber†	L	33	34	3	0	0	58.0	37	4	30	34	4-4	2	2.02
Mel Queen	R	30	17	0	0	0	31.0	31	2	19	19	0-0	0	4.35
Don Rose	R	25	16	4	0	0	42.2	49	9	19	39	1-4	0	4.22
Dave Sells	R	25	10	0	0	0	16.0	11	0	5	2	2-0	0	2.81
Alan Foster	R	25	8	0	0	0	12.2	12	3	6	11	0-1	0	4.97
Tom Dukes	R	29	7	0	0	0	11.0	11	1	0	8	0-1	1	1.64
Tom Murphy†	R	26	6	0	0	0	10.0	13	0	8	2	0-0	0	5.40
Paul Doyle	L	32	2	0	0	0	2.1	2	0	3	4	0-0	0	0.00

1972 Texas Rangers 6th AL West 54-100 .351 38.5 GB

Ted Williams

Player	Gm by Position	B	Age	G	AB	R	H	2B	3B	HR	RBI	BB	SO	SB	Avg	OBP	Slg
Dick Billings	C92,OF41,3B5*	R	29	133	469	41	119	15	1	5	58	29	77	1	.254	.296	.322
Frank Howard†	1B66,OF21	R	35	95	287	28	70	9	0	9	31	42	55	1	.244	.341	.369
Lenny Randle	2B65,SS4,OF2	S	23	74	249	23	48	13	0	2	21	13	51	4	.193	.235	.269
Dave Nelson	3B119,OF15	R	28	145	499	68	113	16	3	2	28	67	81	51	.226	.324	.283
Toby Harrah	SS106	R	23	116	374	47	97	14	3	1	31	34	31	16	.259	.316	.321
Ted Ford	OF119	R	25	129	429	43	101	19	1	14	50	37	80	4	.235	.297	.382
Joe Lovitto	OF103	S	21	117	330	23	74	9	1	1	19	37	54	13	.224	.306	.267
Elliott Maddox	OF94	R	24	98	294	40	74	7	2	0	10	49	53	20	.252	.361	.289
Larry Biittner	1B65,OF65	L	26	137	382	34	99	18	1	3	31	29	37	1	.259	.313	.335
Don Mincher†	1B59	L	34	61	191	23	45	10	0	6	39	46	23	2	.236	.384	.382
Vic Harris	2B58,SS1	S	22	61	186	8	26	5	1	0	10	12	39	7	.140	.192	.177
Dalton Jones†	3B23,2B17,1B7*	L	28	72	151	14	24	2	0	4	19	10	31	1	.159	.207	.252
Jim Mason	SS32,3B10	L	21	46	147	10	29	3	0	0	10	9	39	0	.197	.247	.218
Tom Grieve	OF49	R	24	64	142	12	29	2	1	3	11	11	39	1	.204	.271	.296
Hal King	C38	L	28	50	122	12	22	5	0	4	12	25	35	0	.180	.333	.320
Bill Fahey	C39	L	22	39	119	8	20	2	0	1	10	12	23	4	.168	.250	.210
Ted Kubiak†	2B25,SS15,3B1	S	30	46	116	5	26	3	0	0	7	12	12	0	.224	.300	.250
Jeff Burroughs	OF19,1B1	R	21	22	65	4	12	1	0	1	3	5	22	0	.185	.243	.246
Tom Ragland	2B13,3B5,SS3	R	26	25	58	3	10	2	0	0	2	5	11	0	.172	.238	.207
Marty Martinez†	SS5,3B4,2B1	S	30	26	41	3	6	1	1	0	3	2	8	0	.146	.182	.220
Ken Suarez	C17	R	29	25	33	2	5	1	0	0	4	1	4	0	.152	.167	.182
Jim Driscoll	2B4,3B2	L	28	15	18	0	0	0	0	0	0	2	3	0	.000	.100	.000

D. Billings, 1 G at 1B; D. Jones, 2 G at OF

Pitcher	T	Age	G	GS	CG	ShO	IP	H	HR	BB	SO	W-L	Sv	ERA
Dick Bosman	R	28	29	29	1	1	173.1	183	11	48	105	8-10	0	3.63
Rich Hand	R	23	30	28	2	1	170.2	139	12	103	109	10-14	0	3.32
Pete Broberg	R	22	39	25	3	2	176.1	153	14	85	133	5-12	1	4.29
Bill Gogolewski	R	24	36	21	2	1	150.2	136	9	58	95	4-11	2	4.24
Don Stanhouse	R	21	24	16	1	0	104.2	83	8	73	78	2-9	0	3.78
Paul Lindblad	L	30	66	0	0	0	99.2	95	7	29	51	5-8	9	2.62
Horacio Pina	R	27	60	0	0	0	76.0	61	3	43	60	2-7	15	3.20
Jim Panther	R	27	58	4	0	0	93.2	101	8	46	44	5-9	0	4.13
Mike Paul	L	27	49	20	2	1	161.2	149	4	52	108	8-9	1	2.17
Casey Cox†	R	30	35	4	0	0	65.1	73	7	26	27	3-5	4	4.41
Jim Shellenback	L	28	22	6	0	0	57.0	46	6	16	30	2-4	1	3.47
Steve Lawson	L	21	13	0	0	0	16.0	13	1	10	13	0-0	1	2.81
Rich Hinton†	L	25	5	0	0	0	11.1	7	1	10	4	0-1	0	2.38
Jim Roland†	L	29	5	0	0	0	3.1	7	1	2	4	0-0	0	8.10
Jerry Janeski	R	26	4	1	0	0	12.2	11	0	7	7	0-1	0	2.84
Jan Dukes	L	26	3	0	0	0	2.1	1	0	5	0	0-0	0	3.86

»1972 Pittsburgh Pirates 1st NL East 96-59 .619 —

Bill Virdon

Player	Gm by Position	B	Age	G	AB	R	H	2B	3B	HR	RBI	BB	SO	SB	Avg	OBP	Slg
Manny Sanguillen	C127,OF2	R	28	136	520	55	155	18	8	7	71	21	38	1	.298	.322	.404
Willie Stargell	1B101,OF32	L	32	138	495	75	145	28	2	33	112	65	129	1	.293	.373	.558
Dave Cash	2B97	R	24	99	425	58	120	22	4	3	30	22	31	9	.282	.316	.374
Richie Hebner	3B121	L	24	124	427	63	128	24	4	19	72	52	54	0	.300	.378	.508
Gene Alley	SS114,3B4	R	31	119	347	30	86	12	2	3	36	38	52	0	.248	.321	.320
Al Oliver	OF138,1B3	L	25	140	565	88	176	27	4	12	89	34	44	2	.312	.352	.437
Vic Davalillo	OF97,1B8	L	35	117	368	59	117	19	2	4	28	26	44	14	.318	.367	.413
Roberto Clemente	OF94	R	37	102	378	68	118	19	7	10	60	29	49	0	.312	.356	.479
Rennie Stennett	2B49,OF41,SS6	R	21	109	370	43	106	14	5	3	30	9	43	4	.286	.307	.376
Gene Clines	OF83	R	25	107	311	52	104	15	6	0	17	16	47	12	.334	.369	.421
Bob Robertson	1B89,OF23,3B11	R	25	115	306	25	59	11	0	12	41	41	84	1	.193	.291	.346
Jackie Hernandez	SS68,3B4	R	31	72	176	12	33	7	1	1	14	9	43	0	.188	.227	.256
Milt May	C33	L	21	57	139	12	39	10	0	0	14	10	13	0	.281	.325	.353
Jose Pagan	3B32,OF2	R	37	53	127	11	32	9	0	3	8	5	17	0	.252	.284	.394
Bill Mazeroski	2B15,3B3	R	35	34	64	3	12	4	0	0	3	3	5	0	.188	.217	.250
Richie Zisk	OF12	R	23	17	37	4	7	3	0	0	4	7	10	0	.189	.318	.270
Chuck Goggin	2B1	S	26	5	7	0	2	0	0	0	0	1	1	0	.286	.375	.286
Frank Taveras	SS4	R	22	4	3	0	0	0	0	0	0	1	1	0	.000	.250	.000
Fernando Gonzalez	3B1	R	22	3	2	0	0	0	0	0	0	0	2	0	.000	.000	.000
Charlie Sands		L	24	1	1	0	0	0	0	0	0	0	0	0	.000	.000	.000

Pitcher	T	Age	G	GS	CG	ShO	IP	H	HR	BB	SO	W-L	Sv	ERA
Steve Blass	R	30	33	32	11	2	249.2	227	18	84	117	19-8	0	2.49
Bob Moose	R	24	31	30	6	3	226.0	213	11	47	144	13-10	1	2.91
Nelson Briles	R	28	28	27	9	3	195.2	185	14	43	120	14-11	0	3.08
Dock Ellis	R	27	25	25	4	1	163.1	156	6	33	96	15-7	0	2.70
Bruce Kison	R	22	32	18	6	1	152.0	123	11	69	102	9-7	3	3.26
Dave Giusti	R	32	54	0	0	0	74.2	59	3	20	54	7-4	22	1.93
Ramon Hernandez	L	31	53	0	0	0	70.0	50	3	22	47	5-0	14	1.67
Bob Miller	R	33	36	0	0	0	54.1	54	3	24	18	5-2	3	2.65
Bob Johnson	R	29	31	11	1	0	115.2	98	14	46	79	4-4	3	2.96
Luke Walker	L	28	26	12	2	0	92.2	98	4	34	48	4-6	2	3.40
Bob Veale†	L	36	5	0	0	0	9.0	10	0	7	6	0-0	0	6.00
Gene Garber	R	24	4	0	0	0	6.1	7	3	3	3	0-0	0	7.11
Jim McKee	R	25	2	0	0	0	5.0	2	0	1	4	1-0	0	0.00

1972 Chicago Cubs 2nd NL East 85-70 .548 11.0 GB

Leo Durocher (46-44)/Whitey Lockman (39-26)

Player	Gm by Position	B	Age	G	AB	R	H	2B	3B	HR	RBI	BB	SO	SB	Avg	OBP	Slg
Randy Hundley	C113	R	30	114	357	23	78	12	0	5	30	22	62	1	.218	.261	.294
Jim Hickman	1B77,OF27	R	35	115	368	65	100	15	2	17	64	52	64	3	.272	.364	.462
Glenn Beckert	2B118	R	31	120	474	51	128	22	2	3	43	23	17	2	.270	.304	.344
Ron Santo	3B129,2B3,SS1*	R	32	133	464	68	140	25	5	17	74	69	75	1	.302	.391	.487
Don Kessinger	SS146	S	29	149	577	77	158	20	6	1	39	67	44	8	.274	.351	.334
Billy Williams	OF144,1B5	L	34	150	574	95	191	34	6	37	122	62	59	3	.333	.398	.606
Jose Cardenal	OF137	R	28	143	533	96	155	24	6	17	70	55	58	25	.291	.356	.454
Rick Monday	OF134	L	26	138	434	68	108	22	5	11	42	78	102	12	.249	.362	.399
Carmen Fanzone	3B36,1B21,2B13*	R	28	86	222	26	50	11	0	8	42	35	45	2	.225	.333	.383
Joe Pepitone	1B66	L	31	66	214	23	56	5	0	8	21	13	22	1	.262	.309	.397
Paul Popovich	2B36,SS8,3B1	S	31	58	129	8	25	3	2	1	11	12	8	0	.194	.261	.271
Bill North	OF48	S	24	66	127	22	23	2	3	0	4	13	33	6	.181	.262	.244
Ken Rudolph	C41	R	25	42	106	10	25	1	1	2	9	6	14	1	.236	.283	.321
J.C. Martin	C17	L	35	25	50	3	12	3	0	0	7	5	9	1	.240	.304	.300
Gene Hiser	OF15	L	23	32	46	2	9	0	0	0	4	6	8	1	.196	.288	.196
Ellie Hendricks†	C16	L	31	17	43	7	5	1	0	2	6	13	8	0	.116	.321	.279
Pat Bourque	1B7	L	25	11	27	3	7	1	0	0	5	2	2	0	.259	.310	.296
Tommy Davis†	1B3,OF2	R	33	15	26	3	7	1	0	0	6	2	3	0	.269	.321	.308
Art Shamsky†	1B4	L	30	15	16	1	2	0	0	0	1	3	3	0	.125	.263	.125
Dave Rosello	SS5	R	22	5	12	2	3	0	0	1	3	3	2	0	.250	.400	.500
Al Montreuil	2B5	R	28	5	11	0	1	0	0	0	0	1	4	0	.091	.167	.091
Jim Tyrone	OF4	R	23	13	8	1	0	0	0	0	0	0	3	1	.000	.000	.000
Pete LaCock	OF3	L	20	5	6	3	3	0	0	0	4	0	1	1	.500	.429	.500
Frank Fernandez	C1	R	29	3	3	0	0	0	0	0	0	0	2	0	.000	.000	.000
Chris Ward		L	23	1	1	0	0	0	0	0	0	1	0	0	.000	.000	.000
Frank Coggins		S	28	6	1	1	0	0	0	0	0	1	0	0	.000	.500	.000

R. Santo, 1 G at OF; C. Fanzone, 1 G at SS, 1 G at OF

Pitcher	T	Age	G	GS	CG	ShO	IP	H	HR	BB	SO	W-L	Sv	ERA
Fergie Jenkins	R	28	36	36	23	5	289.1	253	32	62	184	20-12	0	3.20
Burt Hooton	R	22	33	31	9	3	218.1	201	13	81	132	11-14	0	2.80
Milt Pappas	R	33	29	28	10	3	195.0	187	18	29	80	17-7	0	2.77
Bill Hands	R	32	32	28	6	3	189.0	168	12	47	96	11-8	0	3.00
Rick Reuschel	R	23	21	18	5	4	129.0	127	3	29	87	10-8	0	2.93
Jack Aker†	R	31	48	0	0	0	67.0	65	4	23	36	6-6	17	2.96
Dan McGinn	L	28	42	2	0	0	62.2	78	5	29	42	0-5	4	5.89
Tom Phoebus†	R	30	37	1	0	0	83.1	76	9	45	59	3-3	6	3.78
Steve Hamilton	L	36	22	0	0	0	17.0	24	1	8	13	1-0	0	4.76
Bill Bonham	R	23	19	4	0	0	57.2	56	4	25	49	1-1	4	3.12
Juan Pizarro	L	35	16	7	1	0	59.1	66	7	32	24	4-5	1	3.94
Larry Gura	L	24	7	0	0	0	12.1	11	3	3	13	0-0	0	3.65
Joe Decker	R	25	5	1	0	0	12.2	9	1	4	7	1-0	0	2.13
Phil Regan†	R	35	5	0	0	0	4.0	6	0	2	2	0-1	0	2.25
Clint Compton	L	21	1	0	0	0	2.0	2	0	2	0	0-0	0	9.00

1972 New York Mets 3rd NL East 83-73 .532 13.5 GB — Yogi Berra

Player	Gm by Position	B	Age	G	AB	R	H	2B	3B	HR	RBI	BB	SO	SB	Avg	OBP	Slg
Duffy Dyer	C91,OF1	R	26	94	325	33	75	17	3	8	36	28	71	0	.231	.299	.375
Ed Kranepool	1B108,OF1	L	27	122	327	28	88	15	1	8	34	34	35	1	.269	.336	.394
Ken Boswell	2B94	L	26	100	355	35	75	9	1	9	33	32	35	2	.211	.274	.318
Jim Fregosi	3B85,SS6,1B3	R	30	101	340	31	79	15	4	5	32	38	71	0	.232	.311	.344
Bud Harrelson	SS115	S	28	115	418	54	90	10	4	1	24	58	57	12	.215	.313	.266
Tommie Agee	OF109	R	29	114	422	52	96	23	0	13	47	53	92	8	.227	.317	.374
John Milner	OF91,1B10	L	22	117	362	52	86	12	2	17	38	51	74	2	.238	.340	.423
Cleon Jones	OF84,1B20	R	29	106	375	39	92	15	1	5	52	30	83	1	.245	.305	.331
Ted Martinez	2B47,SS42,OF15*	R	24	103	330	22	74	5	5	1	19	12	49	7	.224	.254	.279
Wayne Garrett	3B82,2B22	L	24	111	298	41	69	13	3	2	29	70	58	3	.232	.374	.315
Rusty Staub	OF65	L	28	66	239	32	70	11	0	9	38	31	13	0	.293	.372	.452
Jerry Grote	C59,3B3,OF1	R	29	64	205	15	43	5	1	3	21	26	27	1	.210	.304	.288
Willie Mays†	OF49,1B11	R	41	69	195	27	52	9	1	8	19	43	43	1	.267	.402	.446
Dave Marshall	OF42	L	29	72	156	21	39	5	0	4	11	22	28	3	.250	.346	.359
Dave Schneck	OF33	L	23	37	123	7	23	3	2	3	10	10	26	0	.187	.254	.317
Jim Beauchamp	1B35,OF5	R	32	58	120	10	29	1	0	5	19	7	33	0	.242	.282	.375
Lute Barnes	2B14,SS6	R	25	24	72	5	17	2	2	0	6	6	4	0	.236	.291	.319
Bill Sudakis	1B7,C5	S	26	18	49	3	7	0	0	1	7	6	14	0	.143	.236	.204
Don Hahn	OF10	R	23	17	37	0	6	0	0	0	1	4	12	0	.162	.244	.162
Joe Nolan	C3	L	21	4	10	0	0	0	0	0	0	1	3	0	.000	.091	.000

T. Martinez, 2 G at 3B

Pitcher	T	Age	G	GS	CG	ShO	IP	H	HR	BB	SO	W-L	Sv	ERA
Tom Seaver	R	27	35	35	13	3	262.0	215	23	77	249	21-12	0	2.92
Jon Matlack	L	22	34	32	8	4	244.0	215	14	71	169	15-10	0	2.32
Gary Gentry	R	25	32	26	3	0	164.0	153	20	75	120	7-10	0	4.01
Jerry Koosman	L	29	34	24	4	1	163.0	155	14	52	147	11-12	1	4.14
Jim McAndrew	R	28	28	23	4	0	160.2	133	12	38	81	11-8	1	2.80
Tug McGraw	L	27	54	0	0	0	106.0	71	3	40	92	8-6	27	1.70
Danny Frisella	R	26	39	0	0	0	67.1	63	8	20	46	5-8	9	3.34
Ray Sadecki	L	31	34	2	0	0	75.2	73	3	31	38	2-1	0	3.09
Chuck Taylor†	R	30	20	0	0	0	31.0	44	2	9	9	0-0	2	5.52
Bob Rauch	R	23	19	0	0	0	27.0	27	3	21	23	0-1	1	5.00
Buzz Capra	R	24	14	6	0	0	53.0	50	7	27	45	3-2	0	4.58
Brent Strom	L	23	11	5	0	0	30.1	34	7	15	20	0-3	0	6.82
Hank Webb	R	22	6	2	0	0	18.1	18	1	9	15	0-0	0	4.42
Tommy Moore	R	23	3	1	0	0	12.1	12	1	1	5	0-0	0	2.92

1972 St. Louis Cardinals 4th NL East 75-81 .481 21.5 GB — Red Schoendienst

Player	Gm by Position	B	Age	G	AB	R	H	2B	3B	HR	RBI	BB	SO	SB	Avg	OBP	Slg
Ted Simmons	C135,1B15	S	22	152	594	70	180	36	6	16	96	29	57	1	.303	.336	.465
Matty Alou†	1B66,OF39	L	33	108	404	46	127	17	2	3	31	24	23	11	.314	.353	.389
Ted Sizemore	2B111	R	27	120	439	53	116	17	4	2	38	37	36	8	.264	.324	.335
Joe Torre	3B117,1B27	R	31	149	544	71	157	26	6	11	81	54	64	3	.289	.357	.419
Dal Maxvill†	SS95,2B11	R	33	105	276	22	61	6	1	1	23	31	47	0	.221	.299	.261
Lou Brock	OF149	L	33	153	621	81	193	26	8	3	42	47	93	63	.311	.359	.393
Luis Melendez	OF105	R	22	118	332	32	79	11	3	5	28	25	34	5	.238	.292	.334
Jose Cruz	OF102	L	24	117	332	33	78	14	4	2	23	36	54	9	.235	.309	.319
Bernie Carbo†	OF92,3B1	L	24	99	302	42	78	13	1	7	34	57	56	0	.258	.381	.377
Ed Crosby	SS43,2B38,3B14	L	23	101	276	27	60	9	1	0	19	18	27	1	.217	.269	.257
Donn Clendenon	1B36	R	36	61	136	13	26	4	0	4	9	17	37	1	.191	.279	.309
Dwain Anderson†	SS43,3B13,2B1	R	24	57	135	12	36	4	1	1	8	8	23	0	.267	.313	.333
Ken Reitz	3B20	R	21	21	78	5	28	4	0	0	10	2	4	0	.359	.370	.410
Joe Hague†	1B22,OF3	L	28	27	76	8	18	5	1	3	11	17	18	0	.237	.368	.447
Skip Jutze	C17	R	26	21	71	1	17	2	0	0	5	1	16	0	.239	.247	.268
Jorge Roque	OF24	R	22	32	67	3	7	2	1	1	5	6	19	1	.104	.176	.209
Mick Kelleher	SS23	R	24	23	63	5	10	2	1	0	1	6	15	0	.159	.232	.222
Jerry McNertney	C10	R	35	39	48	3	10	3	1	0	9	6	16	0	.208	.291	.313
Mike Tyson	2B11,SS2	R	22	13	37	1	7	1	0	0	0	1	9	0	.189	.211	.216
Bill Stein	3B4,OF4	R	25	14	35	2	11	0	1	2	3	0	7	1	.314	.314	.543
Brant Alyea†	OF3	R	31	13	19	0	3	1	0	0	1	0	6	0	.158	.158	.211
Bill Voss†	OF2	L	28	11	15	1	4	2	0	0	3	2	2	0	.267	.333	.400
Ron Allen	1B5	S	28	7	11	2	1	0	0	1	1	3	5	0	.091	.286	.364
Mike Fiore†	1B6,OF1	L	27	17	10	0	1	0	0	0	1	2	3	0	.100	.250	.100
Marty Martinez†	SS3,2B2,3B1	S	30	9	7	0	3	0	0	0	2	0	1	0	.429	.429	.429

Pitcher	T	Age	G	GS	CG	ShO	IP	H	HR	BB	SO	W-L	Sv	ERA
Rick Wise	R	26	35	35	20	2	269.0	250	16	71	142	16-16	0	3.11
Bob Gibson	R	36	34	34	23	4	278.0	226	14	88	208	19-11	0	2.46
Reggie Cleveland	R	24	33	33	11	3	230.2	229	21	60	153	14-15	0	3.94
Al Santorini	R	24	30	19	3	3	133.2	136	6	46	72	8-11	0	4.11
Scipio Spinks	R	24	16	16	6	0	118.0	96	5	59	93	5-5	0	2.67
Don Durham	R	23	10	8	1	0	47.2	42	1	22	35	2-7	0	4.34
Jim Bibby	R	27	6	6	0	0	40.1	29	4	19	28	1-3	0	3.35
Diego Segui†	R	34	33	0	0	0	55.2	47	2	32	54	3-1	9	3.07
Joe Grzenda	L	35	30	0	0	0	35.0	46	1	17	15	1-0	0	5.66
Moe Drabowsky†	R	36	30	0	0	0	27.2	29	4	14	22	1-1	2	2.60
Tony Cloninger	R	31	17	0	0	0	26.0	29	2	19	11	0-2	0	5.19
Lowell Palmer†	R	24	16	2	0	0	34.2	30	2	26	25	0-3	0	3.89
Dennis Higgins	R	32	15	1	0	0	22.2	19	0	22	20	1-2	1	3.97
John Cumberland†	L	25	14	1	0	0	21.2	23	6	7	7	1-1	0	6.65
Ray Bare	R	23	14	0	0	0	16.2	18	0	6	5	0-1	1	0.54
Charlie Hudson	L	22	12	0	0	0	12.1	10	0	7	4	1-0	0	5.11
Rich Folkers	L	25	9	0	0	0	13.1	12	0	5	7	1-0	0	3.38
Don Shaw†	L	28	8	0	0	0	3.0	5	1	3	0	0-1	0	9.00
Al Hrabosky	L	22	5	0	0	0	7.0	2	0	3	9	1-0	0	0.00
Lance Clemons	L	24	3	1	0	0	5.1	8	1	5	2	0-1	0	10.13
Santiago Guzman	R	22	1	0	0	0	1.0	1	1	0	0	0-0	0	9.00
Tim Plodinec	R	25	1	0	0	0	0.1	3	0	0	0	0-0	0	27.00

1972 Montreal Expos 5th NL East 70-86 .449 26.5 GB — Gene Mauch

Player	Gm by Position	B	Age	G	AB	R	H	2B	3B	HR	RBI	BB	SO	SB	Avg	OBP	Slg
John Boccabella	C73,1B7,3B1	R	31	83	207	14	47	8	1	1	10	9	29	1	.227	.259	.290
Mike Jorgensen	1B76,OF28	L	23	113	372	48	86	12	3	13	47	53	75	12	.231	.332	.384
Ron Hunt	2B122,3B5	R	31	129	443	56	112	20	0	0	18	51	29	9	.253	.363	.298
Bob Bailey	3B134,OF5,1B3	R	29	143	489	55	114	10	4	16	57	59	112	6	.233	.315	.368
Tim Foli	SS148,2B1	R	21	149	540	45	130	12	2	2	35	25	43	11	.241	.280	.281
Ken Singleton	OF137	S	25	142	507	77	139	23	2	14	50	70	99	5	.274	.363	.410
Boots Day	OF117	L	24	128	386	32	90	7	4	0	30	29	44	3	.233	.288	.272
Clyde Mashore	OF74	R	27	93	176	23	40	7	1	3	23	14	41	6	.227	.278	.330
Ron Fairly	OF70,1B68	L	33	140	446	51	124	15	1	17	68	46	45	3	.278	.348	.430
Tim McCarver†	C45,OF14,3B6	L	30	77	239	19	60	5	1	5	20	19	14	4	.251	.309	.343
Ron Woods	OF73	R	29	97	221	21	57	5	1	10	31	22	33	3	.258	.321	.425
Terry Humphrey	C65	R	22	69	215	13	40	8	0	1	9	16	38	4	.186	.248	.237
Hector Torres	2B60,SS16,OF2*	R	26	83	181	14	28	4	1	2	7	13	26	0	.155	.215	.221
Jim Fairey	OF37	L	27	86	141	9	33	7	0	1	15	10	21	1	.234	.285	.305
Hal Breeden	1B26,OF1	R	28	42	87	6	20	2	0	3	10	7	15	0	.230	.281	.356
Coco Laboy	3B24,2B3,SS2	R	31	28	69	6	18	2	0	3	14	10	16	0	.261	.350	.420
John Bateman†	C7	R	31	18	29	0	7	1	0	0	3	3	4	0	.241	.313	.276
Steve Renko	P30,1B1	R	27	32	24	0	7	0	0	0	0	0	5	0	.292	.292	.292
Bobby Wine	3B21,SS4,2B1	R	33	34	18	2	4	1	0	0	0	0	2	0	.222	.222	.278
Pepe Mangual	OF3	R	20	8	11	2	3	0	0	0	0	1	5	0	.273	.333	.273

H. Torres, 1 G at P, 1 G at 3B

Pitcher	T	Age	G	GS	CG	ShO	IP	H	HR	BB	SO	W-L	Sv	ERA
Bill Stoneman	R	28	36	35	13	4	250.2	213	15	102	171	12-14	0	2.98
Mike Torrez	R	25	34	33	13	0	243.1	215	15	103	112	16-12	0	3.33
Carl Morton	R	28	27	27	3	1	172.0	170	16	53	51	7-13	0	3.92
Ernie McAnally	R	25	29	27	4	2	170.0	165	13	71	102	6-15	0	3.81
Balor Moore	L	21	22	22	6	3	147.2	122	15	59	161	9-9	0	3.47
Mike Marshall	R	29	65	0	0	0	116.0	82	3	47	95	14-8	18	1.78
John Strohmayer	R	25	48	0	0	0	76.2	73	6	31	50	1-2	3	3.52
Tom Walker	R	23	46	0	0	0	74.2	71	4	22	42	2-2	2	2.89
Steve Renko	R	27	30	12	0	0	97.0	96	11	67	66	1-10	0	5.20
Joe Gilbert	L	20	22	0	0	0	33.0	41	3	18	25	0-1	0	8.45
Denny Lemaster	L	33	13	0	0	0	19.2	28	2	6	13	2-0	0	7.78
Hector Torres	R	26	1	0	0	0	0.2	5	0	0	0	0-0	0	27.00

1972 Philadelphia Phillies 6th NL East 59-97 .378 37.5 GB — Frank Lucchesi (26-50)/Paul Owens (33-47)

Player	Gm by Position	B	Age	G	AB	R	H	2B	3B	HR	RBI	BB	SO	SB	Avg	OBP	Slg
John Bateman†	C80	R	31	82	252	10	56	9	0	3	17	8	39	0	.222	.246	.294
Tom Hutton	1B87,OF48	L	26	134	381	40	99	16	2	4	38	56	24	5	.260	.354	.344
Denny Doyle	2B119	L	28	123	442	33	110	14	2	1	26	31	33	6	.249	.295	.296
Don Money	3B151,SS2	R	25	152	536	54	119	16	2	15	52	41	92	5	.222	.278	.343
Larry Bowa	SS150	S	26	152	579	67	145	11	13	1	31	32	51	17	.250	.291	.320
Greg Luzinski	OF145,1B2	R	21	150	563	66	158	33	5	18	68	42	114	0	.281	.332	.453
Willie Montanez	OF130,1B14	L	24	147	531	60	131	39	3	13	64	58	108	1	.247	.320	.405
Bill Robinson	OF72	R	29	82	188	19	45	9	1	8	21	5	30	2	.239	.258	.426
Deron Johnson	1B62	R	33	96	230	19	49	4	1	9	31	26	69	0	.213	.298	.357
Terry Harmon	2B50,SS15,3B5	R	28	73	218	35	62	8	2	2	13	29	28	3	.284	.372	.367
Tim McCarver†	C40	L	30	45	152	14	36	8	0	2	14	17	15	1	.237	.318	.329
Joe Lis	1B30,OF14	R	25	62	140	13	34	6	0	6	18	30	34	0	.243	.380	.414
Oscar Gamble	OF35,1B1	L	22	74	135	17	32	5	2	1	13	19	16	0	.237	.331	.326
Roger Freed	OF46	R	26	73	129	10	29	4	0	6	18	23	39	0	.225	.344	.395
Mike Ryan	C46	R	30	46	106	6	19	4	0	2	10	10	25	0	.179	.254	.274
Mike Anderson	OF35	R	21	36	103	8	20	5	1	2	5	19	36	1	.194	.317	.320
Ron Stone	OF15	L	29	41	54	3	9	0	1	0	3	9	11	0	.167	.286	.204
Bob Boone	C14	R	24	16	51	4	14	1	0	1	4	5	7	1	.275	.333	.353
Pete Koegel	1B8,C5,3B4*	R	24	41	49	3	7	2	0	0	1	6	16	0	.143	.236	.184
Mike Schmidt	3B11,2B1	R	22	13	34	2	7	0	0	1	3	5	15	0	.206	.325	.294
Byron Browne	OF9	R	29	21	21	2	4	0	0	0	0	1	8	0	.190	.227	.190
Craig Robinson	SS4	R	23	5	15	0	3	1	0	0	0	1	2	0	.200	.250	.267

P. Koegel, 2 G at OF

Pitcher	T	Age	G	GS	CG	ShO	IP	H	HR	BB	SO	W-L	Sv	ERA
Steve Carlton	L	27	41	41	30	8	346.1	257	17	87	310	27-10	0	1.97
Ken Reynolds	L	25	33	23	2	0	154.1	149	17	60	87	2-15	0	4.26
Billy Champion	R	24	30	22	2	0	132.2	155	11	54	54	4-14	0	5.09
Woodie Fryman†	L	32	23	17	3	2	119.2	131	15	39	69	4-10	1	4.36
Jim Nash†	R	27	9	8	0	0	37.1	46	5	17	15	0-8	0	6.27
Dave Downs	R	20	4	4	1	1	23.0	25	1	3	5	1-1	0	2.74
Wayne Twitchell	R	24	49	15	1	0	139.2	138	6	56	112	5-9	1	4.06
Dick Selma	R	28	46	10	1	0	98.2	91	13	73	58	2-9	3	5.56
Bucky Brandon	R	31	42	6	0	0	104.1	106	9	46	67	7-7	2	3.45
Barry Lersch	R	27	36	8	3	1	100.2	86	8	33	48	4-6	0	3.04
Mac Scarce	L	23	31	0	0	0	36.2	30	6	20	40	1-2	4	3.44
Billy Wilson	R	29	23	0	0	0	30.0	26	1	11	18	1-1	0	3.30
Chris Short	L	34	19	0	0	0	23.0	24	3	8	20	1-1	1	3.91
Joe Hoerner†	L	35	15	0	0	0	21.2	21	2	5	12	0-2	3	2.08
Gary Neibauer†	R	27	9	2	0	0	18.2	17	1	14	7	0-2	0	5.30
Bob Terlecki	R	27	9	0	0	0	13.1	16	2	10	5	0-0	0	4.73

1972 Cincinnati Reds 1st NL West 95-59 .617 — — Sparky Anderson

Player	Gm by Position	B	Age	G	AB	R	H	2B	3B	HR	RBI	BB	SO	SB	Avg	OBP	Slg
Johnny Bench	C129,OF17,1B7*	R	24	147	538	87	145	22	2	40	125	100	84	6	.270	.379	.541
Tony Perez	1B136	R	30	136	515	64	146	33	7	21	90	55	121	4	.283	.349	.497
Joe Morgan	2B149	L	28	149	552	122	161	23	4	16	73	115	44	58	.292	.417	.435
Denis Menke	3B130,1B11	R	31	140	447	41	104	19	2	9	50	58	76	0	.233	.322	.345
Dave Concepcion	SS114,3B9,2B1	R	24	119	378	40	79	13	2	2	29	32	65	13	.209	.272	.270
Pete Rose	OF154	S	31	154	645	107	198	31	11	6	57	73	46	10	.307	.382	.417
Bobby Tolan	OF149	L	26	149	604	88	171	28	5	8	82	44	88	42	.283	.334	.386
Cesar Geronimo	OF106	L	24	120	255	32	70	9	7	4	29	24	64	2	.275	.344	.412
Darrel Chaney	SS64,2B12,3B10	S	24	83	196	29	49	7	2	2	19	29	28	1	.250	.345	.337
George Foster	OF47	R	23	59	145	15	29	4	1	2	12	5	44	2	.200	.230	.283
Joe Hague†	1B22,OF19	L	28	69	138	17	34	7	1	4	20	20	18	1	.246	.340	.399
Ted Uhlaender	OF27	L	31	73	113	9	18	3	0	0	6	13	11	0	.159	.246	.186
Bill Plummer	C36,1B1,3B1	R	25	38	102	8	19	4	0	2	9	4	20	0	.186	.211	.284
Hal McRae	OF12,3B11	R	26	61	97	9	27	4	0	5	26	2	10	0	.278	.295	.474
Julian Javier	3B19,2B5,1B1	R	35	44	91	3	19	2	0	2	12	6	11	1	.209	.255	.297
Bernie Carbo†	OF4	L	24	19	21	2	3	0	0	0	0	6	3	0	.143	.357	.143
Sonny Ruberto	C2	R	26	2	3	0	0	0	0	0	0	0	1	0	.000	.250	.000
Pat Corrales†	C2	R	31	2	1	0	0	0	0	0	0	2	0	0	.000	.667	.000

J. Bench, 4 G at 3B

Pitcher	T	Age	G	GS	CG	ShO	IP	H	HR	BB	SO	W-L	Sv	ERA
Jack Billingham	R	29	36	31	8	4	217.2	197	18	64	137	12-12	1	3.18
Ross Grimsley	L	22	30	28	4	1	197.1	194	18	50	79	14-8	1	3.06
Gary Nolan	R	24	25	25	6	2	176.0	147	13	30	90	15-5	0	1.99
Wayne Simpson	R	23	24	22	1	0	130.1	124	17	49	70	8-5	0	4.14
Jim McGlothlin	R	28	31	21	3	1	145.0	165	15	49	69	9-8	0	3.91
Don Gullett	L	21	31	16	2	0	134.2	127	15	43	96	9-10	2	3.94
Clay Carroll	R	31	65	0	0	0	96.0	89	5	32	51	6-4	37	2.25
Pedro Borbon	R	25	62	2	0	0	122.0	115	5	32	48	8-3	11	3.17
Tom Hall	L	24	47	7	1	1	124.1	77	13	56	134	10-1	8	2.61
Ed Sprague	R	26	33	1	0	0	56.2	55	6	26	25	3-3	0	4.13
Jim Merritt	L	28	4	1	0	0	8.0	13	1	2	4	1-0	0	4.50
Dave Tomlin	L	23	3	0	0	0	4.0	7	2	1	2	0-0	0	9.00
Joe Gibbon†	L	37	2	0	0	0	0.1	3	1	1	1	0-0	0	54.00

1972 Houston Astros 2nd NL West 84-69 .549 10.5 GB

Harry Walker (67-54)/Salty Parker (1-0)/Leo Durocher (16-15)

Player	Gm by Position	B	Age	G	AB	R	H	2B	3B	HR	RBI	BB	SO	SB	Avg	OBP	Slg
Johnny Edwards	C105	L	34	108	332	33	89	16	2	5	40	50	39	2	.268	.358	.373
Lee May	1B146	R	29	148	592	87	168	31	2	29	98	52	145	3	.284	.343	.490
Tommy Helms	2B139	R	31	139	518	45	134	20	5	5	60	24	27	4	.259	.291	.346
Doug Rader	3B152	R	27	152	553	70	131	24	7	22	90	57	120	5	.237	.309	.425
Roger Metzger	SS153	S	24	153	641	84	142	12	3	2	38	60	71	23	.222	.288	.259
Jimmy Wynn	OF144	R	30	145	542	117	148	29	3	24	90	103	99	17	.273	.389	.470
Bob Watson	OF143,1B2	R	26	147	548	74	171	27	4	16	86	53	83	1	.312	.378	.464
Cesar Cedeno	OF137	R	21	139	559	103	179	39	8	22	82	56	62	55	.320	.385	.537
Larry Howard	C53,OF1	R	27	54	157	16	35	7	0	2	13	17	30	0	.223	.299	.306
Norm Miller	OF29	L	26	67	107	18	26	4	0	4	13	13	23	1	.243	.331	.393
Jimmy Stewart	OF11,1B9,2B8*	S	33	68	96	14	21	5	2	0	9	6	9	0	.219	.257	.313
Jesus Alou	OF23	R	30	52	93	8	29	4	1	0	11	7	5	0	.312	.366	.376
Bobby Fenwick	2B17,SS4,3B2	R	25	36	50	7	9	3	0	0	4	3	13	0	.180	.226	.240
Bob Stinson	C12,OF3	S	26	27	35	3	6	1	0	0	2	1	6	0	.171	.211	.200
Jack Hiatt†	C10	R	29	10	25	2	5	3	0	0	0	5	5	0	.200	.333	.320
Rich Chiles	OF2	L	22	9	11	0	3	1	0	0	2	1	1	0	.273	.333	.364
Gary Sutherland	2B1,3B1	R	27	5	8	0	1	0	0	0	1	0	0	0	.125	.125	.125
Cliff Johnson	C1	R	24	5	4	0	1	0	0	0	0	2	0	0	.250	.500	.250

J. Stewart, 2 G at 3B

Pitcher	T	Age	G	GS	CG	ShO	IP	H	HR	BB	SO	W-L	Sv	ERA
Don Wilson	R	27	33	33	13	3	228.1	196	16	66	172	15-10	0	2.68
Larry Dierker	R	25	31	31	12	5	214.2	209	14	51	115	15-8	0	3.40
Jerry Reuss	L	23	33	30	4	1	192.0	177	14	83	174	9-13	1	4.17
Dave Roberts	L	27	35	28	7	3	192.0	227	18	57	111	12-7	2	4.50
Ken Forsch	R	25	30	24	1	0	156.1	163	19	62	113	6-8	0	3.91
Jim Ray	R	27	54	0	0	0	90.1	77	10	44	50	10-9	8	4.28
George Culver	R	28	45	0	0	0	97.1	73	7	43	82	6-2	2	3.05
Fred Gladding	R	36	42	0	0	0	48.2	38	1	12	18	5-6	14	2.77
Tom Griffin	R	24	39	5	1	1	94.1	92	7	38	83	5-4	3	3.24
Jim York	R	24	26	0	0	0	36.0	45	3	18	25	0-1	0	5.25
Wade Blasingame†	L	28	10	0	0	0	8.1	4	1	8	9	0-0	0	8.64
Joe Gibbon†	L	37	9	0	0	0	7.1	13	2	5	4	0-0	0	9.82
Mike Cosgrove	L	21	7	1	0	0	13.2	16	2	3	7	0-1	1	4.61
J.R. Richard	R	22	4	1	0	0	6.0	10	0	8	8	1-0	0	13.50

1972 Los Angeles Dodgers 3rd NL West 85-70 .548 10.5 GB

Walter Alston

Player	Gm by Position	B	Age	G	AB	R	H	2B	3B	HR	RBI	BB	SO	SB	Avg	OBP	Slg
Chris Cannizzaro	C72	R	34	73	200	14	48	6	0	2	18	31	38	0	.240	.341	.300
Wes Parker	1B120,OF5	S	32	130	427	45	119	14	3	4	59	62	43	3	.279	.367	.354
Lee Lacy	2B58	R	24	60	243	34	63	7	3	0	12	19	37	5	.259	.312	.313
Steve Garvey	3B85,1B3	R	23	96	294	36	79	14	2	9	30	19	36	4	.269	.312	.422
Bill Russell	SS121,OF6	R	23	129	434	47	118	19	5	4	34	34	64	14	.272	.326	.366
Willie Davis	OF146	L	32	149	615	81	178	22	7	19	79	27	61	20	.289	.317	.441
Manny Mota	OF99	R	34	118	371	57	120	16	5	5	48	27	15	4	.323	.375	.434
Frank Robinson	OF95	R	36	103	342	41	86	6	1	19	59	55	76	2	.251	.353	.442
Bobby Valentine	2B49,3B39,OF16*	R	22	119	391	42	107	11	2	3	32	27	33	5	.274	.319	.335
Bill Buckner	OF61,1B35	L	22	105	383	47	122	14	3	5	37	17	13	10	.319	.348	.410
Willie Crawford	OF74	L	25	96	243	28	61	7	3	8	27	35	55	4	.251	.349	.403
Jim Lefebvre	2B33,3B11	S	30	70	169	11	34	8	0	5	24	17	30	0	.201	.271	.337
Duke Sims†	C48	L	31	51	151	7	29	7	0	2	11	17	23	0	.192	.278	.278
Billy Grabarkewitz	3B24,2B19,SS2	R	26	53	144	17	24	4	0	4	16	18	53	3	.167	.265	.278
Maury Wills	SS31,3B26	S	39	71	132	16	17	3	1	0	4	10	18	1	.129	.190	.167
Steve Yeager	C35	R	23	35	106	18	29	0	1	4	15	16	26	0	.274	.374	.406
Dick Dietz	C22	R	30	27	56	4	9	1	0	1	6	14	11	2	.161	.329	.232
Tom Paciorek	1B6,OF6	R	25	11	47	4	12	4	0	1	6	1	7	1	.255	.271	.404
Davey Lopes	2B11	R	27	11	42	6	9	4	0	0	1	7	6	4	.214	.327	.310
Ron Cey	3B11	R	24	11	37	3	10	1	0	1	3	7	10	0	.270	.400	.378
Joe Ferguson	C7,OF2	R	25	8	24	2	7	3	0	1	5	2	4	0	.292	.346	.542
Terry McDermott	1B7	R	21	9	23	2	3	0	0	0	0	2	8	0	.130	.200	.130

B. Valentine, 10 G at SS

Pitcher	T	Age	G	GS	CG	ShO	IP	H	HR	BB	SO	W-L	Sv	ERA
Don Sutton	R	27	33	33	18	9	272.2	186	13	63	207	19-9	0	2.08
Claude Osteen	L	32	33	33	14	4	252.0	232	16	69	100	20-11	0	2.64
Al Downing	L	31	31	30	7	4	202.2	196	13	67	117	9-9	0	2.98
Tommy John	L	29	29	29	4	1	186.2	172	14	40	117	11-5	0	2.89
Bill Singer	R	28	26	25	4	3	169.1	148	8	60	101	6-16	0	3.67
Jim Brewer	L	34	51	0	0	0	78.1	41	6	25	69	8-7	17	1.26
Pete Richert	L	32	37	0	0	0	52.0	42	3	18	38	2-3	6	2.25
Pete Mikkelsen	R	32	33	0	0	0	57.2	65	3	23	41	5-5	5	4.06
Mike Strahler	R	25	19	2	1	0	47.0	42	5	22	25	1-2	0	3.26
Hoyt Wilhelm	R	48	16	0	0	0	25.1	20	0	15	9	0-1	1	4.62
Ron Perranoski†	L	36	9	0	0	0	16.2	19	0	8	5	2-0	0	2.70
Doug Rau	L	23	7	3	2	0	32.2	18	1	11	19	2-2	0	2.20
Jose Pena	R	29	5	0	0	0	7.1	13	1	6	4	0-0	0	8.59
Charlie Hough	R	24	2	0	0	0	2.2	2	0	2	4	0-0	0	3.38

1972 Atlanta Braves 4th NL West 70-84 .455 25.0 GB

Lum Harris (47-57)/Eddie Mathews (23-27)

Player	Gm by Position	B	Age	G	AB	R	H	2B	3B	HR	RBI	BB	SO	SB	Avg	OBP	Slg
Earl Williams	C116,3B21,1B20	R	23	151	565	72	146	24	2	28	87	62	118	0	.258	.336	.457
Hank Aaron	1B109,OF15	R	38	129	449	75	119	10	0	34	77	92	55	4	.265	.390	.514
Felix Millan	2B120	R	28	125	498	46	128	19	3	1	38	23	28	6	.257	.292	.313
Darrell Evans	3B123	L	25	125	418	67	106	12	0	19	71	90	58	4	.254	.384	.419
Marty Perez	SS141	R	25	141	479	33	109	13	1	1	28	30	55	0	.228	.276	.265
Ralph Garr	OF131	L	26	134	554	87	180	22	0	12	53	25	41	25	.325	.359	.430
Dusty Baker	OF123	R	23	127	446	62	143	27	2	17	76	45	68	4	.321	.383	.504
Mike Lum	OF109,1B2	L	26	123	369	40	84	14	2	9	38	50	52	1	.228	.323	.350
Rico Carty	OF78	R	32	86	271	31	75	12	2	6	29	44	33	0	.277	.378	.402
Oscar Brown	OF59	R	26	76	164	19	37	5	1	3	16	4	29	0	.226	.244	.323
Paul Casanova	C43	R	30	49	136	8	28	3	0	2	10	4	28	0	.206	.229	.272
Sonny Jackson	SS17,OF10,3B6	L	27	60	126	20	30	6	3	0	8	7	9	1	.238	.278	.333
Larvell Blanks	2B18,SS4,3B2	R	22	33	85	10	28	5	0	1	7	7	12	0	.329	.376	.424
Jim Breazeale	1B16,3B1	L	22	52	85	10	21	2	0	5	17	6	12	0	.247	.297	.447
Orlando Cepeda†	1B22	R	34	28	84	6	25	3	0	4	9	7	17	0	.298	.352	.476
Gil Garrido	2B21,SS10,3B3	R	31	40	75	11	20	1	0	0	7	11	6	1	.267	.368	.280
Bob Didier	C11	S	23	13	40	5	12	2	1	0	5	2	4	0	.300	.341	.400
Rod Gilbreath	2B7,3B4	R	19	18	38	2	9	1	0	0	1	2	10	1	.237	.293	.263
Rowland Office	OF1	L	19	2	5	1	2	0	0	0	0	1	2	0	.400	.500	.400

Pitcher	T	Age	G	GS	CG	ShO	IP	H	HR	BB	SO	W-L	Sv	ERA
Phil Niekro	R	33	38	36	17	1	282.1	254	22	53	164	16-12	0	3.06
Ron Reed	R	29	31	30	11	1	213.0	222	18	60	111	11-15	0	3.93
George Stone	L	25	31	16	2	1	111.0	143	18	44	63	6-11	1	5.51
Tom Kelley	R	28	27	14	2	1	116.1	122	12	65	59	5-7	0	4.56
Denny McLain†	R	28	15	8	2	0	54.0	60	12	18	21	3-5	1	6.50
Jimmy Freeman	L	21	6	6	1	0	36.0	40	5	22	18	2-2	0	6.00
Cecil Upshaw	R	29	42	0	0	0	53.2	50	5	19	23	3-5	13	3.69
Ron Schueler	R	24	37	18	3	0	144.2	122	16	60	96	5-8	2	3.67
Pat Jarvis	R	31	37	6	0	0	98.2	94	7	44	56	11-7	2	4.10
Jim Hardin	R	28	26	9	1	0	79.2	93	11	24	25	5-2	2	4.41
Joe Hoerner†	L	35	25	0	0	0	23.1	34	4	8	19	1-3	2	6.56
Mike McQueen	L	21	23	7	1	0	78.1	79	11	44	40	0-5	1	4.60
Jim Nash†	R	27	11	4	0	0	31.1	35	2	25	10	1-1	1	5.46
Gary Neibauer†	R	27	8	0	0	0	17.1	27	6	6	8	0-0	0	7.27
Tom House	L	25	8	0	0	0	9.1	7	1	6	7	0-0	2	2.89
Steve Barber†	L	33	5	0	0	0	15.2	18	1	6	6	0-0	0	5.74
Larry Jaster	L	28	5	1	0	0	12.1	12	4	8	6	1-1	0	5.11

1972 San Francisco Giants 5th NL West 69-86 .445 26.5 GB

Charlie Fox

Player	Gm by Position	B	Age	G	AB	R	H	2B	3B	HR	RBI	BB	SO	SB	Avg	OBP	Slg
Dave Rader	C127	L	23	133	459	44	119	14	1	6	41	29	31	1	.259	.306	.333
Willie McCovey	1B74	L	34	81	263	30	56	8	0	14	35	38	45	0	.213	.316	.403
Tito Fuentes	2B152	S	28	152	572	64	151	33	6	7	53	39	56	16	.264	.310	.379
Al Gallagher	3B69	R	26	82	233	19	52	3	1	2	18	33	39	2	.223	.317	.270
Chris Speier	SS150	R	22	150	562	74	151	25	2	15	71	82	92	9	.269	.361	.400
Bobby Bonds	OF153	R	26	153	626	118	162	29	5	26	80	60	137	44	.259	.326	.446
Ken Henderson	OF123	S	26	130	439	60	113	21	2	18	51	38	66	14	.257	.317	.437
Garry Maddox	OF121	R	22	125	458	62	122	26	7	12	58	14	97	13	.266	.293	.432
Dave Kingman	3B59,1B56,OF22	R	23	135	472	65	106	17	4	29	83	51	140	16	.225	.303	.462
Ed Goodson	1B42	L	24	58	150	15	42	1	1	6	30	8	12	0	.280	.319	.420
Jim Howarth	OF25,1B4	L	25	74	119	16	28	4	0	1	7	16	18	3	.235	.326	.294
Fran Healy	C43	R	25	45	99	12	15	4	0	1	8	13	24	0	.152	.257	.222
Chris Arnold	3B17,2B7,SS4	R	24	51	84	8	19	3	1	1	4	8	12	0	.226	.293	.321
Jim Ray Hart	3B20	R	30	24	79	10	24	5	0	5	8	6	10	0	.304	.360	.557
Bernie Williams	OF15	R	23	46	68	12	13	3	1	3	9	7	22	0	.191	.267	.397
Gary Matthews	OF19	R	21	20	62	11	18	1	1	4	14	7	13	0	.290	.357	.532
Willie Mays†	OF14	R	41	19	49	8	9	2	0	0	3	17	5	3	.184	.394	.224
Gary Thomasson	1B7,OF2	L	20	10	27	5	9	1	1	0	1	1	7	0	.333	.357	.444
Damaso Blanco	3B19,SS8,2B3	R	30	39	20	5	7	1	0	0	2	4	3	2	.350	.440	.400
Russ Gibson	C5	R	33	5	12	0	2	0	1	0	3	0	4	0	.167	.167	.333
Jimmy Rosario	OF1	S	27	7	2	1	0	0	0	0	0	0	0	0	.000	.000	.000

Pitcher	T	Age	G	GS	CG	ShO	IP	H	HR	BB	SO	W-L	Sv	ERA
Ron Bryant	L	24	35	28	11	4	214.0	176	20	77	107	14-7	0	2.90
Sam McDowell	L	29	28	25	4	0	164.1	155	12	86	122	10-8	0	4.33
Juan Marichal	R	34	25	24	6	0	165.0	176	15	46	72	6-16	0	3.71
Steve Stone	R	24	27	16	4	1	123.2	97	11	49	85	6-8	0	2.98
Don Carrithers	R	22	25	14	2	0	90.0	108	10	42	42	4-8	1	5.80
Frank Reberger	R	28	20	11	2	0	99.1	97	10	37	52	3-4	0	3.99
Jim Willoughby	R	23	11	11	7	0	87.2	72	8	14	40	6-4	0	2.36
John Cumberland†	L	25	9	6	0	0	25.0	38	6	7	8	0-4	0	8.64
Charlie Williams	R	24	3	2	0	0	9.1	14	3	3	3	0-2	0	8.68
Jerry Johnson	R	28	48	0	0	0	73.1	73	4	40	57	8-6	8	4.42
Jim Barr	R	24	44	18	8	2	179.0	166	16	41	86	8-10	2	2.87
Don McMahon	R	42	44	0	0	0	63.0	46	8	21	45	3-3	5	3.71
Randy Moffitt	R	23	40	0	0	0	70.2	72	5	30	37	1-5	4	3.69
Elias Sosa	R	22	8	0	0	0	15.2	10	0	12	10	0-1	3	2.30
John Morris	L	30	7	0	0	0	6.1	9	2	2	5	0-0	0	4.26

1972 San Diego Padres 6th NL West 58-95 .379 36.5 GB

Preston Gomez (4-7)/Don Zimmer (54-88)

Player	Gm by Position	B	Age	G	AB	R	H	2B	3B	HR	RBI	BB	SO	SB	Avg	OBP	Slg
Fred Kendall	C82,1B1	R	23	91	273	18	59	3	4	6	18	11	42	0	.216	.247	.322
Nate Colbert	1B150	R	26	151	563	87	141	27	2	38	111	70	127	15	.250	.333	.508
Derrel Thomas	2B83,SS49,OF3	R	21	130	500	48	115	15	5	5	36	41	73	9	.230	.290	.310
Dave Roberts	3B84,2B20,SS3*	R	21	100	418	38	102	17	0	5	33	18	64	7	.244	.275	.321
Enzo Hernandez	SS107,OF3	R	23	114	329	33	64	11	2	1	15	22	25	24	.195	.243	.249
Leron Lee	OF96	L	24	101	370	50	111	23	7	12	47	29	58	2	.300	.353	.497
Jerry Morales	OF96,3B4	R	23	115	347	38	83	15	7	4	18	35	54	4	.239	.307	.357
Cito Gaston	OF94	R	28	111	379	30	102	14	0	7	44	22	76	0	.269	.313	.361
Johnny Jeter	OF91	R	27	110	326	25	72	4	3	7	21	18	92	11	.221	.266	.316
Larry Stahl	OF76,1B1	L	31	107	297	31	67	9	3	7	20	31	67	1	.226	.298	.347
Garry Jestadt	2B48,3B25,SS3	R	25	92	256	15	63	5	1	6	22	13	21	0	.246	.281	.344
Pat Corrales†	C43	R	31	44	119	6	23	0	0	0	6	11	26	0	.193	.267	.193
Curt Blefary†	C12,1B6,3B3*	L	28	74	102	10	20	3	0	3	9	19	18	0	.196	.320	.314
Dave Campbell	3B31,2B1	R	30	33	100	6	24	5	0	0	3	11	12	0	.240	.315	.290
Bob Barton	C29	R	30	29	88	1	17	1	0	0	9	2	19	2	.193	.209	.205
Fred Stanley†	2B21,SS17,3B4	R	24	39	85	15	17	2	0	0	2	12	19	1	.200	.306	.224
Ollie Brown†	OF17	R	28	23	70	3	12	2	0	0	3	5	9	0	.171	.224	.200
Randy Elliott	OF13	R	21	14	49	5	10	3	1	0	6	2	11	0	.204	.235	.306
Dave Hilton	3B13	R	21	13	47	2	10	2	1	0	5	3	6	1	.213	.260	.298
Joe Goddard	C12	R	21	12	35	0	7	2	0	0	2	5	9	0	.200	.300	.257
Ed Spiezio†	3B5	R	30	20	29	2	4	2	0	0	4	1	6	1	.138	.161	.207
Rafael Robles	SS15,3B1	R	24	18	24	1	4	0	0	0	0	0	3	0	.167	.167	.167
John Grubb	OF6	L	23	7	21	4	7	1	1	0	1	1	3	0	.333	.364	.476
Don Mason	2B3	L	27	9	11	1	2	0	0	0	0	1	1	0	.182	.250	.182
Ivan Murrell	OF1	R	27	5	7	0	1	0	0	0	1	0	3	0	.143	.143	.143
Mike Fiore†		L	27	7	6	0	0	0	0	0	0	1	3	0	.000	.143	.000

D. Roberts, 1 G at C; C. Blefary, 3 G at OF

Pitcher	T	Age	G	GS	CG	ShO	IP	H	HR	BB	SO	W-L	Sv	ERA
Steve Arlin	R	26	38	37	12	3	250.0	217	19	122	159	10-21	0	3.60
Clay Kirby	R	24	34	34	9	2	238.2	197	21	116	175	12-14	0	3.13
Fred Norman	L	29	42	28	10	6	211.2	195	18	88	167	9-11	2	3.44
Bill Greif	R	22	34	22	2	1	125.1	143	18	47	91	5-16	2	5.60
Tom Phoebus†	R	30	1	1	0	0	5.2	3	2	6	8	0-1	0	7.94
Gary Ross	R	24	60	0	0	0	91.2	87	2	49	46	4-3	3	2.45
Mike Corkins	R	26	47	9	2	1	140.0	125	14	62	108	6-9	6	3.54
Ed Acosta	R	28	46	2	0	0	89.0	105	7	30	53	3-6	0	4.45
Mike Caldwell	L	23	42	20	4	2	163.2	183	10	49	102	7-11	2	4.01
Mark Schaeffer	L	24	41	0	0	0	41.0	52	3	28	25	2-0	1	4.61
Al Severinsen	R	27	17	0	0	0	21.1	13	1	7	9	0-1	1	2.53
Steve Simpson	R	23	9	0	0	0	11.1	10	0	8	9	0-2	2	4.76
Mike Kilkenny†	L	27	5	0	0	0	4.1	7	1	3	5	0-0	0	8.31
Ron Taylor	R	34	4	0	0	0	5.0	9	5	0	0	0-0	0	12.60
Ralph Garcia	R	23	3	0	0	0	5.0	4	0	3	3	0-0	0	1.80

»1973 Baltimore Orioles 1st AL East 97-65 .599 — Earl Weaver

Player	Gm by Position	B	Age	G	AB	R	H	2B	3B	HR	RBI	BB	SO	SB	Avg	OBP	Slg
Earl Williams	C95,1B42	R	24	132	459	58	109	18	1	22	83	66	107	0	.237	.333	.425
Boog Powell	1B111	L	31	114	370	52	98	13	1	11	54	85	64	0	.265	.398	.395
Bobby Grich	2B162	R	24	162	581	82	146	29	7	12	50	107	91	17	.251	.373	.387
Brooks Robinson	3B154	R	36	155	549	53	141	17	2	9	72	55	50	2	.257	.326	.344
Mark Belanger	SS154	R	29	154	470	60	106	15	1	0	27	49	54	13	.226	.302	.262
Paul Blair	OF144,DH1	R	29	146	500	73	140	25	3	10	64	43	72	18	.280	.334	.402
Don Baylor	OF110,1B6,DH1	R	24	118	405	64	116	20	4	11	51	35	48	32	.286	.357	.437
Rich Coggins	OF101,DH1	L	22	110	389	54	124	19	9	7	41	28	24	17	.319	.363	.468
Tommy Davis	DH127,1B4	R	34	137	552	53	169	20	3	7	89	30	56	11	.306	.341	.391
Al Bumbry	OF86,DH7	L	26	110	356	73	120	15	11	7	34	34	49	23	.337	.398	.500
Merv Rettenmund	OF90	R	30	95	321	59	84	17	2	9	44	57	38	11	.262	.378	.411
Andy Etchebarren	C51	R	30	54	152	16	39	9	1	2	23	12	21	1	.257	.317	.368
Terry Crowley	DH23,OF10,1B7	L	26	54	131	16	27	4	0	3	15	16	14	0	.206	.297	.305
Ellie Hendricks	C38	L	32	41	101	9	18	5	1	3	15	10	22	0	.178	.257	.337
Frank Baker	SS32,2B7,1B1*	L	26	44	63	10	12	1	2	1	11	7	7	0	.190	.268	.317
Enos Cabell	1B23,3B1	R	23	32	47	12	10	2	0	1	3	3	7	1	.213	.250	.319
Larry Brown	3B15,2B1	R	33	17	28	4	7	0	0	1	5	5	4	0	.250	.353	.357
Jim Fuller	OF5,1B2,DH1	R	22	9	26	2	3	0	0	2	4	1	17	0	.115	.148	.346
Doug DeCinces	3B8,2B2,SS1	R	22	10	18	2	2	0	0	0	3	1	5	0	.111	.158	.111
Sergio Robles	C8	R	27	8	13	0	1	0	0	0	0	3	1	0	.077	.250	.077
Curt Motton	DH1,OF1	R	32	5	6	2	2	0	0	1	4	1	1	0	.333	.429	.833
Skip Lockwood†		R	26	37	0	0	0	0	0	0	0	0	0	0	—	—	—

F. Baker, 1 G at 3B

Pitcher	T	Age	G	GS	CG	ShO	IP	H	HR	BB	SO	W-L	Sv	ERA
Mike Cuellar	L	36	38	38	17	2	267.0	265	29	84	140	18-13	0	3.27
Dave McNally	L	30	38	38	17	4	266.0	247	16	81	87	17-17	0	3.21
Jim Palmer	R	27	38	37	19	6	296.1	225	16	113	158	22-9	1	2.40
Doyle Alexander	R	22	29	26	10	0	174.2	169	19	52	63	12-8	0	3.86
Jesse Jefferson	R	24	18	15	3	0	100.2	104	15	46	52	6-5	0	4.11
Don Hood	L	23	8	4	1	1	32.1	31	1	6	18	3-2	1	3.90
Grant Jackson	L	30	45	0	0	0	80.1	54	5	24	47	8-0	9	1.90
Bob Reynolds	R	26	42	1	0	0	111.0	88	3	31	77	7-5	9	1.95
Eddie Watt	R	32	30	0	0	0	71.0	62	8	21	38	3-4	5	3.30
Orlando Pena†	R	39	11	2	0	0	44.2	36	10	8	23	1-1	1	4.03
Wayne Garland	R	22	4	1	0	0	16.0	14	1	7	10	0-1	0	3.94
Mickey Scott†	L	25	1	0	0	0	1.2	2	1	2	2	0-0	0	5.40

1973 Boston Red Sox 2nd AL East 89-73 .549 8.0 GB — Eddie Kasko (88-73)/Eddie Popowski (1-0)

Player	Gm by Position	B	Age	G	AB	R	H	2B	3B	HR	RBI	BB	SO	SB	Avg	OBP	Slg
Carlton Fisk	C131,DH3	R	25	135	508	65	125	21	0	26	71	37	99	7	.246	.309	.441
Carl Yastrzemski	1B107,3B31,OF14	L	33	152	540	82	160	25	4	19	95	105	58	9	.296	.407	.463
Doug Griffin	2B113	R	26	113	396	43	101	14	5	1	33	21	42	7	.255	.293	.323
Rico Petrocelli	3B99	R	30	100	356	44	87	13	1	13	45	47	64	0	.244	.333	.396
Luis Aparicio	SS132	R	39	132	499	56	135	17	1	0	49	43	33	13	.271	.324	.309
Tommy Harper	OF143,DH1	R	32	147	566	92	159	23	3	17	71	61	93	54	.281	.351	.422
Rick Miller	OF137	L	25	143	441	65	115	17	7	6	43	51	59	12	.261	.339	.372
Dwight Evans	OF113	R	21	119	282	46	63	13	1	10	32	40	52	5	.223	.320	.383
Orlando Cepeda	DH142	R	35	142	550	51	159	25	0	20	86	50	81	0	.289	.350	.444
Reggie Smith	OF104,DH8,1B1	S	28	115	423	79	128	23	2	21	69	68	49	3	.303	.398	.515
Mario Guerrero	SS46,2B24	R	23	66	219	19	51	5	2	0	11	10	21	2	.233	.272	.274
Danny Cater	1B37,3B21,DH3	R	33	63	195	30	61	12	0	1	24	10	22	0	.313	.348	.390
John Kennedy	2B31,3B24,DH9	R	32	67	155	17	28	9	1	1	16	12	45	0	.181	.246	.271
Ben Oglivie	OF32,DH13	L	24	58	147	16	32	9	1	2	9	9	32	1	.218	.269	.333
Bob Montgomery	C33	R	29	34	128	18	41	6	2	7	25	7	36	0	.320	.353	.563
Cecil Cooper	1B29	L	23	30	101	12	24	2	0	3	11	7	12	1	.238	.284	.347
Buddy Hunter	3B3,2B2,DH1	R	25	13	7	3	3	1	0	0	2	3	1	0	.429	.636	.571

Pitcher	T	Age	G	GS	CG	ShO	IP	H	HR	BB	SO	W-L	Sv	ERA
Luis Tiant	R	32	35	35	23	0	272.0	217	32	78	206	20-13	0	3.34
Bill Lee	L	26	38	33	18	1	284.2	275	20	76	120	17-11	1	2.75
John Curtis	L	25	35	30	10	4	221.1	225	24	83	101	13-13	0	3.58
Marty Pattin	R	30	34	30	11	2	219.1	238	31	69	119	15-15	1	4.31
Roger Moret	L	23	30	15	5	2	156.1	138	19	67	90	13-2	3	3.17
Ray Culp	R	31	10	9	0	0	50.1	46	9	32	32	2-6	0	4.47
Dick Pole	R	22	12	7	0	0	54.2	70	4	18	24	3-2	0	5.60
Lynn McGlothen	R	23	6	3	0	0	23.0	39	6	8	16	1-2	0	8.22
Bobby Bolin	R	34	39	0	0	0	53.1	45	5	13	31	3-4	15	2.70
Bob Veale	L	37	32	0	0	0	36.1	37	2	12	25	2-3	11	3.47
Mike Garman	R	23	12	0	0	0	22.0	32	1	15	9	0-0	0	5.32
Craig Skok	L	25	11	0	0	0	28.2	35	2	11	22	0-1	1	6.28
Don Newhauser	R	25	9	0	0	0	12.0	9	0	13	8	0-0	1	0.00
Sonny Siebert†	R	36	2	0	0	0	2.1	5	1	1	5	0-1	0	7.71
Ken Tatum	R	29	1	0	0	0	4.0	6	2	3	0	0-0	0	9.00

1973 Detroit Tigers 3rd AL East 85-77 .525 12.0 GB — Billy Martin (71-63)/Joe Schultz (14-14)

Player	Gm by Position	B	Age	G	AB	R	H	2B	3B	HR	RBI	BB	SO	SB	Avg	OBP	Slg
Bill Freehan	C98,1B7	R	31	110	380	33	89	10	1	6	29	40	30	0	.234	.323	.313
Norm Cash	1B114,DH3	L	38	121	363	51	95	19	0	19	40	47	73	1	.262	.357	.471
Dick McAuliffe	2B102,SS2,DH1	L	33	106	343	39	94	18	1	12	47	49	52	0	.274	.366	.437
Aurelio Rodriguez	3B160,SS1	R	25	160	555	46	123	27	3	9	58	31	85	3	.222	.266	.330
Ed Brinkman	SS162	R	31	162	515	55	122	16	4	7	40	34	79	0	.237	.284	.324
Mickey Stanley	OF157	R	30	157	602	81	147	23	5	17	57	48	65	0	.244	.297	.384
Jim Northrup	OF116	L	33	119	404	55	124	14	7	12	44	38	41	4	.307	.366	.465
Willie Horton	OF107,DH1	R	30	111	411	42	130	19	3	17	53	23	57	1	.316	.362	.501
Gates Brown	DH119,OF2	L	34	125	377	48	89	11	1	12	50	52	41	1	.236	.328	.366
Al Kaline	OF63,1B36	R	38	91	310	40	79	13	0	10	45	29	28	4	.255	.320	.394
Tony Taylor	2B72,1B6,3B4*	R	37	84	275	35	63	9	3	5	24	17	29	9	.229	.276	.338
Duke Sims†	C68,OF6	L	32	80	252	31	61	10	0	8	30	30	36	1	.242	.324	.377
Frank Howard	DH76,1B2	R	36	85	227	26	58	9	1	12	29	24	28	0	.256	.327	.463
Dick Sharon	OF91	R	23	91	178	20	43	9	0	7	16	10	31	2	.242	.280	.410
Rich Reese†	1B37,OF21	L	31	59	102	10	14	1	0	2	4	7	17	0	.137	.193	.206
Ike Brown	1B21,OF12,DH2*	R	31	42	76	12	22	2	1	1	9	15	13	0	.289	.407	.382
Ron Cash	OF7,3B6	R	23	14	39	8	16	1	1	0	6	5	5	0	.410	.467	.487
John Knox	2B9	L	24	12	32	1	9	1	0	0	3	3	3	1	.281	.343	.313
Bob Didier	C7	S	24	7	22	3	10	1	0	0	1	3	0	0	.455	.520	.500
Tom Veryzer	SS18	R	20	18	20	1	6	0	1	0	2	2	4	0	.300	.364	.400
Joe Staton	1B5	L	25	9	17	2	4	0	0	0	3	0	3	1	.235	.235	.235
Marvin Lane	OF4	R	23	6	8	2	2	0	0	1	2	2	2	0	.250	.400	.625
John Gamble		R	25	7	0	1	0	0	0	0	0	0	0	0	—	—	—

T. Taylor, 1 G at DH, 1 G at OF; I. Brown, 2 G at 3B

Pitcher	T	Age	G	GS	CG	ShO	IP	H	HR	BB	SO	W-L	Sv	ERA
Mickey Lolich	L	32	42	42	17	3	308.2	315	35	79	214	16-15	0	3.82
Joe Coleman	R	26	40	40	13	2	288.1	283	32	93	202	23-15	0	3.53
Jim Perry	R	37	35	34	7	1	203.0	225	22	55	66	14-13	0	4.03
Woodie Fryman	L	33	34	29	1	0	169.2	200	23	64	119	6-13	0	5.36
Mike Strahler	R	26	22	11	1	0	80.1	84	7	39	37	4-5	0	4.37
John Hiller	L	30	65	0	0	0	125.1	89	7	39	124	10-5	38	1.44
Fred Scherman	L	28	34	0	0	0	61.2	59	6	30	28	2-2	1	4.23
Ed Farmer†	R	23	24	0	0	0	45.0	52	3	27	28	3-0	2	5.00
Bob Miller†	R	34	22	0	0	0	42.0	34	3	22	23	4-2	1	3.43
Lerrin LaGrow	R	24	21	3	0	0	54.0	54	8	23	33	1-5	3	4.33
Tom Timmermann†	R	33	17	1	0	0	39.0	39	4	11	21	1-1	1	3.69
Fred Holdsworth	R	21	5	2	0	0	14.2	13	3	6	9	0-1	0	6.75
Chuck Seelbach	R	25	5	0	0	0	7.0	7	1	2	2	1-0	0	3.86
Gary Ignasiak	L	23	3	0	0	0	4.2	5	0	3	4	0-0	0	3.86
Bill Slayback	R	25	3	0	0	0	2.0	5	0	0	1	0-0	0	4.50
Dave Lemanczyk	R	22	1	0	0	0	2.1	4	0	0	0	0-0	0	11.57

1973 New York Yankees 4th AL East 80-82 .494 17.0 GB — Ralph Houk

Player	Gm by Position	B	Age	G	AB	R	H	2B	3B	HR	RBI	BB	SO	SB	Avg	OBP	Slg
Thurman Munson	C142	R	26	147	519	80	156	29	4	20	74	48	64	4	.301	.362	.487
Felipe Alou†	1B67,OF22	R	38	93	280	25	66	12	0	4	27	9	25	0	.236	.256	.321
Horace Clarke	2B147	S	33	148	590	60	155	21	0	2	35	47	48	11	.263	.317	.308
Graig Nettles	3B157,DH2	L	28	160	552	65	129	18	0	22	81	78	76	0	.234	.334	.386
Gene Michael	SS129	S	35	129	418	30	94	11	1	3	47	26	51	1	.225	.270	.278
Roy White	OF162	S	29	162	639	88	157	22	3	18	60	78	81	16	.246	.329	.374
Bobby Murcer	OF160	L	27	160	616	83	187	29	2	22	95	50	67	6	.304	.357	.464
Matty Alou†	OF85,1B40,DH1	L	34	123	497	59	147	22	1	2	28	30	43	5	.296	.338	.356
Jim Ray Hart†	DH106	R	31	114	339	29	86	13	2	13	52	36	45	0	.254	.324	.419
Ron Blomberg	DH55,1B41	L	24	100	301	45	99	13	1	12	57	34	25	2	.329	.395	.498
Johnny Callison	OF32,DH10	L	34	45	136	10	24	4	0	1	10	4	24	1	.176	.197	.228
Mike Hegan†	1B37	L	30	37	131	12	36	3	2	6	14	7	34	0	.275	.309	.466
Hal Lanier	SS26,2B8,3B1	R	30	35	86	9	18	3	0	0	5	3	10	0	.209	.244	.244
Otto Velez	OF23	R	22	23	77	9	15	4	0	2	7	15	24	0	.195	.326	.325
Fred Stanley	SS21,2B3	R	25	26	66	6	14	0	1	1	5	7	16	0	.212	.288	.288
Celerino Sanchez	DH11,3B11,SS2*	R	29	34	64	12	14	3	0	1	9	2	12	1	.219	.239	.313
Jerry Moses	C17,DH1	R	26	21	59	5	15	2	0	0	3	2	6	0	.254	.270	.288
Bernie Allen†	2B13,DH4	L	34	17	57	5	13	3	0	0	4	5	5	0	.228	.290	.281
Ron Swoboda	OF20,DH4	R	29	35	43	6	5	0	0	1	2	4	18	0	.116	.191	.186
Rick Dempsey	C5	R	23	6	11	0	2	0	0	0	0	1	3	0	.182	.250	.182
Duke Sims†	DH2,C1	L	32	4	9	3	3	0	0	1	1	3	1	0	.333	.500	.667

C. Sanchez, 2 G at OF

Pitcher	T	Age	G	GS	CG	ShO	IP	H	HR	BB	SO	W-L	Sv	ERA
Mel Stottlemyre	R	31	38	38	19	4	273.0	259	13	79	95	16-16	0	3.07
Doc Medich	R	24	34	32	11	3	235.0	217	20	74	145	14-9	0	2.95
Fritz Peterson	L	31	31	31	6	1	184.1	207	18	49	59	8-15	0	3.95
Pat Dobson†	R	31	22	21	6	1	142.1	150	22	34	70	9-8	0	4.17
Sam McDowell†	L	30	16	15	2	1	95.2	73	4	64	75	5-8	0	3.95
Steve Kline	R	25	14	13	2	1	74.0	76	5	31	19	4-7	0	4.01
Mike Kekich†	L	28	5	4	0	0	14.2	20	1	14	4	1-1	0	9.20
Sparky Lyle	L	28	51	0	0	0	82.1	66	4	18	63	5-9	27	2.51
Lindy McDaniel	R	37	47	3	1	0	160.1	148	11	49	93	12-6	10	2.86
Fred Beene	R	30	19	4	0	0	91.0	67	5	27	49	6-0	1	1.68
Jim Magnuson	L	26	8	0	0	0	27.1	38	2	9	9	0-1	0	4.28
Tom Buskey	R	26	8	0	0	0	16.2	18	2	4	8	0-1	1	5.40
Wayne Granger†	R	29	7	0	0	0	15.1	19	1	3	10	0-1	0	1.76
Dave Pagan	R	23	4	1	0	0	12.2	16	1	1	9	0-0	0	2.84
Casey Cox	R	31	1	0	0	0	3.0	5	0	1	0	0-0	0	6.00

1973 Milwaukee Brewers 5th AL East 74-88 .457 23.0 GB — Del Crandall

Player	Gm by Position	B	Age	G	AB	R	H	2B	3B	HR	RBI	BB	SO	SB	Avg	OBP	Slg
Darrell Porter	C90,DH19	L	21	117	350	50	89	19	2	16	67	57	85	5	.254	.363	.457
George Scott	1B157,DH1	R	29	158	604	98	185	30	4	24	107	61	94	9	.306	.370	.488
Pedro Garcia	2B160	R	23	160	580	67	142	32	5	15	54	40	119	11	.245	.296	.395
Don Money	3B124,SS21	R	26	145	556	75	158	28	2	11	61	53	53	22	.284	.347	.401
Tim Johnson	SS135	L	23	136	465	39	99	10	2	0	32	29	93	6	.213	.259	.243
Dave May	OF152,DH2	L	29	156	624	96	189	23	4	25	93	44	78	6	.303	.352	.473
John Briggs	OF137,DH1	L	29	142	488	78	120	20	7	18	57	87	83	15	.246	.361	.426
Bob Coluccio	OF108,DH11	R	21	124	438	65	98	21	8	15	58	54	92	13	.224	.311	.411
Ollie Brown	DH82,OF4	R	29	97	296	28	83	10	1	7	32	33	53	1	.280	.355	.392
Ellie Rodriguez	C75,DH14	R	27	94	290	30	78	8	1	0	30	41	28	4	.269	.376	.303
Joe Lahoud	DH41,OF40	L	26	96	225	29	46	9	0	5	26	27	36	5	.204	.302	.311
Gorman Thomas	OF50,DH3,3B1	R	22	59	155	16	29	7	1	2	12	11	61	5	.187	.254	.284
Bobby Mitchell	OF20,DH19	R	29	47	130	12	29	6	0	5	20	5	32	4	.223	.250	.385
John Vukovich	3B40,1B13,SS1	R	25	55	128	10	16	3	0	0	9	9	40	0	.125	.182	.195
Bob Heise	SS29,3B9,1B4*	R	26	49	98	8	20	2	0	0	4	4	4	1	.204	.235	.224
Wilbur Howard	OF12,DH1	S	24	16	39	3	8	0	0	0	1	2	10	0	.205	.244	.205
Charlie Moore	C8	R	20	8	27	0	5	0	1	0	3	2	4	0	.185	.241	.259
John Felske	C7,1B6	R	31	13	22	3	3	0	0	0	4	1	11	0	.136	.167	.227
Rick Auerbach	SS2	R	23	6	10	2	1	1	0	0	0	0	1	0	.100	.100	.200

B. Heise, 4 G at 2B

Pitcher	T	Age	G	GS	CG	ShO	IP	H	HR	BB	SO	W-L	Sv	ERA
Jim Slaton	R	23	38	38	13	3	276.1	266	30	99	134	13-15	0	3.71
Jim Colborn	R	27	43	36	22	4	314.1	297	21	87	135	20-12	1	3.18
Jerry Bell	R	25	31	25	8	0	183.2	185	14	70	57	9-9	1	3.97
Bill Parsons	R	24	20	17	0	0	59.2	59	6	67	30	3-6	0	6.79
Kevin Kobel	L	19	2	1	0	0	8.1	9	2	8	4	0-1	0	8.64
Ken Reynolds	L	26	2	1	0	0	7.1	5	1	10	3	0-1	0	7.36
Chris Short	L	35	42	7	0	0	72.0	86	5	44	44	3-5	2	5.13
Frank Linzy	R	32	42	1	0	0	63.0	68	7	21	21	2-6	13	3.57
Skip Lockwood	R	26	37	15	3	0	154.2	164	10	59	87	5-12	0	3.90
Billy Champion	R	25	37	11	2	0	136.1	139	10	62	67	5-8	1	3.70
Ed Rodriguez	R	21	30	6	2	0	76.1	71	6	47	49	9-7	5	3.30
Carlos Velazquez	R	25	18	0	0	0	38.1	46	5	10	12	2-2	2	2.58
Ray Newman	L	28	11	0	0	0	18.1	19	2	5	16	2-1	1	2.95
Rob Gardner†	L	28	10	0	0	0	12.2	17	0	13	5	1-1	1	9.95
Gary Ryerson	L	25	9	4	0	0	23.0	32	0	7	10	0-1	0	7.83
Ed Sprague†	R	27	7	0	0	0	9.2	13	0	14	3	0-1	1	9.31

1973 Cleveland Indians 6th AL East 71-91 .438 26.0 GB — Ken Aspromonte

Player	Gm by Position	B	Age	G	AB	R	H	2B	3B	HR	RBI	BB	SO	SB	Avg	OBP	Slg
Dave Duncan	C86,DH9	R	27	95	344	43	80	11	1	17	43	35	86	3	.233	.309	.419
Chris Chambliss	1B154	L	24	155	572	70	156	30	2	11	53	58	76	4	.273	.342	.390
Jack Brohamer	2B97	L	23	102	300	29	66	12	1	4	29	32	23	0	.220	.291	.307
Buddy Bell	3B154,OF2	R	21	156	631	86	169	23	7	14	59	49	47	7	.268	.325	.393
Frank Duffy	SS115	R	26	116	361	34	95	16	4	8	50	25	41	6	.263	.312	.396
Rusty Torres	OF114	S	24	122	312	31	64	8	1	7	28	50	62	6	.205	.317	.304
Charlie Spikes	OF111,DH26	R	22	140	506	68	120	12	3	23	73	45	103	5	.237	.303	.409
George Hendrick	OF110	R	23	113	440	64	118	18	0	21	61	25	71	7	.268	.308	.452
Oscar Gamble	DH70,OF37	L	23	113	390	56	104	11	3	20	44	34	37	3	.267	.329	.464
John Ellis	C72,DH38,1B12	R	24	127	437	59	118	12	2	14	68	46	57	0	.270	.339	.403
Walt Williams	OF61,DH26	R	29	104	350	43	101	15	1	8	38	14	29	9	.289	.316	.406
John Lowenstein	OF51,DH25,2B25*	L	26	98	305	42	89	16	1	6	40	23	41	5	.292	.338	.410
Leo Cardenas	SS67,3B5	R	34	72	195	9	42	4	0	0	12	13	42	1	.215	.264	.236
Tom Ragland	2B65,SS2	R	27	67	183	16	47	7	1	0	12	8	31	2	.257	.292	.306
Ron Lolich	OF32,DH12	R	26	61	140	16	32	7	0	2	15	7	27	0	.229	.265	.321
Tommy Smith	OF13	L	24	14	41	6	10	2	0	2	3	1	2	1	.244	.262	.439
Ted Ford	OF10	R	26	11	40	3	9	0	1	0	3	2	7	1	.225	.250	.275
Alan Ashby	C11	S	21	11	29	4	5	1	0	1	3	2	11	0	.172	.226	.310
Jerry Kenney	2B5	L	28	5	16	0	4	0	1	0	2	2	0	0	.250	.316	.375

J. Lowenstein, 8 G at 3B, 1 G at 1B

Pitcher	T	Age	G	GS	CG	ShO	IP	H	HR	BB	SO	W-L	Sv	ERA
Gaylord Perry	R	34	41	41	29	7	344.0	315	34	115	238	19-19	0	3.38
Dick Tidrow	R	26	42	40	13	2	274.2	289	31	95	138	14-16	0	4.42
Milt Wilcox	R	23	26	19	4	0	134.1	143	14	68	82	8-10	0	5.83
Brent Strom	L	24	27	18	2	0	123.0	134	18	47	91	2-10	0	4.61
Dick Bosman†	R	29	22	17	2	0	97.0	130	19	29	41	1-8	0	6.22
Tom Timmermann†	R	33	29	15	4	0	124.1	117	15	54	62	8-7	2	4.92
Steve Dunning†	R	24	4	3	0	0	18.0	17	2	13	10	0-2	0	6.50
Tom Hilgendorf	L	31	48	1	1	0	94.2	87	9	36	58	5-3	6	3.14
Jerry Johnson	R	29	39	1	0	0	59.2	70	7	39	45	5-6	5	6.18
Ray Lamb	R	28	32	1	0	0	86.0	98	7	42	60	3-3	2	4.60
Mike Kekich†	L	28	16	6	0	0	50.0	73	6	35	26	1-4	0	7.02
Ed Farmer†	R	23	16	0	0	0	17.1	25	4	5	10	0-2	1	4.67
Ken Sanders†	R	31	15	0	0	0	27.1	18	2	9	14	5-1	5	1.65
Steve Mingori†	L	29	5	0	0	0	11.2	10	3	10	4	0-0	0	6.17
Mike Kilkenny	L	28	5	0	0	0	2.0	5	1	5	3	0-0	0	22.50
Mike Jackson†	L	27	1	0	0	0	0.2	1	0	0	1	0-0	0	0.00

1973 Oakland Athletics 1st AL West 94-68 .580 — — Dick Williams

Player	Gm by Position	B	Age	G	AB	R	H	2B	3B	HR	RBI	BB	SO	SB	Avg	OBP	Slg
Ray Fosse	C141,DH2	R	26	143	492	37	126	23	2	7	52	25	62	2	.256	.291	.354
Gene Tenace	1B134,C33,DH3*	R	26	160	510	83	132	18	2	24	84	101	94	2	.259	.387	.443
Dick Green	2B133,3B1,SS1	R	32	133	332	33	87	17	0	3	42	21	63	0	.262	.308	.340
Sal Bando	3B159,DH3	R	29	162	592	97	170	32	3	29	98	82	84	4	.287	.375	.498
Bert Campaneris	SS149	R	31	151	601	89	150	17	6	4	46	50	79	34	.250	.308	.318
Reggie Jackson	OF145,DH3	L	27	151	539	99	158	28	2	32	117	76	111	22	.293	.383	.531
Bill North	OF138,DH6	S	25	146	554	98	158	10	5	5	34	78	89	53	.285	.376	.348
Joe Rudi	OF117,DH1,1B1	R	26	120	437	53	118	25	1	12	66	30	72	0	.270	.315	.414
Deron Johnson†	DH107,1B23	R	34	131	464	61	114	14	2	19	81	59	116	0	.246	.330	.407
Angel Mangual	OF50,1B2,2B1	R	26	74	192	20	43	4	1	3	13	8	34	1	.224	.257	.302
Ted Kubiak	2B83,SS26,3B2	S	31	106	182	15	40	6	1	3	17	12	19	1	.220	.267	.313
Billy Conigliaro	OF40,2B1	R	25	48	110	5	22	2	2	0	14	9	26	1	.200	.252	.255
Jesus Alou†	OF21,DH6	R	31	36	108	10	33	3	0	1	11	2	6	0	.306	.318	.361
Mike Hegan†	1B56,DH3,OF3	L	30	75	71	8	13	2	0	1	5	5	17	0	.183	.237	.254
Rich McKinney	3B17,2B7,DH6*	R	26	48	65	9	16	3	0	1	7	7	4	0	.246	.319	.338
Vic Davalillo†	OF19,1B8,DH2	L	36	38	64	5	12	1	0	0	4	3	4	0	.188	.224	.203
Pat Bourque†	DH15,1B5	L	26	23	42	8	8	4	1	2	9	15	10	0	.190	.390	.476
Jay Johnstone	OF7,DH4,2B2	L	27	23	28	1	3	1	0	0	3	2	4	0	.107	.167	.143
Gonzalo Marquez†	2B2,1B1,OF1	L	27	23	25	1	6	1	0	0	2	0	4	0	.240	.240	.280
Mike Andrews†	2B9,DH2	R	29	18	21	1	4	1	0	0	0	3	1	0	.190	.292	.238
Dal Maxvill†	SS18,2B11,3B1	R	34	29	19	0	4	0	0	0	1	1	3	0	.211	.250	.211
Tim Hosley	C13	R	26	13	14	3	3	0	0	0	2	2	3	0	.214	.313	.214
Jose Morales†	DH3	R	28	6	14	0	4	1	0	0	1	1	5	0	.286	.313	.357
Manny Trillo	2B16	R	22	17	12	0	3	2	0	0	3	0	4	0	.250	.250	.417
Rico Carty†	DH1	R	33	7	8	1	2	1	0	1	1	2	1	0	.250	.400	.750
Phil Garner	3B9	R	24	9	5	0	0	0	0	0	0	0	3	0	.000	.000	.000
Larry Haney†	C2	R	30	2	2	0	1	0	0	0	0	0	0	0	.500	.500	.500
Allan Lewis	DH6,OF1	S	31	35	0	16	0	0	0	0	0	0	0	7	—	—	—

G. Tenace, 1 G at 2B; R. McKinney, 3 G at OF

Pitcher	T	Age	G	GS	CG	ShO	IP	H	HR	BB	SO	W-L	Sv	ERA
Ken Holtzman	L	27	40	40	16	4	297.1	275	22	66	157	21-13	0	2.97
Vida Blue	L	23	37	37	13	4	263.2	214	26	105	158	20-9	0	3.28
Catfish Hunter	R	27	36	36	11	3	256.1	222	39	69	124	21-5	0	3.34
Blue Moon Odom	R	28	30	24	3	0	150.1	153	14	67	83	5-12	0	4.49
Dave Hamilton	L	25	16	11	1	0	69.2	74	8	24	34	6-4	0	4.39
Glenn Abbott	R	22	5	3	1	0	18.2	16	3	7	6	1-0	0	3.86
Chuck Dobson	R	29	1	1	0	0	2.1	6	1	2	3	0-1	0	7.71
Rollie Fingers	R	26	62	2	0	0	126.2	107	5	39	110	7-8	22	1.92
Darold Knowles	L	31	52	5	1	1	99.0	87	7	49	46	6-8	9	3.09
Horacio Pina	R	28	47	0	0	0	88.0	58	8	34	41	6-3	8	2.76
Paul Lindblad	L	31	36	3	0	0	78.0	89	8	28	33	1-5	2	3.69
Rob Gardner†	L	28	3	0	0	0	7.1	10	2	4	2	0-0	0	4.91

1973 Kansas City Royals 2nd AL West 88-74 .543 6.0 GB — Jack McKeon

Player	Gm by Position	B	Age	G	AB	R	H	2B	3B	HR	RBI	BB	SO	SB	Avg	OBP	Slg
Fran Healy	C92,DH1	R	26	95	279	25	77	15	2	6	34	31	56	3	.276	.348	.409
John Mayberry	1B149,DH1	L	24	152	510	87	142	20	2	26	100	122	79	3	.278	.417	.478
Cookie Rojas	2B137	R	34	139	551	78	152	29	3	6	69	37	38	18	.276	.320	.372
Paul Schaal	3B121	R	30	121	396	61	114	14	3	8	42	63	45	5	.288	.389	.399
Freddie Patek	SS135	R	28	135	501	82	117	19	5	5	45	54	63	36	.234	.311	.321
Amos Otis	OF135,DH14	R	26	148	583	89	175	21	4	26	93	63	47	13	.300	.368	.484
Lou Piniella	OF128,DH9	R	29	144	513	53	128	28	1	9	69	30	65	5	.250	.291	.361
Ed Kirkpatrick	OF108,C14,DH8	L	28	126	429	61	113	24	3	6	45	46	48	3	.263	.333	.375
Hal McRae	OF64,DH37,3B2	R	27	106	338	36	79	18	3	9	50	34	38	2	.234	.312	.385
Kurt Bevacqua	3B40,2B16,OF10*	R	26	99	276	39	71	8	3	2	40	25	42	2	.257	.317	.330
Steve Hovley	OF79,DH15	L	28	104	232	29	59	8	1	2	24	33	34	6	.254	.346	.323
Carl Taylor	C63,1B2,DH1	R	29	69	145	18	33	6	1	0	16	32	20	2	.228	.363	.283
Frank White	SS37,2B11	R	22	51	139	20	31	6	1	0	5	8	23	3	.223	.262	.281
Gail Hopkins	DH36,1B10	L	30	74	138	17	34	6	1	2	16	29	15	1	.246	.380	.348
Rick Reichardt†	DH31,OF7	R	30	41	127	15	28	5	2	3	17	11	28	0	.220	.279	.362
Jim Wohlford	DH19,OF13	R	22	45	109	21	29	1	3	2	10	11	12	1	.266	.333	.385
Bobby Floyd	2B25,SS24	R	29	51	78	10	26	3	1	0	8	4	14	1	.333	.357	.397
George Brett	3B13	L	20	13	40	2	5	2	0	0	0	0	5	0	.125	.125	.175
Buck Martinez	C14	R	24	14	32	2	8	1	0	1	6	4	5	0	.250	.333	.375
Jerry May†	C11	R	29	11	30	4	4	1	1	0	2	3	5	0	.133	.235	.233
Tom Poquette	OF20	L	21	21	28	4	6	1	0	0	3	1	4	1	.214	.258	.250
Frank Ortenzio	1B7,DH1	R	22	9	25	1	7	2	0	1	6	2	6	0	.280	.333	.480
Keith Marshall	OF8	R	21	8	9	0	2	1	0	0	3	1	4	0	.222	.300	.333

K. Bevacqua, 9 G at 1B

Pitcher	T	Age	G	GS	CG	ShO	IP	H	HR	BB	SO	W-L	Sv	ERA
Paul Splittorff	L	26	38	38	12	3	262.0	279	19	78	110	20-11	0	3.98
Steve Busby	R	23	37	37	7	1	238.1	246	18	105	174	16-15	0	4.23
Dick Drago	R	28	37	33	10	1	212.1	252	16	76	98	12-14	0	4.24
Al Fitzmorris	R	27	15	13	3	1	89.0	88	5	25	26	8-3	0	2.83
Wayne Simpson	R	24	16	10	1	0	59.2	66	1	35	29	3-4	0	5.73
Mark Littell	R	20	8	7	1	0	38.0	44	5	23	16	1-3	0	5.68
Doug Bird	R	23	54	0	0	0	102.1	81	10	30	83	4-4	20	2.99
Gene Garber	R	25	48	8	4	0	152.2	164	14	49	60	9-9	11	4.24
Bruce Dal Canton	R	31	32	3	1	0	97.1	108	8	46	38	4-3	3	4.81
Ken Wright	R	26	25	12	1	0	80.2	60	6	82	75	6-5	0	4.91
Joe Hoerner†	L	36	22	0	0	0	19.1	28	0	13	15	2-0	4	5.12
Steve Mingori†	L	29	19	1	0	0	56.1	59	6	23	46	3-3	1	3.04
Mike Jackson†	L	27	9	0	0	0	22.1	25	3	20	13	0-0	0	6.85
Norm Angelini	L	25	7	0	0	0	3.2	2	0	7	3	0-0	1	4.91
Tom Burgmeier	L	29	6	0	0	0	10.0	13	2	4	4	0-0	1	5.40
Barry Raziano	R	26	2	0	0	0	5.0	6	1	1	0	0-0	0	5.40

1973 Minnesota Twins 3rd AL West 81-81 .500 13.0 GB — Frank Quilici

Player	Gm by Position	B	Age	G	AB	R	H	2B	3B	HR	RBI	BB	SO	SB	Avg	OBP	Slg
George Mitterwald	C122,DH3	R	28	125	432	50	112	15	0	16	64	39	111	3	.259	.326	.405
Joe Lis	1B96,DH1	R	26	103	253	37	62	11	1	9	25	28	66	0	.245	.325	.403
Rod Carew	2B147	L	27	149	580	98	203	30	11	6	62	62	55	41	.350	.411	.471
Steve Braun	3B102,OF6	L	25	115	361	46	102	28	5	6	42	74	48	4	.283	.408	.438
Danny Thompson	SS95,3B1	R	26	99	347	29	78	13	2	1	36	16	41	1	.225	.259	.282
Larry Hisle	OF143	R	26	143	545	88	148	25	6	15	64	64	128	11	.272	.351	.422
Bobby Darwin	OF140,DH1	R	30	145	560	69	141	20	2	18	90	46	137	5	.252	.309	.391
Jim Holt	OF102,1B33	L	29	132	441	52	131	25	3	11	58	29	43	0	.297	.341	.442
Tony Oliva	DH142	L	32	146	571	63	166	20	0	16	92	45	44	2	.291	.345	.410
Jerry Terrell	SS81,DH30,3B30*	R	26	124	438	43	116	15	2	1	32	21	56	13	.265	.297	.315
Steve Brye	OF87,DH1	R	24	92	278	39	73	9	5	6	33	35	43	3	.263	.343	.396
Harmon Killebrew	1B57,DH9	R	37	69	248	29	60	9	1	5	32	41	59	0	.242	.352	.347
Phil Roof	C47	R	32	47	117	10	23	4	1	1	15	13	27	0	.197	.277	.274
Eric Soderholm	3B33,SS1	R	24	35	111	22	33	7	2	1	9	21	16	1	.297	.414	.423
Danny Walton	OF18,DH11,3B1	R	25	37	96	13	17	1	1	4	8	17	28	0	.177	.301	.333
Dan Monzon	2B17,3B14,OF1	R	27	39	76	10	17	1	1	0	4	11	9	1	.224	.326	.263
Mike Adams	OF24,DH2	R	24	55	66	21	14	2	0	3	6	17	18	2	.212	.381	.379
Craig Kusick	1B11,DH2,OF2	R	24	15	48	4	12	2	0	0	4	7	9	0	.250	.357	.292
Glenn Borgmann	C12	R	23	12	34	7	9	2	0	0	9	6	10	0	.265	.375	.324
Rich Reese†	1B17	L	31	22	23	7	4	1	1	1	3	6	6	0	.174	.345	.435

J. Terrell, 14 G at 2B, 1 G at OF

Pitcher	T	Age	G	GS	CG	ShO	IP	H	HR	BB	SO	W-L	Sv	ERA
Bert Blyleven	R	22	40	40	25	9	325.0	296	16	67	258	20-17	0	2.52
Jim Kaat†	L	34	29	28	7	2	181.2	206	26	39	93	11-12	0	4.41
Joe Decker	R	26	29	24	6	3	170.1	167	12	88	109	10-10	0	4.17
Dick Woodson	R	28	23	23	4	2	141.1	137	12	68	53	10-8	0	3.95
Danny Fife	R	23	10	7	1	0	51.2	54	2	29	18	3-2	0	4.35
Ray Corbin	R	24	51	7	1	0	148.1	124	7	60	83	8-5	14	3.03
Bill Hands	R	33	39	15	3	1	142.0	138	14	41	78	7-10	2	3.49
Dave Goltz	R	24	32	10	1	0	106.1	138	11	32	65	6-4	1	5.25
Bill Campbell	R	24	28	2	0	0	51.2	44	5	20	42	3-3	7	3.14
Ken Sanders†	R	31	27	0	0	0	44.1	53	4	21	19	2-4	8	6.09
Eddie Bane	L	21	23	6	0	0	60.1	62	5	30	42	0-5	2	4.92
Vic Albury	L	26	14	0	0	0	23.1	13	1	19	13	1-0	0	2.70
Jim Strickland	L	27	7	0	0	0	5.1	11	0	5	6	0-1	0	11.81

1973 California Angels 4th AL West 79-83 .488 15.0 GB

Bobby Winkles

Player	Gm by Position	B	Age	G	AB	R	H	2B	3B	HR	RBI	BB	SO	SB	Avg	OBP	Slg
Jeff Torborg	C102	R	31	102	255	20	56	7	0	1	18	21	32	0	.220	.278	.259
Mike Epstein†	1B86	L	30	91	312	30	67	8	2	8	32	34	54	0	.215	.300	.330
Sandy Alomar	2B110,SS31	S	29	136	470	45	112	7	1	0	28	34	44	25	.238	.288	.257
Al Gallagher†	3B98,2B1,SS1	R	27	110	311	16	85	6	1	0	26	35	31	1	.273	.345	.299
Rudy Meoli	SS95,3B13,2B8	L	22	120	305	36	68	12	1	2	23	31	38	2	.223	.290	.289
Ken Berry	OF129	R	32	136	415	48	118	11	2	3	36	26	50	1	.284	.327	.342
Vada Pinson	OF120	L	34	124	466	56	121	14	6	8	57	20	55	5	.260	.286	.367
Lee Stanton	OF107	R	27	119	306	41	72	9	2	8	34	27	88	3	.235	.300	.356
Frank Robinson	DH127,OF17	R	37	147	534	85	142	29	0	30	97	82	93	1	.266	.372	.489
Bob Oliver	3B49,OF47,1B32*	R	30	151	544	51	144	24	1	18	89	33	100	1	.265	.311	.412
Tom McCraw	OF34,1B25,DH8	L	32	99	264	25	70	7	0	3	24	30	42	3	.265	.343	.326
Richie Scheinblum†	OF54,DH7	S	30	77	229	28	75	10	2	3	21	35	27	0	.328	.417	.428
Winston Llenas	2B20,3B11,OF4	R	29	78	130	16	35	1	0	1	25	10	16	0	.269	.317	.300
Mickey Rivers	OF29	L	24	30	129	26	45	6	4	0	16	8	11	8	.349	.391	.457
Billy Grabarkewitz†	2B18,3B12,SS1*	R	27	61	129	27	21	6	1	3	9	28	27	2	.163	.316	.295
Bobby Valentine	SS25,OF8	R	23	32	126	12	38	5	2	1	13	5	9	6	.302	.323	.397
John Stephenson	C56	L	32	60	122	9	30	5	0	1	9	7	7	0	.246	.292	.311
Billy Parker	2B32,SS3	R	26	38	102	14	23	2	1	0	7	8	23	0	.225	.286	.265
Jim Spencer†	1B26,DH2	L	26	29	87	10	21	4	2	2	11	9	9	0	.241	.316	.402
Dave Chalk	SS22	R	22	24	69	14	16	2	0	0	6	9	13	0	.232	.329	.261
Art Kusnyer	C41	R	27	41	64	5	8	2	0	0	3	2	12	0	.125	.149	.156
Jerry Davanon	SS14,2B12,3B7	R	27	41	49	6	12	3	0	0	2	3	9	1	.245	.288	.306
Charlie Sands	C10	L	25	17	33	5	9	2	1	1	5	5	10	0	.273	.368	.485
Rick Stelmaszek†	C22	L	24	22	26	2	4	1	0	0	3	6	7	0	.154	.313	.192
Doug Howard	OF6,1B1,3B1	R	25	8	21	2	2	0	0	0	1	1	6	0	.095	.130	.095
Bobby Brooks	OF1	R	27	4	7	0	1	0	0	0	0	0	3	0	.143	.143	.143

B. Oliver, 12 G at DH; B. Grabarkewitz, 1 G at OF

Pitcher	T	Age	G	GS	CG	ShO	IP	H	HR	BB	SO	W-L	Sv	ERA
Bill Singer	R	29	40	40	19	2	315.2	280	15	130	241	20-14	0	3.22
Nolan Ryan	R	26	41	39	26	4	326.0	238	18	162	383	21-16	1	2.87
Clyde Wright	L	32	37	36	13	1	257.0	273	26	76	65	11-19	0	3.68
Rudy May	L	28	34	28	10	4	185.0	177	20	80	134	7-17	0	4.38
Andy Hassler	L	21	7	4	1	0	31.2	33	0	19	19	0-4	0	3.69
Frank Tanana	L	19	4	4	2	1	26.1	20	2	8	22	2-2	0	3.08
Dave Sells	R	26	51	0	0	0	68.0	72	2	35	25	7-2	10	3.71
Steve Barber	L	34	50	1	0	0	89.1	90	5	32	58	3-2	4	3.53
Dick Lange	R	24	17	4	1	0	52.2	61	9	21	27	2-1	0	4.44
Rich Hand†	R	24	16	6	0	0	54.2	58	5	21	19	4-3	0	3.62
Aurelio Monteagudo	R	29	15	0	0	0	30.0	23	2	16	8	2-1	3	4.20
Ron Perranoski	L	37	8	0	0	0	11.0	11	0	7	5	0-2	0	4.09
Lloyd Allen†	R	23	5	0	0	0	8.2	15	0	5	4	0-0	1	10.38
Terry Wilshusen	R	24	1	0	0	0	0.1	0	0	2	0	0-0	0	81.00

1973 Chicago White Sox 5th AL West 77-85 .475 17.0 GB

Chuck Tanner

Player	Gm by Position	B	Age	G	AB	R	H	2B	3B	HR	RBI	BB	SO	SB	Avg	OBP	Slg
Ed Herrmann	C114,DH2	L	26	119	379	42	85	17	1	10	39	31	55	2	.224	.291	.354
Tony Muser	1B89,OF2	L	25	109	309	38	88	14	3	4	30	33	36	8	.285	.352	.388
Jorge Orta	2B122,SS1	L	22	128	425	46	113	9	10	6	40	37	87	8	.266	.323	.376
Bill Melton	3B151,DH1	R	27	152	560	83	155	29	1	20	87	75	66	4	.277	.363	.439
Eddie Leon	SS122,2B3	R	26	127	399	37	91	10	3	3	30	34	103	1	.228	.291	.291
Pat Kelly	OF141,DH1	L	28	144	550	77	154	24	5	1	44	65	91	22	.280	.355	.347
Johnny Jeter	OF72,DH3	R	28	89	300	38	72	14	4	7	26	9	74	4	.240	.260	.383
Carlos May	DH75,OF70,1B2	R	25	149	553	62	148	20	0	20	96	53	73	8	.268	.334	.412
Mike Andrews†	DH30,1B9,2B6*	R	29	52	159	10	32	9	0	0	10	23	28	0	.201	.302	.258
Ken Henderson	OF44,DH26	S	27	73	262	32	68	13	0	6	32	27	49	3	.260	.330	.378
Dick Allen	1B67,2B2,DH1	R	31	72	250	39	79	20	3	16	41	33	51	7	.316	.394	.612
Jerry Hairston	OF33,1B19,DH8	S	21	60	210	25	57	11	1	0	23	33	30	0	.271	.371	.333
Luis Alvarado	2B45,SS18,3B10	R	24	80	203	21	47	7	2	0	20	4	20	6	.232	.250	.286
Bill Sharp	OF70,DH1	L	23	77	196	23	54	8	3	4	22	19	28	2	.276	.345	.408
Buddy Bradford	OF51	R	28	53	168	24	40	3	1	8	15	17	43	4	.238	.316	.411
Rick Reichardt†	OF37,DH6	R	30	46	153	15	42	8	1	3	16	8	29	2	.275	.315	.399
Chuck Brinkman	C63	R	28	63	139	13	26	6	0	1	10	11	37	0	.187	.252	.252
Bucky Dent	SS36,2B3,3B1	R	21	40	117	17	29	2	0	0	10	10	18	2	.248	.308	.265
Brian Downing	OF13,C11,3B8	R	22	34	73	5	13	1	0	2	4	10	17	0	.178	.277	.274
Hank Allen	3B9,1B8,OF5*	R	32	28	39	2	4	2	0	0	0	1	9	0	.103	.125	.154
Sam Ewing	1B4	L	24	11	20	1	3	1	0	0	2	2	6	0	.150	.227	.200
Pete Varney	C5	R	24	5	4	0	0	0	0	0	0	1	0	0	.000	.200	.000
Rich Morales†	3B5,2B2	R	29	7	4	1	0	0	0	0	1	1	1	0	.000	.200	.000
Joe Keough		L	27	5	1	1	0	0	0	0	0	0	0	0	.000	.000	.000

M. Andrews, 5 G at 3B; H. Allen, 1 G at C, 1 G at 2B

Pitcher	T	Age	G	GS	CG	ShO	IP	H	HR	BB	SO	W-L	Sv	ERA
Wilbur Wood	L	31	49	48	21	4	359.1	381	25	91	199	24-20	0	3.46
Stan Bahnsen	R	28	42	42	14	4	282.1	290	20	117	120	18-21	0	3.57
Steve Stone	R	25	36	22	3	0	176.1	163	11	82	138	6-11	1	4.24
Eddie Fisher†	R	36	26	16	2	0	110.2	135	12	38	57	6-7	0	4.88
Jim Kaat†	L	34	7	7	3	1	42.2	44	4	4	16	4-1	0	4.22
Terry Forster	L	21	51	12	4	0	172.2	174	7	78	120	6-11	16	3.23
Cy Acosta	R	26	48	0	0	0	97.0	66	8	39	60	10-6	18	2.23
Bart Johnson	R	23	22	9	0	0	80.2	76	6	40	56	3-3	0	4.13
Goose Gossage	R	21	20	4	1	0	49.2	57	9	37	33	0-4	0	7.43
Ken Frailing	L	25	10	0	0	0	18.1	18	1	7	15	0-0	0	1.96
Steve Kealey	R	26	7	0	0	0	11.1	23	2	7	4	0-0	0	15.09
Denny O'Toole	R	24	6	0	0	0	16.0	23	3	3	8	0-0	0	5.63
Jim Geddes	R	24	6	1	0	0	15.2	14	0	14	7	0-0	0	2.87
Jim McGlothlin†	R	29	5	1	0	0	18.1	13	2	13	14	0-1	0	3.93
Dave Baldwin	R	35	3	0	0	0	5.0	7	0	4	1	0-0	0	3.60

1973 Texas Rangers 6th AL West 57-105 .352 37.0 GB

Whitey Herzog (47-91)/Del Wilber (1-0)/Billy Martin (9-14)

Player	Gm by Position	B	Age	G	AB	R	H	2B	3B	HR	RBI	BB	SO	SB	Avg	OBP	Slg
Ken Suarez	C90	R	30	93	278	25	69	11	0	1	27	33	16	1	.248	.334	.299
Jim Spencer†	1B99,DH1	L	26	102	352	35	94	12	3	4	43	34	41	0	.267	.332	.352
Dave Nelson	2B140	R	29	142	576	71	165	24	4	7	48	34	78	43	.286	.325	.378
Toby Harrah	SS76,3B52	R	24	118	461	64	120	16	1	10	50	46	49	10	.260	.328	.364
Jim Mason	SS74,2B19,3B1	L	22	92	238	23	49	7	2	3	19	23	48	0	.206	.273	.290
Jeff Burroughs	OF148,1B3,DH1	R	22	151	526	71	147	17	1	30	85	67	88	0	.279	.355	.487
Vic Harris	OF113,3B25,2B18	S	23	152	555	71	138	14	7	8	44	55	81	13	.249	.317	.342
Elliott Maddox	OF89,3B7,DH1	R	25	100	172	24	41	1	0	1	17	29	28	5	.238	.356	.262
Alex Johnson	DH116,OF41	R	30	158	624	62	179	26	3	8	68	32	82	10	.287	.322	.377
Rico Carty†	OF53,DH31	R	33	86	306	24	71	12	0	3	33	36	39	2	.232	.311	.301
Dick Billings	C72,OF4,1B3*	R	30	81	280	17	50	11	0	3	32	20	43	1	.179	.237	.250
Larry Biittner	OF57,1B20,DH3	L	27	83	258	19	65	8	2	1	12	20	21	1	.252	.307	.310
Bill Sudakis	3B29,1B24,C9*	S	27	82	235	32	60	11	0	15	43	23	53	0	.255	.320	.494
Jim Fregosi†	3B34,1B10,SS6	R	31	45	157	25	42	6	2	6	16	12	31	0	.268	.318	.446
Tom Grieve	OF59,DH1	R	25	66	123	22	38	6	0	7	21	7	25	1	.309	.348	.528
Pete Mackanin	SS33,3B10	R	21	44	90	3	9	2	0	0	2	4	26	0	.100	.146	.122
Mike Epstein†	1B25	L	30	27	85	9	16	3	0	1	6	14	19	0	.188	.317	.259
Bill Madlock	3B21	R	22	21	77	16	27	5	3	1	5	7	9	3	.351	.412	.532
Joe Lovitto	3B20,OF3	S	22	26	44	3	6	1	0	0	0	5	7	1	.136	.224	.159
Lenny Randle	2B5,OF2	S	24	10	29	3	6	1	1	1	1	0	2	0	.207	.207	.414
Don Castle	DH3	L	23	4	13	0	4	1	0	0	2	1	3	0	.308	.357	.385
Rick Stelmaszek†	C7	L	24	7	9	0	1	0	0	0	0	1	2	0	.111	.200	.111

D. Billings, 2 G at DH; B. Sudakis, 8 G at DH, 2 G at OF

Pitcher	T	Age	G	GS	CG	ShO	IP	H	HR	BB	SO	W-L	Sv	ERA
Jim Bibby†	R	28	26	23	11	2	180.1	121	14	106	155	9-10	1	3.24
Sonny Siebert†	R	36	25	20	1	1	119.2	120	11	37	76	7-11	2	3.99
Pete Broberg	R	23	22	20	6	1	118.2	130	8	66	57	5-9	0	5.61
Jim Merritt	L	29	35	19	8	1	160.0	191	18	34	65	5-13	1	4.05
David Clyde	L	18	18	18	0	0	93.1	106	8	54	74	4-8	0	5.01
Steve Dunning†	R	24	23	12	2	0	94.1	101	11	52	38	2-6	0	5.34
Rich Hand†	R	24	8	7	1	0	41.2	49	2	19	14	2-3	0	5.40
Dick Bosman†	R	29	7	7	1	0	40.1	42	6	17	14	2-5	0	4.24
Jim Kremmel	L	25	4	2	0	0	9.0	15	1	6	6	0-2	0	9.00
Bill Gogolewski	R	25	49	1	0	0	123.2	139	10	48	77	3-6	6	4.22
Mike Paul†	L	28	36	10	1	0	87.1	104	9	36	49	5-4	2	4.95
Steve Foucault	R	23	32	0	0	0	55.2	54	6	31	28	2-4	8	3.88
Jackie Brown	R	30	25	3	2	1	66.2	82	7	25	45	5-5	2	3.92
Charlie Hudson	L	23	25	4	1	1	62.1	59	3	31	34	4-2	1	4.62
Lloyd Allen†	R	23	23	5	0	0	41.0	58	3	39	25	0-6	1	9.22
Don Stanhouse	R	22	21	5	1	0	70.0	70	5	44	42	1-7	1	4.76
Don Durham	R	24	15	4	0	0	40.1	49	7	23	23	0-4	1	7.59
Rick Henninger	R	25	6	2	0	0	23.0	23	1	11	6	1-0	0	2.74
Jim Shellenback	L	29	2	0	0	0	1.2	0	0	0	3	0-0	0	0.00
Rick Waits	L	21	1	0	0	0	1.0	1	0	1	0	0-0	1	9.00

»1973 New York Mets 1st NL East 82-79 .509 —

Yogi Berra

Player	Gm by Position	B	Age	G	AB	R	H	2B	3B	HR	RBI	BB	SO	SB	Avg	OBP	Slg
Jerry Grote	C81,3B2	R	30	84	285	17	73	10	2	1	32	13	23	0	.256	.290	.316
John Milner	1B95,OF29	L	23	129	451	69	108	12	3	23	72	62	84	1	.239	.329	.432
Felix Millan	2B153	R	29	153	638	82	185	23	4	3	37	35	22	2	.290	.332	.353
Wayne Garrett	3B130,SS9,2B6	L	25	140	504	76	129	20	3	16	58	72	74	6	.256	.348	.403
Bud Harrelson	SS103	S	29	106	356	35	92	12	3	0	20	48	49	5	.258	.348	.309
Rusty Staub	OF152	L	29	152	585	77	163	36	1	15	76	74	52	1	.279	.361	.421
Cleon Jones	OF92	R	30	92	339	48	88	13	0	11	48	28	51	1	.260	.315	.395
Don Hahn	OF87	R	24	93	262	22	60	10	0	2	21	22	43	2	.229	.285	.290
Ed Kranepool	1B51,OF32	L	28	100	284	28	68	12	2	1	35	30	28	1	.239	.310	.306
Ted Martinez	SS44,OF21,3B14*	R	25	92	263	34	67	11	0	1	14	13	38	3	.255	.294	.308
Willie Mays	OF45,1B17	R	42	66	209	24	44	10	0	6	25	27	47	1	.211	.303	.344
Duffy Dyer	C60	R	27	70	189	9	35	6	1	1	9	13	40	0	.185	.245	.243
Ron Hodges	C40	L	24	45	127	5	33	2	0	1	18	11	19	0	.260	.314	.299
Jim Fregosi†	3B17,SS17,1B3*	R	31	45	124	7	29	4	1	0	11	20	25	1	.234	.340	.282
George Theodore	OF33,1B4	R	25	45	116	14	30	4	0	1	15	10	13	1	.259	.320	.319
Ken Boswell	3B17,2B3	L	27	76	110	12	25	2	1	2	14	12	11	0	.227	.303	.318
Jim Gosger	OF35	L	30	38	92	9	22	2	0	0	10	9	16	0	.239	.304	.261
Jim Beauchamp	1B11	R	33	50	61	5	17	1	1	0	14	7	11	1	.279	.343	.328
Dave Schneck	OF12	L	24	13	36	2	7	0	1	0	1	1	4	0	.194	.216	.250
Rich Chiles	OF8	L	23	8	25	2	3	2	0	0	1	0	2	0	.120	.120	.200
Jerry May†	C4	R	29	4	8	0	2	0	0	0	0	1	1	0	.250	.333	.250
Brian Ostrosser	SS4	L	24	4	5	0	0	0	0	0	0	0	2	0	.000	.000	.000
Greg Harts		L	23	3	2	0	1	0	0	0	0	0	0	0	.500	.500	.500
Lute Barnes		R	26	3	2	2	1	0	0	0	1	0	1	0	.500	.500	.500

T. Martinez, 5 G at 2B; J. Fregosi, 1 G at OF

Pitcher	T	Age	G	GS	CG	ShO	IP	H	HR	BB	SO	W-L	Sv	ERA
Tom Seaver	R	28	36	36	18	3	290.0	219	23	64	251	19-10	0	2.08
Jerry Koosman	L	30	35	35	12	3	263.0	234	18	76	156	14-15	0	2.84
Jon Matlack	L	23	34	34	14	3	242.0	210	16	99	205	14-16	0	3.20
George Stone	L	26	27	20	2	0	148.0	157	16	31	77	12-3	1	2.80
Jim McAndrew	R	29	23	12	0	0	80.1	109	9	31	38	3-8	1	5.38
Tug McGraw	L	28	60	2	0	0	118.2	106	11	55	81	5-6	25	3.87
Harry Parker	R	25	38	9	0	0	96.2	79	7	36	63	8-4	5	3.35
Ray Sadecki	L	32	31	11	1	1	116.2	109	11	41	87	5-4	1	3.39
Phil Hennigan	R	27	30	0	0	0	43.1	50	6	16	22	0-4	3	6.23
Buzz Capra	R	25	24	0	0	0	42.0	35	4	28	35	2-7	4	3.86
John Strohmayer†	R	26	7	0	0	0	10.0	13	2	4	5	0-0	0	8.10
Craig Swan	R	22	3	1	0	0	8.1	16	2	2	4	0-1	0	8.64
Tommy Moore	R	24	3	1	0	0	3.1	6	1	3	1	0-1	0	10.80
Hank Webb	R	23	2	0	0	0	1.2	2	1	2	1	0-0	0	10.80
Bob Miller†	R	34	1	0	0	0	1.0	0	0	0	1	0-0	0	0.00
Bob Apodaca	R	23	1	0	0	0	0.0	0	0	2	0	0-0	0	—

1973 St. Louis Cardinals 2nd NL East 81-81 .500 1.5 GB — Red Schoendienst

Player	Gm by Position	B	Age	G	AB	R	H	2B	3B	HR	RBI	BB	SO	SB	Avg	OBP	Slg
Ted Simmons	C153,1B6,OF2	S	23	161	619	62	192	36	2	13	91	61	47	2	.310	.370	.438
Joe Torre	1B114,3B58	R	32	141	519	67	149	17	2	13	69	65	78	2	.287	.376	.403
Ted Sizemore	2B139,3B3	R	28	142	521	69	147	22	1	1	54	68	34	6	.282	.365	.334
Ken Reitz	3B135,SS1	R	22	147	426	40	100	20	2	6	42	9	25	0	.235	.256	.333
Mike Tyson	SS128,2B16	R	23	144	469	48	114	15	4	1	33	23	66	2	.243	.279	.299
Lou Brock	OF159	L	34	160	650	110	193	29	8	7	63	71	112	70	.297	.364	.398
Jose Cruz	OF118	L	25	132	406	51	92	22	5	10	57	51	66	10	.227	.310	.379
Luis Melendez	OF95	R	23	121	341	35	91	18	1	2	35	27	50	2	.267	.319	.343
Tim McCarver	1B77,C11	L	31	130	331	30	88	16	4	3	49	38	31	2	.266	.339	.366
Bernie Carbo	OF94	L	25	111	308	42	88	18	0	8	40	58	52	2	.286	.397	.422
Ray Busse†	SS23	R	24	24	70	6	10	4	2	2	5	5	21	0	.143	.200	.343
Bake McBride	OF17	L	24	40	63	8	19	3	0	0	5	4	10	0	.302	.352	.349
Tommie Agee†	OF19	R	30	26	62	8	11	3	1	3	7	5	13	1	.177	.239	.403
Jim Dwyer	OF20	L	23	28	57	7	11	1	1	0	0	1	5	0	.193	.207	.246
Bill Stein	OF10,1B2,3B1	R	26	32	55	4	12	2	0	0	2	7	18	0	.218	.306	.255
Ed Crosby†	SS7,2B5,3B4	L	24	22	39	4	5	2	1	0	1	4	4	0	.128	.209	.231
Mick Kelleher	SS42	R	25	43	38	4	7	2	0	0	2	4	11	0	.184	.279	.237
Tom Heintzelman	2B6	R	26	23	29	5	9	0	0	0	0	3	3	0	.310	.375	.310
Dave Campbell†	2B6	R	31	13	21	1	0	0	0	0	1	1	6	0	.000	.043	.000
Dwain Anderson†	SS3,OF2	R	25	18	17	5	2	0	0	0	0	4	4	0	.118	.286	.118
Terry Hughes	3B5,1B1	R	24	11	14	1	3	1	0	0	1	1	4	0	.214	.267	.286
Heity Cruz	OF5	R	20	11	11	1	0	0	0	0	0	1	3	0	.000	.083	.000
Matty Alou†	1B1,OF1	L	34	11	11	1	3	0	0	0	1	1	0	0	.273	.333	.273
Bobby Fenwick	2B3	R	26	5	6	0	1	0	0	0	1	0	2	0	.167	.167	.167
Marc Hill	C1	R	21	1	3	0	0	0	0	0	0	0	1	0	.000	.000	.000
Larry Haney†	C2	R	30	2	1	0	0	0	0	0	0	0	1	0	.000	.000	.000
Tommy Cruz	OF1	L	22	3	0	1	0	0	0	0	0	0	0	0	—	—	—

Pitcher	T	Age	G	GS	CG	ShO	IP	H	HR	BB	SO	W-L	Sv	ERA
Rick Wise	R	27	35	34	14	5	259.0	259	18	59	144	16-12	0	3.37
Reggie Cleveland	R	25	32	32	6	3	224.0	211	13	61	122	14-10	0	3.01
Alan Foster	R	26	35	29	6	2	203.2	195	17	63	106	13-9	0	3.14
Bob Gibson	R	37	25	25	13	1	195.0	159	12	57	142	12-10	0	2.77
Tom Murphy	R	27	19	13	2	0	88.2	89	5	22	42	3-7	0	3.76
Scipio Spinks	R	25	8	8	0	0	38.2	39	4	25	25	1-5	0	4.89
Mike Nagy	R	25	9	7	0	0	40.2	44	4	15	14	0-2	0	4.20
Jim Bibby†	R	28	6	3	0	0	16.0	19	2	17	12	0-2	0	9.56
Mike Thompson	R	23	2	2	0	0	4.0	1	0	5	3	0-0	0	0.00
Diego Segui	R	35	65	0	0	0	100.1	78	6	53	93	7-6	17	2.78
Al Hrabosky	L	23	44	0	0	0	56.0	45	2	21	57	2-4	5	2.09
Orlando Pena†	R	39	42	0	0	0	62.0	60	3	14	38	4-4	6	2.18
Rich Folkers	L	26	34	9	1	0	82.1	74	10	34	44	4-4	3	3.61
Wayne Granger†	R	29	33	0	0	0	46.2	50	3	21	14	2-4	5	4.24
John Andrews	L	24	16	0	0	0	18.1	16	3	11	5	1-1	0	4.42
Ed Sprague†	R	27	8	0	0	0	8.0	8	1	4	2	0-0	0	2.25
Al Santorini	R	25	6	0	0	0	8.1	14	1	2	2	0-0	0	5.40
Eddie Fisher†	R	36	6	0	0	0	7.0	3	1	1	1	2-1	0	1.29
Lew Krausse	R	30	1	0	0	0	2.0	2	0	1	1	0-0	0	0.00

1973 Pittsburgh Pirates 3rd NL East 80-82 .494 2.5 GB — Bill Virdon (67-69)/Danny Murtaugh (13-13)

Player	Gm by Position	B	Age	G	AB	R	H	2B	3B	HR	RBI	BB	SO	SB	Avg	OBP	Slg
Manny Sanguillen	C89,OF59	R	29	149	589	64	166	26	7	12	65	17	29	2	.282	.301	.411
Bob Robertson	1B107	R	26	119	397	43	95	16	0	14	40	55	77	0	.239	.332	.385
Dave Cash	2B92,3B17	R	25	116	436	59	118	21	2	2	31	38	36	2	.271	.328	.342
Richie Hebner	3B139	L	25	144	509	73	138	28	1	25	74	56	60	0	.271	.346	.477
Dal Maxvill†	SS74	R	34	74	217	19	41	4	3	0	17	22	40	0	.189	.261	.235
Willie Stargell	OF142	L	33	148	522	106	156	43	3	44	119	80	129	0	.299	.392	.646
Al Oliver	OF109,1B50	L	26	158	654	90	191	38	7	20	99	22	52	6	.292	.316	.463
Richie Zisk	OF84	R	24	103	333	44	108	23	7	10	54	21	63	0	.324	.364	.526
Rennie Stennett	2B84,SS43,OF5	R	22	128	466	45	113	18	3	10	55	16	63	2	.242	.265	.358
Gene Clines	OF77	R	26	110	304	42	80	11	3	1	23	26	36	8	.263	.327	.329
Milt May	C79	L	22	101	283	29	76	8	1	7	31	34	26	0	.269	.349	.378
Gene Alley	SS49,3B8	R	32	76	158	25	32	3	2	2	8	20	28	1	.203	.292	.285
Dave Parker	OF39	L	22	54	139	17	40	9	1	4	14	2	27	1	.288	.308	.453
Vic Davalillo†	1B10,OF10	L	36	59	83	9	15	1	0	1	3	2	7	0	.181	.200	.229
Jackie Hernandez	SS49	R	32	54	73	8	18	1	2	0	8	4	12	0	.247	.286	.315
Fernando Gonzalez	3B5	R	23	37	49	5	11	0	1	1	5	1	11	0	.224	.255	.327
Dave Augustine	OF9	R	23	11	7	1	2	1	0	0	0	0	1	0	.286	.286	.429
Jim Campanis		R	29	6	6	0	1	0	0	0	0	0	0	0	.167	.167	.167
Jerry McNertney	C9	R	36	9	4	0	1	0	0	0	0	0	0	0	.250	.250	.250
Chuck Goggin†	C1	S	27	1	1	1	1	0	0	0	0	0	0	0	1.000	1.000	1.000

Pitcher	T	Age	G	GS	CG	ShO	IP	H	HR	BB	SO	W-L	Sv	ERA
Nelson Briles	R	29	33	33	7	1	218.2	201	19	51	94	14-13	0	2.84
Bob Moose	R	25	33	29	6	3	201.1	219	11	70	111	12-13	0	3.53
Dock Ellis	R	28	28	28	3	1	192.0	176	7	55	122	12-14	0	3.05
Steve Blass	R	31	23	18	1	0	88.2	109	11	84	27	3-9	0	9.85
Bruce Kison	R	23	7	7	0	0	43.2	36	4	24	26	3-0	0	3.09
John Morlan	R	25	10	7	1	0	41.0	42	4	23	23	2-2	0	3.95
Dave Giusti	R	33	67	0	0	0	98.2	89	9	37	64	9-2	20	2.37
Ramon Hernandez	L	32	59	0	0	0	89.2	71	5	25	64	4-5	11	2.41
Bob Johnson	R	30	50	2	0	0	92.0	98	12	34	68	4-2	4	3.62
Jim Rooker	L	30	41	18	6	3	170.1	143	12	52	122	10-6	5	2.85
Luke Walker	L	29	37	18	2	1	122.0	129	9	66	74	7-12	1	4.65
John Lamb	R	26	22	0	0	0	29.2	37	3	10	11	0-1	2	6.07
Jim McKee	R	26	15	1	0	0	27.0	31	2	17	13	0-1	0	5.67
Tom Dettore	R	25	12	1	0	0	22.2	33	1	14	13	0-1	0	5.96
Chris Zachary	R	29	6	0	0	0	12.0	10	1	1	6	0-1	1	3.00
Jim Foor	L	24	3	0	0	0	1.1	2	0	1	1	0-0	0	0.00

1973 Montreal Expos 4th NL East 79-83 .488 3.5 GB — Gene Mauch

Player	Gm by Position	B	Age	G	AB	R	H	2B	3B	HR	RBI	BB	SO	SB	Avg	OBP	Slg
John Boccabella	C117,1B1	R	32	118	403	25	94	13	0	7	46	26	57	1	.233	.279	.318
Mike Jorgensen	1B123,OF11	L	24	138	413	49	95	16	2	9	47	64	49	16	.230	.336	.344
Ron Hunt	2B102,3B14	R	32	113	401	61	124	14	0	0	18	52	19	10	.309	.418	.344
Bob Bailey	3B146,OF2	R	30	151	513	77	140	25	4	26	86	88	99	5	.273	.379	.489
Tim Foli	SS123,2B2,OF1	R	22	126	458	37	110	11	0	2	36	28	40	6	.240	.284	.277
Ken Singleton	OF161	S	26	162	560	100	169	26	2	23	103	123	91	2	.302	.425	.479
Ron Fairly	OF121,1B5	L	34	142	413	70	123	13	1	17	49	86	33	2	.298	.422	.458
Ron Woods	OF114	R	30	135	318	45	73	11	3	3	31	56	34	12	.230	.344	.311
Hal Breeden	1B66	R	29	105	258	36	71	10	6	15	43	29	45	0	.275	.353	.535
Pepe Frias	SS46,2B44,3B6*	R	24	100	225	19	52	10	1	0	22	10	24	1	.231	.266	.284
Boots Day	OF51	L	25	101	207	36	57	7	0	4	28	21	28	0	.275	.342	.367
Larry Lintz	2B34,SS15	S	23	52	116	20	29	2	1	0	3	17	18	12	.250	.351	.259
Jim Lyttle	OF36	L	27	49	116	12	30	5	1	4	19	9	14	0	.259	.305	.422
Bob Stinson	C35,3B1	S	27	48	111	12	29	6	1	3	12	17	15	0	.261	.374	.414
Clyde Mashore	OF44,2B1	R	28	67	103	12	21	3	0	3	14	15	28	4	.204	.300	.320
Terry Humphrey	C35	R	23	43	90	5	15	2	0	1	9	5	16	0	.167	.206	.222
Pepe Mangual	OF22	R	21	33	62	9	11	2	1	3	7	6	18	2	.177	.246	.387
Jorge Roque	OF24	R	23	25	61	7	9	2	0	1	6	4	17	2	.148	.212	.230
Bernie Allen†	2B9,3B8	L	34	16	50	5	9	1	0	2	9	5	4	0	.180	.255	.320
Felipe Alou†	OF15,1B1	R	38	19	48	4	10	1	0	1	4	2	4	0	.208	.240	.292
Coco Laboy	3B20,2B1	R	32	22	33	2	4	1	0	1	2	5	8	0	.121	.237	.242
Jim Cox	2B7	R	23	9	15	1	2	1	0	0	0	1	4	0	.133	.188	.200
Barry Foote		R	21	6	6	0	4	0	1	0	1	0	0	0	.667	.667	1.000
Jose Morales†		R	28	5	5	0	2	0	0	0	0	0	0	0	.400	.400	.400
Curtis Brown	OF1	R	27	1	4	0	0	0	0	0	0	0	0	0	.000	.000	.000
Tony Scott	OF3	S	21	11	1	2	0	0	0	0	0	0	1	0	.000	.000	.000

P. Frias, 1 G at OF

Pitcher	T	Age	G	GS	CG	ShO	IP	H	HR	BB	SO	W-L	Sv	ERA
Steve Renko	R	28	36	34	9	0	249.2	201	26	108	164	15-11	1	2.81
Mike Torrez	R	26	35	34	3	1	208.0	207	17	115	90	9-12	0	4.46
Balor Moore	L	22	35	32	3	1	176.1	151	18	109	151	7-16	0	4.49
Ernie McAnally	R	26	27	24	4	0	147.0	158	13	54	72	7-9	0	4.04
Steve Rogers	R	23	17	17	7	3	134.0	93	5	49	64	10-5	0	1.54
Bill Stoneman	R	29	29	17	0	0	96.2	120	12	55	48	4-8	1	6.80
Mike Marshall	R	30	92	0	0	0	179.0	163	10	75	124	14-11	31	2.66
Tom Walker	R	24	54	0	0	0	91.2	95	7	42	68	7-5	4	3.63
Pat Jarvis	R	32	28	0	0	0	39.1	37	6	16	19	2-1	0	3.20
Mickey Scott†	L	25	22	0	0	0	24.0	27	3	9	11	1-2	0	5.25
Joe Gilbert	L	21	21	0	0	0	29.0	30	1	19	17	1-2	1	4.97
John Strohmayer†	R	26	17	3	0	0	34.2	34	4	22	15	0-1	0	5.19
Craig Caskey	L	23	9	1	0	0	14.1	15	3	4	6	0-0	0	5.65
Chuck Taylor	R	31	8	0	0	0	20.1	17	3	2	10	2-0	0	1.77
John Montague	R	25	4	0	0	0	7.2	8	0	2	7	0-0	0	3.52

1973 Chicago Cubs 5th NL East 77-84 .478 5.0 GB — Whitey Lockman

Player	Gm by Position	B	Age	G	AB	R	H	2B	3B	HR	RBI	BB	SO	SB	Avg	OBP	Slg
Randy Hundley	C122	R	31	124	368	35	83	11	1	10	43	30	51	5	.226	.283	.342
Jim Hickman	1B51,OF13	R	36	92	201	27	49	1	2	3	20	42	42	1	.244	.368	.313
Glenn Beckert	2B88	R	32	114	372	38	95	13	0	0	29	30	15	0	.255	.313	.290
Ron Santo	3B146	R	33	149	536	65	143	29	2	20	77	63	97	1	.267	.348	.440
Don Kessinger	SS158	S	30	160	577	52	151	22	3	0	43	57	44	6	.262	.327	.310
Rick Monday	OF148	L	27	149	554	93	148	24	5	26	56	92	124	5	.267	.372	.469
Jose Cardenal	OF142	R	29	145	522	80	158	33	2	11	68	58	62	19	.303	.375	.437
Billy Williams	OF138,1B19	L	35	156	576	72	166	22	2	20	86	76	72	4	.288	.369	.438
Paul Popovich	2B84,SS9,3B1	S	32	99	280	24	66	6	3	2	24	18	27	3	.236	.280	.300
Ken Rudolph	C64	R	26	64	170	12	35	8	1	2	17	7	25	1	.206	.239	.300
Carmen Fanzone	3B25,1B24,OF6	R	29	64	150	22	41	7	0	6	22	20	38	1	.273	.357	.440
Pat Bourque†	1B38	L	26	57	139	11	29	6	0	7	20	16	21	1	.209	.297	.403
Joe Pepitone†	1B28	L	32	31	112	16	30	3	0	3	18	8	6	3	.268	.320	.375
Gene Hiser	OF64	L	24	100	109	15	19	3	0	1	6	11	17	4	.174	.254	.229
Rico Carty†	OF19	R	33	22	70	4	15	0	0	1	8	6	10	0	.214	.276	.257
Gonzalo Marquez†	1B18	L	27	19	58	5	13	2	0	1	4	3	4	0	.224	.270	.310
Adrian Garrett	OF7,C6	L	30	36	54	7	12	0	0	3	8	4	18	1	.222	.267	.389
Cleo James	OF22	R	32	44	45	9	5	0	0	0	0	1	6	5	.111	.130	.111
Dave Rosello	2B13,SS1	R	23	16	38	4	10	2	0	0	2	2	4	2	.263	.300	.316
Andre Thornton	1B9	R	23	17	35	3	7	3	0	0	2	7	9	0	.200	.333	.286
Pete LaCock	OF5	L	21	11	16	1	4	1	0	0	3	1	2	0	.250	.294	.313
Matt Alexander	OF3	S	26	12	5	4	1	0	0	0	1	1	1	2	.200	.333	.200
Tom Lundstedt	C4	S	24	4	5	0	0	0	0	0	0	0	1	0	.000	.000	.000
Tony La Russa		R	28	1	0	1	0	0	0	0	0	0	0	0	—	—	—

Pitcher	T	Age	G	GS	CG	ShO	IP	H	HR	BB	SO	W-L	Sv	ERA
Fergie Jenkins	R	29	38	38	7	2	271.0	267	35	57	170	14-16	0	3.89
Rick Reuschel	R	24	36	36	7	3	237.0	244	15	62	168	14-15	0	3.00
Burt Hooton	R	23	42	34	9	2	239.2	248	12	73	134	14-17	0	3.68
Milt Pappas	R	34	30	29	1	1	162.0	192	20	40	48	7-12	0	4.28
Bob Locker	R	35	63	0	0	0	106.1	96	6	42	76	10-6	18	2.54
Jack Aker	R	32	47	0	0	0	63.2	76	8	23	25	4-5	12	4.10
Dave LaRoche	L	25	45	0	0	0	54.1	55	7	29	34	4-1	4	5.80
Bill Bonham	R	24	44	15	3	0	152.0	126	10	64	121	7-5	6	3.02
Ray Burris	R	22	31	1	0	0	64.2	65	2	27	57	1-1	0	2.92
Larry Gura	L	25	21	7	0	0	64.2	79	10	11	43	2-4	0	4.87
Mike Paul†	L	28	11	1	0	0	18.1	17	2	9	6	0-1	0	3.44
Juan Pizarro†	L	36	2	0	0	0	4.0	6	1	1	3	0-1	0	11.25

1973 Philadelphia Phillies 6th NL East 71-91 .438 11.5 GB

Danny Ozark

Player	Gm by Position	B	Age	G	AB	R	H	2B	3B	HR	RBI	BB	SO	SB	Avg	OBP	Slg
Bob Boone	C145	R	25	145	521	42	136	20	2	10	61	41	36	3	.261	.311	.365
Willie Montanez	1B99,OF51	L	25	146	552	69	145	16	5	11	65	46	80	2	.263	.324	.370
Denny Doyle	2B114	L	29	116	370	45	101	9	3	3	26	31	32	1	.273	.327	.338
Mike Schmidt	3B125,2B4,1B2*	R	23	132	367	43	72	11	0	18	52	62	136	8	.196	.324	.373
Larry Bowa	SS122	S	27	122	446	42	94	11	3	0	23	24	31	10	.211	.252	.249
Greg Luzinski	OF159	R	22	161	610	76	174	26	4	29	97	51	135	3	.285	.346	.484
Del Unser	OF132	L	28	136	440	64	127	20	4	11	52	47	55	5	.289	.354	.427
Bill Robinson	OF113,3B14	R	30	124	452	62	130	32	1	25	65	27	91	5	.288	.326	.529
Cesar Tovar	3B46,OF24,2B22	R	32	97	328	49	88	18	4	1	21	29	35	6	.268	.335	.357
Tom Hutton	1B71	L	27	106	247	31	65	11	0	5	29	32	31	3	.263	.346	.368
Mike Anderson	OF67	R	22	87	193	32	49	9	1	9	28	19	53	0	.254	.321	.451
Terry Harmon	2B43,SS19,3B1	R	29	72	148	17	31	3	0	0	8	13	14	1	.209	.278	.230
Craig Robinson	SS42,2B4	R	24	46	146	11	33	7	0	0	7	0	25	1	.226	.226	.274
Mike Rogodzinski	OF16	L	25	66	80	13	19	3	0	2	7	12	19	0	.238	.333	.350
Jose Pagan	3B16,1B5,OF2*	R	38	46	78	4	16	5	0	0	5	1	15	0	.205	.213	.269
Mike Ryan	C27	R	31	28	69	7	16	1	2	1	5	6	19	0	.232	.289	.348
Billy Grabarkewitz†	2B20,3B3,OF1	R	27	25	66	12	19	2	0	2	7	12	18	3	.288	.397	.409
Deron Johnson†	1B10	R	34	12	36	3	6	2	0	1	5	5	10	0	.167	.279	.306
Jim Essian	C1	R	22	2	3	0	0	0	0	0	0	0	1	0	.000	.000	.000
Larry Cox	C1	R	25	1	0	0	0	0	0	0	0	0	0	0	—	—	—

M. Schmidt, 2 G at SS; J. Pagan, 1 G at 2B

Pitcher	T	Age	G	GS	CG	ShO	IP	H	HR	BB	SO	W-L	Sv	ERA
Steve Carlton	L	28	40	40	18	3	293.1	293	29	113	223	13-20	0	3.90
Jim Lonborg	R	31	38	30	6	0	199.1	218	25	80	106	13-16	0	4.88
Wayne Twitchell	R	25	34	28	10	5	223.1	172	16	99	169	13-9	0	2.50
Ken Brett	L	24	31	25	10	1	211.2	206	19	74	111	13-9	0	3.44
Dick Ruthven	R	22	25	23	3	1	128.1	125	10	75	98	6-9	1	4.21
Larry Christenson	R	19	10	9	1	0	34.1	53	3	20	11	1-4	0	6.55
Mac Scarce	L	24	52	0	0	0	70.2	54	3	47	57	1-8	12	2.42
Billy Wilson	R	30	44	0	0	0	48.2	54	7	29	24	1-3	4	6.66
Barry Lersch	R	28	42	4	0	0	98.1	105	10	27	51	3-6	1	4.39
Bucky Brandon	R	32	36	0	0	0	56.1	54	5	25	25	2-4	2	5.43
Ron Diorio	R	26	23	0	0	0	19.1	18	1	6	11	0-0	1	2.33
Mike Wallace	L	22	20	3	1	0	33.1	38	1	15	20	1-1	1	3.78
George Culver†	R	29	14	0	0	0	18.2	26	0	15	7	3-1	0	4.82
Dick Selma	R	29	6	0	0	0	8.0	6	1	5	4	1-1	0	5.63
Dave Wallace	R	25	4	0	0	0	3.2	13	1	2	2	0-0	0	22.09

1973 Cincinnati Reds 1st NL West 99-63 .611 —

Sparky Anderson

Player	Gm by Position	B	Age	G	AB	R	H	2B	3B	HR	RBI	BB	SO	SB	Avg	OBP	Slg
Johnny Bench	C134,OF23,1B4*	R	25	152	557	83	141	17	3	25	104	83	83	4	.253	.345	.429
Tony Perez	1B151	R	31	151	564	73	177	33	3	27	101	74	117	3	.314	.393	.527
Joe Morgan	2B154	L	29	157	576	116	167	35	2	26	82	111	61	67	.290	.406	.493
Denis Menke	3B123,SS7,2B5*	R	32	139	241	38	46	10	0	3	26	69	53	1	.191	.368	.270
Dave Concepcion	SS88,OF2	R	25	89	328	39	94	18	3	8	46	21	55	22	.287	.327	.433
Pete Rose	OF159	S	32	160	680	115	230	36	8	5	64	65	42	10	.338	.401	.437
Cesar Geronimo	OF130	L	25	139	324	35	68	14	3	4	33	23	74	5	.210	.266	.309
Bobby Tolan	OF120	L	27	129	457	42	94	14	2	9	51	27	68	15	.206	.251	.304
Dan Driessen	3B87,1B35,OF1	L	21	102	366	49	110	15	2	4	47	24	37	8	.301	.346	.385
Darrel Chaney	SS75,2B14,3B12	S	25	105	227	27	41	7	1	0	14	26	50	4	.181	.267	.220
Bill Plummer	C42,3B5	R	26	50	119	8	18	3	0	2	11	18	26	1	.151	.268	.227
Andy Kosco	OF36,1B1	R	31	47	118	17	33	7	0	9	21	13	26	0	.280	.346	.568
Larry Stahl	OF29,1B2	L	32	76	111	17	25	2	2	2	12	14	34	1	.225	.315	.333
Ken Griffey Sr.	OF21	L	23	25	86	19	33	5	1	3	14	6	10	4	.384	.424	.570
Phil Gagliano	3B7,2B4,1B1*	R	31	63	69	8	20	2	0	0	7	13	16	0	.290	.402	.319
Richie Scheinblum†	OF19	S	30	29	54	5	12	2	0	1	8	10	4	0	.222	.338	.315
Ed Crosby†	SS29,2B5	L	24	36	51	4	11	1	1	0	5	7	12	0	.216	.333	.275
Hal King	C9	L	29	35	43	5	8	0	0	4	10	6	10	0	.186	.286	.465
George Foster	OF13	R	24	17	39	6	11	3	0	4	9	4	7	0	.282	.349	.667
Ed Armbrister	OF14	R	24	18	37	5	8	3	1	1	5	2	8	0	.216	.250	.432
Joe Hague	OF5,1B4	L	29	19	33	2	5	2	0	0	1	5	5	1	.152	.256	.212
Gene Locklear†	OF5	L	23	29	26	6	5	0	0	0	0	2	5	0	.192	.276	.192
Bob Barton	C2	R	31	3	1	0	0	0	0	0	0	1	0	0	.000	.500	.000

J. Bench, 1 G at 3B; D. Menke, 1 G at 1B; P. Gagliano, 1 G at OF

Pitcher	T	Age	G	GS	CG	ShO	IP	H	HR	BB	SO	W-L	Sv	ERA
Jack Billingham	R	30	40	40	16	7	293.1	257	20	95	155	19-10	0	3.04
Ross Grimsley	L	23	38	36	8	1	242.1	245	24	68	90	13-10	1	3.23
Don Gullett	L	22	45	30	7	4	228.1	198	24	69	153	18-8	2	3.51
Fred Norman†	L	30	24	24	7	3	166.1	136	18	72	112	12-6	0	3.30
Roger Nelson	R	29	14	8	1	0	54.2	49	4	24	17	3-2	0	3.46
Gary Nolan	R	25	2	2	0	0	10.1	6	1	7	3	0-1	0	3.48
Pedro Borbon	R	26	80	0	0	0	121.0	137	4	35	60	11-4	14	2.16
Tom Hall	L	25	54	7	0	0	103.2	74	13	48	96	8-5	8	3.47
Clay Carroll	R	32	53	5	0	0	92.2	111	5	34	41	8-8	14	3.69
Ed Sprague†	R	27	28	0	0	0	38.2	35	3	22	19	1-3	1	5.12
Jim McGlothlin†	R	29	24	9	0	0	63.1	91	13	23	18	3-3	0	6.68
Dave Tomlin	L	24	16	0	0	0	27.2	24	5	15	20	1-2	1	4.88
Dick Baney	R	26	11	1	0	0	30.2	26	1	6	17	2-1	2	2.93

1973 Los Angeles Dodgers 2nd NL West 95-66 .590 3.5 GB

Walter Alston

Player	Gm by Position	B	Age	G	AB	R	H	2B	3B	HR	RBI	BB	SO	SB	Avg	OBP	Slg
Joe Ferguson	C122,OF20	R	26	136	487	84	128	26	0	25	88	87	81	1	.263	.369	.470
Bill Buckner	1B93,OF48	L	23	140	575	68	158	20	0	8	46	17	34	12	.275	.297	.351
Davey Lopes	2B135,OF5,SS2*	R	28	142	535	77	147	13	5	6	37	62	77	36	.275	.352	.351
Ron Cey	3B146	R	25	152	507	60	124	18	4	15	80	74	77	1	.245	.338	.385
Bill Russell	SS162	R	24	162	615	55	163	26	3	4	56	34	63	15	.265	.301	.337
Willie Davis	OF146	L	33	152	599	82	171	29	9	16	77	29	62	17	.285	.320	.444
Willie Crawford	OF138	L	26	145	457	75	135	26	2	14	66	78	91	12	.295	.396	.453
Tom Paciorek	OF77,1B4	R	26	96	195	26	51	8	0	5	18	11	35	3	.262	.304	.379
Steve Garvey	1B76,OF10	R	24	114	349	37	106	17	3	8	50	11	42	0	.304	.328	.438
Manny Mota	OF74	R	35	89	293	33	92	11	2	0	23	25	12	1	.314	.368	.365
Von Joshua	OF46	L	25	75	159	19	40	4	1	2	17	8	29	7	.252	.288	.327
Lee Lacy	2B41	R	25	57	135	14	28	2	0	0	8	15	34	2	.207	.287	.222
Steve Yeager	C50	R	24	54	134	18	34	5	0	2	10	15	33	1	.254	.340	.336
Ken McMullen	3B24	R	31	42	85	6	21	5	0	5	18	6	13	0	.247	.297	.482
Chris Cannizzaro	C13	R	35	17	21	0	4	0	0	0	3	3	3	0	.190	.280	.190
Jerry Royster	3B6,2B1	R	20	10	19	1	4	0	0	0	2	0	5	1	.211	.211	.211
Jim Fairey		L	28	10	9	0	2	0	0	0	0	1	1	0	.222	.300	.222
Orlando Alvarez		R	21	4	4	0	1	1	0	0	0	0	1	0	.250	.250	.500
Paul Powell	OF1	R	25	2	1	0	0	0	0	0	0	0	1	0	.000	.000	.000

D. Lopes, 1 G at 3B

Pitcher	T	Age	G	GS	CG	ShO	IP	H	HR	BB	SO	W-L	Sv	ERA
Don Sutton	R	28	33	33	14	3	256.1	196	18	56	200	18-10	0	2.42
Andy Messersmith	R	27	33	33	10	3	249.2	196	24	77	177	14-10	0	2.70
Claude Osteen	L	33	33	33	12	3	236.2	227	20	61	86	16-11	0	3.31
Tommy John	L	30	36	31	4	2	218.0	202	16	50	116	16-7	0	3.10
Al Downing	L	32	30	28	5	2	193.0	155	19	68	124	9-9	0	3.31
Jim Brewer	L	35	56	0	0	0	71.2	58	8	25	56	6-8	20	3.01
Pete Richert	L	33	39	0	0	0	51.0	44	5	19	31	3-3	7	3.18
Charlie Hough	R	25	37	0	0	0	71.2	52	3	45	70	4-2	5	2.76
Doug Rau	L	24	31	3	0	0	63.2	64	5	28	51	4-2	3	3.96
George Culver†	R	29	28	0	0	0	42.0	45	4	21	23	4-4	2	3.00
Greg Shanahan	R	25	7	0	0	0	15.2	14	2	4	11	0-0	1	3.45
Geoff Zahn	L	27	6	1	0	0	13.1	5	2	2	9	1-0	0	1.35
Eddie Solomon	R	22	4	0	0	0	6.1	10	3	4	6	0-0	0	7.11
Greg Heydeman	R	21	1	0	0	0	2.0	2	0	1	1	0-0	0	4.50

1973 San Francisco Giants 3rd NL West 88-74 .543 11.0 GB

Charlie Fox

Player	Gm by Position	B	Age	G	AB	R	H	2B	3B	HR	RBI	BB	SO	SB	Avg	OBP	Slg
Dave Rader	C148	L	24	148	462	59	106	15	4	9	41	63	22	0	.229	.326	.338
Willie McCovey	1B117	L	35	130	383	52	102	14	3	29	75	105	78	1	.266	.420	.546
Tito Fuentes	2B160,3B1	S	29	160	656	78	182	25	5	6	63	45	62	12	.277	.328	.358
Ed Goodson	3B93	L	25	102	384	37	116	20	1	12	53	15	44	0	.302	.331	.453
Chris Speier	SS150,2B1	R	23	153	542	58	135	17	4	11	71	66	69	4	.249	.332	.356
Bobby Bonds	OF158	R	27	160	643	131	182	34	4	39	96	87	148	43	.283	.370	.530
Gary Matthews	OF145	R	22	148	540	74	162	22	10	12	58	58	83	17	.300	.367	.444
Garry Maddox	OF140	R	23	144	587	81	187	30	10	11	76	24	73	24	.319	.350	.460
Dave Kingman	3B60,1B46,P2	R	24	112	305	54	62	10	1	24	55	41	122	8	.203	.300	.479
Gary Thomasson	1B47,OF43	L	21	112	235	35	67	10	4	4	30	22	43	2	.285	.345	.413
Mike Phillips	3B28,SS20,2B7	L	22	63	104	18	25	3	4	1	9	6	17	0	.240	.288	.375
Jim Howarth	OF33,1B1	L	26	65	90	8	18	1	1	0	7	7	8	0	.200	.258	.233
Mike Sadek	C35	R	27	39	66	6	11	1	1	0	4	11	8	1	.167	.282	.212
Chris Arnold	C9,2B1,3B1	R	25	49	54	7	16	2	0	1	13	8	11	0	.296	.381	.389
Steve Ontiveros	1B5,OF1	S	21	24	33	3	8	0	0	1	5	4	7	0	.242	.324	.333
Bruce Miller	3B4,2B3,SS1	R	26	12	21	1	3	0	0	0	2	2	3	0	.143	.217	.143
Damaso Blanco	3B7,SS5,2B3	R	31	28	12	4	0	0	0	0	0	1	2	0	.000	.077	.000
Al Gallagher†	3B5	R	27	5	9	1	2	0	0	0	0	1	0	0	.222	.300	.222
Jim Ray Hart†	3B1	R	31	5	3	0	0	0	0	0	0	3	1	0	.000	.429	.000

Pitcher	T	Age	G	GS	CG	ShO	IP	H	HR	BB	SO	W-L	Sv	ERA
Ron Bryant	L	25	41	39	8	0	270.0	240	23	115	143	24-12	0	3.53
Tom Bradley	R	26	35	34	6	1	224.0	212	26	69	136	13-12	0	3.90
Jim Barr	R	25	41	33	8	3	231.1	240	24	49	88	11-17	2	3.81
Juan Marichal	R	35	34	32	9	2	207.1	231	22	37	87	11-15	0	3.82
Elias Sosa	R	23	71	1	0	0	107.0	95	7	41	70	10-4	18	3.28
Randy Moffitt	R	24	60	0	0	0	100.1	86	9	31	65	4-4	14	2.42
Jim Willoughby	R	24	39	12	1	1	123.0	138	21	37	60	4-5	1	4.68
Don Carrithers	R	23	25	3	0	0	58.0	64	2	35	36	1-2	0	4.81
Don McMahon	R	43	22	0	0	0	30.1	21	1	7	20	4-0	6	1.48
Sam McDowell†	L	30	18	3	0	0	40.0	45	4	29	35	1-2	3	4.50
Charlie Williams	R	25	12	2	0	0	23.0	32	2	7	11	3-0	0	6.65
John D'Acquisto	R	21	7	3	1	0	27.2	23	4	19	29	1-1	0	3.58
John Morris	R	31	7	0	0	0	6.1	12	0	3	3	1-0	0	8.53
Dave Kingman	R	24	2	0	0	0	4.0	3	0	6	4	0-0	0	9.00

1973 Houston Astros 4th NL West 82-80 .506 17.0 GB

Leo Durocher

Player	Gm by Position	B	Age	G	AB	R	H	2B	3B	HR	RBI	BB	SO	SB	Avg	OBP	Slg
Skip Jutze	C86	R	27	90	278	18	62	6	0	0	18	19	37	0	.223	.273	.245
Lee May	1B144	R	30	148	545	65	147	24	3	28	105	34	122	1	.270	.310	.479
Tommy Helms	2B145	R	32	146	543	44	156	28	2	4	61	32	21	1	.287	.325	.368
Doug Rader	3B152	R	28	154	574	79	146	26	0	21	89	46	97	4	.254	.310	.409
Roger Metzger	SS149	S	25	154	580	67	145	11	14	1	35	39	70	10	.250	.299	.322
Bob Watson	OF142,1B26,C3	R	27	158	573	97	179	24	3	16	94	85	73	1	.312	.403	.449
Cesar Cedeno	OF136	R	22	139	525	86	168	35	2	25	70	41	79	56	.320	.376	.537
Jimmy Wynn	OF133	R	31	139	481	90	106	14	5	20	55	91	102	14	.220	.347	.395
Johnny Edwards	C76	L	35	79	250	24	61	10	2	5	27	19	23	1	.244	.301	.360
Tommie Agee†	OF67	R	30	83	204	30	48	5	2	8	15	16	55	2	.235	.294	.397
Bob Gallagher	OF42,1B1	L	24	71	148	16	39	3	1	2	10	3	27	0	.264	.275	.338
Jimmy Stewart	3B8,OF3,2B1	S	34	61	68	6	13	0	0	0	3	9	12	0	.191	.293	.191
Hector Torres	SS22,2B13	R	27	38	66	3	6	1	0	0	2	7	13	0	.091	.189	.106
Jesus Alou†	OF14	R	31	28	55	7	13	2	0	1	8	1	6	0	.236	.276	.327
Gary Sutherland	2B14,SS1	R	28	16	54	8	14	5	0	0	3	3	5	0	.259	.298	.352
Larry Howard†	C20	R	28	20	48	3	8	3	0	0	4	5	12	0	.167	.245	.229
Greg Gross	OF9	L	20	14	39	5	9	2	1	0	1	4	4	2	.231	.302	.333
Cliff Johnson	1B5	R	25	7	20	6	6	2	0	2	6	1	7	0	.300	.364	.700
Ray Busse†	SS5,3B3	R	24	15	17	1	1	0	0	0	0	1	12	0	.059	.111	.059
Rafael Batista	1B8	L	25	12	15	2	4	0	0	0	2	1	6	0	.267	.313	.267
Dave Campbell†	3B5,1B2,OF1	R	31	9	15	1	4	2	0	0	2	0	4	0	.267	.267	.400
Mike Easler	OF2	L	22	6	7	1	0	0	0	0	0	2	4	0	.000	.222	.000
Otis Thornton	C2	R	28	2	3	0	0	0	0	0	0	0	2	0	.000	.000	.000
Norm Miller†	OF1	L	27	3	3	0	0	0	0	0	0	0	2	0	.000	.000	.000

Pitcher	T	Age	G	GS	CG	ShO	IP	H	HR	BB	SO	W-L	Sv	ERA
Jerry Reuss	L	24	41	40	12	3	279.1	271	17	117	177	16-13	0	3.74
Dave Roberts	L	28	39	36	12	6	249.1	264	15	62	119	17-11	0	2.85
Don Wilson	R	28	37	32	10	3	239.1	187	21	92	149	11-16	2	3.20
Ken Forsch	R	26	46	26	5	0	201.1	197	18	74	149	9-12	4	4.20
J.R. Richard	R	23	16	10	2	1	72.0	54	2	38	75	6-2	0	4.00
Doug Konieczny	R	21	2	2	0	0	13.0	12	0	4	6	0-1	0	5.54
Jim Crawford	L	22	48	0	0	0	70.0	69	7	33	56	2-4	6	4.50
Jim Ray	R	28	42	0	0	0	69.0	65	5	38	25	6-4	6	4.43
Jim York	R	25	41	0	0	0	53.0	65	4	20	22	3-4	6	4.42
Cecil Upshaw†	R	30	35	0	0	0	38.1	38	3	15	21	2-3	1	4.46
Tom Griffin	R	25	25	12	4	0	99.2	83	10	46	69	4-6	0	4.15
Fred Gladding	R	37	16	0	0	0	16.0	18	4	4	9	2-0	1	4.50
Juan Pizarro†	L	36	15	1	0	0	23.1	28	1	11	10	2-2	0	6.56
Larry Dierker	R	26	14	3	0	0	27.0	27	3	13	18	1-1	0	4.33
Mike Cosgrove	L	22	13	0	0	0	10.0	11	1	8	2	1-1	0	1.80

816 Seasons: Team Rosters

1973 Atlanta Braves 5th NL West 76-85 .472 22.5 GB

Eddie Mathews

Player	Gm by Position	B	Age	G	AB	R	H	2B	3B	HR	RBI	BB	SO	SB	Avg	OBP	Slg
Johnny Oates	C86	L	27	93	322	27	80	6	0	4	27	22	31	1	.248	.299	.304
Mike Lum	1B84,OF64	L	27	138	513	74	151	26	6	16	82	41	89	2	.294	.351	.462
Dave Johnson	2B156	R	30	157	559	84	151	25	0	43	99	81	93	5	.270	.370	.546
Darrell Evans	3B146,1B20	L	26	161	595	114	167	25	8	41	104	124	104	6	.281	.403	.556
Marty Perez	SS139	R	26	141	501	66	125	15	5	8	57	49	66	2	.250	.316	.347
Dusty Baker	OF156	R	24	159	604	101	174	29	4	21	99	67	72	24	.288	.359	.454
Ralph Garr	OF148	L	27	148	668	94	200	32	6	11	55	22	64	35	.299	.323	.415
Hank Aaron	OF105	R	39	120	392	84	118	12	1	40	96	68	51	1	.301	.402	.643
Paul Casanova	C78	R	31	82	236	18	51	7	0	7	18	11	36	0	.216	.254	.335
Sonny Jackson	OF56,SS36	L	28	117	206	29	43	5	2	0	12	22	13	6	.209	.283	.252
Frank Tepedino	1B58	L	25	74	148	20	45	5	0	4	29	13	21	0	.304	.354	.419
Dick Dietz	1B36,C20	R	31	83	139	22	41	8	1	3	24	49	25	0	.295	.474	.432
Chuck Goggin†	2B19,OF6,SS5*	S	27	64	90	18	26	5	0	0	7	9	19	0	.289	.350	.344
Rod Gilbreath	3B22	R	20	29	74	10	21	2	1	0	2	6	10	2	.284	.341	.338
Oscar Brown	OF13	R	27	22	58	3	12	3	0	0	0	3	10	0	.207	.246	.259
Freddie Velazquez	C11	R	35	15	23	2	8	1	0	0	3	1	3	0	.348	.375	.391
Jack Pierce	1B6	L	25	11	20	0	1	0	0	0	0	1	8	0	.050	.095	.050
Larvell Blanks	3B3,2B2,SS2	R	23	17	18	1	4	0	0	0	0	1	3	0	.222	.263	.222
Joe Pepitone†	1B3	L	32	3	11	0	4	0	0	0	1	1	1	0	.364	.417	.364
Larry Howard†	C2	R	28	4	8	0	1	0	0	0	0	2	3	0	.125	.300	.125
Norm Miller†	OF1	L	27	9	8	2	3	1	0	1	6	3	3	0	.375	.500	.875
Leo Foster	SS1	R	22	3	6	1	1	1	0	0	0	0	2	0	.167	.167	.333

C. Goggin, 1 G at C

Pitcher	T	Age	G	GS	CG	ShO	IP	H	HR	BB	SO	W-L	Sv	ERA
Carl Morton	R	29	38	37	10	4	256.1	254	18	70	112	15-10	0	3.41
Phil Niekro	R	34	42	30	9	1	245.0	214	21	89	131	13-10	4	3.31
Roric Harrison	R	26	38	22	3	0	177.1	161	15	98	130	11-8	5	4.16
Ron Schueler	R	25	39	20	4	2	186.0	179	24	66	124	8-7	2	3.87
Ron Reed	R	30	20	19	2	0	116.1	133	7	31	64	4-11	1	4.41
Gary Gentry	R	26	16	14	3	0	86.2	74	7	35	42	4-6	1	3.43
Pat Dobson†	R	31	12	10	1	1	57.2	73	1	19	23	3-7	0	4.99
Wenty Ford	R	26	4	2	1	0	16.1	17	3	8	4	1-2	0	5.51
Tom House	L	26	52	0	0	0	67.1	58	13	31	42	4-2	4	4.68
Danny Frisella	R	27	42	0	0	0	45.0	40	5	23	27	1-2	8	4.20
Adrian Devine	R	21	24	1	0	0	32.1	45	6	12	15	2-3	4	6.40
Jim Panther	R	28	23	0	0	0	30.2	45	3	9	8	2-3	0	7.63
Joe Niekro	R	28	20	0	0	0	24.0	23	2	11	12	2-4	3	4.13
Joe Hoerner†	L	36	20	0	0	0	12.2	17	1	4	10	2-2	2	6.39
Gary Neibauer	R	28	16	1	0	0	21.1	24	3	19	9	2-1	0	7.17
Jimmy Freeman	L	22	13	5	0	0	37.1	50	7	25	20	0-2	1	7.71
Max Leon	R	23	12	1	1	0	27.0	30	6	9	18	2-2	0	5.33
Tom Kelley	R	29	7	0	0	0	12.2	13	0	7	5	0-1	0	2.84
Cecil Upshaw†	R	30	5	0	0	0	3.2	8	0	2	3	0-1	0	9.82
Al Closter	L	30	4	0	0	0	4.1	7	1	4	2	0-0	0	14.54
Dave Cheadle	L	21	2	0	0	0	2.0	2	1	3	2	0-1	0	18.00

1973 San Diego Padres 6th NL West 60-102 .370 39.0 GB

Don Zimmer

Player	Gm by Position	B	Age	G	AB	R	H	2B	3B	HR	RBI	BB	SO	SB	Avg	OBP	Slg
Fred Kendall	C138	R	24	145	507	39	143	22	3	10	59	30	35	3	.282	.320	.396
Nate Colbert	1B144	R	27	145	529	73	143	25	2	22	80	54	146	9	.270	.343	.450
Rich Morales†	2B79,SS10	R	29	90	244	9	40	6	1	0	16	27	36	0	.164	.245	.197
Dave Roberts	3B111,2B12	R	22	127	479	56	137	20	3	21	64	17	83	11	.286	.310	.472
Derrel Thomas	SS74,2B47	R	22	113	404	41	96	7	1	0	22	34	52	15	.238	.299	.260
Cito Gaston	OF119	R	29	133	476	51	119	18	4	16	57	20	88	0	.250	.281	.405
John Grubb	OF102,3B2	L	24	113	389	52	121	22	3	8	37	37	50	9	.311	.373	.445
Jerry Morales	OF100	R	24	122	388	47	109	23	2	9	34	27	55	6	.281	.325	.420
Leron Lee	OF84	L	25	118	333	36	79	7	2	3	30	33	61	4	.237	.306	.297
Enzo Hernandez	SS67	R	24	70	247	26	55	2	1	0	9	17	14	15	.223	.273	.239
Dave Hilton	3B47,2B23	R	22	70	234	21	46	9	0	5	16	19	35	2	.197	.260	.299
Ivan Murrell	OF37,1B24	R	28	93	210	23	48	13	1	9	21	2	52	2	.229	.236	.429
Gene Locklear†	OF37	L	23	67	154	20	37	6	1	3	25	21	22	9	.240	.330	.351
Dave Winfield	OF36,1B1	R	21	56	141	9	39	4	1	3	12	12	19	0	.277	.331	.383
Dwain Anderson†	SS39,3B6	R	25	53	107	11	13	0	0	0	3	14	29	2	.121	.223	.121
Dave Campbell†	2B27,1B3,3B2	R	31	33	98	2	22	3	0	0	8	7	15	1	.224	.271	.255
Pat Corrales	C28	R	32	29	72	7	15	2	1	0	3	6	10	0	.208	.275	.264
Dave Marshall	OF8	L	30	39	49	4	14	5	0	0	4	8	9	0	.286	.390	.388
Bob Davis	C5	R	21	5	11	1	1	0	0	0	0	0	5	0	.091	.091	.091
Don Mason	2B1	L	28	8	8	0	0	0	0	0	0	0	2	0	.000	.000	.000

Pitcher	T	Age	G	GS	CG	ShO	IP	H	HR	BB	SO	W-L	Sv	ERA
Bill Greif	R	23	36	31	9	3	199.1	181	20	62	120	10-17	1	3.21
Clay Kirby	R	25	34	31	4	2	191.2	214	30	66	129	8-18	0	4.79
Steve Arlin	R	27	34	27	7	3	180.0	196	26	72	98	11-14	0	5.10
Randy Jones	L	23	20	19	6	1	139.2	129	13	37	77	7-6	0	3.16
Fred Norman†	L	30	12	11	1	0	74.0	72	9	29	49	1-7	0	4.26
Gary Ross	R	25	58	0	0	0	76.1	93	8	33	44	4-4	0	5.42
Mike Caldwell	L	24	55	13	3	1	149.0	146	8	53	86	5-14	10	3.74
Rich Troedson	L	23	50	18	2	0	152.1	167	12	59	81	7-9	1	4.25
Vicente Romo	R	30	49	1	0	0	87.2	85	11	46	51	2-3	7	3.70
Mike Corkins	R	27	47	11	2	0	122.0	130	12	61	82	5-8	3	4.50
Bob Miller†	R	34	18	0	0	0	30.2	29	4	12	15	0-0	0	4.11
Frank Snook	R	24	18	0	0	0	27.1	19	4	18	13	0-2	1	3.62

»1974 Baltimore Orioles 1st AL East 91-71 .562 —

Earl Weaver

Player	Gm by Position	B	Age	G	AB	R	H	2B	3B	HR	RBI	BB	SO	SB	Avg	OBP	Slg
Earl Williams	C75,1B47,DH1	R	25	118	413	47	105	16	0	14	52	40	79	0	.254	.327	.395
Boog Powell	1B102,DH1	L	32	110	344	37	91	13	1	12	45	52	58	0	.265	.358	.413
Bobby Grich	2B160	R	25	160	582	92	153	29	6	19	82	90	117	17	.263	.376	.431
Brooks Robinson	3B153	R	37	153	553	46	159	27	0	7	59	56	47	2	.288	.353	.374
Mark Belanger	SS155	R	30	155	493	54	111	14	4	5	36	51	69	17	.225	.298	.300
Paul Blair	OF151	R	30	151	552	77	144	27	4	17	62	43	59	27	.261	.313	.417
Don Baylor	OF129,1B8,DH1	R	25	137	489	66	133	22	1	10	59	43	56	29	.272	.341	.382
Rich Coggins	OF105	L	23	113	411	53	100	13	3	4	32	29	31	26	.243	.299	.319
Tommy Davis	DH155	R	35	158	626	67	181	20	1	11	84	34	49	6	.289	.325	.377
Al Bumbry	OF67,DH7	L	27	94	270	35	63	10	3	1	19	21	46	12	.233	.288	.304
Jim Fuller	OF59,1B4,DH2	R	23	64	189	17	42	11	0	7	28	8	68	1	.222	.265	.392
Andy Etchebarren	C60	R	31	62	180	13	40	8	0	2	15	6	26	1	.222	.249	.300
Enos Cabell	1B28,OF22,3B19*	R	24	80	174	24	42	4	2	3	17	7	20	5	.241	.269	.339
Ellie Hendricks	C54,DH1,1B1	L	33	66	159	18	33	8	2	3	8	17	25	0	.208	.283	.340
Frank Baker	SS17,2B3,3B1	L	27	24	29	3	5	1	0	0	0	3	5	0	.172	.250	.207
Mike Reinbach	DH3,OF3	L	24	12	20	2	5	1	0	0	2	2	5	0	.250	.304	.300
Bob Oliver†	1B4,DH2	R	31	9	20	1	3	2	0	0	4	0	5	1	.150	.150	.250
Tim Nordbrook	SS5,2B1	R	24	6	15	4	4	0	0	0	1	2	2	1	.267	.353	.267
Curt Motton	OF2,DH1	R	33	7	8	0	0	0	0	0	0	2	2	0	.000	.200	.000
Jim Northrup†	OF6	L	34	8	7	2	4	0	0	1	3	2	1	0	.571	.667	1.000
Doug DeCinces	3B1	R	23	1	1	0	0	0	0	0	0	1	0	0	.000	.500	.000
Skip Lockwood†		R	27	37	0	0	0	0	0	0	0	0	0	0	—	—	—

E. Cabell, 1 G at 2B

Pitcher	T	Age	G	GS	CG	ShO	IP	H	HR	BB	SO	W-L	Sv	ERA
Ross Grimsley	L	24	40	39	17	4	295.2	267	26	76	158	18-13	1	3.07
Mike Cuellar	L	37	38	38	20	5	269.1	253	17	86	106	22-10	0	3.11
Dave McNally	L	31	39	37	13	4	259.0	260	19	81	111	16-10	1	3.58
Jim Palmer	R	28	26	26	5	2	178.2	176	12	69	84	7-12	0	3.27
Bob Reynolds	R	27	54	0	0	0	69.1	75	4	14	43	7-5	7	2.73
Grant Jackson	L	31	49	0	0	0	66.2	48	7	22	56	6-4	12	2.57
Doyle Alexander	R	23	30	12	2	0	114.1	127	7	43	40	6-9	0	4.01
Wayne Garland	R	23	20	6	0	0	91.0	68	5	26	40	5-5	1	2.97
Don Hood	L	24	20	2	0	0	57.1	47	1	20	26	1-1	1	3.45
Jesse Jefferson	R	25	20	2	0	0	57.1	55	2	38	31	1-0	0	4.40
Dave Johnson	R	25	11	0	0	0	15.1	17	1	5	6	2-2	2	2.93

1974 New York Yankees 2nd AL East 89-73 .549 2.0 GB

Bill Virdon

Player	Gm by Position	B	Age	G	AB	R	H	2B	3B	HR	RBI	BB	SO	SB	Avg	OBP	Slg
Thurman Munson	C137,DH4	R	27	144	517	64	135	19	2	13	60	44	66	2	.261	.316	.381
Chris Chambliss†	1B106	L	25	110	400	38	97	16	3	6	43	23	43	0	.243	.282	.343
Sandy Alomar†	2B76,DH1	S	30	76	279	35	75	8	0	1	27	14	25	6	.269	.302	.308
Graig Nettles	3B154,SS1	L	29	155	566	74	139	21	1	22	75	59	75	1	.246	.316	.403
Jim Mason	SS152	L	23	152	440	41	110	18	6	5	37	35	87	1	.250	.302	.352
Bobby Murcer	OF156	L	28	156	606	69	166	25	4	10	88	57	59	14	.274	.332	.378
Elliott Maddox	OF135,2B2,3B1	R	26	137	466	75	141	26	2	3	45	69	48	6	.303	.395	.386
Lou Piniella	OF130,DH6,1B1	R	30	140	518	71	158	26	0	9	70	32	58	1	.305	.341	.407
Ron Blomberg	DH58,OF19	L	25	90	264	39	82	11	2	10	48	29	33	2	.311	.375	.481
Roy White	OF67,DH53	S	30	136	473	68	130	19	8	7	43	67	44	15	.275	.367	.393
Bill Sudakis	DH39,1B33,3B3*	S	28	89	259	26	60	8	0	7	39	25	48	0	.232	.296	.344
Gene Michael	2B45,SS39,3B2	S	36	81	177	19	46	9	0	0	13	14	24	0	.260	.313	.311
F. Gonzalez†	2B42,3B7,SS3*	R	24	51	121	11	26	5	1	1	7	7	7	0	.215	.258	.298
Rick Dempsey	C31,OF2,DH1	R	24	43	109	12	26	3	0	2	12	8	7	1	.239	.288	.321
Otto Velez	1B21,OF3,3B2	R	23	27	67	9	14	1	1	2	10	15	24	0	.209	.345	.343
Mike Hegan†	1B17	L	31	18	53	3	12	2	0	2	9	5	9	1	.226	.317	.377
Walt Williams	OF24,DH3	R	30	43	53	5	6	0	0	0	3	1	10	1	.113	.127	.113
Horace Clarke†	2B20,DH1	S	34	24	47	3	11	1	0	0	1	4	5	1	.234	.294	.255
Fred Stanley	SS19,2B15	R	26	33	38	2	7	0	0	0	3	3	2	1	.184	.244	.184
Alex Johnson†	DH6,OF1	R	31	10	28	3	6	1	0	1	2	0	3	0	.214	.214	.357
Jim Ray Hart	DH4	R	32	10	19	1	1	0	0	0	0	3	7	0	.053	.182	.053
Duke Sims†	C1	L	33	5	15	1	2	1	0	0	2	1	5	0	.133	.188	.200
Terry Whitfield	OF1	L	21	2	5	0	1	0	0	0	0	0	1	0	.200	.200	.200
Jim Deidel	C2	R	25	2	2	0	0	0	0	0	0	0	0	0	.000	.000	.000
Larry Murray	OF3	S	21	6	1	1	0	0	0	0	0	0	0	0	.000	.000	.000

B. Sudakis, 1 G at C; F. Gonzalez, 1 G at DH

Pitcher	T	Age	G	GS	CG	ShO	IP	H	HR	BB	SO	W-L	Sv	ERA
Pat Dobson	R	32	39	39	12	2	281.0	282	23	75	157	19-15	0	3.07
Doc Medich	R	25	38	38	17	4	279.2	275	24	91	154	19-15	0	3.60
Dick Tidrow†	R	27	33	25	5	0	190.2	205	14	53	100	11-9	1	3.87
Rudy May†	L	29	17	15	8	2	114.1	75	5	48	90	8-4	0	2.28
Mel Stottlemyre	R	32	18	15	6	0	113.0	119	7	37	40	6-7	0	3.58
Larry Gura	L	26	8	8	4	2	56.0	54	2	12	17	5-1	0	2.41
Sam McDowell	L	31	13	7	0	0	48.0	42	6	41	33	1-6	0	4.69
Steve Kline†	R	26	4	4	0	0	26.0	26	3	5	6	2-2	0	3.46
Sparky Lyle	L	29	66	0	0	0	114.0	93	6	43	89	9-3	15	1.66
Cecil Upshaw†	R	31	36	0	0	0	59.2	53	1	24	27	1-5	6	3.02
Mike Wallace†	L	23	23	1	0	0	52.1	42	3	35	34	6-0	0	2.41
Dave Pagan	R	24	16	6	1	0	49.1	49	1	28	39	1-3	0	5.11
Tippy Martinez	L	24	10	0	0	0	12.2	14	0	9	10	0-0	0	4.26
Dick Woodson†	R	29	8	3	0	0	28.0	34	6	12	12	1-2	0	5.79
Fred Beene†	R	31	6	0	0	0	10.0	9	1	2	10	0-0	1	2.70
Tom Buskey†	R	27	4	0	0	0	5.2	10	1	3	3	0-1	1	6.35
Fritz Peterson†	L	32	3	1	0	0	7.2	13	1	2	5	0-0	0	4.70
Ken Wright	R	27	3	0	0	0	5.2	5	0	7	2	0-0	0	3.18
Rick Sawyer	R	26	1	0	0	0	1.2	2	0	1	1	0-0	0	16.20

1974 Boston Red Sox 3rd AL East 84-78 .519 7.0 GB

Darrell Johnson

Player	Gm by Position	B	Age	G	AB	R	H	2B	3B	HR	RBI	BB	SO	SB	Avg	OBP	Slg
Bob Montgomery	C79,DH5	R	30	88	254	26	64	10	0	4	38	13	50	3	.252	.287	.339
Carl Yastrzemski	1B84,OF63,DH4	L	34	148	515	93	155	25	2	15	79	104	48	12	.301	.414	.445
Doug Griffin	2B91,SS1	R	27	93	312	35	83	12	4	0	33	28	21	2	.266	.329	.330
Rico Petrocelli	3B116,DH9	R	31	129	454	53	121	23	1	15	76	48	74	1	.267	.336	.421
Mario Guerrero	SS93	R	24	93	284	18	70	6	2	0	23	13	22	3	.246	.282	.282
Dwight Evans	OF122,DH7	R	22	133	463	60	130	19	8	10	70	38	77	4	.281	.335	.421
Rick Miller	OF105	L	26	114	280	41	73	8	1	5	22	37	47	13	.261	.347	.350
Juan Beniquez	OF97,DH4	R	24	106	389	60	104	14	3	5	33	25	61	19	.267	.313	.357
Tommy Harper	OF61,DH51	R	33	118	443	66	105	15	3	5	24	46	65	28	.237	.312	.318
Cecil Cooper	1B74,DH41	L	24	121	414	55	114	24	1	8	43	32	74	2	.275	.327	.396
Rick Burleson	SS88,2B31,3B2	R	23	114	384	36	109	22	0	4	44	21	34	3	.284	.320	.372
Bernie Carbo	OF87,DH15	L	26	117	338	40	84	20	0	12	61	58	90	4	.249	.364	.414
Dick McAuliffe	2B53,3B40,DH3*	L	34	100	272	32	57	13	1	5	24	39	40	2	.210	.310	.320
Carlton Fisk	C50,DH2	R	26	52	187	36	56	12	1	11	26	24	23	5	.299	.383	.551
Danny Cater	1B23,DH14	R	34	56	126	14	31	5	0	5	20	10	13	1	.246	.309	.405
Tim Blackwell	C44	S	21	44	122	9	30	1	1	0	8	10	21	1	.246	.308	.270
Terry Hughes	3B36,DH1	R	25	41	69	5	14	2	0	1	6	6	18	0	.203	.282	.275
Jim Rice	DH16,OF3	R	21	24	67	6	18	2	1	1	13	4	12	0	.269	.307	.373
Fred Lynn	OF12,DH1	L	22	15	43	5	18	2	2	2	10	6	6	0	.419	.490	.698
Tim McCarver†	C8,DH2	L	32	11	28	3	7	1	0	0	1	4	1	1	.250	.344	.286
Deron Johnson†	DH8	R	35	11	25	0	3	0	0	0	2	0	6	0	.120	.115	.120
John Kennedy	2B6,3B4	R	33	10	15	3	2	0	0	1	1	1	6	0	.133	.188	.333
Bob Didier	C5	S	25	5	14	0	1	0	0	0	1	2	1	0	.071	.176	.071
Chuck Goggin	2B2	S	28	2	1	0	0	0	0	0	0	0	1	0	.000	.000	.000

D. McAuliffe, 3 G at SS

Pitcher	T	Age	G	GS	CG	ShO	IP	H	HR	BB	SO	W-L	Sv	ERA
Luis Tiant	R	33	38	38	25	7	311.1	281	21	82	176	22-13	0	2.92
Bill Lee	L	27	38	37	16	1	282.1	320	25	67	95	17-15	0	3.51
Reggie Cleveland	R	26	41	27	10	0	221.1	234	25	69	103	12-14	0	4.31
Roger Moret	L	24	31	21	10	1	173.1	158	15	79	111	9-10	2	3.74
Dick Drago	R	29	33	18	8	0	175.2	165	17	56	90	7-10	3	3.48
Juan Marichal	R	36	11	9	0	0	57.1	61	3	14	21	5-1	0	4.87
Rick Wise	R	28	9	9	1	0	49.0	47	2	16	25	3-4	0	3.86
Steve Barr	L	22	1	1	1	0	9.0	7	0	6	3	1-0	0	4.00
Diego Segui	R	36	58	0	0	0	108.0	106	9	49	76	6-8	10	4.00
Bob Veale	L	38	18	0	0	0	13.0	15	2	4	16	0-1	2	5.54
Dick Pole	R	23	15	2	0	0	45.0	55	6	13	32	1-1	1	4.20
Lance Clemons	L	26	6	0	0	0	6.1	8	1	4	1	1-0	0	9.95
Don Newhauser	R	26	2	0	0	0	3.2	5	0	4	2	0-1	0	9.82

1974 Cleveland Indians 4th AL East 77-85 .475 14.0 GB

Ken Aspromonte

Player	Gm by Position	B	Age	G	AB	R	H	2B	3B	HR	RBI	BB	SO	SB	Avg	OBP	Slg
Dave Duncan	C134,1B3,DH1	R	28	136	425	45	85	10	1	16	46	42	91	0	.200	.274	.341
John Ellis	1B69,C42,DH21	R	25	128	477	58	136	23	6	10	64	32	53	1	.285	.330	.421
Jack Brohamer	2B99	L	24	101	315	33	85	11	1	2	30	26	22	2	.270	.329	.330
Buddy Bell	3B115,DH1	R	22	116	423	51	111	15	1	7	46	35	29	1	.262	.322	.352
Frank Duffy	SS158	R	27	158	549	62	128	18	0	8	48	30	64	7	.233	.272	.310
Charlie Spikes	OF154	R	23	155	568	63	154	23	1	22	80	34	100	10	.271	.319	.431
George Hendrick	OF133,DH1	R	24	139	495	65	138	23	1	19	67	33	73	6	.279	.322	.444
John Lowenstein	OF100,3B28,1B12*	L	27	140	508	65	123	14	2	8	48	53	85	36	.242	.313	.325
Oscar Gamble	DH115,OF13	L	24	135	454	74	132	16	4	19	59	48	51	5	.291	.363	.469
Leron Lee	OF62,DH2	L	26	79	232	18	54	13	0	5	25	15	42	3	.233	.279	.353
Rusty Torres	OF94,DH1	S	25	108	150	19	28	2	0	3	12	13	24	2	.187	.248	.260
Remy Hermoso	2B45	R	26	48	122	15	27	3	1	0	5	7	7	2	.221	.262	.262
Luis Alvarado†	2B46,SS7,DH3	R	25	61	114	12	25	2	0	0	12	6	14	1	.219	.256	.237
Tom McCraw†	1B38,DH2,OF1	L	33	45	112	17	34	8	0	3	17	5	11	0	.304	.336	.455
Joe Lis†	1B31,DH9,3B9*	R	27	57	109	15	22	3	0	6	16	14	30	1	.202	.293	.394
Rico Carty	DH14,1B8	R	34	33	91	6	33	5	0	1	16	5	9	0	.363	.396	.451
Ed Crosby	3B18,SS13,2B3	L	25	37	86	11	18	3	0	0	6	6	12	0	.209	.258	.244
Chris Chambliss†	1B17	L	25	17	67	8	22	4	0	0	7	5	5	0	.328	.375	.388
Frank Robinson†	DH10,1B4	R	38	15	50	6	10	1	1	2	5	10	10	0	.200	.328	.380
Ossie Blanco	1B16,DH1	R	28	18	36	1	7	0	0	0	2	7	4	0	.194	.326	.194
Tommy Smith	OF17,DH1	L	25	23	31	4	3	1	0	0	0	2	7	0	.097	.176	.129
Duane Kuiper	2B8	L	24	10	22	7	11	2	0	0	4	2	2	1	.500	.542	.591
Johnny Jeter	OF6	R	29	6	17	3	6	1	0	0	1	1	6	1	.353	.389	.412
Jack Heidemann†	3B6,SS4,1B1*	R	24	12	11	2	1	0	0	0	0	0	2	0	.091	.091	.091
Alan Ashby	C9	S	22	10	7	1	1	0	0	0	0	1	2	0	.143	.250	.143
Dwain Anderson	2B1	R	26	2	3	0	1	0	0	0	0	0	1	0	.333	.333	.333
Larry Johnson		R	23	1	0	1	0	0	0	0	0	0	0	0	—	—	—

J. Lowenstein, 4 G at 2B; J. Lis, 1 G at OF; J. Heidemann, 1 G at 2B

Pitcher	T	Age	G	GS	CG	ShO	IP	H	HR	BB	SO	W-L	Sv	ERA
Gaylord Perry	R	35	37	37	28	4	322.1	230	25	99	216	21-13	0	2.51
Jim Perry	R	38	36	36	8	3	252.0	242	11	64	71	17-12	0	2.96
Fritz Peterson†	L	32	29	29	3	0	152.2	187	16	37	52	9-14	0	4.36
Dick Bosman	R	30	25	18	2	1	127.1	126	13	29	56	7-5	0	4.10
Steve Kline†	R	26	16	11	1	0	71.0	70	9	31	17	3-8	0	5.07
Bob Johnson	R	31	14	10	0	0	72.0	75	12	37	36	3-4	0	4.38
Steve Arlin†	R	28	11	10	1	0	43.2	59	1	22	20	2-5	0	6.60
Dick Tidrow†	R	27	4	4	0	0	19.0	21	4	13	8	1-3	0	7.11
Jim Kern	R	25	4	3	1	0	15.1	16	1	14	11	0-1	0	4.70
Tom Buskey†	R	27	51	0	0	0	93.0	93	10	33	40	2-6	17	3.19
Milt Wilcox	R	24	41	2	1	0	71.1	74	10	24	33	2-2	4	4.67
Tom Hilgendorf	L	32	35	0	0	0	48.1	58	6	17	23	4-3	3	4.84
Fred Beene†	R	31	32	0	0	0	73.0	68	7	26	35	4-4	2	4.93
Bruce Ellingsen	L	25	16	2	0	0	42.0	45	5	17	16	1-1	0	3.21
Ken Sanders†	R	32	9	0	0	0	11.0	21	5	5	4	0-1	1	9.82
Cecil Upshaw†	R	31	7	0	0	0	8.0	10	1	4	7	0-1	0	3.38
Bill Gogolewski	R	26	5	0	0	0	13.2	15	1	2	3	0-0	0	4.61
Tom Timmermann	R	34	4	0	0	0	10.0	9	1	5	2	1-1	0	5.40

1974 Milwaukee Brewers 5th AL East 76-86 .469 15.0 GB

Del Crandall

Player	Gm by Position	B	Age	G	AB	R	H	2B	3B	HR	RBI	BB	SO	SB	Avg	OBP	Slg
Darrell Porter	C117,DH9	L	22	131	432	59	104	15	4	12	56	50	88	8	.241	.326	.377
George Scott	1B148,DH9	R	30	158	604	74	170	36	2	17	82	59	90	9	.281	.345	.432
Pedro Garcia	2B140	R	24	141	452	46	90	15	4	12	54	26	67	8	.199	.248	.330
Don Money	3B157,DH1,2B1	R	27	159	629	85	178	32	3	15	65	62	80	19	.283	.346	.415
Robin Yount	SS107	R	18	107	344	48	86	14	5	3	26	12	46	7	.250	.276	.346
John Briggs	OF149,DH2	L	30	154	554	72	140	30	8	17	73	71	102	9	.253	.337	.428
Bob Coluccio	OF131,DH2	R	22	138	394	42	88	13	4	6	31	43	61	15	.223	.305	.322
Dave May	OF121,DH8	L	30	135	477	56	108	15	1	10	42	28	73	4	.226	.273	.325
Bobby Mitchell	DH53,OF26	R	30	88	173	27	42	6	2	5	20	18	46	7	.243	.314	.387
Ken Berry	OF82,DH13	R	33	98	267	21	64	9	2	1	24	18	26	3	.240	.295	.300
Tim Johnson	SS64,2B26,DH1*	L	24	93	245	25	60	7	7	0	25	11	48	4	.245	.278	.331
Charlie Moore	C61,DH6	R	21	72	204	17	50	10	4	0	19	21	34	3	.245	.316	.333
Mike Hegan†	DH37,1B17,OF17	L	31	89	190	21	45	7	1	7	32	33	34	0	.237	.347	.395
Deron Johnson†	DH19,1B2	R	35	49	152	14	23	3	0	6	18	21	41	1	.151	.253	.289
Bob Hansen	DH18,1B3	L	26	58	88	8	26	4	1	2	9	3	16	2	.295	.319	.432
John Vukovich	3B12,SS12,2B11*	R	26	38	80	5	15	1	0	3	11	1	16	2	.188	.193	.313
Sixto Lezcano	OF15	R	20	15	54	5	13	2	0	2	9	4	9	1	.241	.283	.389
Rob Ellis	OF11,DH9,3B1	R	23	22	48	4	14	2	0	0	4	4	11	0	.292	.346	.333
Gorman Thomas	OF13,DH2	R	23	17	46	10	12	4	0	2	11	8	15	4	.261	.357	.478
Jack Lind	SS5,2B4	S	28	9	17	4	4	2	0	0	1	3	2	0	.235	.350	.353
Bob Sheldon	DH4,2B3	L	23	10	17	4	2	1	1	0	0	4	2	0	.118	.286	.294
Felipe Alou	OF1	R	39	3	3	0	0	0	0	0	0	0	2	0	.000	.000	.000

T. Johnson, 1 G at 3B, 1 G at OF; J. Vukovich, 4 G at 1B

Pitcher	T	Age	G	GS	CG	ShO	IP	H	HR	BB	SO	W-L	Sv	ERA
Jim Slaton	R	24	40	35	10	3	250.0	255	22	102	126	13-16	0	3.92
Clyde Wright	L	33	38	32	15	0	232.0	264	22	54	64	9-20	0	4.42
Jim Colborn	R	28	33	31	10	1	224.0	230	27	60	83	10-13	0	4.06
Kevin Kobel	L	20	34	24	3	2	169.1	166	16	54	74	6-14	0	3.99
Billy Champion	R	26	31	23	2	0	161.2	168	12	49	60	11-4	0	3.62
Ed Sprague	R	28	20	10	3	0	94.0	94	3	31	57	7-2	0	2.39
Tom Murphy	R	28	70	0	0	0	123.0	97	6	51	47	10-10	20	1.90
Ed Rodriguez	R	22	43	6	0	0	111.2	97	7	51	58	7-4	4	3.63
Bill Travers	L	21	23	1	0	0	53.0	59	6	30	31	2-3	0	4.92
Bill Castro	R	20	8	0	0	0	18.0	19	2	5	10	0-0	0	4.50
Jerry Bell	R	26	5	0	0	0	14.0	17	2	5	4	1-0	0	2.57
Larry Anderson	R	21	2	0	0	0	2.1	2	0	1	3	0-0	0	0.00
Roger Miller	R	19	2	0	0	0	2.1	3	1	0	2	0-0	0	11.57
Dick Selma†	R	30	2	0	0	0	2.1	5	0	0	2	0-0	0	19.29

1974 Detroit Tigers 6th AL East 72-90 .444 19.0 GB

Ralph Houk

Player	Gm by Position	B	Age	G	AB	R	H	2B	3B	HR	RBI	BB	SO	SB	Avg	OBP	Slg
Jerry Moses	C74	R	27	74	198	19	47	6	3	4	19	11	38	0	.237	.282	.359
Bill Freehan	1B65,C63,DH1	R	32	130	445	58	132	17	5	18	60	42	44	2	.297	.361	.479
Gary Sutherland	2B147,SS10,3B4	R	29	149	619	60	157	20	1	5	49	26	37	1	.254	.282	.313
Aurelio Rodriguez	3B159	R	26	159	571	54	127	23	5	5	49	26	70	2	.222	.255	.306
Ed Brinkman	SS151,3B2	R	32	153	502	55	111	15	3	14	54	29	71	2	.221	.266	.347
Jim Northrup†	OF97	L	34	97	376	41	89	12	1	11	42	36	46	0	.237	.300	.362
Mickey Stanley	OF91,1B12,2B1	R	31	99	394	40	87	13	2	8	34	26	63	5	.221	.270	.325
Willie Horton	OF64,DH1	R	31	72	238	32	71	8	1	15	47	21	36	0	.298	.361	.529
Al Kaline	DH146	R	39	147	558	71	146	28	2	13	64	65	75	2	.262	.337	.389
Ron LeFlore	OF59	R	26	59	254	37	66	8	1	2	13	13	58	23	.260	.301	.323
Ben Oglivie	OF63,1B10,DH4	L	25	92	252	28	68	11	3	4	29	34	38	12	.270	.353	.385
Norm Cash	1B44	L	39	53	149	17	34	3	2	7	12	19	30	1	.228	.327	.416
Jim Nettles	OF41	L	27	43	141	20	32	5	1	6	17	15	26	3	.227	.306	.404
Dick Sharon	OF56	R	24	60	129	12	28	4	0	2	10	14	29	4	.217	.292	.295
Marvin Lane	OF46,DH1	R	24	50	103	16	24	4	1	2	9	19	24	2	.233	.352	.350
Reggie Sanders	1B25,DH1	R	24	26	99	12	27	7	0	3	10	5	20	1	.273	.308	.434
Gates Brown	DH13	L	35	73	99	7	24	2	0	4	17	10	15	0	.242	.312	.384
Gene Lamont	C60	L	27	60	92	9	20	4	0	3	8	7	19	0	.217	.273	.359
John Knox	2B33,DH1,3B1	L	25	55	88	11	27	1	1	0	6	6	13	5	.307	.351	.341
Leon Roberts	OF17	R	23	17	63	5	17	3	2	0	7	3	10	0	.270	.303	.381
Ron Cash	1B15,3B4	R	24	20	62	6	14	2	0	0	5	0	11	0	.226	.222	.258
Tom Veryzer	SS20	R	21	22	55	4	13	2	0	2	9	5	8	1	.236	.300	.382
Dan Meyer	OF12	L	21	13	50	5	10	1	1	3	7	1	1	1	.200	.231	.440
John Wockenfuss	C13	R	25	13	29	1	4	1	0	0	2	3	2	0	.138	.212	.172
Ike Brown	3B2	R	32	2	2	0	0	0	0	0	0	0	0	0	.000	.000	.000

Pitcher	T	Age	G	GS	CG	ShO	IP	H	HR	BB	SO	W-L	Sv	ERA
Mickey Lolich	L	33	41	41	27	3	308.0	310	38	78	202	16-21	0	4.15
Joe Coleman	R	27	41	41	11	2	285.2	272	30	158	177	14-12	0	4.32
Lerrin LaGrow	R	25	37	34	11	0	216.1	245	21	80	85	8-19	0	4.66
Woodie Fryman	L	34	27	22	4	1	141.2	120	16	67	92	6-9	0	4.32
Fred Holdsworth	R	22	8	5	0	0	35.2	40	4	14	16	0-3	0	4.29
Vern Ruhle	R	23	5	3	1	0	33.0	35	1	6	10	2-0	0	2.73
John Hiller	L	31	59	0	0	0	150.0	127	10	62	134	17-14	13	2.64
Luke Walker	L	30	28	9	0	0	92.0	100	9	54	52	5-5	0	4.99
Jim Ray	R	29	28	0	0	0	52.1	49	4	29	26	1-3	2	4.47
Dave Lemanczyk	R	23	22	3	0	0	78.2	79	12	44	52	2-1	0	4.00
Bill Slayback	R	26	16	4	0	0	54.2	57	1	26	23	1-3	0	4.77
Chuck Seelbach	R	26	4	0	0	0	7.2	9	2	3	0	0-0	0	4.70

1974 Oakland Athletics 1st AL West 90-72 .556 —

Alvin Dark

Player	Gm by Position	B	Age	G	AB	R	H	2B	3B	HR	RBI	BB	SO	SB	Avg	OBP	Slg
Gene Tenace	1B106,C79,2B3	R	27	158	484	71	102	17	1	26	73	110	105	2	.211	.367	.411
Pat Bourque†	1B39	L	27	73	96	6	22	4	0	1	16	15	20	0	.229	.327	.302
Dick Green	2B100	R	33	100	287	20	61	8	2	2	22	22	50	2	.213	.269	.275
Sal Bando	3B141,DH3	R	30	146	498	84	121	21	2	22	103	86	79	2	.243	.352	.426
Bert Campaneris	SS133,DH1	R	32	134	527	77	153	18	8	2	41	47	81	34	.290	.347	.366
Joe Rudi	OF140,1B27,DH2	R	27	158	593	73	174	39	4	22	99	34	92	2	.293	.334	.484
Bill North	OF138,DH8	S	26	149	543	79	141	20	5	4	33	69	86	54	.260	.347	.337
Reggie Jackson	OF127,DH19	L	28	148	506	90	146	25	1	29	93	86	105	25	.289	.391	.514
Deron Johnson†	DH50,1B28	R	35	50	174	16	34	1	2	7	23	11	37	1	.195	.239	.345
Angel Mangual	OF74,DH37,3B1	R	27	115	365	37	85	14	4	9	43	17	59	3	.233	.265	.367
C. Washington	DH38,OF32	L	19	73	221	16	63	10	5	0	19	13	44	6	.285	.326	.376
Ted Kubiak	2B71,SS19,3B14*	S	32	99	220	22	46	3	0	0	18	18	15	1	.209	.268	.223
Jesus Alou	DH41,OF25	R	32	96	220	13	59	8	0	2	15	5	9	0	.268	.288	.332
Ray Fosse	C68,DH1	R	27	69	204	20	40	8	3	4	23	11	31	1	.196	.241	.324
Larry Haney	C73,3B3,1B2	R	31	76	121	12	20	4	0	2	3	3	18	1	.165	.185	.248
Dal Maxvill†	2B30,SS29,3B1	R	35	60	52	3	10	0	0	0	2	8	10	0	.192	.300	.192
Jim Holt†	1B17,DH3	L	30	30	42	1	6	0	0	0	0	1	9	0	.143	.182	.143
Gaylen Pitts	3B11,2B6,1B1	R	28	18	41	4	10	3	0	0	3	5	4	0	.244	.326	.317
Manny Trillo	2B21	R	23	21	33	3	5	0	0	0	2	2	8	0	.152	.222	.152
Phil Garner	3B19,SS8,2B3*	R	25	30	28	4	5	1	0	0	1	1	5	1	.179	.207	.214
Champ Summers	OF12,DH2	L	28	20	24	2	3	1	0	0	3	1	5	0	.125	.160	.167
Vic Davalillo	OF6,DH4	L	37	17	23	0	4	0	0	0	1	2	2	0	.174	.231	.174
John Donaldson	2B7,3B3	L	31	10	15	1	2	0	0	0	0	0	0	0	.133	.133	.133
Tim Hosley	C8,1B1	R	27	11	7	3	2	0	0	0	1	1	2	0	.286	.333	.286
Rich McKinney	2B3	R	27	5	7	0	1	0	0	0	0	0	0	0	.143	.143	.143
Herb Washington		R	22	92	0	29	0	0	0	0	0	0	0	29	—	—	—

T. Kubiak, 2 G at DH; P. Garner, 2 G at DH

Pitcher	T	Age	G	GS	CG	ShO	IP	H	HR	BB	SO	W-L	Sv	ERA
Catfish Hunter	R	28	41	41	23	6	318.1	268	25	46	143	25-12	0	2.49
Vida Blue	L	24	40	40	12	1	282.1	246	17	98	174	17-15	0	3.25
Ken Holtzman	L	28	39	38	9	3	255.1	273	14	51	117	19-17	0	3.07
Dave Hamilton	L	26	29	18	1	1	117.0	104	10	48	69	7-4	0	3.15
Glenn Abbott	R	23	19	17	3	0	96.0	89	4	34	38	5-7	0	3.00
Rollie Fingers	R	27	76	0	0	0	119.0	104	5	29	95	9-5	18	2.65
Paul Lindblad	L	32	45	2	0	0	100.2	85	4	30	46	4-4	6	2.06
Darold Knowles	L	32	45	1	0	0	53.1	61	6	35	18	3-3	3	4.22
Blue Moon Odom	R	29	34	5	1	0	87.1	85	4	52	52	1-5	1	3.81
Leon Hooten	R	26	6	0	0	0	8.1	6	1	4	1	0-0	0	3.24
Bill Parsons	R	25	4	0	0	0	2.0	1	0	3	2	0-0	0	0.00

1974 Texas Rangers 2nd AL West 84-76 .525 5.0 GB

Billy Martin

Player	Gm by Position	B	Age	G	AB	R	H	2B	3B	HR	RBI	BB	SO	SB	Avg	OBP	Slg
Jim Sundberg	C132	R	23	132	368	45	91	13	3	3	36	62	61	2	.247	.354	.323
Mike Hargrove	1B91,DH32,OF6	L	24	131	415	57	134	18	6	4	66	49	42	0	.323	.395	.424
Dave Nelson	2B120,DH1	R	30	121	474	71	112	13	1	3	42	34	72	25	.236	.291	.287
Lenny Randle	3B89,2B40,OF21*	S	25	151	520	65	157	17	4	1	49	29	43	26	.302	.338	.356
Toby Harrah	SS158,3B3	R	25	161	573	79	149	23	2	21	74	50	65	15	.260	.319	.417
Jeff Burroughs	OF150,1B2,DH1	R	23	152	554	84	167	33	2	25	118	91	104	2	.301	.397	.504
Cesar Tovar	OF135,DH3	R	33	138	562	78	164	24	6	4	58	47	33	13	.292	.354	.377
Joe Lovitto	OF107,1B5	S	23	113	283	27	63	9	3	2	26	25	36	6	.223	.285	.297
Jim Spencer	1B60,DH54	L	27	118	352	36	98	11	4	7	44	22	27	1	.278	.323	.392
Alex Johnson†	OF81,DH30	R	31	114	453	57	132	14	3	4	41	28	59	20	.291	.338	.362
Tom Grieve	DH40,OF38,1B1	R	26	84	259	30	66	10	4	9	32	20	48	0	.255	.311	.429
Jim Fregosi	1B47,3B32	R	32	78	230	31	60	5	0	12	34	22	41	0	.261	.324	.439
Duke Sims†	C30,DH5,OF1	L	33	39	106	7	22	0	0	3	6	8	24	0	.208	.280	.292
Leo Cardenas	3B21,SS10,DH4	R	35	34	92	5	25	3	0	0	7	2	14	1	.272	.287	.304
Larry Brown	3B47,2B8,SS1	R	34	54	76	10	15	2	0	0	5	9	13	0	.197	.279	.224
Roy Howell	3B12	L	20	13	44	2	11	1	0	1	3	2	10	0	.250	.283	.341
Dick Billings†	C13,DH1,OF1	R	31	16	31	2	7	1	0	0	0	4	6	2	.226	.314	.258
Bill Fahey	C6	L	24	6	16	1	4	0	0	0	0	0	1	0	.250	.250	.250
Mike Cubbage	3B3,2B2	L	23	9	15	0	0	0	0	0	0	0	4	0	.000	.000	.000
Tom Robson	DH5,1B1	R	28	6	13	2	3	1	0	0	2	4	3	0	.231	.412	.308
Pete Mackanin	SS2	R	22	2	6	0	1	0	1	0	0	0	2	0	.167	.167	.500
Bobby Jones	OF2	L	24	2	5	0	0	0	0	0	0	0	1	0	.000	.000	.000
Dave Moates		L	26	1	0	0	0	0	0	0	0	0	0	0	—	—	—

L. Randle, 2 G at DH, 1 G at SS

Pitcher	T	Age	G	GS	CG	ShO	IP	H	HR	BB	SO	W-L	Sv	ERA
Fergie Jenkins	R	30	41	41	29	6	328.1	286	27	45	225	25-12	0	2.82
Jim Bibby	R	29	41	41	11	5	264.0	255	25	113	149	19-19	0	4.74
Steve Hargan	R	31	37	27	8	2	186.2	202	15	48	98	12-9	0	3.95
Jackie Brown	R	31	35	26	9	2	216.2	219	13	74	134	13-12	0	3.57
David Clyde	L	19	28	21	4	0	117.0	129	14	47	52	3-9	0	4.38
Bill Hands†	R	34	2	2	1	1	14.0	11	0	3	4	2-0	0	1.93
Steve Foucault	R	24	69	0	0	0	144.1	123	8	40	106	8-9	12	2.24
Jim Merritt	L	30	26	1	0	0	32.2	46	3	6	18	0-0	0	4.13
Don Stanhouse	R	23	18	0	0	0	31.1	38	4	17	26	1-1	0	4.88
Lloyd Allen†	R	24	14	0	0	0	22.0	24	2	18	18	0-1	0	6.55
Pete Broberg	R	24	12	2	0	0	29.0	29	7	13	15	0-4	0	8.07
Stan Thomas	R	24	12	0	0	0	13.2	22	1	6	8	0-0	0	6.59
Jim Shellenback	L	30	11	0	0	0	24.2	30	5	12	14	0-0	0	5.84
Jeff Terpko	R	23	3	0	0	0	7.0	6	0	4	3	0-0	0	1.29
Steve Dunning	R	25	1	0	0	0	2.1	3	2	3	1	0-0	0	19.29

1974 Minnesota Twins 3rd AL West 82-80 .506 8.0 GB

Frank Quilici

Player	Gm by Position	B	Age	G	AB	R	H	2B	3B	HR	RBI	BB	SO	SB	Avg	OBP	Slg
Glenn Borgmann	C128	R	24	128	345	33	87	8	1	3	45	39	44	2	.252	.323	.307
Craig Kusick	1B75	R	25	76	201	36	48	7	1	8	26	35	36	0	.239	.353	.403
Rod Carew	2B148	L	28	153	599	86	218	30	5	3	55	74	49	38	.364	.433	.446
Eric Soderholm	3B130,SS1	R	25	141	464	63	128	18	3	10	51	48	68	7	.276	.349	.392
Danny Thompson	SS88,3B5,DH1	R	27	97	264	25	66	6	1	4	25	22	29	1	.250	.311	.326
Bobby Darwin	OF142	R	31	152	575	67	152	13	7	25	94	37	127	1	.264	.322	.442
Larry Hisle	OF137	R	27	143	510	68	146	20	7	19	79	48	112	12	.286	.353	.465
Steve Brye	OF129	R	25	135	488	52	138	32	1	2	41	22	59	1	.283	.319	.365
Tony Oliva	DH112	L	33	127	459	43	131	16	2	13	57	27	31	0	.285	.325	.414
Steve Braun	OF108,3B17	L	26	129	453	53	127	12	1	8	40	56	51	4	.280	.361	.364
Harmon Killebrew	DH57,1B33	R	38	122	333	28	74	7	0	13	54	45	61	0	.222	.312	.360
Jerry Terrell	SS34,2B26,3B21*	R	27	116	229	43	56	4	6	0	19	11	27	3	.245	.279	.314
Jim Holt†	1B67,OF5	L	30	79	197	24	50	11	0	0	16	14	16	0	.254	.302	.310
Luis Gomez	SS74,2B2,DH1	R	22	82	168	18	35	1	0	0	3	12	16	2	.208	.261	.214
Phil Roof	C44	R	33	44	97	10	19	1	0	2	13	6	24	0	.196	.257	.268
Randy Hundley	C28	R	32	32	88	2	17	2	0	0	3	4	12	0	.193	.228	.216
Pat Bourque†	1B21,DH8	L	27	23	64	5	14	2	0	1	8	7	11	0	.219	.296	.297
Sergio Ferrer	SS20,2B1	S	23	24	57	12	16	0	2	0	0	8	6	3	.281	.379	.351
Joe Lis†	1B18	R	27	24	41	5	8	0	0	0	3	5	12	0	.195	.298	.195

J. Terrell, 12 G at DH, 3 G at OF, 2 G at 1B

Pitcher	T	Age	G	GS	CG	ShO	IP	H	HR	BB	SO	W-L	Sv	ERA
Bert Blyleven	R	23	37	37	19	3	281.0	244	14	77	249	17-17	0	2.66
Joe Decker	R	27	37	37	11	1	248.2	234	24	97	158	16-14	0	3.29
Dave Goltz	R	25	28	24	5	1	174.1	192	14	45	89	10-10	1	3.25
Vic Albury	L	27	32	22	4	1	164.0	159	19	80	85	8-9	0	4.12
Ray Corbin	R	25	29	15	1	0	112.1	133	8	40	50	7-6	0	5.29
Dick Woodson†	R	29	5	4	0	0	27.0	30	5	4	12	1-1	0	4.33
Jim Hughes	R	22	2	2	1	0	10.0	8	2	4	8	0-2	0	5.40
Bill Campbell	R	25	63	0	0	0	120.1	109	4	55	89	8-7	19	2.62
Tom Burgmeier	L	30	50	0	0	0	91.2	92	7	26	34	5-3	4	4.52
Bill Hands†	R	34	35	10	0	0	115.1	130	9	25	74	4-5	3	4.45
Bill Butler	L	27	26	12	2	0	98.2	91	9	56	79	4-6	1	4.10
Tom Johnson	R	23	4	0	0	0	7.0	4	0	0	4	2-0	1	0.00
Danny Fife	R	24	4	0	0	0	4.2	10	0	4	3	0-0	0	17.36

1974 Chicago White Sox 4th AL West 80-80 .500 9.0 GB

Chuck Tanner

Player	Gm by Position	B	Age	G	AB	R	H	2B	3B	HR	RBI	BB	SO	SB	Avg	OBP	Slg
Ed Herrmann	C107	L	27	107	367	32	95	13	1	10	39	16	49	1	.259	.288	.381
Dick Allen	1B125,DH1,2B1	R	32	128	462	84	139	23	1	32	88	57	89	7	.301	.375	.563
Jorge Orta	2B123,DH10,SS3	L	23	139	525	73	166	31	2	10	67	40	88	9	.316	.365	.440
Bill Melton	3B123,DH11	R	28	136	495	63	120	17	0	21	63	59	60	3	.242	.326	.404
Bucky Dent	SS154	R	22	154	496	55	136	15	3	5	45	28	48	3	.274	.316	.347
Ken Henderson	OF162	S	28	162	602	76	176	35	5	20	95	66	112	12	.292	.360	.467
Carlos May	OF129,DH13	L	26	149	551	66	137	19	2	8	58	46	76	8	.249	.306	.334
Bill Sharp	OF99	L	24	100	320	45	81	13	2	4	24	25	37	0	.253	.309	.344
Pat Kelly	DH67,OF53	L	29	122	424	60	119	16	3	4	21	46	58	18	.281	.354	.361
Ron Santo	DH47,2B39,3B28*	R	34	117	375	29	83	12	1	5	41	37	72	0	.221	.293	.299
Brian Downing	C63,OF39,DH9	R	23	108	293	41	66	12	1	10	39	51	72	0	.225	.344	.375
Tony Muser	1B80,DH13	L	26	103	206	16	60	5	1	1	18	6	22	1	.291	.313	.340
Jerry Hairston	OF22,DH10	S	22	45	109	8	25	7	0	0	8	13	18	0	.229	.311	.294
Buddy Bradford	OF32,DH1	R	29	39	96	16	32	2	0	5	10	13	11	1	.333	.414	.510
Lee Richard	3B12,SS6,DH5*	R	25	32	67	5	11	1	0	0	1	5	8	0	.164	.222	.179
Eddie Leon	SS21,2B7,3B2*	R	27	31	46	1	5	1	0	0	3	2	12	0	.109	.143	.130
Bill Stein	3B11,DH2	R	27	13	43	5	12	1	0	0	5	7	8	0	.279	.380	.302
Lamar Johnson	1B7,DH3	R	23	10	29	1	10	0	0	0	2	0	3	0	.345	.333	.345
Pete Varney	C9	R	25	9	28	1	7	0	0	0	2	1	8	0	.250	.267	.250
Nyls Nyman	OF3	L	20	5	14	5	9	2	1	0	4	0	1	1	.643	.667	.929
Chuck Brinkman†	C8	R	29	8	14	1	2	0	0	0	0	1	3	0	.143	.200	.143
Luis Alvarado†	SS4,2B1,3B1	R	25	8	10	1	1	0	0	0	0	0	1	0	.100	.100	.100
Hugh Yancy	DH1	R	23	1	0	0	0	0	0	0	0	0	0	0	—	—	—

R. Santo, 3 G at 1B, 1 G at SS; L. Richard, 3 G at 2B, 1 G at OF; E. Leon, 1 G at DH

Pitcher	T	Age	G	GS	CG	ShO	IP	H	HR	BB	SO	W-L	Sv	ERA
Wilbur Wood	L	32	42	42	22	1	320.1	305	27	80	169	20-19	0	3.60
Jim Kaat	L	35	42	39	15	3	277.1	263	18	63	142	21-13	0	2.92
Stan Bahnsen	R	29	38	35	10	1	216.1	230	17	110	102	12-15	0	4.70
Bart Johnson	R	24	18	18	8	2	121.2	105	6	32	76	10-4	0	2.74
Jack Kucek	R	21	9	7	0	0	37.2	48	3	21	25	1-4	0	5.26
Joe Henderson	R	27	5	3	0	0	15.0	21	2	11	12	1-0	0	8.40
Stan Perzanowski	R	23	2	1	0	0	2.1	8	1	2	2	0-0	0	19.29
Terry Forster	L	22	59	1	0	0	134.1	120	6	48	105	7-8	24	3.62
Skip Pitlock	L	26	40	5	0	0	105.2	103	7	55	68	3-3	1	4.43
Goose Gossage	R	22	39	3	0	0	89.1	92	4	47	64	4-6	1	4.13
Cy Acosta	R	27	27	0	0	0	45.2	43	3	18	19	0-3	3	3.74
Carl Moran	R	23	15	5	0	0	46.1	57	5	23	17	1-3	0	4.66
Ken Tatum	R	30	10	1	0	0	20.2	23	3	9	5	0-0	0	4.79
Lloyd Allen†	R	24	6	2	0	0	7.0	7	0	12	3	0-1	0	10.29
Jim Otten	R	22	5	1	0	0	16.1	22	0	12	11	0-1	0	5.51
Wayne Granger	R	30	5	0	0	0	7.2	16	1	3	4	0-0	0	8.22
Francisco Barrios	R	21	2	0	0	0	2.0	7	0	2	2	0-0	0	27.00

1974 Kansas City Royals 5th AL West 77-85 .475 13.0 GB

Jack McKeon

Player	Gm by Position	B	Age	G	AB	R	H	2B	3B	HR	RBI	BB	SO	SB	Avg	OBP	Slg
Fran Healy	C138	R	27	139	445	59	112	24	2	9	53	62	73	16	.252	.343	.375
John Mayberry	1B106,DH16	L	25	126	427	63	100	13	1	22	69	77	72	4	.234	.358	.424
Cookie Rojas	2B141	R	35	144	542	52	147	17	1	6	60	30	43	8	.271	.309	.339
George Brett	3B132,SS1	L	21	133	457	49	129	21	5	2	47	21	38	8	.282	.313	.363
Freddie Patek	SS149	R	29	149	537	72	121	18	6	3	38	77	69	33	.225	.324	.298
Amos Otis	OF143,DH2	R	27	146	552	87	157	31	9	12	73	58	67	18	.284	.348	.438
Jim Wohlford	OF138,DH1	R	23	143	501	55	136	16	7	2	44	39	74	16	.271	.327	.343
Vada Pinson	OF110,DH2,1B1	L	35	115	406	46	112	18	2	6	41	21	45	21	.276	.312	.374
Hal McRae	DH90,OF56,3B1	R	28	148	539	71	167	36	4	15	88	54	68	11	.310	.375	.475
Al Cowens	OF102,DH4,3B2	R	22	110	269	28	65	7	1	1	25	23	38	5	.242	.303	.286
Tony Solaita	1B65,DH14,OF1	L	27	96	239	31	64	12	0	7	30	35	70	0	.268	.361	.406
Frank White	2B50,SS29,3B16*	R	23	99	204	19	45	6	3	1	18	5	33	3	.221	.239	.294
Buck Martinez	C38	R	25	43	107	10	23	3	1	1	8	14	19	0	.215	.317	.290
Orlando Cepeda	DH26	R	36	33	107	3	23	5	0	1	18	9	16	1	.215	.282	.290
Kurt Bevacqua†	1B14,3B13,2B7*	R	27	39	90	10	19	0	0	0	3	9	20	1	.211	.290	.211
Richie Scheinblum†	DH18,OF2	S	31	36	83	7	15	2	0	0	2	8	8	0	.181	.253	.205
Paul Schaal†	3B12	R	31	12	34	3	6	2	0	1	4	5	5	0	.176	.286	.324
F. Gonzalez†	3B8	R	24	9	21	1	3	1	0	0	2	0	4	1	.143	.143	.190
Dennis Paepke	C4,OF1	R	29	6	12	0	2	0	0	0	0	1	2	0	.167	.231	.167
Bobby Floyd	2B5,3B2,SS1	R	30	10	9	1	1	0	0	0	0	2	4	0	.111	.273	.111
Rick Reichardt		R	31	1	1	0	1	0	0	0	0	0	0	0	1.000	1.000	1.000

F. White, 3 G at DH; K. Bevacqua, 3 G at DH, 2 G at SS

Pitcher	T	Age	G	GS	CG	ShO	IP	H	HR	BB	SO	W-L	Sv	ERA
Steve Busby	R	24	38	38	20	3	292.1	284	14	92	198	22-14	0	3.39
Paul Splittorff	L	27	36	36	8	1	226.0	252	23	75	90	13-19	0	4.10
Al Fitzmorris	R	28	34	27	9	4	190.0	189	8	63	53	13-6	1	2.79
Bruce Dal Canton	R	32	31	22	9	2	175.1	135	5	82	96	8-10	0	3.13
Nelson Briles	R	30	18	17	3	0	103.0	118	9	21	41	5-7	0	4.02
Dennis Leonard	R	23	5	4	0	0	22.0	28	0	12	8	0-4	0	5.32
Doug Bird	R	24	55	1	1	0	92.1	100	6	27	62	7-6	10	2.73
Lindy McDaniel	R	38	38	5	2	0	106.2	109	6	24	47	1-4	1	3.46
Steve Mingori	L	30	36	0	0	0	67.1	53	4	23	43	2-3	2	2.81
Joe Hoerner	L	37	30	0	0	0	35.1	32	3	12	24	2-3	2	3.82
Marty Pattin	R	31	25	11	2	0	117.1	121	10	28	50	3-7	0	3.99
Gene Garber†	R	26	17	0	0	0	28.0	35	3	13	14	1-2	1	4.82
Aurelio Lopez	R	25	8	1	0	0	16.0	21	0	10	5	0-0	0	5.63

1974 California Angels 6th AL West 68-94 .420 22.0 GB

Bobby Winkles (30-44)/Whitey Herzog (2-2)/Dick Williams (36-48)

Player	Gm by Position	B	Age	G	AB	R	H	2B	3B	HR	RBI	BB	SO	SB	Avg	OBP	Slg
Ellie Rodriguez	C137,DH1	R	28	140	395	48	100	20	0	7	36	69	56	4	.253	.373	.357
John Doherty	1B70,DH2	L	22	74	223	20	57	14	1	3	15	8	13	2	.256	.280	.368
Denny Doyle	2B146,SS2	L	30	147	511	47	133	19	2	1	34	25	49	6	.260	.295	.311
Paul Schaal†	3B51	R	31	53	165	10	41	5	0	2	20	18	27	2	.248	.322	.315
Dave Chalk	SS99,3B38	R	23	133	465	44	117	9	3	5	31	30	57	10	.252	.304	.316
Mickey Rivers	OF116	L	25	118	466	69	133	19	11	3	31	39	47	30	.285	.341	.393
Lee Stanton	OF114	R	28	118	415	48	111	21	2	11	62	33	107	10	.267	.325	.407
Joe Lahoud	OF106,DH10	L	27	127	325	46	88	16	3	13	44	47	57	4	.271	.367	.458
Frank Robinson†	DH124,OF1	R	38	129	427	75	107	26	2	20	63	75	85	5	.251	.371	.461
Bobby Valentine	OF62,SS36,3B15*	R	24	117	371	39	97	10	3	3	39	25	25	8	.261	.308	.329
Bob Oliver†	1B57,3B46,OF4	R	31	110	359	22	89	9	1	8	55	16	51	2	.248	.277	.345
Bruce Bochte	OF39,1B24	L	23	57	196	24	53	4	1	5	26	18	23	6	.270	.332	.378
Morris Nettles	OF54	L	22	56	175	27	48	4	0	0	8	16	38	20	.274	.335	.297
Winston Llenas	OF32,2B15,DH10*	R	30	72	138	16	36	6	0	2	17	11	19	0	.261	.301	.348
Tom McCraw†	1B29,OF12	L	33	56	119	21	34	8	0	3	17	12	13	2	.286	.348	.429
Tom Egan	C41	R	28	43	94	4	11	0	0	0	4	8	40	1	.117	.194	.117
Rudy Meoli	3B20,SS8,1B1*	L	23	36	90	9	22	2	0	0	3	8	10	2	.244	.306	.267
Orlando Ramirez	SS31	R	22	31	86	4	14	0	0	0	7	6	23	2	.163	.215	.163
Charlie Sands	DH21,C5	L	26	43	83	6	16	2	0	4	13	23	17	0	.193	.370	.361
Bob Heise†	2B17,3B6,SS3	R	27	29	75	7	20	7	0	0	6	5	10	0	.267	.313	.360
Mike Epstein	1B18	L	31	18	62	10	10	2	0	4	6	10	13	0	.161	.288	.387
Sandy Alomar†	SS19,2B15,3B5*	S	30	46	54	12	12	0	1	0	1	2	8	2	.222	.250	.259
John Balaz	OF12	R	23	14	42	4	10	0	0	1	5	2	10	0	.238	.289	.310
Doug Howard	OF8,1B5,DH3	R	26	22	39	5	9	0	1	0	5	2	1	1	.231	.268	.282
Richie Scheinblum†	OF8	S	31	10	26	1	4	0	0	0	2	1	2	0	.154	.185	.154

B. Valentine, 4 G at DH, 1 G at 2B; W. Llenas, 2 G at 3B; R. Meoli, 1 G at 2B; S. Alomar, 1 G at OF

Pitcher	T	Age	G	GS	CG	ShO	IP	H	HR	BB	SO	W-L	Sv	ERA
Nolan Ryan	R	27	42	41	26	3	332.2	221	18	202	367	22-16	0	2.89
Frank Tanana	L	20	39	35	12	4	268.2	262	27	77	180	14-19	0	3.12
Andy Hassler	L	22	23	22	10	2	162.0	132	10	79	76	7-11	1	2.61
Dick Lange	R	25	21	18	1	0	113.2	111	10	47	57	3-8	0	3.80
Bill Singer	R	30	14	14	8	0	108.2	102	3	43	77	7-4	0	2.98
Bill Stoneman	R	30	13	11	0	0	58.2	78	8	31	33	1-8	0	6.14
Chuck Dobson	R	30	5	5	2	0	30.0	39	3	13	16	2-3	0	5.70
Skip Lockwood	R	27	37	2	0	0	81.1	81	8	32	39	2-5	1	4.32
Ed Figueroa	R	25	25	12	5	1	105.1	119	3	36	49	2-8	0	3.67
Dave Sells	R	27	20	0	0	0	39.0	48	3	16	14	2-3	2	3.69
Rudy May†	L	29	18	3	0	0	27.0	29	2	10	12	0-1	2	7.00
Dick Selma†	R	30	18	0	0	0	23.0	22	2	17	15	2-2	1	5.09
Luis Quintana	L	22	18	0	0	0	12.2	17	0	14	11	2-1	0	4.26
John Cumberland	L	27	17	0	0	0	21.2	24	2	10	12	0-1	0	3.74
Barry Raziano	R	27	13	0	0	0	16.2	15	1	8	9	1-2	1	6.48
Horacio Pina†	R	29	11	0	0	0	11.2	9	1	3	6	1-2	0	2.31
Ken Sanders†	R	32	9	0	0	0	9.2	10	0	3	4	0-0	1	2.79
Orlando Pena†	R	40	4	0	0	0	8.0	6	0	1	5	0-0	3	0.00
Don Kirkwood	R	24	3	0	0	0	7.1	12	0	6	4	0-0	0	8.59
Bill Gilbreth	L	26	3	0	0	0	1.1	2	0	1	0	0-0	0	13.50

»1974 Pittsburgh Pirates 1st NL East 88-74 .543 —

Danny Murtaugh

Player	Gm by Position	B	Age	G	AB	R	H	2B	3B	HR	RBI	BB	SO	SB	Avg	OBP	Slg
Manny Sanguillen	C151	R	30	151	596	77	171	21	4	7	68	21	27	2	.287	.313	.371
Bob Robertson	1B63	R	27	91	236	25	54	11	0	16	48	33	48	0	.229	.320	.479
Rennie Stennett	2B154,OF2	R	23	157	673	84	196	29	3	7	56	32	51	8	.291	.322	.374
Richie Hebner	3B141	L	26	146	550	97	160	21	6	18	68	60	53	0	.291	.363	.449
Frank Taveras	SS124	R	24	126	333	33	82	4	2	0	26	25	41	13	.246	.300	.270
Richie Zisk	OF141	R	25	149	536	75	168	30	3	17	100	65	91	1	.313	.386	.476
Willie Stargell	OF135,1B1	L	34	140	508	90	153	37	4	25	96	87	106	0	.301	.407	.537
Al Oliver	OF98,1B49	L	27	147	617	96	198	38	12	11	85	33	58	10	.321	.358	.475
Gene Clines	OF78	R	27	107	276	29	62	5	1	0	14	30	40	14	.225	.307	.250
Ed Kirkpatrick	1B59,OF14,C6	L	29	116	271	32	67	9	0	6	38	51	30	1	.247	.367	.347
Dave Parker	OF49,1B6	L	23	73	220	27	62	10	3	4	29	10	53	3	.282	.322	.409
Mario Mendoza	SS87	R	23	91	163	10	36	1	2	0	15	8	35	1	.221	.259	.252
Paul Popovich	2B12,SS10	S	33	59	83	9	18	2	1	0	5	5	10	0	.217	.256	.265
Art Howe	3B20,SS2	R	27	29	74	10	18	4	1	1	5	9	13	0	.243	.321	.365
Kurt Bevacqua†	3B8,OF1	R	27	18	35	1	4	1	0	0	0	2	10	0	.114	.162	.143
Mike Ryan	C15	R	32	15	30	2	3	0	0	0	0	4	16	0	.100	.206	.100
Dave Augustine	OF11	R	24	18	22	3	4	0	0	0	0	0	5	0	.182	.182	.182
Dal Maxvill†	SS8	R	35	8	22	3	4	0	0	0	0	2	4	0	.182	.250	.182
Chuck Brinkman†	C4	R	29	4	7	1	1	0	0	0	1	0	0	0	.143	.125	.143
Ken Macha	C1	R	23	5	5	1	3	1	0	0	1	0	0	0	.600	.600	.800
Ed Ott	OF2	L	22	7	5	1	0	0	0	0	0	0	1	0	.000	.000	.000
Miguel Dilone	OF2	S	19	12	2	3	0	0	0	0	0	1	0	2	.000	.333	.000

Pitcher	T	Age	G	GS	CG	ShO	IP	H	HR	BB	SO	W-L	Sv	ERA
Jerry Reuss	L	25	35	35	14	1	260.0	259	20	101	105	16-11	0	3.50
Jim Rooker	L	31	33	33	15	1	262.2	228	11	83	139	15-11	0	2.78
Ken Brett	L	25	27	27	10	3	191.0	192	9	52	96	13-9	0	3.30
Dock Ellis	R	29	26	26	9	0	176.2	163	13	41	91	12-9	0	3.16
Larry Demery	R	21	19	15	2	0	95.1	95	12	51	51	6-6	0	4.25
Bob Moose	R	26	7	6	0	0	35.2	59	4	7	15	1-5	0	7.57
Dave Giusti	R	34	64	2	0	0	105.2	101	2	40	53	7-5	12	3.32
Ramon Hernandez	L	33	58	0	0	0	68.2	68	3	18	33	5-2	2	2.75
Bruce Kison	R	24	40	16	1	0	129.0	123	8	57	71	9-8	2	3.49
John Morlan	R	26	39	0	0	0	65.0	54	2	48	38	0-3	0	4.29
Daryl Patterson	R	30	14	0	0	0	21.0	35	3	9	8	2-1	1	7.29
Kent Tekulve	R	27	8	0	0	0	9.0	12	1	5	6	1-1	0	6.00
Juan Pizarro	L	37	7	2	0	0	24.0	20	2	11	7	1-1	0	1.88
Jim Minshall	R	26	5	0	0	0	4.1	1	0	2	3	0-1	0	0.00
Jim Sadowski	R	22	4	0	0	0	9.0	7	1	9	1	0-1	0	6.00
Juan Jimenez	R	25	4	0	0	0	4.0	6	0	2	2	0-0	0	6.75
Steve Blass	R	32	1	0	0	0	5.0	5	2	7	2	0-0	0	9.00

1974 St. Louis Cardinals 2nd NL East 86-75 .534 1.5 GB

Red Schoendienst

Player	Gm by Position	B	Age	G	AB	R	H	2B	3B	HR	RBI	BB	SO	SB	Avg	OBP	Slg
Ted Simmons	C141,1B12	S	24	152	599	66	163	33	6	20	103	47	35	0	.272	.327	.447
Joe Torre	1B139,3B18	R	33	147	529	59	149	28	1	11	70	69	88	1	.282	.371	.401
Ted Sizemore	2B128,SS1,OF1	R	29	129	504	68	126	17	0	2	47	70	37	8	.250	.339	.296
Ken Reitz	3B151,SS2,2B1	R	23	154	579	48	157	28	2	7	54	23	63	0	.271	.299	.363
Mike Tyson	SS143,2B12	R	24	151	422	35	94	14	5	1	37	22	70	4	.223	.264	.287
Lou Brock	OF152	L	35	153	635	105	194	25	7	3	48	61	88	118	.306	.368	.381
Bake McBride	OF144	L	25	150	559	81	173	19	5	6	56	43	57	30	.309	.369	.394
Reggie Smith	OF132,1B1	S	29	143	517	79	160	26	9	23	100	71	70	4	.309	.389	.528
Jose Cruz	OF53,1B1	L	26	107	161	24	42	4	3	5	20	20	27	4	.261	.341	.416
Luis Melendez	OF46,SS1	R	24	83	124	15	27	4	3	0	8	11	9	2	.218	.283	.298
Tim McCarver†	C21,1B6	L	32	74	106	13	23	0	1	0	11	22	6	0	.217	.353	.236
Jim Dwyer	OF25,1B3	L	24	74	86	13	24	1	0	2	11	11	16	0	.279	.360	.360
Tom Heintzelman	2B28,3B2,SS1	R	27	38	74	10	17	4	0	1	6	9	14	0	.230	.313	.324
Jack Heidemann†	SS45,3B1	R	24	47	70	8	19	1	0	0	3	5	10	0	.271	.320	.286
Jim Hickman	1B14,3B1	R	37	50	60	5	16	0	0	2	4	8	10	0	.267	.353	.367
Jerry Davanon	SS14,3B8,2B7*	R	28	30	40	4	6	1	0	0	4	4	5	0	.150	.255	.175
Luis Alvarado†	SS17	R	25	17	36	3	5	2	0	0	1	2	6	0	.139	.179	.194
Keith Hernandez	1B9	L	20	14	34	3	10	1	2	0	2	7	8	0	.294	.415	.441
Ron Hunt†	2B5	R	33	12	23	1	4	0	0	0	0	3	2	0	.174	.321	.174
Marc Hill	C9	R	22	10	21	2	5	1	0	0	2	4	5	0	.238	.360	.286
Danny Godby	OF4	R	27	13	13	2	2	0	0	0	1	3	4	0	.154	.294	.154
Bob Heise†	2B3	R	27	3	7	0	1	0	0	0	0	0	0	0	.143	.143	.143
Richie Scheinblum†		S	31	6	6	0	2	0	0	0	0	0	1	0	.333	.333	.333
Dick Billings†	C1	R	31	1	5	0	1	0	0	0	0	0	1	0	.200	.200	.200
Stan Papi	SS7,2B1	R	23	8	4	0	1	0	0	0	1	0	0	0	.250	.250	.250
Jerry Mumphrey	OF1	S	21	5	2	2	0	0	0	0	0	0	0	0	.000	.000	.000
Larry Herndon	OF1	R	20	12	1	3	1	0	0	0	0	0	0	0	1.000	1.000	1.000

J. Davanon, 1 G at OF

Pitcher	T	Age	G	GS	CG	ShO	IP	H	HR	BB	SO	W-L	Sv	ERA
Bob Gibson	R	38	33	33	9	1	240.0	236	24	104	129	11-13	0	3.83
Lynn McGlothen	R	24	31	31	8	3	237.1	212	12	89	142	16-12	0	2.69
John Curtis	L	26	33	29	5	2	195.0	199	15	83	89	10-14	1	3.78
Alan Foster	R	27	31	25	5	1	162.1	167	16	61	78	7-10	0	3.88
Sonny Siebert	R	37	28	20	5	3	133.2	150	8	51	68	8-8	0	3.84
Bob Forsch	R	24	19	14	5	2	100.0	84	5	34	39	7-4	0	2.97
Al Hrabosky	L	24	65	0	0	0	88.1	71	3	38	82	8-1	9	2.95
Mike Garman	R	24	64	0	0	0	81.2	66	4	27	45	7-2	6	2.64
Rich Folkers	L	27	55	0	0	0	90.0	65	4	38	57	6-2	2	3.00
Orlando Pena†	R	40	42	0	0	0	45.0	45	0	20	23	5-2	1	2.60
Mike Thompson†	R	24	19	4	0	0	38.1	37	1	35	25	0-3	0	5.63
Pete Richert†	L	34	13	0	0	0	11.1	10	1	11	4	0-0	1	2.38
Ray Bare	R	25	10	3	0	0	24.1	25	2	9	6	1-2	0	5.92
Claude Osteen†	L	34	8	2	0	0	22.2	26	1	11	6	0-2	0	4.37
John Denny	R	21	2	0	0	0	2.0	3	0	0	1	0-0	0	0.00
Barry Lersch	R	29	1	0	0	0	1.1	3	1	5	0	0-0	0	40.50

1974 Philadelphia Phillies 3rd NL East 80-82 .494 8.0 GB — Danny Ozark

Player	Gm by Position	B	Age	G	AB	R	H	2B	3B	HR	RBI	BB	SO	SB	Avg	OBP	Slg
Bob Boone	C146	R	26	146	488	41	118	24	3	3	52	35	29	3	.242	.295	.322
Willie Montanez	1B137,OF1	L	26	143	527	55	160	33	1	7	79	32	57	3	.304	.343	.410
Dave Cash	2B162	R	26	162	687	89	206	26	11	2	58	46	33	20	.300	.351	.378
Mike Schmidt	3B162	R	24	162	568	108	160	28	7	36	116	106	138	23	.282	.395	.546
Larry Bowa	SS162	S	28	162	669	97	184	19	10	1	36	23	52	39	.275	.298	.338
Del Unser	OF135	L	29	142	454	72	120	18	5	11	61	50	62	6	.264	.337	.399
Mike Anderson	OF133,1B1	R	23	145	395	35	99	22	2	5	34	37	75	2	.251	.313	.354
Bill Robinson	OF87	R	31	100	280	32	66	14	1	5	29	17	61	5	.236	.280	.346
Greg Luzinski	OF82	R	23	85	302	29	82	14	1	7	48	29	76	3	.272	.330	.394
Tom Hutton	1B39,OF33	L	28	96	208	32	50	6	3	4	33	30	13	2	.240	.331	.356
Jay Johnstone	OF59	L	28	64	200	30	59	10	4	6	30	24	28	5	.295	.371	.475
Ollie Brown†	OF33	R	30	43	99	11	24	5	2	4	13	6	20	0	.242	.286	.455
Tony Taylor	1B7,3B5,2B4	R	38	62	64	5	21	4	0	2	13	6	6	0	.328	.389	.484
Larry Cox	C29	R	26	30	53	5	9	2	0	0	4	4	9	0	.170	.241	.208
Billy Grabarkewitz†	OF5,3B1	R	28	34	30	7	4	0	0	1	2	5	10	3	.133	.257	.233
Alan Bannister	OF8,SS2	R	22	26	25	4	3	0	0	0	1	3	7	0	.120	.241	.120
Jim Essian	C15,1B1,3B1	R	23	17	20	1	2	0	0	0	0	2	1	0	.100	.182	.100
Mike Rogodzinski	OF1	L	26	17	15	1	1	0	0	0	1	2	3	0	.067	.176	.067
Terry Harmon	SS7,2B5	R	30	27	15	5	2	0	0	0	0	3	3	0	.133	.278	.133
Jerry Martin	OF11	R	25	13	14	2	3	1	0	0	1	1	5	0	.214	.267	.286
John Stearns	C1	R	22	1	2	0	1	0	0	0	0	0	0	0	.500	.500	.500

Pitcher	T	Age	G	GS	CG	ShO	IP	H	HR	BB	SO	W-L	Sv	ERA
Steve Carlton	L	29	39	39	17	1	291.0	249	21	136	240	16-13	0	3.22
Jim Lonborg	R	32	39	39	16	3	283.0	280	22	70	121	17-13	0	3.21
Dick Ruthven	R	23	35	35	6	0	212.2	182	11	116	153	9-13	0	4.02
Ron Schueler	R	26	44	27	5	0	203.1	202	17	98	109	11-16	1	3.72
Wayne Twitchell	R	26	25	18	2	0	112.1	122	11	65	72	6-9	0	5.21
Mac Scarce	L	25	58	0	0	0	70.1	72	6	35	50	3-8	5	4.99
Eddie Watt	R	33	42	0	0	0	38.1	39	3	26	23	1-1	6	3.99
Gene Garber†	R	26	34	0	0	0	48.0	39	1	31	27	4-0	4	2.06
Jesus Hernaiz	R	29	27	0	0	0	41.1	53	6	25	16	2-3	1	5.88
Frank Linzy	R	33	22	0	0	0	24.2	27	1	7	12	3-2	0	3.28
Pete Richert†	L	34	21	0	0	0	20.1	15	0	4	9	2-1	0	2.21
Ed Farmer	R	24	14	3	0	0	31.0	41	5	27	20	2-1	0	8.42
George Culver	R	30	14	0	0	0	21.2	20	1	16	9	1-0	0	6.65
Larry Christenson	R	20	10	1	0	0	23.0	20	2	15	18	1-1	2	4.30
Mike Wallace†	L	23	8	0	0	0	8.1	12	0	2	1	1-0	0	5.40
Tom Underwood	L	20	7	0	0	0	13.0	15	1	5	8	1-0	0	4.85
Dave Wallace	R	26	3	0	0	0	3.0	4	2	3	3	0-1	0	9.00
Ron Diorio	R	27	2	0	0	0	1.0	2	1	1	0	0-0	0	18.00
Erskine Thomason	R	25	1	0	0	0	1.0	0	0	0	1	0-0	0	0.00

1974 Montreal Expos 4th NL East 79-82 .491 8.5 GB — Gene Mauch

Player	Gm by Position	B	Age	G	AB	R	H	2B	3B	HR	RBI	BB	SO	SB	Avg	OBP	Slg
Barry Foote	C122	R	22	125	420	44	110	23	4	11	60	35	74	2	.262	.315	.414
Mike Jorgensen	1B91,OF29	L	25	131	287	45	89	16	1	11	59	70	39	3	.310	.444	.488
Jim Cox	2B72	R	24	77	236	29	52	9	1	2	26	23	36	2	.220	.288	.292
Ron Hunt†	3B75,2B31,SS1	R	33	115	403	66	108	15	0	0	26	55	17	2	.268	.375	.305
Tim Foli	SS120,3B1	R	23	121	441	41	112	10	3	0	39	28	27	8	.254	.300	.290
Willie Davis	OF151	L	34	153	611	86	180	27	9	12	89	27	69	25	.295	.322	.427
Ken Singleton	OF143	S	27	148	511	68	141	20	2	9	74	93	84	5	.276	.385	.376
Bob Bailey	OF78,3B68	R	31	152	507	69	142	20	2	20	73	100	107	4	.280	.396	.446
Larry Lintz	2B67,SS31,3B1	S	24	113	319	60	76	10	1	0	20	44	50	50	.238	.334	.276
Ron Fairly	1B67,OF20	L	35	101	282	35	69	9	1	12	43	57	28	2	.245	.372	.411
Hal Breeden	1B56	R	30	79	190	14	47	13	0	2	20	24	35	0	.247	.330	.347
Ron Woods	OF61	R	31	90	127	15	26	0	0	1	12	17	17	6	.205	.299	.228
Pepe Frias	SS30,3B27,2B15*	R	25	75	112	12	24	4	1	0	7	7	10	1	.214	.258	.268
Bob Stinson	C29	S	28	38	87	4	15	2	0	1	6	15	16	1	.172	.294	.230
Larry Parrish	3B24	R	20	25	69	9	14	5	0	0	4	6	19	0	.203	.286	.275
Boots Day	OF16	L	26	52	65	8	12	0	0	0	2	5	8	0	.185	.239	.185
Pepe Mangual	OF22	R	22	23	61	10	19	3	0	0	4	5	15	5	.311	.353	.361
Jim Northrup†	OF13	L	34	21	54	3	13	1	0	2	8	5	9	0	.241	.305	.370
Terry Humphrey	C17	R	24	20	52	3	10	3	0	0	3	4	9	0	.192	.246	.250
Gary Carter	C6,OF2	R	20	9	27	5	11	0	1	1	6	1	2	2	.407	.414	.593
Larry Biittner	OF4	L	28	18	26	2	7	1	0	0	3	0	2	0	.269	.269	.308
Jose Morales	C2	R	29	25	26	3	7	4	0	1	5	1	7	0	.269	.296	.538
Warren Cromartie	OF6	L	20	8	17	2	3	0	0	0	0	3	3	1	.176	.300	.176
Jerry White	OF7	S	21	9	10	0	4	1	1	0	2	0	0	3	.400	.400	.700
Jim Lyttle	OF18	L	28	25	9	1	3	0	0	0	2	1	3	0	.333	.364	.333
Tony Scott	OF16	S	22	19	7	2	2	0	0	0	1	1	3	1	.286	.375	.286
Pat Scanlon	3B1	L	21	2	4	1	1	0	0	0	0	0	1	0	.250	.250	.250

P. Frias, 3 G at OF

Pitcher	T	Age	G	GS	CG	ShO	IP	H	HR	BB	SO	W-L	Sv	ERA
Steve Rogers	R	24	38	38	11	1	253.2	255	19	80	154	15-22	0	4.47
Steve Renko	R	29	37	35	8	1	227.2	222	17	81	138	12-16	0	4.03
Mike Torrez	R	27	32	30	6	1	186.1	184	10	84	92	15-8	0	3.57
Dennis Blair	R	20	22	22	4	1	146.0	113	7	72	76	11-7	0	3.27
Ernie McAnally	R	27	25	21	5	2	128.2	126	10	56	79	6-13	0	4.48
Chuck Taylor	R	32	61	0	0	0	107.2	101	8	25	43	6-2	11	2.17
John Montague	R	26	46	1	0	0	82.2	73	5	38	43	3-4	3	3.16
Tom Walker	R	25	33	8	1	0	91.2	96	7	28	70	4-5	2	3.83
Dale Murray	R	24	32	0	0	0	69.2	46	1	23	31	1-1	10	1.03
Don DeMola	R	21	25	1	0	0	57.2	46	7	21	47	1-0	0	3.12
Don Carrithers	R	24	22	3	0	0	60.0	56	6	17	31	5-2	1	3.00
Balor Moore	L	23	8	2	0	0	13.2	13	1	15	16	0-2	0	3.95
Terry Enyart	L	23	2	0	0	0	1.2	4	0	4	2	0-0	0	16.20
Bob Gebhard	R	31	1	0	0	0	2.0	5	1	0	0	0-0	0	4.50

1974 New York Mets 5th NL East 71-91 .438 17.0 GB — Yogi Berra

Player	Gm by Position	B	Age	G	AB	R	H	2B	3B	HR	RBI	BB	SO	SB	Avg	OBP	Slg
Jerry Grote	C94	R	31	97	319	25	82	8	1	5	36	33	33	0	.257	.326	.335
John Milner	1B133	L	24	137	507	70	128	19	0	20	63	66	77	10	.252	.350	.408
Felix Millan	2B134	R	30	136	518	50	139	15	2	1	33	31	14	5	.268	.317	.311
Wayne Garrett	3B144,SS9	L	26	151	522	55	117	14	3	13	53	89	96	4	.224	.337	.337
Bud Harrelson	SS97	S	30	106	331	48	75	10	0	1	13	71	39	9	.227	.366	.266
Rusty Staub	OF147	L	30	151	561	65	145	22	2	19	78	77	39	2	.258	.347	.406
Cleon Jones	OF120	R	31	124	461	62	130	23	1	13	60	38	79	3	.282	.343	.421
Don Hahn	OF106	R	25	110	323	34	81	14	1	4	28	37	34	2	.251	.328	.337
Ted Martinez	SS75,3B12,2B11*	R	26	116	334	32	73	15	7	2	43	14	40	3	.219	.247	.323
Dave Schneck	OF84	L	25	93	254	23	52	11	1	5	25	16	43	4	.205	.254	.315
Ken Boswell	2B28,3B20,OF7	L	28	96	222	19	48	6	1	2	15	18	19	0	.216	.277	.279
Ed Kranepool	OF33,1B24	L	29	94	217	20	65	11	1	4	24	18	14	1	.300	.350	.415
Duffy Dyer	C45	R	28	63	142	14	30	1	1	0	10	18	15	0	.211	.302	.232
Ron Hodges	C44	L	25	59	136	16	30	4	0	4	14	19	11	0	.221	.310	.338
George Theodore	1B14,OF12	R	26	60	76	7	12	1	0	1	1	8	14	0	.158	.247	.211
Bennie Ayala	OF20	R	23	23	68	9	16	1	0	2	8	7	17	0	.235	.308	.338
Jim Gosger	OF24	L	31	26	33	3	3	0	0	0	0	3	2	0	.091	.167	.091
Brock Pemberton	1B4	S	20	11	22	0	4	0	0	0	1	0	3	0	.182	.182	.182
Bruce Boisclair	OF5	L	21	7	12	0	3	1	0	0	1	1	4	0	.250	.308	.333
Rich Puig	2B3,3B1	L	21	4	10	0	0	0	0	0	0	1	2	0	.000	.091	.000
Ike Hampton	C1	S	22	4	4	0	0	0	0	0	1	0	1	0	.000	.000	.000

T. Martinez, 10 G at OF

Pitcher	T	Age	G	GS	CG	ShO	IP	H	HR	BB	SO	W-L	Sv	ERA
Jerry Koosman	L	31	35	35	13	0	265.0	258	16	85	188	15-11	0	3.36
Jon Matlack	L	24	34	34	14	7	265.1	221	8	76	195	13-15	0	2.41
Tom Seaver	R	29	32	32	12	5	236.0	199	19	75	201	11-11	0	3.20
George Stone	L	27	15	13	1	0	77.0	103	10	21	29	2-7	0	5.03
Craig Swan	R	23	7	5	0	0	30.1	28	1	21	10	1-3	0	4.45
Hank Webb	R	24	3	2	0	0	10.0	15	1	10	8	0-2	0	7.20
Randy Sterling	R	23	3	2	0	0	9.1	13	0	3	2	1-1	0	4.82
Nino Espinosa	R	20	2	1	0	0	9.0	12	1	0	2	0-0	0	5.00
Bob Miller	R	35	58	0	0	0	78.0	89	2	39	35	2-2	2	3.58
Tug McGraw	L	29	41	4	1	1	88.2	96	12	32	54	6-11	3	4.16
Harry Parker	R	26	40	16	1	0	131.0	145	10	46	58	4-12	4	3.92
Bob Apodaca	R	24	35	8	1	0	103.0	92	7	42	54	6-6	3	3.50
Ray Sadecki	L	33	34	10	3	1	103.0	107	7	35	46	8-8	0	3.41
Jack Aker†	R	33	24	0	0	0	41.1	33	4	14	18	2-1	2	3.48
Gerald Cram	R	26	10	0	0	0	22.1	22	1	4	8	0-1	0	1.61
John Strohmayer	R	27	1	0	0	0	1.0	0	0	1	0	0-0	0	0.00

1974 Chicago Cubs 6th NL East 66-96 .407 22.0 GB — Whitey Lockman (41-52)/Jim Marshall (25-44)

Player	Gm by Position	B	Age	G	AB	R	H	2B	3B	HR	RBI	BB	SO	SB	Avg	OBP	Slg
Steve Swisher	C90	R	22	90	280	21	60	5	0	5	27	37	63	0	.214	.307	.286
Andre Thornton	1B90,3B1	R	24	107	303	41	79	16	4	10	46	48	50	2	.261	.368	.439
Vic Harris	2B56	S	24	62	200	18	39	6	3	0	11	29	26	9	.195	.294	.255
Bill Madlock	3B121	R	23	128	453	65	142	21	5	9	54	42	39	11	.313	.374	.442
Don Kessinger	SS150	S	31	153	599	83	155	20	7	1	42	62	54	7	.259	.332	.321
Jerry Morales	OF143	R	25	151	534	70	146	21	7	15	82	46	63	2	.273	.330	.423
Rick Monday	OF139	L	28	142	538	84	158	19	7	20	58	70	94	7	.294	.375	.467
Jose Cardenal	OF137	R	30	143	542	75	159	35	3	13	72	56	67	23	.293	.359	.441
Billy Williams	1B65,OF43	L	36	117	404	55	113	22	0	16	68	67	44	4	.280	.382	.453
George Mitterwald	C68	R	29	78	215	17	54	7	0	7	28	18	42	1	.251	.310	.381
Carmen Fanzone	3B35,2B10,1B7*	R	30	65	158	13	30	6	0	4	22	15	27	0	.190	.264	.304
Dave Rosello	2B49,SS12	R	24	62	148	9	30	7	0	0	10	10	28	1	.203	.252	.250
Chris Ward	OF22,1B6	L	25	92	137	8	28	4	0	1	15	18	13	0	.204	.293	.255
Billy Grabarkewitz†	2B45,SS7,3B6	R	28	53	125	21	31	3	2	1	12	21	28	1	.248	.358	.328
Pete LaCock	OF22,1B11	L	22	35	110	9	20	4	1	1	8	12	16	0	.182	.268	.264
Rob Sperring	2B35,SS8	R	24	42	107	9	22	3	0	1	5	9	28	1	.206	.267	.262
Jim Tyrone	OF32,3B1	R	25	57	81	19	15	0	1	3	3	6	8	1	.185	.241	.321
Ron Dunn	2B21,3B6	R	24	23	68	6	20	7	0	2	15	12	8	0	.294	.400	.485
Matt Alexander	3B19,OF4,2B2	S	27	45	54	15	11	2	1	0	0	12	12	8	.204	.358	.278
Rick Stelmaszek	C16	L	25	25	44	2	10	2	0	1	7	10	6	0	.227	.364	.341
Tom Lundstedt	C22	S	25	22	32	1	3	0	0	0	0	5	7	0	.094	.216	.094
Gene Hiser	OF8	L	25	12	17	2	4	1	0	0	1	0	3	0	.235	.235	.294
Gonzalo Marquez	1B1	L	28	11	11	1	0	0	0	0	0	1	2	0	.000	.083	.000
Adrian Garrett	C3,1B1,OF1	L	31	10	8	0	0	0	0	0	0	1	1	0	.000	.111	.000

C. Fanzone, 1 G at OF

Pitcher	T	Age	G	GS	CG	ShO	IP	H	HR	BB	SO	W-L	Sv	ERA
Rick Reuschel	R	25	41	38	8	2	240.2	262	18	83	160	13-12	0	4.30
Bill Bonham	R	25	44	36	10	2	242.2	246	13	109	191	11-22	1	3.86
Steve Stone	R	26	38	23	1	0	169.2	185	19	64	90	8-6	0	4.14
Tom Dettore	R	26	16	9	0	0	64.2	64	4	31	43	3-5	0	4.18
Oscar Zamora	R	29	56	0	0	0	83.2	82	6	19	38	3-9	10	3.12
Ken Frailing	L	26	55	16	1	0	125.1	150	11	43	71	6-9	1	3.88
Dave LaRoche	L	26	49	4	0	0	92.0	103	9	47	49	5-6	5	4.79
Burt Hooton	R	24	48	21	3	1	176.1	214	16	51	94	7-11	1	4.80
Jim Todd	R	26	43	6	0	0	88.0	82	7	41	42	4-2	3	3.89
Ray Burris	R	23	40	5	0	0	75.0	91	8	26	40	3-5	1	6.60
Horacio Pina†	R	29	34	0	0	0	47.1	49	4	28	32	3-4	4	3.99
Jim Kremmel	L	26	23	2	0	0	31.0	37	3	18	22	0-2	0	5.23
Herb Hutson	R	24	20	2	0	0	28.2	24	3	15	22	0-2	0	3.45
Mike Paul	L	29	2	0	0	0	1.1	4	1	1	1	0-1	0	27.00

1974 Los Angeles Dodgers 1st NL West 102-60 .630 —

Walter Alston

Player	Gm by Position	B	Age	G	AB	R	H	2B	3B	HR	RBI	BB	SO	SB	Avg	OBP	Slg
Steve Yeager	C93	R	25	94	316	41	84	16	1	12	41	32	77	2	.266	.334	.437
Steve Garvey	1B156	R	25	156	642	95	200	32	3	21	111	31	66	5	.312	.342	.469
Davey Lopes	2B143	R	29	145	530	95	141	26	3	10	35	66	71	59	.266	.350	.383
Ron Cey	3B158	R	26	159	577	88	151	20	2	18	97	76	68	1	.262	.349	.397
Bill Russell	SS160,OF1	R	25	160	553	61	149	18	6	5	65	53	53	14	.269	.336	.351
Jimmy Wynn	OF148	R	32	150	535	104	145	17	4	32	108	108	104	18	.271	.387	.497
Bill Buckner	OF137,1B6	L	24	145	580	83	182	30	3	7	58	30	24	31	.314	.351	.412
Willie Crawford	OF133	L	27	139	468	73	138	23	4	11	61	64	88	7	.295	.376	.432
Joe Ferguson	C82,OF32	R	27	111	349	54	88	14	1	16	57	75	73	2	.252	.380	.436
Tom Paciorek	OF77,1B1	R	27	85	175	23	42	8	6	1	24	10	32	1	.240	.282	.371
Von Joshua	OF35	L	26	81	124	11	29	5	1	1	16	7	17	3	.234	.276	.315
Lee Lacy	2B34,3B1	R	26	48	78	13	22	6	0	0	8	2	14	2	.282	.293	.359
Rick Auerbach	SS19,2B16,3B3	R	24	45	73	12	25	0	0	1	4	8	9	4	.342	.407	.384
Ken McMullen	3B7,2B3	R	32	44	60	5	15	1	0	3	12	2	12	0	.250	.274	.417
Manny Mota	OF3	R	36	66	57	5	16	2	0	0	16	5	4	0	.281	.328	.316
Gail Hopkins	C2,1B2	L	31	15	18	1	4	0	0	0	0	3	1	0	.222	.333	.222
John Hale	OF3	L	20	4	4	2	4	1	0	0	2	0	0	0	1.000	1.000	1.250
Ivan DeJesus	SS2	R	21	3	3	1	1	0	0	0	0	0	2	0	.333	.333	.333
Charlie Manuel		L	30	4	3	0	1	0	0	0	1	1	0	0	.333	.500	.333
Orlando Alvarez	OF1	R	22	2	1	0	0	0	0	0	0	0	0	0	.000	.000	.000
Jerry Royster	2B1,3B1,OF1	R	21	6	0	2	0	0	0	0	0	0	0	0	—	—	—
Kevin Pasley	C1	R	20	1	0	0	0	0	0	0	0	0	0	0	—	—	—

Pitcher	T	Age	G	GS	CG	ShO	IP	H	HR	BB	SO	W-L	Sv	ERA
Don Sutton	R	29	40	40	10	5	276.0	241	23	80	179	19-9	0	3.23
Andy Messersmith	R	28	39	39	13	3	292.1	227	24	94	221	20-6	0	2.59
Doug Rau	L	25	36	35	3	1	198.1	191	20	70	126	13-11	0	3.72
Tommy John	L	31	22	22	5	3	153.0	133	4	42	78	13-3	0	2.59
Al Downing	L	33	21	16	1	1	98.1	94	7	45	63	5-6	0	3.66
Mike Marshall	R	31	106	0	0	0	208.1	191	9	56	143	15-12	21	2.42
Charlie Hough	R	26	49	0	0	0	96.0	65	12	40	63	9-4	1	3.75
Jim Brewer	L	36	24	0	0	0	39.1	29	5	10	26	4-4	0	2.52
Geoff Zahn	L	28	21	10	1	0	79.2	78	3	16	33	3-5	0	2.03
Rick Rhoden	R	21	4	0	0	0	9.0	5	1	4	7	1-0	0	2.00
Greg Shanahan	R	26	4	0	0	0	7.0	7	1	5	2	0-0	0	3.86
Eddie Solomon	R	23	4	0	0	0	6.0	5	1	2	2	0-0	1	1.50
Rex Hudson	R	20	1	0	0	0	2.0	6	2	0	0	0-0	0	22.50

1974 Cincinnati Reds 2nd NL West 98-64 .605 4.0 GB

Sparky Anderson

Player	Gm by Position	B	Age	G	AB	R	H	2B	3B	HR	RBI	BB	SO	SB	Avg	OBP	Slg
Johnny Bench	C137,3B36,1B5	R	26	160	621	108	174	38	2	33	129	80	90	5	.280	.363	.507
Tony Perez	1B157	R	32	158	596	81	158	28	2	28	101	61	112	1	.265	.331	.460
Joe Morgan	2B142	L	30	149	512	107	150	31	3	22	67	120	69	58	.293	.427	.494
Dan Driessen	3B126,1B47,OF3	L	22	150	470	63	132	23	6	7	56	48	62	10	.281	.347	.400
Dave Concepcion	SS160,OF1	R	26	160	594	70	167	25	1	14	82	44	79	41	.281	.335	.397
Pete Rose	OF163	S	33	163	652	110	185	45	7	3	51	106	54	2	.284	.385	.388
Cesar Geronimo	OF145	L	26	150	474	73	133	17	8	7	54	46	96	9	.281	.345	.395
George Foster	OF98	R	25	106	276	31	73	18	0	7	41	30	52	3	.264	.343	.406
Ken Griffey Sr.	OF70	L	24	88	227	24	57	9	5	2	19	27	43	9	.251	.333	.361
Merv Rettenmund	OF69	R	31	80	208	30	45	6	0	6	28	37	39	5	.216	.337	.332
Darrel Chaney	3B81,2B38,SS12	S	26	117	135	27	27	6	1	2	16	26	33	1	.200	.327	.304
Terry Crowley	OF22,1B7	L	27	84	125	11	30	12	0	1	20	10	16	1	.240	.293	.360
Bill Plummer	C49,3B1	R	27	50	120	7	27	7	0	2	10	6	21	1	.225	.258	.333
Andy Kosco	3B8,OF1	R	32	33	37	3	7	2	0	0	5	7	8	0	.189	.311	.243
Phil Gagliano	2B2,1B1,3B1	R	32	46	31	2	2	0	0	0	0	15	7	0	.065	.370	.065
Junior Kennedy	2B17,3B5	R	23	22	19	2	3	0	0	0	0	6	4	0	.158	.360	.158
Hal King	C5	L	30	20	17	1	3	1	0	0	3	3	4	0	.176	.300	.235
Ray Knight	3B14	R	21	14	11	1	2	1	0	0	2	1	2	0	.182	.250	.273
Ed Armbrister	OF4	R	25	9	7	0	2	0	0	0	0	1	1	0	.286	.375	.286
Roger Freed	1B1	R	28	6	6	1	2	0	0	1	3	1	1	0	.333	.429	.833

Pitcher	T	Age	G	GS	CG	ShO	IP	H	HR	BB	SO	W-L	Sv	ERA
Don Gullett	L	23	36	35	10	3	243.0	201	22	88	183	17-11	0	3.04
Clay Kirby	R	26	36	35	7	1	230.2	210	15	91	160	12-9	0	3.28
Jack Billingham	R	31	36	35	8	3	212.1	233	16	64	103	19-11	0	3.94
Fred Norman	L	31	35	26	8	2	186.1	170	15	68	141	13-12	0	3.14
Tom Carroll	R	21	16	13	0	0	78.1	68	11	44	37	4-3	0	3.68
Roger Nelson	R	30	14	12	1	0	85.1	67	7	35	42	4-4	1	3.38
Pedro Borbon	R	27	73	0	0	0	139.0	133	11	32	53	10-7	14	3.24
Clay Carroll	R	33	57	3	0	0	100.2	96	3	30	46	12-5	6	2.15
Tom Hall	L	26	40	1	0	0	64.0	54	9	30	48	3-1	1	4.08
Will McEnaney	L	22	24	0	0	0	27.0	24	4	9	13	2-1	2	4.33
Dick Baney	R	27	22	1	0	0	41.0	51	4	17	12	1-0	1	5.49
Mike McQueen	L	23	10	0	0	0	15.0	17	4	11	5	0-0	0	5.40
Rawly Eastwick	R	23	8	0	0	0	17.2	12	1	5	14	0-0	2	2.04
Pat Darcy	R	24	6	2	0	0	17.0	17	2	8	14	1-0	0	3.71
Pat Osburn	L	25	6	0	0	0	9.0	11	2	4	4	0-0	0	8.00

1974 Atlanta Braves 3rd NL West 88-74 .543 14.0 GB

Eddie Mathews (50-49)/Clyde King (38-25)

Player	Gm by Position	B	Age	G	AB	R	H	2B	3B	HR	RBI	BB	SO	SB	Avg	OBP	Slg
Johnny Oates	C91	L	28	100	291	22	65	10	0	1	21	23	24	2	.223	.278	.268
Dave Johnson	1B73,2B71	R	31	136	454	56	114	18	0	15	62	75	59	1	.251	.358	.390
Marty Perez	2B102,SS14,3B6	R	27	127	447	51	116	20	5	2	34	35	51	2	.260	.314	.340
Darrell Evans	3B160	L	27	160	571	99	137	21	3	25	79	126	88	4	.240	.381	.419
Craig Robinson	SS142	R	25	145	452	52	104	4	6	0	29	30	57	11	.230	.280	.265
Dusty Baker	OF148	R	25	149	574	80	147	35	0	20	69	71	87	18	.256	.335	.422
Ralph Garr	OF139	L	28	143	606	87	214	24	17	11	54	28	52	26	.353	.383	.503
Rowland Office	OF119	L	21	131	248	20	61	16	1	3	31	16	30	5	.246	.288	.355
Mike Lum	1B60,OF50	L	28	106	361	50	84	11	2	11	50	45	49	0	.233	.319	.366
Hank Aaron	OF89	R	40	112	340	47	91	16	0	20	69	39	29	1	.268	.341	.491
Vic Correll	C59	R	28	73	202	20	48	15	1	4	29	21	38	0	.238	.317	.381
Frank Tepedino	1B46	L	26	78	169	11	39	5	1	0	16	9	13	1	.231	.272	.272
Ivan Murrell	OF32,1B13	R	29	73	133	11	33	1	1	2	12	5	35	0	.248	.273	.316
Leo Foster	SS43,2B10,3B3*	R	23	72	112	16	22	2	0	1	5	9	22	1	.196	.254	.241
Paul Casanova	C33	R	32	42	104	5	21	0	0	0	8	5	17	0	.202	.232	.202
Norm Miller	OF4	L	28	42	41	1	7	1	0	1	5	7	9	0	.171	.292	.268
Jack Pierce	1B2	L	26	6	9	1	1	0	0	0	0	1	0	0	.111	.200	.111
Larvell Blanks	SS2	R	24	3	8	0	2	0	0	0	1	0	0	0	.250	.250	.250
Sonny Jackson	OF1	L	29	5	7	0	3	0	0	0	0	0	0	0	.429	.429	.429
Rod Gilbreath	2B2	R	21	3	6	2	2	0	0	0	0	2	0	0	.333	.500	.333
John Fuller	OF1	L	24	3	3	1	1	0	0	0	0	0	0	0	.333	.333	.333

L. Foster, 1 G at OF

Pitcher	T	Age	G	GS	CG	ShO	IP	H	HR	BB	SO	W-L	Sv	ERA
Phil Niekro	R	35	41	39	18	6	302.1	249	19	88	195	20-13	1	2.38
Carl Morton	R	30	38	38	7	1	274.2	293	10	89	113	16-12	0	3.15
Ron Reed	R	31	28	28	6	2	186.0	171	16	41	78	10-11	0	3.39
Buzz Capra	R	26	39	27	11	5	217.0	163	13	84	137	16-8	1	2.28
Roric Harrison	R	27	20	20	3	0	126.0	148	12	49	46	6-11	0	4.71
Mike Thompson†	R	24	1	1	0	0	4.0	7	0	2	2	0-0	0	4.50
Tom House	L	27	56	0	0	0	102.2	74	5	27	64	6-2	11	1.93
Danny Frisella	R	28	36	1	0	0	41.2	37	4	28	27	3-4	6	5.18
Max Leon	R	24	34	2	1	1	75.0	68	5	14	38	4-7	3	2.64
Lew Krausse	R	31	29	4	0	0	66.2	65	3	32	27	4-3	0	4.19
Joe Niekro	R	29	27	2	0	0	43.0	36	5	18	31	3-2	0	3.56
Jack Aker†	R	33	17	0	0	0	16.2	17	3	9	7	0-1	0	3.78
Mike Beard	L	24	6	0	0	0	9.1	5	1	1	7	0-0	0	2.89
Gary Gentry	R	27	3	1	0	0	6.2	4	1	2	0	0-0	0	1.35
Jamie Easterly	L	21	3	0	0	0	2.2	6	0	4	0	0-0	0	16.88

1974 Houston Astros 4th NL West 81-81 .500 21.0 GB

Preston Gomez

Player	Gm by Position	B	Age	G	AB	R	H	2B	3B	HR	RBI	BB	SO	SB	Avg	OBP	Slg
Milt May	C116	L	23	127	405	47	117	17	4	7	54	39	33	0	.289	.349	.402
Lee May	1B145	R	31	152	556	59	149	26	0	24	85	17	97	1	.268	.294	.444
Tommy Helms	2B133	R	33	137	452	32	126	21	1	5	50	23	27	5	.279	.313	.363
Doug Rader	3B152	R	29	152	533	61	137	27	3	17	78	60	131	7	.257	.334	.415
Roger Metzger	SS143	S	26	143	572	66	145	18	10	0	30	37	73	9	.253	.297	.320
Cesar Cedeno	OF157	R	23	160	610	95	164	29	5	26	102	64	103	57	.269	.338	.461
Greg Gross	OF151	L	21	156	589	78	185	21	8	0	36	76	39	12	.314	.393	.377
Bob Watson	OF140,1B35	R	28	150	524	69	156	19	4	11	67	60	61	3	.298	.370	.412
Cliff Johnson	C28,1B21	R	26	83	171	26	39	4	1	10	29	33	45	0	.228	.357	.439
Larry Milbourne	2B87,SS8,OF4	S	23	112	136	31	38	2	1	0	9	10	14	6	.279	.329	.309
Johnny Edwards	C32	L	36	50	117	8	26	7	1	1	10	11	12	1	.222	.292	.325
Wilbur Howard	OF50	S	25	64	111	19	24	4	0	2	5	5	18	4	.216	.250	.306
Bob Gallagher	OF62,1B4	L	25	102	87	13	15	2	0	0	3	12	23	1	.172	.280	.195
Ollie Brown†	OF20	R	30	27	69	8	15	1	0	3	6	4	15	0	.217	.260	.362
Mick Kelleher	SS18	R	26	19	57	4	9	0	0	0	2	5	10	1	.158	.226	.158
Ray Busse	3B8	R	25	19	34	3	7	1	0	0	0	3	12	0	.206	.270	.235
Denis Menke	1B12,3B7,2B3*	R	33	30	29	2	3	1	0	0	1	4	10	0	.103	.206	.138
Dave Campbell	2B9,1B6,3B2*	R	32	35	23	4	2	1	0	0	2	1	8	1	.087	.125	.130
Mike Easler		L	23	15	15	0	1	0	0	0	0	0	5	0	.067	.067	.067
Skip Jutze	C7	R	28	8	13	0	3	0	0	0	1	1	1	0	.231	.267	.231

D. Menke, 2 G at SS; D. Campbell, 1 G at OF

Pitcher	T	Age	G	GS	CG	ShO	IP	H	HR	BB	SO	W-L	Sv	ERA
Tom Griffin	R	26	34	34	8	3	211.0	202	14	89	110	14-10	0	3.54
Larry Dierker	R	27	33	33	7	3	223.2	189	18	82	150	11-10	0	2.90
Dave Roberts	L	29	34	30	8	2	204.0	216	6	65	72	10-12	1	3.40
Don Wilson	R	29	33	27	5	4	204.2	170	16	100	112	11-13	0	3.08
Claude Osteen†	L	34	23	21	7	2	138.1	158	8	47	45	9-9	0	3.71
J.R. Richard	R	24	15	9	0	0	64.2	58	3	36	42	2-3	0	4.18
Paul Siebert	L	21	5	5	1	1	25.1	21	3	11	10	1-1	0	3.55
Doug Konieczny	R	22	6	3	0	0	16.0	18	0	12	8	0-3	0	7.88
Ken Forsch	R	27	70	0	0	0	103.1	98	3	37	48	8-7	10	2.79
Fred Scherman	L	29	53	0	0	0	61.1	67	5	26	35	2-5	4	4.11
Mike Cosgrove	L	23	45	0	0	0	90.0	76	2	39	47	7-3	2	3.50
Jerry Johnson	R	30	34	0	0	0	45.0	47	2	24	32	2-1	0	4.80
Jim York	R	26	28	0	0	0	38.1	48	1	19	15	2-2	1	3.29
R. De los santos	L	25	12	0	0	0	12.1	11	0	9	7	1-1	0	2.19
Mike Nagy	R	26	9	0	0	0	12.2	17	3	5	5	1-1	0	8.53

1974 San Francisco Giants 5th NL West 72-90 .444 30.0 GB

Charlie Fox (34-42)/Wes Westrum (38-48)

Player	Gm by Position	B	Age	G	AB	R	H	2B	3B	HR	RBI	BB	SO	SB	Avg	OBP	Slg
Dave Rader	C109	L	25	113	323	26	94	16	2	1	26	31	21	1	.291	.351	.362
Dave Kingman	1B91,3B21,OF2	R	25	121	350	41	78	18	2	18	55	37	125	8	.223	.302	.440
Tito Fuentes	2B103	S	30	108	390	33	97	15	2	0	22	22	32	7	.249	.293	.297
Steve Ontiveros	3B75,1B19,OF2	S	22	120	343	45	91	15	1	4	33	57	41	0	.265	.375	.350
Chris Speier	SS135,2B4	R	24	141	501	55	125	19	5	9	53	62	64	3	.250	.336	.361
Gary Matthews	OF151	R	23	154	561	87	161	27	6	16	82	70	69	11	.287	.368	.442
Bobby Bonds	OF148	R	28	150	567	97	145	22	8	21	71	95	134	41	.256	.364	.434
Garry Maddox	OF131	R	24	135	538	74	153	31	3	8	50	29	64	21	.284	.322	.398
Gary Thomasson	OF76,1B15	L	22	120	315	41	77	14	3	2	29	38	56	7	.244	.325	.327
Ed Goodson	1B73,3B8	L	26	98	298	25	81	15	0	6	48	18	22	1	.272	.320	.383
Mike Phillips	3B34,2B30,SS23	L	23	100	283	19	62	6	1	2	20	14	37	4	.219	.258	.269
Bruce Miller	3B41,SS13,2B9	R	27	73	198	19	55	7	1	0	16	11	15	1	.278	.316	.323
Chris Arnold	2B31,3B7,SS1	R	26	78	174	22	42	7	3	1	26	15	27	1	.241	.302	.333
Ken Rudolph	C56	R	27	57	158	11	41	3	0	0	10	21	15	0	.259	.350	.278
John Boccabella	C26	R	33	29	80	6	11	3	0	0	5	4	6	0	.138	.176	.175
Glenn Redmon	2B4	R	26	7	17	0	4	3	0	0	4	1	3	0	.235	.278	.412
Jim Howarth	OF1	L	27	6	4	0	0	0	0	0	0	0	0	0	.000	.000	.000
Damaso Blanco		R	32	5	1	0	0	0	0	0	0	0	1	1	.000	.000	.000

Pitcher	T	Age	G	GS	CG	ShO	IP	H	HR	BB	SO	W-L	Sv	ERA
John D'Acquisto	R	22	38	36	5	1	215.0	182	13	124	167	12-14	0	3.77
Jim Barr	R	26	44	27	11	5	239.2	223	17	47	84	13-9	2	2.74
Mike Caldwell	L	25	31	27	6	2	189.1	176	17	63	83	14-5	0	2.95
Ron Bryant	L	26	41	23	0	0	126.2	142	11	68	75	3-15	0	5.61
Tom Bradley	R	27	30	21	2	0	134.1	152	15	52	72	8-11	0	5.16
Ed Halicki	R	23	16	11	2	0	74.1	84	6	31	40	1-8	0	4.24
John Montefusco	R	24	7	5	1	1	39.0	41	3	19	34	3-2	0	4.85
Elias Sosa	R	24	68	0	0	0	101.0	94	8	45	48	9-7	6	3.48
Randy Moffitt	R	25	61	1	0	0	102.0	99	9	29	49	5-7	15	4.50
Charlie Williams	R	26	39	7	0	0	100.1	93	6	31	48	1-3	0	2.78
Jim Willoughby	R	25	18	4	0	0	40.2	51	7	9	12	1-4	0	4.65
John Morris	L	32	17	0	0	0	20.2	17	1	4	9	1-1	1	3.05
Steve Barber	L	35	13	0	0	0	13.2	13	0	12	13	0-1	1	5.27
Gary Lavelle	L	25	10	0	0	0	16.2	14	1	10	12	0-3	0	2.16
Butch Metzger	R	22	10	0	0	0	12.2	11	0	12	5	1-0	0	3.55
Don McMahon	R	44	9	0	0	0	11.2	13	2	2	5	0-0	0	3.09
Don Rose	R	27	2	0	0	0	1.0	4	0	1	0	0-0	0	9.00

1974 San Diego Padres 6th NL West 60-102 .370 42.0 GB

John McNamara

Player	Gm by Position	B	Age	G	AB	R	H	2B	3B	HR	RBI	BB	SO	SB	Avg	OBP	Slg
Fred Kendall	C133	R	25	141	424	32	98	15	2	8	45	49	33	0	.231	.308	.333
Willie McCovey	1B104	L	36	128	344	53	87	19	1	22	63	96	76	1	.253	.416	.506
Derrel Thomas	2B104,3B22,OF20*	R	23	141	523	48	129	24	6	3	41	51	58	7	.247	.313	.333
Dave Roberts	3B103,SS3,OF1	R	23	113	318	26	53	10	1	5	18	32	69	2	.167	.246	.252
Enzo Hernandez	SS145	R	25	147	512	55	119	19	2	0	34	38	36	37	.232	.285	.277
Dave Winfield	OF131	R	22	145	498	57	132	18	4	20	75	40	96	9	.265	.318	.438
John Grubb	OF122,3B2	L	25	140	444	53	127	20	4	8	42	46	47	4	.286	.355	.403
Bobby Tolan	OF88	L	28	95	357	45	95	16	1	8	40	20	41	7	.266	.320	.384
Nate Colbert	1B79,OF48	R	28	119	368	53	76	16	0	14	54	62	108	10	.207	.319	.364
Cito Gaston	OF63	R	30	106	267	19	57	11	0	6	33	16	51	0	.213	.259	.322
Dave Hilton	3B55,2B15	R	23	74	217	17	52	8	2	1	12	13	28	3	.240	.281	.309
Glenn Beckert	2B36,3B1	R	33	64	172	11	44	1	0	0	7	11	8	0	.256	.301	.262
Horace Clarke†	2B21	S	34	42	90	5	17	1	0	0	4	8	6	0	.189	.255	.200
Bob Barton	C29	R	32	30	81	4	19	1	0	0	7	13	19	0	.235	.333	.247
Matty Alou	OF13,1B2	L	35	48	81	8	16	3	0	0	3	5	6	0	.198	.241	.235
Gene Locklear	OF12	L	24	39	74	7	20	3	2	1	3	4	12	0	.270	.308	.405
Rich Morales	SS29,2B18,3B6*	R	30	54	61	8	12	3	0	1	5	8	6	1	.197	.290	.295
Chris Cannizzaro	C26	R	36	26	60	2	11	1	0	0	4	6	11	0	.183	.258	.200
Jerry Turner	OF13	L	20	17	48	4	14	1	0	0	2	3	5	2	.292	.333	.313
Bill Almon	SS14	R	21	16	38	4	12	1	0	0	3	2	9	1	.316	.350	.342
Mike Ivie	1B11	R	21	12	34	1	3	0	0	1	3	2	8	0	.088	.139	.176
Randy Elliott	OF11,1B1	R	23	13	33	5	7	1	0	1	2	7	9	0	.212	.350	.333
John Scott	OF8	R	22	14	15	3	1	0	0	0	0	0	4	1	.067	.067	.067
Bernie Williams	OF3	R	25	14	15	1	2	0	0	0	0	0	6	0	.133	.133	.133
Rod Gaspar	OF8,1B2	S	28	33	14	4	3	0	0	0	1	4	3	0	.214	.389	.214

D. Thomas, 5 G at SS; R. Morales, 1 G at 1B

Pitcher	T	Age	G	GS	CG	ShO	IP	H	HR	BB	SO	W-L	Sv	ERA
Bill Greif	R	24	43	35	7	1	226.0	244	17	95	137	9-19	1	4.66
Randy Jones	L	24	40	34	4	1	208.1	217	16	78	124	8-22	2	4.45
Dave Freisleben	R	22	33	31	6	2	211.2	194	13	112	130	9-14	0	3.66
Dan Spillner	R	22	30	25	5	2	148.0	153	15	70	95	9-11	0	4.01
Steve Arlin†	R	28	16	12	1	0	64.0	85	5	37	18	1-7	1	5.91
Joe McIntosh	R	22	10	5	0	0	37.1	36	3	17	22	0-4	0	3.62
Larry Hardy	R	26	76	1	0	0	101.2	129	9	44	57	9-4	2	4.69
Vicente Romo	R	31	54	1	0	0	71.0	78	6	37	26	5-5	9	4.56
Dave Tomlin	L	25	47	0	0	0	58.0	59	4	30	29	2-0	2	4.34
Bill Laxton	L	26	30	1	0	0	44.2	37	5	38	40	0-1	0	4.03
Mike Corkins	R	28	25	2	0	0	56.1	53	5	32	41	2-2	0	4.79
Allen Gerhardt	L	23	23	1	0	0	35.2	44	1	17	22	2-1	1	7.07
Lowell Palmer	R	26	22	8	1	0	73.0	68	9	59	52	2-5	0	5.67
Mike Johnson	R	23	18	0	0	0	21.1	29	1	15	15	0-2	0	4.64
Jim McAndrew	R	30	15	5	1	0	41.2	48	7	13	16	1-4	0	5.62
Rich Troedson	L	24	15	1	0	0	18.2	24	6	8	11	1-1	1	8.68
Gary Ross	R	26	9	0	0	0	18.0	23	1	6	11	0-0	0	4.50
Ralph Garcia	R	25	8	0	0	0	10.1	15	1	7	9	0-0	0	6.10

»1975 Boston Red Sox 1st AL East 95-65 .594 —

Darrell Johnson

Player	Gm by Position	B	Age	G	AB	R	H	2B	3B	HR	RBI	BB	SO	SB	Avg	OBP	Slg
Carlton Fisk	C71,DH6	R	27	79	263	47	87	14	4	10	52	27	32	4	.331	.395	.529
Carl Yastrzemski	1B140,OF8,DH2	L	35	149	543	91	146	30	1	14	60	87	67	8	.269	.371	.405
Doug Griffin	2B99,SS1	R	28	100	287	21	69	6	0	1	29	18	29	2	.240	.288	.272
Rico Petrocelli	3B113,DH1	R	32	115	402	31	96	15	1	7	59	41	66	0	.239	.310	.333
Rick Burleson	SS158	R	24	158	580	66	146	25	1	6	62	45	44	8	.252	.305	.329
Fred Lynn	OF144	L	23	145	528	103	175	47	7	21	105	62	90	10	.331	.401	.566
Dwight Evans	OF115,DH7	R	23	128	412	61	113	24	6	13	56	47	60	3	.274	.353	.456
Jim Rice	OF90,DH54	R	22	144	564	92	174	29	4	22	102	36	122	10	.309	.350	.491
Cecil Cooper	DH54,1B35	L	25	106	305	49	95	17	6	14	44	19	33	1	.311	.355	.544
Bernie Carbo	OF85,DH13	L	27	107	319	64	82	21	3	15	50	83	69	2	.257	.409	.483
Denny Doyle†	2B84,3B6,SS2	L	31	89	310	50	96	21	2	4	36	14	11	5	.310	.339	.429
Juan Beniquez	OF44,DH20,3B14	R	25	78	254	43	74	14	4	2	17	25	26	7	.291	.358	.402
Bob Montgomery	C53,1B6,DH3	R	31	62	195	16	44	10	1	2	26	4	37	1	.226	.241	.318
Tim Blackwell	C57,DH2	S	22	59	132	15	26	3	2	0	6	19	13	0	.197	.303	.250
Bob Heise	3B45,2B14,SS4*	R	28	63	126	12	27	3	0	0	21	4	6	0	.214	.246	.238
Rick Miller	OF65	L	27	77	108	21	21	2	1	0	15	21	20	3	.194	.326	.231
Tony Conigliaro	DH15	R	30	21	57	8	7	1	0	2	9	8	9	1	.123	.221	.246
Tim McCarver†	C7,1B1	L	33	12	21	1	8	2	1	0	3	1	3	0	.381	.409	.571
Dick McAuliffe	3B7	L	35	7	15	0	2	0	0	0	1	1	2	0	.133	.188	.133
Deron Johnson†	1B2,DH1	R	36	3	10	2	6	0	0	1	3	2	0	0	.600	.667	.900
Steve Dillard	2B1	R	24	1	5	2	2	0	0	0	0	0	0	1	.400	.400	.400
Butch Hobson	3B1	R	23	2	4	0	1	0	0	0	0	0	2	0	.250	.250	.250
Andy Merchant	C1	L	24	1	4	1	2	0	0	0	0	1	0	0	.500	.600	.500
Kim Andrew	2B2	R	21	2	2	0	1	0	0	0	0	0	0	0	.500	.500	.500
Buddy Hunter	2B1	R	27	1	1	0	0	0	0	0	0	0	0	0	.000	.000	.000

B. Heise, 1 G at 1B

Pitcher	T	Age	G	GS	CG	ShO	IP	H	HR	BB	SO	W-L	Sv	ERA
Luis Tiant	R	34	35	35	18	2	260.0	262	25	72	142	18-14	0	4.02
Rick Wise	R	29	35	35	17	1	255.1	262	34	72	141	19-12	0	3.95
Bill Lee	L	28	41	34	17	4	260.0	274	20	69	78	17-9	0	3.95
Reggie Cleveland	R	27	31	20	3	1	170.2	173	19	52	78	13-9	0	4.43
Dick Pole	R	24	18	11	2	1	89.2	102	11	32	42	4-6	0	4.42
Steve Barr	L	23	3	2	0	0	7.0	11	1	7	2	0-1	0	2.57
Dick Drago	R	30	40	2	0	0	72.2	69	5	31	43	2-2	15	3.84
Roger Moret	L	25	36	16	4	1	145.0	132	8	76	80	14-3	1	3.60
Diego Segui	R	37	33	1	1	0	71.0	71	10	43	45	2-5	6	4.82
Jim Burton	L	25	29	4	0	0	53.0	58	6	19	39	1-2	1	2.89
Jim Willoughby	R	26	24	0	0	0	48.1	46	6	16	29	5-2	8	3.54
Rick Kreuger	L	26	2	0	0	0	4.0	3	0	1	1	0-0	0	4.50

1975 Baltimore Orioles 2nd AL East 90-69 .566 4.5 GB

Earl Weaver

Player	Gm by Position	B	Age	G	AB	R	H	2B	3B	HR	RBI	BB	SO	SB	Avg	OBP	Slg
Dave Duncan	C95	R	29	96	307	30	63	7	0	12	41	16	82	0	.205	.245	.345
Lee May	1B144,DH2	R	32	146	580	67	152	28	3	20	99	36	91	1	.262	.308	.424
Bobby Grich	2B150	R	26	150	524	81	136	26	4	13	57	107	88	14	.260	.389	.399
Brooks Robinson	3B143	R	38	144	482	50	97	15	1	6	53	44	33	0	.201	.267	.274
Mark Belanger	SS152	R	31	152	442	44	100	11	1	3	27	36	53	16	.226	.286	.276
Ken Singleton	OF155	S	28	155	586	88	176	37	4	15	55	118	82	3	.300	.415	.454
Paul Blair	OF138,DH1,1B1	R	31	140	440	51	96	13	4	5	31	25	82	17	.218	.257	.300
Don Baylor	OF135,DH7,1B2	R	26	145	524	79	148	21	6	25	76	53	64	32	.282	.360	.489
Tommy Davis	DH111	R	36	116	460	43	130	14	1	6	57	23	52	2	.283	.315	.357
Al Bumbry	DH48,OF39,3B1	L	28	114	349	47	94	19	4	2	32	32	81	16	.269	.336	.364
Ellie Hendricks	C83	L	34	85	223	32	48	8	2	8	38	34	40	0	.215	.319	.377
Jim Northrup	OF58,DH3	L	35	84	194	27	53	13	0	5	29	22	22	0	.273	.348	.418
Doug DeCinces	3B34,SS13,2B11*	R	24	61	167	20	42	6	3	4	23	13	32	0	.251	.306	.395
Tony Muser†	1B62	L	27	80	82	11	26	3	0	0	11	8	9	0	.317	.374	.354
Tim Nordbrook	SS37,2B3	R	25	40	34	6	4	1	0	0	0	7	7	0	.118	.268	.147
Tom Shopay	OF13,DH3,C1	L	30	40	31	4	5	1	0	0	2	4	7	3	.161	.257	.194
Andy Etchebarren†	C7	R	32	8	20	0	4	1	0	0	3	0	3	0	.200	.200	.250
Royle Stillman	OF2	L	24	13	14	1	6	0	0	0	1	1	3	0	.429	.467	.429
Bob Bailor	SS2,2B1	R	23	5	7	0	1	0	0	0	0	1	0	0	.143	.250	.143
Jim Hutto	C3	R	27	4	5	0	0	0	0	0	0	0	2	0	.000	.000	.000
Larry Harlow	OF4	L	23	4	3	1	1	0	0	0	0	0	1	0	.333	.333	.333

D. DeCinces, 2 G at 1B

Pitcher	T	Age	G	GS	CG	ShO	IP	H	HR	BB	SO	W-L	Sv	ERA
Jim Palmer	R	29	39	38	25	10	323.0	253	20	80	193	23-11	1	2.09
Mike Torrez	R	28	36	36	16	2	270.2	238	15	133	119	20-9	0	3.06
Mike Cuellar	L	38	36	36	17	5	256.0	229	17	84	105	14-12	0	3.66
Ross Grimsley	L	25	35	32	8	1	197.0	210	29	47	89	10-13	0	4.07
Mike Flanagan	L	23	2	1	0	0	9.2	9	0	6	7	0-1	0	2.79
Grant Jackson	L	32	41	0	0	0	48.1	42	3	21	39	4-3	7	3.35
Doyle Alexander	R	24	32	11	3	1	133.1	127	7	47	46	8-8	1	3.04
Dyar Miller	R	29	30	0	0	0	46.1	32	3	16	33	6-3	8	2.72
Wayne Garland	R	24	29	1	0	0	87.1	80	7	31	46	2-5	4	3.71
Paul Mitchell	R	25	11	4	1	0	57.0	41	8	19	31	3-0	0	3.63
Bob Reynolds†	R	28	7	0	0	0	6.0	11	1	1	1	0-1	0	9.00
Dave Johnson	R	26	6	0	0	0	8.2	8	0	7	4	0-1	0	4.15
Jesse Jefferson†	R	26	4	0	0	0	7.2	5	0	8	4	0-2	0	2.35

1975 New York Yankees 3rd AL East 83-77 .519 12.0 GB

Bill Virdon (53-51)/Billy Martin (30-26)

Player	Gm by Position	B	Age	G	AB	R	H	2B	3B	HR	RBI	BB	SO	SB	Avg	OBP	Slg
Thurman Munson	C130,DH22,1B2*	R	28	157	597	83	190	24	3	12	102	45	52	3	.318	.366	.429
Chris Chambliss	1B147	L	26	150	562	66	171	38	4	9	72	29	50	0	.304	.336	.434
Sandy Alomar	2B150,SS1	S	31	151	489	61	117	18	4	2	39	26	58	28	.239	.277	.305
Graig Nettles	3B157	L	30	157	581	71	155	24	4	21	91	51	88	1	.267	.322	.430
Jim Mason	SS93,2B1	L	24	94	223	17	34	3	2	2	16	22	49	0	.152	.228	.211
Roy White	OF135,1B7,DH2	S	31	148	556	81	161	32	5	12	59	72	50	16	.290	.372	.430
Bobby Bonds	OF129,DH12	R	29	145	529	93	143	26	3	32	85	89	137	30	.270	.375	.512
Elliott Maddox	OF55,2B1	R	27	55	218	36	67	10	3	1	23	21	24	9	.307	.382	.394
Ed Herrmann	DH35,C24	L	28	80	200	16	51	9	2	6	30	16	23	0	.255	.309	.410
Fred Stanley	SS83,2B33,3B1	R	27	117	252	34	56	5	1	0	15	21	27	3	.222	.283	.250
Lou Piniella	OF46,DH12	R	31	74	199	7	39	4	1	0	22	16	22	0	.196	.262	.226
Walt Williams	OF31,DH17,2B6	R	31	82	185	27	52	5	1	5	16	8	23	0	.281	.320	.400
Rick Dempsey	C19,DH18,OF8*	R	25	71	145	18	38	8	0	1	11	21	15	0	.262	.353	.338
Alex Johnson	DH28,OF7	R	32	52	119	15	31	5	1	1	15	7	21	2	.261	.297	.345
Rick Bladt	OF51	R	28	52	117	13	26	3	1	1	11	11	8	6	.222	.292	.291
Rich Coggins†	OF36,DH9	L	24	51	107	7	24	1	0	1	6	7	16	3	.224	.272	.262
Ron Blomberg	DH27,OF1	L	26	34	106	18	27	8	2	4	17	13	10	0	.255	.336	.481
Terry Whitfield	OF25,DH1	L	22	28	81	9	22	1	1	0	7	1	17	1	.272	.274	.309
Ed Brinkman†	SS39,2B3,3B3	R	33	44	63	2	11	4	1	0	2	3	6	0	.175	.224	.270
Bob Oliver	1B8,DH3,3B1	R	32	18	38	3	5	1	0	0	1	1	9	0	.132	.154	.158
Kerry Dineen	OF7	L	22	7	22	3	8	1	0	0	1	2	1	0	.364	.417	.409
Dave Bergman	OF6	L	22	7	17	0	0	0	0	0	0	2	4	0	.000	.105	.000
Otto Velez	DH1,1B1	R	24	6	8	0	2	0	0	0	1	2	0	0	.250	.400	.250
Larry Murray	OF4	S	22	6	1	1	0	0	0	0	0	0	0	0	.000	.000	.000
Eddie Leon	SS1	R	28	1	0	0	0	0	0	0	0	0	0	0	—	—	—

T. Munson, 2 G at OF, 1 G at 3B; R. Dempsey, 1 G at 3B

Pitcher	T	Age	G	GS	CG	ShO	IP	H	HR	BB	SO	W-L	Sv	ERA
Catfish Hunter	R	29	39	39	30	7	328.0	248	25	83	177	23-14	0	2.58
Doc Medich	R	26	38	37	15	2	272.1	271	25	72	132	16-16	0	3.50
Rudy May	L	30	32	31	13	1	212.0	179	9	99	145	14-12	0	3.06
Pat Dobson	R	33	33	30	7	1	207.2	205	21	83	129	11-14	0	4.07
Larry Gura	L	27	26	20	5	0	151.1	173	13	41	65	7-8	0	3.51
Sparky Lyle	L	30	49	0	0	0	89.1	94	1	36	65	5-7	6	3.12
Dick Tidrow	R	28	37	0	0	0	69.1	65	5	31	38	6-3	5	3.12
Tippy Martinez	L	25	23	2	0	0	37.0	27	2	32	20	1-2	8	2.68
Dave Pagan	R	25	13	0	0	0	31.0	30	2	13	18	0-0	1	4.06
Ron Guidry	L	24	10	1	0	0	15.2	15	0	9	15	0-1	0	3.45
Rick Sawyer	R	27	4	0	0	0	6.0	7	0	2	3	0-0	0	3.00
Mike Wallace†	L	24	3	0	0	0	4.1	11	1	1	2	0-0	0	14.54

1975 Cleveland Indians 4th AL East 79-80 .497 15.5 GB

Frank Robinson

Player	Gm by Position	B	Age	G	AB	R	H	2B	3B	HR	RBI	BB	SO	SB	Avg	OBP	Slg
Alan Ashby	C87,1B2,DH1*	S	23	90	254	32	57	10	1	5	32	30	42	3	.224	.309	.331
Boog Powell	1B121,DH5	L	33	134	435	64	129	18	0	27	86	59	72	1	.297	.377	.524
Duane Kuiper	2B87,DH1	L	25	90	346	42	101	11	1	0	25	30	26	19	.292	.362	.329
Buddy Bell	3B153	R	23	153	553	66	150	20	4	10	59	51	72	6	.271	.332	.376
Frank Duffy	SS145	R	28	146	482	44	117	22	2	1	47	27	60	10	.243	.283	.303
George Hendrick	OF143	R	25	145	561	82	145	21	2	24	86	40	78	6	.258	.304	.431
Rick Manning	OF118,DH1	L	20	120	480	69	137	16	5	3	35	44	62	19	.285	.347	.358
Charlie Spikes	OF103,DH2	R	24	111	345	41	79	13	3	11	33	30	51	7	.229	.291	.380
Rico Carty	DH72,1B26,OF12	R	35	118	383	57	118	19	1	18	64	45	31	2	.308	.378	.504
Oscar Gamble	OF82,DH29	L	25	121	348	60	91	16	3	15	45	53	39	11	.261	.361	.454
John Ellis	C84,DH3,1B2	R	26	92	296	22	68	11	1	7	32	14	33	0	.230	.266	.345
John Lowenstein	OF36,DH31,3B8*	L	28	91	265	37	64	5	1	12	33	28	28	15	.242	.313	.404
Jack Brohamer	2B66	L	25	69	217	15	53	5	0	6	16	14	14	2	.244	.289	.350
Ed Crosby	SS30,2B19,3B13	L	26	61	128	12	30	3	0	0	7	13	14	0	.234	.305	.258
Frank Robinson	DH42	R	39	49	118	19	28	5	0	9	24	29	15	0	.237	.385	.508
Tom McCraw	1B16,OF3	L	34	23	51	7	14	1	1	2	5	7	7	4	.275	.362	.451
Bill Sudakis†	1B12,C6,DH1	S	29	20	46	4	9	0	0	1	3	4	7	0	.196	.260	.261
Ken Berry	OF18,DH5	R	34	25	40	6	8	1	0	0	1	1	7	0	.200	.238	.225
Leron Lee†	OF5,DH3	L	27	13	23	3	3	1	0	0	0	2	5	1	.130	.231	.174
Joe Lis	1B8,DH1	R	28	9	13	4	4	2	0	2	8	3	3	0	.308	.444	.923
Rick Cerone	C7	R	21	7	12	1	3	1	0	0	0	1	0	0	.250	.308	.333
Tommy Smith	DH3,OF3	L	26	8	8	0	1	0	0	0	2	0	1	0	.125	.111	.125

A. Ashby, 1 G at 3B; J. Lowenstein, 2 G at 2B

Pitcher	T	Age	G	GS	CG	ShO	IP	H	HR	BB	SO	W-L	Sv	ERA
Fritz Peterson	L	33	25	25	6	2	146.1	154	15	40	47	14-8	0	3.94
Dennis Eckersley	R	20	34	24	6	2	186.2	147	16	90	152	13-7	2	2.60
Don Hood	L	25	29	19	2	0	135.1	136	16	57	51	6-10	0	4.39
Roric Harrison†	R	28	19	19	4	0	126.0	137	9	46	52	7-7	0	4.79
Eric Raich	R	23	18	17	2	0	92.2	118	12	31	34	7-8	0	5.54
Gaylord Perry†	R	36	15	15	10	1	121.2	120	16	34	85	6-9	0	3.55
Jim Bibby†	R	30	24	12	2	0	112.2	99	7	50	62	5-9	1	3.20
Jim Kern	R	26	13	7	0	0	71.2	60	5	45	55	1-2	0	3.77
Jim Perry†	R	39	8	6	0	0	37.2	46	8	18	11	1-6	0	6.69
Dick Bosman†	R	31	6	3	0	0	28.2	33	3	8	11	0-2	0	4.08
Dave LaRoche	L	27	61	0	0	0	82.1	61	5	57	94	5-3	17	2.19
Tom Buskey	R	28	50	0	0	0	77.0	69	7	29	29	5-3	7	2.57
Jackie Brown†	R	32	25	3	1	0	69.1	72	9	29	41	1-2	1	4.28
Fred Beene	R	32	19	1	0	0	46.2	63	4	25	20	1-0	1	6.94
Rick Waits	L	23	16	7	3	0	70.1	57	3	25	34	6-2	1	2.94
Bob Reynolds†	R	28	5	0	0	0	9.2	11	0	3	5	0-2	2	4.66
Jim Strickland	L	29	4	0	0	0	4.2	4	0	2	3	0-0	1	1.93
Blue Moon Odom†	R	30	3	1	1	1	10.1	4	1	8	10	1-0	0	2.61
Larry Andersen	R	22	3	0	0	0	5.2	4	0	2	4	0-0	0	4.76

1975 Milwaukee Brewers 5th AL East 68-94 .420 28.0 GB

Del Crandall (67-94)/Harvey Kuenn (1-0)

Player	Gm by Position	B	Age	G	AB	R	H	2B	3B	HR	RBI	BB	SO	SB	Avg	OBP	Slg
Darrell Porter	C124,DH2	L	23	130	409	66	95	12	5	18	60	89	77	2	.232	.371	.418
George Scott	1B144,DH12,3B5	R	31	158	617	86	176	26	4	36	109	51	97	6	.285	.341	.515
Pedro Garcia	2B94,DH1	R	25	98	302	40	68	15	2	6	38	18	59	12	.225	.271	.348
Don Money	3B99,SS7	R	28	109	405	58	112	16	1	15	43	31	51	7	.277	.331	.432
Robin Yount	SS145	R	19	147	558	67	149	28	2	8	52	33	69	12	.267	.307	.367
Sixto Lezcano	OF129,DH2	R	21	134	429	55	106	19	3	11	43	46	93	5	.247	.324	.382
Bill Sharp†	OF124	L	25	125	373	37	95	27	3	1	34	19	26	0	.255	.289	.351
Gorman Thomas	OF113,DH6	R	24	121	240	34	43	12	2	10	28	31	84	4	.179	.268	.371
Hank Aaron	DH128,OF3	R	41	137	465	45	109	16	2	12	60	70	51	0	.234	.332	.355
Kurt Bevacqua	3B60,2B32,SS5*	R	28	104	258	30	59	14	0	2	24	26	45	3	.229	.300	.306
Charlie Moore	C47,OF22,DH1	R	22	73	241	26	70	20	1	1	29	17	31	1	.290	.336	.394
Bobby Mitchell	OF72,DH11	R	31	93	229	39	57	14	3	9	41	25	69	3	.249	.320	.454
Mike Hegan	OF42,1B27,DH5	L	32	93	203	19	51	11	0	5	22	31	42	1	.251	.347	.379
Bobby Darwin†	OF43,DH9	R	32	55	186	19	46	6	2	8	23	11	54	4	.247	.300	.430
Bob Sheldon	2B44,DH6	L	24	53	181	17	52	3	3	0	14	13	14	0	.287	.338	.337
Tim Johnson	2B11,3B11,SS10*	L	25	38	85	6	12	1	0	0	2	6	17	3	.141	.198	.153
John Briggs†	OF21	L	31	28	74	12	22	1	0	3	5	20	13	0	.297	.447	.432
Bob Coluccio†	OF22	R	23	22	62	8	12	0	1	1	5	11	11	1	.194	.320	.274
Tommy Bianco	3B7,1B5,DH2	S	22	18	34	6	6	1	0	0	0	3	7	0	.176	.263	.206
Jack Lind	SS9,3B6,1B1	S	29	17	20	1	1	0	0	0	0	2	12	1	.050	.136	.050
Rob Ellis	OF5,DH1	R	24	6	7	3	2	0	0	0	0	0	0	0	.286	.286	.286

K. Bevacqua, 3 G at 1B, 1 G at DH; T. Johnson, 3 G at DH, 2 G at 1B

Pitcher	T	Age	G	GS	CG	ShO	IP	H	HR	BB	SO	W-L	Sv	ERA
Jim Slaton	R	25	37	33	10	3	217.0	238	28	90	119	11-18	0	4.52
Pete Broberg	R	25	38	32	7	2	220.1	219	17	106	100	14-16	0	4.13
Jim Colborn	R	29	36	29	8	1	206.1	215	18	65	79	11-13	2	4.27
Bill Travers	L	22	28	23	5	0	136.1	130	15	60	57	6-11	1	4.29
Ed Sprague	R	29	18	11	0	0	67.1	81	5	40	21	1-7	1	4.68
Jerry Augustine	L	22	5	3	1	0	26.2	26	2	12	8	2-0	0	3.04
Tom Murphy	R	29	52	0	0	0	72.1	85	5	27	32	1-9	20	4.60
Ed Rodriguez	R	23	43	1	0	0	87.2	77	9	44	65	7-0	7	3.49
Rick Austin	L	28	32	0	0	0	40.0	32	3	32	30	2-3	2	4.05
Tom Hausman	R	22	29	9	1	0	112.0	110	7	47	46	3-6	0	4.10
Billy Champion	R	27	27	13	3	1	110.0	125	11	55	40	6-6	0	5.89
Bill Castro	R	21	18	5	0	0	75.0	78	3	17	25	3-2	1	2.52
Larry Anderson	R	22	8	1	1	1	30.1	36	3	6	13	1-0	0	5.04
Lafayette Currence	L	23	8	1	0	0	18.2	25	5	14	7	0-2	0	7.71
Pat Osburn	L	26	6	1	0	0	11.2	19	2	9	1	0-1	0	5.40

1975 Detroit Tigers 6th AL East 57-102 .358 37.5 GB

Ralph Houk

Player	Gm by Position	B	Age	G	AB	R	H	2B	3B	HR	RBI	BB	SO	SB	Avg	OBP	Slg
Bill Freehan	C113,1B5	R	33	120	427	42	105	17	3	14	47	32	56	2	.246	.306	.398
Jack Pierce	1B49	L	27	53	170	19	40	6	1	8	22	20	40	0	.235	.320	.424
Gary Sutherland	2B128	R	30	129	503	51	130	12	3	6	39	45	41	0	.258	.321	.330
Aurelio Rodriguez	3B151	R	27	151	507	47	124	20	6	13	60	30	63	1	.245	.286	.385
Tom Veryzer	SS128	R	22	128	404	37	102	13	1	5	48	23	76	2	.252	.297	.327
Ron LeFlore	OF134	R	27	136	550	66	142	13	6	8	37	33	139	28	.258	.302	.347
Leon Roberts	OF127,DH1	R	24	129	447	51	115	17	5	10	38	36	94	3	.257	.316	.385
Ben Oglivie	OF86,1B5,DH2	L	26	100	332	45	95	14	1	9	36	16	62	11	.286	.319	.416
Willie Horton	DH159	R	32	159	615	62	169	13	1	25	92	44	109	1	.275	.319	.421
Dan Meyer	OF74,1B46	L	22	122	470	56	111	17	3	8	47	26	25	8	.236	.277	.336
Mickey Stanley	OF28,1B14,3B7*	R	32	52	164	26	42	7	3	3	19	15	27	1	.256	.320	.390
Nate Colbert†	1B44,DH1	R	29	45	156	16	23	4	2	4	18	17	52	0	.147	.231	.276
Gene Michael	SS44,2B7,3B4	S	37	56	145	15	31	2	0	3	13	8	28	0	.214	.253	.290
John Wockenfuss	C34	R	26	35	118	15	27	6	3	4	13	10	15	0	.229	.287	.432
Billy Baldwin	OF25,DH1	L	24	30	95	8	21	3	0	4	8	5	14	2	.221	.260	.379
John Knox	2B23,DH3,3B3	L	26	43	86	8	23	1	0	0	2	10	9	1	.267	.344	.279
Terry Humphrey	C18	R	25	18	41	0	10	0	0	0	0	0	7	0	.244	.279	.244
Art James	OF11	L	22	11	40	2	9	2	0	0	1	1	3	1	.225	.244	.275
Gates Brown		L	36	47	35	1	6	2	0	1	3	9	6	0	.171	.356	.314
Bob Molinaro	OF6	L	25	6	19	2	5	0	1	0	1	1	0	0	.263	.300	.368
Jerry Manuel	2B6	S	21	6	18	0	1	0	0	0	0	0	4	0	.056	.056	.056
Chuck Scrivener	3B3,SS2	R	27	4	16	0	4	1	0	0	0	0	1	1	.250	.250	.313
Gene Lamont	C4	L	28	4	8	1	3	1	0	0	1	0	2	1	.375	.375	.500

M. Stanley, 1 G at DH

Pitcher	T	Age	G	GS	CG	ShO	IP	H	HR	BB	SO	W-L	Sv	ERA
Mickey Lolich	L	34	32	32	19	1	240.2	260	19	64	139	12-18	0	3.78
Joe Coleman	R	28	31	31	6	1	201.0	234	27	85	125	10-18	0	5.55
Vern Ruhle	R	24	32	31	8	3	190.0	199	17	65	67	11-12	0	4.03
Lerrin LaGrow	R	26	32	26	7	2	164.1	183	15	66	75	7-14	0	4.38
Ray Bare	R	26	29	21	6	1	150.2	174	10	47	71	8-13	0	4.48
Tom Walker	R	26	36	9	1	0	115.1	116	16	40	60	3-8	0	4.45
John Hiller	L	32	36	0	0	0	70.2	52	6	36	87	2-3	14	2.17
Dave Lemanczyk	R	24	26	6	4	0	109.0	120	8	46	67	2-7	0	4.46
Bob Reynolds†	R	28	21	0	0	0	34.2	40	8	14	26	0-2	3	4.67
Fredie Arroyo	R	23	14	2	1	0	53.1	56	5	22	25	2-1	0	4.56
Gene Pentz	R	22	13	0	0	0	25.1	27	0	20	21	0-4	0	3.20
Ed Glynn	L	22	3	1	0	0	14.2	11	1	8	8	0-2	0	4.30
Ike Brookens	R	26	3	0	0	0	10.1	11	3	5	8	0-0	0	5.23
Tom Makowski	L	24	3	0	0	0	9.1	10	2	9	3	0-0	0	4.82
Steve Grilli	R	26	3	0	0	0	6.2	3	0	6	5	0-0	0	1.35

1975 Oakland Athletics 1st AL West 98-64 .605 —

Alvin Dark

Player	Gm by Position	B	Age	G	AB	R	H	2B	3B	HR	RBI	BB	SO	SB	Avg	OBP	Slg
Gene Tenace	C125,1B68,DH1	R	28	158	498	83	127	17	0	29	87	106	127	7	.255	.395	.464
Joe Rudi	1B91,OF44,DH2	R	28	126	468	66	130	26	6	21	75	40	56	2	.278	.338	.494
Phil Garner	2B160,SS1	R	26	160	488	46	120	21	6	5	54	30	65	4	.246	.295	.346
Sal Bando	3B160	R	31	160	562	64	129	24	1	15	78	87	80	7	.230	.337	.356
Bert Campaneris	SS137	R	33	137	509	69	135	15	3	4	46	50	71	24	.265	.337	.330
C. Washington	OF148	L	20	148	590	86	182	24	7	10	77	32	80	40	.308	.345	.424
Reggie Jackson	OF147,DH9	L	29	157	593	91	150	39	3	36	104	67	133	17	.253	.329	.511
Bill North	OF138,DH1	S	27	140	524	74	143	17	5	1	43	81	80	30	.273	.373	.330
Billy Williams	DH145,1B7	L	37	155	520	68	127	20	1	23	81	76	68	0	.244	.341	.419
Ray Fosse	C82,1B1,2B1	R	28	82	136	14	19	3	2	0	12	8	19	0	.140	.192	.191
Jim Holt	1B52,DH4,OF2*	L	31	102	123	7	27	3	0	2	16	11	11	0	.220	.292	.293
Angel Mangual	OF39,DH15	R	28	62	109	13	24	3	0	1	5	3	18	0	.220	.241	.275
Ted Martinez†	SS45,2B31,3B14	R	27	86	87	7	15	0	0	0	3	2	9	1	.172	.200	.172
Tommy Harper†	1B16,OF9,DH5*	R	34	34	69	11	22	4	0	2	7	5	9	7	.319	.373	.464
Ted Kubiak†	3B7,SS7,2B6	S	33	20	28	2	7	1	0	0	4	2	6	0	.250	.300	.286
Larry Haney	C43,3B4	R	32	47	26	3	5	0	0	1	2	1	4	0	.192	.222	.308
Cesar Tovar†	DH4,2B4,3B3*	R	34	19	26	5	6	1	0	0	3	3	3	4	.231	.310	.269
Matt Alexander	DH17,OF11,2B3*	S	28	63	10	16	1	0	0	0	0	1	1	17	.100	.182	.100
Dal Maxvill	SS20,2B2	R	36	20	10	1	2	0	0	0	0	0	0	0	.200	.200	.200
Denny Walling	OF3	L	21	6	8	0	1	1	0	0	0	0	4	0	.125	.125	.250
Rich McKinney	DH2,1B1	R	28	8	7	0	1	0	0	0	2	1	2	0	.143	.200	.143
Don Hopkins	DH20,OF5	L	23	82	6	25	1	0	0	0	0	2	0	21	.167	.375	.167
Charlie Chant	OF5,DH1	R	23	5	5	1	0	0	0	0	0	0	0	0	.000	.000	.000
Gaylen Pitts	3B6,SS2,2B1	R	29	10	3	1	1	0	0	0	1	0	0	0	.333	.333	.667
Billy Grabarkewitz	2B4,DH1	R	29	6	2	0	0	0	0	0	0	0	1	0	.000	.000	.000
Charlie Sands	DH1	L	27	3	2	0	1	0	0	0	0	1	1	0	.500	.667	.500
Tommy Sandt	2B1	R	24	1	0	0	0	0	0	0	0	0	0	0	—	—	—
Herb Washington		R	23	13	0	4	0	0	0	0	0	0	0	2	—	—	—

J. Holt, 1 G at C; T. Harper, 2 G at 3B; C. Tovar, 1 G at SS; M. Alexander, 2 G at 3B

Pitcher	T	Age	G	GS	CG	ShO	IP	H	HR	BB	SO	W-L	Sv	ERA
Vida Blue	L	25	39	38	13	2	278.0	243	21	99	189	22-11	1	3.01
Ken Holtzman	L	29	39	38	13	2	266.1	217	16	108	122	18-14	0	3.14
Dick Bosman†	R	31	22	21	2	0	122.2	112	12	24	42	11-4	0	3.52
Stan Bahnsen†	R	30	21	16	2	0	100.0	88	2	37	49	6-7	0	3.24
Glenn Abbott	R	24	30	15	3	1	114.1	109	12	50	51	5-5	0	4.25
Sonny Siebert†	R	38	17	13	0	0	61.0	60	4	31	44	4-4	0	3.69
Jim Perry†	R	39	15	11	2	1	67.2	61	7	26	33	3-4	0	4.66
Mike Norris	R	20	4	3	1	1	16.2	6	0	8	5	1-0	0	0.00
Craig Mitchell	R	21	1	1	0	0	3.2	6	0	2	2	0-1	0	12.27
Rollie Fingers	R	28	75	0	0	0	126.2	95	13	33	115	10-6	24	2.98
Paul Lindblad	L	33	68	0	0	0	122.1	105	6	43	58	9-1	7	2.72
Jim Todd	R	27	58	0	0	0	122.0	104	4	33	50	8-3	12	2.29
Dave Hamilton†	L	27	11	4	0	0	35.2	42	4	18	20	1-2	0	4.04
Blue Moon Odom†	R	30	7	2	0	0	11.0	19	1	11	4	0-2	0	12.27

1975 Kansas City Royals 2nd AL West 91-71 .562 7.0 GB

Jack McKeon (50-46)/Whitey Herzog (41-25)

Player	Gm by Position	B	Age	G	AB	R	H	2B	3B	HR	RBI	BB	SO	SB	Avg	OBP	Slg
Buck Martinez	C79	R	26	80	226	15	51	9	2	3	23	21	28	1	.226	.293	.323
John Mayberry	1B131,DH27	L	26	156	554	95	161	38	1	34	106	119	73	5	.291	.416	.547
Cookie Rojas	2B117,DH1	R	36	120	406	34	103	18	2	2	37	30	24	4	.254	.304	.323
George Brett	3B159,SS1	L	22	159	634	84	195	35	13	11	89	46	49	13	.308	.353	.456
Freddie Patek	SS136,DH1	R	30	136	483	58	110	14	5	5	45	42	65	32	.228	.291	.308
Amos Otis	OF130	R	28	132	470	87	116	26	6	9	46	66	48	39	.247	.342	.385
Hal McRae	OF114,DH12,3B1	R	29	126	480	58	147	38	6	5	71	47	47	11	.306	.366	.442
Al Cowens	OF113,DH2	R	23	120	328	44	91	13	8	4	42	28	36	12	.277	.340	.402
Harmon Killebrew	DH92,1B6	R	39	106	312	25	62	13	0	14	44	54	70	1	.199	.317	.375
Jim Wohlford	OF102,DH4	R	24	116	353	45	90	10	5	0	30	34	37	12	.255	.317	.312
Vada Pinson	OF82,DH5,1B4	L	36	103	319	38	71	14	5	4	22	10	21	5	.223	.248	.335
Frank White	2B67,SS42,3B4*	R	24	111	304	43	76	10	2	7	36	20	39	11	.250	.297	.365
Tony Solaita	DH37,1B35	L	28	93	231	35	60	11	0	16	44	39	79	0	.260	.369	.515
Fran Healy	C51,DH4	R	28	56	188	16	48	5	2	2	18	14	19	4	.255	.307	.335
Bob Stinson	C59,DH1,1B1*	S	29	63	147	18	39	9	1	1	9	18	29	1	.265	.345	.361
Jamie Quirk	OF10,3B2,DH1	L	20	14	39	2	10	0	0	1	5	2	7	0	.256	.293	.333
Rodney Scott	DH22,2B9,SS8	S	21	48	15	13	1	0	0	0	0	1	3	4	.067	.125	.067
Gary Martz	OF1	R	24	1	1	0	0	0	0	0	0	0	0	0	.000	.000	.000

F. White, 2 G at DH, 1 G at C; B. Stinson, 1 G at 2B, 1 G at OF

Pitcher	T	Age	G	GS	CG	ShO	IP	H	HR	BB	SO	W-L	Sv	ERA
Al Fitzmorris	R	29	35	35	11	3	242.0	239	16	76	78	16-12	0	3.57
Steve Busby	R	25	34	34	18	3	260.1	233	18	81	160	18-12	0	3.08
Dennis Leonard	R	24	32	30	8	0	212.1	212	18	90	146	15-7	0	3.77
Paul Splittorff	L	28	35	23	6	3	159.0	156	10	56	76	9-10	1	3.17
Nelson Briles	R	31	24	16	3	0	112.0	127	19	25	73	6-6	2	4.26
Bruce Dal Canton†	R	33	4	2	0	0	8.2	23	0	7	5	0-2	0	15.58
Doug Bird	R	25	51	4	0	0	105.1	100	7	40	81	9-6	11	3.25
Marty Pattin	R	32	44	15	5	1	177.0	173	13	45	89	10-10	5	3.25
Lindy McDaniel	R	39	40	0	0	0	78.0	81	3	24	40	5-1	1	4.15
Steve Mingori	L	31	36	0	0	0	50.1	42	2	20	25	0-3	2	2.50
Bob McClure	L	23	12	0	0	0	15.1	4	0	14	15	1-0	1	0.00
Mark Littell	R	22	7	3	1	0	24.1	19	1	15	19	1-2	0	3.70
George Throop	R	24	7	0	0	0	9.0	8	1	2	8	0-0	2	4.00
Ray Sadecki†	L	34	5	0	0	0	3.0	5	0	3	0	1-0	0	3.00

1975 Texas Rangers 3rd AL West 79-83 .488 19.0 GB

Billy Martin (44-51)/Frank Lucchesi (35-32)

Player	Gm by Position	B	Age	G	AB	R	H	2B	3B	HR	RBI	BB	SO	SB	Avg	OBP	Slg
Jim Sundberg	C155	R	24	155	472	45	94	9	0	6	36	51	77	3	.199	.283	.256
Jim Spencer	1B99,DH25	L	28	132	403	50	107	18	1	11	47	35	43	0	.266	.327	.397
Lenny Randle	2B79,OF66,3B17*	S	26	156	601	85	166	24	7	4	57	57	80	16	.276	.341	.359
Roy Howell	3B115,DH5	L	21	125	383	43	96	15	2	10	51	39	79	2	.251	.322	.379
Toby Harrah	SS118,3B28,2B21	R	26	151	522	81	153	24	1	20	93	98	71	23	.293	.403	.458
Jeff Burroughs	OF148,DH3	R	24	152	585	81	132	20	0	29	94	79	155	4	.226	.315	.409
Mike Hargrove	OF96,1B48,DH12	L	25	145	519	82	157	22	2	11	62	79	66	4	.303	.395	.416
Tom Grieve	OF63,DH45	R	27	118	369	46	102	17	1	14	61	22	74	0	.276	.316	.442
Cesar Tovar†	DH69,OF31,2B1	R	34	102	427	53	110	16	0	3	28	27	25	16	.258	.306	.316
Roy Smalley	SS59,2B19,C1	S	22	78	250	22	57	8	0	3	33	30	42	4	.228	.309	.296
Jim Fregosi	1B54,DH13,3B4	R	33	77	191	25	50	5	0	7	33	20	39	0	.262	.329	.398
Dave Moates	OF51,DH1	L	27	54	175	21	48	9	0	3	14	13	15	9	.274	.321	.377
Willie Davis†	OF42	L	35	42	169	16	42	8	2	5	17	4	25	13	.249	.270	.408
Mike Cubbage	2B37,3B3,DH2	L	24	58	143	12	32	6	0	4	21	18	14	0	.224	.305	.350
Joe Lovitto	OF38,DH2,1B2*	S	24	50	106	17	22	3	0	1	8	13	16	2	.208	.289	.264
Leo Cardenas	3B43,SS5,2B3	R	36	55	102	15	24	2	0	1	5	14	12	0	.235	.328	.284
Dave Nelson	2B23,DH1	R	31	28	80	9	17	1	0	2	10	8	10	6	.213	.289	.300
Bill Fahey	C21	L	25	21	37	3	11	1	1	0	3	1	10	0	.297	.316	.378
Tom Robson	1B5,DH4	R	29	17	35	3	7	0	0	0	2	1	3	0	.200	.216	.200
Ron Pruitt	C13,OF1	R	23	14	17	2	3	0	0	0	0	1	3	0	.176	.222	.176
Bobby Jones	OF5,DH1	L	25	9	11	2	1	0	0	0	0	3	3	0	.091	.286	.091
Ed Brinkman†	3B1	R	33	1	2	0	0	0	0	0	0	0	1	0	.000	.000	.000

L. Randle, 3 G at DH, 1 G at C, 1 G at SS; J. Lovitto, 1 G at C

Pitcher	T	Age	G	GS	CG	ShO	IP	H	HR	BB	SO	W-L	Sv	ERA
Fergie Jenkins	R	31	37	37	22	4	270.0	261	37	56	157	17-18	0	3.93
Steve Hargan	R	32	33	26	8	1	189.1	203	17	62	93	9-10	0	3.80
Gaylord Perry†	R	36	22	22	15	4	184.0	157	12	36	148	12-8	0	3.03
Bill Hands	R	35	18	18	4	1	109.2	118	12	28	67	6-7	0	4.02
Clyde Wright	L	34	25	14	1	0	93.1	105	7	47	32	4-6	0	4.44
Jim Bibby†	R	30	12	12	4	1	68.1	73	2	28	31	2-6	0	5.00
Stan Perzanowski	R	24	12	8	1	0	66.0	59	1	25	26	3-3	0	3.00
David Clyde	L	20	1	1	0	0	7.0	6	0	6	2	0-1	0	2.57
Jim Gideon	R	21	1	1	0	0	5.2	7	1	5	2	0-0	0	7.94
Steve Foucault	R	25	59	0	0	0	107.0	96	10	55	56	8-4	10	4.12
Jim Umbarger	L	22	56	12	3	2	131.0	134	11	59	50	8-7	2	4.12
Stan Thomas	R	25	46	1	0	0	81.1	72	2	34	46	4-4	3	3.10
Mike Kekich	L	30	23	0	0	0	31.1	33	2	21	19	0-0	2	3.73
Jackie Brown†	R	32	17	7	2	1	70.1	70	7	35	35	5-5	0	4.22
Tommy Moore†	R	26	12	0	0	0	21.0	31	1	12	15	0-2	0	8.14
Mike Bacsik	R	23	7	3	0	0	26.2	28	1	9	13	1-2	0	3.71
Jim Merritt	L	31	5	0	0	0	3.2	3	0	0	0	0-0	0	0.00

1975 Minnesota Twins 4th AL West 76-83 .478 20.5 GB

Frank Quilici

Player	Gm by Position	B	Age	G	AB	R	H	2B	3B	HR	RBI	BB	SO	SB	Avg	OBP	Slg
Glenn Borgmann	C125	R	25	125	352	34	73	15	2	2	33	47	59	0	.207	.303	.278
Craig Kusick	1B51	R	26	57	156	14	37	8	0	6	27	21	23	0	.237	.346	.404
Rod Carew	2B123,1B14,DH2	L	29	143	535	89	192	24	4	14	80	64	40	35	.359	.421	.497
Eric Soderholm	3B113,DH3	R	26	117	419	62	120	17	2	11	58	53	66	3	.286	.365	.415
Danny Thompson	SS100,3B7,DH3*	R	28	112	355	25	96	11	2	5	37	18	30	0	.270	.302	.355
Dan Ford	OF120,DH3	R	23	130	440	72	123	21	1	15	59	30	79	6	.280	.333	.434
Steve Braun	OF106,DH9,1B9*	L	27	136	453	70	137	18	3	11	45	66	55	0	.302	.389	.428
Lyman Bostock	OF92,DH1	L	24	98	369	52	104	21	5	0	29	28	42	2	.282	.331	.366
Tony Oliva	DH120	L	34	131	455	46	123	10	0	13	58	41	45	0	.270	.344	.378
Jerry Terrell	SS41,2B39,1B15*	R	28	108	385	48	110	16	2	1	36	19	27	4	.286	.324	.345
John Briggs†	1B49,OF35,DH3	L	31	87	264	44	61	9	2	7	39	60	41	6	.231	.371	.360
Larry Hisle	OF58,DH14	R	28	80	255	37	80	9	2	11	51	27	39	17	.314	.376	.494
Steve Brye	OF72,DH6	R	26	86	246	41	62	13	1	9	34	21	37	2	.252	.315	.423
Bobby Darwin†	OF27,DH19	R	32	48	169	26	37	6	0	5	18	18	44	2	.219	.307	.343
Tom Kelly	1B43,OF2	L	24	49	127	11	23	5	0	1	11	15	22	0	.181	.262	.244
Phil Roof	C63	R	34	63	126	18	38	2	0	7	21	9	28	0	.302	.353	.484
Dave McKay	3B33	S	25	33	125	8	32	4	1	2	16	6	14	1	.256	.291	.352
Sergio Ferrer	SS18,2B10,DH2	S	24	32	81	14	20	3	1	0	2	3	11	3	.247	.279	.309
Luis Gomez	SS70,DH7,2B6	R	23	89	72	7	10	0	0	0	5	4	12	0	.139	.182	.139
Danny Walton	1B7,DH6,C2	R	27	42	63	4	11	2	0	1	8	4	18	0	.175	.224	.254
Mike Poepping	OF13	R	24	14	37	0	5	1	0	0	1	5	7	0	.135	.238	.162
Tom Lundstedt	C14,DH2	S	26	18	28	2	3	0	0	0	1	4	5	0	.107	.219	.107

D. Thompson, 1 G at 2B; S. Braun, 2 G at 3B, 1 G at 2B; J. Terrell, 12 G at 3B, 6 G at OF, 2 G at DH

Pitcher	T	Age	G	GS	CG	ShO	IP	H	HR	BB	SO	W-L	Sv	ERA
Bert Blyleven	R	24	35	35	20	3	275.2	219	24	84	233	15-10	0	3.00
Jim Hughes	R	23	37	34	12	2	250.0	241	17	127	130	16-14	0	3.82
Dave Goltz	R	26	32	32	15	1	243.0	235	18	72	128	14-14	0	3.67
Ray Corbin	R	26	18	11	3	0	89.2	105	13	38	49	5-7	0	5.12
Joe Decker	R	28	10	7	1	0	26.1	25	2	36	8	1-3	0	8.54
Eddie Bane	L	23	4	4	0	0	28.1	28	2	15	14	3-1	0	2.86
Mike Pazik	L	25	5	3	0	0	19.2	28	5	10	8	0-4	0	8.24
Bill Campbell	R	26	47	7	2	1	121.0	119	13	46	76	4-6	5	3.79
Tom Burgmeier	L	31	46	0	0	0	75.2	76	7	23	41	5-8	11	3.09
Vic Albury	L	28	32	15	2	0	135.0	115	16	97	72	6-7	1	4.53
Bill Butler	L	28	23	8	1	0	81.2	100	12	35	55	5-4	0	5.95
Tom Johnson	R	24	18	0	0	0	38.2	40	4	21	17	1-2	3	4.19
Mark Wiley	R	27	15	3	1	0	38.2	50	4	13	15	1-3	2	6.05

1975 Chicago White Sox 5th AL West 75-86 .466 22.5 GB

Chuck Tanner

Player	Gm by Position	B	Age	G	AB	R	H	2B	3B	HR	RBI	BB	SO	SB	Avg	OBP	Slg
Brian Downing	C137,DH1	R	24	138	420	58	101	12	1	7	41	76	75	13	.240	.356	.324
Carlos May	1B63,OF46,DH19	L	27	128	454	55	123	19	2	8	53	67	46	12	.271	.373	.374
Jorge Orta	2B135,DH2	L	24	140	542	64	165	26	10	11	83	48	67	16	.304	.363	.450
Bill Melton	3B138,DH11	R	29	149	512	62	123	16	0	15	70	78	106	5	.240	.346	.359
Bucky Dent	SS157	R	23	157	602	52	159	29	4	3	58	36	48	2	.264	.301	.341
Ken Henderson	OF137,DH1	S	29	140	513	65	129	20	3	9	53	74	65	5	.251	.347	.355
Pat Kelly	OF115,DH14	L	30	133	471	73	129	21	7	9	45	58	69	18	.274	.353	.406
Nyls Nyman	OF94,DH4	L	21	106	327	36	74	6	3	2	28	11	34	10	.226	.255	.281
Deron Johnson†	DH93,1B55	R	36	148	555	66	129	25	1	18	72	48	117	0	.232	.292	.378
Bill Stein	2B28,3B24,DH18*	R	28	76	226	23	61	7	1	3	21	18	32	2	.270	.327	.350
Jerry Hairston	OF59,DH8	S	23	69	219	26	62	8	0	0	23	46	23	1	.283	.407	.320
Bob Coluccio†	OF59,DH1	R	23	61	161	22	33	4	2	4	13	13	34	4	.205	.269	.329
Tony Muser†	1B41	L	27	43	111	11	27	3	0	0	6	7	8	2	.243	.286	.270
Pete Varney	C34,DH2	R	26	36	107	12	29	5	1	2	8	6	28	2	.271	.316	.393
Mike Squires	1B20	L	23	20	65	5	15	0	0	0	4	8	5	3	.231	.311	.231
Buddy Bradford†	OF18,DH4	R	30	25	58	8	9	3	1	2	15	8	22	3	.155	.274	.345
Lee Richard	3B12,SS9,DH5*	R	26	43	45	11	9	0	1	0	5	4	7	2	.200	.265	.244
Chet Lemon	3B6,DH2,OF1	R	20	9	35	2	9	2	0	0	1	2	6	1	.257	.297	.314
Bill Sharp†	OF14	L	25	18	35	1	7	0	0	0	4	2	3	0	.200	.243	.200
Lamar Johnson	1B6,DH2	R	24	8	30	2	6	3	0	1	4	1	5	0	.200	.226	.400
Jerry Moses†	DH1,1B1	R	28	2	2	1	1	0	1	0	0	0	1	0	.500	.500	1.500

B. Stein, 1 G at OF; L. Richard, 5 G at 2B

Pitcher	T	Age	G	GS	CG	ShO	IP	H	HR	BB	SO	W-L	Sv	ERA
Wilbur Wood	L	33	43	43	14	2	291.1	309	26	92	140	16-20	0	4.11
Jim Kaat	L	36	43	41	12	1	303.2	321	20	77	142	20-14	0	3.11
Claude Osteen	L	35	37	37	5	0	204.1	237	16	92	63	7-16	0	4.36
Jesse Jefferson†	R	26	22	21	1	0	107.2	100	10	94	67	5-9	0	5.10
Stan Bahnsen†	R	30	12	12	2	0	67.1	78	9	40	31	4-6	0	6.01
Pete Vuckovich	R	22	4	2	0	0	10.1	17	0	7	5	0-1	0	13.06
Lloyd Allen	R	25	3	2	0	0	5.1	8	2	6	2	0-2	0	11.81
Ken Kravec	L	23	2	1	0	0	4.1	1	0	8	1	0-1	0	6.23
Goose Gossage	R	23	62	0	0	0	141.2	99	3	70	130	9-8	26	1.84
Dave Hamilton†	L	27	30	1	0	0	69.2	63	4	29	51	6-5	6	2.84
Cecil Upshaw	R	32	29	0	0	0	47.1	49	5	21	22	1-1	1	3.23
Danny Osborn	R	29	24	0	0	0	58.0	57	2	37	38	3-0	0	4.50
Bill Gogolewski	R	27	19	0	0	0	55.0	61	5	28	37	0-2	2	5.24
Terry Forster	L	23	17	1	0	0	37.0	30	0	24	32	3-3	4	2.19
Rich Hinton	L	28	15	0	0	0	37.1	41	3	15	30	1-0	0	4.82
Jim Otten	R	23	2	0	0	0	5.1	4	1	7	3	0-0	0	6.75
Jack Kucek	R	22	2	0	0	0	3.1	9	0	4	2	0-0	0	5.40
Chris Knapp	R	21	2	0	0	0	2.0	2	0	4	3	0-0	0	4.50
Tim Stoddard	R	22	1	0	0	0	1.0	2	1	0	0	0-0	0	9.00
Skip Pitlock	L	27	1	0	0	0	0.0	1	0	0	0	0-0	0	—

1975 California Angels 6th AL West 72-89 .447 25.5 GB

Dick Williams

Player	Gm by Position	B	Age	G	AB	R	H	2B	3B	HR	RBI	BB	SO	SB	Avg	OBP	Slg
Ellie Rodriguez	C90	R	29	90	226	20	53	6	0	3	27	49	37	2	.235	.380	.301
Bruce Bochte	1B105,DH1	L	24	107	375	41	107	19	3	3	48	45	43	3	.285	.362	.376
Jerry Remy	2B147	L	22	147	569	82	147	17	5	1	46	45	55	34	.258	.311	.311
Dave Chalk	3B149	R	24	149	513	59	140	24	2	3	56	66	49	6	.273	.353	.345
Mike Miley	SS70	S	22	70	224	17	39	3	2	4	26	16	54	0	.174	.227	.259
Mickey Rivers	OF152,DH1	L	26	155	616	70	175	17	13	1	53	43	42	70	.284	.331	.359
Lee Stanton	OF131,DH1	R	29	137	440	67	115	20	3	14	82	52	85	18	.261	.345	.416
Morris Nettles	OF90,DH9	L	23	112	294	50	68	11	0	0	23	26	57	22	.231	.295	.269
Tommy Harper†	DH55,1B19,OF9	R	34	89	285	40	68	10	1	3	31	38	51	19	.239	.329	.312
Dave Collins	OF75,DH12	S	22	93	319	41	85	13	4	3	29	36	55	24	.266	.340	.361
Joe Lahoud	DH35,OF29	L	28	76	192	21	41	6	2	6	33	48	33	2	.214	.372	.359
Billy Smith	SS50,1B6,DH4*	S	21	59	143	10	29	5	1	0	14	12	27	1	.203	.263	.252
Rudy Meoli	SS28,3B15,2B11*	L	24	70	126	12	27	2	1	0	6	15	20	3	.214	.298	.246
John Balaz	OF27,DH11	R	24	45	120	10	29	8	1	1	10	5	25	0	.242	.270	.350
Winston Llenas	2B12,OF10,DH6*	R	31	56	113	6	21	4	0	0	11	10	11	0	.186	.250	.221
Adrian Garrett†	DH23,1B10,OF2*	L	32	37	107	17	28	5	0	6	18	14	28	3	.262	.344	.477
Orlando Ramirez	SS40	R	23	44	100	10	24	4	1	0	4	11	22	9	.240	.315	.300
Andy Etchebarren†	C31	R	32	31	100	10	28	0	1	3	17	14	19	1	.280	.365	.390
John Doherty	1B26,DH1	L	23	30	94	7	19	3	0	1	12	8	12	1	.202	.262	.266
Tom Egan	C28	R	29	28	70	7	16	3	1	0	3	5	14	0	.229	.280	.300
Ike Hampton	C28,SS2,3B1	S	23	31	66	8	10	3	0	0	4	7	19	0	.152	.243	.197
Bill Sudakis†	DH12,C5,1B2	S	29	30	58	4	7	2	0	1	6	12	15	1	.121	.274	.207
Bobby Valentine†	1B3,3B2,OF2	R	25	26	57	5	16	2	0	0	5	4	3	0	.281	.323	.316
Bob Allietta	C21	R	23	21	45	4	8	1	0	1	2	1	6	0	.178	.196	.267
Ron Jackson	OF9,3B3,DH1	R	22	13	39	2	9	2	0	0	2	2	10	1	.231	.268	.282
Dan Briggs	1B6,OF5,DH2	L	22	13	31	3	7	1	0	1	3	2	6	0	.226	.273	.355
Paul Dade	DH7,OF3,3B1	R	23	11	30	5	6	4	0	0	1	6	7	0	.200	.333	.333
Denny Doyle†	2B6,3B1	L	31	8	15	0	1	0	0	0	0	1	1	0	.067	.125	.067
Danny Goodwin	DH3	L	21	4	10	0	1	0	0	0	0	0	5	0	.100	.100	.100

B. Smith, 2 G at 3B; R. Meoli, 3 G at DH; W. Llenas, 6 G at 1B, 3 G at 3B; A. Garrett, 1 G at C

Pitcher	T	Age	G	GS	CG	ShO	IP	H	HR	BB	SO	W-L	Sv	ERA
Frank Tanana	L	21	34	33	16	5	257.1	211	21	73	269	16-9	0	2.62
Ed Figueroa	R	26	33	32	16	2	244.2	213	14	84	139	16-13	0	2.91
Nolan Ryan	R	28	28	28	10	5	198.0	152	13	132	186	14-12	0	3.45
Bill Singer	R	31	29	27	8	0	179.0	171	18	81	78	7-15	1	4.98
Andy Hassler	L	23	30	18	6	1	133.1	158	12	53	82	3-12	0	5.94
Joe Pactwa	L	27	4	3	0	0	16.1	23	0	10	3	1-0	0	3.86
Sid Monge	L	24	4	2	2	0	23.2	22	3	10	17	0-2	0	4.18
Gary Ross	R	27	1	1	0	0	5.0	6	1	1	4	0-1	0	5.40
Mickey Scott	L	27	50	0	0	0	68.1	59	8	18	31	4-2	1	3.29
Don Kirkwood	R	25	44	2	0	0	84.0	85	6	28	49	6-5	7	3.11
Dick Lange	R	26	30	8	1	0	102.0	119	12	53	45	4-6	1	5.21
Jim Brewer†	L	37	21	0	0	0	34.2	38	2	11	22	1-0	5	1.82
Chuck Hockenbery	R	24	16	4	0	0	41.0	48	3	19	15	0-5	1	5.27
Chuck Dobson	R	31	9	2	0	0	28.0	30	5	13	14	0-2	0	6.75
Orlando Pena	R	41	7	0	0	0	12.2	13	0	8	4	0-2	0	2.13
Dave Sells†	R	28	4	0	0	0	8.1	9	3	8	7	0-0	0	8.64
Luis Quintana	L	23	4	0	0	0	7.0	13	2	6	5	0-2	0	6.43
Charlie Hudson	L	25	3	1	0	0	5.2	7	0	4	0	0-1	0	9.53
Steve Blateric	R	31	2	0	0	0	4.1	9	0	1	5	0-0	0	6.23

»1975 Pittsburgh Pirates 1st NL East 92-69 .571 —

Danny Murtaugh

Player	Gm by Position	B	Age	G	AB	R	H	2B	3B	HR	RBI	BB	SO	SB	Avg	OBP	Slg
Manny Sanguillen	C132	R	31	133	481	60	158	24	4	9	58	48	31	5	.328	.391	.451
Willie Stargell	1B122	L	35	124	461	71	136	32	2	22	90	58	109	0	.295	.375	.516
Rennie Stennett	2B144	R	24	148	616	89	176	25	7	7	62	33	42	5	.286	.324	.383
Richie Hebner	3B126	L	27	128	472	65	116	16	4	15	57	43	48	0	.246	.319	.392
Frank Taveras	SS132	R	25	134	378	44	80	9	4	0	23	37	42	17	.212	.284	.257
Al Oliver	OF153,1B4	L	28	155	628	90	176	39	8	18	84	25	73	4	.280	.309	.454
Dave Parker	OF141	L	24	148	558	75	172	35	10	25	101	38	89	8	.308	.357	.541
Richie Zisk	OF140	R	26	147	504	69	146	27	3	20	75	68	109	0	.290	.374	.474
Bill Robinson	OF57	R	32	92	200	26	56	12	2	6	33	11	36	3	.280	.313	.450
Art Howe	3B42,SS3	R	28	63	146	13	25	9	0	1	10	15	15	1	.171	.248	.253
Ed Kirkpatrick	1B28,OF14	L	30	89	144	15	34	5	0	5	16	18	22	1	.236	.319	.375
Duffy Dyer	C36	R	29	48	132	8	30	5	2	3	16	6	22	0	.227	.266	.364
Bob Robertson	1B27	R	28	75	124	17	34	4	0	6	18	23	25	0	.274	.388	.452
Craig Reynolds	SS30	L	22	31	76	8	17	3	0	0	4	3	5	0	.224	.253	.263
Willie Randolph	2B14,3B1	R	20	30	61	9	10	1	0	0	3	7	6	1	.164	.246	.180
Mario Mendoza	SS53,3B1	R	24	56	50	8	9	1	0	0	2	3	17	0	.180	.226	.200
Paul Popovich	2B8,SS8	S	34	25	40	5	8	1	0	0	1	3	2	0	.200	.273	.225
Miguel Dilone	OF2	S	20	18	6	8	0	0	0	0	0	0	1	2	.000	.000	.000
Omar Moreno	OF1	L	22	6	6	1	1	0	0	0	0	1	1	1	.167	.286	.167
Ed Ott	C2	L	23	5	5	0	1	0	0	0	0	0	0	0	.200	.200	.200

Pitcher	T	Age	G	GS	CG	ShO	IP	H	HR	BB	SO	W-L	Sv	ERA
Jerry Reuss	L	26	32	32	15	6	237.1	224	10	78	131	18-11	0	2.54
Bruce Kison	R	25	33	29	6	0	192.0	160	10	92	89	12-11	0	3.23
Jim Rooker	L	32	28	28	7	1	196.2	177	16	76	102	13-11	0	2.97
Dock Ellis	R	30	27	24	5	2	140.0	163	9	43	69	8-9	0	3.79
John Candelaria	L	21	18	18	4	1	120.2	95	8	36	95	8-6	0	2.76
Ken Brett	L	26	23	16	4	1	118.0	110	10	43	47	9-5	0	3.36
Dave Giusti	R	35	61	0	0	0	91.2	79	3	42	38	5-4	17	2.95
Ramon Hernandez	L	34	46	0	0	0	64.0	62	0	28	43	7-2	5	2.95
Larry Demery	R	22	45	8	1	0	114.2	95	7	43	59	7-5	4	2.90
Kent Tekulve	R	28	34	0	0	0	56.0	43	2	23	28	1-2	5	2.25
Bob Moose	R	27	23	5	1	0	67.2	63	4	25	34	2-2	0	3.72
Sam McDowell	L	32	14	1	0	0	34.2	30	0	20	29	2-1	0	2.86
Odell Jones	R	22	2	0	0	0	3.0	1	0	0	2	0-0	0	0.00
Jim Minshall	R	27	1	0	0	0	1.0	0	0	2	2	0-0	0	0.00

1975 Philadelphia Phillies 2nd NL East 86-76 .531 6.5 GB

Danny Ozark

Player	Gm by Position	B	Age	G	AB	R	H	2B	3B	HR	RBI	BB	SO	SB	Avg	OBP	Slg
Bob Boone	C92,3B3	R	27	97	289	28	71	14	2	2	38	32	14	1	.246	.322	.329
Dick Allen	1B113	R	33	119	416	54	97	21	3	12	62	58	109	11	.233	.327	.385
Dave Cash	2B162	R	27	162	699	111	213	40	3	4	57	56	34	13	.305	.356	.388
Mike Schmidt	3B151,SS10	R	25	158	562	93	140	34	3	38	95	101	180	29	.249	.367	.523
Larry Bowa	SS135	S	29	136	583	79	178	18	9	2	38	24	32	24	.305	.334	.377
Greg Luzinski	OF159	R	24	161	596	85	179	35	3	34	120	89	151	3	.300	.394	.540
Mike Anderson	OF105,1B3	R	24	115	247	24	64	10	3	4	28	17	66	1	.259	.307	.372
Jay Johnstone	OF101	L	29	122	350	50	115	19	2	7	54	42	39	7	.329	.397	.454
Garry Maddox†	OF97	R	25	99	374	50	109	25	8	4	46	36	54	24	.291	.359	.433
Johnny Oates†	C82	L	29	90	269	28	77	14	0	1	25	33	29	1	.286	.359	.349
Tom Hutton	1B71,OF12	L	29	113	165	24	41	6	0	3	24	27	10	2	.248	.352	.339
Ollie Brown	OF63	R	31	84	145	19	44	12	0	6	26	15	29	1	.303	.369	.510
Jerry Martin	OF49	R	26	57	113	15	24	7	1	2	11	11	16	2	.212	.288	.345
Tony Taylor	3B16,1B4,2B3	R	39	79	103	13	25	5	1	1	17	17	18	3	.243	.350	.340
Willie Montanez†	1B21	R	27	21	84	9	24	8	0	2	16	4	12	1	.286	.315	.452
Terry Harmon	SS25,2B7,3B1	R	31	48	72	14	13	1	2	0	5	9	13	0	.181	.280	.250
Alan Bannister	OF18,2B1,SS1	R	23	24	61	10	16	3	1	0	0	1	9	2	.262	.274	.344
Tim McCarver†	C10,1B1	L	33	47	59	6	15	2	0	1	7	14	7	0	.254	.397	.339
Mike Rogodzinski	OF2	L	27	16	19	3	5	1	0	0	4	3	2	0	.263	.364	.316
Larry Cox	C10	R	27	11	5	0	1	0	0	0	1	1	0	0	.200	.286	.200
Don Hahn†	OF7	R	26	9	5	0	0	0	0	0	0	0	2	0	.000	.000	.000
Jim Essian	C2	R	24	2	1	1	1	0	0	0	1	1	0	0	1.000	1.000	1.000
Larry Fritz		L	26	1	1	0	0	0	0	0	0	0	0	0	.000	.000	.000
Ron Clark		R	32	1	1	0	0	0	0	0	0	0	1	0	.000	.000	.000

Pitcher	T	Age	G	GS	CG	ShO	IP	H	HR	BB	SO	W-L	Sv	ERA
Steve Carlton	L	30	37	37	14	3	255.1	217	24	104	192	15-14	0	3.56
Tom Underwood	L	21	35	35	7	2	219.1	221	12	84	123	14-13	0	4.14
Larry Christenson	R	21	29	26	5	2	171.2	149	12	45	88	11-6	1	3.67
Jim Lonborg	R	33	27	26	6	2	159.1	161	12	45	72	8-6	0	4.12
Wayne Twitchell	R	27	36	20	0	0	134.1	132	10	78	101	5-10	0	4.42
Dick Ruthven	R	24	11	7	0	0	40.2	37	2	22	26	2-2	0	4.20
Wayne Simpson	R	26	7	5	0	0	30.2	31	1	11	19	1-0	0	3.23
Gene Garber	R	27	71	0	0	0	110.0	104	13	27	69	10-12	14	3.60
Tug McGraw	L	30	56	0	0	0	102.2	84	6	36	55	9-6	14	2.98
Tom Hilgendorf	L	33	53	0	0	0	96.2	81	6	38	52	7-3	0	2.14
Ron Schueler	R	27	46	6	1	0	92.2	88	6	40	69	4-4	0	5.24
Joe Hoerner	L	38	25	0	0	0	21.0	25	3	8	20	0-0	0	2.57
Cy Acosta	R	28	6	0	0	0	8.2	9	2	3	2	0-0	1	6.23
Randy Lerch	L	20	3	0	0	0	7.0	6	1	1	8	0-0	0	6.43
John Montague†	R	27	3	0	0	0	5.0	8	1	4	1	0-0	0	9.00

1975 New York Mets 3rd NL East 82-80 .506 10.5 GB

Yogi Berra (56-53)/Roy McMillan (26-27)

Player	Gm by Position	B	Age	G	AB	R	H	2B	3B	HR	RBI	BB	SO	SB	Avg	OBP	Slg
Jerry Grote	C111	R	32	119	386	28	114	14	5	2	39	38	23	0	.295	.357	.373
Ed Kranepool	1B82,OF4	L	30	106	325	42	105	16	0	4	43	27	21	1	.323	.370	.409
Felix Millan	2B162	R	31	162	676	81	191	37	2	1	56	36	28	1	.283	.329	.348
Wayne Garrett	3B94,SS3,2B1	L	27	107	274	49	73	8	3	6	34	50	45	3	.266	.379	.383
Mike Phillips†	SS115,2B1	L	24	116	383	31	98	10	7	1	28	25	63	0	.256	.300	.326
Rusty Staub	OF153	L	31	155	574	93	162	30	4	19	105	77	55	2	.282	.371	.448
Del Unser	OF144	L	30	147	531	65	156	18	2	10	53	37	76	4	.294	.337	.392
Dave Kingman	OF71,1B58,3B12	R	26	134	502	65	116	22	1	36	88	34	153	7	.231	.284	.494
Joe Torre	3B83,1B24	R	34	114	361	33	89	16	3	6	35	35	55	0	.247	.317	.357
John Milner	OF31,1B29	L	25	91	220	24	42	11	0	7	29	33	22	1	.191	.302	.336
Gene Clines	OF60	R	28	82	203	25	46	6	3	0	10	11	21	4	.227	.269	.286
John Stearns	C54	R	23	59	169	25	32	5	1	3	10	17	15	4	.189	.268	.284
Mike Vail	OF36	R	23	38	162	17	49	8	1	3	17	9	37	0	.302	.339	.420
Jack Heidemann	SS44,3B4,2B1	R	25	61	145	12	31	4	2	1	16	17	28	1	.214	.291	.290
Jesus Alou	OF20	R	33	62	102	8	27	3	0	0	11	4	5	0	.265	.299	.294
Bud Harrelson	SS34	S	31	34	73	5	16	2	0	0	3	12	13	0	.219	.329	.247
Cleon Jones	OF12	R	32	21	50	2	12	1	0	0	2	3	6	0	.240	.283	.260
Ron Hodges	C9	L	26	9	34	3	7	1	0	2	4	1	6	0	.206	.229	.412
Roy Staiger	3B13	R	25	13	19	2	3	1	0	0	0	0	4	0	.158	.158	.211
Bob Gallagher	OF16	L	26	33	15	5	2	1	0	0	0	1	3	0	.133	.188	.200
Brock Pemberton		S	21	2	2	0	0	0	0	0	0	0	1	0	.000	.000	.000

Pitcher	T	Age	G	GS	CG	ShO	IP	H	HR	BB	SO	W-L	Sv	ERA
Tom Seaver	R	30	36	36	15	5	280.1	217	11	88	243	22-9	0	2.38
Jerry Koosman	L	32	36	34	11	4	239.2	234	19	98	173	14-13	2	3.42
Jon Matlack	L	25	33	32	8	3	228.2	224	15	58	154	16-12	0	3.38
Randy Tate	R	22	26	23	2	0	137.2	121	8	86	99	5-13	0	4.45
Hank Webb	R	25	29	15	3	1	115.0	102	12	62	38	7-6	0	4.07
George Stone	L	28	13	11	1	0	57.0	75	3	21	21	3-3	0	5.05
Craig Swan	R	24	6	6	0	0	31.0	38	4	13	19	1-3	0	6.39
Rick Baldwin	R	22	54	0	0	0	97.1	97	4	34	54	3-5	6	3.33
Bob Apodaca	R	25	46	0	0	0	84.2	66	4	28	45	3-4	13	1.49
Tom Hall†	L	27	34	4	0	0	60.2	58	10	31	48	4-3	1	4.75
Ken Sanders	R	33	29	0	0	0	43.0	31	2	14	8	1-1	5	2.30
Skip Lockwood	R	28	24	0	0	0	48.1	28	3	25	61	1-3	2	1.49
Harry Parker†	R	27	18	1	0	0	34.2	37	2	19	22	2-3	2	4.41
Gerald Cram	R	27	4	0	0	0	5.0	7	2	2	2	0-1	0	5.40
Nino Espinosa	R	21	2	0	0	0	3.0	8	0	1	2	0-1	0	18.00
Mac Scarce	L	26	1	0	0	0	0.0	1	0	0	0	0-0	0	—

1975 St. Louis Cardinals 3rd NL East 82-80 .506 10.5 GB — Red Schoendienst

Player	Gm by Position	B	Age	G	AB	R	H	2B	3B	HR	RBI	BB	SO	SB	Avg	OBP	Slg
Ted Simmons	C154,1B2,OF2	S	25	157	581	80	193	32	3	18	100	63	35	1	.332	.396	.491
Reggie Smith	OF69,1B66,3B1	S	30	135	477	67	144	26	3	19	76	63	59	9	.302	.382	.488
Ted Sizemore	2B153	R	30	153	562	56	135	23	1	3	49	45	37	1	.240	.296	.301
Ken Reitz	3B160	R	24	161	592	43	159	25	1	5	63	22	54	1	.269	.298	.340
Mike Tyson	SS95,2B24,3B5	R	25	122	368	45	98	16	3	2	37	24	39	5	.266	.316	.342
Lou Brock	OF128	L	36	136	528	78	163	27	6	3	47	38	64	56	.309	.359	.400
Bake McBride	OF107	L	26	116	413	70	124	10	9	5	36	34	52	26	.300	.354	.404
Willie Davis†	OF89	L	35	98	350	41	102	19	6	6	50	14	27	10	.291	.319	.431
Luis Melendez	OF89	R	25	110	291	33	77	8	5	2	27	16	25	3	.265	.301	.347
Ron Fairly	1B56,OF20	L	36	107	229	32	69	13	2	7	37	45	22	0	.301	.421	.467
Keith Hernandez	1B56	L	21	64	188	20	47	8	2	3	20	17	26	0	.250	.309	.362
Mario Guerrero	SS64	R	25	64	184	17	44	9	0	0	11	10	7	0	.239	.281	.288
Buddy Bradford†	OF25	R	30	50	81	12	22	1	0	4	15	12	24	0	.272	.366	.432
Ken Rudolph	C31	R	28	44	80	5	16	2	0	1	6	3	10	0	.200	.229	.263
Ed Brinkman†	SS24	R	33	28	75	6	18	4	0	1	6	7	10	0	.240	.306	.333
Heity Cruz	3B12,OF6	R	22	23	48	7	7	2	2	0	6	2	4	0	.146	.176	.271
Danny Cater	1B12	R	35	22	35	3	8	2	0	0	2	1	3	0	.229	.250	.286
Jim Dwyer†	OF9	L	25	21	31	4	6	1	0	0	1	4	6	0	.194	.286	.226
Doug Howard	1B7	R	27	17	29	1	6	0	0	1	1	0	7	0	.207	.207	.310
Ted Martinez†	OF7,2B2,3B1*	R	27	16	21	1	4	2	0	0	2	0	2	0	.190	.190	.286
Larry Lintz†	2B6,SS6	S	25	27	18	6	5	1	0	0	1	3	2	4	.278	.381	.333
Jerry Mumphrey	OF3	S	22	11	16	2	6	2	0	0	1	4	3	0	.375	.500	.500
Don Hahn†	OF4	R	26	7	8	3	1	0	0	0	0	1	1	0	.125	.222	.125
Mick Kelleher	SS7	R	27	7	4	0	0	0	0	0	0	0	1	0	.000	.000	.000
Dick Billings		R	32	3	3	0	0	0	0	0	0	0	2	0	.000	.000	.000

T. Martinez, 1 G at SS

Pitcher	T	Age	G	GS	CG	ShO	IP	H	HR	BB	SO	W-L	Sv	ERA
Lynn McGlothen	R	25	35	34	9	2	239.0	231	21	97	146	15-13	0	3.92
Bob Forsch	R	25	34	34	7	4	230.0	213	14	70	108	15-10	0	2.86
Ron Reed†	R	32	24	24	7	2	175.2	181	4	37	99	9-8	0	3.23
John Denny	R	22	25	24	3	2	136.0	149	5	51	72	10-7	0	3.97
Bob Gibson	R	39	22	14	1	0	109.0	120	10	62	60	3-10	2	5.04
Eric Rasmussen	R	23	14	13	2	1	81.0	86	8	20	59	5-5	0	3.78
Mike Garman	R	25	66	0	0	0	79.0	73	3	48	48	3-8	10	2.39
Al Hrabosky	L	25	65	0	0	0	97.1	72	3	33	82	13-3	22	1.66
John Curtis	L	27	39	18	4	0	146.2	151	13	65	67	8-9	1	3.44
Greg Terlecky	R	23	20	0	0	0	30.1	38	4	12	13	0-1	0	4.45
Elias Sosa†	R	25	14	1	0	0	27.1	22	3	14	15	0-3	0	3.95
Harry Parker†	R	27	14	0	0	0	18.2	21	3	10	13	0-1	1	6.27
Tommy Moore†	R	26	10	0	0	0	18.2	15	2	12	6	0-0	0	3.86
Ken Reynolds	L	28	10	0	0	0	17.0	12	0	11	7	0-1	0	1.59
Ron Bryant	L	27	10	1	0	0	8.2	20	2	7	7	0-1	0	16.62
Mike Wallace†	L	24	9	0	0	0	8.2	9	0	5	6	0-0	0	2.08
Mike Barlow	R	27	9	0	0	0	7.2	11	0	3	2	0-0	0	4.70
Ray Sadecki†	L	34	8	0	0	0	11.0	13	0	7	8	1-0	0	3.27
Ryan Kurosaki	R	22	7	0	0	0	13.0	15	3	7	6	0-0	0	7.62

1975 Chicago Cubs 5th NL East 75-87 .463 17.5 GB — Jim Marshall

Player	Gm by Position	B	Age	G	AB	R	H	2B	3B	HR	RBI	BB	SO	SB	Avg	OBP	Slg
Steve Swisher	C93	R	23	93	254	20	54	16	2	1	22	30	57	1	.213	.301	.303
Andre Thornton	1B113,3B2	R	25	120	372	70	109	21	4	18	60	88	63	3	.293	.428	.516
Manny Trillo	2B153,SS1	R	24	154	545	55	135	12	2	7	70	45	78	1	.248	.306	.316
Bill Madlock	3B128	R	24	130	514	77	182	29	7	7	64	42	34	9	.354	.402	.479
Don Kessinger	SS140,3B13	S	32	154	601	77	146	26	10	0	46	68	47	4	.243	.317	.319
Jerry Morales	OF151	R	26	153	578	62	156	21	0	12	91	50	65	3	.270	.328	.369
Jose Cardenal	OF151	R	31	154	574	85	182	30	2	9	68	77	50	34	.317	.397	.423
Rick Monday	OF131	L	29	136	491	89	131	29	4	17	60	83	95	8	.267	.373	.446
Pete LaCock	1B53,OF26	L	23	106	249	30	57	8	1	6	30	37	27	0	.229	.324	.341
George Mitterwald	C59,1B10	R	30	84	200	19	44	4	3	5	26	19	42	0	.220	.285	.345
Rob Sperring	3B22,2B17,SS16*	R	25	65	144	25	30	4	1	1	9	16	31	0	.208	.288	.271
Tim Hosley	C53	R	28	62	141	22	36	7	0	6	20	27	25	1	.255	.382	.433
Champ Summers	OF18	L	29	76	91	14	21	5	1	1	16	10	13	0	.231	.311	.341
Gene Hiser	OF18,1B1	L	26	45	62	11	15	3	0	0	6	11	7	0	.242	.351	.290
Dave Rosello	SS19	R	25	19	58	7	15	2	0	1	8	9	8	0	.259	.348	.345
Vic Harris	OF11,3B7,2B5	S	25	51	56	6	10	0	0	0	5	6	7	0	.179	.254	.179
Joe Wallis	OF15	S	23	16	56	9	16	2	2	1	4	5	14	2	.286	.344	.446
Ron Dunn	3B11,OF2,2B1	R	25	32	44	2	7	3	0	1	6	6	17	0	.159	.250	.295
Jim Tyrone	OF8	R	26	11	22	0	5	0	1	0	3	1	4	1	.227	.250	.318
Adrian Garrett†	1B4	L	32	16	21	1	2	0	0	1	6	1	8	0	.095	.130	.238

R. Sperring, 8 G at OF

Pitcher	T	Age	G	GS	CG	ShO	IP	H	HR	BB	SO	W-L	Sv	ERA
Rick Reuschel	R	26	38	37	6	0	234.0	244	17	67	155	11-17	1	3.73
Bill Bonham	R	26	38	36	7	2	229.1	254	15	109	165	13-15	0	4.71
Ray Burris	R	24	36	35	8	2	238.1	259	25	73	108	15-10	0	4.12
Steve Stone	R	27	33	32	6	1	214.1	198	24	80	139	12-8	0	3.95
Geoff Zahn†	L	29	16	10	0	0	62.2	67	2	26	21	2-7	1	4.45
Willie Prall	L	25	3	3	0	0	14.2	21	1	8	7	0-2	0	8.59
Burt Hooton†	R	25	3	3	0	0	11.0	18	2	4	5	0-2	0	8.18
Darold Knowles	L	33	58	0	0	0	88.1	107	3	36	63	6-9	15	5.81
Oscar Zamora	R	30	52	0	0	0	71.0	84	17	15	28	5-2	10	5.07
Ken Frailing	L	27	41	0	0	0	53.0	61	6	26	39	2-5	1	5.43
Tom Dettore	R	27	36	5	0	0	85.1	88	8	31	46	5-4	0	5.38
Paul Reuschel	R	28	28	0	0	0	36.0	44	1	13	12	1-3	5	3.50
Milt Wilcox	R	25	25	0	0	0	38.1	50	4	17	21	0-1	0	5.63
Bob Locker	R	37	22	0	0	0	32.2	38	3	16	14	0-1	0	4.96
Ken Crosby	R	27	9	0	0	0	8.1	10	0	7	6	1-0	0	3.24
Eddie Solomon	R	24	6	0	0	0	6.2	7	1	6	3	0-0	0	1.35
Eddie Watt	R	34	6	0	0	0	6.0	14	0	8	6	0-1	0	13.50
Buddy Schultz	L	24	6	0	0	0	5.2	11	0	5	4	2-0	0	6.35
Donnie Moore	R	21	4	1	0	0	8.2	12	1	4	8	0-0	0	4.15

1975 Montreal Expos 5th NL East 75-87 .463 17.5 GB — Gene Mauch

Player	Gm by Position	B	Age	G	AB	R	H	2B	3B	HR	RBI	BB	SO	SB	Avg	OBP	Slg
Barry Foote	C115	R	23	118	387	25	75	16	1	7	30	17	48	0	.194	.229	.295
Mike Jorgensen	1B133,OF6	L	26	144	445	58	116	18	0	18	67	79	75	3	.261	.378	.422
Pete Mackanin	2B127,3B1,SS1	R	23	130	448	59	101	19	6	12	44	31	99	11	.225	.276	.375
Larry Parrish	3B143,2B1,SS1	R	21	145	532	50	146	32	5	10	65	28	74	4	.274	.314	.410
Tim Foli	SS151,2B1	R	24	152	572	64	136	25	2	1	29	36	49	13	.238	.284	.294
Pepe Mangual	OF138	R	23	140	514	84	126	16	2	9	45	74	115	33	.245	.340	.337
Larry Biittner	OF93	L	29	121	346	34	109	13	5	3	28	34	33	2	.315	.376	.408
Gary Carter	OF92,C66,3B1	R	21	144	503	58	136	20	1	17	68	72	83	5	.270	.360	.416
Bob Bailey	OF61,3B3	R	32	106	227	23	62	5	0	5	30	46	38	4	.273	.392	.361
Jim Dwyer†	OF52	L	25	60	175	22	50	7	1	3	20	23	30	4	.286	.365	.389
Jose Morales	1B27,OF6,C5	R	30	93	163	18	49	6	1	2	24	14	21	0	.301	.354	.387
Tony Scott	OF71	S	23	92	143	19	26	4	2	0	11	12	38	5	.182	.258	.238
Larry Lintz†	2B39,SS2	S	25	46	132	18	26	0	0	0	3	23	18	17	.197	.316	.197
Pat Scanlon	3B28,1B1	L	22	60	109	5	20	3	1	2	15	17	25	0	.183	.294	.284
Jerry White	OF30	S	22	39	97	14	29	4	1	2	7	10	7	5	.299	.364	.423
Nate Colbert†	1B22	R	29	38	81	10	14	4	1	4	11	5	31	0	.173	.230	.395
Pepe Frias	SS29,3B11,2B7	R	26	51	64	4	8	2	0	0	4	3	13	0	.125	.162	.156
Jim Lyttle	OF16	L	29	44	55	7	15	4	0	0	6	13	6	0	.273	.406	.345
Rich Coggins†	OF10	L	24	13	37	1	10	3	1	0	4	1	7	0	.270	.289	.405
Hal Breeden	1B12	R	31	24	37	4	5	2	0	0	1	7	5	0	.135	.273	.189
Ellis Valentine	OF11	R	20	12	33	2	12	4	0	1	3	2	4	0	.364	.400	.576
Jim Cox	2B8	R	25	11	27	1	7	1	0	1	5	1	2	0	.259	.276	.407
Bombo Rivera	OF5	R	22	5	9	1	1	0	0	0	0	2	3	0	.111	.273	.111
Larry Johnson	C1	R	24	1	3	0	1	1	0	0	1	1	1	0	.333	.500	.667

Pitcher	T	Age	G	GS	CG	ShO	IP	H	HR	BB	SO	W-L	Sv	ERA
Steve Rogers	R	25	35	35	12	3	251.2	248	13	88	137	11-12	0	3.29
Dennis Blair	R	21	30	27	1	0	163.1	150	14	106	82	8-15	0	3.80
Steve Renko	R	30	31	25	3	1	170.1	175	20	76	99	6-12	1	4.07
Woodie Fryman	L	35	38	20	7	3	157.0	141	10	68	118	9-12	3	3.32
Don Carrithers	R	25	19	14	5	2	101.0	90	7	38	37	5-3	0	3.30
Dave McNally	L	32	12	12	0	0	77.1	88	8	36	36	3-6	0	5.24
Don Stanhouse	R	24	4	3	0	0	13.0	19	1	11	5	0-0	0	8.31
Chip Lang	R	22	1	1	0	0	1.2	2	0	3	2	0-0	0	10.80
Dale Murray	R	25	63	0	0	0	111.1	134	0	39	43	15-8	9	3.96
Don DeMola	R	22	60	0	0	0	97.2	92	8	42	63	4-7	1	4.15
Chuck Taylor	R	33	54	0	0	0	74.0	72	6	24	29	2-2	6	3.53
Dan Warthen	L	22	40	18	2	0	167.2	130	8	87	128	8-6	3	3.11
Fred Scherman†	L	30	34	7	0	0	76.1	84	3	41	43	4-3	0	3.54
John Montague†	R	27	12	0	0	0	17.2	23	4	6	9	0-1	2	5.60

1975 Cincinnati Reds 1st NL West 108-54 .667 — — Sparky Anderson

Player	Gm by Position	B	Age	G	AB	R	H	2B	3B	HR	RBI	BB	SO	SB	Avg	OBP	Slg
Johnny Bench	C121,OF19,1B9	R	27	142	530	83	150	39	1	28	110	65	108	11	.283	.359	.519
Tony Perez	1B132	R	33	137	511	74	144	28	3	20	109	54	101	1	.282	.350	.466
Joe Morgan	2B142	L	31	146	498	107	163	27	6	17	94	132	52	67	.327	.466	.508
Pete Rose	3B137,OF35	S	34	162	662	112	210	47	4	7	74	89	50	0	.317	.406	.432
Dave Concepcion	SS130,3B6	R	27	140	507	62	139	23	1	5	49	39	51	33	.274	.326	.353
Cesar Geronimo	OF148	L	27	148	501	69	129	25	5	6	53	48	97	13	.257	.327	.363
George Foster	OF125,1B1	R	26	134	463	71	139	24	4	23	78	40	73	2	.300	.356	.518
Ken Griffey Sr.	OF119	L	25	132	463	95	141	15	9	4	46	67	67	16	.305	.391	.402
Dan Driessen	1B41,OF29	L	23	88	210	38	59	8	1	7	38	35	30	10	.281	.386	.429
Merv Rettenmund	OF61,3B1	R	32	93	188	24	45	6	1	2	19	35	22	5	.239	.356	.314
Darrel Chaney	SS34,2B23,3B13	S	27	71	160	18	35	6	0	2	26	14	38	3	.219	.280	.294
Bill Plummer	C63	R	28	65	159	17	29	7	0	1	19	24	28	1	.182	.291	.245
Doug Flynn	3B40,2B30,SS17	R	24	89	127	17	34	7	0	1	20	11	13	3	.268	.324	.346
Terry Crowley	1B4,OF4	L	28	66	71	8	19	6	0	1	11	7	6	0	.268	.333	.394
Ed Armbrister	OF19	R	26	59	65	9	12	1	0	0	2	5	19	3	.185	.254	.200
John Vukovich	3B31	R	27	31	38	4	8	3	0	0	2	4	5	0	.211	.286	.289
Don Werner	C7	R	22	7	8	0	1	0	0	0	0	0	0	0	.125	.222	.125

Pitcher	T	Age	G	GS	CG	ShO	IP	H	HR	BB	SO	W-L	Sv	ERA
Gary Nolan	R	27	32	32	5	1	210.2	202	18	29	74	15-9	0	3.16
Jack Billingham	R	32	33	32	5	0	208.0	222	22	76	79	15-10	0	4.11
Fred Norman	L	32	34	26	2	0	188.0	163	23	84	119	12-4	0	3.73
Don Gullett	L	24	22	22	8	3	159.2	127	11	56	98	15-4	0	2.42
Pat Darcy	R	25	27	22	1	0	130.2	134	4	59	46	11-5	1	3.58
Clay Kirby	R	27	26	19	1	0	110.2	113	13	54	48	10-6	0	4.72
Tom Carroll	R	22	12	7	0	0	47.0	52	1	26	14	4-1	0	4.98
Will McEnaney	L	23	70	0	0	0	91.0	92	6	23	48	5-2	15	2.47
Pedro Borbon	R	28	67	0	0	0	125.0	145	6	21	29	9-5	5	2.95
Rawly Eastwick	R	24	58	0	0	0	90.0	77	6	25	61	5-3	22	2.60
Clay Carroll	R	34	56	2	0	0	96.1	93	2	32	44	7-5	7	2.62
Tom Hall†	L	27	2	0	0	0	2.0	2	0	2	3	0-0	0	0.00

1975 Los Angeles Dodgers 2nd NL West 88-74 .543 20.0 GB — Walter Alston

Player	Gm by Position	B	Age	G	AB	R	H	2B	3B	HR	RBI	BB	SO	SB	Avg	OBP	Slg
Steve Yeager	C135	R	26	135	452	34	103	16	1	12	54	40	75	2	.228	.298	.347
Steve Garvey	1B160	R	26	160	659	85	210	38	6	18	95	33	66	11	.319	.351	.476
Davey Lopes	2B137,OF24,SS14	R	30	155	618	108	162	24	6	8	41	91	93	77	.262	.358	.359
Ron Cey	3B158	R	27	158	566	72	160	29	2	25	101	78	74	5	.283	.372	.473
Bill Russell	SS83	R	26	84	252	24	52	9	2	0	14	23	28	5	.206	.277	.258
Jimmy Wynn	OF120	R	33	130	412	80	102	16	0	18	58	110	77	7	.248	.403	.417
Willie Crawford	OF113	L	28	124	373	46	98	15	2	9	46	49	43	5	.263	.345	.386
Bill Buckner	OF72	L	25	92	288	30	70	11	2	6	31	17	15	8	.243	.286	.358
Lee Lacy	2B43,OF43,SS1	R	27	101	306	44	96	11	5	7	40	22	29	5	.314	.356	.451
John Hale	OF68	L	21	71	204	20	43	7	0	6	22	26	51	1	.211	.303	.333
Joe Ferguson	C35,OF34	R	28	66	202	15	42	2	1	5	23	35	47	2	.208	.325	.302
Rick Auerbach	SS81,2B1,3B1	R	25	85	170	18	38	9	0	0	12	18	22	3	.224	.298	.276
Tom Paciorek	OF54	R	28	62	145	14	28	8	0	1	5	11	29	4	.193	.250	.269
Henry Cruz	OF41	L	23	53	94	8	25	3	1	0	5	7	6	1	.266	.317	.319
Ivan DeJesus	SS63	R	22	63	87	10	16	2	1	0	2	11	15	1	.184	.276	.230
Manny Mota	OF5	R	37	52	49	3	13	1	0	0	10	5	1	0	.265	.357	.286
Ken McMullen	3B11,1B3	R	33	39	46	4	11	1	1	2	14	7	12	0	.239	.340	.435
Leron Lee†	OF4	L	27	48	43	2	11	4	0	0	2	3	9	0	.256	.298	.349
Jerry Royster	OF7,2B4,3B3*	R	22	13	36	2	9	2	1	0	1	1	3	1	.250	.270	.361
Charlie Manuel		L	31	15	15	0	2	0	0	0	2	0	3	0	.133	.133	.133
Paul Powell	C7,OF1	R	27	8	10	2	2	1	0	0	0	1	2	0	.200	.273	.300
Joe Simpson	OF6	L	23	9	6	3	2	0	0	0	0	0	2	0	.333	.333	.333
Orlando Alvarez		R	23	4	4	0	0	0	0	0	0	0	1	0	.000	.000	.000

J. Royster, 1 G at SS

Pitcher	T	Age	G	GS	CG	ShO	IP	H	HR	BB	SO	W-L	Sv	ERA
Andy Messersmith	R	29	42	40	19	7	321.2	244	22	96	213	19-14	1	2.29
Doug Rau	L	26	38	38	8	2	257.2	227	18	61	151	15-9	0	3.11
Don Sutton	R	30	35	35	11	4	254.1	202	17	62	175	16-13	0	2.87
Burt Hooton†	R	25	31	30	12	4	223.2	172	16	64	148	18-7	0	2.82
Juan Marichal	R	37	2	2	0	0	6.0	11	2	5	1	0-1	0	13.50
Mike Marshall	R	32	57	0	0	0	109.1	98	8	39	64	9-14	13	3.29
Charlie Hough	R	27	38	0	0	0	61.0	43	3	34	34	3-7	4	2.95
Rick Rhoden	R	22	26	11	1	0	99.1	94	8	32	40	3-3	0	3.08
Al Downing	L	34	22	6	0	0	74.2	59	6	28	39	2-1	1	2.89
Jim Brewer†	L	37	21	0	0	0	33.0	44	2	12	21	3-1	2	5.18
Stan Wall	L	24	10	0	0	0	16.0	12	0	7	6	0-1	0	1.69
Dave Sells†	R	28	5	0	0	0	7.0	6	2	3	1	0-2	0	3.86
Dennis Lewallyn	R	21	2	0	0	0	3.0	1	0	0	0	0-0	0	0.00
Geoff Zahn†	L	29	2	0	0	0	3.0	2	0	5	1	0-1	0	9.00

1975 San Francisco Giants 3rd NL West 80-81 .497 27.5 GB — Wes Westrum

Player	Gm by Position	B	Age	G	AB	R	H	2B	3B	HR	RBI	BB	SO	SB	Avg	OBP	Slg
Dave Rader	C94	L	26	98	292	39	85	15	0	5	31	32	30	1	.291	.360	.394
Willie Montanez†	1B134	L	27	135	518	52	158	26	2	8	85	45	50	5	.305	.359	.409
Derrel Thomas	2B141,OF1	R	24	144	540	99	149	21	9	6	48	57	56	28	.276	.347	.381
Steve Ontiveros	3B89,OF8,1B4	S	23	108	325	21	94	16	0	3	31	55	44	2	.289	.391	.366
Chris Speier	SS136,3B1	R	25	141	487	60	132	30	5	10	69	70	50	4	.271	.362	.415
Bobby Murcer	OF144	L	29	147	526	80	157	29	4	11	91	91	45	9	.298	.396	.432
Von Joshua	OF117	L	27	129	507	75	161	25	10	7	43	32	75	20	.318	.359	.448
Gary Matthews	OF113	R	24	116	425	67	119	22	3	12	58	65	53	13	.280	.377	.431
Gary Thomasson	OF74,1B17	L	23	114	326	44	74	12	3	7	32	37	48	9	.227	.304	.347
Bruce Miller	3B68,2B21,SS6	R	28	99	309	22	74	6	3	1	31	15	26	0	.239	.275	.288
Marc Hill	C60,3B1	R	23	72	182	14	39	4	0	5	23	25	27	0	.214	.305	.319
Ed Goodson†	1B16,3B13	L	27	39	121	10	25	7	0	1	8	7	14	0	.207	.248	.289
Mike Sadek	C38	R	29	42	106	14	25	5	2	0	9	14	14	1	.236	.322	.321
Glenn Adams	OF25	L	27	61	90	10	27	2	1	4	15	11	25	1	.300	.379	.478
Johnnie LeMaster	SS22	R	21	22	74	4	14	4	0	2	9	4	15	2	.189	.241	.324
Garry Maddox†	OF13	R	25	17	52	4	7	1	0	1	4	6	3	1	.135	.237	.212
Jake Brown	OF14	R	27	41	43	6	9	3	0	0	4	5	13	0	.209	.292	.279
Chris Arnold	2B4,OF4	R	27	29	41	4	8	0	0	0	0	4	8	0	.195	.267	.195
Mike Phillips†	2B6,3B6	L	24	10	31	3	6	0	0	0	1	6	4	1	.194	.324	.194
Craig Robinson†	SS12,2B9	R	26	29	29	4	2	1	0	0	0	2	6	0	.069	.129	.103
Jack Clark	OF3,3B2	R	19	8	17	3	4	0	0	0	2	1	2	1	.235	.263	.235
Horace Speed	OF9	R	23	17	15	2	2	1	0	0	1	1	8	0	.133	.235	.200
Gary Alexander	C2	R	22	3	3	1	0	0	0	0	0	1	2	0	.000	.250	.000

Pitcher	T	Age	G	GS	CG	ShO	IP	H	HR	BB	SO	W-L	Sv	ERA
John Montefusco	R	25	35	34	10	4	244.0	210	11	86	215	15-9	0	2.88
Jim Barr	R	27	35	33	12	2	244.0	244	17	58	77	13-14	0	3.06
Pete Falcone	L	21	34	32	3	1	190.0	171	16	111	131	12-11	0	4.17
Ed Halicki	R	24	24	23	7	2	159.2	143	6	59	153	9-13	0	3.49
Mike Caldwell	L	26	38	21	4	0	163.1	194	16	48	57	7-13	1	4.79
John D'Acquisto	R	23	10	6	0	0	28.0	29	5	34	22	2-4	0	10.29
Greg Minton	R	23	4	2	0	0	17.0	19	1	11	6	1-1	0	6.88
Rob Dressler	R	21	3	2	1	0	16.1	17	0	4	6	1-0	0	1.10
Gary Lavelle	L	26	65	0	0	0	82.1	80	3	48	51	6-3	8	2.95
Charlie Williams	R	27	55	2	0	0	98.0	94	2	66	45	5-3	3	3.49
Randy Moffitt	R	26	55	0	0	0	74.0	73	6	32	39	4-5	11	3.89
Dave Heaverlo	R	24	42	0	0	0	64.0	62	2	31	35	3-1	1	2.39
Tom Bradley	R	28	13	6	0	0	42.0	57	6	18	13	2-3	0	6.21
Tommy Toms	R	23	7	0	0	0	10.1	13	1	6	6	0-1	0	6.10

1975 San Diego Padres 4th NL West 71-91 .438 37.0 GB — John McNamara

Player	Gm by Position	B	Age	G	AB	R	H	2B	3B	HR	RBI	BB	SO	SB	Avg	OBP	Slg
Fred Kendall	C85	R	26	103	286	16	57	12	1	0	24	26	28	0	.199	.265	.248
Willie McCovey	1B115	L	37	122	413	43	104	17	0	23	68	57	80	1	.252	.345	.460
Tito Fuentes	2B142	S	31	146	565	57	158	21	3	4	43	25	51	8	.280	.309	.349
Ted Kubiak†	3B64,2B11,1B1	S	33	87	196	13	44	5	0	0	14	24	18	3	.224	.308	.250
Enzo Hernandez	SS111	R	26	116	344	37	75	12	2	0	19	26	25	20	.218	.275	.265
John Grubb	OF139	L	26	144	553	72	149	36	2	4	38	59	59	2	.269	.342	.363
Dave Winfield	OF138	R	23	143	509	74	136	20	2	15	76	69	82	23	.267	.354	.403
Bobby Tolan	OF120,1B27	L	29	147	506	58	129	19	4	5	43	28	45	11	.255	.306	.338
Mike Ivie	1B78,3B61,C1	R	22	111	377	36	94	16	2	8	46	20	63	4	.249	.291	.366
Hector Torres	SS75,3B42,2B16	R	29	112	352	31	91	12	0	5	26	22	32	2	.259	.297	.335
Gene Locklear	OF51	L	25	100	237	31	76	11	1	5	27	22	26	4	.321	.378	.439
Randy Hundley	C51	R	33	74	180	7	37	5	1	2	14	19	29	0	.206	.284	.278
Dick Sharon	OF57	R	25	91	160	14	31	7	0	4	20	26	35	0	.194	.306	.313
Bob Davis	C43	R	23	43	128	6	30	3	2	0	7	11	31	0	.234	.310	.289
Dave Roberts	3B30,2B5	R	24	33	113	7	32	2	0	2	12	13	19	3	.283	.367	.354
Steve Huntz	3B16,2B2	S	29	22	53	3	8	4	0	0	4	7	8	0	.151	.250	.226
Don Hahn†	OF26	R	26	34	26	7	6	1	2	0	3	10	2	1	.231	.444	.423
Jerry Turner	OF4	L	21	11	22	1	6	0	0	0	0	2	1	0	.273	.333	.273
Jerry Moses†	C5	R	28	13	19	1	3	2	0	0	1	2	3	0	.158	.238	.263
Glenn Beckert	3B4	R	34	9	16	2	6	1	0	0	0	1	0	0	.375	.412	.438
Bobby Valentine†	OF4	R	25	7	15	1	2	0	0	1	1	4	0	1	.133	.316	.333
Bill Almon	SS2	R	22	6	10	0	4	0	0	0	0	0	1	0	.400	.400	.400
John Scott	OF1	R	23	25	9	6	0	0	0	0	0	0	2	2	.000	.000	.000
Dave Hilton	3B4	R	24	4	8	0	0	0	0	0	0	0	0	0	.000	.000	.000

Pitcher	T	Age	G	GS	CG	ShO	IP	H	HR	BB	SO	W-L	Sv	ERA
Randy Jones	L	25	37	36	18	6	285.0	242	17	56	103	20-12	0	2.24
Joe McIntosh	R	23	37	28	4	1	183.0	195	14	60	71	8-15	0	3.69
Dave Freisleben	R	23	36	27	4	1	181.0	206	11	82	77	5-14	0	4.28
Dan Spillner	R	23	37	25	3	0	166.2	194	14	63	104	5-13	1	4.27
Brent Strom	L	26	18	16	6	2	120.1	103	6	33	56	8-8	0	2.54
Sonny Siebert†	R	38	6	6	0	0	26.2	37	2	10	10	3-2	0	4.39
Dave Tomlin	L	26	67	0	0	0	83.0	87	5	31	48	4-2	1	3.25
Danny Frisella	R	29	65	0	0	0	97.2	86	7	51	67	1-6	9	3.13
Bill Greif	R	25	59	1	0	0	72.0	74	7	38	43	4-6	9	3.88
Rich Folkers	L	28	45	15	4	0	142.0	155	8	39	87	6-11	0	4.18
Jerry Johnson	R	31	21	4	0	0	54.0	60	3	31	18	3-1	0	5.17
Alan Foster	R	28	17	4	1	0	44.2	41	1	21	20	3-1	0	2.42
Butch Metzger	R	23	4	0	0	0	4.2	6	1	4	6	1-0	0	7.71
Larry Hardy	R	27	3	0	0	0	2.2	8	3	2	3	0-0	0	13.50

1975 Atlanta Braves 5th NL West 67-94 .416 40.5 GB — Clyde King (58-76)/Connie Ryan (9-18)

Player	Gm by Position	B	Age	G	AB	R	H	2B	3B	HR	RBI	BB	SO	SB	Avg	OBP	Slg
Vic Correll	C97	R	29	103	325	37	70	12	1	11	39	42	66	0	.215	.305	.360
Earl Williams	1B90,C11	R	26	111	383	42	92	13	0	11	50	34	63	0	.240	.305	.360
Marty Perez	2B116,SS7	R	28	120	461	50	127	14	2	2	34	37	44	2	.275	.327	.328
Darrell Evans	3B156,1B3	L	28	156	567	82	138	22	2	22	73	105	106	12	.243	.361	.406
Larvell Blanks	SS129,2B12	R	25	141	471	49	110	13	3	3	38	38	43	4	.234	.292	.293
Ralph Garr	OF148	L	29	151	625	74	174	26	11	6	31	44	50	14	.278	.327	.384
Dusty Baker	OF136	R	26	142	494	63	129	18	2	19	72	67	57	12	.261	.346	.421
Rowland Office	OF107	L	22	126	355	30	103	14	1	3	30	23	41	2	.290	.337	.361
Mike Lum	1B60,OF38	L	29	124	364	32	83	8	2	8	36	39	38	2	.228	.302	.327
Dave May	OF53	L	31	82	203	28	56	8	0	12	40	25	27	1	.276	.361	.493
Rod Gilbreath	2B52,3B10,SS1	R	22	90	202	24	49	3	1	2	16	24	26	5	.243	.323	.297
Biff Pocoroba	C62	S	21	67	188	15	48	7	1	1	22	20	11	0	.255	.325	.319
Cito Gaston	OF35,1B1	R	31	64	141	17	34	4	0	6	15	17	33	1	.241	.321	.397
Bob Belloir	SS38,2B1	R	26	43	105	11	23	2	1	0	9	7	8	0	.219	.268	.257
Ed Goodson†	1B13,3B1	L	27	47	76	5	16	2	0	1	8	2	8	0	.211	.228	.276
Bob Beall	1B8	S	27	20	31	2	7	2	0	0	1	6	9	0	.226	.351	.290
Johnny Oates†	C6	L	29	8	18	0	4	1	0	0	0	1	4	0	.222	.263	.278
Craig Robinson†	SS7	R	26	10	17	1	1	0	0	0	0	0	5	0	.059	.059	.059
Frank Tepedino		L	27	8	7	0	0	0	0	0	0	1	2	0	.000	.125	.000
Joe Nolan	C1	L	24	4	4	0	1	0	0	0	0	1	0	0	.250	.400	.250
Dave Johnson		R	32	1	1	0	1	1	0	0	1	0	0	0	1.000	1.000	2.000

Pitcher	T	Age	G	GS	CG	ShO	IP	H	HR	BB	SO	W-L	Sv	ERA
Carl Morton	R	31	39	39	11	2	277.2	302	19	82	78	17-16	0	3.50
Phil Niekro	R	36	39	37	13	1	275.2	285	29	72	144	15-15	0	3.20
Jamie Easterly	L	22	21	13	0	0	68.2	73	5	42	34	2-9	0	4.98
Buzz Capra	R	27	12	12	5	0	78.1	77	8	28	35	4-7	0	4.25
Ron Reed†	R	32	10	10	1	0	74.2	93	1	16	40	4-5	0	4.22
Blue Moon Odom†	R	30	15	10	0	0	56.0	78	5	28	30	1-7	0	7.07
Mike Thompson	R	25	16	10	0	0	51.2	60	2	32	42	0-6	0	4.70
Frank LaCorte	R	23	3	2	0	0	13.2	13	1	6	10	0-3	0	5.27
Tom House	L	28	58	0	0	0	79.1	79	2	36	36	7-7	11	3.18
Max Leon	R	25	50	1	0	0	85.0	90	5	33	53	2-1	6	4.13
Elias Sosa†	R	25	43	0	0	0	62.1	70	3	29	31	2-2	2	4.48
Mike Beard	L	25	34	2	0	0	70.1	71	4	28	27	4-0	0	3.20
Bruce Dal Canton†	R	33	26	9	0	0	67.0	63	2	24	38	2-7	3	3.36
Ray Sadecki†	L	34	25	5	0	0	66.1	73	3	21	24	2-3	1	4.21
Roric Harrison†	R	28	15	7	2	0	54.2	58	7	19	22	3-4	1	4.77
Gary Gentry	R	28	7	2	0	0	20.0	25	3	8	10	1-1	0	4.95
Pablo Torrealba	L	27	6	0	0	0	6.2	7	0	3	5	0-1	0	1.35
Adrian Devine	R	23	5	2	0	0	16.1	19	2	7	8	1-0	0	4.41
Preston Hanna	R	20	4	0	0	0	5.2	7	0	5	2	0-0	0	1.59

1975 Houston Astros 6th NL West 64-97 .398 43.5 GB — Preston Gomez (47-80)/Bill Virdon (17-17)

Player	Gm by Position	B	Age	G	AB	R	H	2B	3B	HR	RBI	BB	SO	SB	Avg	OBP	Slg
Milt May	C102	L	24	111	386	29	93	15	1	4	52	26	41	1	.241	.287	.316
Bob Watson	1B118,OF9	R	29	132	485	67	157	27	1	18	85	40	50	3	.324	.375	.495
Rob Andrews	2B94,SS6	R	22	103	277	29	66	5	4	0	19	31	34	12	.238	.310	.285
Doug Rader	3B124,SS2	R	30	129	448	41	100	23	2	12	48	42	101	5	.223	.296	.364
Roger Metzger	SS126	S	27	127	450	54	102	7	9	2	26	41	39	4	.227	.289	.296
Cesar Cedeno	OF131	R	24	131	500	93	144	31	3	13	63	62	52	50	.288	.371	.440
Greg Gross	OF121	L	22	132	483	67	142	14	10	0	41	63	37	2	.294	.373	.364
Wilbur Howard	OF95	S	26	121	392	62	111	16	8	0	21	21	67	32	.283	.324	.365
Enos Cabell	OF67,1B25,3B22	R	25	117	348	43	92	17	6	2	43	18	53	12	.264	.303	.365
Cliff Johnson	1B47,C41,OF1	R	27	122	340	52	94	16	1	20	65	46	64	1	.276	.370	.506
Jose Cruz	OF94	L	27	120	315	44	81	15	2	9	49	52	44	6	.257	.358	.403
Ken Boswell	2B31,3B23	L	29	86	178	16	43	8	2	0	21	30	12	0	.242	.349	.309
Larry Milbourne	2B43,SS22	S	24	73	151	17	32	1	2	1	9	6	14	1	.212	.245	.265
Tommy Helms	2B42,3B3,SS1	R	34	64	135	7	28	2	0	0	14	10	8	0	.207	.265	.222
Jerry Davanon	SS21,2B9,3B3	R	29	32	97	15	27	4	2	1	10	16	7	2	.278	.386	.392
Skip Jutze	C47	R	29	51	93	9	21	2	0	0	6	2	4	1	.226	.242	.247
Art Gardner	OF8	L	22	13	31	3	6	0	0	0	2	1	8	1	.194	.242	.194
Rafael Batista		L	27	10	10	0	3	1	0	0	0	0	4	0	.300	.300	.400
Mike Easler		L	24	5	5	0	0	0	0	0	0	0	1	0	.000	.000	.000
Jesus De la rosa		R	21	3	3	1	1	1	0	0	0	0	0	0	.333	.333	.667

Pitcher	T	Age	G	GS	CG	ShO	IP	H	HR	BB	SO	W-L	Sv	ERA
Larry Dierker	R	28	34	34	14	2	232.0	225	24	91	127	14-16	0	4.00
J.R. Richard	R	25	33	31	7	1	203.0	178	8	138	176	12-10	0	4.39
Doug Konieczny	R	23	32	29	4	1	171.0	184	15	87	89	6-13	0	4.47
Dave Roberts	L	30	32	27	7	0	198.1	182	16	73	101	8-14	1	4.27
Tom Griffin	R	27	17	13	3	1	79.1	89	11	46	56	3-8	0	5.33
Wayne Granger	R	31	55	0	0	0	74.0	76	7	23	30	2-5	5	3.65
Jim Crawford	L	24	44	2	0	0	86.2	92	0	37	37	3-5	4	3.63
Joe Niekro	R	30	40	4	1	1	88.0	79	3	39	54	6-4	4	3.07
Ken Forsch	R	28	34	9	2	0	109.0	114	9	30	54	4-8	2	3.22
Mike Cosgrove	L	24	32	3	1	0	71.1	62	2	37	32	1-2	5	3.03
Jose Sosa	R	22	25	2	0	0	47.0	51	5	23	31	1-3	1	4.02
Jim York	R	27	19	4	0	0	46.2	43	1	25	17	4-4	0	3.86
Fred Scherman†	L	30	16	0	0	0	16.1	21	4	4	13	0-1	0	4.96
Paul Siebert	L	22	7	2	0	0	18.1	20	0	6	6	0-2	2	2.95
Mike Stanton	R	22	7	2	0	0	17.1	20	1	20	16	0-2	1	7.27

>>1976 New York Yankees 1st AL East 97-62 .610 —

Billy Martin

Player	Gm by Position	B	Age	G	AB	R	H	2B	3B	HR	RBI	BB	SO	SB	Avg	OBP	Slg
Thurman Munson	C121,DH21,OF11	R	29	152	616	79	186	27	1	17	105	29	38	14	.302	.337	.432
Chris Chambliss	1B155,DH1	L	27	156	641	79	188	32	6	17	96	27	80	1	.293	.323	.441
Willie Randolph	2B124	R	21	125	430	59	115	15	4	1	40	58	39	37	.267	.356	.328
Graig Nettles	3B158,SS1	L	31	158	583	88	148	29	2	32	93	62	94	11	.254	.327	.475
Fred Stanley	SS110,2B3	R	28	110	260	32	62	2	2	1	20	34	29	1	.238	.329	.273
Roy White	OF156	S	32	156	626	104	179	29	3	14	65	83	52	31	.286	.365	.409
Mickey Rivers	OF136	L	27	137	590	95	184	31	8	8	67	13	51	43	.312	.327	.432
Oscar Gamble	OF104,DH1	L	26	110	340	43	79	13	1	17	57	38	38	5	.232	.317	.426
Carlos May†	DH71,OF7,1B1	L	28	87	288	38	80	11	2	3	40	34	32	1	.278	.358	.361
Lou Piniella	OF49,DH38	R	32	100	327	36	92	16	6	3	38	18	34	0	.281	.322	.394
Jim Mason	SS93	L	25	93	217	17	39	7	1	1	14	9	37	0	.180	.210	.235
Sandy Alomar	2B38,DH9,SS6*	S	32	67	163	20	39	4	0	1	10	13	12	12	.239	.295	.282
Fran Healy†	C31,DH9	R	29	46	120	10	32	3	0	0	9	9	17	3	.267	.318	.292
Otto Velez	OF24,1B8,DH5*	R	25	49	94	11	25	6	0	2	10	23	26	0	.266	.410	.394
Ellie Hendricks†	C18	L	35	26	53	6	12	1	0	3	5	3	10	0	.226	.263	.415
Elliott Maddox	OF13,DH2	R	28	18	46	4	10	2	0	0	3	4	3	0	.217	.275	.261
Rick Dempsey†	C9,OF4	R	26	21	42	1	5	0	0	0	2	5	4	0	.119	.213	.119
Cesar Tovar†	DH10,2B3	R	35	13	39	2	6	1	0	0	2	4	3	0	.154	.250	.179
Gene Locklear†	DH6,OF3	L	26	13	32	2	7	1	0	0	1	2	7	0	.219	.265	.250
Juan Bernhardt	OF4,DH2,3B1	R	22	10	21	1	4	1	0	0	1	0	4	0	.190	.190	.238
Larry Murray	OF7	S	23	8	10	2	1	0	0	0	2	1	2	2	.100	.182	.100
Kerry Dineen	OF4	L	23	4	7	0	2	0	0	0	1	1	2	1	.286	.375	.286
Rich Coggins†	OF2,DH1	L	25	7	4	1	1	0	0	0	1	0	1	1	.250	.250	.250
Mickey Klutts	SS2	R	21	2	3	0	0	0	0	0	0	0	1	0	.000	.000	.000
Ron Blomberg	DH1	L	27	1	2	0	0	0	0	0	0	0	0	0	.000	.000	.000
Terry Whitfield	OF1	L	23	1	0	0	0	0	0	0	0	0	0	0	—	—	—

S. Alomar, 3 G at 3B, 1 G at 1B, 1 G at OF; O. Velez, 1 G at 3B

Pitcher	T	Age	G	GS	CG	ShO	IP	H	HR	BB	SO	W-L	Sv	ERA
Catfish Hunter	R	30	36	36	21	2	298.2	268	28	68	173	17-15	0	3.53
Ed Figueroa	R	27	34	34	14	4	256.2	237	13	94	119	19-10	0	3.02
Dock Ellis	R	31	32	32	8	1	211.2	195	14	76	65	17-8	0	3.19
Ken Holtzman†	L	30	21	21	10	2	149.0	165	14	35	41	9-7	0	4.17
Doyle Alexander†	R	25	19	19	5	2	136.2	114	9	39	41	10-5	0	3.29
Rudy May†	L	31	11	11	2	1	68.0	49	5	28	38	4-3	0	3.57
Sparky Lyle	L	31	64	0	0	0	103.2	82	5	42	61	7-8	23	2.26
Dick Tidrow	R	29	47	2	0	0	92.1	80	5	24	65	4-5	10	2.63
Grant Jackson†	L	33	21	2	1	1	58.2	38	1	16	25	6-0	1	1.69
Tippy Martinez†	L	26	11	0	0	0	28.0	18	1	14	14	2-0	2	1.93
Dave Pagan†	R	26	7	2	1	0	23.2	18	0	4	13	1-1	0	2.28
Ron Guidry	L	25	7	0	0	0	16.0	20	1	4	12	0-0	0	5.63
Jim York	R	28	3	0	0	0	9.2	14	1	4	6	1-0	0	5.59
Ken Brett†	L	27	2	0	0	0	2.1	2	0	0	1	0-0	1	0.00

1976 Baltimore Orioles 2nd AL East 88-74 .543 10.5 GB

Earl Weaver

Player	Gm by Position	B	Age	G	AB	R	H	2B	3B	HR	RBI	BB	SO	SB	Avg	OBP	Slg
Dave Duncan	C93	R	30	93	284	20	58	7	0	4	17	25	56	0	.204	.271	.271
Tony Muser	1B109,OF12,DH10	L	28	136	326	25	74	7	1	1	30	21	34	1	.227	.270	.264
Bobby Grich	2B140,3B2	R	27	144	518	93	138	31	4	13	54	86	99	14	.266	.373	.417
Doug DeCinces	3B109,2B17,1B11*	R	25	129	440	36	103	17	2	11	42	29	68	8	.234	.284	.357
Mark Belanger	SS153	R	32	153	522	66	141	22	2	1	40	51	64	27	.270	.336	.326
Paul Blair	OF139,DH1	R	32	145	375	29	74	16	0	3	16	22	49	15	.197	.245	.264
Ken Singleton	OF134,DH19	S	29	154	544	62	151	25	2	13	70	79	76	2	.278	.366	.403
Reggie Jackson	OF121,DH11	L	30	134	498	84	138	27	2	27	91	54	108	28	.277	.351	.502
Lee May	1B94,DH52	R	33	148	530	61	137	17	4	25	109	41	104	4	.258	.312	.447
Al Bumbry	OF116,DH10	L	29	133	450	71	113	15	7	9	36	43	76	42	.251	.316	.376
Andres Mora	DH34,OF31	R	21	73	220	18	48	11	0	6	25	13	49	1	.218	.258	.350
Brooks Robinson	3B71	R	39	71	218	16	46	8	2	3	11	8	24	0	.211	.240	.307
Rick Dempsey†	C58,OF3	R	26	59	174	11	37	2	0	0	10	13	17	1	.213	.275	.224
Ellie Hendricks†	C27	L	35	28	79	2	11	1	0	1	4	7	13	0	.139	.209	.190
Tommy Harper	DH27,1B1,OF1	R	35	46	77	8	18	5	0	1	7	10	16	4	.234	.318	.338
Terry Crowley†	DH17,1B1	L	29	33	61	5	15	1	0	0	5	7	11	0	.246	.333	.262
Rich Dauer	2B10	R	23	11	39	0	4	0	0	0	3	1	3	0	.103	.143	.103
Kiko Garcia	SS11	R	22	11	32	2	7	1	1	1	4	0	4	2	.219	.219	.406
Royle Stillman	DH5,1B2	L	25	20	22	0	2	0	0	0	1	3	4	0	.091	.200	.091
Tim Nordbrook†	2B14,SS12	R	26	27	22	4	5	0	0	0	0	3	5	0	.227	.320	.227
Tom Shopay	OF11,C1	L	31	14	20	4	4	0	0	0	1	3	3	1	.200	.304	.200
Bob Bailor	DH1,SS1	R	24	9	6	2	2	0	1	0	0	0	0	0	.333	.333	.667

D. DeCinces, 2 G at SS, 1 G at DH

Pitcher	T	Age	G	GS	CG	ShO	IP	H	HR	BB	SO	W-L	Sv	ERA
Jim Palmer	R	30	40	40	23	6	315.0	255	20	84	159	22-13	0	2.51
Wayne Garland	R	25	38	25	14	4	232.1	224	10	64	113	20-7	1	2.67
Rudy May†	L	31	24	21	5	1	152.1	156	11	42	71	11-7	0	3.78
Ross Grimsley	L	26	28	19	2	0	136.2	143	8	35	41	8-7	0	3.95
Mike Cuellar	L	39	26	19	2	1	107.0	129	8	50	32	4-13	1	4.96
Ken Holtzman†	L	30	13	13	6	1	97.2	100	4	35	25	5-4	0	2.86
Mike Flanagan	L	24	20	10	4	0	85.0	83	7	33	56	3-5	0	4.13
Doyle Alexander†	R	25	11	6	2	1	64.1	58	3	24	17	3-4	0	3.50
Dennis Martinez	R	21	4	2	1	0	27.2	23	1	8	18	1-2	0	2.60
Scott McGregor	L	22	3	2	0	0	14.2	17	0	5	6	0-1	0	3.68
Dyar Miller	R	30	49	0	0	0	88.2	79	5	36	37	2-4	7	2.94
Tippy Martinez†	L	26	28	0	0	0	41.2	32	0	28	31	3-1	8	2.59
Dave Pagan†	R	26	20	5	0	0	46.2	54	2	23	34	1-4	1	5.98
Fred Holdsworth	R	24	16	0	0	0	39.2	24	0	13	24	4-1	2	2.04
Grant Jackson†	L	33	13	0	0	0	19.1	19	1	9	14	1-1	3	5.12

1976 Boston Red Sox 3rd AL East 83-79 .512 15.5 GB

Darrell Johnson (41-45)/Don Zimmer (42-34)

Player	Gm by Position	B	Age	G	AB	R	H	2B	3B	HR	RBI	BB	SO	SB	Avg	OBP	Slg
Carlton Fisk	C133,DH1	R	28	134	487	76	124	17	5	17	58	56	71	12	.255	.336	.415
Carl Yastrzemski	1B94,OF51,DH10	L	36	155	546	71	146	23	2	21	102	80	67	5	.267	.357	.432
Denny Doyle	2B113	L	32	117	432	51	108	15	5	0	26	22	29	8	.250	.285	.308
Butch Hobson	3B76	R	24	76	269	34	63	7	5	8	34	15	62	0	.234	.272	.387
Rick Burleson	SS152	R	25	152	540	75	157	27	1	7	42	60	37	14	.291	.365	.383
Dwight Evans	OF145,DH1	R	24	146	501	61	121	34	5	17	62	57	92	6	.242	.324	.431
Fred Lynn	OF128,DH5	L	24	132	507	76	159	32	8	10	65	48	67	14	.314	.367	.467
Jim Rice	OF98,DH54	R	23	153	581	75	164	25	8	25	85	28	123	8	.282	.315	.482
Cecil Cooper	1B66,DH53	L	26	123	451	66	127	22	6	15	78	16	62	7	.282	.304	.457
Rick Miller	OF82,DH4	L	28	105	269	40	76	15	3	0	27	34	47	11	.283	.359	.361
Rico Petrocelli	3B73,2B5,DH4*	R	33	85	240	17	51	7	1	3	24	34	36	0	.213	.307	.288
Steve Dillard	3B18,2B17,SS12*	R	25	57	167	22	46	14	0	1	15	17	20	6	.275	.341	.377
Doug Griffin	2B44,DH2	R	29	49	127	14	24	2	0	0	4	9	14	2	.189	.248	.205
Bobby Darwin†	OF17,DH16	R	33	43	106	9	19	5	2	3	13	2	35	1	.179	.216	.349
Bob Montgomery	C30,DH1	R	32	31	93	10	23	3	1	3	13	5	20	0	.247	.283	.398
Bob Heise	3B22,SS9,2B1	R	29	32	56	5	15	2	0	0	5	1	2	0	.268	.293	.304
Bernie Carbo†	DH15,OF1	L	28	17	55	5	13	4	0	2	6	8	17	1	.236	.333	.418
Deron Johnson	1B5	R	37	15	38	3	5	1	1	0	0	5	11	0	.132	.233	.211
Jack Baker	1B8,DH1	R	26	12	23	1	3	0	0	1	2	1	5	0	.130	.160	.261
Ernie Whitt	C8	L	24	8	18	4	4	2	0	1	3	2	2	0	.222	.300	.500
Andy Merchant	C1	L	25	2	2	0	0	0	0	0	0	0	2	0	.000	.000	.000

R. Petrocelli, 1 G at 1B, 1 G at SS; S. Dillard, 7 G at DH

Pitcher	T	Age	G	GS	CG	ShO	IP	H	HR	BB	SO	W-L	Sv	ERA
Luis Tiant	R	35	38	38	19	3	279.0	274	25	64	131	21-12	0	3.06
Rick Wise	R	30	34	34	11	4	224.1	218	18	48	93	14-11	0	3.53
Fergie Jenkins	R	32	30	29	12	2	209.0	201	20	43	142	12-11	0	3.27
Rick Jones	L	21	24	14	1	0	104.1	133	6	26	45	5-3	0	3.36
Bill Lee	L	29	24	14	1	0	96.0	124	13	28	29	5-7	3	5.63
Rick Kreuger	L	27	8	4	1	0	31.0	31	3	16	12	2-1	0	4.06
Jim Willoughby	R	27	54	0	0	0	99.0	94	4	31	37	3-12	10	2.82
Reggie Cleveland	R	28	41	14	3	0	170.0	159	3	61	76	10-9	2	3.07
Tom Murphy†	R	30	37	0	0	0	81.0	91	5	25	32	4-5	8	3.44
Tom House	L	29	36	0	0	0	43.2	39	4	19	27	1-3	4	4.33
Dick Pole	R	25	31	15	1	0	120.2	131	8	48	49	6-5	0	4.33

1976 Cleveland Indians 4th AL East 81-78 .509 16.0 GB

Frank Robinson

Player	Gm by Position	B	Age	G	AB	R	H	2B	3B	HR	RBI	BB	SO	SB	Avg	OBP	Slg
Alan Ashby	C86,1B2,3B1	S	24	89	247	26	59	5	1	4	32	27	49	0	.239	.310	.316
Boog Powell	1B89	L	34	95	293	29	63	9	0	9	33	41	43	1	.215	.305	.338
Duane Kuiper	2B128,1B5,DH2	L	26	135	506	47	133	13	6	0	37	30	42	10	.263	.303	.312
Buddy Bell	3B158,1B2	R	24	159	604	75	170	26	2	7	60	44	49	3	.281	.329	.366
Frank Duffy	SS132	R	29	133	392	38	83	11	2	2	30	29	50	10	.212	.268	.265
George Hendrick	OF146	R	26	149	551	72	146	20	3	25	81	51	82	4	.265	.323	.448
Rick Manning	OF136	L	21	138	552	73	161	24	7	6	43	41	75	16	.292	.337	.393
Charlie Spikes	OF98,DH2	R	25	101	334	34	79	11	5	3	31	23	50	5	.237	.294	.326
Rico Carty	DH137,1B12,OF1	R	36	152	552	67	171	34	0	13	83	67	45	1	.310	.379	.442
Larvell Blanks	SS56,2B46,DH3*	R	26	104	328	45	92	8	7	5	41	30	31	1	.280	.337	.393
Ray Fosse	C85,1B3,DH1	R	29	90	276	26	83	9	1	2	30	20	20	1	.301	.347	.362
John Lowenstein	OF61,DH11,1B9	L	29	93	229	33	47	8	2	2	14	25	35	11	.205	.283	.284
Tommy Smith	OF50,DH2	L	27	55	164	17	42	3	1	2	12	8	8	8	.256	.289	.323
Doug Howard	1B32,DH4,OF2	R	28	39	90	7	19	4	0	0	13	3	13	1	.211	.237	.256
Ron Pruitt	OF26,C6,3B6*	R	24	47	86	7	23	1	1	0	5	16	8	2	.267	.375	.302
Orlando Gonzalez	1B15,OF7,DH2	L	24	28	68	5	17	2	0	0	4	5	7	1	.250	.301	.279
Frank Robinson	DH18,1B2,OF1	R	40	36	67	5	15	0	0	3	10	11	12	0	.224	.329	.358
Joe Lis	1B17,DH1	R	29	20	51	4	16	1	0	2	7	8	8	0	.314	.400	.451
Rick Cerone	C6,DH1	R	22	7	16	1	2	0	0	0	1	0	2	0	.125	.125	.125
Alfredo Griffin	SS6,DH4	S	18	12	4	0	1	0	0	0	0	0	2	0	.250	.250	.250
Ed Crosby	DH1,3B1	L	27	2	2	0	1	0	0	0	0	0	0	0	.500	.500	.500

L. Blanks, 2 G at 3B; R. Pruitt, 4 G at DH, 1 G at 1B

Pitcher	T	Age	G	GS	CG	ShO	IP	H	HR	BB	SO	W-L	Sv	ERA
Pat Dobson	R	34	35	35	6	0	217.1	226	13	65	117	16-12	0	3.48
Dennis Eckersley	R	21	36	30	9	3	199.1	155	13	78	200	13-12	1	3.43
Jackie Brown	R	33	32	27	5	2	180.0	193	14	55	104	9-11	0	4.25
Rick Waits	L	24	26	22	4	2	123.2	143	7	54	65	7-9	0	4.00
Jim Bibby	R	31	34	21	4	3	163.1	162	6	56	84	13-7	1	3.20
Fritz Peterson†	L	34	9	9	0	0	47.0	59	3	10	19	0-3	0	5.55
Dave LaRoche	L	28	61	0	0	0	96.1	57	2	49	104	1-4	21	2.24
Jim Kern	R	27	50	2	0	0	117.2	91	2	50	111	10-7	15	2.37
Tom Buskey	R	29	39	0	0	0	94.1	88	9	34	32	5-4	1	3.63
Stan Thomas	R	26	37	7	2	0	105.2	88	5	41	54	4-4	6	2.30
Don Hood	L	26	33	6	0	0	77.2	89	5	41	32	3-5	1	4.87
Harry Parker	R	28	3	0	0	0	7.0	3	0	0	5	0-0	0	0.00
Eric Raich	R	24	1	0	0	0	2.2	7	1	0	1	0-0	0	16.88

1976 Detroit Tigers 5th AL East 74-87 .460 24.0 GB

Ralph Houk

Player	Gm by Position	B	Age	G	AB	R	H	2B	3B	HR	RBI	BB	SO	SB	Avg	OBP	Slg
Bill Freehan	C61,DH3,1B2	R	34	71	237	22	64	10	1	5	27	12	27	0	.270	.303	.384
Jason Thompson	1B117	L	21	123	412	45	90	12	1	17	54	68	72	2	.218	.328	.376
Pedro Garcia†	2B77	R	26	77	227	21	45	10	2	3	20	9	40	2	.198	.239	.300
Aurelio Rodriguez	3B128	R	28	128	480	40	115	13	2	8	50	19	61	0	.240	.267	.325
Tom Veryzer	SS97	R	23	97	354	31	83	8	2	1	25	21	44	1	.234	.286	.277
Ron LeFlore	OF132,DH1	R	28	135	544	93	172	23	8	4	39	51	111	58	.316	.376	.410
Rusty Staub	OF126,DH36	L	32	161	589	73	176	28	3	15	96	83	49	3	.299	.386	.433
Alex Johnson	OF90,DH19	R	33	125	429	41	115	15	2	6	45	19	49	14	.268	.298	.354
Willie Horton	DH105	R	33	114	401	40	105	17	0	14	56	49	63	0	.262	.342	.409
Ben Oglivie	OF64,1B9,DH1	L	27	115	305	36	87	12	3	15	47	11	44	9	.285	.313	.492
Dan Meyer	OF47,1B19	L	23	105	294	37	74	8	4	2	16	17	22	10	.252	.292	.327
Chuck Scrivener	2B43,SS37,3B5	R	28	80	222	28	49	7	1	2	16	19	34	1	.221	.282	.288
Mickey Stanley	OF38,1B17,3B11*	R	33	84	214	34	55	17	1	4	29	14	19	2	.257	.301	.402
Bruce Kimm	C61,DH2	R	25	63	152	13	40	8	0	1	6	15	20	4	.263	.329	.336
John Wockenfuss	C59	R	27	60	144	18	32	7	2	3	10	17	14	0	.222	.309	.361
Gary Sutherland†	2B42	R	31	42	117	10	24	5	2	0	6	7	12	0	.205	.248	.282
Mark Wagner	SS39	R	22	39	115	9	30	2	3	0	12	6	18	0	.261	.298	.330
Phil Mankowski	3B23	L	23	24	85	9	23	2	1	1	4	4	8	0	.271	.300	.353
Marvin Lane	OF15	R	26	18	48	3	9	1	0	0	5	6	11	0	.188	.273	.208
Jerry Manuel	2B47,SS4,DH1	S	22	54	43	4	6	1	0	0	2	3	9	1	.140	.213	.163
Milt May	C6	L	25	6	25	2	7	1	0	0	1	0	1	0	.280	.280	.320

M. Stanley, 3 G at SS, 2 G at 2B

Pitcher	T	Age	G	GS	CG	ShO	IP	H	HR	BB	SO	W-L	Sv	ERA
Dave Roberts	L	31	36	36	18	4	252.0	254	16	63	79	16-17	0	4.00
Vern Ruhle	R	25	32	32	5	1	199.2	227	19	59	88	9-12	0	3.92
Mark Fidrych	R	21	31	29	24	4	250.1	217	12	53	97	19-9	0	2.34
Ray Bare	R	27	30	21	3	2	134.0	157	13	51	59	7-8	0	4.63
Joe Coleman†	R	29	12	12	1	0	66.2	80	1	34	38	2-5	0	4.86
Dave Lemanczyk	R	25	20	10	1	0	81.1	86	7	34	51	4-6	0	5.09
Frank MacCormick	R	21	9	8	0	0	32.2	35	1	34	14	0-5	0	5.79
Ed Glynn	L	23	5	4	1	0	23.2	22	3	20	17	1-3	0	6.08
John Hiller	L	33	56	1	1	1	121.0	93	7	67	117	12-8	13	2.38
Steve Grilli	R	27	36	0	0	0	66.0	63	5	41	36	3-1	3	4.64
Jim Crawford	L	25	32	5	1	0	109.1	115	4	43	68	1-8	2	4.53
Bill Laxton	L	28	26	3	0	0	94.2	77	13	51	74	0-5	2	4.09

1976 Milwaukee Brewers 6th AL East 66-95 .410 32.0 GB

Alex Grammas

Player	Gm by Position	B	Age	G	AB	R	H	2B	3B	HR	RBI	BB	SO	SB	Avg	OBP	Slg
Darrell Porter	C111,DH2	L	24	119	389	43	81	14	1	5	32	51	61	2	.208	.298	.288
George Scott	1B155	R	32	156	606	73	166	21	5	18	77	53	118	0	.274	.334	.414
Tim Johnson	2B100,3B17,1B1*	L	26	105	273	25	75	4	3	0	14	19	32	4	.275	.327	.311
Don Money	3B103,DH10,SS1	R	29	117	439	51	117	18	4	12	62	47	50	6	.267	.333	.408
Robin Yount	SS161,OF1	R	20	161	638	59	161	19	3	2	54	38	69	16	.252	.292	.301
Sixto Lezcano	OF142,DH3	R	22	145	513	53	146	19	5	7	56	51	112	14	.285	.348	.382
Von Joshua†	OF105,DH1	L	28	107	423	44	113	13	5	5	28	18	58	8	.267	.295	.357
Gorman Thomas	OF94,DH1,3B1	R	25	99	227	27	45	9	2	8	36	31	67	2	.198	.294	.361
Hank Aaron	DH74,OF1	R	42	85	271	22	62	8	0	10	35	35	38	0	.229	.315	.369
Charlie Moore	C49,OF28,DH2*	R	23	87	241	33	46	7	4	3	16	43	45	1	.191	.314	.290
Mike Hegan	DH40,OF20,1B10	L	33	80	218	30	54	4	3	5	31	25	54	0	.248	.324	.362
Bernie Carbo†	OF33,DH24	L	28	69	183	20	43	7	0	3	15	33	55	1	.235	.352	.322
Bill Sharp	OF56,DH7	L	26	78	180	16	44	4	0	0	11	10	15	1	.244	.288	.267
Jack Heidemann†	3B40,2B24,DH1	R	26	69	146	11	32	1	0	2	10	7	24	1	.219	.253	.267
Gary Sutherland†	2B45,DH8,1B2	R	31	59	115	9	25	2	0	1	9	8	7	0	.217	.268	.261
Pedro Garcia†	2B39	R	26	41	106	12	23	7	1	1	9	4	23	2	.217	.257	.330
Danny Thomas	OF32	R	25	32	105	13	29	5	1	4	15	14	28	1	.276	.372	.457
Bobby Darwin†	OF21,DH1	R	33	25	73	6	18	3	1	1	5	6	16	0	.247	.321	.356
Jim Gantner	3B24,DH2	L	23	26	69	6	17	1	0	0	7	6	11	1	.246	.316	.261
Bob Hansen	DH14,1B1	L	28	24	61	4	10	1	0	0	4	6	8	0	.164	.239	.180
Steve Bowling	OF13,DH1	R	24	14	42	4	7	2	0	0	2	2	5	0	.167	.205	.214
Jimmy Rosario	OF12,DH2	S	31	15	37	4	7	0	0	1	5	3	8	1	.189	.250	.270
Art Kusnyer	C14	R	30	15	34	2	4	1	0	0	3	1	5	1	.118	.167	.147
Kurt Bevacqua	2B2	R	29	12	7	3	1	0	0	0	0	0	0	0	.143	.143	.143

T. Johnson, 1 G at SS; C. Moore, 1 G at 3B

Pitcher	T	Age	G	GS	CG	ShO	IP	H	HR	BB	SO	W-L	Sv	ERA
Jim Slaton	R	26	38	38	12	2	292.2	287	14	94	138	14-15	0	3.44
Bill Travers	L	23	34	34	15	3	240.0	211	21	95	120	15-16	0	2.81
Jim Colborn	R	30	32	32	7	0	225.2	232	20	54	101	9-15	0	3.71
Jerry Augustine	L	23	39	24	5	3	171.2	167	9	56	59	9-12	0	3.30
Pete Broberg	R	26	20	11	1	0	92.1	99	5	72	28	1-7	0	4.97
Gary Beare	R	23	6	5	2	0	41.0	43	4	15	32	2-3	0	3.29
Ed Rodriguez	R	24	45	12	3	0	136.0	124	10	65	77	5-13	8	3.64
Bill Castro	R	22	39	0	0	0	70.1	70	4	19	23	4-6	8	3.45
Ray Sadecki†	L	35	36	0	0	0	37.1	38	2	20	27	2-0	1	4.34
Danny Frisella†	R	30	32	0	0	0	49.1	30	4	34	43	5-2	9	2.74
Tom Murphy†	R	30	15	0	0	0	18.1	25	2	9	7	0-1	1	7.36
Billy Champion	R	28	10	3	0	0	24.1	35	0	13	8	0-1	0	7.03
Moose Haas	R	20	5	2	0	0	16.0	12	0	12	9	0-1	0	3.94
Ed Sprague	R	30	3	0	0	0	7.2	14	0	3	0	0-2	0	7.04
Rick Austin	L	29	3	0	0	0	5.1	10	1	0	3	0-0	0	5.06
Kevin Kobel	L	22	3	0	0	0	4.0	6	3	3	1	0-1	0	11.25
Tom Hausman	R	23	3	0	0	0	3.1	3	0	3	1	0-0	0	5.40

1976 Kansas City Royals 1st AL West 90-72 .556 —

Whitey Herzog

Player	Gm by Position	B	Age	G	AB	R	H	2B	3B	HR	RBI	BB	SO	SB	Avg	OBP	Slg
Buck Martinez	C94	R	27	95	267	24	61	13	3	5	34	16	45	0	.228	.269	.356
John Mayberry	1B160,DH9	L	27	161	594	76	138	22	2	13	95	82	73	3	.232	.322	.342
Frank White	2B130,SS37	R	25	152	446	39	102	17	6	2	46	19	42	20	.229	.263	.307
George Brett	3B157,SS4	L	23	159	645	94	215	34	14	7	67	49	36	21	.333	.377	.462
Freddie Patek	SS143,DH1	R	31	144	432	58	104	19	3	1	43	50	63	51	.241	.318	.306
Amos Otis	OF152	R	29	153	592	93	165	40	2	18	86	55	100	26	.279	.341	.444
Al Cowens	OF148,DH1	R	24	152	581	71	154	23	6	3	59	26	50	23	.265	.298	.341
Tom Poquette	OF98,DH2	L	24	104	344	43	104	18	10	2	34	29	31	6	.302	.361	.430
Hal McRae	DH117,OF31	R	30	149	527	75	175	34	5	8	73	64	43	22	.332	.407	.461
Jim Wohlford	OF93,DH3,2B1	R	25	107	293	47	73	10	2	1	24	29	24	22	.249	.314	.307
Bob Stinson	C79	S	30	79	209	26	55	7	1	2	25	25	29	3	.263	.342	.335
Dave Nelson	2B46,DH22,1B3	R	32	78	153	24	36	4	2	1	17	14	26	15	.235	.298	.307
Cookie Rojas	2B40,DH9,3B6*	R	37	63	132	11	32	6	0	0	16	8	15	2	.242	.280	.288
Jamie Quirk	DH19,SS12,3B11*	L	21	64	114	11	28	6	0	1	15	2	22	0	.246	.252	.325
Tony Solaita†	DH14,1B5	L	29	31	68	4	16	4	0	0	9	6	17	0	.235	.286	.294
Ruppert Jones	OF17,DH3	L	21	28	51	9	11	1	1	1	7	3	16	0	.216	.259	.333
John Wathan	C23,1B3	R	26	27	42	5	12	1	1	0	5	2	5	0	.286	.333	.310
Fran Healy†	C6,DH1	R	29	8	24	2	3	0	0	0	1	4	10	2	.125	.250	.125
Tommy Davis†	DH3	R	37	8	19	1	5	0	0	0	1	1	0	0	.263	.300	.263
Willie Wilson	OF6	S	20	12	6	0	1	0	0	0	0	0	2	2	.167	.167	.167

C. Rojas, 1 G at 1B; J. Quirk, 2 G at 1B

Pitcher	T	Age	G	GS	CG	ShO	IP	H	HR	BB	SO	W-L	Sv	ERA
Dennis Leonard	R	25	35	34	16	2	259.0	247	16	70	150	17-10	0	3.51
Al Fitzmorris	R	30	35	33	8	2	220.1	227	6	56	80	15-11	0	3.06
Doug Bird	R	26	39	27	2	1	197.2	191	17	31	107	12-10	2	3.37
Paul Splittorff	L	29	26	23	5	1	158.2	169	11	59	59	11-8	0	3.97
Andy Hassler†	L	24	19	14	4	1	99.2	89	2	39	45	5-6	0	2.89
Steve Busby	R	26	13	13	1	0	71.2	58	7	49	29	3-3	0	4.40
Mark Littell	R	23	60	1	0	0	104.0	68	1	60	92	8-4	16	2.08
Steve Mingori	L	32	55	0	0	0	85.1	73	3	25	38	5-5	10	2.32
Marty Pattin	R	33	44	15	4	1	141.0	114	9	38	65	8-14	5	2.49
Tom Hall†	L	28	31	0	0	0	30.1	28	4	18	25	1-1	1	4.45
Larry Gura	L	28	20	2	1	1	62.2	47	4	20	22	4-0	1	2.30
Tom Bruno	R	23	12	0	0	0	17.1	20	3	9	11	1-0	0	6.75
Bob McClure	L	24	8	0	0	0	4.0	3	0	8	3	0-0	0	9.00
Gerald Cram	R	28	4	0	0	0	4.1	8	0	1	2	0-0	0	6.23
Roger Nelson	R	32	3	0	0	0	8.2	4	0	4	4	0-0	0	2.08
Ray Sadecki†	L	35	3	0	0	0	4.2	7	0	3	1	0-0	0	0.00
Ken Sanders†	R	34	3	0	0	0	3.0	3	0	3	2	0-0	0	0.00

1976 Oakland Athletics 2nd AL West 87-74 .540 2.5 GB

Chuck Tanner

Player	Gm by Position	B	Age	G	AB	R	H	2B	3B	HR	RBI	BB	SO	SB	Avg	OBP	Slg
Larry Haney	C87	R	33	88	177	12	40	2	0	0	10	13	26	0	.226	.280	.237
Gene Tenace	1B70,C65,DH2	R	29	128	417	64	104	19	1	22	66	81	91	5	.249	.373	.458
Phil Garner	2B159	R	27	159	555	54	145	29	12	8	74	36	71	35	.261	.307	.400
Sal Bando	3B155,SS5,DH2	R	32	158	550	75	132	18	2	27	84	76	74	20	.240	.335	.427
Bert Campaneris	SS149	R	34	149	536	67	137	14	1	1	52	63	80	54	.256	.331	.291
Bill North	OF144,DH8	S	28	154	590	91	163	20	5	2	31	73	95	75	.276	.356	.337
Joe Rudi	OF126,DH2,1B2	R	29	130	500	54	135	32	3	13	94	41	71	6	.270	.323	.424
C. Washington	OF126,DH6	L	21	134	490	65	126	20	6	5	53	30	90	37	.257	.302	.353
Billy Williams	DH106,OF1	L	38	120	351	36	74	12	0	11	41	58	44	4	.211	.320	.339
Don Baylor	OF76,1B69,DH23	R	27	157	595	85	147	25	1	15	68	58	72	52	.247	.329	.368
Ken McMullen	3B35,1B26,DH23*	R	34	98	186	20	41	6	2	5	23	22	33	1	.220	.305	.355
Jeff Newman	C43	R	27	43	77	5	15	4	0	0	4	4	12	0	.195	.235	.247
Tommy Sandt	SS29,2B9,3B2	R	25	41	67	6	14	1	0	0	3	7	9	0	.209	.284	.224
Tim Hosley†	C37	R	29	37	55	4	9	2	0	1	4	8	12	0	.164	.270	.255
Ron Fairly†	1B15	L	37	15	46	9	11	1	0	3	10	9	12	0	.239	.364	.457
Cesar Tovar†	OF20,DH4	R	35	29	45	1	8	0	0	0	4	4	4	1	.178	.275	.178
Matt Alexander	OF23,DH19	S	29	61	30	16	1	0	0	0	0	0	5	20	.033	.033	.033
Willie McCovey†	DH9	L	38	11	24	0	5	0	0	0	0	3	4	0	.208	.296	.208
Wayne Gross	DH3,1B3,OF2	L	24	10	18	0	4	0	0	0	1	2	1	0	.222	.300	.222
Angel Mangual	OF7	R	29	8	12	0	2	1	0	0	1	0	1	0	.167	.167	.250
Denny Walling	OF3	L	22	3	11	1	3	0	0	0	0	0	3	0	.273	.273	.273
Gary Woods	OF4,DH1	R	21	6	8	0	1	0	0	0	0	0	3	0	.125	.125	.125
Jim Holt	DH2	L	32	4	7	0	2	2	0	0	2	1	2	0	.286	.375	.571
Nate Colbert†	DH2	R	30	2	5	0	0	0	0	0	0	1	3	0	.000	.167	.000
Larry Lintz	DH19,2B5,OF3	S	26	68	1	21	0	0	0	0	0	2	0	31	.000	.667	.000
Don Hopkins	DH2	L	24	3	0	0	0	0	0	0	0	0	0	0	—	—	—

K. McMullen, 5 G at OF, 1 G at 2B

Pitcher	T	Age	G	GS	CG	ShO	IP	H	HR	BB	SO	W-L	Sv	ERA
Mike Torrez	R	29	39	39	13	4	266.1	231	15	87	115	16-12	0	2.50
Vida Blue	L	26	37	37	20	6	298.1	268	9	63	166	18-13	0	2.35
Paul Mitchell	R	26	26	26	4	1	142.0	169	15	30	67	9-7	0	4.25
Mike Norris	R	21	24	19	1	1	96.0	91	10	56	44	4-5	0	4.78
Dick Bosman	R	32	27	15	0	0	112.0	118	13	19	34	4-2	0	4.10
Glenn Abbott	R	25	19	10	0	0	62.1	87	6	16	27	2-4	0	5.49
Chris Batton	R	21	2	1	0	0	4.0	5	1	3	4	0-0	0	9.00
Rollie Fingers	R	29	70	0	0	0	134.2	118	3	40	113	13-11	20	2.47
Paul Lindblad	L	34	65	0	0	0	114.2	111	5	24	37	6-5	5	3.06
Jim Todd	R	28	49	0	0	0	82.2	87	6	34	22	7-8	4	3.81
Stan Bahnsen	R	31	35	14	1	1	143.0	124	13	43	82	8-7	0	3.34
Craig Mitchell	R	22	1	0	0	0	3.1	3	0	0	0	0-0	0	2.70

1976 Minnesota Twins 3rd AL West 85-77 .525 5.0 GB

Gene Mauch

Player	Gm by Position	B	Age	G	AB	R	H	2B	3B	HR	RBI	BB	SO	SB	Avg	OBP	Slg
Butch Wynegar	C137,DH15	S	20	149	534	58	139	21	2	10	69	79	63	0	.260	.356	.363
Rod Carew	1B152,2B7	L	30	156	605	97	200	29	12	9	90	67	52	49	.331	.395	.463
Bob Randall	2B153	R	28	153	475	55	127	18	4	1	34	28	38	3	.267	.317	.328
Mike Cubbage†	3B99,DH2,2B2	L	25	104	342	40	89	19	5	3	49	42	37	1	.260	.344	.371
Roy Smalley†	SS103	S	23	103	384	46	104	16	3	2	36	47	79	0	.271	.353	.344
Larry Hisle	OF154	R	29	155	581	81	158	19	5	14	96	56	93	31	.272	.335	.394
Dan Ford	OF139,DH3	R	24	145	514	87	137	24	7	20	86	36	118	17	.267	.323	.457
Lyman Bostock	OF124	L	25	128	474	75	153	21	9	4	60	33	37	12	.323	.364	.430
Craig Kusick	DH79,1B23	R	27	109	266	33	69	13	0	11	36	35	44	5	.259	.344	.432
Steve Braun	DH71,OF32,3B16	L	28	122	417	73	120	12	3	3	61	67	43	12	.288	.384	.353
Steve Brye	OF78,DH3	R	27	87	258	33	68	11	0	2	23	13	31	1	.264	.295	.329
Jerry Terrell	2B31,3B26,SS16*	R	29	89	171	29	42	3	1	0	8	9	15	11	.246	.286	.275
Dave McKay	3B41,SS2,DH1	S	26	45	138	8	28	2	0	0	8	9	27	1	.203	.272	.217
Danny Thompson†	SS34	R	29	34	124	9	29	4	0	0	6	3	8	1	.234	.256	.266
Tony Oliva	DH32	L	35	67	123	3	26	3	0	1	16	2	13	0	.211	.234	.260
Glenn Borgmann	C24	R	26	24	65	10	16	3	0	1	6	19	7	1	.246	.417	.338
Luis Gomez	SS24,2B8,3B4*	R	24	38	57	5	11	1	0	0	3	3	3	1	.193	.233	.211
Phil Roof†	C12	R	35	18	46	1	10	3	0	0	4	2	6	0	.217	.250	.283

J. Terrell, 12 G at DH, 6 G at OF; L. Gomez, 1 G at DH, 1 G at OF

Pitcher	T	Age	G	GS	CG	ShO	IP	H	HR	BB	SO	W-L	Sv	ERA
Dave Goltz	R	27	36	35	13	4	249.1	239	14	91	133	14-14	0	3.36
Jim Hughes	R	24	37	26	3	0	177.0	190	17	73	87	9-14	0	4.98
Bill Singer†	R	32	26	26	5	3	172.0	177	9	69	63	9-9	0	3.77
Pete Redfern	R	21	23	23	1	1	118.0	105	6	63	74	8-8	0	3.51
Eddie Bane	L	24	17	15	1	0	79.1	92	6	39	24	4-7	0	5.11
Bert Blyleven†	R	25	12	12	4	0	95.1	101	3	35	75	4-5	0	3.12
Joe Decker	R	29	13	12	0	0	58.0	60	3	51	35	2-7	0	5.28
Bill Campbell	R	27	78	0	0	0	167.2	145	9	62	115	17-5	20	3.01
Tom Burgmeier	L	32	57	0	0	0	115.1	95	11	29	45	8-1	1	2.50
Steve Luebber	R	26	38	12	2	1	119.1	109	9	62	45	4-5	2	4.00
Vic Albury	L	29	23	0	0	0	50.1	51	0	24	23	3-1	0	3.58
Tom Johnson	R	25	18	1	0	0	48.1	44	2	8	37	3-1	0	2.61
Mike Pazik	L	26	5	0	0	0	9.0	13	0	4	6	0-0	0	7.00

1976 California Angels 4th AL West 76-86 .469 14.0 GB

Dick Williams (39-57)/Norm Sherry (37-29)

Player	Gm by Position	B	Age	G	AB	R	H	2B	3B	HR	RBI	BB	SO	SB	Avg	OBP	Slg
Andy Etchebarren	C102	R	33	103	247	15	56	9	1	0	21	24	37	0	.227	.305	.271
Bruce Bochte	OF86,1B59,DH1	L	25	146	466	53	120	17	1	2	49	64	53	4	.258	.346	.311
Jerry Remy	2B133,DH5	L	23	143	502	64	132	14	3	0	28	38	43	35	.263	.313	.303
Ron Jackson	3B114,2B7,DH6*	R	23	127	410	44	93	18	3	8	40	30	58	5	.227	.289	.344
Dave Chalk	SS102,3B49	R	25	142	438	39	95	14	1	0	33	49	62	0	.217	.308	.253
Rusty Torres	OF105,DH6,3B1	S	27	120	264	37	54	16	3	6	27	36	39	4	.205	.299	.356
Bobby Bonds	OF98,DH1	R	30	99	378	48	100	10	3	10	54	41	90	30	.265	.337	.386
Lee Stanton	OF79,DH4	R	30	93	231	12	44	13	1	2	25	24	57	2	.190	.266	.281
Tommy Davis†	DH54,1B1	R	37	72	219	16	58	5	0	3	26	15	18	0	.265	.312	.329
Dave Collins	OF71,DH22	S	23	99	365	45	96	12	1	4	28	40	55	32	.263	.335	.334
Bill Melton	DH51,1B30,3B21	R	30	118	341	31	71	17	3	6	42	44	53	2	.208	.300	.328
Mario Guerrero	2B41,SS41,DH7	R	26	83	268	24	76	12	0	1	18	7	12	0	.284	.304	.340
Dan Briggs	1B44,OF40,DH1	L	23	77	248	19	53	13	2	1	14	13	47	0	.214	.254	.294
Tony Solaita†	1B54,DH7	L	29	63	215	25	58	9	0	9	33	34	44	1	.270	.367	.437
Terry Humphrey	C71	R	26	71	196	17	48	10	0	1	19	13	30	0	.245	.306	.311
Bobby Jones	OF62,DH2	L	26	78	166	22	35	6	0	6	17	14	30	3	.211	.273	.355
Joe Lahoud†	OF26,DH3	L	29	42	96	8	17	4	0	0	4	18	16	0	.177	.319	.219
Orlando Ramirez	SS30	R	24	30	70	3	14	1	0	0	5	6	11	3	.200	.263	.214
Mike Easler	DH16	L	25	21	54	6	13	1	1	0	4	2	11	1	.241	.259	.296
Adrian Garrett	C15,DH4,1B1	L	33	29	48	4	6	3	0	0	3	5	16	0	.125	.204	.188
Ed Herrmann†	C27	L	29	29	46	5	8	3	0	2	8	7	8	0	.174	.278	.370
Orlando Alvarez	OF11,DH2	R	24	15	42	4	7	1	0	2	8	0	3	0	.167	.167	.333
Mike Miley	SS14	S	23	14	38	4	7	2	0	0	4	4	8	1	.184	.256	.237
Carlos Lopez	OF4,DH1	R	25	9	10	1	0	0	0	0	0	2	3	2	.000	.167	.000
Paul Dade	OF4,2B2,DH1*	R	24	13	9	2	1	0	0	0	1	3	3	0	.111	.333	.111
Billy Smith	SS10,DH1	S	22	13	8	0	3	0	0	0	0	0	2	0	.375	.375	.375
Tim Nordbrook†	SS4,DH1,2B1	R	26	5	8	1	0	0	0	0	0	1	3	1	.000	.111	.000
Ike Hampton	C2,DH1,SS1	S	24	3	2	0	0	0	0	0	0	0	0	0	.000	.000	.000

R. Jackson, 4 G at OF; P. Dade, 1 G at 3B

Pitcher	T	Age	G	GS	CG	ShO	IP	H	HR	BB	SO	W-L	Sv	ERA
Nolan Ryan	R	29	39	39	21	7	284.1	193	13	183	327	17-18	0	3.36
Frank Tanana	L	22	34	34	23	2	288.1	212	24	73	261	19-10	0	2.43
Gary Ross	R	28	34	31	7	2	225.0	224	12	58	100	8-16	0	3.00
Don Kirkwood	R	26	28	26	4	0	157.2	167	12	57	78	6-12	0	4.62
Dick Drago	R	31	43	0	0	0	79.1	80	7	31	43	7-8	6	4.42
Paul Hartzell	R	22	37	15	7	2	166.0	166	6	43	51	7-4	2	2.77
Mickey Scott	L	28	33	0	0	0	39.0	47	3	12	10	3-0	3	3.23
Sid Monge	L	25	32	13	2	0	117.2	108	10	49	53	6-7	0	3.37
John Verhoeven	R	22	21	0	0	0	37.1	35	2	14	23	0-2	4	3.38
Andy Hassler†	L	24	14	4	0	0	47.1	50	3	17	16	0-6	0	5.13
Jim Brewer	L	38	13	0	0	0	20.0	20	0	6	16	3-1	2	2.70
Mike Overy	R	25	5	0	0	0	7.1	6	1	3	8	0-2	0	6.14
Steve Dunning†	R	27	4	0	0	0	6.0	9	2	6	4	0-0	0	7.50
Gary Wheelock	R	24	2	0	0	0	2.0	6	0	1	2	0-0	0	27.00

1976 Texas Rangers 4th AL West 76-86 .469 14.0 GB

Frank Lucchesi

Player	Gm by Position	B	Age	G	AB	R	H	2B	3B	HR	RBI	BB	SO	SB	Avg	OBP	Slg
Jim Sundberg	C140	R	25	140	448	33	102	24	2	3	34	37	61	0	.228	.285	.310
Mike Hargrove	1B141,DH5	L	26	151	541	80	155	30	1	7	58	97	64	2	.287	.397	.384
Lenny Randle	2B113,OF30,3B2*	S	27	142	539	53	121	11	6	1	51	46	63	30	.224	.286	.273
Roy Howell	3B130,DH8	L	22	140	491	55	124	28	2	8	53	30	106	1	.253	.295	.367
Toby Harrah	SS146,3B5,DH4	R	27	155	584	64	152	21	1	15	67	91	59	8	.260	.360	.377
Jeff Burroughs	OF155,DH3	R	25	158	604	71	143	22	2	18	86	69	93	0	.237	.315	.369
Juan Beniquez	OF141,2B1	R	26	145	478	49	122	14	4	0	33	39	56	17	.255	.315	.301
Gene Clines	OF103,DH10	R	29	116	446	52	123	12	3	0	38	16	52	11	.276	.304	.316
Tom Grieve	DH96,OF52	R	28	149	546	57	139	23	3	20	81	35	119	4	.255	.301	.418
Danny Thompson†	3B39,2B14,SS10	R	29	64	196	12	42	3	0	1	13	13	19	2	.214	.264	.245
Dave Moates	OF66,DH7	L	28	85	137	21	33	7	1	0	13	11	18	6	.241	.293	.307
Jim Fregosi	1B26,DH18,3B5	R	34	58	133	17	31	7	0	2	12	23	33	2	.233	.342	.331
Roy Smalley†	2B38,SS5	S	23	41	129	15	29	2	0	1	8	29	27	2	.225	.363	.264
Joe Lahoud†	DH22,OF5	L	29	38	89	10	20	3	1	1	5	10	16	1	.225	.303	.315
Bill Fahey	C38	L	26	38	80	12	20	2	0	1	9	11	6	1	.250	.348	.313
Mike Cubbage†	DH6,2B5,3B1	L	25	14	32	2	7	0	0	0	0	7	7	0	.219	.359	.219
John Ellis	C7,DH3	R	27	11	31	4	13	2	0	1	8	0	4	0	.419	.419	.581
Ken Pape	SS6,3B4,DH3*	R	24	21	23	7	5	1	0	1	4	3	2	0	.217	.357	.391
Doug Ault	1B4,DH3	R	26	9	20	0	6	1	0	0	1	0	3	0	.300	.333	.350
Greg Pryor	2B3,3B1,SS1	R	26	5	8	2	3	0	0	0	1	0	1	0	.375	.375	.375

L. Randle, 1 G at DH; K. Pape, 1 G at 2B

Pitcher	T	Age	G	GS	CG	ShO	IP	H	HR	BB	SO	W-L	Sv	ERA
Gaylord Perry	R	37	32	32	21	2	250.1	232	14	52	143	15-14	0	3.24
Nelson Briles	R	32	32	31	7	1	210.0	224	17	47	98	11-9	1	3.26
Jim Umbarger	L	23	30	30	10	3	197.1	208	12	54	105	10-12	0	3.15
Bert Blyleven†	R	25	24	24	14	6	202.1	182	11	46	144	9-11	0	2.76
Tommy Boggs	R	20	13	13	3	0	90.1	87	7	34	36	1-7	0	3.49
Steve Barr	L	24	20	10	3	0	67.2	70	10	44	27	2-6	0	5.59
Bill Singer†	R	32	10	10	2	1	64.2	56	4	27	34	4-1	0	3.48
Len Barker	R	20	2	2	1	1	15.0	7	0	6	7	1-0	0	2.40
Fritz Peterson†	L	34	4	2	0	0	15.0	21	0	7	4	1-0	0	3.60
Steve Foucault	R	26	46	0	0	0	75.2	68	9	25	41	8-8	5	3.33
Joe Hoerner	L	39	41	0	0	0	35.0	41	3	19	15	0-4	8	5.14
Steve Hargan	R	33	35	8	2	1	124.1	127	8	38	63	8-8	1	3.62
Jeff Terpko	R	25	32	0	0	0	52.2	42	3	29	24	3-3	0	2.39
Mike Bacsik	R	24	23	0	0	0	55.0	66	3	26	21	3-2	0	4.25
Craig Skok	L	28	9	0	0	0	5.0	13	2	3	5	0-1	0	12.60
Stan Perzanowski	R	25	5	0	0	0	11.2	20	3	4	6	0-0	0	10.03

1976 Chicago White Sox 6th AL West 64-97 .398 25.5 GB

Paul Richards

Player	Gm by Position	B	Age	G	AB	R	H	2B	3B	HR	RBI	BB	SO	SB	Avg	OBP	Slg
Brian Downing	C93,DH11	R	25	104	317	38	81	14	0	3	30	40	55	7	.256	.338	.328
Jim Spencer	1B143,DH2	L	29	150	518	53	131	13	2	14	70	49	52	6	.253	.315	.367
Jack Brohamer	2B117,3B1	L	26	119	354	33	89	12	2	7	40	44	28	1	.251	.333	.356
Kevin Bell	3B67,DH1	R	20	68	230	24	57	7	6	5	20	18	56	2	.248	.302	.396
Bucky Dent	SS158	R	24	158	562	44	138	18	4	2	52	43	45	3	.246	.300	.302
Chet Lemon	OF131	R	21	132	451	46	111	15	5	4	38	28	65	13	.246	.298	.328
Ralph Garr	OF125	L	30	136	527	63	158	22	6	4	36	17	41	14	.300	.322	.387
Jorge Orta	OF77,3B49,DH31	L	25	158	636	74	174	29	8	14	72	38	77	24	.274	.316	.410
Pat Kelly	DH63,OF26	L	31	107	311	42	79	20	3	5	34	45	45	15	.254	.349	.386
Bill Stein	2B58,3B58,DH1*	R	29	117	392	32	105	15	2	4	36	22	67	4	.268	.310	.347
Lamar Johnson	DH35,1B34,OF1	R	25	82	222	29	71	11	1	4	33	19	37	2	.320	.372	.432
Jim Essian	C77,1B2,3B1	R	25	78	199	20	49	7	0	0	21	23	28	2	.246	.326	.281
Buddy Bradford	OF48,DH3	R	31	55	160	20	35	5	2	4	14	19	37	6	.219	.309	.350
Alan Bannister	OF43,SS14,DH4*	R	24	73	145	19	36	6	2	0	8	14	21	12	.248	.317	.317
Jerry Hairston	OF40	S	24	44	119	20	27	2	2	0	10	24	19	1	.227	.352	.277
Rich Coggins†	OF26	L	25	32	96	4	15	2	0	0	5	6	15	3	.156	.206	.177
Carlos May†	DH10,OF9	L	28	20	63	7	11	2	0	0	3	9	5	4	.175	.278	.206
Wayne Nordhagen	OF10,DH6,C5	R	27	22	53	6	10	2	0	0	5	4	12	0	.189	.233	.226
Sam Ewing	DH12,1B1	L	27	19	41	3	9	2	1	0	2	2	8	0	.220	.256	.317
Pete Varney†	C14	R	27	14	41	5	10	2	0	3	5	2	9	0	.244	.279	.512
Cleon Jones	OF8,DH3	R	33	12	40	2	8	1	0	0	3	5	5	0	.200	.304	.225
Nyls Nyman	OF7	L	22	8	15	2	2	1	0	0	1	0	3	1	.133	.133	.200
Hugh Yancy	2B3	R	25	3	10	0	1	1	0	0	0	0	3	0	.100	.100	.200
Phil Roof†	C4,DH1	R	35	4	9	0	1	0	0	0	0	0	3	0	.111	.111	.111
Minnie Minoso	DH3	R	53	3	8	0	1	0	0	0	0	0	2	0	.125	.125	.125
George Enright	C2	R	22	2	1	0	0	0	0	0	0	0	0	0	.000	.000	.000

B. Stein, 1 G at 1B, 1 G at SS, 1 G at OF; A. Bannister, 4 G at 2B, 1 G at 3B

Pitcher	T	Age	G	GS	CG	ShO	IP	H	HR	BB	SO	W-L	Sv	ERA
Bart Johnson	R	26	32	32	8	3	211.1	231	20	62	91	9-16	0	4.73
Goose Gossage	R	24	31	29	15	0	224.0	214	16	90	135	9-17	1	3.94
Ken Brett†	L	27	27	26	16	1	200.2	171	5	76	91	10-12	1	3.32
Terry Forster	L	24	29	16	1	0	111.1	126	7	41	70	2-12	1	4.37
Ken Kravec	L	24	9	8	1	0	49.2	49	3	32	38	1-5	0	4.89
Wilbur Wood	L	34	7	7	5	1	56.1	51	3	11	31	4-3	0	2.24
Chris Knapp	R	22	11	6	1	0	52.1	54	5	32	41	3-1	0	4.82
Blue Moon Odom	R	31	8	4	0	0	28.0	31	2	20	18	2-2	0	5.79
Dave Hamilton	L	28	45	1	0	0	90.1	81	4	45	62	6-6	10	3.59
Francisco Barrios	R	23	35	14	6	0	141.2	136	13	46	81	5-9	3	4.32
Pete Vuckovich	R	23	33	7	1	0	110.1	122	3	60	62	7-4	0	4.65
Clay Carroll	R	35	29	0	0	0	77.1	67	1	24	38	4-4	6	2.56
Jesse Jefferson	R	27	19	9	0	0	62.1	86	3	42	30	2-5	0	8.52
Larry Monroe	R	20	8	2	0	0	21.2	23	0	13	9	0-1	0	4.15
Jim Otten	R	24	2	0	0	0	6.0	9	0	2	3	0-0	0	4.50
Jack Kucek	R	23	2	0	0	0	4.2	9	2	4	2	0-0	0	9.64

»1976 Philadelphia Phillies 1st NL East 101-61 .623 —

Danny Ozark

Player	Gm by Position	B	Age	G	AB	R	H	2B	3B	HR	RBI	BB	SO	SB	Avg	OBP	Slg
Bob Boone	C108,1B4	R	28	121	361	40	98	18	2	4	54	45	44	2	.271	.348	.366
Dick Allen	1B85	R	34	85	298	52	80	16	1	15	49	37	63	11	.268	.346	.480
Dave Cash	2B158	R	28	160	666	92	189	14	12	1	56	54	13	10	.284	.337	.345
Mike Schmidt	3B160	R	26	160	584	112	153	31	4	38	107	100	149	14	.262	.376	.524
Larry Bowa	SS156	S	30	156	624	71	155	15	9	0	49	32	31	30	.248	.283	.301
Greg Luzinski	OF144	R	25	149	533	74	162	28	1	21	95	50	107	1	.304	.369	.478
Garry Maddox	OF144	R	26	146	531	75	175	37	6	6	68	42	59	29	.330	.377	.456
Jay Johnstone	OF122,1B6	L	30	129	440	62	140	38	4	5	53	41	39	5	.318	.373	.457
Bobby Tolan	1B50,OF35	L	30	110	272	32	71	7	0	5	35	7	39	10	.261	.285	.342
Ollie Brown	OF75	R	32	92	209	30	53	10	1	5	30	33	33	2	.254	.350	.383
Tim McCarver	C41,1B2	L	34	90	155	26	43	11	2	3	29	35	14	2	.277	.409	.432
Tom Hutton	1B72,OF1	L	30	95	124	15	25	5	1	1	13	27	11	1	.202	.342	.282
Jerry Martin	OF110,1B1	R	27	130	121	30	30	7	0	2	15	7	28	3	.248	.287	.355
Johnny Oates	C35	L	30	37	99	10	25	2	0	0	8	8	12	0	.253	.308	.273
Terry Harmon	SS19,2B13,3B5	R	32	42	61	12	18	4	1	0	6	3	10	3	.295	.328	.393
Tony Taylor	2B2,3B1	R	40	26	23	2	6	1	0	0	3	1	7	0	.261	.320	.304
Rick Bosetti	OF6	R	22	13	18	6	5	1	0	0	0	1	3	3	.278	.316	.333
Tim Blackwell	C4	S	23	4	8	0	2	0	0	0	1	0	1	0	.250	.250	.250
John Vukovich	3B4,1B1	R	28	4	8	2	1	0	0	1	2	0	2	0	.125	.125	.500
Fred Andrews	2B4	R	24	4	6	1	4	0	0	0	0	2	0	1	.667	.778	.667
Bill Nahorodny	C2	R	22	3	5	0	1	1	0	0	0	0	0	0	.200	.200	.400

Pitcher	T	Age	G	GS	CG	ShO	IP	H	HR	BB	SO	W-L	Sv	ERA
Steve Carlton	L	31	35	35	13	2	252.2	224	19	72	195	20-7	0	3.13
Jim Kaat	L	37	38	35	7	1	227.2	241	21	32	83	12-14	0	3.48
Jim Lonborg	R	34	33	32	8	1	222.0	210	18	50	118	18-10	1	3.08
Larry Christenson	R	22	32	29	2	0	168.2	199	8	42	54	13-8	0	3.68
Tom Underwood	L	22	33	25	3	0	155.2	154	9	63	94	10-5	2	3.53
Ron Reed	R	33	59	4	1	0	128.0	88	8	32	96	8-7	14	2.46
Gene Garber	R	28	59	0	0	0	92.2	78	4	30	92	9-3	11	2.82
Tug McGraw	L	31	58	0	0	0	97.1	81	4	42	76	7-6	11	2.50
Ron Schueler	R	28	35	0	0	0	49.2	44	4	16	43	1-0	3	2.90
Wayne Twitchell	R	28	26	2	0	0	61.2	55	3	18	67	3-1	1	1.75
Randy Lerch	L	21	1	0	0	0	3.0	3	0	0	0	0-0	1	3.00

1976 Pittsburgh Pirates 2nd NL East 92-70 .568 9.0 GB

Danny Murtaugh

Player	Gm by Position	B	Age	G	AB	R	H	2B	3B	HR	RBI	BB	SO	SB	Avg	OBP	Slg
Manny Sanguillen	C111	R	32	114	389	52	113	16	6	2	36	28	18	2	.290	.338	.378
Willie Stargell	1B111	L	36	117	428	54	110	20	3	20	65	50	101	2	.257	.339	.458
Rennie Stennett	2B157,SS4	R	25	157	654	59	168	31	9	2	60	19	32	18	.257	.277	.341
Richie Hebner	3B126	L	28	132	434	60	108	21	3	8	51	47	39	1	.249	.325	.366
Frank Taveras	SS141	R	26	144	519	76	134	8	6	0	24	44	79	58	.258	.321	.297
Richie Zisk	OF152	R	27	155	581	91	168	35	2	21	89	52	96	1	.289	.343	.465
Dave Parker	OF134	L	25	138	537	82	168	28	10	13	90	30	80	19	.313	.349	.475
Al Oliver	OF106,1B3	L	29	121	443	62	143	22	5	12	61	26	29	6	.323	.363	.476
Bill Robinson	OF78,3B37,1B3	R	33	122	393	55	119	22	3	21	64	16	73	2	.303	.329	.534
Duffy Dyer	C58	R	30	69	184	12	41	8	0	3	9	29	35	0	.223	.336	.315
Ed Kirkpatrick	1B25,OF9,3B1	L	31	83	146	14	34	9	0	0	16	14	15	1	.233	.294	.295
Bob Robertson	1B29	R	29	61	129	10	28	5	1	2	25	16	23	0	.217	.299	.318
Omar Moreno	OF42	L	23	48	122	24	33	4	1	2	12	16	24	15	.270	.357	.369
Mario Mendoza	SS45,3B2,2B1	R	25	50	92	6	17	5	0	0	12	4	15	0	.185	.216	.239
Tommy Helms	3B22,2B11,SS1	R	35	62	87	10	24	5	1	1	13	10	5	0	.276	.350	.391
Ed Ott	C8	L	24	27	39	2	12	2	0	0	5	3	5	0	.308	.349	.359
Miguel Dilone	OF3	S	21	16	17	7	4	0	0	0	0	0	0	5	.235	.235	.235
Tony Armas	OF2	R	22	4	6	0	2	0	0	0	1	0	2	0	.333	.333	.333
Craig Reynolds	SS4,2B1	L	23	7	4	1	1	0	0	1	1	0	0	0	.250	.250	1.000

Pitcher	T	Age	G	GS	CG	ShO	IP	H	HR	BB	SO	W-L	Sv	ERA
John Candelaria	L	22	32	31	11	4	220.0	173	22	60	138	16-7	1	3.15
Jerry Reuss	L	27	31	29	11	3	209.1	209	16	51	108	14-9	2	3.53
Jim Rooker	L	33	30	29	10	1	198.2	201	12	72	92	15-8	1	3.35
Bruce Kison	R	26	31	29	6	1	193.0	180	10	52	98	14-9	1	3.08
Doc Medich	R	27	29	26	3	0	179.0	193	10	48	86	8-11	0	3.52
Kent Tekulve	R	29	64	0	0	0	102.2	91	3	25	68	5-3	9	2.45
Bob Moose	R	28	53	2	0	0	88.0	100	4	32	38	3-9	10	3.68
Dave Giusti	R	36	40	0	0	0	58.1	59	5	27	24	5-4	6	4.32
Ramon Hernandez†	L	35	37	0	0	0	43.0	42	3	16	17	2-2	3	3.56
Larry Demery	R	23	36	15	4	1	145.0	123	8	58	72	10-7	2	3.17
Rick Langford	R	24	12	1	0	0	23.0	27	2	14	17	0-1	0	6.26
Doug Bair	R	26	4	0	0	0	6.1	4	0	5	4	0-0	0	5.68

1976 New York Mets 3rd NL East 86-76 .531 15.0 GB

Joe Frazier

Player	Gm by Position	B	Age	G	AB	R	H	2B	3B	HR	RBI	BB	SO	SB	Avg	OBP	Slg
Jerry Grote	C95,OF2	R	33	101	323	30	88	14	2	4	28	38	19	1	.272	.350	.365
Ed Kranepool	1B86,OF31	L	31	123	415	47	121	17	1	10	49	35	38	1	.292	.344	.410
Felix Millan	2B136	R	32	139	531	55	150	25	2	1	35	41	19	2	.282	.341	.343
Roy Staiger	3B93,SS1	R	26	95	304	23	67	8	1	2	26	25	35	3	.220	.278	.273
Bud Harrelson	SS117	S	32	118	359	34	84	12	4	1	26	63	56	9	.234	.351	.298
John Milner	OF112,1B12	L	26	127	443	56	120	25	4	15	78	65	53	0	.271	.362	.447
Dave Kingman	OF111,1B16	R	27	123	474	70	113	14	1	37	86	28	135	7	.238	.286	.506
Bruce Boisclair	OF87	L	23	110	286	42	82	13	3	2	13	28	55	9	.287	.350	.374
Joe Torre	1B78,3B4	R	35	114	310	36	95	10	3	5	31	21	35	1	.306	.358	.406
Del Unser†	OF77	L	31	77	276	28	63	13	2	5	25	18	40	4	.228	.275	.344
Mike Phillips	SS53,2B19,3B10	L	25	87	262	30	67	4	6	4	29	25	29	2	.256	.315	.363
Wayne Garrett†	3B64,2B10,SS1	L	28	80	251	36	56	8	1	4	26	52	26	7	.223	.359	.311
Ron Hodges	C52	L	27	56	155	21	35	6	0	4	24	27	16	2	.226	.339	.342
Mike Vail	OF35	R	24	53	143	8	31	5	1	0	9	6	19	0	.217	.243	.266
John Stearns	C30	R	24	32	103	13	27	6	0	2	10	16	11	1	.262	.364	.379
Pepe Mangual†	OF38	R	24	41	102	15	19	5	2	1	9	10	32	7	.186	.259	.304
Lee Mazzilli	OF23	S	21	24	77	9	15	2	0	2	7	14	10	5	.195	.323	.299
Leon Brown	OF43	R	26	64	70	11	15	3	0	0	2	4	4	2	.214	.257	.257
Leo Foster	3B9,SS7,2B3	R	25	24	59	11	12	2	0	1	15	8	5	3	.203	.299	.288
Bennie Ayala	OF7	R	25	22	26	2	3	0	0	1	2	2	6	0	.115	.179	.231
Billy Baldwin	OF5	L	25	9	22	4	6	1	1	1	5	1	2	0	.273	.292	.545
Jim Dwyer†	OF2	L	26	11	13	2	2	0	0	0	0	2	1	0	.154	.267	.154
Jack Heidemann†	SS3,2B1	R	26	5	12	0	1	0	0	0	0	0	0	0	.083	.083	.083
Jay Kleven	C2	R	26	2	5	0	1	0	0	0	2	0	1	0	.200	.200	.200

Pitcher	T	Age	G	GS	CG	ShO	IP	H	HR	BB	SO	W-L	Sv	ERA
Jon Matlack	L	26	35	35	16	6	262.0	236	18	57	153	17-10	0	2.95
Tom Seaver	R	31	35	34	13	5	271.0	211	14	77	235	14-11	0	2.59
Jerry Koosman	L	33	34	32	17	3	247.1	205	19	66	200	21-10	0	2.69
Mickey Lolich	L	35	31	30	5	2	192.2	184	14	52	120	8-13	0	3.22
Craig Swan	R	25	23	22	2	1	132.1	129	11	44	89	6-9	0	3.54
Skip Lockwood	R	29	56	0	0	0	94.1	62	6	34	108	10-7	19	2.67
Bob Apodaca	R	26	43	3	0	0	89.2	71	4	29	45	3-7	5	2.81
Ken Sanders†	R	34	31	0	0	0	47.0	39	4	12	16	1-2	1	2.87
Bob Myrick	L	23	21	1	0	0	27.2	34	2	13	11	1-1	0	3.25
Nino Espinosa	R	22	12	5	0	0	41.2	41	3	13	30	4-4	0	3.67
Rick Baldwin	R	23	11	0	0	0	22.2	14	0	10	9	0-0	0	2.38
Hank Webb	R	26	8	0	0	0	16.0	17	2	7	7	0-1	0	4.50
Tom Hall†	L	28	5	0	0	0	4.2	5	0	5	2	1-1	0	5.79

1976 Chicago Cubs 4th NL East 75-87 .463 26.0 GB

Jim Marshall

Player	Gm by Position	B	Age	G	AB	R	H	2B	3B	HR	RBI	BB	SO	SB	Avg	OBP	Slg
Steve Swisher	C107	R	24	109	377	25	89	13	3	5	42	20	82	2	.236	.275	.326
Pete LaCock	1B54,OF19	L	24	106	244	34	54	9	2	8	28	42	37	1	.221	.337	.373
Manny Trillo	2B156,SS1	R	25	158	582	42	139	24	3	4	59	53	70	17	.239	.304	.311
Bill Madlock	3B136	R	25	142	514	68	174	36	1	15	84	56	27	15	.339	.412	.500
Mick Kelleher	SS101,3B22,2B5	R	28	124	337	28	77	12	1	0	22	15	32	0	.228	.264	.270
Jerry Morales	OF136	R	27	140	537	66	147	17	0	16	67	41	49	3	.274	.323	.395
Jose Cardenal	OF128	R	32	136	521	64	156	25	2	8	47	32	39	23	.299	.339	.401
Rick Monday	OF103,1B32	L	30	137	534	107	145	20	5	32	77	60	125	5	.272	.346	.507
Joe Wallis	OF90	S	24	121	338	51	86	11	5	5	21	33	62	3	.254	.322	.361
George Mitterwald	C64,1B25	R	31	101	303	19	65	7	0	5	28	16	63	1	.215	.249	.287
Dave Rosello	SS86,2B1	R	26	91	227	27	55	5	1	1	11	41	33	1	.242	.359	.286
Larry Biittner†	1B33,OF24	L	30	78	192	21	47	13	1	0	17	10	6	0	.245	.286	.323
Champ Summers	OF26,1B10,C1	L	30	83	126	11	26	2	0	3	13	13	31	1	.206	.284	.294
Rob Sperring	3B20,SS15,2B4*	R	26	43	93	8	24	3	0	0	7	9	25	0	.258	.320	.290
Andre Thornton†	1B25	R	26	27	85	8	17	6	0	2	14	20	14	2	.200	.361	.341
Wayne Tyrone	OF7,1B5,3B5	R	25	30	57	3	13	1	0	1	8	3	21	0	.228	.262	.298
Mike Adams	OF4,3B3,2B1	R	27	25	29	1	4	2	0	0	2	8	7	0	.138	.342	.207
Jerry Tabb	1B6	L	24	11	24	2	7	0	0	0	0	3	2	0	.292	.370	.292
Randy Hundley	C9	R	34	13	18	3	3	2	0	0	1	1	4	0	.167	.200	.278
Ed Putman	C3,1B1	R	22	5	7	0	3	0	0	0	0	0	0	0	.429	.429	.429
Tim Hosley†		R	29	1	1	0	0	0	0	0	0	0	0	0	.000	.000	.000

R. Sperring, 3 G at OF

Pitcher	T	Age	G	GS	CG	ShO	IP	H	HR	BB	SO	W-L	Sv	ERA
Rick Reuschel	R	27	38	37	9	2	260.0	260	17	64	146	14-12	1	3.46
Ray Burris	R	25	37	36	10	4	249.0	251	22	70	112	15-13	0	3.11
Bill Bonham	R	27	32	31	3	0	196.0	215	11	96	110	9-13	0	4.27
Steve Renko†	R	31	28	27	4	1	163.1	164	12	43	112	8-11	0	3.86
Steve Stone	R	28	17	15	1	1	75.0	70	6	21	33	3-6	0	4.08
Ken Frailing	L	28	6	3	0	0	18.2	20	0	5	10	1-2	0	2.41
Geoff Zahn	L	30	3	2	0	0	8.1	16	0	2	4	0-1	0	10.80
Darold Knowles	L	34	58	0	0	0	71.2	61	6	22	39	5-7	9	2.89
Bruce Sutter	R	23	52	0	0	0	83.1	63	4	26	73	6-3	10	2.70
Paul Reuschel	R	29	50	2	0	0	87.0	94	12	33	55	4-2	3	4.55
Mike Garman	R	26	47	2	0	0	76.1	79	7	35	37	2-4	1	4.95
Oscar Zamora	R	31	40	2	0	0	55.0	70	8	17	27	5-3	3	5.24
Joe Coleman†	R	29	39	4	0	0	79.0	72	9	35	66	2-8	4	4.10
Buddy Schultz	L	25	29	0	0	0	23.2	37	3	9	15	1-1	2	6.08
Ken Crosby	R	28	7	1	0	0	12.0	20	3	8	5	0-0	0	12.00
Tom Dettore	R	28	4	0	0	0	7.0	11	3	2	4	0-1	0	10.29
Mike Krukow	R	24	2	0	0	0	4.1	6	0	2	1	0-0	0	8.31
Ramon Hernandez†	L	35	2	0	0	0	1.2	2	0	0	1	0-0	0	0.00

1976 St. Louis Cardinals 5th NL East 72-90 .444 29.0 GB

Red Schoendienst

Player	Gm by Position	B	Age	G	AB	R	H	2B	3B	HR	RBI	BB	SO	SB	Avg	OBP	Slg
Ted Simmons	C113,1B30,OF7*	S	26	150	546	60	159	35	3	5	75	73	35	0	.291	.371	.394
Keith Hernandez	1B110	L	22	129	374	54	108	21	5	7	46	49	53	4	.289	.376	.428
Mike Tyson	2B74	R	26	76	245	26	70	12	9	3	28	16	34	3	.286	.326	.445
Heity Cruz	3B148	R	23	151	526	54	120	17	1	13	71	42	119	1	.228	.286	.338
Don Kessinger	SS113,2B31,3B2	S	33	145	502	55	120	22	6	1	40	61	51	3	.239	.320	.313
Lou Brock	OF123	L	37	133	498	73	150	24	5	4	67	35	75	56	.301	.344	.394
Willie Crawford	OF107	L	29	120	392	49	119	17	5	9	50	37	53	2	.304	.360	.441
Jerry Mumphrey	OF94	S	23	112	384	51	99	15	5	1	26	37	53	22	.258	.322	.331
Bake McBride	OF66	L	27	72	272	40	91	13	4	3	24	18	28	10	.335	.386	.445
Vic Harris	2B37,OF35,3B12*	S	26	97	259	21	59	12	3	1	19	16	55	1	.228	.275	.309
Garry Templeton	SS53	S	20	53	213	32	62	8	2	1	17	7	33	11	.291	.314	.362
Mike Anderson	OF58,1B5	R	25	86	199	17	58	8	1	1	12	26	30	1	.291	.371	.357
Joe Ferguson†	C48,OF14	R	29	71	189	22	38	8	4	4	21	32	40	4	.201	.317	.349
Reggie Smith†	1B17,OF16,3B13	S	31	47	170	20	37	7	1	8	23	14	28	1	.218	.281	.412
Ron Fairly†	1B27	L	37	73	110	13	29	4	0	0	21	23	12	0	.264	.385	.300
Lee Richard	2B26,SS12,3B1	R	27	66	91	12	16	4	2	0	5	4	9	1	.176	.211	.264
Ken Rudolph	C14	R	29	27	50	1	8	3	0	0	5	1	7	0	.160	.176	.220
Luis Alvarado	2B16	R	27	16	42	5	12	1	0	0	3	3	6	0	.286	.333	.310
Luis Melendez†	OF8	R	26	20	24	0	3	0	0	0	0	0	3	0	.125	.125	.125
Sam Mejias	OF17	R	24	18	21	1	3	1	0	0	0	2	2	2	.143	.217	.190
Mike Potter	OF4	R	25	9	16	0	0	0	0	0	0	1	6	0	.000	.059	.000
Charlie Chant	OF14	R	24	15	14	0	2	0	0	0	0	0	4	0	.143	.143	.143
John Tamargo	C1	S	24	10	10	2	3	0	0	0	1	3	0	0	.300	.429	.300
Doug Clarey	2B7	R	22	9	4	2	1	0	0	1	2	0	1	0	.250	.250	1.000

T. Simmons, 2 G at 3B; V. Harris, 1 G at SS

Pitcher	T	Age	G	GS	CG	ShO	IP	H	HR	BB	SO	W-L	Sv	ERA
Pete Falcone	L	22	32	32	9	2	212.0	173	12	93	138	12-16	0	3.23
Lynn McGlothen	R	26	33	32	10	4	205.0	209	10	68	106	13-15	0	3.91
Bob Forsch	R	26	33	32	2	0	194.0	209	17	71	76	8-10	0	3.94
John Denny	R	23	30	30	8	3	207.0	189	11	74	74	11-9	0	2.52
Al Hrabosky	L	26	68	0	0	0	95.1	89	5	39	73	8-6	13	3.30
Mike Wallace	L	25	49	0	0	0	66.1	66	3	39	40	3-2	2	4.07
Bill Greif†	R	26	47	0	0	0	54.2	60	5	26	32	1-5	6	4.12
Eric Rasmussen	R	24	43	17	2	1	150.1	139	10	54	76	6-12	0	3.53
John Curtis	L	28	37	15	3	1	134.0	139	11	65	52	6-11	1	4.50
Eddie Solomon	R	25	26	2	0	0	37.0	45	2	16	19	1-1	0	4.86
Danny Frisella†	R	30	18	0	0	0	22.2	19	3	13	11	0-0	1	3.97
Mike Proly	R	25	14	0	0	0	17.0	21	0	6	4	1-0	0	3.71
Tom Walker	R	27	10	0	0	0	19.2	22	2	3	11	1-2	3	4.12
Lerrin LaGrow	R	27	8	2	1	0	24.1	21	0	7	10	0-1	0	1.48
Doug Capilla	L	24	7	0	0	0	8.1	8	0	4	5	1-0	0	5.40
Steve Waterbury	R	24	5	0	0	0	6.0	7	0	3	4	0-0	0	6.00

1976 Montreal Expos 6th NL East 55-107 .340 46.0 GB

Karl Kuehl (43-85)/Charlie Fox (12-22)

Player	Gm by Position	B	Age	G	AB	R	H	2B	3B	HR	RBI	BB	SO	SB	Avg	OBP	Slg
Barry Foote	C96,3B2,1B1	R	24	105	350	32	82	12	2	7	27	17	32	2	.234	.272	.340
Mike Jorgensen	1B81,OF41	L	27	125	343	36	87	13	0	6	23	52	48	7	.254	.349	.344
Pete Mackanin	2B100,3B8,SS3*	R	24	114	380	36	85	15	2	8	33	15	66	6	.224	.256	.337
Larry Parrish	3B153	R	22	154	543	65	126	28	5	11	61	41	91	2	.232	.285	.363
Tim Foli	SS146,3B1	R	25	149	546	41	144	36	1	6	54	16	33	6	.264	.281	.366
Jerry White	OF92	S	23	114	278	32	68	11	1	2	21	27	31	15	.245	.316	.313
Ellis Valentine	OF88	R	21	94	305	36	85	15	2	7	39	30	51	14	.279	.339	.410
Del Unser†	OF65	L	31	69	220	29	50	6	2	7	15	11	44	3	.227	.261	.368
Gary Carter	C60,OF36	R	22	91	311	31	68	8	1	6	38	30	43	0	.219	.287	.309
Pepe Mangual†	OF62	R	24	66	215	34	56	9	1	3	16	50	49	17	.260	.403	.353
Earl Williams†	1B47,C13	R	27	61	190	17	45	10	2	8	29	14	32	0	.237	.285	.437
Bombo Rivera	OF56	R	23	68	185	22	51	11	4	2	19	13	32	1	.276	.323	.411
Andre Thornton†	1B43,OF11	R	26	69	183	20	35	5	2	9	24	28	32	2	.191	.304	.388
Wayne Garrett†	2B54,3B2	L	28	59	177	15	43	4	1	2	11	30	20	2	.243	.353	.311
Jose Morales	1B21,C12	R	31	104	158	12	50	11	0	4	37	3	20	0	.316	.333	.462
Pepe Frias	2B35,SS35,3B4*	R	27	76	113	7	28	5	0	0	8	4	14	1	.248	.271	.292
Jim Dwyer†	OF19	L	26	50	92	7	17	3	1	0	5	11	10	0	.185	.269	.239
Gary Roenicke	OF25	R	21	29	90	9	20	3	1	2	5	4	18	0	.222	.260	.344
Andre Dawson	OF24	R	21	24	85	9	20	4	1	0	7	5	13	1	.235	.278	.306
Jim Lyttle†	OF29	L	30	42	85	6	23	4	1	1	8	7	13	0	.271	.326	.376
Warren Cromartie	OF20	L	22	33	81	8	17	1	0	0	2	1	5	1	.210	.220	.222
Nate Colbert†	OF7,1B6	R	30	14	40	5	8	2	0	2	6	9	16	3	.200	.347	.400
Larry Biittner†	OF7	L	30	11	32	2	6	1	0	0	1	0	3	0	.188	.188	.219
Jim Cox	2B11	R	26	13	29	2	5	0	1	0	2	2	2	0	.172	.226	.241
Pat Scanlon	3B7,1B1	L	23	11	27	2	5	1	0	1	2	2	5	0	.185	.241	.333
Roger Freed	1B3,OF1	R	30	8	15	0	3	1	0	0	1	0	3	0	.200	.200	.267
Larry Johnson	C5	R	25	6	13	0	2	1	0	0	0	0	2	0	.154	.154	.231
Rodney Scott	2B6,SS3	S	22	7	10	3	4	0	0	0	0	1	1	2	.400	.455	.400

P. Mackanin, 1 G at OF; P. Frias, 1 G at OF

Pitcher	T	Age	G	GS	CG	ShO	IP	H	HR	BB	SO	W-L	Sv	ERA
Steve Rogers	R	26	33	32	8	4	230.0	212	10	69	150	7-17	1	3.21
Woodie Fryman	L	36	34	32	4	2	216.1	218	14	76	123	13-13	2	3.37
Don Stanhouse	R	25	34	26	8	1	184.0	182	7	92	79	9-12	1	3.77
Don Carrithers	R	26	34	19	2	0	140.1	153	9	78	71	6-12	0	4.43
Dan Warthen	L	23	23	16	2	1	90.0	76	8	66	67	2-10	0	5.30
Clay Kirby	R	28	22	15	0	0	78.2	81	10	63	51	1-8	0	5.72
Dennis Blair	R	22	5	4	1	0	15.2	21	1	11	9	0-2	0	4.02
Gerry Hannahs	L	23	3	3	0	0	16.0	20	2	12	10	2-0	0	6.75
Larry Landreth	R	21	3	3	0	0	11.0	13	1	10	7	1-2	0	4.09
Joe Keener	R	23	2	2	0	0	4.1	7	0	8	1	0-1	0	10.38
Dale Murray	R	26	81	0	0	0	113.1	117	1	37	35	4-9	13	3.26
Joe Kerrigan	R	21	38	0	0	0	56.2	63	3	23	22	2-6	1	3.81
Steve Dunning†	R	27	32	7	1	0	91.1	93	6	33	72	2-6	0	4.14
Chuck Taylor	R	34	31	0	0	0	40.0	38	4	13	14	2-3	0	4.50
Fred Scherman	L	31	31	0	0	0	40.0	42	5	14	18	2-2	1	4.95
Chip Lang	R	23	29	2	0	0	62.1	56	3	34	30	1-3	0	4.19
Wayne Granger	R	32	27	0	0	0	32.0	32	3	16	16	1-0	2	3.66
Steve Renko†	R	31	5	1	0	0	13.0	15	2	3	4	0-1	0	5.54
Bill Atkinson	R	21	4	0	0	0	5.0	3	0	1	4	0-0	0	0.00

1976 Cincinnati Reds 1st NL West 102-60 .630 —

Sparky Anderson

Player	Gm by Position	B	Age	G	AB	R	H	2B	3B	HR	RBI	BB	SO	SB	Avg	OBP	Slg
Johnny Bench	C128,OF5,1B1	R	28	135	465	62	109	24	1	16	74	81	95	13	.234	.348	.394
Tony Perez	1B136	R	34	139	527	77	137	32	6	19	91	50	88	10	.260	.328	.452
Joe Morgan	2B133	L	32	141	472	113	151	30	5	27	111	114	41	60	.320	.444	.576
Pete Rose	3B159,OF1	S	35	162	665	130	215	42	6	10	63	86	54	9	.323	.404	.450
Dave Concepcion	SS150	R	28	152	576	74	162	28	7	9	69	49	68	21	.281	.335	.401
Cesar Geronimo	OF146	L	28	149	486	59	149	24	11	2	49	56	95	22	.307	.382	.414
Ken Griffey Sr.	OF144	L	26	148	562	111	189	28	9	6	74	62	65	34	.336	.401	.450
George Foster	OF142,1B1	R	27	144	562	86	172	21	9	29	121	52	89	17	.306	.364	.530
Dan Driessen	1B40,OF20	L	24	98	219	32	54	11	1	7	44	43	32	14	.247	.362	.402
Doug Flynn	2B55,3B23,SS20	R	25	93	219	20	62	5	2	1	20	10	24	2	.283	.312	.338
Bill Plummer	C54	R	29	56	153	16	38	6	1	4	19	14	36	0	.248	.311	.379
Mike Lum	OF38	L	30	84	136	15	31	5	1	3	20	22	24	0	.228	.331	.346
Bob Bailey	OF31,3B10	R	33	69	124	17	37	6	1	6	23	16	26	0	.298	.376	.508
Ed Armbrister	OF32	R	27	73	78	20	23	3	2	2	7	6	22	7	.295	.341	.462
Joel Youngblood	OF9,3B6,C1*	R	24	55	57	8	11	1	1	0	1	2	8	1	.193	.233	.246
Don Werner	C3	R	23	3	4	0	2	1	0	0	1	1	1	0	.500	.600	.750

J. Youngblood, 1 G at 2B

Pitcher	T	Age	G	GS	CG	ShO	IP	H	HR	BB	SO	W-L	Sv	ERA
Gary Nolan	R	28	34	34	7	1	239.1	232	28	27	113	15-9	0	3.46
Jack Billingham	R	33	34	29	5	2	177.0	190	17	62	76	12-10	1	4.32
Pat Zachry	R	24	38	28	6	1	204.0	170	8	83	143	14-7	0	2.74
Fred Norman	L	33	33	24	8	3	180.1	153	10	70	126	12-7	0	3.09
Santo Alcala	R	23	30	21	3	1	132.0	131	12	67	67	11-4	0	4.70
Don Gullett	L	25	23	20	4	0	126.0	119	8	48	64	11-3	1	3.00
Rawly Eastwick	R	25	71	0	0	0	107.2	93	3	27	70	11-5	26	2.09
Pedro Borbon	R	29	69	1	0	0	121.0	135	4	31	53	4-3	8	3.35
Will McEnaney	L	24	55	0	0	0	72.1	97	3	23	28	2-6	7	4.85
Manny Sarmiento	R	20	22	0	0	0	43.2	36	1	12	20	5-1	0	2.06
Rich Hinton	L	29	12	1	0	0	17.2	30	4	11	8	1-2	0	7.64
Pat Darcy	R	26	11	4	0	0	39.0	41	2	22	15	2-3	2	6.23
Joe Henderson	R	29	4	0	0	0	11.0	9	0	8	7	2-0	0	0.00

1976 Los Angeles Dodgers 2nd NL West 92-70 .568 10.0 GB

Walter Alston (90-68)/Tom Lasorda (2-2)

Player	Gm by Position	B	Age	G	AB	R	H	2B	3B	HR	RBI	BB	SO	SB	Avg	OBP	Slg
Steve Yeager	C115	R	27	117	359	42	77	11	3	11	35	30	84	3	.214	.286	.354
Steve Garvey	1B162	R	27	162	631	85	200	37	4	13	80	50	69	19	.317	.363	.450
Davey Lopes	2B100,OF19	R	31	117	427	72	103	17	7	4	20	56	49	63	.241	.333	.342
Ron Cey	3B144	R	28	145	502	69	139	18	3	23	80	89	74	0	.277	.386	.462
Bill Russell	SS149	R	27	149	554	53	152	17	3	5	65	21	46	15	.274	.301	.343
Bill Buckner	OF153,1B1	L	26	154	642	76	193	28	4	7	60	26	26	28	.301	.326	.389
Dusty Baker	OF106	R	27	112	384	36	93	13	0	4	39	31	54	2	.242	.298	.307
Reggie Smith†	OF58,3B1	S	31	65	225	35	63	8	4	10	26	18	42	2	.280	.335	.484
Ted Sizemore	2B71,3B3,C2	R	31	84	266	18	64	8	1	0	18	15	22	2	.241	.280	.278
Joe Ferguson†	OF39,C17	R	29	54	185	24	41	7	0	6	18	25	41	2	.222	.318	.357
Lee Lacy†	OF37,3B3,2B2	R	28	53	158	17	42	7	1	0	14	16	13	1	.266	.330	.323
Ed Goodson	3B16,1B3,OF2*	L	28	83	118	8	27	4	0	3	17	8	19	0	.229	.273	.339
John Hale	OF37	L	22	44	91	4	14	2	1	0	8	16	14	4	.154	.291	.198
Henry Cruz	OF23	L	24	49	88	8	16	2	1	4	14	9	11	0	.182	.258	.364
Jim Lyttle†	OF18	L	30	23	68	3	15	3	0	0	5	8	12	0	.221	.303	.265
Ellie Rodriguez	C33	R	30	36	66	10	14	0	0	0	9	19	12	0	.212	.400	.212
Manny Mota	OF6	R	38	50	52	1	15	3	0	0	13	7	5	0	.288	.367	.346
Kevin Pasley	C23	R	22	23	52	4	12	2	0	0	2	3	7	0	.231	.273	.269
Rick Auerbach	SS12,3B8,2B7	R	26	36	47	7	6	0	0	0	1	6	6	0	.128	.226	.128
Glenn Burke	OF20	R	23	25	46	9	11	2	0	0	5	3	8	3	.239	.300	.283
Leron Lee	OF10	L	28	23	45	1	6	0	1	0	2	2	9	0	.133	.170	.178
Ivan DeJesus	SS13,3B7	R	23	22	41	4	7	2	1	0	2	4	9	0	.171	.244	.268
Joe Simpson	OF20	L	24	23	30	2	4	1	0	0	0	1	6	0	.133	.161	.167
Danny Walton		R	28	18	15	0	2	0	0	0	2	1	2	0	.133	.176	.133
Sergio Robles	C6	R	30	6	3	0	0	0	0	0	0	0	2	0	.000	.000	.000

E. Goodson, 1 G at 2B

Pitcher	T	Age	G	GS	CG	ShO	IP	H	HR	BB	SO	W-L	Sv	ERA
Don Sutton	R	31	35	34	15	4	267.2	231	22	82	161	21-10	0	3.06
Burt Hooton	R	26	33	33	8	4	226.2	203	16	60	116	11-15	0	3.26
Doug Rau	L	27	34	32	8	3	231.0	221	18	69	98	16-12	0	2.57
Tommy John	L	33	31	31	6	2	207.0	207	7	61	91	10-10	0	3.09
Rick Rhoden	R	23	27	26	10	3	181.0	165	17	53	77	12-3	0	2.98
Dennis Lewallyn	R	22	4	2	0	0	16.2	12	1	6	4	1-1	0	2.16
Rick Sutcliffe	R	20	1	1	0	0	5.0	2	0	1	3	0-0	0	0.00
Charlie Hough	R	28	77	0	0	0	142.2	102	6	77	81	12-8	18	2.21
Stan Wall	L	25	31	0	0	0	50.0	50	5	15	27	2-2	1	3.60
Mike Marshall†	R	33	30	0	0	0	62.2	64	2	25	39	4-3	8	4.45
Elias Sosa†	R	26	24	0	0	0	33.2	30	0	12	20	2-4	1	3.48
Al Downing	L	35	17	3	0	0	46.2	43	3	18	30	1-2	0	3.86

1976 Houston Astros 3rd NL West 80-82 .494 22.0 GB

Bill Virdon

Player	Gm by Position	B	Age	G	AB	R	H	2B	3B	HR	RBI	BB	SO	SB	Avg	OBP	Slg
Ed Herrmann†	C79	L	29	79	265	14	54	8	0	3	25	22	40	0	.204	.273	.268
Bob Watson	1B155	R	30	157	585	76	183	31	3	16	102	62	64	3	.313	.377	.458
Rob Andrews	2B107,SS3	R	23	109	410	42	105	8	5	0	20	33	27	7	.256	.312	.300
Enos Cabell	3B143,1B3	R	26	144	586	85	160	13	7	2	43	29	79	35	.273	.309	.329
Roger Metzger	SS150,2B2	S	28	152	481	37	101	13	8	0	29	52	63	1	.210	.286	.270
Cesar Cedeno	OF146	R	25	150	575	89	171	26	5	18	83	55	51	58	.297	.357	.454
Jose Cruz	OF125	L	28	133	439	49	133	21	5	4	61	53	46	28	.303	.377	.401
Greg Gross	OF115	L	23	128	426	52	122	12	3	0	27	64	39	2	.286	.375	.329
Cliff Johnson	C66,OF20,1B16	R	28	108	318	36	72	21	2	10	49	62	59	0	.226	.359	.399
Leon Roberts	OF60	R	25	87	235	31	68	11	2	7	33	19	43	1	.289	.347	.443
Wilbur Howard	OF63,2B2	S	27	94	191	26	42	7	2	1	18	7	28	7	.220	.245	.293
Larry Milbourne	2B32	S	25	59	145	22	36	4	0	0	7	14	10	6	.248	.319	.276
Ken Boswell	3B16,2B3,OF1	L	30	91	126	12	33	8	1	0	18	8	8	1	.262	.301	.341
Jerry Davanon	2B17,SS17,3B9	R	30	61	107	19	31	3	3	1	20	21	12	0	.290	.408	.402
Skip Jutze	C42	R	30	42	92	7	14	2	3	0	6	4	16	0	.152	.186	.239
Alex Taveras	2B7,SS7	R	20	14	46	3	10	0	0	0	2	2	1	1	.217	.250	.217
Art Howe	3B8,2B2	R	29	21	29	0	4	1	0	0	0	6	6	0	.138	.286	.172
Al Javier	OF7	R	22	8	24	1	5	0	0	0	0	2	5	0	.208	.269	.208
Rich Chiles	OF1	L	26	5	4	1	2	1	0	0	0	0	0	0	.500	.500	.750

Pitcher	T	Age	G	GS	CG	ShO	IP	H	HR	BB	SO	W-L	Sv	ERA
J.R. Richard	R	26	39	39	14	3	291.0	221	14	151	214	20-15	0	2.75
Larry Dierker	R	29	28	28	7	4	187.2	171	9	72	112	13-14	0	3.69
Joaquin Andujar	R	23	28	25	9	4	172.1	163	8	75	59	9-10	0	3.60
Mike Cosgrove	L	25	22	16	1	1	89.2	106	6	58	34	3-4	0	5.52
Dan Larson	R	21	13	13	5	0	92.1	81	3	28	42	5-8	0	3.02
Bo McLaughlin	R	22	17	11	4	2	79.0	71	6	17	32	4-5	1	2.85
Mark Lemongello	R	20	4	4	1	0	29.0	26	2	7	9	3-1	0	2.79
Ken Forsch	R	29	52	0	0	0	92.0	76	5	26	49	4-3	19	2.15
Gene Pentz	R	23	40	0	0	0	63.2	62	5	31	36	3-3	5	2.97
Joe Niekro	R	31	36	13	0	0	118.0	107	8	56	77	4-8	0	3.36
Joe Sambito	L	24	20	4	1	1	53.1	45	4	14	26	3-2	1	3.54
Tom Griffin†	R	28	20	2	0	0	41.2	44	4	37	33	5-3	0	6.05
Gil Rondon	R	22	19	7	0	0	53.2	70	6	39	21	2-2	0	5.70
Paul Siebert	L	23	19	0	0	0	25.2	29	0	18	10	0-2	0	3.16
Mike Barlow	R	28	16	0	0	0	22.0	27	0	17	11	2-2	0	4.50
Larry Hardy	R	28	15	0	0	0	21.2	34	2	10	10	0-0	3	7.06
Jose Sosa	R	23	9	0	0	0	11.2	16	0	6	5	0-0	0	6.94

1976 San Francisco Giants 4th NL West 74-88 .457 28.0 GB

Bill Rigney

Player	Gm by Position	B	Age	G	AB	R	H	2B	3B	HR	RBI	BB	SO	SB	Avg	OBP	Slg
Dave Rader	C81	L	27	88	255	25	67	15	0	1	22	27	21	2	.263	.332	.333
Darrell Evans†	1B83,3B5	L	29	92	257	42	57	9	1	10	36	42	38	6	.222	.329	.381
Marty Perez†	2B89,SS5	R	29	93	332	37	86	13	1	2	26	30	28	3	.259	.318	.322
Ken Reitz	3B155,SS1	R	25	155	577	40	154	21	1	5	66	24	48	5	.267	.293	.333
Chris Speier	SS135,2B7,3B5*	R	26	145	495	51	112	18	4	3	40	60	52	2	.226	.311	.297
Gary Matthews	OF156	R	25	156	587	79	164	28	4	20	84	75	94	12	.279	.359	.443
Bobby Murcer	OF146	L	30	147	533	73	138	20	2	23	90	84	78	12	.259	.362	.433
Larry Herndon	OF110	R	22	115	337	42	97	11	3	2	23	23	45	12	.288	.337	.356
Gary Thomasson	OF54,1B39	L	24	103	328	45	85	20	5	8	38	30	45	8	.259	.321	.424
Derrel Thomas	2B69,OF2,3B1*	R	25	81	272	38	63	5	4	2	19	29	26	10	.232	.313	.301
Willie Montanez†	1B58	L	28	60	230	22	71	15	2	2	20	15	15	2	.309	.351	.417
Von Joshua†	OF35	L	28	42	156	13	41	5	2	0	2	4	20	1	.263	.280	.321
Marc Hill	C49,1B1	R	24	54	131	11	24	5	0	3	15	10	19	0	.183	.243	.290
Jack Clark	OF26	R	20	26	102	14	23	6	2	2	10	8	18	6	.225	.277	.382
Johnnie LeMaster	SS31	R	22	33	100	9	21	3	2	0	9	2	21	2	.210	.223	.280
Mike Sadek	C51	R	30	55	93	8	19	2	0	0	7	11	10	0	.204	.295	.226
Glenn Adams	OF6	L	28	69	74	2	18	4	0	0	3	1	12	1	.243	.253	.297
Steve Ontiveros	3B7,OF7,1B4	S	24	59	74	8	13	3	0	0	5	6	11	0	.176	.244	.216
Gary Alexander	C23	R	23	23	73	12	13	1	1	2	7	10	16	1	.178	.274	.301
Chris Arnold	2B8,3B4,1B1*	R	28	60	69	4	15	0	1	0	5	6	16	0	.217	.276	.246
Bruce Miller	2B8,3B2	R	29	12	25	1	4	1	0	0	2	2	5	0	.160	.222	.200
Craig Robinson†	2B7,3B2,SS1	R	27	15	13	4	4	1	0	0	2	3	4	0	.308	.438	.385

C. Speier, 1 G at 1B; D. Thomas, 1 G at SS; C. Arnold, 1 G at SS

Pitcher	T	Age	G	GS	CG	ShO	IP	H	HR	BB	SO	W-L	Sv	ERA
Jim Barr	R	28	37	37	8	3	252.1	260	9	60	75	15-12	0	2.89
John Montefusco	R	26	37	36	11	6	253.0	224	11	74	172	16-14	0	2.85
Ed Halicki	R	25	32	31	8	4	186.1	171	10	61	130	12-14	0	3.62
Rob Dressler	R	22	25	19	0	0	107.2	125	8	35	33	3-10	0	4.43
John D'Acquisto	R	24	28	19	0	0	106.0	93	5	102	53	3-8	0	5.35
Bob Knepper	L	22	4	4	0	0	25.0	26	0	7	11	1-2	0	3.24
Frank Riccelli	L	23	4	3	0	0	16.0	16	1	5	11	1-1	0	5.63
Gary Lavelle	L	27	65	0	0	0	110.1	102	6	52	71	10-6	12	2.69
Dave Heaverlo	R	25	61	0	0	0	75.0	85	2	15	40	4-4	1	4.44
Randy Moffitt	R	27	58	0	0	0	103.0	92	6	35	50	6-6	14	2.27
Mike Caldwell	L	27	50	9	0	0	107.1	145	5	20	55	1-7	2	4.86
Charlie Williams	R	28	48	2	0	0	85.0	80	4	39	34	2-0	1	2.96
Greg Minton	R	24	10	2	0	0	25.2	32	0	12	7	0-3	0	4.91
Tommy Toms	R	24	7	0	0	0	8.2	13	1	1	4	0-1	1	6.23

1976 San Diego Padres 5th NL West 73-89 .451 29.0 GB

John McNamara

Player	Gm by Position	B	Age	G	AB	R	H	2B	3B	HR	RBI	BB	SO	SB	Avg	OBP	Slg
Fred Kendall	C146	R	27	146	456	30	112	17	0	2	39	36	42	1	.246	.302	.296
Mike Ivie	1B135,C2,3B2	R	23	140	405	51	118	19	5	7	70	30	41	6	.291	.345	.415
Tito Fuentes	2B127	S	32	135	520	48	137	18	0	2	36	18	38	5	.263	.287	.310
Doug Rader	3B137	R	31	139	471	45	121	22	4	9	55	55	102	3	.257	.335	.378
Enzo Hernandez	SS101	R	27	113	340	31	87	13	3	1	24	32	16	12	.256	.319	.321
Dave Winfield	OF134	R	24	137	492	81	139	26	4	13	69	65	78	26	.283	.366	.431
Willie Davis	OF128	L	36	141	493	61	132	18	10	5	46	19	34	14	.268	.295	.375
John Grubb	OF98,1B9,3B3	L	27	109	384	54	109	22	1	5	27	65	53	1	.284	.391	.385
Jerry Turner	OF74	L	22	105	281	41	75	16	5	5	37	32	38	12	.267	.339	.413
Hector Torres	SS63,3B4,2B3	R	30	74	215	8	42	6	0	4	15	16	31	2	.195	.254	.279
Ted Kubiak	3B27,2B25,SS6*	S	34	96	212	16	50	5	2	0	26	25	28	0	.236	.314	.278
Willie McCovey†	1B51	L	38	71	202	20	41	9	0	7	36	21	39	0	.203	.281	.351
Merv Rettenmund	OF43	R	33	86	140	16	32	7	0	2	11	29	23	4	.229	.361	.321
Luis Melendez†	OF60	R	26	72	119	15	29	5	0	0	5	3	12	1	.244	.260	.286
Bob Davis	C47	R	24	51	83	7	17	0	1	0	5	5	13	0	.205	.244	.229
Gene Locklear†	OF11	L	26	43	67	9	15	3	0	0	8	4	15	0	.224	.264	.269
Bill Almon	SS14	R	23	14	57	6	14	3	0	1	6	2	9	3	.246	.271	.351
Bobby Valentine	OF10,1B4	R	26	15	49	3	18	4	0	0	4	6	2	0	.367	.436	.449
Mike Champion	2B11	R	21	11	38	4	9	2	0	1	2	1	3	0	.237	.256	.368
Tucker Ashford	3B1	R	21	4	5	0	3	1	0	0	0	1	0	2	.600	.667	.800

T. Kubiak, 1 G at 1B

Pitcher	T	Age	G	GS	CG	ShO	IP	H	HR	BB	SO	W-L	Sv	ERA
Randy Jones	L	26	40	40	25	5	315.1	274	15	50	93	22-14	0	2.74
Brent Strom	L	27	36	33	8	1	210.2	188	15	73	103	12-16	0	3.29
Dave Freisleben	R	24	34	24	6	3	172.0	163	10	66	81	10-13	1	3.51
Rick Sawyer	R	28	13	11	4	2	81.2	84	2	38	33	5-3	0	2.53
Tom Griffin†	R	28	11	11	2	0	70.1	56	0	42	36	4-3	0	2.94
Bill Greif†	R	26	5	5	0	0	22.1	27	2	11	5	1-3	0	8.06
Dave Wehrmeister	R	23	7	4	0	0	19.1	27	0	11	10	0-4	0	7.45
Bob Owchinko	L	21	2	2	0	0	4.1	11	0	3	4	0-2	0	16.62
Butch Metzger	R	24	77	0	0	0	123.1	119	5	52	89	11-4	16	2.92
Dave Tomlin	L	27	49	1	0	0	73.0	62	4	20	43	0-1	0	2.84
Rich Folkers	L	29	33	3	0	0	59.2	67	10	25	26	2-3	0	5.28
Dan Spillner	R	24	32	14	0	0	106.2	120	11	55	57	2-11	0	5.06
Alan Foster	R	29	26	11	2	0	86.2	75	9	35	22	3-6	0	3.22
Jerry Johnson	R	32	24	1	0	0	39.0	39	0	26	27	1-3	0	5.31
Ken Reynolds	L	29	19	2	0	0	32.1	38	0	29	18	0-3	1	6.40
Mike Dupree	R	23	12	0	0	0	15.2	18	4	7	5	0-0	0	9.19

1976 Atlanta Braves 6th NL West 70-92 .432 32.0 GB

Dave Bristol

Player	Gm by Position	B	Age	G	AB	R	H	2B	3B	HR	RBI	BB	SO	SB	Avg	OBP	Slg
Vic Correll	C65	R	30	69	200	26	45	6	2	5	16	21	37	0	.225	.302	.350
Willie Montanez†	1B103	L	28	103	420	52	135	14	0	9	64	21	32	0	.321	.353	.419
Rod Gilbreath	2B104,3B7,SS1	R	23	116	383	57	96	11	8	1	32	42	36	7	.251	.329	.329
Jerry Royster	3B148,SS2	R	23	149	533	65	132	13	1	5	45	52	53	24	.248	.313	.304
Darrel Chaney	SS151,2B1,3B1	S	28	153	496	42	125	20	8	1	50	54	92	5	.252	.324	.331
Jimmy Wynn	OF138	R	34	148	449	75	93	19	1	17	66	127	111	16	.207	.377	.367
Ken Henderson	OF122	S	30	133	435	52	114	19	0	13	61	62	68	5	.262	.352	.395
Rowland Office	OF92	L	23	99	359	51	101	17	1	4	34	37	49	2	.281	.348	.368
Tom Paciorek	OF84,1B12,3B1	R	29	111	324	39	94	10	4	4	36	19	57	2	.290	.333	.383
Dave May	OF60	L	32	105	214	27	46	5	3	3	23	26	31	5	.215	.300	.308
Earl Williams†	C38,1B17	R	27	61	184	18	39	3	0	9	26	19	33	0	.212	.286	.375
Lee Lacy†	2B44,OF5,3B1	R	28	50	180	25	49	4	2	3	20	6	12	2	.272	.299	.367
Biff Pocoroba	C54	S	22	54	174	16	42	7	0	0	14	19	12	1	.241	.313	.282
Darrell Evans†	1B36,3B7	L	29	44	139	11	24	0	0	1	10	30	33	3	.173	.320	.194
Cito Gaston	OF28,1B2	R	32	69	134	15	39	4	0	4	25	13	21	1	.291	.354	.410
Marty Perez†	2B18,SS17,3B2	R	29	31	96	12	24	4	0	1	6	8	9	0	.250	.305	.323
Dale Murphy	C19	R	20	19	65	3	17	6	0	0	9	7	9	0	.262	.333	.354
Bob Belloir	SS12,3B10,2B5	R	27	30	60	5	12	2	0	0	4	5	7	0	.200	.262	.233
Brian Asselstine	OF9	L	22	11	33	2	7	0	0	1	3	1	2	0	.212	.229	.303
Junior Moore	3B6,2B1,OF1	R	23	20	26	1	7	1	0	0	2	4	4	0	.269	.387	.308
Craig Robinson†	2B5,SS2,3B1	R	27	15	17	4	4	0	0	0	3	5	2	0	.235	.391	.235
Pete Varney†	C5	R	27	5	10	0	1	0	0	0	0	0	2	0	.100	.100	.100
Mike Eden	2B2	S	27	5	8	0	0	0	0	0	1	0	0	0	.000	.000	.000
Terry Crowley†		L	29	7	6	0	0	0	0	0	1	0	0	0	.000	.000	.000
Pat Rockett	SS2	R	21	4	5	0	1	0	0	0	0	0	1	0	.200	.200	.200

Pitcher	T	Age	G	GS	CG	ShO	IP	H	HR	BB	SO	W-L	Sv	ERA
Phil Niekro	R	37	38	37	10	2	270.2	249	18	101	173	17-11	0	3.29
Dick Ruthven	R	25	36	36	8	4	240.1	255	14	90	142	14-17	0	4.19
Andy Messersmith	R	30	29	28	12	3	207.1	166	14	74	135	11-11	1	3.04
Carl Morton	R	32	26	24	1	1	140.1	172	6	45	42	4-9	0	4.17
Frank LaCorte	R	24	19	17	1	0	105.1	97	6	53	79	3-12	0	4.70
Jamie Easterly	L	23	4	4	0	0	22.0	23	0	13	11	1-1	0	4.91
Al Autry	R	24	1	1	0	0	5.0	4	2	3	3	1-0	0	5.40
Adrian Devine	R	24	48	1	0	0	73.0	72	3	26	48	5-6	9	3.21
Bruce Dal Canton	R	34	42	1	0	0	73.1	67	6	42	36	3-5	1	3.56
Pablo Torrealba	L	28	36	0	0	0	53.0	67	0	22	33	0-2	2	3.57
Max Leon	R	26	30	0	0	0	36.0	32	2	15	16	2-4	3	2.75
Mike Beard	L	26	30	0	0	0	33.2	38	1	14	8	0-2	1	4.28
Roger Moret	L	26	27	12	1	0	77.1	84	7	27	30	3-5	1	5.00
Mike Marshall†	R	33	24	0	0	0	36.2	35	4	14	17	2-1	6	3.19
Elias Sosa†	R	26	21	0	0	0	35.1	41	3	13	32	4-4	3	5.35
Rick Camp	R	23	5	1	0	0	11.1	13	0	2	6	0-1	0	6.35
Buzz Capra	R	28	5	0	0	0	9.1	9	0	6	4	0-1	0	8.68
Preston Hanna	R	21	5	0	0	0	8.0	11	0	4	3	0-0	0	4.50

»1977 New York Yankees 1st AL East 100-62 .617 —

Billy Martin

Player	Gm by Position	B	Age	G	AB	R	H	2B	3B	HR	RBI	BB	SO	SB	Avg	OBP	Slg
Thurman Munson	C136,DH10	R	30	149	595	85	183	28	5	18	100	39	55	5	.308	.351	.462
Chris Chambliss	1B157	L	28	157	600	90	172	32	6	17	90	45	73	4	.287	.336	.445
Willie Randolph	2B147	R	22	147	551	91	151	28	11	4	40	64	53	13	.274	.347	.387
Graig Nettles	3B156,DH1	L	32	158	589	99	150	23	4	37	107	68	79	2	.255	.333	.496
Bucky Dent	SS157	R	25	158	477	54	118	18	4	8	49	39	28	1	.247	.300	.352
Mickey Rivers	OF136,DH1	L	28	138	565	79	184	18	5	12	69	18	45	22	.326	.350	.439
Roy White	OF135,DH4	S	33	143	519	72	139	25	2	14	52	75	58	18	.268	.358	.405
Reggie Jackson	OF127,DH18	L	31	146	525	93	150	39	2	32	110	74	129	17	.286	.375	.550
Carlos May†	DH53,OF4	L	29	65	181	21	41	7	1	2	16	17	24	0	.227	.292	.309
Lou Piniella	OF51,DH43,1B1	R	33	103	339	47	112	19	3	12	45	20	31	2	.330	.365	.510
Paul Blair	OF79,DH1	R	33	83	164	20	43	4	3	4	25	9	16	3	.262	.303	.396
Cliff Johnson†	DH25,C15,1B11	R	29	56	142	24	42	8	0	12	31	20	23	0	.296	.405	.606
Jimmy Wynn†	DH15,OF8	R	35	30	77	7	11	2	1	1	3	15	16	1	.143	.283	.234
Fran Healy	C26	R	30	27	67	10	15	5	0	0	7	6	13	1	.224	.288	.299
George Zeber	2B21,DH2,3B2*	S	26	25	65	8	21	3	0	3	10	9	11	0	.323	.405	.508
Fred Stanley	SS42,3B3,2B2	R	29	48	46	6	12	0	0	1	7	8	6	1	.261	.370	.326
Wendell Alston	DH10,OF2	L	24	22	40	10	13	4	0	1	4	3	4	3	.325	.364	.500
Dave Kingman†	DH6	R	28	8	24	5	6	2	0	4	7	2	13	0	.250	.333	.833
Mickey Klutts	3B4,SS1	R	22	5	15	3	4	1	0	1	4	2	1	0	.267	.389	.533
Ellie Hendricks	C6	L	36	10	11	1	3	1	0	1	5	0	2	0	.273	.273	.636
Gene Locklear	OF1	L	27	1	5	1	3	0	0	0	2	0	0	0	.600	.600	.600
Dave Bergman	OF3,1B2	L	24	5	4	1	1	0	0	0	1	0	0	0	.250	.200	.250
Marty Perez†	3B1	R	30	1	4	0	2	0	0	0	0	0	1	0	.500	.500	.500

G. Zeber, 2 G at SS

Pitcher	T	Age	G	GS	CG	ShO	IP	H	HR	BB	SO	W-L	Sv	ERA
Ed Figueroa	R	28	32	32	12	2	239.1	228	19	75	104	16-11	0	3.57
Mike Torrez†	R	30	31	31	15	2	217.0	212	20	75	90	14-12	0	3.82
Ron Guidry	L	26	31	25	9	5	210.2	174	12	65	176	16-7	1	2.82
Don Gullett	L	26	22	22	7	1	158.1	137	14	69	116	14-4	0	3.58
Catfish Hunter	R	31	22	22	8	1	143.1	137	29	47	52	9-9	0	4.71
Ken Holtzman	L	31	18	11	0	0	71.2	105	7	24	14	2-3	0	5.78
Gil Patterson	R	21	10	6	0	0	33.1	38	3	20	29	1-2	1	5.40
Dock Ellis†	R	32	3	3	1	0	19.2	18	1	8	5	1-1	0	1.83
Sparky Lyle	L	32	72	0	0	0	137.0	131	7	33	68	13-5	26	2.17
Dick Tidrow	R	30	49	7	0	0	151.0	143	20	41	83	11-4	5	3.16
Ken Clay	R	23	21	3	0	0	55.2	53	6	24	20	2-3	1	4.37
Stan Thomas†	R	27	3	0	0	0	6.1	7	0	4	1	1-0	0	7.11
Larry McCall	R	24	2	0	0	0	6.0	12	1	1	0	0-1	0	7.50

834 Seasons: Team Rosters

1977 Baltimore Orioles 2nd AL East 97-64 .602 2.5 GB

Earl Weaver

Player	Gm by Position	B	Age	G	AB	R	H	2B	3B	HR	RBI	BB	SO	SB	Avg	OBP	Slg
Rick Dempsey	C91	R	27	91	270	27	61	7	4	3	34	34	34	2	.226	.314	.315
Lee May	1B110,DH39	R	34	150	585	75	148	16	2	27	99	38	119	2	.253	.296	.426
Billy Smith	2B104,SS5,1B2*	S	23	109	367	44	79	12	2	5	29	33	71	3	.215	.281	.300
Doug DeCinces	3B148,DH1,1B1*	R	26	150	522	63	135	28	3	19	69	64	86	8	.259	.339	.433
Mark Belanger	SS142	R	33	144	402	39	83	13	4	2	30	43	68	15	.206	.287	.274
Ken Singleton	OF150,DH1	S	30	152	536	90	176	24	0	24	99	107	101	0	.328	.438	.507
Al Bumbry	OF130	L	30	133	518	74	164	31	3	4	41	45	88	19	.317	.371	.411
Pat Kelly	OF109,DH1	L	32	120	360	50	92	13	0	10	49	53	75	25	.256	.353	.375
Eddie Murray	DH111,1B42,OF3	S	21	160	611	81	173	29	2	27	88	48	104	0	.283	.333	.470
Rich Dauer	2B83,3B9,DH2	R	24	96	304	38	74	15	1	5	25	20	28	1	.243	.294	.349
Andres Mora	OF57,DH5,3B1	R	22	77	233	32	57	8	2	13	44	5	53	0	.245	.261	.464
Dave Skaggs	C80	R	26	80	216	22	62	9	1	1	24	20	34	0	.287	.345	.352
Kiko Garcia	SS61,2B2	R	23	65	131	20	29	6	0	2	10	6	31	2	.221	.255	.313
Tony Muser	1B77,OF11,DH1	L	29	120	118	14	27	6	0	0	7	13	16	1	.229	.301	.280
Elliott Maddox	OF45,3B1	R	29	49	107	14	28	7	0	2	9	13	9	2	.262	.357	.383
Tom Shopay	OF52,DH2	L	32	67	69	15	13	3	0	1	4	8	7	3	.188	.273	.275
Larry Harlow	OF38	L	25	46	48	4	10	0	1	0	0	5	8	6	.208	.283	.250
Brooks Robinson	3B15	R	40	24	47	3	7	2	0	1	4	4	4	0	.149	.212	.255
Terry Crowley	DH2,1B1	L	30	18	22	3	8	1	0	1	9	1	3	0	.364	.391	.545
Ken Rudolph†	C11	R	30	11	14	2	4	1	0	0	2	0	4	0	.286	.286	.357
Dave Criscione	C7	R	25	7	9	1	3	0	0	1	1	0	1	0	.333	.333	.667
Mike Dimmel	OF23	R	22	25	5	8	0	0	0	0	0	0	1	1	.000	.000	.000

B. Smith, 1 G at 3B; D. DeCinces, 1 G at 2B

Pitcher	T	Age	G	GS	CG	ShO	IP	H	HR	BB	SO	W-L	Sv	ERA
Jim Palmer	R	31	39	39	22	3	319.0	263	24	99	193	20-11	0	2.91
Rudy May	L	32	37	37	11	4	251.2	243	25	78	105	18-14	0	3.61
Ross Grimsley	L	27	34	34	11	2	218.1	230	24	74	53	14-10	0	3.96
Mike Flanagan	L	25	36	33	15	2	235.0	235	17	70	149	15-10	1	3.64
Dennis Martinez	R	22	42	13	5	0	166.2	157	10	64	107	14-7	4	4.10
Tippy Martinez	L	27	41	0	0	0	50.0	47	2	27	29	5-1	9	2.70
Dick Drago†	R	32	36	0	0	0	39.2	49	2	15	20	6-3	3	3.63
Scott McGregor	L	23	29	5	1	0	114.0	119	8	30	55	3-5	4	4.42
Dyar Miller†	R	31	12	0	0	0	22.1	25	6	10	9	2-2	1	5.64
Fred Holdsworth†	R	25	12	0	0	0	14.1	17	0	16	4	0-1	0	6.28
Tony Chevez	R	23	4	0	0	0	8.0	10	3	8	7	0-0	0	12.38
Mike Parrott	R	22	3	0	0	0	4.1	4	0	2	2	0-0	0	2.08
Nelson Briles†	R	33	2	0	0	0	4.0	5	2	0	2	0-0	1	6.75
Earl Stephenson	L	29	1	0	0	0	3.0	5	1	0	2	0-0	0	9.00
Randy Miller	R	24	1	0	0	0	0.2	4	0	0	0	0-0	0	40.50
Ed Farmer	R	27	1	0	0	0	0.0	1	0	1	0	0-0	0	—

1977 Boston Red Sox 2nd AL East 97-64 .602 2.5 GB

Don Zimmer

Player	Gm by Position	B	Age	G	AB	R	H	2B	3B	HR	RBI	BB	SO	SB	Avg	OBP	Slg
Carlton Fisk	C151	R	29	152	536	106	169	26	3	26	102	75	85	7	.315	.402	.521
George Scott	1B157	R	33	157	584	103	157	26	5	33	95	57	112	1	.269	.337	.500
Denny Doyle	2B137	L	33	137	455	54	109	13	6	2	49	29	50	2	.240	.289	.308
Butch Hobson	3B159	R	25	159	593	77	157	33	5	30	112	27	162	5	.265	.300	.489
Rick Burleson	SS154	R	26	154	663	80	194	36	7	3	52	47	69	13	.293	.338	.382
Carl Yastrzemski	OF140,1B7,DH6	L	37	150	558	99	165	27	3	28	102	73	40	11	.296	.372	.505
Fred Lynn	OF125,DH1	L	25	129	497	81	129	29	5	18	76	51	63	2	.260	.327	.447
Rick Miller	OF79,DH1	L	29	86	189	34	48	9	3	0	24	22	30	11	.254	.341	.333
Jim Rice	DH116,OF44	R	24	160	644	104	206	29	15	39	114	53	120	5	.320	.376	.593
Dwight Evans	OF63,DH17	R	25	73	230	39	66	9	2	14	36	28	58	4	.287	.363	.526
Bernie Carbo	OF67,DH7	L	29	86	228	36	66	6	1	15	34	47	72	1	.289	.409	.522
Steve Dillard	2B45,SS9,DH6	R	26	66	141	22	34	7	0	1	13	7	13	4	.241	.270	.312
Tommy Helms†	DH13,3B2,2B1	R	36	21	59	5	16	2	0	1	5	4	4	0	.271	.328	.356
Ted Cox	DH13	R	22	13	58	11	21	3	1	1	6	3	6	0	.362	.393	.500
Bob Montgomery	C15	R	33	17	40	6	12	2	0	2	7	4	9	0	.300	.370	.500
Dave Coleman	OF9	R	26	11	12	1	0	0	0	0	0	1	3	0	.000	.077	.000
Bobby Darwin†	DH2,OF1	R	34	4	9	1	2	1	0	0	1	0	4	0	.222	.222	.333
Doug Griffin	2B3	R	30	5	6	0	0	0	0	0	0	0	0	0	.000	.000	.000
Jack Baker	1B1	R	27	2	3	0	0	0	0	0	0	0	1	0	.000	.000	.000
Sam Bowen	OF3	R	24	3	2	0	0	0	0	0	0	0	2	0	.000	.000	.000
Bob Bailey†		R	34	2	2	0	0	0	0	0	0	0	1	0	.000	.000	.000
Bo Diaz	C2	R	24	2	1	0	0	0	0	0	0	0	1	0	.000	.000	.000
Ramon Aviles	2B1	R	25	1	0	0	0	0	0	0	0	0	0	0	—	—	—

Pitcher	T	Age	G	GS	CG	ShO	IP	H	HR	BB	SO	W-L	Sv	ERA
Luis Tiant	R	36	32	32	3	3	188.2	210	26	51	124	12-8	0	4.53
Fergie Jenkins	R	33	28	28	11	1	193.0	190	30	36	105	10-10	0	3.68
Reggie Cleveland	R	29	36	27	9	1	190.1	211	20	43	85	11-8	2	4.26
Rick Wise	R	31	26	20	4	2	128.1	151	19	28	85	11-5	0	4.77
Bill Lee	L	30	27	16	4	0	128.0	155	14	29	31	9-5	1	4.43
Don Aase	R	22	13	13	4	2	92.1	85	6	19	49	6-2	0	3.12
Bill Campbell	R	28	69	0	0	0	140.0	112	13	60	114	13-9	31	2.96
Bob Stanley	R	22	41	13	3	1	151.0	176	10	43	44	8-7	3	3.99
Jim Willoughby	R	28	31	0	0	0	54.2	54	5	18	33	6-2	2	4.94
Mike Paxton	R	23	29	12	2	1	108.0	134	7	25	58	10-5	0	3.83
Tom Murphy†	R	31	16	0	0	0	30.2	44	6	12	13	0-1	0	6.75
Ramon Hernandez†	L	36	12	0	0	0	12.2	14	2	7	8	0-1	1	5.68
Tom House†	L	30	8	0	0	0	7.2	15	0	6	6	1-0	0	12.91
Jim Burton	L	27	1	0	0	0	2.2	2	0	1	3	0-0	0	0.00
Rick Kreuger	L	28	1	0	0	0	0.0	2	0	0	0	0-1	0	—

1977 Detroit Tigers 4th AL East 74-88 .457 26.0 GB

Ralph Houk

Player	Gm by Position	B	Age	G	AB	R	H	2B	3B	HR	RBI	BB	SO	SB	Avg	OBP	Slg
Milt May	C111	L	26	115	397	32	99	9	3	12	46	26	31	0	.249	.291	.378
Jason Thompson	1B158	L	22	158	585	87	158	24	5	31	105	73	91	0	.270	.347	.487
Tito Fuentes	2B151,DH1	S	33	151	615	83	190	19	10	5	51	38	61	4	.309	.348	.397
Aurelio Rodriguez	3B95,SS1	R	29	96	306	30	67	14	1	10	32	16	36	1	.219	.257	.369
Tom Veryzer	SS124	R	24	125	350	31	69	12	1	2	28	16	44	0	.197	.230	.254
Ron LeFlore	OF152	R	29	154	652	100	212	30	10	16	57	37	121	39	.325	.363	.475
Steve Kemp	OF148	L	22	151	552	75	142	29	4	18	88	71	93	3	.257	.343	.422
Ben Oglivie	OF118,DH2	L	28	132	450	63	118	24	2	21	61	40	80	9	.262	.325	.464
Rusty Staub	DH156	L	33	158	623	84	173	34	3	22	101	59	47	1	.278	.336	.448
Phil Mankowski	3B85,2B1	L	24	94	286	21	79	7	3	3	27	16	41	1	.276	.318	.353
Mickey Stanley	OF57,1B3,SS3*	R	34	75	222	30	51	9	1	8	23	18	30	0	.230	.284	.387
John Wockenfuss	C37,OF9,DH3	R	28	53	164	26	45	8	1	9	25	14	18	0	.274	.331	.500
Tim Corcoran	OF18,DH3	L	24	55	103	13	29	3	0	3	15	6	9	0	.282	.315	.398
Chuck Scrivener	SS50,2B8,3B3	R	29	61	72	10	6	0	0	0	2	5	9	0	.083	.143	.083
Mark Wagner	SS21,2B1	R	23	22	48	4	7	0	1	1	3	4	12	0	.146	.222	.250
Lance Parrish	C12	R	21	12	46	10	9	2	0	3	7	5	12	0	.196	.275	.435
Alan Trammell	SS19	R	19	19	43	6	8	0	0	0	0	4	12	0	.186	.255	.186
Lou Whitaker	2B9	L	20	11	32	5	8	1	0	0	2	4	6	2	.250	.333	.281
Bruce Kimm	C12,DH2	R	26	14	25	2	2	1	0	0	1	0	4	0	.080	.115	.120
Bob Adams	1B2,C1	R	25	15	24	2	6	1	0	2	2	0	5	0	.250	.250	.542
Willie Horton†	OF1	R	34	1	4	0	1	0	0	0	0	0	0	0	.250	.250	.250
Bob Molinaro†		L	27	4	4	0	1	1	0	0	0	0	2	0	.250	.250	.500
Luis Alvarado†	3B2	R	28	2	1	0	0	0	0	0	0	0	0	0	.000	.000	.000

M. Stanley, 2 G at DH

Pitcher	T	Age	G	GS	CG	ShO	IP	H	HR	BB	SO	W-L	Sv	ERA
Dave Rozema	R	20	28	28	16	1	218.1	222	25	34	92	15-7	0	3.09
Fredie Arroyo	R	25	38	28	8	1	209.1	227	23	52	60	8-18	0	4.17
Dave Roberts†	L	32	22	22	5	0	129.1	143	20	41	46	4-10	0	5.15
Bob Sykes	L	22	32	20	3	0	132.2	141	15	50	58	5-7	0	4.41
Milt Wilcox	R	27	20	13	1	0	106.1	96	13	37	82	6-2	0	3.64
Mark Fidrych	R	22	11	11	7	1	81.0	82	2	12	42	6-4	0	2.89
Vern Ruhle	R	26	14	10	0	0	66.1	83	9	15	27	3-5	0	5.70
Jack Morris	R	22	7	6	1	0	45.2	38	4	23	28	1-1	0	3.74
Ray Bare	R	28	5	4	0	0	14.1	24	3	7	4	0-2	0	12.56
John Hiller	L	34	45	8	3	0	124.0	120	15	61	115	8-14	7	3.56
Steve Foucault	R	27	44	0	0	0	74.1	64	7	17	58	7-7	13	3.15
Jim Crawford	L	26	37	7	0	0	126.0	156	13	50	91	7-8	1	4.79
Steve Grilli	R	28	30	2	0	0	72.2	71	8	49	49	1-2	0	4.83
Bruce Taylor	R	24	19	0	0	0	29.1	23	2	10	19	1-0	2	3.38
Ed Glynn	L	24	8	3	0	0	27.1	36	3	12	13	2-1	0	5.27

1977 Cleveland Indians 5th AL East 71-90 .441 28.5 GB

Frank Robinson (26-31)/Jeff Torborg (45-59)

Player	Gm by Position	B	Age	G	AB	R	H	2B	3B	HR	RBI	BB	SO	SB	Avg	OBP	Slg
Fred Kendall	C102,DH1	R	28	103	317	18	79	13	1	3	39	16	27	0	.249	.283	.325
Andre Thornton	1B117,DH9	R	27	131	433	77	114	20	5	28	70	70	82	3	.263	.378	.527
Duane Kuiper	2B148	L	27	148	610	62	169	15	8	1	50	37	55	11	.277	.324	.333
Buddy Bell	3B118,OF11	R	25	129	479	64	140	23	4	11	64	45	63	1	.292	.351	.426
Frank Duffy	SS121	R	30	122	334	30	67	13	2	4	31	21	47	8	.201	.247	.287
Jim Norris	OF124,1B3	L	28	133	440	59	119	23	6	2	37	64	57	26	.270	.360	.364
Paul Dade	OF99,3B26,DH7*	R	25	134	461	65	134	15	3	3	45	32	58	16	.291	.333	.356
Bruce Bochte†	OF76,1B36,DH1	L	26	112	392	52	119	19	1	5	43	40	38	3	.304	.364	.395
Rico Carty	DH123,1B2	R	37	127	461	50	129	23	1	15	80	56	51	1	.280	.355	.432
Larvell Blanks	SS66,3B18,2B12*	R	27	105	322	43	92	10	4	6	38	19	37	3	.286	.324	.398
Rick Manning	OF68	L	22	68	252	33	57	7	3	5	18	21	35	9	.226	.282	.337
Ray Fosse†	C77,DH1,1B1	R	30	78	238	25	63	7	1	6	27	7	26	0	.265	.293	.378
Ron Pruitt	OF69,DH4,C4*	R	25	78	219	29	63	10	2	2	32	28	22	2	.288	.369	.379
John Lowenstein	OF39,DH19,1B1	L	30	81	149	24	36	6	1	4	12	21	29	1	.242	.335	.376
Bill Melton	1B15,DH14,3B13	R	31	50	133	17	32	11	0	0	14	17	21	1	.241	.331	.323
Charlie Spikes	OF27,DH2	R	26	32	95	13	22	2	0	3	11	11	17	0	.232	.321	.347
John Grubb	OF28,DH4	L	28	34	93	8	28	3	3	2	14	19	18	0	.301	.425	.462
Alfredo Griffin	SS13,DH1	S	19	14	41	5	6	1	0	0	3	3	5	2	.146	.205	.171
Dave Oliver	2B7	L	26	7	22	2	7	0	1	0	3	4	0	0	.318	.444	.409

P. Dade, 1 G at 2B; L. Blanks, 6 G at DH; R. Pruitt, 1 G at 3B

Pitcher	T	Age	G	GS	CG	ShO	IP	H	HR	BB	SO	W-L	Sv	ERA
Wayne Garland	R	26	38	38	21	1	282.2	281	23	88	118	13-19	0	3.60
Dennis Eckersley	R	22	33	33	12	3	247.1	214	31	54	191	14-13	0	3.53
Jim Bibby	R	32	37	30	9	2	206.2	197	17	73	141	12-13	2	3.57
Al Fitzmorris	R	31	29	21	1	0	133.0	164	12	53	54	6-10	0	5.41
Pat Dobson	R	35	33	17	0	0	133.1	155	23	65	81	3-12	1	6.14
Jim Kern	R	28	60	0	0	0	92.0	85	3	47	91	8-10	18	3.42
Don Hood	L	27	41	5	1	0	105.0	87	3	49	62	2-1	0	3.00
Rick Waits	L	25	37	16	1	0	135.1	132	8	64	62	9-7	2	3.99
Sid Monge†	L	26	33	0	0	0	39.0	47	6	27	25	1-2	3	6.23
Tom Buskey	R	30	21	0	0	0	34.0	45	6	8	15	0-0	0	5.29
Dave LaRoche†	L	29	13	0	0	0	18.2	15	3	7	18	2-2	4	5.30
Larry Andersen	R	24	11	0	0	0	14.1	10	1	9	8	0-1	0	3.14
Cardell Camper	R	24	3	1	0	0	9.1	7	0	4	9	1-0	0	3.86
Bill Laxton†	L	29	2	0	0	0	1.2	2	0	2	1	0-0	0	5.40

1977 Milwaukee Brewers 6th AL East 67-95 .414 33.0 GB

Alex Grammas

Player	Gm by Position	B	Age	G	AB	R	H	2B	3B	HR	RBI	BB	SO	SB	Avg	OBP	Slg
Charlie Moore	C137	R	24	138	375	42	93	15	6	5	45	31	39	1	.248	.306	.360
Cecil Cooper	1B148,DH10	L	27	160	643	86	193	31	7	20	78	28	110	13	.300	.326	.463
Don Money	2B116,OF23,3B15*	R	30	152	570	86	159	28	3	25	83	57	70	8	.279	.348	.470
Sal Bando	3B135,DH24,2B1*	R	33	159	580	65	145	27	3	17	82	75	89	4	.250	.336	.395
Robin Yount	SS153	R	21	154	605	66	174	34	4	4	49	41	80	16	.288	.333	.377
Von Joshua	OF140	L	29	144	536	58	140	25	7	9	49	21	74	12	.261	.286	.384
Jim Wohlford	OF125,DH1,2B1	R	26	129	391	41	97	16	3	2	36	21	49	17	.248	.285	.320
Sixto Lezcano	OF108	R	23	109	400	50	109	21	4	21	49	52	78	6	.273	.358	.503
Jamie Quirk	DH53,OF10,3B8	L	22	93	221	16	48	14	1	3	13	8	47	0	.217	.251	.330
Steve Brye	OF83,DH6	R	28	94	241	27	60	14	3	7	28	16	39	1	.249	.297	.419
Lenn Sakata	2B53	R	23	53	154	13	25	2	0	2	12	9	22	1	.162	.209	.214
Ken McMullen	DH29,1B11,3B7	R	35	63	136	15	31	7	1	5	19	15	33	0	.228	.305	.404
Larry Haney	C63	R	34	63	127	7	29	2	0	0	10	5	30	0	.228	.254	.244
Jimmy Wynn†	OF17,DH15	R	35	36	117	10	23	3	1	0	10	17	31	3	.197	.294	.239
Ed Kirkpatrick†	OF22,DH4,3B1	L	32	29	77	8	21	4	0	0	6	10	8	0	.273	.364	.325
Danny Thomas	DH9,OF9	R	26	22	70	11	19	3	2	2	11	8	11	0	.271	.350	.457
Bob Sheldon	DH17,2B5	L	26	31	64	9	13	4	1	0	3	6	9	0	.203	.268	.297
Mike Hegan	OF8,DH7,1B6	L	34	35	53	8	9	0	0	2	3	10	17	0	.170	.313	.283
Dick Davis	OF12,DH6	R	23	22	51	7	14	2	0	0	6	1	8	0	.275	.278	.314
Jim Gantner	3B14	L	24	14	47	4	14	1	0	1	2	2	5	2	.298	.327	.383
Tim Johnson	2B10,SS6,DH4*	L	27	30	33	5	2	1	0	0	2	5	10	1	.061	.179	.091
Ed Romero	SS10	R	19	10	25	4	7	1	0	0	2	4	3	0	.280	.379	.320
Jack Heidemann	DH3,2B1	R	27	5	1	1	0	0	0	0	0	1	0	0	.000	.500	.000

D. Money, 7 G at DH; S. Bando, 1 G at SS; T. Johnson, 4 G at 3B, 1 G at OF

Pitcher	T	Age	G	GS	CG	ShO	IP	H	HR	BB	SO	W-L	Sv	ERA
Jerry Augustine	L	24	33	33	10	1	209.0	222	23	72	68	12-18	0	4.48
Moose Haas	R	21	32	32	6	0	197.2	195	21	84	113	10-12	0	4.33
Jim Slaton	R	27	32	31	7	1	221.0	223	25	77	104	10-14	0	3.58
Lary Sorensen	R	21	23	20	9	0	142.1	147	10	36	57	7-10	0	4.36
Bill Travers	L	24	19	19	2	1	121.2	140	13	57	49	4-12	0	5.25
Mike Caldwell†	L	28	21	12	2	0	94.1	101	6	36	38	5-8	0	4.58
Bob McClure	L	25	68	0	0	0	71.1	64	2	34	57	2-1	6	2.52
Bill Castro	R	23	51	0	0	0	69.1	76	7	23	28	8-6	13	4.15
Ed Rodriguez	R	25	42	5	1	1	142.2	126	15	56	104	5-6	4	4.35
Sam Hinds	R	23	29	1	0	0	72.1	72	5	40	46	0-3	2	4.73
Gary Beare	R	24	17	6	0	0	58.2	63	6	38	32	3-3	0	6.44
Barry Cort	R	21	7	3	1	0	24.1	25	1	9	17	1-1	0	3.33
Rich Folkers	L	30	3	0	0	0	6.1	7	2	4	6	0-1	0	4.26

1977 Toronto Blue Jays 7th AL East 54-107 .335 45.5 GB

Roy Hartsfield

Player	Gm by Position	B	Age	G	AB	R	H	2B	3B	HR	RBI	BB	SO	SB	Avg	OBP	Slg
Alan Ashby	C124	S	25	124	396	25	83	16	3	2	29	50	50	0	.210	.301	.280
Doug Ault	1B122,DH4	R	27	129	445	44	109	22	3	11	64	39	68	4	.245	.310	.382
Steve Staggs	2B72	R	26	72	290	37	75	11	6	2	28	36	38	5	.259	.339	.359
Roy Howell†	3B87,DH8	L	23	96	364	41	115	17	1	10	44	42	76	4	.316	.386	.451
Hector Torres	SS68,2B23,3B2	R	31	91	266	33	64	7	3	5	26	16	33	1	.241	.282	.346
Al Woods	OF115,DH4	L	23	122	440	58	125	17	4	6	35	36	38	8	.284	.336	.382
Steve Bowling	OF87	R	25	89	194	19	40	8	1	1	13	37	41	2	.206	.330	.273
Otto Velez	OF79,DH28	R	26	120	360	50	92	19	3	16	62	65	87	4	.256	.366	.458
Ron Fairly	DH58,1B40,OF33	L	38	132	458	60	128	24	2	19	64	58	58	0	.279	.362	.465
Bob Bailor	OF63,SS53,DH7	R	25	122	496	62	154	21	5	5	32	17	26	15	.310	.335	.403
Doug Rader†	3B45,DH34,1B7*	R	32	96	313	47	75	18	2	13	40	38	67	2	.240	.323	.435
Dave McKay	2B40,3B32,SS20*	S	27	95	274	18	54	4	3	3	22	7	51	2	.197	.222	.266
Sam Ewing	OF46,DH27,1B2	L	28	97	244	24	70	8	2	4	34	19	42	1	.287	.338	.385
John Scott	OF67,DH2	R	25	79	233	26	56	9	0	2	15	8	39	10	.240	.266	.305
Gary Woods	OF60	R	22	60	227	21	49	9	1	0	17	7	38	5	.216	.246	.264
Pedro Garcia	2B34,DH4	R	27	41	130	10	27	10	1	0	9	5	21	0	.208	.254	.300
Rick Cerone	C31	R	23	31	100	7	20	4	0	1	10	6	12	0	.200	.245	.270
Jim Mason†	SS22	L	26	22	79	10	13	3	0	0	2	7	10	1	.165	.233	.203
Tim Nordbrook†	SS24	R	27	24	63	9	11	0	1	0	1	4	11	1	.175	.224	.206
Ernie Whitt	C14	L	25	23	41	4	7	3	0	0	6	2	12	0	.171	.200	.244
Phil Roof	C3	R	36	3	5	0	0	0	0	0	0	0	1	0	.000	.000	.000

D. Rader, 1 G at OF; D. McKay, 2 G at DH

Pitcher	T	Age	G	GS	CG	ShO	IP	H	HR	BB	SO	W-L	Sv	ERA
Dave Lemanczyk	R	26	34	34	11	0	252.0	278	20	87	105	13-16	0	4.25
Jerry Garvin	L	21	34	34	12	1	244.2	247	33	85	127	10-18	0	4.19
Jesse Jefferson	R	28	33	33	8	0	217.0	224	23	83	114	9-17	0	4.31
Jeff Byrd	R	20	17	17	1	0	87.1	98	5	68	40	2-13	0	6.18
Jim Clancy	R	21	13	13	4	1	76.2	80	7	47	44	4-9	0	5.05
Bill Singer	R	33	13	12	0	0	59.2	71	5	39	33	2-8	0	6.79
Steve Hargan†	R	34	6	5	1	0	29.1	36	2	14	11	1-3	0	5.22
Mike Darr	R	21	1	1	0	0	1.1	3	1	4	1	0-1	0	33.75
Pete Vuckovich	R	24	53	8	3	1	148.0	143	13	59	123	7-7	8	3.47
Mike Willis	L	26	43	3	0	0	107.1	105	15	38	59	2-6	5	3.94
Jerry Johnson	R	33	43	0	0	0	86.0	91	9	54	54	2-4	5	4.60
Tom Murphy†	R	31	19	1	0	0	52.0	63	6	18	26	2-1	2	3.63
Denny DeBarr	L	24	14	0	0	0	21.1	29	1	8	10	0-1	0	5.91
Chuck Hartenstein	R	35	13	0	0	0	27.1	40	8	6	15	0-2	0	6.59
Tom Bruno	R	24	12	0	0	0	18.1	30	4	13	9	0-1	0	7.85

1977 Kansas City Royals 1st AL West 102-60 .630 —

Whitey Herzog

Player	Gm by Position	B	Age	G	AB	R	H	2B	3B	HR	RBI	BB	SO	SB	Avg	OBP	Slg
Darrell Porter	C125,DH1	L	25	130	425	61	117	21	3	16	60	53	70	1	.275	.353	.452
John Mayberry	1B145,DH8	L	28	153	543	73	125	22	1	23	82	83	86	1	.230	.336	.401
Frank White	2B152,SS4	R	26	152	474	59	116	21	5	5	50	25	67	23	.245	.284	.342
George Brett	3B135,DH3,SS1	L	24	139	564	105	176	32	13	22	88	55	24	14	.312	.373	.532
Freddie Patek	SS154	R	32	154	497	72	130	26	6	5	60	41	84	53	.262	.320	.368
Al Cowens	OF159,DH1	R	25	162	606	98	189	32	14	23	112	41	64	16	.312	.361	.525
Amos Otis	OF140	R	30	142	478	85	120	20	8	17	78	71	88	23	.251	.342	.433
Tom Poquette	OF96	L	25	106	342	43	100	23	6	2	33	19	21	1	.292	.337	.412
Hal McRae	DH116,OF46	R	31	162	641	104	191	54	11	21	92	59	43	18	.298	.366	.515
Pete LaCock	1B29,DH26,OF12	L	25	88	218	25	66	12	1	3	29	15	25	2	.303	.345	.408
Joe Zdeb	OF93,DH4,3B1	R	24	105	195	26	58	5	2	2	23	16	23	6	.297	.346	.374
Cookie Rojas	3B31,2B16,DH6	R	38	64	156	8	39	9	1	0	10	8	17	1	.250	.285	.321
John Wathan	C35,1B5,DH2	R	27	55	119	18	39	5	3	2	21	5	8	2	.328	.346	.471
Buck Martinez	C28	R	28	29	80	3	18	4	0	1	9	3	12	0	.225	.253	.313
Joe Lahoud	OF15,DH4	L	30	34	65	8	17	5	0	2	8	11	16	1	.262	.364	.431
Bob Heise	2B21,SS21,3B12*	R	30	54	62	11	16	2	1	0	5	2	8	0	.258	.292	.323
Dave Nelson	2B11,DH7	R	33	27	48	8	9	3	1	0	4	7	11	1	.188	.291	.292
Willie Wilson	OF9,DH2	S	21	13	34	10	11	2	0	0	1	1	8	6	.324	.343	.382
Clint Hurdle	OF9	L	19	9	26	5	8	0	0	2	7	2	7	0	.308	.357	.538
U.L. Washington	SS9,DH1	S	23	10	20	0	4	1	1	0	1	5	4	1	.200	.360	.350

B. Heise, 1 G at 1B

Pitcher	T	Age	G	GS	CG	ShO	IP	H	HR	BB	SO	W-L	Sv	ERA
Dennis Leonard	R	26	38	37	21	5	292.2	246	18	79	244	20-12	1	3.04
Paul Splittorff	L	30	37	37	6	2	229.0	243	11	83	99	16-6	0	3.69
Jim Colborn	R	31	36	35	6	1	239.0	233	22	81	103	18-14	0	3.62
Andy Hassler	L	25	29	27	3	1	156.1	166	7	75	83	9-6	0	4.20
Doug Bird	R	27	53	5	0	0	118.1	120	14	29	83	11-4	14	3.88
Larry Gura	L	29	52	6	1	1	106.1	108	8	28	46	8-5	10	3.13
Mark Littell	R	24	48	5	0	0	104.2	73	6	55	106	8-4	12	3.61
Steve Mingori	L	33	43	0	0	0	64.0	59	4	19	19	2-4	4	3.09
Marty Pattin	R	34	31	10	4	0	128.1	115	16	37	55	10-3	0	3.58
Tom Hall	L	29	6	0	0	0	7.2	4	2	6	10	0-0	0	3.52
George Throop	R	26	4	0	0	0	5.1	1	1	4	1	0-0	1	3.38
Randy McGilberry	R	23	3	0	0	0	7.0	7	1	1	1	0-1	0	5.14
Gary Lance	R	28	1	0	0	0	2.0	2	0	2	0	0-1	0	4.50

1977 Texas Rangers 2nd AL West 94-68 .580 8.0 GB

Frank Lucchesi (31-31)/Eddie Stanky (1-0)/Connie Ryan (2-4)/Billy Hunter (60-33)

Player	Gm by Position	B	Age	G	AB	R	H	2B	3B	HR	RBI	BB	SO	SB	Avg	OBP	Slg
Jim Sundberg	C149	R	26	149	453	61	132	20	3	6	65	53	77	2	.291	.365	.389
Mike Hargrove	1B152	L	27	153	525	98	160	28	4	18	69	103	59	2	.305	.420	.476
Bump Wills	2B150,SS2,DH1*	S	24	152	541	87	155	28	6	9	62	65	96	28	.287	.361	.410
Toby Harrah	3B159,SS1	R	28	159	539	90	142	25	5	27	87	109	73	27	.263	.393	.479
Bert Campaneris	SS149	R	35	150	552	77	140	19	7	5	46	47	86	27	.254	.314	.341
C. Washington	OF127,DH1	L	22	129	521	63	148	31	2	12	68	25	112	21	.284	.318	.420
Juan Beniquez	OF123	R	27	123	424	56	114	19	6	10	50	43	43	26	.269	.336	.413
Dave May	OF111,DH5	L	33	120	340	46	82	14	1	7	42	32	43	4	.241	.311	.350
Willie Horton†	DH128,OF10	R	34	139	519	55	150	23	3	15	75	42	117	2	.289	.337	.432
Ken Henderson	OF65,DH3	S	31	75	244	23	63	14	0	5	23	18	37	2	.258	.317	.377
Tom Grieve	OF60,DH13	R	29	79	236	24	53	9	0	7	30	13	57	1	.225	.273	.352
John Ellis	C16,DH15,1B8	R	28	49	119	7	28	7	0	4	15	8	26	0	.235	.283	.395
Kurt Bevacqua	OF14,3B11,1B5*	R	30	39	96	13	32	7	2	5	28	6	13	0	.333	.365	.604
Sandy Alomar	DH26,2B18,SS6*	S	33	69	83	21	22	3	0	1	11	8	13	4	.265	.333	.337
Bill Fahey	C34	L	27	37	68	3	15	4	0	0	5	1	8	0	.221	.232	.279
Keith Smith	OF22	R	24	23	67	13	16	4	0	2	6	4	7	2	.239	.301	.388
Jim Mason†	SS32,DH1,3B1	L	26	36	55	9	12	3	0	1	7	6	10	0	.218	.290	.327
Ed Kirkpatrick†	OF6,DH4,1B3*	L	32	20	48	2	9	1	0	0	3	4	11	2	.188	.250	.208
Lew Beasley	OF18,DH1,SS1	L	28	25	32	5	7	1	0	0	3	2	2	1	.219	.257	.250
Jim Fregosi†	1B5,DH3	R	35	13	28	4	7	1	0	1	5	3	4	0	.250	.313	.393
Pat Putnam	1B7,DH3	L	23	11	26	3	8	4	0	0	3	1	4	0	.308	.333	.462
Roy Howell†	DH2,OF2,1B1*	L	23	7	17	0	0	0	0	0	0	2	4	0	.000	.105	.000
Eddie Miller	DH3,OF2	S	20	17	6	7	2	0	0	0	1	1	1	3	.333	.429	.333
Gary Gray	OF1	R	24	1	2	0	0	0	0	0	0	0	1	0	.000	.000	.000

B. Wills, 1 G at 1B; K. Bevacqua, 5 G at 2B, 3 G at DH; S. Alomar, 5 G at OF, 4 G at 1B, 1 G at 3B; E. Kirkpatrick, 1 G at C; R. Howell, 1 G at 3B

Pitcher	T	Age	G	GS	CG	ShO	IP	H	HR	BB	SO	W-L	Sv	ERA
Gaylord Perry	R	38	34	34	13	4	238.0	239	21	56	177	15-12	0	3.37
Doyle Alexander	R	26	34	34	12	1	237.0	221	24	82	82	17-11	0	3.65
Bert Blyleven	R	26	30	30	15	5	234.2	181	20	69	182	14-12	0	2.72
Dock Ellis†	R	32	23	22	7	1	167.1	158	13	42	90	10-6	1	2.90
Nelson Briles†	R	33	28	15	2	1	108.1	114	13	30	57	6-4	1	4.07
Tommy Boggs	R	21	6	6	0	0	27.1	40	1	12	15	0-3	0	5.93
Jim Umbarger†	L	24	3	2	0	0	13.0	14	2	4	5	1-1	0	5.54
John Poloni	L	23	2	1	0	0	7.0	8	1	1	5	1-0	0	6.43
Adrian Devine	R	25	56	2	0	0	105.2	102	8	31	67	11-6	15	3.58
Paul Lindblad	L	35	42	1	0	0	98.2	103	16	29	46	4-5	4	4.20
Darold Knowles	L	35	42	0	0	0	50.1	50	3	23	14	5-2	4	3.22
Roger Moret	L	27	18	8	0	0	72.1	59	6	38	39	3-3	4	3.73
Len Barker	R	21	15	3	0	0	47.1	36	1	24	51	4-1	1	2.66
Mike Marshall†	R	34	12	4	0	0	35.2	42	0	13	18	2-2	1	4.04
Steve Hargan†	R	34	6	0	0	0	12.1	22	2	5	10	1-0	0	8.76
Mike Wallace	L	26	5	0	0	0	8.1	10	1	10	2	0-0	0	7.56
Bobby Cuellar	R	24	4	0	0	0	6.2	4	1	2	3	0-0	0	1.35
Mike Bacsik	R	25	2	0	0	0	2.1	9	1	0	1	0-0	0	19.29

836 Seasons: Team Rosters

1977 Chicago White Sox 3rd AL West 90-72 .556 12.0 GB

Bob Lemon

Player	Gm by Position	B	Age	G	AB	R	H	2B	3B	HR	RBI	BB	SO	SB	Avg	OBP	Slg
Jim Essian	C111,3B2	R	26	114	322	50	88	18	2	10	44	52	35	1	.273	.374	.435
Jim Spencer	1B125	L	30	128	470	56	116	16	1	18	69	36	50	1	.247	.300	.400
Jorge Orta	2B139	L	26	144	564	71	159	27	8	11	84	46	49	4	.282	.334	.417
Eric Soderholm	3B126,DH3	R	28	130	460	77	129	20	3	25	67	47	47	2	.280	.350	.500
Alan Bannister	SS133,2B3,OF3	R	25	139	560	87	154	20	3	3	57	54	49	4	.275	.335	.338
Chet Lemon	OF149	R	22	150	553	99	151	38	4	19	67	52	88	8	.273	.343	.459
Ralph Garr	OF126,DH2	L	31	134	543	78	163	29	7	10	54	27	44	12	.300	.333	.435
Richie Zisk	OF109,DH28	R	28	141	531	78	154	17	6	30	101	55	98	0	.290	.355	.514
Oscar Gamble	DH79,OF49	L	27	137	408	75	121	22	2	31	83	54	54	1	.297	.386	.588
Lamar Johnson	DH68,1B45	R	26	118	374	52	113	12	5	18	65	24	53	1	.302	.342	.505
Brian Downing	C61,OF3,DH2	R	26	69	169	28	48	4	2	4	25	34	21	1	.284	.402	.402
Jack Brohamer	3B38,2B18,DH1	L	27	59	152	26	39	10	3	2	20	21	8	0	.257	.347	.401
Wayne Nordhagen	OF46,C3,DH2	R	28	52	124	16	39	7	3	4	22	2	12	1	.315	.323	.516
Royle Stillman	OF26,DH13,1B1	L	26	56	119	18	25	7	1	3	13	17	21	2	.210	.307	.361
Don Kessinger†	SS21,2B13,3B9	S	34	39	119	12	28	3	2	0	11	13	7	2	.235	.308	.294
Bob Coluccio	OF19	R	25	20	37	4	10	0	0	0	7	6	2	0	.270	.356	.270
Kevin Bell	SS5,3B4,OF1	R	21	9	28	4	5	1	0	1	6	3	8	0	.179	.250	.321
Jerry Hairston†	OF11	S	25	13	26	3	8	2	0	0	4	5	7	0	.308	.419	.385
Bill Nahorodny	C7	R	23	7	23	3	6	1	0	1	4	2	3	0	.261	.308	.435
Henry Cruz	OF9	L	25	16	21	3	6	0	0	2	5	1	3	0	.286	.318	.571
Tim Nordbrook†	SS11,DH2,3B1	R	27	15	20	2	5	0	0	0	1	7	4	1	.250	.429	.250
Mike Squires	1B1	L	25	3	3	0	0	0	0	0	0	0	1	0	.000	.000	.000
Bob Molinaro†	OF1	L	27	1	2	0	1	0	0	0	0	0	1	1	.500	.500	.500
John Flannery	SS4,DH1,3B1	R	20	7	2	1	0	0	0	0	0	1	1	0	.000	.333	.000
Tommy Cruz	OF2	L	26	4	2	1	0	0	0	0	0	0	0	0	.000	.000	.000
Nyls Nyman		L	23	1	1	0	0	0	0	0	0	0	0	0	.000	.000	.000

Pitcher	T	Age	G	GS	CG	ShO	IP	H	HR	BB	SO	W-L	Sv	ERA
Francisco Barrios	R	24	33	31	9	0	231.1	241	22	58	119	14-7	0	4.12
Steve Stone	R	29	31	31	8	0	207.1	228	25	80	124	15-12	0	4.51
Chris Knapp	R	23	27	26	4	0	146.1	166	16	61	103	12-7	0	4.80
Ken Kravec	L	25	26	25	6	1	166.2	161	12	57	125	11-8	0	4.10
Wilbur Wood	L	35	24	18	5	1	122.2	139	10	50	42	7-8	0	4.99
Ken Brett†	L	28	13	13	2	0	82.2	101	10	15	39	6-4	0	5.01
Steve Renko†	R	32	8	8	0	0	53.1	55	3	17	36	5-0	0	3.54
Dave Frost	R	24	4	3	0	0	23.2	30	0	3	15	1-1	0	3.04
Lerrin LaGrow	R	28	66	0	0	0	98.2	81	10	35	63	7-3	25	2.46
Dave Hamilton	L	29	55	0	0	0	67.1	71	6	33	45	4-5	9	3.61
Bart Johnson	R	27	29	4	0	0	92.0	114	5	38	46	4-5	2	4.01
Don Kirkwood†	R	27	16	0	0	0	40.0	49	3	10	24	1-1	0	5.18
Silvio Martinez	R	21	10	0	0	0	21.0	28	4	12	10	0-1	1	5.57
Jack Kucek	R	24	8	3	0	0	34.2	35	4	10	25	0-1	0	3.63
Bruce Dal Canton	R	35	8	0	0	0	24.0	20	1	13	9	0-2	2	3.75
Clay Carroll†	R	36	8	0	0	0	11.1	14	3	4	4	1-3	1	4.76
John Verhoeven†	R	23	6	0	0	0	10.1	9	0	2	6	0-0	0	2.61
Larry Anderson	R	24	6	0	0	0	8.2	10	1	15	7	1-3	0	9.35
Randy Wiles	L	25	5	0	0	0	2.2	5	1	3	0	1-1	0	10.13

1977 Minnesota Twins 4th AL West 84-77 .522 17.5 GB

Gene Mauch

Player	Gm by Position	B	Age	G	AB	R	H	2B	3B	HR	RBI	BB	SO	SB	Avg	OBP	Slg
Butch Wynegar	C142,3B1	S	21	144	532	76	139	22	3	10	79	68	61	2	.261	.344	.370
Rod Carew	1B151,2B4,DH1	L	31	155	616	128	239	38	16	14	100	69	55	23	.388	.449	.570
Bob Randall	2B101,DH4,1B1*	R	29	103	306	36	73	13	2	0	22	15	25	1	.239	.289	.294
Mike Cubbage	3B126,DH1	L	26	129	417	60	110	16	5	9	55	37	49	1	.264	.321	.391
Roy Smalley	SS150	S	24	150	584	93	135	21	5	6	56	74	89	5	.231	.316	.315
Lyman Bostock	OF149	L	26	153	593	104	199	36	12	14	90	51	59	16	.336	.389	.508
Dan Ford	OF137,DH3	R	25	144	453	66	121	25	7	11	60	41	79	6	.267	.338	.426
Larry Hisle	OF134,DH6	R	30	141	546	95	165	36	3	28	119	56	106	21	.302	.369	.533
Craig Kusick	DH85,1B23	R	28	115	268	34	68	12	0	12	45	49	60	3	.254	.370	.433
Glenn Adams	DH47,OF44	L	29	95	269	32	91	17	0	6	49	18	30	0	.338	.376	.468
Rich Chiles	DH61,OF22	L	27	108	261	31	69	16	1	3	36	23	17	0	.264	.323	.368
Jerry Terrell	3B59,2B14,DH9*	R	30	93	214	32	48	6	0	1	20	11	21	10	.224	.263	.266
Rob Wilfong	2B66,DH1	L	23	73	171	22	42	1	1	1	13	17	26	10	.246	.321	.281
Bob Gorinski	OF37,DH9	R	25	54	118	14	23	4	1	3	22	5	29	1	.195	.226	.322
Willie Norwood	OF28,DH5	R	26	39	83	15	19	3	0	3	9	6	17	6	.229	.281	.373
Luis Gomez	2B19,SS7,3B4*	R	25	32	65	6	16	4	2	0	11	4	9	0	.246	.290	.369
Glenn Borgmann	C17	R	27	17	43	12	11	1	0	2	7	11	9	0	.256	.407	.419
Bud Bulling	C10,DH3	R	24	15	32	2	5	1	0	0	5	5	5	0	.156	.270	.188
Larry Wolfe	3B8	R	24	8	25	3	6	1	0	0	6	1	0	0	.240	.269	.280
Sam Perlozzo	2B10,3B1	R	26	10	24	6	7	0	2	0	0	2	3	0	.292	.346	.458
Randy Bass	DH6	L	23	9	19	0	2	0	0	0	0	0	5	0	.105	.105	.105

B. Randall, 1 G at 3B; J. Terrell, 7 G at SS, 1 G at 1B, 1 G at OF; L. Gomez, 2 G at DH, 1 G at OF

Pitcher	T	Age	G	GS	CG	ShO	IP	H	HR	BB	SO	W-L	Sv	ERA
Dave Goltz	R	28	39	39	19	2	303.0	284	23	91	186	20-11	0	3.36
Paul Thormodsgard	R	23	37	37	8	1	218.0	236	25	65	94	11-15	0	4.62
Geoff Zahn	L	31	34	32	7	1	198.0	234	20	66	88	12-14	0	4.68
Pete Redfern	R	22	30	28	1	0	137.1	164	13	66	73	6-9	0	5.18
Bill Butler	L	30	6	4	0	0	21.0	19	5	15	5	0-1	0	6.86
Mike Pazik	L	27	3	3	0	0	18.0	18	1	6	6	1-0	0	2.50
Tom Johnson	R	26	71	0	0	0	146.2	152	11	47	87	16-7	15	3.13
Tom Burgmeier	L	33	61	0	0	0	97.1	113	15	33	35	6-4	7	5.09
Ron Schueler	R	29	52	7	0	0	134.2	131	16	61	77	8-7	3	4.41
Dave Johnson	R	28	30	6	0	0	72.2	86	7	23	33	2-5	0	4.58
Jeff Holly	L	24	18	5	0	0	48.1	57	8	12	32	2-3	0	6.89
Gary Serum	R	20	8	0	0	0	22.2	22	4	10	14	0-0	0	4.37
Don Carrithers	R	27	7	0	0	0	14.1	16	2	6	3	0-1	0	6.91
Jim Shellenback	L	33	5	0	0	0	5.2	10	1	5	3	0-0	0	7.94
Jim Hughes	R	25	2	0	0	0	4.0	4	0	1	1	0-0	0	2.25

1977 California Angels 5th AL West 74-88 .457 28.0 GB

Norm Sherry (39-42)/Dave Garcia (35-46)

Player	Gm by Position	B	Age	G	AB	R	H	2B	3B	HR	RBI	BB	SO	SB	Avg	OBP	Slg
Terry Humphrey	C123	R	27	123	304	17	69	11	0	2	34	21	58	1	.227	.283	.283
Tony Solaita	1B91,DH6	L	30	116	324	40	78	15	0	14	53	56	77	1	.241	.349	.417
Jerry Remy	2B152,3B1	L	24	154	575	74	145	19	10	4	44	59	59	41	.252	.322	.341
Dave Chalk	3B141,2B7,SS4	R	26	149	519	58	144	27	2	3	45	52	69	12	.277	.345	.355
Rance Mulliniks	SS77	L	21	78	271	36	73	13	2	3	21	23	36	1	.269	.329	.365
Bobby Bonds	OF140,DH18	R	31	158	592	103	156	23	9	37	115	74	141	41	.264	.342	.520
Gil Flores	OF85,DH8	R	24	104	342	41	95	19	4	1	26	12	39	12	.278	.325	.365
Don Baylor	OF77,DH61,1B18	R	28	154	561	87	141	27	0	25	75	62	76	26	.251	.334	.433
Danny Goodwin	DH23	L	23	35	91	5	19	6	1	1	8	5	19	0	.209	.250	.330
Ron Jackson	1B43,3B30,DH20*	R	24	106	292	38	71	15	2	8	28	24	42	3	.243	.301	.390
Mario Guerrero	SS31,DH19,2B12	R	27	86	244	17	69	8	2	1	28	4	16	0	.283	.292	.344
Joe Rudi	OF61,DH3	R	30	64	242	48	64	13	2	13	53	22	48	1	.264	.333	.496
Thad Bosley	OF55	L	20	58	212	19	63	10	2	0	19	16	32	5	.297	.346	.363
Bobby Grich	SS52	R	28	52	181	24	44	6	0	7	23	37	40	6	.243	.369	.392
Andy Etchebarren	C80	R	34	80	114	11	29	2	2	0	14	12	19	3	.254	.320	.307
Bruce Bochte†	OF24,DH1	L	26	25	100	12	29	4	0	2	8	7	4	3	.290	.336	.390
Willie Aikens	DH13,1B13	L	22	42	91	5	18	4	0	0	6	10	23	1	.198	.277	.242
Rusty Torres	OF54	S	28	58	77	9	12	1	1	3	10	10	18	0	.156	.250	.312
Ken Landreaux	OF22	L	22	23	76	6	19	5	1	0	5	5	15	1	.250	.296	.342
Dan Briggs	1B45,OF13	L	24	59	74	6	12	2	0	1	4	8	14	0	.162	.241	.230
Ike Hampton	C47	S	25	52	44	5	13	1	0	3	9	2	10	0	.295	.340	.523
Dave Kingman†	1B8,OF2	R	28	10	36	4	7	2	0	2	4	1	16	0	.194	.237	.417
Carlos May†	1B3,DH1	L	29	11	18	0	6	0	0	0	1	5	1	0	.333	.478	.333
Bobby Jones	DH6	L	27	14	17	3	3	0	0	1	3	4	5	0	.176	.318	.353
Orlando Ramirez	2B5,SS3,DH1	R	25	25	13	6	1	0	0	0	0	0	3	1	.077	.077	.077

R. Jackson, 3 G at OF, 1 G at SS

Pitcher	T	Age	G	GS	CG	ShO	IP	H	HR	BB	SO	W-L	Sv	ERA
Nolan Ryan	R	30	37	37	22	4	299.0	198	12	204	341	19-16	0	2.77
Frank Tanana	L	23	31	31	20	7	241.1	201	19	61	205	15-9	0	2.54
Paul Hartzell	R	23	41	23	6	0	189.1	200	14	38	79	8-12	4	3.57
Wayne Simpson	R	28	27	23	0	0	122.0	154	14	62	55	6-12	0	5.83
Ken Brett†	L	28	21	21	5	0	142.0	157	15	38	41	7-10	0	4.25
Gary Ross	R	29	14	12	0	0	58.1	83	10	11	30	2-4	0	5.55
Gary Nolan†	R	29	5	5	0	0	18.1	31	5	2	4	0-3	0	8.84
John Caneira	R	24	6	4	0	0	28.2	27	5	16	17	2-2	0	4.08
Mike Cuellar	L	40	2	1	0	0	3.1	9	2	3	3	0-1	0	18.90
Dave LaRoche†	L	29	46	0	0	0	81.1	64	8	37	61	6-5	13	3.10
Dyar Miller†	R	31	41	0	0	0	92.1	81	10	30	49	4-4	4	3.02
Mike Barlow	R	29	20	1	0	0	59.0	53	3	27	25	4-2	1	4.58
Dick Drago†	R	32	13	0	0	0	21.0	22	3	3	15	0-1	2	3.00
Don Kirkwood†	R	27	13	0	0	0	17.2	20	3	9	10	1-0	1	5.09
Mickey Scott	L	29	12	0	0	0	16.0	19	1	4	5	0-2	0	5.63
Balor Moore	L	26	7	3	0	0	22.2	28	7	10	14	0-2	0	3.97
Sid Monge†	L	26	4	0	0	0	12.1	14	2	6	4	0-1	1	2.92
Fred Kuhaulua	L	24	3	1	0	0	6.1	15	1	7	3	0-0	0	15.63
John Verhoeven†	R	23	3	0	0	0	4.2	4	0	4	3	0-2	0	3.86
Tom Walker†	R	28	1	0	0	0	2.0	3	2	0	1	0-0	0	9.00

1977 Seattle Mariners 6th AL West 64-98 .395 38.0 GB

Darrell Johnson

Player	Gm by Position	B	Age	G	AB	R	H	2B	3B	HR	RBI	BB	SO	SB	Avg	OBP	Slg
Bob Stinson	C99,DH1	S	31	105	297	27	80	11	1	8	32	37	50	0	.269	.360	.394
Dan Meyer	1B159	L	24	159	582	75	159	24	4	22	90	43	51	11	.273	.320	.442
Jose Baez	2B77,DH3,3B1	R	23	91	305	39	79	14	1	1	17	19	20	6	.259	.305	.321
Bill Stein	3B147,DH3,SS2	R	30	151	556	53	144	26	5	13	67	29	79	3	.259	.299	.394
Craig Reynolds	SS134	L	24	135	420	41	104	12	3	4	28	15	23	6	.248	.277	.319
Ruppert Jones	OF155,DH4	L	22	160	597	85	157	26	8	24	76	55	120	13	.263	.324	.454
Steve Braun	OF100,DH32,3B1	L	29	139	451	51	106	19	1	5	31	80	59	8	.235	.351	.315
Lee Stanton	OF91,DH33	R	31	133	454	56	125	24	1	27	90	42	115	0	.275	.341	.511
Juan Bernhardt	DH54,3B21,1B8	R	23	89	305	32	74	9	2	7	30	5	26	2	.243	.259	.354
Dave Collins	OF73,DH40	S	24	120	402	46	96	9	3	5	28	33	66	25	.239	.299	.313
Carlos Lopez	OF90,DH2	R	26	99	297	39	84	18	1	8	34	14	61	16	.283	.319	.431
Larry Milbourne	2B41,SS40,DH1*	S	26	86	242	24	53	10	0	2	21	6	20	3	.219	.239	.285
Julio Cruz	2B54,DH1	S	22	60	199	25	51	3	1	1	7	24	29	15	.256	.336	.296
Skip Jutze	C40	R	31	42	109	10	24	2	0	3	15	7	12	0	.220	.267	.321
Larry Cox	C35	R	29	35	93	6	23	6	0	2	6	10	12	1	.247	.320	.376
Jimmy Sexton	SS12	R	25	14	37	5	8	1	1	1	3	2	6	1	.216	.256	.378
Ray Fosse†	C8,DH2	R	30	11	34	3	12	3	0	0	5	2	2	0	.353	.389	.441
Tommy Smith	OF14	L	28	21	27	1	7	1	1	0	4	0	6	0	.259	.259	.370
Puchy Delgado	OF13	R	23	13	22	4	4	0	0	0	2	1	8	0	.182	.217	.182
Kevin Pasley†	C4	R	23	4	13	1	5	0	0	0	2	1	2	0	.385	.429	.385
Joe Lis	1B4,C1	R	30	9	13	1	3	0	0	0	0	1	2	0	.231	.286	.231
Tom McMillan	SS2	R	25	2	5	0	0	0	0	0	0	0	0	0	.000	.000	.000

L. Milbourne, 1 G at 3B

Pitcher	T	Age	G	GS	CG	ShO	IP	H	HR	BB	SO	W-L	Sv	ERA
Glenn Abbott	R	26	36	34	7	0	204.1	212	32	56	100	12-13	0	4.45
Dick Pole	R	26	25	24	3	0	122.1	127	16	57	51	7-12	0	5.15
Gary Wheelock	R	25	17	17	2	0	88.1	94	16	26	47	6-9	0	4.89
Rick Jones	L	22	10	10	0	0	42.1	47	10	37	16	1-4	0	5.10
Stan Thomas†	R	27	13	9	1	0	58.1	74	8	25	14	2-6	0	6.02
Paul Mitchell†	R	27	9	9	0	0	39.2	50	7	16	20	3-3	0	4.99
Bob Galasso	R	25	11	7	0	0	35.0	57	8	8	21	0-6	0	9.00
Doc Medich†	R	28	3	3	1	0	22.1	26	1	4	3	2-0	0	3.63
Frank MacCormick	R	22	3	3	0	0	7.0	4	0	12	4	0-0	0	3.86
Enrique Romo	R	29	58	3	0	0	114.1	93	8	39	105	8-10	16	2.83
John Montague	R	29	47	15	2	0	182.1	193	20	75	98	8-12	4	4.29
Bill Laxton†	L	29	43	0	0	0	72.2	62	10	39	49	3-2	3	4.95
Mike Kekich	L	32	41	2	0	0	90.0	90	11	51	55	5-4	3	5.60
Diego Segui	R	39	40	7	0	0	110.2	108	20	43	91	0-7	2	5.69
Tom House†	L	30	26	11	1	0	89.1	94	12	19	39	4-5	1	3.93
Dave Pagan†	R	27	24	4	1	1	66.0	86	3	26	30	1-1	2	6.14
Tommy Moore	R	28	14	1	0	0	33.0	36	1	21	13	2-1	0	4.91
Rick Honeycutt	L	23	10	3	0	0	29.0	26	7	11	17	0-1	0	4.34
Steve Burke	R	22	6	0	0	0	15.2	12	0	7	6	0-1	0	2.87
Greg Erardi	R	23	5	0	0	0	9.0	12	3	6	5	0-1	0	6.00
Byron McLaughlin	R	21	1	0	0	0	1.1	5	1	0	1	0-0	0	27.00

1977 Oakland Athletics 7th AL West 63-98 .391 38.5 GB

Jack McKeon (26-27)/Bobby Winkles (37-71)

Player	Gm by Position	B	Age	G	AB	R	H	2B	3B	HR	RBI	BB	SO	SB	Avg	OBP	Slg
Jeff Newman	C94,P1	R	28	94	162	17	36	9	0	4	15	4	24	2	.222	.244	.352
Dick Allen	1B50,DH1	R	35	54	171	19	41	4	0	5	31	24	36	1	.240	.330	.351
Marty Perez†	2B105,3B12,SS4	R	30	115	373	32	86	14	5	2	23	29	65	1	.231	.290	.311
Wayne Gross	3B145,1B1	L	25	146	485	66	113	21	1	22	63	86	84	5	.233	.352	.416
Rob Picciolo	SS148	R	24	148	419	35	84	12	3	2	22	9	55	1	.200	.218	.258
Mitchell Page	OF133,DH8	L	25	145	501	85	154	28	8	21	75	78	95	42	.307	.405	.521
Tony Armas	OF112,SS1	R	23	118	363	26	87	8	2	13	53	20	99	1	.240	.274	.380
Jim Tyrone	OF81,DH4,1B1*	R	28	96	294	32	72	11	1	5	26	25	62	3	.245	.300	.340
Manny Sanguillen	C77,DH58,OF9*	R	33	152	571	42	157	17	5	6	58	22	35	2	.275	.302	.354
Rodney Scott	2B71,SS70,3B5*	S	23	133	364	56	95	4	4	0	20	43	50	33	.261	.342	.294
Earl Williams	DH45,C36,1B29	R	28	100	348	39	84	13	0	13	38	18	58	2	.241	.288	.391
Mike Jorgensen†	1B48,OF20,DH2	L	28	66	203	18	50	4	1	8	32	25	44	3	.246	.329	.394
Rich McKinney	1B32,DH18,3B7*	R	30	86	198	13	35	7	0	6	21	16	43	0	.177	.236	.303
Bill North	OF52,DH1	S	29	56	184	32	48	3	3	1	9	32	25	17	.261	.376	.326
Larry Murray	OF78,DH3,SS1	S	24	90	162	19	29	5	2	1	9	17	36	12	.179	.257	.253
Jerry Tabb	1B36,DH5	L	25	51	144	8	32	3	0	6	19	10	26	0	.222	.269	.368
Willie Crawford†	OF22,DH18	L	30	59	136	7	25	7	1	1	16	18	20	0	.184	.277	.272
Sheldon Mallory	OF45,DH7,1B4	L	23	64	126	19	27	4	1	0	5	11	18	12	.214	.291	.262
Tim Hosley	C19,DH12,1B3	R	30	39	78	5	15	0	0	1	10	16	13	0	.192	.333	.231
Matt Alexander	OF31,DH12,SS12*	S	30	90	42	24	10	1	0	0	2	4	6	26	.238	.304	.262
Larry Lintz	2B28,DH5,SS2*	S	27	41	30	11	4	1	0	0	0	8	13	13	.133	.333	.167
Mark Williams	OF1	L	23	3	2	0	0	0	0	0	1	1	1	0	.000	.333	.000

J. Tyrone, 1 G at SS; M. Sanguillen, 7 G at 1B; R. Scott, 1 G at DH, 1 G at OF; R. McKinney, 5 G at OF, 3 G at 2B; M. Alexander, 4 G at 2B, 1 G at 3B; L. Lintz, 1 G at 3B

Pitcher	T	Age	G	GS	CG	ShO	IP	H	HR	BB	SO	W-L	Sv	ERA
Vida Blue	L	27	38	38	16	1	279.2	284	23	86	157	14-19	0	3.83
Rick Langford	R	25	37	31	6	1	208.1	223	18	73	141	8-19	0	4.02
Doc Medich†	R	28	26	25	1	0	147.2	155	19	49	74	10-6	0	4.69
Mike Norris	R	22	16	12	1	1	77.1	77	14	31	35	2-7	0	4.77
Jim Umbarger†	L	24	12	8	1	0	44.0	62	3	28	24	1-5	0	6.55
Dock Ellis†	R	32	7	7	0	0	26.0	35	5	14	11	1-5	0	9.69
Matt Keough	R	21	7	6	0	0	42.2	39	4	22	23	1-3	0	4.85
Mike Torrez†	R	30	4	4	2	0	26.1	23	3	11	12	3-1	0	4.44
Paul Mitchell†	R	27	5	3	0	0	13.2	21	3	7	5	0-3	0	10.54
Steve McCatty	R	23	4	2	0	0	14.1	16	1	7	9	0-0	0	5.02
Bob Lacey	L	23	64	0	0	0	121.2	100	13	43	69	6-8	7	3.03
Doug Bair	R	27	45	0	0	0	83.1	78	11	57	68	4-6	8	3.46
Joe Coleman	R	30	43	12	2	0	127.2	114	11	49	55	4-4	2	2.96
Pablo Torrealba	L	29	41	10	3	0	116.2	127	5	38	51	4-6	2	2.62
Dave Giusti†	R	37	40	0	0	0	60.1	54	4	20	28	3-3	6	2.98
Stan Bahnsen†	R	32	11	2	0	0	22.0	24	5	13	21	1-2	1	6.14
Steve Dunning	R	28	6	0	0	0	18.1	17	2	10	4	1-0	0	3.93
Craig Mitchell	R	23	3	1	0	0	5.2	9	1	2	1	0-1	0	7.94
Jeff Newman	R	28	1	0	0	0	1.0	1	0	0	0	0-0	0	0.00

»1977 Philadelphia Phillies 1st NL East 101-61 .623 —

Danny Ozark

Player	Gm by Position	B	Age	G	AB	R	H	2B	3B	HR	RBI	BB	SO	SB	Avg	OBP	Slg
Bob Boone	C131,3B2	R	29	132	440	55	125	26	4	11	66	42	54	5	.284	.343	.436
Richie Hebner	1B103,3B13,2B1	L	29	118	397	67	113	17	4	18	62	61	46	7	.285	.381	.484
Ted Sizemore	2B152	R	32	152	519	64	146	20	3	4	47	52	40	8	.281	.345	.355
Mike Schmidt	3B149,SS2,2B1	R	27	154	544	114	149	27	11	38	101	104	122	15	.274	.393	.574
Larry Bowa	SS154	S	31	154	624	93	175	19	3	4	41	32	32	32	.280	.313	.340
Greg Luzinski	OF148	R	26	149	554	99	171	35	3	39	130	80	140	3	.309	.394	.594
Garry Maddox	OF138	R	27	139	571	85	167	27	10	14	74	24	58	22	.292	.323	.448
Jerry Martin	OF106,1B1	R	28	116	215	34	56	16	3	6	28	18	42	6	.260	.328	.447
Jay Johnstone	OF91,1B19	L	31	112	363	64	103	18	4	15	59	38	38	3	.284	.349	.479
Bake McBride†	OF73	L	28	85	280	55	95	20	5	11	41	25	25	27	.339	.392	.564
Tim McCarver	C42,1B3	L	35	93	169	28	54	13	2	6	30	28	11	3	.320	.410	.527
Dave Johnson	1B43,2B9,3B6	R	34	78	156	23	50	9	1	8	36	23	20	1	.321	.408	.545
Tom Hutton	1B73,OF9	L	31	107	81	12	25	3	0	2	11	12	10	1	.309	.394	.420
Ollie Brown	OF21	R	33	53	70	5	17	3	1	1	13	4	14	1	.243	.280	.357
Terry Harmon	2B28,SS16,3B3	R	33	46	60	13	11	1	0	2	5	6	9	0	.183	.265	.300
Barry Foote†	C17	R	25	18	32	3	7	1	0	1	3	3	6	0	.219	.286	.344
Dane Iorg†	1B9	L	27	12	30	3	5	1	0	0	2	1	3	0	.167	.194	.200
Fred Andrews	2B7	R	25	12	23	3	4	0	1	0	2	1	5	1	.174	.200	.261
Bobby Tolan†	1B5	L	31	15	16	1	2	0	0	0	1	1	4	0	.125	.176	.125
Jim Morrison	3B5	R	24	5	7	3	3	0	0	0	1	1	1	0	.429	.500	.429
Mike Buskey	SS6	R	28	6	7	1	2	0	1	0	1	0	1	0	.286	.375	.571
John Vukovich		R	29	2	2	0	0	0	0	0	0	0	1	0	.000	.000	.000
Tim Blackwell†	C1	S	24	1	0	1	0	0	0	0	0	0	0	0	—	—	—

Pitcher	T	Age	G	GS	CG	ShO	IP	H	HR	BB	SO	W-L	Sv	ERA
Steve Carlton	L	32	36	36	17	2	283.0	229	25	89	198	23-10	0	2.64
Larry Christenson	R	23	34	34	5	1	219.1	229	21	69	118	19-6	0	4.06
Randy Lerch	L	22	32	28	3	0	168.2	207	20	75	81	10-6	0	5.07
Jim Kaat	L	38	35	27	2	0	160.1	211	20	40	55	6-11	0	5.39
Jim Lonborg	R	35	25	25	4	1	157.2	157	15	50	76	11-4	0	4.11
Wayne Twitchell†	R	29	12	8	0	0	45.2	50	3	25	37	0-5	0	4.53
Manny Seoane	R	22	2	1	0	0	6.0	11	0	3	4	0-0	0	6.00
Gene Garber	R	29	64	0	0	0	103.1	82	6	23	78	8-6	19	2.35
Ron Reed	R	34	60	3	0	0	124.1	101	9	37	84	7-5	15	2.75
Warren Brusstar	R	25	46	0	0	0	71.1	64	7	24	46	7-2	3	2.65
Tug McGraw	L	32	45	0	0	0	79.0	62	6	24	58	7-3	9	2.62
Tom Underwood†	L	23	14	0	0	0	33.1	44	2	18	20	3-2	1	5.13
Dan Warthen†	L	24	3	0	0	0	3.2	4	0	5	1	0-1	0	0.00

1977 Pittsburgh Pirates 2nd NL East 96-66 .593 5.0 GB

Chuck Tanner

Player	Gm by Position	B	Age	G	AB	R	H	2B	3B	HR	RBI	BB	SO	SB	Avg	OBP	Slg
Duffy Dyer	C93	R	31	94	270	27	65	11	1	3	19	54	49	6	.241	.370	.322
Bill Robinson	1B86,OF43,3B17	R	34	137	507	74	154	32	1	26	104	25	92	12	.304	.337	.525
Rennie Stennett	2B113	R	26	116	453	53	152	20	4	5	51	29	24	28	.336	.376	.430
Phil Garner	3B107,2B50,SS12	R	28	153	585	99	152	35	10	17	77	55	65	32	.260	.325	.441
Frank Taveras	SS146	R	27	147	544	72	137	20	10	1	29	38	71	70	.252	.306	.331
Dave Parker	OF158,2B1	L	26	159	637	107	215	44	8	21	88	58	107	17	.338	.397	.531
Al Oliver	OF148	L	30	154	568	75	175	29	6	19	82	40	38	13	.308	.353	.481
Omar Moreno	OF147	L	24	150	492	69	118	19	9	7	34	38	102	53	.240	.295	.358
Ed Ott	C90	L	25	104	311	40	82	14	3	7	38	32	41	7	.264	.334	.395
Willie Stargell	1B55	L	37	63	186	29	51	12	0	13	35	31	55	0	.274	.383	.548
Fernando Gonzalez	3B37,OF16,2B6*	R	27	80	181	17	50	10	0	4	27	13	21	3	.276	.320	.398
Ken Macha	3B17,1B11,OF4	R	26	35	95	2	26	4	0	0	11	6	17	1	.274	.317	.316
Mario Mendoza	SS45,3B19,P1	R	26	70	81	5	16	3	0	0	4	3	10	0	.198	.226	.235
Bobby Tolan†	1B20,OF2	L	31	49	74	7	15	4	0	2	9	4	10	1	.203	.241	.338
Jim Fregosi†	1B15,3B1	R	35	36	56	10	16	1	1	3	16	13	10	2	.286	.408	.500
Jerry Hairston†	OF14,2B1	S	25	51	52	5	10	2	0	2	6	6	10	0	.192	.271	.346
Miguel Dilone	OF17	S	22	29	44	5	6	0	0	0	0	2	3	12	.136	.174	.136
Dale Berra	3B14	R	20	17	40	0	7	1	0	0	3	1	8	0	.175	.195	.200
Ed Kirkpatrick†	1B10,OF2,3B1	L	32	21	28	5	4	2	0	1	4	8	6	1	.143	.324	.321
Terry Forster	P33,OF1	L	25	36	26	2	9	1	1	0	1	0	4	0	.346	.346	.462
Mike Easler	OF4	L	26	10	18	3	8	2	0	1	5	0	1	0	.444	.421	.722
Tommy Helms†		R	36	15	12	0	0	0	0	0	0	0	3	0	.000	.000	.000
Mike Edwards	2B4	R	24	7	6	1	0	0	0	0	0	0	3	0	.000	.143	.000

F. Gonzalez, 2 G at SS

Pitcher	T	Age	G	GS	CG	ShO	IP	H	HR	BB	SO	W-L	Sv	ERA
John Candelaria	L	23	33	33	6	1	230.2	197	29	50	133	20-5	0	2.34
Jerry Reuss	L	28	33	33	8	2	208.0	225	11	71	116	10-13	0	4.11
Bruce Kison	R	27	33	32	3	1	193.0	209	25	55	122	9-10	0	4.90
Jim Rooker	L	34	30	30	7	2	204.1	196	24	64	89	14-9	0	3.08
Goose Gossage	R	25	72	0	0	0	133.0	78	9	49	151	11-9	26	1.62
Kent Tekulve	R	30	72	0	0	0	103.0	89	5	33	59	10-1	7	3.06
Grant Jackson	L	34	49	2	0	0	91.0	81	11	39	41	5-3	4	3.86
Larry Demery	R	24	39	8	0	0	90.1	100	13	47	35	6-5	1	5.08
Odell Jones	R	24	34	15	1	0	108.0	118	14	31	66	3-7	0	5.08
Terry Forster	L	25	33	6	0	0	87.1	90	7	32	58	6-4	1	4.43
Ed Whitson	R	22	5	2	0	0	15.2	11	0	9	10	1-0	0	3.45
Tim Jones	R	23	3	1	0	0	10.0	4	0	3	5	1-0	0	0.00
Al Holland	L	24	2	0	0	0	2.1	4	0	0	1	0-0	0	7.71
Dave Pagan†	R	27	1	0	0	0	3.0	1	0	0	4	0-0	0	0.00
Mario Mendoza	R	26	1	0	0	0	2.0	3	1	2	0	0-0	0	13.50

1977 St. Louis Cardinals 3rd NL East 83-79 .512 18.0 GB

Vern Rapp

Player	Gm by Position	B	Age	G	AB	R	H	2B	3B	HR	RBI	BB	SO	SB	Avg	OBP	Slg
Ted Simmons	C143,OF1	S	27	150	516	82	164	25	3	21	95	79	37	2	.318	.408	.500
Keith Hernandez	1B158	L	23	161	560	90	163	41	4	15	91	79	88	7	.291	.379	.459
Mike Tyson	2B135	R	27	138	418	42	103	15	2	7	57	30	48	3	.246	.299	.342
Ken Reitz	3B157	R	26	157	587	58	153	36	1	17	79	19	74	2	.261	.291	.412
Garry Templeton	SS151	S	21	153	621	94	200	19	18	8	79	15	70	28	.322	.336	.449
Jerry Mumphrey	OF133	S	24	145	463	73	133	20	10	2	38	47	70	22	.287	.354	.387
Lou Brock	OF130	L	38	141	489	69	133	22	6	2	46	30	74	35	.272	.317	.354
Heity Cruz	OF106,3B2	R	24	118	339	50	80	19	2	6	42	46	56	4	.236	.326	.357
Tony Scott	OF89	S	25	95	292	38	85	16	3	3	41	33	48	13	.291	.368	.397
Mike Anderson	OF77	R	26	94	154	18	34	4	1	4	17	14	31	2	.221	.286	.338
Don Kessinger†	SS26,2B24,3B4	S	34	59	134	14	32	4	0	0	7	14	26	0	.239	.309	.269
Bake McBride†	OF33	L	28	43	122	21	32	5	1	4	20	7	19	9	.262	.298	.418
Dave Rader	C38	L	28	66	114	15	30	7	1	1	16	9	10	1	.263	.310	.368
Mike Phillips†	2B31,3B5,SS5	L	26	48	87	17	21	3	2	0	9	9	13	1	.241	.320	.322
Roger Freed	1B18,OF6	R	31	49	83	10	33	2	1	5	21	11	9	0	.398	.463	.627
Rick Bosetti	OF35	R	23	41	69	12	16	0	0	0	3	6	11	4	.232	.303	.232
Dane Iorg†	OF7	L	27	30	32	2	10	1	0	0	4	5	4	0	.313	.395	.344
Jim Dwyer	OF12	L	27	13	31	3	7	1	0	0	2	4	5	0	.226	.351	.258
Joel Youngblood†	OF11,3B6	R	25	25	27	1	5	2	0	0	1	3	5	0	.185	.267	.259
Taylor Duncan	3B5	R	24	8	12	2	4	0	0	1	2	2	1	0	.333	.400	.583
Ken Oberkfell	2B6	L	21	9	9	0	1	0	0	0	1	0	3	0	.111	.111	.111
Jerry Davanon	2B5	R	31	9	8	2	0	0	0	0	0	1	2	0	.000	.111	.000
Mike Potter	OF1	R	26	5	7	0	0	0	0	0	0	0	2	0	.000	.000	.000
John Tamargo	C1	S	25	4	4	0	0	0	0	0	0	0	2	0	.000	.000	.000
Bennie Ayala	OF1	R	26	1	3	0	1	0	0	0	0	0	1	0	.333	.333	.333

Pitcher	T	Age	G	GS	CG	ShO	IP	H	HR	BB	SO	W-L	Sv	ERA
Bob Forsch	R	27	35	35	8	2	217.1	210	20	69	95	20-7	0	3.48
Eric Rasmussen	R	25	34	34	11	3	233.0	223	24	63	120	11-17	0	3.48
John Denny	R	24	26	26	3	1	149.2	165	9	62	60	8-8	0	4.51
Pete Falcone	L	23	27	22	1	1	124.0	130	19	61	75	4-8	1	5.44
Tom Underwood†	L	23	19	17	1	0	100.0	104	7	57	66	6-9	0	4.95
Larry Dierker	R	30	11	9	0	0	39.1	40	7	16	6	2-6	0	4.58
John D'Acquisto†	R	25	3	2	0	0	8.1	5	0	10	9	0-0	0	4.32
Al Hrabosky	L	27	65	0	0	0	86.1	82	12	41	68	6-5	10	4.38
Butch Metzger†	R	25	58	0	0	0	92.2	78	8	38	48	4-2	7	3.11
Clay Carroll†	R	36	51	1	0	0	90.0	77	8	24	34	4-2	4	2.50
John Urrea	R	22	41	12	2	1	139.2	126	13	35	81	7-6	4	3.16
Rawly Eastwick†	R	26	41	1	0	0	53.2	74	6	21	30	3-7	4	4.70
Buddy Schultz	L	26	40	3	0	0	85.1	76	5	24	66	6-1	1	2.32
Johnny Sutton	R	24	14	0	0	0	24.1	28	1	9	9	2-1	0	2.59
Doug Capilla†	L	25	2	0	0	0	2.1	2	0	2	1	0-0	0	15.43

1977 Chicago Cubs 4th NL East 81-81 .500 20.0 GB

Herman Franks

Player	Gm by Position	B	Age	G	AB	R	H	2B	3B	HR	RBI	BB	SO	SB	Avg	OBP	Slg
George Mitterwald	C109,1B1	R	32	110	349	40	83	22	0	9	43	28	69	3	.238	.295	.378
Bill Buckner	1B99	L	27	122	426	40	121	27	0	11	60	21	23	7	.284	.314	.425
Manny Trillo	2B149	R	26	152	504	51	141	18	5	7	57	44	58	3	.280	.339	.377
Steve Ontiveros	3B155	S	25	156	546	54	163	32	3	10	68	81	69	3	.299	.390	.423
Ivan DeJesus	SS154	R	24	155	624	91	166	31	7	3	40	56	90	24	.266	.328	.353
Bobby Murcer	OF150,2B1,SS1	L	31	154	554	90	147	18	3	27	89	80	77	16	.265	.355	.455
Jerry Morales	OF128	R	28	136	490	56	142	34	5	11	69	43	75	0	.290	.348	.447
Greg Gross	OF71	L	24	115	239	43	77	10	4	5	32	33	19	0	.322	.397	.460
Larry Biittner	1B80,OF52,P1	L	31	138	493	74	147	28	1	12	62	35	36	2	.298	.345	.432
Gene Clines	OF63	R	30	101	239	27	70	12	2	3	41	25	25	1	.293	.358	.397
Jose Cardenal	OF62,2B1,SS1	R	33	100	226	33	54	12	1	3	18	28	30	5	.239	.324	.341
Steve Swisher	C72	R	25	74	205	21	39	7	0	5	15	9	47	0	.190	.229	.298
Mick Kelleher	2B40,SS14,3B1	R	29	63	122	14	28	5	2	0	11	9	12	0	.230	.288	.303
Dave Rosello	3B21,SS10,2B3	R	27	56	82	18	18	2	1	1	9	12	12	0	.220	.319	.305
Joe Wallis	OF35	S	25	56	80	14	20	3	0	2	8	16	25	0	.250	.375	.363
Mike Gordon	C8	S	23	8	23	0	1	0	0	0	2	2	8	0	.043	.120	.043
Bobby Darwin†	OF1	R	34	11	12	2	2	1	0	0	0	0	5	0	.167	.167	.250
Mike Sember	2B1	R	24	3	4	0	1	0	0	0	0	0	2	0	.250	.250	.250
Randy Hundley	C2	R	35	2	4	0	0	0	0	0	0	0	1	0	.000	.000	.000
Mike Adams	OF2	R	28	2	2	0	0	0	0	0	0	0	1	0	.000	.000	.000

Pitcher	T	Age	G	GS	CG	ShO	IP	H	HR	BB	SO	W-L	Sv	ERA
Ray Burris	R	26	39	39	5	1	221.0	270	29	67	105	14-16	0	4.72
Rick Reuschel	R	28	39	37	8	4	252.0	233	13	74	166	20-10	1	2.79
Bill Bonham	R	28	34	34	1	0	214.2	207	15	82	134	10-13	0	4.36
Mike Krukow	R	25	34	33	1	1	172.0	195	16	61	106	8-14	0	4.40
Steve Renko†	R	32	13	8	0	0	51.1	51	10	21	34	2-2	1	4.56
Paul Reuschel	R	30	69	0	0	0	107.0	105	9	40	62	5-6	4	4.37
Willie Hernandez	L	22	67	1	0	0	110.0	94	11	28	78	8-7	4	3.03
Bruce Sutter	R	24	62	0	0	0	107.1	69	5	23	129	7-3	31	1.34
Donnie Moore	R	23	27	1	0	0	48.2	51	1	18	34	4-2	0	4.07
Pete Broberg	R	27	22	0	0	0	36.0	34	8	18	20	1-2	0	4.75
Jim Todd	R	29	20	0	0	0	30.2	47	1	19	17	1-1	0	9.10
Dave Giusti†	R	37	20	0	0	0	25.1	30	2	14	15	0-2	1	6.04
Dave Roberts†	L	32	17	6	1	0	53.0	55	1	12	23	1-1	1	3.23
Dennis Lamp	R	24	11	3	0	0	30.0	43	3	8	12	0-2	0	6.30
Ramon Hernandez†	L	36	6	0	0	0	7.2	11	1	3	4	0-0	1	8.22
Larry Biittner	L	31	1	0	0	0	1.1	5	3	1	3	0-0	0	40.50

1977 Montreal Expos 5th NL East 75-87 .463 26.0 GB

Dick Williams

Player	Gm by Position	B	Age	G	AB	R	H	2B	3B	HR	RBI	BB	SO	SB	Avg	OBP	Slg
Gary Carter	C146,OF1	R	23	154	522	86	148	29	2	31	84	58	103	5	.284	.356	.525
Tony Perez	1B148	R	35	154	559	71	158	32	6	19	91	63	111	4	.283	.352	.463
Dave Cash	2B153	R	29	153	650	91	188	42	7	0	43	52	33	21	.289	.343	.375
Larry Parrish	3B115	R	23	123	402	50	99	19	2	11	46	37	71	2	.246	.314	.386
Chris Speier†	SS138	R	27	139	531	58	125	30	6	5	38	67	78	1	.235	.321	.343
Warren Cromartie	OF155	L	23	155	620	64	175	41	7	5	50	33	40	10	.282	.321	.395
Andre Dawson	OF136	R	22	139	525	64	148	26	9	19	65	34	93	21	.282	.326	.474
Ellis Valentine	OF126	R	22	127	508	63	149	28	2	25	76	30	58	13	.293	.331	.504
Del Unser	OF72,1B27	L	32	113	289	33	79	14	1	12	40	33	41	2	.273	.346	.453
Wayne Garrett	3B49,2B1	L	29	68	159	17	43	6	1	2	22	30	18	2	.270	.385	.358
Sam Mejias	OF56	R	25	74	101	14	23	4	1	3	8	2	17	1	.228	.243	.376
Pete Mackanin	2B9,SS8,3B5*	R	25	55	85	9	19	2	2	1	6	4	17	3	.224	.258	.329
Jose Morales	C8,1B8	R	32	65	74	3	15	4	1	1	9	5	12	0	.203	.247	.324
Pepe Frias	2B16,SS14,3B1	R	28	53	70	10	18	1	0	0	5	0	10	1	.257	.257	.271
Tim Foli†	SS13	R	26	13	57	2	10	5	1	0	3	0	4	0	.175	.172	.298
Barry Foote†	C13	R	25	15	49	4	12	3	1	2	8	4	10	0	.245	.302	.469
Stan Papi	3B10,SS2,2B1	R	26	13	43	5	10	2	1	0	4	1	9	1	.233	.250	.326
Tim Blackwell†	C14	S	24	16	22	3	2	1	0	0	0	2	7	0	.091	.167	.136
Jerry White	OF8	S	24	16	21	4	4	0	0	0	1	1	3	1	.190	.227	.190
Mike Jorgensen†	1B5	L	28	19	20	3	4	1	0	0	0	3	4	0	.200	.304	.250

P. Mackanin, 4 G at OF

Pitcher	T	Age	G	GS	CG	ShO	IP	H	HR	BB	SO	W-L	Sv	ERA
Steve Rogers	R	27	40	40	17	4	301.2	272	16	81	206	17-16	0	3.10
Jackie Brown	R	34	42	25	6	2	185.2	189	15	71	89	9-12	0	4.51
Wayne Twitchell†	R	29	22	22	2	0	139.0	116	18	49	93	6-5	0	4.21
Stan Bahnsen†	R	32	23	22	3	1	127.1	142	14	38	58	8-9	0	4.81
Gerry Hannahs	L	24	8	7	0	0	37.0	43	7	17	21	1-5	0	4.86
Dan Warthen†	L	24	12	6	1	0	35.0	33	7	38	26	2-3	0	7.97
Hal Dues	R	22	6	4	0	0	23.0	26	2	9	9	1-1	0	4.30
Dan Schatzeder	L	22	6	3	1	1	21.2	16	0	13	14	2-1	0	2.49
Will McEnaney	L	25	69	0	0	0	86.2	92	6	22	38	3-5	3	3.95
Joe Kerrigan	R	22	66	0	0	0	89.1	80	4	33	43	3-5	11	3.22
Bill Atkinson	R	22	55	0	0	0	83.1	72	12	29	56	7-2	7	3.35
Don Stanhouse	R	26	47	16	1	1	158.1	147	12	84	89	10-10	10	3.41
Santo Alcala†	R	24	31	10	0	0	101.2	104	12	47	64	2-6	2	4.69
Fred Holdsworth†	R	25	14	6	0	0	42.1	35	6	18	21	3-3	0	3.19
Jeff Terpko	R	26	13	0	0	0	20.2	28	2	15	14	0-1	0	5.66
Tom Walker†	R	28	11	0	0	0	19.0	15	2	7	10	1-1	0	4.74
Larry Landreth	R	22	4	1	0	0	9.1	16	0	8	5	0-2	0	9.64

1977 New York Mets 6th NL East 64-98 .395 37.0 GB

Joe Frazier (15-30)/Joe Torre (49-68)

Player	Gm by Position	B	Age	G	AB	R	H	2B	3B	HR	RBI	BB	SO	SB	Avg	OBP	Slg
John Stearns	C127,1B6	R	25	139	431	52	108	25	1	12	55	77	76	9	.251	.370	.397
John Milner	1B87,OF22	L	27	131	388	43	99	20	3	12	57	61	55	6	.255	.353	.415
Felix Millan	2B89	R	33	91	314	40	78	11	2	2	21	18	9	1	.248	.294	.315
Lenny Randle	3B110,2B20,OF6*	S	28	136	513	78	156	22	7	5	27	65	70	33	.304	.383	.404
Bud Harrelson	SS98	S	33	107	269	25	48	6	2	1	12	27	28	5	.178	.255	.227
Lee Mazzilli	OF156	S	22	159	537	66	134	24	3	6	46	72	72	22	.250	.340	.339
Steve Henderson	OF97	R	24	99	350	67	104	16	6	12	65	43	79	6	.297	.372	.480
Bruce Boisclair	OF91,1B9	L	24	127	307	41	90	21	1	4	44	31	57	6	.293	.359	.407
Doug Flynn†	SS65,2B29,3B2	R	26	90	282	14	54	6	1	0	14	11	23	1	.191	.220	.220
Ed Kranepool	OF42,1B41	L	32	108	281	28	79	17	0	10	40	23	20	1	.281	.330	.448
Mike Vail	OF85	R	25	108	279	29	73	12	1	8	35	19	58	0	.262	.310	.398
Dave Kingman†	OF45,1B17	R	28	58	211	22	44	7	0	9	28	13	66	3	.209	.263	.370
Joel Youngblood†	2B33,OF22,3B10	R	25	70	182	16	46	11	1	0	11	13	40	1	.253	.301	.324
Roy Staiger	3B36,SS1	R	27	40	123	16	31	9	0	2	11	4	20	1	.252	.276	.374
Ron Hodges	C27	L	28	66	117	6	31	4	0	1	5	9	17	0	.265	.317	.325
Jerry Grote†	C28,3B11	R	34	42	115	8	31	3	1	0	7	9	12	0	.270	.333	.313
Mike Phillips†	SS24,3B9,2B4	L	26	38	86	5	18	2	1	1	3	2	15	0	.209	.244	.291
Bobby Valentine†	1B15,SS14,3B4	R	27	42	83	8	11	1	0	1	3	6	9	0	.133	.191	.181
Leo Foster	2B20,SS8,3B2	R	26	36	75	6	17	3	0	0	6	5	14	3	.227	.284	.267
Joe Torre	1B16,3B1	R	36	26	51	2	9	3	0	1	9	2	10	0	.176	.204	.294
Luis Rosado	1B7,C1	R	21	9	24	1	5	1	0	0	3	1	3	0	.208	.250	.250
Dan Norman	OF6	R	22	7	16	2	4	1	0	0	0	4	2	0	.250	.400	.313
Pepe Mangual	OF4	R	25	8	7	1	1	0	0	0	2	1	4	0	.143	.250	.143
Luis Alvarado†	2B1	R	28	1	2	0	0	0	0	0	0	0	0	0	.000	.000	.000

L. Randle, 1 G at SS

Pitcher	T	Age	G	GS	CG	ShO	IP	H	HR	BB	SO	W-L	Sv	ERA
Jerry Koosman	L	34	32	32	6	1	226.2	195	17	81	192	8-20	0	3.49
Nino Espinosa	R	23	32	29	7	1	200.0	188	17	55	105	10-13	0	3.42
Jon Matlack	L	27	26	26	5	3	169.0	175	19	43	123	7-15	0	4.21
Craig Swan	R	26	26	24	2	1	146.2	153	10	56	71	9-10	0	4.23
Pat Zachry†	R	25	19	19	2	1	119.2	129	14	48	63	7-6	0	3.76
Tom Seaver†	R	32	13	13	5	3	96.0	79	7	28	72	7-3	0	3.00
Jackson Todd	R	25	19	10	0	0	71.2	78	8	20	39	3-6	0	4.77
Roy Lee Jackson	R	23	4	4	0	0	24.0	25	2	15	13	0-2	0	6.00
Doc Medich†	R	28	1	1	0	0	7.0	6	0	1	3	0-1	0	3.86
Skip Lockwood	R	30	63	0	0	0	104.0	87	5	31	84	4-8	20	3.38
Bob Apodaca	R	27	59	0	0	0	84.0	83	7	30	53	4-8	5	3.43
Bob Myrick	L	24	44	4	0	0	87.1	86	5	33	49	2-2	2	3.61
Rick Baldwin	R	24	40	0	0	0	62.2	62	6	31	23	1-2	1	4.45
Paul Siebert†	L	24	25	0	0	0	28.0	27	0	13	20	2-1	0	3.86
Ray Sadecki	L	36	4	0	0	0	3.0	3	1	3	0	0-1	0	6.00
John Pacella	R	20	3	0	0	0	4.0	2	0	2	1	0-0	0	0.00

1977 Los Angeles Dodgers 1st NL West 98-64 .605 —

Tom Lasorda

Player	Gm by Position	B	Age	G	AB	R	H	2B	3B	HR	RBI	BB	SO	SB	Avg	OBP	Slg
Steve Yeager	C123	R	28	125	387	53	99	21	2	16	55	43	84	1	.256	.334	.444
Steve Garvey	1B160	R	28	162	646	91	192	25	3	33	115	38	90	9	.297	.335	.498
Davey Lopes	2B130	R	32	134	502	85	142	19	5	11	53	73	69	47	.283	.372	.406
Ron Cey	3B153	R	29	153	564	77	136	22	3	30	110	93	106	3	.241	.347	.450
Bill Russell	SS153	R	28	153	634	84	176	28	6	4	51	24	43	16	.278	.304	.360
Dusty Baker	OF152	R	28	153	533	86	155	26	1	30	86	58	89	2	.291	.364	.512
Reggie Smith	OF140	S	32	148	488	104	150	27	4	32	87	104	76	7	.307	.427	.576
Rick Monday	OF115,1B3	L	31	118	392	47	90	13	1	15	48	60	109	1	.230	.330	.383
Lee Lacy	OF32,2B22,3B12	R	29	75	169	28	45	7	0	6	21	10	21	4	.266	.306	.414
Glenn Burke	OF74	R	24	83	169	16	43	8	0	1	13	5	22	13	.254	.280	.320
Johnny Oates	C56	L	31	60	156	18	42	4	0	3	11	11	11	1	.269	.314	.353
Ted Martinez	2B27,SS13,3B12	R	29	67	137	21	41	6	1	1	10	2	20	3	.299	.309	.380
John Hale	OF73	L	23	79	108	10	26	4	1	2	11	15	28	2	.241	.331	.352
Ed Goodson	1B13,3B4	L	29	61	66	3	11	1	0	1	5	3	10	0	.167	.203	.227
Vic Davalillo	OF12	L	40	24	48	3	15	2	0	0	4	0	6	0	.313	.313	.354
Boog Powell	1B4	L	35	50	41	0	10	0	0	0	5	12	9	0	.244	.415	.244
Manny Mota	OF1	R	39	49	38	5	15	1	0	1	4	10	0	1	.395	.521	.500
Jerry Grote†	C16,3B2	R	34	18	27	3	7	0	0	0	4	2	5	0	.259	.310	.259
Joe Simpson	OF28,1B1	L	25	29	23	2	4	0	0	0	1	2	6	1	.174	.240	.174
Ron Washington	SS10	R	25	10	19	4	7	0	0	0	1	0	2	1	.368	.400	.368
Rafael Landestoy	2B8,SS3	S	24	15	18	6	5	0	0	0	0	3	2	2	.278	.381	.278
Jeffrey Leonard	OF10	R	21	11	10	1	3	0	1	0	2	1	4	0	.300	.364	.500
Kevin Pasley†	C2	R	23	2	3	0	1	0	0	0	0	0	0	0	.333	.333	.333

Pitcher	T	Age	G	GS	CG	ShO	IP	H	HR	BB	SO	W-L	Sv	ERA
Don Sutton	R	32	33	33	9	3	240.1	207	23	69	150	14-8	0	3.18
Doug Rau	L	28	32	32	4	2	212.1	232	15	49	126	14-8	0	3.43
Burt Hooton	R	27	32	31	6	2	223.1	184	14	60	153	12-7	1	2.62
Tommy John	L	34	31	31	11	3	220.1	225	12	50	123	20-7	0	2.78
Rick Rhoden	R	24	31	31	4	1	216.1	223	20	63	122	16-10	0	3.74
Charlie Hough	R	29	70	1	0	0	127.1	98	10	70	105	6-12	22	3.32
Mike Garman	R	27	49	0	0	0	62.2	60	7	22	29	4-4	12	2.73
Elias Sosa	R	27	44	0	0	0	63.2	42	7	12	47	2-2	1	1.98
Stan Wall	L	26	25	0	0	0	32.0	36	3	13	22	2-3	0	5.34
Lance Rautzhan	L	24	25	0	0	0	20.2	25	0	7	13	4-1	2	4.35
Al Downing	L	36	12	1	0	0	20.0	22	4	16	23	0-1	0	6.75
Bobby Castillo	R	22	6	0	0	0	11.1	12	2	2	7	1-0	0	3.97
Dennis Lewallyn	R	23	5	1	0	0	17.0	22	1	4	8	3-1	1	4.24
Hank Webb	R	27	5	0	0	0	8.0	5	1	1	2	0-0	0	2.25

1977 Cincinnati Reds 2nd NL West 88-74 .543 10.0 GB

Sparky Anderson

Player	Gm by Position	B	Age	G	AB	R	H	2B	3B	HR	RBI	BB	SO	SB	Avg	OBP	Slg
Johnny Bench	C135,OF8,1B4*	R	29	142	494	67	136	34	2	31	109	58	95	2	.275	.348	.540
Dan Driessen	1B148	L	25	151	536	75	161	31	4	17	91	64	85	31	.300	.375	.468
Joe Morgan	2B151	L	33	153	521	113	150	21	6	22	78	117	58	49	.288	.417	.478
Pete Rose	3B161	S	36	162	655	95	204	38	7	9	64	66	42	16	.311	.377	.432
Dave Concepcion	SS156	R	29	156	572	59	155	26	3	8	64	46	77	29	.271	.322	.369
George Foster	OF158	R	28	158	615	124	197	31	2	52	149	61	107	6	.320	.382	.631
Ken Griffey Sr.	OF147	L	27	154	585	117	186	35	8	12	57	69	84	17	.318	.389	.467
Cesar Geronimo	OF147	L	29	149	492	54	131	22	4	10	52	35	89	10	.266	.321	.388
Mike Lum	OF24,1B8	L	31	81	125	14	20	1	0	5	16	9	33	2	.160	.221	.288
Bill Plummer	C50	R	30	51	117	10	16	5	0	1	7	17	34	1	.137	.244	.205
Ray Knight	3B37,2B17,OF5*	R	24	80	92	8	24	5	1	1	13	9	16	1	.261	.324	.370
Bob Bailey†	1B19,OF3	R	34	49	79	9	20	2	1	2	11	12	10	1	.253	.348	.380
Ed Armbrister	OF27	R	28	65	78	12	20	4	3	1	5	10	21	5	.256	.337	.423
Champ Summers	OF16,3B1	L	31	59	76	11	13	4	0	3	6	6	16	0	.171	.238	.342
Rick Auerbach	2B19,SS12	R	27	33	45	5	7	2	0	0	3	4	7	0	.156	.216	.200
Doug Flynn†	3B25,2B9,SS4	R	26	36	32	0	8	1	1	0	5	0	6	0	.250	.242	.344
Don Werner	C10	R	24	10	23	3	4	0	0	2	4	2	3	0	.174	.231	.435

J. Bench, 1 G at 3B; R. Knight, 3 G at SS

Pitcher	T	Age	G	GS	CG	ShO	IP	H	HR	BB	SO	W-L	Sv	ERA
Fred Norman	L	34	35	34	8	1	221.1	200	28	98	160	14-13	0	3.38
Jack Billingham	R	34	36	23	3	2	161.2	195	16	56	76	10-10	0	5.23
Tom Seaver†	R	32	20	20	14	4	165.1	120	12	38	124	14-3	0	2.34
Paul Moskau	R	23	20	19	2	2	108.0	116	10	40	71	6-6	0	4.00
Doug Capilla†	L	25	22	16	1	0	106.1	94	10	59	74	7-8	0	4.23
Woodie Fryman	L	37	17	12	0	0	75.1	83	13	45	57	5-5	1	5.38
Pat Zachry†	R	25	12	12	3	0	75.0	78	7	29	36	3-7	0	5.04
Mario Soto	R	20	12	10	2	1	60.2	60	12	26	44	2-6	0	5.34
Gary Nolan†	R	29	8	8	0	0	39.1	53	5	12	28	4-1	0	4.81
Pedro Borbon	R	30	73	0	0	0	127.0	131	7	24	48	10-5	18	3.19
Dale Murray	R	27	61	1	0	0	102.0	125	13	46	42	7-2	4	4.94
Manny Sarmiento	R	21	24	0	0	0	40.1	28	6	11	23	0-0	1	2.45
Rawly Eastwick†	R	26	23	0	0	0	43.1	40	3	8	17	2-2	7	2.91
Tom Hume	R	24	14	5	0	0	43.0	54	5	17	22	3-3	0	7.12
Mike Caldwell†	L	28	14	0	0	0	24.2	25	1	8	11	0-0	1	4.01
Joe Hoerner	L	40	8	0	0	0	5.2	9	3	3	5	0-0	0	12.71
Santo Alcala†	R	24	7	2	0	0	15.2	22	1	7	9	1-1	0	5.74
Joe Henderson	R	30	7	0	0	0	9.0	17	2	6	8	0-2	0	12.00
Angel Torres	L	24	5	0	0	0	8.1	7	2	8	8	0-0	0	2.16
Dan Dumoulin	R	23	5	0	0	0	5.1	12	0	3	5	0-0	0	13.50

1977 Houston Astros 3rd NL West 81-81 .500 17.0 GB

Bill Virdon

Player	Gm by Position	B	Age	G	AB	R	H	2B	3B	HR	RBI	BB	SO	SB	Avg	OBP	Slg
Joe Ferguson	C122,1B1	R	30	132	421	59	108	21	3	16	61	85	79	6	.257	.379	.435
Bob Watson	1B146	R	31	151	554	77	160	38	6	22	110	57	69	5	.289	.360	.498
Art Howe	2B96,3B19,SS11	R	30	125	413	44	109	23	7	8	58	41	60	0	.264	.336	.412
Enos Cabell	3B144,1B8,SS1	R	27	150	625	101	176	36	7	16	68	27	55	42	.282	.313	.438
Roger Metzger	SS96,2B1	S	29	97	269	24	50	9	6	0	16	32	24	2	.186	.272	.264
Jose Cruz	OF155	L	29	157	579	87	173	31	10	17	87	69	67	44	.299	.368	.475
Cesar Cedeno	OF137	R	26	141	530	92	148	36	8	14	71	47	50	61	.279	.346	.457
Wilbur Howard	OF62,2B4	S	28	87	187	22	48	6	0	2	13	5	30	11	.257	.276	.321
Julio Gonzalez	SS63,2B45	R	24	110	383	34	94	18	3	1	27	19	45	3	.245	.287	.316
Terry Puhl	OF59	L	20	60	229	40	69	13	5	0	10	30	31	10	.301	.385	.402
Ed Herrmann	C49	L	30	56	158	7	46	7	0	1	17	15	18	1	.291	.352	.354
Cliff Johnson†	OF34,1B10	R	29	51	144	22	43	8	0	10	23	23	30	0	.299	.409	.563
Rob Sperring	SS22,2B20,3B11	R	27	58	129	6	24	3	0	1	9	12	23	0	.186	.254	.233
Willie Crawford†	OF30	L	30	42	114	14	29	3	0	2	18	16	10	0	.254	.341	.333
Jim Fuller	OF27,1B1	R	26	34	100	5	16	6	0	2	9	10	45	0	.160	.243	.280
Ken Boswell	2B26,3B2	L	31	72	97	7	21	1	1	0	12	10	12	0	.216	.287	.247
Art Gardner	OF26	L	24	66	65	7	10	0	0	0	3	3	15	0	.154	.203	.154
Leon Roberts	OF9	R	26	19	27	1	2	0	0	0	2	1	8	0	.074	.107	.074
Denny Walling	OF5	L	23	6	21	1	6	0	1	0	6	2	4	0	.286	.348	.381
Danny Walton	1B5	R	29	13	21	0	4	0	0	0	1	0	5	0	.190	.190	.190
Craig Cacek	1B6	R	22	7	20	0	1	0	0	0	1	1	3	0	.050	.095	.050
Joe Cannon	OF3	L	23	9	17	3	2	2	0	0	1	0	5	1	.118	.118	.235
Mike Fischlin	SS12	R	21	13	15	0	3	0	0	0	0	0	2	0	.200	.200	.200
Luis Pujols	C6	R	21	6	15	0	1	0	0	0	0	0	5	0	.067	.067	.067

Pitcher	T	Age	G	GS	CG	ShO	IP	H	HR	BB	SO	W-L	Sv	ERA
J.R. Richard	R	27	36	36	13	3	267.0	212	18	104	214	18-12	0	2.97
Mark Lemongello	R	21	34	30	5	0	214.2	237	20	52	83	9-14	0	3.48
Joaquin Andujar	R	24	26	25	4	1	158.2	149	11	64	69	11-8	0	3.69
Floyd Bannister	L	22	24	23	4	1	142.2	138	11	68	112	8-9	0	4.04
Doug Konieczny	R	25	4	4	0	0	21.0	26	1	8	7	1-1	0	6.00
Joe Sambito	L	25	54	1	0	0	89.0	77	6	24	67	5-5	7	2.33
Bo McLaughlin	R	23	46	6	0	0	84.2	81	6	34	59	4-7	5	4.25
Joe Niekro	R	32	44	14	9	2	180.2	155	14	64	101	13-8	5	3.04
Ken Forsch	R	30	42	5	0	0	86.0	80	2	28	45	5-8	8	2.72
Gene Pentz	R	24	41	4	0	0	87.0	76	8	44	51	5-2	2	3.83
Dan Larson	R	22	32	10	1	0	97.2	108	13	45	44	1-7	1	5.81
Tom Dixon	R	22	9	4	1	0	30.1	40	0	7	15	1-0	0	3.26
Roy Thomas	R	24	4	0	0	0	6.1	5	0	3	4	0-0	0	2.84

1977 San Francisco Giants 4th NL West 75-87 .463 23.0 GB

Joe Altobelli

Player	Gm by Position	B	Age	G	AB	R	H	2B	3B	HR	RBI	BB	SO	SB	Avg	OBP	Slg
Marc Hill	C102	R	25	108	320	28	80	10	0	9	50	34	34	0	.250	.316	.366
Willie McCovey	1B136	L	39	141	478	54	134	21	0	28	86	67	106	3	.280	.367	.500
Rob Andrews	2B115	R	24	127	436	60	115	11	3	0	25	56	33	5	.264	.345	.303
Bill Madlock	3B126,2B6	R	26	140	533	70	161	28	1	12	46	43	33	13	.302	.360	.426
Tim Foli†	SS102,2B1,3B1*	R	26	104	368	30	84	17	3	4	27	11	16	2	.228	.247	.323
Jack Clark	OF114	R	21	136	413	64	104	17	4	13	51	49	73	12	.252	.332	.407
Gary Thomasson	OF113,1B31	L	25	145	446	63	114	24	6	17	71	75	102	16	.256	.358	.451
Terry Whitfield	OF84	L	24	114	326	41	93	21	3	7	36	20	46	2	.285	.329	.433
Derrel Thomas	OF78,2B27,SS26*	R	26	148	506	75	135	13	10	8	44	46	70	15	.267	.328	.379
Darrell Evans	OF81,1B41,3B35	L	30	144	461	64	117	18	3	17	72	69	50	9	.254	.351	.416
Randy Elliott	OF46	R	26	73	167	17	40	5	1	7	26	8	24	0	.240	.275	.407
Vic Harris	2B27,SS11,3B9*	S	27	69	165	28	43	12	0	2	14	19	36	2	.261	.332	.370
Johnnie LeMaster	SS54,3B2	R	23	68	134	13	20	5	1	0	8	13	27	2	.149	.223	.201
Mike Sadek	C57	R	31	61	126	12	29	7	0	1	15	12	5	2	.230	.297	.310
Gary Alexander	C33,OF1	R	24	51	119	17	36	4	2	5	20	20	33	3	.303	.406	.496
Larry Herndon	OF44	R	23	49	109	13	26	4	3	1	5	5	20	4	.239	.278	.358
Chris Speier†	SS5	R	27	6	17	1	3	1	0	0	0	0	3	0	.176	.176	.235
Skip James	1B9	L	27	10	15	3	4	1	0	0	3	2	3	0	.267	.353	.333
Ken Rudolph†	C11	R	30	11	15	1	3	0	0	0	0	1	3	0	.200	.250	.200
Tom Heintzelman		R	30	2	2	0	0	0	0	0	0	0	0	0	.000	.000	.000

T. Foli, 1 G at OF; D. Thomas, 6 G at 3B, 3 G at 1B; V. Harris, 3 G at OF

Pitcher	T	Age	G	GS	CG	ShO	IP	H	HR	BB	SO	W-L	Sv	ERA
Jim Barr	R	29	38	38	6	2	234.1	286	18	56	97	12-16	0	4.76
Ed Halicki	R	26	37	37	7	2	257.2	241	27	70	168	16-12	0	3.32
Bob Knepper	L	23	27	27	6	2	166.0	151	14	72	100	11-9	0	3.36
John Montefusco	R	27	26	25	4	0	157.0	170	10	46	110	7-12	0	3.50
Lynn McGlothen	R	27	21	15	2	0	80.0	94	9	52	42	2-9	0	5.63
Greg Minton	R	25	2	2	0	0	14.0	14	0	4	5	1-1	0	4.50
Gary Lavelle	L	28	73	0	0	0	118.1	106	4	37	93	7-7	20	2.05
Randy Moffitt	R	28	64	0	0	0	87.2	91	4	39	68	4-9	11	3.59
Dave Heaverlo	R	26	56	0	0	0	98.2	92	10	21	58	5-1	1	2.55
Charlie Williams	R	29	55	8	1	0	119.1	116	9	60	41	6-5	0	4.00
John Curtis	L	29	43	9	1	1	77.0	95	5	48	47	3-3	1	5.49
Terry Cornutt	R	24	28	1	0	0	44.1	38	4	22	23	1-2	0	3.86
Tommy Toms	R	25	4	0	0	0	4.1	7	0	2	2	0-1	0	2.08

1977 San Diego Padres 5th NL West 69-93 .426 29.0 GB

John McNamara (20-28)/Bob Skinner (1-0)/Alvin Dark (48-65)

Player	Gm by Position	B	Age	G	AB	R	H	2B	3B	HR	RBI	BB	SO	SB	Avg	OBP	Slg
Gene Tenace	C99,1B36,3B14	R	30	147	437	66	102	24	4	15	61	125	119	5	.233	.415	.410
Mike Ivie	1B105,3B25	R	24	134	489	66	133	29	2	9	66	39	57	3	.272	.326	.395
Mike Champion	2B149	R	22	150	507	35	116	14	6	1	43	27	85	3	.229	.271	.286
Tucker Ashford	3B74,SS10,2B4	R	22	81	249	25	54	18	0	3	24	21	35	2	.217	.278	.325
Bill Almon	SS155	R	24	155	613	75	160	18	11	2	43	37	114	20	.261	.303	.336
Dave Winfield	OF156	R	25	157	615	104	169	29	7	25	92	58	75	16	.275	.335	.467
George Hendrick	OF142	R	27	152	541	75	168	25	2	23	81	61	74	11	.311	.381	.492
Gene Richards	OF109,1B32	L	23	146	525	79	152	16	11	5	32	60	80	56	.290	.363	.390
Jerry Turner	OF69	L	23	118	289	43	71	16	1	10	48	31	43	12	.246	.316	.412
Dave Roberts	C63,2B2,3B2*	R	26	82	186	15	41	14	1	1	23	11	32	2	.220	.268	.323
Doug Rader†	3B51	R	32	52	170	19	46	8	3	5	27	33	40	0	.271	.392	.441
Dave Kingman†	OF28,1B13,3B2	R	28	56	168	16	40	9	0	11	39	12	48	2	.238	.292	.488
Merv Rettenmund	OF27,3B1	R	34	107	126	23	36	6	1	4	17	33	28	1	.286	.432	.444
Gary Sutherland	2B30,3B21,1B4	R	32	80	103	5	25	3	0	1	11	7	15	0	.243	.291	.301
Bob Davis	C46	R	25	48	94	9	17	2	0	1	10	5	24	0	.181	.235	.234
Pat Scanlon	2B15,3B11,OF1	L	24	47	79	9	15	3	0	1	11	12	20	0	.190	.297	.266
Bobby Valentine†	3B10,SS10,1B1	R	27	44	67	5	12	3	0	1	10	7	10	0	.179	.253	.269
Enzo Hernandez	SS7	R	28	7	3	1	0	0	0	0	0	0	0	0	.000	.000	.000
Luis Melendez	OF2	R	27	8	3	1	0	0	0	0	0	1	1	0	.000	.250	.000
Brian Greer		R	18	1	1	0	0	0	0	0	0	0	1	0	.000	.000	.000

D. Roberts, 1 G at SS

Pitcher	T	Age	G	GS	CG	ShO	IP	H	HR	BB	SO	W-L	Sv	ERA
Bob Shirley	L	23	39	35	1	0	214.0	215	22	100	146	12-18	0	3.70
Bob Owchinko	L	22	30	28	3	2	170.0	191	20	67	101	9-12	0	4.45
Randy Jones	L	27	27	25	1	0	147.1	173	12	36	44	6-12	0	4.58
Dave Freisleben	R	25	33	23	1	0	138.2	140	21	71	72	7-9	0	4.61
Tom Griffin	R	29	38	20	0	0	151.1	144	17	88	79	6-9	0	4.46
John D'Acquisto†	R	25	17	12	0	0	44.0	49	3	47	45	1-2	0	6.95
Rollie Fingers	R	30	78	0	0	0	132.1	123	12	36	113	8-9	35	2.99
Dan Spillner	R	25	76	0	0	0	123.0	130	12	60	74	7-6	6	3.73
Dave Tomlin	L	28	76	0	0	0	101.2	98	3	32	55	4-4	3	3.01
Rick Sawyer	R	29	56	9	0	0	111.0	136	15	55	45	7-6	0	5.84
Dave Wehrmeister	R	24	30	6	0	0	69.2	81	8	44	32	1-3	0	6.07
Butch Metzger†	R	25	17	1	0	0	22.2	27	5	12	6	0-0	0	5.56
Vic Bernal	R	23	15	0	0	0	20.1	23	4	9	6	1-1	0	5.31
Brent Strom	L	28	8	3	0	0	16.2	23	5	12	8	0-2	0	12.42
Paul Siebert†	L	24	4	0	0	0	3.2	3	1	4	1	0-0	0	2.45

1977 Atlanta Braves 6th NL West 61-101 .377 37.0 GB

Dave Bristol (8-21)/Ted Turner (0-1)/Vern Benson (1-0)/Dave Bristol (52-79)

Player	Gm by Position	B	Age	G	AB	R	H	2B	3B	HR	RBI	BB	SO	SB	Avg	OBP	Slg
Biff Pocoroba	C100	S	23	113	321	46	93	24	1	8	44	57	27	3	.290	.394	.445
Willie Montanez	1B134	L	29	136	544	70	156	31	1	20	68	35	60	1	.287	.328	.458
Rod Gilbreath	2B122,3B1	R	24	128	407	47	99	15	2	8	43	45	79	3	.243	.320	.349
Junior Moore	3B104,2B1	R	24	112	361	41	94	9	3	5	34	33	29	4	.260	.323	.343
Pat Rockett	SS84	R	22	93	264	27	67	10	0	1	24	27	32	1	.254	.330	.303
Jeff Burroughs	OF154	R	26	154	579	91	157	19	1	41	114	86	126	4	.271	.362	.520
Gary Matthews	OF145	R	26	148	555	89	157	25	5	17	64	67	90	22	.283	.362	.438
Rowland Office	OF104,1B1	L	24	124	428	42	103	13	1	5	39	23	58	2	.241	.282	.311
Jerry Royster	3B56,SS51,2B38*	R	24	140	445	64	96	10	2	6	28	38	67	28	.216	.278	.288
Barry Bonnell	OF75,3B32	R	23	100	360	41	108	11	0	1	45	37	32	7	.300	.368	.339
Darrel Chaney	SS41,2B24	S	29	74	209	22	42	7	2	3	15	17	44	0	.201	.260	.297
Tom Paciorek	1B32,OF9,3B1	R	30	72	155	20	37	8	0	3	15	6	46	1	.239	.262	.348
Vic Correll	C49	R	31	54	144	16	30	7	0	7	16	22	33	2	.208	.314	.403
Brian Asselstine	OF35	L	23	83	124	12	26	6	0	4	17	9	10	1	.210	.263	.355
Cito Gaston	OF9,1B5	R	33	56	85	6	23	4	0	3	21	5	19	1	.271	.301	.424
Joe Nolan	C19	L	26	62	82	13	23	3	0	3	9	13	12	1	.280	.375	.427
Dale Murphy	C18	R	21	18	76	5	24	8	1	2	14	0	8	0	.316	.316	.526
Craig Robinson	SS23	R	28	27	29	4	6	1	0	0	1	1	6	0	.207	.233	.241
Larry Whisenton		L	20	4	4	1	1	0	0	0	1	0	3	0	.250	.250	.250
Bob Belloir	SS3	R	28	6	1	2	0	0	0	0	0	0	0	0	.000	.000	.000

J. Royster, 1 G at OF

Pitcher	T	Age	G	GS	CG	ShO	IP	H	HR	BB	SO	W-L	Sv	ERA
Phil Niekro	R	38	44	43	20	2	330.1	315	26	164	262	16-20	0	4.03
Dick Ruthven	R	26	25	23	6	2	151.0	158	14	62	84	7-13	0	4.23
Andy Messersmith	R	31	16	16	1	0	102.1	101	12	39	69	5-4	0	4.40
Eddie Solomon	R	26	18	16	0	0	88.2	110	10	34	54	6-6	0	4.57
Preston Hanna	R	22	17	9	1	0	60.0	69	6	34	37	2-6	1	4.95
Frank LaCorte	R	25	14	7	0	0	37.0	67	10	29	28	1-8	0	11.68
Mickey Mahler	L	24	5	5	0	0	23.0	31	4	9	14	1-2	0	6.26
Joey McLaughlin	R	20	3	2	0	0	6.0	10	3	3	0	0-0	0	15.00
Dave Campbell	R	25	65	0	0	0	88.2	78	7	33	42	0-6	13	3.05
Rick Camp	R	24	54	0	0	0	78.2	89	6	47	51	6-3	10	4.00
Buzz Capra	R	29	45	16	0	0	139.1	142	28	80	100	6-11	0	5.36
Don Collins	L	24	40	6	0	0	70.2	82	8	41	27	3-9	2	5.09
Max Leon	R	27	31	9	0	0	81.2	89	9	25	44	4-4	1	3.97
Jamie Easterly	L	24	22	5	0	0	58.2	72	5	30	37	2-4	1	6.14
Duane Theiss	R	23	17	0	0	0	20.2	26	1	16	7	1-1	0	6.53
Steve Hargan†	R	34	16	5	0	0	36.2	49	3	16	18	0-3	0	6.87
Steve Kline	R	29	16	0	0	0	20.1	21	4	12	10	0-0	1	6.64
Mike Davey	L	25	16	0	0	0	16.0	19	1	9	7	0-0	2	5.06
Bob Johnson	R	34	15	0	0	0	22.1	24	7	14	16	0-1	0	7.25
Mike Marshall†	R	34	4	0	0	0	6.0	12	1	2	6	1-0	0	9.00
Mike Beard	L	27	4	0	0	0	4.2	14	3	2	1	0-0	0	9.64
Larry Bradford	L	27	2	0	0	0	3.0	3	1	0	1	0-0	0	3.00

»1978 New York Yankees 1st AL East 100-63 .613 —

Billy Martin (52-42)/Dick Howser (0-1)/Bob Lemon (48-20)

Player	Gm by Position	B	Age	G	AB	R	H	2B	3B	HR	RBI	BB	SO	SB	Avg	OBP	Slg
Thurman Munson	C125,DH14,OF13	R	31	154	617	73	183	27	1	6	71	35	70	2	.297	.332	.373
Chris Chambliss	1B155,DH7	L	29	162	625	81	171	26	3	12	90	41	60	2	.274	.321	.382
Willie Randolph	2B134	R	23	134	499	87	139	18	6	3	42	82	51	36	.279	.381	.357
Graig Nettles	3B159,SS2	L	33	159	587	81	162	23	2	27	93	59	69	1	.276	.343	.460
Bucky Dent	SS123	R	26	123	379	40	92	11	1	5	40	23	24	3	.243	.286	.317
Mickey Rivers	OF138	L	29	141	559	78	148	25	8	11	48	29	51	25	.265	.302	.397
Reggie Jackson	OF104,DH35	L	32	139	511	82	140	13	5	27	97	58	133	14	.274	.356	.477
Lou Piniella	OF103,DH23	R	34	130	472	67	148	34	5	6	69	34	36	3	.314	.361	.445
Cliff Johnson	DH39,C22,1B1	R	30	76	174	20	32	9	1	6	19	30	32	0	.184	.307	.351
Roy White	OF74,DH23	S	34	103	346	44	93	13	3	8	43	42	35	10	.269	.349	.393
Fred Stanley	SS71,2B11,3B4	R	30	81	160	14	35	7	0	1	9	25	31	0	.219	.324	.281
Jim Spencer	DH35,1B15	L	31	71	150	12	34	9	1	7	24	15	32	0	.227	.295	.440
Paul Blair	OF64,2B5,SS4*	R	34	75	125	10	22	5	0	2	13	9	17	1	.176	.231	.264
Gary Thomasson†	OF50,DH1	L	26	55	116	20	32	4	1	3	20	13	22	0	.276	.346	.405
Mike Heath	C33	R	23	33	92	6	21	3	1	0	8	4	9	0	.228	.265	.283
Jay Johnstone†	OF22,DH5	L	32	36	65	6	17	0	0	1	6	4	10	0	.262	.329	.308
Brian Doyle	2B29,SS7,3B5	L	23	39	52	6	10	0	0	0	0	0	3	0	.192	.192	.192
Damaso Garcia	2B16,SS3	R	21	18	41	5	8	0	0	0	1	2	6	1	.195	.227	.195
George Zeber	2B1	S	27	3	6	0	0	0	0	0	0	0	0	0	.000	.000	.000
Wendell Alston†		L	25	3	3	0	0	0	0	0	0	0	2	0	.000	.000	.000
Mickey Klutts	3B1	R	23	1	2	1	2	1	0	0	0	0	0	0	1.000	1.000	1.500
Dennis Sherrill	DH1,3B1	R	22	2	1	1	0	0	0	0	0	0	1	0	.000	.000	.000
Fran Healy	C1	R	31	1	1	0	0	0	0	0	0	0	1	0	.000	.000	.000
Domingo Ramos	SS1	R	20	1	0	0	0	0	0	0	0	0	0	0	—	—	—

P. Blair, 3 G at 3B

Pitcher	T	Age	G	GS	CG	ShO	IP	H	HR	BB	SO	W-L	Sv	ERA
Ron Guidry	L	27	35	35	16	9	273.2	187	13	72	248	25-3	0	1.74
Ed Figueroa	R	29	35	35	12	2	253.0	233	22	77	92	20-9	0	2.99
Dick Tidrow	R	31	31	25	4	0	185.1	191	13	53	73	7-11	0	3.84
Jim Beattie	R	23	25	22	0	0	128.0	123	8	51	65	6-9	0	3.73
Catfish Hunter	R	32	21	20	5	1	118.0	98	16	35	56	12-6	0	3.58
Don Gullett	L	27	8	8	2	0	44.2	46	3	20	28	4-2	0	3.63
Andy Messersmith	R	32	6	5	0	0	22.1	24	7	15	16	0-3	0	5.64
Ken Holtzman†	L	32	5	3	0	0	17.2	21	2	9	3	1-0	0	4.08
Dave Rajsich	L	26	4	2	0	0	13.1	16	0	6	9	0-0	0	4.05
Goose Gossage	R	26	63	0	0	0	134.1	87	9	59	122	10-11	27	2.01
Sparky Lyle	L	33	59	0	0	0	111.2	116	6	33	33	9-3	9	3.47
Ken Clay	R	24	28	6	0	0	75.2	89	3	21	32	3-4	0	4.28
Rawly Eastwick†	R	27	8	0	0	0	24.2	22	2	4	13	2-1	0	3.28
Bob Kammeyer	R	27	7	0	0	0	21.2	24	1	6	11	0-0	0	5.82
Paul Lindblad†	L	36	7	1	0	0	18.1	21	4	8	9	0-0	0	4.42
Larry McCall	R	25	5	1	0	0	16.0	20	2	6	7	1-1	0	5.63
Ron Davis	R	22	4	0	0	0	2.1	3	0	3	0	0-0	0	11.57

1978 Boston Red Sox 2nd AL East 99-64 .607 1.0 GB

Don Zimmer

Player	Gm by Position	B	Age	G	AB	R	H	2B	3B	HR	RBI	BB	SO	SB	Avg	OBP	Slg
Carlton Fisk	C154,DH1,OF1	R	30	157	571	94	162	39	5	20	88	71	83	7	.284	.366	.475
George Scott	1B113,DH7	R	34	120	412	51	96	16	4	12	54	44	86	1	.233	.305	.379
Jerry Remy	2B140,DH4,SS1	L	25	148	583	87	162	24	6	2	44	40	55	30	.278	.321	.350
Butch Hobson	3B133,DH14	R	26	147	512	65	128	26	2	17	80	50	122	1	.250	.312	.408
Rick Burleson	SS144	R	27	145	626	75	155	32	5	5	49	40	71	8	.248	.295	.339
Fred Lynn	OF149	L	26	150	541	75	161	33	3	22	82	75	50	3	.298	.380	.492
Dwight Evans	OF142,DH4	R	26	147	497	75	123	24	2	24	63	65	119	8	.247	.336	.449
Jim Rice	OF114,DH49	R	25	163	677	121	213	25	15	46	139	58	126	7	.315	.370	.600
Bob Bailey	DH34,3B1,OF1	R	35	43	94	12	18	3	0	4	9	19	19	2	.191	.328	.351
Carl Yastrzemski	OF71,1B50,DH27	L	38	144	523	70	145	21	2	17	81	76	44	4	.277	.367	.423
Jack Brohamer	3B30,DH25,2B23	L	28	81	244	34	57	14	1	1	25	25	13	1	.234	.300	.311
Frank Duffy	3B22,SS21,2B12*	R	31	64	104	12	27	5	0	0	4	6	11	1	.260	.306	.308
Gary Hancock	OF19,DH13	L	24	38	80	10	18	3	0	0	4	1	12	0	.225	.232	.263
Bernie Carbo†	OF9,DH8	L	30	17	46	7	12	3	0	1	6	8	8	1	.261	.370	.391
Fred Kendall	1B13,C5	R	29	20	41	3	8	1	0	0	4	1	2	0	.195	.205	.220
Bob Montgomery	C10	R	34	10	29	2	7	1	1	0	5	2	12	0	.241	.290	.345
Sam Bowen	OF4	R	25	6	7	3	1	0	0	1	1	1	2	0	.143	.250	.571

F. Duffy, 6 G at DH

Pitcher	T	Age	G	GS	CG	ShO	IP	H	HR	BB	SO	W-L	Sv	ERA
Mike Torrez	R	31	36	36	15	2	250.0	272	19	99	120	16-13	0	3.96
Dennis Eckersley	R	23	35	35	16	3	268.1	258	30	71	162	20-8	0	2.99
Luis Tiant	R	37	32	31	12	5	212.1	185	26	57	114	13-8	0	3.31
Bill Lee	L	31	28	24	8	1	177.0	198	20	59	44	10-10	0	3.46
Jim Wright	R	27	24	16	5	3	116.0	122	8	24	56	8-4	0	3.57
Allen Ripley	R	25	15	11	1	0	73.0	92	10	22	26	2-5	0	5.55
Bobby Sprowl	L	22	3	3	0	0	12.2	12	3	10	10	0-2	0	6.39
Bob Stanley	R	23	52	3	0	0	141.2	142	5	34	38	15-2	10	2.60
Dick Drago	R	33	37	1	0	0	77.1	71	5	32	42	4-4	7	3.03
Tom Burgmeier	L	34	35	1	0	0	61.1	74	7	23	24	2-1	4	4.40
Bill Campbell	R	29	29	0	0	0	50.2	62	3	17	47	7-5	4	3.91
Andy Hassler†	L	26	13	2	0	0	30.0	38	0	13	23	2-1	1	3.00
John LaRose	L	26	1	0	0	0	2.0	3	1	3	0	0-0	0	22.50
Reggie Cleveland†	R	30	1	0	0	0	0.1	1	0	0	0	0-1	0	0.00

1978 Milwaukee Brewers 3rd AL East 93-69 .574 6.5 GB

George Bamberger

Player	Gm by Position	B	Age	G	AB	R	H	2B	3B	HR	RBI	BB	SO	SB	Avg	OBP	Slg
Charlie Moore	C95	R	25	96	268	30	72	7	1	5	31	12	24	4	.269	.300	.358
Cecil Cooper	1B84,DH19	L	28	107	407	60	127	23	2	13	54	32	72	3	.312	.359	.474
Paul Molitor	2B91,SS31,DH2*	R	21	125	521	73	142	26	4	6	45	19	54	30	.273	.301	.372
Sal Bando	3B134,DH12,1B5	R	34	152	540	85	154	20	6	17	78	72	52	3	.285	.371	.439
Robin Yount	SS125	R	22	127	502	66	147	23	9	9	71	24	43	16	.293	.323	.428
Gorman Thomas	OF137	R	27	137	452	70	111	24	1	32	86	73	133	3	.246	.351	.515
Sixto Lezcano	OF127,DH3	R	24	132	442	62	129	21	4	15	61	64	83	3	.292	.377	.459
Ben Oglivie	OF89,DH27,1B11	L	29	128	469	71	142	29	4	18	72	52	69	11	.303	.370	.497
Larry Hisle	OF87,DH51	R	31	142	520	96	151	24	0	34	115	67	90	10	.290	.374	.533
Don Money	1B61,2B36,3B25*	R	31	137	518	88	152	30	2	14	54	48	70	3	.293	.361	.440
Buck Martinez	C89	R	29	89	256	26	56	10	1	1	20	14	42	1	.219	.255	.277
Dick Davis	DH34,OF28	R	24	69	218	28	54	10	1	5	26	7	23	2	.248	.273	.372
Jim Wohlford	OF35,DH4	R	27	46	118	16	35	7	2	1	19	6	10	3	.297	.325	.415
Jim Gantner	2B21,3B15,1B1*	L	25	43	97	14	21	1	0	1	8	5	10	2	.216	.269	.258
Lenn Sakata	2B29	R	24	30	78	8	15	4	0	0	3	8	11	1	.192	.267	.244
Dave May†	OF16,DH8	L	34	39	77	9	15	4	0	2	11	9	10	0	.195	.295	.325
Tony Muser	1B12	L	30	15	30	0	4	1	1	0	5	3	5	0	.133	.212	.233
Jeff Yurak	OF1	S	24	5	5	0	0	0	0	0	0	1	0	0	.000	.167	.000
Tim Nordbrook†	SS2	R	28	2	5	0	0	0	0	0	0	1	1	0	.000	.167	.000
Larry Haney	C4	R	35	4	5	0	1	0	0	0	1	0	1	0	.200	.200	.200
Andy Etchebarren	C4	R	35	4	5	1	2	1	0	0	2	1	2	0	.400	.500	.600
Tim Johnson†	SS2	L	28	3	3	1	0	0	0	0	0	2	0	0	.000	.400	.000

P. Molitor, 1 G at 3B; D. Money, 15 G at DH, 2 G at SS; J. Gantner, 1 G at SS

Pitcher	T	Age	G	GS	CG	ShO	IP	H	HR	BB	SO	W-L	Sv	ERA
Lary Sorensen	R	22	37	36	17	3	280.2	277	14	50	78	18-12	1	3.21
Mike Caldwell	L	29	37	34	23	6	293.1	258	14	54	131	22-9	1	2.36
Jerry Augustine	L	25	35	30	9	2	188.1	204	14	61	59	13-12	0	4.54
Bill Travers	L	25	28	28	8	3	175.2	184	20	58	66	12-11	0	4.41
Andy Replogle	R	24	32	18	3	2	149.1	177	14	47	41	9-5	0	3.92
Moose Haas	R	22	7	6	2	0	30.2	33	6	8	32	2-3	1	6.16
Mark Bomback	R	25	2	1	0	0	1.2	5	1	1	1	0-0	0	16.20
Bob McClure	L	26	44	0	0	0	65.0	53	8	30	47	2-6	9	3.74
Bill Castro	R	24	42	0	0	0	49.2	43	2	14	17	5-4	8	1.81
Ed Rodriguez	R	26	32	8	0	0	105.1	107	9	26	51	5-5	2	3.93
Randy Stein	R	25	31	1	0	0	72.2	78	5	39	42	3-2	1	5.33
Willie Mueller	R	21	5	0	0	0	12.2	16	1	6	6	1-0	0	6.39
Ed Farmer	R	28	3	0	0	0	11.0	7	1	4	6	1-0	1	0.82

1978 Baltimore Orioles 4th AL East 90-71 .559 9.0 GB

Earl Weaver

Player	Gm by Position	B	Age	G	AB	R	H	2B	3B	HR	RBI	BB	SO	SB	Avg	OBP	Slg
Rick Dempsey	C135	R	28	136	441	41	114	25	0	6	32	48	54	7	.259	.327	.356
Eddie Murray	1B157,3B3,DH1	S	22	161	610	85	174	32	3	27	95	70	97	6	.285	.356	.480
Rich Dauer	2B87,3B52,DH1	R	25	133	459	57	121	23	0	6	46	26	22	0	.264	.301	.353
Doug DeCinces	3B130,2B12	R	27	142	511	72	146	37	1	28	80	46	81	7	.286	.346	.526
Mark Belanger	SS134	R	34	135	348	39	74	13	0	0	16	40	55	6	.213	.299	.250
Ken Singleton	OF141,DH5	S	31	149	502	67	147	21	2	20	81	98	94	0	.293	.409	.462
Larry Harlow	OF138,P1	L	26	147	460	67	112	25	1	8	26	55	72	14	.243	.324	.354
Carlos Lopez	OF114,DH1	R	27	129	193	21	46	6	0	4	20	9	34	5	.238	.273	.332
Lee May	DH140,1B4	R	35	148	556	56	137	16	1	25	80	31	110	5	.246	.286	.414
Pat Kelly	OF80,DH2	L	33	100	274	38	75	12	1	11	40	34	58	10	.274	.357	.445
Billy Smith	2B83,SS2	S	24	85	250	29	65	12	2	5	30	27	40	3	.260	.333	.384
Andres Mora	OF69,DH1	R	23	76	229	21	49	8	0	8	14	13	47	0	.214	.258	.354
Kiko Garcia	SS74,2B3	R	24	79	186	17	49	6	4	0	13	7	43	7	.263	.287	.339
Al Bumbry	OF28	L	31	33	114	21	27	5	2	2	6	17	15	5	.237	.346	.368
Terry Crowley	DH17,OF2,1B1	L	31	62	95	9	24	2	0	0	12	8	12	0	.253	.314	.274
Dave Skaggs	C35	R	27	36	86	6	13	1	1	0	2	9	14	0	.151	.232	.186
Gary Roenicke	OF20	R	23	27	58	5	15	3	0	3	15	8	3	0	.259	.348	.466
Mike Anderson	OF47	R	27	53	32	2	3	0	1	0	3	3	10	0	.094	.171	.156
Ellie Hendricks	C6,DH1,P1	L	37	13	18	4	6	1	0	1	1	3	3	0	.333	.429	.556
Mike Dimmel	OF7	R	23	8	0	2	0	0	0	0	0	0	0	0	—	—	—

Pitcher	T	Age	G	GS	CG	ShO	IP	H	HR	BB	SO	W-L	Sv	ERA
Mike Flanagan	L	26	40	40	17	2	281.1	271	22	87	167	19-15	0	4.03
Jim Palmer	R	32	38	38	19	6	296.0	246	19	97	138	21-12	0	2.46
Dennis Martinez	R	23	40	38	15	2	276.1	257	20	93	142	16-11	0	3.52
Scott McGregor	L	24	35	32	13	4	233.0	217	19	47	94	15-13	1	3.32
Nelson Briles	R	34	16	8	1	0	54.1	58	6	21	30	4-4	0	4.64
Sammy Stewart	R	23	2	2	0	0	11.1	10	0	3	11	1-1	0	3.18
Dave Ford	R	21	2	1	0	0	15.0	10	0	2	5	1-0	0	0.00
Don Stanhouse	R	27	56	0	0	0	74.2	60	0	52	42	6-9	24	2.89
Tippy Martinez	L	28	42	0	0	0	69.0	77	4	40	57	3-3	5	4.83
Joe Kerrigan	R	23	26	2	0	0	71.2	75	10	36	41	3-1	3	4.77
John Flinn	R	23	13	0	0	0	15.2	24	3	13	8	1-1	0	8.04
Tim Stoddard	R	25	8	0	0	0	18.0	22	3	8	14	0-1	0	6.00
Earl Stephenson	L	30	2	0	0	0	9.2	10	0	5	4	0-0	0	2.79
Ellie Hendricks	R	37	1	0	0	0	2.1	1	0	1	0	0-0	0	0.00
Larry Harlow	L	26	1	0	0	0	0.2	2	1	4	1	0-0	0	67.50

1978 Detroit Tigers 5th AL East 86-76 .531 13.5 GB

Ralph Houk

Player	Gm by Position	B	Age	G	AB	R	H	2B	3B	HR	RBI	BB	SO	SB	Avg	OBP	Slg
Milt May	C94	L	27	105	352	24	88	9	0	10	37	27	26	0	.250	.305	.361
Jason Thompson	1B151	L	23	153	589	79	169	25	3	26	96	74	96	0	.287	.364	.472
Lou Whitaker	2B136,DH2	L	21	139	484	71	138	12	7	3	58	61	65	7	.285	.361	.357
Aurelio Rodriguez	3B131	R	30	134	385	40	102	25	2	7	43	19	37	0	.265	.303	.395
Alan Trammell	SS139	R	20	139	448	49	120	14	6	2	34	45	56	3	.268	.335	.339
Steve Kemp	OF157	L	23	159	582	75	161	18	4	15	79	97	87	2	.277	.379	.399
Ron LeFlore	OF155	R	30	155	666	126	198	30	3	12	62	65	104	68	.297	.361	.405
Tim Corcoran	OF109,DH1	L	25	116	324	37	86	13	1	1	27	24	27	3	.265	.322	.321
Rusty Staub	DH162	L	34	162	642	75	175	30	1	24	121	76	35	3	.273	.347	.435
Lance Parrish	C79	R	22	85	288	37	63	11	3	14	41	11	71	0	.219	.254	.424
Phil Mankowski	3B80,DH1	L	25	88	222	28	61	8	0	4	20	22	28	2	.275	.344	.365
John Wockenfuss	OF60,DH2	R	29	71	187	23	53	5	0	7	22	21	14	0	.283	.357	.422
Mickey Stanley	OF34,1B12	R	35	53	151	15	40	9	0	3	8	9	19	0	.265	.306	.384
Steve Dillard	2B41,DH4	R	27	56	130	21	29	5	2	0	7	6	11	1	.223	.257	.292
Mark Wagner	SS35,2B4	R	24	39	109	10	26	1	2	0	6	3	11	1	.239	.272	.284
Charlie Spikes	OF9	R	27	10	28	1	7	1	0	0	2	2	6	0	.250	.344	.286
Dave Stegman	OF7	R	24	8	14	3	4	2	0	1	3	1	2	0	.286	.313	.643

Pitcher	T	Age	G	GS	CG	ShO	IP	H	HR	BB	SO	W-L	Sv	ERA
Jim Slaton	R	28	35	34	11	2	233.2	235	27	85	92	17-11	0	4.12
Jack Billingham	R	35	30	30	10	4	201.2	218	16	65	59	15-8	0	3.88
Dave Rozema	R	21	28	28	11	2	209.1	205	17	41	57	9-12	0	3.14
Milt Wilcox	R	28	29	27	16	2	215.1	208	22	68	132	13-12	0	3.76
Kip Young	R	23	14	13	7	0	105.2	94	9	30	49	6-7	0	2.81
Steve Baker	R	21	15	10	0	0	63.1	66	6	42	39	2-4	0	4.55
Mark Fidrych	R	23	3	3	2	0	22.0	17	1	5	10	2-0	0	2.45
John Hiller	L	35	51	0	0	0	92.1	64	6	35	74	9-4	15	2.34
Jack Morris	R	23	28	7	0	0	106.0	107	8	49	48	3-5	0	4.33
Steve Foucault†	R	28	24	0	0	0	37.1	48	1	21	18	2-4	4	3.13
Bob Sykes	L	23	22	10	3	2	93.2	99	14	34	58	6-6	2	3.94
Jim Crawford	L	27	20	0	0	0	39.1	45	3	19	24	2-3	0	4.35
Ed Glynn	L	25	10	0	0	0	14.2	11	3	4	9	0-0	0	3.07
Dave Tobik	R	25	5	0	0	0	12.0	12	1	3	11	0-0	0	3.75
Fredie Arroyo	R	26	2	0	0	0	4.1	8	1	0	1	0-0	0	8.31
Sheldon Burnside	L	23	2	0	0	0	4.0	4	0	2	3	0-0	0	9.00
Bruce Taylor	R	25	1	0	0	0	1.0	0	0	0	0	0-0	0	0.00

Seasons: Team Rosters 841

1978 Cleveland Indians 6th AL East 69-90 .434 29.0 GB

Jeff Torborg

Player	Gm by Position	B	Age	G	AB	R	H	2B	3B	HR	RBI	BB	SO	SB	Avg	OBP	Slg
Gary Alexander†	C66,DH25	R	25	90	324	39	76	14	3	17	62	35	100	0	.235	.308	.454
Andre Thornton	1B145	R	28	145	508	97	133	22	4	33	105	93	72	4	.262	.377	.516
Duane Kuiper	2B149	L	28	149	547	52	155	18	6	0	43	19	35	4	.283	.311	.338
Buddy Bell	3B139,DH1	R	26	142	556	71	157	27	8	6	62	39	43	1	.282	.328	.392
Tom Veryzer	SS129	R	25	130	421	48	114	18	4	1	32	13	36	1	.271	.298	.340
Rick Manning	OF144	L	23	148	566	65	149	27	3	3	50	38	62	12	.263	.309	.337
John Grubb†	OF110	L	29	113	378	54	100	16	6	14	61	59	60	5	.265	.365	.450
Paul Dade	OF81,DH9	R	26	93	307	37	78	12	1	3	20	34	45	12	.254	.331	.329
Bernie Carbo†	DH49,OF4	L	30	60	174	21	50	8	0	4	16	20	31	1	.287	.362	.402
Jim Norris	OF78,DH15,1B6	L	29	113	315	41	89	14	5	2	27	42	20	12	.283	.364	.378
Ted Cox	OF38,3B20,DH12*	R	23	82	227	14	53	7	0	1	19	16	30	0	.233	.286	.278
Larvell Blanks	SS43,2B17,3B3*	R	28	70	193	19	49	10	0	2	20	10	16	0	.254	.285	.337
Ron Pruitt	C48,OF16,DH5*	R	26	71	187	17	44	6	1	6	17	16	20	2	.235	.296	.374
Willie Horton†	DH48	R	35	50	169	15	42	7	0	5	22	15	25	3	.249	.314	.379
Bo Diaz	C44	R	25	44	127	12	30	4	0	2	11	4	17	0	.236	.260	.315
Horace Speed	OF61,DH3	R	26	70	106	13	24	4	1	0	4	14	31	2	.226	.320	.283
Wayne Cage	DH20,1B11	L	26	36	98	11	24	6	1	4	13	9	28	1	.245	.308	.449
Ron Hassey	C24	L	25	25	74	5	15	0	0	2	9	5	7	2	.203	.256	.284
Dan Briggs	OF15	L	25	15	49	4	8	0	1	1	1	4	9	0	.163	.226	.265
Mike Vail†	OF9,DH1	R	26	14	34	2	8	2	1	0	2	1	9	1	.235	.250	.353
Alfredo Griffin	SS2	S	20	5	4	1	2	1	0	0	0	2	1	0	.500	.667	.750
Larry Lintz	DH1	S	28	3	0	1	0	0	0	0	0	0	0	1	—	—	—

T. Cox, 7 G at 1B, 1 G at SS; L. Blanks, 1 G at DH; R. Pruitt, 2 G at 3B

Pitcher	T	Age	G	GS	CG	ShO	IP	H	HR	BB	SO	W-L	Sv	ERA
Rick Waits	L	26	34	33	15	2	230.1	206	16	86	97	13-15	0	3.20
Rick Wise	R	32	33	31	9	1	211.2	226	22	59	106	9-19	0	4.34
Mike Paxton	R	24	33	27	5	2	191.0	179	13	63	96	12-11	1	3.86
David Clyde	L	23	28	25	5	0	153.1	166	4	60	83	8-11	0	4.28
Don Hood	L	28	36	19	1	0	154.2	166	13	77	73	5-6	0	4.48
Dave Freisleben†	R	26	12	10	0	0	44.1	52	4	31	19	1-4	0	7.11
Wayne Garland	R	27	6	6	0	0	29.2	43	6	16	13	2-3	0	7.89
Jim Kern	R	29	58	0	0	0	99.1	77	4	58	95	10-10	13	3.08
Sid Monge	L	27	48	2	0	0	84.2	71	4	51	54	4-3	6	2.76
Dan Spillner†	R	26	36	0	0	0	56.1	54	2	21	48	3-1	3	3.67
Paul Reuschel†	R	31	18	6	1	0	89.2	95	5	22	24	2-4	0	3.11
Dennis Kinney†	L	26	18	0	0	0	38.2	37	3	14	19	0-2	5	4.42
Al Fitzmorris†	R	32	7	0	0	0	14.1	19	3	7	5	0-1	0	6.28
Rick Kreuger	L	29	6	0	0	0	9.1	6	1	3	7	0-0	0	3.86

1978 Toronto Blue Jays 7th AL East 59-102 .366 40.0 GB

Roy Hartsfield

Player	Gm by Position	B	Age	G	AB	R	H	2B	3B	HR	RBI	BB	SO	SB	Avg	OBP	Slg
Rick Cerone	C84,DH2	R	24	88	282	25	63	8	2	3	20	23	32	0	.223	.284	.298
John Mayberry	1B139,DH7	L	29	152	515	51	129	15	2	22	70	60	57	1	.250	.329	.416
Dave McKay	2B140,SS3,3B2*	S	28	145	504	59	120	20	8	7	45	20	91	4	.238	.268	.351
Roy Howell	3B131,OF5,DH1	L	24	140	551	67	149	28	3	8	61	44	78	0	.270	.325	.376
Luis Gomez	SS153	R	26	153	413	39	92	7	3	0	32	34	41	2	.223	.280	.254
Rick Bosetti	OF135	R	24	136	568	61	147	25	5	5	42	30	65	6	.259	.299	.347
Bob Bailor	OF125,3B28,SS4	R	26	154	621	74	164	29	7	1	52	38	21	5	.264	.310	.338
Otto Velez	OF74,DH9,1B1	R	27	91	248	29	66	14	2	9	38	45	41	1	.266	.380	.448
Rico Carty†	DH101	R	38	104	387	51	110	16	0	20	68	36	41	1	.284	.340	.481
Alan Ashby	C81	S	26	81	264	27	69	15	0	9	29	28	32	1	.261	.333	.420
Willie Upshaw	OF52,DH18,1B10	L	21	95	224	26	53	8	2	1	17	21	35	4	.237	.298	.304
Al Woods	OF60	L	24	62	220	19	53	12	3	3	25	11	23	1	.241	.278	.364
Tom Hutton†	OF55,1B9	L	32	64	173	19	44	9	0	2	9	19	11	1	.254	.328	.341
Willie Horton†	DH30	R	35	33	122	12	25	6	0	3	19	4	29	0	.205	.228	.328
Doug Ault	1B25,OF7,DH5	R	28	54	104	10	25	1	1	3	7	17	14	0	.240	.352	.356
Tim Johnson†	SS49,2B13	L	28	68	79	9	19	2	0	0	3	8	16	0	.241	.315	.266
Sam Ewing	DH9,OF3	L	29	40	56	3	10	0	0	2	9	5	9	0	.179	.242	.286
Garth Iorg	2B18	R	23	19	49	3	8	0	0	0	3	3	4	0	.163	.218	.163
Gary Woods	OF6	R	23	8	19	1	3	1	0	0	0	1	1	1	.158	.200	.211
Butch Alberts	DH4	R	28	6	18	1	5	1	0	0	0	0	2	0	.278	.278	.333
Brian Milner	C2	R	18	2	9	3	4	0	1	0	2	0	1	0	.444	.444	.667
Ernie Whitt	C1	L	26	2	4	0	0	0	0	0	0	1	1	0	.000	.200	.000
Tim Nordbrook†	SS7	R	28	7	0	1	0	0	0	0	0	0	0	0	—	1.000	—

D. McKay, 1 G at DH

Pitcher	T	Age	G	GS	CG	ShO	IP	H	HR	BB	SO	W-L	Sv	ERA
Jesse Jefferson	R	29	31	30	9	2	211.2	214	28	86	97	7-16	0	4.38
Tom Underwood	L	24	31	30	7	1	197.2	201	23	87	139	6-14	0	4.10
Jim Clancy	R	22	31	30	7	0	193.2	199	10	91	106	10-12	0	4.09
Jerry Garvin	L	22	26	22	3	0	144.2	189	20	48	67	4-12	0	5.54
Dave Lemanczyk	R	27	29	20	3	0	136.2	170	16	65	62	4-14	0	6.26
Don Kirkwood	R	28	16	9	3	0	68.0	76	6	25	29	4-5	0	4.24
Tom Murphy	R	32	50	0	0	0	94.0	87	11	37	36	6-9	7	3.93
Mike Willis	L	27	44	2	1	0	100.2	104	11	39	52	3-7	7	4.56
Balor Moore	L	27	37	18	2	0	144.1	165	16	54	75	6-9	0	4.93
Victor Cruz	R	20	32	0	0	0	47.1	28	0	35	51	7-3	9	1.71
Joe Coleman†	R	31	31	0	0	0	60.2	67	6	30	28	2-0	0	4.60
Tom Buskey	R	31	8	0	0	0	13.1	14	1	5	7	0-1	0	3.38
Dave Wallace	R	30	6	0	0	0	14.0	12	1	11	7	0-0	0	3.86
Mark Wiley†	R	30	2	0	0	0	2.2	3	0	1	2	0-0	0	6.75

1978 Kansas City Royals 1st AL West 92-70 .568 —

Whitey Herzog

Player	Gm by Position	B	Age	G	AB	R	H	2B	3B	HR	RBI	BB	SO	SB	Avg	OBP	Slg
Darrell Porter	C145,DH4	L	26	150	520	77	138	27	6	18	78	75	75	0	.265	.358	.444
Pete LaCock	1B106	L	26	118	322	44	95	21	2	5	48	21	27	1	.295	.335	.419
Frank White	2B140	R	27	143	461	66	127	24	6	7	50	26	59	13	.275	.317	.399
George Brett	3B128,SS1	L	25	128	510	79	150	45	8	9	62	39	35	23	.294	.342	.467
Freddie Patek	SS137	R	33	138	440	54	109	23	1	2	46	42	56	38	.248	.312	.318
Amos Otis	OF136,DH1	R	31	141	486	74	145	30	7	22	96	66	54	32	.298	.380	.525
Al Cowens	OF127,3B5,DH2	R	26	132	485	63	133	24	8	5	63	31	54	14	.274	.319	.388
Willie Wilson	OF112,DH6	S	22	127	198	43	43	8	2	0	16	16	33	46	.217	.280	.278
Hal McRae	DH153,OF3	R	32	156	623	90	170	39	5	16	72	56	62	17	.273	.329	.429
Clint Hurdle	OF78,1B52,DH1*	L	20	133	417	48	110	25	5	7	56	56	84	1	.264	.348	.398
Tom Poquette	OF63,DH1	L	26	80	204	16	44	9	2	4	30	14	9	2	.216	.259	.338
John Wathan	1B47,C21	R	28	67	190	19	57	10	1	2	28	3	12	2	.300	.320	.395
Steve Braun†	OF33,3B11	L	30	64	137	16	36	10	1	0	14	28	16	3	.263	.386	.350
Jerry Terrell	2B31,3B25,SS11*	R	31	73	133	14	27	1	0	0	8	4	13	8	.203	.225	.211
U.L. Washington	SS49,2B19,DH1	S	24	69	129	10	34	2	1	0	9	10	20	12	.264	.314	.295
Joe Zdeb	OF52,DH1,2B1*	R	25	60	127	18	32	2	3	0	11	7	18	3	.252	.287	.315
Jamie Quirk	3B10,SS2,DH1	L	23	17	29	3	6	2	0	0	2	5	4	0	.207	.324	.276
Joe Lahoud	DH1,OF1	L	31	13	16	0	2	0	0	0	0	0	1	0	.125	.125	.125
Dave Cripe	3B5	R	27	7	13	1	2	0	0	0	1	0	2	0	.154	.154	.154
Art Kusnyer	C9	R	32	9	13	1	3	1	0	1	2	2	4	0	.231	.333	.538
Luis Silverio	OF6,DH2	R	21	8	11	7	6	2	1	0	3	2	3	1	.545	.615	.909
Jim Gaudet	C3	R	23	3	8	0	0	0	0	0	0	0	3	0	.000	.000	.000
Randy Bass		L	24	2	2	0	0	0	0	0	0	0	0	0	.000	.000	.000

C. Hurdle, 1 G at 3B; J. Terrell, 5 G at 1B; J. Zdeb, 1 G at 3B

Pitcher	T	Age	G	GS	CG	ShO	IP	H	HR	BB	SO	W-L	Sv	ERA
Dennis Leonard	R	27	40	40	20	4	294.2	283	27	78	183	21-17	0	3.33
Paul Splittorff	L	31	39	38	13	2	262.0	244	22	60	76	19-13	0	3.40
Rich Gale	R	24	31	30	9	3	192.1	171	10	100	88	14-8	0	3.09
Larry Gura	L	30	35	26	8	2	221.2	183	13	60	81	16-4	0	2.72
Andy Hassler†	L	26	11	9	1	0	58.1	76	1	24	26	1-4	0	4.32
Steve Busby	R	28	7	5	0	0	21.1	24	2	15	10	1-0	0	7.59
Al Hrabosky	L	28	58	0	0	0	75.0	52	6	35	60	8-7	20	2.88
Steve Mingori	L	34	45	0	0	0	69.0	64	5	16	28	1-4	7	2.74
Doug Bird	R	28	40	6	0	0	98.2	110	8	31	48	6-6	1	5.29
Marty Pattin	R	35	32	5	2	0	78.2	72	8	25	30	3-3	4	3.32
Randy McGilberry	R	24	18	0	0	0	25.2	27	2	18	12	0-1	0	4.21
Jim Colborn†	R	32	8	3	0	0	28.1	31	4	12	8	1-2	0	4.76
Steve Foucault†	R	28	3	0	0	0	2.1	5	0	1	0	0-0	0	3.86
Bill Paschall	R	24	2	0	0	0	8.0	6	0	0	5	0-1	1	3.38
George Throop	R	27	1	0	0	0	3.0	2	0	3	2	1-0	0	0.00

1978 California Angels 2nd AL West 87-75 .537 5.0 GB

Dave Garcia (25-20)/Jim Fregosi (62-55)

Player	Gm by Position	B	Age	G	AB	R	H	2B	3B	HR	RBI	BB	SO	SB	Avg	OBP	Slg
Brian Downing	C128,DH2	R	27	133	412	42	105	15	0	7	46	52	47	3	.255	.345	.342
Ron Fairly	1B78,DH5	L	39	91	235	23	51	5	0	10	40	25	31	0	.217	.289	.366
Bobby Grich	2B144	R	29	144	487	68	122	16	2	6	42	75	83	4	.251	.357	.329
Carney Lansford	3B117,SS2,DH1	R	21	121	453	63	133	23	2	8	52	31	67	20	.294	.339	.406
Dave Chalk	SS97,2B29,3B22*	R	27	135	470	42	119	12	0	1	34	38	34	5	.253	.318	.285
Lyman Bostock	OF146,DH1	L	27	147	568	74	168	24	4	5	71	59	36	15	.296	.362	.379
Rick Miller	OF129	L	30	132	475	66	125	25	4	1	37	54	70	3	.263	.341	.339
Joe Rudi	OF111,DH11,1B10	R	31	133	497	58	127	27	1	17	79	28	82	2	.256	.295	.416
Don Baylor	DH100,OF39,1B17	R	29	158	591	103	151	26	0	34	99	56	71	22	.255	.332	.472
Ron Jackson	1B75,3B31,DH1*	R	25	105	387	49	115	18	6	6	57	16	31	2	.297	.337	.421
Ken Landreaux	OF83,DH1	L	23	93	260	37	58	7	5	5	23	20	20	7	.223	.284	.346
Rance Mulliniks	SS47,DH2	L	22	50	119	6	22	3	1	1	6	8	23	2	.185	.238	.252
Terry Humphrey	C52,2B1,3B1	R	28	53	114	11	25	4	1	1	9	6	12	0	.219	.264	.298
Merv Rettenmund	OF22,DH18	R	35	50	108	16	29	5	1	1	14	30	13	0	.269	.433	.361
Jim Anderson	SS47,2B1	R	21	48	108	6	21	7	0	0	7	11	16	0	.194	.267	.259
Tony Solaita	DH18,1B11	L	31	60	94	10	21	3	0	1	14	16	25	0	.223	.336	.287
Danny Goodwin	DH15	L	24	24	58	9	16	5	0	2	10	10	13	0	.276	.377	.466
Dave Machemer	2B5,3B3,SS1	R	27	10	22	6	6	1	0	1	2	2	1	0	.273	.333	.455
Ike Hampton	C13,DH4,1B1	S	26	19	14	2	3	0	1	1	4	2	7	1	.214	.313	.571

D. Chalk, 1 G at DH; R. Jackson, 1 G at OF

Pitcher	T	Age	G	GS	CG	ShO	IP	H	HR	BB	SO	W-L	Sv	ERA
Frank Tanana	L	24	33	33	10	4	239.0	239	26	60	137	18-12	0	3.65
Nolan Ryan	R	31	31	31	14	3	234.2	183	12	148	260	10-13	0	3.72
Chris Knapp	R	24	30	29	6	0	188.1	178	25	67	126	14-8	0	4.21
Don Aase	R	23	29	29	6	1	178.2	185	14	80	93	11-8	0	4.03
Dave Frost	R	25	11	10	2	1	80.1	71	6	24	30	5-4	0	2.58
John Caneira	R	25	2	2	0	0	7.2	8	2	3	0	0-0	0	7.04
Dave LaRoche	L	30	59	0	0	0	95.2	73	7	48	70	10-9	25	2.82
Paul Hartzell	R	24	54	12	5	0	157.0	168	8	41	55	6-10	6	3.44
Dyar Miller	R	32	41	0	0	0	84.2	85	3	41	34	6-2	1	2.66
Ken Brett	L	29	31	10	1	1	100.0	100	12	42	43	3-5	1	4.95
Tom Griffin	R	30	24	4	0	0	56.0	63	8	31	35	3-4	0	4.02
Al Fitzmorris†	R	32	9	2	0	0	31.2	26	2	14	8	1-0	0	1.71
Mike Barlow	R	30	1	0	0	0	2.0	3	0	0	1	0-0	0	4.50

842 Seasons: Team Rosters

1978 Texas Rangers 2nd AL West 87-75 .537 5.0 GB

Player	Gm by Position	B	Age	G	AB	R	H	2B	3B	HR	RBI	BB	SO	SB	Avg	OBP	Slg
Jim Sundberg	C148,DH1	R	27	149	518	54	144	23	6	6	58	64	70	2	.278	.358	.380
Mike Hargrove	1B140,DH4	L	28	146	494	63	124	24	1	7	40	107	47	2	.251	.388	.346
Bump Wills	2B156	S	25	157	539	78	135	17	4	9	57	63	91	52	.250	.331	.347
Toby Harrah	3B91,SS49	R	29	139	450	56	103	17	3	12	59	83	66	31	.229	.349	.360
Bert Campaneris	SS89,DH4	R	36	98	269	30	50	5	3	1	17	20	36	22	.186	.245	.238
Juan Beniquez	OF126	R	28	127	473	61	123	17	3	11	50	20	59	10	.260	.292	.378
Bobby Bonds†	OF111,DH18	R	32	130	475	85	126	15	4	29	82	69	110	37	.265	.356	.497
Al Oliver	OF107,DH26	L	31	133	525	65	170	35	5	14	89	31	41	8	.324	.358	.490
Richie Zisk	OF90,DH49	R	29	140	511	68	134	19	1	22	85	58	76	3	.262	.338	.432
Kurt Bevacqua	3B49,DH16,2B13*	R	31	90	248	21	55	12	0	6	30	18	31	1	.222	.271	.343
John Lowenstein	3B25,DH21,OF16	L	31	77	176	28	39	8	3	5	21	37	29	16	.222	.363	.386
Bobby Thompson	OF52,DH3	S	24	64	120	23	27	3	3	2	12	9	26	7	.225	.284	.350
Jim Mason	SS42,3B11,DH1*	L	27	55	105	10	20	4	0	0	3	5	17	0	.190	.227	.229
Mike Jorgensen	1B78,OF9,DH1	L	29	96	97	20	19	3	0	1	9	18	10	3	.196	.319	.258
John Ellis	C22,DH7	R	29	34	94	7	23	4	0	3	17	6	20	0	.245	.282	.383
Gary Gray	DH11	R	25	17	50	4	12	1	0	2	6	1	12	1	.240	.255	.380
Pat Putnam	DH12,1B4	L	24	20	46	4	7	1	0	1	2	2	5	0	.152	.188	.239
C. Washington†	OF7,DH4	L	23	12	42	1	7	0	0	0	2	1	12	0	.167	.186	.167
Nelson Norman	SS18,3B6	S	20	23	34	1	9	2	0	0	1	0	5	0	.265	.265	.324
John Grubb†	OF13,DH3	L	29	21	33	8	13	3	0	1	6	11	5	1	.394	.545	.576
Sandy Alomar	1B9,2B6,DH3*	S	34	24	29	3	6	1	0	0	1	1	7	0	.207	.233	.241
Billy Sample	DH3,OF2	R	23	8	15	2	7	2	0	0	3	0	3	0	.467	.467	.600
LaRue Washington	2B2,DH1	R	24	3	3	0	0	0	0	0	0	0	1	0	.000	.000	.000
Greg Mahlberg	C1	R	25	1	1	0	0	0	0	0	0	0	0	0	.000	.000	.000

K. Bevacqua, 1 G at 1B; J. Mason, 1 G at 2B; S. Alomar, 3 G at 3B, 2 G at SS

Billy Hunter (86-75)/Pat Corrales (1-0)

Pitcher	T	Age	G	GS	CG	ShO	IP	H	HR	BB	SO	W-L	Sv	ERA
Jon Matlack	L	28	35	33	18	2	270.0	252	14	51	157	15-13	1	2.27
Fergie Jenkins	R	34	34	30	16	4	249.0	228	21	41	157	18-8	0	3.04
Doyle Alexander	R	27	31	28	7	1	191.0	198	18	71	81	9-10	0	3.86
Doc Medich	R	29	28	22	6	2	171.0	166	10	52	71	9-8	2	3.74
Dock Ellis	R	33	22	22	3	0	141.1	131	15	46	45	9-7	0	4.20
Reggie Cleveland†	R	30	53	0	0	0	75.2	65	5	23	46	5-7	12	3.09
Jim Umbarger	L	25	32	9	1	0	97.2	116	9	36	60	5-8	1	4.88
Steve Comer	R	24	30	11	3	2	117.1	107	5	37	65	11-5	1	2.30
Len Barker	R	22	29	0	0	0	52.1	63	6	29	33	1-5	4	4.82
Paul Lindblad†	L	36	18	0	0	0	39.2	41	2	15	25	1-1	2	3.63
Paul Mirabella	L	24	10	4	0	0	28.0	30	2	17	23	3-2	1	5.79
Roger Moret	L	28	7	2	0	0	14.2	23	1	2	5	0-1	1	4.91
Danny Darwin	R	22	3	1	0	0	8.2	11	0	1	8	1-0	0	4.15

1978 Minnesota Twins 4th AL West 73-89 .451 19.0 GB

Player	Gm by Position	B	Age	G	AB	R	H	2B	3B	HR	RBI	BB	SO	SB	Avg	OBP	Slg
Butch Wynegar	C131,3B1	S	22	135	454	36	104	22	1	4	45	47	42	1	.229	.307	.308
Rod Carew	1B148,2B4,OF1	L	32	152	564	85	188	26	10	5	70	78	62	27	.333	.411	.441
Bob Randall	2B116,3B2,DH1	R	30	119	330	36	89	11	3	0	21	24	22	5	.270	.329	.321
Mike Cubbage	3B115,2B5	L	27	125	394	40	111	12	7	7	57	40	44	3	.282	.348	.401
Roy Smalley	SS157	S	25	158	586	80	160	31	3	19	77	85	70	2	.273	.362	.433
Dan Ford	OF149,DH1	R	26	151	592	78	162	36	10	11	82	48	88	7	.274	.332	.424
Hosken Powell	OF117	L	23	121	381	55	94	20	2	3	31	45	31	11	.247	.323	.333
Willie Norwood	OF115,DH12	R	27	125	428	56	109	22	3	8	46	28	64	25	.255	.301	.376
Glenn Adams	DH101,OF5	L	30	116	310	27	80	18	1	7	35	17	32	0	.258	.297	.390
Bombo Rivera	OF94,DH1	R	25	101	251	35	68	8	2	3	23	35	47	5	.271	.362	.355
Jose Morales	DH77,C1,1B1*	R	33	101	242	22	76	13	1	2	38	20	35	0	.314	.363	.401
Larry Wolfe	3B81,SS7	R	25	88	235	25	55	10	1	3	25	36	27	0	.234	.332	.323
Rob Wilfong	2B80,DH5	L	24	92	199	23	53	8	0	1	11	19	27	8	.266	.336	.322
Rich Chiles	OF61,DH8	L	28	87	198	22	53	12	0	1	22	20	25	1	.268	.333	.343
Craig Kusick	DH35,1B27,OF9	R	29	77	191	23	33	3	2	4	20	37	38	3	.173	.305	.272
Glenn Borgmann	C46,DH1	R	28	49	123	16	26	4	1	3	15	18	17	0	.211	.306	.333
Dave Edwards	OF15	R	24	15	44	7	11	3	0	1	3	7	13	1	.250	.377	.386

J. Morales, 1 G at OF

Gene Mauch

Pitcher	T	Age	G	GS	CG	ShO	IP	H	HR	BB	SO	W-L	Sv	ERA
Roger Erickson	R	21	37	37	14	0	265.2	268	19	79	121	14-13	0	3.96
Geoff Zahn	L	32	35	35	12	1	252.1	260	18	81	106	14-14	0	3.03
Dave Goltz	R	29	29	29	13	2	220.1	209	12	67	116	15-10	0	2.49
Gary Serum	R	21	34	23	6	1	184.1	188	14	44	80	9-9	1	4.10
Darrell Jackson	L	22	19	15	1	1	92.1	89	9	48	54	4-6	0	4.48
Paul Thormodsgard	R	24	12	12	1	0	66.0	81	7	17	23	1-6	0	5.05
Stan Perzanowski	R	27	13	7	1	0	56.2	59	1	26	31	2-7	1	5.24
Pete Redfern	R	23	3	2	0	0	9.2	10	2	6	4	0-2	0	6.52
Mike Marshall	R	35	54	0	0	0	99.0	80	3	37	56	10-12	21	2.45
Greg Thayer	R	28	20	0	0	0	45.0	40	5	30	30	1-1	0	3.80
Tom Johnson	R	27	18	0	0	0	32.2	42	2	17	21	1-4	3	5.51
Johnny Sutton	R	25	17	0	0	0	44.1	46	3	15	18	0-0	0	3.45
Mac Scarce	L	29	17	0	0	0	32.0	35	5	15	17	1-1	0	3.94
Jeff Holly	L	25	15	1	0	0	35.1	28	1	18	12	1-1	0	3.57
Roric Harrison	R	31	9	0	0	0	12.0	18	0	11	7	0-1	0	7.50
Dave Johnson	R	29	6	1	0	0	12.0	15	1	9	7	0-2	0	7.50

1978 Chicago White Sox 5th AL West 71-90 .441 20.5 GB

Player	Gm by Position	B	Age	G	AB	R	H	2B	3B	HR	RBI	BB	SO	SB	Avg	OBP	Slg
Bill Nahorodny	C104,1B4,DH1	R	24	107	347	29	82	11	2	8	35	23	52	1	.236	.285	.349
Lamar Johnson	1B108,DH36	R	27	148	498	52	136	23	2	8	72	43	46	6	.273	.329	.376
Jorge Orta	2B114,DH2	L	27	117	420	45	115	19	2	13	53	42	39	1	.274	.340	.421
Eric Soderholm	3B128,DH11,2B1	R	29	143	457	57	118	17	1	20	67	39	44	2	.258	.318	.431
Don Kessinger	SS123,2B9	S	35	131	431	35	110	18	1	1	31	36	34	2	.255	.312	.309
Ralph Garr	OF109,DH9	L	32	118	443	67	122	18	9	3	29	24	41	7	.275	.314	.377
Chet Lemon	OF95,DH10	R	23	105	357	51	107	24	6	13	55	39	46	5	.300	.377	.510
C. Washington†	OF82,DH1	L	23	86	314	33	83	16	5	6	31	12	57	5	.264	.290	.404
Ron Blomberg	DH36,1B7	L	29	61	156	16	36	7	0	5	22	11	17	0	.231	.280	.372
Bob Molinaro	OF62,DH32	L	28	105	286	39	75	5	5	6	27	19	12	22	.262	.314	.378
Greg Pryor	2B35,SS28,3B20	R	28	82	222	27	58	11	0	2	15	11	18	3	.261	.298	.338
Thad Bosley	OF64	L	21	66	219	25	59	5	1	2	13	13	32	12	.269	.308	.329
Wayne Nordhagen	OF36,DH16,C12	R	29	68	206	28	62	16	0	5	35	5	18	0	.301	.310	.451
Mike Squires	1B45	L	26	46	150	25	42	9	2	0	19	16	21	4	.280	.343	.367
Mike Colbern	C47,DH1	R	23	48	141	11	38	5	1	2	20	1	36	0	.270	.281	.362
Alan Bannister	DH19,OF15,SS8*	R	26	49	107	16	24	3	2	0	8	11	12	3	.224	.303	.290
Bobby Bonds†	OF22,DH3	R	32	26	90	8	25	4	0	2	8	10	10	6	.278	.347	.389
Henry Cruz	OF40,DH1	L	26	53	77	13	17	2	1	2	10	8	11	0	.221	.292	.351
Harry Chappas	SS20	S	20	20	75	11	20	1	0	0	6	6	11	1	.267	.318	.280
Jim Breazeale	1B19,DH4	L	28	25	72	8	15	3	0	3	13	8	10	0	.208	.284	.375
Kevin Bell	3B52,DH1	R	22	54	68	9	13	0	0	2	5	5	19	1	.191	.257	.279
Junior Moore	DH12,3B6,OF5	R	25	24	65	8	19	0	1	0	4	6	7	1	.292	.352	.323
Tom Spencer	OF27,DH2	R	27	29	65	3	12	1	0	0	4	2	9	0	.185	.209	.200
Rusty Torres	OF14	S	29	16	44	7	14	3	0	3	6	6	7	0	.318	.400	.591
Marv Foley	C10	L	24	11	34	3	12	0	0	0	6	4	6	0	.353	.421	.353
Joe Gates	2B8	L	23	8	24	6	6	0	0	0	1	4	6	1	.250	.379	.250
Mike Eden	SS5,2B4	S	29	10	17	1	2	0	0	0	0	4	0	0	.118	.286	.118
Larry Johnson	C2,DH1	R	27	3	8	0	1	0	0	0	0	1	4	0	.125	.222	.125

A. Bannister, 2 G at 2B

Bob Lemon (34-40)/Larry Doby (37-50)

Pitcher	T	Age	G	GS	CG	ShO	IP	H	HR	BB	SO	W-L	Sv	ERA
Francisco Barrios	R	25	33	32	9	2	195.2	180	13	85	79	9-15	0	4.05
Steve Stone	R	30	30	30	6	1	212.0	196	19	84	118	12-12	0	4.37
Ken Kravec	L	26	30	30	7	2	203.0	188	22	95	154	11-16	0	4.08
Wilbur Wood	L	36	28	27	4	0	168.0	187	23	74	69	10-10	0	5.20
Rich Wortham	L	24	8	8	2	0	59.0	59	1	23	25	3-2	0	3.05
Jack Kucek	R	25	10	5	3	0	52.0	42	5	27	30	2-3	1	3.29
Ross Baumgarten	L	23	7	4	1	1	23.0	29	3	9	15	2-2	0	5.87
Steve Trout	L	20	4	3	1	0	22.1	19	0	11	11	3-0	0	4.03
Britt Burns	L	19	2	2	0	0	7.2	14	2	3	3	0-2	0	12.91
Jim Willoughby	R	29	59	0	0	0	93.1	95	6	19	36	1-6	13	3.86
Lerrin LaGrow	R	29	52	0	0	0	88.0	85	9	38	41	6-5	16	4.40
Ron Schueler	R	30	30	7	0	0	81.2	76	10	39	39	3-5	0	4.30
Rich Hinton	L	31	29	4	2	0	80.2	78	5	28	48	2-6	1	4.02
Pablo Torrealba	L	30	25	3	1	1	57.1	69	6	39	23	2-4	1	4.71
Mike Proly	R	27	14	6	2	0	65.2	63	4	12	19	5-2	1	2.74

1978 Oakland Athletics 6th AL West 69-93 .426 23.0 GB

Player	Gm by Position	B	Age	G	AB	R	H	2B	3B	HR	RBI	BB	SO	SB	Avg	OBP	Slg
Jim Essian	C119,DH3,1B3*	R	27	126	278	21	62	9	1	3	26	44	22	2	.223	.326	.295
Dave Revering	1B138,DH3	L	25	152	521	49	141	21	3	16	46	26	55	0	.271	.303	.415
Mike Edwards	2B133,SS9,DH4	R	25	142	414	48	113	16	2	1	23	16	32	27	.273	.303	.329
Wayne Gross	3B106,1B15	L	26	118	285	18	57	10	2	7	23	40	63	0	.200	.308	.323
Mario Guerrero	SS142	R	28	143	505	27	139	18	4	3	38	15	35	0	.275	.302	.345
Mitchell Page	OF114,DH33	L	26	147	516	62	147	25	7	17	70	53	95	23	.285	.355	.459
Miguel Dilone	OF99,3B3,DH1	S	23	135	258	34	59	8	0	1	14	23	30	50	.229	.294	.271
Tony Armas	OF85,DH3	R	24	91	239	17	51	6	1	2	13	10	62	1	.213	.250	.272
Gary Alexander†	DH45,OF6,C1*	R	25	58	174	18	36	6	1	10	22	22	66	0	.207	.298	.425
Taylor Duncan	3B84,2B11,DH7*	R	25	104	319	25	82	15	2	2	37	19	38	1	.257	.296	.335
Joe Wallis†	OF80,DH1	S	26	85	279	28	66	16	1	6	26	26	42	1	.237	.300	.366
Jeff Newman	C61,1B36,DH2	R	29	105	268	25	64	7	1	9	32	18	40	0	.239	.288	.373
Glenn Burke†	OF67,DH2,1B1	R	25	78	200	19	47	6	1	1	14	10	26	15	.235	.270	.290
Wendell Alston†	OF50,1B9,DH3	L	25	58	173	17	36	2	0	1	10	10	21	11	.208	.250	.237
Gary Thomasson†	OF44,1B5	L	26	47	154	17	31	4	1	5	16	15	44	4	.201	.272	.338
Rico Carty†	DH41	R	38	41	141	19	39	5	1	11	31	21	16	0	.277	.368	.560
Willie Horton†	DH27,OF1	R	35	32	102	11	32	8	0	3	19	9	15	0	.314	.369	.480
Rob Picciolo	SS41,2B19,3B13	R	25	78	93	16	21	1	0	2	7	2	13	1	.226	.242	.301
Bruce Robinson	C28	L	24	28	84	5	21	3	1	0	8	3	8	0	.250	.276	.310
Steve Staggs	2B40,DH2,3B2*	R	27	47	78	10	19	2	2	0	0	19	17	2	.244	.392	.321
Bill North†	OF17	S	30	24	52	5	11	4	0	0	5	9	13	3	.212	.344	.288
Dwayne Murphy	OF45,DH5	L	23	60	52	15	10	2	0	0	5	7	14	0	.192	.279	.231
Tito Fuentes	2B13	S	34	13	43	5	6	1	0	0	2	1	6	0	.140	.159	.163
Tim Hosley	C6,DH1	R	31	13	23	1	7	2	0	0	3	1	6	0	.304	.360	.391
Mike Adams	2B6,DH3,3B3	R	29	15	15	5	3	1	0	0	1	7	2	0	.200	.455	.267
Larry Murray	OF6	S	25	11	12	1	1	0	0	0	0	3	2	0	.083	.267	.083
Marty Perez	3B11,SS3,2B1	R	31	16	12	1	0	0	0	0	0	0	5	0	.000	.000	.000
Scott Meyer	C7,DH1	R	20	8	9	1	1	1	0	0	0	0	4	0	.111	.111	.222
Darrell Woodard	2B14,DH1,3B1	R	21	33	9	10	0	0	0	0	0	1	1	3	.000	.100	.000
Jerry Tabb	DH2,1B2	L	26	12	9	0	1	0	0	0	1	2	5	0	.111	.273	.111
Mark Budaska	OF2	S	25	4	4	0	1	1	0	0	0	1	2	0	.250	.400	.500

J. Essian, 1 G at 2B; G. Alexander, 1 G at 1B; T. Duncan, 1 G at SS; S. Staggs, 2 G at SS

Bobby Winkles (24-15)/Jack McKeon (45-78)

Pitcher	T	Age	G	GS	CG	ShO	IP	H	HR	BB	SO	W-L	Sv	ERA
Matt Keough	R	22	32	32	6	0	197.1	178	9	85	108	8-15	0	3.24
John Henry Johnson	L	21	33	30	7	2	186.0	164	18	82	91	11-10	0	3.39
Pete Broberg	R	28	35	26	2	0	165.2	174	16	65	94	10-12	0	4.62
Steve Renko	R	33	27	25	3	1	151.0	152	10	67	89	6-12	0	4.29
Rick Langford	R	26	37	24	4	2	175.2	169	15	56	92	7-13	0	3.43
Alan Wirth	R	21	16	14	2	1	81.1	72	6	34	31	5-6	0	3.43
Mike Morgan	R	18	3	3	1	0	12.1	19	1	8	0	0-3	0	7.30
Tim Conroy	L	18	2	2	0	0	4.2	3	0	9	0	0-0	0	7.71
Bob Lacey	L	24	74	0	0	0	119.2	126	10	35	60	8-9	5	3.01
Dave Heaverlo	R	27	69	0	0	0	130.0	141	11	41	71	3-6	10	3.25
Elias Sosa	R	28	68	0	0	0	109.0	106	5	44	61	8-2	14	2.64
Mike Norris	R	23	14	5	1	0	49.0	46	2	35	36	0-5	0	5.51
Joe Coleman†	R	31	10	0	0	0	19.2	12	1	5	4	3-0	0	1.37
Steve McCatty	R	24	9	0	0	0	20.0	26	1	9	10	0-0	0	4.50
Craig Minetto	L	24	4	1	0	0	12.0	13	1	7	3	0-0	0	3.75

1978 Seattle Mariners 7th AL West 56-104 .350 35.0 GB

Darrell Johnson

Player	Gm by Position	B	Age	G	AB	R	H	2B	3B	HR	RBI	BB	SO	SB	Avg	OBP	Slg
Bob Stinson	C123,DH1	S	32	124	364	46	94	14	3	11	55	45	42	2	.258	.346	.404
Dan Meyer	1B121,OF2,DH1	L	25	123	444	38	101	18	1	8	56	24	39	7	.227	.264	.327
Julio Cruz	2B141,SS5,DH1	S	23	147	550	77	129	14	1	1	25	69	66	59	.235	.319	.269
Bill Stein	3B111,DH1	R	31	114	403	41	105	24	4	4	37	37	56	1	.261	.318	.370
Craig Reynolds	SS146	L	25	148	548	57	160	16	7	5	44	36	41	9	.292	.336	.374
Ruppert Jones	OF128	L	23	129	472	48	111	24	3	6	46	55	85	22	.235	.312	.337
Leon Roberts	OF128,DH2	R	27	134	472	78	142	21	7	22	92	41	52	6	.301	.364	.515
John Hale	OF98,DH3	L	24	107	211	24	36	8	0	4	22	34	64	3	.171	.283	.265
Lee Stanton	DH59,OF30	R	32	93	302	24	55	11	0	3	24	34	80	1	.182	.265	.248
Bruce Bochte	OF91,DH43,1B1	L	27	140	486	58	128	25	3	11	51	60	47	3	.263	.342	.395
Tom Paciorek†	OF54,DH12,1B3	R	31	70	251	32	75	20	3	4	30	15	39	2	.299	.336	.450
Larry Milbourne	3B32,SS23,2B15*	S	27	93	234	31	53	6	2	2	20	9	6	5	.226	.254	.295
Bob Robertson	DH29,1B18	R	31	64	174	17	40	5	2	8	28	24	39	0	.230	.325	.420
Juan Bernhardt	1B25,3B22,DH2	R	24	54	165	13	38	9	0	2	12	9	10	1	.230	.270	.321
Bill Plummer	C40	R	31	41	93	6	20	5	0	2	7	12	19	0	.215	.305	.333
Steve Braun†	DH14,OF4	L	30	32	74	11	17	4	0	3	15	9	5	1	.230	.310	.405
Kevin Pasley	C25	R	24	25	54	3	13	5	0	1	5	2	4	0	.241	.268	.389
Jose Baez	2B14,3B3,DH1	R	24	23	50	8	8	0	1	0	2	6	7	1	.160	.250	.200
Charlie Beamon	DH6,1B2	L	24	10	11	2	2	0	0	0	0	1	1	0	.182	.250	.182

L. Milbourne, 10 G at DH

Pitcher	T	Age	G	GS	CG	ShO	IP	H	HR	BB	SO	W-L	Sv	ERA
Paul Mitchell	R	28	29	29	4	2	168.0	173	21	79	75	8-14	0	4.23
Glenn Abbott	R	27	29	28	8	1	155.1	191	22	44	67	7-15	0	5.27
Rick Honeycutt	L	24	26	24	4	1	134.1	150	12	49	50	5-11	0	4.89
Jim Colborn†	R	32	20	19	3	0	114.1	125	21	38	26	3-10	0	5.35
Dick Pole	R	27	21	18	2	0	98.2	122	16	41	41	4-11	0	6.48
Byron McLaughlin	R	22	20	17	4	0	107.0	97	15	39	87	4-8	0	4.37
Rick Jones	L	23	3	2	0	0	12.1	17	1	7	11	0-2	0	5.84
Enrique Romo	R	30	56	0	0	0	107.1	88	12	39	62	11-7	10	3.69
Shane Rawley	L	22	52	2	0	0	111.1	114	7	51	66	4-9	4	4.12
Jim Todd	R	30	49	2	0	0	106.2	113	4	61	37	3-4	3	3.88
Tom House	L	31	34	9	3	0	116.0	130	10	35	29	5-4	0	4.66
Mike Parrott	R	23	27	10	0	0	82.1	108	8	32	41	1-5	1	5.14
John Montague	R	30	19	0	0	0	43.2	52	2	24	14	1-3	2	6.18
Steve Burke	R	23	18	0	0	0	49.0	46	2	24	16	0-1	0	3.49
Tom Brown	R	28	6	0	0	0	13.0	14	2	4	8	0-0	0	4.15

»1978 Philadelphia Phillies 1st NL East 90-72 .556 —

Danny Ozark

Player	Gm by Position	B	Age	G	AB	R	H	2B	3B	HR	RBI	BB	SO	SB	Avg	OBP	Slg
Bob Boone	C129,1B3,OF1	R	30	132	435	48	123	18	4	12	62	46	37	2	.283	.347	.425
Richie Hebner	1B117,3B19,2B1	L	30	137	435	61	123	22	3	17	71	53	58	4	.283	.369	.464
Ted Sizemore	2B107	R	33	108	351	38	77	12	0	0	25	25	29	8	.219	.270	.254
Mike Schmidt	3B139,SS1	R	28	145	513	93	129	27	2	21	78	91	103	19	.251	.364	.435
Larry Bowa	SS156	S	32	156	654	78	192	31	5	3	43	24	40	27	.294	.319	.370
Garry Maddox	OF154	R	28	155	598	62	172	34	3	11	68	39	89	33	.288	.332	.410
Greg Luzinski	OF154	R	27	155	540	85	143	32	2	35	101	100	135	8	.265	.388	.526
Bake McBride	OF119	L	29	122	472	68	127	20	4	10	49	28	68	28	.269	.315	.392
Jerry Martin	OF112	R	29	128	266	40	72	13	4	9	36	28	65	9	.271	.339	.451
Jose Cardenal	1B50,OF13	R	34	87	201	27	50	12	0	4	33	23	16	2	.249	.323	.368
Tim McCarver	C34,1B11	L	36	90	146	18	36	9	1	1	14	28	24	2	.247	.367	.342
Jim Morrison	2B31,3B3,OF1	R	25	53	108	12	17	1	1	3	10	10	21	1	.157	.235	.269
Bud Harrelson	2B43,SS15	S	34	71	103	16	22	1	0	0	9	18	21	5	.214	.331	.223
Dave Johnson†	2B15,3B9,1B7	R	35	44	89	14	17	2	0	2	14	10	19	0	.191	.284	.281
Barry Foote	C31	R	26	39	57	4	9	0	0	1	4	1	11	0	.158	.172	.211
Jay Johnstone†	1B8,OF7	L	32	35	56	3	10	2	0	0	4	6	9	0	.179	.258	.214
Orlando Gonzalez	OF11,1B3	L	26	26	26	1	5	0	0	0	0	1	1	0	.192	.222	.192
Pete Mackanin	1B1,3B1	R	26	5	8	0	2	0	0	0	1	0	4	0	.250	.250	.250
Kerry Dineen	OF1	L	25	5	8	0	2	1	0	0	0	1	0	0	.250	.333	.375
Todd Cruz	SS2	R	22	3	4	0	2	0	0	0	2	0	0	0	.500	.500	.500
Lonnie Smith	OF11	R	22	17	4	6	0	0	0	0	0	4	3	4	.000	.500	.000
Keith Moreland	C1	R	24	1	2	0	0	0	0	0	0	0	0	0	.000	.000	.000

Pitcher	T	Age	G	GS	CG	ShO	IP	H	HR	BB	SO	W-L	Sv	ERA
Steve Carlton	L	33	34	34	12	3	247.1	228	30	63	161	16-13	0	2.84
Larry Christenson	R	24	33	33	9	3	228.0	209	16	47	131	13-14	0	3.24
Randy Lerch	L	23	33	28	5	0	184.0	183	15	70	96	11-8	0	3.96
Jim Kaat	L	39	26	24	2	1	140.1	150	9	32	48	8-5	0	4.10
Jim Lonborg	R	36	22	22	1	0	113.2	132	16	45	48	8-10	0	5.23
Dick Ruthven†	R	27	20	20	9	2	150.2	136	13	28	75	13-5	0	2.99
Ron Reed	R	35	66	0	0	0	108.2	87	6	23	85	3-4	17	2.24
Warren Brusstar	R	26	58	0	0	0	88.2	74	0	30	60	6-3	0	2.33
Tug McGraw	L	33	55	1	0	0	89.2	82	6	23	63	8-7	9	3.21
Rawly Eastwick†	R	27	22	0	0	0	40.1	31	5	18	14	2-1	0	4.02
Gene Garber†	R	30	22	0	0	0	38.2	26	1	11	24	2-1	3	1.40
Horacio Pina	R	33	2	0	0	0	2.1	0	0	0	4	0-0	0	0.00
Kevin Saucier	L	21	1	0	0	0	2.0	4	0	1	2	0-1	0	18.00
Dan Larson	R	23	1	0	0	0	1.0	1	1	1	2	0-0	0	9.00
Dan Boitano	R	25	1	0	0	0	1.0	0	0	1	0	0-0	0	0.00

1978 Pittsburgh Pirates 2nd NL East 88-73 .547 1.5 GB

Chuck Tanner

Player	Gm by Position	B	Age	G	AB	R	H	2B	3B	HR	RBI	BB	SO	SB	Avg	OBP	Slg
Ed Ott	C97,OF4	L	26	112	379	49	102	18	4	9	38	27	56	4	.269	.315	.409
Willie Stargell	1B112	L	38	122	390	60	115	18	2	28	97	50	93	3	.295	.382	.567
Phil Garner	2B81,3B81,SS4	R	29	154	528	66	138	25	9	10	66	66	71	27	.261	.345	.400
Dale Berra	3B55,SS2	R	21	56	135	16	28	2	0	6	14	13	20	3	.207	.285	.356
Frank Taveras	SS157	R	28	157	654	81	182	31	9	0	38	29	60	46	.278	.313	.353
Omar Moreno	OF152	L	25	155	515	95	121	15	7	2	33	81	104	71	.235	.339	.303
Dave Parker	OF147	L	27	148	581	102	194	32	12	30	117	57	92	20	.334	.394	.585
Bill Robinson	OF127,3B29,1B3	R	35	136	499	70	123	36	2	14	80	35	105	14	.246	.296	.411
Rennie Stennett	2B80,3B6	R	27	106	333	30	81	9	2	3	35	13	22	2	.243	.274	.309
John Milner	OF69,1B28	L	28	108	295	39	80	17	0	6	38	34	25	5	.271	.342	.390
Manny Sanguillen	1B40,C18	R	34	85	220	15	58	5	1	3	16	9	10	2	.264	.296	.336
Duffy Dyer	C55	R	32	58	175	7	37	8	1	0	13	18	32	2	.211	.294	.269
Steve Brye	OF47	R	29	66	115	16	27	7	0	1	9	11	10	2	.235	.305	.322
Mario Mendoza	2B21,3B18,SS14	R	27	57	55	5	12	1	0	1	3	2	9	3	.218	.283	.291
Ken Macha	3B21	R	27	29	52	5	11	1	1	0	5	12	10	2	.212	.354	.269
F. Gonzalez†	2B4,3B3	R	28	9	21	2	4	1	0	0	0	1	3	0	.190	.227	.238
Jim Fregosi	3B5,1B2,2B1	R	36	20	20	3	4	1	0	0	1	6	8	0	.200	.385	.250
Doe Boyland	1B1	L	23	6	8	1	2	0	0	0	0	1	0	1	.250	.250	.250
Steve Nicosia	C1	R	22	3	5	0	0	0	0	0	0	1	0	0	.000	.167	.000
Alberto Lois	OF2	R	22	3	4	0	1	0	1	0	0	0	1	0	.250	.250	.750
Dave May†		L	34	5	4	0	0	0	0	0	0	1	1	1	.000	.200	.000
Cito Gaston†	OF1	R	34	2	2	1	1	0	0	0	0	0	0	0	.500	.500	.500
Matt Alexander		S	31	7	0	2	0	0	0	0	0	0	0	4	—	—	—

Pitcher	T	Age	G	GS	CG	ShO	IP	H	HR	BB	SO	W-L	Sv	ERA
Bert Blyleven	R	27	34	34	11	4	243.2	217	17	66	182	14-10	0	3.03
Don Robinson	R	21	35	32	9	1	228.1	203	20	57	135	14-6	1	3.47
John Candelaria	L	24	30	29	3	1	189.0	191	15	49	94	12-11	1	3.24
Jim Rooker	L	35	28	28	1	0	163.1	160	13	81	76	9-11	0	4.24
Jerry Reuss	L	29	23	12	3	1	82.2	97	5	23	42	3-2	0	4.90
Kent Tekulve	R	31	91	0	0	0	135.0	115	5	55	77	8-7	31	2.33
Grant Jackson	L	35	60	0	0	0	77.1	89	5	32	45	7-5	5	3.26
Ed Whitson	R	23	43	0	0	0	74.1	66	5	37	64	5-6	4	3.27
Jim Bibby	R	33	34	14	3	2	107.0	100	10	39	72	8-7	1	3.53
Bruce Kison	R	28	28	11	0	0	96.0	81	3	39	62	6-6	0	3.19
Dave Hamilton†	L	30	16	0	0	0	26.1	23	2	12	15	0-2	1	3.42
Will McEnaney	L	26	6	0	0	0	8.2	15	3	2	6	0-0	0	10.38
Odell Jones	R	25	3	1	0	0	9.0	7	0	4	10	2-0	0	2.00
Clay Carroll	R	37	2	0	0	0	4.0	2	0	3	0	0-0	0	2.25

1978 Chicago Cubs 3rd NL East 79-83 .488 11.0 GB

Herman Franks

Player	Gm by Position	B	Age	G	AB	R	H	2B	3B	HR	RBI	BB	SO	SB	Avg	OBP	Slg
Dave Rader	C114	L	29	116	305	29	62	13	3	3	36	34	26	1	.203	.281	.295
Bill Buckner	1B105	L	28	117	446	47	144	26	1	5	74	18	17	7	.323	.345	.419
Manny Trillo	2B149	R	27	152	552	53	144	17	5	4	55	50	67	0	.261	.320	.332
Steve Ontiveros	3B77,1B1	S	26	82	276	34	67	14	4	1	22	34	33	0	.243	.321	.333
Ivan DeJesus	SS160	R	25	160	619	104	172	24	7	3	35	74	78	41	.278	.356	.354
Bobby Murcer	OF138	L	32	146	499	66	140	22	6	9	64	80	57	14	.281	.376	.403
Greg Gross	OF111	L	25	124	347	34	92	12	7	1	39	33	19	3	.265	.323	.349
Dave Kingman	OF100,1B6	R	29	119	395	65	105	17	4	28	79	39	111	3	.266	.336	.542
Larry Biittner	1B62,OF29	L	32	120	343	32	88	15	1	4	50	23	37	0	.257	.300	.341
Gene Clines	OF66	R	31	109	229	31	59	10	2	0	17	21	28	4	.258	.321	.319
Rodney Scott	3B59,OF10,2B6*	S	24	78	227	41	64	5	1	0	15	43	41	27	.282	.403	.313
Mike Vail†	OF45,3B1	R	26	74	180	15	60	6	2	4	33	3	24	0	.333	.341	.456
Jerry White†	OF54	S	25	59	136	22	37	6	0	1	10	23	16	4	.272	.373	.338
Larry Cox	C58	R	30	59	121	10	34	5	0	2	18	12	16	0	.281	.346	.372
Tim Blackwell	C49	S	25	49	103	8	23	3	0	0	7	23	17	0	.223	.367	.252
Mick Kelleher	3B37,2B17,SS10	R	30	68	95	8	24	1	0	0	6	7	11	4	.253	.304	.263
Heity Cruz†	OF14,3B7	R	25	30	76	8	18	5	0	2	9	3	6	0	.237	.266	.382
Joe Wallis†	OF25	S	26	28	55	7	17	2	1	1	6	5	13	0	.309	.367	.436
Dave Johnson†	3B12	R	35	24	49	5	15	1	1	2	6	5	9	0	.306	.393	.490
Scot Thompson	OF5,1B2	L	22	19	36	7	15	3	0	0	2	2	4	0	.417	.447	.500
Rudy Meoli	2B6,3B5	L	27	47	29	10	3	0	1	0	2	6	4	1	.103	.257	.172
Ed Putman	3B8,1B3,C2	R	24	17	25	2	5	0	0	0	3	4	6	0	.200	.310	.200
Mike Gordon	C4	S	24	4	5	0	1	0	0	0	0	3	2	0	.200	.556	.200
Mike Sember	3B7,SS1	R	25	9	3	2	1	0	0	0	0	1	1	0	.333	.500	.333
Karl Pagel		L	23	2	2	0	0	0	0	0	0	0	2	0	.000	.000	.000

R. Scott, 6 G at SS

Pitcher	T	Age	G	GS	CG	ShO	IP	H	HR	BB	SO	W-L	Sv	ERA
Dennis Lamp	R	25	37	36	6	3	223.2	221	16	56	73	7-15	0	3.30
Rick Reuschel	R	29	35	35	9	1	242.2	235	16	54	115	14-15	0	3.41
Ray Burris	R	27	40	32	4	1	198.2	210	15	79	94	7-13	1	4.76
Dave Roberts	L	33	35	20	2	1	142.1	159	17	56	54	6-8	1	5.25
Mike Krukow	R	26	27	20	3	1	138.0	125	11	53	81	9-3	0	3.91
Woodie Fryman†	L	38	13	9	0	0	55.2	64	6	37	28	2-4	0	5.17
Donnie Moore	R	24	71	1	0	0	103.0	117	7	31	50	9-7	4	4.11
Bruce Sutter	R	25	64	0	0	0	99.0	82	10	34	106	8-10	27	3.18
Willie Hernandez	L	23	54	0	0	0	59.2	57	6	35	38	8-2	3	3.77
Lynn McGlothen†	R	28	49	1	0	0	80.0	77	7	39	60	5-3	0	3.04
Ken Holtzman†	L	32	23	6	0	0	53.0	61	10	35	36	0-3	2	6.11
Dave Geisel	L	23	18	1	0	0	23.1	27	0	11	15	1-0	0	4.24
Paul Reuschel†	R	31	16	0	0	0	28.0	29	4	13	13	2-0	0	5.14
Manny Seoane	R	23	7	1	0	0	8.1	11	0	6	5	1-0	0	5.40

844 Seasons: Team Rosters

1978 Montreal Expos 4th NL East 76-86 .469 14.0 GB

Dick Williams

Player	Gm by Position	B	Age	G	AB	R	H	2B	3B	HR	RBI	BB	SO	SB	Avg	OBP	Slg
Gary Carter	C152,1B1	R	24	157	533	76	136	27	1	20	72	62	70	10	.255	.336	.422
Tony Perez	1B145	R	36	148	544	63	158	38	3	14	78	38	104	2	.290	.336	.449
Dave Cash	2B159	R	30	159	658	66	166	26	3	3	43	37	29	12	.252	.291	.315
Larry Parrish	3B139	R	24	144	520	68	144	39	4	15	70	32	103	2	.277	.321	.454
Chris Speier	SS148	R	28	150	501	47	126	18	3	5	51	60	75	1	.251	.329	.329
Warren Cromartie	OF158,1B4	L	24	159	607	77	180	32	6	10	56	33	60	8	.297	.337	.418
Andre Dawson	OF153	R	23	157	609	84	154	24	8	25	72	30	128	28	.253	.299	.442
Ellis Valentine	OF146	R	23	151	570	75	165	35	2	25	76	35	88	13	.289	.330	.489
Del Unser	1B64,OF33	L	33	130	179	16	35	5	0	2	15	24	29	2	.196	.293	.257
Stan Papi	SS22,3B15,2B5	R	27	67	152	15	35	11	0	0	11	10	28	0	.230	.285	.303
Wayne Garrett†	3B13	L	30	49	69	6	12	0	0	1	2	8	10	0	.174	.260	.217
Tom Hutton†	1B17,OF5	L	32	39	59	4	12	3	0	0	5	10	5	0	.203	.319	.254
Sam Mejias	OF52,P1	R	26	67	56	9	13	1	0	0	6	2	5	0	.232	.259	.250
Ed Herrmann†	C12	L	31	19	40	1	7	1	0	0	3	1	4	0	.175	.195	.200
Pepe Frias	2B61,SS3	R	29	73	15	5	4	2	1	0	5	0	3	0	.267	.250	.533
Bob Reece	C9	R	27	9	11	2	2	1	0	0	3	0	4	0	.182	.182	.273
Jerry White†	OF3	S	25	18	10	2	2	0	0	0	0	1	3	1	.200	.273	.200
Jerry Fry	C4	R	22	4	9	0	0	0	0	0	0	1	5	0	.000	.100	.000
Bobby Ramos	C1	R	22	2	4	0	0	0	0	0	0	0	1	0	.000	.000	.000

Pitcher	T	Age	G	GS	CG	ShO	IP	H	HR	BB	SO	W-L	Sv	ERA
Ross Grimsley	L	28	36	36	19	3	263.0	237	17	67	84	20-11	0	3.05
Steve Rogers	R	28	30	29	11	1	219.0	186	12	64	126	13-10	1	2.47
Rudy May	L	33	27	23	4	1	144.0	141	15	42	87	8-10	0	3.88
Dan Schatzeder	L	23	29	18	2	0	143.2	108	10	68	69	7-7	0	3.07
Woodie Fryman†	L	38	19	17	4	3	94.2	93	4	37	53	5-7	1	3.61
Scott Sanderson	R	21	10	9	1	1	61.0	52	3	21	50	4-2	0	2.51
Darold Knowles	L	36	60	0	0	0	72.0	63	5	30	34	3-3	6	2.38
Mike Garman†	R	28	47	0	0	0	61.1	54	5	31	23	4-6	13	4.40
Stan Bahnsen	R	33	44	1	0	0	75.0	74	9	31	44	1-5	7	3.84
Wayne Twitchell	R	30	33	15	0	0	112.0	121	16	71	69	4-12	0	5.38
Bill Atkinson	R	23	29	0	0	0	45.1	45	5	28	32	2-2	3	4.37
Hal Dues	R	23	25	12	1	0	99.0	85	5	42	36	5-6	1	2.36
Gerry Pirtle	R	30	19	0	0	0	25.2	33	5	23	14	0-2	0	5.96
Fred Holdsworth	R	26	6	0	0	0	8.2	16	3	8	3	0-0	0	7.27
David Palmer	R	20	5	1	0	0	9.2	9	1	2	7	0-1	0	2.79
Randy Miller	R	25	5	0	0	0	7.0	11	1	3	6	0-1	0	10.29
Bob James	R	19	4	1	0	0	4.0	4	1	4	3	0-1	0	9.00
Sam Mejias	R	26	1	0	0	0	1.0	0	0	0	0	0-0	0	0.00

1978 St. Louis Cardinals 5th NL East 69-93 .426 21.0 GB

Vern Rapp (6-11)/Jack Krol (1-1)/Ken Boyer (62-81)

Player	Gm by Position	B	Age	G	AB	R	H	2B	3B	HR	RBI	BB	SO	SB	Avg	OBP	Slg
Ted Simmons	C134,OF23	S	28	152	516	71	148	40	5	22	80	77	39	1	.287	.377	.512
Keith Hernandez	1B158	L	24	159	542	90	138	32	4	11	64	82	68	13	.255	.351	.389
Mike Tyson	2B124	R	28	125	377	26	88	16	0	3	26	24	41	2	.233	.277	.300
Ken Reitz	3B150	R	27	150	540	41	133	26	2	10	75	23	61	1	.246	.280	.357
Garry Templeton	SS155	S	22	155	647	82	181	31	13	2	47	22	87	34	.280	.303	.377
Jerry Morales	OF126	R	29	130	457	44	109	19	8	4	46	33	44	4	.239	.288	.341
Jerry Mumphrey	OF116	S	25	125	367	41	96	13	4	2	37	30	40	14	.262	.317	.335
George Hendrick†	OF101	R	28	102	382	55	110	27	1	17	67	28	44	1	.288	.337	.497
Lou Brock	OF79	L	39	92	298	31	66	9	0	0	12	17	29	17	.221	.263	.252
Tony Scott	OF77	S	26	96	219	28	50	5	2	1	14	14	41	5	.228	.278	.283
Mike Phillips	2B55,SS10,3B1	L	27	76	164	14	44	8	1	1	28	13	25	0	.268	.317	.348
Steve Swisher	C42	R	26	45	115	11	32	5	1	1	10	8	14	1	.278	.331	.365
Roger Freed	1B15,OF6	R	32	52	92	3	22	6	0	2	20	8	17	1	.239	.297	.370
Dane Iorg	OF25	L	28	35	85	6	23	4	1	0	4	4	10	0	.271	.300	.341
Jim Dwyer†	OF22	L	28	34	65	8	14	3	0	1	4	9	3	1	.215	.320	.308
Wayne Garrett†	3B19	L	30	33	63	11	21	4	0	1	10	11	16	1	.333	.432	.444
Ken Oberkfell	2B17,3B4	L	22	24	50	7	6	1	0	0	0	3	1	0	.120	.170	.140
Terry Kennedy	C10	L	22	10	29	0	5	0	0	0	2	4	3	0	.172	.273	.172
Jim Lentine	OF3	R	23	8	11	1	2	0	0	0	1	0	0	1	.182	.250	.182
John Tamargo†	C1	S	26	6	6	0	0	0	0	0	0	0	2	0	.000	.000	.000
Gary Sutherland	2B1	R	33	10	6	1	1	0	0	0	0	0	0	0	.167	.167	.167
Mike Ramsey	SS4	S	24	12	5	4	1	0	0	0	0	0	1	0	.200	.200	.200
Bob Coluccio	OF2	R	26	5	3	0	0	0	0	0	0	1	2	0	.000	.250	.000

Pitcher	T	Age	G	GS	CG	ShO	IP	H	HR	BB	SO	W-L	Sv	ERA
Bob Forsch	R	28	34	34	7	3	233.2	205	15	97	114	11-17	0	3.70
John Denny	R	25	33	33	11	2	234.0	200	13	74	103	14-11	0	2.96
Pete Vuckovich	R	25	45	23	6	2	198.1	187	9	59	149	12-12	1	2.54
Silvio Martinez	R	22	22	22	5	2	138.1	114	11	71	45	9-8	0	3.64
Pete Falcone	L	24	19	14	0	0	75.0	94	9	48	28	2-7	0	5.76
Eric Rasmussen†	R	26	10	10	2	1	60.1	61	4	20	32	2-5	0	4.18
Rob Dressler	R	24	3	2	0	0	13.0	12	0	4	4	0-1	0	2.08
Mark Littell	R	25	72	2	0	0	106.1	80	8	59	130	4-8	11	2.79
Buddy Schultz	L	27	62	0	0	0	83.0	68	6	36	70	2-4	6	3.80
John Urrea	R	23	27	12	1	0	98.2	108	4	47	61	4-9	0	5.38
Aurelio Lopez	R	29	25	4	0	0	65.0	52	4	32	46	4-2	0	4.29
Tom Bruno	R	25	18	3	0	0	49.2	38	3	17	33	4-3	1	1.99
Roy Thomas	R	25	16	1	0	0	28.1	21	0	16	16	1-1	3	3.81
George Frazier	R	23	14	0	0	0	22.0	22	2	6	8	0-3	0	4.09
Dave Hamilton†	L	30	13	0	0	0	14.0	16	5	6	8	0-0	0	6.43
Dan O'Brien	R	24	7	2	0	0	18.0	22	1	8	12	0-2	0	4.50

1978 New York Mets 6th NL East 66-96 .407 24.0 GB

Joe Torre

Player	Gm by Position	B	Age	G	AB	R	H	2B	3B	HR	RBI	BB	SO	SB	Avg	OBP	Slg
John Stearns	C141,3B1	R	26	143	477	65	126	24	1	15	73	70	57	25	.264	.364	.413
Willie Montanez	1B158	L	30	159	609	66	156	32	0	17	96	60	92	9	.256	.320	.392
Doug Flynn	2B128,SS60	R	27	156	532	37	126	12	8	0	36	30	50	3	.237	.277	.289
Lenny Randle	3B124,2B5	S	29	132	437	53	102	16	8	2	35	64	57	14	.233	.330	.320
Tim Foli	SS112	R	27	113	413	37	106	21	1	1	27	14	30	2	.257	.283	.320
Steve Henderson	OF155	R	25	157	587	83	156	30	9	10	65	60	109	13	.266	.333	.399
Lee Mazzilli	OF144	S	23	148	542	78	148	28	5	16	61	69	82	20	.273	.353	.432
Elliott Maddox	OF79,3B43,1B1	R	30	119	389	43	100	18	2	2	39	71	38	2	.257	.370	.329
Joel Youngblood	OF50,2B39,3B9*	R	26	113	266	40	67	12	8	7	30	16	39	4	.252	.294	.436
Bruce Boisclair	OF69,1B1	L	25	107	214	24	48	7	1	4	15	23	43	3	.224	.293	.322
Bobby Valentine	2B45,3B9	R	28	69	160	17	43	7	0	1	18	19	18	1	.269	.346	.331
Ron Hodges	C30	L	29	47	102	4	26	4	1	0	7	10	11	1	.255	.322	.314
Tom Grieve	OF26,1B2	R	30	54	101	5	21	3	0	2	8	9	23	0	.208	.273	.297
Ed Kranepool	OF12,1B3	L	33	66	81	7	17	2	0	3	19	8	12	0	.210	.280	.346
Dan Norman	OF18	R	23	19	64	7	17	0	1	4	10	2	14	1	.266	.284	.484
Sergio Ferrer	SS29,2B3,3B2	S	27	37	33	8	7	0	1	0	1	4	7	1	.212	.316	.273
Gil Flores	OF8	R	25	11	29	8	8	0	1	0	1	3	5	1	.276	.344	.345
Ken Henderson†	OF7	S	32	7	22	2	5	2	0	1	4	4	4	0	.227	.346	.455
Alex Trevino	C5,3B1	R	20	6	12	3	3	0	0	0	0	1	2	0	.250	.308	.250
Butch Benton	C1	R	20	4	4	1	2	0	0	0	2	0	0	0	.500	.600	.500

J. Youngblood, 1 G at SS

Pitcher	T	Age	G	GS	CG	ShO	IP	H	HR	BB	SO	W-L	Sv	ERA
Jerry Koosman	L	35	38	32	3	0	235.1	221	17	84	160	3-15	2	3.75
Nino Espinosa	R	24	32	32	6	1	203.2	230	24	75	76	11-15	0	4.73
Craig Swan	R	27	29	28	5	1	207.1	164	12	58	125	9-6	0	2.43
Mike Bruhert	R	27	27	22	1	1	133.2	171	6	34	56	4-11	0	4.78
Pat Zachry	R	26	21	21	5	2	138.0	120	9	60	78	10-6	0	3.33
Tom Hausman	R	25	10	10	0	0	51.2	58	6	9	16	3-3	0	4.70
Juan Berenguer	R	23	5	3	0	0	13.0	17	1	11	8	0-2	0	8.31
Roy Lee Jackson	R	24	4	2	0	0	12.2	21	2	6	6	0-0	0	9.24
Skip Lockwood	R	31	57	0	0	0	90.2	78	10	31	73	7-13	15	3.57
Dale Murray†	R	28	53	0	0	0	86.1	85	4	36	37	8-5	5	3.65
Kevin Kobel	L	24	32	11	1	0	108.1	95	9	30	51	5-6	0	2.91
Dwight Bernard	R	26	30	1	0	0	48.0	54	4	27	26	1-4	0	4.31
Paul Siebert	L	25	27	0	0	0	28.0	30	2	21	12	0-2	1	5.14
Butch Metzger	R	26	25	0	0	0	37.1	48	4	22	21	1-3	0	6.51
Mardie Cornejo	R	26	25	0	0	0	36.2	37	1	14	17	4-2	3	2.45
Bob Myrick	L	25	17	0	0	0	24.2	18	3	13	13	0-3	0	3.28

1978 Los Angeles Dodgers 1st NL West 95-67 .586 —

Tom Lasorda

Player	Gm by Position	B	Age	G	AB	R	H	2B	3B	HR	RBI	BB	SO	SB	Avg	OBP	Slg
Steve Yeager	C91	R	29	94	228	19	44	7	0	4	23	36	41	0	.193	.301	.276
Steve Garvey	1B161	R	29	162	639	89	202	36	9	21	113	40	70	10	.316	.353	.499
Davey Lopes	2B147,OF2	R	33	151	587	93	163	25	4	17	58	71	70	45	.278	.355	.421
Ron Cey	3B158	R	30	159	555	84	150	32	0	23	84	96	96	2	.270	.380	.452
Bill Russell	SS155	R	29	155	625	72	179	32	4	3	46	30	34	10	.286	.320	.365
Dusty Baker	OF145	R	29	149	522	62	137	24	1	11	66	47	66	12	.262	.325	.375
Reggie Smith	OF126	S	33	128	447	82	132	27	2	29	93	70	90	12	.295	.382	.559
Rick Monday	OF103,1B1	L	32	119	342	54	87	14	1	19	57	49	100	2	.254	.348	.468
Bill North†	OF103	S	30	110	304	54	71	10	0	0	10	65	48	27	.234	.371	.266
Lee Lacy	OF44,2B24,3B9*	R	30	103	245	29	64	16	4	13	40	27	30	7	.261	.335	.518
Joe Ferguson†	C62,OF3	R	31	67	198	20	47	11	0	7	28	34	41	1	.237	.350	.399
Vic Davalillo	OF25,1B1	L	41	75	77	15	24	1	1	1	11	3	7	2	.312	.333	.390
Johnny Oates	C24	L	32	40	75	5	23	1	0	0	6	5	3	0	.307	.350	.320
Jerry Grote	C32,3B7	R	35	41	70	5	19	5	0	0	9	10	5	0	.271	.354	.343
Ted Martinez	SS17,3B16,2B10	R	30	54	55	13	14	1	0	1	5	4	14	3	.255	.317	.327
Manny Mota		R	40	37	33	2	10	1	0	0	6	3	4	0	.303	.361	.333
Glenn Burke†	OF15	R	25	16	19	2	4	0	0	0	2	0	4	1	.211	.211	.211
Rudy Law	OF6	L	21	11	12	2	3	0	0	0	1	1	2	3	.250	.308	.250
Pedro Guerrero	1B4	R	22	5	8	3	5	0	1	0	1	0	0	0	.625	.625	.875
Joe Simpson	OF10	L	26	10	5	1	2	0	0	0	1	0	2	0	.400	.400	.400
Brad Gulden	C3	L	22	3	4	0	0	0	0	0	0	0	2	0	.000	.000	.000
Myron White	OF4	L	20	7	4	1	2	0	0	0	1	0	1	0	.500	.500	.500
Enzo Hernandez	SS2	R	29	4	3	0	0	0	0	0	0	0	1	0	.000	.000	.000

L. Lacy, 1 G at SS

Pitcher	T	Age	G	GS	CG	ShO	IP	H	HR	BB	SO	W-L	Sv	ERA
Don Sutton	R	33	34	34	12	2	238.1	228	29	54	154	15-11	0	3.55
Burt Hooton	R	28	32	32	10	3	236.0	196	17	61	104	19-10	0	2.71
Tommy John	L	35	33	30	7	0	213.0	230	11	53	124	17-10	1	3.30
Doug Rau	L	29	30	30	7	2	199.0	219	17	68	95	15-9	0	3.26
Rick Rhoden	R	25	30	23	6	3	164.2	160	13	51	79	10-8	0	3.66
Bob Welch	R	21	23	13	4	3	111.1	92	6	26	66	7-4	3	2.02
Charlie Hough	R	30	55	0	0	0	93.1	69	6	48	66	5-5	7	3.28
Terry Forster	L	26	47	0	0	0	65.1	56	2	23	46	5-4	22	1.93
Lance Rautzhan	L	25	43	0	0	0	61.1	61	1	19	25	2-1	4	2.93
Bobby Castillo	R	23	18	0	0	0	34.0	28	2	33	30	0-4	1	3.97
Mike Garman†	R	28	10	0	0	0	16.1	15	3	3	5	0-1	0	4.41
Rick Sutcliffe	R	22	2	0	0	0	1.2	2	0	1	0	0-0	0	0.00
Dennis Lewallyn	R	24	1	0	0	0	2.0	2	0	0	0	0-0	0	0.00
Dave Stewart	R	21	1	0	0	0	2.0	1	0	0	1	0-0	0	0.00
Gerry Hannahs	L	25	1	0	0	0	2.0	3	0	0	5	0-0	0	9.00

1978 Cincinnati Reds 2nd NL West 92-69 .571 2.5 GB

Sparky Anderson

Player	Gm by Position	B	Age	G	AB	R	H	2B	3B	HR	RBI	BB	SO	SB	Avg	OBP	Slg
Johnny Bench	C107,1B11,OF2	R	30	120	393	52	102	17	1	23	73	50	83	4	.260	.340	.483
Dan Driessen	1B151	L	26	153	524	68	131	23	3	16	70	75	79	28	.250	.345	.397
Joe Morgan	2B124	L	34	132	441	68	104	27	0	13	75	79	40	19	.236	.347	.385
Pete Rose	3B156,OF7,1B2	S	37	159	655	103	198	51	3	7	52	62	30	13	.302	.362	.421
Dave Concepcion	SS152	R	30	153	565	75	170	33	4	6	67	51	83	23	.301	.357	.405
George Foster	OF157	R	29	158	604	97	170	26	7	40	120	70	138	4	.281	.360	.546
Ken Griffey Sr.	OF154	L	28	158	614	90	177	33	8	10	63	54	70	23	.288	.344	.417
Cesar Geronimo	OF115	L	30	122	296	28	67	15	1	5	27	43	67	8	.226	.329	.334
Junior Kennedy	2B71,3B4	R	27	89	157	22	40	2	2	0	11	31	28	4	.255	.381	.293
Mike Lum	OF43,1B7	L	32	86	146	15	39	7	1	6	23	22	18	0	.267	.361	.452
Ken Henderson†	OF38	S	32	64	144	10	24	6	1	3	19	23	32	0	.167	.278	.285
Don Werner	C49	R	25	50	113	7	17	2	1	0	11	14	30	1	.150	.242	.186
Vic Correll	C52	R	32	52	105	9	25	7	0	1	6	8	17	0	.238	.292	.333
Dave Collins	OF24	S	25	102	102	13	22	1	0	0	7	15	18	7	.216	.311	.225
Ray Knight	3B60,2B4,OF3*	R	25	83	65	7	13	3	0	1	4	3	13	0	.200	.235	.292
Rick Auerbach	SS26,2B10,3B3	R	28	63	55	17	18	6	0	2	5	7	12	1	.327	.413	.545
Champ Summers	OF12	L	32	13	35	4	9	2	0	1	3	7	4	2	.257	.381	.400
Arturo DeFreitas	1B6	R	25	9	19	1	4	2	1	0	2	1	4	0	.211	.238	.421
Ron Oester	SS6	S	22	6	8	1	3	0	0	0	1	0	2	0	.375	.375	.375
Harry Spilman		L	23	4	4	1	1	0	0	0	0	0	1	0	.250	.250	.250
Mike Grace	3B2	R	22	5	3	0	0	0	0	0	0	0	2	0	.000	.000	.000

R. Knight, 1 G at 1B, 1 G at SS

Pitcher	T	Age	G	GS	CG	ShO	IP	H	HR	BB	SO	W-L	Sv	ERA
Tom Seaver	R	33	36	36	8	1	259.2	218	26	89	226	16-14	0	2.88
Fred Norman	L	35	36	31	0	0	177.1	173	19	82	111	11-9	1	3.70
Paul Moskau	R	24	26	25	2	1	145.0	139	17	57	88	6-4	1	3.97
Tom Hume	R	25	42	23	3	0	174.0	198	12	50	90	8-11	1	4.14
Bill Bonham	R	29	23	23	1	0	140.1	151	9	50	83	11-5	0	3.53
Mike LaCoss	R	22	16	15	2	1	96.0	104	5	46	31	4-8	0	4.50
Doug Capilla	L	26	6	3	0	0	11.0	14	1	11	9	0-1	0	9.82
Doug Bair	R	28	70	0	0	0	100.1	87	6	38	91	7-6	28	1.97
Manny Sarmiento	R	22	63	4	0	0	127.1	109	16	54	72	9-7	5	4.38
Pedro Borbon	R	31	62	0	0	0	99.1	102	6	27	35	8-2	4	4.98
Dave Tomlin	L	29	57	0	0	0	62.1	88	3	30	32	9-1	4	5.78
Dale Murray†	R	28	15	0	0	0	32.2	34	1	17	25	1-1	2	4.13
Mario Soto	R	21	5	1	0	0	18.0	13	1	13	13	1-0	0	2.50
Dan Dumoulin	R	24	3	0	0	0	5.0	7	0	3	2	1-0	0	1.80

1978 San Francisco Giants 3rd NL West 89-73 .549 6.0 GB

Joe Altobelli

Player	Gm by Position	B	Age	G	AB	R	H	2B	3B	HR	RBI	BB	SO	SB	Avg	OBP	Slg
Marc Hill	C116,1B2	R	26	117	358	20	87	15	1	3	36	45	39	1	.243	.329	.316
Willie McCovey	1B97	L	40	108	351	32	80	19	2	12	64	36	57	1	.228	.298	.396
Bill Madlock	2B114,1B3	R	27	122	447	76	138	26	3	15	44	48	39	16	.309	.378	.481
Darrell Evans	3B155	L	31	159	547	82	133	24	2	20	78	105	64	4	.243	.360	.404
Johnnie LeMaster	SS96,2B2	R	24	101	272	23	64	18	3	1	14	21	45	6	.235	.293	.335
Jack Clark	OF152	R	22	156	592	90	181	46	8	25	98	50	72	15	.306	.358	.537
Larry Herndon	OF149	R	24	151	471	52	122	15	9	1	32	35	71	13	.259	.311	.335
Terry Whitfield	OF140	L	25	149	488	70	141	20	2	10	32	33	69	5	.289	.335	.400
Mike Ivie	1B76,OF22	R	25	117	318	34	98	14	3	11	55	27	45	3	.308	.363	.475
Roger Metzger†	SS74	S	30	75	235	17	61	6	1	0	17	12	17	8	.260	.294	.294
Heity Cruz†	OF53,3B14	R	25	79	197	19	44	8	1	6	24	21	39	0	.223	.301	.365
Rob Andrews	2B62,SS1	R	25	79	177	21	39	3	3	1	11	20	18	5	.220	.299	.288
Jim Dwyer†	OF36,1B29	L	28	73	173	22	39	9	2	5	22	28	29	6	.225	.327	.387
Mike Sadek	C37	R	32	40	109	15	26	3	0	2	9	10	11	1	.239	.303	.321
Vic Harris	SS22,2B10,OF6	S	28	53	100	8	15	4	0	1	11	11	24	0	.150	.230	.220
John Tamargo†	C31	S	26	36	92	6	22	4	1	1	8	18	7	1	.239	.360	.337
Tom Heintzelman	2B5,3B3,1B2	R	31	27	35	2	8	1	0	2	6	2	5	0	.229	.270	.429
Skip James	1B27	L	28	41	21	5	2	1	0	0	3	4	5	1	.095	.240	.143
Art Gardner		L	25	7	3	2	0	0	0	0	0	0	2	0	.000	.000	.000
Dennis Littlejohn	C2	R	23	2	0	0	0	0	0	0	0	0	0	0	—	—	—

Pitcher	T	Age	G	GS	CG	ShO	IP	H	HR	BB	SO	W-L	Sv	ERA
John Montefusco	R	28	36	36	3	0	239.0	233	25	68	177	11-9	0	3.80
Bob Knepper	L	24	36	35	16	6	260.0	218	10	85	147	17-11	0	2.63
Vida Blue	L	28	35	35	9	4	258.0	233	12	70	171	18-10	0	2.79
Ed Halicki	R	27	29	28	9	4	199.0	166	11	45	105	9-10	1	2.85
Jim Barr	R	30	32	25	5	2	163.0	180	7	35	44	8-11	1	3.53
Randy Moffitt	R	29	70	0	0	0	81.2	79	5	33	52	8-4	12	3.31
Gary Lavelle	L	29	67	0	0	0	97.2	96	3	44	63	13-10	14	3.32
John Curtis	L	30	46	0	0	0	63.0	60	1	29	38	4-3	1	3.71
Charlie Williams	R	30	25	1	0	0	48.0	60	5	28	22	1-3	0	5.44
Greg Minton	R	26	11	0	0	0	15.2	22	3	8	6	0-1	0	8.04
Lynn McGlothen†	R	28	5	1	0	0	12.2	15	0	4	9	0-0	0	4.97
Eddie Plank	R	26	5	0	0	0	6.2	6	1	2	1	0-0	0	4.05
Phil Nastu	L	23	3	1	0	0	8.0	8	1	2	5	0-1	0	5.63
Terry Cornutt	R	25	1	0	0	0	3.0	1	0	0	0	0-0	0	0.00

1978 San Diego Padres 4th NL West 84-78 .519 11.0 GB

Roger Craig

Player	Gm by Position	B	Age	G	AB	R	H	2B	3B	HR	RBI	BB	SO	SB	Avg	OBP	Slg
Rick Sweet	C76	S	25	88	226	15	50	8	0	1	11	27	22	1	.221	.306	.270
Gene Tenace	1B80,C71,3B1	R	31	142	401	60	90	18	4	16	61	101	98	6	.224	.392	.409
F. Gonzalez†	2B94	R	28	101	320	27	80	10	2	2	29	18	32	4	.250	.286	.313
Bill Almon	3B114,SS15,2B7	R	25	138	405	39	102	19	2	0	21	33	74	17	.252	.308	.309
Ozzie Smith	SS159	S	23	159	590	69	152	17	6	1	46	47	43	40	.258	.311	.312
Dave Winfield	OF154,1B2	R	26	158	587	88	181	30	5	24	97	55	81	21	.308	.367	.499
Gene Richards	OF124,1B26	L	24	154	555	90	171	26	12	4	45	64	80	37	.308	.381	.420
Oscar Gamble	OF107	L	28	126	375	46	103	15	3	7	47	51	45	1	.275	.366	.387
Derrel Thomas	OF77,2B40,3B26*	R	27	128	352	36	80	10	2	3	26	35	37	11	.227	.301	.293
Jerry Turner	OF58	L	24	106	225	28	63	9	1	8	37	21	32	6	.280	.348	.436
Broderick Perkins	1B59	L	23	62	217	14	52	14	1	2	33	5	29	4	.240	.253	.341
Tucker Ashford	3B32,2B18,1B14	R	23	75	155	11	38	11	0	3	26	14	31	1	.245	.301	.374
George Hendrick†	OF33	R	28	36	111	9	27	4	0	3	8	12	16	1	.243	.317	.360
Dave Roberts	C41,1B8,OF2	R	27	54	97	7	21	4	1	1	7	12	25	0	.216	.309	.309
Barry Evans	3B24	R	22	24	90	7	24	1	1	0	4	4	10	0	.267	.295	.300
Don Reynolds	OF25	R	25	57	87	8	22	2	0	0	10	15	14	1	.253	.363	.276
Chuck Baker	2B24,SS12	R	25	44	58	8	12	1	0	0	3	2	15	0	.207	.233	.224
Mike Champion	2B20,3B4	R	23	32	53	3	12	0	2	0	4	5	13	0	.226	.293	.302
Bob Davis	C16	R	26	19	40	3	8	1	0	0	2	1	5	0	.200	.220	.225
Jim Beswick	OF6	S	20	17	20	2	1	0	0	0	0	1	7	0	.050	.095	.050
Jim Wilhelm	OF10	R	25	10	19	2	7	2	0	0	4	0	2	1	.368	.381	.474
Tony Castillo	C5	R	21	5	8	0	1	0	0	0	1	0	2	0	.125	.125	.125

D. Thomas, 14 G at 1B

Pitcher	T	Age	G	GS	CG	ShO	IP	H	HR	BB	SO	W-L	Sv	ERA
Gaylord Perry	R	39	37	37	5	2	260.2	241	9	66	154	21-6	0	2.73
Randy Jones	L	28	37	36	7	2	253.0	263	6	64	71	13-14	0	2.88
Bob Owchinko	L	23	36	33	4	1	202.1	198	14	78	94	10-13	0	3.56
Eric Rasmussen†	R	26	27	24	3	2	146.1	154	16	43	59	12-10	0	4.06
Rollie Fingers	R	31	67	0	0	0	107.1	84	4	29	72	6-13	37	2.52
Mark Lee	R	25	56	0	0	0	85.0	74	2	36	31	5-1	2	3.28
Bob Shirley	L	24	50	20	2	0	166.0	164	10	61	102	8-11	5	3.69
John D'Acquisto	R	26	45	3	0	0	93.0	60	2	56	104	4-3	10	2.13
Mickey Lolich	L	37	20	2	0	0	34.2	30	0	11	13	2-1	1	1.56
Dan Spillner†	R	26	17	0	0	0	25.2	32	2	7	16	1-0	0	4.56
Dave Freisleben†	R	26	12	4	0	0	26.2	41	3	15	16	0-3	0	6.08
Dennis Kinney†	L	26	7	0	0	0	7.0	6	3	4	2	0-1	0	6.43
Steve Mura	R	23	5	2	0	0	7.2	15	1	5	5	0-2	0	11.74
Mark Wiley†	R	30	4	1	0	0	7.2	11	1	1	1	1-0	0	5.87
Dave Wehrmeister	R	25	4	0	0	0	7.1	8	1	5	2	1-0	0	6.14
Juan Eichelberger	R	24	3	0	0	0	3.1	4	0	2	2	0-0	0	10.80

1978 Houston Astros 5th NL West 74-88 .457 21.0 GB

Bill Virdon

Player	Gm by Position	B	Age	G	AB	R	H	2B	3B	HR	RBI	BB	SO	SB	Avg	OBP	Slg
Luis Pujols	C55,1B1	R	22	56	153	11	20	8	1	1	11	12	45	0	.131	.198	.216
Bob Watson	1B128	R	32	139	461	51	133	25	4	14	79	51	57	3	.289	.357	.451
Art Howe	2B107,3B11,1B1	R	31	119	420	46	123	33	3	7	55	34	41	2	.293	.343	.436
Enos Cabell	3B153,1B14,SS1	R	28	162	660	92	195	31	8	7	71	22	80	33	.295	.321	.398
Jimmy Sexton	SS58,3B8,2B3	R	26	88	141	17	29	3	2	2	6	13	28	16	.206	.273	.298
Jose Cruz	OF152,1B2	L	30	153	565	79	178	34	9	10	83	57	57	37	.315	.376	.460
Terry Puhl	OF148	L	21	149	585	87	169	25	6	3	35	48	46	32	.289	.343	.368
Denny Walling	OF78	L	24	120	247	30	62	11	3	3	36	30	24	9	.251	.332	.356
Julio Gonzalez	2B54,SS17,3B4	R	25	78	223	24	52	3	1	1	16	8	31	6	.233	.263	.269
Rafael Landestoy	SS50,OF3,2B2	S	25	59	218	18	58	5	1	0	9	8	23	7	.266	.292	.298
Cesar Cedeno	OF50	R	27	50	192	31	54	8	2	7	23	15	24	23	.281	.333	.453
Dave Bergman	1B66,OF29	L	25	104	186	15	43	5	1	0	12	39	32	2	.231	.361	.269
Bruce Bochy	C53	R	23	54	154	8	41	8	0	3	15	11	35	0	.266	.311	.377
Joe Ferguson†	C51	R	31	51	150	20	31	5	0	7	22	37	30	0	.207	.363	.380
Wilbur Howard	OF16,C3,2B1	S	29	84	148	17	34	4	1	1	13	5	22	6	.230	.268	.291
Jesus Alou	OF28	R	36	77	139	7	45	5	1	2	19	6	5	0	.324	.345	.417
Roger Metzger†	SS42,2B1	S	30	45	123	11	27	4	1	0	6	12	9	0	.220	.287	.268
Mike Fischlin	SS41	R	22	44	86	3	10	1	0	0	0	4	9	1	.116	.165	.128
Reggie Baldwin	C17	R	23	38	67	5	17	5	0	1	11	3	3	0	.254	.286	.373
Keith Drumright	2B17	L	23	17	55	5	9	0	0	0	2	3	4	0	.164	.207	.164
Ed Herrmann†	C14	L	31	16	36	1	4	1	0	0	0	3	3	0	.111	.179	.139
Jeffrey Leonard	OF8	R	22	8	26	2	10	2	0	0	4	1	2	0	.385	.407	.462
Joe Cannon	OF5	L	24	8	18	1	4	0	0	0	1	0	1	0	.222	.222	.222
Jim O'Bradovich	1B3	L	28	10	17	3	3	0	1	0	2	1	3	0	.176	.222	.294

Pitcher	T	Age	G	GS	CG	ShO	IP	H	HR	BB	SO	W-L	Sv	ERA
J.R. Richard	R	28	36	36	16	3	275.1	192	12	141	303	18-11	0	3.11
Mark Lemongello	R	22	33	30	9	1	210.1	204	20	66	77	9-14	1	3.94
Joe Niekro	R	33	35	29	10	1	202.2	190	13	73	97	14-14	0	3.86
Tom Dixon	R	23	30	19	3	2	140.0	140	8	40	66	7-11	1	3.99
Floyd Bannister	L	23	28	16	2	2	110.1	120	13	63	94	3-9	0	4.81
Vern Ruhle	R	27	13	10	2	2	68.0	57	0	20	27	3-3	0	2.12
Joe Sambito	L	26	62	0	0	0	88.0	85	5	32	96	4-9	11	3.07
Ken Forsch	R	31	52	6	4	2	133.1	136	2	37	71	10-6	7	2.70
Joaquin Andujar	R	25	35	13	2	0	110.2	88	3	58	55	5-7	1	3.42
Rick Williams	R	25	17	1	0	0	34.2	43	2	10	17	1-2	0	4.67
Bo McLaughlin	R	24	12	1	0	0	23.1	30	2	16	10	0-1	2	5.01
Gene Pentz	R	25	10	0	0	0	15.0	12	1	13	8	0-0	0	6.00
Oscar Zamora	R	33	10	0	0	0	15.0	20	2	7	6	0-0	0	7.20
Dan Warthen	L	25	5	1	0	0	10.2	10	3	2	2	0-1	0	4.22
Frank Riccelli	L	25	2	0	0	0	3.0	1	0	0	1	0-0	0	0.00

1978 Atlanta Braves 6th NL West 69-93 .426 26.0 GB

Bobby Cox

Player	Gm by Position	B	Age	G	AB	R	H	2B	3B	HR	RBI	BB	SO	SB	Avg	OBP	Slg
Biff Pocoroba	C79	S	24	92	289	21	70	8	0	6	34	29	14	0	.242	.312	.332
Dale Murphy	1B129,C21	R	22	151	530	66	120	14	3	23	79	42	145	11	.226	.284	.394
Jerry Royster	2B75,SS60,3B1	R	25	140	529	67	137	17	8	2	35	56	49	27	.259	.331	.333
Bob Horner	3B89	R	20	89	323	50	86	17	1	23	63	24	42	0	.266	.313	.539
Darrel Chaney	SS77,3B8,2B1	S	30	89	245	27	55	9	1	3	20	25	48	1	.224	.295	.306
Jeff Burroughs	OF146	R	27	153	488	72	147	30	6	23	77	117	92	1	.301	.432	.529
Rowland Office	OF136	L	25	146	404	40	101	13	1	9	40	22	52	8	.250	.297	.354
Gary Matthews	OF127	R	27	129	474	75	135	20	5	18	62	61	92	8	.285	.366	.462
Rod Gilbreath	3B62,2B39	R	25	116	326	22	80	13	3	3	31	26	51	7	.245	.300	.331
Barry Bonnell	OF105,3B15	R	24	117	304	36	73	11	3	1	16	20	30	12	.240	.287	.306
Joe Nolan	C61	L	27	95	213	22	49	7	3	4	22	34	28	3	.230	.339	.347
Bob Beall	1B40,OF8	S	30	108	185	29	45	8	0	1	16	36	27	4	.243	.368	.303
Glenn Hubbard	2B44	R	20	44	163	15	42	4	0	2	13	10	20	2	.258	.309	.319
Pat Rockett	SS51	R	23	55	142	6	20	2	0	0	4	13	12	1	.141	.212	.155
Cito Gaston†	OF29,1B4	R	34	60	118	5	27	1	0	1	9	3	20	0	.229	.244	.263
Brian Asselstine	OF35	L	24	39	103	11	28	3	3	2	13	11	16	2	.272	.339	.417
Bruce Benedict	C22	R	22	22	52	3	13	2	0	0	1	6	6	0	.250	.328	.288
Chico Ruiz	2B14,3B1	R	26	18	46	3	13	3	0	0	2	2	4	0	.283	.313	.348
Eddie Miller	OF5	S	21	6	21	5	3	1	0	0	2	2	4	3	.143	.250	.190
Larry Whisenton	OF4	L	21	6	16	1	3	1	0	0	2	1	2	0	.188	.235	.250
Jerry Maddox	3B5	R	24	7	14	1	3	0	0	0	1	1	2	0	.214	.267	.214
Tom Paciorek†	1B2	R	31	5	9	2	3	0	0	0	0	0	1	0	.333	.333	.333
Hank Small	1B1	R	24	1	4	0	0	0	0	0	0	0	0	0	.000	.000	.000
Bob Belloir	3B1,SS1	R	29	2	1	0	1	1	0	0	0	0	0	0	1.000	1.000	2.000

Pitcher	T	Age	G	GS	CG	ShO	IP	H	HR	BB	SO	W-L	Sv	ERA
Phil Niekro	R	39	44	42	22	4	334.1	295	16	102	248	19-18	1	2.88
Preston Hanna	R	23	29	28	0	0	140.1	132	10	93	90	7-13	0	5.13
Mickey Mahler	L	25	34	21	1	0	134.2	130	16	66	92	4-11	0	4.68
Larry McWilliams	L	24	15	15	3	1	99.1	84	11	35	42	9-3	0	2.81
Dick Ruthven†	R	27	13	13	2	1	81.0	78	8	28	45	2-6	0	4.11
Tommy Boggs	R	22	16	12	1	1	59.0	80	8	26	21	2-8	0	6.71
Jim Bouton	R	39	5	5	0	0	29.0	25	4	21	10	1-3	0	4.97
Frank LaCorte	R	26	2	2	0	0	14.2	9	0	4	7	0-1	0	3.68
Dave Campbell	R	26	53	0	0	0	69.1	67	10	49	45	4-4	1	4.80
Gene Garber†	R	30	43	0	0	0	78.1	58	11	13	61	4-4	22	2.53
Craig Skok	L	30	43	0	0	0	62.0	64	8	27	28	3-2	2	4.35
Rick Camp	R	25	42	4	0	0	74.1	99	5	32	23	2-4	0	3.75
Eddie Solomon	R	27	37	8	0	0	106.0	98	12	50	64	4-6	2	4.08
Jamie Easterly	L	25	37	6	0	0	78.0	91	9	45	42	3-6	1	5.65
Adrian Devine	R	26	31	6	0	0	65.1	84	3	25	26	5-4	3	5.92
Max Leon	R	28	5	0	0	0	5.2	6	1	4	1	0-0	0	6.35
Duane Theiss	R	24	3	0	0	0	6.1	3	0	3	3	0-0	0	1.42
Mike Davey	L	26	3	0	0	0	2.2	1	0	1	0	0-0	0	0.00

»1979 Baltimore Orioles 1st AL East 102-57 .642 —

Earl Weaver

Player	Gm by Position	B	Age	G	AB	R	H	2B	3B	HR	RBI	BB	SO	SB	Avg	OBP	Slg
Rick Dempsey	C124	R	29	124	368	48	88	23	0	6	41	38	37	0	.239	.307	.351
Eddie Murray	1B157,DH2	S	23	159	606	90	179	30	2	25	99	72	78	10	.295	.369	.475
Rich Dauer	2B103,3B44	R	26	142	479	63	123	20	0	9	61	36	36	0	.257	.305	.355
Doug DeCinces	3B120	R	28	120	422	67	97	27	1	16	61	54	68	5	.230	.318	.412
Kiko Garcia	SS113,2B25,3B2*	R	25	126	417	54	103	15	9	5	24	32	87	11	.247	.303	.362
Al Bumbry	OF146	L	32	148	569	80	162	29	1	7	49	43	74	37	.285	.336	.376
Ken Singleton	OF143,DH16	S	32	159	570	93	168	29	1	35	111	109	118	3	.295	.405	.533
Gary Roenicke	OF130,DH2	R	24	133	376	60	98	16	1	25	64	61	74	1	.261	.378	.508
Lee May	DH117,1B2	R	36	124	456	59	116	15	0	19	69	28	100	3	.254	.297	.412
Mark Belanger	SS98	R	35	101	198	28	33	6	2	0	9	29	33	5	.167	.273	.217
John Lowenstein	OF72,DH3,1B1*	L	32	97	197	33	50	8	2	11	34	30	37	16	.254	.351	.482
Billy Smith	2B63,SS5	S	25	68	189	18	47	9	4	6	33	15	33	1	.249	.309	.434
Pat Kelly	OF24,DH18	L	34	68	153	25	44	11	0	9	25	20	25	4	.288	.367	.536
Dave Skaggs	C63	R	28	63	137	9	34	8	0	1	14	13	14	0	.248	.313	.328
Bennie Ayala	OF24,DH10	R	28	42	86	15	22	5	0	6	13	6	9	0	.256	.298	.523
Terry Crowley	DH15,1B2	L	32	61	63	8	20	5	1	1	8	14	13	0	.317	.449	.476
Larry Harlow†	OF31,DH1	L	27	38	41	5	11	1	0	0	1	7	4	1	.268	.375	.293
Wayne Krenchicki	3B7,2B6	L	24	16	21	1	4	1	0	0	0	0	0	0	.190	.190	.238
Mark Corey	OF11,DH1	R	23	13	13	1	2	0	0	0	1	0	4	1	.154	.154	.154
Bob Molinaro	OF5	L	29	8	6	0	0	0	0	0	0	1	3	1	.000	.143	.000
Tom Chism	1B4	L	25	6	3	0	0	0	0	0	0	0	0	0	.000	.000	.000
Ellie Hendricks	C1	L	38	1	1	0	0	0	0	0	0	0	0	0	.000	.000	.000

K. Garcia, 2 G at OF; J. Lowenstein, 1 G at 3B

Pitcher	T	Age	G	GS	CG	ShO	IP	H	HR	BB	SO	W-L	Sv	ERA
Dennis Martinez	R	24	40	39	18	3	292.1	279	28	78	132	15-16	0	3.66
Mike Flanagan	L	27	39	38	16	5	265.2	245	23	70	190	23-9	0	3.08
Steve Stone	R	31	32	32	3	0	186.0	173	31	73	96	11-7	0	3.77
Scott McGregor	L	25	27	23	7	2	174.2	165	19	23	81	13-6	0	3.35
Jim Palmer	R	33	23	22	7	0	155.2	144	12	43	67	10-6	0	3.30
Don Stanhouse	R	28	52	0	0	0	72.2	49	4	51	34	7-3	21	2.85
Tippy Martinez	L	29	39	0	0	0	78.0	59	0	31	61	10-3	3	2.88
Sammy Stewart	R	24	31	3	1	0	117.2	96	11	71	71	8-5	1	3.52
Tim Stoddard	R	26	29	0	0	0	58.0	44	3	19	47	3-1	3	1.71
Dave Ford	R	22	9	2	0	0	30.0	23	2	7	7	2-1	2	2.10
John Flinn	R	24	4	0	0	0	2.2	2	0	1	0	0-0	0	0.00
Jeff Rineer	L	23	1	0	0	0	1.0	0	0	0	0	0-0	0	0.00

1979 Milwaukee Brewers 2nd AL East 95-66 .590 8.0 GB

George Bamberger

Player	Gm by Position	B	Age	G	AB	R	H	2B	3B	HR	RBI	BB	SO	SB	Avg	OBP	Slg
Charlie Moore	C106	R	26	111	337	45	101	16	2	5	38	29	32	8	.300	.355	.404
Cecil Cooper	1B135,DH15	L	29	150	590	83	182	44	1	24	106	56	77	15	.308	.364	.508
Paul Molitor	2B122,SS10,DH8	R	22	140	584	88	188	27	16	9	62	48	48	33	.322	.372	.469
Sal Bando	3B109,DH19,1B4*	R	35	130	476	57	117	14	3	9	43	57	42	2	.246	.330	.345
Robin Yount	SS149	R	23	149	577	72	154	26	5	8	51	35	52	11	.267	.308	.371
Gorman Thomas	OF152,DH4	R	28	156	557	97	136	29	0	45	123	98	175	1	.244	.356	.539
Sixto Lezcano	OF135,DH1	R	25	138	473	84	152	29	3	28	101	77	74	4	.321	.414	.573
Ben Oglivie	OF120,DH13,1B9	L	30	139	514	88	145	30	4	29	81	48	56	12	.282	.343	.525
Dick Davis	DH53,OF35	R	25	91	335	51	89	13	1	12	41	16	46	3	.266	.298	.418
Don Money	DH33,3B26,1B19*	R	32	92	350	52	83	20	1	6	38	40	47	1	.237	.316	.351
Jim Gantner	3B42,2B22,SS3*	L	26	70	208	29	59	10	3	2	22	16	17	3	.284	.336	.389
Buck Martinez	C68,P1	R	30	69	196	17	53	8	0	4	26	8	25	0	.270	.296	.372
Jim Wohlford	OF55,DH5	R	28	63	175	19	46	13	1	1	17	8	28	6	.263	.290	.366
Larry Hisle	DH15,OF10	R	32	26	96	18	27	7	0	3	14	11	19	1	.281	.352	.448
Ray Fosse	C13,DH5,1B1	R	32	19	52	6	12	3	1	0	2	2	6	0	.231	.286	.327
Lenn Sakata	2B4	R	25	4	14	1	7	2	0	0	1	0	1	0	.500	.500	.643
Tim Nordbrook	SS2	R	29	2	2	0	1	0	0	0	0	0	0	0	.500	.500	.500

S. Bando, 1 G at P, 1 G at 2B; D. Money, 16 G at 2B; J. Gantner, 1 G at P

Pitcher	T	Age	G	GS	CG	ShO	IP	H	HR	BB	SO	W-L	Sv	ERA
Lary Sorensen	R	23	34	34	16	2	235.1	250	30	42	63	15-14	0	3.98
Jim Slaton	R	29	32	31	12	3	213.0	229	15	54	80	15-9	0	3.63
Mike Caldwell	L	30	30	30	16	4	235.0	252	18	39	89	16-6	0	3.29
Moose Haas	R	23	29	28	8	1	184.2	198	26	59	95	11-11	0	4.78
Bill Travers	L	26	30	27	9	2	187.1	196	33	45	74	14-8	0	3.89
Jerry Augustine	L	26	43	2	0	0	85.2	95	6	30	41	9-6	5	3.47
Bill Castro	R	25	39	0	0	0	44.1	40	2	13	10	3-1	6	2.03
Bob McClure	L	27	36	0	0	0	51.0	53	6	24	37	5-2	5	3.88
Bob Galasso	R	27	31	0	0	0	51.1	64	5	26	28	3-1	3	4.38
Reggie Cleveland	R	31	29	1	0	0	55.0	77	9	23	22	1-5	4	6.71
Paul Mitchell†	R	29	18	8	0	0	75.0	81	11	10	32	3-3	0	5.76
Dan Boitano	R	26	5	0	0	0	6.0	6	1	3	5	0-0	0	1.50
Andy Replogle	R	25	3	0	0	0	8.0	13	0	2	2	0-0	0	5.63
Lance Rautzhan†	L	26	3	0	0	0	3.0	3	0	10	2	0-0	0	9.00
Sal Bando	R	35	1	0	0	0	3.0	3	0	0	0	0-0	0	6.00
Jim Gantner	R	26	1	0	0	0	1.0	2	0	0	0	0-0	0	0.00
Buck Martinez	R	30	1	0	0	0	1.0	1	0	1	0	0-0	0	9.00

1979 Boston Red Sox 3rd AL East 91-69 .569 11.5 GB

Don Zimmer

Player	Gm by Position	B	Age	G	AB	R	H	2B	3B	HR	RBI	BB	SO	SB	Avg	OBP	Slg
Gary Allenson	C104,3B3	R	24	108	241	27	49	10	2	3	22	20	42	1	.203	.264	.299
Bob Watson†	1B58,DH26	R	33	84	312	48	105	19	4	13	53	29	33	3	.337	.401	.548
Jerry Remy	2B76	L	26	80	306	49	91	11	2	0	29	26	25	14	.297	.350	.346
Butch Hobson	3B142,2B1	R	27	146	528	74	138	26	7	28	93	30	78	3	.261	.298	.496
Rick Burleson	SS153	R	28	153	627	93	174	32	5	5	60	35	54	9	.278	.315	.368
Dwight Evans	OF149	R	27	152	489	69	134	24	1	21	58	69	76	6	.274	.364	.456
Fred Lynn	OF143,DH1	L	27	147	531	116	177	42	1	39	122	82	79	2	.333	.423	.637
Jim Rice	OF125,DH33	R	26	158	619	117	201	39	6	39	130	57	97	9	.325	.381	.596
Carl Yastrzemski	DH56,1B51,OF36	L	39	147	518	69	140	28	1	21	87	62	46	3	.270	.346	.450
Carlton Fisk	DH42,C39,OF1	R	31	91	320	49	87	23	2	10	42	10	38	3	.272	.304	.450
Jack Brohamer	2B36,3B22	L	29	64	192	25	51	7	1	1	11	15	15	0	.266	.316	.328
George Scott†	1B41	R	35	45	156	18	35	9	1	4	23	17	22	0	.224	.299	.372
Tom Poquette†	OF43,DH4	L	27	63	154	14	51	9	0	2	23	8	7	2	.331	.365	.429
Stan Papi	2B26,SS21,DH1	R	28	50	117	9	22	8	0	1	6	5	20	0	.188	.221	.282
Jim Dwyer	1B25,OF19,DH4	L	29	76	113	19	30	7	0	2	14	17	9	3	.265	.361	.381
Ted Sizemore†	2B26,C2	R	34	26	88	12	23	7	0	1	6	4	5	1	.261	.301	.375
Bob Montgomery	C31	R	35	32	86	13	30	4	1	0	7	4	24	1	.349	.374	.419
Larry Wolfe	2B27,3B9,SS2*	R	26	47	78	12	19	4	0	3	15	17	21	0	.244	.378	.410
Mike O'Berry	C43	R	25	43	59	8	10	1	0	1	4	5	16	0	.169	.242	.237
Frank Duffy	2B3,1B1	R	32	6	3	0	0	0	0	0	0	0	1	0	.000	.000	.000

L. Wolfe, 1 G at DH, 1 G at C, 1 G at 1B

Pitcher	T	Age	G	GS	CG	ShO	IP	H	HR	BB	SO	W-L	Sv	ERA
Mike Torrez	R	32	36	36	12	1	252.1	254	20	121	125	16-13	0	4.49
Dennis Eckersley	R	24	33	33	17	2	246.2	234	29	59	150	17-10	0	2.99
Bob Stanley	R	24	40	30	9	4	216.2	250	14	44	56	16-12	1	3.99
Steve Renko	R	34	27	27	4	1	171.0	174	22	53	99	11-9	0	4.11
Chuck Rainey	R	24	20	16	4	1	103.2	97	7	41	41	8-5	1	3.82
John Tudor	L	25	6	6	1	0	28.0	39	2	9	11	1-2	0	6.43
Dick Drago	R	34	53	1	0	0	89.0	85	6	21	67	10-6	13	3.03
Tom Burgmeier	L	35	44	0	0	0	88.2	89	8	16	60	3-2	4	2.74
Bill Campbell	R	30	41	0	0	0	54.2	55	5	23	25	3-4	9	4.28
Allen Ripley	R	26	16	3	0	0	64.2	77	9	25	34	3-1	1	5.15
Joel Finch	R	22	15	7	0	0	57.1	65	5	25	25	0-3	0	4.87
Jim Wright	R	28	11	1	0	0	23.0	19	5	7	15	1-0	0	5.09
Win Remmerswaal	R	25	8	0	0	0	20.1	26	1	12	16	1-0	0	7.08
Andy Hassler†	L	27	8	0	0	0	15.1	23	0	7	7	1-2	0	8.80

1979 New York Yankees 4th AL East 89-71 .556 13.5 GB

Bob Lemon (34-31)/Billy Martin (55-40)

Player	Gm by Position	B	Age	G	AB	R	H	2B	3B	HR	RBI	BB	SO	SB	Avg	OBP	Slg
Thurman Munson	C88,DH5,1B3	R	32	97	382	42	110	18	3	3	39	32	37	1	.288	.340	.374
Chris Chambliss	1B134,DH16	L	30	149	554	61	155	27	3	18	63	34	53	3	.280	.324	.437
Willie Randolph	2B153	R	24	153	574	98	155	15	13	5	61	95	39	33	.270	.374	.368
Graig Nettles	3B144	L	34	145	521	71	132	15	1	20	73	59	53	1	.253	.325	.401
Bucky Dent	SS141	R	27	141	431	47	99	14	2	2	32	37	30	0	.230	.287	.285
Reggie Jackson	OF125,DH11	L	33	131	465	78	138	24	2	29	89	65	107	9	.297	.382	.544
Lou Piniella	OF112,DH16	R	35	130	461	49	137	22	2	11	69	17	31	3	.297	.320	.425
Bobby Murcer†	OF70	L	33	74	264	42	72	12	0	8	33	25	32	1	.273	.339	.409
Jim Spencer	DH71,1B26	L	32	106	295	60	85	15	3	23	53	38	25	0	.288	.367	.593
Mickey Rivers†	OF69	L	30	74	286	37	82	18	5	3	25	13	21	3	.287	.315	.416
Roy White	DH29,OF27	S	35	81	205	24	44	6	0	3	27	23	21	2	.215	.290	.288
Juan Beniquez	OF60,3B3	R	29	62	142	19	36	6	1	4	17	9	17	3	.254	.299	.394
Jerry Narron	C56,DH1	L	23	61	123	17	21	3	1	4	18	9	26	0	.171	.226	.309
Oscar Gamble†	DH27,OF27	L	29	36	113	21	44	4	1	11	32	13	13	0	.389	.452	.735
Fred Stanley	SS31,3B16,2B8*	R	31	57	100	9	20	1	0	2	14	5	17	0	.200	.236	.270
Brad Gulden	C40	L	23	40	92	10	15	4	0	0	6	9	16	0	.163	.238	.207
Bobby Brown†	OF27,DH1	S	25	30	68	7	17	3	1	0	3	2	17	2	.250	.271	.324
Cliff Johnson†	DH22,C4	R	31	28	64	11	17	6	0	2	6	10	7	0	.266	.360	.453
Jay Johnstone†	OF19,DH3	L	33	23	48	7	10	1	0	1	7	2	7	1	.208	.240	.292
Darryl Jones	DH15,OF2	R	28	18	47	6	12	5	1	0	6	2	7	0	.255	.286	.404
George Scott†	DH15,1B1	R	35	16	44	9	14	3	1	1	6	2	7	1	.318	.340	.500
Lenny Randle	OF11	S	30	20	39	2	7	0	0	0	3	3	2	0	.179	.238	.179
Damaso Garcia	SS10,3B1	R	22	11	38	3	10	1	0	0	4	0	2	2	.263	.263	.289
Brian Doyle	2B13,3B6	L	24	20	32	2	4	2	0	0	5	3	1	0	.125	.200	.188
Bruce Robinson	C6	L	25	6	12	0	2	0	0	0	2	1	0	0	.167	.231	.167
Roy Staiger	3B4	R	29	4	11	1	3	1	0	0	1	1	0	0	.273	.308	.364
Paul Blair†	OF2	R	35	2	5	0	1	0	0	0	0	0	1	0	.200	.200	.200
Dennis Werth	1B1	R	26	3	4	1	1	0	0	0	0	0	0	0	.250	.250	.250
Ron Guidry	P33,OF1	L	28	33	0	0	0	0	0	0	0	0	0	0	—	—	—

F. Stanley, 1 G at 1B, 1 G at OF

Pitcher	T	Age	G	GS	CG	ShO	IP	H	HR	BB	SO	W-L	Sv	ERA
Tommy John	L	36	37	36	17	3	276.1	268	9	65	111	21-9	0	2.96
Ron Guidry	L	28	33	30	15	2	236.1	203	20	71	201	18-8	2	2.78
Luis Tiant	R	38	30	30	5	1	195.2	190	22	53	104	13-8	0	3.91
Catfish Hunter	R	33	19	19	1	0	105.0	128	15	34	34	2-9	0	5.31
Ed Figueroa	R	30	16	16	4	1	104.2	109	6	35	42	4-6	0	4.13
Jim Beattie	R	24	15	13	1	1	76.0	85	5	41	32	3-6	0	5.21
Dave Righetti	L	20	3	3	0	0	17.1	10	2	10	13	0-1	0	3.63
Ron Davis	R	23	44	0	0	0	85.1	84	5	28	43	14-2	9	2.85
Jim Kaat†	L	40	40	1	0	0	58.1	64	4	14	23	2-3	2	3.86
Goose Gossage	R	27	36	0	0	0	58.1	48	5	19	41	5-3	18	2.62
Ken Clay	R	25	32	5	0	0	78.1	88	12	25	28	1-7	2	5.40
Don Hood†	L	29	27	6	0	0	67.1	62	3	30	22	3-1	1	3.07
Ray Burris†	R	28	15	0	0	0	27.2	40	5	10	19	1-3	0	6.18
Dick Tidrow†	R	32	14	0	0	0	22.2	38	5	4	7	2-1	2	7.94
Paul Mirabella	L	25	10	1	0	0	14.1	16	3	10	4	0-4	0	8.79
Mike Griffin	R	22	3	0	0	0	4.1	5	0	2	5	0-0	1	4.15
Rick Anderson	R	25	1	0	0	0	2.1	1	0	4	0	0-0	0	3.86
Roger Slagle	R	25	1	0	0	0	2.0	0	0	0	2	0-0	0	0.00
Bob Kammeyer	R	28	1	0	0	0	0.0	7	2	0	0	0-0	0	—

1979 Detroit Tigers 5th AL East 85-76 .528 18.0 GB

Les Moss (27-26)/Dick Tracewski (2-0)/Sparky Anderson (56-50)

Player	Gm by Position	B	Age	G	AB	R	H	2B	3B	HR	RBI	BB	SO	SB	Avg	OBP	Slg
Lance Parrish	C142	R	23	143	493	65	136	26	3	19	65	49	105	6	.276	.343	.456
Jason Thompson	1B140,DH2	L	24	145	492	58	121	16	1	20	79	70	90	2	.246	.338	.404
Lou Whitaker	2B126	L	22	127	423	75	121	14	8	3	42	78	66	20	.286	.395	.378
Aurelio Rodriguez	3B106,1B1	R	31	106	343	27	87	18	0	5	36	11	40	0	.254	.277	.350
Alan Trammell	SS142	R	21	142	460	68	127	11	4	6	50	43	55	17	.276	.335	.357
Steve Kemp	OF120,DH11	L	24	134	490	88	156	26	3	26	105	68	70	5	.318	.398	.543
Jerry Morales	OF119,DH7	R	30	129	440	50	93	23	1	14	56	30	56	10	.211	.260	.364
Ron LeFlore	OF113,DH34	R	31	148	600	110	180	22	10	9	57	52	95	78	.300	.355	.415
Rusty Staub†	DH66	L	35	68	246	32	58	12	1	9	40	32	18	1	.236	.331	.402
Champ Summers†	OF69,DH10,1B4	L	33	90	246	47	77	12	1	20	51	40	33	7	.313	.414	.614
John Wockenfuss	1B31,C20,DH18*	R	30	87	231	27	61	9	1	15	46	18	40	2	.264	.320	.506
Lynn Jones	OF84,DH6	R	26	95	213	33	63	8	0	4	26	17	22	9	.296	.349	.390
Tom Brookens	3B42,2B19,DH1	R	25	60	190	23	50	5	2	4	21	11	40	10	.263	.309	.374
Mark Wagner	SS41,2B29,3B2*	R	25	75	146	16	40	3	0	1	13	16	25	3	.274	.341	.315
Phil Mankowski	3B36,DH1	L	26	42	99	11	22	4	0	0	8	10	16	0	.222	.286	.263
Al Greene	DH15,OF6	L	24	29	59	9	8	1	0	3	6	10	15	0	.136	.257	.305
Ed Putman	C16,1B5	R	25	21	39	4	9	3	0	2	4	4	12	0	.231	.302	.462
Kirk Gibson	OF10	L	22	12	38	3	9	3	0	1	4	1	3	3	.237	.256	.395
Dave Stegman	OF12	R	25	12	31	6	6	0	0	3	5	2	3	1	.194	.242	.484
Dave Machemer	2B11,DH1,OF1	R	28	19	26	8	5	1	0	0	2	3	2	0	.192	.276	.231
Tim Corcoran	OF9,1B5,DH2	L	26	18	22	4	5	1	0	0	6	4	2	1	.227	.333	.273
Ricky Peters	DH3,3B3,2B2*	S	23	12	19	3	5	0	0	0	2	5	3	0	.263	.417	.263
Dan Gonzales	OF3,DH1	L	25	7	18	1	4	1	0	0	2	0	2	1	.222	.222	.278
Milt May†	C5	L	28	6	11	1	3	2	0	0	3	1	1	0	.273	.333	.455

J. Wockenfuss, 6 G at OF; M. Wagner, 1 G at DH; R. Peters, 1 G at OF

Pitcher	T	Age	G	GS	CG	ShO	IP	H	HR	BB	SO	W-L	Sv	ERA
Milt Wilcox	R	29	33	29	7	0	196.1	201	18	73	109	12-10	0	4.35
Jack Morris	R	24	27	27	9	1	197.2	179	19	59	113	17-7	0	3.28
Jack Billingham	R	36	35	19	2	0	158.0	163	13	60	59	10-7	3	3.30
Dave Rozema	R	22	16	16	4	1	97.1	101	12	30	33	4-4	0	3.51
Pat Underwood	L	22	27	15	1	0	121.2	126	17	29	83	6-4	0	4.59
Dan Petry	R	20	15	15	2	0	98.0	90	11	33	43	6-5	0	3.95
Steve Baker	R	22	21	12	0	0	84.0	97	13	51	54	1-7	1	6.64
Bruce Robbins	L	19	10	8	0	0	46.0	45	3	21	22	3-3	0	3.91
Mike Chris	L	21	13	8	0	0	39.0	46	3	21	31	3-3	0	6.92
Kip Young	R	24	13	7	0	0	43.2	60	11	11	22	2-2	0	6.39
Mark Fidrych	R	24	4	4	0	0	14.2	23	3	9	5	0-3	0	10.43
Aurelio Lopez	R	30	61	0	0	0	127.0	95	12	51	106	10-5	21	2.41
John Hiller	L	36	43	0	0	0	79.1	83	14	55	46	4-7	9	5.22
Dave Tobik	R	26	37	0	0	0	68.2	59	12	25	48	3-5	3	4.33
Sheldon Burnside	L	24	10	0	0	0	21.1	28	2	8	13	1-1	0	6.33
Bruce Taylor	R	26	10	0	0	0	18.2	16	1	7	8	1-2	0	4.82
Fredie Arroyo	R	27	6	0	0	0	12.0	17	3	4	7	1-1	0	8.25

1979 Cleveland Indians 6th AL East 81-80 .503 22.0 GB

Jeff Torborg (43-52)/Dave Garcia (38-28)

Player	Gm by Position	B	Age	G	AB	R	H	2B	3B	HR	RBI	BB	SO	SB	Avg	OBP	Slg
Gary Alexander	C91,DH13,OF2	R	26	110	358	54	82	9	2	15	54	46	100	4	.229	.313	.391
Andre Thornton	1B130,DH13	R	29	143	515	89	120	31	1	26	93	90	93	5	.233	.347	.449
Duane Kuiper	2B140	L	29	140	479	46	122	9	5	0	39	37	27	4	.255	.313	.294
Toby Harrah	3B127,SS33,DH9	R	30	149	527	99	147	25	1	20	77	89	60	20	.279	.389	.444
Tom Veryzer	SS148	R	26	149	449	41	99	9	3	0	34	34	54	2	.220	.279	.254
Rick Manning	OF141,DH1	L	24	144	560	67	145	12	2	3	51	55	48	30	.259	.323	.304
Bobby Bonds	OF116,DH29	R	33	146	538	93	148	24	1	25	85	74	135	34	.275	.367	.463
Jim Norris	OF93,DH13	L	30	124	353	50	87	15	6	3	30	44	35	15	.246	.328	.348
Cliff Johnson†	DH62,C1	R	31	72	240	37	65	10	0	18	61	24	39	2	.271	.343	.538
Mike Hargrove†	OF65,1B28,DH7	L	29	100	338	60	110	21	4	10	56	63	40	2	.325	.433	.500
Ron Hassey	C68,1B2,DH1	L	26	75	223	20	64	14	0	4	32	19	19	1	.287	.339	.404
Ted Cox	3B52,OF16,2B4*	R	24	78	189	17	40	6	0	4	22	14	27	3	.212	.272	.307
Paul Dade†	OF37,DH4,3B2	R	27	44	170	22	48	4	1	3	18	12	22	12	.282	.326	.371
Ron Pruitt	OF29,DH14,C11*	R	27	64	166	23	47	7	0	2	21	19	21	2	.283	.355	.361
Dave Rosello	2B33,3B14,SS11	R	29	59	107	20	26	6	1	3	14	15	27	1	.243	.328	.402
Wendell Alston	OF30,DH7	L	26	54	62	10	18	0	2	1	12	10	10	4	.290	.384	.403
Wayne Cage	DH9,1B7	L	27	29	56	6	13	2	0	1	6	5	16	0	.232	.295	.321
Bo Diaz	C15	R	26	15	32	0	5	2	0	0	1	2	6	0	.156	.206	.219
Horace Speed	OF16,DH4	R	27	26	14	6	2	0	0	0	1	5	7	2	.143	.368	.143

T. Cox, 1 G at DH; R. Pruitt, 3 G at 3B

Pitcher	T	Age	G	GS	CG	ShO	IP	H	HR	BB	SO	W-L	Sv	ERA
Rick Wise	R	33	34	34	9	2	231.2	229	24	68	108	15-10	0	3.73
Rick Waits	L	27	34	34	8	3	231.0	230	26	91	91	16-13	0	4.44
Mike Paxton	R	25	33	24	3	0	159.2	210	14	52	70	8-8	0	5.92
Len Barker	R	23	29	19	2	0	137.1	146	6	70	93	6-6	0	4.92
Wayne Garland	R	28	18	14	2	0	94.2	120	11	34	40	4-10	0	5.23
Eric Wilkins	R	22	16	14	0	0	69.2	77	4	38	52	2-4	0	4.39
David Clyde	L	24	9	8	1	0	45.2	50	7	13	17	3-4	0	5.91
Sid Monge	L	28	76	0	0	0	131.0	96	9	64	108	12-10	19	2.40
Victor Cruz	R	21	61	0	0	0	78.2	70	10	44	63	3-9	10	4.23
Dan Spillner	R	27	49	13	3	0	157.2	153	16	64	97	9-5	1	4.62
Paul Reuschel	R	32	17	1	0	0	45.1	73	7	11	22	2-1	1	7.94
Don Hood†	L	29	13	0	0	0	22.0	13	1	14	7	1-0	1	3.68
Larry Andersen	R	26	8	0	0	0	16.2	25	3	4	7	0-0	0	7.56
Sandy Wihtol	R	24	5	0	0	0	10.2	10	0	3	6	0-0	0	3.38

1979 Toronto Blue Jays 7th AL East 53-109 .327 50.5 GB

Roy Hartsfield

Player	Gm by Position	B	Age	G	AB	R	H	2B	3B	HR	RBI	BB	SO	SB	Avg	OBP	Slg
Rick Cerone	C136	R	25	136	469	47	112	27	4	7	61	37	40	1	.239	.294	.358
John Mayberry	1B135	L	30	137	464	61	127	22	1	21	74	69	60	1	.274	.372	.461
Danny Ainge	2B86,DH1	R	20	87	308	26	73	7	1	2	19	12	58	1	.237	.269	.286
Roy Howell	3B133,DH4	L	25	138	511	60	126	28	4	15	72	42	91	1	.247	.310	.405
Alfredo Griffin	SS153	S	21	153	624	81	179	22	10	2	31	40	59	21	.287	.333	.364
Rick Bosetti	OF162	R	25	162	619	59	161	35	2	8	65	22	70	13	.260	.286	.362
Al Woods	OF127,DH2	L	25	132	436	57	121	24	4	5	36	40	28	6	.278	.337	.385
Bob Bailor	OF118,3B9,DH1	R	27	130	414	50	95	11	5	1	38	36	27	14	.229	.297	.287
Rico Carty	DH129	R	39	132	461	48	118	26	0	12	55	46	45	3	.256	.322	.390
Otto Velez	OF73,DH9,1B6	R	28	99	274	45	79	21	0	15	48	46	45	0	.288	.396	.529
Luis Gomez	3B22,2B20,SS15	R	27	59	163	11	39	7	0	0	11	6	17	1	.239	.266	.282
Dave McKay	2B46,3B2	S	29	47	156	19	34	9	0	0	12	7	19	1	.218	.256	.276
Joe Cannon	OF50	L	25	61	142	14	30	1	1	1	5	1	34	12	.211	.217	.254
Tony Solaita†	DH26,1B6	L	32	36	102	14	27	8	1	2	13	17	16	0	.265	.364	.422
Bob Davis	C32	R	27	32	89	6	11	2	0	1	8	6	15	0	.124	.188	.180
Tim Johnson	2B25,3B9,1B7	L	29	43	86	6	16	2	1	0	6	8	15	0	.186	.255	.233
Craig Kusick†	1B20,DH1,P1	R	30	24	54	3	11	1	0	2	7	7	7	0	.204	.302	.333
Bob Robertson	1B9,DH4	R	32	15	29	1	3	0	0	1	1	3	9	0	.103	.188	.207
Ted Wilborn	OF7,DH4	S	20	22	12	3	0	0	0	0	0	1	7	0	.000	.077	.000
Bobby Brown†	OF4	S	25	4	10	1	0	0	0	0	0	2	1	0	.000	.167	.000
Pedro Hernandez	DH2	R	20	3	0	1	0	0	0	0	0	0	0	0	—	—	—

Pitcher	T	Age	G	GS	CG	ShO	IP	H	HR	BB	SO	W-L	Sv	ERA
Tom Underwood	L	25	33	32	12	1	227.0	213	23	95	127	9-16	0	3.69
Phil Huffman	R	21	31	31	2	1	173.0	220	25	68	56	6-18	0	5.77
Dave Lemanczyk	R	28	22	20	11	3	143.0	137	12	45	63	8-10	0	3.71
Dave Stieb	R	21	18	18	7	1	129.1	139	11	48	52	8-8	0	4.31
Jim Clancy	R	23	12	11	2	0	63.2	65	8	31	33	2-7	0	5.51
Mark Lemongello	R	23	18	10	2	0	83.0	97	14	34	40	1-9	0	6.29
Butch Edge	R	22	9	9	1	0	51.2	60	6	24	19	3-4	0	5.23
Tom Buskey	R	32	44	0	0	0	78.2	74	10	25	44	6-10	7	3.43
Dave Freisleben	R	27	42	2	0	0	91.0	101	5	53	35	2-3	3	4.95
Balor Moore	L	28	34	16	5	0	139.1	135	17	79	51	5-7	0	4.84
Jesse Jefferson	R	30	34	10	2	0	116.0	150	19	45	43	2-10	1	5.51
Mike Willis	L	28	17	1	0	0	26.2	35	1	16	8	0-3	0	8.44
Jackson Todd	R	27	12	1	0	0	32.1	40	7	7	14	0-1	0	5.85
Tom Murphy	R	33	10	0	0	0	18.1	23	1	8	6	1-2	0	5.40
Dyar Miller†	R	33	10	0	0	0	15.1	27	3	5	7	0-0	0	10.57
Jerry Garvin	L	23	8	1	0	0	22.2	15	2	10	14	0-1	0	2.78
Craig Kusick	R	30	1	0	0	0	3.2	3	1	0	0	0-0	0	4.91
Steve Grilli	R	30	1	0	0	0	2.1	1	0	0	1	0-0	0	0.00
Steve Luebber	R	29	1	0	0	0	0.0	2	0	1	0	0-0	0	—

1979 California Angels 1st AL West 88-74 .543 —

Jim Fregosi

Player	Gm by Position	B	Age	G	AB	R	H	2B	3B	HR	RBI	BB	SO	SB	Avg	OBP	Slg
Brian Downing	C129,DH18	R	28	148	509	87	166	27	3	12	75	77	57	3	.326	.418	.462
Rod Carew	1B103,DH6	L	33	110	409	78	130	15	3	3	44	73	46	18	.318	.419	.391
Bobby Grich	2B153	R	30	153	534	78	157	30	5	30	101	59	84	1	.294	.365	.537
Carney Lansford	3B157	R	22	157	654	114	188	30	5	19	79	39	115	20	.287	.329	.436
Bert Campaneris†	SS82,DH1	R	37	85	239	27	56	4	4	0	15	19	32	12	.234	.294	.285
Dan Ford	OF141	R	27	142	569	100	165	26	5	21	101	40	86	8	.290	.333	.464
Rick Miller	OF117,DH2	L	31	120	427	60	125	15	5	2	28	50	69	5	.293	.367	.365
Don Baylor	OF97,DH65,1B1	R	30	162	628	120	186	33	3	36	139	71	51	22	.296	.371	.530
Willie Aikens	1B55,DH51	L	24	116	379	59	106	18	0	21	81	61	79	1	.280	.376	.493
Joe Rudi	OF80,1B5,DH3	R	32	90	330	35	80	11	3	11	61	24	61	0	.242	.294	.394
Jim Anderson	SS82,3B10,2B6*	R	22	96	234	33	58	13	1	3	23	17	31	3	.248	.298	.350
Larry Harlow†	OF58	L	27	62	159	22	37	8	2	0	14	25	34	1	.233	.344	.308
Tom Donohue	C38	R	26	38	107	13	24	3	1	3	14	3	29	2	.224	.259	.355
Merv Rettenmund	DH17,OF9	R	36	35	76	7	20	2	0	1	10	11	14	1	.263	.360	.329
Rance Mulliniks	SS22	L	23	22	68	7	10	0	0	1	8	4	14	0	.147	.192	.191
Dickie Thon	2B24,SS8,DH1*	R	21	35	56	6	19	3	0	0	8	5	10	0	.339	.393	.393
Willie Davis	OF7,DH6	L	39	43	56	9	14	2	1	0	2	4	7	1	.250	.300	.321
Bobby Clark	OF19	R	24	19	54	8	16	2	2	1	5	5	11	1	.296	.356	.463
Ralph Garr†	DH6	L	33	6	24	0	3	0	0	0	0	0	3	0	.125	.125	.125
Terry Humphrey	C9	R	29	9	17	2	1	0	0	0	0	1	2	0	.059	.111	.059
Orlando Ramirez	SS10,DH1	R	27	13	12	1	0	0	0	0	0	1	6	1	.000	.143	.000
Ike Hampton	1B2	S	27	4	5	0	2	0	0	0	0	0	1	0	.400	.400	.400
Brian Harper	DH1	R	19	1	2	0	0	0	0	0	0	0	0	0	.000	.000	.000
John Harris	1B1	L	24	1	2	0	0	0	0	0	0	0	0	0	.000	.000	.000

J. Anderson, 3 G at C; D. Thon, 1 G at 3B

Pitcher	T	Age	G	GS	CG	ShO	IP	H	HR	BB	SO	W-L	Sv	ERA
Nolan Ryan	R	32	34	34	17	5	222.2	169	15	114	223	16-14	0	3.60
Dave Frost	R	26	36	33	12	2	239.1	226	17	77	107	16-10	1	3.57
Don Aase	R	24	37	28	7	1	185.1	200	19	77	96	9-10	2	4.81
Jim Barr	R	31	36	25	5	0	197.0	217	22	55	69	10-12	0	4.20
Chris Knapp	R	25	20	18	3	0	98.0	109	8	35	36	5-5	0	5.51
Frank Tanana	L	25	18	17	2	1	90.1	93	9	25	46	7-5	0	3.89
Steve Eddy	R	21	7	4	0	0	32.1	36	1	20	7	1-2	0	4.73
Dave LaRoche	L	31	53	1	0	0	85.2	107	13	32	59	7-11	10	5.57
Mark Clear	R	23	52	0	0	0	109.0	87	6	68	98	11-5	14	3.63
Mike Barlow	R	31	35	0	0	0	86.0	106	8	30	33	1-1	0	5.13
Dyar Miller†	R	33	14	1	0	0	35.1	44	2	13	16	1-0	0	3.31
John Montague†	R	31	14	0	0	0	17.2	16	3	9	6	2-0	6	5.09
Ralph Botting	L	24	12	1	0	0	29.2	46	6	15	22	2-0	0	8.80
Bob Ferris	R	24	2	0	0	0	6.0	5	1	3	2	0-0	0	1.50
Dave Schuler	L	25	1	0	0	0	1.2	2	1	0	0	0-0	0	10.80

1979 Kansas City Royals 2nd AL West 85-77 .525 3.0 GB

Whitey Herzog

Player	Gm by Position	B	Age	G	AB	R	H	2B	3B	HR	RBI	BB	SO	SB	Avg	OBP	Slg
Darrell Porter	C141,DH15	L	27	157	533	101	155	23	10	20	112	121	65	3	.291	.421	.484
Pete LaCock	1B108,DH16	L	27	132	408	54	113	25	4	3	56	37	26	2	.277	.334	.380
Frank White	2B125	R	28	127	467	73	124	26	4	10	48	25	54	28	.266	.300	.403
George Brett	3B149,1B8,DH1	L	26	154	645	119	212	42	20	23	107	51	36	17	.329	.376	.563
Freddie Patek	SS104	R	34	106	306	30	77	17	0	1	37	16	42	11	.252	.293	.317
Willie Wilson	OF152,DH2	S	23	154	588	113	185	18	13	6	49	28	92	83	.315	.351	.420
Amos Otis	OF146,DH4	R	32	151	577	100	170	28	2	18	90	68	92	30	.295	.369	.444
Al Cowens	OF134,DH1	R	27	136	516	69	152	18	7	9	73	40	44	10	.295	.345	.409
Hal McRae	DH100	R	33	101	393	55	113	32	4	10	74	38	46	5	.288	.351	.466
U.L. Washington	SS50,2B46,DH3*	S	25	101	268	32	68	12	5	2	25	20	44	10	.254	.299	.358
John Wathan	1B49,C23,DH11*	R	29	90	199	26	41	7	3	2	28	7	24	2	.206	.227	.302
Clint Hurdle	OF50,DH4,3B1	L	21	59	171	16	41	10	3	3	30	28	24	0	.240	.343	.386
George Scott†	1B41,DH2,3B1	R	35	44	146	19	39	8	2	1	20	12	32	1	.267	.329	.370
Todd Cruz	SS48,3B9	R	23	55	118	9	24	7	0	2	15	3	19	0	.203	.224	.314
Steve Braun	OF18,DH11,3B2	L	31	58	116	15	31	2	0	4	10	22	11	0	.267	.384	.388
Jamie Quirk	DH9,C9,SS5*	L	24	51	79	8	24	6	1	1	11	5	13	0	.304	.353	.443
Jerry Terrell	3B19,2B7,DH2*	R	32	31	40	5	12	3	0	1	2	1	1	1	.300	.317	.450
Tom Poquette†	OF10	L	27	21	26	1	5	0	0	0	3	1	4	0	.192	.214	.192
Jim Nettles	OF8,1B1	L	32	11	23	0	2	0	0	0	1	3	2	0	.087	.192	.087
Joe Zdeb	OF9	R	26	15	23	3	4	1	1	0	0	2	4	1	.174	.240	.304
Jim Gaudet	C3	R	24	3	6	0	1	0	0	0	0	0	0	0	.167	.167	.167
German Barranca	DH1,2B1,3B1	L	22	5	5	3	3	1	0	0	0	0	0	3	.600	.600	.800

U. Washington, 1 G at 3B; J. Wathan, 3 G at OF; J. Quirk, 3 G at 3B; J. Terrell, 1 G at P, 1 G at SS

Pitcher	T	Age	G	GS	CG	ShO	IP	H	HR	BB	SO	W-L	Sv	ERA
Paul Splittorff	L	32	36	35	11	0	240.0	248	25	77	77	15-17	0	4.24
Larry Gura	L	31	39	33	7	1	233.2	226	29	73	85	13-12	0	4.47
Dennis Leonard	R	28	32	32	12	5	236.0	226	33	56	126	14-12	0	4.08
Rich Gale	R	25	34	31	2	1	181.2	197	19	99	103	9-10	0	5.65
Steve Busby	R	29	22	12	4	0	94.1	71	10	64	45	6-6	0	3.63
Craig Chamberlain	R	22	10	10	4	0	69.2	68	7	18	30	4-4	0	3.75
Al Hrabosky	L	29	58	0	0	0	65.0	67	3	41	39	9-4	11	3.74
Dan Quisenberry	R	26	32	0	0	0	40.0	42	5	7	13	3-2	5	3.15
Marty Pattin	R	36	31	7	1	0	94.1	109	11	21	41	5-2	3	4.58
Steve Mingori	L	35	30	1	0	0	46.2	69	10	17	18	3-3	1	5.79
Ed Rodriguez	R	27	29	1	1	0	74.1	79	9	34	26	4-1	2	4.84
Renie Martin	R	23	25	0	0	0	34.2	32	1	14	25	0-3	5	5.19
Bill Paschall	R	25	7	0	0	0	13.2	18	2	5	3	0-1	0	6.59
Gary Christenson	L	26	6	0	0	0	10.2	10	1	2	4	0-0	0	3.38
Craig Eaton	R	24	5	0	0	0	10.0	8	0	3	4	0-0	0	2.70
George Throop†	R	28	4	0	0	0	2.2	7	0	5	1	0-0	0	13.50
Jerry Terrell	R	32	1	0	0	0	1.0	0	0	0	0	0-0	0	0.00

1979 Texas Rangers 3rd AL West 83-79 .512 5.0 GB

Pat Corrales

Player	Gm by Position	B	Age	G	AB	R	H	2B	3B	HR	RBI	BB	SO	SB	Avg	OBP	Slg
Jim Sundberg	C150	R	28	150	495	50	136	23	4	5	64	51	51	3	.275	.345	.368
Pat Putnam	1B96,DH32	L	25	139	426	57	118	19	2	18	64	23	50	1	.277	.319	.458
Bump Wills	2B146	S	26	146	543	90	148	21	3	5	46	53	58	35	.273	.340	.350
Buddy Bell	3B147,SS33	R	27	162	670	89	200	42	3	18	101	30	45	5	.299	.327	.451
Nelson Norman	SS142,2B1	S	21	147	343	36	76	9	3	0	21	19	41	4	.222	.260	.265
Richie Zisk	OF134,DH3	R	30	144	503	69	132	21	1	18	64	57	75	1	.262	.336	.416
Al Oliver	OF119,DH10	L	32	136	492	69	159	28	4	12	76	34	34	4	.323	.367	.470
Billy Sample	OF103,DH9	R	24	128	325	60	95	21	2	5	35	37	28	8	.292	.365	.415
John Ellis	DH62,1B30,C7	R	30	111	316	33	90	12	0	12	61	15	55	2	.285	.318	.437
John Grubb	OF82,DH6	L	30	102	289	42	79	14	0	10	37	34	44	2	.273	.350	.426
Mickey Rivers†	OF57,DH1	L	30	58	247	35	74	9	3	6	25	9	18	7	.300	.323	.433
Oscar Gamble†	DH37,OF21	L	29	64	161	27	54	6	0	8	32	37	15	2	.335	.458	.522
Mike Jorgensen	1B60,OF20,DH2	L	30	90	157	21	35	7	0	6	16	14	29	0	.223	.293	.382
Eric Soderholm†	3B37,DH14,1B2	R	30	63	147	15	40	6	0	4	19	12	9	0	.272	.325	.395
Willie Montanez†	1B19,DH17	L	31	38	144	19	46	6	0	8	24	8	14	0	.319	.357	.528
Larvell Blanks	SS49,2B16,DH1	R	29	68	120	13	24	5	0	1	15	11	9	0	.200	.259	.267
Dave Roberts	C14,OF11,2B8*	R	28	44	84	12	22	2	1	3	14	7	17	1	.262	.319	.417
Gary Gray	DH13	R	26	16	42	4	10	0	0	0	1	2	8	1	.238	.273	.238
LaRue Washington	OF13,DH1,3B1	R	25	25	18	5	5	0	0	0	2	4	0	2	.278	.409	.278
Greg Mahlberg	C7	R	26	7	17	2	2	0	0	1	1	2	4	0	.118	.211	.294
Bert Campaneris†	SS8	R	37	8	9	2	1	0	0	0	0	1	3	1	.111	.200	.111
Dave Chalk†	SS3,DH2,2B1	R	28	9	8	0	2	0	0	0	0	0	0	0	.250	.250	.250
Gary Holle	1B1	R	24	5	6	0	1	1	0	0	0	1	0	0	.167	.286	.333

D. Roberts, 6 G at 1B, 4 G at DH, 1 G at 3B

Pitcher	T	Age	G	GS	CG	ShO	IP	H	HR	BB	SO	W-L	Sv	ERA
Fergie Jenkins	R	35	37	37	10	3	259.0	252	40	81	164	16-14	0	4.07
Steve Comer	R	25	36	36	6	1	242.1	230	24	84	86	17-12	0	3.68
Doc Medich	R	30	29	19	4	1	149.0	156	9	49	58	10-7	0	4.17
Doyle Alexander	R	28	23	18	0	0	113.1	114	3	69	50	5-7	0	4.45
Jon Matlack	L	29	13	13	2	0	85.0	98	9	15	35	5-4	0	4.13
J. Henry Johnson†	L	22	17	12	1	0	82.1	79	12	36	46	2-6	0	4.92
Dock Ellis†	R	34	10	9	0	0	46.2	64	5	16	10	1-5	0	5.98
Brian Allard	R	21	7	4	2	0	33.1	36	4	13	14	1-3	0	4.32
Larry McCall	R	26	2	1	0	0	8.1	7	0	3	3	1-0	0	2.16
Jim Kern	R	30	71	0	0	0	143.0	99	5	62	136	13-5	29	1.57
Sparky Lyle	L	34	67	0	0	0	95.0	78	9	28	48	5-8	13	3.13
Dave Rajsich	L	27	27	3	0	0	53.2	56	7	18	32	1-3	0	3.52
Danny Darwin	R	23	20	6	1	0	78.0	50	5	30	58	4-4	0	4.04
Ed Farmer†	R	29	11	2	0	0	33.0	30	2	19	25	2-0	0	4.36
Jerry Don Gleaton	L	21	5	2	0	0	9.2	15	0	2	2	0-1	0	6.52
Bob Babcock	R	29	4	0	0	0	5.1	7	1	7	6	0-0	0	10.13

1979 Minnesota Twins 4th AL West 82-80 .506 6.0 GB

Gene Mauch

Player	Gm by Position	B	Age	G	AB	R	H	2B	3B	HR	RBI	BB	SO	SB	Avg	OBP	Slg
Butch Wynegar	C146,DH2	S	23	149	504	74	136	20	0	7	57	74	36	2	.270	.363	.351
Ron Jackson	1B157,3B1,SS1*	R	26	159	583	85	158	40	5	14	68	51	59	3	.271	.337	.429
Rob Wilfong	2B133,OF3	L	25	140	419	71	131	22	6	9	59	29	54	11	.313	.352	.458
John Castino	3B143,SS5	R	24	148	393	49	112	13	8	5	52	27	72	5	.285	.331	.397
Roy Smalley	SS161,1B1	S	26	162	621	94	168	28	3	24	95	80	80	2	.271	.353	.441
Ken Landreaux	OF147	L	24	151	564	81	172	27	5	15	83	37	57	10	.305	.347	.450
Bombo Rivera	OF105,DH2	R	26	112	263	37	74	13	5	2	31	17	40	5	.281	.324	.392
Hosken Powell	OF93,DH5	L	24	104	338	49	99	17	3	2	36	33	25	5	.293	.360	.379
Jose Morales	DH77,1B1	R	34	92	191	21	51	5	1	2	27	14	27	0	.267	.319	.335
Glenn Adams	DH55,OF53	L	31	119	326	34	98	13	1	8	50	25	27	2	.301	.350	.420
Willie Norwood	OF71,DH14	R	28	96	270	32	67	13	3	6	30	20	51	9	.248	.299	.385
Mike Cubbage	3B63,DH21,1B1*	L	28	94	243	26	67	10	1	2	23	39	26	1	.276	.371	.350
Dave Edwards	OF86,DH3	R	25	96	229	42	57	8	0	8	35	24	45	6	.249	.323	.389
Bob Randall	2B71,3B7,SS1*	R	31	80	199	25	49	7	0	0	14	15	17	2	.246	.299	.281
Danny Goodwin	DH51,1B8	L	25	58	159	22	46	8	5	5	27	11	23	0	.289	.335	.497
Rick Sofield	OF35	L	22	35	93	8	28	5	0	0	12	12	27	2	.301	.381	.355
Glenn Borgmann	C31	R	29	31	70	4	14	3	0	0	8	12	11	1	.200	.317	.243
Craig Kusick†	DH12,1B8	R	30	24	54	8	13	4	0	3	6	3	11	0	.241	.281	.481
Gary Ward	OF5,DH3	R	25	10	14	2	4	0	0	0	1	3	3	0	.286	.412	.286
Jesus Vega	DH3	R	23	4	7	0	0	0	0	0	0	0	2	0	.000	.000	.000
Dan Graham	DH1	L	24	2	4	0	0	0	0	0	0	0	0	0	.000	.000	.000

R. Jackson, 1 G at OF; M. Cubbage, 1 G at 2B; B. Randall, 1 G at OF

Pitcher	T	Age	G	GS	CG	ShO	IP	H	HR	BB	SO	W-L	Sv	ERA
Jerry Koosman	L	36	37	36	10	2	263.2	268	19	83	157	20-13	0	3.38
Dave Goltz	R	30	36	35	12	1	250.2	282	22	69	132	14-13	0	4.16
Paul Hartzell	R	25	28	26	4	0	163.0	193	18	44	44	6-10	0	5.36
Geoff Zahn	L	33	26	24	4	0	169.0	181	13	41	58	13-7	0	3.57
Roger Erickson	R	22	24	21	0	0	123.0	154	17	48	47	3-10	0	5.63
Mike Marshall	R	36	90	1	0	0	142.2	132	8	48	81	10-15	32	2.65
Pete Redfern	R	24	40	6	0	0	108.1	106	8	35	85	7-3	1	3.49
Mike Bacsik	R	27	31	0	0	0	65.2	61	6	29	33	4-2	0	4.39
Darrell Jackson	L	23	24	8	1	0	69.1	89	5	26	43	4-4	0	4.28
Gary Serum	R	22	20	5	0	0	64.0	93	10	20	31	1-3	0	6.61
Ken Brett†	L	30	9	0	0	0	12.2	16	1	6	3	0-0	0	4.97
Jeff Holly	L	26	6	0	0	0	6.1	10	0	3	5	0-0	0	7.11
Kevin Stanfield	L	23	3	0	0	0	3.0	2	0	0	0	0-0	0	6.00
Terry Felton	R	21	1	0	0	0	2.0	0	0	0	1	0-0	0	0.00
Paul Thormodsgard	R	25	1	0	0	0	1.0	3	1	0	1	0-0	0	9.00

1979 Chicago White Sox 5th AL West 73-87 .456 14.0 GB

Don Kessinger (46-60)/Tony La Russa (27-27)

Player	Gm by Position	B	Age	G	AB	R	H	2B	3B	HR	RBI	BB	SO	SB	Avg	OBP	Slg
Milt May†	C65	L	28	65	202	23	51	13	0	7	28	14	27	0	.252	.306	.421
Mike Squires	1B110,OF1	L	27	122	295	44	78	10	1	2	22	22	9	15	.264	.318	.325
Alan Bannister	2B65,OF47,3B12*	R	27	136	506	71	144	28	8	2	55	43	40	22	.285	.342	.383
Kevin Bell	3B68,SS2	R	23	70	200	20	49	8	1	4	22	15	43	2	.245	.296	.355
Greg Pryor	SS119,2B25,3B22	R	29	143	476	60	131	23	3	3	34	35	41	3	.275	.324	.355
Chet Lemon	OF147,DH1	R	24	148	556	79	177	44	2	17	86	56	68	7	.318	.391	.496
C. Washington	OF122,DH3	L	24	131	471	79	132	33	5	13	66	28	93	19	.280	.322	.454
Rusty Torres	OF85	S	30	90	170	26	43	5	0	8	24	23	37	0	.253	.349	.424
Jorge Orta	DH62,2B41	L	28	113	325	49	85	18	3	11	46	44	33	1	.262	.348	.437
Lamar Johnson	1B94,DH37	R	28	133	479	60	148	29	1	12	74	41	56	8	.309	.363	.449
Ralph Garr†	OF67,DH17	L	33	102	307	34	86	10	2	9	39	17	19	2	.280	.318	.414
Jim Morrison	2B48,3B29	R	26	67	240	38	66	14	0	14	35	15	48	11	.275	.324	.508
Eric Soderholm†	3B56	R	30	56	210	31	53	8	2	6	34	19	19	0	.252	.313	.395
Junior Moore	OF61,DH10,2B2	R	26	88	201	24	53	6	2	1	23	12	20	0	.264	.300	.328
Wayne Nordhagen	DH47,OF12,C5*	R	30	78	193	20	54	15	0	7	25	13	22	0	.280	.324	.466
Bill Nahorodny	C60,DH3	R	25	65	179	20	46	10	0	6	29	18	23	0	.257	.322	.413
Don Kessinger	SS54,1B1,2B1	S	36	56	110	14	22	6	0	1	7	10	12	1	.200	.264	.282
Marv Foley	C33	L	25	34	97	6	24	3	0	2	10	7	5	0	.247	.292	.340
Mike Colbern	C32	R	24	32	83	5	20	5	1	0	8	4	25	0	.241	.276	.325
Thad Bosley	OF28,DH1	L	22	36	77	13	24	1	1	1	8	9	14	4	.312	.384	.390
Harry Chappas	SS23	S	21	26	59	9	17	1	0	1	4	5	5	1	.288	.354	.356
Joe Gates	2B8,DH1,3B1	L	24	16	16	5	1	0	1	0	1	2	3	1	.063	.167	.188
Rusty Kuntz	OF5	R	24	5	11	0	1	0	0	0	0	2	6	0	.091	.231	.091

A. Bannister, 9 G at DH, 1 G at 1B; W. Nordhagen, 2 G at P

Pitcher	T	Age	G	GS	CG	ShO	IP	H	HR	BB	SO	W-L	Sv	ERA
Ken Kravec	L	27	36	35	10	3	250.0	208	20	111	132	15-13	1	3.74
Rich Wortham	L	25	34	33	5	0	204.0	195	21	100	119	14-14	0	4.90
Ross Baumgarten	L	24	28	28	4	3	190.2	175	18	83	72	13-8	0	3.54
Steve Trout	L	21	34	18	6	2	155.0	165	10	59	76	11-8	4	3.89
Francisco Barrios	R	26	15	15	2	0	94.2	88	9	33	28	8-3	0	3.61
Rich Dotson	R	20	5	5	1	1	24.1	28	0	6	13	2-0	0	3.70
Randy Scarbery	R	27	45	5	0	0	101.1	102	9	34	45	2-8	4	4.62
Ed Farmer†	R	29	42	3	0	0	81.1	66	2	34	48	3-7	14	2.43
Mike Proly	R	28	38	6	0	0	88.1	89	6	40	32	3-8	9	3.87
Fred Howard	R	22	28	6	0	0	68.0	73	5	32	36	1-5	0	3.57
Guy Hoffman	L	22	24	0	0	0	30.1	30	0	23	18	0-5	2	5.34
Rich Hinton†	L	32	16	2	0	0	41.2	57	4	8	27	1-2	2	6.05
Lerrin LaGrow†	R	30	11	2	0	0	17.2	27	2	16	9	0-3	1	9.17
Dewey Robinson	R	24	11	0	0	0	14.1	11	1	9	5	0-1	0	6.28
Ron Schueler	R	31	8	1	0	0	19.2	19	3	13	6	0-1	0	7.32
Britt Burns	L	20	6	0	0	0	5.0	10	1	1	2	0-0	0	5.40
Gil Rondon	R	25	4	0	0	0	9.2	11	2	6	3	0-0	0	3.72
Pablo Torrealba	L	31	3	0	0	0	5.2	5	1	2	1	0-0	0	1.59
LaMarr Hoyt	R	24	2	0	0	0	3.0	2	0	0	0	0-0	0	0.00
Wayne Nordhagen	R	30	2	0	0	0	2.0	2	0	1	2	0-0	0	9.00
Mark Esser	L	23	2	0	0	0	1.2	2	0	4	1	0-0	0	16.20
Jack Kucek†	R	26	1	0	0	0	0.2	0	0	3	0	0-0	0	0.00

1979 Seattle Mariners 6th AL West 67-95 .414 21.0 GB — Darrell Johnson

Player	Gm by Position	B	Age	G	AB	R	H	2B	3B	HR	RBI	BB	SO	SB	Avg	OBP	Slg
Larry Cox	C99	R	31	100	293	32	63	11	3	4	36	22	39	2	.215	.266	.314
Bruce Bochte	1B147	L	28	150	554	81	175	38	6	16	100	67	64	2	.316	.385	.493
Julio Cruz	2B107	S	24	107	414	70	112	16	2	1	29	62	61	49	.271	.363	.326
Dan Meyer	3B101,OF31,1B15	L	26	144	525	72	146	21	7	20	74	29	35	11	.278	.317	.459
Mario Mendoza	SS148	R	28	148	373	26	74	10	3	1	29	9	62	3	.198	.216	.249
Ruppert Jones	OF161	L	24	162	622	109	166	29	9	21	78	85	78	33	.267	.356	.444
Leon Roberts	OF136,DH1	R	28	140	450	61	122	24	6	15	54	56	64	3	.271	.352	.451
Joe Simpson	OF105,DH3	L	27	120	265	29	75	11	0	2	27	11	21	6	.283	.312	.347
Willie Horton	DH162	R	36	162	646	77	180	19	5	29	106	42	112	1	.279	.326	.458
Larry Milbourne	SS65,2B49,3B11	S	28	123	356	40	99	13	4	2	26	19	20	5	.278	.313	.354
Tom Paciorek	OF75,1B15	R	32	103	310	38	89	23	4	6	42	28	62	6	.287	.353	.445
Bill Stein	3B67,2B17,SS3	R	32	88	250	28	62	9	2	7	27	17	28	1	.248	.297	.384
Bob Stinson	C91	S	33	95	247	19	60	8	0	6	28	33	38	1	.243	.338	.348
Bobby Valentine	SS29,OF15,2B4*	R	29	62	98	9	27	6	0	0	7	22	5	1	.276	.405	.337
John Hale	OF42,DH2	L	25	54	63	6	14	3	0	2	7	12	26	0	.222	.342	.365
Rodney Craig	OF15	S	21	16	52	9	20	8	1	0	6	1	5	1	.385	.396	.577
Charlie Beamon	1B7,DH5,OF2	L	25	27	25	5	5	1	0	0	0	0	5	1	.200	.200	.240
Juan Bernhardt		R	25	1	1	0	1	0	0	0	0	0	0	0	1.000	1.000	1.000

B. Valentine, 4 G at 3B, 2 G at C, 1 G at DH

Pitcher	T	Age	G	GS	CG	ShO	IP	H	HR	BB	SO	W-L	Sv	ERA
Mike Parrott	R	24	38	30	13	2	229.1	231	17	86	127	14-12	0	3.77
Floyd Bannister	L	24	30	30	6	2	182.1	185	25	68	115	10-15	0	4.05
Rick Honeycutt	L	25	33	28	8	1	194.0	201	22	67	83	11-12	0	4.04
Odell Jones	R	26	25	19	3	0	118.2	151	16	58	72	3-11	0	6.07
Glenn Abbott	R	28	23	19	3	0	116.2	138	19	38	25	4-10	0	5.17
Rob Dressler	R	25	21	11	2	0	104.0	134	11	22	36	3-2	0	4.93
Paul Mitchell†	R	29	10	6	1	0	36.2	46	4	15	18	1-4	0	4.42
Wayne Twitchell†	R	31	4	2	0	0	13.2	11	2	10	5	0-2	0	5.27
Roy Branch	R	25	2	2	0	0	11.1	12	2	7	6	0-1	0	7.94
Shane Rawley	L	23	48	3	0	0	84.1	88	2	40	48	5-9	11	3.84
Byron McLaughlin	R	23	47	7	1	0	123.2	114	13	60	74	7-7	14	4.22
John Montague†	R	31	41	1	0	0	116.1	125	14	47	60	6-4	1	5.57
Randy Stein	R	26	23	1	0	0	41.1	48	7	27	39	2-3	0	5.88
Rich Hinton†	L	32	14	1	0	0	20.0	23	4	5	7	0-2	0	5.40
Joe Decker	R	32	9	2	0	0	27.1	27	2	14	12	0-1	0	4.28
Rafael Vasquez	R	21	9	0	0	0	16.0	23	4	6	9	1-0	0	5.06
Jim Lewis	R	23	2	0	0	0	2.1	10	1	1	0	0-0	0	15.43

1979 Oakland Athletics 7th AL West 54-108 .333 34.0 GB — Jim Marshall

Player	Gm by Position	B	Age	G	AB	R	H	2B	3B	HR	RBI	BB	SO	SB	Avg	OBP	Slg
Jeff Newman	C81,1B46,DH7*	R	30	143	516	53	119	17	2	22	71	27	88	2	.231	.267	.399
Dave Revering	1B104,DH18	L	26	125	472	63	136	25	5	19	77	34	65	1	.288	.334	.483
Mike Edwards	2B113,SS3,DH2	R	26	122	400	35	93	12	2	1	23	15	37	10	.233	.263	.280
Wayne Gross	3B120,1B18,OF2	L	27	138	442	54	99	19	1	14	50	72	62	4	.224	.332	.367
Rob Picciolo	SS105,2B6,3B4*	R	26	115	348	37	88	16	2	2	27	3	45	2	.253	.261	.328
Dwayne Murphy	OF118	L	24	121	388	57	99	10	4	11	40	84	80	15	.255	.387	.387
Larry Murray	OF90,2B3	S	26	105	226	25	42	11	2	2	20	28	34	6	.186	.275	.279
Rickey Henderson	OF88	R	20	89	351	49	96	13	3	1	26	34	39	33	.274	.338	.336
Mitchell Page	DH126,OF4	L	27	133	478	51	118	11	2	9	42	52	93	17	.247	.323	.335
Jim Essian	C70,3B10,1B4*	R	28	98	313	34	76	16	0	8	40	25	29	0	.243	.295	.371
Tony Armas	OF80	R	25	80	278	29	69	9	3	11	34	16	67	1	.248	.290	.421
Mike Heath	OF46,C22,3B7*	R	24	74	258	19	66	8	0	3	27	17	18	1	.256	.304	.322
Dave Chalk†	2B37,3B16,SS16	R	28	66	212	15	47	6	0	2	13	29	14	2	.222	.317	.278
Mario Guerrero	SS43	R	29	46	166	12	38	5	0	0	18	6	7	0	.229	.253	.259
Derek Bryant	OF33,DH2	R	27	39	106	8	19	2	1	0	13	10	10	0	.179	.246	.217
Miguel Dilone†	OF25	S	24	30	91	15	17	1	2	1	6	6	7	6	.187	.237	.275
Glenn Burke	OF23	R	26	23	89	4	19	2	1	0	4	4	10	3	.213	.247	.258
Joe Wallis	OF23	S	27	23	78	6	11	2	0	1	3	10	18	1	.141	.247	.205
Mickey Klutts	SS10,2B8,3B6*	R	24	24	73	3	14	2	1	1	4	7	20	0	.192	.263	.288
Milt Ramirez	3B12,2B11,SS8	R	29	28	62	4	10	1	1	0	3	3	8	0	.161	.200	.210

J. Newman, 7 G at 3B; R. Picciolo, 1 G at OF; J. Essian, 4 G at OF, 3 G at DH; M. Heath, 3 G at DH; M. Klutts, 2 G at DH

Pitcher	T	Age	G	GS	CG	ShO	IP	H	HR	BB	SO	W-L	Sv	ERA
Rick Langford	R	27	34	29	14	1	218.2	233	22	57	101	12-16	0	4.28
Matt Keough	R	23	30	28	7	1	176.2	220	18	78	95	2-17	0	5.04
Steve McCatty	R	25	31	23	8	0	185.2	207	17	80	87	11-12	0	4.22
Mike Norris	R	24	29	18	3	0	146.1	146	11	94	96	5-8	0	4.80
Brian Kingman	R	24	18	17	5	1	112.2	113	10	33	58	8-7	0	4.31
J. Henry Johnson†	L	22	14	13	1	0	84.2	89	13	36	50	2-8	0	4.36
Mike Morgan	R	19	13	13	2	0	77.1	102	7	50	17	2-10	0	5.94
Dave Heaverlo	R	28	62	0	0	0	85.2	97	7	42	40	4-11	9	4.20
Jim Todd	R	31	51	0	0	0	81.0	108	12	51	26	2-5	2	6.56
Bob Lacey	L	25	42	0	0	0	47.2	66	7	24	33	1-5	4	5.85
Dave Hamilton	L	31	40	7	1	0	82.2	80	5	43	52	3-4	5	3.70
Craig Minetto	L	25	36	13	0	0	118.1	131	16	58	64	1-5	0	5.55
Alan Wirth	R	22	5	1	0	0	12.0	14	2	8	7	1-0	0	6.00

»1979 Pittsburgh Pirates 1st NL East 98-64 .605 — — Chuck Tanner

Player	Gm by Position	B	Age	G	AB	R	H	2B	3B	HR	RBI	BB	SO	SB	Avg	OBP	Slg
Ed Ott	C116	L	27	117	403	49	110	20	2	7	51	26	62	0	.273	.314	.385
Willie Stargell	1B113	L	39	126	424	60	119	19	0	32	82	47	105	0	.281	.352	.552
Rennie Stennett	2B102	R	28	108	319	31	76	13	2	0	24	24	25	1	.238	.289	.292
Bill Madlock†	3B85	R	28	85	311	48	102	17	3	7	44	34	22	21	.328	.390	.469
Tim Foli†	SS132	R	28	133	525	70	153	23	1	1	65	28	14	6	.291	.335	.345
Omar Moreno	OF162	L	26	162	695	110	196	21	12	8	69	51	104	77	.282	.333	.381
Dave Parker	OF158	L	28	158	622	109	193	45	7	25	94	67	101	20	.310	.380	.526
Bill Robinson	OF125,1B28,3B3	R	36	148	421	59	111	17	6	24	75	24	81	13	.264	.302	.504
Phil Garner	2B83,3B78,SS14	R	30	150	549	76	161	32	8	11	59	55	74	17	.293	.359	.441
John Milner	OF64,1B48	L	29	128	326	52	90	9	4	16	60	53	37	3	.276	.373	.475
Steve Nicosia	C65	R	23	70	191	22	55	16	0	4	13	23	17	0	.288	.364	.435
Lee Lacy	OF41,2B5	R	31	84	182	17	45	9	3	5	15	22	36	6	.247	.327	.412
Dale Berra	3B22,SS22	R	22	44	123	11	26	5	0	3	15	11	17	0	.211	.272	.325
Manny Sanguillen	C8,1B5	R	35	56	74	8	17	5	2	0	4	2	5	0	.230	.247	.351
Mike Easler	OF4	L	28	55	54	8	15	1	1	2	11	8	13	0	.278	.371	.444
Frank Taveras†	SS11	R	29	11	45	4	11	3	0	0	1	0	2	2	.244	.244	.311
Kent Tekulve	P94,OF1	R	32	94	15	3	2	0	0	0	1	1	8	0	.133	.188	.133
Matt Alexander	OF11,SS1	S	32	44	13	16	7	0	1	0	1	0	0	13	.538	.538	.692
Doe Boyland		L	24	4	3	0	0	0	0	0	0	0	2	0	.000	.000	.000
Gary Hargis		R	22	1	0	0	0	0	0	0	0	0	0	0	—	—	—
Alberto Lois		R	23	11	0	6	0	0	0	0	0	0	0	1	—	—	—

Pitcher	T	Age	G	GS	CG	ShO	IP	H	HR	BB	SO	W-L	Sv	ERA
Bert Blyleven	R	28	37	37	4	0	237.1	238	21	92	172	12-5	0	3.60
John Candelaria	L	25	33	30	8	0	207.0	201	25	41	101	14-9	0	3.22
Bruce Kison	R	29	33	25	3	1	172.1	157	13	45	105	13-7	0	3.19
Don Robinson	R	22	29	25	4	0	160.2	171	12	52	96	8-8	0	3.87
Jim Bibby	R	34	34	17	4	1	137.2	110	9	47	103	12-4	0	2.81
Jim Rooker	L	36	19	17	1	0	103.2	106	11	39	44	4-7	0	4.60
Rick Rhoden	R	26	1	1	0	0	5.0	5	0	2	2	0-1	0	7.20
Kent Tekulve	R	32	94	0	0	0	134.1	109	5	49	75	10-8	31	2.75
Enrique Romo	R	31	84	0	0	0	129.1	122	11	43	106	10-5	5	2.99
Grant Jackson	L	36	72	0	0	0	82.0	67	9	35	39	8-5	14	2.96
Dave Roberts†	L	34	21	3	0	0	38.2	47	1	12	15	5-2	1	3.26
Ed Whitson†	R	24	19	7	0	0	57.2	53	6	36	31	2-3	1	4.37
Joe Coleman†	R	32	10	0	0	0	20.2	29	1	9	14	0-0	0	6.10
Dock Ellis†	R	34	3	1	0	0	7.0	9	1	2	1	0-0	0	2.57

1979 Montreal Expos 2nd NL East 95-65 .594 2.0 GB — Dick Williams

Player	Gm by Position	B	Age	G	AB	R	H	2B	3B	HR	RBI	BB	SO	SB	Avg	OBP	Slg
Gary Carter	C138	R	25	141	505	74	143	26	5	22	75	40	62	3	.283	.338	.485
Tony Perez	1B129	R	37	132	489	58	132	29	4	13	73	38	82	2	.270	.322	.425
Rodney Scott	2B113,SS39	S	25	151	562	69	134	12	5	3	42	66	82	39	.238	.319	.294
Larry Parrish	3B153	R	25	153	544	83	167	39	2	30	82	41	101	5	.307	.357	.551
Chris Speier	SS112	R	29	113	344	31	78	13	1	7	26	43	45	0	.227	.317	.331
Warren Cromartie	OF158	L	25	158	659	84	181	46	5	8	46	38	78	8	.275	.313	.396
Andre Dawson	OF153	R	24	155	639	90	176	24	12	25	92	27	115	35	.275	.309	.468
Ellis Valentine	OF144	R	24	146	548	73	151	29	3	21	82	22	74	11	.276	.303	.454
Dave Cash	2B47	R	31	76	187	24	60	11	1	2	19	12	12	7	.321	.358	.422
Jerry White	OF43	S	26	88	138	30	41	7	1	3	18	21	23	8	.297	.391	.428
Rusty Staub†	1B22,OF1	L	35	38	86	9	23	3	0	3	14	14	10	0	.267	.366	.407
Tom Hutton	1B25,OF9	L	33	86	83	14	21	2	1	1	13	10	7	0	.253	.333	.337
Duffy Dyer	C27	R	33	28	74	4	18	6	0	1	8	9	17	0	.243	.325	.365
Jim Mason	SS33,3B6	L	28	40	71	3	13	5	1	0	6	7	16	0	.183	.256	.282
Tony Solaita†	1B13	L	32	29	42	5	12	4	0	1	7	11	16	0	.286	.434	.452
Tony Bernazard	2B14	S	22	22	40	11	12	2	0	1	8	15	12	1	.300	.500	.425
Ken Macha	3B13,1B2,OF2*	R	28	25	36	8	10	3	1	0	4	2	9	0	.278	.333	.417
John Tamargo†	C4	S	27	12	21	0	8	2	0	0	5	3	3	0	.381	.440	.476
Randy Bass	1B1	L	25	2	1	0	0	0	0	0	0	0	0	0	.000	.000	.000
Tim Raines		S	19	6	0	3	0	0	0	0	0	0	0	2	—	—	—

K. Macha, 1 G at C

Pitcher	T	Age	G	GS	CG	ShO	IP	H	HR	BB	SO	W-L	Sv	ERA
Steve Rogers	R	29	37	37	13	5	248.2	232	14	78	143	13-12	0	3.00
Bill Lee	L	32	33	33	6	3	222.0	230	20	46	59	16-10	0	3.04
Ross Grimsley	L	29	32	27	2	0	151.1	199	18	41	42	10-9	0	5.35
Scott Sanderson	R	22	34	24	5	3	168.0	148	16	54	138	9-8	1	3.43
Dan Schatzeder	L	24	32	21	3	0	162.0	136	17	59	106	10-5	1	2.83
Elias Sosa	R	29	62	0	0	0	96.2	77	2	37	59	8-7	18	1.96
Stan Bahnsen	R	34	55	0	0	0	94.1	80	10	42	71	3-1	5	3.15
Woodie Fryman	L	39	44	0	0	0	58.0	52	4	22	44	3-6	10	2.79
David Palmer	R	21	36	11	2	1	122.2	110	10	30	72	10-2	2	2.64
Rudy May	L	34	33	7	2	1	93.2	88	4	31	67	10-3	0	2.31
Bill Atkinson	R	24	10	0	0	0	13.2	9	0	4	7	2-0	1	1.98
Dale Murray†	R	29	9	0	0	0	13.1	14	1	3	4	1-2	1	2.70
Bob James	R	20	2	0	0	0	2.0	2	0	3	1	0-0	0	13.50
Bill Gullickson	R	20	1	0	0	0	1.0	2	0	0	0	0-0	0	0.00

1979 St. Louis Cardinals 3rd NL East 86-76 .531 12.0 GB — Ken Boyer

Player	Gm by Position	B	Age	G	AB	R	H	2B	3B	HR	RBI	BB	SO	SB	Avg	OBP	Slg
Ted Simmons	C122	S	29	123	448	68	127	22	0	26	87	61	34	0	.283	.369	.507
Keith Hernandez	1B160	L	25	161	610	116	210	48	11	11	105	80	78	11	.344	.417	.513
Ken Oberkfell	2B117,3B17,SS2	L	23	135	369	53	111	19	5	1	35	57	35	4	.301	.396	.388
Ken Reitz	3B158	R	28	159	605	42	162	41	2	8	73	25	85	1	.268	.299	.382
Garry Templeton	SS150	S	23	154	672	105	211	32	19	9	62	18	91	26	.314	.331	.458
Tony Scott	OF151	S	27	153	587	69	152	22	10	6	68	34	92	37	.259	.301	.361
George Hendrick	OF138	R	29	140	493	67	148	27	1	16	75	49	62	2	.300	.359	.456
Jerry Mumphrey	OF114	S	26	124	339	53	100	10	3	3	32	26	39	8	.295	.341	.369
Lou Brock	OF98	L	40	120	405	56	123	15	4	5	38	23	43	21	.304	.342	.398
Mike Tyson	2B71	R	29	75	190	18	42	8	2	5	20	13	28	2	.221	.272	.363
Dane Iorg	OF39,1B10	L	29	79	179	12	52	11	1	1	21	12	28	1	.291	.337	.380
Terry Kennedy	C32	L	23	33	109	11	31	7	0	2	17	6	20	0	.284	.319	.404
Mike Phillips	SS25,2B16,3B1	L	28	44	97	10	22	3	1	1	6	10	9	0	.227	.306	.309
Steve Swisher	C33	R	27	38	73	4	11	1	1	1	3	6	17	0	.151	.213	.233
Bernie Carbo	OF17	L	31	52	64	6	18	1	0	3	12	10	22	1	.281	.368	.438
Roger Freed	1B1	R	33	34	31	2	8	2	0	2	8	5	7	0	.258	.361	.516
Jim Lentine	OF8	R	24	11	23	2	9	1	0	0	1	3	6	0	.391	.462	.435
Tom Grieve	OF5	R	31	9	15	1	3	1	0	0	0	4	1	0	.200	.368	.267
Keith Smith	OF5	R	26	6	13	1	3	0	0	0	0	1	0	0	.231	.231	.231
Tom Herr	2B6	S	23	14	10	4	2	0	0	0	1	2	2	1	.200	.333	.200
Mike Dimmel	OF5	R	24	6	3	1	1	0	0	0	0	0	0	0	.333	.333	.333

Pitcher	T	Age	G	GS	CG	ShO	IP	H	HR	BB	SO	W-L	Sv	ERA
Pete Vuckovich	R	26	34	32	9	0	233.0	229	22	64	145	15-10	0	3.59
Bob Forsch	R	29	33	32	7	1	218.2	215	16	52	92	11-11	0	3.83
John Denny	R	26	31	31	5	2	206.0	206	24	100	99	8-11	0	4.85
Silvio Martinez	R	23	32	29	7	2	206.2	204	14	67	102	15-8	0	3.27
John Fulgham	R	23	20	19	10	2	146.0	123	10	26	75	10-6	0	2.53
Bob Sykes	L	24	13	11	0	0	67.0	86	11	34	35	4-3	0	6.18
John Urrea	R	24	3	2	0	0	11.1	13	0	9	5	0-0	0	3.97
Mark Littell	R	26	63	0	0	0	82.1	60	2	39	67	9-4	13	2.19
Darold Knowles	L	37	48	0	0	0	48.2	54	5	17	22	2-5	6	4.07
Will McEnaney	L	27	45	0	0	0	64.0	60	3	16	15	0-3	2	2.95
Buddy Schultz	L	28	31	0	0	0	42.1	40	7	14	38	4-3	3	4.46
Tom Bruno	R	26	27	1	0	0	38.1	37	1	22	27	2-3	0	4.23
Roy Thomas	R	26	26	6	0	0	77.0	66	9	24	44	3-4	1	2.92
George Frazier	R	24	25	0	0	0	32.1	35	3	12	14	2-4	0	4.45
Dan O'Brien	R	25	6	0	0	0	11.0	21	0	3	5	1-1	0	8.18
Kim Seaman	L	22	1	0	0	0	2.0	0	0	2	3	0-0	0	0.00

1979 Philadelphia Phillies 4th NL East 84-78 .519 14.0 GB

Danny Ozark (65-67)/Dallas Green (19-11)

Player	Gm by Position	B	Age	G	AB	R	H	2B	3B	HR	RBI	BB	SO	SB	Avg	OBP	Slg
Bob Boone	C117,3B2	R	31	119	398	38	114	21	3	9	58	49	33	1	.286	.367	.422
Pete Rose	1B159,3B5,2B1	S	38	163	628	90	208	40	5	4	59	95	32	20	.331	.418	.430
Manny Trillo	2B118	R	28	118	431	40	112	22	1	6	42	20	59	4	.260	.296	.357
Mike Schmidt	3B157,SS2	R	29	160	541	109	137	25	4	45	114	120	115	9	.253	.386	.564
Larry Bowa	SS146	S	33	147	539	74	130	17	11	0	31	61	32	20	.241	.316	.314
Bake McBride	OF147	L	30	151	582	82	163	16	12	12	60	41	77	25	.280	.328	.411
Garry Maddox	OF140	R	29	148	548	70	154	28	6	13	61	17	71	26	.281	.304	.425
Greg Luzinski	OF125	R	28	137	452	47	114	23	1	18	81	56	103	3	.252	.343	.427
Greg Gross	OF73	L	26	111	174	21	58	6	3	0	15	29	5	5	.333	.422	.402
Del Unser	OF30,1B22	L	34	95	141	26	42	8	0	6	29	14	33	2	.298	.354	.482
Tim McCarver	C31,OF1	L	37	79	137	13	33	5	1	1	12	19	12	2	.241	.333	.314
Mike Anderson	OF70,P1	R	28	79	78	12	18	4	0	1	2	13	14	1	.231	.341	.321
Rudy Meoli	SS16,2B15,3B1	L	28	30	73	2	13	4	1	0	6	9	15	2	.178	.268	.260
Bud Harrelson	2B25,SS17,3B9*	S	35	53	71	7	20	6	0	0	7	13	14	3	.282	.395	.366
Ramon Aviles	2B27	R	27	27	61	7	17	2	0	0	12	8	8	0	.279	.371	.311
Dave Rader	C25	L	30	31	54	3	11	1	1	1	5	6	7	0	.204	.283	.315
Jose Cardenal†	OF12,1B1	R	35	29	48	4	10	3	0	0	9	8	8	1	.208	.321	.271
Keith Moreland	C13	R	25	14	48	3	18	3	2	0	8	3	5	0	.375	.412	.521
Lonnie Smith	OF11	R	23	17	30	4	5	2	0	0	3	1	7	2	.167	.194	.233
John Poff	OF4,1B1	L	26	12	19	2	2	1	0	0	1	1	4	0	.105	.150	.158
John Vukovich	3B7,2B3	R	31	10	15	0	3	1	0	0	1	0	3	0	.200	.200	.267
Pete Mackanin	2B2,3B2,SS2	R	27	13	9	2	1	0	0	1	2	1	2	0	.111	.200	.444

B. Harrelson, 1 G at OF

Pitcher	T	Age	G	GS	CG	ShO	IP	H	HR	BB	SO	W-L	Sv	ERA
Steve Carlton	L	34	35	35	13	4	251.0	202	25	89	213	18-11	0	3.62
Randy Lerch	L	24	37	35	6	1	214.0	228	20	60	92	10-13	0	3.74
Nino Espinosa	R	25	33	33	8	3	212.0	211	20	65	88	14-12	0	3.65
Dick Ruthven	R	28	20	20	3	2	122.1	121	10	37	58	7-5	0	4.27
Larry Christenson	R	25	19	17	2	0	106.0	118	9	30	53	5-10	0	4.50
Dickie Noles	R	22	14	14	0	0	90.0	80	6	38	42	3-4	0	3.80
Dan Larson	R	24	3	3	0	0	19.0	17	1	9	9	1-1	0	4.26
Tug McGraw	L	34	65	1	0	0	83.2	83	9	29	57	4-3	16	5.16
Ron Reed	R	36	61	0	0	0	102.0	110	9	32	58	13-8	5	4.15
Rawly Eastwick	R	28	51	0	0	0	82.2	90	8	25	47	3-6	6	4.90
Doug Bird	R	29	32	1	1	0	61.0	73	7	16	33	2-0	0	5.16
Kevin Saucier	L	22	29	2	0	0	62.1	68	4	33	21	1-4	1	4.19
Warren Brusstar	R	27	13	0	0	0	14.1	23	1	4	3	1-0	1	6.91
Jim Lonborg	R	37	4	1	0	0	7.1	14	3	4	7	0-1	0	11.05
Jack Kucek†	R	26	4	0	0	0	4.1	6	2	1	2	1-0	0	8.31
Jim Kaat†	L	40	3	1	0	0	8.1	9	1	5	2	1-0	0	4.32
Mike Anderson	R	28	1	0	0	0	1.0	2	0	0	2	0-0	0	0.00

1979 Chicago Cubs 5th NL East 80-82 .494 18.0 GB

Herman Franks (78-77)/Joey Amalfitano (2-5)

Player	Gm by Position	B	Age	G	AB	R	H	2B	3B	HR	RBI	BB	SO	SB	Avg	OBP	Slg
Barry Foote	C129	R	27	132	429	47	109	26	0	16	56	34	49	5	.254	.316	.427
Bill Buckner	1B140	L	29	149	591	72	168	34	7	14	66	30	28	9	.284	.319	.437
Ted Sizemore†	2B96	R	34	98	330	36	82	17	0	2	24	32	25	3	.248	.319	.318
Steve Ontiveros	3B142,1B1	S	27	152	519	58	148	28	2	4	57	58	68	0	.285	.362	.370
Ivan DeJesus	SS160	R	26	160	636	92	180	26	10	5	52	59	82	24	.283	.345	.379
Jerry Martin	OF144	R	30	150	534	74	145	34	3	19	73	38	85	2	.272	.321	.453
Dave Kingman	OF139	R	30	145	532	97	153	19	5	48	115	45	131	4	.288	.343	.613
Scot Thompson	OF100	L	23	128	346	36	100	13	5	2	29	17	37	4	.289	.322	.373
Larry Biittner	OF44,1B32	L	33	111	272	35	79	13	3	3	50	21	23	1	.290	.339	.393
Bobby Murcer†	OF54	L	33	58	190	22	49	4	1	7	22	36	20	2	.258	.374	.400
Mike Vail	OF39,3B2	R	27	87	179	28	60	8	2	7	35	14	27	0	.335	.379	.520
Steve Dillard	2B60,3B9	R	28	89	166	31	47	6	1	5	24	17	24	1	.283	.351	.422
Mick Kelleher	3B32,2B29,SS14	R	31	73	142	14	36	4	1	0	10	7	9	2	.254	.296	.296
Tim Blackwell	C63	S	26	63	122	8	20	3	1	0	12	32	25	0	.164	.338	.205
Ken Henderson†	OF23	S	33	62	81	11	19	2	0	2	8	15	16	0	.235	.361	.333
Steve Macko	2B10,3B4	L	24	19	40	2	9	1	0	0	3	4	8	0	.225	.295	.250
Miguel Dilone†	OF22	S	24	43	36	14	11	0	0	0	1	2	5	15	.306	.342	.306
Bruce Kimm	C9	R	28	9	11	0	1	0	0	0	0	0	0	0	.091	.091	.091
Sam Mejias†	OF23	R	27	31	11	4	2	0	0	0	0	2	5	0	.182	.308	.182
Gene Clines		R	32	10	10	0	2	0	0	0	0	0	1	0	.200	.200	.200
Steve Davis	2B2,3B1	R	25	3	4	0	0	0	0	0	1	0	0	0	.000	.000	.000
Kurt Seibert	2B1	S	23	7	2	2	0	0	0	0	0	0	1	0	.000	.000	.000
Karl Pagel		L	24	1	1	0	0	0	0	0	0	0	1	0	.000	.000	.000

Pitcher	T	Age	G	GS	CG	ShO	IP	H	HR	BB	SO	W-L	Sv	ERA
Rick Reuschel	R	30	36	36	5	1	239.0	251	16	75	125	18-12	0	3.62
Dennis Lamp	R	26	38	32	6	1	200.1	223	14	46	86	11-10	0	3.50
Lynn McGlothen	R	29	42	29	6	1	212.0	236	27	55	147	13-14	2	4.12
Mike Krukow	R	27	28	28	0	0	164.2	172	13	81	119	9-9	0	4.21
Ken Holtzman	L	33	23	20	3	2	117.2	133	15	53	44	6-9	0	4.59
Dick Tidrow†	R	32	63	0	0	0	102.2	86	5	42	68	11-5	4	2.72
Bruce Sutter	R	26	62	0	0	0	101.1	67	3	32	110	6-6	37	2.22
Willie Hernandez	L	24	51	2	0	0	79.0	85	8	39	53	4-4	0	5.01
Donnie Moore	R	25	39	1	0	0	73.0	95	8	25	43	1-4	1	5.18
Bill Caudill	R	22	29	12	0	0	90.0	89	16	41	104	1-7	0	4.80
Ray Burris†	R	28	14	0	0	0	21.2	23	0	15	14	0-0	0	6.23
Doug Capilla†	L	27	13	1	0	0	17.1	14	1	7	10	0-1	0	2.60
Dave Geisel	L	24	7	0	0	0	15.0	10	0	4	5	0-0	0	0.60
George Riley	L	22	4	1	0	0	13.0	16	1	6	5	0-1	0	5.54

1979 New York Mets 6th NL East 63-99 .389 35.0 GB

Joe Torre

Player	Gm by Position	B	Age	G	AB	R	H	2B	3B	HR	RBI	BB	SO	SB	Avg	OBP	Slg
John Stearns	C121,1B16,3B11*	R	27	155	538	58	131	29	2	9	66	52	57	15	.243	.312	.355
Willie Montanez†	1B108	L	31	109	410	36	96	19	0	5	47	25	48	0	.234	.277	.317
Doug Flynn	2B148,SS20	R	28	157	555	35	135	19	5	4	61	17	46	0	.243	.265	.317
Richie Hebner	3B134,1B6	L	31	136	473	54	127	25	2	10	79	59	59	3	.268	.354	.393
Frank Taveras†	SS153	R	29	153	635	89	167	26	9	1	33	33	72	42	.263	.301	.337
Joel Youngblood	OF147,2B13,3B12	R	27	158	590	90	162	37	5	16	60	60	84	18	.275	.346	.436
Lee Mazzilli	OF143,1B15	S	24	158	597	78	181	34	4	15	79	93	74	34	.303	.395	.449
Steve Henderson	OF94	R	26	98	350	42	107	16	8	5	39	38	58	13	.306	.380	.440
Elliott Maddox	OF65,3B11	R	31	86	224	21	60	13	0	1	12	20	27	3	.268	.335	.339
Alex Trevino	C36,3B27,2B8	R	21	79	207	24	56	11	1	0	20	20	27	2	.271	.338	.333
Ed Kranepool	1B29,OF8	L	34	82	155	7	36	5	0	2	17	13	18	0	.232	.287	.303
Dan Norman	OF33	R	24	44	110	9	27	3	1	3	11	10	26	2	.245	.311	.373
Bruce Boisclair	OF24,1B1	L	26	59	98	7	18	5	1	0	4	3	24	0	.184	.210	.255
Gil Flores	OF32	R	26	70	93	9	18	1	1	1	10	8	17	2	.194	.262	.258
Ron Hodges	C22	L	30	59	86	4	14	4	0	0	5	19	16	0	.163	.311	.209
Kelvin Chapman	2B22,3B1	R	23	35	80	7	12	1	2	0	4	5	15	0	.150	.198	.213
Jose Cardenal†	OF9,1B2	R	35	11	37	8	11	4	0	2	4	6	3	1	.297	.409	.568
Tim Foli†	SS3	R	28	3	7	0	0	0	0	0	0	0	0	0	.000	.000	.000
Sergio Ferrer	3B12,SS5,2B4	S	28	32	7	7	0	0	0	0	0	2	3	0	.000	.222	.000

J. Stearns, 6 G at OF

Pitcher	T	Age	G	GS	CG	ShO	IP	H	HR	BB	SO	W-L	Sv	ERA
Craig Swan	R	28	35	35	10	3	251.1	241	20	57	145	14-13	0	3.29
Pete Falcone	L	25	33	31	1	1	184.0	194	24	76	113	6-14	0	4.16
Kevin Kobel	L	25	30	27	1	1	161.2	169	14	46	67	6-8	0	3.51
Dock Ellis†	R	34	17	14	1	0	85.0	110	9	34	41	3-7	0	6.04
Tom Hausman	R	26	19	10	1	0	78.2	65	6	19	33	2-6	2	2.75
Mike Scott	R	24	18	9	0	0	52.1	59	4	20	21	1-3	0	5.33
Pat Zachry	R	27	7	7	1	0	42.2	44	3	21	17	5-1	0	3.59
Juan Berenguer	R	24	5	5	0	0	30.2	28	2	12	25	1-1	0	2.93
Ray Burris†	R	28	4	4	0	0	21.2	21	2	6	10	0-2	0	3.32
John Pacella	R	22	4	3	0	0	16.1	16	0	4	12	0-2	0	4.41
Dale Murray†	R	29	58	0	0	0	97.0	105	6	52	37	4-8	4	4.82
Neil Allen	R	21	50	5	0	0	99.0	100	4	47	65	6-10	8	3.55
Ed Glynn	L	26	46	0	0	0	60.0	57	3	40	32	1-4	7	3.00
Wayne Twitchell†	R	31	33	2	0	0	63.2	55	6	55	44	5-3	0	5.23
Dwight Bernard	R	27	32	1	0	0	44.0	59	2	26	20	0-3	0	4.70
Andy Hassler†	L	27	29	8	1	0	80.1	74	5	42	53	4-5	4	3.70
Skip Lockwood	R	32	27	0	0	0	42.1	33	3	14	42	2-5	9	1.49
Jesse Orosco	L	22	18	2	0	0	35.0	33	4	22	22	1-2	0	4.89
Jeff Reardon	R	23	18	0	0	0	20.2	12	2	9	10	1-2	2	1.74
Roy Lee Jackson	R	25	8	0	0	0	16.1	11	1	5	10	1-0	0	2.20

1979 Cincinnati Reds 1st NL West 90-71 .559 —

John McNamara

Player	Gm by Position	B	Age	G	AB	R	H	2B	3B	HR	RBI	BB	SO	SB	Avg	OBP	Slg
Johnny Bench	C126,1B2	R	31	130	464	73	128	19	0	22	80	67	73	4	.276	.364	.459
Dan Driessen	1B143	L	27	150	515	72	129	24	3	18	75	62	77	11	.250	.330	.414
Joe Morgan	2B121	L	35	127	436	70	109	26	1	9	32	93	45	28	.250	.379	.376
Ray Knight	3B149	R	26	150	551	64	175	37	4	10	79	38	57	4	.318	.360	.454
Dave Concepcion	SS148	R	31	149	590	91	166	25	3	16	84	64	73	19	.281	.348	.415
Cesar Geronimo	OF118	L	31	123	356	38	85	17	4	4	38	37	56	1	.239	.312	.343
George Foster	OF116	R	30	121	440	68	133	18	3	30	98	59	105	0	.302	.386	.561
Ken Griffey Sr.	OF93	L	29	95	380	62	120	27	4	8	32	36	39	12	.316	.374	.471
Dave Collins	OF91,1B10	S	26	122	396	59	126	16	4	3	35	27	48	16	.318	.364	.402
Junior Kennedy	2B59,SS5,3B4	R	28	83	220	29	60	7	0	1	17	28	31	4	.273	.355	.318
Heity Cruz†	OF69	R	26	74	182	24	44	10	2	4	27	31	39	0	.242	.350	.385
Paul Blair†	OF67	R	35	75	140	7	21	4	1	2	15	11	27	0	.150	.209	.236
Vic Correll	C47	R	33	48	133	14	31	12	0	1	15	14	26	0	.233	.309	.346
Rick Auerbach	3B18,SS16,2B3	R	29	62	100	17	21	8	1	1	12	14	19	0	.210	.304	.340
Champ Summers†	OF13,1B6	L	33	27	60	10	12	2	1	1	11	13	15	0	.200	.351	.317
Harry Spilman	1B12,3B4	L	24	43	56	7	12	3	0	0	5	7	5	0	.214	.323	.268
Arturo DeFreitas	1B6,OF1	R	26	23	34	2	7	2	0	0	4	0	16	0	.206	.206	.265
Ken Henderson†	OF2	S	33	10	13	1	3	1	0	0	2	0	2	0	.231	.231	.308
R. Santo Domingo		S	23	7	6	0	1	0	0	0	0	1	3	0	.167	.286	.167
Ron Oester	SS2	S	23	6	3	0	0	0	0	0	0	0	1	0	.000	.000	.000
Sam Mejias†	OF5	R	27	7	2	1	1	0	0	0	0	0	0	0	.500	.500	.500

Pitcher	T	Age	G	GS	CG	ShO	IP	H	HR	BB	SO	W-L	Sv	ERA
Tom Seaver	R	34	32	32	9	5	215.0	187	16	61	131	16-6	0	3.14
Mike LaCoss	R	23	35	32	6	1	205.2	202	13	79	73	14-8	0	3.50
Fred Norman	L	36	34	31	5	0	195.1	193	14	57	95	11-13	0	3.64
Bill Bonham	R	30	29	29	2	0	175.2	173	14	60	78	9-7	0	3.79
Paul Moskau	R	25	21	15	1	0	106.1	107	9	51	58	5-4	0	3.89
Doug Bair	R	29	65	0	0	0	94.1	93	7	51	86	11-7	16	4.29
Tom Hume	R	26	57	12	2	0	163.0	162	12	33	80	10-9	17	2.76
Dave Tomlin	L	30	53	0	0	0	58.1	59	3	18	30	2-2	1	2.62
Frank Pastore	R	21	30	9	2	1	95.1	102	8	23	63	6-7	4	4.25
Pedro Borbon†	R	32	30	0	0	0	44.2	48	2	8	23	2-2	2	3.43
Mario Soto	R	22	25	0	0	0	37.1	33	2	30	32	3-2	0	5.30
Manny Sarmiento	R	23	23	1	0	0	38.2	47	2	7	23	0-4	0	4.66
Doug Capilla†	L	27	5	0	0	0	6.1	7	1	5	0	1-0	0	8.53
Charlie Leibrandt	L	22	3	0	0	0	4.1	2	0	2	1	0-0	0	0.00

1979 Houston Astros 2nd NL West 89-73 .549 1.5 GB

Bill Virdon

Player	Gm by Position	B	Age	G	AB	R	H	2B	3B	HR	RBI	BB	SO	SB	Avg	OBP	Slg
Alan Ashby	C105	S	27	108	336	25	68	15	2	2	35	26	70	0	.202	.262	.277
Cesar Cedeno	1B91,OF40	R	28	132	470	57	123	27	4	6	54	64	52	30	.262	.348	.374
Rafael Landestoy	2B114,SS3	S	26	129	282	33	76	9	6	0	30	29	24	13	.270	.338	.344
Enos Cabell	3B132,1B51	R	29	155	603	60	164	30	5	6	67	21	68	37	.272	.299	.368
Craig Reynolds	SS143	L	26	146	555	63	147	20	9	0	39	21	49	12	.265	.292	.333
Jose Cruz	OF156	L	31	157	558	73	161	33	7	9	72	72	66	36	.289	.367	.421
Terry Puhl	OF152	L	22	157	600	87	172	22	4	8	49	58	46	30	.287	.352	.377
Jeffrey Leonard	OF123	R	23	134	411	47	119	15	5	0	47	46	68	23	.290	.360	.350
Art Howe	2B68,3B59,1B3	R	32	118	355	32	88	15	2	6	33	36	37	3	.248	.316	.352
Julio Gonzalez	2B32,SS21,3B9	R	26	68	181	16	45	5	2	0	10	5	14	2	.249	.280	.298
Bob Watson†	1B44	R	33	49	163	15	39	4	0	3	18	16	23	0	.239	.304	.319
Denny Walling	OF42	L	25	82	147	21	48	8	4	3	31	17	21	3	.327	.394	.497
Bruce Bochy	C55	R	24	56	129	11	28	4	0	1	6	13	25	0	.217	.294	.271
Luis Pujols	C26	R	23	26	75	7	17	2	1	0	8	2	14	0	.227	.247	.280
Jimmy Sexton	SS11,3B4,2B2	R	27	52	43	8	9	0	0	0	1	3	6	4	.209	.320	.209
Jesus Alou	OF6,1B1	R	37	42	43	3	11	4	0	0	10	6	7	0	.256	.347	.349
Reggie Baldwin	C3,1B1	R	24	14	20	0	4	1	0	0	1	0	4	0	.200	.200	.250
Dave Bergman	1B4	L	26	13	15	4	6	0	0	1	2	0	3	0	.400	.400	.600
Danny Heep	OF2	L	21	14	14	0	2	0	0	0	2	1	4	0	.143	.176	.143
Alan Knicely	C3,3B1	R	24	7	6	0	0	0	0	0	0	2	3	0	.000	.250	.000
Tom Wiedenbauer	OF3	R	20	4	6	0	4	1	0	0	2	0	2	0	.667	.667	.833

Pitcher	T	Age	G	GS	CG	ShO	IP	H	HR	BB	SO	W-L	Sv	ERA
J.R. Richard	R	29	38	38	19	4	292.1	220	13	98	313	18-13	0	2.71
Joe Niekro	R	34	38	38	11	5	263.2	221	17	107	119	21-11	0	3.00
Ken Forsch	R	32	26	24	10	2	177.2	155	14	35	58	11-6	0	3.04
Joaquin Andujar	R	26	46	23	8	0	194.0	168	7	88	77	12-12	4	3.43
Rick Williams	R	26	31	16	2	2	121.1	122	6	30	37	4-7	0	3.26
Vern Ruhle	R	28	13	10	2	2	66.1	64	9	8	33	2-6	0	4.07
Joe Sambito	L	27	63	0	0	0	91.1	80	8	23	83	8-7	22	1.77
Randy Niemann	L	23	26	7	3	2	67.0	68	1	22	24	3-2	1	3.76
Bert Roberge	R	24	26	0	0	0	32.0	20	0	17	13	3-0	4	1.69
Tom Dixon	R	24	19	1	0	0	25.2	39	2	15	9	1-2	0	6.66
George Throop†	R	28	14	0	0	0	22.1	23	4	11	15	1-0	0	3.22
Frank LaCorte†	R	27	12	3	0	0	27.0	21	3	10	24	1-2	0	5.00
Bo McLaughlin†	R	25	12	0	0	0	16.1	22	2	4	12	1-2	0	5.51
Frank Riccelli	L	26	11	2	0	0	22.0	22	0	18	20	2-2	0	4.09
Peter Ladd	R	22	10	0	0	0	12.1	8	1	8	6	1-1	0	2.92
Gary Wilson	R	24	6	0	0	0	7.1	15	2	6	6	0-0	0	12.27
Gordy Pladson	R	22	4	0	0	0	4.0	9	1	2	2	0-0	0	4.50
Bobby Sprowl	L	23	3	0	0	0	4.0	1	0	2	3	0-0	0	2.25
Mike Mendoza	R	23	1	0	0	0	1.0	0	0	0	0	0-0	0	0.00

1979 Los Angeles Dodgers 3rd NL West 79-83 .488 11.5 GB

Tom Lasorda

Player	Gm by Position	B	Age	G	AB	R	H	2B	3B	HR	RBI	BB	SO	SB	Avg	OBP	Slg
Steve Yeager	C103	R	30	105	310	33	67	9	2	13	41	29	68	1	.216	.282	.384
Steve Garvey	1B162	R	30	162	648	92	204	32	1	28	110	37	59	3	.315	.351	.497
Davey Lopes	2B152	R	34	153	582	109	154	20	6	28	73	97	88	44	.265	.372	.464
Ron Cey	3B150	R	31	150	487	77	137	20	1	28	81	86	85	3	.281	.389	.499
Bill Russell	SS150	R	30	153	627	72	170	26	4	7	56	24	43	6	.271	.297	.359
Dusty Baker	OF150	R	30	151	554	86	152	29	1	23	88	56	70	11	.274	.340	.455
Derrel Thomas	OF119,3B18,2B5*	R	28	141	406	47	104	15	4	5	44	41	49	18	.256	.330	.350
Gary Thomasson	OF100,1B1	L	27	115	315	39	78	11	1	14	45	43	70	4	.248	.339	.422
Joe Ferguson	C67,OF52	R	32	122	363	54	95	14	0	20	69	70	68	1	.262	.380	.466
Reggie Smith	OF62	S	34	68	234	41	64	13	1	10	32	31	50	6	.274	.359	.466
Von Joshua	OF46	L	31	94	142	22	40	7	1	3	14	7	23	1	.282	.315	.408
Ted Martinez	3B23,SS21,2B18	R	31	81	112	19	30	5	1	0	2	4	16	3	.268	.293	.330
Mickey Hatcher	OF19,3B17	R	24	33	93	9	25	4	1	1	5	7	12	1	.269	.327	.366
Pedro Guerrero	OF12,1B8,3B3	R	23	25	62	7	15	2	0	2	9	1	14	2	.242	.250	.371
Johnny Oates	C20	L	33	26	46	4	6	2	0	0	2	4	1	0	.130	.200	.174
Manny Mota	OF1	R	41	47	42	1	15	0	0	0	3	3	4	0	.357	.400	.357
Rick Monday	OF10	L	33	12	33	2	10	0	0	0	2	5	6	0	.303	.395	.303
Vic Davalillo	OF3	L	42	29	27	2	7	1	0	0	2	2	0	2	.259	.310	.296

D. Thomas, 3 G at SS, 1 G at 1B

Pitcher	T	Age	G	GS	CG	ShO	IP	H	HR	BB	SO	W-L	Sv	ERA
Don Sutton	R	34	33	32	6	1	226.0	201	21	61	146	12-15	1	3.82
Rick Sutcliffe	R	23	39	30	5	1	242.0	217	16	97	117	17-10	0	3.46
Burt Hooton	R	29	29	29	12	1	212.0	191	11	63	129	11-10	0	2.97
Jerry Reuss	L	30	39	21	4	1	160.0	178	4	60	83	7-14	3	3.54
Andy Messersmith	R	33	11	11	1	0	62.1	55	9	34	26	2-4	0	4.91
Doug Rau	L	30	11	11	1	1	56.0	73	3	22	28	1-5	0	5.30
Gerry Hannahs	L	26	4	2	0	0	16.0	10	2	13	6	0-2	1	3.38
Charlie Hough	R	31	42	14	0	0	151.1	152	16	66	76	7-5	0	4.76
Dave Patterson	R	22	36	0	0	0	53.0	62	5	22	34	4-1	6	5.26
Lerrin LaGrow†	R	30	31	0	0	0	37.0	38	2	18	22	5-1	4	3.41
Ken Brett†	L	30	30	0	0	0	47.0	52	1	12	13	4-3	2	3.45
Bob Welch	R	22	25	12	1	0	81.1	82	7	32	64	5-6	5	3.98
Bobby Castillo	R	24	19	0	0	0	24.1	26	0	13	25	2-0	7	1.11
Joe Beckwith	R	24	17	0	0	0	37.1	42	4	15	28	1-2	2	4.34
Terry Forster	L	27	17	0	0	0	16.1	18	0	11	8	1-2	2	5.51
Lance Rautzhan†	L	26	12	0	0	0	9.2	9	0	11	5	0-2	1	7.45
Dennis Lewallyn	R	25	7	0	0	0	12.1	19	0	5	1	0-1	0	5.11

1979 San Francisco Giants 4th NL West 71-91 .438 19.5 GB

Joe Altobelli (61-79)/Dave Bristol (10-12)

Player	Gm by Position	B	Age	G	AB	R	H	2B	3B	HR	RBI	BB	SO	SB	Avg	OBP	Slg
Dennis Littlejohn	C63	R	24	63	193	15	38	6	1	1	13	21	46	0	.197	.272	.254
Mike Ivie	1B98,OF24,3B4*	R	26	133	402	58	115	18	3	27	89	47	80	5	.286	.359	.547
Joe Strain	2B67,3B1	R	25	67	257	27	62	8	1	1	12	13	21	8	.241	.285	.292
Darrell Evans	3B159	L	32	160	562	68	142	23	2	17	70	91	80	6	.253	.356	.391
Johnnie LeMaster	SS106	R	25	108	343	42	87	11	2	3	29	23	55	9	.254	.304	.324
Jack Clark	OF140,3B2	R	23	143	527	84	144	25	2	26	86	63	95	11	.273	.348	.476
Bill North	OF130	S	31	142	460	87	119	15	4	5	30	96	84	58	.259	.386	.341
Larry Herndon	OF122	R	25	132	354	35	91	14	5	7	36	29	70	8	.257	.313	.384
Terry Whitfield	OF106	L	26	133	394	52	113	20	4	5	44	36	47	5	.287	.349	.396
Willie McCovey	1B89	L	41	117	353	34	88	9	0	15	57	36	70	0	.249	.318	.402
Roger Metzger	SS78,2B10,3B1	S	31	94	259	24	65	7	8	0	31	23	31	11	.251	.311	.340
Bill Madlock†	2B63,1B5	R	28	69	249	37	65	9	2	7	41	18	19	11	.261	.309	.398
Marc Hill	C58,1B1	R	27	63	169	20	35	3	0	3	15	26	25	0	.207	.308	.278
Rob Andrews	2B53,3B3	R	26	75	154	22	40	3	0	2	13	8	9	4	.260	.289	.318
Mike Sadek	C60,OF1	R	33	63	126	14	30	5	0	1	11	15	24	1	.238	.322	.302
Max Venable	OF25	L	22	55	85	12	14	1	1	0	3	10	18	3	.165	.260	.200
Greg Johnston	OF17	L	24	42	74	5	15	2	0	1	7	2	17	0	.203	.224	.270
John Tamargo†	C17	S	27	30	60	7	12	3	0	2	6	4	8	0	.200	.239	.350
Heity Cruz†	OF6,3B2	R	26	16	25	2	3	0	0	0	1	3	7	0	.120	.214	.120
Bob Kearney	C1	R	22	2	0	0	0	0	0	0	0	1	0	0	—	1.000	—

M. Ivie, 1 G at 2B

Pitcher	T	Age	G	GS	CG	ShO	IP	H	HR	BB	SO	W-L	Sv	ERA
Vida Blue	L	29	34	34	10	0	237.0	246	23	111	138	14-14	0	5.01
Bob Knepper	L	25	34	34	6	2	207.1	241	30	77	123	9-12	0	4.64
John Montefusco	R	29	22	22	0	0	137.0	145	15	51	76	3-8	0	3.94
Ed Halicki	R	28	33	19	3	1	125.2	134	12	47	81	5-8	0	4.58
John Curtis	L	31	27	18	3	2	120.2	121	15	42	85	10-9	0	4.18
Ed Whitson†	R	24	18	17	2	0	100.1	98	5	39	62	5-8	0	3.95
Phil Nastu	L	24	25	14	1	0	100.0	105	14	41	47	3-4	0	4.32
Gary Lavelle	L	30	70	0	0	0	96.2	86	5	42	80	7-9	20	2.51
Tom Griffin	R	31	59	3	0	0	94.1	83	9	46	82	5-6	2	3.91
Greg Minton	R	27	46	0	0	0	79.2	59	0	27	33	4-3	4	1.81
Pedro Borbon†	R	32	30	0	0	0	46.0	56	7	13	26	4-3	3	4.89
Randy Moffitt	R	30	28	0	0	0	35.0	53	5	14	16	2-5	2	7.71
Dave Roberts†	L	34	26	1	0	0	42.0	42	3	18	23	0-2	3	2.57
Joe Coleman†	R	32	5	0	0	0	3.2	3	0	2	0	0-0	0	0.00
Eddie Plank	R	27	4	0	0	0	3.2	9	0	2	1	0-0	0	7.36
Al Holland	L	26	3	0	0	0	7.0	3	0	5	7	0-0	0	0.00

1979 San Diego Padres 5th NL West 68-93 .422 22.0 GB

Roger Craig

Player	Gm by Position	B	Age	G	AB	R	H	2B	3B	HR	RBI	BB	SO	SB	Avg	OBP	Slg
Gene Tenace	C94,1B72	R	32	151	463	61	122	16	4	20	67	105	106	2	.263	.403	.445
Dan Briggs	1B50,OF44	L	26	104	227	34	47	4	3	8	30	18	45	2	.207	.277	.357
Fernando Gonzalez	2B103,3B3	R	29	114	323	22	70	13	3	9	34	18	34	0	.217	.258	.359
Paul Dade†	3B70,OF4	R	27	76	283	38	78	19	2	1	19	14	48	13	.276	.311	.367
Ozzie Smith	SS155	S	24	156	587	77	124	18	6	0	27	37	37	28	.211	.260	.262
Dave Winfield	OF157	R	27	159	597	97	184	27	10	34	118	85	71	15	.308	.395	.558
Gene Richards	OF132	L	25	150	545	77	152	17	9	4	41	47	62	24	.279	.343	.365
Jerry Turner	OF115	L	25	138	448	55	111	23	2	9	61	34	58	4	.248	.301	.368
Kurt Bevacqua	3B64,2B16,1B8*	R	32	114	297	23	75	12	4	1	34	38	25	2	.253	.331	.330
Bill Fahey	C68	L	29	73	209	14	60	8	1	3	19	21	17	1	.287	.348	.378
Jay Johnstone†	OF45,1B22	L	33	75	201	10	59	8	2	0	32	18	21	1	.294	.348	.353
Bill Almon	2B61,SS25,OF1	R	26	100	198	20	45	3	0	1	8	21	48	6	.227	.299	.258
Barry Evans	3B53,SS2,2B1	R	23	56	162	9	35	5	0	1	14	5	16	0	.216	.237	.265
Mike Hargrove†	1B37	L	29	52	125	15	24	5	0	0	8	25	15	0	.192	.325	.232
Jim Wilhelm	OF30	R	26	39	103	8	25	4	3	0	8	2	12	1	.243	.255	.340
Fred Kendall	C40,1B2	R	30	46	102	8	17	2	0	1	6	11	7	0	.167	.248	.216
Broderick Perkins	1B28	L	24	57	87	8	23	0	0	0	8	8	12	0	.264	.323	.264
Tim Flannery	2B21	L	21	22	65	2	10	0	1	0	4	4	5	0	.154	.222	.185
Don Reynolds	OF14	R	26	30	45	6	10	1	2	0	6	7	6	0	.222	.321	.333
Bobby Tolan	1B5,OF1	L	33	22	21	2	4	0	1	0	2	0	2	0	.190	.190	.286
Brian Greer	OF4	R	20	4	3	0	0	0	0	0	0	0	1	0	.000	.000	.000
Sam Perlozzo	2B2	R	28	2	2	0	0	0	0	0	0	1	0	0	.000	.333	.000

K. Bevacqua, 8 G at OF

Pitcher	T	Age	G	GS	CG	ShO	IP	H	HR	BB	SO	W-L	Sv	ERA
Randy Jones	L	29	39	39	6	0	263.0	257	17	64	112	11-12	0	3.63
Gaylord Perry	R	40	32	32	10	0	232.2	225	12	67	140	12-11	0	3.06
Bob Shirley	L	25	49	25	4	1	205.0	196	15	59	117	8-16	0	3.38
Juan Eichelberger	R	25	3	3	1	0	21.0	15	1	11	12	1-1	0	3.43
Rollie Fingers	R	32	54	0	0	0	83.2	91	7	37	65	9-9	13	4.52
John D'Acquisto	R	27	51	11	1	1	133.2	140	15	86	97	9-13	2	4.92
Mark Lee	R	26	46	1	0	0	65.0	88	3	25	25	2-4	5	4.29
Eric Rasmussen	R	27	45	20	5	3	156.2	142	9	42	54	6-9	3	3.27
Bob Owchinko	L	24	42	20	2	0	149.1	144	16	55	66	6-12	0	3.74
Steve Mura	R	24	38	5	0	0	73.0	57	6	37	59	4-4	2	3.08
Mickey Lolich	L	38	27	5	0	0	49.1	59	4	22	20	0-2	0	4.74
Dennis Kinney	L	27	13	0	0	0	18.0	17	2	8	11	0-0	0	3.50
Tom Tellmann	R	25	1	0	0	0	2.2	7	1	0	1	0-0	0	16.88

1979 Atlanta Braves 6th NL West 66-94 .413 23.5 GB

Bobby Cox

Player	Gm by Position	B	Age	G	AB	R	H	2B	3B	HR	RBI	BB	SO	SB	Avg	OBP	Slg
Bruce Benedict	C76	R	23	76	204	14	46	11	0	0	15	33	18	1	.225	.331	.279
Dale Murphy	1B76,C27	R	23	104	384	53	106	7	2	21	57	38	67	6	.276	.340	.469
Glenn Hubbard	2B91	R	21	97	325	34	75	12	0	3	29	27	43	0	.231	.290	.295
Bob Horner	3B82,1B45	R	21	121	487	66	153	15	1	33	98	22	74	0	.314	.346	.552
Pepe Frias	SS137	R	30	140	475	41	123	18	4	1	44	20	36	3	.259	.290	.320
Gary Matthews	OF156	R	28	156	631	97	192	34	5	27	90	60	75	18	.304	.363	.502
Barry Bonnell	OF124,3B1	R	25	127	375	47	97	20	3	12	45	26	55	8	.259	.311	.424
Jeff Burroughs	OF110	R	28	116	397	49	89	14	1	11	47	73	75	2	.224	.347	.348
Jerry Royster	3B80,2B77	R	26	154	601	103	164	25	6	3	51	62	59	35	.273	.337	.349
Rowland Office	OF97	L	26	124	277	35	69	14	2	2	37	27	33	5	.249	.320	.336
Joe Nolan	C74	L	28	89	230	28	57	9	3	4	21	27	28	1	.248	.333	.365
Mike Lum	1B51,OF3	L	33	111	217	27	54	6	0	6	27	18	34	0	.249	.304	.359
Darrel Chaney	SS39,2B5,3B4*	S	31	63	117	15	19	5	0	0	10	19	34	2	.162	.277	.205
Eddie Miller	OF27	S	22	27	113	12	35	1	0	0	5	5	24	15	.310	.350	.319
Charlie Spikes	OF15	R	28	66	93	12	26	8	0	3	21	5	30	0	.280	.310	.462
Biff Pocoroba	C7	S	25	28	38	6	12	4	0	0	4	7	0	1	.316	.422	.421
Larry Whisenton	OF13	L	22	13	37	3	9	2	1	0	1	3	3	1	.243	.300	.351
Bob Beall	1B3	S	31	17	15	1	2	2	0	0	1	3	4	0	.133	.263	.267
Mike Macha	3B3	R	25	6	13	2	2	0	0	0	1	1	5	0	.154	.214	.154
Brian Asselstine	OF1	L	25	8	10	1	1	0	0	0	0	1	2	0	.100	.182	.100
Jim Wessinger	2B2	R	23	10	7	2	0	0	0	0	0	1	4	0	.000	.125	.000

D. Chaney, 1 G at C

Pitcher	T	Age	G	GS	CG	ShO	IP	H	HR	BB	SO	W-L	Sv	ERA
Phil Niekro	R	40	44	44	23	1	342.0	311	41	113	208	21-20	0	3.39
Eddie Solomon	R	28	31	30	4	0	186.0	184	19	51	96	7-14	0	4.21
Rick Matula	R	25	28	28	1	0	171.1	193	14	64	67	8-10	0	4.15
Tony Brizzolara	R	22	20	19	2	0	107.1	133	6	33	64	6-9	0	5.28
Mickey Mahler	L	26	26	18	1	0	100.0	123	11	47	71	5-11	0	5.85
Larry McWilliams	L	25	13	13	1	0	66.1	69	4	22	32	3-2	0	5.56
Preston Hanna	R	24	6	4	0	0	24.1	27	1	15	15	1-1	0	2.96
Tommy Boggs	R	23	3	3	0	0	12.2	21	0	4	1	0-2	0	6.39
Gene Garber	R	31	68	0	0	0	106.0	121	10	24	56	6-16	25	4.33
Craig Skok	L	31	44	0	0	0	54.1	58	7	17	30	1-3	2	3.98
Adrian Devine	R	27	40	0	0	0	66.2	84	8	25	22	1-2	0	3.24
Joey McLaughlin	R	22	37	0	0	0	69.0	54	3	34	40	5-3	5	2.48
Bo McLaughlin†	R	25	37	1	0	0	49.2	63	2	16	45	1-1	0	4.89
Larry Bradford	L	29	21	0	0	0	19.0	11	0	10	11	1-0	2	0.95
Rick Mahler	R	25	15	0	0	0	22.0	28	4	11	12	0-0	0	6.14
Frank LaCorte†	R	27	6	0	0	0	8.1	9	2	5	6	0-0	0	7.56
Jamie Easterly	L	26	4	0	0	0	2.2	7	0	3	3	0-0	0	13.50

»1980 New York Yankees 1st AL East 103-59 .636 —

Dick Howser

Player	Gm by Position	B	Age	G	AB	R	H	2B	3B	HR	RBI	BB	SO	SB	Avg	OBP	Slg
Rick Cerone	C147	R	26	147	519	70	144	30	4	14	85	32	56	1	.277	.321	.432
Bob Watson	1B104,DH21	R	34	130	469	62	144	25	3	13	68	48	56	2	.307	.368	.456
Willie Randolph	2B138	R	25	138	513	99	151	23	7	7	46	119	45	30	.294	.427	.407
Graig Nettles	3B88,SS1	L	35	89	324	52	79	14	0	16	45	42	42	0	.244	.331	.435
Bucky Dent	SS141	R	28	141	489	57	128	26	2	5	52	48	37	0	.262	.327	.354
Bobby Brown	OF131,DH1	S	26	137	412	65	107	12	5	14	47	29	82	27	.260	.306	.415
Lou Piniella	OF104,DH7	R	36	116	321	39	92	18	0	2	27	29	20	0	.287	.343	.361
Reggie Jackson	OF94,DH46	L	34	143	514	94	154	22	4	41	111	83	122	1	.300	.398	.597
Eric Soderholm	DH51,3B37	R	31	95	275	38	79	13	1	11	35	27	25	0	.287	.353	.462
Ruppert Jones	OF82	L	25	83	328	38	73	11	3	9	42	34	50	18	.223	.299	.357
Bobby Murcer	OF59,DH33	L	34	100	297	41	80	9	1	13	57	34	28	2	.269	.339	.438
Jim Spencer	1B75,DH15	L	33	97	259	38	61	9	0	13	43	30	44	1	.236	.313	.421
Oscar Gamble	OF49,DH20	L	30	78	194	40	54	10	2	14	50	28	21	2	.278	.376	.567
Aurelio Rodriguez†	3B49,2B6	R	32	52	164	14	36	6	1	3	14	7	35	0	.220	.251	.323
Joe Lefebvre	OF71	L	24	74	150	26	34	1	1	8	21	27	30	0	.227	.345	.407
Fred Stanley	SS19,2B17,3B12	R	32	49	86	13	18	3	0	0	5	5	5	0	.209	.266	.244
Brian Doyle	2B20,SS12,3B2	L	25	34	75	8	13	1	0	1	5	6	7	1	.173	.235	.227
Dennis Werth	1B12,DH8,OF8*	R	27	39	65	15	20	3	0	3	12	12	19	0	.308	.416	.492
Johnny Oates	C39	L	34	39	64	6	12	3	0	1	3	2	3	1	.188	.224	.281
Ted Wilborn	OF3	S	21	8	8	2	2	0	0	0	1	0	1	0	.250	.250	.250
Marshall Brant	1B2,DH1	R	24	3	6	0	0	0	0	0	0	0	3	0	.000	.000	.000
Roger Holt	2B2	S	24	2	6	0	1	0	0	0	1	1	2	0	.167	.286	.167
Bruce Robinson	C3	L	26	4	5	0	0	0	0	0	0	0	4	0	.000	.000	.000
Dennis Sherrill	SS2,2B1	R	24	3	4	0	1	0	0	0	0	0	1	0	.250	.250	.250
Brad Gulden	C2	L	24	2	3	1	1	0	0	1	2	0	0	0	.333	.333	1.333
Paul Blair	OF12	R	36	12	2	2	0	0	0	0	0	0	0	0	.000	.000	.000

D. Werth, 1 G at C, 1 G at 3B

Pitcher	T	Age	G	GS	CG	ShO	IP	H	HR	BB	SO	W-L	Sv	ERA
Tommy John	L	37	36	36	16	6	265.1	270	13	56	78	22-9	0	3.43
Ron Guidry	L	29	37	29	5	3	219.2	215	19	80	166	17-10	1	3.56
Tom Underwood	L	26	38	27	2	2	187.0	163	15	66	116	13-9	2	3.66
Luis Tiant	R	39	25	25	3	0	136.1	139	10	50	84	8-9	0	4.89
Ed Figueroa†	R	31	15	9	0	0	58.0	90	3	24	16	3-3	1	6.98
Mike Griffin	R	23	13	9	0	0	54.0	64	6	23	25	2-4	0	4.83
Gaylord Perry†	R	41	10	8	0	0	50.2	65	2	18	28	4-4	0	4.44
Goose Gossage	R	28	64	0	0	0	99.0	74	5	37	103	6-2	33	2.27
Ron Davis	R	24	53	0	0	0	131.0	121	9	32	65	9-3	7	2.95
Rudy May	L	35	41	17	3	1	175.1	144	14	39	133	15-5	3	2.46
Doug Bird	R	30	22	1	0	0	50.2	47	3	14	17	3-0	1	2.66
Tim Lollar	L	24	14	1	0	0	32.1	33	3	20	13	1-0	2	3.34
Jim Kaat†	L	41	4	0	0	0	5.0	8	0	4	1	0-1	0	7.20

1980 Baltimore Orioles 2nd AL East 100-62 .617 3.0 GB

Earl Weaver

Player	Gm by Position	B	Age	G	AB	R	H	2B	3B	HR	RBI	BB	SO	SB	Avg	OBP	Slg
Rick Dempsey	C112,OF6,1B2*	R	30	119	362	51	95	26	3	9	40	36	45	3	.262	.333	.425
Eddie Murray	1B154,DH1	S	24	158	621	100	186	36	2	32	116	54	71	7	.300	.354	.519
Rich Dauer	2B137,3B35	R	27	152	557	71	158	32	0	2	63	46	19	3	.284	.338	.352
Doug DeCinces	3B142,1B1	R	29	145	489	64	122	23	2	16	64	49	83	11	.249	.319	.403
Mark Belanger	SS109	R	36	113	268	37	61	7	3	0	22	12	25	6	.228	.261	.276
Al Bumbry	OF160	L	33	160	645	118	205	29	9	9	53	78	75	44	.318	.392	.433
Ken Singleton	OF151,DH5	S	33	156	583	85	177	28	3	24	104	92	94	0	.304	.397	.485
Gary Roenicke	OF113	R	25	118	297	40	71	13	0	10	28	41	49	2	.239	.340	.384
Terry Crowley	DH65,1B3	L	33	92	233	33	67	8	0	12	50	29	21	0	.288	.364	.476
Kiko Garcia	SS96,2B27,OF1	R	26	111	311	27	62	8	0	1	27	24	57	8	.199	.255	.235
Dan Graham	C73,3B9,DH2*	L	25	86	266	32	74	7	1	15	54	14	40	0	.278	.310	.481
Lee May	DH58,1B7	R	37	78	222	20	54	10	2	7	31	15	53	2	.243	.289	.401
Pat Kelly	OF36,DH30	L	35	89	200	38	52	10	1	3	26	34	54	16	.260	.363	.365
John Lowenstein	OF91,DH3	L	33	104	196	38	61	8	0	4	27	32	29	7	.311	.403	.413
Bennie Ayala	DH41,OF19	R	29	76	170	28	45	8	1	10	33	19	21	0	.265	.335	.500
Lenn Sakata	2B34,SS4,DH1	R	26	43	83	12	16	3	2	1	9	6	10	2	.193	.244	.313
Mark Corey	OF34	R	24	36	36	7	10	2	0	1	2	5	7	0	.278	.366	.417
Floyd Rayford	3B4,DH1,2B1	R	22	8	18	1	4	0	0	0	1	0	5	0	.222	.222	.222
Wayne Krenchicki	SS6,DH1,2B1	L	25	9	14	1	2	0	0	0	0	1	3	0	.143	.200	.143
Dave Skaggs†	C2	R	29	2	5	0	1	0	0	0	0	0	1	0	.200	.200	.200
Drungo Hazewood	OF3	R	20	6	5	1	0	0	0	0	0	0	4	0	.000	.000	.000
Bobby Bonner	SS3	R	23	4	4	1	0	0	0	0	1	0	0	0	.000	.000	.000

R. Dempsey, 1 G at DH; D. Graham, 1 G at OF

Pitcher	T	Age	G	GS	CG	ShO	IP	H	HR	BB	SO	W-L	Sv	ERA
Mike Flanagan	L	28	37	37	12	2	251.1	278	27	71	128	16-13	0	4.12
Steve Stone	R	32	37	37	9	1	250.2	224	22	101	149	25-7	0	3.23
Scott McGregor	L	26	36	36	12	4	252.0	254	16	58	119	20-8	0	3.32
Jim Palmer	R	34	34	33	4	0	224.0	238	26	74	109	16-10	0	3.98
Mike Boddicker	R	22	1	1	0	0	7.1	6	1	5	4	0-1	0	6.14
Tim Stoddard	R	27	64	0	0	0	86.0	72	2	38	64	5-3	26	2.51
Tippy Martinez	L	30	53	0	0	0	80.2	69	5	34	68	4-4	10	3.01
Sammy Stewart	R	25	33	3	2	0	118.2	103	9	60	78	7-7	3	3.56
Dennis Martinez	R	25	25	12	2	0	99.2	103	12	44	42	6-4	1	3.97
Dave Ford	R	23	25	3	1	0	69.2	66	11	13	22	1-3	1	4.26
Paul Hartzell	R	26	6	0	0	0	17.2	22	3	9	5	0-2	0	6.62
Joe Kerrigan	R	25	1	0	0	0	2.1	3	0	0	1	0-0	0	3.86

1980 Milwaukee Brewers 3rd AL East 86-76 .531 17.0 GB

Buck Rodgers (26-21)/George Bamberger (47-45)/Buck Rodgers (13-10)

Player	Gm by Position	B	Age	G	AB	R	H	2B	3B	HR	RBI	BB	SO	SB	Avg	OBP	Slg
Charlie Moore	C105	R	27	111	320	42	93	13	2	2	30	24	28	10	.291	.336	.363
Cecil Cooper	1B142,DH11	L	30	153	622	96	219	33	4	25	122	39	42	17	.352	.387	.539
Paul Molitor	2B91,SS12,DH7*	R	23	111	450	81	137	29	2	9	37	48	48	34	.304	.372	.438
Jim Gantner	3B69,2B66,SS1	L	27	132	415	47	117	21	3	4	40	30	29	11	.282	.330	.376
Robin Yount	SS133,DH9	R	24	143	611	121	179	49	10	23	87	26	67	20	.293	.321	.519
Gorman Thomas	OF160,DH2	R	29	162	628	78	150	26	3	38	105	58	170	8	.239	.303	.471
Ben Oglivie	OF152,DH4	L	31	156	592	94	180	26	2	41	118	54	71	11	.304	.362	.563
Sixto Lezcano	OF108,DH4	R	26	112	411	51	94	19	3	18	55	39	75	1	.229	.298	.421
Dick Davis	DH63,OF38	R	26	106	365	50	99	26	2	4	30	11	43	5	.271	.297	.386
Don Money	3B55,DH14,1B14*	R	33	86	289	39	74	17	1	17	46	40	36	0	.256	.348	.498
Sal Bando	3B57,DH15,1B7	R	36	78	254	28	50	12	1	5	31	29	35	5	.197	.278	.311
Buck Martinez	C76	R	31	76	219	16	49	9	0	3	17	12	33	1	.224	.266	.306
Mark Brouhard	DH21,OF12,1B10	R	24	45	125	17	29	6	0	5	16	7	24	1	.232	.278	.400
Ed Romero	SS22,2B15,3B3	R	22	42	104	20	27	7	0	1	10	9	11	2	.260	.319	.356
Vic Harris	OF31,3B2,2B1	S	30	34	89	8	19	4	1	1	7	12	13	4	.213	.304	.315
John Poff	DH7,OF7,1B3	L	27	19	68	7	17	1	2	1	7	3	7	0	.250	.282	.368
Larry Hisle	DH17	R	33	17	60	16	17	0	0	6	16	14	7	1	.283	.421	.583
Ned Yost	C15	R	24	15	31	0	5	0	0	0	0	0	6	0	.161	.161	.161

P. Molitor, 1 G at 3B; D. Money, 2 G at 2B

Pitcher	T	Age	G	GS	CG	ShO	IP	H	HR	BB	SO	W-L	Sv	ERA
Moose Haas	R	24	33	33	14	3	252.1	246	25	56	146	16-15	0	3.10
Mike Caldwell	L	31	34	33	11	2	225.1	248	29	56	74	13-11	1	4.03
Larry Sorensen	R	24	35	29	8	2	195.2	242	13	45	54	12-10	1	3.68
Bill Travers	L	27	29	25	7	1	154.1	147	20	47	62	12-6	0	3.91
Paul Mitchell	R	30	17	11	1	1	89.1	92	7	15	29	5-5	1	3.53
Rickey Keeton	R	23	5	5	0	0	28.1	35	4	9	8	2-2	0	4.76
Jim Slaton	R	30	3	3	0	0	16.1	17	3	5	4	1-1	0	4.41
Dave LaPoint	L	20	5	3	0	0	15.0	17	2	13	5	1-0	1	6.00
Bill Castro	R	26	56	0	0	0	84.1	89	2	17	32	2-4	8	2.77
Bob McClure	L	28	52	5	2	0	90.2	83	6	37	47	5-8	10	3.08
Reggie Cleveland	R	32	45	13	5	2	154.1	150	9	49	54	11-9	4	3.73
Jerry Augustine	L	27	39	1	0	0	69.2	83	5	36	22	4-3	2	4.52
John Flinn	R	25	20	1	0	0	37.0	31	3	20	15	2-1	2	3.89
Dan Boitano	R	27	11	0	0	0	17.2	26	7	6	11	0-1	0	8.15
Fred Holdsworth	R	28	9	0	0	0	19.2	24	2	9	12	0-0	0	4.58

1980 Boston Red Sox 4th AL East 83-77 .519 19.0 GB

Don Zimmer (82-73)/Johnny Pesky (1-4)

Player	Gm by Position	B	Age	G	AB	R	H	2B	3B	HR	RBI	BB	SO	SB	Avg	OBP	Slg
Carlton Fisk	C115,DH5,OF5*	R	32	131	478	73	138	25	3	18	62	36	62	11	.289	.353	.467
Tony Perez	1B137,DH13	R	38	151	585	73	161	31	3	25	105	41	93	1	.275	.320	.467
Dave Stapleton	2B94,1B8,OF6*	R	26	106	449	61	144	33	5	7	45	13	32	3	.321	.338	.463
Glenn Hoffman	3B110,SS5,2B2	R	21	114	312	37	89	15	4	4	42	19	41	2	.285	.326	.397
Rick Burleson	SS155	R	29	155	644	89	179	29	2	8	51	62	51	12	.278	.341	.366
Dwight Evans	OF144,DH2	R	28	148	463	72	123	37	5	18	60	64	98	3	.266	.358	.484
Fred Lynn	OF110	L	28	110	415	67	125	32	3	12	61	58	39	12	.301	.383	.480
Jim Rice	OF109,DH15	R	27	124	504	81	148	22	6	24	86	30	87	8	.294	.336	.504
Carl Yastrzemski	DH49,OF39,1B16	L	40	105	364	49	100	21	1	15	50	44	38	0	.275	.350	.462
Butch Hobson	3B57,DH36	R	28	93	324	35	74	6	0	11	39	25	69	1	.228	.281	.349
Jim Dwyer	OF65,DH12,1B9	L	30	93	260	41	74	11	1	9	38	28	23	3	.285	.357	.438
Jerry Remy	2B60,OF1	L	27	63	230	24	72	7	2	0	9	10	14	14	.313	.339	.361
Dave Rader	C34,DH9	L	31	50	137	14	45	11	0	3	17	14	12	1	.328	.388	.474
Gary Hancock	OF27,DH12	L	26	46	115	9	33	6	0	4	19	3	11	0	.287	.300	.443
Gary Allenson	C24,DH6,3B5	R	25	36	70	9	25	6	0	0	10	13	11	2	.357	.452	.443
Jack Brohamer†	3B13,2B4,DH3	L	30	21	57	5	18	2	0	1	6	4	3	0	.316	.361	.404
Chico Walker	2B11,DH7	S	22	19	57	3	12	0	0	1	5	6	10	3	.211	.292	.263
Reid Nichols	OF9,DH1	R	21	12	36	5	8	0	1	0	3	3	8	0	.222	.282	.278
Rich Gedman	DH4,C2	L	20	9	24	2	5	0	0	0	1	0	5	0	.208	.208	.208
Ted Sizemore	2B8	R	35	9	23	1	5	1	0	0	0	0	0	0	.217	.217	.261
Larry Wolfe	3B14,DH4	R	27	18	23	3	3	1	0	1	4	0	5	0	.130	.125	.304
Julio Valdez	SS8	S	24	8	19	4	5	1	0	1	4	0	5	2	.263	.300	.474
Sam Bowen	OF6	R	27	7	13	0	2	0	0	0	0	2	3	1	.154	.267	.154
Stan Papi†	3B1	R	29	1	0	0	0	0	0	0	0	0	0	0	—	—	—
Tom Burgmeier	P62,OF1	L	36	62	0	0	0	0	0	0	0	0	0	0	—	—	—

C. Fisk, 3 G at 1B, 3 G at 3B; D. Stapleton, 3 G at DH, 2 G at 3B

Pitcher	T	Age	G	GS	CG	ShO	IP	H	HR	BB	SO	W-L	Sv	ERA
Mike Torrez	R	33	36	32	6	1	207.1	256	18	75	97	9-16	0	5.08
Dennis Eckersley	R	25	30	30	8	0	197.2	188	25	44	121	12-14	0	4.28
Steve Renko	R	35	32	23	1	0	165.1	180	17	56	90	9-9	0	4.19
John Tudor	L	26	16	13	5	0	92.1	81	4	31	45	8-5	0	3.02
Chuck Rainey	R	25	16	13	2	1	87.0	92	7	41	43	8-3	0	4.86
Bruce Hurst	L	22	12	7	0	0	30.2	39	4	16	16	2-2	0	9.10
Bobby Ojeda	L	22	7	7	0	0	26.0	39	2	14	12	1-1	0	6.92
Steve Crawford	R	22	6	4	2	0	32.1	41	3	8	10	2-0	0	3.62
Jack Billingham†	R	37	7	4	0	0	24.1	45	6	12	4	1-3	0	11.10
Tom Burgmeier	L	36	62	0	0	0	99.0	87	3	20	54	5-4	24	2.00
Bob Stanley	R	25	52	17	5	1	175.0	186	11	52	71	10-8	14	3.39
Dick Drago	R	35	43	7	1	0	132.2	127	17	44	63	7-7	3	4.14
Skip Lockwood	R	33	24	1	0	0	45.2	61	4	17	11	3-1	2	5.32
Bill Campbell	R	31	23	0	0	0	41.1	44	1	22	17	4-0	0	4.79
Keith MacWhorter	R	24	14	2	0	0	42.1	46	3	18	21	0-3	0	5.53
Win Remmerswaal	R	26	14	0	0	0	35.1	39	4	9	20	2-1	0	4.58
Luis Aponte	R	27	4	0	0	0	7.0	6	0	2	1	0-0	0	1.29

1980 Detroit Tigers 5th AL East 84-78 .519 19.0 GB

Sparky Anderson

Player	Gm by Position	B	Age	G	AB	R	H	2B	3B	HR	RBI	BB	SO	SB	Avg	OBP	Slg
Lance Parrish	C121,DH16,1B5*	R	24	144	553	79	158	34	6	24	82	31	109	6	.286	.325	.499
Richie Hebner	1B61,3B32,DH5	L	32	104	341	48	99	10	7	12	82	38	45	0	.290	.360	.466
Lou Whitaker	2B143	L	23	145	477	68	111	19	1	1	45	73	79	8	.233	.331	.283
Tom Brookens	3B138,2B9,DH1*	R	26	151	509	64	140	25	9	10	66	32	71	13	.275	.315	.418
Alan Trammell	SS144	R	22	146	560	107	168	21	5	9	65	69	63	12	.300	.376	.404
Ricky Peters	OF109,DH11	S	24	133	477	79	139	19	7	2	42	54	48	13	.291	.369	.373
Al Cowens†	OF107,DH1	R	28	108	403	58	113	15	3	5	42	37	40	5	.280	.339	.370
Steve Kemp	OF85,DH46	L	25	135	508	88	149	23	3	21	101	69	64	5	.293	.376	.474
Champ Summers	DH64,OF47,1B1	L	34	120	347	61	103	19	1	17	60	52	52	4	.297	.393	.504
John Wockenfuss	1B52,DH28,C25*	R	31	126	372	56	102	13	2	16	65	68	64	1	.274	.390	.449
Kirk Gibson	OF49,DH1	L	23	51	175	23	46	2	1	9	16	10	45	4	.263	.303	.440
Jim Lentine†	OF55,DH9	R	25	67	161	19	42	8	1	1	17	28	30	2	.261	.377	.342
Tim Corcoran	1B48,OF18,DH5	L	27	84	153	20	44	7	1	3	18	22	10	0	.288	.379	.405
Dave Stegman	OF57,DH2	R	26	65	130	12	23	5	0	2	9	14	23	1	.177	.255	.262
Jason Thompson†	1B36	L	25	36	126	10	27	5	0	4	20	13	26	0	.214	.289	.349
Stan Papi†	2B31,3B11,SS5*	R	29	46	114	12	27	3	4	3	17	5	24	0	.237	.267	.412
Duffy Dyer	C37,DH10	R	34	48	108	11	20	1	0	4	11	13	34	0	.185	.273	.306
Mark Wagner	SS28,3B9,2B6	R	26	45	72	5	17	1	0	0	3	7	11	0	.236	.304	.250
Lynn Jones	OF17,DH6	R	27	30	55	9	14	2	2	0	6	10	5	1	.255	.364	.364
Dan Gonzales	DH1,OF1	L	26	2	7	1	1	0	0	0	0	0	1	0	.143	.143	.143

L. Parrish, 5 G at OF; T. Brookens, 1 G at SS; J. Wockenfuss, 23 G at OF; S. Papi, 1 G at 1B

Pitcher	T	Age	G	GS	CG	ShO	IP	H	HR	BB	SO	W-L	Sv	ERA
Jack Morris	R	25	36	36	11	2	250.0	252	20	87	112	16-15	0	4.18
Milt Wilcox	R	30	32	31	13	1	198.2	201	24	68	97	13-11	0	4.48
Dan Schatzeder	L	25	32	26	9	2	192.2	178	23	58	94	11-13	0	4.02
Dan Petry	R	21	27	25	4	3	164.2	156	9	83	88	10-9	0	3.94
Mark Fidrych	R	25	9	9	1	0	44.1	58	5	20	16	2-3	0	5.68
Aurelio Lopez	R	31	67	1	0	0	124.0	125	15	45	97	13-6	21	3.77
Pat Underwood	L	23	49	7	0	0	112.2	121	12	35	60	3-6	5	3.59
Dave Rozema	R	23	42	13	2	1	144.2	152	11	49	49	6-9	4	3.92
Roger Weaver	R	25	19	6	0	0	63.2	56	5	34	42	3-4	0	4.10
Dave Tobik	R	27	17	1	0	0	61.0	61	7	21	34	1-0	0	3.98
Bruce Robbins	L	20	15	6	0	0	51.2	60	12	28	23	4-2	0	6.62
John Hiller	L	37	11	0	0	0	30.2	38	3	14	18	1-0	0	4.40
Jerry Ujdur	R	23	9	2	0	0	21.1	36	5	10	8	1-0	0	7.59
Jack Billingham†	R	37	8	0	0	0	7.1	11	1	6	3	0-0	0	7.36

1980 Cleveland Indians 6th AL East 79-81 .494 23.0 GB

Dave Garcia

Player	Gm by Position	B	Age	G	AB	R	H	2B	3B	HR	RBI	BB	SO	SB	Avg	OBP	Slg
Ron Hassey	C113,DH7,1B3	L	27	130	390	43	124	18	4	8	65	49	51	0	.318	.390	.446
Mike Hargrove	1B160	L	30	160	589	86	179	22	2	11	85	111	36	4	.304	.415	.404
Jack Brohamer†	2B47,DH1	L	30	53	142	13	32	5	1	1	15	14	6	0	.225	.291	.296
Toby Harrah	3B156,DH3,SS2	R	31	160	561	100	150	22	4	11	72	98	60	17	.267	.379	.380
Tom Veryzer	SS108	R	27	109	358	28	97	12	0	2	28	10	25	0	.271	.303	.321
Rick Manning	OF139	L	25	140	471	55	110	17	4	3	52	63	66	12	.234	.321	.306
Jorge Orta	OF120,DH7	L	29	129	481	78	140	18	3	10	64	71	44	6	.291	.379	.403
Miguel Dilone	OF118,DH11	S	25	132	528	82	180	30	9	0	40	28	45	61	.341	.375	.432
Joe Charboneau	OF67,DH57	R	25	131	453	76	131	17	2	23	87	49	70	2	.289	.358	.488
Alan Bannister†	2B41,OF40,3B3*	R	28	81	262	41	86	17	4	1	32	28	25	9	.328	.388	.435
Jerry Dybzinski	SS73,2B29,3B4*	R	24	114	248	32	57	11	1	1	23	13	35	4	.230	.273	.294
Bo Diaz	C75	R	27	76	207	15	47	11	2	3	32	7	27	1	.227	.250	.343
Gary Alexander	DH40,C13,OF2	R	27	76	178	22	40	7	1	5	31	17	52	0	.225	.288	.360
Cliff Johnson†	DH45	R	32	54	174	25	40	3	1	6	28	25	30	0	.230	.320	.362
Duane Kuiper	2B42	L	30	42	149	10	42	5	0	0	9	13	8	0	.282	.337	.315
Dave Rosello	2B43,3B22,SS3*	R	30	71	117	16	29	3	0	2	12	9	19	0	.248	.295	.325
Wendell Alston	OF26,DH6	L	27	52	54	11	12	1	2	0	5	5	7	2	.222	.302	.315
Gary Gray	DH9,1B6,OF6	R	27	28	54	4	8	1	0	2	4	3	13	0	.148	.193	.278
Ron Pruitt†	OF6,DH2,3B2	R	28	23	36	1	11	1	0	0	4	4	6	0	.306	.366	.333
Andres Mora	OF3	R	25	9	18	0	2	0	0	0	0	0	0	0	.111	.111	.111

A. Bannister, 2 G at SS; J. Dybzinski, 2 G at DH; D. Rosello, 1 G at DH

Pitcher	T	Age	G	GS	CG	ShO	IP	H	HR	BB	SO	W-L	Sv	ERA
Len Barker	R	24	36	36	8	1	246.1	237	17	92	187	19-12	0	4.17
Rick Waits	L	28	33	33	9	2	224.1	231	18	82	109	13-14	0	4.45
Dan Spillner	R	28	34	30	7	1	194.1	225	23	74	100	16-11	0	5.28
Wayne Garland	R	29	25	20	4	1	150.1	163	18	48	55	6-9	0	4.61
John Denny	R	27	16	16	4	1	108.2	116	4	47	59	8-6	0	4.39
Ross Grimsley†	L	30	14	11	2	0	74.2	103	11	24	18	4-5	0	6.75
Sid Monge	L	29	67	0	0	0	94.1	80	12	40	61	3-5	14	3.53
Victor Cruz	R	22	55	0	0	0	86.0	71	10	27	88	6-7	12	3.45
Mike Stanton	R	27	51	0	0	0	85.2	98	5	44	74	1-3	5	5.46
Bob Owchinko	L	25	29	14	1	1	114.1	138	13	47	66	2-9	0	5.27
Sandy Wihtol	R	25	17	0	0	0	35.1	35	2	14	20	1-0	1	3.57
Mike Paxton	R	26	4	0	0	0	7.2	13	4	6	6	0-0	0	12.91
Don Collins	L	27	4	0	0	0	6.0	9	0	7	0	0-0	0	7.50

1980 Toronto Blue Jays 7th AL East 67-95 .414 36.0 GB

Bobby Mattick

Player	Gm by Position	B	Age	G	AB	R	H	2B	3B	HR	RBI	BB	SO	SB	Avg	OBP	Slg
Ernie Whitt	C105	L	28	106	295	23	70	12	2	6	34	22	30	1	.237	.288	.353
John Mayberry	1B136,DH8	L	31	149	501	62	124	19	2	30	82	77	80	0	.248	.349	.473
Damaso Garcia	2B138,DH1	R	23	140	543	50	151	30	7	4	46	12	55	13	.278	.296	.381
Roy Howell	3B138,DH2	L	26	142	528	51	142	28	9	10	57	50	92	0	.269	.335	.413
Alfredo Griffin	SS155	S	22	155	653	63	166	26	15	2	41	24	58	18	.254	.283	.349
Barry Bonnell	OF122,DH3	R	26	130	463	55	124	22	4	13	56	37	59	3	.268	.322	.417
Lloyd Moseby	OF104,DH6	L	20	114	389	44	89	24	1	9	46	25	85	4	.229	.281	.365
Bob Bailor	OF98,SS12,3B11*	R	28	117	347	44	82	14	2	1	16	36	33	12	.236	.311	.297
Otto Velez	DH97,1B3	R	29	104	357	54	96	12	3	20	62	54	86	0	.269	.365	.487
Al Woods	OF88,DH13	L	26	109	373	54	112	18	2	15	47	37	35	4	.300	.364	.480
Garth Iorg	2B32,3B20,OF14*	R	25	80	222	24	55	10	1	2	14	12	39	2	.248	.286	.329
Bob Davis	C89	R	28	91	218	18	47	11	0	4	19	12	25	0	.216	.260	.321
Rick Bosetti	OF51	R	26	53	188	24	40	7	1	4	18	15	29	4	.213	.277	.324
Doug Ault	1B32,DH21,OF1	R	30	64	144	12	28	5	1	3	15	14	23	0	.194	.273	.306
Danny Ainge	OF29,3B3,DH2*	R	21	38	111	11	27	6	1	0	4	2	29	3	.243	.263	.315
Willie Upshaw	1B14,DH12,OF1	L	23	34	61	10	13	3	1	1	5	6	14	1	.213	.284	.344
Steve Braun†	DH13,3B1	L	32	37	55	4	15	2	0	1	9	8	5	0	.273	.365	.364
Joe Cannon	OF33,DH1	L	26	70	50	16	4	0	0	0	4	0	14	2	.080	.098	.080
Paul Hodgson	OF11,DH3	R	20	20	41	5	9	0	1	1	5	3	12	0	.220	.273	.341
Domingo Ramos	2B2,SS2,DH1	R	22	5	16	0	2	0	0	0	0	2	5	0	.125	.222	.125
Mike Macha	3B2,C1	R	26	5	8	0	0	0	0	0	0	0	1	0	.000	.000	.000
Pat Kelly	C3	R	24	3	7	0	2	0	0	0	0	0	4	0	.286	.286	.286
Dave Stieb	P34,OF1	R	22	36	1	0	0	0	0	0	0	0	0	0	.000	.000	.000

B. Bailor, 3 G at P, 1 G at DH, 1 G at 2B; G. Iorg, 11 G at 1B, 2 G at DH, 1 G at SS; D. Ainge, 1 G at 2B

Pitcher	T	Age	G	GS	CG	ShO	IP	H	HR	BB	SO	W-L	Sv	ERA
Jim Clancy	R	24	34	34	15	2	250.2	217	19	128	152	13-16	0	3.30
Dave Stieb	R	22	34	32	14	4	242.2	232	12	83	108	12-15	0	3.71
Paul Mirabella	L	26	33	22	3	1	130.2	151	11	66	53	5-12	0	4.34
Jesse Jefferson†	R	31	29	18	2	2	121.2	130	12	52	53	4-13	0	5.47
Jackson Todd	R	28	12	12	4	0	85.0	90	14	30	44	5-2	0	4.02
Jack Kucek	R	27	23	12	0	0	68.0	83	9	41	35	3-8	1	6.75
Luis Leal	R	23	13	10	1	0	59.2	72	6	31	26	3-4	0	4.53
Dave Lemanczyk†	R	29	10	8	0	0	43.1	57	4	15	10	2-5	0	5.40
Jerry Garvin	L	24	61	0	0	0	82.2	70	6	27	52	4-7	8	2.29
Joey McLaughlin	R	23	55	10	0	0	135.2	159	16	53	70	6-9	4	4.51
Mike Barlow	R	32	40	1	0	0	55.0	57	4	21	19	3-1	5	4.09
Tom Buskey	R	33	33	0	0	0	66.2	68	11	26	34	3-1	0	4.46
Balor Moore	L	29	31	3	0	0	64.2	76	6	31	22	1-1	1	5.29
Mike Willis	L	29	20	0	0	0	26.1	25	3	11	14	2-1	3	1.71
Ken Schrom	R	25	17	0	0	0	31.0	32	2	19	13	1-0	1	5.23
Bob Bailor	R	28	3	0	0	0	2.1	4	0	1	0	0-0	0	7.71

1980 Kansas City Royals 1st AL West 97-65 .599 —

Jim Frey

Player	Gm by Position	B	Age	G	AB	R	H	2B	3B	HR	RBI	BB	SO	SB	Avg	OBP	Slg
Darrell Porter	C81,DH34	L	28	118	418	51	104	14	2	7	51	69	50	1	.249	.354	.342
Willie Aikens	1B138,DH13	L	25	151	543	70	151	24	0	20	98	64	88	1	.278	.356	.433
Frank White	2B153	R	29	154	560	70	148	23	4	7	60	19	69	19	.264	.289	.357
George Brett	3B112,1B1	L	27	117	449	87	175	33	9	24	118	58	22	15	.390	.454	.664
U.L. Washington	SS152	S	26	153	549	79	150	16	11	6	53	53	78	20	.273	.336	.375
Willie Wilson	OF159	S	24	161	705	133	230	28	15	3	49	28	81	79	.326	.357	.421
Clint Hurdle	OF126	L	22	130	395	50	116	31	2	10	60	34	61	0	.294	.349	.458
Amos Otis	OF105	R	33	107	394	56	99	16	3	10	53	39	70	16	.251	.316	.383
Hal McRae	DH110,OF9	R	34	124	489	73	145	39	5	14	83	29	56	10	.297	.342	.483
John Wathan	C77,OF35,1B12	R	30	126	453	57	138	14	7	6	58	50	42	17	.305	.377	.406
Dave Chalk	3B33,2B17,DH6*	R	29	69	167	19	42	10	1	1	20	18	27	1	.251	.326	.341
Jamie Quirk	3B28,C15,OF7*	L	25	62	163	13	45	5	0	5	21	7	24	3	.276	.305	.399
Pete LaCock	1B86,OF29	L	28	114	156	14	32	6	0	1	18	17	10	1	.205	.284	.263
Rusty Torres	OF40,DH1	S	31	51	72	10	12	1	0	0	3	8	7	1	.167	.250	.167
Rance Mulliniks	SS18,2B14	L	24	36	54	8	14	3	0	0	6	7	10	0	.259	.339	.315
Jose Cardenal†	OF23	R	36	25	53	8	18	2	0	0	5	5	5	0	.340	.377	.377
Bob Detherage	OF20	R	25	20	26	2	8	2	0	1	7	1	4	1	.308	.333	.500
Steve Braun†	OF5,DH1	L	32	14	23	0	1	0	0	0	1	2	2	0	.043	.120	.043
Jerry Terrell	OF7,1B3,2B3*	R	33	23	16	4	1	0	0	0	0	0	0	0	.063	.063	.063
Onix Concepcion	SS6	R	22	12	15	1	2	0	0	0	2	0	1	0	.133	.133	.133
Manny Castillo	3B3,DH2,2B1	S	23	7	10	1	2	0	0	0	0	0	1	0	.200	.200	.200
Ken Phelps	1B2	L	25	3	4	0	0	0	0	0	0	0	2	0	.000	.000	.000
German Barranca		L	23	7	0	3	0	0	0	0	0	0	0	0	—	—	—

D. Chalk, 1 G at SS; J. Quirk, 1 G at DH, 1 G at 1B; J. Terrell, 1 G at DH, 1 G at P

Pitcher	T	Age	G	GS	CG	ShO	IP	H	HR	BB	SO	W-L	Sv	ERA
Dennis Leonard	R	29	38	38	9	3	280.1	271	30	80	155	20-11	0	3.79
Larry Gura	L	32	36	36	16	4	283.1	272	20	76	113	18-10	0	2.95
Paul Splittorff	L	33	34	33	4	0	204.0	236	17	43	53	14-11	0	4.15
Rich Gale	R	26	32	28	6	1	190.2	169	16	78	97	13-9	1	3.92
Renie Martin	R	24	32	20	2	0	137.1	133	18	70	68	10-10	2	4.39
Steve Busby	R	30	11	6	0	0	42.1	59	3	19	12	1-3	0	6.17
Dan Quisenberry	R	27	75	0	0	0	128.1	129	5	27	37	12-7	33	3.09
Marty Pattin	R	37	37	0	0	0	89.0	97	7	23	40	4-0	4	3.64
Gary Christenson	L	27	24	0	0	0	31.1	35	4	18	16	3-0	1	5.17
Rawly Eastwick	R	29	14	0	0	0	22.0	37	2	8	5	0-1	0	5.32
Jeff Twitty	L	22	13	0	0	0	22.1	33	4	7	9	2-1	0	6.04
Ken Brett	L	31	8	0	0	0	13.1	8	0	5	4	0-0	1	0.00
Craig Chamberlain	R	23	5	0	0	0	9.1	10	3	5	3	0-1	0	6.75
Mike Jones	L	20	3	1	0	0	4.2	6	0	5	2	0-1	0	11.57
Jerry Terrell	R	33	1	0	0	0	1.0	1	0	1	0	0-0	0	0.00

1980 Oakland Athletics 2nd AL West 83-79 .512 14.0 GB

Billy Martin

Player	Gm by Position	B	Age	G	AB	R	H	2B	3B	HR	RBI	BB	SO	SB	Avg	OBP	Slg
Jim Essian	C68,DH11,1B1	R	29	87	285	19	66	11	0	5	29	30	18	1	.232	.302	.323
Dave Revering	1B95,DH5	L	27	106	376	48	109	21	5	15	62	32	37	1	.290	.344	.492
Dave McKay	2B62,3B54,SS10	S	30	123	295	29	72	16	1	1	29	10	57	1	.244	.283	.315
Wayne Gross	3B99,1B10,DH1	L	28	113	366	45	103	20	3	14	61	44	39	5	.281	.355	.467
Mario Guerrero	SS116	R	30	116	381	32	91	16	2	2	23	19	32	3	.239	.273	.307
Tony Armas	OF158	R	26	158	628	87	175	18	8	35	109	29	128	5	.279	.310	.500
Dwayne Murphy	OF158	L	25	159	573	86	157	18	2	13	68	102	96	26	.274	.384	.380
Rickey Henderson	OF157,DH1	R	21	158	591	111	179	22	4	9	53	117	54	100	.303	.420	.399
Mitchell Page	DH101	L	28	110	348	58	85	10	4	17	51	35	87	14	.244	.311	.443
Jeff Newman	1B60,C55,DH9*	R	31	127	438	37	102	19	1	15	56	25	81	3	.233	.273	.384
Mike Heath	C47,DH31,OF8	R	25	92	305	27	74	10	2	1	33	16	28	3	.243	.280	.298
Rob Picciolo	SS49,2B47,OF1	R	27	95	271	32	65	9	2	5	18	2	63	1	.240	.245	.343
Mickey Klutts	3B62,SS8,2B7*	R	25	75	197	20	53	14	0	4	21	13	41	1	.269	.313	.401
Jeff Cox	2B58	R	24	59	169	20	36	3	0	0	9	14	23	8	.213	.273	.231
Mike Davis	OF18,1B7,DH6	L	21	51	95	11	20	2	1	1	8	7	14	2	.211	.262	.284
Orlando Gonzalez	1B11,DH8,OF2	L	28	25	70	10	17	0	0	0	1	9	8	0	.243	.329	.243
Mike Edwards	2B23,DH5,OF1	R	27	46	59	10	14	0	0	0	3	1	5	1	.237	.250	.237
Randy Elliott	DH11	R	29	14	39	4	5	0	0	1	1	1	13	0	.128	.150	.205
Ray Cosey		L	24	9	9	0	1	0	0	0	0	0	0	0	.111	.111	.111

J. Newman, 2 G at 3B, 1 G at 2B; M. Klutts, 1 G at DH

Pitcher	T	Age	G	GS	CG	ShO	IP	H	HR	BB	SO	W-L	Sv	ERA
Rick Langford	R	28	35	33	28	2	290.0	276	29	64	102	19-12	0	3.26
Mike Norris	R	25	33	33	24	1	284.1	215	18	83	180	22-9	0	2.53
Matt Keough	R	24	34	32	20	2	250.0	218	24	94	121	16-13	0	2.92
Steve McCatty	R	26	33	31	11	1	221.2	202	27	99	114	14-14	0	3.86
Brian Kingman	R	25	32	30	10	1	211.1	209	21	82	116	8-20	0	3.83
Bob Lacey	L	26	47	1	1	1	79.2	68	7	21	45	3-2	6	2.94
Jeff Jones	R	23	35	0	0	0	44.1	32	2	26	34	1-3	5	2.84
Dave Hamilton	L	32	21	1	0	0	30.0	44	6	28	23	0-3	0	11.40
Dave Beard	R	20	13	0	0	0	16.0	12	0	7	12	0-1	1	3.38
Craig Minetto	L	26	7	1	0	0	8.0	11	2	3	5	0-2	1	7.88
Rick Lysander	R	27	5	0	0	0	13.2	24	3	4	5	0-0	0	7.90
Ernie Camacho	R	25	5	0	0	0	11.2	20	2	5	9	0-0	0	6.94
Mark Souza	L	26	5	0	0	0	7.0	9	1	5	2	0-0	0	7.71
Alan Wirth	R	23	2	0	0	0	2.0	3	0	1	0	0-0	0	4.50
Rich Bordi	R	21	1	0	0	0	2.0	4	0	0	0	0-0	0	4.50

854 Seasons: Team Rosters

1980 Minnesota Twins 3rd AL West 77-84 .478 19.5 GB

Gene Mauch (54-71)/John Goryl (23-13)

Player	Gm by Position	B	Age	G	AB	R	H	2B	3B	HR	RBI	BB	SO	SB	Avg	OBP	Slg
Butch Wynegar	C142,DH1	S	24	146	486	61	124	18	3	5	57	63	36	3	.255	.339	.335
Ron Jackson	1B119,OF15,3B2*	R	27	131	396	48	105	29	3	5	42	28	41	1	.265	.316	.391
Rob Wilfong	2B120,OF6	L	26	131	416	55	103	16	5	8	45	34	61	10	.248	.308	.368
John Castino	3B138,SS18	R	25	150	546	67	165	17	7	13	64	29	67	7	.302	.336	.430
Roy Smalley	SS125,DH3,1B3	S	27	133	486	64	135	24	1	12	63	65	63	3	.278	.359	.405
Hosken Powell	OF129	L	25	137	485	58	127	17	5	6	35	32	46	14	.262	.312	.355
Rick Sofield	OF126,DH2	L	23	131	417	52	103	18	4	9	49	24	92	4	.247	.287	.374
Ken Landreaux	OF120,DH6	L	25	129	484	56	136	23	11	7	62	39	42	8	.281	.334	.417
Jose Morales	DH86,C2,1B2	R	35	97	241	36	73	17	2	8	36	22	19	0	.303	.361	.490
Pete Mackanin	2B71,SS30,DH5*	R	28	108	319	31	85	18	0	4	35	14	34	6	.266	.296	.361
Mike Cubbage	1B72,3B32,DH1*	L	29	103	285	29	70	9	0	8	42	23	37	0	.246	.301	.361
Glenn Adams	DH81,OF12	L	32	99	262	32	75	11	2	6	38	15	26	2	.286	.320	.412
Dave Edwards	OF72,DH3	R	26	81	200	26	50	9	1	2	20	12	51	2	.250	.294	.335
Danny Goodwin	DH38,1B13	L	26	55	115	12	23	5	0	1	11	17	32	0	.200	.301	.270
Bombo Rivera	OF37,DH1	R	27	44	113	13	25	7	0	3	10	4	20	0	.221	.248	.363
Sal Butera	C32,DH2	R	27	34	85	4	23	1	0	0	2	3	6	0	.271	.300	.282
Willie Norwood	OF17,DH9	R	29	34	73	6	12	2	0	1	8	3	13	1	.164	.197	.233
Gary Ward	OF12	R	26	13	41	11	19	6	2	1	10	3	6	0	.463	.489	.780
Jesus Vega	DH9,1B2	R	24	12	30	3	5	0	0	0	4	3	7	1	.167	.242	.167
Greg Johnston	OF14	L	25	14	27	3	5	3	0	0	1	2	4	0	.185	.233	.296
Bob Randall	3B4,2B1	R	32	5	15	2	3	1	0	0	0	1	0	0	.200	.250	.267
Lenny Faedo	SS5	R	20	5	8	1	2	1	0	0	0	0	0	0	.250	.250	.375

R. Jackson, 1 G at DH; P. Mackanin, 4 G at 1B, 3 G at 3B; M. Cubbage, 1 G at 2B

Pitcher	T	Age	G	GS	CG	ShO	IP	H	HR	BB	SO	W-L	Sv	ERA
Geoff Zahn	L	34	38	35	13	5	232.2	273	17	66	96	14-18	0	4.41
Jerry Koosman	L	37	38	34	8	0	243.1	252	24	69	149	16-13	2	4.03
Roger Erickson	R	23	32	27	7	0	191.1	198	13	56	97	7-13	0	3.25
Darrell Jackson	L	24	32	25	1	0	172.0	161	15	69	90	9-9	1	3.87
Pete Redfern	R	25	23	16	2	0	104.2	117	11	33	73	7-7	2	4.56
Fredie Arroyo	R	28	21	11	1	1	92.1	97	7	32	27	6-6	0	4.68
Al Williams	R	26	18	9	3	0	77.0	73	9	30	35	6-2	1	3.51
Terry Felton	R	22	5	4	0	0	17.2	20	2	9	14	0-3	0	7.13
Doug Corbett	R	27	73	0	0	0	136.1	102	7	42	89	8-6	23	1.98
John Verhoeven	R	26	44	0	0	0	99.2	109	10	29	42	3-4	0	3.97
Mike Kinnunen	L	22	21	0	0	0	24.2	29	1	9	8	0-0	0	5.11
Mike Marshall	R	37	18	0	0	0	32.1	42	2	12	13	1-3	1	6.12
Mike Bacsik	R	28	10	0	0	0	23.0	26	1	11	9	0-0	0	4.30
Bob Veselic	R	24	1	0	0	0	4.0	3	1	1	2	0-0	0	4.50

1980 Texas Rangers 4th AL West 76-85 .472 20.5 GB

Pat Corrales

Player	Gm by Position	B	Age	G	AB	R	H	2B	3B	HR	RBI	BB	SO	SB	Avg	OBP	Slg
Jim Sundberg	C151	R	29	151	505	59	138	24	1	10	63	64	67	2	.273	.353	.384
Pat Putnam	1B137,DH1,3B1	L	26	147	410	42	108	16	2	13	55	36	49	0	.263	.319	.407
Bump Wills	2B144	S	27	146	578	102	152	31	5	5	58	51	71	34	.263	.322	.360
Buddy Bell	3B120,SS3	R	28	129	490	76	161	24	4	17	83	40	39	3	.329	.379	.498
Pepe Frias†	SS106,3B7,2B2	R	31	116	227	27	55	5	1	0	10	4	23	5	.242	.256	.273
Al Oliver	OF157,DH4,1B1	L	33	163	656	96	209	43	3	19	117	39	47	5	.319	.357	.480
Mickey Rivers	OF141,DH4	L	31	147	630	96	210	32	6	7	60	20	34	18	.333	.353	.437
Jim Norris	OF82,1B10,DH1	L	31	119	174	23	43	5	0	0	16	23	16	6	.247	.327	.276
Richie Zisk	DH86,OF37	R	31	135	448	48	130	17	1	19	77	39	72	0	.290	.344	.460
Rusty Staub	DH57,1B30,OF14	L	36	109	340	42	102	23	2	9	55	39	18	1	.300	.370	.459
John Grubb	OF77,DH8	L	31	110	274	40	76	12	1	9	32	42	35	2	.277	.374	.427
Dave Roberts	3B37,SS33,C22*	R	29	101	235	27	56	4	0	10	30	13	38	0	.238	.280	.383
Billy Sample	OF72,DH4	R	25	99	204	29	53	10	0	4	19	18	15	8	.260	.335	.368
John Ellis	1B39,DH20,C3	R	31	73	182	12	43	9	1	1	23	14	23	3	.236	.290	.313
Bud Harrelson	SS87,2B2	S	36	87	180	26	49	6	0	1	9	29	23	4	.272	.373	.322
Mike Richardt	2B20,DH1	R	22	22	71	2	16	2	0	0	8	1	7	0	.225	.236	.254
Tucker Ashford	3B12,SS2	R	25	15	32	2	4	0	0	0	3	3	3	0	.125	.200	.125
Nelson Norman	SS17	S	22	17	32	4	7	0	0	0	1	1	1	0	.219	.242	.219
Danny Walton	DH1	R	32	10	10	2	2	0	0	0	1	3	5	0	.200	.385	.200
Odie Davis	SS13,3B1	R	24	17	8	0	1	0	0	0	0	0	2	0	.125	.125	.125
Mike Hart	OF2	S	28	5	4	1	1	0	0	0	0	1	1	0	.250	.400	.250

D. Roberts, 5 G at OF, 4 G at 1B, 4 G at 2B

Pitcher	T	Age	G	GS	CG	ShO	IP	H	HR	BB	SO	W-L	Sv	ERA
Jon Matlack	L	30	35	34	8	1	234.2	265	17	48	142	10-10	1	3.68
Doc Medich	R	31	34	32	6	0	204.1	230	13	56	91	14-11	0	3.92
Fergie Jenkins	R	36	29	29	12	0	198.0	190	22	52	129	12-12	0	3.77
Gaylord Perry†	R	41	24	24	6	2	155.0	159	12	46	107	6-9	0	3.43
Steve Comer	R	26	12	11	0	0	41.2	65	5	22	9	2-4	0	7.99
Ken Clay	R	26	8	8	0	0	43.0	43	4	29	17	2-3	0	4.60
Ed Figueroa†	R	31	8	8	0	0	39.2	62	9	12	9	0-7	0	5.90
John Butcher	R	23	6	6	1	0	35.1	34	2	13	27	3-3	0	4.08
Don Kainer	R	24	4	3	0	0	19.2	22	0	9	10	0-0	0	1.83
Danny Darwin	R	24	53	2	0	0	109.2	98	4	50	104	13-4	8	2.63
Sparky Lyle†	L	35	49	0	0	0	80.2	97	9	28	43	3-2	8	4.69
Jim Kern	R	31	38	1	0	0	63.1	65	4	45	40	3-11	2	4.83
John Henry Johnson	L	23	33	0	0	0	38.2	27	2	15	44	2-2	4	2.33
Dave Rajsich	L	28	24	1	0	0	48.1	56	7	22	35	2-1	2	5.96
Bob Babcock	R	30	19	0	0	0	23.1	20	3	8	15	1-2	0	4.63
Charlie Hough†	R	32	16	2	2	1	61.1	54	2	37	47	2-2	0	3.96
Adrian Devine	R	28	13	0	0	0	28.0	49	4	9	8	1-1	0	4.82
Brian Allard	R	22	5	2	0	0	14.1	13	0	10	10	0-1	0	5.65
Jerry Don Gleaton	L	22	5	0	0	0	7.0	5	0	4	2	0-0	0	2.57
Dennis Lewallyn	R	26	4	0	0	0	5.2	7	0	4	1	0-0	0	7.94

1980 Chicago White Sox 5th AL West 70-90 .438 26.0 GB

Tony La Russa

Player	Gm by Position	B	Age	G	AB	R	H	2B	3B	HR	RBI	BB	SO	SB	Avg	OBP	Slg
Bruce Kimm	C98	R	29	100	251	20	61	10	1	0	19	17	26	1	.243	.290	.291
Mike Squires	1B114,C2	L	28	131	343	38	97	11	3	2	33	33	24	8	.283	.347	.350
Jim Morrison	2B161,DH1,SS1	R	27	162	604	66	171	40	0	15	57	36	74	9	.283	.329	.424
Kevin Bell	3B83,DH3,SS3	R	24	92	191	16	34	5	2	1	11	29	37	0	.178	.284	.241
Todd Cruz†	SS90	R	24	90	293	23	68	11	1	2	18	9	54	2	.232	.259	.297
Chet Lemon	OF139,DH6,2B1	R	25	147	514	76	150	32	6	11	51	71	56	6	.292	.388	.442
Harold Baines	OF137,DH1	L	21	141	491	55	125	23	6	13	49	19	65	2	.255	.281	.405
Wayne Nordhagen	OF74,DH32	R	31	123	415	45	115	22	4	15	59	10	45	0	.277	.294	.458
Lamar Johnson	1B80,DH66	R	29	147	541	51	150	26	3	13	81	47	53	2	.277	.331	.409
Bob Molinaro	OF49,DH47	L	30	119	344	48	100	16	4	5	36	26	29	18	.291	.348	.404
Greg Pryor	SS76,3B41,2B5*	R	30	122	338	32	81	18	4	1	29	12	35	2	.240	.265	.325
Thad Bosley	OF52	L	23	70	147	12	33	2	0	2	14	10	27	3	.224	.272	.279
Marv Foley	C64,1B3	L	26	68	137	14	29	5	0	4	15	9	22	0	.212	.263	.336
Alan Bannister†	OF23,3B17	R	28	45	130	16	25	6	0	0	9	12	16	5	.192	.259	.238
Junior Moore	3B34,OF3,DH2*	R	27	45	121	9	31	4	1	1	10	7	11	0	.256	.295	.331
C. Washington†	OF23,DH2	L	25	32	90	15	26	4	2	1	12	5	19	4	.289	.333	.411
Leo Sutherland	OF23	L	22	34	89	9	23	3	0	0	5	1	11	4	.258	.264	.292
Glenn Borgmann	C32	R	30	32	87	10	19	2	0	2	14	14	9	0	.218	.320	.310
Ron Pruitt†	OF11,DH7,C5*	R	28	33	70	8	21	2	0	2	11	8	7	0	.300	.372	.414
Rusty Kuntz	OF34	R	25	36	62	5	14	4	0	0	3	5	13	1	.226	.284	.290
Fran Mullins	3B21	R	23	21	62	9	12	4	0	0	3	9	8	0	.194	.292	.258
Ricky Seilheimer	C21	L	19	21	52	4	11	3	1	1	3	4	15	1	.212	.268	.365
Harry Chappas	SS19,DH2,2B1	S	22	26	50	6	8	2	0	0	2	4	10	0	.160	.236	.200
Randy Johnson	DH4,1B1,OF1	L	21	12	20	0	4	0	0	0	3	2	4	0	.200	.280	.200
Minnie Minoso		R	57	2	2	0	0	0	0	0	0	0	0	0	.000	.000	.000

G. Pryor, 1 G at DH; J. Moore, 1 G at 1B; R. Pruitt, 3 G at 3B, 1 G at 1B

Pitcher	T	Age	G	GS	CG	ShO	IP	H	HR	BB	SO	W-L	Sv	ERA
Britt Burns	L	21	34	32	11	1	238.0	213	17	63	133	15-13	0	2.84
Rich Dotson	R	21	33	32	8	0	198.0	185	20	87	109	12-10	0	4.27
Steve Trout	L	22	32	30	7	2	199.2	229	14	49	89	9-16	0	3.70
Ross Baumgarten	L	25	24	23	3	1	136.0	127	10	52	66	2-12	0	3.44
Ken Kravec	L	28	20	15	0	0	81.2	100	13	44	37	3-6	0	6.94
LaMarr Hoyt	R	25	24	13	3	1	112.1	123	8	41	55	9-3	0	4.57
Francisco Barrios	R	27	3	3	0	0	16.1	21	4	8	2	1-1	0	4.96
Ed Farmer	R	30	64	0	0	0	99.2	92	6	56	54	7-9	30	3.34
Mike Proly	R	29	62	3	0	0	146.2	136	7	58	56	5-10	8	3.07
Rich Wortham	L	26	41	10	0	0	92.0	102	4	58	45	4-7	1	5.97
Guy Hoffman	L	23	23	1	0	0	37.2	38	1	17	24	1-0	1	2.63
Dewey Robinson	R	25	15	0	0	0	35.0	26	2	16	28	1-1	0	3.09
Randy Scarbery	R	28	15	0	0	0	28.2	24	1	7	18	1-2	2	4.08
Nardi Contreras	R	28	8	0	0	0	13.2	18	1	7	8	0-0	0	5.93

1980 California Angels 6th AL West 65-95 .406 31.0 GB

Jim Fregosi

Player	Gm by Position	B	Age	G	AB	R	H	2B	3B	HR	RBI	BB	SO	SB	Avg	OBP	Slg
Tom Donohue	C84	R	27	84	218	18	41	4	1	2	14	7	63	5	.188	.216	.243
Rod Carew	1B103,DH32	L	34	144	540	74	179	34	7	3	59	59	38	23	.331	.396	.437
Bobby Grich	2B146,DH3,1B3	R	31	150	498	60	135	22	2	14	62	84	108	3	.271	.377	.408
Carney Lansford	3B150	R	23	151	602	87	157	27	3	15	80	50	93	14	.261	.312	.390
Freddie Patek	SS81	R	35	86	273	41	72	10	5	5	34	15	26	7	.264	.302	.392
Rick Miller	OF118	L	32	129	412	52	113	14	3	2	38	48	71	7	.274	.349	.337
Larry Harlow	OF94,DH1,1B1	L	28	109	301	47	83	13	4	4	27	48	61	3	.276	.376	.385
Joe Rudi	OF90,1B6,DH3	R	33	104	372	42	88	17	1	16	53	17	84	1	.237	.277	.417
Jason Thompson†	1B47,DH45	L	25	102	312	59	99	14	0	17	70	70	60	2	.317	.439	.526
Don Baylor	OF54,DH36	R	31	90	340	39	85	12	2	5	51	24	32	6	.250	.316	.341
Dickie Thon	SS22,2B21,DH15*	R	22	80	267	32	68	12	2	0	15	10	28	7	.255	.282	.315
Bobby Clark	OF77	R	25	78	261	26	60	10	1	5	23	11	42	0	.230	.266	.333
Dan Ford	OF45,DH15	R	28	65	226	22	63	11	0	7	26	19	45	0	.279	.339	.420
Bert Campaneris	SS64,DH2,2B1	R	38	77	210	32	53	8	1	2	18	14	33	10	.252	.300	.329
Al Cowens†	OF30,DH1	R	28	34	119	11	27	5	0	1	17	12	21	1	.227	.303	.294
Brian Downing	C16,DH13	R	29	30	93	5	27	6	0	2	25	12	12	0	.290	.364	.419
Dan Whitmer	C48	R	24	48	87	8	21	3	0	0	7	4	21	1	.241	.269	.276
Dave Skaggs†	C24	R	29	24	66	7	13	0	0	1	9	9	13	0	.197	.289	.242
Gil Kubski	OF20	L	25	22	63	11	16	3	0	0	6	6	10	1	.254	.319	.302
Stan Cliburn	C54	R	23	54	56	7	10	2	0	2	6	3	9	0	.179	.217	.321
Ralph Garr	DH8,OF2	L	34	21	42	5	8	1	0	0	3	4	6	0	.190	.261	.214
John Harris	1B10,OF3	L	25	19	41	8	12	5	0	2	7	7	4	0	.293	.388	.561
Todd Cruz†	SS12,3B4,2B1*	R	24	18	40	5	11	3	0	1	5	5	8	0	.275	.356	.425
Merv Rettenmund	DH1	R	37	2	4	0	1	0	0	0	0	1	1	0	.250	.400	.250

D. Thon, 10 G at 3B, 1 G at 1B; T. Cruz, 1 G at OF

Pitcher	T	Age	G	GS	CG	ShO	IP	H	HR	BB	SO	W-L	Sv	ERA
Frank Tanana	L	26	32	31	7	0	204.0	223	18	45	113	11-12	0	4.15
Fred Martinez	R	23	30	23	4	1	149.1	150	14	59	57	7-9	0	4.52
Don Aase	R	25	40	21	5	1	175.0	193	13	66	74	8-13	2	4.06
Chris Knapp	R	26	32	20	1	0	117.1	133	18	51	46	2-11	1	6.14
Dave Frost	R	27	15	15	2	1	78.1	97	8	21	28	4-8	0	5.29
Bruce Kison	R	30	13	13	2	1	73.1	73	5	32	28	3-6	0	4.91
Ed Halicki†	R	29	10	6	0	0	35.1	39	5	11	16	3-1	0	4.84
Ralph Botting	L	25	6	6	0	0	26.1	40	1	13	12	0-3	0	5.81
Jim Dorsey	R	24	4	4	0	0	15.2	25	2	8	8	1-2	0	9.19
Bob Ferris	R	25	5	3	0	0	15.1	23	2	9	4	0-2	0	5.87
Mark Clear	R	24	58	0	0	0	106.1	82	2	65	105	11-11	9	3.30
Dave LaRoche	L	32	52	9	1	0	128.0	122	14	39	89	3-5	4	4.08
Andy Hassler†	L	28	41	0	0	0	83.0	67	8	37	75	5-1	10	2.49
John Montague	R	32	37	0	0	0	73.2	97	8	21	22	4-2	3	5.13
Jim Barr	R	32	24	7	0	0	68.0	90	12	23	22	1-4	1	5.56
Dave Lemanczyk†	R	29	21	2	0	0	66.2	81	8	27	19	2-4	0	4.32
Dave Schuler	L	26	8	0	0	0	12.2	13	3	2	7	0-1	0	3.55

1980 Seattle Mariners 7th AL West 59-103 .364 38.0 GB

Darrell Johnson (39-65)/Maury Wills (20-38)

Player	Gm by Position	B	Age	G	AB	R	H	2B	3B	HR	RBI	BB	SO	SB	Avg	OBP	Slg
Larry Cox	C104	R	32	105	243	18	49	6	2	4	20	19	36	1	.202	.260	.292
Bruce Bochte	1B133,DH11	L	29	148	520	62	156	34	4	13	78	72	81	2	.300	.381	.456
Julio Cruz	2B115,DH3	S	25	119	422	66	88	9	3	2	16	59	49	45	.209	.306	.258
Ted Cox	3B80	R	25	83	247	17	60	9	0	2	23	19	25	0	.243	.295	.304
Mario Mendoza	SS114	R	29	114	277	27	68	6	3	2	14	16	42	3	.245	.286	.310
Dan Meyer	OF123,DH7,3B5*	L	27	146	531	56	146	25	6	11	71	31	42	8	.275	.314	.407
Joe Simpson	OF119,1B3	L	28	129	365	42	91	15	3	3	34	28	43	17	.249	.302	.332
Leon Roberts	OF104,DH4	R	29	119	374	48	94	18	3	10	33	43	59	8	.251	.325	.396
Willie Horton	DH92	R	37	97	335	32	74	10	1	8	36	39	70	0	.221	.306	.328
Tom Paciorek	OF60,1B36,DH23	R	33	126	418	44	114	19	1	15	59	17	67	3	.273	.301	.431
Jim Anderson	SS65,3B33,DH5*	R	23	116	317	46	72	7	0	8	30	27	39	2	.227	.292	.325
Larry Milbourne	2B38,SS34,DH8*	S	29	106	258	31	68	6	6	0	26	19	13	7	.264	.313	.333
Rodney Craig	OF63	S	22	70	240	30	57	15	1	3	20	17	35	3	.238	.293	.346
Juan Beniquez	OF65,DH1	R	30	70	237	26	54	10	0	6	21	17	25	2	.228	.278	.346
Bill Stein	3B34,2B14,1B8*	R	33	67	198	16	53	5	1	5	27	16	25	1	.268	.321	.379
Bob Stinson	C45	S	34	48	107	6	23	2	0	1	8	9	19	0	.215	.277	.262
Jerry Narron	C39,DH1	L	24	48	107	7	21	3	0	4	18	13	18	0	.196	.279	.336
Dave Edler	3B28	R	23	28	89	11	20	1	0	3	9	8	16	2	.225	.289	.337
Reggie Walton	OF17,DH11	R	27	31	83	8	23	6	0	2	9	3	10	2	.277	.307	.422
Marc Hill†	C29	R	28	29	70	8	16	2	1	2	9	3	10	0	.229	.260	.371
Kim Allen	2B15,OF4,SS1	R	27	23	51	9	12	3	0	0	3	8	3	10	.235	.350	.294

D. Meyer, 4 G at 1B; J. Anderson, 2 G at 2B, 1 G at C; L. Milbourne, 6 G at 3B; B. Stein, 5 G at DH

Pitcher	T	Age	G	GS	CG	ShO	IP	H	HR	BB	SO	W-L	Sv	ERA
Floyd Bannister	L	25	32	32	8	0	217.2	200	24	66	155	9-13	0	3.47
Glenn Abbott	R	29	31	31	7	2	215.0	228	27	49	78	12-12	0	4.10
Rick Honeycutt	L	26	30	30	9	1	203.1	221	22	60	79	10-17	0	3.94
Jim Beattie	R	25	33	29	3	0	187.1	205	19	98	67	5-15	0	4.85
Mike Parrott	R	25	27	16	1	0	94.0	136	16	42	53	1-16	3	7.28
Gary Wheelock	R	28	1	1	0	0	3.0	4	0	1	1	0-0	0	6.00
Dave Heaverlo	R	29	60	0	0	0	78.2	75	9	35	42	6-3	4	3.89
Shane Rawley	L	24	59	0	0	0	113.2	103	3	63	68	7-7	13	3.33
Byron McLaughlin	R	24	45	4	0	0	90.2	124	15	50	41	3-6	2	6.85
Dave Roberts†	L	35	37	4	0	0	80.1	86	7	27	47	2-3	3	4.37
Rob Dressler	R	26	30	14	3	0	149.1	161	14	33	50	4-10	0	3.98
Manny Sarmiento	R	24	9	0	0	0	14.2	14	2	6	15	0-1	1	3.68
Rick Anderson	R	26	5	2	0	0	9.2	8	1	10	7	0-0	0	3.72

»1980 Philadelphia Phillies 1st NL East 91-71 .562 —

Dallas Green

Player	Gm by Position	B	Age	G	AB	R	H	2B	3B	HR	RBI	BB	SO	SB	Avg	OBP	Slg
Bob Boone	C138	R	32	141	480	34	110	23	1	9	55	48	41	3	.229	.299	.338
Pete Rose	1B162	S	39	162	655	95	185	42	1	1	64	66	33	12	.282	.352	.354
Manny Trillo	2B140	R	29	141	531	68	155	25	9	7	43	32	46	8	.292	.334	.412
Mike Schmidt	3B149	R	30	150	548	104	157	25	8	48	121	89	119	12	.286	.380	.624
Larry Bowa	SS147	S	34	147	540	57	144	16	4	2	39	24	28	21	.267	.300	.322
Garry Maddox	OF143	R	30	143	549	59	142	31	3	11	73	18	52	25	.259	.278	.386
Bake McBride	OF133	L	31	137	554	68	171	33	10	9	87	26	58	13	.309	.342	.453
Greg Luzinski	OF105	R	29	106	368	44	84	19	1	19	56	60	100	3	.228	.342	.440
Lonnie Smith	OF82	R	24	100	298	69	101	14	4	3	20	26	48	33	.339	.397	.443
Keith Moreland	C39,3B4,OF2	R	26	62	159	13	50	8	0	4	29	8	14	3	.314	.341	.440
Greg Gross	OF91,1B1	L	27	127	154	19	37	7	2	0	12	24	7	1	.240	.346	.312
Del Unser	1B31,OF23	L	35	96	110	15	29	6	4	0	10	10	21	0	.264	.320	.391
Ramon Aviles	SS29,2B15	R	28	51	101	12	28	6	0	2	9	10	9	0	.277	.336	.396
John Vukovich	3B34,2B9,SS5*	R	32	49	62	4	10	1	1	0	5	2	7	0	.161	.197	.210
George Vukovich	OF28	L	24	78	58	6	13	1	1	0	8	6	9	0	.224	.297	.276
Luis Aguayo	2B14,SS5	R	21	20	47	7	13	1	2	1	8	2	3	1	.277	.300	.447
Bob Dernier	OF3	R	23	10	7	5	4	0	0	0	1	1	0	3	.571	.625	.571
Tim McCarver	1B2	L	38	6	5	2	1	1	0	0	2	1	0	0	.200	.333	.400
Orlando Isales	OF2	R	20	3	5	1	2	0	1	0	3	1	0	0	.400	.500	.800
Jay Loviglio	2B1	R	24	16	5	7	0	0	0	0	0	1	0	1	.000	.167	.000
Ozzie Virgil	C1	R	23	1	5	1	1	1	0	0	0	0	1	0	.200	.200	.400
Don McCormack	C2	R	24	2	1	0	1	0	0	0	0	0	0	0	1.000	1.000	1.000

J. Vukovich, 1 G at 1B

Pitcher	T	Age	G	GS	CG	ShO	IP	H	HR	BB	SO	W-L	Sv	ERA
Steve Carlton	L	35	38	38	13	3	304.0	243	15	90	286	24-9	0	2.34
Dick Ruthven	R	29	33	33	6	1	223.1	241	9	74	86	17-10	0	3.55
Bob Walk	R	23	27	27	2	0	151.2	163	8	71	94	11-7	0	4.57
Randy Lerch	L	25	30	22	2	0	150.0	178	15	55	57	4-14	0	5.16
Larry Christenson	R	26	14	14	0	0	73.2	62	4	27	49	5-1	0	4.03
Nino Espinosa	R	26	12	12	1	0	76.1	73	9	19	13	3-5	0	3.77
Dan Larson	R	25	12	7	0	0	45.2	46	4	24	17	0-5	0	3.15
Marty Bystrom	R	21	6	5	1	1	36.0	26	1	9	21	5-0	0	1.50
Mark Davis	L	19	2	1	0	0	7.0	4	0	5	5	0-0	0	2.57
Tug McGraw	L	35	57	0	0	0	92.1	62	3	23	75	5-4	20	1.46
Ron Reed	R	37	55	0	0	0	91.1	88	4	30	54	7-5	9	4.04
Dickie Noles	R	23	48	3	0	0	81.0	80	5	42	57	1-4	6	3.89
Kevin Saucier	L	23	40	0	0	0	50.0	50	2	20	25	7-3	0	3.42
Warren Brusstar	R	28	26	0	0	0	38.2	42	3	13	21	2-2	0	3.72
Lerrin LaGrow	R	31	25	0	0	0	39.0	42	5	17	21	0-2	3	4.15
Sparky Lyle†	L	35	10	0	0	0	14.0	11	0	6	6	0-0	2	1.93
Scott Munninghoff	R	21	4	0	0	0	6.0	8	0	5	2	0-0	0	4.50

1980 Montreal Expos 2nd NL East 90-72 .556 1.0 GB

Dick Williams

Player	Gm by Position	B	Age	G	AB	R	H	2B	3B	HR	RBI	BB	SO	SB	Avg	OBP	Slg
Gary Carter	C149	R	26	154	549	76	145	25	5	29	101	58	78	3	.264	.331	.486
Warren Cromartie	1B158,OF2	L	26	162	597	74	172	33	5	14	70	51	64	8	.288	.345	.430
Rodney Scott	2B129,SS21	S	26	154	567	84	127	13	13	0	46	70	75	63	.224	.307	.293
Larry Parrish	3B124	R	26	126	452	55	115	27	3	15	72	36	80	2	.254	.310	.427
Chris Speier	SS127,3B1	R	30	128	388	35	103	14	4	1	32	52	38	0	.265	.351	.330
Andre Dawson	OF147	R	25	151	577	96	178	41	7	17	87	44	69	34	.308	.358	.492
Ron LeFlore	OF130	R	32	139	521	95	134	21	11	4	39	62	99	97	.257	.337	.363
Rowland Office	OF97	L	27	116	292	36	78	13	4	6	30	36	39	3	.267	.343	.401
Ellis Valentine	OF83	R	25	86	311	40	98	22	2	13	67	25	44	5	.315	.367	.524
Jerry White	OF84	S	27	110	214	22	56	9	3	7	23	30	37	8	.262	.351	.430
Tony Bernazard	2B39,SS22	S	23	82	183	26	41	7	1	5	18	17	41	9	.224	.289	.355
Ken Macha	3B33,1B2,C1*	R	29	49	107	10	31	5	1	1	8	11	17	0	.290	.361	.383
Brad Mills	3B18	L	23	21	60	1	18	1	0	0	8	5	6	0	.300	.348	.317
Tom Hutton	1B7,OF4,P1	L	34	62	55	2	12	2	0	0	5	4	10	0	.218	.267	.255
John Tamargo	C12	S	28	37	51	4	14	3	0	1	13	6	5	0	.275	.345	.392
Bob Pate	OF18	R	26	23	39	3	10	2	0	0	5	3	6	0	.256	.295	.308
Bill Almon†	SS12,2B1	R	27	18	38	2	10	1	1	0	3	1	5	0	.263	.275	.342
Bobby Ramos	C12	R	24	13	32	5	5	2	0	0	2	5	5	0	.156	.270	.219
Tim Raines	2B7,OF1	S	20	15	20	5	1	0	0	0	0	6	3	5	.050	.269	.050
Willie Montanez†	1B4	L	32	14	19	1	4	0	0	0	1	3	3	0	.211	.318	.211
Tim Wallach	OF3,1B1	R	22	5	11	1	2	0	0	1	2	1	5	0	.182	.250	.455
Jerry Manuel	SS7	S	26	7	6	0	0	0	0	0	0	0	2	0	.000	.000	.000

K. Macha, 1 G at OF

Pitcher	T	Age	G	GS	CG	ShO	IP	H	HR	BB	SO	W-L	Sv	ERA
Steve Rogers	R	30	37	37	14	4	281.0	247	16	85	147	16-11	0	2.98
Scott Sanderson	R	23	33	33	7	3	211.1	206	18	56	125	16-11	0	3.11
Bill Gullickson	R	21	24	19	5	2	141.0	127	6	50	120	10-5	0	3.00
David Palmer	R	22	24	19	3	1	129.2	124	11	30	73	8-6	0	2.98
Charlie Lea	R	23	21	19	0	0	104.0	103	5	55	56	7-5	0	3.72
Bill Lee	L	33	24	18	2	0	118.0	156	13	22	34	4-6	0	4.96
Ross Grimsley†	L	30	11	7	0	0	41.1	61	5	12	11	2-4	0	6.31
Steve Ratzer	R	26	1	1	0	0	4.0	9	0	2	0	0-0	0	11.25
Elias Sosa	R	30	67	0	0	0	93.2	104	5	19	58	9-6	9	3.07
Woodie Fryman	L	40	61	0	0	0	80.0	61	1	30	59	7-4	17	2.25
Stan Bahnsen	R	35	57	0	0	0	91.1	80	7	33	48	7-6	4	3.05
Fred Norman	L	37	48	8	2	0	98.0	96	8	40	58	4-4	4	4.13
Dale Murray	R	30	16	0	0	0	29.1	39	3	12	16	0-1	0	6.14
John D'Acquisto†	R	28	11	0	0	0	20.2	14	0	9	15	0-2	2	2.18
Hal Dues	R	25	6	1	0	0	12.1	17	1	4	2	0-1	0	6.57
Tom Hutton	L	34	1	0	0	0	1.0	3	1	1	1	0-0	0	27.00

1980 Pittsburgh Pirates 3rd NL East 83-79 .512 8.0 GB

Chuck Tanner

Player	Gm by Position	B	Age	G	AB	R	H	2B	3B	HR	RBI	BB	SO	SB	Avg	OBP	Slg
Ed Ott	C117,OF3	L	28	120	392	35	102	14	0	8	41	33	47	1	.260	.317	.357
John Milner	1B70,OF11	L	30	114	238	31	58	6	0	8	34	52	29	2	.244	.378	.370
Phil Garner	2B151,SS1	R	31	151	548	62	142	27	6	5	58	46	53	32	.259	.315	.358
Bill Madlock	3B127,1B12	R	29	137	494	62	137	22	4	10	53	45	33	16	.277	.341	.399
Tim Foli	SS125	R	29	127	495	61	131	22	0	3	38	19	23	11	.265	.296	.327
Omar Moreno	OF162	L	27	162	676	87	168	20	13	2	36	57	101	96	.249	.306	.325
Dave Parker	OF130	L	29	139	518	71	153	31	1	17	79	25	69	10	.295	.327	.458
Mike Easler	OF119	L	29	132	393	66	133	27	3	21	74	43	65	5	.338	.396	.583
Lee Lacy	OF88,3B3	R	32	109	278	45	93	20	4	7	33	28	33	18	.335	.394	.511
Bill Robinson	1B49,OF41	R	37	100	272	28	78	10	1	12	36	15	45	1	.287	.320	.463
Dale Berra	3B48,SS45,2B4	R	23	93	245	21	54	8	2	6	31	16	52	2	.220	.269	.343
Willie Stargell	1B54	L	40	67	202	28	53	10	1	11	38	26	52	0	.262	.351	.485
Steve Nicosia	C58	R	24	60	176	16	38	8	0	1	22	19	16	0	.216	.291	.278
Vance Law	2B11,SS8,3B1	R	23	25	74	11	17	2	2	0	3	3	7	2	.230	.260	.311
Manny Sanguillen	1B5	R	36	47	48	2	12	3	0	0	2	3	1	3	.250	.294	.313
Kurt Bevacqua†	3B9,1B2	R	33	22	43	1	7	1	0	0	4	6	7	0	.163	.280	.186
Tony Pena	C6	R	23	8	21	1	9	1	1	0	1	0	4	0	.429	.429	.571
Bernie Carbo†		L	32	7	6	0	2	0	0	0	1	1	1	0	.333	.429	.333
Bob Beall		S	32	3	3	0	0	0	0	0	0	0	1	0	.000	.000	.000
Matt Alexander	OF4,2B1	S	33	37	3	13	1	1	0	0	0	0	0	10	.333	.333	.667

Pitcher	T	Age	G	GS	CG	ShO	IP	H	HR	BB	SO	W-L	Sv	ERA
Jim Bibby	R	35	35	34	6	1	238.1	210	20	88	144	19-6	0	3.32
John Candelaria	L	26	35	34	7	0	233.1	246	14	50	97	11-14	1	4.01
Bert Blyleven	R	29	34	32	5	2	216.2	219	20	59	168	8-13	0	3.82
Don Robinson	R	23	29	24	3	2	160.1	157	14	45	103	7-10	1	3.99
Rick Rhoden	R	27	20	19	2	0	126.2	133	9	40	70	7-5	0	3.84
Jim Rooker	L	37	4	4	0	0	18.0	16	0	12	8	2-2	0	3.50
Pascual Perez	R	23	2	2	0	0	12.0	15	0	2	7	0-1	0	3.75
Jesse Jefferson†	R	31	1	1	0	0	6.2	3	0	2	4	1-0	0	1.35
Kent Tekulve	R	33	78	0	0	0	93.0	96	6	40	47	8-12	21	3.39
Enrique Romo	R	32	74	0	0	0	123.2	117	10	28	82	5-5	11	3.27
Grant Jackson	L	37	61	0	0	0	71.0	71	4	20	31	8-4	9	2.92
Eddie Solomon	R	29	26	12	2	0	100.1	96	8	37	35	7-3	0	2.69
Rod Scurry	L	24	20	0	0	0	37.2	23	2	17	28	0-2	0	2.15
Andy Hassler†	L	28	6	0	0	0	11.2	9	2	4	4	0-0	0	3.86
Mark Lee	R	27	4	0	0	0	5.2	5	0	3	2	0-1	0	4.76
Dave Roberts†	L	35	2	0	0	0	2.1	2	0	1	1	0-1	0	3.86
Mickey Mahler	L	27	2	0	0	0	1.0	4	1	3	1	0-0	0	63.00

1980 St. Louis Cardinals 4th NL East 74-88 .457 17.0 GB

Ken Boyer (18-33)/Jack Krol (0-1)/Whitey Herzog (38-35)/Red Schoendienst (18-19)

Player	Gm by Position	B	Age	G	AB	R	H	2B	3B	HR	RBI	BB	SO	SB	Avg	OBP	Slg
Ted Simmons	C129,OF5	S	30	145	495	84	150	33	2	21	98	59	45	1	.303	.375	.505
Keith Hernandez	1B157	L	26	159	595	111	191	39	8	16	99	86	73	14	.321	.408	.494
Ken Oberkfell	2B101,3B16	L	24	116	422	58	128	27	6	3	46	51	23	4	.303	.377	.417
Ken Reitz	3B150	R	29	151	523	39	141	33	0	8	58	22	44	0	.270	.300	.379
Garry Templeton	SS115	S	24	118	504	83	161	19	9	4	43	18	43	31	.319	.342	.417
George Hendrick	OF149	R	30	150	572	73	173	33	2	25	109	32	67	6	.302	.342	.498
Tony Scott	OF134	S	28	143	415	51	104	19	3	0	28	35	68	22	.251	.308	.311
Leon Durham	OF78,1B8	L	22	96	303	42	82	15	4	8	42	18	55	8	.271	.309	.426
Dane Iorg	OF63,1B5,3B1	L	30	105	251	33	76	23	1	3	36	20	34	1	.303	.349	.438
Terry Kennedy	C41,OF28	L	24	84	248	28	63	12	3	4	34	28	34	0	.254	.325	.375
Bobby Bonds	OF70	R	34	86	231	37	47	5	3	5	24	33	74	15	.203	.305	.316
Tom Herr	2B58,SS14	S	24	76	222	29	55	12	5	0	15	16	21	9	.248	.299	.347
Mike Phillips	SS37,2B9,3B8	L	29	63	128	13	30	5	0	0	7	9	17	0	.234	.283	.273
Mike Ramsey	2B24,SS20,3B8	S	26	59	126	11	33	8	1	0	8	3	17	0	.262	.279	.341
Tito Landrum	OF29	R	25	35	77	6	19	2	2	0	7	6	17	3	.247	.306	.325
Keith Smith	OF7	R	27	24	31	3	4	1	0	0	2	2	2	0	.129	.182	.161
Steve Swisher	C8	R	28	18	24	2	6	1	0	0	2	1	7	0	.250	.280	.292
Ty Waller	3B5	R	23	5	12	3	1	0	0	0	0	1	5	0	.083	.154	.083
Bernie Carbo†		L	32	14	11	0	2	0	0	0	1	1	2	0	.182	.250	.182
Joe DeSa	1B1,OF1	L	20	7	11	0	3	0	0	0	0	0	2	0	.273	.273	.273
Jim Lentine†	OF6	R	25	9	10	1	1	0	0	0	1	0	2	0	.100	.100	.100

Pitcher	T	Age	G	GS	CG	ShO	IP	H	HR	BB	SO	W-L	Sv	ERA
Bob Forsch	R	30	31	31	8	0	214.2	225	12	33	87	11-10	0	3.77
Pete Vuckovich	R	27	32	30	7	3	222.1	203	18	68	132	12-9	1	3.40
Silvio Martinez	R	24	25	20	2	0	119.2	127	8	48	39	5-10	0	4.81
Bob Sykes	L	25	27	19	4	3	126.0	134	12	54	50	6-10	0	4.64
John Fulgham	R	24	15	14	4	1	85.1	66	7	32	48	4-6	0	3.38
John Martin	L	24	9	5	1	0	42.0	39	1	9	23	2-3	0	4.29
Al Olmsted	L	23	5	5	0	0	34.2	32	2	14	14	1-1	0	2.86
Andy Rincon	R	21	4	4	1	0	31.0	23	1	7	22	3-1	0	2.61
John Littlefield	R	26	52	0	0	0	66.0	71	2	20	22	5-5	9	3.14
Jim Kaat†	L	41	49	14	6	1	129.2	140	6	33	36	8-7	4	3.82
Don Hood	L	30	33	8	1	0	82.1	90	2	34	35	4-6	0	3.39
Jim Otten	R	28	31	4	0	0	55.1	71	3	26	38	0-5	0	5.53
John Urrea	R	25	30	1	0	0	64.2	57	2	41	36	4-1	3	3.48
Kim Seaman	L	23	26	0	0	0	23.2	16	2	13	10	3-2	4	3.42
Roy Thomas	R	27	24	5	0	0	55.0	59	3	25	22	2-3	0	4.75
George Frazier	R	25	22	0	0	0	23.0	24	2	7	11	1-4	3	2.74
Mark Littell	R	27	14	0	0	0	10.2	14	2	7	7	0-2	2	9.28
Donnie Moore	R	26	11	0	0	0	21.2	25	1	5	10	1-1	0	6.23
Pedro Borbon	R	33	10	0	0	0	19.0	17	3	10	4	1-0	1	3.79
Jeff Little	L	25	7	2	0	0	18.2	18	0	9	17	1-1	0	3.86
Darold Knowles	L	38	2	0	0	0	1.2	3	1	0	1	0-1	0	10.80

1980 New York Mets 5th NL East 67-95 .414 24.0 GB — Joe Torre

Player	Gm by Position	B	Age	G	AB	R	H	2B	3B	HR	RBI	BB	SO	SB	Avg	OBP	Slg
Alex Trevino	C86,3B14,2B1	R	22	106	355	26	91	11	2	0	37	13	41	0	.256	.281	.299
Lee Mazzilli	1B92,OF66	S	25	152	578	82	162	31	4	16	76	82	92	41	.280	.370	.431
Doug Flynn	2B128,SS3	R	29	128	443	46	113	9	8	0	24	22	20	2	.255	.288	.312
Elliott Maddox	3B115,OF4,1B2	R	32	130	411	35	101	16	1	4	34	52	44	1	.246	.336	.319
Frank Taveras	SS140	R	30	141	562	65	157	27	0	0	25	23	64	32	.279	.308	.327
Steve Henderson	OF136	R	27	143	513	75	149	17	8	8	58	62	90	23	.290	.368	.402
Joel Youngblood	OF121,3B21,2B6	R	28	146	514	58	142	26	2	8	69	52	69	14	.276	.340	.381
C. Washington†	OF70	L	25	79	284	38	78	16	4	10	42	20	63	17	.275	.324	.465
Mike Jorgensen	1B72,OF31	L	31	119	321	43	82	11	0	7	43	46	55	0	.255	.349	.355
John Stearns	C74,1B16,3B1	R	28	91	319	42	91	25	1	0	45	33	24	7	.285	.346	.370
Jerry Morales	OF63	R	31	94	193	19	49	7	1	3	30	13	31	2	.254	.293	.347
Bill Almon†	SS22,2B18,3B9	R	27	48	112	13	19	3	2	0	4	8	27	2	.170	.225	.232
Mookie Wilson	OF26	S	24	27	105	16	26	5	3	0	4	12	19	7	.248	.325	.352
Wally Backman	2B20,SS8	S	20	27	93	12	30	1	1	0	9	11	14	2	.323	.396	.355
Dan Norman	OF19	R	25	69	92	5	17	1	1	2	9	6	14	5	.185	.235	.283
Hubie Brooks	3B23	R	23	24	81	8	25	2	1	1	10	5	9	1	.309	.364	.395
Jose Moreno	2B4,3B4	S	22	37	46	6	9	2	1	2	9	3	12	1	.196	.240	.413
Jose Cardenal†	OF6,1B5	R	36	26	42	4	7	1	0	0	4	6	4	0	.167	.265	.190
Ron Hodges	C9	L	31	36	42	4	10	2	0	0	5	10	13	1	.238	.377	.286
Mario Ramirez	SS7,2B4,3B3	R	22	18	24	2	5	0	0	0	0	1	7	0	.208	.240	.208
Butch Benton	C8	R	22	12	21	0	1	0	0	0	0	2	4	0	.048	.167	.048
Phil Mankowski	3B3	L	27	8	12	1	2	1	0	0	1	2	4	0	.167	.286	.250
Luis Rosado	1B1	R	24	2	4	0	0	0	0	0	0	0	1	0	.000	.000	.000

Pitcher	T	Age	G	GS	CG	ShO	IP	H	HR	BB	SO	W-L	Sv	ERA
Ray Burris	R	29	29	29	1	0	170.1	181	20	54	83	7-13	0	4.02
Pat Zachry	R	28	28	26	7	3	164.2	145	16	58	88	6-10	0	3.01
Mark Bomback	R	27	36	25	2	1	162.2	191	17	49	68	10-8	0	4.09
Pete Falcone	L	26	37	23	1	0	157.1	163	16	58	109	7-10	1	4.52
Craig Swan	R	29	21	21	4	1	128.1	117	20	30	79	5-9	0	3.58
Mike Scott	R	25	6	6	1	1	29.1	40	1	8	13	1-1	0	4.30
Ed Lynch	R	24	5	4	0	0	19.1	24	0	5	9	1-1	0	5.12
Jeff Reardon	R	24	61	0	0	0	110.1	96	10	47	101	8-7	6	2.61
Neil Allen	R	22	59	0	0	0	97.1	87	7	40	79	7-10	22	3.70
Tom Hausman	R	27	55	4	0	0	122.0	125	12	26	53	6-5	1	3.98
Ed Glynn	L	27	38	0	0	0	52.1	49	5	23	32	3-3	1	4.13
John Pacella	R	23	32	15	0	0	84.0	89	5	59	68	3-4	0	5.14
Dyar Miller	R	34	31	0	0	0	42.0	37	1	11	28	1-2	1	1.93
Roy Lee Jackson	R	26	24	8	1	0	70.2	78	4	20	58	1-7	1	4.20
Kevin Kobel	L	26	14	1	0	0	24.1	36	5	11	8	1-4	0	7.03
Juan Berenguer	R	25	6	0	0	0	9.1	9	1	10	7	0-1	0	5.79
Scott Holman	R	21	4	0	0	0	7.0	6	0	1	3	0-0	0	1.29

1980 Chicago Cubs 6th NL East 64-98 .395 27.0 GB — Preston Gomez (39-51)/Joey Amalfitano (25-47)

Player	Gm by Position	B	Age	G	AB	R	H	2B	3B	HR	RBI	BB	SO	SB	Avg	OBP	Slg
Tim Blackwell	C103	S	27	103	320	24	87	16	4	5	30	41	62	0	.272	.352	.394
Bill Buckner	1B94,OF50	L	30	145	578	69	187	41	3	10	68	30	18	1	.324	.353	.457
Mike Tyson	2B117	R	30	123	341	34	81	19	3	3	23	15	61	1	.238	.273	.337
Lenny Randle	3B111,2B17,OF6	S	31	130	489	67	135	19	6	5	39	50	55	19	.276	.343	.370
Ivan DeJesus	SS156	R	27	157	618	78	160	26	3	3	33	60	81	44	.259	.327	.325
Jerry Martin	OF129	R	31	141	494	57	112	22	2	23	73	38	107	8	.227	.281	.419
Mike Vail	OF77	R	28	114	312	30	93	17	2	6	47	14	77	2	.298	.330	.423
Scot Thompson	OF66,1B12	L	24	102	226	26	48	10	1	2	13	28	31	6	.212	.301	.292
Larry Biittner	1B41,OF38	L	34	127	273	21	68	12	2	1	34	18	33	1	.249	.294	.319
Dave Kingman	OF61,1B2	R	31	81	255	31	71	8	0	18	57	21	44	2	.278	.329	.522
Steve Dillard	3B51,2B38,SS2	R	29	100	244	31	55	8	1	4	27	20	54	2	.225	.285	.316
Barry Foote	C55	R	28	63	202	16	48	13	1	6	28	13	18	1	.238	.282	.401
Jesus Figueroa	OF57	L	23	115	198	20	50	5	0	1	11	14	16	2	.253	.308	.293
Cliff Johnson†	1B46,OF3,C1	R	32	68	196	28	46	8	0	10	34	29	35	0	.235	.335	.429
Jim Tracy	OF31,1B1	L	24	42	122	12	31	3	3	3	9	13	37	2	.254	.326	.402
Mick Kelleher	2B57,3B31,SS17	R	32	105	96	12	14	1	1	0	4	9	17	1	.146	.217	.177
Carlos Lezcano	OF39	R	24	42	88	15	18	4	1	3	12	11	29	1	.205	.294	.375
Ken Henderson	OF22	S	34	44	82	7	16	3	0	2	9	17	19	0	.195	.333	.305
Steve Ontiveros	3B24	S	28	31	77	7	16	3	0	1	3	14	17	0	.208	.330	.286
Mike O'Berry	C19	R	26	19	48	7	10	1	0	0	5	5	13	0	.208	.273	.229
Steve Macko	SS3,3B2,2B1	L	25	6	20	2	6	2	0	0	2	0	3	0	.300	.300	.400
Bill Hayes	C3	R	22	4	9	0	2	1	0	0	0	0	3	0	.222	.222	.333

Pitcher	T	Age	G	GS	CG	ShO	IP	H	HR	BB	SO	W-L	Sv	ERA
Rick Reuschel	R	31	38	38	6	0	257.0	281	13	76	140	11-13	0	3.40
Dennis Lamp	R	27	41	37	2	1	202.2	259	16	82	83	10-14	0	5.20
Mike Krukow	R	28	34	34	3	0	205.0	200	13	80	130	10-15	0	4.39
Lynn McGlothen	R	30	39	27	2	2	182.1	211	24	64	119	12-14	0	4.79
Randy Martz	R	24	6	6	0	0	30.1	28	1	11	5	1-2	0	2.08
Dick Tidrow	R	33	84	0	0	0	116.0	97	10	53	97	6-5	6	2.79
Bill Caudill	R	23	72	2	0	0	127.2	100	10	59	112	4-6	1	2.19
Bruce Sutter	R	27	60	0	0	0	102.1	90	5	34	76	5-8	28	2.64
Willie Hernandez	L	25	53	7	0	0	108.1	115	8	45	75	1-9	0	4.40
Doug Capilla	L	28	39	11	0	0	89.2	82	7	51	51	2-8	0	4.12
George Riley	L	23	22	0	0	0	36.0	41	2	20	18	0-4	0	5.75
Lee Smith	R	22	18	0	0	0	21.2	21	0	14	17	2-0	0	2.91

1980 Houston Astros 1st NL West 93-70 .571 — — Bill Virdon

Player	Gm by Position	B	Age	G	AB	R	H	2B	3B	HR	RBI	BB	SO	SB	Avg	OBP	Slg
Alan Ashby	C114	S	28	116	352	30	90	19	2	3	48	35	40	0	.256	.319	.347
Art Howe	1B77,3B25,SS5*	R	33	110	321	34	91	12	5	10	46	34	29	1	.283	.350	.445
Joe Morgan	2B130	L	36	141	461	66	112	17	5	11	49	93	47	24	.243	.367	.373
Enos Cabell	3B150,1B1	R	30	152	604	69	167	23	8	2	55	26	84	21	.276	.305	.351
Craig Reynolds	SS135	L	27	137	381	34	86	9	6	3	28	20	39	2	.226	.262	.304
Jose Cruz	OF158	L	32	160	612	79	185	29	7	11	91	60	66	36	.302	.360	.426
Cesar Cedeno	OF136	R	29	137	499	71	154	32	8	10	73	66	72	48	.309	.389	.465
Terry Puhl	OF135	L	23	141	535	75	151	24	5	13	55	60	52	27	.282	.357	.419
Rafael Landestoy	2B94,SS65,3B3	S	27	149	393	42	97	13	8	1	27	31	37	23	.247	.306	.328
Denny Walling	1B63,OF19	L	26	100	284	30	85	6	5	3	29	35	26	4	.299	.374	.387
Luis Pujols	C75,3B1	R	24	78	221	15	44	6	1	0	20	13	29	0	.199	.245	.235
Jeffrey Leonard	OF56,1B11	R	24	88	216	29	46	7	5	3	20	19	46	4	.213	.274	.333
Danny Heep	1B22	L	22	33	87	6	24	8	0	0	6	8	9	0	.276	.340	.368
Dave Bergman	1B59,OF5	L	27	90	78	12	20	6	1	0	3	10	10	1	.256	.341	.359
Gary Woods	OF14	R	25	19	53	8	20	5	0	2	15	2	9	1	.377	.400	.585
Julio Gonzalez	SS16,3B11,2B2	R	27	40	52	5	6	1	0	0	1	1	8	1	.115	.132	.135
Bruce Bochy	C10,1B1	R	25	22	22	0	4	1	0	0	0	5	7	0	.182	.357	.227
Scott Loucks	OF4	R	23	8	3	4	1	0	0	0	0	0	2	0	.333	.333	.333
Mike Fischlin	SS1	R	24	1	1	0	0	0	0	0	0	0	1	0	.000	.000	.000
Alan Knicely		R	25	1	1	0	0	0	0	0	0	0	1	0	.000	.000	.000

A. Howe, 3 G at 2B

Pitcher	T	Age	G	GS	CG	ShO	IP	H	HR	BB	SO	W-L	Sv	ERA
Joe Niekro	R	35	37	36	11	2	256.0	268	12	79	127	20-12	0	3.55
Nolan Ryan	R	33	35	35	4	2	233.2	205	10	98	200	11-10	0	3.35
Ken Forsch	R	33	32	32	6	3	222.1	230	15	41	84	12-13	0	3.20
Vern Ruhle	R	29	28	22	6	2	159.1	148	7	29	55	12-4	0	2.37
J.R. Richard	R	30	17	17	4	4	113.2	65	2	40	119	10-4	0	1.90
Gordy Pladson	R	23	12	6	0	0	41.1	38	3	16	13	0-4	0	4.35
Joe Sambito	L	28	64	0	0	0	90.1	65	3	22	75	8-4	17	2.19
Dave Smith	R	25	57	0	0	0	102.2	90	1	32	85	7-5	10	1.93
Frank LaCorte	R	28	55	0	0	0	83.0	61	4	43	66	8-5	11	2.82
Joaquin Andujar	R	27	35	14	0	0	122.0	132	8	43	75	3-8	2	3.91
Randy Niemann	L	24	22	1	0	0	33.0	40	2	12	18	0-1	1	5.45
Bert Roberge	R	25	14	0	0	0	24.1	24	2	10	9	2-0	0	5.92
Bobby Sprowl	L	24	1	0	0	0	1.0	1	0	1	3	0-0	0	0.00

1980 Los Angeles Dodgers 2nd NL West 92-71 .564 1.0 GB — Tom Lasorda

Player	Gm by Position	B	Age	G	AB	R	H	2B	3B	HR	RBI	BB	SO	SB	Avg	OBP	Slg
Steve Yeager	C95	R	31	96	227	20	48	8	0	2	20	20	54	2	.211	.274	.273
Steve Garvey	1B162	R	31	163	658	78	200	27	1	26	106	36	67	6	.304	.341	.467
Davey Lopes	2B140	R	35	141	553	79	139	15	3	10	49	58	71	23	.251	.321	.344
Ron Cey	3B157	R	32	157	551	81	140	25	0	28	77	69	92	2	.254	.342	.452
Bill Russell	SS129	R	31	130	466	38	123	23	2	3	34	18	44	13	.264	.295	.341
Dusty Baker	OF151	R	31	153	579	80	170	26	4	29	97	43	66	12	.294	.339	.503
Rudy Law	OF106	L	23	128	388	55	101	5	4	1	23	23	27	40	.260	.306	.302
Reggie Smith	OF84	S	35	92	311	47	100	13	0	15	55	41	63	5	.322	.392	.508
Derrel Thomas	OF52,SS49,2B18*	R	29	117	297	32	79	18	3	1	22	26	48	7	.266	.326	.357
Jay Johnstone	OF61	L	34	109	251	31	77	15	2	2	20	24	29	3	.307	.372	.406
Rick Monday	OF50	L	34	96	194	35	52	7	1	10	25	28	49	2	.268	.363	.469
Pedro Guerrero	OF40,2B12,3B3*	R	24	75	183	27	59	9	1	7	31	12	31	2	.322	.359	.497
Joe Ferguson	C66,OF1	R	33	77	172	20	41	3	2	9	29	38	46	2	.238	.371	.436
Mike Scioscia	C54	L	21	54	134	8	34	5	1	1	8	12	9	1	.254	.313	.328
Gary Thomasson	OF31,1B1	L	28	80	111	6	24	3	0	1	12	17	26	0	.216	.326	.270
Mickey Hatcher	OF25,3B18	R	25	57	84	4	19	2	0	1	5	2	12	0	.226	.244	.286
Jack Perconte	2B9	L	25	14	17	2	4	0	0	0	2	2	1	3	.235	.316	.235
Pepe Frias†	SS11	R	31	14	9	1	2	1	0	0	0	0	0	0	.222	.222	.333
Bobby Castillo	P61,OF1	R	25	62	9	0	1	0	0	0	0	0	4	0	.111	.111	.111
Manny Mota		R	42	7	7	0	3	0	0	0	2	0	0	0	.429	.429	.429
Vic Davalillo	1B1	L	43	7	6	1	1	0	0	0	0	0	1	0	.167	.167	.167
Bobby Mitchell	OF8	L	25	9	3	1	1	0	0	0	0	1	0	0	.333	.500	.333
Gary Weiss		S	24	8	0	2	0	0	0	0	0	1	0	0	—	—	—

D. Thomas, 5 G at C, 4 G at 3B; P. Guerrero, 2 G at 1B

Pitcher	T	Age	G	GS	CG	ShO	IP	H	HR	BB	SO	W-L	Sv	ERA
Burt Hooton	R	30	34	33	4	2	206.2	194	22	64	118	14-8	1	3.66
Bob Welch	R	23	32	32	3	2	213.2	190	15	79	141	14-9	0	3.29
Don Sutton	R	35	32	31	4	2	212.1	163	20	47	128	13-5	1	2.20
Jerry Reuss	L	31	37	29	10	6	229.1	193	12	40	111	18-6	3	2.51
Dave Goltz	R	31	35	27	2	2	171.1	198	12	59	91	7-11	1	4.31
Bobby Castillo	R	25	61	0	0	0	98.1	70	4	45	60	8-6	5	2.75
Steve Howe	L	22	59	0	0	0	84.2	83	1	22	39	7-9	17	2.66
Rick Sutcliffe	R	24	42	10	1	1	110.0	122	10	55	59	3-9	5	5.56
Joe Beckwith	R	25	38	0	0	0	59.2	60	1	23	40	3-3	0	1.96
Don Stanhouse	R	29	21	0	0	0	25.0	30	4	16	5	2-2	7	5.04
Charlie Hough†	R	32	19	1	0	0	32.1	37	4	21	25	1-3	1	5.57
F. Valenzuela	L	19	10	0	0	0	17.2	8	0	5	16	2-0	1	0.00
Terry Forster	L	28	9	0	0	0	11.2	10	0	4	2	0-0	0	3.09

1980 Cincinnati Reds 3rd NL West 89-73 .549 3.5 GB — John McNamara

Player	Gm by Position	B	Age	G	AB	R	H	2B	3B	HR	RBI	BB	SO	SB	Avg	OBP	Slg
Johnny Bench	C105	R	32	114	360	52	90	12	0	24	68	41	64	4	.250	.327	.483
Dan Driessen	1B151	L	28	154	524	81	139	36	1	14	74	93	68	19	.265	.377	.418
Junior Kennedy	2B103	R	29	104	337	31	88	16	3	1	34	36	34	3	.261	.325	.335
Ray Knight	3B162	R	27	162	618	71	163	39	7	14	78	36	62	1	.264	.307	.417
Dave Concepcion	SS155,2B1	R	32	156	622	72	162	31	8	5	77	37	107	12	.260	.300	.360
Dave Collins	OF141	S	27	144	551	94	167	20	4	3	35	53	68	79	.303	.366	.370
George Foster	OF141	R	31	144	528	79	144	21	5	25	93	75	99	1	.273	.362	.473
Ken Griffey Sr.	OF138	L	30	146	544	89	160	28	10	13	85	62	77	23	.294	.364	.454
Ron Oester	2B79,SS17,3B3	S	24	100	303	40	84	16	2	2	20	26	44	6	.277	.336	.363
Joe Nolan†	C51	L	29	53	154	14	48	7	0	3	24	13	8	0	.312	.353	.416
Cesar Geronimo	OF86	L	32	103	145	16	37	5	0	2	9	14	24	2	.255	.319	.331
Sam Mejias	OF67	R	28	71	108	16	30	5	1	1	10	6	13	4	.278	.322	.370
Harry Spilman	1B18,OF2,C1*	L	25	65	101	14	27	4	0	4	19	9	19	0	.267	.327	.426
Heity Cruz	OF29	R	27	52	75	5	16	4	1	1	5	8	16	0	.213	.289	.333
Don Werner	C24	R	27	24	64	2	11	2	0	0	5	7	10	1	.172	.260	.203
Paul Householder	OF14	S	21	20	45	3	11	1	1	0	7	1	13	1	.244	.261	.311
Rick Auerbach	3B3,SS3,2B1	R	30	24	33	5	11	1	1	1	4	3	5	0	.333	.389	.515
Vic Correll	C10	R	34	10	19	1	8	1	0	0	3	0	2	0	.421	.421	.474
Eddie Milner		L	25	6	3	1	0	0	0	0	0	0	0	0	.000	.000	.000

H. Spilman, 1 G at 3B

Pitcher	T	Age	G	GS	CG	ShO	IP	H	HR	BB	SO	W-L	Sv	ERA
Mike LaCoss	R	24	34	29	4	2	169.1	207	9	68	59	10-12	0	4.62
Frank Pastore	R	22	27	27	9	2	184.2	161	13	42	110	13-7	0	3.27
Charlie Leibrandt	L	23	36	27	5	2	173.2	200	15	54	62	10-9	0	4.25
Tom Seaver	R	35	26	26	5	1	168.0	140	24	59	101	10-8	0	3.64
Paul Moskau	R	26	33	19	2	1	152.2	147	13	41	94	9-7	2	4.01
Joe Price	L	23	24	13	2	0	111.1	95	10	37	44	7-3	0	3.56
Bruce Berenyi	R	25	6	6	0	0	27.2	34	1	23	19	2-2	0	7.81
Bill Bonham	R	31	4	4	0	0	19.0	21	1	5	13	2-1	0	4.74
Tom Hume	R	27	78	0	0	0	137.0	121	6	38	68	9-10	25	2.56
Doug Bair	R	30	61	0	0	0	85.0	91	7	39	62	3-6	6	4.24
Mario Soto	R	23	53	12	3	1	190.1	126	11	84	182	10-8	4	3.07
Dave Tomlin	L	31	27	0	0	0	26.0	38	2	11	6	3-0	0	5.54
Sheldon Burnside	L	25	7	0	0	0	4.2	6	1	1	2	1-0	0	1.93
Jay Howell	R	24	5	0	0	0	3.1	8	0	0	1	0-0	0	13.50
Geoff Combe	R	24	4	0	0	0	6.2	9	0	4	10	0-0	0	10.80

1980 Atlanta Braves 4th NL West 81-80 .503 11.0 GB

Bobby Cox

Player	Gm by Position	B	Age	G	AB	R	H	2B	3B	HR	RBI	BB	SO	SB	Avg	OBP	Slg
Bruce Benedict	C120	R	24	120	359	18	91	14	1	2	34	28	36	3	.253	.308	.315
Chris Chambliss	1B158	L	31	158	602	83	170	37	2	18	72	49	73	7	.282	.338	.440
Glenn Hubbard	2B117	R	22	117	431	55	107	21	3	9	43	49	69	7	.248	.322	.374
Bob Horner	3B121,1B1	R	22	124	463	81	124	14	1	35	89	27	50	3	.268	.307	.529
Luis Gomez	SS119	R	28	121	278	18	53	6	0	0	24	17	27	0	.191	.239	.212
Dale Murphy	OF154,1B1	R	24	156	569	98	160	27	2	33	89	59	133	9	.281	.349	.510
Gary Matthews	OF143	R	29	155	571	79	159	17	3	19	75	42	93	11	.278	.325	.419
Jeff Burroughs	OF73	R	29	99	278	35	73	14	0	13	51	35	57	1	.263	.347	.453
Jerry Royster	2B49,3B48,OF41	R	27	123	392	42	95	17	5	1	20	37	48	22	.242	.309	.319
Larvell Blanks	SS56,3B43,2B1	R	30	88	221	23	45	6	0	2	12	16	27	1	.204	.255	.258
Brian Asselstine	OF61	L	26	87	218	18	62	13	1	3	25	11	37	1	.284	.318	.394
Rafael Ramirez	SS46	R	22	50	165	17	44	6	1	2	11	2	33	2	.267	.292	.352
Bill Nahorodny	C54,1B1	R	26	59	157	14	38	12	0	5	18	8	21	0	.242	.287	.414
Mike Lum	OF19,1B10	L	34	93	83	7	17	3	0	0	5	18	19	0	.205	.343	.241
Biff Pocoroba	C10	S	26	70	83	7	22	4	0	2	8	11	11	1	.265	.347	.386
Terry Harper	OF18	R	24	21	54	3	10	2	1	0	3	6	5	2	.185	.279	.259
Charlie Spikes	OF7	R	29	41	36	6	10	1	0	0	2	3	18	0	.278	.350	.306
Chico Ruiz	3B16,SS4,2B2	R	28	25	26	3	8	2	1	0	2	3	7	0	.308	.379	.462
Joe Nolan†	C6	L	29	17	22	2	6	1	0	0	2	2	4	0	.273	.333	.318
Eddie Miller	OF9	S	23	11	19	3	3	0	0	0	0	0	5	1	.158	.158	.158
Gary Cooper	OF13	S	23	21	2	3	0	0	0	0	0	0	1	2	.000	.000	.000

Pitcher	T	Age	G	GS	CG	ShO	IP	H	HR	BB	SO	W-L	Sv	ERA
Phil Niekro	R	41	40	38	11	3	275.0	256	30	85	176	15-18	1	3.63
Doyle Alexander	R	29	35	35	7	1	231.2	227	20	74	114	14-11	0	4.20
Rick Matula	R	26	33	30	3	1	176.2	195	17	60	62	11-13	0	4.58
Larry McWilliams	L	26	30	30	4	1	163.2	188	27	39	77	9-14	0	4.95
Tommy Boggs	R	24	32	26	4	3	192.1	180	14	46	84	12-9	0	3.42
Rick Camp	R	27	77	0	0	0	108.1	92	3	29	33	6-4	22	1.91
Gene Garber	R	32	68	0	0	0	82.1	95	6	24	51	5-5	7	3.83
Larry Bradford	L	30	56	0	0	0	55.0	49	3	22	32	3-4	4	2.45
Al Hrabosky	L	30	45	0	0	0	59.2	50	8	31	31	4-2	3	3.62
Preston Hanna	R	25	32	2	0	0	79.1	63	3	44	35	2-0	0	3.18
Rick Mahler	R	26	2	0	0	0	3.2	2	0	0	1	0-0	0	2.45

1980 San Francisco Giants 5th NL West 75-86 .466 17.0 GB

Dave Bristol

Player	Gm by Position	B	Age	G	AB	R	H	2B	3B	HR	RBI	BB	SO	SB	Avg	OBP	Slg
Milt May	C103	L	29	111	358	27	93	16	2	6	50	25	40	0	.260	.305	.366
Mike Ivie	1B72	R	27	79	286	21	69	16	1	4	25	19	40	1	.241	.288	.346
Rennie Stennett	2B111	R	29	120	397	34	97	13	2	2	37	22	31	4	.244	.286	.302
Darrell Evans	3B140,1B14	L	33	154	556	69	147	23	0	20	78	83	65	17	.264	.359	.414
Johnnie LeMaster	SS134	R	26	135	405	33	87	16	6	3	31	25	57	0	.215	.257	.306
Larry Herndon	OF122	R	26	139	493	54	127	17	11	8	49	19	91	8	.258	.284	.385
Jack Clark	OF120	R	24	127	437	77	124	20	8	22	82	74	52	2	.284	.382	.517
Bill North	OF115	S	32	128	415	73	104	12	1	1	19	81	78	45	.251	.373	.292
Terry Whitfield	OF95	L	27	118	321	38	95	16	2	4	26	20	44	4	.296	.337	.396
Rich Murray	1B53	R	22	53	194	19	42	8	2	4	24	11	48	2	.216	.259	.340
Jim Wohlford	OF49,3B1	R	29	91	193	17	54	6	4	1	24	13	23	1	.280	.324	.368
Joe Pettini	SS42,3B18,2B8	R	25	63	190	19	44	3	1	1	9	17	33	5	.232	.295	.274
Joe Strain	2B42,3B6,SS1	R	26	77	189	26	54	6	0	0	16	10	10	1	.286	.320	.317
Mike Sadek	C59	R	34	64	151	14	38	4	1	1	16	27	18	0	.252	.363	.311
Max Venable	OF40	L	23	64	138	13	37	5	0	0	10	15	22	8	.268	.333	.304
Willie McCovey	1B27	L	42	48	113	8	23	8	0	1	16	13	23	0	.204	.285	.301
Guy Sularz	2B21,3B5	R	24	25	65	3	16	1	1	0	3	9	6	1	.246	.333	.292
Marc Hill†	C14	R	28	17	41	1	7	2	0	0	0	1	7	0	.171	.190	.220
Dennis Littlejohn	C10	R	25	13	29	2	7	1	0	0	2	7	7	0	.241	.368	.276
Roger Metzger	SS13,2B1	S	32	28	27	5	2	0	0	0	0	3	2	0	.074	.167	.074
Chris Bourjos	OF6	R	25	13	22	4	5	1	0	1	2	2	7	0	.227	.292	.409

Pitcher	T	Age	G	GS	CG	ShO	IP	H	HR	BB	SO	W-L	Sv	ERA
Ed Whitson	R	25	34	34	6	2	211.2	222	7	56	90	11-13	0	3.10
Bob Knepper	L	26	35	33	8	1	215.1	242	15	61	103	9-16	0	4.10
Vida Blue	L	30	31	31	10	3	224.0	202	14	61	129	14-10	0	2.97
Allen Ripley	R	27	23	20	2	0	112.2	119	10	36	65	9-10	0	4.15
John Montefusco	R	30	22	17	1	0	113.0	120	15	39	85	4-8	0	4.38
Alan Hargesheimer	R	23	15	13	0	0	75.0	82	3	32	40	4-6	0	4.32
Bill Bordley	L	22	8	6	0	0	30.2	34	3	21	11	2-3	0	4.70
Jeff Stember	R	22	1	1	0	0	3.0	2	1	2	0	0-0	0	3.00
Greg Minton	R	28	68	0	0	0	91.1	81	0	34	42	4-6	19	2.46
Gary Lavelle	L	31	62	0	0	0	100.0	106	4	36	66	6-8	9	3.42
Al Holland	L	27	54	0	0	0	82.1	71	2	34	65	5-3	7	1.75
Tom Griffin	R	32	42	4	0	0	107.2	80	8	49	79	5-1	0	2.76
Mike Rowland	R	27	19	0	0	0	27.0	20	2	8	8	1-1	0	2.33
Randy Moffitt	R	31	13	0	0	0	16.2	18	2	4	10	1-1	0	4.86
Ed Halicki†	R	29	11	2	0	0	25.0	29	5	10	14	0-0	0	5.40
Phil Nastu	L	25	6	0	0	0	6.0	10	1	5	1	0-0	0	6.00
Fred Breining	R	24	5	0	0	0	6.2	8	0	4	3	0-0	0	5.40

1980 San Diego Padres 6th NL West 73-89 .451 19.5 GB

Jerry Coleman

Player	Gm by Position	B	Age	G	AB	R	H	2B	3B	HR	RBI	BB	SO	SB	Avg	OBP	Slg
Gene Tenace	C104,1B19	R	33	133	316	46	70	11	1	17	50	92	63	4	.222	.399	.424
Willie Montanez†	1B124	L	32	128	481	39	132	12	4	6	63	36	52	3	.274	.325	.353
Dave Cash	2B123	R	32	130	397	25	90	14	2	1	23	35	21	6	.227	.287	.280
Aurelio Rodriguez†	3B88,SS2	R	32	89	175	7	35	7	2	2	13	6	26	1	.200	.227	.297
Ozzie Smith	SS158	S	25	158	609	67	140	18	5	0	35	71	49	57	.230	.313	.276
Dave Winfield	OF159	R	28	162	558	89	154	25	6	20	87	79	83	23	.276	.365	.450
Gene Richards	OF156	L	26	158	642	91	193	26	8	4	41	61	73	61	.301	.363	.385
Jerry Mumphrey	OF153	S	27	160	564	61	168	24	3	4	59	49	90	52	.298	.352	.372
Tim Flannery	2B53,3B41	L	22	95	292	15	70	12	0	0	25	18	30	2	.240	.283	.281
Bill Fahey	C85	L	30	93	241	18	62	4	0	1	22	21	16	2	.257	.314	.286
Luis Salazar	3B42,OF4	R	24	44	169	28	57	4	7	1	25	9	25	11	.337	.372	.462
Jerry Turner	OF34	L	26	85	153	22	44	5	0	3	18	10	18	8	.288	.335	.379
Barry Evans	3B43,2B19,SS4*	R	24	73	125	11	29	3	2	1	14	17	21	1	.232	.317	.312
Broderick Perkins	1B20,OF10	L	25	43	100	18	37	9	0	2	14	11	10	2	.370	.432	.520
Kurt Bevacqua†	3B13,OF4,2B2*	R	33	62	71	4	19	6	1	0	12	6	1	1	.268	.321	.380
Von Joshua	OF12,1B2	L	32	53	63	8	15	2	1	2	7	5	15	0	.238	.294	.397
Paul Dade	3B21,OF8,2B1	R	28	68	53	17	10	0	0	0	3	12	10	4	.189	.338	.189
Craig Stimac	C11,3B2	R	25	20	50	5	11	2	0	0	7	1	6	0	.220	.222	.260
Randy Bass	1B15	L	26	19	49	5	14	0	1	3	8	7	7	0	.286	.386	.510
Fred Kendall	C14,1B1	R	31	19	24	2	7	0	0	0	2	0	3	0	.292	.292	.292
Chuck Baker	SS8	R	27	9	22	0	3	1	0	0	0	0	4	0	.136	.136	.182

B. Evans, 1 G at 1B; K. Bevacqua, 1 G at 1B

Pitcher	T	Age	G	GS	CG	ShO	IP	H	HR	BB	SO	W-L	Sv	ERA
John Curtis	L	32	30	27	6	0	187.0	184	9	67	71	10-8	0	3.51
Rick Wise	R	34	27	27	1	0	154.1	172	14	37	59	6-8	0	3.67
Randy Jones	L	30	24	24	4	3	154.1	165	14	29	53	5-13	0	3.91
Steve Mura	R	25	37	23	3	1	168.2	149	9	86	109	8-7	2	3.68
Juan Eichelberger	R	26	15	13	0	0	88.2	73	8	55	43	4-2	0	3.65
George Stablein	R	22	4	2	0	0	11.2	16	0	3	4	0-1	0	3.09
Rollie Fingers	R	33	66	0	0	0	103.0	101	3	32	69	11-9	23	2.80
Bob Shirley	L	26	59	12	3	0	137.0	143	12	54	67	11-12	7	3.55
Dennis Kinney	L	28	50	0	0	0	82.2	79	3	37	40	4-6	1	4.25
Gary Lucas	L	25	46	18	0	0	150.0	138	8	43	85	5-8	3	3.24
Eric Rasmussen	R	28	40	14	0	0	111.1	130	9	33	50	4-11	1	4.37
John D'Acquisto†	R	28	39	0	0	0	67.0	67	2	36	44	2-3	1	3.76
Mike Armstrong	R	26	11	0	0	0	14.1	16	3	13	14	0-0	0	5.65
Tom Tellmann	R	26	6	2	2	0	22.1	23	0	8	9	3-0	1	1.61
Dennis Blair	R	26	5	1	0	0	14.0	18	3	3	11	0-1	0	6.43

»1981 Milwaukee Brewers AL East 3rd 31-25 .554 3.0 GB (1) 1st 31-22 .585 — (2)

Buck Rodgers

Player	Gm by Position	B	Age	G	AB	R	H	2B	3B	HR	RBI	BB	SO	SB	Avg	OBP	Slg
Ted Simmons	C75,DH22,1B4	S	31	100	380	45	82	13	3	14	61	23	32	0	.216	.262	.376
Cecil Cooper	1B101,DH5	L	31	106	416	70	133	35	1	12	60	28	30	5	.320	.363	.495
Jim Gantner	2B107	L	28	107	352	35	94	14	1	2	33	29	29	3	.267	.325	.330
Don Money	3B56,DH2,1B1	R	34	60	185	17	40	7	0	2	14	19	27	0	.216	.288	.286
Robin Yount	SS93,DH3	R	25	96	377	50	103	15	5	10	49	22	37	4	.273	.312	.419
Ben Oglivie	OF101,DH6	L	32	107	400	53	97	15	2	14	72	37	49	2	.243	.310	.395
Gorman Thomas	OF97,DH6	R	30	103	363	54	94	22	0	21	65	50	85	4	.259	.348	.493
Mark Brouhard	OF51,DH7	R	25	60	186	19	51	6	3	2	20	7	41	1	.274	.305	.371
Larry Hisle	DH24	R	34	27	87	11	20	4	0	4	11	6	17	0	.230	.289	.414
Paul Molitor	OF46,DH16	R	24	64	251	45	67	11	0	2	19	25	29	10	.267	.341	.335
Roy Howell	3B53,DH13,1B3*	L	27	76	244	37	58	13	1	6	33	23	39	0	.238	.306	.373
Charlie Moore	C34,OF8,DH6	R	28	48	156	16	47	8	3	1	9	12	13	1	.301	.351	.410
Thad Bosley	OF37,DH1	L	24	42	105	11	24	2	0	0	3	6	13	2	.229	.270	.248
Ed Romero	SS22,2B18,3B3	R	23	44	91	6	18	3	0	1	10	4	9	0	.198	.227	.264
Sal Bando	3B15,1B9,DH2	R	37	32	65	10	13	4	0	2	9	6	3	1	.200	.268	.354
Marshall Edwards	OF36,DH1	L	28	40	58	10	14	1	1	0	4	0	2	6	.241	.241	.293
Ned Yost	C16	R	25	18	27	4	6	0	0	3	3	3	6	0	.222	.300	.556

R. Howell, 1 G at OF

Pitcher	T	Age	G	GS	CG	ShO	IP	H	HR	BB	SO	W-L	Sv	ERA
Pete Vuckovich	R	28	24	23	2	1	149.2	137	9	57	84	14-4	0	3.55
Mike Caldwell	L	32	24	23	3	0	144.1	151	18	38	41	11-9	0	3.93
Moose Haas	R	25	24	22	5	0	137.1	146	10	40	64	11-7	0	4.46
Jim Slaton	R	31	24	21	0	0	117.1	120	10	50	47	5-7	0	4.37
Randy Lerch	L	26	23	18	1	0	110.2	134	8	43	53	7-9	0	4.31
Rollie Fingers	R	34	47	0	0	0	78.0	55	3	13	61	6-3	28	1.04
Jamie Easterly	L	28	44	0	0	0	62.0	46	0	34	31	3-3	4	3.19
Reggie Cleveland	R	33	35	0	0	0	64.2	57	5	30	18	2-3	1	5.15
Jerry Augustine	L	28	27	2	0	0	61.1	75	4	18	26	2-2	2	4.26
Rickey Keeton	R	24	17	0	0	0	35.1	47	4	11	9	1-0	0	5.09
Dwight Bernard	R	29	6	0	0	0	5.0	5	0	6	1	0-0	0	3.60
Bob McClure	L	29	4	0	0	0	7.2	7	1	4	6	0-0	0	3.52
Chuck Porter	R	26	3	0	0	0	4.1	6	0	1	1	0-0	0	4.15
Donnie Moore	R	27	3	0	0	0	4.0	4	0	4	2	0-0	0	6.75
Frank DiPino	L	24	2	0	0	0	2.1	0	0	3	3	0-0	0	0.00
Willie Mueller	R	24	1	0	0	0	2.0	4	0	0	1	0-0	0	4.50

1981 Baltimore Orioles AL East 2nd 31-23 .574 2.0 GB (1) 4th 28-23 .549 2.0 GB (2)

Earl Weaver

Player	Gm by Position	B	Age	G	AB	R	H	2B	3B	HR	RBI	BB	SO	SB	Avg	OBP	Slg
Rick Dempsey	C90,DH1	R	31	92	251	24	54	10	1	6	15	32	36	0	.215	.306	.335
Eddie Murray	1B99	S	25	99	378	57	111	21	2	22	78	40	43	2	.294	.360	.534
Rich Dauer	2B94,3B4	R	28	96	369	41	97	27	0	4	38	27	18	0	.263	.317	.369
Doug DeCinces	3B100,1B1,OF1	R	30	100	346	49	91	23	2	13	55	41	32	0	.263	.341	.454
Mark Belanger	SS63	R	37	64	139	9	23	3	2	1	10	12	25	2	.165	.242	.237
Al Bumbry	OF100	L	34	101	392	61	107	18	2	1	27	51	51	22	.273	.358	.337
Gary Roenicke	OF83	R	26	85	219	31	59	16	0	3	20	23	29	1	.269	.340	.384
John Lowenstein	OF73,DH4	L	34	83	189	19	47	7	0	6	20	22	32	7	.249	.329	.381
Terry Crowley	DH42,1B4	L	34	68	134	12	33	6	0	4	25	29	12	0	.246	.376	.381
Ken Singleton	OF72,DH30	S	34	103	363	48	101	16	1	13	49	61	59	0	.278	.380	.435
Lenn Sakata	SS42,2B20	R	27	61	150	19	34	4	0	5	15	11	18	4	.227	.282	.353
Dan Graham	C40,DH6,3B4	L	26	55	142	7	25	3	0	2	11	13	32	0	.176	.244	.239
Jim Dwyer	OF59,1B3,DH1	L	31	68	134	16	30	0	1	3	10	20	19	0	.224	.318	.306
Bennie Ayala	DH27,OF4	R	30	44	86	12	24	2	0	3	13	11	9	0	.279	.364	.407
Jose Morales	DH22,1B3	R	36	38	86	6	21	3	0	2	14	3	13	0	.244	.270	.349
Wayne Krenchicki	SS16,2B7,3B6*	L	26	33	56	7	12	4	0	0	6	4	9	0	.214	.267	.286
Cal Ripken Jr.	SS12,3B6	R	20	23	39	1	5	0	0	0	0	1	8	0	.128	.150	.128
Bobby Bonner	SS9	R	24	10	27	6	8	2	0	0	2	1	4	1	.296	.310	.370
Mark Corey	OF9	R	25	10	8	2	0	0	0	0	0	2	2	0	.000	.200	.000
Willie Royster	C4	R	27	4	4	0	0	0	0	0	0	0	2	0	.000	.000	.000
John Shelby	OF4	S	23	7	2	2	0	0	0	0	0	0	1	2	.000	.000	.000
Dallas Williams	OF1	L	23	2	2	0	1	0	0	0	0	0	0	0	.500	.500	.500

W. Krenchicki, 1 G at DH

Pitcher	T	Age	G	GS	CG	ShO	IP	H	HR	BB	SO	W-L	Sv	ERA
Dennis Martinez	R	26	25	24	9	2	179.0	173	10	62	88	14-5	0	3.32
Scott McGregor	L	27	24	22	8	3	160.0	167	13	40	82	13-5	0	3.26
Jim Palmer	R	35	22	22	5	0	127.1	117	14	46	35	7-8	0	3.75
Mike Flanagan	L	29	20	20	3	2	116.0	108	11	37	72	9-6	0	4.19
Steve Stone	R	33	15	12	0	0	62.2	63	7	27	30	4-7	0	4.60
Tippy Martinez	L	31	37	0	0	0	59.0	48	4	32	50	3-3	11	2.90
Tim Stoddard	R	28	31	0	0	0	37.1	38	6	18	32	4-2	7	3.86
Sammy Stewart	R	26	29	3	0	0	112.1	89	8	57	57	4-8	4	2.32
Dave Ford	R	24	15	2	0	0	40.0	61	2	10	12	1-2	0	6.53
Jeff Schneider	L	28	11	0	0	0	24.0	27	4	12	17	0-0	1	4.88
Steve Luebber	R	31	7	0	0	0	16.2	26	3	4	12	0-0	0	7.56
Mike Boddicker	R	23	2	0	0	0	5.2	6	1	2	2	0-0	0	4.76

1981 New York Yankees AL East 1st 34-22 .607 — (1) 6th 25-26 .490 5.0 GB (2)

Gene Michael (48-34)/Bob Lemon (11-14)

Player	Gm by Position	B	Age	G	AB	R	H	2B	3B	HR	RBI	BB	SO	SB	Avg	OBP	Slg
Rick Cerone	C69	R	27	71	234	23	57	13	2	2	21	12	24	0	.244	.276	.342
Bob Watson	1B50,DH6	R	35	59	156	15	33	3	3	6	12	24	17	0	.212	.317	.385
Willie Randolph	2B93	R	26	93	357	59	83	14	3	2	24	57	24	14	.232	.336	.305
Graig Nettles	3B97,DH4	L	36	103	349	46	85	7	1	15	46	47	49	0	.244	.333	.398
Bucky Dent	SS73	R	29	73	227	20	54	11	0	7	27	19	17	0	.238	.300	.379
Dave Winfield	OF102,DH1	R	29	105	388	52	114	25	1	13	68	43	41	11	.294	.360	.464
Jerry Mumphrey	OF79	S	28	80	319	44	98	11	5	6	32	24	27	14	.307	.354	.429
Reggie Jackson	OF61,DH33	L	35	94	334	33	79	17	1	15	54	46	82	0	.237	.330	.428
Oscar Gamble	OF43,DH33	L	31	80	189	24	45	8	0	10	27	35	23	0	.238	.357	.439
Larry Milbourne	SS39,2B14,DH3*	S	30	61	163	24	51	7	2	1	12	9	14	2	.313	.351	.399
Lou Piniella	OF36,DH19	R	37	60	159	16	44	9	0	5	18	13	9	0	.277	.331	.428
Barry Foote†	C34,DH4,1B1	R	29	40	125	12	26	4	0	6	10	8	21	0	.208	.256	.384
Dave Revering†	1B44	L	28	45	119	8	28	4	1	2	7	11	20	0	.235	.300	.336
Bobby Murcer	DH33	L	35	50	117	14	31	6	0	6	24	12	15	0	.265	.331	.470
Jim Spencer†	1B25	L	34	25	63	6	9	2	0	2	4	9	7	0	.143	.250	.270
Bobby Brown	OF29,DH2	S	27	31	62	5	14	1	0	0	6	5	15	4	.226	.279	.242
Dennis Werth	1B19,OF8,DH4*	R	28	34	55	7	6	1	0	0	1	12	12	1	.109	.269	.127
Aurelio Rodriguez	3B20,2B3,DH2*	R	33	27	52	4	18	2	0	2	8	2	10	0	.346	.370	.500
Johnny Oates	C10	L	35	10	26	4	5	1	0	0	0	2	0	0	.192	.250	.231
Andre Robertson	SS8,2B3	R	23	10	19	1	5	1	0	0	0	0	3	1	.263	.263	.316
Mike Patterson†	OF4	L	23	4	9	2	2	0	2	0	0	0	0	0	.222	.222	.667
Steve Balboni	1B3,DH1	R	24	4	7	2	2	1	1	0	2	1	4	0	.286	.375	.714
Tucker Ashford	2B2	R	26	3	0	0	0	0	0	0	0	0	0	0	—	—	—

L. Milbourne, 3 G at 3B; D. Werth, 3 G at C; A. Rodriguez, 1 G at 1B

Pitcher	T	Age	G	GS	CG	ShO	IP	H	HR	BB	SO	W-L	Sv	ERA
Rudy May	L	36	27	22	4	0	147.2	137	10	41	79	6-11	1	4.14
Ron Guidry	L	30	23	21	0	0	127.0	100	12	26	104	11-5	0	2.76
Tommy John	L	38	20	20	7	0	140.1	135	10	39	50	9-8	0	2.63
Dave Righetti	L	22	15	15	2	0	105.1	75	1	38	89	8-4	0	2.05
Rick Reuschel†	R	32	12	11	3	0	70.2	75	4	10	22	4-4	0	2.67
Gene Nelson	R	20	8	7	0	0	39.1	40	5	23	16	3-1	0	4.81
Tom Underwood†	L	27	9	6	0	0	32.2	32	2	13	29	1-4	0	4.41
Ron Davis	R	25	43	0	0	0	73.0	47	6	25	83	4-5	6	2.71
Goose Gossage	R	29	32	0	0	0	46.2	22	2	14	48	3-2	20	0.77
Dave LaRoche	L	33	26	1	0	0	47.0	38	3	16	24	4-1	0	2.49
Doug Bird†	R	31	17	4	0	0	53.1	58	5	16	28	5-1	0	2.70
George Frazier	R	26	16	0	0	0	27.2	26	1	11	17	0-1	3	1.63
Bill Castro	R	27	11	0	0	0	19.0	26	2	5	4	1-1	0	3.79
Dave Wehrmeister	R	28	5	0	0	0	7.0	6	0	7	7	0-0	0	5.14
Andy McGaffigan	R	24	2	0	0	0	7.0	5	1	3	2	0-0	0	2.57
Mike Griffin†	R	24	2	0	0	0	4.1	5	0	0	4	0-0	0	2.08

1981 Detroit Tigers AL East 4th 31-26 .544 3.5 GB (1) 2nd 29-23 .558 1.5 GB (2)

Sparky Anderson

Player	Gm by Position	B	Age	G	AB	R	H	2B	3B	HR	RBI	BB	SO	SB	Avg	OBP	Slg
Lance Parrish	C90,DH5	R	25	96	348	39	85	18	2	10	46	34	52	2	.244	.311	.394
Richie Hebner	1B61,DH11	L	33	78	226	19	51	8	2	5	28	27	28	1	.226	.311	.345
Lou Whitaker	2B108	L	24	109	335	48	88	14	4	5	36	40	42	5	.263	.340	.373
Tom Brookens	3B71	R	27	71	239	19	58	10	1	4	25	14	43	5	.243	.284	.343
Alan Trammell	SS105	R	23	105	392	52	101	15	3	2	31	49	31	10	.258	.342	.327
Steve Kemp	OF92,DH12	L	26	105	372	52	103	18	4	9	49	70	48	9	.277	.389	.419
Al Cowens	OF83	R	29	85	253	27	66	11	4	1	18	22	36	3	.261	.319	.348
Kirk Gibson	OF67,DH9	L	24	83	290	41	95	11	3	9	40	18	64	17	.328	.369	.479
John Wockenfuss	DH39,1B25,C5*	R	32	70	172	20	37	4	0	9	25	28	22	0	.215	.322	.395
Ricky Peters	OF38,DH19	S	25	63	207	26	53	7	3	0	15	29	28	1	.256	.351	.319
Lynn Jones	OF60,DH4	R	28	71	174	19	45	5	0	2	19	18	10	1	.259	.328	.322
Champ Summers	DH37,OF18	L	35	64	165	16	42	8	0	3	21	19	35	1	.255	.339	.358
Ron Jackson†	1B29	R	28	31	95	12	27	8	1	1	12	8	11	4	.284	.337	.421
Stan Papi	3B32,DH3,1B1*	R	30	40	93	8	19	2	1	3	12	3	18	1	.204	.224	.344
Rick Leach	1B32,OF15,DH2	L	24	54	83	9	16	3	1	1	11	16	15	0	.193	.320	.289
Mick Kelleher	3B39,2B11,SS9	R	33	61	77	10	17	4	0	0	6	7	10	0	.221	.282	.273
Bill Fahey	C27	L	31	27	67	5	17	2	0	1	9	2	4	0	.254	.271	.328
Marty Castillo	3B4,C1,OF1	R	24	6	8	1	1	0	0	0	0	0	2	0	.125	.125	.125
Darrell Brown	OF6,DH4	S	25	16	4	4	1	0	0	0	0	0	1	1	.250	.250	.250
Duffy Dyer	C2	R	35	2	0	0	0	0	0	0	0	0	0	0	—	—	—

J. Wockenfuss, 1 G at OF; S. Papi, 1 G at 2B, 1 G at OF

Pitcher	T	Age	G	GS	CG	ShO	IP	H	HR	BB	SO	W-L	Sv	ERA
Jack Morris	R	26	25	25	15	1	198.0	153	14	78	97	14-7	0	3.05
Milt Wilcox	R	31	24	24	8	1	166.1	152	10	52	79	12-9	0	3.03
Dan Petry	R	22	23	22	7	2	141.0	115	10	57	79	10-9	0	3.00
Dan Schatzeder	L	26	17	14	1	0	71.1	74	13	29	20	6-8	0	6.06
Howard Bailey	L	23	9	5	0	0	36.2	45	4	13	17	1-4	0	7.36
Jerry Ujdur	R	24	4	4	0	0	14.0	19	2	5	5	0-0	0	6.43
Kevin Saucier	L	24	38	0	0	0	49.0	26	1	21	23	4-2	13	1.65
Aurelio Lopez	R	32	29	3	0	0	81.2	70	8	31	53	5-2	3	3.64
Dave Rozema	R	24	28	9	2	2	104.0	99	12	25	46	5-5	3	3.63
Dave Tobik	R	28	27	0	0	0	60.1	47	7	33	32	2-2	1	2.69
George Cappuzzello	L	27	18	3	0	0	33.2	28	2	18	19	1-1	1	3.48
Dennis Kinney	L	29	6	0	0	0	3.2	5	0	4	3	0-0	0	9.82
Larry Rothschild	R	27	5	0	0	0	5.2	4	0	6	1	0-0	1	1.59
Dave Rucker	L	23	2	0	0	0	4.0	3	0	1	2	0-0	0	6.75

1981 Boston Red Sox AL East 5th 30-26 .536 4.0 GB (1) 2nd 29-23 .558 1.5 GB (2)

Ralph Houk

Player	Gm by Position	B	Age	G	AB	R	H	2B	3B	HR	RBI	BB	SO	SB	Avg	OBP	Slg
Rich Gedman	C59	L	21	62	205	22	59	15	0	5	26	9	31	0	.288	.317	.434
Tony Perez	1B56,DH23	R	39	84	306	35	77	11	3	9	39	27	66	0	.252	.310	.395
Jerry Remy	2B87	L	28	88	358	55	110	9	1	0	31	36	30	9	.307	.368	.338
Carney Lansford	3B86,DH16	R	24	102	399	61	134	23	3	4	52	34	28	15	.336	.389	.439
Glenn Hoffman	SS78,3B1	R	22	78	242	28	56	10	0	1	20	12	25	0	.231	.271	.285
Jim Rice	OF108	R	28	108	451	51	128	18	1	17	62	34	76	2	.284	.333	.441
Dwight Evans	OF108	R	29	108	412	84	122	19	4	22	71	85	85	3	.296	.415	.522
Rick Miller	OF95	L	33	97	316	38	92	17	2	2	33	28	36	3	.291	.349	.377
Carl Yastrzemski	DH48,1B39	L	41	91	338	36	83	14	1	7	53	49	28	0	.246	.338	.355
Dave Stapleton	SS33,3B25,2B23*	R	27	93	355	45	101	17	1	10	42	21	22	0	.285	.325	.423
Gary Allenson	C47	R	26	47	139	23	31	8	0	5	25	23	33	0	.223	.335	.388
Joe Rudi	DH21,1B5,OF1	R	34	49	122	14	22	3	0	6	24	8	29	0	.180	.239	.352
Reid Nichols	OF27,DH7,3B1	R	22	39	48	13	9	0	1	0	3	2	6	0	.188	.216	.229
Gary Hancock	OF8,DH4	L	27	26	45	4	7	3	0	0	3	2	4	0	.156	.191	.222
Dave Schmidt	C15	R	24	15	42	6	10	1	0	2	3	7	17	0	.238	.347	.405
Julio Valdez	SS17	S	25	17	23	1	5	0	0	0	3	0	2	0	.217	.208	.217
Chico Walker	2B5	S	23	6	17	3	6	0	0	0	2	1	2	0	.353	.389	.353
Tom Poquette†	OF2	L	29	3	2	0	0	0	0	0	0	0	0	0	.000	.000	.000
John Lickert	C1	R	21	1	0	0	0	0	0	0	0	0	0	0	—	—	—

D. Stapleton, 12 G at 1B, 3 G at DH

Pitcher	T	Age	G	GS	CG	ShO	IP	H	HR	BB	SO	W-L	Sv	ERA
Dennis Eckersley	R	26	23	23	8	2	154.0	160	9	35	79	9-8	0	4.27
Frank Tanana	L	27	24	23	5	2	141.1	142	17	43	78	4-10	0	4.01
Mike Torrez	R	34	22	22	2	0	127.1	130	10	51	54	10-3	0	3.68
John Tudor	L	27	18	11	2	0	78.2	74	11	28	44	4-3	1	4.58
Steve Crawford	R	23	14	11	0	0	57.2	69	10	18	29	0-5	0	4.99
Bobby Ojeda	L	23	10	10	2	0	66.1	50	6	25	28	6-2	0	3.12
Bruce Hurst	L	23	5	5	0	0	23.0	23	1	12	11	2-0	0	4.30
Bob Stanley	R	26	35	1	0	0	98.2	110	3	38	28	10-8	0	3.83
Mark Clear	R	25	34	0	0	0	76.2	69	11	51	82	8-3	9	4.11
Tom Burgmeier	L	37	32	0	0	0	59.2	61	5	17	35	4-5	6	2.87
Bill Campbell	R	32	30	0	0	0	48.1	45	5	20	37	1-1	7	3.17
Chuck Rainey	R	26	11	2	0	0	40.0	39	2	13	20	0-1	0	2.70
Luis Aponte	R	28	7	0	0	0	15.2	11	0	3	11	1-0	1	0.57

1981 Cleveland Indians AL East 6th 26-24 .520 5.0 GB (1) 5th 26-27 .491 5.0 GB (2)

Dave Garcia

Player	Gm by Position	B	Age	G	AB	R	H	2B	3B	HR	RBI	BB	SO	SB	Avg	OBP	Slg
Ron Hassey	C56,1B5,DH1	L	28	61	190	8	44	4	0	1	25	17	11	0	.232	.297	.268
Mike Hargrove	1B88,DH4	L	31	94	322	43	102	21	0	2	49	60	16	5	.317	.424	.401
Duane Kuiper	2B72	L	31	72	206	15	53	6	0	0	14	8	13	1	.257	.284	.286
Toby Harrah	3B101,SS3,DH1	R	32	103	361	64	105	12	4	5	44	57	44	12	.291	.382	.388
Tom Veryzer	SS75	R	28	75	221	13	54	4	0	0	14	10	10	1	.244	.278	.262
Rick Manning	OF103	L	26	103	360	47	88	15	3	4	33	40	57	25	.244	.318	.336
Jorge Orta	OF86	L	30	88	338	50	92	14	3	5	34	21	43	4	.272	.312	.376
Miguel Dilone	OF56,DH11	S	26	72	269	33	78	5	5	0	19	18	28	29	.290	.334	.346
Andre Thornton	DH53,1B11	R	31	69	226	22	54	12	0	6	30	23	37	3	.239	.303	.372
Alan Bannister	OF35,2B30,1B2*	R	29	68	232	36	61	11	1	1	17	16	19	16	.263	.309	.332
Bo Diaz	C51,DH3	R	28	63	182	25	57	19	0	7	38	13	23	2	.313	.359	.533
Joe Charboneau	OF27,DH14	R	26	48	138	14	29	7	1	4	18	7	22	1	.210	.247	.362
Von Hayes	DH21,OF13,3B5	L	22	43	109	21	28	8	2	1	17	14	10	8	.257	.346	.394
Dave Rosello	2B26,3B8,DH4*	R	31	43	84	11	20	4	0	1	7	7	12	0	.238	.297	.321
Pat Kelly	DH18,OF8	L	36	48	75	8	16	4	0	1	16	14	9	2	.213	.333	.307
Jerry Dybzinski	SS34,2B3,3B3*	R	25	48	57	10	17	0	0	0	6	5	8	7	.298	.355	.298
Chris Bando	C15,DH2	S	25	21	47	3	10	3	0	0	6	2	2	0	.213	.240	.277
Mike Fischlin	SS19,2B1	R	25	22	43	3	10	1	0	0	5	3	6	3	.233	.277	.256
Larry Littleton	OF24	R	27	26	23	2	0	0	0	0	1	3	6	0	.000	.111	.000
Karl Pagel	1B6,DH1	L	26	14	15	3	4	0	2	1	4	4	1	0	.267	.421	.733
Ron Pruitt	OF3,DH1,C1	R	29	5	9	0	0	0	0	0	0	1	2	0	.000	.100	.000

A. Bannister, 1 G at SS; D. Rosello, 4 G at SS; J. Dybzinski, 1 G at DH

Pitcher	T	Age	G	GS	CG	ShO	IP	H	HR	BB	SO	W-L	Sv	ERA
Len Barker	R	25	22	22	9	3	154.1	150	7	46	127	8-7	0	3.91
Rick Waits	L	29	22	21	5	1	126.1	173	7	44	51	8-10	0	4.92
Bert Blyleven	R	30	20	20	9	1	159.1	145	9	40	107	11-7	0	2.88
John Denny	R	28	19	19	6	3	145.2	139	9	66	94	10-6	0	3.15
Wayne Garland	R	30	12	10	2	1	56.0	89	8	14	15	3-7	0	5.79
Tom Brennan	R	28	7	6	1	0	48.1	49	5	14	15	2-2	0	3.17
Dan Spillner	R	29	32	5	1	0	97.1	86	3	39	59	4-4	7	3.14
Sid Monge	L	30	31	0	0	0	58.0	58	9	21	41	3-5	4	4.34
Mike Stanton	R	28	24	0	0	0	43.1	43	4	18	34	3-3	2	4.36
Bob Lacey†	L	27	14	0	0	0	21.1	36	5	3	11	0-0	0	7.59
Dennis Lewallyn	R	27	7	0	0	0	13.1	16	1	2	11	0-0	0	5.40
Ed Glynn	L	28	4	0	0	0	7.2	5	0	4	4	0-0	0	1.17

1981 Toronto Blue Jays AL East 7th 16-42 .276 19.0 GB (1) 7th 21-27 .438 7.5 GB (2)

Bobby Mattick

Player	Gm by Position	B	Age	G	AB	R	H	2B	3B	HR	RBI	BB	SO	SB	Avg	OBP	Slg
Ernie Whitt	C72	L	29	74	195	16	46	9	0	1	16	20	30	5	.236	.307	.297
John Mayberry	1B80,DH10	L	32	94	290	34	72	6	1	17	43	44	45	1	.248	.360	.452
Damaso Garcia	2B62,DH1	R	24	64	250	24	63	8	1	1	13	9	32	13	.252	.277	.304
Danny Ainge	3B77,SS6,OF4*	R	22	86	246	20	46	6	2	0	14	23	41	8	.187	.258	.228
Alfredo Griffin	SS97,3B4,2B1	S	23	101	388	30	81	19	6	0	21	17	38	8	.209	.243	.289
Lloyd Moseby	OF100	L	21	100	378	36	88	16	2	9	43	24	86	11	.233	.278	.357
Al Woods	OF77,DH2	L	27	85	288	20	71	15	0	1	21	19	31	3	.247	.291	.309
Barry Bonnell	OF66	R	27	66	227	21	50	7	4	4	28	12	25	4	.220	.263	.339
Otto Velez	DH74,1B1	R	30	80	240	32	51	9	2	11	28	55	60	0	.213	.363	.404
Garth Iorg	2B46,3B17,SS2*	R	26	70	215	17	52	11	0	0	10	7	31	2	.242	.269	.293
George Bell	OF44,DH8	R	21	60	163	19	38	2	1	5	12	5	27	3	.233	.256	.350
Buck Martinez	C45	R	32	45	128	13	29	8	1	4	21	11	16	1	.227	.287	.398
Willie Upshaw	DH15,1B14,OF14	L	24	61	111	15	19	3	1	4	10	11	16	2	.171	.252	.324
Jesse Barfield	OF25	R	21	25	95	7	22	3	2	2	9	4	19	4	.232	.270	.368
Ken Macha	3B19,1B16,DH2*	R	30	37	85	4	17	2	0	0	6	8	15	1	.200	.266	.224
Boomer Wells	1B22,DH3	R	27	32	73	7	18	5	0	0	5	5	12	0	.247	.295	.315
Ted Cox	3B14,DH1,1B1	R	26	16	50	6	15	4	0	2	9	5	10	0	.300	.364	.500
Rick Bosetti†	OF19,DH1	R	27	25	47	5	11	2	0	0	4	2	6	0	.234	.265	.277
Fred Manrique	SS11,3B2,DH1	R	19	14	28	1	4	0	0	0	1	0	12	0	.143	.172	.143
Charlie Beamon	DH4,1B1	L	27	8	15	1	3	1	0	0	0	2	2	0	.200	.294	.267
Dan Whitmer	C7	R	25	7	9	0	1	1	0	0	0	1	2	0	.111	.200	.222

D. Ainge, 2 G at 2B, 1 G at DH; G. Iorg, 1 G at DH, 1 G at 1B; K. Macha, 1 G at C

Pitcher	T	Age	G	GS	CG	ShO	IP	H	HR	BB	SO	W-L	Sv	ERA
Dave Stieb	R	23	25	25	11	2	183.2	148	10	61	89	11-10	0	3.19
Jim Clancy	R	25	22	22	2	0	125.0	126	12	64	56	6-12	0	4.90
Luis Leal	R	24	29	19	3	0	129.2	127	8	44	71	7-13	1	3.68
Jackson Todd	R	29	21	13	3	0	97.2	94	10	31	41	2-7	0	3.96
Mark Bomback	R	28	20	11	0	0	90.1	84	6	35	33	5-5	0	3.89
Juan Berenguer†	R	26	12	11	1	0	71.0	62	7	35	29	2-9	0	4.31
Joey McLaughlin	R	24	40	0	0	0	60.0	55	2	21	38	1-5	10	2.85
Roy Lee Jackson	R	27	39	0	0	0	62.0	65	5	25	27	1-2	7	2.61
Jerry Garvin	L	25	35	4	0	0	53.0	46	3	23	25	1-2	0	3.40
Mike Willis	L	30	20	0	0	0	35.0	43	6	20	16	0-4	0	5.91
Mike Barlow	R	33	12	0	0	0	15.0	22	1	6	5	0-0	0	4.20
Dale Murray	R	31	11	0	0	0	15.1	12	0	5	12	1-0	0	1.17
Paul Mirabella	L	27	8	1	0	0	14.2	20	2	7	9	0-0	0	7.36
Nino Espinosa†	R	27	1	0	0	0	1.0	4	0	0	0	0-0	0	9.00

1981 Oakland Athletics AL West 1st 37-23 .617 — (1) 2nd 27-22 .551 1.0 GB (2)

Billy Martin

Player	Gm by Position	B	Age	G	AB	R	H	2B	3B	HR	RBI	BB	SO	SB	Avg	OBP	Slg
Mike Heath	C78,OF6	R	26	84	301	26	71	7	1	8	30	13	36	3	.236	.269	.346
Jim Spencer†	1B48	L	34	54	171	14	35	6	0	2	9	10	20	1	.205	.246	.275
Shooty Babitt	2B52	R	22	54	156	10	40	1	3	0	14	13	13	5	.256	.314	.301
Wayne Gross	3B73,1B2,DH1	L	29	82	243	29	50	7	1	10	31	34	28	2	.206	.304	.366
Rob Picciolo	SS82	R	28	82	179	23	48	5	3	4	13	5	22	0	.268	.290	.397
Tony Armas	OF109	R	27	109	440	51	115	24	3	22	76	19	115	5	.261	.294	.480
Rickey Henderson	OF107	R	22	108	423	89	135	18	7	6	35	64	68	56	.319	.408	.437
Dwayne Murphy	OF106,DH1	L	26	107	390	58	98	10	3	15	60	73	91	10	.251	.369	.408
Cliff Johnson	DH68,1B9	R	33	84	273	40	71	8	0	17	59	28	60	5	.260	.329	.476
Dave McKay	3B43,2B38,SS7	S	31	79	224	25	59	11	1	4	21	16	43	4	.263	.313	.375
Jeff Newman	C37,1B30	R	32	68	216	17	50	12	0	3	15	9	28	0	.231	.260	.329
Fred Stanley	SS62,2B6	R	33	66	145	15	28	4	0	0	7	15	23	2	.193	.269	.221
Mitchell Page	DH29	L	29	34	92	9	13	1	0	4	13	7	29	2	.141	.200	.283
Dave Revering†	1B29,DH2	L	28	31	87	12	20	1	1	2	10	11	12	0	.230	.320	.333
Keith Drumright	2B19,DH5	L	26	31	86	8	25	1	1	0	11	4	4	0	.291	.319	.326
Kelvin Moore	1B13	R	23	14	47	5	12	0	1	1	3	5	15	1	.255	.327	.362
Mickey Klutts	3B14	R	26	15	46	9	17	0	0	5	11	2	9	0	.370	.396	.696
Brian Doyle	2B17	L	26	17	40	2	5	0	0	0	3	1	2	0	.125	.146	.125
Mark Budaska	DH9	S	28	9	32	3	5	1	0	0	2	4	10	0	.156	.250	.188
Mike Patterson†	OF5,DH2	L	23	12	23	4	8	1	1	0	1	2	5	0	.348	.400	.478
Tim Hosley	DH4,1B1	R	34	18	21	2	2	0	0	1	5	2	5	0	.095	.174	.238
Mike Davis	DH3,OF2,1B1	L	22	17	20	0	1	1	0	0	0	2	4	0	.050	.136	.100
Rick Bosetti†	OF5,DH2	R	27	9	19	4	2	0	0	0	1	3	3	0	.105	.227	.105
Jimmy Sexton	DH1,3B1	R	29	7	3	3	0	0	0	0	0	0	2	2	.000	.000	.000
Jim Nettles	OF1	L	34	1	0	0	0	0	0	0	0	0	0	0	—	—	—
Jeff Cox	2B1	R	25	2	0	0	0	0	0	0	0	0	0	0	—	—	—
Bob Kearney	C1	R	24	1	0	0	0	0	0	0	0	0	0	0	—	—	—

Pitcher	T	Age	G	GS	CG	ShO	IP	H	HR	BB	SO	W-L	Sv	ERA
Rick Langford	R	29	24	24	18	2	195.1	190	14	58	84	12-10	0	2.99
Mike Norris	R	26	23	23	12	2	172.2	145	17	63	78	12-9	0	3.75
Steve McCatty	R	27	22	22	16	4	185.2	140	12	61	91	14-7	0	2.33
Matt Keough	R	25	19	19	10	2	140.1	125	11	45	60	10-6	0	3.40
Brian Kingman	R	26	18	15	3	1	100.1	112	10	32	52	3-6	0	3.95
Ed Figueroa	R	32	2	1	0	0	8.1	8	1	6	1	0-0	0	5.40
Jeff Jones	R	24	33	0	0	0	61.0	51	7	40	43	4-1	3	3.39
Bob Owchinko	L	26	29	0	0	0	39.1	34	2	19	26	4-3	2	3.20
Tom Underwood†	L	27	16	5	1	0	51.0	37	4	25	46	3-2	1	3.18
Bo McLaughlin	R	27	11	0	0	0	11.2	17	1	9	3	0-1	1	11.57
Dave Beard	R	21	8	0	0	0	13.0	9	1	4	15	1-1	3	2.77
Craig Minetto	L	27	8	0	0	0	6.2	7	0	4	4	0-0	0	2.70
Dave Heaverlo	R	30	6	0	0	0	5.2	7	0	3	2	1-0	0	1.59
Rich Bordi	R	22	2	0	0	0	2.0	1	0	1	0	0-0	0	0.00

1981 Texas Rangers AL West 2nd 33-22 .600 1.5 GB (1) 3rd 24-26 .480 4.5 GB (2)

Don Zimmer

Player	Gm by Position	B	Age	G	AB	R	H	2B	3B	HR	RBI	BB	SO	SB	Avg	OBP	Slg
Jim Sundberg	C98,OF2	R	30	102	339	42	94	17	2	3	28	50	48	2	.277	.369	.366
Pat Putnam	1B94,OF3	L	27	95	297	33	79	17	2	8	35	17	38	4	.266	.304	.418
Bump Wills	2B101,DH1	S	28	102	410	51	103	13	2	2	41	32	49	12	.251	.304	.307
Buddy Bell	3B96,SS1	R	29	97	360	44	106	16	1	10	64	42	30	3	.294	.364	.428
Mario Mendoza	SS88	R	30	88	229	18	53	6	1	0	22	7	25	2	.231	.254	.266
Mickey Rivers	OF97	L	32	99	399	62	114	21	2	3	26	24	31	9	.286	.327	.371
Leon Roberts	OF71	R	30	72	233	26	65	17	2	4	31	25	38	3	.279	.345	.421
Billy Sample	OF64	R	26	66	230	36	65	16	0	3	25	17	21	4	.283	.346	.391
Al Oliver	DH101,1B1	L	34	102	421	53	130	29	1	4	55	24	28	3	.309	.348	.411
John Grubb	OF58	L	32	67	199	26	46	9	1	3	26	23	25	0	.231	.316	.332
Bill Stein	1B20,OF8,3B7*	R	34	53	115	21	38	6	0	2	22	7	15	1	.330	.360	.435
Mark Wagner	SS43,2B4,3B2	R	27	50	85	15	22	4	1	1	14	8	13	1	.259	.323	.365
Tom Poquette†	OF18	L	29	30	64	2	10	1	0	0	7	5	1	0	.156	.225	.172
John Ellis	1B18,DH1	R	32	23	58	2	8	3	0	1	7	5	10	0	.138	.219	.241
Bobby Jones	OF10	L	31	10	34	4	9	1	0	3	7	1	7	0	.265	.286	.559
Wayne Tolleson	3B6,SS2	S	25	14	24	6	4	0	0	0	1	1	5	2	.167	.200	.167
Bobby Johnson	C5,1B1	R	21	6	18	2	5	0	0	2	4	1	3	0	.278	.316	.611
Dan Duran	OF7,1B1	L	27	13	16	1	4	0	0	0	0	1	3	0	.250	.294	.250
Rick Lisi	OF8	R	25	9	16	6	5	0	0	0	1	4	0	0	.313	.450	.313
Larry Cox	C5	R	33	5	13	0	3	1	0	0	0	0	4	0	.231	.231	.308
Nelson Norman	SS5	S	23	7	13	1	3	1	0	0	2	1	2	0	.231	.267	.308
Don Werner	DH2	R	28	2	8	1	2	0	0	0	0	0	2	0	.250	.250	.250

B. Stein, 3 G at 2B, 1 G at SS

Pitcher	T	Age	G	GS	CG	ShO	IP	H	HR	BB	SO	W-L	Sv	ERA
Danny Darwin	R	25	22	22	6	2	146.0	115	12	57	98	9-9	0	3.64
Doc Medich	R	32	20	20	4	4	143.1	136	8	33	65	10-6	0	3.08
Rick Honeycutt	L	27	20	20	8	2	127.2	120	12	17	40	11-6	0	3.31
Fergie Jenkins	R	37	19	16	1	0	106.0	122	14	40	63	5-8	0	4.50
Jon Matlack	L	31	17	16	1	1	104.1	101	8	41	43	4-7	0	4.14
John Butcher	R	24	5	3	1	1	27.2	18	0	8	19	1-2	0	1.63
Len Whitehouse	L	23	2	1	0	0	3.1	8	1	2	2	0-1	0	16.20
Steve Comer	R	27	36	1	0	0	77.1	70	1	31	22	8-2	6	2.56
John Henry Johnson	L	24	24	0	0	0	23.2	19	2	6	8	3-1	2	2.66
Jim Kern	R	32	23	0	0	0	30.0	21	0	22	20	1-2	6	2.70
Charlie Hough	R	33	21	5	2	0	82.0	61	4	31	69	4-1	1	2.96
Bob Babcock	R	31	16	0	0	0	28.2	21	2	16	18	1-1	0	2.20
Dave Schmidt	R	24	14	1	0	0	31.2	31	1	11	13	0-1	1	3.13
Mark Mercer	L	27	7	0	0	0	7.2	7	1	7	8	0-1	2	4.70
Bob Lacey†	L	27	1	0	0	0	1.0	1	1	0	0	0-0	0	9.00

1981 Chicago White Sox AL West 3rd 31-22 .585 2.5 GB (1) 6th 23-30 .434 7.0 GB (2)

Tony La Russa

Player	Gm by Position	B	Age	G	AB	R	H	2B	3B	HR	RBI	BB	SO	SB	Avg	OBP	Slg
Carlton Fisk	C92,1B1,3B1*	R	33	96	338	44	89	12	0	7	45	38	37	3	.263	.354	.361
Mike Squires	1B88,OF1	L	29	92	294	35	78	9	0	0	25	22	17	7	.265	.312	.296
Tony Bernazard	2B104,SS1	S	24	106	384	53	106	14	4	6	34	54	66	4	.276	.367	.380
Jim Morrison	3B87,DH1,2B1	R	28	90	290	27	68	8	1	10	34	10	29	3	.234	.261	.372
Bill Almon	SS103	R	28	103	349	46	105	10	2	4	41	21	60	16	.301	.341	.375
Chet Lemon	OF93	R	26	94	328	50	99	23	6	9	50	33	48	5	.302	.384	.491
Ron LeFlore	OF82	R	33	82	337	46	83	10	4	0	24	28	70	36	.246	.304	.300
Harold Baines	OF80,DH1	L	22	82	280	42	80	11	7	10	41	12	41	6	.286	.318	.482
Greg Luzinski	DH103	R	30	104	378	55	100	15	1	21	62	58	80	0	.265	.365	.476
Wayne Nordhagen	OF60	R	32	65	208	19	64	8	1	6	33	10	25	0	.308	.338	.442
Lamar Johnson	1B36,DH2	R	30	41	134	10	37	7	0	1	15	5	14	0	.276	.298	.351
Greg Pryor	3B27,SS13,2B5	R	31	47	76	4	17	1	0	0	6	6	8	0	.224	.298	.237
Rusty Kuntz	OF51,DH5	R	26	67	55	15	14	2	0	0	4	6	8	1	.255	.339	.291
Jim Essian	C25,3B2	R	30	27	52	6	16	3	0	0	5	4	5	0	.308	.357	.365
Bob Molinaro	DH4,OF2	L	31	47	42	7	11	1	1	1	9	8	1	1	.262	.377	.405
Jerry Hairston	OF7	S	29	9	25	5	7	1	0	1	6	2	4	0	.280	.345	.440
Jay Loviglio	3B4,2B3,DH2	R	25	14	15	5	4	0	0	0	2	1	1	2	.267	.313	.267
Jerry Turner†	OF1	L	27	10	12	1	2	0	0	0	2	1	2	0	.167	.231	.167
Leo Sutherland	OF7	L	23	11	12	6	2	0	0	0	0	3	1	2	.167	.333	.167
Marc Hill	C14,1B1,3B1	R	29	16	6	0	0	0	0	0	0	0	1	0	.000	.000	.000

C. Fisk, 1 G at OF

Pitcher	T	Age	G	GS	CG	ShO	IP	H	HR	BB	SO	W-L	Sv	ERA
Rich Dotson	R	22	24	24	5	4	141.0	145	13	49	73	9-8	0	3.77
Britt Burns	L	22	24	23	5	1	156.2	139	14	49	108	10-6	0	2.64
Ross Baumgarten	L	26	19	19	2	1	101.2	101	9	40	52	5-9	0	4.07
Steve Trout	L	23	20	18	3	0	124.2	122	7	38	54	8-7	0	3.47
Francisco Barrios	R	28	8	7	1	0	36.1	45	3	14	12	1-3	0	3.96
LaMarr Hoyt	R	26	43	1	0	0	90.2	80	10	28	60	9-3	10	3.57
Ed Farmer	R	31	42	0	0	0	52.2	53	5	34	42	3-3	10	4.61
Kevin Hickey	L	25	41	0	0	0	44.1	38	3	18	17	0-2	3	3.65
Dennis Lamp	R	28	27	10	3	0	127.0	103	4	43	71	7-6	0	2.41
Lynn McGlothen†	R	31	11	0	0	0	21.2	14	0	7	12	0-0	0	4.15
Jerry Koosman†	L	38	8	3	1	0	27.0	27	2	7	21	1-4	0	3.33
Reggie Patterson	R	22	6	1	0	0	7.1	14	1	6	2	0-1	0	13.50
Dewey Robinson	R	26	4	0	0	0	4.0	5	1	3	2	1-0	0	4.50
Juan Agosto	L	23	2	0	0	0	5.2	5	1	0	3	0-0	0	4.76

1981 Kansas City Royals AL West 5th 20-30 .400 12.0 GB (1) 1st 30-23 .566 — (2)

Jim Frey (30-40)/Dick Howser (20-13)

Player	Gm by Position	B	Age	G	AB	R	H	2B	3B	HR	RBI	BB	SO	SB	Avg	OBP	Slg
John Wathan	C73,OF16,1B1	R	31	89	301	24	76	9	3	1	19	19	23	11	.252	.298	.312
Willie Aikens	1B99	L	26	101	349	45	93	16	0	17	53	62	47	0	.266	.377	.458
Frank White	2B93	R	30	94	364	35	91	17	1	9	38	19	50	4	.250	.285	.376
George Brett	3B88	L	28	89	347	42	109	27	7	6	43	27	23	14	.314	.361	.484
U.L. Washington	SS98	S	27	98	339	40	77	19	1	2	29	41	43	10	.227	.310	.307
Willie Wilson	OF101	S	25	102	439	54	133	10	7	1	32	18	42	34	.303	.335	.364
Amos Otis	OF97,DH1	R	34	99	372	49	100	22	3	9	57	31	59	16	.269	.321	.417
Cesar Geronimo	OF57	L	33	59	118	14	29	0	2	2	13	11	16	6	.246	.305	.331
Hal McRae	DH97,OF4	R	35	101	389	38	106	23	2	7	36	34	33	3	.272	.330	.396
Darryl Motley	OF39	R	21	42	125	15	29	4	0	2	8	7	15	1	.232	.276	.312
Jamie Quirk	C22,3B8,DH1*	L	26	46	100	8	25	7	0	0	10	6	17	0	.250	.299	.320
Clint Hurdle	OF28	L	23	28	76	12	25	3	1	4	15	13	10	0	.329	.427	.553
Jerry Grote†	C22	R	38	22	56	4	17	3	1	1	9	3	2	0	.304	.344	.446
Lee May	1B8,DH4	R	38	26	55	3	16	3	0	0	8	3	14	0	.291	.328	.345
Dave Chalk	3B14,2B10,SS1	R	30	27	49	2	11	3	0	0	5	4	2	0	.224	.283	.286
Rance Mulliniks	2B10,SS7,3B5	L	25	24	44	6	10	3	0	0	5	2	7	0	.227	.261	.295
Ken Phelps	DH4,1B2	L	26	21	22	1	3	0	1	0	1	1	13	0	.136	.174	.227
Dan Garcia	OF6,1B2	L	27	12	14	4	2	0	0	0	0	0	2	0	.143	.143	.143
Pat Sheridan	OF3	L	23	3	1	0	0	0	0	0	0	0	1	0	.000	.000	.000
Onix Concepcion	SS1	R	23	2	0	0	0	0	0	0	0	0	0	0	—	—	—
Tim Ireland	1B4	S	28	4	0	1	0	0	0	0	0	0	0	0	—	—	—
Greg Keatley	C2	R	27	2	0	0	0	0	0	0	0	0	0	0	—	—	—

J. Quirk, 1 G at 2B, 1 G at OF

Pitcher	T	Age	G	GS	CG	ShO	IP	H	HR	BB	SO	W-L	Sv	ERA
Dennis Leonard	R	30	26	26	9	2	201.2	202	15	41	107	13-11	0	2.99
Larry Gura	L	33	23	23	12	2	172.1	139	11	35	61	11-8	0	2.72
Rich Gale	R	27	19	15	2	0	101.2	107	14	38	47	6-6	0	5.40
Paul Splittorff	L	34	21	15	1	0	99.0	111	12	23	48	5-5	0	4.36
Mike Jones	L	21	12	11	0	0	75.2	74	7	28	29	6-3	0	3.21
Atlee Hammaker	L	23	10	6	0	0	39.0	44	2	12	11	1-3	0	5.54
Dan Quisenberry	R	28	40	0	0	0	62.1	59	1	15	20	1-4	18	1.73
Renie Martin	R	25	29	0	0	0	61.2	55	2	29	25	4-5	4	2.77
Ken Brett	L	32	22	0	0	0	32.1	35	2	14	7	1-1	2	4.18
Jim Wright	R	26	17	4	0	0	52.0	57	5	21	27	2-3	0	3.46
Juan Berenguer†	R	26	8	3	0	0	19.2	22	4	16	20	0-4	0	8.69
Bill Paschall	R	27	2	0	0	0	2.0	2	0	0	1	0-0	0	4.50
Jeff Schattinger	R	25	1	0	0	0	3.0	2	0	1	1	0-0	0	0.00

1981 California Angels AL West 4th 31-29 .517 6.0 GB (1) 7th 20-30 .400 8.5 GB (2)

Jim Fregosi (22-25)/Gene Mauch (29-34)

Player	Gm by Position	B	Age	G	AB	R	H	2B	3B	HR	RBI	BB	SO	SB	Avg	OBP	Slg
Ed Ott	C72	L	29	75	258	20	56	8	1	2	22	17	42	2	.217	.266	.279
Rod Carew	1B90,DH2	L	35	93	364	57	111	17	1	2	21	45	45	16	.305	.380	.374
Bobby Grich	2B100	R	32	100	352	56	107	14	2	22	61	40	71	2	.304	.378	.543
Butch Hobson	3B83,DH2	R	29	85	268	27	63	7	4	4	36	35	60	1	.235	.321	.336
Rick Burleson	SS109	R	30	109	430	53	126	17	1	5	33	42	38	4	.293	.357	.372
Dan Ford	OF97	R	29	97	375	53	104	14	1	15	48	23	71	2	.277	.327	.440
Fred Lynn	OF69	L	29	76	256	28	56	8	1	5	31	38	42	1	.219	.322	.316
Brian Downing	OF56,C37,DH5	R	30	93	317	47	79	14	0	9	41	46	35	1	.249	.351	.379
Don Baylor	DH97,1B4,OF1	R	32	103	377	52	90	18	1	17	66	42	51	3	.239	.322	.427
Juan Beniquez	OF55,DH1	R	31	58	166	18	30	5	0	3	13	15	16	2	.181	.251	.265
Bobby Clark	OF34	R	26	34	88	12	22	2	1	4	19	7	18	0	.250	.305	.432
Bert Campaneris	3B45,SS3,2B2	R	39	55	82	11	21	2	1	1	10	5	10	5	.256	.295	.341
Larry Harlow	OF39	L	29	43	82	13	17	1	0	0	4	16	25	1	.207	.337	.220
John Harris	1B11,OF10,DH1	L	26	36	77	5	19	3	0	3	9	3	11	0	.247	.275	.403
Daryl Sconiers	1B12,DH3	L	22	15	52	6	14	1	1	1	7	1	10	0	.269	.283	.385
Freddie Patek	2B16,3B7,SS3	R	36	27	47	3	11	1	1	0	5	1	6	1	.234	.250	.298
Tom Brunansky	OF11	R	20	11	33	7	5	0	0	3	6	8	10	1	.152	.317	.424
Joe Ferguson†	C8,OF4	R	34	12	30	5	7	1	0	1	5	9	8	0	.233	.400	.367
Steve Lubratich	3B6	R	26	7	21	2	3	1	0	0	1	0	2	1	.143	.143	.190
Brian Harper	OF2,DH1	R	21	4	11	1	3	0	0	0	1	0	0	1	.273	.250	.273
Bob Davis	C1	R	29	1	2	0	0	0	0	0	0	0	0	0	.000	.000	.000

Pitcher	T	Age	G	GS	CG	ShO	IP	H	HR	BB	SO	W-L	Sv	ERA
Geoff Zahn	L	35	25	25	9	0	161.1	181	18	43	52	10-11	0	4.41
Mike Witt	R	20	22	21	7	1	129.0	123	9	47	75	8-9	0	3.28
Ken Forsch	R	34	20	20	10	4	153.0	143	7	27	55	11-7	0	2.88
Steve Renko	R	36	22	15	0	0	102.0	93	7	42	50	8-4	1	3.44
Dave Frost	R	28	12	9	0	0	47.1	44	3	19	16	1-8	0	5.51
Angel Moreno	L	26	8	4	1	0	31.1	27	2	14	12	1-3	0	2.87
Bill Travers	L	28	4	4	0	0	9.2	14	2	4	5	0-1	0	8.38
Doug Rau	L	32	3	3	0	0	10.1	14	2	4	3	1-2	0	8.71
Andy Hassler	L	29	42	0	0	0	75.2	72	8	33	44	4-3	5	3.21
Don Aase	R	26	39	0	0	0	65.1	56	4	24	38	4-4	11	2.34
Jesse Jefferson	R	32	26	5	0	0	77.0	80	4	24	27	2-4	0	3.62
Luis Sanchez	R	27	17	0	0	0	33.2	39	4	11	13	0-2	2	2.94
Bruce Kison	R	31	11	4	0	0	44.0	40	8	14	19	1-1	0	3.48
John D'Acquisto	R	29	6	0	0	0	19.1	26	2	12	8	0-0	0	10.71
Mickey Mahler	L	28	6	0	0	0	6.1	1	0	2	5	0-0	0	0.00
Fred Martinez	R	24	2	0	0	0	6.0	5	1	3	4	0-0	0	3.00

1981 Seattle Mariners AL West 6th 21-36 .368 14.5 GB (1) 5th 23-29 .442 6.5 GB (2)

Maury Wills (6-18)/Rene Lachemann (38-47)

Player	Gm by Position	B	Age	G	AB	R	H	2B	3B	HR	RBI	BB	SO	SB	Avg	OBP	Slg
Jerry Narron	C65	L	25	76	203	13	45	5	0	3	17	16	35	0	.222	.285	.291
Bruce Bochte	1B82,OF14,DH1	L	30	99	335	39	87	16	0	6	30	47	53	1	.260	.354	.361
Julio Cruz	2B92,SS1	S	26	94	352	57	90	12	3	2	24	39	40	43	.256	.332	.324
Lenny Randle	3B59,2B21,OF5*	S	32	82	273	22	63	9	1	4	25	17	22	11	.231	.276	.315
Jim Anderson	SS68,3B2	R	24	70	162	12	33	7	0	2	19	17	29	3	.204	.283	.284
Tom Paciorek	OF103	R	34	104	405	50	132	28	2	14	66	35	50	13	.326	.379	.509
Joe Simpson	OF88	L	29	91	288	32	64	11	3	2	30	15	41	12	.222	.261	.302
Jeff Burroughs	OF87,DH1	R	30	89	319	32	81	13	1	10	41	41	64	0	.254	.339	.395
Richie Zisk	DH93	R	32	94	357	42	111	12	1	16	43	28	63	0	.311	.366	.485
Dan Meyer	3B49,OF14,DH3*	L	28	83	252	26	66	10	1	3	22	10	16	4	.262	.291	.345
Gary Gray	1B34,DH15,OF4	R	28	69	208	27	51	7	1	13	31	4	44	2	.245	.257	.476
Bud Bulling	C62	R	28	62	154	15	38	3	0	2	15	21	20	0	.247	.341	.305
Dave Henderson	OF58	R	22	59	126	17	21	3	0	6	13	16	24	2	.167	.264	.333
Paul Serna	SS23,2B7	R	22	30	94	11	24	2	0	4	9	3	11	2	.255	.293	.404
Rick Auerbach	SS38	R	31	38	84	12	13	3	0	1	6	4	15	1	.155	.200	.226
Dave Edler	3B26,SS1	R	24	29	78	7	11	3	0	0	5	11	13	3	.141	.250	.179
Jim Maler	1B5,DH2	R	22	12	23	1	8	1	0	0	2	2	1	1	.348	.423	.391
Casey Parsons	OF24,1B1	L	27	36	22	6	5	1	0	1	5	1	4	0	.227	.308	.409
Vance McHenry	SS13,DH1	R	24	15	18	3	4	0	0	0	2	1	1	0	.222	.263	.222
Brad Gulden	C6,DH2	L	25	8	16	0	3	2	0	0	1	0	2	0	.188	.188	.313
Reggie Walton	OF4,DH1	R	28	12	6	1	0	0	0	0	0	1	2	0	.000	.143	.000
Kim Allen	DH2,2B2,OF2	R	28	19	3	1	0	0	0	0	0	0	2	2	.000	.000	.000
Dan Firova	C13	R	24	13	2	0	0	0	0	0	0	0	1	0	.000	.000	.000

L. Randle, 3 G at SS; D. Meyer, 3 G at 1B

Pitcher	T	Age	G	GS	CG	ShO	IP	H	HR	BB	SO	W-L	Sv	ERA
Glenn Abbott	R	30	22	20	1	0	130.1	127	14	28	35	4-9	0	3.94
Floyd Bannister	L	26	21	20	5	2	121.1	128	14	39	85	9-9	0	4.45
Ken Clay	R	27	22	14	0	0	101.0	116	10	42	32	2-7	0	4.63
Jerry Don Gleaton	L	23	20	13	1	0	85.1	88	10	38	31	4-7	0	4.75
Mike Parrott	R	26	24	12	0	0	85.0	102	3	28	43	3-6	1	5.08
Jim Beattie	R	26	13	9	0	0	66.2	59	2	18	36	3-2	1	2.97
Brian Allard	R	23	7	7	1	0	48.0	48	5	8	20	3-2	0	3.75
Bob Stoddard	R	24	5	5	1	0	34.2	35	3	9	22	2-1	0	2.60
Shane Rawley	L	25	46	0	0	0	68.1	64	1	38	35	4-6	8	3.95
Larry Andersen	R	28	41	0	0	0	67.2	57	4	18	40	3-3	5	2.66
Dick Drago	R	36	39	0	0	0	53.2	71	4	15	27	4-6	5	5.53
Bryan Clark	L	24	29	9	1	0	93.1	92	3	55	52	2-5	2	4.34
Bob Galasso	R	29	13	1	0	0	31.2	32	2	13	14	1-1	1	4.83
Randy Stein	R	28	5	0	0	0	9.1	18	1	8	6	0-1	0	10.61
Bud Black	L	24	2	0	0	0	1.0	2	0	3	0	0-0	0	0.00

1981 Minnesota Twins AL West 7th 17-39 .304 18.0 GB (1) 4th 24-29 .453 6.0 GB (2)

John Goryl (11-25)/Billy Gardner (30-43)

Player	Gm by Position	B	Age	G	AB	R	H	2B	3B	HR	RBI	BB	SO	SB	Avg	OBP	Slg
Sal Butera	C59,DH1,1B1	R	28	62	167	13	40	7	1	0	18	22	14	0	.240	.325	.293
Danny Goodwin	1B40,DH5,OF1	L	27	59	151	18	34	6	1	2	17	16	32	3	.225	.298	.318
Rob Wilfong	2B93	L	27	93	305	32	75	11	3	3	19	29	43	2	.246	.311	.331
John Castino	3B98,2B4	R	26	101	381	41	102	13	9	6	36	18	52	4	.268	.301	.396
Roy Smalley	SS37,DH15,1B1	S	28	56	167	24	44	7	1	7	22	31	24	0	.263	.375	.443
Mickey Hatcher	OF91,1B7,3B2*	R	26	99	377	36	96	23	2	3	37	15	29	3	.255	.285	.350
Gary Ward	OF80,DH2	R	27	85	295	42	78	7	6	3	29	28	48	5	.264	.325	.359
Dave Engle	OF76,DH1,3B1	R	24	82	248	29	64	14	4	5	32	13	37	0	.258	.295	.407
Glenn Adams	DH62	L	33	72	220	13	46	10	0	2	24	20	26	0	.209	.273	.282
Hosken Powell	OF64,DH8	L	26	80	264	30	63	11	3	2	25	17	31	7	.239	.286	.326
Pete Mackanin	2B31,SS28,1B10*	R	29	77	225	21	52	7	1	4	18	7	40	1	.231	.256	.324
Ron Jackson†	1B36,OF7,DH6*	R	28	54	175	17	46	9	0	4	28	10	15	2	.263	.305	.383
Butch Wynegar	C37,DH9	S	25	47	150	11	37	5	0	0	10	17	9	0	.247	.322	.280
Rick Sofield	OF34	L	24	41	102	9	18	2	0	0	5	8	22	3	.176	.234	.196
Ron Washington	SS26,OF2	R	29	28	84	8	19	3	1	0	5	4	14	4	.226	.270	.286
Kent Hrbek	1B13,DH8	L	21	24	67	5	16	5	0	1	7	5	9	0	.239	.301	.358
Chuck Baker	SS31,2B3,DH1*	R	28	40	66	6	12	0	3	0	6	1	8	0	.182	.194	.273
Tim Corcoran	1B16,DH3	L	28	22	51	4	9	3	0	0	4	6	7	0	.176	.259	.235
Tim Laudner	C12,DH2	R	23	14	43	4	7	2	0	2	5	3	17	0	.163	.234	.349
Lenny Faedo	SS12	R	21	12	41	3	8	0	1	0	6	1	5	0	.195	.209	.244
Ray Smith	C15	R	25	15	40	4	8	1	0	1	1	0	3	0	.200	.200	.300
Gary Gaetti	3B8,DH1	R	22	9	26	4	5	0	0	2	3	0	6	0	.192	.192	.423
Greg Johnston	OF6	L	26	7	16	2	2	0	0	0	0	2	5	0	.125	.222	.125
Mark Funderburk	OF6,DH1	R	24	8	15	2	3	1	0	0	2	2	1	0	.200	.278	.267

M. Hatcher, 1 G at DH; P. Mackanin, 6 G at DH, 4 G at 3B; R. Jackson, 3 G at 3B; C. Baker, 1 G at 3B

Pitcher	T	Age	G	GS	CG	ShO	IP	H	HR	BB	SO	W-L	Sv	ERA
Pete Redfern	R	26	24	23	3	0	141.2	140	12	52	77	9-8	0	4.07
Al Williams	R	27	23	22	4	0	150.0	160	11	52	76	6-10	0	4.08
Fredie Arroyo	R	29	23	19	2	0	128.1	144	11	34	39	7-10	0	3.93
Roger Erickson	R	24	14	14	1	0	91.1	93	7	31	44	3-8	0	3.84
Jerry Koosman†	L	38	19	13	2	1	94.1	98	8	34	55	3-9	5	4.20
Brad Havens	L	21	14	12	1	1	78.0	76	6	24	43	3-6	0	3.58
Doug Corbett	R	28	54	0	0	0	87.2	80	5	34	60	2-6	17	2.57
Jack O'Connor	L	23	28	0	0	0	35.1	46	3	30	16	3-2	0	5.86
Don Cooper	R	25	27	2	0	0	58.2	61	9	32	33	1-5	0	4.30
John Verhoeven	R	27	25	0	0	0	52.0	57	4	14	16	0-0	0	3.98
Darrell Jackson	L	25	14	5	0	0	32.2	35	1	19	26	3-3	0	4.41
Bob Veselic	R	25	5	0	0	0	22.2	22	1	12	13	1-1	0	3.18
Jack Hobbs	L	25	4	0	0	0	5.2	5	0	6	1	0-0	0	3.18
Terry Felton	R	23	1	0	0	0	1.1	4	1	2	1	0-0	0	40.50

»1981 St. Louis Cardinals NL East 2nd 30-20 .600 1.5 GB (1) 2nd 29-23 .558 0.5 GB (2)

Whitey Herzog

Player	Gm by Position	B	Age	G	AB	R	H	2B	3B	HR	RBI	BB	SO	SB	Avg	OBP	Slg
Darrell Porter	C52	L	29	61	174	22	39	10	2	6	31	39	32	1	.224	.364	.408
Keith Hernandez	1B98,OF3	L	27	103	376	65	115	27	4	8	48	61	45	12	.306	.401	.463
Tom Herr	2B103	S	25	103	411	50	110	14	9	0	46	39	30	23	.268	.329	.345
Ken Oberkfell	3B102,SS1	L	25	102	376	43	110	12	6	2	45	37	28	13	.293	.353	.372
Garry Templeton	SS76	S	25	80	333	47	96	16	8	1	33	14	55	8	.288	.315	.393
George Hendrick	OF101	R	31	101	394	67	112	19	3	18	61	41	44	4	.284	.356	.485
Tito Landrum	OF67	R	26	81	119	13	31	5	4	0	10	6	14	4	.261	.297	.370
Sixto Lezcano	OF65	R	27	72	214	26	57	8	2	5	28	40	40	0	.266	.376	.393
Dane Iorg	OF57,1B8,3B2	L	31	75	217	23	71	11	2	2	39	7	9	2	.327	.344	.424
Tony Scott†	OF44	S	29	45	176	21	40	5	2	2	17	5	22	10	.227	.253	.313
Gene Tenace	C38,1B7	R	34	58	129	26	30	7	0	5	22	38	26	0	.233	.416	.403
Mike Ramsey	SS35,3B5,2B1*	S	27	47	124	19	32	3	0	0	9	8	16	4	.258	.303	.282
Gene Roof	OF20	S	23	23	60	11	18	6	0	0	3	12	16	5	.300	.411	.400
Orlando Sanchez	C18	L	24	27	49	5	14	2	1	0	6	2	6	1	.286	.308	.367
Steve Braun	OF12,3B1	L	33	44	46	9	9	2	1	0	2	15	7	1	.196	.393	.283
David Green	OF18	R	20	21	34	6	5	1	0	0	2	6	5	0	.147	.275	.176
Glenn Brummer	C19	R	26	21	30	2	6	1	0	0	2	1	2	0	.200	.219	.233
Julio Gonzalez	SS5,2B4,3B2	R	28	20	22	2	7	1	0	1	3	1	3	0	.318	.348	.500
Neil Fiala†		L	24	3	3	0	0	0	0	0	0	0	1	0	.000	.000	.000

M. Ramsey, 1 G at OF

Pitcher	T	Age	G	GS	CG	ShO	IP	H	HR	BB	SO	W-L	Sv	ERA
Lary Sorensen	R	25	23	23	3	1	140.1	149	3	26	52	7-7	0	3.27
Bob Forsch	R	31	20	20	1	0	124.1	106	7	29	41	10-5	0	3.18
Silvio Martinez	R	25	18	16	0	0	97.0	95	4	39	34	2-5	0	3.99
John Martin	L	25	17	15	4	0	102.2	85	10	26	36	8-5	0	3.42
Joaquin Andujar†	R	28	11	8	1	0	55.1	56	4	11	19	6-1	0	3.74
Andy Rincon	R	22	5	5	1	1	35.2	27	0	5	13	3-1	0	1.77
Dave LaPoint	L	21	3	2	0	0	10.2	12	1	2	4	1-0	0	4.22
Bruce Sutter	R	28	48	0	0	0	82.1	64	5	24	57	3-5	25	2.62
Jim Kaat	L	42	41	1	0	0	53.0	60	2	17	8	6-6	4	3.40
Bob Shirley	L	27	28	11	1	0	79.1	78	6	34	36	6-4	1	4.08
Mark Littell	R	28	28	1	0	0	41.0	36	2	31	22	1-3	2	4.39
Jim Otten	R	29	24	0	0	0	35.2	44	3	20	20	1-0	0	5.30
Bob Sykes	L	26	22	1	0	0	37.1	37	2	18	14	2-0	0	4.58
Joe Edelen†	R	25	13	0	0	0	17.1	29	2	3	10	1-0	0	9.35
Doug Bair†	R	31	11	0	0	0	15.2	13	0	2	14	2-0	1	3.45
Luis DeLeon	R	22	10	0	0	0	15.1	11	1	3	8	0-1	0	2.35

Seasons: Team Rosters 861

1981 Montreal Expos NL East 3rd 30-25 .545 4.0 GB (1) 1st 30-23 .566 — (2)

Dick Williams (44-37)/Jim Fanning (16-11)

Player	Gm by Position	B	Age	G	AB	R	H	2B	3B	HR	RBI	BB	SO	SB	Avg	OBP	Slg
Gary Carter	C100,1B1	R	27	100	374	48	94	20	2	16	68	35	35	1	.251	.313	.444
Warren Cromartie	1B62,OF38	L	27	99	358	41	109	19	2	6	42	39	27	2	.304	.370	.419
Rodney Scott	2B93	S	27	95	336	43	69	9	3	0	26	50	35	30	.205	.308	.250
Larry Parrish	3B95	R	27	97	349	41	85	19	3	8	44	28	73	0	.244	.297	.384
Chris Speier	SS96	R	31	96	307	33	69	10	2	2	25	38	29	1	.225	.310	.290
Andre Dawson	OF103	R	26	103	394	71	119	21	3	24	64	35	50	26	.302	.365	.553
Tim Raines	OF81,2B1	S	21	88	313	61	95	13	7	5	37	45	31	71	.304	.391	.438
Jerry White	OF39	S	28	59	119	11	26	5	1	3	11	13	17	5	.218	.293	.353
Tim Wallach	OF35,1B16,3B15	R	23	71	212	19	50	9	1	4	13	15	37	0	.236	.299	.344
Terry Francona	OF26,1B1	L	22	34	95	11	26	0	1	1	8	5	6	1	.274	.317	.326
Ellis Valentine†	OF21	R	26	22	76	8	16	3	0	3	15	6	11	0	.211	.259	.368
John Milner†	1B21	L	31	31	76	6	18	5	0	3	9	12	6	0	.237	.341	.421
Willie Montanez†	1B16	L	33	26	62	6	11	0	1	0	5	4	9	0	.177	.227	.210
Jerry Manuel	2B23,SS2	S	27	27	55	10	11	5	0	3	10	6	11	0	.200	.270	.455
Mike Phillips†	SS26,2B6	L	30	34	55	5	12	2	0	0	4	5	15	0	.218	.279	.255
Bobby Ramos	C23	R	25	26	41	4	8	1	0	1	3	3	5	0	.195	.250	.293
Rowland Office	OF15	L	28	26	40	4	7	0	0	0	0	4	6	0	.175	.250	.175
Tom Hutton	1B9,OF2	L	35	31	29	1	3	0	0	0	2	2	1	0	.103	.161	.103
Brad Mills	3B7,2B2	L	24	17	21	3	5	1	0	0	1	2	1	0	.238	.304	.286
Dan Briggs	1B3,OF3	L	28	9	11	0	1	0	0	0	0	0	3	0	.091	.091	.091
Wallace Johnson	2B1	S	24	11	9	1	2	0	1	0	3	1	1	1	.222	.300	.444
Chris Smith	2B1	S	23	7	7	0	0	0	0	0	0	0	2	0	.000	.000	.000
Bob Pate	OF5	R	27	8	6	0	2	0	0	0	0	1	0	0	.333	.429	.333
Dave Hostetler	1B2	R	25	5	6	1	3	0	0	1	1	0	2	0	.500	.500	1.000
Pat Rooney	OF2	R	23	4	5	0	0	0	0	0	0	0	3	0	.000	.000	.000
Mike Gates	2B1	L	24	1	2	1	1	0	1	0	1	0	1	0	.500	.500	1.500
Tony Johnson	OF1	R	25	2	1	0	0	0	0	0	0	0	0	0	.000	.000	.000
Tom Wieghaus	C1	R	24	1	1	0	0	0	0	0	0	0	0	0	.000	.000	.000

Pitcher	T	Age	G	GS	CG	ShO	IP	H	HR	BB	SO	W-L	Sv	ERA
Steve Rogers	R	31	22	22	7	3	160.2	149	7	41	87	12-8	0	3.42
Bill Gullickson	R	22	22	22	3	2	157.1	142	3	34	115	7-9	0	2.80
Scott Sanderson	R	24	22	22	4	1	137.1	122	10	31	77	9-7	0	2.95
Ray Burris	R	30	22	21	4	0	135.2	117	9	41	52	9-7	0	3.05
Charlie Lea	R	24	16	11	2	2	64.1	63	4	26	31	5-4	0	4.62
Woodie Fryman	L	41	35	0	0	0	43.0	38	1	14	25	5-3	7	1.88
Elias Sosa	R	31	32	0	0	0	39.1	46	3	8	18	1-2	3	3.66
Bill Lee	L	34	31	7	0	0	88.2	90	6	14	34	5-6	6	2.94
Stan Bahnsen	R	36	25	3	0	0	49.0	45	7	24	28	2-1	1	4.96
Jeff Reardon†	R	25	25	0	0	0	41.2	21	3	9	21	2-0	6	1.30
Steve Ratzer	R	27	12	0	0	0	17.1	23	2	7	4	1-1	0	6.23
Grant Jackson†	L	38	10	0	0	0	10.2	14	2	9	4	1-0	0	7.59
Tom Gorman	L	23	9	0	0	0	15.0	12	0	6	13	0-0	0	4.20
Bryn Smith	R	25	7	0	0	0	13.0	14	1	3	9	1-0	0	2.77
Rick Engle	L	24	1	0	0	0	2.0	6	0	1	2	0-0	0	18.00

1981 Philadelphia Phillies NL East 1st 34-21 .618 — (1) 3rd 25-27 .481 4.5 GB (2)

Dallas Green

Player	Gm by Position	B	Age	G	AB	R	H	2B	3B	HR	RBI	BB	SO	SB	Avg	OBP	Slg
Bob Boone	C75	R	33	76	227	19	48	7	0	4	24	22	16	2	.211	.279	.295
Pete Rose	1B107	S	40	107	431	73	140	18	5	0	33	46	26	4	.325	.391	.390
Manny Trillo	2B94	R	30	94	349	37	100	14	3	6	36	26	37	10	.287	.338	.395
Mike Schmidt	3B101	R	31	102	354	78	112	19	2	31	91	73	71	12	.316	.435	.644
Larry Bowa	SS102	S	35	103	360	34	102	14	3	0	31	26	17	16	.283	.331	.339
Gary Matthews	OF100	R	30	101	359	62	108	21	3	9	67	59	42	15	.301	.398	.451
Garry Maddox	OF93	R	31	94	323	37	85	7	1	5	40	17	42	9	.263	.295	.337
Bake McBride	OF56	L	32	58	221	26	60	17	1	2	21	11	25	5	.271	.303	.385
Keith Moreland	C50,3B7,1B2*	R	27	61	196	16	50	7	0	6	37	15	13	1	.255	.307	.383
Lonnie Smith	OF51	R	25	62	176	40	57	14	3	2	11	18	14	21	.324	.402	.472
Greg Gross	OF55	L	28	83	102	14	23	6	1	0	7	15	5	2	.225	.319	.304
Dick Davis	OF32	R	27	45	96	12	32	6	1	2	19	8	13	1	.333	.387	.479
Luis Aguayo	2B21,SS21,3B3	R	22	45	84	11	18	4	0	1	7	6	15	1	.214	.283	.298
Del Unser	1B18,OF16	L	36	62	59	5	9	3	0	0	6	13	9	0	.153	.301	.203
Ramon Aviles	2B20,3B13,SS5	R	29	38	28	2	6	1	0	0	3	3	5	0	.214	.290	.250
George Vukovich	OF9	L	25	20	26	5	10	0	0	1	4	1	0	1	.385	.407	.500
Len Matuszek	1B1,3B1	L	26	13	11	1	3	1	0	0	1	3	1	0	.273	.429	.364
Ozzie Virgil	C1	R	24	6	6	0	0	0	0	0	0	0	2	0	.000	.000	.000
Ryne Sandberg	SS5,2B1	R	21	13	6	2	1	0	0	0	0	0	1	0	.167	.167	.167
Bob Dernier	OF5	R	24	10	4	0	3	0	0	0	0	0	0	2	.750	.750	.750
Don McCormack	C3	R	25	3	4	0	1	0	0	0	0	0	1	0	.250	.250	.250
John Vukovich	3B9,1B1,2B1	R	33	11	1	0	0	0	0	0	0	0	1	0	.000	.000	.000

K. Moreland, 2 G at OF

Pitcher	T	Age	G	GS	CG	ShO	IP	H	HR	BB	SO	W-L	Sv	ERA
Steve Carlton	L	36	24	24	10	1	190.0	152	9	62	179	13-4	0	2.42
Dick Ruthven	R	30	23	22	5	0	146.2	162	10	54	80	12-7	0	5.15
Larry Christenson	R	27	20	15	0	0	106.2	108	8	30	70	4-7	1	3.54
Nino Espinosa†	R	27	14	14	2	0	73.2	98	11	24	22	2-5	0	6.11
Marty Bystrom	R	22	9	9	1	0	53.2	55	3	16	24	4-3	0	3.35
Mark Davis	L	20	9	9	0	0	43.0	49	7	24	29	1-4	0	7.74
Dickie Noles	R	24	13	8	0	0	58.1	57	2	23	34	2-2	0	4.17
Dan Larson	R	26	5	4	1	0	28.0	27	4	15	15	3-0	0	4.18
Sparky Lyle	L	36	48	0	0	0	75.0	85	4	33	29	9-6	2	4.44
Ron Reed	R	38	39	0	0	0	61.1	54	6	17	40	5-3	8	3.08
Mike Proly	R	30	35	2	0	0	63.0	66	6	19	19	2-1	2	3.86
Tug McGraw	L	36	34	0	0	0	44.0	35	2	14	26	2-4	10	2.66
Warren Brusstar	R	29	14	0	0	0	12.1	12	0	10	8	0-1	0	4.38
Jerry Reed	R	25	4	0	0	0	4.2	7	0	6	5	0-1	0	7.71

1981 Pittsburgh Pirates NL East 4th 25-23 .521 5.5 GB (1) 6th 21-33 .389 9.5 GB (2)

Chuck Tanner

Player	Gm by Position	B	Age	G	AB	R	H	2B	3B	HR	RBI	BB	SO	SB	Avg	OBP	Slg
Tony Pena	C64	R	24	66	210	16	63	9	1	2	17	8	23	1	.300	.326	.381
Jason Thompson	1B78	L	26	86	223	36	54	13	0	15	42	59	49	0	.242	.396	.502
Phil Garner†	2B50	R	32	56	181	22	46	6	2	1	20	21	21	4	.254	.327	.326
Bill Madlock	3B78	R	30	82	279	35	95	23	1	6	45	34	17	18	.341	.413	.495
Tim Foli	SS81	R	30	86	316	32	78	12	2	0	20	17	10	7	.247	.285	.297
Omar Moreno	OF103	L	28	103	434	62	120	18	8	1	35	26	76	39	.276	.319	.362
Mike Easler	OF90	L	30	95	339	43	97	18	5	7	42	24	45	4	.286	.328	.431
Lee Lacy	OF63,3B1	R	33	78	213	31	57	11	4	2	10	11	29	24	.268	.307	.385
Dave Parker	OF60	L	30	67	240	29	62	14	3	9	48	9	25	6	.258	.287	.454
Dale Berra	3B42,SS30,2B18	R	24	81	232	21	56	12	0	2	27	17	34	11	.241	.302	.319
Steve Nicosia	C52	R	25	54	169	21	39	10	1	2	18	13	10	3	.231	.286	.337
Johnny Ray	2B31	S	24	31	102	10	25	11	0	0	6	6	9	0	.245	.284	.353
Bill Robinson	1B23,OF7,3B1	R	38	39	88	8	19	3	0	2	8	5	18	1	.216	.258	.318
Vance Law	2B19,SS7,3B2	R	24	30	67	1	9	0	1	0	3	2	15	1	.134	.157	.164
Willie Stargell	1B9	L	41	38	60	2	17	4	0	0	9	5	9	0	.283	.333	.350
John Milner†	1B8,OF8	L	31	34	59	6	14	1	0	2	9	5	3	0	.237	.292	.356
Gary Alexander	1B9,OF8	R	28	21	47	6	10	4	1	1	6	3	12	0	.213	.255	.404
Willie Montanez†	1B11	L	33	29	38	2	10	0	0	1	1	1	2	0	.263	.282	.342
Kurt Bevacqua	2B4,3B2	R	34	29	27	2	7	1	0	1	4	4	6	0	.259	.333	.407
Matt Alexander	OF6	S	34	15	11	5	4	0	0	0	0	0	1	3	.364	.364	.364
Doe Boyland		L	26	11	8	0	0	0	0	0	0	1	3	0	.000	.111	.000

Pitcher	T	Age	G	GS	CG	ShO	IP	H	HR	BB	SO	W-L	Sv	ERA
Rick Rhoden	R	28	21	21	4	2	136.1	147	6	53	76	9-4	0	3.89
Eddie Solomon	R	30	22	17	2	0	127.0	133	10	27	38	8-6	1	3.12
Jim Bibby	R	36	14	14	2	2	93.2	79	4	26	48	6-3	0	2.50
Pascual Perez	R	24	17	13	2	0	86.1	92	5	34	46	2-7	0	3.96
Luis Tiant	R	40	9	9	1	0	57.1	54	3	19	32	2-5	0	3.92
Odell Jones	R	28	13	8	0	0	54.1	51	3	23	30	4-5	0	3.31
John Candelaria	L	27	6	6	0	0	40.2	42	3	11	14	2-2	0	3.54
Bob Long	R	26	5	3	0	0	19.2	23	2	10	8	1-2	0	5.95
Kent Tekulve	R	34	45	0	0	0	65.0	61	1	17	34	5-5	3	2.49
Grant Jackson†	L	38	35	0	0	0	32.1	30	1	10	17	1-2	4	2.51
Enrique Romo	R	33	33	0	0	0	41.2	47	5	18	23	1-3	9	4.54
Rod Scurry	L	25	27	7	0	0	74.0	74	6	40	65	4-5	7	3.77
Victor Cruz	R	23	22	0	0	0	34.0	33	6	15	28	1-1	1	2.65
Don Robinson	R	24	16	2	0	0	38.1	47	4	23	17	0-3	2	5.87
Mark Lee	R	28	12	0	0	0	19.2	17	1	5	5	0-2	2	2.75
Ernie Camacho	R	26	7	3	0	0	21.2	23	0	15	11	0-1	0	4.98

1981 New York Mets NL East 5th 17-34 .333 15.0 GB (1) 4th 24-28 .462 5.5 GB (2)

Joe Torre

Player	Gm by Position	B	Age	G	AB	R	H	2B	3B	HR	RBI	BB	SO	SB	Avg	OBP	Slg
John Stearns	C66,1B9,3B4	R	29	80	273	25	74	12	1	1	24	24	17	12	.271	.329	.333
Dave Kingman	1B56,OF48	R	32	100	353	40	78	11	3	22	59	55	105	6	.221	.326	.456
Doug Flynn	2B100,SS5	R	30	105	325	24	72	12	4	1	20	11	19	1	.222	.247	.292
Hubie Brooks	3B93,OF3,SS1	R	24	98	358	34	110	21	2	4	38	23	65	9	.307	.345	.411
Frank Taveras	SS79	R	31	84	283	30	65	11	3	0	11	12	36	16	.230	.263	.290
Lee Mazzilli	OF89	S	26	95	324	36	74	14	5	6	34	46	53	17	.228	.324	.358
Mookie Wilson	OF80	S	25	92	328	49	89	8	8	3	14	20	59	24	.271	.317	.372
Ellis Valentine†	OF47	R	26	48	169	15	35	8	1	5	21	5	38	0	.207	.227	.355
Rusty Staub	1B41	L	37	70	161	9	51	9	0	5	21	22	12	1	.317	.398	.466
Alex Trevino	C45,2B4,OF2*	R	23	56	149	17	39	2	0	0	10	13	19	3	.262	.323	.275
Joel Youngblood	OF41	R	29	43	143	16	50	10	2	4	25	12	19	2	.350	.398	.531
Mike Jorgensen	1B40,OF19	L	32	86	122	8	25	5	2	3	15	12	24	4	.205	.270	.352
Bob Bailor	SS22,2B13,OF13*	R	29	51	81	11	23	3	1	0	8	8	11	2	.284	.352	.346
Mike Cubbage	3B12	L	30	67	80	9	17	2	2	1	4	9	15	0	.213	.289	.325
Ron Gardenhire	SS18,2B6,3B1	R	23	27	48	2	13	1	0	0	3	5	9	2	.271	.340	.292
Ron Hodges	C7	L	32	35	43	5	13	2	0	1	6	5	8	1	.302	.375	.419
Wally Backman	2B11,3B1	S	21	26	36	5	10	2	0	0	0	4	7	1	.278	.350	.333
Mike Howard	OF14	S	23	14	24	4	4	1	0	0	3	4	6	2	.167	.276	.208
Brian Giles	2B2,SS2	R	21	9	7	0	0	0	0	0	0	0	3	0	.000	.000	.000

A. Trevino, 1 G at 3B; B. Bailor, 1 G at 3B

Pitcher	T	Age	G	GS	CG	ShO	IP	H	HR	BB	SO	W-L	Sv	ERA
Pat Zachry	R	29	24	24	3	0	139.0	151	13	56	76	7-14	0	4.14
Mike Scott	R	26	23	23	1	0	136.0	130	11	34	54	5-10	0	3.90
Greg Harris	R	25	16	14	0	0	68.2	65	8	28	54	3-5	1	4.46
Ed Lynch	R	25	17	13	0	0	80.1	79	6	21	27	4-5	0	2.91
Randy Jones	L	31	13	12	0	0	59.1	65	8	38	14	1-8	0	4.85
Dave Roberts	L	36	7	4	0	0	15.1	26	5	5	10	0-3	0	9.39
Craig Swan	R	30	5	3	0	0	13.2	10	0	1	9	0-2	0	3.29
Tim Leary	R	23	1	1	0	0	2.0	0	0	1	3	0-0	0	0.00
Neil Allen	R	23	43	0	0	0	66.2	64	4	26	50	7-6	18	2.97
Pete Falcone	L	27	35	9	3	1	95.1	84	3	36	56	5-3	1	2.55
Ray Searage	L	26	26	0	0	0	36.2	34	2	17	16	1-0	1	3.68
Dyar Miller	R	35	23	0	0	0	38.1	49	2	15	22	1-0	0	3.29
Terry Leach	R	27	21	1	0	0	35.1	26	2	12	16	1-1	0	2.55
Tom Hausman	R	28	20	0	0	0	33.0	28	2	7	13	0-1	0	2.18
Mike Marshall	R	38	20	0	0	0	31.0	26	2	8	8	3-2	0	2.61
Jeff Reardon†	R	25	18	0	0	0	28.2	27	2	12	28	1-0	2	3.45
Dan Boitano	R	28	15	0	0	0	16.1	21	2	5	8	2-1	0	5.51
Jesse Orosco	L	24	8	0	0	0	17.1	13	2	6	18	0-1	1	1.56
Charlie Puleo	R	26	4	1	0	0	13.1	8	0	8	8	0-0	0	0.00

1981 Chicago Cubs NL East 6th 15-37 .288 17.5 GB (1) 5th 23-28 .451 6.0 GB (2)

Joey Amalfitano

Player	Gm by Position	B	Age	G	AB	R	H	2B	3B	HR	RBI	BB	SO	SB	Avg	OBP	Slg
Jody Davis	C56	R	24	56	180	14	46	5	1	4	21	21	28	0	.256	.333	.361
Bill Buckner	1B105	L	31	106	421	45	131	35	3	10	75	26	16	5	.311	.349	.480
Mike Tyson	2B36,SS1	R	31	50	92	6	17	2	0	2	8	7	15	1	.185	.248	.272
Ken Reitz	3B81	R	30	82	260	10	56	9	1	2	28	15	56	0	.215	.261	.281
Ivan DeJesus	SS106	R	28	106	403	49	78	8	4	0	13	46	61	21	.194	.276	.233
Leon Durham	OF83,1B3	L	23	87	328	42	95	14	6	10	35	27	53	25	.290	.344	.460
Steve Henderson	OF77	R	28	82	287	32	84	9	5	5	35	42	61	5	.293	.382	.411
Jerry Morales	OF72	R	32	84	245	27	70	6	2	1	25	22	29	1	.286	.343	.339
Bobby Bonds	OF45	R	35	45	163	26	35	7	1	6	19	24	44	5	.215	.323	.380
Tim Blackwell	C56	S	28	58	158	21	37	10	2	1	11	23	23	2	.234	.331	.342
Steve Dillard	2B32,3B7,SS2	R	30	53	119	18	26	7	1	2	11	8	20	0	.218	.268	.345
Scot Thompson	OF30,1B3	L	25	57	115	8	19	5	0	0	8	7	8	2	.165	.208	.209
Heity Cruz	3B18,OF16	R	28	53	109	15	25	5	0	7	15	17	24	2	.229	.331	.468
Pat Tabler	2B35	R	23	35	101	11	19	3	1	1	5	13	26	0	.188	.281	.267
Joe Strain	2B20	R	27	25	74	7	14	1	0	0	1	5	7	0	.189	.250	.203
Ty Waller	3B22,2B3,OF3	R	24	30	71	10	19	2	1	3	13	4	18	2	.268	.303	.451
Jim Tracy	OF11	L	25	45	63	6	15	2	1	0	5	12	14	1	.238	.355	.302
Mike Lum†	OF14,1B1	L	35	41	58	5	14	1	0	2	7	5	5	0	.241	.308	.362
Scott Fletcher	2B13,SS4,3B1	R	22	19	46	6	10	4	0	0	1	2	4	0	.217	.250	.304
Barry Foote†	C8	R	29	9	22	0	0	0	0	0	1	3	7	0	.000	.115	.000
Carlos Lezcano	OF5	R	25	7	14	1	1	0	0	0	2	0	4	0	.071	.071	.071
Mel Hall	OF3	L	20	10	11	1	1	0	0	1	2	1	4	0	.091	.167	.364
Gary Krug		L	26	7	5	0	2	0	0	0	0	1	1	0	.400	.500	.400
Bill Hayes	C1	R	23	1	0	0	0	0	0	0	0	0	0	0	—	—	—

Pitcher	T	Age	G	GS	CG	ShO	IP	H	HR	BB	SO	W-L	Sv	ERA
Mike Krukow	R	29	25	25	2	1	144.1	146	11	55	101	9-9	0	3.68
Rick Reuschel†	R	32	13	13	1	0	85.2	87	4	23	53	4-7	0	3.47
Ken Kravec	L	29	24	12	0	0	78.1	80	5	39	50	1-6	0	5.06
Doug Bird†	R	31	12	12	2	1	75.1	72	5	16	34	4-5	0	3.58
Mike Griffin†	R	24	16	9	0	0	52.0	64	4	9	20	2-5	1	4.50
Dick Tidrow	R	34	51	0	0	0	74.2	73	6	30	39	3-10	9	5.06
Dave Capilla	L	29	42	0	0	0	51.0	52	1	34	28	1-0	0	3.18
Lee Smith	R	23	40	1	0	0	66.2	57	2	31	50	3-6	1	3.51
Randy Martz	R	25	33	14	1	0	107.2	103	6	49	32	5-7	6	3.68
Bill Caudill	R	24	30	10	0	0	71.0	87	9	31	45	1-5	0	5.83
Rawly Eastwick	R	30	30	0	0	0	43.1	43	2	15	24	0-1	1	2.28
Lynn McGlothen†	R	31	20	6	0	0	54.2	71	1	28	26	1-4	0	4.77
Willie Hernandez	L	26	12	0	0	0	13.2	14	0	8	13	0-0	2	3.95
Dave Geisel	L	26	11	2	0	0	16.0	11	0	10	7	2-0	0	0.56
Jay Howell	R	25	10	2	0	0	22.1	23	3	10	10	2-0	0	4.84

1981 Cincinnati Reds NL West 2nd 35-21 .625 0.5 GB (1) 2nd 31-21 .596 1.5 GB (2)

John McNamara

Player	Gm by Position	B	Age	G	AB	R	H	2B	3B	HR	RBI	BB	SO	SB	Avg	OBP	Slg
Joe Nolan	C81	L	30	81	236	25	73	18	1	1	26	24	19	1	.309	.371	.407
Dan Driessen	1B74	L	29	82	233	35	55	14	0	7	33	40	31	2	.236	.349	.386
Ron Oester	2B103,SS9	S	25	105	354	45	96	16	7	5	42	42	49	2	.271	.342	.398
Ray Knight	3B105	R	28	106	386	43	100	23	1	6	34	33	51	2	.259	.322	.370
Dave Concepcion	SS106	R	33	106	421	57	129	28	0	5	67	37	61	4	.306	.358	.409
George Foster	OF108	R	32	108	414	64	122	23	2	22	90	51	75	4	.295	.373	.519
Ken Griffey Sr.	OF99	L	31	101	396	65	123	21	6	2	34	39	42	12	.311	.370	.409
Dave Collins	OF93	S	28	95	360	63	98	18	6	3	23	41	41	26	.272	.355	.381
Johnny Bench	1B38,C7	R	33	52	178	14	55	8	0	8	25	17	21	0	.309	.369	.489
Mike O'Berry	C55	R	27	55	111	6	20	3	1	1	5	14	19	0	.180	.272	.252
Paul Householder	OF19	S	22	23	69	12	19	4	0	2	9	10	16	3	.275	.367	.420
Larry Biittner	1B8,OF3	L	35	42	61	1	13	4	0	0	8	4	4	0	.213	.258	.279
Sam Mejias	OF58	R	29	66	49	6	14	2	0	0	7	2	9	1	.286	.302	.327
Junior Kennedy	2B16,3B5	R	30	27	44	5	11	1	0	0	5	1	5	0	.250	.255	.273
Mike Vail	OF3	R	29	31	31	1	5	0	0	0	3	0	9	0	.161	.161	.161
Harry Spilman†	3B3,1B2	L	26	23	24	4	4	1	0	0	3	3	7	0	.167	.259	.208
Rafael Landestoy†	2B3	S	28	12	11	2	2	0	0	0	1	1	0	1	.182	.250	.182
German Barranca		L	24	9	6	2	2	0	0	0	1	0	0	0	.333	.333	.333
Eddie Milner	OF4	L	26	8	5	0	1	1	0	0	1	1	1	0	.200	.333	.400
Neil Fiala†		L	24	2	2	1	1	0	0	0	1	0	1	0	.500	.500	.500

Pitcher	T	Age	G	GS	CG	ShO	IP	H	HR	BB	SO	W-L	Sv	ERA
Mario Soto	R	24	25	25	10	3	175.0	142	13	61	151	12-9	0	3.29
Tom Seaver	R	36	23	23	6	1	166.1	120	10	66	87	14-2	0	2.54
Frank Pastore	R	23	22	22	2	1	132.0	125	11	35	81	4-9	0	4.02
Bruce Berenyi	R	26	21	20	5	3	126.0	97	3	77	106	9-6	0	3.50
Mike LaCoss	R	25	20	13	1	1	78.0	102	7	30	22	4-7	1	6.12
Charlie Leibrandt	L	24	7	4	1	1	30.0	28	0	15	9	1-1	0	3.60
Tom Hume	R	28	51	0	0	0	67.2	63	7	31	27	9-4	13	3.46
Joe Price	L	24	41	0	0	0	53.2	42	3	18	41	6-1	4	2.52
Paul Moskau	R	27	27	1	0	0	54.2	54	4	32	32	2-1	2	4.94
Doug Bair†	R	31	24	0	0	0	39.0	42	5	17	16	2-2	0	5.77
Geoff Combe	R	25	14	0	0	0	17.2	27	3	10	9	1-0	0	7.64
Scott Brown	R	24	10	0	0	0	13.0	16	0	1	7	1-0	0	2.77
Joe Edelen†	R	25	5	0	0	0	12.2	5	1	0	5	1-0	0	0.71

1981 Los Angeles Dodgers NL West 1st 36-21 .632 — (1) 4th 27-26 .509 6.0 GB (2)

Tom Lasorda

Player	Gm by Position	B	Age	G	AB	R	H	2B	3B	HR	RBI	BB	SO	SB	Avg	OBP	Slg
Mike Scioscia	C91	L	22	93	290	27	80	10	0	2	29	36	18	0	.276	.353	.331
Steve Garvey	1B110	R	32	110	431	63	122	23	1	10	64	25	49	3	.283	.322	.411
Davey Lopes	2B55	R	36	58	214	35	44	2	0	5	17	22	35	20	.206	.289	.285
Ron Cey	3B84	R	33	85	312	42	90	15	2	13	50	40	55	0	.288	.372	.474
Bill Russell	SS80	R	32	82	262	20	61	9	2	0	22	19	20	2	.233	.284	.282
Dusty Baker	OF101	R	32	103	400	48	128	17	3	9	49	29	43	10	.320	.363	.445
Ken Landreaux	OF95	L	26	99	390	48	98	16	4	7	41	25	42	18	.251	.297	.367
Pedro Guerrero	OF75,3B21,1B1	R	25	98	347	46	104	17	2	12	48	34	57	5	.300	.365	.464
Derrel Thomas	2B30,SS26,OF18*	R	30	80	218	25	54	4	0	4	24	25	23	7	.248	.322	.321
Rick Monday	OF41	L	35	66	130	24	41	1	2	11	25	24	42	1	.315	.423	.608
Steve Sax	2B29	R	21	31	119	15	33	2	0	2	9	7	14	5	.277	.317	.345
Steve Yeager	C40	R	32	42	86	5	18	2	0	3	7	6	14	0	.209	.261	.337
Jay Johnstone	OF16,1B2	L	35	61	83	8	17	3	0	3	6	7	13	0	.205	.267	.349
Ron Roenicke	OF20	S	24	22	47	6	11	0	0	0	0	6	8	1	.234	.321	.234
Pepe Frias	SS15,2B6,3B1	R	32	25	36	6	9	1	0	0	3	1	3	0	.250	.282	.278
Reggie Smith	1B2	S	36	41	35	5	7	1	0	1	8	7	8	0	.200	.318	.314
Mike Marshall	1B3,3B3,OF2	R	21	14	25	2	5	3	0	0	1	1	4	0	.200	.259	.320
Gary Weiss	SS13	S	25	14	19	2	2	0	0	0	1	1	4	0	.105	.143	.105
Joe Ferguson†	OF1	R	34	17	14	2	2	1	0	0	1	2	5	0	.143	.250	.214
Candy Maldonado	OF9	R	20	11	12	0	1	0	0	0	0	0	5	0	.083	.083	.083
Jack Perconte	2B2	L	26	8	9	2	2	0	1	0	1	2	2	1	.222	.364	.444
Bobby Mitchell	OF7	L	26	10	8	0	1	0	0	0	0	1	4	0	.125	.222	.125
Mark Bradley	OF6	R	24	9	6	2	1	1	0	0	0	0	1	0	.167	.167	.333
Jerry Grote†	C1	R	38	2	2	0	0	0	0	0	0	0	1	0	.000	.000	.000

D. Thomas, 10 G at 3B

Pitcher	T	Age	G	GS	CG	ShO	IP	H	HR	BB	SO	W-L	Sv	ERA
F. Valenzuela	L	20	25	25	11	8	192.1	140	11	61	180	13-7	0	2.48
Burt Hooton	R	31	23	23	5	4	142.1	124	3	33	74	11-6	0	2.28
Bob Welch	R	24	23	23	2	1	141.1	141	11	41	88	9-5	0	3.44
Jerry Reuss	L	32	22	22	8	2	152.2	138	6	27	51	10-4	0	2.30
Steve Howe	L	23	41	0	0	0	54.0	51	2	18	32	5-3	8	2.50
Bobby Castillo	R	26	34	1	0	0	50.2	50	5	24	35	2-4	5	5.33
Dave Stewart	R	24	32	0	0	0	43.1	40	3	14	29	4-3	6	2.49
Dave Goltz	R	32	26	8	0	0	77.0	83	4	25	48	2-7	1	4.09
Terry Forster	L	29	21	0	0	0	30.2	37	1	15	17	0-1	0	4.11
Tom Niedenfuer	R	21	17	0	0	0	26.0	25	1	6	12	3-1	2	3.81
Rick Sutcliffe	R	25	14	6	0	0	47.0	41	5	20	16	2-2	0	4.02
Alejandro Pena	R	22	14	0	0	0	25.1	18	2	11	14	1-1	2	2.84
Ted Power	R	26	5	2	0	0	14.1	16	0	7	7	1-3	0	3.14

1981 Houston Astros NL West 3rd 28-29 .491 8.0 GB (1) 1st 33-20 .623 — (2)

Bill Virdon

Player	Gm by Position	B	Age	G	AB	R	H	2B	3B	HR	RBI	BB	SO	SB	Avg	OBP	Slg
Alan Ashby	C81	S	29	83	255	20	69	13	0	4	33	35	33	0	.271	.356	.369
Cesar Cedeno	1B45,OF34	R	30	82	306	42	83	19	0	5	34	24	31	12	.271	.321	.382
Joe Pittman	2B35,3B4	R	27	52	135	11	38	4	2	0	7	11	16	4	.281	.333	.341
Art Howe	3B98,1B2	R	34	103	361	43	107	22	4	3	36	41	23	1	.296	.365	.404
Craig Reynolds	SS85	L	28	87	323	43	84	10	12	4	31	12	31	3	.260	.286	.402
Jose Cruz	OF104	L	33	107	409	53	109	16	5	13	55	35	49	5	.267	.319	.425
Terry Puhl	OF88	L	24	96	350	43	88	19	4	3	28	31	49	22	.251	.315	.354
Tony Scott†	OF55	S	29	55	225	28	66	13	2	2	22	15	32	8	.293	.338	.396
Denny Walling	1B27,OF27	L	27	65	158	23	37	6	0	5	23	28	17	2	.234	.346	.367
Kiko Garcia	SS28,3B13,2B9	R	27	48	136	9	37	6	1	0	15	10	16	2	.272	.324	.331
Luis Pujols	C39	R	25	40	117	5	28	3	1	1	14	10	17	1	.239	.297	.308
Phil Garner†	2B31	R	32	31	113	13	27	3	1	0	6	15	11	6	.239	.326	.283
Gary Woods	OF40	R	26	54	110	10	23	4	1	0	12	11	22	2	.209	.276	.264
Danny Heep	1B22,OF1	L	23	33	96	6	24	3	0	0	11	10	11	0	.250	.321	.281
Dickie Thon	2B28,SS13,3B5	R	23	49	95	13	26	6	0	0	3	9	13	6	.274	.337	.337
Rafael Landestoy†	2B31	S	28	35	74	6	11	1	1	0	4	16	9	4	.149	.300	.189
Dave Roberts	1B10,3B7,2B3*	R	30	27	54	4	13	3	0	1	5	3	6	1	.241	.271	.352
Mike Ivie†	1B10	R	28	19	42	2	10	3	0	0	6	2	11	0	.238	.267	.310
Harry Spilman†	1B13	L	26	28	34	5	10	0	0	0	1	2	3	0	.294	.333	.294
Jeffrey Leonard†	1B2,OF2	R	25	7	18	1	3	1	1	0	3	0	4	1	.167	.158	.333
Tim Tolman	OF3	R	25	4	8	0	1	0	0	0	0	0	0	0	.125	.125	.125
Alan Knicely	C2,OF1	R	26	3	7	2	4	0	0	2	2	0	1	0	.571	.571	1.429
Scott Loucks	OF5	R	24	10	7	2	4	0	0	0	0	1	3	1	.571	.625	.571
Dave Bergman†	1B1	L	28	6	6	1	1	0	0	1	1	0	0	0	.167	.167	.667
Bert Pena	SS3	R	21	4	2	0	1	0	0	0	0	0	0	0	.500	.500	.500

D. Roberts, 1 G at C

Pitcher	T	Age	G	GS	CG	ShO	IP	H	HR	BB	SO	W-L	Sv	ERA
Joe Niekro	R	36	24	24	5	2	166.0	150	8	47	77	9-9	0	2.82
Don Sutton	R	36	23	23	6	3	158.2	132	6	29	104	11-9	0	2.61
Bob Knepper	L	27	22	22	6	5	156.2	128	5	38	75	9-5	0	2.18
Nolan Ryan	R	34	21	21	5	3	149.0	99	2	68	140	11-5	0	1.69
Vern Ruhle	R	30	20	15	1	0	102.0	97	6	20	39	4-6	1	2.91
Joe Sambito	L	29	49	0	0	0	63.2	43	4	22	41	5-5	10	1.84
Dave Smith	R	26	42	0	0	0	75.0	54	2	23	52	5-3	8	2.76
Frank LaCorte	R	29	37	0	0	0	42.0	41	1	21	40	4-2	5	3.64
Bobby Sprowl	L	25	15	1	0	0	28.2	40	1	14	18	0-1	0	5.97
Billy Smith	R	26	10	1	0	0	20.2	20	3	3	3	1-1	1	3.05
Joaquin Andujar†	R	28	9	3	0	0	23.2	29	2	12	18	2-3	0	4.94
Gordy Pladson	R	24	2	0	0	0	4.0	9	0	3	3	0-0	0	9.00

1981 San Francisco Giants NL West 5th 27-32 .458 10.0 GB (1) 3rd 29-23 .558 3.5 GB (2) — Frank Robinson

Player	Gm by Position	B	Age	G	AB	R	H	2B	3B	HR	RBI	BB	SO	SB	Avg	OBP	Slg
Milt May	C93	L	30	97	316	20	98	17	0	2	33	34	29	1	.310	.376	.383
Enos Cabell	1B69,3B22	R	31	96	396	41	101	20	1	2	36	10	47	6	.255	.274	.326
Joe Morgan	2B87	L	37	90	308	47	74	16	1	8	31	66	37	14	.240	.371	.377
Darrell Evans	3B87,1B12	L	34	102	357	51	92	13	4	12	48	54	33	2	.258	.356	.417
Johnnie LeMaster	SS103	R	27	104	324	27	82	9	1	0	28	24	46	3	.253	.306	.287
Jack Clark	OF98	R	25	99	385	60	103	19	2	17	53	45	45	1	.268	.341	.460
Larry Herndon	OF93	R	27	96	364	48	105	15	8	5	41	20	55	15	.288	.325	.415
Jerry Martin	OF64	R	32	72	241	23	58	5	3	4	25	21	52	6	.241	.308	.336
Dave Bergman†	1B33,OF15	L	28	63	145	16	37	9	0	3	13	19	18	2	.255	.339	.379
Bill North	OF37	S	33	46	131	22	29	7	0	1	12	26	28	26	.221	.354	.298
Jeffrey Leonard†	OF28,1B5	R	25	37	127	20	39	11	3	4	26	12	21	4	.307	.371	.535
Rennie Stennett	2B19	R	30	38	87	8	20	0	0	1	7	3	6	2	.230	.264	.264
Jim Wohlford	OF10	R	30	50	68	4	11	3	0	1	7	4	9	0	.162	.205	.250
Billy Smith	SS21,2B5,3B3	S	27	36	61	6	11	0	0	1	5	9	16	0	.180	.282	.230
Bob Brenly	C14,3B3,OF1	R	27	19	45	5	15	2	1	1	4	6	4	0	.333	.423	.489
Mike Sadek	C19	R	35	19	36	5	6	3	0	0	3	8	7	0	.167	.318	.250
Max Venable	OF5	L	24	18	32	2	6	0	2	0	1	4	3	3	.188	.278	.313
Joe Pettini	2B12,SS12,3B9	R	26	35	29	3	2	1	0	0	2	4	5	1	.069	.182	.103
Guy Sularz	2B6,3B1	R	25	10	20	0	4	0	0	0	2	2	4	0	.200	.292	.200
Mike Ivie†	1B5	R	28	7	17	1	5	2	0	0	3	0	1	0	.294	.278	.412
Chili Davis	OF6	S	21	8	15	1	2	0	0	0	0	1	2	2	.133	.188	.133
Jeff Ransom	C5	R	20	5	15	2	4	1	0	0	0	1	1	0	.267	.313	.333

Pitcher	T	Age	G	GS	CG	ShO	IP	H	HR	BB	SO	W-L	Sv	ERA
Doyle Alexander	R	30	24	24	1	1	152.1	156	11	44	77	11-7	0	2.89
Tom Griffin	R	33	22	22	3	1	129.1	121	8	57	83	8-8	0	3.76
Ed Whitson	R	26	22	22	2	1	123.0	130	10	47	65	6-9	0	4.02
Vida Blue	L	31	18	18	1	0	124.2	97	7	54	63	8-6	0	2.45
Allen Ripley	R	28	19	14	1	0	90.2	103	5	27	47	4-4	0	4.07
Alan Hargesheimer	R	24	6	3	0	0	18.2	20	1	9	6	1-2	0	4.34
Greg Minton	R	29	55	0	0	0	84.1	84	0	36	29	4-5	21	2.88
Al Holland	L	28	47	3	0	0	100.2	87	4	44	78	7-5	7	2.41
Fred Breining	R	25	45	1	0	0	77.2	66	4	38	37	5-2	1	2.55
Gary Lavelle	L	32	34	3	0	0	65.2	58	3	23	45	2-6	4	3.84
Bob Tufts	L	25	11	0	0	0	15.1	20	1	6	12	0-0	0	3.52
Randy Moffitt	R	32	10	0	0	0	11.1	15	2	2	11	0-0	0	7.94
Mike Rowland	R	28	9	1	0	0	15.2	13	1	6	8	0-1	0	3.45

1981 Atlanta Braves NL West 4th 25-29 .463 9.5 GB (1) 5th 25-27 .481 7.5 GB (2) — Bobby Cox

Player	Gm by Position	B	Age	G	AB	R	H	2B	3B	HR	RBI	BB	SO	SB	Avg	OBP	Slg
Bruce Benedict	C90	R	25	90	295	26	78	12	1	5	35	33	21	1	.264	.341	.363
Chris Chambliss	1B107	L	32	107	404	44	110	25	2	8	51	44	41	4	.272	.343	.403
Glenn Hubbard	2B98	R	23	99	361	39	85	13	5	6	33	33	59	4	.235	.302	.349
Bob Horner	3B79	R	23	79	300	42	83	10	0	15	42	32	39	2	.277	.345	.460
Rafael Ramirez	SS95	R	23	95	307	30	67	16	2	2	20	24	47	7	.218	.276	.303
Dale Murphy	OF103,1B3	R	25	104	369	43	91	12	1	13	50	44	72	14	.247	.325	.390
C. Washington	OF79	L	26	85	320	37	93	22	3	5	37	15	47	12	.291	.328	.425
Rufino Linares	OF60	R	30	78	253	27	67	9	2	5	25	9	28	8	.265	.289	.375
Eddie Miller	OF36	S	24	50	134	29	31	3	1	0	7	7	29	23	.231	.285	.269
Brett Butler	OF37	L	24	40	126	17	32	2	3	0	4	19	17	9	.254	.352	.317
Biff Pocoroba	3B21,C9	S	27	57	122	4	22	4	0	0	8	12	15	0	.180	.265	.213
Jerry Royster	3B24,2B13	R	28	64	93	13	19	4	1	0	9	7	14	7	.204	.257	.269
Brian Asselstine	OF16	L	27	56	86	8	22	5	0	2	10	5	7	1	.256	.297	.384
Terry Harper	OF27	R	25	40	73	9	19	1	0	2	8	11	17	5	.260	.353	.356
Luis Gomez	SS21,3B9,2B3*	R	29	35	35	4	7	0	0	0	1	6	4	0	.200	.317	.200
Matt Sinatro	C12	R	21	12	32	4	9	1	1	0	4	5	4	1	.281	.378	.375
Paul Runge	SS10	R	23	10	27	2	7	1	0	0	2	4	4	0	.259	.355	.296
Larry Owen	C10	R	26	13	16	0	0	0	0	0	0	1	4	0	.000	.059	.000
Bob Porter		L	21	17	14	2	4	1	0	0	4	2	1	0	.286	.375	.357
Bill Nahorodny	C3,1B1	R	27	14	13	0	3	1	0	0	2	1	3	0	.231	.286	.308
Mike Lum†	OF1	L	35	10	11	1	1	0	0	0	0	2	2	0	.091	.231	.091
Brook Jacoby	3B3	R	21	11	10	0	2	0	0	0	1	0	3	0	.200	.200	.200
Larry Whisenton	OF2	L	24	9	5	1	1	0	0	0	0	2	1	0	.200	.429	.200
Ken Smith	1B4	L	23	5	3	0	1	1	0	0	0	0	1	0	.333	.333	.667
Albert Hall	OF2	S	23	6	2	1	0	0	0	0	0	1	1	0	.000	.333	.000

L. Gomez, 1 G at P

Pitcher	T	Age	G	GS	CG	ShO	IP	H	HR	BB	SO	W-L	Sv	ERA
Tommy Boggs	R	25	25	24	2	0	142.2	140	11	54	81	3-13	0	4.10
Gaylord Perry	R	42	23	23	3	0	150.2	182	9	24	60	8-9	0	3.94
Phil Niekro	R	42	22	22	3	3	139.1	120	6	56	62	7-7	0	3.10
Bob Walk	R	24	12	8	0	0	43.1	41	6	23	16	1-4	0	4.57
Larry McWilliams	L	27	6	5	2	1	37.2	31	2	8	23	2-1	0	3.11
Rick Camp	R	28	48	0	0	0	76.0	68	5	12	47	9-3	17	1.78
Gene Garber	R	33	35	0	0	0	58.2	49	2	20	34	4-6	2	2.61
Rick Mahler	R	27	34	14	1	0	112.1	109	5	43	54	8-6	2	2.80
John Montefusco	R	31	26	9	0	0	77.0	75	9	27	34	2-3	1	3.51
Larry Bradford	L	31	25	0	0	0	27.0	26	1	12	14	2-0	1	3.67
Al Hrabosky	L	31	24	0	0	0	33.2	24	1	9	13	1-1	1	1.07
Preston Hanna	R	26	20	1	0	0	35.1	45	2	23	22	2-1	0	6.37
Steve Bedrosian	R	23	15	1	0	0	24.1	15	2	15	9	1-2	0	4.44
Rick Matula	R	27	5	0	0	0	7.0	8	1	2	0	0-0	0	6.43
Jose Alvarez	R	25	1	0	0	0	2.0	0	0	0	2	0-0	0	0.00
Luis Gomez	R	29	1	0	0	0	1.0	3	0	2	0	0-0	0	27.00

1981 San Diego Padres NL West 6th 23-33 .411 12.5 GB (1) 6th 18-36 .333 15.5 GB (2) — Frank Howard

Player	Gm by Position	B	Age	G	AB	R	H	2B	3B	HR	RBI	BB	SO	SB	Avg	OBP	Slg
Terry Kennedy	C100	L	25	101	382	32	115	24	1	2	41	22	53	0	.301	.341	.385
Broderick Perkins	1B80,OF3	L	26	92	254	27	71	18	3	2	40	14	16	0	.280	.314	.398
Juan Bonilla	2B97	R	25	99	369	30	107	13	2	1	25	25	23	4	.290	.337	.344
Luis Salazar	3B94,OF23	R	25	109	400	37	121	19	6	3	38	16	72	11	.303	.329	.403
Ozzie Smith	SS110	S	26	110	450	53	100	11	2	0	21	41	37	22	.222	.294	.256
Ruppert Jones	OF104	L	26	105	397	53	99	34	1	4	39	43	66	7	.249	.318	.370
Gene Richards	OF101	L	27	104	393	47	113	14	12	3	42	53	44	20	.288	.373	.407
Joe Lefebvre	OF84	L	25	86	246	31	63	13	4	8	31	35	33	6	.256	.352	.439
Randy Bass	1B50	L	27	69	176	13	37	4	1	4	20	20	28	0	.210	.293	.313
Dave Edwards	OF49	R	27	58	112	13	24	4	1	2	13	11	24	3	.214	.282	.321
Barry Evans	3B24,1B10,2B6*	R	25	54	93	11	30	5	0	0	7	9	9	2	.323	.371	.376
Tim Flannery	3B15,2B7	L	23	37	67	4	17	4	1	0	6	2	4	1	.254	.268	.343
Jose Moreno	OF9,2B1	S	23	34	48	5	11	2	0	0	6	1	8	4	.229	.245	.271
Jerry Turner†	OF4	L	27	33	31	5	7	0	0	2	6	4	3	0	.226	.314	.419
Mike Phillips†	2B9,SS1	L	30	14	29	1	6	0	1	0	0	0	3	1	.207	.207	.276
Steve Swisher	C10	R	29	16	28	2	4	0	0	0	0	2	11	0	.143	.200	.143
Doug Gwosdz	C13	R	21	16	24	1	4	2	0	0	3	3	6	0	.167	.241	.250
Alan Wiggins	OF4	S	23	15	14	4	5	0	0	0	0	1	0	2	.357	.400	.357
Mario Ramirez	3B2,SS2	R	23	13	13	1	1	0	0	0	1	2	5	0	.077	.200	.077
Craig Stimac		R	26	9	9	0	1	0	0	0	0	0	3	0	.111	.111	.111

B. Evans, 2 G at SS

Pitcher	T	Age	G	GS	CG	ShO	IP	H	HR	BB	SO	W-L	Sv	ERA
Juan Eichelberger	R	27	25	24	3	1	141.1	136	5	74	81	8-8	0	3.50
Steve Mura	R	26	23	22	2	1	138.2	156	10	50	70	5-14	0	4.28
Chris Welsh	L	26	22	19	4	2	123.2	122	9	41	51	6-7	0	3.78
Rick Wise	R	35	18	18	0	0	98.0	116	10	19	27	4-8	0	3.77
Fred Kuhaulua	L	28	5	4	0	0	29.1	28	1	9	16	1-0	0	2.45
Steve Fireovid	R	24	5	4	0	0	26.1	30	2	7	11	0-1	0	2.73
Gary Lucas	L	26	57	0	0	0	90.0	78	1	36	53	7-7	13	2.00
John Littlefield	R	27	42	0	0	0	64.0	53	5	28	21	2-3	2	3.66
John Urrea	R	26	38	0	0	0	49.0	43	1	28	19	2-2	2	2.39
Dan Boone	L	27	37	0	0	0	63.1	63	2	21	43	1-0	2	2.84
John Curtis	L	33	28	8	0	0	66.2	70	11	30	31	2-6	0	5.13
Tim Lollar	L	25	24	11	0	0	76.2	87	4	51	38	2-8	1	6.10
Eric Show	R	25	15	0	0	0	23.0	17	2	9	22	1-3	3	3.13
Mike Armstrong	R	27	10	0	0	0	12.0	14	1	11	9	0-2	0	6.00

»1982 Milwaukee Brewers 1st AL East 95-67 .586 — — Buck Rodgers (23-24)/Harvey Kuenn (72-43)

Player	Gm by Position	B	Age	G	AB	R	H	2B	3B	HR	RBI	BB	SO	SB	Avg	OBP	Slg
Ted Simmons	C121,DH15	S	32	137	539	73	145	29	0	23	97	32	40	0	.269	.309	.451
Cecil Cooper	1B154,DH1	L	32	155	654	104	205	38	3	32	121	32	53	2	.313	.342	.528
Jim Gantner	2B131	L	29	132	447	48	132	17	2	4	43	26	36	6	.295	.335	.369
Paul Molitor	3B150,DH6,SS4	R	25	160	666	136	201	26	8	19	71	69	93	41	.302	.366	.450
Robin Yount	SS154,DH1	R	26	156	635	129	210	46	12	29	114	54	63	14	.331	.379	.578
Ben Oglivie	OF159	L	33	159	602	92	147	22	1	34	102	70	81	3	.244	.326	.453
Gorman Thomas	OF157	R	31	158	567	96	139	29	1	39	112	84	143	3	.245	.343	.506
Charlie Moore	OF115,C20,2B1	R	29	133	456	53	116	22	4	6	45	29	49	2	.254	.299	.360
Roy Howell	DH84,1B4,OF2	L	28	98	300	31	78	11	2	4	38	21	39	0	.260	.305	.350
Don Money	DH66,3B16,1B11*	R	35	96	275	40	78	14	3	16	55	32	38	0	.284	.360	.531
Marshall Edwards	OF54,DH6	L	29	69	178	24	44	4	1	2	14	4	8	10	.247	.261	.315
Ed Romero	2B39,SS10,3B2*	R	24	52	144	18	36	8	0	1	7	8	16	0	.250	.289	.326
Mark Brouhard	OF30,DH7	R	26	40	108	16	29	4	1	4	10	9	17	0	.269	.336	.435
Ned Yost	C39,DH1	R	26	40	98	13	27	6	3	1	8	7	20	3	.276	.324	.429
Larry Hisle	DH8	R	35	9	31	7	4	0	0	2	5	5	13	0	.129	.250	.323
Rob Picciolo†	2B11,SS6,DH1	R	29	22	21	7	6	1	0	0	1	1	4	0	.286	.318	.333
Kevin Bass†	OF14,DH2	S	23	18	9	4	0	0	0	0	0	1	1	0	.000	.100	.000
Bob Skube	DH1,OF1	L	24	4	3	0	2	0	0	0	0	0	0	0	.667	.667	.667

D. Money, 1 G at 2B; E. Romero, 1 G at OF

Pitcher	T	Age	G	GS	CG	ShO	IP	H	HR	BB	SO	W-L	Sv	ERA
Mike Caldwell	L	33	35	34	12	3	258.0	269	30	58	75	17-13	0	3.91
Pete Vuckovich	R	29	30	30	9	1	223.2	234	14	102	105	18-6	0	3.34
Moose Haas	R	26	32	27	3	0	193.1	232	15	39	104	11-8	1	4.47
Bob McClure	L	30	34	26	5	0	172.2	160	21	74	99	12-7	0	4.22
Randy Lerch†	L	27	21	20	1	1	108.2	123	12	51	33	8-7	0	4.97
Doc Medich†	R	33	10	10	1	0	63.0	57	4	32	36	5-4	0	5.00
Don Sutton†	R	37	7	7	2	1	54.2	55	8	18	36	4-1	0	3.29
Rollie Fingers	R	35	50	0	0	0	79.2	63	5	20	71	5-6	29	2.60
Dwight Bernard	R	30	47	0	0	0	79.0	78	4	27	45	3-1	6	3.76
Jim Slaton	R	32	39	7	0	0	117.2	117	14	41	59	10-6	6	3.29
Jamie Easterly	L	29	28	0	0	0	30.2	39	6	15	16	0-2	2	4.70
Jerry Augustine	L	29	20	2	1	0	62.0	63	13	26	22	1-3	0	5.08
Peter Ladd	R	25	16	0	0	0	18.0	16	5	6	12	1-3	3	4.00
Doug Jones	R	25	4	0	0	0	2.2	5	1	1	1	0-0	0	10.13
Chuck Porter	R	27	3	0	0	0	3.2	3	0	1	3	0-0	0	4.91

1982 Baltimore Orioles 2nd AL East 94-68 .580 1.0 GB — Earl Weaver

Player	Gm by Position	B	Age	G	AB	R	H	2B	3B	HR	RBI	BB	SO	SB	Avg	OBP	Slg
Rick Dempsey	C124,DH1	R	32	125	344	35	88	15	1	5	36	46	37	0	.256	.339	.349
Eddie Murray	1B149,DH2	S	26	151	550	87	174	30	1	32	110	70	82	7	.316	.391	.549
Rich Dauer	2B123,3B61	R	29	158	558	75	156	24	2	8	57	50	34	0	.280	.337	.373
Cal Ripken Jr.	SS94,3B71	R	21	160	598	90	158	32	5	28	93	46	95	3	.264	.317	.475
Lenn Sakata	2B83,SS56	R	28	136	343	40	89	18	1	6	31	30	39	7	.259	.317	.370
Al Bumbry	OF147,DH1	L	35	150	562	77	147	20	4	5	40	44	77	10	.262	.314	.338
Gary Roenicke	OF125,1B10	R	27	137	393	58	106	25	1	21	74	70	73	6	.270	.392	.499
Dan Ford	OF119,DH1	R	30	123	421	46	99	21	3	10	43	23	71	5	.235	.279	.371
Ken Singleton	DH148,OF5	S	35	156	561	71	141	27	2	14	77	86	93	0	.251	.349	.381
John Lowenstein	OF111	L	35	122	322	69	103	15	2	24	66	54	59	7	.320	.415	.602
Joe Nolan	C72	L	31	77	219	24	51	7	1	6	35	16	35	1	.233	.278	.356
Jim Dwyer	OF49,DH1,1B1	L	32	71	148	28	45	4	3	6	15	27	24	2	.304	.407	.493
Glenn Gulliver	3B50	L	27	50	145	24	29	7	0	1	5	37	18	0	.200	.363	.269
Bennie Ayala	OF25,DH17,1B3	R	31	64	128	17	39	6	0	6	24	5	14	1	.305	.331	.492
Terry Crowley	DH14,1B10	L	35	65	93	8	22	2	0	3	17	21	9	0	.237	.377	.355
Bobby Bonner	SS38,2B3	R	25	41	77	8	13	3	1	0	5	3	12	0	.169	.198	.234
Floyd Rayford	3B27,DH2,C2	R	24	34	53	7	7	0	0	3	5	6	14	0	.132	.220	.302
John Shelby	OF24	S	24	26	35	8	11	3	0	3	6	0	5	0	.314	.314	.486
Jose Morales†		R	37	3	3	0	0	0	0	0	0	0	2	0	.000	.000	.000
Leo Hernandez		R	22	2	2	0	0	0	0	0	0	0	2	0	.000	.000	.000
Mike Young	DH2,OF1	S	22	6	2	2	0	0	0	0	0	0	1	0	.000	.000	.000

Pitcher	T	Age	G	GS	CG	ShO	IP	H	HR	BB	SO	W-L	Sv	ERA
Dennis Martinez	R	27	40	39	10	2	252.0	262	30	87	111	16-12	0	4.21
Scott McGregor	L	28	37	37	7	1	226.1	238	31	52	84	14-12	0	4.61
Mike Flanagan	L	30	36	35	11	1	236.0	233	24	76	103	15-11	0	3.97
Jim Palmer	R	36	36	32	8	2	227.0	195	22	63	103	15-5	1	3.13
Tippy Martinez	L	32	76	0	0	0	95.0	81	6	37	78	8-8	16	3.41
Tim Stoddard	R	29	50	0	0	0	56.0	53	4	29	42	3-4	12	4.02
Sammy Stewart	R	27	38	12	1	1	139.0	140	9	62	69	10-9	5	4.14
Storm Davis	R	20	29	8	1	0	100.2	96	8	28	67	8-4	0	3.49
Ross Grimsley	L	32	21	0	0	0	60.0	65	7	22	18	1-2	0	5.25
Don Stanhouse	R	31	17	0	0	0	26.2	29	3	15	8	0-1	0	5.40
Mike Boddicker	R	24	7	0	0	0	25.2	25	2	12	20	1-0	0	3.51
John Flinn	R	27	5	0	0	0	13.2	13	1	3	13	2-0	0	1.32
Don Welchel	R	25	2	0	0	0	4.1	6	0	2	3	1-0	0	8.31

864 Seasons: Team Rosters

1982 Boston Red Sox 3rd AL East 89-73 .549 6.0 GB

Ralph Houk

Player	Gm by Position	B	Age	G	AB	R	H	2B	3B	HR	RBI	BB	SO	SB	Avg	OBP	Slg
Gary Allenson	C91	R	27	92	264	25	54	11	0	6	33	38	39	0	.205	.306	.314
Dave Stapleton	1B106,SS27,2B9*	R	28	150	538	66	142	28	1	14	65	31	40	2	.264	.305	.398
Jerry Remy	2B154	L	29	155	636	89	178	22	3	0	47	55	77	16	.280	.337	.324
Carney Lansford	3B114,DH13	R	25	128	482	65	145	28	4	11	63	46	48	9	.301	.359	.444
Glenn Hoffman	SS150	R	23	150	469	53	98	23	2	7	49	30	69	0	.209	.262	.311
Dwight Evans	OF161,DH1	R	30	162	609	122	178	37	7	32	98	112	125	3	.292	.402	.534
Jim Rice	OF145	R	29	145	573	86	177	24	5	24	97	55	98	0	.309	.375	.494
Rick Miller	OF127	L	34	135	409	50	104	13	2	4	38	40	41	5	.254	.323	.325
Carl Yastrzemski	DH102,1B14,OF2	L	42	131	459	53	126	22	1	16	72	59	50	0	.275	.358	.431
Wade Boggs	1B49,3B44,DH3*	L	24	104	338	51	118	14	1	5	44	35	21	1	.349	.406	.441
Rich Gedman	C86	L	22	92	289	30	72	17	2	4	26	10	37	0	.249	.279	.363
Reid Nichols	OF82,DH4	R	23	92	245	35	74	16	1	7	33	14	28	5	.302	.341	.461
Tony Perez	DH46,1B2	R	40	69	196	18	51	14	2	6	31	19	48	0	.260	.326	.444
Ed Jurak	3B11,OF1	R	24	12	21	3	7	0	0	0	7	2	4	0	.333	.375	.333
Julio Valdez	SS22,DH3	S	26	28	20	3	5	1	0	0	1	0	7	1	.250	.250	.300
Marty Barrett	2B7	R	24	8	18	0	1	0	0	0	0	0	1	0	.056	.056	.056
Gary Hancock	OF7	L	28	11	14	3	0	0	0	0	0	1	1	0	.000	.067	.000
Roger LaFrancois	C8	L	27	8	10	1	4	1	0	0	1	0	0	0	.400	.400	.500
Marc Sullivan	C2	R	23	2	6	0	2	0	0	0	0	0	2	0	.333	.333	.333

D. Stapleton, 5 G at 3B, 4 G at DH, 1 G at OF; W. Boggs, 1 G at OF

Pitcher	T	Age	G	GS	CG	ShO	IP	H	HR	BB	SO	W-L	Sv	ERA
Dennis Eckersley	R	27	33	33	11	3	224.1	228	31	43	127	13-13	0	3.73
Mike Torrez	R	35	31	31	1	0	175.2	196	20	74	84	9-9	0	5.23
John Tudor	L	28	32	30	6	1	195.2	215	20	59	146	13-10	0	3.63
Chuck Rainey	R	27	27	25	3	3	129.0	146	14	63	57	7-5	0	5.02
Bruce Hurst	L	24	28	19	0	0	117.0	161	16	40	53	3-7	0	5.77
Bobby Ojeda	L	24	22	14	0	0	78.1	95	13	29	52	4-6	0	5.63
Brian Denman	R	26	9	9	2	1	49.0	55	6	9	9	3-4	0	4.78
Mark Clear	R	26	55	0	0	0	105.0	92	11	61	109	14-9	14	3.00
Bob Stanley	R	27	48	0	0	0	168.1	161	11	50	83	12-7	14	3.10
Tom Burgmeier	L	38	40	0	0	0	102.1	98	6	22	44	7-0	2	2.29
Luis Aponte	R	29	40	0	0	0	85.0	78	5	25	44	2-2	3	3.18
Steve Crawford	R	24	5	0	0	0	9.0	14	0	0	2	1-0	0	2.00
Oil Can Boyd	R	22	3	1	0	0	8.1	11	2	2	2	0-1	0	5.40
Mike Brown	R	23	3	0	0	0	6.0	7	0	1	4	1-0	0	0.00

1982 Detroit Tigers 4th AL East 83-79 .512 12.0 GB

Sparky Anderson

Player	Gm by Position	B	Age	G	AB	R	H	2B	3B	HR	RBI	BB	SO	SB	Avg	OBP	Slg
Lance Parrish	C132,OF1	R	26	133	486	75	138	19	2	32	87	40	99	3	.284	.338	.529
Enos Cabell	1B83,3B59,OF3	R	32	125	464	45	121	17	3	2	37	15	48	15	.261	.284	.323
Lou Whitaker	2B149,DH1	L	25	152	560	76	160	22	8	15	65	48	58	11	.286	.341	.434
Tom Brookens	3B113,2B26,SS9*	R	28	140	398	40	92	15	3	9	58	27	63	5	.231	.277	.352
Alan Trammell	SS157	R	24	157	489	66	126	34	3	9	57	52	47	19	.258	.325	.395
Larry Herndon	OF155,DH3	R	28	157	614	92	179	21	13	23	88	38	92	12	.292	.332	.480
Chet Lemon	OF121,DH1	R	27	125	436	75	116	20	1	19	52	56	69	1	.266	.368	.447
Glenn Wilson	OF80,DH4	R	23	84	322	39	94	15	1	12	34	15	51	2	.292	.322	.457
Mike Ivie†	DH79	R	29	80	259	35	60	12	1	14	38	24	51	0	.232	.299	.448
Kirk Gibson	OF64,DH4	L	25	69	266	34	74	16	2	8	35	25	41	9	.278	.341	.444
Rick Leach	1B56,OF14,DH4	L	25	82	218	23	52	7	2	3	12	21	29	4	.239	.303	.330
Jerry Turner	DH50,OF13	L	28	85	210	21	52	3	0	8	27	20	37	1	.248	.310	.376
John Wockenfuss	C24,DH17,1B17*	R	33	70	193	28	58	9	0	8	32	29	21	0	.301	.388	.472
Richie Hebner†	1B40,DH20	L	34	68	179	25	49	6	0	8	18	25	21	1	.274	.361	.441
Howard Johnson	3B33,DH10,OF9	S	21	54	155	23	49	5	0	4	14	16	30	7	.316	.384	.426
Lynn Jones	OF56,DH1	R	29	58	139	15	31	3	1	0	14	7	14	0	.223	.259	.259
Mike Laga	1B19,DH8	L	22	27	88	6	23	9	0	3	11	4	23	1	.261	.293	.466
Bill Fahey	C28	L	32	28	67	7	10	2	0	0	4	0	5	1	.149	.147	.179
Eddie Miller	OF8,DH1	S	25	14	25	3	1	0	0	0	0	4	4	0	.040	.250	.040
Mark DeJohn	SS20,3B4,2B1	S	28	24	21	1	4	2	0	0	1	4	4	1	.190	.320	.286
Mick Kelleher†	2B1,3B1	R	34	2	1	0	0	0	0	0	0	0	0	0	.000	.000	.000
Marty Castillo	C1	R	25	1	0	0	0	0	0	0	0	0	0	0	—	—	—

T. Brookens, 1 G at OF; J. Wockenfuss, 10 G at OF, 1 G at 3B

Pitcher	T	Age	G	GS	CG	ShO	IP	H	HR	BB	SO	W-L	Sv	ERA
Jack Morris	R	27	37	37	17	3	266.1	247	37	96	135	17-16	0	4.06
Dan Petry	R	23	35	35	8	1	246.0	220	15	100	132	15-9	0	3.22
Milt Wilcox	R	32	29	29	9	1	193.2	187	18	85	112	12-10	0	3.62
Jerry Ujdur	R	25	25	25	7	0	178.0	150	29	69	86	10-10	0	3.69
Juan Berenguer	R	27	2	1	0	0	6.2	5	0	9	8	0-0	0	6.75
Dave Tobik	R	29	51	1	0	0	98.2	86	8	38	63	4-9	9	3.56
Elias Sosa	R	32	38	0	0	0	61.0	64	11	18	24	3-3	4	4.43
Pat Underwood	L	25	33	12	2	0	99.0	108	17	22	43	4-8	3	4.73
Kevin Saucier	L	25	31	1	0	0	40.1	35	0	29	23	3-1	5	3.12
Larry Pashnick	R	26	28	13	1	0	94.1	110	17	25	19	4-4	0	4.01
Dave Rucker	L	24	27	4	1	0	64.0	62	4	23	31	5-6	0	3.38
Aurelio Lopez	R	33	19	0	0	0	41.0	41	8	19	26	3-1	3	5.27
Bob James†	R	23	12	1	0	0	19.2	22	4	8	20	0-2	0	5.03
Dave Rozema	R	25	8	2	0	0	27.2	17	2	7	15	3-0	1	1.63
Howard Bailey	L	24	8	0	0	0	10.0	6	0	2	3	0-1	0	0.00
Dave Gumpert	R	24	5	1	0	0	2.0	7	1	2	0	0-0	1	27.00
Larry Rothschild	R	28	2	0	0	0	2.2	4	1	2	0	0-0	0	13.50

1982 New York Yankees 5th AL East 79-83 .488 16.0 GB

Bob Lemon (6-8)/Gene Michael (44-42)/Clyde King (29-33)

Player	Gm by Position	B	Age	G	AB	R	H	2B	3B	HR	RBI	BB	SO	SB	Avg	OBP	Slg
Rick Cerone	C89	R	28	89	300	29	68	10	0	5	28	19	27	0	.227	.271	.310
John Mayberry†	1B63,DH4	L	33	69	215	20	45	7	0	8	27	28	38	0	.209	.313	.353
Willie Randolph	2B142,DH1	R	27	144	553	85	155	21	4	3	36	75	35	16	.280	.368	.349
Graig Nettles	3B113,DH3	L	37	122	405	47	94	11	2	18	55	51	49	1	.232	.317	.402
Roy Smalley†	SS89,3B53,DH4*	S	29	142	486	55	125	14	2	20	67	68	100	0	.257	.346	.418
Dave Winfield	OF135,DH4	R	30	140	539	84	151	24	8	37	106	45	64	5	.280	.331	.560
Ken Griffey Sr.	OF125	L	32	127	484	70	134	23	2	12	54	39	58	10	.277	.329	.407
Jerry Mumphrey	OF123	S	29	123	477	76	143	24	10	9	68	50	66	11	.300	.364	.449
Oscar Gamble	DH74,OF29	L	32	108	316	49	86	21	2	18	57	58	47	6	.272	.387	.522
Dave Collins	OF60,1B52,DH1	S	29	111	348	41	88	12	3	3	25	28	49	13	.253	.315	.330
Lou Piniella	DH55,OF40	R	38	102	261	33	80	17	1	6	37	18	18	0	.307	.352	.448
Butch Wynegar†	C62	S	26	63	191	27	56	8	1	3	20	40	21	0	.293	.413	.393
Bucky Dent†	SS58	R	30	59	160	11	27	1	1	0	9	8	11	0	.169	.207	.188
Bobby Murcer	DH47	L	36	65	141	12	32	6	0	7	30	12	15	2	.227	.288	.418
Lee Mazzilli†	1B23,DH9,OF2	S	27	37	128	20	34	2	0	6	17	15	15	2	.266	.347	.422
Andre Robertson	SS27,2B15,3B2	R	24	44	118	16	26	5	0	2	9	8	19	0	.220	.270	.314
Steve Balboni	1B26,DH5	R	25	33	107	8	20	2	1	2	4	6	34	0	.187	.228	.280
Butch Hobson	DH15,1B11	R	30	30	58	2	10	2	0	0	3	1	14	0	.172	.183	.207
Barry Foote	C17	R	30	17	48	4	7	5	0	0	2	1	11	0	.146	.160	.250
Dave Revering†	1B13,DH1	L	29	14	40	2	6	2	0	0	2	3	4	0	.150	.205	.200
Barry Evans	2B8,3B6,SS4	R	26	17	31	2	8	3	0	0	2	6	6	0	.258	.395	.355
Larry Milbourne†	SS9,2B3,3B3	S	31	14	27	2	4	1	0	0	0	1	4	0	.148	.179	.185
Rodney Scott†	SS6,2B4	S	28	10	26	5	5	0	0	0	0	4	2	2	.192	.300	.192
Bob Watson†	1B6,DH1	R	36	7	17	3	4	3	0	0	3	3	0	0	.235	.350	.412
Mike Patterson	OF9,DH1	L	24	11	16	3	3	1	0	1	1	2	6	1	.188	.278	.438
Don Mattingly	OF6,1B1	L	21	7	12	0	2	0	0	0	1	0	1	0	.167	.154	.167
Bobby Ramos	C4	R	26	4	11	1	1	0	0	1	2	0	3	0	.091	.091	.364
Edwin Rodriguez	2B3	R	21	3	9	2	3	0	0	0	0	1	1	0	.333	.400	.333
Juan Espino	C3	R	26	3	2	0	0	0	0	0	0	0	1	0	.000	.000	.000
Dave Stegman		R	28	2	0	0	0	0	0	0	0	0	0	0	—	—	—

R. Smalley, 1 G at 2B

Pitcher	T	Age	G	GS	CG	ShO	IP	H	HR	BB	SO	W-L	Sv	ERA
Ron Guidry	L	31	34	33	6	1	222.0	216	22	69	162	14-8	0	3.81
Dave Righetti	L	23	33	27	4	0	183.0	155	11	108	163	11-10	1	3.79
Tommy John†	L	39	30	26	9	2	186.2	190	11	34	54	10-10	0	3.66
Mike Morgan	R	22	30	23	2	0	150.1	167	15	67	71	7-11	0	4.37
Roger Erickson†	R	25	16	11	0	0	70.2	86	5	17	37	4-5	1	4.46
Doyle Alexander	R	31	16	11	0	0	66.2	81	14	14	26	1-7	0	6.08
Jay Howell	R	26	6	6	0	0	28.0	42	1	13	21	2-3	0	7.71
Stefan Wever	R	24	1	1	0	0	2.2	6	1	3	2	0-1	0	27.00
George Frazier	R	27	63	0	0	0	111.2	103	7	39	69	4-4	1	3.47
Goose Gossage	R	30	56	0	0	0	93.0	63	5	28	102	4-5	30	2.23
Shane Rawley	L	26	47	17	3	0	164.0	165	10	54	111	11-10	3	4.06
Rudy May	L	37	41	6	0	0	106.0	109	4	14	85	6-6	3	2.89
Dave LaRoche	L	34	25	0	0	0	50.0	54	4	11	31	4-2	0	3.42
Curt Kaufman	R	24	7	0	0	0	8.2	9	2	6	1	1-0	0	5.19
Lynn McGlothen	R	32	4	0	0	0	5.0	9	1	2	2	0-0	0	10.80
John Pacella†	R	25	3	1	0	0	10.0	13	0	9	2	0-1	0	7.20
Jim Lewis	R	26	1	0	0	0	0.2	3	0	3	0	0-0	0	54.00

1982 Cleveland Indians 6th AL East 78-84 .481 17.0 GB

Dave Garcia

Player	Gm by Position	B	Age	G	AB	R	H	2B	3B	HR	RBI	BB	SO	SB	Avg	OBP	Slg
Ron Hassey	C105,DH2,1B2	L	29	113	323	33	81	18	0	5	34	53	32	3	.251	.356	.353
Mike Hargrove	1B153,DH5	L	32	160	591	67	160	26	1	4	65	101	58	2	.271	.377	.338
Jack Perconte	2B82,DH2	L	27	93	219	27	52	4	4	0	15	22	25	9	.237	.303	.292
Toby Harrah	3B159,2B3,SS2	R	33	162	602	100	183	29	4	25	78	84	52	17	.304	.398	.490
Mike Fischlin	SS101,3B8,2B6*	R	26	112	276	34	74	12	1	0	21	34	36	9	.268	.351	.319
Rick Manning	OF152	L	27	152	562	71	152	18	2	8	44	54	60	12	.270	.334	.352
Von Hayes	OF139,3B5,1B4	L	23	150	527	65	132	25	3	14	82	42	63	32	.250	.310	.389
Miguel Dilone	OF97,DH1	S	27	104	379	50	89	12	3	3	25	25	36	33	.235	.286	.306
Andre Thornton	DH152,1B8	R	32	161	589	90	161	26	1	32	116	109	81	6	.273	.386	.484
Alan Bannister	OF55,2B48,SS2*	R	30	101	348	40	93	16	1	4	41	42	41	18	.267	.347	.353
Larry Milbourne†	2B63,SS21,3B9*	S	31	82	291	29	80	11	4	2	25	12	20	2	.275	.301	.361
Jerry Dybzinski	SS77,3B3	R	26	80	212	19	49	6	2	0	22	21	25	3	.231	.305	.278
Chris Bando	C63,3B2	S	26	66	184	13	39	6	1	3	16	24	30	0	.212	.299	.304
Carmelo Castillo	OF43,DH2	R	24	47	120	11	25	4	0	2	11	6	17	0	.208	.258	.292
Bill Nahorodny	C35	R	28	39	94	6	21	5	1	4	18	2	9	0	.223	.237	.426
Bake McBride	OF22	L	33	27	85	8	31	3	3	0	13	2	12	2	.365	.375	.471
Rodney Craig	OF22,DH4	S	24	49	65	7	15	2	0	0	1	4	6	3	.231	.275	.262
Joe Charboneau	OF18,DH1	R	27	22	56	7	12	2	1	2	9	5	7	0	.214	.286	.393
Karl Pagel	1B10,DH1	L	27	23	18	3	3	0	0	0	2	7	11	0	.167	.400	.167
Kevin Rhomberg	OF7,DH4,3B1	R	26	16	18	3	6	0	0	1	1	2	4	0	.333	.400	.500

M. Fischlin, 1 G at C; A. Bannister, 1 G at DH, 1 G at 3B; L. Milbourne, 1 G at DH

Pitcher	T	Age	G	GS	CG	ShO	IP	H	HR	BB	SO	W-L	Sv	ERA
Len Barker	R	26	33	33	10	1	244.2	211	17	88	187	15-11	0	3.90
Lary Sorensen	R	26	32	30	6	1	189.1	251	19	55	62	10-15	0	5.61
Rick Sutcliffe	R	26	34	27	6	1	216.0	174	16	98	142	14-8	1	2.96
John Denny†	R	29	21	21	5	0	138.1	126	11	73	94	6-11	0	5.01
Rick Waits	L	30	25	21	2	0	115.0	128	13	57	44	2-13	0	5.40
Neal Heaton	L	22	8	4	0	0	31.0	32	1	16	14	0-2	0	5.23
Bert Blyleven	R	31	4	4	0	0	20.1	16	2	11	19	2-2	0	4.87
John Bohnet	L	21	3	3	0	0	11.2	11	4	7	4	0-0	0	6.94
Dan Spillner	R	30	65	0	0	0	133.2	117	9	45	90	12-10	21	2.49
Ed Glynn	L	29	47	0	0	0	49.2	43	6	30	54	5-2	4	4.17
Ed Whitson	R	27	40	9	1	1	107.2	91	6	58	61	4-2	2	3.26
Tom Brennan	R	29	30	4	0	0	92.2	112	9	10	46	4-2	2	4.27
Bud Anderson	R	26	25	5	1	0	80.2	84	4	30	44	3-4	0	3.35
Jerry Reed†	R	26	6	1	0	0	15.2	15	1	3	10	1-1	0	3.45
Sandy Wihtol	R	27	6	0	0	0	11.2	9	1	7	8	0-0	0	4.63
Dennis Lewallyn	R	28	4	0	0	0	10.1	13	3	1	3	0-1	0	6.97

1982 Toronto Blue Jays 6th AL East 78-84 .481 17.0 GB

Bobby Cox

Player	Gm by Position	B	Age	G	AB	R	H	2B	3B	HR	RBI	BB	SO	SB	Avg	OBP	Slg
Ernie Whitt	C98,DH1	L	30	105	284	28	74	14	2	11	42	26	34	3	.261	.317	.440
Willie Upshaw	1B155,DH5	L	25	160	580	77	155	25	7	21	75	52	91	8	.267	.327	.443
Damaso Garcia	2B141,DH4	R	25	147	597	89	185	32	3	5	42	21	44	54	.310	.338	.399
Rance Mulliniks	3B102,SS16	L	26	112	311	32	76	25	0	4	35	37	49	3	.244	.326	.363
Alfredo Griffin	SS162	S	24	162	539	57	130	20	8	1	48	22	48	10	.241	.269	.314
Lloyd Moseby	OF145	L	22	147	487	51	115	20	9	9	52	33	106	11	.236	.294	.370
Jesse Barfield	OF137,DH1	R	22	139	394	54	97	13	2	18	58	42	79	1	.246	.323	.426
Barry Bonnell	OF125,3B9,DH6	R	28	140	437	59	128	26	3	6	49	32	51	14	.293	.342	.407
Wayne Nordhagen†	DH60,OF10	R	33	72	185	12	50	6	0	1	20	10	22	0	.270	.305	.319
Garth Iorg	3B100,2B30,DH1	R	27	129	417	45	119	20	5	1	36	12	38	3	.285	.307	.365
Hosken Powell	OF75,DH19	L	27	112	265	43	73	13	4	3	26	12	23	4	.275	.304	.389
Buck Martinez	C93	R	33	96	260	26	63	17	0	10	37	24	34	1	.242	.301	.423
Al Woods	OF64,DH10	L	28	85	201	20	47	11	1	3	24	21	20	1	.234	.302	.343
Dave Revering†	DH29,1B4	L	29	55	135	15	29	6	0	5	18	22	30	0	.215	.321	.370
Leon Roberts†	DH21,OF16	R	31	40	105	6	24	4	0	1	5	7	16	1	.229	.274	.295
Tony Johnson	DH28,OF28	R	26	70	98	17	23	2	1	3	14	11	26	3	.235	.309	.367
Glenn Adams	DH27	L	34	30	66	2	17	4	0	1	11	4	5	0	.258	.288	.364
Otto Velez	DH24	R	31	28	52	4	10	1	0	1	5	13	15	1	.192	.354	.269
Geno Petralli	C12,3B3	S	22	16	44	3	16	2	0	0	1	4	6	0	.364	.417	.409
John Mayberry†	DH13,1B4	L	33	17	33	7	9	0	0	2	3	7	5	0	.273	.405	.455
Dave Baker	3B8	L	25	9	20	3	5	1	0	0	2	3	3	0	.250	.400	.300
Pedro Hernandez	DH3,3B2,OF1	R	23	8	9	1	0	0	0	0	0	0	3	0	.000	.000	.000
Dick Davis†	DH1,OF1	R	28	3	7	0	2	0	0	0	2	0	1	0	.286	.250	.286

Pitcher	T	Age	G	GS	CG	ShO	IP	H	HR	BB	SO	W-L	Sv	ERA
Jim Clancy	R	26	40	40	11	3	266.2	251	26	77	139	16-14	0	3.71
Dave Stieb	R	24	38	38	19	5	288.1	271	27	75	141	17-14	0	3.25
Luis Leal	R	25	38	38	10	0	249.2	250	24	79	111	12-15	0	3.93
Jim Gott	R	22	30	23	1	1	136.0	134	15	66	82	5-10	0	4.43
Mark Bomback	R	29	16	8	0	0	59.2	87	10	25	22	1-5	0	6.03
Mark Eichhorn	R	21	7	7	0	0	38.0	40	4	14	16	0-3	0	5.45
Dale Murray	R	32	56	0	0	0	111.0	115	3	32	60	8-7	11	3.16
Roy Lee Jackson	R	28	48	2	0	0	97.0	77	7	31	71	8-8	6	3.06
Joey McLaughlin	R	25	44	0	0	0	70.0	54	7	30	49	8-6	8	3.21
Jerry Garvin	L	26	32	4	0	0	58.1	81	10	26	35	1-1	0	7.25
Dave Geisel	L	27	16	2	0	0	31.2	32	6	17	22	1-1	0	3.98
Steve Senteney	R	26	11	0	0	0	22.0	23	5	6	20	0-0	0	4.91
Ken Schrom	R	27	6	0	0	0	15.1	13	3	15	8	1-0	0	5.87

1982 California Angels 1st AL West 93-69 .574 —

Gene Mauch

Player	Gm by Position	B	Age	G	AB	R	H	2B	3B	HR	RBI	BB	SO	SB	Avg	OBP	Slg
Bob Boone	C143	R	34	143	472	42	121	17	0	7	58	39	34	0	.256	.310	.337
Rod Carew	1B134	L	36	138	523	88	167	25	5	3	44	67	49	10	.319	.396	.403
Bobby Grich	2B142,DH1	R	33	145	506	74	132	28	5	19	65	82	109	3	.261	.371	.449
Doug DeCinces	3B153,SS2	R	31	153	575	94	173	42	5	30	97	66	80	7	.301	.369	.548
Tim Foli	SS139,2B8,3B2	R	31	150	480	46	121	14	2	3	56	14	22	2	.252	.273	.308
Brian Downing	OF158	R	31	158	623	109	175	37	2	28	84	86	58	2	.281	.368	.482
Reggie Jackson	OF139,DH5	L	36	153	530	92	146	17	1	39	101	85	156	4	.275	.375	.532
Fred Lynn	OF133	L	30	138	472	89	141	38	1	21	86	58	72	7	.299	.374	.517
Don Baylor	DH155	R	33	157	608	80	160	24	1	24	93	57	69	10	.263	.329	.424
Juan Beniquez	OF107	R	32	112	196	25	52	11	2	3	24	15	21	3	.265	.321	.388
Ron Jackson	1B37,3B9	R	29	53	142	15	47	6	0	2	19	10	12	0	.331	.381	.415
Rob Wilfong†	2B28,3B5,OF3*	L	28	55	102	17	25	4	2	1	11	7	17	4	.245	.294	.353
Bobby Clark	OF102	R	27	102	90	11	19	1	0	2	8	0	29	1	.211	.209	.289
Joe Ferguson	C32,OF2	R	35	36	84	10	19	2	0	3	8	12	19	0	.226	.323	.357
Mick Kelleher†	SS28,3B6	R	34	34	49	9	8	1	0	0	1	5	5	1	.163	.255	.184
Rick Burleson	SS11	R	31	11	45	4	7	1	0	0	2	6	3	0	.156	.255	.178
Ricky Adams	SS8	R	23	8	14	1	2	0	0	0	0	0	2	1	.143	.200	.143
Daryl Sconiers	1B3,DH1	L	23	12	13	0	2	0	0	0	2	2	1	0	.154	.267	.154
Gary Pettis	OF8	S	24	10	5	5	1	0	0	1	1	0	2	0	.200	.200	.800
Jose Moreno	2B2,DH1	S	24	11	3	3	0	0	0	0	0	2	0	0	.000	.400	.000

R. Wilfong, 2 G at SS, 1 G at DH

Pitcher	T	Age	G	GS	CG	ShO	IP	H	HR	BB	SO	W-L	Sv	ERA
Ken Forsch	R	35	37	35	12	4	228.0	225	25	57	73	13-11	0	3.87
Geoff Zahn	L	36	34	34	12	4	229.1	225	18	65	81	18-8	0	3.73
Mike Witt	R	21	33	26	5	1	179.2	177	8	47	85	8-6	0	3.51
Steve Renko	R	37	31	23	4	0	156.0	163	17	51	81	11-6	0	4.44
Angel Moreno	L	27	13	8	2	0	49.1	55	7	23	22	3-7	1	4.74
Tommy John†	L	39	7	7	1	0	35.0	49	4	5	14	4-2	0	3.86
Luis Tiant	R	41	6	5	0	0	29.2	39	3	8	30	2-2	0	5.76
Andy Hassler	L	30	54	0	0	0	71.1	58	5	40	38	2-1	4	2.78
Luis Sanchez	R	28	46	0	0	0	92.2	89	3	34	58	7-4	5	3.21
Bruce Kison	R	32	33	16	3	1	142.0	120	15	44	86	10-5	1	3.17
Doug Corbett†	R	29	33	0	0	0	57.0	46	8	25	37	1-7	8	5.05
Dave Goltz†	R	33	28	7	1	0	86.0	82	4	32	49	8-5	3	4.08
Don Aase	R	27	24	0	0	0	52.0	45	5	23	40	3-3	4	3.46
Rick Steirer	R	25	10	1	0	0	26.1	25	2	11	14	1-0	0	3.76
John Curtis†	L	34	8	0	0	0	12.0	16	0	3	10	0-1	1	6.00
Stan Bahnsen†	R	37	7	0	0	0	9.2	13	0	8	5	0-1	0	4.66
Mickey Mahler	L	29	6	0	0	0	8.0	9	0	6	5	2-0	0	1.13

1982 Kansas City Royals 2nd AL West 90-72 .556 3.0 GB

Dick Howser

Player	Gm by Position	B	Age	G	AB	R	H	2B	3B	HR	RBI	BB	SO	SB	Avg	OBP	Slg
John Wathan	C120,1B3	R	32	121	448	79	121	11	3	3	51	48	46	36	.270	.343	.328
Willie Aikens	1B128	L	27	134	466	50	131	29	1	17	74	45	70	0	.281	.345	.457
Frank White	2B144	R	31	145	524	71	156	45	6	11	56	16	65	10	.298	.318	.469
George Brett	3B134,OF12	L	29	144	552	101	166	32	9	21	82	71	51	6	.301	.378	.505
U.L. Washington	SS117,DH1	S	28	119	437	64	125	19	3	10	60	38	48	23	.286	.338	.412
Jerry Martin	OF142,DH3	R	33	147	519	52	138	22	1	15	65	38	138	1	.266	.316	.399
Willie Wilson	OF135	S	26	136	585	87	194	19	15	3	46	26	81	37	.332	.365	.431
Amos Otis	OF125	R	35	125	475	73	136	25	3	11	88	37	65	9	.286	.335	.421
Hal McRae	DH158,OF1	R	36	159	613	91	189	46	8	27	133	55	61	4	.308	.369	.542
Onix Concepcion	SS46,2B24,DH1	R	24	74	205	17	48	9	1	0	15	5	18	2	.234	.256	.288
Greg Pryor	3B40,2B15,1B14*	R	32	73	152	23	41	10	1	2	12	10	20	2	.270	.315	.388
Steve Hammond	OF37,DH1	L	25	46	126	14	29	5	1	1	11	4	18	0	.230	.252	.310
Cesar Geronimo	OF44,DH1	L	34	53	119	14	32	6	3	4	23	8	16	2	.269	.305	.471
Don Slaught	C43	R	23	43	115	14	32	6	0	3	8	9	12	0	.278	.331	.409
Lee May	1B32,DH2	R	39	42	91	12	28	5	2	3	12	14	18	0	.308	.393	.505
Jamie Quirk	C29,1B6,3B1*	L	27	36	78	8	18	3	0	1	5	3	15	0	.231	.256	.308
Tom Poquette	OF23	L	30	24	62	4	9	1	0	0	3	4	5	1	.145	.206	.161
Dennis Werth	1B35,C2	R	29	41	15	5	2	0	0	0	2	4	2	0	.133	.316	.133
Ron Johnson	1B7	R	26	8	14	2	4	2	0	0	0	4	3	0	.286	.444	.429
Mark Ryal	OF5	L	21	6	13	0	1	0	0	0	0	1	3	0	.077	.143	.077
Bombo Rivera	OF3	R	29	5	10	1	1	0	0	0	0	0	2	0	.100	.100	.100
Tim Ireland	2B4,OF2,3B1	S	29	7	7	2	1	0	0	0	0	1	1	0	.143	.250	.143
Buddy Biancalana	SS3	S	22	3	2	0	1	0	1	0	0	1	0	0	.500	.667	1.500
Kelly Heath	2B1	R	24	1	1	0	0	0	0	0	0	0	0	0	.000	.000	.000

G. Pryor, 7 G at SS; J. Quirk, 1 G at OF

Pitcher	T	Age	G	GS	CG	ShO	IP	H	HR	BB	SO	W-L	Sv	ERA
Larry Gura	L	34	37	37	8	3	248.0	251	31	64	98	18-12	0	4.03
Vida Blue	L	32	31	31	6	2	181.0	163	20	80	103	13-12	0	3.78
Paul Splittorff	L	35	29	28	0	0	162.0	166	14	57	74	10-10	0	4.28
Dennis Leonard	R	31	21	21	2	0	130.2	145	20	46	58	10-6	0	5.10
Bud Black	L	25	22	14	0	0	88.1	92	10	34	40	4-6	0	4.58
Dave Frost	R	29	21	14	0	0	81.2	103	7	30	26	6-6	0	5.51
Keith Creel	R	23	9	6	0	0	41.2	43	8	25	13	1-4	0	5.40
Derek Botelho	R	25	8	4	0	0	24.0	25	4	8	12	2-1	0	4.13
Dan Quisenberry	R	29	72	0	0	0	136.2	126	12	12	46	9-7	35	2.57
Mike Armstrong	R	28	52	0	0	0	112.2	88	9	43	75	5-5	6	3.20
Don Hood	L	32	30	3	0	0	66.2	71	7	22	31	4-0	1	3.51
Bill Castro	R	28	21	4	0	0	75.2	72	8	20	37	3-2	1	3.45
Grant Jackson†	L	39	20	0	0	0	38.1	42	7	21	15	3-1	0	5.17
Bob Tufts	L	26	10	0	0	0	20.0	24	3	3	13	2-0	2	4.50
Jim Wright	R	27	7	0	0	0	23.2	32	3	6	9	0-0	0	5.32

1982 Chicago White Sox 3rd AL West 87-75 .537 6.0 GB

Tony La Russa

Player	Gm by Position	B	Age	G	AB	R	H	2B	3B	HR	RBI	BB	SO	SB	Avg	OBP	Slg
Carlton Fisk	C133,1B2	R	34	135	476	66	127	17	3	14	65	46	60	17	.267	.336	.403
Mike Squires	1B109	L	30	116	195	33	52	9	3	1	21	14	13	3	.267	.316	.359
Tony Bernazard	2B137	S	25	137	540	90	138	25	9	11	56	67	88	11	.256	.337	.396
Aurelio Rodriguez	3B112,2B3,SS2	R	34	118	257	24	62	15	1	3	31	11	35	0	.241	.275	.342
Bill Almon	SS108,DH1	R	29	111	308	40	79	10	4	4	26	25	49	10	.256	.313	.354
Harold Baines	OF161	L	23	161	608	89	165	29	8	25	105	49	95	10	.271	.321	.469
Steve Kemp	OF154,DH2	L	27	160	580	91	166	23	1	19	98	89	83	7	.286	.381	.428
Rudy Law	OF94,DH3	L	25	121	336	55	107	15	8	3	32	23	41	36	.318	.361	.438
Greg Luzinski	DH156	R	31	159	583	87	170	37	1	18	102	89	120	1	.292	.386	.451
Tom Paciorek	1B102,OF6	R	35	104	382	49	119	27	4	11	55	24	53	3	.312	.361	.490
Vance Law	SS85,3B39,2B10*	R	25	114	359	40	101	20	1	5	54	26	46	4	.281	.327	.384
Ron LeFlore	OF83,DH2	R	34	91	334	58	96	15	4	4	25	22	91	28	.287	.331	.392
Jim Morrison†	3B50,DH1	R	29	51	166	17	37	7	3	7	19	13	15	0	.223	.279	.428
Jerry Hairston	OF36,DH2	S	30	85	90	11	21	5	0	5	18	9	15	0	.233	.294	.456
Marc Hill	C49,1B1,3B1	R	30	53	88	9	23	2	0	3	13	6	13	0	.261	.313	.386
Chris Nyman	1B24,OF2	R	27	28	65	6	16	1	0	0	2	3	9	3	.246	.279	.262
Steve Dillard	2B16	R	31	16	41	1	7	3	1	0	5	1	5	0	.171	.190	.293
Marv Foley	C15,3B2,DH1*	L	28	27	36	1	4	0	0	0	1	6	4	0	.111	.238	.111
Jay Loviglio	2B13,DH2	R	26	15	31	5	6	0	0	0	2	1	4	2	.194	.219	.194
Ron Kittle	OF5,DH3	R	24	20	29	3	7	2	0	1	7	3	12	0	.241	.313	.414
Lorenzo Gray	3B16	R	24	17	28	4	8	1	0	0	0	2	4	1	.286	.333	.321
Rusty Kuntz	OF21	R	27	21	26	4	5	1	0	0	3	2	8	0	.192	.250	.231
Greg Walker	DH4	L	22	11	17	3	7	2	1	2	7	2	3	0	.412	.474	1.000

V. Law, 1 G at OF; M. Foley, 1 G at 1B

Pitcher	T	Age	G	GS	CG	ShO	IP	H	HR	BB	SO	W-L	Sv	ERA
LaMarr Hoyt	R	27	39	32	14	2	239.2	248	17	48	124	19-15	0	3.53
Rich Dotson	R	23	34	31	3	1	196.2	219	19	73	109	11-15	0	3.84
Britt Burns	L	23	28	28	5	1	169.1	168	12	67	116	13-5	0	4.04
Dennis Lamp	R	29	44	27	3	2	189.2	206	9	59	78	11-8	5	3.99
Steve Trout	L	24	25	19	2	0	120.1	130	9	50	62	6-9	0	4.26
Jim Siwy	R	23	2	1	0	0	7.0	10	1	5	3	0-0	0	10.29
Salome Barojas	R	25	61	0	0	0	106.2	96	9	46	56	6-6	21	3.54
Kevin Hickey	L	26	60	0	0	0	78.0	73	4	30	38	4-4	6	3.00
Jerry Koosman	L	39	42	19	3	1	173.1	194	9	38	88	11-7	3	3.84
Chico Escarrega	R	32	38	2	0	0	73.2	73	3	16	33	1-3	1	3.67
Jim Kern†	R	33	13	1	0	0	28.0	20	3	12	23	2-1	3	5.14
Sparky Lyle†	L	37	11	0	0	0	12.0	11	0	7	6	0-0	1	3.00
Warren Brusstar†	R	30	10	0	0	0	18.1	19	2	3	8	2-0	0	3.44
Rich Barnes	L	22	6	2	0	0	17.0	21	1	4	6	0-2	1	4.76
Eddie Solomon†	R	31	6	0	0	0	7.1	7	1	2	2	1-0	0	3.68
Juan Agosto	L	24	1	0	0	0	2.0	7	0	0	1	0-0	0	18.00

1982 Seattle Mariners 4th AL West 76-86 .469 17.0 GB

Rene Lachemann

Player	Gm by Position	B	Age	G	AB	R	H	2B	3B	HR	RBI	BB	SO	SB	Avg	OBP	Slg
Rick Sweet†	C83	S	29	88	258	29	66	6	1	4	24	20	24	3	.256	.311	.333
Gary Gray	1B60,DH14	R	29	80	269	26	69	14	2	7	29	24	59	1	.257	.322	.401
Julio Cruz	2B151,DH2,SS2*	S	27	154	549	83	133	22	5	8	49	57	71	46	.242	.316	.344
Manny Castillo	3B130,2B9	S	25	138	506	49	130	29	1	3	49	22	35	2	.257	.286	.336
Todd Cruz	SS136	R	26	136	492	44	113	20	2	16	57	12	95	2	.230	.246	.376
Al Cowens	OF145,DH1	R	30	146	560	72	151	39	8	20	78	46	81	11	.270	.325	.475
Dave Henderson	OF101	R	23	104	324	47	82	17	1	14	48	36	67	2	.253	.327	.441
Bruce Bochte	OF99,1B34,DH12	L	31	144	509	58	151	21	0	12	70	67	71	8	.297	.380	.409
Richie Zisk	DH130	R	33	131	503	61	147	28	1	21	62	49	89	2	.292	.354	.477
Joe Simpson	OF97	L	30	105	296	39	76	14	4	2	23	22	48	8	.257	.312	.351
Bobby Brown	OF68,DH3	S	28	79	245	29	59	7	1	4	17	17	32	28	.241	.288	.327
Jim Maler	1B57,DH5	R	23	64	221	18	50	8	3	4	26	12	35	0	.226	.274	.344
Paul Serna	SS31,2B18,3B15*	R	23	65	169	15	38	3	0	3	8	4	13	0	.225	.246	.296
Bud Bulling	C56	R	29	56	154	17	34	7	0	1	8	19	16	2	.221	.306	.286
Jim Essian	C48	R	31	48	153	14	42	8	0	3	20	11	7	2	.275	.327	.386
Dave Edler	3B31,DH2,OF2	R	25	40	104	14	29	2	2	2	18	11	13	4	.279	.345	.394
Dave Revering†	1B27	L	29	29	82	8	17	3	1	3	12	9	17	0	.207	.283	.378
Steve Stroughter	DH9,OF3	L	30	26	47	4	8	1	0	1	3	3	9	0	.170	.235	.255
Thad Bosley	OF19	L	25	22	46	3	8	1	0	0	2	4	8	3	.174	.240	.196
Lenny Randle	DH13,3B9,2B6	S	33	30	46	10	8	2	0	0	1	4	4	2	.174	.240	.217
John Moses	OF19	S	24	22	44	7	14	5	1	1	3	4	5	5	.318	.375	.545
Domingo Ramos	SS8	R	24	8	26	3	4	2	0	0	1	3	2	0	.154	.241	.231
Orlando Mercado	C8,DH1	R	20	9	17	1	2	0	0	1	6	0	5	0	.118	.118	.294
Dan Firova	C3	R	25	3	5	0	0	0	0	0	0	0	0	0	.000	.000	.000
Vance McHenry	DH1,SS1	R	25	3	1	0	0	0	0	0	0	0	0	0	.000	.000	.000

J. Cruz, 1 G at 3B; P. Serna, 2 G at DH

Pitcher	T	Age	G	GS	CG	ShO	IP	H	HR	BB	SO	W-L	Sv	ERA
Floyd Bannister	L	27	35	35	5	3	247.0	225	32	77	209	12-13	0	3.43
Gaylord Perry	R	43	32	32	6	0	216.2	245	27	54	116	10-12	0	4.40
Mike Moore	R	22	28	27	1	1	144.1	159	21	79	73	7-14	0	5.36
Jim Beattie	R	27	28	26	6	1	172.1	149	13	65	140	8-12	0	3.34
Gene Nelson	R	21	22	19	2	1	122.2	133	16	60	71	6-9	0	4.62
Bob Stoddard	R	25	9	9	2	1	67.1	48	7	18	24	3-3	0	2.41
Edwin Nunez	R	19	8	5	0	0	35.1	36	7	16	27	1-2	0	4.58
Ed Vande Berg	L	23	78	0	0	0	76.0	54	5	32	60	9-4	5	2.37
Bill Caudill	R	25	70	0	0	0	95.2	65	9	35	111	12-9	26	2.35
Mike Stanton	R	29	56	1	0	0	71.1	70	5	21	49	2-4	7	4.16
Larry Andersen	R	29	40	1	0	0	79.2	100	16	23	32	0-0	1	5.99
Bryan Clark	L	25	37	5	1	1	114.2	104	6	58	70	5-2	0	2.75
Ron Musselman	R	27	12	0	0	0	15.2	18	2	6	9	1-0	0	3.45
Rich Bordi	R	23	7	2	0	0	13.0	18	4	1	10	0-2	0	8.31
Jerry Don Gleaton	L	24	3	0	0	0	4.2	7	3	2	1	0-0	0	13.50

1982 Oakland Athletics 5th AL West 68-94 .420 25.0 GB

Billy Martin

Player	Gm by Position	B	Age	G	AB	R	H	2B	3B	HR	RBI	BB	SO	SB	Avg	OBP	Slg
Mike Heath	C90,OF10,3B5	R	27	101	318	43	77	18	4	3	39	27	36	8	.242	.298	.352
Dan Meyer	1B58,DH38,OF11	L	29	120	383	28	92	17	3	8	59	18	33	1	.240	.271	.363
Davey Lopes	2B125,OF6	R	37	128	450	58	109	19	3	11	42	40	51	28	.242	.304	.371
Wayne Gross	3B108,1B16,DH1	L	30	129	386	43	97	14	0	9	41	53	50	3	.251	.342	.358
Fred Stanley	SS98,2B2	R	34	101	228	33	44	7	0	2	17	29	32	0	.193	.287	.250
Dwayne Murphy	OF147,DH1,SS1	L	27	151	543	84	129	15	1	27	94	94	122	26	.238	.349	.418
Rickey Henderson	OF144,DH4	R	23	149	536	119	143	24	4	10	51	116	94	130	.267	.398	.382
Tony Armas	OF135,DH1	R	28	138	536	58	125	19	2	28	89	33	128	2	.233	.275	.433
Jeff Burroughs	DH48,OF34	R	31	113	285	42	79	13	2	16	48	45	61	1	.277	.372	.505
Jeff Newman	C67,1B3,DH1*	R	33	72	251	19	50	11	0	6	30	14	49	0	.199	.240	.315
Cliff Johnson	DH48,1B11	R	34	73	214	19	51	10	0	7	31	26	41	1	.238	.324	.383
Dave McKay	2B59,3B16,SS3	S	32	78	212	25	42	4	1	4	17	11	35	6	.198	.235	.283
Joe Rudi	1B49,OF14,DH3	R	35	71	193	21	41	6	1	5	18	24	35	0	.212	.301	.332
Mickey Klutts	3B49	R	27	55	157	10	28	8	0	0	14	9	18	0	.178	.222	.229
Jimmy Sexton	SS47,3B8,DH5	R	30	69	139	19	34	4	0	2	14	9	24	16	.245	.289	.317
Jim Spencer	1B32	L	35	33	101	6	17	3	1	2	5	3	20	0	.168	.190	.277
Tony Phillips	SS39	S	23	40	81	11	17	2	2	0	8	12	26	2	.210	.326	.284
Mitchell Page	DH24	L	30	31	78	14	20	5	0	4	7	7	24	3	.256	.333	.474
Mike Davis	OF13,1B7	L	23	23	75	12	30	4	0	1	10	2	8	3	.400	.416	.493
Bob Kearney	C22	R	25	22	71	7	12	3	0	0	5	3	10	0	.169	.218	.211
Kelvin Moore	1B20	R	24	21	67	6	15	1	1	2	6	3	23	0	.224	.250	.358
Danny Goodwin	DH15	L	28	17	52	6	11	2	1	2	8	2	13	0	.212	.236	.404
Rob Picciolo†	SS18	R	29	18	49	3	11	1	0	0	3	1	10	1	.224	.240	.245
Darrell Brown	OF7,DH1	S	26	8	18	2	6	0	1	0	3	1	2	1	.333	.368	.444
Rick Bosetti	OF6	R	28	6	15	1	3	0	0	0	0	0	1	0	.200	.200	.200
Kevin Bell	3B3,DH1	R	26	4	9	1	3	1	0	0	0	0	2	0	.333	.333	.444
Rick Langford	P32,OF1	R	30	33	1	0	0	0	0	0	0	0	0	0	.000	.000	.000

J. Newman, 1 G at 3B

Pitcher	T	Age	G	GS	CG	ShO	IP	H	HR	BB	SO	W-L	Sv	ERA
Matt Keough	R	26	34	34	10	2	209.1	233	38	101	75	11-18	0	5.72
Rick Langford	R	30	32	31	15	2	237.1	265	33	49	79	11-16	0	4.21
Mike Norris	R	27	28	28	7	1	166.1	154	25	84	83	7-11	0	4.76
Steve McCatty	R	28	21	20	2	0	128.2	124	16	70	66	6-3	0	3.99
Brian Kingman	R	27	23	20	3	0	122.2	131	11	57	46	4-12	1	4.48
Tim Conroy	L	22	5	5	1	0	25.1	20	1	18	17	2-2	0	3.55
Steve Baker	R	25	5	3	0	0	25.2	30	3	4	14	1-1	0	4.56
Chris Codiroli	R	24	3	3	0	0	16.2	16	1	4	5	1-2	0	4.32
Tom Underwood	L	28	56	10	2	0	153.0	136	11	68	79	10-6	7	3.29
Bob Owchinko	L	27	54	0	0	0	102.0	111	11	52	67	2-4	3	5.21
Dave Beard	R	22	54	2	0	0	91.2	85	9	35	73	10-9	11	3.44
Preston Hanna†	R	27	23	2	1	0	48.1	54	3	33	32	0-4	0	5.59
Bo McLaughlin	R	28	21	2	1	0	48.1	51	3	27	27	0-4	0	4.84
Jeff Jones	R	25	18	2	0	0	37.0	44	6	26	18	3-1	0	5.11
John D'Acquisto	R	30	11	0	0	0	17.0	20	1	9	7	0-1	0	5.29
Fredie Arroyo†	R	30	10	0	0	0	22.1	23	4	7	9	0-0	0	5.24
Dennis Kinney	L	30	3	0	0	0	4.1	9	1	4	0	0-0	0	8.31

1982 Texas Rangers 6th AL West 64-98 .395 29.0 GB

Don Zimmer (38-58)/Darrell Johnson (26-40)

Player	Gm by Position	B	Age	G	AB	R	H	2B	3B	HR	RBI	BB	SO	SB	Avg	OBP	Slg
Jim Sundberg	C132,OF1	R	31	139	470	37	118	22	5	10	47	49	57	2	.251	.322	.383
Dave Hostetler	1B109,DH3	R	26	113	418	53	97	12	3	22	67	42	113	2	.232	.300	.433
Mike Richardt	2B98,DH15,OF6	R	24	119	402	34	97	10	0	3	43	23	42	9	.241	.281	.289
Buddy Bell	3B145,SS4	R	30	148	537	62	159	27	2	13	67	70	50	5	.296	.376	.426
Mark Wagner	SS60	R	28	60	179	14	43	4	1	0	8	10	28	2	.240	.280	.274
George Wright	OF149	S	23	150	557	69	147	20	5	11	50	30	78	3	.264	.305	.377
Larry Parrish	OF124,3B3,DH2	R	28	128	440	59	116	15	0	17	62	30	84	5	.264	.314	.414
Billy Sample	OF91,DH1	R	27	97	360	56	94	14	2	10	29	27	35	10	.261	.318	.394
Lamar Johnson	DH77,1B12	R	31	105	324	37	84	11	0	7	38	31	40	3	.259	.326	.358
John Grubb	OF77,DH18	L	33	103	308	35	86	13	3	3	26	39	37	0	.279	.368	.370
Doug Flynn†	2B55,SS35	R	31	88	270	13	57	6	2	0	19	4	14	6	.211	.221	.248
Lee Mazzilli†	OF26,DH24	S	27	58	195	23	47	8	0	4	17	28	26	11	.241	.339	.344
Bill Stein	2B34,3B28,SS6*	R	35	85	184	14	44	8	0	1	16	12	23	0	.239	.293	.299
Bucky Dent†	SS45	R	30	46	146	16	32	9	0	1	14	13	10	0	.219	.280	.301
Pat Putnam	1B39,3B1,OF1	L	28	43	122	14	28	8	0	2	9	10	18	0	.230	.293	.344
Leon Roberts†	OF28,DH1	R	31	31	73	7	17	3	0	1	6	4	14	0	.233	.278	.315
Wayne Tolleson	SS26,3B4,2B1	S	26	38	70	6	8	1	0	0	2	5	14	1	.114	.173	.129
Mickey Rivers	DH16	L	33	19	68	6	16	1	1	1	4	0	7	0	.235	.232	.324
Pete O'Brien	OF11,DH4,1B3	L	24	20	67	13	16	4	1	4	13	6	8	1	.239	.297	.507
Terry Bogener	OF16,DH4	L	26	24	60	6	13	2	1	1	4	4	8	2	.217	.288	.333
Don Werner	C22	R	29	22	59	4	12	2	0	0	3	3	7	0	.203	.242	.237
Bobby Johnson	C14,1B3	R	22	20	56	4	7	2	0	2	7	3	22	0	.125	.183	.268
Randy Bass†	DH7,1B6	L	28	16	48	5	10	2	0	1	6	1	7	0	.208	.231	.313
Mario Mendoza	SS12	R	31	12	17	1	2	0	0	0	0	0	4	0	.118	.118	.118
Nick Capra	OF9	R	24	13	15	2	4	0	0	1	1	3	4	2	.267	.421	.467

B. Stein, 3 G at DH, 2 G at 1B, 1 G at OF

Pitcher	T	Age	G	GS	CG	ShO	IP	H	HR	BB	SO	W-L	Sv	ERA
Charlie Hough	R	34	34	34	12	2	228.0	217	21	72	128	16-13	0	3.95
Frank Tanana	L	28	30	30	7	0	194.1	199	16	55	87	7-18	0	4.21
Rick Honeycutt	L	28	30	26	4	1	164.0	201	20	54	64	5-17	0	5.27
Doc Medich†	R	33	21	21	2	0	122.2	146	8	61	37	7-11	0	5.06
John Butcher	R	25	18	13	2	0	94.1	102	10	34	39	1-5	1	4.87
Mike Smithson	R	27	8	8	3	0	46.2	51	5	13	24	3-4	0	5.01
Mike Mason	L	23	4	4	0	0	23.0	21	3	9	8	1-2	0	5.09
Danny Darwin	R	26	56	1	0	0	89.0	95	6	37	61	10-8	7	3.44
Paul Mirabella	L	28	40	0	0	0	50.2	46	4	22	29	1-1	3	4.80
Steve Comer	R	28	37	3	1	0	97.0	133	11	36	23	1-6	6	5.10
Jon Matlack	L	32	33	14	1	0	147.2	158	14	37	78	7-7	1	3.53
Dave Schmidt	R	25	33	8	0	0	109.2	118	5	25	69	4-6	6	3.20
Dan Boitano	R	29	19	0	0	0	30.1	33	5	13	28	0-0	0	5.34
Tom Henke	R	24	8	0	0	0	15.2	14	0	8	9	1-0	0	1.15
Jim Farr	R	26	5	0	0	0	18.0	20	0	7	6	0-0	0	2.50

1982 Minnesota Twins 7th AL West 60-102 .370 33.0 GB

Billy Gardner

Player	Gm by Position	B	Age	G	AB	R	H	2B	3B	HR	RBI	BB	SO	SB	Avg	OBP	Slg
Tim Laudner	C93	R	24	93	306	37	78	19	1	7	33	34	74	0	.255	.328	.392
Kent Hrbek	1B138,DH2	L	22	140	532	82	160	21	4	23	92	54	80	3	.301	.363	.485
John Castino	2B96,3B21,OF6*	R	27	117	410	48	99	12	6	6	37	36	51	2	.241	.304	.344
Gary Gaetti	3B142,SS2	R	23	145	508	59	117	25	4	25	84	37	107	0	.230	.280	.443
Ron Washington	SS91,2B37,3B1	R	30	119	451	48	122	17	6	5	39	14	79	3	.271	.291	.368
Gary Ward	OF150,DH2	R	28	152	570	85	165	33	7	28	91	37	105	13	.289	.330	.519
Tom Brunansky	OF127	R	21	127	463	77	126	30	1	20	46	71	101	1	.272	.377	.471
Bobby Mitchell	OF121	L	27	124	454	48	113	11	6	2	28	54	53	8	.249	.331	.313
Randy Johnson	DH67,OF2	L	23	89	234	26	58	10	0	10	33	30	46	0	.248	.325	.419
Mickey Hatcher	OF47,DH29,3B5	R	27	84	277	23	69	13	2	3	26	8	27	0	.249	.269	.343
Lenny Faedo	SS88,DH1	R	22	90	255	16	62	8	0	3	22	16	22	1	.243	.288	.310
Jesus Vega	DH39,1B18,OF1	R	26	71	199	23	53	6	0	5	29	8	19	6	.266	.289	.372
Dave Engle	OF34,DH20	R	25	58	186	20	42	7	2	4	16	10	22	0	.226	.269	.349
Sal Butera	C53	R	29	54	126	9	32	2	0	0	8	17	12	0	.254	.347	.270
Randy Bush	DH26,OF6	L	23	55	119	13	29	6	1	4	13	8	28	0	.244	.305	.412
Jim Eisenreich	OF30	L	23	34	99	10	30	6	0	2	9	11	13	0	.303	.378	.424
Larry Milbourne†	2B26	S	31	29	98	9	23	1	1	0	1	7	8	1	.235	.283	.265
Butch Wynegar†	C24	S	26	24	86	9	18	4	0	1	8	10	12	0	.209	.292	.291
Rob Wilfong†	2B22	L	28	25	81	7	13	1	0	0	5	7	13	0	.160	.236	.173
Boomer Wells	1B10,DH5	R	28	15	54	5	11	1	2	0	3	1	8	0	.204	.211	.296
Ray Smith	C9	R	26	9	23	1	5	0	1	0	1	1	3	0	.217	.250	.304
Roy Smalley†	SS4	S	29	4	13	2	2	1	0	0	0	3	4	0	.154	.313	.231

J. Castino, 1 G at DH

Pitcher	T	Age	G	GS	CG	ShO	IP	H	HR	BB	SO	W-L	Sv	ERA
Brad Havens	L	22	33	32	4	1	208.2	201	32	80	129	10-14	0	4.31
Al Williams	R	28	26	26	3	0	153.2	166	18	55	61	9-7	0	4.22
Bobby Castillo	R	27	40	25	6	1	218.2	194	26	85	123	13-11	0	3.66
Frank Viola	L	22	22	22	3	1	126.0	152	22	38	84	4-10	0	5.21
Jack O'Connor	L	24	23	19	6	1	126.0	122	13	57	56	8-9	0	4.29
Darrell Jackson	L	26	13	7	0	0	44.2	51	6	24	16	0-5	0	6.25
Roger Erickson†	R	25	7	7	2	0	40.2	56	6	12	12	4-3	0	4.87
Pete Filson	L	23	5	3	0	0	12.1	17	2	8	10	0-2	0	8.76
Ron Davis	R	26	63	0	0	0	106.0	106	16	47	89	3-9	22	4.42
Terry Felton	R	24	48	6	0	0	117.1	99	18	76	92	0-13	3	4.99
Jeff Little	L	27	33	0	0	0	36.1	33	6	27	26	2-0	0	4.21
Pete Redfern	R	27	27	13	2	0	94.1	122	16	51	40	5-11	0	6.58
Paul Boris	R	26	23	0	0	0	49.2	46	8	19	30	1-2	0	3.99
John Pacella†	R	25	21	1	0	0	51.2	61	14	37	20	1-2	2	7.32
Doug Corbett†	R	29	10	0	0	0	22.0	27	3	10	15	0-2	3	5.32
Fredie Arroyo†	R	30	7	0	0	0	13.2	17	2	6	4	0-1	0	5.27
Don Cooper	R	26	6	1	0	0	11.1	14	0	11	5	0-1	0	9.53

»1982 St. Louis Cardinals 1st NL East 92-70 .568 — Whitey Herzog

Player	Gm by Position	B	Age	G	AB	R	H	2B	3B	HR	RBI	BB	SO	SB	Avg	OBP	Slg
Darrell Porter	C111	L	30	120	373	46	86	18	5	12	48	66	66	1	.231	.347	.402
Keith Hernandez	1B158,OF4	L	28	160	579	79	173	33	6	7	94	100	67	19	.299	.397	.413
Tom Herr	2B128	S	26	135	493	83	131	19	4	0	36	57	56	25	.266	.341	.320
Ken Oberkfell	3B135,2B1	L	26	137	470	55	136	22	5	2	34	40	31	11	.289	.345	.370
Ozzie Smith	SS139	S	27	140	488	58	121	24	1	2	43	68	32	25	.248	.339	.314
Lonnie Smith	OF149	R	26	156	592	120	182	35	8	8	69	64	74	68	.307	.381	.434
George Hendrick	OF134	R	32	136	515	65	145	20	5	19	104	37	80	3	.282	.323	.450
Willie McGee	OF117	S	23	123	422	43	125	12	8	4	56	12	58	24	.296	.318	.391
Mike Ramsey	2B43,3B28,SS22*	S	28	112	256	18	59	8	2	1	21	22	34	6	.230	.294	.289
Dane Iorg	OF63,1B10,3B2	L	32	102	238	17	70	14	1	0	34	23	23	0	.294	.352	.361
David Green	OF68	R	21	76	166	21	47	7	1	2	23	8	29	11	.283	.315	.373
Gene Tenace	C37,1B7	R	35	66	124	18	32	9	0	7	18	36	31	1	.258	.436	.500
Julio Gonzalez	3B21,2B9,SS1	R	29	42	87	9	21	3	2	1	7	1	24	1	.241	.258	.356
Tito Landrum	OF56	R	27	79	72	12	20	3	0	2	14	8	18	0	.278	.358	.403
Glenn Brummer	C32	R	27	35	64	4	15	4	0	0	8	0	12	2	.234	.234	.297
Steve Braun	OF8,3B5	L	34	58	62	6	17	4	0	0	4	11	10	0	.274	.384	.339
Orlando Sanchez	C15	L	25	26	37	6	7	0	1	0	3	5	5	0	.189	.286	.243
Kelly Paris	3B5,SS4	R	24	12	29	1	3	0	0	0	1	0	7	0	.103	.100	.103
Gene Roof	OF5	S	24	11	15	3	4	0	0	0	2	1	4	2	.267	.313	.267

M. Ramsey, 2 G at OF

Pitcher	T	Age	G	GS	CG	ShO	IP	H	HR	BB	SO	W-L	Sv	ERA
Joaquin Andujar	R	29	38	37	9	5	265.2	237	11	50	137	15-10	0	2.47
Bob Forsch	R	32	36	34	6	2	233.0	238	16	54	69	15-9	1	3.48
Steve Mura	R	27	35	30	7	1	184.1	196	16	80	84	12-11	0	4.05
Dave LaPoint	L	22	42	21	0	0	152.2	170	8	52	81	9-3	0	3.42
John Stuper	R	25	23	21	2	0	136.2	137	8	55	53	9-7	0	3.36
Andy Rincon	R	23	11	6	1	0	40.0	35	1	25	11	2-3	0	4.73
Bruce Sutter	R	29	70	0	0	0	102.1	88	8	34	61	9-8	36	2.90
Doug Bair	R	32	63	0	0	0	91.2	69	7	36	68	5-3	8	2.55
Jim Kaat	L	43	62	2	0	0	75.0	79	6	23	35	5-3	2	4.08
Jeff Lahti	R	25	33	1	0	0	56.2	53	3	21	22	5-4	0	3.81
John Martin	L	26	24	7	0	0	66.0	56	6	30	21	4-5	0	4.23
Jeff Keener	R	23	19	0	0	0	22.1	19	1	19	25	1-1	0	1.61
Mark Littell	R	29	16	0	0	0	20.2	22	1	15	7	0-1	0	5.23
Eric Rasmussen	R	30	8	3	0	0	18.1	21	2	8	15	1-2	0	4.42

1982 Philadelphia Phillies 2nd NL East 89-73 .549 3.0 GB Pat Corrales

Player	Gm by Position	B	Age	G	AB	R	H	2B	3B	HR	RBI	BB	SO	SB	Avg	OBP	Slg
Bo Diaz	C144	R	29	144	525	69	151	29	1	18	85	36	87	3	.288	.333	.450
Pete Rose	1B162	S	41	162	634	80	172	25	4	3	54	66	32	8	.271	.345	.338
Manny Trillo	2B149	R	31	149	549	52	149	24	1	0	39	33	53	8	.271	.316	.319
Mike Schmidt	3B148	R	32	148	514	108	144	26	3	35	87	107	131	14	.280	.403	.547
Ivan DeJesus	SS154,3B7	R	29	161	536	53	128	21	5	3	59	54	70	14	.239	.309	.313
Gary Matthews	OF162	R	31	162	616	89	173	31	1	19	83	66	87	21	.281	.349	.427
Bob Dernier	OF119	R	25	122	370	56	92	10	2	4	21	36	69	42	.249	.315	.319
Garry Maddox	OF111	R	32	119	412	39	117	27	2	8	61	12	32	7	.284	.303	.417
George Vukovich	OF102	L	26	123	335	41	91	18	2	6	42	32	47	2	.272	.334	.391
Greg Gross	OF71	L	29	119	134	14	40	4	0	0	10	19	8	4	.299	.386	.328
Ozzie Virgil	C35	R	25	49	101	11	24	6	0	3	8	10	26	0	.238	.306	.386
Bill Robinson†	OF19,1B5	R	39	35	69	6	18	6	0	3	19	7	15	1	.261	.321	.478
Dick Davis†	OF16	R	28	28	68	5	19	3	1	2	7	2	9	1	.279	.296	.441
Luis Aguayo	2B21,SS15,3B5	R	23	50	56	11	15	1	2	3	7	5	7	1	.268	.339	.518
Len Matuszek	3B8,1B3	L	27	25	39	1	3	1	0	0	3	1	10	0	.077	.119	.103
Dave Roberts	3B11,C10,2B7	R	31	28	33	2	6	1	0	0	2	2	8	0	.182	.229	.212
Julio Franco	SS11,3B2	R	20	16	29	3	8	1	0	0	3	2	4	0	.276	.323	.310
Willie Montanez†	1B6	L	34	18	16	0	1	0	0	0	1	1	3	0	.063	.118	.063
Del Unser	1B5,OF2	L	37	19	14	0	0	0	0	0	0	3	2	0	.000	.176	.000
Bob Molinaro†		L	32	19	14	0	4	0	0	0	2	3	1	1	.286	.412	.286
Alex Sanchez	OF4	R	23	7	14	3	4	1	0	2	4	0	4	0	.286	.286	.786

Pitcher	T	Age	G	GS	CG	ShO	IP	H	HR	BB	SO	W-L	Sv	ERA
Steve Carlton	L	37	38	38	19	6	295.2	253	17	86	286	23-11	0	3.10
Larry Christenson	R	28	33	33	3	0	223.0	212	15	53	145	9-10	0	3.47
Mike Krukow	R	30	33	33	7	2	208.0	211	8	82	138	13-11	0	3.12
Dick Ruthven	R	31	33	31	8	2	204.1	189	18	59	115	11-11	0	3.79
Marty Bystrom	R	23	19	16	1	0	89.0	93	2	35	50	5-6	0	4.85
John Denny†	R	29	4	4	0	0	22.1	18	1	10	19	0-2	0	4.03
Ron Reed	R	39	57	2	0	0	98.0	85	4	24	57	5-5	14	2.66
Ed Farmer	R	32	47	4	0	0	76.0	66	2	50	58	2-6	6	4.86
Sid Monge	L	31	47	0	0	0	72.0	70	8	22	43	7-1	2	3.75
Tug McGraw	L	37	34	0	0	0	39.2	50	3	12	25	3-3	5	4.31
Sparky Lyle†	L	37	34	0	0	0	36.2	50	3	12	12	3-3	2	5.15
Porfi Altamirano	R	30	29	0	0	0	39.0	41	2	14	26	5-1	2	4.15
Warren Brusstar†	R	30	22	0	0	0	22.2	31	2	5	11	2-3	2	4.76
Stan Bahnsen†	R	37	8	0	0	0	13.1	8	0	3	9	0-0	0	1.35
Jerry Reed†	R	26	7	0	0	0	8.2	11	0	3	1	1-0	0	5.19
Jay Baller	R	21	4	1	0	0	8.0	7	1	2	7	0-0	0	3.38

1982 Montreal Expos 3rd NL East 86-76 .531 6.0 GB Jim Fanning

Player	Gm by Position	B	Age	G	AB	R	H	2B	3B	HR	RBI	BB	SO	SB	Avg	OBP	Slg
Gary Carter	C153	R	28	154	557	91	163	32	1	29	97	78	64	2	.293	.381	.510
Al Oliver	1B159	L	35	160	617	90	204	43	2	22	109	61	59	5	.331	.392	.514
Doug Flynn†	2B58	R	31	58	193	13	47	6	2	0	20	4	23	0	.244	.256	.295
Tim Wallach	3B156,OF2,1B1	R	24	158	596	89	160	31	3	28	97	36	81	6	.268	.313	.471
Chris Speier	SS155	R	32	156	530	41	136	26	4	7	60	47	67	1	.257	.316	.360
Andre Dawson	OF147	R	27	148	608	107	183	37	7	23	83	34	96	39	.301	.343	.498
Warren Cromartie	OF136,1B9	L	28	144	497	59	126	24	3	14	62	69	60	3	.254	.346	.398
Tim Raines	OF120,2B36	S	22	156	647	90	179	32	8	4	43	75	83	78	.277	.353	.369
Terry Francona	OF33,1B16	L	23	46	131	14	42	3	0	0	9	8	11	2	.321	.360	.344
Mike Gates	2B36	L	25	36	121	16	28	2	3	0	8	9	19	0	.231	.280	.298
Jerry White	OF30	S	29	69	115	13	28	6	1	2	13	8	26	3	.243	.304	.365
Joel Youngblood†	OF35	R	30	40	90	16	18	2	0	0	8	9	21	2	.200	.291	.222
Frank Taveras	SS26,2B19	R	32	48	87	9	14	5	1	0	4	7	6	4	.161	.221	.241
Brad Mills	3B13	L	25	54	67	6	15	3	0	1	2	5	11	0	.224	.278	.313
Dan Norman	OF31	R	27	53	66	6	14	3	0	2	7	7	20	0	.212	.288	.348
Wallace Johnson	2B13	S	25	36	57	5	11	0	2	0	2	5	5	4	.193	.258	.263
Tim Blackwell	C18	S	29	23	42	2	8	2	1	0	3	3	11	0	.190	.244	.286
Bryan Little	2B16,SS10	S	22	29	42	6	9	0	0	0	3	4	6	2	.214	.277	.214
Roy Johnson	OF11	L	23	17	32	2	7	2	0	0	2	1	6	0	.219	.235	.281
John Milner†	1B5	L	32	26	28	1	3	0	0	0	2	4	2	0	.107	.212	.107
Rodney Scott†	2B12	S	28	14	25	2	5	0	0	0	1	3	2	5	.200	.286	.200
Mike Phillips	2B10,SS2	L	31	14	8	0	1	0	0	0	1	0	3	0	.125	.111	.125
Ken Phelps		L	27	10	8	0	2	0	0	0	0	0	3	0	.250	.333	.250
Brad Gulden	C2	L	26	5	6	1	0	0	0	0	0	1	1	0	.000	.143	.000
Rowland Office	OF1	L	29	3	3	0	1	1	0	0	0	0	1	0	.333	.333	.667
Chris Smith		S	24	2	2	0	0	0	0	0	0	0	1	0	.000	.000	.000
Mike Stenhouse		L	24	1	1	0	0	0	0	0	0	0	1	0	.000	.000	.000

Pitcher	T	Age	G	GS	CG	ShO	IP	H	HR	BB	SO	W-L	Sv	ERA
Steve Rogers	R	32	35	35	14	4	277.0	245	12	65	179	19-8	0	2.40
Bill Gullickson	R	23	34	34	6	0	236.2	231	25	61	155	12-14	0	3.57
Scott Sanderson	R	25	32	32	7	0	224.0	212	24	58	158	12-12	0	3.46
Charlie Lea	R	25	27	27	4	2	177.2	145	16	56	115	12-10	0	3.24
David Palmer	R	24	13	13	1	0	73.2	60	3	36	46	6-4	0	3.18
Randy Lerch†	L	27	6	4	0	0	23.2	26	0	8	4	2-0	0	3.42
Jeff Reardon	R	26	75	0	0	0	109.0	87	6	36	86	7-4	26	2.06
Woodie Fryman	L	42	60	0	0	0	69.2	66	3	26	46	9-4	12	3.75
Bryn Smith	R	26	47	1	0	0	79.1	81	5	23	50	2-4	3	4.20
Ray Burris	R	31	37	15	2	0	123.2	143	14	53	55	4-14	2	4.73
Dan Schatzeder†	L	27	26	1	0	0	36.0	37	1	12	15	0-2	0	3.50
Bill Lee	L	35	7	0	0	0	12.1	19	1	1	8	0-0	0	4.38
Bob James†	R	23	7	0	0	0	9.0	10	0	8	11	0-0	0	6.00
Tom Gorman†	L	24	5	0	0	0	7.0	8	0	4	6	1-0	0	5.14
Dave Tomlin	L	33	1	0	0	0	2.0	1	0	1	2	0-0	0	4.50

1982 Pittsburgh Pirates 4th NL East 84-78 .519 8.0 GB Chuck Tanner

Player	Gm by Position	B	Age	G	AB	R	H	2B	3B	HR	RBI	BB	SO	SB	Avg	OBP	Slg
Tony Pena	C137	R	25	138	497	53	147	28	4	11	63	17	57	2	.296	.323	.435
Jason Thompson	1B155	L	27	156	550	87	156	32	0	31	101	101	107	1	.284	.391	.511
Johnny Ray	2B162	S	25	162	647	79	182	30	7	7	63	36	34	16	.281	.318	.382
Bill Madlock	3B146,1B3	R	31	154	568	92	181	33	3	19	95	48	39	18	.319	.368	.488
Dale Berra	SS153,3B6	R	25	156	529	64	139	25	5	10	61	33	83	6	.263	.306	.386
Omar Moreno	OF157	L	29	158	645	82	158	18	9	3	44	44	121	60	.245	.292	.315
Mike Easler	OF138	L	31	142	475	52	131	27	2	15	58	40	85	1	.276	.337	.436
Lee Lacy	OF113,3B2	R	34	121	359	66	112	16	3	5	31	32	57	40	.312	.369	.415
Dave Parker	OF63	L	31	73	244	41	66	19	3	6	29	22	45	7	.270	.330	.447
Steve Nicosia	C35,OF3	R	26	39	100	6	28	3	0	1	7	11	13	0	.280	.348	.340
Jim Morrison†	3B26,OF2,2B1*	R	29	44	86	10	24	4	1	4	15	5	14	2	.279	.309	.488
Dick Davis†	OF28	R	28	39	77	7	14	2	1	2	10	5	9	1	.182	.224	.312
Willie Stargell	1B8	L	42	74	73	6	17	4	0	3	17	10	24	0	.233	.318	.411
Bill Robinson†	OF22	R	39	31	71	8	17	3	0	4	12	5	19	0	.239	.286	.451
Richie Hebner†	OF21,1B4,3B1	L	34	25	70	6	21	2	0	2	12	5	3	4	.300	.347	.414
Jim Smith	SS29,2B3,3B1	R	27	42	42	5	10	2	1	0	4	5	7	0	.238	.313	.333
Doug Frobel	OF12	L	23	16	34	5	7	2	0	2	3	1	11	1	.206	.229	.441
Willie Montanez†	1B2,OF2	L	34	36	32	4	9	1	0	0	1	3	3	0	.281	.343	.313
Brian Harper	OF8	R	22	20	29	4	8	1	0	2	4	1	4	0	.276	.300	.517
John Milner†	1B1	L	32	33	25	5	6	2	0	2	8	6	3	1	.240	.406	.560
Reggie Walton	OF2	R	29	13	15	1	3	1	0	0	0	1	1	0	.200	.294	.267
Junior Ortiz	C7	R	22	7	15	1	3	1	0	0	1	0	3	0	.200	.250	.267
Ken Reitz	3B4	R	31	7	10	0	0	0	0	0	0	0	4	0	.000	.091	.000
Hedi Vargas	1B5	R	23	8	8	1	3	1	0	0	3	0	2	0	.375	.333	.500
Wayne Nordhagen†	OF1	R	33	1	4	0	2	0	0	0	2	0	1	0	.500	.500	.500
Nelson Norman	2B2,SS1	S	24	3	3	0	0	0	0	0	0	0	0	0	.000	.000	.000
Rafael Belliard	SS4	R	20	9	2	3	1	0	0	0	0	0	0	1	.500	.500	.500

J. Morrison, 1 G at SS

Pitcher	T	Age	G	GS	CG	ShO	IP	H	HR	BB	SO	W-L	Sv	ERA
Rick Rhoden	R	29	35	35	6	1	230.1	239	14	70	128	11-14	0	4.14
Don Robinson	R	25	38	30	6	0	227.0	213	26	103	165	15-13	0	4.28
John Candelaria	L	28	31	30	1	1	174.2	166	13	37	133	12-7	1	2.94
Larry McWilliams†	L	28	19	18	2	2	121.2	106	9	24	94	6-5	1	3.11
Eddie Solomon†	R	31	11	10	0	0	46.2	69	9	18	18	2-6	0	6.75
Ross Baumgarten	L	27	12	10	0	0	44.0	60	3	27	17	0-5	0	6.55
Tom Griffin	R	34	6	4	0	0	22.1	32	5	15	8	1-3	0	8.87
Lee Tunnell	R	21	5	3	0	0	18.1	17	1	5	4	1-1	0	3.93
Kent Tekulve	R	35	85	0	0	0	128.2	113	7	46	66	12-8	20	2.87
Rod Scurry	L	26	76	0	0	0	103.2	79	3	64	94	4-5	14	1.74
Enrique Romo	R	34	45	0	0	0	86.2	81	11	36	58	9-3	1	4.36
Manny Sarmiento	R	26	35	17	4	0	164.2	153	7	46	81	9-4	1	3.39
Randy Niemann	L	26	20	0	0	0	35.1	34	1	17	26	1-1	1	5.09
Paul Moskau	R	28	13	5	0	0	35.0	43	7	8	15	1-3	0	4.37
Cecilio Guante	R	22	10	0	0	0	27.0	28	1	5	26	0-0	0	3.33
Grant Jackson†	L	39	1	0	0	0	0.2	1	1	0	0	0-0	0	13.50

1982 Chicago Cubs 5th NL East 73-89 .451 19.0 GB

Lee Elia

Player	Gm by Position	B	Age	G	AB	R	H	2B	3B	HR	RBI	BB	SO	SB	Avg	OBP	Slg
Jody Davis	C129	R	25	130	418	41	109	20	2	12	52	36	92	0	.261	.316	.404
Bill Buckner	1B161	L	32	161	657	93	201	34	5	15	105	36	26	15	.306	.342	.441
Bump Wills	2B103	S	29	128	419	64	114	18	4	6	38	46	76	35	.272	.347	.377
Ryne Sandberg	3B133,2B24	R	22	156	635	103	172	33	5	7	54	36	90	32	.271	.312	.372
Larry Bowa	SS140	S	36	142	499	50	123	15	7	0	29	39	38	8	.246	.302	.305
Leon Durham	OF143,1B1	L	24	148	539	84	168	33	7	22	90	66	77	28	.312	.388	.521
Gary Woods	OF103	R	27	117	245	28	66	15	1	4	30	21	48	3	.269	.327	.388
Keith Moreland	OF86,C44,3B2	R	28	138	476	50	124	17	2	15	68	46	71	0	.261	.326	.399
Jay Johnstone†	OF86	L	36	98	269	39	67	13	1	10	43	40	41	0	.249	.343	.416
Steve Henderson	OF70	R	29	92	257	23	60	12	4	2	29	22	64	6	.233	.293	.335
Junior Kennedy	2B71,SS28,3B7	R	31	105	242	22	53	3	1	2	25	21	34	1	.219	.278	.264
Jerry Morales	OF41	R	33	65	116	14	33	2	2	4	30	9	7	1	.284	.333	.440
Pat Tabler	3B25	R	24	25	85	9	20	4	2	1	7	6	20	0	.235	.287	.365
Mel Hall	OF22	L	21	24	80	6	21	3	2	0	4	5	17	0	.263	.318	.350
Scot Thompson	OF23,1B4	L	26	49	74	11	27	5	1	0	7	5	4	0	.365	.405	.459
Bob Molinaro†	OF4	L	32	65	66	6	13	1	0	1	12	6	5	1	.197	.264	.258
Dan Briggs	OF10,1B4	L	29	48	48	1	6	0	0	0	1	0	9	0	.125	.143	.125
Scott Fletcher	SS11	R	23	11	24	4	4	0	0	0	1	4	5	1	.167	.286	.167
Ty Waller	OF7,3B1	R	25	17	21	4	5	0	0	0	1	2	5	0	.238	.304	.238
Heity Cruz	OF4	R	29	17	19	1	4	1	0	0	0	2	4	0	.211	.286	.263
Butch Benton	C4	R	24	4	7	0	1	0	0	0	1	0	1	0	.143	.143	.143
Larry Cox	C2	R	34	2	4	1	0	0	0	0	0	2	1	0	.000	.333	.000

Pitcher	T	Age	G	GS	CG	ShO	IP	H	HR	BB	SO	W-L	Sv	ERA
Fergie Jenkins	R	38	34	34	4	1	217.1	221	19	68	134	14-15	0	3.15
Doug Bird	R	32	35	33	2	1	191.0	230	26	30	71	9-14	0	5.14
Dickie Noles	R	25	31	30	2	2	171.0	180	11	61	85	10-13	0	4.42
Randy Martz	R	26	28	24	1	0	147.2	157	17	36	40	11-10	1	4.21
Allen Ripley	R	29	28	19	0	0	122.2	130	12	38	57	5-7	0	4.26
Tom Filer	R	25	8	8	0	0	40.2	50	5	18	15	1-2	0	5.53
Dan Larson	R	27	12	6	0	0	39.2	51	4	18	22	0-4	0	5.67
Willie Hernandez	L	27	75	0	0	0	75.0	74	3	24	54	4-6	10	3.00
Lee Smith	R	24	72	5	0	0	117.0	105	5	37	99	2-5	17	2.69
Dick Tidrow	R	35	65	0	0	0	103.2	106	6	29	62	8-3	6	3.39
Bill Campbell	R	33	62	0	0	0	100.0	89	6	40	71	3-6	8	3.69
Mike Proly	R	31	44	1	0	0	82.0	77	5	22	24	5-3	1	2.30
Ken Kravec	L	30	13	2	0	0	25.0	27	3	18	20	1-1	0	6.12
Randy Stein	R	29	6	0	0	0	10.1	7	2	7	6	0-0	0	3.48
Herman Segelke	R	24	3	0	0	0	4.1	6	1	6	4	0-0	0	8.31

1982 New York Mets 6th NL East 65-97 .401 27.0 GB

George Bamberger

Player	Gm by Position	B	Age	G	AB	R	H	2B	3B	HR	RBI	BB	SO	SB	Avg	OBP	Slg
John Stearns	C81,3B12	R	30	98	352	46	103	25	3	4	28	30	35	17	.293	.349	.415
Dave Kingman	1B143	R	33	149	535	80	109	9	1	37	99	59	156	4	.204	.285	.432
Wally Backman	2B88,3B6,SS1	S	22	96	261	37	71	13	2	3	22	49	47	8	.272	.387	.372
Hubie Brooks	3B126	R	25	126	457	40	114	21	2	2	40	28	76	6	.249	.297	.317
Ron Gardenhire	SS135,2B1,3B1	R	24	141	384	29	92	17	1	3	33	23	55	5	.240	.279	.313
Mookie Wilson	OF156	S	26	159	639	90	178	25	9	5	55	32	102	58	.279	.314	.369
George Foster	OF138	R	33	151	550	64	136	23	2	13	70	50	123	1	.247	.309	.367
Ellis Valentine	OF98	R	27	111	337	33	97	14	1	8	48	5	38	1	.288	.294	.407
Bob Bailor	SS60,2B56,3B21*	R	30	110	376	44	104	14	1	0	31	20	17	20	.277	.313	.319
Ron Hodges	C74	L	33	80	228	26	56	12	1	5	27	41	40	4	.246	.358	.373
Rusty Staub	OF27,1B18	L	38	112	219	11	53	9	0	3	27	24	10	0	.242	.309	.324
Joel Youngblood†	OF63,2B8,3B1*	R	30	80	202	21	52	12	0	3	21	8	37	0	.257	.302	.361
Gary Rajsich	OF35,1B2	L	27	80	162	17	42	8	3	2	12	17	40	1	.259	.333	.383
Brian Giles	2B45,SS2	R	22	45	138	14	29	5	0	3	10	12	29	6	.210	.270	.312
Mike Jorgensen	1B56,OF16	L	33	120	114	16	29	6	0	2	14	21	24	2	.254	.370	.360
Tom Veryzer	2B26,SS16	R	29	40	54	6	18	2	0	0	4	3	4	1	.333	.362	.370
Bruce Bochy	C16,1B1	R	27	17	49	4	15	4	0	2	8	4	6	0	.306	.358	.510
Mike Howard	OF22,2B3	S	24	33	39	5	7	0	0	1	3	6	7	2	.179	.298	.256
Phil Mankowski	3B13	L	29	13	35	2	8	1	0	0	4	1	6	0	.229	.237	.257
Rusty Tillman	OF3	R	21	12	13	4	2	1	0	0	0	0	4	1	.154	.154	.231
Ronn Reynolds	C2	R	23	2	4	0	0	0	0	0	0	1	1	0	.000	.200	.000
Rick Sweet†		S	29	3	3	0	1	0	0	0	0	0	1	0	.333	.333	.333

B. Bailor, 4 G at OF; J. Youngblood, 1 G at SS

Pitcher	T	Age	G	GS	CG	ShO	IP	H	HR	BB	SO	W-L	Sv	ERA
Charlie Puleo	R	27	36	24	1	1	171.0	179	13	90	98	9-9	1	4.47
Pete Falcone	L	28	40	23	3	0	171.0	159	24	71	101	8-10	2	3.84
Mike Scott	R	27	37	22	1	0	147.0	185	13	60	63	7-13	3	5.14
Craig Swan	R	31	37	21	2	0	166.1	165	13	37	67	11-7	1	3.35
Randy Jones	L	32	28	20	2	1	107.2	130	11	51	44	7-10	0	4.60
Rick Ownbey	R	24	8	8	2	0	50.1	44	3	43	28	1-2	0	3.75
Brent Gaff	R	23	7	5	0	0	31.2	41	3	10	14	0-3	0	4.55
Scott Holman	R	23	4	4	1	0	26.2	23	2	7	11	2-1	0	2.36
Walt Terrell	R	24	3	3	0	0	21.0	22	2	14	8	0-3	0	3.43
Jesse Orosco	L	25	54	2	0	0	109.1	92	7	40	89	4-10	4	2.72
Neil Allen	R	24	50	0	0	0	64.2	65	5	30	59	3-7	19	3.06
Ed Lynch	R	26	43	12	0	0	139.1	145	6	40	51	4-8	2	3.55
Pat Zachry	R	30	36	16	2	0	137.2	149	10	57	69	6-9	1	4.05
Terry Leach	R	28	21	1	1	1	45.1	46	2	18	30	2-1	3	4.17
Tom Hausman†	R	29	21	0	0	0	36.2	44	4	6	16	1-2	0	4.42
Doug Sisk	R	24	8	0	0	0	8.2	5	1	4	4	0-1	1	1.04
Carlos Diaz†	L	24	4	0	0	0	3.2	6	0	4	0	0-0	0	0.00
Tom Gorman†	L	24	3	1	0	0	9.1	8	0	0	7	0-1	0	0.96

1982 Atlanta Braves 1st NL West 89-73 .549 —

Joe Torre

Player	Gm by Position	B	Age	G	AB	R	H	2B	3B	HR	RBI	BB	SO	SB	Avg	OBP	Slg
Bruce Benedict	C118	R	26	118	386	34	95	11	1	3	44	37	40	4	.246	.315	.303
Chris Chambliss	1B151	L	33	157	534	57	144	25	2	20	86	57	57	7	.270	.337	.436
Glenn Hubbard	2B144	R	24	145	532	75	132	25	1	9	59	59	62	4	.248	.324	.350
Bob Horner	3B137	R	24	140	499	85	130	24	0	32	97	66	75	3	.261	.350	.501
Rafael Ramirez	SS157	R	24	157	609	74	169	24	4	10	52	36	49	27	.278	.319	.379
Dale Murphy	OF162	R	26	162	598	113	168	23	2	36	109	93	134	23	.281	.378	.507
C. Washington	OF139	L	27	150	563	94	150	24	6	16	80	50	107	33	.266	.330	.416
Brett Butler	OF77	L	25	89	240	35	52	2	0	0	7	25	35	21	.217	.291	.225
Jerry Royster	3B62,OF25,2B16*	R	29	108	261	43	77	13	2	2	25	22	36	14	.295	.351	.383
Rufino Linares	OF53	R	31	77	191	28	57	7	1	2	17	7	29	5	.298	.325	.377
Terry Harper	OF41	R	26	48	150	16	43	3	0	2	16	14	28	7	.287	.347	.347
Larry Whisenton	OF34	L	25	84	143	21	34	7	2	4	17	23	33	2	.238	.339	.399
Biff Pocoroba	C36,3B2	S	28	56	120	5	33	7	0	2	22	13	12	0	.275	.351	.383
Bob Watson†	1B27,OF2	R	36	57	114	16	28	3	1	5	22	14	20	1	.246	.323	.421
Matt Sinatro	C35	R	22	37	81	10	11	2	0	1	4	4	9	0	.136	.176	.198
Randy Johnson	2B13,3B4	R	26	27	46	5	11	5	0	0	6	6	4	0	.239	.345	.348
Ken Smith	1B6,OF3	L	24	48	41	6	12	1	0	0	3	6	13	0	.293	.383	.317
Bob Porter	OF4,1B1	L	22	24	27	1	3	0	0	0	0	1	9	0	.111	.143	.111
Larry Owen	C2	R	27	2	3	1	1	1	0	0	0	0	1	0	.333	.333	.667
Paul Runge		R	24	4	2	0	0	0	0	0	0	0	0	0	.000	.000	.000
Paul Zuvella	SS1	R	23	2	1	0	0	0	0	0	0	0	0	0	.000	.000	.000
Albert Hall		S	24	5	0	1	0	0	0	0	0	0	0	0	—	—	—

J. Royster, 10 G at SS

Pitcher	T	Age	G	GS	CG	ShO	IP	H	HR	BB	SO	W-L	Sv	ERA
Phil Niekro	R	43	35	35	4	2	234.1	225	23	73	144	17-4	0	3.61
Rick Mahler	R	28	39	33	5	2	205.1	213	18	62	105	9-10	0	4.21
Bob Walk	R	25	32	27	3	1	164.1	179	19	59	84	11-9	0	4.87
Pascual Perez	R	25	16	11	0	0	79.1	85	4	17	29	4-4	0	3.06
Ken Dayley	L	23	20	11	0	0	71.1	79	9	25	34	5-6	0	4.54
Tommy Boggs	R	26	10	10	0	0	46.1	43	2	22	29	2-2	0	3.30
Gene Garber	R	34	69	0	0	0	119.1	100	4	32	68	8-10	30	2.34
Steve Bedrosian	R	24	64	3	0	0	137.2	102	7	57	123	8-6	11	2.42
Rick Camp	R	29	51	21	3	0	177.1	199	18	52	68	11-13	5	3.65
Al Hrabosky	L	32	31	0	0	0	37.1	41	5	17	20	2-1	3	5.54
Larry McWilliams†	L	28	27	2	0	0	37.2	52	3	20	24	2-3	0	6.21
Preston Hanna†	R	27	20	1	0	0	36.0	36	3	28	17	3-0	0	3.75
Carlos Diaz†	L	24	19	0	0	0	25.1	31	3	9	16	3-2	1	4.62
Joe Cowley	R	23	17	8	0	0	52.1	53	6	16	27	1-2	0	4.47
Donnie Moore	R	28	16	0	0	0	27.2	32	1	7	17	3-1	1	4.23
Jose Alvarez	R	26	7	0	0	0	7.2	8	1	2	6	0-0	0	4.70
Tom Hausman†	R	29	3	0	0	0	3.2	6	0	4	2	0-0	0	4.91

1982 Los Angeles Dodgers 2nd NL West 88-74 .543 1.0 GB

Tom Lasorda

Player	Gm by Position	B	Age	G	AB	R	H	2B	3B	HR	RBI	BB	SO	SB	Avg	OBP	Slg
Mike Scioscia	C123	L	23	129	365	31	80	11	1	5	38	44	31	2	.219	.302	.296
Steve Garvey	1B158	R	33	162	625	66	176	35	1	16	86	20	86	5	.282	.301	.418
Steve Sax	2B149	R	22	150	638	88	180	23	7	4	47	49	53	49	.282	.335	.359
Ron Cey	3B149	R	34	150	556	62	141	23	1	24	79	57	99	3	.254	.323	.428
Bill Russell	SS150	R	33	153	497	64	136	20	2	3	46	63	30	10	.274	.357	.340
Dusty Baker	OF144	R	33	147	570	80	171	19	1	23	88	56	62	17	.300	.361	.458
Pedro Guerrero	OF137,3B24	R	26	150	575	87	175	27	5	32	100	65	89	22	.304	.378	.536
Ken Landreaux	OF117	L	27	129	461	71	131	23	7	7	50	39	54	31	.284	.341	.410
Rick Monday	OF57,1B4	L	36	104	210	37	54	6	4	11	42	39	51	2	.257	.372	.481
Steve Yeager	C76	R	33	82	196	13	48	5	2	2	18	13	28	0	.245	.294	.321
Ron Roenicke	OF72	S	25	109	143	18	37	8	0	1	12	21	32	5	.259	.359	.336
Jorge Orta	OF17	L	31	86	115	13	25	5	0	2	8	12	13	0	.217	.295	.313
Derrel Thomas	OF28,2B18,3B14*	R	31	66	98	13	26	2	1	0	2	10	12	2	.265	.333	.306
F. Valenzuela	P37,OF1	L	21	38	95	6	16	0	0	1	9	3	16	0	.168	.190	.200
Mike Marshall	OF19,1B13	R	22	49	95	10	23	3	0	5	9	13	23	2	.242	.336	.432
Bob Welch	P36,OF1	R	25	38	85	5	12	1	0	0	3	3	32	0	.141	.167	.153
Mark Belanger	SS44,2B1	R	38	54	50	6	12	1	0	0	4	5	10	1	.240	.309	.260
Jose Morales†		R	37	35	30	1	9	1	0	1	8	4	8	0	.300	.382	.433
Greg Brock	1B3	L	25	18	17	1	2	1	0	0	1	1	5	0	.118	.167	.176
Jay Johnstone†		L	36	21	13	1	1	1	0	0	2	5	2	0	.077	.316	.154
Candy Maldonado	OF3	R	21	6	4	0	0	0	0	0	0	1	2	0	.000	.200	.000
Don Crow	C4	R	23	4	4	0	0	0	0	0	0	0	3	0	.000	.000	.000
Mark Bradley	OF3	R	25	8	3	1	1	0	0	0	0	0	0	0	.333	.333	.333
Alex Taveras	2B4,3B4,SS2	R	26	11	3	1	1	1	0	0	2	0	1	0	.333	.333	.667
Dave Sax	OF1	R	23	2	2	0	0	0	0	0	0	0	0	0	.000	.000	.000
Manny Mota		R	44	1	1	0	0	0	0	0	0	0	0	0	.000	.000	.000

D. Thomas, 6 G at SS

Pitcher	T	Age	G	GS	CG	ShO	IP	H	HR	BB	SO	W-L	Sv	ERA
F. Valenzuela	L	21	37	37	18	4	285.0	247	13	83	199	19-13	0	2.87
Jerry Reuss	L	33	39	37	8	4	254.2	232	11	50	138	18-11	0	3.11
Bob Welch	R	25	36	36	9	3	235.2	199	19	81	176	16-11	0	3.36
Burt Hooton	R	32	21	21	2	2	120.2	130	5	33	51	4-7	0	4.03
Dave Goltz†	R	33	2	1	0	0	3.2	6	0	0	3	0-1	0	4.91
Steve Howe	L	24	66	0	0	0	99.1	87	3	17	49	7-5	13	2.08
Terry Forster	L	30	56	0	0	0	83.0	66	3	31	52	5-6	3	3.04
Tom Niedenfuer	R	22	55	0	0	0	69.2	71	3	25	60	3-4	9	2.71
Dave Stewart	R	25	45	14	0	0	146.1	137	14	49	80	9-8	1	3.81
Alejandro Pena	R	23	29	0	0	0	35.2	37	2	21	20	0-2	0	4.79
Joe Beckwith	R	27	19	1	0	0	40.0	38	2	14	33	2-1	1	2.70
Vicente Romo	R	39	15	6	0	0	35.2	25	1	14	24	1-2	1	3.03
Ricky Wright	L	23	14	5	0	0	32.2	28	1	20	24	2-1	0	3.03
Ted Power	R	27	12	4	0	0	33.2	38	4	23	15	1-1	0	6.68
Steve Shirley	L	25	11	0	0	0	12.2	15	0	7	8	1-1	0	4.26

1982 San Francisco Giants 3rd NL West 87-75 .537 2.0 GB

Frank Robinson

Player	Gm by Position	B	Age	G	AB	R	H	2B	3B	HR	RBI	BB	SO	SB	Avg	OBP	Slg
Milt May	C110	L	31	114	395	29	104	19	0	9	39	28	38	0	.263	.311	.380
Reggie Smith	1B99	S	37	106	349	51	99	11	0	18	56	46	46	7	.284	.364	.470
Joe Morgan	2B120,3B3	L	38	134	463	68	134	19	4	14	61	85	60	24	.289	.400	.438
Darrell Evans	3B84,1B49,SS13	L	35	141	465	64	119	20	4	16	61	77	64	5	.256	.360	.419
Johnnie LeMaster	SS130	R	28	130	436	34	94	14	1	2	30	31	78	13	.216	.267	.266
Jack Clark	OF155	R	26	157	563	90	154	30	3	27	103	90	91	6	.274	.372	.481
Chili Davis	OF153	S	22	154	641	86	167	27	6	19	76	45	115	24	.261	.308	.410
Jeffrey Leonard	OF74,1B1	R	26	80	278	32	72	16	1	9	49	19	65	18	.259	.306	.421
Tom O'Malley	3B83,2B1,SS1	L	21	92	291	26	80	12	4	2	27	33	39	0	.275	.350	.364
Jim Wohlford	OF72	R	31	97	250	37	64	12	1	2	25	30	36	8	.256	.331	.336
Duane Kuiper	2B51	L	32	107	218	26	61	9	1	0	17	32	24	2	.280	.375	.330
Bob Brenly	C61,3B1	R	28	65	180	26	51	4	1	4	15	18	26	6	.283	.348	.383
Champ Summers	OF31,1B3	L	36	70	125	15	31	5	0	4	19	16	17	0	.248	.342	.384
Max Venable	OF53	L	25	71	125	17	28	2	1	1	7	7	16	9	.224	.265	.280
Dave Bergman	1B69,OF6	L	29	100	121	22	33	3	1	4	14	18	11	3	.273	.364	.413
Guy Sularz	SS37,3B14,2B9	R	26	63	101	15	23	3	0	1	7	9	11	3	.228	.291	.287
Jeff Ransom	C14	R	21	15	44	5	7	0	0	0	3	6	7	0	.159	.255	.159
Joe Pettini	SS26,3B1	R	27	29	39	5	8	1	0	0	2	3	4	0	.205	.262	.231
Jose Barrios	1B7	R	25	10	19	2	3	0	0	0	0	1	4	0	.158	.200	.158
Ron Pruitt	C1,OF1	R	30	5	4	1	2	1	0	0	2	1	1	0	.500	.600	.750
Brad Wellman	2B2	R	22	6	4	1	1	0	0	0	0	0	1	0	.250	.250	.250
John Rabb	OF1	R	22	2	2	0	1	0	1	0	0	0	1	0	.500	.500	1.500

Pitcher	T	Age	G	GS	CG	ShO	IP	H	HR	BB	SO	W-L	Sv	ERA
Bill Laskey	R	24	32	31	7	1	189.1	186	14	43	88	13-12	0	3.14
Rich Gale	R	28	33	29	2	0	170.1	193	9	81	102	7-14	0	4.23
Atlee Hammaker	L	24	29	27	4	1	175.0	189	16	28	102	12-8	0	4.11
Renie Martin	R	26	29	25	1	0	141.1	148	14	64	63	7-10	0	4.65
Alan Fowlkes	R	23	21	15	1	0	85.0	111	12	24	50	4-2	0	5.19
Mike Chris	L	24	9	6	0	0	26.0	23	2	26	10	0-2	0	4.85
Greg Minton	R	30	78	0	0	0	123.0	108	5	42	58	10-4	30	1.83
Gary Lavelle	L	33	68	0	0	0	104.2	97	6	29	76	10-7	8	2.67
Al Holland	L	29	58	7	0	0	129.2	115	12	40	97	7-3	5	3.33
Fred Breining	R	26	54	9	2	0	143.1	146	6	52	98	11-6	0	3.08
Jim Barr	R	34	53	9	1	1	128.2	125	9	20	36	4-3	2	3.29
Dan Schatzeder†	L	27	13	3	0	0	33.1	47	3	12	18	1-4	0	7.29
Andy McGaffigan	R	25	4	0	0	0	8.0	5	0	1	4	1-0	0	0.00
Mark Dempsey	R	24	3	1	0	0	5.2	11	1	2	4	0-0	0	7.94
Scott Garrelts	R	20	1	0	0	0	2.0	3	0	2	4	0-0	0	13.50

1982 San Diego Padres 4th NL West 81-81 .500 8.0 GB

Dick Williams

Player	Gm by Position	B	Age	G	AB	R	H	2B	3B	HR	RBI	BB	SO	SB	Avg	OBP	Slg
Terry Kennedy	C139,1B12	L	26	153	562	75	166	42	1	21	97	26	91	1	.295	.328	.486
Broderick Perkins	1B98,OF11	L	27	125	347	32	94	10	4	2	34	26	20	2	.271	.325	.340
Tim Flannery	2B104,3B5,SS2	L	24	122	379	40	100	11	7	0	30	30	32	1	.264	.317	.330
Luis Salazar	3B129,SS18,OF1	R	26	145	524	55	127	15	5	8	62	23	80	32	.242	.274	.336
Garry Templeton	SS136	S	26	141	563	76	139	25	8	6	64	26	82	27	.247	.279	.352
Sixto Lezcano	OF134	R	28	138	470	73	136	26	6	16	84	78	69	2	.289	.388	.472
Ruppert Jones	OF114	L	27	116	424	69	120	20	2	12	61	62	90	18	.283	.373	.425
Gene Richards	OF103,1B25	L	28	132	521	63	149	13	8	3	28	36	52	30	.286	.333	.359
Alan Wiggins	OF68,2B1	S	24	72	254	40	65	3	3	1	15	13	19	33	.256	.295	.303
Joe Lefebvre	3B39,OF36,C3	L	26	102	239	25	57	9	0	4	21	18	50	0	.238	.292	.326
Tony Gwynn	OF52	L	22	54	190	33	55	12	2	1	17	14	16	8	.289	.337	.389
Juan Bonilla	2B45	R	26	45	182	21	51	6	2	0	8	11	15	0	.280	.325	.335
Kurt Bevacqua	1B30,OF3,3B1	R	35	64	123	15	31	9	0	0	24	17	22	2	.252	.333	.325
Joe Pittman†	2B30,SS13	R	28	55	118	16	30	2	0	0	7	9	13	8	.254	.307	.271
Steve Swisher	C26	R	30	26	58	2	10	1	0	2	3	5	24	0	.172	.238	.293
Dave Edwards	OF45,1B1	R	28	71	55	7	10	2	0	1	2	1	14	0	.182	.196	.273
Rick Lancellotti	1B7,OF3	L	25	17	39	2	7	2	0	0	4	2	8	0	.179	.220	.231
Randy Bass†	1B9	L	28	13	30	1	6	0	0	1	8	2	4	0	.200	.265	.300
Mario Ramirez	SS8,2B1,3B1	R	24	13	23	1	4	1	0	0	1	2	4	0	.174	.240	.217
Jody Lansford	1B9	R	21	13	22	6	4	0	0	0	3	6	4	0	.182	.345	.182
Ron Tingley	C8	R	23	8	20	0	2	0	0	0	0	0	7	0	.100	.100	.100
Doug Gwosdz	C7	R	22	7	17	1	3	0	0	0	0	2	7	0	.176	.263	.176
George Hinshaw	OF6	R	22	6	15	1	4	0	0	0	1	3	5	0	.267	.389	.267
Jerry Manuel	2B1,3B1,SS1	S	28	2	5	0	1	0	1	0	1	1	0	0	.200	.333	.600

Pitcher	T	Age	G	GS	CG	ShO	IP	H	HR	BB	SO	W-L	Sv	ERA
Tim Lollar	L	26	34	34	4	2	232.2	192	20	87	150	16-9	0	3.13
John Montefusco	R	32	32	32	1	0	184.1	177	17	41	83	10-11	0	4.00
Juan Eichelberger	R	28	31	24	8	0	177.2	171	23	72	74	7-14	0	4.20
Chris Welsh	L	27	28	20	3	1	139.1	146	16	63	48	8-8	0	4.91
John Curtis†	L	34	26	18	1	1	116.1	121	15	46	54	8-6	0	4.10
Andy Hawkins	R	22	15	10	1	0	63.2	66	4	27	25	2-5	0	4.10
Gary Lucas	L	27	65	0	0	0	97.1	89	5	29	64	1-10	16	3.24
Luis DeLeon	R	23	61	0	0	0	102.0	77	10	16	60	9-5	15	2.03
Floyd Chiffer	R	26	51	0	0	0	79.1	73	9	34	48	4-3	4	2.95
Eric Show	R	26	47	14	2	2	150.0	117	10	48	88	10-6	3	2.64
Dave Dravecky	L	26	31	10	0	0	105.0	86	8	33	59	5-3	2	2.57
Dan Boone†	L	28	10	0	0	0	16.0	21	2	3	8	1-0	1	5.63
Mike Griffin	R	25	7	0	0	0	10.1	9	0	3	4	0-1	0	3.48
Rick Wise	R	36	1	0	0	0	2.0	3	0	0	0	0-0	0	9.00

1982 Houston Astros 5th NL West 77-85 .475 12.0 GB

Bill Virdon (49-62)/Bob Lillis (28-23)

Player	Gm by Position	B	Age	G	AB	R	H	2B	3B	HR	RBI	BB	SO	SB	Avg	OBP	Slg
Alan Ashby	C95	S	30	100	339	40	87	14	2	12	49	27	53	2	.257	.311	.416
Ray Knight	1B96,3B67	R	29	158	609	72	179	36	6	6	70	48	58	2	.294	.344	.402
Phil Garner	2B136,3B18	R	33	155	588	65	161	33	8	13	83	40	92	24	.274	.320	.423
Art Howe	3B72,1B35	R	35	110	365	29	87	15	1	5	38	41	45	2	.238	.315	.326
Dickie Thon	SS119,3B8,2B1	R	24	136	496	73	137	31	10	3	36	37	48	37	.276	.327	.397
Jose Cruz	OF155	L	34	155	570	62	157	27	2	9	68	60	67	21	.275	.342	.377
Terry Puhl	OF138	L	25	145	507	64	133	17	9	8	50	51	49	17	.262	.331	.379
Tony Scott	OF129	S	30	132	460	43	110	16	3	1	29	15	56	18	.239	.263	.293
Danny Heep	OF39,1B16	L	24	85	198	16	47	14	1	4	22	21	31	0	.237	.311	.379
Luis Pujols	C64	R	26	65	176	8	35	6	2	4	15	10	40	0	.199	.242	.324
Denny Walling	OF32,1B20	L	28	85	146	22	30	4	1	1	14	23	19	4	.205	.312	.267
Alan Knicely	C23,OF16,3B1	R	27	59	133	10	25	2	0	2	12	14	30	0	.188	.270	.248
Craig Reynolds	SS35,3B7	L	29	54	118	16	30	2	3	1	7	11	9	3	.254	.321	.347
Bill Doran	2B26	S	24	26	97	11	27	3	0	0	6	4	11	5	.278	.304	.309
Kiko Garcia	SS21,3B2,2B1	R	28	34	76	5	16	5	0	1	5	3	15	1	.211	.241	.316
Harry Spilman	1B11	L	27	38	61	7	17	2	0	3	11	5	10	0	.279	.333	.459
Scott Loucks	OF37	R	25	44	49	6	11	2	0	0	3	3	17	4	.224	.269	.265
Tim Tolman	OF5,1B1	R	26	15	26	4	5	2	0	1	3	4	3	0	.192	.300	.385
Kevin Bass†	OF7	S	23	12	24	2	1	0	0	0	1	0	8	0	.042	.042	.042
Joe Pittman†	3B3,OF1	R	28	15	10	0	2	1	0	0	0	0	2	0	.200	.200	.300
Mike Ivie†		R	29	7	6	0	2	0	0	0	0	1	0	0	.333	.429	.333
Larry Ray	OF1	L	24	5	6	0	1	0	0	0	1	0	4	0	.167	.143	.167

Pitcher	T	Age	G	GS	CG	ShO	IP	H	HR	BB	SO	W-L	Sv	ERA
Joe Niekro	R	37	35	35	16	5	270.0	224	12	64	130	17-12	0	2.47
Nolan Ryan	R	35	35	35	10	3	250.1	196	20	109	245	16-12	0	3.16
Bob Knepper	L	28	33	29	4	0	180.0	193	14	60	108	5-15	1	4.45
Don Sutton†	R	37	27	27	4	0	195.0	169	10	46	139	13-8	0	3.00
Vern Ruhle	R	31	31	21	3	2	149.0	169	12	24	56	9-13	1	3.93
Frank DiPino	L	25	6	6	0	0	28.1	32	1	11	25	2-2	0	6.04
Frank LaCorte	R	30	55	0	0	0	76.1	71	5	46	51	1-5	7	4.48
Dave Smith	R	27	49	1	0	0	63.1	69	4	31	28	5-4	11	3.84
Mike LaCoss	R	26	41	8	0	0	115.0	107	3	54	51	6-6	0	2.90
Randy Moffitt	R	33	30	0	0	0	41.2	36	3	13	20	2-4	3	3.02
Bert Roberge	R	27	22	0	0	0	25.2	29	0	6	18	1-2	3	4.21
George Cappuzzello	L	28	17	0	0	0	19.1	16	2	7	13	0-1	0	2.79
Dan Boone†	L	28	10	0	0	0	12.2	7	1	4	4	0-1	1	3.55
Joe Sambito	L	30	9	0	0	0	12.2	7	0	2	7	0-0	4	0.71
Mark Ross	R	27	4	0	0	0	6.0	3	0	0	4	0-0	0	1.50
Gordy Pladson	R	25	2	0	0	0	1.1	10	0	2	0	0-0	0	54.00

1982 Cincinnati Reds 6th NL West 61-101 .377 28.0 GB

John McNamara (34-58)/Russ Nixon (27-43)

Player	Gm by Position	B	Age	G	AB	R	H	2B	3B	HR	RBI	BB	SO	SB	Avg	OBP	Slg
Alex Trevino	C116,3B2	R	24	120	355	24	89	10	3	1	33	34	34	3	.251	.318	.304
Dan Driessen	1B144	L	30	149	516	64	139	25	1	17	57	82	62	11	.269	.368	.421
Ron Oester	2B118,SS29,3B13	S	26	151	549	63	143	19	4	9	47	35	82	5	.260	.303	.359
Johnny Bench	3B107,1B8,C1	R	34	119	399	44	103	16	0	13	38	37	58	1	.258	.320	.396
Dave Concepcion	SS145,1B1,3B1	R	34	147	572	48	164	25	4	5	53	45	61	13	.287	.337	.371
Cesar Cedeno	OF131,1B1	R	31	138	492	52	142	35	1	8	57	41	41	16	.289	.346	.413
Paul Householder	OF131	S	23	138	417	40	88	11	5	9	34	30	77	17	.211	.265	.326
Eddie Milner	OF107	L	27	113	407	61	109	23	5	4	31	41	40	18	.268	.338	.378
Duane Walker	OF69	L	25	86	239	26	52	10	0	5	22	27	58	9	.218	.298	.322
Mike Vail	OF52	R	30	78	189	9	48	10	1	4	29	6	33	0	.254	.274	.381
Wayne Krenchicki	3B70,2B9	L	27	94	187	19	53	6	1	2	21	13	23	5	.283	.324	.358
Larry Biittner	OF31,1B15	L	36	97	184	18	57	9	2	2	24	17	16	1	.310	.369	.413
Tom Lawless	2B47	R	25	49	165	19	35	6	0	0	4	9	30	16	.212	.253	.248
Dave Van Gorder	C51	R	25	51	137	4	25	3	1	0	7	14	19	1	.182	.263	.219
Rafael Landestoy	3B21,2B16,OF3*	S	29	73	111	11	21	3	0	1	9	8	14	2	.189	.250	.243
Gary Redus	OF20	R	25	20	83	12	18	3	2	1	7	5	21	11	.217	.258	.337
German Barranca	2B6	L	25	46	51	11	13	1	3	0	2	2	9	2	.255	.283	.392
Mike O'Berry	C21	R	28	21	45	5	10	2	0	0	3	10	13	0	.222	.364	.267
Clint Hurdle	OF17	L	24	19	34	2	7	1	0	0	1	2	6	0	.206	.270	.235

R. Landestoy, 2 G at SS

Pitcher	T	Age	G	GS	CG	ShO	IP	H	HR	BB	SO	W-L	Sv	ERA
Mario Soto	R	25	35	34	13	2	257.2	202	19	71	274	14-13	0	2.79
Bruce Berenyi	R	27	34	34	4	1	222.1	208	8	96	157	9-18	0	3.36
Frank Pastore	R	24	31	29	3	2	188.1	210	13	57	94	8-13	0	3.97
Tom Seaver	R	37	21	21	0	0	111.1	136	14	44	62	5-13	0	5.50
Joe Price	L	25	59	1	0	0	72.2	73	7	32	71	3-4	3	2.85
Jim Kern†	R	33	50	0	0	0	76.0	61	3	48	43	3-5	2	2.84
Tom Hume	R	29	46	0	0	0	63.2	57	2	21	22	2-6	17	3.11
Bob Shirley	L	28	41	20	1	0	152.2	138	17	73	89	8-13	0	3.60
Charlie Leibrandt	L	25	36	11	0	0	107.2	130	4	48	34	5-7	2	5.10
Greg Harris	R	26	34	10	1	0	91.1	96	12	37	67	2-6	1	4.83
Brad Lesley	R	23	28	0	0	0	38.1	27	1	13	29	0-2	4	2.58
Ben Hayes	R	24	26	0	0	0	45.2	37	3	22	38	2-0	2	1.97
Joe Edelen	R	26	9	0	0	0	15.1	22	2	8	11	0-0	0	8.80
Bill Scherrer	L	24	5	2	0	0	17.1	17	0	0	7	0-1	0	2.60

>>1983 Baltimore Orioles 1st AL East 98-64 .605 —

Joe Altobelli

Player	Gm by Position	B	Age	G	AB	R	H	2B	3B	HR	RBI	BB	SO	SB	Avg	OBP	Slg
Rick Dempsey	C128	R	33	128	347	33	80	16	2	4	32	40	54	1	.231	.311	.323
Eddie Murray	1B153,DH2	S	27	156	582	115	178	30	3	33	111	86	90	5	.306	.393	.538
Rich Dauer	2B131,3B17	R	30	140	459	49	108	19	0	5	41	47	29	1	.235	.306	.309
Todd Cruz†	3B79,2B2	R	27	81	221	16	46	9	1	3	27	15	52	3	.208	.259	.299
Cal Ripken Jr.	SS162	R	22	162	663	121	211	47	2	27	102	58	97	0	.318	.371	.517
John Shelby	OF115,DH1	S	25	126	325	52	84	15	2	5	27	18	64	15	.258	.297	.363
John Lowenstein	OF107,DH1,2B1	L	36	122	310	52	87	13	2	15	60	49	55	2	.281	.374	.481
Al Bumbry	OF104,DH11	L	36	124	378	63	104	14	4	3	31	31	33	12	.275	.328	.357
Ken Singleton	DH150	S	36	151	507	52	140	21	3	18	84	99	83	0	.276	.393	.436
Dan Ford	OF103	R	31	103	407	63	114	30	4	9	55	29	55	9	.280	.328	.440
Gary Roenicke	OF100,1B7,DH2*	R	28	115	323	45	84	13	0	19	64	30	35	2	.260	.326	.477
Leo Hernandez	3B64	R	23	64	203	21	50	6	1	6	26	12	19	1	.246	.287	.374
Jim Dwyer	OF56,1B4	L	33	100	196	37	56	17	1	8	38	31	29	1	.286	.382	.505
Joe Nolan	C65	L	32	73	184	25	51	11	1	5	24	16	31	0	.277	.342	.429
Lenn Sakata	2B60,DH1,C1	R	29	66	134	23	34	7	0	3	12	16	17	8	.254	.338	.373
Bennie Ayala	OF24,DH11	R	32	47	104	12	23	7	0	4	13	9	18	0	.221	.278	.404
Aurelio Rodriguez†	3B45	R	35	45	67	0	8	0	0	0	2	0	13	0	.119	.130	.119
Glenn Gulliver	3B21	L	28	23	47	5	10	3	0	0	2	9	5	0	.213	.333	.277
Tito Landrum†	OF26	R	28	26	42	8	13	2	0	1	4	1	11	0	.310	.318	.429
Mike Young	OF22,DH3	S	23	25	36	5	6	2	1	0	2	2	8	1	.167	.231	.278
John Stefero	C9	L	23	9	11	2	5	1	0	0	4	3	2	0	.455	.571	.545
Bobby Bonner	2B5,DH1	R	26	6	0	0	0	0	0	0	0	0	0	0	—	—	—
Dave Huppert	C2	R	26	2	0	0	0	0	0	0	0	0	0	0	—	—	—

G. Roenicke, 2 G at 3B

Pitcher	T	Age	G	GS	CG	ShO	IP	H	HR	BB	SO	W-L	Sv	ERA
Scott McGregor	L	29	36	36	12	2	260.0	271	24	45	86	18-7	0	3.18
Storm Davis	R	21	34	29	6	1	200.1	180	14	64	125	13-7	0	3.59
Mike Boddicker	R	25	27	26	10	5	179.0	141	13	52	120	16-8	0	2.77
Dennis Martinez	R	28	32	25	4	0	153.0	209	21	45	71	7-16	0	5.53
Mike Flanagan	L	31	20	20	3	1	125.1	135	10	31	50	12-4	0	3.30
Jim Palmer	R	37	14	11	0	0	76.2	86	11	19	34	5-4	0	4.23
Allan Ramirez	R	26	11	10	1	0	57.0	46	6	30	20	4-4	0	3.47
Paul Mirabella	L	29	3	2	0	0	9.2	9	1	7	4	0-0	0	5.59
Tippy Martinez	L	33	65	0	0	0	103.1	76	10	37	81	9-3	21	2.35
Sammy Stewart	R	28	58	1	0	0	144.1	138	7	67	95	9-4	7	3.62
Tim Stoddard	R	30	47	0	0	0	57.2	65	10	29	50	4-3	9	6.09
Dan Morogiello	L	28	22	0	0	0	37.2	39	1	10	15	0-1	1	2.39
Don Welchel	R	26	11	0	0	0	26.2	33	1	10	16	0-2	0	5.40
Bill Swaggerty	R	26	7	2	0	0	21.2	23	1	6	7	1-1	0	2.91

1983 Detroit Tigers 2nd AL East 92-70 .568 6.0 GB

Sparky Anderson

Player	Gm by Position	B	Age	G	AB	R	H	2B	3B	HR	RBI	BB	SO	SB	Avg	OBP	Slg
Lance Parrish	C131,DH27	R	27	155	605	80	163	42	3	27	114	44	106	1	.269	.314	.483
Enos Cabell	1B106,DH8,3B4*	R	33	121	392	62	122	23	5	5	46	16	41	4	.311	.335	.434
Lou Whitaker	2B160	L	26	161	643	94	206	40	6	12	72	67	70	17	.320	.380	.457
Tom Brookens	3B103,SS30,2B10*	R	29	138	332	50	71	13	3	6	32	29	46	10	.214	.276	.325
Alan Trammell	SS140	R	25	142	505	83	161	31	2	14	66	57	64	30	.319	.385	.471
Chet Lemon	OF145	R	28	145	491	78	125	21	5	24	69	54	70	0	.255	.350	.464
Glenn Wilson	OF143	R	24	144	503	55	135	25	6	11	65	25	79	1	.268	.306	.408
Larry Herndon	OF133,DH19	R	29	153	603	88	182	28	9	20	92	46	95	9	.302	.351	.478
Kirk Gibson	DH66,OF54	L	26	128	401	60	91	12	9	15	51	53	96	14	.227	.320	.414
John Wockenfuss	DH39,C29,1B13*	R	34	92	245	32	66	8	1	9	44	31	37	1	.269	.349	.420
Rick Leach	1B73,OF13,DH3	L	26	99	242	22	60	17	0	3	26	19	21	2	.248	.305	.355
John Grubb	OF26,DH18	L	34	57	134	20	34	5	2	4	22	28	17	0	.254	.388	.410
Wayne Krenchicki†	3B48,2B6,SS6*	L	28	59	133	18	37	7	0	1	16	11	27	0	.278	.333	.353
Marty Castillo	3B58,C10	R	26	67	119	10	23	4	0	2	10	7	22	2	.193	.238	.277
Howard Johnson	3B21,DH2	S	22	27	66	11	14	0	0	3	5	7	10	0	.212	.297	.348
Lynn Jones	OF31,DH6	R	30	49	64	9	17	1	2	0	6	3	6	1	.266	.299	.344
Mike Ivie	1B12	R	30	12	42	4	9	4	0	0	7	2	4	0	.214	.244	.310
Bill Fahey	C18	L	33	19	22	4	6	1	0	0	2	5	3	0	.273	.407	.318
Julio Gonzalez	SS6,2B5,3B1	R	30	12	21	0	3	1	0	0	2	1	7	0	.143	.182	.190
Mike Laga	DH6,1B5	L	23	12	21	2	4	0	0	0	2	1	9	0	.190	.227	.190
Sal Butera	C4	R	30	4	5	1	1	0	0	0	0	0	0	0	.200	.200	.200
Bob Molinaro†	DH1	L	33	8	2	3	0	0	0	0	0	1	1	1	.000	.333	.000
Bill Nahorodny		R	29	2	1	0	0	0	0	0	0	1	0	0	.000	.500	.000

E. Cabell, 1 G at SS; T. Brookens, 1 G at DH; J. Wockenfuss, 1 G at 3B, 1 G at OF; W. Krenchicki, 3 G at 1B

Pitcher	T	Age	G	GS	CG	ShO	IP	H	HR	BB	SO	W-L	Sv	ERA
Dan Petry	R	24	38	38	9	2	266.1	256	37	99	122	19-11	0	3.92
Jack Morris	R	28	37	37	20	1	293.2	257	30	83	232	20-13	0	3.34
Milt Wilcox	R	33	26	26	9	2	186.0	164	19	74	101	11-10	0	3.97
Juan Berenguer	R	28	37	19	2	1	157.2	110	19	71	129	9-5	1	3.14
Dave Rozema	R	26	29	16	1	0	105.0	100	10	29	63	8-3	2	3.43
Glenn Abbott†	R	32	7	7	1	1	46.2	43	5	7	11	2-1	0	1.93
Larry Pashnick	R	27	12	6	0	0	37.2	48	5	18	17	1-3	0	5.26
Jerry Ujdur	R	26	11	6	0	0	34.0	41	6	20	13	0-4	0	7.15
Dave Rucker†	L	25	4	3	0	0	9.0	18	2	8	6	1-2	0	17.00
Aurelio Lopez	R	34	57	0	0	0	115.1	87	12	49	90	9-8	18	2.81
Howard Bailey	L	25	33	3	0	0	72.0	69	11	25	21	5-5	0	4.88
Doug Bair†	R	33	27	1	0	0	55.2	51	8	19	39	7-3	4	3.88
Dave Gumpert	R	25	26	0	0	0	44.1	43	1	7	14	0-2	2	2.64
John Martin†	L	27	15	0	0	0	13.1	15	2	4	11	0-0	1	7.43
Pat Underwood	L	26	4	0	0	0	10.1	11	1	6	2	0-0	0	8.71
Bob James†	R	24	4	0	0	0	4.0	5	2	3	4	0-0	0	11.25

1983 New York Yankees 3rd AL East 91-71 .562 7.0 GB

Billy Martin

Player	Gm by Position	B	Age	G	AB	R	H	2B	3B	HR	RBI	BB	SO	SB	Avg	OBP	Slg
Butch Wynegar	C93	S	27	94	301	40	89	18	2	6	42	52	29	1	.296	.399	.429
Ken Griffey Sr.	1B101,OF14,DH2	L	33	118	458	60	140	21	3	11	46	34	45	6	.306	.355	.437
Willie Randolph	2B104	R	28	104	420	73	117	21	1	2	38	53	32	12	.279	.361	.348
Graig Nettles	3B126,DH1	L	38	129	462	56	123	17	3	20	75	51	65	0	.266	.341	.446
Roy Smalley	SS91,3B26,1B22	S	30	130	451	70	124	24	1	18	62	58	68	3	.275	.357	.452
Dave Winfield	OF151	R	31	152	598	99	169	26	8	32	116	58	77	15	.283	.345	.513
Steve Kemp	OF101,DH2	L	28	109	373	53	90	17	3	12	49	41	37	1	.241	.318	.399
Jerry Mumphrey†	OF83	S	30	83	267	41	70	11	4	7	36	28	33	2	.262	.327	.412
Don Baylor	DH136,OF5,1B1	R	34	144	534	82	162	33	3	21	85	40	53	17	.303	.361	.494
Andre Robertson	SS78,2B29	R	25	98	322	37	80	16	3	1	22	8	54	2	.248	.271	.326
Don Mattingly	OF48,1B42,2B1	L	22	91	279	34	79	15	4	4	32	21	31	0	.283	.333	.409
Rick Cerone	C78,3B1	R	29	80	246	18	54	7	0	2	22	15	29	0	.220	.267	.272
Oscar Gamble	OF32,DH21	L	33	74	180	26	47	10	2	7	26	25	23	0	.261	.361	.456
Omar Moreno†	OF48	L	30	48	152	17	38	9	1	1	17	8	31	7	.250	.288	.342
Lou Piniella	OF43,DH1	R	39	53	148	19	43	9	1	2	16	11	12	1	.291	.344	.405
Bert Campaneris	2B32,3B24	R	41	60	143	19	46	5	0	0	11	8	9	6	.322	.355	.357
Steve Balboni	1B23,DH4	R	26	32	86	8	20	2	0	5	17	8	23	0	.233	.295	.430
Larry Milbourne†	2B19,SS6,3B4	S	32	31	70	5	14	4	0	0	2	5	10	1	.200	.263	.257
Bobby Meacham	SS18,3B4	S	22	22	51	5	12	2	0	0	4	4	10	8	.235	.304	.275
Brian Dayett	OF9	R	26	11	29	3	6	0	1	0	5	2	4	0	.207	.258	.276
Juan Espino	C10	R	27	10	23	1	6	0	0	1	3	1	5	0	.261	.280	.391
Bobby Murcer	DH5	L	37	9	22	2	4	2	0	1	1	1	1	0	.182	.217	.409
Otis Nixon	OF9	S	24	13	14	2	2	0	0	0	0	1	5	2	.143	.200	.143
Rowland Office	OF2	L	30	2	2	0	0	0	0	0	1	0	0	0	.000	.000	.000
Ron Guidry	P31,OF1	L	32	32	0	0	0	0	0	0	0	0	0	0	—	—	—

Pitcher	T	Age	G	GS	CG	ShO	IP	H	HR	BB	SO	W-L	Sv	ERA
Shane Rawley	L	27	34	33	13	2	238.1	246	19	79	124	14-14	1	3.78
Ron Guidry	L	32	31	31	21	3	250.1	232	26	60	156	21-9	0	3.42
Dave Righetti	L	24	31	31	7	2	217.0	194	12	67	169	14-8	0	3.44
Bob Shirley	L	29	25	17	1	1	108.0	122	10	36	53	5-8	0	5.08
Ray Fontenot	L	25	15	15	3	1	97.1	101	3	25	27	8-2	0	3.33
Jay Howell	R	27	19	12	2	0	82.0	89	7	35	61	1-5	0	5.38
Matt Keough†	R	27	12	12	0	0	55.2	59	12	20	26	3-4	0	5.17
John Montefusco†	R	33	6	6	0	0	38.0	39	3	10	15	5-0	0	3.32
Doyle Alexander†	R	32	8	5	0	0	28.1	31	6	7	17	0-2	0	6.35
George Frazier	R	28	61	0	0	0	115.1	94	5	45	78	4-4	8	3.43
Goose Gossage	R	31	57	0	0	0	87.1	82	5	25	90	13-5	22	2.27
Dale Murray	R	33	40	0	0	0	94.1	113	5	22	45	2-4	1	4.48
Rudy May	L	38	15	0	0	0	18.1	22	1	12	16	1-5	0	6.87
Roger Erickson	R	26	5	0	0	0	16.2	13	1	8	7	0-1	0	4.32
Curt Kaufman	R	25	4	0	0	0	8.2	10	0	4	8	0-0	0	3.12
Dave LaRoche	L	35	1	0	0	0	1.0	2	1	0	0	0-0	0	18.00

1983 Toronto Blue Jays 4th AL East 89-73 .549 9.0 GB

Bobby Cox

Player	Gm by Position	B	Age	G	AB	R	H	2B	3B	HR	RBI	BB	SO	SB	Avg	OBP	Slg
Ernie Whitt	C119	L	31	123	344	53	88	15	2	17	56	50	55	1	.256	.346	.459
Willie Upshaw	1B159,DH1	L	26	160	579	99	177	26	7	27	104	61	98	10	.306	.373	.515
Damaso Garcia	2B130	R	26	131	525	84	161	23	6	3	38	24	34	31	.307	.336	.390
Rance Mulliniks	3B116,SS15,2B2	L	27	129	364	54	100	34	3	10	49	57	43	0	.275	.373	.467
Alfredo Griffin	SS157,2B5,DH1	S	25	162	528	62	132	22	9	4	47	27	44	8	.250	.289	.348
Lloyd Moseby	OF147	L	23	151	539	104	170	31	7	18	81	51	85	27	.315	.376	.499
Jesse Barfield	OF120,DH5	R	23	128	388	58	98	13	3	27	68	22	110	2	.253	.296	.510
Barry Bonnell	OF117,3B4,DH1	R	29	121	377	49	120	21	3	10	54	33	52	10	.318	.369	.469
Cliff Johnson	DH130,1B6	R	35	142	407	59	108	23	1	22	76	67	69	0	.265	.373	.489
Dave Collins	OF112,1B5,DH1	S	30	118	402	55	109	12	4	1	34	43	67	31	.271	.343	.328
Garth Iorg	3B85,2B39,SS1	R	28	122	375	40	103	22	5	2	39	13	45	7	.275	.298	.376
Jorge Orta	DH69,OF17	L	32	103	245	30	58	6	3	10	38	19	29	1	.237	.287	.408
Buck Martinez	C85	R	34	88	221	27	56	14	0	10	33	29	39	0	.253	.337	.452
George Bell	OF34,DH2	R	23	39	112	5	30	5	4	2	17	4	17	1	.268	.305	.438
Hosken Powell	OF33,DH1,1B1	L	28	40	83	6	14	0	0	1	7	5	8	2	.169	.213	.205
Mickey Klutts	3B17,DH2	R	28	22	43	3	11	0	0	3	5	1	11	0	.256	.289	.465
Tony Fernandez	SS13,DH1	S	21	15	34	5	9	1	1	0	2	2	2	0	.265	.324	.353
Mitch Webster	OF7,DH2	S	24	11	11	2	2	0	0	0	0	1	1	0	.182	.250	.182
Geno Petralli	C5,DH1	S	23	6	4	0	0	0	0	0	0	1	1	0	.000	.200	.000

Pitcher	T	Age	G	GS	CG	ShO	IP	H	HR	BB	SO	W-L	Sv	ERA
Dave Stieb	R	25	36	36	14	4	278.0	223	21	93	187	17-12	0	3.04
Luis Leal	R	26	35	35	7	1	217.1	216	23	65	116	13-12	0	4.31
Jim Clancy	R	27	34	34	11	1	223.0	238	23	61	99	15-11	0	3.91
Jim Gott	R	23	34	30	6	1	176.2	195	15	68	121	9-14	0	4.74
Doyle Alexander†	R	32	17	15	5	0	116.2	126	14	26	46	7-6	0	3.93
Matt Williams	R	23	4	3	0	0	8.0	13	5	7	5	1-1	0	14.63
Joey McLaughlin	R	26	50	0	0	0	64.2	63	11	37	47	7-4	9	4.45
Roy Lee Jackson	R	29	49	0	0	0	92.0	92	6	41	48	8-3	7	4.50
Dave Geisel	L	28	47	0	0	0	52.1	47	4	31	50	0-3	5	4.64
Randy Moffitt	R	34	45	0	0	0	57.1	52	5	24	38	6-2	10	3.77
Jim Acker	R	24	38	5	0	0	97.2	103	7	38	44	5-1	1	4.33
Mike Morgan	R	23	16	4	0	0	45.1	48	6	21	22	0-3	0	5.16
Stan Clarke	L	22	10	0	0	0	11.0	10	2	5	7	1-1	0	3.27
Don Cooper	R	27	4	0	0	0	5.1	8	3	0	5	0-0	0	6.75

1983 Milwaukee Brewers 5th AL East 87-75 .537 11.0 GB

Harvey Kuenn

Player	Gm by Position	B	Age	G	AB	R	H	2B	3B	HR	RBI	BB	SO	SB	Avg	OBP	Slg
Ted Simmons	C86,DH66	S	33	153	600	76	185	39	3	13	108	41	51	4	.308	.351	.448
Cecil Cooper	1B158,DH2	L	33	160	661	106	203	37	3	30	126	37	63	2	.307	.341	.508
Jim Gantner	2B158	L	30	161	603	85	170	23	8	11	74	38	46	5	.282	.329	.401
Paul Molitor	3B146,DH2	R	26	152	608	95	164	28	6	15	47	59	74	41	.270	.333	.410
Robin Yount	SS139,DH8	R	27	149	578	102	178	42	10	17	80	72	58	12	.308	.383	.503
Charlie Moore	OF150,C7,DH1	R	30	151	529	65	150	27	6	2	49	55	42	11	.284	.354	.369
Ben Oglivie	OF113,DH8	L	34	125	411	49	115	19	3	13	66	60	64	4	.280	.371	.436
Rick Manning†	OF108	L	28	108	375	40	86	14	4	3	33	26	40	11	.229	.279	.312
Roy Howell	DH54,1B2	L	29	69	194	23	54	9	6	4	25	15	29	1	.278	.330	.448
Ned Yost	C61	R	27	61	196	21	44	5	1	6	28	5	36	1	.224	.243	.352
Mark Brouhard	OF42,DH11	R	27	56	185	25	51	10	1	7	23	9	39	0	.276	.315	.454
Gorman Thomas†	OF46	R	32	46	164	21	30	6	1	5	18	23	50	2	.183	.284	.323
Ed Romero	SS22,OF15,DH5*	R	25	59	145	17	46	7	0	1	18	8	8	1	.317	.348	.386
Don Money	DH28,3B11,1B2	R	36	43	114	5	17	5	0	1	8	11	17	0	.149	.220	.219
Marshall Edwards	OF35,DH4	L	30	51	74	14	22	1	1	0	5	1	9	5	.297	.303	.338
Bill Schroeder	C23	R	24	23	73	7	13	2	1	3	7	3	23	0	.178	.221	.356
Randy Ready	DH6,3B4	R	23	12	37	8	15	3	2	1	6	6	3	0	.405	.488	.676
Rob Picciolo	SS7,2B2,3B2*	R	30	14	27	2	6	3	0	0	1	0	4	0	.222	.214	.333
Bob Skube	OF8,DH2,1B1	L	25	12	25	2	5	1	1	0	9	4	7	0	.200	.310	.320
Dion James	OF9,DH2	L	20	11	20	1	2	0	0	0	1	2	2	1	.100	.182	.100

E. Romero, 5 G at 3B, 3 G at 2B; R. Picciolo, 1 G at DH, 1 G at 1B

Pitcher	T	Age	G	GS	CG	ShO	IP	H	HR	BB	SO	W-L	Sv	ERA
Mike Caldwell	L	34	32	32	10	2	228.1	269	35	51	58	12-11	0	4.53
Don Sutton	R	38	31	31	4	0	220.1	209	21	54	134	8-13	0	4.08
Moose Haas	R	27	25	25	7	3	179.0	170	12	42	75	13-3	0	3.27
Bob McClure	L	31	24	23	4	0	142.0	152	11	68	68	9-9	0	4.50
Chuck Porter	R	28	25	21	6	1	134.0	162	9	38	76	7-9	0	4.50
Tom Candiotti	R	25	10	8	2	1	55.2	62	4	16	21	4-4	0	3.23
Jamie Cocanower	R	26	5	3	1	0	30.0	21	1	12	8	2-0	0	1.80
Pete Vuckovich	R	30	3	3	0	0	14.2	15	0	10	10	0-2	0	4.91
Jim Slaton	R	33	46	0	0	0	112.1	112	12	56	38	14-6	5	4.33
Tom Tellmann	R	29	44	0	0	0	99.2	95	7	35	48	9-4	8	2.80
Peter Ladd	R	26	44	0	0	0	49.1	30	3	16	41	3-4	25	2.55
Jerry Augustine	L	30	34	7	1	0	64.1	89	11	25	40	3-3	2	5.74
Bob Gibson	R	26	27	7	0	0	80.2	71	6	46	46	3-4	2	3.90
Jamie Easterly†	L	30	12	0	0	0	11.2	14	0	10	6	0-1	1	3.86
Rick Waits†	L	31	10	2	0	0	30.0	39	1	11	20	0-2	0	5.10
Andy Beene	R	26	1	0	0	0	2.0	3	0	1	0	0-0	0	4.50

1983 Boston Red Sox 6th AL East 78-84 .481 20.0 GB

Ralph Houk

Player	Gm by Position	B	Age	G	AB	R	H	2B	3B	HR	RBI	BB	SO	SB	Avg	OBP	Slg
Gary Allenson	C84	R	28	84	230	19	53	11	0	3	30	27	43	0	.230	.311	.317
Dave Stapleton	1B145,2B5	R	29	151	542	54	134	31	1	10	66	40	44	1	.247	.297	.363
Jerry Remy	2B144	L	30	146	592	73	163	16	5	0	43	40	35	11	.275	.320	.319
Wade Boggs	3B153	L	25	153	582	100	210	44	7	5	74	92	36	3	.361	.444	.486
Glenn Hoffman	SS143	R	24	143	473	56	123	24	1	4	41	30	76	1	.260	.306	.340
Jim Rice	OF151,DH4	R	30	155	626	90	191	34	1	39	126	52	102	0	.305	.361	.550
Tony Armas	OF116,DH27	R	29	145	574	77	125	23	2	36	107	29	131	0	.218	.254	.453
Dwight Evans	OF99,DH21	R	31	126	470	74	112	19	4	22	58	70	97	3	.238	.338	.436
Carl Yastrzemski	DH107,1B2,OF1	L	43	119	380	38	101	24	0	10	56	54	29	0	.266	.359	.408
Reid Nichols	OF72,DH18,SS1	R	24	100	274	35	78	22	1	6	22	26	36	7	.285	.352	.438
Rick Miller	OF66,DH2,1B2	L	35	104	262	41	75	10	2	2	21	28	30	3	.286	.356	.363
Rich Gedman	C69	L	23	81	204	21	60	16	1	2	18	15	37	0	.294	.345	.412
Ed Jurak	SS38,1B19,3B12*	R	25	75	159	19	44	8	4	0	18	18	25	1	.277	.350	.377
Jeff Newman	C51,DH6	R	34	59	132	11	25	4	0	3	7	10	31	0	.189	.255	.288
Marty Barrett	2B23,DH5	R	25	33	44	7	10	1	1	0	2	3	1	0	.227	.271	.295
Julio Valdez	2B9,SS2,DH1	S	27	12	25	3	3	0	0	0	0	1	4	0	.120	.185	.120
Jackie Gutierrez	SS4	R	23	5	10	2	3	0	0	0	0	1	1	0	.300	.364	.300
Lee Graham	OF3	L	23	5	6	2	0	0	0	0	1	0	0	0	.000	.000	.000
Chico Walker	OF3	S	25	4	5	2	2	0	2	0	1	0	0	0	.400	.400	1.200

E. Jurak, 5 G at DH, 1 G at 2B

Pitcher	T	Age	G	GS	CG	ShO	IP	H	HR	BB	SO	W-L	Sv	ERA
John Tudor	L	29	34	34	7	2	242.0	236	32	81	136	13-12	0	4.09
Bruce Hurst	L	25	33	32	6	2	211.1	241	22	62	115	12-12	0	4.09
Dennis Eckersley	R	28	28	28	2	0	176.1	223	27	39	77	9-13	0	5.61
Bobby Ojeda	L	25	29	28	5	0	173.2	173	15	73	94	12-7	0	4.04
Mike Brown	R	24	19	18	3	1	104.0	110	12	43	35	6-6	0	4.67
Oil Can Boyd	R	23	15	13	5	0	98.2	103	9	23	43	4-8	0	3.28
Al Nipper	R	24	3	2	1	0	16.0	17	0	7	5	1-1	0	2.25
Bob Stanley	R	28	64	0	0	0	145.1	145	7	38	65	8-10	33	2.85
Mark Clear	R	27	48	0	0	0	96.0	101	10	68	81	4-5	4	6.28
Luis Aponte	R	30	34	0	0	0	62.0	74	7	23	32	5-4	3	3.63
John Henry Johnson	L	26	34	1	0	0	53.1	58	3	20	51	3-2	1	3.71
Doug Bird	R	33	22	6	0	0	67.2	91	14	16	33	1-4	1	6.65

1983 Cleveland Indians 7th AL East 70-92 .432 28.0 GB

Mike Ferraro (40-60)/Pat Corrales (30-32)

Player	Gm by Position	B	Age	G	AB	R	H	2B	3B	HR	RBI	BB	SO	SB	Avg	OBP	Slg
Ron Hassey	C113,DH1	L	30	117	341	48	92	21	0	6	42	38	35	2	.270	.342	.384
Mike Hargrove	1B131,DH1	L	33	134	469	57	134	21	4	3	57	78	40	0	.286	.388	.367
Manny Trillo†	2B87	R	32	88	320	33	87	13	1	1	29	21	46	1	.272	.315	.328
Toby Harrah	3B137,DH1,2B1	R	34	138	526	81	140	23	1	9	53	75	49	16	.266	.363	.365
Julio Franco	SS149	R	21	149	560	68	153	24	8	8	80	27	50	32	.273	.306	.388
George Vukovich	OF122	L	27	124	312	31	77	13	2	3	44	24	37	3	.247	.301	.330
Gorman Thomas†	OF106	R	32	106	371	51	82	17	0	17	51	57	98	8	.221	.322	.404
Alan Bannister	OF91,2B27,DH3*	R	31	117	377	51	100	25	4	5	45	31	43	6	.265	.323	.393
Andre Thornton	DH114,1B27	R	33	141	508	78	143	27	1	17	77	87	72	4	.281	.383	.439
Pat Tabler	OF88,3B25,DH6*	R	25	124	430	56	125	23	5	6	65	56	63	2	.291	.370	.409
Bake McBride	OF46,DH15	L	34	70	230	21	67	8	1	1	18	9	26	8	.291	.318	.348
Mike Fischlin	2B71,SS15,3B4*	R	27	95	225	31	47	5	2	2	23	26	32	9	.209	.294	.276
Rick Manning†	OF50	L	28	50	194	20	54	6	0	1	10	12	22	7	.278	.319	.325
Broderick Perkins	1B19,OF17,DH16	L	28	79	184	23	50	10	0	0	24	9	19	1	.272	.299	.326
Chris Bando	C43	S	27	48	121	15	31	3	0	4	15	15	19	0	.256	.336	.380
Jim Essian	C47,3B1	R	32	48	93	11	19	4	0	2	11	16	8	0	.204	.315	.312
Miguel Dilone†	OF19	S	28	32	68	15	13	3	1	0	7	10	5	5	.191	.295	.265
Carmelo Castillo	OF19,DH1	R	25	23	36	9	10	2	1	1	3	4	6	1	.278	.366	.472
Jack Perconte	2B13	L	28	14	26	1	7	1	0	0	0	5	2	3	.269	.387	.308
Otto Velez	DH8	R	32	10	25	1	2	0	0	0	1	3	6	0	.080	.179	.080
Kevin Rhomberg	OF9,DH1	R	27	12	21	2	10	0	0	0	2	2	4	1	.476	.500	.476
Karl Pagel	DH5,OF1	L	28	8	20	1	6	0	0	0	1	0	5	0	.300	.300	.300
Wil Culmer	OF4,DH2	R	24	7	19	0	2	0	0	0	1	0	4	0	.105	.100	.105

A. Bannister, 3 G at 1B; P. Tabler, 2 G at 2B; M. Fischlin, 1 G at DH

Pitcher	T	Age	G	GS	CG	ShO	IP	H	HR	BB	SO	W-L	Sv	ERA
Rick Sutcliffe	R	27	36	35	10	2	243.1	251	23	102	160	17-11	0	4.29
Lary Sorensen	R	27	36	34	8	1	222.2	238	21	65	76	12-11	0	4.24
Bert Blyleven	R	32	24	24	5	0	156.1	160	8	44	123	7-10	0	3.91
Len Barker†	R	27	24	24	4	1	149.2	150	16	52	105	8-13	0	5.11
Juan Eichelberger	R	29	28	15	2	0	134.0	132	10	59	56	4-11	0	4.90
Rick Behenna†	R	23	5	4	0	0	26.0	22	0	14	9	0-2	0	4.15
Rich Barnes	L	23	4	2	0	0	11.2	18	0	10	2	1-1	0	6.94
Dan Spillner	R	31	60	0	0	0	92.1	117	7	38	48	2-9	8	5.07
Jamie Easterly†	L	30	41	0	0	0	57.0	69	4	22	39	4-2	3	3.63
Neal Heaton	L	23	39	16	4	3	149.1	157	11	44	75	11-7	7	4.16
Bud Anderson	R	27	39	1	0	0	68.1	64	8	32	32	1-6	7	4.08
Tom Brennan	R	30	11	5	1	1	39.2	45	3	8	21	2-2	0	3.86
Mike Jeffcoat	L	23	11	2	0	0	32.2	32	1	13	9	1-3	0	3.31
Ed Glynn	L	30	11	0	0	0	12.1	22	2	6	13	0-2	0	5.84
Rick Waits†	L	31	8	0	0	0	19.2	23	1	9	13	0-1	0	4.58
Jerry Reed	R	27	7	0	0	0	21.1	26	4	9	11	0-0	0	7.17
Ernie Camacho	R	28	4	0	0	0	5.1	5	1	2	2	0-1	0	5.06

1983 Chicago White Sox 1st AL West 99-63 .611 —

Tony La Russa

Player	Gm by Position	B	Age	G	AB	R	H	2B	3B	HR	RBI	BB	SO	SB	Avg	OBP	Slg
Carlton Fisk	C133,DH2	R	35	138	488	85	141	26	4	26	86	46	88	9	.289	.355	.518
Mike Squires	1B124,DH5,3B1	L	31	143	153	21	34	4	1	1	11	22	11	3	.222	.326	.281
Julio Cruz†	2B97	S	28	99	334	47	84	9	4	1	40	29	44	24	.251	.311	.311
Vance Law	3B139,2B3,SS2*	R	26	145	408	55	99	21	5	4	42	51	56	3	.243	.325	.348
Jerry Dybzinski	SS118,3B9	R	27	127	256	30	59	10	1	1	32	18	29	11	.230	.283	.289
Harold Baines	OF155	L	24	156	596	76	167	33	2	20	99	49	85	7	.280	.333	.443
Ron Kittle	OF139,DH2	R	25	145	520	75	132	19	3	35	100	39	150	8	.254	.314	.504
Rudy Law	OF132,DH3	L	26	141	501	95	142	20	7	3	34	42	36	77	.283	.340	.369
Greg Luzinski	DH139,1B2	R	32	144	502	73	128	26	1	32	95	70	117	2	.255	.352	.502
Tom Paciorek	1B67,OF55,DH2	R	36	115	420	65	129	32	3	9	63	25	58	6	.307	.347	.462
Greg Walker	1B59,DH21	L	23	118	307	32	83	16	3	10	55	28	57	2	.270	.332	.440
Scott Fletcher	SS100,2B12,3B7*	R	24	114	262	42	62	16	5	3	31	29	22	5	.237	.315	.370
Tony Bernazard†	2B59	S	26	59	233	30	61	16	2	2	26	17	45	2	.262	.306	.373
Marc Hill	C55,DH2,1B1	R	31	58	133	11	30	6	0	1	11	9	24	0	.226	.275	.293
Jerry Hairston	OF32,DH4	S	31	101	126	17	37	9	1	5	22	23	16	0	.294	.397	.500
Lorenzo Gray	3B31,DH7	R	25	41	78	18	14	3	0	1	4	8	16	1	.179	.256	.256
Dave Stegman	OF29	R	29	30	53	5	9	2	0	0	4	10	9	0	.170	.292	.208
Rusty Kuntz†	OF27,DH1	R	28	28	42	6	11	1	0	0	1	6	13	1	.262	.354	.286
Chris Nyman	DH10,1B10	R	28	21	28	12	8	0	0	2	4	4	7	2	.286	.394	.500
Aurelio Rodriguez†	3B22	R	35	22	20	1	4	1	0	1	1	0	3	0	.200	.200	.400
Joel Skinner	C6	R	22	6	11	2	3	0	0	0	1	0	1	0	.273	.273	.273
Casey Parsons	OF3,DH2	L	29	8	5	1	1	0	0	0	0	2	1	0	.200	.429	.200
Tim Hulett	2B6	R	23	6	5	0	1	0	0	0	0	0	0	1	.200	.200	.200
Miguel Dilone†	DH2,OF2	S	28	4	3	1	0	0	0	0	0	0	0	1	.000	.000	.000

V. Law, 1 G at DH, 1 G at OF; S. Fletcher, 1 G at DH

Pitcher	T	Age	G	GS	CG	ShO	IP	H	HR	BB	SO	W-L	Sv	ERA
LaMarr Hoyt	R	28	36	36	11	1	260.2	236	27	31	148	24-10	0	3.66
Rich Dotson	R	24	35	35	8	1	240.0	209	19	106	137	22-7	0	3.23
Floyd Bannister	L	28	34	34	5	2	217.1	191	19	71	193	16-10	0	3.35
Britt Burns	L	24	29	26	8	4	173.2	165	14	55	115	10-11	0	3.58
Jerry Koosman	L	40	37	24	2	1	169.2	176	19	53	90	11-7	2	4.77
Randy Martz	R	27	1	1	0	0	5.0	4	0	4	1	0-0	0	3.60
Salome Barojas	R	26	52	0	0	0	87.1	70	2	32	38	3-3	12	2.47
Dick Tidrow	R	36	50	1	0	0	91.2	86	13	34	66	2-4	7	4.22
Dennis Lamp	R	30	49	5	1	0	116.1	123	6	29	44	7-7	15	3.71
Juan Agosto	L	25	39	0	0	0	41.2	41	2	11	29	2-2	7	4.10
Kevin Hickey	L	27	23	0	0	0	20.2	23	5	11	8	1-2	5	5.23
Guy Hoffman	L	26	11	0	0	0	6.0	14	1	2	2	1-0	0	7.50
Steve Mura	R	28	6	0	0	0	12.1	13	1	6	4	0-0	0	4.38
Al Jones	R	24	2	0	0	0	2.1	3	0	2	2	0-0	0	3.86
Jim Kern	R	34	1	0	0	0	0.2	1	0	0	0	0-0	0	0.00

1983 Kansas City Royals 2nd AL West 79-83 .488 20.0 GB

Dick Howser

Player	Gm by Position	B	Age	G	AB	R	H	2B	3B	HR	RBI	BB	SO	SB	Avg	OBP	Slg
John Wathan	C92,1B37,OF9	R	33	128	437	49	107	18	3	2	32	27	56	28	.245	.289	.314
Willie Aikens	1B112,DH6	L	28	125	410	49	124	26	1	23	72	45	75	0	.302	.373	.539
Frank White	2B145	R	32	146	549	52	143	35	6	11	77	20	51	13	.260	.283	.406
George Brett	3B102,1B14,OF13*	L	30	123	464	90	144	38	2	25	93	57	39	0	.310	.385	.563
U.L. Washington	SS140,DH1	S	29	144	547	76	129	19	6	5	41	48	78	40	.236	.298	.320
Willie Wilson	OF136	S	27	137	576	90	159	22	8	2	33	33	75	59	.276	.316	.352
Pat Sheridan	OF100	L	25	109	333	43	90	12	2	7	36	20	64	12	.270	.312	.381
Amos Otis	OF96,DH1	R	36	98	356	35	93	16	3	4	41	27	63	5	.261	.313	.357
Hal McRae	DH156	R	37	157	589	84	183	41	6	12	82	50	68	2	.311	.372	.462
Don Slaught	C79,DH1	R	24	83	276	21	86	13	4	0	28	11	27	3	.312	.336	.388
Onix Concepcion	3B31,2B28,SS21*	R	25	80	219	22	53	11	3	0	20	12	12	10	.242	.282	.320
Leon Roberts	OF76,DH1	R	32	84	213	24	55	7	0	8	24	17	27	1	.258	.313	.404
Butch Davis	OF33	R	25	33	122	13	42	2	6	2	18	4	19	4	.344	.359	.508
Joe Simpson	1B54,OF38,DH2*	L	31	91	119	16	20	2	2	0	8	11	21	1	.168	.248	.218
Greg Pryor	3B60,1B6,2B3	R	33	68	115	9	25	4	0	1	14	7	8	0	.217	.260	.278
Cesar Geronimo	OF35	L	35	38	87	2	18	4	0	0	4	2	13	0	.207	.242	.253
Darryl Motley	OF18,DH1	R	23	19	68	9	16	1	2	3	11	2	8	2	.235	.264	.441
Jerry Martin	OF13	R	34	13	44	4	14	2	0	2	13	1	7	1	.318	.313	.500
Cliff Pastornicky	3B10	R	24	10	32	4	4	0	0	2	5	0	3	0	.125	.125	.313
Ron Johnson	1B7,C2	R	27	9	27	2	7	0	0	0	1	3	1	0	.259	.333	.259
Buddy Biancalana	SS6	S	23	6	15	2	3	0	0	0	0	0	7	1	.200	.200	.200

G. Brett, 1 G at DH; O. Concepcion, 1 G at DH; J. Simpson, 2 G at P

Pitcher	T	Age	G	GS	CG	ShO	IP	H	HR	BB	SO	W-L	Sv	ERA
Larry Gura	L	35	34	31	5	0	200.1	220	23	76	57	11-18	0	4.90
Paul Splittorff	L	36	27	27	4	0	156.0	159	9	52	61	13-8	0	3.63
Bud Black	L	26	24	24	3	0	161.1	159	19	43	58	10-7	0	3.79
Steve Renko	R	38	25	17	1	0	121.1	144	9	36	54	6-11	1	4.30
Vida Blue	L	33	19	14	1	0	85.1	96	12	35	53	0-5	0	6.01
Gaylord Perry†	R	44	14	14	1	1	84.1	98	6	26	40	4-4	0	4.27
Dennis Leonard	R	32	10	10	1	0	63.0	69	3	19	31	6-3	0	3.71
Eric Rasmussen†	R	31	11	9	2	1	52.2	61	4	22	18	3-6	0	4.78
Frank Wills	R	24	6	4	0	0	34.2	35	2	15	23	2-1	0	4.15
Danny Jackson	L	21	4	3	0	0	19.0	26	1	6	9	1-1	0	5.21
Dan Quisenberry	R	30	69	0	0	0	139.0	118	6	11	48	5-3	45	1.94
Mike Armstrong	R	29	58	0	0	0	102.2	86	11	45	52	10-7	3	3.86
Don Hood	L	33	27	0	0	0	47.2	48	5	14	17	2-3	0	2.27
Keith Creel	R	24	25	10	1	0	89.1	116	17	35	31	2-5	0	6.35
Bill Castro	R	29	18	0	0	0	40.2	51	4	12	17	2-0	0	6.64
Mark Huismann	R	25	13	0	0	0	30.2	29	1	17	20	2-1	0	5.58
Bob Tufts	L	27	6	0	0	0	6.2	16	1	5	3	0-0	0	8.10
Joe Simpson	L	31	2	0	0	0	3.0	4	0	2	1	0-0	0	3.00

1983 Texas Rangers 3rd AL West 77-85 .475 22.0 GB

Doug Rader

Player	Gm by Position	B	Age	G	AB	R	H	2B	3B	HR	RBI	BB	SO	SB	Avg	OBP	Slg
Jim Sundberg	C131	R	32	131	378	30	76	14	0	2	28	35	64	0	.201	.272	.254
Pete O'Brien	1B133,OF27,DH1	L	25	154	524	53	124	24	5	8	53	58	62	5	.237	.313	.347
Wayne Tolleson	2B112,SS26,DH1	S	27	134	470	64	122	13	2	3	20	40	68	33	.260	.319	.315
Buddy Bell	3B154	R	31	156	618	75	171	35	3	14	66	50	48	3	.277	.332	.411
Bucky Dent	SS129,DH1	R	31	131	417	36	99	15	2	2	34	23	31	3	.237	.278	.297
George Wright	OF161	S	24	162	634	79	175	28	6	18	80	41	82	8	.276	.321	.424
Billy Sample	OF146	R	28	147	554	80	152	28	3	12	57	44	46	44	.274	.331	.401
Larry Parrish	OF132,DH13	R	29	145	555	76	151	26	4	26	88	46	91	0	.272	.326	.474
Dave Hostetler	DH88,1B2	R	27	94	304	31	67	9	2	11	46	42	103	0	.220	.323	.372
Mickey Rivers	DH53,OF23	L	34	96	309	37	88	17	0	1	20	11	21	9	.285	.309	.350
Bill Stein	2B32,1B23,3B10*	R	36	78	232	21	72	15	1	2	33	8	31	2	.310	.331	.409
Bobby Johnson	C62,1B10	R	23	72	175	18	37	6	1	5	16	16	55	3	.211	.280	.343
Larry Biittner	1B22,DH9,OF2	L	37	66	116	5	32	5	1	0	18	9	16	0	.276	.323	.336
Jim Anderson	SS27,2B17,3B3*	R	26	50	102	8	22	6	0	0	6	8	6	1	.216	.252	.245
Mike Richardt	2B20	R	25	22	83	9	13	2	1	1	7	2	11	2	.157	.174	.241
Bobby Jones	DH11,OF11,1B1	L	33	41	72	5	16	4	0	1	11	5	17	0	.222	.284	.319
Curtis Wilkerson	SS9,2B2,3B2	S	22	16	35	7	6	0	1	0	1	2	5	3	.171	.216	.229
Tommy Dunbar	OF9,DH1	L	23	12	24	3	6	0	0	0	3	5	7	3	.250	.379	.250
Donnie Scott	C2	S	21	2	4	0	0	0	0	0	0	0	0	0	.000	.000	.000
Mark Wagner	SS2	R	29	2	2	0	0	0	0	0	0	0	1	0	.000	.000	.000
Nick Capra	OF4	R	25	8	2	2	0	0	0	0	0	0	0	0	.000	.000	.000

B. Stein, 6 G at DH; J. Anderson, 3 G at OF, 2 G at DH, 1 G at C

Pitcher	T	Age	G	GS	CG	ShO	IP	H	HR	BB	SO	W-L	Sv	ERA
Charlie Hough	R	35	34	33	11	3	252.0	219	22	95	152	15-13	0	3.18
Mike Smithson	R	28	33	33	10	0	223.1	233	14	71	135	10-14	0	3.91
Danny Darwin	R	27	28	26	9	2	183.0	175	9	62	92	8-13	0	3.49
Rick Honeycutt†	L	29	25	25	5	2	174.2	168	9	37	56	14-8	0	2.42
Frank Tanana	L	29	29	22	3	0	159.1	144	14	49	108	7-9	0	3.16
Dave Stewart†	R	26	8	8	2	0	59.0	50	2	17	24	5-2	0	2.14
Al Lachowicz	R	22	2	1	0	0	8.0	9	0	2	8	0-1	0	2.25
Odell Jones	R	30	42	0	0	0	67.0	56	4	22	50	3-6	10	3.09
John Butcher	R	26	38	6	1	1	123.0	128	8	41	58	6-6	5	3.51
Dave Schmidt	R	26	31	0	0	0	46.1	42	3	14	29	3-3	2	3.88
Dave Tobik	R	30	27	0	0	0	44.0	36	2	13	30	2-1	9	3.68
Jon Matlack	L	33	25	9	2	0	73.1	90	7	27	38	2-4	0	4.66
Victor Cruz	R	25	17	0	0	0	25.0	16	2	10	18	1-3	5	1.44
Tom Henke	R	25	8	0	0	0	16.0	16	1	4	17	1-0	1	3.38
Mike Mason	L	24	5	0	0	0	10.2	10	0	6	9	0-2	0	5.91
Ricky Wright†	L	24	1	0	0	0	2.0	0	0	1	2	0-0	0	0.00

1983 Oakland Athletics 4th AL West 74-88 .457 25.0 GB

Steve Boros

Player	Gm by Position	B	Age	G	AB	R	H	2B	3B	HR	RBI	BB	SO	SB	Avg	OBP	Slg
Bob Kearney	C101,DH3	R	26	108	298	33	76	11	0	8	32	21	50	1	.255	.312	.372
Wayne Gross	1B74,3B67,DH1*	L	31	137	339	34	79	18	0	12	44	36	52	3	.233	.311	.392
Davey Lopes	2B123,DH12,OF7*	R	38	147	494	64	137	13	4	17	67	51	61	22	.277	.341	.423
Carney Lansford	3B78,SS1	R	26	80	299	43	92	16	2	10	45	22	33	3	.308	.357	.475
Tony Phillips	SS101,2B63,3B4*	S	24	148	412	54	102	12	3	4	35	48	70	16	.248	.327	.320
Rickey Henderson	OF142,DH1	R	24	145	513	105	150	25	7	9	48	103	80	108	.292	.414	.421
Dwayne Murphy	OF124,DH7	L	28	130	471	55	107	17	2	17	75	62	105	7	.227	.314	.380
Mike Davis	OF121,DH3	L	24	128	443	61	122	24	4	8	62	27	74	32	.275	.322	.402
Jeff Burroughs	DH114	R	32	121	401	43	108	15	1	10	56	47	79	0	.269	.341	.387
Bill Almon	SS52,3B40,1B38*	R	30	143	451	45	120	29	1	4	63	26	67	26	.266	.302	.361
Mike Heath	C80,OF24,DH2*	R	28	96	345	45	97	17	0	6	33	18	59	3	.281	.318	.383
Gary Hancock	OF67,1B27,DH9	L	29	101	256	29	70	7	3	8	30	5	13	2	.273	.289	.418
Ricky Peters	OF47,DH8	S	27	55	178	20	51	7	0	0	20	12	21	4	.287	.327	.326
Dan Meyer	1B41,DH12,OF11*	L	30	69	169	15	32	9	0	1	13	19	11	0	.189	.268	.260
Donnie Hill	SS53	S	22	53	158	20	42	7	0	2	15	4	21	1	.266	.280	.348
Kelvin Moore	1B40	R	25	41	124	12	26	4	0	5	16	10	39	2	.210	.272	.363
Mitchell Page	DH34,OF10	L	31	57	79	16	19	3	0	0	1	10	22	3	.241	.341	.278
Luis Quinones	2B6,DH4,3B4*	S	21	19	42	5	8	2	1	0	4	1	4	1	.190	.205	.286
Darryl Cias	C19	R	26	20	18	1	6	1	0	0	1	2	4	1	.333	.400	.389
Marshall Brant	1B3,DH1	R	27	5	14	2	2	0	0	0	2	0	3	0	.143	.143	.143
Dave Hudgens	1B3,DH1	L	26	6	7	0	1	0	0	0	0	0	3	0	.143	.143	.143
Rusty McNealy	DH7,OF5	L	24	15	4	5	0	0	0	0	0	0	3	0	.000	.000	.000

W. Gross, 1 G at P; D. Lopes, 5 G at 3B; T. Phillips, 1 G at DH; B. Almon, 23 G at OF, 5 G at 2B, 4 G at DH; M. Heath, 2 G at 3B; D. Meyer, 1 G at 3B; L. Quinones, 4 G at OF, 3 G at SS

Pitcher	T	Age	G	GS	CG	ShO	IP	H	HR	BB	SO	W-L	Sv	ERA
Chris Codiroli	R	25	37	31	7	2	205.2	208	17	72	85	12-12	1	4.46
Steve McCatty	R	29	38	24	3	2	167.0	156	16	82	65	6-9	5	3.99
Bill Krueger	L	25	17	16	2	0	109.2	104	7	53	58	7-6	0	3.61
Mike Norris	R	28	16	16	2	0	88.2	68	11	36	63	4-5	0	3.76
Gorman Heimueller	L	27	16	14	2	1	83.2	93	8	29	31	3-5	0	4.41
Mike Warren	R	22	12	9	3	1	65.2	51	4	18	30	5-3	0	4.11
Rick Langford	R	31	7	7	0	0	20.0	43	4	10	2	0-4	0	12.15
Ben Callahan	R	26	4	2	0	0	9.1	18	0	5	2	1-2	0	12.54
Tom Underwood	L	29	51	15	0	0	144.2	156	13	50	62	9-7	4	4.04
Tom Burgmeier	L	39	49	0	0	0	96.0	89	2	32	39	6-7	4	2.81
Dave Beard	R	23	43	0	0	0	61.0	55	8	36	40	5-5	10	5.61
Tim Conroy	L	23	39	18	3	1	162.1	141	17	98	112	7-10	0	3.94
Steve Baker†	R	26	35	1	0	0	54.0	59	4	26	23	3-3	5	4.33
Keith Atherton	R	24	29	0	0	0	68.1	53	7	23	40	2-5	4	2.77
Matt Keough†	R	27	14	4	0	0	44.0	50	7	31	28	2-3	0	5.52
Jeff Jones	R	26	13	1	0	0	29.2	43	7	8	14	1-1	0	5.76
Mark Smith	R	27	8	1	0	0	14.2	24	0	6	10	1-0	0	6.75
Curt Young	L	23	8	2	0	0	9.0	17	1	5	5	0-1	0	16.00
Bert Bradley	R	26	6	0	0	0	8.1	14	1	4	3	0-0	0	6.48
Ed Farmer†	R	33	5	1	0	0	10.1	15	1	0	7	0-0	0	3.48
Wayne Gross	R	31	1	0	0	0	2.1	2	0	1	0	0-0	0	0.00
Rich Wortham	L	29	1	0	0	0	0.0	3	0	1	0	0-0	0	—

1983 California Angels 5th AL West 70-92 .432 29.0 GB

John McNamara

Player	Gm by Position	B	Age	G	AB	R	H	2B	3B	HR	RBI	BB	SO	SB	Avg	OBP	Slg
Bob Boone	C142	R	35	142	468	46	120	18	0	9	52	24	42	4	.256	.289	.353
Rod Carew	1B89,DH24,2B2	L	37	129	472	66	160	24	2	2	44	57	48	6	.339	.409	.411
Bobby Grich	2B118,SS1	R	34	120	387	65	113	17	0	16	62	76	62	2	.292	.414	.460
Doug DeCinces	3B84,DH10	R	32	95	370	49	104	19	3	18	65	32	56	2	.281	.332	.495
Tim Foli	SS74,3B13	R	32	88	330	29	83	10	0	2	29	5	18	2	.252	.263	.300
Fred Lynn	OF113,DH2	L	31	117	437	56	119	20	3	22	74	55	83	2	.272	.352	.483
Ellis Valentine	OF85	R	28	86	271	30	65	10	2	13	43	18	48	2	.240	.283	.435
Brian Downing	OF84,DH26	R	32	113	403	68	99	15	1	19	53	62	59	1	.246	.352	.429
Reggie Jackson	DH62,OF47	L	37	116	397	43	77	14	1	14	49	52	140	0	.194	.290	.340
Ron Jackson	3B38,1B35,DH16*	R	30	102	348	41	80	16	1	8	39	27	33	2	.230	.291	.351
Juan Beniquez	OF84,DH6	R	33	92	315	44	96	15	0	3	34	15	29	4	.305	.343	.381
Daryl Sconiers	1B57,DH27,OF1	L	24	106	314	49	86	19	3	8	46	17	41	4	.274	.310	.430
Bobby Clark	OF72,DH2,3B1	R	28	76	212	17	49	9	1	5	21	9	45	0	.231	.261	.354
Rob Wilfong	2B39,3B13,SS6*	L	29	65	177	17	45	7	1	2	17	10	25	2	.254	.293	.339
Steve Lubratich	SS23,3B22,2B14	R	28	57	156	12	34	9	0	0	7	4	17	0	.218	.236	.276
Rick Burleson	SS31	R	32	33	119	22	34	7	0	0	11	12	12	0	.286	.348	.345
Ricky Adams	SS38,3B16,2B4	R	24	58	112	22	28	2	0	2	6	5	12	1	.250	.300	.321
Mike Brown	OF31	R	23	31	104	12	24	5	1	3	9	7	20	1	.231	.279	.385
Gary Pettis	OF21	S	25	22	85	19	25	2	3	3	6	7	15	8	.294	.348	.494
Mike O'Berry	C26	R	29	26	60	7	10	1	0	1	5	3	11	0	.167	.206	.233
Dick Schofield	SS21	R	20	21	54	4	11	2	0	3	4	6	8	0	.204	.295	.407
Joe Ferguson	C9,OF3	R	36	12	27	3	2	0	0	0	2	5	8	0	.074	.219	.074
Jerry Narron	C6,DH1	L	27	10	22	1	3	0	0	1	4	1	3	0	.136	.174	.273

R. Jackson, 15 G at OF; R. Wilfong, 1 G at DH

Pitcher	T	Age	G	GS	CG	ShO	IP	H	HR	BB	SO	W-L	Sv	ERA
Tommy John	L	40	34	34	9	0	234.2	287	20	49	65	11-13	0	4.33
Ken Forsch	R	36	31	31	11	1	219.1	226	21	61	81	11-12	0	4.06
Geoff Zahn	L	37	29	28	11	3	203.0	212	22	51	81	9-11	0	3.33
Bruce Kison	R	33	26	17	4	1	126.2	128	13	43	83	11-5	2	4.05
Bill Travers	L	30	10	7	0	0	42.2	58	4	19	24	0-3	0	5.91
Luis Sanchez	R	29	56	1	0	0	98.1	92	6	40	49	10-8	7	3.66
Mike Witt	R	22	43	19	2	0	154.0	173	14	75	77	7-14	5	4.91
Andy Hassler	L	31	42	0	0	0	36.1	42	2	17	20	0-5	4	5.45
John Curtis	L	35	37	3	0	0	90.0	89	5	40	36	1-2	5	3.80
Rick Steirer	R	26	19	5	0	0	61.2	77	3	18	25	3-2	0	4.82
Byron McLaughlin	R	27	16	7	0	0	55.2	63	3	22	45	2-4	0	5.17
Dave Goltz	R	34	15	6	0	0	63.2	81	10	37	27	0-6	0	6.22
Steve Brown	R	26	12	4	2	1	46.0	45	4	16	23	2-3	0	3.52
Doug Corbett	R	30	11	0	0	0	17.1	26	1	4	18	1-1	0	3.63
Curt Brown	R	23	10	0	0	0	16.0	25	1	4	7	1-1	0	7.31
Bob Lacey	L	29	8	0	0	0	8.2	12	1	0	7	1-2	0	5.19

1983 Minnesota Twins 5th AL West 70-92 .432 29.0 GB

Billy Gardner

Player	Gm by Position	B	Age	G	AB	R	H	2B	3B	HR	RBI	BB	SO	SB	Avg	OBP	Slg
Dave Engle	C73,DH29,OF4	R	26	120	374	46	114	22	4	8	43	28	39	2	.305	.350	.449
Kent Hrbek	1B137,DH2	L	23	141	515	75	153	41	5	16	84	57	71	4	.297	.366	.489
John Castino	2B132,3B8,DH1	R	28	142	563	83	156	30	4	11	57	62	54	4	.277	.348	.403
Gary Gaetti	3B154,SS3,DH1	R	24	157	584	81	143	30	3	21	78	54	121	7	.245	.309	.414
Ron Washington	SS81,2B14,DH1*	R	31	99	317	28	78	7	3	4	26	22	50	10	.246	.296	.325
Gary Ward	OF152,DH2	R	29	157	623	76	173	34	5	19	88	44	98	8	.278	.326	.440
Tom Brunansky	OF146,DH4	R	22	151	542	70	123	24	5	28	82	61	95	2	.227	.308	.445
Darrell Brown	OF81,DH3	S	27	91	309	40	84	6	2	0	22	10	28	3	.272	.297	.304
Randy Bush	DH103,1B3	L	24	124	373	43	93	24	3	11	56	34	51	0	.249	.323	.418
Mickey Hatcher	OF56,DH39,1B7*	R	28	106	375	50	119	15	3	9	47	14	19	2	.317	.342	.445
Lenny Faedo	SS51	R	23	51	173	16	48	7	0	1	18	4	19	0	.277	.291	.335
Tim Laudner	C57,DH4	R	25	62	168	20	31	9	0	6	18	15	49	0	.185	.250	.345
Bobby Mitchell	OF44	L	28	59	152	26	35	4	2	1	15	28	21	1	.230	.354	.303
Ray Smith	C59	R	27	59	152	11	34	5	0	0	8	10	12	1	.224	.274	.257
Rusty Kuntz†	OF30	R	28	31	100	13	19	3	0	3	5	12	28	0	.190	.274	.310
Houston Jimenez	SS36	R	25	36	86	5	15	5	1	0	9	4	11	0	.174	.207	.256
Scott Ullger	1B30,3B3,DH1	R	27	35	79	8	15	4	0	0	5	5	21	0	.190	.247	.241
Tim Teufel	2B18,DH1,SS1	R	24	21	78	11	24	7	1	3	6	2	8	0	.308	.325	.538
Greg Gagne	SS10	R	21	10	27	2	3	1	0	0	3	0	6	0	.111	.103	.148
Jim Eisenreich	OF2	L	24	2	7	1	2	1	0	0	0	1	1	0	.286	.375	.429
Tack Wilson	DH2,OF1	R	27	5	4	4	1	1	0	0	1	0	0	0	.250	.250	.500

R. Washington, 1 G at 3B; M. Hatcher, 1 G at 3B

Pitcher	T	Age	G	GS	CG	ShO	IP	H	HR	BB	SO	W-L	Sv	ERA
Frank Viola	L	23	35	34	4	0	210.0	242	34	92	127	7-15	0	5.49
Al Williams	R	29	36	29	4	1	193.1	196	21	68	68	11-14	1	4.14
Ken Schrom	R	28	33	28	6	1	196.1	196	14	80	80	15-8	0	3.71
Bobby Castillo	R	28	27	25	3	0	158.1	170	17	65	90	8-12	0	4.77
Brad Havens	L	23	16	14	1	0	80.1	110	11	38	40	5-8	0	8.18
Bryan Oelkers	L	22	10	8	0	0	34.1	56	7	17	13	0-5	0	8.65
Jay Pettibone	R	26	4	4	1	0	27.0	28	8	8	10	0-4	0	5.33
Ron Davis	R	27	66	0	0	0	89.0	89	6	33	84	5-8	30	3.34
Rick Lysander	R	30	61	4	1	1	125.0	132	8	43	58	5-12	3	3.38
Len Whitehouse	L	25	60	0	0	0	73.2	70	6	44	44	7-1	2	4.15
Jack O'Connor	L	25	27	8	0	0	83.0	107	13	36	56	2-3	0	5.86
Pete Filson	L	24	26	8	0	0	90.0	87	9	29	49	4-1	1	3.40
Mike Walters	R	25	23	0	0	0	59.0	52	4	20	21	1-1	2	4.12
Jim Lewis	R	27	6	0	0	0	18.0	24	5	7	8	0-0	0	6.50

1983 Seattle Mariners 7th AL West 60-102 .370 39.0 GB

Rene Lachemann (26-47)/Del Crandall (34-55)

Player	Gm by Position	B	Age	G	AB	R	H	2B	3B	HR	RBI	BB	SO	SB	Avg	OBP	Slg
Rick Sweet	C85	S	30	93	249	18	55	9	0	1	22	13	26	2	.221	.259	.269
Pat Putnam	1B125,DH11	L	29	144	469	58	126	23	2	19	67	39	57	2	.269	.326	.448
Tony Bernazard†	2B79	S	26	80	300	35	80	18	1	6	30	38	52	21	.267	.351	.393
Jamie Allen	3B82,DH2	R	25	86	273	23	61	10	0	4	21	33	52	6	.223	.309	.304
Spike Owen	SS80	S	22	80	306	36	60	11	3	2	21	24	44	10	.196	.257	.271
Dave Henderson	OF133,DH3	R	24	137	484	50	130	24	5	17	55	28	93	9	.269	.306	.444
Steve Henderson	OF112,DH6	R	30	121	436	50	128	32	3	10	54	44	82	10	.294	.356	.450
Rickey Nelson	OF91,DH1	L	24	98	291	32	74	13	3	5	36	17	50	7	.254	.294	.371
Richie Zisk	DH84	R	34	90	285	30	69	12	0	12	36	30	61	0	.242	.311	.411
Al Cowens	OF70,DH34	R	31	110	356	39	73	19	2	7	35	23	38	10	.205	.255	.329
Todd Cruz†	SS63	R	27	65	216	21	41	4	2	7	21	7	56	1	.190	.221	.324
Manny Castillo	3B55,1B11,DH6*	S	26	91	203	13	42	6	3	0	24	7	20	1	.207	.233	.266
Ron Roenicke†	OF54,1B8,DH1	S	26	59	198	23	50	12	0	4	23	33	22	6	.253	.362	.374
Julio Cruz†	2B60,DH1	S	28	61	181	24	46	10	1	2	12	20	22	33	.254	.332	.354
Orlando Mercado	C65	R	21	66	178	10	35	11	2	1	16	14	27	2	.197	.256	.298
John Moses	OF71,DH10	S	25	93	130	19	27	4	1	0	6	12	20	11	.208	.280	.254
Domingo Ramos	SS28,2B8,3B8*	R	25	53	127	14	36	4	0	2	10	7	12	3	.283	.326	.362
Ken Phelps	1B22,DH19	L	28	50	127	10	30	4	1	7	16	13	25	0	.236	.301	.449
Jamie Nelson	C39	R	23	40	96	9	21	3	0	1	5	13	12	4	.219	.309	.281
Darnell Coles	3B26	R	21	27	92	9	26	7	0	1	6	7	12	0	.283	.333	.391
Phil Bradley	OF21,DH1	R	24	23	67	8	18	2	0	0	5	8	5	3	.269	.342	.299
Al Chambers	DH22,OF3	L	22	31	67	11	14	3	0	1	7	18	20	0	.209	.376	.299
Jim Maler	1B19,DH5	R	24	26	66	5	12	1	0	1	3	5	11	0	.182	.260	.242
Dave Edler	3B13,DH6,1B5*	R	26	29	63	2	12	1	1	1	4	5	11	3	.190	.257	.286
Harold Reynolds	2B18	S	22	20	59	8	12	4	1	0	1	2	9	0	.203	.226	.305
Rod Allen	DH3,OF2	R	23	11	12	1	2	0	0	0	0	0	1	0	.167	.167	.167
Bud Bulling	C5	R	30	5	5	0	0	0	0	0	0	0	0	0	.000	.000	.000

M. Castillo, 5 G at 2B, 1 G at P; D. Ramos, 2 G at DH; D. Edler, 1 G at OF

Pitcher	T	Age	G	GS	CG	ShO	IP	H	HR	BB	SO	W-L	Sv	ERA
Matt Young	L	24	33	32	5	2	203.2	178	17	79	130	11-15	0	3.27
Jim Beattie	R	28	30	29	8	2	196.2	197	12	66	132	10-15	0	3.84
Bob Stoddard	R	26	35	23	2	1	175.2	182	29	58	87	9-17	0	4.41
Mike Moore	R	23	22	21	3	2	128.0	130	10	60	108	6-8	0	4.71
Gaylord Perry†	R	44	16	16	2	0	102.0	116	18	23	42	3-10	0	4.94
Glenn Abbott†	R	32	14	14	2	0	82.1	103	9	15	38	5-3	0	4.59
Gene Nelson	R	22	10	5	1	0	32.0	38	6	21	11	0-3	0	7.88
Ed Vande Berg	L	24	68	0	0	0	64.1	59	6	22	49	2-4	5	3.36
Bill Caudill	R	26	63	0	0	0	72.2	70	10	38	73	2-8	26	4.71
Mike Stanton	R	30	50	0	0	0	65.0	65	3	28	47	2-3	7	3.32
Roy Thomas	R	30	43	0	0	0	88.2	95	3	32	77	3-1	1	3.45
Bryan Clark	L	26	41	17	2	0	162.1	160	14	72	76	7-10	0	3.94
Edwin Nunez	R	20	14	5	0	0	37.0	40	3	22	35	0-4	0	4.38
Karl Best	R	24	4	0	0	0	5.1	14	2	5	3	0-1	0	13.50
Manny Castillo	R	26	1	0	0	0	2.2	8	3	3	2	0-0	0	23.63

»1983 Philadelphia Phillies 1st NL East 90-72 .556 —

Pat Corrales (43-42)/Paul Owens (47-30)

Player	Gm by Position	B	Age	G	AB	R	H	2B	3B	HR	RBI	BB	SO	SB	Avg	OBP	Slg
Bo Diaz	C134	R	30	136	471	49	111	17	0	15	64	38	57	1	.236	.295	.367
Pete Rose	1B112,OF35	S	42	151	493	52	121	14	3	0	45	52	28	7	.245	.316	.286
Joe Morgan	2B117	L	39	123	404	72	93	20	1	16	59	89	54	18	.230	.370	.403
Mike Schmidt	3B153,SS2	R	33	154	534	104	136	16	4	40	109	128	148	7	.255	.399	.524
Ivan DeJesus	SS158	R	30	158	497	60	126	15	7	4	45	53	77	11	.254	.323	.336
Gary Matthews	OF122	R	32	132	446	66	115	18	2	10	50	69	81	13	.258	.352	.374
Greg Gross	OF110,1B1	L	30	136	245	25	74	12	3	0	29	34	16	3	.302	.385	.376
Bob Dernier	OF107	R	26	122	221	41	51	10	0	1	15	18	21	35	.231	.288	.290
Von Hayes	OF103	L	24	124	351	45	93	9	5	6	32	36	55	20	.265	.337	.370
Garry Maddox	OF95	R	33	97	324	27	89	14	2	4	32	17	31	7	.275	.312	.367
Joe Lefebvre†	OF74,3B9,C3	L	27	101	258	34	80	20	8	8	38	31	46	5	.310	.388	.543
Tony Perez	1B69	R	41	91	253	18	61	11	2	6	43	28	57	1	.241	.316	.372
Ozzie Virgil	C51	R	26	55	140	11	30	7	0	6	23	8	34	0	.214	.272	.393
Kiko Garcia	2B52,SS22,3B10	R	29	84	118	22	34	7	1	2	9	9	20	1	.288	.344	.415
Len Matuszek	1B21	L	28	28	80	12	22	6	1	4	16	4	14	0	.275	.306	.525
Larry Milbourne†	2B27,SS8,3B3	S	32	41	66	3	16	0	1	0	4	4	7	2	.242	.282	.273
Juan Samuel	2B18	R	22	18	65	14	18	1	2	2	5	4	16	3	.277	.324	.446
Sixto Lezcano†	OF15	R	29	18	39	8	11	1	0	0	7	5	9	1	.282	.364	.308
Bob Molinaro†		L	33	19	18	1	2	1	0	1	3	0	2	0	.111	.105	.333
Steve Jeltz	2B4,3B2,SS2	S	24	13	8	0	1	0	1	0	1	1	2	0	.125	.222	.375
Bill Robinson	1B3,3B2,OF1	R	40	10	7	0	1	0	0	0	2	1	4	0	.143	.250	.143
Alex Sanchez	OF2	R	24	8	7	2	2	0	0	0	2	0	2	0	.286	.286	.286
Luis Aguayo	SS2	R	24	2	4	1	1	0	0	0	0	1	2	0	.250	.400	.250
Jeff Stone	OF1	L	22	9	4	2	3	0	2	0	3	0	1	4	.750	.750	1.750
Darren Daulton	C2	L	21	2	3	1	1	0	0	0	0	1	1	0	.333	.500	.333
Tim Corcoran	1B3	L	30	3	0	0	0	0	0	0	0	0	0	0	—	—	—

Pitcher	T	Age	G	GS	CG	ShO	IP	H	HR	BB	SO	W-L	Sv	ERA
Steve Carlton	L	38	37	37	8	3	283.2	277	20	84	275	15-16	0	3.11
John Denny	R	30	36	36	7	1	242.2	229	9	53	139	19-6	0	2.37
Charles Hudson	R	24	26	26	3	0	169.1	158	13	53	101	8-8	0	3.35
Marty Bystrom	R	24	24	23	1	1	119.1	136	6	44	87	6-9	0	4.60
Kevin Gross	R	22	17	17	1	1	96.0	100	13	35	66	4-6	0	3.56
Larry Christenson	R	29	9	9	0	0	48.1	42	2	17	44	2-4	0	3.91
Dick Ruthven†	R	32	7	7	0	0	33.2	46	5	10	26	1-3	0	5.61
Tony Ghelfi	R	21	3	3	0	0	14.1	15	2	6	14	1-1	0	3.14
Al Holland	L	30	68	0	0	0	91.2	63	8	30	100	8-4	25	2.26
Willie Hernandez†	L	28	63	0	0	0	95.2	93	9	26	75	8-4	7	3.29
Ron Reed	R	40	61	0	0	0	95.2	89	5	34	73	9-1	8	3.48
Tug McGraw	L	38	34	1	0	0	55.2	58	4	19	30	2-1	0	3.56
Porfi Altamirano	R	31	31	0	0	0	41.1	38	9	15	24	2-3	0	3.70
Larry Andersen	R	30	17	0	0	0	26.1	19	0	9	14	1-0	0	2.39
Sid Monge†	L	32	14	0	0	0	11.2	20	4	6	7	3-0	0	6.94
Ed Farmer†	R	33	12	3	0	0	26.2	35	2	20	16	0-6	0	6.08
Steve Comer	R	29	3	1	0	0	8.2	11	0	3	1	1-0	0	5.19
Don Carman	L	23	1	0	0	0	1.0	0	0	0	0	0-0	1	0.00

1983 Pittsburgh Pirates 2nd NL East 84-78 .519 6.0 GB

Chuck Tanner

Player	Gm by Position	B	Age	G	AB	R	H	2B	3B	HR	RBI	BB	SO	SB	Avg	OBP	Slg
Tony Pena	C149	R	26	151	542	51	163	22	3	15	70	31	73	6	.301	.338	.435
Jason Thompson	1B151	L	28	152	517	70	134	20	1	18	76	99	128	1	.259	.376	.406
Johnny Ray	2B151	S	26	151	576	68	163	38	7	5	53	35	26	18	.283	.323	.399
Bill Madlock	3B126	R	32	130	473	68	153	21	0	12	68	49	24	3	.323	.386	.444
Dale Berra	SS161	R	26	161	537	51	135	25	1	10	52	61	84	8	.251	.327	.358
Dave Parker	OF142	L	32	144	552	68	154	29	4	12	69	28	89	12	.279	.311	.411
Mike Easler	OF105	L	32	115	381	44	117	17	2	10	54	22	64	4	.307	.349	.441
Marvell Wynne	OF102	L	23	103	366	66	89	16	2	7	26	38	52	12	.243	.319	.355
Lee Lacy	OF98	R	35	108	288	40	87	12	3	4	13	22	36	31	.302	.352	.406
Lee Mazzilli	OF57,1B7	S	28	109	246	37	59	9	0	5	24	49	43	15	.240	.365	.337
Richie Hebner	3B40,1B7,OF7	L	35	78	162	23	43	4	1	5	26	17	28	8	.265	.332	.395
Jim Morrison	2B28,3B26,SS7	R	30	66	158	16	48	7	2	6	25	9	25	2	.304	.347	.487
Brian Harper	OF35,1B1	R	23	61	131	16	29	4	1	7	20	2	15	0	.221	.232	.427
Gene Tenace	1B19,C3,OF1	R	36	53	62	7	11	5	0	0	6	12	17	0	.177	.346	.258
Doug Frobel	OF24	L	24	32	60	10	17	4	1	3	11	4	17	1	.283	.328	.533
Steve Nicosia†	C15	R	27	21	46	4	6	2	0	1	1	1	7	0	.130	.149	.239
Milt May†	C4	L	32	7	12	0	3	0	0	0	0	1	1	0	.250	.308	.250
Joe Orsulak	OF4	L	21	7	11	0	2	0	0	0	1	0	2	0	.182	.167	.182
Junior Ortiz†	C4	R	23	5	8	1	1	0	0	0	0	1	0	0	.125	.222	.125
Ron Wotus	SS2,2B1	R	22	5	3	0	0	0	0	0	0	0	1	0	.000	.000	.000
Rafael Belliard	SS3	R	21	4	1	1	0	0	0	0	0	0	1	0	.000	.000	.000
Miguel Dilone†		S	28	7	0	1	0	0	0	0	0	0	0	2	—	—	—

Pitcher	T	Age	G	GS	CG	ShO	IP	H	HR	BB	SO	W-L	Sv	ERA
Rick Rhoden	R	30	36	35	7	2	244.1	256	13	68	153	13-13	1	3.09
Larry McWilliams	L	29	35	35	8	4	238.0	205	19	87	199	15-8	0	3.25
John Candelaria	L	29	33	32	2	0	197.2	191	15	45	157	15-8	0	3.23
Lee Tunnell	R	22	35	25	5	3	177.2	167	15	58	95	11-6	0	3.65
Jose DeLeon	R	22	15	15	3	2	108.0	75	5	47	118	7-3	0	2.83
Don Robinson	R	26	9	6	0	0	36.1	43	5	21	28	2-2	0	4.46
Alfonso Pulido	L	26	1	1	0	0	2.0	4	2	1	1	0-0	0	9.00
Kent Tekulve	R	36	76	0	0	0	99.0	78	1	36	52	7-5	18	1.64
Rod Scurry	L	27	61	0	0	0	68.0	63	6	53	67	4-9	7	5.56
Manny Sarmiento	R	27	52	0	0	0	84.1	74	8	36	49	3-5	4	2.99
Cecilio Guante	R	23	49	0	0	0	100.1	90	5	46	82	2-6	9	3.32
Jim Bibby	R	38	29	12	0	0	78.0	92	10	51	44	5-12	2	6.69
Randy Niemann	L	27	8	1	0	0	13.2	20	2	7	8	0-1	0	9.22
Jim Winn	R	23	7	0	0	0	11.0	12	2	6	3	0-0	0	7.36
Dave Tomlin	L	34	5	0	0	0	4.0	6	0	1	5	0-0	0	6.75
Bob Owchinko	L	28	1	0	0	0	0.0	2	1	0	0	0-0	0	—

874 Seasons: Team Rosters

1983 Montreal Expos 3rd NL East 82-80 .506 8.0 GB

Bill Virdon

Player	Gm by Position	B	Age	G	AB	R	H	2B	3B	HR	RBI	BB	SO	SB	Avg	OBP	Slg
Gary Carter	C144,1B1	R	29	145	541	63	146	37	3	17	79	51	57	1	.270	.336	.444
Al Oliver	1B153,OF1	L	36	157	614	70	184	38	3	8	84	44	44	1	.300	.347	.410
Doug Flynn	2B107,SS37	R	32	143	452	44	107	18	4	0	26	19	38	2	.237	.267	.294
Tim Wallach	3B156	R	25	156	581	54	156	33	3	19	70	55	97	0	.269	.335	.434
Chris Speier	SS74,3B12,2B2	R	33	88	261	31	67	12	2	2	22	29	37	2	.257	.332	.341
Andre Dawson	OF157	R	28	159	633	104	189	36	10	32	113	38	81	25	.299	.338	.539
Tim Raines	OF154,2B7	S	23	156	615	133	183	32	8	11	71	97	70	90	.298	.393	.429
Warren Cromartie	OF101,1B1	L	29	120	360	37	100	26	2	3	43	43	48	8	.278	.352	.386
Bryan Little	SS66,2B51	S	23	106	350	48	91	15	3	1	36	50	22	4	.260	.352	.329
Terry Francona	OF51,1B47	L	24	120	230	21	59	11	1	3	22	6	20	0	.257	.273	.352
Jim Wohlford	OF61	R	32	83	141	7	39	8	0	1	14	5	14	0	.277	.297	.355
Manny Trillo†	2B31	R	32	31	121	16	32	8	0	2	16	10	18	0	.264	.331	.380
Bobby Ramos	C25	R	27	27	61	2	14	3	1	0	5	8	11	0	.230	.329	.311
Mike Vail†	OF15,1B1,3B1	R	31	34	53	5	15	2	0	2	4	8	10	0	.283	.387	.434
Terry Crowley	1B4	L	36	50	44	2	8	0	0	0	3	9	4	0	.182	.327	.182
Mike Stenhouse	OF9,1B5	L	25	24	40	2	5	1	0	0	2	4	10	0	.125	.205	.150
Angel Salazar	SS34	R	21	36	37	5	8	1	1	0	1	1	8	0	.216	.231	.297
Jerry White	OF13	S	30	40	34	4	5	1	0	0	0	12	8	4	.147	.383	.176
Brad Mills	3B3,1B1	L	26	14	20	1	5	0	0	0	1	2	3	0	.250	.318	.250
Tim Blackwell	C5	S	30	6	15	0	3	1	0	0	2	1	3	0	.200	.250	.267
Gene Roof†	OF5	S	25	8	12	2	2	2	0	0	1	1	3	0	.167	.231	.333
Mike Fuentes		R	25	6	4	1	1	0	0	0	0	0	2	0	.250	.250	.250
Mike Phillips	SS3,3B2	L	32	5	2	0	0	0	0	0	0	0	0	0	.000	.000	.000
Wallace Johnson†		S	26	3	2	1	1	0	0	0	0	1	0	1	.500	.667	.500
Razor Shines	OF1	S	26	3	2	0	1	0	0	0	0	0	0	0	.500	.500	.500
Tom Wieghaus	C1	R	26	1	0	0	0	0	0	0	0	0	0	0	—	—	—

Pitcher	T	Age	G	GS	CG	ShO	IP	H	HR	BB	SO	W-L	Sv	ERA
Steve Rogers	R	33	36	36	13	5	273.0	258	14	78	146	17-12	0	3.23
Bill Gullickson	R	24	34	34	10	1	242.1	230	19	59	120	17-12	0	3.75
Charlie Lea	R	26	33	33	8	4	222.0	195	15	84	137	16-11	0	3.12
Scott Sanderson	R	26	18	16	0	0	81.1	98	12	20	55	6-7	1	4.65
Jeff Reardon	R	27	66	0	0	0	92.0	87	7	44	78	7-9	21	3.03
Dan Schatzeder	L	28	58	2	0	0	87.0	88	3	25	48	5-2	2	3.21
Bryn Smith	R	27	49	12	5	3	155.1	142	13	43	101	6-11	3	2.49
Ray Burris	R	32	40	17	2	1	154.0	139	13	56	100	4-7	0	3.68
Bob James†	R	24	27	0	0	0	50.0	37	3	23	56	1-0	7	2.88
Randy Lerch†	L	28	19	5	0	0	38.2	45	6	18	24	1-3	0	6.75
Chris Welsh†	L	28	16	5	0	0	44.2	46	5	18	17	0-1	0	5.04
Greg Bargar	R	24	8	3	0	0	20.0	23	6	8	9	2-0	0	6.75
Woodie Fryman	L	43	6	0	0	0	3.0	8	1	1	1	0-3	0	21.00
Tom Dixon	R	28	4	0	0	0	3.2	6	1	1	4	0-1	0	9.82
Dick Grapenthin	R	25	1	0	0	0	4.0	4	2	1	3	0-1	0	9.00

1983 St. Louis Cardinals 4th NL East 79-83 .488 11.0 GB

Whitey Herzog

Player	Gm by Position	B	Age	G	AB	R	H	2B	3B	HR	RBI	BB	SO	SB	Avg	OBP	Slg
Darrell Porter	C133	L	31	145	443	57	116	24	3	15	66	68	94	1	.262	.363	.431
George Hendrick	1B92,OF51	R	33	144	529	73	168	33	3	18	97	51	76	3	.318	.373	.493
Tom Herr	2B86	S	27	89	313	43	101	14	4	2	31	43	27	6	.323	.403	.412
Ken Oberkfell	3B127,2B32,SS1	L	27	151	488	62	143	26	5	3	38	61	27	12	.293	.371	.385
Ozzie Smith	SS158	S	28	159	552	69	134	30	6	3	50	64	36	34	.243	.321	.335
Willie McGee	OF145	S	24	147	601	75	172	22	8	5	75	26	98	39	.286	.314	.374
David Green	OF136	R	22	146	422	52	120	14	10	8	69	26	76	34	.284	.325	.422
Lonnie Smith	OF126	R	27	130	492	83	158	31	5	8	45	41	55	43	.321	.381	.453
Andy Van Slyke	OF69,3B30,1B9	L	22	101	309	51	81	15	5	8	38	46	64	21	.262	.357	.421
Keith Hernandez†	1B54	L	29	55	218	34	62	15	4	3	26	24	30	1	.284	.352	.431
Mike Ramsey	2B66,SS20,3B8*	S	29	97	175	25	46	4	3	1	16	12	23	4	.263	.309	.337
Dane Iorg	OF22,1B11	L	33	58	116	6	31	9	1	0	11	10	11	1	.267	.321	.362
Floyd Rayford	3B33	R	25	56	104	5	22	4	0	3	14	10	27	1	.212	.278	.337
Steve Braun	OF22,3B4	L	35	78	92	8	25	2	1	3	7	21	7	0	.272	.404	.413
Glenn Brummer	C41	R	28	45	87	7	24	7	0	0	9	10	11	1	.276	.351	.356
Jamie Quirk	C22,3B7,SS1	L	28	48	86	3	18	2	1	2	11	6	27	0	.209	.269	.326
Bill Lyons	2B23,3B8,SS2	R	25	42	60	3	10	1	1	0	3	1	11	3	.167	.180	.217
Jeff Doyle	2B12	S	26	13	37	4	11	1	2	0	2	1	3	0	.297	.316	.432
Jim Adduci	1B6,OF1	L	23	10	20	0	1	0	0	0	0	1	6	0	.050	.095	.050
Rafael Santana	2B9,SS6,3B4	R	25	30	14	1	3	0	0	0	2	2	2	0	.214	.353	.214
Jimmy Sexton	SS4,3B2	R	31	6	9	1	1	1	0	0	0	1	4	0	.111	.200	.222
Orlando Sanchez	C1	L	26	6	6	0	0	0	0	0	0	0	4	0	.000	.000	.000
Tito Landrum†	OF5	R	28	6	5	0	1	0	1	0	0	1	2	1	.200	.333	.600
Gene Roof†	OF1	S	25	6	3	1	0	0	0	0	0	0	0	0	.000	.000	.000

M. Ramsey, 1 G at OF

Pitcher	T	Age	G	GS	CG	ShO	IP	H	HR	BB	SO	W-L	Sv	ERA
Joaquin Andujar	R	30	39	34	5	2	225.0	215	23	75	125	6-16	1	4.16
John Stuper	R	26	40	30	6	1	198.0	202	15	71	81	12-11	1	3.68
Bob Forsch	R	33	34	30	6	2	187.0	190	23	54	56	10-12	0	4.28
Dave LaPoint	L	23	37	29	1	0	191.1	191	12	84	113	12-9	0	3.95
Neil Allen†	R	25	25	18	4	2	121.2	122	6	48	74	10-6	0	3.70
Danny Cox	R	23	12	12	0	0	83.0	92	6	23	36	3-6	0	3.25
Bruce Sutter	R	30	60	0	0	0	89.1	90	8	30	64	9-10	21	4.23
Jeff Lahti	R	26	53	0	0	0	74.0	64	2	29	26	3-3	0	3.16
Dave Von Ohlen	L	24	46	0	0	0	68.1	71	3	25	21	3-2	2	3.29
Dave Rucker†	L	25	34	0	0	0	37.0	36	1	18	22	5-3	0	2.43
John Martin†	L	27	26	5	0	0	66.1	60	6	26	29	3-1	0	3.53
Doug Bair†	R	33	26	0	0	0	29.2	24	4	13	21	1-1	1	3.03
Jim Kaat	L	44	24	0	0	0	34.2	48	5	10	19	0-0	0	3.89
Kevin Hagen	R	23	9	4	0	0	22.1	34	0	7	7	2-2	0	4.84
Steve Baker†	R	26	8	0	0	0	10.0	10	0	4	1	0-1	0	1.80
Ralph Citarella	R	25	6	0	0	0	11.0	8	0	3	4	0-0	0	1.64
Eric Rasmussen†	R	31	6	0	0	0	7.2	16	1	4	6	0-0	1	11.74
Jeff Keener	R	24	4	0	0	0	4.1	6	0	1	4	0-0	0	8.31

1983 Chicago Cubs 5th NL East 71-91 .438 19.0 GB

Lee Elia (54-69)/Charlie Fox (17-22)

Player	Gm by Position	B	Age	G	AB	R	H	2B	3B	HR	RBI	BB	SO	SB	Avg	OBP	Slg
Jody Davis	C150	R	26	151	510	56	138	31	2	24	84	33	93	0	.271	.315	.480
Bill Buckner	1B144,OF15	L	33	153	626	79	175	38	6	16	66	25	30	12	.280	.310	.436
Ryne Sandberg	2B157,SS1	R	23	158	633	94	165	25	4	8	48	51	79	37	.261	.316	.351
Ron Cey	3B157	R	35	159	581	73	160	33	1	24	90	62	85	0	.275	.346	.460
Larry Bowa	SS145	S	37	147	499	73	133	20	5	2	43	35	30	7	.267	.312	.339
Keith Moreland	OF151,C3	R	29	154	533	76	161	30	3	16	70	68	73	0	.302	.378	.460
Mel Hall	OF112	L	22	112	410	60	116	23	5	17	56	42	101	6	.283	.352	.488
Leon Durham	OF95,1B6	L	25	100	337	58	87	18	8	12	55	66	83	12	.258	.381	.466
Gary Woods	OF73,2B1	R	28	93	190	25	46	9	0	4	22	15	27	5	.242	.296	.353
Jay Johnstone	OF44	L	37	86	140	16	36	7	0	6	22	20	24	1	.257	.362	.436
Carmelo Martinez	1B26,3B1,OF1	R	22	29	89	8	23	3	0	6	16	4	19	0	.258	.287	.494
Scot Thompson	OF29,1B1	L	27	53	88	4	17	3	1	0	10	3	14	0	.193	.220	.250
Tom Veryzer	SS28,3B17	R	30	59	88	5	18	3	0	1	3	3	13	0	.205	.231	.273
Jerry Morales	OF29	R	34	63	87	11	17	9	0	0	11	7	19	0	.195	.253	.299
Steve Lake	C32	R	26	38	85	9	22	4	1	1	7	2	6	0	.259	.284	.365
Thad Bosley	OF20	L	26	43	72	12	21	4	1	2	12	10	12	1	.292	.373	.458
Joe Carter	OF16	R	23	23	51	6	9	1	1	0	1	0	21	1	.176	.176	.235
Wayne Nordhagen	OF7	R	34	21	35	1	5	1	0	1	4	0	5	0	.143	.162	.257
Dan Rohn	2B6,SS1	L	27	23	31	3	12	3	2	0	6	2	2	1	.387	.424	.613
Junior Kennedy	2B7,3B4,SS1	R	32	17	22	3	3	0	0	0	3	1	6	0	.136	.167	.136
Dave Owen	SS14,3B3	S	25	16	22	1	2	0	1	0	2	2	7	1	.091	.160	.182
Tom Grant	OF10	L	26	16	20	2	3	1	0	0	2	3	4	0	.150	.261	.200
Fritz Connally	3B3	R	25	8	10	0	1	0	0	0	0	0	5	0	.100	.100	.100
Mike Diaz	C3	R	23	6	7	2	2	1	0	0	1	0	0	0	.286	.286	.429
Jay Loviglio		R	27	1	1	0	0	0	0	0	0	0	1	0	.000	.000	.000

Pitcher	T	Age	G	GS	CG	ShO	IP	H	HR	BB	SO	W-L	Sv	ERA
Chuck Rainey	R	28	34	34	1	1	191.0	219	17	74	84	14-13	0	4.48
Steve Trout	L	25	34	32	1	0	180.0	217	13	59	80	10-14	0	4.65
Fergie Jenkins	R	39	33	29	1	1	167.1	176	19	46	96	6-9	0	4.30
Dick Ruthven†	R	32	25	25	5	2	149.1	156	17	28	73	12-9	0	4.10
Dickie Noles	R	26	24	18	1	1	116.1	133	9	37	59	5-10	0	4.72
Paul Moskau	R	29	8	8	0	0	32.0	44	7	14	16	3-2	0	6.75
Rick Reuschel	R	34	4	4	0	0	20.2	18	1	10	9	1-1	0	3.92
Don Schulze	R	20	4	3	0	0	14.0	19	1	7	8	0-1	0	7.07
Bill Campbell	R	34	82	0	0	0	122.1	128	4	49	97	6-8	8	4.49
Lee Smith	R	25	66	0	0	0	103.1	70	5	41	91	4-10	29	1.65
Mike Proly	R	32	60	0	0	0	83.0	79	5	38	31	1-5	1	3.58
Warren Brusstar	R	31	59	0	0	0	80.1	67	1	37	46	3-1	1	2.35
Craig Lefferts	L	25	56	5	0	0	89.0	80	13	29	60	3-4	1	3.13
Rich Bordi	R	24	11	1	0	0	25.1	34	2	12	20	0-2	1	4.97
Willie Hernandez†	L	28	11	1	0	0	19.2	16	0	6	18	1-0	1	3.20
Bill Johnson	R	22	10	0	0	0	12.1	17	0	3	4	1-0	0	4.38
Reggie Patterson	R	24	5	2	0	0	18.2	17	3	6	10	1-2	0	4.82
Alan Hargesheimer	R	26	5	0	0	0	4.0	6	0	2	5	0-0	0	9.00

1983 New York Mets 6th NL East 68-94 .420 22.0 GB

George Bamberger (16-30)/Frank Howard (52-64)

Player	Gm by Position	B	Age	G	AB	R	H	2B	3B	HR	RBI	BB	SO	SB	Avg	OBP	Slg
Ron Hodges	C96	L	34	110	250	20	65	12	0	0	21	49	42	0	.260	.383	.308
Keith Hernandez†	1B90	L	29	95	320	43	98	8	3	9	37	64	42	8	.306	.424	.434
Brian Giles	2B140,SS12	R	23	145	400	39	98	15	0	2	27	36	77	17	.245	.308	.298
Hubie Brooks	3B145,2B7	R	26	150	586	53	147	18	4	5	58	24	96	6	.251	.284	.321
Jose Oquendo	SS116	S	19	120	328	29	70	7	0	1	17	19	60	8	.213	.260	.244
George Foster	OF153	R	34	157	601	74	145	19	2	28	90	38	111	1	.241	.289	.419
Mookie Wilson	OF148	S	27	152	638	91	176	25	6	7	51	18	103	54	.276	.300	.367
Darryl Strawberry	OF117	L	21	122	420	63	108	15	7	26	74	47	128	19	.257	.336	.512
Bob Bailor	SS75,2B50,3B11*	R	31	118	340	33	85	8	0	1	30	20	23	18	.250	.290	.282
Danny Heep	OF61,1B14	L	25	115	253	30	64	12	0	8	21	29	40	3	.253	.326	.395
Dave Kingman	1B50,OF5	R	34	100	248	25	49	7	0	13	29	22	57	2	.198	.265	.383
Junior Ortiz†	C67	R	23	68	185	10	47	5	0	0	12	3	34	1	.254	.270	.281
Rusty Staub	1B5,OF5	L	39	104	115	5	34	6	0	3	28	14	10	0	.296	.371	.426
Mark Bradley	OF35	R	26	73	104	10	21	4	0	3	5	11	35	4	.202	.278	.327
Ronn Reynolds	C24	R	24	24	66	4	13	1	0	0	2	8	12	0	.197	.280	.212
Tucker Ashford	3B15,2B13,C1	R	28	35	56	3	10	0	1	0	2	7	4	0	.179	.270	.214
Wally Backman	2B14,3B2	S	23	26	42	6	7	0	1	0	3	2	8	0	.167	.205	.214
Gary Rajsich	1B10	L	28	11	36	5	12	3	0	1	3	3	1	0	.333	.400	.500
Clint Hurdle	3B9,OF1	L	25	13	33	3	6	2	0	0	2	2	10	0	.182	.229	.242
Ron Gardenhire	SS15	R	25	17	32	1	2	0	0	0	1	1	4	0	.063	.091	.063
Mike Jorgensen†	1B19	L	34	38	24	5	6	3	0	1	3	2	4	0	.250	.333	.500
Mike Fitzgerald	C8	R	22	8	20	1	2	0	0	1	2	3	6	0	.100	.217	.250
Mike Bishop	C3	R	24	3	8	2	1	1	0	0	0	3	4	0	.125	.364	.250
Mike Howard	OF1	S	25	1	3	0	1	0	0	0	1	0	1	0	.333	.333	.333
John Stearns		R	31	4	0	2	0	0	0	0	0	0	0	0	—	—	—

B. Bailor, 3 G at OF

Pitcher	T	Age	G	GS	CG	ShO	IP	H	HR	BB	SO	W-L	Sv	ERA
Tom Seaver	R	38	34	34	5	2	231.0	201	18	86	135	9-14	0	3.55
Mike Torrez	R	36	39	34	5	0	222.1	227	16	113	94	10-17	0	4.37
Ed Lynch	R	27	30	27	1	0	174.2	208	17	41	44	10-10	0	4.28
Walt Terrell	R	25	21	20	4	2	133.2	123	7	55	59	8-8	0	3.57
Craig Swan	R	32	27	18	0	0	96.1	112	14	42	43	2-8	1	5.51
Ron Darling	R	22	5	5	1	0	35.1	31	0	17	23	1-3	0	2.80
Tim Leary	R	25	2	2	1	0	10.2	15	0	4	9	1-1	0	3.38
Doug Sisk	R	25	67	0	0	0	104.1	88	1	59	33	5-4	11	2.24
Jesse Orosco	L	26	62	0	0	0	110.0	76	3	38	84	13-7	17	1.47
Carlos Diaz	L	25	54	0	0	0	83.1	62	1	35	64	3-1	2	2.05
Scott Holman	R	24	35	10	0	0	101.0	90	7	52	44	1-7	0	3.74
Tom Gorman	L	25	25	4	0	0	49.1	45	3	15	30	1-4	0	4.93
Neil Allen†	R	25	21	4	1	1	54.0	57	6	36	32	2-7	2	4.50
Rick Ownbey	R	25	10	4	0	0	34.2	31	4	21	19	1-3	0	4.67
Brent Gaff	R	24	4	0	0	0	10.1	18	0	1	4	1-0	0	6.10

1983 Los Angeles Dodgers 1st NL West 91-71 .562 —

Tom Lasorda

Player	Gm by Position	B	Age	G	AB	R	H	2B	3B	HR	RBI	BB	SO	SB	Avg	OBP	Slg
Steve Yeager	C112	R	34	113	335	31	68	8	3	15	41	23	57	1	.203	.256	.379
Greg Brock	1B140	L	26	146	455	64	102	14	2	20	66	83	81	5	.224	.343	.396
Steve Sax	2B152	R	23	155	623	94	175	18	5	5	41	58	73	56	.281	.342	.350
Pedro Guerrero	3B157,1B2	R	27	160	584	87	174	28	6	32	103	72	110	23	.298	.373	.531
Bill Russell	SS127	R	34	131	451	47	111	13	1	1	30	33	31	13	.246	.302	.286
Dusty Baker	OF143	R	34	149	531	71	138	25	1	15	73	72	59	7	.260	.346	.395
Ken Landreaux	OF137	L	28	141	481	63	135	25	3	17	66	34	52	30	.281	.328	.451
Mike Marshall	OF109,1B33	R	23	140	465	47	132	17	1	17	65	43	127	7	.284	.347	.434
Derrel Thomas	OF82,SS13,2B9*	R	32	118	192	38	48	6	6	2	8	27	36	9	.250	.345	.375
Rick Monday	OF44,1B4	L	37	99	178	21	44	7	1	6	20	29	42	0	.247	.351	.399
Jack Fimple	C54	R	24	54	148	16	37	8	1	2	22	11	39	1	.250	.300	.358
Ron Roenicke†	OF62	S	26	81	145	12	32	4	0	2	12	14	26	3	.221	.288	.290
Dave Anderson	SS53,3B1	R	22	61	115	12	19	4	2	1	2	12	15	6	.165	.244	.261
Rafael Landestoy†	2B14,3B10,OF10*	S	30	64	64	6	11	1	1	1	1	3	8	0	.172	.209	.266
Candy Maldonado	OF33	R	22	42	62	5	12	1	1	1	6	5	14	0	.194	.254	.290
R.J. Reynolds	OF18	S	24	24	55	5	13	0	0	2	11	3	11	5	.236	.267	.345
Jose Morales	1B4	R	38	47	53	4	15	3	0	3	8	1	11	0	.283	.296	.509
Mike Scioscia	C11	L	24	12	35	3	11	3	0	1	7	5	2	0	.314	.400	.486
Gil Reyes	C19	R	19	19	31	1	5	2	0	0	0	0	5	0	.161	.188	.226
German Rivera	3B8	R	22	13	17	1	6	1	0	0	0	2	2	0	.353	.421	.412
Sid Bream	1B4	L	22	15	11	0	2	0	0	0	2	2	2	0	.182	.308	.182
Cecil Espy	OF15	S	20	20	11	4	3	1	0	0	1	1	2	0	.273	.333	.364
Dave Sax	C4	R	24	7	8	0	0	0	0	0	1	0	0	0	.000	.000	.000
Alex Taveras	SS3,2B2,3B1	R	27	10	4	0	0	0	0	0	0	0	1	0	.000	.000	.000

D. Thomas, 7 G at 3B; R. Landestoy, 1 G at SS

Pitcher	T	Age	G	GS	CG	ShO	IP	H	HR	BB	SO	W-L	Sv	ERA
F. Valenzuela	L	22	35	35	9	4	257.0	245	16	99	189	15-10	0	3.75
Jerry Reuss	L	34	32	31	7	0	223.1	233	12	50	143	12-11	0	2.94
Bob Welch	R	26	31	31	4	3	204.0	164	13	72	156	15-12	0	2.65
Burt Hooton	R	33	33	27	2	0	160.0	156	21	59	87	9-8	0	4.22
Alejandro Pena	R	24	34	26	4	3	177.0	152	7	51	120	12-9	1	2.75
Rick Honeycutt†	L	29	9	7	1	0	39.0	46	6	13	18	2-3	0	5.77
Sid Fernandez	L	20	2	1	0	0	6.0	7	0	7	9	0-1	0	6.00
Tom Niedenfuer	R	23	66	0	0	0	94.2	55	6	29	66	8-3	11	1.90
Dave Stewart†	R	26	46	1	0	0	76.0	67	4	33	54	5-2	8	2.96
Steve Howe	L	25	46	0	0	0	68.2	55	2	12	52	4-7	18	1.44
Joe Beckwith	R	28	42	3	0	0	71.0	73	5	35	50	3-4	1	3.55
Pat Zachry	R	31	40	1	0	0	61.1	63	4	21	36	6-1	0	2.49
Orel Hershiser	R	24	8	0	0	0	8.0	7	1	6	5	0-0	1	3.38
Rich Rodas	L	23	7	0	0	0	4.2	4	0	3	5	0-0	0	1.93
Ricky Wright†	L	24	6	0	0	0	6.1	5	0	2	5	0-0	0	2.84
Larry White	R	24	4	0	0	0	7.0	4	0	3	5	0-0	0	1.29

1983 Atlanta Braves 2nd NL West 88-74 .543 3.0 GB

Joe Torre

Player	Gm by Position	B	Age	G	AB	R	H	2B	3B	HR	RBI	BB	SO	SB	Avg	OBP	Slg
Bruce Benedict	C134	R	27	134	423	43	126	13	1	2	43	61	24	1	.298	.385	.348
Chris Chambliss	1B126	L	34	131	447	59	125	24	3	20	78	63	68	2	.280	.366	.481
Glenn Hubbard	2B148	R	25	148	517	65	136	24	6	12	70	55	71	3	.263	.334	.402
Bob Horner	3B104,1B1	R	25	104	386	75	117	25	1	20	68	50	63	4	.303	.383	.528
Rafael Ramirez	SS152	R	25	152	622	82	185	13	5	7	58	36	48	16	.297	.337	.368
Dale Murphy	OF160	R	27	162	589	131	178	24	4	36	121	90	110	30	.302	.393	.540
Brett Butler	OF143	L	26	151	549	84	154	21	13	5	37	54	56	39	.281	.344	.393
C. Washington	OF128	L	28	134	496	75	138	24	8	9	44	35	103	31	.278	.322	.413
Jerry Royster	3B47,2B26,OF18*	R	30	91	268	32	63	10	3	3	30	28	35	11	.235	.305	.328
Terry Harper	OF60	R	27	80	201	19	53	13	1	3	26	20	43	6	.264	.332	.383
Bob Watson	1B34	R	37	65	149	14	46	9	0	6	37	18	23	0	.309	.376	.490
Randy Johnson	3B53,2B4	R	27	86	144	22	36	3	0	1	17	20	27	1	.250	.345	.292
Biff Pocoroba	C34	S	29	55	120	11	32	6	0	2	16	12	7	0	.267	.331	.367
Mike Jorgensen†	1B19,OF6	L	34	57	48	5	12	1	0	1	8	8	8	0	.250	.351	.333
Gerald Perry	1B7,OF1	L	22	27	39	5	14	2	0	1	6	5	4	0	.359	.422	.487
Brad Komminsk	OF13	R	22	19	36	2	8	2	0	0	4	5	7	0	.222	.317	.278
Larry Owen	C16	R	28	17	17	0	2	0	0	0	1	0	2	0	.118	.118	.118
Matt Sinatro	C7	R	23	7	12	0	2	0	0	0	2	2	1	0	.167	.286	.167
Ken Smith	1B13	L	25	30	12	2	2	0	0	1	2	1	5	1	.167	.231	.417
Albert Hall	OF4	S	25	10	8	2	0	0	0	0	0	2	2	1	.000	.200	.000
Brook Jacoby	3B2	R	23	4	8	0	0	0	0	0	0	0	1	0	.000	.000	.000
Paul Runge	2B2	R	25	5	8	0	2	0	0	0	1	1	4	0	.250	.333	.250
Paul Zuvella	SS2	R	24	3	5	0	0	0	0	0	0	2	1	0	.000	.375	.000

J. Royster, 13 G at SS

Pitcher	T	Age	G	GS	CG	ShO	IP	H	HR	BB	SO	W-L	Sv	ERA
Craig McMurtry	R	23	36	35	6	3	224.2	204	13	88	105	15-9	0	3.08
Pascual Perez	R	26	33	33	7	1	215.1	213	20	51	144	15-8	0	3.43
Phil Niekro	R	44	34	33	2	0	201.2	212	18	105	128	11-10	0	3.97
Ken Dayley	L	24	24	16	0	0	104.2	100	12	39	70	5-8	0	4.30
Len Barker†	R	27	6	6	0	0	33.0	31	0	14	21	1-3	0	3.82
Bob Walk	R	26	1	1	0	0	3.2	7	0	2	4	0-0	0	7.36
Steve Bedrosian	R	25	70	1	0	0	120.0	100	11	51	114	9-10	19	3.60
Terry Forster	L	31	56	0	0	0	79.1	60	3	31	54	3-2	13	2.16
Donnie Moore	R	29	43	0	0	0	68.2	72	6	10	41	2-3	6	3.67
Gene Garber	R	35	43	0	0	0	60.2	72	8	23	45	4-5	9	4.60
Rick Camp	R	30	40	16	1	0	140.0	146	16	38	61	10-9	0	3.79
Pete Falcone	L	29	33	15	2	0	106.2	102	14	60	59	9-4	0	3.63
Rick Behenna†	R	23	14	6	0	0	37.1	37	7	12	17	3-3	0	4.58
Tony Brizzolara	R	26	14	0	0	0	20.1	22	2	6	17	1-0	1	3.54
Rick Mahler	R	29	10	0	0	0	14.1	16	0	9	7	0-0	0	5.02
Tommy Boggs	R	27	5	0	0	0	6.1	8	1	1	5	0-0	0	5.68
Jeff Dedmon	R	23	5	0	0	0	4.0	10	1	0	3	0-0	0	13.50

1983 Houston Astros 3rd NL West 85-77 .525 6.0 GB

Bob Lillis

Player	Gm by Position	B	Age	G	AB	R	H	2B	3B	HR	RBI	BB	SO	SB	Avg	OBP	Slg
Alan Ashby	C85	S	31	87	275	31	63	18	1	8	34	31	38	0	.229	.303	.389
Ray Knight	1B143	R	30	145	507	43	154	36	4	9	70	42	62	0	.304	.355	.444
Bill Doran	2B153	S	25	154	535	70	145	12	7	8	39	86	67	12	.271	.371	.364
Phil Garner	3B154	R	34	154	567	76	135	24	2	14	79	63	84	18	.238	.317	.362
Dickie Thon	SS154	R	25	154	619	81	177	28	9	20	79	54	73	34	.286	.341	.457
Jose Cruz	OF160	L	35	160	594	85	189	28	8	14	92	65	86	30	.318	.385	.463
Terry Puhl	OF124	L	26	137	465	66	136	25	7	8	44	36	48	24	.292	.343	.428
Omar Moreno†	OF97	L	30	97	405	48	98	12	11	0	25	22	72	30	.242	.282	.326
Kevin Bass	OF52	S	24	88	195	25	46	7	3	2	18	6	27	2	.236	.257	.333
Tony Scott	OF61	S	31	80	186	20	42	6	1	2	17	11	39	5	.226	.264	.301
Jerry Mumphrey†	OF43	S	30	44	143	17	48	10	2	1	17	22	23	5	.336	.425	.455
Denny Walling	1B42,3B13,OF13	L	29	100	135	24	40	5	3	3	19	15	16	2	.296	.364	.444
Craig Reynolds	2B26,3B15,SS8*	L	30	65	98	10	21	3	0	1	6	6	10	0	.214	.260	.276
Luis Pujols	C39	R	27	40	87	4	17	2	0	0	12	5	14	0	.195	.234	.218
John Mizerock	C33	L	22	33	85	8	13	4	1	1	10	12	15	0	.153	.263	.259
Harry Spilman	1B19,C6	L	28	42	78	7	13	3	0	1	9	5	12	0	.167	.212	.244
George Bjorkman	C29	R	26	29	75	8	17	4	0	2	14	16	29	0	.227	.370	.360
Tim Tolman	1B7,OF3	R	27	43	56	4	11	4	0	2	10	6	9	0	.196	.270	.375
Scott Loucks	OF6	R	26	7	14	2	3	0	0	0	0	1	4	2	.214	.267	.214
Bert Pena	SS4	R	23	4	8	0	1	0	0	0	0	2	2	0	.125	.300	.125

C. Reynolds, 1 G at OF

Pitcher	T	Age	G	GS	CG	ShO	IP	H	HR	BB	SO	W-L	Sv	ERA
Joe Niekro	R	38	38	38	9	1	263.2	238	15	101	152	15-14	0	3.48
Bob Knepper	L	29	35	29	4	3	203.0	202	12	71	125	6-13	0	3.19
Nolan Ryan	R	36	29	29	5	2	196.1	134	9	101	183	14-9	0	2.98
Mike Scott	R	28	24	24	2	2	145.0	143	8	46	73	10-6	0	3.72
Jeff Heathcock	R	23	6	3	0	0	28.0	19	1	4	12	2-1	1	3.21
Frank DiPino	L	26	53	0	0	0	71.1	52	2	20	67	3-4	20	2.65
Bill Dawley	R	25	48	0	0	0	79.2	51	9	22	60	6-6	14	2.82
Dave Smith	R	28	42	0	0	0	72.2	72	2	36	41	3-1	6	3.10
Vern Ruhle	R	32	41	9	0	0	114.2	107	13	36	43	8-5	3	3.69
Mike LaCoss	R	27	38	17	2	0	138.0	142	10	56	53	5-7	1	4.43
Frank LaCorte	R	31	37	0	0	0	53.1	35	8	28	48	4-4	3	5.06
Mike Madden	L	26	28	13	0	0	94.2	76	4	45	44	9-5	0	3.14
Julio Solano	R	23	4	0	0	0	6.0	5	1	4	3	0-2	0	6.00

1983 San Diego Padres 4th NL West 81-81 .500 10.0 GB

Dick Williams

Player	Gm by Position	B	Age	G	AB	R	H	2B	3B	HR	RBI	BB	SO	SB	Avg	OBP	Slg
Terry Kennedy	C143,1B4	L	27	149	549	47	156	27	2	17	98	51	89	1	.284	.342	.434
Steve Garvey	1B100	R	34	100	388	76	114	22	0	14	59	29	39	4	.294	.344	.459
Juan Bonilla	2B149	R	27	152	556	55	132	17	4	4	45	50	40	3	.237	.301	.304
Luis Salazar	3B118,SS19	R	27	134	481	52	124	16	2	14	45	17	80	24	.258	.285	.387
Garry Templeton	SS123	S	27	126	460	39	121	20	2	3	40	21	57	16	.263	.294	.335
Ruppert Jones	OF111,1B5	L	28	133	335	42	78	12	3	12	49	35	58	11	.233	.305	.394
Alan Wiggins	OF105,1B45	S	25	144	503	83	139	20	2	0	22	65	43	66	.276	.360	.324
Sixto Lezcano†	OF91	R	29	97	317	41	74	11	2	8	49	47	66	0	.233	.331	.356
Tony Gwynn	OF81	L	23	86	304	34	94	12	2	1	37	23	21	7	.309	.355	.372
Gene Richards	OF54	L	29	95	233	37	64	11	3	3	22	17	17	14	.275	.325	.386
Bobby Brown	OF54	S	29	57	225	40	60	5	3	5	22	23	38	27	.267	.333	.382
Tim Flannery	3B52,2B21,SS7	L	25	92	214	24	50	7	3	3	19	20	23	2	.234	.309	.336
Kurt Bevacqua	1B27,3B12,OF12	R	36	74	156	17	38	7	0	2	24	18	33	0	.244	.320	.327
Kevin McReynolds	OF38	R	23	39	140	15	31	3	1	4	14	12	29	2	.221	.277	.343
Mario Ramirez	SS38,3B1	R	25	55	107	11	21	6	3	0	12	20	23	0	.196	.326	.308
Doug Gwosdz	C32	R	23	39	55	7	6	1	0	1	4	7	19	0	.109	.210	.182
Bruce Bochy	C11	R	28	23	42	2	9	1	1	0	3	0	9	0	.214	.205	.286
Jerry Turner	OF1	L	29	25	23	1	3	0	0	0	0	1	8	0	.130	.167	.130
Joe Lefebvre†	OF6,3B4,C2	L	27	18	20	1	5	0	0	0	1	2	3	0	.250	.318	.250
George Hinshaw	3B5,2B1	R	23	7	16	1	7	1	0	0	4	0	4	1	.438	.438	.500
Gerry Davis	OF5	R	24	5	15	3	5	2	0	0	1	3	4	1	.333	.444	.467
Edwin Rodriguez	2B5,SS2,3B1	R	22	7	12	1	2	1	0	0	0	1	3	0	.167	.231	.250
Jody Lansford	1B8	R	22	12	8	1	2	0	0	1	2	0	3	0	.250	.250	.625

Pitcher	T	Age	G	GS	CG	ShO	IP	H	HR	BB	SO	W-L	Sv	ERA
Eric Show	R	27	35	33	4	2	200.2	201	25	74	120	15-12	0	4.17
Tim Lollar	L	27	30	30	1	0	175.2	170	22	85	135	7-12	0	4.61
Dave Dravecky	L	27	28	28	9	1	183.2	181	18	44	74	14-10	0	3.58
Ed Whitson	R	28	31	21	2	0	144.1	143	23	50	81	5-7	1	4.30
Andy Hawkins	R	23	21	19	4	1	119.2	106	8	48	59	5-7	0	2.93
Mark Thurmond	L	26	21	18	2	0	115.1	104	7	33	49	7-3	0	2.65
Luis DeLeon	R	24	63	0	0	0	111.0	89	8	27	90	6-6	13	2.68
Gary Lucas	L	28	62	0	0	0	91.0	85	9	34	60	5-8	17	2.87
Sid Monge†	L	32	47	0	0	0	68.2	65	4	31	32	7-3	7	3.15
Elias Sosa	R	33	41	1	0	0	72.1	72	7	30	45	1-4	1	4.35
John Montefusco†	R	33	31	10	1	0	95.1	94	6	32	52	9-4	4	3.30
Floyd Chiffer	R	27	15	0	0	0	22.2	17	0	10	15	0-2	1	3.18
Mike Couchee	R	25	8	0	0	0	14.0	12	1	6	5	0-1	0	5.14
Chris Welsh†	L	28	7	1	0	0	14.1	13	2	2	5	0-1	0	2.51
Greg Booker	R	23	6	1	0	0	11.2	18	2	9	5	0-1	0	7.71
Dennis Rasmussen	L	24	4	1	0	0	13.2	10	1	8	13	0-0	0	1.98
Marty Decker	R	26	4	0	0	0	8.2	5	1	3	9	0-0	0	2.08
Steve Fireovid	R	26	3	0	0	0	5.0	4	0	2	1	0-0	0	1.80

876 Seasons: Team Rosters

1983 San Francisco Giants 5th NL West 79-83 .488 12.0 GB

Frank Robinson

Player	Gm by Position	B	Age	G	AB	R	H	2B	3B	HR	RBI	BB	SO	SB	Avg	OBP	Slg
Bob Brenly	C90,1B10,OF2	R	29	104	281	36	63	12	2	7	34	37	48	10	.224	.317	.356
Darrell Evans	1B113,3B32,SS9	L	36	142	523	94	145	29	3	30	82	84	81	6	.277	.378	.516
Brad Wellman	2B74,SS2	R	23	82	182	15	39	3	0	1	16	22	39	5	.214	.296	.247
Tom O'Malley	3B117	L	22	135	410	40	106	16	1	5	45	52	47	2	.259	.345	.339
Johnnie LeMaster	SS139	R	29	141	534	81	128	16	1	6	30	60	96	39	.240	.317	.307
Jeffrey Leonard	OF136	R	27	139	516	74	144	17	7	21	87	35	116	26	.279	.323	.461
Jack Clark	OF133,1B2	R	27	135	492	82	132	25	0	20	66	74	79	5	.268	.361	.441
Chili Davis	OF133	S	23	137	486	54	113	21	2	11	59	55	108	10	.233	.305	.352
Joel Youngblood	2B64,3B28,OF22	R	31	124	373	59	109	20	3	17	53	33	59	7	.292	.356	.499
Max Venable	OF66	L	26	94	228	28	50	7	4	6	27	22	34	15	.219	.295	.364
Milt May†	C56	L	32	66	186	18	46	6	0	6	20	21	23	2	.247	.324	.376
Duane Kuiper	2B64	L	33	72	176	14	44	2	2	0	14	27	13	0	.250	.353	.284
Dave Bergman	1B50,OF6	L	30	90	140	16	40	4	1	6	24	24	21	2	.286	.394	.457
John Rabb	C31,OF2	R	23	40	104	10	24	9	0	1	14	9	17	1	.231	.292	.346
Joe Pettini	SS26,2B14,3B12	R	28	61	86	11	16	0	1	0	7	9	11	4	.186	.260	.209
Chris Smith	1B15,OF4,3B1	S	25	22	67	13	22	6	1	1	11	7	12	0	.328	.403	.493
Dan Gladden	OF18	R	25	18	63	6	14	2	0	1	9	5	11	4	.222	.275	.302
Steve Nicosia†	C9	R	27	15	33	4	11	0	0	0	6	3	2	0	.333	.389	.333
Mike Vail†	1B4,OF2	R	31	18	26	1	4	1	0	0	3	0	7	0	.154	.185	.192
Champ Summers	OF1	L	37	29	22	3	3	0	0	0	3	7	8	0	.136	.333	.136
Guy Sularz	SS6,3B4	R	27	10	20	3	2	0	0	0	0	3	2	0	.100	.217	.100
Jeff Ransom	C6	R	22	6	20	3	4	0	0	1	3	4	7	0	.200	.333	.350
Rich Murray	1B3	R	25	4	10	0	2	0	0	0	1	0	3	0	.200	.200	.200
Wallace Johnson†	2B1	S	26	7	8	0	1	0	0	0	1	0	0	0	.125	.125	.125
Ron Pruitt		R	31	1	1	0	0	0	0	0	0	0	0	0	.000	.000	.000

Pitcher	T	Age	G	GS	CG	ShO	IP	H	HR	BB	SO	W-L	Sv	ERA
Fred Breining	R	27	32	32	6	0	202.2	202	15	60	117	11-12	0	3.82
Mike Krukow	R	31	31	31	2	1	184.1	189	17	76	136	11-11	0	3.95
Bill Laskey	R	25	25	25	1	0	148.1	151	18	45	81	13-10	0	4.19
Atlee Hammaker	L	25	23	23	8	3	172.1	147	9	32	127	10-9	0	2.25
Mark Davis	L	22	20	20	2	2	111.0	93	14	50	83	6-4	0	3.49
Scott Garrelts	R	21	5	5	1	1	35.2	33	4	19	16	2-2	0	2.52
Greg Minton	R	31	73	0	0	0	106.2	117	6	47	38	7-11	22	3.54
Gary Lavelle	L	34	56	0	0	0	87.0	73	4	19	68	7-4	20	2.59
Jim Barr	R	35	53	0	0	0	92.2	106	7	20	47	5-3	2	3.98
Andy McGaffigan	R	26	43	16	0	0	134.1	131	17	39	93	3-9	2	4.29
Renie Martin	R	27	37	6	0	0	94.1	95	11	51	43	2-4	1	4.20
Mark Calvert	R	26	18	4	0	0	37.1	46	2	34	14	1-4	0	6.27
Mike Chris	L	25	7	0	0	0	13.1	16	1	16	5	0-0	0	8.10
Randy Lerch†	L	28	7	0	0	0	10.2	9	1	8	6	1-0	0	3.38
Pat Larkin	L	23	5	0	0	0	10.1	13	1	3	6	0-0	0	4.35
Brian Kingman	R	28	3	0	0	0	4.2	10	0	1	1	0-0	0	7.71

1983 Cincinnati Reds 6th NL West 74-88 .457 17.0 GB

Russ Nixon

Player	Gm by Position	B	Age	G	AB	R	H	2B	3B	HR	RBI	BB	SO	SB	Avg	OBP	Slg
Dann Bilardello	C105	R	24	109	298	27	71	18	0	9	38	15	49	2	.238	.274	.389
Dan Driessen	1B112	L	31	122	386	57	107	17	1	12	57	75	51	6	.277	.390	.420
Ron Oester	2B154	S	27	157	549	63	145	23	5	11	58	49	106	2	.264	.322	.384
Nick Esasky	3B84	R	23	85	302	41	80	10	5	12	46	27	99	6	.265	.328	.450
Dave Concepcion	SS139,3B6,1B1	R	35	143	528	54	123	22	0	1	47	56	81	14	.233	.303	.280
Eddie Milner	OF139	L	28	146	502	77	131	23	6	9	33	68	60	41	.261	.350	.384
Gary Redus	OF120	R	26	125	453	90	112	20	9	17	51	71	111	39	.247	.352	.444
Paul Householder	OF112	S	24	123	380	40	97	24	4	6	43	44	60	12	.255	.335	.387
Cesar Cedeno	OF73,1B17	R	32	98	332	40	77	16	0	9	39	33	53	13	.232	.302	.361
Johnny Bench	3B42,1B32,C5*	R	35	110	310	32	79	15	2	12	54	24	38	0	.255	.308	.432
Duane Walker	OF60	L	26	109	225	14	53	12	1	2	29	20	43	6	.236	.296	.324
Alex Trevino	C63,3B4,2B1	R	25	74	167	14	36	8	1	1	13	17	20	0	.216	.285	.293
Kelly Paris	3B16,2B10,SS7*	R	25	56	120	13	30	6	0	0	7	15	22	8	.250	.336	.300
Alan Knicely	C31,OF8,1B2	R	28	59	98	11	22	3	0	2	10	16	28	0	.224	.333	.316
Tom Foley	SS37,2B5	L	23	68	98	7	20	4	1	0	9	13	17	1	.204	.297	.265
Wayne Krenchicki†	3B39,2B1	L	28	51	77	6	21	2	0	0	11	8	4	0	.273	.345	.299
Jeff Jones	OF13,1B1	R	25	16	44	6	10	3	0	0	5	11	13	2	.227	.379	.295
Dallas Williams	OF12	L	25	18	36	2	2	0	0	0	1	3	6	0	.056	.128	.056
Skeeter Barnes	1B7,3B7	R	26	15	34	5	7	0	0	1	4	7	3	2	.206	.372	.294
Steve Christmas	C7	L	25	9	17	0	1	0	0	0	1	1	3	0	.059	.105	.059
Rafael Landestoy†	1B2,3B1,OF1	S	30	7	5	0	0	0	0	0	0	0	0	0	.000	.000	.000

J. Bench, 1 G at OF; K. Paris, 3 G at 1B

Pitcher	T	Age	G	GS	CG	ShO	IP	H	HR	BB	SO	W-L	Sv	ERA
Mario Soto	R	26	34	34	18	3	273.2	207	28	95	242	17-13	0	2.70
Bruce Berenyi	R	28	32	31	4	1	186.1	173	9	102	151	9-14	0	3.86
Frank Pastore	R	25	36	29	4	1	184.1	207	20	64	93	9-12	0	4.88
Charlie Puleo	R	28	27	24	0	0	143.2	145	18	91	71	6-12	0	4.89
Joe Price	L	26	21	21	5	0	144.0	118	12	46	83	10-6	0	2.88
Jeff Russell	R	21	10	10	2	0	68.1	58	7	22	40	4-5	0	3.03
Bill Scherrer	L	25	73	0	0	0	92.0	73	6	33	57	2-3	10	2.74
Ben Hayes	R	25	60	0	0	0	69.1	82	8	37	44	4-6	7	6.49
Ted Power	R	28	49	6	1	0	111.0	120	10	49	57	5-6	2	4.54
Tom Hume	R	30	48	0	0	0	66.0	66	8	41	34	3-5	9	4.77
Rich Gale	R	29	33	7	0	0	89.2	103	8	43	53	4-6	1	5.82
Brad Lesley	R	24	5	0	0	0	8.1	9	1	0	5	0-0	0	2.16
Keefe Cato	R	25	4	0	0	0	3.2	2	0	1	3	1-0	0	2.45
Greg Harris	R	27	1	0	0	0	1.0	2	0	3	1	0-0	0	27.00

»1984 Detroit Tigers 1st AL East 104-58 .642 —

Sparky Anderson

Player	Gm by Position	B	Age	G	AB	R	H	2B	3B	HR	RBI	BB	SO	SB	Avg	OBP	Slg
Lance Parrish	C127,DH22	R	28	147	578	75	137	16	2	33	98	41	120	2	.237	.287	.443
Dave Bergman	1B114,OF2	L	31	120	271	42	74	8	5	7	44	33	40	3	.273	.351	.417
Lou Whitaker	2B142	L	27	143	558	90	161	25	1	13	56	62	63	6	.289	.357	.407
Howard Johnson	3B108,SS9,DH4*	S	23	116	355	43	88	14	1	12	50	40	67	10	.248	.324	.394
Alan Trammell	SS114,DH22	R	26	139	555	85	174	34	5	14	69	60	63	19	.314	.382	.468
Chet Lemon	OF140,DH1	R	29	141	509	77	146	34	6	20	76	51	83	5	.287	.357	.495
Kirk Gibson	OF139,DH6	L	27	149	531	92	150	23	10	27	91	63	103	29	.282	.363	.516
Larry Herndon	OF117,DH4	R	30	125	407	52	114	18	5	7	43	32	63	6	.280	.333	.400
Darrell Evans	DH62,1B47,3B19	L	37	131	401	60	93	11	1	16	63	77	70	2	.232	.353	.384
Barbaro Garbey	1B65,3B20,DH18*	R	27	110	327	45	94	17	1	5	52	17	35	6	.287	.325	.391
Tom Brookens	3B68,SS28,2B26*	R	30	113	224	32	55	11	4	5	26	19	33	6	.246	.306	.397
Ruppert Jones	OF73,DH2	L	29	79	215	26	61	12	1	12	37	21	47	2	.284	.346	.516
John Grubb	OF36,DH33	L	35	86	176	25	47	5	0	8	17	36	36	1	.267	.395	.432
Marty Castillo	C36,3B33,DH1	R	27	70	141	16	33	5	2	4	17	10	33	1	.234	.285	.383
Rusty Kuntz	OF67,DH10	R	29	84	140	32	40	12	0	2	22	25	28	2	.286	.393	.414
Doug Baker	SS39,2B5	S	23	43	108	15	20	4	1	0	12	7	22	3	.185	.241	.241
Dwight Lowry	C31	L	26	32	45	8	11	2	0	2	7	3	11	0	.244	.292	.422
Scott Earl	2B14	R	23	14	35	3	4	0	1	0	1	0	9	1	.114	.114	.171
Nelson Simmons	OF5,DH4	S	21	9	30	4	13	2	0	0	3	2	5	1	.433	.469	.500
Rod Allen	DH11,OF2	R	24	15	27	6	8	1	0	0	3	2	8	1	.296	.367	.333
Mike Laga	DH4,1B4	L	24	9	11	1	6	0	0	0	1	1	2	0	.545	.583	.545

H. Johnson, 1 G at 1B, 1 G at OF; B. Garbey, 10 G at OF, 3 G at 2B; T. Brookens, 1 G at DH

Pitcher	T	Age	G	GS	CG	ShO	IP	H	HR	BB	SO	W-L	Sv	ERA
Jack Morris	R	29	35	35	9	1	240.1	221	20	87	148	19-11	0	3.60
Dan Petry	R	25	35	35	7	2	233.1	231	21	66	144	18-8	0	3.24
Milt Wilcox	R	34	33	33	0	0	193.2	183	13	66	119	17-8	0	4.00
Juan Berenguer	R	29	31	27	2	1	168.1	146	14	79	118	11-10	0	3.48
Dave Rozema	R	27	29	16	0	0	101.0	110	13	18	48	7-6	0	3.74
Glenn Abbott	R	33	13	8	1	0	44.0	62	9	8	8	3-4	0	5.93
Randy O'Neal	R	23	4	3	0	0	18.2	16	0	6	12	2-1	0	3.38
Willie Hernandez	L	29	80	0	0	0	140.1	96	6	36	112	9-3	32	1.92
Aurelio Lopez	R	35	71	0	0	0	137.2	109	16	52	94	10-1	14	2.94
Doug Bair	R	34	47	1	0	0	93.2	82	10	36	57	5-3	4	3.75
Sid Monge†	L	33	19	0	0	0	36.0	40	5	12	19	1-0	0	4.25
Bill Scherrer†	L	26	18	0	0	0	19.0	14	1	8	16	1-0	0	1.89
Carl Willis†	R	23	10	2	0	0	16.0	25	1	5	4	0-2	0	7.31
Roger Mason	R	25	5	2	0	0	22.0	23	1	10	15	1-1	1	4.50

1984 Toronto Blue Jays 2nd AL East 89-73 .549 15.0 GB

Bobby Cox

Player	Gm by Position	B	Age	G	AB	R	H	2B	3B	HR	RBI	BB	SO	SB	Avg	OBP	Slg
Ernie Whitt	C118	L	32	124	315	35	75	12	1	15	46	43	49	0	.238	.327	.425
Willie Upshaw	1B151,DH1	L	27	152	569	79	158	31	9	19	84	55	86	10	.278	.345	.464
Damaso Garcia	2B149,DH1	R	27	152	633	79	180	32	5	5	46	16	46	46	.284	.310	.374
Rance Mulliniks	3B119,SS3,2B1	L	28	125	343	41	111	21	5	3	42	33	44	2	.324	.383	.440
Alfredo Griffin	SS115,2B21,DH5	S	26	140	419	53	101	8	2	4	30	4	33	11	.241	.248	.298
Lloyd Moseby	OF156	L	24	158	592	97	166	28	15	18	92	78	122	39	.280	.368	.470
George Bell	OF147,DH7,3B3	R	24	159	606	85	177	39	4	26	87	24	86	11	.292	.326	.498
Dave Collins	OF108,1B6,DH4	S	31	128	441	59	136	24	15	2	44	33	41	60	.308	.366	.444
Cliff Johnson	DH109,1B2	R	36	127	359	51	109	23	1	16	61	50	62	0	.304	.390	.507
Jesse Barfield	OF88,DH9	R	24	110	320	51	91	14	1	14	49	35	81	8	.284	.357	.466
Garth Iorg	3B112,2B7,SS2*	R	29	121	247	24	56	10	3	1	25	5	16	1	.227	.244	.304
Willie Aikens	DH81,1B2	L	29	93	234	21	48	7	0	11	26	29	56	0	.205	.298	.376
Tony Fernandez	SS73,3B10,DH1	S	22	88	233	29	63	5	3	3	19	17	15	5	.270	.317	.356
Buck Martinez	C98,DH1	R	35	102	232	24	51	13	1	5	37	29	49	0	.220	.301	.349
Rick Leach	OF23,1B15,DH6*	L	27	65	88	11	23	6	2	0	7	8	14	0	.261	.320	.375
Mitch Webster	OF10,DH9,1B1	S	25	26	22	9	5	2	1	0	4	1	7	0	.227	.261	.409
Kelly Gruber	3B12,OF2,SS1	R	22	15	16	1	1	0	0	1	2	0	5	0	.063	.063	.250
Fred Manrique	2B9,DH1	R	22	10	9	0	3	0	0	0	1	0	1	0	.333	.333	.333
Ron Shepherd	OF5,DH4	R	23	12	4	0	0	0	0	0	0	0	3	0	.000	.000	.000
Geno Petralli	DH1,C1	S	24	3	3	0	0	0	0	0	0	0	0	0	.000	.000	.000
Toby Hernandez	C3	R	25	3	2	1	1	0	0	0	0	0	0	0	.500	.500	.500

G. Iorg, 1 G at DH; R. Leach, 1 G at P

Pitcher	T	Age	G	GS	CG	ShO	IP	H	HR	BB	SO	W-L	Sv	ERA
Jim Clancy	R	28	36	36	5	0	219.2	249	25	88	118	13-15	0	5.12
Dave Stieb	R	26	35	35	11	2	267.0	215	19	88	198	16-8	0	2.83
Doyle Alexander	R	33	36	35	11	2	261.2	238	21	59	139	17-6	0	3.13
Luis Leal	R	27	35	35	6	2	222.1	221	27	77	134	13-8	0	3.89
Jimmy Key	L	23	63	0	0	0	62.0	70	8	32	44	4-5	10	4.65
Dennis Lamp	R	31	56	4	0	0	85.0	97	9	38	45	8-8	9	4.55
Roy Lee Jackson	R	30	54	0	0	0	86.0	73	12	31	58	7-8	10	3.56
Jim Gott	R	24	35	12	1	1	109.2	93	7	49	73	7-6	2	4.02
Jim Acker	R	25	32	3	0	0	72.0	79	3	25	33	3-5	1	4.38
Bryan Clark	L	27	20	3	0	0	45.2	66	6	22	21	1-2	0	5.91
Ron Musselman	R	29	11	0	0	0	21.1	18	2	10	9	0-2	1	2.11
Joey McLaughlin†	R	27	6	0	0	0	10.2	12	0	7	3	0-0	0	2.53
Rick Leach	L	27	1	0	0	0	1.0	2	1	2	0	0-0	0	27.00

1984 New York Yankees 3rd AL East 87-75 .537 17.0 GB

Yogi Berra

Player	Gm by Position	B	Age	G	AB	R	H	2B	3B	HR	RBI	BB	SO	SB	Avg	OBP	Slg
Butch Wynegar	C126	S	28	129	442	48	118	13	1	6	45	65	35	1	.267	.360	.342
Don Mattingly	1B133,OF19	L	23	153	603	91	207	44	2	23	110	41	33	1	.343	.381	.537
Willie Randolph	2B142	R	29	142	564	86	162	24	2	2	31	86	42	10	.287	.377	.348
Toby Harrah	3B74,2B4,OF1	R	35	88	253	40	55	9	4	1	26	42	28	3	.217	.331	.296
Bobby Meacham	SS96,2B2	S	23	99	360	62	91	13	4	2	25	32	70	9	.253	.312	.328
Dave Winfield	OF140	R	32	141	567	106	193	34	4	19	100	53	71	6	.340	.393	.515
Omar Moreno	OF108,DH1	L	31	117	355	37	92	12	6	4	38	18	48	20	.259	.294	.361
Ken Griffey Sr.	OF82,1B27,DH2	L	34	120	399	44	109	20	1	7	56	29	32	2	.273	.321	.381
Don Baylor	DH127,OF5	R	35	134	493	84	129	29	1	27	89	38	68	1	.262	.341	.489
Steve Kemp	OF75,DH12	L	29	94	313	37	91	12	1	7	41	40	54	4	.291	.369	.403
Roy Smalley†	3B35,SS13,DH5*	S	31	67	209	17	50	8	1	7	26	15	35	2	.239	.286	.388
Mike Pagliarulo	3B67	L	24	67	201	24	48	15	3	7	34	15	46	0	.239	.288	.448
Tim Foli	SS28,2B21,3B10*	R	33	61	163	8	41	11	0	0	16	2	16	0	.252	.265	.319
Andre Robertson	SS49,2B6	R	26	52	140	10	30	5	1	0	6	4	20	0	.214	.236	.264
Brian Dayett	OF62,DH1	R	27	64	127	14	31	8	0	4	23	9	14	0	.244	.295	.402
Oscar Gamble	DH26,OF12	L	34	54	125	17	23	2	0	10	27	25	18	1	.184	.318	.440
Rick Cerone	C38	R	30	38	120	8	25	3	0	2	13	9	15	1	.208	.269	.283
Lou Piniella	OF24,DH2	R	40	29	86	8	26	4	1	1	6	7	5	0	.302	.355	.407
Victor Mata	OF28	R	23	30	70	8	23	5	0	1	6	0	12	1	.329	.333	.443
Mike O'Berry	C12,3B1	R	30	13	32	3	8	2	0	0	5	2	2	0	.250	.294	.313
Scott Bradley	OF5,C3	L	24	9	21	3	6	1	0	0	2	1	1	0	.286	.318	.333
Stan Javier	OF5	S	20	7	7	1	1	0	0	0	0	0	1	0	.143	.143	.143
Rex Hudler	2B9	R	23	9	7	2	1	1	0	0	0	1	5	0	.143	.333	.286
Keith Smith	SS2	S	22	2	4	0	0	0	0	0	0	0	2	0	.000	.200	.000

R. Smalley, 5 G at 1B; T. Foli, 2 G at 1B

Pitcher	T	Age	G	GS	CG	ShO	IP	H	HR	BB	SO	W-L	Sv	ERA
Phil Niekro	R	45	32	31	5	1	215.2	219	15	76	136	16-8	0	3.09
Ron Guidry	L	33	29	28	5	1	195.2	223	24	44	127	10-11	0	4.51
Ray Fontenot	L	26	35	24	0	0	169.1	189	8	58	85	8-9	0	3.61
Dennis Rasmussen	L	25	24	24	1	0	147.2	127	16	60	110	9-6	0	4.57
Joe Cowley	R	25	16	11	3	1	83.1	75	12	31	71	9-2	0	3.56
John Montefusco	R	34	11	11	0	0	55.1	55	5	13	23	5-3	0	3.58
Shane Rawley†	L	28	11	10	0	0	42.0	46	0	27	24	2-3	0	6.21
Marty Bystrom†	R	25	7	7	0	0	39.1	34	3	13	24	2-2	0	2.97
Jim Deshaies	L	24	2	2	0	0	7.0	14	1	7	5	0-1	0	11.57
Dave Righetti	L	25	64	0	0	0	96.1	79	5	37	90	5-6	31	2.34
Jay Howell	R	28	61	1	0	0	103.2	86	5	34	109	9-4	7	2.69
Bob Shirley	L	30	41	7	1	0	114.1	119	8	38	48	3-3	0	3.38
Mike Armstrong	R	30	36	0	0	0	54.1	47	6	26	43	3-2	1	3.48
Jose Rijo	R	19	24	5	0	0	62.1	74	5	33	47	2-8	2	4.76
Clay Christiansen	R	26	24	1	0	0	38.2	50	4	12	27	2-4	2	6.05
Dale Murray	R	34	19	0	0	0	23.2	30	2	5	13	1-2	0	4.94
Curt Brown	R	24	13	0	0	0	16.2	18	1	4	10	1-1	0	2.70

1984 Boston Red Sox 4th AL East 86-76 .531 18.0 GB

Ralph Houk

Player	Gm by Position	B	Age	G	AB	R	H	2B	3B	HR	RBI	BB	SO	SB	Avg	OBP	Slg
Rich Gedman	C125	L	24	133	449	54	121	26	4	24	72	29	72	0	.269	.312	.506
Bill Buckner†	1B113	L	34	114	439	51	122	21	2	11	67	24	38	2	.278	.321	.410
Marty Barrett	2B136	R	26	139	475	56	144	23	3	3	45	42	25	5	.303	.358	.383
Wade Boggs	3B156,DH2	L	26	158	625	109	203	31	4	6	55	89	44	3	.325	.407	.416
Jackie Gutierrez	SS150	R	24	151	449	55	118	12	3	2	29	15	49	12	.263	.284	.316
Dwight Evans	OF161,DH1	R	32	162	630	121	186	37	8	32	104	96	115	3	.295	.388	.532
Jim Rice	OF157,DH2	R	31	159	657	98	184	25	7	28	122	44	102	4	.280	.323	.467
Tony Armas	OF126,DH31	R	30	157	639	107	171	29	5	43	123	32	156	1	.268	.300	.531
Mike Easler	DH126,1B29	L	33	156	601	87	188	31	5	27	91	58	134	1	.313	.376	.516
Reid Nichols	OF48,DH1	R	25	74	124	14	28	5	1	1	14	12	18	2	.226	.307	.306
Rick Miller	OF31,1B8	L	36	95	123	17	32	5	1	0	12	17	22	1	.260	.348	.317
Jerry Remy	2B24	L	31	30	104	8	26	1	1	0	8	7	11	4	.250	.297	.279
Gary Allenson	C35	R	29	35	83	9	19	2	0	2	8	9	14	0	.229	.304	.325
Glenn Hoffman	SS56,3B4,2B2	R	25	64	74	8	14	4	0	0	4	5	10	0	.189	.241	.243
Ed Jurak	1B19,2B14,3B9*	R	26	47	66	6	16	3	1	1	7	12	12	0	.242	.359	.364
Jeff Newman	C24	R	35	24	63	5	14	2	0	1	3	5	16	0	.222	.275	.302
Dave Stapleton	1B10,DH1	R	30	13	39	4	9	2	0	0	1	3	3	0	.231	.286	.282
Marc Sullivan	C2	R	25	2	6	1	3	0	0	0	1	1	0	0	.500	.571	.500
Chico Walker	2B1	S	26	3	2	0	0	0	0	0	0	0	1	0	.000	.000	.000

E. Jurak, 2 G at SS

Pitcher	T	Age	G	GS	CG	ShO	IP	H	HR	BB	SO	W-L	Sv	ERA
Bruce Hurst	L	26	33	33	9	2	218.0	232	25	88	136	12-12	0	3.92
Bobby Ojeda	L	26	33	32	8	5	216.2	211	17	96	137	12-12	0	3.99
Oil Can Boyd	R	24	29	26	10	3	197.2	207	18	53	134	12-12	0	4.37
Al Nipper	R	25	29	24	6	0	182.2	183	18	52	84	11-6	0	3.89
Roger Clemens	R	21	21	20	5	1	133.1	146	13	29	126	9-4	0	4.32
Mike Brown	R	25	15	11	0	0	67.0	104	9	19	32	1-8	0	6.85
Dennis Eckersley†	R	29	9	9	2	0	64.2	71	10	13	33	4-4	0	5.01
Bob Stanley	R	29	57	0	0	0	106.2	113	9	23	52	9-10	22	3.54
Mark Clear	R	28	47	0	0	0	67.0	47	2	70	76	8-3	8	4.03
Steve Crawford	R	26	35	0	0	0	62.0	69	6	21	21	5-0	1	3.34
John Henry Johnson	L	27	30	3	0	0	63.2	64	7	27	57	1-2	1	3.53
Rich Gale	R	30	13	4	0	0	43.2	57	6	18	28	2-3	0	5.56
Charlie Mitchell	R	22	10	0	0	0	16.1	14	1	6	7	0-0	0	2.76
Jim Dorsey	R	28	2	0	0	0	2.2	6	0	2	4	0-0	0	10.13

1984 Baltimore Orioles 5th AL East 85-77 .525 19.0 GB

Joe Altobelli

Player	Gm by Position	B	Age	G	AB	R	H	2B	3B	HR	RBI	BB	SO	SB	Avg	OBP	Slg
Rick Dempsey	C108	R	34	109	330	37	76	11	0	11	34	40	58	1	.230	.312	.364
Eddie Murray	1B159,DH3	S	28	162	588	97	180	26	3	29	110	107	87	10	.306	.410	.509
Rich Dauer	2B123,3B3	R	31	127	397	29	101	26	0	2	24	24	23	1	.254	.296	.335
Wayne Gross	3B117,1B3,DH1	L	32	127	342	53	74	9	1	22	64	68	69	1	.216	.346	.442
Cal Ripken Jr.	SS162	R	23	162	641	103	195	37	7	27	86	71	89	2	.304	.374	.510
John Shelby	OF124	S	26	128	383	44	80	12	5	6	30	20	71	12	.209	.248	.313
Gary Roenicke	OF117	R	29	121	326	36	73	19	1	10	44	58	43	1	.224	.346	.380
Mike Young	OF115,DH1	S	24	123	401	59	101	17	2	17	52	58	110	6	.252	.355	.431
Ken Singleton	DH103	S	37	111	363	28	78	7	1	6	36	37	60	0	.215	.286	.289
Al Bumbry	OF99,DH9	L	37	119	344	47	93	12	1	3	24	25	35	9	.270	.317	.337
John Lowenstein	OF67,DH22,1B2	L	37	105	270	34	64	13	0	8	28	33	54	1	.237	.319	.374
Floyd Rayford	C66,3B22,1B1	R	26	86	250	24	64	14	0	4	27	12	51	0	.256	.296	.360
Jim Dwyer	OF52,DH3	L	34	76	161	22	41	9	1	2	21	23	24	0	.255	.337	.360
Lenn Sakata	2B76,OF1	R	30	81	157	23	30	1	0	3	11	6	15	4	.191	.221	.255
Todd Cruz	3B89,DH1,P1	R	28	96	142	15	31	4	0	3	9	8	33	1	.218	.263	.310
Bennie Ayala	DH34,OF13	R	33	60	118	9	25	6	0	4	24	8	24	1	.212	.258	.364
Dan Ford	OF15,DH8	R	32	25	91	7	21	4	0	1	5	7	13	1	.231	.286	.308
Joe Nolan	DH11,C6	L	33	35	62	2	18	1	1	1	9	12	10	0	.290	.400	.387
Ron Jackson†	3B10	R	31	12	28	0	8	2	0	0	2	0	4	0	.286	.286	.357
Jim Traber	DH9	L	22	10	21	3	5	0	0	0	2	2	4	0	.238	.292	.238
Vic Rodriguez	2B7,DH3	R	22	11	17	4	7	3	0	0	2	0	2	0	.412	.412	.588
Larry Sheets	OF7	L	24	8	16	3	7	1	0	1	2	1	3	0	.438	.471	.688
Orlando Sanchez†	C4	L	27	4	8	0	2	0	0	0	1	0	2	0	.250	.250	.250

Pitcher	T	Age	G	GS	CG	ShO	IP	H	HR	BB	SO	W-L	Sv	ERA
Mike Boddicker	R	26	34	34	16	4	261.1	218	23	81	128	20-11	0	2.79
Mike Flanagan	L	32	34	34	10	2	226.2	213	24	81	115	13-13	0	3.53
Storm Davis	R	22	35	31	10	2	225.0	205	7	71	105	14-9	1	3.12
Scott McGregor	L	30	30	30	10	3	196.1	216	18	54	67	15-12	0	3.94
Dennis Martinez	R	29	34	20	2	0	141.2	145	26	37	77	6-9	0	5.02
Jim Palmer	R	38	5	3	0	0	17.2	22	2	17	4	0-3	0	9.17
Ken Dixon	R	23	2	2	0	0	13.0	14	1	4	8	0-1	0	4.15
Sammy Stewart	R	29	60	0	0	0	93.0	81	7	47	56	7-4	13	3.29
Tippy Martinez	L	34	55	0	0	0	89.2	88	9	51	72	4-9	17	3.91
Tom Underwood	L	30	37	1	0	0	71.2	78	8	31	39	1-0	1	3.52
Bill Swaggerty	R	27	23	6	0	0	57.0	68	7	21	18	3-2	0	5.21
Mark Brown	R	24	9	0	0	0	23.0	22	2	7	10	1-2	0	3.91
John Pacella	R	27	6	1	0	0	14.2	15	2	9	8	0-1	0	6.75
Nate Snell	R	31	5	0	0	0	7.2	8	1	1	7	1-1	0	2.35
Todd Cruz	R	28	1	0	0	0	1.0	0	0	0	0	0-0	0	0.00

1984 Cleveland Indians 6th AL East 75-87 .463 29.0 GB

Pat Corrales

Player	Gm by Position	B	Age	G	AB	R	H	2B	3B	HR	RBI	BB	SO	SB	Avg	OBP	Slg
Jerry Willard	C76,DH1	L	24	87	246	21	55	8	1	10	37	26	55	1	.224	.295	.386
Mike Hargrove	1B124	L	34	133	352	44	94	14	2	2	44	53	38	0	.267	.361	.335
Tony Bernazard	2B136,DH1	S	27	140	439	44	97	15	4	2	38	43	70	20	.221	.290	.287
Brook Jacoby	3B126,SS1	R	24	126	439	64	116	19	3	7	40	32	73	3	.264	.314	.369
Julio Franco	SS159,DH1	R	22	160	658	82	188	22	5	3	79	43	68	19	.286	.331	.348
Brett Butler	OF156	L	27	159	602	108	162	25	9	3	49	86	62	52	.269	.361	.355
George Vukovich	OF130	L	28	134	437	38	133	22	5	9	60	34	61	1	.304	.354	.439
Carmelo Castillo	OF70,DH2	R	26	87	211	36	55	9	2	10	36	21	32	1	.261	.329	.464
Andre Thornton	DH144,1B11	R	34	155	587	91	159	26	0	33	99	91	79	6	.271	.366	.484
Pat Tabler	1B67,OF43,3B36*	R	26	144	473	66	137	21	3	10	68	47	62	3	.290	.354	.410
Mel Hall†	OF69,DH9	L	23	83	257	43	66	13	1	7	30	35	55	1	.257	.344	.397
Joe Carter	OF59,1B7	R	24	66	244	32	67	6	1	13	41	11	48	2	.275	.307	.467
Chris Bando	C63,DH1,1B1*	S	28	75	220	38	64	11	0	12	41	33	35	1	.291	.377	.505
Ron Hassey†	C44,DH1,1B1	L	31	48	149	11	38	5	1	0	19	15	26	1	.255	.321	.302
Mike Fischlin	2B55,3B17,SS15	R	28	85	133	17	30	4	2	1	14	12	20	2	.226	.290	.308
Otis Nixon	OF46	S	25	49	91	16	14	0	0	0	1	8	11	12	.154	.220	.154
Broderick Perkins	DH10,1B2	L	29	58	66	5	13	1	0	0	4	7	10	0	.197	.276	.212
Jeff Moronko	3B6,DH1	R	24	7	19	1	3	1	0	0	3	3	5	0	.158	.273	.211
Junior Noboa	2B19,DH1	R	19	23	11	3	4	0	0	0	0	0	2	1	.364	.364	.364
Kevin Rhomberg	OF7,DH1,1B1*	R	28	13	8	0	2	0	0	0	0	0	3	0	.250	.250	.250
Jamie Quirk†	C1	L	29	1	1	1	1	0	0	1	1	0	0	0	1.000	1.000	4.000

P. Tabler, 1 G at DH, 1 G at 2B; C. Bando, 1 G at 3B; K. Rhomberg, 1 G at 2B

Pitcher	T	Age	G	GS	CG	ShO	IP	H	HR	BB	SO	W-L	Sv	ERA
Neal Heaton	L	24	38	34	4	1	198.2	231	21	75	75	12-15	0	5.21
Bert Blyleven	R	33	33	32	12	4	245.0	204	19	74	170	19-7	0	2.87
Steve Comer	R	30	22	20	1	0	117.1	146	11	39	39	4-8	0	5.68
Steve Farr	R	27	31	16	0	0	116.0	106	14	46	83	3-11	1	4.58
Rick Sutcliffe†	R	28	15	15	2	0	94.1	111	7	46	58	4-5	0	5.15
Roy Smith	R	22	22	14	0	0	86.1	91	14	40	55	5-5	0	4.59
Don Schulze†	R	21	19	14	2	0	85.2	105	9	27	39	3-6	0	4.83
Dan Spillner†	R	32	14	8	0	0	51.0	70	3	22	23	0-5	1	5.65
Jerry Ujdur	R	27	4	3	0	0	14.1	22	1	6	6	1-2	0	6.91
Rick Behenna	R	24	3	3	0	0	9.2	17	5	8	6	0-3	0	13.97
Jose Roman	R	21	3	2	0	0	6.0	9	1	11	3	0-2	0	18.00
Ernie Camacho	R	29	69	0	0	0	100.0	83	6	37	48	5-9	23	2.43
Mike Jeffcoat	L	24	63	1	0	0	75.1	82	7	24	41	5-2	1	2.99
Tom Waddell	R	25	58	0	0	0	97.0	68	12	37	59	7-4	6	3.06
Jamie Easterly	L	31	26	1	0	0	69.1	74	3	23	42	3-1	2	3.38
Luis Aponte	R	31	25	0	0	0	50.1	53	5	15	25	1-0	0	4.11
George Frazier†	R	29	22	0	0	0	44.1	45	3	14	24	3-2	1	3.65
Jeff Barkley	R	24	3	0	0	0	4.0	6	0	1	4	0-0	0	6.75
Ramon Romero	L	25	1	0	0	0	3.0	0	0	0	3	0-0	0	0.00

1984 Milwaukee Brewers 7th AL East 67-94 .416 36.5 GB

Rene Lachemann

Player	Gm by Position	B	Age	G	AB	R	H	2B	3B	HR	RBI	BB	SO	SB	Avg	OBP	Slg
Jim Sundberg	C109	R	33	110	348	43	91	19	4	7	43	38	63	1	.261	.332	.399
Cecil Cooper	1B122,DH26	L	34	148	603	63	166	28	3	11	67	27	59	8	.275	.307	.386
Jim Gantner	2B153	L	31	153	613	61	173	27	1	3	56	30	51	6	.282	.314	.344
Ed Romero	3B59,SS39,2B11*	R	26	116	357	36	90	12	0	1	31	29	43	3	.252	.307	.294
Robin Yount	SS120,DH39	R	28	160	624	105	186	27	7	16	80	67	67	14	.298	.362	.441
Ben Oglivie	OF125,DH1	L	35	131	461	49	121	16	2	12	60	44	56	0	.262	.327	.384
Dion James	OF118	L	21	128	387	52	114	19	5	1	30	32	41	10	.295	.351	.377
Rick Manning	OF114,DH1	L	29	119	341	53	85	10	5	7	31	34	32	5	.249	.318	.370
Ted Simmons	DH77,1B37,3B14	S	34	132	497	44	110	23	2	4	52	30	40	3	.221	.269	.300
Bill Schroeder	C58,DH3,1B1	R	25	61	210	29	54	6	0	14	25	8	54	0	.257	.288	.486
Mark Brouhard	OF52,DH8	R	28	66	197	20	47	7	0	6	22	16	36	0	.239	.298	.365
Charlie Moore	OF61,C7	R	31	70	188	13	44	7	1	2	17	10	26	0	.234	.275	.314
Bobby Clark	OF56	R	29	58	169	17	44	7	2	2	16	16	35	1	.260	.326	.361
Roy Howell	3B46,DH8,1B4	L	30	68	164	12	38	5	1	4	17	8	32	0	.232	.284	.348
Randy Ready	3B36	R	24	37	123	13	23	6	1	3	13	14	18	0	.187	.270	.325
Willie Lozado	3B36,SS6,DH1*	R	25	43	107	15	29	8	2	1	20	12	23	0	.271	.339	.411
Doug Loman	OF23	L	26	23	76	13	21	4	0	2	12	15	7	0	.276	.402	.408
Paul Molitor	3B7,DH4	R	27	13	46	3	10	1	0	0	6	2	8	1	.217	.245	.239

E. Romero, 4 G at 1B, 2 G at DH, 1 G at OF; W. Lozado, 1 G at 2B

Pitcher	T	Age	G	GS	CG	ShO	IP	H	HR	BB	SO	W-L	Sv	ERA
Don Sutton	R	39	33	33	1	0	212.2	224	24	51	143	14-12	0	3.77
Moose Haas	R	28	31	30	4	0	189.1	205	15	43	84	9-11	0	3.99
Jamie Cocanower	R	27	33	27	1	0	174.2	188	13	78	65	8-16	0	4.02
Mike Caldwell	L	35	26	19	4	1	126.0	160	11	21	34	6-13	0	4.64
Chuck Porter	R	29	17	12	1	0	81.1	92	8	12	48	6-4	0	3.87
Bob Gibson	R	27	18	9	1	1	69.0	61	10	47	54	2-5	0	4.96
Tom Candiotti	R	26	8	6	0	0	32.1	38	5	10	23	2-2	0	5.29
Andy Beene	R	27	5	3	0	0	18.2	28	1	9	11	0-2	0	11.09
Peter Ladd	R	27	54	1	0	0	91.0	94	16	38	75	4-9	3	5.24
Tom Tellmann	R	30	50	0	0	0	81.0	82	6	31	28	6-3	4	2.78
Rick Waits	L	32	47	1	0	0	73.0	84	7	24	49	3-2	3	3.58
Bob McClure	L	32	39	18	1	0	139.2	154	9	52	68	4-8	1	4.38
Rollie Fingers	R	37	33	0	0	0	46.0	38	5	13	40	1-2	23	1.96
Ray Searage	L	29	21	0	0	0	38.1	20	0	16	29	2-1	6	0.70
Jack Lazorko	R	28	15	1	0	0	39.2	37	7	22	24	0-1	0	4.31
Jim Kern†	R	35	6	0	0	0	4.2	6	0	3	4	1-0	0	0.00
Paul Hartzell	R	30	4	1	0	0	10.1	17	0	6	3	0-1	0	7.84
Jerry Augustine	L	31	4	0	0	0	5.1	4	0	4	3	0-0	0	0.00

1984 Kansas City Royals 1st AL West 84-78 .519 —

Dick Howser

Player	Gm by Position	B	Age	G	AB	R	H	2B	3B	HR	RBI	BB	SO	SB	Avg	OBP	Slg
Don Slaught	C123,DH1	R	25	124	409	48	108	27	4	4	42	20	55	0	.264	.297	.379
Steve Balboni	1B125,DH1	R	27	126	438	58	107	23	2	28	77	45	139	0	.244	.320	.498
Frank White	2B129	R	33	129	479	58	130	22	5	17	56	27	72	5	.271	.311	.445
Greg Pryor	3B105,2B22,SS2*	R	34	123	270	32	71	11	1	4	25	12	28	0	.263	.301	.356
Onix Concepcion	SS85,2B6,3B1	R	26	90	287	36	81	9	2	1	23	14	33	9	.282	.319	.338
Darryl Motley	OF138	R	24	146	522	64	148	25	6	15	70	28	73	10	.284	.319	.441
Pat Sheridan	OF134	L	26	138	481	64	136	24	4	8	53	41	91	19	.283	.338	.399
Willie Wilson	OF128	S	28	128	541	81	163	24	9	2	44	39	56	47	.301	.350	.390
Hal McRae	DH94	R	38	106	317	30	96	13	4	3	42	34	47	0	.303	.363	.397
Jorge Orta	DH83,OF26,2B1	L	33	122	403	50	120	23	7	9	50	28	39	0	.298	.343	.457
George Brett	3B101	L	31	104	377	42	107	21	3	13	69	38	37	0	.284	.344	.459
Dane Iorg†	1B43,OF22,3B1	L	34	78	235	27	60	16	2	5	30	13	15	0	.255	.287	.404
John Wathan	C59,1B33,DH4*	R	34	97	171	17	31	7	1	2	10	21	34	6	.181	.271	.269
U.L. Washington	SS61	S	30	63	170	18	38	6	0	1	10	14	31	4	.224	.281	.276
Buddy Biancalana	SS33,2B29,DH1	S	24	66	134	18	26	6	1	2	9	6	44	1	.194	.229	.299
Butch Davis	OF35,DH2	R	26	41	116	11	17	3	0	2	12	10	19	4	.147	.211	.224
Lynn Jones	OF45	R	31	47	103	11	31	6	0	1	10	4	9	1	.301	.330	.388
Leon Roberts	OF16,DH3,P1	R	33	29	45	4	10	1	1	0	3	4	3	0	.222	.300	.289
Tucker Ashford	3B9	R	29	9	13	1	2	1	0	0	0	1	2	0	.154	.214	.231
Orlando Sanchez†	C1	L	27	10	10	0	1	1	0	0	2	0	2	0	.100	.100	.200
Bucky Dent	SS9,3B2	R	32	11	9	2	3	0	0	0	1	1	2	0	.333	.400	.333
Dave Leeper	OF2,DH1	L	24	4	6	1	0	0	0	0	0	0	1	0	.000	.000	.000
Luis Pujols	C4	R	28	4	5	0	1	0	0	0	1	0	0	0	.200	.200	.200
Jim Scranton	3B1,SS1	R	24	2	2	0	0	0	0	0	0	0	0	0	.000	.000	.000

G. Pryor, 1 G at DH, 1 G at 1B; J. Wathan, 1 G at OF

Pitcher	T	Age	G	GS	CG	ShO	IP	H	HR	BB	SO	W-L	Sv	ERA
Bud Black	L	27	35	35	8	1	257.0	226	22	64	140	17-12	0	3.12
Mark Gubicza	R	21	29	29	4	2	189.0	172	13	75	111	10-14	0	4.05
Larry Gura	L	36	31	25	3	0	168.2	175	26	67	68	12-9	0	5.18
Charlie Leibrandt	L	27	23	23	0	0	143.2	158	11	38	53	11-7	0	3.63
Mike Jones	L	24	23	12	0	0	81.0	86	10	36	43	2-3	0	4.89
Danny Jackson	L	22	15	11	1	0	76.0	84	4	35	40	2-6	0	4.26
Frank Wills	R	25	10	5	0	0	37.0	39	3	13	21	2-3	0	5.11
Dan Quisenberry	R	31	72	0	0	0	129.1	121	10	12	41	6-3	44	2.64
Joe Beckwith	R	29	49	1	0	0	100.2	92	13	25	75	8-4	2	3.40
Bret Saberhagen	R	20	38	18	2	1	157.2	138	13	36	73	10-11	1	3.48
Mark Huismann	R	26	38	0	0	0	75.0	84	7	21	54	3-3	3	4.20
Paul Splittorff	L	37	12	3	0	0	28.0	47	3	10	4	1-3	0	7.71
Leon Roberts	R	33	1	0	0	0	1.0	4	1	1	1	0-0	0	27.00

1984 California Angels 2nd AL West 81-81 .500 3.0 GB

John McNamara

Player	Gm by Position	B	Age	G	AB	R	H	2B	3B	HR	RBI	BB	SO	SB	Avg	OBP	Slg
Bob Boone	C137	R	36	139	450	33	91	16	1	3	32	25	45	3	.202	.242	.262
Rod Carew	1B83,DH1	L	38	93	329	42	97	8	1	3	31	40	39	4	.295	.367	.353
Rob Wilfong	2B97,SS4,DH1	L	30	108	307	31	76	13	2	6	33	20	53	3	.248	.296	.362
Doug DeCinces	3B140,DH5	R	33	146	547	77	147	23	3	20	82	53	79	4	.269	.327	.431
Dick Schofield	SS140	R	21	140	400	39	77	10	3	4	21	33	79	5	.193	.264	.263
Fred Lynn	OF140	L	32	142	517	84	140	28	4	23	79	77	97	2	.271	.366	.474
Gary Pettis	OF134	S	26	140	397	63	90	11	6	2	29	60	115	48	.227	.332	.300
Brian Downing	OF131,DH21	R	33	156	539	65	148	28	2	23	91	70	66	0	.275	.360	.462
Reggie Jackson	DH134,OF3	L	38	143	525	67	117	17	2	25	81	55	141	8	.223	.300	.406
Bobby Grich	2B91,1B25,3B21	R	35	116	363	60	93	15	1	18	58	57	70	2	.256	.357	.452
Juan Beniquez	OF98	R	34	110	354	60	119	17	0	8	39	18	43	0	.336	.370	.452
Daryl Sconiers	1B41,DH1	L	25	57	160	14	39	4	0	4	17	13	17	1	.244	.301	.344
Jerry Narron	C46,1B7	L	28	69	150	9	37	5	0	3	17	8	12	0	.247	.286	.340
Mike Brown	OF44,DH3	R	24	62	148	19	42	8	3	7	22	13	23	0	.284	.342	.520
Rob Picciolo	SS66,3B13,2B9*	R	31	87	119	18	24	6	0	1	9	0	21	0	.202	.200	.277
Ron Jackson†	1B21,3B9,OF1	R	31	33	91	5	15	2	1	0	5	7	13	0	.165	.222	.209
Darrell Miller	1B16,OF1	R	26	17	41	5	7	0	0	0	1	4	9	0	.171	.244	.171
Derrel Thomas†	OF7,SS4,3B3	R	33	14	29	3	4	0	1	0	2	3	4	0	.138	.219	.207
Rick Burleson		R	33	7	4	2	0	0	0	0	0	0	2	0	.000	.000	.000

R. Picciolo, 1 G at OF

Pitcher	T	Age	G	GS	CG	ShO	IP	H	HR	BB	SO	W-L	Sv	ERA
Mike Witt	R	23	34	34	9	2	246.2	227	17	84	196	15-11	0	3.47
Ron Romanick	R	23	33	33	8	2	229.2	240	23	61	87	12-12	0	3.76
Tommy John	L	41	32	29	4	1	181.1	223	15	56	47	7-13	0	4.52
Geoff Zahn	L	38	28	27	9	5	199.1	200	11	48	61	13-10	0	3.12
Jim Slaton	R	34	32	22	5	1	163.0	192	22	56	67	7-10	0	4.97
Steve Brown	R	27	3	3	0	0	11.0	16	0	9	5	0-1	0	9.00
Ken Forsch	R	37	2	2	1	0	16.1	14	2	3	10	1-1	0	2.20
Craig Swan†	R	33	2	1	0	0	5.0	8	3	0	2	0-1	0	10.80
Rick Steirer	R	27	1	1	0	0	2.2	6	0	2	2	0-1	0	16.88
Luis Sanchez	R	30	49	0	0	0	83.2	84	10	33	62	9-7	11	3.33
Doug Corbett	R	31	45	1	0	0	85.0	76	2	30	48	5-1	4	2.12
Curt Kaufman	R	26	29	1	0	0	69.0	68	13	20	41	2-3	1	4.57
Don Aase	R	29	23	0	0	0	39.0	30	1	19	28	4-1	8	1.62
Bruce Kison	R	34	20	7	0	0	65.1	72	10	28	66	4-5	2	5.37
John Curtis	L	36	17	0	0	0	28.2	30	4	11	18	1-2	0	4.40
Frank LaCorte	R	32	13	1	0	0	29.1	33	9	13	13	1-2	0	7.06
Stew Cliburn	R	27	1	0	0	0	2.0	3	0	1	1	0-0	0	13.50
Dave Smith	R	26	1	0	0	0	1.0	4	1	0	0	0-0	0	18.00

1984 Minnesota Twins 2nd AL West 81-81 .500 3.0 GB

Billy Gardner

Player	Gm by Position	B	Age	G	AB	R	H	2B	3B	HR	RBI	BB	SO	SB	Avg	OBP	Slg
Dave Engle	C86,DH22	R	27	109	391	56	104	20	1	4	38	26	22	0	.266	.308	.353
Kent Hrbek	1B148,DH1	L	24	149	559	80	174	31	3	27	107	65	87	1	.311	.383	.522
Tim Teufel	2B157	R	25	157	568	76	149	30	3	14	61	76	73	1	.262	.349	.400
Gary Gaetti	3B154,OF8,SS2	R	25	162	588	55	154	29	4	5	65	44	81	11	.262	.315	.350
Houston Jimenez	SS107	R	26	108	298	28	60	11	1	0	19	15	34	0	.201	.238	.245
Tom Brunansky	OF153,DH1	R	23	155	567	75	144	21	0	32	85	57	94	4	.254	.320	.460
Kirby Puckett	OF128	R	23	128	557	63	165	12	5	0	31	16	69	14	.296	.320	.336
Mickey Hatcher	OF100,DH37,1B17*	R	29	152	576	61	174	35	5	5	69	37	34	0	.302	.342	.406
Randy Bush	DH89,1B2	L	25	113	311	46	69	17	1	11	43	31	60	1	.222	.292	.389
Tim Laudner	C81,DH2	R	26	87	262	31	54	16	1	10	35	18	78	0	.206	.258	.389
Darrell Brown	OF55,DH13	S	28	95	260	36	71	9	3	1	19	14	16	4	.273	.309	.342
Ron Washington	SS71,2B9,DH4*	R	32	88	197	25	58	11	5	3	23	4	31	1	.294	.307	.447
Dave Meier	OF50,DH4,3B1	R	24	59	147	18	35	8	1	0	13	6	9	0	.238	.271	.306
Lenny Faedo	SS15,DH1	R	24	16	52	6	13	1	0	1	6	4	3	0	.250	.304	.327
Andre David	OF14,DH2	L	26	33	48	5	12	2	0	1	5	7	11	0	.250	.351	.354
Pat Putnam†	DH11	L	30	14	38	1	3	1	0	0	4	4	12	0	.079	.163	.105
Chris Speier†	SS12	R	34	12	33	2	7	0	0	0	1	3	7	0	.212	.278	.212
Jim Eisenreich	DH6,OF3	L	25	12	32	1	7	1	0	0	3	2	4	2	.219	.250	.250
Mike Hart	OF11	L	26	13	29	0	5	0	0	0	5	1	2	0	.172	.194	.172
John Castino	3B8	R	29	8	27	5	12	1	0	0	3	5	2	0	.444	.531	.481
Jeff Reed	C18	L	21	18	21	3	3	3	0	0	1	2	6	0	.143	.217	.286
Greg Gagne		R	22	2	1	0	0	0	0	0	0	0	0	0	.000	.000	.000
Alvaro Espinoza	SS1	R	22	1	0	0	0	0	0	0	0	0	0	0	—	—	—

M. Hatcher, 1 G at 3B; R. Washington, 2 G at 3B

Pitcher	T	Age	G	GS	CG	ShO	IP	H	HR	BB	SO	W-L	Sv	ERA
Mike Smithson	R	29	36	36	10	1	252.0	246	35	54	144	15-13	0	3.68
Frank Viola	L	24	35	35	10	4	257.2	225	28	73	149	18-12	0	3.21
John Butcher	R	27	34	34	8	1	225.0	242	18	53	83	13-11	0	3.44
Ken Schrom	R	29	25	21	3	0	137.0	156	15	41	49	5-11	0	4.47
Ed Hodge	L	26	25	15	0	0	100.0	116	13	29	59	4-3	0	4.77
Al Williams	R	30	17	11	1	0	68.2	75	9	22	22	3-5	0	5.77
Ron Davis	R	28	64	0	0	0	83.0	79	11	41	74	7-11	29	4.55
Pete Filson	L	25	55	7	0	0	118.2	106	14	54	59	6-5	1	4.10
Rick Lysander	R	31	36	0	0	0	56.2	62	2	27	22	4-3	5	3.49
Len Whitehouse	L	26	30	0	0	0	31.1	29	3	17	18	2-2	1	3.16
Mike Walters	R	26	23	0	0	0	29.0	31	1	14	10	0-3	2	3.72
Larry Pashnick	R	28	13	1	0	0	38.1	38	3	11	10	2-1	0	3.52
Bobby Castillo	R	29	10	2	0	0	25.1	14	2	19	7	2-1	0	1.78
Keith Comstock	L	28	4	0	0	0	6.1	6	2	4	2	0-0	0	8.53
Jack O'Connor	L	26	2	0	0	0	4.2	1	1	4	0	0-0	0	1.93
Curt Wardle	L	23	2	0	0	0	4.0	3	2	0	5	0-0	0	4.50

1984 Oakland Athletics 4th AL West 77-85 .475 7.0 GB

Steve Boros (20-24)/Jackie Moore (57-61)

Player	Gm by Position	B	Age	G	AB	R	H	2B	3B	HR	RBI	BB	SO	SB	Avg	OBP	Slg
Mike Heath	C108,OF45,3B2*	R	29	140	475	49	118	21	5	13	64	26	72	7	.248	.287	.396
Bruce Bochte	1B144,DH2	L	33	148	469	58	124	23	0	5	52	52	59	2	.264	.333	.345
Joe Morgan	2B100	L	40	116	365	50	89	21	0	6	43	66	39	8	.244	.356	.351
Carney Lansford	3B151	R	27	151	597	70	179	31	5	14	74	40	62	9	.300	.342	.439
Tony Phillips	SS91,2B90,OF1	S	25	154	451	62	120	24	3	4	37	42	86	10	.266	.325	.359
Dwayne Murphy	OF153	L	29	153	559	93	143	18	2	33	88	74	111	4	.256	.342	.472
Rickey Henderson	OF140	R	25	142	502	113	147	27	4	16	58	86	81	66	.293	.399	.458
Mike Davis	OF127,DH4	L	25	134	382	47	88	18	3	9	46	31	66	14	.230	.285	.364
Dave Kingman	DH139,1B9	R	35	147	549	68	147	23	1	35	118	44	119	2	.268	.321	.505
Davey Lopes†	OF42,2B17,DH9*	R	39	72	230	32	59	11	1	9	36	31	36	12	.257	.343	.430
Bill Almon	OF48,1B44,DH12*	R	31	106	211	24	47	11	0	7	16	10	42	5	.223	.253	.374
Donnie Hill	SS66,2B4,DH2*	S	23	73	174	21	40	6	0	2	16	5	12	1	.230	.249	.299
Jim Essian	C59,DH1,3B1	R	33	63	136	17	32	9	0	2	10	23	17	1	.235	.348	.346
Mark Wagner	SS57,3B15,2B8*	R	30	82	87	8	20	5	1	0	12	7	11	2	.230	.284	.310
Mickey Tettleton	C32	S	23	33	76	10	20	2	1	1	5	11	21	0	.263	.352	.355
Jeff Burroughs	DH23,OF4	R	33	58	71	5	15	1	0	2	8	18	23	0	.211	.367	.310
Gary Hancock	OF18,DH5,1B4*	L	30	51	60	2	13	2	0	0	8	0	1	0	.217	.217	.250
Steve Kiefer	SS17,DH3,3B2	R	23	23	40	7	7	1	2	0	2	2	10	2	.175	.209	.300
Dan Meyer	1B3,DH2	L	31	20	22	1	7	3	1	0	4	0	2	0	.318	.318	.545

M. Heath, 1 G at SS; D. Lopes, 5 G at 3B; B. Almon, 4 G at 3B, 1 G at C, 1 G at SS; D. Hill, 2 G at 3B; M. Wagner, 3 G at DH, 1 G at P; G. Hancock, 1 G at P

Pitcher	T	Age	G	GS	CG	ShO	IP	H	HR	BB	SO	W-L	Sv	ERA
Steve McCatty	R	30	33	30	4	0	179.2	206	24	71	63	8-14	0	4.76
Ray Burris	R	33	34	28	5	1	211.2	193	15	90	93	13-10	0	3.15
Bill Krueger	L	26	26	24	1	0	142.0	156	9	85	61	10-10	0	4.75
Curt Young	L	24	20	17	2	1	108.2	118	9	31	41	9-4	0	4.06
Chris Codiroli	R	26	28	14	1	0	89.1	111	16	34	44	6-4	1	5.84
Mike Warren	R	23	24	12	0	0	90.0	104	11	44	61	3-6	0	4.90
Rick Langford	R	32	3	2	0	0	8.2	15	2	2	2	0-0	0	8.31
Bill Caudill	R	27	68	0	0	0	96.1	77	9	31	89	9-7	36	2.71
Keith Atherton	R	25	57	0	0	0	104.0	110	13	39	58	7-6	2	4.33
Lary Sorensen	R	28	46	21	2	0	183.1	240	21	44	63	6-13	1	4.91
Tim Conroy	L	24	38	14	0	0	93.0	82	11	63	69	1-6	0	5.23
Tom Burgmeier	L	40	17	0	0	0	23.0	15	2	8	8	3-0	2	2.35
Chuck Rainey†	R	29	16	0	0	0	30.2	43	2	17	10	1-1	1	6.75
Jeff Jones	R	27	13	0	0	0	33.0	31	4	12	19	0-3	0	3.55
Dave Leiper	L	22	8	0	0	0	7.0	12	2	5	3	1-0	0	9.00
Gorman Heimueller	L	28	6	0	0	0	14.2	21	2	7	3	0-1	0	6.14
Jeff Bettendorf	R	23	3	0	0	0	9.2	9	3	5	5	0-0	1	4.66
Mike Torrez†	R	37	2	0	0	0	2.1	9	0	3	2	0-0	0	27.00
Mark Wagner	R	30	1	0	0	0	1.2	2	0	1	1	0-0	0	0.00
Gary Hancock	L	30	1	0	0	0	1.1	0	0	0	0	0-0	0	0.00

1984 Chicago White Sox 5th AL West 74-88 .457 10.0 GB

Tony La Russa

Player	Gm by Position	B	Age	G	AB	R	H	2B	3B	HR	RBI	BB	SO	SB	Avg	OBP	Slg
Carlton Fisk	C90,DH5	R	36	102	359	54	83	20	1	21	43	26	60	6	.231	.289	.468
Greg Walker	1B101,DH21	L	24	136	442	62	130	29	2	24	75	35	66	8	.294	.346	.532
Julio Cruz	2B141	S	29	143	415	42	92	14	4	5	43	45	58	14	.222	.295	.311
Vance Law	3B137,2B22,OF5*	R	27	151	481	60	121	18	2	17	59	41	75	4	.252	.309	.403
Scott Fletcher	SS134,2B28,3B3	R	25	149	456	46	114	13	3	3	35	46	46	10	.250	.328	.311
Harold Baines	OF147	L	25	147	569	72	173	28	10	29	94	54	75	1	.304	.361	.541
Rudy Law	OF130	L	27	136	487	68	122	14	7	6	37	39	42	29	.251	.309	.345
Ron Kittle	OF124,DH7	R	26	139	466	67	100	15	0	32	74	49	137	3	.215	.295	.453
Greg Luzinski	DH114	R	33	125	412	47	98	13	0	13	58	56	80	5	.238	.329	.364
Tom Paciorek	1B67,OF41	R	37	111	363	35	93	21	2	4	29	25	69	6	.256	.308	.358
Jerry Hairston	OF37,DH20	S	32	115	227	41	59	13	2	5	19	41	29	2	.260	.373	.401
Marc Hill	C72,1B2	R	32	77	193	15	45	10	1	5	20	9	26	0	.233	.275	.373
Roy Smalley†	3B38,SS3,DH2*	S	31	47	135	15	23	4	0	4	13	22	30	1	.170	.285	.289
Jerry Dybzinski	SS76,3B14,DH1*	R	28	94	132	17	31	5	1	1	10	13	12	7	.235	.311	.311
Dave Stegman	OF46,DH3	R	30	55	92	13	24	1	2	2	11	4	18	3	.261	.306	.380
Daryl Boston	OF34,DH1	L	21	35	83	8	14	3	1	0	3	4	20	6	.169	.207	.229
Mike Squires	1B77,3B13,OF3*	L	32	104	82	9	15	1	0	0	6	6	7	2	.183	.239	.195
Joel Skinner	C43	R	23	43	80	4	17	2	0	0	3	7	19	1	.213	.273	.238
Tom O'Malley†	3B6	L	23	12	16	0	2	0	0	0	3	0	5	0	.125	.125	.125
Steve Christmas	C1	L	26	12	11	1	4	1	0	1	4	0	2	0	.364	.364	.727
Tim Hulett	3B4,2B3	R	24	8	7	1	0	0	0	0	0	1	4	1	.000	.125	.000
Jamie Quirk†	3B1	L	29	3	2	0	0	0	0	0	1	0	2	0	.000	.000	.000
Casey Parsons		L	30	1	1	0	0	0	0	0	0	0	1	0	.000	.000	.000
LaMarr Hoyt	P34,OF1	R	29	35	0	0	0	0	0	0	0	0	0	0	—	—	—

V. Law, 4 G at SS; R. Smalley, 1 G at 1B; J. Dybzinski, 1 G at 2B; M. Squires, 1 G at P

Pitcher	T	Age	G	GS	CG	ShO	IP	H	HR	BB	SO	W-L	Sv	ERA
LaMarr Hoyt	R	29	34	34	11	1	235.2	244	31	43	126	13-18	0	4.47
Tom Seaver	R	39	34	33	10	4	236.2	216	27	61	131	15-11	0	3.95
Floyd Bannister	L	29	34	33	4	0	218.0	211	30	80	152	14-11	0	4.83
Rich Dotson	R	25	32	32	14	1	245.2	216	24	103	120	14-15	0	3.59
Bob Fallon	L	24	3	3	0	0	14.2	12	0	11	10	0-0	0	3.68
Ron Reed	R	41	51	0	0	0	73.0	67	7	14	57	0-6	12	3.08
Juan Agosto	L	26	49	0	0	0	55.1	54	2	34	26	2-1	7	3.09
Britt Burns	L	25	34	16	2	0	117.0	130	7	45	85	4-12	3	5.00
Salome Barojas†	R	27	24	0	0	0	39.1	48	3	19	18	3-2	1	4.58
Dan Spillner†	R	32	22	0	0	0	48.1	51	7	14	26	1-0	1	4.10
Bert Roberge	R	29	21	0	0	0	40.2	36	2	15	25	3-3	0	3.76
Gene Nelson	R	23	20	9	2	0	74.2	72	9	17	36	3-5	1	4.46
Al Jones	R	25	20	0	0	0	20.1	23	3	11	15	1-1	5	4.43
Jerry Don Gleaton	L	26	11	1	0	0	18.1	20	2	6	4	1-2	2	3.44
Randy Niemann	L	28	5	0	0	0	5.1	5	0	5	5	0-0	0	1.69
Tom Brennan	R	31	4	1	0	0	6.2	8	1	3	3	0-1	0	4.05
Jim Siwy	R	25	1	0	0	0	4.1	3	0	2	1	0-0	0	2.08
Mike Squires	L	32	1	0	0	0	0.1	0	0	0	0	0-0	0	0.00

1984 Seattle Mariners 5th AL West 74-88 .457 10.0 GB

Del Crandall (59-76)/Chuck Cottier (15-12)

Player	Gm by Position	B	Age	G	AB	R	H	2B	3B	HR	RBI	BB	SO	SB	Avg	OBP	Slg
Bob Kearney	C133	R	27	133	431	39	97	24	1	7	43	18	72	7	.225	.257	.334
Alvin Davis	1B147,DH7	L	23	152	567	80	161	34	3	27	116	97	78	5	.284	.391	.497
Jack Perconte	2B150	L	29	155	612	93	180	24	4	0	31	57	47	29	.294	.357	.346
Jim Presley	3B69,DH1	R	22	70	251	27	57	12	1	10	36	6	63	1	.227	.247	.402
Spike Owen	SS151	S	23	152	530	67	130	18	8	3	43	46	63	16	.245	.308	.326
Al Cowens	OF130,DH7	R	32	139	524	60	145	34	2	15	78	27	83	9	.277	.312	.435
Phil Bradley	OF117,DH3	R	25	124	322	49	97	12	4	0	24	34	61	21	.301	.373	.363
Dave Henderson	OF97,DH10	R	25	112	350	42	98	23	0	14	43	19	56	5	.280	.320	.466
Ken Phelps	DH84,1B9	L	29	101	290	52	70	9	0	24	51	61	73	3	.241	.378	.521
Barry Bonnell	OF94,3B10,1B5	R	30	110	363	42	96	15	4	8	48	25	51	5	.264	.315	.394
Steve Henderson	OF53,DH51	R	31	109	325	42	85	12	3	10	35	38	62	2	.262	.341	.409
Larry Milbourne	3B40,2B14,DH6*	S	33	79	211	22	56	5	1	1	22	12	16	0	.265	.304	.313
Pat Putnam†	DH30,OF13,1B6	L	30	64	155	11	31	6	0	2	16	12	27	3	.200	.254	.277
Darnell Coles	3B42,DH3,OF3	R	22	48	143	15	23	3	1	0	6	17	26	2	.161	.259	.196
Gorman Thomas	OF34,DH1	R	33	35	108	6	17	3	0	1	13	28	27	0	.157	.322	.213
Domingo Ramos	3B38,SS13,1B5*	R	26	59	81	6	15	2	0	0	2	5	12	2	.185	.233	.210
Orlando Mercado	C29	R	22	30	78	5	17	3	1	0	5	4	12	1	.218	.265	.282
Al Chambers	OF13,DH1	L	23	22	49	4	11	1	0	1	4	3	12	1	.224	.269	.306
John Moses	OF19,DH1	S	26	19	35	3	12	1	1	0	2	2	5	1	.343	.395	.429
Dave Valle	C13	R	23	13	27	4	8	1	0	1	4	1	5	0	.296	.321	.444
Bill Nahorodny	C10,1B1	R	30	12	25	2	6	0	0	1	3	1	7	0	.240	.310	.360
Ivan Calderon	OF11	R	22	11	24	2	5	1	0	1	1	2	5	1	.208	.269	.375
Danny Tartabull	SS8,2B1	R	21	10	20	3	6	1	0	2	7	2	3	0	.300	.375	.650
Rickey Nelson	DH3,OF2	L	25	9	15	2	3	0	0	1	2	2	4	0	.200	.294	.400
Harold Reynolds	2B6	S	23	10	10	3	3	0	0	0	0	0	1	1	.300	.364	.300

L. Milbourne, 5 G at SS; D. Ramos, 3 G at 2B

Pitcher	T	Age	G	GS	CG	ShO	IP	H	HR	BB	SO	W-L	Sv	ERA
Mark Langston	L	23	35	33	5	2	225.0	188	16	118	204	17-10	0	3.40
Mike Moore	R	24	34	33	6	0	212.0	236	16	85	158	7-17	0	4.97
Jim Beattie	R	29	32	32	12	2	211.0	206	13	75	119	12-16	0	3.41
Matt Young	L	25	22	22	1	0	113.1	141	11	57	73	6-8	0	5.72
Salome Barojas†	R	27	19	14	0	0	95.1	88	12	41	37	6-5	1	3.97
Mike Stanton	R	31	54	0	0	0	61.0	55	3	22	55	4-4	8	3.54
Paul Mirabella	L	30	52	1	0	0	68.0	74	6	32	41	2-5	3	4.37
Ed Vande Berg	L	25	50	17	2	0	130.1	165	18	50	71	8-12	7	4.76
Dave Beard	R	24	43	0	0	0	76.0	88	15	33	40	3-2	5	5.80
Edwin Nunez	R	21	37	0	0	0	67.2	55	8	21	57	2-2	7	3.19
Bob Stoddard	R	27	27	6	0	0	79.0	86	10	37	39	2-3	0	5.13
Roy Thomas	R	31	21	1	0	0	49.2	52	8	37	42	3-2	1	5.26
Dave Geisel	L	29	20	3	0	0	43.1	47	2	9	28	1-1	3	4.15
Karl Best	R	25	5	0	0	0	6.0	7	0	0	6	1-1	0	3.00
Lee Guetterman	L	25	3	0	0	0	4.1	9	0	2	2	0-0	0	4.15

1984 Texas Rangers 7th AL West 69-92 .429 14.5 GB

Doug Rader

Player	Gm by Position	B	Age	G	AB	R	H	2B	3B	HR	RBI	BB	SO	SB	Avg	OBP	Slg
Donnie Scott	C80	S	22	81	235	16	52	9	0	3	20	20	44	0	.221	.280	.298
Pete O'Brien	1B141,OF1	L	26	142	520	57	149	26	2	18	80	53	50	3	.287	.348	.448
Wayne Tolleson	2B109,SS7,3B5*	S	28	118	338	35	72	9	2	0	9	27	47	22	.213	.276	.251
Buddy Bell	3B147	R	32	148	553	88	174	36	5	11	83	63	54	2	.315	.382	.458
Curtis Wilkerson	SS116,2B47	S	23	153	484	47	120	12	0	1	26	22	72	12	.248	.282	.279
Gary Ward	OF148,DH5	R	30	155	602	97	171	21	7	21	79	55	95	7	.284	.343	.447
Billy Sample	OF122,DH2	R	29	130	489	67	121	20	2	5	33	29	46	18	.247	.286	.327
Larry Parrish	OF81,DH63,3B12	R	30	156	613	72	175	42	1	22	101	42	116	2	.285	.336	.465
Mickey Rivers	DH48,OF30	L	35	102	313	40	94	13	1	4	33	9	23	5	.300	.320	.387
George Wright	OF80,DH18	S	25	101	383	40	93	19	4	9	48	15	54	0	.243	.273	.384
Ned Yost	C78	R	28	80	242	15	44	4	0	6	25	6	47	1	.182	.201	.273
Bobby Jones	OF22,1B15,DH4	L	34	64	143	14	37	4	0	4	22	10	19	1	.259	.308	.371
Jeff Kunkel	SS48,DH1	R	22	50	142	13	29	2	3	3	7	2	35	4	.204	.218	.324
Marv Foley	C36,DH4,1B1*	L	30	63	115	13	25	2	0	6	19	15	24	0	.217	.306	.391
Alan Bannister†	2B25,DH9,OF3*	R	32	47	112	20	33	2	1	2	9	21	17	3	.295	.407	.384
Tommy Dunbar	OF20,DH5	L	24	34	97	9	25	2	0	2	10	6	16	1	.258	.301	.340
Dave Hostetler	1B14,DH13	R	28	37	82	7	18	2	1	3	10	13	27	0	.220	.326	.378
Jim Anderson	SS31,3B6,2B1	R	27	39	47	2	5	0	0	0	1	4	7	0	.106	.176	.106
Bill Stein	2B11,DH4,1B3*	R	37	27	43	3	12	1	0	0	3	5	9	0	.279	.354	.302
Mike Richardt†	2B4	R	26	6	9	0	1	0	0	0	0	1	1	0	.111	.200	.111
Kevin Buckley	DH3	R	25	5	7	1	2	1	0	0	0	2	4	0	.286	.444	.429

W. Tolleson, 1 G at DH, 1 G at OF; M. Foley, 1 G at 3B; A. Bannister, 1 G at 1B, 1 G at 3B; B. Stein, 3 G at 3B

Pitcher	T	Age	G	GS	CG	ShO	IP	H	HR	BB	SO	W-L	Sv	ERA
Charlie Hough	R	36	36	36	17	1	266.0	260	26	94	164	16-14	0	3.76
Frank Tanana	L	30	35	35	9	1	246.1	234	30	81	141	15-15	0	3.25
Danny Darwin	R	28	35	32	5	1	223.2	249	19	54	123	8-12	0	3.94
Dave Stewart	R	27	32	27	3	0	192.1	193	26	87	119	7-14	0	4.73
Mike Mason	L	25	36	24	4	0	184.1	159	18	51	113	9-13	0	3.61
Dave Schmidt	R	27	43	0	0	0	70.1	69	3	20	46	6-6	12	2.56
Odell Jones	R	31	33	0	0	0	59.1	62	7	23	28	2-4	2	3.64
Tom Henke	R	26	25	0	0	0	28.1	36	0	20	25	1-1	2	6.35
Dave Tobik	R	31	24	0	0	0	42.1	44	5	17	30	1-6	5	3.61
Dickie Noles†	R	27	18	6	0	0	57.2	60	6	30	39	2-3	0	5.15
Joey McLaughlin†	R	27	15	0	0	0	32.2	33	4	13	21	2-1	0	4.41
Jim Bibby	R	39	8	0	0	0	16.1	19	1	10	6	0-0	0	4.41
Ricky Wright	L	25	8	1	0	0	14.2	20	3	11	6	0-2	0	6.14
Dwayne Henry	R	22	3	0	0	0	4.1	5	0	7	2	0-1	0	8.31

»1984 Chicago Cubs 1st NL East 96-65 .596 —

Jim Frey

Player	Gm by Position	B	Age	G	AB	R	H	2B	3B	HR	RBI	BB	SO	SB	Avg	OBP	Slg
Jody Davis	C146	R	27	150	523	55	134	25	2	19	94	47	99	5	.256	.315	.421
Leon Durham	1B130	L	26	137	473	86	132	30	4	23	96	69	86	16	.279	.369	.505
Ryne Sandberg	2B156	R	24	156	636	114	200	36	19	19	84	52	101	32	.314	.367	.520
Ron Cey	3B144	R	36	146	505	71	121	27	0	25	97	61	108	3	.240	.324	.442
Larry Bowa	SS132	S	38	133	391	33	87	14	2	0	17	28	24	10	.223	.274	.269
Gary Matthews	OF145	R	33	147	491	101	143	21	2	14	82	103	97	17	.291	.410	.428
Bob Dernier	OF140	R	27	143	536	94	149	26	5	3	32	63	60	45	.278	.356	.362
Keith Moreland	OF103,1B29,3B8*	R	30	140	495	59	138	17	3	16	80	34	71	1	.279	.326	.422
Mel Hall†	OF46	L	23	48	150	25	42	11	3	4	22	12	23	2	.280	.329	.473
Henry Cotto	OF88	R	23	105	146	24	40	5	0	0	8	10	23	9	.274	.325	.308
Thad Bosley	OF33	L	27	55	98	17	29	2	2	2	14	13	22	5	.296	.375	.418
Gary Woods	OF62,2B3	R	29	87	98	13	23	4	1	3	10	15	21	2	.235	.333	.388
Dave Owen	SS35,3B6,2B4	S	26	47	93	8	18	2	2	1	10	8	15	1	.194	.269	.290
Richie Hebner	3B14,1B3,OF3	L	36	44	81	12	27	3	0	2	8	10	15	1	.333	.407	.444
Tom Veryzer	SS36,3B5,2B4	R	31	44	74	5	14	1	0	0	4	3	11	0	.189	.259	.203
Jay Johnstone	OF15	L	38	52	73	8	21	2	2	0	3	7	18	0	.288	.350	.370
Steve Lake	C24	R	27	25	54	4	12	4	0	2	7	0	7	0	.222	.232	.407
Bill Buckner†	1B7,OF2	L	34	21	43	3	9	0	0	0	2	1	1	0	.209	.239	.209
Ron Hassey†	C6,1B4	L	31	19	33	5	11	0	0	2	5	4	6	0	.333	.405	.515
Dan Rohn	3B7,2B5,SS5	L	28	25	31	1	4	0	0	1	3	1	6	0	.129	.152	.226
Davey Lopes†	OF9,2B2	R	39	16	17	5	4	1	0	0	0	6	5	3	.235	.435	.294
Billy Hatcher	OF4	R	23	8	9	1	1	0	0	0	0	1	0	2	.111	.200	.111

K. Moreland, 3 G at C

Pitcher	T	Age	G	GS	CG	ShO	IP	H	HR	BB	SO	W-L	Sv	ERA
Steve Trout	L	26	32	31	6	2	190.0	205	7	59	81	13-7	0	3.41
Dennis Eckersley†	R	29	24	24	2	0	160.1	152	11	36	81	10-8	0	3.03
Scott Sanderson	R	27	24	24	3	0	140.2	140	5	24	76	8-5	0	3.14
Dick Ruthven	R	33	23	22	0	0	126.2	154	14	41	55	6-10	0	5.04
Rick Sutcliffe†	R	28	20	20	7	3	150.1	123	9	39	155	16-1	0	2.69
Chuck Rainey†	R	29	17	16	0	0	88.1	102	4	38	45	5-7	0	4.28
Rick Reuschel	R	35	19	14	1	0	92.1	123	7	23	43	5-5	0	5.17
Don Schulze†	R	21	1	1	0	0	3.0	8	0	1	2	0-0	0	12.00
Lee Smith	R	26	69	0	0	0	101.0	98	6	35	86	9-7	33	3.65
Tim Stoddard	R	31	58	0	0	0	92.0	77	9	57	87	10-6	7	3.82
Warren Brusstar	R	32	41	0	0	0	63.2	57	4	21	36	1-1	3	3.11
George Frazier†	R	29	37	0	0	0	63.2	53	4	26	58	6-3	3	4.10
Rich Bordi	R	25	31	7	0	0	83.1	78	11	20	41	5-2	4	3.46
Dickie Noles†	R	27	21	1	0	0	50.2	60	4	16	14	2-2	0	5.15
Porfi Altamirano	R	32	5	0	0	0	11.1	8	2	1	7	0-0	0	4.76
Bill Johnson	R	23	4	0	0	0	5.1	4	0	1	3	0-0	0	1.69
Reggie Patterson	R	25	3	1	0	0	6.0	10	1	2	5	0-1	0	10.50
Ron Meridith	L	27	3	0	0	0	5.1	6	1	2	4	0-0	0	3.38

1984 New York Mets 2nd NL East 90-72 .556 6.5 GB — Davey Johnson

Player	Gm by Position	B	Age	G	AB	R	H	2B	3B	HR	RBI	BB	SO	SB	Avg	OBP	Slg
Mike Fitzgerald	C107	R	23	112	360	20	87	15	1	2	33	24	71	1	.242	.288	.306
Keith Hernandez	1B153	L	30	154	550	83	171	31	0	15	94	97	89	2	.311	.409	.449
Wally Backman	2B115,SS8	S	24	128	436	68	122	19	2	1	26	56	63	32	.280	.360	.339
Hubie Brooks	3B129,SS26	R	27	153	561	61	159	23	2	16	73	48	79	6	.283	.341	.417
Jose Oquendo	SS67	S	20	81	189	23	42	5	0	0	10	15	26	10	.222	.284	.249
Mookie Wilson	OF146	S	28	154	587	88	162	28	10	10	54	26	90	46	.276	.308	.409
Darryl Strawberry	OF146	L	22	147	522	75	131	27	4	26	97	75	131	27	.251	.343	.467
George Foster	OF141	R	35	146	553	67	149	22	1	24	86	30	122	2	.269	.311	.443
Ron Gardenhire	SS49,2B18,3B7	R	26	74	207	20	51	7	1	1	10	9	43	6	.246	.276	.304
Danny Heep	OF48,1B10	L	26	99	199	36	46	9	2	1	12	27	22	3	.231	.319	.312
Kelvin Chapman	2B57,3B3	R	28	75	197	27	57	13	0	3	23	19	30	8	.289	.356	.401
Rafael Santana	SS50	R	26	51	152	14	42	11	1	1	12	9	17	0	.276	.317	.382
Ron Hodges	C35	L	35	64	106	5	22	3	0	1	11	23	18	1	.208	.351	.264
Ray Knight†	3B27,1B3	R	31	27	93	13	26	4	0	1	6	7	13	0	.280	.337	.355
Jerry Martin	OF30,1B3	R	35	51	91	6	14	1	0	3	5	6	29	0	.154	.206	.264
Junior Ortiz	C32	R	24	40	91	6	18	3	0	0	11	5	15	1	.198	.235	.231
Rusty Staub	1B3	L	40	78	72	2	19	4	0	1	18	4	9	0	.264	.291	.361
John Gibbons	C9	R	22	10	31	1	2	0	0	0	1	3	11	0	.065	.171	.065
Herm Winningham	OF10	L	22	14	27	5	11	1	1	0	5	1	7	2	.407	.429	.519
John Stearns	C4,1B2	R	32	8	17	6	3	1	0	0	1	4	2	1	.176	.333	.235
Kevin Mitchell	3B5	R	22	7	14	0	3	0	0	0	1	0	3	0	.214	.214	.214
John Christensen	OF5	R	23	5	11	2	3	2	0	0	3	1	2	0	.273	.308	.455
Ross Jones	SS6,2B1,3B1	R	24	17	10	2	1	1	0	0	1	3	4	0	.100	.308	.200
Billy Beane	OF5	R	22	5	10	0	1	0	0	0	0	0	2	0	.100	.100	.100

Pitcher	T	Age	G	GS	CG	ShO	IP	H	HR	BB	SO	W-L	Sv	ERA
Walt Terrell	R	26	33	33	3	1	215.0	232	16	80	114	11-12	0	3.52
Ron Darling	R	23	33	33	2	2	205.2	179	17	104	136	12-9	0	3.81
Dwight Gooden	R	19	31	31	7	3	218.0	161	7	73	276	17-9	0	2.60
Bruce Berenyi†	R	29	19	19	0	0	115.0	100	6	53	81	9-6	0	3.76
Sid Fernandez	L	21	15	15	0	0	90.0	74	8	34	62	6-6	0	3.50
Mike Torrez†	R	37	9	8	0	0	37.2	55	3	18	16	1-5	0	5.02
Calvin Schiraldi	R	22	5	3	0	0	17.1	20	3	10	16	0-2	0	5.71
Jesse Orosco	L	27	60	0	0	0	87.0	58	7	34	85	10-6	31	2.59
Doug Sisk	R	26	50	0	0	0	77.2	57	1	54	32	1-3	15	2.09
Brent Gaff	R	25	47	0	0	0	84.1	77	4	36	42	3-2	1	3.63
Ed Lynch	R	28	40	13	0	0	124.0	169	14	24	62	9-8	2	4.50
Tom Gorman	L	26	36	0	0	0	57.2	51	6	13	40	6-0	0	2.97
Wes Gardner	R	23	21	0	0	0	25.1	34	0	8	19	1-1	1	6.39
Tim Leary	R	26	20	7	0	0	53.2	61	2	18	29	3-3	0	4.02
Dick Tidrow	R	37	11	0	0	0	15.2	25	5	7	8	0-0	0	9.19
Craig Swan†	R	33	10	0	0	0	18.2	18	5	7	10	1-0	0	8.20

1984 St. Louis Cardinals 3rd NL East 84-78 .519 12.5 GB — Whitey Herzog

Player	Gm by Position	B	Age	G	AB	R	H	2B	3B	HR	RBI	BB	SO	SB	Avg	OBP	Slg
Darrell Porter	C122	L	32	127	422	56	98	16	3	11	68	60	79	5	.232	.331	.363
David Green	1B117,OF14	R	23	126	452	49	121	14	4	15	65	20	105	17	.268	.297	.416
Tom Herr	2B144	S	28	145	558	67	154	23	2	4	49	49	56	13	.276	.335	.346
Terry Pendleton	3B66	S	23	67	262	37	85	16	3	1	33	16	32	20	.324	.357	.420
Ozzie Smith	SS124	S	29	124	412	53	106	20	5	1	44	56	17	35	.257	.347	.337
Willie McGee	OF141	S	25	145	571	82	166	19	11	6	50	29	80	43	.291	.325	.394
Lonnie Smith	OF140	R	28	145	504	77	126	20	4	6	49	70	90	50	.250	.349	.341
George Hendrick	OF116,1B1	R	34	120	441	57	122	28	1	9	69	32	75	0	.277	.324	.406
Andy Van Slyke	OF81,3B32,1B30	L	23	137	361	45	88	16	4	7	50	63	71	28	.244	.354	.368
Tito Landrum	OF88	R	29	105	173	21	47	9	1	3	26	10	27	3	.272	.306	.387
Ken Oberkfell†	3B46,2B2,SS1	L	28	50	152	17	47	11	1	0	11	16	10	1	.309	.379	.395
Art Howe	3B45,1B11,2B8*	R	37	89	139	17	30	5	0	2	12	18	18	0	.216	.300	.295
Chris Speier†	SS34,3B2	R	34	38	118	9	21	7	1	3	8	9	19	0	.178	.242	.331
Steve Braun	OF19,3B1	L	36	86	98	6	27	3	1	0	16	17	17	0	.276	.383	.327
Mike Jorgensen†	1B39	L	35	59	98	5	24	4	2	1	12	10	17	0	.245	.315	.357
Tom Nieto	C32	R	23	33	86	7	24	4	0	3	12	5	18	0	.279	.312	.430
Bill Lyons	2B25,SS11,3B3	R	26	46	73	13	16	3	0	0	3	9	13	3	.219	.305	.260
Glenn Brummer	C26	R	29	28	58	3	12	0	0	1	3	3	7	0	.207	.246	.259
Dane Iorg†	1B6,OF5	L	34	15	28	3	4	2	0	0	3	2	6	0	.143	.200	.214
Mark Salas	C4,OF3	L	23	14	20	1	2	1	0	0	1	0	3	0	.100	.100	.150
Jose Uribe	SS5,2B1	S	25	8	19	4	4	0	0	0	3	0	2	1	.211	.211	.211
Mike Ramsey†	2B7,SS7,3B1	S	30	21	15	1	1	1	0	0	0	1	3	0	.067	.125	.133
Paul Householder†	OF8	S	25	13	14	1	2	0	0	0	0	0	3	0	.143	.143	.143
Gary Rajsich	1B3	L	29	7	7	1	1	0	0	0	2	2	1	0	.143	.300	.143

A. Howe, 5 G at SS

Pitcher	T	Age	G	GS	CG	ShO	IP	H	HR	BB	SO	W-L	Sv	ERA
Joaquin Andujar	R	31	36	36	12	4	261.1	218	20	70	147	20-14	0	3.34
Dave LaPoint	L	24	33	33	2	1	193.0	205	9	77	130	12-10	0	3.96
Danny Cox	R	24	29	27	1	1	156.1	171	9	54	70	9-11	0	4.03
Kurt Kepshire	R	24	17	16	2	2	109.0	100	7	44	71	6-5	0	3.30
John Stuper	R	27	15	12	0	0	61.1	73	4	20	19	3-5	0	5.28
Bob Forsch	R	34	16	11	1	0	52.1	64	6	19	21	2-5	0	6.02
Rick Ownbey	R	26	4	4	0	0	19.0	23	1	8	11	0-3	0	4.74
Ken Dayley†	L	25	3	2	0	0	5.0	16	1	5	0	0-2	0	18.00
Bruce Sutter	R	31	71	0	0	0	122.2	109	9	23	77	5-7	45	1.54
Jeff Lahti	R	27	63	0	0	0	84.2	69	6	34	45	4-2	1	3.72
Neil Allen	R	26	57	1	0	0	119.0	105	6	49	66	9-6	3	3.55
Dave Rucker	L	26	50	0	0	0	73.0	62	0	34	38	2-3	0	2.10
Ricky Horton	L	24	37	18	1	1	125.2	140	14	39	76	9-4	1	3.44
Dave Von Ohlen	L	25	27	0	0	0	34.2	39	0	8	19	1-0	1	3.12
Ralph Citarella	R	26	10	2	0	0	22.1	20	0	7	15	0-1	0	3.63
Kevin Hagen	R	24	4	0	0	0	7.1	9	0	1	2	1-0	0	2.45
Andy Hassler	L	32	3	0	0	0	2.1	4	2	2	1	1-0	0	11.57

1984 Philadelphia Phillies 4th NL East 81-81 .500 15.5 GB — Paul Owens

Player	Gm by Position	B	Age	G	AB	R	H	2B	3B	HR	RBI	BB	SO	SB	Avg	OBP	Slg
Ozzie Virgil	C137	R	27	141	456	61	119	21	2	18	68	45	91	1	.261	.331	.434
Len Matuszek	1B81,OF1	L	29	101	262	40	65	17	1	12	43	39	54	4	.248	.350	.458
Juan Samuel	2B160	R	23	160	701	105	191	36	19	15	69	28	168	72	.272	.307	.442
Mike Schmidt	3B145,1B2,SS1	R	34	151	528	93	146	23	3	36	106	92	116	5	.277	.383	.536
Ivan DeJesus	SS141	R	31	144	435	40	112	15	3	0	35	43	76	12	.257	.325	.306
Von Hayes	OF148	L	25	152	561	85	164	27	6	16	67	59	84	48	.292	.359	.447
Glenn Wilson	OF109,3B4	R	25	132	341	28	82	21	3	6	31	17	56	7	.240	.276	.372
Sixto Lezcano	OF87	R	30	109	256	36	71	6	2	14	40	38	43	0	.277	.371	.480
Garry Maddox	OF69	R	34	77	241	29	68	11	0	5	19	13	29	3	.282	.316	.390
Tim Corcoran	1B51,OF17	L	31	102	208	30	71	13	1	5	36	37	27	0	.341	.440	.486
Greg Gross	OF48,1B28	L	31	112	202	19	65	9	1	0	16	24	11	1	.322	.393	.376
Jeff Stone	OF46	L	23	51	185	27	67	4	6	1	15	9	26	27	.362	.394	.465
John Wockenfuss	1B39,C21,3B2	R	35	86	180	20	52	3	1	6	24	30	24	1	.289	.390	.417
Joe Lefebvre	OF47,3B1	L	28	52	160	22	40	9	0	3	18	23	37	0	.250	.348	.363
John Russell	OF29,C2	R	23	39	99	11	28	8	1	2	11	12	33	0	.283	.351	.444
Al Oliver†	1B19,OF5	L	37	28	93	9	29	7	0	0	14	7	9	1	.312	.360	.387
Bo Diaz	C23	R	31	27	75	5	16	4	0	1	9	5	13	0	.213	.256	.307
Luis Aguayo	3B14,2B12,SS10	R	25	58	72	15	20	4	0	3	11	8	16	0	.278	.350	.458
Steve Jeltz	SS27,3B1	S	25	28	68	7	14	0	1	1	7	7	11	2	.206	.276	.279
Kiko Garcia	SS30,3B23,2B1	R	30	57	60	6	14	2	0	0	5	4	11	0	.233	.281	.267
Rick Schu	3B15	R	22	17	29	12	8	2	1	2	5	6	6	0	.276	.389	.621
Francisco Melendez	1B10	L	20	21	23	0	3	0	0	0	2	1	5	0	.130	.167	.130
Mike LaValliere	C6	L	23	6	7	0	0	0	0	0	0	2	2	0	.000	.222	.000

Pitcher	T	Age	G	GS	CG	ShO	IP	H	HR	BB	SO	W-L	Sv	ERA
Jerry Koosman	L	41	36	34	3	1	224.0	232	8	60	137	14-15	0	3.25
Steve Carlton	L	39	33	33	1	0	229.0	214	14	79	163	13-7	0	3.58
Charles Hudson	R	25	30	30	1	1	173.2	181	12	52	94	9-11	0	4.04
John Denny	R	31	22	22	2	0	154.1	122	11	29	94	7-7	0	2.45
Shane Rawley†	L	28	18	18	3	0	120.1	117	13	27	58	10-6	0	3.81
Marty Bystrom†	R	25	11	11	0	0	56.2	66	5	22	36	4-4	0	5.08
Al Holland	L	31	68	0	0	0	98.1	82	14	30	61	5-10	29	3.39
Larry Andersen	R	31	64	0	0	0	90.2	85	5	25	54	3-7	4	2.38
Bill Campbell	R	35	57	0	0	0	81.1	68	2	35	52	6-5	1	3.43
Kevin Gross	R	23	44	14	1	0	129.0	140	8	44	84	8-5	1	4.12
Tug McGraw	L	39	25	0	0	0	38.0	36	1	10	26	2-0	0	3.79
Don Carman	L	24	11	0	0	0	13.1	14	2	6	16	0-1	0	5.40
Renie Martin†	R	28	9	0	0	0	15.2	17	2	12	5	0-2	0	4.60
Jim Kern†	R	35	8	0	0	0	13.1	20	3	10	8	0-1	0	10.13
Dave Wehrmeister	R	31	7	0	0	0	15.0	18	1	7	13	0-0	0	7.20
Steve Fireovid	R	27	6	0	0	0	5.2	4	0	0	3	0-0	0	1.59

1984 Montreal Expos 5th NL East 78-83 .484 18.0 GB — Bill Virdon (64-67)/Jim Fanning (14-16)

Player	Gm by Position	B	Age	G	AB	R	H	2B	3B	HR	RBI	BB	SO	SB	Avg	OBP	Slg
Gary Carter	C143,1B25	R	30	159	596	75	175	32	1	27	106	64	57	2	.294	.366	.487
Terry Francona	1B50,OF6	L	25	58	214	18	74	19	2	1	18	5	12	0	.346	.360	.467
Doug Flynn	2B88,SS34	R	33	124	366	23	89	12	1	0	17	12	41	0	.243	.267	.281
im Wallach	3B160,SS1	R	26	160	582	55	143	25	4	18	72	50	101	3	.246	.311	.395
Angel Salazar	SS80	R	22	80	174	12	27	4	2	0	12	4	38	1	.155	.178	.201
Tim Raines	OF160,2B2	S	24	160	622	106	192	38	9	8	60	87	69	75	.309	.393	.437
Andre Dawson	OF134	R	29	138	533	73	132	23	6	17	86	41	80	13	.248	.301	.409
Jim Wohlford	OF59,3B2	R	33	95	213	20	64	13	2	5	29	14	19	3	.300	.342	.451
Pete Rose†	1B40,OF28	S	43	95	278	34	72	6	2	0	23	31	20	1	.259	.334	.295
Bryan Little	2B77,SS2	S	24	85	266	31	65	11	1	0	9	34	19	2	.244	.332	.293
Derrel Thomas†	SS62,OF48,2B15*	R	33	108	243	26	62	12	2	0	20	20	33	0	.255	.308	.321
Mike Stenhouse	OF48,1B14	L	26	80	175	14	32	8	0	4	16	26	32	0	.183	.289	.297
Miguel Dilone	OF41	S	29	88	169	28	47	8	2	1	10	17	18	27	.278	.346	.367
Dan Driessen†	1B45	L	32	51	169	20	43	11	0	9	32	17	15	0	.254	.321	.479
Bobby Ramos	C31	R	28	31	83	8	16	1	0	2	5	6	13	0	.193	.244	.277
Tony Scott†	OF17	S	32	45	71	8	18	4	0	0	5	7	21	1	.254	.316	.310
Max Venable	OF27	L	27	38	71	7	17	2	0	2	7	3	7	1	.239	.276	.352
Mike Ramsey†	SS26,2B12	S	30	37	70	2	15	1	0	0	3	0	13	0	.214	.214	.229
Chris Speier†	SS13,3B4	R	34	25	40	1	6	0	0	0	1	1	8	0	.150	.171	.150
Roy Johnson	OF10	L	25	16	33	2	5	2	0	1	2	7	10	1	.152	.300	.303
Rene Gonzales	SS27	R	23	29	30	5	7	1	0	0	2	2	5	0	.233	.303	.267
Wallace Johnson	1B4	S	27	17	24	3	5	0	0	0	4	5	4	0	.208	.345	.208
Razor Shines	1B3,3B1	S	27	12	20	0	6	1	0	0	2	0	3	0	.300	.286	.350
Tom Lawless†	2B9	R	27	11	17	1	3	1	0	0	0	0	4	1	.176	.176	.235
Ron Johnson	1B2,OF1	R	28	5	5	0	1	0	0	0	1	0	2	0	.200	.200	.200
Mike Fuentes	OF1	R	26	3	4	0	1	0	0	0	0	1	2	0	.250	.400	.250
Sal Butera	C2	R	31	3	3	0	0	0	0	0	0	1	0	0	.000	.250	.000

D. Thomas, 4 G at 3B, 1 G at 1B

Pitcher	T	Age	G	GS	CG	ShO	IP	H	HR	BB	SO	W-L	Sv	ERA
Bill Gullickson	R	25	32	32	3	0	226.2	230	27	37	100	12-9	0	3.61
Charlie Lea	R	27	30	30	8	0	224.1	198	19	68	123	15-10	0	2.89
Bryn Smith	R	28	28	28	4	2	179.0	178	15	51	101	12-13	0	3.32
Steve Rogers	R	34	31	28	1	0	169.1	171	12	78	64	6-15	0	4.31
David Palmer	R	26	20	19	1	1	105.1	101	5	44	66	7-3	0	3.84
Jeff Reardon	R	28	68	0	0	0	87.0	70	5	37	79	7-7	23	2.90
Bob James	R	25	62	0	0	0	96.0	92	6	45	91	6-6	10	3.66
Gary Lucas	L	29	55	0	0	0	53.0	54	4	20	42	0-3	8	2.72
Dan Schatzeder	L	29	36	14	1	1	136.0	112	13	36	89	7-7	1	2.71
Andy McGaffigan†	R	27	21	3	0	0	46.0	37	2	15	39	3-4	1	2.54
Greg Harris†	R	28	15	0	0	0	17.2	10	0	7	15	0-1	2	2.04
Dick Grapenthin	R	26	13	1	0	0	23.0	19	3	7	9	1-2	2	3.52
Joe Hesketh	L	25	11	5	1	1	45.0	38	2	15	32	2-2	1	1.80
Randy St. Claire	R	23	4	0	0	0	8.0	11	0	2	4	0-0	0	4.50
Fred Breining	R	28	4	0	0	0	6.2	4	0	5	5	0-0	0	1.35
Greg Bargar	R	25	3	1	0	0	8.0	8	1	7	2	0-1	0	7.88

1984 Pittsburgh Pirates 6th NL East 75-87 .463 21.5 GB

Chuck Tanner

Player	Gm by Position	B	Age	G	AB	R	H	2B	3B	HR	RBI	BB	SO	SB	Avg	OBP	Slg
Tony Pena	C146	R	27	147	546	77	156	27	2	15	78	36	79	12	.286	.333	.425
Jason Thompson	1B152	L	29	154	543	61	138	22	0	17	74	87	73	0	.254	.357	.389
Johnny Ray	2B149	S	27	155	555	75	173	38	6	6	67	37	31	11	.312	.354	.434
Bill Madlock	3B98,1B1	R	33	103	403	38	102	16	0	4	44	26	29	3	.253	.297	.323
Dale Berra	SS135,3B1	R	27	136	450	31	100	16	0	9	52	34	78	1	.222	.273	.318
Marvell Wynne	OF154	L	24	154	653	77	174	24	11	0	39	42	81	24	.266	.310	.337
Lee Lacy	OF127,2B2	R	36	138	474	66	152	26	3	12	70	32	61	21	.321	.362	.464
Doug Frobel	OF112	L	25	126	276	33	56	9	3	12	28	24	84	7	.203	.271	.388
Jim Morrison	3B61,2B26,SS2*	R	31	100	304	38	87	14	2	11	45	20	52	0	.286	.328	.454
Lee Mazzilli	OF74,1B5	S	29	111	266	37	63	11	1	4	21	40	42	8	.237	.338	.331
Brian Harper	OF37,C2	R	24	46	112	4	29	4	0	2	11	5	11	0	.259	.300	.348
Amos Otis	OF32	R	37	40	97	6	16	4	0	0	10	7	15	0	.165	.213	.206
Milt May	C26	L	33	50	96	4	17	3	0	1	8	10	15	0	.177	.255	.240
Denny Gonzalez	3B11,SS10,OF3	R	20	26	82	9	15	3	1	0	4	7	21	1	.183	.247	.244
Benny Distefano	OF20,1B17	L	22	45	78	10	13	1	2	3	9	5	13	0	.167	.226	.346
Joe Orsulak	OF25	L	22	32	67	12	17	1	2	0	3	1	7	3	.254	.271	.328
Ron Wotus	SS17,2B7	R	23	27	55	4	12	6	0	0	2	6	8	0	.218	.290	.327
Don Robinson	P51,OF1	R	27	53	31	6	9	0	0	1	5	4	9	0	.290	.371	.387
Hedi Vargas	1B13	R	25	18	31	3	7	2	0	0	2	3	5	0	.226	.294	.290
Rafael Belliard	SS12,2B1	R	22	20	22	3	5	0	0	0	0	0	1	4	.227	.227	.227
Mitchell Page		L	32	16	12	2	4	1	0	0	0	3	4	0	.333	.467	.417

J. Morrison, 1 G at 1B

Pitcher	T	Age	G	GS	CG	ShO	IP	H	HR	BB	SO	W-L	Sv	ERA
Rick Rhoden	R	31	33	33	6	3	238.1	216	13	62	136	14-9	0	2.72
Larry McWilliams	L	30	34	32	7	2	227.1	226	18	78	149	12-11	1	2.93
John Tudor	L	30	32	32	6	1	212.0	200	19	56	117	12-11	0	3.27
Jose DeLeon	R	23	30	28	5	1	192.1	147	10	92	153	7-13	0	3.74
John Candelaria	L	30	33	28	3	1	185.1	179	19	34	133	12-11	2	2.72
Bob Walk	R	27	2	2	0	0	10.1	8	1	4	10	1-1	0	2.61
Kent Tekulve	R	37	72	0	0	0	88.0	86	4	33	36	3-9	13	2.66
Don Robinson	R	27	51	1	0	0	122.0	99	6	49	110	5-6	10	3.02
Rod Scurry	L	28	43	0	0	0	46.1	28	1	22	48	5-6	4	2.53
Cecilio Guante	R	24	27	0	0	0	41.1	32	3	16	30	2-3	2	2.61
Lee Tunnell	R	23	26	6	0	0	68.1	81	6	40	51	1-7	1	5.27
Jim Winn	R	24	9	0	0	0	18.2	19	2	9	11	1-0	1	3.86
Ray Krawczyk	R	24	4	0	0	0	5.1	7	0	4	3	0-0	0	3.38
Mike Bielecki	R	24	4	0	0	0	4.1	4	0	0	1	0-0	0	0.00
Chris Green	L	23	4	0	0	0	3.0	5	0	1	3	0-0	0	6.00
Jeff Zaske	R	23	3	0	0	0	5.0	4	0	1	2	0-0	0	0.00
Alfonso Pulido	L	27	1	0	0	0	2.0	3	0	1	2	0-0	0	9.00

1984 San Diego Padres 1st NL West 92-70 .568 —

Dick Williams

Player	Gm by Position	B	Age	G	AB	R	H	2B	3B	HR	RBI	BB	SO	SB	Avg	OBP	Slg
Terry Kennedy	C147	L	28	148	530	54	127	16	1	14	57	33	99	1	.240	.284	.353
Steve Garvey	1B159	R	35	161	617	72	175	27	2	8	86	24	64	1	.284	.307	.373
Alan Wiggins	2B157	S	26	158	596	106	154	19	7	3	34	75	57	70	.258	.342	.329
Graig Nettles	3B119	L	39	124	395	56	90	11	1	20	65	58	55	0	.228	.329	.413
Garry Templeton	SS146	S	28	148	493	40	127	19	3	2	35	39	81	8	.258	.312	.320
Tony Gwynn	OF156	L	24	158	606	88	213	21	10	5	71	59	23	33	.351	.410	.444
Kevin McReynolds	OF143	R	24	147	525	68	146	26	6	20	75	34	69	3	.278	.317	.465
Carmelo Martinez	OF142,1B2	R	23	149	488	64	122	28	2	13	66	68	82	1	.250	.340	.395
Luis Salazar	3B58,OF24,SS4	R	28	93	228	20	55	7	2	3	17	6	38	11	.241	.261	.329
Bobby Brown	OF53	S	30	85	171	28	43	7	2	3	29	11	33	16	.251	.292	.368
Tim Flannery	2B22,3B14,SS14	L	26	86	128	24	35	3	3	2	10	12	17	4	.273	.347	.391
Bruce Bochy	C36	R	29	37	92	10	21	5	1	4	15	3	21	0	.228	.250	.435
Kurt Bevacqua	1B20,3B10,OF3	R	37	59	80	7	16	3	0	1	9	14	19	0	.200	.326	.275
Mario Ramirez	SS33,3B6,2B2	R	26	48	59	12	7	1	0	2	9	13	14	0	.119	.278	.237
Champ Summers	1B8	L	38	47	54	5	10	3	0	1	12	4	15	0	.185	.254	.296
Ron Roenicke	OF10	S	27	12	20	4	6	1	0	1	2	2	5	0	.300	.364	.500
Eddie Miller	OF8	S	27	13	14	4	4	0	1	1	2	0	4	4	.286	.286	.643
Doug Gwosdz	C6	R	24	7	8	0	2	0	0	0	1	2	5	0	.250	.400	.250

Pitcher	T	Age	G	GS	CG	ShO	IP	H	HR	BB	SO	W-L	Sv	ERA
Eric Show	R	28	32	32	3	1	206.2	175	18	88	104	15-9	0	3.40
Tim Lollar	L	28	31	31	3	2	195.2	168	18	105	131	11-13	0	3.91
Ed Whitson	R	29	31	31	1	0	189.0	181	16	42	103	14-8	0	3.24
Mark Thurmond	L	27	32	29	1	1	178.2	174	12	55	57	14-8	0	2.97
Andy Hawkins	R	24	36	22	2	1	146.0	143	13	72	77	8-9	0	4.68
Craig Lefferts	L	26	62	0	0	0	105.2	88	4	24	56	3-4	10	2.13
Goose Gossage	R	32	62	0	0	0	102.1	75	6	36	84	10-6	25	2.90
Dave Dravecky	L	28	50	14	3	2	156.2	125	12	51	71	9-8	8	2.93
Greg Booker	R	24	32	1	0	0	57.1	67	4	27	28	1-1	0	3.30
Luis DeLeon	R	25	32	0	0	0	42.2	44	12	12	44	2-2	0	5.48
Greg Harris†	R	28	19	1	0	0	36.2	28	3	18	30	2-1	1	2.70
Floyd Chiffer	R	28	15	1	0	0	28.0	42	1	16	20	1-0	0	7.71
Sid Monge†	L	33	13	0	0	0	15.0	17	3	17	7	2-1	0	4.80

1984 Atlanta Braves 2nd NL West 80-82 .494 12.0 GB

Joe Torre

Player	Gm by Position	B	Age	G	AB	R	H	2B	3B	HR	RBI	BB	SO	SB	Avg	OBP	Slg
Bruce Benedict	C95	R	28	95	300	26	67	8	1	4	25	34	25	1	.223	.301	.297
Chris Chambliss	1B109	L	35	135	389	47	100	14	0	9	44	58	54	1	.257	.350	.362
Glenn Hubbard	2B117	R	26	120	397	53	93	27	2	9	43	55	61	4	.234	.331	.380
Randy Johnson	3B81	R	28	91	294	28	82	13	0	5	30	21	21	4	.279	.329	.374
Rafael Ramirez	SS145	R	26	145	591	51	157	22	4	2	48	26	70	14	.266	.295	.327
Dale Murphy	OF160	R	28	162	607	94	176	32	8	36	100	79	134	19	.290	.372	.547
C. Washington	OF107	L	29	120	416	62	119	21	2	17	61	59	77	21	.286	.374	.469
Brad Komminsk	OF80	R	23	90	301	37	61	10	0	8	36	29	77	18	.203	.276	.316
Gerald Perry	1B64,OF53	L	23	122	347	52	92	12	2	7	47	61	38	15	.265	.372	.372
Alex Trevino†	C79	R	26	79	266	36	65	16	0	3	28	16	27	5	.244	.289	.338
Jerry Royster	2B29,3B17,SS16*	R	31	81	227	22	47	13	2	1	21	15	41	6	.207	.257	.295
Ken Oberkfell†	3B45,2B4	L	28	50	172	21	40	8	1	1	10	15	17	1	.233	.289	.308
Albert Hall	OF66	S	26	87	142	25	37	6	1	1	9	10	18	6	.261	.309	.338
Bob Horner	3B32	R	26	32	113	15	31	8	0	3	19	14	17	0	.274	.349	.425
Terry Harper	OF29	R	28	40	102	4	16	3	1	0	8	4	21	4	.157	.194	.206
Milt Thompson	OF25	L	25	25	99	16	30	1	0	2	4	11	11	14	.303	.373	.374
Paul Runge	2B22,SS7,3B3	R	26	28	90	5	24	3	1	0	3	10	14	5	.267	.340	.322
Bob Watson	1B19	R	38	49	85	4	18	4	0	2	12	9	12	0	.212	.287	.329
Rufino Linares	OF13	R	33	34	58	4	12	3	0	1	10	6	12	0	.207	.273	.310
Mike Jorgensen†	1B8,OF4	L	35	31	26	4	7	1	0	0	5	3	6	0	.269	.333	.308
Paul Zuvella	2B6,SS6	R	25	11	25	2	5	1	0	0	1	2	3	0	.200	.259	.240
Matt Sinatro	C2	R	24	2	4	0	0	0	0	0	0	0	0	0	.000	.000	.000
Biff Pocoroba		S	30	4	2	1	0	0	0	0	0	2	0	0	.000	.500	.000

J. Royster, 11 G at OF

Pitcher	T	Age	G	GS	CG	ShO	IP	H	HR	BB	SO	W-L	Sv	ERA
Pascual Perez	R	27	30	30	4	1	211.2	208	26	51	145	14-8	0	3.74
Craig McMurtry	R	24	37	30	0	0	183.1	184	16	102	99	9-17	0	4.32
Rick Mahler	R	30	38	29	9	1	222.0	209	13	62	106	13-10	0	3.12
Rick Camp	R	31	31	21	1	0	148.2	134	11	63	69	8-6	0	3.27
Len Barker	R	28	21	20	1	0	126.1	120	10	38	95	7-8	0	3.85
Ken Dayley†	L	25	4	4	0	0	18.2	28	5	6	10	0-3	0	5.30
Zane Smith	L	23	3	3	0	0	20.0	16	1	13	16	1-0	0	2.25
Gene Garber	R	36	62	0	0	0	106.0	103	7	24	55	3-6	11	3.06
Jeff Dedmon	R	24	54	0	0	0	81.0	86	5	35	51	4-3	4	3.78
Donnie Moore	R	30	47	0	0	0	64.1	63	3	18	47	4-5	16	2.94
Steve Bedrosian	R	26	40	4	0	0	83.2	65	5	33	81	9-6	11	2.37
Pete Falcone	L	30	35	16	2	1	120.0	115	15	57	55	5-7	2	4.13
Terry Forster	L	32	25	0	0	0	26.2	30	1	7	10	2-0	5	2.70
Tony Brizzolara	R	27	10	4	0	0	29.0	33	4	13	17	1-2	0	5.28
Mike Payne	R	22	3	1	0	0	5.2	7	0	3	3	0-1	0	6.35

1984 Houston Astros 2nd NL West 80-82 .494 12.0 GB

Bob Lillis

Player	Gm by Position	B	Age	G	AB	R	H	2B	3B	HR	RBI	BB	SO	SB	Avg	OBP	Slg
Mark Bailey	C108	S	22	108	344	38	73	16	1	9	34	53	71	0	.212	.318	.343
Enos Cabell	1B112	R	34	127	436	52	135	17	3	8	44	21	47	8	.310	.341	.417
Bill Doran	2B139,SS13	S	26	147	548	92	143	18	11	4	41	66	69	21	.261	.341	.356
Phil Garner	3B82,2B35	R	35	128	374	60	104	17	6	4	45	43	63	3	.278	.355	.388
Craig Reynolds	SS143,3B1	L	31	146	527	61	137	15	11	6	60	22	53	7	.260	.286	.364
Jose Cruz	OF160	L	36	160	600	96	187	28	13	12	95	73	68	22	.312	.381	.462
Jerry Mumphrey	OF137	S	31	151	524	66	152	20	3	9	83	56	79	15	.290	.355	.391
Terry Puhl	OF126	L	27	132	449	66	135	19	7	9	55	59	45	13	.301	.380	.434
Kevin Bass	OF81	S	25	121	331	33	86	17	5	2	29	6	57	5	.260	.279	.360
Ray Knight†	3B54,1B24	R	31	88	278	15	62	10	0	2	29	14	30	0	.223	.259	.281
Denny Walling	3B52,1B16,OF6	L	30	87	249	37	70	11	5	3	31	16	28	7	.281	.325	.402
Alan Ashby	C63	S	32	66	191	16	50	7	0	4	27	20	22	0	.262	.330	.361
Jim Pankovits	2B15,SS4,OF3	R	28	53	81	6	23	7	0	1	14	2	20	2	.284	.298	.407
Harry Spilman	1B18,C8	L	29	32	72	14	19	2	0	2	15	12	10	0	.264	.356	.375
Glenn Davis	1B16	R	23	18	61	6	13	5	0	2	8	4	12	0	.213	.258	.393
Bert Pena	SS21	R	24	24	39	3	8	1	0	1	4	3	8	0	.205	.262	.308
Tony Scott†	OF6	S	32	25	21	2	4	1	0	0	0	4	3	0	.190	.320	.238
Alan Bannister†	SS4,OF1	R	32	9	20	2	4	2	0	0	0	2	2	0	.200	.273	.300
Dickie Thon	SS5	R	26	5	17	3	6	0	1	0	1	0	4	0	.353	.389	.471
Tim Tolman	OF3,1B1	R	28	14	17	2	3	1	0	0	0	0	3	0	.176	.176	.235
Mike Richardt†		R	26	16	15	1	4	1	0	0	2	0	1	0	.267	.267	.333
Tom Wieghaus	C6	R	27	6	10	0	0	0	0	0	1	1	3	0	.000	.083	.000

Pitcher	T	Age	G	GS	CG	ShO	IP	H	HR	BB	SO	W-L	Sv	ERA
Joe Niekro	R	39	38	38	6	1	248.1	223	16	89	127	16-12	0	3.04
Bob Knepper	L	30	35	34	11	3	233.2	223	26	55	140	15-10	0	3.20
Nolan Ryan	R	37	30	30	5	2	183.2	143	12	69	197	12-11	0	3.04
Mike Scott	R	29	31	29	0	0	154.0	179	7	43	83	5-11	0	4.68
Bill Dawley	R	26	60	0	0	0	98.0	82	5	35	47	11-4	5	1.93
Frank DiPino	L	27	57	0	0	0	75.1	74	3	36	65	4-9	14	3.35
Dave Smith	R	29	53	0	0	0	77.1	60	5	20	45	5-4	5	2.21
Vern Ruhle	R	33	40	6	0	0	90.1	112	5	29	60	1-9	2	4.58
Mike LaCoss	R	28	39	18	2	1	132.0	132	3	55	86	7-5	3	4.02
Joe Sambito	L	32	32	0	0	0	47.2	39	5	16	26	0-0	0	3.02
Julio Solano	R	24	31	0	0	0	50.2	31	3	18	33	1-3	0	1.95
Mike Madden	L	27	17	7	0	0	40.2	46	1	35	29	2-3	0	5.53
Jeff Calhoun	L	26	9	0	0	0	15.1	5	0	2	11	0-1	0	1.17
Mark Ross	R	29	2	0	0	0	2.1	1	0	0	1	1-0	0	0.00

1984 Los Angeles Dodgers 4th NL West 79-83 .488 13.0 GB

Tom Lasorda

Player	Gm by Position	B	Age	G	AB	R	H	2B	3B	HR	RBI	BB	SO	SB	Avg	OBP	Slg
Mike Scioscia	C112	L	25	114	341	29	93	18	0	5	38	52	26	2	.273	.367	.370
Greg Brock	1B83	L	27	88	271	33	61	6	0	14	34	39	37	8	.225	.319	.402
Steve Sax	2B141	R	24	145	569	70	138	24	4	1	35	47	53	34	.243	.300	.304
German Rivera	3B90	R	23	94	227	20	59	12	2	2	17	21	30	1	.260	.321	.357
Dave Anderson	SS111,3B11	R	23	121	374	51	94	16	2	3	34	45	55	15	.251	.331	.329
Ken Landreaux	OF129	L	29	134	438	39	110	11	5	11	47	29	35	10	.251	.295	.374
Mike Marshall	OF118,1B15	R	24	134	495	68	127	27	0	21	65	40	93	4	.257	.315	.438
Candy Maldonado	OF102,3B4	R	23	116	254	25	68	14	0	5	28	19	29	0	.268	.318	.382
Pedro Guerrero	3B76,OF58,1B16	R	28	144	535	85	162	29	4	16	72	49	105	9	.303	.358	.462
Bill Russell	SS65,OF18,2B5	R	35	89	262	25	70	12	1	0	19	25	24	4	.267	.329	.321
R.J. Reynolds	OF63	S	25	73	240	24	62	12	2	2	24	14	38	7	.258	.300	.350
Franklin Stubbs	1B51,OF20	L	23	87	217	22	42	2	3	8	17	24	63	2	.194	.273	.341
Steve Yeager	C65	R	35	74	197	16	45	4	0	4	29	20	38	1	.228	.295	.310
Terry Whitfield	OF58	L	31	87	180	15	44	8	0	4	18	17	35	1	.244	.313	.356
Bob Bailor	2B23,3B17,SS16	R	32	65	131	11	36	4	0	0	8	8	1	3	.275	.317	.305
Rafael Landestoy	2B14,3B11,OF5	S	31	53	54	10	10	0	0	1	2	1	6	2	.185	.200	.241
Sid Bream	1B14	L	23	27	49	2	9	3	0	0	6	6	9	1	.184	.263	.245
Rick Monday	1B10,OF2	L	38	31	47	4	9	2	0	1	7	8	16	0	.191	.309	.298
Ed Amelung	OF23	L	25	34	46	7	10	0	0	0	4	2	4	3	.217	.250	.217
Tony Brewer	OF10	R	26	24	37	3	4	1	0	1	4	4	9	1	.108	.195	.216
Jack Fimple	C12	R	25	12	26	2	5	1	0	0	3	1	6	0	.192	.214	.231
Jose Morales		R	39	22	19	0	3	0	0	0	0	1	2	0	.158	.200	.158
Mike Vail	OF1	R	32	16	16	1	1	0	0	0	2	1	7	0	.063	.118	.063
Lemmie Miller	OF5	R	24	8	12	1	2	0	0	0	0	1	2	0	.167	.231	.167
Gil Reyes	C2	R	20	4	5	0	0	0	0	0	0	0	3	0	.000	.000	.000

Pitcher	T	Age	G	GS	CG	ShO	IP	H	HR	BB	SO	W-L	Sv	ERA
F. Valenzuela	L	23	34	34	12	2	261.0	218	14	106	240	12-17	0	3.03
Bob Welch	R	27	31	29	3	1	178.2	191	11	58	126	13-13	0	3.78
Alejandro Pena	R	25	28	28	8	4	199.1	186	7	46	135	12-6	0	2.48
Rick Honeycutt	L	30	29	28	6	2	183.2	180	11	51	75	10-9	0	2.84
Jerry Reuss	L	35	30	15	2	0	99.0	102	4	31	44	5-7	1	3.82
Pat Zachry	R	32	58	0	0	0	82.2	84	3	51	55	5-6	2	3.81
Burt Hooton	R	34	54	6	0	0	110.0	109	5	43	62	3-6	4	3.44
Orel Hershiser	R	25	45	20	8	4	189.2	160	9	50	150	11-8	2	2.66
Carlos Diaz	L	26	37	0	0	0	41.0	47	4	24	36	1-0	1	5.49
Tom Niedenfuer	R	24	33	0	0	0	47.1	39	3	23	45	2-5	11	2.47
Ken Howell	R	23	32	1	0	0	51.1	51	1	9	54	5-5	6	3.33
Larry White	R	25	7	1	0	0	12.0	9	2	6	10	0-1	0	3.00
Rich Rodas	L	24	3	0	0	0	5.0	5	2	1	1	0-0	0	5.40

1984 Cincinnati Reds 5th NL West 70-92 .432 22.0 GB

Vern Rapp (51-70)/Pete Rose (19-22)

Player	Gm by Position	B	Age	G	AB	R	H	2B	3B	HR	RBI	BB	SO	SB	Avg	OBP	Slg
Brad Gulden	C100	L	28	107	292	31	66	8	2	4	33	33	35	2	.226	.307	.308
Dan Driessen†	1B70	L	32	81	218	27	61	13	0	7	28	37	25	2	.280	.378	.436
Ron Oester	2B147,SS1	S	28	150	553	54	134	26	3	3	38	41	97	7	.242	.295	.316
Nick Esasky	3B82,1B25	R	24	113	322	30	62	10	5	10	45	52	103	1	.193	.301	.348
Dave Concepcion	SS104,3B54,1B6	R	36	154	531	46	130	26	1	4	58	52	72	22	.245	.307	.320
Dave Parker	OF151	L	33	156	607	73	173	28	0	16	94	41	89	11	.285	.328	.410
Gary Redus	OF114	R	27	123	394	69	100	21	3	7	22	52	71	48	.254	.338	.376
Eddie Milner	OF108	L	29	117	336	44	78	8	4	7	29	51	50	21	.232	.333	.342
Cesar Cedeno	OF77,1B44	R	33	110	380	59	105	24	2	10	47	25	54	19	.276	.321	.429
Tom Foley	SS83,2B10,3B1	L	24	106	277	26	70	8	3	5	27	24	36	3	.253	.310	.357
Duane Walker	OF68	L	27	83	195	35	57	10	3	10	28	33	35	7	.292	.391	.528
Dann Bilardello	C68	R	25	68	182	16	38	7	0	2	10	19	34	0	.209	.287	.280
Wayne Krenchicki	3B62,1B3,2B3	L	29	97	181	18	54	9	2	6	22	19	23	0	.298	.358	.470
Eric Davis	OF51	R	22	57	174	33	39	10	1	10	30	24	48	10	.224	.320	.466
Tony Perez	1B31	R	42	71	137	9	33	6	1	2	15	11	21	0	.241	.295	.343
Dave Van Gorder	C36,1B1	R	27	38	101	10	23	2	0	0	6	12	17	0	.228	.310	.248
Pete Rose†	1B23	S	43	26	96	9	35	9	0	0	11	9	7	0	.365	.430	.458
Tom Lawless†	2B23,3B6	R	27	43	80	10	20	2	0	1	2	8	12	6	.250	.318	.313
Skeeter Barnes	3B11,OF3	R	27	32	42	5	5	0	0	1	3	4	6	0	.119	.196	.190
Alan Knicely	1B8,C1	R	29	10	29	0	4	0	0	0	5	3	6	0	.138	.200	.138
Paul Householder†	OF10	S	25	14	12	3	1	1	0	0	0	3	3	1	.083	.267	.167
Wade Rowdon	3B1,SS1	R	23	4	7	0	2	0	0	0	0	0	1	0	.286	.286	.286
Alex Trevino†	C4	R	26	6	6	0	1	0	0	0	0	0	2	0	.167	.167	.167

Pitcher	T	Age	G	GS	CG	ShO	IP	H	HR	BB	SO	W-L	Sv	ERA
Mario Soto	R	27	33	33	13	0	237.1	181	26	87	185	18-7	0	3.53
Jeff Russell	R	22	33	30	4	2	181.2	186	15	65	101	6-18	0	4.26
Joe Price	L	27	30	30	3	1	171.2	176	19	61	129	7-13	0	4.19
Frank Pastore	R	26	24	16	1	0	98.1	110	10	40	53	3-8	0	6.50
Jay Tibbs	R	22	14	14	3	1	100.2	87	4	33	40	6-2	0	2.86
Bruce Berenyi†	R	29	13	11	0	0	51.0	63	0	42	53	3-7	0	6.00
Charlie Puleo	R	29	5	4	0	0	22.0	27	2	15	6	1-2	0	5.73
Tom Browning	L	24	3	3	0	0	23.1	27	0	5	14	1-0	0	1.54
Ted Power	R	29	78	0	0	0	108.2	93	4	46	81	9-7	11	2.82
Tom Hume	R	31	54	8	0	0	113.1	142	14	41	59	4-13	3	5.64
John Franco	L	23	54	0	0	0	79.1	74	3	36	55	6-2	4	2.61
Bob Owchinko	L	29	49	4	0	0	94.0	91	10	39	60	3-5	2	4.12
Bill Scherrer†	L	26	36	0	0	0	52.1	64	6	15	35	1-1	1	4.99
Brad Lesley	R	25	16	0	0	0	19.1	17	3	14	7	0-1	2	5.12
Ron Robinson	R	22	12	5	1	0	39.2	35	3	13	24	1-2	0	2.72
Andy McGaffigan†	R	27	9	3	0	0	23.0	23	2	8	18	0-2	0	5.48
Keefe Cato	R	26	8	0	0	0	15.2	22	5	4	12	0-1	1	8.04
Mike Smith	R	23	8	0	0	0	10.1	12	1	5	7	1-0	0	5.23
Carl Willis†	R	23	7	0	0	0	9.2	8	1	2	3	0-1	1	3.72
Fred Toliver	R	23	3	1	0	0	10.0	7	0	7	4	0-0	0	0.90

1984 San Francisco Giants 6th NL West 66-96 .407 26.0 GB

Frank Robinson (42-64)/Danny Ozark (24-32)

Player	Gm by Position	B	Age	G	AB	R	H	2B	3B	HR	RBI	BB	SO	SB	Avg	OBP	Slg
Bob Brenly	C127,1B22,OF3	R	30	145	506	74	147	28	0	20	80	48	52	6	.291	.352	.464
Scot Thompson	1B87,OF6	L	28	120	245	30	75	7	1	1	31	30	26	5	.306	.376	.355
Manny Trillo	2B96,3B4	R	33	98	401	45	102	21	1	4	36	25	55	0	.254	.300	.342
Joel Youngblood	3B117,OF11,2B5	R	32	134	469	50	119	17	1	10	51	48	86	5	.254	.328	.358
Johnnie LeMaster	SS129	R	30	132	451	46	98	13	2	4	32	31	97	17	.217	.265	.282
Jeffrey Leonard	OF131	R	28	136	514	76	155	27	2	21	86	47	123	17	.302	.357	.484
Chili Davis	OF123	S	24	137	499	87	157	21	6	21	81	42	74	12	.315	.368	.507
Dan Gladden	OF85	R	26	86	342	71	120	17	2	4	31	33	37	31	.351	.410	.447
Al Oliver†	1B82	L	37	91	339	27	101	19	2	0	34	20	27	2	.298	.339	.366
Brad Wellman	2B54,SS34,3B9	R	24	93	265	23	60	9	1	2	25	19	41	10	.226	.274	.291
Dusty Baker	OF62	R	35	100	243	31	71	7	2	3	32	40	27	4	.292	.387	.374
Jack Clark	OF54,1B4	R	28	57	203	33	65	9	1	11	44	43	29	1	.320	.434	.537
Gene Richards	OF26	L	30	87	135	18	34	4	0	0	4	18	28	5	.252	.340	.281
Steve Nicosia	C41	R	28	48	132	9	40	11	2	2	19	8	14	1	.303	.336	.462
Duane Kuiper	2B31,1B1	L	34	83	115	8	23	1	0	0	11	12	10	0	.200	.273	.209
Fran Mullins	3B28,SS28,2B4	R	27	57	110	8	24	8	0	2	10	9	29	3	.218	.277	.345
Chris Brown	3B23	R	22	23	84	6	24	7	0	1	11	9	19	2	.286	.358	.405
John Rabb	1B13,OF8,C6	R	24	54	82	10	16	1	0	3	9	10	33	1	.195	.283	.317
Alex Sanchez	OF11	R	25	13	41	3	8	0	1	0	2	0	12	2	.195	.195	.244
Randy Gomez	C14	R	27	14	30	0	5	1	0	0	0	8	3	0	.167	.342	.200
Tom O'Malley†	3B7	L	23	13	25	2	3	0	0	0	0	2	2	0	.120	.185	.120
Rob Deer	OF9	R	23	13	24	5	4	0	0	3	3	7	10	1	.167	.375	.542
Joe Pittman	SS6,2B5,3B2	R	30	17	22	2	5	0	0	0	2	0	6	1	.227	.217	.227

Pitcher	T	Age	G	GS	CG	ShO	IP	H	HR	BB	SO	W-L	Sv	ERA
Bill Laskey	R	26	35	34	2	0	207.2	222	20	50	71	9-14	0	4.33
Mike Krukow	R	32	35	33	3	1	199.1	234	22	78	141	11-12	1	4.56
Jeff Robinson	R	23	34	33	1	1	171.2	195	12	52	102	7-15	0	4.56
Mark Davis	L	23	46	27	1	0	174.2	201	25	54	124	5-17	0	5.36
Mark Grant	R	20	11	10	0	0	53.2	56	6	19	32	1-4	1	6.37
Atlee Hammaker	L	26	6	6	0	0	33.0	32	2	9	24	2-0	0	2.18
Mark Calvert	R	27	10	5	1	0	32.0	40	4	9	5	2-4	0	5.06
George Riley	L	27	5	4	0	0	29.1	39	1	7	12	1-0	0	3.99
Gary Lavelle	L	35	77	0	0	0	101.0	92	5	42	71	5-4	12	2.76
Greg Minton	R	32	74	1	0	0	124.1	130	6	57	48	4-9	19	3.76
Frank Williams	R	26	61	1	1	1	106.1	88	2	51	91	9-4	3	3.55
Randy Lerch	L	29	37	4	0	0	72.1	80	3	36	48	5-3	2	4.23
Bob Lacey	L	30	34	1	0	0	51.0	55	5	13	26	1-3	0	3.88
Jeff Cornell	R	27	23	0	0	0	38.1	51	4	22	19	1-3	0	6.10
Scott Garrelts	R	22	21	3	0	0	43.0	45	6	34	32	2-3	0	5.65
Renie Martin†	R	28	12	0	0	0	23.1	29	2	16	8	1-1	0	3.86

>>1985 Toronto Blue Jays 1st AL East 99-62 .615 —

Bobby Cox

Player	Gm by Position	B	Age	G	AB	R	H	2B	3B	HR	RBI	BB	SO	SB	Avg	OBP	Slg
Ernie Whitt	C134	L	33	139	412	55	101	21	2	19	64	47	59	3	.245	.323	.444
Willie Upshaw	1B147,DH1	L	28	148	501	79	138	31	5	15	65	48	71	8	.275	.342	.447
Damaso Garcia	2B143	R	28	146	600	70	169	25	4	8	65	15	41	28	.282	.302	.377
Rance Mulliniks	3B119	L	29	129	366	55	108	26	1	10	57	55	54	2	.295	.383	.454
Tony Fernandez	SS160	S	23	161	564	71	163	31	10	2	51	43	41	13	.289	.340	.390
George Bell	OF157,3B2	R	25	157	607	87	167	28	6	28	95	43	90	21	.275	.327	.479
Jesse Barfield	OF154	R	25	155	539	94	156	34	9	27	84	66	143	22	.289	.369	.536
Lloyd Moseby	OF152	L	25	152	584	92	151	30	7	18	70	76	91	37	.259	.345	.426
Jeff Burroughs	DH75	R	34	86	191	19	49	9	3	6	28	34	36	0	.257	.366	.429
Garth Iorg	3B104,2B23	R	30	131	288	33	90	22	1	7	37	21	26	3	.313	.358	.469
Al Oliver†	DH59,1B1	L	38	61	187	20	47	6	1	5	23	7	13	0	.251	.282	.374
Len Matuszek†	DH54,1B5	L	30	62	151	23	32	6	2	2	15	11	24	2	.212	.259	.318
Buck Martinez	C42	R	36	42	99	11	16	3	0	4	14	10	12	0	.162	.239	.313
Cecil Fielder	1B25	R	21	30	74	6	23	4	0	4	16	6	16	0	.311	.358	.527
Cliff Johnson†	DH21,1B3	R	37	24	73	4	20	0	0	1	10	9	15	0	.274	.349	.315
Lou Thornton	OF35,DH16	L	22	56	72	18	17	1	1	1	8	2	24	1	.236	.267	.319
Manuel Lee	2B38,DH8,SS8*	S	20	64	40	9	8	0	0	0	0	2	9	1	.200	.238	.200
Ron Shepherd	OF16,DH15	R	24	38	35	7	4	2	0	0	1	2	12	3	.114	.162	.171
Rick Leach	1B10,OF4	L	28	16	35	2	7	0	1	0	1	3	9	0	.200	.263	.257
Gary Allenson	C14	R	30	14	34	2	4	1	0	0	3	0	10	0	.118	.118	.147
Willie Aikens	DH11	L	30	12	20	2	4	1	0	1	5	3	6	0	.200	.292	.400
Steve Nicosia†	C6	R	29	6	15	0	4	0	0	0	1	0	0	0	.267	.267	.267
Kelly Gruber	3B5,2B1	R	23	5	13	0	3	0	0	0	1	0	3	0	.231	.231	.231
Jeff Hearron	C4	R	23	4	7	0	1	0	0	0	0	0	2	0	.143	.143	.143
Mitch Webster†	DH2,OF2	S	26	4	1	0	0	0	0	0	0	0	0	0	.000	.000	.000

M. Lee, 5 G at 3B

Pitcher	T	Age	G	GS	CG	ShO	IP	H	HR	BB	SO	W-L	Sv	ERA
Dave Stieb	R	27	36	36	8	2	265.0	206	22	96	167	14-13	0	2.48
Doyle Alexander	R	34	36	36	6	1	260.2	268	28	67	142	17-10	0	3.45
Jimmy Key	L	24	35	32	3	0	212.2	188	22	50	85	14-6	0	3.00
Jim Clancy	R	29	23	23	1	0	128.2	117	15	37	66	9-6	0	3.78
Luis Leal	R	28	15	14	0	0	67.1	82	13	24	33	3-6	0	5.75
Tom Filer	R	28	11	9	0	0	48.2	38	6	18	24	7-0	0	3.88
Steve Davis	L	24	10	5	0	0	28.0	23	5	13	22	2-1	0	3.54
Gary Lavelle	L	36	69	0	0	0	72.2	54	5	36	50	5-7	8	3.10
Bill Caudill	R	28	67	0	0	0	69.1	53	9	35	46	4-6	14	2.99
Jim Acker	R	26	61	0	0	0	86.1	86	7	43	42	7-2	10	3.23
Dennis Lamp	R	32	53	1	0	0	105.2	96	7	27	68	11-0	2	3.32
Tom Henke	R	27	28	0	0	0	40.0	29	4	8	42	3-3	13	2.03
Ron Musselman	R	30	25	4	0	0	52.1	59	2	24	29	3-0	0	4.47
John Cerutti	L	25	4	1	0	0	6.2	10	1	4	5	0-2	0	5.40
Stan Clarke	L	24	4	0	0	0	4.0	3	1	2	2	0-0	0	4.50

1985 New York Yankees 2nd AL East 97-64 .602 2.0 GB

Yogi Berra (6-10)/Billy Martin (91-54)

Player	Gm by Position	B	Age	G	AB	R	H	2B	3B	HR	RBI	BB	SO	SB	Avg	OBP	Slg
Butch Wynegar	C96	S	29	102	309	27	69	15	0	5	32	64	43	0	.223	.356	.320
Don Mattingly	1B159	L	24	159	652	107	211	48	3	35	145	56	41	2	.324	.371	.567
Willie Randolph	2B143	R	30	143	497	75	137	21	2	5	40	85	39	16	.276	.382	.356
Mike Pagliarulo	3B134	L	25	138	380	55	91	16	2	19	62	45	86	0	.239	.324	.442
Bobby Meacham	SS155	S	24	156	481	70	105	16	2	1	47	54	102	25	.218	.302	.266
Dave Winfield	OF152,DH2	R	33	155	633	105	174	34	6	26	114	52	96	19	.275	.328	.471
Rickey Henderson	OF141,DH1	R	26	143	547	146	172	28	5	24	72	99	65	80	.314	.419	.516
Ken Griffey Sr.	OF110,DH7,1B1	L	35	127	438	68	120	28	4	10	69	41	51	7	.274	.331	.425
Don Baylor	DH140	R	36	142	477	70	110	24	1	23	91	52	90	0	.231	.330	.430
Ron Hassey	C69,DH2,1B2	L	32	92	267	31	79	16	1	13	42	28	21	0	.296	.369	.509
Dan Pasqua	OF37,DH14	L	23	60	148	17	31	3	1	9	25	16	38	0	.209	.289	.426
Billy Sample	OF55	R	30	59	139	18	40	5	0	1	15	9	10	2	.288	.336	.345
Andre Robertson	3B33,SS14,2B2	R	27	50	125	16	41	5	0	2	17	6	24	1	.328	.358	.416
Dale Berra	3B41,SS6	R	28	48	109	8	25	5	1	1	8	7	20	1	.229	.276	.321
Omar Moreno†	OF26,DH1	L	32	34	66	12	13	4	1	1	4	1	16	1	.197	.209	.333
Henry Cotto	OF30	R	24	34	56	4	17	1	0	1	6	3	12	1	.304	.339	.375
Rex Hudler	2B16,1B1,SS1	R	24	20	51	4	8	0	1	0	1	1	9	0	.157	.173	.196
Scott Bradley	DH9,C3	L	25	19	49	4	8	2	1	0	1	1	5	0	.163	.196	.245
Juan Bonilla	2B7	R	29	8	16	0	2	1	0	0	2	0	3	0	.125	.125	.188
Juan Espino	C9	R	29	9	11	0	4	0	0	0	0	0	0	0	.364	.364	.364
Victor Mata	OF3	R	24	6	7	1	1	0	0	0	0	0	0	0	.143	.143	.143
Keith Smith	SS3	S	23	4	0	1	0	0	0	0	0	0	0	0	—	—	—

Pitcher	T	Age	G	GS	CG	ShO	IP	H	HR	BB	SO	W-L	Sv	ERA
Ron Guidry	L	34	34	33	11	2	259.0	243	28	42	143	22-6	0	3.27
Phil Niekro	R	46	33	33	7	1	220.0	203	29	120	149	16-12	0	4.09
Ed Whitson	R	30	30	30	2	2	158.2	201	19	43	89	10-8	0	4.88
Joe Cowley	R	26	30	26	1	0	159.2	132	29	85	97	12-6	0	3.95
Dennis Rasmussen	L	26	22	16	2	0	101.2	97	10	42	63	3-5	0	3.98
Marty Bystrom	R	26	8	8	0	0	41.0	44	8	19	16	3-2	0	5.71
Joe Niekro†	R	40	3	3	0	0	12.1	14	3	8	4	2-1	0	5.84
Dave Righetti	L	26	74	0	0	0	107.0	96	5	45	92	12-7	29	2.78
Brian Fisher	R	23	55	0	0	0	98.1	77	4	29	85	4-4	14	2.38
Rich Bordi	R	26	51	3	0	0	98.0	95	5	29	64	6-8	2	3.21
Bob Shirley	L	31	48	8	2	0	109.0	103	5	26	55	5-5	2	2.64
Neil Allen†	R	27	17	0	0	0	29.1	26	1	13	16	1-0	1	2.76
Mike Armstrong	R	31	9	0	0	0	14.2	9	4	2	11	0-0	0	3.07
Don Cooper	R	29	7	0	0	0	10.0	12	2	3	4	0-0	0	5.40
Rod Scurry†	L	29	5	0	0	0	12.2	5	2	10	17	1-0	1	2.84
John Montefusco	R	35	3	1	0	0	7.0	12	3	2	2	0-0	0	10.29
Dale Murray†	R	35	3	0	0	0	2.0	4	0	0	0	0-0	0	13.50

1985 Detroit Tigers 3rd AL East 84-77 .522 15.0 GB

Sparky Anderson

Player	Gm by Position	B	Age	G	AB	R	H	2B	3B	HR	RBI	BB	SO	SB	Avg	OBP	Slg
Lance Parrish	C120,DH22	R	29	140	549	64	150	27	1	28	98	41	90	2	.273	.323	.479
Darrell Evans	1B113,DH33,3B7	L	38	151	505	81	125	17	0	40	94	85	85	0	.248	.356	.519
Lou Whitaker	2B150	L	28	152	609	102	170	29	8	21	73	80	56	6	.279	.362	.456
Tom Brookens	3B151,SS8,2B3*	R	31	156	485	54	115	34	6	7	47	27	78	14	.237	.277	.375
Alan Trammell	SS149	R	27	149	605	79	156	21	7	13	57	50	71	14	.258	.312	.380
Kirk Gibson	OF144,DH8	L	28	154	581	96	167	37	5	29	97	71	137	30	.287	.364	.518
Chet Lemon	OF144	R	30	145	517	69	137	28	4	18	68	45	93	0	.265	.334	.439
Larry Herndon	OF136	R	31	137	442	45	108	12	7	12	37	33	79	2	.244	.298	.385
John Grubb	DH33,OF18	L	36	78	155	19	38	7	1	5	25	24	25	0	.245	.342	.400
Nelson Simmons	OF38,DH31	S	22	75	251	31	60	11	0	10	33	26	41	1	.239	.306	.402
Barbaro Garbey	1B37,OF24,DH21*	R	28	86	237	27	61	9	1	6	29	15	37	3	.257	.305	.380
Dave Bergman	1B44,DH5,OF1	L	32	69	140	8	25	2	0	3	7	14	15	0	.179	.250	.257
Alex Sanchez	OF31,DH28	R	26	71	133	19	33	6	2	6	12	0	39	2	.248	.248	.459
Marty Castillo	C32,3B25	R	28	57	84	4	10	2	0	2	5	2	19	0	.119	.138	.214
Bob Melvin	C41	R	23	41	82	10	18	4	1	0	4	3	21	0	.220	.247	.293
Chris Pittaro	3B22,2B4,DH1	S	23	28	62	10	15	3	1	0	7	5	13	1	.242	.299	.323
Doug Flynn†	2B20,SS8,3B4	R	34	32	51	2	13	2	1	0	2	0	3	0	.255	.250	.333
Mike Laga	DH5,1B4	L	25	9	36	3	6	1	0	2	6	0	9	0	.167	.167	.361
Doug Baker	SS12,2B1	S	24	15	27	4	5	1	0	0	1	0	9	0	.185	.185	.222
Scotti Madison	DH3,C1	S	25	6	11	0	0	0	0	0	1	2	0	0	.000	.143	.000
Jim Weaver	DH4,OF4	L	25	12	7	2	1	1	0	0	0	1	4	0	.143	.250	.286
Rusty Kuntz	DH3,1B1	R	30	5	5	0	0	0	0	0	0	2	2	0	.000	.286	.000

T. Brookens, 1 G at DH, 1 G at C; B. Garbey, 1 G at 3B

Pitcher	T	Age	G	GS	CG	ShO	IP	H	HR	BB	SO	W-L	Sv	ERA
Jack Morris	R	30	35	35	13	4	257.0	212	21	110	191	16-11	0	3.33
Dan Petry	R	26	34	34	8	0	238.2	190	24	81	109	15-13	0	3.36
Walt Terrell	R	27	34	34	5	3	229.0	221	9	95	130	15-10	0	3.85
Frank Tanana†	L	31	20	20	4	0	137.1	131	13	34	107	10-7	0	3.34
Milt Wilcox	R	35	8	8	0	0	39.0	51	6	14	20	1-3	0	4.85
Mickey Mahler†	L	32	3	2	0	0	20.2	19	2	4	14	1-2	0	1.74
Willie Hernandez	L	30	74	0	0	0	106.2	82	13	14	76	8-10	31	2.70
Aurelio Lopez	R	36	51	0	0	0	86.1	82	15	41	53	3-7	5	4.80
Bill Scherrer	L	27	48	0	0	0	66.0	62	10	41	46	3-2	0	4.36
Juan Berenguer	R	30	31	13	0	0	95.0	96	12	48	82	5-6	0	5.59
Randy O'Neal	R	24	28	12	1	0	94.1	82	8	36	52	5-5	1	3.24
Doug Bair†	R	35	21	3	0	0	49.0	54	3	25	30	2-0	0	6.24
Chuck Cary	L	25	16	0	0	0	23.2	16	2	8	22	0-1	2	3.42
Bob Stoddard	R	28	8	0	0	0	13.1	15	3	5	11	0-0	1	6.75

1985 Baltimore Orioles 4th AL East 83-78 .516 16.0 GB

Joe Altobelli (29-26)/Cal Ripken (1-0)/Earl Weaver (53-52)

Player	Gm by Position	B	Age	G	AB	R	H	2B	3B	HR	RBI	BB	SO	SB	Avg	OBP	Slg
Rick Dempsey	C131	R	35	132	362	54	92	19	0	12	52	50	87	0	.254	.345	.406
Eddie Murray	1B154,DH2	S	29	156	583	111	173	37	1	31	124	84	68	5	.297	.383	.523
Alan Wiggins†	2B76	S	27	76	298	43	85	11	4	0	21	29	16	30	.285	.353	.349
Floyd Rayford	3B78,C29,DH1	R	27	105	359	55	110	21	1	18	48	10	69	3	.306	.324	.521
Cal Ripken Jr.	SS161	R	24	161	642	116	181	32	5	26	110	67	68	2	.282	.347	.469
Fred Lynn	OF123	L	33	124	448	59	118	12	1	23	68	53	100	7	.263	.339	.449
Lee Lacy	OF115,DH5	R	37	121	492	69	144	22	4	9	48	39	95	10	.293	.343	.409
Mike Young	OF90,DH37	S	25	139	450	72	123	22	1	28	81	48	104	1	.273	.348	.513
Larry Sheets	DH93,OF9,1B1	L	25	113	328	43	86	8	0	17	50	28	52	0	.262	.323	.442
Jim Dwyer	OF78,DH3	L	35	101	233	35	58	8	3	7	36	37	31	0	.249	.353	.399
Gary Roenicke	OF89,DH17	R	30	114	225	36	49	9	0	15	43	44	36	2	.218	.342	.458
Wayne Gross	3B67,DH10,1B9	L	33	103	217	31	51	8	0	11	18	46	48	1	.235	.369	.424
Rich Dauer	2B73,3B17,1B1	R	32	85	208	25	42	7	0	2	14	20	7	0	.202	.275	.264
John Shelby	OF59,DH3,2B1	S	27	69	205	28	58	6	2	7	27	7	44	5	.283	.307	.434
Fritz Connally	3B46,1B2,DH1	R	27	50	112	16	26	4	0	3	15	19	21	0	.232	.346	.348
Lenn Sakata	2B50,DH1	R	31	55	97	15	22	3	0	3	6	6	15	3	.227	.279	.351
Dan Ford	DH28	R	33	28	75	4	14	2	0	1	1	7	17	0	.187	.256	.253
Al Pardo	C29	S	22	34	75	3	10	1	0	0	1	3	15	0	.133	.167	.147
Joe Nolan	C5,DH4	L	34	31	38	1	5	2	0	0	6	5	5	0	.132	.227	.184
John Lowenstein	DH6,OF4	L	38	12	26	0	2	0	0	0	2	2	3	0	.077	.138	.077
Leo Hernandez	DH8,1B1,OF1	R	25	12	21	0	1	0	0	0	0	0	4	0	.048	.048	.048
Tom O'Malley	3B3	L	24	8	14	1	1	0	0	1	2	0	2	0	.071	.071	.286
Kelly Paris	DH2,2B2	R	27	5	9	0	0	0	0	0	0	0	1	0	.000	.000	.000

Pitcher	T	Age	G	GS	CG	ShO	IP	H	HR	BB	SO	W-L	Sv	ERA
Scott McGregor	L	31	35	34	8	1	204.0	226	34	65	86	14-14	0	4.81
Mike Boddicker	R	27	32	32	9	2	203.1	227	13	89	135	12-17	0	4.07
Dennis Martinez	R	30	33	31	3	1	180.0	203	29	63	68	13-11	0	5.15
Storm Davis	R	23	31	28	8	1	175.0	172	11	70	93	10-8	0	4.53
Ken Dixon	R	24	34	18	3	1	162.0	144	20	64	108	8-4	1	3.67
Mike Flanagan	L	33	15	15	1	0	86.0	101	14	28	42	4-5	0	5.13
Phil Huffman	R	27	2	1	0	0	4.2	7	1	5	2	0-0	0	15.43
Sammy Stewart	R	30	56	1	0	0	129.2	117	15	66	77	5-7	9	3.61
Don Aase	R	30	54	0	0	0	88.0	83	6	35	67	10-6	14	3.78
Tippy Martinez	L	35	49	0	0	0	70.0	70	8	37	47	3-3	4	5.40
Nate Snell	R	32	43	0	0	0	100.1	100	4	30	41	3-2	5	2.69
Brad Havens	L	25	8	1	0	0	14.1	20	4	10	19	0-1	0	8.79
Eric Bell	L	21	4	0	0	0	5.2	4	1	4	4	0-0	0	4.76
John Habyan	R	21	2	0	0	0	2.2	3	0	0	2	1-0	0	0.00
Bill Swaggerty	R	28	1	0	0	0	1.2	3	0	2	2	0-0	0	5.40

1985 Boston Red Sox 5th AL East 81-81 .500 18.5 GB

John McNamara

Player	Gm by Position	B	Age	G	AB	R	H	2B	3B	HR	RBI	BB	SO	SB	Avg	OBP	Slg
Rich Gedman	C139	L	25	144	498	66	147	30	5	18	80	50	79	2	.295	.362	.484
Bill Buckner	1B162	L	35	162	673	89	201	46	3	16	110	30	36	18	.299	.325	.447
Marty Barrett	2B155	R	27	156	534	59	142	26	0	5	56	56	50	7	.266	.336	.343
Wade Boggs	3B161	L	27	161	653	107	240	42	3	8	78	96	61	2	.368	.450	.478
Jackie Gutierrez	SS99	R	25	103	275	33	60	5	2	2	21	12	37	10	.218	.250	.273
Dwight Evans	OF152,DH7	R	33	159	617	110	162	29	1	29	78	114	105	7	.263	.378	.454
Jim Rice	OF130,DH7	R	32	140	546	85	159	20	3	27	103	51	75	2	.291	.349	.487
Steve Lyons	OF114,DH5,3B1*	L	25	133	371	52	98	14	3	5	30	32	64	12	.264	.322	.358
Mike Easler	DH130,OF20	L	34	155	568	71	149	29	4	16	74	53	129	0	.262	.325	.412
Tony Armas	OF79,DH19	R	31	103	385	50	102	17	5	23	64	18	90	0	.265	.298	.514
Glenn Hoffman	SS93,2B3,3B3	R	26	96	279	40	77	17	2	6	34	25	40	2	.276	.343	.416
Marc Sullivan	C32	R	26	32	69	10	12	2	0	2	3	6	15	0	.174	.240	.290
Dave Stapleton	2B14,1B8,DH5	R	31	30	66	4	15	6	0	0	2	4	11	0	.227	.271	.318
Rick Miller	OF8,DH4	L	37	41	45	5	15	2	0	0	9	5	6	1	.333	.392	.378
Dave Sax	C16,OF4	R	26	22	36	2	11	3	0	0	6	3	3	0	.306	.350	.389
Reid Nichols†	OF10,DH4,2B3	R	26	21	32	3	6	1	0	1	3	2	4	1	.188	.250	.313
Mike Greenwell	OF17	L	21	17	31	7	10	1	0	4	8	3	4	1	.323	.382	.742
Kevin Romine	OF23,DH1	R	24	24	28	3	6	2	0	0	1	1	4	1	.214	.241	.286
Ed Jurak	3B7,SS3,DH2*	R	27	26	13	4	3	0	0	0	0	1	3	0	.231	.286	.231

S. Lyons, 1 G at SS; E. Jurak, 1 G at 1B, 1 G at OF

Pitcher	T	Age	G	GS	CG	ShO	IP	H	HR	BB	SO	W-L	Sv	ERA
Oil Can Boyd	R	25	35	35	13	3	272.1	273	26	67	154	15-13	0	3.70
Bruce Hurst	L	27	35	31	6	1	229.1	243	31	70	189	11-13	0	4.51
Al Nipper	R	26	25	25	5	0	162.0	157	14	82	85	9-12	0	4.06
Bobby Ojeda	L	27	39	22	5	0	157.2	166	11	48	102	9-11	1	4.00
Roger Clemens	R	22	15	15	3	1	98.1	83	5	37	74	7-5	0	3.29
Tim Lollar†	L	29	16	10	1	0	67.0	57	9	40	44	5-5	1	4.57
Jeff Sellers	R	21	4	4	1	0	22.1	24	1	7	6	2-0	0	3.63
Jim Dorsey	R	29	2	1	0	0	5.1	12	2	10	2	0-1	0	20.25
Mike Brown	R	26	2	1	0	0	3.1	9	0	3	3	0-0	0	21.60
Bob Stanley	R	30	48	0	0	0	87.2	76	7	30	46	6-6	10	2.87
Steve Crawford	R	27	44	1	0	0	91.0	103	5	28	58	6-5	12	3.76
Mark Clear	R	29	41	0	0	0	55.2	45	1	50	55	1-3	3	3.72
Mike Trujillo	R	25	27	7	1	0	84.0	112	7	23	19	4-4	1	4.82
Bruce Kison	R	35	22	9	0	0	92.0	98	9	32	56	5-3	1	4.11
Rob Woodward	R	22	5	2	0	0	26.2	17	0	9	16	1-0	0	1.69
Tom McCarthy	R	24	3	0	0	0	5.0	7	1	4	2	0-0	0	10.80
Charlie Mitchell	R	23	2	0	0	0	1.2	5	1	0	2	0-0	0	16.20

1985 Milwaukee Brewers 6th AL East 71-90 .441 28.0 GB

George Bamberger

Player	Gm by Position	B	Age	G	AB	R	H	2B	3B	HR	RBI	BB	SO	SB	Avg	OBP	Slg
Charlie Moore	C102,OF3	R	32	105	349	35	81	13	4	0	31	27	53	4	.232	.288	.292
Cecil Cooper	1B123,DH30	L	35	154	631	82	185	39	8	16	99	30	77	10	.293	.322	.456
Jim Gantner	2B124,3B24,SS1	L	32	143	523	63	133	15	4	5	44	33	42	11	.254	.300	.327
Paul Molitor	3B135,DH4	R	28	140	576	93	171	28	3	10	48	54	80	21	.297	.356	.408
Ernest Riles	SS115,DH1	L	24	116	448	54	128	12	7	5	45	36	54	2	.286	.339	.377
Robin Yount	OF108,DH12,1B2	R	29	122	466	76	129	26	3	15	68	49	56	10	.277	.342	.442
Ben Oglivie	OF91,DH4	L	36	101	341	40	99	17	2	10	61	37	51	0	.290	.354	.440
Paul Householder	OF91,DH3	S	26	95	299	41	77	15	0	11	34	27	60	1	.258	.320	.418
Ted Simmons	DH99,1B28,C15*	S	35	143	528	60	144	28	2	12	76	57	32	1	.273	.342	.402
Ed Romero	SS43,2B31,OF14*	R	27	88	251	24	63	11	1	0	21	26	20	1	.251	.321	.303
Rick Manning	OF74,DH2	L	30	79	216	19	47	9	1	2	18	14	19	1	.218	.265	.296
Bill Schroeder	C48,DH4,1B1	R	26	53	194	18	47	8	0	8	25	12	61	0	.242	.290	.407
Randy Ready	OF37,3B7,2B3*	R	25	48	181	29	48	9	5	1	21	14	23	0	.265	.318	.387
Mark Brouhard	OF29,DH1	R	29	37	108	11	28	7	2	1	13	5	26	0	.259	.298	.389
Bobby Clark	OF27	R	30	29	93	6	21	3	0	0	8	7	19	1	.226	.277	.258
Doug Loman	OF20	L	27	24	66	10	14	3	2	0	7	1	12	0	.212	.221	.318
Carlos Ponce	1B10,OF6,DH3	R	26	21	62	4	10	2	0	1	5	1	9	0	.161	.169	.242
Brian Giles	SS20,2B13,DH2	R	25	34	58	6	10	1	0	1	1	7	16	2	.172	.262	.241
Mike Felder	OF14	S	23	15	56	8	11	1	0	0	0	5	6	4	.196	.262	.214
Billy Joe Robidoux	OF11,1B6,DH1	L	21	18	51	5	9	2	0	3	8	12	16	0	.176	.333	.392
Dion James	OF11,DH3	L	22	18	49	5	11	1	0	0	3	6	6	0	.224	.309	.245
Dave Huppert	C15	R	28	15	21	1	1	0	0	0	0	2	7	0	.048	.130	.048

T. Simmons, 2 G at 3B; E. Romero, 1 G at 3B; R. Ready, 2 G at DH

Pitcher	T	Age	G	GS	CG	ShO	IP	H	HR	BB	SO	W-L	Sv	ERA
Teddy Higuera	L	26	32	30	7	2	212.1	186	22	63	127	15-8	0	3.90
Danny Darwin	R	29	39	29	11	1	217.2	212	34	65	125	8-18	2	3.80
Ray Burris	R	34	29	28	6	1	170.1	182	25	53	81	9-13	0	4.81
Moose Haas	R	29	27	26	6	1	161.2	165	21	25	78	8-8	0	3.84
Pete Vuckovich	R	32	22	22	1	0	112.2	134	16	48	55	6-10	0	5.51
Jamie Cocanower	R	28	24	15	3	1	116.1	122	6	73	44	6-8	0	4.33
Tim Leary	R	27	5	5	0	0	33.1	40	5	8	29	1-4	0	4.05
Bill Wegman	R	22	3	3	0	0	17.2	17	3	3	6	2-0	0	3.57
Rollie Fingers	R	38	47	0	0	0	55.1	59	9	19	24	1-6	17	5.04
Bob Gibson	R	28	41	1	0	0	92.1	86	10	49	53	6-7	11	3.90
Bob McClure	L	33	38	1	0	0	85.2	91	10	30	57	4-1	3	4.31
Ray Searage	L	30	33	0	0	0	38.0	54	2	24	36	1-4	1	5.92
Peter Ladd	R	28	29	0	0	0	45.2	58	5	10	22	0-2	2	4.53
Rick Waits	L	33	24	0	0	0	47.0	67	3	20	24	3-2	1	6.51
Chuck Porter	R	30	6	1	0	0	13.2	15	1	2	8	0-0	0	1.98
Jim Kern	R	36	5	0	0	0	11.0	14	1	5	3	0-1	0	6.55
Brad Lesley	R	26	5	0	0	0	6.1	8	2	2	5	1-0	0	9.95

1985 Cleveland Indians 7th AL East 60-102 .370 39.5 GB

Pat Corrales

Player	Gm by Position	B	Age	G	AB	R	H	2B	3B	HR	RBI	BB	SO	SB	Avg	OBP	Slg
Jerry Willard	C96,DH1	L	25	104	300	39	81	13	0	7	36	28	59	0	.270	.333	.383
Pat Tabler	1B92,DH18,3B4*	R	27	117	404	47	111	18	3	5	59	27	55	0	.275	.321	.371
Tony Bernazard	2B147,SS1	S	28	153	500	73	137	26	3	11	59	69	72	17	.274	.361	.404
Brook Jacoby	3B161,2B1	R	25	161	606	72	166	26	3	20	87	48	120	2	.274	.324	.426
Julio Franco	SS151,2B8,DH1	R	23	160	636	97	183	33	4	6	90	54	74	13	.288	.343	.381
Brett Butler	OF150,DH1	L	28	152	591	106	184	28	14	5	50	63	42	47	.311	.377	.431
George Vukovich	OF137	L	29	149	434	43	106	22	0	8	45	30	75	2	.244	.292	.350
Joe Carter	OF135,1B11,DH7*	R	25	143	489	64	128	27	0	15	59	25	74	24	.262	.298	.409
Andre Thornton	DH122	R	35	124	461	49	109	13	0	22	88	47	75	3	.236	.304	.408
Mike Hargrove	1B84,DH2,OF1	L	35	107	284	31	81	14	1	1	27	39	29	1	.285	.370	.352
Carmelo Castillo	OF51,DH9	R	27	67	184	27	45	5	1	11	25	11	40	3	.245	.298	.462
Chris Bando	C67	S	29	73	173	11	24	4	1	0	13	22	21	0	.139	.234	.173
Otis Nixon	OF80,DH11	S	26	104	162	34	38	4	0	3	9	8	27	20	.235	.271	.315
Bennie Ayala	OF20,DH3	R	34	46	76	10	19	7	0	2	15	4	17	0	.250	.284	.421
Butch Benton	C26	R	27	31	67	5	12	4	0	0	7	3	9	0	.179	.208	.239
Mel Hall	OF15,DH5	L	24	23	66	7	21	6	0	0	12	8	12	0	.318	.387	.409
Mike Fischlin	2B31,SS22,1B6*	R	29	73	60	12	12	4	1	0	2	5	7	0	.200	.262	.300
Johnnie LeMaster†	SS10	R	31	11	20	0	3	0	0	0	0	0	3	0	.150	.150	.150
Jim Wilson	DH2,1B2	R	24	4	14	2	5	0	0	0	4	1	3	0	.357	.400	.357

P. Tabler, 1 G at 2B; J. Carter, 1 G at 2B; M. Fischlin, 5 G at DH, 3 G at 3B

Pitcher	T	Age	G	GS	CG	ShO	IP	H	HR	BB	SO	W-L	Sv	ERA
Neal Heaton	L	25	36	33	5	1	207.2	244	19	80	82	9-17	0	4.90
Bert Blyleven†	R	34	23	23	15	4	179.2	163	14	49	129	9-11	0	3.26
Don Schulze	R	22	19	18	1	0	94.1	128	10	19	37	4-10	0	6.01
Curt Wardle†	L	24	15	12	0	0	66.0	78	11	34	37	7-6	0	6.68
Roy Smith	R	23	12	11	1	0	62.1	84	8	17	28	1-4	0	5.34
Ramon Romero	L	26	19	10	0	0	64.1	69	13	38	38	2-3	0	6.58
Keith Creel	R	26	15	8	0	0	62.0	73	7	23	31	2-5	0	4.79
Rick Behenna	R	25	4	4	0	0	19.2	29	3	8	4	0-2	0	7.78
Jose Roman	R	22	5	3	0	0	16.1	13	3	14	12	0-4	0	6.61
Rich Thompson	R	26	57	0	0	0	80.0	95	8	48	30	3-8	5	6.30
Jamie Easterly	L	32	50	7	0	0	98.2	96	9	53	58	4-1	0	3.92
Tom Waddell	R	26	49	9	1	0	112.2	104	20	39	53	8-6	9	4.87
Vern Ruhle	R	34	42	16	1	0	125.0	139	16	30	54	2-10	3	4.32
Jerry Reed	R	29	33	5	0	0	72.1	67	12	19	37	3-5	8	4.11
Bryan Clark	L	28	31	3	0	0	62.2	78	8	34	24	3-4	2	6.32
Dave Von Ohlen	L	26	26	0	0	0	43.1	47	5	20	12	3-2	0	2.91
Jeff Barkley	R	25	21	0	0	0	41.0	37	5	15	30	0-3	1	5.27
Mike Jeffcoat†	L	25	9	0	0	0	9.2	8	1	6	4	0-0	0	2.79
Ernie Camacho	R	30	2	0	0	0	3.1	4	0	1	2	0-1	0	8.10

1985 Kansas City Royals 1st AL West 91-71 .562 —

Dick Howser

Player	Gm by Position	B	Age	G	AB	R	H	2B	3B	HR	RBI	BB	SO	SB	Avg	OBP	Slg
Jim Sundberg	C112	R	34	115	367	38	90	12	4	10	35	33	67	0	.245	.308	.381
Steve Balboni	1B160	R	28	160	600	74	146	28	2	36	88	52	166	1	.243	.307	.477
Frank White	2B149	R	34	149	563	62	140	25	1	22	69	28	86	10	.249	.284	.414
George Brett	3B152,DH1	L	32	155	550	108	184	38	5	30	112	103	49	9	.335	.436	.585
Onix Concepcion	SS128,2B2	R	27	131	314	32	64	5	1	2	20	16	29	4	.204	.255	.245
Willie Wilson	OF140	S	29	141	605	87	168	25	21	4	43	29	94	43	.278	.316	.408
Lonnie Smith†	OF119	R	29	120	448	77	115	23	4	6	41	41	69	40	.257	.321	.366
Darryl Motley	OF114,DH7	R	25	123	383	45	85	20	1	17	49	18	57	6	.222	.257	.413
Hal McRae	DH106	R	39	112	320	41	83	19	0	14	70	44	45	0	.259	.349	.450
Jorge Orta	DH85	L	34	110	300	32	80	21	1	4	45	22	28	2	.267	.317	.383
Pat Sheridan	OF69,DH1	L	27	78	206	18	47	9	2	3	17	23	38	11	.228	.307	.335
Lynn Jones	OF100,DH2	R	32	110	152	12	32	7	0	0	9	8	15	0	.211	.261	.257
John Wathan	C49,1B6,DH2	R	35	60	145	11	34	8	1	1	9	17	15	1	.234	.319	.324
Buddy Biancalana	SS74,2B4,DH2	S	25	81	138	21	26	5	1	1	6	17	34	1	.188	.277	.261
Dane Iorg	OF32,DH2,1B2*	L	35	64	130	7	29	9	1	1	21	8	16	0	.223	.268	.331
Greg Pryor	3B26,2B20,SS13*	R	35	63	114	8	25	3	0	1	3	8	12	0	.219	.270	.272
Omar Moreno†	OF21	L	32	24	70	9	17	1	3	2	12	3	8	0	.243	.280	.429
Jamie Quirk	C17,1B1	L	30	19	57	3	16	3	1	0	4	2	9	0	.281	.305	.368
Dave Leeper	OF8	L	25	15	34	1	3	0	0	0	4	1	3	0	.088	.114	.088
Jim Scranton	SS5	R	25	6	4	1	0	0	0	0	0	0	0	0	.000	.000	.000
Bob Hegman	2B1	R	27	1	0	0	0	0	0	0	0	0	0	0	—	—	—

D. Iorg, 1 G at 3B; G. Pryor, 1 G at DH, 1 G at 1B

Pitcher	T	Age	G	GS	CG	ShO	IP	H	HR	BB	SO	W-L	Sv	ERA
Charlie Leibrandt	L	28	33	33	8	3	237.2	223	17	68	108	17-9	0	2.69
Bud Black	L	28	33	33	5	2	205.2	216	17	59	122	10-15	0	4.33
Bret Saberhagen	R	21	32	32	10	1	235.1	211	19	38	158	20-6	0	2.87
Danny Jackson	L	23	32	32	4	3	208.0	209	7	76	114	14-12	0	3.42
Mark Gubicza	R	22	29	28	0	0	177.1	160	14	77	99	14-10	0	4.06
Dan Quisenberry	R	32	84	0	0	0	129.0	142	8	16	54	8-9	37	2.37
Joe Beckwith	R	30	49	0	0	0	95.0	99	9	32	80	1-5	1	4.07
Mike Jones	L	25	33	1	0	0	64.0	62	6	39	32	3-3	0	4.78
Mike LaCoss	R	29	21	0	0	0	40.2	49	2	29	26	1-1	1	5.09
Steve Farr	R	28	16	3	0	0	37.2	34	2	20	36	2-1	1	3.11
Mark Huismann	R	27	9	0	0	0	18.2	14	1	3	9	1-0	0	1.93
Larry Gura†	L	37	3	0	0	0	4.1	7	1	4	2	0-0	1	12.46
Tony Ferreira	L	22	2	0	0	0	5.2	6	0	2	5	0-0	0	7.94
Dennis Leonard	R	34	2	0	0	0	2.0	1	0	0	1	0-0	0	0.00

1985 California Angels 2nd AL West 90-72 .556 1.0 GB

Gene Mauch

Player	Gm by Position	B	Age	G	AB	R	H	2B	3B	HR	RBI	BB	SO	SB	Avg	OBP	Slg
Bob Boone	C147	R	37	150	460	37	114	17	0	5	55	37	35	1	.248	.306	.317
Rod Carew	1B116	L	39	127	443	69	124	17	3	2	39	64	47	5	.280	.371	.345
Bobby Grich	2B116,1B16,3B15*	R	36	144	479	74	116	17	3	13	53	81	77	3	.242	.355	.372
Doug DeCinces	3B111,DH3	R	34	120	427	50	104	22	1	20	78	47	71	1	.244	.317	.440
Dick Schofield	SS147	R	22	147	438	50	96	19	3	8	41	35	70	11	.219	.287	.331
Gary Pettis	OF122	S	27	125	443	67	114	10	8	1	32	62	125	56	.257	.347	.323
Brian Downing	OF121,DH25	R	34	150	520	80	137	23	1	20	85	78	61	5	.263	.371	.427
Reggie Jackson	OF81,DH52	L	39	143	460	64	116	27	0	27	85	78	138	1	.252	.360	.487
Ruppert Jones	OF73,DH43	L	30	125	389	66	90	17	2	21	67	57	82	7	.231	.328	.447
Juan Beniquez	OF71,1B46,DH14*	R	35	132	411	54	125	13	5	8	42	34	46	4	.304	.364	.418
Rob Wilfong	2B69,DH2	L	31	83	217	16	41	3	0	4	13	16	32	4	.189	.243	.258
Mike Brown†	OF48,DH7	R	25	60	153	23	41	9	1	4	20	7	21	0	.268	.304	.418
Jack Howell	3B42	L	23	43	137	19	27	4	0	5	18	16	33	1	.197	.279	.336
Jerry Narron	C45,DH7,1B1	L	29	67	132	12	29	4	0	5	14	11	17	0	.220	.280	.364
Daryl Sconiers	DH20,1B6	L	26	44	98	14	28	6	1	2	12	15	18	2	.286	.371	.429
Craig Gerber	SS53,3B9,DH1*	L	26	65	91	8	24	1	2	0	6	2	3	0	.264	.277	.319
Darrell Miller	OF45,DH4,C1*	R	27	51	48	8	18	2	1	2	7	1	10	0	.375	.400	.583
Rufino Linares	DH14,OF2	R	34	18	43	7	11	2	0	3	11	2	5	2	.256	.283	.512
George Hendrick†	OF12,DH1	R	35	16	41	5	5	1	0	2	6	4	8	0	.122	.196	.293
Devon White	OF16	S	22	21	7	7	1	0	0	0	0	1	3	3	.143	.333	.143
Pat Keedy	3B2,OF1	R	27	3	4	1	2	1	0	1	1	0	0	0	.500	.500	1.500
Gus Polidor	SS1,OF1	R	23	2	1	1	1	0	0	0	0	0	0	0	1.000	1.000	1.000

B. Grich, 6 G at DH; J. Beniquez, 1 G at 3B, 1 G at SS; C. Gerber, 1 G at 2B; D. Miller, 1 G at 3B

Pitcher	T	Age	G	GS	CG	ShO	IP	H	HR	BB	SO	W-L	Sv	ERA
Mike Witt	R	24	35	35	6	1	250.0	228	22	98	180	15-9	0	3.56
Ron Romanick	R	24	31	31	6	1	195.0	210	29	62	64	14-9	0	4.11
Kirk McCaskill	R	24	30	29	6	1	189.2	189	23	64	102	12-12	0	4.70
Jim Slaton	R	35	29	24	1	0	148.1	162	22	63	60	6-10	1	4.37
John Candelaria†	L	31	13	13	1	1	71.0	70	7	24	53	7-3	0	3.80
Urbano Lugo	R	22	20	10	1	0	83.0	86	10	29	42	3-4	0	3.69
Geoff Zahn	L	39	7	7	1	1	37.0	44	5	14	14	2-2	0	4.38
Tommy John†	L	42	12	6	0	0	38.1	51	3	15	17	2-4	0	4.70
Don Sutton†	R	40	5	5	0	0	31.2	27	6	8	16	2-2	0	3.69
Bob Kipper†	L	20	2	1	0	0	3.1	7	1	3	0	0-1	0	21.60
Tony Mack	R	24	1	1	0	0	2.1	8	0	0	0	0-1	0	15.43
Donnie Moore	R	31	65	0	0	0	103.0	91	9	21	72	8-8	31	1.92
Stew Cliburn	R	28	44	0	0	0	99.0	87	5	26	48	9-3	6	2.09
Pat Clements†	L	23	41	0	0	0	62.0	47	4	25	19	5-0	1	3.34
Doug Corbett	R	32	30	0	0	0	46.0	49	7	20	24	3-3	0	4.89
Luis Sanchez	R	31	26	0	0	0	61.1	67	9	27	34	2-0	2	5.72
Al Holland†	L	32	15	0	0	0	24.1	17	4	10	14	0-1	0	1.48
Dave Smith	R	27	4	0	0	0	5.0	5	1	1	3	0-0	0	7.20
Alan Fowlkes	R	26	2	0	0	0	7.0	8	4	4	5	0-0	0	9.00

1985 Chicago White Sox 3rd AL West 85-77 .525 6.0 GB

Tony La Russa

Player	Gm by Position	B	Age	G	AB	R	H	2B	3B	HR	RBI	BB	SO	SB	Avg	OBP	Slg
Carlton Fisk	C130,DH28	R	37	153	543	85	129	23	1	37	107	52	81	17	.238	.320	.488
Greg Walker	1B151,DH7	L	25	163	601	77	155	38	4	24	92	44	100	5	.258	.308	.454
Julio Cruz	2B87,DH2	S	30	91	234	28	46	2	3	0	15	32	40	8	.197	.297	.231
Tim Hulett	3B115,2B28,OF1	R	25	141	395	52	106	19	4	5	37	30	81	6	.268	.324	.375
Ozzie Guillen	SS150	L	21	150	491	71	134	21	9	1	33	12	36	7	.273	.291	.358
Harold Baines	OF159,DH1	L	26	160	640	86	198	29	3	22	113	42	89	1	.309	.348	.467
Rudy Law	OF120,DH3	L	28	125	390	62	101	21	6	4	36	27	40	29	.259	.311	.374
Daryl Boston	OF93,DH2	L	22	95	232	20	53	13	1	3	15	14	44	8	.228	.271	.332
Ron Kittle	DH57,OF57	R	27	116	379	51	87	12	0	26	58	31	92	1	.230	.295	.467
Luis Salazar	OF84,3B39,DH8*	R	29	122	327	39	80	18	2	10	45	12	60	14	.245	.267	.404
Scott Fletcher	3B55,SS44,2B37*	R	26	119	301	38	77	8	1	2	31	35	47	5	.256	.332	.309
Bryan Little	2B68,3B2,SS1	S	25	73	188	35	47	9	1	2	27	26	21	0	.250	.345	.340
Oscar Gamble	DH48	L	35	70	148	20	30	5	0	4	20	34	22	0	.203	.353	.318
Jerry Hairston	DH29,OF5	S	33	95	140	9	34	8	0	2	20	29	18	0	.243	.371	.343
Tom Paciorek†	OF23,DH12,1B6	R	38	46	122	14	30	2	0	0	9	8	22	2	.246	.293	.262
Reid Nichols†	OF48,DH1	R	26	51	118	20	35	7	1	1	15	15	13	5	.297	.373	.398
Marc Hill	C37,3B1	R	33	40	75	5	10	2	0	0	4	12	9	0	.133	.253	.160
Joel Skinner	C21	R	24	22	44	9	15	4	1	1	5	5	13	0	.341	.408	.545
Joe DeSa	1B9,DH4,OF1	L	25	28	44	5	8	2	0	2	7	3	6	0	.182	.234	.364
Mark Ryal	OF12	L	24	12	33	4	5	3	0	0	3	3	3	0	.152	.222	.242
Mark Gilbert	OF7	S	28	7	22	3	6	1	0	0	3	4	5	0	.273	.385	.318
John Cangelosi	OF3,DH2	S	22	5	2	2	0	0	0	0	0	0	1	0	.000	.333	.000
Mike Squires		L	33	2	0	1	0	0	0	0	0	0	0	0	—	—	—

L. Salazar, 6 G at 1B; S. Fletcher, 2 G at DH

Pitcher	T	Age	G	GS	CG	ShO	IP	H	HR	BB	SO	W-L	Sv	ERA
Britt Burns	L	26	36	34	8	4	227.0	206	26	79	172	18-11	0	3.96
Floyd Bannister	L	30	34	34	4	1	210.2	211	30	100	198	10-14	0	4.87
Tom Seaver	R	40	35	33	6	1	238.2	223	22	69	134	16-11	0	3.17
Tom Lollar†	L	29	18	13	0	1	83.0	83	10	58	61	3-5	0	4.66
Joel Davis	R	20	12	11	1	0	71.1	71	6	26	37	3-3	0	4.16
Rich Dotson	R	26	9	9	0	0	52.1	53	5	17	33	3-4	0	4.47
Bill Long	R	25	4	3	0	0	14.0	25	4	5	13	0-1	0	10.29
Bob James	R	26	69	0	0	0	110.0	90	5	23	88	8-7	32	2.13
Juan Agosto	L	27	54	0	0	0	60.1	45	3	23	39	4-3	1	3.58
Dan Spillner	R	33	52	3	0	0	91.2	83	10	33	41	4-3	1	3.44
Gene Nelson	R	24	46	18	1	0	145.2	144	23	67	101	10-10	2	4.26
Jerry Don Gleaton	L	27	31	0	0	0	29.2	37	3	13	22	1-0	1	5.76
Dave Wehrmeister	R	32	23	0	0	0	39.1	35	4	10	32	2-2	2	3.43
Mike Stanton†	R	32	11	0	0	0	11.2	15	2	8	12	0-1	0	9.26
Bruce Tanner	R	23	10	4	0	0	27.0	34	1	13	9	1-2	0	5.33
Bob Fallon	L	25	10	0	0	0	16.0	25	5	9	17	0-0	0	6.19
Edwin Correa	R	19	5	1	0	0	10.1	11	2	11	10	1-0	0	6.97
Al Jones	R	26	5	0	0	0	6.0	3	0	3	2	1-0	0	1.50
Steve Fireovid	R	28	4	0	0	0	7.0	17	0	2	2	0-0	0	5.14

1985 Minnesota Twins 4th AL West 77-85 .475 14.0 GB

Billy Gardner (27-35)/Ray Miller (50-50)

Player	Gm by Position	B	Age	G	AB	R	H	2B	3B	HR	RBI	BB	SO	SB	Avg	OBP	Slg
Mark Salas	C115,DH3	L	24	120	360	51	108	20	5	9	41	18	37	0	.300	.332	.458
Kent Hrbek	1B156,DH2	L	25	158	593	78	165	31	2	21	93	67	87	1	.278	.351	.444
Tim Teufel	2B137,DH1	R	26	138	434	58	113	24	3	10	50	48	70	4	.260	.335	.399
Gary Gaetti	3B156,OF4,DH1*	R	26	160	560	71	138	31	0	20	63	37	89	13	.246	.301	.409
Greg Gagne	SS106,DH5	R	23	114	293	37	66	15	3	2	23	20	57	10	.225	.279	.317
Kirby Puckett	OF161	R	24	161	691	80	199	29	13	4	74	41	87	21	.288	.330	.385
Tom Brunansky	OF155	R	24	157	567	71	137	28	4	27	90	71	86	5	.242	.320	.448
Mickey Hatcher	OF97,DH11,1B4	R	30	116	444	46	125	28	0	3	49	16	23	0	.282	.308	.365
Roy Smalley	DH56,SS49,3B14*	S	32	129	388	57	100	20	0	12	45	60	65	0	.258	.357	.402
Randy Bush	OF41,DH28,1B1	L	26	97	234	26	56	13	3	10	35	24	30	3	.239	.321	.449
Mike Stenhouse	DH27,OF16,1B8	L	27	81	179	23	40	5	0	5	21	29	18	1	.223	.330	.335
Dave Engle	DH38,C17,OF3	R	28	70	172	28	44	8	2	7	25	21	28	2	.256	.333	.448
Tim Laudner	C68,1B1	R	27	72	164	16	39	5	0	7	19	12	45	0	.238	.292	.396
Ron Washington	SS31,2B24,DH7*	R	33	70	135	24	37	6	4	1	14	8	15	5	.274	.308	.400
Dave Meier	OF63,DH3	R	25	71	104	15	27	6	0	1	8	18	12	0	.260	.374	.346
Mark Funderburk	DH15,OF5,1B1	R	28	23	70	7	22	7	1	2	13	5	12	0	.314	.351	.529
Alvaro Espinoza	SS31	R	23	32	57	5	15	2	0	0	9	1	9	0	.263	.288	.298
Steve Lombardozzi	2B26	R	25	28	54	10	20	4	1	0	6	6	6	3	.370	.426	.481
Jeff Reed	C7	L	22	7	10	2	2	0	0	0	0	0	3	0	.200	.200	.200

G. Gaetti, 1 G at 1B; R. Smalley, 1 G at 1B; R. Washington, 7 G at 3B, 1 G at 1B

Pitcher	T	Age	G	GS	CG	ShO	IP	H	HR	BB	SO	W-L	Sv	ERA
Mike Smithson	R	30	37	37	8	3	257.0	264	25	78	127	15-14	0	4.34
Frank Viola	L	25	36	36	9	0	250.2	262	26	68	135	18-14	0	4.09
John Butcher	R	28	34	33	8	2	207.2	239	24	43	92	11-14	0	4.98
Ken Schrom	R	30	29	26	6	0	160.2	164	28	59	74	9-12	0	4.99
Bert Blyleven†	R	34	14	14	9	1	114.0	101	9	26	77	8-5	0	3.00
Mark Portugal	R	22	6	4	0	0	24.1	24	3	14	12	1-3	0	5.55
Rich Yett	R	22	1	1	0	0	0.1	1	0	2	0	0-0	0	27.00
Ron Davis	R	29	57	0	0	0	64.2	55	7	35	72	2-6	25	3.48
Pete Filson	L	26	40	6	1	0	95.2	93	13	30	42	4-5	2	3.67
Frank Eufemia	R	25	39	0	0	0	61.2	56	7	21	30	4-2	2	3.79
Rick Lysander	R	32	35	1	0	0	61.0	72	3	22	26	0-2	3	6.05
Curt Wardle†	L	24	35	0	0	0	49.0	49	9	28	47	1-3	1	5.51
Steve Howe†	L	27	13	0	0	0	19.0	28	1	7	10	2-3	0	6.16
Tom Klawitter	L	27	7	2	0	0	9.1	7	2	13	5	0-0	0	6.75
Mark Brown	R	25	6	0	0	0	15.2	21	1	7	5	0-0	0	6.89
Dennis Burtt	R	27	5	2	0	0	28.1	20	2	7	9	2-2	0	3.81
Len Whitehouse	L	27	5	0	0	0	7.1	12	4	2	4	0-0	1	11.05

1985 Oakland Athletics 4th AL West 77-85 .475 14.0 GB

Jackie Moore

Player	Gm by Position	B	Age	G	AB	R	H	2B	3B	HR	RBI	BB	SO	SB	Avg	OBP	Slg
Mike Heath	C112,OF35,3B13	R	30	138	436	71	109	18	6	13	55	41	63	7	.250	.313	.408
Bruce Bochte	1B128	L	34	137	424	48	125	17	1	14	60	49	58	3	.295	.367	.439
Donnie Hill	2B122	S	24	123	393	45	112	13	2	3	48	23	33	9	.285	.321	.351
Carney Lansford	3B97	R	28	98	401	51	111	18	2	13	46	18	27	2	.277	.311	.429
Alfredo Griffin	SS162	S	27	162	614	75	166	18	7	2	64	20	50	24	.270	.290	.332
Mike Davis	OF151	L	26	154	547	92	157	34	1	24	82	50	99	24	.287	.348	.484
Dwayne Murphy	OF150	L	30	152	523	77	122	21	3	20	59	84	123	4	.233	.340	.400
Dave Collins	OF91	S	32	112	379	52	95	16	4	4	29	29	37	29	.251	.303	.346
Dave Kingman	DH149,1B9	R	36	158	592	66	141	16	0	30	91	62	114	3	.238	.309	.417
Dusty Baker	1B58,OF35,DH13	R	36	111	343	48	92	15	1	14	52	50	47	2	.268	.359	.440
Mickey Tettleton	C76,DH1	S	24	78	211	23	53	12	0	3	15	28	59	2	.251	.344	.351
Steve Henderson	OF58,DH1	R	32	85	193	25	58	8	3	3	31	18	34	0	.301	.358	.420
Tony Phillips	3B31,2B24	S	26	42	161	23	45	12	2	4	17	13	34	3	.280	.331	.453
Rob Picciolo	3B19,2B17,1B13*	R	32	71	102	19	28	2	0	1	8	2	17	3	.275	.288	.324
Jose Canseco	OF26	R	20	29	96	16	29	3	0	5	13	4	31	1	.302	.330	.490
Mike Gallego	2B42,SS21,3B12	R	24	76	77	13	16	5	1	1	9	12	14	1	.208	.319	.338
Steve Kiefer	3B34,DH2	R	24	40	66	8	13	1	1	1	10	1	18	0	.197	.203	.288
Dan Meyer	DH1,3B1,OF1	L	32	14	12	2	0	0	0	0	0	1	0	0	.000	.077	.000
Charlie O'Brien	C16	R	25	16	11	3	3	1	0	0	1	3	3	0	.273	.429	.364

R. Picciolo, 10 G at DH, 9 G at SS

Pitcher	T	Age	G	GS	CG	ShO	IP	H	HR	BB	SO	W-L	Sv	ERA
Chris Codiroli	R	27	37	37	4	0	226.0	228	23	78	111	14-14	0	4.46
Don Sutton†	R	40	29	29	1	1	194.1	194	19	51	91	13-8	0	3.89
Tim Birtsas	L	24	29	25	2	0	141.1	124	18	91	94	10-6	0	4.01
Bill Krueger	L	27	32	23	2	0	151.1	165	13	69	56	9-10	0	4.52
Tommy John†	L	42	11	11	0	0	48.0	66	6	13	8	2-6	0	6.19
Jose Rijo	R	20	12	9	0	0	63.2	57	6	28	65	6-4	0	3.53
Jay Howell	R	29	63	0	0	0	98.0	98	5	31	68	9-8	29	2.85
Keith Atherton	R	26	56	0	0	0	104.2	89	17	42	77	4-7	3	4.30
Steve Ontiveros	R	24	39	0	0	0	74.2	45	4	19	36	1-3	8	1.93
Steve McCatty	R	31	30	9	1	0	85.2	95	10	41	36	4-4	0	5.57
Rick Langford	R	33	23	3	0	0	59.0	60	8	15	21	3-5	0	3.51
Steve Mura	R	30	23	1	0	0	48.0	41	3	25	29	1-1	1	4.13
Curt Young	L	25	19	7	0	0	46.0	57	15	22	19	0-4	0	7.24
Mike Warren	R	24	16	6	0	0	49.0	52	13	38	48	1-4	0	6.61
Tim Conroy	L	25	16	2	0	0	25.1	25	3	15	8	0-1	0	4.26
Jeff Kaiser	L	24	15	0	0	0	16.2	25	6	20	10	0-0	0	14.58
Tom Tellmann	R	31	11	0	0	0	21.1	33	3	9	8	0-0	0	5.06

Seasons: Team Rosters 885

1985 Seattle Mariners 6th AL West 74-88 .457 17.0 GB

Chuck Cottier

Player	Gm by Position	B	Age	G	AB	R	H	2B	3B	HR	RBI	BB	SO	SB	Avg	OBP	Slg
Bob Kearney	C108	R	28	108	305	24	74	14	1	6	27	11	59	1	.243	.277	.354
Alvin Davis	1B154	L	24	155	578	78	166	33	1	18	78	90	71	1	.287	.381	.441
Jack Perconte	2B125	L	30	125	485	60	128	17	7	2	23	50	36	31	.264	.335	.340
Jim Presley	3B154	R	23	155	570	71	157	33	1	28	84	44	100	2	.275	.324	.484
Spike Owen	SS117	S	24	118	352	41	91	10	6	6	37	34	27	11	.259	.322	.372
Phil Bradley	OF159	R	26	159	641	100	192	33	8	26	88	55	129	22	.300	.365	.498
Dave Henderson	OF138	R	26	139	502	70	121	28	2	14	68	48	104	6	.241	.310	.388
Al Cowens	OF110,DH5	R	33	122	452	59	120	32	5	14	69	30	56	0	.265	.310	.451
Gorman Thomas	DH133	R	34	135	484	76	104	16	1	32	87	84	126	3	.215	.330	.450
Ivan Calderon	OF53,DH3,1B2	R	23	67	210	37	60	16	4	8	28	19	45	4	.286	.349	.514
Donnie Scott	C74	S	23	80	185	18	41	13	0	4	23	15	41	1	.222	.275	.357
Domingo Ramos	SS36,2B20,1B14*	R	27	75	168	19	33	6	0	1	15	17	23	0	.196	.267	.250
Ken Phelps	DH25,1B8	L	30	61	116	18	24	3	0	9	24	24	33	2	.207	.343	.466
Barry Bonnell	OF22,1B5,DH2	R	31	48	111	9	27	8	0	1	10	6	19	1	.243	.282	.342
Harold Reynolds	2B61	S	24	67	104	15	15	3	1	0	6	17	14	3	.144	.264	.192
Dave Valle	C31	R	24	31	70	2	11	1	0	0	4	1	17	0	.157	.181	.171
John Moses	OF29	S	27	33	62	4	12	0	0	0	3	2	8	5	.194	.219	.194
Danny Tartabull	SS16,3B4	R	22	19	61	8	20	7	1	1	7	8	14	1	.328	.406	.525
Darnell Coles	SS15,3B7,DH2*	R	23	27	59	8	14	4	0	1	5	9	17	0	.237	.338	.356
Al Chambers		L	24	4	4	0	0	0	0	0	0	0	2	0	.000	.000	.000
Rickey Nelson	OF3	L	26	6	2	2	0	0	0	0	0	0	1	0	.000	.000	.000

D. Ramos, 7 G at 3B; D. Coles, 2 G at OF

Pitcher	T	Age	G	GS	CG	ShO	IP	H	HR	BB	SO	W-L	Sv	ERA
Matt Young	L	26	37	35	5	2	218.1	242	23	76	136	12-19	1	4.91
Mike Moore	R	25	35	34	14	2	247.0	230	18	70	155	17-10	0	3.46
Mark Langston	L	24	24	24	2	0	126.2	122	22	91	72	7-14	0	5.47
Bill Swift	R	23	23	21	0	0	120.2	131	8	48	55	6-10	0	4.77
Frank Wills	R	26	24	18	1	0	123.0	122	18	68	67	5-11	1	6.00
Jim Beattie	R	30	18	15	1	1	70.1	93	9	33	45	5-6	0	7.29
Mike Morgan	R	25	2	2	0	0	6.0	11	2	5	2	1-1	0	12.00
Bill Wilkinson	L	20	2	2	0	0	6.0	8	2	6	5	0-2	0	13.50
Jim Lewis	R	29	2	1	0	0	4.2	8	1	1	1	0-1	0	7.71
Ed Vande Berg	L	26	76	0	0	0	67.2	71	4	31	34	2-1	3	3.72
Edwin Nunez	R	22	70	0	0	0	90.1	79	13	34	58	7-3	16	3.09
Roy Thomas	R	32	40	0	0	0	93.2	66	8	48	70	7-0	1	3.36
Bob Long	R	30	28	0	0	0	38.1	30	7	17	29	0-0	0	3.76
Mike Stanton†	R	32	24	0	0	0	29.0	32	4	21	17	1-2	1	5.28
Salome Barojas	R	28	17	4	0	0	52.2	65	6	33	27	0-5	0	5.98
Brian Snyder	L	27	15	6	0	0	35.1	44	2	19	23	1-2	1	6.37
Karl Best	R	26	15	0	0	0	32.1	25	1	6	32	2-1	4	1.95
Jack Lazorko	R	29	15	0	0	0	20.1	23	1	8	7	0-0	1	3.54
Dave Geisel	L	30	12	0	0	0	27.0	35	3	15	17	0-0	0	6.33
Paul Mirabella	L	31	10	0	0	0	13.2	9	0	4	8	0-0	0	1.32
Dave Tobik	R	32	8	0	0	0	9.0	10	2	3	8	1-0	1	6.00

1985 Texas Rangers 7th AL West 62-99 .385 28.5 GB

Doug Rader (9-23)/Bobby Valentine (53-76)

Player	Gm by Position	B	Age	G	AB	R	H	2B	3B	HR	RBI	BB	SO	SB	Avg	OBP	Slg
Don Slaught	C102	R	26	102	343	34	96	17	4	8	35	20	41	5	.280	.331	.423
Pete O'Brien	1B159	L	27	159	573	69	153	34	3	22	92	69	53	5	.267	.342	.452
Toby Harrah	2B122,SS2,DH1	R	36	126	396	65	107	18	1	9	44	113	60	11	.270	.432	.389
Buddy Bell†	3B83	R	33	84	313	33	74	13	3	4	32	33	21	3	.236	.308	.335
Curtis Wilkerson	SS110,2B19,DH2	S	24	129	360	35	88	11	6	0	22	22	63	14	.244	.293	.308
Gary Ward	OF153,DH1	R	31	154	593	77	170	28	7	15	70	39	97	26	.287	.329	.433
Oddibe McDowell	OF103,DH4	L	22	111	406	63	97	14	5	18	42	36	85	25	.239	.304	.431
George Wright	OF102,DH4	S	26	109	363	21	69	13	0	2	18	25	49	4	.190	.241	.242
Cliff Johnson†	DH82	R	37	82	296	31	76	17	1	12	56	31	44	0	.257	.330	.443
Larry Parrish	OF69,DH22,3B2	R	31	94	346	44	86	11	1	17	51	33	77	0	.249	.314	.434
Wayne Tolleson	SS81,2B29,3B12*	S	29	123	323	45	101	9	5	1	18	21	46	21	.313	.353	.381
Steve Buechele	3B69,2B1	R	23	69	219	22	48	6	3	6	21	14	38	3	.219	.271	.356
Bobby Jones	OF30,DH10,1B4	L	35	83	134	14	30	2	0	5	23	11	30	1	.224	.284	.351
Duane Walker†	OF32,DH10	L	28	53	132	14	23	2	0	5	11	15	29	2	.174	.264	.303
Alan Bannister	DH21,OF14,2B10*	R	33	57	122	17	32	4	1	1	6	14	17	8	.262	.338	.336
Glenn Brummer	C47,DH1,OF1	R	30	49	108	7	30	4	0	0	5	11	22	1	.278	.355	.315
Tommy Dunbar	DH18,OF14	L	25	45	104	7	21	4	0	1	5	12	9	0	.202	.291	.269
Geno Petralli	C41	S	25	42	100	7	27	2	0	0	11	8	12	1	.270	.319	.290
Bill Stein	3B11,1B8,DH6*	R	38	44	79	5	20	3	1	1	12	1	15	0	.253	.272	.354
Ellis Valentine	OF7,DH4	R	30	11	38	5	8	1	0	2	4	2	8	0	.211	.250	.395
Nick Capra	OF8	R	27	8	8	1	1	0	0	0	0	0	0	0	.125	.125	.125
Jeff Kunkel	SS2	R	23	2	4	1	1	0	0	0	0	0	3	0	.250	.250	.250
Luis Pujols	C1	R	29	1	1	0	1	0	0	0	0	0	0	0	1.000	1.000	1.000

W. Tolleson, 6 G at DH; A. Bannister, 5 G at 3B, 4 G at 1B; B. Stein, 3 G at 2B, 3 G at OF

Pitcher	T	Age	G	GS	CG	ShO	IP	H	HR	BB	SO	W-L	Sv	ERA
Charlie Hough	R	37	34	34	14	1	250.1	198	23	83	141	14-16	0	3.31
Mike Mason	L	26	38	30	1	1	179.0	212	22	73	92	8-15	0	4.83
Burt Hooton	R	35	29	20	2	0	124.0	149	18	40	62	5-8	0	5.23
Frank Tanana†	L	31	13	13	0	0	77.2	89	15	23	52	2-7	0	5.91
Jeff Russell	R	23	13	13	0	0	62.0	85	10	27	44	3-6	0	7.55
Glen Cook	R	25	9	7	0	0	40.0	53	12	18	19	2-3	0	9.45
Jose Guzman	R	22	5	5	0	0	32.2	27	3	14	24	3-2	0	2.76
Bob Sebra	R	23	7	4	0	0	20.1	26	4	14	13	0-2	0	7.52
Matt Williams	R	25	6	3	0	0	26.0	20	3	10	22	2-1	0	2.42
Greg Harris	R	29	58	0	0	0	113.0	74	7	43	111	5-4	11	2.47
Dave Schmidt	R	28	51	4	1	1	85.2	81	6	22	46	7-6	5	3.15
Dave Stewart†	R	28	42	5	0	0	81.1	86	13	37	64	0-6	4	5.42
Dave Rozema	R	28	34	4	0	0	88.0	100	10	22	42	3-7	7	4.19
Dickie Noles	R	28	28	13	0	0	110.1	129	11	33	59	4-8	1	5.06
Chris Welsh	L	30	25	6	0	0	76.1	101	11	25	31	2-5	0	4.13
Dwayne Henry	R	23	16	0	0	0	21.0	16	0	7	20	2-2	3	2.57
Rich Surhoff†	R	22	7	0	0	0	8.1	12	2	3	8	0-1	2	7.56
Ricky Wright	L	26	5	0	0	0	7.2	5	0	5	7	0-0	0	4.70
Tommy Boggs	R	29	4	0	0	0	7.0	13	3	2	6	0-0	0	11.57
Dale Murray†	R	35	1	0	0	0	1.0	3	0	0	0	0-0	0	18.00

»1985 St. Louis Cardinals 1st NL East 101-61 .623 —

Whitey Herzog

Player	Gm by Position	B	Age	G	AB	R	H	2B	3B	HR	RBI	BB	SO	SB	Avg	OBP	Slg
Tom Nieto	C95	R	24	95	253	15	57	10	2	0	34	26	37	0	.225	.305	.281
Jack Clark	1B121,OF12	R	29	126	442	71	124	26	3	22	87	83	88	1	.281	.393	.502
Tom Herr	2B158	S	29	159	596	97	180	38	3	8	110	80	55	31	.302	.379	.416
Terry Pendleton	3B149	S	24	149	559	56	134	16	3	5	69	37	75	17	.240	.285	.306
Ozzie Smith	SS158	S	30	158	537	70	148	22	3	6	54	65	27	31	.276	.355	.361
Vince Coleman	OF150	S	23	151	636	107	170	20	10	1	40	50	115	110	.267	.320	.335
Willie McGee	OF149	S	26	152	612	114	216	26	18	10	82	34	86	56	.353	.384	.503
Andy Van Slyke	OF142,1B2	L	24	146	424	61	110	25	6	13	55	47	54	34	.259	.335	.439
Darrell Porter	C82	L	33	84	240	30	53	12	2	10	36	41	48	6	.221	.335	.413
Tito Landrum	OF73	R	30	85	161	21	45	8	2	4	21	19	30	1	.280	.356	.429
Mike Jorgensen	1B49,OF2	L	36	72	112	14	22	6	0	0	11	31	27	2	.196	.375	.250
Lonnie Smith†	OF28	R	29	28	96	15	25	2	2	0	7	15	20	12	.260	.377	.323
Cesar Cedeno†	1B23,OF2	R	34	28	76	14	33	4	1	6	19	5	7	5	.434	.463	.750
Ivan DeJesus	3B20,SS13	R	32	59	72	11	16	5	0	0	7	4	16	2	.222	.260	.292
Steve Braun	OF14	L	37	64	67	7	16	4	0	1	6	10	9	0	.239	.342	.343
Tom Lawless	3B13,2B11	R	28	47	58	8	12	3	1	0	8	5	4	2	.207	.270	.293
Brian Harper	OF13,3B6,C2*	R	25	43	52	5	13	4	0	0	8	2	3	0	.250	.273	.327
Mike LaValliere	C12	L	24	12	34	2	5	1	0	0	6	7	3	0	.147	.273	.176
Randy Hunt	C13	R	25	14	19	1	3	0	0	0	1	0	5	0	.158	.158	.158
Curt Ford	OF4	L	24	11	12	2	6	2	0	0	3	4	1	1	.500	.625	.667
Art Howe	1B1,3B1	R	38	4	3	0	0	0	0	0	0	0	0	0	.000	.000	.000

B. Harper, 1 G at 1B

Pitcher	T	Age	G	GS	CG	ShO	IP	H	HR	BB	SO	W-L	Sv	ERA
Joaquin Andujar	R	32	38	38	10	2	269.2	265	15	82	112	21-12	0	3.40
John Tudor	L	31	36	36	14	10	275.0	209	14	49	169	21-8	0	1.93
Danny Cox	R	25	35	35	10	4	241.0	226	19	64	131	18-9	0	2.88
Kurt Kepshire	R	25	32	29	0	0	153.1	155	16	71	67	10-9	0	4.75
Bob Forsch	R	35	34	19	3	1	136.0	132	11	47	48	9-6	2	3.90
Ken Dayley	L	26	57	0	0	0	65.1	65	2	18	62	4-4	11	2.76
Jeff Lahti	R	28	52	0	0	0	68.1	63	3	26	41	5-2	19	1.84
Bill Campbell	R	36	50	0	0	0	64.1	55	5	21	41	5-3	4	3.50
Ricky Horton	L	25	49	3	0	0	89.2	84	5	34	59	3-2	1	2.91
Neil Allen†	R	27	23	1	0	0	29.0	32	3	17	10	1-4	2	5.59
Todd Worrell	R	25	17	0	0	0	21.2	17	2	7	17	3-0	5	2.91
Joe Boever	R	24	13	0	0	0	16.1	17	3	4	20	0-0	0	4.41
Andy Hassler	L	33	10	0	0	0	10.0	9	0	4	5	0-1	0	1.80
Pat Perry	L	26	6	0	0	0	12.1	3	0	3	6	1-0	0	0.00
Matt Keough	R	29	4	1	0	0	10.0	10	0	4	10	0-1	0	4.50
Doug Bair†	R	35	2	0	0	0	2.0	1	0	2	0	0-0	0	0.00

1985 New York Mets 2nd NL East 98-64 .605 3.0 GB

Davey Johnson

Player	Gm by Position	B	Age	G	AB	R	H	2B	3B	HR	RBI	BB	SO	SB	Avg	OBP	Slg
Gary Carter	C143,1B6,OF1	R	31	149	555	83	156	17	1	32	100	69	46	1	.281	.365	.488
Keith Hernandez	1B157	L	31	158	593	87	183	34	4	10	91	77	59	3	.309	.384	.430
Wally Backman	2B140,SS1	S	25	145	520	77	142	24	5	1	38	36	72	30	.273	.320	.344
Howard Johnson	3B113,SS7,OF1	S	24	126	389	38	94	18	4	11	46	34	78	6	.242	.300	.393
Rafael Santana	SS153	R	27	154	529	41	136	19	1	1	29	29	54	1	.257	.295	.302
George Foster	OF123	R	36	129	452	57	119	24	1	21	77	46	87	0	.263	.331	.460
Darryl Strawberry	OF110	L	23	111	393	78	109	15	4	29	79	73	96	26	.277	.389	.557
Mookie Wilson	OF83	S	29	93	337	56	93	16	8	6	26	28	52	24	.276	.331	.424
Ray Knight	3B73,2B2,1B1	R	32	90	271	22	59	12	0	6	36	13	32	1	.218	.252	.328
Danny Heep	OF78,1B4	L	27	95	271	26	76	17	0	7	42	27	27	2	.280	.341	.421
Lenny Dykstra	OF74	L	22	83	236	40	60	9	3	1	19	30	24	15	.254	.338	.331
Kelvin Chapman	2B48,3B1	R	29	62	144	16	25	3	0	0	7	9	15	5	.174	.231	.194
Tom Paciorek†	OF29,1B8	R	38	46	116	14	33	3	1	1	11	6	14	1	.284	.325	.353
John Christensen	OF38	R	24	51	113	10	21	4	1	3	13	19	23	1	.186	.303	.319
Clint Hurdle	C17,OF10	L	27	43	82	7	16	4	0	3	7	13	20	0	.195	.313	.354
Rusty Staub	OF1	L	41	54	45	2	12	3	0	1	8	10	4	0	.267	.400	.400
Ronn Reynolds	C25	R	26	28	43	4	9	2	0	0	1	0	18	0	.209	.227	.256
Ron Gardenhire	SS13,2B5,3B2	R	27	26	39	5	7	2	1	0	2	8	11	0	.179	.319	.282
Larry Bowa†	SS9,2B4	S	39	14	19	2	2	1	0	0	2	2	2	0	.105	.190	.158
Terry Blocker	OF5	L	25	18	15	1	1	0	0	0	0	1	2	0	.067	.125	.067
Billy Beane	OF2	R	23	8	8	0	2	1	0	0	1	0	3	0	.250	.250	.375

Pitcher	T	Age	G	GS	CG	ShO	IP	H	HR	BB	SO	W-L	Sv	ERA
Dwight Gooden	R	20	35	35	16	8	276.2	198	13	69	268	24-4	0	1.53
Ron Darling	R	24	36	35	4	2	248.0	214	21	114	167	16-6	0	2.90
Ed Lynch	R	29	31	29	6	1	191.0	188	19	27	65	10-8	0	3.44
Sid Fernandez	L	22	26	26	3	0	170.1	108	14	80	180	9-9	0	2.80
Rick Aguilera	R	23	21	19	2	0	122.1	118	8	37	74	10-7	0	3.24
Bruce Berenyi	R	30	3	3	0	0	13.2	8	0	10	10	1-0	0	2.63
Roger McDowell	R	24	62	2	0	0	127.1	108	9	37	70	6-5	17	2.83
Jesse Orosco	L	28	54	0	0	0	79.0	66	6	34	68	8-6	17	2.73
Doug Sisk	R	27	42	0	0	0	73.0	86	3	40	26	4-5	2	5.30
Tom Gorman	L	27	34	2	0	0	52.2	56	8	18	32	4-4	0	5.13
Terry Leach	R	31	22	4	1	1	55.2	48	3	14	30	3-4	1	2.91
Calvin Schiraldi	R	23	10	4	0	0	26.1	43	4	11	21	2-1	0	8.89
Wes Gardner	R	24	9	0	0	0	12.0	18	1	8	11	0-2	0	5.25
Joe Sambito	L	33	8	0	0	0	10.2	21	1	8	3	0-0	0	12.66
Bill Latham	L	24	7	3	0	0	22.2	21	1	7	10	1-3	0	3.97
Randy Niemann	L	29	4	0	0	0	4.2	5	0	0	2	0-0	0	0.00
Randy Myers	L	22	1	0	0	0	2.0	0	0	1	2	0-0	0	0.00

886 Seasons: Team Rosters

1985 Montreal Expos 3rd NL East 84-77 .522 16.5 GB

Buck Rodgers

Player	Gm by Position	B	Age	G	AB	R	H	2B	3B	HR	RBI	BB	SO	SB	Avg	OBP	Slg
Mike Fitzgerald	C108	R	24	108	295	25	61	7	1	5	34	38	55	5	.207	.297	.288
Dan Driessen†	1B88	L	33	91	312	31	78	18	0	6	25	33	29	2	.250	.324	.365
Vance Law	2B126,1B20,3B11*	R	28	147	519	75	138	30	6	10	52	86	96	6	.266	.369	.405
Tim Wallach	3B154	R	27	155	569	70	148	36	3	22	81	38	79	9	.260	.310	.450
Hubie Brooks	SS155	R	28	156	605	67	163	34	7	13	100	34	79	6	.269	.310	.413
Tim Raines	OF146	S	25	150	575	115	184	30	13	11	41	81	60	70	.320	.405	.475
Andre Dawson	OF131	R	30	139	529	65	135	27	2	23	91	29	92	13	.255	.295	.444
Herm Winningham	OF116	L	23	125	312	30	74	6	5	3	21	28	72	20	.237	.297	.317
Terry Francona	1B57,OF28,3B1	L	26	107	281	19	75	15	1	2	31	12	12	5	.267	.299	.349
Mitch Webster†	OF64	S	26	74	212	32	58	8	2	11	30	20	33	15	.274	.335	.486
U.L. Washington	2B43,SS9,3B3	S	31	68	193	24	48	9	4	1	17	15	33	6	.249	.301	.352
Jim Wohlford	OF43	R	34	70	125	7	24	5	1	1	15	16	18	0	.192	.284	.272
Sal Butera	C66,P1	R	32	67	120	11	24	1	0	3	12	13	12	0	.200	.281	.283
Miguel Dilone†	OF22	S	30	51	84	10	16	0	2	0	6	6	11	7	.190	.242	.238
Andres Galarraga	1B23	R	24	24	75	9	14	1	0	2	4	3	18	1	.187	.228	.280
Steve Nicosia†	C23,1B2	R	29	42	71	4	12	2	0	0	1	7	11	1	.169	.244	.197
Razor Shines	1B5,P1	S	28	47	50	0	6	0	0	0	3	4	9	0	.120	.185	.120
Scot Thompson†	1B3,OF3	L	29	34	32	2	9	1	0	0	4	3	7	0	.281	.333	.313
Al Newman	2B15,SS2	S	25	25	29	7	5	1	0	0	1	3	4	2	.172	.250	.207
Skeeter Barnes	3B4,OF3,1B1	R	28	19	26	0	4	1	0	0	0	0	2	0	.154	.154	.192
Doug Frobel†	OF6	L	26	12	23	3	3	1	0	1	4	2	6	0	.130	.200	.304
Mike O'Berry	C20	R	31	20	21	2	4	0	0	0	0	4	3	1	.190	.320	.190
Fred Manrique	2B2,SS2,3B1	R	23	9	13	5	4	1	1	1	1	1	3	0	.308	.357	.769
Ned Yost	C5	R	29	5	11	1	2	0	0	0	0	0	2	0	.182	.182	.182
Doug Flynn†	2B6,SS1	R	34	9	6	0	1	0	0	0	0	0	0	0	.167	.167	.167
Roy Johnson	OF3	L	26	3	5	0	0	0	0	0	0	0	3	0	.000	.000	.000

V. Law, 1 G at OF

Pitcher	T	Age	G	GS	CG	ShO	IP	H	HR	BB	SO	W-L	Sv	ERA
Bryn Smith	R	29	32	32	4	2	222.1	193	12	41	127	18-5	0	2.91
Bill Gullickson	R	26	29	29	4	1	181.1	187	8	47	68	14-12	0	3.52
Joe Hesketh	L	26	25	25	2	1	155.1	125	10	45	113	10-5	0	2.49
David Palmer	R	27	24	23	0	0	135.2	128	5	67	106	7-10	0	3.71
Dan Schatzeder	L	30	24	15	1	0	104.1	101	13	31	64	3-5	0	3.80
Floyd Youmans	R	21	14	12	0	0	77.0	57	3	49	54	4-3	0	2.45
Mickey Mahler†	L	32	9	7	1	1	48.1	40	3	24	32	1-4	1	3.54
Steve Rogers	R	35	8	7	1	0	38.0	51	1	20	18	2-4	0	5.68
Bill Laskey†	R	27	11	7	0	0	34.1	55	9	14	18	0-5	0	9.44
John Dopson	R	21	4	3	0	0	13.0	25	4	4	4	0-2	0	11.08
Tim Burke	R	26	78	0	0	0	120.1	86	9	44	87	9-4	8	2.39
Jeff Reardon	R	29	63	0	0	0	87.2	68	7	26	67	2-8	41	3.18
Gary Lucas	L	30	49	0	0	0	67.2	63	6	24	31	6-2	1	3.19
Randy St. Claire	R	24	42	0	0	0	68.2	69	3	26	25	5-3	0	3.93
Bert Roberge	R	30	42	0	0	0	68.0	58	5	22	34	3-3	2	3.44
Jack O'Connor	L	27	20	1	0	0	23.2	21	1	13	16	0-2	0	4.94
Dick Grapenthin	R	27	5	0	0	0	7.0	13	0	8	4	0-0	0	14.14
Ed Glynn	L	32	3	0	0	0	2.1	5	0	4	2	0-0	0	19.29
Sal Butera	R	32	1	0	0	0	1.0	0	0	0	0	0-0	0	0.00
Razor Shines	R	28	1	0	0	0	1.0	1	0	0	0	0-0	0	0.00

1985 Chicago Cubs 4th NL East 77-84 .478 23.5 GB

Jim Frey

Player	Gm by Position	B	Age	G	AB	R	H	2B	3B	HR	RBI	BB	SO	SB	Avg	OBP	Slg
Jody Davis	C138	R	28	142	482	47	112	30	0	17	58	48	83	1	.232	.300	.400
Leon Durham	1B151	L	27	153	542	58	153	32	2	21	75	64	99	7	.282	.357	.465
Ryne Sandberg	2B153,SS1	R	25	153	609	113	186	31	6	26	83	57	97	54	.305	.364	.504
Ron Cey	3B140	R	37	145	500	64	116	18	2	22	63	58	106	1	.232	.316	.408
Shawon Dunston	SS73	R	22	74	250	40	65	12	4	4	18	19	42	11	.260	.310	.388
Keith Moreland	OF148,1B12,3B11*	R	31	161	587	74	180	30	3	14	106	68	58	12	.307	.374	.440
Bob Dernier	OF116	R	28	121	469	63	119	20	3	1	21	40	44	31	.254	.315	.316
Gary Matthews	OF85	R	34	97	298	45	70	12	0	13	40	59	64	2	.235	.362	.406
Davey Lopes	OF79,3B4,2B1	R	40	99	275	52	78	11	0	11	44	46	37	47	.284	.383	.444
Chris Speier	SS58,3B31,2B13	R	35	106	218	16	53	11	0	4	24	17	34	1	.243	.295	.349
Larry Bowa†	SS66	S	39	72	195	13	48	6	4	0	13	11	20	5	.246	.285	.318
Thad Bosley	OF55	L	28	108	180	25	59	6	3	7	27	20	29	5	.328	.391	.511
Billy Hatcher	OF44	R	24	53	163	24	40	12	1	2	10	8	12	2	.245	.290	.368
Richie Hebner	1B12,3B7,OF1	L	37	83	120	10	26	2	0	3	22	7	15	0	.217	.266	.308
Steve Lake	C55	R	28	58	119	5	18	2	0	1	11	3	21	1	.151	.177	.193
Gary Woods	OF56	R	30	81	82	11	20	3	0	0	4	14	18	0	.244	.354	.280
Brian Dayett	OF10	R	28	22	26	1	6	0	0	1	4	0	6	0	.231	.259	.346
Dave Owen	3B7,SS7,2B4	S	27	22	19	6	7	0	0	0	4	1	5	1	.368	.400	.368
Chico Walker	OF6,2B2	S	27	21	12	3	1	0	0	0	0	0	5	1	.083	.083	.083
Darrin Jackson	OF4	R	21	5	11	0	1	0	0	0	0	0	3	0	.091	.091	.091

K. Moreland, 2 G at C

Pitcher	T	Age	G	GS	CG	ShO	IP	H	HR	BB	SO	W-L	Sv	ERA
Dennis Eckersley	R	30	25	25	6	2	169.1	145	15	19	117	11-7	0	3.08
Steve Trout	L	27	24	24	3	1	140.2	142	8	63	44	9-7	0	3.39
Ray Fontenot	L	27	38	23	0	0	154.2	177	23	45	70	6-10	0	4.36
Rick Sutcliffe	R	29	20	20	6	3	130.0	119	12	44	102	8-8	0	3.18
Scott Sanderson	R	28	19	19	2	0	121.0	100	13	27	80	5-6	0	3.12
Dick Ruthven	R	34	20	15	0	0	87.1	103	6	37	26	4-7	0	4.53
Steve Engel	L	23	11	8	1	0	51.2	61	10	26	29	1-5	1	5.57
Derek Botelho	R	28	11	7	1	0	44.0	52	8	23	23	1-3	0	5.32
Reggie Patterson	R	26	8	5	1	0	39.0	36	2	10	17	3-0	0	3.00
Johnny Abrego	R	22	6	5	0	0	24.0	32	3	12	13	1-1	0	6.38
Larry Gura†	L	37	5	4	0	0	20.1	34	4	6	7	0-3	0	8.41
Lee Smith	R	27	65	0	0	0	97.2	87	9	32	112	7-4	33	3.04
George Frazier	R	30	51	0	0	0	76.0	88	11	52	46	7-8	2	6.39
Warren Brusstar	R	33	51	0	0	0	74.1	87	8	36	34	4-3	4	6.05
Lary Sorensen	R	29	45	3	0	0	82.1	86	8	24	34	3-7	0	4.26
Ron Meridith	L	28	32	0	0	0	46.1	53	3	24	23	3-2	1	4.47
Jay Baller	R	24	20	4	0	0	52.0	52	8	17	31	2-3	1	3.46
Dave Beard	R	25	9	0	0	0	12.2	16	2	7	4	0-0	0	6.39
Dave Gumpert	R	27	9	0	0	0	10.1	12	0	7	4	1-0	0	3.48
Jon Perlman	R	28	6	0	0	0	8.2	10	3	8	4	1-0	0	11.42

1985 Philadelphia Phillies 5th NL East 75-87 .463 26.0 GB

John Felske

Player	Gm by Position	B	Age	G	AB	R	H	2B	3B	HR	RBI	BB	SO	SB	Avg	OBP	Slg
Ozzie Virgil	C120	R	28	131	426	47	105	16	3	19	55	49	85	0	.246	.330	.432
Mike Schmidt	1B106,3B54,SS1	R	35	158	549	89	152	31	5	33	93	87	117	1	.277	.375	.532
Juan Samuel	2B159	R	24	161	663	101	175	31	13	19	74	33	141	53	.264	.303	.436
Rick Schu	3B111	R	23	112	416	54	105	21	4	7	24	38	78	8	.252	.318	.373
Steve Jeltz	SS86	S	26	89	196	17	37	4	1	0	12	26	55	1	.189	.283	.219
Glenn Wilson	OF158	R	26	161	608	73	167	39	5	14	102	35	117	7	.275	.311	.424
Von Hayes	OF146	L	26	152	570	76	150	30	4	13	70	61	99	21	.263	.332	.398
Garry Maddox	OF94	R	35	105	218	22	52	8	1	4	23	13	26	4	.239	.281	.339
Jeff Stone	OF69	L	24	88	264	36	70	4	3	3	11	15	50	15	.265	.307	.337
John Russell	OF49,1B18	R	24	81	216	22	47	12	0	9	23	18	72	2	.218	.278	.398
Tim Corcoran	1B59,OF3	L	32	103	182	11	39	6	1	0	22	29	20	0	.214	.312	.258
Greg Gross	OF52,1B8	L	32	93	169	21	44	5	2	0	14	32	9	1	.260	.374	.314
Luis Aguayo	SS60,2B17,3B7	R	26	91	165	27	46	7	3	6	21	22	26	1	.279	.378	.467
Tom Foley†	SS45	L	25	46	158	17	42	8	0	3	17	13	18	1	.266	.322	.373
Darren Daulton	C28	L	23	36	103	14	21	3	1	4	11	16	37	3	.204	.311	.369
Derrel Thomas	SS21,OF7,C1*	R	34	63	92	16	19	2	0	4	12	11	14	2	.207	.291	.359
Bo Diaz†	C24	R	32	26	76	9	16	5	1	2	16	6	7	0	.211	.268	.382
John Wockenfuss	1B7,C2	R	36	32	37	1	6	0	0	0	2	8	7	0	.162	.311	.162
Alan Knicely†	1B1	R	30	7	7	0	0	0	0	0	0	0	4	0	.000	.000	.000
Kiko Garcia	SS3,3B1	R	31	4	3	0	0	0	0	0	0	0	1	0	.000	.000	.000

D. Thomas, 1 G at 2B, 1 G at 3B

Pitcher	T	Age	G	GS	CG	ShO	IP	H	HR	BB	SO	W-L	Sv	ERA
John Denny	R	32	33	33	6	2	230.2	252	15	83	123	11-14	0	3.82
Kevin Gross	R	24	38	31	6	2	205.2	194	11	81	151	15-13	0	3.41
Shane Rawley	L	29	36	31	6	2	198.2	188	16	81	106	13-8	0	3.31
Charles Hudson	R	26	38	26	3	0	193.0	188	23	74	122	8-13	0	3.78
Jerry Koosman	L	42	19	18	3	1	99.1	107	14	34	60	6-4	0	4.62
Steve Carlton	L	40	16	16	0	0	92.0	84	6	53	48	1-8	0	3.33
Don Carman	L	25	71	0	0	0	86.1	52	6	38	87	9-4	7	2.08
Kent Tekulve†	R	38	58	0	0	0	72.1	67	4	25	36	4-10	14	2.99
Larry Andersen	R	32	57	0	0	0	73.0	78	5	26	50	3-3	3	4.32
Dave Rucker	L	27	39	3	0	0	79.1	83	6	40	41	3-2	1	4.31
Dave Shipanoff	R	25	26	0	0	0	36.1	33	3	16	26	1-2	3	3.22
Rocky Childress	R	23	16	1	0	0	33.1	45	3	9	14	0-1	0	6.21
Fred Toliver	R	24	11	3	0	0	25.0	27	2	17	23	0-4	1	4.68
Pat Zachry	R	33	10	0	0	0	12.2	14	1	11	8	0-0	0	4.26
Dave Stewart†	R	28	4	0	0	0	4.1	5	0	4	2	0-0	0	6.23
Al Holland†	L	32	3	0	0	0	4.0	5	0	4	1	0-1	1	4.50
Rich Surhoff†	R	22	2	0	0	0	1.0	2	0	0	1	1-0	0	0.00

1985 Pittsburgh Pirates 6th NL East 57-104 .354 43.5 GB

Chuck Tanner

Player	Gm by Position	B	Age	G	AB	R	H	2B	3B	HR	RBI	BB	SO	SB	Avg	OBP	Slg
Tony Pena	C146,1B1	R	28	147	546	53	136	27	2	10	59	29	67	12	.249	.284	.361
Jason Thompson	1B114	L	30	123	402	42	97	17	1	12	61	84	58	0	.241	.369	.378
Johnny Ray	2B151	S	28	154	594	67	163	33	3	7	70	46	24	13	.274	.325	.375
Bill Madlock†	3B98,1B12	R	34	110	399	49	100	23	1	10	41	39	42	3	.251	.323	.388
Sammy Khalifa	SS95	R	21	95	320	30	76	14	3	2	31	34	56	5	.238	.307	.319
Joe Orsulak	OF115	L	23	121	397	54	119	14	6	0	21	26	27	24	.300	.342	.365
Marvell Wynne	OF99	L	25	103	337	21	69	6	3	2	18	18	48	10	.205	.247	.258
George Hendrick†	OF65	R	35	69	256	23	59	15	0	2	25	18	42	1	.230	.278	.313
Bill Almon	SS43,OF32,1B7*	R	32	88	244	33	66	17	0	6	29	22	61	10	.270	.330	.414
Jim Morrison	3B59,2B15,OF1	R	32	92	244	17	62	10	0	4	22	8	44	3	.254	.277	.344
Steve Kemp	OF63	L	30	92	236	19	59	13	2	2	21	25	54	1	.250	.317	.347
Mike Brown†	OF56	R	25	57	205	29	68	18	2	5	33	22	27	2	.332	.391	.512
R.J. Reynolds†	OF31	S	26	31	130	22	40	5	3	3	17	9	18	12	.308	.357	.462
Denny Gonzalez	3B21,OF13,2B6	R	21	35	124	11	28	4	0	4	12	13	27	2	.226	.299	.355
Lee Mazzilli	1B19,OF5	S	30	92	117	20	33	8	0	1	9	29	17	4	.282	.425	.376
Sixto Lezcano	OF40	R	31	72	116	16	24	2	0	3	9	35	17	0	.207	.392	.302
Doug Frobel†	OF36	L	26	53	109	14	22	5	0	0	7	19	24	4	.202	.320	.248
Sid Bream†	1B25	L	24	26	95	14	27	7	0	3	15	11	14	0	.284	.355	.453
Junior Ortiz	C23	R	25	23	72	4	21	2	0	1	5	3	17	1	.292	.320	.361
Johnnie LeMaster†	SS21	R	31	22	58	4	9	0	0	1	6	5	12	1	.155	.222	.207
Tim Foli	SS13	R	34	19	37	1	7	0	0	0	2	4	2	0	.189	.268	.189
Rafael Belliard	SS12	R	23	17	20	1	4	0	0	0	1	0	5	0	.200	.200	.200
Scott Loucks	OF4	R	28	4	7	1	2	2	0	0	1	2	2	0	.286	.444	.571
Trench Davis	OF2	L	24	2	7	1	1	0	0	0	0	0	0	1	.143	.143	.143
Jerry Dybzinski	SS5	R	29	5	4	0	0	0	0	0	0	0	0	0	.000	.000	.000

B. Almon, 7 G at 3B

Pitcher	T	Age	G	GS	CG	ShO	IP	H	HR	BB	SO	W-L	Sv	ERA
Rick Rhoden	R	32	35	35	2	0	213.1	254	18	69	128	10-15	0	4.47
Rick Reuschel	R	36	31	26	9	1	194.0	153	7	52	138	14-8	1	2.27
Jose DeLeon	R	24	31	25	1	0	162.2	138	15	89	149	2-19	3	4.70
Lee Tunnell	R	24	24	23	0	0	132.1	126	11	57	74	4-10	0	4.01
Larry McWilliams	L	31	30	19	2	0	126.1	139	9	62	52	7-9	0	4.70
Bob Walk	R	28	9	9	1	1	58.2	60	3	18	40	2-3	0	3.68
Mike Bielecki	R	25	12	7	0	0	45.2	45	5	31	22	2-3	0	4.53
Bob Kipper†	L	20	5	4	0	0	24.2	21	4	7	13	1-2	0	5.11
Cecilio Guante	R	25	63	0	0	0	109.0	84	5	40	92	4-6	5	2.72
Don Robinson	R	28	44	6	0	0	95.1	95	6	42	65	5-11	3	3.87
Al Holland†	L	32	38	0	0	0	58.2	48	5	17	47	1-3	4	3.38
John Candelaria†	L	31	37	0	0	0	54.1	57	7	14	47	2-4	9	3.64
Jim Winn	R	25	30	7	0	0	75.2	77	4	31	22	3-6	0	5.23
Rod Scurry†	L	29	30	0	0	0	47.2	42	4	28	43	0-1	2	3.21
Pat Clements†	L	23	27	0	0	0	34.1	39	2	15	17	0-2	2	3.67
Ray Krawczyk	R	25	8	0	0	0	8.1	20	1	6	9	0-2	0	14.04
Kent Tekulve†	R	38	3	0	0	0	3.1	7	1	5	4	0-0	0	16.20
Dave Tomlin	L	36	1	0	0	0	1.0	1	0	1	0	0-0	0	0.00

1985 Los Angeles Dodgers 1st NL West 95-67 .586 —

Tom Lasorda

Player	Gm by Position	B	Age	G	AB	R	H	2B	3B	HR	RBI	BB	SO	SB	Avg	OBP	Slg
Mike Scioscia	C139	L	26	141	429	47	127	26	3	7	53	77	21	3	.296	.407	.420
Greg Brock	1B122	L	28	129	438	64	110	19	0	21	66	54	72	4	.251	.332	.438
Steve Sax	2B135,3B1	R	25	136	488	62	136	8	4	1	42	54	43	27	.279	.352	.318
Dave Anderson	3B51,SS25,2B2	R	24	77	221	24	44	6	0	4	18	35	42	5	.199	.310	.281
Mariano Duncan	SS123,2B19	S	22	142	562	74	137	24	6	6	39	38	113	38	.244	.293	.340
Ken Landreaux	OF140	L	30	147	482	70	129	26	2	12	50	33	37	15	.268	.311	.405
Mike Marshall	OF125,1B7	R	25	135	518	72	152	27	2	28	95	37	137	3	.293	.342	.515
Candy Maldonado	OF113	R	24	121	213	20	48	7	1	5	19	19	40	1	.225	.288	.338
Pedro Guerrero	OF81,3B44,1B12	R	29	137	487	99	156	22	2	33	87	83	68	12	.320	.422	.577
R.J. Reynolds†	OF54	S	26	73	207	22	55	10	4	0	25	13	31	6	.266	.308	.353
Enos Cabell†	3B32,1B21,OF4	R	35	57	192	20	56	11	0	0	22	14	21	6	.292	.340	.349
Bill Russell	SS23,OF21,2B8*	R	36	76	169	19	44	6	1	0	13	18	9	4	.260	.333	.308
Steve Yeager	C48	R	36	53	121	4	25	4	1	0	9	7	24	0	.207	.246	.256
Bob Bailor	3B45,2B16,SS5*	R	33	74	118	8	29	3	1	0	7	3	5	1	.246	.270	.288
Bill Madlock†	3B32	R	34	34	114	20	41	4	0	2	15	10	11	7	.360	.422	.447
Terry Whitfield	OF28	L	32	79	104	8	27	7	0	3	16	6	27	0	.260	.300	.413
Al Oliver†	OF17	L	38	35	79	1	20	5	0	0	8	5	11	1	.253	.294	.316
Len Matuszek†	OF17,1B10,3B1	L	30	43	63	10	14	2	1	3	13	8	14	0	.222	.307	.429
Sid Bream†	1B16	L	24	24	53	4	7	0	0	3	6	7	10	0	.132	.230	.302
Jay Johnstone		L	39	17	15	0	2	1	0	0	2	1	2	0	.133	.188	.200
Mike Ramsey	SS4,2B2	S	31	9	15	1	2	1	0	0	0	2	4	0	.133	.235	.200
Jose Gonzalez	OF18	R	20	23	11	6	3	2	0	0	0	1	3	1	.273	.333	.455
Franklin Stubbs	1B4	L	24	10	9	0	2	0	0	0	2	0	3	0	.222	.222	.222
Reggie Williams	OF15	R	24	22	9	4	3	0	0	0	0	0	4	1	.333	.333	.333
Ralph Bryant	OF3	L	24	6	6	0	2	0	0	0	1	0	2	0	.333	.333	.333
Stuart Pederson	OF5	L	25	8	4	1	0	0	0	0	0	0	2	0	.000	.000	.000
Gil Reyes	C6	R	21	6	1	0	0	0	0	0	0	1	1	0	.000	.667	.000

B. Russell, 5 G at 3B; B. Bailor, 1 G at OF

Pitcher	T	Age	G	GS	CG	ShO	IP	H	HR	BB	SO	W-L	Sv	ERA
F. Valenzuela	L	24	35	35	14	5	272.1	211	14	101	208	17-10	0	2.45
Orel Hershiser	R	26	36	34	9	5	239.2	179	8	68	157	19-3	0	2.03
Jerry Reuss	L	36	34	33	5	3	212.2	210	13	58	84	14-10	0	2.92
Rick Honeycutt	L	31	31	25	1	0	142.0	141	9	49	67	8-12	1	3.42
Bob Welch	R	28	23	23	8	3	167.1	141	16	35	96	14-4	0	2.31
Alejandro Pena	R	26	2	1	0	0	4.1	7	1	3	2	0-1	0	8.31
Tom Niedenfuer	R	25	64	0	0	0	106.1	86	6	24	102	7-9	19	2.71
Ken Howell	R	24	56	0	0	0	86.0	66	8	35	85	4-7	12	3.77
Carlos Diaz	L	27	46	0	0	0	79.1	70	7	18	73	6-3	0	2.61
Bobby Castillo	R	30	35	5	0	0	68.0	59	9	41	57	2-2	0	5.43
Steve Howe†	L	27	19	0	0	0	22.0	30	2	5	11	1-1	3	4.91
Dennis Powell	L	21	16	2	0	0	29.1	30	7	13	19	1-1	1	5.22
Tom Brennan	R	32	12	4	0	0	31.2	41	2	11	17	1-3	0	7.39
Brian Holton	R	25	3	0	0	0	4.0	9	0	1	1	1-1	0	9.00

1985 Cincinnati Reds 2nd NL West 89-72 .553 5.5 GB

Pete Rose

Player	Gm by Position	B	Age	G	AB	R	H	2B	3B	HR	RBI	BB	SO	SB	Avg	OBP	Slg
Dave Van Gorder	C70	R	28	73	151	12	36	7	0	2	24	9	19	0	.238	.280	.325
Pete Rose	1B110	S	44	119	405	60	107	12	2	2	46	86	35	8	.264	.395	.319
Ron Oester	2B149	S	29	152	526	59	155	26	3	1	34	51	65	5	.295	.354	.361
Buddy Bell†	3B67	R	33	67	247	28	54	15	2	6	36	34	27	0	.219	.311	.368
Dave Concepcion	SS151,3B5	R	37	155	560	59	141	19	2	7	48	50	67	16	.252	.314	.330
Dave Parker	OF159	L	34	160	635	88	198	42	4	34	125	52	80	5	.312	.365	.551
Eddie Milner	OF135	L	30	145	453	82	115	19	7	3	33	61	31	35	.254	.342	.347
Gary Redus	OF85	R	28	101	246	51	62	14	4	6	28	44	52	48	.252	.366	.415
Nick Esasky	3B62,OF54,1B12	R	25	125	413	61	108	21	0	21	66	41	102	3	.262	.332	.465
Cesar Cedeno†	OF53,1B34	R	34	83	220	24	53	12	0	3	30	19	35	9	.241	.307	.336
Tony Perez	1B50	R	43	72	183	25	60	8	0	6	33	22	22	0	.328	.396	.470
Wayne Krenchicki	3B52,2B3	L	30	90	173	16	47	9	0	4	25	28	20	0	.272	.369	.393
Bo Diaz†	C51	R	32	51	161	12	42	8	0	3	15	15	18	0	.261	.324	.366
Alan Knicely†	C46	R	30	48	158	17	40	9	0	5	26	16	34	0	.253	.322	.405
Max Venable	OF39	L	28	77	135	21	39	12	3	0	10	6	17	11	.289	.315	.422
Eric Davis	OF47	R	23	56	122	26	30	3	3	8	18	7	39	16	.246	.287	.516
Dann Bilardello	C42	R	26	42	102	6	17	0	0	1	9	4	15	0	.167	.206	.196
Tom Foley†	2B18,SS15,3B1	L	25	43	92	7	18	5	1	0	6	6	16	1	.196	.245	.272
Duane Walker†	OF10	L	28	37	48	5	8	2	1	2	6	6	18	1	.167	.259	.375
Tom Runnells	SS11,2B1	S	30	28	35	3	7	1	0	0	0	3	4	0	.200	.263	.229
Paul O'Neill	OF2	L	22	5	12	1	4	1	0	0	1	0	2	0	.333	.333	.417
Wade Rowdon	3B4	R	24	5	9	2	2	0	0	0	2	1	2	0	.222	.364	.222

Pitcher	T	Age	G	GS	CG	ShO	IP	H	HR	BB	SO	W-L	Sv	ERA
Tom Browning	L	25	38	38	6	4	261.1	242	29	73	155	20-9	0	3.55
Mario Soto	R	28	36	36	9	1	256.2	196	30	104	214	12-15	0	3.58
Jay Tibbs	R	23	35	34	5	2	218.0	216	14	83	98	10-16	0	3.92
Andy McGaffigan	R	28	15	15	2	0	94.1	88	4	30	83	3-3	0	3.72
John Franco	L	24	67	0	0	0	99.0	83	5	40	61	12-3	12	2.18
Ted Power	R	30	64	0	0	0	80.0	65	2	45	42	8-6	27	2.70
Tom Hume	R	32	56	0	0	0	80.0	65	7	35	50	3-5	3	3.26
Ron Robinson	R	23	33	12	0	0	108.1	107	11	32	76	7-7	1	3.99
John Stuper	R	28	33	13	1	0	99.0	116	8	37	38	8-5	0	4.55
Joe Price	L	28	26	8	0	0	64.2	59	10	23	52	2-2	1	3.90
Frank Pastore	R	27	17	6	1	0	54.0	60	1	16	29	2-1	0	3.83
Bob Buchanan	L	24	14	0	0	0	16.0	25	4	9	3	1-0	0	8.44
Carl Willis	R	24	11	0	0	0	13.2	21	3	5	6	1-0	1	9.22
Mike Smith	R	24	2	0	0	0	3.1	2	2	1	2	0-0	0	5.40
Rob Murphy	L	25	2	0	0	0	3.0	2	1	2	1	0-0	0	6.00

1985 Houston Astros 3rd NL West 83-79 .512 12.0 GB

Bob Lillis

Player	Gm by Position	B	Age	G	AB	R	H	2B	3B	HR	RBI	BB	SO	SB	Avg	OBP	Slg
Mark Bailey	C110,1B2	S	23	114	332	47	88	14	0	10	45	67	70	0	.265	.389	.398
Glenn Davis	1B89,OF9	R	24	100	350	51	95	11	0	20	64	27	68	0	.271	.332	.474
Bill Doran	2B147	S	27	148	578	84	166	31	6	14	59	71	69	23	.287	.362	.434
Phil Garner	3B123,2B15	R	36	135	463	65	124	23	10	6	51	34	72	4	.268	.317	.400
Craig Reynolds	SS102,2B1	L	32	107	379	43	103	18	8	4	32	12	30	4	.272	.293	.393
Kevin Bass	OF141	S	26	150	539	72	145	27	5	16	68	31	63	19	.269	.315	.427
Jose Cruz	OF137	L	37	141	544	69	163	34	4	9	79	43	74	16	.300	.349	.426
Jerry Mumphrey	OF126	S	32	130	444	52	123	25	2	8	61	37	57	6	.277	.329	.396
Denny Walling	3B51,1B46,OF13	L	31	119	345	44	93	20	1	7	45	25	26	5	.270	.316	.394
Dickie Thon	SS79	R	27	84	251	26	63	6	1	6	29	18	50	8	.251	.299	.355
Terry Puhl	OF53	L	28	57	194	34	55	14	3	2	23	18	23	6	.284	.343	.418
Alan Ashby	C60	S	33	65	189	20	53	8	0	8	25	24	27	0	.280	.363	.450
Jim Pankovits	OF33,2B21,3B1*	R	29	75	172	24	42	3	0	4	14	17	29	1	.244	.316	.331
Enos Cabell†	1B49	R	35	60	143	20	35	8	1	2	14	16	15	3	.245	.321	.357
Harry Spilman	1B19,C2	L	30	44	66	3	9	1	0	1	4	3	7	0	.136	.174	.197
Tim Tolman	OF9,1B6	R	29	31	43	4	6	1	0	2	8	1	10	0	.140	.178	.302
John Mizerock	C15	L	24	15	38	6	9	4	0	0	6	2	8	0	.237	.293	.342
Ty Gainey	OF9	L	24	13	37	5	6	0	0	0	0	2	9	0	.162	.244	.162
German Rivera	3B11	R	24	13	36	3	7	2	1	0	2	4	8	0	.194	.275	.306
Bert Pena	3B7,SS6,2B2	R	25	20	29	7	8	2	0	0	4	1	6	0	.276	.290	.345
Eric Bullock	OF7	L	25	18	25	3	7	2	0	0	2	1	3	0	.280	.308	.360
Chris Jones	OF15	L	27	31	25	0	5	0	0	0	1	3	7	0	.200	.286	.200

J. Pankovits, 1 G at SS

Pitcher	T	Age	G	GS	CG	ShO	IP	H	HR	BB	SO	W-L	Sv	ERA
Bob Knepper	L	31	37	37	4	0	241.0	253	21	54	131	15-13	0	3.55
Nolan Ryan	R	38	35	35	4	0	232.0	205	12	95	209	10-12	0	3.80
Mike Scott	R	30	36	35	4	2	221.2	194	20	80	137	18-8	0	3.29
Joe Niekro†	R	40	32	32	4	1	213.0	197	21	99	117	9-12	0	3.72
Jeff Heathcock	R	25	14	7	1	0	56.1	50	9	13	25	3-1	1	3.36
Charlie Kerfeld	R	21	11	6	0	0	44.1	44	2	25	30	4-2	0	4.06
Mark Knudson	R	24	2	2	0	0	11.0	21	0	3	4	0-2	0	9.00
Dave Smith	R	30	64	0	0	0	79.1	69	3	17	40	9-5	27	2.27
Frank DiPino	L	28	54	0	0	0	76.0	69	7	43	49	3-7	6	4.03
Bill Dawley	R	27	49	0	0	0	81.0	76	7	37	48	5-3	2	3.56
Jeff Calhoun	L	27	44	0	0	0	63.2	56	2	24	47	2-5	4	2.54
Ron Mathis	R	26	23	8	0	0	70.0	83	7	27	34	3-5	1	6.04
Julio Solano	R	25	20	0	0	0	33.2	34	5	13	17	2-2	0	3.48
Mike Madden	L	28	13	0	0	0	19.0	29	1	11	16	0-0	0	4.26
Mark Ross	R	30	8	0	0	0	13.0	12	2	2	3	0-2	1	4.85
Jim Deshaies	L	25	2	0	0	0	3.0	1	0	0	2	0-0	0	0.00

1985 San Diego Padres 3rd NL West 83-79 .512 12.0 GB

Dick Williams

Player	Gm by Position	B	Age	G	AB	R	H	2B	3B	HR	RBI	BB	SO	SB	Avg	OBP	Slg
Terry Kennedy	C140,1B5	L	29	143	532	54	139	27	1	10	74	31	102	0	.261	.301	.372
Steve Garvey	1B162	R	36	162	654	80	184	34	6	17	81	35	67	0	.281	.318	.430
Tim Flannery	2B121,3B1	L	27	126	384	50	108	14	3	1	40	58	39	2	.281	.386	.341
Graig Nettles	3B130	L	40	137	440	66	115	23	1	15	61	72	59	0	.261	.363	.420
Garry Templeton	SS148	L	29	148	546	63	154	30	2	6	55	41	88	16	.282	.332	.377
Tony Gwynn	OF152	L	25	154	622	90	197	29	5	6	46	45	33	14	.317	.364	.408
Kevin McReynolds	OF150	R	25	152	564	61	132	24	4	15	75	43	81	4	.234	.290	.371
Carmelo Martinez	OF150,1B3	R	24	150	514	64	130	28	1	21	72	87	82	0	.253	.362	.434
Jerry Royster	2B58,3B29,SS7*	R	32	90	249	31	70	13	2	5	31	32	31	6	.281	.363	.410
Kurt Bevacqua	3B33,1B9,OF1	R	38	71	138	17	33	6	0	3	25	25	17	0	.239	.349	.348
Bruce Bochy	C46	R	30	48	112	16	30	2	0	6	13	6	30	0	.268	.305	.446
Al Bumbry	OF17	L	38	68	95	6	19	3	0	1	10	7	9	2	.200	.255	.263
Bobby Brown	OF28	S	31	79	84	8	13	3	0	0	6	5	20	6	.155	.200	.190
Mario Ramirez	SS27,2B7	R	27	37	60	6	17	0	0	2	5	3	11	0	.283	.317	.383
Gerry Davis	OF23	R	26	44	58	10	17	3	1	0	2	5	7	0	.293	.349	.379
Miguel Dilone†	OF14	S	30	27	46	8	10	0	1	0	1	4	8	10	.217	.280	.261
Alan Wiggins†	2B9	S	27	10	37	3	2	1	0	0	0	2	4	0	.054	.103	.081
Edwin Rodriguez		R	24	1	1	0	0	0	0	0	0	0	0	0	.000	.000	.000

J. Royster, 2 G at OF

Pitcher	T	Age	G	GS	CG	ShO	IP	H	HR	BB	SO	W-L	Sv	ERA
Eric Show	R	29	35	35	5	2	233.0	212	27	87	141	12-11	0	3.09
Andy Hawkins	R	25	33	33	5	2	228.2	229	18	65	69	18-8	0	3.15
Dave Dravecky	L	29	34	31	7	2	214.2	200	18	57	105	13-11	0	2.93
LaMarr Hoyt	R	30	31	31	8	3	210.1	210	20	20	83	16-8	0	3.47
Mark Thurmond	L	28	36	23	1	1	138.1	154	9	44	57	7-11	2	3.97
Craig Lefferts	L	27	60	0	0	0	83.1	75	7	30	48	7-6	2	3.35
Goose Gossage	R	33	50	0	0	0	79.0	64	1	17	52	5-3	26	1.82
Tim Stoddard	R	32	44	0	0	0	60.0	63	3	37	42	1-6	1	4.65
Luis DeLeon	R	26	29	0	0	0	38.2	39	6	10	31	0-3	3	4.19
Roy Lee Jackson	R	31	22	2	0	0	40.0	32	4	13	28	2-3	2	2.70
Lance McCullers	R	21	21	0	0	0	35.0	23	3	16	27	0-2	5	2.31
Greg Booker	R	25	17	0	0	0	22.1	20	3	17	7	0-1	0	6.85
Ed Wojna	R	24	15	7	0	0	42.0	53	6	19	18	2-4	0	5.79
Gene Walter	L	24	15	0	0	0	22.0	12	0	8	18	0-2	3	2.05
Bob Patterson	L	26	3	0	0	0	4.0	13	2	3	1	0-0	0	24.75

1985 Atlanta Braves 5th NL West 66-96 .407 29.0 GB

Eddie Haas (50-71)/Bobby Wine (16-25)

Player	Gm by Position	B	Age	G	AB	R	H	2B	3B	HR	RBI	BB	SO	SB	Avg	OBP	Slg
Rick Cerone	C91	R	31	96	282	15	61	9	0	3	25	29	25	0	.216	.288	.280
Bob Horner	1B87,3B40	R	27	130	483	61	129	25	3	27	89	50	57	1	.267	.333	.499
Glenn Hubbard	2B140	R	27	142	439	51	102	21	0	5	39	56	54	4	.232	.321	.314
Ken Oberkfell	3B117,2B16	L	29	134	412	30	112	19	4	3	35	51	38	1	.272	.359	.359
Rafael Ramirez	SS133	R	27	138	568	54	141	25	4	5	58	20	63	2	.248	.272	.333
Dale Murphy	OF161	R	29	162	616	118	185	32	2	37	111	90	141	10	.300	.388	.539
Terry Harper	OF131	R	29	138	492	58	130	15	2	17	72	44	76	9	.264	.327	.407
C. Washington	OF99	L	30	122	398	62	110	16	6	15	43	40	66	14	.276	.342	.455
Brad Komminsk	OF92	R	24	106	300	52	68	12	3	4	21	38	71	10	.227	.314	.327
Gerald Perry	1B55,OF1	L	24	110	238	22	51	5	0	3	13	23	28	9	.214	.282	.273
Bruce Benedict	C70	R	29	70	208	12	42	6	0	0	20	22	12	0	.202	.279	.231
Paul Zuvella	2B42,SS33,3B5	R	26	81	190	16	48	8	1	0	4	16	14	2	.253	.311	.305
Milt Thompson	OF49	L	26	73	182	17	55	7	2	0	6	7	36	9	.302	.339	.363
Chris Chambliss	1B39	L	36	101	170	16	40	7	0	3	21	18	22	0	.235	.307	.329
Paul Runge	3B28,SS5,2B2	R	27	50	87	15	19	3	0	1	5	18	18	0	.218	.349	.287
Larry Owen	C25	R	30	26	71	7	17	3	0	2	12	8	17	0	.239	.313	.366
Albert Hall	OF13	S	27	54	47	5	7	0	1	0	3	9	12	1	.149	.286	.191
Andres Thomas	SS10	R	21	15	18	6	5	0	0	0	2	0	2	0	.278	.278	.278
John Rabb	OF1	R	25	3	2	0	0	0	0	0	0	0	1	0	.000	.000	.000

Pitcher	T	Age	G	GS	CG	ShO	IP	H	HR	BB	SO	W-L	Sv	ERA
Rick Mahler	R	31	39	39	6	1	266.2	272	24	79	107	17-15	0	3.48
Steve Bedrosian	R	27	37	37	0	0	206.2	198	17	111	134	7-15	0	3.83
Pascual Perez	R	28	22	22	0	0	95.1	115	10	57	57	1-13	0	6.14
Len Barker	R	29	20	18	0	0	73.2	84	10	37	47	2-9	0	6.35
Joe Johnson	R	23	15	14	1	0	85.2	95	9	24	34	4-4	0	4.10
Rick Camp	R	32	66	2	0	0	127.2	130	8	61	49	4-6	3	3.95
Jeff Dedmon	R	25	60	0	0	0	86.0	84	5	49	41	6-3	0	4.08
Gene Garber	R	37	59	0	0	0	97.1	98	8	25	66	6-6	1	3.61
Bruce Sutter	R	32	58	0	0	0	88.1	91	13	29	52	7-7	23	4.48
Terry Forster	L	33	46	0	0	0	59.1	49	7	28	37	2-3	1	2.28
Zane Smith	L	24	42	18	2	2	147.0	135	4	80	85	9-10	0	3.80
Steve Shields	R	26	23	6	0	0	68.0	86	9	32	29	1-2	0	5.16
Craig McMurtry	R	25	17	6	0	0	45.0	56	6	27	28	0-3	1	6.60
Dave Schuler	L	31	9	0	0	0	10.2	19	4	3	10	0-0	0	6.75

888 Seasons: Team Rosters

1985 San Francisco Giants 6th NL West 62-100 .383 33.0 GB

Jim Davenport (56-88)/Roger Craig (6-12)

Player	Gm by Position	B	Age	G	AB	R	H	2B	3B	HR	RBI	BB	SO	SB	Avg	OBP	Slg
Bob Brenly	C110,3B17,1B10	R	31	133	440	41	97	16	1	19	56	57	62	1	.220	.311	.391
David Green	1B78,OF12	R	24	106	294	36	73	10	2	5	20	22	58	6	.248	.301	.347
Manny Trillo	2B120,3B1	R	34	125	451	36	101	16	2	3	25	40	44	2	.224	.287	.288
Chris Brown	3B120	R	23	131	432	50	117	20	3	16	61	38	78	2	.271	.345	.442
Jose Uribe	SS145,2B1	S	26	147	476	46	113	20	4	3	26	30	57	8	.237	.285	.315
Jeffrey Leonard	OF126	R	29	133	507	49	122	20	3	17	62	21	107	11	.241	.272	.393
Chili Davis	OF126	S	25	136	481	53	130	25	2	13	56	62	74	15	.270	.349	.412
Dan Gladden	OF124	R	27	142	502	64	122	15	8	7	41	40	78	32	.243	.307	.347
Joel Youngblood	OF56,3B1	R	33	95	230	24	62	6	0	4	24	30	37	3	.270	.355	.348
Dan Driessen†	1B49	L	33	54	181	22	42	8	0	3	22	17	22	0	.232	.297	.326
Brad Wellman	2B36,3B25,SS3	R	25	71	174	16	41	11	1	0	16	4	33	5	.236	.268	.310
Rob Deer	OF37,1B10	R	24	78	162	22	30	5	1	8	20	23	71	0	.185	.283	.377
Alex Trevino	C55,3B1	R	27	57	157	17	34	10	1	6	19	20	24	0	.217	.303	.408
Ron Roenicke	OF35	S	28	65	133	23	34	9	1	3	13	35	27	6	.256	.408	.406
Ricky Adams	SS25,3B16,2B6	R	26	54	121	12	23	3	1	2	10	5	23	1	.190	.228	.281
Scot Thompson†	1B24	L	29	64	111	8	23	5	0	0	6	2	10	0	.207	.221	.252
Gary Rajsich	1B23	L	30	51	91	5	15	6	0	0	10	17	22	0	.165	.296	.231
Mike Woodard	2B23	L	25	24	82	12	20	1	0	0	9	5	3	6	.244	.287	.256
Matt Nokes	C14	L	21	19	53	3	11	2	0	2	5	1	9	0	.208	.236	.358
Johnnie LeMaster†	SS10	R	31	12	16	1	0	0	0	0	0	1	5	0	.000	.059	.000
Duane Kuiper		L	35	9	5	0	3	0	0	0	0	1	0	0	.600	.667	.600

Pitcher	T	Age	G	GS	CG	ShO	IP	H	HR	BB	SO	W-L	Sv	ERA
Dave LaPoint	L	25	31	31	2	1	206.2	215	18	74	122	7-17	0	3.57
Atlee Hammaker	L	27	29	29	1	1	170.2	161	17	47	100	5-12	0	3.74
Mike Krukow	R	33	28	28	6	1	194.2	176	19	49	150	8-11	0	3.38
Jim Gott	R	25	26	26	2	0	148.1	144	10	51	78	7-10	0	3.88
Vida Blue	L	35	33	20	1	0	131.0	115	17	80	103	8-8	0	4.47
Bill Laskey†	R	27	19	19	0	0	114.0	110	10	39	42	5-11	0	3.55
Roger Mason	R	26	5	5	1	1	29.2	28	1	11	26	1-3	0	2.12
Mark Davis	L	24	77	1	0	0	114.1	89	13	41	131	5-12	7	3.54
Scott Garrelts	R	23	74	0	0	0	105.2	76	2	58	106	9-6	13	2.30
Greg Minton	R	33	68	0	0	0	96.2	98	6	54	37	5-4	4	3.54
Frank Williams	R	27	49	0	0	0	73.0	65	5	35	54	2-4	0	4.19
Mike Jeffcoat†	L	25	19	1	0	0	22.0	27	4	6	10	0-2	0	5.32
Bob Moore	R	26	11	0	0	0	16.2	18	1	10	10	0-0	0	3.24
Jeff Robinson	R	24	8	0	0	0	12.1	16	2	10	8	0-0	0	5.11
Colin Ward	L	24	6	2	0	0	12.1	10	0	7	8	0-0	0	4.38

»1986 Boston Red Sox 1st AL East 95-66 .590 —

John McNamara

Player	Gm by Position	B	Age	G	AB	R	H	2B	3B	HR	RBI	BB	SO	SB	Avg	OBP	Slg
Rich Gedman	C134	L	26	135	462	49	119	29	0	16	65	37	61	1	.258	.315	.424
Bill Buckner	1B138,DH15	L	36	153	629	73	168	39	2	18	102	40	25	6	.267	.311	.421
Marty Barrett	2B158	R	28	158	625	94	179	39	4	4	60	65	31	15	.286	.353	.381
Wade Boggs	3B149	L	28	149	580	107	207	47	2	8	71	105	44	0	.357	.453	.486
Ed Romero	SS75,3B18,2B4*	R	28	100	233	41	49	11	0	2	23	18	16	2	.210	.270	.283
Jim Rice	OF156,DH1	R	33	157	618	98	200	39	2	20	110	62	78	0	.324	.384	.490
Dwight Evans	OF149,DH1	R	34	152	529	86	137	33	2	26	97	97	117	3	.259	.376	.476
Tony Armas	OF117,DH1	R	32	121	425	40	112	21	4	11	58	24	77	0	.264	.305	.409
Don Baylor	DH143,1B13,OF3	R	37	160	585	93	139	23	1	31	94	62	111	3	.238	.344	.439
Rey Quinones†	SS62	R	22	62	190	26	45	12	1	2	15	19	26	3	.237	.315	.342
Spike Owen†	SS42	S	25	42	126	21	23	2	1	1	10	17	9	3	.183	.283	.238
Steve Lyons†	OF55	L	26	59	124	20	31	7	2	1	14	12	23	2	.250	.312	.363
Marc Sullivan	C41	R	27	41	119	15	23	4	0	1	14	7	32	0	.193	.260	.252
Dave Henderson†	OF32	R	27	36	51	8	10	3	0	1	3	2	15	1	.196	.226	.314
Dave Stapleton	1B29,2B6,3B2	R	32	39	39	4	5	1	0	0	3	2	10	0	.128	.171	.154
Kevin Romine	OF33	R	25	35	35	6	9	2	0	0	2	3	9	2	.257	.316	.314
Mike Greenwell	OF15,DH3	L	22	31	35	4	11	2	0	0	4	5	7	0	.314	.400	.371
Laschelle Tarver	OF9	L	27	13	25	3	3	0	0	0	1	1	4	0	.120	.154	.120
Glenn Hoffman	SS11,3B1	R	27	12	23	1	5	2	0	0	1	2	3	0	.217	.269	.304
Mike Stenhouse	OF4,1B3	L	28	21	21	1	2	1	0	0	1	12	5	0	.095	.424	.143
Pat Dodson	1B7	L	26	9	12	3	5	2	0	1	3	3	3	0	.417	.533	.833
Dave Sax	C2,1B1	R	27	4	11	1	5	1	0	1	1	0	1	0	.455	.455	.818

E. Romero, 1 G at OF

Pitcher	T	Age	G	GS	CG	ShO	IP	H	HR	BB	SO	W-L	Sv	ERA
Roger Clemens	R	23	33	33	10	1	254.0	179	21	67	238	24-4	0	2.48
Oil Can Boyd	R	26	30	30	10	0	214.1	222	32	45	129	16-10	0	3.78
Al Nipper	R	27	26	26	3	0	159.0	186	24	47	79	10-12	0	5.38
Bruce Hurst	L	28	25	25	11	4	174.1	169	18	50	167	13-8	0	2.99
Tom Seaver†	R	41	16	16	1	0	104.1	114	8	29	72	5-7	0	3.80
Jeff Sellers	R	22	14	13	1	0	82.0	90	13	40	51	3-7	0	4.94
Mike Brown†	R	27	15	10	0	0	57.1	72	10	25	32	4-4	0	5.34
Rob Woodward	R	23	9	6	0	0	35.2	46	4	11	14	2-3	0	5.30
Bob Stanley	R	31	66	1	0	0	82.1	109	9	22	54	6-6	16	4.37
Joe Sambito	L	34	53	0	0	0	44.2	54	4	16	30	2-0	12	4.84
Steve Crawford	R	28	40	0	0	0	57.1	69	5	19	32	0-2	4	3.92
Tim Lollar	L	30	32	1	0	0	43.0	51	7	34	28	2-0	0	6.91
Sammy Stewart	R	31	27	0	0	0	63.2	64	7	48	47	4-1	0	4.38
Calvin Schiraldi	R	24	25	0	0	0	51.0	36	5	15	55	4-2	9	1.41
Mike Trujillo†	R	26	3	0	0	0	5.2	7	0	6	4	0-0	0	9.53
Wes Gardner	R	25	1	0	0	0	1.0	1	0	0	1	0-0	0	9.00

1986 New York Yankees 2nd AL East 90-72 .556 5.5 GB

Lou Piniella

Player	Gm by Position	B	Age	G	AB	R	H	2B	3B	HR	RBI	BB	SO	SB	Avg	OBP	Slg
Butch Wynegar	C57	S	30	61	194	19	40	4	1	7	29	30	21	0	.206	.310	.345
Don Mattingly	1B160,3B3,DH1	L	25	162	677	117	238	53	2	31	113	53	35	0	.352	.394	.573
Willie Randolph	2B139,DH1	R	31	141	492	76	136	15	2	5	50	94	49	15	.276	.393	.346
Mike Pagliarulo	3B143,SS2	L	26	149	504	71	120	24	3	28	71	54	120	4	.238	.316	.464
Wayne Tolleson†	SS56,3B7,2B3	S	30	60	215	22	61	9	2	0	14	14	33	4	.284	.332	.344
Rickey Henderson	OF146,DH5	R	27	153	608	130	160	31	5	28	74	89	81	87	.263	.358	.469
Dave Winfield	OF145,DH6,3B2	R	34	154	565	90	148	31	5	24	104	77	106	6	.262	.349	.462
Dan Pasqua	OF81,1B5,DH3	L	24	102	280	44	82	17	0	16	45	47	78	2	.293	.399	.525
Mike Easler	DH129,OF11	L	35	146	490	64	148	26	2	14	78	49	87	3	.302	.362	.449
Ken Griffey Sr.†	OF51,DH2	L	36	59	198	33	60	7	0	9	26	15	24	2	.303	.349	.475
Ron Hassey†	C51,DH3	L	33	64	191	23	57	14	0	6	29	24	16	1	.298	.381	.466
Joel Skinner†	C54	R	25	54	166	6	43	4	0	1	17	7	40	0	.259	.287	.301
Bobby Meacham	SS56	S	25	56	161	19	36	7	1	0	10	17	39	3	.224	.309	.280
Gary Roenicke	OF37,DH15,3B3*	R	31	69	136	11	36	5	0	3	18	27	30	1	.265	.388	.368
C. Washington†	OF39	L	31	54	135	19	32	5	0	6	16	7	33	6	.237	.285	.407
Dale Berra	SS19,3B18,DH4	R	29	42	108	10	25	7	0	2	13	9	14	0	.231	.294	.352
Mike Fischlin	SS42,2B27	R	30	71	102	9	21	2	0	0	3	8	29	0	.206	.261	.225
Ron Kittle†	DH24,OF1	R	28	30	80	8	19	2	0	4	12	7	23	2	.238	.292	.413
Henry Cotto	OF29,DH1	R	25	35	80	11	17	3	0	1	6	2	17	3	.213	.229	.288
Paul Zuvella	SS21	R	27	21	48	2	4	1	0	0	2	5	4	0	.083	.170	.104
Bryan Little†	2B14	S	26	14	41	3	8	1	0	0	0	2	7	0	.195	.233	.220
Juan Espino	C27	R	30	27	37	1	6	2	0	0	5	2	9	0	.162	.200	.216
Phil Lombardi	OF8,C3	R	23	20	36	6	10	3	0	2	6	4	7	0	.278	.366	.528
Leo Hernandez	3B7,2B1	R	26	7	22	2	5	2	0	1	4	1	8	0	.227	.261	.455
Ivan DeJesus	SS7	R	33	7	4	1	0	0	0	0	0	1	1	0	.000	.200	.000

G. Roenicke, 2 G at 1B

Pitcher	T	Age	G	GS	CG	ShO	IP	H	HR	BB	SO	W-L	Sv	ERA
Dennis Rasmussen	L	27	31	31	3	1	202.0	160	28	74	131	18-6	0	3.88
Ron Guidry	L	35	30	30	5	0	192.1	202	28	38	140	9-12	0	3.98
Joe Niekro	R	41	25	25	0	0	125.2	139	15	63	59	9-10	0	4.87
Doug Drabek	R	23	27	21	0	0	131.2	126	13	50	76	7-8	0	4.10
Bob Tewksbury	R	25	23	20	2	0	130.1	144	8	31	49	9-5	0	3.31
Tommy John	L	43	13	10	1	0	70.2	73	8	15	28	5-3	0	2.93
Scott Nielsen	R	27	10	9	2	2	56.0	66	12	12	20	4-4	0	4.02
Brad Arnsberg	R	22	2	1	0	0	8.0	13	1	1	3	0-0	0	3.38
Dave Righetti	L	27	74	0	0	0	106.2	88	4	35	83	8-8	46	2.45
Brian Fisher	R	24	62	0	0	0	96.2	105	14	37	67	9-5	6	4.93
Bob Shirley	L	32	39	6	0	0	105.1	108	13	40	64	0-4	3	5.04
Rod Scurry	L	30	31	0	0	0	39.1	38	1	22	36	1-2	2	3.66
Al Holland	L	33	25	1	0	0	40.2	44	5	9	37	1-0	0	5.09
Tim Stoddard†	R	33	24	0	0	0	49.1	41	6	23	34	4-1	0	3.83
Ed Whitson†	R	31	14	4	0	0	37.0	54	5	23	27	5-2	0	7.54
Alfonso Pulido	L	29	10	3	0	0	30.2	38	8	9	13	1-1	1	4.70
Mike Armstrong	R	32	7	1	0	0	8.2	13	4	5	8	0-1	0	9.35
John Montefusco	R	36	4	0	0	0	12.1	9	2	5	3	0-0	0	2.19

1986 Detroit Tigers 3rd AL East 87-75 .537 8.5 GB

Sparky Anderson

Player	Gm by Position	B	Age	G	AB	R	H	2B	3B	HR	RBI	BB	SO	SB	Avg	OBP	Slg
Lance Parrish	C85,DH6	R	30	91	327	53	84	6	1	22	62	38	83	0	.257	.340	.483
Darrell Evans	1B105,DH42,3B2	L	39	151	507	78	122	15	0	29	85	91	105	3	.241	.356	.442
Lou Whitaker	2B141	L	29	144	584	95	157	26	6	20	73	63	70	13	.269	.338	.437
Darnell Coles	3B133,DH7,SS2*	R	24	142	521	67	142	30	2	20	86	45	84	6	.273	.333	.453
Alan Trammell	SS149,DH2	R	28	151	574	107	159	33	7	21	75	59	57	25	.277	.347	.469
Chet Lemon	OF124	R	31	126	403	45	101	21	3	12	53	39	53	2	.251	.326	.407
Kirk Gibson	OF114,DH4	L	29	119	441	84	118	11	2	28	86	68	107	34	.268	.371	.492
Dave Collins	OF94,DH24	S	33	124	419	44	113	18	2	1	27	44	49	27	.270	.340	.329
John Grubb	DH52,OF19	L	37	81	210	32	70	13	1	13	51	28	28	0	.333	.412	.590
Larry Herndon	OF83,DH18	R	32	106	283	33	70	13	1	8	37	27	40	2	.247	.310	.385
Tom Brookens	3B35,2B31,DH14*	R	32	98	281	42	76	11	2	3	25	20	42	11	.270	.319	.356
Pat Sheridan	OF90,DH5	L	28	98	236	41	56	9	1	6	19	21	57	9	.237	.300	.360
Dwight Lowry	C55,1B1,OF1	L	28	56	150	21	46	4	0	3	18	17	19	0	.307	.392	.393
Dave Bergman	1B41,DH8,OF2	L	33	65	130	14	30	6	1	1	9	21	16	0	.231	.338	.315
Mike Heath†	C29,3B1	R	31	30	98	11	26	3	0	4	11	4	17	4	.265	.291	.418
Dave Engle	1B23,DH5,OF4*	R	29	35	86	6	22	7	0	0	4	7	13	0	.256	.312	.337
Harry Spilman†	DH11,3B2,C1*	L	31	24	49	6	12	2	0	3	8	3	8	0	.245	.288	.469
Mike Laga†	1B12,DH3	L	26	15	45	6	9	1	0	3	8	5	13	0	.200	.280	.422
Bruce Fields	OF14,DH1	L	25	16	43	4	12	1	1	0	6	1	6	1	.279	.283	.349
Brian Harper	OF11,DH6,C2*	R	26	19	36	2	5	1	0	0	3	3	3	0	.139	.200	.167
Tim Tolman	DH9,OF4,1B3	R	30	16	34	4	6	1	0	0	2	6	4	1	.176	.293	.206
Doug Baker	SS10,2B2,DH1	S	25	13	24	1	3	1	0	0	0	2	7	0	.125	.192	.167
Matt Nokes	C7	L	22	7	24	2	8	1	0	1	2	1	1	0	.333	.360	.500
Scotti Madison	DH1,3B1	S	26	2	7	0	0	0	0	0	1	0	3	0	.000	.000	.000

D. Coles, 2 G at OF; T. Brookens, 14 G at SS, 3 G at OF; D. Engle, 3 G at C; H. Spilman, 1 G at 1B; B. Harper, 2 G at 1B

Pitcher	T	Age	G	GS	CG	ShO	IP	H	HR	BB	SO	W-L	Sv	ERA
Jack Morris	R	31	35	35	15	6	267.0	229	40	82	223	21-8	0	3.27
Walt Terrell	R	28	34	33	9	2	217.1	199	30	98	93	15-12	0	4.56
Frank Tanana	L	32	32	31	3	1	188.1	196	23	65	119	12-9	0	4.16
Dan Petry	R	27	20	20	2	0	116.0	122	15	53	56	5-10	0	4.66
Dave LaPoint†	L	26	16	8	0	0	67.2	85	11	32	36	3-6	0	5.72
Bryan Kelly	R	27	6	4	0	0	20.0	21	4	10	18	1-2	0	4.50
Willie Hernandez	L	31	64	0	0	0	88.2	87	13	21	77	8-7	24	3.55
Randy O'Neal	R	25	37	11	1	0	122.2	121	13	44	68	3-7	2	4.33
Bill Campbell	R	37	34	0	0	0	55.2	46	5	21	37	3-6	3	3.88
Eric King	R	22	33	16	3	1	138.1	108	11	63	79	11-4	3	3.51
Mark Thurmond†	L	29	25	4	0	0	51.2	44	7	17	17	4-1	3	1.92
Jim Slaton†	R	36	22	0	0	0	40.0	46	5	11	12	0-0	2	4.05
Chuck Cary	L	26	22	0	0	0	31.2	33	3	15	21	1-2	0	3.41
Bill Scherrer	L	28	13	0	0	0	21.0	19	3	22	16	0-1	0	7.29
John Pacella	R	29	5	0	0	0	11.0	10	0	13	5	0-0	1	4.09
Jack Lazorko	R	30	3	0	0	0	6.2	8	0	4	3	0-0	0	4.05

1986 Toronto Blue Jays 4th AL East 86-76 .531 9.5 GB

Jimy Williams

Player	Gm by Position	B	Age	G	AB	R	H	2B	3B	HR	RBI	BB	SO	SB	Avg	OBP	Slg
Ernie Whitt	C129	L	34	131	395	48	106	19	2	16	56	35	39	0	.268	.326	.448
Willie Upshaw	1B154,DH1	L	29	155	573	85	144	28	6	9	60	78	87	23	.251	.341	.368
Damaso Garcia	2B106,DH11,1B1	R	29	122	424	57	119	22	0	6	46	13	32	9	.281	.306	.375
Rance Mulliniks	3B110,DH5,2B1	L	30	117	348	50	90	22	0	11	45	43	60	1	.259	.340	.417
Tony Fernandez	SS163	S	24	163	687	91	213	33	9	10	65	27	52	25	.310	.338	.428
Jesse Barfield	OF157	R	26	158	589	107	170	35	2	40	108	69	146	8	.289	.368	.559
George Bell	OF147,DH11,3B2	R	26	159	641	101	198	38	6	31	108	41	62	7	.309	.349	.532
Lloyd Moseby	OF147,DH3	L	26	152	589	89	149	24	5	21	86	64	122	32	.253	.329	.418
Cliff Johnson	DH95,1B1	R	38	107	336	48	84	12	1	15	55	52	57	0	.250	.355	.426
Garth Iorg	3B90,2B52,SS2	R	31	137	327	30	85	19	1	3	44	20	47	3	.260	.303	.352
Rick Leach	DH42,OF39,1B7	L	29	110	246	35	76	14	1	5	39	13	24	0	.309	.335	.435
Buck Martinez	C78,DH1	R	37	81	160	13	29	8	0	2	12	20	25	0	.181	.271	.269
Kelly Gruber	3B42,DH14,2B14*	R	24	87	143	20	28	4	1	5	15	5	27	2	.196	.220	.343
Cecil Fielder	DH22,1B7,3B2*	R	22	34	83	7	13	2	0	4	13	6	27	0	.157	.222	.325
Manuel Lee	2B29,SS5,3B2	S	21	35	78	8	16	0	1	1	7	4	10	0	.205	.241	.269
Ron Shepherd	OF32,DH16	R	25	65	69	16	14	4	0	2	4	3	22	0	.203	.236	.348
Jeff Hearron	C12	R	24	12	23	2	5	1	0	0	4	3	7	0	.217	.300	.261
Fred McGriff	DH2,1B1	L	22	3	5	1	1	0	0	0	0	0	2	0	.200	.200	.200

K. Gruber, 9 G at OF, 5 G at SS; C. Fielder, 1 G at OF

Pitcher	T	Age	G	GS	CG	ShO	IP	H	HR	BB	SO	W-L	Sv	ERA
Jimmy Key	L	25	36	35	4	2	232.0	222	24	74	141	14-11	0	3.57
Jim Clancy	R	30	34	34	6	3	219.1	202	24	63	126	14-14	0	3.94
Dave Stieb	R	28	37	34	1	1	205.0	239	29	87	127	7-12	1	4.74
John Cerutti	L	26	34	20	2	1	145.1	150	25	47	89	9-4	1	4.15
Doyle Alexander†	R	35	17	17	3	0	111.0	120	18	20	65	5-4	0	4.46
Joe Johnson†	R	24	16	15	0	0	88.0	94	3	22	39	7-2	0	3.89
Duane Ward†	R	22	2	1	0	0	2.0	3	0	4	1	0-1	0	13.50
Mark Eichhorn	R	25	69	0	0	0	157.0	105	8	45	166	14-6	10	1.72
Tom Henke	R	28	63	0	0	0	91.1	63	6	32	118	9-5	27	3.35
Dennis Lamp	R	33	40	2	0	0	73.0	93	5	23	30	2-6	2	5.05
Bill Caudill	R	29	40	0	0	0	36.1	36	6	17	32	2-4	2	6.19
Jim Acker†	R	27	23	5	0	0	60.0	63	6	22	32	2-4	0	4.35
Don Gordon	R	26	14	0	0	0	21.2	28	1	8	13	0-1	1	7.06
Stan Clarke	L	25	10	0	0	0	12.2	18	4	10	9	0-1	0	9.24
Luis Aquino	R	22	7	0	0	0	11.1	14	2	3	5	1-1	0	6.35
Jeff Musselman	L	23	6	0	0	0	5.1	8	1	5	4	0-0	0	10.13
Steve Davis	L	25	3	0	0	0	3.2	8	2	5	5	0-0	0	17.18
Mickey Mahler†	L	33	2	0	0	0	1.0	1	0	0	0	0-0	0	0.00

1986 Cleveland Indians 5th AL East 84-78 .519 11.5 GB

Pat Corrales

Player	Gm by Position	B	Age	G	AB	R	H	2B	3B	HR	RBI	BB	SO	SB	Avg	OBP	Slg
Andy Allanson	C99	R	24	101	293	30	66	7	3	1	29	14	36	10	.225	.260	.280
Pat Tabler	1B107,DH18	R	28	130	473	61	154	29	2	6	48	29	75	3	.326	.368	.433
Tony Bernazard	2B146	S	29	146	562	88	169	28	4	17	73	53	77	17	.301	.362	.456
Brook Jacoby	3B158	R	26	158	583	83	168	30	4	17	80	56	137	2	.288	.350	.441
Julio Franco	SS134,2B13,DH3	R	24	149	599	80	183	30	5	10	74	32	66	10	.306	.338	.422
Brett Butler	OF159	L	29	161	587	92	163	17	14	4	51	70	65	32	.278	.356	.375
Mel Hall	OF126,DH7	L	25	140	442	68	131	29	2	18	77	33	65	6	.296	.346	.493
Joe Carter	OF104,1B70	R	26	162	663	108	200	36	9	29	121	32	95	29	.302	.335	.514
Andre Thornton	DH110	R	36	120	401	49	92	14	0	17	66	65	67	4	.229	.333	.392
Cory Snyder	OF74,SS34,3B11*	R	23	103	416	58	113	21	1	24	69	16	123	2	.272	.299	.500
Chris Bando	C86	S	30	92	254	28	68	9	0	2	26	22	49	0	.268	.325	.327
Carmelo Castillo	OF37,DH35	R	28	85	205	34	57	9	0	8	32	9	48	2	.278	.310	.439
Otis Nixon	OF95,DH5	S	27	105	95	33	25	4	1	0	8	13	12	23	.263	.352	.326
Dave Clark	OF10,DH7	L	23	18	58	10	16	1	0	3	9	7	11	1	.276	.348	.448
Fran Mullins	2B13,SS11,DH1*	R	29	28	40	3	7	4	0	0	5	2	11	0	.175	.209	.275
Jay Bell	DH2,2B2	R	20	5	14	3	5	2	0	1	4	2	3	0	.357	.438	.714
Dan Rohn	2B2,3B2,SS1	L	30	6	10	1	2	0	0	0	2	1	1	0	.200	.273	.200
Eddie Williams	OF4	R	21	5	7	2	1	0	0	0	1	0	3	0	.143	.143	.143

C. Snyder, 1 G at DH; F. Mullins, 1 G at 1B

Pitcher	T	Age	G	GS	CG	ShO	IP	H	HR	BB	SO	W-L	Sv	ERA
Tom Candiotti	R	28	36	34	17	3	252.1	234	18	106	167	16-12	0	3.57
Ken Schrom	R	31	34	33	3	1	206.0	217	34	49	87	14-7	0	4.54
Phil Niekro	R	47	34	32	5	0	210.1	241	24	95	81	11-11	0	4.32
Don Schulze	R	23	19	13	1	0	84.2	88	9	34	33	4-4	0	5.00
Neal Heaton†	L	26	12	12	2	0	74.1	73	8	34	24	3-6	0	4.24
Greg Swindell	L	21	9	9	1	0	61.2	57	9	15	46	5-2	0	4.23
John Butcher†	R	29	13	8	1	1	50.2	86	6	13	16	1-5	0	6.93
Jose Roman	R	23	6	5	0	0	22.0	23	3	17	9	1-2	0	6.55
Scott Bailes	L	24	62	10	0	0	112.2	123	12	43	60	10-10	7	4.95
Ernie Camacho	R	31	51	0	0	0	57.1	60	1	31	36	2-4	20	4.08
Rich Yett	R	23	39	3	1	1	78.2	84	10	37	50	5-3	1	5.15
Bryan Oelkers	L	25	35	4	0	0	69.0	70	13	40	33	3-3	1	4.70
Dickie Noles	R	29	32	0	0	0	54.2	56	9	30	32	3-2	0	5.10
Frank Wills	R	27	26	0	0	0	40.1	43	6	16	32	4-4	4	4.91
Jim Kern	R	37	16	0	0	0	27.1	34	1	23	11	1-1	0	7.90
Jamie Easterly	L	33	13	0	0	0	17.2	27	3	12	9	0-2	0	7.64
Doug Jones	R	29	11	0	0	0	18.0	18	0	6	12	1-0	1	2.50
Reggie Ritter	R	26	5	0	0	0	10.0	14	1	4	6	0-0	0	6.30

1986 Milwaukee Brewers 6th AL East 77-84 .478 18.0 GB

George Bamberger (71-81)/Tom Trebelhorn (6-3)

Player	Gm by Position	B	Age	G	AB	R	H	2B	3B	HR	RBI	BB	SO	SB	Avg	OBP	Slg
Charlie Moore	C72,OF4,DH2*	R	33	80	235	24	61	12	3	3	39	21	38	5	.260	.317	.374
Cecil Cooper	1B90,DH44	L	36	134	542	46	140	24	1	12	75	41	87	1	.258	.310	.373
Jim Gantner	2B135,3B3,DH1*	L	33	139	497	58	136	25	1	7	38	26	50	13	.274	.313	.370
Paul Molitor	3B91,DH10,OF4	R	29	105	437	62	123	24	6	9	55	40	81	20	.281	.340	.426
Ernest Riles	SS142	L	25	145	524	69	132	24	2	9	47	54	80	7	.252	.321	.357
Robin Yount	OF131,DH6,1B3	R	30	140	522	82	163	31	7	9	46	62	73	14	.312	.388	.450
Rob Deer	OF131,1B4	R	25	134	466	75	108	17	3	33	86	72	179	5	.232	.336	.494
Rick Manning	OF83,DH5	L	31	89	205	31	52	7	3	8	27	17	20	5	.254	.310	.434
Ben Oglivie	OF50,DH42	L	37	103	346	31	98	20	1	5	53	30	33	1	.283	.336	.390
Dale Sveum	3B65,2B13,SS13	S	22	91	317	35	78	13	2	7	35	32	63	4	.246	.316	.366
Bill Schroeder	C35,1B19,DH10	R	27	64	217	32	46	14	0	7	19	9	59	1	.212	.262	.373
Rick Cerone	C68	R	32	68	216	22	56	14	0	4	18	15	28	1	.259	.304	.380
Glenn Braggs	OF56,DH2	R	23	58	215	19	51	8	2	4	18	11	47	1	.237	.274	.349
Billy Joe Robidoux	1B43,DH10	L	22	56	181	15	41	8	0	1	21	33	36	0	.227	.344	.287
Mike Felder	OF42,DH1	S	24	44	155	24	37	2	4	1	13	13	16	16	.239	.289	.323
Gorman Thomas†	DH36,1B6	R	35	44	145	21	26	4	1	6	10	31	50	2	.179	.324	.345
Randy Ready†	OF11,2B7,3B3*	R	26	23	79	8	15	4	0	1	4	9	9	2	.190	.273	.278
Paul Householder	OF22,DH3	S	27	26	78	4	17	3	1	1	16	7	16	1	.218	.284	.321
Juan Castillo	2B17,SS4,DH2*	S	24	26	54	6	9	0	1	0	5	5	12	1	.167	.250	.204
Edgar Diaz	SS5	R	22	5	13	0	3	0	0	0	0	1	3	0	.231	.286	.231
Jim Adduci	1B3	L	26	3	11	2	1	1	0	0	0	1	2	0	.091	.167	.182
Steve Kiefer	SS2	R	25	2	6	0	0	0	0	0	0	0	4	0	.000	.000	.000

C. Moore, 1 G at 2B; J. Gantner, 1 G at SS; R. Ready, 1 G at DH; J. Castillo, 2 G at 3B, 1 G at OF

Pitcher	T	Age	G	GS	CG	ShO	IP	H	HR	BB	SO	W-L	Sv	ERA
Teddy Higuera	L	27	34	34	15	4	248.1	226	26	74	207	20-11	0	2.79
Juan Nieves	L	21	35	33	4	3	184.2	224	17	77	116	11-12	0	4.92
Bill Wegman	R	23	35	32	2	0	198.1	217	32	43	82	5-12	0	5.13
Tim Leary	R	28	33	30	3	2	188.1	216	20	53	110	12-12	0	4.21
Danny Darwin†	R	30	27	14	5	1	130.1	120	13	35	80	6-8	0	3.52
Pete Vuckovich	R	33	6	6	0	0	32.1	33	3	11	12	2-4	0	3.06
Mike Birkbeck	R	25	7	4	0	0	22.0	24	0	12	13	1-1	0	4.50
Mark Clear	R	30	59	0	0	0	73.2	53	4	36	85	5-5	16	2.20
Dan Plesac	L	24	51	0	0	0	91.0	81	5	29	75	10-7	14	2.97
Bryan Clutterbuck	R	26	20	0	0	0	56.2	68	8	16	38	0-1	0	4.29
John Henry Johnson	L	29	19	0	0	0	44.0	43	2	10	42	2-1	1	2.66
Jamie Cocanower	R	29	17	2	0	0	44.2	40	1	38	22	0-1	0	4.43
Ray Searage†	L	31	17	0	0	0	22.0	29	6	9	10	0-1	1	6.95
Bob McClure†	L	34	13	0	0	0	16.1	18	2	10	11	2-1	0	3.86
Bob Gibson	R	29	11	1	0	0	26.2	23	3	23	11	1-2	0	4.73
Chris Bosio	R	23	10	4	0	0	34.2	41	9	13	29	0-4	0	7.01
Mark Knudson†	R	25	4	1	0	0	17.2	22	7	5	9	0-1	0	7.64

1986 Baltimore Orioles 7th AL East 73-89 .451 22.5 GB

Earl Weaver

Player	Gm by Position	B	Age	G	AB	R	H	2B	3B	HR	RBI	BB	SO	SB	Avg	OBP	Slg
Rick Dempsey	C121	R	36	122	327	42	68	15	1	13	29	45	78	1	.208	.309	.379
Eddie Murray	1B119,DH16	S	30	137	495	61	151	25	1	17	84	78	49	3	.305	.396	.463
Juan Bonilla	2B70,3B33,DH2	R	30	102	284	33	69	10	1	1	18	25	21	0	.243	.311	.296
Floyd Rayford	3B72,C10,DH1	R	28	81	210	15	37	4	0	8	19	15	50	0	.176	.231	.310
Cal Ripken Jr.	SS162	R	25	162	627	98	177	35	1	25	81	70	60	4	.282	.355	.461
John Shelby	OF121,DH2	S	28	135	404	54	92	14	4	11	49	18	75	18	.228	.263	.364
Lee Lacy	OF120,DH3	R	38	130	491	77	141	18	0	11	47	37	71	4	.287	.334	.391
Fred Lynn	OF107,DH1	L	34	112	397	67	114	13	1	23	67	53	59	2	.287	.371	.499
Larry Sheets	DH58,OF32,C6*	L	26	112	338	42	92	17	1	18	60	21	56	2	.272	.317	.488
Mike Young	OF69,DH38	S	26	117	369	43	93	15	1	9	42	49	90	3	.252	.342	.371
Juan Beniquez	OF54,3B25,DH16*	R	36	113	343	48	103	15	0	6	36	40	49	2	.300	.372	.397
Alan Wiggins	2B66,DH1	S	28	71	239	30	60	3	1	0	11	22	20	21	.251	.309	.272
Jim Traber	1B29,DH21,OF8	L	24	65	212	28	54	7	0	13	44	18	31	0	.255	.321	.472
Tom O'Malley	3B55	L	25	56	181	19	46	9	0	1	18	17	21	0	.254	.317	.320
Jim Dwyer	DH24,OF24,1B1	L	36	94	160	18	39	13	1	8	31	23	31	0	.244	.339	.488
Jackie Gutierrez	2B53,3B6,DH1	R	26	61	145	8	27	3	0	0	4	3	27	0	.186	.207	.207
John Stefero	C50,2B1	L	26	52	120	14	28	2	0	2	13	16	25	0	.233	.321	.300
Ken Gerhart	OF20	R	25	20	69	4	16	2	0	1	7	4	18	0	.232	.267	.304
Al Pardo	C14,DH1	S	23	16	51	3	7	1	0	1	3	0	14	0	.137	.137	.216
Ricky Jones	2B11,3B6	R	28	16	33	2	6	2	0	0	4	6	8	0	.182	.308	.242
Tom Dodd	DH6,3B1	R	27	8	13	1	3	0	0	1	2	2	2	0	.231	.375	.462
Kelly Paris	3B3,DH2	R	28	5	10	0	2	0	0	0	0	0	3	0	.200	.200	.200
Carl Nichols	C5	R	23	5	5	0	0	0	0	0	0	1	4	0	.000	.167	.000
Rex Hudler	2B13,3B1	R	25	14	1	1	0	0	0	0	0	0	0	1	.000	.000	.000

L. Sheets, 4 G at 1B, 2 G at 3B; J. Beniquez, 14 G at 1B

Pitcher	T	Age	G	GS	CG	ShO	IP	H	HR	BB	SO	W-L	Sv	ERA
Mike Boddicker	R	28	33	33	7	0	218.1	214	30	74	175	14-12	0	4.70
Scott McGregor	L	32	34	33	4	2	203.0	216	35	57	95	11-15	0	4.52
Ken Dixon	R	25	35	33	2	0	202.1	194	33	83	170	11-13	0	4.58
Mike Flanagan	L	34	29	28	2	0	172.0	179	15	66	96	7-11	0	4.24
Storm Davis	R	24	25	25	2	0	154.0	166	16	49	96	9-12	0	3.62
John Habyan	R	22	6	5	0	0	26.1	24	3	18	14	1-3	0	4.44
Eric Bell	L	22	4	4	0	0	23.1	23	4	14	18	1-2	0	5.01
Don Aase	R	31	66	0	0	0	81.2	71	6	28	67	6-7	34	2.98
Rich Bordi	R	27	52	1	0	0	107.0	105	13	41	83	6-4	3	4.46
Brad Havens	L	26	46	0	0	0	71.0	64	7	29	57	3-3	1	4.56
Nate Snell	R	33	34	0	0	0	72.1	69	9	22	29	2-1	0	3.86
Odell Jones	R	33	21	0	0	0	49.1	58	4	23	32	2-2	0	3.83
Tippy Martinez	L	36	14	0	0	0	16.0	18	1	12	8	0-2	1	5.63
Tony Arnold	R	27	11	0	0	0	25.1	25	0	11	7	0-2	0	3.55
Mike Kinnunen	L	28	9	0	0	0	7.0	8	1	5	1	0-0	0	6.43
Dennis Martinez‡	R	31	4	0	0	0	6.2	11	0	2	2	0-0	0	6.75
Bill Swaggerty	R	29	1	0	0	0	1.0	6	0	1	1	0-0	0	18.00

1986 California Angels 1st AL West 92-70 .568 —

Gene Mauch

Player	Gm by Position	B	Age	G	AB	R	H	2B	3B	HR	RBI	BB	SO	SB	Avg	OBP	Slg
Bob Boone	C144	R	38	144	442	48	98	12	2	7	49	43	30	1	.222	.287	.305
Wally Joyner	1B152	L	24	154	593	82	172	27	3	22	100	57	58	5	.290	.348	.457
Rob Wilfong	2B90	L	32	92	288	25	63	11	3	3	33	16	34	1	.219	.263	.330
Doug DeCinces	3B132,DH3,SS1	R	35	140	512	69	131	20	3	26	96	52	74	2	.256	.325	.459
Dick Schofield	SS137	R	23	139	458	67	114	17	6	13	57	48	55	23	.249	.321	.397
Gary Pettis	OF153,DH1	S	28	154	539	93	139	23	4	5	58	69	132	50	.258	.339	.343
Brian Downing	OF138,DH10	R	35	152	513	90	137	27	4	20	95	90	84	4	.267	.389	.452
Ruppert Jones	OF121	L	31	126	393	73	90	21	3	17	49	64	87	10	.229	.339	.427
Reggie Jackson	DH121,OF4	L	40	132	419	65	101	12	2	18	58	92	115	1	.241	.379	.408
Bobby Grich	2B87,1B11,3B2	R	37	98	313	42	84	18	0	9	30	39	54	1	.268	.354	.412
George Hendrick	OF93,1B7,DH4	R	36	102	283	45	77	13	1	14	47	26	41	1	.272	.332	.473
Rick Burleson	DH38,SS37,2B6*	R	35	93	271	35	77	14	0	5	29	33	32	1	.284	.363	.391
Jack Howell	3B39,OF8,DH2	L	24	63	151	26	41	14	2	4	21	19	28	2	.272	.349	.470
Jerry Narron	C51,DH2	L	30	57	95	5	21	3	1	1	8	9	14	0	.221	.292	.305
Darrell Miller	OF23,C10,DH2	R	28	33	57	6	13	2	1	0	4	4	8	0	.228	.274	.298
Devon White	OF28	S	23	29	51	8	12	1	1	1	3	6	8	6	.235	.316	.353
Mark Ryal	OF6,1B4,DH2	L	25	13	32	6	12	0	0	2	5	2	4	1	.375	.412	.563
Gus Polidor	2B4,3B1,SS1	R	24	6	19	1	5	1	0	0	1	1	0	0	.263	.300	.316
Mark McLemore	2B2	S	21	5	4	0	0	0	0	0	0	1	2	0	.000	.200	.000

R. Burleson, 4 G at 3B

Pitcher	T	Age	G	GS	CG	ShO	IP	H	HR	BB	SO	W-L	Sv	ERA
Mike Witt	R	25	34	34	14	3	269.0	218	22	73	208	18-10	0	2.84
Don Sutton	R	41	34	34	3	1	207.0	192	31	49	116	15-11	0	3.74
Kirk McCaskill	R	25	34	33	10	2	246.1	207	19	92	202	17-10	0	3.36
Ron Romanick	R	25	18	18	1	1	106.1	124	13	44	38	5-8	0	5.50
John Candelaria	L	32	16	16	1	1	91.2	68	4	26	81	10-2	0	2.55
Jim Slaton†	R	36	14	12	0	0	73.1	84	9	29	31	4-6	0	5.65
Ray Chadwick	R	23	7	7	0	0	27.1	39	5	15	9	0-5	0	7.24
Urbano Lugo	R	23	6	3	0	0	21.1	21	4	6	9	1-1	0	3.80
Willie Fraser	R	22	1	1	0	0	4.1	6	0	1	2	0-0	0	8.31
Donnie Moore	R	32	49	0	0	0	72.2	60	10	22	53	4-5	21	2.97
Doug Corbett	R	33	46	0	0	0	78.2	66	11	22	36	4-2	10	3.66
Terry Forster	L	34	41	0	0	0	41.0	47	2	17	28	4-1	5	3.51
Gary Lucas	L	31	27	0	0	0	45.2	45	1	6	31	4-1	2	3.15
Chuck Finley	L	23	25	0	0	0	46.1	40	2	23	37	3-1	0	3.30
Vern Ruhle	R	35	16	3	0	0	47.2	46	5	7	23	1-3	1	4.15
T.R. Bryden	R	27	16	0	0	0	34.1	38	4	21	25	2-1	0	6.55
Ken Forsch	R	39	10	0	0	0	17.0	24	4	10	13	0-1	1	9.53
Todd Fischer	R	25	9	0	0	0	17.0	18	4	8	7	0-0	0	4.24
Mike Cook	R	22	5	1	0	0	9.0	13	3	7	6	0-2	0	9.00

1986 Texas Rangers 2nd AL West 87-75 .537 5.0 GB

Bobby Valentine

Player	Gm by Position	B	Age	G	AB	R	H	2B	3B	HR	RBI	BB	SO	SB	Avg	OBP	Slg
Don Slaught	C91,DH2	R	27	95	314	39	83	17	1	13	46	16	59	3	.264	.308	.449
Pete O'Brien	1B155	L	28	156	551	86	160	23	3	23	90	87	66	4	.290	.385	.468
Toby Harrah	2B93	R	37	95	289	36	63	18	2	7	41	44	53	2	.218	.322	.367
Steve Buechele	3B137,2B33,OF2	R	24	153	461	54	112	19	2	18	54	35	98	5	.243	.302	.410
Scott Fletcher	SS136,3B12,2B11*	R	27	147	530	82	159	34	5	3	50	47	59	12	.300	.360	.400
Oddibe McDowell	OF148,DH1	L	23	154	572	105	152	24	7	18	49	65	112	33	.266	.341	.427
Pete Incaviglia	OF114,DH36	R	22	153	540	82	135	21	2	30	88	55	185	3	.250	.320	.463
Ruben Sierra	OF107,DH3	S	20	113	382	50	101	13	10	16	55	22	65	7	.264	.302	.476
Larry Parrish	DH99,3B30	R	32	129	464	67	128	22	1	28	94	52	114	3	.276	.347	.509
Gary Ward	OF104,DH1	R	32	105	380	54	120	15	2	5	51	31	72	12	.316	.372	.405
Curtis Wilkerson	2B60,SS56,DH2	S	25	110	236	27	56	10	3	0	15	11	42	9	.237	.273	.305
Tom Paciorek	OF25,1B23,3B21*	R	39	88	213	17	61	7	0	4	22	3	41	1	.286	.305	.376
Darrell Porter	C25,DH19	L	34	68	155	21	41	6	0	12	29	22	51	1	.265	.360	.535
Geno Petralli	C41,3B15,DH2*	S	26	69	137	17	35	9	3	2	18	5	14	3	.255	.282	.409
George Wright†	OF42,DH1	S	27	49	106	10	23	3	1	2	7	4	23	3	.217	.250	.321
Orlando Mercado	C45	R	24	46	102	7	24	1	1	1	7	6	13	0	.235	.279	.294
Mike Stanley	3B7,C4,DH3*	R	23	15	30	4	10	3	0	1	1	3	7	1	.333	.394	.533
Jerry Browne	2B8	S	20	12	24	6	10	2	0	0	3	1	4	0	.417	.440	.500
Bobby Jones	OF9,1B2	L	36	13	21	1	2	0	0	0	3	2	5	0	.095	.174	.095
Jeff Kunkel	SS5,DH1	R	24	8	13	3	3	0	0	1	2	0	2	0	.231	.231	.462
Bob Brower	OF17,DH1	R	26	21	9	3	1	1	0	0	0	0	3	1	.111	.111	.222

S. Fletcher, 1 G at DH; T. Paciorek, 9 G at DH, 1 G at SS; G. Petralli, 2 G at 2B; M. Stanley, 1 G at OF

Pitcher	T	Age	G	GS	CG	ShO	IP	H	HR	BB	SO	W-L	Sv	ERA
Charlie Hough	R	38	33	33	7	2	230.1	188	32	89	146	17-10	0	3.79
Edwin Correa	R	20	32	32	4	2	202.1	167	15	126	189	12-14	0	4.23
Bobby Witt	R	22	31	31	0	0	157.2	130	18	143	174	11-9	0	5.48
Jose Guzman	R	23	29	29	2	0	172.1	199	23	60	87	9-15	0	4.54
Mike Mason	L	27	27	22	2	1	135.0	135	11	56	85	7-3	0	4.33
Mike Loynd	R	22	9	8	0	0	42.0	49	4	19	33	2-2	1	5.36
Kevin Brown	R	21	1	1	0	0	5.0	6	0	0	4	1-0	0	3.60
Mitch Williams	L	21	80	0	0	0	98.0	69	8	79	90	8-6	8	3.58
Greg Harris	R	30	73	0	0	0	111.1	103	12	42	95	10-8	20	2.83
Dale Mohorcic	R	30	58	0	0	0	79.0	86	5	15	29	2-4	7	2.51
Jeff Russell	R	24	37	0	0	0	82.0	74	11	31	54	5-2	2	3.40
Mickey Mahler†	L	33	29	5	0	0	63.0	71	3	29	28	0-2	3	4.14
Ricky Wright	L	27	21	1	0	0	39.1	44	1	21	23	1-0	0	5.03
Dwayne Henry	R	24	19	0	0	0	19.1	14	1	22	17	1-0	0	4.66
Dave Rozema	R	29	6	0	0	0	10.2	19	1	3	3	0-0	0	5.91
Ron Meridith	L	29	5	0	0	0	3.0	2	0	1	2	1-0	0	3.00

1986 Kansas City Royals 3rd AL West 76-86 .469 16.0 GB

Dick Howser (40-48)/Mike Ferraro (36-38)

Player	Gm by Position	B	Age	G	AB	R	H	2B	3B	HR	RBI	BB	SO	SB	Avg	OBP	Slg
Jim Sundberg	C134	R	35	140	429	41	91	9	1	12	42	57	91	1	.212	.303	.322
Steve Balboni	1B137	R	29	138	512	54	117	25	1	29	88	43	146	0	.229	.286	.451
Frank White	2B151,3B1,SS1	R	35	151	566	76	154	37	3	22	84	43	88	4	.272	.322	.465
George Brett	3B115,DH7,SS2	L	33	124	441	70	128	28	4	16	73	80	45	1	.290	.401	.481
Angel Salazar	SS115,2B1	R	24	117	298	24	73	20	2	0	24	7	47	1	.245	.266	.326
Willie Wilson	OF155	S	30	156	631	77	170	20	7	9	44	31	97	34	.269	.313	.366
Lonnie Smith	OF118,DH10	R	30	134	508	80	146	25	7	8	44	46	78	26	.287	.357	.411
Rudy Law	OF77,DH2	L	29	87	307	42	80	26	5	1	36	29	22	14	.261	.327	.388
Jorge Orta	DH87	L	35	106	336	35	93	14	2	9	46	23	34	0	.277	.321	.411
Hal McRae	DH75	R	40	112	278	22	70	14	0	7	37	18	39	0	.252	.298	.378
Jamie Quirk	C41,3B24,1B6*	L	31	80	219	24	47	10	0	8	26	17	41	0	.215	.273	.370
Darryl Motley†	OF66,DH2	R	26	72	217	22	44	9	1	7	20	11	31	0	.203	.241	.350
Mike Kingery	OF59	L	25	62	209	25	54	8	5	3	14	12	30	7	.258	.296	.388
Buddy Biancalana	SS89,2B12	S	26	100	190	24	46	4	4	2	8	15	50	5	.242	.298	.337
Greg Pryor	3B35,SS17,2B12*	R	36	63	112	7	19	4	0	0	7	3	14	1	.170	.191	.205
Kevin Seitzer	1B22,OF5,3B3	R	24	28	96	16	31	4	1	2	11	19	14	0	.323	.440	.448
Bo Jackson	OF23,DH1	R	23	25	82	9	17	2	1	2	9	7	34	3	.207	.286	.329
Lynn Jones	OF62,DH3,2B1	R	33	67	47	1	6	2	0	0	1	6	5	0	.128	.226	.170
Rondin Johnson	2B11	S	27	11	31	1	8	0	1	0	2	0	3	0	.258	.258	.323
Bill Pecota	3B12,SS2	R	26	12	29	3	6	2	0	0	2	3	3	0	.207	.294	.276
Mike Brewer	OF9,DH1	R	26	12	18	0	3	1	0	0	0	2	6	0	.167	.250	.222
Terry Bell	C8	R	23	8	3	0	0	0	0	0	0	2	1	0	.000	.400	.000
Dwight Taylor	DH2,OF1	L	26	4	2	1	0	0	0	0	0	0	0	0	.000	.000	.000

J. Quirk, 1 G at OF; G. Pryor, 1 G at 1B

Pitcher	T	Age	G	GS	CG	ShO	IP	H	HR	BB	SO	W-L	Sv	ERA
Charlie Leibrandt	L	29	35	34	8	1	231.1	238	18	63	108	14-11	0	4.09
Dennis Leonard	R	35	33	30	5	2	192.2	207	22	51	114	8-13	0	4.44
Danny Jackson	L	24	32	27	4	1	185.2	177	13	79	115	11-12	1	3.20
Bret Saberhagen	R	22	30	25	4	2	156.0	165	15	29	112	7-12	0	4.15
Mark Gubicza	R	23	35	24	3	2	180.2	155	8	84	118	12-6	0	3.64
Scott Bankhead	R	22	24	17	0	0	121.0	121	14	37	94	8-9	0	4.61
Dan Quisenberry	R	33	62	0	0	0	81.1	92	2	24	36	3-7	12	2.77
Bud Black	L	29	56	4	0	0	121.0	100	14	43	68	5-10	9	3.20
Steve Farr	R	29	56	0	0	0	109.1	90	10	39	83	8-4	8	3.13
David Cone	R	23	11	0	0	0	22.2	29	2	13	21	0-0	0	5.56
Mark Huismann†	R	28	10	0	0	0	17.1	18	1	6	13	0-1	1	4.15
Alan Hargesheimer	R	29	5	1	0	0	13.0	18	1	7	4	0-1	0	6.23
Steve Shields†	R	27	3	0	0	0	8.2	3	1	4	2	0-0	0	2.08

1986 Oakland Athletics 3rd AL West 76-86 .469 16.0 GB

Jackie Moore (29-44)/Jeff Newman (2-8)/Tony La Russa (45-34)

Player	Gm by Position	B	Age	G	AB	R	H	2B	3B	HR	RBI	BB	SO	SB	Avg	OBP	Slg
Mickey Tettleton	C89	S	25	90	211	26	43	9	0	10	35	39	51	7	.204	.325	.389
Bruce Bochte	1B115,DH1	L	35	125	407	57	104	13	1	6	43	65	68	3	.256	.357	.337
Tony Phillips	2B88,3B30,OF4*	S	27	118	441	76	113	14	5	5	52	76	82	15	.256	.367	.345
Carney Lansford	3B100,1B60,DH2*	R	29	151	591	80	168	16	4	19	72	39	51	16	.284	.332	.421
Alfredo Griffin	SS162	S	28	162	594	74	169	23	6	4	51	35	52	33	.285	.323	.364
Jose Canseco	OF155,DH1	R	21	157	600	85	144	29	1	33	117	65	175	15	.240	.318	.457
Mike Davis	OF139	L	27	142	489	77	131	28	3	19	55	34	91	27	.268	.314	.454
Dwayne Murphy	OF97,DH1	L	31	98	329	50	83	11	3	9	39	56	80	3	.252	.364	.386
Dave Kingman	DH140,1B3	R	37	144	561	70	118	19	0	35	94	33	126	3	.210	.255	.431
Donnie Hill	2B68,3B33,DH3*	S	25	108	339	37	96	16	2	4	29	23	38	5	.283	.329	.378
Dusty Baker	OF55,DH15,1B3	R	37	83	242	25	58	8	0	4	19	27	37	0	.240	.314	.322
Jerry Willard	C71,DH7	L	26	75	161	17	43	7	0	4	26	22	28	0	.267	.354	.385
Stan Javier	OF51,DH2	S	22	59	114	13	23	8	0	0	8	16	27	8	.202	.305	.272
Bill Bathe	C39	R	25	39	103	9	19	3	0	5	11	2	20	0	.184	.208	.359
Mark McGwire	3B16	R	22	18	53	10	10	1	0	3	9	4	18	0	.189	.259	.377
Rusty Tillman	OF17	R	25	22	39	6	10	1	0	1	6	3	11	2	.256	.310	.359
Ricky Peters	OF27,DH4,2B1	S	30	44	38	7	7	1	0	0	1	7	7	2	.184	.311	.211
Mike Gallego	2B19,3B2,SS1	R	25	20	37	2	10	2	0	0	4	1	6	0	.270	.289	.324
Lenn Sakata	2B16,DH1	R	32	17	34	4	12	2	0	0	5	3	6	0	.353	.395	.412
Steve Henderson	OF7,DH1	R	33	11	26	2	2	1	0	0	3	0	5	0	.077	.074	.115
Terry Steinbach	C5	R	24	6	15	3	5	0	0	2	4	1	0	0	.333	.375	.733
Rob Nelson	1B2,DH1	L	22	5	9	1	2	1	0	0	0	1	4	0	.222	.300	.333
Wayne Gross	3B1	L	34	3	2	0	0	0	0	0	0	1	0	0	.000	.333	.000

T. Phillips, 2 G at DH, 1 G at SS; C. Lansford, 1 G at 2B; D. Hill, 2 G at SS

Pitcher	T	Age	G	GS	CG	ShO	IP	H	HR	BB	SO	W-L	Sv	ERA
Curt Young	L	26	29	27	5	2	198.0	176	19	57	116	13-9	0	3.45
Jose Rijo	R	21	39	26	4	1	193.2	172	24	108	176	9-11	1	4.65
Joaquin Andujar	R	33	28	26	7	1	155.1	139	23	56	72	12-7	1	3.82
Dave Stewart†	R	29	29	17	4	1	149.1	137	15	65	102	9-5	0	3.74
Chris Codiroli	R	28	16	16	1	0	91.2	91	15	38	43	5-8	0	4.03
Eric Plunk	R	22	26	15	0	0	120.1	91	14	102	98	4-7	0	5.31
Moose Haas	R	30	12	12	1	0	72.1	58	4	19	40	7-2	0	2.74
Rick Langford	R	34	16	11	0	0	55.0	69	13	18	30	1-10	0	7.36
Rick Rodriguez	R	25	3	3	0	0	16.1	17	4	7	2	1-2	0	6.61
Steve Ontiveros	R	25	46	0	0	0	72.2	72	10	25	54	2-2	10	4.71
Bill Mooneyham	R	25	45	6	0	0	99.2	103	4	67	75	4-5	2	4.52
Jay Howell	R	30	38	0	0	0	53.1	53	3	23	42	3-6	16	3.38
Dave Leiper	L	24	33	0	0	0	31.2	28	3	18	15	2-2	1	4.83
Doug Bair	R	36	31	0	0	0	45.0	37	5	18	40	2-3	4	3.00
Dave Von Ohlen	L	27	24	0	0	0	15.1	18	0	7	4	0-3	1	3.52
Keith Atherton†	R	27	13	0	0	0	15.1	18	2	11	8	1-2	0	5.87
Bill Krueger	L	28	11	3	0	0	34.1	40	4	13	10	1-2	1	6.03
Tom Dozier	R	24	4	0	0	0	6.1	6	1	5	4	0-0	0	5.68
Darrel Akerfelds	R	24	2	0	0	0	5.1	7	2	3	5	0-0	0	6.75
Tim Birtsas	L	25	2	0	0	0	2.0	2	1	4	1	0-0	0	22.50
Fredie Arroyo	R	34	1	0	0	0	0.0	0	0	3	0	0-0	0	—

1986 Chicago White Sox 5th AL West 72-90 .444 20.0 GB

Tony La Russa (26-38)/Doug Rader (1-1)/Jim Fregosi (45-51)

Player	Gm by Position	B	Age	G	AB	R	H	2B	3B	HR	RBI	BB	SO	SB	Avg	OBP	Slg
Carlton Fisk	C71,OF31,DH22	R	38	125	457	42	101	11	0	14	63	22	92	2	.221	.263	.337
Greg Walker	1B77,DH1	L	26	78	282	37	78	10	6	13	51	29	44	1	.277	.345	.493
Julio Cruz	2B78,DH3	S	31	81	209	38	45	2	0	0	19	42	28	7	.215	.343	.225
Tim Hulett	3B89,2B66	R	26	150	520	53	120	16	5	17	44	21	91	4	.231	.260	.379
Ozzie Guillen	SS157,DH1	L	22	159	547	58	137	19	4	2	47	12	52	8	.250	.265	.311
Harold Baines	OF141,DH3	L	27	145	570	72	169	29	2	21	88	38	89	2	.296	.338	.465
John Cangelosi	OF129,DH3	S	23	137	438	65	103	16	3	2	32	71	61	50	.235	.349	.299
Daryl Boston	OF53,DH1	L	23	56	199	29	53	11	3	5	22	21	33	9	.266	.335	.427
Ron Kittle†	DH62,OF20	R	28	86	296	34	63	11	0	17	48	28	87	2	.213	.282	.422
Wayne Tolleson†	3B65,SS18,DH2*	S	30	81	260	39	65	7	3	3	29	38	43	13	.250	.342	.335
Bobby Bonilla†	OF43,1B30	S	23	75	234	27	63	10	2	2	26	33	49	4	.269	.361	.355
Jerry Hairston	DH29,1B19,OF11	S	34	101	225	32	61	15	0	5	26	26	26	0	.271	.348	.404
Russ Morman	1B47	R	24	49	159	18	40	5	0	4	17	16	36	1	.252	.324	.358
Ron Hassey†	DH34,C11	L	33	49	150	22	53	11	1	3	20	22	11	0	.353	.437	.500
Joel Skinner†	C60	R	25	60	149	17	30	5	1	4	20	9	43	1	.201	.250	.329
Reid Nichols	OF53,DH3,2B2	R	27	74	136	9	31	4	0	2	18	11	23	5	.228	.282	.301
Steve Lyons†	OF35,3B3,DH1*	L	26	42	123	10	25	2	1	0	6	7	24	2	.203	.248	.236
Ron Karkovice	C37	R	22	37	97	13	24	7	0	4	13	9	37	1	.247	.315	.443
Jack Perconte	2B24	L	31	24	73	6	16	1	0	0	4	11	10	2	.219	.321	.233
Dave Cochrane	3B18,SS1	S	23	19	62	4	12	2	0	1	2	5	22	0	.194	.254	.274
George Foster†	OF11,DH3	R	37	15	51	2	11	0	2	1	4	3	8	0	.216	.259	.353
Bryan Little†	2B12,SS7,3B1	S	26	20	35	3	6	1	0	0	2	4	4	0	.171	.256	.200
Ivan Calderon†	DH6,OF5	R	24	13	33	3	10	2	1	0	2	3	6	0	.303	.361	.424
Kenny Williams	OF10,DH1	R	22	15	31	2	4	0	0	1	1	1	11	1	.129	.182	.226
Scott Bradley†	DH6,OF1	L	26	9	21	3	6	0	0	0	0	1	0	0	.286	.375	.286
Marc Hill	C22	R	34	22	19	2	3	0	0	0	0	1	3	0	.158	.238	.158
Brian Giles	2B7,SS1	R	26	9	11	0	3	0	0	0	1	0	2	0	.273	.273	.273
Rodney Craig	OF2	S	28	10	10	3	2	0	0	0	0	2	2	0	.200	.333	.200
Luis Salazar	DH2	R	30	4	7	1	1	0	0	0	0	1	3	0	.143	.250	.143

W. Tolleson, 2 G at OF; S. Lyons, 1 G at 1B

Pitcher	T	Age	G	GS	CG	ShO	IP	H	HR	BB	SO	W-L	Sv	ERA
Rich Dotson	R	27	34	34	3	1	197.0	226	24	69	110	10-17	0	5.48
Floyd Bannister	L	31	28	27	6	1	165.1	162	17	48	92	10-14	0	3.54
Joe Cowley	R	27	27	27	4	0	162.1	133	20	83	132	11-11	0	3.88
Joel Davis	R	21	19	19	1	0	105.1	115	9	51	54	4-5	0	4.70
Neil Allen	R	28	22	17	2	2	113.0	101	8	38	57	7-2	0	3.82
Jose DeLeon†	R	25	13	13	1	0	79.0	49	7	42	68	4-5	0	2.96
Tom Seaver†	R	41	12	12	1	0	72.0	66	9	27	31	2-6	0	4.38
Steve Carlton†	L	41	10	10	0	0	63.1	58	6	25	40	4-3	0	3.69
Gene Nelson	R	25	54	1	0	0	114.2	118	7	41	70	6-6	6	3.85
Dave Schmidt	R	29	49	1	0	0	92.1	94	10	27	67	3-6	8	3.31
Bob James	R	27	49	0	0	0	58.1	61	8	23	32	5-4	14	5.25
Bill Dawley	R	28	46	0	0	0	97.2	91	10	28	66	0-7	2	3.32
Joel McKeon	L	23	30	0	0	0	33.0	18	2	17	18	3-1	1	2.45
Ray Searage†	L	31	29	0	0	0	29.0	15	1	19	26	1-0	0	0.62
Bobby Thigpen	R	22	20	0	0	0	35.2	26	1	12	20	2-0	7	1.77
Juan Agosto†	L	28	9	0	0	0	4.2	6	0	4	3	0-2	0	7.71
Bryan Clark	L	29	5	0	0	0	8.0	8	0	2	5	0-0	0	4.50
Pete Filson†	L	27	3	1	0	0	11.2	14	4	5	4	0-1	0	6.17

Seasons: Team Rosters 891

1986 Minnesota Twins 6th AL West 71-91 .438 21.0 GB

Ray Miller (59-80)/Tom Kelly (12-11)

Player	Gm by Position	B	Age	G	AB	R	H	2B	3B	HR	RBI	BB	SO	SB	Avg	OBP	Slg
Mark Salas	C69,DH8	L	25	91	258	28	60	7	4	8	33	18	32	3	.233	.282	.384
Kent Hrbek	1B147,DH1	L	26	149	550	85	147	27	1	29	91	71	81	2	.267	.353	.478
Steve Lombardozzi	2B155	R	26	156	453	53	103	20	5	8	33	52	76	3	.227	.308	.347
Gary Gaetti	3B156,SS2,2B1*	R	27	157	596	91	171	34	1	34	108	52	108	14	.287	.347	.518
Greg Gagne	SS155,2B4	R	24	156	472	63	118	22	6	12	54	30	108	12	.250	.301	.398
Kirby Puckett	OF160	R	25	161	680	119	223	37	6	31	96	34	99	20	.328	.366	.537
Tom Brunansky	OF152,DH2	R	25	157	593	69	152	28	1	23	75	53	98	12	.256	.315	.423
Randy Bush	OF102,DH6,1B3	L	27	130	357	50	96	19	7	7	45	39	63	5	.269	.347	.420
Roy Smalley	DH114,SS19,3B8	S	33	143	459	59	113	20	4	20	57	68	80	1	.246	.342	.438
Mickey Hatcher	OF46,DH28,1B22*	R	31	115	317	40	88	13	3	3	32	19	26	2	.278	.315	.366
Tim Laudner	C68	R	28	76	193	21	47	10	0	10	29	24	56	1	.244	.333	.451
Billy Beane	OF67,DH5	R	24	80	183	20	39	6	0	3	15	11	54	2	.213	.258	.295
Jeff Reed	C64	L	23	68	165	13	39	6	1	2	9	16	19	1	.236	.308	.321
Ron Washington	2B16,DH15,SS7*	R	34	48	74	15	19	3	0	4	11	3	21	1	.257	.278	.459
Mark Davidson	OF31,DH3	R	25	36	68	5	8	3	0	0	2	6	22	2	.118	.189	.162
Alvaro Espinoza	2B19,SS18	R	24	37	42	4	9	1	0	0	1	1	10	0	.214	.233	.238
Al Woods	DH7	L	32	23	28	5	9	1	0	2	8	3	5	0	.321	.375	.571
Chris Pittaro	2B8,SS4	S	24	11	21	0	2	0	0	0	0	0	8	0	.095	.095	.095
Alex Sanchez	DH3,OF1	R	27	8	16	1	2	0	0	0	1	1	8	0	.125	.176	.125
Andre David		L	28	5	5	0	1	0	0	0	0	0	2	0	.200	.333	.200

G. Gaetti, 1 G at OF; M. Hatcher, 3 G at 3B; R. Washington, 3 G at 3B

Pitcher	T	Age	G	GS	CG	ShO	IP	H	HR	BB	SO	W-L	Sv	ERA
Frank Viola	L	26	37	37	7	1	245.2	257	37	83	191	16-13	0	4.51
Bert Blyleven	R	35	36	36	16	3	271.2	262	50	58	215	17-14	0	4.01
Mike Smithson	R	31	34	33	8	1	198.0	234	26	57	114	13-14	0	4.77
Neal Heaton†	L	26	21	17	3	0	124.1	128	18	47	66	4-9	1	3.98
Mark Portugal	R	23	27	15	3	0	112.2	112	10	50	67	6-10	1	4.31
John Butcher†	R	29	16	10	1	0	70.0	82	11	24	29	0-3	0	6.30
Keith Atherton†	R	27	47	0	0	0	81.2	82	9	35	59	5-8	10	3.75
Ron Davis†	R	30	36	0	0	0	38.2	55	7	29	30	2-6	2	9.08
Frank Pastore	R	28	33	1	0	0	49.1	54	4	24	18	3-1	2	4.01
Roy Lee Jackson	R	32	28	0	0	0	58.1	57	7	16	32	0-1	1	3.86
Allan Anderson	L	22	21	10	1	0	84.1	106	11	30	51	3-6	0	5.55
Juan Agosto†	L	28	17	1	0	0	20.1	43	1	14	9	1-2	1	8.85
George Frazier†	R	31	15	0	0	0	26.2	23	2	16	25	1-1	6	4.39
Ray Fontenot†	L	28	15	0	0	0	16.1	27	3	4	10	0-0	0	9.92
Bill Latham	L	25	7	2	0	0	16.0	24	1	6	8	0-1	0	7.31
Roy Smith	R	24	5	0	0	0	10.1	13	1	5	8	0-2	0	6.97
Pete Filson†	L	27	4	0	0	0	6.1	13	1	2	4	0-0	0	5.68
Dennis Burtt	R	28	3	0	0	0	2.0	7	1	3	1	0-0	0	31.50

1986 Seattle Mariners 7th AL West 67-95 .414 25.0 GB

Chuck Cottier (9-19)/Marty Martinez (0-1)/Dick Williams (58-75)

Player	Gm by Position	B	Age	G	AB	R	H	2B	3B	HR	RBI	BB	SO	SB	Avg	OBP	Slg
Bob Kearney	C79	R	29	81	204	23	49	10	0	6	25	12	35	0	.240	.281	.377
Alvin Davis	1B101,DH32	L	25	135	479	66	130	18	1	18	72	76	68	0	.271	.373	.426
Harold Reynolds	2B126	S	25	126	445	46	99	19	4	1	24	29	42	30	.222	.275	.290
Jim Presley	3B155	R	24	155	616	83	163	33	4	27	107	32	172	0	.265	.303	.463
Spike Owen†	SS112	S	25	112	402	46	99	22	6	0	35	34	42	1	.246	.305	.331
Phil Bradley	OF140	R	27	143	526	88	163	27	4	12	50	77	134	21	.310	.405	.445
Danny Tartabull	OF101,2B31,DH3*	R	23	137	511	76	138	25	6	25	96	61	157	4	.270	.347	.489
John Moses	OF93,1B7,DH4	S	28	103	399	56	102	16	3	3	34	34	65	25	.256	.311	.333
Ken Phelps	1B55,DH52	L	31	125	344	69	85	16	4	24	64	88	96	2	.247	.406	.526
Dave Henderson†	OF80,DH22	R	27	103	337	51	93	19	4	14	44	37	95	1	.276	.350	.481
Scott Bradley†	C59,DH3	L	26	68	199	17	60	8	3	5	28	12	7	1	.302	.344	.447
Gorman Thomas†	DH52	R	35	57	170	24	33	4	0	10	26	27	55	1	.194	.308	.394
Ivan Calderon†	OF32	R	24	37	131	13	31	5	0	2	13	6	33	3	.237	.275	.321
Steve Yeager	C49	R	37	50	130	10	27	2	0	2	12	12	23	0	.208	.273	.269
Rey Quinones†	SS36	R	22	36	122	6	23	4	0	0	7	5	31	1	.189	.219	.221
Mickey Brantley	OF25	R	25	27	102	12	20	3	2	3	7	10	21	1	.196	.268	.353
Domingo Ramos	SS21,2B16,3B8*	R	28	49	99	8	18	2	0	0	5	8	13	0	.182	.250	.202
Al Cowens	OF19,DH1	R	34	28	82	5	15	4	0	0	6	3	18	1	.183	.209	.232
Dave Hengel	DH11,OF8	R	24	21	63	3	12	1	0	1	6	1	13	0	.190	.215	.254
Dave Valle	C12,1B4	R	25	22	53	10	18	3	0	5	15	7	7	0	.340	.417	.679
Barry Bonnell	OF9,1B8,DH2	R	32	17	51	4	10	2	0	0	4	1	13	0	.196	.208	.235
Ross Jones	SS4,2B3,3B2*	R	26	11	21	0	2	0	0	0	0	0	4	0	.095	.095	.095
Rickey Nelson	DH4,OF1	L	27	10	12	2	2	0	0	0	1	0	4	1	.167	.167	.167

D. Tartabull, 1 G at 3B; D. Ramos, 2 G at DH; R. Jones, 1 G at DH

Pitcher	T	Age	G	GS	CG	ShO	IP	H	HR	BB	SO	W-L	Sv	ERA
Mike Moore	R	26	38	37	11	1	266.0	279	28	94	146	11-13	1	4.30
Mark Langston	L	25	37	36	9	0	239.1	234	30	123	245	12-14	0	4.85
Mike Morgan	R	26	37	33	9	1	216.1	243	24	86	116	11-17	1	4.53
Bill Swift	R	24	29	17	1	0	115.1	148	5	55	55	2-9	0	5.46
Milt Wilcox	R	36	13	10	0	0	55.2	74	11	28	26	0-8	0	5.50
Jim Beattie	R	31	9	7	0	0	40.1	57	7	14	24	0-6	0	6.02
Matt Young	L	27	65	5	1	0	103.2	108	9	46	82	8-6	13	3.82
Peter Ladd	R	29	52	0	0	0	70.2	69	10	18	53	8-6	6	3.82
Lee Guetterman	L	27	41	4	1	0	76.0	108	7	30	38	0-4	0	7.34
Mark Huismann†	R	28	36	1	0	0	80.0	80	18	19	59	3-3	4	3.71
Karl Best	R	27	26	0	0	0	35.2	35	3	21	23	2-3	1	4.04
Edwin Nunez	R	23	14	1	0	0	21.2	25	5	5	17	1-2	0	5.82
Mike Trujillo†	R	26	11	4	1	1	41.1	32	5	15	19	3-2	1	2.40
Jerry Reed	R	30	11	4	0	0	34.2	38	3	13	16	4-0	0	3.12
Steve Fireovid	R	29	10	1	0	0	21.0	28	1	4	10	2-0	0	4.29
Paul Mirabella	L	32	8	0	0	0	6.1	13	1	3	6	0-0	0	8.53
Mike Brown†	R	27	6	2	0	0	15.2	19	4	11	9	0-2	0	7.47

»1986 New York Mets 1st NL East 108-54 .667 —

Davey Johnson

Player	Gm by Position	B	Age	G	AB	R	H	2B	3B	HR	RBI	BB	SO	SB	Avg	OBP	Slg
Gary Carter	C122,1B9,OF4*	R	32	132	490	81	125	14	2	24	105	62	63	1	.255	.337	.439
Keith Hernandez	1B149	L	32	149	551	94	171	34	1	13	83	94	69	2	.310	.413	.446
Wally Backman	2B113	S	26	124	387	67	124	18	2	1	27	36	32	13	.320	.376	.385
Ray Knight	3B132,1B1	R	33	137	486	51	145	24	2	11	76	40	63	2	.298	.351	.424
Rafael Santana	SS137,2B1	R	28	139	394	38	86	11	0	1	28	36	43	0	.218	.285	.254
Lenny Dykstra	OF139	L	23	147	431	77	127	27	7	8	45	58	55	31	.295	.377	.445
Darryl Strawberry	OF131	L	24	136	475	76	123	27	5	27	93	72	141	28	.259	.358	.507
Mookie Wilson	OF114	S	30	123	381	61	110	17	5	9	45	32	72	25	.289	.345	.430
Kevin Mitchell	OF68,SS24,3B7*	R	24	108	328	51	91	22	2	12	43	33	61	3	.277	.344	.466
Tim Teufel	2B84,1B3,3B1	R	27	93	279	35	69	20	1	4	31	32	42	1	.247	.324	.369
George Foster†	OF62	R	37	72	233	28	53	6	1	13	38	21	53	1	.227	.289	.429
Howard Johnson	3B45,SS34,OF1	S	25	88	220	30	54	14	0	10	39	31	64	8	.245	.341	.445
Danny Heep	OF56	L	28	86	195	24	55	8	2	5	33	30	31	1	.282	.379	.421
Ed Hearn	C45	R	25	49	136	16	36	5	0	4	10	12	19	0	.265	.322	.390
Lee Mazzilli†	OF10,1B8	S	31	39	58	10	16	3	0	2	7	12	11	1	.276	.417	.431
Kevin Elster	SS19	R	21	19	30	3	5	1	0	0	0	3	8	0	.167	.242	.200
Stan Jefferson	OF7	S	23	14	24	6	5	1	0	1	3	2	8	0	.208	.296	.375
John Gibbons	C8	R	24	8	19	4	9	4	0	1	1	3	5	0	.474	.545	.842
Roger McDowell	P75,OF1	R	25	75	18	1	5	0	0	0	3	1	4	0	.278	.316	.278
Dave Magadan	1B9	L	23	10	18	3	8	0	0	0	3	3	1	0	.444	.524	.444
Barry Lyons	C3	R	26	6	9	1	0	0	0	0	2	1	2	0	.000	.100	.000
Tim Corcoran	1B1	L	33	6	7	1	0	0	0	0	0	2	0	0	.000	.222	.000
Jesse Orosco	P58,OF1	R	29	58	3	1	0	0	0	0	1	2	0	0	.000	.333	.000

G. Carter, 1 G at 3B; K. Mitchell, 2 G at 1B

Pitcher	T	Age	G	GS	CG	ShO	IP	H	HR	BB	SO	W-L	Sv	ERA
Ron Darling	R	25	34	34	4	2	237.0	203	21	81	184	15-6	0	2.81
Dwight Gooden	R	21	33	33	12	2	250.0	197	17	80	200	17-6	0	2.84
Sid Fernandez	L	23	32	31	2	1	204.1	161	13	91	200	16-6	1	3.52
Bobby Ojeda	L	28	32	30	7	2	217.1	185	15	52	148	18-5	0	2.57
Rick Aguilera	R	24	28	20	2	0	141.2	145	15	36	104	10-7	0	3.88
Bruce Berenyi	R	31	14	7	0	0	39.2	47	5	22	30	2-2	0	6.35
Roger McDowell	R	25	75	0	0	0	128.0	107	4	42	65	14-9	22	3.02
Jesse Orosco	L	29	58	0	0	0	81.0	64	6	35	62	8-6	21	2.33
Doug Sisk	R	28	41	0	0	0	70.2	77	0	31	31	4-2	1	3.06
Randy Niemann	L	30	31	1	0	0	35.2	44	2	12	18	2-3	0	3.79
Rick Anderson	R	29	15	5	0	0	49.2	45	3	11	21	2-1	1	2.72
Randy Myers	L	23	10	0	0	0	10.2	11	1	9	13	0-0	0	4.22
Terry Leach	R	32	6	0	0	0	6.2	6	0	3	4	0-0	0	2.70
John Mitchell	R	20	4	1	0	0	10.0	10	1	4	2	0-1	0	3.60
Ed Lynch†	R	30	1	0	0	0	1.2	2	0	0	1	0-0	0	0.00

1986 Philadelphia Phillies 2nd NL East 86-75 .534 21.5 GB

John Felske

Player	Gm by Position	B	Age	G	AB	R	H	2B	3B	HR	RBI	BB	SO	SB	Avg	OBP	Slg
John Russell	C89	R	25	93	315	35	76	21	2	13	60	25	103	0	.241	.300	.444
Von Hayes	1B134,OF31	L	27	158	610	107	186	46	2	19	98	74	77	24	.305	.379	.480
Juan Samuel	2B143	R	25	145	591	90	157	36	12	16	78	26	142	42	.266	.302	.448
Mike Schmidt	3B124,1B35	R	36	160	552	97	160	29	1	37	119	89	84	1	.290	.390	.547
Steve Jeltz	SS141	S	27	145	439	44	96	11	4	0	36	65	97	6	.219	.320	.262
Glenn Wilson	OF154	R	27	155	584	70	158	30	4	15	84	42	91	5	.271	.319	.413
Gary Redus	OF89	R	29	90	340	62	84	22	4	11	33	47	78	25	.247	.343	.432
Milt Thompson	OF89	L	27	96	299	38	75	7	1	6	23	26	62	19	.251	.311	.341
Ron Roenicke	OF83	S	29	102	275	42	68	13	1	5	42	61	52	2	.247	.381	.356
Jeff Stone	OF58	L	25	82	249	32	69	6	4	6	19	20	52	19	.277	.341	.406
Rick Schu	3B58	R	24	92	208	32	57	10	1	8	25	18	44	2	.274	.335	.447
Darren Daulton	C48	L	24	49	138	18	31	4	0	8	21	38	41	2	.225	.391	.428
Luis Aguayo	2B31,SS20,3B1	R	27	62	133	17	28	6	1	4	13	8	26	1	.211	.267	.361
Ronn Reynolds	C42	R	27	43	126	8	27	4	0	3	10	5	30	0	.214	.242	.317
Greg Gross	OF27,1B5,P1	L	33	87	101	11	25	5	0	0	8	21	11	1	.248	.379	.297
Tom Foley†	SS24,2B1,3B1	L	26	39	61	8	18	2	1	0	5	10	11	2	.295	.389	.361
Chris James	OF11	R	23	16	46	5	13	3	0	1	5	1	13	0	.283	.298	.413
Greg Legg	2B4,SS1	R	26	11	20	2	9	1	0	0	1	0	3	0	.450	.450	.500
Joe Lefebvre	OF3	L	30	14	18	0	2	0	0	0	0	3	5	0	.111	.238	.111
Francisco Melendez	1B2	L	22	9	8	0	2	0	0	0	0	0	2	0	.250	.250	.250
Garry Maddox	OF3	R	36	6	7	1	3	0	0	0	1	2	1	0	.429	.556	.429

Pitcher	T	Age	G	GS	CG	ShO	IP	H	HR	BB	SO	W-L	Sv	ERA
Kevin Gross	R	25	37	36	7	2	241.2	240	28	94	154	12-12	0	4.02
Shane Rawley	L	30	23	23	7	1	157.2	166	13	50	73	11-7	0	3.54
Charles Hudson	R	27	33	23	0	0	144.0	165	20	58	82	7-10	0	4.94
Bruce Ruffin	L	22	21	21	6	0	146.1	138	6	44	70	9-4	0	2.46
Steve Carlton†	L	41	16	16	0	0	83.0	102	15	45	62	4-8	0	6.18
Mike Maddux	R	24	16	16	0	0	78.0	88	6	34	44	3-7	0	5.42
Fred Toliver	R	25	5	5	0	0	25.2	28	0	11	20	0-2	0	3.51
Marvin Freeman	R	23	3	3	0	0	16.0	6	0	10	8	2-0	0	2.25
Jeff Bittiger	R	24	3	3	0	0	14.2	16	2	7	8	1-1	0	5.52
Kent Tekulve	R	39	73	0	0	0	110.0	99	2	25	57	11-5	4	2.54
Steve Bedrosian	R	28	68	0	0	0	90.1	79	12	34	82	8-6	29	3.39
Don Carman	L	26	50	14	2	1	134.1	113	11	52	98	10-5	1	3.22
Tom Hume	R	33	48	1	0	0	94.1	89	5	34	51	4-1	4	2.77
Dan Schatzeder†	L	31	25	0	0	0	29.1	28	3	16	14	3-3	1	3.38
Dave Rucker	L	28	19	0	0	0	25.0	34	4	14	14	0-2	0	5.76
Larry Andersen†	R	33	10	0	0	0	12.2	19	0	3	9	0-0	0	4.26
Mike Jackson	R	21	9	0	0	0	13.1	12	2	4	3	0-0	0	3.38
Dave Stewart†	R	29	8	0	0	0	12.1	15	1	4	9	0-0	0	6.57
Tom Gorman	L	28	8	0	0	0	11.2	21	0	5	8	0-1	0	7.71
Randy Lerch	L	31	4	0	0	0	8.0	10	0	7	5	1-1	0	7.88
Rocky Childress	R	24	2	0	0	0	2.2	4	0	1	1	0-0	0	6.75
Greg Gross	L	33	1	0	0	0	0.2	1	0	1	2	0-0	0	0.00

1986 St. Louis Cardinals 3rd NL East 79-82 .491 28.5 GB

Whitey Herzog

Player	Gm by Position	B	Age	G	AB	R	H	2B	3B	HR	RBI	BB	SO	SB	Avg	OBP	Slg
Mike LaValliere	C108	L	25	110	303	18	71	10	2	3	30	36	37	0	.234	.318	.310
Jack Clark	1B64	R	30	65	232	34	55	12	2	9	23	45	61	1	.237	.362	.422
Tom Herr	2B152	S	30	152	559	48	141	30	4	2	61	73	75	22	.252	.342	.331
Terry Pendleton	3B156,OF1	S	25	159	578	56	138	26	5	1	59	34	59	24	.239	.279	.306
Ozzie Smith	SS144	S	31	153	514	67	144	19	4	0	54	79	27	31	.280	.376	.333
Vince Coleman	OF149	S	24	154	600	94	139	13	8	0	29	60	98	107	.232	.301	.280
Willie McGee	OF121	S	27	124	497	65	127	22	7	7	48	37	82	19	.256	.306	.370
Andy Van Slyke	OF110,1B38	L	25	137	418	48	113	23	7	13	61	47	85	21	.270	.343	.452
Curt Ford	OF64	L	25	85	214	30	53	15	2	2	29	23	29	13	.248	.318	.364
Tito Landrum	OF78	R	31	96	205	24	43	7	1	2	17	20	41	3	.210	.279	.283
Mike Heath†	C63,OF2	R	31	65	190	19	39	8	1	4	25	23	36	2	.205	.293	.321
Clint Hurdle	1B39,OF10,C5*	L	28	78	154	18	30	5	1	3	15	26	38	0	.195	.311	.299
Jose Oquendo	SS29,2B21,3B1*	S	22	76	138	20	41	4	1	0	13	15	20	2	.297	.359	.341
John Morris	OF31	L	25	39	100	8	24	0	1	1	14	7	15	6	.240	.287	.290
Alan Knicely	1B29,C2	R	31	34	82	8	16	3	0	1	6	17	21	1	.195	.330	.268
Jim Lindeman	1B17,3B1,OF1	R	24	19	55	7	14	1	0	1	6	2	10	1	.255	.276	.327
Steve Lake†	C26	R	29	26	49	4	12	1	0	2	10	2	5	0	.245	.275	.388
Mike Laga†	1B16	L	26	18	46	7	10	4	0	3	8	5	18	0	.217	.308	.500
Tom Lawless	3B12,2B7,OF1	R	29	46	39	5	11	1	0	0	3	2	8	8	.282	.310	.308
Jerry White	OF6	S	33	25	24	1	3	0	0	1	3	2	3	0	.125	.179	.250
Fred Manrique	3B4,2B1	R	24	13	17	2	3	0	0	1	1	1	1	1	.176	.222	.353
Todd Worrell	P74,OF2	R	26	74	7	0	1	0	1	0	0	0	5	0	.143	.143	.429

C. Hurdle, 4 G at 3B; J. Oquendo, 1 G at OF

Pitcher	T	Age	G	GS	CG	ShO	IP	H	HR	BB	SO	W-L	Sv	ERA
Bob Forsch	R	36	33	33	3	0	230.0	211	19	68	104	14-10	0	3.25
Danny Cox	R	26	32	32	8	0	220.0	189	14	60	108	12-13	0	2.90
John Tudor	L	32	30	30	3	0	219.0	197	22	53	107	13-7	0	2.92
Greg Mathews	L	24	23	22	1	0	145.1	139	15	44	67	11-8	0	3.65
Tim Conroy	L	26	25	21	1	0	115.1	122	15	56	79	5-11	0	5.23
Kurt Kepshire	R	26	2	1	0	0	8.0	8	2	4	6	0-1	0	4.50
Todd Worrell	R	26	74	0	0	0	103.2	86	9	41	73	9-10	36	2.08
Pat Perry	L	27	46	0	0	0	68.2	59	5	34	29	2-3	2	3.80
Ricky Horton	L	26	42	9	1	0	100.1	77	7	26	49	4-3	3	2.24
Ken Dayley	L	27	31	0	0	0	38.2	42	1	11	33	0-3	5	3.26
Ray Soff	R	27	30	0	0	0	38.1	37	4	13	22	4-2	0	3.29
Ray Burris	R	35	23	10	0	0	82.0	92	13	32	34	4-5	0	5.60
Greg Bargar	R	27	22	0	0	0	27.1	36	3	10	12	0-2	0	5.60
Rick Ownbey	R	28	17	3	0	0	42.2	47	4	19	25	1-3	0	3.80
Joe Boever	R	25	11	0	0	0	21.2	19	2	11	8	0-1	0	1.66
Jeff Lahti	R	29	4	0	0	0	2.1	3	0	1	3	0-0	0	0.00
Bill Earley	L	30	3	0	0	0	3.0	0	0	2	2	0-0	0	0.00

1986 Montreal Expos 4th NL East 78-83 .484 29.5 GB

Buck Rodgers

Player	Gm by Position	B	Age	G	AB	R	H	2B	3B	HR	RBI	BB	SO	SB	Avg	OBP	Slg
Dann Bilardello	C77	R	27	79	191	12	37	5	0	4	17	14	32	1	.194	.249	.283
Andres Galarraga	1B102	R	25	105	321	39	87	13	0	10	42	30	79	6	.271	.338	.405
Vance Law	2B94,1B20,3B13*	R	29	112	360	37	81	17	2	5	44	37	66	3	.225	.298	.325
Tim Wallach	3B132	R	28	134	480	50	112	22	1	18	71	44	72	8	.233	.308	.396
Hubie Brooks	SS80	R	29	80	306	50	104	18	5	14	58	25	60	4	.340	.388	.569
Tim Raines	OF147	S	26	151	580	91	194	35	10	9	62	78	60	70	.334	.413	.476
Mitch Webster	OF146	S	27	151	576	89	167	31	13	8	49	57	78	36	.290	.355	.431
Andre Dawson	OF127	R	31	130	496	65	141	32	2	20	78	37	79	18	.284	.338	.478
Wayne Krenchicki	1B41,3B24,2B1*	L	31	101	221	21	53	6	2	2	23	22	32	2	.240	.306	.312
Mike Fitzgerald	C71	R	25	73	209	20	59	13	1	6	37	27	34	3	.282	.364	.440
Tom Foley†	SS29,2B25,3B15	L	26	64	202	18	52	13	2	1	18	20	26	8	.257	.320	.356
Herm Winningham	OF66,SS1	L	24	90	185	23	40	6	3	4	11	18	51	12	.216	.286	.346
Al Newman	2B59,SS22	S	26	95	185	23	37	3	0	1	8	21	20	11	.200	.279	.232
Luis Rivera	SS55	R	22	55	166	20	34	11	1	0	13	17	33	1	.205	.285	.283
Wallace Johnson	1B27	S	29	61	127	13	36	3	1	1	10	7	9	6	.283	.321	.346
George Wright†	OF32	S	27	56	117	12	22	5	2	0	5	11	28	1	.188	.258	.265
Casey Candaele	2B24,3B4	S	25	30	104	9	24	4	1	0	6	5	15	3	.231	.264	.288
Jim Wohlford	OF22,3B6	R	35	70	94	10	25	4	2	1	11	9	17	0	.266	.327	.383
Tom Nieto	C30	R	25	30	65	5	13	3	1	1	7	6	21	0	.200	.278	.323
Jason Thompson	1B15	L	31	30	51	6	10	4	0	0	4	18	12	0	.196	.406	.275
Randy Hunt	C21	R	26	21	48	4	10	0	0	2	5	5	16	0	.208	.283	.333
Rene Gonzales	SS6,3B5	R	25	11	26	1	3	0	0	0	0	2	7	0	.115	.179	.115
Wilfredo Tejada	C10	R	23	10	25	1	6	1	0	0	2	2	8	0	.240	.296	.280
Bill Moore	1B3,OF1	R	25	6	12	0	2	0	0	0	0	0	4	0	.167	.167	.167

V. Law, 3 G at P, 1 G at OF; W. Krenchicki, 1 G at OF

Pitcher	T	Age	G	GS	CG	ShO	IP	H	HR	BB	SO	W-L	Sv	ERA
Floyd Youmans	R	22	33	32	6	2	219.0	145	14	118	202	13-12	0	3.53
Jay Tibbs	R	24	35	31	3	2	190.1	181	12	70	117	7-9	0	3.97
Bryn Smith	R	30	30	30	1	0	187.1	182	15	63	105	10-8	0	3.94
Dennis Martinez†	R	31	19	15	1	1	98.0	103	11	28	63	3-6	0	4.59
Joe Hesketh	L	27	15	15	0	0	82.2	92	11	31	67	6-5	0	5.01
Bob Sebra	R	24	17	13	3	1	91.1	82	9	25	66	5-5	0	3.55
Sergio Valdez	R	21	5	5	0	0	25.0	39	2	11	20	0-4	0	6.84
Bob Owchinko	L	31	3	3	0	0	15.0	17	1	3	6	1-0	0	3.60
Tim Burke	R	27	68	2	0	0	101.1	103	7	46	82	9-7	4	2.93
Jeff Reardon	R	30	62	0	0	0	89.0	83	12	26	67	7-9	35	3.94
Bob McClure†	L	34	52	0	0	0	62.2	53	2	23	42	2-5	6	3.02
Andy McGaffigan	R	29	48	14	1	1	142.2	114	9	55	104	10-5	2	2.65
Dan Schatzeder†	L	31	30	1	0	0	59.0	53	6	19	33	3-2	1	3.20
Bert Roberge	R	31	21	0	0	0	28.2	33	2	10	20	0-4	1	6.28
Jeff Parrett	R	24	12	0	0	0	20.1	19	3	13	21	0-1	0	4.87
Randy St. Claire	R	25	11	0	0	0	19.0	13	2	6	21	2-0	1	2.37
George Riley	L	29	10	0	0	0	8.2	7	0	8	5	0-0	0	4.15
Dave Tomlin	L	37	7	0	0	0	10.1	13	1	7	6	0-0	0	5.23
Curt Brown	R	26	6	0	0	0	12.0	15	0	2	4	0-1	0	3.00
Vance Law	R	29	3	0	0	0	4.0	3	0	2	0	0-0	0	2.25

1986 Chicago Cubs 5th NL East 70-90 .438 37.0 GB

Jim Frey (23-33)/John Vukovich (1-1)/Gene Michael (46-56)

Player	Gm by Position	B	Age	G	AB	R	H	2B	3B	HR	RBI	BB	SO	SB	Avg	OBP	Slg
Jody Davis	C145,1B1	R	29	148	528	61	132	27	2	21	74	41	110	0	.250	.300	.428
Leon Durham	1B141	L	28	141	484	66	127	18	7	20	65	67	98	8	.262	.350	.452
Ryne Sandberg	2B153	R	26	154	627	68	178	28	5	14	76	46	79	34	.284	.330	.411
Ron Cey	3B77	R	38	97	256	42	70	21	0	13	36	44	66	0	.273	.384	.508
Shawon Dunston	SS149	R	23	150	581	66	145	37	3	17	68	21	114	13	.250	.278	.411
Keith Moreland	OF121,3B24,C13*	R	32	156	586	72	159	30	0	12	79	53	48	3	.271	.326	.384
Gary Matthews	OF105	R	35	123	370	49	96	16	1	21	46	60	59	3	.259	.361	.478
Bob Dernier	OF105	R	29	108	324	32	73	14	1	4	18	22	41	27	.225	.275	.312
Jerry Mumphrey	OF92	S	33	111	309	37	94	11	2	5	32	26	45	2	.304	.355	.401
Davey Lopes†	3B32,OF22	R	41	59	157	38	47	8	2	6	22	31	16	17	.299	.419	.490
Chris Speier	3B53,SS23,2B7	R	36	95	155	21	44	8	0	6	23	15	32	2	.284	.349	.452
Manny Trillo	3B53,1B11,2B6	R	35	81	152	22	45	10	0	1	19	16	21	0	.296	.359	.382
Terry Francona	OF30,1B23	L	27	86	124	13	31	3	0	2	8	6	8	0	.250	.286	.323
Thad Bosley	OF41	L	29	87	120	15	33	4	1	1	9	18	24	3	.275	.370	.350
Dave Martinez	OF46	L	21	53	108	13	15	1	1	1	7	6	22	4	.139	.190	.194
Chico Walker	OF26	S	28	28	101	21	28	3	2	1	7	10	20	15	.277	.339	.376
Rafael Palmeiro	OF20	L	21	22	73	9	18	4	0	3	12	4	6	1	.247	.295	.425
Brian Dayett	OF24	R	29	24	67	7	18	4	0	4	11	6	10	0	.269	.316	.507
Steve Lake†	C10	R	29	10	19	4	8	1	0	0	4	1	2	0	.421	.450	.474
Mike Martin	C8	L	27	8	13	1	1	1	0	0	0	2	4	0	.077	.200	.154
Steve Christmas	C1,1B1	L	28	3	9	0	1	1	0	0	2	0	1	0	.111	.111	.222

K. Moreland, 12 G at 1B

Pitcher	T	Age	G	GS	CG	ShO	IP	H	HR	BB	SO	W-L	Sv	ERA
Dennis Eckersley	R	31	33	32	1	0	201.0	226	21	43	137	6-11	0	4.57
Scott Sanderson	R	29	37	28	1	1	169.2	165	21	37	124	9-11	1	4.19
Rick Sutcliffe	R	30	28	27	4	1	176.2	166	18	96	122	5-14	0	4.64
Steve Trout	L	28	37	25	0	0	161.0	184	6	78	69	5-7	0	4.75
Jamie Moyer	L	23	16	16	1	1	87.1	107	10	42	45	7-4	0	5.05
Ed Lynch†	R	30	23	13	1	1	99.2	105	10	23	57	7-5	0	3.79
Greg Maddux	R	20	6	5	1	0	31.0	44	3	11	20	2-4	0	5.52
Drew Hall	L	23	5	4	1	0	23.2	24	3	10	21	1-2	1	4.56
Lee Smith	R	28	66	0	0	0	90.1	69	7	42	93	9-9	31	3.09
Ray Fontenot†	L	28	42	0	0	0	56.0	57	5	21	24	3-5	2	3.86
Dave Gumpert	R	28	38	0	0	0	59.2	60	4	28	45	2-0	2	4.37
Jay Baller	R	25	36	0	0	0	53.2	58	7	28	42	2-4	5	5.37
George Frazier†	R	31	35	0	0	0	51.2	63	5	34	41	2-4	0	5.40
Guy Hoffman	L	29	32	8	1	0	84.0	92	6	29	47	6-2	0	3.86
Frank DiPino†	L	29	30	0	0	0	40.0	47	6	14	43	2-4	0	5.18
Matt Keough†	R	30	19	2	0	0	29.0	36	4	12	19	2-2	0	4.97
Ron Davis†	R	30	17	0	0	0	20.0	31	3	3	10	0-2	0	7.65
Dick Ruthven	R	35	6	0	0	0	10.2	12	4	6	3	0-0	0	5.06

1986 Pittsburgh Pirates 6th NL East 64-98 .395 44.0 GB

Jim Leyland

Player	Gm by Position	B	Age	G	AB	R	H	2B	3B	HR	RBI	BB	SO	SB	Avg	OBP	Slg
Tony Pena	C139,1B4	R	29	144	510	56	147	26	2	10	52	53	69	9	.288	.356	.406
Sid Bream	1B153,OF2	L	25	154	522	73	140	37	5	16	77	60	73	13	.268	.341	.450
Johnny Ray	2B151	S	29	155	579	67	174	33	0	7	78	58	47	6	.301	.363	.394
Jim Morrison	3B151,2B1,SS1	R	33	154	537	58	147	35	4	23	88	47	88	9	.274	.334	.482
Rafael Belliard	SS96,2B23	R	24	117	309	33	72	5	2	0	31	26	54	12	.233	.298	.262
Joe Orsulak	OF120	L	24	138	401	60	100	19	6	2	19	28	38	24	.249	.299	.342
R.J. Reynolds	OF112	S	27	118	402	63	108	30	2	9	48	40	78	16	.269	.335	.420
Barry Bonds	OF110	L	21	113	413	72	92	26	3	16	48	65	102	36	.223	.330	.416
Mike Brown	OF71	R	26	87	243	18	53	7	0	4	26	27	32	2	.218	.293	.296
Mike Diaz	OF38,1B20,3B5*	R	26	97	209	22	56	9	0	12	36	19	43	0	.268	.330	.483
Bill Almon	OF54,3B28,SS19*	R	33	102	196	29	43	7	2	7	27	30	38	11	.219	.319	.383
Bobby Bonilla†	OF51,1B4,3B4	S	23	63	192	28	46	6	2	1	17	29	39	4	.240	.342	.307
Sammy Khalifa	SS60,2B6	R	22	64	151	8	28	6	0	0	4	19	28	0	.185	.276	.225
U.L. Washington	SS51,2B3	S	32	72	135	14	27	0	4	0	10	15	27	6	.200	.278	.259
Junior Ortiz	C36	R	26	49	110	11	37	6	0	0	14	9	13	0	.336	.380	.391
Lee Mazzilli†	OF18,1B7	S	31	61	93	18	21	2	1	1	8	26	25	3	.226	.392	.301
Benny Distefano	OF9,1B1	L	24	31	39	3	7	1	0	1	5	1	5	0	.179	.190	.282
Trench Davis	OF7	L	25	15	23	2	3	0	0	0	1	0	4	0	.130	.125	.130
Steve Kemp	OF4	L	31	13	16	1	3	0	0	1	1	4	6	1	.188	.350	.375
Rich Renteria	3B1	R	24	10	12	2	3	1	0	0	1	0	4	0	.250	.250	.333
Ruben Rodriguez	C2	R	21	2	3	0	0	0	0	0	0	0	1	0	.000	.000	.000

M. Diaz, 1 G at C; B. Almon, 4 G at 1B

Pitcher	T	Age	G	GS	CG	ShO	IP	H	HR	BB	SO	W-L	Sv	ERA
Rick Rhoden	R	33	34	34	12	1	253.2	211	17	76	159	15-12	0	2.84
Rick Reuschel	R	37	35	34	4	2	215.2	232	20	57	125	9-16	0	3.96
Mike Bielecki	R	26	31	27	0	0	148.2	149	10	83	83	6-11	0	4.66
Bob Kipper	L	21	20	19	0	0	114.0	123	17	34	81	6-8	0	4.03
Stan Fansler	R	21	5	5	0	0	24.0	20	2	15	13	0-3	0	3.75
Richard Sauveur	L	22	3	3	0	0	12.0	17	3	6	6	0-0	0	6.00
Pat Clements	L	24	65	0	0	0	61.0	53	1	32	31	0-4	2	2.80
Cecilio Guante	R	26	52	0	0	0	78.0	65	11	29	63	5-2	4	3.35
Jim Winn	R	26	50	3	0	0	88.0	85	9	38	70	3-5	3	3.58
Don Robinson	R	29	50	0	0	0	69.1	61	5	27	53	3-4	14	3.38
Larry McWilliams	L	32	49	15	0	0	122.1	129	16	49	80	3-11	0	5.15
Bob Walk	R	29	44	15	1	1	141.2	129	14	64	78	7-8	2	3.75
Barry Jones	R	23	26	0	0	0	37.1	29	3	21	29	3-4	3	2.89
Ray Krawczyk	R	26	12	0	0	0	12.1	17	3	10	7	0-1	0	7.30
John Smiley	L	21	12	0	0	0	11.2	4	2	4	9	1-0	0	3.86
Bob Patterson	L	27	11	5	0	0	36.1	49	0	5	20	2-3	0	4.95
Hipolito Pena	L	22	10	1	0	0	8.1	7	3	3	6	0-3	1	8.64
Jose DeLeon†	R	25	9	1	0	0	16.1	17	2	17	11	1-3	1	8.27

Seasons: Team Rosters 893

1986 Houston Astros 1st NL West 96-66 .593 —

Hal Lanier

Player	Gm by Position	B	Age	G	AB	R	H	2B	3B	HR	RBI	BB	SO	SB	Avg	OBP	Slg
Alan Ashby	C103	S	34	120	315	24	81	15	0	7	38	39	56	1	.257	.333	.371
Glenn Davis	1B156	R	25	158	574	91	152	32	3	31	101	64	72	3	.265	.344	.493
Bill Doran	2B144	S	28	145	550	92	152	29	3	6	37	81	57	42	.276	.368	.373
Denny Walling	3B102,OF11,1B4	L	32	130	382	54	119	23	1	13	58	36	31	1	.312	.367	.479
Dickie Thon	SS104	R	28	106	278	24	69	13	1	3	21	29	49	6	.248	.318	.335
Kevin Bass	OF155	S	27	157	591	83	184	33	5	20	79	38	72	22	.311	.357	.486
Jose Cruz	OF134	L	38	141	479	48	133	22	4	10	72	55	86	3	.278	.351	.403
Billy Hatcher	OF121	R	25	127	419	55	108	15	4	6	36	22	52	38	.258	.302	.356
Craig Reynolds	SS98,1B5,3B4*	L	33	114	313	32	78	7	3	6	41	12	31	3	.249	.274	.348
Phil Garner	3B84,2B7	R	37	107	313	43	83	14	3	9	41	30	45	12	.265	.329	.415
Terry Puhl	OF47	L	29	81	172	17	42	10	0	3	14	15	24	3	.244	.302	.355
Mark Bailey	C53,1B1	S	24	57	153	9	27	5	0	4	15	28	45	1	.176	.302	.288
Jim Pankovits	2B26,OF5,C1	R	30	70	113	12	32	6	1	1	7	11	25	1	.283	.347	.381
Davey Lopes†	OF19,3B5	R	41	37	98	11	23	2	1	1	13	12	9	8	.235	.315	.306
Tony Walker	OF68	R	26	84	90	19	20	7	0	2	10	11	15	11	.222	.307	.367
John Mizerock	C42	L	25	44	81	9	15	1	1	1	6	24	16	0	.185	.374	.259
Ty Gainey	OF19	L	25	26	50	6	15	3	1	1	6	6	19	3	.300	.375	.460
Bert Pena	SS10,3B2,2B1	R	26	15	29	3	6	1	0	0	2	5	5	1	.207	.324	.241
Dan Driessen†	1B12	L	34	17	24	5	7	1	0	1	3	5	2	0	.292	.414	.458
Eric Bullock	OF6	L	26	6	21	0	1	0	0	0	1	0	3	2	.048	.048	.048
Robbie Wine	C8	R	23	9	12	2	3	1	0	0	0	1	4	0	.250	.308	.333
Louie Meadows	OF1	L	25	6	6	1	2	0	0	0	0	0	0	1	.333	.333	.333

C. Reynolds, 2 G at OF, 1 G at P

Pitcher	T	Age	G	GS	CG	ShO	IP	H	HR	BB	SO	W-L	Sv	ERA
Bob Knepper	L	32	40	38	8	5	258.0	232	19	62	143	17-12	0	3.14
Mike Scott	R	31	37	37	7	5	275.1	182	17	72	306	18-10	0	2.22
Nolan Ryan	R	39	30	30	1	0	178.0	119	14	82	194	12-8	0	3.34
Jim Deshaies	L	26	26	26	1	1	144.0	124	16	59	128	12-5	0	3.25
Danny Darwin†	R	30	12	8	1	0	54.1	50	3	9	40	5-2	0	2.32
Mark Knudson†	R	25	9	7	0	0	42.2	48	5	15	20	1-5	0	4.22
Matt Keough†	R	30	10	5	0	0	35.0	22	5	18	25	3-2	0	3.09
Charlie Kerfeld	R	22	61	0	0	0	93.2	71	5	42	77	11-2	7	2.59
Dave Smith	R	31	54	0	0	0	56.0	39	5	22	46	4-7	33	2.73
Aurelio Lopez	R	37	45	0	0	0	78.0	64	6	25	44	3-3	7	3.46
Larry Andersen†	R	33	38	0	0	0	64.2	64	2	23	33	2-1	1	2.78
Frank DiPino†	L	29	31	0	0	0	40.1	27	5	16	27	1-3	3	3.57
Jeff Calhoun	L	28	20	0	0	0	26.2	28	3	12	14	1-0	0	3.71
Julio Solano	R	26	16	1	0	0	32.0	39	5	22	21	3-1	0	7.59
Mike Madden	L	29	13	6	0	0	39.2	47	3	22	30	1-2	0	4.08
Manny Hernandez	R	25	9	4	0	0	27.2	33	2	12	9	2-3	0	3.90
Tom Funk	L	24	8	0	0	0	8.1	10	1	6	2	0-0	0	6.48
Craig Reynolds	R	33	1	0	0	0	1.0	3	0	2	1	0-0	0	27.00
Rafael Montalvo	R	22	1	0	0	0	1.0	1	0	2	0	0-0	0	9.00

1986 Cincinnati Reds 2nd NL West 86-76 .531 10.0 GB

Pete Rose

Player	Gm by Position	B	Age	G	AB	R	H	2B	3B	HR	RBI	BB	SO	SB	Avg	OBP	Slg
Bo Diaz	C134	R	33	134	474	50	129	21	0	10	56	40	52	1	.272	.327	.380
Nick Esasky	1B70,OF42,3B1	R	26	102	330	35	76	17	2	12	41	47	97	0	.230	.325	.403
Ron Oester	2B151	S	30	153	523	52	135	23	2	8	44	52	84	9	.258	.325	.356
Buddy Bell	3B151,2B1	R	34	155	568	89	158	29	3	20	75	73	49	2	.278	.362	.445
Kurt Stillwell	SS80	S	21	104	279	31	64	6	1	0	26	30	47	6	.229	.309	.258
Dave Parker	OF159	L	35	162	637	89	174	31	3	31	116	56	126	1	.273	.330	.477
Eddie Milner	OF127	L	31	145	424	70	110	22	6	15	47	36	56	18	.259	.317	.446
Eric Davis	OF121	R	24	132	415	97	115	15	3	27	71	68	100	80	.277	.378	.523
Dave Concepcion	SS60,1B12,2B10*	R	38	90	311	42	81	13	2	3	30	26	43	13	.260	.314	.344
Pete Rose	1B61	S	45	72	237	15	52	8	2	0	25	30	31	3	.219	.316	.270
Tony Perez	1B55	R	44	77	200	14	51	12	1	2	29	25	25	0	.255	.333	.355
Kal Daniels	OF47	L	22	74	181	34	58	10	4	6	23	22	30	15	.320	.398	.519
Barry Larkin	SS36,2B3	R	22	41	159	27	45	4	3	3	19	9	21	8	.283	.320	.403
Max Venable	OF57	L	29	108	147	17	31	7	1	2	15	17	24	7	.211	.289	.313
Sal Butera	C53,P1	R	33	56	113	14	27	6	1	2	16	21	10	0	.239	.356	.363
Tracy Jones	OF24,1B2	R	25	46	86	16	30	3	0	2	10	9	5	7	.349	.406	.453
Wade Rowdon	3B7,SS6,OF5*	R	25	38	80	9	20	5	1	0	10	9	17	2	.250	.330	.338
Tom Runnells	2B4,3B3	S	31	12	11	1	1	1	0	0	0	0	2	0	.091	.091	.182
Dave Van Gorder	C7	R	29	9	10	0	0	0	0	0	0	1	2	0	.000	.091	.000
Paul O'Neill		L	23	3	2	0	0	0	0	0	0	1	1	0	.000	.333	.000

D. Concepcion, 10 G at 3B; W. Rowdon, 3 G at 2B

Pitcher	T	Age	G	GS	CG	ShO	IP	H	HR	BB	SO	W-L	Sv	ERA
Tom Browning	L	26	39	39	4	2	243.1	225	26	70	147	14-13	0	3.81
Bill Gullickson	R	27	37	37	6	2	244.2	245	24	60	121	15-12	0	3.38
John Denny	R	33	27	27	2	1	171.1	179	15	56	115	11-10	0	4.20
Chris Welsh	L	31	24	24	1	0	139.1	163	9	40	40	6-9	0	4.78
Mario Soto	R	29	19	19	1	1	105.0	113	15	46	67	5-10	0	4.71
Mike Smith	R	25	2	1	0	0	3.1	7	0	1	1	0-0	0	13.50
John Franco	L	25	74	0	0	0	101.0	90	7	44	84	6-6	29	2.94
Ron Robinson	R	24	70	0	0	0	116.2	110	10	43	117	10-3	14	3.24
Ted Power	R	31	56	10	0	0	129.0	115	13	52	95	10-6	1	3.70
Rob Murphy	L	26	34	0	0	0	50.1	26	0	21	36	6-0	1	0.72
Carl Willis	R	25	29	0	0	0	52.1	54	4	32	24	1-3	0	4.47
Scott Terry	R	26	28	3	0	0	55.2	66	8	32	32	1-2	0	6.14
Joe Price	L	29	25	2	0	0	41.2	49	5	22	30	1-2	0	5.40
Bill Landrum	R	28	10	0	0	0	13.1	23	0	4	14	0-0	0	6.75
Sal Butera	R	33	1	0	0	0	1.0	0	0	1	1	0-0	0	0.00

1986 San Francisco Giants 3rd NL West 83-79 .512 13.0 GB

Roger Craig

Player	Gm by Position	B	Age	G	AB	R	H	2B	3B	HR	RBI	BB	SO	SB	Avg	OBP	Slg
Bob Brenly	C101,3B45,1B19	R	32	149	472	60	116	26	0	16	62	74	97	10	.246	.350	.403
Will Clark	1B102	L	22	111	408	66	117	27	2	11	41	34	76	4	.287	.343	.444
Robby Thompson	2B149,SS1	R	24	149	549	73	149	27	3	7	47	42	112	12	.271	.328	.370
Chris Brown	3B111,SS2	R	24	116	416	57	132	16	3	7	49	33	43	13	.317	.376	.421
Jose Uribe	SS156	S	27	157	453	46	101	15	1	3	43	61	76	22	.223	.315	.280
Chili Davis	OF148	S	26	153	526	71	146	28	3	13	70	84	96	16	.278	.375	.416
Candy Maldonado	OF101,3B1	R	25	133	405	49	102	31	3	18	85	20	77	4	.252	.289	.477
Dan Gladden	OF89	R	28	102	351	55	97	16	1	4	29	39	59	27	.276	.357	.362
Jeffrey Leonard	OF87	R	30	89	341	48	95	11	3	6	42	20	62	16	.279	.322	.381
Bob Melvin	C84,3B1	R	24	89	268	24	60	14	2	5	25	15	69	3	.224	.262	.347
Mike Aldrete	1B37,OF31	L	25	84	216	27	54	18	3	2	25	33	34	1	.250	.353	.389
Randy Kutcher	OF51,SS13,3B4*	R	26	71	186	28	44	9	1	7	16	11	41	6	.237	.279	.409
Joel Youngblood	OF45,1B7,3B5*	R	34	97	184	20	47	12	0	5	28	18	34	1	.255	.320	.402
Luis Quinones	SS33,3B31,2B8	S	24	71	106	13	19	1	3	0	11	3	17	3	.179	.207	.245
Harry Spilman†	1B19,3B5,C1*	L	31	58	94	12	27	7	0	2	22	12	13	0	.287	.368	.426
Mike Woodard	2B23,3B2,SS2	L	26	48	79	14	20	2	1	1	5	10	9	7	.253	.337	.342
Phil Ouellette	C9	S	24	10	23	1	4	0	0	0	0	3	3	0	.174	.269	.174
Brad Gulden	C10	L	30	17	22	2	2	0	0	0	1	2	5	0	.091	.167	.091
Rick Lancellotti	1B1,OF1	L	29	15	18	2	4	0	0	2	6	0	7	0	.222	.222	.556
Dan Driessen†	1B4	L	34	15	16	2	3	2	0	0	0	4	4	0	.188	.350	.313
Jeff Robinson	P64,OF1	R	25	65	15	0	1	0	0	0	2	0	7	0	.067	.063	.067
Brad Wellman	SS8,2B1,3B1	R	26	12	13	0	2	0	0	0	1	1	2	0	.154	.214	.154
Chris Jones		L	28	3	1	0	0	0	0	0	0	0	0	1	.000	.000	.000
Randy Bockus	P5,OF1	L	25	6	1	0	0	0	0	0	0	0	1	0	.000	.000	.000

R. Kutcher, 3 G at 2B; J. Youngblood, 4 G at 2B, 1 G at SS; H. Spilman, 1 G at 2B, 1 G at OF

Pitcher	T	Age	G	GS	CG	ShO	IP	H	HR	BB	SO	W-L	Sv	ERA
Mike Krukow	R	34	34	34	10	2	245.0	204	24	55	178	20-9	0	3.05
Mike LaCoss	R	30	37	31	4	1	204.1	179	14	70	86	10-13	0	3.57
Vida Blue	L	36	28	28	0	0	156.2	137	19	77	100	10-10	0	3.27
Kelly Downs	R	25	14	14	1	0	88.1	78	5	30	64	4-4	0	2.75
Roger Mason	R	27	11	11	1	0	60.0	56	5	30	43	3-4	0	4.80
Terry Mulholland	L	23	15	10	0	0	54.2	51	3	35	27	1-7	0	4.94
Steve Carlton†	L	41	6	6	0	0	30.0	36	4	16	18	1-3	0	5.10
Mark Davis	L	25	67	2	0	0	84.1	63	6	34	90	5-7	4	2.99
Jeff Robinson	R	25	64	1	0	0	104.1	92	8	32	90	6-3	8	3.36
Scott Garrelts	R	24	53	18	2	0	173.2	144	17	74	125	13-9	10	3.11
Greg Minton	R	34	48	0	0	0	68.2	63	4	34	34	4-4	5	3.93
Juan Berenguer	R	31	46	4	0	0	73.1	64	4	44	72	2-3	4	2.70
Frank Williams	R	28	36	0	0	0	52.1	35	0	21	33	3-1	1	1.20
Bill Laskey	R	28	20	0	0	0	27.1	28	5	13	8	1-1	1	4.28
Chuck Hensley	L	27	11	0	0	0	7.1	5	2	2	6	0-0	1	2.45
Jim Gott	R	26	9	2	0	0	13.0	16	0	13	9	0-0	1	7.62
Randy Bockus	R	25	5	0	0	0	7.0	7	1	6	4	0-0	0	2.57
Mark Grant	R	22	4	1	0	0	10.0	6	0	5	5	0-1	0	3.60

1986 San Diego Padres 4th NL West 74-88 .457 22.0 GB

Steve Boros

Player	Gm by Position	B	Age	G	AB	R	H	2B	3B	HR	RBI	BB	SO	SB	Avg	OBP	Slg
Terry Kennedy	C123	L	30	141	432	46	114	22	1	12	57	37	74	0	.264	.324	.403
Steve Garvey	1B148	R	37	155	557	58	142	22	0	21	81	23	72	1	.255	.284	.408
Tim Flannery	2B108,3B23,SS8	L	28	134	368	48	103	11	2	3	28	54	61	3	.280	.378	.345
Graig Nettles	3B114	L	41	126	354	36	77	9	0	16	55	41	62	0	.218	.300	.379
Garry Templeton	SS144	S	30	147	510	42	126	21	2	2	44	35	86	10	.247	.296	.308
Tony Gwynn	OF160	L	26	160	642	107	211	33	7	14	59	52	35	37	.329	.381	.467
Kevin McReynolds	OF154	R	26	158	560	89	161	31	6	26	96	66	83	8	.288	.358	.504
Marvell Wynne	OF125	L	26	137	288	34	76	19	2	7	37	15	45	11	.264	.300	.417
John Kruk	OF74,1B9	L	25	122	278	33	86	16	2	4	38	45	58	2	.309	.403	.424
Jerry Royster	3B59,SS24,2B21*	R	33	118	257	31	66	12	0	5	26	32	45	3	.257	.336	.362
Carmelo Martinez	OF60,1B26,3B1	R	25	113	244	28	58	10	0	9	25	35	46	1	.238	.333	.389
Bip Roberts	2B87	S	22	101	241	34	61	5	2	1	12	14	29	14	.253	.293	.303
Bruce Bochy	C48	R	31	63	127	16	32	9	0	8	22	14	23	1	.252	.326	.512
Dane Iorg	1B10,3B6,OF3*	L	36	90	106	10	24	2	1	2	11	2	21	0	.226	.239	.321
Benito Santiago	C17	R	21	17	62	10	18	2	0	3	6	2	12	0	.290	.308	.468
Randy Asadoor	3B15,2B2	R	23	15	55	9	20	5	0	0	7	3	13	1	.364	.397	.455
Tim Pyznarski	1B13	R	26	15	42	3	10	1	0	0	0	4	11	2	.238	.319	.262
Gary Green	SS13	R	24	13	33	2	7	1	0	0	2	1	11	0	.212	.235	.242
Mark Parent	C3	R	24	8	14	1	2	0	0	0	0	1	3	0	.143	.200	.143
Mark Wasinger	3B3,2B1	R	24	3	8	0	0	0	0	0	1	0	2	0	.000	.000	.000
Randy Ready†	3B1	R	26	1	3	0	0	0	0	0	0	0	1	0	.000	.000	.000

J. Royster, 7 G at OF; D. Iorg, 2 G at P

Pitcher	T	Age	G	GS	CG	ShO	IP	H	HR	BB	SO	W-L	Sv	ERA
Andy Hawkins	R	26	37	35	3	1	209.1	218	24	75	117	10-8	0	4.30
Dave Dravecky	L	30	26	26	3	1	161.1	149	17	54	87	9-11	0	3.07
LaMarr Hoyt	R	31	35	25	1	0	159.0	170	27	68	85	8-11	0	5.15
Eric Show	R	30	24	22	2	0	136.1	109	11	69	94	9-5	0	2.97
Mark Thurmond†	L	29	17	15	2	1	70.2	96	7	27	32	3-7	0	6.50
Ed Whitson†	R	31	17	12	0	0	75.2	85	8	37	46	1-7	0	5.59
Ed Wojna	R	25	7	7	1	0	39.0	42	2	16	19	2-2	0	3.23
Jimmy Jones	R	22	3	3	1	1	18.0	10	1	3	15	2-0	0	2.50
Ed Vosberg	L	24	5	3	0	0	13.2	17	1	9	8	0-1	0	6.59
Ray Hayward	L	25	3	3	0	0	10.0	16	1	4	6	0-2	0	9.00
Craig Lefferts	L	28	83	0	0	0	107.2	98	7	44	72	9-8	4	3.09
Lance McCullers	R	22	70	7	0	0	136.0	103	12	58	92	10-10	5	2.78
Gene Walter	L	25	57	0	0	0	98.0	89	7	49	84	2-2	1	3.86
Goose Gossage	R	34	45	0	0	0	64.2	69	8	20	63	5-7	21	4.45
Tim Stoddard†	R	33	30	0	0	0	45.1	33	6	34	47	1-3	0	3.77
Dave LaPoint†	L	26	24	4	0	0	61.1	67	8	24	41	1-4	0	4.26
Bob Stoddard	R	29	18	0	0	0	23.1	20	1	11	17	1-0	1	2.31
Greg Booker	R	26	9	0	0	0	11.0	10	0	4	7	1-0	0	1.64
Dane Iorg	R	36	2	0	0	0	3.0	5	2	1	2	0-0	0	12.00

1986 Los Angeles Dodgers 5th NL West 73-89 .451 23.0 GB

Tom Lasorda

Player	Gm by Position	B	Age	G	AB	R	H	2B	3B	HR	RBI	BB	SO	SB	Avg	OBP	Slg
Mike Scioscia	C119	L	27	122	374	36	94	18	1	5	26	62	23	3	.251	.359	.345
Greg Brock	1B99	L	29	115	325	33	76	13	0	16	52	37	60	2	.234	.309	.422
Steve Sax	2B154	R	26	157	633	91	210	43	4	6	56	59	58	40	.332	.390	.441
Bill Madlock	3B101,1B2	R	35	111	379	38	106	17	0	10	60	30	43	3	.280	.336	.404
Mariano Duncan	SS106	S	23	109	407	47	93	7	0	8	30	30	78	48	.229	.284	.305
Franklin Stubbs	OF124,1B13	L	25	132	420	55	95	11	1	23	58	37	107	7	.226	.291	.421
Reggie Williams	OF124	R	25	128	303	35	84	14	2	4	32	23	57	9	.277	.331	.376
Mike Marshall	OF97	R	26	103	330	47	77	11	0	19	53	27	90	4	.233	.298	.439
Ken Landreaux	OF85	L	31	103	283	34	74	13	2	4	29	22	39	10	.261	.313	.364
Enos Cabell	1B61,OF16,3B7	R	36	107	277	27	71	11	0	2	29	14	26	10	.256	.294	.318
Bill Russell	OF48,SS32,2B8*	R	37	105	216	21	54	11	0	0	18	15	23	7	.250	.302	.301
Dave Anderson	3B51,SS34,2B5	R	25	92	216	31	53	9	0	1	15	22	39	5	.245	.314	.301
Alex Trevino	C63,1B1	R	28	89	202	31	53	13	0	4	26	27	35	0	.262	.351	.386
Len Matuszek	OF37,1B31	L	31	91	199	26	52	7	0	9	28	21	47	2	.261	.333	.432
Jeff Hamilton	3B66,SS2	R	22	71	147	22	33	5	0	5	19	2	43	0	.224	.232	.361
Jose Gonzalez	OF57	R	21	57	93	15	20	5	1	2	6	7	29	4	.215	.270	.355
Cesar Cedeno	OF31	R	35	37	78	5	18	2	1	0	6	7	13	1	.231	.294	.282
Ralph Bryant	OF26	L	25	27	75	15	19	4	2	6	13	5	25	0	.253	.305	.600
Pedro Guerrero	OF10,1B4	R	30	31	61	7	15	3	0	5	10	2	19	0	.246	.281	.541
Craig Shipley	SS10,2B1,3B1	R	23	12	27	3	3	1	0	0	4	2	5	0	.111	.200	.148
Larry See	1B9	R	26	13	20	1	5	2	0	0	2	2	7	0	.250	.318	.350
Terry Whitfield	OF1	L	33	19	14	0	1	0	0	0	0	5	2	0	.071	.316	.071
Jack Fimple	C7,1B1,2B1	R	27	13	13	2	1	0	0	0	2	6	6	0	.077	.350	.077
Ed Amelung	OF4	L	27	8	11	0	1	0	0	0	0	0	4	0	.091	.091	.091

B. Russell, 1 G at 3B

Pitcher	T	Age	G	GS	CG	ShO	IP	H	HR	BB	SO	W-L	Sv	ERA
Orel Hershiser	R	27	35	35	8	1	231.1	213	13	86	153	14-14	0	3.85
F. Valenzuela	L	25	34	34	20	3	269.1	226	18	85	242	21-11	0	3.14
Bob Welch	R	29	33	33	7	3	235.2	227	14	55	183	7-13	0	3.28
Rick Honeycutt	L	32	32	28	0	0	171.0	164	9	45	100	11-9	0	3.32
Jerry Reuss	L	37	19	13	0	0	74.0	96	13	17	29	2-6	1	5.84
Ken Howell	R	25	62	0	0	0	97.2	86	7	63	104	6-12	12	3.87
Tom Niedenfuer	R	26	60	0	0	0	80.0	86	11	29	55	6-6	11	3.71
Ed Vande Berg	L	27	60	0	0	0	71.1	83	8	33	42	1-5	0	3.41
Dennis Powell	L	22	27	6	0	0	65.1	65	5	25	31	2-7	0	4.27
Alejandro Pena	R	27	24	10	0	0	70.0	74	6	30	46	1-2	1	4.89
Carlos Diaz	L	28	19	0	0	0	25.1	33	2	7	18	0-0	0	4.26
Joe Beckwith	R	31	15	0	0	0	18.1	28	5	6	13	0-0	0	6.87
Brian Holton	R	26	12	3	0	0	24.1	28	1	6	24	2-3	0	4.44
Balvino Galvez	R	22	10	0	0	0	20.2	19	3	12	11	0-1	0	3.92

1986 Atlanta Braves 6th NL West 72-89 .447 23.5 GB

Chuck Tanner

Player	Gm by Position	B	Age	G	AB	R	H	2B	3B	HR	RBI	BB	SO	SB	Avg	OBP	Slg
Ozzie Virgil	C111	R	29	114	359	45	80	9	0	15	48	63	73	1	.223	.343	.373
Bob Horner	1B139	R	28	141	517	70	141	22	0	27	87	52	72	1	.273	.336	.472
Glenn Hubbard	2B142	R	28	143	408	42	94	16	1	4	36	66	74	3	.230	.340	.304
Ken Oberkfell	3B130,2B41	L	30	151	503	62	136	24	3	5	48	83	40	7	.270	.373	.360
Andres Thomas	SS97	R	22	102	323	26	81	17	2	6	32	8	49	4	.251	.267	.372
Dale Murphy	OF159	R	30	160	614	89	163	29	7	29	83	75	141	7	.265	.347	.477
Omar Moreno	OF97	L	33	118	359	46	84	18	6	4	27	21	77	17	.234	.276	.351
Terry Harper	OF83	R	30	106	265	26	68	12	0	8	30	29	39	3	.257	.330	.392
Rafael Ramirez	SS86,3B57,OF3	R	28	134	496	57	119	21	1	8	33	21	60	19	.240	.273	.335
Ken Griffey Sr.†	OF77,1B1	L	36	80	292	36	90	15	3	12	32	20	43	12	.308	.351	.503
Billy Sample	OF56,2B1	R	31	92	200	23	57	11	0	6	14	14	26	4	.285	.338	.430
Bruce Benedict	C57	R	30	64	160	11	36	10	1	0	13	15	10	1	.225	.298	.300
C. Washington†	OF38	L	31	40	137	17	37	11	0	5	14	14	26	4	.270	.336	.460
Ted Simmons	1B14,C10,3B9	S	36	76	127	14	32	5	0	4	25	12	14	1	.252	.313	.386
Chris Chambliss	1B20	L	37	97	122	13	38	8	0	2	14	15	24	0	.311	.384	.426
Gerald Perry	OF21,1B1	L	25	29	70	6	19	2	0	2	11	8	4	0	.271	.342	.386
Albert Hall	OF14	S	28	16	50	6	12	2	0	0	1	5	6	8	.240	.309	.280
Jeff Dedmon	P57,OF1	L	26	57	16	2	2	0	0	0	1	0	7	0	.125	.125	.125
Darryl Motley†	OF3	R	26	5	10	1	2	1	0	0	0	1	1	0	.200	.273	.300
Paul Runge	2B5	R	28	7	8	1	2	0	0	0	0	2	4	0	.250	.400	.250
Brad Komminsk	3B2,OF2	R	25	5	5	1	2	0	0	0	1	0	1	0	.400	.400	.400

Pitcher	T	Age	G	GS	CG	ShO	IP	H	HR	BB	SO	W-L	Sv	ERA
Rick Mahler	R	32	39	39	7	1	237.2	283	25	95	137	14-18	0	4.88
David Palmer	R	28	35	35	2	0	209.2	181	17	102	170	11-10	0	3.65
Zane Smith	L	25	38	32	3	1	204.2	209	8	105	139	8-16	1	4.05
Doyle Alexander†	R	35	17	17	2	0	117.1	135	9	17	74	6-6	0	3.84
Joe Johnson†	R	24	17	15	2	0	87.0	101	8	35	49	6-7	0	4.97
Jim Acker†	R	27	21	14	0	0	95.0	100	7	26	37	3-8	0	3.79
Charlie Puleo	R	31	5	3	1	0	24.1	13	4	12	18	1-2	0	2.96
Gene Garber	R	38	61	0	0	0	78.0	76	3	20	56	5-5	24	2.54
Paul Assenmacher	L	25	61	0	0	0	68.1	61	5	26	56	7-3	7	2.50
Jeff Dedmon	R	26	57	0	0	0	99.2	90	8	39	58	6-6	3	2.98
Craig McMurtry	R	26	37	5	0	0	79.2	82	7	43	50	1-6	0	4.74
Ed Olwine	L	28	37	0	0	0	47.2	35	5	17	37	0-0	1	3.40
Bruce Sutter	R	33	16	0	0	0	18.2	17	3	9	16	2-0	3	4.34
Cliff Speck	R	29	13	1	0	0	28.1	25	2	15	21	2-1	0	4.13
Duane Ward†	R	22	10	0	0	0	16.0	22	2	8	8	0-1	0	7.31
Steve Shields†	R	27	6	0	0	0	12.2	13	4	7	6	0-0	0	7.11

»1987 Detroit Tigers 1st AL East 98-64 .605 —

Sparky Anderson

Player	Gm by Position	B	Age	G	AB	R	H	2B	3B	HR	RBI	BB	SO	SB	Avg	OBP	Slg
Matt Nokes	C109,DH18,OF3*	L	23	135	461	69	133	14	2	32	87	35	70	2	.289	.345	.536
Darrell Evans	1B105,DH44,3B7	L	40	150	499	90	128	20	0	34	99	100	84	6	.257	.379	.501
Lou Whitaker	2B148	L	30	149	604	110	160	38	6	16	59	71	108	13	.265	.341	.427
Tom Brookens	3B122,SS16,2B11	R	33	143	444	59	107	15	3	13	59	33	63	7	.241	.295	.376
Alan Trammell	SS149	R	29	151	597	109	205	34	3	28	105	60	47	21	.343	.402	.551
Chet Lemon	OF145	R	32	146	470	75	130	30	3	20	75	70	82	0	.277	.376	.481
Pat Sheridan	OF137	L	29	141	421	57	109	19	3	6	49	44	90	18	.259	.327	.361
Kirk Gibson	OF121,DH4	L	30	128	487	95	135	25	3	24	79	71	117	26	.277	.372	.489
Bill Madlock†	DH64,1B22,3B1	R	36	87	326	56	91	17	0	14	50	28	45	4	.279	.351	.460
Mike Heath	C67,OF24,1B4*	R	32	93	270	34	76	16	0	8	33	21	42	1	.281	.339	.430
Larry Herndon	OF57,DH23	R	33	89	225	32	73	13	2	9	47	23	35	1	.324	.378	.520
Dave Bergman	1B65,DH7,OF7	L	34	91	172	25	47	7	3	6	22	30	23	0	.273	.379	.453
Darnell Coles†	3B36,1B9,OF8*	R	25	53	149	14	27	5	1	4	15	15	23	0	.181	.263	.309
Jim Morrison†	3B16,DH8,2B3*	R	34	34	117	15	24	1	1	4	19	2	26	2	.205	.221	.333
John Grubb	OF31,DH16,3B1	L	38	59	114	9	23	6	0	2	13	15	16	0	.202	.290	.307
Billy Bean	OF24	L	23	26	66	6	17	2	0	0	4	5	11	1	.258	.310	.288
Terry Harper†	DH15,OF14	R	31	31	64	4	13	3	0	3	10	9	8	1	.203	.301	.391
Jim Walewander	2B24,3B17,SS3	S	25	53	54	24	13	3	1	1	4	7	6	2	.241	.328	.389
Scott Lusader	OF22,DH1	L	22	23	47	8	15	3	1	1	8	5	7	1	.319	.377	.489
Dwight Lowry	C12,1B1	L	29	13	25	0	5	2	0	0	1	0	6	0	.200	.200	.280
Orlando Mercado†	C10	R	25	10	22	2	3	0	0	0	1	2	0	0	.136	.208	.136
Tim Tolman	OF7,DH2	R	31	9	12	3	1	1	0	0	1	7	2	0	.083	.429	.167
Doug Baker	SS6,2B1,3B1	S	26	8	1	0	0	0	0	0	0	0	1	0	.000	.000	.000

M. Nokes, 2 G at 3B; M. Heath, 4 G at 3B, 2 G at SS, 1 G at DH, 1 G at 2B; D. Coles, 3 G at DH, 1 G at SS; J. Morrison, 3 G at SS, 3 G at OF, 1 G at 1B

Pitcher	T	Age	G	GS	CG	ShO	IP	H	HR	BB	SO	W-L	Sv	ERA
Walt Terrell	R	29	35	35	10	1	244.2	254	30	94	143	17-10	0	4.05
Jack Morris	R	32	34	34	13	0	266.0	227	39	93	208	18-11	0	3.38
Frank Tanana	L	33	34	34	5	3	218.2	216	27	56	146	15-10	0	3.91
Dan Petry	R	28	30	21	0	0	134.2	148	22	76	93	9-7	0	5.61
Jeff Robinson	R	25	29	21	2	1	127.1	132	16	54	98	9-6	0	5.37
Doyle Alexander†	R	36	11	11	3	3	88.1	63	3	26	44	9-0	0	1.53
Eric King	R	23	55	4	0	0	116.0	111	15	60	89	6-9	9	4.89
Mike Henneman	R	25	55	0	0	0	96.2	86	8	30	75	11-3	7	2.98
Mark Thurmond	L	30	48	0	0	0	61.2	83	5	24	21	0-1	5	4.23
Willie Hernandez	L	32	45	0	0	0	49.0	53	8	20	30	3-4	8	3.67
Nate Snell	R	34	22	2	0	0	38.2	39	5	19	19	1-2	0	3.96
Bryan Kelly	R	28	5	0	0	0	10.2	12	2	7	10	0-1	0	5.06
Dickie Noles†	R	30	4	0	0	0	2.0	2	0	1	0	0-0	2	4.50
Morris Madden	L	26	2	0	0	0	1.2	4	0	3	0	0-0	0	16.20

1987 Toronto Blue Jays 2nd AL East 96-66 .593 2.0 GB

Jimy Williams

Player	Gm by Position	B	Age	G	AB	R	H	2B	3B	HR	RBI	BB	SO	SB	Avg	OBP	Slg
Ernie Whitt	C131	L	35	135	446	57	120	24	1	19	75	44	50	0	.269	.334	.455
Willie Upshaw	1B146	L	30	150	512	68	125	22	4	15	58	58	78	10	.244	.324	.391
Garth Iorg	2B91,3B28,DH5	R	32	122	310	35	65	11	0	4	30	21	52	2	.210	.262	.284
Kelly Gruber	3B119,SS21,2B7*	R	25	138	341	50	80	14	3	12	36	17	70	12	.235	.283	.399
Tony Fernandez	SS146	S	25	146	578	90	186	29	8	5	67	51	48	32	.322	.379	.426
Jesse Barfield	OF158	R	27	159	590	89	155	25	3	28	84	58	141	3	.263	.331	.458
Lloyd Moseby	OF153,DH2	L	27	155	592	106	167	27	4	26	96	70	124	39	.282	.358	.473
George Bell	OF148,DH7,2B1*	R	27	156	610	111	188	32	4	47	134	39	75	5	.308	.352	.605
Fred McGriff	DH90,1B14	L	23	107	295	58	73	16	0	20	43	60	104	3	.247	.376	.505
Rance Mulliniks	3B96,DH22,SS1	L	31	124	332	37	103	28	1	11	44	34	55	1	.310	.371	.500
Rick Leach	OF43,DH30,1B5	L	30	98	195	26	55	13	1	3	25	25	25	0	.282	.371	.405
Cecil Fielder	DH55,1B16,3B2	R	23	82	175	30	47	7	1	14	32	20	48	0	.269	.345	.560
Nelson Liriano	2B37	S	23	37	158	29	38	6	2	2	10	16	22	13	.241	.310	.342
Manuel Lee	2B27,SS26	S	22	56	121	14	31	2	3	1	11	6	13	2	.256	.289	.347
Charlie Moore	C44,OF5	R	34	51	107	15	23	10	1	1	7	13	12	0	.215	.306	.355
Mike Sharperson†	2B32	R	25	32	96	4	20	4	1	0	9	7	15	2	.208	.269	.271
Juan Beniquez†	DH15,OF7,1B2	R	37	39	81	6	23	5	1	5	21	5	13	0	.284	.330	.556
Rob Ducey	OF28	L	22	34	48	12	9	1	0	1	6	8	10	2	.188	.298	.271
Jeff DeWillis	C13	R	22	13	25	2	3	1	0	1	2	2	12	0	.120	.185	.280
Matt Stark	C5	R	22	5	12	0	1	0	0	0	0	0	0	0	.083	.083	.083
Greg Myers	C7	L	21	7	9	1	1	0	0	0	0	0	3	0	.111	.111	.111
Lou Thornton	OF4	L	24	12	2	5	1	0	0	0	0	1	0	0	.500	.667	.500
Alexis Infante		R	25	1	0	0	0	0	0	0	0	0	0	0	—	—	—

K. Gruber, 2 G at OF; G. Bell, 1 G at 3B

Pitcher	T	Age	G	GS	CG	ShO	IP	H	HR	BB	SO	W-L	Sv	ERA
Jim Clancy	R	31	37	37	5	1	241.1	234	24	80	180	15-11	0	3.54
Jimmy Key	L	26	36	36	8	1	261.0	210	24	66	161	17-8	0	2.76
Dave Stieb	R	29	33	31	3	1	185.0	164	16	87	115	13-9	0	4.09
Joe Johnson	R	25	14	14	0	0	66.2	77	10	18	27	3-5	0	5.13
Mike Flanagan†	L	35	7	7	0	0	49.1	46	3	15	43	3-2	0	2.37
Phil Niekro†	R	48	3	3	0	0	12.0	15	4	7	7	0-2	0	8.25
Mark Eichhorn	R	26	89	0	0	0	127.2	110	14	52	96	10-6	4	3.17
Tom Henke	R	29	72	0	0	0	94.0	62	10	25	128	0-6	34	2.49
Jeff Musselman	L	24	68	1	0	0	89.0	75	7	54	54	12-5	3	4.15
John Cerutti	L	27	44	21	2	0	151.1	144	30	59	92	11-4	0	4.40
Jose Nunez	R	23	37	9	0	0	97.0	91	12	58	99	5-2	0	5.01
Gary Lavelle†	L	38	23	0	0	0	27.2	36	2	19	17	2-3	1	5.53
David Wells	L	24	18	2	0	0	29.1	37	0	12	32	4-3	1	3.99
Duane Ward	R	23	12	1	0	0	11.2	14	0	12	10	1-0	0	6.94
Don Gordon†	R	27	5	0	0	0	11.0	8	2	3	3	0-0	0	4.09

1987 Milwaukee Brewers 3rd AL East 91-71 .562 7.0 GB

Tom Trebelhorn

Player	Gm by Position	B	Age	G	AB	R	H	2B	3B	HR	RBI	BB	SO	SB	Avg	OBP	Slg
B.J. Surhoff	C98,3B10,DH7*	L	22	115	395	50	118	22	3	7	68	36	30	11	.299	.350	.423
Greg Brock	1B141	L	30	141	532	81	159	29	3	13	85	57	63	5	.299	.371	.438
Juan Castillo	2B97,SS13,3B7	S	25	116	321	44	72	11	4	3	28	33	76	15	.224	.302	.312
Ernest Riles	3B65,SS21	L	26	83	276	38	72	11	1	4	38	30	47	3	.261	.329	.351
Dale Sveum	SS142,2B13	S	23	153	535	86	135	27	3	25	95	40	133	2	.252	.303	.454
Robin Yount	OF150,DH8	R	31	158	635	99	198	25	9	21	103	76	94	19	.312	.384	.479
Glenn Braggs	OF123,DH7	R	24	132	505	67	136	28	7	13	77	47	96	12	.269	.332	.430
Rob Deer	OF123,1B12,DH4	R	26	134	474	71	113	15	2	28	80	86	186	12	.238	.360	.456
Cecil Cooper	DH62	L	37	63	250	25	62	13	0	6	36	17	51	1	.248	.293	.372
Paul Molitor	DH58,3B41,2B19	R	30	118	465	114	164	41	5	16	75	69	67	45	.353	.438	.566
Mike Felder	OF99,DH3,2B1	S	25	108	289	48	77	5	7	2	31	28	23	34	.266	.329	.353
Jim Gantner	2B57,3B38,DH1	L	34	81	265	37	72	14	0	4	30	19	22	6	.272	.331	.370
Bill Schroeder	C67,1B4,DH2	R	28	75	250	35	83	12	0	14	42	16	56	5	.332	.379	.548
Rick Manning	OF78,DH2	L	32	97	114	21	26	7	1	0	13	12	18	4	.228	.299	.307
Jim Paciorek	1B21,3B15,OF5*	R	27	48	101	16	23	5	0	2	10	12	20	1	.228	.302	.337
Steve Kiefer	3B26,2B4	R	26	28	99	17	20	4	0	5	17	7	28	0	.202	.257	.394
Billy Joe Robidoux	DH10,1B10	L	23	23	62	9	12	0	0	0	4	8	17	0	.194	.286	.194
Charlie O'Brien	C10	R	27	10	35	2	7	3	1	0	0	4	4	0	.200	.282	.343
Brad Komminsk	OF5,DH1	R	26	7	15	0	1	0	0	0	0	1	7	1	.067	.125	.067
Steve Stanicek	DH1	R	26	4	7	2	2	0	0	0	0	0	2	0	.286	.286	.286

B. Surhoff, 1 G at 1B; J. Paciorek, 2 G at DH

Pitcher	T	Age	G	GS	CG	ShO	IP	H	HR	BB	SO	W-L	Sv	ERA
Teddy Higuera	L	28	35	35	14	3	261.2	236	24	87	240	18-10	0	3.85
Bill Wegman	R	24	34	33	7	0	225.0	229	31	53	102	12-11	0	4.24
Juan Nieves	L	22	34	33	3	1	195.2	199	24	100	163	14-8	0	4.88
Len Barker	R	31	11	11	0	0	43.2	54	6	17	22	2-1	0	5.36
Mike Birkbeck	R	26	10	10	1	0	45.0	63	8	19	25	1-4	0	6.20
Mark Knudson	R	26	15	8	1	0	62.0	88	7	14	26	4-4	0	5.37
Mark Ciardi	R	25	4	3	0	0	16.1	26	5	9	8	1-1	0	9.37
Mark Clear	R	31	58	1	0	0	78.1	70	9	55	81	8-5	6	4.48
Dan Plesac	L	25	57	0	0	0	79.1	63	8	23	89	5-6	23	2.61
Chuck Crim	R	25	53	5	0	0	130.0	133	15	39	56	6-8	12	3.67
Chris Bosio	R	24	46	19	2	1	170.0	187	18	50	150	11-8	2	5.24
Jay Aldrich	R	26	31	0	0	0	58.1	71	8	13	22	3-1	0	4.94
Paul Mirabella	L	33	29	0	0	0	29.1	30	0	16	14	2-1	2	4.91
John Henry Johnson	L	30	10	2	0	0	26.1	42	1	18	18	0-1	0	9.57
Ray Burris	R	36	10	2	0	0	23.0	33	4	12	8	2-2	0	5.87
Dave Stapleton	L	25	4	0	0	0	14.2	13	0	3	14	2-0	0	1.84
Alex Madrid	R	24	3	0	0	0	5.1	11	1	1	1	0-0	0	15.19

1987 New York Yankees 4th AL East 89-73 .549 9.0 GB

Lou Piniella

Player	Gm by Position	B	Age	G	AB	R	H	2B	3B	HR	RBI	BB	SO	SB	Avg	OBP	Slg
Rick Cerone	C111,P2,1B2	R	33	113	284	28	69	12	1	4	23	30	46	0	.243	.320	.335
Don Mattingly	1B140,DH1	L	26	141	569	93	186	38	2	30	115	51	38	1	.327	.378	.559
Willie Randolph	2B119,DH1	R	32	120	449	96	137	24	2	7	67	82	25	11	.305	.411	.414
Mike Pagliarulo	3B147,1B1	L	27	150	522	76	122	26	3	32	87	53	111	1	.234	.305	.479
Wayne Tolleson	SS119,3B3	S	31	121	349	48	77	4	0	1	22	43	72	5	.221	.306	.241
Dave Winfield	OF145,DH8	R	35	156	575	83	158	22	1	27	97	76	96	5	.275	.358	.457
Gary Ward	OF94,DH36,1B15	R	33	146	529	65	131	22	1	16	78	33	101	9	.248	.291	.384
Dan Pasqua	OF74,DH20,1B12	L	25	113	318	42	74	7	1	17	42	40	99	0	.233	.319	.421
Ron Kittle	DH49,OF2	R	29	59	159	21	44	5	0	12	28	10	36	0	.277	.318	.535
Rickey Henderson	OF69,DH24	R	28	95	358	78	104	17	3	17	37	80	52	41	.291	.423	.497
C. Washington	OF72,DH13	L	32	102	312	42	87	17	0	9	44	27	54	10	.279	.336	.420
Bobby Meacham	SS56,2B25,DH1	S	26	77	203	28	55	11	1	5	21	19	33	6	.271	.349	.409
Mike Easler†	DH32,OF15	L	36	65	167	13	47	6	0	4	21	14	32	1	.281	.337	.389
Henry Cotto	OF57	R	26	68	149	21	35	10	0	5	20	6	35	4	.235	.269	.403
Joel Skinner	C64	R	26	64	139	9	19	4	0	3	14	8	46	0	.137	.187	.230
Mark Salas†	C41,DH4,OF1	L	26	50	115	13	23	4	0	3	12	10	17	0	.200	.279	.313
Juan Bonilla	2B22,DH1,3B1	R	31	23	55	6	14	3	0	1	3	5	6	0	.255	.317	.364
Roberto Kelly	OF17,DH2	R	22	23	52	12	14	3	0	1	7	5	15	9	.269	.328	.385
Lenn Sakata	3B12,2B6	R	33	19	45	5	12	0	1	2	4	2	4	0	.267	.313	.444
Jerry Royster†	3B13,2B1,SS1*	R	34	18	42	1	15	2	0	0	4	4	4	2	.357	.413	.405
Paul Zuvella	2B7,SS6,3B1	R	28	14	34	2	6	0	0	0	0	0	4	0	.176	.176	.176
Randy Velarde	SS8	R	24	8	22	1	4	0	0	0	1	0	6	0	.182	.182	.182
Jay Buhner	OF7	R	22	7	22	0	5	2	0	0	1	1	6	0	.227	.261	.318
Orestes Destrade	1B3,DH2	S	25	9	19	5	5	0	0	0	1	5	5	0	.263	.417	.263
Jeff Moronko	3B3,SS2,OF2	R	27	7	11	0	1	0	0	0	0	0	2	0	.091	.167	.091
Phil Lombardi	C3	R	24	5	8	0	1	0	0	0	0	0	2	0	.125	.125	.125
Keith Hughes†		L	23	4	4	0	0	0	0	0	0	0	2	0	.000	.000	.000

J. Royster, 1 G at OF

Pitcher	T	Age	G	GS	CG	ShO	IP	H	HR	BB	SO	W-L	Sv	ERA
Tommy John	L	44	33	33	3	1	187.2	212	12	47	63	13-6	0	4.03
Rick Rhoden	R	34	30	29	4	0	181.2	184	22	61	107	16-10	0	3.86
D. Rasmussen†	L	28	26	25	2	0	146.0	145	31	55	89	9-7	0	4.75
Ron Guidry	L	36	22	17	2	0	117.2	111	14	38	96	5-8	0	3.67
Steve Trout†	L	29	14	9	0	0	46.1	51	4	37	27	0-4	0	6.60
Joe Niekro†	R	42	8	8	1	0	50.2	40	4	19	30	3-4	0	3.55
Bill Gullickson†	R	28	8	8	1	0	48.0	46	7	11	28	4-2	0	4.88
Bob Tewksbury†	R	26	8	6	0	0	33.1	47	5	7	12	1-4	0	6.75
Al Leiter	L	21	4	4	0	0	22.2	24	2	15	28	2-2	0	6.35
Dave Righetti	L	28	60	0	0	0	95.0	95	9	44	77	8-6	31	3.51
Tim Stoddard	R	34	57	0	0	0	92.2	83	13	30	78	4-3	8	3.50
Pat Clements	L	25	55	0	0	0	80.0	91	4	30	36	3-3	7	4.95
Charles Hudson	R	28	35	16	6	2	154.2	137	19	57	100	11-7	0	3.61
Cecilio Guante	R	27	23	0	0	0	44.0	42	8	20	46	3-2	1	5.73
Rich Bordi	R	28	16	1	0	0	33.0	42	7	12	23	3-1	0	7.64
Bob Shirley†	L	33	12	1	0	0	34.0	36	4	16	12	1-0	0	4.50
Neil Allen†	R	29	8	1	0	0	24.2	23	2	10	16	0-1	0	3.65
Pete Filson	L	28	7	2	0	0	22.0	26	2	9	10	1-0	0	3.27
Brad Arnsberg	R	23	6	2	0	0	19.1	22	5	13	14	1-3	0	5.59
Al Holland	L	34	3	0	0	0	6.1	9	1	9	5	0-0	0	14.21
Bill Fulton	R	23	3	0	0	0	4.2	9	4	1	2	1-0	0	11.57
Rick Cerone	R	33	2	0	0	0	2.0	0	0	1	1	0-0	0	0.00

1987 Boston Red Sox 5th AL East 78-84 .481 20.0 GB

John McNamara

Player	Gm by Position	B	Age	G	AB	R	H	2B	3B	HR	RBI	BB	SO	SB	Avg	OBP	Slg
Marc Sullivan	C60	R	28	60	160	11	27	5	0	2	10	4	43	0	.169	.198	.238
Dwight Evans	1B79,OF77,DH4	R	35	154	541	109	165	37	2	34	123	106	98	4	.305	.417	.569
Marty Barrett	2B137	R	29	137	559	72	164	23	0	3	43	51	38	15	.293	.351	.351
Wade Boggs	3B145,DH1,1B1	L	29	147	551	108	200	40	6	24	89	105	48	1	.363	.461	.588
Spike Owen	SS130	S	26	132	437	50	113	17	7	2	48	53	43	11	.259	.337	.343
Ellis Burks	OF132	R	22	133	558	94	152	30	2	20	59	41	98	27	.272	.324	.441
Jim Rice	OF94,DH13	R	34	108	404	66	112	14	0	13	62	45	77	1	.277	.357	.408
Mike Greenwell	OF91,DH15,C1	L	23	125	412	71	135	31	6	19	89	35	40	5	.328	.386	.570
Don Baylor†	DH92	R	38	108	339	64	81	8	0	16	57	40	47	5	.239	.355	.404
Bill Buckner†	1B74	L	37	75	286	23	78	6	1	2	42	13	19	1	.273	.299	.322
Ed Romero	2B29,3B24,SS24*	R	29	88	235	23	64	5	0	0	14	18	22	0	.272	.322	.294
Todd Benzinger	OF61,1B2	S	24	73	223	36	62	11	1	8	43	22	41	5	.278	.344	.444
Dave Henderson†	OF64	R	28	75	184	30	43	10	0	8	25	22	48	1	.234	.313	.418
John Marzano	C52	R	24	52	168	20	41	11	0	5	24	7	41	0	.244	.283	.399
Sam Horn	DH40	L	23	46	158	31	44	7	0	14	34	17	55	0	.278	.356	.589
Rich Gedman	C51	L	27	52	151	11	31	8	0	1	13	10	24	0	.205	.250	.278
Danny Sheaffer	C25	R	25	25	66	5	8	1	0	1	5	0	14	0	.121	.119	.182
Glenn Hoffman†	SS16,3B3,2B2	R	28	21	55	5	11	3	0	0	6	3	9	0	.200	.267	.255
Pat Dodson	1B21,DH1	L	27	26	42	4	7	3	0	2	6	8	13	0	.167	.288	.381
Jody Reed	SS4,2B2,3B1	R	24	9	30	4	9	1	1	0	8	4	0	1	.300	.382	.400
Kevin Romine	OF7,DH2	R	26	9	24	5	7	2	0	0	2	2	6	0	.292	.346	.375
Dave Sax	C2	R	28	2	3	0	0	0	0	0	0	0	1	0	.000	.000	.000

E. Romero, 8 G at 1B

Pitcher	T	Age	G	GS	CG	ShO	IP	H	HR	BB	SO	W-L	Sv	ERA
Roger Clemens	R	24	36	36	18	7	281.2	248	19	83	256	20-9	0	2.97
Bruce Hurst	L	29	33	33	15	3	238.2	239	35	76	190	15-13	0	4.41
Al Nipper	R	28	30	30	6	0	174.0	196	30	62	89	11-12	0	5.43
Jeff Sellers	R	23	25	22	4	2	139.2	161	10	61	99	7-8	0	5.28
Bob Stanley	R	32	34	20	4	1	152.2	198	17	42	67	4-15	0	5.01
Oil Can Boyd	R	27	7	7	0	0	36.2	47	6	9	12	1-3	0	5.89
Rob Woodward	R	24	9	6	0	0	37.0	53	6	15	15	1-1	0	7.05
John Leister	R	26	8	6	0	0	30.1	49	9	12	16	0-2	0	9.20
Calvin Schiraldi	R	25	62	1	0	0	83.2	75	15	40	93	8-5	6	4.41
Wes Gardner	R	26	49	1	0	0	89.2	98	17	42	70	3-6	10	5.42
Joe Sambito	L	35	47	0	0	0	37.2	46	8	16	35	2-6	0	6.93
Steve Crawford	R	29	29	0	0	0	72.2	91	13	32	43	5-4	0	5.33
Tom Bolton	L	25	29	0	0	0	61.2	83	5	27	49	1-0	0	4.38

1987 Baltimore Orioles 6th AL East 67-95 .414 31.0 GB

Cal Ripken

Player	Gm by Position	B	Age	G	AB	R	H	2B	3B	HR	RBI	BB	SO	SB	Avg	OBP	Slg
Terry Kennedy	C142	L	31	143	512	51	128	13	1	18	62	35	112	1	.250	.299	.385
Eddie Murray	1B156,DH4	S	31	160	618	89	171	28	3	30	91	73	80	1	.277	.352	.477
Billy Ripken	2B58	R	22	58	234	27	72	9	0	2	20	21	23	4	.308	.363	.372
Ray Knight	3B130,DH14,1B6	R	34	150	563	46	144	24	0	14	65	39	90	0	.256	.310	.373
Cal Ripken Jr.	SS162	R	26	162	624	97	157	28	3	27	98	81	77	3	.252	.333	.436
Larry Sheets	OF124,DH7,1B3	L	27	135	469	74	148	23	0	31	94	31	67	1	.316	.358	.563
Fred Lynn	OF101,DH8	L	35	111	396	49	100	24	0	23	60	39	72	3	.253	.320	.487
Ken Gerhart	OF91	R	26	92	284	41	69	10	2	14	34	17	53	9	.243	.286	.440
Mike Young	OF60,DH47	S	27	110	363	46	87	10	1	16	39	46	91	10	.240	.328	.405
Alan Wiggins	DH44,2B33,OF5	S	29	85	306	37	71	4	2	1	15	28	34	20	.232	.298	.268
Lee Lacy	OF80,DH4	R	39	87	258	35	63	13	3	7	28	32	49	3	.244	.326	.399
Jim Dwyer	DH41,OF30	L	37	92	241	54	66	7	1	15	33	37	57	4	.274	.371	.498
Rick Burleson	2B55,DH7	R	36	62	206	26	43	14	1	2	14	17	30	0	.209	.279	.316
Pete Stanicek	2B19,DH10,3B2	S	24	30	113	9	31	3	0	0	9	8	19	8	.274	.333	.301
Ron Washington	3B20,2B3,DH2*	R	35	26	79	7	16	3	1	1	6	1	15	0	.203	.213	.304
Mike Hart	OF32	L	29	34	76	7	12	2	0	4	12	6	19	1	.158	.217	.342
Rene Gonzales	3B29,2B6,SS1	R	26	37	60	14	16	2	1	1	7	3	11	1	.267	.302	.383
Floyd Rayford	C17,3B1	R	29	20	50	5	11	0	0	2	3	2	9	0	.220	.250	.340
Nelson Simmons	OF13,DH1	S	24	16	49	3	13	1	1	1	4	3	8	0	.265	.296	.388
John Shelby†	OF19,DH1	S	29	21	32	4	6	0	0	1	3	1	13	0	.188	.212	.281
Dave Van Gorder	C12	R	30	12	21	4	5	0	0	1	1	3	6	0	.238	.333	.381
Carl Nichols	C13	R	24	13	21	4	8	1	0	0	3	1	4	0	.381	.409	.429
Jackie Gutierrez	2B1,3B1	R	27	3	1	0	0	0	0	0	0	0	0	0	.000	.000	.000

R. Washington, 2 G at OF, 1 G at SS

Pitcher	T	Age	G	GS	CG	ShO	IP	H	HR	BB	SO	W-L	Sv	ERA
Mike Boddicker	R	29	33	33	7	2	226.0	212	29	78	152	10-12	0	4.18
Eric Bell	L	23	33	29	2	0	165.0	174	32	78	111	10-13	0	5.45
Mike Flanagan†	L	35	16	16	4	0	94.2	102	9	36	50	3-6	0	4.94
Scott McGregor	L	33	26	15	1	1	85.1	112	15	35	39	2-7	0	6.64
Jeff Ballard	L	23	14	14	0	0	69.2	100	15	35	27	2-8	0	6.59
Jose Mesa	R	21	6	5	0	0	31.1	38	7	15	17	1-3	0	6.03
Mark Williamson	R	27	61	2	0	0	125.0	122	12	41	73	8-9	3	4.03
Tom Niedenfuer†	R	27	45	0	0	0	52.1	55	11	22	37	3-5	13	4.99
Dave Schmidt	R	30	35	14	2	2	124.0	128	13	26	70	10-5	1	3.77
Ken Dixon	R	26	34	15	0	0	105.0	128	31	27	91	7-10	5	6.43
Jack O'Connor	L	29	29	0	0	0	46.0	46	5	23	33	1-1	2	4.30
John Habyan	R	23	27	13	0	0	116.1	110	20	40	64	6-7	1	4.80
Tony Arnold	R	28	27	0	0	0	53.0	71	8	17	18	0-0	0	5.77
Mike Griffin	R	30	23	6	1	0	74.1	78	9	33	42	3-5	1	4.36
Mike Kinnunen	L	29	18	0	0	0	20.0	27	3	16	14	0-0	0	4.95
Doug Corbett	R	34	11	0	0	0	23.0	25	5	13	16	0-2	1	7.83
Luis DeLeon	R	28	11	0	0	0	20.2	19	1	8	13	0-2	1	4.79
Don Aase	R	32	7	0	0	0	8.0	8	1	4	3	1-0	2	2.25

1987 Cleveland Indians 7th AL East 61-101 .377 37.0 GB

Pat Corrales (31-56)/Doc Edwards (30-45)

Player	Gm by Position	B	Age	G	AB	R	H	2B	3B	HR	RBI	BB	SO	SB	Avg	OBP	Slg
Chris Bando	C86	S	31	89	211	20	46	9	0	5	16	12	28	0	.218	.260	.332
Joe Carter	1B84,OF62,DH5	R	27	149	588	83	155	27	2	32	106	27	105	31	.264	.304	.480
Tony Bernazard†	2B78	S	30	79	293	39	70	12	1	11	30	25	49	7	.239	.300	.399
Brook Jacoby	3B144,1B7,DH4	R	27	155	540	73	162	26	4	32	69	75	73	2	.300	.387	.541
Julio Franco	SS111,2B9,DH8	R	25	128	495	86	158	24	3	8	52	57	56	32	.319	.389	.428
Cory Snyder	OF139,SS18	R	24	157	577	74	136	24	2	33	82	31	166	5	.236	.273	.456
Brett Butler	OF136	L	30	137	522	91	154	25	8	9	41	91	55	33	.295	.399	.425
Mel Hall	OF122,DH14	L	26	142	485	57	136	21	1	18	76	20	68	5	.280	.309	.439
Pat Tabler	1B82,DH66	R	29	151	553	66	170	34	3	11	86	51	84	5	.307	.369	.439
Tommy Hinzo	2B67	S	23	67	257	31	68	9	3	3	21	10	47	9	.265	.296	.358
Carmelo Castillo	DH43,OF23	R	29	89	220	27	55	17	0	11	31	16	52	1	.250	.296	.477
Andy Allanson	C50	R	25	50	154	17	41	6	0	3	16	9	30	1	.266	.298	.364
Rick Dempsey	C59	R	37	60	141	16	25	10	0	1	9	23	29	0	.177	.295	.270
Jay Bell	SS38	R	21	38	125	14	27	9	1	2	13	8	31	2	.216	.269	.352
Dave Clark	OF13,DH12	L	24	29	87	11	18	5	0	3	12	2	24	1	.207	.225	.368
Andre Thornton	DH21	R	37	36	85	8	10	2	0	0	5	10	25	1	.118	.206	.141
Junior Noboa	2B21,SS8,3B5	R	22	39	80	7	18	2	1	0	7	3	6	1	.225	.253	.275
Eddie Williams	3B22	R	22	22	64	9	11	4	0	1	4	9	19	0	.172	.280	.281
Doug Frobel	OF12,DH5	L	28	29	40	5	4	0	0	2	5	5	13	0	.100	.196	.250
Dave Gallagher	OF14	R	26	15	36	2	4	1	1	0	1	2	5	2	.111	.158	.194
Casey Parsons	DH5,OF2,1B1	L	33	18	25	2	4	0	0	1	5	0	5	0	.160	.160	.280
Otis Nixon	OF17	S	28	19	17	2	1	0	0	0	1	3	4	2	.059	.200	.059
Brian Dorsett	C4	R	26	5	11	2	3	0	0	1	3	0	3	0	.273	.333	.545

Pitcher	T	Age	G	GS	CG	ShO	IP	H	HR	BB	SO	W-L	Sv	ERA
Tom Candiotti	R	29	32	32	7	2	201.2	193	28	93	111	7-18	0	4.78
Ken Schrom	R	32	32	29	4	1	153.2	185	29	57	61	6-13	0	6.50
Phil Niekro†	R	48	22	22	2	0	123.2	142	18	53	57	7-11	0	5.89
Greg Swindell	L	22	16	15	4	1	102.1	112	18	37	97	3-8	0	5.10
Steve Carlton†	L	42	23	14	3	0	109.0	111	17	63	71	5-9	1	5.37
Darrel Akerfelds	R	25	16	13	1	0	74.2	84	18	38	42	2-6	0	6.75
John Farrell	R	24	10	9	1	0	69.0	68	7	22	28	5-1	0	3.39
Ed Vande Berg	L	28	55	0	0	0	72.1	96	9	21	40	1-0	0	5.10
Doug Jones	R	30	49	0	0	0	91.1	101	4	24	87	6-5	8	3.15
Scott Bailes	L	25	39	17	0	0	120.1	145	21	47	65	7-8	6	4.64
Rich Yett	R	24	37	11	2	0	97.2	96	21	49	59	3-9	1	5.25
Sammy Stewart	R	32	25	0	0	0	27.0	25	4	21	25	4-2	3	5.67
Don Gordon†	R	27	21	0	0	0	39.2	49	3	12	20	0-3	1	4.08
Mark Huismann†	R	29	20	0	0	0	35.1	38	6	8	23	2-3	2	5.09
Jamie Easterly	L	34	16	0	0	0	31.2	26	4	13	22	1-1	0	4.55
Ernie Camacho	R	32	15	0	0	0	13.2	21	1	5	9	0-1	1	9.22
Reggie Ritter	R	27	14	0	0	0	26.2	33	5	16	11	1-1	0	6.08
Mike Armstrong	R	33	14	0	0	0	18.2	27	4	10	9	1-0	1	8.68
Tom Waddell	R	28	6	0	0	0	5.2	7	1	7	6	0-1	0	14.29
Frank Wills	R	28	6	0	0	0	5.1	3	0	7	4	0-1	1	5.06
Jeff Kaiser	L	26	2	0	0	0	3.1	4	1	3	2	0-0	0	16.20

1987 Minnesota Twins 1st AL West 85-77 .525 —

Tom Kelly

Player	Gm by Position	B	Age	G	AB	R	H	2B	3B	HR	RBI	BB	SO	SB	Avg	OBP	Slg
Tim Laudner	C101,1B7,DH2	R	29	113	288	30	55	7	1	16	43	23	80	1	.191	.252	.389
Kent Hrbek	1B137,DH1	L	27	143	477	85	136	20	1	34	90	84	60	5	.285	.389	.545
Steve Lombardozzi	2B133	R	27	136	432	51	103	19	3	8	38	33	66	5	.238	.298	.352
Gary Gaetti	3B150,DH2	R	28	154	584	95	150	36	2	31	109	37	92	10	.257	.303	.485
Greg Gagne	SS136,OF4,DH1*	R	25	137	437	68	116	28	7	10	40	25	84	6	.265	.310	.430
Kirby Puckett	OF147,DH8	R	26	157	624	96	207	32	5	28	99	32	91	12	.332	.367	.534
Tom Brunansky	OF138,DH17	R	26	155	532	83	138	22	2	32	85	74	104	11	.259	.352	.489
Dan Gladden	OF111,DH4	R	29	121	438	69	109	21	2	8	38	38	72	25	.249	.312	.361
Roy Smalley	DH73,3B14,SS4	S	34	110	309	32	85	16	1	8	34	36	52	2	.275	.352	.411
Al Newman	SS55,2B47,3B12*	S	27	110	307	44	68	15	5	0	29	34	27	15	.221	.298	.303
Randy Bush	OF75,DH9,1B9	L	28	122	293	46	74	10	2	11	46	43	49	10	.253	.349	.413
Gene Larkin	DH40,1B26	S	24	85	233	23	62	11	2	4	28	25	31	1	.266	.340	.382
Mark Davidson	OF86,DH9	R	26	102	150	32	40	4	1	1	14	13	26	9	.267	.321	.327
Sal Butera†	C51	R	34	51	111	7	19	5	0	1	12	7	16	0	.171	.217	.243
Tom Nieto	C40,DH1	R	26	41	105	7	21	7	1	1	12	8	24	0	.200	.276	.314
Don Baylor†	DH14	R	38	20	49	3	14	1	0	0	6	5	12	0	.286	.397	.306
Mark Salas†	C14	L	26	22	45	8	17	2	0	3	9	5	6	0	.378	.431	.622
Billy Beane	OF7	R	25	12	15	1	4	2	0	0	1	0	6	0	.267	.267	.400
Chris Pittaro	2B8	S	25	14	12	6	4	0	0	0	0	1	0	1	.333	.385	.333

G. Gagne, 1 G at 2B; A. Newman, 5 G at DH, 2 G at OF

Pitcher	T	Age	G	GS	CG	ShO	IP	H	HR	BB	SO	W-L	Sv	ERA
Bert Blyleven	R	36	37	37	8	1	267.0	249	46	101	196	15-12	0	4.01
Frank Viola	L	27	36	36	7	1	251.2	230	29	66	197	17-10	0	2.90
Les Straker	R	27	31	26	1	0	154.1	150	24	59	76	8-10	0	4.37
Mike Smithson	R	32	21	20	0	0	109.0	126	17	38	53	4-7	0	5.94
Joe Niekro†	R	42	19	18	0	0	96.1	115	11	45	54	4-9	0	6.26
Mark Portugal	R	24	13	7	0	0	44.0	58	13	24	28	1-3	0	7.77
Steve Carlton†	L	42	9	7	0	0	43.0	54	7	23	20	1-5	0	6.70
Allan Anderson	L	23	4	2	0	0	12.1	20	3	10	3	1-0	0	10.95
Jeff Reardon	R	31	63	0	0	0	80.1	70	14	28	83	8-8	31	4.48
Keith Atherton	R	28	59	0	0	0	79.1	81	10	30	51	7-5	2	4.54
George Frazier	R	32	54	0	0	0	81.1	77	9	51	58	5-5	2	4.98
Juan Berenguer	R	32	47	6	0	0	112.0	100	10	47	110	8-1	4	3.94
Dan Schatzeder†	L	32	30	1	0	0	43.2	64	8	18	30	3-1	0	6.39
Joe Klink	L	25	12	0	0	0	23.0	37	4	11	17	0-1	0	6.65
Roy Smith	R	25	7	1	0	0	16.1	20	3	6	8	1-0	0	4.96
Randy Niemann	L	31	6	0	0	0	5.1	3	0	7	1	1-0	0	8.44
Jeff Bittiger	R	25	3	1	0	0	8.1	11	2	0	5	1-0	0	5.40

1987 Kansas City Royals 2nd AL West 83-79 .512 2.0 GB

Billy Gardner (62-64)/John Wathan (21-15)

Player	Gm by Position	B	Age	G	AB	R	H	2B	3B	HR	RBI	BB	SO	SB	Avg	OBP	Slg
Jamie Quirk	C108,SS1	L	32	109	296	24	70	17	0	5	33	28	56	1	.236	.307	.345
George Brett	1B83,DH21,3B11	L	34	115	427	71	124	18	2	22	78	72	47	6	.290	.388	.496
Frank White	2B152,DH1	R	36	154	563	67	138	32	2	17	78	51	86	1	.245	.308	.400
Kevin Seitzer	3B141,1B25,OF3*	R	25	161	641	105	207	33	8	15	83	80	85	12	.323	.399	.470
Angel Salazar	SS116	R	25	116	317	24	65	7	0	2	21	6	46	4	.205	.219	.246
Danny Tartabull	OF149,DH6	R	24	158	582	95	180	27	3	34	101	79	136	9	.309	.390	.541
Willie Wilson	OF143,DH2	S	31	146	610	97	170	18	15	4	30	32	88	59	.279	.320	.377
Bo Jackson	OF113,DH1	R	24	116	396	46	93	17	2	22	53	30	158	10	.235	.296	.455
Steve Balboni	1B55,DH52	R	30	121	386	44	80	11	1	24	60	34	97	0	.207	.273	.427
Juan Beniquez†	OF22,DH15,1B6*	R	37	57	174	14	41	7	0	3	26	11	26	0	.236	.282	.328
Lonnie Smith	OF32,DH15	R	31	48	167	26	42	7	1	3	8	24	31	9	.251	.355	.359
Larry Owen	C75	R	32	76	164	17	31	6	0	5	14	16	51	0	.189	.260	.317
Bill Pecota	SS36,3B17,2B15	R	27	66	156	22	43	5	1	3	14	15	25	5	.276	.343	.378
Thad Bosley	OF28,DH13	L	30	80	140	13	39	6	1	1	16	9	26	0	.279	.318	.357
Ross Jones	SS36,2B3	R	27	39	114	10	29	4	2	0	10	5	15	1	.254	.285	.325
Jim Eisenreich	DH26	L	28	44	105	10	25	8	2	4	21	7	13	1	.238	.278	.467
Gary Thurman	OF27	R	22	27	81	12	24	2	0	0	5	8	20	7	.296	.360	.321
Jorge Orta	DH12	L	36	21	50	3	9	4	0	2	4	3	8	0	.180	.226	.380
Buddy Biancalana†	SS22,2B12	S	27	37	47	4	10	1	0	1	7	1	10	0	.213	.229	.298
Hal McRae	DH7	R	41	18	32	5	10	3	0	1	9	5	1	0	.313	.405	.500
Mike Macfarlane	C8	R	23	8	19	0	4	1	0	0	3	2	2	0	.211	.286	.263
Ed Hearn	C5	R	26	6	17	2	5	2	0	0	3	4	2	0	.294	.429	.412
Scotti Madison	1B4,C3	S	27	7	15	4	4	3	0	0	0	1	5	0	.267	.313	.467

K. Seitzer, 1 G at DH; J. Beniquez, 6 G at 3B

Pitcher	T	Age	G	GS	CG	ShO	IP	H	HR	BB	SO	W-L	Sv	ERA
Mark Gubicza	R	24	35	35	10	2	241.2	231	18	120	166	13-18	0	3.98
Charlie Leibrandt	L	30	35	35	8	3	240.1	235	23	74	151	16-11	0	3.41
Danny Jackson	L	25	36	34	11	2	224.0	219	11	109	152	9-18	0	4.02
Bret Saberhagen	R	23	33	33	15	4	257.0	246	27	53	163	18-10	0	3.36
Bud Black	L	30	29	18	0	0	122.1	126	16	35	61	8-6	1	3.60
Melido Perez	R	21	3	3	0	0	10.1	18	2	5	5	1-1	0	7.84
Jerry Don Gleaton	L	29	48	0	0	0	50.2	38	4	28	44	4-4	5	4.26
Steve Farr	R	30	47	0	0	0	91.0	97	9	44	88	4-3	1	4.15
Dan Quisenberry	R	34	47	0	0	0	49.0	58	3	10	17	4-1	8	2.76
John Davis	R	24	27	0	0	0	43.2	29	0	26	24	5-2	2	2.27
Bob Stoddard	R	30	17	2	0	0	40.0	51	3	22	23	1-3	1	4.28
Gene Garber†	R	39	13	0	0	0	14.1	13	1	1	3	0-0	8	2.51
Dave Gumpert	R	29	8	0	0	0	19.1	27	3	6	13	0-0	0	6.05
Rick Anderson	R	30	6	2	0	0	13.0	26	3	9	12	0-2	0	13.85
Bob Shirley†	L	33	3	0	0	0	7.1	10	5	6	1	0-0	0	14.73

1987 Oakland Athletics 3rd AL West 81-81 .500 4.0 GB

Tony La Russa

Player	Gm by Position	B	Age	G	AB	R	H	2B	3B	HR	RBI	BB	SO	SB	Avg	OBP	Slg
Terry Steinbach	C107,3B10,DH8*	R	25	122	391	66	111	16	3	16	56	32	66	1	.284	.349	.463
Mark McGwire	1B145,3B8,OF3	R	23	151	557	97	161	28	4	49	118	71	131	1	.289	.370	.618
Tony Phillips	2B87,3B11,SS9*	S	28	111	379	48	91	20	0	10	46	57	76	7	.240	.337	.372
Carney Lansford	3B142,1B17,DH4	R	30	151	554	89	160	27	4	19	76	60	44	27	.289	.366	.455
Alfredo Griffin	SS137,2B1	S	29	144	494	69	130	23	5	3	60	28	41	26	.263	.306	.348
Jose Canseco	OF130,DH30	R	22	159	630	81	162	35	3	31	113	50	157	15	.257	.310	.470
Mike Davis	OF124,DH14	L	28	139	494	69	131	32	1	22	72	42	94	19	.265	.320	.468
Luis Polonia	OF104,DH18	L	22	125	435	78	125	16	10	4	49	32	64	29	.287	.335	.398
Reggie Jackson	DH79,OF20	L	41	115	336	42	74	14	1	15	43	33	97	2	.220	.297	.402
Dwayne Murphy	OF79,1B1,2B1	L	32	82	219	39	51	7	0	8	35	58	61	4	.233	.388	.374
Tony Bernazard†	2B59,DH3	S	30	61	214	34	57	14	1	3	19	30	30	4	.266	.354	.383
Mickey Tettleton	C80,DH1,1B1	S	26	82	211	19	41	3	0	8	26	30	65	1	.194	.292	.322
Stan Javier	OF71,1B6,DH1	S	23	81	151	22	28	3	1	2	9	19	33	3	.185	.276	.258
Mike Gallego	2B31,3B24,SS17	R	26	72	124	18	31	6	0	2	14	12	21	0	.250	.319	.347
Steve Henderson	OF31,DH9	R	34	46	114	14	33	7	0	3	9	12	19	0	.289	.357	.430
Ron Cey	DH30,1B7,3B3	R	39	45	104	12	23	6	0	4	11	22	32	0	.221	.359	.394
Walt Weiss	SS11	S	23	16	26	3	12	4	0	0	1	2	2	1	.462	.500	.615
Johnnie LeMaster	3B8,SS7,2B5	R	33	20	24	3	2	0	0	0	1	1	4	0	.083	.120	.083
Rob Nelson†	1B7	L	23	7	24	1	4	1	0	0	0	0	12	0	.167	.167	.208
Brian Harper	DH7,OF1	R	27	11	17	1	4	1	0	0	3	0	4	0	.235	.222	.294
Jerry Willard	DH3,1B1,3B1	L	27	7	6	1	1	0	0	0	0	2	1	0	.167	.375	.167
Alex Sanchez	OF1	R	28	2	3	0	0	0	0	0	0	0	1	0	.000	.000	.000
Matt Sinatro	C6	R	27	6	3	0	0	0	0	0	0	0	1	0	.000	.000	.000
Alex Sanchez	DH1	R	21	1	0	0	0	0	0	0	0	0	0	0	—	—	—

T. Steinbach, 1 G at 1B; T. Phillips, 2 G at OF, 1 G at DH

Pitcher	T	Age	G	GS	CG	ShO	IP	H	HR	BB	SO	W-L	Sv	ERA
Dave Stewart	R	30	37	37	8	1	261.1	224	24	105	205	20-13	0	3.68
Curt Young	L	27	31	31	6	0	203.0	194	38	44	124	13-7	0	4.08
Steve Ontiveros	R	26	35	22	2	1	150.2	141	19	50	97	10-8	1	4.00
Jose Rijo	R	22	21	14	1	0	82.1	106	10	41	67	2-7	0	5.90
Joaquin Andujar	R	34	13	13	1	0	60.2	63	11	26	32	3-5	0	6.08
Moose Haas	R	31	9	9	0	0	40.2	57	7	9	13	2-2	0	5.75
Storm Davis†	R	25	5	5	0	0	30.1	28	3	11	28	1-1	0	3.26
Rick Honeycutt†	L	33	7	4	0	0	23.2	25	3	9	10	1-4	0	5.32
Chris Codiroli	R	29	3	3	0	0	11.1	12	1	8	4	0-2	0	8.74
Gene Nelson	R	26	54	6	0	0	123.2	120	12	35	94	6-5	3	3.93
Dennis Eckersley	R	32	54	2	0	0	115.2	99	11	17	113	6-8	16	3.03
Dave Leiper†	L	25	45	0	0	0	52.1	49	6	18	33	2-1	1	3.78
Dennis Lamp	R	34	36	5	0	0	56.2	76	5	22	36	1-3	0	5.08
Jay Howell	R	31	36	0	0	0	44.1	48	6	21	35	3-4	16	5.89
Eric Plunk	R	23	32	11	0	0	95.0	91	8	62	90	4-6	2	4.74
Greg Cadaret	L	25	29	0	0	0	39.2	37	6	24	30	6-2	0	4.54
Rick Rodriguez	R	26	15	0	0	0	24.1	32	1	15	9	1-0	0	2.96
Bill Krueger†	L	29	9	0	0	0	5.2	9	0	8	2	0-3	0	9.53
Bill Caudill	R	30	6	0	0	0	8.0	10	3	1	8	0-0	1	9.00
Gary Lavelle†	L	38	6	0	0	0	4.1	4	0	3	6	0-0	0	8.31
Dave Von Ohlen	L	28	4	0	0	0	6.0	10	1	1	3	0-0	0	7.50
Dave Otto	L	22	3	0	0	0	6.0	7	1	1	3	0-0	0	9.00

1987 Seattle Mariners 4th AL West 78-84 .481 7.0 GB

Dick Williams

Player	Gm by Position	B	Age	G	AB	R	H	2B	3B	HR	RBI	BB	SO	SB	Avg	OBP	Slg
Scott Bradley	C82,3B8,DH6*	L	27	102	342	34	95	15	1	5	43	15	18	0	.278	.310	.371
Alvin Davis	1B157	L	26	157	580	86	171	37	2	29	100	72	84	0	.295	.370	.516
Harold Reynolds	2B160	S	26	160	530	73	146	31	8	1	35	39	34	60	.275	.325	.370
Jim Presley	3B148,SS4,DH1	R	25	152	575	78	142	23	6	24	88	38	157	2	.247	.296	.433
Rey Quinones	SS135	R	23	135	478	55	132	18	2	12	56	26	71	1	.276	.317	.397
Phil Bradley	OF158	R	28	158	603	101	179	38	10	14	67	84	119	40	.297	.387	.463
Mike Kingery	OF114,DH4	L	26	120	354	38	99	25	4	9	52	27	43	7	.280	.329	.449
John Moses	OF100,1B16,DH5	S	29	116	390	58	96	16	4	3	38	29	49	23	.246	.301	.331
Ken Phelps	DH114,1B1	L	32	120	332	68	86	13	1	27	68	80	75	1	.259	.410	.548
Mickey Brantley	OF82,DH9	R	26	92	351	52	106	23	2	14	54	24	44	13	.302	.344	.499
Dave Valle	C75,DH14,1B2*	R	26	95	324	40	83	16	3	12	53	15	46	2	.256	.292	.435
John Christensen	OF43,DH8	R	26	53	132	19	32	6	1	2	12	12	28	2	.242	.306	.348
Donell Nixon	OF32,DH6	R	25	46	132	17	33	4	0	3	12	13	28	21	.250	.327	.348
Gary Matthews†	DH39	R	36	45	119	10	28	1	0	3	15	15	22	0	.235	.319	.319
Domingo Ramos	SS25,3B7,2B6*	R	29	42	103	9	32	6	0	2	11	3	12	0	.311	.336	.427
Bob Kearney	C24	R	30	24	47	5	8	4	1	0	1	1	9	0	.170	.188	.298
Edgar Martinez	3B12,DH1	R	24	13	43	6	16	5	2	0	5	2	5	0	.372	.413	.581
Mario Diaz	SS10	R	25	11	23	4	7	0	1	0	3	0	4	0	.304	.304	.391
Dave Hengel	OF7,DH1	R	25	10	19	2	6	0	0	1	4	0	4	0	.316	.316	.474
Rich Renteria	DH4,2B4,SS1	R	25	12	10	2	1	1	0	0	0	1	2	1	.100	.182	.200
Jerry Narron	C3	L	31	4	8	0	0	0	0	0	0	0	2	0	.000	.000	.000
Brick Smith	1B3,DH1	R	28	5	8	1	1	0	0	0	0	2	4	0	.125	.300	.125
Jim Weaver	OF4	L	27	7	4	2	0	0	0	0	0	2	3	1	.000	.333	.000

S. Bradley, 2 G at OF; D. Valle, 1 G at OF; D. Ramos, 2 G at DH

Pitcher	T	Age	G	GS	CG	ShO	IP	H	HR	BB	SO	W-L	Sv	ERA
Mark Langston	L	26	35	35	14	3	272.0	242	30	114	262	19-13	0	3.84
Mike Moore	R	27	33	33	12	0	231.0	268	29	84	115	9-19	0	4.71
Mike Morgan	R	27	34	31	8	2	207.0	245	25	53	85	12-17	0	4.65
Scott Bankhead	R	23	27	25	2	0	149.1	168	35	37	95	9-8	0	5.42
Lee Guetterman	L	28	25	17	2	1	113.1	117	13	35	42	11-4	0	3.81
Mike Campbell	R	23	9	9	1	0	49.1	41	9	25	35	1-4	0	4.74
Bill Wilkinson	L	22	56	0	0	0	76.1	61	8	21	73	3-4	10	3.66
Edwin Nunez	R	24	48	0	0	0	47.1	45	7	18	34	3-4	12	3.80
Jerry Reed	R	31	39	1	0	0	81.2	79	7	24	51	1-2	7	3.42
Mike Trujillo	R	27	28	7	0	0	65.2	70	12	26	36	4-4	1	6.17
Stan Clarke	L	26	22	0	0	0	23.0	31	7	10	13	2-2	0	5.48
Steve Shields	R	28	20	0	0	0	30.0	43	7	12	22	2-0	3	6.60
Dennis Powell	L	23	16	3	0	0	34.1	32	3	15	17	1-3	0	3.15
Roy Thomas	R	34	8	0	0	0	20.2	23	2	11	14	1-0	0	5.23
Mark Huismann†	R	29	6	0	0	0	14.2	10	1	4	15	0-0	0	4.91
Clay Parker	R	24	3	1	0	0	7.2	15	2	4	8	0-0	0	10.57
Rich Monteleone	R	24	3	0	0	0	7.0	10	2	4	2	0-0	0	6.43
Mike Brown	R	28	1	0	0	0	0.1	3	0	0	0	0-0	0	54.00

1987 Chicago White Sox 5th AL West 77-85 .475 8.0 GB

Jim Fregosi

Player	Gm by Position	B	Age	G	AB	R	H	2B	3B	HR	RBI	BB	SO	SB	Avg	OBP	Slg
Carlton Fisk	C122,1B9,DH7*	R	39	135	454	68	116	22	1	23	71	39	72	1	.256	.321	.460
Greg Walker	1B154,DH3	L	27	157	566	85	145	33	2	27	94	75	112	2	.256	.346	.465
Fred Manrique	2B92,SS23	R	25	115	298	30	77	13	3	4	29	19	69	5	.258	.302	.362
Tim Hulett	3B61,2B8	R	27	68	240	20	52	10	0	7	28	10	41	0	.217	.246	.346
Ozzie Guillen	SS149	L	23	149	560	64	156	22	7	2	51	22	52	25	.279	.303	.354
Ivan Calderon	OF139,DH3	R	25	144	542	93	159	38	2	28	83	60	109	10	.293	.362	.526
Gary Redus	OF123,DH4	R	30	130	475	78	112	26	6	12	48	69	90	52	.236	.328	.392
Kenny Williams	OF115	R	23	116	391	48	110	18	2	11	50	10	83	21	.281	.314	.422
Harold Baines	DH117,OF8	L	28	132	505	59	148	26	4	20	93	46	82	0	.293	.352	.479
Donnie Hill	2B84,3B32,DH1	S	26	111	410	57	98	14	6	9	46	30	35	1	.239	.290	.368
Daryl Boston	OF92,DH5	L	24	103	337	51	87	21	2	10	29	25	68	12	.258	.307	.421
Steve Lyons	3B51,OF15,DH6*	L	27	76	193	26	54	11	1	1	19	12	37	3	.280	.320	.363
Jerry Royster†	3B30,OF13,2B5*	R	34	55	154	25	37	11	0	7	23	19	28	2	.240	.324	.448
Ron Hassey	C24,DH18	L	34	49	145	15	31	9	0	3	12	17	11	0	.214	.303	.338
Jerry Hairston	DH13,OF13,1B7	S	35	66	126	14	29	8	0	5	20	25	25	0	.230	.357	.413
Ron Karkovice	C37	R	23	39	85	7	6	0	0	2	7	7	40	3	.071	.160	.141
Pat Keedy	3B11,1B2,DH1*	R	29	17	41	6	7	1	0	2	2	2	14	1	.171	.209	.341
Bill Lindsey	C9	R	27	9	16	2	3	0	0	0	1	0	3	0	.188	.176	.188

C. Fisk, 2 G at OF; S. Lyons, 1 G at 2B; J. Royster, 4 G at DH; P. Keedy, 1 G at 2B, 1 G at SS, 1 G at OF

Pitcher	T	Age	G	GS	CG	ShO	IP	H	HR	BB	SO	W-L	Sv	ERA
Floyd Bannister	L	32	34	34	11	2	228.2	216	38	49	124	16-11	0	3.58
Rich Dotson	R	28	31	31	7	2	211.1	201	24	86	114	11-12	0	4.17
Jose DeLeon	R	26	33	31	2	0	206.0	177	24	97	153	11-12	0	4.02
Bill Long	R	27	29	23	5	2	169.0	179	20	28	72	8-8	1	4.37
Dave LaPoint†	L	27	14	12	2	1	82.2	69	7	31	43	6-3	0	2.94
Neil Allen†	R	29	15	10	0	0	49.2	74	6	26	26	0-7	0	7.07
Joel Davis	R	22	13	9	1	0	55.0	56	7	29	25	1-5	0	5.73
Jack McDowell	R	21	4	4	0	0	28.0	16	1	6	15	3-0	0	1.93
Adam Peterson	R	21	1	1	0	0	4.0	8	1	3	1	0-0	0	13.50
Ray Searage	L	32	58	0	0	0	55.2	56	9	24	33	2-3	2	4.20
Jim Winn	R	27	56	0	0	0	94.0	95	10	62	44	4-6	6	4.79
Bobby Thigpen	R	23	51	0	0	0	89.0	86	10	24	52	7-5	16	2.73
Bob James	R	28	43	0	0	0	54.0	54	10	17	34	4-6	10	4.67
Scott Nielsen	R	28	19	7	1	1	66.1	83	9	25	23	3-5	2	6.24
Joel McKeon	L	24	13	0	0	0	21.0	27	8	15	14	1-2	0	9.43
Bryan Clark	L	30	11	0	0	0	18.2	19	1	8	8	0-0	0	2.41
Ralph Citarella	R	29	5	0	0	0	11.0	13	4	4	9	0-0	0	7.36
John Pawlowski	R	23	2	0	0	0	3.2	7	0	3	2	0-0	0	4.91

1987 California Angels 6th AL West 75-87 .463 10.0 GB

Gene Mauch

Player	Gm by Position	B	Age	G	AB	R	H	2B	3B	HR	RBI	BB	SO	SB	Avg	OBP	Slg
Bob Boone	C127,DH1	R	39	128	389	42	94	18	0	3	33	35	36	0	.242	.304	.311
Wally Joyner	1B149	L	25	149	564	100	161	33	1	34	117	72	64	8	.285	.366	.528
Mark McLemore	2B132,SS6,DH3	S	22	138	433	61	102	13	3	3	41	48	72	25	.236	.310	.300
Doug DeCinces†	3B128,1B4,SS1	R	36	133	453	65	106	23	0	16	63	70	87	3	.234	.337	.391
Dick Schofield	SS131,2B2,DH1	R	24	134	479	52	120	17	3	9	46	37	63	19	.251	.305	.355
Devon White	OF159	S	24	159	639	103	168	33	5	24	87	39	135	32	.263	.306	.443
Gary Pettis	OF131	S	29	133	394	49	82	13	2	1	17	52	124	24	.208	.302	.259
Jack Howell	OF89,3B48,2B13	L	25	138	449	64	110	18	5	23	64	57	118	4	.245	.331	.461
Brian Downing	DH118,OF34	R	36	155	567	110	154	29	3	29	77	106	85	5	.272	.400	.487
Ruppert Jones	OF66,DH1	L	32	85	192	25	47	8	2	8	28	20	38	2	.245	.316	.432
Bill Buckner†	DH39,1B5	L	37	57	183	16	56	12	1	3	32	9	7	1	.306	.337	.432
George Hendrick	OF45,1B9,DH5	R	37	65	162	14	39	10	0	5	25	14	18	0	.241	.301	.395
Gus Polidor	SS46,3B11,2B3	R	25	63	137	12	36	3	0	2	15	2	15	0	.263	.277	.328
Johnny Ray†	2B29,DH1	S	30	30	127	16	44	11	0	0	15	3	10	0	.346	.359	.433
Darrell Miller	C33,OF18,3B1	R	29	53	108	14	26	5	0	4	16	9	13	1	.241	.303	.398
Mark Ryal	OF21,DH5,1B4	L	26	58	100	7	20	6	0	5	18	3	15	0	.200	.223	.410
Butch Wynegar	C28,DH1	S	31	31	92	4	19	2	0	0	5	9	13	0	.207	.277	.228
Tony Armas	OF27	R	33	28	81	8	16	3	1	3	9	1	11	1	.198	.205	.370
Jack Fimple	C13	R	28	13	10	1	2	0	0	0	1	1	2	0	.200	.273	.200
Jim Eppard	OF1	L	27	8	9	2	3	0	0	0	0	2	0	0	.333	.455	.333
Tack Wilson	OF4,DH2	R	31	7	2	5	1	0	0	0	0	1	0	0	.500	.667	.500

Pitcher	T	Age	G	GS	CG	ShO	IP	H	HR	BB	SO	W-L	Sv	ERA
Mike Witt	R	26	36	36	10	0	247.0	252	34	84	192	16-14	0	4.01
Don Sutton	R	42	35	34	1	0	191.2	199	38	41	99	11-11	0	4.70
Willie Fraser	R	23	36	23	5	1	176.2	160	26	63	106	10-10	1	3.92
John Candelaria†	L	33	20	20	0	0	116.2	127	17	20	74	8-6	0	4.71
Jerry Reuss†	L	38	17	16	1	1	82.1	112	16	17	37	4-5	0	5.25
Kirk McCaskill	R	26	14	13	1	1	74.2	84	14	34	56	4-6	0	5.67
Urbano Lugo	R	24	7	5	0	0	28.0	42	8	18	24	0-2	0	9.32
DeWayne Buice	R	29	57	0	0	0	114.0	87	12	40	109	6-7	17	3.39
Gary Lucas	L	32	48	0	0	0	74.1	66	7	35	44	1-5	3	3.63
Greg Minton†	R	35	41	0	0	0	76.0	71	4	29	35	5-4	10	3.08
Chuck Finley	L	24	35	3	0	0	90.2	102	7	43	63	2-7	0	4.67
Jack Lazorko	R	31	26	11	2	0	117.2	108	20	44	55	5-6	0	4.59
Mike Cook	R	23	16	1	0	0	34.1	34	7	18	27	1-2	0	5.50
Donnie Moore	R	33	14	0	0	0	26.2	28	2	13	17	2-2	5	2.70
Bryan Harvey	R	24	3	0	0	0	5.0	6	0	2	3	0-0	0	0.00
Miguel Garcia†	L	20	1	0	0	0	1.2	3	0	3	0	0-0	0	16.20

1987 Texas Rangers 6th AL West 75-87 .463 10.0 GB

Bobby Valentine

Player	Gm by Position	B	Age	G	AB	R	H	2B	3B	HR	RBI	BB	SO	SB	Avg	OBP	Slg
Don Slaught	C85,DH5	R	28	95	237	25	53	15	2	8	16	24	51	0	.224	.298	.405
Pete O'Brien	1B158,OF2	L	29	159	569	84	163	26	1	23	88	59	61	0	.286	.348	.457
Jerry Browne	2B130,DH1	S	21	132	454	63	123	16	6	1	38	61	50	27	.271	.358	.339
Steve Buechele	3B123,2B18,OF2	R	25	136	363	45	86	20	0	13	50	28	66	2	.237	.290	.399
Scott Fletcher	SS155,DH1	R	28	156	588	82	169	28	4	5	63	61	66	13	.287	.358	.374
Ruben Sierra	OF157	S	21	158	643	97	169	35	4	30	109	39	114	16	.263	.302	.470
Pete Incaviglia	OF132,DH7	R	23	139	509	85	138	26	4	27	80	48	168	9	.271	.332	.497
Oddibe McDowell	OF125	L	24	128	407	65	98	26	4	14	52	51	99	24	.241	.324	.428
Larry Parrish	DH122,3B28,OF1	R	33	152	557	79	149	22	1	32	100	49	154	3	.268	.328	.483
Bob Brower	OF106,DH7	R	27	127	303	63	79	10	3	14	46	36	66	15	.261	.338	.452
Mike Stanley	C61,1B12,DH5*	R	24	78	216	34	59	8	1	6	37	31	48	3	.273	.361	.403
Geno Petralli	C63,3B17,1B5*	S	27	101	202	28	61	11	2	7	31	27	29	0	.302	.388	.480
Curtis Wilkerson	SS33,2B28,3B18*	S	26	85	138	28	37	5	3	2	14	6	16	6	.268	.308	.391
Darrell Porter	DH35,C7,1B5	L	35	85	130	19	31	3	0	7	21	30	43	0	.238	.387	.423
Tom O'Malley	3B40,2B1	L	26	45	117	10	32	8	0	1	12	15	9	0	.274	.351	.368
Tom Paciorek	1B12,OF12,DH3	R	40	27	60	6	17	3	0	3	12	1	19	0	.283	.302	.483
Jeff Kunkel	2B10,3B3,OF3*	R	25	15	32	1	7	0	0	1	2	0	10	0	.219	.242	.313
Dave Meier	OF8	R	27	13	21	4	6	1	0	0	0	0	4	0	.286	.286	.333
Greg Tabor	2B4,DH1	R	26	9	9	4	1	1	0	0	1	0	4	0	.111	.111	.222
Cecil Espy	OF8	S	24	14	8	1	0	0	0	0	0	1	3	2	.000	.111	.000

M. Stanley, 1 G at OF; G. Petralli, 4 G at 2B, 3 G at OF, 2 G at DH; C. Wilkerson, 4 G at DH; J. Kunkel, 1 G at DH, 1 G at 1B, 1 G at SS

Pitcher	T	Age	G	GS	CG	ShO	IP	H	HR	BB	SO	W-L	Sv	ERA
Charlie Hough	R	39	40	40	13	0	285.1	238	36	124	223	18-13	0	3.79
Jose Guzman	R	24	37	30	6	0	208.1	196	30	82	143	14-14	0	4.67
Bobby Witt	R	23	26	25	1	0	143.0	114	10	140	160	8-10	0	4.91
Edwin Correa	R	21	15	15	0	0	70.0	83	17	52	61	3-5	0	7.59
Mike Mason†	L	28	8	6	0	0	29.0	37	6	22	21	0-2	0	5.59
Bob Malloy	R	22	2	2	0	0	11.0	13	6	3	8	0-0	0	6.55
Mike Jeffcoat	L	27	2	2	0	0	7.0	11	4	4	1	0-1	0	12.86
Mitch Williams	L	22	85	1	0	0	108.2	63	9	94	129	8-6	6	3.23
Dale Mohorcic	R	31	74	0	0	0	99.1	88	11	19	48	7-6	16	2.99
Jeff Russell	R	25	52	2	0	0	97.1	109	9	52	56	5-4	3	4.44
Greg Harris	R	31	42	19	0	0	140.2	157	18	56	106	5-10	0	4.86
Mike Loynd	R	23	26	8	0	0	69.1	82	14	38	48	1-5	1	6.10
Paul Kilgus	L	25	25	12	0	0	89.1	95	14	31	42	2-7	0	4.13
Steve Howe	L	29	24	0	0	0	31.1	33	2	8	19	3-3	1	4.31
Ron Meridith	L	30	11	0	0	0	20.2	25	7	12	17	1-0	0	6.10
Scott Anderson	R	24	8	0	0	0	11.1	17	0	8	6	0-1	0	9.53
Keith Creel	R	28	6	0	0	0	9.2	12	2	5	5	0-0	0	4.66
Dwayne Henry	R	25	5	0	0	0	10.0	12	2	9	7	0-0	0	9.00
Gary Mielke	R	24	3	0	0	0	3.0	3	2	1	3	0-0	0	6.00

»1987 St. Louis Cardinals 1st NL East 95-67 .586 —

Whitey Herzog

Player	Gm by Position	B	Age	G	AB	R	H	2B	3B	HR	RBI	BB	SO	SB	Avg	OBP	Slg
Tony Pena	C112,1B4,OF2	R	30	116	384	40	82	13	4	5	44	36	54	6	.214	.281	.307
Jack Clark	1B126,OF1	R	31	131	419	93	120	23	1	35	106	136	139	1	.286	.459	.597
Tom Herr	2B137	S	31	141	510	73	134	29	0	2	83	68	62	19	.263	.346	.331
Terry Pendleton	3B158	S	26	159	583	82	167	29	4	12	96	70	74	19	.286	.360	.412
Ozzie Smith	SS158	S	32	158	600	104	182	40	4	0	75	89	36	43	.303	.392	.383
Willie McGee	OF152,SS1	S	28	153	620	76	177	37	11	11	105	24	90	16	.285	.312	.434
Vince Coleman	OF150	S	25	151	623	121	180	14	10	3	43	70	126	109	.289	.363	.358
Curt Ford	OF75	L	26	89	228	32	65	9	5	3	26	14	32	11	.285	.325	.408
Jose Oquendo	OF46,2B32,SS23*	S	23	116	248	43	71	9	0	1	24	54	29	4	.286	.408	.335
Jim Lindeman	OF49,1B20	R	25	75	207	20	43	13	0	8	28	11	56	3	.208	.253	.386
Steve Lake	C59	R	30	74	179	19	45	7	2	2	19	10	18	0	.251	.289	.346
John Morris	OF74	L	26	101	157	22	41	6	4	3	23	11	22	5	.261	.314	.408
Dan Driessen	1B21	L	35	24	60	5	14	2	0	1	11	7	8	0	.233	.309	.317
Lance Johnson	OF25	L	23	33	59	4	13	2	1	0	7	4	6	6	.220	.270	.288
Tito Landrum†	OF23,1B1	R	32	30	50	5	10	1	0	0	6	7	14	1	.200	.298	.220
Tom Pagnozzi	C25,1B1	R	24	27	48	8	9	1	0	2	9	4	13	1	.188	.250	.333
Rod Booker	2B18,3B4,SS1	L	28	44	47	9	13	1	1	0	8	7	7	2	.277	.370	.340
David Green	OF10,1B3	R	26	14	30	4	8	2	1	1	1	2	5	0	.267	.313	.500
Mike Laga	1B12	L	27	17	29	4	4	1	0	1	4	2	7	0	.138	.182	.276
Ricky Horton	P67,OF1	L	27	68	29	2	5	1	0	0	0	1	9	0	.172	.200	.207
Tom Lawless	2B7,3B3,OF1	R	30	19	25	5	2	1	0	0	0	3	5	2	.080	.179	.120
Todd Worrell	P75,OF1	R	27	75	10	0	1	0	0	0	0	0	6	0	.100	.100	.100
Doug DeCinces†	3B3	R	36	4	9	1	2	2	0	0	1	0	2	0	.222	.222	.444
Skeeter Barnes	3B1	R	30	4	4	1	1	0	0	1	3	0	0	0	.250	.250	1.000

J. Oquendo, 8 G at 3B, 3 G at 1B, 1 G at P

Pitcher	T	Age	G	GS	CG	ShO	IP	H	HR	BB	SO	W-L	Sv	ERA
Greg Mathews	L	25	32	32	2	1	197.2	184	17	71	108	11-11	0	3.73
Danny Cox	R	27	31	31	2	0	199.1	224	17	71	101	11-9	0	3.88
Bob Forsch	R	37	33	30	2	1	179.0	189	15	45	89	11-7	0	4.32
Joe Magrane	L	22	27	26	4	2	170.1	157	9	60	101	9-7	0	3.54
John Tudor	L	33	16	16	0	0	96.0	100	11	32	54	10-2	0	3.84
Tim Conroy	L	27	10	9	0	0	40.2	48	0	25	22	3-2	0	5.53
Randy O'Neal†	R	26	1	1	0	0	5.0	2	0	2	4	0-0	0	1.80
Todd Worrell	R	27	75	0	0	0	94.2	86	8	34	92	8-6	33	2.66
Ricky Horton	L	27	67	6	0	0	125.0	127	15	42	55	8-3	7	3.82
Bill Dawley	R	29	60	0	0	0	96.2	93	15	38	65	5-8	2	4.47
Ken Dayley	L	28	53	0	0	0	61.0	52	2	33	63	9-5	4	2.66
Pat Perry†	L	28	45	0	0	0	65.2	54	7	21	33	4-2	1	4.39
Lee Tunnell	R	26	32	9	0	0	74.1	90	5	34	49	4-4	0	4.84
Ray Soff	R	28	12	0	0	0	15.1	18	3	5	9	1-0	0	6.46
Steve Peters	L	24	12	0	0	0	15.0	17	1	6	11	0-0	1	1.80
Scott Terry	R	27	11	0	0	0	13.1	13	0	8	9	0-0	0	3.38
Dave LaPoint†	L	27	6	2	0	0	16.0	26	4	5	8	1-1	0	6.75
Jose Oquendo	R	23	1	0	0	0	1.0	4	0	1	0	0-0	0	27.00

898 Seasons: Team Rosters

1987 New York Mets 2nd NL East 92-70 .568 3.0 GB

Davey Johnson

Player	Gm by Position	B	Age	G	AB	R	H	2B	3B	HR	RBI	BB	SO	SB	Avg	OBP	Slg
Gary Carter	C135,1B4,OF1	R	33	139	523	55	123	18	2	20	83	42	73	0	.235	.290	.392
Keith Hernandez	1B154	L	33	154	587	87	170	28	2	18	89	81	104	0	.290	.377	.436
Tim Teufel	2B92,1B1	R	28	97	299	55	92	29	0	14	61	44	53	3	.308	.398	.545
Howard Johnson	3B140,SS38,OF2	S	26	157	554	93	147	22	1	36	99	83	113	32	.265	.364	.504
Rafael Santana	SS138	R	29	139	439	41	112	21	2	5	44	29	57	1	.255	.302	.346
Darryl Strawberry	OF151	L	25	154	532	108	151	32	5	39	104	97	122	36	.284	.398	.583
Kevin McReynolds	OF150	R	27	151	590	86	163	32	5	29	95	39	70	14	.276	.318	.495
Lenny Dykstra	OF118	L	24	132	431	86	123	37	3	10	43	40	67	27	.285	.352	.455
Mookie Wilson	OF109	S	31	124	385	58	115	19	7	9	34	35	85	21	.299	.359	.455
Wally Backman	2B87	S	27	94	300	43	75	6	1	1	23	25	43	11	.250	.307	.287
Dave Magadan	3B50,1B13	L	24	85	192	21	61	13	1	3	24	22	22	0	.318	.386	.443
Barry Lyons	C49	R	27	53	130	15	33	4	1	4	24	8	24	0	.254	.301	.392
Lee Mazzilli	OF25,1B13	S	32	88	124	26	38	8	1	3	24	21	14	5	.306	.399	.460
Bill Almon†	SS22,2B10,1B2*	R	34	49	54	8	13	3	0	0	4	8	16	1	.241	.339	.296
Keith Miller	2B16	R	24	25	51	14	19	2	2	0	1	2	6	8	.373	.407	.490
Mark Carreon	OF5	R	23	9	12	0	3	0	0	0	1	1	1	0	.250	.308	.250
Kevin Elster	SS3	R	22	5	10	1	4	2	0	0	1	0	1	0	.400	.400	.600
Al Pedrique†	SS4,2B1	R	26	5	6	1	0	0	0	0	0	1	2	0	.000	.143	.000
Gregg Jefferies		S	19	6	6	0	3	1	0	0	2	0	0	0	.500	.500	.667
Clint Hurdle	1B1	L	29	3	3	1	1	0	0	0	0	0	1	0	.333	.333	.333
Randy Milligan		R	25	3	1	0	0	0	0	0	0	1	1	0	.000	.500	.000

B. Almon, 1 G at OF

Pitcher	T	Age	G	GS	CG	ShO	IP	H	HR	BB	SO	W-L	Sv	ERA
Ron Darling	R	26	32	32	2	0	207.2	183	24	96	167	12-8	0	4.29
Sid Fernandez	L	24	28	27	3	1	156.0	130	16	67	134	12-8	0	3.81
Dwight Gooden	R	22	25	25	7	3	179.2	162	11	53	148	15-7	0	3.21
John Mitchell	R	21	20	19	1	0	111.2	124	6	36	57	3-6	0	4.11
Rick Aguilera	R	25	18	17	1	0	115.0	124	12	33	77	11-3	0	3.60
David Cone	R	24	21	13	1	0	99.1	87	11	44	68	5-6	1	3.71
Bobby Ojeda	L	29	10	7	0	0	46.1	45	5	10	21	3-5	0	3.88
Don Schulze	R	24	5	4	0	0	21.2	24	4	6	5	1-2	0	6.23
John Candelaria†	L	33	3	3	0	0	12.1	17	1	3	10	2-0	0	5.84
Tom Edens	R	26	2	2	0	0	8.0	15	2	4	4	0-0	0	6.75
Jesse Orosco	L	30	58	0	0	0	77.0	78	5	31	78	3-9	16	4.44
Roger McDowell	R	26	56	0	0	0	88.2	95	7	28	32	7-5	25	4.16
Doug Sisk	R	29	55	0	0	0	78.0	83	5	22	37	3-1	3	3.46
Randy Myers	L	24	54	0	0	0	75.0	61	6	30	92	3-6	6	3.96
Terry Leach	R	33	44	12	1	1	131.1	132	14	29	61	11-1	0	3.22
Gene Walter	L	26	21	0	0	0	19.2	18	1	13	11	1-2	0	3.20
Jeff Innis	R	24	17	1	0	0	25.2	29	5	4	28	0-1	0	3.16
Bob Gibson	R	30	1	0	0	0	1.0	0	0	1	2	0-0	0	0.00

1987 Montreal Expos 3rd NL East 91-71 .562 4.0 GB

Buck Rodgers

Player	Gm by Position	B	Age	G	AB	R	H	2B	3B	HR	RBI	BB	SO	SB	Avg	OBP	Slg
Mike Fitzgerald	C104,1B1,2B1	R	26	107	287	32	69	11	0	3	36	42	54	3	.240	.338	.310
Andres Galarraga	1B146	R	26	147	551	72	168	40	3	13	90	41	127	7	.305	.361	.459
Vance Law	2B106,3B22,1B17*	R	30	133	436	52	119	27	1	12	56	51	62	8	.273	.347	.422
Tim Wallach	3B150,P1	R	29	153	593	89	177	42	4	26	123	37	98	9	.298	.343	.514
Hubie Brooks	SS109	R	30	112	430	57	113	22	3	14	72	24	72	4	.263	.301	.426
Mitch Webster	OF153	S	28	156	588	101	165	30	8	15	63	70	95	33	.281	.361	.435
Tim Raines	OF139	S	27	139	530	123	175	34	8	18	68	90	52	50	.330	.429	.526
Herm Winningham	OF131	L	25	137	347	34	83	20	3	4	41	34	68	29	.239	.304	.349
Casey Candaele	2B68,OF67,SS25*	S	26	138	449	62	122	23	4	1	23	38	28	7	.272	.330	.347
Tom Foley	SS49,2B39,3B9	L	27	106	280	35	82	18	3	5	28	11	40	6	.293	.322	.432
Jeff Reed	C74	L	24	75	207	15	44	11	0	1	21	12	20	0	.213	.254	.280
Reid Nichols	OF59,3B3	R	28	77	147	22	39	8	2	4	20	14	13	2	.265	.329	.429
Wallace Johnson	1B9	S	30	75	85	7	21	5	0	1	14	7	6	5	.247	.298	.341
Dave Engle	OF11,C6,1B2*	R	30	59	84	7	19	4	0	1	14	6	11	1	.226	.278	.310
John Stefero	C17	L	27	18	56	4	11	0	0	1	3	3	17	0	.196	.237	.250
Alonzo Powell	OF11	R	22	14	41	3	8	3	0	0	4	5	17	0	.195	.283	.268
Luis Rivera	SS15	R	23	18	32	0	5	2	0	0	1	1	8	0	.156	.182	.219
Jack Daugherty	1B1	S	26	11	10	1	1	1	0	0	1	0	3	0	.100	.100	.200
Razor Shines	1B2	S	30	6	9	0	2	0	0	0	0	1	0	1	.222	.364	.222
Nelson Norman	SS1	S	29	1	4	0	0	0	0	0	0	0	1	0	.000	.000	.000
Tom Romano	OF3	R	28	7	3	1	0	0	0	0	0	0	1	0	.000	.000	.000
Nelson Santovenia	C1	R	25	2	1	0	0	0	0	0	0	0	0	0	.000	.000	.000

V. Law, 3 G at P; C. Candaele, 1 G at 1B; D. Engle, 1 G at 3B

Pitcher	T	Age	G	GS	CG	ShO	IP	H	HR	BB	SO	W-L	Sv	ERA
Neal Heaton	L	27	32	32	3	1	193.1	207	25	37	105	13-10	0	4.52
Bob Sebra	R	25	36	27	4	1	177.1	184	15	67	156	6-15	0	4.42
Bryn Smith	R	31	26	26	2	0	150.1	164	16	31	94	10-9	0	4.37
Floyd Youmans	R	23	23	23	3	3	116.1	112	13	47	94	9-8	0	4.64
Dennis Martinez	R	32	22	22	2	1	144.2	133	9	40	84	11-4	0	3.30
Jay Tibbs	R	25	19	12	0	0	83.0	95	10	34	54	4-5	0	4.99
Pascual Perez	R	30	10	10	2	0	70.1	52	5	16	58	7-0	0	2.30
Jeff Fischer	R	23	4	2	0	0	13.2	21	3	5	6	0-1	0	8.56
Ubaldo Heredia	R	31	2	2	0	0	10.0	10	2	3	6	0-1	0	5.40
Charlie Lea	R	30	1	1	0	0	1.0	4	1	2	1	0-1	0	36.00
Andy McGaffigan	R	30	69	0	0	0	120.1	105	5	42	100	5-2	12	2.39
Tim Burke	R	28	55	0	0	0	91.0	64	3	17	58	7-0	18	1.19
Bob McClure	L	35	52	0	0	0	52.1	47	8	20	33	6-1	5	3.44
Jeff Parrett	R	25	45	0	0	0	62.0	53	8	30	56	7-6	6	4.21
Randy St. Claire	R	26	44	0	0	0	67.0	64	9	20	43	3-3	7	4.03
Lary Sorensen	R	31	23	5	0	0	47.2	56	7	12	21	3-4	1	4.72
Joe Hesketh	L	28	18	0	0	0	28.2	23	2	15	31	0-0	1	3.14
Bill Campbell	R	38	7	0	0	0	10.0	18	2	4	4	0-0	0	8.10
Curt Brown	R	27	5	0	0	0	7.0	10	2	4	6	0-1	0	7.71
Vance Law	R	30	3	0	0	0	3.1	5	0	0	2	0-0	0	5.40
Tim Wallach	R	29	1	0	0	0	1.0	1	0	0	0	0-0	0	0.00

1987 Philadelphia Phillies 4th NL East 80-82 .494 15.0 GB

John Felske (29-32)/Lee Elia (51-50)

Player	Gm by Position	B	Age	G	AB	R	H	2B	3B	HR	RBI	BB	SO	SB	Avg	OBP	Slg
Lance Parrish	C127	R	31	130	466	42	114	21	0	17	67	47	104	0	.245	.313	.399
Von Hayes	1B144,OF32	L	28	158	556	84	154	36	5	21	84	121	77	16	.277	.404	.473
Juan Samuel	2B160	R	26	160	655	113	178	37	15	28	100	60	162	35	.272	.335	.502
Mike Schmidt	3B138,1B9,SS3	R	37	147	522	88	153	28	0	35	113	83	80	2	.293	.388	.548
Steve Jeltz	SS114,OF1	S	28	114	293	37	68	9	6	0	12	39	54	1	.232	.324	.304
Glenn Wilson	OF154,P1	R	28	154	569	55	150	21	2	14	54	38	82	3	.264	.308	.381
Milt Thompson	OF146	L	28	150	527	86	159	26	9	7	43	42	87	46	.302	.351	.425
Chris James	OF108	R	24	115	358	48	105	20	6	17	54	27	67	3	.293	.344	.525
Luis Aguayo	SS78,2B6,3B2	R	28	94	209	25	43	9	1	12	21	15	56	0	.206	.273	.431
Rick Schu	3B45,1B28	R	25	92	196	24	46	6	3	7	23	20	36	0	.235	.311	.403
Greg Gross	OF50,1B11	L	34	114	133	14	38	4	1	1	12	25	12	0	.286	.395	.353
Darren Daulton	C40,1B1	L	25	53	129	10	25	6	0	3	13	16	37	0	.194	.281	.310
Jeff Stone	OF25	L	26	66	125	19	32	7	1	1	16	8	38	3	.256	.316	.352
Mike Easler†	OF30	L	36	33	110	7	31	4	0	1	10	6	20	0	.282	.316	.345
Ron Roenicke	OF26	S	30	63	78	9	13	3	1	1	4	14	15	1	.167	.293	.269
Keith Hughes†	OF19	L	23	37	76	8	20	2	0	0	10	7	11	0	.263	.333	.289
John Russell	OF10,C7	R	26	24	62	5	9	1	0	3	8	3	17	0	.145	.185	.306
Ken Dowell	SS15	R	26	15	39	4	5	0	0	0	1	2	5	0	.128	.171	.128
Ken Jackson	SS8	R	23	8	16	1	4	2	0	0	2	1	4	0	.250	.333	.375
Greg Jelks	3B4,1B2,OF1	R	25	10	11	2	1	1	0	0	0	3	4	0	.091	.286	.182
Greg Legg	2B1,3B1,SS1	R	27	3	2	1	0	0	0	0	0	0	0	0	.000	.000	.000

Pitcher	T	Age	G	GS	CG	ShO	IP	H	HR	BB	SO	W-L	Sv	ERA
Shane Rawley	L	31	36	36	4	1	229.2	250	23	86	123	17-11	0	4.39
Don Carman	L	27	35	35	3	2	211.0	194	34	69	125	13-11	0	4.22
Bruce Ruffin	L	23	35	35	3	1	204.2	236	17	73	93	11-14	0	4.35
Kevin Gross	R	26	34	33	3	1	200.2	205	26	87	110	9-16	0	4.35
Joe Cowley	R	28	5	4	0	0	11.2	21	2	17	5	0-4	0	15.43
Kent Tekulve	R	40	90	0	0	0	105.0	96	8	29	60	6-4	3	3.09
Steve Bedrosian	R	29	65	0	0	0	89.0	79	11	28	74	5-3	40	2.83
Mike Jackson	R	22	55	7	0	0	109.1	88	16	56	93	3-10	1	4.20
Wally Ritchie	L	21	49	0	0	0	62.1	60	8	29	45	3-2	3	3.75
Jeff Calhoun	L	29	42	0	0	0	42.2	25	1	26	31	3-1	1	1.48
Tom Hume†	R	34	38	6	0	0	70.2	75	10	41	29	1-4	0	5.60
Dan Schatzeder†	L	32	26	0	0	0	37.2	40	4	14	28	3-1	0	4.06
Doug Bair	R	37	11	0	0	0	13.2	17	4	5	10	2-0	0	5.93
Fred Toliver	R	26	10	4	0	0	30.1	34	2	17	25	1-1	0	5.64
Todd Frohwirth	R	24	10	0	0	0	11.0	12	0	2	9	1-0	0	0.00
Mike Maddux	R	25	7	2	0	0	17.0	17	0	5	15	2-0	0	2.65
Tom Newell	R	24	2	0	0	0	1.0	4	1	3	1	0-0	0	36.00
Glenn Wilson	R	28	1	0	0	0	1.0	0	0	0	1	0-0	0	0.00

1987 Pittsburgh Pirates 4th NL East 80-82 .494 15.0 GB

Jim Leyland

Player	Gm by Position	B	Age	G	AB	R	H	2B	3B	HR	RBI	BB	SO	SB	Avg	OBP	Slg
Mike LaValliere	C112	L	26	121	340	33	102	19	0	1	36	43	32	0	.300	.377	.365
Sid Bream	1B144	L	26	149	516	64	142	25	3	13	65	49	69	13	.275	.336	.411
Johnny Ray†	2B119	S	30	123	472	48	129	19	3	5	54	41	36	4	.273	.328	.358
Bobby Bonilla	3B89,OF46,1B6	S	24	141	466	58	140	33	3	15	77	39	64	3	.300	.351	.481
Al Pedrique†	SS76,3B3,2B2	R	26	88	246	23	74	10	1	1	27	18	27	5	.301	.354	.362
Andy Van Slyke	OF150,1B1	L	26	157	564	93	165	36	11	21	82	56	122	34	.293	.359	.507
Barry Bonds	OF145	L	22	150	551	99	144	34	9	25	59	54	88	32	.261	.329	.492
R.J. Reynolds	OF99	S	28	117	335	47	87	24	1	7	51	34	80	14	.260	.323	.400
Jim Morrison†	3B82,SS17,2B9	R	34	96	348	41	92	22	1	9	46	27	57	8	.264	.315	.411
Mike Diaz	OF37,1B32,C8	R	27	103	241	28	58	8	2	16	48	31	42	1	.241	.326	.490
Rafael Belliard	SS71,2B7	R	25	81	203	26	42	4	3	1	15	20	25	5	.207	.286	.271
Junior Ortiz	C72	R	27	75	192	16	52	8	1	1	22	15	23	0	.271	.322	.339
John Cangelosi	OF47	S	24	104	182	44	50	8	3	4	18	46	33	21	.275	.427	.418
Jose Lind	2B35	R	23	35	143	21	46	8	4	0	11	8	12	2	.322	.358	.434
Darnell Coles†	OF26,3B10,1B1	R	25	40	119	20	27	8	0	6	24	19	20	1	.227	.333	.445
Felix Fermin	SS23	R	23	23	68	6	17	0	0	0	4	4	9	0	.250	.301	.250
Terry Harper†	OF20	R	31	36	66	8	19	3	0	1	7	7	11	0	.288	.356	.379
Mackey Sasser†	C5	L	24	12	23	2	5	0	0	0	2	0	2	0	.217	.217	.217
Bill Almon†	SS4,OF2,3B1	R	34	19	20	5	4	1	0	0	1	1	5	0	.200	.238	.250
Sammy Khalifa	SS5	R	23	5	17	1	3	0	0	0	2	0	2	0	.176	.176	.176
U.L. Washington	3B1,SS1	S	33	10	10	1	3	0	0	0	0	2	3	0	.300	.417	.300
Tom Prince	C4	R	22	4	9	1	2	1	0	1	2	0	2	0	.222	.222	.667
Tommy Gregg	OF4	L	23	10	8	3	2	1	0	0	0	0	2	0	.250	.250	.375
Butch Davis	OF1	R	29	7	7	3	1	1	0	0	0	1	3	0	.143	.250	.286
Denny Gonzalez	SS1	R	23	5	7	1	0	0	0	0	0	1	2	0	.000	.125	.000
Houston Jimenez	2B2,SS2	R	29	5	6	0	0	0	0	0	0	1	2	0	.000	.143	.000
Onix Concepcion		R	29	1	1	0	1	0	0	0	0	0	0	0	1.000	1.000	1.000

Pitcher	T	Age	G	GS	CG	ShO	IP	H	HR	BB	SO	W-L	Sv	ERA
Doug Drabek	R	24	29	28	1	1	176.1	165	22	46	120	11-12	0	3.88
Brian Fisher	R	25	37	26	6	3	185.1	185	27	72	117	11-9	0	4.52
Rick Reuschel†	R	38	25	25	9	3	177.0	163	12	35	80	8-6	0	2.75
Mike Dunne	R	24	23	23	5	1	163.1	143	10	68	72	13-6	0	3.03
Bob Kipper	L	22	24	20	1	1	110.2	117	25	52	83	5-9	0	5.94
Dorn Taylor	R	28	14	8	0	0	53.1	48	10	28	37	2-3	0	5.74
Mike Bielecki	R	27	8	8	2	0	45.2	43	6	12	25	2-3	0	4.73
Vicente Palacios	R	23	6	4	0	0	29.1	27	1	9	13	2-1	0	4.30
John Smiley	L	22	63	0	0	0	75.0	69	7	50	58	5-5	4	5.76
Don Robinson†	R	30	42	0	0	0	65.1	66	6	22	53	6-6	12	3.86
Bob Walk	R	30	39	12	1	1	117.0	107	11	51	78	8-2	0	3.31
Barry Jones	R	24	32	0	0	0	43.1	55	6	23	28	2-4	1	5.61
Brett Gideon	R	23	29	0	0	0	36.2	34	6	10	31	1-5	3	4.66
Jim Gott†	R	27	25	0	0	0	31.0	28	0	8	27	0-2	13	1.45
Jeff Robinson†	R	26	18	0	0	0	26.2	20	1	6	19	2-1	4	3.04
Logan Easley	R	25	17	0	0	0	26.1	23	5	17	21	1-1	1	5.47
Hipolito Pena	L	23	16	1	0	0	25.2	16	2	26	16	0-3	1	4.56
Bob Patterson	L	28	15	7	0	0	43.0	49	5	22	27	1-4	0	6.70
Tim Drummond	R	22	6	0	0	0	6.0	5	0	3	5	0-0	0	4.50
Dave Johnson	R	27	5	0	0	0	6.1	13	1	2	4	0-0	0	9.95
Mark Ross	R	32	1	0	0	0	1.0	1	1	0	0	0-0	0	9.00
Miguel Garcia†	L	20	1	0	0	0	0.2	0	0	0	0	0-0	0	0.00

1987 Chicago Cubs 6th NL East 76-85 .472 18.5 GB

Gene Michael (68-68)/Frank Lucchesi (8-17)

Player	Gm by Position	B	Age	G	AB	R	H	2B	3B	HR	RBI	BB	SO	SB	Avg	OBP	Slg
Jody Davis	C123	R	30	125	428	57	106	12	2	19	51	52	91	1	.248	.331	.418
Leon Durham	1B123	L	29	131	439	70	120	22	1	27	63	51	92	2	.273	.348	.513
Ryne Sandberg	2B131	R	27	132	523	81	154	25	2	16	59	59	79	21	.294	.367	.442
Keith Moreland	3B150,1B1	R	33	153	563	63	150	29	1	27	88	39	66	3	.266	.309	.465
Shawon Dunston	SS94	R	24	95	346	40	85	18	3	5	22	10	68	12	.246	.267	.358
Andre Dawson	OF152	R	32	153	621	90	178	24	2	49	137	32	103	11	.287	.328	.568
Dave Martinez	OF139	L	22	142	459	70	134	18	8	8	36	57	96	16	.292	.372	.418
Jerry Mumphrey	OF85	S	34	118	309	41	103	19	2	13	44	35	47	1	.333	.400	.534
Rafael Palmeiro	OF45,1B18	L	22	84	221	32	61	15	1	14	30	20	26	2	.276	.336	.543
Manny Trillo	1B47,3B35,2B10*	R	36	108	214	27	63	8	0	8	26	25	37	0	.294	.367	.444
Bob Dernier	OF71	R	30	93	199	38	63	4	4	8	21	19	19	16	.317	.379	.497
Paul Noce	2B36,SS35,3B2	R	27	70	180	17	41	9	2	3	14	6	49	5	.228	.261	.350
Brian Dayett	OF78	R	30	97	177	20	49	14	1	5	25	20	37	0	.277	.348	.452
Jim Sundberg	C57	R	36	61	139	9	28	2	0	4	15	19	40	0	.201	.306	.302
Chico Walker	OF33,3B2	S	29	47	105	15	21	4	0	0	7	12	23	11	.200	.277	.238
Mike Brumley	SS34,2B1	S	24	39	104	8	21	2	2	1	9	10	30	7	.202	.276	.288
Luis Quinones	SS28,2B4,3B1	S	25	49	101	12	22	6	0	0	8	10	16	0	.218	.288	.277
Gary Matthews†	OF2	R	36	44	42	3	11	3	0	0	8	4	11	0	.262	.326	.333
Wade Rowdon	3B9	R	26	11	31	2	7	1	1	1	4	3	10	0	.226	.294	.419
Damon Berryhill	C11	S	23	12	28	2	5	1	0	0	1	3	5	0	.179	.258	.214
Darrin Jackson	OF5	R	23	7	5	2	4	1	0	0	0	0	0	0	.800	.800	1.000

M. Trillo, 6 G at SS

Pitcher	T	Age	G	GS	CG	ShO	IP	H	HR	BB	SO	W-L	Sv	ERA
Rick Sutcliffe	R	31	34	34	6	1	237.1	223	24	106	174	18-10	0	3.68
Jamie Moyer	L	24	35	33	1	0	201.0	210	28	97	147	12-15	0	5.10
Greg Maddux	R	21	30	27	1	1	155.2	181	17	74	101	6-14	0	5.61
Scott Sanderson	R	30	32	22	0	0	144.2	156	23	50	106	8-9	2	4.29
Les Lancaster	R	25	27	18	0	0	132.1	138	14	51	78	8-3	0	4.90
Steve Trout†	L	29	11	11	3	2	75.0	72	3	27	32	6-3	0	3.00
Frank DiPino	L	30	69	0	0	0	80.0	75	7	34	61	3-3	4	3.15
Lee Smith	R	29	62	0	0	0	83.2	84	4	32	96	4-10	36	3.12
Ed Lynch	R	31	58	8	0	0	110.1	130	17	48	80	2-9	4	5.38
Dickie Noles†	R	30	41	1	0	0	64.1	59	1	27	33	4-2	2	3.50
Jay Baller	R	26	23	0	0	0	29.1	38	4	20	27	0-1	0	6.75
Drew Hall	L	24	21	0	0	0	32.2	40	4	14	20	1-1	0	6.89
Ron Davis†	R	31	21	0	0	0	32.1	43	8	12	31	0-0	0	5.85
Mike Mason†	L	28	17	4	0	0	38.0	43	4	23	28	4-1	0	5.68
Bob Tewksbury†	R	26	7	3	0	0	18.0	32	1	13	10	0-4	0	6.50

1987 San Francisco Giants 1st NL West 90-72 .556 —

Roger Craig

Player	Gm by Position	B	Age	G	AB	R	H	2B	3B	HR	RBI	BB	SO	SB	Avg	OBP	Slg
Bob Brenly	C108,1B6,3B2	R	33	123	375	55	100	19	1	18	51	47	85	10	.267	.348	.467
Will Clark	1B139	L	23	150	529	89	163	29	5	35	91	49	98	5	.308	.371	.580
Robby Thompson	2B126	R	25	132	420	62	110	26	5	10	44	40	91	16	.262	.338	.419
Kevin Mitchell†	3B68,OF3,SS1	R	25	69	268	49	82	13	1	15	44	28	50	9	.306	.376	.530
Jose Uribe	SS95	S	28	95	309	44	90	16	5	5	30	24	35	12	.291	.343	.424
Chili Davis	OF135	S	27	149	500	80	125	22	1	24	76	72	109	16	.250	.344	.442
Jeffrey Leonard	OF127	R	31	131	503	70	141	29	4	19	63	21	68	16	.280	.309	.467
Candy Maldonado	OF116	R	26	118	442	69	129	28	4	20	85	34	78	8	.292	.346	.509
Mike Aldrete	OF79,1B33	L	26	126	357	50	116	18	2	9	51	43	50	6	.325	.396	.462
Chris Speier	2B55,3B44,SS22	R	37	111	317	39	79	13	0	11	39	42	51	4	.249	.342	.394
Bob Melvin	C78,1B1	R	25	84	246	31	49	8	0	11	31	17	44	0	.199	.249	.366
Matt Williams	SS70,3B17	R	21	84	245	28	46	9	2	8	21	16	68	4	.188	.240	.339
Eddie Milner	OF84	L	32	101	214	38	54	14	0	4	19	24	33	10	.252	.328	.374
Chris Brown†	3B37,SS1	R	25	38	132	17	32	6	0	6	17	9	16	1	.242	.306	.424
Joel Youngblood	OF22,3B2	R	35	69	91	9	23	3	0	3	11	5	13	1	.253	.296	.385
Harry Spilman	3B10,1B9,C1	L	32	83	90	5	24	5	0	1	14	9	20	1	.267	.327	.356
Mark Wasinger	3B21,2B10,SS2	R	25	44	80	16	22	3	0	1	3	8	14	2	.275	.341	.350
Dave Henderson†	OF9	R	28	15	21	2	5	2	0	0	1	8	5	2	.238	.448	.333
Mike Woodard	2B8	L	27	10	19	0	4	1	0	0	1	0	1	0	.211	.211	.263
Francisco Melendez	1B5	L	23	12	16	2	5	0	0	1	1	0	3	0	.313	.313	.500
Randy Kutcher	OF6,2B2,3B2*	R	27	14	16	7	3	1	1	0	1	1	5	1	.188	.235	.375
Ivan DeJesus	SS9	R	34	9	10	0	2	0	0	0	1	0	2	0	.200	.200	.200
Rob Wilfong	2B2	L	33	2	8	2	1	0	0	1	2	1	2	1	.125	.222	.500
Jessie Reid	OF3	L	25	6	8	1	1	0	0	1	1	1	5	0	.125	.222	.500
Kirt Manwaring	C6	R	21	6	7	0	1	0	0	0	0	0	1	0	.143	.250	.143
Mackey Sasser†	C1	L	24	2	4	0	0	0	0	0	0	0	0	0	.000	.000	.000
Keith Comstock†	P15,OF1	L	31	15	1	0	0	0	0	0	0	0	1	0	.000	.000	.000

R. Kutcher, 1 G at SS

Pitcher	T	Age	G	GS	CG	ShO	IP	H	HR	BB	SO	W-L	Sv	ERA
Kelly Downs	R	26	41	28	4	3	186.0	185	14	67	137	12-9	1	3.63
Mike Krukow	R	35	30	28	3	0	163.0	182	24	46	104	5-6	0	4.80
Atlee Hammaker	L	29	31	27	2	0	168.1	159	22	57	107	10-10	0	3.58
Mike LaCoss	R	31	39	26	2	1	171.0	184	16	63	79	13-10	0	3.68
Dave Dravecky†	L	31	18	18	4	3	112.1	115	8	33	78	7-5	0	3.20
Mark Davis†	L	26	20	11	1	0	70.2	72	9	28	51	4-5	0	4.71
Mark Grant†	R	23	16	8	0	0	61.0	66	6	21	32	1-2	1	3.54
Rick Reuschel†	R	38	9	8	3	1	50.0	44	1	7	27	5-3	0	4.32
Roger Mason	R	28	5	5	0	0	26.0	30	4	10	18	1-1	0	4.50
Scott Garrelts	R	25	64	0	0	0	106.1	70	10	55	127	11-7	12	3.22
Jeff Robinson†	R	26	63	0	0	0	96.2	69	10	48	82	6-8	10	2.79
Craig Lefferts†	L	29	44	0	0	0	47.1	36	4	18	18	3-3	4	3.23
Jim Gott†	R	27	30	3	0	0	56.0	53	4	32	63	1-0	0	4.50
Don Robinson†	R	30	25	0	0	0	42.2	39	1	18	26	5-1	7	2.74
Joe Price	L	30	20	0	0	0	35.0	19	5	13	42	2-2	1	2.57
Greg Minton†	R	35	15	0	0	0	23.1	30	2	10	9	1-0	1	3.47
Keith Comstock†	L	31	15	0	0	0	20.2	19	1	10	21	2-0	1	3.05
Randy Bockus	R	26	12	0	0	0	17.1	17	2	4	9	1-0	0	3.63
Jon Perlman	R	30	10	0	0	0	11.1	11	1	4	3	0-0	0	3.97
John Burkett	R	22	3	0	0	0	6.0	7	2	3	5	0-0	0	4.50

1987 Cincinnati Reds 2nd NL West 84-78 .519 6.0 GB

Pete Rose

Player	Gm by Position	B	Age	G	AB	R	H	2B	3B	HR	RBI	BB	SO	SB	Avg	OBP	Slg
Bo Diaz	C137	R	34	140	496	49	134	28	1	15	82	19	73	1	.270	.300	.421
Nick Esasky	1B93,3B1,OF1	R	27	100	346	48	94	19	2	22	59	29	76	0	.272	.327	.529
Ron Oester	2B69	S	31	69	237	28	60	9	6	2	23	22	51	2	.253	.317	.367
Buddy Bell	3B142	R	35	143	522	74	148	19	2	17	70	71	39	4	.284	.369	.425
Barry Larkin	SS119	R	23	125	439	64	107	16	2	12	43	36	52	21	.244	.306	.371
Dave Parker	OF142,1B9	L	36	153	589	77	149	28	0	26	97	44	104	7	.253	.311	.433
Eric Davis	OF128	R	25	129	474	120	139	23	4	37	100	84	134	50	.293	.399	.593
Tracy Jones	OF95	R	26	117	359	53	104	17	3	10	44	23	40	31	.290	.333	.437
Kurt Stillwell	SS51,2B37,3B20	S	22	131	395	54	102	20	7	4	33	32	50	4	.258	.316	.375
Kal Daniels	OF94	L	23	108	368	73	123	24	1	26	64	60	62	26	.334	.429	.617
Dave Concepcion	2B59,1B26,3B13*	R	39	104	279	32	89	15	0	1	33	28	24	4	.319	.377	.384
Terry Francona	1B57,OF8	L	28	102	207	16	47	5	0	3	12	10	12	2	.227	.266	.295
Paul O'Neill	OF42,1B2,P1	L	24	84	160	24	41	14	1	7	28	18	29	2	.256	.331	.488
Terry McGriff	C33	R	23	34	89	6	20	3	0	2	11	8	17	0	.225	.289	.326
Dave Collins	OF21	S	34	57	85	19	25	5	0	0	5	11	12	9	.294	.388	.353
Jeff Treadway	2B21	L	24	23	84	9	28	4	0	2	4	2	6	1	.333	.356	.452
Lloyd McClendon	C12,1B5,3B1*	R	28	45	72	8	15	5	0	2	13	4	15	1	.208	.247	.361
Leo Garcia	OF14	L	24	31	30	8	6	0	0	1	2	4	8	3	.200	.286	.300
Sal Butera†	C5	R	34	5	11	1	2	0	0	1	2	1	6	0	.182	.250	.455
Max Venable	OF4	L	30	7	7	2	1	0	0	0	2	0	0	0	.143	.143	.143

D. Concepcion, 2 G at SS; L. McClendon, 1 G at OF

Pitcher	T	Age	G	GS	CG	ShO	IP	H	HR	BB	SO	W-L	Sv	ERA
Ted Power	R	32	34	34	2	1	204.0	213	28	71	133	10-13	0	4.50
Tom Browning	L	27	32	31	2	0	183.0	201	27	61	117	10-13	0	5.02
Bill Gullickson†	R	28	27	27	3	1	165.0	172	33	39	89	10-11	0	4.85
Guy Hoffman	L	30	36	22	0	0	158.2	160	20	49	87	9-10	0	4.37
D. Rasmussen†	L	28	7	7	0	0	45.1	39	5	12	39	4-1	0	3.97
Pat Pacillo	R	23	12	7	0	0	39.2	41	7	19	23	3-3	0	6.13
Jerry Reuss†	L	38	7	7	0	0	34.2	52	2	12	10	0-5	0	7.79
Mario Soto	R	30	6	6	0	0	31.2	34	7	12	11	3-2	0	5.12
Rob Murphy	L	27	87	0	0	0	100.2	91	7	32	99	8-5	3	3.04
Frank Williams	R	29	85	0	0	0	105.2	101	5	39	60	4-0	2	2.30
John Franco	L	26	68	0	0	0	82.0	76	6	27	61	8-5	32	2.52
Ron Robinson	R	25	48	18	0	0	154.0	148	14	43	99	7-5	4	3.68
Bill Landrum	R	29	44	2	0	0	65.0	68	3	34	42	3-2	2	4.71
Bill Scherrer	L	29	23	0	0	0	33.0	43	3	16	24	1-1	0	4.36
Jeff Montgomery	R	25	14	1	0	0	19.1	25	2	9	13	2-2	0	6.52
Pat Perry†	L	28	12	0	0	0	15.1	6	0	4	6	1-0	1	0.00
Tom Hume†	R	34	11	0	0	0	13.1	14	0	2	4	1-0	0	4.05
Paul O'Neill	L	24	1	0	0	0	2.0	2	1	4	2	0-0	0	13.50

1987 Houston Astros 3rd NL West 76-86 .469 14.0 GB

Hal Lanier

Player	Gm by Position	B	Age	G	AB	R	H	2B	3B	HR	RBI	BB	SO	SB	Avg	OBP	Slg
Alan Ashby	C110	S	35	125	386	53	111	16	0	14	63	50	52	0	.288	.367	.438
Glenn Davis	1B151	R	26	151	578	70	145	35	2	27	93	47	84	4	.251	.310	.458
Bill Doran	2B162,SS3	S	29	162	625	82	177	23	3	16	79	82	64	31	.283	.365	.406
Denny Walling	3B79,1B16,OF7	L	33	110	325	45	92	21	4	5	33	39	37	5	.283	.356	.418
Craig Reynolds	SS129,3B2	L	34	135	374	35	95	17	3	4	28	30	44	5	.254	.303	.348
Kevin Bass	OF155	S	28	157	592	83	168	31	5	19	85	53	77	21	.284	.344	.449
Billy Hatcher	OF140	R	26	141	564	96	167	28	3	11	63	42	70	53	.296	.352	.415
Jose Cruz	OF97	L	39	126	365	47	88	17	4	11	38	36	65	4	.241	.307	.400
Gerald Young	OF67	S	22	71	274	44	88	9	2	1	15	26	27	26	.321	.380	.380
Ken Caminiti	3B61	S	24	63	203	10	50	7	1	3	23	12	44	0	.246	.287	.335
Terry Puhl	OF40	L	30	90	122	9	28	5	0	2	15	11	16	1	.230	.293	.320
Phil Garner†	3B36,2B2	R	38	43	112	15	25	5	0	3	15	8	20	1	.223	.268	.348
Ronn Reynolds	C38	R	28	38	102	5	17	4	0	1	7	3	29	0	.167	.189	.235
Chuck Jackson	3B16,OF13,SS1	R	24	35	71	3	15	3	0	1	6	7	19	1	.211	.282	.296
Dickie Thon	SS31	R	29	32	66	6	14	1	0	1	3	16	13	3	.212	.366	.273
Mark Bailey	C27	S	25	35	64	5	13	1	0	0	3	10	21	1	.203	.311	.219
Jim Pankovits	2B9,OF6,3B4	R	31	50	61	7	14	2	0	1	8	6	13	2	.230	.299	.311
Bert Pena	SS19,3B1	R	27	21	46	5	7	0	0	0	0	2	7	0	.152	.204	.152
Dale Berra	SS18,2B3	R	30	19	45	3	8	3	0	0	2	8	12	0	.178	.296	.244
Davey Lopes	OF5	R	42	47	43	4	10	2	0	1	6	13	8	2	.233	.411	.349
Robbie Wine	C12	R	24	14	29	1	3	1	0	0	0	1	10	0	.103	.133	.138
Buddy Biancalana†	SS16,2B3	S	27	18	24	1	1	0	0	0	0	1	12	0	.042	.080	.042
Ty Gainey	OF6	L	26	18	24	1	3	0	0	0	1	2	9	1	.125	.192	.125
Troy Afenir	C10	R	23	10	20	1	6	1	0	0	1	0	12	0	.300	.300	.350
Paul Householder	OF7	S	28	14	12	2	1	1	0	0	1	4	2	0	.083	.313	.167
Ty Waller	OF3	R	30	11	6	1	1	1	0	0	0	0	3	0	.167	.167	.333

Pitcher	T	Age	G	GS	CG	ShO	IP	H	HR	BB	SO	W-L	Sv	ERA
Mike Scott	R	32	36	36	8	3	247.2	199	21	79	233	16-13	0	3.23
Nolan Ryan	R	40	34	34	0	0	211.2	154	14	87	270	8-16	0	2.76
Bob Knepper	L	33	33	31	1	0	177.2	226	26	54	76	8-17	0	5.27
Danny Darwin	R	31	33	30	3	1	195.2	184	17	69	134	9-10	0	3.59
Jim Deshaies	L	27	26	25	1	0	152.0	149	22	57	104	11-6	0	4.62
Manny Hernandez	R	26	6	3	0	0	21.2	25	1	5	12	0-4	0	5.40
Larry Andersen	R	34	67	0	0	0	101.2	95	7	41	94	9-5	5	3.45
Dave Smith	R	32	50	0	0	0	60.0	39	0	21	73	2-3	24	1.65
Dave Meads	L	23	45	0	0	0	48.2	60	8	16	32	5-3	0	5.55
Rocky Childress	R	25	32	0	0	0	48.1	46	4	18	26	1-2	0	2.98
Juan Agosto	L	29	27	0	0	0	27.1	26	1	10	6	1-1	2	2.63
Aurelio Lopez	R	38	26	0	0	0	38.0	39	6	12	21	2-1	1	4.50
Charlie Kerfeld	R	23	21	0	0	0	29.2	34	3	21	17	0-2	0	6.67
Jeff Heathcock	R	27	19	2	0	0	42.2	44	4	9	15	4-2	1	3.16
Julio Solano	R	27	11	0	0	0	20.0	25	5	9	12	0-0	0	7.65
Ron Mathis	R	28	8	0	0	0	12.0	10	2	11	8	0-1	0	5.25
Rob Mallicoat	L	22	4	1	0	0	6.2	8	0	6	4	0-0	0	6.75

1987 Los Angeles Dodgers 4th NL West 73-89 .451 17.0 GB

Tom Lasorda

Player	Gm by Position	B	Age	G	AB	R	H	2B	3B	HR	RBI	BB	SO	SB	Avg	OBP	Slg
Mike Scioscia	C138	L	28	142	461	44	122	26	1	6	38	55	23	7	.265	.343	.364
Franklin Stubbs	1B111,OF18	L	26	129	386	48	90	16	3	16	52	31	85	8	.233	.290	.415
Steve Sax	2B152,3B1,OF1	R	27	157	610	84	171	22	7	6	46	44	61	37	.280	.331	.369
Mickey Hatcher	3B49,1B37,OF7	R	32	101	287	27	81	19	1	7	42	20	19	2	.282	.328	.429
Mariano Duncan	SS67,2B7,OF2	S	24	76	261	31	56	8	1	6	18	17	62	11	.215	.267	.322
John Shelby†	OF117	S	29	120	476	61	132	26	0	21	69	31	97	16	.277	.317	.464
Pedro Guerrero	OF109,1B40	R	31	152	545	89	184	25	2	27	89	74	85	9	.338	.416	.539
Mike Marshall	OF102	R	27	104	402	45	118	19	0	16	72	18	79	0	.294	.327	.460
Dave Anderson	SS65,3B35,2B5	R	26	108	265	32	62	12	3	1	13	24	43	9	.234	.299	.313
Ken Landreaux	OF63	L	32	115	182	17	37	4	0	6	23	16	28	5	.203	.269	.324
Alex Trevino	C45,OF2,3B1	R	29	72	144	16	32	7	1	3	16	6	28	1	.222	.271	.347
Tracy Woodson	3B45,1B7	R	24	53	136	14	31	8	1	1	11	9	21	1	.228	.284	.324
Glenn Hoffman†	SS40	R	28	40	132	10	29	5	0	0	10	7	23	0	.220	.270	.258
Phil Garner†	3B46,2B12,SS2	R	38	70	126	14	24	4	0	2	8	20	24	5	.190	.299	.270
Mike Ramsey	OF43	S	26	48	125	18	29	4	2	0	12	10	32	2	.232	.287	.296
Danny Heep	OF22,1B6	L	29	60	98	7	16	4	0	0	9	8	10	1	.163	.226	.204
Jeff Hamilton	3B31,SS1	R	23	35	83	5	18	3	0	0	1	7	22	0	.217	.286	.253
Ralph Bryant	OF19	L	26	46	69	7	17	2	1	2	10	10	24	2	.246	.346	.391
Tito Landrum†	OF31	R	32	51	67	8	16	3	0	1	4	3	16	1	.239	.282	.328
Bill Madlock†	3B16,1B1	R	36	21	61	5	11	1	0	3	7	6	5	0	.180	.265	.344
Mike Devereaux	OF18	R	24	19	54	7	12	3	0	0	4	3	10	3	.222	.263	.278
Reggie Williams	OF30	R	26	39	36	6	4	0	0	0	4	5	9	1	.111	.214	.111
Craig Shipley	SS18,3B6	R	24	26	35	3	9	1	0	0	2	0	6	0	.257	.257	.286
Mike Sharperson†	3B7,2B6	R	25	10	33	7	9	2	0	0	1	4	5	0	.273	.351	.333
Chris Gwynn	OF10	L	22	17	32	2	7	1	0	0	2	1	7	0	.219	.242	.250
Jose Gonzalez	OF16	R	22	19	16	2	3	2	0	0	1	1	2	5	.188	.222	.313
Len Matuszek	1B3	L	32	16	15	0	1	0	0	0	0	1	4	0	.067	.125	.067
Orlando Mercado†	C7	R	25	7	5	1	3	1	0	0	1	1	1	0	.600	.667	.800
Brad Wellman	2B1,3B1,SS1	R	27	3	4	1	1	0	0	0	1	0	1	0	.250	.250	.250
Gil Reyes	C1	R	23	1	0	0	0	0	0	0	0	0	0	0	—	—	—

Pitcher	T	Age	G	GS	CG	ShO	IP	H	HR	BB	SO	W-L	Sv	ERA
Orel Hershiser	R	28	37	35	10	1	264.2	247	17	74	190	16-16	1	3.06
Bob Welch	R	30	35	35	6	4	251.2	204	21	86	196	15-9	0	3.22
F. Valenzuela	L	26	34	34	12	1	251.0	254	25	124	190	14-14	0	3.98
Rick Honeycutt†	L	33	27	20	1	1	115.2	133	10	45	92	2-12	0	4.59
Shawn Hillegas	R	22	12	10	0	0	58.0	52	5	31	51	4-3	0	3.57
Tim Belcher	R	25	6	5	0	0	34.0	30	2	7	23	4-2	0	2.38
Brian Holton	R	27	53	1	0	0	83.1	87	11	32	58	3-2	2	3.89
Matt Young	L	28	47	0	0	0	54.1	62	3	17	42	5-8	11	4.47
Ken Howell	R	26	40	2	0	0	55.0	54	7	29	60	3-4	1	4.91
Tim Leary	R	29	39	12	0	0	107.2	121	15	36	61	3-11	1	4.76
Alejandro Pena	R	28	37	7	0	0	87.1	82	9	37	76	2-7	11	3.50
Brad Havens	L	27	31	1	0	0	35.1	30	2	23	23	0-0	1	4.33
Tim Crews	R	26	20	0	0	0	29.0	30	2	8	20	1-1	3	2.48
Tom Niedenfuer†	R	27	15	0	0	0	16.1	13	1	9	10	1-0	1	2.76
Ron Davis†	R	31	4	0	0	0	4.0	7	0	6	1	0-0	0	6.75
Jack Savage	R	23	3	0	0	0	3.1	4	0	0	0	0-0	0	2.70
Bill Krueger†	L	29	2	0	0	0	2.1	3	0	1	2	0-0	0	0.00
Jerry Reuss†	L	38	1	0	0	0	2.0	2	0	0	2	0-0	0	4.50

1987 Atlanta Braves 5th NL West 69-92 .429 20.5 GB

Chuck Tanner

Player	Gm by Position	B	Age	G	AB	R	H	2B	3B	HR	RBI	BB	SO	SB	Avg	OBP	Slg
Ozzie Virgil	C122	R	30	123	429	57	106	13	1	27	72	47	81	0	.247	.331	.471
Gerald Perry	1B136,OF7	L	26	142	533	77	144	35	2	12	74	48	63	42	.270	.329	.411
Glenn Hubbard	2B139	R	29	141	443	69	117	33	2	5	38	77	57	1	.264	.378	.381
Ken Oberkfell	3B126,2B11	L	31	135	508	59	142	29	2	3	48	48	29	3	.280	.342	.362
Andres Thomas	SS81	R	23	82	324	29	75	11	0	5	39	14	50	6	.231	.268	.312
Dale Murphy	OF159	R	31	159	566	115	167	27	1	44	105	115	136	16	.295	.417	.580
Dion James	OF126	L	24	134	494	80	154	37	6	10	61	70	63	10	.312	.397	.472
Ken Griffey Sr.	OF107,1B3	L	37	122	399	65	114	24	1	14	64	46	54	4	.286	.358	.456
Albert Hall	OF69	S	29	92	292	54	83	20	4	3	24	38	36	33	.284	.369	.411
Rafael Ramirez	SS38,3B12	R	29	56	179	22	47	12	0	1	21	8	16	6	.263	.300	.346
Ted Simmons	1B28,C15,3B2	S	37	73	177	20	49	8	0	4	30	21	23	1	.277	.350	.390
Graig Nettles	3B40,1B6	L	42	112	177	16	37	8	1	5	33	22	25	1	.209	.294	.350
Jeff Blauser	SS50	R	21	51	165	11	40	6	3	2	15	18	34	7	.242	.328	.352
Gary Roenicke	OF44,1B9	R	32	67	151	25	33	8	0	9	28	32	23	0	.219	.353	.450
Bruce Benedict	C35	R	31	37	95	4	14	1	0	1	5	17	15	0	.147	.277	.189
Ron Gant	2B20	R	22	21	83	9	22	4	0	2	9	1	11	4	.265	.271	.386
Paul Runge	3B10,SS9,2B2	R	29	27	47	9	10	1	0	3	8	5	10	0	.213	.288	.426
Darryl Motley	OF2	R	27	6	8	0	0	0	0	0	1	0	1	0	.000	.000	.000
Trench Davis		L	26	6	3	0	0	0	0	0	0	0	1	0	.000	.000	.000
Terry Bell		R	24	1	1	0	0	0	0	0	0	0	1	0	.000	.000	.000
Mike Fischlin		R	31	1	0	0	0	0	0	0	0	0	0	0	—	—	—

Pitcher	T	Age	G	GS	CG	ShO	IP	H	HR	BB	SO	W-L	Sv	ERA
Zane Smith	L	26	36	36	9	3	242.0	245	19	91	130	15-10	0	4.09
Rick Mahler	R	33	39	28	3	1	197.0	212	24	85	95	8-13	0	4.98
David Palmer	R	29	28	28	0	0	152.1	169	17	64	111	8-11	0	4.90
Doyle Alexander†	R	36	16	16	3	0	117.2	115	21	27	64	5-10	0	4.13
Randy O'Neal†	R	26	16	10	0	0	61.0	79	12	24	33	4-2	0	5.61
Tom Glavine	L	21	9	9	0	0	50.1	55	5	33	20	2-4	0	5.54
Pete Smith	R	21	6	6	0	0	31.2	39	3	14	11	1-2	0	4.83
Kevin Coffman	R	22	5	5	0	0	25.1	31	2	22	14	2-3	0	4.62
Phil Niekro†	R	48	1	1	0	0	3.0	6	0	6	0	0-0	0	15.00
Jim Acker	R	28	68	0	0	0	114.2	109	11	51	68	4-9	14	4.16
Jeff Dedmon	R	27	53	3	0	0	89.2	82	8	42	40	3-4	4	3.91
Paul Assenmacher	L	26	52	0	0	0	54.2	58	8	24	39	1-1	2	5.10
Gene Garber†	R	39	49	0	0	0	69.1	87	7	28	48	8-10	10	4.41
Charlie Puleo	R	32	35	16	1	0	123.1	122	11	40	99	6-8	0	4.23
Ed Olwine	L	29	27	0	0	0	23.1	25	4	8	12	0-1	1	5.01
Joe Boever	R	26	14	0	0	0	18.1	29	4	12	18	1-0	0	7.36
Chuck Cary	L	27	13	0	0	0	16.2	17	3	4	15	1-1	1	3.78
Larry McWilliams	L	33	9	2	0	0	20.1	25	2	7	13	0-1	0	5.75
Marty Clary	R	25	7	1	0	0	14.2	20	2	4	7	0-1	0	6.14
Steve Ziem	R	25	2	0	0	0	2.1	4	0	1	0	0-1	0	7.71

1987 San Diego Padres 6th NL West 65-97 .401 25.0 GB

Larry Bowa

Player	Gm by Position	B	Age	G	AB	R	H	2B	3B	HR	RBI	BB	SO	SB	Avg	OBP	Slg
Benito Santiago	C146	R	22	146	546	64	164	33	2	18	79	16	112	21	.300	.324	.467
John Kruk	1B101,OF29	L	26	138	447	72	140	14	2	20	91	73	93	18	.313	.406	.488
Tim Flannery	2B84,3B8,SS2	L	29	106	276	23	63	5	1	0	20	42	30	2	.228	.332	.254
Randy Ready	3B52,2B51,OF16	R	27	124	350	69	108	26	6	12	54	67	44	7	.309	.423	.520
Garry Templeton	SS146	S	31	148	510	42	113	13	5	5	48	42	92	14	.222	.281	.296
Tony Gwynn	OF156	L	27	157	589	119	218	36	13	7	54	82	35	56	.370	.447	.511
Stan Jefferson	OF107	S	24	116	422	59	97	8	7	8	29	39	92	34	.230	.296	.339
Shane Mack	OF91	R	23	105	238	28	57	11	3	4	25	18	47	4	.239	.299	.361
Carmelo Martinez	OF78,1B65	R	26	139	447	59	122	21	2	15	70	70	82	5	.273	.372	.430
Joey Cora	2B66,SS6	S	22	77	241	23	57	7	2	0	13	28	26	15	.237	.317	.282
Kevin Mitchell†	3B51,OF3	R	25	62	196	19	48	7	1	7	26	20	38	0	.245	.313	.398
Luis Salazar	3B38,SS22,OF10*	R	31	84	189	13	48	5	0	3	17	14	30	3	.254	.302	.328
Marvell Wynne	OF71	L	27	98	188	17	47	8	2	2	24	20	37	11	.250	.321	.346
Chris Brown†	3B43	R	25	44	155	17	36	3	0	6	23	11	30	3	.232	.294	.368
Steve Garvey	1B20	R	38	27	76	5	16	2	0	1	9	1	10	0	.211	.231	.276
Bruce Bochy	C23	R	32	38	75	8	12	3	0	2	11	11	21	0	.160	.264	.280
James Steels	OF28	L	26	62	68	9	13	1	1	0	6	11	14	3	.191	.300	.235
Shawn Abner	OF14	R	21	16	47	5	13	3	1	2	7	2	8	1	.277	.306	.511
Mark Parent	C10	R	25	12	25	0	2	0	0	0	2	0	9	0	.080	.080	.080
Randy Byers	OF5	L	22	10	16	1	5	1	0	0	1	1	5	1	.313	.353	.375
Rob Nelson†	1B2	L	23	10	11	0	1	0	0	0	1	1	8	0	.091	.167	.091

L. Salazar, 2 G at P, 1 G at 1B

Pitcher	T	Age	G	GS	CG	ShO	IP	H	HR	BB	SO	W-L	Sv	ERA
Eric Show	R	31	34	34	5	3	206.1	188	26	85	117	8-16	0	3.84
Ed Whitson	R	32	36	34	3	1	205.2	197	36	64	135	10-13	0	4.73
Jimmy Jones	R	23	30	22	2	1	145.2	154	14	54	51	9-7	0	4.14
Andy Hawkins	R	27	24	20	0	0	117.2	131	16	49	51	3-10	0	5.05
Mark Grant†	R	23	17	17	2	1	102.1	104	16	52	58	6-7	0	4.66
Eric Nolte	L	23	12	12	1	0	67.1	57	6	36	44	2-6	0	3.21
Ed Wojna	R	26	5	3	0	0	18.1	25	2	6	13	0-3	0	5.89
Lance McCullers	R	23	78	0	0	0	123.1	115	11	59	126	8-10	16	3.72
Greg Booker	R	27	44	0	0	0	68.1	62	5	30	17	1-1	1	3.16
Mark Davis†	L	26	43	0	0	0	62.1	51	5	31	47	5-3	2	3.18
Goose Gossage	R	35	40	0	0	0	52.0	47	4	19	44	5-4	11	3.12
Craig Lefferts†	L	29	33	0	0	0	51.1	56	9	15	39	2-2	2	4.38
Dave Dravecky†	L	31	30	10	1	0	79.0	71	10	31	60	3-7	0	3.76
Keith Comstock†	L	31	26	0	0	0	36.0	33	4	21	38	0-1	0	5.50
Storm Davis†	R	25	21	10	0	0	62.2	70	5	36	37	2-7	0	6.18
Dave Leiper†	L	25	12	0	0	0	16.0	16	2	5	10	1-0	1	4.50
Tom Gorman	L	29	6	0	0	0	11.0	11	1	5	8	0-0	0	4.09
Ray Hayward	L	26	4	0	0	0	6.0	12	3	3	2	0-0	0	16.50
Luis Salazar	R	31	2	0	0	0	2.0	2	0	1	0	0-0	0	4.50

»1988 Boston Red Sox 1st AL East 89-73 .549 —

John McNamara (43-42)/Joe Morgan (46-31)

Player	Gm by Position	B	Age	G	AB	R	H	2B	3B	HR	RBI	BB	SO	SB	Avg	OBP	Slg
Rich Gedman	C93,DH1	L	28	95	299	33	69	14	0	9	39	18	49	0	.231	.279	.368
Todd Benzinger	1B85,OF48,DH1	S	25	120	405	47	103	28	1	13	70	22	80	2	.254	.293	.425
Marty Barrett	2B150	R	30	150	612	83	173	28	1	1	65	40	35	7	.283	.330	.337
Wade Boggs	3B151,DH3	L	30	155	584	128	214	45	6	5	58	125	34	2	.366	.476	.490
Jody Reed	SS94,2B11,3B4	R	25	109	338	60	99	23	1	1	28	45	21	1	.293	.380	.376
Mike Greenwell	OF147,DH11	L	24	158	590	86	192	39	8	22	119	87	38	16	.325	.416	.531
Ellis Burks	OF142,DH2	R	23	144	540	93	159	37	5	18	92	62	89	25	.294	.367	.481
Dwight Evans	OF85,1B64,DH6	R	36	149	559	96	164	31	7	21	111	76	99	5	.293	.375	.487
Jim Rice	DH111,OF19	R	35	135	485	57	128	18	3	15	72	48	89	1	.264	.330	.406
Rick Cerone	C83,DH1	R	34	84	264	31	71	13	1	3	27	20	32	0	.269	.326	.360
Spike Owen	SS76,DH7	S	27	89	257	40	64	14	1	5	18	27	27	0	.249	.324	.370
Larry Parrish†	1B36,DH14	R	34	52	158	10	41	5	0	7	26	8	32	0	.259	.298	.424
Brady Anderson†	OF41	L	24	41	148	14	34	5	3	0	12	15	35	4	.230	.315	.304
Kevin Romine	OF45,DH5	R	27	57	78	17	15	2	1	1	6	7	15	2	.192	.259	.282
Ed Romero	3B15,SS8,2B5*	R	30	31	75	3	18	3	0	0	5	3	8	0	.240	.272	.280
Sam Horn	DH16	L	24	24	61	4	9	0	0	2	8	11	20	0	.148	.274	.246
Pat Dodson	1B17	L	28	17	45	5	8	3	1	1	1	6	17	0	.178	.275	.356
John Marzano	C10	R	25	10	29	3	4	1	0	0	1	1	3	0	.138	.167	.172
Randy Kutcher	OF7,3B2	R	28	19	12	2	2	1	0	0	0	0	2	0	.167	.167	.250
Carlos Quintana	OF3,DH1	R	22	5	6	1	2	0	0	0	2	2	3	0	.333	.500	.333

E. Romero, 1 G at DH, 1 G at 1B

Pitcher	T	Age	G	GS	CG	ShO	IP	H	HR	BB	SO	W-L	Sv	ERA
Roger Clemens	R	25	35	35	14	8	264.0	217	17	62	291	18-12	0	2.93
Bruce Hurst	L	30	33	32	7	1	216.2	222	21	65	166	18-6	0	3.66
Oil Can Boyd	R	28	23	23	1	0	129.2	147	25	41	71	9-7	0	5.34
Wes Gardner	R	27	36	18	1	0	149.0	119	17	64	106	8-6	2	3.50
Mike Smithson	R	33	31	18	1	0	126.2	149	25	37	73	9-6	0	5.97
Mike Boddicker†	R	30	15	14	1	1	89.0	85	3	26	56	7-3	0	2.63
Jeff Sellers	R	24	18	12	1	0	85.2	89	9	56	70	1-7	0	4.83
Steve Ellsworth	R	27	8	7	0	0	36.0	47	7	16	16	1-6	0	6.75
Steve Curry	R	22	3	3	0	0	11.0	15	0	14	4	0-1	0	8.18
Lee Smith	R	30	64	0	0	0	83.2	72	7	37	96	4-5	29	2.80
Bob Stanley	R	33	57	0	0	0	101.2	90	6	29	57	6-4	5	3.19
Dennis Lamp	R	35	46	0	0	0	82.2	92	3	19	49	7-6	0	3.48
Tom Bolton	L	26	28	0	0	0	30.1	35	1	14	21	1-3	1	4.75
John Trautwein	R	25	9	0	0	0	16.0	26	2	9	8	0-1	0	9.00
Zach Crouch	L	22	3	0	0	0	1.1	4	0	2	0	0-0	0	6.75
Mike Rochford	L	25	2	0	0	0	2.1	4	0	1	1	0-0	0	0.00
Rob Woodward	R	25	1	0	0	0	0.2	2	0	1	0	0-0	0	13.50

1988 Detroit Tigers 2nd AL East 88-74 .543 1.0 GB

Sparky Anderson

Player	Gm by Position	B	Age	G	AB	R	H	2B	3B	HR	RBI	BB	SO	SB	Avg	OBP	Slg
Matt Nokes	C110,DH2	L	24	122	382	53	96	18	0	16	53	34	58	0	.251	.313	.424
Darrell Evans	DH72,1B65	L	41	144	437	48	91	9	0	22	64	84	89	1	.208	.337	.380
Lou Whitaker	2B110	L	31	115	403	54	111	18	2	12	55	66	61	2	.275	.376	.419
Tom Brookens	3B136,SS3,2B1	R	34	136	441	62	107	23	5	5	38	44	74	4	.243	.313	.351
Alan Trammell	SS125	R	30	128	466	73	145	24	1	15	69	46	46	7	.311	.373	.464
Chet Lemon	OF144	R	33	144	512	67	135	29	4	17	64	59	65	1	.264	.346	.436
Gary Pettis	OF126,DH2	S	30	129	458	65	96	14	4	3	36	47	85	44	.210	.285	.277
Pat Sheridan	OF111,DH3	L	30	127	347	47	88	9	5	11	47	44	64	8	.254	.339	.403
Larry Herndon	DH53,OF15	R	34	76	174	16	39	5	0	4	20	23	37	0	.224	.313	.322
Luis Salazar	OF68,SS37,3B31*	R	32	130	452	61	122	14	1	12	62	21	70	6	.270	.305	.385
Ray Knight	1B64,DH25,3B11*	R	35	105	299	34	65	12	2	3	33	20	30	1	.217	.271	.301
Dave Bergman	1B64,DH30,OF13	L	35	116	289	37	85	14	0	5	35	38	34	0	.294	.372	.394
Mike Heath	C75,OF9	R	33	86	219	24	54	7	2	5	18	18	32	1	.247	.307	.365
Jim Walewander	2B61,DH9,SS8*	S	26	88	175	23	37	5	0	0	6	12	26	11	.211	.261	.240
Dwayne Murphy	OF43,DH3	L	33	49	144	14	36	5	0	4	19	24	26	1	.250	.361	.368
Fred Lynn†	OF22,DH3	L	36	27	90	9	20	1	0	7	19	5	16	0	.222	.265	.467
Jim Morrison†	DH14,1B4,3B4*	R	35	24	74	7	16	5	0	0	6	0	14	0	.216	.216	.284
Torey Lovullo	2B9,3B3	S	22	12	21	2	8	1	1	1	2	1	2	0	.381	.409	.667
Ivan DeJesus	SS7	R	35	7	17	1	3	0	0	0	0	1	4	0	.176	.222	.176
Scott Lusader	DH6,OF4	L	23	16	16	3	1	0	0	1	3	1	4	0	.063	.111	.250
Billy Bean	OF4,1B2,DH1	L	24	10	11	2	2	0	1	0	0	0	2	0	.182	.182	.364
Billy Beane	OF6	R	20	6	6	1	1	0	0	0	1	0	2	0	.167	.167	.167
Chris Bando†	C1	S	32	1	0	0	0	0	0	0	0	0	0	0	—	—	—

L. Salazar, 5 G at 2B, 4 G at 1B; R. Knight, 2 G at OF; J. Walewander, 3 G at 3B; J. Morrison, 2 G at OF, 1 G at SS

Pitcher	T	Age	G	GS	CG	ShO	IP	H	HR	BB	SO	W-L	Sv	ERA
Jack Morris	R	33	34	34	10	2	235.0	225	20	83	168	15-13	0	3.94
Doyle Alexander	R	37	34	34	5	1	229.0	260	30	46	126	14-11	0	4.32
Frank Tanana	L	34	32	32	2	0	203.0	213	25	64	127	14-11	0	4.21
Walt Terrell	R	30	29	29	11	1	206.1	199	20	78	84	7-16	0	3.97
Jeff Robinson	R	26	24	23	6	2	172.0	121	19	72	114	13-6	0	2.98
Ted Power†	R	33	4	2	0	0	18.2	23	1	8	13	1-1	0	5.79
Steve Searcy	L	24	2	2	0	0	8.0	8	3	4	5	0-2	0	5.63
Mike Henneman	R	26	65	0	0	0	91.1	72	7	24	58	9-6	22	1.87
Willie Hernandez	L	33	63	0	0	0	67.2	50	8	31	59	6-5	10	3.06
Paul Gibson	R	28	40	1	0	0	92.0	83	6	34	50	4-2	0	2.93
Eric King	R	24	23	5	0	0	68.2	60	5	34	45	4-1	3	3.41
Don Heinkel	R	28	21	0	0	0	36.1	30	4	12	30	0-0	1	3.96
Mike Trujillo	R	28	6	0	0	0	12.1	11	2	5	5	0-0	0	5.11
Mark Huismann	R	30	5	0	0	0	5.1	6	0	2	6	1-0	0	5.06

1988 Milwaukee Brewers 3rd AL East 87-75 .537 2.0 GB

Tom Trebelhorn

Player	Gm by Position	B	Age	G	AB	R	H	2B	3B	HR	RBI	BB	SO	SB	Avg	OBP	Slg
B.J. Surhoff	C106,3B31,1B2*	L	23	139	493	47	121	21	0	5	38	31	49	21	.245	.292	.318
Greg Brock	1B114,DH1	L	31	115	364	53	77	16	1	6	50	63	48	6	.212	.329	.310
Jim Gantner	2B154,3B1	L	35	155	539	67	149	28	2	0	47	34	50	20	.276	.322	.336
Paul Molitor	3B105,DH49,2B1	R	31	154	609	115	190	34	6	13	60	71	54	41	.312	.384	.452
Dale Sveum	SS127,DH1,2B1	S	24	129	467	41	113	14	4	9	51	21	122	1	.242	.274	.347
Robin Yount	OF158,DH4	R	32	162	621	92	190	38	11	13	91	63	63	22	.306	.369	.465
Rob Deer	OF133,DH1	R	27	135	492	71	124	24	0	23	85	51	153	9	.252	.328	.441
Jeffrey Leonard†	OF91,DH2	R	32	94	374	45	88	19	0	8	44	16	68	10	.235	.270	.350
Joey Meyer	DH66,1B33	R	26	103	327	22	86	18	0	11	45	23	88	0	.263	.313	.419
Glenn Braggs	OF54,DH18	R	25	72	272	30	71	14	0	10	42	14	60	6	.261	.307	.423
Ernest Riles†	3B28,SS9,DH5	L	27	41	127	7	32	6	1	1	9	7	26	2	.252	.291	.339
Bill Schroeder	C30,1B10,DH1	R	29	41	122	9	19	2	0	5	10	6	36	0	.156	.208	.295
Charlie O'Brien	C40	R	28	40	118	12	26	6	0	2	9	5	16	0	.220	.252	.322
Darryl Hamilton	OF37,DH3	L	23	44	103	14	19	4	0	1	11	12	9	7	.184	.274	.252
Jim Adduci	OF24,DH12,1B3	L	28	44	94	8	25	6	1	1	15	0	15	0	.266	.258	.383
Billy Joe Robidoux	1B30,DH1	L	24	33	91	9	23	5	0	0	5	8	14	1	.253	.307	.308
Juan Castillo	2B18,3B17,SS13*	S	26	54	90	10	20	0	0	0	2	3	14	2	.222	.247	.222
Mike Felder	OF28,DH8,2B1	S	26	50	81	14	14	1	0	0	5	0	11	8	.173	.183	.185
Gary Sheffield	SS24	R	19	24	80	12	19	1	0	4	12	7	7	3	.238	.295	.400
Mike Young†	DH5,OF2	S	28	8	14	2	0	0	0	0	0	2	5	0	.000	.176	.000
Steve Kiefer	2B4,3B4	R	27	7	10	2	3	1	0	1	1	2	3	0	.300	.462	.700

B. Surhoff, 1 G at SS, 1 G at OF; J. Castillo, 3 G at DH, 1 G at OF

Pitcher	T	Age	G	GS	CG	ShO	IP	H	HR	BB	SO	W-L	Sv	ERA
Teddy Higuera	L	29	31	31	8	1	227.1	168	15	59	192	16-9	0	2.45
Bill Wegman	R	25	32	31	4	1	199.0	207	24	50	84	13-13	0	4.12
Mike Birkbeck	R	27	23	23	0	0	124.0	141	10	37	64	10-8	0	4.72
Chris Bosio	R	25	38	22	9	1	182.0	190	13	38	84	7-15	6	3.36
Don August	R	24	24	22	6	1	148.1	137	12	48	66	13-7	0	3.09
Tom Filer	R	31	19	16	2	1	101.2	108	8	33	39	5-8	0	4.43
Juan Nieves	L	23	25	15	1	1	110.1	84	13	50	73	7-5	1	4.08
Chuck Crim	R	26	70	0	0	0	105.0	95	11	28	58	7-6	9	2.91
Dan Plesac	L	26	50	0	0	0	52.1	46	2	12	52	1-2	30	2.41
Paul Mirabella	L	34	38	0	0	0	60.0	44	3	21	33	2-2	4	1.65
Odell Jones	R	35	28	2	0	0	80.2	75	8	29	48	5-0	1	4.35
Mark Clear	R	32	25	0	0	0	29.0	23	4	21	26	1-0	0	2.79
Dave Stapleton	L	26	6	0	0	0	13.2	20	1	9	6	0-0	0	5.93
Mark Knudson	R	27	5	0	0	0	16.0	17	1	2	7	0-0	0	1.13

1988 Toronto Blue Jays 3rd AL East 87-75 .537 2.0 GB

Jimy Williams

Player	Gm by Position	B	Age	G	AB	R	H	2B	3B	HR	RBI	BB	SO	SB	Avg	OBP	Slg
Ernie Whitt	C123	L	36	127	398	63	100	11	2	16	70	61	38	4	.251	.348	.410
Fred McGriff	1B153	L	24	154	536	100	151	35	4	34	82	79	149	6	.282	.376	.552
Manuel Lee	2B98,SS23,3B8*	S	23	116	381	38	111	16	3	2	38	26	64	3	.291	.333	.365
Kelly Gruber	3B156,2B7,OF2*	R	26	158	569	75	158	33	5	16	81	38	92	23	.278	.328	.438
Tony Fernandez	SS154	S	26	154	648	76	186	41	4	5	70	45	65	15	.287	.335	.386
George Bell	OF149,DH7	R	28	156	614	78	165	27	5	24	97	34	66	4	.269	.304	.446
Jesse Barfield	OF136,DH1	R	28	137	468	62	114	21	5	18	56	41	108	7	.244	.302	.425
Lloyd Moseby	OF125,DH1	L	28	128	472	77	113	17	7	10	42	70	93	31	.239	.343	.369
Rance Mulliniks	DH108,3B7	L	32	119	337	49	101	21	1	12	48	56	57	1	.300	.395	.475
Nelson Liriano	2B80,DH11,3B1	S	24	99	276	36	73	6	2	3	23	11	40	12	.264	.297	.333
Rick Leach	OF49,DH25,1B4	L	31	87	199	21	55	13	1	0	23	18	27	0	.276	.336	.352
Cecil Fielder	DH50,1B17,3B3*	R	24	74	174	24	40	6	1	9	23	14	53	0	.230	.289	.431
Pat Borders	C43,DH7,2B1*	R	25	56	154	15	42	6	3	5	21	3	24	0	.273	.285	.448
Sil Campusano	OF69,DH2	R	22	73	142	14	31	10	2	2	12	9	33	0	.218	.282	.359
Sal Butera	C23	R	35	23	60	3	14	2	1	1	6	1	9	0	.233	.246	.350
Juan Beniquez	DH19,OF1	R	38	27	58	9	17	2	0	1	8	8	6	0	.293	.373	.379
Rob Ducey	OF26	L	23	27	54	15	17	4	1	0	6	5	7	1	.315	.361	.426
Alexis Infante	3B9,SS2	R	26	19	15	7	3	0	0	0	0	2	4	0	.200	.294	.200
Lou Thornton	OF10	L	25	11	2	1	0	0	0	0	0	0	0	0	.000	.000	.000

M. Lee, 1 G at DH; K. Gruber, 1 G at SS; C. Fielder, 2 G at 2B; P. Borders, 1 G at 3B

Pitcher	T	Age	G	GS	CG	ShO	IP	H	HR	BB	SO	W-L	Sv	ERA
Mike Flanagan	L	36	34	34	2	1	211.0	220	23	80	99	13-13	0	4.18
Dave Stieb	R	30	32	31	8	4	207.1	157	15	79	147	16-8	0	3.04
Jim Clancy	R	32	36	31	4	0	196.1	207	26	47	118	11-13	1	4.49
Jimmy Key	L	27	21	21	2	2	131.1	127	13	30	65	12-5	0	3.29
Todd Stottlemyre	R	23	28	16	0	0	98.0	109	15	46	67	4-8	0	5.69
Jeff Musselman	L	25	15	15	0	0	85.0	80	4	30	39	8-5	0	3.18
Duane Ward	R	24	64	0	0	0	111.2	101	5	60	91	9-3	15	3.30
Tom Henke	R	30	52	0	0	0	68.0	60	6	24	66	4-4	25	2.91
John Cerutti	L	28	46	12	0	0	123.2	120	12	42	65	6-7	1	3.13
David Wells	L	25	41	0	0	0	64.1	65	12	31	56	3-5	4	4.62
Mark Eichhorn	R	27	37	0	0	0	66.2	79	3	27	28	0-3	1	4.19
Tony Castillo	L	25	14	0	0	0	15.0	10	2	2	14	1-0	0	3.00
Jose Nunez	R	24	13	2	0	0	29.1	28	3	17	18	0-1	0	3.07
Frank Wills	R	29	10	0	0	0	20.2	22	2	6	19	0-0	0	5.23
Doug Bair	R	38	10	0	0	0	13.1	14	2	3	8	0-0	0	4.05
Mark Ross	R	33	3	0	0	0	7.1	5	0	4	4	0-0	0	4.91

1988 New York Yankees 5th AL East 85-76 .528 3.5 GB

Billy Martin (40-28)/Lou Piniella (45-48)

Player	Gm by Position	B	Age	G	AB	R	H	2B	3B	HR	RBI	BB	SO	SB	Avg	OBP	Slg
Don Slaught	C94,DH1	R	29	97	322	33	91	25	1	9	43	24	54	1	.283	.334	.450
Don Mattingly	1B143,DH1,OF1	L	27	144	599	94	186	37	0	18	88	41	29	1	.311	.353	.462
Willie Randolph	2B110	R	33	110	404	43	93	20	1	2	34	55	39	8	.230	.322	.300
Mike Pagliarulo	3B124	L	28	125	444	46	96	20	1	15	67	37	104	1	.216	.276	.367
Rafael Santana	SS148	R	30	148	480	50	115	12	1	4	38	33	61	1	.240	.289	.294
Dave Winfield	OF141,DH4	R	36	149	559	96	180	37	2	25	107	69	88	9	.322	.398	.530
Rickey Henderson	OF136,DH3	R	29	140	554	118	169	30	2	6	50	82	54	93	.305	.394	.399
C. Washington	OF117	L	33	126	455	62	140	22	3	11	64	24	74	15	.308	.342	.442
Jack Clark	DH112,OF19,1B10	R	32	150	496	81	120	14	0	27	93	113	141	3	.242	.381	.433
Joel Skinner	C85,OF2,1B1	R	27	88	251	23	57	15	0	4	23	14	72	0	.227	.267	.335
Gary Ward	OF54,1B11,DH9*	R	34	91	231	26	52	8	0	4	24	24	41	0	.225	.302	.312
Luis Aguayo†	3B33,2B13,SS6	R	29	50	140	12	35	4	0	3	8	7	33	0	.250	.289	.343
Bobby Meacham	SS24,2B21,3B5	S	27	47	115	18	25	9	0	0	7	14	22	7	.217	.308	.296
Randy Velarde	2B24,SS14,3B11	R	25	48	115	18	20	6	0	5	12	8	24	1	.174	.240	.357
Ken Phelps†	DH28,1B1	L	33	45	107	17	24	5	0	10	22	19	26	0	.224	.339	.551
Jose Cruz	DH12,OF8	L	40	38	80	9	16	2	0	1	7	8	8	0	.200	.273	.263
Roberto Kelly	OF30,DH3	R	23	38	77	9	19	4	1	1	7	3	15	5	.247	.272	.364
Jay Buhner†	OF22	R	23	25	69	8	13	0	0	3	13	3	25	0	.188	.250	.319
Wayne Tolleson	2B12,3B10,SS1	S	32	21	59	8	15	2	0	0	5	8	12	1	.254	.338	.288
Hal Morris	OF4,DH1	L	23	15	20	1	2	0	0	0	0	0	9	0	.100	.100	.100
Bob Geren	C10	R	26	10	10	0	1	0	0	0	0	2	3	0	.100	.250	.100
Alvaro Espinoza	2B2,SS1	R	26	3	3	0	0	0	0	0	0	0	0	0	.000	.000	.000
Chris Chambliss		L	39	1	1	0	0	0	0	0	0	0	1	0	.000	.000	.000

G. Ward, 2 G at 3B

Pitcher	T	Age	G	GS	CG	ShO	IP	H	HR	BB	SO	W-L	Sv	ERA
Tommy John	L	45	35	32	0	0	176.1	221	11	46	81	9-8	0	4.49
Rick Rhoden	R	35	30	30	5	1	197.0	206	20	56	94	12-12	0	4.29
Rich Dotson	R	29	32	29	4	0	171.0	178	27	72	77	12-9	0	5.00
John Candelaria	L	34	25	24	6	2	157.0	150	18	23	121	13-7	1	3.38
Al Leiter	L	22	14	14	0	0	57.1	49	7	33	60	4-4	0	3.92
Ron Guidry	L	37	12	10	0	0	56.0	57	7	15	32	2-3	0	4.18
Dave Eiland	R	21	3	3	0	0	12.2	15	6	4	7	0-0	0	6.39
Dave Righetti	L	29	60	0	0	0	87.0	86	5	37	70	5-4	25	3.52
Cecilio Guante†	R	28	56	0	0	0	75.0	59	10	22	61	5-6	11	2.88
Neil Allen	R	30	41	2	0	1	117.1	121	14	37	61	5-3	0	3.84
Steve Shields	R	29	39	0	0	0	82.1	96	8	30	55	5-5	0	4.37
Charles Hudson	R	29	28	12	1	0	106.1	93	9	36	58	6-6	2	4.49
Tim Stoddard	R	35	28	0	0	0	55.0	62	5	27	33	2-2	3	6.38
Lee Guetterman	L	29	20	2	0	0	40.2	49	2	14	15	1-2	0	4.65
Hipolito Pena	L	24	16	0	0	0	14.1	10	1	9	10	1-1	0	3.14
Dale Mohorcic†	R	32	13	0	0	0	22.2	21	1	9	19	2-2	1	2.78
Scott Nielsen	R	29	7	2	0	0	19.2	27	5	13	4	1-2	0	6.86
Pat Clements	L	26	6	1	0	0	8.1	12	1	4	3	0-0	0	6.48

1988 Cleveland Indians 6th AL East 78-84 .481 11.0 GB

Doc Edwards

Player	Gm by Position	B	Age	G	AB	R	H	2B	3B	HR	RBI	BB	SO	SB	Avg	OBP	Slg
Andy Allanson	C133	R	26	133	434	44	114	11	0	5	50	25	63	5	.263	.305	.323
Willie Upshaw	1B144	L	31	149	493	58	121	22	3	11	50	62	66	12	.245	.330	.369
Julio Franco	2B151,DH1	R	26	152	613	88	186	23	6	10	54	56	72	25	.303	.361	.409
Brook Jacoby	3B151	R	28	152	552	59	133	25	0	9	49	48	101	2	.241	.300	.335
Jay Bell	SS72	R	22	73	211	23	46	5	1	2	21	21	53	4	.218	.289	.280
Joe Carter	OF156	R	28	157	621	85	168	36	6	27	98	35	82	27	.271	.314	.478
Mel Hall	OF141,DH6	L	27	150	515	69	144	32	4	6	71	28	50	7	.280	.312	.392
Cory Snyder	OF141	R	25	142	511	71	139	24	3	26	75	42	101	5	.272	.326	.483
Ron Kittle	DH63	R	30	75	225	31	58	8	0	18	43	16	65	0	.258	.323	.533
Ron Washington	SS54,3B8,2B7*	R	36	69	223	30	57	14	2	2	21	9	35	3	.256	.298	.363
Terry Francona	DH38,1B5,OF5	L	29	62	212	24	66	8	0	1	12	5	18	0	.311	.324	.363
Carmelo Castillo	OF45,DH9	R	30	66	176	12	48	8	0	4	14	5	31	6	.273	.297	.386
Dave Clark	DH27,OF23	L	25	63	156	11	41	4	1	3	18	17	28	0	.263	.333	.359
Pat Tabler†	DH29,1B10	R	30	41	143	16	32	5	1	1	17	23	27	1	.224	.333	.294
Paul Zuvella	SS49	R	29	51	130	9	30	5	1	0	7	8	13	0	.231	.275	.285
Chris Bando†	C32	S	32	32	72	6	9	1	0	1	8	8	12	0	.125	.217	.181
Luis Medina	1B16	R	25	16	51	10	13	0	0	6	8	2	18	0	.255	.309	.608
Domingo Ramos†	2B11,1B5,SS4*	R	30	22	46	7	12	1	0	0	5	3	7	0	.261	.308	.283
Reggie Williams	OF11	R	27	11	31	7	7	2	0	1	3	0	6	0	.226	.226	.387
Ron Tingley	C9	R	29	9	24	1	4	0	0	1	2	2	8	0	.167	.231	.292
Houston Jimenez	2B7,SS2	R	30	9	21	1	1	0	0	0	1	0	2	0	.048	.048	.048
Eddie Williams	3B10	R	23	10	21	3	4	0	0	0	1	0	3	0	.190	.227	.190
Rod Allen	DH4	R	28	5	11	1	1	1	0	0	0	0	2	0	.091	.091	.182
Scott Jordan	OF6	R	25	7	9	0	1	0	0	0	1	0	3	0	.111	.111	.111
Tom Lampkin	C3	L	24	4	4	0	0	0	0	0	0	1	0	0	.000	.200	.000
Dan Firova	C1	R	31	1	0	0	0	0	0	0	0	0	0	0	—	—	—

R. Washington, 1 G at DH; D. Ramos, 2 G at 3B

Pitcher	T	Age	G	GS	CG	ShO	IP	H	HR	BB	SO	W-L	Sv	ERA
Greg Swindell	L	23	33	33	12	4	242.0	234	18	45	180	18-14	0	3.20
Tom Candiotti	R	30	31	31	11	1	216.2	225	15	53	137	14-8	0	3.28
John Farrell	R	25	31	30	4	0	210.1	216	15	67	92	14-10	0	4.24
Rich Yett	R	25	23	22	0	0	134.1	146	11	55	71	9-6	0	4.62
Scott Bailes	L	26	37	21	5	2	145.0	149	22	46	53	9-14	0	4.90
Rod Nichols	R	23	11	10	3	0	69.1	73	5	23	31	1-7	0	5.06
Rick Rodriguez	R	27	10	5	0	0	33.0	43	4	17	9	1-2	0	7.09
Doug Jones	R	31	51	0	0	0	83.1	69	1	16	72	3-4	37	2.27
Don Gordon	R	28	38	0	0	0	59.1	65	5	19	20	3-4	1	4.40
Brad Havens†	L	28	28	0	0	0	57.1	62	7	17	30	2-3	1	3.14
Jeff Dedmon	R	28	21	0	0	0	33.2	35	3	21	17	1-0	1	4.54
Bill Laskey	R	30	17	0	0	0	24.1	32	0	6	17	1-0	1	5.18
Bud Black†	L	31	16	7	0	0	59.0	59	6	23	44	2-3	1	5.03
Dan Schatzeder†	L	33	15	0	0	0	16.0	26	6	2	10	0-2	3	9.56
Chris Codiroli	R	30	14	2	0	0	19.1	32	2	10	12	0-4	1	9.31
Jon Perlman	R	31	10	0	0	0	19.2	25	0	11	10	0-2	0	5.49
Mike Walker	R	21	3	1	0	0	8.2	8	0	10	7	0-1	0	7.27
Jeff Kaiser	L	27	3	0	0	0	2.2	2	0	1	0	0-0	0	0.00

1988 Baltimore Orioles 7th AL East 54-107 .335 34.5 GB

Cal Ripken (0-6)/Frank Robinson (54-101)

Player	Gm by Position	B	Age	G	AB	R	H	2B	3B	HR	RBI	BB	SO	SB	Avg	OBP	Slg
Mickey Tettleton	C80	S	27	86	283	31	74	11	1	11	37	28	70	0	.261	.330	.424
Eddie Murray	1B103,DH58	S	32	161	603	75	171	27	2	28	84	75	78	5	.284	.361	.474
Billy Ripken	2B149,3B2	R	23	150	512	52	106	18	1	2	34	33	63	8	.207	.260	.258
Rene Gonzales	3B80,2B14,SS2*	R	27	92	237	13	51	6	0	2	15	13	32	2	.215	.263	.266
Cal Ripken Jr.	SS161	R	27	161	575	87	152	25	1	23	81	102	69	2	.264	.372	.431
Joe Orsulak	OF117	L	26	125	379	48	109	21	3	8	27	23	30	9	.288	.331	.422
Ken Gerhart	OF93,DH3	R	27	103	262	27	51	10	1	9	23	21	57	7	.195	.256	.344
Fred Lynn†	OF83,DH2	L	36	87	301	37	76	13	1	18	37	28	66	2	.252	.312	.482
Larry Sheets	OF76,DH50,1B3	L	28	136	452	38	104	19	1	10	47	42	72	1	.230	.302	.343
Jim Traber	1B57,DH30,OF11	L	26	103	352	25	78	6	0	10	45	19	42	1	.222	.261	.324
Rick Schu	3B72,DH9,1B4	R	26	89	270	22	69	9	4	4	20	21	49	6	.256	.316	.363
Terry Kennedy	C79	L	32	85	265	20	60	10	0	3	16	15	53	0	.226	.269	.298
Pete Stanicek	OF65,2B16,DH1	S	25	83	261	29	60	7	1	4	17	28	45	12	.230	.313	.310
Brady Anderson†	OF49	L	24	53	177	17	35	8	1	1	9	8	40	6	.198	.232	.271
Keith Hughes	OF31	L	24	41	108	10	21	4	2	2	14	16	27	1	.194	.294	.324
Craig Worthington	3B26	R	23	26	81	5	15	2	0	2	4	9	24	1	.185	.267	.284
Jeff Stone	OF21,DH1	L	27	26	61	4	10	1	0	0	1	4	11	4	.164	.215	.180
Jim Dwyer†	DH17,OF2	L	38	35	53	3	12	0	0	0	3	12	11	0	.226	.364	.226
Carl Nichols	C13,OF3	R	25	18	47	2	9	1	0	0	1	3	10	0	.191	.235	.213
Wade Rowdon	3B8,DH5,OF5	R	27	20	30	1	3	0	0	0	0	0	6	1	.100	.100	.100
Butch Davis	OF10,DH1	R	30	13	25	2	6	1	0	0	0	0	8	1	.240	.240	.280
Tito Landrum	OF12,DH1	R	33	13	24	2	3	0	1	0	2	4	6	0	.125	.250	.208

R. Gonzales, 1 G at 1B, 1 G at OF

Pitcher	T	Age	G	GS	CG	ShO	IP	H	HR	BB	SO	W-L	Sv	ERA
Jose Bautista	R	23	33	25	3	0	171.2	171	21	45	76	6-15	0	4.30
Jeff Ballard	L	24	25	25	6	1	153.1	167	15	42	41	8-12	0	4.40
Jay Tibbs	R	26	30	24	1	0	158.2	184	18	63	82	4-15	0	5.39
Mike Boddicker†	R	30	21	21	4	0	147.0	149	14	51	100	6-12	0	3.86
Oswaldo Peraza	R	25	19	15	1	0	86.0	98	10	37	61	5-7	0	5.55
Scott McGregor	L	34	4	4	0	0	17.1	27	3	7	10	0-3	0	8.83
Curt Schilling	R	21	4	4	0	0	14.2	22	3	10	4	0-3	0	9.82
Bob Milacki	R	23	3	3	1	1	25.0	9	1	9	18	2-0	0	0.72
Pete Harnisch	R	21	2	2	0	0	13.0	13	1	9	10	0-2	0	5.54
Dickie Noles	R	31	2	2	0	0	3.1	11	2	0	1	0-2	0	24.30
Gordon Dillard	L	24	2	1	0	0	3.0	3	1	4	2	0-0	0	6.00
Doug Sisk	R	30	52	0	0	0	94.1	109	3	45	26	3-3	0	3.72
Tom Niedenfuer	R	28	52	0	0	0	59.0	59	8	19	40	3-4	18	3.51
Mark Thurmond	L	31	43	6	0	0	74.2	80	10	27	29	1-8	3	4.58
Dave Schmidt	R	31	41	9	0	0	129.2	129	14	38	67	8-5	2	3.40
Mark Williamson	R	28	37	10	2	0	117.2	125	14	40	69	5-8	2	4.90
Don Aase	R	33	35	0	0	0	46.2	40	4	37	28	0-0	0	4.05
Mike Morgan	R	28	22	10	2	0	71.1	70	6	23	29	1-6	1	5.43
Gregg Olson	R	21	10	0	0	0	11.0	10	1	10	9	1-1	0	3.27
John Habyan	R	24	7	0	0	0	14.2	22	2	4	4	1-0	0	4.30
Bill Scherrer†	L	30	4	0	0	0	4.0	8	2	3	3	0-1	0	13.50

1988 Oakland Athletics 1st AL West 104-58 .642 —

Tony La Russa

Player	Gm by Position	B	Age	G	AB	R	H	2B	3B	HR	RBI	BB	SO	SB	Avg	OBP	Slg
Ron Hassey	C91,DH9	L	35	107	323	32	83	15	0	7	45	30	42	2	.257	.323	.368
Mark McGwire	1B154,OF1	R	24	155	550	87	143	22	1	32	99	76	117	0	.260	.352	.478
Glenn Hubbard	2B104,DH1	R	30	105	294	35	75	12	2	3	33	33	50	1	.255	.334	.340
Carney Lansford	3B143,1B9,DH1*	R	31	150	556	80	155	20	2	7	57	35	35	29	.279	.327	.360
Walt Weiss	SS147	S	24	147	452	44	113	17	3	3	39	35	56	4	.250	.312	.321
Jose Canseco	OF144,DH13	R	23	158	610	120	187	34	0	42	124	78	128	40	.307	.391	.569
Dave Henderson	OF143	R	29	146	507	100	154	38	1	24	94	47	92	2	.304	.363	.525
Stan Javier	OF115,1B4,DH2	S	24	125	397	49	102	13	3	2	35	32	63	20	.257	.313	.320
Don Baylor	DH80	R	39	92	264	28	58	7	0	7	34	34	44	0	.220	.332	.326
Dave Parker	DH61,OF34,1B1	L	37	101	377	43	97	18	1	12	55	32	70	0	.257	.314	.406
Terry Steinbach	C84,3B9,1B8*	R	26	104	351	42	93	19	1	9	51	33	47	3	.265	.334	.402
Luis Polonia	OF76,DH2	L	23	84	288	51	84	11	4	2	27	21	40	24	.292	.338	.378
Mike Gallego	2B83,SS42,3B16	R	27	129	277	38	58	8	0	2	20	34	53	2	.209	.298	.260
Tony Phillips	3B32,OF31,2B27*	S	29	79	212	32	43	8	4	2	17	36	50	0	.203	.320	.307
Doug Jennings	OF23,1B14,DH2	L	23	71	101	9	21	6	0	1	15	21	28	0	.208	.346	.297
Orlando Mercado	C16	R	26	16	24	3	3	0	0	1	1	3	8	0	.125	.222	.250
Matt Sinatro	C9	R	28	10	9	1	3	2	0	0	5	0	1	0	.333	.300	.556
Felix Jose	OF6	S	23	8	6	2	2	1	0	0	1	0	1	1	.333	.333	.500
Lance Blankenship	2B4	R	24	10	3	1	0	0	0	0	0	0	1	0	.000	.000	.000
Ed Jurak	3B1	R	30	3	1	1	0	0	0	0	0	0	0	0	.000	.000	.000

C. Lansford, 1 G at 2B; T. Steinbach, 7 G at DH, 1 G at OF; T. Phillips, 10 G at SS, 3 G at 1B

Pitcher	T	Age	G	GS	CG	ShO	IP	H	HR	BB	SO	W-L	Sv	ERA
Dave Stewart	R	31	37	37	14	2	275.2	240	14	110	192	21-12	0	3.23
Bob Welch	R	31	36	36	4	2	244.2	237	22	81	158	17-9	0	3.64
Storm Davis	R	26	33	33	1	0	201.2	211	16	91	127	16-7	0	3.70
Curt Young	L	28	26	26	1	0	156.1	162	23	50	69	11-8	0	4.14
Todd Burns	R	24	17	14	2	0	102.2	93	8	34	57	8-2	1	3.16
Steve Ontiveros	R	27	10	10	0	0	54.2	57	4	21	30	3-4	0	4.61
Dave Otto	L	23	3	2	0	0	10.0	9	0	6	7	0-0	0	1.80
Rick Bordi	R	29	2	2	0	0	7.2	6	0	5	6	0-1	0	4.70
Dennis Eckersley	R	33	60	0	0	0	72.2	52	5	11	70	4-2	45	2.35
Greg Cadaret	L	26	58	0	0	0	71.2	60	2	36	64	5-2	3	2.89
Rick Honeycutt	L	34	55	0	0	0	79.2	74	6	25	47	3-2	7	3.50
Gene Nelson	R	27	54	1	0	0	111.2	93	9	38	67	9-6	3	3.06
Eric Plunk	R	24	49	0	0	0	78.0	62	6	39	79	7-2	5	3.00
Jim Corsi	R	26	11	1	0	0	21.1	20	1	6	10	0-1	0	3.80
Jeff Shaver	R	24	1	0	0	0	1.0	0	0	0	0	0-0	0	0.00

1988 Minnesota Twins 2nd AL West 91-71 .562 13.0 GB

Tom Kelly

Player	Gm by Position	B	Age	G	AB	R	H	2B	3B	HR	RBI	BB	SO	SB	Avg	OBP	Slg
Tim Laudner	C109,DH4,1B3	R	30	117	375	38	94	18	1	13	54	36	89	0	.251	.316	.408
Kent Hrbek	1B105,DH37	L	28	143	510	75	159	31	0	25	76	67	54	0	.312	.387	.520
Steve Lombardozzi	2B90,SS12,3B5	R	28	103	287	34	60	15	2	3	27	35	48	2	.209	.295	.307
Gary Gaetti	3B115,DH5,SS2	R	29	133	468	66	141	29	2	28	88	36	85	7	.301	.353	.551
Greg Gagne	SS146,OF2,2B1	R	26	149	461	70	109	20	6	14	48	27	110	15	.236	.288	.397
Kirby Puckett	OF158	R	27	158	657	109	234	42	5	24	121	23	83	6	.356	.375	.545
Dan Gladden	OF140,P1,2B1*	R	30	141	576	91	155	32	6	11	62	46	74	28	.269	.325	.403
Randy Bush	OF109,DH17,1B6	L	29	136	394	51	103	20	3	14	51	58	49	8	.261	.365	.434
Gene Larkin	DH86,1B60	S	25	149	505	56	135	30	2	8	70	68	55	3	.267	.368	.382
Tom Herr†	2B73,DH3,SS2	S	32	86	304	42	80	16	0	1	21	40	47	10	.263	.349	.326
Al Newman	3B60,SS28,2B23	S	28	105	260	35	58	7	0	0	19	29	34	12	.223	.301	.250
John Moses	OF82,DH2	S	30	105	206	33	65	10	3	2	12	15	21	11	.316	.366	.422
Brian Harper	C48,DH5,3B2	R	28	60	166	15	49	11	1	3	20	10	12	0	.295	.344	.428
Mark Davidson	OF91,3B1	R	27	100	106	22	23	7	0	1	10	10	20	3	.217	.288	.311
Tom Nieto	C24	R	27	24	60	1	4	0	0	0	0	1	17	0	.067	.097	.067
Tom Brunansky†	OF13,DH1	R	27	14	49	5	9	1	0	1	6	7	11	1	.184	.286	.265
Jim Dwyer†	DH13	L	38	20	41	6	12	1	0	2	15	13	8	0	.293	.464	.463
John Christensen	OF17	R	27	23	38	5	10	4	0	0	5	3	5	0	.263	.349	.368
Eric Bullock	OF4,DH2	L	28	16	17	3	5	0	0	0	3	3	1	1	.294	.400	.294
Kelvin Torve	1B4	L	28	12	16	1	3	0	0	1	2	1	2	0	.188	.235	.375
Dwight Lowry	C5	L	30	7	7	0	0	0	0	0	0	0	2	0	.000	.000	.000
Doug Baker	SS9,2B1,3B1	S	27	11	7	1	0	0	0	0	0	0	5	0	.000	.000	.000

D. Gladden, 1 G at 3B

Pitcher	T	Age	G	GS	CG	ShO	IP	H	HR	BB	SO	W-L	Sv	ERA
Frank Viola	L	28	35	35	7	2	255.1	236	20	54	193	24-7	0	2.64
Bert Blyleven	R	37	33	33	7	0	207.1	240	21	51	145	10-17	0	5.43
Allan Anderson	L	24	30	30	3	1	202.1	199	14	37	83	16-9	0	2.45
Charlie Lea	R	31	24	23	0	0	130.0	156	19	50	72	7-7	0	4.85
Fred Toliver	R	27	21	19	0	0	114.2	116	8	52	69	7-6	0	4.24
Les Straker	R	28	16	14	1	1	82.2	86	8	25	23	2-5	1	3.92
Jeff Reardon	R	32	63	0	0	0	73.0	68	6	15	56	2-4	42	2.47
Juan Berenguer	R	33	57	1	0	0	100.0	74	7	61	99	8-4	2	3.96
Keith Atherton	R	29	49	0	0	0	74.0	65	10	22	43	7-5	3	3.41
Mark Portugal	R	25	26	0	0	0	57.2	60	11	17	31	3-3	3	4.53
German Gonzalez	R	26	16	0	0	0	21.1	20	4	8	19	0-0	1	3.38
Karl Best	R	29	11	0	0	0	12.0	15	1	7	9	0-0	0	6.00
Dan Schatzeder†	L	33	10	0	0	0	10.1	8	1	5	7	0-1	0	1.74
Roy Smith	R	26	9	4	0	0	37.0	29	3	12	17	3-0	0	2.68
Jim Winn	R	28	9	0	0	0	21.0	33	4	10	9	1-0	0	6.00
Joe Niekro	R	43	5	2	0	0	11.2	16	2	9	7	1-1	0	10.03
Mike Mason	L	29	5	0	0	0	6.2	8	1	9	7	0-1	0	10.80
Steve Carlton	L	43	4	1	0	0	9.2	20	5	5	5	0-1	0	16.76
Tippy Martinez	L	38	3	0	0	0	4.0	8	1	4	3	0-0	0	18.00
Dan Gladden	R	30	1	0	0	0	1.0	0	0	0	0	0-0	0	0.00

1988 Kansas City Royals 3rd AL West 84-77 .522 19.5 GB

John Wathan

Player	Gm by Position	B	Age	G	AB	R	H	2B	3B	HR	RBI	BB	SO	SB	Avg	OBP	Slg
Jamie Quirk	C79,1B1,3B1	L	33	84	196	22	47	7	1	8	25	28	41	1	.240	.333	.408
George Brett	1B124,DH33,SS1	L	35	157	589	90	180	42	3	24	103	82	51	14	.306	.389	.509
Frank White	2B148,DH3	R	37	150	537	48	126	25	1	8	58	21	67	7	.235	.266	.330
Kevin Seitzer	3B147,DH1,OF1	R	26	149	559	90	170	32	5	5	60	72	64	10	.304	.388	.406
Kurt Stillwell	SS124	S	23	128	459	63	115	28	5	10	53	47	76	6	.251	.322	.399
Willie Wilson	OF142	S	32	147	591	81	155	17	11	1	37	22	106	35	.262	.289	.333
Danny Tartabull	OF130,DH13	R	25	146	507	80	139	38	3	26	102	76	119	8	.274	.369	.515
Bo Jackson	OF121,DH1	R	25	124	439	63	108	16	4	25	68	25	146	27	.246	.287	.472
Bill Buckner†	DH42,1B21	L	38	89	242	18	62	14	0	3	34	13	19	3	.256	.290	.351
Pat Tabler†	DH40,OF37,1B7*	R	30	89	301	37	93	17	2	1	49	23	41	2	.309	.358	.389
Mike Macfarlane	C68	R	24	70	211	25	56	15	0	4	26	21	37	0	.265	.332	.393
Jim Eisenreich	OF64,DH13	L	29	82	202	26	44	8	1	1	19	6	31	9	.218	.236	.282
Bill Pecota	SS41,3B21,1B11*	R	28	90	178	25	37	3	3	1	15	18	34	7	.208	.286	.275
Brad Wellman	2B46,SS15,3B4*	R	28	71	107	11	29	3	0	1	6	6	23	1	.271	.322	.327
Larry Owen	C37	R	33	37	81	5	17	1	0	1	3	9	23	0	.210	.304	.259
Gary Thurman	OF32,DH1	R	23	35	66	6	11	1	0	0	2	4	20	5	.167	.214	.182
Steve Balboni†	1B13,DH6	R	31	21	63	2	9	2	0	2	5	1	20	0	.143	.156	.270
Scotti Madison	DH4,C4,OF3*	S	28	16	35	4	6	2	0	0	2	4	5	1	.171	.256	.229
Nick Capra	OF11	R	30	14	29	3	4	1	0	0	0	2	3	1	.138	.194	.172
Luis de los Santos	1B5,DH3	R	21	11	22	1	2	1	1	0	1	4	4	0	.091	.231	.227
Thad Bosley†	OF6,DH4	L	31	15	21	1	4	0	0	0	2	2	6	0	.190	.250	.190
Ed Hearn	C4,DH2	R	27	7	18	1	4	2	0	0	1	0	1	0	.222	.222	.333
Rey Palacios	C3,3B1	R	25	5	11	2	1	0	0	0	0	0	4	0	.091	.091	.091
Dave Owen	SS7	S	30	7	5	0	0	0	0	0	0	0	3	0	.000	.000	.000

P. Tabler, 1 G at 3B; B. Pecota, 9 G at OF, 4 G at DH, 3 G at 2B, 1 G at C; B. Wellman, 1 G at DH; S. Madison, 2 G at 1B

Pitcher	T	Age	G	GS	CG	ShO	IP	H	HR	BB	SO	W-L	Sv	ERA
Mark Gubicza	R	25	35	35	8	4	269.2	237	11	83	183	20-8	0	2.70
Bret Saberhagen	R	24	35	35	9	0	260.2	271	18	59	171	14-16	0	3.80
Charlie Leibrandt	L	31	35	35	7	2	243.0	244	20	62	125	13-12	0	3.19
Floyd Bannister	L	33	31	31	2	0	189.1	182	22	68	113	12-13	0	4.33
Ted Power†	R	33	22	12	2	2	80.1	98	7	30	44	5-6	0	5.94
Luis Aquino	R	24	7	5	1	1	29.0	33	1	17	11	1-0	0	2.79
Jose DeJesus	R	23	2	1	0	0	2.2	6	0	5	2	0-1	0	27.00
Steve Farr	R	31	62	1	0	0	82.2	74	5	30	72	5-4	20	2.50
Jeff Montgomery	R	26	45	0	0	0	62.2	54	6	30	47	7-2	1	3.45
Jerry Don Gleaton	L	30	42	0	0	0	38.0	33	2	17	29	0-4	3	3.55
Gene Garber	R	40	26	0	0	0	32.2	29	4	13	20	0-4	6	3.58
Dan Quisenberry†	R	35	20	0	0	0	25.1	32	0	5	9	0-1	1	3.55
Zip Sanchez	L	24	19	1	0	0	35.2	36	0	18	14	3-2	1	4.54
Bud Black†	L	31	17	0	0	0	22.0	23	2	11	19	2-1	0	4.91
Rick Anderson	R	31	7	3	0	0	34.0	41	3	9	9	2-1	0	4.24
Tom Gordon	R	20	5	2	0	0	15.2	16	1	7	18	0-2	0	5.17
Mark Lee	L	23	4	0	0	0	5.0	6	0	1	0	0-0	0	3.60

1988 California Angels 4th AL West 75-87 .463 29.0 GB

Cookie Rojas (75-79)/Moose Stubing (0-8)

Player	Gm by Position	B	Age	G	AB	R	H	2B	3B	HR	RBI	BB	SO	SB	Avg	OBP	Slg
Bob Boone	C121	R	40	122	352	38	104	17	0	5	39	29	26	2	.295	.352	.386
Wally Joyner	1B156	L	26	158	597	81	176	31	2	13	85	55	51	8	.295	.356	.419
Johnny Ray	2B104,OF40,DH6	S	31	153	602	75	184	42	7	6	83	36	38	4	.306	.345	.429
Jack Howell	3B152,OF2	L	26	154	500	59	127	32	2	16	63	46	130	2	.254	.323	.422
Dick Schofield	SS155	R	25	155	527	61	126	11	6	6	34	40	57	20	.239	.303	.317
Chili Davis	OF153,DH3	S	28	158	600	81	161	29	3	21	93	56	118	9	.268	.326	.432
Devon White	OF116	S	25	122	455	76	118	22	2	11	51	23	84	17	.259	.297	.389
Tony Armas	OF113,DH5	R	34	120	368	42	100	20	2	13	49	22	87	1	.272	.311	.443
Brian Downing	DH132	R	37	135	484	80	117	18	2	25	64	81	63	3	.242	.362	.442
Mark McLemore	2B63,3B5,DH1	S	23	77	233	38	56	11	2	2	16	25	28	13	.240	.312	.330
Darrell Miller	C53,OF8,DH1	R	30	70	140	21	31	4	1	2	7	9	29	2	.221	.292	.307
George Hendrick	OF24,1B12,DH3	R	38	69	127	12	31	1	0	3	19	7	20	0	.244	.283	.323
Jim Eppard	OF17,DH10,1B6	L	28	56	113	7	32	3	1	0	14	11	15	0	.283	.347	.327
Gus Polidor	SS25,3B22,2B3	R	26	54	81	4	12	3	0	0	4	3	11	0	.148	.179	.185
Chico Walker	OF17,2B7,3B2	S	30	33	78	8	12	1	0	0	2	6	15	2	.154	.214	.167
Thad Bosley†	OF26,DH2	L	31	35	75	9	21	5	0	0	7	6	12	1	.280	.321	.347
Butch Wynegar	C26	S	32	27	55	8	14	4	1	1	8	8	7	0	.255	.338	.418
Mike Brown	OF18	R	28	18	50	4	11	2	0	0	3	1	12	0	.220	.235	.260
Dante Bichette	OF21	R	24	21	46	1	12	2	0	0	8	0	7	0	.261	.240	.304
Bill Buckner†	DH11,1B1	L	38	19	43	1	9	0	0	0	9	4	0	2	.209	.271	.209
Junior Noboa	2B9,SS3,3B2	R	23	21	16	4	1	0	0	0	0	0	1	0	.063	.063	.063
Domingo Ramos†	3B8,OF1	R	30	10	15	3	2	0	0	0	0	0	0	0	.133	.133	.133
Doug Davis	C3,3B3	R	25	6	12	1	0	0	0	0	0	0	3	0	.000	.077	.000
Brian Dorsett	C7	R	27	7	11	0	1	0	0	0	2	1	5	0	.091	.167	.091
Joe Redfield	3B1	R	27	2	2	0	0	0	0	0	0	0	0	0	.000	.000	.000

Pitcher	T	Age	G	GS	CG	ShO	IP	H	HR	BB	SO	W-L	Sv	ERA
Mike Witt	R	27	34	34	12	2	249.2	263	14	87	133	13-16	0	4.15
Willie Fraser	R	24	34	32	2	0	194.2	203	33	80	86	12-13	0	5.41
Chuck Finley	L	25	31	31	2	0	194.1	191	15	82	111	9-15	0	4.17
Kirk McCaskill	R	27	23	23	4	2	146.1	155	9	61	98	8-6	0	4.31
Dan Petry	R	29	22	22	4	1	139.2	139	18	59	64	3-9	0	4.38
Terry Clark	R	27	15	15	2	1	94.0	120	8	31	39	6-6	0	5.07
Bryan Harvey	R	25	50	0	0	0	76.0	59	4	20	67	7-5	17	2.13
Greg Minton	R	36	44	0	0	0	79.0	67	1	34	46	4-5	7	2.85
Stew Cliburn	R	31	40	1	0	0	84.0	83	11	32	42	4-2	0	4.07
Sherm Corbett	L	25	34	0	0	0	45.2	47	2	23	28	2-1	1	4.14
DeWayne Buice	R	30	32	0	0	0	41.1	45	5	19	38	2-4	3	5.88
Donnie Moore	R	34	27	0	0	0	33.0	48	4	8	22	5-2	4	4.91
Ray Krawczyk	R	28	14	1	0	0	24.1	29	2	8	17	0-1	1	4.81
Jack Lazorko	R	32	10	3	0	0	37.2	37	5	16	19	0-1	0	3.35
Frank DiMichele	L	23	4	0	0	0	4.2	5	2	2	1	0-0	0	9.64
Rich Monteleone	R	25	3	0	0	0	4.1	4	0	1	3	0-0	0	0.00
Mike Cook	R	24	3	0	0	0	3.2	4	0	1	2	0-1	0	4.91
Vance Lovelace	L	24	3	0	0	0	1.1	2	1	3	0	0-0	0	13.50
Urbano Lugo	R	25	1	0	0	0	2.0	2	1	1	1	0-0	0	9.00

1988 Chicago White Sox 5th AL West 71-90 .441 32.5 GB

Jim Fregosi

Player	Gm by Position	B	Age	G	AB	R	H	2B	3B	HR	RBI	BB	SO	SB	Avg	OBP	Slg
Carlton Fisk	C74	R	40	76	253	37	70	8	1	19	50	37	40	0	.277	.377	.542
Greg Walker	1B98	L	28	99	377	45	93	22	1	8	42	29	77	0	.247	.304	.374
Fred Manrique	2B129,SS12	R	26	140	345	43	81	10	6	5	37	21	54	6	.235	.283	.342
Steve Lyons	3B128,OF14,2B4*	L	28	146	472	59	127	28	3	5	45	32	59	1	.269	.313	.373
Ozzie Guillen	SS156	L	24	156	566	58	148	16	7	0	39	25	40	25	.261	.294	.314
Dan Pasqua	OF112,1B7,DH2	L	26	129	422	48	96	16	2	20	50	46	100	1	.227	.307	.417
Dave Gallagher	OF95,DH2	R	27	101	347	59	105	15	3	5	31	29	40	5	.303	.354	.406
Daryl Boston	OF85,DH5	L	25	105	281	37	61	12	2	15	31	21	44	9	.217	.271	.434
Harold Baines	DH147,OF9	L	29	158	599	55	166	39	1	13	81	67	109	0	.277	.347	.411
Ivan Calderon	OF67,DH3	R	26	73	264	40	56	14	0	14	35	34	66	4	.212	.299	.424
Gary Redus†	OF68,DH2	R	31	77	262	42	69	10	4	6	34	33	52	26	.263	.342	.401
Donnie Hill	2B59,3B12,DH5	S	27	83	221	17	48	6	1	2	20	26	32	3	.217	.296	.281
Kenny Williams	OF38,3B32,DH3	R	24	73	220	18	35	4	2	8	28	10	64	6	.159	.221	.305
Mark Salas	C69,DH1	L	27	75	196	17	49	7	0	3	9	12	17	0	.250	.303	.332
Mike Diaz†	1B39,DH1	R	28	40	152	12	36	6	0	3	12	5	30	0	.237	.266	.336
Lance Johnson	OF31,DH1	L	24	33	124	11	23	4	1	0	6	6	11	6	.185	.223	.234
Ron Karkovice	C46	R	24	46	115	10	20	4	0	3	9	7	30	4	.174	.228	.287
Russ Morman	1B22,OF10,DH3	R	26	40	75	8	18	2	0	0	3	3	17	0	.240	.269	.267
Carlos Martinez	3B15	R	23	17	55	5	9	1	0	0	0	0	12	1	.164	.164	.182
Mike Woodard	2B14	L	28	18	45	3	6	0	1	0	4	1	5	1	.133	.170	.178
Kelly Paris	1B9,3B4	R	30	14	44	6	11	0	0	3	6	0	6	0	.250	.250	.455
Sap Randall	1B2,DH1,OF1	S	27	4	12	1	0	0	0	0	1	2	3	0	.000	.133	.000
Jerry Hairston		S	36	2	2	0	0	0	0	0	0	0	0	0	.000	.000	.000

S. Lyons, 2 G at C, 1 G at 1B

Pitcher	T	Age	G	GS	CG	ShO	IP	H	HR	BB	SO	W-L	Sv	ERA
Melido Perez	R	22	32	32	3	1	197.0	186	26	72	138	12-10	0	3.79
Jerry Reuss	L	39	32	29	2	0	183.0	183	15	43	73	13-9	0	3.44
Jack McDowell	R	22	26	26	1	0	158.2	147	12	68	84	5-10	0	3.97
Dave LaPoint†	L	28	25	25	1	1	161.1	151	10	47	79	10-11	0	3.40
Shawn Hillegas†	R	23	6	6	0	0	40.0	30	4	18	26	3-2	0	3.15
Ravelo Manzanillo	L	24	2	2	0	0	9.1	7	1	12	10	0-1	0	5.79
Adam Peterson	R	22	2	2	0	0	6.0	6	0	6	5	0-1	0	13.50
Bobby Thigpen	R	24	68	0	0	0	90.0	96	6	33	62	5-8	34	3.30
Ricky Horton†	L	28	52	9	1	0	109.1	120	6	36	28	6-10	2	4.86
Bill Long	R	28	47	18	3	0	174.0	187	21	43	77	8-11	2	4.03
John Davis	R	25	34	1	0	0	63.2	77	5	50	37	2-5	1	6.64
Steve Rosenberg	L	23	33	0	0	0	46.0	53	5	19	28	0-1	1	4.30
Jeff Bittiger	R	26	25	7	0	0	61.2	59	11	29	33	2-4	0	4.23
Donn Pall	R	26	17	0	0	0	28.2	39	1	8	16	0-2	0	3.45
Barry Jones†	R	25	17	0	0	0	26.0	15	3	17	17	2-2	1	2.42
Ken Patterson	L	23	9	2	0	0	20.2	25	2	7	8	0-2	1	4.79
John Pawlowski	R	24	6	0	0	0	14.0	20	2	3	10	1-0	0	8.36
Tom McCarthy	R	27	6	0	0	0	13.0	9	0	2	5	2-0	1	1.38
Carl Willis	R	27	6	0	0	0	12.0	17	3	7	6	0-0	0	8.25
Joel Davis	R	23	5	2	0	0	16.0	21	4	5	10	0-1	0	6.75
Jose Segura	R	25	4	0	0	0	8.2	19	1	8	2	0-0	0	13.50

1988 Texas Rangers 6th AL West 70-91 .435 33.5 GB

Bobby Valentine

Player	Gm by Position	B	Age	G	AB	R	H	2B	3B	HR	RBI	BB	SO	SB	Avg	OBP	Slg
Geno Petralli	C85,DH23,3B9*	S	28	129	351	35	99	14	2	7	36	41	52	0	.282	.356	.393
Pete O'Brien	1B155,DH1	L	30	156	547	57	149	24	1	16	71	72	73	1	.272	.352	.408
Curtis Wilkerson	2B87,SS24,3B11*	S	27	117	338	41	99	12	5	0	28	26	43	9	.293	.345	.358
Steve Buechele	3B153,2B2	R	26	155	503	68	126	21	4	16	58	65	79	2	.250	.342	.404
Scott Fletcher	SS139	R	29	140	515	59	142	19	4	0	47	62	34	8	.276	.364	.328
Ruben Sierra	OF153,DH1	S	22	156	615	77	156	32	2	23	91	44	91	18	.254	.301	.424
Oddibe McDowell	OF113,DH2	L	25	120	437	55	108	19	5	6	37	41	89	33	.247	.311	.355
Cecil Espy	OF98,DH12,SS3*	S	25	123	347	46	86	17	6	2	39	20	83	33	.248	.288	.349
Larry Parrish†	DH67	R	34	68	248	22	47	9	1	7	26	20	79	0	.190	.253	.319
Pete Incaviglia	OF93,DH20	R	24	116	418	59	104	19	3	22	54	39	153	6	.249	.321	.467
Mike Stanley	C64,DH18,1B7*	R	25	94	249	21	57	8	0	3	27	37	62	0	.229	.323	.297
Jerry Browne	2B70,DH1	S	22	73	214	26	49	9	2	1	17	25	32	7	.229	.308	.304
Bob Brower	OF59,DH13	R	28	82	201	29	45	7	0	1	11	27	38	10	.224	.316	.274
Jeff Kunkel	2B28,SS19,3B10*	R	26	55	154	14	35	8	3	2	15	4	35	0	.227	.250	.357
Jim Sundberg†	C36	R	37	38	91	13	26	4	0	4	13	5	17	0	.286	.323	.462
Barbaro Garbey	OF8,DH7,1B7*	R	31	30	62	4	12	2	0	0	5	4	11	0	.194	.239	.226
James Steels	OF17,DH7,1B6	L	27	36	53	4	10	1	0	0	5	0	15	2	.189	.185	.208
Chad Kreuter	C16	S	23	16	51	3	14	2	1	1	5	7	13	0	.275	.362	.412
Steve Kemp	DH7,OF5,1B1	L	33	16	36	2	8	0	0	0	2	2	9	1	.222	.256	.222
Kevin Reimer	DH5,OF1	L	24	12	25	2	3	0	0	1	2	0	6	0	.120	.115	.240
Larry See	DH7,C2,1B2*	R	28	13	23	0	3	0	0	0	0	1	8	0	.130	.167	.130

G. Petralli, 2 G at 1B, 2 G at 2B; C. Wilkerson, 1 G at DH; C. Espy, 2 G at C, 1 G at 1B, 1 G at 2B; M. Stanley, 2 G at 3B; J. Kunkel, 6 G at OF, 3 G at DH, 1 G at P; B. Garbey, 3 G at 3B; L. See, 1 G at 3B

Pitcher	T	Age	G	GS	CG	ShO	IP	H	HR	BB	SO	W-L	Sv	ERA
Charlie Hough	R	40	34	34	10	0	252.0	202	20	126	174	15-16	0	3.32
Paul Kilgus	L	26	32	32	5	3	203.1	190	18	71	88	12-15	0	4.16
Jose Guzman	R	25	30	30	6	2	206.2	180	20	82	157	11-13	0	3.70
Jeff Russell	R	26	34	24	5	0	188.2	183	15	66	88	10-9	0	3.82
Bobby Witt	R	24	22	22	13	2	174.1	134	13	101	148	8-10	0	3.92
Ray Hayward	L	27	12	12	1	1	62.2	63	6	35	37	4-6	0	5.46
Kevin Brown	R	23	4	4	1	0	23.1	33	2	8	12	1-1	0	4.24
Mitch Williams	L	23	67	0	0	0	68.0	48	4	47	61	2-7	18	4.63
Dale Mohorcic†	R	32	43	0	0	0	52.0	62	6	20	25	2-6	5	4.85
Craig McMurtry	R	28	32	0	0	0	60.0	37	5	24	35	3-3	3	2.25
Ed Vande Berg	L	29	26	0	0	0	37.0	44	2	11	18	2-2	2	4.14
Jose Cecena	R	24	22	0	0	0	26.1	20	2	23	27	0-0	1	4.78
Guy Hoffman	L	31	11	0	0	0	22.1	22	5	8	9	0-0	0	5.24
Dwayne Henry	R	26	11	0	0	0	10.1	15	1	9	10	0-1	1	8.71
DeWayne Vaughn	R	28	8	0	0	0	15.1	24	4	4	8	0-0	0	7.63
Cecilio Guante†	R	28	7	0	0	0	4.2	8	1	4	4	0-0	1	1.93
Mike Jeffcoat	L	28	5	2	0	0	10.0	19	1	5	5	0-2	0	11.70
Tony Fossas	L	30	5	0	0	0	5.2	11	0	2	0	0-0	0	4.76
Steve Wilson	L	23	3	0	0	0	7.2	7	1	4	1	0-0	0	5.87
Scott May	R	26	3	1	0	0	7.1	8	3	4	4	0-0	0	8.59
Jeff Kunkel	R	26	1	0	0	0	1.0	0	0	0	1	0-0	0	0.00

1988 Seattle Mariners 7th AL West 68-93 .422 35.5 GB

Dick Williams (23-33)/Jimmy Snyder (45-60)

Player	Gm by Position	B	Age	G	AB	R	H	2B	3B	HR	RBI	BB	SO	SB	Avg	OBP	Slg
Scott Bradley	C85,DH4,OF4*	L	28	103	335	45	86	17	1	4	33	17	16	1	.257	.295	.349
Alvin Davis	1B115,DH25	L	27	140	478	67	141	24	1	18	69	95	53	1	.295	.412	.462
Harold Reynolds	2B158	S	27	158	598	61	169	26	11	4	41	51	51	35	.283	.340	.383
Jim Presley	3B146,DH4	R	26	150	544	50	125	26	0	14	62	36	114	3	.230	.280	.355
Rey Quinones	SS135,DH4	R	24	140	499	63	124	30	3	12	52	23	71	0	.248	.284	.393
Mickey Brantley	OF147	R	27	149	577	76	152	25	4	15	56	26	64	18	.263	.296	.399
Henry Cotto	OF120,DH2	R	27	133	386	50	100	18	1	8	33	23	53	27	.259	.302	.373
Glenn Wilson†	OF75,DH2	R	29	78	284	28	71	10	1	3	17	15	52	1	.250	.286	.324
Ken Phelps†	DH64,1B3	L	33	72	190	37	54	8	0	14	32	51	35	1	.284	.434	.547
Steve Balboni†	DH56,1B40	R	31	97	350	44	88	15	1	21	61	23	67	0	.251	.298	.480
Dave Valle	C84,DH3,1B1	R	27	93	290	29	67	15	2	10	50	18	38	0	.231	.295	.400
Darnell Coles†	OF47,DH7,1B1	R	26	55	195	32	57	10	1	10	34	17	26	3	.292	.356	.508
Jay Buhner†	OF59	R	23	60	192	28	43	13	1	10	25	25	68	1	.224	.320	.458
Mike Kingery	OF44,1B10	L	27	57	123	21	25	6	0	1	9	19	23	3	.203	.313	.276
Rich Renteria	SS11,3B5,2B4	R	26	31	88	6	18	9	0	0	6	2	8	1	.205	.222	.307
Mario Diaz	SS21,2B4,1B1*	R	26	28	72	6	22	5	0	0	9	3	5	0	.306	.329	.375
Bruce Fields	OF23,DH6	L	27	39	67	8	18	5	0	1	5	4	11	0	.269	.310	.388
Dave Hengel	DH12,OF12	R	26	26	60	3	10	1	0	2	7	1	15	0	.167	.177	.283
Greg Briley	OF11	L	23	13	36	6	9	2	0	1	4	5	6	0	.250	.333	.389
Edgar Martinez	3B13	R	25	14	32	0	9	4	0	0	5	4	7	0	.281	.351	.406
Bill McGuire	C9	R	24	9	16	1	3	0	0	0	2	3	2	0	.188	.316	.188
John Rabb	DH5,OF2,1B1	R	28	9	14	2	5	2	0	0	4	0	1	0	.357	.357	.500
Brick Smith	1B4	R	29	4	10	1	1	0	0	0	1	0	1	0	.100	.100	.100

S. Bradley, 3 G at 3B, 2 G at 1B; M. Diaz, 1 G at 3B

Pitcher	T	Age	G	GS	CG	ShO	IP	H	HR	BB	SO	W-L	Sv	ERA
Mark Langston	L	27	35	35	9	3	261.1	222	32	110	235	15-11	0	3.34
Mike Moore	R	28	37	32	9	3	228.2	196	24	63	182	9-15	1	3.78
Bill Swift	R	26	38	24	6	1	174.2	199	10	65	47	8-12	0	4.59
Scott Bankhead	R	24	21	21	2	1	135.0	115	8	38	102	7-9	0	3.07
Mike Campbell	R	24	20	20	2	0	114.2	128	18	43	63	6-10	0	5.89
Steve Trout	L	30	15	13	0	0	56.1	86	6	31	14	4-7	0	7.83
Erik Hanson	R	23	6	6	0	0	41.2	35	4	12	36	2-3	0	3.24
Terry Taylor	R	23	5	5	0	0	23.0	26	2	11	9	0-1	0	6.26
Mike Jackson	R	23	62	0	0	0	99.1	74	10	43	76	6-5	4	2.63
Jerry Reed	R	32	46	0	0	0	86.1	82	8	33	48	1-1	1	3.96
Mike Schooler	R	25	40	0	0	0	48.1	45	4	24	54	5-8	15	3.54
Rod Scurry	L	32	39	0	0	0	31.1	32	6	18	33	0-2	2	4.02
Bill Wilkinson	L	23	30	0	0	0	31.0	28	3	15	25	2-2	2	3.48
Julio Solano	R	28	17	0	0	0	22.0	22	3	12	10	0-0	3	4.09
Gene Walter†	L	27	16	0	0	0	26.1	21	0	15	13	1-0	0	5.13
Edwin Nunez†	R	25	14	3	0	0	29.1	45	4	14	19	1-4	0	7.98
Dennis Powell	L	24	12	2	0	0	18.2	29	2	11	15	1-3	0	8.68

»1988 New York Mets 1st NL East 100-60 .625 —

Davey Johnson

Player	Gm by Position	B	Age	G	AB	R	H	2B	3B	HR	RBI	BB	SO	SB	Avg	OBP	Slg
Gary Carter	C119,1B10,3B1	R	34	130	455	39	110	16	2	11	46	34	52	0	.242	.301	.358
Keith Hernandez	1B93	L	34	95	348	43	96	16	0	11	55	31	57	2	.276	.333	.417
Wally Backman	2B92	S	28	99	294	44	89	12	0	0	17	41	49	9	.303	.388	.344
Howard Johnson	3B131,SS52	S	27	148	495	85	114	21	1	24	68	86	104	23	.230	.343	.422
Kevin Elster	SS148	R	23	149	406	41	87	11	1	9	37	35	47	2	.214	.282	.313
Darryl Strawberry	OF150	L	26	153	543	101	146	27	3	39	101	85	127	29	.269	.366	.545
Kevin McReynolds	OF147	R	28	147	552	82	159	30	2	27	99	38	56	21	.288	.336	.496
Lenny Dykstra	OF112	L	25	126	429	57	116	19	3	8	33	30	43	30	.270	.321	.385
Mookie Wilson	OF104	S	32	112	378	61	112	17	5	8	41	27	63	15	.296	.345	.431
Dave Magadan	1B71,3B48	L	25	112	314	39	87	15	0	1	35	60	39	0	.277	.393	.334
Tim Teufel	2B84,1B3	R	29	90	273	35	64	20	0	4	31	29	41	0	.234	.306	.352
Mackey Sasser	C42,3B1,OF1	L	25	60	123	9	35	10	1	1	17	6	9	0	.285	.313	.407
Lee Mazzilli	OF18,1B16	S	33	68	116	9	17	2	0	0	12	12	16	4	.147	.227	.164
Gregg Jefferies	3B20,2B10	S	20	29	109	19	35	8	2	6	17	8	10	5	.321	.364	.596
Barry Lyons	C32,1B1	R	28	50	91	5	21	7	1	0	11	3	12	0	.231	.253	.330
Keith Miller	2B16,SS8,3B6*	R	25	40	70	9	15	1	1	1	5	6	10	0	.214	.276	.300
Mark Carreon	OF4	R	24	7	9	5	5	2	0	1	1	2	1	0	.556	.636	1.111

K. Miller, 1 G at OF

Pitcher	T	Age	G	GS	CG	ShO	IP	H	HR	BB	SO	W-L	Sv	ERA
Dwight Gooden	R	23	34	34	10	3	248.1	242	8	57	175	18-9	0	3.19
Ron Darling	R	27	34	34	7	4	240.2	218	24	60	161	17-9	0	3.25
Sid Fernandez	L	25	31	31	1	1	187.0	127	15	70	189	12-10	0	3.03
Bobby Ojeda	L	30	29	29	5	5	190.1	158	6	33	133	10-13	0	2.88
David Cone	R	25	35	28	8	4	231.1	178	10	80	213	20-3	0	2.22
David West	L	23	2	1	0	0	6.0	6	0	3	3	1-0	0	3.00
Roger McDowell	R	27	62	0	0	0	89.0	80	1	31	46	5-5	16	2.63
Randy Myers	L	25	55	0	0	0	68.0	45	5	17	69	7-3	26	1.72
Terry Leach	R	34	52	0	0	0	92.0	95	5	24	51	7-2	3	2.54
Gene Walter†	L	27	19	0	0	0	16.2	21	0	11	14	0-1	0	3.78
Bob McClure†	L	36	14	0	0	0	11.0	12	1	2	7	1-0	1	4.09
Jeff Innis	R	25	12	0	0	0	19.0	19	0	2	14	1-1	0	1.89
Rick Aguilera	R	26	11	3	0	0	24.2	29	2	10	16	0-4	0	6.93
Edwin Nunez†	R	25	10	0	0	0	14.0	21	1	3	8	1-0	0	4.50
John Mitchell	R	22	1	0	0	0	1.0	2	0	1	1	0-0	0	0.00

1988 Pittsburgh Pirates 2nd NL East 85-75 .531 15.0 GB

Jim Leyland

Player	Gm by Position	B	Age	G	AB	R	H	2B	3B	HR	RBI	BB	SO	SB	Avg	OBP	Slg
Mike LaValliere	C114	L	27	120	352	24	92	18	0	2	47	50	34	3	.261	.353	.330
Sid Bream	1B138	L	27	148	462	50	122	37	0	10	65	47	64	9	.264	.328	.409
Jose Lind	2B153	R	24	154	611	82	160	24	4	2	49	42	75	15	.262	.308	.324
Bobby Bonilla	3B159	S	25	159	584	87	160	32	7	24	100	85	82	3	.274	.366	.476
Rafael Belliard	SS117,2B3	R	26	122	286	28	61	0	4	0	11	26	47	7	.213	.288	.241
Andy Van Slyke	OF152	L	27	154	587	101	169	23	15	25	100	57	126	30	.288	.345	.506
Barry Bonds	OF136	L	23	144	538	97	152	30	5	24	58	72	82	17	.283	.368	.491
R.J. Reynolds	OF95	S	29	130	323	35	80	14	2	6	51	20	62	15	.248	.288	.359
Darnell Coles†	OF55,1B1,3B1	R	26	68	211	20	49	13	1	5	36	20	41	1	.232	.299	.374
Al Pedrique	SS46,3B5	R	27	50	128	7	23	5	0	0	4	8	17	0	.180	.234	.219
Glenn Wilson†	OF35	R	29	37	126	11	34	8	0	2	15	3	18	0	.270	.288	.381
Junior Ortiz	C40	R	28	49	118	8	33	6	0	2	18	9	9	1	.280	.336	.381
John Cangelosi	OF24,P1	S	25	75	118	18	30	4	1	0	8	17	16	9	.254	.353	.305
Felix Fermin	SS43	R	24	43	87	9	24	0	2	0	2	8	10	3	.276	.354	.322
Randy Milligan	1B25,OF1	R	26	40	82	10	18	5	0	3	8	20	24	1	.220	.379	.390
Mike Diaz†	OF19,1B6,C1	R	28	47	74	6	17	3	0	0	5	16	13	0	.230	.367	.270
Tom Prince	C28	R	23	29	74	3	13	2	0	0	6	4	15	0	.176	.218	.203
Gary Redus†	OF19	R	31	30	71	12	14	2	0	2	4	15	19	5	.197	.341	.310
Ken Oberkfell†	2B11,SS3,3B2*	L	32	20	54	7	12	2	0	0	2	5	6	0	.222	.288	.259
Orestes Destrade	1B8	S	26	36	47	2	7	1	0	1	3	5	17	0	.149	.226	.234
Denny Gonzalez	SS14,2B4,3B2	R	24	24	32	5	6	1	0	0	1	6	10	0	.188	.316	.219
Benny Distefano	1B5,OF2	L	26	16	29	6	10	3	1	1	6	3	4	0	.345	.394	.621
Tommy Gregg†	OF6	L	24	14	15	4	3	1	0	1	3	1	4	0	.200	.235	.467
Dave Hostetler	1B4,C1	R	32	6	8	0	2	0	0	0	0	0	3	0	.250	.250	.250
Ruben Rodriguez	C2	R	23	2	5	1	1	0	1	0	1	0	2	0	.200	.200	.600

K. Oberkfell, 1 G at 1B

Pitcher	T	Age	G	GS	CG	ShO	IP	H	HR	BB	SO	W-L	Sv	ERA
Doug Drabek	R	25	33	32	3	1	219.1	194	21	50	127	15-7	0	3.08
Bob Walk	R	31	32	32	1	1	212.2	183	6	65	81	12-10	0	2.71
John Smiley	L	23	34	32	5	1	205.0	185	15	46	129	13-11	0	3.25
Mike Dunne	R	25	30	28	1	0	170.0	163	15	88	70	7-11	0	3.92
Brian Fisher	R	26	33	22	1	1	146.1	157	13	57	66	8-10	1	4.61
Dave LaPoint†	L	28	8	8	1	0	52.0	54	4	10	19	4-2	0	2.77
Rick Reed	R	23	2	2	0	0	12.0	10	1	2	6	1-0	0	3.00
Jeff Robinson	R	27	75	0	0	0	124.2	113	6	39	87	11-5	9	3.03
Jim Gott	R	28	67	0	0	0	77.1	68	9	22	76	6-6	34	3.49
Bob Kipper	L	23	50	0	0	0	65.0	54	7	26	39	2-6	0	3.74
Barry Jones†	R	25	42	0	0	0	56.1	57	3	21	31	1-1	2	3.04
Dave Rucker	L	30	31	0	0	0	28.1	39	2	9	16	0-2	0	4.76
Scott Medvin	R	26	17	0	0	0	27.2	23	1	9	16	3-0	0	4.88
Vicente Palacios	R	24	7	3	0	0	24.1	28	3	15	15	1-2	0	6.66
Randy Kramer	R	27	5	1	0	0	10.0	12	1	1	7	1-2	0	5.40
Morris Madden	L	27	5	0	0	0	5.2	5	0	7	3	0-0	0	0.00
John Cangelosi	L	25	1	0	0	0	2.0	1	0	0	0	0-0	0	0.00
Miguel Garcia	L	21	1	0	0	0	2.0	3	1	2	2	0-0	0	4.50

1988 Montreal Expos 3rd NL East 81-81 .500 20.0 GB

Buck Rodgers

Player	Gm by Position	B	Age	G	AB	R	H	2B	3B	HR	RBI	BB	SO	SB	Avg	OBP	Slg
Nelson Santovenia	C86,1B1	R	26	92	309	26	73	20	2	8	41	24	77	2	.236	.294	.392
Andres Galarraga	1B156	R	27	157	609	99	184	42	8	29	92	39	153	13	.302	.352	.540
Tom Foley	2B89,SS32,3B9	L	28	127	377	33	100	21	3	5	43	30	49	2	.265	.319	.377
Tim Wallach	3B153,2B1	R	30	159	592	52	152	32	5	12	69	38	88	2	.257	.302	.389
Luis Rivera	SS116	R	24	123	371	35	83	17	3	4	30	24	69	3	.224	.271	.318
Hubie Brooks	OF149	R	31	151	588	61	164	35	2	20	90	35	108	7	.279	.318	.447
Tim Raines	OF108	S	28	109	429	66	116	19	7	12	48	53	44	33	.270	.350	.431
Otis Nixon	OF82	S	29	90	271	47	66	8	2	0	15	28	42	46	.244	.312	.288
Mitch Webster†	OF71	S	29	81	259	33	66	5	2	2	13	36	37	12	.255	.354	.313
Rex Hudler	2B41,SS27,OF4	R	27	77	216	38	59	14	2	4	14	10	34	29	.273	.303	.412
Dave Martinez†	OF60	L	23	63	191	24	49	3	5	2	12	17	48	16	.257	.316	.356
Mike Fitzgerald	C47,OF4	R	27	63	155	17	42	6	1	5	23	19	22	2	.271	.347	.419
Tracy Jones†	OF43	R	27	53	141	20	47	5	1	2	15	12	12	9	.333	.390	.426
Jeff Reed†	C39	L	25	43	123	10	27	3	2	0	9	13	22	1	.220	.292	.276
Casey Candaele†	2B35	S	27	36	116	9	20	5	1	0	4	10	11	1	.172	.238	.233
Wallace Johnson	1B13,2B1	S	31	86	94	7	29	5	1	0	3	12	15	0	.309	.387	.383
Graig Nettles	3B12,1B5	L	43	80	93	5	16	4	0	1	14	9	19	0	.172	.240	.247
Johnny Paredes	2B28,OF1	R	25	35	91	6	17	2	0	1	10	9	17	5	.187	.282	.242
Herm Winningham†	OF30	L	26	47	90	10	21	2	1	0	6	12	18	4	.233	.320	.278
Jeff Huson	SS15,2B2,3B1*	L	23	20	42	7	13	2	0	0	3	4	3	2	.310	.370	.357
Dave Engle	C9,OF4,3B1	R	31	34	37	4	8	3	0	0	1	5	5	0	.216	.310	.297
Tom O'Malley	3B7	L	27	14	27	3	7	0	0	0	2	3	4	0	.259	.323	.259
Wilfredo Tejada	C7	R	25	8	15	1	4	2	0	0	2	0	4	0	.267	.250	.400

J. Huson, 1 G at OF

Pitcher	T	Age	G	GS	CG	ShO	IP	H	HR	BB	SO	W-L	Sv	ERA
Dennis Martinez	R	33	34	34	9	2	235.1	215	21	55	120	15-13	0	2.72
Bryn Smith	R	32	32	32	1	0	198.0	179	15	32	122	12-10	0	3.00
Pascual Perez	R	31	27	27	4	2	188.0	133	15	44	131	12-8	0	2.44
John Dopson	R	24	26	26	1	0	168.2	150	15	58	101	3-11	0	3.04
Brian Holman	R	23	18	16	1	1	100.1	101	3	34	58	4-8	0	3.23
Floyd Youmans	R	24	14	13	1	1	84.0	64	8	41	54	3-6	0	3.21
Randy Johnson	L	24	4	4	1	0	26.0	23	3	7	25	3-0	0	2.42
Andy McGaffigan	R	31	63	0	0	0	91.1	81	4	37	71	6-0	4	2.76
Jeff Parrett	R	26	61	0	0	0	91.2	66	8	45	62	12-4	6	2.65
Tim Burke	R	29	61	0	0	0	82.0	84	7	25	42	3-5	18	3.40
Joe Hesketh	L	29	60	0	0	0	72.2	63	1	35	64	4-3	9	2.85
Neal Heaton	L	28	32	11	0	0	97.1	98	14	43	43	3-10	2	4.99
Bob McClure†	L	36	19	0	0	0	19.0	23	3	6	12	1-3	2	6.16
Randy St. Claire†	R	27	6	0	0	0	7.1	11	2	5	6	0-0	0	6.14
Mike Smith	R	27	5	0	0	0	8.2	6	0	5	4	0-0	1	3.12
Tim Barrett	R	27	4	0	0	0	9.1	10	2	2	5	0-0	1	5.79
Richard Sauveur	L	24	4	0	0	0	3.0	3	1	2	3	0-0	0	6.00

1988 Chicago Cubs 4th NL East 77-85 .475 24.0 GB

Don Zimmer

Player	Gm by Position	B	Age	G	AB	R	H	2B	3B	HR	RBI	BB	SO	SB	Avg	OBP	Slg
Damon Berryhill	C90	S	24	95	309	19	80	19	1	7	38	17	56	1	.259	.295	.395
Mark Grace	1B133	L	24	134	486	65	144	23	4	7	57	60	43	3	.296	.371	.403
Ryne Sandberg	2B153	R	28	155	618	77	163	23	8	19	69	54	91	25	.264	.322	.419
Vance Law	3B150,OF1	R	31	151	556	73	163	29	2	11	78	55	79	1	.293	.358	.412
Shawon Dunston	SS151	R	25	155	575	69	143	23	6	9	56	16	108	30	.249	.271	.357
Andre Dawson	OF147	R	33	157	591	78	179	31	8	24	79	37	73	12	.303	.344	.504
Rafael Palmeiro	OF147,1B5	L	23	152	580	75	178	41	5	8	53	38	34	12	.307	.349	.436
Darrin Jackson	OF74	R	24	100	188	29	50	11	3	6	20	5	28	4	.266	.287	.452
Mitch Webster†	OF65	S	29	70	264	36	70	11	6	4	26	19	50	10	.265	.319	.398
Dave Martinez†	OF72	L	23	75	256	27	65	10	1	4	34	21	46	7	.254	.311	.348
Jody Davis†	C74	R	31	88	249	19	57	9	0	6	33	29	51	0	.229	.309	.337
Manny Trillo	1B24,3B17,2B13*	R	37	76	164	15	41	5	0	1	14	8	32	2	.250	.283	.299
Doug Dascenzo	OF20	S	24	26	75	9	16	3	0	0	4	9	4	6	.213	.298	.253
Leon Durham†	1B20	L	30	24	73	10	16	6	1	3	6	9	20	0	.219	.305	.452
Gary Varsho	OF18	L	27	46	73	6	20	3	0	0	5	1	6	5	.274	.280	.315
Jerry Mumphrey	OF4	S	35	63	66	3	9	2	0	0	9	7	16	0	.136	.219	.167
Angel Salazar	SS29,2B2,3B1	R	26	34	60	4	15	1	1	0	1	1	11	0	.250	.262	.300
Jim Sundberg†	C20	R	37	24	54	8	13	1	0	2	9	8	15	0	.241	.333	.370
Rolando Roomes	OF5	R	26	17	16	3	3	0	0	0	0	0	4	0	.188	.188	.188
Rick Wrona	C2	R	24	4	6	0	0	0	0	0	0	0	1	0	.000	.000	.000
Dave Meier	3B1	R	28	2	5	0	2	0	0	0	1	0	1	0	.400	.400	.400

M. Trillo, 7 G at SS

Pitcher	T	Age	G	GS	CG	ShO	IP	H	HR	BB	SO	W-L	Sv	ERA
Greg Maddux	R	22	34	34	9	3	249.0	230	13	81	140	18-8	0	3.18
Rick Sutcliffe	R	32	32	32	12	2	226.0	232	18	70	144	13-14	0	3.86
Jamie Moyer	L	25	34	30	3	1	202.0	212	20	55	121	9-15	0	3.48
Calvin Schiraldi	R	26	29	27	2	1	166.1	166	13	63	140	9-13	1	4.38
Al Nipper	R	29	22	12	0	0	80.0	72	9	34	27	2-4	1	3.04
Mike Harkey	R	21	5	5	0	0	34.2	33	0	15	18	0-3	0	2.60
Kevin Blankenship†	R	25	1	1	0	0	5.0	7	2	1	4	1-0	0	7.20
Bob Tewksbury	R	27	1	1	0	0	3.1	6	1	2	1	0-0	0	8.10
Frank DiPino	L	31	63	0	0	0	90.1	102	6	32	69	2-3	6	4.98
Goose Gossage	R	36	46	0	0	0	43.2	50	3	15	30	4-4	13	4.33
Les Lancaster	R	26	44	3	1	0	85.2	89	4	34	36	4-6	5	3.78
Pat Perry†	L	29	35	0	0	0	38.0	40	5	7	24	2-2	1	3.32
Jeff Pico	R	22	29	13	3	2	112.2	108	6	37	57	6-7	1	4.15
Mike Capel	R	26	22	0	0	0	29.1	34	5	13	19	2-1	0	4.91
Mike Bielecki	R	28	19	5	0	0	48.1	55	4	16	33	2-2	0	3.35
Drew Hall	L	25	19	0	0	0	22.1	26	4	9	22	1-1	1	7.66
Scott Sanderson	R	31	11	0	0	0	15.1	13	1	3	6	1-2	0	5.28
Bill Landrum	R	30	7	0	0	0	12.1	19	1	3	6	1-0	0	5.84

1988 St. Louis Cardinals 5th NL East 76-86 .469 25.0 GB

Whitey Herzog

Player	Gm by Position	B	Age	G	AB	R	H	2B	3B	HR	RBI	BB	SO	SB	Avg	OBP	Slg
Tony Pena	C142,1B3	R	31	149	505	55	133	23	1	10	51	33	60	6	.263	.308	.372
Bob Horner	1B57	R	30	60	206	15	53	9	1	3	33	32	23	0	.257	.348	.354
Luis Alicea	2B91	S	22	93	297	20	63	10	4	1	24	25	32	1	.212	.276	.283
Terry Pendleton	3B101	S	27	110	391	44	99	20	2	6	53	21	51	3	.253	.293	.361
Ozzie Smith	SS150	S	33	153	575	80	155	27	1	3	51	74	43	57	.270	.350	.336
Vince Coleman	OF150	S	26	153	616	77	160	20	10	3	38	49	111	81	.260	.313	.339
Tom Brunansky†	OF143	R	27	143	523	69	128	22	4	22	79	79	82	16	.245	.345	.428
Willie McGee	OF135	S	29	137	562	73	164	24	6	3	50	32	84	41	.292	.329	.372
Jose Oquendo	2B69,3B47,SS17*	S	24	148	451	36	125	10	1	7	46	52	40	4	.277	.350	.350
Tom Pagnozzi	C28,1B28,3B5	R	25	81	195	17	55	9	0	0	15	11	32	0	.282	.319	.328
Pedro Guerrero†	1B37,OF7	R	32	44	149	16	40	7	1	5	30	21	26	2	.268	.358	.430
Curt Ford	OF40,1B7	L	27	91	128	11	25	6	0	1	18	8	26	6	.195	.239	.266
Mike Laga	1B37	L	28	41	100	5	13	0	0	1	4	2	21	0	.130	.147	.160
Jose DeLeon	P34,OF1	R	27	35	72	1	10	1	0	0	2	1	19	0	.139	.162	.153
Tom Lawless	3B24,OF6,2B5*	R	31	54	65	9	10	2	1	1	3	7	9	6	.154	.236	.262
Denny Walling†	OF11,3B5,1B1	L	34	19	58	3	13	3	0	0	1	2	7	1	.224	.250	.276
Steve Lake	C19	R	31	36	54	5	15	3	0	1	4	3	15	0	.278	.339	.389
Tim Jones	SS9,2B8,3B1	L	25	31	52	2	14	0	0	0	3	4	10	4	.269	.321	.269
Tom Herr†	2B15	S	32	15	50	4	13	0	0	1	3	11	4	3	.260	.393	.320
Mike Fitzgerald	1B12	R	24	13	46	4	9	1	0	0	1	0	9	0	.196	.213	.217
Jim Lindeman	OF12,1B3	R	26	17	43	3	9	1	0	2	7	2	9	0	.209	.244	.372
John Morris	OF16	L	27	20	38	3	11	2	1	0	3	1	7	0	.289	.308	.395
Rod Booker	3B13,2B1	L	29	18	35	6	12	3	0	0	3	4	3	2	.343	.410	.429
Duane Walker	OF4,1B1	L	31	24	22	1	4	1	0	0	3	2	7	0	.182	.250	.227

J. Oquendo, 16 G at 1B, 15 G at OF, 1 G at P, 1 G at C; T. Lawless, 1 G at 1B

Pitcher	T	Age	G	GS	CG	ShO	IP	H	HR	BB	SO	W-L	Sv	ERA
Jose DeLeon	R	27	34	34	3	1	225.1	198	13	86	208	13-10	0	3.67
Joe Magrane	L	23	24	24	4	3	165.1	133	6	51	100	5-9	0	2.18
John Tudor†	L	34	21	21	4	1	145.1	131	5	31	55	6-5	0	2.29
Danny Cox	R	28	13	13	0	0	86.0	89	6	25	47	3-8	0	3.98
Greg Mathews	L	26	13	13	1	0	68.0	61	4	33	31	4-6	0	4.24
Randy O'Neal	R	27	10	8	0	0	53.0	57	7	10	20	2-3	0	4.58
Cris Carpenter	R	23	8	8	1	0	47.2	56	3	9	24	2-3	0	4.72
Todd Worrell	R	28	68	0	0	0	90.0	69	7	34	78	5-9	32	3.00
Ken Dayley	L	29	54	0	0	0	55.1	48	2	19	38	2-7	5	2.77
Scott Terry	R	28	51	11	1	0	129.1	119	5	34	65	9-6	3	2.92
Steve Peters	L	25	44	0	0	0	45.0	57	8	22	30	3-3	0	6.40
Larry McWilliams	L	34	42	17	2	1	136.0	130	10	45	70	6-9	1	3.90
John Costello	R	27	36	0	0	0	49.2	44	3	25	38	5-2	1	1.81
Dan Quisenberry†	R	35	33	0	0	0	38.0	54	4	6	19	2-0	0	6.16
Bob Forsch†	R	38	30	12	1	1	108.2	111	8	38	40	9-4	0	3.73
Scott Arnold	R	25	6	0	0	0	6.2	9	0	4	8	0-0	0	5.40
Ken Hill	R	22	4	1	0	0	14.0	16	0	6	6	0-1	0	5.14
Gibson Alba	L	28	3	0	0	0	3.1	1	0	2	3	0-0	0	2.70
Jose Oquendo	R	24	1	0	0	0	4.0	4	0	6	1	0-1	0	4.50

1988 Philadelphia Phillies 6th NL East 65-96 .404 35.5 GB

Lee Elia (60-92)/John Vukovich (5-4)

Player	Gm by Position	B	Age	G	AB	R	H	2B	3B	HR	RBI	BB	SO	SB	Avg	OBP	Slg
Lance Parrish	C117,1B1	R	32	123	424	44	91	17	2	15	60	47	93	0	.215	.293	.370
Von Hayes	1B85,OF16,3B3	L	29	104	367	43	100	28	2	6	45	49	59	20	.272	.355	.409
Juan Samuel	2B152,OF3,3B1	R	27	157	629	68	153	32	9	12	67	39	151	33	.243	.298	.380
Mike Schmidt	3B104,1B3	R	38	108	390	52	97	21	2	12	62	49	42	3	.249	.337	.405
Steve Jeltz	SS148	S	29	148	379	39	71	11	4	0	27	59	58	3	.187	.295	.237
Phil Bradley	OF153	R	29	154	569	77	150	30	5	11	56	54	106	11	.264	.341	.392
Chris James	OF116,3B31	R	25	150	566	57	137	24	1	19	66	31	73	7	.242	.283	.389
Milt Thompson	OF112	L	29	122	378	53	109	16	2	2	33	39	59	17	.288	.354	.357
Ricky Jordan	1B69	R	23	69	273	41	84	15	1	11	43	7	39	1	.308	.324	.491
Bob Dernier	OF54	R	31	68	166	19	48	3	1	1	10	9	19	13	.289	.330	.337
Mike Young†	OF42	S	28	75	146	13	33	14	0	1	14	26	43	0	.226	.343	.342
Darren Daulton	C44,1B1	L	26	58	144	13	30	6	0	1	12	17	26	2	.208	.288	.271
Greg Gross	OF37,1B14	L	35	98	133	10	27	1	0	0	5	16	3	0	.203	.291	.211
Ron Jones	OF32	L	24	33	124	15	36	6	1	8	26	2	14	0	.290	.295	.548
Luis Aguayo†	SS27,3B13,2B2	R	29	49	97	9	24	3	0	3	5	13	17	2	.247	.336	.371
Jackie Gutierrez	SS22,3B13	R	28	33	77	8	19	4	0	0	9	2	9	0	.247	.259	.299
Tom Barrett	2B10	S	28	36	54	5	11	1	0	0	3	7	8	0	.204	.306	.222
John Russell	C15	R	27	22	49	5	12	1	0	2	4	3	15	0	.245	.302	.388
Keith Miller	OF4,3B3,SS1	S	25	47	48	4	8	3	0	0	6	5	13	0	.167	.245	.229
Shane Turner	3B8,SS5	L	25	18	35	1	6	0	0	0	1	5	9	0	.171	.275	.171
Bill Almon	3B9,SS5,1B1	R	35	20	26	1	3	2	0	0	1	3	11	0	.115	.207	.192
Al Pardo	C2	S	25	2	2	0	0	0	0	0	0	0	2	0	.000	.000	.000

Pitcher	T	Age	G	GS	CG	ShO	IP	H	HR	BB	SO	W-L	Sv	ERA
Kevin Gross	R	27	33	33	5	1	231.2	209	18	89	162	12-14	0	3.69
Don Carman	L	28	36	32	2	0	201.1	211	20	70	116	10-14	0	4.29
Shane Rawley	L	32	32	32	4	1	198.0	220	27	78	87	8-16	0	4.18
David Palmer	R	30	22	22	1	1	129.0	129	8	48	85	7-9	0	4.47
Marvin Freeman	R	25	11	11	0	0	51.2	55	2	43	37	2-3	0	6.10
Bob Sebra	R	26	3	3	0	0	11.1	15	0	10	7	1-2	0	7.94
Kent Tekulve	R	41	70	0	0	0	80.0	87	3	22	43	3-7	4	3.60
Greg Harris	R	32	66	1	0	0	107.0	80	7	52	71	4-6	1	2.36
Steve Bedrosian	R	30	57	0	0	0	74.1	75	6	27	61	6-6	28	3.75
Bruce Ruffin	L	24	55	15	3	0	144.1	151	7	80	82	6-10	3	4.43
Mike Maddux	R	26	25	11	0	0	88.2	91	6	34	59	4-3	0	3.76
Wally Ritchie	L	22	19	0	0	0	26.0	19	1	17	8	0-0	0	3.12
Danny Clay	R	26	17	0	0	0	24.0	27	5	21	12	0-1	0	6.00
Todd Frohwirth	R	25	12	0	0	0	12.0	16	2	11	11	1-2	0	8.25
Bill Dawley	R	30	8	0	0	0	8.2	16	3	4	3	0-2	0	13.50
Bill Scherrer†	L	30	8	0	0	0	6.2	7	0	2	3	0-0	0	5.40
Salome Barojas	R	31	6	0	0	0	8.2	7	1	8	1	0-0	0	8.31
Alex Madrid	R	25	5	2	1	0	16.1	15	0	6	2	1-1	0	2.76
Brad Moore	R	24	5	0	0	0	5.2	4	0	4	2	0-0	0	0.00
Scott Service	R	21	5	0	0	0	5.1	7	0	1	6	0-0	0	1.69
Jeff Calhoun	L	30	3	0	0	0	2.1	6	2	1	1	0-0	0	15.43

1988 Los Angeles Dodgers 1st NL West 94-67 .584 —

Tom Lasorda

Player	Gm by Position	B	Age	G	AB	R	H	2B	3B	HR	RBI	BB	SO	SB	Avg	OBP	Slg
Mike Scioscia	C123	L	29	130	408	29	105	18	0	3	35	38	31	0	.257	.318	.324
Franklin Stubbs	1B84,OF13	L	27	115	242	30	54	13	0	8	34	23	61	11	.223	.288	.376
Steve Sax	2B158	R	28	160	632	70	175	19	4	5	57	45	51	42	.277	.325	.343
Jeff Hamilton	3B105,SS2,1B1	R	24	111	309	34	73	14	2	6	33	10	51	0	.236	.268	.353
Alfredo Griffin	SS93	S	30	95	316	39	63	8	3	1	27	24	30	7	.199	.259	.253
Kirk Gibson	OF148	L	31	150	542	106	157	28	1	25	76	73	120	31	.290	.377	.483
John Shelby	OF140	S	30	140	494	65	130	23	6	10	64	44	128	16	.263	.320	.395
Mike Marshall	OF90,1B53	R	28	144	542	63	150	27	2	20	82	24	93	4	.277	.314	.445
Dave Anderson	SS82,3B12,2B11	R	27	116	285	31	71	10	2	2	20	32	45	4	.249	.325	.319
Mike Davis	OF76	L	29	108	281	29	55	11	2	2	17	25	59	7	.196	.260	.270
Pedro Guerrero†	3B45,1B15,OF2	R	32	59	215	24	64	7	1	5	35	25	33	2	.298	.374	.409
Mickey Hatcher	OF29,1B25,3B3	R	33	88	191	22	56	8	0	1	25	7	7	0	.293	.322	.351
Tracy Woodson	3B41,1B25	R	25	65	173	15	43	4	1	3	15	7	32	1	.249	.279	.335
Rick Dempsey	C74	R	38	77	167	25	42	13	0	7	30	25	44	1	.251	.338	.455
Danny Heep	OF32,1B12,P1	L	30	95	149	14	36	2	0	0	11	22	13	2	.242	.341	.255
Mike Sharperson	2B20,3B6,SS4	R	26	46	59	8	16	1	0	0	4	1	12	0	.271	.290	.288
Mike Devereaux	OF26	R	25	30	43	4	5	1	0	0	2	2	10	0	.116	.156	.140
Jose Gonzalez	OF24	R	23	37	24	7	2	1	0	0	0	2	10	3	.083	.154	.125
Chris Gwynn	OF4	L	23	12	11	1	2	0	0	0	0	1	2	0	.182	.250	.182
Gil Reyes	C5	R	24	5	9	1	1	0	0	0	0	0	3	0	.111	.111	.111

Pitcher	T	Age	G	GS	CG	ShO	IP	H	HR	BB	SO	W-L	Sv	ERA
Orel Hershiser	R	29	35	34	15	8	267.0	208	18	73	178	23-8	1	2.26
Tim Leary	R	30	35	34	9	6	228.2	201	13	56	180	17-11	0	2.91
Tim Belcher	R	26	36	27	4	1	179.2	143	8	51	152	12-6	4	2.91
F. Valenzuela	L	27	23	22	3	0	142.1	142	11	76	64	5-8	1	4.24
Don Sutton	R	43	16	16	0	0	87.1	91	7	30	44	3-6	0	3.92
Shawn Hillegas†	R	23	11	10	0	0	56.2	54	5	17	30	3-4	0	4.13
John Tudor†	L	34	9	9	1	0	52.1	58	5	10	32	4-3	0	2.41
Ramon Martinez	R	20	9	6	0	0	35.2	27	0	22	23	1-3	0	3.79
Bill Brennan	R	25	4	2	0	0	9.1	13	0	6	7	0-1	0	6.75
Bill Krueger	L	30	1	1	0	0	2.1	4	0	2	1	0-0	0	11.57
Alejandro Pena	R	29	60	0	0	0	94.1	75	4	27	83	6-7	12	1.91
Jesse Orosco	L	31	55	0	0	0	53.0	41	4	30	43	3-2	9	2.72
Jay Howell	R	32	50	0	0	0	65.0	44	1	21	70	5-3	21	2.08
Brian Holton	R	28	45	0	0	0	84.2	69	1	26	49	7-3	1	1.70
Tim Crews	R	27	42	0	0	0	71.2	77	3	16	45	4-0	0	3.14
Ricky Horton†	L	28	12	0	0	0	9.0	11	2	2	8	1-1	0	5.00
Brad Havens†	L	28	9	0	0	0	9.2	15	1	4	8	0-0	0	4.66
Ken Howell	R	27	4	1	0	0	12.2	16	0	4	12	0-1	0	6.39
Danny Heep	L	30	1	0	0	0	2.0	2	1	0	0	0-0	0	9.00

1988 Cincinnati Reds 2nd NL West 87-74 .540 7.0 GB

Pete Rose (11-12)/Tommy Helms (12-15)/Pete Rose (64-47)

Player	Gm by Position	B	Age	G	AB	R	H	2B	3B	HR	RBI	BB	SO	SB	Avg	OBP	Slg
Bo Diaz	C88	R	35	92	315	26	69	9	0	10	35	7	41	0	.219	.236	.343
Nick Esasky	1B116	R	28	122	391	40	95	17	2	15	62	48	104	7	.243	.327	.412
Jeff Treadway	2B97,3B2	L	25	103	301	30	76	19	4	2	23	27	30	2	.252	.315	.362
Chris Sabo	3B135,SS2	R	26	137	538	74	146	40	2	11	44	29	52	46	.271	.314	.414
Barry Larkin	SS148	R	24	151	588	91	174	32	5	12	56	41	24	40	.296	.347	.429
Kal Daniels	OF137	L	24	140	495	95	144	29	1	18	64	87	94	27	.291	.397	.463
Eric Davis	OF130	R	26	135	472	81	129	18	3	26	93	65	124	35	.273	.363	.489
Paul O'Neill	OF118,1B21	L	25	145	485	58	122	25	3	16	73	38	65	8	.252	.306	.414
Dave Concepcion	2B46,1B16,SS13*	R	40	84	197	11	39	9	0	0	8	18	23	3	.198	.265	.244
Dave Collins	OF35,1B3	S	35	99	174	12	41	6	2	0	14	11	27	7	.236	.286	.293
Ron Oester	2B49,SS5	S	32	54	150	20	42	7	0	0	10	9	24	0	.280	.319	.327
Jeff Reed†	C49	L	25	49	142	10	33	6	0	1	7	15	19	0	.232	.306	.296
Lloyd McClendon	C23,OF17,1B12*	R	29	72	137	9	30	4	0	3	14	15	22	4	.219	.301	.314
Herm Winningham†	OF42	L	26	53	113	6	26	1	3	0	15	5	27	8	.230	.261	.292
Terry McGriff	C32	R	24	35	96	9	19	3	0	1	4	12	31	1	.198	.284	.260
Tracy Jones†	OF25	R	27	37	83	9	19	1	0	1	9	8	6	9	.229	.304	.277
Buddy Bell†	3B13,1B2	R	36	21	54	3	10	0	0	0	3	7	3	0	.185	.270	.185
Luis Quinones	SS10,2B4,3B4	S	26	23	52	4	12	3	0	1	11	2	11	1	.231	.255	.346
Leon Durham†	1B17	L	30	21	51	4	11	3	0	1	2	5	12	0	.216	.286	.333
Eddie Milner	OF15	L	33	23	51	3	9	1	0	0	2	4	9	2	.176	.236	.196
Ken Griffey Sr.†	1B10	L	38	25	50	5	14	1	0	2	4	2	5	0	.280	.308	.420
Lenny Harris	3B10,2B6	L	23	16	43	7	16	1	0	0	8	5	4	4	.372	.420	.395
Ron Roenicke	OF14	S	31	14	37	4	5	1	0	0	5	4	8	0	.135	.238	.162
Leo Garcia	OF9	L	25	23	28	2	4	1	0	0	0	4	5	0	.143	.250	.179
Van Snider	OF8	L	24	11	28	4	6	1	0	1	6	0	13	0	.214	.207	.357
Marty Brown	3B8	R	25	10	16	0	3	1	0	0	2	1	2	0	.188	.235	.250

D. Concepcion, 9 G at 3B, 1 G at P; L. McClendon, 2 G at 3B

Pitcher	T	Age	G	GS	CG	ShO	IP	H	HR	BB	SO	W-L	Sv	ERA
Tom Browning	L	28	36	36	5	2	250.2	205	36	64	124	18-5	0	3.41
Danny Jackson	L	26	35	35	15	6	260.2	206	13	71	161	23-8	0	2.73
Ron Robinson	R	26	17	16	0	0	78.2	88	5	26	38	3-7	0	4.12
Mario Soto	R	31	14	14	3	1	87.0	88	8	28	34	3-7	0	4.66
Jack Armstrong	R	23	14	13	0	0	65.1	63	8	38	45	4-7	0	5.79
D. Rasmussen†	L	29	11	11	1	1	56.1	68	8	22	27	2-6	0	5.75
Norm Charlton	L	25	10	10	0	0	61.1	60	6	20	39	4-5	0	3.96
Keith Brown	R	24	4	3	0	0	16.1	14	1	4	6	2-1	0	2.76
Rob Murphy	L	28	76	0	0	0	84.2	69	3	38	74	0-6	3	3.08
John Franco	L	27	70	0	0	0	86.0	60	3	27	46	6-6	39	1.57
Frank Williams	R	30	60	0	0	0	62.2	59	6	35	43	3-2	1	2.59
Jose Rijo	R	23	49	19	0	0	162.0	120	7	63	160	13-8	0	2.39
Rob Dibble	R	24	37	0	0	0	59.1	43	2	21	59	1-1	0	1.82
Tim Birtsas	L	27	36	4	0	0	64.1	61	6	24	38	1-3	0	4.20
Pat Perry†	L	29	12	0	0	0	20.2	21	4	9	11	2-2	0	5.66
Randy St. Claire†	R	27	10	0	0	0	13.2	13	3	5	8	1-0	0	2.63
Pat Pacillo	R	24	6	0	0	0	10.2	14	2	4	11	1-0	0	5.06
Jeff Gray	R	25	5	0	0	0	9.1	12	0	4	5	0-0	0	3.86
Candy Sierra†	R	21	1	0	0	0	4.0	5	0	1	4	0-0	0	4.50
Dave Concepcion	R	40	1	0	0	0	1.1	2	0	0	1	0-0	0	0.00

1988 San Diego Padres 3rd NL West 83-78 .516 11.0 GB

Larry Bowa (16-30)/Jack McKeon (67-48)

Player	Gm by Position	B	Age	G	AB	R	H	2B	3B	HR	RBI	BB	SO	SB	Avg	OBP	Slg
Benito Santiago	C136	R	23	139	492	49	122	22	2	10	46	24	82	15	.248	.282	.362
Keith Moreland	1B73,OF64,3B2	R	34	143	511	40	131	23	0	5	64	40	51	2	.256	.305	.331
Roberto Alomar	2B143	S	20	143	545	84	145	24	6	9	41	47	83	24	.266	.328	.382
Chris Brown	3B72	R	26	80	247	14	58	6	0	2	19	19	49	0	.235	.295	.283
Garry Templeton	SS105,3B2	S	32	110	362	35	90	15	7	3	36	20	50	8	.249	.286	.354
Tony Gwynn	OF133	L	28	133	521	64	163	22	5	7	70	51	40	26	.313	.373	.415
Marvell Wynne	OF113	L	28	128	333	37	88	13	4	11	42	31	62	3	.264	.325	.426
Carmelo Martinez	OF64,1B41	R	27	121	365	48	86	12	0	18	65	35	57	1	.236	.301	.416
John Kruk	1B63,OF55	L	27	120	378	54	91	17	1	9	44	80	68	5	.241	.369	.362
Randy Ready	3B57,2B26,OF16	R	28	114	331	43	88	16	2	7	39	39	38	6	.266	.346	.390
Dickie Thon	SS70,2B2,3B1	R	30	95	258	36	68	12	2	1	18	33	49	19	.264	.347	.337
Tim Flannery	3B51,2B2,SS1	L	30	79	170	16	45	5	4	0	19	24	32	3	.265	.365	.341
Shane Mack	OF55	R	24	56	119	13	29	3	0	0	12	14	21	5	.244	.336	.269
Mark Parent	C36	R	26	41	118	9	23	3	0	6	15	6	23	0	.195	.232	.373
Stan Jefferson	OF38	S	25	49	111	16	16	1	2	1	4	9	22	5	.144	.211	.216
Shawn Abner	OF35	R	22	37	83	6	15	3	0	2	5	4	19	0	.181	.225	.289
Rob Nelson	1B5	L	24	7	21	4	4	0	0	1	3	2	9	0	.190	.261	.333
Jerald Clark	OF4	R	24	6	15	0	3	1	0	0	3	0	4	0	.200	.200	.267
Randy Byers	OF2	L	23	11	10	0	2	1	0	0	0	0	5	0	.200	.200	.300
Bip Roberts	3B2,2B1	S	24	5	9	1	3	0	0	0	0	1	2	0	.333	.400	.333
Sandy Alomar Jr.		R	22	1	1	0	0	0	0	0	0	0	1	0	.000	.000	.000

Pitcher	T	Age	G	GS	CG	ShO	IP	H	HR	BB	SO	W-L	Sv	ERA
Andy Hawkins	R	28	33	33	4	2	217.2	196	16	76	91	14-11	0	3.35
Ed Whitson	R	33	34	33	3	1	205.1	202	17	45	118	13-11	0	3.77
Eric Show	R	32	32	32	13	1	234.2	201	22	53	144	16-11	0	3.26
Jimmy Jones	R	24	29	29	3	0	179.0	192	14	44	82	9-14	0	4.12
D. Rasmussen†	L	29	20	20	6	0	148.1	131	9	36	85	14-4	0	2.55
Mark Davis	L	27	62	0	0	0	98.1	70	2	42	102	5-10	28	2.01
Lance McCullers	R	24	60	0	0	0	97.2	70	8	55	81	3-6	10	2.49
Dave Leiper	L	26	35	0	0	0	54.0	45	1	14	33	3-0	1	2.17
Greg Booker	R	28	34	2	0	0	63.2	68	5	19	43	2-2	0	3.39
Mark Grant	R	24	33	11	0	0	97.2	97	14	36	61	2-8	0	3.69
Candy Sierra†	R	21	15	0	0	0	23.2	36	2	11	20	0-1	0	5.70
Keith Comstock	L	32	7	0	0	0	8.0	8	1	3	9	0-0	0	6.75
Greg Harris	R	24	3	1	1	0	18.0	13	0	3	15	2-0	0	1.50
Eric Nolte	L	24	2	0	0	0	3.0	3	1	2	1	0-0	0	6.00

1988 San Francisco Giants 4th NL West 83-79 .512 11.5 GB

Roger Craig

Player	Gm by Position	B	Age	G	AB	R	H	2B	3B	HR	RBI	BB	SO	SB	Avg	OBP	Slg
Bob Melvin	C89,1B1	R	26	92	273	23	64	13	1	8	27	13	46	0	.234	.268	.377
Will Clark	1B158	L	24	162	575	102	162	31	6	29	109	100	129	9	.282	.386	.508
Robby Thompson	2B134	R	26	138	477	66	126	24	6	7	48	40	111	14	.264	.323	.384
Kevin Mitchell	3B102,OF40	R	26	148	505	60	127	25	7	19	80	48	85	5	.251	.319	.442
Jose Uribe	SS140	S	29	141	493	47	124	10	7	3	35	36	69	14	.252	.301	.318
Brett Butler	OF155	L	31	157	568	109	163	27	9	6	43	97	64	43	.287	.393	.398
Candy Maldonado	OF139	R	27	142	499	53	127	23	1	12	68	37	89	6	.255	.311	.377
Mike Aldrete	OF115,1B10	L	27	139	389	44	104	15	0	3	50	56	65	6	.267	.357	.329
Bob Brenly	C69	R	34	73	206	13	39	7	0	5	22	20	40	1	.189	.265	.296
Ernest Riles†	3B30,2B17,SS16	L	27	79	187	26	55	7	2	3	28	10	33	1	.294	.323	.401
Chris Speier	2B45,3B22,SS12	R	38	82	171	26	37	9	1	3	18	23	39	3	.216	.311	.333
Jeffrey Leonard†	OF43	R	32	44	160	12	41	8	1	2	20	9	24	7	.256	.292	.356
Matt Williams	3B43,SS14	R	22	52	156	17	32	6	1	8	19	8	41	0	.205	.251	.410
Joel Youngblood	OF45	R	36	83	123	12	31	4	0	0	16	10	17	1	.252	.307	.285
Kirt Manwaring	C40	R	22	40	116	12	29	7	0	1	15	2	21	0	.250	.279	.336
Donell Nixon	OF46	R	26	59	78	15	27	3	0	0	6	10	12	11	.346	.420	.385
Harry Spilman†	1B6,C2,OF1	L	33	40	40	4	7	1	1	1	3	4	6	0	.175	.250	.325
Francisco Melendez	1B6,OF1	L	24	23	26	1	5	0	0	0	3	3	2	0	.192	.276	.192
Phil Garner	3B2	R	39	15	13	0	2	0	0	0	1	1	3	0	.154	.214	.154
Charlie Hayes	OF4,3B3	R	23	7	11	0	1	0	0	0	0	0	3	0	.091	.091	.091
Tony Perezchica	2B6	R	22	7	8	1	1	0	0	0	1	2	1	0	.125	.273	.125
Rusty Tillman	OF1	R	27	4	4	1	1	0	0	1	3	2	1	0	.250	.500	1.000
Angel Escobar	3B1,SS1	S	23	3	3	1	1	0	0	0	0	0	0	0	.333	.333	.333
Mark Wasinger	3B1	R	26	3	2	1	0	0	0	0	0	0	0	0	.000	.000	.000
Jessie Reid		L	26	2	2	0	0	0	0	0	0	0	1	0	.000	.000	.000

Pitcher	T	Age	G	GS	CG	ShO	IP	H	HR	BB	SO	W-L	Sv	ERA
Rick Reuschel	R	39	36	36	7	2	245.0	242	11	42	92	19-11	0	3.12
Kelly Downs	R	27	27	26	6	3	168.0	140	11	47	118	13-9	0	3.32
Mike Krukow	R	36	20	20	1	0	124.2	111	13	31	75	7-4	0	3.54
Mike LaCoss	R	32	19	19	1	1	114.1	99	5	47	70	7-7	0	3.62
Dave Dravecky	L	32	7	7	1	0	37.0	33	4	8	19	2-2	0	3.16
Terry Mulholland	L	25	9	6	2	1	46.0	50	3	7	18	2-1	0	3.72
Trevor Wilson	L	22	4	4	0	0	22.0	25	1	8	15	0-2	0	4.09
Dennis Cook	L	25	4	4	1	1	22.0	9	1	11	13	2-1	0	2.86
Scott Garrelts	R	26	65	0	0	0	98.0	80	3	46	86	5-9	13	3.58
Craig Lefferts	L	30	64	0	0	0	92.1	74	7	23	58	3-8	11	2.92
Don Robinson	R	31	51	19	3	2	176.2	152	11	49	122	10-5	6	2.45
Atlee Hammaker	L	30	43	17	3	1	144.2	136	11	41	65	9-9	5	3.73
Joe Price	L	31	38	3	0	0	61.2	59	5	27	49	1-6	4	3.94
Randy Bockus	R	27	20	0	0	0	32.0	35	2	13	18	1-1	0	4.78
Roger Samuels	L	27	15	0	0	0	23.1	17	4	7	22	1-2	0	3.47
Lary Sorensen	R	32	12	0	0	0	16.2	24	1	3	9	0-0	2	4.86
Jeff Brantley	R	24	9	1	0	0	20.2	22	2	6	11	0-1	1	5.66
Ron Davis	R	32	9	0	0	0	17.1	15	4	6	15	1-1	0	4.67

1988 Houston Astros 5th NL West 82-80 .506 12.5 GB

Hal Lanier

Player	Gm by Position	B	Age	G	AB	R	H	2B	3B	HR	RBI	BB	SO	SB	Avg	OBP	Slg
Alex Trevino	C74,OF1	R	30	78	193	19	48	17	0	2	13	24	29	5	.249	.341	.368
Glenn Davis	1B151	R	27	152	561	78	152	26	0	30	99	53	77	4	.271	.341	.478
Bill Doran	2B130	S	30	132	480	66	119	18	1	7	53	65	60	17	.248	.338	.333
Buddy Bell†	3B66,1B7	R	36	74	269	24	68	10	1	7	37	19	29	1	.253	.301	.375
Rafael Ramirez	SS154	R	30	155	566	51	156	30	5	6	59	18	61	3	.276	.298	.378
Kevin Bass	OF147	S	29	157	541	57	138	27	2	14	72	42	65	31	.255	.314	.390
Gerald Young	OF145	S	23	149	576	79	148	21	9	0	37	66	66	65	.257	.334	.325
Billy Hatcher	OF142	R	27	145	530	79	142	25	4	7	52	37	56	32	.268	.321	.370
Terry Puhl	OF78	L	31	113	234	42	71	7	2	3	19	35	30	22	.303	.395	.389
Alan Ashby	C66	S	36	73	227	19	54	10	0	7	33	29	36	0	.238	.319	.374
Denny Walling†	3B51,1B3,OF1	L	34	65	176	19	43	10	2	1	20	15	18	1	.244	.304	.341
Craig Reynolds	SS22,3B19,2B11*	L	35	78	161	20	41	7	0	1	14	8	23	3	.255	.290	.317
Jim Pankovits	2B31,3B11,1B2	R	32	68	140	13	31	7	1	2	12	8	28	2	.221	.272	.329
Craig Biggio	C50	R	22	50	123	14	26	6	1	3	5	7	29	6	.211	.254	.350
Chuck Jackson	3B32,SS3,OF3	R	25	46	83	7	19	5	1	1	8	7	16	1	.229	.286	.349
Ken Caminiti	3B28	S	25	30	83	5	15	2	0	1	7	5	18	0	.181	.225	.241
Steve Henderson	OF8,1B1	R	35	42	46	4	10	2	0	0	5	7	14	1	.217	.321	.261
Louie Meadows	OF10	L	27	35	42	5	8	0	1	2	3	6	8	4	.190	.292	.381
Casey Candaele†	2B10,OF5,3B1	S	27	21	31	2	5	3	0	0	1	1	6	0	.161	.188	.258
John Fishel	OF6	R	25	19	26	1	6	0	0	1	2	3	6	0	.231	.310	.346
Mark Bailey	C8	S	26	8	23	1	3	0	0	0	0	5	6	0	.130	.286	.130
Cameron Drew	OF5	L	24	7	16	1	3	0	1	0	1	0	1	0	.188	.188	.313
Harry Spilman†	1B1	L	33	7	5	0	0	0	0	0	0	0	3	0	.000	.000	.000
Craig Smajstrla	2B2	S	26	8	3	2	0	0	0	0	0	0	1	0	.000	.000	.000

C. Reynolds, 10 G at 1B

Pitcher	T	Age	G	GS	CG	ShO	IP	H	HR	BB	SO	W-L	Sv	ERA
Nolan Ryan	R	41	33	33	4	1	220.0	186	18	87	228	12-11	0	3.52
Mike Scott	R	33	32	32	8	5	218.2	162	19	53	190	14-8	0	2.92
Jim Deshaies	L	28	31	31	3	2	207.0	164	20	72	127	11-14	0	3.00
Bob Knepper	L	34	27	27	3	2	175.0	156	13	67	103	14-5	0	3.14
Bob Forsch†	R	38	6	6	0	0	27.2	42	2	6	14	1-4	0	6.51
Juan Agosto	L	30	75	0	0	0	91.2	74	6	30	33	10-2	4	2.26
Larry Andersen	R	35	53	0	0	0	82.2	82	3	20	66	2-4	5	2.94
Dave Smith	R	33	51	0	0	0	57.1	60	1	19	38	4-5	27	2.67
Danny Darwin	R	32	44	20	3	0	192.0	189	20	48	129	8-13	3	3.84
Joaquin Andujar	R	35	23	10	0	0	78.2	94	9	21	35	2-5	0	4.00
Dave Meads	L	24	22	2	0	0	39.2	37	4	14	27	3-1	0	3.18
Jeff Heathcock	R	28	17	1	0	0	31.0	33	2	16	12	0-5	0	5.81
Ernie Camacho	R	33	13	0	0	0	17.2	25	1	12	13	0-3	1	7.64
Rocky Childress	R	26	11	0	0	0	23.1	26	3	9	24	1-0	0	6.17
Brian Meyer	R	25	8	0	0	0	12.1	9	2	4	10	0-0	0	1.46

1988 Atlanta Braves 6th NL West 54-106 .338 39.5 GB

Chuck Tanner (12-27)/Russ Nixon (42-79)

Player	Gm by Position	B	Age	G	AB	R	H	2B	3B	HR	RBI	BB	SO	SB	Avg	OBP	Slg
Ozzie Virgil	C96	R	31	107	320	23	82	10	0	9	31	22	54	2	.256	.313	.372
Gerald Perry	1B141	L	27	141	547	61	164	29	1	8	74	36	49	29	.300	.338	.400
Ron Gant	2B122,3B22	R	23	146	563	85	146	28	8	19	60	46	118	19	.259	.317	.439
Ken Oberkfell†	3B113,2B1	L	32	120	422	42	117	20	4	3	40	32	28	4	.277	.325	.365
Andres Thomas	SS150	R	24	153	606	54	153	22	2	13	68	14	95	7	.252	.268	.360
Dale Murphy	OF156	R	32	156	592	77	134	35	4	24	77	74	125	3	.226	.313	.421
Dion James	OF120	L	25	132	386	46	99	17	5	3	30	58	59	9	.256	.353	.350
Albert Hall	OF63	S	30	85	231	27	57	7	1	1	15	21	35	15	.247	.314	.299
Bruce Benedict	C89	R	32	90	236	11	57	7	0	0	19	19	26	0	.242	.296	.271
Terry Blocker	OF61	L	28	66	198	13	42	4	2	2	10	10	20	1	.212	.250	.283
Ken Griffey Sr.†	OF42,1B11	L	38	69	193	21	48	5	0	2	19	17	26	1	.249	.307	.306
Gary Roenicke	OF35,1B1	R	33	49	114	11	26	5	0	1	7	8	15	0	.228	.279	.298
Lonnie Smith	OF35	R	32	43	114	14	27	3	0	3	9	10	25	4	.237	.296	.342
Ted Simmons	1B19,C10	S	38	78	107	6	21	6	0	2	11	15	9	0	.196	.293	.308
Jerry Royster	OF26,3B10,2B2*	R	35	68	102	8	18	3	0	0	1	6	16	0	.176	.222	.206
Jim Morrison†	3B20,OF4,P3	R	35	51	92	6	14	2	0	2	13	10	13	0	.152	.229	.239
Paul Runge	3B19,2B7,SS6	R	30	52	76	11	16	5	0	0	7	14	21	0	.211	.330	.276
Jeff Blauser	2B9,SS8	R	22	18	67	7	16	3	1	2	7	2	11	0	.239	.268	.403
Damaso Garcia	2B13	R	31	21	60	3	7	1	0	1	4	3	10	1	.117	.159	.183
Mark Lemke	2B16	S	22	16	58	8	13	4	0	0	2	4	5	0	.224	.274	.293
Tommy Gregg†	OF7	L	24	11	29	1	10	3	0	0	4	2	2	0	.345	.387	.448
Jody Davis†	C2	R	31	2	8	2	2	0	0	1	3	0	1	0	.250	.250	.625

J. Royster, 2 G at SS

Pitcher	T	Age	G	GS	CG	ShO	IP	H	HR	BB	SO	W-L	Sv	ERA
Rick Mahler	R	34	39	34	5	0	249.0	279	17	42	131	9-16	0	3.69
Tom Glavine	L	22	34	34	1	0	195.1	201	12	63	84	7-17	0	4.56
Pete Smith	R	22	32	32	5	3	195.1	183	15	88	124	7-15	0	3.69
Zane Smith	L	27	23	22	3	0	140.1	159	8	44	59	5-10	0	4.30
John Smoltz	R	21	12	12	0	0	64.0	74	10	33	37	2-7	0	5.48
Kevin Coffman	R	23	18	11	0	0	67.0	62	3	54	24	2-6	0	5.78
German Jimenez	L	25	15	9	0	0	55.2	65	4	12	26	1-6	0	5.01
Kevin Blankenship†	R	25	2	2	0	0	10.2	7	0	7	5	0-1	0	3.38
Paul Assenmacher	L	27	64	0	0	0	79.1	72	4	32	71	8-7	5	3.06
Jose Alvarez	R	32	60	0	0	0	102.1	88	7	53	81	5-6	3	2.99
Charlie Puleo	R	33	53	3	0	0	106.1	101	9	47	70	5-5	1	3.47
Bruce Sutter	R	35	38	0	0	0	45.1	49	4	11	40	1-4	14	4.76
Jim Acker	R	29	21	1	0	0	42.0	45	6	14	25	0-4	0	4.71
Juan Eichelberger	R	34	20	0	0	0	37.1	44	3	10	13	2-0	0	3.86
Joe Boever	R	27	16	0	0	0	20.1	12	1	1	7	0-2	1	1.77
Ed Olwine	L	30	16	0	0	0	18.2	22	4	4	5	0-0	1	6.75
Chuck Cary	L	28	7	0	0	0	8.1	8	1	4	7	0-0	0	6.48
Gary Eave	R	24	5	0	0	0	5.0	7	0	3	0	0-0	0	9.00
Jim Morrison	R	35	3	0	0	0	3.2	3	0	2	1	0-0	0	0.00

»1989 Toronto Blue Jays 1st AL East 89-73 .549 —

Jimy Williams (12-24)/Cito Gaston (77-49)

Player	Gm by Position	B	Age	G	AB	R	H	2B	3B	HR	RBI	BB	SO	SB	Avg	OBP	Slg
Ernie Whitt	C115,DH8	L	37	129	385	42	101	24	1	11	53	52	53	5	.262	.349	.416
Fred McGriff	1B159,DH2	L	25	161	551	98	148	27	3	36	92	119	132	7	.269	.399	.525
Nelson Liriano	2B122,DH5	S	25	132	418	51	110	26	3	5	53	43	51	16	.263	.331	.376
Kelly Gruber	3B119,OF16,DH1*	R	27	135	545	83	158	24	4	18	73	30	60	10	.290	.328	.448
Tony Fernandez	SS140	S	27	140	573	64	147	25	9	11	64	29	51	22	.257	.291	.389
George Bell	OF134,DH19	R	29	153	613	88	182	41	2	18	104	33	60	4	.297	.330	.458
Lloyd Moseby	OF120,DH14	L	29	135	502	72	111	25	3	11	43	56	101	24	.221	.306	.349
Junior Felix	OF107,DH1	S	21	110	415	62	107	14	8	9	46	33	101	18	.258	.315	.395
Rance Mulliniks	DH73,3B29	L	33	103	273	25	65	11	2	3	29	34	40	0	.238	.320	.326
Manuel Lee	2B40,SS28,3B17*	S	24	99	300	27	78	9	2	3	34	20	60	4	.260	.305	.333
Pat Borders	C68,DH18	R	26	94	241	22	62	11	1	3	29	11	45	2	.257	.290	.349
Mookie Wilson†	OF54	S	33	54	238	32	71	9	1	2	17	3	37	12	.298	.311	.370
Bob Brenly†	DH28,C13,1B5	R	35	48	88	9	15	3	1	1	6	10	17	1	.170	.255	.261
Jesse Barfield†	OF21	R	29	21	80	8	16	4	0	5	11	5	28	0	.200	.256	.438
Rob Ducey	OF35,DH1	L	24	41	76	5	16	4	0	0	7	9	25	2	.211	.294	.263
Tom Lawless	OF16,DH12,3B12*	R	32	59	70	20	16	1	0	0	3	7	12	12	.229	.295	.243
Lee Mazzilli†	DH19,1B2,OF2	S	34	28	66	12	15	3	0	4	11	17	16	2	.227	.395	.455
Glenallen Hill	OF16,DH3	R	24	19	52	4	15	0	0	1	7	3	12	2	.288	.327	.346
Greg Myers	C11,DH6	L	23	17	44	0	5	2	0	0	1	2	9	0	.114	.152	.159
Alexis Infante	SS9,3B4,2B1	R	27	20	12	1	2	0	0	0	0	0	1	1	.167	.167	.167
Francisco Cabrera†	DH3	R	22	3	12	1	2	1	0	0	0	1	3	0	.167	.231	.250
Ozzie Virgil	DH6,C1	R	32	9	11	2	2	1	0	1	2	4	3	0	.182	.400	.545
Kevin Batiste	OF5	R	22	6	8	1	2	0	0	0	0	0	5	0	.250	.250	.250
John Olerud	1B5,DH1	L	20	6	8	2	3	0	0	0	0	0	1	0	.375	.375	.375

K. Gruber, 1 G at SS; M. Lee, 13 G at DH, 1 G at OF; T. Lawless, 7 G at 2B, 1 G at C

Pitcher	T	Age	G	GS	CG	ShO	IP	H	HR	BB	SO	W-L	Sv	ERA
Jimmy Key	L	28	33	33	5	1	216.0	226	18	27	118	13-14	0	3.88
Dave Stieb	R	31	33	33	3	2	206.2	164	12	76	101	17-8	0	3.35
John Cerutti	L	29	33	31	3	1	205.1	214	19	53	69	11-11	0	3.07
Mike Flanagan	L	37	30	30	1	1	171.2	186	10	47	47	8-10	0	3.93
Todd Stottlemyre	R	24	27	18	0	0	127.2	137	11	44	63	7-7	0	3.88
Alex Sanchez	R	23	4	3	0	0	11.2	16	1	14	4	0-1	0	10.03
Jeff Musselman†	L	26	5	3	0	0	11.0	19	2	9	3	0-1	0	10.64
Al Leiter†	L	23	1	1	0	0	6.2	9	1	2	4	0-0	0	4.05
Duane Ward	R	25	66	0	0	0	114.2	94	4	58	122	4-10	15	3.77
Tom Henke	R	31	64	0	0	0	89.0	66	5	25	116	8-3	20	1.92
David Wells	L	26	54	0	0	0	86.1	66	5	28	78	7-4	2	2.40
Frank Wills	R	30	24	4	0	0	71.1	65	4	30	41	3-1	0	3.66
Tony Castillo†	L	26	17	0	0	0	17.2	23	0	10	10	1-1	1	6.11
Jim Acker†	R	30	14	0	0	0	28.1	24	1	12	24	2-1	0	1.59
Mauro Gozzo	R	23	9	3	0	0	31.2	35	1	9	10	4-1	0	4.83
Xavier Hernandez	R	23	7	0	0	0	22.2	25	2	8	7	1-0	0	4.76
DeWayne Buice	R	31	7	0	0	0	17.0	13	2	13	10	1-0	0	5.82
Jose Nunez	R	25	6	1	0	0	10.2	8	0	2	14	0-0	0	2.53
Steve Cummings	R	24	5	2	0	0	21.0	18	1	11	8	2-0	0	3.00

1989 Baltimore Orioles 2nd AL East 87-75 .537 2.0 GB

Frank Robinson

Player	Gm by Position	B	Age	G	AB	R	H	2B	3B	HR	RBI	BB	SO	SB	Avg	OBP	Slg
Mickey Tettleton	C75,DH43	S	28	117	411	72	106	21	2	26	65	73	117	3	.258	.369	.509
Randy Milligan	1B117	R	27	124	365	56	98	23	5	12	45	74	75	9	.268	.394	.458
Billy Ripken	2B114	R	24	115	318	31	76	11	2	2	26	22	53	1	.239	.284	.305
Craig Worthington	3B145	R	24	145	497	57	123	23	0	15	70	61	114	1	.247	.334	.384
Cal Ripken Jr.	SS162	R	28	162	646	80	166	30	0	21	93	57	72	3	.257	.317	.401
Phil Bradley	OF140,DH2	R	30	144	545	83	151	23	10	11	55	70	103	20	.277	.364	.417
Mike Devereaux	OF112,DH5	R	26	122	391	55	104	14	3	8	46	36	60	22	.266	.329	.379
Joe Orsulak	OF109,DH5	L	27	123	390	59	111	22	5	7	55	41	35	5	.285	.351	.421
Larry Sheets	DH88	L	29	102	304	33	74	12	1	7	33	26	58	1	.243	.305	.359
Bob Melvin	C75,DH9	R	27	85	278	22	67	10	1	1	32	15	53	1	.241	.279	.295
Brady Anderson	OF79,DH8	L	25	94	266	44	55	12	2	4	16	43	45	16	.207	.324	.312
Jim Traber	1B69,DH5	L	27	86	234	14	49	8	0	4	26	19	41	4	.209	.266	.295
Steve Finley	OF76,DH3	L	24	81	217	35	54	5	2	2	25	15	30	17	.249	.298	.318
Rene Gonzales	2B54,3B17,SS1	R	28	71	166	16	36	4	0	1	11	12	30	5	.217	.268	.259
Stan Jefferson†	OF32,DH2	S	26	35	127	19	33	7	0	4	20	4	22	9	.260	.284	.409
Keith Moreland†	DH29	R	35	33	107	11	23	4	0	1	10	4	12	0	.215	.243	.280
Tim Hulett	2B23,3B11	R	29	33	97	12	27	5	0	3	18	10	17	0	.278	.343	.423
Jamie Quirk†	C24	L	34	25	51	5	11	2	0	0	9	9	11	0	.216	.328	.255
Francisco Melendez	1B5	L	25	9	11	1	3	0	0	0	3	1	2	0	.273	.308	.273
Chris Hoiles	DH3,C3	R	24	6	9	0	1	1	0	0	1	1	3	0	.111	.200	.222
Butch Davis	OF3	R	31	5	6	1	1	1	0	0	0	0	3	0	.167	.167	.333
Juan Bell	DH4,2B2,SS2	R	21	8	4	2	0	0	0	0	0	0	1	1	.000	.000	.000
Rick Schu†	2B1	R	27	1	0	0	0	0	0	0	0	0	0	0	—	—	—

Pitcher	T	Age	G	GS	CG	ShO	IP	H	HR	BB	SO	W-L	Sv	ERA
Bob Milacki	R	24	37	36	3	2	243.0	233	21	88	113	14-12	0	3.74
Jeff Ballard	L	25	35	35	4	1	215.1	240	16	57	62	18-8	0	3.43
Dave Schmidt	R	32	38	26	2	0	156.2	196	24	36	46	10-13	0	5.69
Pete Harnisch	R	22	18	17	2	0	103.1	97	10	64	70	5-9	0	4.62
Dave Johnson	R	29	14	14	4	0	89.1	90	11	28	26	4-7	0	4.23
Jose Bautista	R	24	15	10	0	0	78.0	84	17	15	30	3-4	0	5.31
Jay Tibbs	R	27	10	8	1	0	54.1	62	2	20	30	5-0	0	2.82
Mark Williamson	R	29	65	0	0	0	107.1	105	4	30	55	10-5	9	2.93
Gregg Olson	R	22	64	0	0	0	85.0	57	1	46	90	5-2	27	1.69
Kevin Hickey	L	33	51	0	0	0	49.1	38	3	23	28	2-3	2	2.92
Mark Thurmond	L	32	49	2	0	0	90.0	102	6	17	34	2-4	4	3.90
Brian Holton	R	29	39	12	0	0	116.1	140	11	39	51	5-7	0	4.02
Michael Smith	R	25	13	1	0	0	20.0	25	3	14	12	2-0	0	7.65
Mark Huismann	R	31	8	0	0	0	11.1	13	0	0	13	0-0	1	6.35
Mickey Weston	R	28	7	0	0	0	13.0	18	1	2	7	1-0	1	5.54
Ben McDonald	R	21	6	0	0	0	7.1	8	2	4	3	1-0	0	8.59
Curt Schilling	R	22	5	1	0	0	8.2	10	2	3	6	0-1	0	6.23

1989 Boston Red Sox 3rd AL East 83-79 .512 6.0 GB

Joe Morgan

Player	Gm by Position	B	Age	G	AB	R	H	2B	3B	HR	RBI	BB	SO	SB	Avg	OBP	Slg
Rick Cerone	C97,DH1,OF1	R	35	102	296	28	72	16	1	4	48	34	40	0	.243	.320	.345
Nick Esasky	1B153,OF1	R	29	154	564	79	156	26	5	30	108	66	117	1	.277	.355	.500
Marty Barrett	2B80,DH4	R	31	86	336	31	86	18	0	1	27	32	12	4	.256	.320	.318
Wade Boggs	3B152,DH3	L	31	156	621	113	205	51	7	3	54	107	51	2	.330	.430	.449
Luis Rivera	SS90,DH1,2B1	R	25	93	323	35	83	17	1	5	29	20	60	2	.257	.301	.362
Mike Greenwell	OF139,DH5	L	25	145	578	87	178	36	0	14	95	56	44	13	.308	.370	.443
Ellis Burks	OF95,DH1	R	24	97	399	73	121	19	6	12	61	36	52	21	.303	.365	.471
Kevin Romine	OF89,DH2	R	28	92	274	30	75	13	0	1	23	21	53	1	.274	.327	.332
Dwight Evans	OF77,DH69	R	37	146	520	82	148	27	3	20	100	99	84	3	.285	.397	.463
Jody Reed	SS77,2B70,3B4*	R	26	146	524	76	151	42	2	3	40	73	44	4	.288	.376	.393
Danny Heep	OF75,1B19,DH9	L	31	113	320	36	96	17	0	5	49	29	26	0	.300	.356	.400
Rich Gedman	C91	L	29	93	260	24	55	9	0	4	16	23	47	0	.212	.273	.292
Jim Rice	DH55	R	36	56	209	22	49	10	2	3	28	13	39	1	.234	.276	.344
Randy Kutcher	OF57,DH6,3B6*	R	29	77	160	28	36	10	3	2	18	11	46	3	.225	.273	.363
Ed Romero†	2B22,3B14,SS10	R	31	46	113	14	24	4	0	0	6	7	7	0	.212	.260	.248
Carlos Quintana	OF21,DH7,1B1	R	23	34	77	6	16	5	0	0	6	7	12	0	.208	.274	.273
Sam Horn	DH14,1B2	L	25	33	54	1	8	2	0	0	4	8	16	0	.148	.258	.185
John Marzano	C7	R	26	7	18	5	8	3	0	1	3	0	2	0	.444	.421	.778
Jeff Stone†	OF11,DH3	L	28	18	15	3	3	0	0	0	1	1	2	1	.200	.235	.200
Dana Williams	DH2,OF1	R	26	8	5	1	1	1	0	0	0	0	1	0	.200	.333	.400

J. Reed, 1 G at DH, 1 G at OF; R. Kutcher, 1 G at C

Pitcher	T	Age	G	GS	CG	ShO	IP	H	HR	BB	SO	W-L	Sv	ERA
Roger Clemens	R	26	35	35	8	3	253.1	215	20	93	230	17-11	0	3.13
Mike Boddicker	R	31	34	34	3	2	211.2	217	19	71	145	15-11	0	4.00
John Dopson	R	25	29	28	2	0	169.1	166	14	69	95	12-8	0	3.99
Wes Gardner	R	28	22	16	0	0	86.0	97	10	47	81	3-7	0	5.97
Eric Hetzel	R	25	12	11	0	0	50.1	61	7	28	33	2-3	0	6.26
Oil Can Boyd	R	29	10	10	0	0	59.0	57	8	19	26	3-2	0	4.42
Tom Bolton	L	27	4	4	0	0	17.1	21	1	10	9	0-4	0	8.31
Rob Murphy	L	29	74	0	0	0	105.0	97	7	41	107	5-7	9	2.74
Lee Smith	R	31	64	0	0	0	70.2	53	6	33	96	6-1	25	3.57
Bob Stanley	R	34	43	0	0	0	79.1	102	4	26	32	5-2	4	4.88
Dennis Lamp	R	36	42	0	0	0	112.1	96	4	27	61	4-2	2	2.32
Mike Smithson	R	34	40	19	1	1	143.2	170	21	35	61	7-14	2	4.95
Joe Price†	L	32	31	5	0	0	70.1	71	8	30	52	2-5	0	4.35
Greg Harris†	R	33	15	0	0	0	28.0	21	1	15	25	2-2	0	2.57
Mike Rochford	L	26	4	0	0	0	4.0	4	1	4	1	0-0	0	6.75

1989 Milwaukee Brewers 4th AL East 81-81 .500 8.0 GB

Tom Trebelhorn

Player	Gm by Position	B	Age	G	AB	R	H	2B	3B	HR	RBI	BB	SO	SB	Avg	OBP	Slg
B.J. Surhoff	C106,DH12,3B6	L	24	126	436	42	108	17	4	5	55	25	29	14	.248	.287	.339
Greg Brock	1B100,DH7	L	32	107	373	40	99	16	0	12	52	43	49	6	.265	.345	.405
Jim Gantner	2B114,DH2	L	36	116	409	51	112	18	3	0	34	21	33	20	.274	.321	.333
Paul Molitor	3B112,DH28,2B16	R	32	155	615	84	194	35	4	11	56	64	67	27	.315	.379	.439
Bill Spiers	SS89,3B12,DH4*	L	23	114	345	44	88	9	3	4	33	21	63	10	.255	.298	.333
Robin Yount	OF143,DH17	R	33	160	614	101	195	38	9	21	103	63	71	19	.318	.384	.511
Glenn Braggs	OF132,DH14	R	26	144	514	77	127	12	3	15	66	42	111	17	.247	.305	.370
Rob Deer	OF125,DH5	R	28	130	466	72	98	18	2	26	65	60	158	4	.210	.305	.425
Joey Meyer	DH31,1B18	R	27	53	147	13	33	6	0	7	29	12	36	1	.224	.274	.408
Gary Sheffield	SS70,3B21,DH4	R	20	95	368	34	91	18	0	5	32	27	33	10	.247	.303	.337
Mike Felder	OF93,2B10,DH8	S	27	117	315	50	76	11	3	3	23	23	38	26	.241	.293	.324
Terry Francona	1B46,DH23,OF16*	L	30	90	233	26	54	10	1	3	23	8	20	2	.232	.255	.322
Charlie O'Brien	C62	R	29	62	188	22	44	10	0	6	35	21	11	0	.234	.339	.383
Gus Polidor	3B30,2B29,SS21*	R	27	79	175	15	34	7	0	0	14	6	18	3	.194	.230	.234
Greg Vaughn	OF24,DH13	R	23	38	113	18	30	3	0	5	23	13	23	4	.265	.336	.425
Dave Engle	1B18,DH3,C3	R	32	27	65	5	14	3	0	2	8	4	13	0	.215	.261	.354
Ed Romero†	2B11,3B4,DH2*	R	31	15	50	3	10	3	0	0	3	0	10	0	.200	.200	.260
George Canale	1B11	L	23	13	26	5	5	1	0	1	3	2	3	0	.192	.250	.346
Billy Bates	2B7	L	25	7	14	3	3	0	0	0	0	0	1	2	.214	.214	.214
Juan Castillo	2B3	S	27	3	4	0	0	0	0	0	3	0	2	0	.000	.000	.000
Lavel Freeman	DH2	L	26	2	3	1	0	0	0	0	0	0	2	0	.000	.000	.000
Chuck Crim	P76,1B1	R	27	76	0	0	0	0	0	0	0	0	0	0	—	—	—

B. Spiers, 4 G at 2B, 2 G at 1B; T. Francona, 1 G at P; G. Polidor, 2 G at DH; E. Romero, 1 G at SS

Pitcher	T	Age	G	GS	CG	ShO	IP	H	HR	BB	SO	W-L	Sv	ERA
Chris Bosio	R	26	33	33	8	2	234.2	225	16	48	173	15-10	0	2.95
Don August	R	25	31	25	2	1	142.1	175	17	58	51	12-12	0	5.31
Teddy Higuera	L	30	22	22	2	1	135.1	125	9	48	91	9-6	0	3.46
Jaime Navarro	R	22	19	17	1	0	109.2	119	6	32	56	7-8	0	3.12
Tom Filer	R	32	13	13	0	0	72.1	74	6	23	20	7-3	0	3.61
Bryan Clutterbuck	R	29	14	11	1	0	67.1	73	11	16	29	2-5	0	4.14
Mike Birkbeck	R	28	9	9	1	0	44.2	57	4	22	31	0-4	0	5.44
Bill Wegman	R	26	11	8	0	0	51.0	69	6	21	27	2-6	0	6.71
Jerry Reuss†	L	40	7	7	0	0	33.2	36	7	13	13	1-4	0	5.35
Jeff Peterek	R	25	7	4	0	0	31.1	31	3	14	16	0-2	0	4.02
Chuck Crim	R	27	76	0	0	0	117.2	114	7	36	59	9-7	7	2.83
Dan Plesac	L	27	52	0	0	0	61.1	47	6	17	52	3-4	33	2.35
Tony Fossas	L	31	51	0	0	0	61.0	57	3	22	42	2-2	1	3.54
Mark Knudson	R	28	40	7	1	0	123.2	110	15	29	47	8-5	0	3.35
Bill Krueger	L	31	34	5	0	0	93.2	96	9	33	72	3-2	3	3.84
Jay Aldrich†	R	28	16	0	0	0	26.0	24	3	13	12	1-0	1	3.81
Paul Mirabella	L	35	13	0	0	0	15.1	18	1	7	6	0-0	0	7.63
Randy Veres	R	23	3	1	0	0	8.1	9	0	4	8	0-1	0	4.32
Ray Krawczyk	R	29	1	0	0	0	2.0	4	0	1	6	0-0	0	13.50
Terry Francona	L	30	1	0	0	0	1.0	0	0	0	1	0-0	0	0.00

1989 New York Yankees 5th AL East 74-87 .460 14.5 GB

Dallas Green (56-65)/Bucky Dent (18-22)

Player	Gm by Position	B	Age	G	AB	R	H	2B	3B	HR	RBI	BB	SO	SB	Avg	OBP	Slg
Don Slaught	C105,DH3	R	30	117	350	34	88	21	3	5	38	30	57	1	.251	.315	.371
Don Mattingly	1B145,DH17,OF1	L	28	158	631	79	191	37	2	23	113	51	30	3	.303	.351	.477
Steve Sax	2B158	R	29	158	651	88	205	26	3	5	63	52	44	43	.315	.364	.387
Mike Pagliarulo†	3B69,DH1	L	29	74	223	19	44	10	0	4	16	19	43	1	.197	.266	.296
Alvaro Espinoza	SS146	R	27	146	503	51	142	23	1	0	41	14	60	3	.282	.301	.332
Roberto Kelly	OF137	R	24	137	441	65	133	18	3	9	48	41	89	35	.302	.369	.417
Jesse Barfield†	OF129	R	29	129	441	71	106	19	1	18	56	82	122	5	.240	.360	.410
Mel Hall	OF75,DH34	L	28	113	361	54	94	9	0	17	58	21	37	0	.260	.295	.427
Steve Balboni	DH82,1B20	R	32	110	300	33	71	12	2	17	59	25	67	0	.237	.296	.460
Rickey Henderson†	OF65	R	30	65	235	41	58	13	1	3	22	56	29	25	.247	.392	.349
Luis Polonia†	OF53,DH9	L	24	66	227	39	71	11	2	2	29	16	29	9	.313	.359	.405
Bob Geren	C60,DH2	R	27	65	205	26	59	5	1	9	27	12	44	0	.288	.329	.454
Ken Phelps†	DH56,1B8	L	34	86	185	26	46	3	0	7	29	27	47	0	.249	.340	.378
Tom Brookens	3B51,SS7,2B5*	R	35	66	168	14	38	6	0	4	14	11	27	1	.226	.272	.333
Wayne Tolleson	3B28,SS28,2B13*	S	33	79	140	16	23	5	2	1	9	16	23	5	.164	.255	.250
Randy Velarde	3B27,SS9	R	26	33	100	12	34	4	2	2	11	7	14	0	.340	.389	.480
Bob Brower	OF25,DH1	R	29	26	69	9	16	3	0	2	3	6	11	3	.232	.293	.362
Deion Sanders	OF14	L	21	14	47	7	11	2	0	2	7	3	8	1	.234	.280	.404
Mike Blowers	3B13	R	24	13	38	2	10	0	0	0	3	3	13	0	.263	.317	.263
Hensley Meulens	3B8	R	22	8	28	2	5	0	0	0	1	2	8	0	.179	.233	.179
Jamie Quirk†	C6,DH1,SS1	L	34	13	24	0	2	0	0	0	0	3	5	0	.083	.185	.083
Brian Dorsett	C8	R	28	8	22	3	8	1	0	0	4	1	3	0	.364	.391	.409
Hal Morris	OF5,1B2,DH1	L	24	15	18	2	5	0	0	0	4	1	4	0	.278	.316	.278
Gary Ward†	OF6,DH1	R	35	8	17	3	5	1	0	0	1	3	5	0	.294	.400	.353
Marcus Lawton	OF8,DH1	S	23	10	14	1	3	0	0	0	0	0	3	1	.214	.214	.214
Stan Jefferson†	OF7,DH1	S	26	10	12	1	1	0	0	0	1	0	4	1	.083	.083	.083
Steve Kiefer	3B5	R	28	5	8	0	1	0	0	0	0	0	5	0	.125	.125	.125

T. Brookens, 3 G at DH, 3 G at OF; W. Tolleson, 10 G at DH

Pitcher	T	Age	G	GS	CG	ShO	IP	H	HR	BB	SO	W-L	Sv	ERA
Andy Hawkins	R	29	34	34	5	2	208.1	238	23	76	98	15-15	0	4.80
Dave LaPoint	L	29	20	20	0	0	113.2	146	12	45	51	6-9	0	5.62
Clay Parker	R	26	22	17	2	0	120.0	123	12	31	53	4-5	0	3.68
Greg Cadaret†	L	27	20	13	3	1	92.1	109	7	38	66	5-5	0	4.58
Walt Terrell†	R	31	13	13	1	1	83.0	102	9	24	30	6-5	0	5.20
Chuck Cary	L	29	22	11	2	0	99.1	78	13	29	79	4-4	0	3.26
Tommy John	L	46	10	10	0	0	63.2	87	6	22	18	2-7	0	5.80
Rich Dotson†	R	30	11	9	1	0	51.2	69	8	17	14	2-5	0	5.57
John Candelaria†	L	35	10	6	1	0	49.0	49	8	12	37	3-3	0	5.14
Jimmy Jones	R	25	11	6	0	0	48.0	56	7	16	25	2-1	0	5.25
Dave Eiland	R	22	6	6	0	0	34.1	44	5	13	11	1-3	0	5.77
Al Leiter†	L	23	4	4	0	0	26.2	23	1	21	22	1-2	0	6.08
Don Schulze†	R	26	2	2	0	0	11.0	12	1	5	5	1-1	0	4.09
Kevin Mmahat	L	24	4	2	0	0	7.2	13	2	8	3	0-2	0	12.91
Lee Guetterman	L	30	70	0	0	0	103.0	98	6	26	51	5-5	13	2.45
Dave Righetti	L	30	55	0	0	0	69.0	73	3	26	51	2-6	25	3.00
Lance McCullers	R	25	52	1	0	0	84.2	83	9	37	82	4-3	3	4.57
Dale Mohorcic	R	33	32	0	0	0	57.2	65	8	18	24	2-1	2	4.99
Eric Plunk†	R	25	27	7	0	0	75.2	65	9	52	61	7-5	0	3.69
Goose Gossage†	R	37	11	0	0	0	14.1	14	0	3	6	1-0	1	3.77
Scott Nielsen	R	30	2	0	0	0	0.2	2	0	1	0	1-0	0	13.50
Bob Davidson	R	26	1	0	0	0	1.0	1	1	1	0	0-0	0	18.00

1989 Cleveland Indians 6th AL East 73-89 .451 16.0 GB

Doc Edwards (65-78)/John Hart (8-11)

Player	Gm by Position	B	Age	G	AB	R	H	2B	3B	HR	RBI	BB	SO	SB	Avg	OBP	Slg
Andy Allanson	C111	R	27	111	323	30	75	9	1	3	17	23	47	4	.232	.289	.294
Pete O'Brien	1B154,DH1	L	31	155	554	75	144	24	1	12	55	83	48	3	.260	.356	.372
Jerry Browne	2B151,DH2	S	23	153	598	83	179	31	4	5	45	68	64	14	.299	.370	.390
Brook Jacoby	3B144,DH3	R	29	147	519	49	141	26	5	13	64	62	90	2	.272	.348	.416
Felix Fermin	SS153,2B2	R	25	156	484	50	115	9	1	0	21	41	27	6	.238	.302	.260
Joe Carter	OF146,1B11,DH8	R	29	162	651	84	158	32	4	35	105	39	112	13	.243	.292	.465
Cory Snyder	OF125,SS7,DH2	R	26	132	489	49	105	17	0	18	59	23	134	6	.215	.251	.360
Brad Komminsk	OF68	R	28	71	198	27	47	8	2	8	33	24	55	8	.237	.319	.419
Dave Clark	DH55,OF21	L	26	102	253	21	60	12	0	8	29	30	63	0	.237	.317	.379
Dion James†	OF37,DH27,1B2	L	26	71	245	26	75	11	0	4	29	24	26	1	.306	.368	.400
Oddibe McDowell†	OF64	L	26	69	239	33	53	5	2	3	22	25	36	12	.222	.296	.297
Albert Belle	OF44,DH17	R	22	62	218	22	49	8	4	7	37	12	55	2	.225	.269	.394
Joel Skinner	C79	R	28	79	178	10	41	10	0	1	13	9	42	1	.230	.271	.303
Luis Aguayo	3B19,SS15,2B10*	R	30	47	97	7	17	4	1	1	8	7	19	0	.175	.239	.268
Luis Medina	DH25,OF3,1B1	R	26	30	83	8	17	1	0	4	8	6	35	0	.205	.258	.361
Mark Salas	DH20,C5	L	28	30	77	4	17	4	1	2	7	5	13	0	.221	.277	.377
Mike Young	DH15,OF1	S	29	32	59	2	11	0	0	1	5	6	13	1	.186	.273	.237
Paul Zuvella	SS15,3B5,DH3	R	30	24	58	10	16	2	0	2	6	1	11	0	.276	.300	.414
Dave Hengel	OF9,DH3	R	27	12	25	2	3	1	0	0	1	2	4	0	.120	.185	.160
Beau Allred	OF5,DH2	L	24	13	24	0	6	3	0	0	1	2	10	0	.250	.308	.375
Denny Gonzalez	DH6,3B1	R	25	8	17	3	5	1	0	0	1	0	4	0	.294	.333	.353
Tommy Hinzo	2B6,SS1	S	25	18	17	4	0	0	0	0	0	2	6	1	.000	.105	.000
Danny Sheaffer	DH3,3B2,OF1	R	27	7	16	1	1	0	0	0	0	2	2	0	.063	.167	.063
Pat Keedy	OF3,3B2,DH1*	R	31	9	14	3	3	2	0	0	1	2	5	0	.214	.313	.357
Mark Higgins	1B5	R	25	6	10	1	1	0	0	0	0	1	6	0	.100	.182	.100
Tom Magrann	C9	R	25	9	10	0	0	0	0	0	0	0	4	0	.000	.000	.000
Pete Dalena	DH1	L	29	5	7	0	1	1	0	0	0	0	3	0	.143	.143	.286

L. Aguayo, 2 G at DH; P. Keedy, 1 G at 1B, 1 G at SS

Pitcher	T	Age	G	GS	CG	ShO	IP	H	HR	BB	SO	W-L	Sv	ERA
Bud Black	L	32	33	32	6	3	222.1	213	14	52	88	12-11	0	3.36
John Farrell	R	26	31	31	7	2	208.0	196	14	71	132	9-14	0	3.63
Tom Candiotti	R	31	31	31	4	0	206.0	188	10	55	124	13-10	0	3.10
Greg Swindell	L	24	28	28	5	2	184.1	170	16	51	129	13-6	0	3.37
Rod Nichols	R	24	15	11	0	0	71.2	81	9	24	42	4-6	0	4.40
Joe Skalski	R	24	2	1	0	0	6.2	7	0	4	3	0-2	0	6.75
Jesse Orosco	L	32	69	0	0	0	78.0	54	7	26	79	3-4	3	2.08
Doug Jones	R	32	59	0	0	0	80.2	76	4	13	65	7-10	32	2.34
Scott Bailes	L	27	34	11	0	0	113.2	116	7	29	47	5-9	0	4.28
Rich Yett	R	26	32	12	1	0	99.0	111	10	47	47	5-6	0	5.00
Keith Atherton	R	30	32	0	0	0	39.0	48	7	13	13	0-3	2	4.15
Steve Olin	R	23	25	0	0	0	36.0	35	1	14	24	1-4	1	3.75
Tim Stoddard	R	36	14	0	0	0	21.1	25	1	7	12	0-0	0	2.95
Steve Davis	L	28	12	2	0	0	25.2	34	2	14	12	1-1	0	8.06
Ed Wojna	R	28	9	3	0	0	33.0	31	0	14	10	0-1	0	4.09
Brad Havens†	L	29	7	0	0	0	13.1	18	3	7	6	0-0	0	4.05
Jeff Kaiser	L	28	6	0	0	0	3.2	5	1	5	4	0-1	0	7.36
Rudy Seanez	R	20	5	0	0	0	5.0	1	0	4	7	0-0	0	3.60
Neil Allen	R	31	3	0	0	0	3.0	8	1	0	0	0-1	0	15.00
Kevin Wickander	L	24	2	0	0	0	2.2	6	0	2	0	0-0	0	3.38

1989 Detroit Tigers 7th AL East 59-103 .364 30.0 GB

Sparky Anderson

Player	Gm by Position	B	Age	G	AB	R	H	2B	3B	HR	RBI	BB	SO	SB	Avg	OBP	Slg
Mike Heath	C117,3B4,OF3*	R	34	122	396	38	104	16	2	10	43	24	71	7	.263	.308	.389
Dave Bergman	1B123,DH7,OF1	L	36	137	385	38	103	13	1	7	37	44	44	1	.268	.345	.361
Lou Whitaker	2B146,DH2	L	32	148	509	77	128	21	1	28	85	89	59	6	.251	.361	.462
Rick Schu†	3B83,DH9,2B5*	R	27	98	266	25	57	11	0	7	21	24	37	1	.214	.278	.335
Alan Trammell	SS117,DH2	R	31	121	449	54	109	20	3	5	43	45	45	10	.243	.314	.334
Gary Pettis	OF119	S	31	119	444	77	114	8	6	1	18	84	106	43	.257	.375	.309
Chet Lemon	OF111,DH13	R	34	127	414	45	98	19	2	7	47	46	71	1	.237	.323	.343
Kenny Williams	OF87,DH1,1B1	R	25	94	258	29	53	5	1	6	23	18	63	9	.205	.269	.302
Keith Moreland†	DH51,1B31,3B12*	R	35	90	318	34	95	16	0	5	35	27	33	3	.299	.357	.396
Fred Lynn	OF68,DH46	L	37	117	353	44	85	11	1	11	46	47	71	1	.241	.328	.371
Gary Ward†	OF51,1B26,DH20	R	35	105	275	24	69	10	2	9	29	21	54	1	.251	.300	.400
Matt Nokes	C51,DH33	L	25	87	268	15	67	10	0	9	39	17	37	1	.250	.298	.388
Mike Brumley	SS42,2B24,3B11*	S	26	92	212	33	42	5	2	1	11	14	45	8	.198	.251	.255
Doug Strange	3B54,2B9,SS9*	S	25	64	196	16	42	4	1	1	14	17	36	3	.214	.280	.260
Tracy Jones†	OF36,DH8	R	28	46	158	17	41	10	0	3	26	16	16	1	.259	.326	.380
Pat Sheridan†	OF35,DH8	L	31	50	120	16	29	3	0	3	15	17	21	4	.242	.333	.342
Scott Lusader	OF33,DH1	L	24	40	103	15	26	4	0	1	8	9	21	3	.252	.310	.320
Torey Lovullo	1B18,3B11	S	23	29	87	8	10	2	0	1	4	14	20	0	.115	.233	.172
Al Pedrique	3B12,SS12,2B8	R	28	31	69	1	14	3	0	0	5	2	15	0	.203	.225	.246
Chris Brown	3B17	R	27	17	57	3	11	3	0	0	4	1	17	0	.193	.203	.246
Rob Richie	OF13,DH4	L	23	19	49	6	13	4	2	1	10	5	10	0	.265	.333	.490
Matt Sinatro	C13	R	29	13	25	2	3	0	0	0	1	1	8	0	.120	.185	.120
Billy Bean†	OF6,1B2	L	25	9	11	0	0	0	0	0	0	2	3	0	.000	.214	.000
Jeff Datz	C6,DH1	R	29	7	10	0	2	0	0	0	0	1	1	0	.200	.333	.200

M. Heath, 1 G at DH; R. Schu, 3 G at 1B, 3 G at SS; K. Moreland, 1 G at C; M. Brumley, 8 G at DH, 4 G at OF; D. Strange, 1 G at DH

Pitcher	T	Age	G	GS	CG	ShO	IP	H	HR	BB	SO	W-L	Sv	ERA
Frank Tanana	L	35	33	33	6	1	223.2	227	21	74	147	10-14	0	3.58
Doyle Alexander	R	38	33	33	5	1	223.0	245	28	76	95	6-18	0	4.44
Jack Morris	R	34	24	24	10	0	170.1	189	23	59	115	6-14	0	4.86
Jeff Robinson	R	27	16	16	1	1	78.0	76	10	46	40	4-5	0	4.73
Kevin Ritz	R	24	12	12	1	0	74.0	75	2	44	56	4-6	0	4.38
Brian DuBois	L	24	6	5	0	0	36.0	29	2	17	13	0-4	1	1.75
David Palmer	R	31	5	5	0	0	17.1	25	1	11	12	0-3	0	7.79
Mike Trujillo	R	29	8	4	1	0	25.2	35	3	13	13	1-2	0	5.96
Randy Nosek	R	22	2	2	0	0	5.1	7	2	10	4	0-2	0	13.50
Dave Beard	R	29	2	1	0	0	5.1	9	2	2	1	0-2	0	5.06
Mike Henneman	R	27	60	0	0	0	90.0	84	4	51	69	11-4	8	3.70
Paul Gibson	R	29	45	13	0	0	132.0	129	11	57	77	4-8	0	4.64
Frank Williams	R	31	42	0	0	0	71.2	70	5	46	33	3-3	1	3.64
Willie Hernandez	L	34	32	0	0	0	31.1	36	4	16	30	2-2	15	5.74
Edwin Nunez	R	26	27	0	0	0	54.0	49	6	36	41	3-4	1	4.17
Charles Hudson	R	30	18	7	0	0	66.2	75	14	31	23	1-5	0	6.35
Mike Schwabe	R	24	13	4	0	0	44.2	58	6	16	13	2-4	0	6.04
Brad Havens†	L	29	13	1	0	0	22.2	28	3	14	15	1-2	0	5.56
Steve Searcy	L	25	8	2	0	0	22.1	27	3	12	11	1-1	0	6.04
Ramon Pena	R	27	8	0	0	0	18.0	26	0	8	12	0-0	0	6.00
Shawn Holman	R	24	5	0	0	0	10.0	8	0	11	9	0-0	0	1.80
Randy Bockus	R	28	2	0	0	0	5.1	7	0	2	2	0-0	0	5.06

Seasons: Team Rosters 909

1989 Oakland Athletics 1st AL West 99-63 .611 —

Tony La Russa

Player	Gm by Position	B	Age	G	AB	R	H	2B	3B	HR	RBI	BB	SO	SB	Avg	OBP	Slg
Terry Steinbach	C103,OF14,1B10*	R	27	130	454	37	124	13	1	7	42	30	66	1	.273	.319	.352
Mark McGwire	1B141,DH2	R	25	143	490	74	113	17	0	33	95	83	94	1	.231	.339	.467
Tony Phillips	2B84,3B49,SS17*	S	30	143	451	48	118	15	6	4	47	58	66	3	.262	.345	.348
Carney Lansford	3B136,1B15,DH3	R	32	148	551	81	185	28	2	2	52	51	25	37	.336	.398	.405
Mike Gallego	SS94,2B41,3B3*	R	28	133	357	45	90	14	2	3	30	35	43	7	.252	.327	.328
Dave Henderson	OF149,DH2	R	30	152	579	77	145	24	3	15	80	54	131	8	.250	.315	.380
Stan Javier	OF107,1B1,2B1	S	25	112	310	42	77	12	3	1	28	31	45	12	.248	.317	.316
Rickey Henderson†	OF82,DH3	R	30	85	306	72	90	13	2	9	35	70	39	52	.294	.425	.438
Dave Parker	DH140,OF1	L	38	144	553	56	146	27	0	22	97	38	91	0	.264	.308	.432
Ron Hassey	C78,DH2,1B1	L	36	97	268	29	61	12	0	5	23	24	45	1	.228	.290	.328
Walt Weiss	SS84	S	25	84	236	30	55	11	0	3	21	21	39	6	.233	.298	.318
Jose Canseco	OF56,DH5	R	24	65	227	40	61	9	1	17	57	23	69	6	.269	.333	.542
Luis Polonia†	OF55	L	24	59	206	31	59	6	4	1	17	9	15	13	.286	.315	.369
Glenn Hubbard	2B48,DH3	R	31	53	131	12	26	6	0	3	12	19	20	2	.198	.296	.313
Lance Blankenship	OF25,2B24,DH10	R	25	58	125	22	29	5	1	1	4	8	31	5	.232	.276	.312
Billy Beane	OF25,DH4,1B4*	R	27	37	79	8	19	5	0	0	11	0	13	3	.241	.238	.304
Felix Jose	OF19	S	24	20	57	3	11	2	0	0	5	4	13	0	.193	.246	.228
Jamie Quirk†	3B3,C2,1B1*	L	34	9	10	1	2	0	0	1	1	0	4	0	.200	.200	.500
Ken Phelps†	1B1	L	34	11	9	0	1	1	0	0	0	4	0	0	.111	.385	.222
Larry Arndt	1B1,3B1	R	26	2	6	1	1	0	0	0	0	0	1	0	.167	.167	.167
Doug Jennings	OF3	L	24	4	4	0	0	0	0	0	0	0	2	0	.000	.000	.000
Dann Howitt	1B1,OF1	L	25	3	3	0	0	0	0	0	0	0	2	0	.000	.000	.000
Chris Bando	C1	S	33	1	2	0	1	0	0	0	1	0	1	0	.500	.500	.500
Dick Scott	SS3	R	26	3	2	0	0	0	0	0	1	0	0	0	.000	.000	.000
Scott Hemond		R	23	4	0	2	0	0	0	0	0	0	0	0	—	—	—

T. Steinbach, 4 G at DH, 3 G at 3B; T. Phillips, 16 G at OF, 1 G at 1B; M. Gallego, 1 G at DH; B. Beane, 1 G at C, 1 G at 3B; J. Quirk, 1 G at OF

Pitcher	T	Age	G	GS	CG	ShO	IP	H	HR	BB	SO	W-L	Sv	ERA
Dave Stewart	R	32	36	36	8	0	257.2	260	23	69	155	21-9	0	3.32
Mike Moore	R	29	35	35	6	3	241.2	193	14	83	172	19-11	0	2.61
Bob Welch	R	32	33	33	1	0	209.2	191	13	78	137	17-8	0	3.00
Storm Davis	R	27	31	31	1	0	169.1	187	19	68	91	19-7	0	4.36
Curt Young	L	29	25	20	1	0	111.0	117	10	47	55	5-9	0	3.73
Dave Otto	L	24	1	1	0	0	6.2	6	0	2	4	0-0	0	2.70
Rick Honeycutt	L	35	64	0	0	0	76.2	56	5	26	52	2-2	12	2.35
Dennis Eckersley	R	34	51	0	0	0	57.2	32	5	3	55	4-0	33	1.56
Todd Burns	R	25	50	2	0	0	96.1	66	3	28	49	6-5	8	2.24
Gene Nelson	R	28	50	0	0	0	80.0	60	5	30	70	3-5	3	3.26
Matt Young	L	30	26	4	0	0	37.1	42	2	31	27	1-4	0	6.75
Greg Cadaret†	L	27	26	0	0	0	27.2	21	0	19	14	0-0	0	2.28
Eric Plunk†	R	25	23	0	0	0	28.2	17	1	12	24	1-1	1	2.20
Jim Corsi	R	27	22	0	0	0	38.1	26	2	10	21	1-2	0	1.88
Bill Dawley	R	31	4	0	0	0	9.0	11	0	2	3	0-0	0	4.00
Brian Snyder	L	31	2	0	0	0	0.2	2	1	2	1	0-0	0	27.00

1989 Kansas City Royals 2nd AL West 92-70 .568 7.0 GB

John Wathan

Player	Gm by Position	B	Age	G	AB	R	H	2B	3B	HR	RBI	BB	SO	SB	Avg	OBP	Slg
Bob Boone	C129	R	41	131	405	33	111	13	2	1	43	49	37	3	.274	.351	.323
George Brett	1B104,DH17,OF2	L	36	124	457	67	129	26	3	12	80	59	47	14	.282	.362	.431
Frank White	2B132,OF1	R	38	135	418	34	107	22	1	2	36	30	52	3	.256	.307	.328
Kevin Seitzer	3B159,SS6,OF3*	R	27	160	597	78	168	17	2	4	48	102	76	17	.281	.387	.337
Kurt Stillwell	SS130	S	24	130	463	52	121	20	7	7	54	42	64	9	.261	.325	.380
Jim Eisenreich	OF123,DH10	L	30	134	475	64	139	33	7	9	59	37	44	27	.293	.341	.448
Bo Jackson	OF110,DH25	R	26	135	515	86	132	15	6	32	105	39	172	26	.256	.310	.495
Willie Wilson	OF108,DH1	S	33	112	383	58	97	17	7	3	43	27	78	24	.253	.300	.358
Danny Tartabull	OF71,DH55	R	26	133	441	54	118	22	0	18	62	69	123	4	.268	.369	.440
Pat Tabler	OF55,DH39,1B20*	R	31	123	390	36	101	11	1	2	42	37	42	0	.259	.325	.308
Brad Wellman	2B64,SS34,3B3	R	29	103	178	30	41	4	0	2	12	7	36	5	.230	.263	.287
Bill Buckner	1B24,DH19	L	39	79	176	7	38	4	1	1	16	6	11	1	.216	.240	.267
Mike Macfarlane	C59,DH4	R	25	69	157	13	35	6	0	2	19	7	27	0	.223	.263	.299
Matt Winters	OF31,DH3	L	29	42	107	14	25	6	0	2	9	14	23	0	.234	.320	.346
Gary Thurman	OF60,DH4	R	24	72	87	24	17	2	1	0	5	15	26	16	.195	.311	.241
Luis de los Santos	1B27	R	22	28	87	6	22	3	1	0	6	5	14	0	.253	.293	.310
Bill Pecota	SS29,OF15,2B12*	R	29	65	83	21	17	4	2	3	5	7	9	5	.205	.275	.410
Rey Palacios	3B21,1B18,C13*	R	26	55	47	12	8	2	0	1	8	2	14	0	.170	.216	.277
Jeff Schulz	OF5	L	28	7	9	0	2	0	0	0	1	0	2	0	.222	.222	.222

K. Seitzer, 2 G at 1B; P. Tabler, 3 G at 2B, 1 G at 3B; B. Pecota, 7 G at 3B, 4 G at 1B; R. Palacios, 1 G at OF

Pitcher	T	Age	G	GS	CG	ShO	IP	H	HR	BB	SO	W-L	Sv	ERA
Mark Gubicza	R	26	36	36	8	2	255.0	252	10	63	173	15-11	0	3.04
Bret Saberhagen	R	25	36	35	12	4	262.1	209	13	43	193	23-6	0	2.16
Charlie Leibrandt	L	32	33	27	3	1	161.0	196	13	54	73	5-11	0	5.14
Floyd Bannister	L	34	14	14	0	0	75.1	87	8	18	35	4-1	0	4.66
Larry McWilliams†	L	35	8	5	1	0	32.2	31	2	8	24	2-2	0	4.13
Kevin Appier	R	21	6	5	0	0	21.2	34	3	12	10	1-4	0	9.14
Stan Clarke	L	28	2	2	0	0	7.0	14	2	4	2	0-2	0	15.43
Jeff Montgomery	R	27	63	0	0	0	92.0	66	3	25	94	7-3	18	1.37
Steve Farr	R	32	51	2	0	0	63.1	75	5	22	56	2-5	18	4.12
Tom Gordon	R	21	49	16	1	1	163.0	122	10	86	153	17-9	1	3.64
Luis Aquino	R	25	34	16	2	1	141.1	148	6	35	68	6-8	0	3.50
Terry Leach†	R	35	30	3	0	0	73.2	78	4	36	34	5-6	0	4.15
Steve Crawford	R	31	25	0	0	0	54.0	48	2	19	33	3-1	0	2.83
Rick Luecken	R	28	19	0	0	0	23.2	23	3	13	16	2-1	1	3.42
Jerry Don Gleaton	L	31	15	0	0	0	14.1	20	0	6	9	0-0	0	5.65
Jose DeJesus	R	24	3	1	0	0	8.0	7	1	8	2	0-0	0	4.50
Bob Buchanan	L	28	2	0	0	0	3.1	5	1	3	3	0-0	0	16.20

1989 California Angels 3rd AL West 91-71 .562 8.0 GB

Doug Rader

Player	Gm by Position	B	Age	G	AB	R	H	2B	3B	HR	RBI	BB	SO	SB	Avg	OBP	Slg
Lance Parrish	C122,DH2	R	33	124	433	48	103	12	1	17	50	42	104	1	.238	.306	.388
Wally Joyner	1B159	L	27	159	593	78	167	30	2	16	79	46	58	3	.282	.335	.420
Johnny Ray	2B130	S	32	134	530	52	153	16	3	5	62	36	30	6	.289	.327	.358
Jack Howell	3B142,OF4	L	27	144	474	56	108	19	4	20	52	52	125	0	.228	.308	.411
Dick Schofield	SS90	R	26	91	302	42	69	11	2	4	26	28	47	9	.228	.299	.318
Devon White	OF154,DH1	S	26	156	636	86	156	18	13	12	56	31	129	44	.245	.282	.371
Chili Davis	OF147,DH6	S	29	154	560	81	152	24	1	22	90	61	109	3	.271	.340	.436
C. Washington	OF100,DH7	L	34	110	418	53	114	18	4	13	42	27	84	13	.273	.319	.428
Brian Downing	DH141	R	38	142	544	59	154	25	2	14	59	56	87	0	.283	.354	.414
Kent Anderson	SS70,2B7,3B5*	R	25	86	223	27	51	6	1	0	17	17	42	1	.229	.285	.265
Tony Armas	OF47,DH6,1B2	R	35	60	202	22	52	7	1	11	30	7	48	0	.257	.280	.465
Bill Schroeder	C33,1B8	R	30	41	138	16	28	2	0	6	15	3	44	0	.203	.220	.348
Dante Bichette	OF40,DH1	R	25	48	138	13	29	7	0	3	15	6	24	3	.210	.240	.326
Glenn Hoffman	SS23,3B18,2B4*	R	30	48	104	9	22	3	0	1	3	3	13	0	.212	.241	.269
Mark McLemore	2B27,DH1	S	24	32	103	12	25	3	1	0	14	7	19	6	.243	.295	.291
Max Venable	OF13	L	32	20	53	7	19	4	0	0	4	1	16	0	.358	.370	.434
John Orton	C16	R	23	16	39	4	7	1	0	0	4	2	17	0	.179	.220	.205
Bobby Rose	3B10,2B3	R	22	14	38	4	8	1	2	1	3	2	10	0	.211	.268	.421
Jim Eppard	1B4	L	29	12	12	0	3	0	0	0	2	1	4	0	.250	.308	.250
Ron Tingley	C4	R	30	4	3	0	1	0	0	0	0	1	0	0	.333	.500	.333
Brian Brady	OF1	L	26	2	2	0	1	1	0	0	1	0	1	0	.500	.500	1.000
Gary DiSarcina	SS1	R	21	2	0	0	0	0	0	0	0	0	0	0	—	—	—

K. Anderson, 2 G at OF, 1 G at DH; G. Hoffman, 1 G at DH, 1 G at 1B

Pitcher	T	Age	G	GS	CG	ShO	IP	H	HR	BB	SO	W-L	Sv	ERA
Bert Blyleven	R	38	33	33	8	5	241.0	225	14	44	131	17-5	0	2.73
Mike Witt	R	28	33	33	5	0	220.0	252	26	48	123	9-15	0	4.54
Kirk McCaskill	R	28	32	32	6	4	212.0	202	16	59	107	15-10	0	2.93
Chuck Finley	L	26	29	29	9	1	199.2	171	13	82	156	16-9	0	2.57
Jim Abbott	L	21	29	29	4	2	181.1	190	13	74	115	12-12	0	3.92
Terry Clark	R	28	4	2	0	0	11.0	13	0	3	7	0-2	0	4.91
Greg Minton	R	37	62	0	0	0	90.0	76	4	37	42	4-3	8	2.20
Bryan Harvey	R	26	51	0	0	0	55.0	36	6	41	78	3-3	25	3.44
Bob McClure	L	37	48	0	0	0	52.1	39	2	15	36	6-1	3	1.55
Willie Fraser	R	25	44	0	0	0	91.2	80	6	23	46	4-7	2	3.24
Rich Monteleone	R	26	24	0	0	0	39.2	39	3	13	27	2-2	0	3.18
Dan Petry	R	30	19	4	0	0	51.0	53	8	23	21	3-2	0	5.47
Sherm Corbett	L	26	4	0	0	0	5.1	3	1	1	3	0-0	0	3.38
Mike Fetters	R	24	1	0	0	0	3.1	5	1	1	4	0-0	0	8.10
Vance Lovelace	L	25	1	0	0	0	1.0	0	0	1	1	0-0	0	0.00

1989 Texas Rangers 4th AL West 83-79 .512 16.0 GB

Bobby Valentine

Player	Gm by Position	B	Age	G	AB	R	H	2B	3B	HR	RBI	BB	SO	SB	Avg	OBP	Slg
Chad Kreuter	C85	S	24	87	158	16	24	3	0	5	9	27	40	0	.152	.274	.266
Rafael Palmeiro	1B147,DH6	L	24	156	559	76	154	23	4	8	64	63	48	4	.275	.354	.374
Julio Franco	2B140,DH10	R	27	150	548	80	173	31	5	13	92	66	69	21	.316	.386	.462
Steve Buechele	3B145,2B18,SS1	R	27	155	486	60	114	22	2	16	59	36	107	1	.235	.294	.387
Scott Fletcher†	SS81,DH1	R	30	83	314	47	75	14	1	0	22	38	41	1	.239	.323	.290
Ruben Sierra	OF162	S	23	162	634	101	194	35	14	29	119	43	82	8	.306	.347	.543
Cecil Espy	OF133,DH3	S	26	142	475	65	122	12	7	3	31	38	99	45	.257	.313	.331
Pete Incaviglia	OF125,DH5	R	25	133	453	48	107	27	4	21	81	32	136	5	.236	.293	.453
Harold Baines†	DH46,OF1	L	30	50	172	18	49	9	0	3	16	13	27	0	.285	.333	.390
Jeff Kunkel	SS59,OF30,2B8*	R	27	108	293	39	79	21	2	8	29	20	75	3	.270	.323	.437
Rick Leach	DH44,OF41,1B4	L	32	110	239	32	65	14	1	1	23	32	33	2	.272	.358	.351
Fred Manrique†	SS37,2B17,3B6	R	27	54	191	23	55	12	0	2	22	9	33	4	.288	.318	.382
Geno Petralli	C49,DH16	S	29	70	184	18	56	7	0	4	23	17	24	0	.304	.368	.408
Jim Sundberg	C73,DH1	R	38	76	147	13	29	7	1	2	8	23	37	0	.197	.304	.299
Mike Stanley	C25,DH21,1B7*	R	26	67	122	9	30	3	1	1	11	12	29	1	.246	.324	.311
Jack Daugherty	1B23,DH8,OF5	S	28	52	106	15	32	4	2	1	10	11	21	2	.302	.364	.406
Sammy Sosa†	OF19,DH3	R	20	25	84	8	20	3	0	1	3	0	20	0	.238	.238	.310
Buddy Bell	DH22,3B9,1B1	R	37	34	82	4	15	4	0	0	3	7	10	0	.183	.247	.232
Juan Gonzalez	OF24	R	19	24	60	6	9	3	0	1	7	6	17	0	.150	.227	.250
Scott Coolbaugh	3B23,DH2	R	23	25	51	7	14	1	0	2	7	4	12	0	.275	.321	.412
Thad Bosley	OF8,DH5	L	32	37	40	5	9	2	0	1	9	3	11	2	.225	.273	.350
Jeff Stone†	DH15,OF3	L	28	22	36	5	6	1	2	0	5	3	5	2	.167	.250	.306
Dean Palmer	DH6,3B6,SS1*	R	20	16	19	0	2	2	0	0	1	0	12	0	.105	.100	.211
Kevin Reimer	DH1	L	25	3	5	0	0	0	0	0	0	0	1	0	.000	.000	.000

J. Kunkel, 5 G at DH, 4 G at 3B, 1 G at P; M. Stanley, 3 G at 3B; D. Palmer, 1 G at OF

Pitcher	T	Age	G	GS	CG	ShO	IP	H	HR	BB	SO	W-L	Sv	ERA
Nolan Ryan	R	42	32	32	6	2	239.1	162	17	98	301	16-10	0	3.20
Bobby Witt	R	25	31	31	5	1	194.1	182	14	114	166	12-13	0	5.14
Charlie Hough	R	41	30	30	5	1	182.0	168	28	95	94	10-13	0	4.35
Kevin Brown	R	24	28	28	7	0	191.0	167	10	70	104	12-9	0	3.35
Mike Jeffcoat	L	29	22	22	2	2	130.2	139	7	33	64	9-6	0	3.58
Jamie Moyer	L	26	15	15	1	0	76.0	84	10	33	44	4-9	0	4.86
John Barfield	L	24	4	2	0	0	11.2	15	0	4	9	0-1	0	6.17
Wilson Alvarez	L	19	1	1	0	0	0.0	3	2	2	0	0-1	0	—
Kenny Rogers	L	24	73	0	0	0	73.2	60	2	42	63	3-4	2	2.93
Jeff Russell	R	27	71	0	0	0	72.2	45	4	24	77	6-4	38	1.98
Cecilio Guante	R	29	50	0	0	0	69.0	66	7	36	69	6-6	2	3.91
Gary Mielke	R	26	43	0	0	0	49.2	52	4	25	26	1-0	1	3.26
Drew Hall	L	26	38	0	0	0	58.1	42	3	33	45	2-1	0	3.70
Craig McMurtry	R	29	19	0	0	0	23.0	29	3	13	14	0-0	0	7.43
Brad Arnsberg	R	25	16	1	0	0	48.0	45	6	22	26	2-1	1	4.13
Darrel Akerfelds	R	27	6	0	0	0	11.0	11	1	5	9	0-1	0	3.27
Paul Wilmet	R	30	3	0	0	0	2.1	5	0	2	1	0-0	0	15.43
Jeff Kunkel	R	27	1	0	0	0	1.2	4	1	3	0	0-0	0	21.60

1989 Minnesota Twins 5th AL West 80-82 .494 19.0 GB

Tom Kelly

Player	Gm by Position	B	Age	G	AB	R	H	2B	3B	HR	RBI	BB	SO	SB	Avg	OBP	Slg
Brian Harper	C101,DH19,OF3*	R	29	126	385	43	125	24	0	8	57	13	16	2	.325	.353	.449
Kent Hrbek	1B89,DH18	L	29	109	375	59	102	17	0	25	84	53	35	3	.272	.360	.517
Al Newman	2B84,3B37,SS31*	S	29	141	446	62	113	18	2	0	38	59	46	25	.253	.341	.303
Gary Gaetti	3B125,DH3,1B2	R	30	130	498	63	125	11	4	19	75	25	87	6	.251	.286	.404
Greg Gagne	SS146,OF1	R	27	149	460	69	125	29	7	9	48	17	80	11	.272	.298	.424
Kirby Puckett	OF157,DH2	R	28	159	635	75	215	45	4	9	85	41	59	11	.339	.379	.465
Dan Gladden	OF117,DH2,P1	R	31	121	461	69	136	23	3	8	46	23	53	23	.295	.331	.410
Randy Bush	OF109,1B25,DH5	L	30	141	391	60	103	17	4	14	54	48	73	5	.263	.347	.435
Jim Dwyer†	DH74,OF1	L	39	88	225	34	71	11	0	3	23	28	23	2	.316	.390	.404
Gene Larkin	1B67,DH41,OF32	S	26	136	446	61	119	25	1	6	46	54	57	5	.267	.353	.368
Wally Backman	2B84,DH1	S	29	87	299	33	69	9	2	1	26	32	45	1	.231	.306	.284
John Moses	OF108,DH3,1B2*	S	31	129	242	33	68	12	3	1	31	19	23	14	.281	.333	.368
Tim Laudner	C68,DH19,1B11	R	31	100	239	24	53	11	1	6	27	25	65	1	.222	.293	.351
Carmelo Castillo	OF67,DH16	R	31	94	218	23	56	13	3	8	33	15	40	1	.257	.305	.454
Doug Baker	2B25,SS19	S	28	43	78	17	23	5	1	0	9	9	18	0	.295	.378	.385
Chip Hale	2B16,3B9,DH2	L	24	28	67	6	14	3	0	0	4	1	6	0	.209	.214	.254
Orlando Mercado	C19	R	27	19	38	1	4	0	0	0	1	4	4	1	.105	.190	.105
Terry Jorgensen	3B9	R	22	10	23	1	4	1	0	0	2	4	5	0	.174	.296	.217
Paul Sorrento	DH5,1B5	L	23	14	21	2	5	0	0	0	1	5	4	0	.238	.370	.238
Lenny Webster	C14	R	24	14	20	3	6	2	0	0	1	3	2	0	.300	.391	.400
Vic Rodriguez	3B5	R	27	6	11	2	5	2	0	0	0	0	1	0	.455	.455	.636
Greg Olson	C3	R	28	3	2	0	1	0	0	0	0	0	0	0	.500	.500	.500

B. Harper, 2 G at 1B, 2 G at 3B; A. Newman, 4 G at OF, 2 G at DH; J. Moses, 1 G at P

Pitcher	T	Age	G	GS	CG	ShO	IP	H	HR	BB	SO	W-L	Sv	ERA
Allan Anderson	L	25	33	33	4	1	196.2	214	15	53	69	17-10	0	3.80
Roy Smith	R	27	32	26	2	0	172.1	180	22	51	92	10-6	1	3.92
Shane Rawley	L	33	27	25	1	0	145.0	167	19	60	68	5-12	0	5.21
Frank Viola†	L	29	24	24	7	1	175.2	171	17	47	138	8-12	0	3.79
Mike Dyer	R	22	16	12	1	0	71.0	74	2	37	37	4-7	0	4.82
Rick Aguilera†	R	27	11	11	3	0	75.2	71	5	17	57	3-5	0	3.21
Mark Guthrie	R	23	13	8	0	0	57.1	66	7	21	38	2-4	0	4.55
Francisco Oliveras	R	26	12	8	1	0	55.2	64	8	15	24	3-4	0	4.53
David West†	L	24	10	5	0	0	39.1	48	5	19	31	3-2	0	6.41
Kevin Tapani†	R	25	5	5	0	0	32.2	34	2	8	21	2-2	0	3.86
Fred Toliver†	R	28	7	5	0	0	29.0	39	2	15	11	1-3	0	7.76
Jeff Reardon	R	33	65	0	0	0	73.0	68	8	12	46	5-4	31	4.07
Gary Wayne	L	26	60	0	0	0	71.0	55	4	36	41	3-4	1	3.30
Juan Berenguer	R	34	56	0	0	0	106.0	96	11	47	93	9-3	3	3.48
German Gonzalez	R	27	22	0	0	0	29.0	32	2	11	25	3-2	0	4.66
Mike Cook	R	25	15	0	0	0	21.1	22	1	17	15	0-1	0	5.06
Randy St. Claire	R	28	14	0	0	0	22.1	19	4	10	14	1-0	1	5.24
Steve Shields	R	30	11	0	0	0	17.1	28	3	6	12	0-1	0	7.79
Lee Tunnell	R	28	10	0	0	0	12.0	18	1	6	7	1-0	0	6.00
Tim Drummond	R	24	8	0	0	0	16.1	16	0	8	9	0-0	1	3.86
Greg Booker†	R	29	6	0	0	0	8.2	11	1	2	3	0-0	0	4.15
John Moses	L	31	1	0	0	0	1.0	0	0	1	0	0-0	0	0.00
Dan Gladden	R	31	1	0	0	0	1.0	2	0	1	0	0-0	0	9.00

1989 Seattle Mariners 6th AL West 73-89 .451 26.0 GB

Jim Lefebvre

Player	Gm by Position	B	Age	G	AB	R	H	2B	3B	HR	RBI	BB	SO	SB	Avg	OBP	Slg
Dave Valle	C93	R	28	94	316	32	75	10	3	7	34	29	32	0	.237	.311	.354
Alvin Davis	1B125,DH14	L	28	142	498	84	152	30	1	21	95	101	49	0	.305	.424	.496
Harold Reynolds	2B151,DH1	S	28	153	613	87	184	24	9	0	43	55	45	25	.300	.359	.369
Jim Presley	3B90,1B30,DH1	R	27	117	390	42	92	20	1	12	41	21	107	0	.236	.275	.385
Omar Vizquel	SS143	S	22	143	387	45	85	7	3	1	20	28	40	1	.220	.273	.261
Ken Griffey Jr.	OF127	L	19	127	455	61	120	23	0	16	61	44	83	16	.264	.329	.420
Greg Briley	OF105,2B10,DH2	L	24	115	394	52	105	22	4	13	52	39	82	11	.266	.336	.442
Henry Cotto	OF90,DH2	R	28	100	295	44	78	11	2	9	33	12	44	10	.264	.300	.407
Jeffrey Leonard	DH123,OF26	R	33	150	566	69	144	20	1	24	93	38	125	6	.254	.301	.420
Darnell Coles	OF89,3B26,1B18*	R	27	146	535	54	135	21	3	10	59	27	61	5	.252	.294	.359
Scott Bradley	C70,DH6,1B2*	L	29	103	270	21	74	16	0	3	37	21	23	1	.274	.322	.367
Jay Buhner	OF57	R	24	58	204	27	56	15	1	9	33	19	55	1	.275	.341	.490
Edgar Martinez	3B61	R	26	65	171	20	41	5	0	2	20	17	26	2	.240	.314	.304
Mickey Brantley	OF23,DH6	R	28	34	108	14	17	5	0	0	8	7	7	2	.157	.207	.204
Dave Cochrane	SS30,1B9,3B9*	S	26	54	102	13	24	4	1	3	7	14	27	0	.235	.333	.382
Mike Kingery	OF23	L	28	31	76	14	17	3	0	2	6	7	14	1	.224	.286	.342
Mario Diaz	SS37,2B14,3B3	R	27	52	74	9	10	0	0	1	7	7	7	0	.135	.210	.176
Bill McGuire	C14	R	25	14	28	2	5	0	0	1	4	2	6	0	.179	.233	.286
Rey Quinones†	SS7	R	25	7	19	2	2	0	0	0	0	1	1	0	.105	.150	.105
Jim Wilson	DH5	R	28	5	8	0	0	0	0	0	1	0	3	0	.000	.000	.000
Bruce Fields	OF1	L	28	3	3	2	1	1	0	0	0	0	1	0	.333	.333	.667

D. Coles, 12 G at DH; S. Bradley, 1 G at OF; D. Cochrane, 4 G at 2B, 3 G at OF, 2 G at C

Pitcher	T	Age	G	GS	CG	ShO	IP	H	HR	BB	SO	W-L	Sv	ERA
Scott Bankhead	R	25	33	33	3	2	210.1	187	19	63	140	14-6	0	3.34
Brian Holman†	R	24	23	22	6	2	159.2	160	9	62	82	8-10	0	3.44
Randy Johnson†	L	25	22	22	2	0	131.0	118	11	70	104	7-9	0	4.40
Erik Hanson	R	24	17	17	1	0	113.1	103	7	32	75	9-5	0	3.18
Mike Dunne†	R	26	15	15	1	0	85.1	104	7	37	38	2-9	0	5.27
Mark Langston†	L	28	10	10	2	1	73.1	60	3	19	60	4-5	0	3.56
Clint Zavaras	R	22	10	10	0	0	52.0	49	4	30	31	1-6	0	5.19
Gene Harris†	R	24	10	6	0	0	33.1	47	3	15	14	1-4	1	6.48
Mike Campbell	R	25	5	5	0	0	21.0	28	4	10	6	1-2	0	7.29
Luis DeLeon	R	30	1	1	0	0	4.0	5	1	1	2	0-0	0	2.25
Mike Schooler	R	26	67	0	0	0	77.0	81	2	19	69	1-7	33	2.81
Mike Jackson	R	24	65	0	0	0	99.1	81	8	54	94	4-6	7	3.17
Jerry Reed	R	33	52	1	0	0	101.2	89	10	43	50	7-7	0	3.19
Dennis Powell	L	25	43	1	0	0	45.0	49	6	21	27	2-2	2	5.00
Bill Swift	R	27	37	16	0	0	130.0	140	7	38	45	7-3	1	4.43
Keith Comstock	L	33	31	0	0	0	25.2	26	2	10	22	1-2	0	2.81
Tom Niedenfuer	R	29	25	0	0	0	36.1	46	7	15	15	0-3	0	6.69
Steve Trout	L	31	19	3	0	0	30.0	43	3	17	17	4-3	0	6.60
Julio Solano	R	29	7	0	0	0	9.2	6	1	4	6	0-0	0	5.59

1989 Chicago White Sox 7th AL West 69-92 .429 29.5 GB

Jeff Torborg

Player	Gm by Position	B	Age	G	AB	R	H	2B	3B	HR	RBI	BB	SO	SB	Avg	OBP	Slg
Carlton Fisk	C90,DH13	R	41	103	375	47	110	25	2	13	68	36	60	1	.293	.356	.475
Greg Walker	1B48,DH23	L	29	77	233	25	49	14	0	5	26	23	50	0	.210	.286	.335
Steve Lyons	2B70,1B40,3B28*	L	29	140	443	51	117	21	3	2	50	35	68	9	.264	.317	.339
Carlos Martinez	3B68,1B34,OF10	R	24	109	350	44	105	22	0	5	32	21	57	4	.300	.340	.406
Ozzie Guillen	SS155	L	25	155	597	63	151	20	8	1	54	15	48	36	.253	.270	.318
Dave Gallagher	OF160,DH1	R	28	161	601	74	160	22	2	1	46	46	79	5	.266	.320	.314
Ivan Calderon	OF103,DH36,1B26	R	27	157	622	83	178	34	9	14	87	43	94	7	.286	.332	.437
Daryl Boston	OF75,DH9	L	26	101	218	34	55	3	4	5	23	24	31	7	.252	.325	.372
Harold Baines†	DH70,OF25	L	30	96	333	55	107	20	1	13	56	60	52	0	.321	.423	.505
Dan Pasqua	OF66,DH5	L	27	73	246	26	61	9	1	11	47	25	58	1	.248	.315	.427
Scott Fletcher†	2B53,SS8	R	30	59	232	30	63	11	1	1	21	26	19	1	.272	.344	.341
Eddie Williams	3B65	R	24	66	201	25	55	8	0	3	10	18	31	1	.274	.341	.358
Fred Manrique†	2B57,SS2,3B1	R	27	65	187	23	56	13	1	2	30	8	30	0	.299	.333	.412
Ron Karkovice	C68,DH2	R	25	71	182	21	48	9	2	3	24	10	56	0	.264	.306	.385
Lance Johnson	OF45,DH1	L	25	50	180	28	54	8	2	0	16	17	24	16	.300	.360	.367
Ron Kittle	1B27,DH17,OF5	R	31	51	169	26	51	10	0	11	37	22	42	0	.302	.378	.556
Sammy Sosa†	OF33	R	20	33	99	19	27	5	0	3	10	11	27	7	.273	.351	.414
Matt Merullo	C27,DH1	L	23	31	81	5	18	1	0	1	8	6	14	0	.222	.273	.272
Russ Morman	1B35	R	27	37	58	5	13	2	0	0	8	6	16	1	.224	.292	.259
Robin Ventura	3B16	L	21	16	45	5	8	3	0	0	7	8	6	0	.178	.298	.244
Billy Joe Robidoux	1B15,OF1	L	25	16	39	2	5	2	0	0	1	4	9	0	.128	.209	.179
Jeff Schaefer	SS5,2B4,3B4*	R	29	15	10	2	1	0	0	0	0	0	2	1	.100	.100	.100
Jerry Hairston	DH2	S	37	3	3	0	1	1	0	0	0	0	0	0	.333	.333	.333

S. Lyons, 20 G at OF, 3 G at SS, 1 G at C; J. Schaefer, 1 G at DH

Pitcher	T	Age	G	GS	CG	ShO	IP	H	HR	BB	SO	W-L	Sv	ERA
Melido Perez	R	23	31	31	2	0	183.1	187	23	90	141	11-14	0	5.01
Eric King	R	25	25	25	1	1	159.1	144	13	64	72	9-10	0	3.39
Greg Hibbard	L	24	23	23	2	0	137.1	142	5	41	55	6-7	0	3.21
Steve Rosenberg	L	24	38	21	2	0	142.0	148	14	58	77	4-13	0	4.94
Jerry Reuss†	L	40	23	19	1	1	106.2	135	12	21	27	8-5	0	5.06
Rich Dotson†	R	30	17	17	1	0	99.2	112	8	41	55	3-7	0	3.88
Adam Peterson	R	23	3	2	0	0	5.1	13	1	2	3	0-1	0	15.19
Jeff Bittiger	R	27	2	1	0	0	9.2	9	2	6	7	0-1	0	6.52
Bobby Thigpen	R	25	61	0	0	0	79.0	62	10	40	47	2-6	34	3.76
Donn Pall	R	27	53	0	0	0	87.0	90	9	19	58	4-5	6	3.31
Shawn Hillegas	R	24	50	13	0	0	119.2	132	12	51	76	7-11	3	4.74
Ken Patterson	L	24	50	1	0	0	65.2	64	11	28	43	6-1	0	4.52
Tom McCarthy	R	28	31	0	0	0	66.2	72	8	20	27	1-2	0	3.51
Bill Long	R	29	30	8	0	0	98.2	101	8	37	51	5-5	1	3.92
Barry Jones	R	26	22	0	0	0	30.1	22	2	8	17	3-2	1	2.37
Wayne Edwards	L	25	7	0	0	0	7.1	7	1	3	9	0-0	0	3.68
Jose Segura	R	26	7	0	0	0	6.0	13	2	3	4	0-1	0	15.00
Jack Hardy	R	29	5	0	0	0	12.1	14	1	5	4	0-0	0	6.57
John Davis	R	26	4	0	0	0	6.0	5	2	2	5	0-1	1	4.50

>>1989 Chicago Cubs 1st NL East 93-69 .574 —

Don Zimmer

Player	Gm by Position	B	Age	G	AB	R	H	2B	3B	HR	RBI	BB	SO	SB	Avg	OBP	Slg
Damon Berryhill	C89	S	25	91	334	37	86	13	0	5	41	16	54	1	.257	.291	.341
Mark Grace	1B142	L	25	142	510	74	160	28	3	13	79	80	42	14	.314	.405	.457
Ryne Sandberg	2B155	R	29	157	606	104	176	25	5	30	76	59	85	15	.290	.356	.497
Vance Law	3B119,OF1	R	32	130	408	38	96	22	3	7	42	38	73	2	.235	.296	.355
Shawon Dunston	SS138	R	26	138	471	52	131	20	6	9	60	30	86	19	.278	.320	.403
Jerome Walton	OF115	R	23	116	475	64	139	23	3	5	46	27	77	24	.293	.335	.385
Andre Dawson	OF112	R	34	118	416	62	105	18	6	21	77	35	62	8	.252	.307	.476
Dwight Smith	OF102	L	25	109	343	52	111	19	6	9	52	31	51	9	.324	.382	.493
Mitch Webster	OF74	S	30	98	272	40	70	12	4	3	19	30	55	14	.257	.331	.364
Lloyd McClendon	OF45,1B28,3B6*	R	30	92	259	47	74	12	1	12	40	37	31	6	.286	.368	.479
Domingo Ramos	SS42,3B30	R	31	85	179	18	47	6	2	1	19	17	23	1	.263	.333	.335
Curtis Wilkerson	3B26,2B15,SS7*	S	28	77	160	18	39	4	2	1	10	8	33	4	.244	.278	.313
Joe Girardi	C59	R	24	59	157	15	39	10	0	1	14	11	26	2	.248	.304	.331
Doug Dascenzo	OF45	S	25	47	139	20	23	1	0	1	12	13	13	6	.165	.234	.194
Rick Wrona	C37	R	25	38	92	11	26	2	1	2	14	2	21	0	.283	.299	.391
Gary Varsho	OF21	L	28	61	87	10	16	4	2	0	6	4	13	3	.184	.220	.276
Darrin Jackson†	OF39	R	25	45	83	7	19	4	0	1	8	6	17	1	.229	.281	.313
Luis Salazar†	3B25,OF2	R	33	26	80	7	26	5	0	1	12	4	13	0	.325	.357	.425
Marvell Wynne†	OF13	L	29	20	48	8	9	2	1	1	4	1	7	2	.188	.220	.333
Phil Stephenson†	OF3	L	28	17	21	0	3	0	0	0	0	2	3	1	.143	.217	.143
Greg Smith	2B2	S	22	4	5	1	2	0	0	0	2	0	0	0	.400	.500	.400

L. McClendon, 5 G at C; C. Wilkerson, 1 G at OF

Pitcher	T	Age	G	GS	CG	ShO	IP	H	HR	BB	SO	W-L	Sv	ERA
Greg Maddux	R	23	35	35	7	1	238.1	222	13	82	135	19-12	0	2.95
Rick Sutcliffe	R	33	35	34	5	1	229.0	202	18	69	153	16-11	0	3.66
Mike Bielecki	R	29	33	33	4	3	212.1	187	16	81	147	18-7	0	3.14
Scott Sanderson	R	32	37	23	2	0	146.1	155	16	31	86	11-9	0	3.94
Paul Kilgus	L	27	35	23	0	0	145.2	164	9	49	61	6-10	2	4.39
Joe Kraemer	L	24	1	1	0	0	3.2	7	0	2	5	0-1	0	4.91
Mitch Williams	L	24	76	0	0	0	81.2	71	6	52	67	4-4	36	2.64
Calvin Schiraldi†	R	27	54	0	0	0	78.2	60	7	50	54	3-6	4	3.78
Jeff Pico	R	23	53	5	0	0	90.2	99	8	31	38	3-1	2	3.77
Steve Wilson	L	24	53	8	0	0	85.2	83	6	31	65	6-4	2	4.20
Les Lancaster	R	27	42	0	0	0	72.2	60	2	15	56	4-2	8	1.36
Pat Perry	L	30	19	0	0	0	35.2	23	2	16	20	0-1	1	1.77
Paul Assenmacher†	L	28	14	0	0	0	19.0	19	1	12	15	2-1	0	5.21
Dean Wilkins	R	22	11	0	0	0	15.2	13	2	9	14	1-0	0	5.17
Kevin Blankenship	R	26	2	0	0	0	5.1	4	0	2	2	0-0	0	1.69

1989 New York Mets 2nd NL East 87-75 .537 6.0 GB

Davey Johnson

Player	Gm by Position	B	Age	G	AB	R	H	2B	3B	HR	RBI	BB	SO	SB	Avg	OBP	Slg
Barry Lyons	C76	R	29	79	235	15	58	13	0	3	27	11	28	0	.247	.283	.340
Dave Magadan	1B87,3B28	L	26	127	374	47	107	22	3	4	41	49	37	1	.286	.367	.393
Gregg Jefferies	2B123,3B20	S	21	141	508	72	131	28	2	12	56	39	46	21	.258	.314	.392
Howard Johnson	3B143,SS31	S	28	153	571	104	164	41	3	36	101	77	126	41	.287	.369	.559
Kevin Elster	SS150	R	24	151	458	52	106	25	2	10	55	34	77	4	.231	.283	.360
Kevin McReynolds	OF145	R	29	148	545	74	148	25	3	22	85	46	74	15	.272	.326	.450
Darryl Strawberry	OF131	L	27	134	476	69	107	26	1	29	77	61	105	11	.225	.312	.466
Juan Samuel†	OF84	R	28	86	333	37	76	13	1	3	28	24	75	31	.228	.299	.300
Mookie Wilson†	OF71	S	33	80	249	22	51	10	1	3	18	10	47	7	.205	.237	.289
Tim Teufel	2B40,1B33	R	30	83	219	27	56	7	2	2	15	32	50	1	.256	.350	.333
Keith Hernandez	1B58	L	35	75	215	18	50	8	0	4	19	27	39	0	.233	.324	.326
Mackey Sasser	C62,3B1	L	26	72	182	17	53	14	2	1	22	7	15	0	.291	.316	.407
Lenny Dykstra†	OF51	L	26	56	159	27	43	12	1	3	13	23	15	13	.270	.362	.415
Gary Carter	C47,1B1	R	35	50	153	14	28	8	0	2	15	12	15	0	.183	.241	.275
Keith Miller	2B23,OF14,SS8*	R	26	57	143	15	33	7	0	1	7	5	27	6	.231	.262	.301
Mark Carreon	OF39	R	25	68	133	20	41	6	0	6	16	12	17	2	.308	.370	.489
Lee Mazzilli†	OF10,1B8	S	34	48	60	10	11	2	0	2	7	17	19	3	.183	.364	.317
Phil Lombardi	C16,1B1	R	26	18	48	4	11	1	0	1	3	5	8	0	.229	.302	.313
Lou Thornton	OF6	L	26	13	13	5	4	1	0	0	1	0	1	2	.308	.308	.385
Jeff McKnight	2B4,1B1,3B1*	S	26	6	12	2	3	0	0	0	0	2	1	0	.250	.357	.250
Tom O'Malley	3B3	L	28	9	11	2	6	2	0	0	8	0	2	0	.545	.545	.727
Craig Shipley	SS3,3B2	R	26	4	7	3	1	0	0	0	0	0	1	0	.143	.143	.143

K. Miller, 2 G at 3B; J. McKnight, 1 G at SS

Pitcher	T	Age	G	GS	CG	ShO	IP	H	HR	BB	SO	W-L	Sv	ERA
David Cone	R	26	34	33	7	2	219.2	183	20	74	190	14-8	0	3.52
Ron Darling	R	28	33	33	4	0	217.1	214	19	70	153	14-14	0	3.52
Sid Fernandez	L	26	35	32	6	2	219.1	157	21	75	198	14-5	0	2.83
Bobby Ojeda	L	31	31	31	5	2	192.0	179	16	78	95	13-11	0	3.47
Dwight Gooden	R	24	19	17	0	0	118.1	93	9	47	101	9-4	1	2.89
Frank Viola†	L	29	12	12	2	1	85.1	75	5	27	73	5-5	0	3.38
Blaine Beatty	L	25	2	1	0	0	6.0	5	1	2	3	0-0	0	1.50
Randy Myers	L	26	65	0	0	0	84.1	62	4	40	88	7-4	24	2.35
Don Aase	R	34	49	0	0	0	59.1	56	5	26	34	1-5	2	3.94
Rick Aguilera†	R	27	36	0	0	0	69.1	59	3	21	80	6-6	7	2.34
Jeff Innis	R	26	29	0	0	0	39.2	38	2	8	16	0-1	0	3.18
Roger McDowell†	R	28	25	0	0	0	35.1	34	1	16	15	1-5	4	3.31
Jeff Musselman†	L	26	20	0	0	0	26.1	27	1	14	11	3-2	0	3.08
David West†	L	24	11	2	0	0	24.1	25	4	14	19	0-2	0	7.40
Terry Leach†	R	35	10	0	0	0	21.1	19	1	4	2	0-0	0	4.22
Julio Machado	R	23	10	0	0	0	11.0	9	0	3	14	0-1	0	3.27
Wally Whitehurst	R	25	9	1	0	0	14.0	17	2	5	9	0-1	0	4.50
Kevin Tapani†	R	25	3	0	0	0	7.1	5	1	4	2	0-0	0	3.68
John Mitchell	R	23	2	0	0	0	3.0	3	0	4	4	0-1	0	6.00
Manny Hernandez	R	28	1	0	0	0	1.0	0	0	0	1	0-0	0	0.00

1989 St. Louis Cardinals 3rd NL East 86-76 .531 7.0 GB

Whitey Herzog

Player	Gm by Position	B	Age	G	AB	R	H	2B	3B	HR	RBI	BB	SO	SB	Avg	OBP	Slg
Tony Pena	C134,OF1	R	32	141	424	36	110	17	2	4	37	35	33	5	.259	.318	.337
Pedro Guerrero	1B160	R	33	162	570	60	177	42	1	17	117	79	84	2	.311	.391	.477
Jose Oquendo	2B156,SS7,1B1	S	25	163	556	59	162	28	7	1	48	79	59	3	.291	.375	.372
Terry Pendleton	3B161	S	28	162	613	83	162	28	5	13	74	44	81	9	.264	.313	.390
Ozzie Smith	SS153	S	34	155	593	82	162	30	8	2	50	55	37	29	.273	.335	.361
Tom Brunansky	OF155,1B1	R	28	158	556	67	133	29	3	20	85	59	107	5	.239	.312	.410
Milt Thompson	OF147	L	30	155	545	60	158	28	8	4	68	39	91	27	.290	.340	.393
Vince Coleman	OF142	S	27	145	563	94	143	21	9	2	28	50	90	65	.254	.316	.334
Willie McGee	OF47	S	30	58	199	23	47	10	2	3	17	10	34	8	.236	.275	.352
John Morris	OF51	L	28	96	117	8	28	4	1	2	14	4	22	1	.239	.264	.342
Todd Zeile	C23	R	23	28	82	7	21	3	1	1	8	9	14	0	.256	.326	.354
Tom Pagnozzi	C38,1B2,3B1	R	26	52	80	3	12	2	0	0	3	6	19	0	.150	.216	.175
Denny Walling	1B20,3B9,OF6	L	35	69	79	9	24	7	0	1	11	14	12	0	.304	.409	.430
Tim Jones	2B12,SS12,3B5*	L	26	42	75	11	22	6	0	0	7	7	8	1	.293	.353	.373
Jim Lindeman	1B42,OF5	R	27	73	45	8	5	1	0	0	2	3	18	0	.111	.163	.133
Leon Durham	1B18	L	31	29	18	2	1	1	0	0	1	2	4	0	.056	.182	.111
Rod Booker	2B5,3B1	L	30	10	8	1	2	0	0	0	0	0	1	0	.250	.250	.250
Craig Wilson	3B2	R	24	6	4	1	1	0	0	0	1	1	2	0	.250	.400	.250
Todd Worrell	P47,OF1	R	29	47	1	0	0	0	0	0	0	0	1	0	.000	.000	.000

T. Jones, 1 G at C, 1 G at OF

Pitcher	T	Age	G	GS	CG	ShO	IP	H	HR	BB	SO	W-L	Sv	ERA
Jose DeLeon	R	28	36	36	5	3	244.2	173	10	80	201	16-12	0	3.05
Joe Magrane	L	24	34	33	9	3	234.2	219	5	72	127	18-9	0	2.91
Ken Hill	R	23	33	33	2	1	196.2	186	9	99	112	7-15	0	3.80
Scott Terry	R	29	31	24	1	0	148.2	142	14	43	69	8-10	2	3.57
Ted Power	R	34	23	15	0	0	97.0	96	7	21	43	7-7	0	3.71
Ricky Horton†	L	29	11	8	0	0	45.2	50	2	10	14	0-3	0	4.73
Don Heinkel	R	29	7	5	0	0	26.1	40	2	7	16	1-1	0	5.81
Bob Tewksbury	R	28	7	4	1	1	30.0	25	2	10	17	1-0	0	3.30
Ken Dayley	L	30	71	0	0	0	75.1	63	3	30	40	4-3	12	2.87
Frank DiPino	L	32	67	0	0	0	88.1	73	6	20	44	9-0	0	2.45
Dan Quisenberry	R	36	63	0	0	0	78.1	78	2	14	37	3-1	6	2.64
John Costello	R	28	48	0	0	0	62.1	48	5	20	40	5-4	3	3.32
Todd Worrell	R	29	47	0	0	0	51.2	42	4	26	41	3-5	20	2.96
Cris Carpenter	R	24	36	5	0	0	68.0	70	4	26	35	4-4	0	3.18
Matt Kinzer	R	26	8	1	0	0	13.1	25	3	4	8	0-2	0	12.83

1989 Montreal Expos 4th NL East 81-81 .500 12.0 GB

Buck Rodgers

Player	Gm by Position	B	Age	G	AB	R	H	2B	3B	HR	RBI	BB	SO	SB	Avg	OBP	Slg
Nelson Santovenia	C89,1B1	R	27	97	304	30	76	14	1	5	31	24	37	2	.250	.307	.352
Andres Galarraga	1B147	R	28	152	572	76	147	30	1	23	85	48	158	12	.257	.327	.434
Tom Foley	2B108,3B16,SS14*	L	29	122	375	34	86	19	2	7	39	45	53	2	.229	.314	.347
Tim Wallach	3B153,P1	R	31	154	573	76	159	42	0	13	77	58	81	3	.277	.341	.419
Spike Owen	SS142	S	28	142	437	52	102	17	4	6	41	76	44	3	.233	.349	.332
Hubie Brooks	OF140	R	32	148	542	56	145	30	1	14	70	39	108	6	.268	.317	.404
Tim Raines	OF139	S	29	145	517	76	148	29	6	9	60	93	48	41	.286	.395	.418
Dave Martinez	OF118	L	24	126	361	41	99	16	7	3	27	27	57	23	.274	.324	.382
Mike Fitzgerald	C77,3B8,OF6	R	28	100	290	33	69	18	2	7	42	35	61	3	.238	.322	.386
Otis Nixon	OF98	S	30	126	258	41	56	7	2	0	21	33	36	37	.217	.306	.260
Damaso Garcia	2B62,3B1	R	32	80	203	26	55	9	1	3	18	15	20	5	.271	.317	.369
Rex Hudler	2B38,OF23,SS18	R	28	92	155	21	38	7	0	6	13	6	23	15	.245	.278	.406
Mike Aldrete	OF37,1B10	L	28	76	136	12	30	8	1	1	12	19	30	1	.221	.316	.316
Wallace Johnson	1B18	S	32	85	114	9	31	3	1	2	17	7	12	1	.272	.309	.368
Jeff Huson	SS20,2B9,3B1	L	24	32	74	1	12	5	0	0	2	6	6	3	.162	.225	.230
Marquis Grissom	OF23	R	22	26	74	16	19	2	0	1	2	12	21	1	.257	.360	.324
Larry Walker	OF15	L	22	20	47	4	8	0	0	0	4	5	13	1	.170	.264	.170
Junior Noboa	2B13,SS4,3B1	R	24	21	44	3	10	0	0	0	1	1	3	0	.227	.244	.227
Marty Pevey	C11,OF1	L	26	13	41	2	9	1	1	0	3	0	8	0	.220	.220	.293
Jim Dwyer†		L	39	13	10	1	3	1	0	0	2	1	1	0	.300	.364	.400
Gil Reyes	C4	R	25	4	5	0	1	0	0	0	1	0	1	0	.200	.200	.200

T. Foley, 1 G at P

Pitcher	T	Age	G	GS	CG	ShO	IP	H	HR	BB	SO	W-L	Sv	ERA
Dennis Martinez	R	34	34	33	5	2	232.0	227	21	49	142	16-7	0	3.18
Bryn Smith	R	33	33	32	3	1	215.2	177	16	54	129	10-11	0	2.84
Kevin Gross	R	28	31	31	4	3	201.1	188	20	88	158	11-12	0	4.38
Pascual Perez	R	32	33	28	2	0	198.1	178	15	45	152	9-13	0	3.31
Mark Langston†	L	28	24	24	6	4	176.2	138	13	93	175	12-9	0	2.39
Randy Johnson†	L	25	7	6	0	0	29.2	29	2	26	26	0-4	0	6.67
Mark Gardner	R	27	7	4	0	0	26.1	26	2	11	21	0-3	0	5.13
Tim Burke	R	30	68	0	0	0	84.2	68	6	22	54	9-3	28	2.55
Andy McGaffigan	R	32	57	0	0	0	75.0	85	3	30	40	3-5	2	4.68
Joe Hesketh	L	30	43	0	0	0	48.1	54	5	26	44	6-4	3	5.77
Zane Smith†	L	28	31	0	0	0	48.0	39	2	19	35	0-1	2	1.50
Steve Frey	L	25	20	0	0	0	21.1	29	4	11	15	3-2	0	5.48
Rich Thompson	R	30	19	1	0	0	33.0	27	2	11	15	0-2	0	2.18
John Candelaria†	L	35	12	0	0	0	16.1	17	3	4	14	0-2	0	3.31
Gene Harris†	R	24	11	0	0	0	20.0	16	1	10	11	1-1	0	4.95
Brian Holman†	R	24	10	3	0	0	31.2	34	2	15	23	1-2	0	4.83
Brett Gideon	R	25	4	0	0	0	4.2	5	1	5	2	0-0	0	1.93
Urbano Lugo	R	26	3	0	0	0	4.0	4	1	0	3	0-0	0	6.75
Tim Wallach	R	31	1	0	0	0	1.0	2	0	0	0	0-0	0	9.00
Tom Foley	R	29	1	0	0	0	0.1	1	1	0	0	0-0	0	27.00

1989 Pittsburgh Pirates 5th NL East 74-88 .457 19.0 GB

Jim Leyland

Player	Gm by Position	B	Age	G	AB	R	H	2B	3B	HR	RBI	BB	SO	SB	Avg	OBP	Slg
Junior Ortiz	C84	R	29	91	230	16	50	6	1	1	22	20	20	2	.217	.282	.265
Gary Redus	1B72,OF16	R	32	98	279	42	79	18	7	6	33	40	51	25	.283	.372	.462
Jose Lind	2B151	R	25	153	578	52	134	21	3	2	48	39	64	15	.232	.280	.289
Bobby Bonilla	3B156,1B8,OF1	S	26	163	616	96	173	37	10	24	86	76	93	8	.281	.358	.490
Jay Bell	SS78	R	23	78	271	33	70	13	3	2	27	19	47	5	.258	.307	.351
Barry Bonds	OF156	L	24	159	580	96	144	34	6	19	58	93	93	32	.248	.351	.426
Andy Van Slyke	OF123,1B2	L	28	130	476	64	113	18	9	9	53	47	100	16	.237	.308	.370
R.J. Reynolds	OF98	S	30	125	363	45	98	16	2	6	48	34	66	22	.270	.331	.375
Glenn Wilson†	OF85,1B10	R	30	100	330	42	93	20	4	9	49	32	39	1	.282	.342	.448
Rey Quinones†	SS69	R	25	71	225	21	47	11	0	3	29	15	40	0	.209	.253	.298
Jeff King	1B46,3B13,2B7*	R	24	75	215	31	42	13	3	5	19	20	34	4	.195	.266	.353
Mike LaValliere	C65	L	28	68	190	15	60	10	0	2	23	29	24	0	.316	.406	.400
John Cangelosi	OF46	S	26	112	160	18	35	4	2	0	9	35	20	11	.219	.365	.269
Rafael Belliard	SS40,2B20,3B6	R	27	67	154	10	33	4	0	0	8	8	22	5	.214	.253	.240
Benny Distefano	1B48,C3,OF1	L	27	96	154	12	38	8	0	2	15	17	30	1	.247	.333	.338
Billy Hatcher†	OF20	R	28	27	86	10	21	4	0	1	7	0	9	2	.244	.253	.326
Dann Bilardello	C33	R	30	33	80	11	18	6	0	2	8	2	18	1	.225	.244	.375
Tom Prince	C21	R	24	21	52	1	7	4	0	0	5	6	12	1	.135	.220	.212
Ken Oberkfell†	1B9,2B3	L	33	14	40	2	5	1	0	0	2	2	2	0	.125	.163	.150
Sid Bream	1B13	L	28	19	36	3	8	3	0	0	4	12	10	0	.222	.417	.306
Albert Hall	OF12	S	31	20	33	4	6	2	1	0	1	3	5	3	.182	.250	.303
Steve Carter	OF5	L	24	9	16	2	2	1	0	1	3	2	5	0	.125	.222	.375
Scott Little	OF1	R	26	3	4	0	1	0	0	0	0	0	1	0	.250	.250	.250

J. King, 1 G at SS

Pitcher	T	Age	G	GS	CG	ShO	IP	H	HR	BB	SO	W-L	Sv	ERA
Doug Drabek	R	26	35	34	8	5	244.1	215	21	69	123	14-12	0	2.80
Bob Walk	R	32	33	31	2	0	196.0	208	15	65	83	13-10	0	4.41
John Smiley	L	24	28	28	8	1	205.1	174	22	49	123	12-8	0	2.81
Mike Dunne†	R	26	3	3	0	0	14.1	21	1	9	4	1-1	0	7.53
Bill Landrum	R	31	56	0	0	0	81.0	60	2	28	51	2-3	26	1.67
Bob Kipper	L	24	52	0	0	0	83.0	55	5	33	58	3-4	4	2.93
Jeff Robinson	R	28	50	19	0	0	141.1	161	14	59	95	7-13	4	4.58
Doug Bair	R	39	44	0	0	0	67.1	52	4	28	56	2-3	1	2.27
Neal Heaton	L	29	42	18	1	0	147.1	127	12	55	67	6-7	0	3.05
Randy Kramer	R	28	35	15	1	1	111.1	90	10	61	52	5-9	2	3.96
Mike Smith	R	28	16	0	0	0	24.0	28	1	10	12	0-1	0	3.75
Rick Reed	R	24	15	7	0	0	54.2	62	5	11	34	1-4	0	5.60
Bob Patterson	L	30	12	3	0	0	26.2	23	3	8	20	4-3	1	4.05
Miguel Garcia	L	22	11	0	0	0	16.0	25	2	7	9	0-2	0	8.44
Logan Easley	R	27	10	0	0	0	12.1	8	1	7	6	1-0	1	4.38
Brian Fisher	R	27	9	3	0	0	17.0	25	2	10	8	0-3	1	7.94
Morris Madden	L	28	9	3	0	0	14.0	17	0	13	6	2-2	0	7.07
Dorn Taylor	R	30	9	0	0	0	10.2	14	0	5	3	1-1	0	5.06
Stan Belinda	R	22	8	0	0	0	10.1	13	0	2	10	0-1	0	6.10
Scott Medvin	R	27	6	0	0	0	6.1	6	0	5	4	0-1	0	5.68
Roger Samuels	L	28	5	0	0	0	3.2	9	1	4	2	0-0	0	9.82
Jim Gott	R	29	1	0	0	0	0.2	1	0	1	1	0-0	0	0.00

1989 Philadelphia Phillies 6th NL East 67-95 .414 26.0 GB

Nick Leyva

Player	Gm by Position	B	Age	G	AB	R	H	2B	3B	HR	RBI	BB	SO	SB	Avg	OBP	Slg
Darren Daulton	C126	L	27	131	368	29	74	12	2	8	44	52	58	2	.201	.303	.310
Ricky Jordan	1B140	R	24	144	523	63	149	22	3	12	75	23	62	4	.285	.317	.407
Tom Herr	2B144	S	33	151	561	65	161	25	6	2	37	54	63	10	.287	.352	.364
Charlie Hayes†	3B82	R	24	84	299	26	77	15	1	8	43	11	49	3	.258	.281	.395
Dickie Thon	SS129	R	31	136	435	45	118	18	4	15	60	33	81	6	.271	.321	.434
Von Hayes	OF128,1B30,3B10	L	30	154	540	93	140	27	2	26	78	101	103	28	.259	.376	.461
Lenny Dykstra†	OF88	L	26	90	352	39	78	20	3	4	19	37	38	17	.222	.297	.330
Bob Dernier	OF74	R	32	107	187	26	32	5	0	1	13	14	28	4	.171	.225	.214
John Kruk†	OF72,1B7	L	28	81	281	46	93	13	6	5	38	27	39	3	.331	.386	.473
Steve Jeltz	SS63,3B30,2B23*	S	30	116	263	28	64	7	3	4	25	45	44	4	.243	.356	.338
Juan Samuel†	OF50	R	28	51	199	32	49	3	1	8	20	18	45	11	.246	.311	.392
Randy Ready†	OF36,3B14,2B7	R	29	72	187	33	50	11	1	8	21	31	31	4	.267	.372	.465
Chris James†	OF37,3B11	R	26	45	179	14	37	4	0	2	19	4	23	3	.207	.223	.263
Dwayne Murphy	OF52	L	34	98	156	20	34	5	0	9	27	29	44	0	.218	.341	.423
Steve Lake	C55	R	32	58	155	9	39	5	1	2	14	12	20	0	.252	.304	.335
Mike Schmidt	3B42	R	39	42	148	19	30	7	0	6	28	21	17	0	.203	.297	.372
Curt Ford	OF52,1B1,2B1	L	28	108	142	13	31	5	1	1	13	16	33	5	.218	.298	.289
Mark Ryal	1B4,OF4	L	28	29	33	2	8	2	0	0	5	1	6	0	.242	.265	.303
Ron Jones	OF12	L	25	12	31	7	9	0	0	2	4	9	1	1	.290	.450	.484
Tom Barrett	2B9	S	29	14	27	3	6	0	0	0	1	1	7	0	.222	.250	.222
Tom Nieto	C11	R	28	11	20	1	3	0	0	0	0	6	7	0	.150	.370	.150
Jim Adduci	1B4,OF1	L	29	13	19	1	7	1	0	0	0	0	4	0	.368	.368	.421
Keith Miller	OF2	S	26	8	10	0	3	1	0	0	0	0	3	0	.300	.300	.400
Steve Stanicek		R	28	9	9	0	1	0	0	0	1	0	3	0	.111	.111	.111
Eric Bullock	OF3	L	29	6	4	1	0	0	0	0	0	0	2	0	.000	.000	.000
Al Pardo	C1	S	26	1	1	0	0	0	0	0	0	0	0	0	.000	.000	.000

S. Jeltz, 1 G at OF

Pitcher	T	Age	G	GS	CG	ShO	IP	H	HR	BB	SO	W-L	Sv	ERA
Ken Howell	R	28	33	32	1	1	204.0	155	11	86	164	12-12	0	3.44
Bruce Ruffin	L	25	24	23	1	0	125.2	152	10	62	70	6-10	0	4.44
Terry Mulholland†	L	26	20	17	2	1	104.1	122	8	32	60	4-7	0	5.00
Dennis Cook†	L	26	21	16	1	1	106.0	97	17	33	58	6-8	0	3.99
Floyd Youmans	R	25	10	10	0	0	42.2	50	7	25	20	1-5	0	5.70
Pat Combs	L	22	6	6	1	1	38.2	36	2	6	30	4-0	0	2.09
Bob Sebra†	R	27	6	5	0	0	34.1	41	6	10	21	2-3	0	4.46
Steve Ontiveros	R	28	6	5	0	0	30.2	34	2	15	12	2-1	0	3.82
Jason Grimsley	R	21	4	4	0	0	18.1	19	2	19	7	1-3	0	5.89
Alex Madrid	R	26	6	3	0	0	24.2	32	3	14	13	1-2	0	5.47
Marvin Freeman	R	26	1	1	0	0	3.0	2	0	5	0	0-0	0	6.00
Jeff Parrett	R	27	72	0	0	0	105.2	90	6	44	98	12-6	6	2.98
Don Carman	L	29	49	20	0	0	149.1	152	21	86	81	5-15	0	5.24
Todd Frohwirth	R	26	45	0	0	0	62.2	56	4	18	39	1-0	0	3.59
Greg Harris†	R	33	44	0	0	0	75.1	64	7	43	51	2-2	1	3.58
Roger McDowell†	R	28	44	0	0	0	56.2	45	2	22	32	3-3	19	1.11
Larry McWilliams†	L	35	40	16	2	1	120.2	123	3	49	54	2-11	0	4.10
Steve Bedrosian†	R	31	28	0	0	0	33.2	21	7	17	24	2-3	6	3.21
Randy O'Neal	R	28	20	1	0	0	39.0	46	5	9	29	0-1	0	6.23
Mike Maddux	R	27	16	4	2	1	43.2	52	3	14	26	1-3	1	5.15
Chuck McElroy	L	21	11	0	0	0	10.1	12	1	4	8	0-0	0	1.74
Gordon Dillard	L	25	5	0	0	0	4.0	7	0	0	2	0-0	0	6.75

1989 San Francisco Giants 1st NL West 92-70 .568 —

Roger Craig

Player	Gm by Position	B	Age	G	AB	R	H	2B	3B	HR	RBI	BB	SO	SB	Avg	OBP	Slg
Terry Kennedy	C121,1B2	L	33	125	355	19	85	15	0	5	34	35	56	1	.239	.306	.324
Will Clark	1B158	L	25	159	588	104	196	38	9	23	111	74	103	8	.333	.407	.546
Robby Thompson	2B148	R	27	148	547	91	132	26	11	13	50	51	133	12	.241	.321	.400
Ernest Riles	3B83,2B18,SS7*	L	28	122	302	43	84	13	2	7	40	28	50	0	.278	.339	.404
Jose Uribe	SS150	S	30	151	453	34	100	12	6	1	30	34	74	6	.221	.273	.280
Brett Butler	OF152	L	32	154	594	100	168	22	4	4	36	59	69	31	.283	.349	.354
Kevin Mitchell	OF147,3B2	R	27	154	543	100	158	34	6	47	125	87	115	3	.291	.388	.635
Candy Maldonado	OF116	R	28	129	345	39	75	23	0	9	41	37	69	4	.217	.296	.362
Matt Williams	3B73,SS30	R	23	84	292	31	59	18	1	18	50	14	72	1	.202	.242	.455
Kirt Manwaring	C81	R	23	85	200	14	42	4	2	0	18	11	28	2	.210	.264	.250
Donell Nixon	OF64	R	27	95	166	23	44	2	0	1	15	11	30	10	.265	.311	.295
Pat Sheridan†	OF66	L	31	70	161	20	33	3	4	3	14	13	45	4	.205	.264	.329
Greg Litton	3B34,2B15,SS9*	R	24	71	143	12	36	5	3	4	17	7	29	0	.252	.291	.413
Ken Oberkfell†	3B38,1B7,2B7	L	33	83	116	17	37	5	1	2	15	8	8	0	.319	.367	.431
Tracy Jones†	OF30	R	28	40	97	5	18	4	0	0	12	5	14	2	.186	.233	.227
Ed Jurak	SS6,3B5,2B4*	R	31	30	42	2	10	0	0	0	1	5	5	0	.238	.319	.238
Chris Speier	3B9,SS9,2B4*	R	39	28	37	7	9	4	0	0	2	5	9	0	.243	.333	.351
Bill Bathe	C7	R	28	30	32	3	9	1	0	0	6	0	7	0	.281	.273	.313
Bob Brenly†	C12	R	35	12	22	2	4	2	0	0	3	1	7	0	.182	.208	.273
Mike Laga	1B4	L	29	17	20	1	4	1	0	1	7	1	6	0	.200	.238	.400
Jim Weaver	OF8	L	29	12	20	2	4	3	0	0	2	0	7	1	.200	.200	.350
James Steels	1B3,OF1	L	28	13	12	0	1	0	0	0	0	2	4	0	.083	.214	.083
Mike Benjamin	SS8	R	23	14	6	6	1	0	0	0	0	0	1	0	.167	.167	.167
Charlie Hayes†	3B3	R	24	3	5	0	1	0	0	0	0	0	1	0	.200	.200	.200

E. Riles, 5 G at OF; G. Litton, 6 G at OF, 2 G at C; E. Jurak, 2 G at OF, 1 G at 1B; C. Speier, 1 G at 1B

Pitcher	T	Age	G	GS	CG	ShO	IP	H	HR	BB	SO	W-L	Sv	ERA
Rick Reuschel	R	40	32	32	2	0	208.1	195	18	54	111	17-8	0	2.94
Don Robinson	R	32	34	32	5	1	197.0	184	22	37	96	12-11	0	3.43
Scott Garrelts	R	27	30	29	2	1	193.1	149	11	46	119	14-5	0	2.28
Kelly Downs	R	28	18	15	0	0	82.2	82	7	26	49	4-8	0	4.79
Mike Krukow	R	37	8	8	0	0	43.0	37	5	18	18	4-3	0	3.98
Dennis Cook†	L	26	2	2	1	0	15.0	13	1	5	9	1-0	0	1.80
Dave Dravecky	L	33	2	2	0	0	13.0	8	2	4	5	2-0	0	3.46
Russ Swan	L	25	2	2	0	0	6.2	11	4	4	2	0-2	0	10.80
Craig Lefferts	L	31	70	0	0	0	107.0	93	11	22	71	2-4	20	2.69
Jeff Brantley	R	25	59	1	0	0	97.1	101	10	37	69	7-1	0	4.07
Mike LaCoss	R	33	45	18	1	0	150.1	143	3	65	78	10-10	6	3.17
Steve Bedrosian†	R	31	40	0	0	0	51.0	35	5	22	34	1-4	17	2.65
Goose Gossage†	R	37	31	0	0	0	43.2	32	2	27	24	2-1	4	2.68
Atlee Hammaker	L	31	28	9	0	0	76.2	78	5	23	30	6-6	0	3.76
Randy McCament	R	26	25	0	0	0	36.2	32	4	23	12	1-1	0	3.93
Trevor Wilson	L	23	14	4	0	0	39.1	28	2	24	22	2-3	0	4.35
Bob Knepper†	L	35	13	6	1	1	52.0	55	4	15	19	3-2	0	3.46
Ernie Camacho	R	34	13	0	0	0	16.1	10	1	11	14	3-0	0	2.76
Joe Price†	L	32	7	1	0	0	14.0	16	3	4	10	1-1	0	5.79
Terry Mulholland†	L	26	5	1	0	0	11.0	15	0	4	6	0-0	0	4.09
Stu Tate	R	27	2	0	0	0	2.2	3	0	0	4	0-0	0	3.38

1989 San Diego Padres 2nd NL West 89-73 .549 3.0 GB

Jack McKeon

Player	Gm by Position	B	Age	G	AB	R	H	2B	3B	HR	RBI	BB	SO	SB	Avg	OBP	Slg
Benito Santiago	C127	R	24	129	462	50	109	16	3	16	62	26	89	11	.236	.277	.387
Jack Clark	1B131,OF12	R	33	142	455	76	110	19	1	26	94	132	145	6	.242	.410	.459
Roberto Alomar	2B157	S	21	158	623	82	184	27	1	7	56	53	76	42	.295	.347	.376
Luis Salazar†	3B72,OF14,SS9*	R	33	95	246	27	66	7	2	8	22	11	44	1	.268	.302	.411
Garry Templeton	SS140	S	33	142	506	43	129	26	3	6	40	23	80	1	.255	.286	.354
Tony Gwynn	OF157	L	29	158	604	82	203	27	7	4	62	56	30	40	.336	.389	.424
Marvell Wynne†	OF96	L	29	105	294	19	74	11	1	6	35	12	41	4	.252	.282	.357
Chris James†	OF79,3B6	R	26	87	303	41	80	13	2	11	46	22	45	2	.264	.314	.429
Bip Roberts	OF54,3B37,SS14*	S	25	117	329	81	99	15	8	3	25	49	45	21	.301	.391	.422
Carmelo Martinez	OF65,1B32	R	28	111	267	23	59	12	2	6	39	32	54	0	.221	.302	.348
Mike Pagliarulo†	3B49	L	29	50	148	12	29	7	0	3	14	18	39	2	.196	.287	.304
Mark Parent	C41,1B1	R	27	52	141	12	27	4	0	7	21	8	34	1	.191	.229	.369
Tim Flannery	3B33,2B1	L	31	73	130	9	30	5	0	0	8	13	20	2	.231	.299	.269
Shawn Abner	OF51	R	23	57	102	13	18	4	0	2	14	5	20	1	.176	.213	.275
Darrin Jackson†	OF24	R	25	25	87	10	18	3	0	3	12	7	17	0	.207	.260	.345
Rob Nelson	1B31	L	25	42	82	6	16	0	1	3	7	20	29	1	.195	.353	.329
John Kruk†	OF27	L	28	31	76	7	14	0	0	3	6	17	14	0	.184	.333	.303
Randy Ready†	3B18,2B2,OF1	R	29	28	67	4	17	2	1	0	5	11	6	0	.254	.354	.313
Jerald Clark	OF14	R	25	17	41	5	8	2	0	1	7	3	9	0	.195	.250	.317
Gary Green	SS11,3B1	R	27	15	27	4	7	3	0	0	0	1	1	0	.259	.286	.370
Joey Cora	SS7,3B2,2B1	S	24	12	19	5	6	1	0	0	1	1	0	1	.316	.350	.368
Sandy Alomar Jr.	C6	R	23	7	19	1	4	1	0	1	6	3	3	0	.211	.318	.421
Phil Stephenson†	1B8	L	28	10	17	4	6	0	0	2	2	3	2	0	.353	.450	.706

L. Salazar, 2 G at 1B; B. Roberts, 9 G at 2B

Pitcher	T	Age	G	GS	CG	ShO	IP	H	HR	BB	SO	W-L	Sv	ERA
Bruce Hurst	L	31	33	33	10	2	244.2	214	16	66	179	15-11	0	2.69
Ed Whitson	R	34	33	33	5	1	227.0	198	22	48	117	16-11	0	2.66
Dennis Rasmussen	L	30	33	33	1	0	183.2	190	18	72	87	10-10	0	4.26
Walt Terrell†	R	31	19	19	4	1	123.1	134	14	26	63	5-13	0	4.01
Eric Show	R	33	16	16	1	0	106.1	113	9	39	66	8-6	0	4.23
Andy Benes	R	21	10	10	0	0	66.2	51	7	31	66	6-3	0	3.51
Don Schulze†	R	26	7	4	0	0	24.1	38	6	6	15	2-1	0	5.55
Calvin Schiraldi†	R	27	5	4	0	0	21.1	12	1	13	17	3-1	0	2.53
Mark Davis	L	28	70	0	0	0	92.2	66	6	31	92	4-3	44	1.85
Greg Harris	R	25	56	8	0	0	135.0	106	8	52	106	8-9	6	2.60
Mark Grant	R	25	50	0	0	0	116.1	105	11	32	69	8-2	2	3.33
Pat Clements	L	27	23	1	0	0	39.0	39	4	15	18	4-1	0	3.92
Dave Leiper	L	27	22	0	0	0	28.2	40	2	20	7	0-1	0	5.02
Greg Booker†	R	29	11	0	0	0	19.0	15	2	10	8	0-1	0	4.26
Fred Toliver†	R	28	9	0	0	0	14.0	17	5	9	14	0-0	0	7.07
Dan Murphy	R	24	7	0	0	0	6.1	6	1	4	1	0-0	0	5.68
Eric Nolte	L	25	3	1	0	0	9.0	15	1	7	8	0-0	0	11.00

1989 Houston Astros 3rd NL West 86-76 .531 6.0 GB

Art Howe

Player	Gm by Position	B	Age	G	AB	R	H	2B	3B	HR	RBI	BB	SO	SB	Avg	OBP	Slg
Craig Biggio	C125,OF5	R	23	134	443	64	114	21	2	13	60	49	64	21	.257	.336	.402
Glenn Davis	1B156	R	28	158	581	87	156	26	1	34	89	69	123	4	.269	.350	.492
Bill Doran	2B138	S	31	142	507	65	111	25	2	8	58	59	63	22	.219	.301	.323
Ken Caminiti	3B160	S	26	161	585	71	149	31	3	10	72	51	93	4	.255	.316	.369
Rafael Ramirez	SS149	R	31	151	537	46	132	20	2	6	54	29	64	3	.246	.283	.324
Gerald Young	OF143	S	24	146	533	71	124	17	3	0	38	74	60	34	.233	.326	.276
Billy Hatcher†	OF104	R	28	108	395	49	90	15	3	3	44	30	53	22	.228	.281	.304
Terry Puhl	OF103,1B3	L	32	121	354	41	96	25	4	0	27	45	39	9	.271	.353	.364
Kevin Bass	OF84	S	30	87	313	42	94	19	4	5	44	29	44	11	.300	.357	.435
Craig Reynolds	2B29,SS26,3B10*	L	36	101	189	16	38	4	0	2	14	19	18	1	.201	.274	.254
Alex Trevino	C32,1B2,3B2	R	31	59	131	15	38	7	1	2	16	7	18	0	.290	.329	.405
Glenn Wilson†	OF25	R	30	28	102	8	22	6	0	2	15	5	14	0	.216	.250	.333
Eric Yelding	SS15,2B13,OF8	R	24	70	90	19	21	2	0	0	9	7	19	11	.233	.290	.256
Greg Gross	OF12,1B6,P1	L	36	60	75	2	15	0	0	0	4	11	6	0	.200	.310	.200
Mark Davidson	OF23	R	28	33	65	7	13	2	1	1	5	7	14	1	.200	.278	.308
Alan Ashby	C19	S	37	22	61	4	10	1	1	0	3	7	8	0	.164	.257	.213
Eric Anthony	OF21	L	21	25	61	7	11	2	0	4	7	9	16	0	.180	.286	.410
Louie Meadows	OF14,1B1	L	28	31	51	5	9	0	0	3	10	1	14	1	.176	.189	.353
Steve Lombardozzi	2B18,3B1	R	29	21	37	5	8	3	1	1	3	4	9	0	.216	.293	.432
Harry Spilman	1B9,C1	L	34	32	36	7	10	3	0	0	3	7	2	0	.278	.395	.361
Carl Nichols	C6	R	26	8	13	0	1	0	0	0	2	0	3	0	.077	.077	.077
Ron Washington	2B1,3B1	R	37	7	7	1	1	1	0	0	0	0	4	0	.143	.143	.286

C. Reynolds, 5 G at 1B, 1 G at P, 1 G at OF

Pitcher	T	Age	G	GS	CG	ShO	IP	H	HR	BB	SO	W-L	Sv	ERA
Jim Deshaies	L	29	34	34	6	3	225.2	180	15	79	153	15-10	0	2.91
Mike Scott	R	34	33	32	9	2	229.0	180	23	62	172	20-10	0	3.10
Jim Clancy	R	33	33	26	1	0	147.0	155	13	66	91	7-14	0	5.08
Bob Knepper†	L	35	22	20	0	0	113.0	135	12	60	45	4-10	0	5.89
Rick Rhoden	R	36	20	17	0	0	96.2	108	7	41	41	2-6	0	4.28
Mark Portugal	R	26	20	15	2	1	108.0	91	7	37	86	7-1	0	2.75
Jose Cano	R	27	6	3	1	0	23.0	24	2	7	8	1-1	0	5.09
Juan Agosto	L	31	71	0	0	0	83.0	81	3	32	46	4-5	1	2.93
Danny Darwin	R	33	68	0	0	0	122.0	92	8	33	104	11-4	7	2.36
Larry Andersen	R	36	60	0	0	0	87.2	63	2	24	85	4-4	3	1.54
Dave Smith	R	34	52	0	0	0	58.0	49	1	19	31	3-4	25	2.64
Bob Forsch	R	39	37	15	0	0	108.1	133	10	46	40	4-5	0	5.32
Dan Schatzeder	L	34	36	0	0	0	56.2	64	2	28	46	4-1	1	4.45
Brian Meyer	R	26	12	0	0	0	18.0	16	0	13	13	0-1	1	4.50
Roger Mason	R	30	2	0	0	0	1.1	2	0	2	3	0-0	0	20.25
Greg Gross	L	36	1	0	0	0	1.0	3	0	1	1	0-0	0	18.00
Craig Reynolds	R	36	1	0	0	0	1.0	3	0	1	0	0-0	0	27.00

1989 Los Angeles Dodgers 4th NL West 77-83 .481 14.0 GB — Tom Lasorda

Player	Gm by Position	B	Age	G	AB	R	H	2B	3B	HR	RBI	BB	SO	SB	Avg	OBP	Slg
Mike Scioscia	C130	L	30	133	408	40	102	16	0	10	44	52	29	0	.250	.338	.363
Eddie Murray	1B159,3B2	S	33	160	594	66	147	29	1	20	88	87	85	7	.247	.342	.401
Willie Randolph	2B140	R	34	145	549	62	155	18	0	2	36	71	51	7	.282	.366	.326
Jeff Hamilton	3B147,P1,2B1*	R	25	151	548	45	134	35	1	12	56	20	71	0	.245	.272	.378
Alfredo Griffin	SS131	S	31	136	506	49	125	27	2	0	29	29	57	10	.247	.287	.308
Mike Marshall	OF102	R	29	105	377	41	98	21	1	11	42	33	78	2	.260	.325	.408
John Shelby	OF98	S	31	108	345	28	63	11	1	1	12	25	92	10	.183	.237	.229
Jose Gonzalez	OF87	R	24	95	261	31	70	11	2	3	18	23	53	9	.268	.326	.360
Kirk Gibson	OF70	L	32	71	253	35	54	8	2	9	28	35	55	12	.213	.312	.368
Mickey Hatcher	OF48,3B16,1B5*	R	34	94	224	18	66	9	2	2	25	13	16	1	.295	.328	.379
Mike Davis	OF48	L	30	67	173	21	43	7	1	5	19	16	28	6	.249	.309	.387
Rick Dempsey	C62	R	39	79	151	16	27	7	0	4	16	30	37	1	.179	.319	.305
Lenny Harris†	OF21,2B14,3B8*	L	24	54	147	19	37	6	1	1	15	11	13	4	.252	.308	.327
Dave Anderson	SS33,3B18,2B7	R	28	87	140	15	32	2	0	1	14	17	26	2	.229	.310	.264
Franklin Stubbs	OF28,1B7	L	28	69	103	11	30	6	0	4	15	16	27	3	.291	.387	.466
Mariano Duncan†	SS16,2B8,OF7	S	26	49	84	9	21	5	1	0	8	0	15	3	.250	.267	.333
Billy Bean†	OF44	L	25	51	71	7	14	4	0	0	3	4	10	0	.197	.250	.254
Chris Gwynn	OF19	L	24	32	68	8	16	4	1	0	7	2	9	1	.235	.254	.324
F. Valenzuela	P31,1B1	L	28	34	66	3	12	2	0	0	6	0	11	0	.182	.182	.212
Kal Daniels†	OF11	L	25	11	38	7	13	2	0	2	8	7	5	3	.342	.435	.553
Mike Sharperson	2B4,1B2,3B2*	R	27	27	28	2	7	3	0	0	5	4	7	0	.250	.333	.357
Mike Huff	OF9	R	25	12	25	4	5	1	0	1	2	3	6	0	.200	.310	.360
Jose Vizcaino	SS5	S	21	7	10	2	2	0	0	0	0	0	1	0	.200	.200	.200
Darrin Fletcher	C5	L	22	5	8	1	4	0	0	1	2	1	0	0	.500	.556	.875
Tracy Woodson	3B1	R	26	4	6	0	0	0	0	0	0	0	1	0	.000	.000	.000

J. Hamilton, 1 G at SS; M. Hatcher, 1 G at P; L. Harris, 1 G at SS; M. Sharperson, 1 G at SS

Pitcher	T	Age	G	GS	CG	ShO	IP	H	HR	BB	SO	W-L	Sv	ERA
Orel Hershiser	R	30	35	33	8	4	256.2	226	9	77	178	15-15	0	2.31
F. Valenzuela	L	28	31	31	3	0	196.2	185	11	98	116	10-13	0	3.43
Tim Belcher	R	27	39	30	10	8	230.0	182	20	80	200	15-12	1	2.82
Tim Leary†	R	31	19	17	2	0	117.1	107	9	37	59	6-7	0	3.38
Ramon Martinez	R	21	15	15	2	2	98.2	79	11	41	89	6-4	0	3.19
John Tudor	L	35	6	3	0	0	14.1	17	1	6	9	0-0	0	3.14
Jay Howell	R	33	56	0	0	0	79.2	60	3	22	55	5-3	28	1.58
Alejandro Pena	R	30	53	0	0	0	76.0	62	6	18	75	4-3	5	2.13
Tim Crews	R	28	44	0	0	0	61.2	69	7	23	56	0-1	1	3.21
Ray Searage	L	34	41	0	0	0	35.2	29	1	18	24	3-4	0	3.53
Mike Morgan	R	29	40	19	0	0	152.2	130	6	33	72	8-11	0	2.53
John Wetteland	R	22	31	12	0	0	102.2	81	8	34	96	5-8	1	3.77
Ricky Horton†	L	29	23	0	0	0	26.2	35	1	11	12	0-0	0	5.06
Mike Hartley	R	27	5	0	0	0	6.0	2	0	0	4	0-1	0	1.50
Mike Munoz	L	23	3	0	0	0	2.2	5	1	2	3	0-0	0	16.88
Jeff Fischer	R	25	2	0	0	0	3.1	7	1	0	2	0-0	0	13.50
Jeff Hamilton	R	25	1	0	0	0	1.2	2	0	1	2	0-1	0	5.40
Mickey Hatcher	R	34	1	0	0	0	1.0	0	0	3	0	0-0	0	9.00

1989 Cincinnati Reds 5th NL West 75-87 .463 17.0 GB — Pete Rose (59-66)/Tommy Helms (16-21)

Player	Gm by Position	B	Age	G	AB	R	H	2B	3B	HR	RBI	BB	SO	SB	Avg	OBP	Slg
Jeff Reed	C99	L	26	102	287	16	64	11	0	3	23	34	46	0	.223	.306	.293
Todd Benzinger	1B158	S	26	161	628	79	154	28	3	17	76	44	120	3	.245	.293	.381
Ron Oester	2B102,SS2	S	33	109	305	23	75	15	0	1	14	32	47	1	.246	.318	.305
Chris Sabo	3B76	R	27	82	304	40	79	21	1	6	29	25	33	14	.260	.316	.395
Barry Larkin	SS82	R	25	97	325	47	111	14	4	4	36	20	23	10	.342	.375	.446
Eric Davis	OF125	R	27	131	462	74	130	14	2	34	101	68	116	21	.281	.367	.541
Paul O'Neill	OF115	L	26	117	428	49	118	24	2	15	74	46	64	20	.276	.346	.446
Rolando Roomes	OF100	R	27	107	315	36	83	18	5	7	34	13	100	12	.263	.296	.419
Luis Quinones	2B53,3B50,SS5	S	27	97	340	43	83	13	4	12	34	25	46	2	.244	.300	.412
Herm Winningham	OF85	L	27	115	251	40	63	11	3	3	13	24	50	14	.251	.316	.355
Ken Griffey Sr.	OF58,1B9	L	39	106	236	26	62	8	3	8	30	29	42	4	.263	.346	.424
Lenny Harris†	2B32,SS17,3B16	L	24	61	188	17	42	4	0	2	11	9	20	10	.223	.263	.277
Mariano Duncan†	SS44,2B5	S	26	45	174	23	43	10	1	3	13	8	36	6	.247	.292	.368
Joe Oliver	C47	R	23	49	151	13	41	8	0	3	23	6	28	0	.272	.300	.384
Kal Daniels†	OF38	L	25	44	133	26	29	11	0	2	9	36	28	6	.218	.390	.346
Bo Diaz	C43	R	36	43	132	6	27	5	0	1	8	6	7	0	.205	.239	.265
Jeff Richardson	SS39,3B8	R	23	53	125	10	21	4	0	2	11	10	23	1	.168	.234	.248
Joel Youngblood	OF45	R	37	76	118	13	25	5	0	3	13	13	21	0	.212	.299	.331
Dave Collins	OF16	S	36	78	106	12	25	4	0	0	7	10	17	3	.236	.302	.274
Scotti Madison	3B26	S	29	40	98	13	17	7	0	1	7	8	9	0	.173	.241	.276
Manny Trillo	2B10,1B3,SS1	R	38	17	39	3	8	0	0	0	0	2	9	0	.205	.262	.205
Marty Brown	3B11	R	26	16	30	2	5	1	0	0	4	4	9	0	.167	.257	.200
Terry McGriff	C6	R	25	6	11	1	3	0	0	0	2	2	3	0	.273	.385	.273
Van Snider	OF6	L	25	8	7	1	1	0	0	0	0	0	5	0	.143	.143	.143
Skeeter Barnes		R	32	5	3	1	0	0	0	0	0	0	0	0	.000	.000	.000

Pitcher	T	Age	G	GS	CG	ShO	IP	H	HR	BB	SO	W-L	Sv	ERA
Tom Browning	L	29	37	37	9	2	249.2	241	31	64	118	15-12	0	3.39
Rick Mahler	R	35	40	31	5	2	220.2	242	15	51	102	9-13	0	3.83
Danny Jackson	L	27	20	20	1	0	115.2	122	10	57	70	6-11	0	5.60
Jose Rijo	R	24	19	19	1	1	111.0	101	6	48	86	7-6	0	2.84
Scott Scudder	R	21	23	17	0	0	100.1	91	14	61	66	4-9	0	4.49
Ron Robinson	R	27	15	15	0	0	83.1	80	8	28	36	5-3	0	3.35
Tim Leary†	R	31	14	14	0	0	89.2	98	8	31	64	2-7	0	3.71
Jack Armstrong	R	24	9	8	0	0	42.2	40	5	21	23	2-3	0	4.64
Rob Dibble	R	25	74	0	0	0	99.0	62	4	39	141	10-5	2	2.09
Norm Charlton	L	26	69	0	0	0	95.1	67	5	40	98	8-3	0	2.93
John Franco	L	28	60	0	0	0	80.2	77	3	36	60	4-8	32	3.12
Tim Birtsas	L	28	42	1	0	0	69.2	68	5	27	57	2-2	1	3.75
Kent Tekulve	R	42	37	0	0	0	52.0	56	5	23	31	0-3	1	5.02
Mike Roesler	R	25	17	0	0	0	25.0	22	4	9	14	0-1	0	3.96
Bob Sebra†	R	27	15	0	0	0	21.0	24	2	18	14	0-0	1	6.43
Rosario Rodriguez	L	19	7	0	0	0	4.1	3	0	3	0	1-1	0	4.15
Mike Griffin	R	32	3	0	0	0	4.1	10	0	3	1	0-0	0	12.46

1989 Atlanta Braves 6th NL West 63-97 .394 28.0 GB — Russ Nixon

Player	Gm by Position	B	Age	G	AB	R	H	2B	3B	HR	RBI	BB	SO	SB	Avg	OBP	Slg
Jody Davis	C72,1B2	R	32	78	231	12	39	5	0	4	19	23	61	0	.169	.246	.242
Gerald Perry	1B72	L	28	72	266	24	67	11	0	4	21	32	28	10	.252	.337	.338
Jeff Treadway	2B123,3B6	L	26	134	473	58	131	18	3	8	40	30	38	3	.277	.317	.378
Jeff Blauser	3B78,2B39,SS30*	R	23	142	456	63	123	24	2	12	46	38	101	5	.270	.325	.410
Andres Thomas	SS138	R	25	141	554	41	118	18	0	13	57	12	62	3	.213	.228	.316
Dale Murphy	OF151	R	33	154	574	60	131	16	0	20	84	65	142	3	.228	.306	.361
Lonnie Smith	OF132	R	33	134	482	89	152	34	4	21	79	76	95	25	.315	.415	.533
Oddibe McDowell†	OF68	L	26	76	280	56	85	18	4	7	24	27	37	15	.304	.365	.471
Darrell Evans	1B50,3B28	L	42	107	276	31	57	6	1	11	39	41	46	0	.207	.303	.355
Tommy Gregg	OF48,1B37	L	25	102	276	24	67	8	0	6	23	18	45	3	.243	.288	.337
Ron Gant	3B53,OF14	R	24	75	260	26	46	8	3	9	25	20	63	9	.177	.237	.335
Dion James†	OF46,1B8	L	26	63	170	15	44	7	0	1	11	25	23	1	.259	.355	.318
Bruce Benedict	C65	R	33	66	160	12	31	3	0	1	6	23	18	0	.194	.299	.231
John Russell	C45,OF14,1B2*	R	28	74	159	14	29	2	0	2	9	8	53	0	.182	.225	.233
Geronimo Berroa	OF34	R	24	81	136	7	36	4	0	2	9	7	32	0	.265	.301	.338
Ed Whited	3B29,1B3	R	25	36	74	5	12	3	0	1	4	6	15	1	.162	.222	.243
Mark Lemke	2B14	S	23	14	55	4	10	2	1	2	10	5	7	0	.182	.250	.364
David Justice	OF16	L	23	16	51	7	12	3	0	1	3	3	9	2	.235	.291	.353
Jeff Wetherby	OF9	L	25	52	48	5	10	2	1	1	7	4	6	1	.208	.264	.354
Drew Denson	1B12	S	23	12	36	1	9	1	0	0	5	3	9	1	.250	.308	.278
Terry Blocker	OF8,P1	L	29	26	31	1	7	1	0	0	1	1	5	1	.226	.250	.258
John Mizerock	C11	L	28	11	27	1	6	0	0	0	2	0	3	0	.222	.222	.222
Kelly Mann	C7	R	21	7	24	1	5	2	0	0	1	0	6	0	.208	.240	.292
Ed Romero†	2B4,SS2,3B1	R	31	7	19	1	5	1	0	1	1	0	0	0	.263	.263	.474
Francisco Cabrera†	1B2,C1	R	22	4	14	0	3	2	0	0	0	0	3	0	.214	.214	.357

J. Blauser, 2 G at OF; J. Russell, 2 G at 3B, 1 G at P

Pitcher	T	Age	G	GS	CG	ShO	IP	H	HR	BB	SO	W-L	Sv	ERA
Derek Lilliquist	L	23	32	30	0	0	165.2	202	16	34	79	8-10	0	3.97
John Smoltz	R	22	29	29	5	0	208.0	160	15	72	168	12-11	0	2.94
Tom Glavine	L	23	29	29	6	4	186.0	172	20	40	90	14-8	0	3.68
Pete Smith	R	23	28	27	1	0	142.0	144	13	57	115	5-14	0	4.75
Marty Clary	R	27	18	17	2	1	108.2	103	6	31	30	4-3	0	3.15
Zane Smith†	L	28	17	17	0	0	99.0	102	5	33	58	1-12	0	4.45
Tommy Greene	R	22	4	4	1	1	26.1	22	5	6	17	1-2	0	4.10
Gary Eave	R	25	3	3	0	0	20.2	15	0	12	9	2-0	0	1.31
Rusty Richards	R	24	2	2	0	0	9.1	10	2	6	4	0-0	0	4.82
Kent Mercker	L	21	2	1	0	0	4.1	8	0	6	4	0-0	0	12.46
Joe Boever	R	28	66	0	0	0	82.1	78	6	34	68	4-11	21	3.94
Jim Acker†	R	30	59	0	0	0	97.2	84	5	20	68	0-6	2	2.67
Paul Assenmacher†	L	28	49	0	0	0	57.2	55	2	16	64	1-3	0	3.59
Mark Eichhorn	R	28	45	0	0	0	68.1	70	6	19	49	5-5	0	4.35
Jose Alvarez	R	33	30	0	0	0	50.1	44	4	24	45	3-3	2	2.86
Mike Stanton	L	22	20	0	0	0	24.0	17	0	8	27	0-1	7	1.50
Sergio Valdez	R	24	19	1	0	0	32.2	31	5	17	26	1-2	0	6.06
Charlie Puleo	R	34	15	1	0	0	29.0	26	2	16	17	1-1	0	4.66
Dwayne Henry	R	27	12	0	0	0	12.2	12	2	5	16	0-2	1	4.26
Tony Castillo†	L	26	12	0	0	0	9.1	8	0	4	5	0-1	0	4.82
Jay Aldrich†	R	28	8	0	0	0	12.1	7	0	6	7	1-2	0	2.19
Terry Blocker	L	29	1	0	0	0	1.0	0	0	2	0	0-0	0	0.00
John Russell	R	28	1	0	0	0	0.1	0	0	0	0	0-0	0	0.00

»1990 Boston Red Sox 1st AL East 88-74 .543 — — Joe Morgan

Player	Gm by Position	B	Age	G	AB	R	H	2B	3B	HR	RBI	BB	SO	SB	Avg	OBP	Slg
Tony Pena	C142,1B1	R	33	143	491	62	129	19	1	7	56	43	71	8	.263	.322	.348
Carlos Quintana	1B148,OF3	R	24	149	512	56	147	28	0	7	67	52	74	1	.287	.354	.383
Jody Reed	2B119,SS50,DH1	R	27	155	598	70	173	45	0	5	51	75	65	4	.289	.371	.390
Wade Boggs	3B152,DH3	L	32	155	619	89	187	44	5	6	63	87	68	0	.302	.386	.418
Luis Rivera	SS112,2B3,3B1	R	26	118	346	38	78	20	0	7	45	25	58	4	.225	.279	.344
Mike Greenwell	OF159	L	26	159	610	71	181	30	6	14	73	65	43	8	.297	.367	.434
Ellis Burks	OF143,DH6	R	25	152	588	89	174	33	8	21	89	48	82	9	.296	.349	.486
Tom Brunansky†	OF121,DH7	R	29	129	461	61	123	24	5	15	71	54	105	5	.267	.342	.438
Dwight Evans	DH122	R	38	123	445	66	111	18	3	13	63	67	73	3	.249	.349	.391
Marty Barrett	2B60,DH1,3B1	R	32	62	159	15	36	4	0	0	13	15	13	4	.226	.294	.252
Kevin Romine	OF64,DH1	R	29	70	136	21	37	7	0	2	14	12	27	4	.272	.331	.368
Mike Marshall†	DH14,1B8,OF8	R	30	30	112	10	32	6	1	4	12	4	26	0	.286	.316	.464
Tim Naehring	SS19,3B5,2B1	R	23	24	85	10	23	6	0	2	12	8	15	0	.271	.333	.412
John Marzano	C32	R	27	32	83	8	20	4	0	0	6	5	10	0	.241	.281	.289
Randy Kutcher	OF34,3B11,DH5*	R	30	63	74	18	17	4	1	1	5	13	18	3	.230	.345	.351
Danny Heep	OF14,DH6,1B5*	L	32	41	69	3	12	1	1	0	8	7	14	0	.174	.256	.217
Billy Joe Robidoux	1B11,DH4	L	26	27	44	3	8	4	0	1	4	6	14	0	.182	.288	.341
Bill Buckner	1B15	L	40	22	43	4	8	0	0	1	3	3	2	0	.186	.234	.256
Rich Gedman†	C9	L	30	10	15	3	3	0	0	0	0	5	6	0	.200	.429	.200
Phil Plantier	DH4,OF1	L	21	14	15	1	2	1	0	0	3	4	6	0	.133	.333	.200
Rick Lancellotti	1B2	L	33	4	8	0	0	0	0	0	0	1	3	0	.000	.000	.000
Jeff Stone	DH2	L	29	10	2	1	1	0	0	0	1	0	1	0	.500	.500	.500
Scott Cooper		L	22	2	1	0	0	0	0	0	1	0	1	0	.000	.000	.000
Jim Pankovits	2B2	R	34	2	0	0	0	0	0	0	0	0	0	0	—	—	—

R. Kutcher, 5 G at 2B; D. Heep, 1 G at P

Pitcher	T	Age	G	GS	CG	ShO	IP	H	HR	BB	SO	W-L	Sv	ERA
Mike Boddicker	R	32	34	34	4	0	228.0	225	16	69	143	17-8	0	3.36
Roger Clemens	R	27	31	31	7	4	228.1	193	7	54	209	21-6	0	1.93
Greg Harris	R	34	34	30	1	0	184.1	186	13	77	117	13-9	0	4.00
Dana Kiecker	R	29	32	25	0	0	152.0	145	7	54	93	8-9	0	3.97
Tom Bolton	L	28	21	16	3	0	119.2	111	6	47	65	10-5	0	3.38
Eric Hetzel	R	26	9	8	0	0	35.0	39	3	21	20	1-4	0	5.91
John Dopson	R	26	4	4	0	0	17.2	13	2	9	9	0-0	0	2.04
John Leister	R	29	2	1	0	0	5.2	7	0	4	3	0-0	0	4.76
Mike Rochford	L	27	2	1	0	0	4.0	10	1	4	0	0-1	0	18.00
Rob Murphy	L	30	68	0	0	0	57.0	85	10	32	54	0-6	7	6.32
Dennis Lamp	R	37	47	1	0	0	105.2	114	10	30	49	3-5	0	4.68
Jeff Reardon	R	34	47	0	0	0	51.1	39	5	19	33	5-3	21	3.16
Jeff Gray	R	27	41	0	0	0	50.2	53	3	15	50	2-4	9	4.44
Wes Gardner	R	29	34	9	0	0	77.1	77	6	35	58	3-7	0	4.89
Jerry Reed†	R	34	29	0	0	0	45.0	55	1	16	17	2-1	2	4.80
Larry Andersen†	R	37	15	0	0	0	22.0	18	0	3	25	0-0	1	1.23
Joe Hesketh†	L	31	12	2	0	0	25.2	37	2	11	26	0-4	0	3.51
Daryl Irvine	R	25	11	0	0	0	17.1	15	0	10	9	1-1	0	4.67
Lee Smith†	R	32	11	0	0	0	14.1	13	0	9	17	2-1	4	1.88
Danny Heep	L	32	1	0	0	0	1.0	4	0	0	0	0-0	0	9.00

1990 Toronto Blue Jays 2nd AL East 86-76 .531 2.0 GB

Cito Gaston

Player	Gm by Position	B	Age	G	AB	R	H	2B	3B	HR	RBI	BB	SO	SB	Avg	OBP	Slg
Pat Borders	C115,DH1	R	27	125	346	36	99	24	2	15	49	18	57	0	.286	.319	.497
Fred McGriff	1B147,DH6	L	26	153	557	91	167	21	1	35	88	94	108	5	.300	.400	.530
Manuel Lee	2B112,SS9	S	25	117	391	45	95	12	4	6	41	26	90	3	.243	.288	.340
Kelly Gruber	3B145,OF6,DH1	R	28	150	592	92	162	36	6	31	118	48	94	14	.274	.330	.512
Tony Fernandez	SS161	S	28	161	635	84	175	27	17	4	66	71	70	26	.276	.352	.391
Mookie Wilson	OF141,DH6	S	34	147	588	81	156	36	4	3	51	31	102	23	.265	.300	.355
Junior Felix	OF125,DH1	S	22	127	463	73	122	23	7	15	65	45	99	13	.263	.328	.441
George Bell	OF106,DH36	R	30	142	562	67	149	25	0	21	86	32	80	3	.265	.303	.422
John Olerud	DH90,1B18	L	21	111	358	43	95	15	1	14	48	57	75	0	.265	.364	.430
Glenallen Hill	OF60,DH20	R	25	84	260	47	60	11	3	12	32	18	62	8	.231	.281	.435
Greg Myers	C87	L	24	87	250	33	59	7	1	5	22	22	33	0	.236	.293	.332
Nelson Liriano†	2B49	S	26	50	170	16	36	7	2	1	15	16	20	3	.212	.282	.294
Rance Mulliniks	3B22,DH10,1B3	L	34	57	97	11	28	4	0	2	16	22	19	2	.289	.417	.392
Mark Whiten	OF30,DH2	S	23	33	88	12	24	1	1	2	7	7	14	2	.273	.323	.375
Luis Sojo	2B15,SS5,OF5*	R	24	33	80	14	18	3	0	1	9	5	5	1	.225	.271	.300
Kenny Williams†	OF30,DH9	R	26	49	72	13	14	6	1	0	8	7	18	7	.194	.272	.306
Rob Ducey	OF19	L	25	19	53	7	16	5	0	0	7	7	15	1	.302	.387	.396
Tom Lawless	DH5,3B4,OF2*	R	33	15	12	1	1	0	0	0	1	0	1	0	.083	.083	.083
Ozzie Virgil	C2,DH1	R	33	3	5	0	0	0	0	0	0	0	3	0	.000	.000	.000
Jim Eppard		L	30	6	5	0	1	0	0	0	0	0	2	0	.200	.333	.200
Carlos Diaz	C9	R	25	9	3	1	1	0	0	0	0	0	2	0	.333	.333	.333
Tom Quinlan	3B1	R	22	1	2	0	1	0	0	0	0	0	1	0	.500	.667	.500

L. Sojo, 4 G at 3B, 3 G at DH; T. Lawless, 1 G at 2B

Pitcher	T	Age	G	GS	CG	ShO	IP	H	HR	BB	SO	W-L	Sv	ERA
Dave Stieb	R	32	33	33	2	2	208.2	179	11	64	125	18 6	0	2.93
Todd Stottlemyre	R	25	33	33	4	0	203.0	214	18	69	115	13-17	0	4.34
Jimmy Key	L	29	27	27	0	0	154.2	169	20	22	88	13-7	0	4.25
David Wells	L	27	43	25	0	0	189.0	165	14	45	115	11-6	3	3.14
John Cerutti	L	30	30	23	0	0	140.0	162	23	49	49	9-9	0	4.76
Mike Flanagan	L	38	5	5	0	0	20.1	28	3	8	5	2-2	0	5.31
Bud Black†	L	33	3	2	0	0	15.2	10	2	3	3	2-1	0	4.02
Duane Ward	R	26	73	0	0	0	127.2	101	9	42	112	2-8	11	3.45
Tom Henke	R	32	61	0	0	0	74.2	58	8	19	75	2-4	32	2.17
Jim Acker	R	31	59	0	0	0	91.2	103	9	30	54	4-4	1	3.83
Frank Wills	R	31	44	4	0	0	99.0	101	13	38	72	6-4	0	4.73
Willie Blair	R	24	27	6	0	0	68.2	66	4	28	43	3-5	0	4.06
John Candelaria†	L	36	13	2	0	0	21.1	32	2	11	19	0-3	1	5.48
Paul Kilgus	L	28	11	0	0	0	16.1	19	2	7	7	0-0	0	6.06
Steve Cummings	R	25	6	2	0	0	12.1	22	4	5	4	0-0	0	5.11
Al Leiter	L	24	4	0	0	0	6.1	1	0	2	5	0-0	0	0.00
Bob MacDonald	L	25	4	0	0	0	2.1	0	0	2	0	0-0	0	0.00
Tom Gilles	R	27	2	0	0	0	1.1	2	0	0	1	1-0	0	6.75
Rick Luecken†	R	29	1	0	0	0	1.0	2	1	1	0	0-0	0	9.00

1990 Detroit Tigers 3rd AL East 79-83 .488 9.0 GB

Sparky Anderson

Player	Gm by Position	B	Age	G	AB	R	H	2B	3B	HR	RBI	BB	SO	SB	Avg	OBP	Slg
Mike Heath	C117,OF3,DH2*	R	35	122	370	46	100	18	2	7	38	19	71	7	.270	.311	.386
Cecil Fielder	1B143,DH15	R	26	159	573	104	159	25	1	51	132	90	182	0	.277	.377	.592
Lou Whitaker	2B130,DH1	L	33	132	472	75	112	22	2	18	60	74	71	8	.237	.338	.407
Tony Phillips	3B104,2B47,SS11*	S	31	152	573	97	144	23	5	8	55	99	85	19	.251	.364	.351
Alan Trammell	SS142,DH3	R	32	146	559	71	170	37	1	14	89	68	55	12	.304	.377	.449
Lloyd Moseby	OF116,DH4	L	30	122	431	64	107	16	5	14	51	48	77	17	.248	.329	.406
Chet Lemon	OF96,DH6	R	35	104	322	39	83	16	4	5	32	48	61	3	.258	.359	.379
Gary Ward	OF85,DH10,1B2	R	36	106	309	32	79	11	2	9	46	30	50	2	.256	.322	.392
Dave Bergman	DH51,1B27,OF5	L	37	100	205	21	57	10	1	2	26	33	17	3	.278	.375	.366
Larry Sheets	OF79,DH44	L	30	131	360	40	94	17	2	10	52	24	42	1	.261	.308	.403
Travis Fryman	3B48,SS17,DH1	R	21	66	232	32	69	11	1	9	27	17	51	3	.297	.348	.470
John Shelby†	OF68,DH5	S	32	78	222	22	55	9	3	4	20	10	51	3	.248	.280	.369
Mark Salas	C57,DH3,3B1	L	29	74	164	18	38	3	0	9	24	21	28	0	.232	.323	.415
Tracy Jones†	DH27,OF27	R	29	50	118	15	27	4	1	4	9	6	13	1	.229	.283	.381
Matt Nokes†	DH24,C19	L	26	44	111	12	30	5	1	3	8	4	14	0	.270	.305	.414
Darnell Coles†	DH31,OF11,3B8	R	28	52	108	13	22	2	0	1	4	12	21	0	.204	.281	.250
Scott Lusader	OF42,DH2	L	25	45	87	13	21	2	0	2	16	12	8	0	.241	.324	.333
Kenny Williams†	OF47,DH6	R	26	57	83	10	11	2	0	0	5	3	24	2	.133	.170	.157
Ed Romero	3B27,DH3	R	32	32	70	8	16	3	0	0	4	6	4	0	.229	.286	.271
Milt Cuyler	OF17	S	21	19	51	8	13	3	1	0	8	5	10	1	.255	.316	.353
Jim Lindeman	DH10,1B1,OF1	R	28	12	32	5	7	1	0	2	8	2	13	0	.219	.265	.438
Rich Rowland	C5,DH2	R	26	7	19	3	3	1	0	0	0	2	4	0	.158	.238	.211
Johnny Paredes†	2B4	R	27	6	8	2	1	0	0	0	0	1	0	0	.125	.222	.125

M. Heath, 1 G at SS; T. Phillips, 8 G at OF, 4 G at DH

Pitcher	T	Age	G	GS	CG	ShO	IP	H	HR	BB	SO	W-L	Sv	ERA
Jack Morris	R	35	36	36	11	3	249.2	231	26	97	162	15-18	0	4.51
Frank Tanana	L	36	34	29	1	0	176.1	190	25	66	114	9-8	1	5.31
Jeff Robinson	R	28	27	27	1	1	145.0	141	23	88	76	10-9	0	5.96
Dan Petry	R	31	32	23	1	0	149.2	148	14	77	73	10-9	0	4.45
Walt Terrell†	R	32	13	12	0	0	75.1	86	7	24	30	6-4	0	4.54
Steve Searcy	L	26	16	12	1	0	75.1	76	9	51	66	2-7	0	4.66
Brian DuBois	L	25	12	11	0	0	58.1	70	9	22	34	3-5	0	5.09
Kevin Ritz	R	25	4	4	0	0	7.1	14	0	14	3	0-4	0	11.05
Scott Aldred	L	22	4	3	0	0	14.1	13	0	10	7	1-2	0	3.77
Randy Nosek	R	23	3	2	0	0	7.0	7	1	9	3	1-1	0	7.71
Mike Henneman	R	28	69	0	0	0	94.1	90	4	33	50	8-6	22	3.05
Paul Gibson	R	30	61	0	0	0	97.1	99	10	44	56	5-4	3	3.05
Jerry Don Gleaton	L	32	57	0	0	0	82.2	62	5	25	56	1-3	13	2.94
Edwin Nunez	R	27	42	0	0	0	80.1	65	4	37	66	3-1	6	2.24
Clay Parker†	R	27	24	1	0	0	51.0	45	6	25	20	2-2	0	3.18
Urbano Lugo	R	27	13	1	0	0	24.1	30	9	13	12	2-0	0	7.03
Lance McCullers†	R	26	9	1	0	0	29.2	18	2	13	20	1-0	0	2.73
Steve Wapnick	R	24	4	0	0	0	7.0	8	0	10	6	0-0	0	6.43
Mike Schwabe	R	25	1	0	0	0	3.2	5	0	0	1	0-0	0	2.45
Matt Kinzer	R	27	1	0	0	0	1.2	3	0	3	1	0-0	0	16.20

1990 Cleveland Indians 4th AL East 77-85 .475 11.0 GB

John McNamara

Player	Gm by Position	B	Age	G	AB	R	H	2B	3B	HR	RBI	BB	SO	SB	Avg	OBP	Slg
Sandy Alomar Jr.	C129	R	24	132	445	60	129	26	2	9	66	25	46	4	.290	.326	.418
Brook Jacoby	3B99,1B78	R	30	155	553	77	162	24	4	14	75	63	58	1	.293	.365	.427
Jerry Browne	2B139	S	24	140	513	92	137	26	5	6	50	72	46	12	.267	.353	.372
Carlos Baerga	3B50,SS48,2B8	S	21	108	312	46	81	17	2	7	47	16	57	0	.260	.300	.394
Felix Fermin	SS147,2B1	R	26	148	414	47	106	13	2	1	40	26	22	3	.256	.297	.304
Candy Maldonado	OF134,DH20	R	29	155	590	76	161	32	2	22	95	49	134	3	.273	.330	.446
Cory Snyder	OF120,SS5	R	27	123	438	46	102	27	3	14	55	21	118	1	.233	.268	.404
Mitch Webster	OF118,DH3,1B3	S	31	128	437	58	110	20	6	12	55	20	61	22	.252	.285	.407
Chris James	DH124,OF14	R	27	140	528	62	158	32	4	12	70	31	71	4	.299	.341	.443
Dion James	1B35,OF33,DH10	L	27	87	248	28	68	15	2	1	22	27	23	5	.274	.347	.363
Alex Cole	OF59,DH1	L	24	63	227	43	68	5	4	0	13	28	38	40	.300	.379	.357
Tom Brookens	3B35,2B21,SS3*	R	36	64	154	18	41	7	2	1	20	14	25	0	.266	.322	.357
Joel Skinner	C49	R	29	49	139	16	35	4	1	2	16	7	44	0	.252	.288	.338
Keith Hernandez	1B42	L	36	43	130	7	26	2	0	1	8	14	17	0	.200	.283	.238
Stan Jefferson†	OF34,DH6	S	27	49	98	21	27	8	0	2	10	8	18	8	.276	.333	.418
Jeff Manto	1B25,3B5	R	25	30	76	12	17	5	1	2	14	21	18	0	.224	.392	.395
Ken Phelps†	1B14,DH6	L	35	24	61	4	7	0	0	0	0	10	11	1	.115	.239	.115
Turner Ward	OF13,DH1	S	25	14	46	10	16	2	1	1	10	3	8	3	.348	.388	.500
Albert Belle	DH6,OF1	R	23	9	23	1	4	0	0	1	3	1	6	0	.174	.208	.304
Beau Allred	OF4	L	25	4	16	2	3	1	0	1	2	2	3	0	.188	.278	.438
Rafael Santana	SS7	R	32	7	13	3	3	0	0	1	3	0	0	0	.231	.231	.462
Mark McLemore†	3B4,2B3	S	25	8	12	2	2	0	0	0	0	0	6	0	.167	.167	.167
Steve Springer	3B3,DH1	R	29	4	12	1	2	0	0	0	1	0	6	0	.167	.154	.167

T. Brookens, 2 G at 1B, 1 G at DH

Pitcher	T	Age	G	GS	CG	ShO	IP	H	HR	BB	SO	W-L	Sv	ERA
Greg Swindell	L	25	34	34	3	0	214.2	245	27	47	135	12-9	0	4.40
Tom Candiotti	R	32	31	29	3	1	202.0	207	23	55	128	15-11	0	3.65
Bud Black†	L	33	29	29	5	2	191.0	171	17	58	103	11-10	0	3.53
John Farrell	R	27	17	17	1	0	96.2	108	10	33	44	4-5	0	4.28
Sergio Valdez†	R	25	24	13	0	0	102.1	109	17	35	63	6-6	0	4.75
Mike Walker	R	23	18	11	0	0	75.2	82	6	42	34	2-6	0	4.88
Jeff Shaw	R	23	12	9	0	0	48.2	73	11	20	25	3-4	0	6.66
Charles Nagy	R	23	9	8	0	0	45.2	58	7	21	26	2-4	0	5.91
Al Nipper	R	31	9	5	0	0	24.0	35	2	19	12	2-3	0	6.75
Kevin Bearse	L	24	3	3	0	0	7.2	16	2	5	2	0-2	0	12.91
Rod Nichols	R	25	4	2	0	0	16.0	24	5	6	3	0-3	0	7.88
Doug Jones	R	33	66	0	0	0	84.1	66	5	22	55	5-5	43	2.56
Jesse Orosco	L	33	55	0	0	0	64.2	58	9	38	55	5-4	2	3.90
Steve Olin	R	24	50	1	0	0	92.1	96	3	26	64	4-4	1	3.41
Cecilio Guante	R	30	26	1	0	0	46.2	38	10	18	30	2-3	0	5.01
Rudy Seanez	R	21	24	0	0	0	27.1	22	2	25	24	2-1	0	5.60
Colby Ward	R	26	22	0	0	0	36.0	31	3	21	23	1-3	1	4.25
Efrain Valdez	L	24	13	0	0	0	23.2	20	2	14	13	1-1	0	3.04
Kevin Wickander	L	25	10	0	0	0	12.1	14	0	4	10	0-1	0	3.65
Jeff Kaiser	L	29	5	0	0	0	12.2	16	2	7	9	0-0	0	3.55
Mauro Gozzo	R	24	2	0	0	0	3.0	2	0	2	2	0-0	0	0.00

1990 Baltimore Orioles 5th AL East 76-85 .472 11.5 GB

Frank Robinson

Player	Gm by Position	B	Age	G	AB	R	H	2B	3B	HR	RBI	BB	SO	SB	Avg	OBP	Slg
Mickey Tettleton	C90,DH40,1B5*	S	29	135	444	68	99	21	2	15	51	106	160	2	.223	.376	.381
Randy Milligan	1B98,DH9	R	28	109	362	64	96	20	1	20	60	88	68	6	.265	.408	.492
Billy Ripken	2B127	R	25	129	406	48	118	28	1	3	38	28	43	5	.291	.342	.387
Craig Worthington	3B131,DH2	R	25	133	425	46	96	17	0	8	44	63	96	1	.226	.328	.322
Cal Ripken Jr.	SS161	R	29	161	600	78	150	28	4	21	84	82	66	3	.250	.341	.415
Steve Finley	OF133,DH2	L	25	142	464	46	119	16	4	3	37	32	53	22	.256	.304	.328
Joe Orsulak	OF109,DH5	L	28	124	413	49	111	14	3	11	57	46	48	6	.269	.343	.397
Mike Devereaux	OF104,DH3	R	27	108	367	48	88	18	1	12	49	28	48	13	.240	.291	.392
Sam Horn	DH63,1B10	L	26	79	246	30	61	13	0	14	45	32	62	0	.248	.332	.472
Bob Melvin	C76,DH10,1B1	R	28	93	301	30	73	14	1	5	37	11	53	0	.243	.267	.346
Phil Bradley†	OF70,DH2	R	31	72	289	39	78	9	1	4	26	30	35	10	.270	.352	.349
Brady Anderson	OF63,DH11	L	26	89	234	24	54	5	2	3	24	31	46	15	.231	.327	.308
Tim Hulett	3B24,2B16,DH8	R	30	53	153	16	39	7	1	3	16	15	41	1	.255	.321	.373
David Segui	1B36,DH4	S	23	40	123	14	30	7	0	2	15	11	15	0	.244	.311	.350
Rene Gonzales	2B43,3B16,SS9*	R	29	67	103	13	22	3	1	1	12	12	14	1	.214	.296	.291
Brad Komminsk†	OF40,DH2	R	29	46	101	18	24	4	0	3	8	14	29	1	.238	.342	.366
Jeff McKnight	1B15,OF8,2B5*	S	27	29	75	11	15	2	0	1	4	5	17	0	.200	.259	.267
Chris Hoiles	DH7,C7,1B6	R	25	23	63	7	12	3	0	1	6	5	12	0	.190	.250	.286
Ron Kittle†	DH13,1B5	R	32	22	61	4	10	2	0	2	3	2	14	0	.164	.203	.295
Dave Gallagher†	OF20	R	29	23	51	7	11	1	0	0	2	4	3	1	.216	.268	.235
Leo Gomez	3B12	R	24	12	39	3	9	0	0	0	1	8	7	0	.231	.362	.231
Greg Walker†	DH11	L	30	14	34	2	5	0	0	0	2	3	9	1	.147	.237	.147
Donell Nixon	OF4,DH3	R	28	8	20	1	5	2	0	0	2	1	7	5	.250	.286	.350
Stan Jefferson†	OF5	S	27	10	19	1	0	0	0	0	0	2	8	1	.000	.095	.000
Marty Brown	DH4,2B3,3B2	R	27	9	15	1	3	0	0	0	0	1	7	0	.200	.250	.200
Juan Bell	DH1,SS1	R	22	5	2	1	0	0	0	0	0	0	1	0	.000	.000	.000

M. Tettleton, 1 G at OF; R. Gonzales, 1 G at OF; J. McKnight, 1 G at DH, 1 G at SS

Pitcher	T	Age	G	GS	CG	ShO	IP	H	HR	BB	SO	W-L	Sv	ERA
Pete Harnisch	R	23	31	31	3	0	188.2	189	17	86	122	11-11	0	4.34
Dave Johnson	R	30	30	29	3	0	180.0	196	30	43	68	13-9	0	4.10
Bob Milacki	R	25	27	24	1	1	135.1	143	18	61	60	5-8	0	4.46
John Mitchell	R	24	24	17	0	0	114.1	133	7	48	43	6-6	0	4.64
Ben McDonald	R	22	21	15	3	2	118.2	88	9	35	65	8-5	0	2.43
Jay Tibbs†	R	28	10	10	0	0	50.2	55	8	14	23	2-7	0	5.68
Anthony Telford	R	24	8	8	0	0	36.1	43	4	19	20	3-3	0	4.95
Jose Mesa	R	24	7	7	0	0	46.2	37	2	27	24	3-2	0	3.86
Gregg Olson	R	23	64	0	0	0	74.1	57	3	31	74	6-5	37	2.42
Joe Price	L	33	50	0	0	0	65.1	62	8	24	54	3-4	0	3.58
Mark Williamson	R	30	49	0	0	0	85.1	65	8	28	60	8-2	1	2.21
Jeff Ballard	L	26	44	17	0	0	133.1	152	22	42	50	2-11	0	4.93
Kevin Hickey	L	34	37	0	0	0	26.1	26	3	13	17	1-3	1	5.13
Curt Schilling	R	23	35	0	0	0	46.0	38	1	19	32	1-2	3	2.54
Brian Holton	R	30	33	0	0	0	58.0	68	7	21	27	2-3	0	4.50
Jose Bautista	R	25	22	0	0	0	26.2	28	4	7	15	1-0	0	4.05
Mickey Weston	R	29	9	2	0	0	21.0	28	6	6	9	0-1	0	7.71
Jay Aldrich	R	29	7	0	0	0	12.0	17	1	7	5	1-2	1	8.25
Dan Boone	L	36	4	1	0	0	9.2	12	1	3	2	0-0	0	2.79
Dorn Taylor	R	31	4	0	0	0	3.2	4	0	2	4	0-1	0	2.45
Michael Smith	R	26	2	0	0	0	3.0	4	2	1	2	0-0	0	12.00

1990 Milwaukee Brewers 6th AL East 74-88 .457 14.0 GB

Tom Trebelhorn

Player	Gm by Position	B	Age	G	AB	R	H	2B	3B	HR	RBI	BB	SO	SB	Avg	OBP	Slg
B.J. Surhoff	C125,3B11	L	25	135	474	55	131	21	4	6	59	41	37	18	.276	.331	.376
Greg Brock	1B115	L	33	123	367	42	91	23	0	7	50	43	45	4	.248	.324	.368
Jim Gantner	2B80,3B9	L	37	88	323	36	85	8	5	0	25	29	19	18	.263	.328	.319
Gary Sheffield	3B125	R	21	125	487	67	143	30	1	10	67	44	41	25	.294	.350	.421
Bill Spiers	SS111	L	24	112	363	44	88	15	3	2	36	16	45	11	.242	.274	.317
Robin Yount	OF157,DH1	R	34	158	587	98	145	17	5	17	77	78	89	15	.247	.337	.380
Rob Deer	OF117,1B21,DH1	R	29	134	440	57	92	15	1	27	69	64	147	2	.209	.313	.432
Mike Felder	OF109,2B1,3B1	S	28	121	237	38	65	7	2	3	27	22	17	20	.274	.330	.359
Dave Parker	DH153,1B3	L	39	157	610	71	176	30	3	21	92	41	102	4	.289	.330	.451
Paul Molitor	2B60,1B37,DH4*	R	33	103	418	64	119	27	6	12	45	37	51	18	.285	.343	.464
Greg Vaughn	OF106,DH8	R	24	120	382	51	84	26	2	17	61	33	91	7	.220	.280	.432
Edgar Diaz	SS65,2B15,3B7*	R	26	86	218	27	59	2	2	0	14	21	32	3	.271	.338	.298
Darryl Hamilton	OF72,DH9	L	25	89	156	27	46	5	0	1	18	9	12	10	.295	.333	.346
Charlie O'Brien†	C46	R	30	46	145	11	27	7	2	0	11	11	26	0	.186	.253	.262
Dale Sveum	3B22,2B16,1B5*	S	26	48	117	15	23	7	0	1	12	12	30	0	.197	.278	.282
Glenn Braggs†	OF32,DH2	R	27	37	113	17	28	5	0	3	13	12	21	5	.248	.328	.372
Billy Bates†	2B14	L	26	14	29	6	3	1	0	0	2	4	7	4	.103	.206	.138
Gus Polidor	3B14,2B2,SS2	R	28	18	15	0	1	0	0	0	1	0	1	0	.067	.067	.067
George Canale	1B6,DH3	L	24	10	13	4	1	1	0	0	0	2	6	0	.077	.200	.154
Tim McIntosh	C4	R	25	5	5	1	1	0	0	1	1	0	2	0	.200	.200	.800
Terry Francona	1B2,DH1	L	31	3	4	1	0	0	0	0	0	0	0	0	.000	.000	.000

P. Molitor, 2 G at 3B; E. Diaz, 1 G at DH; D. Sveum, 5 G at SS

Pitcher	T	Age	G	GS	CG	ShO	IP	H	HR	BB	SO	W-L	Sv	ERA
Teddy Higuera	L	31	27	27	4	1	170.0	167	16	50	129	11-10	0	3.76
Mark Knudson	R	29	30	27	4	2	168.1	187	14	40	56	10-9	0	4.12
Jaime Navarro	R	23	32	22	3	0	149.1	176	11	41	75	8-7	1	4.46
Ron Robinson†	R	28	22	22	7	2	148.1	158	5	37	57	12-5	0	2.91
Chris Bosio	R	27	20	20	4	1	132.2	131	15	38	76	4-9	0	4.00
Bill Krueger	L	32	30	17	0	0	129.0	137	10	54	64	6-8	0	3.98
Dennis Powell†	L	26	9	7	0	0	39.1	59	0	19	23	0-4	0	6.86
Bill Wegman	R	27	8	5	1	1	29.2	37	6	6	20	2-2	0	4.85
Tom Filer	R	33	7	4	0	0	22.0	26	2	9	8	2-3	0	6.14
Kevin Brown†	L	24	5	3	0	0	21.0	14	1	7	12	1-1	0	2.57
Chuck Crim	R	28	67	0	0	0	85.2	88	7	23	39	3-5	11	3.47
Dan Plesac	L	28	66	0	0	0	69.0	67	5	31	65	3-7	24	4.43
Paul Mirabella	L	36	44	2	0	0	59.0	66	9	27	28	4-2	0	3.97
Tom Edens	R	29	35	6	0	0	89.0	89	8	33	40	4-5	2	4.45
Tony Fossas	L	32	32	0	0	0	29.1	44	5	10	24	2-3	0	6.44
Randy Veres	R	24	26	0	0	0	41.2	38	5	16	16	0-3	1	3.67
Mark Lee	L	25	11	0	0	0	21.1	20	1	4	14	1-0	0	2.11
Julio Machado†	R	24	10	0	0	0	13.0	9	0	8	12	0-0	3	0.69
Bob Sebra	R	28	10	0	0	0	11.0	20	1	5	4	1-2	0	8.18
Don August	R	26	5	0	0	0	11.0	13	0	5	2	0-3	0	6.55
Narciso Elvira	L	22	4	0	0	0	5.0	6	0	5	6	0-0	0	5.40
Mike Capel	R	28	2	0	0	0	0.1	6	0	1	1	0-0	0	135.00

1990 New York Yankees 7th AL East 67-95 .414 21.0 GB

Bucky Dent (18-31)/Stump Merrill (49-64)

Player	Gm by Position	B	Age	G	AB	R	H	2B	3B	HR	RBI	BB	SO	SB	Avg	OBP	Slg
Bob Geren	C107,DH1	R	28	110	277	21	59	7	0	8	31	13	73	0	.213	.259	.325
Don Mattingly	1B89,DH13,OF1	L	29	102	394	40	101	16	0	5	42	28	20	1	.256	.308	.335
Steve Sax	2B154	R	30	155	615	70	160	24	2	4	42	49	46	43	.260	.316	.325
Randy Velarde	3B74,SS15,OF5*	R	27	95	229	21	48	6	2	5	19	20	53	0	.210	.275	.319
Alvaro Espinoza	SS150	R	28	150	438	31	98	12	2	2	20	16	54	1	.224	.258	.274
Roberto Kelly	OF160,DH1	R	25	162	641	85	183	32	4	15	61	33	148	42	.285	.323	.418
Jesse Barfield	OF151	R	30	153	476	69	117	21	2	25	78	82	150	4	.246	.359	.456
Oscar Azocar	OF57,DH1	L	25	65	214	18	53	8	0	5	19	2	15	7	.248	.257	.355
Steve Balboni	DH72,1B28	R	33	116	266	24	51	6	0	17	34	35	91	0	.192	.291	.406
Mel Hall	DH54,OF50	L	29	113	360	41	93	23	2	12	46	6	46	0	.258	.272	.433
Jim Leyritz	3B69,OF14,C11	R	26	92	303	28	78	13	1	5	25	27	51	2	.257	.331	.356
Kevin Maas	1B57,DH18	L	25	79	254	42	64	9	0	21	41	43	76	1	.252	.367	.535
Matt Nokes†	C46,DH30,OF2	L	26	92	240	21	57	4	0	8	32	20	33	2	.238	.307	.354
Mike Blowers	3B45,DH2	R	25	48	144	16	27	4	0	5	21	12	50	1	.188	.255	.319
Rick Cerone	C35,DH6,2B1	R	36	49	139	12	42	6	0	2	11	5	13	0	.302	.324	.388
Deion Sanders	OF42,DH4	L	22	57	133	24	21	2	2	3	9	13	27	8	.158	.236	.271
Hensley Meulens	OF23	R	23	23	83	12	20	7	0	3	10	9	25	1	.241	.337	.434
C. Washington†	OF21,DH2	L	35	33	80	4	13	1	1	0	6	2	17	3	.163	.181	.200
Wayne Tolleson	SS45,2B13,DH5*	S	34	73	74	12	11	1	1	0	4	6	21	1	.149	.210	.189
Dave Winfield†	OF12,DH7	R	38	20	61	7	13	3	0	2	6	4	13	0	.213	.269	.361
Brian Dorsett	C9,DH5	R	29	14	35	2	5	2	0	0	0	2	4	0	.143	.189	.200
Luis Polonia†	DH4	L	25	11	22	2	7	0	0	0	3	0	1	1	.318	.304	.318
Jim Walewander	DH2,2B2,3B2*	S	28	9	5	1	1	1	0	0	1	0	0	1	.200	.200	.400

R. Velarde, 3 G at DH, 3 G at 2B; W. Tolleson, 3 G at 3B; J. Walewander, 1 G at SS

Pitcher	T	Age	G	GS	CG	ShO	IP	H	HR	BB	SO	W-L	Sv	ERA
Tim Leary	R	32	31	31	6	1	208.0	202	18	78	138	9-19	0	4.11
Dave LaPoint	L	30	28	27	2	0	157.2	180	11	57	67	7-10	0	4.11
Chuck Cary	L	30	28	27	2	0	156.2	155	21	55	134	6-12	0	4.19
Andy Hawkins	R	30	28	26	2	1	157.2	156	20	82	74	5-12	0	5.37
Mike Witt†	R	29	16	16	2	1	96.2	87	8	34	60	5-6	0	4.47
Dave Eiland	R	23	5	5	0	0	30.1	31	2	5	16	2-1	0	3.56
Steve Adkins	L	25	5	5	0	0	24.0	19	4	29	14	1-2	0	6.38
Pascual Perez	R	33	3	3	0	0	14.0	8	0	3	12	1-2	0	1.29
Lee Guetterman	L	31	64	0	0	0	93.0	80	6	26	48	11-7	2	3.39
Greg Cadaret	L	28	54	6	0	0	121.1	120	8	64	80	5-4	3	4.15
Jeff Robinson	R	29	54	4	1	0	88.2	82	8	34	43	3-6	0	3.45
Dave Righetti	L	31	53	0	0	0	53.0	48	8	26	43	1-1	36	3.57
Eric Plunk	R	26	47	0	0	0	72.2	58	6	43	67	6-3	0	2.72
Alan Mills	R	23	36	0	0	0	41.2	48	4	33	24	1-5	0	4.10
Jimmy Jones	R	26	17	7	0	0	50.0	72	8	23	25	1-2	0	6.30
Lance McCullers†	R	26	11	0	0	0	15.0	14	2	6	11	1-0	0	3.60
Mark Leiter	R	27	8	3	0	0	26.1	33	5	9	21	1-1	0	6.84
John Habyan	R	26	6	0	0	0	8.2	10	0	2	4	0-0	0	2.08
Clay Parker†	R	27	5	2	0	0	22.0	19	5	7	20	1-1	0	4.50
Rich Monteleone	R	27	5	0	0	0	7.1	8	0	2	8	0-1	0	6.14

1990 Oakland Athletics 1st AL West 103-59 .636 —

Tony La Russa

Player	Gm by Position	B	Age	G	AB	R	H	2B	3B	HR	RBI	BB	SO	SB	Avg	OBP	Slg
Terry Steinbach	C83,DH25,1B3	R	28	114	379	32	95	15	2	9	57	19	66	0	.251	.291	.372
Mark McGwire	1B154,DH2	R	26	156	523	87	123	16	0	39	108	110	116	2	.235	.370	.489
Willie Randolph†	2B84,DH6	R	35	93	292	37	75	9	3	1	21	32	25	6	.257	.331	.318
Carney Lansford	3B126,DH5,1B5	R	33	134	507	58	136	15	1	3	50	45	50	16	.268	.333	.320
Walt Weiss	SS137	S	26	138	445	50	118	17	1	2	35	46	53	9	.265	.337	.321
Rickey Henderson	OF118,DH15	R	31	136	489	119	159	33	3	28	61	97	60	65	.325	.439	.577
Dave Henderson	OF116,DH6	R	31	127	450	65	122	28	0	20	63	40	105	3	.271	.331	.467
Felix Jose†	OF92,DH7	S	25	101	341	42	90	12	0	8	39	16	65	8	.264	.306	.370
Jose Canseco	OF88,DH43	R	25	131	481	83	132	14	2	37	101	72	158	19	.274	.371	.543
Mike Gallego	2B83,SS38,3B27*	R	29	140	389	36	80	13	2	3	34	35	50	5	.206	.277	.272
Ron Hassey	C59,DH15,1B3	L	37	94	254	18	54	7	0	5	22	27	29	0	.213	.288	.299
Doug Jennings	OF45,DH8,1B4	L	25	64	156	19	30	7	2	2	14	17	48	0	.192	.275	.301
Lance Blankenship	3B28,OF28,2B20*	R	26	86	136	18	26	3	0	0	10	20	23	3	.191	.295	.213
Jamie Quirk	C37,1B8,3B8*	L	35	56	121	12	34	5	1	3	26	14	34	0	.281	.353	.413
Willie McGee†	OF28,DH1	S	31	29	113	23	31	3	2	0	15	10	18	3	.274	.333	.336
Harold Baines†	DH30	L	31	32	94	11	25	5	0	3	21	20	17	0	.266	.381	.415
Ken Phelps†	DH15,1B5	L	35	32	59	6	11	2	0	1	6	12	10	0	.186	.319	.271
Steve Howard	OF14,DH7	R	26	21	52	5	12	4	0	0	1	4	17	0	.231	.286	.308
Darren Lewis	OF23,DH2	R	22	25	35	4	8	0	0	0	1	7	4	2	.229	.372	.229
Stan Javier†	OF13,DH2	S	26	19	33	4	8	0	2	0	3	3	6	0	.242	.306	.364
Dann Howitt	OF11,1B5,3B1	L	26	14	22	3	3	0	1	0	1	3	12	0	.136	.240	.227
Ozzie Canseco	DH4,OF2	R	25	9	19	1	2	1	0	0	1	1	10	0	.105	.150	.158
Troy Afenir	C12	R	26	14	14	0	2	0	0	0	2	0	6	0	.143	.133	.143
Mike Bordick	3B10,SS9,2B7	R	24	25	14	0	1	0	0	0	0	1	4	0	.071	.133	.071
Scott Hemond	3B7,2B1	R	24	7	13	0	2	0	0	0	1	0	5	0	.154	.154	.154

M. Gallego, 1 G at DH, 1 G at OF; L. Blankenship, 6 G at DH, 1 G at 1B; J. Quirk, 1 G at OF

Pitcher	T	Age	G	GS	CG	ShO	IP	H	HR	BB	SO	W-L	Sv	ERA
Dave Stewart	R	33	36	36	11	4	267.0	226	16	83	166	22-11	0	2.56
Bob Welch	R	33	35	35	2	2	238.0	214	26	77	127	27-6	0	2.95
Scott Sanderson	R	33	34	34	2	1	206.1	205	27	66	128	17-11	0	3.88
Mike Moore	R	30	33	33	3	0	199.1	204	14	84	73	13-15	0	4.65
Curt Young	L	30	26	21	0	0	124.1	124	17	53	56	9-6	0	4.85
Dennis Eckersley	R	35	63	0	0	0	73.1	41	2	4	73	4-2	48	0.61
Rick Honeycutt	L	36	63	0	0	0	63.1	46	2	22	38	2-2	7	2.70
Gene Nelson	R	29	51	0	0	0	74.2	55	5	17	38	3-3	5	1.57
Todd Burns	R	26	43	2	0	0	78.2	78	8	32	43	3-3	3	2.97
Joe Klink	L	28	40	0	0	0	39.2	34	1	18	19	0-0	1	2.04
Reggie Harris	R	21	16	1	0	0	41.1	25	5	21	31	1-0	0	3.48
Mike Norris	R	35	14	0	0	0	27.0	24	0	9	16	1-0	0	3.00
Steve Chitren	R	23	8	0	0	0	17.2	7	0	4	19	1-0	0	1.02
Dave Otto	L	25	2	0	0	0	2.1	3	0	3	2	0-0	0	7.71
Joe Bitker†	R	26	1	0	0	0	3.0	1	0	1	2	0-0	0	0.00

1990 Chicago White Sox 2nd AL West 94-68 .580 9.0 GB

Jeff Torborg

Player	Gm by Position	B	Age	G	AB	R	H	2B	3B	HR	RBI	BB	SO	SB	Avg	OBP	Slg
Carlton Fisk	C116,DH14	R	42	137	452	65	129	21	0	18	65	61	73	7	.285	.378	.451
Carlos Martinez	1B82,DH1,OF1	R	25	92	272	18	61	6	5	4	24	10	40	0	.224	.252	.327
Scott Fletcher	2B151	R	31	151	509	54	123	18	3	4	56	45	63	1	.242	.304	.312
Robin Ventura	3B147,1B1	L	22	150	493	48	123	17	1	5	54	55	53	1	.249	.324	.318
Ozzie Guillen	SS159	L	26	160	516	61	144	21	4	1	58	26	37	13	.279	.312	.341
Sammy Sosa	OF152	R	21	153	532	72	124	26	10	15	70	33	150	32	.233	.282	.404
Lance Johnson	OF148,DH1	L	26	151	541	76	154	18	9	1	51	33	45	36	.285	.325	.357
Ivan Calderon	OF130,DH27,1B2	R	28	158	607	85	166	44	2	14	74	51	79	32	.273	.327	.422
Dan Pasqua	DH57,OF43	L	28	112	325	43	89	27	3	13	58	37	66	1	.274	.347	.495
Ron Kittle†	DH54,1B25	R	32	83	277	29	68	14	0	16	43	24	77	0	.245	.311	.469
Frank Thomas	1B51,DH8	R	22	60	191	39	63	11	3	7	31	44	54	0	.330	.454	.529
Ron Karkovice	C64,DH1	R	26	68	183	30	45	10	0	6	20	16	52	2	.246	.308	.399
Steve Lyons	1B61,2B15,OF7*	L	30	94	146	22	28	6	1	1	11	10	41	1	.192	.245	.267
Phil Bradley†	OF38,DH7	R	31	45	133	20	30	5	1	0	5	20	26	7	.226	.344	.278
Craig Grebeck	3B35,SS16,2B6	R	25	59	119	7	20	3	1	1	9	8	24	0	.168	.227	.235
Dave Gallagher†	OF37,DH4	R	29	45	75	5	21	3	1	0	5	3	9	0	.280	.316	.347
Matt Stark	DH6	R	25	8	16	0	4	1	0	0	3	1	6	0	.250	.294	.313
Rodney McCray	OF13,DH7	R	26	32	6	8	0	0	0	0	0	1	4	6	.000	.143	.000
Greg Walker†	DH1,1B1	L	30	2	5	0	1	0	0	0	0	0	2	0	.200	.200	.200
Jerry Willard	C1	L	30	3	3	0	0	0	0	0	0	0	2	0	.000	.000	.000
Daryl Boston†	DH3,OF1	L	27	5	1	0	0	0	0	0	0	0	0	1	.000	.000	.000

S. Lyons, 5 G at 3B, 3 G at DH, 1 G at P, 1 G at SS

Pitcher	T	Age	G	GS	CG	ShO	IP	H	HR	BB	SO	W-L	Sv	ERA
Melido Perez	R	24	35	35	3	3	197.0	177	14	86	161	13-14	0	4.61
Greg Hibbard	L	25	33	33	3	1	211.0	202	11	55	92	14-9	0	3.16
Jack McDowell	R	24	33	33	4	0	205.0	189	20	77	165	14-9	0	3.82
Eric King	R	26	25	25	2	2	151.0	135	10	40	70	12-4	0	3.28
Alex Fernandez	R	20	13	13	3	0	87.2	89	6	34	61	5-5	0	3.80
Adam Peterson	R	24	20	11	2	0	85.0	90	12	26	29	2-5	0	4.55
Jerry Kutzler	R	25	7	7	0	0	31.1	38	2	14	21	2-1	0	6.03
Bobby Thigpen	R	26	77	0	0	0	88.2	60	5	32	70	4-6	57	1.83
Barry Jones	R	27	65	0	0	0	74.0	62	2	33	45	11-4	1	2.31
Scott Radinsky	L	22	62	0	0	0	52.1	47	1	36	46	6-1	4	4.82
Donn Pall	R	28	56	0	0	0	76.0	63	7	24	39	3-5	2	3.32
Ken Patterson	L	25	43	0	0	0	66.1	58	6	34	40	2-1	2	3.39
Wayne Edwards	L	26	42	5	0	0	95.0	81	6	41	63	5-3	2	3.22
Shawn Hillegas	R	25	7	0	0	0	11.1	4	0	5	5	0-0	0	0.79
Steve Rosenberg	L	25	6	0	0	0	10.0	10	2	5	4	1-0	0	5.40
Bill Long†	R	30	4	0	0	0	5.2	6	2	2	2	0-1	0	6.35
Steve Lyons	R	30	1	0	0	0	2.0	2	0	4	1	0-0	0	4.50

1990 Texas Rangers 3rd AL West 83-79 .512 20.0 GB

Bobby Valentine

Player	Gm by Position	B	Age	G	AB	R	H	2B	3B	HR	RBI	BB	SO	SB	Avg	OBP	Slg
Geno Petralli	C118,3B7,2B3	S	30	133	325	28	83	13	1	0	21	50	49	0	.255	.357	.302
Rafael Palmeiro	1B146,DH6	L	25	154	598	72	191	35	6	14	89	40	59	3	.319	.361	.468
Julio Franco	2B152,DH3	R	28	157	582	96	172	27	1	11	69	82	83	31	.296	.383	.402
Steve Buechele	3B88,2B4	R	28	91	251	30	54	10	0	7	30	27	63	1	.215	.294	.339
Jeff Huson	SS119,3B36,2B12	L	25	145	396	57	95	12	2	0	28	46	54	12	.240	.320	.280
Ruben Sierra	OF151,DH7	S	24	159	608	70	170	37	2	16	96	49	86	9	.280	.330	.426
Pete Incaviglia	OF145,DH1	R	26	153	529	59	123	27	0	24	85	45	146	3	.233	.302	.420
Gary Pettis	OF128,DH2	S	32	136	423	66	101	16	8	3	31	57	118	38	.239	.333	.336
Harold Baines†	DH95,OF2	L	31	103	321	41	93	10	1	13	44	47	63	0	.290	.377	.449
Jack Daugherty	OF42,1B30,DH21	S	29	125	310	36	93	20	2	6	47	22	49	0	.300	.347	.435
Jeff Kunkel	SS67,3B15,2B13*	R	28	99	200	17	34	11	1	3	17	11	66	2	.170	.221	.280
Mike Stanley	C63,DH14,3B8*	R	27	103	189	21	47	8	1	2	19	30	25	1	.249	.350	.333
Scott Coolbaugh	3B66	R	24	67	180	21	36	6	0	2	13	15	47	1	.200	.264	.267
John Russell	C31,DH19,OF6*	R	29	68	128	16	35	4	0	2	8	11	41	1	.273	.331	.352
Kevin Reimer	DH21,OF9	L	26	64	100	5	26	9	1	2	15	10	22	0	.260	.333	.430
Juan Gonzalez	OF16,DH9	R	20	25	90	11	26	7	1	4	12	2	18	0	.289	.316	.522
Gary Green	SS58	R	28	62	88	10	19	3	0	0	8	6	18	1	.216	.263	.250
Cecil Espy	OF39,DH4,2B1	S	27	52	71	10	9	0	0	0	1	10	20	11	.127	.235	.127
Thad Bosley	OF9,DH4	L	33	30	29	3	4	0	0	1	3	4	7	1	.138	.242	.241
Chad Kreuter	C20	S	25	22	22	2	1	1	0	0	2	8	9	0	.045	.290	.091
Kevin Belcher	OF9	R	22	16	15	4	2	1	0	0	0	2	6	0	.133	.235	.200
Bill Haselman	DH3,C1	R	24	7	13	0	2	0	0	0	3	1	5	0	.154	.214	.154

J. Kunkel, 5 G at OF; M. Stanley, 6 G at 1B; J. Russell, 3 G at 1B, 1 G at 3B

Pitcher	T	Age	G	GS	CG	ShO	IP	H	HR	BB	SO	W-L	Sv	ERA
Bobby Witt	R	26	33	32	7	1	222.0	197	12	110	221	17-10	0	3.36
Charlie Hough	R	42	32	32	5	0	218.2	190	24	119	114	12-12	0	4.07
Nolan Ryan	R	43	30	30	5	2	204.0	137	18	74	232	13-9	0	3.44
Kevin Brown	R	25	26	26	6	2	180.0	175	13	60	88	12-10	0	3.60
Scott Chiamparino	R	23	6	6	0	0	37.2	36	1	12	19	1-2	0	2.63
Brian Bohanon	L	21	11	6	0	0	34.0	40	6	18	15	0-3	0	6.62
Gerald Alexander	R	22	3	2	0	0	7.0	14	0	5	8	0-0	0	7.71
Kenny Rogers	L	25	69	3	0	0	97.2	93	6	42	74	10-6	15	3.13
Brad Arnsberg	R	26	53	0	0	0	62.2	56	4	33	44	6-1	5	2.15
Mike Jeffcoat	L	30	44	12	1	0	110.2	122	12	28	58	5-6	5	4.47
Jamie Moyer	L	27	33	10	1	0	102.1	115	6	39	58	2-6	0	4.66
John Barfield	L	25	33	0	0	0	44.1	42	2	13	17	4-3	1	4.67
Gary Mielke	R	27	33	0	0	0	41.0	42	4	15	13	0-3	0	3.73
Jeff Russell	R	28	27	0	0	0	25.1	23	1	16	16	1-5	10	4.26
Craig McMurtry	R	30	23	3	0	0	41.2	43	4	30	14	0-3	0	4.32
Joe Bitker†	R	26	5	0	0	0	9.0	7	0	3	6	0-0	0	3.00
John Hoover	R	27	2	0	0	0	4.2	8	0	3	0	0-0	0	11.57
Ramon Manon	R	22	1	0	0	0	2.0	3	0	3	0	0-0	0	13.50

1990 California Angels 4th AL West 80-82 .494 23.0 GB

Doug Rader

Player	Gm by Position	B	Age	G	AB	R	H	2B	3B	HR	RBI	BB	SO	SB	Avg	OBP	Slg
Lance Parrish	C131,1B4,DH1	R	34	133	470	54	126	14	0	24	70	46	107	2	.268	.338	.451
Wally Joyner	1B83	L	28	83	310	35	83	15	0	8	41	41	34	2	.268	.350	.394
Johnny Ray	2B100,DH1	S	33	105	404	47	112	23	0	5	43	19	44	2	.277	.308	.371
Jack Howell	3B102,1B1,SS1	L	28	105	316	35	72	19	1	8	33	46	61	3	.228	.326	.370
Dick Schofield	SS99	R	27	99	310	41	79	8	1	1	18	52	61	3	.255	.363	.297
Devon White	OF122	S	27	125	443	57	96	17	3	11	44	44	116	21	.217	.290	.343
Dave Winfield†	OF108,DH3	R	38	112	414	63	114	18	2	19	72	48	68	0	.275	.348	.466
Dante Bichette	OF105	R	26	109	349	40	89	15	1	15	53	16	79	5	.255	.292	.433
Brian Downing	DH87	R	39	96	330	47	90	18	2	14	51	50	45	0	.273	.374	.467
Chili Davis	DH60,OF52	S	30	113	412	58	109	17	1	12	58	61	89	1	.265	.357	.398
Luis Polonia†	OF85,DH11	L	25	109	381	50	128	7	9	2	32	25	42	20	.336	.376	.417
Donnie Hill	2B60,SS24,3B21*	S	29	103	352	36	93	18	2	3	32	29	27	1	.264	.319	.352
Lee Stevens	1B67	L	22	67	248	28	53	10	0	7	32	22	75	1	.214	.275	.339
Max Venable	OF77,DH1	L	33	93	189	26	49	9	3	4	21	24	31	5	.259	.340	.402
Rick Schu	3B38,1B15,OF4*	R	28	61	157	19	42	8	0	6	14	11	25	0	.268	.314	.433
Kent Anderson	SS28,3B16,2B5	R	26	49	143	16	44	6	1	1	5	13	19	0	.308	.369	.385
John Orton	C31	R	24	31	84	8	16	5	0	1	6	5	31	0	.190	.244	.286
Bill Schroeder	C15,1B3	R	31	18	58	7	13	3	0	4	9	1	10	0	.224	.237	.483
Gary DiSarcina	SS14,2B3	R	22	18	57	8	8	1	1	0	0	3	10	1	.140	.183	.193
Mark McLemore†	2B8,SS8,DH2	S	25	20	48	4	7	2	0	0	2	4	9	1	.146	.212	.188
Pete Coachman	3B9,DH2,2B2	R	28	16	45	3	14	3	0	0	5	1	7	0	.311	.354	.378
C. Washington†	OF9	L	35	12	34	3	6	1	0	1	3	2	8	1	.176	.222	.294
Bobby Rose	2B4,3B3	R	23	7	13	5	5	0	0	1	2	2	1	0	.385	.467	.615
Ron Tingley	C5	R	31	5	3	0	0	0	0	0	0	1	1	0	.000	.250	.000

D. Hill, 3 G at 1B, 1 G at DH, 1 G at P; R. Schu, 1 G at 2B

Pitcher	T	Age	G	GS	CG	ShO	IP	H	HR	BB	SO	W-L	Sv	ERA
Mark Langston	L	29	33	33	5	1	223.0	215	13	104	195	10-17	0	4.40
Jim Abbott	L	22	33	33	4	1	211.2	246	16	72	105	10-14	0	4.51
Chuck Finley	L	27	32	32	7	2	236.0	210	17	81	177	18-9	0	2.40
Kirk McCaskill	R	29	29	29	2	1	174.1	161	9	72	78	12-11	0	3.25
Bert Blyleven	R	39	23	23	2	0	134.0	163	15	25	69	8-7	0	5.24
Joe Grahe	R	23	8	8	0	0	43.1	51	3	23	25	3-4	0	4.98
Scott Lewis	R	24	2	2	1	0	16.1	10	2	2	9	1-1	0	2.20
Mark Eichhorn	R	29	60	0	0	0	84.2	98	2	23	69	2-5	13	3.08
Bryan Harvey	R	27	54	0	0	0	64.1	45	4	35	82	4-4	25	3.22
Willie Fraser	R	26	45	0	0	0	76.0	69	4	24	32	5-4	2	3.08
Scott Bailes	L	28	27	0	0	0	35.1	46	8	20	16	2-0	0	6.37
Mike Fetters	R	25	26	2	0	0	67.2	77	9	20	35	1-1	1	4.12
Cliff Young	L	25	17	0	0	0	30.2	40	2	7	19	1-1	0	3.52
Greg Minton	R	38	11	0	0	0	15.1	11	1	7	4	1-1	0	2.35
Bob McClure	L	38	11	0	0	0	7.0	7	0	3	6	2-0	0	6.43
Mike Witt†	R	29	10	0	0	0	20.1	19	1	13	14	0-3	1	1.77
Mark Clear	R	34	4	0	0	0	7.2	5	0	9	6	0-0	0	5.87
Sherm Corbett	L	27	4	0	0	0	5.0	8	0	3	2	0-0	0	9.00
Donnie Hill	R	29	1	0	0	0	1.0	0	0	1	1	0-0	0	0.00
Jeff Richardson	R	26	1	0	0	0	0.1	1	0	0	0	0-0	0	0.00

1990 Seattle Mariners 5th AL West 77-85 .475 26.0 GB

Jim Lefebvre

Player	Gm by Position	B	Age	G	AB	R	H	2B	3B	HR	RBI	BB	SO	SB	Avg	OBP	Slg
Dave Valle	C104,1B1	R	29	107	308	37	66	15	0	7	33	45	48	1	.214	.328	.331
Pete O'Brien	1B97,DH6,OF6	L	32	108	366	32	82	18	0	5	27	44	33	0	.224	.308	.314
Harold Reynolds	2B160	S	29	160	642	100	162	36	5	5	55	81	52	31	.252	.336	.347
Edgar Martinez	3B143,DH2	R	27	144	487	71	147	27	2	11	49	74	62	1	.302	.397	.433
Omar Vizquel	SS81	S	23	81	255	19	63	3	2	2	18	18	22	4	.247	.295	.298
Ken Griffey Jr.	OF151,DH2	L	20	155	597	91	179	28	7	22	80	63	81	16	.300	.366	.481
Henry Cotto	OF118,DH3	R	29	127	355	40	92	14	3	4	33	22	52	21	.259	.307	.349
Greg Briley	OF107,DH4	L	25	125	337	40	83	18	2	5	29	37	48	16	.246	.319	.356
Alvin Davis	DH87,1B52	L	29	140	494	63	140	21	0	17	68	85	68	0	.283	.387	.429
Jeffrey Leonard	OF79,DH48	R	34	134	478	39	120	20	0	10	75	37	97	4	.251	.305	.356
Scott Bradley	C63,DH6,3B5*	L	30	101	233	11	52	9	0	1	28	15	20	0	.223	.264	.275
Jay Buhner	OF40,DH10	R	25	51	163	16	45	12	0	7	33	17	50	2	.276	.357	.479
Mike Brumley	SS47,2B6,3B3*	S	27	62	147	19	36	5	4	0	7	10	22	2	.244	.272	.313
Darnell Coles†	OF20,3B6,1B4	R	28	37	107	9	23	5	1	2	16	4	17	0	.215	.248	.336
Jeff Schaefer	3B26,SS24,2B3	R	30	55	107	11	22	3	0	0	6	3	11	4	.206	.239	.234
Brian Giles	SS37,2B2,DH1*	R	30	45	95	15	22	6	0	4	11	15	24	2	.232	.336	.421
Tracy Jones†	DH18,OF18	R	29	25	86	8	26	4	0	2	15	3	12	0	.302	.341	.419
Ken Griffey Sr.†	OF20	L	40	21	77	13	29	2	0	3	18	10	3	0	.377	.443	.519
Tino Martinez	1B23	L	22	24	68	4	15	4	0	0	5	9	9	0	.221	.308	.279
Matt Sinatro	C28	R	30	30	50	2	15	1	0	0	4	4	10	1	.300	.352	.320
Dave Cochrane	SS5,1B3,3B3*	S	27	15	20	0	3	0	0	0	0	0	8	0	.150	.150	.150

S. Bradley, 1 G at 1B; M. Brumley, 2 G at OF, 1 G at DH; B. Giles, 1 G at 3B; D. Cochrane, 1 G at C

Pitcher	T	Age	G	GS	CG	ShO	IP	H	HR	BB	SO	W-L	Sv	ERA
Erik Hanson	R	25	33	33	5	1	236.0	205	15	68	211	18-9	0	3.24
Matt Young	L	31	34	33	7	1	225.1	198	15	107	176	8-18	0	3.51
Randy Johnson	L	26	33	33	5	2	219.2	174	26	120	194	14-11	0	3.65
Brian Holman	R	25	28	28	3	0	189.2	188	17	66	121	11-11	0	4.03
Russ Swan†	L	26	11	8	0	0	47.0	42	3	18	15	2-3	0	3.64
Rich DeLucia	R	25	5	5	1	0	36.0	30	2	9	20	1-2	0	2.00
Gary Eave	R	26	8	5	0	0	30.0	27	5	20	16	0-3	0	4.20
Scott Bankhead	R	26	4	4	0	0	13.0	18	2	7	10	0-2	0	11.08
Mike Gardiner	R	24	5	3	0	0	12.2	22	1	5	6	0-2	0	10.66
Mike Jackson	R	25	63	0	0	0	77.1	64	8	44	69	5-7	3	4.54
Keith Comstock	L	34	60	0	0	0	56.0	40	4	26	50	7-4	2	2.89
Bill Swift	R	28	55	8	0	0	128.0	135	4	21	42	6-4	6	2.39
Mike Schooler	R	27	49	0	0	0	56.0	47	5	16	45	1-4	30	2.25
Gene Harris	R	25	25	0	0	0	38.0	31	5	30	43	1-2	0	4.74
Brent Knackert	R	20	24	2	0	0	37.1	50	5	21	28	1-1	0	6.51
Bryan Clark	L	33	12	0	0	0	11.0	9	0	10	3	2-0	0	3.27
Dave Burba	R	23	6	0	0	0	8.0	8	0	2	4	0-0	0	4.50
Scott Medvin	R	28	5	0	0	0	4.1	7	0	2	1	0-1	0	6.23
Vance Lovelace	L	26	5	0	0	0	2.1	3	0	6	1	0-0	0	3.86
Jerry Reed†	R	34	4	0	0	0	7.1	8	1	3	2	0-1	0	4.91
Jose Melendez	R	24	3	0	0	0	5.1	8	2	3	7	0-0	0	11.81
Dennis Powell†	L	26	2	0	0	0	3.0	5	0	2	0	0-0	0	9.00

1990 Kansas City Royals 6th AL West 75-86 .466 27.5 GB

John Wathan

Player	Gm by Position	B	Age	G	AB	R	H	2B	3B	HR	RBI	BB	SO	SB	Avg	OBP	Slg
Mike Macfarlane	C112,DH5	R	26	124	400	37	102	24	4	6	58	25	69	1	.255	.306	.380
George Brett	1B102,DH32,OF9*	L	37	142	544	82	179	45	7	14	87	56	63	9	.329	.387	.515
Frank White	2B79,OF1	R	39	82	241	20	52	14	1	2	21	10	32	1	.216	.253	.307
Kevin Seitzer	3B152,2B10	R	28	158	622	91	171	31	5	6	38	67	66	7	.275	.346	.370
Kurt Stillwell	SS141	S	25	144	506	60	126	35	4	3	51	39	60	0	.249	.304	.352
Jim Eisenreich	OF138,DH2	L	31	142	496	61	139	29	7	5	51	42	51	12	.280	.335	.397
Willie Wilson	OF106,DH1	S	34	115	307	49	89	13	3	2	42	30	57	24	.290	.354	.371
Bo Jackson	OF97,DH10	R	27	111	405	74	110	16	1	28	78	44	128	15	.272	.342	.523
Gerald Perry	DH68,1B51	L	29	133	465	57	118	22	2	8	57	39	56	17	.254	.313	.361
Danny Tartabull	OF52,DH32	R	27	88	313	41	84	19	0	15	60	36	93	1	.268	.341	.473
Bill Pecota	2B50,SS21,3B11*	R	30	87	240	43	58	15	2	5	20	33	39	8	.242	.336	.383
Pat Tabler†	OF42,DH15,3B6*	R	32	75	195	12	53	14	0	1	19	20	21	0	.272	.338	.359
Brian McRae	OF45	S	22	46	168	21	48	8	3	2	23	9	29	4	.286	.318	.405
Bob Boone	C40	R	42	40	117	11	28	3	0	0	9	17	12	1	.239	.336	.265
Steve Jeltz	2B34,SS23,OF13*	S	31	74	103	11	16	4	0	0	10	6	21	1	.155	.200	.194
Terry Shumpert	2B27,DH3	R	23	32	91	7	25	6	1	0	8	2	17	3	.275	.292	.363
Jeff Schulz	OF22,DH1	L	29	30	66	5	17	5	1	0	6	6	13	0	.258	.319	.364
Gary Thurman	OF21	R	25	23	60	5	14	3	0	0	3	2	12	1	.233	.258	.283
Rey Palacios	C27,1B7,3B3*	R	27	41	56	8	13	3	0	2	9	5	24	2	.232	.295	.393
Russ Morman	OF8,1B3,DH1	R	28	12	37	5	10	4	2	1	3	3	3	0	.270	.317	.568
Sean Berry	3B8	R	24	8	23	2	5	1	1	0	4	2	5	0	.217	.280	.348
Jeff Conine	1B9	R	24	9	20	3	5	2	0	0	2	2	5	0	.250	.318	.350
Brent Mayne	C5	L	22	5	13	2	3	0	0	0	1	3	3	0	.231	.375	.231

G. Brett, 1 G at 3B; B. Pecota, 6 G at OF, 4 G at 1B, 2 G at DH; P. Tabler, 5 G at 1B; S. Jeltz, 3 G at DH, 3 G at 3B; R. Palacios, 1 G at OF

Pitcher	T	Age	G	GS	CG	ShO	IP	H	HR	BB	SO	W-L	Sv	ERA
Tom Gordon	R	22	32	32	6	1	195.1	192	17	99	175	12-11	0	3.73
Kevin Appier	R	22	32	24	3	3	185.2	179	13	54	127	12-8	0	2.76
Bret Saberhagen	R	26	20	20	5	0	135.0	146	9	28	87	5-9	0	3.27
Storm Davis	R	28	21	20	0	0	112.0	129	9	35	62	7-10	0	4.74
Mark Gubicza	R	27	16	16	2	0	94.0	101	5	38	71	4-7	0	4.50
Pete Filson	L	31	8	7	0	0	35.0	42	6	13	9	0-4	0	5.91
Rich Dotson	R	31	8	7	0	0	28.2	43	3	14	9	0-4	0	8.48
Hector Wagner	R	21	5	5	0	0	23.1	32	4	11	14	0-2	0	8.10
Jim Campbell	L	24	2	2	0	0	9.2	15	1	1	2	1-0	0	8.38
Daryl Smith	R	29	2	1	0	0	6.2	5	0	4	6	0-1	0	4.05
Jeff Montgomery	R	28	73	0	0	0	94.1	81	6	34	94	6-5	24	2.39
Steve Farr	R	33	57	6	1	1	127.0	99	6	48	94	13-7	1	1.98
Mark Davis	L	29	53	3	0	0	68.2	71	9	52	73	2-7	6	5.11
Steve Crawford	R	32	46	0	0	0	80.0	79	7	23	54	5-4	1	4.16
Andy McGaffigan†	R	33	24	11	0	0	78.2	75	6	28	49	4-3	1	3.09
Luis Aquino	R	26	20	3	1	0	68.1	59	6	27	28	4-1	0	3.16
Mel Stottlemyre Jr.	R	26	13	2	0	0	31.1	35	3	12	14	0-1	0	4.88
Larry McWilliams	L	36	13	0	0	0	8.1	10	2	9	7	0-0	0	9.72
Zip Sanchez	L	26	11	0	0	0	9.2	16	1	3	5	0-0	0	8.38
Chris Codiroli	R	32	6	2	0	0	10.1	13	1	17	8	0-1	0	9.58
Luis Encarnacion	R	26	4	0	0	0	10.1	14	1	4	8	0-0	0	7.84
Carlos Maldonado	R	23	4	0	0	0	6.0	9	0	4	9	0-0	0	9.00
Jay Baller	R	29	3	0	0	0	2.1	4	1	2	1	0-1	0	15.43

1990 Minnesota Twins 7th AL West 74-88 .457 29.0 GB

Tom Kelly

Player	Gm by Position	B	Age	G	AB	R	H	2B	3B	HR	RBI	BB	SO	SB	Avg	OBP	Slg
Brian Harper	C120,DH11,3B3*	R	30	134	479	61	141	42	3	6	54	19	27	3	.294	.328	.432
Kent Hrbek	1B120,DH20,3B1	L	30	143	492	61	141	26	0	22	79	69	45	5	.287	.377	.474
Al Newman	2B89,SS48,3B28*	S	30	144	388	43	94	14	0	0	30	33	34	13	.242	.304	.278
Gary Gaetti	3B151,1B2,SS2	R	31	154	577	61	132	27	5	16	85	36	101	6	.229	.274	.376
Greg Gagne	SS135,DH2,OF1	R	28	138	388	38	91	22	3	7	38	24	76	8	.235	.280	.361
Kirby Puckett	OF141,DH4,2B1*	R	29	146	551	82	164	40	3	12	80	57	73	5	.298	.365	.446
Dan Gladden	OF133,DH2	R	32	136	534	64	147	27	6	5	40	26	67	25	.275	.314	.376
Shane Mack	OF109,DH4	R	26	125	313	50	102	10	4	8	44	29	69	13	.326	.392	.460
Gene Larkin	OF47,DH43,1B28	S	27	119	401	46	108	26	4	5	42	42	55	5	.269	.343	.392
Fred Manrique	2B67,DH1	R	28	69	228	22	54	10	0	5	29	4	35	2	.237	.254	.346
Nelson Liriano†	2B50,DH2,SS1	S	26	53	185	30	47	5	7	0	13	22	24	5	.254	.332	.357
Randy Bush	OF32,DH29,1B6	L	31	73	181	17	44	8	0	6	18	21	27	0	.243	.338	.387
John Moses	OF85,DH10,1B6*	S	32	115	172	26	38	3	1	1	14	19	19	2	.221	.303	.267
Junior Ortiz	C68,DH3	R	30	71	170	18	57	7	1	0	18	12	16	0	.335	.384	.388
Carmelo Castillo	DH35,OF21	R	32	64	137	11	30	4	0	0	12	3	23	0	.219	.239	.248
Paul Sorrento	DH23,1B15	L	24	41	121	11	25	4	1	5	13	12	31	1	.207	.281	.380
Pedro Munoz	OF21,DH1	R	21	22	85	13	23	4	1	0	5	2	16	3	.271	.281	.341
Jim Dwyer	DH23,OF2	L	40	37	63	7	12	0	0	1	5	12	7	0	.190	.320	.238
Scott Leius	SS12,3B1	R	24	14	25	4	6	1	0	1	4	2	2	0	.240	.296	.400
Lenny Webster	C2	R	25	2	6	1	2	1	0	0	0	1	1	0	.333	.429	.500
Chip Hale	2B1	L	25	1	2	0	0	0	0	0	2	0	1	0	.000	.000	.000
Doug Baker	2B3	S	29	3	1	0	0	0	0	0	0	0	0	0	.000	.000	.000

B. Harper, 2 G at 1B; A. Newman, 3 G at OF; K. Puckett, 1 G at 3B, 1 G at SS; J. Moses, 2 G at P

Pitcher	T	Age	G	GS	CG	ShO	IP	H	HR	BB	SO	W-L	Sv	ERA
Allan Anderson	L	26	31	31	5	1	188.2	214	20	39	82	7-18	0	4.53
Kevin Tapani	R	26	28	28	1	1	159.1	164	12	29	101	12-8	0	4.07
David West	L	25	29	27	2	0	146.1	142	21	78	92	7-9	0	5.10
Roy Smith	R	28	32	23	1	1	153.1	191	20	47	87	5-10	0	4.81
Mark Guthrie	R	24	24	21	3	1	144.2	154	8	39	101	7-9	0	3.79
Scott Erickson	R	22	19	17	1	0	113.0	108	9	51	53	8-4	0	2.87
Paul Abbott	R	22	7	7	0	0	34.2	37	0	28	25	0-5	0	5.97
Larry Casian	L	24	5	3	0	0	22.1	26	2	4	11	2-1	0	3.22
Rick Aguilera	R	28	56	0	0	0	65.1	55	5	19	61	5-3	32	2.76
Terry Leach	R	36	55	0	0	0	81.2	84	2	21	46	2-5	2	3.20
Juan Berenguer	R	35	51	0	0	0	100.1	85	9	58	77	8-5	0	3.41
Gary Wayne	L	27	38	0	0	0	38.2	38	5	13	28	1-1	1	4.19
Tim Drummond	R	25	35	4	0	0	91.0	104	8	36	49	3-5	1	4.35
John Candelaria†	L	36	34	1	0	0	58.1	55	9	9	44	7-3	4	3.39
Jack Savage	R	26	17	0	0	0	26.0	37	3	11	12	0-2	1	8.31
Rich Garces	R	19	5	0	0	0	5.2	4	0	4	1	0-0	2	1.59
Rich Yett	R	27	4	0	0	0	4.1	6	1	1	2	0-0	0	2.08
John Moses	L	32	2	0	0	0	2.0	5	0	2	0	0-0	0	13.50

»1990 Pittsburgh Pirates 1st NL East 95-67 .586 —

Jim Leyland

Player	Gm by Position	B	Age	G	AB	R	H	2B	3B	HR	RBI	BB	SO	SB	Avg	OBP	Slg
Mike LaValliere	C95	L	29	96	279	27	72	15	0	3	31	44	20	0	.258	.362	.344
Sid Bream	1B142	L	29	147	389	39	105	23	2	15	67	48	65	8	.270	.349	.455
Jose Lind	2B152	R	26	152	514	46	134	28	5	1	48	35	52	8	.261	.305	.340
Jeff King	3B115,1B1	R	25	127	371	46	91	17	1	14	53	21	50	3	.245	.283	.410
Jay Bell	SS159	R	24	159	583	93	148	28	7	7	52	65	109	10	.254	.329	.362
Barry Bonds	OF150	L	25	151	519	104	156	32	3	33	114	93	83	52	.301	.406	.565
Bobby Bonilla	OF149,3B14,1B3	S	27	160	625	112	175	39	7	32	120	45	103	4	.280	.322	.518
Andy Van Slyke	OF133	L	29	136	493	67	140	26	6	17	77	66	89	14	.284	.367	.465
Wally Backman	3B71,2B15	S	30	104	315	62	92	21	3	2	28	42	53	6	.292	.374	.397
Don Slaught	C78	R	31	84	230	27	69	18	3	4	29	27	27	0	.300	.375	.457
Gary Redus	1B72,OF7	R	33	96	227	32	56	15	3	6	23	33	38	11	.247	.341	.419
R.J. Reynolds	OF59	S	31	95	215	25	62	10	1	0	19	23	35	12	.288	.354	.344
John Cangelosi	OF12	S	27	58	76	13	15	2	0	0	1	11	12	7	.197	.307	.224
Rafael Belliard	2B21,SS10,3B5	R	28	47	54	10	11	3	0	0	6	5	13	1	.204	.283	.259
Dann Bilardello	C19	R	31	19	37	1	2	0	0	0	3	4	10	0	.054	.146	.054
Orlando Merced	C1,OF1	S	23	25	24	3	5	1	0	0	0	1	9	0	.208	.240	.250
Carmelo Martinez†	1B5,OF2	R	29	12	19	3	4	1	0	2	4	1	5	0	.211	.250	.579
Mark Ryal	OF4	L	29	9	12	0	1	0	0	0	0	0	3	0	.083	.083	.083
Tom Prince	C3	R	25	4	10	1	1	0	0	0	0	1	2	0	.100	.182	.100
Steve Carter	OF3	L	25	5	5	0	1	0	0	0	0	0	1	0	.200	.200	.200
Moises Alou†	OF2	R	23	2	5	0	1	0	0	0	0	0	0	0	.200	.200	.200
Carlos Garcia	SS3	R	22	4	4	1	2	0	0	0	0	0	2	0	.500	.500	.500
Lloyd McClendon†	OF1	R	31	4	3	1	1	0	0	1	2	0	1	0	.333	.333	1.333

Pitcher	T	Age	G	GS	CG	ShO	IP	H	HR	BB	SO	W-L	Sv	ERA
Doug Drabek	R	27	33	33	9	3	231.1	190	15	56	131	22-6	0	2.76
John Smiley	L	25	26	25	2	0	149.1	161	15	36	86	9-10	0	4.64
Neal Heaton	L	30	30	24	0	0	146.0	143	17	38	68	12-9	0	3.45
Bob Walk	R	33	26	24	1	1	129.2	136	17	36	73	7-5	1	3.75
Walt Terrell†	R	32	16	16	0	0	82.2	98	13	33	34	2-7	0	5.88
Randy Tomlin	L	24	12	12	2	0	77.2	62	5	12	42	4-4	0	2.55
Zane Smith†	L	29	11	10	3	2	76.0	55	4	9	50	6-2	0	1.30
Rick Reed	R	25	13	8	1	1	53.2	62	6	12	27	2-3	1	4.36
Bob Patterson	L	31	55	5	0	0	94.2	88	9	21	70	8-5	5	2.95
Stan Belinda	R	23	55	0	0	0	58.1	48	4	29	55	3-4	8	3.55
Bill Landrum	R	32	54	0	0	0	71.2	69	4	21	39	7-3	13	2.13
Scott Ruskin†	L	27	44	0	0	0	47.2	50	2	28	34	2-2	2	3.02
Bob Kipper	L	25	41	1	0	0	62.2	44	7	26	35	5-2	3	3.02
Ted Power	R	35	40	0	0	0	51.2	50	5	17	42	1-3	7	3.66
Doug Bair	R	40	22	0	0	0	24.1	30	3	11	19	0-0	0	4.81
Randy Kramer†	R	29	12	2	0	0	25.2	27	3	9	15	0-1	0	4.91
Mark Ross	R	35	9	0	0	0	12.2	11	2	4	5	1-0	0	3.55
Vicente Palacios	R	26	7	0	0	0	15.0	4	0	2	8	0-0	3	0.00
Jay Tibbs†	R	28	5	0	0	0	7.0	7	0	2	4	1-0	0	2.57
Mike Roesler	R	26	5	0	0	0	6.0	5	1	2	4	1-0	0	3.00
Mike York	R	25	4	1	0	0	12.2	13	0	5	4	1-1	0	2.84
Jerry Reuss	L	41	4	1	0	0	7.2	8	1	3	1	0-0	0	3.52
Mark Huismann	R	32	2	0	0	0	3.0	6	2	1	2	1-0	0	9.00

1990 New York Mets 2nd NL East 91-71 .562 4.0 GB

Davey Johnson (20-22)/Bud Harrelson (71-49)

Player	Gm by Position	B	Age	G	AB	R	H	2B	3B	HR	RBI	BB	SO	SB	Avg	OBP	Slg
Mackey Sasser	C87,1B1	L	27	100	270	31	83	14	0	6	41	15	19	0	.307	.344	.426
Dave Magadan	1B113,3B19	L	27	144	451	74	148	28	6	6	72	74	55	2	.328	.417	.457
Gregg Jefferies	2B118,3B34	S	22	153	604	96	171	40	3	15	68	46	40	11	.283	.337	.434
Howard Johnson	3B92,SS73	S	29	154	590	89	144	37	3	23	90	69	100	34	.244	.319	.434
Kevin Elster	SS92	R	25	92	314	36	65	20	1	9	45	30	54	2	.207	.274	.363
Darryl Strawberry	OF149	L	28	152	542	92	150	18	1	37	108	70	110	15	.277	.361	.518
Kevin McReynolds	OF144	R	30	147	521	75	140	23	1	24	82	71	61	9	.269	.353	.455
Daryl Boston†	OF109	L	27	115	366	65	100	21	2	12	45	28	50	18	.273	.328	.440
Keith Miller	OF61,2B11,SS4	R	27	88	233	42	60	8	0	1	12	23	46	16	.258	.327	.305
Mark Carreon	OF60	R	26	82	188	30	47	12	0	10	26	15	29	1	.250	.312	.473
Tim Teufel	1B24,2B24,3B10	R	31	80	175	28	43	11	0	10	24	15	33	0	.246	.304	.480
Mike Marshall†	1B42,OF1	R	30	53	163	24	39	8	1	6	27	7	40	0	.239	.278	.411
Tom O'Malley	3B38,1B3	L	29	82	121	14	27	7	0	3	14	11	20	0	.223	.286	.355
Tom Herr†	2B26	S	34	27	100	9	25	5	0	1	10	14	11	0	.250	.342	.330
Orlando Mercado†	C40	R	28	42	90	10	19	1	0	3	7	8	11	0	.211	.290	.322
Barry Lyons†	C23	R	30	24	80	8	19	0	0	2	7	2	9	0	.238	.265	.313
Charlie O'Brien†	C28	R	30	28	68	6	11	3	0	0	9	10	8	0	.162	.272	.206
Todd Hundley	C36	S	21	36	67	8	14	6	0	0	2	6	18	0	.209	.274	.299
Pat Tabler†	OF10	R	32	17	43	6	12	1	1	1	10	3	8	0	.279	.340	.419
Darren Reed	OF14	R	24	26	39	5	8	4	1	1	2	3	11	1	.205	.262	.436
Kelvin Torve	1B9,OF1	L	30	20	38	0	11	4	0	0	2	4	9	0	.289	.386	.395
Mario Diaz	SS10,2B1	R	28	16	22	0	3	1	0	0	1	0	3	0	.136	.130	.182
Kevin Baez	SS4	R	23	5	12	0	2	1	0	0	0	0	0	0	.167	.167	.250
Chris Jelic	OF4	R	26	4	11	2	1	0	0	1	1	0	3	0	.091	.091	.364
Alex Trevino†	C7	R	32	9	10	0	3	1	0	0	2	1	0	0	.300	.333	.400
Keith Hughes	OF5	L	26	8	9	0	0	0	0	0	0	0	4	0	.000	.000	.000
Chuck Carr	OF1	S	21	4	2	0	0	0	0	0	0	0	2	1	.000	.000	.000
Dave Liddell	C1	R	24	1	1	1	1	0	0	0	0	0	0	0	1.000	1.000	1.000
Lou Thornton	OF2	L	27	3	0	0	0	0	0	0	0	0	0	0	—	—	—

Pitcher	T	Age	G	GS	CG	ShO	IP	H	HR	BB	SO	W-L	Sv	ERA
Frank Viola	L	30	35	35	7	3	249.2	227	15	60	182	20-12	0	2.67
Dwight Gooden	R	25	34	34	2	1	232.2	229	10	70	223	19-7	0	3.83
David Cone	R	27	31	30	6	2	211.2	177	21	65	233	14-10	0	3.23
Sid Fernandez	L	27	30	30	2	1	179.1	130	18	67	181	9-14	0	3.46
Ron Darling	R	29	33	18	1	0	126.0	135	20	44	99	7-9	0	4.50
Julio Valera	R	21	3	3	0	0	13.0	20	1	7	4	1-1	0	6.92
John Franco	L	29	55	0	0	0	67.2	66	4	21	56	5-3	33	2.53
Alejandro Pena	R	31	52	0	0	0	76.0	71	4	22	76	3-3	5	3.20
Bobby Ojeda	L	32	38	12	0	0	118.0	123	10	40	62	7-6	0	3.66
Wally Whitehurst	R	26	38	0	0	0	65.2	63	5	9	46	1-0	2	3.29
Jeff Musselman	L	27	28	0	0	0	32.0	40	3	11	14	0-2	0	5.63
Julio Machado†	R	24	27	0	0	0	34.1	32	4	17	27	4-1	0	3.15
Jeff Innis	R	27	18	0	0	0	26.1	19	4	10	12	1-3	1	2.39
Dan Schatzeder†	L	35	6	0	0	0	5.2	5	0	0	2	0-0	0	0.00
Kevin Brown†	L	24	2	0	0	0	2.0	2	0	1	0	0-0	0	0.00

1990 Montreal Expos 3rd NL East 85-77 .525 10.0 GB

Buck Rodgers

Player	Gm by Position	B	Age	G	AB	R	H	2B	3B	HR	RBI	BB	SO	SB	Avg	OBP	Slg
Mike Fitzgerald	C98,OF6	R	29	111	313	36	76	18	1	9	41	60	60	8	.243	.365	.393
Andres Galarraga	1B154	R	29	155	579	65	148	29	0	20	87	40	169	10	.256	.306	.409
Delino DeShields	2B128	L	21	129	499	69	144	28	6	4	45	66	96	42	.289	.375	.393
Tim Wallach	3B161	R	32	161	626	69	185	37	5	21	98	42	80	6	.296	.339	.471
Spike Owen	SS148	S	29	149	453	55	106	24	5	5	35	70	60	8	.234	.333	.342
Larry Walker	OF124	L	23	133	419	59	101	18	3	19	51	49	112	21	.241	.326	.434
Tim Raines	OF123	S	30	130	457	65	131	11	5	9	62	70	43	49	.287	.379	.392
Dave Martinez	OF108,P1	L	25	118	391	60	109	13	5	11	39	24	48	13	.279	.321	.422
Marquis Grissom	OF87	R	23	98	288	42	74	14	2	3	29	27	40	22	.257	.320	.351
Otis Nixon	OF88,SS1	S	31	119	231	46	58	6	2	1	20	28	33	50	.251	.331	.307
Tom Foley	SS45,2B20,3B7*	L	30	73	164	11	35	2	1	0	12	12	22	0	.213	.266	.238
Nelson Santovenia	C51	R	28	59	163	13	31	3	1	6	28	8	31	0	.190	.222	.331
Mike Aldrete	OF38,1B18	L	29	96	161	22	39	7	1	1	18	37	31	1	.242	.385	.317
Junior Noboa	2B31,OF9,3B8*	R	25	81	158	15	42	7	2	0	14	7	14	4	.266	.294	.335
Jerry Goff	C38,1B3,3B3	L	26	52	119	14	27	1	0	3	7	21	36	0	.227	.343	.311
Wallace Johnson	1B7	S	33	47	49	6	8	1	0	1	5	7	6	1	.163	.281	.245
Moises Alou†	OF5	R	23	14	15	4	3	0	1	0	0	0	3	0	.200	.200	.333
Rolando Roomes†	OF6	R	28	16	14	1	4	0	1	0	1	1	6	0	.286	.333	.429
Orlando Mercado†	C8	R	28	8	8	0	2	0	0	0	0	0	1	0	.250	.250	.250
Johnny Paredes†	2B2	R	27	3	6	0	2	1	0	0	1	1	0	0	.333	.429	.500
Rex Hudler†		R	29	4	3	1	1	0	0	0	0	0	1	0	.333	.333	.333
Eric Bullock		L	30	4	2	0	1	0	0	0	0	1	0	0	.500	.500	.500

T. Foley, 1 G at 1B; J. Noboa, 7 G at SS, 1 G at P

Pitcher	T	Age	G	GS	CG	ShO	IP	H	HR	BB	SO	W-L	Sv	ERA
Dennis Martinez	R	35	32	32	7	2	226.0	191	16	49	156	10-11	0	2.95
Oil Can Boyd	R	30	31	31	3	3	190.2	164	19	52	113	10-6	0	2.93
Kevin Gross	R	29	31	26	2	1	163.1	171	9	65	111	9-12	0	4.57
Mark Gardner	R	28	27	26	3	3	152.2	129	13	61	135	7-9	0	3.42
Zane Smith†	L	29	22	21	1	0	139.1	141	11	41	80	6-7	0	3.23
Chris Nabholz	L	23	11	11	1	1	70.0	43	6	32	53	6-2	0	2.83
Brian Barnes	L	23	4	4	1	0	28.0	25	2	7	23	1-1	0	2.89
Howard Farmer	R	23	6	4	0	0	23.0	26	9	10	14	0-3	0	7.04
Scott Anderson	R	27	4	3	0	0	18.0	12	1	5	16	0-1	0	3.00
Bill Sampen	R	27	59	4	0	0	90.1	94	7	33	69	12-7	2	2.99
Tim Burke	R	31	58	0	0	0	75.0	71	6	21	47	3-3	20	2.52
Steve Frey	L	26	51	0	0	0	55.2	44	4	29	29	8-2	9	2.10
Drew Hall	L	27	42	0	0	0	58.1	52	6	29	40	4-7	3	5.09
Dale Mohorcic	R	34	34	0	0	0	53.0	56	6	18	29	1-2	2	3.23
Dave Schmidt	R	33	34	0	0	0	48.0	58	3	13	22	3-3	13	4.31
Mel Rojas	R	23	23	0	0	0	40.0	34	5	24	26	3-1	1	3.60
Scott Ruskin†	L	27	23	0	0	0	27.2	25	2	10	23	1-0	0	2.28
John Costello†	R	29	4	0	0	0	6.1	5	2	1	1	0-0	0	5.68
Joe Hesketh†	L	31	2	0	0	0	3.0	2	0	2	3	1-0	0	0.00
Bob Malloy	R	25	1	0	0	0	2.0	1	0	1	1	0-0	0	0.00
Rich Thompson	R	31	1	0	0	0	1.0	1	0	0	0	0-0	0	0.00
Brett Gideon	R	26	1	0	0	0	1.0	2	0	4	0	0-0	0	9.00
Junior Noboa	R	25	1	0	0	0	0.2	0	0	1	0	0-0	0	0.00
Dave Martinez	L	25	1	0	0	0	0.1	2	0	2	0	0-0	0	54.00

1990 Chicago Cubs 4th NL East 77-85 .475 18.0 GB — Don Zimmer

Player	Gm by Position	B	Age	G	AB	R	H	2B	3B	HR	RBI	BB	SO	SB	Avg	OBP	Slg
Joe Girardi	C133	R	25	133	419	36	113	24	2	1	38	17	50	8	.270	.300	.344
Mark Grace	1B153	L	26	157	589	72	182	32	1	9	82	59	54	15	.309	.372	.413
Ryne Sandberg	2B154	R	30	155	615	116	188	30	3	40	100	50	84	25	.306	.354	.559
Luis Salazar	3B91,OF28	R	34	115	410	44	104	13	3	12	47	19	59	3	.254	.293	.388
Shawon Dunston	SS144	R	27	146	545	73	143	22	8	17	66	15	87	25	.262	.283	.426
Andre Dawson	OF139	R	35	147	529	72	164	28	5	27	100	42	65	16	.310	.358	.535
Doug Dascenzo	OF107,P1	S	26	113	241	27	61	9	5	1	26	21	18	15	.253	.312	.344
Jerome Walton	OF98	R	24	101	392	63	103	16	2	2	21	50	70	14	.263	.350	.329
Dwight Smith	OF81	L	26	117	290	34	76	15	0	6	27	28	46	11	.262	.329	.376
Domingo Ramos	3B66,SS21,2B1	R	32	98	226	22	60	5	0	2	17	27	29	0	.265	.342	.314
Curtis Wilkerson	3B52,2B14,SS1*	S	29	77	186	21	41	5	1	0	16	7	36	2	.220	.249	.258
Marvell Wynne	OF66	L	30	92	186	21	38	8	2	4	19	14	25	3	.204	.264	.333
Dave Clark	OF39	L	27	84	171	22	47	4	2	5	20	8	40	7	.275	.304	.409
Hector Villanueva	C23,1B14	R	25	52	114	14	31	4	1	7	18	4	27	1	.272	.308	.509
Lloyd McClendon†	OF23,C8,1B8	R	31	49	107	5	17	3	0	1	10	14	21	1	.159	.254	.215
Derrick May	OF17	L	21	17	61	8	15	3	0	1	11	2	7	1	.246	.270	.344
Damon Berryhill	C15	S	26	17	53	6	10	4	0	1	9	5	14	0	.189	.254	.321
Gary Varsho	OF3	L	29	46	48	10	12	4	0	0	1	1	6	2	.250	.265	.333
Greg Smith	2B7,SS7	S	23	18	44	4	9	2	1	0	5	2	5	1	.205	.234	.295
Rick Wrona	C16	R	26	16	29	3	5	0	0	0	0	2	11	1	.172	.226	.172
Les Lancaster	P55,OF1	R	28	55	20	1	1	0	0	0	0	3	11	0	.050	.174	.050

C. Wilkerson, 1 G at OF

Pitcher	T	Age	G	GS	CG	ShO	IP	H	HR	BB	SO	W-L	Sv	ERA
Greg Maddux	R	24	35	35	8	2	237.0	242	11	71	144	15-15	0	3.46
Mike Bielecki	R	30	36	29	0	0	168.0	188	13	70	103	8-11	1	4.93
Mike Harkey	R	23	27	27	2	1	173.2	153	14	59	94	12-6	0	3.26
Shawn Boskie	R	23	15	15	1	0	97.2	99	8	31	49	5-6	0	3.69
Rick Sutcliffe	R	34	5	5	0	0	21.1	25	2	12	7	0-2	0	5.91
Lance Dickson	L	20	3	3	0	0	13.2	20	2	4	4	0-3	0	7.24
Kevin Blankenship	R	27	3	2	0	0	12.1	13	1	6	5	0-2	0	5.84
Paul Assenmacher	L	29	74	1	0	0	103.0	90	10	36	95	7-2	10	2.80
Mitch Williams	L	25	59	2	0	0	66.1	60	4	50	55	1-8	16	3.93
Les Lancaster	R	28	55	6	1	1	109.0	121	11	40	65	9-5	6	4.62
Steve Wilson	L	25	45	15	1	0	139.0	140	17	43	95	4-9	1	4.79
Bill Long†	R	30	42	0	0	0	55.2	66	8	21	32	6-1	5	4.37
Jeff Pico	R	24	31	8	0	0	92.0	120	7	37	37	4-4	2	4.79
Jose Nunez	R	26	21	10	0	0	60.2	61	5	34	40	4-7	0	6.53
Joe Kraemer	L	25	18	0	0	0	25.0	31	2	14	16	0-1	0	7.20
Dave Pavlas	R	27	13	0	0	0	21.1	23	2	6	12	2-0	0	2.11
Randy Kramer†	R	29	10	2	0	0	20.1	20	3	12	12	0-2	0	3.98
Kevin Coffman	R	25	8	2	0	0	18.1	26	0	19	9	0-2	0	11.29
Dean Wilkins	R	23	7	0	0	0	7.1	11	1	7	3	0-0	1	9.82
Doug Dascenzo	L	26	1	0	0	0	1.0	1	0	0	0	0-0	0	0.00

1990 Philadelphia Phillies 4th NL East 77-85 .475 18.0 GB — Nick Leyva

Player	Gm by Position	B	Age	G	AB	R	H	2B	3B	HR	RBI	BB	SO	SB	Avg	OBP	Slg
Darren Daulton	C139	L	28	143	459	62	123	30	1	12	57	72	72	7	.268	.367	.416
Ricky Jordan	1B84	R	25	92	324	32	78	21	0	5	44	13	39	2	.241	.277	.352
Tom Herr†	2B114	S	34	119	447	39	118	21	3	4	50	36	47	7	.264	.320	.351
Charlie Hayes	3B146,1B4,2B1	R	25	152	561	56	145	20	0	10	57	28	91	4	.258	.293	.348
Dickie Thon	SS148	R	32	149	552	54	141	20	4	8	48	37	77	12	.255	.305	.350
Lenny Dykstra	OF149	L	27	149	590	106	192	35	3	9	60	89	48	33	.325	.418	.441
Von Hayes	OF127	L	31	129	467	70	122	14	3	17	73	87	81	16	.261	.375	.413
John Kruk	OF87,1B61	L	29	142	443	52	129	25	8	7	67	69	70	10	.291	.386	.431
Randy Ready	OF30,2B28	R	30	101	217	26	53	9	1	1	26	29	35	3	.244	.332	.309
Dale Murphy†	OF55	R	34	57	214	22	57	9	1	7	28	20	46	0	.266	.328	.416
Carmelo Martinez†	1B43,OF20	R	29	71	198	23	48	8	0	8	31	29	37	2	.242	.339	.404
Rod Booker	SS27,2B23,3B10	L	31	73	131	19	29	5	2	0	10	15	26	3	.221	.301	.290
Dave Hollins	3B30,1B1	S	24	72	114	14	21	0	0	5	15	10	28	0	.184	.252	.316
Sil Campusano	OF47	R	24	66	85	10	18	1	1	2	9	6	16	1	.212	.269	.318
Steve Lake	C28	R	33	29	80	4	20	2	0	0	6	3	12	0	.250	.286	.275
Mickey Morandini	2B25	L	24	25	79	9	19	4	0	1	3	6	19	3	.241	.294	.329
Ron Jones	OF16	L	26	24	58	5	16	2	0	3	7	9	9	0	.276	.373	.466
Jim Vatcher†	OF24	R	24	36	46	5	12	1	0	1	4	4	6	0	.261	.320	.348
Wes Chamberlain	OF10	R	24	18	46	9	13	3	0	2	4	1	9	4	.283	.298	.478
Tom Nieto	C17	R	29	17	30	1	5	0	0	0	4	3	11	0	.167	.265	.167
Darrin Fletcher†	C6	L	23	9	22	3	3	1	0	0	1	1	5	0	.136	.174	.182
Curt Ford	OF3	L	29	22	18	0	2	0	0	0	0	1	5	0	.111	.158	.111
Louie Meadows†	OF4	L	29	15	14	1	1	0	0	0	0	1	3	0	.071	.133	.071

Pitcher	T	Age	G	GS	CG	ShO	IP	H	HR	BB	SO	W-L	Sv	ERA
Pat Combs	L	23	32	31	3	2	183.1	179	12	86	108	10-10	0	4.07
Terry Mulholland	L	27	33	26	6	1	180.2	172	15	42	75	9-10	0	3.34
Bruce Ruffin	L	26	32	25	2	1	149.0	178	14	62	79	6-13	0	5.38
Jose DeJesus	R	25	22	22	3	1	130.0	97	10	73	87	7-8	0	3.74
Ken Howell	R	29	18	18	2	0	106.2	106	12	49	70	8-7	0	4.64
Jason Grimsley	R	22	11	11	0	0	57.1	47	1	43	41	3-2	0	3.30
Tommy Greene†	R	23	10	7	0	0	39.0	36	5	17	17	2-3	0	4.15
Roger McDowell	R	29	72	0	0	0	86.1	92	2	35	39	6-8	22	3.86
Darrel Akerfelds	R	28	71	0	0	0	93.0	65	10	54	42	5-2	3	3.77
Don Carman	L	30	59	1	0	0	86.2	69	13	38	58	6-2	1	4.15
Jeff Parrett†	R	28	47	5	0	0	81.2	92	10	36	69	4-9	1	5.18
Dennis Cook†	L	27	42	13	2	1	141.2	132	13	54	58	8-3	1	3.56
Joe Boever†	R	29	34	0	0	0	46.0	37	0	16	40	2-3	6	2.15
Marvin Freeman†	R	27	16	3	0	0	32.1	34	5	14	26	0-2	1	5.57
Chuck McElroy	L	22	16	0	0	0	14.0	24	0	10	16	0-1	0	7.71
Chuck Malone	R	24	7	0	0	0	7.1	3	1	11	7	1-0	0	3.68
Steve Ontiveros	R	29	5	0	0	0	10.0	9	1	3	6	0-0	0	2.70
Todd Frohwirth	R	27	5	0	0	0	1.0	3	0	6	1	0-1	0	18.00
Brad Moore	R	26	3	0	0	0	2.2	4	0	2	1	0-0	0	3.38
Dickie Noles	R	33	1	0	0	0	0.1	2	0	0	0	0-1	0	27.00

1990 St. Louis Cardinals 6th NL East 70-92 .432 25.0 GB — Whitey Herzog (33-47)/Red Schoendienst (13-11)/Joe Torre (24-34)

Player	Gm by Position	B	Age	G	AB	R	H	2B	3B	HR	RBI	BB	SO	SB	Avg	OBP	Slg
Todd Zeile	C105,3B24,1B11*	R	24	144	495	62	121	25	3	15	57	67	77	2	.244	.333	.398
Pedro Guerrero	1B132	R	34	136	498	42	140	31	1	13	80	44	70	1	.281	.334	.426
Jose Oquendo	2B150,SS4	S	26	156	469	38	118	17	5	1	37	74	46	1	.252	.350	.316
Terry Pendleton	3B117	S	29	121	447	46	103	20	2	6	58	30	58	7	.230	.277	.324
Ozzie Smith	SS140	S	35	143	512	61	130	21	1	1	50	61	33	32	.254	.330	.305
Willie McGee†	OF124	S	31	125	501	76	168	32	5	3	62	38	86	28	.335	.382	.437
Vince Coleman	OF120	S	28	124	497	73	145	18	9	6	39	35	88	77	.292	.340	.400
Milt Thompson	OF116	L	31	135	418	42	91	14	7	6	30	39	60	25	.218	.292	.328
Tom Pagnozzi	C63,1B2	R	27	69	220	20	61	15	0	2	23	14	37	1	.277	.321	.373
Rex Hudler†	OF45,2B10,1B6*	R	29	89	217	30	61	11	2	7	22	12	31	18	.281	.323	.447
Tim Jones	SS29,2B19,3B6*	L	27	67	128	9	28	7	1	1	12	12	20	3	.219	.291	.313
Denny Walling	1B15,3B11,OF8	L	36	78	127	7	28	5	0	1	19	8	15	0	.220	.265	.283
Ray Lankford	OF35	L	23	39	126	12	36	10	1	3	12	13	27	8	.286	.353	.452
Craig Wilson	3B13,OF13,2B9*	R	25	55	121	13	30	2	0	0	7	8	14	0	.248	.290	.264
Felix Jose†	OF23	S	25	25	85	12	23	4	1	3	13	8	16	4	.271	.333	.447
Bernard Gilkey	OF18	R	23	18	64	11	19	5	2	1	3	8	5	6	.297	.375	.484
Dave Collins	1B49,OF12	S	37	99	58	12	13	1	0	0	3	13	10	7	.224	.366	.241
Tom Brunansky†	OF17	R	29	19	57	5	9	3	0	1	2	12	10	0	.158	.310	.263
Geronimo Pena	2B11	S	23	18	45	5	11	2	0	0	2	4	14	1	.244	.314	.289
Rod Brewer	1B9	L	24	14	25	4	6	1	0	0	2	0	4	0	.240	.240	.280
John Morris	OF6	L	29	18	18	0	2	0	0	0	0	3	6	0	.111	.238	.111
Ray Stephens	C5	R	27	5	15	2	2	1	0	1	1	0	3	0	.133	.133	.400

T. Zeile, 1 G at OF; R. Hudler, 6 G at 3B, 1 G at SS; T. Jones, 1 G at P; C. Wilson, 1 G at 1B

Pitcher	T	Age	G	GS	CG	ShO	IP	H	HR	BB	SO	W-L	Sv	ERA
Jose DeLeon	R	29	32	32	0	0	182.2	168	15	86	164	7-19	0	4.43
Joe Magrane	L	25	31	31	3	2	203.1	204	10	59	100	10-17	0	3.59
Bryn Smith	R	34	26	25	0	0	141.1	160	11	30	78	9-8	0	4.27
John Tudor	L	36	25	22	1	1	146.1	120	10	30	63	12-4	0	2.40
Bob Tewksbury	R	29	28	20	3	2	145.1	151	7	15	50	10-9	1	3.47
Ken Hill	R	24	17	14	1	0	78.2	79	7	33	58	5-6	0	5.49
Greg Mathews	L	28	11	10	0	0	50.2	53	2	30	18	0-5	0	5.33
Omar Olivares	R	22	9	6	0	0	49.1	45	2	17	20	1-1	0	2.92
Frank DiPino	L	33	62	0	0	0	81.0	92	8	31	49	5-2	3	4.56
Ken Dayley	L	31	58	0	0	0	73.1	63	5	30	51	4-4	2	3.56
Lee Smith†	R	32	53	0	0	0	68.2	58	3	20	70	3-4	27	2.10
Tom Niedenfuer	R	30	52	0	0	0	65.0	66	3	25	32	0-6	2	3.46
Scott Terry	R	30	50	2	0	0	72.0	75	7	27	35	2-6	2	4.75
Ricky Horton	L	30	32	0	0	0	42.0	52	3	22	18	1-1	1	4.93
Mike Perez	R	25	13	0	0	0	13.2	12	0	3	5	1-0	1	3.95
Tim Sherrill	L	24	8	0	0	0	4.1	10	0	3	3	0-0	0	6.23
Ernie Camacho†	R	35	6	0	0	0	5.2	7	2	6	7	0-0	0	7.94
Cris Carpenter	R	25	4	0	0	0	8.0	5	2	2	6	0-0	0	4.50
John Costello†	R	29	4	0	0	0	4.1	7	1	1	1	0-0	0	6.23
Stan Clarke	L	29	2	0	0	0	3.1	2	0	0	3	0-0	0	2.70
Howard Hilton	R	26	2	0	0	0	3.0	2	0	3	2	0-0	0	0.00
Tim Jones	R	27	1	0	0	0	1.1	1	0	2	0	0-0	0	6.75

1990 Cincinnati Reds 1st NL West 91-71 .562 — — Lou Piniella

Player	Gm by Position	B	Age	G	AB	R	H	2B	3B	HR	RBI	BB	SO	SB	Avg	OBP	Slg
Joe Oliver	C118	R	24	121	364	34	84	23	0	8	52	37	75	1	.231	.304	.360
Todd Benzinger	1B95,OF10	S	27	118	376	35	95	14	2	5	46	19	69	3	.253	.291	.340
Mariano Duncan	2B115,SS12,OF1	R	27	125	435	67	133	22	11	10	55	24	67	13	.306	.345	.476
Chris Sabo	3B146	R	28	148	567	95	153	38	2	25	71	61	58	25	.270	.343	.476
Barry Larkin	SS156	R	26	158	614	85	185	25	6	7	67	49	49	30	.301	.358	.396
Paul O'Neill	OF141	L	27	145	503	59	136	28	0	16	78	53	103	13	.270	.339	.421
Billy Hatcher	OF131	R	29	139	504	68	139	28	5	5	25	33	42	30	.276	.327	.381
Eric Davis	OF122	R	28	127	453	84	118	26	2	24	86	60	100	21	.260	.347	.486
Hal Morris	1B80,OF6	L	25	107	309	50	105	22	3	7	36	21	32	9	.340	.381	.498
Glenn Braggs†	OF60	R	27	72	201	22	60	9	1	6	28	26	43	3	.299	.385	.443
Jeff Reed	C70	L	27	72	175	12	44	8	1	3	16	24	26	0	.251	.340	.360
Herm Winningham	OF64	L	28	84	160	20	41	8	5	3	17	14	31	6	.256	.314	.425
Ron Oester	2B50,3B3	S	34	64	154	10	46	10	1	0	13	10	29	1	.299	.339	.377
Luis Quinones	3B22,2B13,SS9*	S	28	83	145	10	35	7	0	2	17	13	29	1	.241	.301	.331
Ken Griffey Sr.†	1B9,OF6	L	40	46	63	6	13	2	0	1	8	2	5	2	.206	.235	.286
Rolando Roomes†	OF19	R	28	30	61	5	13	0	0	2	7	0	20	0	.213	.213	.311
Bill Doran†	2B12,3B4	S	32	17	59	10	22	8	0	1	5	8	5	3	.373	.448	.559
Terry Lee	1B6	R	28	12	19	1	4	1	0	0	3	2	2	0	.211	.273	.263
Alex Trevino†	C2	R	32	7	7	0	3	1	0	0	1	0	0	0	.429	.500	.571
Billy Bates†	2B1	L	26	8	5	2	0	0	0	0	0	0	2	2	.000	.000	.000
Terry McGriff†	C1	R	26	2	4	0	0	0	0	0	0	0	1	0	.000	.000	.000
Paul Noce		R	30	1	1	0	1	0	0	0	0	0	0	0	1.000	1.000	1.000
Glenn Sutko	C1	R	22	1	1	0	0	0	0	0	0	0	1	0	.000	.000	.000

L. Quinones, 1 G at 1B

Pitcher	T	Age	G	GS	CG	ShO	IP	H	HR	BB	SO	W-L	Sv	ERA
Tom Browning	L	30	35	35	2	1	227.2	235	24	52	99	15-9	0	3.80
Jose Rijo	R	25	29	29	7	1	197.0	151	10	78	152	14-8	0	2.70
Jack Armstrong	R	25	29	27	2	1	166.0	151	9	59	110	12-9	0	3.42
Danny Jackson	L	28	22	21	0	0	117.1	119	11	40	76	6-6	0	3.61
Ron Robinson†	R	28	6	5	0	0	31.1	36	2	14	14	2-2	0	4.88
Chris Hammond	L	24	3	3	0	0	11.1	13	2	12	4	0-2	0	6.35
Rob Dibble	R	26	68	0	0	0	98.0	62	3	34	136	8-3	11	1.74
Randy Myers	L	27	66	0	0	0	86.2	59	6	38	98	4-6	31	2.08
Norm Charlton	L	27	56	16	1	1	154.1	131	10	70	117	12-9	2	2.74
Tim Layana	R	26	55	0	0	0	80.0	71	7	44	53	5-3	2	3.49
Rick Mahler	R	36	35	16	2	1	134.2	134	16	39	68	7-6	4	4.28
Tim Birtsas	L	29	29	0	0	0	51.1	69	7	24	41	1-3	0	3.86
Scott Scudder	R	22	21	10	0	0	71.2	74	12	30	42	5-5	0	4.90
Rosario Rodriguez	L	20	9	0	0	0	10.1	15	3	2	8	0-0	0	6.10
Keith Brown	R	26	8	0	0	0	11.1	12	2	3	8	0-0	0	4.76
Kip Gross	R	25	5	0	0	0	6.1	6	0	2	3	0-0	0	4.26
Gino Minutelli	L	26	2	0	0	0	1.0	0	0	2	0	0-0	0	9.00

1990 Los Angeles Dodgers 2nd NL West 86-76 .531 5.0 GB

Tom Lasorda

Player	Gm by Position	B	Age	G	AB	R	H	2B	3B	HR	RBI	BB	SO	SB	Avg	OBP	Slg
Mike Scioscia	C132	L	31	135	435	46	115	25	0	12	66	55	31	4	.264	.348	.405
Eddie Murray	1B150	S	34	155	558	96	184	22	3	26	95	82	64	8	.330	.414	.520
Juan Samuel	2B108,OF31	R	29	143	492	62	119	24	3	13	52	51	126	38	.242	.316	.382
Mike Sharperson	3B106,SS15,2B9*	R	28	129	357	42	106	14	2	3	36	46	39	15	.297	.376	.373
Alfredo Griffin	SS139	S	32	141	461	38	97	11	3	1	35	29	65	6	.210	.258	.254
Hubie Brooks	OF150	R	33	153	568	74	151	28	1	20	91	33	108	2	.266	.307	.424
Kal Daniels	OF127	L	26	130	450	81	133	23	1	27	94	68	104	4	.296	.389	.531
Stan Javier†	OF87	S	26	104	276	56	84	9	4	3	24	37	44	15	.304	.384	.399
Lenny Harris	3B94,2B44,OF2*	L	25	137	431	61	131	16	4	2	29	29	31	15	.304	.348	.374
Kirk Gibson	OF81	L	33	89	315	59	82	20	0	8	38	39	65	26	.260	.345	.400
Chris Gwynn	OF44	L	25	101	141	19	40	2	1	5	22	7	28	0	.284	.311	.418
Mickey Hatcher	1B25,3B10,OF10	R	35	85	132	12	28	3	1	0	13	6	22	0	.212	.248	.250
Rick Dempsey	C53	R	40	62	128	13	25	5	0	2	15	23	29	1	.195	.318	.281
Jose Gonzalez	OF81	R	25	106	99	15	23	5	3	2	8	6	27	3	.232	.280	.404
Willie Randolph†	2B26	R	35	26	96	15	26	4	0	1	9	13	9	1	.271	.364	.344
Jose Offerman	SS27	S	21	29	58	7	9	0	0	1	7	4	14	1	.155	.210	.207
Jose Vizcaino	SS11,2B6	S	22	37	51	3	14	1	1	0	2	4	8	1	.275	.327	.333
John Shelby†	OF12	S	32	25	24	2	6	1	0	0	2	0	7	1	.250	.250	.292
Jeff Hamilton	3B7	R	26	7	24	1	3	0	0	0	1	0	3	0	.125	.125	.125
Carlos Hernandez	C10	R	23	10	20	2	4	1	0	0	1	0	2	0	.200	.200	.250
Brian Traxler	1B3	L	22	9	11	0	1	1	0	0	0	0	4	0	.091	.091	.182
Dave Hansen	3B2	L	21	5	7	0	1	0	0	0	1	0	3	0	.143	.143	.143
Luis Lopez	1B1	R	25	6	6	0	0	0	0	0	0	0	2	0	.000	.000	.000
Barry Lyons†	C2	R	30	3	5	1	1	0	0	1	2	0	1	0	.200	.200	.800
Darrin Fletcher†	C1	L	23	2	1	0	0	0	0	0	0	0	1	0	.000	.000	.000

M. Sharperson, 6 G at 1B; L. Harris, 1 G at SS

Pitcher	T	Age	G	GS	CG	ShO	IP	H	HR	BB	SO	W-L	Sv	ERA
Ramon Martinez	R	22	33	33	12	3	234.1	191	22	67	223	20-6	0	2.92
Mike Morgan	R	30	33	33	6	4	211.0	216	19	60	106	11-15	0	3.75
F. Valenzuela	L	29	33	33	5	2	204.0	223	19	77	115	13-13	0	4.59
Tim Belcher	R	28	24	24	5	2	153.0	136	17	48	102	9-9	0	4.00
Jim Neidlinger	R	25	12	12	0	0	74.0	67	4	15	46	5-3	0	3.28
Terry Wells	L	26	5	5	0	0	20.2	25	4	14	18	1-2	0	7.84
Orel Hershiser	R	31	4	4	0	0	25.1	26	1	4	16	1-1	0	4.26
Dennis Cook†	L	27	5	3	0	0	14.1	23	7	2	6	1-1	0	7.53
Tim Crews	R	29	66	2	0	0	107.1	98	9	24	76	4-5	5	2.77
Jim Gott	R	30	50	0	0	0	62.0	59	5	34	44	3-5	3	2.90
Jay Howell	R	34	45	0	0	0	66.0	59	5	20	59	5-5	16	2.18
Mike Hartley	R	28	32	6	1	1	79.1	58	7	30	76	6-3	1	2.95
Don Aase	R	35	32	0	0	0	38.0	33	5	19	24	3-1	3	4.97
Ray Searage	L	35	29	0	0	0	32.1	30	1	10	19	1-0	0	2.78
John Wetteland	R	23	22	5	0	0	43.0	44	6	17	36	2-4	0	4.81
David Walsh	L	29	20	0	0	0	16.1	15	1	6	15	1-0	1	3.86
Jim Poole	L	24	16	0	0	0	10.2	7	1	8	6	0-0	0	4.22
Darren Holmes	R	24	14	0	0	0	17.1	15	1	11	19	0-1	0	5.19
Mike Maddux	R	28	11	2	0	0	20.2	24	3	4	11	0-1	0	6.53
Mike Munoz	L	24	8	0	0	0	5.2	6	0	3	2	0-1	0	3.18
Pat Perry	L	31	7	0	0	0	6.2	9	0	5	2	0-0	0	8.10

1990 San Francisco Giants 3rd NL West 85-77 .525 6.0 GB

Roger Craig

Player	Gm by Position	B	Age	G	AB	R	H	2B	3B	HR	RBI	BB	SO	SB	Avg	OBP	Slg
Terry Kennedy	C103	L	34	107	303	25	84	22	0	2	26	31	38	1	.277	.342	.370
Will Clark	1B153	L	26	154	600	91	177	25	5	19	95	62	97	8	.295	.357	.448
Robby Thompson	2B142	R	28	144	498	67	122	22	3	15	56	34	96	14	.245	.299	.392
Matt Williams	3B159	R	24	159	617	87	171	27	2	33	122	33	138	7	.277	.319	.488
Jose Uribe	SS134	S	31	138	415	35	103	8	6	1	24	29	49	5	.248	.297	.304
Brett Butler	OF159	L	33	160	622	108	192	20	9	3	44	90	62	51	.309	.397	.384
Kevin Mitchell	OF138	R	28	140	524	90	152	24	2	35	93	58	87	4	.290	.360	.544
Mike Kingery	OF95	L	29	105	207	24	61	7	1	0	24	12	19	6	.295	.335	.338
Gary Carter	C80,1B3	R	36	92	244	24	62	10	0	9	27	25	31	1	.254	.324	.406
Kevin Bass	OF55	S	31	61	214	25	54	9	1	7	32	14	26	2	.252	.303	.402
Greg Litton	OF56,2B18,SS7*	R	25	93	204	17	50	9	1	1	24	11	45	1	.245	.284	.314
Rick Leach	OF52,1B7	L	33	78	174	24	51	13	0	2	16	21	20	0	.293	.372	.402
Ernest Riles	SS26,2B24,3B10	L	29	92	155	22	31	2	1	8	21	26	26	0	.200	.313	.381
Rick Parker	OF35,2B3,3B1*	R	27	54	107	19	26	5	0	2	14	10	15	6	.243	.314	.346
Dave Anderson	SS29,2B13,1B3*	R	29	60	100	14	35	5	1	1	6	3	20	1	.350	.369	.450
Mike Benjamin	SS21	R	24	22	56	7	12	3	1	2	3	3	10	1	.214	.254	.411
Steve Decker	C15	R	24	15	54	5	16	2	0	3	8	1	10	0	.296	.309	.500
Bill Bathe	C8	R	29	52	48	3	11	0	1	3	12	7	12	0	.229	.321	.458
Mike Laga	1B10	L	30	23	27	4	5	1	0	2	4	1	7	0	.185	.241	.444
Mark Leonard	OF7	L	25	11	17	3	3	1	0	1	2	3	8	0	.176	.300	.412
Kirt Manwaring	C8	R	24	8	13	0	2	0	1	0	1	0	3	0	.154	.154	.308
Mark Bailey	C1	S	28	5	7	1	1	0	0	1	3	0	2	0	.143	.143	.571
Brad Komminsk†	OF7	R	29	8	5	2	1	0	0	0	0	1	2	0	.200	.333	.200
Tony Perezchica	2B2,SS2	R	24	4	3	1	1	0	0	0	0	1	2	0	.333	.500	.333
Andres Santana	SS3	S	22	6	2	0	0	0	0	0	1	0	0	0	.000	.000	.000

G. Litton, 5 G at 3B; R. Parker, 1 G at SS; D. Anderson, 2 G at 3B

Pitcher	T	Age	G	GS	CG	ShO	IP	H	HR	BB	SO	W-L	Sv	ERA
John Burkett	R	25	33	32	2	0	204.0	201	18	61	118	14-7	1	3.79
Scott Garrelts	R	28	31	31	4	2	182.0	190	16	70	80	12-11	0	4.15
Don Robinson	R	33	26	25	4	0	157.2	173	18	41	78	10-7	0	4.57
Trevor Wilson	L	24	27	17	3	2	110.1	87	11	49	66	8-7	0	4.00
Rick Reuschel	R	41	15	13	0	0	87.0	102	8	31	49	3-6	1	3.93
Mike LaCoss	R	34	13	12	1	0	77.2	75	5	39	39	6-4	0	3.94
Kelly Downs	R	29	13	9	0	0	63.0	56	2	20	31	3-2	0	3.43
Bob Knepper	L	36	12	7	0	0	44.1	56	7	19	24	3-3	0	5.68
Eric Gunderson	L	24	7	4	0	0	19.2	24	2	11	14	1-2	0	5.49
Russ Swan†	L	26	2	1	0	0	2.1	6	0	4	1	0-1	0	3.86
Steve Bedrosian	R	32	68	0	0	0	79.1	72	6	44	43	9-9	17	4.20
Jeff Brantley	R	26	55	0	0	0	86.2	77	3	33	61	5-3	19	1.56
Mark Thurmond	L	33	43	0	0	0	56.2	53	6	18	24	2-3	4	3.34
Francisco Oliveras	R	27	33	2	0	0	55.1	47	5	21	41	2-2	2	2.77
Randy O'Neal	R	29	26	0	0	0	47.0	58	3	18	30	1-0	0	3.83
Atlee Hammaker†	L	32	25	6	0	0	67.1	69	7	21	28	4-5	0	4.28
Ed Vosberg	L	28	18	0	0	0	24.1	21	3	12	12	1-1	0	5.55
Mark Dewey	R	25	14	0	0	0	22.2	22	1	5	11	1-1	0	2.78
Ernie Camacho†	R	35	8	0	0	0	10.0	10	1	3	8	0-0	0	3.60
Rafael Novoa	L	22	7	2	0	0	18.2	21	3	13	14	0-1	1	6.75
Dan Quisenberry	R	37	5	0	0	0	6.2	13	1	3	2	0-1	0	13.50
Paul McClellan	R	24	4	1	0	0	7.2	14	3	6	2	0-1	0	11.74
Andy McGaffigan†	R	33	4	0	0	0	4.2	10	2	4	4	0-0	0	17.36
Randy McCament	R	27	3	0	0	0	6.0	8	0	5	5	0-0	0	3.00
Rick Rodriguez	R	29	3	0	0	0	3.1	5	0	2	2	0-0	0	8.10
Greg Booker	R	30	2	0	0	0	2.0	7	0	0	1	0-0	0	13.50

1990 Houston Astros 4th NL West 75-87 .463 16.0 GB

Art Howe

Player	Gm by Position	B	Age	G	AB	R	H	2B	3B	HR	RBI	BB	SO	SB	Avg	OBP	Slg
Craig Biggio	C113,OF50	R	24	150	555	53	153	24	2	4	42	53	79	25	.276	.342	.348
Glenn Davis	1B91	R	29	93	327	44	82	15	4	22	64	46	54	8	.251	.357	.523
Bill Doran†	2B99	S	32	109	344	49	99	21	2	6	32	71	53	18	.288	.405	.413
Ken Caminiti	3B149	S	27	153	541	52	131	20	2	4	51	48	97	9	.242	.302	.309
Rafael Ramirez	SS129	R	32	132	445	44	116	19	3	2	37	24	46	10	.261	.299	.330
Glenn Wilson	OF108,1B1	R	31	118	368	42	90	14	0	10	55	26	64	0	.245	.293	.364
Eric Yelding	OF94,SS40,2B10*	R	25	142	511	69	130	9	5	1	28	39	87	64	.254	.305	.297
Franklin Stubbs	1B72,OF71	L	29	146	448	59	117	23	2	23	71	48	114	19	.261	.334	.475
Casey Candaele	OF58,2B49,SS13*	S	29	130	262	30	75	8	6	3	22	31	42	7	.286	.364	.397
Eric Anthony	OF71	L	22	84	239	26	46	8	0	10	29	29	78	5	.192	.279	.351
Gerald Young	OF50	S	25	57	154	15	27	4	1	1	4	20	23	6	.175	.269	.234
Ken Oberkfell	3B24,1B11,2B11	L	34	77	150	10	31	6	1	1	12	15	17	1	.207	.281	.280
Mark Davidson	OF51	R	29	57	130	12	38	5	1	1	11	10	18	0	.292	.340	.369
Rich Gedman†	C39	L	30	40	104	4	21	7	0	1	10	15	24	0	.202	.300	.298
Dave Rohde	2B32,3B4,SS2	S	26	59	98	8	18	4	0	0	5	9	20	0	.184	.283	.224
Karl Rhodes	OF30	L	21	38	86	12	21	6	1	1	3	13	12	4	.244	.340	.372
Javier Ortiz	OF25	R	27	30	77	7	21	5	1	1	10	12	11	1	.273	.367	.403
Alex Trevino†	C30,1B1	R	32	42	69	3	13	3	0	1	10	6	11	0	.188	.266	.275
Carl Nichols	C15,1B3,OF1	R	27	32	49	7	10	3	0	0	11	8	11	0	.204	.317	.265
Terry Puhl	OF8,1B1	L	33	37	41	5	12	1	0	0	8	5	7	1	.293	.375	.317
Luis Gonzalez	3B4,1B2	L	22	12	21	1	4	2	0	0	0	2	5	0	.190	.261	.286
Louie Meadows†	OF9	L	29	15	14	3	2	0	0	0	0	2	4	0	.143	.250	.143
Mike Simms	1B6	R	23	12	13	3	4	1	0	1	2	0	4	0	.308	.308	.615
Jeff Baldwin	OF3	L	24	7	8	1	0	0	0	0	0	1	2	0	.000	.111	.000
Andujar Cedeno	SS3	R	20	7	8	0	0	0	0	0	0	0	5	0	.000	.000	.000
Terry McGriff†	C4	R	26	4	5	0	0	0	0	0	0	0	2	0	.000	.000	.000
Steve Lombardozzi		R	30	2	1	0	0	0	0	0	0	1	1	0	.000	.500	.000

E. Yelding, 3 G at 3B; C. Candaele, 1 G at 3B

Pitcher	T	Age	G	GS	CG	ShO	IP	H	HR	BB	SO	W-L	Sv	ERA
Jim Deshaies	L	30	34	34	2	0	209.1	186	21	84	119	7-12	0	3.78
Mike Scott	R	35	32	32	4	2	205.2	194	27	66	121	9-13	0	3.81
Mark Portugal	R	27	32	32	1	0	196.2	187	21	67	136	11-10	0	3.62
Bill Gullickson	R	31	32	32	2	1	193.1	221	21	61	73	10-14	0	3.82
Terry Clark	R	29	1	1	0	0	4.0	9	0	3	2	0-0	0	13.50
Juan Agosto	L	32	82	0	0	0	92.1	91	4	39	50	9-8	4	4.29
Larry Andersen†	R	37	50	0	0	0	73.2	61	2	24	68	5-2	6	1.95
Dave Smith	R	35	49	0	0	0	60.1	45	4	20	50	6-6	23	2.39
Danny Darwin	R	34	48	17	3	0	162.2	136	11	31	109	11-4	2	2.21
Dan Schatzeder†	L	35	45	2	0	0	64.0	61	2	23	37	1-3	0	2.39
Xavier Hernandez	R	24	34	1	0	0	62.1	60	8	24	24	2-1	0	4.62
Jim Clancy	R	34	33	10	0	0	76.0	100	4	33	44	2-8	1	6.51
Brian Meyer	R	27	14	0	0	0	20.1	16	3	6	6	0-4	1	2.21
Al Osuna	L	24	12	0	0	0	11.1	10	1	6	6	2-0	0	4.76
Charlie Kerfeld†	R	26	5	0	0	0	3.1	9	0	6	4	0-2	0	16.20
Brian Fisher	R	28	4	0	0	0	5.0	9	1	0	1	0-0	0	7.20
Randy Hennis	R	24	3	1	0	0	9.2	1	0	3	4	0-0	0	0.00

1990 San Diego Padres 4th NL West 75-87 .463 16.0 GB

Jack McKeon (37-43)/Greg Riddoch (38-44)

Player	Gm by Position	B	Age	G	AB	R	H	2B	3B	HR	RBI	BB	SO	SB	Avg	OBP	Slg
Benito Santiago	C98	R	25	100	344	42	93	8	5	11	53	27	55	5	.270	.323	.419
Jack Clark	1B109	R	34	115	334	59	89	12	1	25	62	104	91	4	.266	.441	.533
Roberto Alomar	2B137,SS5	S	22	147	586	80	168	27	5	6	60	48	72	24	.287	.340	.381
Mike Pagliarulo	3B116	L	30	128	398	29	101	23	2	7	38	39	66	1	.254	.322	.374
Garry Templeton	SS135	S	34	144	505	45	125	25	3	9	59	24	59	1	.248	.280	.362
Joe Carter	OF150,1B14	R	30	162	634	79	147	27	1	24	115	48	93	22	.232	.290	.391
Tony Gwynn	OF141	L	30	141	573	79	177	29	10	4	72	44	23	17	.309	.357	.415
Bip Roberts	OF75,3B56,SS18*	S	26	149	556	104	172	36	3	9	44	55	65	46	.309	.375	.433
Fred Lynn	OF55	L	38	90	196	18	47	3	1	6	23	22	44	1	.240	.315	.357
Mark Parent	C60	R	28	65	189	13	42	11	0	3	16	16	29	1	.222	.283	.328
Shawn Abner	OF62	R	24	91	184	17	45	9	0	1	15	9	28	2	.245	.286	.310
Phil Stephenson	1B60	L	29	103	182	26	38	9	1	4	19	30	43	2	.209	.319	.335
Darrin Jackson	OF39	R	26	58	113	10	29	3	0	3	9	5	24	3	.257	.286	.363
Jerald Clark	1B15,OF13	R	26	52	101	12	27	4	1	5	11	5	24	0	.267	.299	.475
Joey Cora	SS21,2B15,C1	S	25	51	100	12	27	3	0	0	2	6	9	8	.270	.311	.300
Tom Lampkin	C20	L	26	26	63	4	14	0	1	1	4	4	9	0	.222	.269	.302
Thomas Howard	OF13	S	25	20	44	4	12	2	0	0	0	0	11	0	.273	.273	.318
Eddie Williams	3B13	R	25	14	42	5	12	3	0	3	4	5	6	0	.286	.362	.571
Paul Faries	2B7,SS4,3B1	R	25	14	37	4	7	1	0	0	2	4	7	0	.189	.279	.216
Ronn Reynolds	C8	R	31	8	15	1	1	1	0	0	1	1	6	0	.067	.125	.133
Rob Nelson		L	26	5	5	0	0	0	0	0	0	0	4	0	.000	.000	.000

B. Roberts, 8 G at 2B

Pitcher	T	Age	G	GS	CG	ShO	IP	H	HR	BB	SO	W-L	Sv	ERA
Bruce Hurst	L	32	33	33	9	4	223.2	188	21	63	162	11-9	0	3.14
Ed Whitson	R	35	32	32	6	3	228.2	215	13	47	127	14-9	0	2.60
Dennis Rasmussen	L	31	32	32	3	1	187.2	217	28	62	86	11-15	0	4.51
Andy Benes	R	22	32	31	2	0	192.1	177	18	69	140	10-11	0	3.60
Mike Dunne	R	27	10	6	0	0	28.2	28	4	17	15	0-3	0	5.65
Greg Harris	R	26	73	0	0	0	117.1	92	6	49	97	8-8	9	2.30
Craig Lefferts	L	32	56	0	0	0	78.2	68	10	22	60	7-5	23	2.52
Calvin Schiraldi	R	28	42	8	0	0	104.0	105	11	60	74	3-8	1	4.41
Eric Show	R	34	39	12	0	0	106.1	131	16	41	55	6-8	1	5.76
Rich Rodriguez	L	27	32	0	0	0	47.2	52	2	16	22	1-1	1	2.83
Mark Grant†	R	26	26	0	0	0	39.0	47	5	19	29	1-1	0	4.85
Derek Lilliquist†	L	24	16	7	1	1	60.1	61	6	23	29	3-3	0	4.33
Atlee Hammaker†	L	32	9	1	0	0	19.1	16	1	6	16	0-4	0	4.66
Pat Clements	L	28	9	0	0	0	13.0	20	1	7	6	0-0	0	4.15
John Davis	R	27	6	0	0	0	9.1	9	1	4	7	0-1	0	5.79
Rafael Valdez	R	21	3	0	0	0	5.2	11	4	2	3	0-1	0	11.12

1990 Atlanta Braves 6th NL West 65-97 .401 26.0 GB

Russ Nixon (25-40)/Bobby Cox (40-57)

Player	Gm by Position	B	Age	G	AB	R	H	2B	3B	HR	RBI	BB	SO	SB	Avg	OBP	Slg
Greg Olson	C97,3B1	R	29	100	298	36	78	12	1	7	36	30	51	1	.262	.332	.379
David Justice	1B69,OF61	L	24	127	439	76	124	23	2	28	78	64	92	11	.282	.373	.535
Jeff Treadway	2B122	L	27	128	474	56	134	20	2	11	59	25	42	3	.283	.320	.403
Jim Presley	3B133,1B17	R	28	140	541	59	131	34	1	19	72	29	130	1	.242	.282	.414
Jeff Blauser	SS93,2B14,3B9*	R	24	115	386	46	104	24	3	8	39	35	70	3	.269	.338	.409
Ron Gant	OF146	R	25	152	575	107	174	34	3	32	84	50	86	33	.303	.357	.539
Lonnie Smith	OF122	R	34	135	466	72	142	27	9	9	42	58	69	10	.305	.384	.459
Dale Murphy†	OF97	R	34	97	349	38	81	14	0	17	55	41	84	9	.232	.312	.418
Oddibe McDowell	OF72	L	27	113	305	47	74	14	0	7	25	21	53	13	.243	.295	.357
Andres Thomas	SS72,3B5	R	26	84	278	26	61	8	0	5	30	11	43	2	.219	.248	.302
Tommy Gregg	1B50,OF20	L	26	124	239	18	63	13	1	5	32	20	39	4	.264	.322	.389
Mark Lemke	3B45,2B44,SS1	S	24	102	239	22	54	13	0	0	21	21	22	0	.226	.286	.280
Ernie Whitt	C59	L	38	67	180	14	31	8	0	2	10	23	27	0	.172	.265	.250
Francisco Cabrera	1B48,C3	R	23	63	137	14	38	5	1	7	25	5	21	1	.277	.301	.482
Jimmy Kremers	C27	L	24	29	73	7	8	1	1	1	2	6	27	0	.110	.177	.192
Mike Bell	1B24	L	22	36	45	8	11	5	1	1	5	2	9	0	.244	.292	.467
Nick Esasky	1B9	R	30	9	35	2	6	0	0	0	0	4	14	0	.171	.256	.171
Jody Davis	1B6,C4	R	33	12	28	0	2	0	0	0	1	3	3	0	.071	.161	.071
Alexis Infante	2B10,3B4,SS3	R	28	20	28	3	1	0	0	0	0	0	7	0	.036	.069	.071
Kelly Mann	C10	R	22	11	28	2	4	1	0	1	2	0	6	0	.143	.143	.286
Jim Vatcher†	OF6	R	24	21	27	2	7	1	1	0	3	1	9	0	.259	.286	.370
Victor Rosario	SS3,2B1	R	23	9	7	3	1	0	0	0	0	1	1	0	.143	.250	.143
Geronimo Berroa	OF3	R	25	7	4	0	0	0	0	0	0	1	1	0	.000	.200	.000

J. Blauser, 1 G at OF

Pitcher	T	Age	G	GS	CG	ShO	IP	H	HR	BB	SO	W-L	Sv	ERA
John Smoltz	R	23	34	34	6	2	231.1	206	20	90	170	14-11	0	3.85
Tom Glavine	L	24	33	33	1	0	214.1	232	18	78	129	10-12	0	4.28
Charlie Leibrandt	L	33	24	24	5	2	162.1	164	9	35	76	9-11	0	3.16
Steve Avery	L	20	21	20	1	1	99.0	121	7	45	75	3-11	0	5.64
Pete Smith	R	24	13	13	3	0	77.0	77	11	24	56	5-6	0	4.79
Derek Lilliquist†	L	24	12	11	0	0	61.2	75	10	19	34	2-8	0	6.28
Paul Marak	R	24	7	7	1	1	39.0	39	2	19	15	1-2	0	3.69
Tony Castillo	L	27	52	3	0	0	76.2	93	5	20	64	5-1	1	4.23
Rick Luecken†	R	29	36	0	0	0	53.0	73	5	30	35	1-4	1	5.77
Kent Mercker	L	22	36	0	0	0	48.1	43	6	24	39	4-7	7	3.17
Dwayne Henry	R	28	34	0	0	0	38.1	41	3	25	34	2-2	0	5.63
Marty Clary	R	28	33	14	0	0	101.2	128	9	39	44	1-10	0	5.67
Mark Grant†	R	26	33	1	0	0	52.1	61	4	18	40	1-2	3	4.64
Joe Boever†	R	29	33	0	0	0	42.1	40	6	35	35	1-3	8	4.68
Joe Hesketh†	L	31	31	0	0	0	31.0	30	5	12	21	0-2	5	5.81
Charlie Kerfeld†	R	26	25	0	0	0	30.2	31	2	23	27	3-1	2	5.58
Jeff Parrett†	R	28	20	0	0	0	27.0	27	1	19	17	1-1	1	3.00
Marvin Freeman†	R	27	9	0	0	0	15.2	7	0	3	12	1-0	0	1.72
Mike Stanton	L	23	7	0	0	0	7.0	16	1	4	7	0-3	2	18.00
Sergio Valdez†	R	25	6	0	0	0	5.1	6	0	3	3	0-0	0	6.75
Tommy Greene†	R	23	5	2	0	0	12.1	14	3	9	4	1-0	0	8.03
Doug Sisk	R	32	3	0	0	0	2.1	1	0	4	1	0-0	0	3.86
Rusty Richards	R	25	1	0	0	0	1.0	2	1	1	0	0-0	0	27.00

»1991 Toronto Blue Jays 1st AL East 91-71 .562 —

Cito Gaston (66-54)/Gene Tenace (19-14)/Cito Gaston (6-3)

Player	Gm by Position	B	Age	G	AB	R	H	2B	3B	HR	RBI	BB	SO	SB	Avg	OBP	Slg
Greg Myers	C104	L	25	107	309	25	81	22	0	8	36	21	45	0	.262	.306	.411
John Olerud	1B135,DH1	L	22	139	454	64	116	30	1	17	68	68	84	0	.256	.353	.438
Roberto Alomar	2B160	S	23	161	637	88	188	41	11	9	69	57	86	53	.295	.354	.436
Kelly Gruber	3B111,DH2	R	29	113	429	58	108	18	2	20	65	31	70	12	.252	.308	.443
Manuel Lee	SS138	S	26	138	445	41	104	18	3	0	29	24	107	7	.234	.274	.288
Devon White	OF156	S	28	156	642	110	181	40	10	17	60	55	135	33	.282	.342	.455
Joe Carter	OF151,DH11	R	31	162	638	89	174	42	3	33	108	49	112	20	.273	.330	.503
Candy Maldonado†	OF52	R	30	52	177	26	49	9	0	7	28	23	53	3	.277	.375	.446
Rance Mulliniks	DH81,3B5	L	35	97	240	27	60	12	1	2	24	44	44	0	.250	.364	.333
Pat Borders	C102	R	28	105	291	22	71	17	0	5	36	11	45	0	.244	.271	.354
Mookie Wilson	OF41,DH34	S	35	86	241	26	58	12	4	2	28	8	35	11	.241	.277	.349
Pat Tabler	DH67,1B20,OF1	R	33	82	185	20	40	5	1	1	21	29	21	0	.216	.318	.270
Ed Sprague	3B35,1B22,DH2*	R	23	61	160	17	44	7	0	4	20	19	43	0	.275	.361	.394
Mark Whiten†	OF42	S	24	46	149	12	33	4	3	2	19	11	35	0	.221	.274	.329
Rene Gonzales	SS36,3B26,2B11*	R	30	71	118	16	23	3	0	1	6	12	22	0	.195	.289	.246
Glenallen Hill†	DH16,OF13	R	26	35	99	14	25	5	2	3	11	7	24	2	.253	.296	.434
Rob Ducey	OF24,DH2	L	26	39	68	8	16	2	2	1	4	6	26	2	.235	.297	.368
Cory Snyder†	OF14,1B4,3B3	R	28	21	49	4	7	0	1	0	6	3	19	0	.143	.189	.184
Dave Parker†	DH12	L	40	13	36	2	12	4	0	0	3	4	7	0	.333	.400	.444
Kenny Williams†	OF9,DH2	R	27	13	29	5	6	2	0	1	3	4	5	1	.207	.314	.379
Derek Bell	OF13	R	22	18	28	5	4	0	0	0	1	6	5	3	.143	.314	.143
Eddie Zosky	SS18	R	23	18	27	2	4	1	1	0	2	0	8	0	.148	.148	.259
Ray Giannelli	3B9	L	25	9	24	2	4	1	0	0	0	5	9	1	.167	.310	.208
Turner Ward†	OF6	S	26	8	13	1	4	0	0	0	2	1	2	0	.308	.357	.308
Randy Knorr	C3	R	22	3	1	0	0	0	0	0	0	1	1	0	.000	.500	.000

E. Sprague, 2 G at C; R. Gonzales, 2 G at 1B

Pitcher	T	Age	G	GS	CG	ShO	IP	H	HR	BB	SO	W-L	Sv	ERA
Todd Stottlemyre	R	26	34	34	1	0	219.0	194	21	75	116	15-8	0	3.78
Jimmy Key	L	30	33	33	2	2	209.1	207	12	44	125	16-12	0	3.05
David Wells	L	28	40	28	2	0	198.1	188	24	49	106	15-10	1	3.72
Juan Guzman	R	24	23	23	1	0	138.2	98	6	66	123	10-3	0	2.99
Tom Candiotti†	R	33	19	19	3	0	129.2	114	6	45	81	6-7	0	2.98
Dave Stieb	R	33	9	9	1	0	59.2	52	4	23	29	4-3	0	3.17
Denis Boucher†	L	23	7	7	0	0	35.1	39	6	16	16	0-3	0	4.58
Duane Ward	R	27	81	0	0	0	107.1	80	3	33	132	7-6	23	2.77
Mike Timlin	R	25	63	3	0	0	108.1	94	6	50	85	11-6	3	3.16
Jim Acker	R	32	54	4	0	0	88.1	77	16	36	44	3-5	1	5.20
Tom Henke	R	33	49	0	0	0	50.1	33	4	11	53	0-2	32	2.32
Bob MacDonald	L	26	45	0	0	0	53.2	51	5	25	24	3-3	0	2.85
Dave Weathers	R	21	15	0	0	0	14.2	15	1	17	13	1-0	0	4.91
Willie Fraser†	R	27	13	1	0	0	26.1	33	4	11	12	0-2	0	6.15
Ken Dayley	L	32	8	0	0	0	4.1	7	0	5	3	0-0	0	6.23
Frank Wills	R	32	4	0	0	0	4.1	8	2	5	2	0-1	0	16.62
Vince Horsman	L	24	4	0	0	0	4.0	2	0	3	2	0-0	0	0.00
Pat Hentgen	R	22	3	1	0	0	7.1	5	1	3	3	0-0	0	2.45
Al Leiter	L	25	3	0	0	0	1.2	3	0	5	1	0-0	0	27.00
Mickey Weston	R	30	2	0	0	0	2.0	1	0	1	1	0-0	0	0.00

1991 Boston Red Sox 2nd AL East 84-78 .519 7.0 GB

Joe Morgan

Player	Gm by Position	B	Age	G	AB	R	H	2B	3B	HR	RBI	BB	SO	SB	Avg	OBP	Slg
Tony Pena	C140	R	34	141	464	45	107	23	2	5	48	37	53	8	.231	.291	.321
Carlos Quintana	1B138,OF13,DH1	R	25	149	478	69	141	21	1	11	71	61	66	1	.295	.375	.412
Jody Reed	2B152,SS6	R	28	153	618	87	175	42	2	5	60	60	53	6	.283	.349	.382
Wade Boggs	3B140	L	33	144	546	93	181	42	2	8	51	89	32	1	.332	.421	.460
Luis Rivera	SS129	R	27	129	414	64	107	22	3	8	40	35	86	4	.258	.318	.384
Mike Greenwell	OF143,DH1	L	27	147	544	76	163	26	6	9	83	43	35	15	.300	.350	.419
Tom Brunansky	OF137,DH1	R	30	142	459	54	105	24	1	16	70	49	72	1	.229	.303	.390
Ellis Burks	OF126,DH2	R	26	130	474	56	119	33	3	14	56	39	81	6	.251	.314	.422
Jack Clark	DH135	R	35	140	481	75	120	18	1	28	87	96	133	0	.249	.374	.466
Mo Vaughn	1B49,DH16	L	23	74	219	21	57	12	0	4	32	26	43	2	.260	.339	.370
Steve Lyons	OF45,2B16,3B12*	L	31	87	212	15	51	10	1	4	17	11	35	10	.241	.277	.354
Phil Plantier	OF40,DH5	L	22	53	148	27	49	7	1	11	35	23	38	1	.331	.420	.615
Mike Brumley	SS31,3B17,2B7*	S	28	63	118	16	25	5	0	0	5	10	22	2	.212	.273	.254
John Marzano	C48	R	28	49	114	10	30	8	0	0	9	1	16	0	.263	.271	.333
Mike Marshall†	DH7,1B5,OF4	R	31	22	62	4	18	4	0	1	7	0	19	0	.290	.290	.403
Kevin Romine	OF23,DH14	R	30	44	55	7	9	2	0	1	7	3	10	1	.164	.207	.255
Tim Naehring	SS17,3B2,2B1	R	24	20	55	1	6	1	0	0	3	6	15	0	.109	.197	.127
Scott Cooper	3B13	L	23	14	35	6	16	4	2	0	7	2	2	0	.457	.486	.686
Bob Zupcic	OF16	R	24	18	25	3	4	0	0	1	3	1	6	0	.160	.192	.280
Wayne Housie	OF4	S	26	11	8	2	2	1	0	0	0	1	3	1	.250	.333	.375
Eric Wedge	DH1	R	23	1	1	0	1	0	0	0	0	0	0	0	1.000	1.000	1.000

S. Lyons, 2 G at DH, 2 G at 1B, 1 G at P, 1 G at SS; M. Brumley, 4 G at OF, 2 G at DH

Pitcher	T	Age	G	GS	CG	ShO	IP	H	HR	BB	SO	W-L	Sv	ERA
Roger Clemens	R	28	35	35	13	4	271.1	219	15	65	241	18-10	0	2.62
Mike Gardiner	R	25	22	22	0	0	130.0	140	18	47	91	9-10	0	4.85
Tom Bolton	L	29	25	19	0	0	110.0	136	16	51	64	8-9	0	5.24
Matt Young	L	32	19	16	0	0	88.2	92	4	53	69	3-7	0	5.18
Kevin Morton	L	22	16	15	1	0	86.1	93	9	40	45	6-5	0	4.59
Danny Darwin	R	35	12	12	0	0	68.0	71	15	15	42	3-6	0	5.16
Tony Fossas	L	33	64	0	0	0	57.0	49	3	28	29	3-2	1	3.47
Jeff Reardon	R	35	57	0	0	0	59.1	54	9	16	44	1-4	40	3.03
Greg Harris	R	35	53	21	1	0	173.0	157	13	69	127	11-12	2	3.85
Dennis Lamp	R	38	51	0	0	0	92.0	100	8	31	57	6-3	0	4.70
Jeff Gray	R	28	50	0	0	0	61.2	39	7	10	41	2-3	1	2.34
Joe Hesketh	L	32	39	17	0	0	153.1	142	19	53	104	12-4	0	3.29
Dana Kiecker	R	30	18	5	0	0	40.1	56	6	23	21	2-3	0	7.36
Dan Petry†	R	32	13	0	0	0	22.1	21	3	12	12	0-0	1	4.03
Daryl Irvine	R	26	9	0	0	0	18.0	25	2	9	8	0-0	0	6.00
Jeff Plympton	R	25	4	0	0	0	5.1	5	0	4	2	0-0	0	0.00
Steve Lyons	R	31	1	0	0	0	1.0	2	0	0	1	0-0	0	0.00
John Dopson	R	27	1	0	0	0	1.0	2	0	1	0	0-0	0	18.00
Josias Manzanillo	R	23	1	0	0	0	1.0	2	0	3	1	0-0	0	18.00

1991 Detroit Tigers 2nd AL East 84-78 .519 7.0 GB

Sparky Anderson

Player	Gm by Position	B	Age	G	AB	R	H	2B	3B	HR	RBI	BB	SO	SB	Avg	OBP	Slg
Mickey Tettleton	C125,DH24,OF3*	S	30	154	501	85	132	17	2	31	89	101	131	3	.263	.387	.491
Cecil Fielder	1B122,DH42	R	27	162	624	102	163	25	0	44	133	78	151	0	.261	.347	.513
Lou Whitaker	2B135,DH3	L	34	138	470	94	131	26	2	23	78	90	45	4	.279	.391	.489
Travis Fryman	3B86,SS71	R	22	149	557	65	144	36	3	21	91	40	149	12	.259	.309	.447
Alan Trammell	SS92,DH6	R	33	101	375	57	93	20	0	9	55	37	39	11	.248	.320	.373
Milt Cuyler	OF151	S	22	154	475	77	122	15	7	3	33	52	92	41	.257	.335	.337
Rob Deer	OF132,DH2	R	30	134	448	64	80	14	2	25	64	89	175	1	.179	.314	.386
Lloyd Moseby	OF64,DH7	L	31	74	260	37	68	15	1	6	35	21	43	8	.262	.321	.396
Pete Incaviglia	OF54,DH42	R	27	97	337	38	72	12	1	11	38	36	92	1	.214	.290	.353
Tony Phillips	OF56,3B46,2B36*	S	32	146	564	87	160	28	4	17	72	79	95	10	.284	.371	.438
Dave Bergman	1B49,DH13,OF4	L	38	86	194	23	46	10	1	7	29	35	40	1	.237	.351	.407
Skeeter Barnes	OF33,3B17,1B9*	R	34	75	159	28	46	13	2	5	17	9	24	10	.289	.325	.491
Andy Allanson	C56,1B2,DH1	R	29	60	151	10	35	10	0	1	16	7	31	0	.232	.266	.318
John Shelby	OF47,DH4	S	33	53	143	19	22	8	1	3	8	8	23	0	.154	.204	.287
Scott Livingstone	3B43	L	25	44	127	19	37	5	0	2	11	10	25	2	.291	.341	.378
Mark Salas	C11,DH8,1B5	L	30	33	57	2	5	1	0	1	7	0	10	0	.088	.117	.158
Luis de los Santos	DH9,OF3,1B2*	R	24	16	30	1	5	2	0	0	0	2	4	0	.167	.219	.233
John Moses	OF12	S	33	13	21	5	1	1	0	0	1	2	7	4	.048	.130	.095
Shawn Hare	OF6,DH2	L	24	9	19	0	1	1	0	0	0	2	1	0	.053	.143	.105
Johnny Paredes	2B7,DH2,3B1*	R	28	16	18	4	6	0	0	0	0	0	1	1	.333	.333	.333
Tony Bernazard	DH2,2B2	S	34	6	12	0	2	0	0	0	0	0	4	0	.167	.167	.167
Rich Rowland	C2,DH1	R	27	4	4	0	1	0	0	0	1	1	2	0	.250	.333	.250

M. Tettleton, 1 G at 1B; T. Phillips, 18 G at DH, 13 G at SS; S. Barnes, 7 G at 2B, 3 G at DH; L. de los Santos, 2 G at 3B; J. Paredes, 1 G at SS

Pitcher	T	Age	G	GS	CG	ShO	IP	H	HR	BB	SO	W-L	Sv	ERA
Bill Gullickson	R	32	35	35	4	0	226.1	256	22	44	91	20-9	0	3.90
Walt Terrell	R	33	35	33	8	2	218.2	257	16	79	80	12-14	0	4.24
Frank Tanana	L	37	33	33	3	2	217.1	217	26	78	107	13-12	0	3.69
Scott Aldred	L	23	11	11	1	0	57.1	58	9	30	35	2-4	0	5.18
Paul Gibson	R	31	68	0	0	0	96.0	112	10	48	52	5-7	8	4.59
Mike Henneman	R	29	60	0	0	0	84.1	81	2	34	61	10-2	21	2.88
Jerry Don Gleaton	L	33	47	0	0	0	75.1	74	7	39	47	3-2	2	4.06
Mark Leiter	R	28	38	15	1	0	134.2	125	16	50	103	9-7	1	4.21
John Cerutti	L	31	38	8	1	0	88.2	94	9	37	29	3-6	2	4.57
Dan Gakeler	R	27	31	7	0	0	73.2	73	5	39	43	1-4	2	5.74
Dan Petry†	R	32	17	6	0	0	54.2	66	9	19	18	2-3	0	4.94
Steve Searcy†	L	27	16	5	0	0	40.2	52	8	30	32	1-2	0	8.41
Kevin Ritz	R	26	11	5	0	0	15.1	17	1	22	9	0-3	0	11.74
Dave Haas	R	25	11	0	0	0	10.2	8	1	12	6	1-0	0	6.75
Rusty Meacham	R	23	10	4	0	0	27.2	35	4	11	14	2-1	0	5.20
Jeff Kaiser	L	30	10	0	0	0	5.0	6	1	5	4	0-1	2	9.00
John Kiely	R	26	7	0	0	0	6.2	13	0	9	1	0-1	0	14.85
Mike Munoz	L	25	6	0	0	0	9.1	14	0	5	3	0-0	0	9.64
Mike Dalton	L	28	4	0	0	0	8.0	12	2	2	4	0-0	0	3.38

1991 Milwaukee Brewers 4th AL East 83-79 .512 8.0 GB

Tom Trebelhorn

Player	Gm by Position	B	Age	G	AB	R	H	2B	3B	HR	RBI	BB	SO	SB	Avg	OBP	Slg
B.J. Surhoff	C127,DH6,3B5*	L	26	143	505	57	146	19	4	5	68	26	33	5	.289	.319	.372
Franklin Stubbs	1B92,DH4,OF4	L	30	103	362	48	71	16	2	11	38	35	71	13	.213	.282	.359
Willie Randolph	2B121,DH2	R	36	124	431	60	141	14	3	0	54	75	38	4	.327	.424	.374
Jim Gantner	3B90,2B59	L	38	140	526	63	149	27	4	2	47	27	34	4	.283	.320	.361
Bill Spiers	SS128,OF1	L	25	133	414	71	117	13	6	8	54	34	55	14	.283	.337	.401
Greg Vaughn	OF135,DH10	R	25	145	542	81	132	24	5	27	98	62	125	2	.244	.319	.456
Dante Bichette	OF127,3B1	R	27	134	445	53	106	18	3	15	59	22	107	14	.238	.272	.393
Robin Yount	OF117,DH13	R	35	130	503	66	131	20	4	10	77	54	79	6	.260	.332	.376
Paul Molitor	DH112,1B46	R	34	158	665	133	216	32	13	17	75	77	62	19	.325	.399	.489
Darryl Hamilton	OF117	L	26	122	405	64	126	15	6	1	57	33	38	16	.311	.361	.385
Dale Sveum	SS51,3B38,DH3*	S	27	90	266	33	64	19	1	4	43	32	78	2	.241	.320	.365
Gary Sheffield	3B43,DH5	R	22	50	175	25	34	12	2	2	22	19	15	5	.194	.277	.320
Rick Dempsey	C56,P2,1B1	R	41	61	147	15	34	5	0	4	21	23	20	0	.231	.329	.347
Candy Maldonado†	OF24,DH9	R	30	34	111	11	23	6	0	5	20	13	23	1	.207	.288	.396
Greg Brock	1B25	L	34	31	60	9	17	4	0	1	6	14	9	1	.283	.419	.400
George Canale	1B19	L	25	21	34	6	6	2	0	3	10	8	6	0	.176	.318	.500
Tim McIntosh	OF4,DH2,1B1	R	26	7	11	2	4	1	0	1	1	0	4	0	.364	.364	.727
Jim Olander	OF9,DH3	R	28	12	9	2	0	0	0	0	0	2	5	0	.000	.182	.000
Matias Carrillo	OF3	L	28	3	0	0	0	0	0	0	0	0	0	0	—	—	—

B. Surhoff, 2 G at OF, 1 G at 2B; D. Sveum, 2 G at 2B

Pitcher	T	Age	G	GS	CG	ShO	IP	H	HR	BB	SO	W-L	Sv	ERA
Jaime Navarro	R	24	34	34	10	2	234.0	237	18	73	114	15-12	0	3.92
Chris Bosio	R	28	32	32	5	1	204.2	187	15	58	117	14-10	0	3.25
Bill Wegman	R	28	28	28	7	2	193.1	176	16	40	89	15-7	0	2.84
Don August	R	27	28	23	1	1	138.1	166	18	47	62	9-8	0	5.47
Kevin Brown	L	25	15	10	0	0	63.2	66	6	34	30	2-4	0	5.51
Mark Knudson	R	30	12	7	0	0	35.0	54	8	15	23	1-3	0	7.97
Teddy Higuera	L	32	7	6	0	0	36.1	37	2	10	33	3-2	0	4.46
Jim Hunter	R	27	8	6	0	0	31.0	45	3	17	14	0-5	0	7.26
Cal Eldred	R	23	3	3	0	0	16.0	20	2	6	10	2-0	0	4.50
Chris George	R	24	2	1	0	0	6.0	8	0	0	2	0-0	0	3.00
Ron Robinson	R	29	1	1	0	0	4.1	6	0	3	0	0-1	0	6.23
Chuck Crim	R	29	66	0	0	0	91.1	115	9	25	39	8-5	3	4.63
Mark Lee	L	26	62	0	0	0	67.2	72	10	31	43	2-5	1	3.86
Julio Machado	R	25	54	0	0	0	88.2	65	12	55	98	3-3	3	3.45
Dan Plesac	L	29	45	10	0	0	92.1	92	12	39	61	2-7	8	4.29
Darren Holmes	R	25	40	0	0	0	76.1	90	6	27	59	1-4	3	4.72
Doug Henry	R	27	32	0	0	0	36.0	16	1	14	28	2-1	15	1.00
Edwin Nunez	R	28	23	0	0	0	25.1	28	6	13	24	2-1	8	6.04
James Austin	R	27	5	0	0	0	8.2	8	1	11	3	0-0	0	8.31
Mike Ignasiak	R	25	4	1	0	0	12.2	7	2	8	10	2-1	0	5.68
Rick Dempsey	R	41	2	0	0	0	2.0	3	0	1	0	0-0	0	4.50

1991 New York Yankees 5th AL East 71-91 .438 20.0 GB

Stump Merrill

Player	Gm by Position	B	Age	G	AB	R	H	2B	3B	HR	RBI	BB	SO	SB	Avg	OBP	Slg
Matt Nokes	C130,DH3	L	27	135	456	52	122	20	0	24	77	25	49	3	.268	.308	.469
Don Mattingly	1B127,DH22	L	30	152	587	64	169	35	0	9	68	46	42	2	.288	.339	.394
Steve Sax	2B149,3B5,DH4	R	31	158	652	85	198	38	2	10	56	41	38	31	.304	.345	.414
Pat Kelly	3B80,2B19	R	23	96	298	35	72	12	4	3	23	15	52	12	.242	.288	.339
Alvaro Espinoza	SS147,3B2,P1	R	29	148	480	51	123	23	2	5	33	16	57	4	.256	.282	.344
Roberto Kelly	OF125	R	26	126	486	68	130	22	2	20	69	45	77	32	.267	.333	.444
Mel Hall	OF120,DH10	L	30	141	492	67	140	23	2	19	80	26	40	0	.285	.321	.455
Bernie Williams	OF85	S	22	85	320	43	76	19	4	3	34	48	57	10	.238	.336	.350
Kevin Maas	DH109,1B36	L	26	148	500	69	110	14	1	23	63	83	128	5	.220	.333	.390
Hensley Meulens	OF73,DH13,1B7	R	24	96	288	37	64	8	1	6	29	18	97	3	.222	.276	.319
Jesse Barfield	OF81	R	31	84	284	37	64	12	0	17	48	36	80	1	.225	.312	.447
Randy Velarde	3B50,SS31,OF2	R	28	80	184	19	45	11	1	1	15	18	43	3	.245	.322	.332
Bob Geren	C63	R	29	64	128	7	28	3	0	2	12	9	31	0	.219	.270	.289
Pat Sheridan	OF34,DH2	L	33	62	113	13	23	3	0	4	7	13	30	1	.204	.286	.336
Jim Leyritz	3B18,C5,1B3*	R	27	32	77	8	14	3	0	0	4	13	15	0	.182	.300	.221
Torey Lovullo	3B22	S	25	22	51	0	9	2	0	0	2	5	7	0	.176	.250	.216
Mike Humphreys	OF9,DH7,3B6	R	24	25	40	9	8	0	0	0	3	9	7	2	.200	.347	.200
Carlos Rodriguez	SS11,2B3	S	23	15	37	1	7	0	0	0	2	1	2	0	.189	.211	.189
Mike Blowers	3B14	R	26	15	35	3	7	0	0	1	1	4	3	0	.200	.282	.286
John Ramos	C5,DH4	R	25	10	26	4	8	1	0	0	3	1	3	0	.308	.310	.346
Scott Lusader	OF4,DH1	L	26	11	7	2	1	0	0	0	1	1	3	0	.143	.250	.143

J. Leyritz, 1 G at DH

Pitcher	T	Age	G	GS	CG	ShO	IP	H	HR	BB	SO	W-L	Sv	ERA
Scott Sanderson	R	34	34	34	2	2	208.0	200	22	29	130	16-10	0	3.81
Jeff Johnson	L	24	23	23	0	0	127.0	156	15	33	62	6-11	0	5.88
Wade Taylor	R	25	23	22	0	0	116.1	144	13	53	72	7-12	0	6.27
Tim Leary	R	33	28	18	1	0	120.2	150	20	57	83	4-10	0	6.49
Pascual Perez	R	34	14	14	0	0	73.2	68	7	24	41	2-4	0	3.18
Dave Eiland	R	24	18	13	0	0	72.2	87	10	23	18	2-5	0	5.33
Scott Kamieniecki	R	27	9	9	0	0	55.1	54	8	22	34	4-4	0	3.90
Chuck Cary	L	31	10	9	0	0	53.1	61	6	32	34	1-6	0	5.91
Andy Hawkins†	R	31	4	3	0	0	12.2	23	5	6	5	0-2	0	9.95
Mike Witt	R	30	2	2	0	0	5.1	8	1	1	0	0-1	0	10.13
Greg Cadaret	L	29	68	5	0	0	121.2	110	8	59	105	8-6	3	3.62
John Habyan	R	27	66	0	0	0	90.0	73	2	20	70	4-2	2	2.30
Lee Guetterman	L	32	64	0	0	0	88.0	91	6	25	35	3-4	6	3.68
Steve Farr	R	34	60	0	0	0	70.0	57	4	20	60	5-5	23	2.19
Eric Plunk	R	27	43	8	0	0	111.2	128	18	62	103	2-5	0	4.76
Steve Howe	L	33	37	0	0	0	48.1	39	1	7	34	3-1	3	1.68
Rich Monteleone	R	28	26	0	0	0	47.0	42	5	19	34	3-1	0	3.64
Alan Mills	R	24	6	2	0	0	16.1	16	1	8	11	1-1	0	4.41
Darrin Chapin	R	25	3	0	0	0	5.1	3	0	6	5	0-1	0	5.06
Alvaro Espinoza	R	29	1	0	0	0	0.2	0	0	0	0	0-0	0	0.00

1991 Baltimore Orioles 6th AL East 67-95 .414 24.0 GB

Frank Robinson (13-24)/Johnny Oates (54-71)

Player	Gm by Position	B	Age	G	AB	R	H	2B	3B	HR	RBI	BB	SO	SB	Avg	OBP	Slg
Chris Hoiles	C89,DH13,1B2	R	26	107	341	36	83	15	0	11	31	29	61	0	.243	.304	.384
Randy Milligan	1B106,DH25,OF9	R	29	141	483	57	127	17	2	16	70	84	108	0	.263	.373	.406
Billy Ripken	2B103	R	26	104	287	24	62	11	1	0	14	15	31	0	.216	.253	.261
Leo Gomez	3B105,DH10,1B3	R	25	118	391	40	91	17	2	16	45	40	82	1	.233	.302	.409
Cal Ripken Jr.	SS162	R	30	162	650	99	210	46	5	34	114	53	46	6	.323	.374	.566
Mike Devereaux	OF149	R	28	149	608	82	158	27	10	19	59	47	115	16	.260	.313	.431
Joe Orsulak	OF132,DH2	L	29	143	486	57	135	22	1	5	43	28	45	6	.278	.321	.358
Brady Anderson	OF101,DH3	L	27	113	256	40	59	12	3	2	27	38	44	12	.230	.338	.324
Sam Horn	DH102	L	27	121	317	45	74	16	0	23	61	41	99	0	.233	.326	.502
Dwight Evans	OF67,DH21	R	39	101	270	35	73	9	1	6	38	54	54	2	.270	.393	.378
Bob Melvin	C72,DH4	R	29	79	228	11	57	10	0	1	23	11	46	0	.250	.279	.307
Chito Martinez	OF54,DH4,1B1	L	25	67	216	32	58	12	1	13	33	11	51	1	.269	.303	.514
David Segui	1B42,OF33,DH4	S	24	86	212	15	59	7	0	2	22	12	19	1	.278	.316	.340
Juan Bell	2B77,SS15,DH4*	R	23	100	209	26	36	9	2	1	15	8	51	0	.172	.201	.249
Tim Hulett	3B39,2B26,DH15*	R	31	79	206	29	42	9	0	7	18	13	49	0	.204	.255	.350
Glenn Davis	1B36,DH12	R	30	49	176	29	40	9	1	10	28	16	29	4	.227	.307	.460
Craig Worthington	3B30	R	26	31	102	11	23	3	0	4	12	12	14	0	.225	.313	.373
Ernie Whitt	C20,DH2	L	39	35	62	5	15	2	0	0	3	8	12	0	.242	.329	.274
Luis Mercedes	OF15,DH1	R	23	19	54	10	11	2	0	0	2	4	9	0	.204	.259	.241
Jeff McKnight	OF7,DH4,1B2	S	28	16	41	2	7	1	0	0	2	2	7	1	.171	.209	.195
Jeff Tackett	C6	R	25	6	8	1	1	0	0	0	0	2	2	0	.125	.300	.125
Shane Turner	DH1,2B1	L	28	4	1	0	0	0	0	0	0	0	0	0	.000	.000	.000

J. Bell, 1 G at OF; T. Hulett, 1 G at SS

Pitcher	T	Age	G	GS	CG	ShO	IP	H	HR	BB	SO	W-L	Sv	ERA
Bob Milacki	R	26	31	26	3	1	184.0	175	17	53	108	10-9	0	4.01
Jose Mesa	R	25	23	23	2	1	123.2	151	11	62	64	6-11	0	5.97
Jeff Ballard	L	27	26	22	0	0	123.2	153	16	28	37	6-12	0	5.60
Ben McDonald	R	23	21	21	1	0	126.1	126	16	43	85	6-8	0	4.84
Jeff Robinson	R	29	21	19	0	0	104.1	119	12	51	65	4-9	0	5.18
Dave Johnson	R	31	22	14	0	0	84.0	127	18	24	38	4-8	0	7.07
Roy Smith	R	29	17	14	0	0	80.1	99	9	24	25	5-4	0	5.60
Mike Mussina	R	22	12	12	2	0	87.2	77	7	21	52	4-5	0	2.87
Arthur Rhodes	L	21	8	8	0	0	36.0	47	4	23	23	0-3	0	8.00
Gregg Olson	R	24	72	0	0	0	73.2	74	1	29	72	4-6	31	3.18
Mark Williamson	R	31	65	0	0	0	80.1	87	9	35	53	5-5	4	4.48
Mike Flanagan	L	39	64	1	0	0	98.1	84	6	25	55	2-7	3	2.38
Todd Frohwirth	R	28	51	0	0	0	96.1	64	2	29	77	7-3	3	1.87
Paul Kilgus	L	29	38	0	0	0	62.0	60	8	24	32	0-2	1	5.08
Jim Poole†	L	25	24	0	0	0	36.0	19	3	9	34	3-2	0	2.00
Kevin Hickey	L	35	19	0	0	0	14.0	15	3	6	10	1-0	0	9.00
Anthony Telford	R	25	9	1	0	0	26.2	27	3	6	24	0-0	0	4.05
Jose Bautista	R	26	5	0	0	0	5.1	13	1	5	3	0-1	0	16.88
Stacy Jones	R	24	4	1	0	0	11.0	11	1	5	10	0-0	0	4.09
F. de la Rosa	R	25	2	0	0	0	4.0	6	0	2	1	0-0	0	4.50

1991 Cleveland Indians 7th AL East 57-105 .352 34.0 GB

John McNamara (25-52)/Mike Hargrove (32-53)

Player	Gm by Position	B	Age	G	AB	R	H	2B	3B	HR	RBI	BB	SO	SB	Avg	OBP	Slg
Joel Skinner	C99	R	30	99	284	23	69	14	0	1	24	14	67	0	.243	.279	.303
Brook Jacoby†	1B55,3B15	R	31	66	231	14	54	9	1	4	24	16	32	0	.234	.289	.333
Carlos Baerga	3B89,2B75,SS2	S	22	158	593	80	171	28	2	11	69	48	74	3	.288	.346	.398
Jeff Manto	3B32,1B14,C5*	R	26	47	128	15	27	7	0	2	13	14	22	2	.211	.306	.313
Felix Fermin	SS129	R	27	129	424	30	111	13	2	0	31	26	27	5	.262	.307	.302
Alex Cole	OF107,DH6	L	25	122	387	58	114	17	3	0	21	58	47	27	.295	.386	.354
Albert Belle	OF89,DH32	R	24	123	461	60	130	31	2	28	95	25	99	3	.282	.323	.540
Mark Whiten†	OF67,DH3	S	24	70	258	34	66	14	4	7	26	19	50	4	.256	.310	.422
Chris James	DH60,OF39,1B15	R	28	115	437	31	104	16	2	5	41	18	61	3	.238	.273	.318
Mark Lewis	2B50,SS36	R	21	84	314	29	83	15	1	0	30	15	45	2	.264	.293	.318
Jerry Browne	2B47,OF17,3B15*	S	25	107	290	28	66	5	2	1	29	27	29	2	.228	.292	.269
Carlos Martinez	DH41,1B31	R	26	72	257	22	73	14	0	5	30	10	43	3	.284	.310	.397
Sandy Alomar Jr.	C46,DH4	R	25	51	184	10	40	9	0	0	7	8	24	0	.217	.264	.266
Mike Aldrete†	1B47,OF16,DH7	L	30	85	183	22	48	6	1	1	19	36	37	1	.262	.380	.322
Mike Huff†	OF48,2B2	R	27	51	146	28	35	6	1	2	10	25	30	11	.240	.364	.336
Beau Allred	OF42,DH1	L	26	48	125	17	29	3	0	3	12	25	35	2	.232	.359	.328
Glenallen Hill†	OF33,DH1	R	26	37	122	15	32	3	0	5	14	16	30	4	.262	.345	.410
Reggie Jefferson†	1B26	S	22	26	101	10	20	3	0	2	12	3	22	0	.198	.219	.287
Turner Ward†	OF38	S	26	40	100	11	23	7	0	0	5	10	16	0	.230	.300	.300
Jim Thome	3B27	L	20	27	98	7	25	4	2	1	9	5	16	1	.255	.298	.367
Luis Lopez	C12,1B10,DH6*	R	26	35	82	7	18	4	1	0	7	4	7	0	.220	.261	.293
Jose Gonzalez†	OF32	R	26	33	69	10	11	2	1	1	4	11	27	8	.159	.284	.261
Eddie Taubensee	C25	L	22	26	66	5	16	2	1	0	8	5	16	0	.242	.288	.303
Wayne Kirby	OF21	L	27	21	43	4	9	2	0	0	5	2	6	1	.209	.239	.256
Mitch Webster†	OF10	S	32	13	32	2	4	0	0	0	0	3	9	2	.125	.200	.125
Tony Perezchica†	SS6,3B3,2B2	R	25	17	22	4	8	2	0	0	0	3	5	0	.364	.440	.455
Luis Medina	DH5	R	28	5	16	0	1	0	0	0	0	1	7	0	.063	.118	.063
Jose Escobar	SS5,2B4,3B1	R	30	10	15	0	3	0	0	0	1	1	4	0	.200	.250	.200
Ever Magallanes	SS2	L	25	3	2	0	0	0	0	0	0	1	1	0	.000	.333	.000

J. Manto, 1 G at OF; J. Browne, 7 G at DH; L. Lopez, 1 G at 3B, 1 G at OF

Pitcher	T	Age	G	GS	CG	ShO	IP	H	HR	BB	SO	W-L	Sv	ERA
Greg Swindell	L	26	33	33	7	0	238.0	241	21	31	169	9-16	0	3.48
Charles Nagy	R	24	33	33	6	1	211.1	228	15	66	109	10-15	0	4.13
Eric King	R	27	25	24	2	1	150.2	166	7	44	59	6-11	0	4.60
Rod Nichols	R	26	31	16	3	1	137.1	145	6	30	76	2-11	1	3.54
Tom Candiotti†	R	33	15	15	3	0	108.1	88	6	28	86	7-6	0	2.24
Dave Otto	L	26	18	14	1	0	100.0	108	7	27	47	2-8	0	4.23
Denis Boucher†	L	23	5	5	0	0	22.2	35	6	8	13	1-4	0	8.34
Jeff Mutis	L	24	3	3	0	0	12.1	23	1	7	6	0-3	0	11.68
Mauro Gozzo	R	25	2	2	0	0	4.2	9	0	7	3	0-0	0	19.29
Shawn Hillegas	R	26	51	3	0	0	83.0	67	7	46	66	3-4	7	4.34
Steve Olin	R	25	48	0	0	0	56.1	61	2	23	38	3-6	17	3.36
Jesse Orosco	L	34	47	0	0	0	45.2	52	4	15	36	2-0	0	3.74
Doug Jones	R	34	36	4	0	0	63.1	87	7	17	48	4-8	7	5.54
Jeff Shaw	R	24	29	1	0	0	72.1	72	6	27	31	0-5	1	3.36
Mike York	R	26	14	4	0	0	34.2	45	2	19	19	1-4	0	6.75
Willie Blair	R	25	11	5	0	0	36.0	58	7	10	13	2-3	0	6.75
Eric Bell	L	27	10	0	0	0	18.0	5	0	5	7	4-0	0	0.50
Efrain Valdez	L	25	7	0	0	0	6.0	5	0	3	1	0-0	0	1.50
Garland Kiser	L	22	7	0	0	0	4.2	7	0	4	3	0-0	0	9.64
Sergio Valdez	R	26	6	0	0	0	16.1	15	3	5	11	1-0	0	5.51
Bruce Egloff	R	26	6	0	0	0	5.2	8	0	4	8	0-0	0	4.76
Rudy Seanez	R	22	5	0	0	0	5.0	10	2	7	7	0-0	0	16.20
Mike Walker	R	24	5	0	0	0	4.1	6	0	2	2	0-1	0	2.08
Tom Kramer	R	23	4	0	0	0	4.2	10	1	6	4	0-0	0	17.36

1991 Minnesota Twins 1st AL West 95-67 .586 —

Tom Kelly

Player	Gm by Position	B	Age	G	AB	R	H	2B	3B	HR	RBI	BB	SO	SB	Avg	OBP	Slg
Brian Harper	C119,DH2,1B1*	R	31	123	441	54	137	28	1	10	69	14	22	1	.311	.336	.447
Kent Hrbek	1B128	L	31	132	462	72	131	20	1	20	89	67	48	4	.284	.373	.461
Chuck Knoblauch	2B148,SS2	R	22	151	565	78	159	24	6	1	50	59	40	25	.281	.351	.350
Mike Pagliarulo	3B118,2B1	L	31	121	365	38	102	20	0	6	36	21	55	1	.279	.322	.384
Greg Gagne	SS137,DH1	R	29	139	408	52	108	23	3	8	42	26	72	11	.265	.310	.395
Kirby Puckett	OF152	R	30	152	611	92	195	29	6	15	89	31	78	11	.319	.352	.460
Shane Mack	OF140,DH1	R	27	143	442	79	137	27	8	18	74	34	79	13	.310	.363	.529
Dan Gladden	OF126	R	33	126	461	65	114	14	9	6	52	36	60	15	.247	.306	.356
Chili Davis	DH150,OF2	S	31	153	534	84	148	34	1	29	93	95	117	5	.277	.385	.507
Gene Larkin	OF47,1B39,DH4*	S	28	98	255	34	73	14	1	2	19	30	21	2	.286	.361	.373
Al Newman	SS55,2B35,3B35*	S	31	118	246	25	47	5	0	0	19	23	21	4	.191	.260	.211
Scott Leius	3B79,SS19,OF2	R	25	109	199	35	57	7	2	5	20	30	35	5	.286	.378	.417
Randy Bush	OF38,1B12,DH10	L	32	93	165	21	50	10	1	6	23	24	25	0	.303	.401	.485
Pedro Munoz	OF44,DH2	R	22	51	138	15	39	7	1	7	26	9	31	3	.283	.327	.500
Junior Ortiz	C60	R	31	61	134	9	28	5	1	0	11	15	12	0	.209	.293	.261
Paul Sorrento	1B13,DH2	L	25	26	47	6	12	2	0	4	13	4	11	0	.255	.314	.553
Jarvis Brown	OF32,DH4	R	24	38	37	10	8	0	0	0	0	2	8	7	.216	.256	.216
Lenny Webster	C17	R	26	18	34	7	10	1	0	3	8	6	10	0	.294	.390	.588
Carmelo Castillo	OF4,DH2	R	33	9	12	0	2	0	1	0	0	0	2	0	.167	.231	.333

B. Harper, 1 G at OF; G. Larkin, 1 G at 2B, 1 G at 3B; A. Newman, 3 G at DH, 1 G at 1B, 1 G at OF

Pitcher	T	Age	G	GS	CG	ShO	IP	H	HR	BB	SO	W-L	Sv	ERA
Jack Morris	R	36	35	35	10	2	246.2	226	18	92	163	18-12	0	3.43
Kevin Tapani	R	27	34	34	4	1	244.0	225	23	40	135	16-9	0	2.99
Scott Erickson	R	23	32	32	5	3	204.0	189	13	71	108	20-8	0	3.18
Allan Anderson	L	27	29	22	2	0	134.1	148	24	42	51	5-11	0	4.96
David West	L	26	15	12	0	0	71.1	66	13	28	52	4-4	0	4.54
Tom Edens	R	30	8	6	0	0	33.0	34	2	10	19	2-2	0	4.09
Willie Banks	R	22	5	3	0	0	17.1	21	1	12	16	1-1	0	5.71
Rick Aguilera	R	29	63	0	0	0	69.0	44	3	30	61	4-5	42	2.35
Steve Bedrosian	R	33	56	0	0	0	77.1	70	11	35	44	5-3	6	4.42
Terry Leach	R	37	50	0	0	0	67.1	82	3	14	32	1-2	0	3.61
Mark Guthrie	R	25	41	12	0	0	98.0	116	11	41	72	7-5	2	4.32
Carl Willis	R	30	40	0	0	0	89.0	76	4	19	53	8-3	2	2.63
Paul Abbott	R	23	15	3	0	0	47.1	38	5	36	43	3-1	0	4.75
Larry Casian	L	25	15	0	0	0	18.1	28	4	7	6	0-0	0	7.36
Gary Wayne	L	28	8	0	0	0	12.1	11	1	4	7	1-0	1	5.11
Denny Neagle	L	22	7	3	0	0	20.0	28	3	7	14	0-1	0	4.05

1991 Chicago White Sox 2nd AL West 87-75 .537 8.0 GB

Jeff Torborg

Player	Gm by Position	B	Age	G	AB	R	H	2B	3B	HR	RBI	BB	SO	SB	Avg	OBP	Slg
Carlton Fisk	C106,DH13,1B12	R	43	134	460	42	111	25	0	18	74	32	86	1	.241	.299	.413
Dan Pasqua	1B83,OF59,DH8	L	29	134	417	71	108	22	5	18	66	62	86	0	.259	.358	.465
Scott Fletcher	2B86,3B4	R	32	90	248	14	51	10	1	1	28	17	26	0	.206	.262	.266
Robin Ventura	3B151,1B31	L	23	157	606	92	172	25	1	23	100	80	67	2	.284	.367	.442
Ozzie Guillen	SS149	L	27	154	524	52	143	20	3	3	49	11	38	21	.273	.284	.340
Lance Johnson	OF158	L	27	160	588	72	161	14	13	0	49	26	58	26	.274	.304	.342
Tim Raines	OF133,DH19	S	31	155	609	102	163	20	6	5	50	83	68	51	.268	.359	.345
Sammy Sosa	OF111,DH2	R	22	116	316	39	64	10	1	10	33	14	98	13	.203	.240	.335
Frank Thomas	DH101,1B56	R	23	158	559	104	178	31	2	32	109	138	112	1	.318	.453	.553
Joey Cora	2B80,SS5,DH2	S	26	100	228	37	55	2	3	0	18	20	21	11	.241	.313	.276
Craig Grebeck	3B49,2B36,SS26	R	26	107	224	37	63	16	3	6	31	38	40	1	.281	.386	.460
Ron Karkovice	C69,OF1	R	27	75	167	25	41	13	0	5	22	15	42	0	.246	.310	.413
Matt Merullo	C27,1B16,DH6	L	25	80	140	8	32	1	0	5	21	9	18	0	.229	.268	.343
Warren Newson	OF50,DH3	L	26	71	132	20	39	5	0	4	25	28	34	2	.295	.419	.424
Cory Snyder†	OF29,1B18,DH3	R	28	50	117	10	22	4	0	3	11	6	41	0	.188	.228	.299
Mike Huff†	OF48,DH2,2B2	R	27	51	97	14	26	4	1	1	15	12	18	3	.268	.357	.361
Bo Jackson	DH21	R	28	23	71	8	16	4	0	3	14	12	25	0	.225	.333	.408
Ron Kittle	1B15	R	33	17	47	7	9	0	0	2	7	5	9	0	.191	.291	.319
Don Wakamatsu	C18	R	28	18	31	2	7	0	0	0	0	1	6	0	.226	.250	.226
Rodney McCray	OF8,DH6	R	27	17	7	2	2	0	0	0	0	0	2	1	.286	.286	.286
Esteban Beltre	SS8	R	23	8	6	0	1	0	0	0	0	1	1	1	.167	.286	.167

Pitcher	T	Age	G	GS	CG	ShO	IP	H	HR	BB	SO	W-L	Sv	ERA
Jack McDowell	R	25	35	35	15	3	253.2	212	19	82	191	17-10	0	3.41
Alex Fernandez	R	21	34	32	2	0	191.2	186	16	88	145	9-13	0	4.51
Charlie Hough	R	43	31	29	4	1	199.1	167	21	94	107	9-10	0	4.02
Greg Hibbard	L	26	32	29	5	0	194.0	196	23	57	71	11-11	0	4.31
Ramon Garcia	R	22	16	15	0	0	78.1	79	13	31	40	4-4	0	5.40
Wilson Alvarez	L	21	10	9	2	1	56.1	47	9	29	32	3-2	0	3.51
Scott Radinsky	L	23	67	0	0	0	71.1	53	4	23	49	5-5	8	2.02
Bobby Thigpen	R	27	67	0	0	0	69.2	63	10	38	47	7-5	30	3.49
Donn Pall	R	29	51	0	0	0	71.0	59	7	20	40	7-2	0	2.41
Melido Perez	R	25	49	8	0	0	135.2	111	15	52	128	8-7	1	3.12
Ken Patterson	L	26	43	0	0	0	63.2	48	5	35	32	3-0	1	2.83
Brian Drahman	R	24	28	0	0	0	30.2	21	4	13	18	3-2	0	3.23
Wayne Edwards	L	27	13	0	0	0	23.1	22	2	17	12	0-2	0	3.86
Roberto Hernandez	R	26	9	3	0	0	15.0	18	1	7	6	1-0	0	7.80
Steve Wapnick	R	25	6	0	0	0	5.0	2	0	4	1	0-1	0	1.80
Jeff Carter	R	26	5	2	0	0	12.0	8	1	5	2	0-1	0	5.25
Tom Drees	L	28	4	0	0	0	7.1	10	4	6	2	0-0	0	12.27

1991 Texas Rangers 3rd AL West 85-77 .525 10.0 GB

Bobby Valentine

Player	Gm by Position	B	Age	G	AB	R	H	2B	3B	HR	RBI	BB	SO	SB	Avg	OBP	Slg
Ivan Rodriguez	C88	R	19	88	280	24	74	16	0	3	27	5	42	0	.264	.276	.354
Rafael Palmeiro	1B157,DH2	L	26	159	631	115	203	49	3	26	88	68	72	4	.322	.389	.532
Julio Franco	2B146	R	29	146	589	108	201	27	3	15	78	65	78	36	.341	.408	.474
Steve Buechele†	3B111,2B13,SS4	R	29	121	416	58	111	17	2	18	66	39	69	0	.267	.335	.447
Jeff Huson	SS116,2B2,3B1	L	26	119	268	36	57	8	3	2	26	39	32	8	.213	.312	.287
Ruben Sierra	OF161	S	25	161	661	110	203	44	5	25	116	56	91	16	.307	.357	.502
Juan Gonzalez	OF136,DH4	R	21	142	545	78	144	34	1	27	102	42	118	4	.264	.321	.479
Gary Pettis	OF126,DH3	S	33	137	282	37	61	7	5	0	19	54	91	29	.216	.341	.277
Brian Downing	DH109	R	40	123	407	76	113	17	2	17	49	58	70	1	.278	.377	.455
Kevin Reimer	OF66,DH56	L	27	136	394	46	106	22	0	20	69	33	93	0	.269	.332	.477
Dean Palmer	3B50,OF29,DH5	R	22	81	268	38	50	9	2	15	37	32	98	0	.187	.281	.403
Geno Petralli	C66,3B7,DH5	S	31	87	199	21	54	8	1	2	20	21	25	2	.271	.339	.352
Mario Diaz	SS65,2B20,3B8*	R	29	96	182	24	48	7	0	1	22	15	18	0	.264	.318	.319
Mike Stanley	C58,1B12,DH6*	R	28	95	181	25	45	13	1	3	25	34	44	0	.249	.372	.381
Jack Daugherty	OF37,1B11,DH1	S	30	58	144	8	28	3	2	1	11	16	23	1	.194	.270	.264
Jose Hernandez	SS44,3B1	R	21	45	98	8	18	2	1	0	4	3	31	0	.184	.208	.224
Denny Walling	3B14,OF5	L	37	24	44	1	4	1	0	0	2	3	8	0	.091	.184	.114
Monty Fariss	OF8,2B4,DH3	R	23	19	31	6	8	1	0	1	6	7	11	0	.258	.395	.387
John Russell	OF8,DH5,C5	R	30	22	27	3	3	0	0	0	1	1	7	0	.111	.138	.111
Gary Green	SS8	R	29	8	20	0	3	1	0	0	1	1	6	0	.150	.190	.200
Rob Maurer	1B4,DH2	L	24	13	16	0	1	1	0	0	2	2	6	0	.063	.211	.125
Donald Harris	OF12,DH3	R	23	18	8	4	3	0	0	1	2	1	3	1	.375	.444	.750
Tony Scruggs	OF5	R	25	5	6	1	0	0	0	0	0	0	1	0	.000	.000	.000
Chad Kreuter	C1	S	26	3	4	0	0	0	0	0	0	0	1	0	.000	.000	.000
Mark Parent	C3	R	29	3	1	0	0	0	0	0	0	0	1	0	.000	.000	.000
Nick Capra	OF2	R	33	2	0	1	0	0	0	0	0	1	0	0	—	1.000	—

M. Diaz, 1 G at DH; M. Stanley, 6 G at 3B, 1 G at OF

Pitcher	T	Age	G	GS	CG	ShO	IP	H	HR	BB	SO	W-L	Sv	ERA
Kevin Brown	R	26	33	33	0	0	210.2	233	17	90	96	9-12	0	4.40
Nolan Ryan	R	44	27	27	2	2	173.0	102	12	72	203	12-6	0	2.91
Jose Guzman	R	28	25	25	5	1	169.2	152	10	84	125	13-7	0	3.08
Bobby Witt	R	27	17	16	1	1	88.2	84	4	74	82	3-7	0	6.09
Oil Can Boyd†	R	31	12	12	0	0	62.0	81	12	17	33	2-7	0	6.68
Brian Bohanon	L	22	11	11	1	0	61.1	66	4	23	34	4-3	0	4.84
Scott Chiamparino	R	24	5	5	0	0	22.1	26	1	12	8	1-0	0	4.03
Hector Fajardo†	R	20	4	3	0	0	19.0	25	2	4	15	0-2	0	5.68
Mike Jeffcoat	L	31	70	0	0	0	79.2	104	8	25	43	5-3	1	4.63
Jeff Russell	R	29	68	0	0	0	79.1	71	11	26	52	6-4	30	3.29
Kenny Rogers	L	26	63	9	0	0	109.2	121	14	61	73	10-10	5	5.42
Goose Gossage	R	39	44	0	0	0	40.1	33	4	16	28	4-2	1	3.57
Wayne Rosenthal	R	26	36	0	0	0	70.1	72	9	36	61	1-4	1	5.25
Terry Mathews	R	26	34	2	0	0	57.1	54	5	18	51	4-0	1	3.61
Gerald Alexander	R	23	30	9	0	0	89.1	93	11	48	50	5-3	0	5.24
John Barfield	L	26	28	9	0	0	83.1	96	11	22	27	4-4	1	4.54
Joe Bitker	R	27	9	0	0	0	14.2	17	4	8	16	1-0	0	6.75
Brad Arnsberg	R	27	9	0	0	0	9.2	10	5	5	8	0-1	0	8.38
Barry Manuel	R	25	8	0	0	0	16.0	7	0	6	5	1-0	0	1.13
Jim Poole†	L	25	5	0	0	0	6.0	10	0	3	4	0-0	1	4.50
Mark Petkovsek	R	25	4	1	0	0	9.1	21	4	4	6	0-1	0	14.46
Calvin Schiraldi	R	29	3	0	0	0	4.2	5	3	5	1	0-1	0	11.57
Eric Nolte†	L	27	3	0	0	0	2.2	3	0	3	1	0-0	0	3.38

1991 Oakland Athletics 4th AL West 84-78 .519 11.0 GB

Tony La Russa

Player	Gm by Position	B	Age	G	AB	R	H	2B	3B	HR	RBI	BB	SO	SB	Avg	OBP	Slg
Terry Steinbach	C117,1B9,DH2	R	29	129	456	50	125	31	1	6	67	22	70	2	.274	.312	.386
Mark McGwire	1B152	R	27	154	483	62	97	22	0	22	75	93	116	2	.201	.330	.383
Mike Gallego	2B135,SS55	R	30	159	482	67	119	15	4	12	49	67	84	6	.247	.343	.369
Ernest Riles	3B69,SS20,2B7*	L	30	108	281	30	60	8	4	5	32	31	42	3	.214	.290	.324
Mike Bordick	SS84,2B5,3B1	R	25	90	235	21	56	5	1	0	21	14	37	3	.238	.289	.268
Dave Henderson	OF140,DH7,2B1	R	32	150	572	86	158	33	0	25	85	58	113	6	.276	.346	.465
Jose Canseco	OF131,DH24	R	26	154	572	115	152	32	1	44	122	78	152	26	.266	.359	.556
Rickey Henderson	OF119,DH10	R	32	134	470	105	126	17	1	18	57	98	73	58	.268	.400	.423
Harold Baines	DH125,OF12	L	32	141	488	76	144	25	1	20	90	72	67	0	.295	.383	.473
Willie Wilson	OF87,DH9	S	35	113	294	38	70	14	4	0	28	18	43	20	.238	.290	.313
Jamie Quirk	C54,1B8,DH1*	L	36	76	203	16	53	4	0	1	17	16	28	0	.261	.321	.296
Brook Jacoby†	3B52,1B3	R	31	56	188	14	40	12	0	0	20	11	22	0	.213	.255	.277
Lance Blankenship	2B45,OF28,3B14*	R	27	90	185	33	46	8	0	3	21	23	42	12	.249	.336	.341
Vance Law	3B67,SS3,OF3*	R	34	74	134	11	28	7	1	0	9	18	27	0	.209	.303	.276
Walt Weiss	SS40	S	27	40	133	15	30	6	1	0	13	12	14	6	.226	.286	.286
Scott Brosius	2B18,OF13,3B7*	R	24	36	68	9	16	5	0	2	4	3	11	3	.235	.268	.397
Dann Howitt	OF20,1B1	L	27	21	42	5	7	1	0	1	3	1	12	0	.167	.182	.262
Brad Komminsk	OF22	R	30	24	25	1	3	1	0	0	2	2	9	1	.120	.185	.160
Scott Hemond	C8,2B7,DH4*	R	25	23	23	4	5	0	0	0	0	1	7	1	.217	.250	.217
Fred Manrique	SS7,2B2	R	29	9	21	2	3	0	0	0	0	2	1	0	.143	.217	.143
Ron Witmeyer	1B8	L	24	11	19	0	1	0	0	0	0	0	5	0	.053	.053	.053
Carney Lansford	3B4,DH1	R	34	5	16	0	1	0	0	0	1	0	2	0	.063	.063	.063
Troy Afenir	C4,DH1	R	27	5	11	0	1	0	0	0	0	0	2	0	.091	.091	.091
Doug Jennings	OF6	L	26	8	9	0	1	0	0	0	0	2	2	0	.111	.273	.111

E. Riles, 5 G at 1B; J. Quirk, 1 G at 3B; L. Blankenship, 6 G at DH; V. Law, 1 G at P, 1 G at 1B; S. Brosius, 1 G at DH; S. Hemond, 2 G at 3B, 1 G at SS

Pitcher	T	Age	G	GS	CG	ShO	IP	H	HR	BB	SO	W-L	Sv	ERA
Dave Stewart	R	34	35	35	2	1	226.0	245	24	105	144	11-11	0	5.18
Bob Welch	R	34	35	35	7	1	220.0	220	25	91	101	12-13	0	4.58
Mike Moore	R	31	33	33	3	1	210.0	176	11	105	153	17-8	0	2.96
Joe Slusarski	R	24	20	19	1	0	109.1	121	14	52	60	5-7	0	5.27
Andy Hawkins†	R	31	15	14	1	0	77.0	68	5	36	40	4-4	0	4.79
Ron Darling†	R	30	12	12	0	0	75.0	64	7	38	60	3-7	0	4.08
Kirk Dressendorfer	R	22	7	7	0	0	34.2	33	5	21	17	3-3	0	5.45
Todd Van Poppel	R	19	1	1	0	0	4.2	7	1	2	6	0-0	0	9.64
Dennis Eckersley	R	36	67	0	0	0	76.0	60	11	9	87	5-4	43	2.96
Joe Klink	L	29	62	0	0	0	62.0	60	4	21	34	10-3	2	4.35
Steve Chitren	R	24	56	0	0	0	60.1	59	8	32	47	1-4	4	4.33
Gene Nelson	R	30	44	0	0	0	48.2	60	12	23	23	1-5	0	6.84
Rick Honeycutt	L	37	43	0	0	0	37.2	37	3	20	26	2-4	0	3.58
Curt Young	L	31	41	1	0	0	68.1	74	8	34	27	4-2	0	5.00
Eric Show	R	35	23	5	0	0	51.2	62	5	17	20	1-2	0	5.92
Kevin Campbell	R	26	14	0	0	0	23.0	13	4	14	16	1-0	0	2.74
Bruce Walton	R	28	12	0	0	0	13.0	11	3	6	10	1-0	0	6.23
John Briscoe	R	23	11	0	0	0	14.0	12	3	10	9	0-0	0	7.07
Dana Allison	L	24	11	0	0	0	11.0	16	0	5	4	1-1	0	7.36
Todd Burns	R	27	9	0	0	0	13.1	10	2	8	3	1-0	0	3.38
Johnny Guzman	L	20	5	0	0	0	5.0	11	0	2	3	1-0	0	9.00
Reggie Harris	R	22	2	0	0	0	3.0	5	0	3	2	0-0	0	12.00
Vance Law	R	34	1	0	0	0	0.2	1	0	1	0	0-0	0	0.00

1991 Seattle Mariners 5th AL West 83-79 .512 12.0 GB

Jim Lefebvre

Player	Gm by Position	B	Age	G	AB	R	H	2B	3B	HR	RBI	BB	SO	SB	Avg	OBP	Slg
Dave Valle	C129,1B2	R	30	132	324	38	63	8	1	8	32	34	49	0	.194	.286	.299
Pete O'Brien	1B132,DH18,OF13	L	33	152	560	58	139	29	3	17	88	44	61	0	.248	.300	.402
Harold Reynolds	2B159,DH1	S	30	161	631	95	160	34	6	3	57	72	63	28	.254	.332	.341
Edgar Martinez	3B144,DH2	R	28	150	544	98	167	35	1	14	52	84	72	0	.307	.405	.452
Omar Vizquel	SS138,2B1	S	24	142	426	42	98	16	4	1	41	45	37	7	.230	.302	.293
Ken Griffey Jr.	OF152,DH1	L	21	154	548	76	179	42	1	22	100	71	82	18	.327	.399	.527
Jay Buhner	OF131	R	26	137	406	64	99	14	4	27	77	53	117	0	.244	.337	.498
Greg Briley	OF125,DH2,2B1*	L	26	139	381	39	99	17	3	2	26	27	51	23	.260	.307	.336
Alvin Davis	DH126,1B14	L	30	145	462	39	102	15	1	12	69	56	78	0	.221	.299	.335
Dave Cochrane	OF26,C19,3B13*	S	28	65	178	16	44	13	0	2	22	9	38	0	.247	.286	.354
Henry Cotto	OF56,DH6	R	30	66	177	35	54	6	2	6	23	10	27	16	.305	.347	.463
Tracy Jones	DH37,OF36	R	30	79	175	30	44	8	1	3	24	18	22	2	.251	.321	.360
Scott Bradley	C65,3B4,DH2*	L	31	83	172	10	35	7	0	0	11	19	19	0	.203	.280	.244
Jeff Schaefer	SS46,3B30,2B11	R	31	84	164	19	41	7	1	1	11	5	25	3	.250	.272	.323
Tino Martinez	1B29,DH5	L	23	36	112	11	23	2	0	4	9	11	24	0	.205	.272	.330
Alonzo Powell	OF40,DH7,1B7	R	26	57	111	16	24	6	1	3	12	11	24	0	.216	.288	.369
Ken Griffey Sr.	OF26,DH1	L	41	30	85	10	24	7	0	1	9	13	13	0	.282	.380	.400
Rich Amaral	2B5,DH2,3B2*	R	29	14	16	2	1	0	0	0	0	1	5	0	.063	.167	.063
Matt Sinatro	C5	R	31	5	8	1	2	0	0	0	1	1	1	0	.250	.333	.250
Patrick Lennon	DH5,OF1	R	23	9	8	2	1	1	0	0	1	3	1	0	.125	.364	.250
Chris Howard	C9	R	25	9	6	1	1	1	0	0	0	1	2	0	.167	.286	.333

G. Briley, 1 G at 3B; D. Cochrane, 4 G at 1B, 1 G at DH; S. Bradley, 1 G at 1B; R. Amaral, 2 G at SS, 1 G at 1B

Pitcher	T	Age	G	GS	CG	ShO	IP	H	HR	BB	SO	W-L	Sv	ERA
Randy Johnson	L	27	33	33	2	1	201.1	151	15	152	228	13-10	0	3.98
Rich DeLucia	R	26	32	31	0	0	182.0	176	31	78	98	12-13	0	5.09
Brian Holman	R	26	30	30	5	3	195.1	199	16	77	108	13-14	0	3.69
Erik Hanson	R	26	27	27	2	1	174.2	182	16	56	143	8-8	0	3.81
Bill Krueger	L	33	35	25	1	0	175.0	194	15	60	91	11-8	0	3.60
Scott Bankhead	R	27	17	9	0	0	60.2	73	8	21	28	3-6	0	4.90
Mike Jackson	R	26	72	0	0	0	88.2	64	5	34	74	7-7	14	3.25
Bill Swift	R	29	71	0	0	0	90.1	74	3	26	48	1-2	17	1.99
Russ Swan	L	27	63	0	0	0	78.2	81	8	28	33	6-2	2	3.43
Rob Murphy	L	31	57	0	0	0	48.0	47	4	19	34	0-1	4	3.00
Mike Schooler	R	28	34	0	0	0	34.1	25	2	10	31	3-3	7	3.67
Calvin Jones	R	27	27	0	0	0	46.1	33	0	29	42	2-2	2	2.53
Dave Burba	R	24	22	2	0	0	36.2	34	6	14	16	2-2	1	3.68
Dave Fleming	L	21	9	3	0	0	17.2	19	3	3	11	1-0	0	6.62
Gene Harris	R	26	8	0	0	0	13.1	15	1	10	6	0-0	1	4.05
Pat Rice	R	27	7	2	0	0	21.0	18	3	10	12	1-1	0	3.00
Keith Comstock	L	35	1	0	0	0	0.1	2	0	1	0	0-0	0	54.00

1991 Kansas City Royals 6th AL West 82-80 .506 13.0 GB

John Wathan (15-22)/Bob Schaefer (1-0)/Hal McRae (66-58)

Player	Gm by Position	B	Age	G	AB	R	H	2B	3B	HR	RBI	BB	SO	SB	Avg	OBP	Slg
Brent Mayne	C80,DH1	L	23	85	231	22	58	8	0	3	31	23	42	2	.251	.315	.325
Todd Benzinger†	1B75,DH1	S	28	78	293	29	86	15	3	2	40	17	46	2	.294	.338	.386
Terry Shumpert	2B144	R	24	144	369	45	80	16	4	5	34	30	75	17	.217	.283	.322
Bill Pecota	3B102,2B34,SS9*	R	31	125	398	53	114	23	2	6	45	41	45	16	.286	.356	.399
Kurt Stillwell	SS118	S	26	122	385	44	102	17	1	6	51	33	56	3	.265	.322	.361
Brian McRae	OF150	S	23	152	629	86	164	28	9	8	64	24	99	20	.261	.288	.372
Danny Tartabull	OF124,DH6	R	28	132	484	78	153	35	3	31	100	65	121	6	.316	.397	.593
Jim Eisenreich	OF105,1B15,DH1	L	32	135	375	47	113	22	3	2	47	20	35	5	.301	.333	.392
George Brett	DH118,1B10	L	38	131	505	77	129	40	2	10	61	58	75	2	.255	.327	.402
Kirk Gibson	OF94,DH30	L	34	132	462	81	109	17	6	16	55	69	103	18	.236	.341	.403
Mike Macfarlane	C69,DH4	R	27	84	267	34	74	18	2	13	41	17	52	1	.277	.330	.506
Dave Howard	SS63,2B26,DH1*	S	24	94	236	20	51	7	0	1	17	16	45	3	.216	.267	.258
Kevin Seitzer	3B68,DH3	R	29	85	234	28	62	11	3	1	25	29	21	4	.265	.350	.350
Gary Thurman	OF72	R	26	80	184	24	51	9	0	2	13	11	42	15	.277	.320	.359
Warren Cromartie	1B29,OF6,DH1	L	37	69	131	13	41	7	2	1	20	15	18	1	.313	.381	.420
Carmelo Martinez†	1B43,DH1	R	30	44	121	17	25	6	0	4	17	27	25	0	.207	.351	.355
Tim Spehr	C37	R	24	37	74	7	14	5	0	3	14	9	18	1	.189	.282	.378
Sean Berry	3B30	R	25	31	60	5	8	3	0	0	1	5	23	0	.133	.212	.183
Harvey Pulliam	OF15	R	23	18	33	4	9	1	0	3	4	3	9	0	.273	.333	.576
Russ Morman	1B8,OF2,DH1	R	29	12	23	1	6	0	0	0	1	1	5	0	.261	.292	.261
Nelson Liriano	2B10	S	27	10	22	5	9	0	0	0	1	0	2	0	.409	.409	.409
Jorge Pedre	C9,1B1	R	24	10	19	2	5	1	1	0	3	3	5	0	.263	.364	.421
Terry Puhl	DH2,OF1	L	34	15	18	0	4	0	0	0	3	3	2	0	.222	.333	.222
Bobby Moore	OF13	R	25	18	14	3	5	1	0	0	0	1	2	3	.357	.400	.429
Dave Clark	DH1,OF1	L	28	11	10	1	2	0	0	0	1	1	1	0	.200	.273	.200
Stu Cole	2B5,DH2,SS1	R	25	9	7	1	1	0	0	0	0	2	2	0	.143	.333	.143
Paul Zuvella	3B2	R	32	2	0	0	0	0	0	0	0	0	0	0	—	—	—

B. Pecota, 8 G at 1B, 2 G at DH, 1 G at P, 1 G at OF; D. Howard, 1 G at 3B, 1 G at OF

Pitcher	T	Age	G	GS	CG	ShO	IP	H	HR	BB	SO	W-L	Sv	ERA
Kevin Appier	R	23	34	31	6	3	207.2	205	13	61	158	13-10	0	3.42
Mike Boddicker	R	33	30	29	1	0	180.2	188	13	59	79	12-12	0	4.08
Bret Saberhagen	R	27	28	28	7	2	196.1	165	12	45	136	13-8	0	3.07
Mark Gubicza	R	28	26	26	0	0	133.0	168	10	42	89	9-12	0	5.68
Hector Wagner	R	22	2	2	0	0	10.0	16	2	3	5	1-1	0	7.20
Jeff Montgomery	R	29	67	0	0	0	90.0	83	6	28	77	4-4	33	2.90
Storm Davis	R	29	51	9	1	1	114.1	140	11	46	53	3-9	2	4.96
Tom Gordon	R	23	45	14	1	0	158.0	129	16	87	167	9-14	1	3.87
Luis Aquino	R	27	38	18	1	1	157.0	152	10	47	80	8-4	3	3.44
Mike Magnante	L	26	38	0	0	0	55.0	55	3	23	42	0-1	0	2.45
Steve Crawford	R	33	33	0	0	0	46.2	60	3	18	38	3-2	1	5.98
Mark Davis	L	30	29	5	0	0	62.2	55	6	39	47	6-3	1	4.45
Joel Johnston	R	24	13	0	0	0	22.1	9	0	9	21	1-0	0	0.40
Dan Schatzeder	L	36	8	0	0	0	6.2	11	0	7	4	0-0	0	9.45
Carlos Maldonado	R	24	5	0	0	0	7.2	11	0	9	1	0-0	0	8.22
Andy McGaffigan	R	34	4	0	0	0	8.0	14	0	2	3	0-0	0	4.50
Wes Gardner†	R	30	3	0	0	0	5.2	5	0	2	3	0-0	0	1.59
Archie Corbin	R	23	2	0	0	0	2.1	3	0	2	1	0-0	0	3.86
Bill Pecota	R	31	1	0	0	0	2.0	4	0	0	0	0-0	0	4.50

1991 California Angels 7th AL West 81-81 .500 14.0 GB

Doug Rader (61-63)/Buck Rodgers (20-18)

Player	Gm by Position	B	Age	G	AB	R	H	2B	3B	HR	RBI	BB	SO	SB	Avg	OBP	Slg
Lance Parrish	C111,DH5,1B3	R	35	119	402	38	87	12	0	19	51	35	117	0	.216	.285	.388
Wally Joyner	1B141	L	29	143	551	79	166	34	3	21	96	52	66	2	.301	.360	.488
Luis Sojo	2B107,SS2,DH1*	R	25	113	364	38	94	14	1	3	20	14	26	4	.258	.295	.327
Gary Gaetti	3B152	R	32	152	586	58	144	22	1	18	66	33	104	5	.246	.293	.379
Dick Schofield	SS133	R	28	134	427	44	96	9	3	0	31	50	69	8	.225	.310	.260
Luis Polonia	OF143,DH4	L	26	150	604	92	179	28	8	2	50	52	74	48	.296	.352	.379
Dave Winfield	OF115,DH34	R	39	150	568	75	149	27	4	28	86	56	109	7	.262	.326	.472
Dave Gallagher	OF87,DH2	R	30	90	270	32	79	17	0	1	30	24	43	2	.293	.355	.367
Dave Parker†	DH119	L	40	119	466	45	108	22	2	11	56	29	91	3	.232	.279	.358
Junior Felix	OF65	S	23	66	230	32	65	10	2	2	26	11	55	7	.283	.321	.370
Donnie Hill	2B39,SS29,1B3	S	30	77	209	36	50	8	1	1	20	30	21	1	.239	.335	.301
Max Venable	OF65,DH3	L	34	82	187	24	46	8	2	3	21	11	30	2	.246	.292	.358
Ron Tingley	C45	R	32	45	115	11	23	7	0	1	13	8	34	1	.200	.258	.287
Shawn Abner†	OF38	R	25	41	101	12	23	6	1	2	9	4	18	1	.228	.257	.366
Jack Howell†	2B12,3B8,OF5*	L	29	32	81	11	17	2	0	2	7	11	11	1	.210	.304	.309
John Orton	C28	R	25	29	69	7	14	4	0	0	3	10	17	0	.203	.313	.261
Bobby Rose	2B8,OF7,3B4*	R	24	22	65	5	18	5	1	1	8	3	13	0	.277	.304	.431
Lee Stevens	1B11,OF9	L	23	18	58	8	17	7	0	0	9	6	12	1	.293	.354	.414
Gary DiSarcina	SS10,2B7,3B2	R	23	18	57	5	12	2	0	0	3	3	4	0	.211	.274	.246
Ruben Amaro	OF5,2B4,DH1	S	26	10	23	0	5	1	0	0	2	3	3	0	.217	.308	.261
Chris Cron	1B5,DH1	R	27	6	15	0	2	0	0	0	0	2	5	0	.133	.235	.133
Kevin Flora	2B3	R	22	3	8	1	1	0	0	0	0	1	5	1	.125	.222	.125
Mike Marshall†	DH1,1B1	R	31	2	7	0	0	0	0	0	0	0	1	0	.000	.000	.000
Barry Lyons†	1B2	R	31	2	5	0	1	0	0	0	0	0	0	0	.200	.200	.200
Mark Davis	OF3	R	26	3	2	0	0	0	0	0	0	0	0	0	.000	.000	.000

L. Sojo, 1 G at 3B, 1 G at OF; J. Howell, 3 G at 1B, 1 G at DH; B. Rose, 3 G at 1B

Pitcher	T	Age	G	GS	CG	ShO	IP	H	HR	BB	SO	W-L	Sv	ERA
Mark Langston	L	30	34	34	7	0	246.1	190	30	96	183	19-8	0	3.00
Jim Abbott	L	23	34	34	5	1	243.0	222	14	73	158	18-11	0	2.89
Chuck Finley	L	28	34	34	4	2	227.1	205	23	101	171	18-9	0	3.80
Kirk McCaskill	R	30	30	30	1	0	177.2	193	19	66	71	10-19	0	4.26
Scott Lewis	R	25	16	11	0	0	60.1	81	9	21	37	3-5	0	6.27
Joe Grahe	R	24	18	10	1	0	73.0	84	2	33	40	3-7	0	4.81
Kyle Abbott	L	23	5	3	0	0	19.2	22	2	13	12	1-2	0	4.58
F. Valenzuela	L	30	2	2	0	0	6.2	14	3	3	5	0-2	0	12.15
Mark Eichhorn	R	30	70	0	0	0	81.2	63	2	13	49	3-3	1	1.98
Bryan Harvey	R	28	67	0	0	0	78.2	51	6	17	101	2-4	46	1.60
Scott Bailes	L	29	42	0	0	0	51.2	41	5	22	41	1-2	0	4.18
Jeff Robinson	R	30	39	0	0	0	57.0	56	9	29	57	0-3	3	5.37
Chris Beasley	R	29	22	0	0	0	26.2	26	2	10	14	0-1	0	3.38
Mike Fetters	R	26	19	4	0	0	44.2	53	4	28	24	2-5	0	4.84
Floyd Bannister	L	36	16	0	0	0	25.0	25	5	10	16	0-0	0	3.96
Bob McClure†	L	39	13	0	0	0	9.2	13	3	5	5	0-0	0	9.31
Cliff Young	L	26	11	0	0	0	12.2	12	3	3	6	1-0	0	4.26

»1991 Pittsburgh Pirates 1st NL East 98-64 .605 —

Jim Leyland

Player	Gm by Position	B	Age	G	AB	R	H	2B	3B	HR	RBI	BB	SO	SB	Avg	OBP	Slg
Mike LaValliere	C105	L	30	108	336	25	97	11	2	3	41	33	27	2	.289	.351	.360
Orlando Merced	1B105,OF7	S	24	120	411	83	113	17	2	10	50	64	81	8	.275	.373	.399
Jose Lind	2B149	R	27	150	502	53	133	16	6	3	54	30	56	7	.265	.306	.339
Bobby Bonilla	OF104,3B67,1B4	S	28	157	577	102	174	44	6	18	100	90	67	2	.302	.391	.492
Jay Bell	SS156	R	25	157	608	96	164	32	8	16	67	52	99	10	.270	.330	.428
Barry Bonds	OF150	L	26	153	510	95	149	28	5	25	116	107	73	43	.292	.410	.514
Andy Van Slyke	OF135	L	30	138	491	87	130	24	7	17	83	71	85	10	.265	.355	.446
Gary Varsho	OF54,1B3	L	30	99	187	23	51	11	2	4	23	19	34	9	.273	.344	.417
Gary Redus	1B47,OF33	R	34	98	252	45	62	12	2	7	24	28	39	17	.246	.324	.393
Don Slaught	C69,3B1	R	32	77	220	19	65	17	1	1	29	21	32	1	.295	.363	.395
Curtis Wilkerson	2B30,SS15,3B14	S	30	85	191	20	36	9	1	2	18	15	40	2	.188	.243	.277
Lloyd McClendon	OF32,1B22,C2	R	32	85	163	24	47	7	0	7	24	18	23	2	.288	.366	.460
Steve Buechele†	3B31	R	29	31	114	16	28	5	1	4	19	10	28	0	.246	.315	.412
Jeff King	3B33	R	26	33	109	16	26	1	1	4	18	14	15	3	.239	.328	.376
John Wehner	3B36	R	24	37	106	15	36	7	0	0	7	7	17	3	.340	.381	.406
Mitch Webster†	OF29	S	32	36	97	9	17	3	4	1	9	9	31	0	.175	.245	.320
Cecil Espy	OF35	S	28	43	82	7	20	4	0	1	11	5	17	4	.244	.281	.329
Tom Prince	C19,1B1	R	26	26	34	4	9	3	0	1	2	7	3	0	.265	.405	.441
Carlos Garcia	SS9,3B2,2B1	R	23	12	24	2	6	0	2	0	1	1	8	0	.250	.280	.417
Jose Gonzalez†	OF14	R	26	16	20	2	2	0	0	1	3	0	6	0	.100	.095	.250
Joe Redfield	3B9	R	30	11	18	1	2	0	0	0	0	4	1	0	.111	.273	.111
Carmelo Martinez†	1B8	R	30	11	16	1	4	0	0	0	0	1	2	0	.250	.294	.250
Jeff Richardson	3B3,SS2	R	25	6	4	0	1	0	0	0	0	0	3	0	.250	.250	.250
Scott Bullett	OF3	S	22	11	4	2	0	0	0	0	0	0	3	1	.000	.200	.000
Jeff Schulz		L	30	3	3	0	0	0	0	0	0	0	2	0	.000	.000	.000
Jeff Banister		R	26	1	1	0	1	0	0	0	0	0	0	0	1.000	1.000	1.000

Pitcher	T	Age	G	GS	CG	ShO	IP	H	HR	BB	SO	W-L	Sv	ERA
Doug Drabek	R	28	35	35	5	2	234.2	245	16	62	142	15-14	0	3.07
Zane Smith	L	30	35	35	6	3	228.0	234	15	29	120	16-10	0	3.20
John Smiley	L	26	33	32	2	1	207.2	194	17	44	129	20-8	0	3.08
Randy Tomlin	L	25	31	27	4	2	175.0	170	9	54	104	8-7	0	2.98
Bob Walk	R	34	25	20	0	0	115.0	104	10	35	67	9-2	0	3.60
Hector Fajardo†	R	20	2	2	0	0	6.1	10	0	7	8	0-0	0	9.95
Paul Miller	R	26	1	1	0	0	5.0	4	0	3	2	0-0	0	5.40
Rick Reed	R	26	1	1	0	0	4.1	8	1	1	2	0-0	0	10.38
Bill Landrum	R	33	61	0	0	0	76.1	76	4	19	45	4-4	17	3.18
Stan Belinda	R	24	60	0	0	0	78.1	50	10	35	71	7-5	16	3.45
Bob Patterson	L	32	54	1	0	0	65.2	67	7	15	57	4-3	2	4.11
Bob Kipper	L	26	52	0	0	0	60.0	66	7	22	38	2-2	4	4.65
Neal Heaton	L	31	42	1	0	0	68.2	72	6	21	34	3-3	0	4.33
Vicente Palacios	R	27	36	7	1	1	81.2	69	12	38	64	6-3	3	3.75
Roger Mason	R	32	24	0	0	0	29.2	21	2	6	21	3-2	3	3.03
Rosario Rodriguez	L	21	18	0	0	0	15.1	14	1	8	10	1-1	6	4.11
Mark Huismann	R	33	5	0	0	0	5.0	7	0	2	5	0-0	0	7.20

1991 St. Louis Cardinals 2nd NL East 84-78 .519 14.0 GB

Joe Torre

Player	Gm by Position	B	Age	G	AB	R	H	2B	3B	HR	RBI	BB	SO	SB	Avg	OBP	Slg
Tom Pagnozzi	C139,1B3	R	28	140	459	38	121	24	5	2	57	36	63	9	.264	.319	.351
Pedro Guerrero	1B112	R	35	115	427	41	116	12	1	8	70	37	46	4	.272	.326	.361
Jose Oquendo	2B118,SS22,1B3*	S	27	127	366	37	88	11	4	1	26	67	48	1	.240	.357	.301
Todd Zeile	3B154	R	25	155	565	76	158	36	3	11	81	62	94	17	.280	.353	.412
Ozzie Smith	SS150	S	36	150	550	96	157	30	3	3	50	83	36	35	.285	.380	.367
Felix Jose	OF153	S	26	154	568	69	173	40	6	8	77	50	113	20	.305	.360	.438
Ray Lankford	OF149	L	24	151	566	83	142	23	15	9	69	41	114	44	.251	.301	.392
Milt Thompson	OF91	L	32	115	326	55	100	16	5	6	34	32	53	16	.307	.368	.442
Bernard Gilkey	OF74	R	24	81	268	28	58	7	2	5	20	39	33	14	.216	.316	.313
Gerald Perry	1B61,OF5	L	30	109	242	29	58	8	4	6	36	22	34	15	.240	.300	.380
Rex Hudler	OF58,1B12,2B5	R	30	101	207	21	47	10	2	1	15	10	29	12	.227	.260	.309
Geronimo Pena	2B83,OF4	S	24	104	185	38	45	8	3	5	17	18	45	15	.243	.322	.400
Rich Gedman	C43	L	31	46	94	7	10	1	0	3	8	4	15	0	.106	.140	.213
Craig Wilson	3B12,OF5,1B4*	R	26	60	82	5	14	2	0	0	13	6	10	0	.171	.222	.195
Luis Alicea	2B11,3B2,SS1	S	25	56	68	5	13	3	0	0	0	8	19	0	.191	.276	.235
Tim Jones	SS14,2B4	L	28	16	24	1	4	2	0	0	2	2	6	0	.167	.222	.250
Stan Royer	3B5	R	23	9	21	1	6	1	0	0	1	1	2	0	.286	.318	.333
Rod Brewer	1B15,OF3	L	25	19	13	0	1	0	0	0	1	0	5	0	.077	.077	.077
Ray Stephens	C6	R	28	6	7	0	2	0	0	0	0	1	3	0	.286	.375	.286

J. Oquendo, 1 G at P; C. Wilson, 3 G at 2B

Pitcher	T	Age	G	GS	CG	ShO	IP	H	HR	BB	SO	W-L	Sv	ERA
Bryn Smith	R	35	31	31	3	0	198.2	188	16	45	94	12-9	0	3.85
Bob Tewksbury	R	30	30	30	3	0	191.0	206	13	38	75	11-12	0	3.25
Ken Hill	R	25	30	30	0	0	181.1	147	15	67	121	11-10	0	3.57
Jose DeLeon	R	30	28	28	1	0	162.2	144	15	61	118	5-9	0	2.71
Omar Olivares	R	23	28	24	0	0	167.1	148	13	61	91	11-7	1	3.71
Rheal Cormier	L	24	11	10	2	0	67.2	74	5	8	38	4-5	0	4.12
Jamie Moyer	L	28	8	7	0	0	31.1	38	5	16	20	0-5	0	5.74
Juan Agosto	L	33	72	0	0	0	86.0	92	4	39	34	5-3	2	4.81
Lee Smith	R	33	67	0	0	0	73.0	70	5	13	67	6-3	47	2.34
Scott Terry	R	31	65	0	0	0	80.1	76	1	32	52	4-4	1	2.80
Cris Carpenter	R	26	59	0	0	0	66.0	53	6	20	47	10-4	0	4.23
Willie Fraser†	R	27	35	0	0	0	49.1	44	9	21	25	3-3	0	4.93
Bob McClure†	L	39	32	0	0	0	23.0	24	1	8	15	1-1	0	3.13
Mike Perez	R	26	14	0	0	0	17.0	19	1	7	7	0-2	0	5.82
Tim Sherrill	L	25	10	0	0	0	14.1	20	2	3	4	0-0	0	8.16
Mark Clark	R	23	7	2	0	0	22.1	17	3	11	13	1-1	0	4.03
Mark Grater	R	27	3	0	0	0	3.0	5	0	2	0	0-0	0	0.00
Jose Oquendo	R	27	1	0	0	0	1.0	2	0	2	1	0-0	0	27.00

1991 Philadelphia Phillies 3rd NL East 78-84 .481 20.0 GB

Nick Leyva (4-9)/Jim Fregosi (74-75)

Player	Gm by Position	B	Age	G	AB	R	H	2B	3B	HR	RBI	BB	SO	SB	Avg	OBP	Slg
Darren Daulton	C88	L	29	89	285	36	56	12	0	12	42	41	66	5	.196	.297	.365
John Kruk	1B102,OF52	L	30	152	538	84	158	27	6	21	92	67	100	7	.294	.367	.483
Mickey Morandini	2B97	L	25	98	325	38	81	11	4	1	20	29	45	13	.249	.313	.317
Charlie Hayes	3B138,SS2	R	26	142	460	34	106	23	1	12	53	16	75	3	.230	.257	.363
Dickie Thon	SS146	R	33	146	539	44	136	18	4	9	44	25	84	11	.252	.283	.351
Dale Murphy	OF147	R	35	153	544	66	137	33	1	18	81	48	93	1	.252	.309	.415
Wes Chamberlain	OF98	R	25	101	383	51	92	16	3	13	50	31	73	9	.240	.300	.399
Von Hayes	OF72	L	32	77	284	43	64	15	1	0	21	31	42	9	.225	.303	.285
Ricky Jordan	1B72	R	26	101	301	38	82	21	3	9	49	14	49	0	.272	.304	.452
Lenny Dykstra	OF63	L	28	63	246	48	73	13	5	3	12	37	20	24	.297	.391	.427
Randy Ready	2B66	R	31	76	205	32	51	10	1	1	20	47	25	2	.249	.385	.322
Wally Backman	2B36,3B20	S	31	94	185	20	45	12	0	0	15	30	30	3	.243	.344	.308
Steve Lake	C58	R	34	58	158	12	36	4	1	1	11	2	26	0	.228	.238	.285
Dave Hollins	3B36,1B6	S	25	56	151	18	45	10	2	6	21	17	26	1	.298	.378	.510
Darrin Fletcher	C45	L	24	46	136	5	31	8	0	1	12	5	15	0	.228	.255	.309
John Morris	OF57	L	30	85	127	15	28	2	1	1	6	12	25	2	.220	.293	.276
Jim Lindeman	OF30,1B1	R	29	65	95	13	32	5	0	0	12	13	14	0	.337	.413	.389
Rod Booker	SS20,3B3	L	32	28	53	3	12	1	0	0	7	1	7	0	.226	.236	.245
Braulio Castillo	OF26	R	23	28	52	3	9	3	0	0	2	1	15	1	.173	.189	.231
Sil Campusano	OF15	R	25	15	35	2	4	0	0	1	2	1	10	0	.114	.139	.200
Kim Batiste	SS7	R	23	10	27	2	6	0	0	0	1	1	8	0	.222	.250	.222
Ron Jones		L	27	28	26	0	4	2	0	0	3	2	9	0	.154	.214	.231
Rick Schu	3B3,1B1	R	29	17	22	1	2	0	0	0	2	1	7	0	.091	.125	.091
Doug Lindsey	C1	R	23	1	3	0	0	0	0	0	0	0	3	0	.000	.000	.000

Pitcher	T	Age	G	GS	CG	ShO	IP	H	HR	BB	SO	W-L	Sv	ERA
Terry Mulholland	L	28	34	34	8	3	232.0	231	15	49	142	16-13	0	3.61
Jose DeJesus	R	26	31	29	3	0	181.2	147	7	128	118	10-9	1	3.42
Tommy Greene	R	24	36	27	3	2	207.2	177	19	66	154	13-7	0	3.38
Danny Cox	R	31	23	17	0	0	102.1	98	14	39	46	4-6	0	4.57
Pat Combs	L	24	14	13	1	0	64.1	64	7	43	41	2-6	0	4.90
Jason Grimsley	R	23	12	12	0	0	61.0	54	4	41	42	1-7	0	4.87
Andy Ashby	R	23	8	8	0	0	42.0	41	5	19	26	1-5	0	6.00
Cliff Brantley	R	23	6	5	0	0	31.2	26	0	19	25	2-2	0	3.41
Dave LaPoint	L	31	2	2	0	0	5.0	10	0	6	3	0-1	0	16.20
Mitch Williams	L	26	69	0	0	0	88.1	56	4	62	84	12-5	30	2.34
Joe Boever	R	30	68	0	0	0	98.1	90	10	54	89	3-5	0	3.84
Wally Ritchie	L	25	39	0	0	0	50.1	44	4	17	26	1-2	0	2.50
Roger McDowell†	R	30	38	0	0	0	59.0	61	1	32	28	3-6	3	3.20
Bruce Ruffin	L	27	31	15	1	1	119.0	125	6	38	85	4-7	0	3.78
Darrel Akerfelds	R	29	30	0	0	0	49.2	49	5	27	31	2-1	0	5.26
Steve Searcy†	L	27	18	0	0	0	30.1	29	2	14	21	2-1	0	4.15
Mike Hartley†	R	29	18	0	0	0	26.1	21	4	10	19	2-1	1	3.76
Tim Mauser	R	24	3	0	0	0	10.2	18	3	3	6	0-0	0	7.59
Amalio Carreno	R	27	3	0	0	0	3.1	5	1	3	2	0-0	0	16.20

1991 Chicago Cubs 4th NL East 77-83 .481 20.0 GB

Don Zimmer (18-19)/Joe Altobelli (0-1)/Jim Essian (59-63)

Player	Gm by Position	B	Age	G	AB	R	H	2B	3B	HR	RBI	BB	SO	SB	Avg	OBP	Slg
Rick Wilkins	C82	L	24	86	203	21	45	9	0	6	22	19	56	3	.222	.307	.355
Mark Grace	1B160	L	27	160	619	87	169	28	5	8	58	70	53	3	.273	.346	.373
Ryne Sandberg	2B157	R	31	158	585	104	170	32	2	26	100	87	89	22	.291	.379	.485
Luis Salazar	3B86,1B7,OF1	R	35	103	333	34	86	14	1	14	38	15	45	0	.258	.292	.432
Shawon Dunston	SS142	R	28	142	492	59	128	22	7	12	50	23	64	21	.260	.292	.407
George Bell	OF146	R	31	149	558	63	159	27	0	25	86	32	62	2	.285	.323	.468
Andre Dawson	OF137	R	36	149	563	69	153	21	4	31	104	22	80	4	.272	.302	.488
Jerome Walton	OF101	R	25	123	270	42	59	13	1	5	17	19	55	7	.219	.275	.330
Chico Walker	3B57,OF53,2B6	S	33	124	374	51	96	10	1	6	34	33	57	13	.257	.315	.337
Doug Dascenzo	OF86,P3	S	27	118	239	40	61	11	0	1	18	24	26	14	.255	.327	.314
Hector Villanueva	C55,1B6	R	26	71	192	23	53	10	1	13	32	21	30	0	.276	.346	.542
Dwight Smith	OF42	L	27	90	167	16	38	7	2	3	21	11	32	2	.228	.279	.347
Damon Berryhill†	C48	S	27	62	159	13	30	7	0	5	14	11	41	1	.189	.244	.327
Jose Vizcaino	3B57,SS33,2B9	S	23	93	145	7	38	5	0	0	10	5	18	2	.262	.283	.297
Ced Landrum	OF44	L	27	56	86	28	20	2	1	0	6	10	18	27	.233	.313	.279
Gary Scott	3B31	R	22	31	79	8	13	3	0	1	5	13	14	0	.165	.305	.241
Joe Girardi	C21	R	26	21	47	3	9	2	0	0	6	6	6	0	.191	.283	.234
Rey Sanchez	SS10,2B2	R	23	13	23	1	6	0	0	0	2	4	3	0	.261	.370	.261
Derrick May	OF7	L	22	15	22	4	5	2	0	1	3	2	1	0	.227	.280	.455
Erik Pappas	C6	R	25	7	17	1	3	0	0	0	2	1	5	0	.176	.222	.176
Doug Strange	3B3	S	27	3	9	0	4	1	0	0	1	0	1	1	.444	.455	.556

Pitcher	T	Age	G	GS	CG	ShO	IP	H	HR	BB	SO	W-L	Sv	ERA
Greg Maddux	R	25	37	37	7	2	263.0	232	18	66	198	15-11	0	3.35
Mike Bielecki†	R	31	39	25	0	0	172.0	169	18	54	72	13-11	0	4.50
Shawn Boskie	R	24	28	20	0	0	129.0	150	14	52	62	4-9	0	5.23
Frank Castillo	R	22	18	18	4	0	111.2	107	5	33	73	6-7	0	4.35
Rick Sutcliffe	R	35	19	18	0	0	96.2	96	4	45	52	6-5	0	4.10
Danny Jackson	L	29	17	14	0	0	70.2	89	8	48	31	1-5	0	6.75
Mike Harkey	R	24	4	4	0	0	18.2	21	3	6	15	0-2	0	5.30
Paul Assenmacher	L	30	75	0	0	0	102.2	85	10	31	117	7-8	15	3.24
Chuck McElroy	L	23	71	0	0	0	101.1	73	7	57	92	6-2	3	1.95
Les Lancaster	R	29	64	11	1	0	156.0	150	13	49	102	9-7	3	3.52
Heathcliff Slocumb	R	25	52	0	0	0	62.2	53	3	30	34	2-1	1	3.45
Bob Scanlan	R	24	40	13	0	0	111.0	114	5	40	44	7-8	1	3.89
Dave Smith	R	36	35	0	0	0	33.0	39	6	19	16	0-6	17	6.00
Steve Wilson†	L	26	8	0	0	0	12.1	13	1	5	9	0-0	0	4.38
Laddie Renfroe	R	29	4	0	0	0	4.2	11	1	2	4	0-1	0	13.50
Yorkis Perez	L	23	3	0	0	0	4.1	2	0	2	3	1-0	0	2.08
Doug Dascenzo	L	27	3	0	0	0	4.0	2	0	2	2	0-0	0	0.00
Scott May	R	29	2	0	0	0	2.0	6	0	1	1	0-0	0	18.00
Dave Pavlas	R	28	1	0	0	0	1.0	3	1	0	0	0-0	0	18.00

1991 New York Mets 5th NL East 77-84 .478 20.5 GB

Bud Harrelson (74-80)/Mike Cubbage (3-4)

Player	Gm by Position	B	Age	G	AB	R	H	2B	3B	HR	RBI	BB	SO	SB	Avg	OBP	Slg
Rick Cerone	C81	R	37	90	227	18	62	13	0	2	16	30	24	1	.273	.360	.357
Dave Magadan	1B122	L	28	124	418	58	108	23	0	4	51	83	50	1	.258	.378	.342
Gregg Jefferies	2B77,3B51	S	23	136	486	59	132	19	2	9	62	47	38	26	.272	.336	.374
Howard Johnson	3B104,OF30,SS28	S	30	156	564	108	146	34	4	38	117	78	120	30	.259	.342	.535
Kevin Elster	SS107	R	26	115	348	33	84	16	2	6	36	40	53	2	.241	.318	.351
Kevin McReynolds	OF141	R	31	143	522	65	135	32	1	16	74	49	46	6	.259	.322	.416
Daryl Boston	OF115	L	28	137	255	40	70	16	4	4	21	30	42	15	.275	.350	.416
Hubie Brooks	OF100	R	34	103	357	48	85	11	1	16	50	44	62	3	.238	.324	.409
Vince Coleman	OF70	S	29	72	278	45	71	7	5	1	17	39	47	37	.255	.347	.327
Keith Miller	2B60,OF28,3B2*	R	28	98	275	41	77	22	1	4	23	23	44	14	.280	.345	.411
Mark Carreon	OF77	R	27	106	254	18	66	6	0	4	21	12	26	2	.260	.297	.331
Mackey Sasser	C43,OF21,1B10	L	28	96	228	18	62	14	2	5	35	9	19	0	.272	.298	.417
Garry Templeton†	SS40,1B25,3B2*	S	35	80	219	20	50	9	1	2	20	9	29	3	.228	.257	.306
Charlie O'Brien	C67	R	31	69	168	16	31	6	0	2	14	17	25	0	.185	.272	.256
Tom Herr†	2B57,OF1	S	35	70	155	17	30	7	0	1	14	32	21	7	.194	.328	.258
Chris Donnels	1B15,3B11	L	25	37	89	7	20	2	0	0	5	14	19	1	.225	.330	.247
Todd Hundley	C20	S	22	21	60	5	8	0	1	1	7	6	14	0	.133	.221	.217
Jeff Gardner	SS8,2B3	L	27	13	37	3	6	0	0	0	1	4	6	0	.162	.238	.162
Tim Teufel†	1B6,3B5,2B1	R	32	20	34	2	4	0	0	1	2	2	8	1	.118	.167	.206
Terry McDaniel	OF14	S	24	23	29	3	6	1	0	0	2	1	11	2	.207	.233	.241
Chuck Carr	OF9	S	22	12	11	1	2	0	0	0	1	0	2	1	.182	.182	.182
Kelvin Torve	1B1	L	31	10	8	0	0	0	0	0	0	0	1	0	.000	.000	.000

K. Miller, 2 G at SS; G. Templeton, 2 G at OF

Pitcher	T	Age	G	GS	CG	ShO	IP	H	HR	BB	SO	W-L	Sv	ERA
Frank Viola	L	31	35	35	3	0	231.1	259	25	54	132	13-15	0	3.97
David Cone	R	28	34	34	5	2	232.2	204	13	73	241	14-14	0	3.29
Dwight Gooden	R	26	27	27	3	1	190.0	185	12	56	150	13-7	0	3.60
Wally Whitehurst	R	27	36	20	0	0	133.1	142	12	25	87	7-12	1	4.19
Ron Darling†	R	30	17	17	0	0	102.1	96	9	28	58	5-6	0	3.87
Anthony Young	R	25	10	8	0	0	49.1	48	4	12	20	2-5	0	3.10
Sid Fernandez	L	28	8	8	0	0	44.0	36	4	9	31	1-3	0	2.86
Jeff Innis	R	28	69	0	0	0	84.2	66	2	23	47	0-2	0	2.66
John Franco	L	30	52	0	0	0	55.1	61	2	18	45	5-9	30	2.93
Alejandro Pena†	R	32	44	0	0	0	63.0	63	5	19	49	6-1	4	2.71
Doug Simons	L	24	42	1	0	0	60.2	55	5	19	38	2-3	1	5.19
Pete Schourek	L	22	35	8	1	1	86.1	82	7	43	67	5-4	2	4.27
Tim Burke†	R	32	35	0	0	0	55.2	55	5	12	34	3-3	1	2.75
Tony Castillo†	L	28	10	3	0	0	23.2	27	1	6	10	1-0	0	1.90
Terry Bross	R	25	8	0	0	0	10.0	7	1	3	5	0-0	0	1.80
Richard Sauveur	L	27	6	0	0	0	3.1	7	1	2	4	0-0	0	10.80
Blaine Beatty	L	27	5	0	0	0	9.2	9	0	4	7	0-0	0	2.79
Julio Valera	R	22	2	0	0	0	2.0	1	0	4	3	0-0	0	0.00

1991 Montreal Expos 6th NL East 71-90 .441 26.5 GB

Buck Rodgers (20-29)/Tom Runnells (51-61)

Player	Gm by Position	B	Age	G	AB	R	H	2B	3B	HR	RBI	BB	SO	SB	Avg	OBP	Slg
Gil Reyes	C80	R	27	83	207	11	45	9	0	0	13	19	51	2	.217	.285	.261
Andres Galarraga	1B105	R	30	107	375	34	82	13	2	9	33	23	86	5	.219	.268	.336
Delino DeShields	2B148	L	22	151	563	83	134	15	4	10	51	95	151	56	.238	.347	.332
Tim Wallach	3B149	R	33	151	577	60	130	22	1	13	73	50	100	2	.225	.292	.334
Spike Owen	SS133	S	30	139	424	39	108	22	8	3	26	42	61	2	.255	.321	.366
Marquis Grissom	OF138	R	24	148	558	73	149	23	9	6	39	34	89	76	.267	.310	.373
Ivan Calderon	OF122,1B4	R	29	134	470	69	141	22	3	19	75	53	64	31	.300	.368	.481
Dave Martinez	OF112	L	26	124	396	47	117	18	5	7	42	20	54	16	.295	.332	.419
Larry Walker	OF102,1B39	L	24	137	487	59	141	30	2	16	64	42	102	14	.290	.349	.458
Mike Fitzgerald	C54,1B3,OF3	R	30	71	198	17	40	5	2	4	28	22	35	4	.202	.278	.308
Tom Foley	SS43,1B31,3B6*	L	31	86	168	12	35	11	1	0	15	14	30	2	.208	.269	.286
Bret Barberie	SS19,2B10,3B10*	S	23	57	136	16	48	12	2	2	18	20	22	0	.353	.435	.515
Ron Hassey	C34	L	38	52	119	5	27	8	0	1	14	13	16	1	.227	.301	.319
Nelson Santovenia	C30,1B7	R	29	41	96	7	24	5	0	2	14	2	18	0	.250	.255	.365
Junior Noboa	OF7,2B6,3B2*	R	26	67	95	5	23	3	0	1	2	1	8	2	.242	.250	.305
Eric Bullock	OF9,1B3	L	31	73	72	6	16	4	0	1	6	9	13	6	.222	.305	.319
Kenny Williams†	OF24	R	27	34	70	11	19	5	2	0	1	3	22	2	.271	.311	.400
John VanderWal	OF17	L	25	21	61	4	13	4	1	1	8	1	18	0	.213	.222	.361
Nikco Riesgo	OF2	R	24	4	7	1	1	0	0	0	0	3	1	0	.143	.400	.143

T. Foley, 2 G at 2B; B. Barberie, 1 G at 1B; J. Noboa, 2 G at SS, 1 G at 1B

Pitcher	T	Age	G	GS	CG	ShO	IP	H	HR	BB	SO	W-L	Sv	ERA
Dennis Martinez	R	36	31	31	9	5	222.0	187	9	62	123	14-11	0	2.39
Mark Gardner	R	29	27	27	0	0	168.1	139	17	75	107	9-11	0	3.85
Brian Barnes	L	24	28	27	1	0	160.0	135	16	84	117	5-8	0	4.22
Chris Nabholz	L	24	24	24	1	0	153.2	134	5	57	99	8-7	0	3.63
Oil Can Boyd†	R	31	19	19	1	1	120.1	115	9	40	82	6-8	0	3.52
Chris Haney	L	22	16	16	0	0	84.2	94	6	43	51	3-7	0	4.04
Rick Mahler†	R	37	10	6	0	0	37.1	37	2	15	17	1-3	0	3.62
Ron Darling†	R	30	3	3	0	0	17.0	25	6	5	11	0-2	0	7.41
Barry Jones	R	28	77	0	0	0	88.2	76	8	33	46	4-9	13	3.35
Scott Ruskin	L	28	64	0	0	0	63.2	57	4	30	46	4-4	6	4.24
Jeff Fassero	L	28	51	0	0	0	55.1	39	1	17	42	2-5	8	2.44
Bill Sampen	R	28	43	8	0	0	92.1	96	13	46	52	9-5	0	4.00
Mel Rojas	R	24	37	0	0	0	48.0	42	4	13	37	3-3	6	3.75
Tim Burke†	R	32	37	0	0	0	46.0	41	3	14	25	3-4	5	4.11
Steve Frey	L	27	31	0	0	0	39.2	43	3	23	21	0-1	1	4.99
Doug Piatt	R	25	21	0	0	0	34.2	29	3	17	29	0-0	0	2.60
Dave Schmidt	R	34	4	0	0	0	4.1	9	2	2	3	0-1	0	10.38
Bill Long	R	31	3	0	0	0	1.2	4	0	4	0	0-0	0	10.80
David Wainhouse	R	23	2	0	0	0	2.2	2	0	4	1	0-1	0	6.75

Seasons: Team Rosters 925

1991 Atlanta Braves 1st NL West 94-68 .580 — Bobby Cox

Player	Gm by Position	B	Age	G	AB	R	H	2B	3B	HR	RBI	BB	SO	SB	Avg	OBP	Slg
Greg Olson	C127	R	30	133	411	46	99	25	0	6	44	44	48	1	.241	.316	.345
Brian Hunter	1B85,OF6	R	23	97	271	32	68	16	1	12	50	17	48	0	.251	.296	.450
Mark Lemke	2B110,3B15	S	25	136	269	36	63	11	2	2	23	29	27	1	.234	.305	.312
Terry Pendleton	3B148	S	30	153	586	94	187	34	8	22	86	43	70	10	.319	.363	.517
Rafael Belliard	SS145	R	29	149	353	36	88	9	2	0	27	22	63	3	.249	.296	.286
Ron Gant	OF148	R	26	154	561	101	141	35	3	32	105	71	104	34	.251	.338	.496
Otis Nixon	OF115	S	32	124	401	81	119	10	1	0	26	47	40	72	.297	.371	.327
David Justice	OF106	L	25	109	396	67	109	25	1	21	87	65	81	8	.275	.377	.503
Lonnie Smith	OF99	R	35	122	353	58	97	19	1	7	44	50	64	9	.275	.377	.394
Jeff Blauser	SS85,2B32,3B18	R	25	129	352	49	91	14	3	11	54	54	59	5	.259	.358	.409
Jeff Treadway	2B93	L	28	106	306	41	98	17	2	3	32	23	19	2	.320	.368	.418
Sid Bream	1B85	L	30	91	265	32	67	12	0	11	45	25	31	0	.253	.313	.423
Mike Heath	C45	R	36	49	139	4	29	3	1	1	12	7	26	0	.209	.250	.266
Deion Sanders	OF44	L	23	54	110	16	21	1	2	4	13	12	23	11	.191	.270	.345
Tommy Gregg	OF14,1B13	L	27	72	107	13	20	8	1	1	4	12	24	2	.187	.275	.308
Francisco Cabrera	C17,1B14	R	24	44	95	7	23	6	0	4	23	6	20	1	.242	.284	.432
Keith Mitchell	OF34	R	21	48	66	11	21	0	0	2	5	8	12	3	.318	.392	.409
Mike Bell	1B14	L	23	17	30	4	4	0	0	1	1	2	7	1	.133	.188	.233
Jerry Willard	C1	L	31	17	14	1	3	0	0	1	4	2	5	0	.214	.313	.429
Danny Heep	1B1,OF1	L	33	14	12	4	5	1	0	0	3	1	4	0	.417	.462	.500
Vinny Castilla	SS12	R	23	12	5	1	1	0	0	0	0	0	2	0	.200	.200	.200
Damon Berryhill†	C1	S	27	1	1	0	0	0	0	0	0	0	1	0	.000	.000	.000
Rico Rossy	SS1	R	27	5	1	0	0	0	0	0	0	0	1	0	.000	.000	.000

Pitcher	T	Age	G	GS	CG	ShO	IP	H	HR	BB	SO	W-L	Sv	ERA
Charlie Leibrandt	L	34	36	36	1	1	229.2	212	18	56	128	15-13	0	3.49
John Smoltz	R	24	36	36	5	0	229.2	206	16	77	148	14-13	0	3.80
Steve Avery	L	21	35	35	3	1	210.1	189	21	65	137	18-8	0	3.38
Tom Glavine	L	25	34	34	9	1	246.2	201	17	69	192	20-11	0	2.55
Pete Smith	R	25	14	10	0	0	48.0	48	5	22	29	1-3	0	5.06
Armando Reynoso	R	25	6	5	0	0	23.1	26	4	10	10	2-1	0	6.17
Mike Stanton	L	24	74	0	0	0	78.0	62	6	21	54	5-5	7	2.88
Kent Mercker	L	23	50	4	0	0	73.1	56	5	35	62	5-3	6	2.58
Juan Berenguer	R	36	49	0	0	0	64.1	43	5	20	53	0-3	17	2.24
Marvin Freeman	R	28	34	0	0	0	48.0	37	2	13	34	1-0	1	3.00
Jim Clancy†	R	35	24	0	0	0	34.2	36	3	14	17	3-2	3	5.71
Randy St. Claire	R	30	19	0	0	0	28.2	31	4	9	30	0-0	0	4.08
Jeff Parrett	R	29	18	0	0	0	21.1	31	2	12	14	1-2	1	6.33
Mark Wohlers	R	21	17	0	0	0	19.2	17	1	13	13	3-1	2	3.20
Alejandro Pena†	R	32	15	0	0	0	19.1	11	1	3	13	2-0	11	1.40
Doug Sisk	R	33	14	0	0	0	14.1	21	1	8	5	2-1	0	5.02
Rick Mahler†	R	37	13	2	0	0	28.2	33	2	13	10	1-1	0	5.65
Dan Petry†	R	32	10	0	0	0	24.1	29	2	14	9	0-0	0	5.55
Tony Castillo†	L	28	7	0	0	0	8.2	13	3	5	8	1-1	0	7.27
Mike Bielecki†	R	31	2	0	0	0	1.2	2	0	2	3	0-0	0	0.00

1991 Los Angeles Dodgers 2nd NL West 93-69 .574 1.0 GB Tom Lasorda

Player	Gm by Position	B	Age	G	AB	R	H	2B	3B	HR	RBI	BB	SO	SB	Avg	OBP	Slg
Mike Scioscia	C115	L	32	119	345	39	91	16	2	8	40	47	32	4	.264	.353	.391
Eddie Murray	1B149,3B1	S	35	153	576	69	150	23	1	19	96	55	74	10	.260	.321	.403
Juan Samuel	2B152	R	30	153	594	74	161	22	6	12	58	49	133	23	.271	.328	.389
Lenny Harris	3B113,2B27,SS20*	L	26	145	429	59	123	16	1	3	38	37	32	12	.287	.349	.350
Alfredo Griffin	SS109	S	33	109	350	27	85	6	2	0	27	22	49	5	.243	.286	.271
Brett Butler	OF161	L	34	161	615	112	182	13	5	2	38	108	79	38	.296	.401	.343
Darryl Strawberry	OF136	L	29	139	505	86	134	22	4	28	99	75	125	10	.265	.361	.491
Kal Daniels	OF132	L	27	137	461	54	115	15	1	17	73	63	116	6	.249	.337	.397
Gary Carter	C68,1B10	R	37	101	248	22	61	14	0	6	26	22	26	2	.246	.323	.375
Mike Sharperson	3B68,SS16,1B10*	R	29	105	216	24	60	11	2	2	20	25	24	1	.278	.355	.375
Stan Javier	OF69,1B2	S	27	121	176	21	36	5	3	1	11	16	36	7	.205	.268	.284
Chris Gwynn	OF41	L	26	94	139	18	35	5	1	5	22	10	23	1	.252	.301	.410
Jose Offerman	SS50	S	22	52	113	10	22	2	0	0	3	25	32	3	.195	.345	.212
Jeff Hamilton	3B33,SS1	R	27	41	94	4	21	4	0	1	14	4	21	0	.223	.255	.298
Mitch Webster†	OF36,1B1	S	32	58	74	12	21	5	1	1	10	9	21	0	.284	.361	.419
Dave Hansen	3B21,SS1	L	22	53	56	3	15	4	0	1	5	2	12	1	.268	.293	.393
Jose Gonzalez†	OF27	R	26	42	28	3	0	0	0	0	0	2	9	0	.000	.067	.000
Carlos Hernandez	C13,3B1	R	24	15	14	1	3	1	0	0	1	0	5	1	.214	.250	.286
Eric Karros	1B10	R	23	14	14	0	1	1	0	0	1	1	6	0	.071	.133	.143
Barry Lyons†	C6	R	31	9	9	0	0	0	0	0	0	0	2	0	.000	.000	.000
Tom Goodwin	OF5	L	22	16	7	3	1	0	0	0	0	0	0	1	.143	.143	.143
Greg Smith	2B1	S	24	5	3	1	0	0	0	0	0	0	2	0	.000	.000	.000
Butch Davis		R	33	1	1	0	0	0	0	0	0	0	0	0	.000	.000	.000
Roger McDowell†	P33,OF2	R	30	34	0	0	0	0	0	0	0	0	0	0	—	—	—

L. Harris, 1 G at OF; M. Sharperson, 5 G at 2B

Pitcher	T	Age	G	GS	CG	ShO	IP	H	HR	BB	SO	W-L	Sv	ERA
Mike Morgan	R	31	34	33	5	1	236.1	197	12	61	140	14-10	1	2.78
Ramon Martinez	R	23	33	33	6	4	220.1	190	18	69	150	17-13	0	3.27
Tim Belcher	R	29	33	33	2	1	209.1	189	10	75	156	10-9	0	2.62
Bobby Ojeda	L	33	31	31	2	1	189.1	181	15	70	120	12-9	0	3.18
Orel Hershiser	R	32	21	21	0	0	112.0	112	3	32	73	7-2	0	3.46
Tim Crews	R	30	60	0	0	0	76.0	75	7	19	53	2-3	6	3.43
John Candelaria	L	37	59	0	0	0	33.2	31	3	11	38	1-1	2	3.74
Jim Gott	R	31	55	0	0	0	76.0	63	5	32	73	4-3	2	2.96
Kevin Gross	R	30	46	10	0	0	115.2	123	10	50	95	10-11	3	3.58
Jay Howell	R	35	44	0	0	0	51.0	39	3	11	40	6-5	16	3.18
Mike Hartley†	R	29	40	0	0	0	57.0	53	7	37	44	2-0	1	4.42
Roger McDowell†	R	30	33	0	0	0	42.1	39	3	16	22	6-3	7	2.55
Dennis Cook	L	28	20	1	0	0	17.2	12	0	7	8	1-0	0	0.51
Steve Wilson†	L	26	11	0	0	0	8.1	1	0	4	5	0-0	2	0.00
John Wetteland	R	24	6	0	0	0	9.0	5	0	3	9	1-0	0	0.00
Mike Christopher	R	27	3	0	0	0	4.0	2	0	3	2	0-0	0	0.00

1991 San Diego Padres 3rd NL West 84-78 .519 10.0 GB Greg Riddoch

Player	Gm by Position	B	Age	G	AB	R	H	2B	3B	HR	RBI	BB	SO	SB	Avg	OBP	Slg
Benito Santiago	C151,OF1	R	26	152	580	60	155	22	3	17	87	23	114	8	.267	.296	.403
Fred McGriff	1B153	L	27	153	528	84	147	19	1	31	106	105	135	4	.278	.396	.494
Bip Roberts	2B68,OF46	S	27	117	424	66	119	13	3	3	32	37	71	26	.281	.342	.347
Scott Coolbaugh	3B54	R	25	60	180	12	39	8	1	2	15	19	45	0	.217	.294	.306
Tony Fernandez	SS145	S	29	145	558	81	152	27	5	4	38	55	74	23	.272	.337	.360
Tony Gwynn	OF134	L	31	134	530	69	168	27	11	4	62	34	19	8	.317	.355	.432
Darrin Jackson	OF98,P1	R	27	122	359	51	94	12	1	21	49	27	66	5	.262	.315	.476
Jerald Clark	OF96,1B16	R	27	118	369	26	84	16	0	10	47	31	90	2	.228	.295	.352
Tim Teufel†	2B65,3B48	R	32	97	307	39	70	16	0	11	42	49	69	8	.228	.334	.388
Thomas Howard	OF86	S	26	106	281	30	70	12	3	4	22	24	57	10	.249	.309	.356
Jack Howell†	3B54	L	29	58	160	24	33	3	1	6	16	18	33	0	.206	.287	.350
Paul Faries	2B36,3B12,SS8	R	26	57	130	13	23	3	1	0	7	14	21	3	.177	.262	.215
Shawn Abner†	OF39	R	25	53	115	15	19	4	1	1	5	7	25	0	.165	.218	.243
Kevin Ward	OF33	R	29	44	107	13	26	7	2	2	8	9	27	1	.243	.308	.402
Craig Shipley	SS19,2B14	R	28	37	91	6	25	3	0	1	6	2	14	0	.275	.298	.341
Jim Presley	3B16	R	29	20	59	3	8	0	0	1	5	4	16	0	.136	.200	.186
Tom Lampkin	C11	L	27	38	58	4	11	3	1	0	3	3	9	0	.190	.230	.276
Garry Templeton†	3B15,SS1	S	35	32	57	5	11	1	1	1	6	1	9	0	.193	.203	.298
Oscar Azocar	OF13,1B1	L	26	38	57	5	14	2	0	0	9	1	9	2	.246	.267	.281
Jose Mota	2B13,SS3	S	26	17	36	4	8	0	0	0	2	2	7	0	.222	.282	.222
Dann Bilardello	C13	R	32	15	26	4	7	2	1	0	5	3	4	0	.269	.345	.423
Jim Vatcher	OF11	R	25	17	20	3	4	0	0	0	2	4	6	1	.200	.333	.200
Marty Barrett	2B2,3B2	R	33	12	16	1	3	1	0	1	3	0	3	0	.188	.235	.438
Mike Aldrete†	OF5	L	30	12	15	2	0	0	0	0	1	3	4	0	.000	.167	.000
Brian Dorsett	1B2	R	30	11	12	0	1	0	0	0	1	0	3	0	.083	.083	.083
Phil Stephenson		L	30	11	7	0	2	0	0	0	0	2	3	0	.286	.444	.286

Pitcher	T	Age	G	GS	CG	ShO	IP	H	HR	BB	SO	W-L	Sv	ERA
Andy Benes	R	23	33	33	4	1	223.0	194	23	59	167	15-11	0	3.03
Bruce Hurst	L	33	31	31	4	0	221.2	201	17	59	141	15-8	0	3.29
Dennis Rasmussen	L	32	24	24	1	1	146.2	155	12	49	75	6-13	0	3.74
Greg Harris	R	27	20	20	3	2	133.0	116	16	27	95	9-5	0	2.23
Ed Whitson	R	36	13	12	2	0	78.2	93	13	17	40	4-6	0	5.03
Adam Peterson	R	25	13	11	0	0	54.2	50	10	28	37	3-4	0	4.45
Ricky Bones	R	22	11	11	0	0	54.0	57	3	18	31	4-6	0	4.83
Eric Nolte†	L	27	6	6	0	0	22.0	37	6	10	15	3-2	0	11.05
Atlee Hammaker	L	33	1	1	0	0	4.2	8	0	3	1	0-1	0	5.79
Mike Maddux	R	29	64	1	0	0	98.2	78	4	27	57	7-2	5	2.46
Rich Rodriguez	L	28	64	1	0	0	80.0	66	8	44	40	3-1	0	3.26
Craig Lefferts	L	33	54	0	0	0	69.0	74	5	14	48	1-6	23	3.91
Larry Andersen	R	38	38	0	0	0	47.0	39	0	13	40	3-4	13	2.30
Jose Melendez	R	25	31	9	0	0	93.2	77	11	24	60	8-5	3	3.27
John Costello	R	30	27	0	0	0	35.0	37	2	17	24	1-0	0	3.09
Wes Gardner†	R	30	14	0	0	0	20.1	27	1	12	9	0-1	1	7.08
Pat Clements	L	29	12	0	0	0	14.1	13	0	9	8	1-0	0	3.77
Jim Lewis	R	26	12	0	0	0	13.0	14	0	11	10	0-0	0	4.15
Steve Rosenberg	L	26	10	0	0	0	11.2	11	3	5	6	1-1	0	6.94
Jeremy Hernandez	R	24	9	0	0	0	14.1	8	0	5	9	0-0	2	0.00
Derek Lilliquist	L	25	6	2	0	0	14.1	25	3	4	7	0-2	0	8.79
Tim Scott	R	24	2	0	0	0	1.0	2	0	0	1	0-0	0	9.00
Darrin Jackson	R	27	1	0	0	0	2.0	3	0	2	0	0-0	0	9.00

1991 San Francisco Giants 4th NL West 75-87 .463 19.0 GB Roger Craig

Player	Gm by Position	B	Age	G	AB	R	H	2B	3B	HR	RBI	BB	SO	SB	Avg	OBP	Slg
Steve Decker	C78	R	25	79	233	11	48	7	1	5	24	16	44	0	.206	.262	.300
Will Clark	1B144	L	27	148	565	84	170	32	7	29	116	51	91	4	.301	.359	.536
Robby Thompson	2B144	R	29	144	492	74	129	24	5	19	48	63	95	14	.262	.352	.447
Matt Williams	3B155,SS4	R	25	157	589	72	158	24	5	34	98	33	128	5	.268	.310	.499
Jose Uribe	SS87	S	32	90	231	23	51	8	4	1	12	20	33	3	.221	.283	.303
Willie McGee	OF128	S	32	131	497	67	155	30	3	4	43	34	74	17	.312	.357	.408
Mike Felder	OF107,3B3,2B1	S	29	132	348	51	92	10	6	0	18	30	31	21	.264	.325	.328
Kevin Bass	OF101	S	32	124	361	43	84	10	4	10	40	36	56	7	.233	.307	.366
Kevin Mitchell	OF100,1B1	R	29	113	371	52	95	13	1	27	69	43	57	2	.256	.338	.515
Dave Anderson	SS63,1B16,3B11*	R	30	100	226	24	56	5	2	2	13	12	35	2	.248	.286	.314
Darren Lewis	OF68	R	23	72	222	41	55	5	3	1	15	36	30	13	.248	.358	.311
Kirt Manwaring	C67	R	25	67	178	16	40	9	0	0	19	9	22	1	.225	.271	.275
Terry Kennedy	C58,1B2	L	35	69	171	12	40	7	1	3	13	11	31	0	.234	.283	.339
Mark Leonard	OF34	L	26	64	129	14	31	7	1	2	14	12	25	0	.240	.306	.357
Greg Litton	1B15,2B15,3B11*	R	26	59	127	13	23	7	1	1	15	11	25	0	.181	.250	.276
Mike Kingery	OF38,1B6	L	30	91	110	13	20	2	2	0	8	15	21	1	.182	.280	.236
Mike Benjamin	SS51,3B1	R	25	54	106	12	13	3	0	2	8	7	26	3	.123	.188	.208
Tom Herr†	2B15,3B3	S	35	32	60	6	15	1	1	0	7	13	7	2	.250	.384	.300
Tony Perezchica†	SS13,2B6	R	25	23	48	2	11	4	1	0	3	2	12	0	.229	.260	.354
Royce Clayton	SS8	R	21	9	26	0	3	1	0	0	2	1	6	0	.115	.148	.154
Ted Wood	OF8	L	24	10	25	0	3	0	0	0	1	2	11	0	.120	.185	.120
Darnell Coles	OF3,1B1	R	29	11	14	1	3	0	0	0	0	0	2	0	.214	.214	.214
Rick Parker	OF4	R	28	13	14	0	1	0	0	0	1	1	5	0	.071	.133	.071

D. Anderson, 6 G at 2B; G. Litton, 9 G at SS, 6 G at OF, 1 G at P, 1 G at C

Pitcher	T	Age	G	GS	CG	ShO	IP	H	HR	BB	SO	W-L	Sv	ERA
Bud Black	L	34	34	34	3	3	214.1	201	25	71	104	12-16	0	3.99
John Burkett	R	26	36	34	3	1	206.2	223	19	60	131	12-11	0	4.18
Trevor Wilson	L	25	44	29	2	1	202.0	173	13	77	139	13-11	0	3.56
Paul McClellan	R	25	13	12	1	0	71.0	68	12	25	44	3-6	0	4.56
Mike Remlinger	L	25	8	6	1	1	35.0	36	5	20	19	2-1	0	4.37
Gil Heredia	R	25	7	4	0	0	33.0	27	4	7	13	0-2	0	3.82
Jeff Brantley	R	27	67	0	0	0	95.1	78	8	52	81	5-2	15	2.45
Dave Righetti	L	32	61	0	0	0	71.2	64	4	28	51	2-7	24	3.39
Francisco Oliveras	R	28	55	1	0	0	79.1	69	12	22	48	6-6	3	3.86
Kelly Downs	R	30	45	11	0	0	111.2	99	12	53	62	10-4	0	4.19
Don Robinson	R	34	34	16	0	0	121.1	123	12	50	78	5-9	1	4.38
Rod Beck	R	22	31	0	0	0	52.1	53	4	13	38	1-1	1	3.78
Mike LaCoss	R	35	18	5	0	0	47.1	61	4	24	30	1-5	0	7.23
Bryan Hickerson	L	27	17	6	0	0	50.0	53	3	17	43	2-2	0	3.60
Jose Segura	R	28	11	0	0	0	16.1	20	1	5	10	0-1	0	4.41
Scott Garrelts	R	29	8	3	0	0	19.2	25	5	9	8	1-1	0	6.41
Rick Reuschel	R	42	4	1	0	0	10.2	17	0	7	4	0-2	0	4.22
Eric Gunderson	L	25	2	0	0	0	3.1	6	0	1	2	0-0	1	5.40
Greg Litton	R	26	1	0	0	0	1.0	1	0	3	0	0-0	0	9.00

1991 Cincinnati Reds 5th NL West 74-88 .457 20.0 GB

Lou Piniella

Player	Gm by Position	B	Age	G	AB	R	H	2B	3B	HR	RBI	BB	SO	SB	Avg	OBP	Slg
Joe Oliver	C90	R	25	94	269	21	58	11	0	11	41	18	53	0	.216	.265	.379
Hal Morris	1B128,OF1	L	26	136	478	72	152	33	1	14	59	46	61	10	.318	.374	.479
Bill Doran	2B88,OF6,1B4	S	33	111	361	51	101	12	2	6	35	46	39	5	.280	.359	.374
Chris Sabo	3B151	R	29	153	582	91	175	35	3	26	88	44	79	19	.301	.354	.505
Barry Larkin	SS119	R	27	123	464	88	140	27	4	20	69	55	64	24	.302	.378	.506
Paul O'Neill	OF150	L	28	152	532	71	136	36	0	28	91	73	107	12	.256	.346	.481
Billy Hatcher	OF121	R	30	138	442	45	116	25	3	4	41	26	55	11	.262	.312	.360
Eric Davis	OF82	R	29	89	285	39	67	10	0	11	33	48	92	14	.235	.353	.386
Mariano Duncan	2B62,SS32,OF7	S	28	100	333	46	86	7	4	12	40	12	57	5	.258	.288	.411
Jeff Reed	C89	L	28	91	270	20	72	15	2	3	31	23	38	0	.267	.321	.370
Glenn Braggs	OF74	R	28	85	250	36	65	10	0	11	39	23	46	11	.260	.323	.432
Luis Quinones	2B33,3B19,SS5	S	29	97	212	15	47	4	3	4	20	21	31	1	.222	.297	.325
Herm Winningham	OF66	L	29	98	169	17	38	6	1	1	4	11	40	4	.225	.272	.290
Carmelo Martinez†	1B25,OF16	R	30	53	138	12	32	5	0	6	19	15	37	0	.232	.301	.399
Todd Benzinger†	1B21,OF15	S	28	51	123	7	23	3	2	1	11	10	20	2	.187	.244	.268
Chris Jones	OF26	R	25	52	89	14	26	1	2	2	6	2	31	2	.292	.304	.416
Freddie Benavides	SS20,2B3	R	25	24	63	11	18	1	0	0	3	1	15	1	.286	.303	.302
Reggie Sanders	OF9	R	23	9	40	6	8	0	0	1	3	0	9	1	.200	.200	.275
Donnie Scott	C8	S	29	10	19	0	3	0	0	0	0	0	2	0	.158	.158	.158
Stan Jefferson	OF5	S	28	13	19	2	1	0	0	0	0	1	3	2	.053	.100	.053
Glenn Sutko	C9	R	23	10	10	0	1	0	0	0	1	2	6	0	.100	.250	.100
Reggie Jefferson†	1B2	S	22	5	7	1	1	0	0	1	1	1	2	0	.143	.250	.571
Terry Lee	1B2	R	29	3	6	0	0	0	0	0	0	0	2	0	.000	.000	.000

Pitcher	T	Age	G	GS	CG	ShO	IP	H	HR	BB	SO	W-L	Sv	ERA
Tom Browning	L	31	36	36	1	0	230.1	241	32	56	115	14-14	0	4.18
Jose Rijo	R	26	30	30	3	1	204.1	165	8	55	172	15-6	0	2.51
Jack Armstrong	R	26	27	24	1	0	139.2	158	25	54	93	7-13	0	5.48
Chris Hammond	L	25	20	18	0	0	99.2	92	4	48	50	7-7	0	4.06
Scott Scudder	R	23	27	14	0	0	101.1	91	6	56	51	6-9	1	4.35
Mo Sanford	R	24	5	5	0	0	28.0	19	3	15	31	1-2	0	3.86
Ted Power	R	36	68	0	0	0	87.0	87	6	31	51	5-3	3	3.62
Rob Dibble	R	27	67	0	0	0	82.1	67	5	25	124	3-5	31	3.17
Randy Myers	L	28	58	12	1	0	132.0	116	8	80	108	6-13	6	3.55
Norm Charlton	L	28	39	11	0	0	108.1	92	6	34	77	3-5	1	2.91
Kip Gross	R	26	29	9	1	0	85.2	93	8	40	40	6-4	0	3.47
Don Carman	L	31	28	0	0	0	36.0	40	8	19	15	0-2	1	5.25
Milt Hill	R	25	22	0	0	0	33.1	36	1	8	20	1-1	0	3.78
Tim Layana	R	27	22	0	0	0	20.2	23	1	11	14	0-2	0	6.97
Gino Minutelli	L	27	16	3	0	0	25.1	30	5	18	21	0-2	0	6.04
Steve Foster	R	24	11	0	0	0	14.0	7	1	4	11	0-0	0	1.93
Keith Brown	R	27	11	0	0	0	12.0	15	0	6	4	0-0	0	2.25

1991 Houston Astros 6th NL West 65-97 .401 29.0 GB

Art Howe

Player	Gm by Position	B	Age	G	AB	R	H	2B	3B	HR	RBI	BB	SO	SB	Avg	OBP	Slg
Craig Biggio	C139,2B3,OF2	R	25	149	546	79	161	23	4	4	46	53	71	19	.295	.358	.374
Jeff Bagwell	1B155	R	23	156	554	79	163	26	4	15	82	75	116	7	.294	.387	.437
Casey Candaele	2B109,OF26,3B11	S	30	151	461	44	121	20	7	4	50	40	49	9	.262	.319	.362
Ken Caminiti	3B152	S	28	152	574	65	145	30	3	13	80	46	85	4	.253	.312	.383
Eric Yelding	SS72,OF4	R	26	78	276	19	67	11	1	1	20	13	46	11	.243	.276	.301
Steve Finley	OF153	L	26	159	596	84	170	28	10	8	54	42	65	34	.285	.331	.406
Luis Gonzalez	OF133	L	23	137	473	51	120	28	9	13	69	40	101	10	.254	.320	.433
Gerald Young	OF84	S	26	108	142	26	31	3	1	1	11	24	17	16	.218	.327	.275
Andujar Cedeno	SS66	R	21	67	251	27	61	13	2	9	36	9	74	4	.243	.270	.418
Rafael Ramirez	SS45,2B27,3B2	R	33	101	233	17	55	10	0	1	20	13	40	3	.236	.274	.292
Mark Davidson	OF63	R	30	85	142	10	27	6	0	2	15	12	28	0	.190	.263	.275
Karl Rhodes	OF44	L	22	44	136	7	29	3	1	1	12	14	26	2	.213	.289	.272
Mike Simms	OF41	R	24	49	123	18	25	5	0	3	16	18	38	1	.203	.301	.317
Eric Anthony	OF37	L	23	39	118	11	18	6	0	1	7	12	41	1	.153	.227	.229
Andy Mota	2B27	R	25	27	90	4	17	2	0	1	6	1	17	2	.189	.198	.244
Javier Ortiz	OF24	R	28	47	83	7	23	4	1	1	5	14	14	0	.277	.381	.386
Kenny Lofton	OF20	L	24	20	74	9	15	1	0	0	0	5	19	2	.203	.253	.216
Ken Oberkfell	1B13,3B4	L	35	53	70	7	16	4	0	0	14	14	8	0	.229	.357	.286
Mark McLemore	2B19	S	26	21	61	6	9	1	0	0	2	6	13	0	.148	.221	.164
Jose Tolentino	1B10,OF1	L	30	44	54	6	14	4	0	1	6	4	9	0	.259	.305	.389
Carl Nichols	C17	R	28	20	51	3	10	3	0	0	1	5	17	0	.196	.268	.255
Dave Rohde	2B4,3B3,SS3*	S	27	29	41	3	5	0	0	0	0	5	8	0	.122	.217	.122
Scott Servais	C14	R	24	16	37	0	6	3	0	0	6	4	8	0	.162	.244	.243
Tony Eusebio	C9	R	24	10	19	4	2	1	0	0	0	6	8	0	.105	.320	.158
Gary Cooper	3B4	R	26	9	16	1	4	1	0	0	2	3	6	0	.250	.368	.313

D. Rohde, 1 G at 1B

Pitcher	T	Age	G	GS	CG	ShO	IP	H	HR	BB	SO	W-L	Sv	ERA
Pete Harnisch	R	24	33	33	4	2	216.2	169	14	83	172	12-9	0	2.70
Jim Deshaies	L	31	28	28	1	0	161.0	156	19	72	98	5-12	0	4.98
Mark Portugal	R	28	32	27	1	0	168.1	163	19	59	120	10-12	1	4.49
Darryl Kile	R	22	37	22	0	0	153.2	144	16	84	100	7-11	0	3.69
Jimmy Jones	R	27	26	22	1	1	135.1	143	9	51	88	6-8	0	4.39
Ryan Bowen	R	23	14	13	0	0	71.2	73	4	36	49	6-4	0	5.15
Chris Gardner	R	22	5	4	0	0	24.2	19	5	14	12	1-2	0	4.01
Jeff Juden	R	20	4	3	0	0	18.0	19	3	7	11	0-2	0	6.00
Brian Williams	R	22	2	2	0	0	12.0	11	2	4	4	0-1	0	3.75
Mike Scott	R	36	2	2	0	0	7.0	11	2	4	3	0-2	0	12.86
Al Osuna	L	25	71	0	0	0	81.2	59	5	46	68	7-6	12	3.42
Curt Schilling	R	24	56	0	0	0	75.2	79	2	39	71	3-5	8	3.81
Dwayne Henry	R	29	52	0	0	0	67.2	51	7	39	51	3-2	2	3.19
Jim Corsi	R	29	47	0	0	0	77.2	76	6	23	53	0-5	0	3.71
Xavier Hernandez	R	25	32	6	0	0	63.0	66	6	32	55	2-7	3	4.71
Jim Clancy†	R	35	30	0	0	0	55.0	37	5	20	33	0-3	5	2.78
Mike Capel	R	29	25	0	0	0	32.2	33	3	15	23	1-3	3	3.03
Rob Mallicoat	L	26	24	0	0	0	23.1	22	2	13	18	0-2	1	3.86
Dean Wilkins	R	24	7	0	0	0	8.0	16	0	10	4	2-1	1	11.25

»1992 Toronto Blue Jays 1st AL East 96-66 .593 —

Cito Gaston

Player	Gm by Position	B	Age	G	AB	R	H	2B	3B	HR	RBI	BB	SO	SB	Avg	OBP	Slg
Pat Borders	C137	R	29	138	480	47	116	26	2	13	53	33	75	1	.242	.290	.385
John Olerud	1B133,DH1	L	23	138	458	68	130	28	0	16	66	70	61	1	.284	.375	.450
Roberto Alomar	2B150,DH1	S	24	152	571	105	177	27	8	8	76	87	52	49	.310	.405	.427
Kelly Gruber	3B120	R	30	120	446	42	102	16	3	11	43	26	72	7	.229	.275	.352
Manuel Lee	SS128	S	27	128	396	49	104	10	1	3	39	50	73	6	.263	.343	.316
Devon White	OF152,DH1	S	29	153	641	98	159	26	7	17	60	47	133	37	.248	.303	.390
Candy Maldonado	OF132,DH4	R	31	137	489	64	133	25	4	20	66	59	112	2	.272	.357	.462
Joe Carter	OF129,DH24,1B4	R	32	158	622	97	164	30	7	34	119	36	109	12	.264	.309	.498
Dave Winfield	DH130,OF26	R	40	156	583	92	169	33	3	26	108	82	89	2	.290	.377	.491
Jeff Kent†	3B49,2B17,1B3	R	24	65	192	36	46	13	1	8	35	20	47	2	.240	.324	.443
Derek Bell	OF56,DH1	R	23	61	161	23	39	6	3	2	15	15	34	7	.242	.324	.354
Alfredo Griffin	SS48,2B16	S	34	63	150	21	35	7	0	0	10	9	19	3	.233	.273	.280
Pat Tabler	1B34,OF8,DH2*	R	34	49	135	11	34	5	0	0	16	11	14	0	.252	.306	.289
Greg Myers†	C18,DH1	L	26	22	61	4	14	6	0	1	13	5	5	0	.230	.279	.377
Ed Sprague	C15,1B4,DH2*	R	24	22	47	6	11	2	0	1	7	3	7	0	.234	.280	.340
Turner Ward	OF12	S	27	18	29	7	10	3	0	1	3	4	4	0	.345	.424	.552
Rob Ducey†	OF13,DH4	L	27	23	21	3	1	1	0	0	0	0	10	0	.048	.048	.095
Randy Knorr	C8,DH1	R	23	8	19	1	5	0	0	1	2	1	5	0	.263	.300	.421
Tom Quinlan	3B13	R	24	13	15	2	1	1	0	0	2	2	9	0	.067	.176	.133
Domingo Martinez	1B7	R	24	7	8	2	5	0	0	1	3	0	1	0	.625	.625	1.000
Eddie Zosky	SS8	R	24	8	7	1	2	0	1	0	1	0	2	0	.286	.250	.571
Mike Maksudian	1B1	L	26	3	3	0	0	0	0	0	0	0	0	0	.000	.000	.000
Rance Mulliniks	DH2	L	36	3	2	1	1	0	0	0	0	1	0	0	.500	.667	.500

P. Tabler, 1 G at 3B; E. Sprague, 1 G at 3B

Pitcher	T	Age	G	GS	CG	ShO	IP	H	HR	BB	SO	W-L	Sv	ERA
Jack Morris	R	37	34	34	6	1	240.2	222	18	80	132	21-6	0	4.04
Jimmy Key	L	31	33	33	4	2	216.2	205	24	59	117	13-13	0	3.53
Juan Guzman	R	25	28	28	1	0	180.2	135	6	72	165	16-5	0	2.64
Todd Stottlemyre	R	27	28	27	6	2	174.0	175	20	63	98	12-11	0	4.50
Dave Stieb	R	34	21	14	1	0	96.1	98	9	43	45	4-6	0	5.04
David Cone†	R	29	8	7	0	0	53.0	39	3	29	47	4-3	0	2.55
Duane Ward	R	28	79	0	0	0	101.1	76	5	39	103	7-4	12	1.95
Tom Henke	R	34	57	0	0	0	55.2	40	5	22	46	3-2	34	2.26
David Wells	L	29	41	14	0	0	120.0	138	16	36	62	7-9	2	5.40
Pat Hentgen	R	23	28	2	0	0	50.1	49	7	32	39	5-2	0	5.36
Bob MacDonald	L	27	27	0	0	0	47.1	50	4	16	26	1-0	0	4.37
Mike Timlin	R	26	26	0	0	0	43.2	45	0	20	35	0-2	1	4.12
Mark Eichhorn†	R	31	23	0	0	0	31.0	35	1	7	19	2-0	0	4.35
Doug Linton	R	27	8	3	0	0	24.0	31	5	17	16	1-3	0	8.63
Dave Weathers	R	22	2	0	0	0	3.1	5	1	2	3	0-0	0	8.10
Ricky Trlicek	R	23	2	0	0	0	1.2	2	0	2	1	0-0	0	10.80
Al Leiter	L	26	1	0	0	0	1.0	1	0	2	0	0-0	0	9.00

1992 Milwaukee Brewers 2nd AL East 92-70 .568 4.0 GB

Phil Garner

Player	Gm by Position	B	Age	G	AB	R	H	2B	3B	HR	RBI	BB	SO	SB	Avg	OBP	Slg
B.J. Surhoff	C109,1B17,DH9*	L	27	139	480	63	121	19	1	4	62	46	41	14	.252	.314	.321
Franklin Stubbs	1B68,DH16,OF1	L	31	92	288	37	66	11	1	9	42	27	68	11	.229	.297	.368
Scott Fletcher	2B106,SS22,3B1	R	33	123	386	53	106	18	3	3	51	30	33	17	.275	.335	.360
Kevin Seitzer	3B146,2B2,1B1	R	30	148	540	74	146	35	1	5	71	57	44	13	.270	.337	.367
Pat Listach	SS148,2B1,OF1	S	24	149	579	93	168	19	6	1	47	55	124	54	.290	.352	.349
Robin Yount	OF139,DH11	R	36	150	557	71	147	40	3	8	77	53	81	15	.264	.325	.390
Greg Vaughn	OF131,DH7	R	26	141	501	77	114	18	2	23	78	60	123	15	.228	.313	.409
Darryl Hamilton	OF124	L	27	128	470	67	140	19	7	5	62	45	42	41	.298	.356	.400
Paul Molitor	DH108,1B48	R	35	158	609	89	195	36	7	12	89	73	66	31	.320	.389	.461
Dante Bichette	OF101,DH4	R	28	112	387	37	111	27	2	5	41	16	74	18	.287	.318	.406
Jim Gantner	2B68,3B31,DH2*	L	39	101	256	22	63	12	1	1	18	12	17	6	.246	.278	.313
Dave Nilsson	C46,1B3,DH2	L	22	51	164	15	38	8	0	4	25	17	18	2	.232	.304	.354
John Jaha	1B38,DH8,OF1	R	26	47	133	17	30	3	1	2	10	12	30	10	.226	.291	.308
Tim McIntosh	C14,OF10,1B7*	R	27	35	77	7	14	3	0	0	6	3	9	1	.182	.229	.221
Andy Allanson	C9	R	30	9	25	6	8	1	0	0	0	1	2	3	.320	.346	.360
Bill Spiers	SS5,2B4,DH1*	L	26	12	16	2	5	2	0	0	2	1	4	1	.313	.353	.438
William Suero	2B15,DH2,SS1	R	25	18	16	4	3	1	0	0	0	2	1	1	.188	.316	.250
Alex Diaz	OF11,DH2	S	23	22	9	5	1	0	0	0	1	0	0	3	.111	.111	.111
Jimmy Tatum	3B5	R	24	5	8	0	1	0	0	0	0	1	2	0	.125	.222	.125
Jose Valentin	2B1,SS1	S	22	4	3	1	0	0	0	0	1	0	0	0	.000	.000	.000

B. Surhoff, 7 G at OF, 3 G at 3B; J. Gantner, 2 G at 1B; T. McIntosh, 3 G at DH; B. Spiers, 1 G at 3B

Pitcher	T	Age	G	GS	CG	ShO	IP	H	HR	BB	SO	W-L	Sv	ERA
Bill Wegman	R	29	35	35	7	0	261.2	251	28	55	127	13-14	0	3.20
Jaime Navarro	R	25	34	34	5	3	246.0	224	14	64	100	17-11	0	3.33
Chris Bosio	R	29	33	33	4	2	231.1	223	21	44	120	16-6	0	3.62
Ricky Bones	R	23	31	28	0	0	163.1	169	27	48	65	9-10	0	4.57
Cal Eldred	R	24	14	14	2	1	100.1	76	4	23	62	11-2	0	1.79
Ron Robinson	R	30	8	8	0	0	35.1	51	3	14	12	1-4	0	5.86
Doug Henry	R	28	68	0	0	0	65.0	64	6	24	52	1-4	29	4.02
Jesse Orosco	L	35	59	0	0	0	39.0	33	5	13	40	3-1	1	3.23
Mike Fetters	R	27	50	0	0	0	62.2	38	3	24	43	5-1	2	1.87
James Austin	R	28	47	0	0	0	58.1	38	2	32	30	5-2	0	1.85
Dan Plesac	L	30	44	4	0	0	79.0	64	5	35	54	5-4	1	2.96
Darren Holmes	R	26	41	0	0	0	42.1	35	1	11	31	4-4	6	2.55
Bruce Ruffin	L	28	25	6	1	0	58.0	66	7	41	45	1-6	0	6.67
Edwin Nunez†	R	29	10	0	0	0	13.2	12	1	6	10	1-1	0	2.63
Neal Heaton†	L	32	1	0	0	0	1.0	0	0	1	2	0-0	0	0.00

1992 Baltimore Orioles 3rd AL East 89-73 .549 7.0 GB

Johnny Oates

Player	Gm by Position	B	Age	G	AB	R	H	2B	3B	HR	RBI	BB	SO	SB	Avg	OBP	Slg
Chris Hoiles	C95,DH1	R	27	96	310	49	85	10	1	20	40	55	60	0	.274	.384	.506
Randy Milligan	1B129,DH6	R	30	137	462	71	111	21	1	11	53	106	81	0	.240	.383	.361
Billy Ripken	2B108,DH2	R	27	111	330	35	76	15	0	4	36	18	26	2	.230	.275	.312
Leo Gomez	3B137	R	26	137	468	62	124	24	0	17	64	63	78	2	.265	.356	.425
Cal Ripken Jr.	SS162	R	31	162	637	73	160	29	1	14	72	64	50	4	.251	.323	.366
Brady Anderson	OF158	L	28	159	623	100	169	28	10	21	80	98	98	53	.271	.373	.449
Mike Devereaux	OF155	R	29	156	653	76	180	29	11	24	107	44	94	10	.276	.321	.464
Joe Orsulak	OF110,DH1	L	30	117	391	45	113	18	3	4	39	28	34	5	.289	.342	.381
Glenn Davis	DH103,1B2	R	31	106	398	46	110	15	2	13	48	37	65	1	.276	.338	.422
Mark McLemore	2B70,DH16	S	27	101	228	40	56	7	2	0	27	21	26	11	.246	.308	.294
Chito Martinez	OF52,DH4	L	26	83	198	26	53	10	1	5	25	31	47	0	.268	.366	.404
David Segui	1B95,OF18	S	25	115	189	21	44	9	0	1	17	20	23	1	.233	.306	.296
Jeff Tackett	C64,3B1	R	26	65	179	21	43	8	1	5	24	17	28	0	.240	.307	.380
Sam Horn	DH46	L	28	63	162	13	38	10	1	5	19	21	60	0	.235	.324	.401
Tim Hulett	3B27,DH13,2B10*	R	32	57	142	11	41	7	2	2	21	10	31	0	.289	.340	.408
Luis Mercedes	OF16,DH7	R	24	23	50	7	7	2	0	0	4	8	9	0	.140	.267	.180
Mark Parent	C16	R	30	17	34	4	8	1	0	2	4	3	7	0	.235	.316	.441
Steve Scarsone†	2B5,3B2,SS1	R	26	11	17	2	3	0	0	0	0	1	6	0	.176	.222	.176
Rick Dempsey	C8	R	42	8	9	2	1	0	0	0	0	2	1	0	.111	.273	.111
Manny Alexander	SS3	R	21	4	5	1	1	0	0	0	0	0	3	0	.200	.200	.200
Tommy Shields		L	27	2	0	0	0	0	0	0	0	0	0	0	—	—	—
Jack Voigt		R	26	1	0	0	0	0	0	0	0	0	0	0	—	—	—

T. Hulett, 5 G at SS

Pitcher	T	Age	G	GS	CG	ShO	IP	H	HR	BB	SO	W-L	Sv	ERA
Rick Sutcliffe	R	36	36	36	5	2	237.1	251	20	74	109	16-15	0	4.47
Ben McDonald	R	24	35	35	4	2	227.0	213	32	74	158	13-13	0	4.24
Mike Mussina	R	23	32	32	8	4	241.0	212	16	48	130	18-5	0	2.54
Bob Milacki	R	27	23	20	0	0	115.2	140	16	44	51	6-8	1	5.84
Arthur Rhodes	L	22	15	15	2	1	94.1	87	6	38	77	7-5	0	3.63
Jose Mesa†	R	26	13	12	0	0	67.2	77	9	27	22	3-8	0	5.19
Craig Lefferts†	L	34	5	5	1	0	33.0	34	3	6	23	1-3	0	4.09
Richie Lewis	R	26	2	2	0	0	6.2	13	1	7	4	1-1	0	10.80
Todd Frohwirth	R	29	65	0	0	0	106.0	97	4	41	58	4-3	4	2.46
Gregg Olson	R	25	60	0	0	0	61.1	46	3	24	58	1-5	36	2.05
Storm Davis	R	30	48	2	0	0	89.1	79	5	36	53	7-3	4	3.43
Mike Flanagan	L	40	42	0	0	0	34.2	50	3	23	17	0-0	0	8.05
Alan Mills	R	25	35	3	0	0	103.1	78	5	54	60	10-4	2	2.61
Pat Clements†	L	30	23	0	0	0	24.2	23	0	11	9	2-0	0	3.28
Mark Williamson	R	32	12	0	0	0	18.2	16	1	10	14	0-0	1	0.96
Jim Poole	L	26	6	0	0	0	3.1	3	0	1	3	0-0	0	0.00

1992 Cleveland Indians 4th AL East 76-86 .469 20.0 GB

Mike Hargrove

Player	Gm by Position	B	Age	G	AB	R	H	2B	3B	HR	RBI	BB	SO	SB	Avg	OBP	Slg
Sandy Alomar Jr.	C88,DH1	R	26	89	299	22	75	16	0	2	26	13	32	3	.251	.293	.324
Paul Sorrento	1B121,DH11	L	26	140	458	52	123	24	1	18	60	51	89	0	.269	.341	.443
Carlos Baerga	2B160,DH1	S	23	161	657	92	205	32	1	20	105	35	76	10	.312	.354	.455
Brook Jacoby	3B111,1B10	R	32	120	291	30	76	7	0	4	36	28	54	0	.261	.324	.326
Mark Lewis	SS121,3B1	R	22	122	413	44	109	21	0	5	30	25	69	4	.264	.308	.351
Mark Whiten	OF144,DH2	S	25	148	508	73	129	19	4	9	43	72	102	16	.254	.347	.360
Kenny Lofton	OF143	L	25	148	576	96	164	15	8	5	42	68	54	66	.285	.362	.365
Thomas Howard†	OF97,DH2	S	27	117	358	36	99	15	2	2	32	17	60	15	.277	.308	.346
Albert Belle	DH100,OF52	R	25	153	585	81	152	23	1	34	112	52	128	8	.260	.320	.477
Glenallen Hill	OF59,DH34	R	27	102	369	38	89	16	1	18	49	20	73	9	.241	.287	.436
Junior Ortiz	C86	R	32	86	244	20	61	7	0	0	24	12	23	1	.250	.296	.279
Carlos Martinez	1B37,3B28,DH4	R	27	69	228	23	60	9	1	5	35	7	21	1	.263	.283	.377
Felix Fermin	SS55,3B17,2B7*	R	28	79	215	27	58	7	2	0	13	18	10	0	.270	.326	.321
Jim Thome	3B40	L	21	40	117	8	24	3	1	2	12	10	34	2	.205	.275	.299
Alex Cole†	OF24,DH3	L	26	41	97	11	20	1	0	0	5	10	21	9	.206	.284	.216
Reggie Jefferson	1B15,DH7	S	23	24	89	8	30	6	2	1	6	1	17	0	.337	.352	.483
Jesse Levis	C21,DH1	L	24	28	43	2	12	4	0	1	3	0	5	0	.279	.279	.442
Craig Worthington	3B9	R	27	9	24	0	4	0	0	0	2	2	4	0	.167	.231	.167
Tony Perezchica	3B9,2B4,SS4*	R	26	18	20	2	2	1	0	0	1	2	6	0	.100	.182	.150
Wayne Kirby	DH4,OF2	L	28	21	18	9	3	1	0	1	1	3	2	0	.167	.286	.389
Dave Rohde	3B5	S	28	5	7	0	0	0	0	0	0	2	3	0	.000	.222	.000
Jose Hernandez	SS3	R	22	3	4	0	0	0	0	0	0	0	2	0	.000	.000	.000

F. Fermin, 2 G at 1B; T. Perezchica, 1 G at DH

Pitcher	T	Age	G	GS	CG	ShO	IP	H	HR	BB	SO	W-L	Sv	ERA
Charles Nagy	R	25	33	33	10	3	252.0	245	11	57	169	17-10	0	2.96
Dennis Cook	L	29	32	25	1	0	158.0	156	29	50	96	5-7	0	3.82
Jack Armstrong	R	27	35	23	1	0	166.2	176	23	67	114	6-15	0	4.64
Scott Scudder	R	24	23	22	0	0	109.0	134	10	55	66	6-10	0	5.28
Dave Otto	L	27	18	16	0	0	80.1	110	12	33	32	5-9	0	7.06
Jose Mesa†	R	26	15	15	1	1	93.0	92	5	43	40	4-4	0	4.16
Denis Boucher	L	24	8	7	0	0	41.0	48	9	20	17	2-2	0	6.37
Dave Mlicki	R	24	4	4	0	0	21.2	23	3	16	16	0-2	0	4.98
Alan Embree	L	22	4	4	0	0	18.0	19	3	8	12	0-2	0	7.00
Jeff Mutis	L	25	3	2	0	0	11.1	24	4	6	8	0-2	0	9.53
Jeff Shaw	R	25	2	1	0	0	7.2	7	2	4	3	0-1	0	8.22
Steve Olin	R	26	72	0	0	0	88.1	80	8	27	47	8-5	29	2.34
Derek Lilliquist	L	26	71	0	0	0	61.2	39	5	18	47	5-3	6	1.75
Ted Power	R	37	64	0	0	0	99.1	88	7	35	51	3-3	6	2.54
Eric Plunk	R	28	58	0	0	0	71.2	61	5	38	50	9-6	4	3.64
Kevin Wickander	L	27	44	0	0	0	41.0	39	1	28	38	2-0	1	3.07
Rod Nichols	R	27	30	9	0	0	105.1	114	13	31	56	4-3	0	4.53
Mike Christopher	R	28	10	0	0	0	18.0	17	2	10	13	0-0	0	3.00
Brad Arnsberg	R	28	8	0	0	0	10.2	13	6	11	5	0-0	0	11.81
Eric Bell	L	28	7	1	0	0	15.1	22	1	9	10	0-2	0	7.63

1992 New York Yankees 4th AL East 76-86 .469 20.0 GB

Buck Showalter

Player	Gm by Position	B	Age	G	AB	R	H	2B	3B	HR	RBI	BB	SO	SB	Avg	OBP	Slg
Matt Nokes	C111	L	28	121	384	42	86	9	1	22	59	37	62	0	.224	.293	.424
Don Mattingly	1B143,DH15	L	31	157	640	89	184	40	0	14	86	39	43	3	.288	.327	.416
Pat Kelly	2B101,DH1	R	24	106	318	38	72	22	2	7	27	25	72	8	.226	.301	.374
Charlie Hayes	3B139,1B4	R	27	142	509	52	131	19	2	18	66	28	100	3	.257	.297	.409
Andy Stankiewicz	SS81,2B34,DH1	R	27	116	400	52	107	22	2	2	25	38	42	9	.268	.338	.348
Roberto Kelly	OF146	R	27	152	580	81	158	31	2	10	66	41	96	28	.272	.322	.384
Mel Hall	OF136,DH11	L	31	152	583	67	163	36	3	15	81	29	53	4	.280	.310	.429
Danny Tartabull	OF69,DH53	R	29	123	421	72	112	19	0	25	85	103	115	2	.266	.409	.489
Kevin Maas	DH62,1B22	L	27	98	286	35	71	12	0	11	35	25	63	3	.248	.305	.406
Randy Velarde	SS75,3B26,OF23*	R	29	121	412	57	112	24	1	7	46	38	78	7	.272	.333	.386
Bernie Williams	OF62	S	23	62	261	39	73	14	2	5	26	29	36	7	.280	.354	.406
Mike Gallego	2B40,SS14	R	31	53	173	24	44	7	1	3	14	20	22	0	.254	.343	.358
Mike Stanley	C55,DH6,1B4	R	29	68	173	24	43	7	0	8	27	33	45	0	.249	.372	.428
Dion James	OF46,DH5	L	29	67	145	24	38	8	0	3	17	22	15	1	.262	.359	.379
Jim Leyritz	DH31,C18,1B2*	R	28	63	144	17	37	6	0	7	26	14	22	0	.257	.341	.444
Jesse Barfield	OF30	R	32	30	95	8	13	2	0	2	7	9	27	1	.137	.210	.221
Gerald Williams	OF12	R	25	15	27	7	8	2	0	3	6	0	3	2	.296	.296	.704
J.T. Snow	1B6	S	24	7	14	1	2	1	0	0	2	5	5	0	.143	.368	.214
Dave Silvestri	SS6	R	24	7	13	3	4	0	2	0	1	0	3	0	.308	.308	.615
Mike Humphreys	OF2,DH1	R	25	4	10	0	1	0	0	0	0	0	1	0	.100	.100	.100
Hensley Meulens	3B2	R	25	2	5	1	3	0	0	1	1	1	0	0	.600	.667	1.200

R. Velarde, 3 G at 2B; J. Leyritz, 2 G at 3B, 2 G at OF, 1 G at 2B

Pitcher	T	Age	G	GS	CG	ShO	IP	H	HR	BB	SO	W-L	Sv	ERA
Melido Perez	R	26	33	33	10	1	247.2	212	16	93	218	13-16	0	2.87
Scott Sanderson	R	35	33	33	2	1	193.1	220	28	64	104	12-11	0	4.93
Scott Kamieniecki	R	28	28	28	4	0	188.0	193	13	74	88	6-14	0	4.36
Tim Leary†	R	34	18	15	2	0	97.0	84	9	57	34	5-6	0	5.57
Sam Militello	R	22	9	9	0	0	60.0	43	6	32	42	3-3	0	3.45
Jeff Johnson	L	25	13	8	0	0	52.2	71	4	23	14	2-3	0	6.66
Bob Wickman	R	23	8	8	0	0	50.1	51	2	20	21	6-1	0	4.11
Sterling Hitchcock	L	21	3	3	0	0	13.0	23	2	6	6	0-2	0	8.31
John Habyan	R	28	56	0	0	0	72.2	84	6	21	44	5-6	7	3.84
Steve Farr	R	35	50	0	0	0	52.0	34	2	19	37	2-2	30	1.56
Rich Monteleone	R	29	47	0	0	0	92.2	82	7	27	62	7-3	0	3.30
Greg Cadaret	L	30	46	11	1	0	103.2	104	12	74	73	4-8	1	4.25
Tim Burke†	R	33	23	0	0	0	27.2	26	2	15	8	2-2	0	3.25
Shawn Hillegas†	R	27	21	9	1	1	78.1	96	12	33	46	1-8	0	5.51
Steve Howe	L	34	20	0	0	0	22.0	9	1	3	12	3-0	6	2.45
Jerry Nielsen	L	25	20	0	0	0	19.2	17	1	18	12	1-0	0	4.58
Lee Guetterman†	L	33	15	0	0	0	22.2	35	5	13	5	1-1	0	9.53
Russ Springer	R	23	14	0	0	0	16.0	18	0	10	12	0-0	0	6.19
Curt Young†	L	32	13	5	0	0	43.1	51	1	10	13	3-0	0	3.32

1992 Detroit Tigers 6th AL East 75-87 .463 21.0 GB

Sparky Anderson

Player	Gm by Position	B	Age	G	AB	R	H	2B	3B	HR	RBI	BB	SO	SB	Avg	OBP	Slg
Mickey Tettleton	C113,DH40,1B3*	S	31	157	525	82	125	25	0	32	83	122	137	0	.238	.379	.469
Cecil Fielder	1B114,DH43	R	28	155	594	80	145	22	0	35	124	73	151	0	.244	.325	.458
Lou Whitaker	2B119,DH10	L	35	130	453	77	126	26	0	19	71	81	46	6	.278	.386	.461
Scott Livingstone	3B112	L	26	117	354	43	100	21	0	4	46	21	36	1	.282	.319	.376
Travis Fryman	SS137,3B26	R	23	161	659	87	175	31	4	20	96	45	144	8	.266	.316	.416
Dan Gladden	OF108,DH2	R	34	113	417	57	106	20	1	7	42	30	64	4	.254	.304	.357
Rob Deer	OF106,DH2	R	31	110	393	66	97	20	1	32	64	51	131	4	.247	.337	.547
Milt Cuyler	OF89	S	23	89	291	39	70	11	1	3	28	10	62	8	.241	.275	.316
Tony Phillips	OF69,2B57,DH34*	S	33	159	606	114	167	32	3	10	64	114	93	12	.276	.387	.388
Mark Carreon	OF83,DH13	R	28	101	336	34	78	11	1	10	41	22	57	3	.232	.278	.360
Chad Kreuter	C62,DH1	S	27	67	190	22	48	9	0	2	16	20	38	0	.253	.321	.332
Dave Bergman	1B55,DH12,OF1	L	39	87	181	17	42	3	0	1	10	20	19	1	.232	.305	.265
Skeeter Barnes	3B39,1B17,OF15*	R	35	95	165	27	45	8	1	3	25	10	18	3	.273	.318	.388
Gary Pettis†	OF46	S	34	48	129	27	26	4	3	1	12	27	34	13	.202	.338	.302
Alan Trammell	SS27	R	34	29	102	11	28	7	1	1	11	15	4	2	.275	.370	.392
Phil Clark	OF13,DH7	R	24	23	54	3	22	4	0	1	5	6	9	1	.407	.467	.537
Shawn Hare	OF9,1B4	L	25	15	26	0	3	1	0	0	5	2	4	0	.115	.172	.154
Rico Brogna	1B8,DH2	L	22	9	26	3	5	1	0	1	3	3	5	0	.192	.276	.346
Rich Rowland	C3,DH2,1B1*	R	26	6	14	2	3	0	0	0	0	3	3	0	.214	.353	.214

M. Tettleton, 2 G at OF; T. Phillips, 20 G at 3B, 1 G at SS; S. Barnes, 7 G at DH, 7 G at 2B; R. Rowland, 1 G at 3B

Pitcher	T	Age	G	GS	CG	ShO	IP	H	HR	BB	SO	W-L	Sv	ERA
Bill Gullickson	R	33	34	34	4	1	221.2	228	35	50	64	14-13	0	4.34
Frank Tanana	L	38	32	31	3	0	186.2	188	22	90	91	13-11	0	4.39
Eric King	R	28	17	14	0	0	79.1	90	12	28	45	4-6	1	5.22
Scott Aldred	L	24	16	13	0	0	65.0	80	12	33	34	3-8	0	6.78
Dave Haas	R	26	12	11	1	1	61.2	68	8	16	29	5-3	0	3.94
Buddy Groom	L	26	12	7	0	0	38.2	48	4	22	15	0-5	1	5.82
Mike Munoz	L	26	65	0	0	0	48.0	44	3	25	23	1-2	2	3.00
Mike Henneman	R	30	60	0	0	0	77.1	75	6	20	58	2-6	24	3.96
Kurt Knudsen	R	25	48	1	0	0	70.2	70	9	41	51	2-3	5	4.58
John Doherty	R	25	47	11	0	0	116.0	131	4	25	37	7-4	3	3.88
Les Lancaster	R	30	41	1	0	0	86.2	101	11	51	35	3-4	0	6.33
John Kiely	R	27	39	0	0	0	55.0	44	2	28	18	4-2	0	2.13
Walt Terrell	R	34	36	14	1	0	136.2	163	14	48	61	7-10	0	5.20
Mark Leiter	R	29	35	14	1	0	112.0	116	9	43	75	8-5	0	4.18
Kevin Ritz	R	27	23	11	0	0	80.1	88	4	44	57	2-5	0	5.60

1992 Boston Red Sox 7th AL East 73-89 .451 23.0 GB

Butch Hobson

Player	Gm by Position	B	Age	G	AB	R	H	2B	3B	HR	RBI	BB	SO	SB	Avg	OBP	Slg
Tony Pena	C132	R	35	133	410	39	99	21	1	1	38	24	61	3	.241	.284	.305
Mo Vaughn	1B85,DH20	L	24	113	355	42	83	16	2	13	57	47	67	3	.234	.326	.400
Jody Reed	2B142,DH1	R	29	143	550	64	136	27	1	3	40	62	44	7	.247	.321	.316
Wade Boggs	3B117,DH21	L	34	143	514	62	133	22	4	7	50	74	31	1	.259	.353	.358
Luis Rivera	SS93,DH1,2B1*	R	28	102	288	17	62	11	1	0	29	26	56	4	.215	.287	.260
Bob Zupcic	OF114,DH5	R	25	124	392	46	108	19	1	3	43	25	60	2	.276	.322	.352
Tom Brunansky	OF92,1B28,DH17	R	31	138	458	47	122	31	3	15	74	66	96	2	.266	.354	.445
Phil Plantier	OF76,DH23	L	23	108	349	46	86	19	0	7	30	44	83	2	.246	.332	.361
Jack Clark	DH64,1B13	R	36	81	257	32	54	11	0	5	33	56	87	1	.210	.350	.311
Scott Cooper	1B62,3B47,DH2*	L	24	123	337	34	93	21	0	5	33	37	33	1	.276	.346	.383
Billy Hatcher†	OF75	R	31	75	315	37	75	16	2	1	23	17	41	4	.238	.283	.311
Ellis Burks	OF63,DH1	R	27	66	235	35	60	8	3	8	30	25	48	5	.255	.327	.417
Herm Winningham	OF67,DH6	L	30	105	234	27	55	8	1	1	14	10	53	6	.235	.266	.291
Tim Naehring	SS30,2B23,3B10*	R	25	72	186	12	43	8	0	3	14	18	31	0	.231	.308	.323
John Valentin	SS58	R	25	58	185	21	51	13	0	5	25	20	17	1	.276	.351	.427
Mike Greenwell	OF41,DH6	L	28	49	180	16	42	2	0	2	18	18	19	2	.233	.307	.278
Eric Wedge	DH20,C5	R	24	27	68	11	17	2	0	5	11	13	18	0	.250	.370	.500
John Flaherty	C34	R	24	35	66	3	13	2	0	0	2	3	7	0	.197	.229	.227
John Marzano	C18,DH1	R	29	19	50	4	4	2	1	0	1	2	12	0	.080	.132	.160
Steve Lyons†	1B8,OF5,DH2*	L	32	21	28	3	7	0	1	0	2	2	9	0	.250	.300	.321
Tom Barrett	2B2	S	32	4	3	1	0	0	0	0	0	2	0	0	.000	.400	.000
Mike Brumley		S	29	2	1	0	0	0	0	0	0	0	1	0	.000	.000	.000

L. Rivera, 1 G at 3B, 1 G at OF; S. Cooper, 1 G at 2B, 1 G at SS; T. Naehring, 4 G at DH, 1 G at OF; S. Lyons, 1 G at 2B

Pitcher	T	Age	G	GS	CG	ShO	IP	H	HR	BB	SO	W-L	Sv	ERA
Frank Viola	L	32	35	35	6	1	238.0	214	13	89	121	13-12	0	3.44
Roger Clemens	R	29	32	32	11	5	246.2	203	11	62	208	18-11	0	2.41
Joe Hesketh	L	33	30	25	1	0	148.2	162	15	58	104	8-9	1	4.36
John Dopson	R	28	25	25	0	0	141.1	159	17	38	55	7-11	0	4.08
Mike Gardiner	R	26	28	18	0	0	130.2	126	12	58	79	4-10	0	4.75
Greg Harris	R	36	70	2	1	0	107.2	82	6	60	73	4-9	4	2.51
Tony Fossas	L	34	60	0	0	0	29.2	31	1	14	19	1-2	2	2.43
Danny Darwin	R	36	51	15	2	0	161.1	159	11	53	124	9-9	3	3.96
Jeff Reardon†	R	36	46	0	0	0	42.1	53	6	7	32	2-2	27	4.25
Matt Young	L	33	28	8	1	0	70.2	69	7	42	57	0-4	0	4.58
Paul Quantrill	R	23	27	0	0	0	49.1	55	1	15	24	2-3	1	2.19
Tom Bolton†	L	30	21	1	0	0	29.0	34	0	14	23	1-2	0	3.41
Daryl Irvine	R	27	21	0	0	0	28.0	31	1	14	10	3-4	0	6.11
Ken Ryan	R	23	7	0	0	0	7.0	4	2	5	5	0-0	1	6.43
Peter Hoy	R	26	5	0	0	0	3.2	8	0	2	2	0-0	0	7.36
Scott Taylor	L	24	4	1	0	0	14.2	13	4	4	7	1-1	0	4.91

1992 Oakland Athletics 1st AL West 96-66 .593 —

Tony La Russa

Player	Gm by Position	B	Age	G	AB	R	H	2B	3B	HR	RBI	BB	SO	SB	Avg	OBP	Slg
Terry Steinbach	C124,1B5,DH2	R	30	128	438	48	122	20	1	12	53	45	58	2	.279	.345	.411
Mark McGwire	1B139,DH1	R	28	139	467	87	125	22	0	42	104	90	105	0	.268	.385	.585
Mike Bordick	2B95,SS70	R	26	154	504	62	151	19	4	3	48	40	59	12	.300	.358	.371
Carney Lansford	3B119,1B18,DH2*	R	35	135	496	65	130	30	1	7	75	43	39	7	.262	.325	.369
Walt Weiss	SS103	S	28	103	316	36	67	5	2	0	21	43	39	6	.212	.305	.241
Willie Wilson	OF120,DH5	S	36	132	396	38	107	15	5	0	37	35	65	28	.270	.329	.333
Rickey Henderson	OF108,DH6	R	33	117	396	77	112	18	3	15	46	95	56	48	.283	.426	.457
Jose Canseco†	OF77,DH20	R	27	97	366	66	90	11	0	22	72	48	104	5	.246	.335	.456
Harold Baines	DH116,OF23	L	33	140	478	58	121	18	0	16	76	59	61	1	.253	.331	.391
Lance Blankenship	2B78,OF51,1B7*	R	28	123	349	59	84	24	1	3	34	82	57	21	.241	.393	.341
Jerry Browne	3B58,OF43,2B19*	S	26	111	324	43	93	12	2	3	40	40	40	3	.287	.366	.364
Jamie Quirk	C59,1B9,3B2*	L	37	78	177	13	39	7	1	2	11	16	28	0	.220	.294	.305
Eric Fox	OF43,DH3	S	28	51	143	24	34	5	2	3	13	13	29	3	.238	.299	.364
Randy Ready	DH24,OF24,3B7*	R	32	61	125	17	25	2	0	3	17	25	23	1	.200	.329	.288
Ruben Sierra†	OF25,DH2	S	26	27	101	17	28	4	1	3	17	14	9	2	.277	.359	.426
Scott Brosius	OF20,3B12,1B3*	R	25	38	87	13	19	2	0	4	13	3	13	3	.218	.258	.379
Dave Henderson	OF12,DH4	R	33	20	63	1	9	1	0	0	2	2	16	0	.143	.169	.159
Troy Neel	DH9,OF9,1B2	L	26	24	53	8	14	3	0	3	9	5	15	0	.264	.339	.491
Dann Howitt†	OF19,1B4,DH1	L	28	22	48	1	6	0	0	1	2	5	4	0	.125	.208	.188
Mike Kingery	OF10	L	31	12	28	3	3	0	0	0	1	1	3	0	.107	.138	.107
Scott Hemond†	C8,SS3,3B2*	R	26	17	27	7	6	1	0	0	1	3	7	1	.222	.300	.259
Henry Mercedes	C9	R	22	9	5	1	4	0	1	0	1	0	1	0	.800	.800	1.200
Ron Darling	P33,DH1	R	31	33	0	0	0	0	0	0	0	0	0	0	—	—	—

C. Lansford, 1 G at SS; L. Blankenship, 3 G at DH; J. Browne, 1 G at DH, 1 G at SS; J. Quirk, 1 G at DH; R. Ready, 4 G at 1B, 4 G at 2B; S. Brosius, 1 G at DH, 1 G at SS; S. Hemond, 2 G at OF, 1 G at DH

Pitcher	T	Age	G	GS	CG	ShO	IP	H	HR	BB	SO	W-L	Sv	ERA
Mike Moore	R	32	36	36	2	0	223.0	229	20	103	117	17-12	0	4.12
Ron Darling	R	31	33	33	4	3	206.1	198	15	72	99	15-10	0	3.66
Dave Stewart	R	35	31	31	2	0	199.1	175	25	79	130	12-10	0	3.66
Bob Welch	R	35	20	20	0	0	123.2	114	13	43	47	11-7	0	3.27
Joe Slusarski	R	25	15	14	0	0	76.0	85	15	27	38	5-5	0	5.45
Kelly Downs†	R	31	18	13	0	0	82.0	72	4	46	38	5-5	0	3.29
Bobby Witt†	R	28	6	6	0	0	31.2	31	2	19	25	1-1	0	3.41
John Briscoe	R	24	2	2	0	0	7.0	12	0	9	4	0-1	0	6.43
Dennis Eckersley	R	37	69	0	0	0	80.0	62	5	11	93	7-1	51	1.91
Jeff Parrett	R	30	66	0	0	0	98.1	81	7	42	78	9-1	0	3.02
Vince Horsman	L	25	58	0	0	0	43.1	39	3	21	18	2-1	1	2.49
Rick Honeycutt	L	38	54	0	0	0	39.0	41	2	10	32	1-4	3	3.69
Kevin Campbell	R	27	32	5	0	0	65.0	66	4	45	38	2-3	1	5.12
Jim Corsi	R	30	32	0	0	0	44.0	44	2	18	19	4-2	0	1.43
Goose Gossage	R	40	30	0	0	0	38.0	32	5	19	26	0-2	0	2.84
Gene Nelson	R	31	28	2	0	0	51.2	68	5	22	23	3-1	0	6.45
Jeff Russell†	R	30	8	0	0	0	9.2	4	0	3	5	2-0	2	0.00
Mike Raczka	L	29	8	0	0	0	6.1	8	0	5	2	0-0	0	8.53
Bruce Walton	R	29	7	0	0	0	10.0	17	1	3	7	0-0	0	9.90
Shawn Hillegas†	R	27	5	0	0	0	7.2	8	1	4	3	0-0	0	2.35
Johnny Guzman	L	21	2	0	0	0	3.0	8	0	0	0	0-0	0	12.00
Todd Revenig	R	23	2	0	0	0	2.0	2	0	0	1	0-0	0	0.00

1992 Minnesota Twins 2nd AL West 90-72 .556 6.0 GB

Tom Kelly

Player	Gm by Position	B	Age	G	AB	R	H	2B	3B	HR	RBI	BB	SO	SB	Avg	OBP	Slg
Brian Harper	C133,DH2	R	32	140	502	58	154	25	0	9	73	26	22	0	.307	.343	.410
Kent Hrbek	1B104,DH8	L	32	112	394	52	96	20	0	15	58	71	56	5	.244	.357	.409
Chuck Knoblauch	2B154,DH1,SS1	R	23	155	600	104	178	19	6	2	56	88	60	34	.297	.384	.358
Scott Leius	3B125,SS10	R	26	129	409	50	102	18	2	2	35	34	61	6	.249	.309	.318
Greg Gagne	SS141	R	30	146	439	53	108	23	0	7	39	19	83	6	.246	.280	.346
Shane Mack	OF155	R	28	156	600	101	189	31	6	16	75	64	106	26	.315	.394	.467
Kirby Puckett	OF149,DH9,2B2*	R	31	160	639	104	210	38	4	19	110	44	97	17	.329	.374	.490
Pedro Munoz	OF122,DH3	R	23	127	418	44	113	16	3	12	71	17	90	4	.270	.298	.409
Chili Davis	DH125,OF4,1B1	S	32	138	444	63	128	27	2	12	66	73	76	4	.288	.386	.439
Gene Larkin	1B55,OF43,DH4	S	29	115	337	38	83	18	1	6	42	28	43	7	.246	.308	.359
Randy Bush	DH24,OF24,1B8	L	33	100	182	14	39	8	1	2	22	11	37	1	.214	.263	.302
Jeff Reboulet	SS36,3B22,2B13*	R	28	73	137	15	26	7	1	1	16	23	26	3	.190	.311	.277
Lenny Webster	C49,DH1	R	27	53	118	10	33	10	1	1	13	9	11	0	.280	.331	.407
Mike Pagliarulo	3B37,DH1	L	32	42	105	10	21	4	0	0	9	1	17	1	.200	.213	.238
J.T. Bruett	OF45,DH2	L	24	56	76	7	19	4	0	0	2	6	12	6	.250	.313	.303
Terry Jorgensen	1B13,3B9,SS2	R	25	22	58	5	18	1	0	0	5	3	11	1	.310	.349	.328
Donnie Hill	SS10,2B7,3B5*	S	31	25	51	7	15	3	0	0	2	5	6	0	.294	.368	.353
Darren Reed†	OF13,DH1	R	26	14	33	2	6	2	0	0	4	2	11	0	.182	.216	.242
Jarvis Brown	OF31,DH1	R	25	35	15	8	1	0	0	0	0	2	4	2	.067	.222	.067
Bernardo Brito	OF3,DH1	R	28	8	14	1	2	1	0	0	2	0	4	0	.143	.133	.214
Derek Parks	C7	R	23	7	6	1	2	0	0	0	0	1	1	0	.333	.500	.333
Luis Quinones	DH1,3B1,SS1	S	30	3	5	0	1	0	0	0	1	0	0	0	.200	.167	.200

K. Puckett, 2 G at 3B, 1 G at SS; J. Reboulet, 7 G at OF, 1 G at DH; D. Hill, 1 G at OF

Pitcher	T	Age	G	GS	CG	ShO	IP	H	HR	BB	SO	W-L	Sv	ERA
John Smiley	L	27	34	34	5	2	241.0	205	17	65	163	16-9	0	3.21
Kevin Tapani	R	28	34	34	4	1	220.0	226	17	48	138	16-11	0	3.97
Scott Erickson	R	24	32	32	5	3	212.0	197	18	83	101	13-12	0	3.40
Bill Krueger†	L	34	27	27	2	2	161.1	166	18	46	86	10-6	0	4.30
Pat Mahomes	R	21	14	13	0	0	69.2	73	5	37	44	3-4	0	5.04
Willie Banks	R	23	16	12	0	0	71.0	80	6	37	37	4-4	0	5.70
Mike Trombley	R	25	10	7	0	0	46.1	43	5	17	38	3-2	0	3.30
Rick Aguilera	R	30	64	0	0	0	66.2	60	7	17	52	2-6	41	2.84
Carl Willis	R	31	59	0	0	0	79.1	73	4	11	45	7-3	1	2.72
Mark Guthrie	R	26	54	0	0	0	75.0	59	7	23	76	2-3	5	2.88
Tom Edens	R	31	52	0	0	0	76.1	65	1	36	57	6-3	3	2.83
Gary Wayne	L	29	41	0	0	0	48.0	46	2	19	29	3-3	0	2.63
Bob Kipper	L	27	25	0	0	0	38.2	40	8	14	22	3-3	0	4.42
David West	L	27	9	3	0	0	28.1	32	3	20	19	1-3	0	6.99
Paul Abbott	R	24	6	0	0	0	11.0	12	1	5	13	0-0	0	3.27
Larry Casian	L	26	6	0	0	0	6.2	7	0	1	2	1-0	0	2.70
Mauro Gozzo	R	26	2	0	0	0	1.2	7	2	0	1	0-0	0	27.00

1992 Chicago White Sox 3rd AL West 86-76 .531 10.0 GB

Gene Lamont

Player	Gm by Position	B	Age	G	AB	R	H	2B	3B	HR	RBI	BB	SO	SB	Avg	OBP	Slg
Ron Karkovice	C119,OF1	R	28	123	342	39	81	12	1	13	50	30	89	10	.237	.302	.392
Frank Thomas	1B158,DH2	R	24	160	573	108	185	46	2	24	115	122	88	6	.323	.439	.536
Steve Sax	2B141,DH1	R	32	143	567	74	134	26	4	4	47	43	42	30	.236	.290	.317
Robin Ventura	3B157,1B2	L	24	157	592	85	167	38	1	16	93	93	71	2	.282	.375	.431
Craig Grebeck	SS85,3B7,OF2	R	27	88	287	24	77	21	2	3	35	30	34	0	.268	.341	.387
Lance Johnson	OF157	L	28	157	567	67	158	15	12	3	47	34	33	41	.279	.318	.363
Tim Raines	OF129,DH14	S	32	144	551	102	162	22	9	7	54	81	48	45	.294	.380	.405
Shawn Abner	OF94,DH1	R	26	97	208	21	58	10	1	1	16	12	35	1	.279	.323	.351
George Bell	DH140,OF15	R	32	155	627	74	160	27	0	25	112	31	97	5	.255	.294	.418
Dan Pasqua	OF81,1B5,DH1	L	30	93	265	26	56	16	1	6	33	36	57	0	.211	.305	.347
Carlton Fisk	C54,DH2	R	44	62	188	12	43	4	1	3	21	23	38	3	.229	.313	.309
Warren Newson	OF50,DH4	L	27	63	136	19	30	3	0	1	11	37	38	3	.221	.387	.265
Joey Cora	2B28,DH16,SS6*	S	27	68	122	27	30	7	1	0	9	22	13	10	.246	.371	.320
Mike Huff	OF56,DH1	R	28	60	115	13	24	5	0	0	8	10	24	1	.209	.273	.252
Dale Sveum†	SS37,1B2,3B2	S	28	40	114	15	25	9	0	2	12	12	29	1	.219	.287	.351
Esteban Beltre	SS43,DH4	R	24	49	110	21	21	2	0	1	10	3	18	1	.191	.211	.236
Matt Merullo	C16,DH1	L	26	24	50	3	9	1	1	0	3	1	8	0	.180	.208	.240
Ozzie Guillen	SS12	L	28	12	40	5	8	4	0	0	7	1	5	1	.200	.214	.300
Shawn Jeter	OF8,DH2	L	26	13	18	1	2	0	0	0	0	0	7	0	.111	.111	.111
Scott Hemond†	DH4,OF2,C1*	R	26	8	13	1	3	1	0	0	1	1	6	0	.231	.267	.308
Chris Cron	1B5,OF1	R	28	6	10	0	0	0	0	0	0	0	4	0	.000	.000	.000
Nelson Santovenia	C2	R	30	2	3	1	1	0	0	1	2	0	0	0	.333	.333	1.333

J. Cora, 5 G at 3B; S. Hemond, 1 G at 3B

Pitcher	T	Age	G	GS	CG	ShO	IP	H	HR	BB	SO	W-L	Sv	ERA
Jack McDowell	R	26	34	34	13	1	260.2	247	21	75	178	20-10	0	3.18
Kirk McCaskill	R	31	34	34	0	0	209.0	193	11	95	109	12-13	0	4.18
Alex Fernandez	R	22	29	29	4	2	187.2	199	21	50	95	8-11	0	4.27
Greg Hibbard	L	27	31	28	0	0	176.0	187	17	57	69	10-7	1	4.40
Charlie Hough	R	44	27	27	4	0	176.1	160	19	66	76	7-12	0	3.93
Scott Radinsky	L	24	68	0	0	0	59.1	54	3	34	48	3-7	15	2.73
Bobby Thigpen	R	28	55	0	0	0	55.0	58	4	33	45	1-3	22	4.75
Terry Leach	R	38	51	0	0	0	73.2	57	2	20	22	6-5	0	1.95
Roberto Hernandez	R	27	43	0	0	0	71.0	45	4	20	68	7-3	12	1.65
Donn Pall	R	30	39	0	0	0	73.0	79	9	27	27	5-2	1	4.93
Wilson Alvarez	L	22	34	9	0	0	100.1	103	12	65	66	5-3	1	5.20
Brian Drahman	R	25	5	0	0	0	7.0	6	0	2	1	0-0	0	2.57
Mike Dunne	R	29	4	1	0	0	12.2	12	0	6	6	2-0	0	4.26

1992 Texas Rangers 4th AL West 77-85 .475 19.0 GB

Bobby Valentine (45-41)/Toby Harrah (32-44)

Player	Gm by Position	B	Age	G	AB	R	H	2B	3B	HR	RBI	BB	SO	SB	Avg	OBP	Slg
Ivan Rodriguez	C116,DH2	R	20	123	420	39	109	16	1	8	37	24	73	0	.260	.300	.360
Rafael Palmeiro	1B156,DH2	L	27	159	608	84	163	27	4	22	85	72	83	2	.268	.352	.434
Al Newman	2B72,3B28,SS20*	S	32	116	246	25	54	5	0	0	12	34	26	9	.220	.317	.240
Dean Palmer	3B150	R	23	152	541	74	124	25	0	26	72	62	154	10	.229	.311	.420
Dickie Thon	SS87	R	34	95	275	30	68	15	3	4	37	20	40	12	.247	.293	.367
Juan Gonzalez	OF148,DH4	R	22	155	584	77	152	24	2	43	109	35	143	0	.260	.304	.529
Ruben Sierra†	OF119,DH4	S	26	124	500	66	139	30	6	14	70	31	59	12	.278	.315	.446
Kevin Reimer	OF110,DH32	L	28	148	494	56	132	32	2	16	58	42	103	2	.267	.336	.437
Brian Downing	DH93	R	41	107	320	53	89	18	0	10	39	62	58	1	.278	.407	.428
Jeff Huson	SS82,2B47,OF2*	L	27	123	318	49	83	14	3	4	24	41	43	18	.261	.342	.362
Jeff Frye	2B67	R	25	67	199	24	51	9	1	1	12	16	27	1	.256	.320	.327
Geno Petralli	C54,DH14,3B4*	L	32	94	192	11	38	12	0	1	18	20	34	0	.198	.274	.276
Monty Fariss	OF49,2B17,DH4*	R	24	67	166	13	36	7	1	3	21	17	51	0	.217	.297	.325
Jack Daugherty	OF26,DH13,1B8	S	31	59	127	13	26	9	0	0	9	16	21	2	.205	.295	.276
Julio Franco	DH15,2B9,OF4	R	30	35	107	19	25	7	0	2	8	15	17	1	.234	.328	.355
David Hulse	OF31,DH1	L	24	32	92	14	28	4	0	0	2	3	18	3	.304	.326	.348
John Cangelosi	OF65,DH6	S	29	73	85	12	16	2	0	1	6	18	16	6	.188	.330	.247
Jose Canseco†	OF13,DH8	R	27	22	73	8	17	4	0	4	15	15	24	1	.233	.385	.452
Cris Colon	SS14	S	23	14	36	5	6	0	0	0	1	1	8	0	.167	.189	.167
Donald Harris	OF24	R	24	24	33	3	6	1	0	0	1	0	15	1	.182	.182	.212
Russ McGinnis	C10,1B2,3B2	R	29	14	33	2	8	4	0	0	4	3	7	0	.242	.306	.364
Mario Diaz	SS16,2B3,3B1	R	30	19	31	2	7	1	0	0	1	1	2	0	.226	.250	.258
Dan Peltier	OF10	L	24	12	24	1	4	0	0	0	2	0	3	0	.167	.167	.167
Ray Stephens	C6,DH1	R	29	8	13	0	2	0	0	0	0	0	5	0	.154	.154	.154
John Russell	C4,OF2,DH1	R	31	7	10	1	1	0	0	0	2	1	4	0	.100	.231	.100
Rob Maurer	1B3,DH1	L	25	8	9	1	2	0	0	0	1	1	2	0	.222	.300	.222
Doug Davis	C1	R	29	1	1	0	1	0	0	0	0	0	0	0	1.000	1.000	1.000

A. Newman, 1 G at DH, 1 G at OF; J. Huson, 1 G at DH; G. Petralli, 2 G at 2B; M. Fariss, 1 G at 1B

Pitcher	T	Age	G	GS	CG	ShO	IP	H	HR	BB	SO	W-L	Sv	ERA
Kevin Brown	R	27	35	35	11	1	265.2	262	11	76	173	21-11	0	3.32
Jose Guzman	R	29	33	33	5	0	224.0	229	17	73	179	16-11	0	3.66
Nolan Ryan	R	45	27	27	2	0	157.1	138	9	69	157	5-9	0	3.72
Bobby Witt†	R	28	25	25	0	0	161.1	152	14	95	100	9-13	0	4.46
Roger Pavlik	R	24	13	12	1	0	62.0	66	3	34	45	4-4	0	4.21
Scott Chiamparino	R	25	4	4	0	0	25.1	25	2	5	13	0-4	0	3.55
Mike Jeffcoat	L	32	6	3	0	0	19.2	28	2	5	6	0-1	0	7.32
Dan Smith	L	23	4	2	0	0	14.1	18	1	8	5	0-3	0	5.02
Kenny Rogers	L	27	81	0	0	0	78.2	80	7	26	70	3-6	6	3.09
Jeff Russell†	R	30	51	0	0	0	56.2	51	3	22	43	2-3	28	1.91
Terry Mathews	R	27	40	0	0	0	42.1	48	4	31	26	2-4	0	5.95
Edwin Nunez†	R	29	39	0	0	0	45.2	51	5	16	39	0-2	3	5.52
Floyd Bannister	L	37	36	0	0	0	37.0	39	3	21	30	1-1	0	6.32
Todd Burns	R	28	35	10	0	0	103.0	97	8	32	55	3-5	1	3.84
Matt Whiteside	R	24	20	0	0	0	28.0	26	1	11	13	1-1	4	1.93
Brian Bohanon	L	23	18	7	0	0	45.2	57	7	25	29	1-1	0	6.31
Jeff Robinson†	R	30	16	4	0	0	45.2	50	6	21	18	4-4	0	5.72
Danilo Leon	R	25	15	0	0	0	18.1	18	5	10	15	1-1	0	5.89
Wayne Rosenthal	R	27	6	0	0	0	4.2	7	1	2	1	0-0	0	7.71
Lance McCullers	R	28	5	0	0	0	5.0	1	0	8	3	1-0	0	5.40
Steve Fireovid	R	35	3	0	0	0	6.2	10	0	4	0	1-0	0	4.05
Barry Manuel	R	26	3	0	0	0	5.2	6	2	1	9	1-0	0	4.76
Gerald Alexander	R	24	3	0	0	0	1.2	5	1	1	1	1-0	0	27.00
Don Carman	L	32	2	0	0	0	2.1	4	0	0	2	0-0	0	7.71
Mike Campbell	R	28	1	0	0	0	3.2	3	1	2	2	0-1	0	9.82

1992 California Angels 5th AL West 72-90 .444 24.0 GB

Buck Rodgers (19-20)/John Wathan (39-50)/Buck Rodgers (14-20)

Player	Gm by Position	B	Age	G	AB	R	H	2B	3B	HR	RBI	BB	SO	SB	Avg	OBP	Slg
Mike Fitzgerald	C74,OF11,3B3*	R	31	95	189	19	40	2	0	6	17	22	34	2	.212	.294	.317
Lee Stevens	1B91,DH2	L	24	106	312	25	69	19	0	7	37	29	64	1	.221	.288	.349
Luis Sojo	2B96,3B9,SS5	R	26	106	368	37	100	12	3	7	43	14	24	7	.272	.299	.378
Gary Gaetti	3B67,1B44,DH17	R	33	130	456	41	103	13	2	12	48	21	79	3	.226	.267	.342
Gary DiSarcina	SS157	R	24	157	518	48	128	19	0	3	42	20	50	9	.247	.283	.301
Chad Curtis	OF135,DH1	R	23	139	441	59	114	16	2	10	46	51	71	43	.259	.341	.372
Junior Felix	OF128,DH8	S	24	139	509	63	125	22	5	9	72	33	128	8	.246	.289	.361
Luis Polonia	OF99,DH47	L	27	149	577	83	165	17	4	0	35	45	64	51	.286	.337	.329
Hubie Brooks	DH70,1B6	R	35	82	306	28	66	13	0	8	36	12	46	3	.216	.247	.337
Rene Gonzales	3B53,2B42,1B13*	R	31	104	329	47	91	17	1	7	38	41	46	7	.277	.363	.398
Von Hayes	OF85,DH5,1B4	L	33	94	307	35	69	17	1	4	29	37	54	11	.225	.305	.326
Damion Easley	3B45,SS3	R	22	47	151	14	39	5	0	1	12	8	26	9	.258	.307	.311
Ron Tingley	C69	R	33	71	127	15	25	2	1	3	8	13	35	0	.197	.282	.299
John Orton	C43	R	26	43	114	11	25	3	0	2	12	7	32	1	.219	.276	.298
Alvin Davis	1B22,DH9	L	31	40	104	5	26	8	0	0	16	13	9	0	.250	.331	.327
Ken Oberkfell	2B21,DH5,1B2	L	36	41	91	6	24	1	0	0	10	8	5	0	.264	.317	.275
Bobby Rose	2B28,1B2	R	25	30	84	10	18	5	0	2	10	8	9	1	.214	.295	.345
Lance Parrish†	C22,DH2	R	36	24	83	7	19	2	0	4	11	5	22	0	.229	.270	.398
Tim Salmon	OF21	R	23	23	79	8	14	1	0	2	6	11	23	1	.177	.283	.266
Rob Ducey†	OF20,DH1	L	27	31	59	4	14	3	0	0	2	5	12	2	.237	.292	.288
John Morris	OF14,DH6	L	31	43	57	4	11	1	0	1	3	4	11	1	.193	.258	.263
Jose Gonzalez	OF22,DH1	R	27	33	55	4	10	2	0	0	2	7	20	0	.182	.270	.218
Reggie Williams	OF12,DH1	S	26	14	26	5	6	1	1	0	2	1	10	0	.231	.259	.346
Greg Myers†	C8	L	26	8	17	0	4	1	0	0	0	0	6	0	.235	.235	.294
Dick Schofield†	SS1	R	29	1	3	0	1	0	0	0	0	1	0	0	.333	.500	.333
Mark Langston	P32,DH1	R	31	33	2	1	0	0	0	0	0	0	2	0	.000	.000	.000

M. Fitzgerald, 2 G at 1B, 1 G at DH, 1 G at 2B; R. Gonzales, 8 G at SS

Pitcher	T	Age	G	GS	CG	ShO	IP	H	HR	BB	SO	W-L	Sv	ERA
Mark Langston	L	31	32	32	9	2	229.0	206	14	74	174	13-14	0	3.66
Chuck Finley	L	29	31	31	4	1	204.1	212	24	98	124	7-12	0	3.96
Jim Abbott	L	24	29	29	7	0	211.0	208	12	68	130	7-15	0	2.77
Julio Valera	R	23	30	28	4	2	188.0	188	15	64	113	8-11	0	3.73
Bert Blyleven	R	41	25	24	1	0	133.0	150	17	29	70	8-12	0	4.74
Don Robinson†	R	35	3	3	0	0	16.1	19	1	3	9	1-0	0	2.20
Hilly Hathaway	L	22	2	1	0	0	5.2	8	1	3	1	0-0	0	7.94
Chuck Crim	R	30	57	0	0	0	87.0	100	11	29	30	7-6	1	5.17
Steve Frey	L	28	51	0	0	0	45.1	39	6	22	24	4-2	4	3.57
Joe Grahe	R	25	46	7	0	0	94.2	85	5	39	39	5-6	21	3.52
Mark Eichhorn†	R	31	42	0	0	0	56.2	51	2	18	42	2-4	2	2.38
Scott Bailes	L	30	32	0	0	0	38.2	59	7	28	25	3-1	0	7.45
Bryan Harvey	R	29	25	0	0	0	28.2	22	4	11	34	0-4	13	2.83
Scott Lewis	R	26	21	2	0	0	38.1	36	3	14	18	4-0	0	3.99
Mike Butcher	R	27	19	0	0	0	27.2	29	3	13	24	2-2	0	3.25
Tim Fortugno	L	30	14	5	1	1	41.2	37	5	19	31	1-1	1	5.18

1992 Kansas City Royals 5th AL West 72-90 .444 24.0 GB

Hal McRae

Player	Gm by Position	B	Age	G	AB	R	H	2B	3B	HR	RBI	BB	SO	SB	Avg	OBP	Slg
Mike Macfarlane	C104,DH13	R	28	129	402	51	94	28	3	17	48	30	89	1	.234	.310	.445
Wally Joyner	1B145,DH4	L	30	149	572	66	154	36	2	9	66	55	50	11	.269	.336	.386
Keith Miller	2B93,OF16,DH1	R	29	106	416	57	118	24	4	4	38	31	46	16	.284	.352	.389
Gregg Jefferies	3B146,DH11,2B1	S	24	152	604	66	172	36	3	10	75	43	29	19	.285	.329	.404
Dave Howard	SS74,OF2	S	25	74	219	19	49	6	2	1	18	15	43	3	.224	.271	.283
Brian McRae	OF148,DH1	S	24	149	533	63	119	23	5	4	52	42	88	18	.223	.285	.308
Kevin McReynolds	OF106,DH1	R	32	109	373	45	92	25	0	13	49	67	48	7	.247	.357	.418
Jim Eisenreich	OF88,DH8	L	33	113	353	31	95	13	3	2	28	24	36	11	.269	.313	.340
George Brett	DH132,1B15,3B3	L	39	152	592	55	169	35	5	7	61	35	69	8	.285	.330	.397
Curtis Wilkerson	SS69,2B39,3B5*	S	31	111	296	27	74	10	1	2	29	18	47	18	.250	.292	.311
Brent Mayne	C62,3B8,DH1	L	24	82	213	16	48	10	0	0	18	11	26	0	.225	.260	.272
Gary Thurman	OF67,DH8	R	27	88	200	25	49	6	3	0	20	9	34	9	.245	.281	.305
Rico Rossy	SS51,3B9,2B3	R	28	59	149	21	32	8	1	1	12	20	20	0	.215	.310	.302
Kevin Koslofski	OF52	L	25	55	133	20	33	0	2	3	13	12	23	2	.248	.313	.346
Juan Samuel†	OF18,2B10	R	31	29	102	15	29	5	3	0	8	7	27	6	.284	.336	.392
Terry Shumpert	2B33,DH1,SS1	R	25	36	94	6	14	5	1	1	11	3	17	2	.149	.175	.255
Jeff Conine	OF23,1B4,DH1	R	26	28	91	10	23	5	2	0	9	8	23	0	.253	.313	.352
Chris Gwynn	OF19,DH2	L	27	34	84	10	24	3	2	1	7	3	10	0	.286	.303	.405
Bob Melvin	C21,1B3	R	30	32	70	5	22	5	0	0	6	5	13	0	.314	.351	.386
Harvey Pulliam	DH2,OF1	R	24	4	5	2	1	1	0	0	0	1	3	0	.200	.333	.400

C. Wilkerson, 1 G at DH

Pitcher	T	Age	G	GS	CG	ShO	IP	H	HR	BB	SO	W-L	Sv	ERA
Kevin Appier	R	24	30	30	3	0	208.1	167	10	68	150	15-8	0	2.46
Hipolito Pichardo	R	22	31	24	1	1	143.2	148	9	49	59	9-6	0	3.95
Mark Gubicza	R	29	18	18	2	1	111.1	110	8	36	81	7-6	0	3.72
Rick Reed	R	27	19	18	1	1	100.1	105	10	20	49	3-7	0	3.68
Luis Aquino	R	28	15	13	0	0	67.2	81	5	20	11	3-6	0	4.52
Chris Haney†	L	23	7	7	1	1	42.0	35	5	16	27	2-3	0	3.86
D. Rasmussen†	L	33	5	5	1	1	37.2	25	0	6	12	4-1	0	1.43
Dennis Moeller	L	24	5	4	0	0	18.0	24	5	11	6	0-3	0	7.00
Eddie Pierce	L	23	2	1	0	0	5.1	9	1	4	3	0-0	0	3.38
Jeff Montgomery	R	30	65	0	0	0	82.2	61	5	27	69	1-6	39	2.18
Rusty Meacham	R	24	64	0	0	0	101.2	88	5	21	64	10-4	2	2.74
Mike Magnante	L	27	44	12	0	0	89.1	115	5	35	31	4-9	0	4.94
Tom Gordon	R	24	40	11	0	0	117.2	116	9	55	98	6-10	0	4.59
Steve Shifflett	R	26	34	0	0	0	52.0	55	6	17	25	1-4	0	2.60
Neal Heaton†	L	32	31	0	0	0	41.0	43	5	22	29	3-1	0	4.17
Mike Boddicker	R	34	29	8	0	0	86.2	92	5	37	47	1-4	3	4.98
Juan Berenguer†	R	37	19	2	0	0	44.2	42	3	20	26	1-4	0	5.64
Mark Davis†	L	31	13	6	0	0	36.1	42	6	28	19	1-3	0	7.18
Curt Young†	L	32	10	2	0	0	24.1	29	1	7	7	1-2	0	5.18
Bill Sampen†	R	29	8	1	0	0	19.2	21	0	3	14	0-2	0	3.66
Richard Sauveur	L	28	8	0	0	0	14.1	15	1	8	7	0-1	0	4.40
Joel Johnston	R	25	5	0	0	0	2.2	3	2	2	0	0-0	0	13.50

1992 Seattle Mariners 7th AL West 64-98 .395 32.0 GB

Bill Plummer

Player	Gm by Position	B	Age	G	AB	R	H	2B	3B	HR	RBI	BB	SO	SB	Avg	OBP	Slg
Dave Valle	C122	R	31	124	367	39	88	16	1	9	30	27	58	0	.240	.305	.362
Pete O'Brien	1B81,DH35	L	34	134	396	40	88	15	1	14	52	40	27	2	.222	.289	.371
Harold Reynolds	2B134,DH1,OF1	S	31	140	458	55	113	23	3	3	33	45	41	15	.247	.316	.330
Edgar Martinez	3B103,DH28,1B2	R	29	135	528	100	181	46	3	18	73	54	61	14	.343	.404	.544
Omar Vizquel	SS136	S	25	136	483	49	142	20	4	0	21	32	38	15	.294	.340	.352
Jay Buhner	OF150	R	27	152	543	69	132	16	3	25	79	71	146	0	.243	.333	.422
Ken Griffey Jr.	OF137,DH3	L	22	142	565	83	174	39	4	27	103	44	67	10	.308	.361	.535
Henry Cotto	OF92,DH3	R	31	108	294	42	76	11	1	5	27	14	49	23	.259	.294	.354
Tino Martinez	1B78,DH47	L	24	136	460	53	118	19	2	16	66	42	77	2	.257	.316	.411
Kevin Mitchell	OF69,DH26	R	30	99	360	48	103	24	0	9	67	35	46	0	.286	.351	.428
Greg Briley	OF42,DH12,2B4*	L	27	86	200	18	55	10	0	5	12	4	31	9	.275	.290	.400
Lance Parrish†	C34,1B16,DH14	R	36	69	192	19	45	11	1	8	21	19	48	1	.234	.304	.427
Dave Cochrane	OF25,C21,3B10*	S	29	65	152	10	38	5	0	2	12	12	34	1	.250	.309	.322
Bret Boone	2B32,3B6	R	23	33	129	15	25	4	0	4	15	4	34	1	.194	.224	.318
Rich Amaral	3B17,SS17,OF3*	R	30	35	100	9	24	3	0	1	7	5	16	4	.240	.276	.300
Shane Turner	3B18,OF15	L	29	34	74	8	20	5	0	0	5	9	15	2	.270	.341	.338
Mike Blowers	3B29,1B3	R	27	31	73	7	14	3	0	1	2	6	20	0	.192	.253	.274
Jeff Schaefer	SS33,3B21,2B7*	R	32	65	70	5	8	2	0	1	3	2	10	0	.114	.139	.186
Dann Howitt†	OF11	L	28	13	37	6	10	4	1	1	8	3	5	1	.270	.302	.514
Matt Sinatro	C18	R	32	18	28	0	3	0	0	0	0	0	5	0	.107	.107	.107
John Moses	OF18,DH1	S	34	21	22	3	3	1	0	0	1	5	4	0	.136	.296	.182
Bill Haselman	C5,OF2	R	26	8	19	1	5	0	0	0	0	0	7	0	.263	.263	.263
Bert Heffernan	C5	L	27	8	11	0	1	1	0	0	1	0	1	0	.091	.091	.182
Patrick Lennon	1B1	R	24	1	2	0	0	0	0	0	0	0	0	0	.000	.000	.000
Scott Bradley†	C1	L	32	2	1	0	0	0	0	0	0	1	1	0	.000	.500	.000

G. Briley, 4 G at 3B; D. Cochrane, 3 G at 1B, 3 G at SS, 2 G at DH, 1 G at 2B; R. Amaral, 2 G at 1B, 1 G at 2B; J. Schaefer, 1 G at DH

Pitcher	T	Age	G	GS	CG	ShO	IP	H	HR	BB	SO	W-L	Sv	ERA
Dave Fleming	L	22	33	33	7	4	228.1	225	13	60	112	17-10	0	3.39
Randy Johnson	L	28	31	31	6	2	210.1	154	13	144	241	12-14	0	3.77
Erik Hanson	R	27	31	30	6	1	186.2	209	14	57	112	8-17	0	4.82
Brian Fisher	R	30	22	14	0	0	91.1	80	9	47	26	4-3	1	4.53
Tim Leary†	R	34	8	8	1	0	44.0	47	3	30	12	3-4	0	4.91
Clay Parker	R	29	8	6	0	0	33.1	47	6	11	20	0-2	0	7.56
Randy Kramer	R	31	4	4	0	0	16.1	30	2	7	6	0-1	0	7.71
Mike Walker	R	27	5	3	0	0	14.2	21	4	9	5	0-3	0	7.36
Jeff Nelson	R	25	66	0	0	0	81.0	71	7	44	46	1-7	6	3.44
Russ Swan	L	28	55	9	1	0	104.1	104	8	45	45	3-10	9	4.74
Mike Schooler	R	29	53	0	0	0	51.2	55	7	24	33	2-7	13	4.70
Dennis Powell	L	28	49	0	0	0	57.0	49	5	29	35	4-2	0	4.58
Calvin Jones	R	28	38	1	0	0	61.2	50	8	47	49	3-5	0	5.69
Rich DeLucia	R	27	30	11	0	0	83.2	100	13	35	66	3-6	1	5.49
Mark Grant	R	28	23	10	0	0	81.0	100	6	22	42	2-4	0	3.89
Jim Acker	R	33	17	0	0	0	30.2	45	4	12	11	0-0	0	5.28
Juan Agosto†	L	34	17	1	0	0	18.1	27	0	3	12	0-0	0	5.89
Shawn Barton	L	29	14	0	0	0	12.1	10	1	7	4	0-1	0	2.92
Eric Gunderson	L	26	9	0	0	0	9.1	12	1	5	2	2-1	0	8.68
Kerry Woodson	R	23	8	1	0	0	13.2	12	0	11	6	0-1	0	3.29
Gene Harris†	R	27	8	0	0	0	9.0	8	3	6	6	0-0	0	7.00
Dave Schmidt	R	35	3	0	0	0	3.1	7	1	3	1	0-0	0	18.90
Kevin Brown	L	26	2	0	0	0	3.0	4	1	3	2	0-0	0	9.00

»1992 Pittsburgh Pirates 1st NL East 96-66 .593 —

Jim Leyland

Player	Gm by Position	B	Age	G	AB	R	H	2B	3B	HR	RBI	BB	SO	SB	Avg	OBP	Slg
Mike LaValliere	C92,3B1	L	31	95	293	22	75	13	1	2	29	44	21	0	.256	.350	.328
Orlando Merced	1B114,OF17	S	25	134	405	50	100	28	5	6	60	52	63	5	.247	.332	.385
Jose Lind	2B134	R	28	135	468	38	110	14	1	0	39	26	29	3	.235	.275	.269
Steve Buechele†	3B80	R	30	80	285	27	71	14	1	8	43	34	61	0	.249	.331	.389
Jay Bell	SS159	R	26	159	632	87	167	36	6	9	55	55	103	7	.264	.326	.383
Andy Van Slyke	OF154	L	31	154	614	103	199	45	12	14	89	58	99	12	.324	.381	.505
Barry Bonds	OF139	L	27	140	473	109	147	36	5	34	103	127	69	39	.311	.456	.624
Cecil Espy	OF82	S	29	112	194	21	50	7	3	1	20	15	40	6	.258	.310	.340
Jeff King	3B73,1B32,2B32*	R	27	130	480	56	111	21	2	14	65	27	56	4	.231	.272	.371
Don Slaught	C79	R	33	87	255	26	88	17	3	4	37	17	23	2	.345	.384	.482
Alex Cole†	OF53	L	26	64	205	33	57	3	7	0	10	18	46	7	.278	.335	.361
Lloyd McClendon	OF60,1B18	R	33	84	190	26	48	8	1	3	20	28	24	1	.253	.350	.353
Gary Redus	1B36,OF15	R	35	76	176	26	45	7	3	3	12	17	25	11	.256	.321	.381
Gary Varsho	OF44	L	31	103	162	22	36	6	3	4	22	10	32	5	.222	.266	.370
John Wehner	3B34,1B13,2B5	R	25	55	123	11	22	6	0	0	4	12	22	3	.179	.252	.228
Kirk Gibson	OF13	L	35	16	56	6	11	0	0	2	5	3	12	3	.196	.237	.304
Tom Prince	C19,3B1	R	27	27	44	1	4	2	0	0	5	6	9	1	.091	.192	.136
Carlos Garcia	2B14,SS8	R	24	22	39	4	8	1	0	0	4	0	9	0	.205	.195	.231
Dave Clark	OF8	L	29	23	33	3	7	0	0	2	7	6	8	0	.212	.325	.394
Al Martin	OF7	L	24	12	12	1	2	0	1	0	2	0	5	0	.167	.154	.333
W. Pennyfeather	OF10	R	24	15	9	2	2	0	0	0	0	0	3	0	.222	.222	.222
Kevin Young	3B7,1B1	R	23	10	7	2	4	0	0	0	4	2	0	1	.571	.667	.571

J. King, 6 G at SS, 1 G at OF

Pitcher	T	Age	G	GS	CG	ShO	IP	H	HR	BB	SO	W-L	Sv	ERA
Doug Drabek	R	29	34	34	10	4	256.2	218	17	54	177	15-11	0	2.77
Randy Tomlin	L	26	35	33	1	1	208.2	226	11	42	90	14-9	0	3.41
Zane Smith	L	31	23	22	4	3	141.0	138	8	19	56	8-8	0	3.06
Bob Walk	R	35	36	19	1	0	135.0	132	10	43	60	10-6	2	3.20
Danny Jackson†	L	30	15	15	0	0	88.1	94	1	29	46	4-4	0	3.36
Tim Wakefield	R	25	13	13	4	1	92.0	76	3	35	51	8-1	0	2.15
Jeff Robinson†	R	30	8	7	0	0	36.1	33	2	15	14	3-1	0	4.46
Victor Cole	R	24	8	4	0	0	23.0	23	1	14	12	0-2	0	5.48
Roger Mason	R	33	65	0	0	0	88.0	80	11	33	56	5-7	8	4.09
Bob Patterson	L	33	60	0	0	0	64.2	59	7	23	43	6-3	9	2.92
Stan Belinda	R	25	59	0	0	0	71.1	58	8	29	57	6-4	18	3.15
Denny Neagle	L	23	55	6	0	0	86.1	81	9	43	77	4-6	2	4.48
Jerry Don Gleaton	L	34	23	0	0	0	31.2	34	4	19	18	1-0	0	4.26
Dennis Lamp	R	39	21	0	0	0	28.0	33	3	9	15	1-1	0	5.14
Vicente Palacios	R	28	20	8	0	0	53.0	56	1	27	33	3-2	0	4.25
Danny Cox†	R	32	16	0	0	0	24.1	20	2	8	18	3-1	3	3.33
Steve Cooke	L	22	11	0	0	0	23.0	22	2	4	10	2-0	1	3.52
Paul Wagner	R	24	6	1	0	0	13.0	9	0	5	5	2-0	0	0.69
Paul Miller	R	27	6	0	0	0	11.1	11	0	1	5	1-0	0	2.38
Miguel Batista	R	21	1	0	0	0	2.0	4	1	3	1	0-0	0	9.00
Blas Minor	R	24	1	0	0	0	2.0	3	0	0	0	0-0	0	4.50

1992 Montreal Expos 2nd NL East 87-75 .537 9.0 GB

Tom Runnells (17-20)/Felipe Alou (70-55)

Player	Gm by Position	B	Age	G	AB	R	H	2B	3B	HR	RBI	BB	SO	SB	Avg	OBP	Slg
Gary Carter	C85,1B5	R	38	95	285	24	62	18	1	5	29	33	37	0	.218	.299	.340
Tim Wallach	3B85,1B71	R	34	150	537	53	120	29	1	9	59	50	90	2	.223	.296	.331
Delino DeShields	2B134	L	23	135	530	82	155	19	8	7	56	54	108	46	.292	.359	.398
Bret Barberie	3B63,2B26,SS1	S	24	111	285	26	66	11	0	1	24	47	62	9	.232	.354	.281
Spike Owen	SS116	S	31	122	386	52	104	16	3	7	40	50	30	9	.269	.348	.381
Marquis Grissom	OF157	R	25	159	653	99	180	39	6	14	66	42	81	78	.276	.322	.418
Larry Walker	OF139	L	25	143	528	85	159	31	4	23	93	41	97	18	.301	.353	.506
Moises Alou	OF100	R	25	115	341	53	96	28	2	9	56	25	46	16	.282	.328	.455
Archi Cianfrocco	1B56,3B19,OF5	R	25	86	232	25	56	5	2	6	30	11	66	3	.241	.276	.358
Darrin Fletcher	C69	L	25	83	222	13	54	10	2	2	26	14	28	0	.243	.289	.333
John VanderWal	OF57,1B7	L	26	105	213	21	51	8	2	4	20	24	36	3	.239	.316	.352
Ivan Calderon	OF46	R	30	48	170	19	45	14	2	3	24	14	22	1	.265	.323	.424
Greg Colbrunn	1B47	R	22	52	168	12	45	8	0	2	18	6	34	3	.268	.294	.351
Wil Cordero	SS35,2B9	R	20	45	126	17	38	4	1	2	8	9	31	0	.302	.353	.397
Tom Foley	SS33,2B13,1B12*	L	32	72	115	7	20	3	1	0	5	8	21	3	.174	.230	.217
Darren Reed†	OF29	R	26	42	81	10	14	2	0	5	10	6	23	0	.173	.239	.383
Rick Cerone	C28	R	38	33	63	10	17	4	0	1	7	3	5	1	.270	.313	.381
Sean Berry	3B20	R	26	24	57	5	19	1	0	1	4	1	11	2	.333	.345	.404
Tim Laker	C28	R	22	28	46	8	10	3	0	0	4	2	14	1	.217	.250	.283
Matt Stairs	OF10	L	23	13	30	2	5	2	0	0	5	7	7	0	.167	.316	.233
Jerry Willard†	1B5	L	32	21	25	0	3	0	0	0	1	1	7	0	.120	.154	.120
Steve Lyons†	OF8,1B1	L	32	16	13	2	3	0	0	0	1	1	3	1	.231	.286	.231
Todd Haney	2B5	R	26	7	10	0	3	1	0	0	1	0	0	0	.300	.300	.400
Bob Natal	C4	R	26	5	6	0	0	0	0	0	0	1	1	0	.000	.143	.000
Eric Bullock		L	32	8	5	0	0	0	0	0	0	0	1	0	.000	.000	.000
Jerry Goff		L	28	3	3	0	0	0	0	0	0	0	3	0	.000	.000	.000

T. Foley, 4 G at 3B, 1 G at OF

Pitcher	T	Age	G	GS	CG	ShO	IP	H	HR	BB	SO	W-L	Sv	ERA
Ken Hill	R	26	33	33	3	3	218.0	187	13	75	150	16-9	0	2.68
Dennis Martinez	R	37	32	32	6	0	226.1	172	12	60	147	16-11	0	2.47
Chris Nabholz	L	25	32	32	1	1	195.0	176	11	74	130	11-12	0	3.32
Mark Gardner	R	30	33	30	0	0	179.2	179	15	60	132	12-10	0	4.36
Brian Barnes	L	25	21	17	0	0	100.0	77	9	46	65	6-6	0	2.97
Chris Haney†	L	23	9	6	1	1	38.0	40	6	10	27	2-3	0	5.45
Jon Hurst	R	25	3	3	0	0	16.1	18	1	7	4	1-1	0	5.51
Bill Risley	R	25	1	1	0	0	5.0	4	0	1	2	1-0	0	1.80
Jeff Fassero	L	29	70	0	0	0	85.2	81	1	34	63	8-7	1	2.84
Mel Rojas	R	25	68	0	0	0	100.2	71	2	34	70	7-1	10	1.43
John Wetteland	R	25	67	0	0	0	83.1	64	6	36	99	4-4	37	2.92
Bill Sampen†	R	29	44	1	0	0	63.1	62	4	29	23	1-4	0	3.13
Sergio Valdez	R	27	27	0	0	0	37.1	25	2	12	32	0-2	0	2.41
Bill Landrum	R	34	18	0	0	0	20.0	27	3	9	7	1-1	0	7.20
Pete Young	R	24	13	0	0	0	20.1	18	0	9	11	0-0	0	3.98
Kent Bottenfield	R	23	10	4	0	0	32.1	26	1	11	14	1-2	1	2.23
Bill Krueger†	L	34	9	2	0	0	17.1	23	0	7	13	0-2	0	6.75
Gil Heredia†	R	26	7	1	0	0	14.2	12	1	4	7	0-0	0	1.84
Doug Simons	L	25	7	0	0	0	5.1	15	3	2	6	0-0	0	23.63
Scott Service	R	25	5	0	0	0	7.0	15	1	5	11	0-0	0	14.14
Matt Maysey	R	25	2	0	0	0	2.1	4	1	0	1	0-0	0	3.86

1992 St. Louis Cardinals 3rd NL East 83-79 .512 13.0 GB

Joe Torre

Player	Gm by Position	B	Age	G	AB	R	H	2B	3B	HR	RBI	BB	SO	SB	Avg	OBP	Slg
Tom Pagnozzi	C138	R	29	139	485	33	121	26	3	7	44	28	64	2	.249	.290	.359
Andres Galarraga	1B90	R	31	95	325	38	79	14	2	10	39	11	69	5	.243	.282	.391
Luis Alicea	2B75,SS4	S	26	85	265	26	65	9	11	2	32	27	40	2	.245	.320	.385
Todd Zeile	3B124	R	26	126	439	51	113	18	4	7	48	68	70	7	.257	.352	.364
Ozzie Smith	SS132	S	37	132	518	73	153	20	2	0	31	59	34	43	.295	.367	.342
Ray Lankford	OF153	L	25	153	598	87	175	40	6	20	86	72	147	42	.293	.371	.480
Felix Jose	OF127	S	27	131	509	62	150	22	3	14	75	40	100	28	.295	.347	.432
Bernard Gilkey	OF111	R	25	131	384	56	116	19	4	7	43	39	52	18	.302	.364	.427
Milt Thompson	OF45	L	33	109	208	31	61	9	1	4	17	16	39	18	.293	.350	.404
Geronimo Pena	2B57	S	25	62	203	31	62	12	1	7	31	24	37	13	.305	.386	.478
Brian Jordan	OF53	R	25	55	193	17	40	9	4	5	22	10	48	7	.207	.250	.373
Pedro Guerrero	1B28,OF10	R	36	43	146	10	32	6	1	1	16	11	25	2	.219	.270	.295
Tim Jones	SS34,2B28,3B2*	L	29	67	145	9	29	4	0	0	3	11	29	5	.200	.256	.228
Gerald Perry	1B29	L	31	87	143	13	34	8	0	1	18	15	23	3	.238	.311	.315
Tracy Woodson	3B26,1B3	R	29	31	114	9	35	8	0	1	22	3	10	0	.307	.331	.404
Craig Wilson	3B18,2B11,OF3	R	27	61	106	6	33	6	0	0	13	10	18	1	.311	.368	.368
Rich Gedman	C40	L	32	41	105	5	23	4	0	1	8	11	22	0	.219	.291	.286
Rod Brewer	1B27,OF4	L	26	29	103	11	31	6	0	0	10	8	12	0	.301	.354	.359
Rex Hudler	2B16,OF12,1B8	R	31	61	98	17	24	4	0	3	5	2	23	2	.245	.265	.378
Chuck Carr	OF19	S	23	22	64	8	14	3	0	0	3	9	6	10	.219	.315	.266
Jose Oquendo	2B9,SS5	S	28	14	35	3	9	3	1	0	3	5	3	0	.257	.350	.400
Stan Royer	3B5,1B4	R	24	13	31	6	10	2	0	2	9	1	4	0	.323	.333	.581
Ozzie Canseco	OF8	R	27	9	29	7	8	5	0	0	3	7	4	0	.276	.417	.448
Bien Figueroa	SS9,2B3	R	28	12	11	1	2	1	0	0	4	1	2	0	.182	.250	.273

T. Jones, 1 G at OF

Pitcher	T	Age	G	GS	CG	ShO	IP	H	HR	BB	SO	W-L	Sv	ERA
Bob Tewksbury	R	31	33	32	5	0	233.0	217	15	20	91	16-5	0	2.16
Omar Olivares	R	24	32	30	1	0	197.0	189	20	63	124	9-9	0	3.84
Rheal Cormier	L	25	31	30	3	0	186.0	194	15	33	117	10-10	0	3.68
Donovan Osborne	L	23	34	29	0	0	179.0	193	14	38	104	11-9	0	3.77
Mark Clark	R	24	20	20	1	1	113.1	117	12	36	44	3-10	0	4.45
Jose DeLeon†	R	31	29	15	0	0	102.1	95	7	43	72	2-7	0	4.57
Joe Magrane	L	27	5	5	0	0	31.1	34	2	15	20	1-2	0	4.02
Mike Perez	R	27	77	0	0	0	93.0	70	4	32	46	9-3	0	1.84
Cris Carpenter	R	27	73	0	0	0	88.0	69	10	27	46	5-4	1	2.97
Bob McClure	L	40	71	0	0	0	54.0	52	6	25	24	2-2	0	3.17
Lee Smith	R	34	70	0	0	0	75.0	62	4	26	60	4-9	43	3.12
Todd Worrell	R	32	67	0	0	0	64.0	45	4	25	64	5-3	3	2.11
Juan Agosto†	L	34	22	0	0	0	31.2	39	2	9	13	2-4	0	6.25
Bryn Smith	R	36	13	1	0	0	21.1	20	3	5	9	4-2	0	4.64
Frank DiPino	L	35	9	0	0	0	11.0	9	0	3	8	0-0	0	1.64

1992 Chicago Cubs 4th NL East 78-84 .481 18.0 GB

Jim Lefebvre

Player	Gm by Position	B	Age	G	AB	R	H	2B	3B	HR	RBI	BB	SO	SB	Avg	OBP	Slg
Joe Girardi	C86	R	27	91	270	19	73	3	1	1	12	19	38	0	.270	.320	.300
Mark Grace	1B157	L	28	158	603	72	185	37	5	9	79	72	36	6	.307	.380	.430
Ryne Sandberg	2B157	R	32	158	612	100	186	32	8	26	87	68	73	17	.304	.371	.510
Steve Buechele†	3B63,2B2	R	30	65	239	25	66	9	3	1	21	18	44	1	.276	.338	.351
Rey Sanchez	SS68,2B4	R	24	74	255	24	64	14	3	1	19	10	17	2	.251	.285	.341
Andre Dawson	OF139	R	37	143	542	60	150	27	2	22	90	30	70	6	.277	.316	.456
Doug Dascenzo	OF122	S	28	139	376	37	96	13	4	0	20	27	32	6	.255	.304	.311
Derrick May	OF108	L	23	124	351	33	96	11	0	8	45	14	40	5	.274	.306	.373
Jose Vizcaino	SS50,3B29,2B5	S	24	86	285	25	64	10	4	1	17	14	35	3	.225	.260	.298
Sammy Sosa	OF67	R	23	67	262	41	68	7	2	8	25	19	63	15	.260	.317	.393
Luis Salazar	3B40,OF34,SS12*	R	36	98	255	20	53	7	2	5	25	11	34	1	.208	.237	.310
Rick Wilkins	C73	L	25	83	244	20	66	9	1	8	22	28	53	0	.270	.344	.414
Dwight Smith	OF63	L	28	109	217	28	60	10	3	3	24	13	40	9	.276	.318	.392
Hector Villanueva	C28,1B6	R	27	51	112	9	17	6	0	2	13	11	24	0	.152	.228	.259
Kal Daniels†	OF28	L	28	48	108	12	27	6	0	4	17	12	24	0	.250	.328	.417
Alex Arias	SS30	R	24	32	99	14	29	6	0	0	7	11	13	0	.293	.375	.354
Gary Scott	3B30,SS2	R	23	36	96	8	15	2	0	2	11	5	14	0	.156	.198	.240
Doug Strange	3B33,2B12	S	28	52	94	7	15	1	0	1	5	10	15	1	.160	.240	.202
Shawon Dunston	SS18	R	29	18	73	8	23	3	1	0	2	3	13	2	.315	.342	.384
Jerome Walton	OF24	R	26	30	55	7	7	0	1	0	1	9	13	1	.127	.273	.164
Jeff Kunkel	SS6,2B3,OF3	R	30	20	29	0	4	2	0	0	1	0	8	0	.138	.138	.207
Chico Walker†	OF6,2B2,3B2	S	34	19	26	2	3	0	0	0	2	3	4	1	.115	.200	.115
Fernando Ramsey	OF15	R	26	18	25	0	3	0	0	0	2	0	6	0	.120	.120	.120
Jorge Pedre	C4	R	25	4	4	0	0	0	0	0	0	0	1	0	.000	.000	.000

L. Salazar, 5 G at 1B

Pitcher	T	Age	G	GS	CG	ShO	IP	H	HR	BB	SO	W-L	Sv	ERA
Greg Maddux	R	26	35	35	9	4	268.0	201	7	70	199	20-11	0	2.18
Mike Morgan	R	32	34	34	6	1	240.0	203	14	79	123	16-8	0	2.55
Frank Castillo	R	23	33	33	0	0	205.1	179	19	63	135	10-11	0	3.46
Danny Jackson†	L	30	19	19	0	0	113.0	117	5	48	51	4-9	0	4.22
Shawn Boskie	R	25	23	18	0	0	91.2	96	14	36	39	5-11	0	5.01
Mike Harkey	R	25	7	7	0	0	38.0	34	4	15	21	4-0	0	1.89
Chuck McElroy	L	24	72	0	0	0	83.2	73	5	51	83	4-7	6	3.55
Paul Assenmacher	L	31	70	0	0	0	68.0	72	6	26	67	4-4	8	4.10
Bob Scanlan	R	25	69	0	0	0	87.1	76	4	30	42	3-6	14	2.89
Jeff Robinson	R	31	49	5	0	0	78.0	76	5	40	46	4-3	1	3.00
Jim Bullinger	R	26	39	9	1	0	85.0	72	9	54	36	2-8	7	4.66
Ken Patterson	L	27	32	1	0	0	41.2	41	7	27	23	2-3	0	3.89
Heathcliff Slocumb	R	26	30	0	0	0	36.0	52	3	21	27	0-3	1	6.50
Dave Smith	R	37	11	0	0	0	14.1	15	0	4	3	0-0	0	2.51
Jeff Hartsock	R	25	4	0	0	0	9.1	15	2	4	6	0-0	0	6.75
Jessie Hollins	R	22	4	0	0	0	4.2	8	1	5	0	0-0	0	13.50
D. Rasmussen†	L	33	3	1	0	0	5.0	7	2	2	0	0-0	0	10.80

1992 New York Mets 5th NL East 72-90 .444 24.0 GB

Jeff Torborg

Player	Gm by Position	B	Age	G	AB	R	H	2B	3B	HR	RBI	BB	SO	SB	Avg	OBP	Slg
Todd Hundley	C121	S	23	123	358	32	75	17	0	7	32	19	76	3	.209	.256	.316
Eddie Murray	1B154	S	36	156	551	64	144	37	2	16	93	66	74	4	.261	.336	.423
Willie Randolph	2B79	R	37	90	286	29	72	11	1	2	15	40	34	1	.252	.352	.318
Dave Magadan	3B93,1B2	L	29	99	321	33	91	9	1	3	28	56	44	1	.283	.390	.346
Dick Schofield†	SS141	R	29	142	420	52	86	18	2	4	36	60	82	11	.205	.309	.286
Bobby Bonilla	OF121,1B6	S	29	128	438	62	109	23	0	19	70	66	73	4	.249	.348	.432
Howard Johnson	OF98	S	31	100	350	48	78	19	0	7	43	55	79	22	.223	.329	.337
Daryl Boston	OF95	L	29	130	289	37	72	14	2	11	35	38	60	12	.249	.338	.426
Bill Pecota	3B48,SS39,2B38*	R	32	117	269	28	61	13	0	2	26	25	40	9	.227	.293	.297
Vince Coleman	OF61	S	30	71	229	37	63	11	1	2	21	27	41	24	.275	.355	.358
Chico Walker†	3B36,2B16,OF15	S	34	107	227	24	70	12	1	4	36	24	46	14	.308	.369	.423
Dave Gallagher	OF76	R	31	98	175	20	42	11	1	1	21	19	16	4	.240	.307	.331
Charlie O'Brien	C64	R	32	68	156	15	33	12	0	2	13	16	18	0	.212	.289	.327
Mackey Sasser	C27,1B12,OF9	L	29	92	141	7	34	6	0	2	18	3	10	0	.241	.248	.326
Kevin Bass†	OF39	S	33	46	137	15	37	12	2	2	9	7	17	7	.270	.303	.431
Chris Donnels	3B29,2B12	L	26	45	121	8	21	4	0	0	6	17	25	1	.174	.275	.207
Jeff Kent†	2B34,3B1,SS1	R	24	37	113	16	27	8	1	3	15	7	29	0	.239	.289	.407
Ryan Thompson	OF29	R	24	30	108	15	24	7	1	3	10	8	24	2	.222	.274	.389
Jeff McKnight	2B14,1B9,3B3*	S	29	31	85	10	23	3	1	2	13	2	8	0	.271	.287	.400
Pat Howell	OF28	S	23	31	75	9	14	1	0	0	1	2	15	4	.187	.218	.200
Junior Noboa	2B16,3B3,SS2	R	27	46	47	7	7	0	0	0	3	3	8	0	.149	.212	.149
D.J. Dozier	OF17	R	26	25	47	4	9	2	0	0	2	4	19	4	.191	.264	.234
Kevin Elster	SS5	R	27	6	18	0	4	0	0	0	0	0	2	0	.222	.222	.222
Kevin Baez	SS5	R	25	6	13	0	2	0	0	0	0	0	0	0	.154	.154	.154
Steve Springer	2B1,3B1	R	31	4	5	0	2	1	0	0	0	0	1	0	.400	.400	.600
Rodney McCray	OF13	R	28	18	1	3	1	0	0	0	1	0	0	2	1.000	1.000	1.000

B. Pecota, 1 G at P, 1 G at 1B; J. McKnight, 3 G at SS, 1 G at OF

Pitcher	T	Age	G	GS	CG	ShO	IP	H	HR	BB	SO	W-L	Sv	ERA
Sid Fernandez	L	29	32	32	5	2	214.2	162	12	67	193	14-11	0	2.73
Dwight Gooden	R	27	31	31	3	0	206.0	197	11	70	145	10-13	0	3.67
David Cone†	R	29	27	27	7	5	196.2	162	12	82	214	13-7	0	2.88
Pete Schourek	L	23	22	21	0	0	136.0	137	9	44	60	6-8	0	3.64
Bret Saberhagen	R	28	17	15	1	1	97.2	84	6	27	81	3-5	0	3.50
Eric Hillman	L	26	11	8	0	0	52.1	67	9	10	16	2-2	0	5.33
Mike Birkbeck	R	31	1	1	0	0	7.0	12	3	1	2	0-1	0	9.00
Jeff Innis	R	29	76	0	0	0	88.0	85	4	36	39	6-9	1	2.86
Anthony Young	R	26	52	13	1	0	121.0	134	8	31	64	2-14	15	4.17
Wally Whitehurst	R	28	44	11	0	0	97.0	99	4	33	70	3-9	0	3.62
Paul Gibson	R	32	43	1	0	0	62.0	70	7	25	49	0-1	0	5.23
Lee Guetterman†	L	33	43	0	0	0	43.1	57	5	14	15	3-4	2	5.82
John Franco	L	31	31	0	0	0	33.0	24	1	11	20	6-2	15	1.64
Mark Dewey	R	27	20	0	0	0	33.1	37	2	10	24	1-0	0	4.32
Barry Jones†	R	29	17	0	0	0	15.1	20	0	11	11	2-0	1	9.39
Tim Burke†	R	33	15	0	0	0	15.2	26	1	3	7	1-2	0	5.74
Tom Filer	R	35	9	1	0	0	22.0	18	2	6	9	0-1	0	2.05
Joe Vitko	R	22	3	1	0	0	4.2	12	1	1	6	0-1	0	13.50
Bill Pecota	R	32	1	0	0	0	1.0	1	1	0	0	0-0	0	9.00

Seasons: Team Rosters 931

1992 Philadelphia Phillies 6th NL East 70-92 .432 26.0 GB — Jim Fregosi

Player	Gm by Position	B	Age	G	AB	R	H	2B	3B	HR	RBI	BB	SO	SB	Avg	OBP	Slg
Darren Daulton	C141	L	30	145	485	80	131	32	5	27	109	88	103	11	.270	.385	.524
John Kruk	1B121,OF35	L	31	144	507	86	164	30	4	10	70	92	88	3	.323	.423	.458
Mickey Morandini	2B124,SS3	L	26	127	422	47	112	8	8	3	30	25	64	8	.265	.305	.344
Dave Hollins	3B156,1B1	S	26	156	586	104	158	28	4	27	93	76	110	9	.270	.369	.469
Juan Bell	SS46	R	24	46	147	12	30	3	1	1	8	18	29	5	.204	.292	.259
Ruben Amaro	OF113	S	27	126	374	43	82	15	6	7	34	37	54	11	.219	.303	.348
Lenny Dykstra	OF85	L	29	85	345	53	104	18	0	6	39	40	32	30	.301	.375	.406
Stan Javier†	OF74	S	28	74	276	36	72	14	1	0	24	31	43	17	.261	.338	.319
Mariano Duncan	OF65,2B52,SS42*	S	29	142	574	71	153	40	3	8	50	17	108	23	.267	.292	.389
Ricky Jordan	1B54,OF11	R	27	94	276	33	84	19	0	4	34	5	44	3	.304	.313	.417
Wes Chamberlain	OF73	R	26	76	275	26	71	18	0	9	41	10	55	4	.258	.285	.422
Kim Batiste	SS41	R	24	44	136	9	28	4	0	1	10	4	18	0	.206	.224	.257
Dale Sveum†	SS34,3B5,1B4	S	28	54	135	13	24	4	0	2	16	16	39	0	.178	.261	.252
Tom Marsh	OF35	R	26	42	125	7	25	3	2	2	16	2	23	0	.200	.215	.304
Joe Millette	SS26,3B3,2B1	R	25	33	78	5	16	0	0	0	2	5	10	1	.205	.271	.205
Braulio Castillo	OF24	R	24	28	76	12	15	3	1	2	7	4	15	1	.197	.238	.342
Jeff Grotewold	C2,OF2,1B1	L	26	72	65	7	13	2	0	3	5	9	16	0	.200	.307	.369
Dale Murphy	OF16	R	36	18	62	5	10	1	0	2	7	1	13	0	.161	.175	.274
Steve Lake	C17	R	35	20	53	3	13	2	0	1	2	1	8	0	.245	.255	.340
Wally Backman	2B10,3B2	S	32	42	48	6	13	1	0	0	6	6	9	1	.271	.352	.292
Todd Pratt	C11	R	25	16	46	6	13	1	0	2	10	4	12	0	.283	.340	.435
Jim Lindeman	OF9	R	30	29	39	6	10	1	0	1	6	3	11	0	.256	.310	.359
Steve Scarsone†	2B3	R	26	7	13	1	2	0	0	0	0	1	6	0	.154	.214	.154
Julio Peguero	OF14	S	23	14	9	3	2	0	0	0	0	3	3	0	.222	.417	.222

M. Duncan, 4 G at 3B

Pitcher	T	Age	G	GS	CG	ShO	IP	H	HR	BB	SO	W-L	Sv	ERA
Terry Mulholland	L	29	32	32	12	2	229.0	227	14	46	125	13-11	0	3.81
Curt Schilling	R	25	42	26	10	4	226.1	165	11	59	147	14-11	2	2.35
Kyle Abbott	L	24	31	19	0	0	133.1	147	20	45	88	1-14	0	5.13
Ben Rivera†	R	24	20	14	4	1	102.0	78	8	32	66	7-3	0	2.82
Tommy Greene	R	25	13	12	0	0	64.1	75	5	34	39	3-3	0	5.32
Don Robinson†	R	35	8	8	0	0	43.2	49	6	4	17	1-4	0	6.18
Andy Ashby	R	24	10	8	0	0	37.0	42	6	21	24	1-3	0	7.54
Greg Mathews	L	30	14	7	0	0	52.1	54	7	24	27	2-3	0	5.16
Brad Brink	R	27	8	7	0	0	41.1	53	2	13	16	0-4	0	4.14
Danny Cox†	R	32	9	7	0	0	38.1	46	3	19	30	2-2	0	5.40
Mike Williams	R	23	5	5	1	0	28.2	29	3	7	5	1-1	0	5.34
Pat Combs	L	25	4	4	0	0	18.2	20	0	12	11	1-1	0	7.71
Jose DeLeon†	R	31	3	3	0	0	15.0	16	0	5	7	0-1	0	3.00
Mickey Weston	R	31	1	1	0	0	3.2	7	1	1	0	0-1	0	12.27
Mitch Williams	L	27	66	0	0	0	81.0	69	4	64	74	5-8	29	3.78
Mike Hartley	R	30	46	0	0	0	55.0	54	5	23	53	7-6	0	3.44
Barry Jones†	R	29	44	0	0	0	54.1	65	3	24	19	5-6	0	4.64
Wally Ritchie	L	26	40	0	0	0	39.0	44	3	17	19	2-1	1	3.00
Bob Ayrault	R	26	30	0	0	0	43.1	32	0	17	27	2-2	0	3.12
Cliff Brantley	R	24	28	9	0	0	76.1	71	6	58	32	2-6	0	4.60
Keith Shepherd	R	24	12	0	0	0	22.0	19	0	6	10	1-1	2	3.27
Steve Searcy	L	28	10	0	0	0	10.1	13	0	8	5	0-0	0	6.10
Jay Baller	R	31	8	0	0	0	11.0	10	5	10	9	0-0	0	8.18
Darrin Chapin	R	26	1	0	0	0	2.0	2	1	0	1	0-0	0	9.00

1992 Atlanta Braves 1st NL West 98-64 .605 — — Bobby Cox

Player	Gm by Position	B	Age	G	AB	R	H	2B	3B	HR	RBI	BB	SO	SB	Avg	OBP	Slg
Greg Olson	C94	R	31	95	302	27	72	14	2	3	27	34	31	2	.238	.316	.328
Sid Bream	1B120	L	31	125	372	30	97	25	1	10	61	46	51	6	.261	.340	.414
Mark Lemke	2B145,3B13	S	26	155	427	38	97	7	4	6	26	50	39	0	.227	.307	.304
Terry Pendleton	3B158	S	31	160	640	98	199	39	1	21	105	37	67	5	.311	.345	.473
Rafael Belliard	SS139,2B1	R	30	144	285	20	60	6	1	0	14	14	43	0	.211	.255	.239
Ron Gant	OF147	R	27	153	544	74	141	22	6	17	80	45	101	32	.259	.321	.415
David Justice	OF140	L	26	144	484	78	124	19	5	21	72	79	85	2	.256	.359	.446
Otis Nixon	OF111	S	33	120	456	79	134	14	2	2	22	39	54	41	.294	.348	.346
Jeff Blauser	SS106,2B21,3B1	R	26	123	343	61	90	19	3	14	46	46	82	5	.262	.354	.458
Damon Berryhill	C84	S	28	101	307	21	70	16	1	10	43	17	67	0	.228	.268	.384
Deion Sanders	OF75	L	24	97	303	54	92	6	14	8	28	18	52	26	.304	.346	.495
Brian Hunter	1B92,OF6	R	24	102	238	34	57	13	2	14	41	21	50	1	.239	.292	.487
Lonnie Smith	OF35	R	36	84	158	23	39	8	2	6	33	17	37	4	.247	.324	.437
Jeff Treadway	2B45,3B1	L	29	61	126	5	28	6	1	0	5	9	16	1	.222	.274	.286
Jerry Willard†	C1	L	32	26	23	2	8	1	0	2	7	1	3	0	.348	.375	.652
Tommy Gregg	OF9	L	28	18	19	1	5	0	0	1	1	1	7	1	.263	.300	.421
Melvin Nieves	OF6	S	20	12	19	0	4	1	0	0	1	2	7	0	.211	.286	.263
Vinny Castilla	3B4,SS4	R	24	9	16	1	4	1	0	0	1	1	4	0	.250	.333	.313
Javy Lopez	C9	R	21	9	16	3	6	2	0	0	2	0	1	0	.375	.375	.500
Steve Lyons†	OF6,2B2	L	32	11	14	0	1	0	1	0	1	0	4	0	.071	.071	.214
Ryan Klesko	1B5	L	21	13	14	0	0	0	0	0	1	0	5	0	.000	.067	.000
Francisco Cabrera	C1	R	25	12	10	2	3	0	0	2	3	1	1	0	.300	.364	.900

Pitcher	T	Age	G	GS	CG	ShO	IP	H	HR	BB	SO	W-L	Sv	ERA
John Smoltz	R	25	35	35	9	3	246.2	206	17	80	215	15-12	0	2.85
Steve Avery	L	22	35	35	2	2	233.2	216	14	71	129	11-11	0	3.20
Tom Glavine	L	26	33	33	7	5	225.0	197	6	70	129	20-8	0	2.76
Charlie Leibrandt	L	35	32	31	5	2	193.0	191	9	42	104	15-7	0	3.36
Mike Bielecki	R	32	19	14	1	1	80.2	77	2	27	62	2-4	0	2.57
Pete Smith	R	26	12	11	2	1	79.0	63	3	28	43	7-0	0	2.05
Mike Stanton	L	25	65	0	0	0	63.2	59	6	20	44	5-4	8	4.10
Marvin Freeman	R	29	58	0	0	0	64.1	61	7	29	41	7-5	3	3.22
Kent Mercker	L	24	53	0	0	0	68.1	51	4	35	49	3-2	6	3.42
Alejandro Pena	R	33	41	0	0	0	42.0	40	7	13	34	1-6	15	4.07
Mark Wohlers	R	22	32	0	0	0	35.1	28	0	14	17	1-2	4	2.55
Juan Berenguer†	R	37	28	0	0	0	33.1	35	7	16	19	3-1	1	5.13
Mark Davis†	L	31	14	0	0	0	16.2	22	3	13	15	1-0	0	7.02
Jeff Reardon†	R	36	14	0	0	0	15.2	14	0	2	7	3-0	3	1.15
Randy St. Claire	R	31	10	0	0	0	15.1	17	1	8	7	0-0	0	5.87
Ben Rivera†	R	24	8	0	0	0	15.1	21	1	13	11	0-1	0	4.70
Dave Nied	R	23	6	2	0	0	23.0	10	0	5	19	3-0	0	1.17
Armando Reynoso	R	26	3	1	0	0	7.2	11	2	2	2	1-0	1	4.70
Pedro Borbon	L	24	2	0	0	0	1.1	2	0	1	1	0-1	0	6.75

1992 Cincinnati Reds 2nd NL West 90-72 .556 8.0 GB — Lou Piniella

Player	Gm by Position	B	Age	G	AB	R	H	2B	3B	HR	RBI	BB	SO	SB	Avg	OBP	Slg
Joe Oliver	C141,1B1	R	26	143	485	42	131	25	1	10	57	35	75	2	.270	.316	.388
Hal Morris	1B109	L	27	115	395	41	107	21	3	6	53	45	53	6	.271	.347	.385
Bill Doran	2B104,1B25	S	34	132	387	48	91	16	2	8	47	64	40	7	.235	.342	.349
Chris Sabo	3B93	R	30	96	344	42	84	19	3	12	43	30	54	4	.244	.302	.422
Barry Larkin	SS140	R	28	140	533	76	162	32	6	12	78	63	58	15	.304	.377	.454
Paul O'Neill	OF143	L	29	148	496	59	122	19	1	14	66	77	85	6	.246	.346	.373
Dave Martinez	OF111,1B21	L	27	135	393	47	100	20	5	3	31	42	54	12	.254	.323	.354
Reggie Sanders	OF110	R	24	116	385	62	104	26	6	12	36	48	98	16	.270	.356	.462
Bip Roberts	OF79,2B42,3B36	S	28	147	532	92	172	34	6	4	45	62	54	44	.323	.393	.432
Glenn Braggs	OF79	R	29	92	266	40	63	16	3	8	38	36	48	3	.237	.330	.410
Freddie Benavides	2B37,SS34,3B1	R	26	74	173	14	40	10	1	1	17	10	34	0	.231	.277	.318
Darnell Coles	3B23,1B20,OF5	R	30	55	141	16	44	11	2	3	18	3	15	1	.312	.322	.482
Jeff Branson	2B33,3B8,SS1	L	25	72	115	12	34	7	1	0	15	5	16	0	.296	.322	.374
Billy Hatcher†	OF23	R	31	43	94	10	27	3	0	2	10	5	11	0	.287	.314	.383
Willie Greene	3B25	L	20	29	93	10	25	5	2	2	13	10	23	0	.269	.337	.430
Cesar Hernandez	OF18	R	25	34	51	6	14	4	0	0	4	0	10	3	.275	.275	.353
Tim Costo	1B12	R	23	12	36	3	8	2	0	0	2	5	6	0	.222	.310	.278
Troy Afenir	C15	R	28	16	34	3	6	1	2	0	4	5	12	0	.176	.282	.324
Jacob Brumfield	OF16	R	27	24	30	6	4	0	0	0	2	2	4	6	.133	.212	.133
Jeff Reed	C6	L	29	15	25	2	4	0	0	0	2	1	4	0	.160	.192	.160
Dan Wilson	C9	R	23	12	25	2	9	1	0	0	3	3	8	0	.360	.429	.400
Rick Wrona	C10,1B1	R	28	11	23	0	4	0	0	0	0	0	3	0	.174	.174	.174
Geronimo Berroa	OF3	R	27	13	15	2	4	1	0	0	0	2	1	0	.267	.389	.333
Gary Green	SS6,3B1	R	30	8	12	3	4	1	0	0	0	0	2	0	.333	.333	.417
Scott Bradley†	C2	L	32	5	5	1	2	0	0	0	1	1	0	0	.400	.500	.400

Pitcher	T	Age	G	GS	CG	ShO	IP	H	HR	BB	SO	W-L	Sv	ERA
Tim Belcher	R	30	35	34	2	1	227.2	201	17	80	149	15-14	0	3.91
Jose Rijo	R	27	33	33	2	0	211.0	185	15	44	171	15-10	0	2.56
Greg Swindell	L	27	31	30	5	3	213.2	210	14	41	138	12-8	0	2.70
Chris Hammond	L	26	28	26	0	0	147.1	149	13	55	79	7-10	0	4.21
Tom Browning	L	32	16	16	0	0	87.0	108	6	28	33	6-5	0	5.07
Tom Bolton†	L	30	16	8	0	0	46.1	52	9	23	27	3-3	0	5.24
Tim Pugh	R	25	7	7	0	0	45.1	47	2	13	18	4-2	0	2.58
Bobby Ayala	R	22	5	5	0	0	29.0	33	1	13	23	2-1	0	4.34
Keith Brown	R	28	2	2	0	0	8.0	10	2	5	5	0-1	0	4.50
Norm Charlton	L	29	64	0	0	0	81.1	79	7	26	90	4-2	26	2.99
Rob Dibble	R	28	63	0	0	0	70.1	48	3	31	110	3-5	25	3.07
Dwayne Henry	R	30	60	0	0	0	83.2	59	4	44	72	3-3	0	3.33
Scott Ruskin	L	29	57	0	0	0	53.2	56	6	20	43	4-3	0	5.03
Scott Bankhead	R	28	54	0	0	0	70.2	57	4	29	53	10-4	1	2.93
Steve Foster	R	25	31	1	0	0	50.0	52	4	13	34	1-1	2	2.88
Milt Hill	R	26	14	0	0	0	20.0	15	1	5	10	0-0	1	3.15
Tony Menendez	R	27	3	0	0	0	4.2	1	1	0	5	1-0	0	1.93

1992 San Diego Padres 3rd NL West 82-80 .506 16.0 GB — Greg Riddoch (78-72)/Jim Riggleman (4-8)

Player	Gm by Position	B	Age	G	AB	R	H	2B	3B	HR	RBI	BB	SO	SB	Avg	OBP	Slg
Benito Santiago	C103	R	27	106	386	37	97	21	0	10	42	21	52	2	.251	.287	.383
Fred McGriff	1B151	L	28	152	531	79	152	30	4	35	104	96	108	8	.286	.394	.556
Kurt Stillwell	2B111	S	27	114	379	35	86	15	3	2	24	26	58	4	.227	.274	.298
Gary Sheffield	3B144	R	23	146	557	87	184	34	3	33	100	48	40	5	.330	.385	.580
Tony Fernandez	SS154	S	30	155	622	84	171	32	4	4	37	56	62	20	.275	.337	.359
Darrin Jackson	OF153	R	28	155	587	72	146	23	5	17	70	26	106	14	.249	.283	.392
Jerald Clark	OF134,1B11	R	28	146	496	45	120	22	6	12	58	22	97	3	.242	.278	.383
Tony Gwynn	OF127	L	32	128	520	77	165	27	3	6	41	46	16	3	.317	.371	.415
Tim Teufel	2B52,3B26,1B5	R	33	101	246	23	55	10	0	6	25	31	45	2	.224	.312	.337
Dan Walters	C55	R	25	57	179	14	45	11	1	4	22	10	28	1	.251	.295	.391
Oscar Azocar	OF37	L	27	99	168	15	32	6	0	0	8	9	12	1	.190	.230	.226
Kevin Ward	OF51	R	30	81	147	12	29	5	0	3	12	14	38	2	.197	.274	.293
Craig Shipley	SS23,2B11,3B8	R	29	52	105	7	26	6	0	0	7	2	21	1	.248	.262	.305
Phil Stephenson	OF15,1B7	L	31	53	71	5	11	2	1	0	8	10	11	0	.155	.259	.211
Dann Bilardello	C14	R	33	17	33	2	4	1	0	0	1	4	8	0	.121	.216	.152
Gary Pettis†	OF14	S	34	30	30	0	6	1	0	0	0	2	11	1	.200	.250	.233
G. Velasquez	1B3,OF2	L	24	15	23	1	7	0	0	1	5	1	7	0	.304	.333	.435
Jeff Gardner	2B11	L	28	15	19	0	2	0	0	0	0	1	8	0	.105	.150	.105
Tom Lampkin	C7,OF1	L	28	9	17	3	4	0	0	0	0	6	1	2	.235	.458	.235
Jim Vatcher	OF13	R	26	13	16	1	4	1	0	0	2	3	6	0	.250	.368	.313
Paul Faries	2B4,3B2,SS1	R	27	10	11	3	5	1	0	0	1	1	2	0	.455	.500	.545
Thomas Howard†		S	27	5	3	1	1	0	0	0	0	0	0	0	.333	.333	.333

Pitcher	T	Age	G	GS	CG	ShO	IP	H	HR	BB	SO	W-L	Sv	ERA
Andy Benes	R	24	34	34	2	2	231.1	230	14	61	169	13-14	0	3.35
Bruce Hurst	L	34	32	32	6	4	217.1	223	22	51	131	14-9	0	3.85
Craig Lefferts†	L	34	27	27	0	0	163.1	180	16	35	81	13-9	0	3.69
Greg Harris	R	28	20	20	1	0	118.0	113	13	35	66	4-8	0	4.12
Frank Seminara	R	25	19	18	0	0	100.1	98	5	46	61	9-4	0	3.68
Jim Deshaies	L	32	15	15	0	0	96.0	92	6	33	46	4-7	0	3.28
Dave Eiland	R	25	7	7	0	0	27.0	33	1	5	10	0-2	0	5.67
Doug Brocail	R	25	3	3	0	0	14.0	17	2	5	15	0-0	0	6.43
Randy Myers	L	29	66	0	0	0	79.2	84	7	34	66	3-6	38	4.29
Rich Rodriguez	L	29	61	1	0	0	91.0	77	4	29	64	6-3	0	2.37
Jose Melendez	R	26	56	3	0	0	89.1	82	9	20	82	6-7	0	2.92
Mike Maddux	R	30	50	1	0	0	79.2	71	2	24	60	2-2	5	2.37
Tim Scott	R	25	34	0	0	0	37.2	39	4	21	30	4-1	0	5.26
Larry Andersen	R	39	34	0	0	0	35.0	26	2	8	35	1-1	2	3.34
Pat Clements†	L	30	27	0	0	0	23.2	25	0	12	11	2-1	0	2.66
Jeremy Hernandez	R	25	26	0	0	0	36.2	39	4	11	25	1-4	1	4.17
Gene Harris†	R	27	14	1	0	0	21.1	15	0	9	19	0-2	0	2.95

1992 Houston Astros 4th NL West 81-81 .500 17.0 GB

Art Howe

Player	Gm by Position	B	Age	G	AB	R	H	2B	3B	HR	RBI	BB	SO	SB	Avg	OBP	Slg
Eddie Taubensee	C103	L	23	104	297	23	66	15	0	5	28	31	78	2	.222	.299	.323
Jeff Bagwell	1B159	R	24	162	586	87	160	34	6	18	96	84	97	10	.273	.368	.444
Craig Biggio	2B161	R	26	162	613	96	170	32	3	6	39	94	95	38	.277	.378	.369
Ken Caminiti	3B129	S	29	135	506	68	149	31	2	13	62	44	68	10	.294	.350	.441
Andujar Cedeno	SS70	R	22	71	220	15	38	13	2	2	13	14	71	2	.173	.232	.277
Steve Finley	OF160	L	27	162	607	84	177	29	13	5	55	58	63	44	.292	.355	.407
Eric Anthony	OF115	L	24	137	440	45	105	15	1	19	80	38	98	5	.239	.298	.407
Luis Gonzalez	OF111	L	24	122	387	40	94	19	3	10	55	24	52	7	.243	.289	.385
Pete Incaviglia	OF98	R	28	113	349	31	93	22	1	11	44	25	99	2	.266	.319	.430
Casey Candaele	SS65,3B29,OF21*	S	31	135	320	19	68	12	1	1	18	24	36	7	.213	.269	.266
Scott Servais	C73	R	25	77	205	12	49	9	0	0	15	11	25	0	.239	.294	.283
Rafael Ramirez	SS57,3B1	R	34	73	176	17	44	6	0	1	13	7	24	0	.250	.283	.301
Juan Guerrero	SS19,3B12,OF3*	R	25	79	125	8	25	4	2	1	14	10	32	1	.200	.261	.288
Gerald Young	OF57	S	27	74	76	14	14	1	1	0	4	10	11	6	.184	.279	.224
Chris Jones	OF43	R	26	54	63	7	12	2	1	1	4	7	21	3	.190	.271	.302
Ernest Riles	SS6,3B5,1B4*	L	31	39	61	5	16	1	0	1	4	2	11	1	.262	.281	.328
Benny Distefano	OF12,1B6	L	30	52	60	4	14	0	2	0	7	5	14	0	.233	.303	.300
Scooter Tucker	C19	R	25	20	50	5	6	1	0	0	3	3	13	1	.120	.200	.140
Mike Simms	OF9,1B1	R	25	15	24	1	6	1	0	1	3	2	9	0	.250	.333	.417
Eric Yelding	SS2,OF2	R	27	9	8	1	2	0	0	0	0	0	3	0	.250	.250	.250
Karl Rhodes	OF1	L	23	5	4	0	0	0	0	0	0	0	2	0	.000	.000	.000
Denny Walling		L	38	3	3	1	1	0	0	0	0	0	0	0	.333	.333	.333

C. Candaele, 9 G at 2B; J. Guerrero, 2 G at 2B; E. Riles, 2 G at 2B

Pitcher	T	Age	G	GS	CG	ShO	IP	H	HR	BB	SO	W-L	Sv	ERA
Pete Harnisch	R	25	34	34	0	0	206.2	182	18	64	164	9-10	0	3.70
Butch Henry	L	23	28	28	2	1	165.2	185	16	41	96	6-9	0	4.02
Jimmy Jones	R	28	25	23	0	0	139.1	135	13	39	69	10-6	0	4.07
Darryl Kile	R	23	22	22	2	0	125.1	124	8	63	90	5-10	0	3.95
Mark Portugal	R	29	18	16	1	1	101.1	76	7	41	62	6-3	0	2.66
Brian Williams	R	23	16	16	0	0	96.1	92	10	42	54	7-6	0	3.92
Ryan Bowen	R	24	11	9	0	0	33.2	48	8	30	22	0-7	0	10.96
Shane Reynolds	R	24	8	5	0	0	25.1	42	2	6	10	1-3	0	7.11
Joe Boever	R	31	81	0	0	0	111.1	103	3	45	67	3-6	2	2.51
Doug Jones	R	35	80	0	0	0	111.2	96	5	17	93	11-8	36	1.85
Xavier Hernandez	R	26	77	0	0	0	111.0	81	5	42	96	9-1	7	2.11
Al Osuna	L	26	66	0	0	0	61.2	52	8	38	37	6-3	0	4.23
Rob Murphy	L	32	59	0	0	0	55.2	56	2	21	42	3-1	0	4.04
Willie Blair	R	26	29	8	0	0	78.2	74	5	25	48	5-7	0	4.00
Rob Mallicoat	L	27	23	0	0	0	23.2	26	2	19	20	0-0	0	7.23
Rich Scheid	L	27	7	1	0	0	12.0	14	2	6	8	0-1	0	6.00

1992 San Francisco Giants 5th NL West 72-90 .444 26.0 GB

Roger Craig

Player	Gm by Position	B	Age	G	AB	R	H	2B	3B	HR	RBI	BB	SO	SB	Avg	OBP	Slg
Kirt Manwaring	C108	R	26	109	349	24	85	10	5	4	26	29	42	2	.244	.311	.335
Will Clark	1B141	L	28	144	513	69	154	40	1	16	73	73	82	12	.300	.384	.476
Robby Thompson	2B120	R	30	128	443	54	115	25	1	14	49	43	75	5	.260	.333	.415
Matt Williams	3B144	R	26	146	529	58	120	13	5	20	66	39	109	7	.227	.286	.384
Royce Clayton	SS94,3B1	R	22	98	321	31	72	7	4	4	24	26	63	8	.224	.281	.308
Willie McGee	OF119	S	33	138	474	56	141	20	2	1	36	29	88	13	.297	.339	.354
Mike Felder	OF105,2B3	S	30	145	322	44	92	13	3	4	23	21	29	14	.286	.330	.382
Darren Lewis	OF94	R	24	100	320	38	74	8	1	1	18	29	46	28	.231	.295	.272
Cory Snyder	OF70,1B27,3B14*	R	29	124	390	48	105	22	2	14	57	23	96	4	.269	.311	.444
Kevin Bass†	OF72	S	33	89	265	25	71	11	3	7	30	16	53	7	.268	.310	.411
Chris James	OF62	R	29	111	248	25	60	10	4	5	32	14	45	2	.242	.285	.375
Jose Uribe	SS62	S	33	66	162	24	39	9	1	2	13	14	25	2	.241	.299	.346
Greg Litton	2B31,3B10,1B8*	R	27	68	140	9	32	5	0	4	15	11	33	0	.229	.285	.350
Mark Leonard	OF37	L	27	55	128	13	30	7	0	4	16	16	31	0	.234	.331	.383
Craig Colbert	C35,3B9,2B2	R	27	49	126	10	29	5	2	1	16	9	22	1	.230	.277	.325
John Patterson	2B22,OF5	S	25	32	103	10	19	1	1	0	4	5	24	5	.184	.229	.214
Mike Benjamin	SS33,3B2	R	26	40	75	4	13	2	1	1	3	4	15	1	.173	.215	.267
Jim McNamara	C30	L	27	30	74	6	16	1	0	1	9	6	25	0	.216	.275	.270
Ted Wood	OF16	L	25	24	58	5	12	2	0	1	3	6	15	0	.207	.292	.293
Steve Hosey	OF18	R	23	21	56	6	14	1	0	1	6	0	15	1	.250	.241	.321
Steve Decker	C15	R	26	15	43	3	7	1	0	0	1	6	7	0	.163	.280	.186
Mark Bailey	C7	S	30	13	26	0	4	1	0	0	1	3	7	0	.154	.241	.192

C. Snyder, 4 G at 2B, 3 G at SS; G. Litton, 3 G at SS, 1 G at OF

Pitcher	T	Age	G	GS	CG	ShO	IP	H	HR	BB	SO	W-L	Sv	ERA
John Burkett	R	27	32	32	3	1	189.2	194	13	45	107	13-9	0	3.84
Bud Black	L	35	28	28	2	1	177.0	178	23	59	82	10-12	0	3.97
Trevor Wilson	L	26	26	26	1	1	154.0	152	18	64	88	8-14	0	4.21
Bill Swift	R	30	30	22	3	2	164.2	144	6	43	77	10-4	1	2.08
Kevin Rogers	L	23	6	6	0	0	34.0	37	4	13	26	0-2	0	4.24
Larry Carter	R	27	6	6	0	0	33.0	34	6	18	21	1-5	0	4.64
Pat Rapp	R	24	3	2	0	0	10.0	8	0	6	3	0-2	0	7.20
Mike Jackson	R	27	67	0	0	0	82.0	76	7	33	80	6-6	2	3.73
Rod Beck	R	23	65	0	0	0	92.0	62	4	15	87	3-3	17	1.76
Bryan Hickerson	L	28	61	1	0	0	87.1	74	7	21	68	5-3	0	3.09
Jeff Brantley	R	28	56	4	0	0	91.2	67	8	45	86	7-7	7	2.95
Dave Righetti	L	33	54	4	0	0	78.1	79	4	36	47	2-7	3	5.06
Jim Pena	L	27	25	2	0	0	44.0	49	4	20	32	1-1	0	3.48
Dave Burba	R	25	23	11	0	0	70.2	80	4	31	47	2-7	0	4.97
Kelly Downs†	R	31	19	7	0	0	62.1	65	4	24	33	1-2	0	3.47
Steve Reed	R	26	18	0	0	0	15.2	13	2	3	11	1-0	0	2.30
Francisco Oliveras	R	29	16	7	0	0	44.2	41	11	10	17	0-3	0	3.63
Gil Heredia†	R	26	13	4	0	0	30.0	32	3	16	15	2-3	0	5.40

1992 Los Angeles Dodgers 6th NL West 63-99 .389 35.0 GB

Tom Lasorda

Player	Gm by Position	B	Age	G	AB	R	H	2B	3B	HR	RBI	BB	SO	SB	Avg	OBP	Slg
Mike Scioscia	C108	L	33	117	348	19	77	6	3	3	24	32	31	3	.221	.286	.282
Eric Karros	1B143	R	24	149	545	63	140	30	1	20	88	37	103	2	.257	.304	.426
Lenny Harris	2B81,3B33,OF15*	L	27	135	347	28	94	11	0	0	30	24	24	19	.271	.318	.303
Dave Hansen	3B108	L	23	132	341	30	73	11	0	6	22	34	49	0	.214	.286	.299
Jose Offerman	SS149	S	23	149	534	67	139	20	8	1	30	57	98	23	.260	.331	.333
Brett Butler	OF155	L	35	157	553	86	171	14	11	3	39	95	67	41	.309	.413	.391
Mitch Webster	OF90	S	33	135	262	33	70	12	5	6	35	27	49	11	.267	.334	.420
Eric Davis	OF74	R	30	76	267	21	61	8	1	5	32	36	71	19	.228	.325	.322
Mike Sharperson	2B63,3B60,SS2	R	30	128	317	48	95	21	0	3	36	47	33	2	.300	.387	.394
Todd Benzinger	OF51,1B42	S	29	121	293	24	70	16	2	4	31	15	54	2	.239	.272	.348
Carlos Hernandez	C63	R	25	69	173	11	45	4	0	3	17	11	21	0	.260	.316	.335
Darryl Strawberry	OF42	L	30	43	156	20	37	8	0	5	25	19	34	3	.237	.322	.385
Henry Rodriguez	OF48,1B1	L	24	53	146	11	32	7	0	3	14	8	30	0	.219	.258	.329
Eric Young	2B43	R	25	49	132	9	34	1	0	1	11	8	9	6	.258	.300	.288
Juan Samuel†	2B38,OF1	R	31	47	122	7	32	3	1	0	15	7	22	2	.262	.303	.303
Kal Daniels†	OF21,1B8	L	28	35	104	9	24	5	0	2	8	10	30	0	.231	.302	.337
Billy Ashley	OF27	R	21	29	95	6	21	5	0	2	6	5	34	0	.221	.260	.337
Dave Anderson	3B26,SS7	R	31	51	84	10	24	4	0	3	8	4	11	0	.286	.311	.440
Tom Goodwin	OF45	L	23	57	73	15	17	1	1	0	3	6	10	7	.233	.291	.274
Mike Piazza	C16	R	23	21	69	5	16	3	0	1	7	4	12	0	.232	.284	.319
Stan Javier†	OF27	S	28	56	58	6	11	3	0	1	5	6	11	1	.190	.277	.293
Rafael Bournigal	SS9	R	26	10	20	1	3	1	0	0	0	1	2	0	.150	.227	.200

L. Harris, 10 G at SS

Pitcher	T	Age	G	GS	CG	ShO	IP	H	HR	BB	SO	W-L	Sv	ERA
Orel Hershiser	R	33	33	33	1	0	210.2	209	15	69	130	10-15	0	3.67
Kevin Gross	R	31	34	30	4	3	204.2	182	11	77	158	8-13	0	3.17
Tom Candiotti	R	34	32	30	6	2	203.2	177	13	63	152	11-15	0	3.00
Bobby Ojeda	L	34	29	29	2	1	166.1	169	8	81	94	6-9	0	3.63
Ramon Martinez	R	24	25	25	1	1	150.2	141	11	69	101	8-11	0	4.00
Pedro Astacio	R	23	11	11	4	4	82.0	80	1	20	43	5-5	0	1.98
Pedro Martinez	R	20	2	1	0	0	8.0	6	0	1	8	0-1	0	2.25
Jim Gott	R	32	68	0	0	0	88.0	72	4	41	75	3-3	6	2.45
Roger McDowell	R	31	65	0	0	0	83.2	103	3	42	50	6-10	14	4.09
Steve Wilson	L	27	60	0	0	0	66.2	74	6	29	54	2-5	0	4.19
John Candelaria	L	38	50	0	0	0	25.1	20	1	13	23	2-5	5	2.84
Tim Crews	R	31	49	2	0	0	78.0	95	6	20	43	0-3	0	5.19
Jay Howell	R	36	41	0	0	0	46.2	41	2	18	36	1-3	4	1.54
Kip Gross	R	27	16	1	0	0	23.2	32	1	10	14	1-1	0	4.18

»1993 Toronto Blue Jays 1st AL East 95-67 .586 —

Cito Gaston

Player	Gm by Position	B	Age	G	AB	R	H	2B	3B	HR	RBI	BB	SO	SB	Avg	OBP	Slg
Pat Borders	C138	R	30	138	488	38	124	30	0	9	55	20	66	2	.254	.285	.371
John Olerud	1B137,DH20	L	24	158	551	109	200	54	2	24	107	114	65	0	.363	.473	.599
Roberto Alomar	2B151	S	25	153	589	109	192	35	6	17	93	80	67	55	.326	.408	.492
Ed Sprague	3B150	R	25	150	546	50	142	31	1	12	73	32	85	1	.260	.310	.386
Tony Fernandez†	SS94	S	31	94	353	45	108	18	9	4	50	31	26	15	.306	.361	.442
Joe Carter	OF151,DH3	R	33	155	603	92	153	33	5	33	121	47	113	8	.254	.312	.489
Devon White	OF145	S	30	146	598	116	163	42	6	15	52	57	127	34	.273	.341	.438
Turner Ward	OF65,1B1	S	28	72	167	20	32	4	2	4	28	23	26	3	.192	.287	.311
Paul Molitor	DH137,1B23	R	36	160	636	121	211	37	5	22	111	77	71	22	.332	.402	.509
Darnell Coles	OF44,3B16,DH1*	R	31	64	194	26	49	9	1	4	26	16	29	1	.253	.319	.371
Darrin Jackson†	OF46	R	29	46	176	15	38	8	0	5	19	8	53	0	.216	.250	.347
Rickey Henderson†	OF44	R	34	44	163	37	35	3	1	4	12	35	19	22	.215	.356	.319
Dick Schofield	SS36	R	30	36	110	11	21	1	2	0	5	16	25	3	.191	.294	.236
Randy Knorr	C39	R	24	39	101	11	25	3	2	4	20	9	29	0	.248	.309	.436
Alfredo Griffin	SS20,2B11,3B6	S	35	46	95	15	20	3	0	0	3	3	13	0	.211	.235	.242
Rob Butler	OF16	L	23	17	48	8	13	4	0	0	2	7	12	2	.271	.375	.354
Luis Sojo	2B8,SS8,3B3	R	27	19	47	5	8	2	0	0	6	4	2	0	.170	.231	.213
Willie Canate	OF31,DH1	R	21	38	47	12	10	0	0	1	3	6	15	1	.213	.309	.277
Domingo Cedeno	SS10,2B5	S	24	15	46	5	8	0	0	0	7	1	10	1	.174	.188	.174
Domingo Martinez	1B7,3B1	R	25	8	14	2	4	0	0	1	3	1	7	0	.286	.333	.500
Shawn Green	OF2,DH1	L	20	3	6	0	0	0	0	0	0	0	1	0	.000	.000	.000
Carlos Delgado	DH1,C1	L	21	2	1	0	0	0	0	0	0	1	0	0	.000	.500	.000

D. Coles, 1 G at 1B

Pitcher	T	Age	G	GS	CG	ShO	IP	H	HR	BB	SO	W-L	Sv	ERA
Juan Guzman	R	26	33	33	2	1	221.0	211	17	110	194	14-3	0	3.99
Pat Hentgen	R	24	34	32	3	0	216.1	215	27	74	122	19-9	0	3.87
Todd Stottlemyre	R	28	30	28	1	1	176.2	204	11	69	98	11-12	0	4.84
Jack Morris	R	38	27	27	4	1	152.2	189	18	65	103	7-12	0	6.19
Dave Stewart	R	36	26	26	0	0	162.0	146	23	72	96	12-8	0	4.44
Scott Brow	R	24	6	3	0	0	18.0	19	2	10	7	1-1	0	6.00
Duane Ward	R	29	71	0	0	0	71.2	49	4	25	97	2-3	45	2.13
Mark Eichhorn	R	32	54	0	0	0	72.2	74	3	22	47	3-1	0	2.72
Mike Timlin	R	27	54	0	0	0	55.2	63	7	27	49	4-2	1	4.69
Tony Castillo	L	30	51	0	0	0	50.2	44	4	22	28	3-2	0	3.38
Danny Cox	R	33	44	0	0	0	83.2	73	8	29	84	7-6	2	3.12
Al Leiter	L	27	34	12	1	1	105.0	93	8	56	66	9-6	2	4.11
Woody Williams	R	26	30	0	0	0	37.0	40	2	22	24	3-1	0	4.38
Huck Flener	L	24	6	0	0	0	6.2	7	0	4	2	0-0	0	4.05
Doug Linton†	R	28	4	1	0	0	11.0	11	0	9	4	0-1	0	6.55
Ken Dayley	L	34	2	0	0	0	0.2	1	0	4	2	0-0	0	0.00

1993 New York Yankees 2nd AL East 88-74 .543 7.0 GB

Buck Showalter

Player	Gm by Position	B	Age	G	AB	R	H	2B	3B	HR	RBI	BB	SO	SB	Avg	OBP	Slg
Mike Stanley	C122,DH2	R	30	130	423	70	129	17	1	26	84	57	85	1	.305	.389	.534
Don Mattingly	1B130,DH5	L	32	134	530	78	154	27	2	17	86	61	42	0	.291	.364	.445
Pat Kelly	2B125	R	25	127	406	49	111	24	1	7	51	24	68	14	.273	.317	.389
Wade Boggs	3B134,DH8	L	35	143	560	83	169	26	1	2	59	74	49	0	.302	.378	.363
Spike Owen	SS96,DH1	S	32	103	334	41	78	16	2	2	20	29	30	3	.234	.294	.311
Bernie Williams	OF139	S	24	139	567	67	152	31	4	12	68	53	106	9	.268	.333	.400
Paul O'Neill	OF138,DH2	L	30	141	498	71	155	34	1	20	75	44	69	2	.311	.367	.504
Dion James	OF103,DH1,1B1	L	30	115	343	62	114	21	2	7	36	31	31	0	.332	.390	.466
Danny Tartabull	DH88,OF50	R	30	138	513	87	128	33	2	31	102	92	156	0	.250	.363	.503
Mike Gallego	SS55,2B52,3B27*	R	32	119	403	63	114	20	1	10	54	50	65	3	.283	.364	.412
Jim Leyritz	1B29,OF28,DH21*	R	29	95	259	43	80	14	0	14	53	37	59	0	.309	.410	.525
Randy Velarde	OF50,SS26,3B16*	R	30	85	226	28	68	13	2	7	24	18	39	2	.301	.360	.469
Matt Nokes	C56,DH11	L	29	76	217	25	54	8	0	10	35	16	31	0	.249	.303	.424
Kevin Maas	DH31,1B17	L	28	59	151	20	31	4	0	9	25	24	32	1	.205	.316	.411
Gerald Williams	OF37	R	26	42	67	11	10	2	3	0	6	1	14	2	.149	.183	.269
Hensley Meulens	OF24,1B3,3B1	R	26	30	53	8	9	1	1	2	5	8	19	0	.170	.279	.340
Mike Humphreys	OF21,DH3	R	26	25	35	6	6	2	1	1	6	4	11	2	.171	.250	.371
Dave Silvestri	SS4,3B3	R	25	7	21	4	6	1	0	1	4	5	3	0	.286	.423	.476
Andy Stankiewicz	2B6,3B4,DH1*	R	28	16	9	5	0	0	0	0	0	1	1	0	.000	.100	.000

M. Gallego, 1 G at DH; J. Leyritz, 12 G at C; R. Velarde, 1 G at DH; A. Stankiewicz, 1 G at SS

Pitcher	T	Age	G	GS	CG	ShO	IP	H	HR	BB	SO	W-L	Sv	ERA
Jimmy Key	L	32	34	34	4	2	236.2	219	26	43	173	18-6	0	3.00
Jim Abbott	L	25	32	32	4	1	214.0	221	22	73	95	11-14	0	4.37
Melido Perez	R	27	25	25	0	0	163.0	173	22	64	148	6-14	0	5.19
Scott Kamieniecki	R	29	30	20	2	0	154.1	163	17	59	72	10-7	1	4.08
Mike Witt	R	32	9	9	0	0	41.0	39	7	22	30	3-2	0	5.27
Domingo Jean	R	24	10	6	0	0	40.1	37	7	19	20	1-1	0	4.46
Sterling Hitchcock	L	22	6	6	0	0	31.0	32	4	14	26	1-2	0	4.65
Mark Hutton	R	23	7	4	0	0	22.0	24	2	17	12	1-1	0	5.73
Frank Tanana†	L	39	3	3	0	0	19.2	18	2	7	12	0-2	0	3.20
Sam Militello	R	23	3	2	0	0	9.1	10	1	7	5	1-1	0	6.75
Jeff Johnson	L	26	2	2	0	0	2.2	12	1	2	0	0-2	0	30.38
Steve Howe	L	35	51	0	0	0	50.2	58	7	10	19	3-5	4	4.97
Steve Farr	R	36	49	0	0	0	47.0	44	8	28	39	2-2	25	4.21
Rich Monteleone	R	30	42	0	0	0	85.2	85	14	35	50	7-4	0	4.94
Bob Wickman	R	24	41	19	1	1	140.0	156	13	69	70	14-4	4	4.63
Bobby Munoz	R	25	38	0	0	0	45.2	48	1	26	33	3-3	0	5.32
John Habyan†	R	29	36	0	0	0	42.1	45	5	16	29	2-1	1	4.04
Paul Assenmacher†	L	32	26	0	0	0	17.1	10	0	9	11	2-2	0	3.12
Paul Gibson†	R	33	20	0	0	0	35.1	31	4	9	25	2-0	0	3.06
Neal Heaton	L	33	18	0	0	0	27.0	34	6	11	15	1-0	0	6.00
Lee Smith†	R	35	8	0	0	0	8.0	4	0	5	11	0-0	3	0.00
Andy Cook	R	25	4	0	0	0	5.1	4	1	7	4	0-1	0	5.06

1993 Baltimore Orioles 3rd AL East 85-77 .525 10.0 GB

Johnny Oates

Player	Gm by Position	B	Age	G	AB	R	H	2B	3B	HR	RBI	BB	SO	SB	Avg	OBP	Slg
Chris Hoiles	C124,DH2	R	28	126	419	80	130	28	0	29	82	69	94	1	.310	.416	.585
David Segui	1B144,DH1	S	26	146	450	54	123	27	0	10	60	58	53	2	.273	.351	.400
Harold Reynolds	2B141,DH1	S	32	145	485	64	122	20	4	4	47	66	47	12	.252	.343	.334
Tim Hulett	3B75,SS8,2B4*	R	33	85	260	40	78	15	0	2	23	23	56	1	.300	.361	.381
Cal Ripken Jr.	SS162	R	32	162	641	87	165	26	3	24	90	65	58	1	.257	.329	.420
Brady Anderson	OF140,DH2	L	29	142	560	87	147	36	8	13	66	82	99	24	.263	.363	.425
Mike Devereaux	OF130	R	30	131	527	72	132	31	3	14	75	43	99	3	.250	.306	.400
Mark McLemore	OF124,2B25,3B4*	S	28	148	581	81	165	27	5	4	72	64	92	21	.284	.353	.368
Harold Baines	DH116	L	34	118	416	64	130	22	0	20	78	57	52	0	.313	.390	.510
Leo Gomez	3B70,DH1	R	27	71	244	30	48	7	0	10	25	32	60	0	.197	.295	.348
Jack Voigt	OF43,DH8,1B5*	R	27	64	152	32	45	11	1	6	23	25	33	1	.296	.395	.500
Mike Pagliarulo†	3B28,1B4	L	33	33	117	24	38	9	0	6	21	8	15	0	.325	.373	.556
Glenn Davis	1B22,DH7	R	32	30	113	8	20	3	0	1	9	7	29	0	.177	.230	.230
Jeffrey Hammonds	OF23,DH7	R	22	33	105	10	32	8	0	3	19	2	16	4	.305	.312	.467
Sherman Obando	DH21,OF8	R	23	31	92	8	25	2	0	3	15	4	26	0	.272	.309	.391
Jeff Tackett	C38,P1	R	27	39	87	8	15	3	0	0	9	13	28	0	.172	.277	.207
Damon Buford	OF30,DH16	R	23	53	79	18	18	5	0	2	9	9	19	2	.228	.315	.367
Mark Parent	C21,DH1	R	31	22	54	7	14	2	0	4	12	3	14	0	.259	.293	.519
Paul Carey	1B9,DH5	R	25	18	47	1	10	1	0	0	3	5	14	0	.213	.288	.234
Lonnie Smith†	DH5,OF4	R	37	9	24	8	5	1	0	2	3	8	10	0	.208	.406	.500
Luis Mercedes†	OF8,DH2	R	25	10	24	1	7	2	0	0	0	5	4	1	.292	.414	.375
Mark Leonard	OF4,DH3	L	28	10	15	1	1	1	0	0	3	3	7	0	.067	.190	.133
Chito Martinez	OF5,DH2	L	27	8	15	0	0	0	0	0	0	4	4	0	.000	.211	.000
Manny Alexander	DH1	R	22	3	0	1	0	0	0	0	0	0	0	0	—	—	—

T. Hulett, 2 G at DH; M. McLemore, 1 G at DH; J. Voigt, 3 G at 3B

Pitcher	T	Age	G	GS	CG	ShO	IP	H	HR	BB	SO	W-L	Sv	ERA
Ben McDonald	R	25	34	34	7	1	220.1	185	17	86	171	13-14	0	3.39
F. Valenzuela	L	32	32	31	5	2	178.2	179	18	79	78	8-10	0	4.94
Rick Sutcliffe	R	37	29	28	3	0	166.0	212	23	74	80	10-10	0	5.75
Mike Mussina	R	24	25	25	3	2	167.2	163	20	44	117	14-6	0	4.46
Jamie Moyer	L	30	25	25	3	1	152.0	154	11	38	90	12-9	0	3.43
Arthur Rhodes	L	23	17	17	0	0	85.2	91	16	49	49	5-6	0	6.51
Todd Frohwirth	R	30	70	0	0	0	96.1	91	7	44	50	6-7	3	3.83
Jim Poole	L	27	55	0	0	0	50.1	30	2	21	29	2-1	2	2.15
Gregg Olson	R	26	50	0	0	0	45.0	37	1	18	44	0-2	29	1.60
Mark Williamson	R	33	48	1	0	0	88.0	106	5	25	45	7-5	0	4.91
Alan Mills	R	26	45	0	0	0	100.1	80	14	51	68	5-4	4	3.23
Brad Pennington	L	24	34	0	0	0	33.0	34	7	25	39	3-2	4	6.55
John O'Donoghue	L	24	11	1	0	0	19.2	22	4	10	16	0-1	0	4.58
Kevin McGehee	R	24	5	0	0	0	16.2	18	5	7	7	0-0	0	5.94
Mike Oquist	R	25	5	0	0	0	11.2	12	0	4	8	0-0	0	3.86
Anthony Telford	R	27	3	0	0	0	7.1	11	3	1	6	0-0	0	9.82
Mike Cook	R	29	2	0	0	0	3.0	1	0	2	3	0-0	0	0.00
Jeff Tackett	R	27	1	0	0	0	1.0	1	0	1	0	0-0	0	0.00

1993 Detroit Tigers 3rd AL East 85-77 .525 10.0 GB

Sparky Anderson

Player	Gm by Position	B	Age	G	AB	R	H	2B	3B	HR	RBI	BB	SO	SB	Avg	OBP	Slg
Chad Kreuter	C112,DH2,1B1	S	28	119	374	59	107	23	3	15	51	49	92	2	.286	.371	.484
Cecil Fielder	1B119,DH36	R	29	154	573	80	153	23	0	30	117	90	125	0	.267	.368	.464
Lou Whitaker	2B110	L	36	119	383	72	111	32	1	9	67	78	46	3	.290	.412	.449
Travis Fryman	SS81,3B69,DH1	R	24	151	607	98	182	37	5	22	97	77	128	9	.300	.379	.486
Alan Trammell	SS63,3B35,OF8*	R	35	112	401	72	132	25	3	12	60	38	38	12	.329	.388	.496
Tony Phillips	OF108,2B51,DH4*	S	34	151	566	113	177	27	0	7	57	132	102	16	.313	.443	.398
Dan Gladden	OF86,DH5	R	35	91	356	52	95	16	2	13	56	21	50	8	.267	.312	.433
Rob Deer†	OF86,DH4	R	32	90	323	48	70	11	0	14	39	38	120	3	.217	.302	.381
Kirk Gibson	DH76,OF32	L	36	116	403	62	105	18	6	13	62	44	87	15	.261	.337	.432
Mickey Tettleton	1B59,C56,OF55*	S	32	152	522	79	128	25	4	32	110	109	139	3	.245	.372	.492
Scott Livingstone	3B62,DH32	L	27	98	304	39	89	10	2	2	39	19	32	1	.293	.328	.359
Milt Cuyler	OF80	S	24	82	249	46	53	11	7	0	19	19	53	13	.213	.276	.313
Skeeter Barnes	1B27,OF18,DH13*	R	36	84	160	24	45	8	1	2	27	11	19	5	.281	.318	.381
Chris Gomez	SS29,2B17,DH1	R	22	46	128	11	32	7	1	0	11	9	17	2	.250	.304	.320
Gary Thurman	OF53,DH6	R	28	75	89	22	19	2	2	0	13	11	30	7	.213	.297	.281
Eric Davis†	OF18,DH5	R	31	23	75	14	19	1	1	6	15	14	18	2	.253	.371	.533
Danny Bautista	OF16,DH1	R	21	17	61	6	19	3	0	1	9	1	10	3	.311	.317	.410
Rich Rowland	C17,DH3	R	29	21	46	2	10	3	0	0	4	5	16	0	.217	.294	.283

A. Trammell, 6 G at DH; T. Phillips, 1 G at 3B; M. Tettleton, 4 G at DH; S. Barnes, 13 G at 3B, 10 G at 2B, 2 G at SS

Pitcher	T	Age	G	GS	CG	ShO	IP	H	HR	BB	SO	W-L	Sv	ERA
Mike Moore	R	33	36	36	4	3	213.2	227	35	89	89	13-9	0	5.22
John Doherty	R	26	32	31	3	2	184.2	205	19	48	63	14-11	0	4.44
David Wells	L	30	32	30	0	0	187.0	183	26	42	139	11-9	0	4.19
Bill Gullickson	R	34	28	28	2	0	159.1	186	28	44	70	13-9	0	5.37
Sean Bergman	R	23	9	6	1	0	39.2	47	6	23	19	1-4	0	5.67
Bob MacDonald	L	28	68	0	0	0	65.2	67	8	33	39	3-3	3	5.35
Mike Henneman	R	31	63	0	0	0	71.2	69	4	32	58	5-3	24	2.64
Tom Bolton	L	31	43	8	0	0	102.2	113	5	45	66	6-6	0	4.47
Bill Krueger	L	35	32	7	0	0	82.0	90	6	30	60	6-4	0	3.40
Kurt Knudsen	R	26	30	0	0	0	37.2	41	9	16	29	3-2	2	4.78
Mark Leiter	R	30	27	13	1	0	106.2	111	17	44	70	6-6	0	4.73
Storm Davis†	R	31	24	0	0	0	35.1	25	4	15	36	0-2	4	3.06
Dave Haas	R	27	20	0	0	0	28.0	45	9	8	17	1-2	0	6.11
Buddy Groom	L	27	19	3	0	0	36.2	48	4	13	15	0-2	0	6.14
Joe Boever†	R	32	19	0	0	0	23.0	14	1	11	14	2-1	3	2.74
Greg Gohr	R	25	16	0	0	0	22.2	26	1	14	23	0-0	0	5.96
Mike Gardiner†	R	27	10	0	0	0	11.1	12	0	7	4	0-0	0	3.97
John Kiely	R	28	8	0	0	0	11.2	13	2	13	5	0-2	0	7.71
Mike Munoz†	L	27	8	0	0	0	3.0	4	1	6	1	0-1	0	6.00
Dave Johnson	R	33	6	0	0	0	8.1	13	3	5	7	1-1	0	12.96
Mark Grater	R	29	6	0	0	0	5.0	6	0	4	4	0-0	0	5.40
John DeSilva†	R	25	1	0	0	0	1.0	2	0	0	0	0-0	0	9.00

1993 Boston Red Sox 5th AL East 80-82 .494 15.0 GB

Butch Hobson

Player	Gm by Position	B	Age	G	AB	R	H	2B	3B	HR	RBI	BB	SO	SB	Avg	OBP	Slg
Tony Pena	C125	R	36	126	304	20	55	11	0	4	19	25	46	1	.181	.246	.257
Mo Vaughn	1B131,DH19	L	25	152	539	86	160	34	1	29	101	79	130	4	.297	.390	.525
Scott Fletcher	2B116,SS2,DH1*	R	34	121	480	81	137	31	5	5	45	37	35	16	.285	.341	.402
Scott Cooper	3B154,1B2,SS1	L	25	156	526	67	147	29	3	9	63	58	81	5	.279	.355	.397
John Valentin	SS144	R	26	144	468	50	130	40	3	11	66	49	77	3	.278	.346	.447
Mike Greenwell	OF134,DH10	L	29	146	540	77	170	38	6	13	72	54	46	5	.315	.379	.480
Billy Hatcher	OF130,2B2	R	32	136	508	71	146	24	3	9	57	28	46	14	.287	.336	.400
Bob Zupcic	OF122,DH5	R	26	141	286	40	69	24	2	2	26	27	54	5	.241	.308	.360
Andre Dawson	DH97,OF20	R	38	121	461	44	126	29	1	13	67	17	49	2	.273	.313	.425
Carlos Quintana	1B53,OF51	R	27	101	303	31	74	5	0	1	19	31	52	1	.244	.317	.271
Ivan Calderon†	OF47,DH18	R	31	73	213	25	47	8	2	1	19	21	28	4	.221	.291	.291
Bob Melvin	C76,1B1	R	31	77	176	13	39	7	0	3	23	7	44	0	.222	.251	.313
Rob Deer†	OF36,DH2	R	32	38	143	18	28	6	1	7	16	20	49	2	.196	.303	.399
Ernest Riles	2B20,DH15,3B11*	L	32	94	143	15	27	8	0	5	20	20	40	1	.189	.292	.350
Luis Rivera	2B27,SS27,DH5*	R	29	62	130	13	27	8	1	1	7	11	36	1	.208	.273	.308
Tim Naehring	2B15,DH10,3B9*	R	26	39	127	14	42	10	0	1	17	10	26	1	.331	.377	.433
Jeff McNeely	OF13,DH2	R	23	21	37	10	11	1	1	0	1	7	9	6	.297	.409	.378
Greg Blosser	OF9,DH1	L	22	17	28	1	2	1	0	0	1	2	7	1	.071	.133	.107
John Flaherty	C13	R	25	13	25	3	3	2	0	0	2	2	6	0	.120	.214	.200
Jeff Richardson	2B8,SS5,DH1*	R	27	15	24	3	5	2	0	0	2	1	3	0	.208	.240	.292
Steve Lyons	OF10,2B9,DH1*	L	33	28	23	4	3	1	0	0	0	2	5	1	.130	.200	.174
Luis Ortiz	3B5,DH2	R	23	9	12	0	3	0	0	0	1	0	2	0	.250	.250	.250
Jim Byrd	DH1	R	24	2	0	0	0	0	0	0	0	0	0	0	—	—	—

S. Fletcher, 1 G at 3B; E. Riles, 1 G at 1B; L. Rivera, 2 G at 3B; T. Naehring, 4 G at SS; J. Richardson, 1 G at 3B; S. Lyons, 1 G at C, 1 G at 1B, 1 G at 3B

Pitcher	T	Age	G	GS	CG	ShO	IP	H	HR	BB	SO	W-L	Sv	ERA
Danny Darwin	R	37	34	34	2	1	229.1	196	31	49	130	15-11	0	3.26
Roger Clemens	R	30	29	29	2	1	191.2	175	17	67	160	11-14	0	4.46
Frank Viola	L	33	29	29	2	1	183.2	180	12	72	91	11-8	0	3.14
John Dopson	R	29	34	28	1	1	155.2	170	16	59	89	7-11	0	4.97
Aaron Sele	R	23	18	18	0	0	111.2	100	5	48	93	7-2	0	2.74
Nate Minchey	R	23	5	5	1	0	33.0	35	5	8	18	1-2	0	3.55
Greg Harris	R	37	80	0	0	0	112.1	95	7	60	103	6-7	8	3.77
Tony Fossas	L	35	71	0	0	0	40.0	38	4	15	39	1-1	0	5.18
Jeff Russell	R	31	51	0	0	0	46.2	39	1	14	45	1-4	33	2.70
Paul Quantrill	R	24	49	14	1	1	138.0	151	13	44	66	6-12	1	3.91
Ken Ryan	R	24	47	0	0	0	50.0	43	2	29	49	7-2	1	3.60
Scott Bankhead	R	29	40	0	0	0	64.1	59	7	29	47	2-1	0	3.50
Joe Hesketh	L	34	28	5	0	0	53.1	62	4	29	34	3-4	1	5.06
Scott Taylor	L	25	16	0	0	0	11.0	14	1	12	8	0-1	0	8.18
Cory Bailey	R	22	11	0	0	0	15.2	12	0	12	11	0-1	0	3.45
Jose Melendez	R	27	9	0	0	0	16.0	10	2	5	14	2-1	0	2.25

1993 Cleveland Indians 6th AL East 76-86 .469 19.0 GB

Mike Hargrove

Player	Gm by Position	B	Age	G	AB	R	H	2B	3B	HR	RBI	BB	SO	SB	Avg	OBP	Slg
Junior Ortiz	C95	R	33	95	249	19	55	13	0	0	20	11	26	1	.221	.267	.273
Paul Sorrento	1B144,OF3,DH1	L	27	148	463	75	119	26	1	18	65	58	121	3	.257	.340	.434
Carlos Baerga	2B150,DH4	S	24	154	624	105	200	28	6	21	114	34	68	15	.321	.355	.486
Alvaro Espinoza	3B99,SS35,2B2	R	31	129	263	34	73	15	0	4	27	8	36	2	.278	.298	.380
Felix Fermin	SS140	R	29	140	480	48	126	16	2	2	45	24	14	4	.263	.303	.317
Albert Belle	OF150,DH9	R	26	159	594	93	172	36	3	38	129	76	96	23	.290	.370	.552
Kenny Lofton	OF146	L	26	148	569	116	185	28	8	1	42	81	83	70	.325	.408	.408
Wayne Kirby	OF123,DH5	L	29	131	458	71	123	19	5	6	60	37	58	17	.269	.323	.371
Reggie Jefferson	DH88,1B15	S	24	113	366	35	91	11	2	10	34	28	78	1	.249	.310	.372
Carlos Martinez	3B35,1B22,DH19	R	28	80	262	26	64	10	0	5	31	20	29	1	.244	.295	.340
Jeff Treadway	3B42,2B19,DH4	L	30	97	221	25	67	14	1	2	27	14	21	1	.303	.347	.403
Sandy Alomar Jr.	C64	R	27	64	215	24	58	7	1	6	32	11	28	3	.270	.318	.395
Thomas Howard†	OF47,DH7	S	28	74	178	26	42	7	0	3	23	12	42	5	.236	.278	.326
Glenallen Hill†	OF39,DH18	R	28	66	174	19	39	7	2	5	25	11	50	7	.224	.268	.374
Jim Thome	3B47	L	22	47	154	28	41	11	0	7	22	29	36	2	.266	.385	.474
Candy Maldonado†	OF26,DH2	R	32	28	81	11	20	2	0	5	20	11	18	0	.247	.333	.457
Jesse Levis	C29	L	25	31	63	7	11	2	0	0	4	2	10	0	.175	.197	.206
Manny Ramirez	DH20,OF1	R	21	22	53	5	9	1	0	2	5	2	8	0	.170	.200	.302
Mark Lewis	SS13	R	23	14	52	6	13	2	0	1	5	0	7	3	.250	.250	.346
Randy Milligan†	1B18,DH1	R	31	19	47	7	20	7	0	0	7	14	4	0	.426	.557	.574
Sam Horn	DH11	L	29	12	33	8	15	1	0	4	8	1	5	0	.455	.472	.848
Lance Parrish	C10	R	37	10	20	2	4	1	0	1	2	4	5	1	.200	.333	.400

Pitcher	T	Age	G	GS	CG	ShO	IP	H	HR	BB	SO	W-L	Sv	ERA
Jose Mesa	R	27	34	33	3	0	208.2	232	21	62	118	10-12	0	4.92
Mark Clark	R	25	26	15	1	0	109.1	119	18	25	57	7-5	0	4.28
Jeff Mutis	L	26	17	13	1	1	81.0	93	14	33	29	3-6	0	5.78
Mike Bielecki	R	33	13	13	0	0	68.2	90	8	23	38	4-5	0	5.90
Albie Lopez	R	21	9	9	0	0	49.2	49	7	32	25	3-1	0	5.98
Charles Nagy	R	26	9	9	1	0	48.2	66	6	13	30	2-6	0	6.29
Bobby Ojeda	L	35	9	7	0	0	43.0	48	5	21	27	2-1	0	4.40
Julian Tavarez	R	20	8	7	0	0	37.0	53	7	13	19	2-2	0	6.57
Jason Grimsley	R	25	10	6	0	0	42.1	52	3	20	27	3-4	0	5.31
Paul Abbott	R	25	5	5	0	0	18.1	19	5	11	7	0-1	0	6.38
Dave Mlicki	R	25	3	3	0	0	13.1	11	2	6	7	0-0	0	3.38
Scott Scudder	R	25	2	1	0	0	4.0	5	0	4	1	0-1	0	9.00
Eric Plunk	R	29	70	0	0	0	71.0	61	5	30	77	4-5	15	2.79
Derek Lilliquist	L	27	56	2	0	0	64.0	64	5	19	40	4-4	10	2.25
Jeremy Hernandez†	R	26	49	0	0	0	77.1	75	12	27	44	6-5	8	3.14
Jerry Dipoto	R	25	46	0	0	0	56.1	57	0	30	41	4-4	11	2.40
Tom Kramer	R	25	39	16	1	0	121.0	126	19	59	71	7-3	0	4.02
Bill Wertz	R	26	34	0	0	0	59.2	54	5	32	53	2-3	0	3.62
Dennis Cook	L	30	25	6	0	0	54.0	62	9	16	34	5-5	0	5.67
Matt Young	L	34	22	8	0	0	74.1	75	8	57	65	1-6	0	5.21
Cliff Young	L	28	21	7	0	0	60.1	74	9	18	31	3-3	1	4.62
Heathcliff Slocumb†	R	27	20	0	0	0	27.1	28	3	16	18	3-1	0	4.28
Ted Power†	R	38	20	0	0	0	20.0	30	2	8	11	0-2	0	7.20
Kevin Wickander†	L	28	11	0	0	0	8.2	15	3	3	3	0-0	0	4.15
Mike Christopher	R	29	9	0	0	0	11.2	14	3	2	8	0-0	0	3.86
Bob Milacki	R	28	5	2	0	0	16.0	19	3	11	7	1-1	0	3.38

1993 Milwaukee Brewers 7th AL East 69-93 .426 26.0 GB

Phil Garner

Player	Gm by Position	B	Age	G	AB	R	H	2B	3B	HR	RBI	BB	SO	SB	Avg	OBP	Slg
Dave Nilsson	C91,DH4,1B4	L	23	100	296	35	76	10	2	7	40	37	36	3	.257	.336	.375
John Jaha	1B150,2B1,3B1	R	27	153	515	78	136	21	0	19	70	51	109	13	.264	.337	.416
Bill Spiers	2B104,OF7,SS4*	L	27	113	340	43	81	8	4	2	36	29	51	9	.238	.302	.303
B.J. Surhoff	3B121,OF24,1B8*	L	28	148	552	66	151	38	3	7	79	36	47	12	.274	.318	.391
Pat Listach	SS95,OF6	S	25	98	356	50	87	15	1	3	30	37	70	18	.244	.319	.317
Darryl Hamilton	OF129	L	28	135	520	74	161	21	1	9	48	45	62	21	.310	.367	.406
Robin Yount	OF114,1B7,DH6	R	37	127	454	62	117	25	3	8	51	44	93	9	.258	.326	.379
Greg Vaughn	OF94,DH58	R	27	154	569	97	152	28	2	30	97	89	118	10	.267	.369	.482
Kevin Reimer	DH83,OF37	L	29	125	437	53	109	22	1	13	60	30	72	5	.249	.303	.394
Juan Bell†	2B47,SS40,OF3*	R	25	91	286	42	67	6	2	5	29	36	64	6	.234	.321	.322
Dickie Thon	SS28,3B25,2B22*	R	35	85	245	23	66	10	1	1	33	22	39	6	.269	.324	.331
Tom Brunansky	OF71,DH6	R	32	80	224	20	41	7	3	6	29	25	59	3	.183	.265	.321
Kevin Seitzer†	3B33,1B7,DH3*	R	31	47	162	21	47	6	0	7	30	17	15	3	.290	.359	.457
Tom Lampkin	C60,OF3,DH1	L	29	73	162	22	32	8	0	4	25	20	26	7	.198	.280	.321
Joe Kmak	C50	R	30	51	110	9	24	5	0	0	7	14	13	6	.218	.317	.264
Alex Diaz	OF28,DH1	S	24	32	69	9	22	2	0	0	1	0	12	5	.319	.319	.348
Bill Doran	2B17,1B4	S	35	28	60	7	13	4	0	0	6	6	3	1	.217	.284	.283
Matt Mieske	OF22	R	25	23	58	9	14	0	0	3	7	4	14	0	.241	.290	.397
Jose Valentin	SS19	S	23	19	53	10	13	1	2	1	7	7	16	1	.245	.344	.396
Troy O'Leary	OF19	L	23	19	41	3	12	3	0	0	3	5	9	0	.293	.370	.366
William Suero	2B8,3B1	R	26	15	14	0	4	0	0	0	0	1	3	0	.286	.333	.286
Tim McIntosh†	C1	R	28	1	0	0	0	0	0	0	0	0	0	0	—	—	—
Ricky Bones	P32,OF1	R	24	32	0	0	0	0	0	0	0	0	0	0	—	—	—

B. Spiers, 1 G at DH; B. Surhoff, 3 G at C, 1 G at DH; J. Bell, 2 G at DH; D. Thon, 14 G at DH; K. Seitzer, 1 G at 2B, 1 G at OF

Pitcher	T	Age	G	GS	CG	ShO	IP	H	HR	BB	SO	W-L	Sv	ERA
Cal Eldred	R	25	36	36	8	1	258.0	232	32	91	180	16-16	0	4.01
Jaime Navarro	R	26	35	34	5	1	214.1	254	21	73	114	11-12	0	5.33
Ricky Bones	R	24	32	31	3	0	203.2	222	28	63	63	11-11	0	4.86
Bill Wegman	R	30	20	18	5	0	120.2	135	13	34	50	4-14	0	4.48
Angel Miranda	L	23	22	17	2	0	120.0	100	12	52	88	4-5	0	3.30
Mike Boddicker	R	35	10	10	1	0	54.0	77	6	15	24	3-5	0	5.67
Teddy Higuera	L	34	8	8	0	0	30.0	43	4	16	27	1-3	0	7.20
Jesse Orosco	L	36	57	0	0	0	56.2	47	2	17	67	3-5	8	3.18
Graeme Lloyd	L	26	55	0	0	0	63.2	64	5	13	31	3-4	0	2.83
Doug Henry	R	29	54	0	0	0	55.0	67	7	25	38	4-4	17	5.56
Mike Fetters	R	28	45	0	0	0	59.1	59	4	22	23	3-3	0	3.34
James Austin	R	29	31	0	0	0	33.0	28	3	13	15	1-2	0	3.82
Carlos Maldonado	R	26	29	0	0	0	37.1	40	2	17	18	2-2	1	4.58
Mike Ignasiak	R	27	27	0	0	0	37.0	32	2	21	28	1-1	0	3.65
Matt Maysey	R	26	23	0	0	0	22.0	28	4	13	10	1-2	1	5.73
Rafael Novoa	L	25	15	7	2	0	56.0	58	7	22	17	0-3	0	4.50
Josias Manzanillo†	R	25	10	1	0	0	17.0	22	1	10	10	1-1	1	9.53
Mark Kiefer	R	24	6	0	0	0	9.1	3	0	5	7	0-0	1	0.00

1993 Chicago White Sox 1st AL West 94-68 .580 —

Gene Lamont

Player	Gm by Position	B	Age	G	AB	R	H	2B	3B	HR	RBI	BB	SO	SB	Avg	OBP	Slg
Ron Karkovice	C127	R	29	128	403	60	92	17	1	20	54	29	126	2	.228	.287	.424
Frank Thomas	1B150,DH4	R	25	153	549	106	174	36	0	41	128	112	54	4	.317	.426	.607
Joey Cora	2B151,3B3	S	28	153	579	95	155	15	13	2	51	67	63	20	.268	.351	.349
Robin Ventura	3B155,1B4	L	25	157	554	85	145	27	1	22	94	105	82	1	.262	.379	.433
Ozzie Guillen	SS133	L	29	134	457	44	128	23	4	4	50	10	41	5	.280	.292	.374
Lance Johnson	OF146	L	29	147	540	75	168	18	14	0	47	36	33	35	.311	.354	.396
Ellis Burks	OF146	R	28	146	499	75	137	24	4	17	74	60	97	6	.275	.352	.441
Tim Raines	OF112	S	33	115	415	75	127	16	4	16	54	64	35	21	.306	.401	.480
George Bell	DH102	R	33	102	410	36	89	17	2	13	64	13	49	1	.217	.243	.363
Bo Jackson	OF47,DH36	R	30	85	284	32	66	9	0	16	45	23	106	0	.232	.289	.433
Craig Grebeck	SS46,2B16,3B14	R	28	72	190	25	43	5	0	1	12	26	26	1	.226	.319	.268
Dan Pasqua	OF37,1B32,DH6	L	31	78	176	22	36	10	1	5	20	26	51	2	.205	.302	.358
Steve Sax	OF32,DH20,2B1	R	33	57	119	20	28	5	0	1	8	8	6	7	.235	.283	.303
Mike LaValliere†	C37	L	32	37	97	6	25	2	0	0	8	4	14	0	.258	.282	.278
Carlton Fisk	C25	R	45	25	53	2	10	0	0	1	4	2	11	0	.189	.228	.245
Mike Huff	OF43	R	29	43	44	4	8	2	0	1	6	9	15	1	.182	.321	.295
Warren Newson	DH10,OF5	L	28	26	40	9	12	0	0	2	6	9	12	0	.300	.429	.450
Ivan Calderon†	DH6	R	31	9	26	1	3	2	0	0	3	0	5	0	.115	.115	.192
Matt Merullo	DH6	L	27	8	20	1	1	0	0	0	0	0	1	0	.050	.050	.050
Norberto Martin	2B5,DH1	R	26	8	14	3	5	0	0	0	2	1	1	0	.357	.400	.357
Rick Wrona	C4	R	29	4	8	0	1	0	0	0	1	0	4	0	.125	.125	.125
Drew Denson	1B3	S	27	4	5	0	1	0	0	0	0	0	2	0	.200	.200	.200
Doug Lindsey†	C2	R	25	2	1	0	0	0	0	0	0	0	1	0	.000	.000	.000

Pitcher	T	Age	G	GS	CG	ShO	IP	H	HR	BB	SO	W-L	Sv	ERA
Jack McDowell	R	27	34	34	10	4	256.2	261	20	69	158	22-10	0	3.37
Alex Fernandez	R	23	34	34	3	1	247.1	221	27	67	169	18-9	0	3.13
Wilson Alvarez	L	23	31	31	1	1	207.2	168	14	122	155	15-8	0	2.95
Jason Bere	R	22	24	24	1	0	142.2	109	12	81	129	12-5	0	3.47
Tim Belcher†	R	31	12	11	1	1	71.2	64	8	27	34	3-5	0	4.40
Rodney Bolton	R	24	9	8	0	0	42.1	55	4	16	17	2-6	0	7.44
Dave Stieb	R	35	4	4	0	0	22.1	27	1	14	11	1-3	0	6.04
Scott Ruffcorn	R	23	3	2	0	0	10.0	9	2	10	2	0-2	0	8.10
Scott Radinsky	L	25	73	0	0	0	54.2	61	3	19	44	8-2	4	4.28
Roberto Hernandez	R	28	70	0	0	0	78.2	66	6	20	71	3-4	38	2.29
Jeff Schwarz	R	29	41	0	0	0	51.0	35	1	38	41	2-2	0	3.71
Donn Pall†	R	31	39	0	0	0	58.2	62	5	11	29	2-3	1	3.22
Kirk McCaskill	R	32	30	14	0	0	113.2	144	12	36	65	4-8	2	5.23
Bobby Thigpen†	R	29	25	0	0	0	34.2	51	5	12	19	0-0	1	5.71
Chuck Cary	L	33	16	0	0	0	20.2	22	1	11	10	1-0	0	5.23
Terry Leach	R	39	14	0	0	0	16.0	15	0	2	3	0-0	1	2.81
Jose DeLeon†	R	32	11	0	0	0	10.1	5	2	3	6	0-0	0	1.74
Barry Jones	R	30	6	0	0	0	7.1	14	2	3	7	0-1	0	8.59
Brian Drahman	R	26	5	0	0	0	5.1	7	0	2	3	0-0	1	0.00
Chris Howard	L	27	3	0	0	0	2.1	2	0	3	1	1-0	0	0.00

1993 Texas Rangers 2nd AL West 86-76 .531 8.0 GB

Kevin Kennedy

Player	Gm by Position	B	Age	G	AB	R	H	2B	3B	HR	RBI	BB	SO	SB	Avg	OBP	Slg
Ivan Rodriguez	C134,DH1	R	21	137	473	56	129	28	4	10	66	29	70	8	.273	.315	.412
Rafael Palmeiro	1B160	L	28	160	597	124	176	40	2	37	105	73	85	22	.295	.371	.554
Doug Strange	2B135,3B9,SS1	S	29	145	484	58	124	29	0	7	60	43	69	6	.256	.318	.360
Dean Palmer	3B148,SS1	R	24	148	519	88	127	31	2	33	96	53	154	11	.245	.321	.503
Manuel Lee	SS72	S	28	73	205	31	45	3	1	1	12	22	39	2	.220	.300	.259
Juan Gonzalez	OF129,DH10	R	23	140	536	105	166	33	1	46	118	37	99	4	.310	.368	.632
David Hulse	OF112,DH2	L	25	114	407	71	118	9	10	1	29	26	57	29	.290	.333	.369
Doug Dascenzo	OF68,DH2	S	29	76	146	20	29	5	1	2	10	8	22	2	.199	.239	.288
Julio Franco	DH140	R	31	144	532	85	154	31	3	14	84	62	95	9	.289	.360	.438
Jose Canseco	OF49,DH9,P1	R	28	60	231	30	59	14	1	10	46	16	62	6	.255	.308	.455
Gary Redus	OF61,1B5,DH1*	R	36	77	222	28	64	12	4	6	31	23	35	4	.288	.351	.459
Mario Diaz	SS57,3B12,1B1	R	31	71	205	24	56	10	1	2	24	8	13	1	.273	.297	.361
Dan Peltier	OF55,1B5	L	25	65	160	23	43	7	1	1	17	20	27	0	.269	.352	.344
Butch Davis	OF44,DH11	R	35	62	159	24	39	10	4	3	20	5	28	3	.245	.273	.415
Geno Petralli	C39,DH2,2B1*	S	33	59	133	16	32	5	0	1	13	22	17	2	.241	.348	.301
Billy Ripken	2B34,SS18,3B1	R	28	50	132	12	25	4	0	0	11	11	19	0	.189	.270	.220
Rob Ducey	OF26	L	28	27	85	15	24	6	3	2	9	10	17	2	.282	.351	.494
Donald Harris	OF38,DH2	R	25	40	76	10	15	2	0	1	8	5	18	0	.197	.253	.263
Benji Gil	SS22	R	20	22	57	3	7	0	0	0	2	5	22	1	.123	.194	.123
Jon Shave	SS9,2B8	R	25	17	47	3	15	2	0	0	7	0	8	1	.319	.306	.362
Jeff Huson	SS12,2B5,DH2*	L	28	23	45	3	6	1	1	0	2	0	10	0	.133	.133	.200
Chris James†	OF7	R	30	8	31	5	11	1	0	3	7	3	6	0	.355	.412	.677
John Russell	C11,1B1,3B1*	R	32	18	22	1	5	1	0	1	3	2	10	0	.227	.292	.409
Steve Balboni	DH2	R	36	2	5	0	3	0	0	0	0	0	2	0	.600	.600	.600

G. Redus, 1 G at 2B; G. Petralli, 1 G at 3B; J. Huson, 2 G at 3B; J. Russell, 1 G at OF

Pitcher	T	Age	G	GS	CG	ShO	IP	H	HR	BB	SO	W-L	Sv	ERA
Kevin Brown	R	28	34	34	12	3	233.0	228	14	74	142	15-12	0	3.59
Kenny Rogers	L	28	35	33	5	0	208.1	210	18	71	140	16-10	0	4.10
Roger Pavlik	R	25	26	26	2	0	166.1	151	18	80	131	12-6	0	3.41
Charlie Leibrandt	L	36	26	26	1	0	150.1	169	15	45	89	9-10	0	4.55
Nolan Ryan	R	46	13	13	0	0	66.1	54	5	40	46	5-5	0	4.88
Steve Dreyer	R	23	10	6	0	0	41.0	48	7	20	23	3-3	0	5.71
Tom Henke	R	35	66	0	0	0	74.1	55	7	27	79	5-5	40	2.91
Matt Whiteside	R	25	60	0	0	0	73.0	78	7	23	39	2-1	1	4.32
Craig Lefferts	L	35	52	8	0	0	83.1	102	17	28	58	3-9	0	6.05
Bob Patterson	L	34	52	0	0	0	52.2	59	8	11	46	2-4	1	4.78
Brian Bohanon	L	24	36	8	0	0	92.2	107	8	46	45	4-4	0	4.76
Cris Carpenter†	R	28	27	0	0	0	32.0	35	4	12	27	4-1	1	4.22
Todd Burns†	R	29	25	5	0	0	65.0	63	6	32	35	0-4	0	4.57
Jeff Bronkey	R	27	21	0	0	0	36.0	39	4	11	18	1-1	1	4.00
Mike Schooler	R	30	17	0	0	0	24.1	30	3	10	16	3-0	0	5.55
Robb Nen†	R	23	9	3	0	0	22.2	28	1	26	12	1-1	0	6.35
Gene Nelson†	R	32	6	0	0	0	8.0	10	0	1	4	0-0	1	3.38
Rick Reed†	R	28	2	0	0	0	4.0	6	1	1	2	1-0	0	2.25
Darren Oliver	L	22	2	0	0	0	3.1	2	1	1	4	0-0	0	2.70
Jose Canseco	R	28	1	0	0	0	1.0	2	0	3	0	0-0	0	27.00
Hector Fajardo	R	22	1	0	0	0	0.2	0	0	0	1	0-0	0	0.00

1993 Kansas City Royals 3rd AL West 84-78 .519 10.0 GB

Hal McRae

Player	Gm by Position	B	Age	G	AB	R	H	2B	3B	HR	RBI	BB	SO	SB	Avg	OBP	Slg
Mike Macfarlane	C114	R	29	117	388	55	106	27	0	20	67	40	83	2	.273	.360	.497
Wally Joyner	1B140	L	31	141	497	83	145	36	3	15	65	66	67	5	.292	.375	.467
Jose Lind	2B136	R	29	136	431	33	107	13	2	0	37	13	36	3	.248	.271	.288
Gary Gaetti†	3B72,1B18,DH1	R	34	82	281	37	72	18	1	14	46	16	75	0	.256	.309	.477
Greg Gagne	SS159	R	31	159	540	66	151	32	3	10	57	33	93	10	.280	.319	.406
Brian McRae	OF153	S	25	153	627	78	177	28	9	12	69	37	105	23	.282	.325	.413
Felix Jose	OF144,DH1	S	28	149	499	64	126	24	3	6	43	36	95	31	.253	.303	.349
Kevin McReynolds	OF104,DH1	R	33	110	351	44	86	22	4	11	42	37	56	2	.245	.316	.425
George Brett	DH140	L	40	145	560	69	149	31	3	19	75	39	67	7	.266	.312	.434
Chris Gwynn	OF83,DH5,1B1	L	28	103	287	36	86	14	4	1	25	24	34	0	.300	.354	.387
Phil Hiatt	3B70,DH9	R	24	81	238	30	52	12	1	7	36	16	82	6	.218	.285	.366
Brent Mayne	C68,DH1	L	25	71	205	22	52	9	1	2	22	18	31	3	.254	.317	.337
Hubie Brooks	OF40,DH9,1B3	R	36	75	168	14	48	12	0	1	24	11	27	0	.286	.331	.375
Keith Miller	3B21,DH6,OF4*	R	30	37	108	9	18	3	0	0	3	8	19	3	.167	.229	.194
Rico Rossy	2B24,3B16,SS11	R	29	46	86	10	19	4	0	2	12	9	11	0	.221	.302	.337
Harvey Pulliam	OF26	R	25	27	62	7	16	5	0	1	6	2	14	0	.258	.292	.387
Craig Wilson	3B15,2B1,OF1	R	28	21	49	6	13	1	0	1	3	7	6	1	.265	.357	.347
Bob Hamelin	1B15	L	25	16	49	2	11	3	0	2	5	6	15	0	.224	.309	.408
Curtis Wilkerson	2B10,SS4	S	32	12	28	1	4	0	0	0	0	1	6	2	.143	.172	.143
Kevin Koslofski	OF13,DH1	L	26	15	26	4	7	0	0	1	2	4	5	0	.269	.387	.385
Dave Howard	2B7,SS3,3B2*	S	26	15	24	5	8	0	1	0	2	2	5	1	.333	.370	.417
Terry Shumpert	2B8	R	26	8	10	0	1	0	0	0	0	2	2	1	.100	.250	.100
Nelson Santovenia	C4	R	31	4	8	0	1	0	0	0	0	1	2	0	.125	.222	.125

K. Miller, 3 G at 2B; D. Howard, 1 G at OF

Pitcher	T	Age	G	GS	CG	ShO	IP	H	HR	BB	SO	W-L	Sv	ERA
David Cone	R	30	34	34	6	1	254.0	205	20	114	191	11-14	0	3.33
Kevin Appier	R	25	34	34	5	1	238.2	183	8	81	186	18-8	0	2.56
Hipolito Pichardo	R	23	30	25	2	0	165.0	183	10	53	70	7-8	0	4.04
Chris Haney	L	24	23	23	1	1	124.0	141	13	53	65	9-9	0	6.02
Mark Gardner	R	31	17	16	0	0	91.2	92	17	36	54	4-6	0	6.19
Mike Magnante	L	28	7	6	0	0	35.1	37	3	11	16	1-2	0	4.08
Jeff Montgomery	R	31	69	0	0	0	87.1	65	3	23	66	7-5	45	2.27
Mark Gubicza	R	30	49	6	0	0	104.1	128	2	43	80	5-8	2	4.66
Tom Gordon	R	25	48	14	2	0	155.2	125	11	77	143	12-6	1	3.58
Billy Brewer	L	25	46	0	0	0	39.0	31	6	20	28	2-2	0	3.46
Stan Belinda†	R	26	23	0	0	0	27.1	30	2	6	25	1-1	0	4.28
Bill Sampen	R	30	18	0	0	0	18.1	25	1	9	9	2-2	0	5.89
Rusty Meacham	R	25	15	0	0	0	21.0	31	2	5	13	2-2	0	5.57
Greg Cadaret†	L	31	13	0	0	0	15.1	14	0	7	2	1-1	0	2.93
John Habyan†	R	29	12	0	0	0	14.0	14	1	4	10	0-0	0	4.50
Frank DiPino	L	36	11	0	0	0	15.2	21	2	6	5	1-1	0	6.89
Dennis Rasmussen	L	34	9	4	0	0	29.0	40	4	14	12	1-2	0	7.45
Enrique Burgos	L	27	5	0	0	0	5.0	5	0	6	6	0-1	0	9.00
Rick Reed†	R	28	1	0	0	0	3.2	6	0	1	3	0-0	0	9.82
Jeff Granger	L	21	1	0	0	0	1.0	3	0	2	1	0-0	0	27.00

1993 Seattle Mariners 4th AL West 82-80 .506 12.0 GB

Lou Piniella

Player	Gm by Position	B	Age	G	AB	R	H	2B	3B	HR	RBI	BB	SO	SB	Avg	OBP	Slg
Dave Valle	C135	R	32	135	423	48	109	19	0	13	63	48	56	1	.258	.354	.395
Tino Martinez	1B103,DH6	L	25	109	408	48	108	25	1	17	60	45	56	0	.265	.343	.456
Rich Amaral	2B77,3B19,SS14*	R	31	110	373	53	108	24	1	1	44	33	54	19	.290	.348	.367
Mike Blowers	3B117,DH2,OF2*	R	28	127	379	55	106	23	3	15	57	44	98	1	.280	.357	.475
Omar Vizquel	SS155,DH2	S	26	158	560	68	143	14	2	2	31	50	71	12	.255	.319	.298
Jay Buhner	OF148,DH10	R	28	158	563	91	153	28	3	27	98	100	144	2	.272	.379	.476
Ken Griffey Jr.	OF139,DH19,1B1	L	23	156	582	113	180	38	3	45	109	96	91	17	.309	.408	.617
Mike Felder	OF95,DH6,3B2	S	31	109	342	31	72	7	5	1	20	22	34	15	.211	.262	.269
Pete O'Brien	DH52,1B9,OF1	L	35	72	210	30	54	7	0	7	27	26	21	0	.257	.335	.390
Bret Boone	2B74,DH1	R	24	76	271	31	68	12	2	12	38	17	52	2	.251	.301	.443
Dave Magadan†	1B41,3B27,DH2	L	30	71	228	27	59	11	0	1	21	36	33	2	.259	.356	.320
Mackey Sasser	OF37,DH19,C4*	L	30	83	188	18	41	10	2	1	21	15	30	1	.218	.274	.309
Greg Litton	OF22,2B17,1B13*	R	28	72	174	25	52	17	0	3	25	18	30	0	.299	.366	.448
Brian Turang	OF38,3B2,DH1*	R	26	40	140	22	35	11	1	0	7	17	20	6	.250	.340	.343
Bill Haselman	C49,DH4,OF2	R	27	58	137	21	35	8	0	5	16	12	19	2	.255	.316	.423
Edgar Martinez	DH24,3B16	R	30	42	135	20	32	7	0	4	13	28	19	0	.237	.366	.378
Henry Cotto†	OF34,DH14	R	32	54	105	10	20	1	0	2	7	2	22	5	.190	.213	.257
Dann Howitt	OF29,DH2	L	29	32	76	6	16	3	1	2	8	4	18	0	.211	.250	.355
Marc Newfield	DH15,OF5	R	20	22	66	5	15	3	0	1	7	2	8	0	.227	.257	.318
Fernando Vina	2B16,SS4,DH2	L	24	24	45	5	10	2	0	0	2	4	3	6	.222	.327	.267
Wally Backman	3B9,2B1	S	33	10	29	2	4	0	0	0	0	1	8	0	.138	.167	.138
Greg Pirkl	1B5,DH2	R	22	7	23	1	4	0	0	1	4	0	4	0	.174	.174	.304
Lee Tinsley	OF6,DH2	S	24	11	19	2	3	1	0	1	2	2	9	0	.158	.238	.368
Larry Sheets	DH5,OF1	L	33	11	17	0	2	1	0	0	1	2	1	0	.118	.250	.176
Chris Howard	C4	R	27	4	1	0	0	0	0	0	0	0	0	0	.000	.000	.000
Chris Bosio	P29,DH1	R	30	29	0	0	0	0	0	0	0	0	0	0	—	—	—
Erik Hanson	P31,DH1	R	28	33	0	2	0	0	0	0	0	0	0	0	—	—	—
Randy Johnson	P35,OF1	R	29	35	0	0	0	0	0	0	0	0	0	0	—	—	—
Jeff Nelson	P71,OF1	R	26	71	0	0	0	0	0	0	0	0	0	0	—	—	—

R. Amaral, 9 G at DH, 3 G at 1B; M. Blowers, 1 G at C, 1 G at 1B; M. Sasser, 1 G at 1B; G. Litton, 12 G at DH, 7 G at 3B, 5 G at SS; B. Turang, 1 G at 2B

Pitcher	T	Age	G	GS	CG	ShO	IP	H	HR	BB	SO	W-L	Sv	ERA
Randy Johnson	L	29	35	34	10	3	255.1	185	22	99	308	19-8	1	3.24
Erik Hanson	R	28	31	30	7	0	215.0	215	17	60	163	11-12	0	3.47
Tim Leary	R	35	33	27	0	0	169.1	202	21	58	68	11-9	0	5.05
Dave Fleming	L	23	26	26	1	1	167.1	189	15	67	75	12-5	0	4.36
Chris Bosio	R	30	29	24	3	1	164.1	138	14	59	119	9-9	1	3.45
John Cummings	L	24	10	8	1	0	46.1	59	6	16	19	0-6	0	6.02
Jim Converse	R	21	4	4	0	0	20.1	23	0	14	10	1-3	0	5.31
Roger Salkeld	R	22	3	2	0	0	14.1	13	0	4	13	0-0	0	2.51
Jeff Nelson	R	26	71	0	0	0	60.0	57	5	34	61	5-3	1	4.35
Norm Charlton	L	30	34	0	0	0	34.2	22	4	17	48	1-3	18	2.34
Dennis Powell	L	29	33	2	0	0	47.2	42	7	24	32	0-0	0	4.15
Dwayne Henry†	R	31	31	1	0	0	54.0	56	6	35	35	2-1	2	6.67
Rich DeLucia	R	28	30	1	0	0	42.2	46	5	23	48	3-6	0	4.64
Ted Power†	R	38	25	0	0	0	25.1	27	1	9	16	2-2	13	3.91
Russ Swan	L	29	23	0	0	0	19.2	25	2	18	10	3-3	0	9.15
Erik Plantenberg	L	24	20	0	0	0	9.2	11	0	12	3	0-0	1	6.52
Brad Holman	R	25	19	0	0	0	36.1	27	1	16	17	1-3	3	3.72
Bob Ayrault†	R	27	14	0	0	0	19.2	18	1	6	7	1-1	0	3.20
Steve Ontiveros	R	32	14	0	0	0	18.0	18	0	6	13	0-2	0	1.00
Mike Hampton	L	20	13	3	0	0	17.0	28	3	17	8	1-3	1	9.53
Kevin King	L	24	13	0	0	0	11.2	9	3	4	8	0-1	0	6.17
David Wainhouse	R	25	3	0	0	0	2.1	7	1	5	2	0-0	0	27.00
Zak Shinall	R	24	1	0	0	0	2.2	4	1	2	0	0-0	0	3.38

1993 California Angels 5th AL West 71-91 .438 23.0 GB

Buck Rodgers

Player	Gm by Position	B	Age	G	AB	R	H	2B	3B	HR	RBI	BB	SO	SB	Avg	OBP	Slg
Greg Myers	C97,DH2	L	27	108	290	27	74	10	0	7	40	17	47	3	.255	.298	.362
J.T. Snow	1B129	S	25	129	419	60	101	18	2	16	57	55	88	3	.241	.328	.408
Torey Lovullo	2B91,3B14,SS9*	S	27	116	367	42	92	20	0	6	30	36	49	7	.251	.318	.354
Rene Gonzales	3B79,1B31,SS5*	R	32	118	335	34	84	17	0	2	31	49	45	5	.251	.346	.319
Gary DiSarcina	SS126	R	25	126	416	44	99	20	1	3	45	15	38	5	.238	.273	.313
Chad Curtis	OF151,2B3	R	24	152	583	94	166	25	3	6	59	70	89	48	.285	.361	.369
Luis Polonia	OF141,DH3	L	28	152	576	75	156	17	6	1	32	48	53	55	.271	.328	.326
Tim Salmon	OF140,DH1	R	24	142	515	93	146	35	1	31	95	82	135	5	.283	.382	.536
Chili Davis	DH150,P1	S	33	153	573	74	139	32	0	27	112	71	135	4	.243	.327	.440
Stan Javier	OF64,1B12,2B2*	S	29	92	237	33	69	10	4	3	28	27	33	12	.291	.362	.405
Damion Easley	2B54,3B14,DH1	R	23	73	230	33	72	13	2	2	22	28	35	6	.313	.392	.413
Eduardo Perez	3B45,DH3	R	23	52	180	16	45	6	2	4	30	9	39	5	.250	.292	.372
Rod Correia	SS40,2B11,DH3*	R	25	64	128	12	34	5	0	0	9	6	20	2	.266	.319	.305
John Orton	C35,OF1	R	27	37	95	5	18	5	0	1	4	7	24	1	.189	.252	.274
Ron Tingley	C58	R	34	58	90	7	18	7	0	0	12	9	22	1	.200	.277	.278
Chris Turner	C25	R	24	25	75	9	21	5	0	1	13	9	16	1	.280	.360	.387
Kelly Gruber	3B17,DH1,OF1	R	31	18	65	10	18	3	0	3	9	2	11	0	.277	.309	.462
Kurt Stillwell†	2B18,SS7	S	28	22	61	2	16	2	2	0	3	4	11	2	.262	.299	.361
Jim Edmonds	OF17	L	23	18	61	5	15	4	1	0	4	2	16	0	.246	.270	.344
Gary Gaetti†	3B7,1B6,DH5	R	34	20	50	3	9	2	0	0	4	5	12	1	.180	.250	.220
Ty Van Burkleo	1B12	L	29	12	33	2	5	3	0	1	1	6	9	1	.152	.282	.333
Jim Walewander	SS6,DH2,2B2	S	31	12	8	2	1	0	0	0	3	5	1	1	.125	.429	.125
Jerome Walton	DH3,OF1	R	27	5	2	2	0	0	0	0	1	1	2	1	.000	.333	.000
Larry Gonzales	C2	R	26	2	2	0	1	0	0	0	1	1	0	0	.500	.667	.500

T. Lovullo, 2 G at OF, 1 G at 1B; R. Gonzales, 4 G at 2B, 1 G at P; S. Javier, 1 G at DH; R. Correia, 3 G at 3B

Pitcher	T	Age	G	GS	CG	ShO	IP	H	HR	BB	SO	W-L	Sv	ERA
Mark Langston	L	32	35	35	7	0	256.1	220	22	85	196	16-11	0	3.20
Chuck Finley	L	30	35	35	13	2	251.1	243	22	82	187	16-14	0	3.15
Scott Sanderson†	R	36	21	21	4	1	135.1	153	15	27	66	7-11	0	4.46
John Farrell	R	30	21	17	0	0	90.2	110	22	44	45	3-12	0	7.35
Phil Leftwich	R	24	12	12	1	0	80.2	81	5	27	31	4-6	0	3.79
Hilly Hathaway	L	23	11	11	0	0	57.1	71	6	26	11	4-3	0	5.02
Russ Springer	R	24	14	9	1	0	60.0	73	11	32	31	1-6	0	7.20
Joe Magrane†	L	28	8	8	0	0	48.0	48	4	21	24	3-2	0	3.94
Mark Holzemer	L	23	5	4	0	0	23.1	34	2	13	10	0-3	0	8.87
Steve Frey	L	29	55	0	0	0	48.1	41	1	26	22	2-3	13	2.98
Ken Patterson	L	28	46	0	0	0	59.0	54	7	35	36	1-1	1	4.58
Gene Nelson†	R	32	46	0	0	0	52.2	50	3	23	31	0-5	4	3.08
Joe Grahe	R	26	45	0	0	0	56.2	54	5	25	31	4-1	11	2.86
Mike Butcher	R	28	23	0	0	0	28.1	21	2	15	24	1-0	8	2.86
Julio Valera	R	24	19	5	0	0	53.0	77	8	15	28	3-6	4	6.62
Doug Linton†	R	28	19	0	0	0	25.2	35	8	14	19	2-0	0	7.71
Darryl Scott	R	24	16	0	0	0	20.0	19	1	11	13	1-2	0	5.85
Scott Lewis	R	27	15	4	0	0	32.0	37	3	12	10	1-2	0	4.22
Chuck Crim	R	31	11	0	0	0	15.1	17	2	5	10	2-2	0	5.87
Jerry Nielsen	L	26	10	0	0	0	12.1	18	1	4	8	0-0	0	8.03
Paul Swingle	R	26	9	0	0	0	9.2	15	2	6	6	0-1	0	8.38
Brian Anderson	L	21	4	1	0	0	11.1	11	1	2	4	0-0	0	3.97
Chili Davis	R	33	1	0	0	0	2.0	0	0	0	0	0-0	0	0.00
Rene Gonzales	R	32	1	0	0	0	1.0	0	0	0	0	0-0	0	0.00

1993 Minnesota Twins 5th AL West 71-91 .438 23.0 GB

Tom Kelly

Player	Gm by Position	B	Age	G	AB	R	H	2B	3B	HR	RBI	BB	SO	SB	Avg	OBP	Slg
Brian Harper	C134,DH7	R	33	147	530	52	161	26	1	12	73	29	29	1	.304	.347	.425
Kent Hrbek	1B115,DH2	L	33	123	392	60	95	11	1	25	83	71	57	4	.242	.357	.467
Chuck Knoblauch	2B148,SS6,OF1	R	24	153	602	82	167	27	4	2	41	65	44	29	.277	.354	.346
Mike Pagliarulo†	3B79	L	33	83	253	31	74	16	4	3	23	18	34	6	.292	.350	.423
Pat Meares	SS111	R	24	111	346	33	87	14	3	0	33	7	52	4	.251	.266	.309
Kirby Puckett	OF139,DH17	R	32	156	622	89	184	39	3	22	89	47	93	8	.296	.349	.474
Shane Mack	OF128	R	29	128	503	66	139	30	4	10	61	41	76	15	.276	.335	.412
Pedro Munoz	OF102	R	24	104	326	34	76	11	1	13	38	25	97	1	.233	.294	.393
Dave Winfield	DH105,OF31,1B5	R	41	143	547	72	148	27	2	21	76	45	106	2	.271	.325	.442
Dave McCarty	OF67,1B36,DH2	R	23	98	350	36	75	15	2	2	21	19	80	2	.214	.257	.286
Jeff Reboulet	SS62,3B35,2B11*	R	29	109	240	33	62	8	0	1	15	35	37	5	.258	.356	.304
Chip Hale	2B21,DH19,3B19*	L	28	69	186	25	62	6	1	3	27	18	17	2	.333	.408	.425
Terry Jorgensen	3B45,1B9,SS6	R	26	59	152	15	34	7	0	1	12	10	11	1	.224	.270	.289
Gene Larkin	OF28,1B18,DH3*	S	30	56	144	17	38	7	1	1	19	21	16	0	.264	.357	.347
Lenny Webster	C45,DH1	R	28	49	106	14	21	2	0	1	8	11	8	1	.198	.274	.245
Scott Stahoviak	3B19	L	23	20	57	1	11	4	0	0	1	3	22	0	.193	.233	.263
Bernardo Brito	OF10,DH7	R	29	27	54	8	13	2	0	4	9	1	20	0	.241	.255	.500
Randy Bush	DH5,1B4,OF1	L	34	35	45	1	7	2	0	0	3	7	13	0	.156	.269	.200
Denny Hocking	SS12,2B1	S	23	15	36	7	5	1	0	0	0	6	8	1	.139	.262	.167
Derek Lee	OF13	L	26	15	33	3	5	1	0	0	4	1	4	0	.152	.176	.182
J.T. Bruett	OF13	L	25	17	20	2	5	1	0	0	1	2	4	0	.250	.318	.350
Derek Parks	C7	R	24	7	20	3	4	0	0	0	1	1	2	0	.200	.238	.200
Scott Leius	SS9	R	27	10	18	4	3	0	0	0	2	2	4	0	.167	.227	.167
Mike Maksudian	1B4,3B1	L	27	5	12	2	2	1	0	0	2	4	2	0	.167	.353	.250
Rich Becker	OF3	S	21	3	7	3	2	2	0	0	0	5	4	1	.286	.583	.571

J. Reboulet, 3 G at OF, 1 G at DH; C. Hale, 1 G at 1B, 1 G at SS; G. Larkin, 2 G at 3B

Pitcher	T	Age	G	GS	CG	ShO	IP	H	HR	BB	SO	W-L	Sv	ERA
Kevin Tapani	R	29	36	35	3	1	225.2	243	21	57	150	12-15	0	4.43
Scott Erickson	R	25	34	34	1	0	218.2	266	17	71	116	8-19	0	5.19
Willie Banks	R	24	31	30	0	0	171.1	186	17	78	138	11-12	0	4.04
Jim Deshaies†	L	33	27	27	1	0	167.1	159	24	51	80	11-13	0	4.41
Eddie Guardado	L	22	19	16	0	0	94.2	123	13	36	46	3-8	0	6.18
Greg Brummett†	R	26	5	5	0	0	26.2	29	3	15	10	2-1	0	5.74
Rick Aguilera	R	31	65	0	0	0	72.1	60	9	14	59	4-3	34	3.11
Larry Casian	L	27	54	0	0	0	56.2	59	1	14	31	5-3	1	3.02
Mike Hartley	R	31	53	0	0	0	81.0	86	4	36	57	1-2	1	4.00
Carl Willis	R	32	53	0	0	0	58.0	56	2	17	44	3-0	5	3.10
Mike Trombley	R	26	44	10	0	0	114.1	131	15	41	85	6-6	2	4.88
George Tsamis	L	26	41	0	0	0	68.1	86	9	27	30	1-2	1	6.19
Mark Guthrie	R	27	22	0	0	0	21.0	20	2	16	15	2-1	0	4.71
Brett Merriman	R	26	19	0	0	0	27.0	36	3	23	14	1-1	0	9.67
Pat Mahomes	R	22	12	5	0	0	37.1	47	8	16	23	1-5	0	7.71
Rich Garces	R	22	3	0	0	0	4.0	4	0	2	3	0-0	0	0.00

936

Seasons: Team Rosters

1993 Oakland Athletics 7th AL West 68-94 .420 26.0 GB

Tony La Russa

Player	Gm by Position	B	Age	G	AB	R	H	2B	3B	HR	RBI	BB	SO	SB	Avg	OBP	Slg
Terry Steinbach	C86,1B15,DH6	R	31	104	389	47	111	19	1	10	43	25	65	3	.285	.333	.416
Mike Aldrete	1B59,OF20,DH6	L	32	95	255	40	68	13	1	10	33	34	45	1	.267	.353	.443
Brent Gates	2B139	S	23	139	535	64	155	29	2	7	69	56	75	7	.290	.357	.391
Craig Paquette	3B104,DH1,OF1	R	24	105	393	35	86	20	4	12	46	14	108	4	.219	.245	.382
Mike Bordick	SS159,2B1	R	27	159	546	60	136	21	2	3	48	60	58	10	.249	.332	.311
Ruben Sierra	OF133,DH25	S	27	158	630	77	147	23	5	22	101	52	97	25	.233	.288	.390
Dave Henderson	OF76,DH28	R	34	107	382	37	84	19	0	20	53	32	113	0	.220	.275	.427
Rickey Henderson†	OF74,DH16	R	34	90	318	77	104	19	1	17	47	85	46	31	.327	.469	.553
Troy Neel	DH85,1B34	L	27	123	427	59	124	21	0	19	63	49	101	3	.290	.367	.473
Jerry Browne	OF56,3B13,2B3*	S	27	76	260	27	65	13	0	2	19	22	17	4	.250	.306	.323
Kevin Seitzer†	3B46,1B24,DH3*	R	31	73	255	24	65	10	2	4	27	27	33	4	.255	.324	.357
Lance Blankenship	OF66,2B19,1B6*	R	29	94	252	43	48	8	1	2	23	67	64	13	.190	.363	.254
Scott Hemond	C75,OF6,DH3*	R	27	91	215	31	55	16	0	6	26	32	55	14	.256	.353	.414
Scott Brosius	OF46,1B11,3B10*	R	26	70	213	26	53	10	1	6	25	14	37	6	.249	.296	.390
Scott Lydy	OF38,DH2	R	24	41	102	11	23	5	0	2	7	8	39	2	.225	.288	.333
Mark McGwire	1B25	R	29	27	84	16	28	6	0	9	24	21	19	0	.333	.467	.726
Dale Sveum	1B14,3B7,2B4*	S	29	30	79	12	14	2	1	2	6	16	21	0	.177	.316	.304
Kurt Abbott	OF13,SS6,2B2	R	24	20	61	11	15	1	0	3	9	3	20	2	.246	.281	.410
Eric Fox	OF26,DH1	S	29	29	56	5	8	1	0	1	5	2	7	0	.143	.172	.214
Henry Mercedes	C18,DH1	R	23	20	47	5	10	2	0	0	3	2	15	1	.213	.260	.255
Marcos Armas	1B12,DH2,OF1	R	23	15	31	7	6	2	0	1	1	1	12	1	.194	.242	.355
Eric Helfand	C5	L	24	8	13	1	3	0	0	0	1	0	1	0	.231	.231	.231

J. Browne, 2 G at 1B; K. Seitzer, 3 G at OF, 2 G at 2B, 1 G at P, 1 G at SS; L. Blankenship, 5 G at DH, 2 G at SS; S. Hemond, 1 G at 1B, 1 G at 2B; S. Brosius, 6 G at SS, 2 G at DH; D. Sveum, 2 G at DH, 1 G at SS, 1 G at OF

Pitcher	T	Age	G	GS	CG	ShO	IP	H	HR	BB	SO	W-L	Sv	ERA
Bobby Witt	R	29	35	33	5	1	220.0	226	16	91	131	14-13	0	4.21
Ron Darling	R	32	31	29	3	0	178.0	198	22	72	95	5-9	0	5.16
Bob Welch	R	36	30	28	0	0	166.2	208	25	56	63	9-11	0	5.29
Todd Van Poppel	R	21	16	16	0	0	84.0	76	10	62	47	6-6	0	5.04
Shawn Hillegas	R	28	18	11	0	0	60.2	78	8	33	29	3-6	0	6.97
Steve Karsay	R	21	8	8	0	0	49.0	49	4	16	33	3-3	0	4.04
Miguel Jimenez	R	23	5	4	0	0	27.0	27	5	16	13	1-0	0	4.00
Curt Young	L	33	3	3	0	0	14.2	14	5	6	4	1-1	0	4.30
Joe Slusarski	R	26	2	1	0	0	8.2	9	1	11	1	0-0	0	5.19
Dennis Eckersley	R	38	64	0	0	0	67.0	67	7	13	80	2-4	36	4.16
Edwin Nunez	R	30	56	0	0	0	75.2	89	2	29	58	3-6	1	3.81
Rick Honeycutt	L	39	52	0	0	0	41.2	30	2	20	21	1-4	1	2.81
Kelly Downs	R	32	42	12	0	0	119.2	135	14	60	66	5-10	0	5.64
Joe Boever†	R	32	42	0	0	0	79.1	87	8	33	49	4-2	0	3.86
Mike Mohler	L	24	42	9	0	0	64.1	57	10	44	42	1-6	0	5.60
Vince Horsman	L	26	40	0	0	0	25.0	25	2	15	17	2-0	0	5.40
Goose Gossage	R	41	39	0	0	0	47.2	49	6	26	40	4-5	1	4.53
Storm Davis†	R	31	19	8	0	0	62.2	68	5	33	37	2-6	0	6.18
John Briscoe	R	25	17	0	0	0	24.2	26	2	26	24	1-0	0	8.03
Roger Smithberg	R	27	13	0	0	0	19.2	13	2	7	4	1-2	3	2.75
Kevin Campbell	R	28	11	0	0	0	16.0	20	1	11	9	0-0	0	7.31
Kevin Seitzer	R	31	1	0	0	0	0.1	0	0	0	1	0-0	0	0.00

»1993 Philadelphia Phillies 1st NL East 97-65 .599 —

Jim Fregosi

Player	Gm by Position	B	Age	G	AB	R	H	2B	3B	HR	RBI	BB	SO	SB	Avg	OBP	Slg
Darren Daulton	C146	L	31	147	510	90	131	35	4	24	105	117	111	5	.257	.392	.482
John Kruk	1B144	L	32	150	535	100	169	33	5	14	85	111	87	6	.316	.430	.475
Mickey Morandini	2B111	L	27	120	425	57	105	19	9	3	33	34	73	13	.247	.309	.355
Dave Hollins	3B143	S	27	143	543	104	148	30	4	18	93	85	109	2	.273	.372	.442
Kevin Stocker	SS70	S	23	70	259	46	84	12	3	2	31	30	43	5	.324	.409	.417
Lenny Dykstra	OF160	L	30	161	637	143	194	44	6	19	66	129	64	37	.305	.420	.482
Jim Eisenreich	OF137,1B1	L	34	153	362	51	115	17	4	7	54	26	36	5	.318	.363	.445
Milt Thompson	OF106	L	34	129	340	42	89	14	2	4	44	40	57	9	.262	.341	.350
Mariano Duncan	2B65,SS59	S	30	124	496	68	140	26	4	11	73	12	88	6	.282	.304	.417
Pete Incaviglia	OF97	R	29	116	368	60	101	16	3	24	89	21	82	1	.274	.318	.530
Wes Chamberlain	OF76	R	27	96	284	34	80	20	2	12	45	17	51	2	.282	.320	.493
Ricky Jordan	1B33	R	28	90	159	21	46	4	1	5	18	8	32	0	.289	.324	.421
Kim Batiste	3B58,SS24	R	25	79	156	14	44	7	1	5	29	3	29	0	.282	.298	.436
Todd Pratt	C26	R	26	33	87	8	25	6	0	5	13	5	19	0	.287	.330	.529
Juan Bell†	SS22	R	25	24	65	5	13	6	1	0	7	5	12	0	.200	.268	.323
Ruben Amaro	OF16	S	28	25	48	7	16	2	2	1	6	6	5	0	.333	.400	.521
Jeff Manto	3B6,SS1	R	28	8	18	0	1	0	0	0	0	0	3	0	.056	.105	.056
Tony Longmire	OF2	L	24	11	13	1	3	0	0	0	1	0	1	0	.231	.231	.231
Joe Millette	SS7,3B3	R	26	10	10	3	2	0	0	0	2	1	2	0	.200	.273	.200
Doug Lindsey†	C2	R	25	2	2	0	1	0	0	0	0	0	1	0	.500	.500	.500

Pitcher	T	Age	G	GS	CG	ShO	IP	H	HR	BB	SO	W-L	Sv	ERA
Curt Schilling	R	26	34	34	7	2	235.1	234	23	57	186	16-7	0	4.02
Danny Jackson	L	31	32	32	2	1	210.1	214	12	80	120	12-11	0	3.77
Tommy Greene	R	26	31	30	7	2	200.0	175	12	62	167	16-4	0	3.42
Terry Mulholland	L	30	29	28	7	2	191.0	177	20	40	116	12-9	0	3.25
Ben Rivera	R	25	30	28	1	1	163.0	175	16	85	123	13-9	0	5.02
Tyler Green	R	23	3	2	0	0	7.1	16	1	5	7	0-0	0	7.36
Kevin Foster	R	24	2	1	0	0	6.2	13	3	7	6	0-1	0	14.85
David West	L	28	76	0	0	0	86.1	60	6	51	87	6-4	3	2.92
Mitch Williams	L	28	65	0	0	0	62.0	56	3	44	60	3-7	43	3.34
Larry Andersen	R	40	64	0	0	0	61.2	54	4	21	67	3-2	0	2.92
Roger Mason†	R	34	34	0	0	0	49.2	47	9	16	32	5-5	0	4.89
Mark Davis†	L	32	25	0	0	0	31.1	35	4	24	28	1-2	0	5.17
Jose DeLeon†	R	32	24	3	0	0	47.0	39	5	27	34	3-0	0	3.26
Mike Williams	R	24	17	4	0	0	51.0	50	5	22	33	1-3	0	5.29
Bobby Thigpen†	R	29	17	0	0	0	19.1	23	2	9	10	3-1	0	6.05
Bob Ayrault†	R	27	10	0	0	0	10.1	18	1	10	8	2-0	0	9.58
Donn Pall†	R	31	8	0	0	0	17.2	15	1	3	11	1-0	0	2.55
Tim Mauser†	R	26	8	0	0	0	16.1	15	1	7	14	0-0	0	4.96
Brad Brink	R	28	2	0	0	0	6.0	3	1	3	8	0-0	0	3.00
Paul Fletcher	R	26	1	0	0	0	0.1	0	0	0	0	0-0	0	0.00

1993 Montreal Expos 2nd NL East 94-68 .580 3.0 GB

Felipe Alou

Player	Gm by Position	B	Age	G	AB	R	H	2B	3B	HR	RBI	BB	SO	SB	Avg	OBP	Slg
Darrin Fletcher	C127	L	26	133	396	33	101	20	1	9	60	34	40	0	.255	.320	.379
Greg Colbrunn	1B61	R	23	70	153	15	39	9	0	4	23	6	33	4	.255	.282	.392
Delino DeShields	2B123	L	24	123	481	75	142	17	7	2	29	72	64	43	.295	.389	.372
Sean Berry	3B96	R	27	122	299	50	78	15	2	14	49	41	70	12	.261	.348	.465
Wil Cordero	SS134,3B2	R	21	138	475	56	118	32	2	10	58	34	60	12	.248	.308	.387
Marquis Grissom	OF157	R	26	157	630	104	188	27	2	19	95	52	76	53	.298	.351	.438
Moises Alou	OF136	R	26	136	482	70	138	29	6	18	85	38	53	17	.286	.340	.483
Larry Walker	OF132,1B4	L	26	138	490	85	130	24	5	22	86	80	76	29	.265	.371	.469
Mike Lansing	3B81,SS51,2B25	R	25	141	491	64	141	29	1	3	45	46	56	23	.287	.352	.369
John VanderWal	1B42,OF38	L	27	106	215	34	50	7	4	5	30	27	30	6	.233	.320	.372
Frank Bolick	1B51,3B24	S	27	95	213	25	45	13	0	4	24	23	37	1	.211	.298	.329
Lou Frazier	OF60,1B8,2B1	S	28	112	189	27	54	7	1	1	16	16	24	17	.286	.340	.349
Randy Ready	2B28,1B13,3B3	R	33	40	134	22	34	8	1	1	10	23	8	2	.254	.367	.351
Tim Spehr	C49	R	26	53	87	14	20	6	0	2	10	6	20	2	.230	.281	.368
Tim Laker	C43	R	23	43	86	3	17	2	1	0	7	2	16	2	.198	.222	.244
Oreste Marrero	1B32	L	23	32	81	10	17	5	1	1	4	14	16	1	.210	.326	.333
Rondell White	OF21	R	21	23	73	9	19	3	1	2	15	7	16	1	.260	.321	.411
Derrick White	1B17	R	23	17	49	6	11	3	0	2	4	2	12	2	.224	.269	.408
Cliff Floyd	1B10	L	20	10	31	3	7	0	0	1	2	0	9	0	.226	.226	.323
Ted Wood	OF8	L	26	13	26	4	5	1	0	0	3	3	3	0	.192	.276	.231
Tim McIntosh†	OF7,C5	R	28	20	21	2	2	1	0	0	2	0	7	0	.095	.095	.143
Joe Siddall	C15,1B1,OF1	L	25	19	20	0	2	1	0	0	1	1	5	0	.100	.143	.150
Archi Cianfrocco†	1B11	R	26	12	17	3	4	1	0	1	1	0	5	0	.235	.235	.471
Curtis Pride	OF2	L	24	10	9	3	4	1	1	1	5	0	3	1	.444	.444	1.111
Matt Stairs	OF1	L	24	6	8	1	3	1	0	0	2	0	1	0	.375	.375	.500
Charlie Montoyo	2B3	R	27	4	5	1	2	1	0	0	3	0	0	0	.400	.400	.600

Pitcher	T	Age	G	GS	CG	ShO	IP	H	HR	BB	SO	W-L	Sv	ERA
Dennis Martinez	R	38	35	34	2	0	224.2	211	27	64	138	15-9	1	3.85
Ken Hill	R	27	28	28	2	0	183.2	163	7	74	90	9-7	0	3.23
Chris Nabholz	L	26	26	21	1	0	116.2	100	9	63	74	9-8	0	4.09
Kirk Rueter	L	22	14	14	1	0	85.2	85	5	18	31	8-0	0	2.73
Jimmy Jones	R	29	12	6	0	0	39.2	47	6	9	21	4-1	0	6.35
Denis Boucher	L	25	5	5	0	0	28.1	24	1	3	14	3-1	0	1.91
John Wetteland	R	26	70	0	0	0	85.1	58	3	28	113	9-3	43	1.37
Mel Rojas	R	26	66	0	0	0	88.1	80	6	30	48	5-8	10	2.95
Jeff Fassero	L	30	56	15	1	0	149.2	119	7	54	140	12-5	1	2.29
Jeff Shaw	R	26	55	8	0	0	95.2	91	12	32	50	2-7	0	4.14
Brian Barnes	L	26	52	8	0	0	100.0	105	9	48	60	2-6	3	4.41
Tim Scott†	R	26	32	0	0	0	34.0	31	3	19	35	5-2	1	3.71
Mike Gardiner†	R	27	24	2	0	0	38.0	40	3	19	21	2-3	0	5.21
Kent Bottenfield†	R	24	23	11	0	0	83.0	93	11	33	33	2-5	0	4.12
Gil Heredia	R	27	20	9	1	0	57.1	66	4	14	40	4-2	2	3.92
Butch Henry†	L	24	10	1	0	0	18.1	18	1	4	8	1-1	0	3.93
Bruce Walton	R	30	4	0	0	0	5.2	11	1	3	0	0-0	0	9.53
Pete Young	R	25	4	0	0	0	5.1	4	1	0	3	1-0	0	3.38
Sergio Valdez	R	28	4	0	0	0	3.0	4	1	1	2	0-0	0	9.00
Brian Looney	L	23	3	1	0	0	6.0	8	0	2	7	0-0	0	3.00
Scott Aldred†	L	25	3	0	0	0	5.1	9	1	1	4	1-0	0	6.75
Bill Risley	R	26	2	0	0	0	3.0	2	1	2	2	0-0	0	6.00

1993 St. Louis Cardinals 3rd NL East 87-75 .537 10.0 GB

Joe Torre

Player	Gm by Position	B	Age	G	AB	R	H	2B	3B	HR	RBI	BB	SO	SB	Avg	OBP	Slg
Tom Pagnozzi	C92	R	30	92	330	31	85	15	1	7	41	19	30	1	.258	.296	.373
Gregg Jefferies	1B140,2B1	S	25	142	544	89	186	24	3	16	83	62	32	46	.342	.408	.485
Luis Alicea	2B96,OF4,3B1	S	27	115	362	50	101	19	3	3	46	47	54	11	.279	.362	.373
Todd Zeile	3B153	R	27	157	571	82	158	36	1	17	103	70	76	5	.277	.352	.433
Ozzie Smith	SS134	S	38	141	545	75	157	22	6	1	53	43	18	21	.288	.337	.356
Mark Whiten	OF148	S	26	152	562	81	142	13	4	25	99	58	110	15	.253	.323	.423
Bernard Gilkey	OF134,1B3	R	26	137	557	99	170	40	5	16	70	56	66	15	.305	.370	.481
Ray Lankford	OF121	L	26	127	407	64	97	17	3	7	45	81	111	14	.238	.366	.346
Geronimo Pena	2B64	S	26	74	254	34	65	19	2	5	30	25	71	13	.256	.330	.406
Erik Pappas	C63,OF16,1B2	R	27	82	228	25	63	12	0	1	28	35	35	1	.276	.368	.342
Brian Jordan	OF65	R	26	67	223	33	69	10	6	10	44	12	35	6	.309	.351	.543
Rod Brewer	OF33,1B32,P1	L	27	110	147	15	42	8	0	2	20	17	26	1	.286	.359	.381
Gerald Perry	1B15,OF1	L	32	96	98	21	33	5	0	4	16	18	23	1	.337	.440	.510
Tracy Woodson	3B28,1B11	R	30	62	77	4	16	2	0	0	2	1	14	0	.208	.215	.234
Jose Oquendo	SS22,2B16	S	29	46	73	7	15	0	0	0	4	12	8	0	.205	.314	.205
Tim Jones	SS21,2B7	L	30	29	61	13	16	6	0	0	1	9	8	2	.262	.366	.361
Hector Villanueva	C17	R	28	17	55	7	8	1	0	3	9	4	17	0	.145	.203	.327
Stan Royer	3B10,1B2	R	25	24	46	4	14	2	0	1	8	2	14	0	.304	.333	.413
Tripp Cromer	SS9	R	25	10	23	1	2	0	0	0	0	1	6	0	.087	.125	.087
Ozzie Canseco	OF5	R	28	6	17	0	3	0	0	0	0	1	3	0	.176	.222	.176
Lonnie Maclin	OF5	L	26	12	13	2	1	0	0	0	1	0	5	1	.077	.071	.077
Marc Ronan	C6	L	23	6	12	0	1	0	0	0	0	0	5	0	.083	.083	.083

Pitcher	T	Age	G	GS	CG	ShO	IP	H	HR	BB	SO	W-L	Sv	ERA
Bob Tewksbury	R	32	32	32	2	0	213.2	258	15	20	97	17-10	0	3.83
Rene Arocha	R	27	32	29	1	0	188.0	197	20	31	96	11-8	0	3.78
Donovan Osborne	L	24	26	26	1	0	155.2	153	18	47	83	10-7	0	3.76
Rheal Cormier	L	26	38	21	1	0	145.1	163	18	27	75	7-6	0	4.33
Joe Magrane†	L	28	22	20	0	0	116.0	127	15	37	38	8-10	0	4.97
Allen Watson	L	22	16	15	0	0	86.0	90	11	28	49	6-7	0	4.60
Tom Urbani	L	25	18	9	0	0	62.0	73	4	26	33	1-3	0	4.65
Rob Murphy	L	33	73	0	0	0	64.2	73	8	20	41	5-7	1	4.87
Mike Perez	R	28	65	0	0	0	72.2	65	4	20	58	7-2	7	2.48
Omar Olivares	R	25	58	9	0	0	118.2	134	10	54	63	5-3	1	4.17
Lee Smith†	R	35	55	0	0	0	50.0	49	11	9	49	2-4	43	4.50
Les Lancaster	R	31	50	0	0	0	61.1	56	5	21	36	4-1	0	2.93
Lee Guetterman	L	34	40	0	0	0	46.0	41	1	16	19	3-3	1	2.93
Todd Burns†	R	29	24	0	0	0	30.2	32	8	9	10	0-4	0	6.16
Paul Kilgus	L	31	22	1	0	0	28.2	18	1	8	21	1-0	1	0.63
Richard Batchelor	R	26	9	0	0	0	10.0	14	1	3	4	0-0	0	8.10
Steve Dixon	L	23	4	0	0	0	2.2	7	1	5	2	0-0	0	33.75
Rod Brewer	L	27	1	0	0	0	1.0	3	1	2	1	0-0	0	45.00

1993 Chicago Cubs 4th NL East 84-78 .519 13.0 GB — Jim Lefebvre

Player	Gm by Position	B	Age	G	AB	R	H	2B	3B	HR	RBI	BB	SO	SB	Avg	OBP	Slg
Rick Wilkins	C133	L	26	136	446	78	135	23	1	30	73	50	99	2	.303	.376	.561
Mark Grace	1B154	L	29	155	594	86	193	39	4	14	98	71	32	8	.325	.393	.475
Ryne Sandberg	2B115	R	33	117	456	67	141	20	0	9	45	37	62	9	.309	.359	.412
Steve Buechele	3B129,1B6	R	31	133	460	53	125	27	2	15	65	48	87	1	.272	.345	.437
Rey Sanchez	SS98	R	25	105	344	35	97	11	2	0	28	15	22	1	.282	.316	.326
Sammy Sosa	OF158	R	24	159	598	92	156	25	5	33	93	38	135	36	.261	.309	.485
Derrick May	OF122	L	24	128	465	62	137	25	2	10	77	31	41	10	.295	.336	.422
Dwight Smith	OF89	L	29	111	310	51	93	17	5	11	35	25	51	8	.300	.355	.494
Jose Vizcaino	SS81,3B44,2B34	S	25	151	551	74	158	19	4	4	54	46	71	12	.287	.340	.358
Willie Wilson	OF82	S	37	105	221	29	57	11	3	1	11	11	40	7	.258	.301	.348
Kevin Roberson	OF51	S	25	62	180	23	34	4	1	9	27	12	48	0	.189	.251	.372
Candy Maldonado†	OF41	R	32	70	140	8	26	5	0	3	15	13	40	0	.186	.260	.286
Steve Lake	C41	R	36	44	120	11	27	6	0	5	13	4	19	0	.225	.250	.400
Eric Yelding	2B32,3B7,SS1*	R	28	69	108	14	22	5	1	1	10	11	22	3	.204	.277	.296
Glenallen Hill†	OF21	R	28	31	87	14	30	7	0	10	22	6	21	1	.345	.387	.770
Doug Jennings	1B10	L	28	42	52	8	13	3	1	2	8	3	10	0	.250	.316	.462
Karl Rhodes†	OF14	L	24	15	52	12	15	2	1	3	7	11	9	2	.288	.413	.538
Tommy Shields	2B7,3B7,1B1*	L	28	20	34	4	6	1	0	0	1	2	10	0	.176	.222	.206
Matt Walbeck	C11	S	23	11	30	2	6	2	0	1	6	1	6	0	.200	.226	.367
Eddie Zambrano	OF4,1B2	R	27	8	17	1	5	0	0	0	2	1	3	0	.294	.333	.294
Shawon Dunston	SS2	R	30	7	10	3	4	2	0	0	2	0	1	0	.400	.400	.600

E. Yelding, 1 G at OF; T. Shields, 1 G at OF

Pitcher	T	Age	G	GS	CG	ShO	IP	H	HR	BB	SO	W-L	Sv	ERA
Mike Morgan	R	33	32	32	1	1	207.2	206	15	74	111	10-15	0	4.03
Greg Hibbard	L	28	31	31	1	0	191.0	209	19	47	82	15-11	0	3.96
Jose Guzman	R	30	30	30	2	1	191.0	188	25	74	163	12-10	0	4.34
Mike Harkey	R	26	28	28	1	0	157.1	187	17	43	67	10-10	0	5.26
Frank Castillo	R	24	29	25	2	0	141.1	162	20	39	84	5-8	0	4.84
Turk Wendell	R	26	7	4	0	0	22.2	24	0	8	15	1-2	0	4.37
Steve Trachsel	R	22	3	3	0	0	19.2	16	4	3	14	0-2	0	4.58
Randy Myers	L	30	73	0	0	0	75.1	65	7	26	86	2-4	53	3.11
Bob Scanlan	R	26	70	0	0	0	75.1	79	6	28	44	4-5	0	4.54
Jose Bautista	R	28	58	7	1	0	111.2	105	11	27	63	10-3	2	2.82
Dan Plesac	L	31	57	0	0	0	62.2	74	10	21	47	2-1	0	4.74
Chuck McElroy	L	25	49	0	0	0	47.1	51	4	25	31	2-2	0	4.56
Paul Assenmacher†	L	32	46	0	0	0	38.2	44	5	13	34	2-1	0	3.49
Shawn Boskie	R	26	39	2	0	0	65.2	63	7	21	39	5-3	0	3.43
Jim Bullinger	R	27	15	0	0	0	16.2	18	1	9	10	1-0	1	4.32
Heathcliff Slocumb†	R	27	10	0	0	0	10.2	7	0	4	4	1-0	0	3.38
Bill Brennan	R	30	8	1	0	0	15.0	16	2	8	11	2-1	0	4.20

1993 Pittsburgh Pirates 5th NL East 75-87 .463 22.0 GB — Jim Leyland

Player	Gm by Position	B	Age	G	AB	R	H	2B	3B	HR	RBI	BB	SO	SB	Avg	OBP	Slg
Don Slaught	C105	R	34	116	377	34	113	19	2	10	55	29	56	2	.300	.356	.440
Kevin Young	1B135,3B6	R	24	141	449	38	106	24	3	6	47	36	82	2	.236	.300	.343
Carlos Garcia	2B140,SS3	R	25	141	546	77	147	25	5	12	47	31	67	18	.269	.316	.399
Jeff King	3B156,2B2,SS2	R	28	158	611	82	180	35	3	9	98	59	54	8	.295	.356	.406
Jay Bell	SS154	R	27	154	604	102	187	32	9	9	51	77	122	16	.310	.392	.437
Al Martin	OF136	L	25	143	480	85	135	26	8	18	64	42	122	16	.281	.338	.481
Orlando Merced	OF109,1B42	S	26	137	447	68	140	26	4	8	70	77	64	3	.313	.414	.443
Dave Clark	OF91	L	30	110	277	43	75	11	2	11	46	38	58	1	.271	.358	.444
Andy Van Slyke	OF78	L	32	83	323	42	100	13	4	8	50	24	40	11	.310	.357	.449
Lonnie Smith†	OF60	R	37	94	199	35	57	5	4	6	24	43	42	9	.286	.422	.442
Tom Foley	2B35,1B12,3B7*	L	33	86	194	18	49	11	1	3	22	11	26	0	.253	.287	.366
Lloyd McClendon	OF61,1B6	R	34	88	181	21	40	11	1	2	19	23	17	0	.221	.306	.326
Tom Prince	C59	R	28	66	179	14	35	14	0	2	24	13	38	1	.196	.272	.307
Scott Bullett	OF19	S	24	23	55	2	11	0	2	0	4	3	15	3	.200	.237	.273
Andy Tomberlin	OF7	L	26	27	42	4	12	0	1	1	5	2	14	0	.286	.333	.405
Jerry Goff	C14	L	29	14	37	5	11	2	0	2	6	8	9	0	.297	.422	.514
Midre Cummings	OF11	S	21	13	36	5	4	1	0	0	3	4	9	0	.111	.195	.139
John Wehner	OF13,2B3,3B3	R	26	29	35	3	5	0	0	0	0	6	10	0	.143	.268	.143
W. Pennyfeather	OF17	R	25	21	34	4	7	1	0	0	2	0	6	0	.206	.206	.235
Rich Aude	1B7,OF1	R	21	13	26	1	3	1	0	0	4	1	7	0	.115	.148	.154
Ben Shelton	OF6,1B2	R	23	15	24	3	6	1	0	2	7	3	3	0	.250	.333	.542
Tony Womack	SS6	L	23	15	24	5	2	0	0	0	0	3	3	2	.083	.185	.083
Glenn Wilson	OF5	R	34	10	14	0	2	0	0	0	0	0	9	0	.143	.143	.143
Mike LaValliere†	C1	L	32	1	5	0	1	0	0	0	0	0	0	0	.200	.200	.200

T. Foley, 6 G at SS

Pitcher	T	Age	G	GS	CG	ShO	IP	H	HR	BB	SO	W-L	Sv	ERA
Steve Cooke	L	23	32	32	3	1	210.2	207	22	59	132	10-10	0	3.89
Bob Walk	R	36	32	32	3	0	187.0	214	23	70	80	13-14	0	5.68
Tim Wakefield	R	26	24	20	3	2	128.1	145	14	75	59	6-11	0	5.61
Randy Tomlin	L	27	18	18	1	0	98.1	109	11	15	44	4-8	0	4.85
Zane Smith	L	32	14	14	1	0	83.0	97	5	22	32	3-7	0	4.55
John Hope	R	22	7	7	0	0	38.0	47	2	8	8	0-2	0	4.03
Paul Miller	R	28	3	2	0	0	10.0	15	2	2	2	0-0	0	5.40
Blas Minor	R	25	65	0	0	0	94.1	94	8	26	84	8-6	2	4.10
Denny Neagle	L	24	50	7	0	0	81.1	82	10	37	73	3-5	1	5.31
Paul Wagner	R	25	44	17	1	1	141.1	143	15	42	114	8-8	2	4.27
Stan Belinda†	R	26	40	0	0	0	42.1	35	4	11	30	3-1	19	3.61
Joel Johnston	R	26	33	0	0	0	53.1	38	7	19	31	2-4	2	3.38
Dave Otto	L	28	28	8	0	0	68.0	85	9	28	30	3-4	0	5.03
Mark Petkovsek	R	27	26	0	0	0	32.1	43	7	9	14	3-0	0	6.96
Jeff Ballard	L	29	25	5	0	0	53.2	70	3	15	16	4-1	0	4.86
John Candelaria	L	39	24	0	0	0	19.2	25	2	9	17	0-3	1	8.24
Mark Dewey	R	28	21	0	0	0	26.2	14	0	10	14	1-2	7	2.36
Tony Menendez	R	28	14	0	0	0	21.0	20	4	4	13	2-0	0	3.00
Fred Toliver	R	32	12	0	0	0	21.2	20	2	8	14	1-0	0	3.74
Dennis Moeller	L	25	10	0	0	0	16.1	26	2	7	13	1-0	0	9.92
Rich Robertson	L	24	9	0	0	0	9.0	15	0	4	5	0-1	0	6.00
Danny Miceli	R	22	9	0	0	0	5.1	6	0	3	4	0-0	0	5.06
Brian Shouse	L	24	6	0	0	0	4.0	7	1	2	3	0-0	0	9.00

1993 Florida Marlins 6th NL East 64-98 .395 33.0 GB — Rene Lachemann

Player	Gm by Position	B	Age	G	AB	R	H	2B	3B	HR	RBI	BB	SO	SB	Avg	OBP	Slg
Benito Santiago	C136,OF1	R	28	139	469	49	108	19	6	13	50	37	88	10	.230	.291	.380
Orestes Destrade	1B152	S	31	153	569	61	145	20	3	20	87	58	130	0	.255	.324	.406
Bret Barberie	2B97	S	25	99	375	45	104	16	2	5	33	33	58	2	.277	.344	.371
Gary Sheffield†	3B66	R	24	72	236	33	69	8	3	10	37	29	34	12	.292	.378	.479
Walt Weiss	SS153	S	29	158	500	50	133	14	2	1	39	79	73	7	.266	.367	.308
Jeff Conine	OF147,1B43	R	27	162	595	75	174	24	3	12	79	52	135	2	.292	.351	.403
Chuck Carr	OF139	S	24	142	551	75	147	19	2	4	41	49	74	58	.267	.327	.330
Darrell Whitmore	OF69	L	24	76	250	24	51	8	2	4	19	10	72	4	.204	.249	.300
Rich Renteria	2B45,3B25,OF1	R	31	103	263	27	67	9	2	2	30	21	31	0	.255	.314	.327
Alex Arias	2B30,3B22,SS18	R	25	96	249	27	67	5	1	2	20	27	18	1	.269	.344	.321
Dave Magadan†	3B63,1B2	L	30	66	227	22	65	12	0	4	29	44	30	0	.286	.400	.392
Junior Felix	OF52	S	25	57	214	25	51	11	1	7	22	10	50	2	.238	.276	.397
Greg Briley	OF67	L	28	120	170	17	33	6	0	3	12	12	42	6	.194	.250	.282
Henry Cotto†	OF46	R	32	54	135	15	40	7	0	3	14	3	18	11	.296	.312	.415
Bob Natal	C38	R	27	41	117	3	25	4	1	1	6	6	22	1	.214	.273	.291
Matias Carrillo	OF16	L	30	24	55	4	14	6	0	0	3	1	7	0	.255	.281	.364
Scott Pose	OF10	L	26	15	41	0	8	2	0	0	3	2	4	0	.195	.233	.244
Geronimo Berroa	OF9	R	28	14	34	3	4	1	0	0	0	2	7	0	.118	.167	.147
Monty Fariss	OF8	R	25	18	29	3	5	2	1	0	2	5	13	0	.172	.294	.310
Carl Everett	OF8	S	23	11	19	0	2	0	0	0	0	1	9	1	.105	.150	.105
Nigel Wilson	OF3	L	23	7	16	0	0	0	0	0	0	0	11	0	.000	.000	.000
Steve Decker	C5	R	27	8	15	0	0	0	0	0	1	3	3	0	.000	.158	.000
Mitch Lyden	C2	R	28	6	10	2	3	0	0	1	1	0	3	0	.300	.300	.600
Terry McGriff	C3	R	29	3	7	0	0	0	0	0	0	1	2	0	.000	.125	.000
Gus Polidor	2B1,3B1	R	31	7	6	0	1	1	0	0	0	0	2	0	.167	.167	.333

Pitcher	T	Age	G	GS	CG	ShO	IP	H	HR	BB	SO	W-L	Sv	ERA
Charlie Hough	R	45	34	34	0	0	204.1	202	20	71	126	9-16	0	4.27
Jack Armstrong	R	28	36	33	0	0	196.1	210	29	78	118	9-17	0	4.49
Chris Hammond	L	27	32	32	1	0	191.0	207	18	66	108	11-12	0	4.66
Ryan Bowen	R	25	27	27	2	1	156.2	156	11	87	98	8-12	0	4.42
Pat Rapp	R	25	16	16	1	0	94.0	101	7	39	57	4-6	0	4.02
Bryan Harvey	R	30	59	0	0	0	69.0	45	4	13	73	1-5	45	1.70
Joe Klink	L	31	59	0	0	0	37.2	37	0	24	22	0-2	0	5.02
Richie Lewis	R	27	57	0	0	0	77.1	68	7	43	65	6-3	0	3.26
Matt Turner	R	26	55	0	0	0	68.0	55	7	26	59	4-5	0	2.91
Luis Aquino	R	29	38	13	0	0	110.2	115	6	40	67	6-8	0	3.42
Rich Rodriguez†	L	30	36	0	0	0	46.0	39	8	24	21	0-1	1	4.11
Cris Carpenter†	R	28	29	0	0	0	37.1	29	1	13	26	0-1	0	2.89
Trevor Hoffman†	R	25	28	0	0	0	35.2	24	5	19	26	2-2	2	3.28
Robb Nen†	R	23	15	1	0	0	33.1	35	5	20	27	1-0	0	7.02
Jim Corsi	R	31	15	0	0	0	20.1	28	1	10	7	0-2	0	6.64
Dave Weathers	R	23	14	6	0	0	45.2	57	3	13	34	2-3	0	5.12
Bob McClure	L	41	14	0	0	0	6.1	13	2	5	6	1-1	0	7.11
John Johnstone	R	24	7	0	0	0	10.2	16	1	7	5	0-2	0	5.91

1993 New York Mets 7th NL East 59-103 .364 38.0 GB — Jeff Torborg (13-25)/Dallas Green (46-78)

Player	Gm by Position	B	Age	G	AB	R	H	2B	3B	HR	RBI	BB	SO	SB	Avg	OBP	Slg
Todd Hundley	C123	S	24	130	417	40	95	17	2	11	53	23	62	1	.228	.269	.357
Eddie Murray	1B154	S	37	154	610	77	174	28	1	27	100	40	61	2	.285	.325	.467
Jeff Kent	2B127,3B12,SS2	R	25	140	496	65	134	24	0	21	80	30	88	4	.270	.320	.446
Howard Johnson	3B67	S	32	72	235	32	56	8	2	7	26	43	43	6	.238	.354	.379
Tim Bogar	SS66,3B7,2B6	R	26	78	205	19	50	13	0	3	25	14	29	0	.244	.300	.351
Joe Orsulak	OF114,1B4	L	31	134	409	59	116	15	4	8	35	28	25	5	.284	.331	.399
Vince Coleman	OF90	S	31	92	373	64	104	14	8	2	25	21	58	38	.279	.316	.375
Bobby Bonilla	OF85,3B52,1B6	S	30	139	502	81	133	21	3	34	87	72	96	3	.265	.352	.522
Ryan Thompson	OF76	R	25	80	288	34	72	19	2	11	26	19	81	2	.250	.302	.444
Jeromy Burnitz	OF79	L	24	86	263	49	64	10	6	13	38	38	66	3	.243	.339	.475
Chico Walker	2B24,3B23,OF15	S	35	115	213	18	48	7	1	5	19	14	29	7	.225	.271	.338
Dave Gallagher	OF72,1B9	R	32	99	201	34	55	12	2	6	28	20	18	1	.274	.338	.443
Charlie O'Brien	C65	R	33	67	188	15	48	11	0	4	23	14	14	1	.255	.312	.378
Tony Fernandez†	SS48	S	31	48	173	20	39	5	2	1	14	25	19	6	.225	.323	.295
Jeff McKnight	SS29,2B15,1B10*	S	30	105	164	19	42	3	1	2	13	13	31	0	.256	.311	.323
Kevin Baez	SS52	R	26	52	126	10	23	9	0	0	7	13	17	0	.183	.259	.254
Darrin Jackson†	OF26	R	29	31	87	4	17	1	0	1	7	2	22	0	.195	.211	.241
Doug Saunders	2B22,3B4,SS1	R	23	28	67	8	14	2	0	0	0	3	4	0	.209	.243	.239
Butch Huskey	3B13	R	21	13	41	2	6	1	0	0	3	1	13	0	.146	.159	.171
Ced Landrum	OF3	L	29	22	19	2	5	1	0	0	1	0	5	0	.263	.263	.316
Tito Navarro	SS2	R	22	12	17	1	1	0	0	0	1	0	4	0	.059	.059	.059
Wayne Housie	OF2	S	28	18	16	2	3	1	0	0	1	1	1	0	.188	.235	.250

J. McKnight, 9 G at 3B, 1 G at C

Pitcher	T	Age	G	GS	CG	ShO	IP	H	HR	BB	SO	W-L	Sv	ERA
Dwight Gooden	R	28	29	29	7	2	208.2	188	16	61	149	12-15	0	3.45
Frank Tanana†	L	39	29	29	0	0	183.0	198	26	48	104	7-15	0	4.48
Eric Hillman	L	27	27	22	3	1	145.0	173	12	24	60	2-9	0	3.97
Bret Saberhagen	R	29	19	19	4	1	139.1	131	11	17	93	7-7	0	3.29
Sid Fernandez	L	30	18	18	1	1	119.2	82	17	36	81	5-6	0	2.93
Bobby Jones	R	23	9	9	0	0	61.2	61	6	22	35	2-4	0	3.65
Jeff Innis	R	30	67	0	0	0	76.2	81	5	38	36	2-3	3	4.11
Mike Maddux	R	31	58	0	0	0	75.0	67	3	27	57	3-8	5	3.60
Pete Schourek	L	24	41	18	0	0	128.1	168	13	45	72	5-12	0	5.96
Anthony Young	R	27	39	10	1	0	100.1	103	8	42	62	1-16	3	3.77
John Franco	L	32	35	0	0	0	36.1	46	6	19	29	4-3	10	5.20
Mike Draper	R	26	29	1	0	0	42.1	53	2	14	16	1-1	0	4.25
Dave Telgheder	R	26	24	7	0	0	75.2	82	10	21	35	6-2	0	4.76
Mauro Gozzo	R	27	10	0	0	0	14.0	11	1	5	6	0-1	1	2.57
Paul Gibson†	R	33	8	0	0	0	8.2	14	1	2	12	1-1	0	5.19
Josias Manzanillo†	R	25	6	0	0	0	12.0	8	1	9	11	0-0	0	3.00
Jeff Kaiser†	L	32	6	0	0	0	4.2	6	1	3	5	0-0	0	11.57
Mickey Weston	R	32	4	0	0	0	5.2	11	0	1	2	0-0	0	7.94
Ken Greer	R	26	1	0	0	0	1.0	0	0	0	2	1-0	0	0.00

1993 Atlanta Braves 1st NL West 104-58 .642 —

Bobby Cox

Player	Gm by Position	B	Age	G	AB	R	H	2B	3B	HR	RBI	BB	SO	SB	Avg	OBP	Slg
Damon Berryhill	C105	S	29	115	335	24	82	18	2	8	43	21	64	0	.245	.291	.382
Sid Bream	1B90	L	32	117	277	33	72	14	1	9	35	31	43	4	.260	.332	.415
Mark Lemke	2B150	S	27	151	493	52	124	19	2	7	49	65	50	1	.252	.335	.341
Terry Pendleton	3B161	S	32	161	633	81	172	33	1	17	84	36	97	5	.272	.311	.408
Jeff Blauser	SS161	R	27	161	597	110	182	29	2	15	73	85	109	16	.305	.401	.436
David Justice	OF157	L	27	157	585	90	158	15	4	40	120	78	90	3	.270	.357	.515
Ron Gant	OF155	R	28	157	606	113	166	27	4	36	117	67	117	26	.274	.345	.510
Otis Nixon	OF116	S	34	134	461	77	124	12	3	1	24	61	63	47	.269	.351	.315
Deion Sanders	OF60	L	25	95	272	42	75	18	6	6	28	16	42	19	.276	.321	.452
Greg Olson	C81	R	32	83	262	23	59	10	0	4	24	29	27	1	.225	.304	.309
Fred McGriff†	1B66	L	29	68	255	59	79	18	1	19	55	34	51	1	.310	.392	.612
Francisco Cabrera	1B12,C2	R	26	70	83	8	20	3	0	4	11	8	21	0	.241	.308	.422
Brian Hunter	1B29,OF2	R	25	37	80	4	11	3	1	0	8	2	15	0	.138	.153	.200
Rafael Belliard	SS58,2B24	R	31	91	79	6	18	5	0	0	6	4	13	0	.228	.291	.291
Bill Pecota	3B23,2B4,OF1	R	33	72	62	17	20	2	1	0	5	2	5	1	.323	.344	.387
Tony Tarasco	OF12	L	22	24	35	6	8	2	0	0	2	0	5	0	.229	.243	.286
Ryan Klesko	1B3,OF2	L	22	22	17	3	6	1	0	2	5	3	4	0	.353	.450	.765
Javy Lopez	C7	R	22	8	16	1	6	1	1	1	2	0	2	0	.375	.412	.750
Chipper Jones	SS3	S	21	8	3	2	2	1	0	0	0	1	1	0	.667	.750	1.000
Ramon Caraballo	2B5	S	24	6	0	0	0	0	0	0	0	0	0	0	—	—	—

Pitcher	T	Age	G	GS	CG	ShO	IP	H	HR	BB	SO	W-L	Sv	ERA
Greg Maddux	R	27	36	36	8	1	267.0	228	14	52	197	20-10	0	2.36
Tom Glavine	L	27	36	36	4	2	239.1	236	16	90	120	22-6	0	3.20
John Smoltz	R	26	35	35	3	1	243.2	208	23	100	208	15-11	0	3.62
Steve Avery	L	23	35	35	3	1	223.1	216	14	43	125	18-6	0	2.94
Pete Smith	R	27	20	14	0	0	90.2	92	15	36	53	4-8	0	4.37
Greg McMichael	R	26	74	0	0	0	91.2	68	3	29	89	2-3	19	2.06
Mike Stanton	L	26	63	0	0	0	52.0	51	4	29	43	4-6	27	4.67
Jay Howell	R	37	54	0	0	0	58.1	48	3	16	37	3-3	0	2.31
Steve Bedrosian	R	35	49	0	0	0	49.2	34	4	14	33	5-2	0	1.63
Mark Wohlers	R	23	46	0	0	0	48.0	37	2	22	45	6-2	0	4.50
Kent Mercker	L	25	43	6	0	0	66.0	52	2	36	59	3-1	0	2.86
Marvin Freeman	R	30	21	0	0	0	23.2	24	1	10	25	2-0	0	6.08
Pedro Borbon	L	25	3	0	0	0	1.2	3	0	3	2	0-0	0	21.60

1993 San Francisco Giants 2nd NL West 103-59 .636 1.0 GB

Dusty Baker

Player	Gm by Position	B	Age	G	AB	R	H	2B	3B	HR	RBI	BB	SO	SB	Avg	OBP	Slg
Kirt Manwaring	C130	R	27	130	432	48	119	15	1	5	49	41	76	1	.275	.345	.350
Will Clark	1B129	L	29	132	491	82	139	27	2	14	73	63	68	2	.283	.367	.432
Robby Thompson	2B128	R	31	128	494	85	154	30	2	19	65	45	97	10	.312	.375	.496
Matt Williams	3B144	R	27	145	579	105	170	33	4	38	110	27	80	1	.294	.325	.561
Royce Clayton	SS153	R	23	153	549	54	155	21	5	6	70	38	91	11	.282	.331	.372
Barry Bonds	OF157	L	28	159	539	129	181	38	4	46	123	126	79	29	.336	.458	.677
Darren Lewis	OF131	R	25	136	522	84	132	17	7	2	48	30	40	46	.253	.302	.324
Willie McGee	OF126	S	34	130	475	53	143	28	1	4	46	38	67	10	.301	.353	.389
Dave Martinez	OF73	L	28	91	241	28	58	12	1	5	27	27	39	6	.241	.317	.361
Todd Benzinger	1B40,OF7,3B1	S	30	86	177	25	51	7	2	6	26	13	35	0	.288	.332	.452
Mark Carreon	OF41,1B3	R	29	78	150	22	49	9	1	7	33	13	16	1	.327	.373	.540
Mike Benjamin	2B23,SS23,3B16	R	27	63	146	22	29	7	0	4	16	9	23	0	.199	.264	.329
Jeff Reed	C37	L	30	66	119	10	31	3	0	6	12	16	22	0	.261	.346	.437
Steve Scarsone	2B20,3B8,1B6	R	27	44	103	16	26	9	0	2	15	4	32	0	.252	.278	.398
Craig Colbert	C10,2B2,3B1	R	28	23	37	2	6	2	0	1	5	3	13	0	.162	.225	.297
Paul Faries	2B7,SS4,3B1	R	28	15	36	6	8	2	1	0	4	1	4	2	.222	.237	.333
Luis Mercedes†	OF5	R	25	18	25	1	4	0	1	0	3	1	3	0	.160	.250	.240
Andy Allanson	C8,1B2	R	31	13	24	3	4	1	0	0	2	1	2	0	.167	.200	.208
John Patterson		S	26	16	16	1	3	0	0	1	2	0	5	0	.188	.188	.375
J.R. Phillips	1B5	L	23	11	16	1	5	1	1	1	4	0	5	0	.313	.313	.688
Rikkert Faneyte	OF6	R	24	7	15	2	2	0	0	0	0	2	4	0	.133	.235	.133
Jim McNamara	C4	L	28	4	7	0	1	0	0	0	1	0	1	0	.143	.143	.143
Erik Johnson	2B2,3B1,SS1	R	27	4	5	1	2	2	0	0	0	0	1	0	.400	.400	.800
Steve Hosey	OF1	R	24	3	2	0	1	1	0	0	1	1	1	0	.500	.667	1.000

Pitcher	T	Age	G	GS	CG	ShO	IP	H	HR	BB	SO	W-L	Sv	ERA
Bill Swift	R	31	34	34	1	1	232.2	195	18	55	157	21-8	0	2.82
John Burkett	R	28	34	34	2	1	231.2	224	18	40	145	22-7	0	3.65
Trevor Wilson	L	27	22	18	1	0	110.0	110	8	40	57	7-5	0	3.60
Bud Black	L	36	16	16	0	0	93.2	89	13	33	45	8-2	0	3.56
Scott Sanderson†	R	36	11	8	0	0	48.2	48	12	7	36	4-2	0	3.51
Greg Brummett†	R	26	8	8	0	0	46.0	53	9	13	20	2-3	0	4.70
Salomon Torres	R	21	8	8	0	0	44.2	37	5	27	23	3-5	0	4.03
Jim Deshaies†	L	33	5	4	0	0	17.0	24	2	6	5	2-2	0	4.24
Mike Jackson	R	28	81	0	0	0	77.1	58	7	24	70	6-6	1	3.03
Rod Beck	R	24	76	0	0	0	79.1	57	11	13	86	3-1	48	2.16
Kevin Rogers	L	24	64	0	0	0	80.2	71	3	28	62	2-2	0	2.68
Dave Burba	R	26	54	5	0	0	95.1	95	14	37	88	10-3	0	4.25
Jeff Brantley	R	29	53	12	0	0	113.2	112	19	46	76	5-6	0	4.28
Dave Righetti	L	34	51	0	0	0	47.1	58	11	17	31	1-1	1	5.70
Bryan Hickerson	L	29	47	15	0	0	120.1	137	14	39	69	7-5	0	4.26
Gino Minutelli	L	29	9	0	0	0	14.1	7	2	15	10	0-1	0	3.77
Terry Bross	R	27	2	0	0	0	2.0	3	1	1	1	0-0	0	9.00
Tim Layana	R	29	1	0	0	0	2.0	7	1	1	1	0-0	0	22.50

1993 Houston Astros 3rd NL West 85-77 .525 19.0 GB

Art Howe

Player	Gm by Position	B	Age	G	AB	R	H	2B	3B	HR	RBI	BB	SO	SB	Avg	OBP	Slg
Eddie Taubensee	C90	L	24	94	288	26	72	11	1	9	42	21	44	1	.250	.299	.389
Jeff Bagwell	1B140	R	25	142	535	76	171	37	4	20	88	62	73	13	.320	.388	.516
Craig Biggio	2B155	R	27	155	610	98	175	41	5	21	64	77	93	15	.287	.373	.474
Ken Caminiti	3B143	S	30	143	543	75	142	31	0	13	75	49	88	8	.262	.321	.390
Andujar Cedeno	SS149,3B1	R	23	149	505	69	143	24	4	11	56	48	97	9	.283	.346	.412
Luis Gonzalez	OF149	L	25	154	540	82	162	34	3	15	72	47	83	20	.300	.361	.457
Steve Finley	OF140	L	28	142	545	69	145	15	13	8	44	28	65	19	.266	.304	.385
Eric Anthony	OF131	L	25	145	486	70	121	19	4	15	66	49	88	3	.249	.319	.397
Scott Servais	C82	R	26	85	258	24	63	11	0	11	32	22	45	0	.244	.313	.415
Kevin Bass	OF64	S	34	111	229	31	65	18	0	3	37	26	31	7	.284	.359	.402
Chris Donnels	3B31,1B23,2B1	L	27	88	179	18	46	14	2	2	24	19	33	2	.257	.327	.391
Chris James†	OF34	R	30	65	129	19	33	10	1	6	19	15	34	2	.256	.333	.488
Casey Candaele	2B19,OF17,SS14*	S	32	75	121	18	29	8	0	1	7	10	14	2	.240	.298	.331
Jose Uribe	SS41	S	34	45	53	4	13	1	0	0	3	8	5	1	.245	.355	.264
Rick Parker	OF16,2B1,SS1	R	30	45	45	11	15	3	0	0	4	3	8	1	.333	.375	.400
Scooter Tucker	C8	R	26	9	26	1	5	1	0	0	3	2	3	0	.192	.250	.231
Jim Lindeman	1B9	R	31	9	23	2	8	3	0	0	0	0	7	0	.348	.348	.478
Mike Brumley	3B1,SS1,OF1	S	30	8	10	1	3	0	0	0	2	1	3	0	.300	.364	.300
Jack Daugherty†	1B1,OF1	S	32	4	3	0	1	0	0	0	0	0	0	0	.333	.333	.333
Karl Rhodes†	OF4	L	24	5	2	0	0	0	0	0	0	0	0	0	.000	.000	.000

C. Candaele, 4 G at 3B

Pitcher	T	Age	G	GS	CG	ShO	IP	H	HR	BB	SO	W-L	Sv	ERA
Doug Drabek	R	30	34	34	7	2	237.2	242	18	60	157	9-18	0	3.79
Pete Harnisch	R	26	33	33	5	4	217.2	171	20	79	185	16-9	0	2.98
Mark Portugal	R	30	33	33	1	1	208.0	194	10	77	131	18-4	0	2.77
Greg Swindell	L	28	31	30	1	1	190.1	215	24	40	124	12-13	0	4.16
Darryl Kile	R	24	32	26	4	2	171.2	152	12	69	141	15-8	0	3.51
Xavier Hernandez	R	27	72	0	0	0	96.2	75	6	28	101	4-5	9	2.61
Doug Jones	R	36	71	0	0	0	85.1	102	7	21	66	4-10	26	4.54
Al Osuna	L	27	44	0	0	0	25.1	17	3	13	21	1-1	2	3.20
Brian Williams	R	24	42	5	0	0	82.0	76	7	38	56	4-4	3	4.83
Tom Edens	R	32	38	0	0	0	49.0	47	4	19	21	1-1	0	3.12
Todd Jones	R	25	27	0	0	0	37.1	28	4	15	25	1-2	2	3.13
Eric Bell	L	29	10	0	0	0	7.1	10	0	2	2	0-1	0	6.14
Mark Grant†	R	29	6	0	0	0	11.0	11	0	5	6	0-0	0	0.82
Juan Agosto	L	35	6	0	0	0	6.0	8	1	0	3	0-0	0	6.00
Shane Reynolds	R	25	5	1	0	0	11.0	11	0	6	10	0-0	0	0.82
Jeff Juden	R	22	2	0	0	0	5.0	4	1	4	7	0-1	0	5.40

1993 Los Angeles Dodgers 4th NL West 81-81 .500 23.0 GB

Tom Lasorda

Player	Gm by Position	B	Age	G	AB	R	H	2B	3B	HR	RBI	BB	SO	SB	Avg	OBP	Slg
Mike Piazza	C146,1B1	R	24	149	547	81	174	24	2	35	112	46	86	3	.318	.370	.561
Eric Karros	1B157	R	25	158	619	74	153	27	2	23	80	34	82	0	.247	.287	.409
Jody Reed	2B132	R	30	132	445	48	123	21	2	2	31	38	40	1	.276	.333	.346
Tim Wallach	3B130,1B1	R	35	133	477	42	106	19	1	12	62	32	70	0	.222	.271	.342
Jose Offerman	SS158	S	24	158	590	77	159	21	6	1	62	71	75	30	.269	.346	.331
Brett Butler	OF155	L	36	156	607	80	181	21	10	1	42	86	69	39	.298	.387	.371
Cory Snyder	OF115,3B23,1B12*	R	30	143	516	61	137	33	1	11	56	47	147	4	.266	.331	.397
Eric Davis†	OF103	R	31	108	376	57	88	17	0	14	53	41	88	33	.234	.308	.391
Henry Rodriguez	OF48,1B13	L	25	76	176	20	39	10	0	8	23	11	39	1	.222	.266	.415
Mitch Webster	OF56	S	34	88	172	26	42	6	2	2	14	11	24	4	.244	.293	.337
Lenny Harris	2B35,3B17,SS3*	L	28	107	160	20	38	6	1	2	11	15	15	3	.238	.303	.325
Dave Hansen	3B18	L	24	84	105	13	38	3	0	4	30	21	13	0	.362	.465	.505
Darryl Strawberry	OF29	L	31	32	100	12	14	2	0	5	12	16	19	1	.140	.267	.310
Carlos Hernandez	C43	R	26	50	99	6	25	5	0	2	7	2	11	0	.253	.267	.364
Mike Sharperson	2B17,3B6,SS3*	R	31	73	90	13	23	4	0	2	10	5	17	2	.256	.299	.367
Raul Mondesi	OF40	R	22	42	86	13	25	3	1	4	10	4	16	4	.291	.322	.488
Orel Hershiser	P33,3B1	R	34	34	73	11	26	4	0	0	6	2	5	0	.356	.373	.411
Billy Ashley	OF11	R	22	14	37	0	9	0	0	0	0	2	11	0	.243	.282	.243
Rafael Bournigal	2B4,SS4	R	27	8	18	0	9	1	0	0	3	0	2	0	.500	.500	.556
Tom Goodwin	OF12	L	24	30	17	6	5	1	0	0	1	1	4	1	.294	.333	.353
Jerry Brooks	OF2	R	26	9	9	2	2	1	0	1	1	0	2	0	.222	.222	.667
Pedro Martinez	P65,3B1	R	21	66	4	0	0	0	0	0	0	0	3	0	.000	.000	.000

C. Snyder, 2 G at SS; L. Harris, 2 G at OF; M. Sharperson, 1 G at 1B, 1 G at OF

Pitcher	T	Age	G	GS	CG	ShO	IP	H	HR	BB	SO	W-L	Sv	ERA
Orel Hershiser	R	34	33	33	5	1	215.2	201	17	72	141	12-14	0	3.59
Tom Candiotti	R	35	33	32	2	0	213.2	192	12	71	155	8-10	0	3.12
Ramon Martinez	R	25	32	32	4	3	211.2	202	15	104	127	10-12	0	3.44
Kevin Gross	R	32	33	32	3	0	202.1	224	15	74	150	13-13	0	4.14
Pedro Astacio	R	24	31	31	3	2	186.1	165	14	68	122	14-9	0	3.57
Pedro Martinez	R	21	65	2	0	0	107.0	76	5	57	119	10-5	2	2.61
Jim Gott	R	33	62	0	0	0	77.2	71	6	17	67	4-8	25	2.32
Roger McDowell	R	32	54	0	0	0	68.0	76	2	30	27	5-3	2	2.25
Omar Daal	L	21	47	0	0	0	35.1	36	5	21	19	2-3	0	5.09
Ricky Trlicek	R	24	41	0	0	0	64.0	59	3	21	41	1-2	1	4.08
Todd Worrell	R	33	35	0	0	0	38.2	46	6	11	31	1-1	5	6.05
Steve Wilson	L	28	25	0	0	0	25.2	30	2	14	23	1-0	1	4.56
Kip Gross	R	28	10	0	0	0	15.0	13	0	4	12	0-0	0	0.60
Rod Nichols	R	28	4	0	0	0	6.1	9	1	2	3	0-1	0	5.68
John DeSilva†	R	25	3	0	0	0	5.1	6	0	1	6	0-0	0	6.75

1993 Cincinnati Reds 5th NL West 73-89 .451 31.0 GB

Tony Perez (20-24)/Davey Johnson (53-65)

Player	Gm by Position	B	Age	G	AB	R	H	2B	3B	HR	RBI	BB	SO	SB	Avg	OBP	Slg
Joe Oliver	C133,1B12,OF1	R	27	139	482	40	115	28	0	14	75	27	91	0	.239	.276	.384
Hal Morris	1B98	L	28	101	379	48	120	18	0	7	49	34	51	2	.317	.371	.420
Juan Samuel	2B70,1B6,3B4*	R	32	103	261	31	60	10	4	4	26	23	53	9	.230	.298	.345
Chris Sabo	3B148	R	31	148	552	86	143	33	2	21	82	43	105	6	.259	.315	.440
Barry Larkin	SS99	R	29	100	384	57	121	20	3	8	51	51	33	14	.315	.394	.445
Reggie Sanders	OF137	R	25	138	496	90	136	16	4	20	83	51	118	27	.274	.343	.444
Jacob Brumfield	OF96,2B4	R	28	103	272	40	73	17	3	6	23	21	47	20	.268	.321	.419
Kevin Mitchell	OF87	R	31	93	323	56	110	21	3	19	64	25	48	1	.341	.385	.601
Jeff Branson	SS59,2B45,3B14*	L	26	125	381	40	92	15	1	3	22	19	73	4	.241	.275	.310
Roberto Kelly	OF77	R	28	78	320	44	102	17	3	9	35	17	43	21	.319	.354	.475
Bip Roberts	2B64,OF11,3B3*	S	29	83	292	46	70	13	0	1	18	38	46	26	.240	.330	.295
Randy Milligan†	1B61,OF9	R	31	83	234	30	64	11	1	6	29	46	49	0	.274	.394	.406
Thomas Howard†	OF37	S	28	38	141	22	39	8	3	4	13	12	21	5	.277	.331	.461
Tim Costo	OF26,1B2,3B2	R	24	31	98	13	22	5	0	3	12	4	17	0	.224	.250	.367
Gary Varsho	OF22	L	32	77	95	8	22	6	0	2	11	9	19	1	.232	.302	.358
Dan Wilson	C35	R	24	36	76	6	17	3	0	0	8	9	16	0	.224	.302	.263
Brian Dorsett	C18,1B3	R	32	25	63	7	16	4	0	2	12	3	14	0	.254	.288	.413
Cecil Espy	OF18	S	30	40	60	6	14	2	0	0	5	14	13	2	.233	.368	.267
Jack Daugherty†	OF16,1B2	S	32	46	59	7	13	2	0	2	9	11	15	0	.220	.338	.356
Greg Tubbs	OF21	R	30	35	59	10	11	0	0	1	2	14	10	3	.186	.351	.237
Willie Greene	SS10,3B5	L	21	15	50	7	8	1	1	2	5	2	19	0	.160	.189	.340
Keith Kessinger	SS11	S	26	11	27	4	7	1	0	1	3	4	4	0	.259	.344	.407
Cesar Hernandez	OF23	R	26	27	24	3	2	0	0	0	1	1	8	1	.083	.120	.083
Brian Koelling	2B3,SS2	R	24	7	15	2	1	0	0	0	0	0	2	0	.067	.125	.067
Tommy Gregg	OF4	L	29	10	12	1	2	0	0	0	1	0	0	0	.167	.154	.167
Keith Gordon	OF2	R	24	3	6	0	1	0	0	0	0	0	2	0	.167	.167	.167
Keith Hughes	OF2	L	29	3	4	0	0	0	0	0	0	0	0	0	.000	.000	.000

J. Samuel, 3 G at OF; J. Branson, 1 G at 1B; B. Roberts, 1 G at SS

Pitcher	T	Age	G	GS	CG	ShO	IP	H	HR	BB	SO	W-L	Sv	ERA
Jose Rijo	R	28	36	36	2	1	257.1	218	19	62	227	14-9	0	2.48
Tim Pugh	R	26	31	27	3	1	164.1	200	19	59	94	10-15	0	5.26
Tim Belcher†	R	31	22	22	4	2	137.0	134	11	47	101	9-6	0	4.47
Tom Browning	L	33	21	20	0	0	114.0	159	15	20	53	7-7	0	4.74
John Smiley	L	28	18	18	2	0	105.2	117	15	31	60	3-9	0	5.62
John Roper	R	21	16	15	0	0	80.0	92	10	36	54	2-5	0	5.63
Larry Luebbers	R	23	14	14	0	0	77.1	74	7	38	38	2-5	0	4.54
Jeff Reardon	R	37	58	0	0	0	61.2	66	4	10	35	4-6	8	4.09
Rob Dibble	R	29	45	0	0	0	41.2	34	8	42	49	1-4	19	6.48
Bobby Ayala	R	23	43	9	0	0	98.0	106	16	45	65	7-10	3	5.60
Jerry Spradlin	R	26	37	0	0	0	49.0	44	4	9	24	2-1	2	3.49
Greg Cadaret†	L	31	34	0	0	0	32.2	40	3	23	23	2-1	1	4.96
Kevin Wickander†	L	28	33	0	0	0	25.1	32	5	19	20	1-0	0	6.75
Scott Service†	R	26	26	0	0	0	41.1	36	5	15	40	2-2	2	3.70
Johnny Ruffin	R	21	21	0	0	0	37.2	36	4	11	30	2-1	2	3.58
Milt Hill	R	27	19	0	0	0	28.2	34	5	9	23	3-0	0	5.65
Bill Landrum	R	35	18	0	0	0	21.2	18	1	6	14	0-2	0	3.74
Steve Foster	R	26	17	0	0	0	25.2	23	1	5	16	2-2	0	1.75
Ross Powell	L	25	9	1	0	0	16.1	13	1	6	17	0-3	0	4.41
Chris Bushing	R	25	6	0	0	0	4.1	9	1	4	3	0-0	0	12.46
Scott Ruskin	L	30	4	0	0	0	1.0	3	1	2	0	0-0	0	18.00
Mike Anderson	R	26	3	0	0	0	5.1	12	3	3	4	0-0	0	18.56
Dwayne Henry†	R	31	3	0	0	0	4.2	6	0	4	2	0-1	0	3.86
Jeff Kaiser†	L	32	3	0	0	0	3.1	4	0	2	4	0-0	0	2.70

1993 Colorado Rockies 6th NL West 67-95 .414 37.0 GB

Don Baylor

Player	Gm by Position	B	Age	G	AB	R	H	2B	3B	HR	RBI	BB	SO	SB	Avg	OBP	Slg
Joe Girardi	C84	R	28	86	310	35	90	14	5	3	31	24	41	6	.290	.346	.397
Andres Galarraga	1B119	R	32	120	470	71	174	35	4	22	98	24	73	2	.370	.403	.602
Eric Young	2B79,OF52	R	26	144	490	82	132	16	8	3	42	63	41	42	.269	.355	.353
Charlie Hayes	3B154,SS1	R	28	157	573	89	175	45	2	25	98	43	82	11	.305	.355	.522
Vinny Castilla	SS104	R	25	105	337	36	86	9	7	9	30	13	45	2	.255	.283	.404
Dante Bichette	OF137	R	29	141	538	93	167	43	5	21	89	28	99	14	.310	.348	.526
Jerald Clark	OF96,1B37	R	29	140	478	65	135	26	6	13	67	20	60	9	.282	.324	.444
Alex Cole	OF93	L	27	126	348	50	89	9	4	0	24	43	58	30	.256	.339	.305
Daryl Boston	OF79	L	30	124	291	46	76	15	1	14	40	26	57	1	.261	.325	.464
Roberto Mejia	2B65	R	21	65	229	31	53	14	5	5	20	13	63	4	.231	.275	.402
Danny Sheaffer	C65,1B7,OF2*	R	31	82	216	26	60	9	1	4	32	8	15	2	.278	.299	.384
Freddie Benavides	SS48,2B19,3B5*	R	27	74	213	20	61	10	3	3	26	6	27	3	.286	.305	.404
Chris Jones	OF70	R	27	86	209	29	57	11	4	6	31	10	48	9	.273	.305	.450
Nelson Liriano	SS35,2B16,3B1	S	29	48	151	28	46	6	3	2	15	18	22	6	.305	.376	.424
Jimmy Tatum	1B12,3B6,OF3	R	25	92	98	7	20	5	0	1	12	5	27	0	.204	.245	.286
Jayhawk Owens	C32	R	24	33	86	12	18	5	0	3	6	6	30	1	.209	.277	.372
Pedro Castellano	3B13,1B10,SS5*	R	23	34	71	12	13	2	0	3	7	8	16	1	.183	.266	.338
Dale Murphy	OF13	R	37	26	42	1	6	1	0	0	7	5	15	0	.143	.224	.167
Jay Gainer	1B7	L	26	23	41	4	7	0	0	3	6	4	12	1	.171	.244	.390
Gerald Young	OF11	S	28	19	19	5	1	0	0	0	1	4	1	0	.053	.217	.053
Eric Wedge	C1	R	25	9	11	2	2	0	0	0	1	0	4	0	.182	.182	.182

D. Sheaffer, 1 G at 3B; F. Benavides, 1 G at 1B; P. Castellano, 4 G at 2B

Pitcher	T	Age	G	GS	CG	ShO	IP	H	HR	BB	SO	W-L	Sv	ERA
Armando Reynoso	R	27	30	30	4	0	189.0	206	22	63	117	12-11	0	4.00
Dave Nied	R	24	16	16	1	0	87.0	99	8	42	46	5-9	0	5.17
Butch Henry†	L	24	20	15	1	0	84.2	117	14	24	39	2-8	0	6.59
Kent Bottenfield†	R	24	14	14	1	0	76.2	86	13	38	30	3-5	0	6.10
Greg Harris†	R	29	13	13	0	0	73.1	88	15	30	40	1-8	0	6.50
Lance Painter	L	25	10	6	1	0	39.0	52	5	9	16	2-2	0	6.00
Mo Sanford	R	26	11	6	0	0	35.2	37	4	27	36	1-2	0	5.30
Bruce Hurst†	L	35	3	3	0	0	8.2	6	1	3	6	0-1	0	5.19
Gary Wayne	L	30	65	0	0	0	62.1	68	8	26	49	5-3	1	5.05
Steve Reed	R	27	64	0	0	0	84.1	80	13	30	51	9-5	3	4.48
Darren Holmes	R	27	62	0	0	0	66.2	56	6	20	60	3-3	25	4.05
Bruce Ruffin	L	29	59	12	0	0	139.2	145	10	69	126	6-5	2	3.87
Willie Blair	R	27	46	18	1	0	146.0	184	20	42	84	6-10	0	4.75
Jeff Parrett	R	31	40	6	0	0	73.2	78	6	45	66	3-3	1	5.38
Marcus Moore	R	22	27	0	0	0	26.1	30	4	20	13	3-1	0	6.84
Scott Fredrickson	R	25	25	0	0	0	29.0	33	3	17	20	0-1	0	6.21
Mike Munoz†	L	27	21	0	0	0	18.0	21	1	9	16	2-1	0	4.50
Andy Ashby†	R	25	20	9	0	0	54.0	89	5	32	33	0-4	1	8.50
Curt Leskanic	R	25	18	8	0	0	57.0	59	7	27	30	1-5	0	5.37
Keith Shepherd	R	25	14	1	0	0	19.1	26	4	4	7	1-3	1	6.98
Mark Grant†	R	29	14	0	0	0	14.1	23	4	6	8	0-1	1	12.56
Bryn Smith	R	37	11	5	0	0	29.2	47	2	11	9	2-4	0	8.49
Scott Aldred†	L	25	5	0	0	0	6.2	10	1	9	5	0-0	0	10.80
Mark Knudson	R	32	4	0	0	0	5.2	16	4	5	3	0-0	0	22.24
Scott Service†	R	26	3	0	0	0	4.2	8	1	1	3	0-0	0	9.64

1993 San Diego Padres 7th NL West 61-101 .377 43.0 GB

Jim Riggleman

Player	Gm by Position	B	Age	G	AB	R	H	2B	3B	HR	RBI	BB	SO	SB	Avg	OBP	Slg
Kevin Higgins	C59,3B4,1B3*	L	26	71	181	17	40	4	1	0	13	16	17	0	.221	.294	.254
Fred McGriff†	1B83	L	29	83	302	52	83	11	1	18	46	42	55	4	.275	.361	.497
Jeff Gardner	2B133,3B1,SS1	L	29	140	404	53	106	21	7	1	24	45	69	2	.262	.337	.356
Gary Sheffield†	3B67	R	24	68	258	34	76	12	2	10	36	18	30	5	.295	.344	.473
Ricky Gutierrez	SS117,2B6,OF5*	R	23	133	438	76	110	10	5	5	26	50	97	4	.251	.334	.331
Phil Plantier	OF134	L	24	138	462	67	111	20	1	34	100	61	124	4	.240	.335	.509
Derek Bell	OF125,3B19	R	24	150	542	73	142	19	1	21	72	23	122	26	.262	.303	.417
Tony Gwynn	OF121	L	33	122	489	70	175	41	3	7	59	36	19	14	.358	.398	.497
Archi Cianfrocco†	3B64,1B31	R	26	84	279	27	68	10	2	11	47	17	64	2	.244	.289	.412
Phil Clark	OF36,1B24,C11*	R	25	102	240	33	75	17	0	9	33	8	31	2	.313	.345	.496
Craig Shipley	SS38,3B37,2B12*	R	30	105	230	25	54	9	0	4	22	10	31	12	.235	.275	.326
Tim Teufel	2B52,3B9,1B8	R	34	96	200	26	50	11	2	7	31	27	39	2	.250	.338	.430
Billy Bean	OF54,1B12	L	29	88	177	19	46	9	0	5	32	6	29	2	.260	.284	.395
Brad Ausmus	C49	R	24	49	160	18	41	8	1	5	12	6	28	2	.256	.283	.413
Bob Geren	C49,1B1,3B1	R	31	58	145	8	31	6	0	3	6	13	28	0	.214	.278	.317
G. Velasquez	1B38,OF6	L	25	79	143	7	30	2	0	3	20	13	35	0	.210	.274	.287
Jarvis Brown	OF43	R	26	47	133	21	31	9	2	0	8	15	26	3	.233	.335	.331
Kurt Stillwell†	SS30,3B3	S	28	57	121	9	26	4	0	1	11	11	22	4	.215	.286	.273
Dan Walters	C26	R	27	27	94	6	19	3	0	1	10	7	13	0	.202	.255	.266
Darrell Sherman	OF26	L	25	37	63	8	14	1	0	0	2	6	8	2	.222	.315	.238
Melvin Nieves	OF15	S	21	19	47	4	9	0	0	2	3	3	21	0	.191	.255	.319
Luis Lopez	2B15	S	22	17	43	1	5	1	0	0	1	0	8	0	.116	.114	.140
Dave Staton	1B12	R	25	17	42	7	11	3	0	5	9	3	12	0	.262	.326	.690

K. Higgins, 3 G at OF, 1 G at 2B; R. Gutierrez, 4 G at 3B; P. Clark, 5 G at 3B; C. Shipley, 5 G at OF

Pitcher	T	Age	G	GS	CG	ShO	IP	H	HR	BB	SO	W-L	Sv	ERA
Andy Benes	R	25	34	34	4	2	230.2	200	23	86	179	15-15	0	3.78
Doug Brocail	R	26	24	24	0	0	128.1	143	16	42	70	4-13	0	4.56
Greg Harris†	R	29	22	22	4	0	152.0	151	18	39	83	10-9	0	3.67
Wally Whitehurst	R	29	21	19	0	0	105.2	109	11	30	57	4-7	0	3.83
Tim Worrell	R	25	21	16	0	0	100.2	104	11	43	52	2-7	0	4.92
Andy Ashby†	R	25	12	12	0	0	69.0	79	14	24	44	3-6	0	5.48
Scott Sanders	R	24	9	9	0	0	52.1	54	4	23	37	3-3	0	4.13
Dave Eiland	R	26	10	9	0	0	48.1	58	5	17	14	0-3	0	5.21
Bruce Hurst†	L	35	2	2	0	0	4.1	9	0	3	3	0-1	0	12.46
Gene Harris	R	28	59	0	0	0	59.1	57	3	37	39	6-6	23	3.03
Trevor Hoffman†	R	25	39	0	0	0	54.1	56	5	20	53	2-4	3	4.31
Kerry Taylor	R	22	36	7	0	0	68.1	72	5	49	45	0-5	0	6.45
Mark Davis†	L	32	35	0	0	0	38.1	44	6	20	42	0-3	4	3.52
Roger Mason†	R	34	34	0	0	0	50.0	43	1	18	39	0-7	0	3.24
Rich Rodriguez†	L	30	34	0	0	0	30.0	34	2	9	22	2-3	2	3.30
Pedro A. Martinez	L	24	32	0	0	0	37.0	23	4	13	32	3-1	0	2.43
Tim Mauser†	R	26	28	0	0	0	37.2	36	5	17	32	0-1	0	3.58
Pat Gomez	L	25	27	1	0	0	31.2	35	2	19	26	1-2	0	5.12
Tim Scott†	R	26	24	0	0	0	37.2	38	1	15	30	2-0	0	2.39
Jeremy Hernandez†	R	26	21	0	0	0	34.1	41	2	7	26	0-2	0	4.72
Frank Seminara	R	26	18	7	0	0	46.1	53	5	21	22	3-3	0	4.47
Mark Ettles	R	26	14	0	0	0	18.0	23	4	4	9	1-0	0	6.50
Rudy Seanez	R	24	3	0	0	0	3.1	8	1	2	1	0-0	0	13.50

>>1994 New York Yankees 1st AL East 70-43 .619 —

Buck Showalter

Player	Gm by Position	B	Age	G	AB	R	H	2B	3B	HR	RBI	BB	SO	SB	Avg	OBP	Slg
Mike Stanley	C72,1B7,DH4	R	31	82	290	54	87	20	0	17	57	39	56	0	.300	.384	.545
Don Mattingly	1B97	L	33	97	372	62	113	20	1	6	51	60	24	0	.304	.397	.411
Pat Kelly	2B93	R	26	93	286	35	80	21	2	3	41	19	51	6	.280	.330	.399
Wade Boggs	3B93,1B4	L	36	97	366	61	125	19	1	11	55	61	29	2	.342	.433	.489
Mike Gallego	SS72,2B26	R	33	89	306	39	73	17	1	6	41	38	46	0	.239	.327	.359
Bernie Williams	OF107	S	25	108	408	80	118	29	1	12	57	61	54	16	.289	.384	.453
Paul O'Neill	OF99,DH4	L	31	103	368	68	132	25	1	21	83	72	56	5	.359	.460	.603
Luis Polonia	OF84,DH2	L	29	95	350	62	109	21	6	1	36	37	36	20	.311	.383	.414
Danny Tartabull	DH78,OF26	R	31	104	399	68	102	24	1	19	67	66	111	1	.256	.360	.464
Randy Velarde	SS49,3B27,OF7*	R	31	77	280	47	78	16	1	9	34	22	61	4	.279	.338	.439
Jim Leyritz	C37,DH25,1B10	R	30	75	249	47	66	12	0	17	58	35	61	0	.265	.365	.518
Gerald Williams	OF43,DH2	R	27	57	86	19	25	8	0	4	13	4	17	1	.291	.319	.523
Matt Nokes	C17,DH5,1B4	L	30	28	79	11	23	3	0	7	19	5	16	0	.291	.329	.595
Daryl Boston	OF16,DH9	L	31	52	77	11	14	2	0	4	14	6	20	0	.182	.250	.364
Kevin Elster	SS7	R	29	7	20	0	0	0	0	0	0	1	6	0	.000	.048	.000
Dave Silvestri	2B9,3B2,SS1	R	26	12	18	3	2	0	1	0	2	4	9	0	.111	.261	.389
Bob Melvin†	C4,1B4,DH1	R	32	9	14	2	4	0	0	1	3	0	3	0	.286	.286	.500
Russ Davis	3B4	R	24	4	14	0	2	0	0	0	1	0	4	0	.143	.143	.143
Robert Eenhoorn	SS3	R	26	3	4	1	2	1	0	0	0	0	0	0	.500	.500	.750

R. Velarde, 5 G at 2B

Pitcher	T	Age	G	GS	CG	ShO	IP	H	HR	BB	SO	W-L	Sv	ERA
Jimmy Key	L	33	25	25	1	0	168.0	177	10	52	97	17-4	0	3.27
Jim Abbott	L	26	24	24	2	0	160.1	167	24	64	90	9-8	0	4.55
Melido Perez	R	28	22	22	1	0	151.1	134	16	58	109	9-4	0	4.10
Terry Mulholland	L	31	24	19	2	0	120.2	150	24	37	72	6-7	0	6.49
Scott Kamieniecki	R	30	22	16	1	0	117.1	115	13	59	71	8-6	0	3.76
Bobby Ojeda	L	36	2	2	0	0	3.0	11	1	6	3	0-0	0	24.00
Bob Wickman	R	25	53	0	0	0	70.0	54	3	27	56	5-4	6	3.09
Steve Howe	L	36	40	0	0	0	40.0	28	2	7	18	3-0	15	1.80
Xavier Hernandez	R	28	31	0	0	0	40.0	48	7	21	37	4-4	6	5.85
Paul Gibson	L	34	30	0	0	0	29.0	26	5	17	21	1-1	0	4.97
Donn Pall†	R	32	26	0	0	0	35.0	43	3	9	21	1-2	0	3.60
Sterling Hitchcock	L	23	23	5	1	0	49.1	48	3	29	37	4-1	2	4.20
Joe Ausanio	R	28	13	0	0	0	15.2	16	3	6	15	2-1	0	5.17
Jeff Reardon	R	38	11	0	0	0	9.2	17	3	3	4	1-0	2	8.38
Greg Harris†	R	38	3	0	0	0	5.0	4	1	3	4	0-1	0	5.40
Rob Murphy†	L	34	3	0	0	0	1.2	3	2	0	0	0-0	0	16.20
Mark Hutton	R	24	2	0	0	0	3.2	4	0	0	1	0-0	0	4.91

1994 Baltimore Orioles 2nd AL East 63-49 .563 6.5 GB

Johnny Oates

Player	Gm by Position	B	Age	G	AB	R	H	2B	3B	HR	RBI	BB	SO	SB	Avg	OBP	Slg
Chris Hoiles	C98	R	29	99	332	45	82	10	0	19	53	63	73	2	.247	.371	.449
Rafael Palmeiro	1B111	L	29	111	436	82	139	32	0	23	76	54	63	7	.319	.392	.550
Mark McLemore	2B96,OF7,DH1	S	29	104	343	44	88	11	1	3	29	51	50	20	.257	.354	.321
Leo Gomez	3B78,DH5,1B1	R	28	84	285	46	78	20	0	15	56	41	55	0	.274	.366	.502
Cal Ripken Jr.	SS112	R	33	112	444	71	140	19	3	13	75	32	41	1	.315	.364	.459
Brady Anderson	OF109	L	30	111	453	78	119	25	5	12	48	57	75	31	.263	.356	.419
Mike Devereaux	OF84,DH1	R	31	85	301	35	61	8	2	9	33	22	72	1	.203	.256	.332
Jeffrey Hammonds	OF66	R	23	68	250	45	74	18	2	8	31	17	39	5	.296	.339	.480
Harold Baines	DH91	L	35	94	326	44	96	12	1	16	54	30	49	0	.294	.356	.485
Chris Sabo	3B37,OF22,DH10	R	32	68	258	41	66	15	3	11	42	20	38	1	.256	.320	.465
Jack Voigt	OF54,1B6,DH2	R	28	59	141	15	34	5	0	3	20	18	25	0	.241	.327	.340
Tim Hulett	2B23,3B9,SS6	R	34	36	92	11	21	2	1	2	15	12	24	0	.228	.314	.337
Dwight Smith†	OF22,DH3	L	30	28	74	12	23	2	1	3	12	5	17	0	.311	.363	.486
Lonnie Smith	DH30,OF2	R	38	35	59	13	12	3	0	0	2	11	18	1	.203	.333	.254
Jeff Tackett	C26	R	28	26	53	5	12	3	1	2	9	5	13	0	.226	.317	.434
Mark Smith	OF3	R	24	3	7	0	1	0	0	0	2	0	2	0	.143	.143	.143
Damon Buford	DH1,OF1	R	24	4	2	2	1	0	0	0	0	0	1	0	.500	.500	.500

Pitcher	T	Age	G	GS	CG	ShO	IP	H	HR	BB	SO	W-L	Sv	ERA
Mike Mussina	R	25	24	24	3	0	176.1	163	19	42	99	16-5	0	3.06
Ben McDonald	R	26	24	24	5	1	157.1	151	14	54	94	14-7	0	4.06
Jamie Moyer	L	31	23	23	0	0	149.0	158	23	38	87	5-7	0	4.77
Sid Fernandez	L	31	19	19	2	0	115.1	109	27	46	95	6-6	0	5.15
Arthur Rhodes	L	24	10	10	3	2	52.2	51	8	30	47	3-5	0	5.81
Mike Oquist	R	26	15	9	0	0	58.1	75	7	30	39	3-3	0	6.17
Scott Klingenbeck	R	23	1	1	0	0	7.0	6	1	4	5	1-0	0	3.86
Alan Mills	R	27	47	0	0	0	45.1	43	7	24	44	3-3	2	5.16
Mark Eichhorn	R	33	43	0	0	0	71.0	62	1	19	35	6-5	1	2.15
Lee Smith	R	36	41	0	0	0	38.1	34	6	11	42	1-4	33	3.29
Jim Poole	L	28	38	0	0	0	20.1	32	4	11	18	1-0	0	6.64
Mark Williamson	R	34	28	2	0	0	67.1	75	9	17	28	3-1	1	4.01
Tom Bolton	L	32	22	0	0	0	23.1	29	3	13	12	1-2	0	5.40
Brad Pennington	L	25	8	0	0	0	6.0	9	2	8	7	0-1	0	12.00
Armando Benitez	R	21	3	0	0	0	10.0	8	0	4	14	0-0	0	0.90

1994 Toronto Blue Jays 3rd AL East 55-60 .478 16.0 GB

Cito Gaston

Player	Gm by Position	B	Age	G	AB	R	H	2B	3B	HR	RBI	BB	SO	SB	Avg	OBP	Slg
Pat Borders	C85	R	31	85	295	24	73	13	1	3	26	15	50	1	.247	.284	.329
John Olerud	1B104,DH3	L	25	108	384	47	114	29	2	12	67	61	53	1	.297	.393	.477
Roberto Alomar	2B106	S	26	107	392	78	120	25	4	8	38	51	41	19	.306	.386	.452
Ed Sprague	3B107,1B3	R	26	109	405	38	97	19	1	11	44	23	95	1	.240	.296	.373
Dick Schofield	SS95	R	31	95	325	38	83	14	1	4	32	34	62	7	.255	.332	.342
Joe Carter	OF110,DH1	R	34	111	435	70	118	25	2	27	103	33	64	11	.271	.317	.524
Devon White	OF98	S	31	100	403	67	109	24	6	13	49	21	80	11	.270	.313	.457
Mike Huff	OF76	R	30	80	207	31	63	15	3	3	25	27	27	2	.304	.392	.449
Paul Molitor	DH110,1B5	R	37	115	454	86	155	30	4	14	75	55	48	20	.341	.410	.518
Darnell Coles	OF29,1B10,3B7*	R	32	48	143	15	30	6	1	4	15	10	25	0	.210	.263	.350
Carlos Delgado	OF41,C1	L	22	43	130	17	28	2	0	9	24	25	46	1	.215	.352	.438
Randy Knorr	C40	R	25	40	124	20	30	2	0	7	19	10	35	0	.242	.301	.427
Domingo Cedeno	2B28,SS8,3B6*	S	25	47	97	14	19	2	3	0	10	10	31	1	.196	.261	.278
Rob Butler	OF31,DH1	L	24	41	74	13	13	0	1	0	5	7	8	0	.176	.250	.203
Alex Gonzalez	SS15	R	21	15	53	7	8	3	1	0	1	4	17	3	.151	.224	.245
Shawn Green	OF14	L	21	14	33	1	3	1	0	0	1	1	8	1	.091	.118	.121
Robert Perez	OF4	R	25	4	8	0	1	0	0	0	0	0	1	0	.125	.125	.125

D. Coles, 1 G at DH; D. Cedeno, 1 G at OF

Pitcher	T	Age	G	GS	CG	ShO	IP	H	HR	BB	SO	W-L	Sv	ERA
Juan Guzman	R	27	25	25	2	0	147.1	165	20	76	124	12-11	0	5.68
Pat Hentgen	R	25	24	24	6	3	174.2	158	21	59	147	13-8	0	3.40
Dave Stewart	R	37	22	22	1	0	133.1	151	26	62	111	7-8	0	5.87
Al Leiter	L	28	20	20	1	0	111.2	125	6	65	100	6-7	0	5.08
Todd Stottlemyre	R	29	26	19	3	1	140.2	149	19	48	105	7-7	1	4.22
Paul Spoljaric	L	23	2	1	0	0	2.1	5	3	9	2	0-1	0	38.57
Tony Castillo	L	31	41	0	0	0	68.0	66	7	28	43	5-2	1	2.51
Woody Williams	R	27	38	0	0	0	59.1	44	5	33	56	1-3	0	3.64
Mike Timlin	R	28	34	0	0	0	40.0	41	5	20	38	0-1	2	5.18
Darren Hall	R	29	30	0	0	0	31.2	26	3	14	28	2-3	17	3.41
Greg Cadaret†	L	32	21	0	0	0	20.0	24	4	17	15	0-1	0	5.85
Scott Brow	R	25	18	0	0	0	29.0	34	4	19	15	0-3	2	5.90
Dave Righetti†	L	35	13	0	0	0	13.1	9	2	10	10	0-1	0	6.75
Danny Cox	R	34	10	0	0	0	18.2	7	0	7	14	1-1	3	1.45
Brad Cornett	R	25	9	4	0	0	31.0	40	1	11	22	1-3	0	6.68
Randy St. Claire	R	33	2	0	0	0	2.0	4	0	2	2	0-0	0	9.00
Aaron Small	R	22	1	0	0	0	2.0	5	1	2	0	0-0	0	9.00

1994 Boston Red Sox 4th AL East 54-61 .470 17.0 GB

Butch Hobson

Player	Gm by Position	B	Age	G	AB	R	H	2B	3B	HR	RBI	BB	SO	SB	Avg	OBP	Slg
Damon Berryhill	C67,DH6	S	30	82	255	30	67	17	2	6	34	19	59	0	.263	.312	.416
Mo Vaughn	1B106,DH1	L	26	111	394	65	122	25	1	26	82	57	112	4	.310	.408	.576
Scott Fletcher	2B53,DH4	R	35	63	185	31	42	9	1	3	11	16	14	8	.227	.296	.335
Scott Cooper	3B104	L	26	104	369	49	104	16	4	13	53	30	65	0	.282	.333	.453
John Valentin	SS83	R	27	84	301	53	95	26	2	9	49	42	38	3	.316	.400	.505
Otis Nixon	OF103	S	35	103	398	60	109	15	1	0	25	55	65	42	.274	.360	.317
Mike Greenwell	OF84,DH6	L	30	95	327	60	88	25	1	11	45	38	26	2	.269	.348	.453
Lee Tinsley	OF60,DH10	S	25	78	144	27	32	4	0	2	14	19	36	13	.222	.315	.292
Andre Dawson	DH74	R	39	75	292	34	70	18	0	16	48	9	53	2	.240	.271	.466
Tim Naehring	2B49,3B11,1B8*	R	27	80	297	41	82	18	1	7	42	30	56	1	.276	.349	.414
Tom Brunansky†	OF42,1B5,DH3	R	33	48	177	22	42	10	1	10	34	23	48	0	.237	.319	.475
Carlos Rodriguez	SS32,2B20,3B4	S	26	57	174	15	50	14	1	1	13	11	13	1	.287	.330	.397
Billy Hatcher†	OF43,DH1	R	33	44	164	24	40	9	1	1	18	11	14	4	.244	.292	.329
Wes Chamberlain†	OF34,DH12	R	28	51	164	13	42	9	1	4	20	12	38	0	.256	.307	.396
Rich Rowland	C39,DH4,1B1	R	30	46	118	14	27	3	0	9	20	11	35	0	.229	.295	.483
Dave Valle†	C28,1B2	R	33	30	76	6	12	2	1	1	5	9	18	0	.158	.256	.250
Andy Tomberlin	OF11,DH5,P1	L	27	18	36	1	7	0	1	1	1	6	12	1	.194	.310	.333
Greg Litton	2B4,1B3,3B2*	R	29	11	21	2	2	0	0	0	1	0	5	0	.095	.091	.095
Luis Ortiz	DH6	R	24	7	18	3	3	2	0	0	6	1	5	0	.167	.182	.278
Greg Blosser	OF3,DH1	L	23	5	11	2	1	0	0	0	1	4	4	0	.091	.333	.091
Stan Royer†	3B3,1B1	R	26	4	9	0	1	0	0	0	1	0	3	0	.111	.111	.111
Eric Wedge	DH2	R	26	2	6	0	0	0	0	0	0	1	3	0	.000	.143	.000
Bob Zupcic†	OF2,DH1	R	27	4	4	0	0	0	0	0	0	0	1	0	.000	.000	.000

T. Naehring, 8 G at SS, 7 G at DH; G. Litton, 1 G at DH

Pitcher	T	Age	G	GS	CG	ShO	IP	H	HR	BB	SO	W-L	Sv	ERA
Roger Clemens	R	31	24	24	3	1	170.2	124	15	71	168	9-7	0	2.85
Aaron Sele	R	24	22	22	2	0	143.1	140	13	60	105	8-7	0	3.83
Joe Hesketh	L	35	25	20	0	0	114.0	117	9	46	83	8-5	0	4.26
Danny Darwin	R	38	13	13	0	0	75.2	101	13	24	54	7-5	0	6.30
Chris Nabholz†	L	27	8	8	0	0	42.0	44	5	29	23	3-4	0	6.64
Gar Finnvold	R	26	8	8	0	0	36.1	45	4	15	17	0-4	0	5.94
Tim VanEgmond	R	25	7	7	1	0	38.1	38	7	21	22	2-3	0	6.34
Frank Viola	L	34	6	6	0	0	31.0	34	2	17	9	1-1	0	4.65
Nate Minchey	R	24	6	5	0	0	23.0	44	1	14	15	2-3	0	8.61
Tony Fossas	L	36	44	0	0	0	34.0	35	6	15	31	2-0	1	4.76
Ken Ryan	R	25	42	0	0	0	48.0	46	1	17	32	2-3	13	2.44
Chris Howard	L	28	37	0	0	0	39.2	35	5	12	22	1-0	1	3.63
Greg Harris†	R	38	35	0	0	0	45.2	60	8	23	44	3-4	2	8.28
Jeff Russell†	R	32	29	0	0	0	28.0	30	3	13	18	0-5	12	5.14
Scott Bankhead	R	30	27	0	0	0	37.2	34	5	12	25	3-2	0	4.54
Todd Frohwirth	R	31	22	0	0	0	26.2	40	3	17	13	0-3	1	10.80
Paul Quantrill†	R	25	17	0	0	0	23.0	25	4	5	15	1-1	0	3.52
Ricky Trlicek	R	25	12	1	0	0	22.1	32	5	16	7	1-1	0	8.06
Sergio Valdez	R	29	12	1	0	0	14.1	25	4	8	4	0-1	0	8.16
Steve Farr†	R	37	11	0	0	0	13.0	24	2	8	8	1-0	0	6.23
Jose Melendez	R	28	10	0	0	0	16.1	20	3	8	9	0-1	0	6.06
Cory Bailey	R	23	5	0	0	0	4.1	10	2	3	4	0-1	0	12.46
Andy Tomberlin	L	27	1	0	0	0	2.0	1	0	1	1	0-0	0	0.00

1994 Detroit Tigers 5th AL East 53-62 .461 18.0 GB

Sparky Anderson

Player	Gm by Position	B	Age	G	AB	R	H	2B	3B	HR	RBI	BB	SO	SB	Avg	OBP	Slg
Chad Kreuter	C64,1B1,OF1	S	29	65	170	17	38	8	0	1	19	28	36	0	.224	.327	.288
Cecil Fielder	1B102,DH7	R	30	109	425	67	110	16	2	28	90	50	110	0	.259	.337	.504
Lou Whitaker	2B83,DH5	L	37	92	322	67	97	21	2	12	43	41	47	2	.301	.377	.491
Travis Fryman	3B114	R	25	114	464	66	122	34	5	18	85	45	128	2	.263	.326	.474
Alan Trammell	SS63,DH11	R	36	76	292	38	78	17	1	8	28	16	35	3	.267	.307	.414
Tony Phillips	OF104,2B12,DH6	S	35	114	438	91	123	19	3	19	61	95	105	13	.281	.409	.468
Junior Felix	OF81,DH2	S	26	86	301	54	92	25	1	13	49	26	76	1	.306	.372	.525
Milt Cuyler	OF45	S	25	48	116	20	28	3	1	1	11	13	21	5	.241	.318	.310
Kirk Gibson	DH56,OF38	L	37	98	330	71	91	17	2	23	72	42	69	4	.276	.358	.548
Mickey Tettleton	C53,1B24,DH22*	S	33	107	339	57	84	18	2	17	51	97	98	0	.248	.419	.463
Chris Gomez	SS57,2B30	R	23	84	296	32	76	19	0	8	53	33	64	5	.257	.336	.402
Juan Samuel	OF27,DH10,2B8*	R	33	59	136	32	42	9	5	5	21	10	26	5	.309	.364	.559
Eric Davis	OF35	R	32	37	120	19	22	4	0	3	13	18	45	5	.183	.290	.292
Danny Bautista	OF30,DH1	R	22	31	99	12	23	4	1	4	15	3	18	1	.232	.255	.414
John Flaherty	C33,DH1	R	26	34	40	2	6	1	0	0	4	1	11	0	.150	.167	.175
Scott Livingstone†	DH5,1B5,3B1	L	28	15	23	0	5	1	0	0	1	1	4	0	.217	.250	.261
Riccardo Ingram	OF8,DH1	R	27	12	23	3	5	0	0	0	2	1	2	0	.217	.240	.217
Skeeter Barnes	1B15,OF4,DH1	R	37	24	21	4	6	0	0	1	4	0	2	0	.286	.286	.429

M. Tettleton, 18 G at OF; J. Samuel, 2 G at 1B

Pitcher	T	Age	G	GS	CG	ShO	IP	H	HR	BB	SO	W-L	Sv	ERA
Tim Belcher	R	32	25	25	3	0	162.0	192	21	78	76	7-15	0	5.89
Mike Moore	R	34	25	25	4	0	154.1	152	27	89	62	11-10	0	5.42
Bill Gullickson	R	35	21	19	1	0	115.1	156	24	25	65	4-5	0	5.93
John Doherty	R	27	18	17	2	0	101.1	139	13	26	28	6-7	0	6.48
David Wells	L	31	16	16	5	1	111.1	113	13	24	71	5-7	0	3.96
Greg Gohr	R	26	8	6	0	0	34.0	36	3	21	21	2-2	0	4.50
Sean Bergman	R	24	3	3	0	0	17.2	22	2	7	12	2-1	0	5.60
Joe Boever	R	33	46	0	0	0	81.1	80	12	37	49	9-2	3	3.98
Buddy Groom	L	28	40	0	0	0	32.0	31	4	13	27	0-1	1	3.94
Mike Gardiner	R	28	38	1	0	0	58.2	53	10	23	31	2-2	5	4.14
Storm Davis	R	32	35	0	0	0	48.0	36	3	34	38	2-4	0	3.56
Mike Henneman	R	32	30	0	0	0	34.2	43	5	17	27	1-3	8	5.19
Greg Cadaret†	L	32	17	0	0	0	20.0	17	0	16	14	1-0	2	3.60
Bill Krueger†	L	36	16	2	0	0	19.2	26	3	17	17	0-2	0	9.61
Gene Harris†	R	29	11	0	0	0	11.1	13	1	4	10	0-0	1	7.15
Phil Stidham	R	25	5	0	0	0	4.1	12	3	4	4	0-0	0	24.92
Kurt Knudsen	R	27	4	0	0	0	5.1	7	2	11	1	1-0	0	13.50
Jose Lima	R	21	3	1	0	0	6.2	11	2	3	7	0-1	0	13.50

1994 Chicago White Sox 1st AL Central 67-46 .593 —

Gene Lamont

Player	Gm by Position	B	Age	G	AB	R	H	2B	3B	HR	RBI	BB	SO	SB	Avg	OBP	Slg
Ron Karkovice	C76	R	30	77	207	33	44	9	1	11	29	36	68	0	.213	.325	.425
Frank Thomas	1B99,DH13	R	26	113	399	106	141	34	1	38	101	109	61	2	.353	.487	.729
Joey Cora	2B84,DH1	S	29	90	312	55	86	13	4	2	30	38	32	8	.276	.353	.362
Robin Ventura	3B108,1B3,SS1	L	26	109	401	57	113	15	1	18	78	61	69	3	.282	.373	.459
Ozzie Guillen	SS99	L	30	100	365	46	105	9	5	1	39	14	35	5	.288	.311	.348
Lance Johnson	OF103,DH1	L	30	106	412	56	114	11	14	3	54	26	23	26	.277	.321	.393
Darrin Jackson	OF102	R	30	104	369	43	115	17	3	10	51	27	56	7	.312	.362	.455
Tim Raines	OF96	S	34	101	384	80	102	15	5	10	52	61	43	13	.266	.365	.409
Julio Franco	DH99,1B14	R	32	112	433	72	138	19	2	20	98	62	75	8	.319	.406	.510
Mike LaValliere	C57	L	33	59	139	6	39	4	0	1	24	20	15	0	.281	.368	.331
Norberto Martin	2B28,SS6,3B5*	R	27	45	131	19	36	7	1	1	16	9	16	4	.275	.317	.366
Warren Newson	OF34,DH3	L	29	63	102	16	26	5	0	2	7	14	23	1	.255	.345	.363
Craig Grebeck	2B14,SS14,3B7	R	29	35	97	17	30	5	0	0	5	12	5	0	.309	.391	.361
Bob Zupcic†	OF28,3B2,1B1	R	27	32	88	10	18	4	1	1	8	4	16	0	.205	.237	.307
Joe Hall	OF9,DH2	R	28	17	28	6	11	3	0	1	5	2	4	0	.393	.452	.607
Dan Pasqua	OF5,1B3	L	32	11	23	2	5	2	0	2	4	0	9	0	.217	.217	.565
Bob Melvin†	C11	R	32	11	19	3	3	0	0	0	1	1	4	0	.158	.200	.158
Dann Howitt	OF7,1B4	L	30	10	14	4	5	3	0	0	0	1	7	0	.357	.400	.571
Olmedo Saenz	3B5	R	23	5	14	2	2	0	1	0	0	0	5	0	.143	.143	.286
Ron Tingley†	C5	R	35	5	5	0	0	0	0	0	0	0	2	0	.000	.000	.000

N. Martin, 2 G at OF, 1 G at DH

Pitcher	T	Age	G	GS	CG	ShO	IP	H	HR	BB	SO	W-L	Sv	ERA
Jack McDowell	R	28	25	25	6	2	181.0	186	12	42	127	10-9	0	3.73
Alex Fernandez	R	24	24	24	4	3	170.1	163	25	50	122	11-7	0	3.86
Wilson Alvarez	L	24	24	24	2	1	161.2	147	16	62	108	12-8	0	3.45
Jason Bere	R	23	24	24	0	0	141.2	119	17	80	127	12-2	0	3.81
Scott Sanderson	R	37	18	14	1	0	92.0	110	20	12	36	8-4	0	5.09
Scott Ruffcorn	R	24	2	2	0	0	6.1	15	1	5	3	0-2	0	12.79
Roberto Hernandez	R	29	45	0	0	0	47.2	44	5	19	50	4-4	14	4.91
Paul Assenmacher	L	33	44	0	0	0	33.0	26	2	13	29	1-2	1	3.55
Jose DeLeon	R	33	42	0	0	0	67.0	48	5	31	67	3-2	2	3.36
Kirk McCaskill	R	33	40	0	0	0	52.2	51	6	22	37	1-4	3	3.42
Dennis Cook	L	31	38	0	0	0	33.0	29	4	14	26	3-1	0	3.55
Dane Johnson	R	31	15	0	0	0	12.1	16	2	11	7	2-1	0	6.57
Jeff Schwarz†	R	30	9	0	0	0	11.1	9	0	16	14	0-0	0	6.35
Atlee Hammaker	L	36	2	0	0	0	1.1	1	0	0	1	0-0	0	0.00

1994 Cleveland Indians 2nd AL Central 66-47 .584 1.0 GB

Mike Hargrove

Player	Gm by Position	B	Age	G	AB	R	H	2B	3B	HR	RBI	BB	SO	SB	Avg	OBP	Slg
Sandy Alomar Jr.	C78	R	28	80	292	44	84	15	1	14	43	25	31	8	.288	.347	.490
Paul Sorrento	1B86,DH8	L	28	95	322	43	90	14	0	14	62	34	68	0	.280	.345	.453
Carlos Baerga	2B102,DH1	S	25	103	442	81	139	32	2	19	80	10	45	8	.314	.333	.525
Jim Thome	3B94	L	23	98	321	58	86	20	1	20	52	46	84	3	.268	.359	.523
Omar Vizquel	SS69	S	27	69	286	39	78	10	1	1	33	23	23	13	.273	.325	.325
Kenny Lofton	OF112	L	27	112	459	105	160	32	9	12	57	52	56	60	.349	.412	.536
Albert Belle	OF104,DH2	R	27	106	412	90	147	35	2	36	101	58	71	9	.357	.438	.714
Manny Ramirez	OF84,DH5	R	22	91	290	51	78	22	0	17	60	42	72	4	.269	.357	.521
Eddie Murray	DH82,1B26	S	38	108	433	57	110	21	1	17	76	31	53	8	.254	.302	.425
Alvaro Espinoza	3B37,SS36,2B20*	R	32	90	231	27	55	13	0	1	19	6	33	1	.238	.258	.307
Wayne Kirby	OF68,DH2	L	30	78	191	33	56	6	0	5	23	13	30	11	.293	.341	.403
Tony Pena	C40	R	37	40	112	18	33	8	1	2	10	9	11	0	.295	.341	.438
Candy Maldonado	DH25,OF5	R	33	42	92	14	18	5	1	5	12	19	31	1	.196	.333	.435
Mark Lewis	SS13,3B6,2B1	R	24	20	73	6	15	5	0	1	8	2	13	1	.205	.227	.315
Rene Gonzales	3B13,1B4,SS4*	R	33	22	23	6	8	1	1	1	5	5	3	2	.348	.448	.609
Ruben Amaro	OF12,DH3	S	29	26	23	5	5	1	0	2	5	2	3	2	.217	.280	.522
Matt Merullo	C4	L	28	4	10	1	1	0	0	0	0	2	1	0	.100	.250	.100
Herbert Perry	1B2,3B2	R	24	4	9	1	1	0	0	0	1	3	1	0	.111	.357	.111
Jesse Levis		L	26	1	1	0	1	0	0	0	0	0	0	0	1.000	1.000	1.000

A. Espinoza, 3 G at 1B; R. Gonzales, 1 G at 2B

Pitcher	T	Age	G	GS	CG	ShO	IP	H	HR	BB	SO	W-L	Sv	ERA
Dennis Martinez	R	39	24	24	7	3	176.2	166	14	44	92	11-6	0	3.52
Charles Nagy	R	27	23	23	3	0	169.1	175	15	48	108	10-8	0	3.45
Jack Morris	R	39	23	23	1	0	141.1	163	14	67	100	10-6	0	5.60
Mark Clark	R	26	20	20	4	1	127.1	133	14	40	60	11-3	0	3.82
Jason Grimsley	R	26	14	13	1	0	82.2	91	7	34	59	5-2	0	4.57
Albie Lopez	R	22	4	4	1	1	17.0	20	3	6	18	1-2	0	4.24
Chris Nabholz†	L	27	6	4	0	0	11.0	23	1	9	5	0-1	0	11.45
Julian Tavarez	R	21	1	1	0	0	1.2	6	1	1	0	0-1	0	21.60
Jose Mesa	R	28	51	0	0	0	73.0	71	3	26	63	7-5	2	3.82
Eric Plunk	R	30	41	0	0	0	71.0	61	3	37	73	7-2	3	2.54
Derek Lilliquist	L	28	36	0	0	0	29.1	34	6	8	15	1-3	1	4.91
Steve Farr†	R	37	19	0	0	0	15.1	17	3	15	12	1-1	4	5.28
Paul Shuey	R	23	14	0	0	0	11.2	14	1	12	16	0-1	5	8.49
Jeff Russell†	R	32	13	0	0	0	12.2	13	2	3	10	1-1	5	4.97
Russ Swan	L	30	12	0	0	0	8.0	13	1	7	2	0-1	0	11.25
Matt Turner	R	27	9	0	0	0	12.2	13	0	7	5	1-0	1	2.13
Jerry Dipoto	R	26	7	0	0	0	15.2	26	1	10	9	0-0	0	8.04
Larry Casian†	L	28	7	0	0	0	8.1	16	1	4	2	0-2	0	8.64
Brian Barnes†	L	27	6	0	0	0	13.1	12	2	15	5	0-1	0	5.40
Chad Ogea	R	23	4	1	0	0	16.1	21	2	10	11	0-1	0	6.06
Bill Wertz	R	27	1	0	0	0	4.1	9	0	1	1	0-0	0	10.38

1994 Kansas City Royals 3rd AL Central 64-51 .557 4.0 GB

Hal McRae

Player	Gm by Position	B	Age	G	AB	R	H	2B	3B	HR	RBI	BB	SO	SB	Avg	OBP	Slg
Mike Macfarlane	C81,DH8	R	30	92	314	53	80	17	3	14	47	35	71	1	.255	.359	.462
Wally Joyner	1B86,DH11	L	32	97	363	52	113	20	3	8	57	47	43	3	.311	.386	.449
Jose Lind	2B84,DH1	R	30	85	290	34	78	16	2	1	31	16	34	9	.269	.306	.348
Gary Gaetti	3B85,1B9	R	35	90	327	53	94	15	3	12	57	19	63	0	.287	.328	.462
Greg Gagne	SS106	R	32	107	375	39	97	23	3	7	51	27	79	10	.259	.314	.392
Brian McRae	OF110,DH4	S	26	114	436	71	119	22	6	4	40	54	67	28	.273	.359	.378
Vince Coleman	OF99,DH5	S	32	104	438	61	105	14	12	2	33	29	72	50	.240	.285	.340
Felix Jose	OF98	S	29	99	366	56	111	28	1	11	55	35	75	10	.303	.362	.475
Bob Hamelin	DH70,1B24	L	26	101	312	64	88	25	1	24	65	56	62	4	.282	.388	.599
Dave Henderson	OF40,DH16	R	35	56	198	27	49	14	1	5	31	16	28	2	.247	.304	.404
Terry Shumpert	2B38,3B24,DH2*	R	27	64	183	28	44	6	2	8	24	13	39	18	.240	.289	.426
Brent Mayne	C42,DH3	L	26	46	144	19	37	5	1	2	20	14	27	1	.257	.323	.347
Dave Howard	3B25,SS15,2B3*	S	27	46	83	9	19	4	0	1	13	11	23	3	.229	.309	.313
Hubie Brooks	DH19,1B4	R	37	34	61	5	14	2	0	1	14	2	10	1	.230	.239	.311
Keith Miller	OF4,3B2	R	31	5	15	1	2	0	0	0	0	0	3	0	.133	.133	.133
Kevin Koslofski	OF2	L	27	2	4	2	1	0	0	0	0	2	1	0	.250	.500	.250
Tom Goodwin	DH1,OF1	L	25	2	2	0	0	0	0	0	0	0	1	0	.000	.000	.000

T. Shumpert, 1 G at SS; D. Howard, 2 G at DH, 1 G at P, 1 G at OF

Pitcher	T	Age	G	GS	CG	ShO	IP	H	HR	BB	SO	W-L	Sv	ERA
Tom Gordon	R	26	24	24	0	0	155.1	136	15	87	126	11-7	0	4.35
David Cone	R	31	23	23	4	3	171.2	130	15	54	132	16-5	0	2.94
Kevin Appier	R	26	23	23	1	0	155.0	137	11	63	145	7-6	0	3.83
Mark Gubicza	R	31	22	22	0	0	130.0	158	11	26	59	7-9	0	4.50
Bob Milacki	R	29	10	10	0	0	55.2	68	6	20	17	0-5	0	6.14
Chris Haney	L	25	6	6	0	0	28.1	36	2	11	18	2-2	0	7.31
Jose DeJesus	R	29	5	4	0	0	26.2	27	2	13	12	3-1	0	4.73
Jeff Granger	L	22	2	2	0	0	9.1	13	2	6	3	0-1	0	6.75
Billy Brewer	L	26	50	0	0	0	38.2	28	4	16	25	4-1	3	2.56
Hipolito Pichardo	R	24	45	0	0	0	67.2	82	4	24	36	5-3	3	4.92
Jeff Montgomery	R	32	42	0	0	0	44.2	48	5	15	50	2-3	27	4.03
Stan Belinda	R	27	37	0	0	0	49.0	47	6	24	37	2-2	1	5.14
Rusty Meacham	R	26	36	0	0	0	50.2	51	7	12	36	3-3	4	3.73
Mike Magnante	L	29	36	1	0	0	47.0	55	5	16	21	2-3	0	4.60
Dave Howard	R	27	1	0	0	0	2.0	2	0	5	0	0-0	0	4.50

1994 Minnesota Twins 4th AL Central 53-60 .469 14.0 GB

Tom Kelly

Player	Gm by Position	B	Age	G	AB	R	H	2B	3B	HR	RBI	BB	SO	SB	Avg	OBP	Slg
Matt Walbeck	C95,DH1	S	24	97	338	31	69	12	0	5	35	17	37	1	.204	.246	.284
Kent Hrbek	1B72,DH4	L	34	81	274	34	74	11	0	10	53	37	28	0	.270	.353	.420
Chuck Knoblauch	2B109,SS1	R	25	109	445	85	139	45	3	5	51	41	56	35	.312	.381	.461
Scott Leius	3B95,SS2	R	28	97	350	57	86	16	1	14	49	37	58	2	.246	.318	.417
Pat Meares	SS79	R	25	80	229	29	61	12	1	2	24	14	50	5	.266	.310	.354
Alex Cole	OF100,DH1	L	28	105	345	68	102	15	5	4	23	44	60	29	.296	.375	.403
Kirby Puckett	OF95,DH13	R	33	108	439	79	139	32	3	20	112	28	47	6	.317	.362	.540
Shane Mack	OF75,DH4	R	30	81	303	55	101	21	2	15	61	32	51	4	.333	.402	.564
Dave Winfield	DH76,OF1	R	42	77	294	35	74	15	3	10	43	31	51	2	.252	.321	.425
Pedro Munoz	OF58,DH12	R	25	75	244	35	72	15	2	11	36	19	67	0	.295	.348	.508
Jeff Reboulet	SS42,2B14,1B10*	R	30	74	189	28	49	11	1	3	23	18	23	0	.259	.327	.376
Dave McCarty	1B32,OF14	R	24	44	131	21	34	8	2	1	12	7	32	2	.260	.322	.374
Chip Hale	3B21,DH10,1B7*	L	29	67	118	13	31	9	0	1	11	16	14	0	.263	.350	.364
Rich Becker	OF26,DH1	S	22	28	98	12	26	3	0	1	8	13	25	6	.265	.351	.327
Derek Parks	C31	R	25	31	89	6	17	6	0	1	9	4	20	0	.191	.242	.292
Steve Dunn	1B12	L	24	14	35	2	8	5	0	0	4	1	12	0	.229	.250	.371
Denny Hocking	SS10	S	24	11	31	3	10	3	0	0	2	0	4	2	.323	.323	.419
Pat Mahomes	P21,DH1	R	23	22	0	1	0	0	0	0	0	0	0	0	—	—	—

J. Reboulet, 6 G at 3B, 4 G at OF, 1 G at DH; C. Hale, 5 G at 2B, 1 G at OF

Pitcher	T	Age	G	GS	CG	ShO	IP	H	HR	BB	SO	W-L	Sv	ERA
Jim Deshaies	L	34	25	25	0	0	130.1	170	30	54	78	6-12	0	7.39
Kevin Tapani	R	30	24	24	4	1	156.0	181	13	39	91	11-7	0	4.62
Scott Erickson	R	26	23	23	2	1	144.0	173	15	59	104	8-11	0	5.44
Pat Mahomes	R	23	21	21	0	0	120.0	121	22	62	53	9-5	0	4.73
Carlos Pulido	L	22	19	14	0	0	84.1	87	17	40	32	3-7	0	5.98
Eddie Guardado	L	23	4	4	0	0	17.0	26	3	4	8	0-2	0	8.47
Mark Guthrie	R	28	50	2	0	0	51.1	65	8	18	38	4-2	1	6.14
Carl Willis	R	33	49	0	0	0	59.1	89	6	12	37	2-4	3	5.92
Rick Aguilera	R	32	44	0	0	0	44.2	57	7	10	46	1-4	23	3.63
Larry Casian†	L	28	33	0	0	0	40.2	57	11	12	18	1-3	1	7.08
Mike Trombley	R	27	24	0	0	0	48.1	56	10	18	32	2-0	0	6.33
Dave Stevens	R	24	24	0	0	0	45.0	55	6	23	24	5-2	0	6.80
Brett Merriman	R	27	15	0	0	0	17.0	18	0	14	10	0-1	0	6.35
Kevin Campbell	R	29	14	0	0	0	24.2	20	2	5	15	1-0	0	2.92
Erik Schullstrom	R	25	9	0	0	0	13.0	13	0	5	13	0-0	1	2.77
Keith Garagozzo	L	24	7	0	0	0	9.1	9	3	13	3	0-0	0	9.64

1994 Milwaukee Brewers 5th AL Central 53-62 .461 15.0 GB

Phil Garner

Player	Gm by Position	B	Age	G	AB	R	H	2B	3B	HR	RBI	BB	SO	SB	Avg	OBP	Slg
Dave Nilsson	C60,DH43,1B5	L	24	109	397	51	109	28	3	12	69	34	61	1	.275	.326	.451
John Jaha	1B73,DH11	R	28	84	291	45	70	14	0	12	39	32	75	3	.241	.332	.412
Jody Reed	2B106	R	31	108	399	48	108	22	0	2	37	57	34	5	.271	.362	.341
Kevin Seitzer	3B43,1B35,DH4	R	32	80	309	44	97	24	2	5	49	30	38	2	.314	.375	.453
Jose Valentin	SS83,2B18,DH1*	S	24	97	285	47	68	19	0	11	46	38	75	12	.239	.330	.421
Turner Ward	OF99,3B1	S	29	102	367	55	85	15	2	9	45	52	68	6	.232	.328	.357
Greg Vaughn	OF81,DH14	R	28	95	370	59	94	24	1	19	55	51	93	9	.254	.345	.478
Matt Mieske	OF80,DH1	R	26	84	259	39	67	13	1	10	38	21	62	3	.259	.320	.432
Brian Harper	DH36,C25,OF3	R	34	64	251	23	73	15	0	4	32	9	18	0	.291	.318	.398
Bill Spiers	3B35,SS35,DH3*	L	28	73	214	27	54	10	1	0	17	19	42	7	.252	.316	.308
Alex Diaz	OF73,2B2,DH1	S	25	79	187	17	47	5	7	1	17	10	19	5	.251	.285	.369
Darryl Hamilton	OF32,DH4	L	29	36	141	23	37	10	1	1	13	15	17	3	.262	.331	.369
B.J. Surhoff	3B18,C12,1B8*	L	29	40	134	20	35	11	2	5	22	16	14	0	.261	.336	.485
Jeff Cirillo	3B37,2B1	R	24	39	126	17	30	9	0	3	12	11	16	0	.238	.309	.381
Troy O'Leary	OF21,DH1	L	24	27	66	9	18	1	1	2	7	5	12	1	.273	.329	.409
Pat Listach	SS16	S	26	16	54	8	16	3	0	0	2	3	8	2	.296	.333	.352
Mike Matheny	C27	R	23	28	53	3	12	3	0	1	2	3	13	0	.226	.293	.340
Dave Valle†	C12,DH2	R	33	16	36	8	14	6	0	1	5	9	4	0	.389	.522	.639
Tom Brunansky†	OF6,DH2,1B2	R	33	16	28	2	6	2	0	0	0	1	9	0	.214	.241	.286
Rick Wrona	C5,1B1	R	30	6	10	2	5	4	0	1	3	1	1	0	.500	.545	1.200
Duane Singleton	OF2	L	21	2	0	0	0	0	0	0	0	0	0	0	—	—	—

J. Valentin, 1 G at 3B; B. Spiers, 2 G at OF, 1 G at 1B; B. Surhoff, 3 G at OF, 1 G at DH

Pitcher	T	Age	G	GS	CG	ShO	IP	H	HR	BB	SO	W-L	Sv	ERA
Cal Eldred	R	26	25	25	6	0	179.0	158	23	84	98	11-11	0	4.68
Ricky Bones	R	25	24	24	4	1	170.2	166	17	45	57	10-9	0	3.43
Bill Wegman	R	31	19	19	0	0	115.2	140	14	26	59	8-4	0	4.51
Teddy Higuera	L	35	17	12	0	0	58.2	74	13	36	35	1-5	0	7.06
Angel Miranda	L	24	8	8	1	0	46.0	39	8	27	24	2-5	0	5.28
Graeme Lloyd	L	27	43	0	0	0	47.0	49	4	15	31	2-3	3	5.17
Mike Fetters	R	29	42	0	0	0	46.0	41	0	27	31	1-4	17	2.54
Jesse Orosco	L	37	40	0	0	0	39.0	32	4	26	36	3-1	0	5.08
Bob Scanlan	R	27	30	12	0	0	103.0	117	11	28	65	2-6	2	4.11
Jaime Navarro	R	27	29	10	0	0	89.2	115	10	35	65	4-9	0	6.62
Doug Henry	R	30	25	0	0	0	31.1	32	7	23	20	2-3	0	4.60
Mike Ignasiak	R	28	23	5	0	0	47.2	51	5	13	24	3-1	0	4.53
Jose Mercedes	R	23	19	0	0	0	31.0	22	4	16	11	2-0	0	2.32
Jeff Bronkey	R	28	16	0	0	0	20.2	20	3	12	13	1-1	1	4.35
Mark Kiefer	R	25	7	0	0	0	10.2	15	4	8	8	1-0	0	8.44

1994 Texas Rangers 1st AL West 52-62 .456 —

Kevin Kennedy

Player	Gm by Position	B	Age	G	AB	R	H	2B	3B	HR	RBI	BB	SO	SB	Avg	OBP	Slg
Ivan Rodriguez	C99	R	22	99	363	56	108	19	1	16	57	31	42	6	.298	.360	.488
Will Clark	1B107,DH1	L	30	110	389	73	128	24	2	13	80	71	59	5	.329	.431	.501
Jeff Frye	2B54,DH1,3B1	R	27	57	205	37	67	20	3	0	18	29	23	6	.327	.408	.454
Dean Palmer	3B91	R	25	93	342	50	84	14	2	19	59	26	89	3	.246	.302	.465
Manuel Lee	SS85,2B13	S	29	95	335	41	93	18	2	2	38	21	66	3	.278	.319	.361
Juan Gonzalez	OF107	R	24	107	422	57	116	18	4	19	85	30	66	6	.275	.330	.472
David Hulse	OF76,DH1	L	26	77	310	58	79	8	4	1	19	21	53	18	.255	.305	.316
Rusty Greer	OF73,1B9	L	25	80	277	36	87	16	1	10	46	46	46	0	.314	.410	.487
Jose Canseco	DH111	R	29	111	429	88	121	19	2	31	90	69	114	15	.282	.386	.552
Doug Strange	2B53,3B13,OF3	S	30	73	226	26	48	12	1	5	26	15	38	1	.212	.268	.341
Oddibe McDowell	OF53,DH2	L	31	59	183	34	48	5	1	1	15	28	39	14	.262	.355	.317
Chris James	OF48	R	31	52	133	28	34	8	4	7	19	20	38	0	.256	.361	.534
Esteban Beltre	SS41,3B5,2B1	R	26	48	131	12	37	5	0	0	12	16	25	2	.282	.358	.321
Billy Ripken	3B18,2B12,SS2*	R	29	32	81	9	25	5	0	0	6	3	11	2	.309	.333	.370
Junior Ortiz	C28	R	34	29	76	3	21	2	0	0	9	5	11	0	.276	.329	.303
Gary Redus	OF7,1B5	R	37	18	33	2	9	1	0	0	2	4	6	0	.273	.351	.303
Rob Ducey	OF10	L	29	11	29	1	5	1	0	0	1	2	1	0	.172	.226	.207
Butch Davis	OF4	R	36	4	17	2	4	3	0	0	0	0	3	1	.235	.235	.412
Chuck Jackson	3B1	R	31	1	2	0	0	0	0	0	0	0	0	0	.000	.000	.000

B. Ripken, 1 G at 1B

Pitcher	T	Age	G	GS	CG	ShO	IP	H	HR	BB	SO	W-L	Sv	ERA
Kevin Brown	R	29	26	25	3	0	170.0	218	18	50	123	7-9	0	4.82
Kenny Rogers	L	29	24	24	6	2	167.1	169	24	52	120	11-8	0	4.46
Hector Fajardo	R	23	18	12	0	0	83.1	95	15	26	45	5-7	0	6.91
Roger Pavlik	R	26	11	11	0	0	50.1	61	8	30	31	2-5	0	7.69
John Dettmer	R	24	11	9	0	0	54.0	63	10	20	27	0-6	0	4.33
Rick Helling	R	23	9	9	1	1	52.0	62	14	18	25	3-2	0	5.88
Bruce Hurst	L	36	8	8	0	0	38.0	53	8	16	24	2-1	0	7.11
Tim Leary	R	36	6	3	0	0	21.0	26	4	11	9	1-1	0	8.14
Steve Dreyer	R	24	5	3	0	0	17.1	19	1	8	11	1-1	0	5.71
Rick Reed	R	29	4	3	0	0	16.2	17	3	7	12	1-1	0	5.94
Jack Armstrong	R	29	2	2	0	0	10.0	9	3	2	7	0-1	0	3.60
Matt Whiteside	R	26	47	0	0	0	61.0	68	6	28	37	2-2	1	5.02
Cris Carpenter	R	29	47	0	0	0	59.0	69	7	20	39	2-5	5	5.03
Darren Oliver	L	23	43	0	0	0	50.0	40	4	35	50	4-0	2	3.42
Rick Honeycutt	L	40	42	0	0	0	25.0	37	4	9	18	1-2	1	7.20
Jay Howell	R	38	40	0	0	0	43.0	44	10	16	22	4-1	2	5.44
Tom Henke	R	36	37	0	0	0	38.0	33	6	12	39	3-6	15	3.79
Dan Smith	L	25	13	0	0	0	14.2	18	2	12	9	1-2	0	4.30
Brian Bohanon	L	25	11	5	0	0	37.1	51	7	8	26	2-2	0	7.23
James Hurst	L	27	8	0	0	0	10.2	17	1	8	5	0-0	0	10.13
Duff Brumley	R	23	2	0	0	0	3.1	6	1	5	4	0-0	0	16.20
Terry Burrows	L	25	1	0	0	0	1.0	1	1	1	0	0-0	0	9.00

942 Seasons: Team Rosters

1994 Oakland Athletics 2nd AL West 51-63 .447 1.0 GB

Tony La Russa

Player	Gm by Position	B	Age	G	AB	R	H	2B	3B	HR	RBI	BB	SO	SB	Avg	OBP	Slg
Terry Steinbach	C93,DH6,1B6	R	32	103	369	51	105	21	2	11	57	26	62	2	.285	.327	.442
Troy Neel	1B45,DH35	L	28	83	278	43	74	13	0	15	48	38	61	2	.266	.357	.475
Brent Gates	2B63,1B1	S	24	64	233	29	66	11	1	2	24	21	32	3	.283	.337	.365
Scott Brosius	3B93,OF7,1B1	R	27	96	324	31	77	14	1	14	49	24	57	2	.238	.289	.417
Mike Bordick	SS112,2B4	R	28	114	391	38	99	18	4	2	37	38	44	7	.253	.320	.335
Stan Javier	OF108,1B1,3B1	S	30	109	419	75	114	23	0	10	44	49	76	24	.272	.349	.399
Ruben Sierra	OF98,DH10	S	28	110	426	71	114	21	1	23	92	23	64	8	.268	.298	.484
Rickey Henderson	OF71,DH13	R	35	87	296	66	77	13	0	6	20	72	45	22	.260	.411	.365
Geronimo Berroa	DH44,OF42,1B9	R	29	96	340	55	104	18	2	13	65	41	62	7	.306	.379	.485
Scott Hemond	C39,2B25,3B12*	R	28	91	198	23	44	11	0	3	20	16	51	7	.222	.280	.323
Mike Aldrete	OF35,1B27,DH1	L	33	76	178	23	43	5	0	4	18	20	35	2	.242	.313	.337
Mark McGwire	1B40,DH5	R	30	47	135	26	34	3	0	9	25	37	40	0	.252	.413	.474
Craig Paquette	3B14	R	25	14	49	0	7	2	0	0	0	0	14	1	.143	.143	.184
Eric Fox	OF24	S	30	26	44	7	9	2	0	1	1	3	8	2	.205	.255	.318
Junior Noboa†	2B14,SS1	R	29	17	40	3	13	1	1	0	6	2	5	1	.325	.357	.400
Ernie Young	OF10,DH1	R	24	11	30	2	2	1	0	0	3	1	8	0	.067	.097	.100
Fausto Cruz	SS10,3B4,2B1	R	22	17	28	2	3	0	0	0	0	4	6	0	.107	.219	.107
Francisco Matos	2B12,DH2	R	24	14	28	1	7	1	0	0	2	1	2	1	.250	.267	.286
Mike Brumley	2B4,3B4,OF3*	S	31	11	25	0	6	0	0	0	2	1	8	0	.240	.269	.240
Steve Sax	2B6	R	34	7	24	2	6	0	1	0	1	0	2	0	.250	.250	.333
Jim Bowie	1B6	L	29	6	14	0	3	0	0	0	0	0	2	0	.214	.214	.214
Jeff Schaefer	3B3,SS2,1B1	R	34	6	8	0	1	0	0	0	0	0	1	0	.125	.125	.125
Eric Helfand	C6	L	25	7	6	1	1	0	0	0	1	0	1	0	.167	.167	.167

S. Hemond, 7 G at 1B, 3 G at DH, 2 G at OF; M. Brumley, 1 G at SS

Pitcher	T	Age	G	GS	CG	ShO	IP	H	HR	BB	SO	W-L	Sv	ERA
Ron Darling	R	33	25	25	4	0	160.0	162	18	59	108	10-11	0	4.50
Bobby Witt	R	30	24	24	5	3	135.2	151	22	70	111	8-10	0	5.04
Todd Van Poppel	R	22	23	23	0	0	116.2	108	20	89	83	7-10	0	6.09
Miguel Jimenez	R	24	8	7	0	0	34.0	38	9	32	22	1-4	0	7.41
Steve Karsay	R	22	4	4	1	0	28.0	26	1	8	15	1-1	0	2.57
Mike Mohler	L	25	1	1	0	0	2.1	2	1	2	4	0-1	0	7.71
Dennis Eckersley	R	39	45	0	0	0	44.1	49	5	13	47	5-4	19	4.26
Billy Taylor	R	32	41	0	0	0	46.1	38	4	18	48	1-3	1	3.50
John Briscoe	R	26	37	0	0	0	49.1	31	7	39	45	4-2	1	4.01
Mark Acre	R	25	34	0	0	0	34.1	24	4	23	21	5-1	0	3.41
Vince Horsman	L	27	33	0	0	0	29.1	29	2	11	20	0-1	0	4.91
Steve Ontiveros	R	33	27	13	2	0	115.1	93	7	26	56	6-4	0	2.65
Carlos Reyes	R	25	27	9	0	0	78.0	71	10	44	57	0-3	1	4.15
Dave Leiper	L	32	26	0	0	0	18.2	13	0	6	14	0-0	1	1.93
Bob Welch	R	37	25	8	0	0	68.2	79	10	43	44	3-6	0	7.08
Ed Vosberg	L	32	16	0	0	0	13.2	16	2	5	12	0-2	0	3.95
Edwin Nunez	R	31	15	0	0	0	15.0	26	2	10	15	0-0	0	12.00
Dave Righetti†	L	35	7	0	0	0	7.0	13	3	9	4	0-0	0	16.71
Steve Phoenix	R	26	2	0	0	0	4.1	4	0	2	3	0-0	0	6.23
Roger Smithberg	R	28	2	0	0	0	2.1	6	1	1	3	0-0	0	15.43

1994 Seattle Mariners 3rd AL West 49-63 .438 2.0 GB

Lou Piniella

Player	Gm by Position	B	Age	G	AB	R	H	2B	3B	HR	RBI	BB	SO	SB	Avg	OBP	Slg
Dan Wilson	C91	R	25	91	282	24	61	14	2	3	27	10	57	1	.216	.244	.312
Tino Martinez	1B82,DH8	L	26	97	329	42	86	21	0	20	61	29	52	1	.261	.320	.508
Rich Amaral	2B42,OF16,SS7*	R	32	77	228	37	60	10	2	4	18	24	28	5	.263	.333	.377
Edgar Martinez	3B64,DH23	R	31	89	326	47	93	23	1	13	51	53	42	6	.285	.387	.482
Felix Fermin	SS77,2B25	R	30	101	379	52	120	21	0	1	35	11	22	4	.317	.338	.380
Ken Griffey Jr.	OF103,DH9	L	24	111	433	94	140	24	4	40	90	56	73	11	.323	.402	.674
Jay Buhner	OF96,DH4	R	29	101	358	74	100	23	4	21	68	66	63	0	.279	.394	.542
Eric Anthony	OF71,DH4	L	26	79	262	31	62	14	1	10	30	23	66	6	.237	.297	.412
Reggie Jefferson	DH32,1B13,OF2	S	25	63	162	24	53	11	0	8	32	17	32	0	.327	.392	.543
Mike Blowers	3B48,1B20,DH9*	R	29	85	270	37	78	13	0	9	49	25	60	2	.289	.348	.437
Luis Sojo	2B40,SS24,DH2*	R	28	63	213	32	59	9	2	6	22	8	25	2	.277	.308	.423
Keith Mitchell	OF38,DH6	R	24	46	128	21	29	2	0	5	15	18	22	0	.227	.324	.359
Brian Turang	OF30,2B5,DH4	R	27	38	112	9	21	5	1	1	8	7	25	3	.188	.242	.277
Bill Haselman	C33,DH3,OF2	R	28	38	83	11	16	7	1	1	8	3	11	1	.193	.230	.337
Torey Lovullo	2B20,3B5,DH2	S	28	36	72	9	16	5	0	2	7	9	13	1	.222	.309	.375
Alex Rodriguez	SS17	R	18	17	54	4	11	0	0	0	2	3	20	3	.204	.241	.204
Greg Pirkl	DH10,1B7	R	23	19	53	7	14	3	0	6	11	1	12	0	.264	.286	.660
Marc Newfield	DH9,OF3	R	21	12	38	3	7	1	0	1	4	2	4	0	.184	.225	.289
Dale Sveum	DH4,3B3	S	30	10	27	3	5	0	0	1	2	2	10	0	.185	.241	.296
Chris Howard	C9	R	28	9	25	2	5	1	0	0	2	1	6	0	.200	.250	.240
Quinn Mack	OF4,DH1	L	28	5	21	1	5	3	0	0	2	1	3	2	.238	.273	.381
Darren Bragg	DH3,OF3	L	24	8	19	4	3	1	0	0	2	2	5	0	.158	.238	.211
Jerry Willard	DH1,C1	L	34	6	5	1	1	0	0	1	3	1	1	0	.200	.333	.800
Mackey Sasser	C1,OF1	L	31	3	4	0	0	0	0	0	0	0	0	0	.000	.000	.000

R. Amaral, 6 G at DH, 2 G at 1B; M. Blowers, 9 G at OF; L. Sojo, 1 G at 3B

Pitcher	T	Age	G	GS	CG	ShO	IP	H	HR	BB	SO	W-L	Sv	ERA
Randy Johnson	L	30	23	23	9	4	172.0	132	14	72	204	13-6	0	3.19
Dave Fleming	L	24	23	23	0	0	117.0	152	17	65	65	7-11	0	6.46
Chris Bosio	R	31	19	19	4	0	125.0	137	15	40	67	4-10	0	4.32
Greg Hibbard	L	29	15	14	0	0	80.2	115	11	31	39	1-5	0	6.69
Roger Salkeld	R	23	13	13	0	0	59.0	76	7	45	46	2-5	0	7.17
Jim Converse	R	22	13	8	0	0	48.2	73	5	40	39	0-5	0	8.69
George Glinatsis	R	25	2	2	0	0	5.1	9	2	6	1	0-1	0	13.50
Shawn Boskie†	R	27	2	1	0	0	2.2	4	1	1	0	0-1	0	6.75
Bobby Ayala	R	24	46	0	0	0	56.2	42	2	26	76	4-3	18	2.86
Tim Davis	L	23	42	1	0	0	49.1	57	4	25	28	2-2	2	4.01
Bill Risley	R	27	37	0	0	0	52.1	31	7	19	61	9-6	0	3.44
Goose Gossage	R	42	36	0	0	0	47.1	44	6	15	29	3-0	1	4.18
Jeff Nelson	R	27	28	0	0	0	42.1	35	3	20	44	0-0	0	2.76
Kevin King	L	25	19	0	0	0	15.1	21	0	17	6	0-2	0	7.04
John Cummings	L	25	17	8	0	0	64.0	66	7	37	33	2-4	0	5.63
Milt Hill†	R	28	13	0	0	0	23.2	30	4	11	16	1-0	0	6.46
Bobby Thigpen	R	30	7	0	0	0	7.2	12	3	5	4	0-2	0	9.39
Erik Plantenberg	L	25	6	0	0	0	7.0	4	0	7	1	0-0	0	0.00
Jeff Darwin	R	24	2	0	0	0	4.0	7	1	3	1	0-0	0	13.50
Bob Wells†	R	27	1	0	0	0	4.0	4	0	1	3	1-0	0	2.25

1994 California Angels 4th AL West 47-68 .409 5.5 GB

Buck Rodgers (16-23)/Bobby Knoop (1-1)/Marcel Lachemann (30-44)

Player	Gm by Position	B	Age	G	AB	R	H	2B	3B	HR	RBI	BB	SO	SB	Avg	OBP	Slg
Chris Turner	C57	R	25	58	149	23	36	7	1	1	12	10	29	3	.242	.290	.322
J.T. Snow	1B61	S	26	61	223	22	49	4	0	8	30	19	48	0	.220	.289	.345
Harold Reynolds	2B65,DH3	S	33	74	207	33	48	10	1	0	11	23	18	10	.232	.310	.290
Spike Owen	3B70,SS5,1B4*	S	33	82	268	30	83	17	2	3	37	49	17	2	.310	.418	.422
Gary DiSarcina	SS110	R	26	112	389	53	101	14	2	3	33	18	28	3	.260	.294	.329
Chad Curtis	OF114	R	25	114	453	67	116	23	4	11	50	37	69	25	.256	.317	.397
Tim Salmon	OF99	R	25	100	373	67	107	18	2	23	70	54	102	1	.287	.382	.531
Jim Edmonds	OF77,1B22	L	24	94	289	35	79	13	1	5	37	30	72	4	.273	.343	.377
Chili Davis	DH106,OF2	S	34	108	392	72	122	18	1	26	84	69	84	3	.311	.410	.561
Damion Easley	3B47,2B40	R	24	88	316	41	68	16	1	6	30	29	48	4	.215	.258	.329
Bo Jackson	OF46,DH9	R	31	75	201	23	56	7	0	13	43	20	72	1	.279	.344	.507
Eduardo Perez	1B38	R	24	38	129	10	27	7	0	5	16	12	29	3	.209	.275	.380
Jorge Fabregas	C41	L	24	43	127	12	36	3	0	0	16	7	18	2	.283	.321	.307
Greg Myers	C41,DH1	L	28	45	126	10	31	6	0	2	8	10	27	0	.246	.299	.341
Rex Hudler	2B22,OF18,DH4*	R	33	56	124	17	37	8	0	8	20	6	28	2	.298	.326	.556
Dwight Smith†	OF31,DH2	L	30	45	122	19	32	5	1	5	18	7	20	2	.262	.300	.443
Mark Dalesandro	C11,3B5,OF2	R	26	19	25	5	5	1	0	1	2	2	4	0	.200	.259	.360
Rod Correia	2B5,SS1	R	26	6	17	4	4	1	0	0	0	0	0	0	.235	.316	.294
Garret Anderson	OF4	L	22	5	13	0	5	0	0	0	1	0	2	0	.385	.385	.385

S. Owen, 2 G at DH, 1 G at 2B; R. Hudler, 4 G at 3B, 1 G at 1B

Pitcher	T	Age	G	GS	CG	ShO	IP	H	HR	BB	SO	W-L	Sv	ERA
Chuck Finley	L	31	25	25	7	2	183.1	178	21	71	148	10-10	0	4.32
Phil Leftwich	R	25	20	20	1	0	114.0	127	16	42	67	5-10	0	5.68
Mark Langston	L	33	18	18	2	1	119.1	121	19	54	109	7-8	0	4.68
Brian Anderson	L	22	18	18	0	0	101.2	120	13	27	47	7-5	0	5.22
Joe Magrane	L	29	20	11	1	0	74.0	89	18	51	33	2-6	0	7.30
Andrew Lorraine	L	21	4	3	0	0	18.2	30	7	11	10	0-2	0	10.61
John Farrell	R	31	3	3	0	0	13.0	16	2	8	10	1-2	0	9.00
Bob Patterson	L	35	47	0	0	0	42.0	35	6	15	30	2-3	1	4.07
Mark Leiter	R	31	40	7	0	0	95.1	99	13	35	71	4-7	2	4.72
Joe Grahe	R	27	40	0	0	0	43.1	68	5	18	26	2-5	13	6.65
Mike Butcher	R	29	33	0	0	0	29.2	31	2	23	19	2-1	1	6.67
Craig Lefferts	L	36	30	0	0	0	34.2	50	7	12	27	1-1	1	4.67
John Dopson	R	30	21	5	0	0	58.2	67	6	26	33	1-4	1	6.14
Scott Lewis	R	28	20	0	0	0	31.0	46	5	10	10	0-1	0	6.10
Russ Springer	R	25	18	5	0	0	45.2	53	9	14	28	2-2	2	5.52
Bill Sampen	R	31	10	0	0	0	15.1	14	1	13	9	1-1	0	6.46
Jeff Schwarz†	R	30	4	0	0	0	6.2	5	0	6	4	0-0	0	4.05
Ken Patterson	L	29	1	0	0	0	0.2	0	0	0	1	0-0	0	0.00

>>1994 Montreal Expos 1st NL East 74-40 .649 —

Felipe Alou

Player	Gm by Position	B	Age	G	AB	R	H	2B	3B	HR	RBI	BB	SO	SB	Avg	OBP	Slg
Darrin Fletcher	C81	L	27	94	285	28	74	18	1	10	57	25	23	0	.260	.314	.435
Cliff Floyd	1B77,OF26	L	21	100	334	43	94	19	4	4	41	24	63	10	.281	.332	.398
Mike Lansing	2B82,3B27,SS12	R	26	106	394	44	105	21	2	5	35	30	37	12	.266	.328	.368
Sean Berry	3B100	R	28	103	320	43	89	19	2	11	41	32	50	14	.278	.347	.453
Wil Cordero	SS109	R	22	110	415	65	122	30	3	15	63	41	62	16	.294	.363	.489
Marquis Grissom	OF109	R	27	110	475	96	137	25	4	11	45	41	66	36	.288	.344	.427
Moises Alou	OF106	R	27	107	422	81	143	31	5	22	78	42	63	7	.339	.397	.592
Larry Walker	OF68,1B35	L	27	103	395	76	127	44	2	19	86	47	74	15	.322	.394	.587
Lenny Webster	C46	R	29	57	143	13	39	10	0	5	23	16	24	0	.273	.370	.448
Lou Frazier	OF36,2B6,1B1	S	29	76	140	25	38	3	1	0	14	18	23	20	.271	.358	.307
Juan Bell	2B25,3B3,SS1	R	26	38	97	12	27	4	0	2	10	15	21	4	.278	.372	.381
Rondell White	OF29	R	22	40	97	16	27	10	1	2	13	9	18	1	.278	.358	.464
Freddie Benavides	2B36,3B5,1B3*	R	28	47	85	8	16	5	1	0	6	3	15	0	.188	.222	.271
Randy Milligan	1B33	R	32	47	82	10	19	2	0	2	12	14	21	0	.232	.337	.329
Tim Spehr	C46,OF2	R	27	52	36	8	9	3	1	0	5	4	11	2	.250	.325	.389
Jeff Gardner	3B9,2B4	L	30	18	32	4	7	0	1	0	1	3	5	0	.219	.286	.281

F. Benavides, 3 G at SS

Pitcher	T	Age	G	GS	CG	ShO	IP	H	HR	BB	SO	W-L	Sv	ERA
Ken Hill	R	28	23	23	2	1	154.2	145	12	44	85	16-5	0	3.32
Pedro Martinez	R	22	24	23	1	1	144.2	115	11	45	142	11-5	1	3.42
Jeff Fassero	L	31	21	21	1	0	138.2	119	13	40	119	8-6	0	2.99
Kirk Rueter	L	23	20	20	0	0	92.1	106	11	23	35	7-3	0	5.17
Butch Henry	L	25	24	15	0	0	107.1	97	10	20	70	8-3	1	2.43
Gabe White	L	22	7	5	0	0	23.2	24	4	11	17	1-1	1	6.08
Rodney Henderson	R	23	3	2	0	0	6.2	9	1	7	3	0-1	0	9.45
Mel Rojas	R	27	58	0	0	0	84.0	71	11	21	84	3-2	16	3.32
John Wetteland	R	27	52	0	0	0	63.2	46	5	21	68	4-6	25	2.83
Jeff Shaw	R	27	46	0	0	0	67.1	67	8	15	47	5-2	1	3.88
Tim Scott	R	27	40	0	0	0	53.1	51	0	18	37	5-2	1	2.70
Gil Heredia	R	28	39	3	0	0	75.1	85	7	13	62	6-3	0	3.46
Denis Boucher	L	26	10	2	0	0	18.2	24	6	7	17	0-1	0	6.75
Heath Haynes	R	25	4	0	0	0	3.2	3	0	3	1	0-0	0	0.00
Brian Looney	L	24	1	0	0	0	2.0	4	1	0	2	0-0	0	22.50
Joey Eischen	L	24	1	0	0	0	0.2	4	0	0	1	0-0	0	54.00

1994 Atlanta Braves 2nd NL East 68-46 .596 6.0 GB

Bobby Cox

Player	Gm by Position	B	Age	G	AB	R	H	2B	3B	HR	RBI	BB	SO	SB	Avg	OBP	Slg
Javy Lopez	C75	R	23	80	277	27	68	9	0	13	35	17	61	0	.245	.299	.419
Fred McGriff	1B112	L	30	113	424	81	135	25	1	34	94	50	76	7	.318	.389	.623
Mark Lemke	2B103	S	28	104	350	40	103	15	0	3	31	38	37	0	.294	.363	.363
Terry Pendleton	3B77	S	33	77	309	25	78	18	3	7	30	12	57	2	.252	.280	.398
Jeff Blauser	SS96	R	28	96	380	56	98	21	4	6	45	38	64	1	.258	.329	.382
David Justice	OF102	L	28	104	352	61	110	16	2	19	59	69	45	2	.313	.427	.531
Dave Gallagher	OF77,1B1	R	33	89	152	27	34	5	0	2	14	22	17	0	.224	.326	.296
Ryan Klesko	OF74,1B6	L	23	92	245	42	68	13	3	17	47	26	48	1	.278	.344	.563
Roberto Kelly†	OF63	R	29	63	255	44	73	15	3	6	24	24	36	10	.286	.345	.439
Deion Sanders†	OF46	L	26	46	191	32	55	10	0	4	21	16	28	19	.288	.343	.403
Charlie O'Brien	C48	R	34	51	152	24	37	11	0	8	28	15	24	0	.243	.322	.474
Tony Tarasco	OF45	L	23	87	132	16	36	6	0	5	19	9	17	5	.273	.313	.432
Rafael Belliard	SS26,2B18	R	32	46	120	9	29	7	1	0	9	2	29	0	.242	.264	.317
Bill Pecota	3B31,2B1,OF1	R	34	64	112	11	24	5	0	2	16	16	16	1	.214	.310	.313
Mike Kelly	OF25	R	24	30	77	14	21	10	1	2	9	2	17	0	.273	.300	.506
Jose Oliva	3B16	R	23	19	59	9	17	5	0	6	11	7	10	0	.288	.364	.678
Jarvis Brown	OF9	R	27	17	15	3	2	1	0	1	1	0	2	0	.133	.133	.400
Mike Mordecai	SS4	S	26	4	4	1	1	0	0	1	3	1	0	0	.250	.400	1.000

Pitcher	T	Age	G	GS	CG	ShO	IP	H	HR	BB	SO	W-L	Sv	ERA
Greg Maddux	R	28	25	25	10	3	202.0	150	4	31	156	16-6	0	1.56
Tom Glavine	L	28	25	25	2	0	165.1	173	10	70	140	13-9	0	3.97
Steve Avery	L	24	24	24	1	0	151.2	127	15	55	122	8-3	0	4.04
John Smoltz	R	27	21	21	1	0	134.2	120	15	48	113	6-10	0	4.14
Kent Mercker	L	26	20	17	2	1	112.1	90	16	45	111	9-4	0	3.45
Brad Woodall	L	25	1	1	0	0	6.0	5	2	2	2	0-1	0	4.50
Greg McMichael	R	27	51	0	0	0	58.2	66	1	19	47	4-6	21	3.84
Mark Wohlers	R	24	51	0	0	0	51.0	51	1	33	58	7-2	1	4.59
Mike Stanton	L	27	49	0	0	0	45.2	41	2	26	35	3-1	3	3.55
Steve Bedrosian	R	36	46	0	0	0	46.0	41	4	18	43	0-2	0	3.33
Mike Bielecki	R	34	19	1	0	0	27.0	28	2	12	18	2-0	0	4.00
Gregg Olson	R	27	16	0	0	0	14.2	19	1	13	10	0-2	1	9.20
Milt Hill†	R	28	10	0	0	0	11.1	18	3	6	10	0-0	0	7.94

Seasons: Team Rosters

943

1994 New York Mets 3rd NL East 55-58 .487 18.5 GB

Dallas Green

Player	Gm by Position	B	Age	G	AB	R	H	2B	3B	HR	RBI	BB	SO	SB	Avg	OBP	Slg
Todd Hundley	C82	S	25	91	291	45	69	10	1	16	42	25	73	2	.237	.303	.443
David Segui	1B78,OF21	S	27	92	336	46	81	17	1	10	43	33	43	0	.241	.308	.387
Jeff Kent	2B107	R	26	107	415	53	121	24	5	14	68	23	84	1	.292	.341	.475
Bobby Bonilla	3B107	S	31	108	403	60	117	24	1	20	67	55	101	1	.290	.374	.504
Jose Vizcaino	SS102	S	26	103	410	47	105	13	3	3	33	33	62	1	.256	.310	.324
Ryan Thompson	OF98	R	26	98	334	39	75	14	1	18	59	28	94	1	.225	.301	.434
Joe Orsulak	OF90,1B6	L	32	96	292	39	76	3	0	8	42	16	21	4	.260	.299	.353
John Cangelosi	OF50	S	31	62	111	14	28	4	0	0	4	19	20	5	.252	.371	.288
Kevin McReynolds	OF47	R	34	51	180	23	46	11	2	4	21	20	34	2	.256	.328	.406
Kelly Stinnett	C44	R	24	47	150	20	38	6	2	2	14	11	28	2	.253	.323	.360
Jeromy Burnitz	OF42	L	25	45	143	26	34	4	0	3	15	23	45	1	.238	.347	.329
Jim Lindeman	OF33,1B4	R	32	52	137	18	37	8	1	7	20	6	35	0	.270	.303	.496
Rico Brogna	1B35	L	24	39	131	16	46	11	2	7	20	6	29	1	.351	.380	.626
Fernando Vina	2B13,3B12,SS9*	L	25	79	124	20	31	6	0	0	6	12	11	3	.250	.372	.298
Tim Bogar	3B22,1B14,SS7*	R	27	50	52	5	8	0	0	2	5	4	11	1	.154	.211	.269
Luis Rivera	SS11,2B5	R	30	32	43	11	12	2	1	3	5	4	14	0	.279	.367	.581
Shawn Hare	OF14	L	27	22	40	7	9	1	1	0	2	4	11	0	.225	.295	.300
Jeff McKnight	1B2	S	31	31	27	1	4	1	0	0	2	4	12	0	.148	.250	.185
Rick Parker	OF6	R	31	8	16	1	1	0	0	0	0	0	2	0	.063	.063	.063

F. Vina, 6 G at OF; T. Bogar, 1 G at 2B, 1 G at OF

Pitcher	T	Age	G	GS	CG	ShO	IP	H	HR	BB	SO	W-L	Sv	ERA
Bret Saberhagen	R	30	24	24	4	0	177.1	169	13	13	143	14-4	0	2.74
Bobby Jones	R	24	24	24	1	1	160.0	157	10	56	80	12-7	0	3.15
Pete Smith	R	28	21	21	1	0	131.1	145	25	42	62	4-10	0	5.55
Mike Remlinger	L	28	10	9	0	0	54.2	55	9	35	33	1-5	0	4.61
Jason Jacome	L	23	8	8	1	1	54.0	54	3	17	30	4-3	0	2.67
Dwight Gooden	R	29	7	7	0	0	41.1	46	9	15	40	3-4	0	6.31
Eric Hillman	L	28	11	6	0	0	34.2	45	9	11	20	0-3	0	7.79
Juan Castillo	R	24	2	2	0	0	11.2	17	2	5	1	0-0	0	6.94
John Franco	L	33	47	0	0	0	50.0	47	2	19	42	1-4	30	2.70
Roger Mason†	R	35	41	0	0	0	51.1	44	6	20	26	2-4	1	3.51
Josias Manzanillo	R	26	37	0	0	0	47.1	34	4	13	48	3-2	2	2.66
Doug Linton	R	29	32	3	0	0	50.1	74	4	20	29	6-2	0	4.47
Mike Maddux	R	32	27	0	0	0	44.0	45	7	13	32	2-1	2	5.11
Mauro Gozzo	R	28	23	8	0	0	69.0	86	5	28	33	3-5	0	4.83
Eric Gunderson	L	28	14	0	0	0	9.0	5	0	4	4	0-0	0	0.00
Frank Seminara	R	27	10	1	0	0	17.0	20	2	8	7	0-2	0	5.82
Jon Hurst	R	27	7	0	0	0	10.0	15	5	5	6	0-1	0	12.60
Dave Telgheder	R	27	6	0	0	0	10.0	11	2	8	4	0-1	0	7.20

1994 Philadelphia Phillies 4th NL East 54-61 .470 20.5 GB

Jim Fregosi

Player	Gm by Position	B	Age	G	AB	R	H	2B	3B	HR	RBI	BB	SO	SB	Avg	OBP	Slg
Darren Daulton	C68	L	32	69	257	43	77	17	1	15	56	33	43	4	.300	.380	.549
John Kruk	1B69	L	33	75	255	35	77	17	0	5	38	42	51	4	.302	.395	.427
Mickey Morandini	2B79	L	28	87	274	40	80	16	5	2	26	34	33	10	.292	.378	.409
Dave Hollins	3B43,OF1	S	28	44	162	28	36	7	1	4	26	23	32	1	.222	.328	.352
Kevin Stocker	SS82	S	24	82	271	38	74	11	2	2	28	44	41	2	.273	.383	.351
Jim Eisenreich	OF93	L	35	104	290	42	87	15	4	4	43	33	31	6	.300	.371	.421
Lenny Dykstra	OF82	L	31	84	315	68	86	26	5	5	24	68	44	15	.273	.404	.435
Milt Thompson†	OF79	L	35	87	220	29	60	7	0	3	30	23	28	7	.273	.348	.345
Mariano Duncan	2B37,3B28,SS19*	S	31	88	347	49	93	22	1	8	48	17	72	10	.268	.306	.406
Pete Incaviglia	OF63	R	30	80	244	28	56	10	1	13	32	16	71	1	.230	.278	.439
Ricky Jordan	1B49	R	29	72	220	29	62	14	2	8	37	6	32	0	.282	.303	.473
Kim Batiste	3B42,SS17	R	26	64	209	17	49	6	0	1	13	1	32	1	.234	.239	.278
Tony Longmire	OF32	L	25	69	139	10	33	11	0	0	17	10	27	2	.237	.289	.317
Billy Hatcher†	OF40	R	33	43	134	15	33	5	1	2	13	6	14	4	.246	.271	.343
Todd Pratt	C28	R	27	28	102	10	20	6	1	2	9	12	29	0	.196	.281	.333
Mike Lieberthal	C22	R	22	24	79	6	21	3	1	1	5	3	5	0	.266	.301	.367
Wes Chamberlain†	OF18	R	28	24	69	7	19	5	0	2	6	3	12	0	.275	.306	.435
Randy Ready	2B11,3B1	R	34	17	42	5	16	1	0	1	3	8	6	0	.381	.480	.476
Tom Quinlan	3B20	R	26	24	35	6	7	2	0	1	3	3	13	0	.200	.263	.343
Tom Marsh	OF7	R	28	8	18	3	5	1	1	0	3	1	1	0	.278	.316	.444

M. Duncan, 6 G at 1B

Pitcher	T	Age	G	GS	CG	ShO	IP	H	HR	BB	SO	W-L	Sv	ERA
Danny Jackson	L	32	25	25	4	1	179.1	183	13	46	129	14-6	0	3.26
Bobby Munoz	R	26	21	14	1	0	104.1	101	8	35	59	7-5	1	2.67
Shawn Boskie†	R	27	18	14	1	0	84.1	85	14	29	59	4-6	0	5.23
Curt Schilling	R	27	13	13	1	0	82.1	87	10	28	58	2-8	0	4.48
Mike Williams	R	25	12	8	0	0	50.1	61	7	20	29	2-4	0	5.01
F. Valenzuela	L	33	8	7	0	0	45.0	42	8	7	19	1-2	0	3.00
Ben Rivera	R	26	9	7	0	0	38.0	40	7	22	19	3-4	0	6.87
Tommy Greene	R	27	7	7	0	0	35.2	37	5	22	28	2-0	0	4.54
Jeff Juden	R	23	6	5	0	0	27.2	29	4	12	22	1-4	0	6.18
Heathcliff Slocumb	R	28	52	0	0	0	72.1	75	0	28	58	5-1	0	2.86
Doug Jones	R	37	47	0	0	0	54.0	55	2	6	38	2-4	27	2.17
David West	L	29	31	14	0	0	99.0	74	7	61	83	4-10	0	3.55
Larry Andersen	R	41	29	0	0	0	32.2	33	2	15	27	1-2	0	4.41
Toby Borland	R	25	24	0	0	0	34.1	31	1	14	26	1-0	1	2.36
Andy Carter	L	25	20	0	0	0	34.1	34	5	12	18	0-2	0	4.46
Paul Quantrill†	R	25	18	1	0	0	30.0	39	3	10	13	2-2	1	6.00
Roger Mason†	R	35	6	0	0	0	8.2	11	2	5	7	1-1	0	5.19
Bob Wells†	R	27	6	0	0	0	5.0	4	0	3	3	1-0	0	1.80
Tom Edens†	R	33	3	0	0	0	4.0	4	0	1	1	1-0	0	2.25
Ricky Bottalico	R	24	3	0	0	0	3.0	3	0	1	3	0-0	0	0.00

1994 Florida Marlins 5th NL East 51-64 .443 23.5 GB

Rene Lachemann

Player	Gm by Position	B	Age	G	AB	R	H	2B	3B	HR	RBI	BB	SO	SB	Avg	OBP	Slg
Benito Santiago	C97	R	29	101	337	35	92	14	2	11	41	25	57	1	.273	.322	.424
Jeff Conine	OF97,1B46	R	28	115	451	60	144	27	6	18	82	40	92	1	.319	.373	.525
Bret Barberie	2B106	S	26	107	372	40	112	20	2	5	31	23	65	2	.301	.356	.406
Jerry Browne	3B62,OF30,2B15	S	28	101	329	42	97	17	4	3	30	52	23	3	.295	.392	.398
Kurt Abbott	SS99	R	25	101	345	41	86	17	3	9	33	16	98	3	.249	.291	.394
Chuck Carr	OF104	S	25	106	433	61	114	19	2	2	30	22	71	32	.263	.305	.330
Gary Sheffield	OF87	R	25	87	322	61	89	16	1	27	78	51	50	12	.276	.380	.584
Matias Carrillo	OF49	L	31	80	136	13	34	7	0	0	9	9	31	3	.250	.295	.301
Dave Magadan	3B48,1B16	L	31	74	211	30	58	7	0	1	17	39	25	0	.275	.386	.322
Greg Colbrunn	1B41	R	24	47	155	17	47	10	0	6	31	9	27	1	.303	.345	.484
Orestes Destrade	1B37	S	32	39	130	12	27	4	0	5	15	19	32	1	.208	.316	.354
Alex Arias	SS20,3B15	R	26	59	113	4	27	5	0	0	15	9	19	0	.239	.298	.283
Mario Diaz	3B11,2B7,SS7	R	32	32	77	10	25	4	2	0	11	6	6	0	.325	.376	.429
Ron Tingley†	C18	R	35	19	52	4	9	3	1	1	2	5	18	0	.173	.246	.327
Carl Everett	OF16	S	24	16	51	7	11	1	0	2	6	3	15	4	.216	.259	.353
Rich Renteria	3B14,2B6,OF2	R	32	28	49	5	11	0	0	2	4	1	4	0	.224	.269	.347
Jesus Tavarez	OF11	S	23	17	39	4	7	0	0	0	4	1	5	1	.179	.200	.179
Russ Morman	1B8	R	32	13	33	2	7	0	1	1	2	2	9	0	.212	.278	.364
Bob Natal	C8	R	28	10	29	2	8	2	0	0	2	5	5	1	.276	.382	.345
Darrell Whitmore	OF6	L	25	9	22	1	5	1	0	0	0	3	5	0	.227	.320	.273
Charles Johnson	C4	R	22	4	11	5	5	1	0	1	4	1	4	0	.455	.462	.818
Greg O'Halloran	C1	L	26	12	11	1	2	0	0	0	1	0	1	0	.182	.167	.182

Pitcher	T	Age	G	GS	CG	ShO	IP	H	HR	BB	SO	W-L	Sv	ERA
Dave Weathers	R	24	24	24	0	0	135.0	166	13	59	72	8-12	0	5.27
Pat Rapp	R	26	24	23	2	1	133.1	132	13	69	75	7-8	0	3.85
Charlie Hough	R	46	21	21	1	1	113.2	118	17	52	65	5-9	0	5.15
Mark Gardner	R	32	20	14	0	0	92.1	97	14	30	57	4-4	0	4.87
Chris Hammond	L	28	13	13	1	1	73.1	79	5	23	40	4-4	0	3.07
Ryan Bowen	R	26	8	8	1	0	47.1	50	9	19	32	1-5	0	4.94
Rich Scheid	L	29	8	5	0	0	32.1	35	6	8	17	1-3	0	3.34
Kurt Miller	R	21	4	4	0	0	20.0	26	3	7	11	1-3	0	8.10
Richie Lewis	R	28	45	0	0	0	54.0	62	7	38	45	1-4	0	5.67
Robb Nen	R	24	44	0	0	0	58.0	46	6	17	60	5-5	15	2.95
Yorkis Perez	L	26	44	0	0	0	40.2	33	4	14	41	3-0	0	3.54
Jeff Mutis	L	27	35	0	0	0	38.1	51	6	15	30	1-0	0	5.40
Luis Aquino	R	30	29	1	0	0	50.2	39	3	22	22	2-1	0	3.73
Terry Mathews	R	29	24	2	0	0	43.0	45	4	9	21	2-1	0	3.35
Jeremy Hernandez	R	27	21	0	0	0	23.1	16	0	14	13	3-3	9	2.70
John Johnstone	R	25	17	0	0	0	21.1	23	4	16	23	1-2	0	5.91
Bryan Harvey	R	31	12	0	0	0	10.1	12	1	4	10	0-0	6	5.23
Brian Drahman	R	27	9	0	0	0	13.0	15	2	6	7	0-0	0	6.23
Willie Fraser	R	30	9	0	0	0	12.1	20	1	6	7	2-0	0	5.84
Mike Jeffcoat	L	34	4	0	0	0	2.2	4	2	0	1	0-0	0	10.13

1994 Cincinnati Reds 1st NL Central 66-48 .579 —

Davey Johnson

Player	Gm by Position	B	Age	G	AB	R	H	2B	3B	HR	RBI	BB	SO	SB	Avg	OBP	Slg
Brian Dorsett	C73,1B1	R	33	76	216	21	53	8	0	5	26	21	33	0	.245	.313	.352
Hal Morris	1B112	L	29	112	436	60	146	30	4	10	78	34	62	6	.335	.385	.491
Bret Boone	2B106,3B2	R	25	108	381	59	122	25	2	12	68	24	74	3	.320	.368	.491
Tony Fernandez	3B93,SS9,2B5	S	32	104	366	50	102	18	6	8	50	44	40	12	.279	.361	.426
Barry Larkin	SS110	R	30	110	427	78	119	23	5	9	52	64	58	26	.279	.369	.419
Reggie Sanders	OF104	R	26	107	400	66	105	20	8	17	62	41	114	21	.263	.332	.480
Kevin Mitchell	OF89,1B1	R	32	95	310	57	101	18	1	30	77	59	62	2	.326	.429	.681
Thomas Howard	OF57	S	29	83	178	24	47	11	0	5	24	10	30	4	.264	.302	.410
Deion Sanders†	OF45	L	26	46	184	26	51	7	4	0	7	16	35	19	.277	.342	.359
Roberto Kelly†	OF47	R	29	47	179	29	54	8	0	3	21	11	35	9	.302	.351	.397
Eddie Taubensee†	C61	L	25	61	177	29	52	8	2	8	21	15	28	2	.294	.345	.497
Jacob Brumfield	OF43	R	29	68	122	36	38	10	2	4	11	15	18	6	.311	.381	.525
Jeff Branson	2B19,3B18,SS8*	L	27	58	109	18	31	4	1	6	16	5	16	0	.284	.316	.505
Lenny Harris	3B15,1B4,OF3*	L	29	66	100	13	31	3	1	0	14	5	13	7	.310	.340	.360
Jerome Walton	OF26,1B7	R	28	46	68	10	21	4	0	1	9	4	12	1	.309	.347	.412
Willie Greene	3B13,OF1	L	22	16	37	5	8	2	0	0	3	6	14	0	.216	.318	.270
Brian Hunter†	OF5,1B1	R	26	9	23	6	7	1	0	4	10	2	1	0	.304	.346	.870
Joe Oliver	C6	R	28	6	19	1	4	0	0	1	5	2	3	0	.211	.286	.368
Steve Pegues†	OF4	R	26	11	10	1	3	0	0	0	0	1	3	0	.300	.364	.300

J. Branson, 2 G at 1B; L. Harris, 2 G at 2B

Pitcher	T	Age	G	GS	CG	ShO	IP	H	HR	BB	SO	W-L	Sv	ERA
Jose Rijo	R	29	26	26	2	0	172.1	177	16	52	171	9-6	0	3.08
John Smiley	L	29	24	24	1	1	158.2	169	18	37	112	11-10	0	3.86
Erik Hanson	R	29	22	21	0	0	122.2	137	10	23	101	5-5	0	4.11
John Roper	R	22	16	15	0	0	92.0	90	16	30	51	6-2	0	4.50
Tim Pugh	R	27	10	9	1	0	47.2	60	5	26	24	3-3	0	6.04
Tom Browning	L	34	7	7	2	1	40.2	34	8	13	22	3-1	0	4.20
Kevin Jarvis	R	24	6	3	0	0	17.2	22	4	5	10	1-1	0	7.13
Chuck McElroy	L	26	52	0	0	0	57.2	52	3	15	38	1-2	5	2.34
Johnny Ruffin	R	22	51	0	0	0	70.0	57	7	27	44	7-2	1	3.09
Jeff Brantley	R	30	50	0	0	0	65.1	46	6	28	63	6-6	15	2.48
Hector Carrasco	R	24	45	0	0	0	56.1	42	3	30	41	5-6	6	2.24
Tim Fortugno	L	32	25	0	0	0	30.0	32	2	14	29	1-0	0	4.20
Pete Schourek	L	25	22	10	0	0	81.1	90	11	29	69	7-2	0	4.09
Rich DeLucia	R	29	8	0	0	0	10.2	9	4	5	15	0-0	0	4.22
Jerry Spradlin	R	27	6	0	0	0	8.0	12	2	2	4	0-0	0	10.13
Scott Service	R	27	6	0	0	0	7.1	8	2	3	5	1-2	0	7.36

1994 Houston Astros 2nd NL Central 66-49 .574 0.5 GB

Terry Collins

Player	Gm by Position	B	Age	G	AB	R	H	2B	3B	HR	RBI	BB	SO	SB	Avg	OBP	Slg
Scott Servais	C78	R	27	78	251	27	49	15	1	9	41	10	44	0	.195	.235	.371
Jeff Bagwell	1B109,OF1	R	26	110	400	104	147	32	2	39	116	65	65	15	.368	.451	.750
Craig Biggio	2B113	R	28	114	437	88	139	44	5	6	56	62	58	39	.318	.411	.483
Ken Caminiti	3B108	S	31	111	406	63	115	28	2	18	75	43	71	4	.283	.352	.495
Andujar Cedeno	SS95	R	24	98	342	38	90	26	0	9	49	29	79	1	.263	.334	.418
Luis Gonzalez	OF111	L	26	112	392	57	107	29	4	8	67	49	57	15	.273	.353	.429
James Mouton	OF96	R	25	99	310	43	76	11	0	2	16	27	69	24	.245	.315	.300
Steve Finley	OF92	L	29	94	373	64	103	16	5	11	33	28	52	13	.276	.329	.434
Kevin Bass	OF57	S	35	82	203	37	63	15	1	6	35	28	24	2	.310	.393	.483
Tony Eusebio	C52	R	27	55	159	18	47	9	1	5	30	8	33	0	.296	.320	.459
Mike Felder	OF32	S	32	58	117	10	28	2	2	0	13	4	12	3	.239	.264	.291
Chris Donnels	3B14,1B4,2B4	L	28	54	86	12	23	5	0	3	5	13	18	1	.267	.364	.430
Sid Bream	1B10	L	33	46	61	7	21	5	0	0	7	9	9	0	.344	.429	.426
Andy Stankiewicz	SS17,2B6,3B1	R	29	37	54	10	14	3	0	1	5	12	12	1	.259	.403	.370
Orlando Miller	SS11,2B3	R	25	16	40	3	13	0	1	2	9	2	12	1	.325	.386	.525
Brian Hunter	OF6	R	23	6	24	2	6	1	0	0	0	1	6	2	.250	.280	.292
Milt Thompson†	OF6	L	35	9	21	5	6	0	0	1	3	1	2	2	.286	.318	.429
Mike Simms	OF3	R	27	6	12	1	1	1	0	0	0	0	5	1	.083	.083	.167
Eddie Taubensee†	C5	L	25	5	10	0	1	0	0	0	0	0	3	0	.100	.100	.100
Roberto Petagine	1B2	L	23	8	7	0	0	0	0	0	0	1	3	0	.000	.125	.000

Pitcher	T	Age	G	GS	CG	ShO	IP	H	HR	BB	SO	W-L	Sv	ERA
Greg Swindell	L	29	24	24	1	0	148.1	175	20	26	74	8-9	0	4.37
Darryl Kile	R	25	24	24	0	0	147.2	153	13	82	105	9-6	0	4.57
Doug Drabek	R	31	23	23	6	2	164.2	132	14	45	121	12-6	0	2.84
Pete Harnisch	R	27	17	17	1	0	95.0	100	13	39	62	8-5	0	5.40
Brian Williams	R	25	20	13	0	0	78.1	112	9	41	49	6-5	0	5.74
Todd Jones	R	26	48	0	0	0	72.2	52	3	26	63	5-2	5	2.72
Mike Hampton	L	21	44	0	0	0	41.1	46	4	16	24	2-1	0	3.70
John Hudek	R	27	42	0	0	0	39.1	24	5	18	39	0-2	16	2.97
Tom Edens†	R	33	39	0	0	0	50.0	55	3	17	38	4-1	1	4.50
Shane Reynolds	R	26	33	14	1	1	124.0	128	10	21	110	8-5	0	3.05
Dave Veres	R	27	32	0	0	0	41.0	39	4	7	28	3-3	1	2.41
Mitch Williams	L	29	25	0	0	0	20.0	21	4	24	21	1-4	6	7.65
Ross Powell	L	26	12	0	0	0	7.1	6	0	5	5	0-0	0	1.23

944 Seasons: Team Rosters

1994 Pittsburgh Pirates 3rd NL Central 53-61 .465 13.0 GB

Jim Leyland

Player	Gm by Position	B	Age	G	AB	R	H	2B	3B	HR	RBI	BB	SO	SB	Avg	OBP	Slg
Don Slaught	C74	R	35	76	240	21	69	7	0	2	21	34	31	0	.288	.381	.342
Brian Hunter†	1B59,OF5	R	26	76	233	28	53	15	1	11	47	15	55	0	.227	.270	.442
Carlos Garcia	2B98	R	26	98	412	49	114	15	2	6	28	16	67	18	.277	.309	.367
Jeff King	3B91,2B1	R	29	94	339	36	89	23	0	5	42	30	38	3	.263	.316	.375
Jay Bell	SS110	R	28	110	424	68	117	35	4	9	45	49	82	2	.276	.353	.441
Andy Van Slyke	OF99	L	33	105	374	41	92	18	3	6	30	52	72	7	.246	.340	.358
Al Martin	OF77	L	26	82	276	48	79	12	4	9	33	34	56	15	.286	.367	.457
Orlando Merced	OF68,1B55	S	27	108	386	48	105	21	3	9	51	42	58	4	.272	.343	.412
Dave Clark	OF57	L	31	86	223	37	66	11	1	10	46	22	48	2	.296	.355	.489
Lance Parrish	C38,1B1	R	38	40	126	10	34	5	0	3	16	18	28	1	.270	.363	.381
Tom Foley	2B17,3B14,SS8*	L	34	59	123	13	29	7	0	3	15	13	18	0	.236	.307	.366
Kevin Young	1B37,3B17,OF1	R	25	59	122	15	25	7	2	1	11	8	34	0	.205	.258	.320
Lloyd McClendon	OF20,1B2	R	35	51	92	9	22	4	0	4	12	4	11	0	.239	.278	.413
Midre Cummings	OF24	S	22	24	86	11	21	4	0	1	12	4	18	0	.244	.283	.326
Gary Varsho	OF36,1B1	L	33	67	82	15	21	6	3	0	5	4	19	0	.256	.307	.402
Steve Pegues†	OF7	R	26	7	26	1	10	2	0	0	2	1	2	1	.385	.407	.462
Jerry Goff	C7	L	30	8	25	0	2	0	0	0	1	0	11	0	.080	.080	.080
Tony Womack	2B3,SS2	L	24	5	12	4	4	0	0	0	1	2	3	0	.333	.429	.333
John Wehner	3B1	R	27	2	4	1	1	1	0	0	3	0	1	0	.250	.250	.500
W. Pennyfeather	OF1	R	26	4	3	0	0	0	0	0	0	0	0	0	.000	.000	.000
Junior Noboa†	SS1	R	29	2	2	0	0	0	0	0	0	0	0	0	.000	.000	.000

T. Foley, 3 G at 1B

Pitcher	T	Age	G	GS	CG	ShO	IP	H	HR	BB	SO	W-L	Sv	ERA
Zane Smith	L	33	25	24	2	1	157.0	162	18	34	57	10-8	0	3.27
Denny Neagle	L	25	24	24	2	0	137.0	135	18	49	122	9-10	0	5.12
Steve Cooke	L	24	25	23	2	0	134.1	157	21	46	74	4-11	0	5.02
Paul Wagner	R	26	29	17	1	0	119.2	136	7	50	86	7-8	0	4.59
Jon Lieber	R	24	17	17	1	0	108.2	116	12	25	71	6-7	0	3.73
Ravelo Manzanillo	L	30	46	0	0	0	50.0	45	4	42	39	4-2	1	4.14
Mark Dewey	R	29	45	0	0	0	51.1	61	4	19	30	2-1	1	3.68
Rick White	R	25	43	5	0	0	75.1	79	9	17	38	4-5	6	3.82
Danny Miceli	R	23	28	0	0	0	27.1	28	5	11	27	2-1	2	5.93
Jeff Ballard	L	30	28	0	0	0	24.1	32	5	10	11	1-1	2	6.66
Alejandro Pena	R	35	22	0	0	0	28.2	22	4	10	27	3-2	7	5.02
Blas Minor	R	26	17	0	0	0	19.0	27	4	9	17	0-1	1	8.05
Mike Dyer	R	27	14	0	0	0	15.1	15	1	12	13	1-1	4	5.87
Randy Tomlin	L	28	10	4	0	0	20.2	23	1	10	17	0-3	0	3.92
John Hope	R	23	9	0	0	0	14.0	18	1	4	6	0-0	0	5.79
Rich Robertson	L	25	8	0	0	0	15.2	20	2	10	8	0-0	0	6.89
Jeff Tabaka†	L	30	5	0	0	0	4.0	4	1	8	2	0-0	0	18.00
Joel Johnston	R	27	4	0	0	0	3.1	14	0	4	5	0-0	0	29.70

1994 St. Louis Cardinals 3rd NL Central 53-61 .465 13.0 GB

Joe Torre

Player	Gm by Position	B	Age	G	AB	R	H	2B	3B	HR	RBI	BB	SO	SB	Avg	OBP	Slg
Tom Pagnozzi	C70,1B1	R	31	70	243	21	66	12	1	7	40	21	39	0	.272	.327	.416
Gregg Jefferies	1B102	S	26	103	397	52	129	27	1	12	55	45	26	12	.325	.391	.489
Geronimo Pena	2B59,3B1	S	27	83	213	33	54	13	1	11	34	24	54	9	.254	.344	.479
Todd Zeile	3B112	R	28	113	415	62	111	25	1	19	75	52	56	1	.267	.348	.470
Ozzie Smith	SS96	S	39	98	381	51	100	18	3	3	30	38	26	6	.262	.326	.349
Ray Lankford	OF104	L	27	109	416	89	111	25	5	19	57	58	113	11	.267	.359	.488
Bernard Gilkey	OF102	R	27	105	380	52	96	22	1	6	45	39	65	15	.253	.336	.363
Mark Whiten	OF90	S	27	92	334	57	98	18	2	14	53	37	75	10	.293	.364	.485
Luis Alicea	2B53,OF2	S	28	88	205	32	57	12	5	5	29	30	38	4	.278	.373	.459
Brian Jordan	OF46,1B1	R	27	53	178	14	46	8	2	5	15	16	40	4	.258	.320	.410
Jose Oquendo	SS28,2B16	S	30	55	129	13	34	2	2	0	9	21	16	1	.264	.364	.310
Terry McGriff	C39	R	30	42	114	10	25	6	0	0	13	13	11	0	.219	.308	.272
Gerald Perry	1B13	L	33	60	77	12	25	7	0	3	18	15	12	1	.325	.435	.532
Stan Royer†	1B11,3B5	R	26	39	57	3	10	5	0	1	2	0	18	0	.175	.175	.316
Erik Pappas	C15	R	28	15	44	8	4	1	0	0	5	10	13	0	.091	.259	.114
Gerald Young	OF11	S	29	16	41	5	13	3	2	0	3	3	8	2	.317	.364	.488
John Mabry	OF6	L	23	6	23	2	7	3	0	0	3	2	4	0	.304	.360	.435
Scott Coolbaugh	1B4,3B4	R	28	15	21	4	4	0	0	2	6	1	4	0	.190	.217	.476
Tripp Cromer	SS2	R	26	2	0	1	0	0	0	0	0	0	0	0	—	—	—

Pitcher	T	Age	G	GS	CG	ShO	IP	H	HR	BB	SO	W-L	Sv	ERA
Bob Tewksbury	R	33	24	24	4	1	155.2	190	19	22	79	12-10	0	5.32
Allen Watson	L	23	22	22	0	0	115.2	130	15	53	74	6-5	0	5.52
Vicente Palacios	R	30	31	17	1	1	117.2	104	16	43	95	3-8	1	4.44
Rick Sutcliffe	R	38	16	14	0	0	67.2	93	11	32	26	6-4	0	6.52
Omar Olivares	R	26	14	12	1	0	73.2	84	10	37	26	3-4	1	5.74
Tom Urbani	L	26	20	10	0	0	80.1	98	12	21	43	3-7	0	5.15
Rheal Cormier	L	27	7	7	0	0	39.2	40	6	7	26	3-2	0	5.45
John Frascatore	R	24	1	1	0	0	3.1	7	2	2	2	0-1	0	16.20
Rich Rodriguez	L	31	56	0	0	0	60.1	62	6	26	43	3-5	0	4.03
John Habyan	R	30	52	0	0	0	47.1	50	2	20	46	1-0	1	3.23
Rob Murphy†	L	34	50	0	0	0	40.1	35	7	13	25	4-3	2	3.79
Rene Arocha	R	28	45	7	1	1	83.0	94	9	21	62	4-4	11	4.01
Bryan Eversgerd	L	25	40	1	0	0	67.2	75	8	20	47	2-3	0	4.52
Mike Perez	R	29	36	0	0	0	31.0	52	5	10	20	2-3	12	8.71
Frank Cimorelli	R	25	11	0	0	0	13.1	20	0	10	1	0-0	1	8.78
Gary Buckels	R	28	10	0	0	0	12.0	8	2	7	9	0-1	0	2.25
Willie Smith	R	26	8	0	0	0	7.0	9	4	3	7	1-1	0	9.00
Steve Dixon	L	24	2	0	0	0	2.1	3	0	8	1	0-0	0	23.14

1994 Chicago Cubs 5th NL Central 49-64 .434 16.5 GB

Tom Trebelhorn

Player	Gm by Position	B	Age	G	AB	R	H	2B	3B	HR	RBI	BB	SO	SB	Avg	OBP	Slg
Rick Wilkins	C95,1B2	L	27	100	313	44	71	25	2	7	39	40	86	4	.227	.317	.387
Mark Grace	1B103	L	30	106	403	55	120	23	3	6	44	48	41	0	.298	.370	.414
Ryne Sandberg	2B57	R	34	57	223	36	53	9	5	5	24	23	40	2	.238	.312	.390
Steve Buechele	3B99,1B6,2B1	R	32	104	339	33	82	11	1	14	52	39	80	1	.242	.325	.404
Shawon Dunston	SS84	R	31	88	331	38	92	19	0	11	35	16	48	3	.278	.313	.435
Sammy Sosa	OF105	R	25	105	426	59	128	17	6	25	70	25	92	22	.300	.339	.545
Derrick May	OF92	L	25	100	345	43	98	19	2	8	51	30	34	3	.284	.340	.420
Glenallen Hill	OF78	R	29	89	269	48	80	12	1	10	38	29	57	19	.297	.365	.461
Rey Sanchez	2B50,SS30,3B17	R	26	96	291	26	83	13	1	0	24	20	29	2	.285	.345	.337
Karl Rhodes	OF76	L	25	95	269	39	63	17	0	8	19	33	64	6	.234	.318	.387
Jose Hernandez	3B28,SS21,2B8*	R	24	56	132	18	32	2	3	1	9	8	29	2	.242	.291	.326
Eddie Zambrano	OF27,1B9,3B4	R	28	67	116	17	30	7	0	6	18	16	29	2	.259	.353	.474
Mark Parent	C37	R	32	44	99	8	26	4	0	3	16	13	24	0	.263	.348	.394
Kevin Roberson	OF9	S	26	44	55	8	12	4	0	4	9	2	14	0	.218	.271	.509
Todd Haney	2B11,3B3	R	28	17	37	6	6	0	0	1	2	3	3	2	.162	.238	.243
Mike Maksudian	1B3,C2,3B2	L	28	26	26	6	7	2	0	0	4	10	4	0	.269	.472	.346
Willie Wilson	OF10	S	38	17	21	4	5	0	2	0	0	1	6	1	.238	.273	.429

J. Hernandez, 1 G at OF

Pitcher	T	Age	G	GS	CG	ShO	IP	H	HR	BB	SO	W-L	Sv	ERA
Willie Banks	R	25	23	23	1	1	138.1	139	16	56	91	8-12	0	5.40
Steve Trachsel	R	23	22	22	1	0	146.0	133	19	54	108	9-7	0	3.21
Anthony Young	R	28	20	19	0	0	114.2	103	12	46	65	4-6	0	3.92
Mike Morgan	R	34	15	15	1	0	80.2	111	12	35	57	2-10	0	6.69
Kevin Foster	R	25	13	13	0	0	81.0	70	7	35	75	3-4	0	2.89
Frank Castillo	R	25	4	4	1	0	23.0	25	3	5	19	2-1	0	4.30
Jose Guzman	R	31	4	4	0	0	19.2	22	1	13	11	2-2	0	9.15
Jose Bautista	R	29	58	0	0	0	69.1	75	10	17	45	4-5	1	3.89
Dan Plesac	L	32	54	0	0	0	54.2	61	9	13	53	2-3	1	4.61
Chuck Crim	R	32	49	1	0	0	64.1	69	9	24	43	5-4	2	4.48
Randy Myers	L	31	38	0	0	0	40.1	40	3	16	32	1-5	21	3.79
Dave Otto	L	29	36	0	0	0	45.0	49	4	22	19	0-1	0	3.80
Jim Bullinger	R	28	33	10	1	0	100.0	87	6	34	72	6-2	2	3.60
Blaise Ilsley	L	30	10	0	0	0	15.0	25	2	9	9	0-0	0	7.80
Randy Veres	R	28	10	0	0	0	9.2	12	3	2	5	1-1	0	5.59
Turk Wendell	R	27	6	2	0	0	14.1	22	3	10	9	0-1	0	11.93
Donn Pall†	R	32	2	0	0	0	4.0	8	1	1	2	0-0	0	4.50
Shawn Boskie†	R	27	2	0	0	0	3.2	3	0	0	2	0-0	0	0.00

1994 Los Angeles Dodgers 1st NL West 58-56 .509 —

Tom Lasorda

Player	Gm by Position	B	Age	G	AB	R	H	2B	3B	HR	RBI	BB	SO	SB	Avg	OBP	Slg
Mike Piazza	C104	R	25	107	405	64	129	18	0	24	92	33	65	1	.319	.370	.541
Eric Karros	1B109	R	26	111	406	51	108	21	1	14	46	29	53	2	.266	.310	.426
Delino DeShields	2B88,SS10	L	25	89	320	51	80	11	3	2	33	54	53	27	.250	.357	.322
Tim Wallach	3B113	R	36	113	414	68	116	21	1	23	78	46	80	0	.280	.356	.502
Jose Offerman	SS72	S	25	72	243	27	51	8	4	1	25	38	38	2	.210	.314	.288
Raul Mondesi	OF112	R	23	112	434	63	133	27	8	16	56	16	78	11	.306	.333	.516
Brett Butler	OF111	L	37	111	417	79	131	13	9	8	33	68	52	27	.314	.411	.446
Henry Rodriguez	OF86,1B17	L	26	104	306	33	82	14	2	8	49	17	58	0	.268	.307	.405
Cory Snyder	OF50,1B9,3B6*	R	31	73	153	18	36	6	0	6	18	14	47	1	.235	.300	.392
Rafael Bournigal	SS40	R	28	40	116	2	26	3	1	0	11	9	5	0	.224	.291	.267
Mitch Webster	OF48	S	35	82	84	16	23	4	0	4	12	8	13	1	.274	.344	.464
Garey Ingram	2B23	R	23	26	78	10	22	1	0	3	8	7	22	0	.282	.341	.410
Chris Gwynn	OF20	L	29	58	71	9	19	0	0	3	13	7	7	0	.268	.333	.394
Jeff Treadway	2B24,3B3	L	31	52	67	14	20	3	0	0	5	5	8	1	.299	.351	.343
Carlos Hernandez	C27	R	27	32	64	6	14	2	0	2	6	1	14	0	.219	.231	.344
Dave Hansen	3B7	L	25	40	44	3	15	3	0	0	5	5	5	0	.341	.408	.409
Eddie Pye	2B3,SS3	R	27	7	10	2	1	0	0	0	1	1	4	0	.100	.182	.100
Tom Prince	C3	R	29	3	6	2	2	0	0	0	1	1	3	0	.333	.429	.333
Billy Ashley	OF2	R	23	2	6	0	2	1	0	0	0	0	2	0	.333	.333	.500

C. Snyder, 4 G at SS, 3 G at 2B

Pitcher	T	Age	G	GS	CG	ShO	IP	H	HR	BB	SO	W-L	Sv	ERA
Ramon Martinez	R	26	24	24	4	3	170.0	160	18	56	119	12-7	0	3.97
Kevin Gross	R	33	25	23	1	0	157.1	162	11	43	124	9-7	1	3.60
Pedro Astacio	R	25	23	23	3	1	149.0	142	18	47	108	6-8	0	4.29
Tom Candiotti	R	36	23	22	5	0	153.0	149	9	54	102	7-7	0	4.12
Orel Hershiser	R	35	21	21	1	0	135.1	146	15	42	72	6-6	0	3.79
Todd Worrell	R	34	38	0	0	0	42.0	37	4	12	44	6-5	11	4.29
Jim Gott	R	34	37	0	0	0	36.1	46	3	20	29	5-3	2	5.94
Roger McDowell	R	33	32	0	0	0	41.1	50	3	22	29	0-3	0	5.23
Darren Dreifort	R	22	27	0	0	0	29.0	45	0	15	22	0-5	6	6.21
Omar Daal	L	22	24	0	0	0	13.2	12	1	5	9	0-0	0	3.29
Ismael Valdes	R	20	21	1	0	0	28.1	21	2	10	28	3-1	0	3.18
Gary Wayne	L	31	19	0	0	0	17.1	19	2	6	10	1-3	0	4.67
Rudy Seanez	R	25	17	0	0	0	23.2	24	2	9	18	1-1	0	2.66
Al Osuna	L	28	15	0	0	0	8.2	13	0	4	7	2-0	0	6.23
Brian Barnes†	L	27	5	0	0	0	5.0	10	1	4	5	0-0	0	7.20
Chan Ho Park	R	21	2	0	0	0	4.0	5	1	5	6	0-0	0	11.25

1994 San Francisco Giants 2nd NL West 55-60 .478 3.5 GB

Dusty Baker

Player	Gm by Position	B	Age	G	AB	R	H	2B	3B	HR	RBI	BB	SO	SB	Avg	OBP	Slg
Kirt Manwaring	C97	R	28	97	316	30	79	17	1	1	29	25	50	1	.250	.308	.320
Todd Benzinger	1B99	S	31	107	328	32	87	13	2	9	31	17	84	2	.265	.304	.399
John Patterson	2B63	S	27	85	240	36	57	10	1	3	32	16	43	13	.238	.315	.325
Matt Williams	3B110	R	28	112	445	74	119	16	3	43	96	33	87	1	.267	.319	.607
Royce Clayton	SS108	R	24	108	385	38	91	14	6	3	30	30	74	23	.236	.295	.327
Darren Lewis	OF113	R	26	114	451	70	116	15	9	4	29	53	50	30	.257	.340	.357
Barry Bonds	OF112	L	29	112	391	89	122	18	1	37	81	74	43	29	.312	.426	.647
Dave Martinez	OF58,1B25	L	29	97	235	23	58	9	3	4	27	21	22	3	.247	.314	.362
Willie McGee	OF42	S	35	45	156	19	44	3	0	5	23	15	24	3	.282	.337	.397
Robby Thompson	2B35	R	32	35	129	13	27	8	2	2	7	15	32	3	.209	.290	.349
Jeff Reed	C33	L	31	50	103	11	18	3	0	1	7	11	21	0	.175	.254	.233
Steve Scarsone	2B22,3B8,1B6*	R	28	52	103	21	28	8	0	2	13	10	20	0	.272	.330	.408
Mark Carreon	OF33	R	30	51	100	8	27	4	0	3	20	7	20	0	.270	.324	.400
Darryl Strawberry	OF27	L	32	29	92	13	22	3	1	4	17	19	22	0	.239	.363	.424
Mike Benjamin	SS18,2B10,3B5	R	28	38	62	9	16	5	1	1	9	5	16	5	.258	.343	.419
J.R. Phillips	1B10	L	24	15	38	1	5	0	0	1	3	1	13	1	.132	.150	.211
Rikkert Faneyte	OF6	R	25	19	26	1	3	3	0	0	4	3	11	0	.115	.207	.231
Erik Johnson	2B2,SS1	R	28	5	13	0	2	0	0	0	0	0	0	0	.154	.154	.154
Mark Leonard	OF2	L	29	14	11	2	4	1	1	0	2	3	2	0	.364	.500	.636

S. Scarsone, 1 G at SS

Pitcher	T	Age	G	GS	CG	ShO	IP	H	HR	BB	SO	W-L	Sv	ERA
John Burkett	R	29	25	25	0	0	159.1	176	14	36	85	6-8	0	3.62
Mark Portugal	R	31	21	21	1	0	137.1	135	17	45	87	10-8	0	3.93
Bill Swift	R	32	17	17	0	0	109.1	109	10	31	62	8-7	0	3.38
Bryan Hickerson	L	30	28	14	0	0	98.1	118	20	38	59	4-8	1	5.40
Salomon Torres	R	22	16	14	1	0	84.1	95	10	34	42	2-8	0	5.44
W. VanLandingham	R	23	16	14	0	0	84.0	70	4	43	56	8-2	0	3.54
Bud Black	L	37	10	10	0	0	54.1	50	9	16	28	4-2	0	4.47
Dave Burba	R	27	57	0	0	0	74.0	59	5	45	84	3-6	0	4.38
Rod Beck	R	25	48	0	0	0	48.2	49	10	13	39	2-4	28	2.77
Steve Frey	L	30	44	0	0	0	31.0	37	6	15	20	1-0	1	4.94
Rich Monteleone	R	31	39	0	0	0	45.1	43	6	13	16	4-3	0	3.18
Mike Jackson	R	29	36	0	0	0	42.1	23	4	11	51	3-2	4	1.49
Pat Gomez	L	26	26	0	0	0	33.1	23	2	20	14	0-1	0	3.78
Kevin Rogers	L	25	9	0	0	0	10.1	10	1	6	7	0-0	0	3.48
Tony Menendez	R	29	6	0	0	0	3.1	8	2	2	2	0-1	0	21.60
Brad Brink	R	29	4	0	0	0	8.1	4	1	4	3	0-0	0	1.08
Kent Bottenfield†	R	25	1	0	0	0	1.2	5	1	0	0	0-0	0	10.80

1994 Colorado Rockies 3rd NL West 53-64 .453 6.5 GB

Don Baylor

Player	Gm by Position	B	Age	G	AB	R	H	2B	3B	HR	RBI	BB	SO	SB	Avg	OBP	Slg
Joe Girardi	C93	R	29	93	330	47	91	9	4	4	34	21	48	3	.276	.321	.364
Andres Galarraga	1B103	R	33	103	417	77	133	21	0	31	85	19	93	8	.319	.356	.592
Nelson Liriano	2B79,SS3,3B2	S	30	87	255	39	65	17	5	3	31	42	44	0	.255	.357	.396
Charlie Hayes	3B110	R	29	113	423	46	122	23	4	10	50	36	71	3	.288	.348	.433
Walt Weiss	SS110	S	30	110	423	58	106	11	4	1	32	56	58	12	.251	.336	.303
Dante Bichette	OF116	R	30	116	484	74	147	33	2	27	95	19	70	21	.304	.334	.548
Mike Kingery	OF98,1B1	L	33	105	301	56	105	27	8	4	41	30	26	5	.349	.402	.532
Howard Johnson	OF62,1B1	S	33	93	227	30	48	10	2	10	40	39	73	11	.211	.323	.405
Eric Young	OF60,2B1	R	27	90	228	37	62	13	1	7	30	38	17	18	.272	.378	.430
Ellis Burks	OF39	R	29	42	149	33	48	8	3	13	24	16	39	3	.322	.388	.678
Vinny Castilla	SS18,2B14,3B9*	R	26	52	130	16	43	11	1	3	18	7	23	2	.331	.357	.500
Roberto Mejia	2B34	R	22	38	116	11	28	8	1	4	14	15	33	3	.241	.326	.431
Danny Sheaffer	C30,1B2,OF1	R	32	44	110	11	24	4	0	1	12	10	11	0	.218	.283	.282
John VanderWal	1B14,OF7	L	28	91	110	12	27	3	1	5	15	16	31	2	.245	.339	.427
Chris Jones	OF14	R	28	21	40	6	12	2	1	0	2	2	14	0	.300	.333	.400
Trent Hubbard	OF5	R	28	18	25	3	7	1	1	1	3	3	4	0	.280	.357	.520
Jayhawk Owens	C6	R	25	6	12	4	3	0	1	0	1	3	3	0	.250	.400	.417
Ty Van Burkleo	1B2	L	30	2	5	0	0	0	0	0	0	0	1	0	.000	.000	.000

V. Castilla, 2 G at 1B

Pitcher	T	Age	G	GS	CG	ShO	IP	H	HR	BB	SO	W-L	Sv	ERA
Dave Nied	R	25	22	22	2	1	122.0	137	15	47	74	9-7	0	4.80
Greg Harris	R	30	29	19	1	0	130.0	154	22	52	82	3-12	1	6.65
Marvin Freeman	R	31	19	18	0	0	112.2	113	10	23	67	10-2	0	2.80
Kevin Ritz	R	29	15	15	0	0	73.2	88	5	35	53	5-6	0	5.62
Lance Painter	L	26	15	14	0	0	73.2	91	9	26	41	4-6	0	6.11
Mike Harkey	R	27	24	13	0	0	91.2	125	10	35	39	1-6	0	5.79
Armando Reynoso	R	28	9	9	1	0	52.1	54	5	22	25	3-4	0	4.82
Mark Thompson	R	23	2	2	0	0	9.0	16	2	8	5	1-1	0	9.00
Steve Reed	R	28	61	0	0	0	64.0	79	9	26	51	3-2	3	3.94
Mike Munoz	L	28	57	0	0	0	45.2	37	3	31	32	4-2	1	3.74
Bruce Ruffin	L	30	56	0	0	0	55.2	55	6	30	65	4-5	16	4.04
Willie Blair	R	28	47	1	0	0	77.2	98	9	39	68	0-5	3	5.79
Marcus Moore	R	23	29	0	0	0	33.2	33	4	21	33	1-1	0	6.15
Darren Holmes	R	28	29	0	0	0	28.1	35	5	24	33	0-3	3	6.35
Kent Bottenfield†	R	25	15	1	0	0	24.2	28	1	10	15	3-1	1	5.84
Curt Leskanic	R	26	8	3	0	0	22.1	27	2	10	17	1-1	0	5.64
Jim Czajkowski	R	30	5	0	0	0	8.2	9	2	6	2	0-0	0	4.15
Bruce Walton	R	31	4	0	0	0	5.1	6	1	3	1	1-0	0	8.44

1994 San Diego Padres 4th NL West 47-70 .402 12.5 GB

Jim Riggleman

Player	Gm by Position	B	Age	G	AB	R	H	2B	3B	HR	RBI	BB	SO	SB	Avg	OBP	Slg
Brad Ausmus	C99,1B1	R	25	101	327	45	82	12	1	7	24	30	63	5	.251	.314	.358
Eddie Williams	1B46,3B1	R	29	49	175	32	58	11	1	11	42	15	26	0	.331	.392	.594
Bip Roberts	2B90,OF20	S	30	105	403	52	129	15	5	2	31	39	57	21	.320	.383	.397
Craig Shipley	3B53,SS14,2B13*	R	31	81	240	32	80	14	4	4	30	9	28	6	.333	.362	.475
Ricky Gutierrez	SS78,2B7	R	24	90	275	27	66	11	2	1	28	32	54	2	.240	.321	.305
Derek Bell	OF108	R	25	108	434	54	135	20	0	14	54	29	88	24	.311	.354	.454
Tony Gwynn	OF106	L	34	110	419	79	165	35	1	12	64	48	19	5	.394	.454	.568
Phil Plantier	OF91	L	25	96	341	44	75	21	0	18	41	36	91	3	.220	.302	.440
Luis Lopez	SS43,2B29,3B5	S	23	77	235	29	65	16	1	2	20	15	39	3	.277	.325	.379
Scott Livingstone†	3B50	L	28	57	180	11	49	12	1	2	10	6	22	2	.272	.294	.383
Phil Clark	1B24,OF17,C5*	R	26	61	149	14	32	6	0	5	20	5	17	1	.215	.250	.356
Archi Cianfrocco	3B37,1B16,SS1	R	27	59	146	9	32	8	0	4	13	3	39	2	.219	.252	.356
Billy Bean	OF39,1B16	L	30	84	135	7	29	5	1	0	14	7	25	0	.215	.248	.267
Tim Hyers	1B41,OF2	L	22	52	118	13	30	3	0	0	7	9	15	3	.254	.307	.280
Brian Johnson	C24,1B5	R	26	36	93	7	23	4	1	3	16	5	21	0	.247	.283	.409
Dave Staton	1B20	R	26	29	66	6	12	2	0	4	6	10	18	0	.182	.289	.394
Keith Lockhart	3B13,2B5,SS1*	L	29	27	43	4	9	0	0	2	6	4	10	1	.209	.286	.349
Ray McDavid	OF7	L	22	9	28	2	7	1	0	0	2	1	8	1	.250	.276	.286
Melvin Nieves	OF6	S	22	10	19	2	5	1	0	1	4	3	10	0	.263	.364	.474
Ray Holbert	SS1	R	23	5	5	1	1	0	0	0	0	0	4	0	.200	.200	.200

C. Shipley, 2 G at OF, 1 G at 1B; P. Clark, 1 G at 3B; K. Lockhart, 1 G at OF

Pitcher	T	Age	G	GS	CG	ShO	IP	H	HR	BB	SO	W-L	Sv	ERA
Andy Benes	R	26	25	25	2	2	172.1	155	20	51	189	6-14	0	3.86
Andy Ashby	R	26	24	24	4	0	164.1	145	16	43	121	6-11	0	3.40
Scott Sanders	R	25	23	20	0	0	111.0	103	10	48	109	4-8	1	4.78
Joey Hamilton	R	23	16	16	1	1	108.2	98	7	29	61	9-6	0	2.98
Wally Whitehurst	R	30	13	13	0	0	64.0	84	8	26	43	4-7	0	4.92
Bill Krueger†	L	36	8	7	1	0	41.0	42	5	7	30	3-2	0	4.83
Tim Worrell	R	26	3	3	0	0	14.2	9	0	5	14	0-1	0	3.68
Mike Campbell	R	30	3	2	0	0	8.1	13	5	5	10	1-1	0	12.96
Kerry Taylor	R	23	1	1	0	0	4.1	9	1	1	3	0-0	0	8.31
Pedro A. Martinez	L	25	48	1	0	0	68.1	52	4	49	52	3-2	3	2.90
Trevor Hoffman	R	26	47	0	0	0	56.0	39	4	20	68	4-4	20	2.57
Tim Mauser	R	27	35	0	0	0	49.0	50	3	19	32	2-4	2	3.49
Jeff Tabaka†	L	30	34	0	0	0	37.0	28	0	19	30	3-1	1	3.89
Donnie Elliott	R	25	30	1	0	0	33.0	31	3	21	24	0-1	0	3.27
A.J. Sager	R	29	22	3	0	0	46.2	62	4	16	26	1-4	0	5.98
Mark Davis	L	33	20	0	0	0	16.1	20	4	13	15	0-1	0	8.82
Gene Harris†	R	29	13	0	0	0	12.1	21	2	8	9	1-1	0	8.03
Doug Brocail	R	27	12	0	0	0	17.0	21	1	5	11	0-0	0	5.82
Bryce Florie	R	24	9	0	0	0	9.1	8	0	3	8	0-0	0	0.96
Jose Martinez	R	23	4	1	0	0	12.0	18	2	5	7	0-2	0	6.75

»1995 Boston Red Sox 1st AL East 86-58 .597 —

Kevin Kennedy

Player	Gm by Position	B	Age	G	AB	R	H	2B	3B	HR	RBI	BB	SO	SB	Avg	OBP	Slg
Mike Macfarlane	C111,DH3	R	31	115	364	45	82	18	1	15	51	38	78	2	.225	.319	.404
Mo Vaughn	1B138,DH2	L	27	140	550	98	165	28	3	39	126	68	150	11	.300	.388	.575
Luis Alicea	2B132	S	29	132	419	64	113	20	3	6	44	63	61	13	.270	.367	.375
Tim Naehring	3B124,DH1	R	28	126	433	61	133	27	2	10	57	77	66	0	.307	.415	.448
John Valentin	SS135	R	28	135	520	108	155	37	2	27	102	81	67	20	.298	.399	.533
Mike Greenwell	OF118,DH2	L	31	120	481	67	143	25	4	15	76	38	35	9	.297	.349	.459
Troy O'Leary	OF105,DH3	L	25	112	399	60	123	31	6	10	49	29	64	5	.308	.355	.491
Lee Tinsley	OF97	S	26	100	341	61	97	17	1	7	41	39	74	18	.284	.359	.402
Jose Canseco	DH101,OF1	R	30	102	396	64	121	25	1	24	81	42	93	4	.306	.378	.556
Willie McGee	OF64	S	36	67	200	32	57	11	3	2	15	9	41	5	.285	.311	.400
Bill Haselman	C48,DH11,1B1*	R	29	64	152	22	37	6	1	5	23	17	30	0	.243	.322	.395
Reggie Jefferson	DH32,1B7,OF2	S	26	46	121	21	35	8	0	5	26	9	24	0	.289	.333	.479
Mark Whiten†	OF31,DH1	S	28	32	108	13	20	3	0	1	10	8	23	1	.185	.239	.241
Chris Donnels†	3B27,1B8,2B3	L	29	40	91	13	23	2	2	2	11	9	18	0	.253	.317	.385
Matt Stairs	OF23,DH2	L	26	39	88	8	23	7	1	1	17	4	14	0	.261	.298	.398
Dwayne Hosey	OF21,DH1	S	28	24	68	20	23	8	1	3	7	8	16	6	.338	.408	.618
Terry Shumpert	2B8,3B5,SS3*	R	28	21	47	6	11	3	0	0	3	4	13	3	.234	.294	.298
Wes Chamberlain	OF12,DH5	R	29	19	42	4	5	1	0	1	1	3	11	1	.119	.178	.214
Carlos Rodriguez	2B7,SS6,3B1	S	27	13	30	5	10	2	0	0	5	2	2	0	.333	.394	.400
Rich Rowland	C11,DH3	R	31	14	29	1	5	1	0	0	1	0	11	0	.172	.172	.207
Juan Bell	SS6,2B5,3B1	R	27	17	26	7	4	2	0	1	2	2	10	0	.154	.207	.346
Karl Rhodes†	OF9	L	26	10	25	2	2	1	0	0	1	3	4	0	.080	.179	.120
Chris James†	OF8,DH5	R	32	16	24	2	4	1	0	0	1	1	4	0	.167	.200	.208
Ron Mahay	OF5	L	24	5	20	3	4	2	0	1	3	1	6	0	.200	.273	.450
Dave Hollins†	DH3,OF2	S	29	5	13	2	2	0	0	0	1	4	7	0	.154	.353	.154
Steve Rodriguez†	SS4,DH1,2B1	R	24	6	8	1	1	0	0	0	0	1	1	1	.125	.222	.125
Scott Hatteberg	C2	L	25	2	2	1	1	0	0	0	0	0	0	0	.500	.500	.500

B. Haselman, 1 G at 3B; T. Shumpert, 1 G at DH

Pitcher	T	Age	G	GS	CG	ShO	IP	H	HR	BB	SO	W-L	Sv	ERA
Erik Hanson	R	30	29	29	1	1	186.2	187	17	59	139	15-5	0	4.24
Tim Wakefield	R	28	27	27	6	1	195.1	163	22	68	119	16-8	0	2.95
Roger Clemens	R	32	23	23	0	0	140.0	141	15	60	132	10-5	0	4.18
Zane Smith	L	34	24	21	0	0	110.2	144	7	23	47	8-8	0	5.61
Vaughn Eshelman	L	26	23	14	0	0	81.2	86	3	36	41	6-3	0	4.85
Aaron Sele	R	25	6	6	0	0	32.1	32	3	14	21	3-1	0	3.06
Matt Murray†	R	24	2	1	0	0	3.1	11	1	3	1	0-1	0	18.90
Stan Belinda	R	28	63	0	0	0	69.2	51	5	28	57	8-1	10	3.10
Rheal Cormier	L	28	48	12	0	0	115.0	131	12	31	69	7-5	0	4.07
Joe Hudson	R	24	39	0	0	0	46.0	53	2	23	29	0-1	1	4.11
Mike Maddux†	R	33	36	4	0	0	89.2	86	5	15	65	4-1	1	3.61
Rick Aguilera†	R	33	30	0	0	0	30.1	26	4	7	23	2-2	20	2.67
Ken Ryan	R	26	28	0	0	0	32.2	34	4	24	34	0-4	7	4.96
Derek Lilliquist	L	29	28	0	0	0	23.0	27	7	9	9	2-1	0	6.26
Mike Stanton†	L	28	22	0	0	0	21.0	17	3	8	10	1-0	0	3.00
Eric Gunderson†	L	29	19	0	0	0	12.1	13	0	9	9	2-1	0	5.11
Alejandro Pena†	R	36	17	0	0	0	24.1	33	5	12	25	1-1	0	7.40
Jeff Pierce	R	26	12	0	0	0	15.0	16	0	14	12	0-3	0	6.60
Frank Rodriguez†	R	22	9	2	0	0	15.1	21	3	10	14	0-2	0	10.57
Jeff Suppan	R	20	8	3	0	0	22.2	29	4	5	19	1-2	0	5.96
Mike Hartley†	R	33	5	0	0	0	7.0	8	1	2	2	0-0	0	9.00
Tim VanEgmond	R	26	4	1	0	0	6.2	9	2	6	5	0-1	0	9.45
Joel Johnston	R	28	4	0	0	0	4.0	2	1	3	4	0-1	0	11.25
Brian Looney	L	25	3	1	0	0	4.2	12	1	4	2	0-1	0	17.36
Brian Bark	L	26	3	0	0	0	2.1	2	0	1	0	0-0	0	0.00
Keith Shepherd	R	27	2	0	0	0	1.0	4	0	2	0	0-0	0	36.00

1995 New York Yankees 2nd AL East 79-65 .549 7.0 GB

Buck Showalter

Player	Gm by Position	B	Age	G	AB	R	H	2B	3B	HR	RBI	BB	SO	SB	Avg	OBP	Slg
Mike Stanley	C107,DH10	R	32	118	399	63	107	29	1	18	83	57	106	1	.268	.360	.481
Don Mattingly	1B125,DH1	L	34	128	458	59	132	32	2	7	49	40	35	0	.288	.341	.413
Pat Kelly	2B87,DH1	R	27	89	270	32	64	12	1	4	29	23	65	8	.237	.307	.333
Wade Boggs	3B117,1B9	L	37	126	460	76	149	22	4	5	63	74	50	1	.324	.412	.422
Tony Fernandez	SS103,2B4	S	33	108	384	57	94	20	2	5	45	42	40	6	.245	.322	.346
Bernie Williams	OF144	S	26	144	563	93	173	29	9	18	82	75	98	8	.307	.392	.487
Paul O'Neill	OF121,DH4	L	32	127	460	82	138	30	4	22	96	71	76	1	.300	.387	.526
Gerald Williams	OF92,DH1	R	28	100	182	33	45	18	2	6	28	22	34	4	.247	.327	.467
Ruben Sierra†	DH46,OF10	S	29	56	215	33	56	15	0	7	44	22	34	1	.260	.322	.428
Randy Velarde	2B62,SS28,OF20*	R	32	111	367	60	102	19	1	7	46	55	64	5	.278	.375	.392
Jim Leyritz	C46,1B18,DH15	R	31	77	264	37	71	12	0	7	37	37	73	1	.269	.374	.394
Luis Polonia†	OF64	L	30	67	238	37	62	9	3	2	15	25	29	10	.261	.326	.349
Dion James	OF29,DH27,1B6	L	32	85	209	22	60	6	1	2	26	20	16	4	.287	.346	.354
Danny Tartabull†	DH39,OF18	R	32	59	192	25	43	12	0	6	28	33	54	0	.224	.335	.380
Russ Davis	3B34,DH4,1B2	R	25	40	98	14	27	5	2	2	12	10	26	0	.276	.349	.429
Darryl Strawberry	DH15,OF11	L	33	32	87	15	24	4	1	3	13	10	22	0	.276	.364	.448
Derek Jeter	SS15	R	21	15	48	5	12	4	1	0	7	3	11	0	.250	.294	.375
Dave Silvestri†	2B7,DH4,1B4*	R	27	17	21	4	2	0	0	1	4	4	9	0	.095	.259	.238
Kevin Elster†	SS10,2B1	R	30	10	17	1	2	1	0	0	0	1	5	0	.118	.167	.176
Robert Eenhoorn	2B3,SS2	R	27	5	14	1	2	1	0	0	2	1	3	0	.143	.200	.214
Ruben Rivera	OF4	R	21	5	1	0	0	0	0	0	0	0	1	0	.000	.000	.000
Jorge Posada	C1	S	23	1	0	0	0	0	0	0	0	0	0	0	—	—	—

R. Velarde, 19 G at 3B; D. Silvestri, 1 G at SS

Pitcher	T	Age	G	GS	CG	ShO	IP	H	HR	BB	SO	W-L	Sv	ERA
Jack McDowell	R	29	30	30	8	2	217.2	211	25	78	157	15-10	0	3.93
Sterling Hitchcock	L	24	27	27	4	1	168.1	155	22	68	121	11-10	0	4.70
Andy Pettitte	L	23	31	26	3	0	175.0	183	15	63	114	12-9	0	4.17
Scott Kamieniecki	R	31	17	16	1	0	89.2	83	8	49	43	7-6	0	4.01
David Cone†	R	32	13	13	1	0	99.0	82	12	47	89	9-2	0	3.82
Melido Perez	R	29	13	12	1	0	69.1	70	10	31	44	5-5	0	5.58
Mariano Rivera	R	25	19	10	0	0	67.0	71	11	30	51	5-3	0	5.51
Jimmy Key	L	34	5	5	0	0	30.1	40	3	6	14	1-2	0	5.64
Bob Wickman	R	26	63	1	0	0	80.0	77	6	33	51	2-4	1	4.05
John Wetteland	R	28	60	0	0	0	61.1	40	6	14	66	1-5	31	2.93
Steve Howe	L	37	56	0	0	0	49.0	66	7	17	28	6-3	2	4.96
Bob MacDonald	L	30	33	0	0	0	46.1	50	7	22	41	1-1	0	4.86
Joe Ausanio	R	29	28	0	0	0	37.2	42	9	23	36	2-0	1	5.73
Scott Bankhead	R	31	20	1	0	0	39.0	44	9	16	20	1-1	0	6.00
Josias Manzanillo†	R	27	11	0	0	0	17.1	19	1	9	11	0-0	0	2.08
Brian Boehringer	R	25	7	3	0	0	17.2	24	5	22	10	0-3	0	13.75
Dave Eiland	R	28	4	1	0	0	10.0	16	1	3	6	1-1	0	6.30
Dave Pavlas	R	32	4	0	0	0	5.2	8	0	0	3	0-0	0	3.18
Jeff Patterson	R	26	3	0	0	0	3.1	3	1	3	3	0-0	0	2.70
Rick Honeycutt†	L	41	3	0	0	0	1.0	2	1	1	0	0-0	0	27.00

1995 Baltimore Orioles 3rd AL East 71-73 .493 15.0 GB

Player	Gm by Position	B	Age	G	AB	R	H	2B	3B	HR	RBI	BB	SO	SB	Avg	OBP	Slg
Chris Hoiles	C107,DH6	R	30	114	352	53	88	15	1	19	58	67	80	1	.250	.373	.460
Rafael Palmeiro	1B142	L	30	143	554	89	172	30	2	39	104	62	65	3	.310	.380	.583
Manny Alexander	2B81,SS7,3B2*	R	24	94	242	35	57	9	1	3	23	20	30	11	.236	.299	.318
Jeff Manto	3B69,DH13,1B4	R	30	89	254	31	65	9	0	17	38	24	69	0	.256	.325	.492
Cal Ripken Jr.	SS144	R	34	144	550	71	144	33	2	17	88	52	59	0	.262	.324	.422
Brady Anderson	OF142	L	31	143	554	108	145	33	10	16	64	87	111	26	.262	.371	.444
Curtis Goodwin	OF84,DH2	L	22	87	289	40	76	11	3	1	24	15	53	22	.263	.301	.332
Kevin Bass	OF77,DH19	S	36	111	295	32	72	12	0	5	32	24	47	8	.244	.303	.336
Harold Baines	DH122	L	36	127	385	60	115	19	1	24	63	70	45	0	.299	.403	.540
Bobby Bonilla†	OF39,3B24	S	32	61	237	47	79	12	4	10	46	23	31	0	.333	.392	.544
Bret Barberie	2B74,DH5,3B3	S	27	90	237	32	57	14	0	2	25	36	50	3	.241	.351	.325
Jeffrey Hammonds	OF46,DH5	R	24	57	178	18	43	9	1	4	23	9	30	4	.242	.279	.371
Jeff Huson	3B33,2B21,DH2*	L	30	66	161	24	40	4	2	1	19	15	20	5	.248	.315	.317
Leo Gomez	3B44,DH5,1B3	R	29	53	127	16	30	5	0	4	12	18	23	0	.236	.336	.370
Mark Smith	OF32,DH3	R	25	37	104	11	24	5	0	3	15	12	22	3	.231	.314	.365
Greg Zaun	C39	S	24	40	104	18	27	5	0	3	14	16	14	1	.260	.358	.394
Andy Van Slyke†	OF17	L	34	17	63	6	10	1	0	3	8	5	15	0	.159	.221	.317
Matt Nokes†	C16,DH2	L	31	26	49	4	6	1	0	2	6	4	11	0	.122	.185	.265
Sherman Obando	DH7,OF7	R	25	16	38	0	10	1	0	0	3	2	12	1	.263	.293	.289
Damon Buford†	OF24	R	25	24	32	6	2	0	0	0	2	6	7	3	.063	.205	.063
Jarvis Brown	OF17	R	28	18	27	2	4	1	0	0	1	7	9	1	.148	.324	.185
Cesar Devarez	C6	R	25	6	4	0	0	0	0	0	0	0	0	0	.000	.000	.000
Jack Voigt†	DH1,1B1	R	29	3	1	1	1	0	0	0	0	0	0	0	1.000	1.000	1.000

M. Alexander, 1 G at DH; J. Huson, 1 G at SS

Phil Regan

Pitcher	T	Age	G	GS	CG	ShO	IP	H	HR	BB	SO	W-L	Sv	ERA
Mike Mussina	R	26	32	32	7	4	221.2	187	24	50	158	19-9	0	3.29
Kevin Brown	R	30	26	26	3	1	172.1	155	10	48	117	10-9	0	3.60
Jamie Moyer	L	32	27	18	0	0	115.2	117	18	30	65	8-6	0	5.21
Scott Erickson†	R	27	17	16	7	2	108.2	111	7	35	61	9-4	0	3.89
Ben McDonald	R	27	14	13	1	0	80.0	67	10	38	62	3-6	0	4.16
Rick Krivda	L	25	13	13	1	0	75.1	76	9	25	53	2-7	0	4.54
Sid Fernandez†	L	32	8	7	0	0	28.0	36	9	17	31	0-4	0	7.39
Scott Klingenbeck†	R	24	6	5	0	0	31.1	32	6	18	15	2-2	0	4.88
Jimmy Haynes	R	22	4	3	0	0	24.0	11	2	12	22	2-1	0	2.25
John DeSilva	R	27	2	2	0	0	8.2	8	3	7	1	1-0	0	7.27
Jesse Orosco	L	38	65	0	0	0	49.2	28	4	27	58	2-4	3	3.26
Doug Jones	R	38	52	0	0	0	46.2	55	6	16	42	0-4	22	5.01
Armando Benitez	R	22	44	0	0	0	47.2	37	8	37	56	1-5	2	5.66
Mark Lee	L	30	39	0	0	0	33.1	31	5	18	27	2-0	1	4.86
Terry Clark†	R	34	38	0	0	0	39.0	40	3	15	18	2-5	1	3.46
Mike Oquist	R	27	27	0	0	0	54.0	51	6	41	27	2-1	0	4.17
Alan Mills	R	28	21	0	0	0	23.0	30	4	18	16	3-0	0	7.43
Arthur Rhodes	L	25	19	9	0	0	75.1	68	13	48	77	2-5	0	6.21
Brad Pennington†	L	26	8	0	0	0	6.2	3	1	11	10	0-1	0	8.10
Jim Dedrick	R	27	6	0	0	0	7.2	8	1	6	3	0-0	0	2.35
Joe Borowski	R	24	6	0	0	0	7.1	5	0	4	3	0-0	0	1.23
Mike Hartley†	R	33	3	0	0	0	7.0	5	0	1	4	1-0	0	1.29
Gene Harris†	R	30	3	0	0	0	4.0	4	0	1	4	0-0	0	4.50

1995 Detroit Tigers 4th AL East 60-84 .417 26.0 GB

Player	Gm by Position	B	Age	G	AB	R	H	2B	3B	HR	RBI	BB	SO	SB	Avg	OBP	Slg
John Flaherty	C112	R	27	112	354	39	86	22	1	11	40	18	47	0	.243	.284	.404
Cecil Fielder	1B77,DH58	R	31	136	494	70	120	18	1	31	82	75	116	0	.243	.346	.472
Lou Whitaker	2B63,DH8	L	38	84	249	36	73	14	0	14	44	31	41	4	.293	.372	.518
Travis Fryman	3B144	R	26	144	567	79	156	21	5	15	81	63	100	4	.275	.347	.409
Chris Gomez	SS97,2B31,DH1	R	24	123	431	49	96	20	2	11	50	41	96	4	.223	.292	.355
Chad Curtis	OF144	R	26	144	586	96	157	29	3	21	67	70	93	27	.268	.349	.435
Bob Higginson	OF123,DH2	L	24	131	410	61	92	17	5	14	43	62	107	6	.224	.329	.393
Danny Bautista	OF86	R	23	89	271	28	55	9	0	7	27	12	68	4	.203	.237	.314
Kirk Gibson	DH63,OF1	L	38	70	227	37	59	12	2	9	35	33	61	9	.260	.358	.449
Alan Trammell	SS60,DH6	R	37	74	223	28	60	12	0	2	23	27	19	3	.269	.345	.350
Scott Fletcher	2B63,SS3,1B1	R	36	67	182	19	42	10	1	1	17	19	27	1	.231	.312	.313
Juan Samuel†	1B37,DH16,OF9*	R	34	76	171	28	48	10	1	10	34	24	38	5	.281	.376	.526
Ron Tingley	C53,1B1	R	36	54	124	14	28	8	1	4	18	15	38	0	.226	.307	.403
Franklin Stubbs	1B20,OF20,DH3	L	34	62	116	13	29	11	0	2	19	19	27	0	.250	.358	.397
Tony Clark	1B27	S	23	27	101	10	24	5	1	3	11	8	30	0	.238	.294	.396
Phil Nevin†	OF27,DH2	R	24	29	96	9	21	3	1	2	12	11	27	0	.219	.318	.333
Milt Cuyler	OF36,DH2	S	26	41	88	15	18	1	4	0	5	8	16	2	.205	.271	.307
Derrick White	1B16,OF9,DH8	R	25	39	48	3	9	2	0	0	2	0	7	1	.188	.188	.229
Todd Steverson	OF27,DH1	R	23	30	42	11	11	0	0	2	6	6	10	2	.262	.340	.405
Steve Rodriguez†	2B12,SS1	R	24	12	31	4	6	1	0	0	0	5	9	1	.194	.306	.226
Rudy Pemberton	OF8,DH3	R	25	12	30	3	9	3	1	0	3	1	5	0	.300	.344	.467
Joe Hall	OF5,DH1	R	29	7	15	2	2	0	0	0	0	2	3	0	.133	.235	.133
Shannon Penn	2B3	S	25	3	9	0	3	0	0	0	0	1	2	0	.333	.400	.333

J. Samuel, 6 G at 2B

Sparky Anderson

Pitcher	T	Age	G	GS	CG	ShO	IP	H	HR	BB	SO	W-L	Sv	ERA
Sean Bergman	R	25	28	28	1	1	135.1	169	19	67	86	7-10	0	5.12
Mike Moore	R	35	25	25	1	0	132.2	179	24	68	64	5-15	0	7.53
Felipe Lira	R	23	37	22	0	0	146.1	151	17	56	89	9-13	1	4.31
David Wells†	L	32	18	18	3	0	130.1	120	17	37	83	10-3	0	3.04
Jose Lima	R	22	15	15	0	0	73.2	85	10	18	37	3-9	0	6.11
C.J. Nitkowski†	L	22	11	11	0	0	39.1	53	7	20	13	1-4	0	7.09
Clint Sodowsky	R	22	6	6	0	0	23.1	24	4	18	14	2-2	0	5.01
Pat Ahearne	R	25	4	3	0	0	10.0	20	2	5	4	0-2	0	11.70
Joe Boever	R	34	60	0	0	0	98.2	128	17	44	71	5-7	3	6.39
Brian Bohanon	L	26	52	10	0	0	105.2	121	10	41	63	1-1	1	5.54
John Doherty	R	28	48	2	0	0	113.0	130	10	37	46	5-9	6	5.10
Brian Maxcy	R	24	41	0	0	0	52.1	61	6	31	20	4-5	0	6.88
Mike Christopher	R	31	36	0	0	0	61.1	71	8	14	34	4-0	1	3.82
Mike Henneman†	R	33	29	0	0	0	29.1	24	0	9	24	0-1	18	1.53
Buddy Groom†	L	29	23	4	0	0	40.2	55	6	26	23	1-3	1	7.52
Kevin Wickander†	L	30	21	0	0	0	17.1	18	1	9	9	0-0	1	2.60
Ben Blomdahl	R	24	14	0	0	0	24.1	36	5	13	15	0-0	1	7.77
Mike Myers†	L	26	11	0	0	0	6.1	10	1	4	4	1-0	0	9.95
Greg Gohr	R	27	10	0	0	0	10.1	9	0	3	12	1-0	0	0.87
Dwayne Henry	R	33	10	0	0	0	8.2	11	0	10	9	1-0	5	6.23
Mike Gardiner	R	29	9	0	0	0	12.1	27	5	2	7	0-0	0	14.59
Sean Whiteside	L	24	2	0	0	0	3.2	7	1	4	2	0-0	0	14.73

1995 Toronto Blue Jays 5th AL East 56-88 .389 30.0 GB

Player	Gm by Position	B	Age	G	AB	R	H	2B	3B	HR	RBI	BB	SO	SB	Avg	OBP	Slg
Lance Parrish	C67,DH1	R	39	70	178	15	36	9	0	4	22	15	52	0	.202	.265	.320
John Olerud	1B133	L	26	135	492	72	143	32	0	8	54	84	54	0	.291	.398	.404
Roberto Alomar	2B128	S	27	130	517	71	155	24	7	13	66	47	45	30	.300	.354	.449
Ed Sprague	3B139,1B7,DH2	R	27	144	521	77	127	27	2	18	74	58	96	0	.244	.333	.407
Alex Gonzalez	SS97,3B9,DH3	R	22	111	367	51	89	19	4	10	42	44	114	4	.243	.322	.398
Joe Carter	OF128,1B7,DH5	R	35	139	558	70	141	23	0	25	76	37	87	12	.253	.300	.428
Shawn Green	OF109	L	22	121	379	52	109	31	4	15	54	20	68	1	.288	.326	.509
Devon White	OF99	S	32	101	427	61	121	23	5	10	53	29	97	11	.283	.334	.431
Paul Molitor	DH129	R	38	130	525	63	142	31	2	15	60	61	57	12	.270	.350	.423
Sandy Martinez	C61	L	22	62	191	12	46	12	0	2	25	7	45	0	.241	.270	.335
Domingo Cedeno	SS30,2B20,3B1	S	26	51	161	18	38	6	1	4	14	10	35	0	.236	.289	.360
Candy Maldonado†	OF58,DH1	R	34	61	160	22	43	13	0	7	25	25	45	1	.269	.368	.481
Mike Huff	OF55	R	31	61	138	14	32	9	1	1	9	22	21	1	.232	.337	.333
Randy Knorr	C45	R	26	45	132	18	28	8	0	3	16	11	28	0	.212	.273	.341
Tomas Perez	SS31,2B7,3B1	S	21	41	98	12	24	3	1	1	8	7	18	0	.245	.292	.327
Carlos Delgado	OF17,DH7,1B4	L	23	37	91	7	15	3	0	3	11	6	26	0	.165	.212	.297
Robert Perez	OF15	R	26	17	48	2	9	2	0	1	3	0	5	0	.188	.188	.292
Shannon Stewart	OF12	S	21	12	38	2	8	0	0	0	1	5	5	2	.211	.318	.211
Howard Battle	3B6,DH1	R	23	9	15	3	3	0	0	0	0	4	8	1	.200	.368	.200

Cito Gaston

Pitcher	T	Age	G	GS	CG	ShO	IP	H	HR	BB	SO	W-L	Sv	ERA
Pat Hentgen	R	26	30	30	2	0	200.2	236	24	90	135	10-14	0	5.11
Al Leiter	L	29	28	28	2	1	183.0	162	15	108	153	11-11	0	3.64
Juan Guzman	R	28	24	24	3	0	135.1	151	13	73	94	4-14	0	6.32
David Cone†	R	32	17	17	5	2	130.1	113	12	41	102	9-6	0	3.38
Danny Darwin†	R	39	13	11	1	0	65.0	91	13	24	36	1-8	0	7.62
Edwin Hurtado	R	25	14	10	1	0	77.2	81	11	40	33	5-2	0	5.45
Giovanni Carrara	R	27	12	7	1	0	48.2	64	10	25	27	2-4	0	7.21
Jeff Ware	R	24	5	5	0	0	26.1	28	2	21	18	2-1	0	5.47
Tony Castillo	L	32	55	0	0	0	72.2	64	7	24	38	1-5	13	3.22
Mike Timlin	R	29	31	0	0	0	42.0	38	1	17	36	4-3	5	2.14
Tim Crabtree	R	25	31	0	0	0	32.0	30	1	13	21	0-2	0	3.09
Danny Cox	R	35	24	0	0	0	45.0	57	4	33	38	1-3	0	7.40
Woody Williams	R	28	23	3	0	0	53.2	44	6	28	41	1-2	0	3.69
Paul Menhart	R	26	21	9	1	0	78.2	72	9	47	50	1-4	0	4.92
Ken Robinson	R	25	21	0	0	0	39.0	25	7	22	31	1-2	0	3.69
Jimmy Rogers	R	28	19	0	0	0	23.2	21	4	18	13	2-4	0	5.70
Darren Hall	R	30	17	0	0	0	16.1	21	2	9	11	0-2	3	4.41
Ricardo Jordan	L	25	15	0	0	0	15.0	18	3	13	10	1-0	1	6.60
Brad Cornett	R	26	5	0	0	0	5.0	9	1	3	4	0-0	0	9.00
Duane Ward	R	31	4	0	0	0	2.2	11	0	5	3	0-1	0	27.00

1995 Cleveland Indians 1st AL Central 100-44 .694 —

Player	Gm by Position	B	Age	G	AB	R	H	2B	3B	HR	RBI	BB	SO	SB	Avg	OBP	Slg
Tony Pena	C91	R	38	91	263	25	69	15	0	5	28	14	44	1	.262	.302	.376
Paul Sorrento	1B91,DH11	L	29	104	323	50	76	14	0	25	79	51	71	1	.235	.336	.511
Carlos Baerga	2B134,DH1	S	26	135	557	87	175	28	2	15	90	35	31	11	.314	.355	.452
Jim Thome	3B134,DH1	L	24	137	452	92	142	29	3	25	73	97	113	4	.314	.438	.558
Omar Vizquel	SS136	S	28	136	542	87	144	28	0	6	56	59	59	29	.266	.333	.351
Albert Belle	OF142,DH1	R	28	143	546	121	173	52	1	50	126	73	80	5	.317	.401	.690
Manny Ramirez	OF131,DH5	R	23	137	484	85	149	26	1	31	107	75	112	6	.308	.402	.558
Kenny Lofton	OF114,DH2	L	28	118	481	93	149	22	13	7	53	40	49	54	.310	.362	.453
Eddie Murray	DH95,1B18	S	39	113	436	68	141	21	0	21	82	39	65	5	.323	.375	.516
Sandy Alomar Jr.	C61	R	29	66	203	32	61	6	0	10	35	7	26	3	.300	.332	.478
Wayne Kirby	OF68,DH7	L	31	101	188	29	39	10	2	1	14	13	32	10	.207	.260	.298
Herbert Perry	1B45,DH5,3B1	R	25	52	162	23	51	13	1	3	23	13	28	1	.315	.376	.463
Alvaro Espinoza	2B22,3B22,SS19*	R	33	66	143	15	36	4	0	2	17	2	16	0	.252	.264	.322
Dave Winfield	DH39	R	43	46	115	11	22	5	0	2	4	14	26	1	.191	.285	.287
Ruben Amaro	OF22,DH3	S	30	28	60	5	12	3	0	1	7	4	6	1	.200	.273	.300
Scooter Tucker†	C17	R	28	17	20	2	0	0	0	0	0	5	4	0	.000	.231	.000
Jesse Levis	C12	L	27	12	18	1	6	2	0	0	3	1	0	0	.333	.333	.444
Billy Ripken	2B7,3B1	R	30	8	17	4	7	0	0	2	3	0	3	0	.412	.412	.765
Brian Giles	OF3,DH1	L	24	6	9	6	5	0	0	1	3	0	1	0	.556	.556	.889
Jeromy Burnitz	OF6,DH2	L	26	9	7	4	4	1	0	0	0	0	0	0	.571	.571	.714
David Bell†	3B2	R	22	2	2	0	0	0	0	0	0	0	0	0	.000	.000	.000

A. Espinoza, 2 G at 1B, 1 G at DH

Mike Hargrove

Pitcher	T	Age	G	GS	CG	ShO	IP	H	HR	BB	SO	W-L	Sv	ERA
Charles Nagy	R	28	29	29	2	1	178.0	194	20	61	139	16-6	0	4.55
Dennis Martinez	R	40	28	28	3	2	187.0	174	17	46	99	12-5	0	3.08
Orel Hershiser	R	36	26	26	1	1	167.1	151	21	51	111	16-6	0	3.87
Mark Clark	R	27	22	21	2	0	124.2	143	13	42	68	9-7	0	5.27
Chad Ogea	R	24	20	14	1	0	106.1	95	11	29	57	8-3	0	3.05
Ken Hill†	R	29	12	11	1	0	74.2	77	5	32	48	4-1	0	3.98
Bud Black	L	38	11	10	0	0	47.1	63	8	16	34	4-2	0	6.85
Joe Roa	R	23	1	1	0	0	6.0	9	1	2	0	0-1	0	6.00
Jose Mesa	R	29	62	0	0	0	64.0	49	3	17	58	3-0	46	1.13
Julian Tavarez	R	22	57	0	0	0	85.0	76	7	21	68	10-2	0	2.44
Eric Plunk	R	31	56	0	0	0	64.0	48	5	27	71	6-2	2	2.67
Paul Assenmacher	L	34	47	0	0	0	38.1	32	3	12	40	6-2	0	2.82
Jim Poole	L	29	42	0	0	0	50.1	40	7	17	41	3-3	0	3.75
Alan Embree	L	25	23	0	0	0	24.2	23	2	16	23	3-2	1	5.11
Jason Grimsley	R	27	15	2	0	0	34.0	37	4	32	25	0-0	1	6.09
Dennis Cook†	L	32	11	0	0	0	12.2	16	3	10	13	0-0	0	6.39
Paul Shuey	R	24	7	0	0	0	6.1	5	0	5	5	0-2	0	4.26
Albie Lopez	R	23	6	2	0	0	23.0	17	4	7	22	0-0	0	3.13
Gregg Olson†	R	28	3	0	0	0	2.2	5	1	2	0	0-0	0	13.50
John Farrell	R	32	1	0	0	0	4.2	7	0	0	4	0-0	0	3.86

1995 Kansas City Royals 2nd AL Central 70-74 .486 30.0 GB

Bob Boone

Player	Gm by Position	B	Age	G	AB	R	H	2B	3B	HR	RBI	BB	SO	SB	Avg	OBP	Slg
Brent Mayne	C103	L	27	110	307	23	77	18	1	1	27	25	41	0	.251	.313	.326
Wally Joyner	1B126,DH2	L	33	131	465	69	144	28	0	12	83	69	65	3	.310	.394	.447
Keith Lockhart	2B61,3B17,DH14	L	30	94	274	41	88	19	3	6	33	14	21	8	.321	.355	.478
Gary Gaetti	3B123,1B11,DH6	R	36	137	514	76	134	27	0	35	96	47	91	3	.261	.329	.518
Greg Gagne	SS118,DH2	R	33	120	430	58	110	25	4	6	49	38	60	3	.256	.316	.374
Tom Goodwin	OF130,DH2	L	26	133	480	72	138	16	3	4	28	38	72	50	.288	.346	.358
Jon Nunnally	OF107,DH4	L	23	119	303	51	74	15	6	14	42	51	86	6	.244	.357	.472
Vince Coleman†	OF69,DH4	S	33	75	293	39	84	13	4	4	20	27	48	26	.287	.348	.399
Bob Hamelin	DH56,1B8	L	27	72	208	20	35	7	1	7	25	26	56	0	.168	.278	.313
Dave Howard	2B41,SS33,OF30*	S	28	95	255	23	62	13	4	0	19	24	41	6	.243	.310	.325
Johnny Damon	OF47	L	21	47	188	32	53	11	5	3	23	12	22	7	.282	.324	.441
Michael Tucker	OF36,DH22	L	24	62	177	23	46	10	0	4	17	18	51	2	.260	.332	.384
Pat Borders†	C45,DH3	R	32	52	143	14	33	8	1	4	13	7	22	0	.231	.267	.385
Joe Vitiello	DH38,1B8	R	25	53	130	13	33	4	0	7	21	8	25	0	.254	.317	.446
Edgar Caceres	2B36,SS8,1B6*	S	31	55	117	13	28	6	2	1	17	8	15	2	.239	.291	.350
Phil Hiatt	OF47,DH2	R	26	52	113	11	23	6	0	4	12	9	37	1	.204	.262	.363
Jose Lind†	2B29	R	31	29	97	4	26	3	0	0	6	3	8	0	.268	.290	.299
Joe Randa	3B22,2B9,DH2	R	25	34	70	6	12	2	0	1	5	6	17	0	.171	.237	.243
Chris James†	DH14,OF5	R	32	26	58	6	18	3	0	2	7	6	10	1	.310	.373	.466
Henry Mercedes	C22	R	25	23	43	7	11	2	0	0	9	8	13	0	.256	.370	.302
Les Norman	OF17,DH5	R	26	24	40	6	9	0	1	0	4	6	6	0	.225	.326	.275
Jeff Grotewold	DH11,1B1	L	29	15	36	4	10	1	0	1	6	9	7	0	.278	.422	.389
Chris Stynes	2B17,DH1	R	22	22	35	7	6	1	0	0	2	4	3	0	.171	.256	.200
Brent Cookson	OF12,DH2	R	25	22	35	2	5	1	0	0	5	2	7	1	.143	.189	.171
Juan Samuel†	DH7,OF5,1B1	R	34	15	34	3	6	0	0	2	5	5	11	1	.176	.282	.353
Felix Jose	OF7	S	30	9	30	2	4	1	0	0	1	2	9	0	.133	.188	.167
Keith Miller	DH4,OF4	R	32	9	15	2	5	0	0	1	3	2	4	0	.333	.412	.533
Russ McGinnis	1B1,3B1,OF1	R	32	3	5	1	0	0	0	0	0	1	1	0	.000	.167	.000
Mike Sweeney	C4	R	21	4	4	1	1	0	0	0	0	0	0	0	.250	.250	.250
Jose Mota	2B2	S	30	2	2	0	0	0	0	0	0	0	0	0	.000	.000	.000

D. Howard, 1 G at DH, 1 G at 1B; E. Caceres, 3 G at DH, 3 G at 3B

Pitcher	T	Age	G	GS	CG	ShO	IP	H	HR	BB	SO	W-L	Sv	ERA
Mark Gubicza	R	32	33	33	3	2	213.1	222	21	62	81	12-14	0	3.75
Kevin Appier	R	27	31	31	4	1	201.1	163	14	80	185	15-10	0	3.89
Tom Gordon	R	27	31	31	2	0	189.0	204	12	89	119	12-12	0	4.43
Jason Jacome†	L	24	15	14	1	0	84.0	101	15	21	39	4-6	0	5.36
Chris Haney	L	26	16	13	1	0	81.1	78	7	33	31	3-4	0	3.65
Dave Fleming†	L	25	9	5	0	0	32.0	27	4	19	14	0-1	0	3.66
Scott Anderson	R	32	6	4	0	0	25.1	29	3	8	6	1-0	0	5.33
Tom Browning	L	35	2	2	0	0	10.0	13	2	5	3	0-2	0	8.10
Jim Pittsley	R	21	1	1	0	0	3.1	7	3	1	0	0-0	0	13.50
Jeff Montgomery	R	33	54	0	0	0	65.2	60	7	25	49	2-3	31	3.43
Rusty Meacham	R	27	49	0	0	0	59.2	72	6	19	30	4-3	2	4.98
Billy Brewer	L	27	48	0	0	0	45.1	54	9	20	31	2-4	0	5.56
Hipolito Pichardo	R	25	44	0	0	0	64.0	66	4	30	43	8-4	1	4.36
Mike Magnante	L	30	28	0	0	0	44.2	45	6	16	28	1-1	0	4.23
Dilson Torres	R	25	24	2	0	0	44.1	56	6	17	28	1-2	0	6.09
Gregg Olson†	R	28	20	0	0	0	30.1	23	3	17	21	3-3	3	3.26
Mel Bunch	R	23	13	5	0	0	40.0	42	11	14	19	1-3	0	5.63
Jim Converse†	R	23	9	0	0	0	12.1	12	0	8	5	1-0	0	5.84
Doug Linton	R	30	7	2	0	0	22.1	22	4	10	13	0-1	0	7.25
Rick Huisman	R	26	7	0	0	0	9.2	14	2	1	12	0-0	0	7.45
Dennis Rasmussen	L	36	5	1	0	0	10.0	13	3	8	6	0-1	0	9.00

1995 Chicago White Sox 3rd AL Central 68-76 .472 32.0 GB

Gene Lamont (11-20)/Terry Bevington (57-56)

Player	Gm by Position	B	Age	G	AB	R	H	2B	3B	HR	RBI	BB	SO	SB	Avg	OBP	Slg
Ron Karkovice	C113	R	31	113	323	44	70	14	1	13	51	39	84	2	.217	.306	.387
Frank Thomas	1B91,DH53	R	27	145	493	102	152	27	0	40	111	136	74	3	.308	.454	.606
Ray Durham	2B122,DH1	S	23	125	471	68	121	27	6	7	51	31	83	18	.257	.309	.384
Robin Ventura	3B121,1B18,DH1	L	27	135	492	79	145	22	0	26	93	75	98	4	.295	.384	.498
Ozzie Guillen	SS120,DH1	L	31	122	415	50	103	20	3	1	41	13	25	6	.248	.270	.318
Lance Johnson	OF140,DH1	L	31	142	607	98	186	18	12	10	57	32	31	40	.306	.341	.425
Tim Raines	OF107,DH22	S	35	133	502	81	143	25	4	12	67	70	52	13	.285	.374	.422
Mike Devereaux†	OF90	R	32	92	333	48	102	21	1	10	55	25	51	6	.306	.352	.465
John Kruk	DH42,1B1	L	34	45	159	13	49	7	0	2	23	26	33	0	.308	.399	.390
Dave Martinez	OF59,1B47,DH4*	L	30	119	303	49	93	16	4	5	37	32	41	8	.307	.371	.436
Lyle Mouton	OF53,DH2	R	26	58	179	23	54	16	0	5	27	19	46	1	.302	.373	.475
Norberto Martin	2B17,OF12,DH10*	R	28	72	160	17	43	7	4	2	17	3	25	5	.269	.281	.400
Craig Grebeck	SS31,3B18,2B8	R	30	53	154	19	40	12	0	1	18	21	23	0	.260	.360	.357
Mike LaValliere	C46	L	34	46	98	7	24	6	0	1	19	9	15	0	.245	.303	.337
Warren Newson†	OF24,DH7	L	30	51	85	19	20	0	2	3	9	23	27	1	.235	.404	.388
Chris Sabo†	DH15,1B1,3B1	R	33	20	71	10	18	5	0	1	8	3	12	2	.254	.295	.366
Chris Snopek	3B17,SS6	R	24	22	68	12	22	4	0	1	7	9	12	1	.324	.403	.426
Barry Lyons	C16,DH7,1B4	R	35	27	64	8	17	2	0	5	16	4	14	0	.266	.304	.531
Mike Cameron	OF28	R	22	28	38	4	7	2	0	1	2	3	15	0	.184	.244	.316
Chris Tremie	C9,DH1	R	25	10	24	0	4	0	0	0	0	1	2	0	.167	.200	.167
Doug Brady	2B6,DH2	S	25	12	21	4	4	1	0	0	3	2	4	0	.190	.261	.238

D. Martinez, 1 G at P; N. Martin, 9 G at 3B, 7 G at SS

Pitcher	T	Age	G	GS	CG	ShO	IP	H	HR	BB	SO	W-L	Sv	ERA
Alex Fernandez	R	25	30	30	5	2	203.2	200	19	65	159	12-8	0	3.80
Wilson Alvarez	L	25	29	29	3	0	175.0	171	21	93	118	8-11	0	4.32
Jason Bere	R	24	27	27	1	0	137.2	151	21	106	110	8-15	0	7.19
Jim Abbott††	L	27	17	17	3	0	112.1	116	10	35	45	6-4	0	3.36
Dave Righetti	L	36	10	9	0	0	49.1	65	6	18	29	3-2	0	4.20
Mike Sirotka	L	24	6	6	0	0	34.1	39	2	17	19	1-2	0	4.19
Luis Andujar	R	22	5	5	0	0	30.1	26	4	14	9	2-1	0	3.26
James Baldwin	R	23	6	4	0	0	14.2	32	6	9	10	0-1	0	12.89
Mike Bertotti	L	25	4	4	0	0	14.1	23	6	11	15	1-1	0	12.56
Roberto Hernandez	R	30	60	0	0	0	59.2	63	9	28	84	3-7	32	3.92
Kirk McCaskill	R	34	55	1	0	0	81.0	97	10	33	50	6-4	2	4.89
Scott Radinsky	L	27	46	0	0	0	38.0	46	7	17	14	2-1	1	5.45
Jose DeLeon†	R	34	38	0	0	0	67.2	60	10	28	53	5-3	0	5.19
Tim Fortugno	L	33	37	0	0	0	38.2	30	7	19	24	1-3	0	5.59
Matt Karchner	R	28	31	0	0	0	32.0	33	2	12	24	4-2	0	1.69
Brian Keyser	R	28	23	10	0	0	92.1	114	10	27	48	5-6	0	4.97
Larry Thomas	L	25	17	0	0	0	13.2	8	1	6	12	0-0	0	1.32
Rob Dibble†	R	31	16	0	0	0	14.1	7	1	27	16	0-1	1	6.28
Bill Simas	R	23	14	0	0	0	14.0	15	1	10	16	1-1	0	2.57
Atlee Hammaker	L	37	13	0	0	0	6.1	11	2	8	3	0-0	0	12.79
Jeff Shaw†	R	28	9	0	0	0	9.2	12	2	1	6	0-0	0	6.52
Rodney Bolton	R	26	8	3	0	0	22.0	33	4	14	10	0-2	0	8.18
Isidro Marquez	R	30	7	0	0	0	6.2	9	3	2	8	0-1	0	6.75
Andrew Lorraine	L	22	5	0	0	0	8.0	3	0	2	5	0-0	0	3.38
Scott Ruffcorn	R	25	4	0	0	0	8.0	10	0	13	5	0-0	0	7.88
Dave Martinez	L	30	1	0	0	0	1.0	0	0	2	0	0-0	0	0.00

1995 Milwaukee Brewers 4th AL Central 65-79 .451 35.0 GB

Phil Garner

Player	Gm by Position	B	Age	G	AB	R	H	2B	3B	HR	RBI	BB	SO	SB	Avg	OBP	Slg
Joe Oliver	C91,DH6,1B2	R	29	97	337	43	92	20	0	12	51	27	66	2	.273	.332	.439
John Jaha	1B81,DH6	R	29	88	316	59	99	20	2	20	65	36	66	2	.313	.389	.579
Fernando Vina	2B99,SS6,3B2	L	26	113	288	46	74	7	7	3	29	22	28	6	.257	.327	.361
Jeff Cirillo	3B108,2B25,1B3*	R	25	125	328	57	91	19	4	9	39	47	42	7	.277	.371	.442
Jose Valentin	SS104,DH3,3B1	S	25	112	338	62	74	23	3	11	49	37	83	16	.219	.293	.402
David Hulse	OF115	L	27	119	339	46	85	11	6	3	47	18	60	15	.251	.285	.345
Darryl Hamilton	OF109,DH2	L	30	112	398	54	108	20	6	5	44	47	35	11	.271	.350	.389
Matt Mieske	OF108,DH2	R	27	117	267	42	67	13	1	12	48	27	45	2	.251	.323	.442
Greg Vaughn	DH104	R	29	108	392	67	88	19	1	17	59	55	89	10	.224	.317	.408
Kevin Seitzer	3B88,1B36,DH14	R	33	132	492	56	153	33	3	5	69	64	57	2	.311	.395	.421
B.J. Surhoff	OF60,1B55,C18*	L	30	117	415	72	133	26	3	13	73	37	43	7	.320	.378	.492
Pat Listach	2B59,SS36,OF11*	S	27	101	334	35	73	8	2	0	25	25	61	13	.219	.276	.254
Dave Nilsson	OF58,DH14,1B7*	L	25	81	263	41	73	12	1	12	53	24	41	2	.278	.337	.468
Mike Matheny	C80	R	24	80	166	13	41	9	1	0	21	12	28	2	.247	.306	.313
Turner Ward	OF40,DH1	S	30	44	129	19	34	3	1	4	16	14	21	6	.264	.338	.395
Derrick May†	OF32	L	26	32	113	15	28	3	1	1	9	5	18	0	.248	.286	.319
Mark Loretta	SS13,2B4,DH1	R	23	19	50	13	13	3	0	1	3	4	7	1	.260	.327	.380
Duane Singleton	OF11	L	22	13	31	0	2	0	0	0	0	1	10	1	.065	.094	.065
Tim Unroe	1B2	R	24	2	4	0	1	0	0	0	0	0	0	0	.250	.250	.250
Bill Wegman	P37,OF1	R	32	37	0	0	0	0	0	0	0	0	0	0	—	—	—

J. Cirillo, 2 G at SS; B. Surhoff, 3 G at DH; P. Listach, 2 G at 3B; D. Nilsson, 2 G at C

Pitcher	T	Age	G	GS	CG	ShO	IP	H	HR	BB	SO	W-L	Sv	ERA
Ricky Bones	R	26	32	31	3	0	200.1	218	26	83	77	10-12	0	4.63
Steve Sparks	R	29	33	27	3	0	202.0	210	17	86	96	9-11	0	4.63
Brian Givens	L	29	19	19	0	0	107.1	116	11	54	73	5-7	0	4.95
Scott Karl	L	23	25	18	1	0	124.0	141	10	50	59	6-7	0	4.14
Bob Scanlan	R	28	17	14	0	0	83.1	101	9	44	29	4-7	0	6.59
Sid Roberson	L	23	26	13	0	0	84.1	102	16	37	40	6-4	0	5.76
Cal Eldred	R	27	4	4	0	0	23.2	24	4	10	18	1-1	0	3.42
Mike Fetters	R	30	40	0	0	0	34.2	40	3	20	33	0-3	22	3.38
Bill Wegman	R	32	37	4	0	0	70.2	89	14	21	50	5-7	2	5.35
Ron Rightnowar	R	30	34	0	0	0	36.2	35	3	18	22	2-1	1	5.40
Graeme Lloyd	L	28	33	0	0	0	32.0	28	4	8	13	0-5	4	4.50
Angel Miranda	L	25	30	10	0	0	74.0	83	8	49	45	4-5	1	5.23
Al Reyes	R	24	27	0	0	0	33.1	19	3	18	29	1-1	1	2.43
Mike Ignasiak	R	29	25	0	0	0	39.2	51	5	23	26	4-1	0	5.90
Mark Kiefer	R	26	24	0	0	0	49.2	37	6	27	41	4-1	0	3.44
Rob Dibble†	R	31	15	0	0	0	12.0	9	1	19	10	1-1	0	8.25
Joe Slusarski	R	28	12	0	0	0	15.0	21	3	6	6	1-1	0	5.40
Jamie McAndrew	R	27	10	4	0	0	36.1	37	2	12	19	2-3	0	4.71
Jeff Bronkey	R	29	8	0	0	0	12.1	15	0	6	5	0-0	0	3.65
Kevin Wickander†	L	30	8	0	0	0	6.0	1	0	3	2	0-0	0	0.00
Jose Mercedes	R	24	5	0	0	0	7.1	12	1	8	6	0-1	0	9.82
Mike Thomas	L	25	1	0	0	0	1.1	2	0	1	0	0-0	0	0.00

1995 Minnesota Twins 5th AL Central 56-88 .389 44.0 GB

Tom Kelly

Player	Gm by Position	B	Age	G	AB	R	H	2B	3B	HR	RBI	BB	SO	SB	Avg	OBP	Slg
Matt Walbeck	C113	S	25	115	393	40	101	18	1	1	44	25	71	3	.257	.302	.316
Scott Stahoviak	1B69,3B22,DH1	L	25	94	263	28	70	19	0	3	23	30	61	5	.266	.341	.373
Chuck Knoblauch	2B136,SS2	R	26	136	538	107	179	34	8	11	63	78	95	46	.333	.424	.487
Scott Leius	3B112,SS7,DH3	R	29	117	372	51	92	16	5	4	45	49	54	2	.247	.335	.349
Pat Meares	SS114,OF3	R	26	116	390	57	105	19	4	12	49	15	68	10	.269	.311	.431
Marty Cordova	OF137	R	25	137	512	81	142	27	4	24	84	52	111	20	.277	.352	.486
Kirby Puckett	OF109,DH28,2B1*	R	34	137	538	83	169	39	0	23	99	56	89	3	.314	.379	.515
Rich Becker	OF105	S	23	106	392	45	93	15	1	2	33	34	95	8	.237	.303	.296
Pedro Munoz	DH77,OF25,1B3	R	26	104	376	45	113	17	0	18	58	19	86	0	.301	.338	.489
Jeff Reboulet	SS39,3B22,1B17*	R	31	87	216	39	63	11	0	4	23	27	34	1	.292	.373	.398
Dan Masteller	1B48,OF22,DH8	L	27	71	198	21	47	12	0	3	21	18	19	1	.237	.303	.343
Matt Merullo	C46,DH13,1B2	L	29	76	195	19	55	14	1	1	27	14	27	0	.282	.335	.379
Jerald Clark	OF23,1B11,DH3	L	31	36	109	17	37	8	3	3	15	2	11	3	.339	.354	.550
Chip Hale	DH27,2B7,3B5*	L	30	69	103	10	27	4	0	2	18	11	20	0	.262	.333	.359
Ron Coomer	1B22,3B13,DH4*	R	28	37	101	15	26	3	1	5	19	9	11	0	.257	.324	.455
Alex Cole	OF23,DH2	L	29	28	79	10	27	3	2	1	14	8	15	1	.342	.409	.468
Matt Lawton	OF19,DH1	L	23	21	60	11	19	4	1	1	12	7	11	1	.317	.414	.467
Kevin Maas	DH12,1B8	L	30	22	57	5	11	4	0	1	5	7	11	0	.193	.281	.316
Dave McCarty†	1B18,OF5	R	25	25	55	10	12	3	1	0	4	4	18	0	.218	.279	.309
Denny Hocking	SS6	S	25	9	25	4	5	0	2	0	3	2	2	1	.200	.259	.360
Brian Raabe	2B4,3B2	R	27	6	14	4	3	0	0	0	1	1	0	0	.214	.267	.214
Riccardo Ingram	DH3	R	28	4	8	0	1	0	0	0	1	2	0	0	.125	.300	.125
Steve Dunn	1B3	L	25	5	6	0	0	0	0	0	0	1	3	0	.000	.143	.000
Bernardo Brito	DH3	R	31	5	5	1	1	0	0	1	1	0	3	0	.200	.333	.800

K. Puckett, 1 G at 3B, 1 G at SS; J. Reboulet, 15 G at 2B, 1 G at C; C. Hale, 3 G at 1B; R. Coomer, 1 G at OF

Pitcher	T	Age	G	GS	CG	ShO	IP	H	HR	BB	SO	W-L	Sv	ERA
Brad Radke	R	22	29	28	2	1	181.0	195	32	47	75	11-14	0	5.32
Kevin Tapani†	R	31	20	20	3	1	133.2	155	21	34	88	6-11	0	4.92
Mike Trombley	R	28	20	18	0	0	97.2	107	18	42	68	4-8	0	5.62
Frank Rodriguez†	R	22	16	16	0	0	90.1	93	8	47	45	5-6	0	5.38
Scott Erickson†	R	27	15	15	0	0	87.2	102	11	32	45	4-6	0	5.95
Jose Parra†	R	22	12	12	0	0	61.2	83	11	22	29	1-5	0	7.59
Greg Harris	R	31	7	6	0	0	32.2	50	5	16	21	0-5	0	8.82
LaTroy Hawkins	R	22	6	6	1	0	27.0	39	3	12	9	2-3	0	8.67
Dave Stevens	R	25	56	0	0	0	65.2	74	14	32	47	5-4	10	5.07
Eddie Guardado	L	24	51	5	0	0	91.1	99	13	45	71	4-9	2	5.12
Pat Mahomes	R	24	47	7	0	0	94.2	100	22	47	67	4-10	3	6.37
Erik Schullstrom	R	26	37	0	0	0	47.0	66	8	22	21	0-0	0	6.89
Mark Guthrie†	R	29	36	0	0	0	42.1	47	5	16	48	5-3	0	4.46
Scott Watkins	L	25	27	0	0	0	21.2	22	2	11	11	0-0	0	5.40
Rich Robertson	L	26	25	4	1	0	51.2	48	4	31	38	2-0	0	3.83
Rick Aguilera†	R	33	22	0	0	0	25.0	20	2	6	29	1-1	12	2.52
Scott Klingenbeck†	R	24	18	4	0	0	48.1	69	16	24	27	0-2	0	8.57
Mo Sanford	R	28	11	0	0	0	18.2	16	7	16	17	0-0	0	5.30
Oscar Munoz	R	25	10	3	0	0	35.1	40	6	17	25	2-1	0	5.60
Kevin Campbell	R	30	6	0	0	0	9.2	8	0	5	5	0-0	0	4.66
Vince Horsman	L	28	6	0	0	0	9.0	12	2	4	4	0-0	0	7.00
Carl Willis	R	34	3	0	0	0	0.2	5	0	5	0	0-0	0	94.50

1995 Seattle Mariners 1st AL West 79-66 .545 —

Lou Piniella

Player	Gm by Position	B	Age	G	AB	R	H	2B	3B	HR	RBI	BB	SO	SB	Avg	OBP	Slg
Dan Wilson	C119	R	26	119	399	40	111	22	3	9	51	33	63	2	.278	.336	.416
Tino Martinez	1B139,DH1	L	27	141	519	92	152	35	3	31	111	62	91	0	.293	.369	.551
Joey Cora	2B112,SS1	S	30	120	427	64	127	19	2	3	39	37	31	18	.297	.359	.372
Mike Blowers	3B126,1B7,OF5	R	30	134	439	59	113	24	1	23	96	53	128	2	.257	.335	.474
Luis Sojo	SS80,2B19,OF6	R	29	102	339	50	98	18	2	7	39	23	19	4	.289	.335	.416
Jay Buhner	OF120,DH4	R	30	126	470	86	123	23	0	40	121	60	120	0	.262	.343	.566
Alex Diaz	OF88	S	26	103	270	44	67	14	0	3	27	13	27	18	.248	.286	.333
Rich Amaral	OF73,DH1	R	33	90	238	45	67	14	2	2	19	21	33	21	.282	.342	.382
Edgar Martinez	DH138,3B4,1B3	R	32	145	511	121	182	52	0	29	113	116	87	4	.356	.479	.628
Ken Griffey Jr.	OF70,DH2	L	25	72	260	52	67	7	0	17	42	52	53	4	.258	.379	.481
Felix Fermin	SS46,2B29	R	31	73	200	21	39	6	0	0	15	6	6	2	.195	.232	.225
Vince Coleman†	OF38	S	33	40	162	27	47	10	2	1	9	10	32	16	.290	.335	.395
Doug Strange	3B41,2B5,OF4*	S	31	74	155	19	42	9	2	2	21	10	25	0	.271	.323	.394
Darren Bragg	OF47,DH1	L	25	52	145	20	34	5	1	3	12	18	37	9	.234	.331	.345
Alex Rodriguez	SS46,DH1	R	19	48	142	15	33	6	2	5	19	6	42	4	.232	.264	.408
Marc Newfield†	OF24	R	22	24	85	7	16	3	0	3	14	3	16	0	.188	.225	.329
Chad Kreuter	C23	S	30	26	75	12	17	5	0	1	8	5	22	0	.227	.293	.333
Warren Newson†	OF23	L	30	33	72	15	21	2	0	2	6	16	18	1	.292	.420	.403
Chris Widger	C19,OF3,DH1	R	24	23	45	2	9	0	0	1	2	3	11	0	.200	.245	.267
Gary Thurman	OF9	R	30	13	25	3	8	2	0	0	3	1	3	5	.320	.333	.400
Greg Pirkl	1B6,DH1	R	24	10	17	2	4	0	0	0	0	1	7	0	.235	.278	.235
Arquimedez Pozo	2B1	R	21	1	1	0	0	0	0	0	0	0	0	0	.000	.000	.000

D. Strange, 1 G at DH

Pitcher	T	Age	G	GS	CG	ShO	IP	H	HR	BB	SO	W-L	Sv	ERA
Chris Bosio	R	32	31	31	0	0	170.0	211	18	69	85	10-8	0	4.92
Randy Johnson	L	31	30	30	6	3	214.1	159	12	65	294	18-2	0	2.48
Tim Belcher	R	33	28	28	1	0	179.1	188	19	88	96	10-12	0	4.52
Salomon Torres†	R	23	16	13	1	0	72.0	87	12	42	45	3-8	0	6.00
Andy Benes†	R	27	12	12	0	0	63.0	72	8	33	45	7-2	0	5.86
Bob Wolcott	R	21	7	6	0	0	36.2	43	6	14	19	3-2	0	4.42
Tim Davis	L	24	5	5	0	0	24.0	30	2	18	19	2-1	0	6.38
Bill Krueger†	L	37	6	5	0	0	20.0	37	4	4	10	2-1	0	5.85
Bobby Ayala	R	25	63	0	0	0	71.0	73	9	30	77	6-5	19	4.44
Jeff Nelson	R	28	62	0	0	0	78.2	58	4	27	96	7-3	2	2.17
Bill Risley	R	28	45	0	0	0	60.1	55	7	18	65	2-1	1	3.13
Bob Wells	R	28	30	4	0	0	76.2	88	11	39	38	4-3	0	5.75
Norm Charlton†	L	32	30	0	0	0	47.2	23	2	16	58	2-1	14	1.51
Lee Guetterman	L	36	23	0	0	0	17.0	21	1	11	11	0-0	1	6.88
Ron Villone†	L	25	19	0	0	0	19.1	20	6	23	26	0-2	0	7.91
Dave Fleming†	L	25	16	7	1	0	48.0	57	15	34	26	1-5	0	7.50
Rafael Carmona	R	22	15	3	0	0	47.2	55	9	34	28	2-4	1	5.66
Steve Frey†	L	31	13	0	0	0	11.1	16	0	6	7	0-3	0	4.76
Jim Converse†	R	23	6	1	0	0	11.0	16	2	8	9	0-3	1	7.36
John Cummings†	L	26	4	0	0	0	5.1	8	0	7	4	0-0	0	11.81
Scott Davison	R	24	3	0	0	0	4.1	7	1	1	3	0-0	0	6.23
Jim Mecir	R	25	2	0	0	0	4.2	5	0	2	3	0-0	0	0.00
Kevin King	L	26	2	0	0	0	3.2	7	0	1	3	0-0	0	12.27
Tim Harikkala	R	23	1	0	0	0	3.1	7	1	1	1	0-0	0	16.20

1995 California Angels 2nd AL West 78-67 .538 1.0 GB

Marcel Lachemann

Player	Gm by Position	B	Age	G	AB	R	H	2B	3B	HR	RBI	BB	SO	SB	Avg	OBP	Slg
Jorge Fabregas	C73	L	25	73	227	24	56	10	0	1	22	17	28	0	.247	.298	.304
J.T. Snow	1B143	S	27	143	544	80	157	22	1	24	102	52	91	2	.289	.353	.465
Damion Easley	2B88,SS25	R	25	114	357	35	77	14	2	4	35	32	47	5	.216	.288	.300
Tony Phillips	3B88,OF48,DH2	S	36	139	525	119	137	21	1	27	61	113	135	13	.261	.394	.459
Gary DiSarcina	SS98	R	27	99	362	61	111	28	6	5	41	20	25	7	.307	.344	.459
Tim Salmon	OF142,DH1	R	26	143	537	111	177	34	3	34	105	91	111	5	.330	.429	.594
Jim Edmonds	OF139	L	25	141	558	120	162	30	4	33	107	51	130	1	.290	.352	.536
Garret Anderson	OF100,DH1	L	23	106	374	50	120	19	1	16	69	19	65	6	.321	.352	.505
Chili Davis	DH119	S	35	119	424	81	135	23	0	20	86	89	79	3	.318	.429	.514
Greg Myers	C61,DH16	L	29	85	273	35	71	12	2	9	38	17	49	0	.260	.304	.418
Rex Hudler	2B52,OF22,DH3*	R	34	84	223	30	59	16	0	6	27	10	48	13	.265	.310	.417
Spike Owen	3B29,SS25,2B16	S	34	82	218	17	50	9	3	1	28	18	22	3	.229	.288	.312
Andy Allanson	C35	R	33	35	82	5	14	3	0	3	10	7	12	0	.171	.244	.317
Eduardo Perez	3B23,DH1	R	25	29	71	9	12	4	1	1	7	12	9	0	.169	.302	.296
Carlos Martinez	3B16,1B4,DH2	R	30	26	61	7	11	1	0	1	9	6	7	0	.180	.265	.246
Jose Lind†	2B15	R	31	15	43	5	7	2	0	0	1	3	4	0	.163	.217	.209
Mike Aldrete†	DH2,OF2,1B1	L	34	18	24	1	6	0	0	0	3	0	8	0	.250	.240	.250
Rod Correia	SS7,2B3,3B2*	R	27	14	21	3	5	1	1	0	3	0	5	0	.238	.238	.381
Dick Schofield†	SS12	R	32	12	20	1	5	0	0	0	2	4	2	0	.250	.375	.250
Orlando Palmeiro	OF7,DH1	L	26	15	20	3	7	0	0	0	1	1	1	0	.350	.381	.350
Rene Gonzales	3B18,2B6,SS1	R	34	30	18	1	6	1	0	1	3	0	4	0	.333	.333	.556
Dave Gallagher†	OF6,DH1	R	34	11	16	1	3	1	0	0	0	2	1	0	.188	.278	.250
Chris Turner	C4	R	26	5	10	0	1	0	0	0	1	0	3	0	.100	.100	.100
Mark Dalesandro	C8,DH1,OF1	R	27	11	10	1	1	1	0	0	0	0	2	0	.100	.100	.200
Kevin Flora†	DH1	R	26	2	1	1	0	0	0	0	0	0	1	0	.000	.000	.000

R. Hudler, 2 G at 1B; R. Correia, 1 G at DH

Pitcher	T	Age	G	GS	CG	ShO	IP	H	HR	BB	SO	W-L	Sv	ERA
Chuck Finley	L	32	32	32	2	1	203.0	192	20	93	195	15-12	0	4.21
Mark Langston	L	34	31	31	2	1	200.1	212	21	64	142	15-7	0	4.63
Shawn Boskie	R	28	20	20	1	0	111.2	127	16	25	51	7-7	0	5.64
Brian Anderson	L	23	18	17	1	0	99.2	110	24	30	45	6-8	0	5.87
Jim Abbott†	L	27	13	13	1	1	84.2	93	4	29	41	5-4	0	4.15
Mike Bielecki	R	35	22	11	0	0	75.1	80	15	31	45	4-6	0	5.97
Mike Harkey†	R	28	12	8	1	0	61.1	80	12	16	28	4-3	0	4.55
Scott Sanderson	R	38	7	7	0	0	39.1	48	6	4	23	1-3	0	4.12
Troy Percival	R	25	62	0	0	0	74.0	37	6	26	94	3-2	3	1.95
Bob Patterson	L	36	62	0	0	0	53.1	48	6	13	41	5-2	0	3.04
Lee Smith	R	37	52	0	0	0	49.1	42	3	25	43	0-5	37	3.47
Mike James	R	27	46	0	0	0	55.2	49	6	26	36	3-0	1	3.88
Mike Butcher	R	30	40	0	0	0	51.1	49	7	31	29	6-1	0	4.73
John Habyan†	R	31	28	0	0	0	32.2	36	2	12	25	1-2	0	4.13
Mitch Williams	L	30	20	0	0	0	10.2	13	1	21	9	1-2	0	6.75
Russ Springer†	R	26	19	6	0	0	51.2	60	11	25	38	1-2	1	6.10
Mark Holzemer	L	25	12	0	0	0	8.1	11	1	7	5	0-1	0	5.40
Rich Monteleone	R	32	9	0	0	0	9.0	8	1	3	5	1-0	0	2.00
Ken Edenfield	R	28	7	0	0	0	12.2	15	1	5	6	0-0	0	4.26
Erik Bennett	R	26	1	0	0	0	0.1	0	0	0	0	0-0	0	0.00

1995 Texas Rangers 3rd AL West 74-70 .514 4.5 GB

Johnny Oates

Player	Gm by Position	B	Age	G	AB	R	H	2B	3B	HR	RBI	BB	SO	SB	Avg	OBP	Slg
Ivan Rodriguez	C127,DH1	R	23	130	492	56	149	32	2	12	67	16	48	0	.303	.327	.449
Will Clark	1B122,DH1	L	31	123	454	85	137	27	3	16	92	68	50	0	.302	.389	.480
Jeff Frye	2B83	R	28	90	313	38	87	15	2	4	29	24	45	3	.278	.335	.377
Mike Pagliarulo	3B68,1B11	L	35	86	241	27	56	16	0	4	27	15	49	0	.232	.277	.349
Benji Gil	SS130	R	22	130	415	36	91	20	3	9	46	26	147	2	.219	.266	.347
Otis Nixon	OF138	S	36	139	589	87	174	21	2	0	45	58	85	50	.295	.357	.338
Rusty Greer	OF125,1B3	L	26	131	417	58	113	21	2	13	61	55	66	3	.271	.355	.424
Mark McLemore	OF73,2B66,DH1	S	30	129	467	73	122	20	5	5	41	59	71	21	.261	.346	.358
Juan Gonzalez	DH83,OF5	R	25	90	352	57	104	20	2	27	82	17	66	0	.295	.324	.594
Mickey Tettleton	OF63,DH58,1B9*	S	34	134	429	76	102	19	1	32	78	107	110	0	.238	.396	.510
Dean Palmer	3B36	R	26	36	119	30	40	6	0	9	24	21	21	1	.336	.448	.613
Luis Ortiz	3B35,DH3	R	25	41	108	10	25	5	2	1	18	6	18	0	.231	.270	.343
Lou Frazier†	OF47,DH2	S	30	49	99	19	21	2	0	0	8	7	20	9	.212	.278	.232
Esteban Beltre	SS36,2B15,3B1	R	27	54	92	7	20	8	0	0	7	4	15	0	.217	.250	.304
Dave Valle	C29,1B7	R	34	36	75	7	18	3	0	0	5	6	18	1	.240	.305	.280
Craig Worthington†	3B26	R	30	26	68	4	15	4	0	2	6	7	8	0	.221	.293	.368
Jack Voigt†	OF25,1B5,DH1	R	29	33	62	8	10	3	0	2	8	10	14	0	.161	.274	.306
Candy Maldonado†	OF11	R	34	13	30	6	7	3	0	2	5	7	5	0	.233	.378	.533
Steve Buechele†	3B9	R	33	9	24	0	3	0	0	0	0	4	3	0	.125	.250	.125
Shawn Hare	OF9,DH2,1B1	L	28	18	24	2	6	1	0	0	2	4	6	0	.250	.357	.292
Eric Fox	OF8,DH1	S	31	10	15	2	0	0	0	0	0	3	4	0	.000	.167	.000
Billy Hatcher	OF5,DH1	R	34	6	12	2	1	1	0	0	0	1	1	0	.083	.154	.167
Sam Horn	DH1	L	31	11	9	0	1	0	0	0	0	1	6	0	.111	.200	.111
John Marzano	C2	R	32	2	6	1	2	0	0	0	0	0	0	0	.333	.333	.333

M. Tettleton, 3 G at C

Pitcher	T	Age	G	GS	CG	ShO	IP	H	HR	BB	SO	W-L	Sv	ERA
Kenny Rogers	L	30	31	31	3	1	208.0	192	26	76	140	17-7	0	3.38
Roger Pavlik	R	27	31	31	2	1	191.2	174	19	90	149	10-10	0	4.37
Kevin Gross	R	34	31	30	4	0	183.2	200	27	89	106	9-15	0	5.54
Bob Tewksbury	R	34	21	21	4	1	129.2	169	8	20	53	8-7	0	4.58
Bobby Witt†	R	31	10	10	1	0	61.1	81	4	21	46	3-4	0	4.55
Danny Darwin†	R	39	7	4	0	0	34.0	40	12	7	22	2-2	0	7.15
Scott Taylor	R	28	3	3	0	0	15.1	25	6	5	10	1-2	0	9.39
Rick Helling	R	24	3	3	0	0	12.1	17	2	8	5	0-2	0	6.57
Roger McDowell	R	34	64	0	0	0	85.0	86	5	34	49	7-4	4	4.02
Ed Vosberg	L	33	44	0	0	0	36.0	32	3	16	36	5-5	4	3.00
Matt Whiteside	R	27	40	0	0	0	53.0	48	5	19	46	5-4	3	4.08
Jeff Russell	R	33	37	0	0	0	32.2	36	3	9	21	1-0	20	3.03
Dennis Cook†	L	32	35	1	0	0	45.0	47	6	16	40	0-2	2	4.00
Terry Burrows	L	26	28	3	0	0	44.2	60	11	19	22	2-2	1	6.45
Darren Oliver	L	24	17	7	0	0	49.0	47	3	32	39	4-2	0	4.22
Chris Nichting	R	29	13	0	0	0	24.1	36	1	13	6	0-0	0	7.03
Jose Alberro	R	26	12	0	0	0	20.2	26	2	12	10	0-0	0	7.40
Mark Brandenburg	R	24	11	0	0	0	27.1	36	5	7	21	0-1	0	5.93
Wilson Heredia	R	23	6	0	0	0	12.0	9	2	15	6	0-1	0	3.75
Hector Fajardo	R	24	5	0	0	0	15.0	19	2	5	9	0-0	0	7.80
Chris Howard	L	29	4	0	0	0	4.0	3	0	1	2	0-0	0	0.00
John Dettmer	R	25	1	0	0	0	0.1	2	0	0	0	0-0	0	27.00

1995 Oakland Athletics 4th AL West 67-77 .465 11.5 GB

Tony La Russa

Player	Gm by Position	B	Age	G	AB	R	H	2B	3B	HR	RBI	BB	SO	SB	Avg	OBP	Slg
Terry Steinbach	C111,1B2	R	33	114	406	43	113	26	1	15	65	25	74	1	.278	.322	.458
Mark McGwire	1B91,DH10	R	31	104	317	75	87	13	0	39	90	88	77	1	.274	.441	.685
Brent Gates	2B132,DH3,1B1	S	25	136	524	60	133	24	4	5	56	46	84	3	.254	.308	.344
Craig Paquette	3B75,OF20,SS8*	R	26	105	283	42	64	13	1	13	49	12	88	5	.226	.256	.417
Mike Bordick	SS126,DH1	R	29	126	428	46	113	13	0	8	44	35	48	11	.264	.325	.350
Stan Javier	OF124,3B1	S	31	130	442	81	123	20	2	8	56	49	63	36	.278	.353	.387
Rickey Henderson	OF90,DH19	R	36	112	407	67	122	31	1	9	54	72	66	32	.300	.407	.447
Geronimo Berroa	DH72,OF71	R	30	141	546	87	152	22	3	22	88	63	98	7	.278	.351	.451
Danny Tartabull†	DH22,OF1	R	32	24	88	9	23	4	0	2	7	10	28	0	.261	.337	.375
Scott Brosius	3B60,OF49,1B18*	R	28	123	389	69	102	19	2	17	46	41	67	4	.262	.342	.452
Ruben Sierra†	OF62,DH7	S	29	70	264	40	70	17	0	12	42	24	42	4	.265	.323	.466
Jason Giambi	3B30,1B26,DH2	L	24	54	176	27	45	7	0	6	25	28	31	2	.256	.364	.398
Mike Aldrete†	1B35,OF16	L	34	60	125	18	34	8	0	4	21	19	23	0	.272	.367	.432
Mike Gallego	2B18,SS14,3B12	R	34	43	120	11	28	0	0	0	8	9	24	0	.233	.292	.233
Eric Helfand	C36	L	26	38	86	9	14	2	1	0	7	11	25	0	.163	.265	.209
Andy Tomberlin	OF42,DH1	L	28	46	85	15	18	0	0	4	10	5	22	4	.212	.256	.353
George Williams	C13,DH10	S	26	29	79	13	23	5	1	3	14	11	21	0	.291	.383	.494
Jose Herrera	OF25,DH5	L	22	33	70	9	17	1	2	0	2	6	11	1	.243	.299	.314
Ernie Young	OF24	R	25	26	50	9	10	3	0	2	5	8	12	0	.200	.310	.380
Fausto Cruz	SS8	R	23	8	23	0	5	0	0	0	5	3	5	1	.217	.286	.217
Brian Harper	C2	R	35	2	7	0	0	0	0	0	0	0	1	0	.000	.000	.000

C. Paquette, 3 G at 1B; S. Brosius, 3 G at 2B, 3 G at SS, 2 G at DH

Pitcher	T	Age	G	GS	CG	ShO	IP	H	HR	BB	SO	W-L	Sv	ERA
Todd Stottlemyre	R	30	31	31	2	0	209.2	228	26	80	205	14-7	0	4.55
Steve Ontiveros	R	34	22	22	2	1	129.2	144	12	38	77	9-6	0	4.37
Ron Darling	R	34	21	21	1	0	104.0	124	16	46	69	4-7	0	6.23
Dave Stewart	R	38	16	16	0	0	81.0	101	11	39	58	3-7	0	6.89
Mike Harkey†	R	28	14	12	0	0	66.0	75	12	31	28	4-6	0	6.27
Ariel Prieto	R	25	14	9	1	0	58.0	57	4	32	37	2-6	0	4.97
Doug Johns	L	27	11	9	1	1	54.2	44	5	26	25	5-3	0	4.61
S. Wojciechowski	L	24	14	7	0	0	48.2	51	7	28	13	2-3	0	5.18
Dennis Eckersley	R	40	52	0	0	0	50.1	53	5	11	40	4-6	29	4.83
Rick Honeycutt†	L	41	49	0	0	0	44.2	37	5	9	21	5-1	2	2.42
Mark Acre	R	26	43	0	0	0	52.0	52	7	28	47	1-2	0	5.71
Carlos Reyes	R	26	40	1	0	0	69.0	71	10	28	48	4-6	0	5.09
Jim Corsi	R	33	38	0	0	0	45.0	31	2	26	26	2-4	2	2.20
Todd Van Poppel	R	23	36	14	1	0	138.1	125	16	56	122	4-8	0	4.88
Mike Mohler	L	26	28	0	0	0	23.2	16	0	18	15	1-1	1	3.04
Dave Leiper†	L	33	24	0	0	0	22.2	23	3	13	10	1-1	0	3.57
Don Wengert	R	25	19	0	0	0	29.2	30	3	12	16	1-1	0	3.34
John Briscoe	R	27	16	0	0	0	18.1	25	4	21	19	0-1	0	8.35
Chris Eddy	L	25	6	0	0	0	3.2	7	0	2	2	0-0	0	7.36
John Wasdin	R	22	5	2	0	0	17.1	14	4	3	6	1-1	0	4.67
Scott Baker	L	25	1	0	0	0	3.2	5	0	5	3	0-0	0	9.82
Steve Phoenix	R	27	1	0	0	0	1.2	3	1	3	3	0-0	0	32.40
Ramon Fermin	R	22	1	0	0	0	1.1	4	0	1	0	0-0	0	13.50

»1995 Atlanta Braves 1st NL East 90-54 .625 —

Bobby Cox

Player	Gm by Position	B	Age	G	AB	R	H	2B	3B	HR	RBI	BB	SO	SB	Avg	OBP	Slg
Javy Lopez	C93	R	24	100	333	37	105	11	4	14	51	14	57	0	.315	.344	.498
Fred McGriff	1B144	L	31	144	528	85	148	27	1	27	93	65	99	3	.280	.361	.489
Mark Lemke	2B115	S	29	116	399	42	101	16	5	5	38	44	40	2	.253	.325	.356
Chipper Jones	3B123,OF20	S	23	140	524	87	139	22	3	23	86	73	99	8	.265	.353	.450
Jeff Blauser	SS115	R	29	115	431	60	91	16	2	12	31	57	107	8	.211	.319	.341
Marquis Grissom	OF136	R	28	139	551	80	142	23	3	12	42	47	61	29	.258	.317	.376
David Justice	OF120	L	29	120	411	73	104	17	2	24	78	73	68	4	.253	.365	.479
Ryan Klesko	OF102,1B4	L	24	107	329	48	102	25	2	23	70	47	72	5	.310	.396	.608
Charlie O'Brien	C64	R	35	67	198	18	45	7	0	9	23	29	40	0	.227	.343	.399
Rafael Belliard	SS40,2B32	R	33	75	180	12	40	2	1	0	7	6	28	2	.222	.255	.244
Mike Kelly	OF83	R	25	97	137	26	26	6	1	3	17	11	49	7	.190	.258	.314
Dwight Smith	OF25	L	31	103	131	16	33	8	2	3	21	13	35	0	.252	.327	.412
Jose Oliva†	3B25,1B1	R	24	48	109	7	17	4	0	5	12	7	22	0	.156	.207	.330
Mike Mordecai	2B21,1B9,3B6*	S	27	69	75	10	21	6	0	3	11	9	16	0	.280	.353	.480
Mike Devereaux†	OF27	R	32	29	55	7	14	3	0	1	8	2	11	2	.255	.281	.364
Luis Polonia†	OF15	L	30	28	53	6	14	7	0	0	2	3	9	3	.264	.304	.396
Brian Kowitz	OF8	L	25	10	24	3	4	1	0	0	3	2	5	0	.167	.259	.208
Ed Giovanola	2B7,3B3,SS1	L	26	13	14	2	1	0	0	0	0	3	5	0	.071	.235	.071
Eddie Perez	C5,1B1	R	27	7	13	1	4	1	0	1	4	0	2	0	.308	.308	.615
Mike Sharperson	3B1	R	33	7	7	1	1	1	0	0	2	0	2	0	.143	.143	.286

M. Mordecai, 6 G at SS, 1 G at OF

Pitcher	T	Age	G	GS	CG	ShO	IP	H	HR	BB	SO	W-L	Sv	ERA
Tom Glavine	L	29	29	29	3	1	198.2	182	9	66	127	16-7	0	3.08
John Smoltz	R	28	29	29	2	1	192.2	166	15	72	193	12-7	0	3.18
Steve Avery	L	25	29	29	3	1	173.1	165	22	52	141	7-13	0	4.67
Greg Maddux	R	29	28	28	10	3	209.2	147	8	23	181	19-2	0	1.63
Kent Mercker	L	27	29	26	0	0	143.0	140	16	61	102	7-8	0	4.15
Greg McMichael	R	28	67	0	0	0	80.2	64	8	32	74	7-2	2	2.79
Mark Wohlers	R	25	65	0	0	0	64.2	51	2	24	90	7-3	25	2.09
Brad Clontz	R	24	59	0	0	0	69.0	71	5	22	55	8-1	4	3.65
Pedro Borbon	L	27	41	0	0	0	32.0	29	2	17	33	2-2	2	3.09
Steve Bedrosian	R	37	29	0	0	0	28.0	40	6	12	22	1-2	0	6.11
Mike Stanton†	L	28	26	0	0	0	19.1	31	3	6	13	1-1	1	5.59
Alejandro Pena†	R	36	14	0	0	0	13.0	11	1	4	18	0-0	0	4.15
Jason Schmidt	R	22	9	2	0	0	25.0	27	2	18	19	2-2	0	5.76
Brad Woodall	L	26	9	0	0	0	10.1	13	1	8	5	1-1	0	6.10
Rod Nichols	R	30	5	0	0	0	6.2	14	3	5	3	0-0	0	5.40
Matt Murray†	R	24	4	1	0	0	10.2	10	3	5	3	0-2	0	6.75
Terrell Wade	L	22	3	0	0	0	4.0	3	1	4	3	0-1	0	4.50
Terry Clark†	R	34	3	0	0	0	3.2	3	0	5	2	0-0	0	4.91
Tom Thobe	L	25	3	0	0	0	3.1	7	0	0	2	0-0	0	10.80
Darrell May	L	23	2	0	0	0	4.0	10	0	0	1	0-0	0	11.25

1995 New York Mets 2nd NL East 69-75 .479 21.0 GB

Dallas Green

Player	Gm by Position	B	Age	G	AB	R	H	2B	3B	HR	RBI	BB	SO	SB	Avg	OBP	Slg
Todd Hundley	C89	S	26	90	275	39	77	11	0	15	51	42	64	1	.280	.382	.484
Rico Brogna	1B131	L	25	134	495	72	143	27	2	22	76	39	111	0	.289	.342	.485
Jeff Kent	2B122	R	27	125	472	65	131	22	3	20	65	29	89	3	.278	.327	.464
Edgardo Alfonzo	3B58,2B29,SS6	R	21	101	335	26	93	13	5	4	41	12	37	1	.278	.301	.382
Jose Vizcaino	SS134,2B1	S	27	135	509	66	146	21	5	3	56	35	76	8	.287	.332	.365
Brett Butler†	OF90	L	38	90	367	54	114	13	7	1	25	43	42	21	.311	.381	.392
Joe Orsulak	OF86,1B1	L	33	108	290	41	82	19	2	1	37	19	35	1	.283	.323	.372
Carl Everett	OF77	S	25	79	289	48	75	13	1	12	54	39	67	2	.260	.352	.436
Bobby Bonilla†	3B46,OF31,1B10	S	32	80	317	49	103	25	4	18	53	31	48	0	.325	.385	.599
Ryan Thompson	OF74	R	27	75	267	39	67	13	0	7	31	19	77	3	.251	.306	.378
Kelly Stinnett	C67	R	25	77	196	23	43	8	1	4	18	29	65	2	.219	.338	.332
Chris Jones	OF52,1B5	R	29	79	182	33	51	6	2	8	31	13	45	2	.280	.327	.467
Tim Bogar	SS27,3B25,1B10*	R	28	78	145	17	42	7	0	1	21	9	25	1	.290	.329	.359
Damon Buford†	OF39	R	25	44	136	24	32	5	0	4	12	19	28	7	.235	.346	.360
Butch Huskey	3B27,OF1	R	23	28	90	8	17	1	0	3	11	10	16	1	.189	.267	.300
David Segui†	OF18,1B7	S	28	33	73	9	24	3	1	2	11	12	9	1	.329	.420	.479
Bill Spiers	3B11,2B6	L	29	63	72	5	15	2	1	0	11	12	15	0	.208	.314	.264
Ricky Otero	OF23	S	23	35	51	5	7	2	0	0	1	3	10	2	.137	.185	.176
Alex Ochoa	OF10	R	23	11	37	7	11	1	0	0	0	2	10	1	.297	.333	.324
Aaron Ledesma	3B10,1B2,SS2	R	24	21	33	4	8	0	0	0	3	6	7	0	.242	.359	.242
Alberto Castillo	C12	R	25	13	29	2	3	0	0	0	0	3	9	1	.103	.212	.103
Jeff Barry	OF2	S	26	15	15	2	2	1	0	0	0	1	8	0	.133	.188	.200
Brook Fordyce		R	25	4	2	1	1	1	0	0	0	1	0	0	.500	.667	1.000

T. Bogar, 7 G at 2B, 1 G at OF

Pitcher	T	Age	G	GS	CG	ShO	IP	H	HR	BB	SO	W-L	Sv	ERA
Bobby Jones	R	25	30	30	3	1	195.2	209	20	53	127	10-10	0	4.19
Dave Mlicki	R	27	29	25	0	0	160.2	160	23	54	123	9-7	0	4.26
Pete Harnisch	R	28	18	18	0	0	110.0	111	13	24	82	2-8	0	3.68
Bill Pulsipher	L	21	17	17	2	0	126.2	122	11	45	81	5-7	0	3.98
Bret Saberhagen†	R	31	16	16	3	0	110.0	105	13	20	71	5-5	0	3.35
Jason Isringhausen	R	22	14	14	1	0	93.0	88	6	31	55	9-2	0	2.81
Reid Cornelius†	R	25	10	10	0	0	57.2	64	8	25	35	3-7	0	5.15
Jason Jacome†	L	24	5	5	0	0	21.0	33	3	15	11	0-4	0	10.29
Mike Birkbeck	R	34	4	4	0	0	27.2	22	2	2	14	0-1	0	1.63
Dave Telgheder	R	28	7	4	0	0	25.2	34	4	7	16	1-2	0	5.61
Jerry Dipoto	R	27	58	0	0	0	78.2	77	2	29	49	4-6	2	3.78
Doug Henry	R	31	51	0	0	0	67.0	48	7	25	62	3-6	4	2.96
John Franco	L	34	48	0	0	0	51.2	48	4	17	41	5-3	29	2.44
Blas Minor	R	27	35	0	0	0	46.2	44	6	13	43	4-2	1	3.66
Eric Gunderson†	L	29	30	0	0	0	24.1	25	2	8	19	1-1	0	3.70
Paul Byrd	R	24	17	0	0	0	22.0	18	1	7	26	2-0	0	2.05
Don Florence	L	28	14	0	0	0	12.0	17	0	6	5	3-0	0	1.50
Pete Walker	R	26	13	0	0	0	17.2	24	3	5	5	1-0	0	4.58
Josias Manzanillo†	R	27	12	0	0	0	16.0	18	3	6	14	1-2	0	7.88
Kevin Lomon	R	23	6	0	0	0	9.1	17	0	5	6	0-1	0	6.75
Mike Remlinger†	L	29	5	0	0	0	5.2	7	1	2	6	0-1	0	6.35
Robert Person	R	25	3	1	0	0	12.0	5	1	2	10	1-0	0	0.75

1995 Philadelphia Phillies 2nd NL East 69-75 .479 21.0 GB

Jim Fregosi

Player	Gm by Position	B	Age	G	AB	R	H	2B	3B	HR	RBI	BB	SO	SB	Avg	OBP	Slg
Darren Daulton	C95	L	33	98	342	44	85	19	3	9	55	55	52	3	.249	.359	.401
Dave Hollins†	1B61	S	29	65	205	46	47	12	2	7	25	53	38	1	.229	.393	.410
Mickey Morandini	2B122	L	29	127	494	65	140	34	7	6	49	42	80	9	.283	.350	.417
Charlie Hayes	3B141	R	30	141	529	58	146	30	3	11	85	50	88	5	.276	.340	.406
Kevin Stocker	SS125	S	25	125	412	42	90	14	3	1	32	43	75	6	.218	.304	.274
Jim Eisenreich	OF111	L	36	129	377	46	119	22	2	10	55	38	44	10	.316	.375	.464
Lenny Dykstra	OF61	L	32	62	254	37	67	15	1	2	18	33	28	10	.264	.353	.354
Andy Van Slyke†	OF56	L	34	63	214	26	52	10	2	3	16	28	41	7	.243	.333	.350
Gregg Jefferies	1B59,OF55	S	27	114	480	69	147	31	2	11	56	35	26	9	.306	.349	.448
Mark Whiten†	OF55	S	28	60	212	38	57	10	1	11	37	31	63	7	.269	.365	.481
Mariano Duncan†	2B24,SS14,1B12*	S	32	52	196	20	56	12	1	3	23	0	43	1	.286	.285	.403
Dave Gallagher†	OF55	R	34	62	157	12	50	12	0	1	12	16	20	0	.318	.379	.414
Lenny Webster	C43	R	30	49	150	18	40	9	0	4	14	16	27	0	.267	.337	.407
Tom Marsh	OF29	R	29	43	109	13	32	3	1	3	15	4	25	0	.294	.316	.422
Tony Longmire	OF23	L	26	59	104	21	37	7	0	3	19	11	19	1	.356	.419	.510
Gary Varsho	OF25	L	34	72	103	7	26	1	1	0	11	7	17	2	.252	.310	.282
Kevin Flora†	OF20	R	26	24	75	12	16	3	0	2	7	4	22	1	.213	.253	.333
Gene Schall	1B14,OF4	R	25	24	65	2	15	2	0	0	5	6	16	0	.231	.306	.262
Kevin Jordan	2B9,3B1	R	25	24	54	6	10	1	0	2	6	2	9	0	.185	.228	.315
Kevin Elster†	SS19,1B4,3B2	R	30	26	53	10	11	4	1	1	9	7	14	0	.208	.302	.377
Mike Lieberthal	C14	R	23	16	47	1	12	2	0	0	4	5	5	0	.255	.327	.298
Randy Ready	1B3,2B1	R	35	23	29	3	4	0	0	0	0	3	6	0	.138	.219	.138
Kevin Sefcik	3B2	R	24	5	4	1	0	0	0	0	0	0	2	0	.000	.000	.000
Gary Bennett		R	23	1	1	0	0	0	0	0	0	0	1	0	.000	.000	.000

M. Duncan, 1 G at 3B

Pitcher	T	Age	G	GS	CG	ShO	IP	H	HR	BB	SO	W-L	Sv	ERA
Paul Quantrill	R	26	33	29	0	0	179.1	212	20	44	103	11-12	0	4.67
Tyler Green	R	25	26	25	4	2	140.2	157	15	66	85	8-9	0	5.31
Michael Mimbs	L	26	35	19	2	1	136.2	127	10	75	93	9-7	1	4.15
Curt Schilling	R	28	17	17	1	0	116.0	96	12	26	114	7-5	0	3.57
Sid Fernandez†	L	32	11	11	0	0	64.2	48	11	21	79	6-1	0	3.34
Jeff Juden	R	24	13	10	1	0	62.2	53	6	31	47	2-4	0	4.02
David West	L	30	8	8	0	0	38.0	34	5	19	25	3-2	0	3.79
Tommy Greene	R	28	11	6	0	0	33.2	45	6	20	24	0-5	0	8.29
Dennis Springer	R	30	4	4	0	0	22.1	21	3	9	15	0-3	0	4.84
Bobby Munoz	R	27	3	3	0	0	15.2	15	2	9	6	0-2	0	5.74
Mike Grace	R	25	2	2	0	0	11.1	10	0	4	7	1-1	0	3.18
Jim Deshaies	L	35	2	2	0	0	5.1	15	3	1	6	0-1	0	20.25
Ricky Bottalico	R	25	62	0	0	0	87.2	50	7	42	87	5-3	1	2.46
Heathcliff Slocumb	R	29	61	0	0	0	65.1	64	2	35	63	5-6	32	2.89
Toby Borland	R	26	50	0	0	0	74.0	81	3	37	59	1-3	6	3.77
Mike Williams	R	26	33	8	0	0	87.2	78	10	29	57	3-3	0	3.29
Norm Charlton†	L	32	25	0	0	0	22.0	23	2	15	12	2-5	0	7.36
Gene Harris†	R	30	21	0	0	0	19.0	19	2	8	9	2-2	0	4.26
Kyle Abbott	L	27	18	0	0	0	28.1	28	3	16	21	2-0	0	3.81
Russ Springer†	R	26	14	0	0	0	26.2	22	5	10	32	0-0	0	3.71
Paul Fletcher	R	28	10	0	0	0	13.1	15	2	9	10	1-0	0	5.40
Steve Frey†	L	31	9	0	0	0	10.2	3	1	2	2	0-0	1	0.84
Chuck Ricci	R	26	7	0	0	0	10.0	9	0	3	9	1-0	0	1.80
Omar Olivares†	R	27	5	0	0	0	10.0	11	1	2	7	0-1	0	5.40
Andy Carter	L	26	4	0	0	0	7.1	4	3	2	6	0-0	0	6.14
Ryan Karp	L	25	1	0	0	0	2.0	1	0	3	2	0-0	0	4.50

1995 Florida Marlins 4th NL East 67-76 .469 22.5 GB

Rene Lachemann

Player	Gm by Position	B	Age	G	AB	R	H	2B	3B	HR	RBI	BB	SO	SB	Avg	OBP	Slg
Charles Johnson	C97	R	23	97	315	40	79	15	1	11	39	46	71	0	.251	.351	.410
Greg Colbrunn	1B134	R	25	138	528	70	146	22	1	23	89	22	69	11	.277	.311	.453
Quilvio Veras	2B122,OF2	S	24	124	440	86	115	20	7	5	32	80	68	56	.261	.384	.373
Terry Pendleton	3B129	S	34	133	513	70	149	32	1	14	78	38	84	1	.290	.339	.439
Kurt Abbott	SS115	R	26	120	420	60	107	18	7	17	60	36	110	4	.255	.318	.452
Jeff Conine	OF118,1B14	R	29	133	483	72	146	26	2	25	105	66	94	2	.302	.379	.520
Chuck Carr	OF103	S	26	105	308	54	70	20	0	2	20	46	49	25	.227	.330	.312
Gary Sheffield	OF61	R	26	63	213	46	69	8	0	16	46	55	45	19	.324	.467	.587
Andre Dawson	OF59	R	40	79	226	30	58	10	3	8	37	9	45	0	.257	.305	.434
Alex Arias	SS36,3B21,2B6	R	27	94	216	22	58	9	2	3	26	22	20	1	.269	.337	.370
Jesus Tavarez	OF61	S	24	63	190	31	55	6	2	2	13	16	27	7	.289	.346	.374
Jerry Browne	OF29,2B27,3B7	S	29	77	184	21	47	4	0	1	17	25	20	1	.255	.346	.293
Tommy Gregg	OF38,1B2	L	31	72	156	20	37	5	0	6	20	16	33	3	.237	.313	.385
Steve Decker	C46,1B2	R	29	51	133	12	30	2	1	3	13	19	22	1	.226	.318	.323
Mario Diaz	2B9,SS5,3B3	R	33	49	87	5	20	3	0	1	6	1	12	0	.230	.239	.299
Russ Morman	OF18,1B3	R	33	34	72	9	20	2	1	3	7	3	12	0	.278	.316	.458
Darrell Whitmore	OF16	L	26	27	58	6	11	2	0	1	2	5	15	0	.190	.250	.276
Bob Natal	C13	R	29	16	43	2	10	2	1	2	6	1	9	0	.233	.244	.465
Eddie Zosky	SS4,2B1	R	27	6	5	0	1	0	0	0	0	0	0	0	.200	.200	.200

Pitcher	T	Age	G	GS	CG	ShO	IP	H	HR	BB	SO	W-L	Sv	ERA
John Burkett	R	30	30	30	4	0	188.1	208	22	57	126	14-14	0	4.30
Pat Rapp	R	27	28	28	3	2	167.1	158	10	76	102	14-7	0	3.44
Chris Hammond	L	29	25	24	3	2	161.0	157	17	47	126	9-6	0	3.80
Bobby Witt†	R	31	19	19	1	0	110.2	104	8	47	95	2-7	0	3.90
Dave Weathers	R	25	28	15	0	0	90.1	104	8	52	60	4-5	0	5.98
Willie Banks†	R	26	9	9	0	0	50.0	43	7	30	30	2-3	0	4.32
Ryan Bowen	R	27	4	3	0	0	16.2	23	3	12	15	2-0	0	3.78
Marc Valdes	R	23	3	3	0	0	7.0	17	1	9	2	0-0	0	14.14
Yorkis Perez	L	27	69	0	0	0	46.2	35	6	28	47	2-6	1	5.21
Robb Nen	R	25	62	0	0	0	65.2	62	6	23	68	0-7	23	3.29
Terry Mathews	R	30	57	0	0	0	82.2	70	9	27	72	4-4	3	3.38
Randy Veres	R	29	47	0	0	0	48.2	46	6	22	31	4-4	1	3.88
Mark Gardner	R	33	39	11	1	1	102.1	109	14	43	87	5-5	1	4.49
Richie Lewis	R	29	21	1	0	0	36.0	30	9	15	32	0-1	0	3.75
Buddy Groom†	L	29	14	0	0	0	15.0	26	2	6	12	1-2	0	7.20
Alejandro Pena†	R	36	13	0	0	0	18.0	11	2	3	21	2-0	0	1.50
Matt Mantei	R	21	12	0	0	0	13.1	12	1	13	15	0-1	0	4.73
Rich Garces†	R	24	11	0	0	0	13.1	14	1	8	16	0-2	0	5.40
Jay Powell	R	23	9	0	0	0	8.1	7	0	6	4	0-0	0	1.08
Rob Murphy†	L	35	8	0	0	0	7.1	8	1	5	5	1-1	0	9.82
Matt Dunbar	L	26	8	0	0	0	7.0	12	0	11	5	0-1	0	11.57
Jeremy Hernandez	R	28	7	0	0	0	7.0	12	2	3	5	0-0	0	11.57
Aaron Small	R	23	7	0	0	0	6.1	7	1	6	5	1-0	0	1.42
Rich Scheid	L	30	6	0	0	0	10.1	14	1	7	10	0-0	0	6.10
John Johnstone	R	26	4	0	0	0	4.2	7	1	2	3	0-0	0	3.86
Mike Myers†	L	26	2	0	0	0	2.0	1	0	3	0	0-0	0	0.00
Bryan Harvey	R	32	1	0	0	0	0.0	2	1	1	0	0-0	0	—

1995 Montreal Expos 5th NL East 66-78 .458 24.0 GB

Felipe Alou

Player	Gm by Position	B	Age	G	AB	R	H	2B	3B	HR	RBI	BB	SO	SB	Avg	OBP	Slg
Darrin Fletcher	C98	L	28	110	350	42	100	21	1	11	45	32	23	0	.286	.351	.446
David Segui†	1B97,OF2	S	28	97	383	59	117	22	3	10	57	28	38	1	.305	.355	.457
Mike Lansing	2B127,SS2	R	27	127	467	47	119	30	2	10	62	28	65	27	.255	.299	.392
Sean Berry	3B83,1B3	R	29	103	314	38	100	22	1	14	55	25	53	3	.318	.367	.529
Wil Cordero	SS105,OF26	R	23	131	514	64	147	35	2	10	49	36	88	9	.286	.341	.420
Rondell White	OF119	R	23	130	474	87	140	33	4	13	57	41	87	25	.295	.356	.464
Tony Tarasco	OF116	L	24	126	438	64	109	18	4	14	40	51	78	24	.249	.329	.404
Moises Alou	OF92	R	28	93	344	48	94	22	0	14	58	29	56	4	.273	.342	.459
Mark Grudzielanek	SS34,3B31,2B13	R	25	78	269	27	66	12	2	1	20	14	47	8	.245	.300	.316
Shane Andrews	3B51,1B29	R	23	84	220	27	47	10	1	8	31	17	68	1	.214	.271	.377
Tim Laker	C61	R	25	64	141	17	33	8	1	3	20	14	38	0	.234	.306	.369
F.P. Santangelo	OF25,2B5	S	27	35	98	11	29	5	1	1	9	12	9	1	.296	.384	.398
Roberto Kelly†	OF24	R	30	24	95	11	26	4	0	1	9	7	14	4	.274	.337	.347
Dave Silvestri†	SS9,3B8,1B4*	R	27	39	72	12	19	6	0	2	7	9	27	2	.264	.341	.431
Cliff Floyd	1B18,OF4	L	22	29	69	6	9	1	0	1	8	7	22	3	.130	.221	.188
Lou Frazier†	OF25,2B1	S	30	35	63	6	12	2	0	0	3	8	12	4	.190	.297	.222
Curtis Pride	OF24	L	26	48	63	10	11	1	0	0	2	5	16	3	.175	.235	.190
Henry Rodriguez†	1B10,OF8	L	27	24	58	7	12	0	0	1	5	6	11	0	.207	.277	.259
Jeff Treadway†	2B11,3B1	L	32	41	50	4	12	2	0	0	10	5	2	0	.240	.309	.280
Yamil Benitez	OF14	R	23	14	39	8	15	2	1	2	7	1	7	0	.385	.400	.641
Tim Spehr	C38	R	28	41	35	4	9	5	0	1	3	6	7	0	.257	.366	.486
Tom Foley	1B4,2B3	L	35	11	24	2	5	2	0	0	2	2	4	1	.208	.269	.292
Chad Fonville†	2B2	S	24	14	12	2	4	0	0	0	0	0	3	0	.333	.333	.333
Joe Siddall	C7	L	27	7	10	4	3	0	0	0	1	3	3	0	.300	.500	.300

D. Silvestri, 3 G at 2B, 3 G at OF

Pitcher	T	Age	G	GS	CG	ShO	IP	H	HR	BB	SO	W-L	Sv	ERA
Pedro Martinez	R	23	30	30	2	2	194.2	158	21	66	174	14-10	0	3.51
Jeff Fassero	L	32	30	30	1	0	189.0	207	15	74	164	13-14	0	4.33
Carlos Perez	L	24	28	23	2	1	141.1	142	18	28	106	10-8	0	3.69
Butch Henry	L	26	21	21	1	1	126.2	133	11	28	60	7-9	0	2.84
Kirk Rueter	L	24	9	9	1	1	47.1	38	3	9	28	5-3	0	3.23
Tavo Alvarez	R	23	8	8	0	0	37.1	46	2	14	17	1-5	0	6.75
Ugueth Urbina	R	21	7	4	0	0	23.1	26	6	14	15	2-2	0	6.17
Tim Scott	R	28	62	0	0	0	63.1	52	6	23	57	2-0	2	3.98
Mel Rojas	R	28	59	0	0	0	67.2	69	2	29	61	1-4	30	4.12
Jeff Shaw†	R	28	50	0	0	0	62.1	58	4	26	45	1-6	3	4.62
Greg Harris	S	39	45	0	0	0	48.1	45	6	16	47	2-3	0	2.61
Gil Heredia	R	29	40	18	0	0	119.0	137	7	21	74	5-6	1	4.31
Luis Aquino†	R	31	29	0	0	0	37.1	47	4	11	22	0-2	2	3.86
Dave Leiper†	L	33	26	0	0	0	22.0	16	2	6	12	0-2	2	2.86
Bryan Eversgerd	L	26	25	0	0	0	21.0	22	2	9	8	0-0	0	5.14
Willie Fraser	R	31	22	0	0	0	25.2	25	6	9	12	2-1	2	5.61
Gabe White	L	23	19	1	0	0	25.2	26	7	9	25	1-2	0	7.01
Curt Schmidt	R	25	11	0	0	0	10.1	15	1	9	7	0-0	0	6.97
Reid Cornelius†	R	25	8	0	0	0	9.0	11	3	5	4	0-0	0	8.00
Jose DeLeon†	R	34	7	0	0	0	8.1	7	2	7	12	0-1	0	7.56
J.J. Thobe	R	24	4	0	0	0	4.0	6	0	3	0	0-0	0	9.00

1995 Cincinnati Reds 1st NL Central 85-59 .590 —

Davey Johnson

Player	Gm by Position	B	Age	G	AB	R	H	2B	3B	HR	RBI	BB	SO	SB	Avg	OBP	Slg
Benito Santiago	C75,1B8	R	30	81	266	40	76	20	0	11	44	24	48	2	.286	.351	.485
Hal Morris	1B99	L	30	101	359	53	100	25	2	11	51	29	58	1	.279	.333	.451
Bret Boone	2B138	R	26	138	513	63	137	34	2	15	68	41	84	5	.267	.326	.429
Jeff Branson	3B98,SS32,2B6*	L	28	122	331	43	86	18	2	12	45	44	69	2	.260	.345	.435
Barry Larkin	SS130	R	31	131	496	98	158	29	6	15	66	61	49	51	.319	.394	.492
Reggie Sanders	OF130	R	27	133	484	91	148	36	6	28	99	69	122	36	.306	.397	.579
Ron Gant	OF117	R	30	119	410	79	113	19	4	29	88	74	108	23	.276	.386	.554
Jerome Walton	OF89,1B3	R	29	102	162	32	47	12	1	8	22	17	25	10	.290	.368	.525
Thomas Howard	OF82	S	30	113	281	42	85	15	2	3	26	20	37	17	.302	.350	.402
Eddie Taubensee	C65,1B3	L	26	80	218	32	62	14	2	9	44	22	52	2	.284	.354	.491
Lenny Harris	3B24,1B23,OF8*	L	30	101	197	32	41	8	3	2	16	14	20	10	.208	.259	.310
Mark Lewis	3B72,2B2,SS2	R	25	81	171	25	58	13	1	3	30	21	33	0	.339	.407	.480
Darren Lewis†	OF57	R	27	58	163	19	40	3	0	0	8	17	20	11	.245	.324	.264
Eric Anthony	OF24,1B17	L	27	47	134	19	36	6	0	5	23	13	30	2	.269	.327	.425
Deion Sanders†	OF33	L	27	33	129	19	31	2	3	1	10	9	18	16	.240	.296	.326
Damon Berryhill	C29,1B1	S	31	34	82	6	15	3	0	2	11	10	19	0	.183	.260	.293
Brian Hunter	1B23,OF4	R	27	40	79	9	17	6	0	1	9	11	21	2	.215	.312	.329
Mariano Duncan†	2B7,1B6,SS6*	S	32	29	69	16	20	2	1	3	13	5	19	0	.290	.329	.478
Willie Greene	3B7	L	23	8	19	1	2	0	0	0	0	3	7	0	.105	.227	.105
Craig Worthington†	1B4,3B2	R	30	10	18	1	5	1	0	1	2	2	1	0	.278	.350	.500
Nigel Wilson	OF2	L	25	5	7	0	0	0	0	0	0	0	4	0	.000	.000	.000
Steve Gibralter	OF2	R	22	4	3	0	1	0	0	0	0	0	0	0	.333	.333	.333
Eric Owens	3B2	R	24	2	2	0	2	0	0	0	1	0	0	0	1.000	1.000	1.000

J. Branson, 1 G at 1B; L. Harris, 1 G at 2B; M. Duncan, 3 G at OF

Pitcher	T	Age	G	GS	CG	ShO	IP	H	HR	BB	SO	W-L	Sv	ERA
Pete Schourek	L	26	29	29	2	0	190.1	158	17	45	160	18-7	0	3.22
John Smiley	L	30	28	27	1	0	176.2	173	11	39	124	12-5	0	3.46
Mark Portugal†	R	32	14	14	0	0	77.2	79	7	22	33	6-5	0	3.82
Jose Rijo	R	30	14	14	0	0	69.0	76	6	22	62	5-4	0	4.17
Kevin Jarvis	R	25	19	11	1	1	79.0	91	13	32	33	3-4	0	5.70
David Wells†	L	32	11	11	3	0	72.2	74	6	16	50	6-5	0	3.59
Dave Burba†	R	28	15	9	1	1	63.1	52	4	26	50	6-2	0	3.27
C.J. Nitkowski†	L	22	9	7	0	0	32.1	41	4	15	18	1-3	0	6.12
Rick Reed	R	30	4	3	0	0	17.0	18	5	3	10	0-0	0	5.82
Frank Viola	L	35	3	3	0	0	14.1	20	3	3	4	0-1	0	6.28
John Roper†	R	23	2	2	0	0	7.0	13	3	4	6	0-0	0	10.29
Hector Carrasco	R	25	64	0	0	0	87.1	86	1	46	64	2-7	5	4.12
Xavier Hernandez	R	29	59	0	0	0	90.0	95	8	31	84	7-2	3	4.60
Jeff Brantley	R	31	56	0	0	0	70.1	53	11	20	62	3-2	28	2.82
Chuck McElroy	L	27	44	0	0	0	40.1	46	5	15	27	3-4	0	6.02
Mike Jackson	R	30	40	0	0	0	49.0	38	5	19	41	6-1	2	2.39
Tim Pugh	R	28	28	12	0	0	98.1	100	13	32	38	6-5	0	3.84
Pete Smith	R	29	11	2	0	0	24.1	30	8	7	14	1-2	0	6.66
Johnny Ruffin	R	23	10	0	0	0	13.1	4	0	11	11	0-0	0	1.35
Brad Pennington†	L	26	6	0	0	0	9.2	9	0	11	7	0-0	0	5.59
Scott Sullivan	R	24	3	0	0	0	3.2	4	0	2	2	0-0	0	4.91
Matt Grott	L	27	2	0	0	0	1.2	6	1	0	2	0-0	0	21.60
Mike Remlinger†	L	29	2	0	0	0	1.0	2	0	3	1	0-0	0	9.00
John Courtright	L	25	1	0	0	0	1.0	2	0	0	0	0-0	0	9.00

1995 Houston Astros 2nd NL Central 76-68 .528 9.0 GB

Terry Collins

Player	Gm by Position	B	Age	G	AB	R	H	2B	3B	HR	RBI	BB	SO	SB	Avg	OBP	Slg
Tony Eusebio	C103	R	28	113	368	46	110	21	1	6	58	31	59	0	.299	.354	.410
Jeff Bagwell	1B114	R	27	114	448	88	130	29	0	21	87	79	102	12	.290	.399	.496
Craig Biggio	2B141	R	29	141	553	123	167	30	2	22	77	80	85	33	.302	.406	.483
Dave Magadan	3B100,1B11	L	32	127	348	44	109	24	0	2	51	71	56	2	.313	.428	.399
Orlando Miller	SS89	R	26	92	324	36	85	20	1	5	36	22	71	3	.262	.319	.377
Derek Bell	OF110	R	26	112	452	63	151	21	2	8	86	33	71	27	.334	.385	.442
James Mouton	OF94	R	26	104	298	42	78	18	2	4	27	25	59	25	.262	.326	.376
Brian Hunter	OF74	R	24	78	321	52	97	14	5	2	28	21	52	24	.302	.346	.396
Craig Shipley	3B65,SS11,2B4*	R	32	92	232	23	61	8	1	3	24	8	28	6	.263	.291	.345
Luis Gonzalez†	OF55	L	27	56	209	35	54	10	4	6	35	18	30	1	.258	.322	.431
Derrick May†	OF55,1B1	L	26	78	206	29	62	15	1	8	41	19	24	5	.301	.358	.500
John Cangelosi	OF59,P1	S	32	90	201	46	64	5	2	2	18	48	42	21	.318	.457	.393
Ricky Gutierrez	SS44,3B2	R	25	52	156	22	43	6	0	0	12	10	33	5	.276	.321	.314
Milt Thompson	OF34	L	36	92	132	14	29	9	0	2	19	14	37	4	.220	.297	.333
Mike Simms	1B25,OF12	R	28	50	121	14	31	4	0	9	24	13	28	1	.256	.341	.512
Scott Servais†	C28	R	28	28	89	7	20	10	0	1	12	9	15	0	.225	.300	.371
Phil Plantier†	OF20	L	26	22	68	12	17	2	0	4	15	11	19	0	.250	.349	.456
Phil Nevin†	3B16	R	24	18	60	4	7	1	0	0	1	7	13	1	.117	.221	.133
Andy Stankiewicz	SS14,2B6,3B3	R	30	43	52	6	6	1	0	0	7	12	19	4	.115	.281	.135
Rick Wilkins†	C13	L	28	15	40	6	10	1	0	1	5	10	10	0	.250	.392	.350
Pat Borders†	C11	R	32	11	35	1	4	0	0	0	0	2	7	0	.114	.162	.114
Chris Donnels†	3B9,2B1	L	29	19	30	4	9	0	0	0	2	3	6	0	.300	.364	.300
Jerry Goff	C11	L	31	12	26	2	4	2	0	1	3	4	13	0	.154	.267	.346
Mike Brumley	SS3,OF3,1B1*	S	32	18	18	1	1	0	0	1	2	0	6	1	.056	.056	.222
Scooter Tucker†	C3	R	28	5	7	1	2	0	0	1	1	0	0	0	.286	.286	.714
Dave Hajek		R	27	5	2	0	0	0	0	0	0	1	1	1	.000	.333	.000

C. Shipley, 1 G at 1B; M. Brumley, 1 G at 3B

Pitcher	T	Age	G	GS	CG	ShO	IP	H	HR	BB	SO	W-L	Sv	ERA
Doug Drabek	R	32	31	31	2	1	185.0	205	18	54	143	10-9	0	4.77
Shane Reynolds	R	27	30	30	3	2	189.1	196	15	37	175	10-11	0	3.47
Greg Swindell	L	30	33	26	1	1	153.0	180	21	39	96	10-9	0	4.47
Mike Hampton	L	22	24	24	0	0	150.2	141	13	49	115	9-8	0	3.35
Darryl Kile	R	26	25	21	0	0	127.0	114	5	73	113	4-12	0	4.96
Donne Wall	R	27	6	5	0	0	24.1	33	5	5	16	3-1	0	5.55
Dave Veres	R	28	72	0	0	0	103.1	89	5	30	94	5-1	1	2.26
Todd Jones	R	27	68	0	0	0	99.2	89	8	52	96	6-5	15	3.07
Jim Dougherty	R	27	56	0	0	0	67.2	76	7	25	49	8-4	0	4.92
Dean Hartgraves	L	28	40	0	0	0	36.1	30	2	16	24	2-0	0	3.22
Doug Brocail	R	28	36	7	0	0	77.1	87	10	22	39	6-4	1	4.19
Pedro A. Martinez	L	26	25	0	0	0	20.2	29	3	16	17	0-0	0	7.40
Jeff Tabaka†	L	31	24	0	0	0	24.1	17	1	12	19	1-0	0	2.22
Mike Henneman†	R	33	21	0	0	0	21.0	21	1	4	19	0-1	8	3.00
John Hudek	R	28	19	0	0	0	20.0	19	3	5	29	2-2	7	5.40
Ross Powell†	L	27	15	0	0	0	9.0	16	1	11	8	0-0	0	11.00
Craig McMurtry	R	35	11	0	0	0	10.1	15	0	9	4	0-1	0	7.84
John Cangelosi	L	32	1	0	0	0	1.0	0	0	1	0	0-0	0	0.00
Billy Wagner	L	24	1	0	0	0	0.1	0	0	0	0	0-0	0	0.00

1995 Chicago Cubs 3rd NL Central 73-71 .507 12.0 GB

Jim Riggleman

Player	Gm by Position	B	Age	G	AB	R	H	2B	3B	HR	RBI	BB	SO	SB	Avg	OBP	Slg
Scott Servais†	C52	R	28	52	175	31	50	12	0	12	35	23	37	2	.286	.371	.560
Mark Grace	1B143	L	31	143	552	97	180	51	3	16	92	65	46	6	.326	.395	.516
Rey Sanchez	2B111,SS4	R	27	114	428	57	119	22	2	3	27	14	48	6	.278	.301	.360
Todd Zeile†	3B75,OF2,1B1	R	29	79	299	34	68	16	0	9	30	16	53	0	.227	.271	.371
Shawon Dunston	SS125	R	32	127	477	58	141	30	6	14	69	10	75	10	.296	.317	.472
Sammy Sosa	OF143	R	26	144	564	89	151	17	3	36	119	58	134	34	.268	.340	.500
Brian McRae	OF137	S	27	137	580	92	167	38	7	12	48	47	92	27	.288	.348	.440
Luis Gonzalez†	OF76	L	27	77	262	34	76	19	4	7	34	39	33	5	.290	.384	.473
Jose Hernandez	SS43,2B29,3B20	R	25	93	245	37	60	11	4	13	40	13	69	1	.245	.281	.482
Ozzie Timmons	OF55	R	24	77	171	30	45	10	1	8	28	13	32	3	.263	.314	.474
Howard Johnson	3B34,OF13,2B8*	S	34	87	169	26	33	4	1	7	22	34	46	1	.195	.330	.355
Rick Wilkins†	C49,1B2	L	28	50	162	24	31	2	0	6	14	36	51	0	.191	.340	.315
Scott Bullett	OF64	S	26	104	150	19	41	5	7	3	22	12	30	8	.273	.331	.460
Steve Buechele†	3B32	R	33	32	106	10	20	2	0	1	9	11	19	0	.189	.265	.236
Todd Haney	2B17,3B4	R	29	25	73	11	30	8	0	2	6	7	11	0	.411	.463	.603
Todd Pratt	C25	R	28	25	60	3	8	2	0	0	4	6	21	0	.133	.209	.167
Joe Kmak	C18,3B1	R	32	19	53	7	13	3	0	1	6	6	12	0	.245	.328	.358
Kevin Roberson	OF11	S	27	32	38	5	7	1	0	4	6	6	14	0	.184	.311	.526
Mark Parent†	C10	R	33	12	32	5	8	2	0	3	5	3	7	0	.250	.314	.594
Mike Hubbard	C9	R	24	15	23	2	4	0	0	0	1	2	2	0	.174	.240	.174
Matt Franco	2B3,1B1,3B1	L	25	16	17	3	5	1	0	0	1	0	4	0	.294	.294	.353
Karl Rhodes†	OF11	L	26	13	16	2	2	0	0	0	2	0	4	0	.125	.118	.125

H. Johnson, 3 G at 1B, 1 G at SS

Pitcher	T	Age	G	GS	CG	ShO	IP	H	HR	BB	SO	W-L	Sv	ERA
Jaime Navarro	R	28	29	29	1	1	200.1	194	19	56	128	14-6	0	3.28
Frank Castillo	R	26	29	29	2	2	188.0	179	22	52	135	11-10	0	3.21
Steve Trachsel	R	24	30	29	2	0	160.2	174	25	76	117	7-13	0	5.15
Kevin Foster	R	26	30	28	0	0	167.2	149	32	65	146	12-11	0	4.51
Jim Bullinger	R	29	24	24	1	0	150.0	152	14	65	93	12-8	0	4.14
Mike Morgan†	R	35	4	4	0	0	24.2	19	2	9	15	2-1	0	2.19
Mike Perez	R	30	68	0	0	0	71.1	72	8	27	49	2-6	2	3.66
Randy Myers	L	32	57	0	0	0	55.2	49	7	28	59	1-2	38	3.88
Turk Wendell	R	28	43	0	0	0	60.1	71	11	24	50	3-1	0	4.92
Mike Walker	R	28	42	0	0	0	44.2	45	2	24	20	1-3	1	3.22
Larry Casian	L	29	42	0	0	0	23.1	23	1	15	11	1-0	0	1.93
Bryan Hickerson†	L	31	38	0	0	0	31.2	36	3	15	28	2-3	1	6.82
Chris Nabholz	L	28	34	0	0	0	23.1	22	4	14	21	0-1	0	5.40
Anthony Young	R	29	32	1	0	0	41.1	47	5	14	15	3-4	2	3.70
Terry Adams	R	22	18	0	0	0	18.0	22	0	10	15	1-1	1	6.50
Willie Banks†	R	26	10	0	0	0	11.2	27	5	12	9	0-1	0	15.43
Rich Garces†	R	24	7	0	0	0	11.0	11	0	3	6	0-0	0	3.27
Dave Swartzbaugh	R	27	7	0	0	0	7.1	5	0	3	5	0-0	0	0.00
Roberto Rivera	L	26	7	0	0	0	5.0	8	1	2	2	0-0	0	5.40
Tom Edens	R	34	5	0	0	0	3.0	6	0	3	2	1-0	0	6.00
Tanyon Sturtze	R	24	2	0	0	0	2.0	2	1	1	0	0-0	0	9.00

1995 St. Louis Cardinals 4th NL Central 62-81 .434 22.5 GB

Joe Torre (20-27)/Mike Jorgensen (42-54)

Player	Gm by Position	B	Age	G	AB	R	H	2B	3B	HR	RBI	BB	SO	SB	Avg	OBP	Slg
Danny Sheaffer	C67,1B3,3B1	R	33	76	208	24	48	10	1	5	30	23	38	0	.231	.306	.361
John Mabry	1B73,OF39	L	24	129	388	35	119	21	1	5	41	24	45	0	.307	.347	.405
Jose Oquendo	2B62,SS24,3B2*	S	31	88	220	31	46	8	3	2	17	35	21	1	.209	.316	.300
Scott Cooper	3B110	L	27	118	374	29	86	18	2	3	40	49	85	0	.230	.321	.313
Tripp Cromer	SS95,2B11	R	27	105	345	36	78	19	0	5	18	14	66	0	.226	.261	.325
Ray Lankford	OF129	L	28	132	483	81	134	35	2	25	82	63	110	24	.277	.360	.513
Brian Jordan	OF126	R	28	131	490	83	145	20	4	22	81	22	79	24	.296	.339	.488
Bernard Gilkey	OF118	R	28	121	480	73	143	33	4	17	69	42	70	12	.298	.358	.490
Tom Pagnozzi	C61	R	32	62	219	17	47	14	1	2	15	11	31	0	.215	.254	.315
Ozzie Smith	SS41	S	40	44	156	16	31	5	1	0	11	17	12	4	.199	.282	.244
David Bell†	2B37,3B3	R	22	39	144	13	36	7	2	2	19	4	25	1	.250	.278	.368
Darnell Coles	3B22,1B18,OF1	R	33	63	138	13	31	7	0	3	16	16	20	0	.225	.316	.341
Todd Zeile†	1B34	R	29	34	127	16	37	6	0	5	22	18	23	1	.291	.378	.457
Scott Hemond	C38,2B6	R	29	57	118	11	17	1	0	3	9	12	31	0	.144	.233	.229
Allen Battle	OF32	R	26	61	118	13	32	5	0	0	2	15	26	3	.271	.358	.314
Geronimo Pena	2B25	S	28	32	101	20	27	6	1	1	8	16	30	3	.267	.367	.376
Ramon Caraballo	2B24	S	26	34	99	10	20	4	1	2	3	6	33	3	.202	.269	.323
Gerald Perry	1B11	L	34	65	79	4	13	4	0	0	5	6	12	0	.165	.224	.215
Mark Sweeney	1B19,OF1	L	25	37	77	5	21	2	0	2	13	10	15	1	.273	.348	.377
Jose Oliva†	3B18,1B2	R	24	22	74	8	9	1	0	2	8	5	24	0	.122	.195	.216
Terry Bradshaw	OF10	L	26	19	44	6	10	1	1	0	2	2	10	1	.227	.261	.295
Chris Sabo†	1B2,3B1	R	33	5	13	0	2	1	0	0	3	1	2	1	.154	.214	.231
Tim Hulett	2B2,SS1	R	35	4	11	0	2	0	0	0	0	0	3	0	.182	.182	.182
Ray Giannelli	1B2,OF2	L	29	9	11	0	1	0	0	0	0	3	4	0	.091	.286	.091
Manuel Lee	2B1	S	30	1	1	1	1	0	0	0	0	0	0	0	1.000	1.000	1.000

J. Oquendo, 1 G at OF

Pitcher	T	Age	G	GS	CG	ShO	IP	H	HR	BB	SO	W-L	Sv	ERA
Mark Petkovsek	R	29	26	21	1	1	137.1	136	11	35	71	6-6	0	4.00
Allen Watson	L	24	21	19	0	0	114.1	126	17	41	49	7-9	0	4.96
Donovan Osborne	L	26	19	19	0	0	113.1	112	17	34	82	4-6	0	3.81
Danny Jackson	L	33	19	19	2	1	100.2	120	10	48	52	2-12	0	5.90
Ken Hill†	R	29	18	18	0	0	110.1	125	16	45	50	6-7	0	5.06
Mike Morgan†	R	35	17	17	1	0	106.2	114	10	25	46	5-6	0	3.88
Tom Urbani	L	27	24	13	0	0	82.2	99	11	21	52	3-5	0	3.70
Alan Benes	R	23	3	3	0	0	16.0	24	2	4	20	1-2	0	8.44
Jeff Parrett	R	33	59	0	0	0	76.2	71	8	28	71	4-7	0	3.64
Tony Fossas	L	37	58	0	0	0	36.2	28	1	10	40	3-0	0	1.47
Rich DeLucia	R	30	56	1	0	0	82.1	63	9	36	76	8-7	0	3.39
Tom Henke	R	37	52	0	0	0	54.1	42	2	18	48	1-1	36	1.82
Rene Arocha	R	29	41	0	0	0	49.2	55	6	18	25	3-5	0	3.99
John Habyan†	R	31	31	0	0	0	40.2	32	0	15	35	3-2	0	2.88
T.J. Mathews	R	25	23	0	0	0	29.2	21	1	11	28	1-1	2	1.52
Vicente Palacios	R	31	20	5	0	0	40.1	48	7	19	34	2-3	0	5.80
John Frascatore	R	25	14	4	0	0	32.2	39	3	16	21	1-1	0	4.41
Brian Barber	R	22	9	4	0	0	29.1	31	4	16	27	2-1	0	5.22
Doug Creek	L	26	6	0	0	0	6.2	2	0	3	10	0-0	0	0.00
Cory Bailey	R	24	3	0	0	0	3.2	2	0	2	5	0-0	0	7.36
Rich Rodriguez	L	32	1	0	0	0	1.2	0	0	0	0	0-0	0	0.00

1995 Pittsburgh Pirates 5th NL Central 58-86 .403 27.0 GB

Jim Leyland

Player	Gm by Position	B	Age	G	AB	R	H	2B	3B	HR	RBI	BB	SO	SB	Avg	OBP	Slg
Mark Parent†	C67	R	33	69	233	25	54	9	0	15	33	23	62	0	.232	.301	.464
Mark Johnson	1B70	L	27	79	221	32	46	6	1	13	28	37	66	5	.208	.326	.421
Carlos Garcia	2B92,SS15	R	27	104	367	41	108	24	2	6	50	25	55	8	.294	.340	.420
Jeff King	3B84,1B35,2B8*	R	30	122	445	61	118	27	2	18	87	55	63	7	.265	.342	.456
Jay Bell	SS136,3B3	R	29	138	530	79	139	28	4	13	55	55	110	2	.262	.336	.404
Al Martin	OF121	L	27	124	439	70	124	25	3	13	41	44	92	20	.282	.351	.442
Orlando Merced	OF107,1B35	S	28	132	487	75	146	29	4	15	83	52	74	7	.300	.365	.468
Jacob Brumfield	OF104	R	30	116	402	64	109	23	2	4	26	37	71	22	.271	.339	.368
Nelson Liriano	2B67,3B5,SS1	S	31	107	259	29	74	12	1	5	38	24	34	2	.286	.347	.398
Dave Clark	OF61	L	32	77	196	30	55	6	0	4	24	24	38	3	.281	.359	.372
Kevin Young	3B48,1B6	R	26	56	181	13	42	9	0	6	22	8	53	1	.232	.268	.381
Steve Pegues	OF53	R	27	82	171	17	42	8	0	6	16	4	36	1	.246	.263	.398
Angelo Encarnacion	C55	R	22	58	159	18	36	7	2	2	10	13	28	1	.226	.285	.333
Midre Cummings	OF41	S	23	59	152	13	37	7	1	2	15	13	30	1	.243	.303	.342
Don Slaught	C33	R	36	35	112	13	34	6	0	0	13	9	8	0	.304	.361	.357
Rich Aude	1B32	R	23	42	109	10	27	8	0	2	19	6	20	1	.248	.287	.376
John Wehner	OF23,3B19,C1*	R	28	52	107	13	33	0	3	0	5	10	17	3	.308	.361	.364
Freddy Garcia	OF10,3B8	R	22	42	57	5	8	1	1	0	1	8	17	0	.140	.246	.193
Mackey Sasser	C11	L	32	14	26	1	4	1	0	0	0	0	0	0	.154	.154	.192

J. King, 2 G at SS; J. Wehner, 1 G at SS

Pitcher	T	Age	G	GS	CG	ShO	IP	H	HR	BB	SO	W-L	Sv	ERA
Denny Neagle	L	26	31	31	5	1	209.2	221	20	45	150	13-8	0	3.43
Esteban Loaiza	R	23	32	31	1	0	172.2	205	21	55	85	8-9	0	5.16
Paul Wagner	R	27	33	25	3	1	165.0	174	18	72	120	5-16	1	4.80
John Ericks	R	27	19	18	1	0	106.0	108	7	50	80	3-9	0	4.58
Steve Parris	R	27	15	15	1	1	82.0	89	12	33	61	6-6	0	5.38
Jon Lieber	R	25	21	12	0	0	72.2	103	7	14	45	4-7	0	6.32
Rick White	R	26	15	9	0	0	55.0	66	3	18	29	2-3	0	4.75
Jason Christiansen	L	25	63	0	0	0	56.1	49	5	34	53	1-3	0	4.15
Dan Plesac	L	33	58	0	0	0	60.1	53	3	27	57	4-4	3	3.58
Danny Miceli	R	24	58	0	0	0	58.0	61	7	28	56	4-4	21	4.66
Mike Dyer	R	28	55	0	0	0	74.2	81	9	30	53	4-5	0	4.34
Jeff McCurry	R	25	55	0	0	0	61.0	82	9	30	27	1-4	1	5.02
Jim Gott	R	35	25	0	0	0	31.1	38	2	12	19	2-4	3	6.03
Ross Powell†	L	27	12	3	0	0	20.2	20	5	10	12	0-2	0	5.23
Lee Hancock	L	28	11	0	0	0	14.0	10	0	2	6	0-0	0	1.93
Gary Wilson	R	25	10	0	0	0	14.1	13	2	5	8	0-1	0	5.02
Mike Maddux†	R	33	8	0	0	0	9.0	14	0	3	4	1-0	0	9.00
Ramon Morel	R	20	5	0	0	0	6.1	6	0	2	3	0-1	0	2.84
Ravelo Manzanillo	L	31	5	0	0	0	3.2	3	0	2	1	0-0	0	4.91
John Hope	R	24	3	0	0	0	2.1	8	0	4	2	0-0	0	30.86
D. Konuszewski	R	24	1	0	0	0	0.1	3	0	1	0	0-0	0	54.00

1995 Los Angeles Dodgers 1st NL West 78-66 .542 —

Tom Lasorda

Player	Gm by Position	B	Age	G	AB	R	H	2B	3B	HR	RBI	BB	SO	SB	Avg	OBP	Slg
Mike Piazza	C112	R	26	112	434	82	150	17	0	32	93	39	80	1	.346	.400	.606
Eric Karros	1B143	R	27	143	551	83	164	29	3	32	105	61	115	4	.298	.369	.535
Delino DeShields	2B113	L	26	127	425	66	109	18	3	8	37	63	83	39	.256	.353	.369
Tim Wallach	3B96,1B1	R	37	97	327	24	87	22	2	9	38	27	69	0	.266	.326	.428
Jose Offerman	SS115	S	26	119	429	69	123	14	6	4	33	69	67	2	.287	.389	.375
Raul Mondesi	OF138	R	24	139	536	91	153	23	6	26	88	33	96	27	.285	.328	.496
Roberto Kelly†	OF110	R	30	112	409	47	114	19	2	6	48	15	65	15	.279	.306	.379
Billy Ashley	OF69	R	24	81	215	17	51	5	0	8	27	25	88	0	.237	.320	.372
Chad Fonville†	SS38,2B36,OF11	S	24	88	308	41	85	6	1	0	16	23	39	20	.276	.328	.302
Dave Hansen	3B58	L	26	100	181	19	52	10	0	1	14	28	28	0	.287	.384	.359
Brett Butler†	OF38	L	38	39	146	24	40	5	2	0	13	24	9	11	.274	.368	.336
Todd Hollandsworth	OF37	L	22	41	103	16	24	2	0	5	13	10	29	2	.233	.304	.398
Carlos Hernandez	C41	R	28	45	94	3	14	1	0	2	8	7	25	0	.149	.216	.223
Chris Gwynn	OF17,1B2	L	30	67	84	8	18	3	2	1	10	6	23	0	.214	.272	.333
Henry Rodriguez†	OF20,1B1	L	27	21	80	6	21	4	1	1	10	5	17	0	.263	.306	.375
Mitch Webster	OF25	S	36	54	56	6	10	1	1	1	3	4	14	0	.179	.246	.286
Garey Ingram	3B12,2B7,OF4	R	24	44	55	5	11	2	0	0	3	9	8	3	.200	.313	.236
Roger Cedeno	OF36	S	20	40	42	4	10	2	0	0	3	3	10	1	.238	.283	.286
Tom Prince	C17	R	30	18	40	3	8	2	1	1	4	4	10	0	.200	.273	.375
Rick Parker	OF21,3B2,SS2	R	32	27	29	3	8	0	0	0	4	2	4	1	.276	.323	.276
Karim Garcia	OF5	L	19	13	20	1	4	0	0	0	0	0	4	0	.200	.200	.200
Jeff Treadway†	3B2,2B1	L	32	17	17	2	2	0	1	0	3	0	2	0	.118	.118	.235
Mike Busch	3B10,1B2	R	26	13	17	3	4	0	0	3	6	0	7	0	.235	.235	.765
Reggie Williams	OF14	S	29	15	11	2	1	0	0	0	1	2	3	0	.091	.231	.091
Dick Schofield†	SS3,3B1	R	32	9	10	0	1	0	0	0	0	1	3	0	.100	.182	.100
Eddie Pye	3B2	R	28	7	8	0	0	0	0	0	0	0	4	0	.000	.000	.000
Juan Castro	3B7,SS4	R	23	11	4	0	1	0	0	0	0	1	1	0	.250	.400	.250
Noe Munoz	C2	R	24	2	1	0	0	0	0	0	0	0	0	0	.000	.000	.000

Pitcher	T	Age	G	GS	CG	ShO	IP	H	HR	BB	SO	W-L	Sv	ERA
Ramon Martinez	R	27	30	30	4	2	206.1	176	19	81	138	17-7	0	3.66
Tom Candiotti	R	37	30	30	1	1	190.1	187	18	58	141	7-14	0	3.50
Hideo Nomo	R	26	28	28	4	3	191.1	124	14	78	236	13-6	0	2.54
Ismael Valdes	R	21	33	27	6	2	197.2	168	17	51	150	13-11	1	3.05
Kevin Tapani†	R	31	13	11	0	0	57.0	72	8	14	43	4-2	0	5.05
Willie Banks†	R	26	6	6	0	0	29.0	36	2	16	23	0-2	0	4.03
Chan Ho Park	R	22	2	1	0	0	4.0	2	1	2	7	0-0	0	4.50
Todd Worrell	R	35	59	0	0	0	62.1	50	4	19	61	4-1	32	2.02
Pedro Astacio	R	26	48	11	1	1	104.0	103	12	29	80	7-8	0	4.24
Antonio Osuna	R	22	39	0	0	0	44.2	39	5	20	46	2-4	0	4.43
Rudy Seanez	R	26	37	0	0	0	34.2	39	5	18	29	1-3	3	6.75
John Cummings†	L	26	35	0	0	0	39.0	38	3	10	21	3-1	0	3.00
Omar Daal	L	23	28	0	0	0	20.0	29	1	15	11	4-0	0	7.20
Mark Guthrie†	R	29	24	0	0	0	19.2	19	1	9	19	0-2	0	3.66
Greg Hansell	R	24	20	0	0	0	19.1	29	5	6	13	0-1	0	7.45
Joey Eischen	L	25	17	0	0	0	20.1	19	1	11	15	0-0	0	3.10
Todd Williams	R	24	16	0	0	0	19.1	19	3	7	8	2-2	0	5.12
Felix Rodriguez	R	22	11	0	0	0	10.2	11	2	5	5	1-1	0	2.53
Jim Bruske	R	30	9	0	0	0	10.0	12	0	4	5	0-0	1	4.50
Jose Parra†	R	22	8	0	0	0	10.1	10	2	6	7	0-0	0	4.35
Rob Murphy†	L	35	6	0	0	0	5.0	6	2	3	2	0-1	0	12.60

1995 Colorado Rockies 2nd NL West 77-67 .535 1.0 GB

Don Baylor

Player	Gm by Position	B	Age	G	AB	R	H	2B	3B	HR	RBI	BB	SO	SB	Avg	OBP	Slg
Joe Girardi	C122	R	30	125	462	63	121	17	2	8	55	29	76	3	.262	.308	.359
Andres Galarraga	1B142	R	34	143	554	89	155	29	3	31	106	32	146	12	.280	.331	.511
Jason Bates	2B82,SS20,3B15	S	24	116	322	42	86	17	4	8	46	42	70	3	.267	.355	.419
Vinny Castilla	3B137,SS5	R	27	139	527	82	163	34	2	32	90	30	87	2	.309	.347	.564
Walt Weiss	SS136	S	31	137	427	65	111	17	3	1	25	98	57	15	.260	.403	.321
Dante Bichette	OF136	R	31	139	579	102	197	38	2	40	128	22	96	13	.340	.364	.620
Larry Walker	OF129	L	28	131	494	96	151	31	5	36	101	49	72	16	.306	.381	.607
Mike Kingery	OF108,1B5	L	34	119	350	66	94	18	4	8	37	45	40	13	.269	.351	.411
Eric Young	2B77,OF19	R	28	120	366	68	116	21	9	6	36	49	29	35	.317	.404	.473
Ellis Burks	OF80	R	30	103	278	41	74	10	6	14	49	39	72	7	.266	.359	.496
John VanderWal	1B10,OF10	L	29	105	101	15	35	8	1	5	21	16	23	1	.347	.432	.594
Trent Hubbard	OF16	R	29	24	58	13	18	4	0	3	9	8	6	2	.310	.394	.534
Roberto Mejia	2B16	R	23	23	52	5	8	1	0	1	4	0	17	0	.154	.167	.231
Jorge Brito	C18	R	29	18	51	5	11	3	0	0	7	2	17	1	.216	.259	.275
Jayhawk Owens	C16	R	26	18	45	7	11	2	0	4	12	2	15	0	.244	.286	.556
Jimmy Tatum	OF2,C1	R	27	34	34	4	8	1	1	0	4	1	7	0	.235	.257	.324
Matt Nokes†	C3	L	31	10	11	1	2	1	0	0	0	1	4	0	.182	.250	.273
Harvey Pulliam	OF1	R	27	5	5	1	2	1	0	1	3	0	2	0	.400	.400	1.200
Pedro Castellano	3B3	R	25	4	5	0	0	0	0	0	0	2	3	0	.000	.286	.000
Craig Counsell	SS3	L	24	3	1	0	0	0	0	0	0	1	0	0	.000	.500	.000
Quinton McCracken	OF1	S	25	3	1	0	0	0	0	0	0	0	1	0	.000	.000	.000

Pitcher	T	Age	G	GS	CG	ShO	IP	H	HR	BB	SO	W-L	Sv	ERA
Kevin Ritz	R	30	31	28	0	0	173.1	171	16	65	120	11-11	2	4.21
Bill Swift	R	33	19	19	0	0	105.2	122	12	43	68	9-3	0	4.94
Marvin Freeman	R	32	22	18	0	0	94.2	122	15	41	61	3-7	0	5.89
Armando Reynoso	R	29	20	18	0	0	93.0	116	12	36	40	7-7	0	5.32
Bryan Rekar	R	23	15	14	1	0	85.0	95	11	24	60	4-6	0	4.98
Juan Acevedo	R	25	17	11	0	0	65.2	82	15	20	40	4-6	0	6.44
Joe Grahe	R	28	17	9	0	0	56.2	69	6	27	27	4-3	0	5.08
Bret Saberhagen†	R	31	9	9	0	0	43.0	60	8	13	29	2-1	0	6.28
Omar Olivares†	R	27	11	6	0	0	31.2	44	4	21	15	1-3	0	7.39
Curt Leskanic	R	27	76	0	0	0	98.0	83	7	33	107	6-3	10	3.40
Steve Reed	R	29	71	0	0	0	84.0	61	8	21	79	5-2	3	2.14
Darren Holmes	R	29	68	0	0	0	66.2	59	3	28	61	6-1	14	3.24
Mike Munoz	L	29	64	0	0	0	43.2	54	9	27	37	2-4	2	7.42
Roger Bailey	R	24	39	6	0	0	81.1	88	9	39	33	7-6	0	4.98
Bruce Ruffin	L	31	37	0	0	0	34.0	26	1	19	23	0-1	11	2.12
Lance Painter	L	27	33	1	0	0	45.1	55	9	10	36	3-0	1	4.37
Mark Thompson	R	24	21	5	0	0	51.0	73	7	22	30	2-3	0	6.53
Bryan Hickerson†	L	31	18	0	0	0	16.2	33	5	13	12	1-0	0	11.88
A.J. Sager	R	30	10	0	0	0	14.2	19	1	7	10	0-0	0	7.36
Dave Nied	R	26	2	0	0	0	4.1	11	2	3	3	0-0	0	20.77

1995 San Diego Padres 3rd NL West 70-74 .486 8.0 GB

Bruce Bochy

Player	Gm by Position	B	Age	G	AB	R	H	2B	3B	HR	RBI	BB	SO	SB	Avg	OBP	Slg
Brad Ausmus	C100,1B1	R	26	103	328	44	96	16	4	5	34	31	56	16	.293	.353	.412
Eddie Williams	1B81	R	30	97	296	35	77	11	1	12	47	23	47	0	.260	.320	.426
Jody Reed	2B130,SS5	R	32	131	445	58	114	18	1	4	40	59	38	6	.256	.348	.328
Ken Caminiti	3B143	S	32	143	526	74	159	33	0	26	94	69	94	12	.302	.380	.513
Andujar Cedeno	SS116,3B1	R	25	120	390	42	82	16	2	6	31	28	92	5	.210	.271	.308
Steve Finley	OF138	L	30	139	562	104	167	23	8	10	44	59	62	36	.297	.366	.420
Tony Gwynn	OF133	L	35	135	535	82	197	33	1	9	90	35	15	17	.368	.404	.484
Melvin Nieves	OF79,1B2	S	23	98	234	32	48	6	1	14	38	19	88	2	.205	.276	.419
Bip Roberts	OF50,2B25,SS7	S	31	73	296	40	90	14	0	2	25	17	36	20	.304	.346	.372
Brian Johnson	C55,1B2	R	27	68	207	20	52	9	0	3	29	11	39	0	.251	.287	.338
Scott Livingstone	1B43,3B13,2B4	L	29	99	196	26	66	15	0	5	32	15	22	2	.337	.380	.490
Phil Plantier†	OF39	L	26	54	148	21	38	4	0	5	19	17	29	1	.257	.333	.385
Roberto Petagine	1B51,OF2	L	24	89	124	15	29	8	0	3	17	26	41	0	.234	.367	.371
Archi Cianfrocco	1B30,SS15,OF7*	R	28	51	118	22	31	7	0	5	31	11	28	0	.263	.333	.449
Phil Clark	OF34,1B2	R	27	75	97	12	21	3	0	2	7	8	18	0	.216	.278	.309
Ray Holbert	SS30,2B7,OF1	R	24	63	73	11	13	2	1	2	5	8	20	4	.178	.277	.315
Marc Newfield†	OF19	R	22	21	55	6	17	5	1	1	7	2	8	0	.309	.333	.491
Ray McDavid	OF7	L	23	11	17	2	3	0	0	0	0	2	6	1	.176	.263	.176
Billy Bean	OF4	L	31	4	7	1	0	0	0	0	0	1	4	0	.000	.125	.000
Tim Hyers	1B1	L	23	6	5	0	0	0	0	0	0	0	1	0	.000	.000	.000

A. Cianfrocco, 3 G at 2B, 3 G at 3B

Pitcher	T	Age	G	GS	CG	ShO	IP	H	HR	BB	SO	W-L	Sv	ERA
Andy Ashby	R	27	31	31	2	2	192.2	180	17	62	150	12-10	0	2.94
Joey Hamilton	R	24	31	30	2	2	204.1	189	17	56	123	6-9	0	3.08
Andy Benes†	R	27	19	19	1	1	118.2	121	10	45	126	4-7	0	4.17
Glenn Dishman	L	24	19	16	0	0	97.0	104	11	34	43	4-8	0	5.01
F. Valenzuela	L	34	29	15	0	0	90.1	101	16	34	57	8-3	0	4.98
Scott Sanders	R	26	17	15	1	0	90.0	79	14	31	88	5-5	0	4.30
Trevor Hoffman	R	27	55	0	0	0	53.1	48	10	14	52	7-4	31	3.88
Bryce Florie	R	25	47	0	0	0	68.2	49	8	38	68	2-2	1	3.01
Brian Williams	R	26	44	6	0	0	72.0	79	3	38	75	3-10	0	6.00
Willie Blair	R	29	40	12	0	0	114.0	112	11	45	83	7-5	0	4.34
Andres Berumen	R	24	37	0	0	0	44.1	37	3	36	42	2-3	1	5.68
Doug Bochtler	R	24	34	0	0	0	45.1	38	5	19	45	4-4	1	3.57
Dustin Hermanson	R	22	26	0	0	0	31.2	35	8	22	19	3-1	0	6.82
Ron Villone†	L	25	19	0	0	0	25.2	24	5	11	37	2-1	1	4.21
Jeff Tabaka†	L	31	10	0	0	0	6.1	10	1	5	6	0-0	0	7.11
Tim Worrell	R	27	9	0	0	0	13.1	16	2	6	13	1-0	0	4.73
Bill Krueger†	L	37	6	0	0	0	7.2	13	1	4	6	0-0	0	7.04
Tim Mauser	R	28	5	0	0	0	5.2	4	0	9	9	0-1	0	9.53
Marc Kroon	R	22	2	0	0	0	1.2	1	0	2	2	0-1	0	10.80
Donnie Elliott	R	26	1	0	0	0	2.0	2	0	1	3	0-0	0	0.00

1995 San Francisco Giants 4th NL West 67-77 .465 11.0 GB

Dusty Baker

Player	Gm by Position	B	Age	G	AB	R	H	2B	3B	HR	RBI	BB	SO	SB	Avg	OBP	Slg
Kirt Manwaring	C118	R	29	118	379	21	95	15	2	4	36	27	72	1	.251	.314	.332
Mark Carreon	1B81,OF22	R	31	117	396	53	119	24	0	17	65	23	37	0	.301	.343	.490
Robby Thompson	2B91	R	33	95	336	51	75	15	0	8	23	42	76	1	.223	.317	.339
Matt Williams	3B74	R	29	76	283	53	95	17	1	23	65	30	58	2	.336	.399	.647
Royce Clayton	SS136	R	25	138	509	56	124	29	3	5	58	38	109	24	.244	.298	.342
Barry Bonds	OF143	L	30	144	506	109	149	30	7	33	104	120	83	31	.294	.431	.577
Glenallen Hill	OF125	R	30	132	497	71	131	29	4	24	86	39	98	25	.264	.317	.483
Darren Lewis†	OF73	R	27	74	309	47	78	10	3	1	16	17	37	21	.252	.303	.314
Steve Scarsone	3B50,2B13,1B11	R	29	80	233	33	62	10	3	11	29	18	82	3	.266	.333	.476
J.R. Phillips	1B79,OF1	L	25	92	231	27	45	9	0	9	28	19	69	1	.195	.256	.351
Deion Sanders†	OF52	L	27	52	214	29	61	9	5	5	18	18	42	8	.285	.346	.444
John Patterson	2B53	S	28	95	205	27	42	5	3	1	14	14	41	4	.205	.294	.273
Mike Benjamin	3B43,SS16,2B8	R	29	68	186	19	41	6	0	3	12	8	51	11	.220	.256	.301
Jeff Reed	C42	L	32	66	113	12	30	2	0	0	9	20	17	0	.265	.376	.283
Rikkert Faneyte	OF34	R	26	46	86	7	17	4	1	0	4	11	27	1	.198	.289	.267
Tom Lampkin	C17,OF6	L	31	65	76	8	21	2	0	1	9	9	8	2	.276	.360	.342
Marvin Benard	OF7	L	25	13	34	5	13	2	0	1	4	1	7	1	.382	.400	.529
Mark Leonard	OF6	L	30	14	21	4	4	1	0	1	4	5	2	0	.190	.346	.381
Dave McCarty†	OF4,1B2	R	25	12	20	1	5	1	0	0	2	2	4	1	.250	.318	.300
Rich Aurilia	SS6	R	23	9	19	4	9	3	0	2	4	1	2	1	.474	.476	.947
Todd Benzinger	1B5	S	32	9	10	2	2	0	0	1	2	2	3	0	.200	.308	.500

Pitcher	T	Age	G	GS	CG	ShO	IP	H	HR	BB	SO	W-L	Sv	ERA
Mark Leiter	R	32	30	29	7	1	195.2	185	19	55	129	10-12	0	3.82
Terry Mulholland	L	32	29	24	2	0	149.0	190	25	38	65	5-13	0	5.80
W. VanLandingham	R	24	18	18	1	0	122.2	124	14	40	95	6-3	0	3.67
Mark Portugal†	R	32	17	17	1	0	104.0	106	10	34	63	5-5	0	4.15
Trevor Wilson	L	29	17	17	0	0	82.2	82	8	38	38	3-4	0	3.92
Jamie Brewington	R	23	13	13	0	0	75.1	68	8	45	45	6-4	0	4.54
Sergio Valdez	R	30	13	11	1	0	66.1	78	12	17	29	4-5	0	4.75
Joe Rosselli	L	23	9	5	0	0	30.0	39	5	20	7	2-1	0	8.70
Shawn Estes	L	22	3	3	0	0	17.1	16	2	5	14	0-3	0	6.75
Rod Beck	R	26	60	0	0	0	58.2	60	7	21	42	5-6	33	4.45
Jose Bautista	R	30	52	6	0	0	100.2	120	24	26	45	3-8	0	6.44
Shawn Barton	L	32	52	0	0	0	44.1	37	3	19	22	4-1	1	4.26
Chris Hook	R	26	45	0	0	0	52.1	55	7	29	40	5-1	0	5.50
Dave Burba†	R	28	37	0	0	0	43.1	38	5	25	46	4-2	0	4.98
Scott Service	R	28	28	0	0	0	31.0	18	4	20	30	3-1	0	3.19
Mark Dewey	R	30	27	0	0	0	31.2	30	2	17	32	1-0	0	3.13
Pat Gomez	L	27	18	0	0	0	14.0	16	2	12	15	0-0	0	5.14
Steve Mintz	R	26	14	0	0	0	19.1	26	4	12	7	1-2	0	7.45
Carlos Valdez	R	23	11	0	0	0	14.2	19	1	8	7	0-1	0	6.14
Steve Frey†	L	31	9	0	0	0	6.1	7	1	2	5	0-1	0	4.26
Ken Greer	R	28	8	0	0	0	12.0	15	3	5	7	0-2	0	5.25
Enrique Burgos	L	29	5	0	0	0	8.1	14	1	6	12	0-0	0	8.64
Luis Aquino†	R	31	5	0	0	0	5.0	10	2	2	4	0-1	0	14.40
Salomon Torres†	R	23	4	1	0	0	8.0	13	4	7	2	0-1	0	9.00
John Roper†	R	23	1	0	0	0	1.0	2	0	2	0	0-0	0	27.00

›› 1996 New York Yankees 1st AL East 92-70 .568 —

Joe Torre

Player	Gm by Position	B	Age	G	AB	R	H	2B	3B	HR	RBI	BB	SO	SB	Avg	OBP	Slg
Joe Girardi	C120,DH2	R	31	124	422	55	124	22	3	2	45	30	55	13	.294	.346	.374
Tino Martinez	1B151,DH3	L	28	155	595	82	174	28	0	25	117	68	85	2	.292	.364	.466
Mariano Duncan	2B104,3B3,OF3*	S	33	109	400	62	136	34	3	8	56	9	77	4	.340	.352	.500
Wade Boggs	3B123,DH4	L	38	132	501	80	156	29	2	2	41	67	32	1	.311	.389	.389
Derek Jeter	SS157	R	22	157	582	104	183	25	6	10	78	48	102	14	.314	.370	.430
Paul O'Neill	OF146,DH3,1B1	L	33	150	546	89	165	35	1	19	91	102	76	0	.302	.411	.474
Bernie Williams	OF140,DH2	S	27	143	551	108	168	26	7	29	102	82	72	17	.305	.391	.535
Gerald Williams†	OF92,DH2	R	29	99	233	37	63	15	4	5	30	15	39	7	.270	.319	.433
Ruben Sierra†	DH61,OF33	S	30	96	360	39	93	17	1	11	52	40	58	1	.258	.327	.403
Jim Leyritz	C55,DH13,3B13*	R	32	88	265	23	70	10	0	7	40	30	68	2	.264	.355	.381
Darryl Strawberry	OF34,DH26	L	34	63	202	35	53	13	0	11	36	31	55	6	.262	.359	.490
Tim Raines	OF50,DH2	S	36	59	201	45	57	10	0	9	33	34	29	10	.284	.383	.468
Cecil Fielder†	DH43,1B9	R	32	53	200	30	52	8	0	13	37	24	48	0	.260	.342	.495
Andy Fox	2B72,3B31,SS9*	L	25	113	189	26	37	4	0	3	13	20	28	11	.196	.276	.265
Ruben Rivera	OF45	R	22	46	88	17	25	6	1	2	16	13	26	6	.284	.381	.443
Mike Aldrete†	DH9,OF9,1B8*	L	35	32	68	11	17	5	0	3	12	9	15	0	.250	.338	.456
Charlie Hayes†	3B19	R	31	20	67	7	19	3	0	2	13	1	12	0	.284	.294	.418
Matt Howard	2B30,3B6	R	28	35	54	9	11	1	0	1	9	2	8	1	.204	.228	.278
Luis Sojo†	2B14,SS4,3B1	R	30	18	40	3	11	2	0	0	5	1	4	0	.275	.286	.325
Pat Kelly	2B10,DH3	R	28	13	21	4	3	0	0	0	2	2	9	0	.143	.217	.143
Robert Eenhoorn†	2B10,3B2	R	28	12	14	2	1	0	0	0	2	2	3	0	.071	.167	.071
Jorge Posada	C4,DH3	S	24	8	14	1	1	0	0	0	0	1	6	0	.071	.133	.071
Dion James	OF4,DH1	L	33	6	12	1	2	0	0	0	0	1	2	1	.167	.231	.167
Tim McIntosh	C1,1B1,3B1	R	31	3	3	0	0	0	0	0	0	0	0	0	.000	.000	.000
Matt Luke	DH1	L	25	1	0	1	0	0	0	0	0	0	0	0	—	—	—

M. Duncan, 2 G at DH; J. Leyritz, 5 G at 1B, 3 G at OF, 2 G at 2B; A. Fox, 3 G at DH, 1 G at OF; M. Aldrete, 1 G at P

Pitcher	T	Age	G	GS	CG	ShO	IP	H	HR	BB	SO	W-L	Sv	ERA
Andy Pettitte	L	24	35	34	2	0	221.0	229	23	72	162	21-8	0	3.87
Kenny Rogers	L	31	30	30	2	1	179.0	179	16	83	92	12-8	0	4.68
Jimmy Key	L	35	30	30	0	0	169.1	171	21	58	116	12-11	0	4.68
Dwight Gooden	R	31	29	29	1	1	170.2	169	19	88	126	11-7	0	5.01
David Cone	R	33	11	11	1	0	72.0	50	3	34	71	7-2	0	2.88
Ramiro Mendoza	R	24	12	11	0	0	53.0	80	5	10	34	4-5	0	6.79
Scott Kamieniecki	R	32	7	5	0	0	22.2	36	6	19	15	1-2	0	11.12
Wally Whitehurst	R	32	2	2	0	0	8.0	11	1	2	1	1-1	0	6.75
Jeff Nelson	R	29	73	0	0	0	74.1	75	6	36	91	4-4	2	4.36
John Wetteland	R	29	62	0	0	0	63.2	54	9	21	69	2-3	43	2.83
Mariano Rivera	R	26	61	0	0	0	107.2	73	1	34	130	8-3	5	2.09
Bob Wickman†	R	27	58	0	0	0	79.0	94	7	34	61	4-1	0	4.67
Dale Polley	L	31	32	0	0	0	21.2	23	5	11	14	1-3	0	7.89
Jim Mecir	R	26	26	0	0	0	40.1	42	6	23	38	1-1	0	5.13
Steve Howe	L	38	25	0	0	0	17.0	19	1	6	5	0-1	1	6.35
Dave Pavlas	R	33	16	0	0	0	23.0	23	0	7	18	0-0	1	2.35
Brian Boehringer	R	26	15	3	0	0	46.1	46	6	21	37	2-4	0	5.44
Graeme Lloyd†	L	29	13	0	0	0	5.2	12	1	5	6	0-2	0	17.47
Mark Hutton†	R	26	12	2	0	0	30.1	32	3	18	25	0-2	0	5.04
Dave Weathers†	R	26	11	4	0	0	17.1	23	1	14	13	0-2	0	9.35
Ricky Bones†	R	27	4	1	0	0	7.0	14	2	6	4	0-0	0	14.14
Billy Brewer	L	28	4	0	0	0	5.2	7	0	8	8	1-0	0	9.53
Paul Gibson	R	36	4	0	0	0	4.1	6	1	0	3	0-0	0	6.23
Mike Aldrete	L	35	1	0	0	0	1.0	1	0	0	0	0-0	0	0.00

1996 Baltimore Orioles 2nd AL East 88-74 .543 4.0 GB

Davey Johnson

Player	Gm by Position	B	Age	G	AB	R	H	2B	3B	HR	RBI	BB	SO	SB	Avg	OBP	Slg
Chris Hoiles	C126,1B1	R	31	127	407	64	105	13	0	25	73	57	97	0	.258	.356	.474
Rafael Palmeiro	1B159,DH3	L	31	162	626	110	181	40	2	39	142	95	96	8	.289	.381	.546
Roberto Alomar	2B141,DH10	S	28	153	588	132	193	43	4	22	94	90	65	17	.328	.411	.527
B.J. Surhoff	3B106,OF27,DH10*	L	31	143	537	74	157	27	6	21	82	47	79	0	.292	.352	.482
Cal Ripken Jr.	SS158,3B6	R	35	163	640	94	178	40	1	26	102	59	78	1	.278	.341	.466
Brady Anderson	OF143,DH2	L	32	149	579	117	172	37	5	50	110	76	106	21	.297	.396	.637
Mike Devereaux	OF112,DH10	R	33	127	323	49	74	11	2	8	34	34	53	8	.229	.305	.350
Bobby Bonilla	OF108,DH44,1B9*	S	33	159	595	107	171	27	5	28	116	75	85	1	.287	.363	.491
Eddie Murray†	DH62	S	40	64	230	36	59	12	0	10	34	27	42	1	.257	.327	.439
Jeffrey Hammonds	OF70,DH1	R	25	71	248	38	56	10	1	9	27	23	53	3	.226	.301	.383
Luis Polonia†	OF34,DH18	L	31	58	175	25	42	4	1	2	14	10	20	8	.240	.285	.309
Billy Ripken	2B30,3B25,1B1	R	31	57	135	19	31	8	0	2	12	9	18	0	.230	.281	.333
Todd Zeile†	3B29	R	30	29	117	17	28	8	0	5	19	15	16	0	.239	.326	.436
Greg Zaun†	C49	S	25	50	108	16	25	8	1	1	13	11	15	0	.231	.309	.352
Tony Tarasco	OF23,DH5	L	25	31	84	14	20	3	0	1	9	7	15	5	.238	.297	.310
Mark Smith	OF20,DH6	R	26	27	78	9	19	2	0	4	10	3	20	0	.244	.298	.423
Manny Alexander	SS21,2B7,3B7*	R	25	54	68	6	7	0	0	0	4	3	27	3	.103	.141	.103
Brent Bowers	OF21	L	25	21	39	6	12	2	0	0	3	0	7	0	.308	.308	.359
Pete Incaviglia†	OF7,DH4	R	32	12	33	4	10	2	0	2	8	0	7	0	.303	.314	.545
Mark Parent†	C18	R	34	18	33	4	6	1	0	2	6	2	10	0	.182	.229	.394
Jeff Huson	2B12,3B3,OF1	L	31	17	28	5	9	1	0	0	2	1	3	0	.321	.333	.357
Cesar Devarez	C10	R	26	10	18	3	2	0	1	0	0	1	3	0	.111	.158	.222
Gene Kingsale	OF2	S	19	3	0	0	0	0	0	0	0	0	0	0	—	—	—

B. Surhoff, 2 G at 1B; B. Bonilla, 4 G at 3B; M. Alexander, 3 G at OF, 1 G at DH, 1 G at P

Pitcher	T	Age	G	GS	CG	ShO	IP	H	HR	BB	SO	W-L	Sv	ERA
Mike Mussina	R	27	36	36	4	1	243.1	264	31	69	204	19-11	0	4.81
David Wells	L	33	34	34	3	0	224.1	247	32	51	130	11-14	0	5.14
Scott Erickson	R	28	34	34	6	0	222.1	262	21	66	100	13-12	0	5.02
Rocky Coppinger	R	22	23	22	0	0	125.0	126	25	60	104	10-6	0	5.18
Kent Mercker†	L	28	14	12	0	0	58.0	73	12	35	22	3-6	0	7.76
Rick Krivda	L	26	22	11	0	0	81.2	89	14	39	54	3-5	0	4.96
Jesse Orosco	L	39	66	0	0	0	55.2	42	5	28	52	3-1	0	3.40
Randy Myers	L	33	62	0	0	0	58.2	60	7	29	74	4-4	31	3.53
Alan Mills	R	29	49	0	0	0	54.2	40	10	35	50	3-2	3	4.28
Roger McDowell	R	35	41	0	0	0	59.1	69	7	23	20	1-1	4	4.25
Arthur Rhodes	L	26	28	2	0	0	53.0	48	6	23	62	9-1	1	4.08
Jimmy Haynes	R	23	26	11	0	0	89.0	122	14	58	65	3-6	1	8.29
Archie Corbin	R	28	18	0	0	0	27.1	22	2	22	20	2-0	0	2.30
Armando Benitez	R	23	18	0	0	0	14.1	7	2	6	20	1-0	4	3.77
Terry Mathews†	R	31	14	0	0	0	18.2	20	3	7	13	2-2	0	3.38
Keith Shepherd	R	28	13	0	0	0	20.2	31	6	18	17	0-1	0	8.71
Mike Milchin†	L	28	13	0	0	0	11.0	13	0	5	10	1-0	0	5.73
Jimmy Myers	R	27	11	0	0	0	14.0	18	4	3	6	0-0	0	7.07
Nerio Rodriguez	R	23	8	1	0	0	16.2	18	2	7	12	0-1	0	4.32
Esteban Yan	R	22	4	0	0	0	9.1	13	3	3	7	0-0	0	5.79
Garrett Stephenson	R	24	3	0	0	0	6.1	13	1	3	3	0-1	0	12.79
Brian Sackinsky	R	25	3	0	0	0	4.2	6	1	3	2	0-0	0	3.86
Manny Alexander	R	25	1	0	0	0	0.2	1	1	4	0	0-0	0	67.50

1996 Boston Red Sox 3rd AL East 85-77 .525 7.0 GB

Kevin Kennedy

Player	Gm by Position	B	Age	G	AB	R	H	2B	3B	HR	RBI	BB	SO	SB	Avg	OBP	Slg
Mike Stanley	C105,DH10	R	33	121	397	73	107	20	1	24	69	69	62	2	.270	.383	.506
Mo Vaughn	1B146,DH15	L	28	161	635	118	207	29	1	44	143	95	154	2	.326	.420	.583
Jeff Frye	2B100,OF5,SS3*	R	29	105	419	74	120	27	2	4	41	54	57	18	.286	.372	.389
Tim Naehring	3B116,2B1	R	29	116	430	77	124	16	0	17	65	49	63	2	.288	.363	.444
John Valentin	SS118,3B12,DH1	R	29	131	527	84	156	29	3	13	59	63	59	9	.296	.374	.436
Troy O'Leary	OF146	L	26	149	497	68	129	28	5	15	81	47	80	3	.260	.327	.427
Lee Tinsley†	OF83	S	27	92	192	28	47	6	1	3	14	13	56	6	.245	.298	.333
Mike Greenwell	OF76	L	32	77	295	35	87	20	1	7	44	18	27	4	.295	.336	.441
Jose Canseco	DH84,OF11	R	31	96	360	68	104	22	1	28	82	63	82	3	.289	.400	.589
Reggie Jefferson	DH49,OF45,1B16	S	27	122	386	67	134	30	4	19	74	25	89	0	.347	.388	.593
Bill Haselman	C69,DH2,1B2	R	30	77	237	33	65	13	1	8	34	19	52	4	.274	.331	.439
Darren Bragg†	OF58	L	26	58	222	38	56	14	1	3	22	36	39	6	.252	.357	.365
Wil Cordero	2B37,DH13,1B1	R	24	59	198	29	57	14	0	3	37	11	31	2	.288	.330	.404
Milt Cuyler	OF45,DH1	S	27	50	110	19	22	1	2	2	12	13	19	7	.200	.299	.300
Jose Malave	OF38	R	25	41	102	12	24	3	0	4	17	2	25	0	.235	.257	.382
Bill Selby	2B14,3B14,OF6*	L	26	40	95	12	26	4	0	3	6	9	11	1	.274	.337	.411
Kevin Mitchell†	OF21,DH4	R	34	27	92	9	28	4	0	2	13	11	14	0	.304	.385	.413
Nomar Garciaparra	SS22,DH1,2B1	R	22	24	87	11	21	2	3	4	16	4	14	5	.241	.272	.471
Dwayne Hosey	OF26,DH1	S	29	28	78	13	17	2	2	1	3	7	17	6	.218	.282	.333
Alex Cole	OF24	L	30	24	72	13	16	5	1	0	7	8	11	5	.222	.296	.319
Tony Rodriguez	SS21,3B5	R	25	27	67	7	16	1	0	1	9	4	8	0	.239	.292	.299
Esteban Beltre	3B13,2B8,SS6*	R	28	27	62	6	16	2	0	0	6	4	14	1	.258	.299	.290
Arquimedez Pozo	2B10,3B10,DH1	R	22	21	58	4	10	3	1	1	11	2	10	1	.172	.210	.310
Jeff Manto†	3B10,2B4,SS4*	R	31	22	48	8	10	3	1	2	6	8	12	0	.208	.333	.438
Rudy Pemberton	OF13	R	26	13	41	11	21	8	0	1	10	2	4	3	.512	.556	.780
Alex Delgado	C14,OF6,3B4*	R	25	26	20	5	5	0	0	0	1	3	3	0	.250	.348	.250
Scott Hatteberg	C10	L	26	10	11	3	2	1	0	0	0	3	2	0	.182	.357	.273
Jimmy Tatum†	3B2	R	28	2	8	1	1	0	0	0	0	0	2	0	.125	.125	.125
Trot Nixon	OF2	L	22	2	4	2	2	1	0	0	0	0	1	1	.500	.500	.750
Phil Clark	DH1,1B1,3B1	R	28	3	3	0	0	0	0	0	0	0	1	0	.000	.000	.000
Greg Pirkl†		R	25	2	2	0	0	0	0	0	0	0	1	0	.000	.000	.000
Walt McKeel	C1	R	24	1	0	0	0	0	0	0	0	0	0	0	—	—	—

J. Frye, 1 G at DH; B. Selby, 1 G at DH; E. Beltre, 1 G at DH; J. Manto, 1 G at 1B; A. Delgado, 1 G at 1B, 1 G at 2B

Pitcher	T	Age	G	GS	CG	ShO	IP	H	HR	BB	SO	W-L	Sv	ERA
Roger Clemens	R	33	34	34	6	2	242.2	216	19	106	257	10-13	0	3.63
Tom Gordon	R	28	34	34	4	1	215.2	249	28	105	171	12-9	0	5.59
Tim Wakefield	R	29	32	32	6	0	211.2	238	38	90	140	14-13	0	5.14
Aaron Sele	R	26	29	29	1	0	157.1	192	14	67	137	7-11	0	5.32
Jeff Suppan	R	21	8	4	0	0	22.2	29	3	13	13	1-1	0	7.54
Nate Minchey	R	26	2	2	0	0	6.0	16	1	5	4	0-2	0	15.00
Heathcliff Slocumb	R	30	75	0	0	0	83.1	68	2	55	88	5-5	31	3.02
Mike Stanton†	L	29	59	0	0	0	56.1	58	9	23	46	4-3	1	3.83
Vaughn Eshelman	L	27	39	10	0	0	87.2	112	13	58	59	6-3	0	7.08
Rich Garces	R	25	37	0	0	0	44.0	42	5	33	55	3-2	0	4.91
Joe Hudson	R	25	36	0	0	0	45.0	57	4	32	19	3-5	1	5.40
Stan Belinda	R	29	31	0	0	0	28.2	31	3	20	18	2-1	2	6.59
Mark Brandenburg†	R	25	29	0	0	0	28.1	28	5	8	29	4-2	0	3.81
Eric Gunderson	L	30	28	0	0	0	17.1	21	5	8	7	0-1	0	8.31
Jamie Moyer†	L	33	23	10	0	0	90.0	111	14	27	50	7-1	0	4.50
Mike Maddux	R	34	23	7	0	0	64.1	76	12	27	32	3-2	0	4.48
Brad Pennington†	L	27	14	0	0	0	13.0	6	1	15	13	0-2	0	2.77
Pat Mahomes†	R	25	11	0	0	0	12.1	9	3	6	6	2-0	2	5.84
Kerry Lacy	R	23	11	0	0	0	10.2	15	2	8	9	2-0	0	3.38
Brent Knackert	R	26	8	0	0	0	10.0	16	1	7	5	0-1	0	9.00
Reggie Harris	R	27	4	0	0	0	4.1	7	2	5	4	0-0	0	12.46
John Doherty	R	29	3	0	0	0	6.1	8	1	4	3	0-0	0	5.68
Ken Grundt	L	26	1	0	0	0	0.1	1	0	0	0	0-0	0	27.00

1996 Toronto Blue Jays 4th AL East 74-88 .457 18.0 GB

Cito Gaston

Player	Gm by Position	B	Age	G	AB	R	H	2B	3B	HR	RBI	BB	SO	SB	Avg	OBP	Slg
Charlie O'Brien	C105	R	36	109	324	33	77	17	0	13	44	29	68	0	.238	.331	.410
John Olerud	1B101,DH15	L	27	125	398	59	109	25	0	18	61	60	37	1	.274	.382	.472
Tomas Perez	2B75,3B11,SS5	S	22	91	295	24	74	13	4	1	19	25	29	1	.251	.311	.332
Ed Sprague	3B148,DH10	R	28	159	591	88	146	35	2	36	101	60	146	0	.247	.325	.496
Alex Gonzalez	SS147	R	23	147	527	64	124	30	5	14	64	45	127	16	.235	.300	.391
Shawn Green	OF127,DH1	L	23	132	422	52	118	32	3	11	45	33	75	5	.280	.342	.448
Otis Nixon	OF125	S	37	125	496	87	142	15	1	1	29	71	68	54	.286	.377	.327
Joe Carter	OF115,1B41,DH15	R	36	157	625	84	158	35	7	30	107	44	106	7	.253	.306	.475
Carlos Delgado	DH108,1B27	L	24	138	488	68	132	28	2	25	92	58	139	0	.270	.353	.490
Jacob Brumfield†	OF83,DH5	R	31	90	308	52	79	19	2	12	52	24	58	12	.256	.316	.448
Domingo Cedeno†	2B62,3B6,SS5	S	27	77	282	44	79	10	2	2	17	15	60	5	.280	.320	.351
Sandy Martinez	C75	L	23	76	229	17	52	9	3	3	18	16	58	0	.227	.288	.332
Robert Perez	OF79,DH2	R	27	86	202	30	66	10	0	2	21	8	17	3	.327	.354	.406
Juan Samuel	DH24,OF24,1B17	R	35	69	188	34	48	8	3	8	26	15	65	9	.255	.319	.457
Tilson Brito	2B18,SS5,DH2	R	24	26	80	10	19	7	0	1	7	10	18	1	.238	.344	.363
Felipe Crespo	2B10,3B6,1B2	S	23	22	49	6	9	4	0	0	4	12	13	1	.184	.375	.265
Mike Huff	OF9,3B3	R	32	11	29	5	5	0	1	0	0	1	5	0	.172	.200	.241
Miguel Cairo	2B9	R	22	9	27	5	6	2	0	0	1	2	9	0	.222	.300	.296
Julio Mosquera	C8	R	24	8	22	2	5	2	0	0	2	0	3	0	.227	.261	.318
Shannon Stewart	OF6	S	22	7	17	2	3	1	0	0	2	1	4	1	.176	.222	.235

Pitcher	T	Age	G	GS	CG	ShO	IP	H	HR	BB	SO	W-L	Sv	ERA
Pat Hentgen	R	27	35	35	10	3	265.2	238	20	94	177	20-10	0	3.22
Erik Hanson	R	31	35	35	4	1	214.2	243	26	102	156	13-17	0	5.41
Juan Guzman	R	29	27	27	4	1	187.2	158	20	53	165	11-8	0	2.93
Paul Quantrill	R	27	38	20	0	0	134.1	172	27	51	86	5-14	0	5.43
Marty Janzen	R	23	15	11	0	0	73.2	95	16	38	47	4-6	0	7.33
Huck Flener	L	27	15	11	0	0	70.2	68	9	33	44	3-2	0	4.58
Woody Williams	R	29	12	10	1	0	59.0	64	8	21	43	4-5	0	4.73
Frank Viola	L	36	6	6	0	0	30.1	43	6	21	18	1-3	0	7.71
Luis Andujar†	R	23	3	2	0	0	14.1	14	4	1	5	1-1	0	5.02
Mike Timlin	R	30	59	0	0	0	56.2	47	4	18	52	1-6	31	3.65
Tim Crabtree	R	26	53	0	0	0	67.1	59	4	22	57	5-3	1	2.54
Tony Castillo†	L	33	40	0	0	0	72.1	72	9	20	48	2-3	1	4.23
Paul Spoljaric	L	25	28	0	0	0	38.0	30	6	19	38	2-2	1	3.08
Bill Risley	R	29	25	0	0	0	41.2	33	7	25	29	0-1	0	3.89
Brian Bohanon	L	27	20	0	0	0	22.0	27	4	19	17	0-1	1	7.77
Scott Brow	R	27	18	1	0	0	38.2	45	5	25	23	1-0	0	5.59
Jeff Ware	R	25	13	4	0	0	32.2	35	6	31	11	1-5	0	9.09
Giovanni Carrara†	R	28	11	0	0	0	15.0	23	5	12	10	0-1	0	11.40
Dane Johnson	R	33	10	0	0	0	9.0	5	0	5	7	0-0	0	3.00
Jose Silva	R	22	2	0	0	0	2.0	5	1	0	0	0-0	0	13.50

1996 Detroit Tigers 5th AL East 53-109 .327 39.0 GB

Buddy Bell

Player	Gm by Position	B	Age	G	AB	R	H	2B	3B	HR	RBI	BB	SO	SB	Avg	OBP	Slg
Brad Ausmus†	C73	R	27	75	226	30	56	12	0	4	22	26	45	3	.248	.328	.354
Tony Clark	1B86,DH12	S	24	100	376	56	94	14	0	27	72	29	127	0	.250	.299	.503
Mark Lewis	2B144,DH1	R	26	145	545	69	147	30	3	11	55	42	109	6	.270	.326	.396
Travis Fryman	3B128,SS29	R	27	157	616	90	165	32	3	22	100	57	118	4	.268	.329	.437
Andujar Cedeno†	SS51,3B1	R	26	52	179	19	35	4	2	7	20	4	37	2	.196	.213	.358
Bob Higginson	OF123,DH4	L	25	130	440	75	141	35	0	26	81	65	66	6	.320	.404	.577
Melvin Nieves	OF105,DH11	S	24	120	431	71	106	23	4	24	60	44	158	1	.246	.322	.485
Chad Curtis†	OF104	R	27	104	400	65	105	20	1	10	37	53	73	16	.263	.346	.393
Eddie Williams	DH52,1B7,3B3*	R	31	77	215	22	43	5	0	6	26	18	50	0	.200	.267	.307
Cecil Fielder†	1B71,DH36	R	32	107	391	55	97	12	0	26	80	63	91	2	.248	.354	.478
Curtis Pride	OF48,DH31	L	27	95	267	52	80	17	5	10	31	31	63	11	.300	.372	.513
Kimera Bartee	OF99,DH2	R	23	110	217	32	55	6	1	1	14	17	77	20	.253	.308	.304
Alan Trammell	SS43,2B11,3B8*	R	38	66	193	16	45	2	0	1	16	10	27	6	.233	.267	.259
Ruben Sierra†	OF23,DH20	S	30	46	158	22	35	9	1	1	20	20	25	3	.222	.306	.310
John Flaherty†	C46	R	28	47	152	18	38	12	0	4	23	8	25	1	.250	.290	.408
Chris Gomez†	SS47	R	25	48	128	21	31	5	0	1	16	18	20	1	.242	.340	.305
Phil Nevin	3B24,OF9,C4*	R	25	38	120	15	35	5	0	8	19	8	39	1	.292	.338	.533
Mark Parent†	C33,1B1	R	34	38	104	13	25	6	0	7	17	3	27	0	.240	.259	.500
Raul Casanova	C22,DH3	S	23	25	85	6	16	1	0	4	9	6	18	0	.188	.242	.341
Damion Easley†	2B8,SS8,3B2*	R	26	21	67	10	23	1	0	2	10	4	13	3	.343	.384	.448
Danny Bautista†	OF22,DH1	R	24	25	64	12	16	2	0	2	8	9	15	1	.250	.342	.375
Duane Singleton	OF15	L	23	18	56	5	9	1	0	0	3	4	15	0	.161	.230	.179
Fausto Cruz	2B8,SS4,DH1	R	24	14	38	5	9	2	0	0	0	1	11	0	.237	.256	.289
Tim Hyers	1B9,DH2,OF1	L	24	17	26	1	2	1	0	0	0	4	5	0	.077	.200	.115
Phil Hiatt	3B3,OF2,DH1	R	27	7	21	3	4	0	1	0	1	2	11	0	.190	.261	.286
Shannon Penn	DH4,OF1	S	26	6	14	0	1	0	0	0	1	0	3	0	.071	.071	.071

E. Williams, 2 G at OF; A. Trammell, 1 G at OF; P. Nevin, 1 G at DH; D. Easley, 1 G at DH

Pitcher	T	Age	G	GS	CG	ShO	IP	H	HR	BB	SO	W-L	Sv	ERA
Felipe Lira	R	24	32	32	3	2	194.2	204	30	66	113	6-14	0	5.22
Omar Olivares	R	28	25	25	4	0	160.0	169	16	75	81	7-11	0	4.89
Greg Gohr†	R	28	17	16	0	0	91.2	129	24	34	60	4-8	0	7.17
Justin Thompson	L	23	11	11	0	0	59.0	62	7	31	44	1-6	0	4.58
Todd Van Poppel†	R	24	9	9	1	1	36.1	53	11	29	16	2-4	0	11.39
C.J. Nitkowski	L	23	11	8	0	0	45.2	62	7	38	36	2-3	0	8.08
Scott Aldred†	L	28	11	8	0	0	43.1	60	9	26	36	0-4	0	9.35
Clint Sodowsky	R	23	7	7	0	0	24.1	40	5	20	9	1-3	0	11.84
Trever Miller	L	23	5	4	0	0	16.2	28	3	9	8	0-4	0	9.18
Brian Moehler	R	24	2	2	0	0	10.1	11	1	8	2	0-1	0	4.35
John Farrell	R	33	2	2	0	0	6.1	11	2	5	0	0-2	0	14.21
Mike Myers	L	27	83	0	0	0	64.2	70	6	34	69	1-5	6	5.01
Richie Lewis	R	30	72	0	0	0	90.1	78	9	65	78	4-6	2	4.18
Gregg Olson†	R	29	43	0	0	0	43.0	43	6	28	29	3-0	8	5.02
Brian Williams	R	27	40	17	2	1	121.0	145	21	85	72	3-10	2	6.77
Jose Lima	R	23	39	4	0	0	72.2	87	13	22	59	5-6	3	5.70
Greg Keagle	R	25	26	6	0	0	87.2	104	13	68	70	3-6	0	7.39
Randy Veres	R	30	25	0	0	0	30.1	38	6	23	28	0-4	0	8.31
Joey Eischen†	L	26	24	0	0	0	25.0	27	3	14	15	1-1	0	3.24
A.J. Sager	R	31	22	9	0	0	79.0	91	10	29	52	4-5	0	5.01
John Cummings†	L	27	21	0	0	0	31.2	36	3	20	24	3-3	0	5.12
Mike Walker	R	29	20	0	0	0	27.2	40	10	17	13	0-0	1	8.46
Tom Urbani†	L	28	16	2	0	0	23.2	31	8	14	20	2-2	0	8.37
Mike Christopher	R	32	13	0	0	0	30.0	47	12	11	19	1-1	0	9.30
Bob Scanlan†	R	29	8	0	0	0	11.0	16	1	9	3	0-0	0	10.64
Jeff McCurry	R	26	2	0	0	0	3.1	9	3	2	0	0-0	0	24.30
Brian Maxcy	R	25	2	0	0	0	3.1	8	2	2	1	0-0	0	13.50

1996 Cleveland Indians 1st AL Central 99-62 .615 —

Mike Hargrove

Player	Gm by Position	B	Age	G	AB	R	H	2B	3B	HR	RBI	BB	SO	SB	Avg	OBP	Slg
Sandy Alomar Jr.	C124,1B1	R	30	127	418	53	110	23	0	11	50	19	42	1	.263	.299	.397
Julio Franco	1B97,DH13	R	34	112	432	72	139	20	1	14	76	61	82	8	.322	.407	.470
Carlos Baerga†	2B100	S	27	100	424	54	113	25	0	10	55	16	25	1	.267	.302	.396
Jim Thome	3B150,DH1	L	25	151	505	122	157	28	5	38	116	123	141	2	.311	.450	.612
Omar Vizquel	SS150	S	29	151	542	98	161	36	1	9	64	56	42	35	.297	.362	.417
Kenny Lofton	OF152	L	29	154	662	132	210	35	4	14	67	61	82	75	.317	.372	.446
Albert Belle	OF152,DH6	R	29	158	602	124	187	38	3	48	148	99	87	11	.311	.410	.623
Manny Ramirez	OF149,DH3	R	24	152	550	94	170	45	3	33	112	85	104	8	.309	.399	.582
Eddie Murray†	DH87,1B1	S	40	88	336	33	88	9	1	12	45	34	45	3	.262	.326	.402
Jose Vizcaino†	2B45,SS4,DH1	S	28	48	179	23	51	5	2	0	13	7	24	6	.285	.310	.335
Tony Pena	C67	R	39	67	174	14	34	4	0	1	27	15	25	0	.195	.255	.236
Mark Carreon†	1B34,OF5,DH2	R	32	38	142	16	46	12	0	2	14	11	9	1	.324	.385	.451
Jeromy Burnitz†	OF30,DH15	L	27	71	128	30	36	10	0	7	26	25	31	2	.281	.406	.523
Brian Giles	DH21,OF16	L	25	51	121	26	43	14	1	5	27	19	13	3	.355	.434	.612
Alvaro Espinoza†	3B20,1B18,SS16*	R	34	59	112	12	25	4	2	4	11	6	18	1	.223	.279	.402
Jeff Kent†	1B20,2B9,3B6*	R	28	39	102	16	27	7	0	3	16	10	22	2	.265	.328	.422
Kevin Seitzer†	DH17,1B5	R	34	22	83	11	32	10	0	1	16	14	11	0	.386	.480	.542
Casey Candaele	2B11,3B3,SS1	S	35	24	44	8	11	2	0	1	4	1	9	0	.250	.267	.364
Scott Leius	3B8,1B7,2B6*	R	30	27	43	3	6	4	0	1	3	2	8	0	.140	.178	.302
Ryan Thompson	OF8	R	28	8	22	2	7	0	0	1	5	1	6	0	.318	.348	.455
Wayne Kirby†	OF18,DH3	L	32	27	16	3	4	1	0	0	1	2	2	0	.250	.333	.313
Nigel Wilson	DH3,OF1	L	26	10	12	2	3	0	0	2	5	1	6	0	.250	.308	.750
Herbert Perry	1B5,3B1	R	26	7	12	1	1	1	0	0	0	1	2	1	.083	.154	.167
Damian Jackson	SS5	R	22	5	10	2	3	2	0	0	1	1	4	0	.300	.364	.500
Geronimo Pena	3B3,2B1	S	29	5	9	1	1	0	0	1	2	1	4	0	.111	.200	.444
Einar Diaz	C4	R	23	4	1	0	0	0	0	0	0	0	0	0	.000	.000	.000

A. Espinoza, 5 G at 2B, 1 G at DH; J. Kent, 5 G at DH; S. Leius, 1 G at DH

Pitcher	T	Age	G	GS	CG	ShO	IP	H	HR	BB	SO	W-L	Sv	ERA
Orel Hershiser	R	37	33	33	1	0	206.0	238	21	58	125	15-9	0	4.24
Charles Nagy	R	29	32	32	5	0	222.0	217	21	61	167	17-5	0	3.41
Jack McDowell	R	30	30	30	5	1	192.0	214	22	67	141	13-9	0	5.11
Chad Ogea	R	25	29	21	1	1	146.2	151	22	42	101	10-6	0	4.79
Dennis Martinez	R	41	20	20	1	1	112.0	122	12	37	48	9-6	0	4.50
Albie Lopez	R	24	13	10	0	0	62.0	80	14	22	45	5-4	0	6.39
Brian Anderson	L	24	10	9	0	0	51.1	58	9	14	21	3-1	0	4.91
Jose Mesa	R	30	69	0	0	0	72.1	69	6	28	64	2-7	39	3.73
Paul Assenmacher	L	35	63	0	0	0	46.2	46	1	14	44	4-2	1	3.09
Eric Plunk	R	32	56	0	0	0	77.2	56	6	34	85	3-2	2	2.43
Julian Tavarez	R	23	51	4	0	0	80.2	101	9	22	46	4-7	0	5.36
Paul Shuey	R	25	42	0	0	0	53.2	45	6	26	44	5-2	4	2.85
Jim Poole†	L	30	32	0	0	0	26.2	29	3	14	19	4-0	0	3.04
Alan Embree	L	26	24	0	0	0	31.0	30	10	21	33	1-1	0	6.39
Danny Graves	R	22	15	0	0	0	29.2	29	2	10	22	2-0	0	4.55
Greg Swindell†	L	31	13	2	0	0	28.2	31	8	8	21	1-1	0	6.59
Kent Mercker†	L	28	10	0	0	0	11.2	10	1	3	7	1-0	0	3.09
Joe Roa	R	24	1	0	0	0	1.2	4	0	3	0	0-0	0	10.80

1996 Chicago White Sox 2nd AL Central 85-77 .525 14.5 GB

Terry Bevington

Player	Gm by Position	B	Age	G	AB	R	H	2B	3B	HR	RBI	BB	SO	SB	Avg	OBP	Slg
Ron Karkovice	C111	R	32	111	355	44	78	22	0	10	38	24	93	0	.220	.270	.366
Frank Thomas	1B139	R	28	141	527	110	184	26	0	40	134	109	70	1	.349	.459	.626
Ray Durham	2B150,DH3	S	24	156	557	79	153	33	5	10	65	58	95	30	.275	.350	.406
Robin Ventura	3B150,1B14	L	28	158	586	96	168	31	2	34	105	78	81	1	.287	.368	.520
Ozzie Guillen	SS146,OF2	L	32	150	499	62	131	24	8	4	45	10	27	6	.263	.273	.367
Tony Phillips	OF150,2B2,1B1	S	37	153	581	119	161	29	3	12	63	125	132	13	.277	.404	.399
Darren Lewis	OF138	R	28	141	337	55	77	12	2	4	53	45	40	21	.228	.321	.312
Danny Tartabull	OF122,DH10	R	33	132	472	58	120	23	3	27	101	64	128	1	.254	.340	.487
Harold Baines	DH141	L	37	143	495	80	154	29	0	22	95	73	62	3	.311	.399	.503
Dave Martinez	OF121,1B23	L	31	146	440	85	140	20	8	10	53	52	52	15	.318	.393	.468
Lyle Mouton	OF47,DH28	R	27	87	214	25	63	8	1	7	39	22	50	3	.294	.361	.439
Norberto Martin	SS24,DH19,2B10*	R	29	70	140	30	49	7	0	1	14	6	17	10	.350	.374	.421
Chad Kreuter	C38,1B2,DH1	S	31	46	114	14	25	8	0	3	18	13	29	0	.219	.308	.368
Chris Snopek	3B27,SS12,DH3	R	25	46	104	18	27	6	1	6	18	6	16	0	.260	.304	.510
Pat Borders†	C30,DH1	R	33	31	94	6	26	1	0	3	6	5	18	0	.277	.313	.383
Don Slaught†	C12,DH1	R	37	14	36	2	9	1	0	0	4	2	2	0	.250	.289	.278
Jose Munoz	2B7,DH2,SS2*	S	28	17	27	7	7	0	0	0	1	4	1	0	.259	.355	.259
Greg Norton	SS6,3B2,DH1	S	23	11	23	4	5	0	0	2	3	4	6	0	.217	.333	.478
Domingo Cedeno†	2B2,SS2,DH1	S	27	12	19	2	3	2	0	0	3	0	4	1	.158	.143	.263
Mike Cameron	OF8,DH1	R	23	11	11	1	1	0	0	0	0	1	3	0	.091	.167	.091
Mike Robertson	1B2,DH1	L	25	6	7	0	1	1	0	0	0	0	1	0	.143	.143	.286
Robert Machado	C4	R	23	4	6	1	4	1	0	0	2	0	0	0	.667	.667	.833

N. Martin, 3 G at 3B; J. Munoz, 1 G at 3B, 1 G at OF

Pitcher	T	Age	G	GS	CG	ShO	IP	H	HR	BB	SO	W-L	Sv	ERA
Alex Fernandez	R	26	35	35	6	1	258.0	248	34	72	200	16-10	0	3.45
Wilson Alvarez	L	26	35	35	0	0	217.1	216	21	97	181	15-10	0	4.22
Kevin Tapani	R	32	34	34	1	0	225.1	236	34	76	150	13-10	0	4.59
James Baldwin	R	24	28	28	0	0	169.0	168	24	57	127	11-6	0	4.42
Luis Andujar†	R	23	5	5	0	0	23.0	32	4	15	6	0-2	0	8.22
Jason Bere	R	25	5	5	0	0	16.2	26	3	18	19	0-1	0	10.26
Marvin Freeman†	R	33	1	1	0	0	2.0	4	0	1	1	0-0	0	13.50
Roberto Hernandez	R	31	72	0	0	0	84.2	65	2	38	85	6-5	38	1.91
Bill Simas	R	24	64	0	0	0	72.2	75	5	39	65	2-8	2	4.58
Larry Thomas	L	26	57	0	0	0	30.2	32	1	14	20	2-3	0	3.23
Matt Karchner	R	29	50	0	0	0	59.1	61	10	41	46	7-4	1	5.76
Kirk McCaskill	R	35	29	4	0	0	51.2	72	6	31	28	5-5	0	6.97
Brian Keyser	R	29	28	0	0	0	59.2	78	3	28	19	1-2	1	4.98
Jeff Darwin	R	26	22	0	0	0	30.2	26	5	9	15	0-1	0	2.93
Joe Magrane	L	31	19	8	0	0	53.2	70	10	25	21	1-5	0	6.88
Al Levine	R	28	16	0	0	0	18.1	22	1	7	12	0-1	0	5.40
Mike Bertotti	L	26	15	2	0	0	28.0	28	5	20	19	2-0	0	5.14
Mike Sirotka	L	25	15	4	0	0	26.1	34	3	12	11	1-2	0	7.18
Tony Castillo†	L	33	15	0	0	0	22.2	23	1	4	9	3-1	1	1.59
Scott Ruffcorn	R	26	3	1	0	0	6.1	10	1	6	3	0-1	0	11.37
Richard Sauveur	L	32	3	0	0	0	3.0	3	1	5	1	0-0	0	15.00
Stacy Jones	R	29	2	0	0	0	2.0	0	0	1	1	0-0	0	0.00

1996 Milwaukee Brewers 3rd AL Central 80-82 .494 19.5 GB

Phil Garner

Player	Gm by Position	B	Age	G	AB	R	H	2B	3B	HR	RBI	BB	SO	SB	Avg	OBP	Slg
Mike Matheny	C104,DH1	R	25	106	313	31	64	15	2	8	46	14	80	3	.204	.243	.342
John Jaha	1B85,DH63	R	30	148	543	108	163	28	1	34	118	85	118	3	.300	.398	.543
Fernando Vina	2B137	L	27	140	554	94	157	19	10	7	46	38	35	16	.283	.342	.392
Jeff Cirillo	3B154,DH3,1B2*	R	26	158	566	101	184	46	5	15	83	58	69	4	.325	.391	.504
Jose Valentin	SS151	S	26	154	552	90	143	33	7	24	95	66	145	17	.259	.336	.475
Matt Mieske	OF122	R	28	127	374	46	104	24	3	14	64	26	76	1	.278	.324	.471
Greg Vaughn†	OF100,DH1	R	30	102	375	78	105	16	0	31	95	58	99	5	.280	.378	.571
Pat Listach	OF68,2B12,SS7*	S	28	87	317	51	76	16	2	1	33	36	51	25	.240	.317	.312
Kevin Seitzer†	1B65,DH56,3B12	R	34	132	490	74	155	25	3	12	62	73	68	6	.316	.406	.453
Dave Nilsson	OF61,DH40,1B24*	L	26	123	453	81	150	33	2	17	84	57	68	2	.331	.407	.525
Jesse Levis	C90,DH6	L	28	104	233	27	55	6	1	1	21	38	15	0	.236	.348	.283
Marc Newfield†	OF49	R	23	49	179	21	55	15	0	7	31	11	26	0	.307	.354	.508
Mark Loretta	2B28,3B23,SS21	R	24	73	154	20	43	3	0	1	13	14	15	2	.279	.339	.318
David Hulse	OF68,DH3	L	28	81	117	18	26	3	0	0	6	8	16	4	.222	.272	.248
Chuck Carr	OF27	S	27	27	106	18	29	6	1	1	11	6	21	5	.274	.310	.377
Gerald Williams†	OF26	R	29	26	92	6	19	4	0	0	4	4	18	3	.207	.247	.250
Jeromy Burnitz†	OF22	L	27	23	72	8	17	4	0	2	14	8	16	2	.236	.321	.375
Turner Ward	OF32,DH1	S	31	43	67	7	12	2	1	2	10	13	17	3	.179	.309	.328
Kevin Koslofski	OF22,DH1	L	29	25	42	5	9	3	2	0	6	4	12	0	.214	.298	.381
Kelly Stinnett	C14,DH1	R	26	14	26	1	2	0	0	0	0	2	11	0	.077	.172	.077
Tim Unroe	1B11,3B3,DH1*	R	25	14	16	5	3	0	0	0	0	4	5	0	.188	.350	.188
Todd Dunn	OF6	R	25	6	10	2	3	1	0	0	1	0	3	0	.300	.300	.400
Brian Banks	OF3,1B1	S	25	4	7	2	4	2	0	1	2	1	2	0	.571	.625	1.286
Danny Perez	OF3,DH1	R	25	4	4	0	0	0	0	0	0	0	0	0	.000	.000	.000

J. Cirillo, 1 G at 2B; P. Listach, 1 G at DH; D. Nilsson, 2 G at C; T. Unroe, 1 G at OF

Pitcher	T	Age	G	GS	CG	ShO	IP	H	HR	BB	SO	W-L	Sv	ERA
Ben McDonald	R	28	35	35	2	0	221.1	228	25	67	146	12-10	0	3.90
Scott Karl	L	24	32	32	3	1	207.1	220	29	72	121	13-9	0	4.86
Ricky Bones†	R	27	32	23	0	0	145.0	170	28	62	59	7-14	0	5.83
Jeff D'Amico	R	20	17	17	0	0	86.0	88	21	31	53	6-6	0	5.44
Cal Eldred	R	28	15	15	0	0	84.2	82	8	38	50	4-4	0	4.46
Steve Sparks	R	30	20	13	1	0	88.2	103	19	52	21	4-7	0	6.60
Tim VanEgmond	R	27	12	9	0	0	54.2	58	6	23	33	3-5	0	5.27
Brian Givens	L	30	4	4	0	0	14.0	32	3	7	10	1-3	0	12.86
Mike Fetters	R	31	61	0	0	0	61.1	65	4	26	53	3-3	32	3.38
Graeme Lloyd†	L	29	52	0	0	0	51.0	49	3	17	24	2-4	0	2.82
Angel Miranda	L	26	46	12	0	0	109.1	116	12	69	78	7-6	1	4.94
Ramon Garcia	R	27	37	2	0	0	75.2	84	17	21	40	4-4	4	6.66
Marshall Boze	R	25	25	0	0	0	32.1	47	5	25	19	0-2	1	7.79
Mike Potts	L	25	24	0	0	0	45.1	58	7	30	21	1-2	1	7.15
Doug Jones†	R	39	24	0	0	0	31.2	31	3	13	34	5-0	1	3.41
Ron Villone†	L	26	23	0	0	0	24.2	14	4	18	19	0-0	2	3.28
Kevin Wickander	L	31	21	0	0	0	25.1	26	2	17	19	2-0	0	4.97
Bryce Florie†	R	26	15	0	0	0	19.0	20	3	13	12	0-1	0	6.63
Bob Wickman†	R	27	12	0	0	0	16.2	12	3	10	14	3-0	0	3.24
Jose Mercedes	R	25	11	0	0	0	16.2	20	6	5	6	0-2	0	9.18
Terry Burrows	L	27	8	0	0	0	12.2	12	2	10	5	2-0	0	2.84
Cris Carpenter	R	31	8	0	0	0	8.1	12	1	2	2	0-0	0	7.56
Mark Kiefer	R	27	7	0	0	0	10.0	15	1	5	5	0-0	0	8.10
Al Reyes	R	25	5	0	0	0	5.2	8	1	2	2	1-0	0	7.94

1996 Minnesota Twins 4th AL Central 78-84 .481 21.5 GB

Tom Kelly

Player	Gm by Position	B	Age	G	AB	R	H	2B	3B	HR	RBI	BB	SO	SB	Avg	OBP	Slg
Greg Myers	C90	L	30	97	329	37	94	22	3	6	47	19	52	0	.286	.320	.426
Scott Stahoviak	1B114,DH9	L	26	130	405	72	115	30	3	13	61	59	114	3	.284	.376	.469
Chuck Knoblauch	2B151,DH1	R	27	153	578	140	197	35	14	13	72	98	74	45	.341	.448	.517
Dave Hollins†	3B116,DH3,SS1	S	30	121	422	71	102	26	0	13	53	71	102	6	.242	.364	.396
Pat Meares	SS150,OF1	R	27	152	517	66	138	26	7	8	67	17	90	9	.267	.298	.391
Rich Becker	OF146	S	24	148	525	92	153	31	4	12	71	68	118	19	.291	.372	.434
Marty Cordova	OF145	R	26	145	569	97	176	46	1	16	111	53	96	11	.309	.371	.478
Roberto Kelly	OF93,DH2	R	31	98	322	41	104	17	4	6	47	23	53	10	.323	.375	.457
Paul Molitor	DH143,1B17	R	39	161	660	99	225	41	8	9	113	56	72	18	.341	.390	.468
Matt Lawton	OF75,DH1	L	24	79	252	34	65	7	1	6	42	28	28	4	.258	.339	.365
Jeff Reboulet	SS37,3B36,2B22*	R	32	107	234	20	52	9	0	0	23	25	34	4	.222	.298	.261
Ron Coomer	1B57,OF23,3B9*	R	29	95	233	34	69	12	1	12	41	17	24	3	.296	.340	.511
Matt Walbeck	C61	S	26	63	215	25	48	10	0	2	24	9	34	3	.223	.252	.298
Denny Hocking	OF33,SS6,2B2*	S	26	49	127	16	25	6	0	1	10	8	24	3	.197	.243	.268
Chip Hale	2B14,DH10,1B6*	L	31	85	87	8	24	5	0	1	16	10	6	0	.276	.347	.368
Todd Walker	3B20,2B4,DH1	L	23	25	82	8	21	6	0	0	6	4	13	2	.256	.281	.329
Mike Durant	C37	R	26	40	81	15	17	3	0	0	5	10	15	3	.210	.293	.247
Brent Brede	OF7	L	24	10	20	2	6	0	1	0	2	1	5	0	.300	.333	.400
Brian Raabe	3B6,2B1	R	28	7	9	0	2	0	0	0	1	0	1	0	.222	.200	.222
Tom Quinlan	3B4	R	28	4	6	0	0	0	0	0	0	0	3	0	.000	.000	.000

J. Reboulet, 13 G at 1B, 7 G at OF, 3 G at DH; R. Coomer, 3 G at DH; D. Hocking, 1 G at DH, 1 G at 1B; C. Hale, 3 G at 3B, 3 G at OF

Pitcher	T	Age	G	GS	CG	ShO	IP	H	HR	BB	SO	W-L	Sv	ERA
Brad Radke	R	23	35	35	3	0	232.0	231	40	57	148	11-16	0	4.46
Frank Rodriguez	R	23	38	33	3	0	206.2	218	27	78	110	13-14	2	5.05
Rich Robertson	L	27	36	31	5	3	186.1	197	22	116	114	7-17	0	5.12
Rick Aguilera	R	34	19	19	2	0	111.1	124	20	27	83	8-6	0	5.42
Scott Aldred†	L	28	25	17	0	0	122.0	134	20	42	75	6-5	0	5.09
Travis Miller	L	23	7	7	0	0	26.1	45	7	9	15	1-2	0	9.23
LaTroy Hawkins	R	23	7	6	0	0	26.1	42	8	9	24	1-1	0	8.20
Dan Serafini	L	22	1	1	0	0	4.1	7	1	2	1	0-1	0	10.38
Eddie Guardado	L	25	83	0	0	0	73.2	61	12	33	74	6-5	4	5.25
Greg Hansell	R	25	50	0	0	0	74.1	83	14	31	46	3-0	3	5.69
Dave Stevens	R	26	49	0	0	0	58.0	58	12	25	29	3-3	11	4.66
Dan Naulty	R	26	49	0	0	0	57.0	43	5	35	56	3-2	4	3.79
Mike Trombley	R	29	43	0	0	0	68.2	61	2	25	57	5-1	6	3.01
Jose Parra	R	23	27	5	0	0	70.0	88	15	27	50	5-5	0	6.04
Mike Milchin†	L	28	26	0	0	0	21.2	31	6	12	19	2-1	0	8.31
Erik Bennett	R	27	24	0	0	0	27.1	33	7	16	13	2-0	1	7.90
Pat Mahomes†	R	25	20	5	0	0	45.0	63	10	27	30	1-4	0	7.20
Scott Klingenbeck	R	25	10	3	0	0	28.2	42	5	10	15	1-1	0	7.85

1996 Kansas City Royals 5th AL Central 75-86 .466 24.0 GB

Bob Boone

Player	Gm by Position	B	Age	G	AB	R	H	2B	3B	HR	RBI	BB	SO	SB	Avg	OBP	Slg
Mike Macfarlane	C99,DH9	R	32	112	379	58	104	24	2	19	54	31	57	3	.274	.339	.499
Jose Offerman	1B96,2B38,SS36*	S	27	151	561	85	170	33	8	5	47	74	98	24	.303	.384	.417
Keith Lockhart	2B84,3B55,DH1	L	31	138	433	49	118	33	3	7	55	30	40	11	.273	.319	.411
Joe Randa	3B92,2B15,1B7*	R	26	110	337	36	102	24	1	6	47	26	47	13	.303	.351	.433
Dave Howard	SS135,2B3,1B2*	S	29	143	420	51	92	14	5	4	48	40	74	5	.219	.291	.305
Johnny Damon	OF144,DH1	L	22	145	517	61	140	22	5	6	50	31	64	25	.271	.313	.368
Tom Goodwin	OF136,DH5	L	27	143	524	80	148	14	4	1	35	39	79	66	.282	.334	.330
Michael Tucker	OF98,1B9,DH4	L	25	108	339	55	88	18	4	12	53	40	69	10	.260	.346	.442
Joe Vitiello	DH70,1B9,OF1	R	26	85	257	29	62	15	1	8	40	38	69	2	.241	.342	.401
Craig Paquette	3B51,OF47,1B19*	R	27	118	429	61	111	15	1	22	67	23	101	5	.259	.296	.452
Bip Roberts	2B63,DH16,OF11	S	32	90	339	39	96	21	2	0	52	25	38	12	.283	.331	.357
Bob Hamelin	DH47,1B33	L	28	89	239	31	61	14	1	9	40	54	58	5	.255	.391	.435
Mike Sweeney	C26,DH22	R	22	50	165	23	46	10	0	4	24	18	21	1	.279	.358	.412
Sal Fasano	C51	R	24	51	143	20	29	2	0	6	19	14	25	1	.203	.283	.343
Kevin Young	1B27,OF17,3B7*	R	27	55	132	20	32	6	0	8	23	11	32	3	.242	.301	.470
Chris Stynes	OF19,2B5,DH3*	R	23	36	92	8	27	6	0	0	6	2	5	5	.293	.309	.359
Jon Nunnally	OF29,DH4	L	24	35	90	16	19	5	1	5	17	13	25	0	.211	.308	.456
Rod Myers	OF19	L	23	22	63	9	18	7	0	1	11	7	16	3	.286	.357	.444
Les Norman	OF38,DH7	R	27	54	49	9	6	0	0	0	0	6	14	1	.122	.232	.122
Patrick Lennon	OF11,DH1	R	28	14	30	5	7	3	0	0	1	7	10	0	.233	.378	.333
Henry Mercedes	C4	R	26	4	4	1	1	0	0	0	0	0	1	0	.250	.250	.250

J. Offerman, 1 G at OF; J. Randa, 1 G at DH; D. Howard, 1 G at DH, 1 G at OF; C. Paquette, 11 G at SS, 6 G at DH; K. Young, 2 G at DH; C. Stynes, 2 G at 3B

Pitcher	T	Age	G	GS	CG	ShO	IP	H	HR	BB	SO	W-L	Sv	ERA
Tim Belcher	R	34	35	35	4	1	238.2	262	28	68	113	15-11	0	3.92
Chris Haney	L	27	35	35	4	1	228.0	267	29	51	115	10-14	0	4.70
Kevin Appier	R	28	32	32	5	1	211.1	192	17	75	207	14-11	0	3.62
Mark Gubicza	R	33	19	19	2	1	119.1	132	22	34	55	4-12	0	5.13
Doug Linton	R	31	21	18	0	0	104.0	111	13	26	87	7-9	0	5.02
Jose Rosado	L	21	16	16	2	1	106.2	101	7	26	64	8-6	0	3.21
Hipolito Pichardo	R	26	57	0	0	0	68.0	74	5	26	43	3-5	3	5.43
Jason Jacome	L	25	49	2	0	0	47.2	67	5	22	32	0-4	1	4.72
Jeff Montgomery	R	34	48	0	0	0	63.1	59	14	19	45	4-6	24	4.26
Mike Magnante	L	31	38	0	0	0	54.0	58	5	24	32	2-2	0	5.67
Julio Valera	R	27	31	2	0	0	61.1	75	7	27	31	3-2	1	6.46
Rick Huisman	R	27	22	0	0	0	29.1	25	4	18	23	2-1	1	4.60
Tim Pugh†	R	29	19	1	0	0	36.1	42	9	12	27	0-1	0	5.45
Jaime Bluma	R	24	17	0	0	0	20.0	18	2	4	14	0-0	5	3.60
Jeff Granger	L	24	15	0	0	0	16.1	21	3	10	11	0-0	0	6.61
Terry Clark†	R	35	12	0	0	0	17.1	28	3	7	12	1-1	0	7.79
Bob Scanlan†	R	29	9	0	0	0	11.1	13	1	3	3	0-1	0	3.18
Ken Robinson	R	26	5	0	0	0	6.0	9	0	3	5	1-0	0	6.00
Brian Bevil	R	24	3	1	0	0	11.0	9	2	5	7	1-0	0	5.73

1996 Texas Rangers 1st AL West 90-72 .556 —

Johnny Oates

Player	Gm by Position	B	Age	G	AB	R	H	2B	3B	HR	RBI	BB	SO	SB	Avg	OBP	Slg
Ivan Rodriguez	C146,DH6	R	24	153	639	116	192	47	3	19	86	38	55	5	.300	.342	.473
Will Clark	1B117	L	32	117	436	69	124	25	1	13	72	64	67	2	.284	.377	.436
Mark McLemore	2B147,OF1	S	31	147	517	84	150	23	4	5	46	87	69	27	.290	.389	.379
Dean Palmer	3B154,DH1	R	27	154	582	98	163	26	2	38	107	59	145	2	.280	.348	.527
Kevin Elster	SS157	R	31	157	515	79	130	32	2	24	99	52	138	4	.252	.317	.462
Darryl Hamilton	OF147	L	31	148	627	94	184	29	4	6	51	54	66	15	.293	.348	.381
Rusty Greer	OF137,DH1,1B1	L	27	139	542	96	180	41	6	18	100	62	86	9	.332	.397	.530
Juan Gonzalez	OF102,DH32	R	26	134	541	89	170	33	2	47	144	45	82	2	.314	.368	.643
Mickey Tettleton	DH115,1B23	S	35	143	491	78	121	26	1	24	83	95	137	2	.246	.366	.450
Warren Newson	OF66,DH8	L	31	91	235	34	60	14	1	10	31	37	82	3	.255	.355	.451
Damon Buford	OF80,DH3	R	26	90	145	30	41	9	0	6	20	15	34	8	.283	.348	.469
Rene Gonzales	1B23,3B15,SS10*	R	35	51	92	19	20	4	0	2	5	10	11	0	.217	.288	.326
Dave Valle	C35,1B5,DH1	R	35	42	86	14	26	6	1	3	17	9	17	0	.302	.368	.500
Lee Stevens	1B18,OF5	L	28	27	78	6	18	2	3	3	12	6	22	0	.231	.291	.449
Kurt Stillwell	2B21,SS9,3B6*	S	31	46	77	12	21	4	0	1	4	10	11	0	.273	.364	.364
Lou Frazier	OF15,DH11,2B1	S	31	30	50	5	13	2	1	0	5	8	10	4	.260	.373	.340
Craig Worthington	3B7,1B6	R	31	13	19	2	3	0	0	1	4	6	3	0	.158	.333	.316
Jack Voigt	OF3,3B1	R	30	5	9	1	1	0	0	0	0	0	2	0	.111	.111	.111
Luis Ortiz	DH1	R	26	3	7	1	2	0	1	1	1	0	1	0	.286	.286	1.000
Benji Gil	SS5	R	23	5	5	0	2	0	0	0	1	1	1	0	.400	.500	.400
Rikkert Faneyte	OF6,DH2	R	27	8	5	0	1	0	0	0	1	0	0	0	.200	.200	.200
Kevin L. Brown	C2,DH1	R	23	3	4	1	0	0	0	0	1	2	2	0	.000	.375	.000

R. Gonzales, 5 G at 2B, 1 G at OF; K. Stillwell, 1 G at DH, 1 G at 1B

Pitcher	T	Age	G	GS	CG	ShO	IP	H	HR	BB	SO	W-L	Sv	ERA
Ken Hill	R	30	35	35	7	3	250.2	250	19	95	170	16-10	0	3.63
Roger Pavlik	R	28	34	34	7	0	201.0	216	28	81	127	15-8	0	5.19
Bobby Witt	R	32	33	32	2	0	199.2	235	28	96	157	16-12	0	5.41
Darren Oliver	L	25	30	30	1	1	173.2	190	20	76	112	14-6	0	4.66
Kevin Gross	R	35	28	19	1	0	129.1	151	19	50	78	11-8	0	5.22
John Burkett†	R	31	10	10	1	1	68.2	75	4	16	47	5-2	0	4.06
Dennis Cook	L	33	60	0	0	0	70.1	53	2	35	64	5-2	0	4.09
Jeff Russell	R	34	55	0	0	0	56.0	58	5	22	23	3-3	3	3.38
Ed Vosberg	L	34	52	0	0	0	44.0	51	4	21	32	1-1	8	3.27
Mike Henneman	R	34	49	0	0	0	42.0	41	6	17	34	0-7	31	5.79
Gil Heredia	R	30	44	0	0	0	73.1	91	12	14	43	2-5	1	5.89
Mark Brandenburg†	R	25	26	0	0	0	47.2	48	3	25	37	1-3	0	3.21
Mike Stanton†	L	29	22	0	0	0	22.1	20	2	4	14	0-1	0	3.22
Matt Whiteside	R	28	14	0	0	0	32.1	43	8	11	15	0-1	0	6.68
Danny Patterson	R	25	7	0	0	0	8.2	10	0	3	5	0-0	0	0.00
Rick Helling†	R	25	6	2	0	0	20.1	23	7	9	16	1-2	0	7.52
Jose Alberro	R	27	5	1	0	0	9.1	14	1	7	2	0-1	0	5.79

1996 Seattle Mariners 2nd AL West 85-76 .528 4.5 GB

Lou Piniella

Player	Gm by Position	B	Age	G	AB	R	H	2B	3B	HR	RBI	BB	SO	SB	Avg	OBP	Slg
Dan Wilson	C135	R	27	138	491	51	140	24	0	18	83	32	88	1	.285	.330	.444
Paul Sorrento	1B138	L	30	143	471	67	136	32	1	23	93	57	103	0	.289	.370	.507
Joey Cora	2B140,3B1	S	31	144	530	90	154	37	6	6	45	35	32	5	.291	.340	.417
Russ Davis	3B51	R	26	51	167	24	39	9	0	5	18	17	50	2	.234	.312	.377
Alex Rodriguez	SS146	R	20	146	601	141	215	54	1	36	123	59	104	15	.358	.414	.631
Jay Buhner	OF142,DH8	R	31	150	564	107	153	29	0	44	138	84	159	0	.271	.369	.557
Ken Griffey Jr.	OF137,DH5	L	26	140	545	125	165	26	2	49	140	78	104	16	.303	.392	.628
Rich Amaral	OF91,2B15,1B10*	R	34	118	312	69	91	11	3	1	29	47	55	25	.292	.392	.356
Edgar Martinez	DH134,1B4,3B2	R	33	139	499	121	163	52	2	26	103	123	84	3	.327	.464	.595
Luis Sojo†	3B33,2B27,SS19	R	30	77	247	20	52	8	1	1	16	10	13	2	.211	.244	.263
Brian Hunter	1B41,OF29,DH2	R	28	75	198	21	53	10	0	7	28	15	43	0	.268	.327	.424
Darren Bragg†	OF63	L	26	69	195	36	53	12	1	7	25	33	35	8	.272	.376	.451
Doug Strange	3B39,OF11,DH10*	S	32	88	183	19	43	7	1	3	23	14	31	1	.235	.290	.333
Mark Whiten†	OF39	S	29	40	140	31	42	7	0	12	33	21	40	2	.300	.399	.607
Andy Sheets	3B25,2B18,SS7	R	24	47	110	18	21	8	0	0	9	10	41	2	.191	.262	.264
John Marzano	C39	R	33	41	106	8	26	6	0	0	6	7	15	0	.245	.316	.302
Dave Hollins†	3B28,1B1	S	30	28	94	17	33	3	0	3	25	13	15	0	.351	.438	.479
Alex Diaz	OF28,DH1	S	27	38	79	11	19	2	0	1	5	2	8	6	.241	.274	.304
Jeff Manto†	3B16,DH2,OF1	R	31	21	54	7	10	3	0	1	4	9	12	0	.185	.302	.296
Ricky Jordan	1B9,DH2	R	31	15	28	4	7	0	0	1	4	1	6	0	.250	.290	.357
Greg Pirkl†	DH3,1B2	R	25	7	21	2	4	1	0	1	1	0	3	0	.190	.190	.381
Manny Martinez†	OF8	R	25	9	17	3	4	2	1	0	3	3	5	2	.235	.350	.471
Chris Widger	C7	R	25	8	11	1	2	0	0	0	0	0	5	0	.182	.250	.182
Raul Ibanez	DH2	L	24	4	5	0	0	0	0	0	0	0	1	0	.000	.167	.000

R. Amaral, 4 G at DH, 1 G at 3B; D. Strange, 3 G at 1B, 3 G at 2B

Pitcher	T	Age	G	GS	CG	ShO	IP	H	HR	BB	SO	W-L	Sv	ERA
Sterling Hitchcock	L	25	35	35	0	0	196.2	245	27	73	132	13-9	0	5.35
Bob Wolcott	R	22	30	28	1	0	149.1	179	26	54	78	7-10	0	5.73
Matt Wagner	R	24	15	14	1	0	80.0	91	15	38	41	3-5	0	6.86
Terry Mulholland†	L	33	12	12	0	0	69.1	75	5	28	34	5-4	0	4.67
Jamie Moyer†	L	33	11	11	0	0	70.2	66	9	19	29	6-2	0	3.31
Chris Bosio	R	33	18	9	0	0	60.2	72	8	24	39	4-4	0	5.93
Randy Johnson	L	32	14	8	0	0	61.1	48	8	25	85	5-0	1	3.67
Salomon Torres	R	24	10	7	1	1	49.0	44	5	23	36	3-3	0	4.59
Paul Menhart	R	27	11	6	0	0	42.0	55	9	25	18	2-2	0	7.29
Bob Milacki	R	31	7	4	0	0	21.0	30	3	15	13	1-4	0	6.86
Tim Harikkala	R	24	1	1	0	0	4.1	4	1	2	1	0-1	0	12.46
Mike Jackson	R	31	73	0	0	0	72.0	61	11	24	70	1-1	6	3.63
Norm Charlton	L	33	70	0	0	0	75.2	68	7	38	73	4-7	20	4.04
Rafael Carmona	R	23	53	1	0	0	90.1	95	11	55	62	8-3	1	4.28
Bobby Ayala	R	26	50	0	0	0	67.1	65	10	25	61	6-3	3	5.88
Tim Davis	L	25	40	0	0	0	42.2	43	4	17	34	2-2	0	4.01
Bob Wells	R	29	36	16	1	1	130.2	141	25	46	94	12-7	0	5.30
Lee Guetterman	L	37	17	0	0	0	11.0	11	0	10	6	0-2	0	4.09
Edwin Hurtado	R	26	16	4	0	0	47.2	61	10	30	36	2-5	2	7.74
Rusty Meacham	R	28	15	5	0	0	42.1	57	9	13	25	1-1	1	5.74
Blas Minor†	R	28	11	0	0	0	25.1	27	6	11	14	0-1	0	4.97
Greg McCarthy	L	27	10	0	0	0	9.2	8	0	4	7	0-0	0	1.86
Scott Davison	R	25	5	0	0	0	9.0	11	6	3	9	0-0	0	9.00
Joe Klink	L	34	3	0	0	0	2.1	3	1	1	2	0-0	0	3.86
Makoto Suzuki	R	21	1	0	0	0	1.1	2	0	2	1	0-0	0	20.25

1996 Oakland Athletics 3rd AL West 78-84 .481 12.0 GB

Art Howe

Player	Gm by Position	B	Age	G	AB	R	H	2B	3B	HR	RBI	BB	SO	SB	Avg	OBP	Slg
Terry Steinbach	C137,DH4,1B1	R	34	145	514	79	140	25	1	35	100	49	115	0	.272	.342	.529
Mark McGwire	1B109,DH18	R	32	130	423	104	132	21	0	52	113	116	112	0	.312	.467	.730
Rafael Bournigal	2B64,SS23	R	30	88	252	33	61	14	2	0	18	16	19	4	.242	.290	.313
Scott Brosius	3B109,1B10,OF4	R	29	114	428	73	130	25	0	22	71	59	85	7	.304	.393	.516
Mike Bordick	SS155	R	30	155	525	46	126	18	4	5	54	52	59	5	.240	.307	.318
Ernie Young	OF140	R	26	141	462	72	112	19	4	19	64	52	118	7	.242	.326	.424
Jose Herrera	OF100,DH1	L	23	108	320	44	86	15	1	6	30	20	59	8	.269	.318	.378
Phil Plantier	OF68,DH1	L	27	73	231	29	49	8	1	7	31	28	56	2	.212	.304	.346
Geronimo Berroa	DH91,OF61	R	31	153	586	101	170	32	1	36	106	47	122	0	.290	.344	.532
Jason Giambi	1B45,OF45,3B39*	L	25	140	536	84	156	40	1	20	79	51	95	0	.291	.355	.481
Brent Gates	2B63	S	26	64	247	26	65	19	2	2	30	18	35	1	.263	.316	.381
Tony Batista	2B52,3B18,DH4*	R	22	74	238	38	71	10	2	6	25	19	49	7	.298	.350	.433
Matt Stairs	OF44,DH5,1B1	L	27	61	137	21	38	5	1	10	23	19	23	1	.277	.367	.547
George Williams	C43,DH11	S	27	56	132	17	20	5	0	3	10	28	32	0	.152	.311	.258
Allen Battle	OF47	R	27	47	130	20	25	3	0	1	5	17	26	10	.192	.293	.238
Pedro Munoz	DH18,OF14	R	27	34	121	17	31	5	0	6	18	9	31	0	.256	.308	.446
Damon Mashore	OF48	R	26	50	105	20	28	7	1	3	12	16	31	4	.267	.366	.438
Torey Lovullo	1B42,3B11,DH4*	S	30	65	82	15	18	4	0	3	9	11	17	1	.220	.323	.378
Brian Lesher	OF25,1B1	R	25	26	82	11	19	3	0	5	16	5	17	0	.232	.281	.451
Scott Spiezio	3B5,DH4	S	23	9	29	6	9	2	0	2	8	4	4	0	.310	.394	.586
Izzy Molina	C12,DH1	R	25	14	25	0	5	2	0	0	1	1	3	0	.200	.231	.280
Kerwin Moore	OF18,DH1	S	25	22	16	4	1	1	0	0	0	2	6	1	.063	.167	.125
Webster Garrison	2B3,1B1	R	30	5	9	0	0	0	0	0	0	1	0	0	.000	.100	.000
S. Wojciechowski	P16,DH1	L	25	16	0	0	0	0	0	0	0	0	0	0	—	—	—

J. Giambi, 12 G at DH; T. Batista, 4 G at SS; T. Lovullo, 2 G at 2B, 1 G at SS, 1 G at OF

Pitcher	T	Age	G	GS	CG	ShO	IP	H	HR	BB	SO	W-L	Sv	ERA
Don Wengert	R	26	36	25	1	1	161.1	200	29	60	75	7-11	0	5.58
Doug Johns	L	28	40	23	1	0	158.0	187	21	69	71	6-12	1	5.98
John Wasdin	R	23	25	21	1	0	131.1	145	24	50	75	8-7	0	5.96
Ariel Prieto	R	26	21	21	2	0	125.2	130	9	54	75	6-7	0	4.15
S. Wojciechowski	L	25	16	15	0	0	79.2	97	10	28	30	5-5	0	5.65
Dave Telgheder	R	29	16	14	1	1	79.1	92	12	26	43	4-7	0	4.65
Willie Adams	R	23	12	12	1	1	76.1	76	11	23	68	3-4	0	4.01
Bobby Chouinard	R	24	13	11	0	0	59.0	75	10	32	32	4-2	0	6.10
Mike Mohler	L	27	72	0	0	0	81.0	79	9	41	64	6-3	7	3.67
Buddy Groom	L	30	72	1	0	0	77.1	85	8	34	57	5-0	2	3.84
Jim Corsi	R	34	56	0	0	0	73.2	71	6	34	43	6-0	3	4.03
Billy Taylor	R	34	55	0	0	0	60.1	52	5	25	67	6-3	17	4.33
Carlos Reyes	R	27	46	10	0	0	122.1	134	19	61	78	7-10	0	4.78
Todd Van Poppel†	R	24	28	6	0	0	63.0	86	13	33	37	1-5	1	7.71
Mark Acre	R	27	22	0	0	0	25.0	38	4	9	18	1-3	2	6.12
John Briscoe	R	28	17	0	0	0	26.1	18	2	24	14	0-1	1	3.76
Aaron Small	R	24	12	3	0	0	28.2	37	3	22	17	1-3	0	8.16
Jay Witasick	R	23	12	0	0	0	13.0	12	5	5	12	1-1	0	6.23
Steve Montgomery	R	25	8	0	0	0	13.2	18	5	13	8	1-0	0	9.22
Paul Fletcher	R	29	1	0	0	0	1.1	6	0	1	0	0-0	0	20.25

1996 California Angels 4th AL West 70-91 .435 19.5 GB

Marcel Lachemann (53-64)/John McNamara (17-27)

Player	Gm by Position	B	Age	G	AB	R	H	2B	3B	HR	RBI	BB	SO	SB	Avg	OBP	Slg
Jorge Fabregas	C89,DH1	L	26	90	254	18	73	6	0	2	26	17	27	0	.287	.326	.335
J.T. Snow	1B154	S	28	155	575	69	148	20	1	17	67	56	96	1	.257	.327	.384
Randy Velarde	2B114,3B28,SS7	R	33	136	530	82	151	27	3	14	54	70	118	7	.285	.372	.426
George Arias	3B83,DH1	R	24	84	252	19	60	8	1	6	28	16	50	2	.238	.284	.349
Gary DiSarcina	SS150	R	28	150	536	62	137	26	4	5	48	21	36	2	.256	.286	.347
Tim Salmon	OF153,DH3	R	27	156	581	90	166	27	4	30	98	93	125	4	.286	.386	.501
Garret Anderson	OF146,DH1	L	24	150	607	79	173	33	2	12	72	27	84	7	.285	.314	.405
Jim Edmonds	OF111,DH1	L	26	114	431	73	131	28	3	27	66	46	101	4	.304	.375	.571
Chili Davis	DH143	S	36	145	530	73	155	24	0	28	95	86	99	5	.292	.387	.496
Rex Hudler	2B53,OF21,DH7*	R	35	92	302	60	94	20	3	16	40	9	54	14	.311	.337	.556
Darin Erstad	OF48	L	22	57	208	34	59	5	1	4	20	17	29	3	.284	.333	.375
Don Slaught†	C59,DH1	R	37	62	207	23	67	9	0	6	32	13	20	0	.324	.366	.454
Tim Wallach†	3B46,DH8,1B3	R	38	57	190	23	45	7	0	8	20	18	47	1	.237	.306	.400
Jack Howell	3B43,DH4,1B2*	L	34	66	126	20	34	4	1	8	21	10	30	0	.270	.324	.508
Orlando Palmeiro	OF31,DH4	L	27	50	87	6	25	6	1	0	6	8	13	0	.287	.361	.379
Todd Greene	C26,DH1	R	25	29	79	9	15	1	0	2	9	4	11	2	.190	.238	.278
Pat Borders†	C19	R	33	19	57	6	13	3	0	2	8	3	11	0	.228	.267	.386
Damion Easley†	SS13,2B9,3B3*	R	26	28	45	4	7	1	0	2	7	6	12	0	.156	.255	.311
Mike Aldrete†	DH6,OF6,1B1	L	35	31	40	5	6	1	0	3	8	5	4	0	.150	.239	.400
Dick Schofield	SS7,2B2,3B1	R	33	13	16	3	4	0	0	0	0	1	1	1	.250	.294	.250
Robert Eenhoorn†	SS4,2B2	R	28	6	15	1	4	0	0	0	0	0	2	0	.267	.267	.267
Chris Pritchett	1B5	L	26	5	13	1	2	0	0	0	1	0	3	0	.154	.154	.154
Chris Turner	C3,OF1	R	27	4	3	1	1	0	0	0	1	1	0	0	.333	.400	.333
Shawn Boskie	P37,DH1	R	29	37	0	0	0	0	0	0	0	0	0	0	—	—	—

R. Hudler, 7 G at 1B; J. Howell, 1 G at 2B; D. Easley, 2 G at DH, 2 G at OF

Pitcher	T	Age	G	GS	CG	ShO	IP	H	HR	BB	SO	W-L	Sv	ERA
Chuck Finley	L	33	35	35	4	1	238.0	241	27	94	215	15-16	0	4.16
Shawn Boskie	R	29	37	28	1	0	189.1	226	40	67	133	12-11	0	5.32
Jim Abbott	L	28	27	23	1	0	142.0	171	23	78	58	2-18	0	7.48
Jason Grimsley	R	28	35	20	2	1	130.1	150	14	74	82	5-7	0	6.84
Mark Langston	L	35	18	18	2	0	123.1	116	18	45	83	6-5	0	4.82
Dennis Springer	R	31	20	15	2	1	94.2	91	24	43	64	5-6	0	5.51
Jason Dickson	R	23	7	7	0	0	43.1	52	6	18	20	1-4	0	4.57
Scott Sanderson	R	39	5	4	0	0	18.0	39	5	4	7	0-2	0	7.50
Phil Leftwich	R	27	2	2	0	0	7.1	12	1	3	4	0-1	0	7.36
Mike James	R	28	69	0	0	0	81.0	62	7	42	65	5-5	1	2.67
Troy Percival	R	26	62	0	0	0	74.0	38	8	31	100	0-2	36	2.31
Chuck McElroy†	L	28	40	0	0	0	36.2	32	2	13	32	5-1	0	2.95
Mike Holtz	L	23	30	0	0	0	29.1	21	1	19	31	3-3	0	2.45
Mark Holzemer	L	26	25	0	0	0	24.2	35	7	8	20	1-0	0	8.76
Mark Eichhorn	R	35	24	0	0	0	30.1	36	3	11	24	1-2	0	5.04
Greg Gohr†	R	28	15	0	0	0	24.0	34	7	10	15	1-1	1	7.50
Shad Williams	R	25	13	2	0	0	28.1	42	7	21	26	0-2	0	8.89
Rich Monteleone	R	33	12	0	0	0	15.1	23	5	2	5	0-3	0	5.87
Pep Harris	R	23	11	3	0	0	32.1	31	4	17	20	2-0	0	3.90
Ryan Hancock	R	24	11	4	0	0	27.2	34	2	17	19	4-1	0	7.48
Lee Smith†	R	38	11	0	0	0	11.0	8	0	3	6	0-0	0	2.45
Jeff Schmidt	R	25	9	0	0	0	8.0	13	2	8	2	2-0	0	7.88
Brad Pennington†	L	27	8	0	0	0	7.1	5	1	16	7	0-0	0	12.27
Darrell May†	L	24	5	0	0	0	2.2	3	1	2	1	0-0	0	10.13
Todd Frohwirth	R	33	4	0	0	0	5.2	10	1	4	1	0-0	0	11.12
Robert Ellis	R	25	3	0	0	0	5.0	0	0	4	5	0-0	0	0.00
Kyle Abbott	L	28	3	0	0	0	4.0	10	1	5	3	0-1	0	20.25
Ken Edenfield	R	29	2	0	0	0	4.1	10	2	2	4	0-0	0	10.38
Ben VanRyn	L	24	1	0	0	0	1.0	1	0	1	0	0-0	0	0.00

»1996 Atlanta Braves 1st NL East 96-66 .593 — Bobby Cox

Player	Gm by Position	B	Age	G	AB	R	H	2B	3B	HR	RBI	BB	SO	SB	Avg	OBP	Slg
Javy Lopez	C135	R	25	138	489	56	138	19	1	23	69	28	84	1	.282	.322	.466
Fred McGriff	1B158	L	32	159	617	81	182	37	1	28	107	68	116	7	.295	.365	.494
Mark Lemke	2B133	S	30	135	498	64	127	17	0	5	37	53	48	5	.255	.323	.319
Chipper Jones	3B118,SS38,OF1	S	24	157	598	114	185	32	5	30	110	87	88	14	.309	.393	.530
Jeff Blauser	SS79	R	30	83	265	48	65	14	1	10	35	40	54	6	.245	.356	.419
Marquis Grissom	OF158	R	29	158	671	106	207	32	10	23	74	41	73	28	.308	.349	.489
Ryan Klesko	OF144,1B2	L	25	153	528	90	149	21	4	34	93	68	129	6	.282	.364	.530
Jermaine Dye	OF92	R	22	98	292	32	82	16	0	12	37	8	67	1	.281	.304	.459
Terry Pendleton†	3B41	S	35	42	162	21	33	6	0	4	17	15	36	2	.204	.271	.315
Eddie Perez	C54,1B7	R	28	68	156	19	40	9	1	4	17	8	19	0	.256	.293	.404
Dwight Smith	OF29	L	32	101	153	16	31	5	0	3	16	17	42	1	.203	.285	.294
Rafael Belliard	SS63,2B15	R	34	87	142	9	24	7	0	0	3	2	22	3	.169	.179	.218
David Justice	OF40	L	30	40	140	23	45	9	0	6	25	21	22	1	.321	.409	.514
Mike Mordecai	2B20,3B10,SS6*	S	28	66	108	12	26	5	0	2	8	9	24	1	.241	.297	.343
Andruw Jones	OF29	R	19	31	106	11	23	7	1	5	13	7	29	3	.217	.265	.443
Mark Whiten†	OF29	S	29	36	90	12	23	5	1	3	17	16	25	2	.256	.364	.433
Ed Giovanola	SS25,3B6,2B5	L	27	43	82	10	19	2	0	0	7	8	13	1	.232	.304	.256
Jerome Walton	OF28	R	30	37	47	9	16	5	0	1	4	5	10	0	.340	.389	.511
Tony Graffanino	2B18	R	24	22	46	7	8	1	1	0	2	4	13	0	.174	.250	.239
Luis Polonia†	OF7	L	31	22	31	3	13	0	0	0	2	1	3	1	.419	.424	.419
Tyler Houston†	1B11,OF1	L	25	33	27	3	6	2	1	1	8	1	9	0	.222	.250	.481
Danny Bautista†	OF14	R	24	17	20	1	3	0	0	0	1	2	5	0	.150	.261	.150
Joe Ayrault	C7	R	24	7	5	0	1	0	0	0	0	0	1	0	.200	.333	.200
Pablo Martinez	SS1	S	27	4	2	1	1	0	0	0	0	0	0	0	.500	.500	.500

M. Mordecai, 1 G at 1B

Pitcher	T	Age	G	GS	CG	ShO	IP	H	HR	BB	SO	W-L	Sv	ERA
Tom Glavine	L	30	36	36	1	0	235.1	222	14	85	181	15-10	0	2.98
John Smoltz	R	29	35	35	6	2	253.2	199	19	55	276	24-8	0	2.94
Greg Maddux	R	30	35	35	5	1	245.0	225	11	28	172	15-11	0	2.72
Steve Avery	L	26	24	23	1	0	131.0	146	10	40	86	7-10	0	4.47
Jason Schmidt†	R	23	13	11	0	0	58.2	69	8	32	48	3-4	0	6.75
Denny Neagle†	L	27	6	6	1	0	38.2	40	5	14	18	2-3	0	5.59
Brad Clontz	R	25	81	0	0	0	80.2	78	11	33	49	6-3	1	5.69
Mark Wohlers	R	26	77	0	0	0	77.1	71	8	21	100	2-4	39	3.03
Greg McMichael	R	29	73	0	0	0	86.2	84	4	27	78	5-3	2	3.22
Terrell Wade	L	23	44	8	0	0	69.2	57	9	47	79	5-0	1	2.97
Pedro Borbon	L	28	43	0	0	0	36.0	26	1	7	31	3-0	1	2.75
Mike Bielecki	R	36	40	5	0	0	75.1	63	8	33	71	4-3	2	2.63
Joe Borowski	R	25	22	0	0	0	26.0	33	4	13	15	2-4	0	4.85
Dean Hartgraves†	L	29	20	0	0	0	18.2	16	3	7	14	1-0	0	4.34
Brad Woodall	L	27	8	3	0	0	19.2	28	4	4	20	2-2	0	7.32
Kevin Lomon	R	24	6	0	0	0	7.1	7	0	3	1	0-0	0	4.91
Tom Thobe	L	26	4	0	0	0	6.0	5	1	0	1	0-1	0	1.50
Carl Schutz	L	24	3	0	0	0	3.1	3	0	2	5	0-0	0	2.70

1996 Montreal Expos 2nd NL East 88-74 .543 8.0 GB Felipe Alou

Player	Gm by Position	B	Age	G	AB	R	H	2B	3B	HR	RBI	BB	SO	SB	Avg	OBP	Slg
Darrin Fletcher	C112	L	29	127	394	41	105	22	0	12	57	27	42	0	.266	.321	.414
David Segui	1B113	S	29	115	416	69	119	30	1	11	58	60	54	4	.286	.375	.442
Mike Lansing	2B159,SS2	R	28	159	641	99	183	40	2	11	53	44	85	23	.285	.341	.406
Shane Andrews	3B123	R	24	127	375	43	85	15	2	19	64	35	119	3	.227	.295	.429
Mark Grudzielanek	SS153	R	26	153	657	99	201	34	4	6	49	26	83	33	.306	.340	.397
Moises Alou	OF142	R	29	143	540	87	152	28	2	21	96	49	83	9	.281	.339	.457
F.P. Santangelo	OF124,3B23,2B5*	S	28	152	393	54	109	20	5	7	56	49	61	5	.277	.369	.407
Henry Rodriguez	OF89,1B51	L	28	145	532	81	147	42	1	36	103	37	160	2	.276	.325	.562
Rondell White	OF86	R	24	88	334	35	98	19	4	6	41	22	53	14	.293	.340	.428
Cliff Floyd	OF85,1B2	L	23	117	227	29	55	15	4	6	26	30	52	7	.242	.340	.423
Sherman Obando	OF47	R	26	89	178	30	44	9	0	8	22	22	48	2	.247	.332	.433
Lenny Webster	C63	R	31	78	174	18	40	10	0	2	17	25	21	0	.230	.332	.322
Dave Silvestri	3B47,SS10,OF2*	R	28	86	162	16	33	4	0	1	17	34	41	2	.204	.340	.247
Andy Stankiewicz	2B19,SS13,3B1	R	31	64	77	12	22	5	1	0	9	6	12	1	.286	.356	.377
Tim Spehr	C58,OF1	R	29	63	44	4	4	1	0	1	3	3	15	1	.091	.167	.182
Vladimir Guerrero	OF8	R	20	9	27	2	5	0	0	1	1	0	3	0	.185	.185	.296
Yamil Benitez	OF4	R	24	11	12	0	2	0	0	0	2	0	4	0	.167	.167	.167
Raul Chavez	C3	R	23	4	5	1	1	0	0	0	0	1	1	1	.200	.333	.200
Rick Schu	3B1	R	34	1	4	0	0	0	0	0	0	0	0	0	.000	.000	.000
Rob Lukachyk		L	27	2	2	0	0	0	0	0	0	0	1	0	.000	.000	.000
Tony Barron		R	29	1	1	0	0	0	0	0	0	0	1	0	.000	.000	.000

F. Santangelo, 1 G at SS; D. Silvestri, 1 G at 1B, 1 G at 2B

Pitcher	T	Age	G	GS	CG	ShO	IP	H	HR	BB	SO	W-L	Sv	ERA
Jeff Fassero	L	33	34	34	5	1	231.2	217	20	55	222	15-11	0	3.30
Pedro Martinez	R	24	33	33	4	1	216.2	189	19	70	222	13-10	0	3.70
Rheal Cormier	L	29	33	27	1	1	159.2	165	16	41	100	7-10	0	4.17
Ugueth Urbina	R	22	33	17	0	0	114.0	102	18	44	108	10-5	0	3.71
Kirk Rueter†	L	25	16	16	0	0	78.2	91	12	22	30	5-6	0	4.58
Mark Leiter†	R	33	12	12	1	0	69.2	68	12	19	46	4-2	0	4.39
Jose Paniagua	R	22	13	11	0	0	51.0	55	7	23	27	2-4	0	3.53
Mel Rojas	R	29	74	0	0	0	81.0	56	5	28	92	7-4	36	3.22
Mike Dyer	R	29	70	1	0	0	75.2	79	7	34	51	5-5	2	4.40
Dave Veres	R	29	68	0	0	0	77.2	85	10	32	81	6-3	4	4.17
Omar Daal	L	24	64	6	0	0	87.1	74	10	37	82	4-5	0	4.02
Barry Manuel	R	30	53	0	0	0	86.0	70	10	26	62	4-1	0	3.24
Tim Scott†	R	29	45	0	0	0	46.1	41	3	21	37	3-5	1	3.11
Jeff Juden†	R	25	22	0	0	0	32.2	22	1	14	26	1-0	0	2.20
Tavo Alvarez	R	24	11	5	0	0	21.0	19	0	12	9	2-1	0	3.00
Dave Leiper†	L	34	7	0	0	0	4.0	9	0	2	3	0-1	0	11.25
Alex Pacheco	R	22	5	0	0	0	5.2	8	2	1	7	0-0	0	11.12
Derek Aucoin	R	26	2	0	0	0	2.2	3	0	1	1	0-1	0	3.38

1996 Florida Marlins 3rd NL East 80-82 .494 16.0 GB Rene Lachemann (39-47)/Cookie Rojas (1-0)/John Boles (40-35)

Player	Gm by Position	B	Age	G	AB	R	H	2B	3B	HR	RBI	BB	SO	SB	Avg	OBP	Slg
Charles Johnson	C120	R	24	120	386	34	84	13	1	13	37	40	91	1	.218	.292	.358
Greg Colbrunn	1B134	R	26	141	511	60	146	26	2	16	69	25	76	4	.286	.333	.438
Quilvio Veras	2B67	S	25	73	253	40	64	8	1	4	14	51	42	8	.253	.381	.340
Terry Pendleton†	3B108	S	35	111	406	30	102	20	1	7	58	26	75	0	.251	.298	.357
Edgar Renteria	SS106	R	20	106	431	68	133	18	3	5	31	33	68	16	.309	.358	.399
Gary Sheffield	OF161	R	27	161	519	118	163	33	1	42	120	142	66	16	.314	.465	.624
Devon White	OF139	S	33	146	552	77	151	37	6	17	84	38	99	22	.274	.325	.455
Jeff Conine	OF128,1B48	R	30	157	597	84	175	32	2	26	95	62	121	1	.293	.360	.484
Kurt Abbott	SS44,3B33,2B20	R	27	109	320	37	81	18	7	8	33	22	99	3	.253	.307	.428
Alex Arias	3B59,SS20,1B1*	R	28	100	224	27	62	11	2	3	26	17	28	2	.277	.335	.384
Joe Orsulak	OF59,1B2	L	34	120	217	23	48	6	1	2	19	16	38	1	.221	.274	.286
Luis Castillo	2B41	S	20	41	164	26	43	2	1	1	8	14	46	17	.262	.320	.305
Jesus Tavarez	OF65	S	25	98	114	14	25	3	0	0	6	7	18	5	.219	.264	.246
Craig Grebeck	2B29,SS2,3B1	R	31	50	95	8	20	1	0	1	9	4	14	0	.211	.245	.253
Bob Natal	C43	R	30	44	90	4	12	1	1	0	2	15	31	0	.133	.257	.167
Ralph Milliard	2B24	R	22	24	62	7	10	2	0	0	1	14	16	2	.161	.312	.194
Andre Dawson	OF6	R	41	42	58	6	16	2	0	2	14	2	13	0	.276	.311	.414
Billy McMillon	OF15	L	24	28	51	4	11	0	0	0	4	5	14	0	.216	.286	.216
Joe Siddall	C18	L	28	18	47	0	7	1	0	0	3	2	8	0	.149	.184	.170
Greg Zaun†	C10	S	25	10	31	4	9	1	0	1	2	3	5	1	.290	.353	.419
Russ Morman	1B2	R	34	6	6	0	1	1	0	0	0	1	2	0	.167	.286	.333
Jerry Brooks	OF2,1B1	R	29	8	5	2	2	0	1	0	3	1	1	0	.400	.571	.800
Josh Booty	3B1	R	21	2	2	1	1	0	0	0	0	0	0	0	.500	.500	.500

A. Arias, 1 G at 2B

Pitcher	T	Age	G	GS	CG	ShO	IP	H	HR	BB	SO	W-L	Sv	ERA
Al Leiter	L	30	33	33	2	1	215.1	153	14	119	200	16-12	0	2.93
Kevin Brown	R	31	32	32	5	3	233.0	187	8	33	159	17-11	0	1.89
Pat Rapp	R	28	30	29	0	0	162.1	184	12	91	86	8-16	0	5.10
John Burkett†	R	31	24	24	1	0	154.0	154	15	42	108	6-10	0	4.32
Mark Hutton†	R	26	13	9	0	0	56.1	47	6	18	31	5-1	0	3.67
Marc Valdes	R	24	11	8	0	0	48.2	63	5	23	13	1-3	0	4.81
Rick Helling†	R	25	5	4	0	0	27.2	14	2	7	26	2-1	0	1.95
Andy Larkin	R	22	1	1	0	0	5.0	3	0	4	2	0-0	0	1.80
Robb Nen	R	26	75	0	0	0	83.0	67	2	21	92	5-1	35	1.95
Jay Powell	R	24	67	0	0	0	71.1	71	5	36	52	4-3	2	4.54
Yorkis Perez	L	28	64	0	0	0	47.2	51	2	31	47	3-4	0	5.29
Terry Mathews†	R	31	57	0	0	0	55.0	59	7	27	49	2-4	4	4.91
Chris Hammond	L	30	38	9	0	0	81.0	104	14	27	50	5-8	0	6.56
Dave Weathers†	R	26	31	8	0	0	71.1	85	7	28	40	2-2	0	4.54
Kurt Miller	R	23	26	5	0	0	46.1	57	5	33	30	1-3	0	6.80
Felix Heredia	L	20	21	0	0	0	16.2	21	1	10	10	1-1	0	4.32
Matt Mantei	R	22	14	0	0	0	18.1	13	2	21	25	1-0	0	6.38
Donn Pall	R	34	12	0	0	0	18.2	16	3	9	9	1-1	0	5.79
Miguel Batista	R	25	9	0	0	0	11.1	9	0	7	6	0-0	0	5.56
Joel Adamson	L	24	9	0	0	0	11.0	18	1	7	7	0-0	0	7.36
Alejandro Pena	R	37	4	0	0	0	4.0	4	2	1	5	0-1	0	4.50
Bill Hurst	R	26	2	0	0	0	2.0	3	0	1	1	0-0	0	0.00
Livan Hernandez	R	21	1	0	0	0	3.0	3	0	2	2	0-0	0	0.00

1996 New York Mets 4th NL East 71-91 .438 25.0 GB Dallas Green (59-72)/Bobby Valentine (12-19)

Player	Gm by Position	B	Age	G	AB	R	H	2B	3B	HR	RBI	BB	SO	SB	Avg	OBP	Slg
Todd Hundley	C150	S	27	153	540	85	140	32	1	41	112	79	146	1	.259	.356	.550
Butch Huskey	1B75,OF40,3B6	R	24	118	414	43	115	16	2	15	60	27	77	1	.278	.319	.435
Jose Vizcaino†	2B93	S	28	96	363	47	110	12	6	1	32	28	58	9	.303	.356	.377
Jeff Kent†	3B89	R	28	89	335	45	97	20	1	9	39	21	56	4	.290	.331	.436
Rey Ordonez	SS150	R	23	151	502	51	129	12	4	1	30	22	53	1	.257	.289	.303
Lance Johnson	OF157	L	32	160	682	117	227	31	21	9	69	33	40	50	.333	.362	.479
Bernard Gilkey	OF151	R	29	153	571	108	181	44	3	30	117	73	125	17	.317	.393	.562
Alex Ochoa	OF76	R	24	82	282	37	83	19	3	4	33	17	30	4	.294	.336	.426
Edgardo Alfonzo	2B66,3B36,SS15	R	22	123	368	36	96	15	2	4	40	25	56	2	.261	.304	.345
Carl Everett	OF55	S	26	101	192	29	46	8	1	1	16	21	53	6	.240	.326	.307
Rico Brogna	1B52	L	26	55	188	18	48	10	1	7	30	19	50	0	.255	.318	.431
Chris Jones	OF66,1B5	R	30	89	149	22	36	7	0	4	18	12	42	1	.242	.307	.369
Alvaro Espinoza†	3B38,SS7,2B2*	R	34	48	134	19	41	7	2	4	16	4	19	0	.306	.324	.478
Brent Mayne	C21	L	28	70	99	9	26	6	0	1	6	12	22	0	.263	.342	.354
Roberto Petagine	1B40	L	25	50	99	10	23	3	0	4	17	9	27	0	.232	.313	.384
Tim Bogar	1B32,3B25,SS19*	R	29	91	89	17	19	4	0	0	6	8	20	1	.213	.287	.258
Carlos Baerga†	1B16,3B6,2B1	S	27	26	83	5	16	3	0	2	11	5	2	0	.193	.253	.301
Andy Tomberlin	OF17,1B1	L	29	63	66	12	17	4	0	3	10	9	27	0	.258	.355	.455
Jason Hardtke	2B18	S	24	19	57	3	11	5	0	0	6	2	12	0	.193	.233	.281
Kevin Roberson	OF10	S	28	27	36	8	8	1	0	3	9	7	17	0	.222	.348	.500
Matt Franco	3B8,1B2	L	26	14	31	3	6	1	0	1	2	1	5	0	.194	.235	.323
Alberto Castillo	C6	R	26	6	11	1	4	0	0	0	0	0	4	0	.364	.364	.364
Charlie Greene	C1	R	25	2	1	0	0	0	0	0	0	0	0	0	.000	.000	.000

A. Espinoza, 1 G at 1B; T. Bogar, 8 G at 2B

Pitcher	T	Age	G	GS	CG	ShO	IP	H	HR	BB	SO	W-L	Sv	ERA
Mark Clark	R	28	32	32	2	0	212.1	217	20	48	142	14-11	0	3.43
Bobby Jones	R	26	31	31	3	1	195.2	219	26	46	116	12-8	0	4.42
Pete Harnisch	R	29	31	31	2	1	194.2	195	30	61	114	8-12	0	4.21
Jason Isringhausen	R	23	27	27	2	1	171.2	190	13	73	114	6-14	0	4.77
Paul Wilson	R	23	26	26	1	0	149.0	157	15	71	109	5-12	0	5.38
Doug Henry	R	32	58	0	0	0	75.0	82	7	36	58	2-8	9	4.68
Jerry Dipoto	R	28	57	0	0	0	77.1	91	5	45	52	7-2	0	4.19
Dave Mlicki	R	28	51	2	0	0	90.0	95	9	33	83	6-7	1	3.30
John Franco	L	35	51	0	0	0	54.0	54	2	21	48	4-3	28	1.83
Paul Byrd	R	25	38	0	0	0	46.2	48	7	21	31	1-2	0	4.24
Robert Person	R	26	27	13	0	0	89.2	86	16	35	76	4-5	0	4.52
Bob MacDonald	L	31	20	0	0	0	19.0	16	2	9	12	0-2	0	4.26
Derek Wallace	R	24	19	0	0	0	24.2	29	2	14	15	2-3	3	4.01
Blas Minor†	R	28	17	0	0	0	25.2	23	4	6	20	0-0	0	3.51
Pedro A. Martinez†	L	27	5	0	0	0	7.0	8	1	7	6	0-0	0	6.43
Ricky Trlicek	R	27	5	0	0	0	5.1	3	0	3	3	0-1	0	3.38
Mike Fyhrie	R	26	2	0	0	0	2.1	4	0	3	0	0-1	0	15.43

1996 Philadelphia Phillies 5th NL East 67-95 .414 29.0 GB

Jim Fregosi

Player	Gm by Position	B	Age	G	AB	R	H	2B	3B	HR	RBI	BB	SO	SB	Avg	OBP	Slg
Benito Santiago	C114,1B14	R	31	136	481	71	127	21	2	30	85	49	104	2	.264	.332	.503
Gregg Jefferies	1B53,OF51	S	28	104	404	59	118	17	3	7	51	36	21	20	.292	.348	.401
Mickey Morandini	2B137	L	30	140	539	64	135	24	6	3	32	49	87	26	.250	.321	.334
Todd Zeile†	3B106,1B28	R	30	134	500	61	134	24	0	20	80	67	88	1	.268	.353	.436
Kevin Stocker	SS119	S	26	119	394	46	100	22	6	5	41	43	89	6	.254	.336	.378
Ricky Otero	OF100	S	24	104	411	54	112	11	7	2	32	34	30	16	.273	.330	.348
Jim Eisenreich	OF91	L	37	113	338	45	122	24	3	3	41	31	32	11	.361	.413	.476
Pete Incaviglia†	OF71	R	32	99	269	33	63	7	2	16	42	30	82	2	.234	.318	.454
Mark Whiten†	OF51	S	29	60	182	33	43	8	0	7	21	33	62	13	.236	.356	.396
Mike Lieberthal	C43	R	24	50	166	21	42	8	0	7	23	10	30	0	.253	.297	.428
Wendell Magee	OF37	R	23	38	142	9	29	7	0	2	14	9	33	0	.204	.252	.296
Lenny Dykstra	OF39	L	33	40	134	21	35	6	3	3	13	26	25	3	.261	.387	.418
Kevin Jordan	1B30,2B7,3B1	R	26	43	131	15	37	10	0	3	12	5	20	2	.282	.309	.427
Scott Rolen	3B37	R	21	37	130	10	33	7	0	4	18	13	27	0	.254	.322	.400
Ruben Amaro	OF35,1B1	S	31	61	117	14	37	10	0	2	15	9	18	0	.316	.380	.453
Kevin Sefcik	SS21,3B20,2B1	R	25	44	116	10	33	5	3	0	9	9	16	3	.284	.341	.379
David Doster	2B24,3B1	R	25	39	105	14	28	8	0	1	8	7	21	0	.267	.313	.371
Mike Benjamin	SS31,2B1	R	30	35	103	13	23	5	1	4	13	12	21	3	.223	.316	.408
Glenn Murray	OF27	R	25	38	97	8	19	3	0	2	6	7	36	1	.196	.250	.289
Jon Zuber	1B22	L	26	30	91	7	23	4	0	1	10	6	11	1	.253	.296	.330
J.R. Phillips†	OF15,1B11	L	26	35	79	9	12	5	0	5	10	10	38	0	.152	.256	.405
Gene Schall	1B19	R	26	28	66	7	18	5	1	2	10	12	15	0	.273	.392	.470
Lee Tinsley†	OF22	S	27	31	52	1	7	0	0	0	2	4	22	2	.135	.196	.135
Desi Relaford	SS9,2B4	S	22	15	40	2	7	2	0	0	1	3	9	1	.175	.233	.225
Manny Martinez†	OF11	R	25	13	36	2	8	0	2	0	0	1	11	2	.222	.263	.333
Bobby Estalella	C4	R	21	7	17	5	6	0	0	2	4	1	6	1	.353	.389	.706
Gary Bennett	C5	R	24	6	16	0	4	0	0	0	1	2	6	0	.250	.333	.250
Darren Daulton	OF5	L	34	5	12	3	2	0	0	0	0	7	5	0	.167	.500	.167
Howard Battle	3B1	R	24	5	5	0	0	0	0	0	0	0	2	0	.000	.000	.000

Pitcher	T	Age	G	GS	CG	ShO	IP	H	HR	BB	SO	W-L	Sv	ERA
Mike Williams	R	27	32	29	0	0	167.0	188	25	67	103	6-14	0	5.44
Curt Schilling	R	29	26	26	8	2	183.1	149	16	50	182	9-10	0	3.19
Terry Mulholland†	L	33	21	21	3	0	133.1	157	17	21	52	8-7	0	4.66
Michael Mimbs	L	27	21	17	0	0	99.1	116	13	41	56	3-9	0	5.53
Rich Hunter	R	21	14	14	0	0	69.1	84	10	33	32	3-7	0	6.49
Mike Grace	R	26	12	12	1	1	80.0	72	9	16	49	7-2	0	3.49
Sid Fernandez	L	33	11	11	0	0	63.0	50	5	26	77	3-6	0	3.43
Matt Beech	L	24	8	8	0	0	41.1	49	8	11	33	1-4	0	6.97
David West	L	31	7	6	0	0	28.1	31	0	11	22	2-2	0	4.76
Bobby Munoz	R	28	6	6	0	0	25.1	42	5	7	8	0-3	0	7.82
Calvin Maduro	R	21	4	2	0	0	15.1	13	1	3	11	0-1	0	3.52
Carlos Crawford	R	24	1	1	0	0	3.2	7	1	2	4	0-1	0	4.91
Rafael Quirico	L	26	1	1	0	0	1.2	4	1	5	1	0-1	0	37.80
Toby Borland	R	27	69	0	0	0	90.2	83	9	43	76	7-3	0	4.07
Ken Ryan	R	27	62	0	0	0	89.0	71	4	45	70	3-5	8	2.43
Ricky Bottalico	R	26	61	0	0	0	67.2	47	6	23	74	4-5	34	3.19
Russ Springer	R	27	51	7	0	0	96.2	106	12	38	94	3-10	0	4.66
Steve Frey	L	32	31	0	0	0	34.1	38	4	18	12	0-1	0	4.72
Ron Blazier	R	24	27	0	0	0	38.1	49	6	10	25	3-1	0	5.87
Ricardo Jordan	L	26	26	0	0	0	25.0	18	0	12	17	2-2	0	1.80
Dave Leiper†	L	34	26	0	0	0	21.0	31	4	7	10	2-0	0	6.43
Jeff Parrett†	R	34	18	0	0	0	24.0	24	0	11	22	1-1	0	1.88
Larry Mitchell	R	24	7	0	0	0	12.0	14	1	5	7	0-0	0	4.50
Glenn Dishman†	L	25	4	1	0	0	7.0	9	2	2	3	0-0	0	7.71
Bronson Heflin	R	24	3	0	0	0	6.2	11	1	3	4	0-0	0	6.75

1996 St. Louis Cardinals 1st NL Central 88-74 .543 —

Tony La Russa

Player	Gm by Position	B	Age	G	AB	R	H	2B	3B	HR	RBI	BB	SO	SB	Avg	OBP	Slg
Tom Pagnozzi	C116,1B1	R	33	119	407	48	110	23	0	13	55	24	78	4	.270	.311	.423
John Mabry	1B146,OF14	L	25	151	543	63	161	30	2	13	74	37	84	3	.297	.342	.431
Luis Alicea	2B125	S	30	129	380	54	98	26	3	5	42	52	78	11	.258	.350	.382
Gary Gaetti	3B133,1B14	R	37	141	522	71	143	27	4	23	80	35	97	2	.274	.326	.473
Royce Clayton	SS113	R	26	129	491	64	136	20	4	6	35	33	89	33	.277	.321	.371
Ray Lankford	OF144	L	29	149	545	100	150	36	8	21	86	79	133	35	.275	.366	.486
Brian Jordan	OF136,1B1	R	29	140	513	82	159	36	1	17	104	29	84	22	.310	.349	.483
Ron Gant	OF116	R	31	122	419	74	103	14	2	30	82	73	98	13	.246	.359	.504
Willie McGee	OF83,1B6	S	37	123	309	52	95	15	2	5	41	18	60	5	.307	.348	.417
Ozzie Smith	SS52	S	41	82	227	36	64	10	2	2	18	25	9	7	.282	.358	.370
Danny Sheaffer	C47,3B17,1B6*	R	34	79	198	10	45	9	3	2	20	9	25	3	.227	.271	.333
Mark Sweeney	OF43,1B15	L	26	98	170	32	45	9	0	3	22	33	29	3	.265	.387	.371
David Bell	3B45,2B20,SS1	R	23	62	145	12	31	6	0	1	9	10	22	1	.214	.268	.276
Mike Gallego	2B43,3B7,SS1	R	35	51	143	12	30	2	0	0	4	12	31	0	.210	.276	.224
Pat Borders†	C17,1B1	R	33	26	69	3	22	3	0	0	4	1	14	0	.319	.329	.362
Dmitri Young	1B10	S	22	16	29	3	7	0	0	0	2	4	5	0	.241	.353	.241
Miguel Mejia	OF21	R	21	45	23	10	2	0	0	0	0	0	10	6	.087	.087	.087
Terry Bradshaw	OF7	L	27	15	21	4	7	1	0	0	3	3	2	0	.333	.417	.381
Mike Difelice	C4	R	27	4	7	0	2	1	0	0	2	0	1	0	.286	.286	.429
Aaron Holbert	2B1	R	23	1	3	0	0	0	0	0	0	0	0	0	.000	.000	.000

D. Sheaffer, 3 G at OF

Pitcher	T	Age	G	GS	CG	ShO	IP	H	HR	BB	SO	W-L	Sv	ERA
Andy Benes	R	28	36	34	3	1	230.1	215	28	77	160	18-10	1	3.83
Todd Stottlemyre	R	31	34	33	5	2	223.1	191	30	93	194	14-11	0	3.87
Alan Benes	R	24	34	32	3	1	191.0	192	27	87	131	13-10	0	4.90
Donovan Osborne	L	27	30	30	2	1	198.2	191	22	57	134	13-9	0	3.53
Mike Morgan†	R	36	18	18	0	0	103.0	118	14	40	55	4-8	0	5.24
Tom Urbani†	L	28	3	2	0	0	11.2	15	3	4	1	1-0	0	7.71
Mike Busby	R	23	1	1	0	0	4.0	9	4	4	4	0-1	0	18.00
Brian Barber	R	23	1	1	0	0	3.0	4	0	6	1	0-0	0	15.00
T.J. Mathews	R	26	67	0	0	0	83.2	62	8	32	80	2-6	6	3.01
Tony Fossas	L	38	65	0	0	0	47.0	43	7	21	36	0-4	2	2.68
Dennis Eckersley	R	41	63	0	0	0	60.0	65	8	6	49	0-6	30	3.30
Rick Honeycutt	L	42	61	0	0	0	47.1	42	3	7	30	2-1	4	2.85
Cory Bailey	R	25	51	0	0	0	57.0	57	1	30	38	5-2	0	3.00
Mark Petkovsek	R	30	48	6	0	0	88.2	83	9	35	45	11-2	0	3.55
Jeff Parrett†	R	34	33	0	0	0	42.1	40	2	20	42	2-2	0	4.25
Danny Jackson	L	34	13	4	0	0	36.1	33	3	16	27	1-1	0	4.46
Richard Batchelor	R	29	11	0	0	0	15.0	9	0	1	11	2-0	0	1.20
Eric Ludwick	R	24	6	1	0	0	10.0	11	4	3	12	0-1	0	9.00

1996 Houston Astros 2nd NL Central 82-80 .506 6.0 GB

Terry Collins

Player	Gm by Position	B	Age	G	AB	R	H	2B	3B	HR	RBI	BB	SO	SB	Avg	OBP	Slg
Rick Wilkins†	C82	L	29	84	254	34	54	8	2	6	23	46	81	0	.213	.330	.331
Jeff Bagwell	1B162	R	28	162	568	111	179	48	2	31	120	135	114	21	.315	.451	.570
Craig Biggio	2B162	R	30	162	605	113	174	24	4	15	75	75	72	25	.288	.386	.415
Sean Berry	3B110	R	30	132	431	55	121	38	1	17	95	23	58	12	.281	.328	.492
Orlando Miller	SS117,3B29	R	27	139	468	43	120	26	2	15	58	14	116	3	.256	.291	.417
Derek Bell	OF157	R	27	158	627	84	165	40	3	17	113	40	123	29	.263	.311	.418
Brian Hunter	OF127	R	25	132	526	74	145	27	2	5	35	17	92	35	.276	.297	.363
James Mouton	OF108	R	27	122	300	40	79	15	1	3	34	38	55	21	.263	.343	.350
John Cangelosi	OF78	S	33	108	262	49	69	11	4	1	16	44	41	17	.263	.378	.347
Derrick May	OF71	L	27	109	259	24	65	12	3	5	33	30	33	2	.251	.330	.378
Bill Spiers	3B77,2B7,1B4*	L	30	122	218	27	55	10	1	6	26	20	34	7	.252	.320	.390
Ricky Gutierrez	SS74,3B6,2B5	R	26	89	218	28	62	8	1	1	15	23	42	6	.284	.359	.344
Tony Eusebio	C47	R	29	58	152	15	41	7	2	1	19	18	20	0	.270	.343	.362
Randy Knorr	C33	R	27	37	87	7	17	5	0	1	7	5	18	0	.195	.245	.287
Kirt Manwaring†	C37	R	30	37	82	5	18	3	0	0	4	3	16	0	.220	.264	.256
Mike Simms	OF12,1B5	R	29	49	68	6	12	2	1	1	8	4	16	1	.176	.233	.279
Bob Abreu	OF7	L	22	15	22	1	5	1	0	0	1	2	3	0	.227	.292	.273
Ray Montgomery	OF6	R	26	12	14	4	3	1	0	1	4	1	5	0	.214	.267	.500
Dave Hajek	3B3,2B2	R	28	8	10	3	3	1	0	0	0	2	0	0	.300	.417	.400
Jerry Goff	C1	L	32	1	4	1	2	0	0	1	2	0	1	0	.500	.500	1.250
Andujar Cedeno†	SS2,3B1	R	26	3	2	1	0	0	0	0	0	2	1	0	.000	.500	.000

B. Spiers, 4 G at SS, 2 G at OF

Pitcher	T	Age	G	GS	CG	ShO	IP	H	HR	BB	SO	W-L	Sv	ERA
Shane Reynolds	R	28	35	35	4	1	239.0	227	20	44	204	16-10	0	3.65
Darryl Kile	R	27	35	33	4	0	219.0	233	16	97	219	12-11	0	4.19
Doug Drabek	R	33	30	30	1	0	175.1	208	21	60	137	7-9	0	4.57
Mike Hampton	L	23	27	27	2	1	160.1	175	12	49	101	10-10	0	3.59
Donne Wall	R	28	26	23	2	1	150.0	170	17	34	99	9-8	0	4.56
Greg Swindell†	L	31	8	4	0	0	23.0	35	5	11	15	0-3	0	7.83
Xavier Hernandez†	R	30	58	0	0	0	74.2	69	11	26	78	5-5	6	4.22
Alvin Morman	L	27	53	0	0	0	42.0	43	8	24	31	4-1	0	4.93
Todd Jones	R	28	51	0	0	0	57.1	61	5	32	44	6-3	17	4.40
Billy Wagner	L	25	37	0	0	0	51.2	28	6	30	67	2-2	9	2.44
Anthony Young	R	30	28	0	0	0	33.1	36	4	22	19	3-3	0	4.59
Doug Brocail	R	29	23	4	0	0	53.0	58	7	23	34	1-5	0	4.58
Dean Hartgraves†	L	29	19	0	0	0	19.0	18	1	16	16	0-0	0	5.21
Jeff Tabaka	L	32	18	0	0	0	20.1	28	5	14	18	0-2	1	6.64
Mark Small	R	28	16	0	0	0	24.1	33	1	13	16	0-1	0	5.92
Danny Darwin†	R	40	15	6	0	0	42.1	43	7	11	27	3-2	0	5.95
John Hudek	R	29	15	0	0	0	16.0	12	2	5	14	2-0	2	2.81
Jim Dougherty	R	28	12	0	0	0	13.0	14	2	11	6	0-2	0	9.00
John Johnstone	R	27	9	0	0	0	13.0	17	2	5	5	1-0	0	5.54
Gregg Olson†	R	29	9	0	0	0	9.1	12	1	7	8	1-0	0	4.82
Terry Clark†	R	35	5	0	0	0	6.1	16	1	2	5	0-2	0	11.37
Chris Holt	R	24	4	0	0	0	4.2	5	0	3	0	0-1	0	5.79

1996 Cincinnati Reds 3rd NL Central 81-81 .500 7.0 GB

Ray Knight

Player	Gm by Position	B	Age	G	AB	R	H	2B	3B	HR	RBI	BB	SO	SB	Avg	OBP	Slg
Joe Oliver	C97,1B3,OF3	R	30	106	289	31	70	12	1	11	46	28	54	2	.242	.311	.405
Hal Morris	1B140	L	31	142	528	82	165	32	4	16	80	50	76	7	.313	.374	.479
Bret Boone	2B141	R	27	142	520	56	121	21	3	12	69	31	100	3	.233	.275	.354
Willie Greene	3B74,OF10,1B2*	L	24	115	287	48	70	5	5	19	63	36	88	0	.244	.327	.495
Barry Larkin	SS151	R	32	152	517	117	154	32	4	33	89	96	52	36	.298	.410	.567
Eric Davis	OF126,1B1	R	34	129	415	81	119	20	0	26	83	70	121	23	.287	.394	.523
Thomas Howard	OF103	S	31	121	360	50	98	19	10	6	42	17	51	6	.272	.307	.431
Reggie Sanders	OF80	R	28	81	287	49	72	17	1	14	33	44	86	24	.251	.353	.463
Eddie Taubensee	C94	L	27	108	327	46	95	20	0	12	48	26	64	3	.291	.338	.462
Jeff Branson	3B64,SS38,2B31	L	29	129	311	34	76	16	4	9	37	31	67	2	.244	.312	.408
Lenny Harris	OF37,3B24,1B16*	L	31	125	302	33	86	17	2	5	32	21	31	14	.285	.330	.404
Eric Owens	OF52,2B6,3B5	R	25	88	205	26	41	6	0	0	9	23	38	16	.200	.281	.229
Curtis Goodwin	OF42	L	23	49	136	20	31	3	0	0	5	19	34	15	.228	.323	.250
Chris Sabo	3B43	R	34	54	125	15	32	7	1	3	16	18	27	2	.256	.354	.400
Eric Anthony†	OF37	L	28	47	123	22	30	6	0	8	13	22	36	0	.244	.359	.488
Kevin Mitchell†	OF31,1B3	R	34	37	114	18	37	11	0	6	26	26	16	0	.325	.447	.579
Vince Coleman	OF20	S	34	33	84	10	13	1	1	1	4	9	31	12	.155	.237	.226
Chad Mottola	OF31	R	24	35	79	10	17	3	0	3	6	6	16	2	.215	.271	.367
Mike Kelly	OF17	R	26	19	49	5	9	4	0	1	7	9	11	4	.184	.333	.327
Eduardo Perez	1B8,3B3	R	26	18	36	8	8	0	0	3	5	5	9	0	.222	.317	.472
Keith Mitchell	OF5	R	26	11	15	2	4	1	0	1	3	1	3	0	.267	.313	.533
Tim Belk	1B6	R	26	7	15	2	3	0	0	0	0	1	2	0	.200	.250	.200
Brook Fordyce	C4	R	26	4	7	0	2	1	0	0	1	3	1	0	.286	.500	.429
Steve Gibralter	OF2	R	23	2	2	0	0	0	0	0	0	0	2	0	.000	.000	.000

W. Greene, 1 G at SS; L. Harris, 8 G at 2B

Pitcher	T	Age	G	GS	CG	ShO	IP	H	HR	BB	SO	W-L	Sv	ERA
John Smiley	L	31	35	34	2	2	217.1	207	20	54	171	13-14	0	3.64
Dave Burba	R	29	34	33	0	0	195.0	179	18	97	148	11-13	0	3.83
Mark Portugal	R	33	27	26	1	1	156.0	146	20	42	93	8-9	0	3.98
Kevin Jarvis	R	26	24	20	2	1	120.1	152	17	43	63	8-9	0	5.98
Roger Salkeld	R	25	29	19	1	1	116.0	114	18	54	82	8-5	0	5.20
Pete Schourek	L	27	12	12	0	0	67.1	79	7	24	54	4-5	0	6.01
Mike Morgan†	R	36	5	5	0	0	27.1	28	2	7	19	2-3	0	2.30
Giovanni Carrara†	R	28	8	5	0	0	23.0	31	6	13	13	1-0	0	5.87
Curt Lyons	R	21	3	3	0	0	16.0	17	1	7	14	2-0	0	4.50
Jeff Shaw	R	29	78	0	0	0	104.2	99	8	29	69	8-6	4	2.49
Jeff Brantley	R	32	66	0	0	0	71.0	54	7	28	76	1-2	44	2.41
Hector Carrasco	R	26	56	0	0	0	74.1	58	6	45	59	4-3	0	3.75
Johnny Ruffin	R	24	49	0	0	0	62.1	71	10	37	69	1-3	0	5.49
Lee Smith†	R	38	43	0	0	0	44.1	49	4	23	35	3-4	2	4.06
Scott Service	R	29	34	1	0	0	48.0	51	7	18	46	1-0	0	3.94
Marcus Moore	R	25	23	0	0	0	26.1	26	3	22	27	3-3	2	5.81
Mike Remlinger	L	30	19	4	0	0	27.1	24	4	19	19	0-1	0	5.60
Chuck McElroy†	L	28	12	0	0	0	12.1	13	2	10	13	2-0	0	6.57
Tim Pugh†	R	29	10	0	0	0	15.2	24	3	11	9	1-1	0	11.49
Scott Sullivan	R	25	7	0	0	0	8.0	7	0	5	3	0-0	0	2.25
Derek Lilliquist	L	30	5	0	0	0	3.2	5	1	0	1	0-0	0	7.36
Pedro A. Martinez†	L	27	4	0	0	0	3.0	5	1	1	3	0-0	0	6.00
Xavier Hernandez†	R	30	3	0	0	0	3.1	8	2	2	3	0-0	0	13.50
Jerry Spradlin	R	29	1	0	0	0	0.1	0	0	0	0	0-0	0	0.00

958 Seasons: Team Rosters

1996 Chicago Cubs 4th NL Central 76-86 .469 12.0 GB — Jim Riggleman

Player	Gm by Position	B	Age	G	AB	R	H	2B	3B	HR	RBI	BB	SO	SB	Avg	OBP	Slg
Scott Servais	C128,1B1	R	29	129	445	42	118	20	0	11	63	30	75	0	.265	.327	.384
Mark Grace	1B141	L	32	142	547	88	181	39	1	9	75	62	41	2	.331	.396	.455
Ryne Sandberg	2B146	R	36	150	554	85	135	28	4	25	92	54	116	12	.244	.316	.444
Leo Gomez	3B124,1B8,SS1	R	30	136	362	44	86	19	0	17	56	53	94	1	.238	.344	.431
Rey Sanchez	SS92	R	28	95	289	28	61	9	0	1	12	22	42	7	.211	.272	.253
Brian McRae	OF155	S	28	157	624	111	172	32	5	17	66	73	84	37	.276	.360	.425
Luis Gonzalez	OF139,1B2	L	28	146	483	70	131	30	4	15	79	61	49	9	.271	.354	.443
Sammy Sosa	OF124	R	27	124	498	84	136	21	2	40	100	34	134	18	.273	.323	.564
Jose Hernandez	SS87,3B43,2B1*	R	26	131	331	52	80	14	1	10	41	24	97	4	.242	.293	.381
Dave Magadan	3B51,1B10	L	33	78	169	23	43	10	0	3	17	29	23	0	.254	.360	.367
Scott Bullett	OF58	S	27	109	165	26	35	5	0	3	16	10	54	7	.212	.256	.297
Ozzie Timmons	OF47	R	25	65	140	18	28	4	0	7	16	15	30	1	.200	.282	.379
Tyler Houston†	C27,3B9,2B2*	L	25	46	115	18	39	7	0	2	19	8	18	3	.339	.382	.452
Doug Glanville	OF35	R	25	49	83	10	20	5	1	1	10	3	11	2	.241	.264	.361
Todd Haney	2B23,3B4,SS3	R	30	49	82	11	11	1	0	0	3	7	15	1	.134	.200	.146
Brant Brown	1B18	L	25	29	69	11	21	1	0	5	9	2	17	3	.304	.329	.536
Robin Jennings	OF11	L	24	31	58	7	13	5	0	0	4	3	9	1	.224	.274	.310
Brian Dorsett	C15	R	35	17	41	3	5	0	0	1	3	4	8	0	.122	.196	.195
Mike Hubbard	C14	R	25	21	38	1	4	0	0	1	4	0	15	0	.105	.103	.184
Terry Shumpert	3B10,2B4,SS1	R	29	27	31	5	7	1	0	2	6	2	11	0	.226	.286	.452
Bret Barberie	2B6,3B2,SS1	S	28	15	29	4	1	0	0	1	2	5	11	0	.034	.176	.138
Brooks Kieschnick	OF8	L	24	25	29	6	10	2	0	1	6	3	8	0	.345	.406	.517
Felix Fermin	2B6,SS2	R	32	11	16	4	2	1	0	0	1	2	0	0	.125	.222	.188
Pedro Valdes	OF2	L	23	9	8	2	1	1	0	0	1	1	5	0	.125	.222	.250

J. Hernandez, 1 G at OF; T. Houston, 1 G at 1B

Pitcher	T	Age	G	GS	CG	ShO	IP	H	HR	BB	SO	W-L	Sv	ERA
Jaime Navarro	R	29	35	35	4	1	236.2	244	25	72	158	15-12	0	3.92
Frank Castillo	R	27	33	33	1	1	182.1	209	28	46	139	7-16	0	5.28
Steve Trachsel	R	25	31	31	3	2	205.0	181	30	62	132	13-9	0	3.03
Jim Bullinger	R	30	37	20	1	1	129.1	144	15	68	90	6-10	1	6.54
Amaury Telemaco	R	22	25	17	0	0	97.1	108	20	31	64	5-7	0	5.46
Kevin Foster	R	27	17	16	1	0	87.0	98	16	35	53	7-6	0	6.21
Dave Swartzbaugh	R	28	6	5	0	0	24.0	26	3	14	13	0-2	0	6.38
Bob Patterson	L	37	79	0	0	0	54.2	46	6	22	53	3-3	8	3.13
Turk Wendell	R	29	70	0	0	0	79.1	58	8	44	75	4-5	18	2.84
Terry Adams	R	23	69	0	0	0	101.0	84	6	49	78	3-6	4	2.94
Kent Bottenfield	R	27	48	0	0	0	61.2	59	3	19	33	3-5	1	2.63
Rodney Myers	R	27	45	0	0	0	67.1	61	6	38	50	2-1	0	4.68
Larry Casian	L	30	35	0	0	0	24.0	14	2	11	15	1-1	0	1.88
Doug Jones†	R	39	28	0	0	0	32.1	41	4	7	26	2-2	2	5.01
Mike Perez	R	31	24	0	0	0	27.0	29	2	13	22	1-0	0	4.67
Mike Campbell	R	32	13	5	0	0	36.1	29	7	10	19	3-1	0	4.46
Tanyon Sturtze	R	25	6	0	0	0	11.0	16	3	5	7	1-0	0	9.00

1996 Pittsburgh Pirates 5th NL Central 73-89 .451 15.0 GB — Jim Leyland

Player	Gm by Position	B	Age	G	AB	R	H	2B	3B	HR	RBI	BB	SO	SB	Avg	OBP	Slg
Jason Kendall	C129	R	22	130	414	54	124	23	5	3	42	35	30	5	.300	.372	.401
Mark Johnson	1B100,OF1	L	28	127	343	55	94	24	0	13	47	44	64	6	.274	.361	.458
Carlos Garcia	2B77,SS19,3B14	R	28	101	390	66	111	18	4	6	44	23	58	16	.285	.329	.397
Charlie Hayes†	3B124	R	31	128	459	51	114	21	2	10	62	36	78	6	.248	.301	.368
Jay Bell	SS151	R	30	151	527	65	132	29	3	13	71	54	108	6	.250	.323	.391
Al Martin	OF152	L	28	155	630	101	189	40	1	18	72	54	116	38	.300	.354	.452
Orlando Merced	OF115,1B1	S	29	120	453	69	130	24	1	17	80	51	74	8	.287	.357	.457
Mike Kingery	OF83	L	35	117	276	32	68	12	2	3	27	23	29	2	.246	.304	.337
Jeff King	1B92,2B71,3B17	R	31	155	591	91	160	36	4	30	111	70	95	15	.271	.346	.497
J. Allensworth	OF61	R	24	61	229	32	60	9	3	4	31	23	50	11	.262	.337	.380
Nelson Liriano	2B36,3B9,SS5	S	32	112	217	23	58	14	2	3	30	14	22	2	.267	.308	.392
Dave Clark†	OF61	L	33	92	211	28	58	12	2	8	35	31	51	2	.275	.366	.464
Keith Osik	C41,3B2,OF2	R	27	48	140	18	41	14	1	1	14	14	22	1	.293	.361	.429
John Wehner	OF29,3B24,2B12*	R	29	86	139	19	36	9	1	2	13	8	22	1	.259	.299	.381
Midre Cummings	OF21	S	24	24	85	11	19	3	1	3	7	0	16	0	.224	.221	.388
Jacob Brumfield†	OF22	R	31	29	80	11	20	9	0	2	8	5	17	3	.250	.291	.438
Trey Beamon	OF14	L	22	24	51	7	11	2	0	0	6	4	6	1	.216	.273	.255
Dale Sveum	3B10	S	32	12	34	9	12	5	0	1	5	6	6	0	.353	.450	.588
Tony Womack	OF6,2B4	L	26	17	30	11	10	3	1	0	7	6	1	2	.333	.459	.500
Angelo Encarnacion	C7	R	23	7	22	3	7	2	0	0	1	0	5	0	.318	.318	.409
Rich Aude	1B4	R	24	7	16	0	4	0	0	0	1	0	8	0	.250	.250	.250

J. Wehner, 1 G at C

Pitcher	T	Age	G	GS	CG	ShO	IP	H	HR	BB	SO	W-L	Sv	ERA
Denny Neagle†	L	27	27	27	1	0	182.2	186	21	34	131	14-6	0	3.05
Danny Darwin†	R	40	19	19	0	0	122.1	117	9	16	69	7-9	0	3.02
Zane Smith	L	35	16	16	1	1	83.1	104	7	21	47	4-6	0	5.08
Paul Wagner	R	28	16	15	1	0	81.2	86	10	39	81	4-8	0	5.40
Chris Peters	L	24	16	10	0	0	64.0	72	9	25	28	2-4	0	5.63
Esteban Loaiza	R	24	10	10	1	1	52.2	65	11	19	32	2-3	0	4.96
Jason Schmidt†	R	23	6	6	1	0	37.2	39	2	21	26	2-2	0	4.06
Steve Parris	R	28	8	4	0	0	26.1	35	4	11	27	0-3	0	7.18
John Hope	R	25	5	4	0	0	19.1	17	5	11	13	1-3	0	6.98
Rich Loiselle	R	24	5	3	0	0	20.2	22	3	8	9	1-0	0	3.05
Dan Plesac	L	34	73	0	0	0	70.1	67	4	24	76	6-5	11	4.09
Francisco Cordova	R	24	59	6	0	0	99.0	103	11	20	95	4-7	12	4.09
Jon Lieber	R	26	51	15	0	0	142.0	156	19	28	94	9-5	1	3.99
Marc Wilkins	R	25	47	2	0	0	75.0	75	6	36	62	4-3	1	3.84
Danny Miceli	R	25	44	9	0	0	85.2	99	15	45	66	2-10	1	5.78
Jason Christiansen	L	26	33	0	0	0	44.1	56	7	19	38	3-3	0	6.70
Ramon Morel	R	21	29	0	0	0	42.0	57	4	19	22	2-1	0	5.36
John Ericks	R	28	28	4	0	0	46.2	56	11	19	46	4-5	8	5.79
Matt Ruebel	L	26	26	7	0	0	58.2	64	7	25	22	1-1	1	4.60
David Wainhouse	R	28	17	0	0	0	23.2	22	3	10	16	1-0	0	5.70
Elmer Dessens	R	24	15	3	0	0	25.0	40	2	4	13	0-2	0	8.28
Lee Hancock	L	29	13	0	0	0	18.1	21	5	10	13	0-0	0	6.38
Joe Boever	R	35	13	0	0	0	15.0	17	2	6	6	0-2	2	5.40
Darrell May†	L	24	5	2	0	0	8.2	15	5	4	5	0-1	0	9.35
Steve Cooke	L	26	3	0	0	0	8.1	11	1	5	7	0-0	0	7.56

1996 San Diego Padres 1st NL West 91-71 .562 — Bruce Bochy

Player	Gm by Position	B	Age	G	AB	R	H	2B	3B	HR	RBI	BB	SO	SB	Avg	OBP	Slg
John Flaherty†	C72	R	28	72	264	22	80	12	0	9	41	9	36	2	.303	.327	.451
Wally Joyner	1B119	L	34	121	433	59	120	29	1	8	65	69	71	5	.277	.377	.404
Jody Reed	2B145	R	33	146	495	45	121	20	0	2	49	59	53	2	.244	.325	.297
Ken Caminiti	3B145	S	33	146	546	109	178	37	2	40	130	78	99	11	.326	.408	.621
Chris Gomez†	SS89	R	25	89	328	32	86	16	1	3	29	39	64	2	.262	.349	.345
Steve Finley	OF160	L	31	161	655	126	195	45	9	30	95	56	87	22	.298	.354	.531
Rickey Henderson	OF134	R	37	148	465	110	112	17	2	9	29	125	90	37	.241	.410	.344
Tony Gwynn	OF111	L	36	116	451	67	159	27	2	3	50	39	17	11	.353	.400	.441
Brian Johnson	C66,1B1,3B1	R	28	82	243	18	66	13	1	8	35	4	36	0	.272	.290	.432
Archi Cianfrocco	1B33,3B11,SS10*	R	29	79	192	21	54	13	3	2	32	8	56	1	.281	.315	.411
Marc Newfield†	OF51,1B2	R	23	84	191	27	48	11	0	5	26	16	44	1	.251	.311	.387
Scott Livingstone	1B22,3B16	L	30	102	172	20	51	4	1	2	20	9	22	0	.297	.331	.366
Andujar Cedeno†	SS47,3B2	R	26	49	154	10	36	2	1	3	18	9	32	3	.234	.279	.318
Brad Ausmus†	C46	R	27	50	149	16	27	4	0	1	13	13	27	1	.181	.261	.228
Greg Vaughn†	OF39	R	30	43	141	20	29	3	1	10	22	24	31	4	.206	.329	.454
Luis Lopez	SS35,2B22,3B2	S	25	63	139	10	25	3	0	2	11	9	35	0	.180	.233	.245
Craig Shipley	2B17,SS7,3B4*	R	33	33	92	13	29	5	0	1	7	2	15	7	.315	.337	.402
Chris Gwynn	OF29,1B1	L	31	81	90	8	16	4	0	1	10	10	28	0	.178	.260	.256
Rob Deer	OF18	R	35	25	50	9	9	3	0	4	9	14	30	0	.180	.359	.480
Jason Thompson	1B13	L	25	13	49	4	11	4	0	2	6	1	14	0	.224	.235	.429
Doug Dascenzo	OF10	S	32	21	9	3	1	0	0	0	0	1	2	0	.111	.200	.111
Jimmy Tatum†	3B1	R	28	5	3	0	0	0	0	0	0	0	1	0	.000	.000	.000
Todd Steverson		R	24	1	1	0	0	0	0	0	0	0	1	0	.000	.000	.000
Sean Mulligan		R	26	2	1	0	0	0	0	0	0	0	0	0	.000	.000	.000

A. Cianfrocco, 8 G at OF, 6 G at 2B, 1 G at C; C. Shipley, 3 G at OF

Pitcher	T	Age	G	GS	CG	ShO	IP	H	HR	BB	SO	W-L	Sv	ERA
Joey Hamilton	R	25	34	33	3	1	211.2	206	19	83	184	15-9	0	4.17
Bob Tewksbury	R	35	36	33	1	0	206.2	224	17	43	126	10-10	0	4.31
F. Valenzuela	L	35	33	31	0	0	171.2	177	17	67	95	13-8	0	3.62
Andy Ashby	R	28	24	24	1	0	150.2	147	17	34	85	9-5	0	3.23
Trevor Hoffman	R	28	70	0	0	0	88.0	50	6	31	111	9-5	42	2.25
Doug Bochtler	R	25	63	0	0	0	65.2	45	6	39	68	2-4	3	3.02
Willie Blair	R	30	60	0	0	0	88.0	80	13	29	67	2-6	1	4.60
Tim Worrell	R	28	50	11	0	0	121.0	109	9	39	99	9-7	1	3.05
Scott Sanders	R	27	46	16	0	0	144.0	117	10	48	157	9-5	0	3.38
Sean Bergman	R	26	41	14	0	0	113.1	119	14	33	85	6-8	0	4.37
Bryce Florie†	R	26	39	0	0	0	49.1	45	1	27	51	2-2	0	4.01
Dario Veras	R	23	23	0	0	0	29.0	24	3	10	23	3-1	0	2.79
Ron Villone†	L	26	21	0	0	0	18.1	17	2	7	19	1-1	0	2.95
Al Osuna	L	30	10	0	0	0	4.0	5	0	2	4	0-0	0	2.25
Dustin Hermanson	R	23	8	0	0	0	13.2	18	3	4	11	1-0	0	8.56
Mike Oquist	R	28	8	0	0	0	7.2	6	0	4	4	0-0	0	2.35
Andres Berumen	R	25	3	0	0	0	3.1	3	1	2	4	0-0	0	5.40
Glenn Dishman†	L	25	3	0	0	0	2.1	3	0	1	0	0-0	0	7.71
Pete Walker	R	27	1	0	0	0	0.2	0	0	3	1	0-0	0	0.00

1996 Los Angeles Dodgers 2nd NL West 90-72 .556 1.0 GB — Tom Lasorda (41-35)/Bill Russell (49-37)

Player	Gm by Position	B	Age	G	AB	R	H	2B	3B	HR	RBI	BB	SO	SB	Avg	OBP	Slg
Mike Piazza	C146	R	27	148	547	87	184	16	0	36	105	81	93	0	.336	.422	.563
Eric Karros	1B154	R	28	154	608	84	158	29	1	34	111	53	121	8	.260	.316	.479
Delino DeShields	2B154	L	27	154	581	75	130	12	8	5	41	53	124	48	.224	.288	.298
Mike Blowers	3B90,1B6,SS1	R	31	92	317	31	84	19	2	6	38	37	77	0	.265	.341	.394
Greg Gagne	SS127	R	34	128	428	48	109	13	2	10	55	50	93	4	.255	.333	.364
Raul Mondesi	OF157	R	25	157	634	98	188	40	7	24	88	32	122	14	.297	.334	.495
Todd Hollandsworth	OF142	L	23	149	478	64	139	26	4	12	59	41	93	21	.291	.348	.437
Roger Cedeno	OF71	S	21	86	211	26	52	11	1	2	18	24	47	5	.246	.326	.336
Chad Fonville	OF35,2B23,SS20*	S	25	103	201	34	41	4	1	0	13	17	31	7	.204	.266	.234
Wayne Kirby†	OF53	L	32	65	188	23	51	10	1	1	11	17	17	4	.271	.333	.351
Tim Wallach†	3B45	R	38	45	162	14	37	3	1	4	22	12	32	0	.228	.286	.333
Juan Castro	SS30,3B23,2B9*	R	24	70	132	16	26	5	3	0	5	10	27	1	.197	.254	.280
Brett Butler	OF34	L	39	34	131	22	35	1	1	0	8	9	22	8	.267	.313	.290
Billy Ashley	OF38	R	25	71	110	18	22	2	1	9	25	21	44	0	.200	.331	.482
Dave Hansen	3B19,1B8	L	27	80	104	7	23	1	0	0	6	11	22	0	.221	.293	.231
Chad Curtis†	OF40	R	27	43	104	20	22	5	0	2	9	17	15	2	.212	.322	.317
Mike Busch	3B23,1B1	R	27	38	83	8	18	4	0	4	17	5	33	0	.217	.261	.410
Tom Prince	C35	R	31	40	64	6	19	6	0	1	11	6	15	0	.297	.365	.438
Milt Thompson†	OF17	L	37	48	51	2	6	1	0	0	1	6	10	1	.118	.211	.137
Dave Clark†	OF1	L	33	15	15	0	3	0	0	0	1	3	2	0	.200	.333	.200
Carlos Hernandez	C9	R	29	13	14	1	4	0	0	0	0	2	2	0	.286	.375	.286
Rick Parker	OF4	R	33	16	14	2	4	1	0	0	1	0	2	1	.286	.333	.357
Oreste Marrero	1B1	L	26	10	8	2	3	1	0	0	1	1	3	0	.375	.444	.500
Wilton Guerrero		R	21	5	2	1	0	0	0	0	0	0	2	0	.000	.000	.000
Karim Garcia		L	20	1	1	0	0	0	0	0	0	0	1	0	.000	.000	.000

C. Fonville, 2 G at 3B; J. Castro, 1 G at OF

Pitcher	T	Age	G	GS	CG	ShO	IP	H	HR	BB	SO	W-L	Sv	ERA
Hideo Nomo	R	27	33	33	3	2	228.1	180	23	85	234	16-11	0	3.19
Ismael Valdes	R	22	33	33	0	0	225.0	219	20	54	173	15-7	0	3.32
Pedro Astacio	R	27	35	32	0	0	211.2	207	18	67	130	9-8	0	3.44
Ramon Martinez	R	28	28	27	2	2	168.2	153	12	86	133	15-6	0	3.42
Tom Candiotti	R	38	28	27	1	0	152.1	172	18	43	79	9-11	0	4.49
Antonio Osuna	R	23	73	0	0	0	84.0	65	6	32	85	9-6	4	3.00
Todd Worrell	R	36	72	0	0	0	65.1	70	5	15	66	4-6	44	3.03
Mark Guthrie	R	30	66	0	0	0	73.0	65	3	22	56	2-3	1	2.22
Scott Radinsky	L	28	58	0	0	0	52.1	52	2	17	48	5-1	1	2.41
Chan Ho Park	R	23	48	10	0	0	108.2	82	7	71	119	5-5	0	3.64
Joey Eischen†	L	26	28	0	0	0	43.1	48	4	20	36	0-1	0	4.78
Darren Dreifort	R	24	19	0	0	0	23.2	23	2	12	24	1-4	0	4.94
Jim Bruske	R	31	11	0	0	0	12.2	17	2	3	12	0-0	0	5.68
Darren Hall	R	31	9	0	0	0	12.0	13	2	5	12	0-2	0	6.00
John Cummings†	L	27	4	0	0	0	5.1	12	1	2	5	0-1	0	6.75

1996 Colorado Rockies 3rd NL West 83-79 .512 8.0 GB

Don Baylor

Player	Gm by Position	B	Age	G	AB	R	H	2B	3B	HR	RBI	BB	SO	SB	Avg	OBP	Slg
Jeff Reed	C111	L	33	116	341	34	97	20	1	8	37	43	65	2	.284	.365	.419
Andres Galarraga	1B159,3B1	R	35	159	626	119	190	39	3	47	150	40	157	18	.304	.357	.601
Eric Young	2B139	R	29	141	568	113	184	23	4	8	74	47	31	53	.324	.393	.421
Vinny Castilla	3B160	R	28	160	629	97	191	34	0	40	113	35	88	7	.304	.343	.548
Walt Weiss	SS155	S	32	155	517	89	146	20	2	8	48	80	78	10	.282	.381	.375
Dante Bichette	OF156	R	32	159	633	114	198	39	3	31	141	45	105	31	.313	.359	.531
Ellis Burks	OF152	R	31	156	613	142	211	45	8	40	128	61	114	32	.344	.408	.639
Quinton McCracken	OF93	S	26	124	283	50	82	13	6	3	40	32	62	17	.290	.363	.410
Larry Walker	OF83	L	29	83	272	58	75	18	4	18	58	20	58	18	.276	.342	.570
Jayhawk Owens	C68	R	27	73	180	31	43	9	1	4	17	27	56	4	.239	.338	.367
Jason Bates	2B37,SS18,3B12	S	25	88	160	19	33	8	1	1	9	23	34	2	.206	.312	.288
John VanderWal	OF26,1B10	L	30	104	151	20	38	6	2	5	31	19	38	2	.252	.335	.417
Eric Anthony†	OF19	L	28	32	62	10	15	2	0	4	9	10	20	0	.242	.342	.468
Trent Hubbard†	OF19	R	30	45	60	12	13	5	1	1	12	9	22	2	.217	.329	.383
Neifi Perez	SS14,2B4	S	21	17	45	4	7	2	0	0	3	0	8	2	.156	.156	.200
Steve Decker†	C10	R	30	10	25	8	8	2	0	1	8	3	3	1	.320	.393	.520
Angel Echevarria	OF11	R	25	26	21	2	6	0	0	0	6	2	5	0	.286	.346	.286
Pedro Castellano	2B3,3B1,OF1	R	26	13	17	1	2	0	0	0	2	3	6	0	.118	.286	.118
Milt Thompson†	OF1	L	37	14	15	1	1	1	0	0	2	1	3	0	.067	.125	.133
Harvey Pulliam	OF3	R	28	10	15	2	2	0	0	0	0	2	6	0	.133	.235	.133
Jorge Brito	C8	R	30	8	14	1	1	0	0	0	0	1	8	0	.071	.235	.071
Terry Jones	OF4	S	25	12	10	6	3	0	0	0	1	0	3	0	.300	.273	.300
Alan Cockrell	OF1	R	33	9	8	0	2	1	0	0	2	0	4	0	.250	.222	.375

Pitcher	T	Age	G	GS	CG	ShO	IP	H	HR	BB	SO	W-L	Sv	ERA
Kevin Ritz	R	31	35	35	2	0	213.0	236	24	105	105	17-11	0	5.28
Armando Reynoso	R	30	30	30	0	0	168.2	195	27	49	88	8-9	0	4.96
Mark Thompson	R	25	34	28	3	1	169.2	189	25	74	99	9-11	0	5.30
Marvin Freeman†	R	33	26	23	0	0	129.2	151	21	57	71	7-9	0	6.04
Jamey Wright	R	21	16	15	0	0	91.1	105	8	41	45	4-4	0	4.93
Bryan Rekar	R	24	14	11	0	0	58.1	87	11	26	25	2-4	0	8.95
Mike Farmer	L	27	7	4	0	0	28.0	32	8	13	16	0-1	0	7.71
Bruce Ruffin	L	32	71	0	0	0	69.2	55	5	29	74	7-5	24	4.00
Steve Reed	R	30	70	0	0	0	75.0	66	11	19	51	4-3	0	3.96
Curt Leskanic	R	28	70	0	0	0	73.2	82	12	38	76	7-5	6	6.23
Darren Holmes	R	30	62	0	0	0	77.0	78	8	28	73	5-4	1	3.97
Mike Munoz	L	30	54	0	0	0	44.2	55	4	16	45	2-2	0	6.65
Lance Painter	L	28	34	1	0	0	50.2	56	12	25	48	4-2	0	5.86
Roger Bailey	R	25	24	11	0	0	83.2	94	7	52	45	2-3	1	6.24
John Habyan	R	32	19	0	0	0	24.0	34	4	14	25	1-1	0	7.13
John Burke	R	26	11	0	0	0	15.2	21	3	7	19	2-1	0	7.47
Ryan Hawblitzel	R	25	8	0	0	0	15.0	18	2	6	7	0-1	0	6.00
Bill Swift	R	34	7	3	0	0	18.1	23	1	5	5	1-1	2	5.40
Garvin Alston	R	24	6	0	0	0	6.0	9	1	3	5	1-0	0	9.00
Dave Nied	R	27	6	1	0	0	5.1	5	1	8	4	0-2	0	13.50
Robbie Beckett	L	23	5	0	0	0	5.1	6	3	9	6	0-0	0	13.50

1996 San Francisco Giants 4th NL West 68-94 .420 23.0 GB

Dusty Baker

Player	Gm by Position	B	Age	G	AB	R	H	2B	3B	HR	RBI	BB	SO	SB	Avg	OBP	Slg
Tom Lampkin	C53	L	32	66	177	26	41	8	0	6	29	20	22	1	.232	.324	.379
Mark Carreon†	1B73,OF5	R	32	81	292	40	76	22	3	9	51	22	33	2	.260	.317	.449
Steve Scarsone	2B74,3B14,1B1*	R	30	105	283	28	62	12	1	5	23	25	91	2	.219	.286	.322
Matt Williams	3B92,1B13,SS1	R	30	105	404	69	122	16	1	22	85	39	91	1	.302	.367	.510
Rich Aurilia	SS93,2B11	R	24	105	318	27	76	7	1	3	26	25	52	4	.239	.295	.296
Barry Bonds	OF152	L	31	158	517	122	159	27	3	42	129	151	76	40	.308	.461	.615
Marvin Benard	OF132	L	26	135	488	89	121	17	4	5	27	59	84	25	.248	.333	.330
Glenallen Hill	OF98	R	31	98	379	56	106	26	0	19	67	33	95	6	.280	.344	.499
Shawon Dunston	SS78	R	33	82	287	27	86	12	2	5	25	13	40	8	.300	.331	.408
Stan Javier	OF71	S	32	71	274	44	74	25	0	2	22	25	51	14	.270	.336	.383
Robby Thompson	2B62	R	34	63	227	35	48	11	1	5	21	24	69	2	.211	.301	.335
Bill Mueller	3B45,2B8	S	25	55	200	31	66	15	1	0	19	24	26	0	.330	.401	.415
Dave McCarty	1B51,OF20	R	26	91	175	16	38	3	0	6	24	18	43	2	.217	.294	.337
Rick Wilkins†	C42,1B7	L	29	52	157	19	46	10	0	8	36	21	40	0	.293	.366	.510
Kirt Manwaring†	C49	R	30	49	145	9	34	6	0	1	14	16	24	0	.234	.319	.297
Kim Batiste	3B25,SS7	R	28	54	130	17	27	6	0	3	11	5	33	3	.208	.235	.323
Steve Decker†	C30,1B3,3B2	R	30	57	122	16	28	1	0	1	12	15	26	0	.230	.309	.262
Jay Canizaro	2B35,SS7	R	22	43	120	11	24	4	1	2	8	9	38	0	.200	.260	.300
Desi Wilson	1B33	L	27	41	118	10	32	2	0	2	12	12	27	0	.271	.338	.339
Jacob Cruz	OF23	L	23	33	77	10	18	3	0	3	10	12	24	0	.234	.352	.390
Dan Peltier	1B13,OF1	L	28	31	59	3	15	2	0	0	9	7	9	0	.254	.328	.288
Dax Jones	OF33	R	25	34	58	7	10	0	2	1	7	8	12	2	.172	.269	.293
Trent Hubbard†	OF9	R	30	10	29	3	6	0	1	1	2	2	5	0	.207	.258	.379
Mel Hall	OF4	L	35	25	25	3	3	0	0	0	5	1	4	0	.120	.148	.120
J.R. Phillips†	1B10	L	26	15	25	3	5	0	0	2	5	1	13	0	.200	.231	.440
Wilson Delgado	SS6	S	20	6	22	3	8	0	0	0	2	1	5	1	.364	.440	.364
Keith Williams	OF4	R	24	9	20	0	5	0	0	0	0	0	6	0	.250	.250	.250
Marcus Jensen	C7	S	23	9	19	4	4	1	0	0	4	8	7	0	.211	.444	.263
Doug Mirabelli	C8	R	25	9	18	2	4	1	0	0	1	3	4	0	.222	.333	.278

S. Scarsone, 1 G at SS

Pitcher	T	Age	G	GS	CG	ShO	IP	H	HR	BB	SO	W-L	Sv	ERA
W. VanLandingham	R	25	32	32	0	0	181.2	196	17	78	97	9-14	0	5.40
Allen Watson	L	25	29	29	2	0	185.2	189	28	69	128	8-12	0	4.61
Mark Gardner	R	34	30	28	4	1	179.1	200	28	57	145	12-7	0	4.42
Osvaldo Fernandez	R	27	30	28	2	0	171.2	193	20	57	106	7-13	0	4.61
Mark Leiter†	R	33	23	22	1	0	135.1	151	25	50	118	4-10	0	5.19
Shawn Estes	L	23	11	11	0	0	70.0	63	3	39	60	3-5	0	3.60
Kirk Rueter†	L	25	4	3	0	0	23.1	18	0	5	16	1-2	0	1.93
Steve Soderstrom	R	24	3	3	0	0	13.2	16	1	6	9	2-0	0	5.27
Mark Dewey	R	31	78	0	0	0	83.1	79	9	41	57	6-3	0	4.21
Rod Beck	R	27	63	0	0	0	62.0	56	9	10	48	0-9	35	3.34
Doug Creek	L	27	63	0	0	0	48.1	45	11	32	38	0-2	0	6.52
Rich DeLucia	R	31	56	0	0	0	61.2	62	8	31	55	3-6	0	5.84
Jose Bautista	R	31	37	1	0	0	69.2	66	10	15	28	3-4	0	3.36
Jeff Juden†	R	25	36	0	0	0	41.2	39	7	20	35	4-0	0	4.10
Jim Poole†	L	30	35	0	0	0	23.2	15	2	13	19	2-1	0	2.66
Tim Scott†	R	29	20	0	0	0	19.2	24	5	9	10	2-2	0	8.24
Steve Bourgeois	R	21	15	5	0	0	40.0	60	4	21	17	1-3	0	6.30
Chris Hook	R	27	10	0	0	0	13.1	16	3	14	4	0-1	0	7.43
Shawn Barton	L	33	7	0	0	0	8.1	19	2	1	3	0-0	0	9.72
Dan Carlson	R	26	5	0	0	0	10.0	13	2	2	4	1-0	0	2.70

»1997 Baltimore Orioles 1st AL East 98-64 .605 —

Davey Johnson

Player	Gm by Position	B	Age	G	AB	R	H	2B	3B	HR	RBI	BB	SO	SB	Avg	OBP	Slg
Lenny Webster	C97,DH1	R	32	98	259	29	66	8	1	7	37	22	46	0	.255	.317	.375
Rafael Palmeiro	1B155,DH3	L	32	158	614	95	156	24	2	38	110	67	109	5	.254	.329	.485
Roberto Alomar	2B109,DH2	S	29	112	412	64	137	23	2	14	60	40	43	9	.333	.390	.500
Cal Ripken Jr.	3B162,SS3	R	36	162	615	79	166	30	0	17	84	56	73	1	.270	.331	.402
Mike Bordick	SS153	R	31	153	509	55	120	19	1	7	46	33	66	0	.236	.283	.318
B.J. Surhoff	OF133,DH9,1B3*	L	32	147	528	80	150	30	4	18	88	49	60	1	.284	.345	.458
Brady Anderson	OF124,DH25	L	33	151	590	97	170	39	7	18	73	84	105	18	.288	.393	.469
Jeffrey Hammonds	OF114,DH4	R	26	118	397	71	105	19	3	21	55	32	73	15	.264	.323	.486
Geronimo Berroa†	DH42,OF40	R	32	83	300	48	78	13	0	10	48	40	62	1	.260	.347	.403
Chris Hoiles	C87,DH8,1B4*	R	32	99	320	45	83	15	0	12	49	51	86	1	.259	.375	.419
Jeff Reboulet	2B63,SS22,3B12*	R	33	99	228	26	54	9	0	4	27	23	44	3	.237	.307	.329
Tony Tarasco	OF81,DH2	L	26	100	166	26	34	8	1	7	26	25	33	2	.205	.313	.392
Eric Davis	OF30,DH12	R	35	42	158	29	48	11	0	8	25	14	47	6	.304	.358	.525
Pete Incaviglia†	DH26,OF18	R	33	48	138	18	34	4	0	5	12	11	43	0	.246	.314	.384
Harold Baines†	DH35	L	38	44	134	15	39	5	0	4	15	14	15	0	.291	.356	.418
Aaron Ledesma	2B22,3B11,1B5*	R	26	43	88	24	31	5	1	2	11	13	9	1	.352	.437	.500
Jerome Walton	OF19,1B5,DH2	R	31	26	68	8	20	1	0	3	9	4	10	0	.294	.333	.441
David Dellucci	OF9,DH5	L	23	17	27	3	6	1	0	1	3	4	7	0	.222	.344	.370
Tim Laker	C7	R	27	7	14	0	0	0	0	0	1	2	9	0	.000	.118	.000
Mel Rosario	C4	S	24	4	3	0	0	0	0	0	0	0	1	0	.000	.000	.000
Danny Clyburn	OF1	R	23	2	3	0	0	0	0	0	0	0	2	0	.000	.000	.000
Charlie Greene	C4	R	26	5	2	0	0	0	0	0	1	0	1	0	.000	.000	.000

B. Surhoff, 3 G at 3B; C. Hoiles, 1 G at 3B; J. Reboulet, 1 G at OF; A. Ledesma, 4 G at SS

Pitcher	T	Age	G	GS	CG	ShO	IP	H	HR	BB	SO	W-L	Sv	ERA
Jimmy Key	L	36	34	34	1	1	212.1	210	24	82	141	16-10	0	3.43
Mike Mussina	R	28	33	33	4	1	224.2	197	27	54	218	15-8	0	3.20
Scott Erickson	R	29	34	33	3	2	221.2	218	16	61	131	16-7	0	3.69
Scott Kamieniecki	R	33	30	30	0	0	179.1	179	20	67	109	10-6	0	4.01
Rick Krivda	L	27	10	10	0	0	50.0	67	7	18	29	4-2	0	6.30
Rocky Coppinger	R	23	5	4	0	0	20.0	21	2	16	22	1-1	0	6.30
Esteban Yan	R	23	3	2	0	0	9.2	20	3	7	4	0-1	0	15.83
Armando Benitez	R	24	71	0	0	0	73.1	49	7	43	106	4-5	9	2.45
Jesse Orosco	L	40	71	0	0	0	50.1	29	6	30	46	6-3	0	2.32
Randy Myers	L	34	61	0	0	0	59.2	47	2	22	56	2-3	45	1.51
Terry Mathews	R	32	57	0	0	0	63.1	63	8	36	39	4-4	1	4.41
Arthur Rhodes	L	27	53	0	0	0	95.1	75	9	26	102	10-3	1	3.02
Alan Mills	R	30	39	0	0	0	38.2	41	5	33	32	2-3	0	4.89
Shawn Boskie	R	30	28	9	0	0	77.0	95	14	26	50	6-6	1	6.43
Mike Johnson†	R	21	14	5	0	0	39.2	52	12	16	29	0-1	2	7.94
Brian Williams	R	28	13	0	0	0	24.0	20	0	18	14	0-0	0	3.00
Nerio Rodriguez	R	24	6	2	0	0	22.0	21	2	8	11	2-1	0	4.91

1997 New York Yankees 2nd AL East 96-66 .593 2.0 GB

Joe Torre

Player	Gm by Position	B	Age	G	AB	R	H	2B	3B	HR	RBI	BB	SO	SB	Avg	OBP	Slg
Joe Girardi	C111	R	32	112	398	38	105	23	1	1	50	26	53	2	.264	.311	.334
Tino Martinez	1B150,DH7	L	29	158	594	96	176	31	2	44	141	75	75	3	.296	.371	.577
Luis Sojo	2B72,SS4,3B3*	R	31	77	215	27	66	6	1	2	25	16	14	3	.307	.355	.372
Charlie Hayes	3B98,2B5	R	32	100	353	39	91	16	0	11	53	40	66	3	.258	.332	.397
Derek Jeter	SS159	R	23	159	654	116	190	31	7	10	70	74	125	23	.291	.370	.405
Paul O'Neill	OF146,DH2,1B2	L	34	149	553	89	179	42	0	21	117	75	92	10	.324	.399	.514
Bernie Williams	OF128	S	28	129	509	107	167	35	6	21	100	73	80	15	.328	.408	.544
Chad Curtis†	OF92	R	28	93	320	51	93	21	1	12	50	36	49	12	.291	.362	.475
Cecil Fielder	DH89,1B8	R	33	98	361	40	94	15	0	13	61	51	87	0	.260	.358	.410
Wade Boggs	3B76,DH19,P1	L	39	104	353	55	103	23	1	4	28	48	38	0	.292	.373	.397
Tim Raines	OF57,DH13	S	37	74	271	56	87	20	2	4	38	41	34	8	.321	.403	.454
Mark Whiten	OF57,DH7	S	30	69	215	34	57	11	0	5	24	30	47	4	.265	.360	.386
Jorge Posada	C60	S	25	60	188	29	47	12	0	6	25	30	33	1	.250	.359	.410
Mariano Duncan†	2B41,OF6,DH2	S	34	50	172	16	42	8	0	1	13	6	39	2	.244	.270	.308
Rey Sanchez†	2B37,SS6	R	29	38	138	21	43	12	0	1	15	5	21	0	.312	.338	.420
Pat Kelly	2B48,DH16	R	29	67	120	25	29	6	1	2	10	14	37	8	.242	.324	.358
Mike Stanley†	DH16,1B12	R	34	28	87	16	25	8	0	3	12	15	22	0	.287	.388	.483
Scott Pose	OF45,DH5	L	30	54	87	19	19	2	1	0	5	9	11	3	.218	.292	.264
Andy Fox	3B11,2B5,DH2*	L	26	22	31	13	7	1	0	0	1	7	9	2	.226	.368	.258
Darryl Strawberry	DH4,OF4	L	35	11	29	1	3	1	0	0	2	3	9	0	.103	.188	.138
Ivan Cruz	DH4,1B3,OF1	L	29	11	20	0	5	1	0	0	3	2	4	0	.250	.318	.300
Pete Incaviglia†	DH5	R	33	5	16	1	4	0	0	0	0	0	3	0	.250	.250	.250
Homer Bush	2B8	R	24	10	11	2	4	0	0	0	3	0	0	0	.364	.364	.364
Mike Figga	DH1,C1	R	26	2	4	0	0	0	0	0	0	0	3	0	.000	.000	.000

L. Sojo, 2 G at 1B; A. Fox, 2 G at SS, 2 G at OF

Pitcher	T	Age	G	GS	CG	ShO	IP	H	HR	BB	SO	W-L	Sv	ERA
Andy Pettitte	L	25	35	35	4	1	240.1	233	7	65	166	18-7	0	2.88
David Wells	L	34	32	32	5	2	218.0	239	24	45	156	16-10	0	4.21
David Cone	R	34	29	29	1	0	195.0	155	17	86	222	12-6	0	2.82
Kenny Rogers	L	32	31	22	1	0	145.0	161	18	62	78	6-7	0	5.65
Dwight Gooden	R	32	20	19	0	0	106.1	116	14	53	66	9-5	0	4.91
Hideki Irabu	R	28	13	9	0	0	53.1	69	15	20	56	5-4	0	7.09
Jeff Nelson	R	30	77	0	0	0	78.2	53	7	37	81	3-7	2	2.86
Mariano Rivera	R	27	66	0	0	0	71.2	65	5	20	68	6-4	43	1.88
Mike Stanton	L	30	64	0	0	0	66.2	50	3	34	70	6-1	3	2.57
Graeme Lloyd	L	30	46	0	0	0	49.0	55	6	20	26	1-1	1	3.31
Ramiro Mendoza	R	25	39	15	0	0	133.2	157	15	28	82	8-6	2	4.24
Brian Boehringer	R	27	34	0	0	0	48.0	39	4	32	53	3-2	0	2.63
Jim Mecir	R	27	25	0	0	0	33.2	36	5	10	25	0-4	0	5.88
Dave Weathers†	R	27	10	0	0	0	9.0	15	1	7	4	0-1	0	10.00
Willie Banks	R	28	5	1	0	0	14.0	9	0	6	8	3-0	0	1.93
Danny Rios	R	24	2	0	0	0	2.1	9	3	2	1	0-0	0	19.29
Joe Borowski†	R	26	1	0	0	0	2.0	2	0	4	2	0-1	0	9.00
Wade Boggs	R	39	1	0	0	0	1.0	0	0	1	1	0-0	0	0.00

1997 Detroit Tigers 3rd AL East 79-83 .488 19.0 GB

Buddy Bell

Player	Gm by Position	B	Age	G	AB	R	H	2B	3B	HR	RBI	BB	SO	SB	Avg	OBP	Slg
Raul Casanova	C92,DH1	S	24	101	304	27	74	10	1	5	24	26	48	1	.243	.308	.332
Tony Clark	1B158,DH1	S	25	159	580	105	160	28	3	32	117	93	144	1	.276	.376	.500
Damion Easley	2B137,SS21,DH4	R	27	151	527	97	139	37	3	22	72	68	102	28	.264	.362	.471
Travis Fryman	3B153	R	28	154	595	90	163	27	3	22	102	46	113	16	.274	.326	.440
Deivi Cruz	SS147	R	22	147	436	35	105	26	0	2	40	14	55	3	.241	.263	.314
Brian Hunter	OF162	R	26	162	658	112	177	29	7	4	45	66	121	74	.269	.334	.353
Bob Higginson	OF143,DH1	L	26	146	546	94	163	30	5	27	101	70	85	12	.299	.379	.520
Melvin Nieves	OF99,DH12	S	25	116	359	46	82	18	1	20	64	39	157	1	.228	.311	.451
Bob Hamelin	DH95,1B7	L	29	110	318	47	86	15	0	18	52	48	72	2	.270	.366	.487
Phil Nevin	OF40,DH30,3B17*	R	26	93	251	32	59	16	1	9	35	25	68	0	.235	.306	.414
Curtis Pride†	OF35,DH23	L	28	79	162	21	34	4	4	2	19	24	45	6	.210	.314	.321
Brian Johnson†	C43,DH2	R	29	45	139	13	33	6	1	2	18	5	19	1	.237	.262	.338
Matt Walbeck	C44	S	27	47	137	18	38	3	0	3	10	12	19	3	.277	.331	.365
Bubba Trammell	OF28,DH14	R	25	44	123	14	28	5	0	4	13	15	35	3	.228	.307	.366
Jody Reed	2B41,DH5	R	34	52	112	6	22	2	0	0	8	10	15	3	.196	.278	.214
Orlando Miller	SS31,DH11,3B4*	R	28	50	111	13	26	7	1	2	10	5	24	1	.234	.289	.369
Juan Encarnacion	OF10	R	21	11	33	3	7	1	1	1	5	3	12	3	.212	.316	.394
Frank Catalanotto	2B6,DH3	L	23	13	26	2	8	2	0	0	3	3	7	0	.308	.379	.385
Jimmy Hurst	OF12,DH1	R	25	13	17	1	3	1	0	1	1	2	6	0	.176	.263	.412
Vince Coleman	OF3,DH1	S	35	6	14	0	1	0	0	0	0	1	3	0	.071	.133	.071
Marcus Jensen†	C8	S	24	8	11	1	2	0	0	0	1	1	5	0	.182	.250	.182
Kimera Bartee	OF6,DH3	R	24	12	5	4	1	0	0	0	0	2	2	3	.200	.500	.200
Joe Hall	OF1	R	31	2	4	1	2	1	0	0	3	0	0	0	.500	.500	.750

P. Nevin, 7 G at 1B, 1 G at C; O. Miller, 3 G at 1B

Pitcher	T	Age	G	GS	CG	ShO	IP	H	HR	BB	SO	W-L	Sv	ERA
Justin Thompson	L	24	32	32	4	0	223.1	188	20	66	151	15-11	0	3.02
Brian Moehler	R	25	31	31	2	1	175.1	198	22	61	97	11-12	0	4.67
Willie Blair	R	31	29	27	2	0	175.0	186	18	46	90	16-8	0	4.17
Omar Olivares†	R	29	19	19	3	2	115.0	110	8	53	74	5-6	0	4.70
Felipe Lira†	R	25	20	15	1	1	92.0	101	15	45	64	5-7	0	5.77
Scott Sanders†	R	28	14	14	1	1	74.1	79	14	24	58	3-8	0	5.33
Greg Keagle	R	26	11	10	0	0	45.1	58	9	18	33	3-5	0	6.55
Glenn Dishman	L	26	7	4	0	0	29.0	30	4	8	20	1-2	0	5.28
Tim Pugh	R	30	2	2	0	0	9.0	6	0	5	4	1-1	0	5.00
Mike Myers	L	28	88	0	0	0	53.2	58	12	25	50	0-4	2	5.70
Danny Miceli	R	26	71	0	0	0	82.2	77	13	38	79	3-2	3	5.01
Todd Jones	R	29	68	0	0	0	70.0	60	3	35	70	5-4	31	3.09
Doug Brocail	R	30	61	4	0	0	78.0	74	10	36	60	3-4	2	3.23
A.J. Sager	R	32	38	1	0	0	84.0	81	10	24	53	3-4	3	4.18
Jose Bautista†	R	32	21	0	0	0	40.1	55	6	12	19	2-2	0	6.69
John Cummings	L	28	19	0	0	0	24.2	32	3	14	8	2-0	0	5.47
Kevin Jarvis†	R	27	17	3	0	0	41.2	55	9	14	27	0-3	0	5.40
Eddie Gaillard	R	26	16	0	0	0	20.1	16	2	10	12	1-0	1	5.31
Roberto Duran	L	24	13	0	0	0	10.2	7	0	15	11	0-0	0	7.59
F.Hernandez	R	26	2	0	0	0	1.1	5	0	3	2	0-0	0	40.50

1997 Boston Red Sox 4th AL East 78-84 .481 20.0 GB

Jimy Williams

Player	Gm by Position	B	Age	G	AB	R	H	2B	3B	HR	RBI	BB	SO	SB	Avg	OBP	Slg
Scott Hatteberg	C106,DH1	L	27	114	350	46	97	23	1	10	44	40	70	0	.277	.354	.434
Mo Vaughn	1B131,DH9	L	29	141	527	91	166	24	0	35	96	86	154	2	.315	.420	.560
Jeff Frye	2B80,3B18,OF13*	R	30	127	404	56	126	36	2	3	51	27	44	19	.312	.352	.433
Tim Naehring	3B68,DH1	R	30	70	259	38	74	18	1	9	40	38	40	1	.286	.375	.467
Nomar Garciaparra	SS153	R	23	153	684	122	209	44	11	30	98	35	92	22	.306	.342	.534
Darren Bragg	OF150,3B1	L	27	153	513	65	132	35	2	9	57	61	102	10	.257	.337	.386
Troy O'Leary	OF142,DH1	L	27	146	499	65	154	32	4	15	80	39	70	0	.309	.358	.479
Wil Cordero	OF137,DH2,2B1	R	25	140	570	82	160	26	3	18	72	31	122	1	.281	.320	.432
Reggie Jefferson	DH119,1B12	S	28	136	489	74	156	33	1	13	67	24	93	1	.319	.358	.470
John Valentin	2B79,3B64	R	30	143	575	95	176	47	5	18	77	58	66	7	.306	.372	.499
Mike Stanley†	DH53,1B31,C15	R	34	97	260	45	78	17	0	13	53	39	50	0	.300	.394	.515
Bill Haselman	C66	R	31	67	212	22	50	15	0	6	26	15	44	0	.236	.290	.392
Shane Mack	OF45,DH5	R	33	60	130	13	41	7	0	3	17	9	24	2	.315	.368	.438
Mike Benjamin	3B19,SS16,2B5*	R	31	49	116	12	27	9	1	0	7	4	27	2	.233	.262	.328
Jesus Tavarez	OF35,DH2	S	26	42	69	12	12	3	1	0	9	4	9	0	.174	.216	.246
Rudy Pemberton	OF23	R	27	27	63	8	15	2	0	2	10	4	13	0	.238	.314	.365
Michael Coleman	OF7	R	21	8	24	2	4	1	0	0	2	0	11	1	.167	.167	.208
Arquimedez Pozo	3B4	R	23	4	15	0	4	1	0	0	3	0	5	0	.267	.250	.333
Jose Malave	OF4	R	26	4	4	0	0	0	0	0	0	0	2	0	.000	.000	.000
Walt McKeel	C4,1B1	R	25	5	3	0	0	0	0	0	0	0	1	0	.000	.000	.000
Curtis Pride†		L	28	2	2	1	1	0	0	1	1	0	1	0	.500	.500	2.000
Jason Varitek	C1	S	25	1	1	0	1	0	0	0	0	0	0	0	1.000	1.000	1.000

J. Frye, 11 G at DH, 3 G at SS, 1 G at 1B; M. Benjamin, 4 G at 1B, 1 G at DH, 1 G at P

Pitcher	T	Age	G	GS	CG	ShO	IP	H	HR	BB	SO	W-L	Sv	ERA
Aaron Sele	R	27	33	33	1	0	177.1	196	25	80	122	13-12	0	5.38
Tim Wakefield	R	30	35	29	4	2	201.1	193	24	87	151	12-15	0	4.25
Tom Gordon	R	29	42	25	2	1	182.2	155	10	78	159	6-10	11	3.74
Jeff Suppan	R	22	23	22	0	0	112.1	140	12	36	67	7-3	0	5.69
Steve Avery	L	27	22	18	0	0	96.2	127	15	49	51	6-7	0	6.42
Bret Saberhagen	R	33	6	6	0	0	26.0	30	5	10	14	0-1	0	6.58
Brian Rose	R	21	1	1	0	0	3.0	5	0	2	3	0-0	0	12.00
John Wasdin	R	24	53	7	0	0	124.2	121	18	38	84	4-6	0	4.40
Jim Corsi	R	35	52	0	0	0	57.2	56	1	21	40	5-3	2	3.43
Heathcliff Slocumb†	R	31	49	0	0	0	46.2	58	4	34	36	0-5	17	5.79
Butch Henry	L	28	36	5	0	0	84.1	89	6	19	51	7-3	6	3.52
Kerry Lacy	R	24	33	0	0	0	45.2	60	7	22	18	1-1	3	6.11
Mark Brandenburg	R	26	31	0	0	0	41.0	49	3	16	34	0-2	0	5.49
Chris Hammond	L	31	29	8	0	0	65.1	81	5	27	48	3-4	1	5.92
Ron Mahay	L	26	28	0	0	0	25.0	19	3	11	22	3-0	0	2.52
Joe Hudson	R	26	26	0	0	0	35.2	39	1	14	14	3-1	0	3.53
Vaughn Eshelman	L	28	21	6	0	0	42.2	58	3	17	18	3-3	0	6.33
Ricky Trlicek†	R	28	18	0	0	0	23.1	26	2	18	10	3-4	0	4.63
Rich Garces	R	26	12	0	0	0	13.2	14	2	9	12	0-1	0	4.61
Pat Mahomes	R	26	10	0	0	0	10.0	15	2	10	5	1-0	0	8.10
Derek Lowe†	R	24	8	0	0	0	16.0	15	0	3	13	0-2	0	3.38
Robinson Checo	R	25	5	2	0	0	13.1	12	0	3	14	1-1	0	3.38
Toby Borland†	R	28	3	0	0	0	3.1	6	1	7	1	0-0	0	13.50
Ken Grundt	L	27	2	0	0	0	3.0	5	0	0	0	0-0	0	9.00
Mike Benjamin	R	31	1	0	0	0	1.0	0	0	0	0	0-0	0	0.00

1997 Toronto Blue Jays 5th AL East 76-86 .469 22.0 GB

Cito Gaston (72-85)/Mel Queen (4-1)

Player	Gm by Position	B	Age	G	AB	R	H	2B	3B	HR	RBI	BB	SO	SB	Avg	OBP	Slg
Benito Santiago	C95,DH1	R	32	97	341	31	83	10	0	13	42	17	80	1	.243	.279	.387
Carlos Delgado	1B119,DH33	L	25	153	519	79	136	42	3	30	91	64	133	0	.262	.350	.528
Carlos Garcia	2B96,SS5,3B4	R	29	103	350	29	77	18	2	3	23	15	60	11	.220	.253	.309
Ed Sprague	3B129,DH8	R	29	138	504	63	115	29	4	14	48	51	102	0	.228	.306	.385
Alex Gonzalez	SS125	R	24	126	426	46	102	23	2	12	35	34	94	15	.239	.302	.387
Otis Nixon†	OF102,DH1	S	38	103	401	54	105	12	1	1	26	52	54	47	.262	.343	.304
Orlando Merced	OF96,DH1,1B1	S	30	98	368	45	98	23	2	9	40	47	62	7	.266	.352	.413
Shawn Green	OF91,DH35	L	24	135	429	57	123	22	4	16	53	36	99	14	.287	.340	.469
Joe Carter	DH64,OF51,1B42	R	37	157	612	76	143	30	4	21	102	40	105	8	.234	.284	.399
Charlie O'Brien	C69	R	37	69	225	22	49	15	1	4	27	22	45	0	.218	.311	.347
Jose Cruz Jr.†	OF55	S	23	55	212	31	49	7	0	14	34	28	72	6	.231	.316	.462
Jacob Brumfield	OF47,DH4	R	32	58	174	22	36	5	1	2	20	14	31	4	.207	.268	.282
Shannon Stewart	OF41,DH1	S	23	44	168	25	48	13	7	0	22	19	24	10	.286	.368	.446
Mariano Duncan†	2B39	S	34	39	167	20	38	6	0	0	12	6	39	4	.228	.267	.263
Tilson Brito†	2B25,3B17,SS8	R	25	49	126	9	28	3	0	0	8	9	28	1	.222	.281	.246
Tomas Perez	SS32,2B8	S	23	40	123	9	24	3	2	0	9	11	28	1	.195	.267	.252
Juan Samuel	DH16,3B9,1B7*	R	36	45	95	13	27	5	4	3	15	10	28	5	.284	.364	.516
Robert Perez	OF25,DH7	R	28	37	78	4	15	4	1	2	6	0	16	0	.192	.192	.346
Ruben Sierra†	OF7,DH6	S	31	14	48	4	10	0	2	1	5	3	13	0	.208	.250	.354
Tom Evans	3B12	R	22	12	38	7	11	2	0	1	2	2	10	0	.289	.341	.421
Felipe Crespo	3B7,DH2,2B1	S	24	12	28	3	8	0	1	1	5	2	4	0	.286	.333	.464
Rich Butler	OF3,DH1	L	24	7	14	3	4	1	0	0	2	2	3	0	.286	.375	.357
Julio Mosquera	C3	R	25	3	8	0	2	1	0	0	0	0	2	0	.250	.250	.375
Sandy Martinez	C3	L	24	3	2	1	0	0	0	0	0	1	1	0	.000	.333	.000

J. Samuel, 4 G at 2B, 2 G at OF

Pitcher	T	Age	G	GS	CG	ShO	IP	H	HR	BB	SO	W-L	Sv	ERA
Pat Hentgen	R	28	35	35	9	3	264.0	253	31	71	160	15-10	0	3.68
Roger Clemens	R	34	34	34	9	3	264.0	204	9	68	292	21-7	0	2.05
Woody Williams	R	30	31	31	0	0	194.2	201	31	66	124	9-14	0	4.35
Robert Person	R	27	23	22	0	0	128.1	125	19	60	99	5-10	0	5.61
Chris Carpenter	R	22	14	13	1	1	81.1	108	7	37	55	3-7	0	5.09
Juan Guzman	R	30	13	13	0	0	60.0	48	14	31	52	3-6	0	4.95
Erik Hanson	R	32	3	2	0	0	15.0	15	3	6	18	0-0	0	7.80
Paul Quantrill	R	28	77	0	0	0	88.0	103	5	17	56	6-7	5	1.94
Dan Plesac	L	35	73	0	0	0	50.1	47	8	19	61	2-4	1	3.58
Mike Timlin†	R	31	38	0	0	0	47.0	41	6	15	36	3-2	9	2.87
Paul Spoljaric†	L	26	37	0	0	0	48.0	37	3	21	43	0-3	3	3.19
Tim Crabtree	R	27	37	0	0	0	40.2	65	7	17	26	3-3	2	7.08
Kelvim Escobar	R	21	27	0	0	0	31.0	28	1	19	36	3-2	14	2.90
Luis Andujar	R	24	17	8	0	0	50.0	76	9	21	28	0-6	0	6.48
Marty Janzen	R	24	12	0	0	0	25.0	23	4	13	17	2-1	0	3.60
Omar Daal†	L	25	9	3	0	0	27.0	34	3	6	28	1-1	0	4.00
Huck Flener	L	28	8	1	0	0	17.1	40	3	6	9	0-1	0	9.87
Carlos Almanzar	R	23	4	0	0	0	3.1	1	1	1	4	0-1	0	2.70
Bill Risley	R	30	3	0	0	0	4.1	3	2	2	2	0-1	0	8.31
Ken Robinson	R	27	3	0	0	0	3.1	1	1	1	4	0-0	0	2.70

1997 Cleveland Indians 1st AL Central 86-75 .534 —

Mike Hargrove

Player	Gm by Position	B	Age	G	AB	R	H	2B	3B	HR	RBI	BB	SO	SB	Avg	OBP	Slg
Sandy Alomar Jr.	C119,DH1	R	31	125	451	63	146	37	0	21	83	19	48	0	.324	.354	.545
Jim Thome	1B145	L	26	147	496	104	142	25	0	40	102	120	146	1	.286	.423	.579
Tony Fernandez	2B109,SS10,DH1	S	35	120	409	55	117	21	1	11	44	22	47	6	.286	.323	.423
Matt Williams	3B151	R	31	151	596	86	157	32	3	32	105	34	108	12	.263	.307	.488
Omar Vizquel	SS152	S	30	153	565	89	158	23	6	5	49	57	58	43	.280	.347	.368
Manny Ramirez	OF146,DH4	R	25	150	561	99	184	40	0	26	88	79	115	2	.328	.415	.538
Marquis Grissom	OF144	R	30	144	558	74	146	27	6	12	66	43	89	22	.262	.317	.396
Brian Giles	OF115,DH9	L	26	130	377	62	101	15	3	17	61	63	50	13	.268	.368	.459
David Justice	OF78,DH61	L	31	139	495	84	163	31	1	33	101	80	79	3	.329	.418	.596
Julio Franco†	DH42,2B35,1B1	R	35	78	289	46	82	13	1	3	25	38	75	8	.284	.367	.367
Kevin Seitzer	DH24,1B19,3B13	R	35	64	198	27	53	14	0	2	24	18	25	0	.268	.326	.369
Pat Borders	C53	R	34	55	159	17	47	7	1	4	15	9	27	0	.296	.341	.428
Bip Roberts†	2B13,OF10	S	33	23	85	19	23	3	0	3	8	7	14	3	.271	.333	.412
Jeff Branson†	2B19,3B6,SS2*	L	30	29	72	5	19	4	0	2	7	7	17	0	.264	.329	.403
Kevin Mitchell	DH16,OF1	R	35	20	59	7	9	1	0	4	11	9	11	1	.153	.275	.373
Jeff Manto	3B7,1B6,OF1	R	32	16	30	3	8	3	0	2	7	1	10	0	.267	.290	.567
Chad Curtis†	OF19	R	28	22	29	8	6	1	0	3	5	7	10	0	.207	.361	.552
Casey Candaele	2B9,DH1,3B1	S	36	14	26	5	8	1	0	0	4	1	1	1	.308	.333	.346
Bruce Aven	OF13	R	25	13	19	4	4	1	0	0	2	1	5	0	.211	.250	.263
Enrique Wilson	SS4,2B1	S	21	5	15	2	5	0	0	0	1	0	2	0	.333	.333	.333
Trent Hubbard	OF6	R	31	7	12	3	3	1	0	0	0	1	3	2	.250	.308	.333
Richie Sexson	1B2,DH1	R	22	5	11	1	3	0	0	0	0	0	2	0	.273	.273	.273
Sean Casey	DH3,1B1	L	22	6	10	1	2	0	0	0	1	1	2	0	.200	.333	.200
Damian Jackson†	SS5,2B1	R	23	8	9	2	1	0	0	0	0	0	1	1	.111	.200	.111
Einar Diaz	C5	R	24	5	7	1	1	1	0	0	1	0	2	0	.143	.143	.286

J. Branson, 1 G at DH

Pitcher	T	Age	G	GS	CG	ShO	IP	H	HR	BB	SO	W-L	Sv	ERA
Charles Nagy	R	30	34	34	1	1	227.0	253	27	77	149	15-11	0	4.28
Orel Hershiser	R	38	32	32	1	0	195.1	199	26	69	107	14-6	0	4.47
Chad Ogea	R	26	21	21	1	0	126.1	139	13	47	80	8-9	0	4.99
Bartolo Colon	R	22	19	17	1	0	94.0	107	12	45	66	4-7	0	5.65
Jaret Wright	R	21	16	16	0	0	90.1	81	9	35	63	8-3	0	4.38
Brian Anderson	L	25	8	8	0	0	48.0	55	7	11	22	4-2	0	4.69
Jack McDowell	R	31	8	6	0	0	40.2	44	6	18	38	3-3	0	5.09
John Smiley†	L	32	6	6	0	0	37.1	45	9	10	26	2-4	0	5.54
Jeff Juden†	R	26	8	5	0	0	31.1	32	6	15	29	0-1	0	5.46
Terry Clark†	R	36	4	4	0	0	26.1	29	3	13	13	0-3	0	6.15
Paul Assenmacher	L	36	75	0	0	0	49.0	43	5	15	53	5-0	4	2.94
Mike Jackson	R	32	71	0	0	0	75.0	59	3	29	74	2-5	15	3.24
Jose Mesa	R	31	66	0	0	0	82.1	83	7	28	69	4-4	16	2.40
Eric Plunk	R	33	55	0	0	0	65.2	62	12	36	66	4-5	0	4.66
Paul Shuey	R	26	40	0	0	0	45.0	52	5	28	46	4-2	2	6.20
Albie Lopez	R	25	37	6	0	0	76.2	101	11	40	63	3-7	0	6.93
Alvin Morman	L	28	34	0	0	0	18.1	19	2	14	13	0-0	2	5.89
Jason Jacome†	L	26	21	4	0	0	42.2	45	8	15	24	2-0	0	5.27
Steve Kline†	L	24	20	1	0	0	26.1	42	6	13	17	3-1	0	5.81
Dave Weathers†	R	27	9	1	0	0	16.2	23	2	8	14	1-2	0	7.56
Danny Graves†	R	23	5	0	0	0	11.1	15	2	9	4	0-0	0	4.76

1997 Chicago White Sox 2nd AL Central 80-81 .497 6.0 GB

Terry Bevington

Player	Gm by Position	B	Age	G	AB	R	H	2B	3B	HR	RBI	BB	SO	SB	Avg	OBP	Slg
Jorge Fabregas†	C92,1B1	L	27	100	322	31	90	10	1	7	48	11	43	1	.280	.302	.382
Frank Thomas	1B97,DH49	R	29	146	530	110	184	35	0	35	125	109	69	1	.347	.456	.611
Ray Durham	2B153,DH1	S	25	155	634	106	172	27	5	11	53	61	96	33	.271	.337	.382
Chris Snopek	3B82,SS4	R	26	86	298	27	65	15	0	5	35	18	51	3	.218	.263	.319
Ozzie Guillen	SS139	L	33	142	490	59	120	21	6	4	52	22	24	5	.245	.275	.337
Albert Belle	OF154,DH7	R	30	161	634	90	174	45	1	30	116	53	105	4	.274	.332	.491
Mike Cameron	OF112,DH3	R	24	116	379	63	98	18	3	14	55	55	105	23	.259	.356	.433
Dave Martinez	OF105,1B52	L	32	145	504	78	144	16	6	12	55	55	69	12	.286	.356	.413
Harold Baines†	DH86,OF1	L	38	93	318	40	97	18	0	12	52	41	47	0	.305	.382	.475
Lyle Mouton	OF67,DH11	R	28	88	242	26	65	9	0	5	23	14	66	4	.269	.308	.368
Norberto Martin	SS28,3B17,2B9*	R	30	71	213	24	64	7	1	2	27	6	31	1	.300	.320	.371
Robin Ventura	3B54	L	29	54	183	27	48	10	1	6	26	34	21	0	.262	.373	.426
Ron Karkovice	C51	R	33	51	138	10	25	3	0	6	18	11	32	0	.181	.248	.333
Tony Phillips†	OF28,3B9	S	38	36	129	23	40	6	0	2	9	29	29	4	.310	.440	.403
Mario Valdez	1B47,DH2,3B1	L	22	54	115	11	28	7	0	1	13	17	39	1	.243	.350	.330
Darren Lewis†	OF64,DH6	R	29	81	77	15	18	1	0	0	5	11	14	11	.234	.330	.247
Magglio Ordonez	OF19	R	23	21	69	12	22	6	0	4	11	2	8	1	.319	.338	.580
Tony Pena†	C30,3B1	R	40	31	67	4	11	1	0	0	8	8	13	0	.164	.250	.179
Jeff Abbott	OF10,DH3	R	24	19	38	8	10	1	0	1	2	0	6	0	.263	.263	.368
Chad Kreuter†	C13,1B2	S	32	19	37	6	8	2	1	1	3	8	9	0	.216	.356	.405
Greg Norton	3B11,DH2	S	24	18	34	5	9	2	2	0	1	2	8	0	.265	.306	.441
Robert Machado	C10	R	24	10	15	1	3	0	1	0	2	1	6	0	.200	.250	.333
Chad Fonville†	OF3,2B2,SS2*	S	26	9	9	1	1	0	0	0	1	1	1	2	.111	.200	.111

N. Martin, 6 G at DH; C. Fonville, 1 G at DH

Pitcher	T	Age	G	GS	CG	ShO	IP	H	HR	BB	SO	W-L	Sv	ERA
Jaime Navarro	R	30	33	33	2	0	209.2	267	22	73	142	9-14	0	5.79
James Baldwin	R	25	32	32	1	0	200.0	205	19	83	140	12-15	0	5.27
Doug Drabek	R	34	31	31	0	0	169.1	170	30	69	85	12-11	0	5.74
Wilson Alvarez†	L	27	22	22	2	1	145.2	126	9	55	110	9-8	0	3.03
Danny Darwin†	R	41	21	17	1	0	113.1	130	21	31	62	4-8	0	4.13
Scott Eyre	L	25	11	11	0	0	60.2	62	11	31	36	4-4	0	5.04
Jason Bere	R	26	6	6	0	0	28.2	20	4	17	21	4-2	0	4.71
Mike Sirotka	L	26	7	4	0	0	32.0	36	4	5	24	3-0	0	2.25
Tony Castillo	L	34	64	0	0	0	62.1	74	6	23	42	4-4	4	4.91
Matt Karchner	R	30	52	0	0	0	52.2	50	4	26	30	3-1	15	2.91
Chuck McElroy†	L	29	48	0	0	0	59.1	56	3	19	44	1-3	1	3.94
R. Hernandez†	R	32	46	0	0	0	48.0	38	5	24	47	5-1	27	2.44
Bill Simas	R	25	40	0	0	0	41.1	46	6	24	38	3-1	1	4.14
Carlos Castillo	R	22	37	2	0	0	66.1	68	9	33	43	2-1	1	4.48
Al Levine	R	29	25	0	0	0	27.1	35	4	16	22	2-2	0	6.91
Nelson Cruz	R	24	19	0	0	0	26.1	29	6	9	23	0-2	0	6.49
Keith Foulke†	R	24	16	0	0	0	28.2	28	4	5	21	3-0	3	3.45
Jeff Darwin	R	27	14	0	0	0	13.2	17	1	7	9	0-1	0	5.27
Mike Bertotti	L	27	9	0	0	0	3.2	9	0	2	4	0-0	0	7.36
Tom Fordham	L	23	7	1	0	0	17.1	17	2	10	10	0-1	0	6.23
Chris Clemons	R	24	5	2	0	0	12.2	19	4	11	8	0-2	0	8.53
Larry Thomas	L	27	5	0	0	0	3.1	3	1	2	0	0-0	0	8.10

1997 Milwaukee Brewers 3rd AL Central 78-83 .484 8.0 GB

Phil Garner

Player	Gm by Position	B	Age	G	AB	R	H	2B	3B	HR	RBI	BB	SO	SB	Avg	OBP	Slg
Mike Matheny	C121,1B2	R	26	123	320	29	78	16	1	4	32	17	68	0	.244	.294	.338
Dave Nilsson	1B74,DH59,OF22	L	27	156	554	71	154	33	0	20	81	65	88	2	.278	.352	.446
Fernando Vina	2B77,DH1	L	28	79	324	37	89	12	2	4	28	12	23	8	.275	.312	.361
Jeff Cirillo	3B150,DH2	R	27	154	580	74	167	46	2	10	82	60	74	4	.288	.367	.426
Jose Valentin	SS134,DH1	S	27	136	494	58	125	23	1	17	58	39	109	19	.253	.310	.407
Gerald Williams	OF154,DH1	R	30	155	566	73	143	32	2	10	41	19	90	23	.253	.282	.369
Jeromy Burnitz	OF149	L	28	153	494	85	139	37	8	27	85	75	111	20	.281	.382	.553
Matt Mieske	OF74,DH5	R	29	84	253	39	63	15	3	5	21	19	50	1	.249	.300	.391
Julio Franco†	DH28,1B13	R	35	42	141	22	34	3	0	4	19	31	41	7	.241	.373	.348
Mark Loretta	2B63,SS44,1B19*	R	25	132	418	56	120	17	5	5	47	47	60	5	.287	.354	.388
Jesse Levis	C78,DH8	L	29	99	200	19	57	7	0	1	19	24	17	1	.285	.361	.335
John Jaha	1B27,DH20	R	31	46	162	25	40	7	0	11	26	25	40	1	.247	.354	.494
Marc Newfield	OF28,DH18	R	24	50	157	14	36	8	0	1	18	14	27	0	.229	.295	.299
Jack Voigt	OF40,1B19,3B6*	R	31	72	151	20	37	9	2	8	22	19	36	1	.245	.331	.490
Jeff Huson	2B32,1B21,OF9*	L	32	84	143	12	29	3	0	0	11	5	15	3	.203	.238	.224
Todd Dunn	OF27,DH14	R	26	44	118	17	27	5	0	3	9	2	39	3	.229	.242	.347
Darrin Jackson†	OF26	R	33	26	81	7	22	7	0	2	15	2	10	2	.272	.289	.432
Brian Banks	OF15,1B5,DH1*	S	26	28	68	9	14	1	0	1	8	6	17	0	.206	.267	.265
Antone Williamson	1B14,DH4	L	23	24	54	2	11	3	0	0	6	4	8	0	.204	.254	.259
Eddy Diaz	2B14,3B1,SS1	R	25	16	50	4	11	2	1	0	7	1	5	0	.220	.235	.300
Chuck Carr†	OF23	S	28	26	46	3	6	3	0	0	0	2	11	1	.130	.184	.196
Kelly Stinnett	C25,DH1	R	27	30	36	2	9	4	0	0	3	3	9	0	.250	.308	.361
Tim Unroe	1B23,3B2,OF2*	R	26	32	16	3	4	1	0	2	5	2	9	2	.250	.333	.688

M. Loretta, 15 G at 3B; J. Voigt, 1 G at DH; J. Huson, 4 G at DH, 2 G at 3B; B. Banks, 1 G at 3B; T. Unroe, 1 G at 2B

Pitcher	T	Age	G	GS	CG	ShO	IP	H	HR	BB	SO	W-L	Sv	ERA
Cal Eldred	R	29	34	34	1	1	202.0	207	31	89	122	13-15	0	4.99
Scott Karl	L	25	32	32	1	0	193.1	212	23	67	119	10-13	0	4.47
Jose Mercedes	R	26	29	23	2	1	159.0	146	24	53	80	7-10	0	3.79
Jeff D'Amico	R	21	23	23	1	1	135.2	139	25	43	94	9-7	0	4.71
Ben McDonald	R	29	21	21	1	0	133.0	120	13	36	110	8-7	0	4.06
Steve Woodard	R	22	7	7	0	0	36.2	39	5	6	32	3-3	0	5.15
Jamie McAndrew	R	29	5	4	0	0	19.1	24	1	23	8	1-1	0	8.38
Pete Harnisch†	R	30	4	3	0	0	14.0	13	1	12	10	1-1	0	5.14
Doug Jones	R	40	75	0	0	0	80.1	62	4	9	82	6-6	36	2.02
Bob Wickman	R	28	74	0	0	0	95.2	89	8	41	78	7-6	1	2.73
Mike Fetters	R	32	51	0	0	0	70.1	62	4	33	62	1-5	6	3.45
Ron Villone	L	27	50	0	0	0	52.2	54	4	36	40	1-0	0	3.42
Bryce Florie	R	27	32	8	0	0	75.0	74	4	42	53	4-4	0	4.32
Joel Adamson	L	25	30	6	0	0	76.1	78	13	19	56	5-3	0	3.54
Al Reyes	R	26	19	0	0	0	29.2	32	4	9	28	1-2	1	5.46
Mark Davis	L	36	19	0	0	0	16.1	21	4	5	14	0-0	0	5.51
Angel Miranda	L	27	10	0	0	0	14.0	17	1	9	8	0-0	0	3.86
Mike Misuraca	R	28	5	0	0	0	10.1	15	5	7	10	0-0	0	11.32
Sean Maloney	R	26	3	0	0	0	7.0	7	1	2	5	0-0	0	5.14
Greg Hansell	R	26	3	0	0	0	4.2	5	1	1	5	0-0	0	9.64
Paul Wagner†	R	29	2	0	0	0	2.0	3	1	0	0	1-0	0	9.00

1997 Minnesota Twins 4th AL Central 68-94 .420 18.5 GB

Tom Kelly

Player	Gm by Position	B	Age	G	AB	R	H	2B	3B	HR	RBI	BB	SO	SB	Avg	OBP	Slg
Terry Steinbach	C116,1B2,DH1	R	35	122	447	60	111	27	1	12	54	35	106	6	.248	.302	.394
Scott Stahoviak	1B81,DH5	L	27	91	275	33	63	17	0	10	33	24	73	5	.229	.301	.400
Chuck Knoblauch	2B153,DH1,SS1	R	28	156	611	117	178	26	10	9	58	84	84	62	.291	.390	.411
Ron Coomer	3B119,1B9,DH7*	R	30	140	523	63	156	30	2	13	85	22	91	4	.298	.324	.438
Pat Meares	SS134	R	28	134	439	63	121	23	3	10	60	18	86	7	.276	.323	.410
Matt Lawton	OF138	L	25	142	460	74	114	29	3	14	60	76	81	7	.248	.366	.415
Rich Becker	OF128	S	25	132	443	61	117	22	3	10	45	62	130	17	.264	.354	.395
Marty Cordova	OF101,DH2	R	27	103	378	44	93	18	4	15	51	30	92	5	.246	.305	.434
Paul Molitor	DH122,1B12	R	40	135	538	63	164	32	4	10	89	45	73	11	.305	.351	.435
Denny Hocking	SS44,3B39,OF20*	S	27	115	253	28	65	12	4	2	25	18	51	3	.257	.308	.360
Roberto Kelly†	OF59,DH12	R	32	75	247	39	71	19	2	5	37	17	50	7	.287	.336	.441
Greg Colbrunn†	1B64,DH2	R	27	70	217	24	61	14	0	5	26	8	38	1	.281	.307	.415
Brent Brede	OF42,1B15,DH1	L	25	61	190	25	52	11	1	3	21	21	38	7	.274	.347	.389
Greg Myers†	C38,DH10	L	31	62	165	24	44	11	1	5	28	16	29	0	.267	.328	.436
Todd Walker	3B40,2B8,DH2	L	24	52	156	15	37	7	1	3	16	11	30	7	.237	.288	.353
Darrin Jackson†	OF44	R	33	49	130	19	33	2	1	3	21	4	21	2	.254	.272	.354
Damian Miller	C20,DH3	R	27	25	66	5	18	1	0	2	13	2	12	0	.273	.282	.379
David Ortiz	1B11	L	21	15	49	10	16	3	0	1	6	2	19	0	.327	.353	.449
Chris Latham	OF10	S	24	15	22	4	4	1	0	0	1	0	8	0	.182	.182	.227
Javier Valentin	C4	S	21	4	7	1	2	0	0	0	0	0	3	0	.286	.286	.286
Torii Hunter		R	21	1	0	0	0	0	0	0	0	0	0	0	—	—	—

R. Coomer, 7 G at OF; D. Hocking, 15 G at 2B, 1 G at DH, 1 G at 1B

Pitcher	T	Age	G	GS	CG	ShO	IP	H	HR	BB	SO	W-L	Sv	ERA
Brad Radke	R	24	35	35	4	1	239.2	238	28	48	174	20-10	0	3.87
Bob Tewksbury	R	36	26	26	5	2	168.2	200	12	31	92	8-13	0	4.22
Rich Robertson	L	28	31	26	0	0	147.0	169	19	70	69	8-12	0	5.69
LaTroy Hawkins	R	24	20	20	0	0	103.1	134	19	47	58	6-12	0	5.84
Scott Aldred	L	29	17	15	0	0	77.1	102	20	28	33	2-10	0	7.68
Travis Miller	L	24	13	7	0	0	48.1	64	8	23	26	1-5	0	7.63
Dave Stevens†	R	27	6	6	0	0	23.0	41	8	17	16	1-3	0	9.00
Shane Bowers	R	25	5	5	0	0	19.0	27	2	8	7	0-3	0	8.05
Dan Serafini	L	23	6	4	1	0	26.1	27	1	11	15	2-1	0	3.42
Eddie Guardado	L	26	69	0	0	0	46.0	45	7	17	54	0-4	1	3.91
Mike Trombley	R	30	67	0	0	0	82.1	77	7	31	74	2-3	1	4.37
Greg Swindell	L	32	65	1	0	0	115.2	102	12	25	75	7-4	1	3.58
Rick Aguilera	R	35	61	0	0	0	68.1	65	9	22	68	5-4	26	3.82
Frank Rodriguez	R	24	43	15	0	0	142.1	147	12	60	65	3-6	0	4.62
Todd Ritchie	R	25	42	0	0	0	74.2	87	11	28	44	2-3	0	4.58
Dan Naulty	R	27	29	0	0	0	30.2	29	8	10	23	1-1	1	5.87
Gregg Olson†	R	30	11	0	0	0	8.1	19	0	11	6	0-0	0	18.36
Kevin Jarvis†	R	27	6	2	0	0	13.0	23	4	8	9	0-0	0	12.46

1997 Kansas City Royals 5th AL Central 67-94 .416 19.0 GB

Bob Boone (36-46)/Tony Muser (31-48)

Player	Gm by Position	B	Age	G	AB	R	H	2B	3B	HR	RBI	BB	SO	SB	Avg	OBP	Slg
Mike Macfarlane	C81	R	33	82	257	34	61	14	2	8	35	24	47	0	.237	.316	.401
Jeff King	1B150,DH2	R	32	155	543	84	129	30	1	28	112	89	96	16	.238	.341	.451
Jose Offerman	2B101,DH1	S	28	106	424	59	126	23	6	2	39	41	64	9	.297	.359	.394
Craig Paquette	3B72,OF4	R	28	77	252	26	58	15	1	8	33	10	57	2	.230	.263	.393
Jay Bell	SS149,3B4	R	31	153	573	89	167	28	3	21	92	71	101	10	.291	.368	.461
Johnny Damon	OF136,DH5	L	23	146	472	70	130	12	8	8	48	42	70	16	.275	.338	.386
Tom Goodwin†	OF96	L	28	97	367	51	100	13	4	2	22	19	51	34	.272	.311	.346
Bip Roberts†	OF84,3B10	S	33	97	346	44	107	17	2	1	36	21	53	15	.309	.348	.379
Chili Davis	DH133	S	37	140	477	71	133	20	0	30	90	85	96	6	.279	.386	.509
Jermaine Dye	OF75	R	23	75	263	26	62	14	0	7	22	17	51	2	.236	.284	.369
Mike Sweeney	C76,DH3	R	23	84	240	30	58	8	0	7	31	17	33	3	.242	.306	.363
Yamil Benitez	OF52	R	25	53	191	22	51	7	1	8	21	10	49	2	.267	.307	.440
Dean Palmer†	3B48,DH1	R	28	49	187	23	52	10	1	9	31	15	50	1	.278	.335	.487
Dave Howard	2B34,OF23,SS9*	S	30	80	162	24	39	8	1	1	13	10	31	2	.241	.287	.321
Scott Cooper	3B39,1B8,DH5	L	29	75	159	12	32	6	1	3	15	17	32	1	.201	.283	.308
Joe Vitiello	OF28,DH12,1B1	R	27	51	130	11	31	6	0	5	18	14	37	0	.238	.322	.400
Shane Halter	OF32,2B18,3B12*	R	27	74	123	16	34	5	1	2	10	10	28	4	.276	.341	.382
Rod Myers	OF26	L	24	31	101	14	26	7	0	2	9	17	22	4	.257	.370	.386
Jed Hansen	2B31	R	24	34	94	11	29	6	1	1	14	13	29	3	.309	.394	.426
Larry Sutton	1B12,DH3,OF1	L	27	27	69	9	20	2	0	2	8	5	12	0	.290	.338	.406
Sal Fasano	C12,DH1	R	25	13	38	4	8	2	0	1	1	1	12	0	.211	.231	.342
Tim Spehr†	C17	R	30	17	35	3	6	0	0	1	2	2	12	0	.171	.237	.257
Felix Martinez	SS12	S	23	16	31	3	7	1	1	0	3	6	8	0	.226	.351	.323
Jon Nunnally†	OF9	L	25	13	29	8	7	0	1	1	4	5	7	0	.241	.353	.414
Ryan Long	OF5,DH1	R	24	6	9	2	2	0	0	0	2	0	3	0	.222	.300	.222
Andy Stewart	C4,DH1	R	26	5	8	1	2	1	0	0	0	0	0	0	.250	.250	.375

D. Howard, 7 G at 3B, 5 G at DH; S. Halter, 5 G at SS, 4 G at DH

Pitcher	T	Age	G	GS	CG	ShO	IP	H	HR	BB	SO	W-L	Sv	ERA
Kevin Appier	R	29	34	34	4	1	235.2	215	24	74	196	9-13	0	3.40
Jose Rosado	L	22	33	33	2	0	203.1	208	26	73	129	9-12	0	4.69
Tim Belcher	R	35	32	32	3	1	213.1	242	31	70	113	13-12	0	5.02
Glendon Rusch	L	22	30	27	1	0	170.1	206	28	52	116	6-9	0	5.50
Jim Pittsley	R	23	21	21	0	0	112.0	120	15	54	52	5-8	0	5.46
Ricky Bones†	R	28	21	11	1	0	78.1	102	10	25	36	4-7	0	5.97
Jeff Montgomery	R	35	55	0	0	0	59.1	53	9	18	48	1-4	14	3.49
Jamie Walker	L	25	50	0	0	0	43.0	46	6	20	24	3-3	0	5.44
Hipolito Pichardo	R	27	47	0	0	0	49.0	51	7	24	34	3-5	11	4.22
Gregg Olson†	R	30	34	0	0	0	41.2	39	3	17	28	4-3	1	3.02
Larry Casian†	L	31	32	0	0	0	26.2	32	5	6	16	0-2	0	5.06
Hector Carrasco†	R	27	28	0	0	0	34.2	29	4	16	30	1-6	0	5.45
Randy Veres	R	31	24	0	0	0	35.1	36	4	7	28	4-0	1	3.31
Matt Whisenant†	L	26	24	0	0	0	19.0	15	0	12	16	1-0	0	2.84
Brian Bevil	R	25	18	0	0	0	16.1	16	1	9	13	1-2	1	6.61
Mike Perez	R	32	16	0	0	0	20.1	15	2	8	17	2-0	0	3.54
Scott Service†	R	30	12	0	0	0	17.0	17	1	5	19	0-3	0	4.76
Mike Williams	R	28	10	0	0	0	14.0	20	1	8	10	0-2	1	6.43
Chris Haney	L	28	8	3	0	0	24.2	29	1	5	16	1-2	0	4.38
Mitch Williams	L	32	7	0	0	0	6.2	11	2	7	10	0-1	0	10.80
Jason Jacome†	L	26	7	0	0	0	6.2	13	2	5	3	0-0	0	9.45
Jose Santiago	R	22	4	0	0	0	4.2	7	0	2	1	0-0	0	1.93
Jim Converse	R	25	3	0	0	0	5.0	4	2	5	3	0-0	0	3.60
Allen McDill	L	25	3	0	0	0	4.0	3	1	8	2	0-0	0	13.50
Roland de la Maza	R	25	1	0	0	0	2.0	1	1	1	1	0-0	0	4.50

1997 Seattle Mariners 1st AL West 90-72 .556 —

Lou Piniella

Player	Gm by Position	B	Age	G	AB	R	H	2B	3B	HR	RBI	BB	SO	SB	Avg	OBP	Slg
Dan Wilson	C144	R	28	146	508	66	137	31	1	15	74	39	72	7	.270	.326	.423
Paul Sorrento	1B139,DH1	L	31	146	457	68	123	19	0	31	80	51	112	0	.269	.345	.514
Joey Cora	2B142	S	32	149	574	105	172	40	4	11	54	53	49	6	.300	.359	.441
Russ Davis	3B117,DH1	R	27	119	420	57	114	29	1	20	63	27	100	6	.271	.317	.488
Alex Rodriguez	SS140,DH1	R	21	141	587	100	176	40	3	23	84	41	99	29	.300	.350	.496
Jay Buhner	OF154,DH2	R	32	157	540	104	131	18	2	40	109	119	175	0	.243	.383	.506
Ken Griffey Jr.	OF153,DH4	L	27	157	608	125	185	34	3	56	147	76	121	15	.304	.382	.646
Rob Ducey	OF69	L	32	76	143	25	41	15	2	5	10	6	31	3	.287	.311	.524
Edgar Martinez	DH144,1B7,3B1	R	34	155	542	104	179	35	1	28	108	119	86	2	.330	.456	.554
Rich Amaral	OF52,1B14,2B11*	R	35	89	190	34	54	5	0	1	21	10	34	12	.284	.327	.326
Jose Cruz Jr.†	OF49	S	23	49	183	28	49	12	1	12	34	13	45	1	.268	.315	.541
Brent Gates	3B32,2B21,SS5*	S	27	65	151	18	36	8	0	3	20	14	21	0	.238	.298	.351
Mike Blowers	1B49,3B10,OF6*	R	32	68	150	22	44	5	0	5	20	21	33	0	.293	.376	.427
Lee Tinsley	OF41,DH4	S	28	49	122	12	24	6	2	0	6	11	34	2	.197	.263	.279
Roberto Kelly†	OF29,DH1	R	32	30	121	19	36	7	0	7	22	5	17	2	.298	.328	.529
Andy Sheets	3B21,SS9,2B2	R	25	32	89	18	22	3	0	4	9	7	34	2	.247	.299	.416
John Marzano	C37,DH1	R	34	39	87	7	25	3	0	1	10	7	15	0	.287	.340	.356
Alvaro Espinoza	SS17,2B14,3B1	R	35	33	72	3	13	1	0	0	7	2	12	1	.181	.213	.194
Raul Ibanez	OF8,DH1	L	25	11	26	3	4	0	1	1	4	0	6	0	.154	.154	.346
Rick Wilkins†	C3,DH2	L	30	5	12	2	3	1	0	1	4	1	2	0	.250	.286	.583
Dan Rohrmeier	DH4,1B3	R	32	7	9	4	3	0	0	0	2	2	4	0	.333	.455	.333
Giomar Guevara	DH2,2B2,SS1	R	24	5	4	0	0	0	0	0	0	0	2	1	.000	.000	.000
Brian Raabe†	3B2,2B1	R	29	2	3	0	0	0	0	0	0	1	2	0	.000	.250	.000

R. Amaral, 3 G at DH, 1 G at 3B, 1 G at SS; B. Gates, 1 G at DH, 1 G at 1B, 1 G at OF; M. Blowers, 1 G at DH

Pitcher	T	Age	G	GS	CG	ShO	IP	H	HR	BB	SO	W-L	Sv	ERA
Jeff Fassero	L	34	35	35	2	1	234.1	226	21	84	189	16-9	0	3.61
Jamie Moyer	L	34	30	30	2	0	188.2	187	21	43	113	17-5	0	3.86
Randy Johnson	L	33	30	29	5	2	213.0	147	20	77	291	20-4	0	2.28
Bob Wolcott	R	23	19	18	0	0	100.0	129	22	29	58	5-6	0	6.03
Omar Olivares†	R	29	13	12	0	0	62.1	81	10	28	29	1-4	0	5.49
Derek Lowe†	R	24	12	9	0	0	53.0	59	11	20	39	2-4	0	6.96
Ken Cloude	R	22	10	9	0	0	51.0	41	8	26	46	4-2	0	5.12
Dennis Martinez	R	42	9	9	0	0	49.0	65	8	29	17	1-5	0	7.71
Bobby Ayala	R	27	71	0	0	0	96.2	91	14	41	92	10-5	8	3.82
Norm Charlton	L	34	71	0	0	0	69.1	89	7	47	55	3-8	14	7.27
Bob Wells	R	30	46	1	0	0	67.1	88	11	18	51	2-0	2	5.75
Greg McCarthy	L	28	37	0	0	0	29.2	26	4	16	34	1-1	0	5.46
Scott Sanders†	R	28	33	6	0	0	65.1	73	16	38	62	3-6	2	6.47
Heathcliff Slocumb†	R	31	27	0	0	0	28.1	26	2	15	28	0-4	10	4.13
Mike Timlin†	R	31	26	0	0	0	25.2	28	2	5	9	3-2	1	3.86
Paul Spoljaric†	L	26	20	0	0	0	22.2	24	1	15	27	0-0	0	4.76
Josias Manzanillo	R	29	16	0	0	0	18.1	19	3	17	18	0-1	0	5.40
Mark Holzemer	L	27	14	0	0	0	9.0	9	0	8	7	0-0	1	6.00
Edwin Hurtado	R	27	13	1	0	0	19.0	25	5	15	10	1-2	0	9.00
Felipe Lira†	R	25	8	3	0	0	18.2	31	3	10	9	0-4	0	9.16
Mike Maddux	R	35	6	0	0	0	10.2	20	1	8	7	1-0	0	10.13
Rafael Carmona	R	24	4	0	0	0	5.2	3	1	2	6	0-0	0	3.18
Tim Davis	L	26	2	0	0	0	6.2	6	1	4	10	0-0	0	6.75
Salomon Torres†	R	25	2	0	0	0	3.1	7	0	3	0	0-0	0	27.00

1997 Anaheim Angels 2nd AL West 84-78 .519 6.0 GB

Terry Collins

Player	Gm by Position	B	Age	G	AB	R	H	2B	3B	HR	RBI	BB	SO	SB	Avg	OBP	Slg
Chad Kreuter†	C67,DH2	S	32	70	218	19	51	7	1	4	18	21	57	0	.234	.301	.330
Darin Erstad	1B126,DH9,OF1	L	23	139	539	99	161	34	4	16	77	51	86	23	.299	.360	.466
Luis Alicea	2B105,3B12,DH6	S	31	128	388	59	98	16	7	5	37	69	65	22	.253	.375	.369
Dave Hollins	3B135,1B14	S	31	149	572	101	165	29	2	16	85	62	124	16	.288	.363	.430
Gary DiSarcina	SS153	R	29	154	549	52	135	28	2	4	47	17	29	7	.246	.271	.326
Tim Salmon	OF153,DH4	R	28	157	582	95	172	28	1	33	129	95	142	9	.296	.394	.517
Garret Anderson	OF148,DH4	L	25	154	624	76	189	36	3	8	92	30	70	10	.303	.334	.409
Jim Edmonds	OF115,1B11,DH8	L	27	133	502	82	146	27	0	26	80	60	80	5	.291	.368	.500
Eddie Murray†	DH45	S	41	46	160	13	35	7	0	3	15	13	24	1	.219	.273	.319
Tony Phillips†	2B43,OF35,DH26*	S	38	105	405	73	107	28	2	6	48	73	89	9	.264	.376	.388
Jim Leyritz†	C58,1B15,DH13	R	33	84	294	47	81	7	0	11	50	37	56	1	.276	.357	.412
Jack Howell	3B24,DH22,1B12	L	35	77	174	25	45	7	0	14	34	13	36	1	.259	.305	.540
Orlando Palmeiro	OF52,DH11	L	28	74	134	19	29	2	2	0	8	17	11	2	.216	.307	.261
Craig Grebeck	2B26,SS20,3B15*	R	32	63	126	12	34	9	0	1	6	18	11	0	.270	.359	.365
Todd Greene	C26,DH8	R	26	34	124	24	36	6	0	9	24	7	25	2	.290	.328	.556
Rickey Henderson†	DH19,OF13	R	38	32	115	21	21	3	0	2	7	26	23	16	.183	.343	.261
Jorge Fabregas†	C21	L	27	21	38	2	3	1	0	0	3	3	3	0	.079	.146	.105
Chris Turner	C8,1B2,DH1*	R	28	13	23	4	6	1	1	1	2	5	8	0	.261	.393	.522
Robert Eenhoorn	3B5,2B3,SS2	R	29	11	20	2	7	1	0	1	6	0	2	0	.350	.333	.550
Angelo Encarnacion	C11	R	24	11	17	2	7	1	0	1	4	0	1	2	.412	.412	.647
George Arias†	DH1,3B1	R	25	3	6	1	2	0	0	0	1	0	0	0	.333	.333	.333
Randy Velarde		R	34	1	0	0	0	0	0	0	0	0	0	0	—	—	—

T. Phillips, 1 G at 3B; C. Grebeck, 3 G at OF; C. Turner, 1 G at OF

Pitcher	T	Age	G	GS	CG	ShO	IP	H	HR	BB	SO	W-L	Sv	ERA
Allen Watson	L	26	35	34	0	0	199.0	220	37	73	141	12-12	0	4.93
Jason Dickson	R	24	33	32	2	1	203.2	236	32	56	115	13-9	0	4.29
Dennis Springer	R	32	32	28	3	1	194.2	199	32	73	75	9-9	0	5.18
Chuck Finley	L	34	25	25	3	1	164.0	152	20	65	155	13-6	0	4.23
Ken Hill†	R	31	12	12	1	0	79.0	65	8	39	38	4-4	0	3.65
Mark Langston	L	36	9	9	0	0	47.2	61	8	29	30	2-4	0	5.85
Matt Perisho	L	22	11	8	0	0	45.0	59	6	28	35	0-2	0	6.00
Mark Gubicza	R	34	2	2	0	0	4.2	13	2	3	5	0-1	0	25.07
Mike Holtz	L	24	66	0	0	0	43.1	38	7	15	40	3-4	2	3.32
Pep Harris	R	24	61	0	0	0	79.2	82	7	38	56	5-4	0	3.62
Mike James	R	29	58	0	0	0	62.2	69	3	28	57	5-5	7	4.31
Troy Percival	R	27	55	0	0	0	52.0	40	6	22	72	5-5	27	3.46
S. Hasegawa	R	28	50	7	0	0	116.2	118	14	46	83	3-7	0	3.93
Rich DeLucia†	R	32	33	0	0	0	42.1	29	5	27	42	6-4	3	3.61
Darrell May	L	25	29	2	0	0	51.2	56	6	25	42	2-1	0	5.23
Greg Cadaret	L	35	15	0	0	0	13.2	11	1	8	11	0-0	0	3.29
Chuck McElroy†	L	29	13	0	0	0	15.2	17	2	3	18	0-0	0	3.45
Kevin Gross	R	36	12	3	0	0	25.1	30	4	20	20	2-1	0	6.75
Anthony Chavez	R	26	7	0	0	0	9.2	7	1	5	10	0-0	0	0.93
Mike Bovee	R	23	3	0	0	0	3.1	3	1	1	5	0-0	0	5.40
Shad Williams	R	26	1	0	0	0	1.0	1	0	1	0	0-0	0	0.00

1997 Texas Rangers 3rd AL West 77-85 .475 13.0 GB

Johnny Oates

Player	Gm by Position	B	Age	G	AB	R	H	2B	3B	HR	RBI	BB	SO	SB	Avg	OBP	Slg
Ivan Rodriguez	C143,DH5	R	25	150	597	98	187	34	4	20	77	38	89	7	.313	.360	.484
Will Clark	1B100,DH7	L	33	110	393	56	128	29	1	12	51	49	62	0	.326	.400	.496
Mark McLemore	2B89,OF1	S	32	89	349	47	91	17	2	1	25	40	54	7	.261	.338	.330
Dean Palmer†	3B93	R	28	94	355	47	87	21	0	14	55	26	84	1	.245	.296	.423
Benji Gil	SS106,DH3	R	24	110	317	35	71	13	2	5	31	17	96	1	.224	.263	.325
Rusty Greer	OF153,DH2	L	28	157	601	112	193	42	3	26	87	83	87	9	.321	.405	.531
Damon Buford	OF117,DH3	R	27	122	366	49	82	18	0	8	39	30	83	18	.224	.287	.339
Juan Gonzalez	DH69,OF64	R	27	133	533	87	158	24	3	42	131	33	107	0	.296	.335	.589
Lee Stevens	1B62,DH38,OF22	L	29	137	426	58	128	24	2	21	74	23	83	1	.300	.336	.514
Domingo Cedeno	2B65,SS43,3B3*	S	28	113	365	49	103	19	6	4	36	27	77	3	.282	.334	.400
Fernando Tatis	3B60	R	22	60	223	29	57	9	0	8	29	14	42	3	.256	.297	.404
Tom Goodwin†	OF51	L	28	53	207	39	49	13	2	0	17	25	37	16	.237	.319	.319
Billy Ripken	SS31,2B25,3B13*	R	32	71	203	18	56	9	1	3	24	9	32	0	.276	.300	.374
Warren Newson	OF58,DH9	L	32	81	169	23	36	10	1	10	23	31	53	3	.213	.333	.462
Mike Simms	DH28,OF19,1B2	R	30	59	111	13	28	8	0	5	22	8	27	0	.252	.298	.459
Alex Diaz	OF23,1B1,2B1	S	28	28	90	8	20	4	0	2	12	5	13	1	.222	.268	.333
Jim Leyritz†	C11,DH9,1B9	R	33	37	85	11	24	4	0	0	14	23	22	1	.282	.446	.329
Mike Devereaux	OF28	R	34	29	72	8	15	3	0	0	7	7	10	1	.208	.275	.250
Henry Mercedes	C23	R	27	23	47	4	10	4	0	0	4	6	25	0	.213	.302	.298
Mickey Tettleton	DH13	S	36	17	44	5	4	1	0	3	4	3	12	0	.091	.167	.318
Marc Sagmoen	OF17,1B1	L	26	21	43	2	6	2	0	1	4	2	13	0	.140	.174	.256
Hanley Frias	SS12,2B1	S	23	14	26	4	5	1	0	0	1	1	4	0	.192	.222	.231
Kevin L. Brown	C4	R	24	4	5	1	2	0	0	1	1	0	0	0	.400	.400	1.000
Dave Silvestri	3B1,SS1	R	29	2	4	0	0	0	0	0	0	0	1	0	.000	.000	.000

D. Cedeno, 2 G at DH; B. Ripken, 9 G at 1B

Pitcher	T	Age	G	GS	CG	ShO	IP	H	HR	BB	SO	W-L	Sv	ERA
Bobby Witt	R	33	34	32	3	0	209.0	245	33	74	121	12-12	0	4.82
Darren Oliver	L	26	32	32	3	1	201.1	213	29	82	104	13-12	0	4.20
John Burkett	R	32	30	30	2	0	189.1	240	20	30	139	9-12	0	4.56
Ken Hill†	R	31	19	19	0	0	111.0	129	11	56	68	5-8	0	5.19
Roger Pavlik	R	29	11	11	0	0	57.2	59	7	31	35	3-5	0	4.37
Rick Helling†	R	26	10	8	0	0	55.0	47	5	21	46	3-3	0	4.58
Tanyon Sturtze	R	26	9	5	0	0	32.2	45	6	18	18	1-1	0	8.27
Terry Clark†	R	36	9	5	0	0	30.2	41	3	10	11	1-4	0	5.87
John Wetteland	R	30	61	0	0	0	65.0	43	5	21	63	7-2	31	1.94
Eric Gunderson	L	31	60	0	0	0	49.2	45	5	15	31	2-1	1	3.26
Danny Patterson	R	26	54	0	0	0	71.0	70	3	23	69	10-6	1	3.42
Xavier Hernandez	R	31	44	0	0	0	49.1	51	7	22	36	0-4	0	4.56
Matt Whiteside	R	29	42	1	0	0	72.2	85	4	26	44	4-1	0	5.08
Ed Vosberg†	L	35	42	0	0	0	41.0	44	3	15	29	1-2	0	4.61
Julio Santana	R	24	30	14	0	0	104.0	141	16	49	64	4-6	0	6.75
Scott Bailes	L	35	24	0	0	0	22.0	18	2	10	14	1-0	0	2.86
Jose Alberro	R	28	10	4	0	0	28.1	37	4	17	11	0-3	0	7.94
Wilson Heredia	R	25	10	0	0	0	19.2	14	2	16	8	1-0	0	3.20
Eric Moody	R	26	10	1	0	0	19.0	26	4	2	12	0-1	0	4.26
Bryan Eversgerd	L	28	3	0	0	0	1.1	5	0	3	2	0-2	0	20.25

1997 Oakland Athletics 4th AL West 65-97 .401 25.0 GB

Art Howe

Player	Gm by Position	B	Age	G	AB	R	H	2B	3B	HR	RBI	BB	SO	SB	Avg	OBP	Slg
Brent Mayne	C83	L	29	85	256	29	74	12	0	6	22	18	33	1	.289	.343	.406
Mark McGwire†	1B101	R	33	105	366	48	104	24	0	34	81	58	98	1	.284	.383	.628
Scott Spiezio	2B146,3B1	S	24	147	538	58	131	28	4	14	65	44	75	9	.243	.300	.388
Scott Brosius	3B107,SS30,OF22	R	30	129	479	59	97	20	1	11	41	34	102	9	.203	.259	.317
Rafael Bournigal	SS74,2B7	R	31	79	222	29	62	9	0	1	20	16	19	2	.279	.339	.333
Matt Stairs	OF89,DH17,1B7	L	28	133	352	62	105	19	0	27	73	50	60	3	.298	.386	.582
Damon Mashore	OF89	R	27	92	279	55	69	10	2	3	18	50	82	5	.247	.370	.330
Jason McDonald	OF74	S	25	78	236	47	62	11	4	4	14	36	49	13	.263	.361	.394
Jose Canseco	DH60,OF44	R	32	108	388	56	91	19	0	23	74	51	122	8	.235	.325	.461
Jason Giambi	OF68,1B51,DH25	L	26	142	519	66	152	41	2	20	81	55	89	0	.293	.362	.495
Dave Magadan	3B49,1B30,DH25	L	34	128	271	38	82	10	1	4	30	50	40	1	.303	.414	.391
Geronimo Berroa†	OF43,DH27	R	32	73	261	40	81	12	0	16	42	36	58	3	.310	.395	.540
Mark Bellhorn	3B40,2B17,DH3*	S	22	68	224	33	51	9	1	6	19	32	70	7	.228	.324	.357
George Williams	C67,DH1	S	28	76	201	30	58	9	1	3	22	35	46	0	.289	.397	.388
Tony Batista	SS61,3B4,DH1*	R	23	68	188	22	38	10	1	4	18	14	31	2	.202	.265	.330
Ernie Young	OF66	R	27	71	175	22	39	7	0	5	15	19	57	1	.223	.303	.349
Brian Lesher	OF32,DH3,1B3	R	26	46	131	17	30	4	1	4	16	9	30	4	.229	.275	.366
Patrick Lennon	OF36,DH17	R	29	56	116	14	34	6	1	1	14	15	35	0	.293	.374	.388
Izzy Molina	C48	R	26	48	111	6	22	3	1	3	7	3	17	0	.198	.219	.324
Miguel Tejada	SS26	R	21	26	99	10	20	3	2	2	10	2	22	2	.202	.240	.333
Ben Grieve	OF24	L	21	24	93	12	29	6	0	3	24	13	25	0	.312	.402	.473
Tilson Brito†	3B10,SS6,2B2	R	25	17	46	8	13	2	1	2	6	1	10	0	.283	.298	.500
Scott Sheldon	SS12,2B1,3B1	R	28	13	24	2	6	0	0	1	2	1	6	0	.250	.308	.375

M. Bellhorn, 1 G at SS; T. Batista, 1 G at 2B

Pitcher	T	Age	G	GS	CG	ShO	IP	H	HR	BB	SO	W-L	Sv	ERA
Steve Karsay	R	25	24	24	0	0	132.2	166	20	47	92	3-12	0	5.77
Ariel Prieto	R	27	22	22	0	0	125.0	155	16	70	90	6-8	0	5.04
Dave Telgheder	R	30	20	19	0	0	101.0	134	15	35	55	4-6	0	6.06
Mike Oquist	R	29	19	17	1	0	107.2	111	15	43	72	4-6	0	5.02
Brad Rigby	R	24	14	14	0	0	77.2	92	14	22	34	1-7	0	4.87
Jimmy Haynes	R	24	13	13	0	0	73.1	74	7	40	65	3-6	0	4.42
Willie Adams	R	24	13	12	0	0	58.1	73	9	32	37	3-5	0	8.18
Andrew Lorraine	L	24	12	6	0	0	29.2	45	2	15	18	3-1	0	6.37
Eric Ludwick†	R	25	6	5	0	0	24.0	32	7	16	14	1-4	0	8.25
S. Wojciechowski	L	26	2	2	0	0	10.1	17	2	1	5	0-2	0	7.84
Buddy Groom	L	31	78	0	0	0	64.2	75	9	24	45	2-2	3	5.15
Billy Taylor	R	35	72	0	0	0	73.0	70	3	36	66	3-4	23	3.82
Aaron Small	R	25	71	0	0	0	96.2	109	6	40	57	9-5	4	4.28
Mike Mohler	L	28	62	10	0	0	101.2	116	11	54	66	1-10	1	5.13
Don Wengert	R	27	49	12	1	0	134.0	177	21	41	68	5-11	2	6.04
Dane Johnson	R	34	38	0	0	0	45.2	49	4	31	43	4-1	2	4.53
Carlos Reyes	R	28	37	6	0	0	77.1	101	13	25	43	3-4	0	5.82
T.J. Mathews†	R	27	24	0	0	0	28.2	34	5	12	24	6-2	3	4.40
Mark Acre	R	28	15	0	0	0	15.2	21	1	8	12	2-0	0	5.74
Richie Lewis†	R	31	14	0	0	0	18.2	24	7	15	12	2-0	0	9.64
Tim Kubinski	L	25	11	0	0	0	12.2	12	2	6	10	0-0	0	5.68
Jay Witasick	R	24	8	0	0	0	11.0	14	2	6	8	0-0	0	5.73
Gary Haught	R	26	6	0	0	0	11.1	12	3	6	11	0-0	0	7.15
John Johnstone†	R	28	5	0	0	0	6.1	7	0	7	4	0-0	0	2.84
Steve Montgomery	R	26	4	0	0	0	6.1	10	2	8	1	0-1	0	9.95
Billy Brewer†	L	29	3	0	0	0	2.0	4	1	2	1	0-0	0	13.50

>>1997 Atlanta Braves 1st NL East 101-61 .623 —

Bobby Cox

Player	Gm by Position	B	Age	G	AB	R	H	2B	3B	HR	RBI	BB	SO	SB	Avg	OBP	Slg
Javy Lopez	C117	R	26	123	414	52	122	28	1	23	68	40	82	1	.295	.361	.534
Fred McGriff	1B149	L	33	152	564	77	156	25	1	22	97	68	112	5	.277	.356	.441
Mark Lemke	2B104	S	31	109	351	33	86	17	1	2	26	33	51	2	.245	.306	.316
Chipper Jones	3B152,OF5	S	25	157	597	100	176	41	3	21	111	76	88	20	.295	.371	.479
Jeff Blauser	SS149,DH1	R	31	151	519	90	160	31	4	17	70	70	101	5	.308	.405	.482
Andruw Jones	OF147	R	20	153	399	60	92	18	1	18	70	56	107	20	.231	.329	.416
Ryan Klesko	OF130,1B22	L	26	143	467	67	122	23	6	24	84	48	130	4	.261	.334	.490
Michael Tucker	OF129	L	26	138	499	80	141	25	7	14	56	44	116	12	.283	.347	.445
Kenny Lofton	OF122	L	30	122	493	90	164	20	6	5	48	64	83	27	.333	.409	.428
Eddie Perez	C64,1B6	R	29	73	191	20	41	5	0	6	18	10	35	0	.215	.259	.335
Tony Graffanino	2B75,3B2,SS2*	R	25	104	186	33	48	9	1	8	20	26	46	6	.258	.344	.446
Keith Lockhart	2B20,3B11,DH4	L	32	96	147	25	41	5	3	6	32	14	17	0	.279	.337	.476
Danny Bautista	OF57	R	25	64	103	14	25	3	2	3	9	5	24	2	.243	.282	.398
Mike Mordecai	3B19,2B4,SS4*	S	29	61	81	8	14	2	1	0	3	6	16	0	.173	.227	.222
Rafael Belliard	SS53,2B7	R	35	72	71	9	15	3	0	1	3	1	17	0	.211	.219	.296
Greg Colbrunn†	1B14,DH3	R	27	28	54	3	15	3	0	2	9	2	11	0	.278	.316	.444
Tommy Gregg	OF6,1B1	L	33	13	19	1	5	2	0	0	0	1	2	1	.263	.300	.368
Tim Spehr†	C7	R	30	8	14	2	3	1	0	1	4	0	4	1	.214	.214	.500
Randall Simon	1B6	L	22	13	14	2	6	1	0	0	1	1	2	0	.429	.467	.500
Greg Myers†	C2	L	31	9	9	0	1	0	0	0	1	1	3	0	.111	.200	.111
Ed Giovanola	3B8,2B1,SS1	L	28	14	8	0	2	0	0	0	0	2	1	0	.250	.400	.250

T. Graffanino, 1 G at 1B; M. Mordecai, 3 G at 1B, 1 G at DH, 1 G at OF

Pitcher	T	Age	G	GS	CG	ShO	IP	H	HR	BB	SO	W-L	Sv	ERA
John Smoltz	R	30	35	35	7	2	256.0	234	21	63	241	15-12	0	3.02
Denny Neagle	L	28	34	34	4	4	233.1	204	18	49	172	20-5	0	2.97
Tom Glavine	L	31	33	33	5	2	240.0	197	20	79	152	14-7	0	2.96
Greg Maddux	R	31	33	33	5	2	232.2	200	9	20	177	19-4	0	2.20
Terrell Wade	L	24	12	9	0	0	42.0	60	6	16	35	2-3	0	5.36
Kevin Millwood	R	22	12	8	0	0	51.1	55	1	21	42	5-3	0	4.03
Chris Brock	R	27	7	6	0	0	30.2	34	2	19	16	0-0	0	5.58
Mark Wohlers	R	27	71	0	0	0	69.1	57	4	38	92	5-7	33	3.50
Alan Embree	L	27	66	0	0	0	46.0	36	1	20	45	3-1	0	2.54
Brad Clontz	R	26	51	0	0	0	48.0	52	3	18	42	5-1	1	3.75
Mike Bielecki	R	37	50	0	0	0	57.1	56	9	21	60	3-7	2	4.08
Mike Cather	R	26	35	0	0	0	37.2	23	1	19	29	2-4	0	2.39
Paul Byrd	R	26	31	4	0	0	53.0	47	6	28	37	4-4	0	5.26
Chad Fox	R	26	30	0	0	0	27.1	24	4	16	28	0-1	0	3.29
Joe Borowski†	R	26	20	0	0	0	24.0	27	2	16	6	2-2	0	3.75
Kerry Ligtenberg	R	26	15	0	0	0	15.0	12	4	4	19	1-0	1	3.00
John LeRoy	R	22	1	0	0	0	2.0	1	0	3	3	1-0	0	0.00

1997 Florida Marlins 2nd NL East 92-70 .568 9.0 GB

Jim Leyland

Player	Gm by Position	B	Age	G	AB	R	H	2B	3B	HR	RBI	BB	SO	SB	Avg	OBP	Slg
Charles Johnson	C123	R	25	124	416	43	104	26	1	19	63	60	109	0	.250	.347	.454
Jeff Conine	1B145,OF1	R	31	151	405	46	98	13	1	17	61	57	89	2	.242	.337	.405
Luis Castillo	2B70	S	21	75	263	27	63	8	0	0	8	27	53	16	.240	.310	.270
Bobby Bonilla	3B149,DH3,1B2	S	34	153	562	77	167	39	3	17	96	73	94	6	.297	.378	.468
Edgar Renteria	SS153	R	21	154	617	90	171	21	3	4	52	45	108	32	.277	.327	.340
Moises Alou	OF150	R	30	150	538	88	157	29	5	23	115	70	85	9	.292	.373	.493
Gary Sheffield	OF132,DH1	R	28	135	444	86	111	22	1	21	71	121	79	11	.250	.424	.446
Devon White	OF71	S	34	74	265	37	65	13	1	6	34	32	65	13	.245	.338	.370
Jim Eisenreich	OF55,1B29,DH4	L	38	120	293	36	82	19	1	2	34	30	28	0	.280	.345	.372
Kurt Abbott	2B54,OF10,SS7*	R	28	94	252	35	69	18	2	6	30	14	68	3	.274	.315	.433
John Cangelosi	OF58,P1	S	34	103	192	28	47	8	0	1	12	19	33	5	.245	.321	.302
Craig Counsell†	2B51	L	26	51	164	20	49	9	2	1	16	18	17	1	.299	.376	.396
Greg Zaun	C50,1B1	S	26	58	143	21	43	10	2	2	20	26	18	1	.301	.415	.441
Cliff Floyd	OF38,1B9	L	24	61	137	23	32	9	1	6	19	24	33	6	.234	.354	.445
Darren Daulton†	1B39,OF3,DH1	L	35	52	126	22	33	8	2	3	21	22	17	2	.262	.371	.429
Alex Arias	3B37,SS11	R	29	74	93	13	23	2	0	1	11	12	12	0	.247	.352	.301
Mark Kotsay	OF14	L	21	14	52	5	10	1	1	0	4	4	7	3	.192	.250	.250
Todd Dunwoody	OF14	L	22	19	50	7	13	2	2	2	7	7	21	2	.260	.362	.500
John Wehner	OF27,3B6	R	30	44	36	8	10	2	0	0	2	2	5	1	.278	.333	.333
Ralph Milliard	2B8	R	23	8	30	2	6	0	0	0	2	3	3	1	.200	.314	.200
Billy McMillon†	OF2	L	25	13	18	0	2	1	0	0	1	0	7	0	.111	.111	.167
Russ Morman	OF2,1B1	R	35	4	7	3	2	1	0	1	2	0	2	1	.286	.286	.857
Josh Booty	3B4	R	22	4	5	2	3	0	0	0	1	1	1	0	.600	.667	.600
Bob Natal	C4	R	31	4	4	2	2	1	0	1	3	2	0	0	.500	.571	1.500

K. Abbott, 4 G at 3B, 2 G at DH

Pitcher	T	Age	G	GS	CG	ShO	IP	H	HR	BB	SO	W-L	Sv	ERA
Kevin Brown	R	32	33	33	6	2	237.1	214	10	66	205	16-8	0	2.69
Alex Fernandez	R	27	32	32	5	1	220.2	193	25	69	183	17-12	0	3.59
Al Leiter	L	31	27	27	0	0	151.1	133	13	91	132	11-9	0	4.34
Tony Saunders	L	23	22	21	0	0	111.1	99	12	64	102	4-6	0	4.61
Pat Rapp†	R	29	19	19	1	1	108.2	121	11	51	64	4-6	0	4.47
Livan Hernandez	R	22	17	17	0	0	96.1	81	5	38	72	9-3	0	3.18
Kirt Ojala	L	28	7	5	0	0	28.2	28	4	18	19	1-2	0	3.14
Jay Powell	R	25	74	0	0	0	79.2	71	3	30	65	7-2	2	3.28
Robb Nen	R	27	73	0	0	0	74.0	72	7	40	81	9-3	35	3.89
Dennis Cook	L	34	59	0	0	0	62.1	64	4	28	63	1-2	0	3.90
Felix Heredia	L	21	56	0	0	0	56.2	53	3	30	54	5-3	0	4.29
Robby Stanifer	R	25	36	0	0	0	45.0	43	9	16	28	1-2	1	4.60
Mark Hutton†	R	27	32	0	0	0	47.2	50	7	19	29	3-1	0	3.78
Rick Helling†	R	26	31	8	0	0	76.0	61	12	48	53	2-6	0	4.38
Antonio Alfonseca	R	25	17	0	0	0	25.2	36	3	10	19	1-3	0	4.91
Ed Vosberg†	L	35	17	0	0	0	12.0	15	0	6	8	1-1	1	3.75
Kurt Miller	R	24	7	0	0	0	7.1	12	2	7	7	0-1	0	9.82
Matt Whisenant†	L	26	4	0	0	0	2.2	4	0	6	4	0-0	0	16.88
Donn Pall	R	35	2	0	0	0	2.1	3	1	1	0	0-0	0	3.86
John Cangelosi	L	34	1	0	0	0	1.0	0	0	1	0	0-0	0	0.00

1997 New York Mets 3rd NL East 88-74 .543 13.0 GB

Bobby Valentine

Player	Gm by Position	B	Age	G	AB	R	H	2B	3B	HR	RBI	BB	SO	SB	Avg	OBP	Slg
Todd Hundley	C122,DH2	S	28	132	417	78	114	21	2	30	86	83	116	2	.273	.394	.549
John Olerud	1B146	L	28	154	524	90	154	34	1	22	102	85	67	0	.294	.400	.489
Carlos Baerga	2B131	S	28	133	467	53	131	25	1	9	52	20	54	2	.281	.311	.396
Edgardo Alfonzo	3B143,SS12,2B3	R	23	151	518	84	163	27	2	10	72	63	56	11	.315	.391	.432
Rey Ordonez	SS118	R	24	120	356	35	77	5	3	1	33	18	36	11	.216	.255	.256
Bernard Gilkey	OF136,DH2	R	30	145	518	85	129	31	1	18	78	70	111	7	.249	.338	.417
Carl Everett	OF128	S	27	142	443	58	110	28	3	14	57	32	102	17	.248	.308	.420
Butch Huskey	OF92,1B22,3B15*	R	25	142	471	61	135	26	2	24	81	25	84	8	.287	.319	.503
Lance Johnson†	OF66	L	33	72	265	43	82	10	6	1	24	33	21	15	.309	.385	.404
Alex Ochoa	OF88,DH1	R	25	113	238	31	58	14	1	3	22	18	32	3	.244	.300	.349
Luis Lopez	SS45,2B20,3B4	S	26	78	178	19	48	12	1	1	19	12	42	2	.270	.330	.365
Matt Franco	3B39,1B13,DH1*	L	27	112	163	21	45	5	0	5	21	13	23	1	.276	.330	.399
Manny Alexander†	2B31,SS26,3B1	R	26	54	149	26	37	9	3	2	15	9	38	11	.248	.294	.389
Brian McRae†	OF41	S	29	45	145	23	36	5	2	5	15	13	22	3	.248	.317	.414
Todd Pratt	C36	R	30	39	106	12	30	6	0	2	19	13	32	0	.283	.372	.396
Steve Bieser	OF21,C2	L	29	47	69	16	17	3	0	0	4	7	20	2	.246	.346	.290
Iberto Castillo	C34	R	27	35	59	3	12	1	0	0	7	9	16	0	.203	.304	.220
Jason Hardtke	2B21,3B1	S	25	30	56	9	15	2	0	2	8	4	6	1	.268	.323	.411
Shawn Gilbert	2B8,SS6,3B3*	R	29	29	22	3	3	0	0	1	1	1	8	1	.136	.174	.273
Roberto Petagine	1B6,OF1	L	26	12	15	2	1	0	0	0	2	3	6	0	.067	.222	.067
Carlos Mendoza	OF3	L	22	15	12	6	3	0	0	0	1	4	2	0	.250	.500	.250
Andy Tomberlin	OF2	L	30	6	7	0	2	0	0	0	0	1	3	0	.286	.375	.286
Gary Thurman	OF7	R	32	11	6	0	1	0	0	0	0	0	0	0	.167	.167	.167
Kevin Morgan	3B1	R	27	1	1	0	0	0	0	0	0	0	0	0	.000	.000	.000

B. Huskey, 4 G at DH; M. Franco, 1 G at OF; S. Gilbert, 1 G at OF

Pitcher	T	Age	G	GS	CG	ShO	IP	H	HR	BB	SO	W-L	Sv	ERA
Dave Mlicki	R	29	32	32	1	1	193.2	194	21	76	157	8-12	0	4.00
Rick Reed	R	32	33	31	2	0	208.1	186	19	31	113	13-9	0	2.89
Bobby Jones	R	27	30	30	2	1	193.1	177	24	63	125	15-9	0	3.63
Mark Clark†	R	29	23	22	1	0	142.0	158	18	47	72	8-7	0	4.25
Armando Reynoso	R	31	16	16	1	1	91.1	95	7	29	47	6-3	0	4.53
Brian Bohanon	L	28	19	14	0	0	94.1	95	9	34	66	6-4	0	3.82
Jason Isringhausen	R	24	6	6	0	0	29.2	40	3	22	25	2-2	0	7.58
Pete Harnisch†	R	30	6	5	0	0	25.2	35	5	11	12	0-1	0	8.06
Greg McMichael	R	30	73	0	0	0	87.2	73	8	27	81	7-10	7	2.98
John Franco	L	36	59	0	0	0	60.0	49	3	20	53	5-3	36	2.55
Cory Lidle	R	25	54	2	0	0	81.2	86	7	20	54	7-2	2	3.53
Takashi Kashiwada	L	26	35	0	0	0	31.1	35	4	18	19	3-1	0	4.31
Juan Acevedo	R	27	25	2	0	0	47.2	52	6	22	33	3-1	0	3.59
Mel Rojas†	R	30	23	0	0	0	26.1	24	4	6	32	0-2	2	5.13
Ricardo Jordan	L	27	22	0	0	0	27.0	31	1	15	19	1-2	0	5.33
Joe Crawford	L	27	19	2	0	0	46.1	36	7	13	25	4-3	0	3.30
Barry Manuel	R	31	19	0	0	0	25.2	35	6	13	21	0-1	0	5.26
Turk Wendell†	R	30	13	0	0	0	16.1	15	3	14	10	0-0	1	4.96
Toby Borland†	R	28	13	0	0	0	13.1	11	1	14	7	0-1	1	6.08
Ricky Trlicek†	R	28	9	0	0	0	9.0	10	2	5	4	0-0	0	8.00
Yorkis Perez	L	29	9	0	0	0	8.2	15	2	4	7	0-1	0	8.31

1997 Montreal Expos 4th NL East 78-84 .481 23.0 GB

Felipe Alou

Player	Gm by Position	B	Age	G	AB	R	H	2B	3B	HR	RBI	BB	SO	SB	Avg	OBP	Slg
Chris Widger	C85	R	26	91	278	30	65	20	3	7	37	22	59	2	.234	.290	.403
David Segui	1B125	S	30	125	459	75	141	22	3	21	68	57	66	1	.307	.380	.505
Mike Lansing	2B144	R	29	144	572	86	161	45	2	20	70	45	92	11	.281	.338	.472
Doug Strange	3B105,2B3,OF2*	S	33	118	327	40	84	16	2	12	47	36	76	0	.257	.332	.428
Mark Grudzielanek	SS156	R	27	156	649	76	177	54	3	4	51	23	76	25	.273	.307	.384
Rondell White	OF151	R	25	151	592	84	160	29	5	28	82	31	111	16	.270	.316	.478
Henry Rodriguez	OF126,1B3	L	29	132	476	55	116	28	3	26	83	42	149	3	.244	.306	.479
F.P. Santangelo	OF99,3B32,2B7*	S	29	130	350	56	87	19	5	5	31	50	73	8	.249	.379	.374
Vladimir Guerrero	OF85	R	21	90	325	44	98	22	2	11	40	19	39	3	.302	.350	.483
Darrin Fletcher	C83	L	30	96	310	39	86	20	1	17	55	17	35	1	.277	.323	.513
Ryan McGuire	OF44,1B30,DH3	L	25	84	199	22	51	15	2	3	17	19	34	1	.256	.320	.397
Jose Vidro	3B36,DH5,2B5	S	22	67	169	19	42	12	1	2	17	11	20	1	.249	.297	.367
Joe Orsulak	OF63,1B15,DH1	L	35	106	150	13	34	12	1	1	7	18	17	0	.227	.310	.340
Andy Stankiewicz	2B25,SS14,3B3*	R	32	76	107	11	24	9	0	1	5	4	22	1	.224	.250	.336
Shane Andrews	3B18	R	25	18	64	10	13	3	0	4	9	3	20	0	.203	.232	.438
Sherman Obando	OF15,DH2	R	27	41	47	3	6	1	0	2	9	6	14	0	.128	.241	.277
Brad Fullmer	1B8,OF2	L	22	19	40	4	12	2	0	3	8	2	7	0	.300	.349	.575
Raul Chavez	C13	R	24	13	26	0	7	0	0	0	2	0	5	1	.269	.259	.269
Hensley Meulens	OF8,1B3	R	30	16	24	6	7	1	0	2	6	4	10	0	.292	.379	.583
Orlando Cabrera	SS6,2B4	R	22	16	18	4	4	0	0	0	2	1	3	1	.222	.263	.222

D. Strange, 1 G at 1B; F. Santangelo, 1 G at SS; A. Stankiewicz, 2 G at DH

Pitcher	T	Age	G	GS	CG	ShO	IP	H	HR	BB	SO	W-L	Sv	ERA
Carlos Perez	L	26	33	32	8	5	206.2	206	21	48	110	12-13	0	3.88
Pedro Martinez	R	25	31	31	13	4	241.1	158	16	67	305	17-8	0	1.90
Dustin Hermanson	R	24	32	28	1	1	158.1	134	15	66	136	8-8	0	3.69
Jim Bullinger	R	31	36	25	2	2	155.1	165	17	74	87	7-12	0	5.56
Jeff Juden†	R	26	22	22	3	0	130.0	125	17	57	107	11-5	0	4.22
Mike Johnson†	R	21	11	11	0	0	50.0	54	8	21	28	2-5	0	5.94
Rheal Cormier	L	30	1	1	0	0	1.1	4	1	1	0	0-1	0	33.75
Anthony Telford	R	31	65	0	0	0	89.0	77	11	33	61	4-6	1	3.24
Ugueth Urbina	R	23	63	0	0	0	64.1	52	9	29	84	5-8	27	3.78
Dave Veres	R	30	53	0	0	0	62.0	68	5	27	47	2-3	1	3.48
Marc Valdes	R	25	48	7	0	0	95.0	84	2	39	54	4-4	2	3.13
Omar Daal†	L	25	33	0	0	0	30.1	48	4	15	16	1-2	1	9.79
Steve Kline†	L	24	26	0	0	0	26.1	31	4	10	20	1-3	0	6.15
Lee Smith	R	39	25	0	0	0	21.2	28	2	8	15	0-1	5	5.82
Rick DeHart	L	27	23	0	0	0	29.1	33	7	14	29	2-1	0	5.52
Shayne Bennett	R	25	16	0	0	0	22.2	21	2	9	8	0-1	0	3.18
Salomon Torres†	R	25	12	0	0	0	22.1	25	2	12	11	0-0	0	7.25
Jose Paniagua	R	23	9	3	0	0	18.0	29	2	16	8	1-2	0	12.00
Mike Thurman	R	23	5	2	0	0	11.2	8	3	4	8	1-0	0	5.40
Steve Falteisek	R	25	5	0	0	0	8.0	8	0	3	2	0-0	0	3.38
Everett Stull	R	25	3	0	0	0	3.1	7	1	4	2	0-1	0	16.20

964 Seasons: Team Rosters

1997 Philadelphia Phillies 5th NL East 68-94 .420 33.0 GB

Terry Francona

Player	Gm by Position	B	Age	G	AB	R	H	2B	3B	HR	RBI	BB	SO	SB	Avg	OBP	Slg
Mike Lieberthal	C129,DH1	R	25	134	455	59	112	27	1	20	77	44	76	3	.246	.314	.442
Rico Brogna	1B145	L	27	148	543	68	137	36	1	20	81	33	116	12	.252	.293	.433
Mickey Morandini	2B146,SS1	L	31	150	553	83	163	40	2	1	39	62	91	16	.295	.371	.380
Scott Rolen	3B155	R	22	156	561	93	159	35	3	21	92	76	138	16	.283	.377	.469
Kevin Stocker	SS147	S	27	149	504	51	134	23	5	4	40	51	91	11	.266	.335	.355
Gregg Jefferies	OF124	S	29	130	476	68	122	25	3	11	48	53	27	12	.256	.333	.391
Ruben Amaro	OF72,1B1	S	32	117	175	18	41	6	1	2	21	21	24	1	.234	.320	.314
Darren Daulton†	OF70,DH6,1B3	L	35	84	269	46	71	13	6	11	42	54	57	4	.264	.381	.480
Midre Cummings†	OF54	S	25	63	208	24	63	16	4	1	23	23	30	2	.303	.369	.433
Tony Barron	OF53	R	30	57	189	22	54	12	1	4	24	12	38	0	.286	.330	.423
Kevin Jordan	1B25,3B12,2B6*	R	27	84	177	19	47	8	0	6	30	3	26	0	.266	.273	.412
Ricky Otero	OF42	S	25	50	151	20	38	6	2	0	3	19	15	0	.252	.339	.318
Derrick May	OF56	L	28	83	149	8	34	5	1	1	13	8	26	4	.228	.266	.295
Rex Hudler	OF35,2B6	R	36	50	122	17	27	4	0	5	10	6	28	1	.221	.264	.377
Kevin Sefcik	2B22,SS10,3B4	R	26	61	119	11	32	3	0	2	6	4	9	1	.269	.298	.345
Wendell Magee	OF38	R	24	38	115	7	23	4	0	1	9	9	20	1	.200	.254	.261
Mark Parent	C38	R	35	39	113	4	17	3	0	0	8	7	39	0	.150	.198	.177
Rob Butler	OF25	L	27	43	89	10	26	9	1	0	13	5	8	1	.292	.326	.416
Billy McMillon†	OF21	L	25	24	72	10	21	4	1	2	13	6	17	2	.292	.333	.458
Desi Relaford	SS12	S	23	15	38	3	7	1	2	0	6	5	6	3	.184	.279	.316
Mike Robertson	1B5,OF5,DH1	L	26	22	38	3	8	2	1	0	4	0	6	1	.211	.268	.316
Bobby Estalella	C11	R	22	13	29	9	10	1	0	4	9	7	7	0	.345	.472	.793
Danny Tartabull	OF3	R	34	3	7	2	0	0	0	0	0	4	4	0	.000	.364	.000

K. Jordan, 1 G at DH

Pitcher	T	Age	G	GS	CG	ShO	IP	H	HR	BB	SO	W-L	Sv	ERA
Curt Schilling	R	30	35	35	7	2	254.1	208	25	58	319	17-11	0	2.97
Mark Leiter	R	34	31	31	3	0	182.2	216	25	64	148	10-17	0	5.67
Matt Beech	L	25	24	24	0	0	136.2	147	25	57	120	4-9	0	5.07
Garrett Stephenson	R	25	20	18	2	0	117.0	104	11	38	81	8-6	0	3.15
Tyler Green	R	27	14	14	0	0	76.2	72	8	45	58	4-4	0	4.93
Calvin Maduro	R	22	15	13	0	0	71.0	83	12	41	31	3-7	0	7.23
Bobby Munoz	R	29	8	7	0	0	33.1	47	4	15	20	1-5	0	8.91
Mike Grace	R	27	6	6	1	1	39.0	32	3	10	26	3-2	0	3.46
Mark Portugal	R	34	3	3	0	0	13.2	17	0	5	2	0-2	0	4.61
Edgar Ramos	R	22	4	2	0	0	14.0	15	3	6	4	0-2	0	5.14
Ryan Nye	R	24	4	2	0	0	12.0	20	2	9	7	0-2	0	8.25
Jerry Spradlin	R	30	76	0	0	0	81.2	86	9	27	67	4-8	1	4.74
Ricky Bottalico	R	27	69	0	0	0	74.0	68	7	42	89	2-5	34	3.65
Reggie Harris	R	28	50	0	0	0	54.1	55	1	43	45	1-3	0	5.30
Wayne Gomes	R	24	37	0	0	0	42.2	45	4	24	24	5-1	0	5.27
Ron Blazier	R	25	36	0	0	0	53.2	62	8	21	42	1-1	0	5.03
Erik Plantenberg	L	28	35	0	0	0	25.2	25	1	12	12	0-0	0	4.91
Billy Brewer†	L	29	25	0	0	0	22.0	15	2	11	16	1-2	0	3.27
Ken Ryan	R	28	22	0	0	0	20.2	31	5	13	10	1-0	0	9.58
Scott Ruffcorn	R	27	18	4	0	0	39.2	42	4	36	33	0-3	0	7.71
Michael Mimbs	L	28	17	1	0	0	28.2	31	6	27	29	0-3	0	7.53
Ryan Karp	L	27	15	1	0	0	15.0	12	2	9	18	1-1	0	5.40
Darrin Winston	L	30	7	1	0	0	12.0	8	4	3	8	2-0	0	5.25

1997 Houston Astros 1st NL Central 84-78 .519 —

Larry Dierker

Player	Gm by Position	B	Age	G	AB	R	H	2B	3B	HR	RBI	BB	SO	SB	Avg	OBP	Slg
Brad Ausmus	C129	R	28	130	425	45	113	25	1	4	44	38	78	14	.266	.326	.358
Jeff Bagwell	1B159,DH1	R	29	162	566	109	162	40	2	43	135	127	122	31	.286	.425	.592
Craig Biggio	2B160,DH1	R	31	162	619	146	191	37	8	22	81	84	107	47	.309	.415	.501
Sean Berry	3B85,DH3	R	31	96	301	37	77	24	1	8	43	25	53	1	.256	.318	.422
Tim Bogar	SS80,3B14,1B1	R	30	97	241	30	60	14	4	4	30	24	42	4	.249	.320	.390
Luis Gonzalez	OF146,1B1	L	29	152	550	78	142	31	2	10	68	71	67	10	.258	.345	.376
Derek Bell	OF125,DH1	R	28	129	493	67	136	29	3	15	71	40	94	15	.276	.344	.438
Thomas Howard	OF62	S	32	107	255	24	63	16	1	3	22	26	48	1	.247	.323	.353
Ricky Gutierrez	SS64,3B22,2B9	R	27	102	303	33	79	14	4	3	34	21	50	5	.261	.315	.363
Bill Spiers	3B84,SS28,1B8*	L	31	132	291	51	93	27	4	4	48	61	42	10	.320	.438	.481
Chuck Carr†	OF59	S	28	63	192	34	53	11	2	4	17	15	37	11	.276	.333	.417
Bob Abreu	OF53	L	23	59	188	22	47	10	2	3	26	21	48	7	.250	.329	.372
James Mouton	OF61	R	28	86	180	24	38	9	1	3	23	18	30	9	.211	.287	.322
Tony Eusebio	C43	R	30	60	164	12	45	2	0	1	18	19	27	0	.274	.364	.305
Pat Listach	SS31,OF6	S	29	52	132	13	24	2	2	0	6	11	24	4	.182	.247	.227
Ray Montgomery	OF18	R	27	29	68	8	16	4	1	0	4	5	18	0	.235	.276	.324
Richard Hidalgo	OF19	R	21	19	62	8	19	5	0	2	6	4	18	1	.306	.358	.484
Russ Johnson	3B14,2B3	R	24	21	60	7	18	1	0	2	9	6	14	1	.300	.364	.417
Tony Pena†	C8	R	40	9	19	2	4	3	0	0	2	2	3	0	.211	.273	.368
J.R. Phillips	1B3,OF3	L	27	13	15	2	2	0	0	1	4	0	7	0	.133	.125	.333
Luis Rivera	SS6,2B1	R	33	7	13	2	3	0	1	0	3	1	6	0	.231	.286	.385
Ken Ramos	OF2	L	30	14	12	0	0	0	0	0	1	2	0	0	.000	.133	.000
Randy Knorr	C3,1B2	R	28	4	8	1	3	0	0	1	1	0	2	0	.375	.375	.750

B. Spiers, 4 G at 2B

Pitcher	T	Age	G	GS	CG	ShO	IP	H	HR	BB	SO	W-L	Sv	ERA
Darryl Kile	R	28	34	34	6	4	255.2	208	19	94	205	19-7	0	2.57
Mike Hampton	L	24	34	34	7	2	223.0	217	16	77	139	15-10	0	3.83
Chris Holt	R	25	33	32	0	0	209.2	211	17	61	95	8-12	0	3.52
Shane Reynolds	R	29	30	30	2	0	181.0	189	19	47	152	9-10	0	4.23
Donne Wall	R	29	8	8	0	0	41.2	53	8	16	25	2-5	0	6.26
Tommy Greene	R	30	2	2	0	0	9.0	10	2	5	11	0-1	0	7.00
Sid Fernandez	L	34	1	1	0	0	5.0	4	1	2	3	1-0	0	3.60
Billy Wagner	L	26	62	0	0	0	66.1	49	5	30	106	7-8	23	2.85
Tom Martin	L	27	55	0	0	0	56.0	52	2	23	36	5-3	2	2.09
Russ Springer	R	28	54	0	0	0	55.1	48	4	27	74	3-3	3	4.23
Jose Lima	R	24	52	1	0	0	75.0	79	9	16	63	1-6	2	5.28
Ramon Garcia	R	28	42	20	1	1	158.2	155	20	52	120	9-8	1	3.69
Mike Magnante	L	32	40	0	0	0	47.2	39	2	11	43	3-1	1	2.27
John Hudek	R	30	40	0	0	0	40.2	38	8	33	36	1-3	4	5.98
Jose Cabrera	R	25	12	0	0	0	15.1	6	1	6	18	0-0	0	1.17
Blas Minor	R	29	11	0	0	0	12.0	13	1	5	6	1-0	1	4.50
Oscar Henriquez	R	23	4	0	0	0	4.0	2	0	3	3	0-1	0	4.50
Manuel Barrios	R	22	2	0	0	0	3.0	6	0	3	3	0-0	0	12.00

1997 Pittsburgh Pirates 2nd NL Central 79-83 .488 5.0 GB

Gene Lamont

Player	Gm by Position	B	Age	G	AB	R	H	2B	3B	HR	RBI	BB	SO	SB	Avg	OBP	Slg
Jason Kendall	C142	R	23	144	486	71	143	36	4	8	49	49	53	18	.294	.391	.434
Kevin Young	1B77,3B12,OF11	R	28	97	333	59	100	18	3	18	74	16	89	11	.300	.332	.535
Tony Womack	2B152,SS4	L	27	155	641	85	178	26	9	6	50	43	109	60	.278	.326	.374
Joe Randa	3B120,2B13	R	27	126	443	58	134	27	9	7	60	41	64	4	.302	.366	.451
Kevin Polcovich	SS80,2B2,3B1	R	27	84	245	37	67	16	1	4	21	21	45	2	.273	.350	.396
Jose Guillen	OF136	R	21	143	498	58	133	20	5	14	70	17	88	1	.267	.300	.412
Al Martin	OF110	L	29	113	423	64	123	24	7	13	59	45	83	23	.291	.359	.473
J. Allensworth	OF104	R	25	108	369	55	94	18	2	3	43	44	79	14	.255	.340	.339
Dale Sveum	3B47,SS28,1B21*	S	33	126	306	30	80	20	1	12	47	27	81	0	.261	.319	.451
Mark Johnson	1B63,DH1	L	29	78	219	30	47	10	0	4	29	43	78	1	.215	.345	.315
Mark Smith	OF42,1B9,DH5	R	27	71	193	29	55	13	1	9	35	28	36	3	.285	.374	.503
Turner Ward	OF54	S	32	71	167	33	59	16	1	7	33	18	17	4	.353	.420	.587
Adrian Brown	OF38	S	23	48	147	17	28	6	0	1	10	13	18	8	.190	.273	.252
Kevin Elster	SS39	R	32	39	138	14	31	6	2	7	25	21	39	0	.225	.327	.449
Midre Cummings†	OF25	S	25	52	106	11	20	6	2	3	8	8	26	0	.189	.252	.368
Keith Osik	C32,2B4,1B1*	R	28	49	105	10	27	9	1	0	7	9	21	0	.257	.322	.362
Emil Brown	OF42	R	22	66	95	16	17	2	1	2	6	10	32	5	.179	.304	.284
Eddie Williams†	1B26	R	32	30	89	12	22	5	0	3	11	10	24	1	.247	.333	.404
Shawon Dunston†	SS18	R	34	18	71	14	28	4	1	5	16	0	11	3	.394	.389	.690
Freddy Garcia	3B10,1B2	R	24	20	40	4	6	1	0	3	5	2	17	0	.150	.190	.400
Abraham Nunez	SS12,2B9	S	21	19	40	3	9	2	2	0	6	3	10	1	.225	.289	.375
Lou Collier	SS18	R	23	18	37	3	5	0	0	0	3	1	11	1	.135	.158	.135

D. Sveum, 2 G at 2B; K. Osik, 1 G at 3B

Pitcher	T	Age	G	GS	CG	ShO	IP	H	HR	BB	SO	W-L	Sv	ERA
Esteban Loaiza	R	25	33	32	1	0	196.1	214	17	56	122	11-11	0	4.13
Jon Lieber	R	27	33	32	1	0	188.1	193	23	51	160	11-14	0	4.49
Jason Schmidt	R	24	32	32	2	0	187.2	193	16	76	136	10-9	0	4.60
Steve Cooke	L	27	32	32	1	0	167.1	184	15	77	109	9-15	0	4.30
Francisco Cordova	R	25	29	29	2	2	178.2	175	14	49	121	11-8	0	3.63
Rich Loiselle	R	25	72	0	0	0	72.2	76	7	24	66	1-5	29	3.10
Marc Wilkins	R	26	70	0	0	0	75.2	65	7	33	47	9-5	2	3.69
Ricardo Rincon	L	27	62	0	0	0	60.0	51	5	24	71	4-8	4	3.45
Clint Sodowsky	R	24	45	0	0	0	52.0	49	6	34	51	2-2	0	3.63
Matt Ruebel	L	27	44	0	0	0	62.2	77	8	27	50	3-2	0	6.32
Jason Christiansen	L	27	39	0	0	0	33.2	37	2	17	37	3-0	0	2.94
Chris Peters	L	25	31	1	0	0	37.1	38	6	21	17	2-2	0	4.58
David Wainhouse	R	29	25	0	0	0	28.0	34	2	17	21	0-1	0	8.04
Paul Wagner†	R	29	14	0	0	0	16.0	17	3	13	9	0-0	0	3.94
Jose Silva	R	23	11	4	0	0	36.1	52	4	16	30	2-1	0	5.94
Jeff Wallace	L	21	11	0	0	0	12.0	8	0	8	14	0-0	0	0.75
John Ericks	R	29	10	0	0	0	9.1	7	1	4	6	1-0	6	1.93
Jeff Granger	L	25	9	0	0	0	5.0	10	3	8	4	0-0	0	18.00
Ramon Morel†	R	22	5	0	0	0	7.2	11	2	4	4	0-0	0	4.70
Jason Johnson	R	23	3	0	0	0	6.0	10	2	1	3	0-0	0	6.00
Elmer Dessens	R	25	3	0	0	0	3.1	2	0	0	2	0-0	0	0.00

1997 Cincinnati Reds 3rd NL Central 76-86 .469 8.0 GB

Ray Knight (42-54)/Jack McKeon (34-32)

Player	Gm by Position	B	Age	G	AB	R	H	2B	3B	HR	RBI	BB	SO	SB	Avg	OBP	Slg
Joe Oliver	C106,1B4	R	31	111	349	28	90	13	0	14	43	25	58	1	.258	.313	.415
Hal Morris	1B89	L	32	96	333	42	92	20	1	1	33	23	43	3	.276	.328	.351
Bret Boone	2B136	R	28	139	443	40	99	25	1	7	46	45	101	5	.223	.298	.332
Willie Greene	3B103,OF39,1B7*	L	25	151	495	62	125	22	1	26	91	78	111	6	.253	.354	.459
Pokey Reese	SS110,2B8,3B8	R	24	128	397	48	87	15	0	4	26	31	82	25	.219	.284	.287
Deion Sanders	OF113	L	29	115	465	53	127	13	7	5	23	34	67	56	.273	.329	.363
Reggie Sanders	OF85	R	29	86	312	52	79	19	2	19	56	42	93	13	.253	.347	.510
Curtis Goodwin	OF71	L	24	85	265	27	67	11	0	1	12	24	53	22	.253	.316	.306
Eduardo Perez	1B67,OF12,3B8*	R	27	106	297	44	75	18	0	16	52	29	76	5	.253	.321	.475
Eddie Taubensee	C64,OF11,1B7*	L	28	108	254	26	68	18	0	10	34	22	66	0	.268	.323	.457
Lenny Harris	OF42,2B20,3B13*	L	32	120	238	32	65	13	1	3	28	18	18	4	.273	.327	.374
Barry Larkin	SS63,DH2	R	33	73	224	34	71	17	3	4	20	47	24	14	.317	.440	.473
Jon Nunnally†	OF60	L	25	65	201	38	64	12	3	13	35	26	51	7	.318	.400	.602
Chris Stynes	OF38,2B8,3B3	R	24	49	198	31	69	7	1	6	28	11	13	11	.348	.394	.485
Mike Kelly	OF59	R	27	73	140	27	41	13	2	6	19	10	30	6	.293	.338	.543
Terry Pendleton	3B32	S	36	50	113	11	28	9	0	1	17	12	14	2	.248	.320	.354
Jeff Branson†	3B27,2B14,SS11	L	30	65	98	9	15	3	1	1	5	7	23	1	.153	.210	.235
Brook Fordyce	C30,DH1	R	27	47	96	7	20	5	0	1	8	8	15	2	.208	.267	.292
Ruben Sierra†	OF24	S	31	25	90	6	22	5	1	2	7	6	21	0	.244	.292	.389
Eric Owens	OF18,2B2	R	26	27	57	8	15	0	0	0	3	4	11	3	.263	.311	.263
Aaron Boone	3B13,2B1	R	24	16	49	5	12	1	0	0	5	2	5	1	.245	.275	.265
Pat Watkins	OF15	R	24	17	29	2	6	2	0	0	0	0	5	1	.207	.207	.276
Damian Jackson†	SS6,2B3	R	23	12	27	6	6	2	1	1	2	4	7	1	.222	.323	.481
Pete Rose Jr.	3B2,1B1	L	27	11	14	2	2	0	0	0	0	2	9	0	.143	.250	.143
Ozzie Timmons	OF1	R	26	6	9	1	3	1	0	0	0	0	1	0	.333	.333	.444

W. Greene, 3 G at SS; E. Perez, 1 G at DH; E. Taubensee, 3 G at DH; L. Harris, 11 G at 1B

Pitcher	T	Age	G	GS	CG	ShO	IP	H	HR	BB	SO	W-L	Sv	ERA
Mike Morgan	R	37	31	30	1	0	162.0	165	13	49	103	9-12	0	4.78
Dave Burba	R	30	30	27	2	0	160.0	157	22	73	131	11-10	0	4.73
Kent Mercker	L	29	28	25	0	0	144.2	135	16	62	75	8-11	0	3.92
Mike Smiley†	L	32	20	20	0	0	117.0	139	17	31	94	9-10	0	5.23
Brett Tomko	R	24	22	19	0	0	126.0	106	14	47	95	11-7	0	3.43
Pete Schourek	L	28	18	17	0	0	84.2	78	18	38	59	5-8	0	5.42
Gabe White	L	25	12	6	0	0	41.0	39	6	8	25	2-2	1	4.39
Giovanni Carrara	R	29	2	2	0	0	10.1	14	4	6	5	0-1	0	7.84
Jim Crowell	L	23	2	1	0	0	6.1	12	2	5	3	0-1	0	9.95
Stan Belinda	R	30	84	0	0	0	99.1	84	11	33	114	1-5	1	3.71
Jeff Shaw	R	30	78	0	0	0	94.2	79	7	12	74	4-2	42	2.38
Mike Remlinger	L	31	69	12	2	0	124.0	100	11	60	145	8-8	2	4.14
Scott Sullivan	R	26	59	0	0	0	97.1	79	12	30	96	5-3	1	3.24
Hector Carrasco†	R	27	38	0	0	0	51.1	51	3	25	46	1-2	0	3.68
Felix Rodriguez	R	24	26	1	0	0	46.0	48	2	28	34	0-0	0	4.30
Jeff Brantley	R	33	13	0	0	0	11.2	9	2	7	16	1-1	1	3.86
Danny Graves†	R	23	10	0	0	0	14.2	26	0	11	7	0-0	0	6.14
Ricky Bones†	R	28	9	2	0	0	17.2	31	2	11	8	0-1	0	10.19
Kevin Jarvis†	R	27	9	0	0	0	13.1	21	4	7	12	0-1	1	10.13
Pedro A. Martinez	L	28	8	0	0	0	6.2	8	1	7	4	1-1	0	9.45
Scott Winchester	R	24	5	0	0	0	6.0	9	1	2	3	0-0	0	6.00
Richie Lewis†	R	31	4	0	0	0	5.2	4	3	3	4	0-0	0	6.35
Scott Service†	R	30	4	0	0	0	5.1	11	1	1	3	0-0	0	11.81
Jeff Tabaka	L	33	3	0	0	0	2.0	1	1	1	1	0-0	0	4.50
Joey Eischen	L	27	1	0	0	0	1.1	2	0	1	2	0-0	0	6.75

1997 St. Louis Cardinals 4th NL Central 73-89 .451 11.0 GB

Tony La Russa

Player	Gm by Position	B	Age	G	AB	R	H	2B	3B	HR	RBI	BB	SO	SB	Avg	OBP	Slg
Mike Difelice	C91,1B1	R	28	93	260	16	62	10	1	4	30	19	61	1	.238	.297	.331
Dmitri Young	1B74,OF17,DH1	S	23	110	333	38	86	14	3	5	34	38	63	6	.258	.335	.363
Delino DeShields	2B147	L	28	150	572	92	169	26	14	11	58	55	72	55	.295	.357	.448
Gary Gaetti	3B132,1B20,P1	R	38	148	502	63	126	24	1	17	69	36	88	7	.251	.305	.404
Royce Clayton	SS153	R	27	154	576	75	153	39	5	9	61	33	109	30	.266	.306	.398
Ray Lankford	OF131	L	30	133	465	94	137	36	3	31	98	95	125	21	.295	.411	.585
Ron Gant	OF128,DH1	R	32	139	502	68	115	21	4	17	62	58	162	14	.229	.310	.388
Willie McGee	OF81,DH3	S	38	122	300	29	90	19	4	3	38	22	59	8	.300	.347	.420
John Mabry	OF78,1B49,3B1	L	26	116	388	40	110	19	0	5	36	39	77	0	.284	.352	.371
Tom Lampkin	C86	L	33	108	229	28	56	8	1	7	22	28	30	2	.245	.335	.380
Mark McGwire†	1B50	R	33	51	174	38	44	3	0	24	42	43	61	2	.253	.411	.684
Brian Jordan	OF44	R	30	47	145	17	34	5	0	0	10	10	21	6	.234	.311	.269
David Bell	3B35,2B23,SS13	R	24	66	142	9	30	7	2	1	12	10	28	1	.211	.261	.310
Danny Sheaffer	3B30,OF22,C9*	R	35	76	132	10	33	5	0	0	11	8	17	1	.250	.296	.288
Phil Plantier†	OF32	L	28	42	113	13	29	8	0	5	18	11	27	0	.257	.333	.460
Mark Sweeney†	OF25,1B4	L	27	44	61	5	13	3	0	0	4	9	14	0	.213	.319	.262
Tom Pagnozzi	C13,1B2,3B1	R	34	25	50	4	11	3	0	1	8	1	7	0	.220	.235	.340
Eli Marrero	C17	R	23	17	45	4	11	2	0	2	7	2	13	4	.244	.271	.422
Mike Gallego	2B11,SS10,3B7	R	36	27	43	6	7	2	0	0	1	1	6	0	.163	.178	.209
Scott Livingstone†	3B2,DH1,OF1	L	31	42	41	3	7	1	0	0	3	1	10	1	.171	.182	.195
Micah Franklin	OF13	S	25	17	34	6	11	0	0	2	2	3	10	0	.324	.378	.500
Scarborough Green	OF19	R	23	20	31	5	3	0	0	0	1	2	5	0	.097	.152	.097
Luis Ordaz	SS11	R	21	12	22	3	6	1	0	0	1	1	2	3	.273	.304	.318
Roberto Mejia	2B3,OF1	R	25	7	14	0	1	1	0	0	2	0	5	0	.071	.067	.143
Steve Scarsone	2B2,OF2,3B1	R	31	5	10	0	1	0	0	0	0	2	5	1	.100	.250	.100
Mike Gulan	3B3	R	26	5	9	2	0	0	0	0	1	1	5	0	.000	.100	.000
Jeff Berblinger	2B4	R	26	7	5	1	0	0	0	0	0	0	1	0	.000	.000	.000

D. Sheaffer, 3 G at 2B

Pitcher	T	Age	G	GS	CG	ShO	IP	H	HR	BB	SO	W-L	Sv	ERA
Matt Morris	R	22	33	33	3	0	217.0	208	12	69	149	12-9	0	3.19
Todd Stottlemyre	R	32	28	28	0	0	181.0	155	16	65	160	12-9	0	3.88
Andy Benes	R	29	26	26	0	0	177.0	149	9	61	175	10-7	0	3.10
Alan Benes	R	25	23	23	2	0	161.2	128	13	68	160	9-9	0	2.89
Donovan Osborne	L	28	14	14	0	0	80.1	84	10	23	51	3-7	0	4.93
Manny Aybar	R	22	12	12	0	0	68.0	66	8	29	41	2-4	0	4.24
F. Valenzuela†	L	36	5	5	0	0	22.2	22	2	14	10	0-4	0	5.56
Danny Jackson†	L	35	4	4	0	0	18.2	26	3	8	13	1-2	0	7.71
Sean Lowe	R	26	6	4	0	0	17.1	27	2	10	8	0-2	0	9.35
Mike Busby	R	24	3	3	0	0	14.1	24	2	4	6	0-2	0	8.79
Tony Fossas	L	39	71	0	0	0	51.2	62	7	26	41	2-7	0	3.83
John Frascatore	R	27	59	0	0	0	80.0	74	5	33	58	5-2	0	2.48
Dennis Eckersley	R	42	57	0	0	0	53.0	49	9	8	45	1-5	36	3.91
Mark Petkovsek	R	31	55	2	0	0	96.0	109	14	31	51	4-7	2	5.06
T.J. Mathews†	R	27	40	0	0	0	46.0	41	4	18	46	4-4	0	2.15
Rigo Beltran	L	27	35	4	0	0	54.1	47	3	17	50	1-2	1	3.48
Curtis King	R	26	30	0	0	0	29.1	38	0	11	13	4-2	0	2.76
Brady Raggio	R	24	15	4	0	0	31.1	44	1	16	21	1-2	0	6.89
Lance Painter	L	29	14	0	0	0	17.0	13	1	8	11	1-1	0	4.76
Jose Bautista†	R	32	11	0	0	0	12.1	15	2	2	4	0-0	0	6.57
Richard Batchelor†	R	30	10	0	0	0	16.0	21	0	7	8	1-1	0	4.50
Eric Ludwick†	R	25	5	0	0	0	6.2	12	1	6	7	0-1	0	9.45
Rick Honeycutt	L	43	2	0	0	0	2.0	5	0	1	2	0-0	0	13.50
Tom McGraw	L	29	2	0	0	0	1.2	2	0	1	0	0-0	0	0.00
Gary Gaetti	R	38	1	0	0	0	0.1	1	0	0	0	0-0	0	0.00

1997 Chicago Cubs 5th NL Central 68-94 .420 16.0 GB

Jim Riggleman

Player	Gm by Position	B	Age	G	AB	R	H	2B	3B	HR	RBI	BB	SO	SB	Avg	OBP	Slg
Scott Servais	C118,DH2,1B1	R	30	122	385	36	100	21	0	6	45	24	56	0	.260	.311	.361
Mark Grace	1B148	L	33	151	555	87	177	32	5	13	78	88	45	2	.319	.409	.465
Ryne Sandberg	2B126,DH1	R	37	135	447	54	118	26	0	12	64	28	94	7	.264	.308	.403
Kevin Orie	3B112,SS3	R	24	114	364	40	100	23	5	8	44	39	57	2	.275	.350	.431
Shawon Dunston†	SS108,OF7	R	34	114	419	57	119	18	4	9	41	8	64	29	.284	.300	.411
Sammy Sosa	OF161	R	28	162	642	90	161	31	4	36	119	45	174	22	.251	.300	.480
Doug Glanville	OF138	R	26	146	474	79	142	22	5	4	35	24	46	19	.300	.333	.392
Brian McRae†	OF107	S	29	108	417	63	100	27	5	6	28	52	62	14	.240	.329	.372
Rey Sanchez†	SS63,2B32,3B1	R	29	97	205	14	51	9	0	1	12	11	26	4	.249	.287	.307
Tyler Houston	C41,3B12,1B2*	L	26	72	196	15	51	10	0	2	28	9	35	1	.260	.290	.342
Jose Hernandez	3B47,SS21,2B20*	R	27	121	183	33	50	8	5	7	26	14	42	2	.273	.323	.486
Dave Hansen	3B51,1B4,2B1	L	28	90	151	19	47	8	2	3	21	31	32	1	.311	.429	.450
Lance Johnson†	OF39,DH1	L	33	39	145	17	44	6	2	4	15	9	10	5	.303	.342	.455
Dave Clark	OF25,DH4	L	34	102	143	19	43	8	0	5	32	19	34	1	.301	.386	.462
Brant Brown	OF27,1B12	L	26	46	137	15	32	7	1	5	15	7	28	2	.234	.286	.409
Manny Alexander†	SS28,2B4	R	26	33	99	11	29	3	1	1	7	8	16	2	.293	.358	.374
Brooks Kieschnick	OF27	L	25	39	90	9	18	2	0	4	12	12	21	1	.200	.294	.356
Mike Hubbard	C20,3B1	R	26	29	64	4	13	0	0	1	2	2	21	0	.203	.227	.250
Miguel Cairo	2B9,SS2	R	23	16	29	7	7	1	0	0	1	2	3	0	.241	.313	.276
Robin Jennings	OF5	L	25	9	18	1	3	1	0	0	2	0	2	0	.167	.158	.222
Terrell Lowery	OF6	R	26	9	14	2	4	0	0	0	0	3	3	1	.286	.412	.286

T. Houston, 1 G at 2B, 1 G at SS; J. Hernandez, 6 G at OF, 1 G at DH, 1 G at 1B

Pitcher	T	Age	G	GS	CG	ShO	IP	H	HR	BB	SO	W-L	Sv	ERA
Steve Trachsel	R	26	34	34	0	0	201.1	225	32	69	160	8-12	0	4.51
Terry Mulholland†	L	34	25	25	1	0	157.0	162	20	45	74	6-12	0	4.07
Kevin Foster	R	28	26	25	1	0	146.1	141	27	66	118	10-7	0	4.61
Jeremi Gonzalez	R	22	23	23	1	1	144.0	126	16	69	93	11-9	0	4.25
Frank Castillo†	R	28	20	19	0	0	98.0	113	9	44	67	6-9	0	5.42
Kevin Tapani	R	33	13	13	1	1	85.0	77	7	23	55	9-3	0	3.39
Mark Clark†	R	29	9	9	2	0	63.0	55	6	12	51	6-1	0	2.86
Miguel Batista	R	26	11	6	0	0	36.1	36	4	24	27	0-5	0	5.70
Amaury Telemaco	R	23	10	5	0	0	38.0	47	4	11	29	0-3	0	6.16
Dave Swartzbaugh	R	29	2	2	0	0	8.0	12	1	7	4	0-1	0	9.00
Bob Patterson	L	38	76	0	0	0	59.1	47	9	10	58	1-6	0	3.34
Terry Adams	R	24	74	0	0	0	74.0	91	3	40	64	2-9	18	4.62
Kent Bottenfield	R	28	64	0	0	0	84.0	82	13	35	74	2-3	2	3.86
Ramon Tatis	L	24	56	0	0	0	55.2	66	13	29	33	1-1	0	5.34
Mel Rojas†	R	30	54	0	0	0	59.0	54	11	30	61	0-4	13	4.42
Turk Wendell†	R	30	52	0	0	0	60.0	53	4	39	54	3-5	4	4.20
Marc Pisciotta	R	26	24	0	0	0	28.1	20	1	16	21	3-1	0	3.18
Larry Casian†	L	31	12	0	0	0	9.2	16	3	2	7	0-1	0	7.45
Dave Stevens†	R	27	10	0	0	0	9.1	13	0	9	13	0-2	0	9.64
Rodney Myers	R	28	5	1	0	0	9.0	12	1	7	6	0-0	0	6.00
Ramon Morel†	R	22	3	0	0	0	3.2	3	1	3	3	0-0	0	4.91

1997 San Francisco Giants 1st NL West 90-72 .556 —

Dusty Baker

Player	Gm by Position	B	Age	G	AB	R	H	2B	3B	HR	RBI	BB	SO	SB	Avg	OBP	Slg
Rick Wilkins†	C57	L	30	66	190	18	37	5	0	6	23	17	65	0	.195	.257	.316
J.T. Snow	1B156	S	29	157	531	81	149	36	1	28	104	96	124	6	.281	.387	.510
Jeff Kent	2B148,1B13	R	29	155	580	90	145	38	2	29	121	48	133	11	.250	.316	.472
Bill Mueller	3B122	S	26	128	390	51	114	26	3	7	44	48	71	4	.292	.369	.428
Jose Vizcaino	SS147,2B5	S	29	151	568	77	151	19	7	5	50	48	87	8	.266	.323	.350
Barry Bonds	OF159	L	32	159	532	123	155	26	5	40	101	145	87	37	.291	.446	.585
Stan Javier	OF130,1B3	S	33	142	440	69	126	16	4	8	50	56	70	25	.286	.368	.395
Darryl Hamilton	OF118	L	32	125	460	78	124	23	3	5	43	61	61	15	.270	.354	.365
Glenallen Hill	OF97,DH7	R	32	128	398	47	104	28	4	11	64	19	87	7	.261	.297	.435
Mark Lewis	3B69,2B29,DH1	R	27	118	341	50	91	14	6	10	42	23	62	3	.267	.318	.431
Brian Johnson†	C55,1B2	R	29	56	179	19	50	7	2	11	27	14	26	0	.279	.333	.525
Damon Berryhill	C51,1B1	S	33	73	167	17	43	8	0	3	23	20	29	0	.257	.335	.359
Marvin Benard	OF36,DH1	L	27	84	114	13	26	4	0	1	13	13	29	3	.228	.315	.289
Rich Aurilia	SS36	R	25	46	102	16	28	8	0	5	19	8	15	1	.275	.321	.500
Marcus Jensen†	C28	S	24	30	74	5	11	2	0	1	3	7	23	0	.149	.222	.216
Dante Powell	OF22	R	23	27	39	8	12	1	0	1	3	4	11	1	.308	.372	.410
Jacob Cruz	OF11	L	24	16	25	3	4	1	0	0	3	3	4	0	.160	.241	.200
Doug Mirabelli	C6	R	26	6	7	0	1	0	0	0	0	1	3	0	.143	.250	.143
Wilson Delgado	2B3,SS1	S	21	8	7	1	1	1	0	0	0	0	2	0	.143	.143	.286

Pitcher	T	Age	G	GS	CG	ShO	IP	H	HR	BB	SO	W-L	Sv	ERA
Shawn Estes	L	24	32	32	3	2	201.0	162	12	100	181	19-5	0	3.18
Kirk Rueter	L	26	32	32	0	0	190.2	194	17	51	115	13-6	0	3.45
Mark Gardner	R	35	30	30	2	1	180.1	188	28	57	136	12-9	0	4.29
W. VanLandingham	R	26	18	17	0	0	89.0	80	11	59	52	4-7	0	4.96
Wilson Alvarez†	L	27	11	11	0	0	66.1	54	9	36	69	4-3	0	4.48
Osvaldo Fernandez	R	28	11	11	0	0	56.1	74	9	15	31	3-4	0	4.95
Keith Foulke†	R	24	11	8	0	0	44.2	60	9	18	33	1-5	0	8.26
Danny Darwin†	R	41	10	7	0	0	44.0	51	5	14	30	1-3	0	4.91
Pat Rapp†	R	29	8	6	0	0	33.0	37	5	21	28	1-2	0	6.00
Doug Creek	L	28	3	3	0	0	13.1	12	1	14	14	1-2	0	6.75
Julian Tavarez	R	24	89	0	0	0	88.1	91	6	34	38	6-4	0	3.87
Doug Henry	R	33	75	0	0	0	70.2	70	5	41	69	4-5	3	4.71
Rod Beck	R	28	73	0	0	0	70.0	67	7	8	53	7-4	37	3.47
Rich Rodriguez	L	34	71	0	0	0	65.1	65	7	21	32	4-3	1	3.17
Jim Poole	L	31	63	0	0	0	49.1	73	6	25	26	3-1	0	7.11
Joe Roa	R	25	28	3	0	0	65.2	86	8	20	34	2-5	0	5.21
R. Hernandez†	R	32	28	0	0	0	32.2	29	2	14	35	5-2	4	2.48
Terry Mulholland†	L	34	15	2	0	0	29.2	28	4	6	25	0-1	0	5.16
John Johnstone†	R	28	13	0	0	0	18.2	15	1	7	15	0-0	0	3.38
Cory Bailey	R	26	7	0	0	0	9.2	15	1	4	5	0-1	0	8.38
Dan Carlson	R	27	6	0	0	0	15.1	20	5	8	14	0-0	0	7.63
Rene Arocha	R	31	6	0	0	0	10.1	17	2	5	7	0-0	0	11.32
Rich DeLucia†	R	32	3	0	0	0	1.2	6	0	0	2	0-0	0	10.80

1997 Los Angeles Dodgers 2nd NL West 88-74 .543 2.0 GB

Bill Russell

Player	Gm by Position	B	Age	G	AB	R	H	2B	3B	HR	RBI	BB	SO	SB	Avg	OBP	Slg
Mike Piazza	C139,DH7	R	28	152	556	104	201	32	1	40	124	69	77	5	.362	.431	.638
Eric Karros	1B162	R	29	162	628	86	167	28	0	31	104	61	116	15	.266	.329	.459
Wilton Guerrero	2B90,SS5	R	22	111	357	39	104	10	9	4	32	8	52	6	.291	.305	.403
Todd Zeile	3B160	R	31	160	575	89	154	17	0	31	90	85	112	8	.268	.365	.459
Greg Gagne	SS143	R	35	144	514	49	129	20	3	9	57	31	120	2	.251	.298	.354
Raul Mondesi	OF159	R	26	159	616	95	191	42	5	30	87	44	105	32	.310	.360	.541
Todd Hollandsworth	OF99	L	24	106	296	39	73	20	2	4	31	17	60	5	.247	.286	.368
Brett Butler	OF91,DH1	L	40	105	343	52	97	8	3	0	18	42	40	15	.283	.363	.324
Roger Cedeno	OF71	S	22	80	194	31	53	10	2	3	17	25	44	9	.273	.362	.392
Otis Nixon†	OF42	S	38	42	175	30	48	6	2	1	18	13	24	12	.274	.323	.349
Eric Young†	2B37	R	30	37	154	28	42	4	2	2	16	14	17	13	.273	.347	.364
Billy Ashley	OF35	R	26	71	131	12	32	7	0	6	19	8	46	0	.244	.293	.435
Tom Prince	C45	R	32	47	100	17	22	5	0	3	14	5	15	0	.220	.275	.360
Nelson Liriano	2B17,1B2,3B1*	S	33	76	88	10	20	6	0	1	11	6	12	0	.227	.274	.330
Tripp Cromer	2B17,SS10,3B1	R	29	28	86	8	25	3	0	4	20	6	16	0	.291	.333	.465
Darren Lewis†	OF25	R	29	26	77	7	23	3	1	1	10	6	17	3	.299	.349	.403
Juan Castro	SS22,2B14,3B3	R	25	40	75	3	11	3	1	0	4	7	20	0	.147	.220	.213
Eric Anthony	OF21	L	29	47	74	8	18	3	2	2	5	12	18	2	.243	.349	.419
Wayne Kirby	OF26	L	33	46	65	6	11	2	0	0	4	10	12	0	.169	.280	.200
Karim Garcia	OF12	L	21	15	39	5	5	0	0	1	8	6	14	0	.128	.239	.205
Adam Riggs	2B8	R	24	9	20	3	4	1	0	0	1	4	3	1	.200	.333	.250
Chad Fonville†	2B3	S	26	9	14	1	2	0	0	0	1	2	3	0	.143	.250	.143
Chip Hale	3B2	L	32	14	12	0	1	0	0	0	0	2	4	0	.083	.214	.083
Garey Ingram	OF7	R	26	12	9	2	4	0	0	0	1	1	3	1	.444	.500	.444
Eddie Murray†		S	41	9	7	0	2	0	0	0	3	2	2	0	.286	.444	.286
Eddie Williams†		R	32	8	7	0	1	0	0	0	1	1	1	0	.143	.250	.143
Paul Konerko	1B1,3B1	R	21	6	7	0	1	0	0	0	0	1	2	0	.143	.250	.143
Henry Blanco	1B1,3B1	R	25	3	5	1	2	0	0	1	1	0	1	0	.400	.400	1.000

N. Liriano, 1 G at SS

Pitcher	T	Age	G	GS	CG	ShO	IP	H	HR	BB	SO	W-L	Sv	ERA
Hideo Nomo	R	28	33	33	1	0	207.1	193	23	92	233	14-12	0	4.25
Ismael Valdes	R	23	30	30	0	0	196.2	171	16	47	140	10-11	0	2.65
Chan Ho Park	R	24	32	29	2	0	192.0	149	24	70	166	14-8	0	3.38
Pedro Astacio†	R	28	26	24	2	1	153.2	151	15	47	115	7-9	0	4.10
Ramon Martinez	R	29	22	22	1	0	133.2	123	14	68	120	10-5	0	3.64
Scott Radinsky	L	29	75	0	0	0	62.1	54	4	21	44	5-1	3	2.89
Todd Worrell	R	37	65	0	0	0	59.2	60	12	23	61	2-6	35	5.28
Darren Hall	R	32	63	0	0	0	54.2	58	3	26	39	3-2	2	2.30
Mark Guthrie	R	31	62	0	0	0	69.1	71	12	30	42	1-4	1	5.32
Darren Dreifort	R	25	48	0	0	0	63.0	45	3	34	63	5-2	4	2.86
Antonio Osuna	R	24	48	0	0	0	61.2	46	6	19	68	3-4	0	2.19
Tom Candiotti	R	39	41	18	0	0	135.0	128	21	40	89	10-7	0	3.60
Dennis Reyes	L	20	14	5	0	0	47.0	51	4	18	36	2-3	0	3.83
Mike Harkey	R	30	10	0	0	0	14.2	12	3	5	6	1-0	0	4.30
Rick Gorecki	R	23	4	1	0	0	6.0	9	3	6	6	1-0	0	15.00
Mike Judd	R	22	1	0	0	0	2.2	4	0	0	4	0-0	0	0.00

1997 Colorado Rockies 3rd NL West 83-79 .512 7.0 GB — Don Baylor

Player	Gm by Position	B	Age	G	AB	R	H	2B	3B	HR	RBI	BB	SO	SB	Avg	OBP	Slg
Kirt Manwaring	C100	R	31	104	337	22	76	6	4	1	27	30	78	1	.226	.291	.276
Andres Galarraga	1B154	R	36	154	600	120	191	31	3	41	140	54	141	15	.318	.389	.585
Eric Young†	2B117	R	30	118	468	78	132	29	6	6	45	57	37	32	.282	.363	.408
Vinny Castilla	3B157	R	29	159	612	94	186	25	2	40	113	44	108	2	.304	.356	.547
Walt Weiss	SS119	S	33	121	393	52	106	23	5	4	38	66	56	5	.270	.377	.384
Larry Walker	OF151,1B3,DH1	L	30	153	568	143	208	46	4	49	130	78	90	33	.366	.452	.720
Dante Bichette	OF139,DH5	R	33	151	561	81	173	31	2	26	118	30	90	6	.308	.343	.510
Quinton McCracken	OF132	S	27	147	325	69	95	11	1	3	36	42	62	28	.292	.374	.360
Ellis Burks	OF112	R	32	119	424	91	123	19	2	32	82	47	75	7	.290	.363	.571
Neifi Perez	SS45,2B41,3B2	S	22	83	313	46	91	13	10	5	31	21	43	4	.291	.333	.444
Jeff Reed	C78	L	34	90	256	43	76	10	0	17	47	35	55	2	.297	.386	.535
Jason Bates	2B22,SS16,3B6	S	26	62	121	17	29	10	0	3	11	15	27	0	.240	.338	.397
Todd Helton	1B8	L	23	35	93	13	26	2	1	5	11	8	11	0	.280	.337	.484
John VanderWal	OF9,1B5,DH2	L	31	76	92	7	16	2	0	1	11	10	33	1	.174	.255	.228
Harvey Pulliam	OF33	R	29	59	67	15	19	3	0	3	9	5	15	0	.284	.333	.463
Darnell Coles	3B3,OF2	R	35	21	22	1	7	1	0	1	2	0	6	0	.318	.348	.500
Angel Echevarria	OF7	R	26	15	20	4	5	2	0	0	0	2	5	0	.250	.318	.350
Brian Raabe†	2B1	R	29	2	3	0	1	0	0	0	0	0	1	0	.333	.333	.333
Rene Gonzales	3B1	R	36	2	2	0	1	0	0	0	1	0	0	0	.500	.500	.500
Craig Counsell†		L	26	1	0	0	0	0	0	0	0	0	0	0	—	—	—

Pitcher	T	Age	G	GS	CG	ShO	IP	H	HR	BB	SO	W-L	Sv	ERA
Roger Bailey	R	26	29	29	5	2	191.0	210	27	70	84	9-10	0	4.29
John Thomson	R	23	27	27	2	1	166.1	193	15	51	106	7-9	0	4.71
Jamey Wright	R	22	26	26	1	0	149.2	198	19	71	59	8-12	0	6.25
Kevin Ritz	R	32	18	18	1	0	107.1	142	16	46	56	6-8	0	5.87
Frank Castillo†	R	28	14	14	0	0	86.1	107	16	25	59	6-3	0	5.42
Bill Swift	R	35	14	13	0	0	65.1	85	11	26	29	4-6	0	6.34
John Burke	R	27	17	9	0	0	59.0	83	13	26	39	2-5	0	6.56
Pedro Astacio†	R	28	7	7	0	0	48.2	49	9	14	51	5-1	0	4.25
Mark Thompson	R	26	6	6	0	0	29.2	40	8	13	9	3-3	0	7.89
Bobby M. Jones	L	25	4	4	0	0	19.1	30	2	12	5	1-1	0	8.38
Bryan Rekar	R	25	2	2	0	0	9.1	11	3	6	4	1-0	0	5.79
Jerry Dipoto	R	29	74	0	0	0	95.2	108	6	33	74	5-3	16	4.70
Mike Munoz	L	31	64	0	0	0	45.2	52	4	13	26	3-3	2	4.53
Steve Reed	R	31	63	0	0	0	62.1	49	10	27	43	4-6	6	4.04
Mike DeJean	R	26	55	0	0	0	67.2	74	4	24	38	5-0	2	3.99
Curt Leskanic	R	29	55	0	0	0	58.1	59	8	24	53	4-0	2	5.55
Darren Holmes	R	31	42	6	0	0	89.1	113	12	36	70	9-2	3	5.34
Jeff McCurry	R	27	33	0	0	0	40.2	43	7	20	19	1-4	0	4.43
Bruce Ruffin	L	33	23	0	0	0	22.0	18	3	18	31	0-2	7	5.32
Mark Hutton†	R	27	8	1	0	0	12.2	22	3	7	10	0-1	0	7.11
Tim Scott†	R	30	3	0	0	0	2.2	5	0	2	2	0-0	0	10.13
Nate Minchey	R	27	2	0	0	0	2.0	5	0	1	1	0-0	0	13.50
Robbie Beckett	L	24	2	0	0	0	1.2	1	0	1	2	0-0	0	5.40

1997 San Diego Padres 4th NL West 76-86 .469 14.0 GB — Bruce Bochy

Player	Gm by Position	B	Age	G	AB	R	H	2B	3B	HR	RBI	BB	SO	SB	Avg	OBP	Slg
John Flaherty	C124	R	29	129	439	38	120	21	1	9	46	33	62	4	.273	.323	.387
Wally Joyner	1B131	L	35	135	455	59	149	29	2	13	83	51	51	3	.327	.390	.486
Quilvio Veras	2B142	S	26	145	539	74	143	23	1	3	45	72	84	33	.265	.357	.328
Ken Caminiti	3B133	S	34	137	486	92	141	28	0	26	90	80	118	11	.290	.389	.508
Chris Gomez	SS149	R	26	150	522	62	132	19	2	5	54	53	114	5	.253	.326	.326
Tony Gwynn	OF143,DH3	L	37	149	592	97	220	49	2	17	119	43	28	12	.372	.409	.547
Steve Finley	OF140	L	32	143	560	101	146	26	5	28	92	43	92	15	.261	.313	.475
Greg Vaughn	OF94,DH3	R	31	120	361	60	78	10	0	18	57	56	110	7	.216	.322	.393
Rickey Henderson†	OF78,DH2	R	38	88	288	63	79	11	0	6	27	71	62	29	.274	.422	.375
Archi Cianfrocco	1B39,3B38,2B12*	R	30	89	220	25	54	12	0	4	26	25	80	7	.245	.328	.355
Chris Jones	OF61	R	31	92	152	24	37	9	0	7	25	16	45	7	.243	.322	.441
Craig Shipley	SS21,2B16,1B4*	R	34	63	139	22	38	9	0	5	19	7	20	1	.273	.306	.446
Carlos Hernandez	C44,1B4	R	30	50	134	15	42	7	1	3	14	3	27	0	.313	.328	.448
Mark Sweeney†	OF20,1B7	L	27	71	103	11	33	4	0	2	19	11	18	2	.320	.383	.417
Trey Beamon	OF20	L	23	43	65	5	18	3	0	0	7	2	17	1	.277	.309	.323
Derrek Lee	1B21	R	21	22	54	9	14	3	0	1	4	9	24	0	.259	.365	.370
Mandy Romero	C19	S	29	21	48	7	10	0	0	2	4	2	18	1	.208	.240	.333
Terry Shumpert	2B7,OF3,3B2	R	30	13	33	4	9	3	0	1	6	3	4	0	.273	.324	.455
Jorge Velandia	SS6,2B5,3B3	R	22	14	29	0	3	2	0	0	1	7	0		.103	.133	.172
Scott Livingstone†	3B3,1B2,2B1	L	31	23	26	1	4	1	0	0	3	2	1	0	.154	.214	.192
George Arias†	3B8	R	25	11	22	2	5	1	0	0	2	0	1	0	.227	.227	.273
Don Slaught	C6	R	38	20	20	2	0	0	0	0	0	5	4	0	.000	.200	.000
Ruben Rivera	OF7	R	23	17	20	2	5	1	0	1	2	9	2		.250	.318	.300
Phil Plantier†	OF3	L	28	10	8	0	1	0	0	0	0	2	3	0	.125	.300	.125

Pitcher	T	Age	G	GS	CG	ShO	IP	H	HR	BB	SO	W-L	Sv	ERA
Andy Ashby	R	29	30	30	2	0	200.2	207	17	49	144	9-11	0	4.13
Joey Hamilton	R	26	31	29	1	0	192.2	199	22	69	124	12-7	0	4.25
Sterling Hitchcock	L	26	32	28	1	0	161.0	172	24	55	106	10-11	0	5.20
F. Valenzuela†	L	36	13	13	1	0	66.1	84	10	32	51	2-8	0	4.75
Danny Jackson†	L	35	13	9	0	0	49.0	72	8	20	19	1-7	0	7.53
Paul Menhart	R	28	9	8	0	0	44.0	42	6	13	22	2-3	0	4.70
Trevor Hoffman	R	29	70	0	0	0	81.1	59	9	24	111	2-3	37	2.66
Tim Worrell	R	29	60	10	0	0	106.1	116	14	50	81	4-8	3	5.16
Will Cunnane	R	23	54	8	0	0	91.1	114	11	49	79	6-3	0	5.81
Doug Bochtler	R	26	54	0	0	0	60.1	51	3	50	46	3-6	2	4.77
Sean Bergman	R	27	44	9	0	0	99.0	126	11	38	74	2-4	0	6.09
Pete Smith	R	31	37	15	0	0	118.0	120	16	52	68	7-6	1	4.81
Jim Bruske	R	32	28	0	0	0	44.2	37	4	25	32	4-1	0	3.63
Dario Veras	R	24	24	0	0	0	24.2	28	5	12	21	2-1	0	5.11
Heath Murray	L	24	17	3	0	0	33.1	50	3	21	16	1-2	0	6.75
Tim Scott†	R	30	14	0	0	0	18.1	25	2	5	14	1-1	0	7.85
Richard Batchelor†	R	30	13	0	0	0	12.2	19	2	7	10	2-0	0	7.82
Terry Burrows	L	28	13	0	0	0	10.1	12	1	8	8	0-2	0	10.45
Marc Kroon	R	24	12	0	0	0	11.1	14	2	5	12	0-1	0	7.15
Todd Erdos	R	23	11	0	0	0	13.2	17	1	4	13	2-0	0	5.27
Joey Long	L	26	10	0	0	0	11.0	17	1	8	8	0-0	0	8.18

A. Cianfrocco, 5 G at SS, 2 G at OF; C. Shipley, 2 G at 3B.

Leaders

Career

We list the top 100 career totals in 32 batting and 28 pitching categories. Minimums for the percentage categories are 3,000 plate appearances for hitters and 200 decisions (winning percentage only) or 1,500 innings for pitchers.

Season

As with the Career leaders, we provide the top 100 single-season performances in 32 hitting and 28 pitching categories. Minimums for the percentage categories are 3.1 plate appearances per team game for batters and 15 decisions (winning percentage only) or one inning per team game for pitchers, regardless of the qualifying rules in use at that time. Several of the Season pitching leader boards were dominated by pitchers from the 1800s, so we have a separate listing for 20th- century pitchers for 12 categories.

Rookie

We show the top 20 rookie leaders in 16 hitting and 16 pitching categories, using the same minimums for percentage categories detailed in the Season section. A player's rookie season is defined as the year in which he exceeds 130 at-bats or 50 innings pitched for his career.

Decade

For each decade in major league history, we provide the top 10 performances in 28 batting and 28 pitching categories, both for the decade as a whole and for a single season. For the entire decade, minimums for the percentage categories are 3,000 plate appearances for hitters and 100 decisions (winning percentage only) or 1,000 innings for pitchers. For single seasons, we use the same minimums detailed in the Season section. Because the National League played just four seasons in the 1870s, we combined that decade with the 1880s.

Age

We also show the top 10 leaders by age in 12 hitting and 12 pitching categories, from both a career and season standpoint. We have career leaders through each age from 18-42, as well as after ages 29, 34, 39 and 42. Minimums for the percentage categories increase as the ages do and are explained on the leader boards. For seasons, we show leaders for age 18 or younger, each age from 19-42 and after ages 30, 35, 40 and 43. The minimums for these percentage categories are the same as in the Season section.

Period

For 28 batting and 24 pitching categories, we show leaders over every period of time from two to 10 years. Sixteen batting and sixteen pitching leader boards are top 15s, while the others list only the top performer. Minimums for the percentage categories increase as the periods do and are explained on the leader boards. To qualify for a period, a played had to play in the first and last year of the span but not necessarily in between.

RC/27

For each league each year, we display the top hitter in terms of runs created per 27 outs at each of the eight non-pitching positions (including the top three outfielders rather than one left, center and right fielder). We also include a designated hitter for the American League since 1973, when the DH was used for the first time. The minimum to qualify at any position is 3.1 plate appearances per team game.

Relativity

In this section, we identify the top 50 players at eight positions: catcher, first baseman, second baseman, third baseman, shortstop, outfielder, starting pitcher and relief pitcher. Hitters are ranked in order of the ratio of their of runs created per 27 outs to their league runs created per 27 outs over the course of their career. Pitchers are ranked in order of the ratio of their league earned run average to their component earned run average. Both of these ratios are expressed as a relativity quotient (RQ), with an RQ of 100 indicating an average performer. League runs created per 27 outs or earned run average is weighted on the batter or pitcher's playing time each year of his career. The minimums to qualify for this section are 750 games for catchers, 1,000 games for other position players, 1,500 innings for starting pitchers and 300 games for relief pitchers. Hitters are listed at their primary position. A starting pitcher is defined as a pitcher who started in at least half his career appearances.

Fielding

We provide fielding leaders for seven basic categories for each of the seven positions (pitcher, catcher, first baseman, second baseman, third baseman, shortstop and outfielder). We also include passed balls for catchers and range factors for second basemen, third basemen, shortstop and outfielders. We list the top 100 performers for a career and the top 20 for a season. We also break down baseball into six eras and provide top 20 career and single-season lists for each. Overall career minimums for percentage categories are 500 games for pitchers, 750 games for catchers and 1,000 games for other positions. Era career minimums are 150 games for pitchers, 500 games for catchers and 750 games for other positions. Season minimums for percentage categories are 25 games for pitchers and 100 games for other positions for both the overall and era lists.

Abbreviations & Formulas

A complete list of team and statistical abbreviations are listed in the back of the book, along with an appendix explaining formulas and the availability of certain statistics.

Batting Leaders—Career

	Games			At-Bats			Runs			Hits	
1	Pete Rose	3,562	1	Pete Rose	14,053	1	Ty Cobb	2,245	1	Pete Rose	4,256
2	Carl Yastrzemski	3,308	2	Hank Aaron	12,364	2	Hank Aaron	2,174	2	Ty Cobb	4,190
3	Hank Aaron	3,298	3	Carl Yastrzemski	11,988		Babe Ruth	2,174	3	Hank Aaron	3,771
4	Ty Cobb	3,034	4	Ty Cobb	11,434	4	Pete Rose	2,165	4	Stan Musial	3,630
5	Eddie Murray	3,026	5	Eddie Murray	11,336	5	Willie Mays	2,062	5	Tris Speaker	3,514
	Stan Musial	3,026	6	Robin Yount	11,008	6	Stan Musial	1,949	6	Carl Yastrzemski	3,419
7	Willie Mays	2,992	7	Dave Winfield	11,003	7	Rickey Henderson	1,913	7	Honus Wagner	3,415
8	Dave Winfield	2,973	8	Stan Musial	10,972	8	Lou Gehrig	1,888	8	Eddie Collins	3,312
9	Rusty Staub	2,951	9	Willie Mays	10,881	9	Tris Speaker	1,882	9	Willie Mays	3,283
10	Brooks Robinson	2,896	10	Brooks Robinson	10,654	10	Mel Ott	1,859	10	Eddie Murray	3,255
11	Robin Yount	2,856	11	Honus Wagner	10,430	11	Frank Robinson	1,829	11	Nap Lajoie	3,242
12	Al Kaline	2,834	12	George Brett	10,349	12	Eddie Collins	1,821	12	Paul Molitor	3,178
13	Eddie Collins	2,826	13	Paul Molitor	10,333	13	Carl Yastrzemski	1,816	13	George Brett	3,154
14	Reggie Jackson	2,820	14	Lou Brock	10,332	14	Ted Williams	1,798	14	Paul Waner	3,152
15	Frank Robinson	2,808	15	Luis Aparicio	10,230	15	Charlie Gehringer	1,774	15	Robin Yount	3,142
16	Honus Wagner	2,792	16	Tris Speaker	10,195	16	Jimmie Foxx	1,751	16	Dave Winfield	3,110
17	Tris Speaker	2,789	17	Al Kaline	10,116	17	Honus Wagner	1,736	17	Rod Carew	3,053
18	Tony Perez	2,777	18	Rabbit Maranville	10,078	18	Jesse Burkett	1,720	18	Lou Brock	3,023
19	Mel Ott	2,730	19	Frank Robinson	10,006	19	Willie Keeler	1,719	19	Al Kaline	3,007
20	George Brett	2,707	20	Eddie Collins	9,948		Cap Anson	1,719	20	Roberto Clemente	3,000
21	Graig Nettles	2,700	21	Andre Dawson	9,927	21	Paul Molitor	1,707	21	Cap Anson	2,995
22	Darrell Evans	2,687	22	Reggie Jackson	9,864	22	Billy Hamilton	1,690	22	Sam Rice	2,987
23	Rabbit Maranville	2,670	23	Cal Ripken Jr.	9,832	23	Bid McPhee	1,678	23	Sam Crawford	2,961
24	Joe Morgan	2,649	24	Tony Perez	9,778	24	Mickey Mantle	1,677	24	Frank Robinson	2,943
25	Andre Dawson	2,627	25	Rusty Staub	9,720	25	Dave Winfield	1,669	25	Willie Keeler	2,932
26	Lou Brock	2,616	26	Vada Pinson	9,645	26	Joe Morgan	1,650	26	Rogers Hornsby	2,930
27	Dwight Evans	2,606	27	Nap Lajoie	9,589	27	Jimmy Ryan	1,642		Jake Beckley	2,930
28	Luis Aparicio	2,599	28	Sam Crawford	9,571	28	George Van Haltren	1,639	28	Al Simmons	2,927
29	Willie McCovey	2,588	29	Jake Beckley	9,526	29	Robin Yount	1,632	29	Zack Wheat	2,884
30	Ozzie Smith	2,573	30	Paul Waner	9,459	30	Eddie Murray	1,627	30	Frankie Frisch	2,880
31	Paul Molitor	2,557	31	Mel Ott	9,456	31	Paul Waner	1,626	31	Mel Ott	2,876
32	Paul Waner	2,549	32	Roberto Clemente	9,454	32	Al Kaline	1,622	32	Babe Ruth	2,873
33	Cal Ripken Jr.	2,543	33	Ernie Banks	9,421	33	Roger Connor	1,620	33	Jesse Burkett	2,850
34	Ernie Banks	2,528	34	Bill Buckner	9,397	34	Fred Clarke	1,619	34	Brooks Robinson	2,848
35	Bill Buckner	2,517	35	Ozzie Smith	9,396	35	Lou Brock	1,610	35	Charlie Gehringer	2,839
	Sam Crawford	2,517	36	Max Carey	9,363	36	Jake Beckley	1,600	36	George Sisler	2,812
37	Babe Ruth	2,503	37	Dave Parker	9,358	37	Ed Delahanty	1,599	37	Wade Boggs	2,800
38	Carlton Fisk	2,499	38	Billy Williams	9,350	38	Bill Dahlen	1,589	38	Tony Gwynn	2,780
39	Dave Concepcion	2,488	39	Rod Carew	9,315	39	George Brett	1,583	39	Andre Dawson	2,774
	Billy Williams	2,488	40	Joe Morgan	9,277	40	Rogers Hornsby	1,579	40	Vada Pinson	2,757
41	Nap Lajoie	2,480	41	Sam Rice	9,269	41	Hugh Duffy	1,552	41	Luke Appling	2,749
42	Max Carey	2,476	42	Nellie Fox	9,232	42	Reggie Jackson	1,551	42	Al Oliver	2,743
43	Rod Carew	2,469	43	Willie Davis	9,174	43	Max Carey	1,545	43	Goose Goslin	2,735
	Vada Pinson	2,469	44	Doc Cramer	9,140	44	George Davis	1,539	44	Tony Perez	2,732
45	Dave Parker	2,466	45	Frankie Frisch	9,112	45	Frankie Frisch	1,532	45	Lou Gehrig	2,721
46	Harold Baines	2,463	46	Zack Wheat	9,106	46	Dan Brouthers	1,523	46	Rusty Staub	2,716
47	Rickey Henderson	2,460	47	Cap Anson	9,101	47	Tom Brown	1,521	47	Bill Buckner	2,715
48	Ted Simmons	2,456	48	Lave Cross	9,068	48	Sam Rice	1,514		Cal Ripken Jr.	2,715
49	Bill Dahlen	2,443	49	Al Oliver	9,049	49	Eddie Mathews	1,509	49	Dave Parker	2,712
50	Ron Fairly	2,442	50	Bill Dahlen	9,031	50	Al Simmons	1,507	50	Billy Williams	2,711
51	Harmon Killebrew	2,435		George Davis	9,031	51	Mike Schmidt	1,506	51	Doc Cramer	2,705
52	Roberto Clemente	2,433	52	Dwight Evans	8,996	52	Nap Lajoie	1,504	52	Luis Aparicio	2,677
53	Willie Davis	2,429	53	Buddy Bell	8,995	53	Harry Stovey	1,492	53	Fred Clarke	2,672
54	Luke Appling	2,422	54	Graig Nettles	8,986	54	Goose Goslin	1,483	54	Max Carey	2,665
55	Zack Wheat	2,410	55	Darrell Evans	8,973	55	Arlie Latham	1,478	55	Nellie Fox	2,663
56	Mickey Vernon	2,409	56	Rickey Henderson	8,931	56	Tim Raines	1,475	56	Harry Heilmann	2,660
57	Buddy Bell	2,405	57	Charlie Gehringer	8,860	57	Dwight Evans	1,470		George Davis	2,660
58	Mike Schmidt	2,404	58	Luke Appling	8,857	58	Herman Long	1,455	58	Ted Williams	2,654
	Sam Rice	2,404	59	Steve Garvey	8,835	59	Jim O'Rourke	1,446	59	Jimmie Foxx	2,646
60	Mickey Mantle	2,401	60	Harold Baines	8,818	60	Cal Ripken Jr.	1,445	60	Lave Cross	2,644
61	Eddie Mathews	2,391	61	Tommy Corcoran	8,804	61	Harry Hooper	1,429	61	Rabbit Maranville	2,605
62	Lou Whitaker	2,390	62	Harry Hooper	8,785	62	Dummy Hoy	1,426	62	Steve Garvey	2,599
63	Jake Beckley	2,386	63	Al Simmons	8,761	63	Rod Carew	1,424	63	Ed Delahanty	2,597
64	Bobby Wallace	2,383	64	Carlton Fisk	8,756	64	Wade Boggs	1,422	64	Reggie Jackson	2,584
65	Enos Slaughter	2,380	65	Mickey Vernon	8,731	65	Joe Kelley	1,421	65	Ernie Banks	2,583
66	Al Oliver	2,368	66	Dave Concepcion	8,723	66	Roberto Clemente	1,416	66	Richie Ashburn	2,574
	George Davis	2,368	67	Bert Campaneris	8,684	67	Billy Williams	1,410	67	Harold Baines	2,561
68	Nellie Fox	2,367	68	Ted Simmons	8,680	68	Monte Ward	1,408		Willie Davis	2,561
69	Willie Stargell	2,360	69	Goose Goslin	8,656	69	Mike Griffin	1,405	69	Rickey Henderson	2,550
70	Jose Cruz	2,353	70	Bobby Wallace	8,618	70	Sam Crawford	1,391	70	George Van Haltren	2,532
71	Brian Downing	2,344	71	Willie Keeler	8,591	71	Joe DiMaggio	1,390	71	Heinie Manush	2,524
72	Steve Garvey	2,332	72	Lou Whitaker	8,570	72	Lou Whitaker	1,386	72	Joe Morgan	2,517
73	Bert Campaneris	2,328	73	Fred Clarke	8,568	73	Andre Dawson	1,373	73	Buddy Bell	2,514
74	Frank White	2,324	74	Eddie Mathews	8,537	74	Vada Pinson	1,366	74	Jimmy Ryan	2,502
75	Charlie Gehringer	2,323	75	Red Schoendienst	8,479	75	Brett Butler	1,359	75	Mickey Vernon	2,495
76	Jimmie Foxx	2,317	76	Wade Boggs	8,453	76	Doc Cramer	1,357	76	Ted Simmons	2,472
77	Frankie Frisch	2,311	77	Jesse Burkett	8,421		King Kelly	1,357	77	Joe Medwick	2,471
78	Harry Hooper	2,308	78	Larry Bowa	8,418	78	Tommy Leach	1,355	78	Roger Connor	2,467
79	Gary Carter	2,296	79	Babe Ruth	8,399	79	Darrell Evans	1,344	79	Harry Hooper	2,466
80	Alan Trammell	2,293	80	Ryne Sandberg	8,385	80	Pee Wee Reese	1,338	80	Ozzie Smith	2,460
81	Don Baylor	2,292	81	Richie Ashburn	8,365	81	Luis Aparicio	1,335	81	Lloyd Waner	2,459
	Ted Williams	2,292	82	Mike Schmidt	8,352	82	Lave Cross	1,332	82	Bill Dahlen	2,457
83	Goose Goslin	2,287	83	Bid McPhee	8,291	83	George Gore	1,327	83	Jim Rice	2,452
84	Jimmy Dykes	2,282	84	Alan Trammell	8,288	84	Richie Ashburn	1,322	84	Red Schoendienst	2,449
85	Cap Anson	2,276	85	George Sisler	8,267	85	Luke Appling	1,319	85	Dwight Evans	2,446
86	Lave Cross	2,275	86	Tim Raines	8,238	86	Ryne Sandberg	1,318	86	Tim Raines	2,439
87	Bob Boone	2,264	87	Gary Gaetti	8,227		Patsy Donovan	1,318	87	Pie Traynor	2,416
88	Gary Gaetti	2,261	88	Jim Rice	8,225	88	Mike Tiernan	1,313	88	Mickey Mantle	2,415
89	Chris Speier	2,260	89	Don Baylor	8,198	89	Ernie Banks	1,305	89	Stuffy McInnis	2,406
90	Rogers Hornsby	2,259	90	Willie McCovey	8,197		Kiki Cuyler	1,305	90	Ryne Sandberg	2,386
91	Chili Davis	2,255	91	Tony Gwynn	8,187	91	Jimmy Sheckard	1,296	91	Enos Slaughter	2,383
92	Larry Bowa	2,247	92	Brett Butler	8,180	92	Harry Heilmann	1,291	92	Edd Roush	2,376
93	Ron Santo	2,243	93	Rogers Hornsby	8,173	93	Zack Wheat	1,289	93	Brett Butler	2,375
94	Fred Clarke	2,242	94	Jimmy Ryan	8,164	94	Heinie Manush	1,287	94	Lou Whitaker	2,369
95	Doc Cramer	2,239	95	Harmon Killebrew	8,147	95	George Sisler	1,284	95	Alan Trammell	2,365
96	Wade Boggs	2,227	96	Ron Santo	8,143	96	Harmon Killebrew	1,283	96	Carlton Fisk	2,356
97	Red Schoendienst	2,216	97	Jimmie Foxx	8,134	97	Donie Bush	1,280	97	Joe Judge	2,352
98	Al Simmons	2,215	98	Mickey Mantle	8,102	98	Nellie Fox	1,279	98	Orlando Cepeda	2,351
99	Brett Butler	2,213	99	Tim Wallach	8,099	99	Fred Tenney	1,278	99	Billy Herman	2,345
100	Tim Wallach	2,212	100	Chili Davis	8,094	100	Carlton Fisk	1,276	100	Joe Torre	2,342

Doubles

Rank	Player	2B
1	Tris Speaker	792
2	Pete Rose	746
3	Stan Musial	725
	Ty Cobb	725
5	George Brett	665
6	Nap Lajoie	657
7	Carl Yastrzemski	646
8	Honus Wagner	640
9	Hank Aaron	624
10	Paul Waner	603
11	Robin Yount	583
12	Paul Molitor	576
13	Charlie Gehringer	574
14	Eddie Murray	560
15	Harry Heilmann	542
16	Wade Boggs	541
	Rogers Hornsby	541
18	Dave Winfield	540
	Joe Medwick	540
20	Al Simmons	539
21	Lou Gehrig	535
22	Al Oliver	529
23	Frank Robinson	528
	Cap Anson	528
25	Dave Parker	526
26	Ted Williams	525
27	Willie Mays	523
28	Ed Delahanty	522
29	Cal Ripken Jr.	517
30	Joe Cronin	515
31	Babe Ruth	506
32	Tony Perez	505
33	Andre Dawson	503
34	Goose Goslin	500
35	Rusty Staub	499
36	Bill Buckner	498
	Al Kaline	498
38	Sam Rice	497
39	Heinie Manush	491
40	Mickey Vernon	490
41	Mel Ott	488
42	Lou Brock	486
	Billy Herman	486
44	Vada Pinson	485
45	Hal McRae	484
46	Ted Simmons	483
	Dwight Evans	483
48	Brooks Robinson	482
49	Zack Wheat	476
50	Jake Beckley	473
51	Frankie Frisch	466
52	Jim Bottomley	465
53	Reggie Jackson	463
54	Tony Gwynn	460
	Dan Brouthers	460
56	Jimmie Foxx	458
	Sam Crawford	458
58	Jimmy Dykes	453
59	George Davis	451
	Jimmy Ryan	451
61	Joe Morgan	449
62	Rod Carew	445
63	George Burns	444
64	Don Mattingly	442
	Dick Bartell	442
66	Roger Connor	441
67	Steve Garvey	440
	Roberto Clemente	440
	Luke Appling	440
70	Harold Baines	439
71	Eddie Collins	438
72	Cesar Cedeno	436
	Joe Sewell	436
74	Wally Moses	435
75	Billy Williams	434
76	Joe Judge	433
77	Tim Wallach	432
78	Red Schoendienst	427
79	Keith Hernandez	426
	Rickey Henderson	426
81	Buddy Bell	425
	George Sisler	425
	Sherry Magee	425
84	Willie Stargell	423
85	Carlton Fisk	421
86	Lou Whitaker	420
87	Max Carey	419
88	Orlando Cepeda	417
89	Cecil Cooper	415
90	Kirby Puckett	414
	Jim O'Rourke	414
92	Enos Slaughter	413
	Bill Dahlen	413
94	Alan Trammell	412
	Joe Kuhel	412
96	Lave Cross	411
97	Joe Carter	410
98	Mike Schmidt	408
99	3 tied with	407

Triples

Rank	Player	3B
1	Sam Crawford	309
2	Ty Cobb	296
3	Honus Wagner	252
4	Jake Beckley	243
5	Roger Connor	233
6	Tris Speaker	222
7	Fred Clarke	220
8	Dan Brouthers	205
9	Joe Kelley	194
10	Paul Waner	190
11	Bid McPhee	188
12	Eddie Collins	186
13	Ed Delahanty	185
14	Sam Rice	184
15	Edd Roush	182
	Jesse Burkett	182
17	Ed Konetchy	181
18	Buck Ewing	178
19	Stan Musial	177
	Rabbit Maranville	177
21	Harry Stovey	174
22	Goose Goslin	173
23	Zack Wheat	172
	Tommy Leach	172
25	Rogers Hornsby	169
26	Joe Jackson	168
27	Roberto Clemente	166
	Sherry Magee	166
29	Jake Daubert	165
30	Pie Traynor	164
	George Sisler	164
	Elmer Flick	164
33	Nap Lajoie	163
	Bill Dahlen	163
	George Davis	163
36	Lou Gehrig	162
	Mike Tiernan	162
38	George Van Haltren	161
39	Heinie Manush	160
	Harry Hooper	160
	Sam Thompson	160
42	Joe Judge	159
	Max Carey	159
44	Ed McKean	158
45	Kiki Cuyler	157
	Jimmy Ryan	157
47	Tommy Corcoran	155
48	Earle Combs	154
49	Jim Bottomley	151
	Harry Heilmann	151
51	Al Simmons	149
	Kip Selbach	149
53	Enos Slaughter	148
	Wally Pipp	148
55	Willie Wilson	147
	Bobby Veach	147
57	Charlie Gehringer	146
	Harry Davis	146
59	Willie Keeler	145
60	Bobby Wallace	143
61	Lou Brock	141
62	Willie Mays	140
63	John Reilly	139
64	Willie Davis	138
	Frankie Frisch	138
	Jimmy Williams	138
	Tom Brown	138
68	George Brett	137
69	Babe Ruth	136
	Jimmy Sheckard	136
	Elmer Smith	136
72	Pete Rose	135
	Lave Cross	135
74	Shano Collins	133
75	George Wood	132
	Jim O'Rourke	132
77	Brett Butler	131
	Joe DiMaggio	131
	Buck Freeman	131
80	Buddy Myer	130
81	Larry Gardner	129
	Oyster Burns	129
83	Arky Vaughan	128
	Earl Averill	128
85	Vada Pinson	127
86	Robin Yount	126
	Hardy Richardson	126
88	Jimmie Foxx	125
89	Hal Chase	124
	Wildfire Schulte	124
	John Anderson	124
	Cap Anson	124
93	Larry Doyle	123
	Duke Farrell	123
95	Dummy Hoy	121
96	Mickey Vernon	120
97	Hugh Duffy	119
	Fred Pfeffer	119
99	3 tied with	118

Home Runs

Rank	Player	HR
1	Hank Aaron	755
2	Babe Ruth	714
3	Willie Mays	660
4	Frank Robinson	586
5	Harmon Killebrew	573
6	Reggie Jackson	563
7	Mike Schmidt	548
8	Mickey Mantle	536
9	Jimmie Foxx	534
10	Willie McCovey	521
	Ted Williams	521
12	Ernie Banks	512
	Eddie Mathews	512
14	Mel Ott	511
15	Eddie Murray	504
16	Lou Gehrig	493
17	Willie Stargell	475
19	Dave Winfield	465
20	Carl Yastrzemski	452
21	Dave Kingman	442
22	Andre Dawson	438
23	Billy Williams	426
24	Darrell Evans	414
25	Duke Snider	407
26	Al Kaline	399
27	Dale Murphy	398
28	Graig Nettles	390
29	Johnny Bench	389
30	Mark McGwire	387
31	Dwight Evans	385
32	Jim Rice	382
	Frank Howard	382
34	Tony Perez	379
	Orlando Cepeda	379
36	Joe Carter	378
37	Norm Cash	377
38	Carlton Fisk	376
39	Barry Bonds	374
	Rocky Colavito	374
41	Cal Ripken Jr.	370
	Gil Hodges	370
43	Ralph Kiner	369
44	Joe DiMaggio	361
45	Johnny Mize	359
46	Yogi Berra	358
47	Lee May	354
48	Jose Canseco	351
	Dick Allen	351
50	George Foster	348
51	Ron Santo	342
52	Jack Clark	340
53	Dave Parker	339
	Harold Baines	339
	Fred McGriff	339
	Boog Powell	339
57	Don Baylor	338
58	Joe Adcock	336
59	Bobby Bonds	332
	Gary Gaetti	332
61	Hank Greenberg	331
62	Chili Davis	328
63	Willie Horton	325
64	Gary Carter	324
	Lance Parrish	324
66	Roy Sievers	318
67	George Brett	317
68	Ron Cey	316
69	Reggie Smith	314
70	Darryl Strawberry	308
71	Greg Luzinski	307
	Al Simmons	307
73	Fred Lynn	306
74	Cecil Fielder	302
75	Rogers Hornsby	301
76	Chuck Klein	300
77	Ken Griffey Jr.	294
78	Kent Hrbek	293
79	Rusty Staub	292
80	Jimmy Wynn	291
81	Andres Galarraga	288
	Del Ennis	288
	Hank Sauer	288
	Bob Johnson	288
85	Frank Thomas	286
86	Ryne Sandberg	282
	Ken Boyer	282
88	Matt Williams	279
	Ted Kluszewski	279
90	Rudy York	277
91	Brian Downing	275
	Roger Maris	275
93	Steve Garvey	272
	Albert Belle	272
95	Tom Brunansky	271
	Rafael Palmeiro	271
	George Scott	271
98	Gorman Thomas	268
	Joe Morgan	268
	Brooks Robinson	268

Home Runs (Home)

Rank	Player	HR
1	Hank Aaron	385
2	Babe Ruth	347
3	Willie Mays	335
4	Mel Ott	323
5	Frank Robinson	321
6	Jimmie Foxx	299
7	Harmon Killebrew	291
8	Ernie Banks	290
9	Reggie Jackson	280
10	Mickey Mantle	266
11	Mike Schmidt	265
12	Willie McCovey	264
13	Stan Musial	252
14	Lou Gehrig	251
15	Ted Williams	248
16	Billy Williams	245
17	Eddie Murray	242
18	Eddie Mathews	238
19	Carl Yastrzemski	237
20	Al Kaline	226
21	Duke Snider	224
22	Willie Stargell	221
23	Darrell Evans	219
24	Dave Winfield	218
25	Dave Kingman	217
	Dale Murphy	217
27	Graig Nettles	216
	Ron Santo	216
29	Norm Cash	213
30	Johnny Mize	212
31	Yogi Berra	210
	Ralph Kiner	210
	Gil Hodges	210
34	Andre Dawson	207
	Jim Rice	207
36	Hank Greenberg	205
37	Dwight Evans	203
38	Joe Carter	202
39	Johnny Bench	195
40	Rocky Colavito	193
41	Chuck Klein	190
42	Carlton Fisk	188
43	Frank Howard	186
44	George Foster	184
45	Cal Ripken Jr.	183
	Dick Allen	183
47	Tony Perez	182
	Barry Bonds	182
	Orlando Cepeda	182
50	Greg Luzinski	179
	Lee May	179
	Mark McGwire	179
53	Fred Lynn	177
54	Bobby Bonds	173
55	Dave Parker	170
	Hank Sauer	170
57	Bob Johnson	168
58	Jose Canseco	167
59	Ron Cey	166
60	Chili Davis	164
	Ryne Sandberg	164
	Fred McGriff	164
63	Harold Baines	163
	Rogers Hornsby	163
65	Gary Carter	162
	Gary Gaetti	162
	Ted Kluszewski	162
	Al Simmons	162
69	Cy Williams	161
70	Lance Parrish	160
	Cecil Fielder	160
72	Reggie Smith	158
	Rudy York	158
74	Don Baylor	156
	Kent Hrbek	156
	Darryl Strawberry	156
77	Jack Clark	155
	Ken Griffey Jr.	155
79	Willie Horton	154
80	Steve Garvey	151
	Andres Galarraga	151
	Vada Pinson	151
83	George Scott	150
	Boog Powell	150
	Roy Sievers	150
86	Ken Boyer	148
	Joe DiMaggio	148
88	Lou Whitaker	146
	Del Ennis	146
90	Bobby Doerr	145
91	Rusty Staub	144
	Earl Averill	144
93	Dolph Camilli	143
94	Bobby Murcer	142
	Bob Horner	142
	Rafael Palmeiro	142
	Ken Williams	142
98	Roy Campanella	140
99	Brian Downing	138
	Andre Thornton	138

Home Runs (Road)

#	Player	HR
1	Hank Aaron	370
2	Babe Ruth	367
3	Willie Mays	325
4	Reggie Jackson	283
	Mike Schmidt	283
6	Harmon Killebrew	282
7	Eddie Mathews	274
8	Ted Williams	273
9	Mickey Mantle	270
10	Frank Robinson	265
11	Eddie Murray	262
12	Willie McCovey	257
13	Willie Stargell	254
14	Dave Winfield	247
15	Lou Gehrig	242
16	Jimmie Foxx	235
17	Andre Dawson	231
18	Dave Kingman	225
19	Stan Musial	223
20	Ernie Banks	222
21	Carl Yastrzemski	215
22	Joe DiMaggio	213
23	Mark McGwire	208
24	Joe Adcock	199
25	Tony Perez	197
	Orlando Cepeda	197
27	Frank Howard	196
28	Darrell Evans	195
29	Johnny Bench	194
30	Barry Bonds	192
31	Boog Powell	189
32	Carlton Fisk	188
	Mel Ott	188
34	Cal Ripken Jr.	187
35	Jack Clark	185
36	Jose Canseco	184
37	Duke Snider	183
38	Don Baylor	182
	Dwight Evans	182
40	George Brett	181
	Dale Murphy	181
	Billy Williams	181
	Rocky Colavito	181
44	Harold Baines	176
	Joe Carter	176
46	Lee May	175
	Jim Rice	175
	Fred McGriff	175
49	Graig Nettles	174
50	Al Kaline	173
51	Willie Horton	171
52	Gary Gaetti	170
53	Dave Parker	169
54	Dick Allen	168
	Roy Sievers	168
56	George Foster	164
	Lance Parrish	164
	Chili Davis	164
	Norm Cash	164
60	Gary Carter	162
61	Frank Thomas	160
	Gil Hodges	160
63	Bobby Bonds	159
	Ralph Kiner	159
65	Tim Wallach	157
66	Reggie Smith	156
	Goose Goslin	156
68	Jimmy Wynn	154
69	Roger Maris	153
70	Darryl Strawberry	152
71	Ron Cey	150
72	Rusty Staub	148
	Yogi Berra	148
74	Bobby Bonilla	147
	Johnny Mize	147
76	Joe Morgan	146
77	George Bell	145
	Danny Tartabull	145
	Al Simmons	145
80	Larry Parrish	144
81	Matt Williams	143
	Albert Belle	143
83	Tom Brunansky	142
	Cecil Fielder	142
	Del Ennis	142
86	Juan Gonzalez	140
87	John Mayberry	139
	Ken Griffey Jr.	139
89	Roberto Clemente	138
	Rogers Hornsby	138
91	Brian Downing	137
	Gorman Thomas	137
	Kent Hrbek	137
	Andres Galarraga	137
	Jay Buhner	137
96	Kirk Gibson	136
	Joe Torre	136
	Bill Nicholson	136
99	3 tied with	134

At-Bats/Home Run

(minimum 3,000 Plate Appearances)

#	Player	AB/HR
1	Babe Ruth	11.76
2	Mark McGwire	11.94
3	Ralph Kiner	14.11
4	Harmon Killebrew	14.22
5	Juan Gonzalez	14.31
6	Ted Williams	14.79
7	Frank Thomas	14.87
8	Albert Belle	14.98
9	Dave Kingman	15.11
10	Mickey Mantle	15.12
11	Jimmie Foxx	15.23
12	Mike Schmidt	15.24
13	Ron Kittle	15.39
14	Jose Canseco	15.55
15	Ken Griffey Jr.	15.62
16	Hank Greenberg	15.69
17	Cecil Fielder	15.70
18	Willie McCovey	15.73
19	Jay Buhner	16.18
20	Barry Bonds	16.23
21	Lou Gehrig	16.23
22	Jim Gentile	16.32
23	Hank Aaron	16.38
24	Darryl Strawberry	16.47
25	Willie Mays	16.49
26	Hank Sauer	16.65
27	Eddie Mathews	16.67
28	Willie Stargell	16.69
29	Fred McGriff	16.79
30	Rob Deer	16.87
31	Mo Vaughn	16.94
32	Matt Williams	16.97
33	Frank Howard	16.98
34	Frank Robinson	17.08
35	Steve Balboni	17.24
36	Kevin Mitchell	17.27
37	Bob Horner	17.33
38	David Justice	17.37
39	Roy Campanella	17.38
40	Rocky Colavito	17.39
41	Gus Zernial	17.43
42	Tim Salmon	17.43
43	Gorman Thomas	17.45
44	Reggie Jackson	17.52
45	Dick Stuart	17.53
46	Duke Snider	17.59
47	Norm Cash	17.79
48	Eric Davis	17.86
49	Johnny Mize	17.95
50	Dean Palmer	17.99
51	Dick Allen	18.04
52	Larry Walker	18.32
53	Ernie Banks	18.40
54	Mel Ott	18.50
55	Roger Maris	18.55
56	Chris Hoiles	18.77
57	Joe DiMaggio	18.89
58	Gil Hodges	19.00
59	Greg Vaughn	19.02
60	Wally Post	19.08
61	Danny Tartabull	19.13
62	Mickey Tettleton	19.18
63	Al Rosen	19.40
64	Tony Conigliaro	19.40
65	Sammy Sosa	19.43
66	Paul Sorrento	19.44
67	Hack Wilson	19.51
68	Jeff Bagwell	19.56
69	Glenn Davis	19.57
70	Tino Martinez	19.65
71	Bob Allison	19.66
72	Joe Adcock	19.66
73	Johnny Bench	19.69
74	Boog Powell	19.71
75	Jesse Barfield	19.75
76	Nate Colbert	19.78
77	Dale Murphy	20.00
78	Charlie Keller	20.05
79	Roy Sievers	20.08
80	Cliff Johnson	20.13
81	Don Mincher	20.13
82	Jack Clark	20.14
83	George Foster	20.18
84	Ron Gant	20.28
85	Gary Sheffield	20.33
86	Pete Incaviglia	20.40
87	Tony Armas	20.57
88	Andre Thornton	20.91
89	Orlando Cepeda	20.92
90	Leon Wagner	20.98
91	Jim Lemon	21.01
92	Andres Galarraga	21.09
93	Yogi Berra	21.10
94	Don Demeter	21.12
95	Kent Hrbek	21.13
96	Larry Doby	21.14
97	Greg Luzinski	21.19
98	Bobby Bonds	21.21
99	Ted Kluszewski	21.25
100	Joe Carter	21.25

Extra Base Hits

#	Player	XBH
1	Hank Aaron	1,477
2	Stan Musial	1,377
3	Babe Ruth	1,356
4	Willie Mays	1,323
5	Lou Gehrig	1,190
6	Frank Robinson	1,186
7	Carl Yastrzemski	1,157
8	Ty Cobb	1,138
9	Tris Speaker	1,131
10	George Brett	1,119
11	Ted Williams	1,117
	Jimmie Foxx	1,117
13	Eddie Murray	1,099
14	Dave Winfield	1,093
15	Reggie Jackson	1,075
16	Mel Ott	1,071
17	Pete Rose	1,041
18	Andre Dawson	1,039
19	Mike Schmidt	1,015
20	Rogers Hornsby	1,011
21	Ernie Banks	1,009
22	Al Simmons	995
23	Honus Wagner	993
24	Al Kaline	972
25	Tony Perez	963
26	Robin Yount	960
27	Willie Stargell	953
28	Mickey Mantle	952
29	Billy Williams	948
30	Dwight Evans	941
31	Dave Parker	940
32	Eddie Mathews	938
33	Cal Ripken Jr.	930
34	Goose Goslin	921
35	Willie McCovey	920
36	Paul Molitor	915
37	Paul Waner	906
38	Charlie Gehringer	904
39	Nap Lajoie	902
40	Harmon Killebrew	887
41	Joe DiMaggio	881
42	Harry Heilmann	876
43	Vada Pinson	868
44	Sam Crawford	864
45	Joe Medwick	858
46	Duke Snider	850
47	Roberto Clemente	846
48	Carlton Fisk	844
49	Joe Carter	840
50	Rusty Staub	838
51	Jim Bottomley	835
52	Jim Rice	834
53	Harold Baines	826
54	Al Oliver	825
55	Orlando Cepeda	823
56	Brooks Robinson	818
57	Joe Morgan	813
58	Roger Connor	812
59	Johnny Mize	809
60	Ed Delahanty	808
61	Joe Cronin	803
62	Jake Beckley	802
63	Johnny Bench	794
64	Barry Bonds	789
65	Dale Murphy	787
66	Mickey Vernon	782
67	Hank Greenberg	781
68	Zack Wheat	780
69	Darrell Evans	779
	Bob Johnson	779
71	Ted Simmons	778
72	Lou Brock	776
73	Ron Santo	774
74	Chuck Klein	772
75	Dan Brouthers	771
76	Gary Gaetti	769
77	Earl Averill	767
78	Ryne Sandberg	761
	Heinie Manush	761
80	Steve Garvey	755
81	Dick Allen	750
82	Chili Davis	749
	Cap Anson	749
84	Hal McRae	741
85	Fred Lynn	737
	Rickey Henderson	737
88	Reggie Smith	734
89	Don Baylor	732
90	Enos Slaughter	730
91	Lou Whitaker	729
92	Tim Wallach	728
	Yogi Berra	728
94	Gary Carter	726
	Jimmy Ryan	726
96	Lee May	725
97	Bill Buckner	721
98	Willie Davis	715
	Del Ennis	715
	Sam Rice	715

Total Bases

#	Player	TB
1	Hank Aaron	6,856
2	Stan Musial	6,134
3	Willie Mays	6,066
4	Ty Cobb	5,858
5	Babe Ruth	5,793
6	Pete Rose	5,752
7	Carl Yastrzemski	5,539
8	Eddie Murray	5,397
9	Frank Robinson	5,373
10	Dave Winfield	5,221
11	Tris Speaker	5,101
12	Lou Gehrig	5,059
13	George Brett	5,044
14	Mel Ott	5,041
15	Jimmie Foxx	4,956
16	Ted Williams	4,884
17	Honus Wagner	4,862
18	Al Kaline	4,852
19	Reggie Jackson	4,834
20	Andre Dawson	4,787
21	Robin Yount	4,730
22	Rogers Hornsby	4,712
23	Ernie Banks	4,706
24	Al Simmons	4,685
25	Paul Molitor	4,662
26	Billy Williams	4,599
27	Tony Perez	4,532
28	Mickey Mantle	4,511
29	Roberto Clemente	4,492
30	Paul Waner	4,474
31	Nap Lajoie	4,471
32	Cal Ripken Jr.	4,428
33	Dave Parker	4,405
34	Mike Schmidt	4,404
35	Eddie Mathews	4,349
36	Sam Crawford	4,328
37	Goose Goslin	4,325
38	Brooks Robinson	4,270
39	Vada Pinson	4,264
40	Eddie Collins	4,263
41	Charlie Gehringer	4,257
42	Lou Brock	4,238
43	Dwight Evans	4,230
44	Willie McCovey	4,219
45	Willie Stargell	4,190
46	Rusty Staub	4,185
47	Jake Beckley	4,147
48	Harmon Killebrew	4,143
49	Jim Rice	4,129
50	Harold Baines	4,113
51	Zack Wheat	4,100
52	Al Oliver	4,083
53	Cap Anson	4,062
54	Harry Heilmann	4,053
55	Carlton Fisk	3,999
56	Rod Carew	3,998
57	Joe Morgan	3,962
58	Orlando Cepeda	3,959
59	Sam Rice	3,954
60	Joe DiMaggio	3,948
61	Steve Garvey	3,941
62	Frankie Frisch	3,937
63	George Sisler	3,871
64	Darrell Evans	3,866
65	Duke Snider	3,865
66	Joe Medwick	3,852
67	Rickey Henderson	3,850
68	Bill Buckner	3,833
69	Ted Simmons	3,793
70	Ed Delahanty	3,792
71	Roger Connor	3,788
72	Ryne Sandberg	3,787
73	Wade Boggs	3,780
74	Graig Nettles	3,779
	Ron Santo	3,779
76	Willie Davis	3,778
77	Jesse Burkett	3,760
78	Mickey Vernon	3,741
79	Jim Bottomley	3,737
80	Dale Murphy	3,733
81	Joe Carter	3,731
82	Tony Gwynn	3,729
83	Fred Clarke	3,674
84	Heinie Manush	3,665
85	Chili Davis	3,656
	George Davis	3,656
87	Buddy Bell	3,654
88	Lou Whitaker	3,651
89	Johnny Bench	3,644
90	Yogi Berra	3,643
91	Johnny Mize	3,621
	Jimmy Ryan	3,621
93	Max Carey	3,612
94	Enos Slaughter	3,599
95	Don Baylor	3,571
	Gary Gaetti	3,571
97	Willie Keeler	3,563
98	Joe Torre	3,560
99	Joe Cronin	3,546
100	Tim Raines	3,539

RBI

#	Player	RBI
1	Hank Aaron	2,297
2	Babe Ruth	2,210
3	Lou Gehrig	1,995
4	Stan Musial	1,951
5	Ty Cobb	1,933
6	Jimmie Foxx	1,921
7	Eddie Murray	1,917
8	Willie Mays	1,903
9	Cap Anson	1,879
10	Mel Ott	1,860
11	Carl Yastrzemski	1,844
12	Ted Williams	1,839
13	Dave Winfield	1,833
14	Al Simmons	1,827
15	Frank Robinson	1,812
16	Honus Wagner	1,732
17	Reggie Jackson	1,702
18	Tony Perez	1,652
19	Ernie Banks	1,636
20	Goose Goslin	1,609
21	Nap Lajoie	1,599
22	George Brett	1,595
	Mike Schmidt	1,595
24	Andre Dawson	1,591
25	Harmon Killebrew	1,584
	Rogers Hornsby	1,584
27	Al Kaline	1,583
28	Jake Beckley	1,575
29	Willie McCovey	1,555
30	Willie Stargell	1,540
31	Harry Heilmann	1,539
32	Joe DiMaggio	1,537
	Tris Speaker	1,537
34	Sam Crawford	1,525
35	Mickey Mantle	1,509
36	Dave Parker	1,493
37	Billy Williams	1,475
38	Rusty Staub	1,466
39	Ed Delahanty	1,464
40	Cal Ripken Jr.	1,453
	Eddie Mathews	1,453
42	Jim Rice	1,451
43	George Davis	1,437
44	Yogi Berra	1,430
45	Charlie Gehringer	1,427
46	Joe Cronin	1,424
47	Harold Baines	1,423
48	Jim Bottomley	1,422
49	Robin Yount	1,406
50	Ted Simmons	1,389
51	Dwight Evans	1,384
52	Joe Medwick	1,383
53	Joe Carter	1,382
54	Johnny Bench	1,376
55	Lave Cross	1,371
56	Orlando Cepeda	1,365
57	Brooks Robinson	1,357
58	Darrell Evans	1,354
59	Johnny Mize	1,337
60	Duke Snider	1,333
61	Ron Santo	1,331
62	Carlton Fisk	1,330
63	Al Oliver	1,326
64	Roger Connor	1,322
65	Graig Nettles	1,314
	Pete Rose	1,314
67	Mickey Vernon	1,311
68	Paul Waner	1,309
69	Steve Garvey	1,308
70	Roberto Clemente	1,305
71	Enos Slaughter	1,304
72	Hugh Duffy	1,302
73	Eddie Collins	1,300
74	Sam Thompson	1,299
75	Dan Brouthers	1,296
76	Chili Davis	1,285
77	Del Ennis	1,284
78	Bob Johnson	1,283
79	Don Baylor	1,276
	Hank Greenberg	1,276
81	Gil Hodges	1,274
82	Pie Traynor	1,273
83	Dale Murphy	1,266
84	Zack Wheat	1,248
85	Bobby Doerr	1,247
86	Lee May	1,244
	Frankie Frisch	1,244
88	George Foster	1,239
89	Paul Molitor	1,238
90	Bill Dahlen	1,233
91	Gary Carter	1,225
92	Gary Gaetti	1,224
93	Dave Kingman	1,210
94	Bill Dickey	1,209
95	Bill Buckner	1,208
96	Chuck Klein	1,201
97	Bob Elliott	1,195
98	Joe Kelley	1,194
99	Tony Lazzeri	1,191
100	Boog Powell	1,187

Walks

#	Player	Walks
1	Babe Ruth	2,056
2	Ted Williams	2,019
3	Joe Morgan	1,865
4	Carl Yastrzemski	1,845
5	Rickey Henderson	1,772
6	Mickey Mantle	1,733
7	Mel Ott	1,708
8	Eddie Yost	1,614
9	Darrell Evans	1,605
10	Stan Musial	1,599
11	Pete Rose	1,566
12	Harmon Killebrew	1,559
13	Lou Gehrig	1,508
14	Mike Schmidt	1,507
15	Eddie Collins	1,503
16	Willie Mays	1,463
17	Jimmie Foxx	1,452
18	Eddie Mathews	1,444
19	Frank Robinson	1,420
20	Hank Aaron	1,402
21	Dwight Evans	1,391
22	Tris Speaker	1,381
23	Reggie Jackson	1,375
24	Willie McCovey	1,345
25	Eddie Murray	1,333
26	Wade Boggs	1,328
27	Luke Appling	1,302
28	Al Kaline	1,277
29	Ken Singleton	1,263
30	Jack Clark	1,262
31	Rusty Staub	1,255
32	Ty Cobb	1,249
33	Willie Randolph	1,243
34	Barry Bonds	1,227
35	Jimmy Wynn	1,224
36	Dave Winfield	1,216
37	Pee Wee Reese	1,210
38	Tim Raines	1,209
39	Tony Phillips	1,201
40	Richie Ashburn	1,198
41	Brian Downing	1,197
	Lou Whitaker	1,197
43	Billy Hamilton	1,187
44	Charlie Gehringer	1,185
45	Donie Bush	1,158
46	Toby Harrah	1,153
	Max Bishop	1,153
48	Harry Hooper	1,136
49	Jimmy Sheckard	1,135
50	Brett Butler	1,129
51	Ron Santo	1,108
52	Chili Davis	1,107
53	George Brett	1,096
54	Stan Hack	1,092
	Lu Blue	1,092
56	Paul Waner	1,091
57	Graig Nettles	1,088
58	Bobby Grich	1,087
59	Bob Johnson	1,075
60	Ozzie Smith	1,072
61	Keith Hernandez	1,070
	Harlond Clift	1,070
63	Bill Dahlen	1,064
64	Joe Cronin	1,059
65	Ron Fairly	1,052
66	Paul Molitor	1,049
67	Billy Williams	1,045
68	Norm Cash	1,043
	Eddie Joost	1,043
70	Roy Thomas	1,042
71	Max Carey	1,040
72	Rogers Hornsby	1,038
73	Jim Gilliam	1,036
74	Sal Bando	1,031
75	Jesse Burkett	1,029
76	Rod Carew	1,018
	Enos Slaughter	1,018
78	Cal Ripken Jr.	1,016
79	Ron Cey	1,012
80	Ralph Kiner	1,011
81	Dummy Hoy	1,004
82	Miller Huggins	1,003
83	Roger Connor	1,002
84	Boog Powell	1,001
85	Eddie Stanky	996
86	Cupid Childs	991
87	Dale Murphy	986
88	Gene Tenace	984
89	Bid McPhee	981
90	Earl Torgeson	980
	Joe Kuhel	980
92	Augie Galan	979
93	Duke Snider	971
94	Bob Elliott	967
95	Robin Yount	966
96	Mike Hargrove	965
	Buddy Myer	965
	Joe Judge	965
99	Honus Wagner	963
100	Jimmy Dykes	958

Walks/PA

(minimum 3,000 Plate Appearances)

#	Player	Walks/PA
1	Ted Williams	.206
2	Max Bishop	.200
3	Babe Ruth	.194
4	Ferris Fain	.184
5	Frank Thomas	.184
6	Eddie Stanky	.183
7	Gene Tenace	.178
8	Roy Cullenbine	.178
9	Jack Crooks	.176
10	Eddie Yost	.176
11	Mickey Mantle	.175
12	Bill Joyce	.173
13	Eddie Lake	.171
14	Charlie Keller	.170
15	John McGraw	.169
16	Barry Bonds	.166
17	Mickey Tettleton	.165
18	Joe Morgan	.165
19	Rickey Henderson	.163
20	Earl Torgeson	.162
21	Bernie Carbo	.162
22	Ralph Kiner	.162
23	Yank Robinson	.159
24	Harmon Killebrew	.159
25	Roy Thomas	.158
26	Mark McGwire	.158
27	Billy Hamilton	.156
28	Lou Gehrig	.156
29	Harlond Clift	.155
30	Joe Ferguson	.155
31	Elmer Valo	.155
32	Eddie Joost	.154
33	Jack Clark	.153
34	Jimmy Wynn	.153
35	Lu Blue	.152
36	Mel Ott	.151
37	Jimmie Foxx	.150
38	Mike Schmidt	.150
39	Darrell Evans	.149
40	Dolph Camilli	.149
41	Ken Singleton	.148
42	Miller Huggins	.148
43	Joe Cunningham	.148
44	Edgar Martinez	.147
45	Cupid Childs	.147
46	George Selkirk	.146
47	Elbie Fletcher	.146
48	Dave Magadan	.146
49	Jim McTamany	.145
50	Darren Daulton	.145
51	Merv Rettenmund	.145
52	Topsy Hartsel	.145
53	Mike Hargrove	.144
54	Tony Phillips	.144
55	Jason Thompson	.144
56	Wayne Garrett	.143
57	Eddie Mathews	.143
58	Dwayne Murphy	.143
59	Jeff Bagwell	.142
60	John Kruk	.141
61	Solly Hemus	.140
62	Augie Galan	.140
63	Hank Greenberg	.140
64	Andre Thornton	.139
65	Gene Woodling	.139
66	Willie McCovey	.139
67	John Olerud	.139
68	Larry Doby	.138
69	Hank Thompson	.138
70	Mickey Cochrane	.138
71	Darrell Porter	.138
72	John Briggs	.137
73	Alvin Davis	.137
74	John Mayberry	.137
75	Jim Gentile	.137
76	Paul Radford	.136
77	Bill North	.136
78	David Justice	.135
79	Tim Salmon	.135
80	Steve Braun	.135
81	Norm Siebern	.134
82	Bob Allison	.134
83	Al Rosen	.134
84	Wade Boggs	.134
85	Bob Johnson	.134
86	Lee Mazzilli	.133
87	Roger Bresnahan	.133
88	Donie Bush	.133
89	Fred McGriff	.132
90	Bobby Grich	.132
91	Wally Schang	.132
92	Sammy Strang	.132
93	Mike Epstein	.132
94	Mike Jorgensen	.132
95	Carl Yastrzemski	.132
96	Norm Cash	.132
97	Rick Ferrell	.132
98	Tommy Henrich	.132
99	Dwight Evans	.132
100	Albie Pearson	.132

Intentional Walks

#	Player	IW
1	Hank Aaron	293
2	Willie McCovey	260
	Barry Bonds	260
4	George Brett	229
5	Willie Stargell	227
6	Eddie Murray	222
7	Frank Robinson	218
8	Mike Schmidt	201
9	Ernie Banks	198
10	Rusty Staub	193
11	Willie Mays	192
12	Carl Yastrzemski	190
13	Tony Gwynn	189
14	Ted Simmons	188
15	Billy Williams	182
16	Chili Davis	180
17	Harold Baines	173
18	Dave Winfield	172
	Wade Boggs	172
20	Dave Parker	170
21	Pete Rose	167
	Roberto Clemente	167
23	Reggie Jackson	164
24	Harmon Killebrew	160
25	Dale Murphy	159
26	Orlando Cepeda	154
27	Tony Perez	150
28	Will Clark	145
29	Rod Carew	144
	Garry Templeton	144
31	Andre Dawson	143
32	Jose Cruz	142
	Tim Raines	142
	Ken Griffey Jr.	142
35	Darrell Evans	141
36	Boog Powell	140
37	Dick Allen	138
38	Don Mattingly	136
39	Johnny Bench	135
	Frank Howard	135
41	Tony Oliva	131
	Al Kaline	131
43	Keith Hernandez	130
44	Ron Fairly	129
45	Jack Clark	127
	Darryl Strawberry	127
	Joe Torre	127
	Stan Musial	127
49	Mickey Mantle	126
50	Ken Singleton	125
51	Lou Brock	124
52	Leo Cardenas	122
53	Bill Madlock	121
54	Brooks Robinson	120
55	Tim McCarver	119
	Al Oliver	119
57	Bobby Bonilla	118
	Frank Thomas	118
	Johnny Edwards	118
60	Ron Cey	117
61	Fred McGriff	116
62	Pedro Guerrero	115
	Reggie Smith	115
64	Steve Garvey	113
65	Norm Cash	112
66	Bill Buckner	111
67	Kent Hrbek	110
	John Roseboro	110
	Bill Mazeroski	110
70	Rick Monday	107
	Eddie Mathews	107
72	Gary Carter	106
	George Foster	106
	John Mayberry	106
	Darrell Porter	106
	Chris Speier	106
	Bill Russell	106
78	Carlton Fisk	105
	Ben Oglivie	105
	Howard Johnson	105
	Mo Vaughn	105
82	Duke Snider	104
83	Willie Montanez	103
	Cal Ripken Jr.	103
85	Mike Scioscia	101
86	Dan Driessen	100
87	Chris Chambliss	99
	Paul O'Neill	99
88	Bob Watson	98
90	Jeff Bagwell	97
	Ken Boyer	97
92	Manny Sanguillen	96
	Bobby Murcer	96
	Leon Durham	96
	Tom Haller	96
96	6 tied with	95

Strikeouts

#	Player	Total
1	Reggie Jackson	2,597
2	Willie Stargell	1,936
3	Mike Schmidt	1,883
4	Tony Perez	1,867
5	Dave Kingman	1,816
6	Bobby Bonds	1,757
7	Dale Murphy	1,748
8	Lou Brock	1,730
9	Mickey Mantle	1,710
10	Harmon Killebrew	1,699
11	Dwight Evans	1,697
12	Dave Winfield	1,686
13	Chili Davis	1,580
14	Lee May	1,570
15	Dick Allen	1,556
16	Willie McCovey	1,550
17	Dave Parker	1,537
18	Frank Robinson	1,532
19	Lance Parrish	1,527
20	Willie Mays	1,526
21	Eddie Murray	1,516
22	Rick Monday	1,513
23	Andre Dawson	1,509
24	Greg Luzinski	1,495
25	Eddie Mathews	1,487
26	Gary Gaetti	1,486
27	Jose Canseco	1,471
28	Andres Galarraga	1,469
29	Frank Howard	1,460
30	Jack Clark	1,441
31	Juan Samuel	1,429
32	Jimmy Wynn	1,427
33	Jim Rice	1,423
34	George Foster	1,419
35	George Scott	1,418
36	Darrell Evans	1,410
37	Rob Deer	1,409
38	Carl Yastrzemski	1,393
39	Carlton Fisk	1,386
40	Hank Aaron	1,383
41	Danny Tartabull	1,362
42	Larry Parrish	1,359
43	Tony Phillips	1,355
44	Robin Yount	1,350
45	Ron Santo	1,343
46	Gorman Thomas	1,339
47	Babe Ruth	1,330
48	Joe Carter	1,326
49	Deron Johnson	1,318
50	Willie Horton	1,313
51	Jimmie Foxx	1,311
52	Tim Wallach	1,307
	Mickey Tettleton	1,307
54	Harold Baines	1,287
55	Kirk Gibson	1,285
56	Bobby Grich	1,278
	Johnny Bench	1,278
58	Rickey Henderson	1,276
59	Pete Incaviglia	1,267
60	Claudell Washington	1,266
61	Ryne Sandberg	1,260
62	Fred McGriff	1,247
63	Ken Singleton	1,246
	Darryl Strawberry	1,246
65	Duke Snider	1,237
66	Ernie Banks	1,236
67	Ron Cey	1,235
68	Jesse Barfield	1,234
69	Roberto Clemente	1,230
70	Boog Powell	1,226
71	Devon White	1,211
72	Graig Nettles	1,209
73	Cecil Fielder	1,205
74	Paul Molitor	1,203
75	Tony Armas	1,201
76	Vada Pinson	1,196
77	Tom Brunansky	1,187
78	Dave Concepcion	1,186
79	Orlando Cepeda	1,169
80	Willie Wilson	1,144
81	Pete Rose	1,143
	Eric Davis	1,143
83	Bert Campaneris	1,142
84	Donn Clendenon	1,140
85	Gil Hodges	1,137
86	Jeff Burroughs	1,135
	Lloyd Moseby	1,135
	Leo Cardenas	1,135
89	Willie McGee	1,129
90	Jay Buhner	1,128
91	Brian Downing	1,127
92	Bob Bailey	1,126
93	Gary Matthews	1,125
94	Greg Gagne	1,121
95	Fred Lynn	1,116
96	Cal Ripken Jr.	1,106
97	Dave Henderson	1,105
98	Mark McGwire	1,104
99	Lou Whitaker	1,099
100	Jim Fregosi	1,097

Hit By Pitch

#	Player	Total
1	Hughie Jennings	287
2	Tommy Tucker	272
3	Don Baylor	267
4	Ron Hunt	243
5	Dan McGann	230
6	Frank Robinson	198
7	Minnie Minoso	192
8	Jake Beckley	183
9	Curt Welch	173
10	Kid Elberfeld	165
11	Fred Clarke	153
12	Chet Lemon	151
13	Carlton Fisk	143
14	Nellie Fox	142
15	Art Fletcher	141
16	Bill Dahlen	140
17	Frank Chance	137
18	Nap Lajoie	134
19	Dummy Hoy	133
20	John McGraw	132
	Steve Brodie	132
22	Brian Downing	129
	Willie Keeler	129
24	Honus Wagner	124
25	Buck Herzog	120
26	Craig Biggio	119
27	Sherm Lollar	115
28	Bill Freehan	114
	Frankie Crosetti	114
30	Andres Galarraga	112
31	Andre Dawson	111
	Steve Evans	111
33	George Burns	110
34	Jimmy Dykes	109
	Sherry Magee	109
36	Bill Joyce	108
37	Pete Rose	107
	Wally Schang	107
39	Dan Brouthers	105
40	Tris Speaker	103
41	Orlando Cepeda	102
42	Henry Larkin	100
43	Eddie Yost	99
	Bucky Harris	99
	Elmer Flick	99
46	Brady Anderson	97
	Dick Bartell	97
	Dick Padden	97
49	Reggie Jackson	96
50	Ty Cobb	94
	John Titus	94
	Jake Stahl	94
	Ed Delahanty	94
	John Reilly	94
55	Lonnie Smith	92
	Mike Macfarlane	92
	Doc Gessler	92
	Jim Delahanty	92
59	Gene Tenace	91
	John Warner	91
	Chief Zimmer	91
62	Norm Cash	90
	Jimmy Sheckard	90
64	Jack Fournier	89
	Billy Hamilton	89
66	Joe Carter	88
	Cesar Tovar	88
68	Bid McPhee	87
69	Bobby Grich	86
	Cy Williams	86
71	Joe Torre	85
	Kiki Cuyler	85
	Boileryard Clarke	85
	Arlie Latham	85
75	Greg Luzinski	84
	Gary Gaetti	84
	Art Devlin	84
	Jimmy Collins	84
	Deacon McGuire	84
80	Heine Groh	83
	Patsy Donovan	83
	Jimmy Ryan	83
83	Al Oliver	82
	Monte Cross	82
	Joe Kelley	82
	Denny Lyons	82
87	Bing Miller	80
	Clyde Milan	80
89	Mike Schmidt	79
	Rusty Staub	79
	Hal McRae	79
	Rickey Henderson	79
	Joe Sewell	79
	Harry Steinfeldt	79
95	Willie Stargell	78
	Tony Taylor	78
	Dick Harley	78
98	5 tied with	77

Sac Hits

#	Player	Total
1	Eddie Collins	511
2	Jake Daubert	392
3	Stuffy McInnis	383
4	Willie Keeler	366
5	Ray Chapman	340
6	Donie Bush	337
7	Bill Wambsganss	323
8	Roger Peckinpaugh	314
9	Larry Gardner	311
10	Tris Speaker	310
11	Rabbit Maranville	300
12	Ty Cobb	296
13	Max Carey	290
14	Jimmy Sheckard	287
15	Joe Tinker	285
16	Jack Barry	284
17	Wildfire Schulte	279
18	Harry Heilmann	277
	Jimmy Austin	277
	Fred Tenney	277
21	Joe Sewell	275
	Everett Scott	275
23	Wally Pipp	271
	Bobby Veach	271
25	Dick Bartell	269
26	Terry Turner	268
27	George Cutshaw	266
28	Otto Knabe	265
29	Duffy Lewis	263
30	Howard Shanks	262
31	Sherry Magee	260
32	Ossie Vitt	259
33	Shano Collins	258
34	Joe Judge	257
35	Edd Roush	256
	Johnny Evers	256
37	Ed Konetchy	253
	Bill Bradley	253
39	Fielder Jones	251
40	Bucky Harris	249
41	Harry Hooper	248
	Harry Steinfeldt	248
43	Buck Weaver	242
	Sam Crawford	242
45	Tommy Leach	240
46	Willie Kamm	238
47	Dots Miller	235
48	Milt Stock	234
49	Del Pratt	233
50	Pie Traynor	231
	Hans Lobert	231
52	Frankie Frisch	229
53	Jimmy Dykes	228
54	Mule Haas	227
55	George Sisler	226
56	George McBride	225
57	Dode Paskert	224
	Claude Ritchey	224
59	Fred Clarke	222
60	Honus Wagner	221
	Nap Lajoie	221
62	Charlie Grimm	219
	Wally Gerber	219
	Doc Hoblitzell	219
65	Ossie Bluege	218
66	Amos Strunk	217
	Mickey Doolan	217
68	Rogers Hornsby	216
	Buck Herzog	216
	Hal Chase	216
71	Ozzie Smith	214
72	Sam Rice	213
	Ray Schalk	213
74	Dave Bancroft	212
	Kid Gleason	212
76	Bing Miller	210
77	Nellie Fox	208
78	Freddy Parent	203
79	Frank Isbell	202
80	Bert Campaneris	199
81	Marty McManus	198
	Ivy Olson	198
83	Larry Doyle	195
	Danny Murphy	195
	Monte Cross	195
86	Lee Magee	194
87	Phil Rizzuto	193
88	Miller Huggins	191
89	Earl Sheely	189
	Bibb Falk	189
91	Hughie Critz	187
	George Burns	187
	Hi Myers	187
	Clyde Milan	187
95	Heinie Manush	186
	Mike Mowrey	186
97	Doc Johnston	185
	Harry Lord	185
99	Solly Hofman	184
	George Davis	184

Sac Flies

#	Player	Total
1	Eddie Murray	128
2	Robin Yount	123
3	Hank Aaron	121
4	George Brett	120
5	Rusty Staub	119
6	Andre Dawson	118
7	Don Baylor	115
8	Brooks Robinson	114
9	Cal Ripken Jr.	109
10	Mike Schmidt	108
11	Tony Perez	106
12	Carl Yastrzemski	105
13	Al Kaline	104
14	Amos Otis	103
15	Frank Robinson	102
16	Joe Carter	101
	Ruben Sierra	101
18	Ted Simmons	100
19	Gary Carter	99
	Paul Molitor	99
21	Bill Buckner	97
22	Joe Morgan	96
	Don Mattingly	96
	Willie Davis	96
	Ernie Banks	96
26	Dave Winfield	95
	Al Oliver	95
28	Jim Rice	94
	Gary Gaetti	94
	Ron Santo	94
31	Harold Baines	92
32	Lou Whitaker	91
	Willie Mays	91
34	Darrell Evans	90
	Steve Garvey	90
	Graig Nettles	90
	Johnny Bench	90
	Chili Davis	90
	Wade Boggs	90
40	Bobby Bonilla	88
41	Will Clark	87
42	Dave Concepcion	86
	George Hendrick	86
	Fred Lynn	86
	Dave Parker	86
	Reggie Smith	86
47	Dusty Baker	85
	Hal McRae	85
49	Jack Clark	83
	George Bell	83
51	Ron Cey	82
	Jose Cruz	82
53	Bobby Murcer	81
	Wally Joyner	81
55	Buddy Bell	80
56	Cecil Cooper	79
	Carlton Fisk	79
	Greg Luzinski	79
	Pete Rose	79
60	Bob Boone	78
	Vada Pinson	78
62	Carney Lansford	77
	Dwight Evans	77
	Tim Wallach	77
	Harmon Killebrew	77
66	Alan Trammell	76
	Luis Aparicio	76
68	Dave Kingman	75
	Willie Stargell	75
70	Jimmy Wynn	74
	Orlando Cepeda	74
72	Pedro Guerrero	73
	Billy Williams	73
74	Toby Harrah	72
	Tom Brunansky	72
	Boog Powell	72
77	Cesar Cedeno	71
	Keith Hernandez	71
	Andre Thornton	71
	Ryne Sandberg	71
81	Brian Downing	70
	Willie McCovey	70
	Tony Gwynn	70
	B.J. Surhoff	70
	Bill Mazeroski	70
	Frank Thomas	70
87	Bill Madlock	69
	Ben Oglivie	69
	Roy White	69
90	George Foster	68
	Reggie Jackson	68
	Julio Franco	68
	Pete O'Brien	68
	Tommy Davis	68
95	Mike Hargrove	67
	Richie Hebner	67
	Jorge Orta	67
	Tim Raines	67
99	3 tied with	66

Stolen Bases

#	Player	SB
1	Rickey Henderson	1,231
2	Lou Brock	938
3	Billy Hamilton	912
4	Ty Cobb	892
5	Tim Raines	795
6	Vince Coleman	752
7	Eddie Collins	745
8	Arlie Latham	739
9	Max Carey	738
10	Honus Wagner	723
11	Joe Morgan	689
12	Willie Wilson	668
13	Tom Brown	657
14	Bert Campaneris	649
15	George Davis	616
16	Dummy Hoy	594
17	Maury Wills	586
18	George Van Haltren	583
19	Ozzie Smith	580
20	Hugh Duffy	574
21	Bid McPhee	568
22	Brett Butler	558
23	Davey Lopes	557
	Otis Nixon	557
25	Cesar Cedeno	550
26	Bill Dahlen	547
27	Monte Ward	540
28	Herman Long	534
29	Patsy Donovan	518
30	Jack Doyle	516
31	Harry Stovey	509
32	Luis Aparicio	506
	Fred Clarke	506
34	Paul Molitor	495
	Clyde Milan	495
	Willie Keeler	495
37	Omar Moreno	487
38	Mike Griffin	473
39	Tommy McCarthy	468
40	Jimmy Sheckard	465
41	Bobby Bonds	461
42	Ron LeFlore	455
	Ed Delahanty	455
44	Curt Welch	453
45	Steve Sax	444
46	Joe Kelley	443
47	Sherry Magee	441
48	John McGraw	436
49	Tris Speaker	434
50	Mike Tiernan	428
51	Bob Bescher	427
52	Frankie Frisch	419
	Charlie Comiskey	419
54	Jimmy Ryan	418
55	Barry Bonds	417
56	Tommy Harper	408
57	Donie Bush	403
58	Frank Chance	401
59	Bill Lange	399
60	Willie Davis	398
61	Sam Mertes	396
62	Dave Collins	395
	Bill North	395
64	Jesse Burkett	389
65	Tommy Corcoran	387
66	Freddie Patek	385
	Tom Daly	385
68	Juan Samuel	383
	George Burns	383
	Hugh Nicol	383
71	Fred Pfeffer	382
72	Walt Wilmot	381
73	Nap Lajoie	380
74	George Sisler	375
	Harry Hooper	375
76	Jack Glasscock	372
77	Lonnie Smith	370
78	King Kelly	368
79	Sam Crawford	366
	Tommy Dowd	366
81	Hal Chase	363
82	Tommy Leach	361
83	Fielder Jones	359
	Hughie Jennings	359
85	Delino DeShields	356
86	Gary Pettis	354
	Kenny Lofton	354
	Buck Ewing	354
89	Rod Carew	353
90	Tommy Tucker	352
91	Sam Rice	351
92	George Case	349
93	Paul Radford	346
94	Marquis Grissom	345
95	Ryne Sandberg	344
96	Julio Cruz	343
97	Amos Otis	341
98	Willie McGee	338
	Willie Mays	338
	John Anderson	338

Caught Stealing

#	Player	CS
1	Lou Brock	307
2	Rickey Henderson	288
3	Brett Butler	257
4	Ty Cobb	212
5	Maury Wills	208
6	Bert Campaneris	199
7	Rod Carew	187
8	Omar Moreno	182
9	Cesar Cedeno	179
10	Steve Sax	178
11	Vince Coleman	177
12	George Burns	174
13	Eddie Collins	173
14	Otis Nixon	172
15	Bobby Bonds	169
16	Max Carey	167
17	Bill North	162
	Joe Morgan	162
19	Pete Rose	149
20	Ozzie Smith	148
21	Harry Hooper	146
22	Sam Rice	143
23	Ron LeFlore	142
	Tim Raines	142
25	Clyde Milan	141
26	Lonnie Smith	140
27	Jose Cardenal	139
	Dave Collins	139
29	Harold Reynolds	138
30	Jose Cruz	136
	Luis Aparicio	136
32	Juan Samuel	135
	Ben Chapman	135
34	Alfredo Griffin	134
	Claudell Washington	134
	Willie Wilson	134
37	Freddie Patek	131
	Willie Davis	131
39	Minnie Minoso	130
40	Garry Templeton	129
	Paul Molitor	129
	Luis Polonia	129
	Tris Speaker	129
44	George Sisler	127
45	Enos Cabell	124
46	Vada Pinson	122
47	Tony Gwynn	121
48	Don Baylor	120
	Tony Fernandez	120
50	Pat Kelly	118
	Barry Bonds	118
	Babe Ruth	118
53	Roy White	117
54	Carl Yastrzemski	116
	Delino DeShields	116
	Tommy Harper	116
57	Reggie Jackson	115
	Willie McGee	115
59	Davey Lopes	114
60	Dave Parker	113
61	Lenny Randle	112
62	Tony Taylor	111
	Jim Gilliam	111
64	Tony Phillips	110
65	Dave Concepcion	109
	Andre Dawson	109
	Alan Trammell	109
	George Case	109
	Buddy Myer	109
70	Cesar Tovar	108
	Luke Appling	108
	Del Pratt	108
73	Ryne Sandberg	107
	Charlie Jamieson	107
75	Frank Taveras	106
	Johnny Mostil	106
77	Larry Bowa	105
	Robin Yount	105
	Phil Garner	105
	Don Buford	105
	Ken Williams	105
82	Carney Lansford	104
	Gary Pettis	104
84	Willie Mays	103
	Bob Meusel	103
86	Julio Franco	101
	Ozzie Guillen	101
	Jimmy Wynn	101
	Lou Gehrig	101
90	Bobby Tolan	100
91	Terry Puhl	99
	Jerry Remy	99
93	Mookie Wilson	98
94	George Brett	97
	Von Hayes	97
96	Dave Winfield	96
	Chili Davis	96
	Greg Gagne	96
	Lance Johnson	96
	Ray Lankford	96

SB Percentage
(minimum 200 attempts)

#	Player	Pct
1	Eric Davis	.861
2	Tim Raines	.848
3	Stan Javier	.847
4	Barry Larkin	.843
5	Willie Wilson	.833
6	Davey Lopes	.830
7	Julio Cruz	.815
8	Rickey Henderson	.810
9	Marquis Grissom	.810
10	Joe Morgan	.810
11	Vince Coleman	.809
12	Andy Van Slyke	.806
13	Lenny Dykstra	.798
14	Ozzie Smith	.797
15	Kenny Lofton	.796
16	Gary Redus	.795
17	Paul Molitor	.793
18	Roberto Alomar	.791
19	Devon White	.789
20	Luis Aparicio	.788
21	Amos Otis	.786
22	Kirk Gibson	.785
23	Chuck Knoblauch	.782
24	Alan Wiggins	.781
25	Barry Bonds	.779
26	Tommy Harper	.779
27	Rudy Law	.778
28	Mike Felder	.778
29	Joe Carter	.777
30	Bob Dernier	.776
31	Larry Walker	.775
32	Miguel Dilone	.774
33	Gary Pettis	.773
34	Gregg Jefferies	.770
35	Mookie Wilson	.769
36	Rodney Scott	.768
37	Hank Aaron	.767
38	Willie Mays	.766
39	Craig Biggio	.766
40	Bert Campaneris	.765
41	Milt Thompson	.764
42	Otis Nixon	.764
43	Ryne Sandberg	.763
44	Ron LeFlore	.762
45	George Case	.762
46	Oddibe McDowell	.761
47	Lance Johnson	.759
48	Deion Sanders	.756
49	Brady Anderson	.756
50	Cesar Cedeno	.754
51	Delino DeShields	.754
52	Lou Brock	.753
53	Mariano Duncan	.753
54	Lloyd Moseby	.753
55	Willie Davis	.752
56	Larry Bowa	.752
57	Bump Wills	.751
58	Howard Johnson	.750
59	Mickey Rivers	.748
60	Steve Finley	.747
61	Dave Concepcion	.747
62	Willie McGee	.746
63	Freddie Patek	.746
64	Tom Herr	.746
65	Bake McBride	.744
66	Willie Randolph	.742
67	Andre Dawson	.742
68	Dave Collins	.740
69	Sandy Alomar	.739
70	Juan Samuel	.739
71	Frank Taveras	.739
72	Roberto Kelly	.739
73	Tom Goodwin	.738
74	Maury Wills	.738
75	Gene Richards	.735
76	Eric Young	.734
77	Al Bumbry	.734
78	Bobby Bonds	.732
79	Bip Roberts	.732
80	Garry Maddox	.729
81	Omar Moreno	.728
82	Jeffrey Leonard	.728
83	Dickie Thon	.726
84	Frank Robinson	.726
85	Lonnie Smith	.725
86	John Cangelosi	.724
87	Von Hayes	.723
88	Horace Clarke	.722
89	Shawon Dunston	.721
	Darren Lewis	.721
91	Robin Yount	.721
92	Julio Franco	.720
93	Phil Rizzuto	.720
94	Dave Nelson	.719
95	Brian McRae	.719
96	Tony Gwynn	.718
97	Toby Harrah	.717
98	Alex Cole	.715
99	Bill Buckner	.715
100	Billy Hatcher	.715

GDP

#	Player	GDP
1	Hank Aaron	328
2	Carl Yastrzemski	323
3	Dave Winfield	319
4	Eddie Murray	316
5	Jim Rice	315
6	Cal Ripken Jr.	302
7	Rusty Staub	297
	Brooks Robinson	297
9	Ted Simmons	287
10	Joe Torre	284
11	George Scott	277
12	Roberto Clemente	275
13	Al Kaline	271
14	Frank Robinson	269
15	Tony Perez	268
16	Dave Concepcion	266
17	Ernie Lombardi	261
18	Harold Baines	257
19	Ron Santo	256
20	Buddy Bell	255
	Julio Franco	255
22	Al Oliver	254
23	Steve Garvey	251
	Willie Mays	251
25	Ken Singleton	248
26	Bill Buckner	247
	Pete Rose	247
28	Harmon Killebrew	243
	Stan Musial	243
30	George Brett	235
31	Tony Pena	234
32	Ernie Banks	229
33	Dwight Evans	227
34	Tony Gwynn	226
35	Joe Adcock	223
36	Dick Groat	220
37	Lee May	219
	Gary Gaetti	219
	Tommy Davis	219
	Frank Howard	219
41	Willie Randolph	218
	Orlando Cepeda	218
43	Andre Dawson	217
	Robin Yount	217
45	Rod Carew	216
46	Chili Davis	214
47	Del Ennis	212
48	George Hendrick	211
49	Lou Piniella	209
	Dave Parker	209
	Dale Murphy	209
	Wade Boggs	209
53	Carl Furillo	207
54	Rico Carty	206
55	Carlton Fisk	204
56	Joe Medwick	203
57	Johnny Bench	201
58	Billy Williams	200
59	Brian Downing	197
	Lance Parrish	197
	Graig Nettles	197
	Ted Williams	197
63	Don Baylor	196
	George Foster	196
65	Willie Horton	195
	Bob Bailey	195
	Billy Jurges	195
68	Bill Mazeroski	194
69	Tim Wallach	192
	Bill Skowron	192
71	Bob Boone	191
	Don Mattingly	191
	Frank Thomas	191
	Billy Herman	191
75	Bill Madlock	190
	Paul Molitor	190
	Dave Philley	190
78	Kirby Puckett	188
	George Kell	188
80	Larry Parrish	187
	Bob Elliott	187
82	Hal McRae	186
83	Ron Cey	185
	Minnie Minoso	185
	Ken Boyer	185
	Jackie Jensen	185
87	Luis Aparicio	184
	Sherm Lollar	184
89	Reggie Jackson	183
	Chris Speier	183
	Mickey Vernon	183
92	Rocky Colavito	182
	Bobby Doerr	182
94	Cookie Rojas	181
95	Gary Carter	180
	Red Schoendienst	180
97	Gary Matthews	179
98	Doug DeCinces	177
99	4 tied with	176

Runs Created

1	Babe Ruth	2,579
2	Ty Cobb	2,566
3	Hank Aaron	2,434
4	Stan Musial	2,418
5	Willie Mays	2,278
6	Ted Williams	2,259
7	Tris Speaker	2,200
8	Pete Rose	2,165
9	Lou Gehrig	2,161
10	Honus Wagner	2,152
11	Mel Ott	2,127
12	Cap Anson	2,108
13	Carl Yastrzemski	2,079
14	Frank Robinson	2,037
15	Jimmie Foxx	2,025
16	Eddie Collins	2,006
17	Mickey Mantle	1,950
18	Eddie Murray	1,908
19	Rogers Hornsby	1,896
20	Roger Connor	1,891
21	Jesse Burkett	1,855
22	Dan Brouthers	1,804
23	Paul Molitor	1,802
24	Rickey Henderson	1,799
25	Nap Lajoie	1,797
26	Al Kaline	1,794
27	Paul Waner	1,793
	Ed Delahanty	1,793
29	George Brett	1,787
30	Charlie Gehringer	1,766
31	Jake Beckley	1,759
32	Joe Morgan	1,754
33	Dave Winfield	1,748
34	Reggie Jackson	1,744
35	Billy Hamilton	1,725
36	Al Simmons	1,711
37	George Davis	1,706
38	Jimmy Ryan	1,691
39	Goose Goslin	1,687
40	Sam Crawford	1,685
41	Fred Clarke	1,676
42	Robin Yount	1,665
	George Van Haltren	1,665
44	Eddie Mathews	1,663
45	Mike Schmidt	1,662
46	Billy Williams	1,628
47	Hugh Duffy	1,609
48	Harry Heilmann	1,600
	Bid McPhee	1,600
50	Willie Keeler	1,594
51	Bill Dahlen	1,587
52	Willie McCovey	1,584
53	Rod Carew	1,574
54	Harmon Killebrew	1,564
55	Dwight Evans	1,562
56	Wade Boggs	1,558
57	Joe DiMaggio	1,554
58	Joe Kelley	1,544
59	Jim O'Rourke	1,515
60	Rusty Staub	1,513
61	Lou Brock	1,510
62	Zack Wheat	1,500
63	Tim Raines	1,499
	Luke Appling	1,499
65	Sam Rice	1,492
66	Roberto Clemente	1,487
67	Frankie Frisch	1,482
68	Cal Ripken Jr.	1,481
	Ernie Banks	1,481
70	Tony Perez	1,475
71	Andre Dawson	1,470
72	Harry Stovey	1,462
73	Darrell Evans	1,459
74	Willie Stargell	1,451
75	Duke Snider	1,436
76	Dummy Hoy	1,424
77	Joe Cronin	1,419
78	Tony Gwynn	1,418
79	Johnny Mize	1,417
80	Max Carey	1,414
81	Dave Parker	1,413
82	Barry Bonds	1,404
	George Sisler	1,404
84	Lou Whitaker	1,398
85	Harold Baines	1,395
86	Heinie Manush	1,393
87	Enos Slaughter	1,386
88	Vada Pinson	1,377
89	Sam Thompson	1,361
90	King Kelly	1,357
91	Carlton Fisk	1,356
	Mickey Vernon	1,356
93	Mike Tiernan	1,353
94	Harry Hooper	1,349
95	Joe Medwick	1,347
96	Bob Johnson	1,346
	Jim Bottomley	1,346
98	Herman Long	1,344
	Lave Cross	1,344
100	3 tied with	1,341

Runs Created/27 Outs
(minimum 3,000 Plate Appearances)

1	Babe Ruth	11.73
2	Ted Williams	11.49
3	Billy Hamilton	10.70
4	Dan Brouthers	10.68
5	Lou Gehrig	10.29
6	John McGraw	9.88
7	Bill Joyce	9.63
8	Pete Browning	9.60
9	Tip O'Neill	9.59
10	Frank Thomas	9.54
11	Jimmie Foxx	9.35
12	Ed Delahanty	9.31
13	Roger Connor	9.31
14	Dave Orr	9.24
15	Cap Anson	9.07
16	Hank Greenberg	9.00
17	Rogers Hornsby	8.95
18	Mickey Mantle	8.93
19	Bill Lange	8.93
20	Jake Stenzel	8.90
21	Harry Stovey	8.87
22	King Kelly	8.82
23	Sam Thompson	8.78
24	Charley Jones	8.71
25	Joe DiMaggio	8.67
26	Ty Cobb	8.66
27	George Gore	8.64
28	Mike Tiernan	8.54
29	Hugh Duffy	8.54
30	Jesse Burkett	8.44
31	Stan Musial	8.41
32	Mel Ott	8.34
33	Joe Jackson	8.33
34	Henry Larkin	8.33
35	Johnny Mize	8.32
36	Barry Bonds	8.26
37	Buck Ewing	8.23
38	Oyster Burns	8.22
39	Charlie Keller	8.21
40	Lefty O'Doul	8.10
41	Elmer Smith	8.07
42	Tris Speaker	8.06
43	Joe Kelley	8.04
44	Mike Griffin	8.00
45	Bug Holliday	7.96
46	Jim O'Rourke	7.89
47	George Van Haltren	7.73
48	Earl Averill	7.70
49	Jeff Bagwell	7.67
50	Willie Mays	7.65
51	Jimmy Ryan	7.63
52	Harry Heilmann	7.63
53	Paul Hines	7.63
54	Honus Wagner	7.62
55	Mickey Cochrane	7.61
56	Edgar Martinez	7.57
57	Hardy Richardson	7.57
58	Fred Carroll	7.57
59	John Reilly	7.49
60	Hub Collins	7.49
61	Hack Wilson	7.49
62	Ralph Kiner	7.48
63	Mark McGwire	7.46
64	Al Simmons	7.43
65	Tim Salmon	7.41
66	Charlie Gehringer	7.38
67	Ken Griffey Jr.	7.36
68	Bill Terry	7.35
69	George Selkirk	7.35
70	Mike Donlin	7.34
71	Mo Vaughn	7.33
72	Frank Robinson	7.32
73	Chuck Klein	7.30
74	Hughie Jennings	7.29
75	Jackie Robinson	7.28
76	Yank Robinson	7.27
77	Jocko Milligan	7.26
78	Darby O'Brien	7.24
79	Arky Vaughan	7.24
80	Elmer Flick	7.23
81	Duke Snider	7.22
82	Hank Aaron	7.21
83	Abner Dalrymple	7.20
84	David Justice	7.19
85	Dolph Camilli	7.19
86	Riggs Stephenson	7.18
87	Joe Start	7.16
88	Goose Goslin	7.16
89	Fred Dunlap	7.15
90	Paul Waner	7.15
91	Eddie Collins	7.14
92	Frank Chance	7.11
93	Tommy Henrich	7.10
94	Will Clark	7.09
95	Ed McKean	7.09
96	Dummy Hoy	7.07
97	Bill Dickey	7.07
98	Babe Herman	7.07
99	Dick Allen	7.07
100	Bob Johnson	7.06

Batting Average
(minimum 3,000 Plate Appearances)

1	Ty Cobb	.366
2	Rogers Hornsby	.358
3	Joe Jackson	.356
4	Lefty O'Doul	.349
5	Ed Delahanty	.346
6	Tris Speaker	.345
7	Ted Williams	.344
8	Billy Hamilton	.344
9	Dave Orr	.342
10	Dan Brouthers	.342
11	Babe Ruth	.342
12	Harry Heilmann	.342
13	Pete Browning	.341
14	Willie Keeler	.341
15	Bill Terry	.341
16	George Sisler	.340
17	Lou Gehrig	.340
18	Tony Gwynn	.340
19	Jake Stenzel	.339
20	Jesse Burkett	.338
21	Nap Lajoie	.338
22	Riggs Stephenson	.336
23	Al Simmons	.334
24	John McGraw	.334
25	Paul Waner	.333
26	Eddie Collins	.333
27	Mike Donlin	.333
28	Wade Boggs	.331
29	Stan Musial	.331
30	Sam Thompson	.331
31	Bill Lange	.330
32	Frank Thomas	.330
33	Heinie Manush	.330
34	Cap Anson	.329
35	Rod Carew	.328
36	Honus Wagner	.327
37	Tip O'Neill	.326
38	Bob Fothergill	.325
39	Jimmie Foxx	.325
40	Earle Combs	.325
41	Joe DiMaggio	.325
42	Babe Herman	.324
43	Hugh Duffy	.324
44	Joe Medwick	.324
45	Edd Roush	.323
46	Sam Rice	.322
47	Ross Youngs	.322
48	Kiki Cuyler	.321
49	Charlie Gehringer	.320
50	Chuck Klein	.320
51	Pie Traynor	.320
52	Mickey Cochrane	.320
53	Ken Williams	.319
54	Kirby Puckett	.318
55	Earl Averill	.318
56	Arky Vaughan	.318
57	Bill Everitt	.317
58	Roberto Clemente	.317
59	Joe Harris	.317
60	Chick Hafey	.317
61	Edgar Martinez	.317
62	Joe Kelley	.317
63	Zack Wheat	.317
64	Roger Connor	.317
65	Lloyd Waner	.316
66	Frankie Frisch	.316
67	Goose Goslin	.316
68	Kenny Lofton	.316
69	Lew Fonseca	.316
70	George Van Haltren	.316
71	Bibb Falk	.314
72	Cecil Travis	.314
73	Hank Greenberg	.313
74	Jack Fournier	.313
75	Elmer Flick	.313
76	Eddie Morgan	.313
77	Bill Dickey	.313
78	Dale Mitchell	.312
79	Johnny Mize	.312
80	Joe Sewell	.312
81	Fred Clarke	.312
82	Barney McCosky	.312
83	Bing Miller	.312
84	Johnny Hodapp	.311
85	Hughie Jennings	.311
86	Freddy Lindstrom	.311
87	Jackie Robinson	.311
88	Baby Doll Jacobson	.311
89	Taffy Wright	.311
90	Rip Radcliff	.311
91	Bug Holliday	.311
92	Ginger Beaumont	.311
93	Benny Kauff	.311
94	Mike Tiernan	.311
95	Denny Lyons	.310
96	Irish Meusel	.310
97	Luke Appling	.310
98	Elmer Smith	.310
99	Bobby Veach	.310
100	Jim O'Rourke	.310

On-Base Percentage
(minimum 3,000 Plate Appearances)

1	Ted Williams	.482
2	Babe Ruth	.474
3	John McGraw	.465
4	Billy Hamilton	.455
5	Frank Thomas	.452
6	Lou Gehrig	.447
7	Bill Joyce	.435
8	Rogers Hornsby	.434
9	Ty Cobb	.433
10	Jimmie Foxx	.428
11	Tris Speaker	.428
12	Eddie Collins	.424
13	Ferris Fain	.424
14	Dan Brouthers	.423
15	Joe Jackson	.423
16	Edgar Martinez	.423
17	Max Bishop	.423
18	Mickey Mantle	.421
19	Wade Boggs	.420
20	Mickey Cochrane	.419
21	Stan Musial	.417
22	Cupid Childs	.416
23	Jesse Burkett	.415
24	Mel Ott	.414
25	Roy Thomas	.413
26	Lefty O'Doul	.413
27	Hank Greenberg	.412
28	Ed Delahanty	.412
29	Charlie Keller	.410
30	Eddie Stanky	.410
31	Harry Heilmann	.410
32	Jeff Bagwell	.409
33	Jackie Robinson	.409
34	Jake Stenzel	.408
35	Roy Cullenbine	.408
36	Barry Bonds	.408
37	Denny Lyons	.407
38	Riggs Stephenson	.407
39	Rickey Henderson	.406
40	Arky Vaughan	.406
41	Joe Harris	.404
42	Paul Waner	.404
43	Charlie Gehringer	.404
44	Joe Cunningham	.403
45	Pete Browning	.403
46	Lu Blue	.402
47	Joe Kelley	.402
48	Bill Lange	.401
49	George Selkirk	.400
50	Luke Appling	.399
51	Ross Youngs	.399
52	Elmer Valo	.398
53	Joe DiMaggio	.398
54	Ralph Kiner	.398
55	Eddie Morgan	.398
56	Elmer Smith	.398
57	Johnny Mize	.397
58	Roger Connor	.397
59	Earle Combs	.397
60	John Kruk	.397
61	Richie Ashburn	.396
62	John Olerud	.396
63	Mike Hargrove	.396
64	Hack Wilson	.395
65	Earl Averill	.395
66	Cap Anson	.395
67	Johnny Pesky	.394
68	Stan Hack	.394
69	Eddie Yost	.394
70	Frank Chance	.394
71	Ken Williams	.393
72	Wally Schang	.393
73	Rod Carew	.393
74	Dave Magadan	.393
75	Bob Johnson	.393
76	Bill Terry	.393
77	Mo Vaughn	.393
78	George Grantham	.392
79	Tim Salmon	.392
80	Tip O'Neill	.392
81	Joe Morgan	.392
82	Jack Fournier	.392
83	Mike Tiernan	.392
84	Joe Sewell	.391
85	Honus Wagner	.391
86	Chuck Knoblauch	.391
87	Augie Galan	.390
88	Tony Gwynn	.390
89	Hughie Jennings	.390
90	Harlond Clift	.390
91	Solly Hemus	.390
92	Joe Cronin	.390
93	Buddy Myer	.389
94	Frank Robinson	.389
95	Elmer Flick	.389
96	Benny Kauff	.389
97	Minnie Minoso	.389
98	Dolph Camilli	.388
99	Mike Griffin	.388
100	Ken Singleton	.388

Slugging Percentage

(minimum 3,000 Plate Appearances)

#	Player	SLG
1	Babe Ruth	.690
2	Ted Williams	.634
3	Lou Gehrig	.632
4	Jimmie Foxx	.609
5	Hank Greenberg	.605
6	Frank Thomas	.600
7	Joe DiMaggio	.579
8	Rogers Hornsby	.577
9	Albert Belle	.566
10	Johnny Mize	.562
11	Ken Griffey Jr.	.562
12	Stan Musial	.559
13	Willie Mays	.557
14	Juan Gonzalez	.557
15	Mickey Mantle	.557
16	Mark McGwire	.556
17	Hank Aaron	.555
18	Barry Bonds	.551
19	Ralph Kiner	.548
20	Hack Wilson	.545
21	Chuck Klein	.543
22	Larry Walker	.542
23	Duke Snider	.540
24	Frank Robinson	.537
25	Jeff Bagwell	.536
26	Al Simmons	.535
27	Dick Allen	.534
28	Earl Averill	.533
29	Mel Ott	.533
30	Mo Vaughn	.532
31	Lefty O'Doul	.532
32	Babe Herman	.532
33	Ken Williams	.531
34	Willie Stargell	.529
35	Mike Schmidt	.527
36	Tim Salmon	.527
37	Chick Hafey	.526
38	Kevin Mitchell	.525
39	Hal Trosky	.522
40	Wally Berger	.522
41	Fred McGriff	.521
42	Harry Heilmann	.520
43	Dan Brouthers	.519
44	Joe Jackson	.518
45	Charlie Keller	.518
46	Jose Canseco	.516
47	Willie McCovey	.515
48	Edgar Martinez	.513
49	David Justice	.513
50	Ty Cobb	.512
51	Eddie Mathews	.509
52	Jeff Heath	.509
53	Harmon Killebrew	.509
54	Bob Johnson	.506
55	Bill Terry	.506
56	Ed Delahanty	.505
57	Sam Thompson	.505
58	Joe Medwick	.505
59	Darryl Strawberry	.502
60	Jim Rice	.502
61	Dave Orr	.502
62	Tris Speaker	.500
63	Jim Bottomley	.500
64	Goose Goslin	.500
65	Roy Campanella	.500
66	Ernie Banks	.500
67	Orlando Cepeda	.499
68	Bob Horner	.499
69	Frank Howard	.499
70	Jay Buhner	.499
71	Ellis Burks	.498
72	Dante Bichette	.498
73	Ted Kluszewski	.498
74	Matt Williams	.497
75	Bob Meusel	.497
76	Rafael Palmeiro	.496
77	Hank Sauer	.496
78	Danny Tartabull	.496
79	Andres Galarraga	.496
80	Al Rosen	.495
81	Gary Sheffield	.495
82	Will Clark	.493
83	Billy Williams	.492
84	Ripper Collins	.492
85	Dolph Camilli	.492
86	Tommy Henrich	.491
87	Larry Doby	.490
88	Reggie Jackson	.490
89	Dick Stuart	.489
90	Moises Alou	.489
91	Reggie Smith	.489
92	Gabby Hartnett	.489
93	Cecil Fielder	.489
94	Rocky Colavito	.489
95	Norm Cash	.488
96	Tino Martinez	.488
97	Zeke Bonura	.487
98	George Brett	.487
99	Gil Hodges	.487
100	Jim Gentile	.486

OBP+Slugging

(minimum 3,000 Plate Appearances)

#	Player	OPS
1	Babe Ruth	1.163
2	Ted Williams	1.115
3	Lou Gehrig	1.080
4	Frank Thomas	1.053
5	Jimmie Foxx	1.038
6	Hank Greenberg	1.017
7	Rogers Hornsby	1.010
8	Mickey Mantle	.977
	Joe DiMaggio	.977
10	Stan Musial	.976
11	Johnny Mize	.959
	Barry Bonds	.959
13	Mel Ott	.947
14	Ralph Kiner	.946
15	Ty Cobb	.945
	Lefty O'Doul	.945
	Jeff Bagwell	.945
18	Ken Griffey Jr.	.943
19	Dan Brouthers	.942
20	Willie Mays	.941
	Joe Jackson	.941
22	Hack Wilson	.940
23	Mark McGwire	.938
24	Edgar Martinez	.936
25	Harry Heilmann	.930
	Albert Belle	.930
27	Hank Aaron	.928
	Tris Speaker	.928
	Earl Averill	.928
	Charlie Keller	.928
31	Frank Robinson	.926
32	Mo Vaughn	.925
33	Ken Williams	.924
34	Chuck Klein	.922
35	Duke Snider	.919
	Tim Salmon	.919
37	Ed Delahanty	.917
38	Larry Walker	.916
39	Babe Herman	.915
	Al Simmons	.915
41	Dick Allen	.912
42	Mike Schmidt	.908
43	Bill Joyce	.902
	Fred McGriff	.902
45	Bob Johnson	.899
	Bill Terry	.899
47	Chick Hafey	.898
48	Mickey Cochrane	.897
49	David Justice	.893
50	Hal Trosky	.892
51	Juan Gonzalez	.891
52	Willie McCovey	.889
	Willie Stargell	.889
54	Jake Stenzel	.888
	Sam Thompson	.888
	Kevin Mitchell	.888
57	Billy Hamilton	.887
	Goose Goslin	.887
59	Eddie Mathews	.885
60	Harmon Killebrew	.884
	Charlie Gehringer	.884
62	Roger Connor	.883
	George Selkirk	.883
	Jackie Robinson	.883
65	Wally Berger	.881
66	Gary Sheffield	.880
	Dolph Camilli	.880
	Riggs Stephenson	.880
69	Al Rosen	.879
	Jeff Heath	.879
71	Paul Waner	.877
	Joe Harris	.877
73	Larry Doby	.876
74	John McGraw	.875
	Jack Fournier	.875
76	Will Clark	.873
	Tommy Henrich	.873
78	John Olerud	.870
79	Jim Bottomley	.869
	Pete Browning	.869
	Jose Canseco	.869
82	Bill Dickey	.868
	Dave Orr	.868
84	Zeke Bonura	.867
	Joe Medwick	.867
	Wade Boggs	.867
87	Danny Tartabull	.864
	Eddie Morgan	.864
89	Norm Cash	.862
	Jesse Burkett	.862
91	Rafael Palmeiro	.860
	Roy Campanella	.860
	Kiki Cuyler	.860
94	Arky Vaughan	.859
	Bill Lange	.859
	Earle Combs	.859
97	Gabby Hartnett	.858
98	4 tied with	.857

Secondary Average

(minimum 3,000 Plate Appearances)

#	Player	SecA
1	Babe Ruth	.607
2	Ted Williams	.555
3	Barry Bonds	.533
4	Frank Thomas	.505
5	Lou Gehrig	.493
6	Mickey Mantle	.491
7	Mark McGwire	.491
8	Rickey Henderson	.482
9	Jimmie Foxx	.473
10	Bill Joyce	.471
11	Ralph Kiner	.468
12	Hank Greenberg	.467
13	Mike Schmidt	.461
14	Charlie Keller	.450
15	Harmon Killebrew	.446
16	Eric Davis	.443
17	Darryl Strawberry	.434
18	Jeff Bagwell	.433
19	Joe Morgan	.431
20	Billy Hamilton	.423
21	Willie Mays	.421
22	Gene Tenace	.420
23	Mel Ott	.419
24	Eddie Mathews	.415
25	Mickey Tettleton	.415
26	Ken Griffey Jr.	.412
27	Willie McCovey	.412
28	Frank Robinson	.405
29	Jack Clark	.404
30	Dick Allen	.404
31	Jimmy Wynn	.404
32	Tim Salmon	.403
33	Dolph Camilli	.403
34	Fred McGriff	.402
35	Jose Canseco	.401
36	John McGraw	.401
37	Larry Walker	.401
38	Albert Belle	.400
39	David Justice	.399
40	Bobby Bonds	.398
41	Gary Sheffield	.395
42	Jay Buhner	.394
43	Duke Snider	.394
44	Ray Lankford	.392
45	Bob Allison	.391
46	Reggie Jackson	.391
47	Hack Wilson	.390
48	Jim Gentile	.390
49	Johnny Mize	.387
50	Gary Redus	.387
51	Mo Vaughn	.385
52	George Selkirk	.384
53	Howard Johnson	.384
54	Danny Tartabull	.384
55	Gorman Thomas	.383
56	Hank Aaron	.382
57	Rob Deer	.382
58	Roy Cullenbine	.382
59	Edgar Martinez	.381
60	Stan Musial	.381
61	Jack Crooks	.379
62	Norm Cash	.379
63	Bob Johnson	.379
64	Larry Doby	.378
65	Al Rosen	.378
66	Tim Raines	.377
67	Earl Torgeson	.376
68	Joe DiMaggio	.374
69	Darrell Evans	.373
70	Andre Thornton	.373
71	Tommy Henrich	.372
72	Rocky Colavito	.372
73	Bernie Carbo	.370
74	Ron Gant	.369
75	Darren Daulton	.368
76	Kirk Gibson	.368
77	Cecil Fielder	.368
78	Kevin Mitchell	.368
79	Harland Clift	.368
80	Willie Stargell	.367
81	Joe Ferguson	.364
82	Brady Anderson	.364
83	Greg Vaughn	.364
84	Harry Stovey	.363
85	Bill Lange	.363
86	Chris Hoiles	.362
87	Dwight Evans	.362
88	Max Bishop	.362
89	Rogers Hornsby	.362
90	Hank Thompson	.361
91	Ken Williams	.359
92	Don Mincher	.357
93	Gil Hodges	.357
94	Roy Campanella	.356
95	Stan Lopata	.356
96	Gavy Cravath	.355
97	Yank Robinson	.355
98	Jackie Robinson	.355
99	Jim McTamany	.354
100	Leon Durham	.352

Isolated Power

(minimum 3,000 Plate Appearances)

#	Player	ISO
1	Babe Ruth	.348
2	Mark McGwire	.296
3	Lou Gehrig	.292
4	Hank Greenberg	.292
5	Ted Williams	.289
6	Jimmie Foxx	.284
7	Albert Belle	.274
8	Juan Gonzalez	.272
9	Frank Thomas	.270
10	Ralph Kiner	.269
11	Barry Bonds	.262
12	Mike Schmidt	.260
13	Ken Griffey Jr.	.259
14	Mickey Mantle	.259
15	Willie Mays	.256
16	Joe DiMaggio	.254
17	Harmon Killebrew	.252
18	Johnny Mize	.250
19	Hank Aaron	.250
20	Jose Canseco	.247
21	Willie Stargell	.247
22	Willie McCovey	.245
23	Larry Walker	.245
24	Duke Snider	.244
25	Darryl Strawberry	.244
26	Frank Robinson	.243
27	Dave Kingman	.242
28	Dick Allen	.242
29	Jay Buhner	.241
30	Kevin Mitchell	.240
31	Eddie Mathews	.238
32	Hack Wilson	.238
33	Fred McGriff	.236
34	Mo Vaughn	.234
35	Ron Kittle	.234
36	Tim Salmon	.234
37	Matt Williams	.233
38	Cecil Fielder	.232
39	Jeff Bagwell	.232
40	Charlie Keller	.231
41	David Justice	.230
42	Hank Sauer	.230
43	Mel Ott	.229
44	Stan Musial	.228
45	Reggie Jackson	.228
46	Jim Gentile	.227
47	Dick Stuart	.225
48	Ernie Banks	.225
49	Frank Howard	.225
50	Roy Campanella	.224
51	Danny Tartabull	.223
52	Chuck Klein	.223
53	Gorman Thomas	.223
54	Rob Deer	.223
55	Rocky Colavito	.223
56	Bob Horner	.222
57	Dean Palmer	.222
58	Steve Balboni	.222
59	Wally Berger	.221
60	Gus Zernial	.221
61	Wally Post	.220
62	Eric Davis	.220
63	Hal Trosky	.219
64	Rogers Hornsby	.218
65	Norm Cash	.217
66	Bob Allison	.217
67	Roger Maris	.216
68	Jeff Heath	.216
69	Earl Averill	.216
70	Dolph Camilli	.215
71	Gil Hodges	.214
72	Tony Conigliaro	.212
73	Tino Martinez	.211
74	Ken Williams	.211
75	Ron Gant	.211
76	Sammy Sosa	.211
77	Greg Vaughn	.211
78	Jesse Barfield	.210
79	Al Rosen	.210
80	Bob Johnson	.210
81	Tommy Henrich	.209
82	Chick Hafey	.209
83	Jack Clark	.209
84	Ellis Burks	.209
85	Johnny Bench	.208
86	Gary Sheffield	.208
87	Roy Sievers	.208
88	Rudy York	.208
89	Mickey Tettleton	.208
90	Glenn Davis	.208
91	Joe Adcock	.208
92	Paul Sorrento	.208
93	Nate Colbert	.207
94	Babe Herman	.207
95	Andres Galarraga	.207
96	Larry Doby	.207
97	George Foster	.206
98	Joe Carter	.205
99	Chris Hoiles	.204
100	Jim Rice	.204

Leaders: Career Hitting

Pitching Leaders—Career

Wins

#	Player	Wins
1	Cy Young	511
2	Walter Johnson	417
3	Pete Alexander	373
	Christy Mathewson	373
5	Warren Spahn	363
6	Kid Nichols	361
7	Pud Galvin	360
8	Tim Keefe	341
9	Steve Carlton	329
10	John Clarkson	328
11	Eddie Plank	326
12	Don Sutton	324
	Nolan Ryan	324
14	Phil Niekro	318
15	Gaylord Perry	314
16	Tom Seaver	311
17	Old Hoss Radbourn	309
	Mickey Welch	309
19	Early Wynn	300
	Lefty Grove	300
21	Tommy John	288
22	Bert Blyleven	287
23	Robin Roberts	286
24	Fergie Jenkins	284
	Tony Mullane	284
26	Jim Kaat	283
27	Red Ruffing	273
28	Burleigh Grimes	270
29	Jim Palmer	268
30	Bob Feller	266
	Eppa Rixey	266
32	Jim McCormick	265
33	Gus Weyhing	264
34	Ted Lyons	260
35	Jack Morris	254
	Red Faber	254
37	Carl Hubbell	253
38	Bob Gibson	251
39	Vic Willis	249
40	Jack Quinn	247
41	Joe McGinnity	246
42	Jack Powell	245
	Amos Rusie	245
44	Juan Marichal	243
45	Dennis Martinez	241
	Herb Pennock	241
47	Frank Tanana	240
48	Three Finger Brown	239
49	Waite Hoyt	237
	Clark Griffith	237
51	Whitey Ford	236
52	Charlie Buffinton	233
53	Luis Tiant	229
	Sad Sam Jones	229
	Will White	229
56	George Mullin	227
57	Catfish Hunter	224
	Jim Bunning	224
59	Paul Derringer	223
	Mel Harder	223
61	Jerry Koosman	222
	Hooks Dauss	222
63	Joe Niekro	221
64	Jerry Reuss	220
65	Earl Whitehill	218
	Bob Caruthers	218
67	Mickey Lolich	217
	Freddie Fitzsimmons	217
69	Charlie Hough	216
	Wilbur Cooper	216
71	Jim Perry	215
	Stan Coveleski	215
73	Rick Reuschel	214
74	Roger Clemens	213
75	Chief Bender	212
76	Bob Welch	211
	Billy Pierce	211
	Bobo Newsom	211
79	Jesse Haines	210
80	Vida Blue	209
	Milt Pappas	209
	Don Drysdale	209
	Eddie Cicotte	209
84	Bob Lemon	207
	Hal Newhouser	207
	Carl Mays	207
87	Al Orth	205
88	Jack Stivetts	204
89	Lew Burdette	203
	Silver King	203
91	Charlie Root	201
	Rube Marquard	201
93	George Uhle	200
94	Bucky Walters	198
	Jack Chesbro	198
	Adonis Terry	198
97	Bob Friend	197
	Larry French	197
	Dazzy Vance	197
	Jesse Tannehill	197

Losses

#	Player	Losses
1	Cy Young	316
2	Pud Galvin	308
3	Nolan Ryan	292
4	Walter Johnson	279
5	Phil Niekro	274
6	Gaylord Perry	265
7	Don Sutton	256
	Jack Powell	256
9	Eppa Rixey	251
10	Bert Blyleven	250
11	Robin Roberts	245
	Warren Spahn	245
13	Steve Carlton	244
	Early Wynn	244
15	Jim Kaat	237
16	Frank Tanana	236
17	Gus Weyhing	232
18	Tommy John	231
19	Bob Friend	230
	Ted Lyons	230
21	Fergie Jenkins	226
22	Red Ruffing	225
	Tim Keefe	225
24	Bobo Newsom	222
25	Tony Mullane	220
26	Jack Quinn	218
27	Sad Sam Jones	217
28	Charlie Hough	216
29	Jim McCormick	214
30	Red Faber	213
	Chick Fraser	213
32	Paul Derringer	212
	Burleigh Grimes	212
34	Mickey Welch	211
35	Jerry Koosman	209
36	Pete Alexander	208
	Kid Nichols	208
38	Tom Seaver	205
	Vic Willis	205
40	Joe Niekro	204
	Jim Whitney	204
42	George Mullin	196
	Adonis Terry	196
44	Claude Osteen	195
	Old Hoss Radbourn	195
46	Eddie Plank	194
47	Rick Reuschel	191
	Jerry Reuss	191
	Mickey Lolich	191
	Tom Zachary	191
51	Al Orth	189
52	Christy Mathewson	188
53	Dennis Martinez	187
54	Jack Morris	186
	Mel Harder	186
56	Earl Whitehill	185
57	Jim Bunning	184
58	Larry Jackson	183
	Curt Simmons	183
	Joe Bush	183
61	Waite Hoyt	182
	Hooks Dauss	182
63	Rick Wise	181
	Murry Dickson	181
	Dutch Leonard	181
66	Lee Meadows	180
67	Dolf Luque	179
	Pink Hawley	179
69	Wilbur Cooper	178
70	Rube Marquard	177
	Bill Dinneen	177
	John Clarkson	177
73	Mike Moore	176
74	Red Donahue	175
75	Doyle Alexander	174
	Jim Perry	174
	Bob Gibson	174
	Long Tom Hughes	174
	Amos Rusie	174
80	Danny Darwin	172
	Luis Tiant	172
82	Larry French	171
83	Dennis Eckersley	170
	Camilo Pascual	170
	Ted Breitenstein	170
86	Billy Pierce	169
87	Jim Clancy	167
	Mike Morgan	167
	Red Ames	167
	Red Ehret	167
	Bert Cunningham	167
92	Catfish Hunter	166
	Don Drysdale	166
	George Uhle	166
	Howard Ehmke	166
	Will White	166
97	Si Johnson	165
	Bump Hadley	165
	Mark Baldwin	165
100	3 tied with	164

Winning Percentage

(minimum 200 decisions)

#	Player	Pct.
1	Dave Foutz	.690
2	Whitey Ford	.690
3	Bob Caruthers	.688
4	Lefty Grove	.680
5	Larry Corcoran	.665
6	Christy Mathewson	.665
7	Sam Leever	.661
8	Sandy Koufax	.655
9	Johnny Allen	.654
10	Ron Guidry	.651
11	John Clarkson	.650
12	Lefty Gomez	.649
13	Three Finger Brown	.649
14	Dwight Gooden	.646
15	Dizzy Dean	.644
16	Roger Clemens	.644
17	Pete Alexander	.642
18	Jim Palmer	.638
19	Kid Nichols	.634
20	Deacon Phillippe	.634
21	Joe McGinnity	.634
22	David Cone	.632
23	Ed Reulbach	.632
24	Juan Marichal	.631
25	Mort Cooper	.631
26	Greg Maddux	.630
27	Allie Reynolds	.630
28	Jesse Tannehill	.629
29	Ray Kremer	.627
30	Eddie Plank	.627
31	Tommy Bond	.627
32	Chief Bender	.625
33	Don Newcombe	.623
34	Nig Cuppy	.623
35	Firpo Marberry	.623
36	Addie Joss	.623
37	Carl Hubbell	.622
	Carl Mays	.622
39	Bob Feller	.621
40	Clark Griffith	.619
41	Bob Lemon	.618
42	Cy Young	.618
43	Monte Ward	.617
44	Urban Shocker	.615
45	Jim Maloney	.615
46	Lon Warneke	.613
47	Old Hoss Radbourn	.613
48	Jimmy Key	.612
49	Schoolboy Rowe	.610
50	Carl Erskine	.610
51	Ed Walsh	.607
52	Dave McNally	.607
53	Tom Glavine	.607
	Jack Stivetts	.607
55	Hooks Wiltse	.607
56	Art Nehf	.605
57	Charlie Buffinton	.605
58	Jack McDowell	.604
59	Tom Seaver	.603
60	Tim Keefe	.602
61	Stan Coveleski	.602
62	Preacher Roe	.602
63	Wes Ferrell	.601
64	Jack Chesbro	.600
65	Walter Johnson	.599
66	Herb Pennock	.598
67	Freddie Fitzsimmons	.598
68	Ed Lopat	.597
69	Warren Spahn	.597
70	Rip Sewell	.596
71	Mickey Welch	.594
72	Mike Garcia	.594
73	Jim Bagby	.593
74	Pat Malone	.593
75	Orel Hershiser	.593
76	General Crowder	.592
77	John Candelaria	.592
78	Harry Brecheen	.591
79	Bob Welch	.591
80	Bob Gibson	.591
81	Dutch Ruether	.591
82	Denny McLain	.590
83	Eddie Rommel	.590
84	Jack Coombs	.590
85	Mike Cuellar	.587
86	Jeff Pfeffer	.585
87	Lew Burdette	.585
88	Amos Rusie	.585
89	Dazzy Vance	.585
90	Tommy Bridges	.584
91	Eddie Cicotte	.584
92	Ed Morris	.584
93	Bret Saberhagen	.583
94	Babe Adams	.581
95	Noodles Hahn	.580
96	Hal Newhouser	.580
97	Will White	.580
98	Larry Jansen	.578
99	Tom Browning	.577
100	2 tied with	.577

Games

#	Player	Games
1	Hoyt Wilhelm	1,070
2	Kent Tekulve	1,050
3	Lee Smith	1,022
4	Dennis Eckersley	1,021
5	Goose Gossage	1,002
6	Lindy McDaniel	987
7	Jesse Orosco	956
8	Rollie Fingers	944
9	Gene Garber	931
10	Cy Young	906
11	Sparky Lyle	899
12	Jim Kaat	898
13	Jeff Reardon	880
14	Don McMahon	874
15	Phil Niekro	864
16	Charlie Hough	858
17	Roy Face	848
18	Tug McGraw	824
19	Nolan Ryan	807
20	Walter Johnson	802
21	Rick Honeycutt	797
22	Gaylord Perry	777
23	Don Sutton	774
24	John Franco	771
25	Darold Knowles	765
26	Tommy John	760
	Paul Assenmacher	760
28	Jack Quinn	755
29	Ron Reed	751
30	Warren Spahn	750
31	Gary Lavelle	745
	Tom Burgmeier	745
33	Willie Hernandez	744
34	Steve Carlton	741
35	Ron Perranoski	737
36	Ron Kline	736
37	Steve Bedrosian	732
38	Clay Carroll	731
39	Mike Marshall	723
	Roger McDowell	723
41	Dave Righetti	718
42	Johnny Klippstein	711
43	Greg Minton	710
44	Stu Miller	704
45	Greg Harris	703
46	Joe Niekro	702
47	Bill Campbell	700
48	Larry Andersen	699
49	Bob McClure	698
50	Pud Galvin	697
51	Craig Lefferts	696
	Pete Alexander	696
53	Mike Jackson	694
	Bob Miller	694
55	Bert Blyleven	692
	Grant Jackson	692
	Eppa Rixey	692
58	Early Wynn	691
59	Eddie Fisher	690
60	Danny Darwin	683
61	Ted Abernathy	681
62	Dan Plesac	680
63	Robin Roberts	676
64	Dan Quisenberry	674
	Waite Hoyt	674
66	Red Faber	669
67	Dave Giusti	668
68	Randy Myers	666
69	Fergie Jenkins	664
70	Bruce Sutter	661
71	Tom Seaver	656
72	Paul Lindblad	655
73	Doug Jones	653
74	Wilbur Wood	651
75	Dave LaRoche	647
	Sad Sam Jones	647
77	Tom Henke	642
78	Gerry Staley	640
	Dutch Leonard	640
80	Dennis Lamp	639
	Dennis Martinez	639
	Diego Segui	639
83	Frank Tanana	638
84	Bob Stanley	637
85	Christy Mathewson	635
86	Charlie Root	632
87	Jim Perry	630
88	Jerry Reuss	628
89	Lew Burdette	626
90	Woodie Fryman	625
	Murry Dickson	625
92	Mark Davis	624
	Red Ruffing	624
94	Eddie Plank	623
95	Dick Tidrow	620
	Kid Nichols	620
97	Mitch Williams	619
98	Todd Worrell	617
	Herb Pennock	617
100	2 tied with	616

Games Started

1	Cy Young	815
2	Nolan Ryan	773
3	Don Sutton	756
4	Phil Niekro	716
5	Steve Carlton	709
6	Tommy John	700
7	Gaylord Perry	690
8	Bert Blyleven	685
9	Pud Galvin	682
10	Walter Johnson	666
11	Warren Spahn	665
12	Tom Seaver	647
13	Jim Kaat	625
14	Frank Tanana	616
15	Early Wynn	612
16	Robin Roberts	609
17	Pete Alexander	599
18	Fergie Jenkins	594
19	Tim Keefe	593
20	Kid Nichols	561
21	Dennis Martinez	557
22	Eppa Rixey	552
23	Christy Mathewson	551
24	Mickey Welch	549
25	Jerry Reuss	547
26	Red Ruffing	536
27	Eddie Plank	530
28	Rick Reuschel	529
29	Jack Morris	527
	Jerry Koosman	527
31	Jim Palmer	521
32	Jim Bunning	519
33	John Clarkson	518
34	Jack Powell	516
35	Tony Mullane	504
36	Old Hoss Radbourn	503
	Gus Weyhing	503
38	Joe Niekro	500
39	Bob Friend	497
40	Mickey Lolich	496
41	Burleigh Grimes	495
42	Claude Osteen	488
43	Sad Sam Jones	487
44	Jim McCormick	485
45	Luis Tiant	484
	Bob Feller	484
	Ted Lyons	484
48	Bobo Newsom	483
	Red Faber	483
50	Bob Gibson	482
51	Catfish Hunter	476
52	Vida Blue	473
	Earl Whitehill	473
54	Vic Willis	471
55	Milt Pappas	465
	Don Drysdale	465
57	Doyle Alexander	464
58	Bob Welch	462
59	Curt Simmons	461
60	Mike Torrez	458
61	Juan Marichal	457
	Lefty Grove	457
63	Rick Wise	455
64	Jim Perry	447
65	Paul Derringer	445
66	Jack Quinn	443
67	Charlie Hough	440
	Mike Moore	440
69	Whitey Ford	438
70	Mel Harder	433
71	Billy Pierce	432
72	Carl Hubbell	431
73	Larry Jackson	429
74	George Mullin	428
75	Amos Rusie	427
76	Freddie Fitzsimmons	426
77	Fernando Valenzuela	424
78	Bob Forsch	422
	Waite Hoyt	422
80	Frank Viola	420
	Herb Pennock	420
82	Roger Clemens	416
83	Bob Knepper	413
84	Ken Holtzman	410
85	Dave Stieb	409
86	Tom Zachary	408
87	Scott Sanderson	407
	Mark Langston	407
	Adonis Terry	407
90	Wilbur Cooper	406
91	Mike Flanagan	404
	Camilo Pascual	404
	Lee Meadows	404
	Rube Marquard	404
95	Will White	401
96	Bucky Walters	398
97	Dave McNally	396
	Charlie Buffinton	396
	Jim Whitney	396
100	2 tied with	394

Complete Games

1	Cy Young	749
2	Pud Galvin	639
3	Tim Keefe	553
4	Walter Johnson	531
	Kid Nichols	531
6	Mickey Welch	525
7	Old Hoss Radbourn	489
8	John Clarkson	485
9	Tony Mullane	468
10	Jim McCormick	466
11	Gus Weyhing	448
12	Pete Alexander	438
13	Christy Mathewson	434
14	Jack Powell	422
15	Eddie Plank	410
16	Will White	394
17	Amos Rusie	392
18	Vic Willis	388
19	Warren Spahn	382
20	Jim Whitney	377
21	Adonis Terry	368
22	Ted Lyons	356
23	George Mullin	353
24	Charlie Buffinton	351
25	Chick Fraser	342
26	Clark Griffith	337
27	Red Ruffing	335
28	Silver King	329
29	Al Orth	324
30	Bill Hutchison	321
31	Burleigh Grimes	314
	Joe McGinnity	314
33	Red Donahue	312
34	Guy Hecker	310
35	Bill Dinneen	306
36	Robin Roberts	305
37	Gaylord Perry	303
38	Lefty Grove	300
	Ted Breitenstein	300
40	Bob Caruthers	298
41	Ed Morris	297
	Pink Hawley	297
43	Mark Baldwin	296
44	Tommy Bond	294
45	Brickyard Kennedy	293
46	Early Wynn	290
	Eppa Rixey	290
48	Wild Bill Donovan	289
	Bobby Mathews	289
50	Bert Cunningham	286
51	Bob Feller	279
	Wilbur Cooper	279
	Sadie McMahon	279
54	Jack Taylor	278
	Jack Stivetts	278
56	Charlie Getzien	277
57	Red Faber	274
58	Three Finger Brown	271
	Frank Dwyer	271
60	Jouett Meekin	270
61	Fergie Jenkins	267
62	Elton Chamberlin	264
	Matt Kilroy	264
64	Jesse Tannehill	263
65	Doc White	262
66	Rube Waddell	261
67	Carl Hubbell	260
	Jack Chesbro	260
	Red Ehret	260
70	Chief Bender	257
71	Larry Corcoran	256
72	Bob Gibson	255
73	Steve Carlton	254
74	Frank Killen	253
75	Win Mercer	252
76	Paul Derringer	251
77	Sad Sam Jones	250
	Ed Walsh	250
79	Eddie Cicotte	249
	Stump Wiedman	249
81	Herb Pennock	247
82	Bobo Newsom	246
83	Phil Niekro	245
	Hooks Dauss	245
	George Bradley	245
86	Juan Marichal	244
	Monte Ward	244
	Harry Howell	244
89	Bert Blyleven	242
	Bucky Walters	242
	Jack Quinn	242
	Deacon Phillippe	242
93	Sam Leever	241
94	Kid Gleason	240
95	Addie Joss	234
96	George Uhle	232
97	Tom Seaver	231
	Carl Mays	231
	Harry Staley	231
100	Earl Moore	230

Shutouts

1	Walter Johnson	110
2	Pete Alexander	90
3	Christy Mathewson	79
4	Cy Young	76
5	Eddie Plank	69
6	Warren Spahn	63
7	Tom Seaver	61
	Nolan Ryan	61
9	Bert Blyleven	60
10	Don Sutton	58
11	Ed Walsh	57
12	Bob Gibson	56
	Three Finger Brown	56
	Pud Galvin	56
15	Steve Carlton	55
16	Gaylord Perry	53
	Jim Palmer	53
18	Juan Marichal	52
19	Rube Waddell	50
	Vic Willis	50
21	Fergie Jenkins	49
	Luis Tiant	49
	Don Drysdale	49
	Early Wynn	49
25	Kid Nichols	48
26	Jack Powell	47
27	Tommy John	46
	Doc White	46
29	Phil Niekro	45
	Whitey Ford	45
	Robin Roberts	45
	Red Ruffing	45
	Addie Joss	45
34	Bob Feller	44
	Babe Adams	44
36	Milt Pappas	43
37	Catfish Hunter	42
	Bucky Walters	42
39	Roger Clemens	41
	Mickey Lolich	41
	Hippo Vaughn	41
	Chief Bender	41
	Mickey Welch	41
44	Mel Stottlemyre	40
	Claude Osteen	40
	Jim Bunning	40
	Sandy Koufax	40
	Larry French	40
	Ed Reulbach	40
50	Jerry Reuss	39
	Eppa Rixey	39
	Tim Keefe	39
	Sam Leever	39
54	Billy Pierce	38
	Stan Coveleski	38
	Nap Rucker	38
57	Vida Blue	37
	Steve Rogers	37
	Larry Jackson	37
	John Clarkson	37
61	Mike Cuellar	36
	Camilo Pascual	36
	Bob Friend	36
	Curt Simmons	36
	Allie Reynolds	36
	Carl Hubbell	36
	Sad Sam Jones	36
	Bill Doak	36
	Wilbur Cooper	36
	Will White	36
71	Lefty Grove	35
	Burleigh Grimes	35
	Joe Bush	35
	Herb Pennock	35
	Eddie Cicotte	35
	George Mullin	35
	Jack Chesbro	35
	Wild Bill Donovan	35
	Old Hoss Radbourn	35
	Jack Coombs	35
	Tommy Bond	35
82	Frank Tanana	34
	Earl Moore	34
	Jesse Tannehill	34
85	Jerry Koosman	33
	Dave McNally	33
	Dean Chance	33
	Lew Burdette	33
	Virgil Trucks	33
	Hal Newhouser	33
	Tommy Bridges	33
	Bob Shawkey	33
	Dutch Leonard	33
	Lefty Leifield	33
	Jim McCormick	33
96	Jim Perry	32
	Mort Cooper	32
	Paul Derringer	32
	Lefty Tyler	32
	Joe McGinnity	32

Saves

1	Lee Smith	478
2	Dennis Eckersley	389
3	Jeff Reardon	367
4	John Franco	359
5	Rollie Fingers	341
6	Randy Myers	319
7	Tom Henke	311
8	Goose Gossage	310
9	Bruce Sutter	300
10	Doug Jones	278
11	Todd Worrell	256
	Jeff Montgomery	256
13	Dave Righetti	252
14	Dan Quisenberry	244
15	Sparky Lyle	238
16	Rick Aguilera	237
17	Hoyt Wilhelm	227
18	Gene Garber	218
19	Dave Smith	216
20	John Wetteland	211
21	Bobby Thigpen	201
22	Rod Beck	199
23	Mike Henneman	193
	Roy Face	193
25	Mitch Williams	192
26	Mike Marshall	188
27	Jeff Russell	186
28	Kent Tekulve	184
	Steve Bedrosian	184
30	Tug McGraw	180
31	Ron Perranoski	179
32	Bryan Harvey	177
33	Gregg Olson	173
34	Lindy McDaniel	172
35	Roberto Hernandez	165
36	Roger McDowell	159
37	Jay Howell	155
38	Stu Miller	154
39	Don McMahon	153
40	Greg Minton	150
41	Dan Plesac	149
42	Ted Abernathy	148
43	Willie Hernandez	147
44	Dave Giusti	145
45	Darold Knowles	143
	Clay Carroll	143
47	Gary Lavelle	136
48	Trevor Hoffman	135
49	Jesse Orosco	133
50	Bob Stanley	132
	Steve Farr	132
	Jim Brewer	132
53	Ron Davis	130
	Jeff Brantley	130
55	Terry Forster	127
56	Bill Campbell	126
	Dave LaRoche	126
58	John Hiller	125
59	Mel Rojas	124
60	Jack Aker	123
61	Dick Radatz	122
62	Duane Ward	121
63	Tippy Martinez	115
64	Frank Linzy	111
65	Al Worthington	110
66	Fred Gladding	109
67	Robb Nen	108
	Wayne Granger	108
	Ron Kline	108
70	Johnny Murphy	107
71	Bill Caudill	106
72	Mark Wohlers	104
73	Ron Reed	103
	Jose Mesa	103
	John Wyatt	103
76	Tom Burgmeier	102
	Tim Burke	102
	Ellis Kinder	102
79	Craig Lefferts	101
	Firpo Marberry	101
81	Joe Hoerner	99
82	Mike Schooler	98
83	Al Hrabosky	97
	Tom Niedenfuer	97
85	Mark Davis	96
	Randy Moffitt	96
	Clem Labine	96
88	Norm Charlton	95
	Bob Locker	95
90	Aurelio Lopez	93
91	Tom Hume	92
	Heathcliff Slocumb	92
	Phil Regan	92
94	Steve Howe	91
	Jim Gott	91
96	Bill Henry	90
97	Donnie Moore	89
	Rob Dibble	89
99	Jim Kern	88
100	2 tied with	86

Games Finished

1	Lee Smith	802
2	Rollie Fingers	709
3	Jeff Reardon	695
4	Goose Gossage	681
5	Hoyt Wilhelm	651
6	Kent Tekulve	638
7	Sparky Lyle	634
8	John Franco	623
9	Gene Garber	609
10	Lindy McDaniel	577
11	Roy Face	574
12	Dennis Eckersley	564
13	Dan Quisenberry	553
14	Mike Marshall	549
15	Tom Henke	548
16	Tug McGraw	541
	Doug Jones	541
18	Bruce Sutter	512
19	Randy Myers	506
	Don McMahon	506
21	Dave Righetti	474
22	Jeff Montgomery	459
23	Ron Perranoski	458
24	Todd Worrell	456
25	Bill Campbell	455
26	Steve Bedrosian	439
27	Jesse Orosco	435
28	Dave Smith	432
	Mike Henneman	432
30	Roger McDowell	430
31	Willie Hernandez	419
	Mitch Williams	419
33	Darold Knowles	417
34	Ted Abernathy	416
35	Greg Minton	415
36	Rick Aguilera	408
37	Stu Miller	405
38	Gary Lavelle	399
39	Dave LaRoche	381
40	Dave Giusti	380
41	Bob Stanley	376
42	Clay Carroll	373
43	Tom Burgmeier	370
44	John Hiller	363
45	Jay Howell	360
46	Dan Plesac	359
47	Bobby Thigpen	356
48	Jim Brewer	351
49	John Wetteland	348
50	Rod Beck	346
51	Eddie Fisher	344
52	Gregg Olson	343
53	Frank Linzy	342
54	Jeff Russell	340
55	Ron Davis	339
56	Mark Clear	338
	Ron Kline	338
58	Elias Sosa	330
59	Jack Aker	321
60	Tippy Martinez	320
61	Terry Forster	318
62	Al Worthington	314
63	Steve Farr	313
64	Al Hrabosky	307
65	Randy Moffitt	306
	Roberto Hernandez	306
67	Turk Farrell	301
68	Ron Reed	300
69	Doug Bair	299
70	Dick Radatz	297
71	Bill Caudill	293
	Johnny Murphy	293
73	Grant Jackson	291
	John Wyatt	291
75	Bob Miller	290
76	Phil Regan	289
77	Dale Murray	288
	Bob Locker	288
	Clem Labine	288
80	Craig Lefferts	286
81	Ken Sanders	285
82	Jeff Brantley	283
83	Ron Taylor	282
84	Aurelio Lopez	281
85	Pedro Borbon	278
	Bryan Harvey	278
	Fred Gladding	278
88	Tom Niedenfuer	276
89	Johnny Klippstein	275
90	Joe Sambito	274
91	Duane Ward	272
92	Firpo Marberry	271
93	Wayne Granger	270
	Claude Raymond	270
95	Joe Hoerner	268
96	Tom Hume	267
	Larry Andersen	267
	Jack Baldschun	267
	Jim Konstanty	267
100	Greg Harris	266

Batters Faced

1	Cy Young	30,058
2	Pud Galvin	25,234
3	Walter Johnson	23,749
4	Phil Niekro	22,677
5	Nolan Ryan	22,575
6	Gaylord Perry	21,953
7	Steve Carlton	21,683
8	Don Sutton	21,631
9	Warren Spahn	21,547
10	Kid Nichols	21,243
11	Tim Keefe	20,975
12	Pete Alexander	20,928
13	Bert Blyleven	20,491
14	Mickey Welch	20,190
15	Tommy John	19,692
16	Early Wynn	19,408
17	Tom Seaver	19,369
18	Robin Roberts	19,174
19	Christy Mathewson	19,136
20	John Clarkson	19,069
21	Jim Kaat	19,021
	Tony Mullane	19,021
23	Old Hoss Radbourn	18,910
24	Gus Weyhing	18,817
25	Eppa Rixey	18,754
26	Red Ruffing	18,579
27	Fergie Jenkins	18,400
28	Jack Powell	18,316
29	Eddie Plank	18,225
30	Burleigh Grimes	17,959
31	Ted Lyons	17,846
32	Jim McCormick	17,658
33	Frank Tanana	17,641
34	Red Faber	17,360
35	Sad Sam Jones	16,820
36	Lefty Grove	16,633
37	Jack Quinn	16,603
38	Vic Willis	16,598
39	Bobo Newsom	16,467
40	Dennis Martinez	16,358
41	Bob Feller	16,180
42	Charlie Hough	16,170
43	Waite Hoyt	16,123
44	Jack Morris	16,120
45	Jim Palmer	16,112
46	Bob Gibson	16,068
47	Jerry Koosman	15,996
48	Amos Rusie	15,972
49	Earl Whitehill	15,795
50	George Mullin	15,647
51	Jim Bunning	15,618
52	Jerry Reuss	15,582
53	Paul Derringer	15,391
54	Herb Pennock	15,246
55	Bob Friend	15,214
56	Adonis Terry	15,189
57	Joe Niekro	15,166
58	Mickey Lolich	15,140
59	Rick Reuschel	14,888
60	Mel Harder	14,862
61	Will White	14,829
62	Carl Hubbell	14,805
63	Chick Fraser	14,710
64	Jim Whitney	14,638
65	Charlie Buffinton	14,510
66	Joe McGinnity	14,495
67	Claude Osteen	14,433
	Hooks Dauss	14,433
69	Wilbur Cooper	14,377
70	Clark Griffith	14,368
71	Luis Tiant	14,365
72	Juan Marichal	14,236
73	Doyle Alexander	14,162
74	Curt Simmons	14,144
75	Al Orth	14,130
76	Don Drysdale	14,097
77	Catfish Hunter	14,032
78	Billy Pierce	13,853
79	Vida Blue	13,837
80	Jim Perry	13,732
81	Rube Marquard	13,677
82	Jesse Haines	13,644
83	George Uhle	13,639
84	Larry Jackson	13,593
85	Tom Zachary	13,551
86	Charlie Root	13,529
87	Dutch Leonard	13,487
88	Dolf Luque	13,470
89	Larry French	13,465
90	Silver King	13,439
91	Freddie Fitzsimmons	13,410
92	Lee Meadows	13,371
93	Dennis Eckersley	13,363
94	Brickyard Kennedy	13,256
95	Joe Bush	13,249
96	Red Ames	13,214
97	Milt Pappas	13,198
98	Mike Torrez	13,179
99	Rick Wise	13,157
100	Bucky Walters	13,140

Innings Pitched

1	Cy Young	7,355.2
2	Pud Galvin	5,941.1
3	Walter Johnson	5,914.2
4	Phil Niekro	5,404.1
5	Nolan Ryan	5,386.0
6	Gaylord Perry	5,350.1
7	Don Sutton	5,282.1
8	Warren Spahn	5,243.2
9	Steve Carlton	5,217.1
10	Pete Alexander	5,190.0
11	Kid Nichols	5,056.1
12	Tim Keefe	5,052.1
13	Bert Blyleven	4,970.0
14	Mickey Welch	4,802.0
15	Tom Seaver	4,782.2
16	Christy Mathewson	4,780.2
17	Tommy John	4,710.1
18	Robin Roberts	4,688.2
19	Early Wynn	4,564.0
20	John Clarkson	4,536.1
21	Old Hoss Radbourn	4,535.1
22	Tony Mullane	4,531.1
23	Jim Kaat	4,530.1
24	Fergie Jenkins	4,500.2
25	Eddie Plank	4,495.2
26	Eppa Rixey	4,494.2
27	Jack Powell	4,389.0
28	Red Ruffing	4,344.0
29	Gus Weyhing	4,324.1
30	Jim McCormick	4,275.2
31	Frank Tanana	4,188.1
32	Burleigh Grimes	4,179.2
33	Ted Lyons	4,161.0
34	Red Faber	4,087.2
35	Vic Willis	3,996.0
36	Jim Palmer	3,948.0
37	Lefty Grove	3,940.1
38	Jack Quinn	3,926.1
39	Dennis Martinez	3,908.2
40	Bob Gibson	3,884.1
41	Sad Sam Jones	3,883.0
42	Jerry Koosman	3,839.1
43	Bob Feller	3,827.0
44	Jack Morris	3,824.0
45	Charlie Hough	3,801.1
46	Amos Rusie	3,769.2
47	Waite Hoyt	3,762.1
48	Jim Bunning	3,760.1
49	Bobo Newsom	3,759.0
50	George Mullin	3,686.2
51	Jerry Reuss	3,669.2
52	Paul Derringer	3,645.0
53	Mickey Lolich	3,638.1
54	Bob Friend	3,611.0
55	Carl Hubbell	3,590.1
56	Joe Niekro	3,584.0
57	Earl Whitehill	3,565.0
58	Herb Pennock	3,558.0
59	Rick Reuschel	3,548.1
60	Will White	3,542.2
61	Adonis Terry	3,523.0
62	Juan Marichal	3,507.1
63	Jim Whitney	3,496.1
64	Luis Tiant	3,486.1
65	Wilbur Cooper	3,480.0
66	Claude Osteen	3,460.1
67	Catfish Hunter	3,449.1
68	Joe McGinnity	3,441.1
69	Don Drysdale	3,432.0
70	Mel Harder	3,426.1
71	Charlie Buffinton	3,404.0
72	Hooks Dauss	3,390.2
73	Clark Griffith	3,386.1
74	Doyle Alexander	3,367.2
75	Chick Fraser	3,356.0
76	Al Orth	3,354.2
77	Curt Simmons	3,348.1
78	Vida Blue	3,343.1
79	Billy Pierce	3,306.2
	Rube Marquard	3,306.2
81	Jim Perry	3,285.2
82	Larry Jackson	3,262.2
83	Dennis Eckersley	3,246.0
84	Eddie Cicotte	3,225.1
85	Freddie Fitzsimmons	3,223.2
86	Dolf Luque	3,220.1
87	Dutch Leonard	3,218.1
88	Jesse Haines	3,208.2
89	Red Ames	3,198.0
90	Charlie Root	3,197.1
91	Silver King	3,190.2
92	Milt Pappas	3,186.0
93	Three Finger Brown	3,172.0
94	Whitey Ford	3,170.1
95	Larry French	3,152.0
96	Lee Meadows	3,151.2
97	Rick Wise	3,127.0
98	Tom Zachary	3,126.1
99	George Uhle	3,119.2
100	Bucky Walters	3,104.2

Hits Allowed

1	Cy Young	7,092
2	Pud Galvin	6,352
3	Phil Niekro	5,044
4	Gaylord Perry	4,938
5	Kid Nichols	4,912
6	Walter Johnson	4,907
7	Pete Alexander	4,868
8	Warren Spahn	4,830
9	Tommy John	4,783
10	Don Sutton	4,692
11	Steve Carlton	4,672
12	Eppa Rixey	4,633
13	Bert Blyleven	4,632
14	Jim Kaat	4,620
15	Mickey Welch	4,587
16	Robin Roberts	4,582
17	Gus Weyhing	4,562
18	Ted Lyons	4,489
19	Tim Keefe	4,442
20	Burleigh Grimes	4,412
21	Old Hoss Radbourn	4,335
22	Jack Powell	4,319
23	John Clarkson	4,295
24	Early Wynn	4,291
25	Red Ruffing	4,284
26	Jack Quinn	4,238
27	Christy Mathewson	4,218
28	Tony Mullane	4,195
29	Fergie Jenkins	4,142
30	Red Faber	4,106
31	Jim McCormick	4,092
32	Sad Sam Jones	4,084
33	Frank Tanana	4,063
34	Waite Hoyt	4,037
35	Tom Seaver	3,971
36	Eddie Plank	3,958
37	Nolan Ryan	3,923
38	Earl Whitehill	3,917
39	Paul Derringer	3,912
40	Herb Pennock	3,900
41	Lefty Grove	3,849
42	Dennis Martinez	3,788
43	Bob Friend	3,772
44	Bobo Newsom	3,769
45	Jerry Reuss	3,734
46	Mel Harder	3,706
47	Clark Griffith	3,670
48	Jerry Koosman	3,635
49	Vic Willis	3,621
50	Jim Whitney	3,598
51	Rick Reuschel	3,588
52	Tom Zachary	3,580
53	Jack Morris	3,567
54	Al Orth	3,564
55	Adonis Terry	3,521
56	George Mullin	3,518
57	Claude Osteen	3,471
58	Joe Niekro	3,466
59	Carl Hubbell	3,461
60	Jesse Haines	3,460
	Chick Fraser	3,460
62	Will White	3,440
63	Jim Bunning	3,433
64	George Uhle	3,417
65	Wilbur Cooper	3,415
66	Hooks Dauss	3,407
67	Amos Rusie	3,384
68	Doyle Alexander	3,376
	Red Donahue	3,376
70	Larry French	3,375
71	Mickey Lolich	3,366
72	Jim Palmer	3,349
73	Charlie Buffinton	3,344
74	Freddie Fitzsimmons	3,335
75	Pink Hawley	3,334
76	Curt Simmons	3,313
77	Frank Dwyer	3,312
78	Dutch Leonard	3,304
79	Charlie Hough	3,283
80	Lee Meadows	3,280
81	Bob Gibson	3,279
82	Joe McGinnity	3,276
	Brickyard Kennedy	3,276
84	Bob Feller	3,271
85	Charlie Root	3,252
86	Rube Marquard	3,233
87	Dolf Luque	3,231
88	Rick Wise	3,227
89	Larry Jackson	3,206
90	Lew Burdette	3,186
91	Red Ehret	3,172
92	Juan Marichal	3,153
93	Jim Perry	3,127
94	Bill Hutchison	3,123
95	Silver King	3,105
96	Ted Breitenstein	3,091
97	Don Drysdale	3,084
98	Luis Tiant	3,075
99	Bert Cunningham	3,063
100	Win Mercer	3,057

Runs Allowed	Earned Runs Allowed	Home Runs Allowed	Walks

Runs Allowed

Rank	Player	Total
1	Pud Galvin	3,318
2	Cy Young	3,167
3	Gus Weyhing	2,788
4	Mickey Welch	2,556
5	Tony Mullane	2,523
6	Kid Nichols	2,477
7	Tim Keefe	2,468
8	John Clarkson	2,376
9	Phil Niekro	2,337
10	Adonis Terry	2,298
11	Old Hoss Radbourn	2,275
12	Nolan Ryan	2,178
13	Steve Carlton	2,130
14	Gaylord Perry	2,128
15	Red Ruffing	2,117
16	Don Sutton	2,104
17	Jim McCormick	2,095
18	Amos Rusie	2,066
19	Ted Lyons	2,056
20	Burleigh Grimes	2,048
21	Jim Kaat	2,038
22	Early Wynn	2,037
23	Bert Blyleven	2,029
24	Jim Whitney	2,026
25	Earl Whitehill	2,018
26	Tommy John	2,017
27	Warren Spahn	2,016
28	Sad Sam Jones	2,007
29	Chick Fraser	1,995
30	Jack Powell	1,991
31	Eppa Rixey	1,986
32	Robin Roberts	1,962
33	Bert Cunningham	1,938
34	Pink Hawley	1,927
35	Bill Hutchison	1,913
36	Frank Tanana	1,910
37	Bobo Newsom	1,908
38	Walter Johnson	1,902
39	Red Ehret	1,881
40	Brickyard Kennedy	1,859
41	Fergie Jenkins	1,853
42	Clark Griffith	1,852
43	Pete Alexander	1,851
44	Ted Breitenstein	1,845
45	Will White	1,844
46	Jack Stivetts	1,836
47	Jack Quinn	1,835
48	Charlie Buffinton	1,824
49	Mark Baldwin	1,817
50	Jack Morris	1,815
51	Red Faber	1,813
52	Charlie Hough	1,807
	Silver King	1,807
54	Dennis Martinez	1,782
	Frank Dwyer	1,782
56	Waite Hoyt	1,780
57	Bobby Mathews	1,758
58	Win Mercer	1,744
59	Kid Carsey	1,722
60	Guy Hecker	1,715
61	Mel Harder	1,714
62	Al Orth	1,704
	Jouett Meekin	1,704
64	Jerry Reuss	1,700
65	Herb Pennock	1,692
66	Tom Seaver	1,674
67	Bob Friend	1,652
	Paul Derringer	1,652
69	Red Donahue	1,638
70	George Mullin	1,636
71	George Uhle	1,635
72	Vic Willis	1,628
73	Joe Niekro	1,620
74	Christy Mathewson	1,616
75	Bump Hadley	1,609
76	Jerry Koosman	1,608
77	Hooks Dauss	1,599
78	Lefty Grove	1,594
79	Sadie McMahon	1,593
80	Frank Killen	1,571
81	Eddie Plank	1,569
82	Elton Chamberlin	1,560
83	Bob Feller	1,557
84	Jesse Haines	1,556
85	Charlie Getzien	1,555
86	Tom Zachary	1,552
87	Curt Simmons	1,551
88	Doyle Alexander	1,541
89	Matt Kilroy	1,539
90	Mickey Lolich	1,537
91	Stump Wiedman	1,536
92	Jim Bunning	1,527
93	Mike Moore	1,516
94	Kid Gleason	1,511
95	Freddie Fitzsimmons	1,505
96	Mike Torrez	1,501
97	Rick Reuschel	1,494
98	Willis Hudlin	1,491
	Lee Meadows	1,491
100	Harry Staley	1,472

Earned Runs Allowed

Rank	Player	Total
1	Cy Young	2,146
2	Phil Niekro	2,012
3	Don Sutton	1,914
4	Nolan Ryan	1,911
5	Pud Galvin	1,895
6	Gus Weyhing	1,867
7	Steve Carlton	1,864
8	Gaylord Perry	1,846
9	Red Ruffing	1,833
10	Bert Blyleven	1,830
11	Warren Spahn	1,798
12	Early Wynn	1,796
13	Robin Roberts	1,774
14	Tommy John	1,749
15	Jim Kaat	1,738
16	Earl Whitehill	1,726
17	Frank Tanana	1,702
18	Ted Lyons	1,696
19	Fergie Jenkins	1,669
20	Bobo Newsom	1,664
21	Kid Nichols	1,660
22	Jack Morris	1,657
23	Sad Sam Jones	1,656
24	Burleigh Grimes	1,636
25	Dennis Martinez	1,598
26	Charlie Hough	1,582
27	Eppa Rixey	1,572
28	Tony Mullane	1,537
29	Tom Seaver	1,521
30	Waite Hoyt	1,500
31	Jerry Reuss	1,483
32	Pete Alexander	1,476
33	Tim Keefe	1,472
34	Adonis Terry	1,456
35	Jack Powell	1,450
36	Mel Harder	1,447
	Mickey Welch	1,447
38	Bob Friend	1,438
39	Jerry Koosman	1,433
	Jack Quinn	1,433
41	Joe Niekro	1,431
42	Red Faber	1,430
43	Herb Pennock	1,428
44	Walter Johnson	1,424
45	John Clarkson	1,417
46	Doyle Alexander	1,406
47	Paul Derringer	1,401
48	Mickey Lolich	1,390
49	Bump Hadley	1,389
50	Bob Feller	1,384
	George Uhle	1,384
52	Mike Moore	1,381
53	Chick Fraser	1,371
54	Jim Bunning	1,366
55	Old Hoss Radbourn	1,348
56	Mike Torrez	1,340
57	Lefty Grove	1,339
58	Rick Reuschel	1,330
	Ted Breitenstein	1,330
60	Brickyard Kennedy	1,329
61	Pink Hawley	1,326
62	Curt Simmons	1,318
63	Jesse Haines	1,298
64	Tom Zachary	1,295
65	Amos Rusie	1,287
66	Rick Wise	1,281
	Willis Hudlin	1,281
68	Luis Tiant	1,280
69	Bert Cunningham	1,279
70	Charlie Root	1,274
71	Claude Osteen	1,268
72	Jim Perry	1,258
	Bob Gibson	1,258
74	Dennis Eckersley	1,257
	Freddie Fitzsimmons	1,257
76	Al Orth	1,256
77	Jim Palmer	1,253
78	Hooks Dauss	1,250
79	Catfish Hunter	1,248
80	Lew Burdette	1,246
	Clark Griffith	1,246
82	Murry Dickson	1,240
83	Larry Jackson	1,233
84	Red Ehret	1,229
85	Bill Hutchison	1,228
86	Rube Walberg	1,224
87	Rick Sutcliffe	1,223
	Kid Carsey	1,223
89	Mark Langston	1,217
90	Vida Blue	1,211
91	Larry French	1,206
92	Joe Bush	1,205
93	Frank Dwyer	1,204
94	Milt Pappas	1,203
95	Jim Slaton	1,202
96	Billy Pierce	1,201
97	Mike Flanagan	1,199
	Jack Stivetts	1,199
99	Danny Darwin	1,195
100	3 tied with	1,191

Home Runs Allowed

Rank	Player	Total
1	Robin Roberts	505
2	Fergie Jenkins	484
3	Phil Niekro	482
4	Don Sutton	472
5	Frank Tanana	448
6	Warren Spahn	434
7	Bert Blyleven	430
8	Steve Carlton	414
9	Gaylord Perry	399
10	Jim Kaat	395
11	Jack Morris	389
12	Charlie Hough	383
13	Tom Seaver	380
14	Catfish Hunter	374
15	Jim Bunning	372
16	Dennis Martinez	364
17	Mickey Lolich	347
18	Luis Tiant	346
19	Dennis Eckersley	341
20	Early Wynn	338
21	Doyle Alexander	324
22	Nolan Ryan	321
23	Juan Marichal	320
24	Pedro Ramos	315
25	Jim Perry	308
26	Jim Palmer	303
27	Tommy John	302
	Murry Dickson	302
29	Danny Darwin	298
	Milt Pappas	298
31	Scott Sanderson	297
32	Frank Viola	294
33	Mudcat Grant	292
34	Floyd Bannister	291
	Mike Moore	291
	Mark Langston	291
37	Jerry Koosman	290
38	Lew Burdette	289
39	Bob Friend	286
40	Billy Pierce	284
41	Bill Gullickson	282
42	Don Drysdale	280
43	Jim Slaton	277
44	Vida Blue	276
45	Vern Law	268
46	Bob Welch	267
47	Dave Stewart	264
48	Vida Blue	263
49	Rick Wise	261
50	Larry Jackson	259
51	Bruce Hurst	258
52	Bob Gibson	257
53	Camilo Pascual	256
54	Mike McCormick	255
	Curt Simmons	255
56	Red Ruffing	254
57	Don Newcombe	252
58	Mike Flanagan	251
59	Jimmy Key	249
	Ken Holtzman	249
	Claude Osteen	249
62	Steve Renko	248
63	John Candelaria	245
	Jerry Reuss	245
65	Jim Clancy	244
66	Denny McLain	242
	Johnny Podres	242
68	Ray Sadecki	240
	Harvey Haddix	240
70	Ron Darling	239
71	Bob Buhl	238
72	Rick Sutcliffe	236
	Tom Browning	236
	Earl Wilson	236
75	Scott McGregor	235
76	Joe Coleman	234
77	Jim Lonborg	233
78	Kevin Gross	230
	Dave McNally	230
80	Bob Knepper	228
	Whitey Ford	228
82	Carl Hubbell	227
83	Fernando Valenzuela	226
	Ron Guidry	226
	Doug Drabek	226
86	Don Cardwell	225
87	Bob Feller	224
88	Stan Bahnsen	223
	Mike Torrez	223
	Ted Lyons	223
91	Mike Cuellar	222
92	Rick Reuschel	221
	Ray Burris	221
94	Dave Stieb	219
95	Mike Caldwell	218
	Dan Petry	218
	Ron Kline	218
98	Bud Black	217
99	Bob Forsch	216
	Ralph Terry	216

Walks

Rank	Player	Total
1	Nolan Ryan	2,795
2	Steve Carlton	1,833
3	Phil Niekro	1,809
4	Early Wynn	1,775
5	Bob Feller	1,764
6	Bobo Newsom	1,732
7	Amos Rusie	1,704
8	Charlie Hough	1,665
9	Gus Weyhing	1,566
10	Red Ruffing	1,541
11	Bump Hadley	1,442
12	Warren Spahn	1,434
13	Earl Whitehill	1,431
14	Tony Mullane	1,408
15	Sad Sam Jones	1,396
16	Tom Seaver	1,390
	Jack Morris	1,390
18	Gaylord Perry	1,379
19	Mike Torrez	1,371
20	Walter Johnson	1,363
21	Don Sutton	1,343
22	Bob Gibson	1,336
23	Chick Fraser	1,332
24	Bert Blyleven	1,322
25	Sam McDowell	1,312
26	Jim Palmer	1,311
27	Mark Baldwin	1,307
28	Adonis Terry	1,301
29	Mickey Welch	1,297
30	Burleigh Grimes	1,295
31	Kid Nichols	1,268
32	Joe Bush	1,263
33	Joe Niekro	1,262
34	Allie Reynolds	1,261
35	Tommy John	1,259
36	Frank Tanana	1,255
37	Bob Lemon	1,251
38	Hal Newhouser	1,249
39	George Mullin	1,238
40	Tim Keefe	1,224
41	Mark Langston	1,219
42	Cy Young	1,217
43	Red Faber	1,213
44	Vic Willis	1,212
45	Ted Breitenstein	1,203
46	Brickyard Kennedy	1,201
47	Jerry Koosman	1,198
48	Bobby Witt	1,195
49	Tommy Bridges	1,192
50	John Clarkson	1,191
51	Lefty Grove	1,187
52	Vida Blue	1,185
53	Billy Pierce	1,178
54	Mike Moore	1,156
55	Jack Stivetts	1,155
56	Fernando Valenzuela	1,151
57	Dennis Martinez	1,146
58	Johnny Vander Meer	1,132
	Bill Hutchison	1,132
60	Jerry Reuss	1,127
61	Bucky Walters	1,121
	Ted Lyons	1,121
63	Mel Harder	1,118
64	Earl Moore	1,108
65	Bob Buhl	1,105
66	Luis Tiant	1,104
67	Mickey Lolich	1,099
68	Lefty Gomez	1,095
69	Virgil Trucks	1,088
70	Whitey Ford	1,086
71	Jim Kaat	1,083
72	Eppa Rixey	1,082
73	Rick Sutcliffe	1,081
74	Eddie Plank	1,072
75	Camilo Pascual	1,069
76	Bob Turley	1,068
77	Elton Chamberlin	1,065
78	Hooks Dauss	1,064
	Bert Cunningham	1,064
80	Curt Simmons	1,063
81	Wild Bill Donovan	1,059
82	Murry Dickson	1,058
	Jouett Meekin	1,058
84	Vern Kennedy	1,049
85	Dizzy Trout	1,046
86	Howard Ehmke	1,042
87	Wes Ferrell	1,040
88	Tommy Byrne	1,037
89	Bob Welch	1,034
	Dave Stewart	1,034
	Red Ames	1,034
92	Rube Walberg	1,031
93	Jack Powell	1,021
94	Bob Shawkey	1,018
95	Dave Stieb	1,017
96	Steve Renko	1,010
97	Jim Slaton	1,004
98	Joe Coleman	1,003
	Waite Hoyt	1,003
100	Jim Bunning	1,000

Leaders: Career Pitching

Leaders: Career Pitching

Intentional Walks

1	Kent Tekulve	179
2	Gaylord Perry	164
3	Gene Garber	155
4	Steve Carlton	150
5	Lindy McDaniel	136
6	Greg Minton	131
7	Tug McGraw	128
8	Gary Lavelle	126
9	Ron Reed	124
10	Don Drysdale	123
11	Jerry Koosman	121
	Ron Perranoski	121
13	Jerry Reuss	118
	Bob Gibson	118
	Ron Kline	118
16	Rick Reuschel	117
17	Jim Kaat	116
	Tom Seaver	116
	Fergie Jenkins	116
	Frank Tanana	116
21	Bob Friend	115
22	Stu Miller	114
23	Dick Tidrow	112
	Clay Carroll	112
25	Bob Miller	111
26	Rollie Fingers	109
	Dave Giusti	109
28	Larry Jackson	106
	Roy Face	106
30	Don Sutton	102
	Tommy John	102
32	Mike McCormick	101
33	Lee Smith	100
	Bill Campbell	100
	Greg Maddux	100
36	Jack Morris	99
37	Orel Hershiser	98
	Roger McDowell	98
	Jim Bunning	98
40	Danny Darwin	97
	Jack Billingham	97
	Frank Linzy	97
43	Jim Perry	93
	Claude Osteen	93
45	John Curtis	92
46	Goose Gossage	90
47	Don Robinson	89
	Milt Pappas	89
49	Randy Jones	88
	Dennis Eckersley	88
	Paul Lindblad	88
52	Tom Hume	87
	Bob Stanley	87
54	Mike LaCoss	86
	Dennis Lamp	86
	Phil Niekro	86
	Greg Harris	86
	Steve Renko	86
	Diego Segui	86
60	Darold Knowles	85
61	Bob Forsch	84
	Mike Krukow	84
	Mike Torrez	84
	Don McMahon	84
65	Bruce Sutter	83
	Pedro Borbon	83
	Rick Wise	83
68	Bill Gullickson	82
	Mike Henneman	82
	Juan Marichal	82
	Ray Sadecki	82
	Turk Farrell	82
73	Sparky Lyle	81
	Rick Honeycutt	81
	Dave LaRoche	81
76	Dale Murray	80
	Dave Roberts	80
	Bob Locker	80
	Joe Gibbon	80
	Don Cardwell	80
	Ted Abernathy	80
82	Woodie Fryman	79
	Willie Hernandez	79
	Fred Norman	79
	Nelson Briles	79
	Phil Regan	79
87	Bob Knepper	78
	Nolan Ryan	78
89	Doug Bair	77
	Jim Brewer	77
	Harvey Haddix	77
92	Ray Burris	76
	Kevin Gross	76
	Pat Dobson	76
	Ron Taylor	76
	Pedro Ramos	76
97	9 tied with	75

Strikeouts

1	Nolan Ryan	5,714
2	Steve Carlton	4,136
3	Bert Blyleven	3,701
4	Tom Seaver	3,640
5	Don Sutton	3,574
6	Gaylord Perry	3,534
7	Walter Johnson	3,509
8	Phil Niekro	3,342
9	Fergie Jenkins	3,192
10	Bob Gibson	3,117
11	Roger Clemens	2,882
12	Jim Bunning	2,855
13	Mickey Lolich	2,832
14	Cy Young	2,802
15	Frank Tanana	2,773
16	Warren Spahn	2,583
17	Bob Feller	2,581
18	Jerry Koosman	2,556
19	Tim Keefe	2,521
20	Christy Mathewson	2,502
21	Don Drysdale	2,486
22	Jack Morris	2,478
23	Jim Kaat	2,461
24	Sam McDowell	2,453
25	Luis Tiant	2,416
26	Sandy Koufax	2,396
27	Dennis Eckersley	2,379
28	Mark Langston	2,365
29	Charlie Hough	2,362
30	Robin Roberts	2,357
31	Early Wynn	2,334
32	Rube Waddell	2,316
33	Juan Marichal	2,303
34	Lefty Grove	2,266
35	Eddie Plank	2,246
36	Tommy John	2,245
37	Jim Palmer	2,212
38	Pete Alexander	2,198
39	Vida Blue	2,175
40	Camilo Pascual	2,167
41	Dennis Martinez	2,087
42	Bobo Newsom	2,082
43	Fernando Valenzuela	2,074
44	Dwight Gooden	2,067
45	Dazzy Vance	2,045
46	David Cone	2,034
47	Rick Reuschel	2,015
48	Catfish Hunter	2,012
49	Randy Johnson	2,000
50	Billy Pierce	1,999
51	Red Ruffing	1,987
52	John Clarkson	1,978
53	Bob Welch	1,969
54	Whitey Ford	1,956
55	Amos Rusie	1,934
56	Jerry Reuss	1,907
57	Kid Nichols	1,868
58	Danny Darwin	1,861
59	Mickey Welch	1,850
60	Frank Viola	1,844
61	Old Hoss Radbourn	1,830
62	Greg Maddux	1,820
63	Tony Mullane	1,803
64	Pud Galvin	1,799
65	Hal Newhouser	1,796
66	Orel Hershiser	1,786
67	Ron Guidry	1,778
68	John Smoltz	1,769
69	Rudy May	1,760
70	Joe Niekro	1,747
71	Sid Fernandez	1,743
72	Dave Stewart	1,741
73	Chuck Finley	1,739
74	Bobby Witt	1,737
75	Ed Walsh	1,736
76	Bob Friend	1,734
77	Joe Coleman	1,728
	Milt Pappas	1,728
79	Kevin Gross	1,727
80	Floyd Bannister	1,723
81	Chief Bender	1,711
82	Larry Jackson	1,709
83	Jim McCormick	1,704
84	Bob Veale	1,703
85	Red Ames	1,702
86	Charlie Buffinton	1,700
87	Curt Simmons	1,697
88	Bruce Hurst	1,689
89	Rick Sutcliffe	1,679
90	Carl Hubbell	1,677
91	Tommy Bridges	1,674
92	John Candelaria	1,673
93	Mike Moore	1,667
94	Gus Weyhing	1,665
95	Vic Willis	1,651
96	Rick Wise	1,647
97	Dave Stieb	1,642
98	Al Downing	1,639
99	Mike Cuellar	1,632
100	Chris Short	1,629

Strikeouts/9 Innings

(minimum 1,500 Innings Pitched)

1	Randy Johnson	10.38
2	Nolan Ryan	9.55
3	Sandy Koufax	9.28
4	Sam McDowell	8.86
5	Roger Clemens	8.53
6	Sid Fernandez	8.40
7	J.R. Richard	8.37
8	David Cone	8.36
9	Bob Veale	7.96
10	Jose Rijo	7.84
11	Jim Maloney	7.81
12	John Smoltz	7.73
13	Tom Gordon	7.73
14	Dwight Gooden	7.60
15	Jose DeLeon	7.56
16	Mark Langston	7.55
17	Mario Soto	7.54
18	Sam Jones	7.54
19	Andy Benes	7.47
20	Goose Gossage	7.47
21	Bobby Witt	7.41
22	Kevin Appier	7.37
23	Bob Gibson	7.22
24	Steve Carlton	7.13
25	Rube Waddell	7.04
26	Mickey Lolich	7.01
27	Chuck Finley	6.99
28	Erik Hanson	6.89
29	Rollie Fingers	6.87
30	Tom Seaver	6.85
31	Jim Bunning	6.83
32	Ramon Martinez	6.75
33	Juan Pizarro	6.73
34	Bobby Bolin	6.71
35	Bert Blyleven	6.70
36	Ron Guidry	6.69
37	Ray Culp	6.69
38	Stan Williams	6.66
39	Camilo Pascual	6.65
40	Bob Turley	6.65
41	Don Wilson	6.60
42	Dennis Eckersley	6.60
43	Tug McGraw	6.59
44	Denny Lemaster	6.57
45	Andy Messersmith	6.56
46	Don Drysdale	6.52
47	Alex Fernandez	6.51
48	Al Downing	6.50
49	Floyd Bannister	6.49
50	Toad Ramsey	6.49
51	Diego Segui	6.46
52	Dean Chance	6.43
53	Hoyt Wilhelm	6.43
54	Mike Scott	6.39
55	Fergie Jenkins	6.38
56	Moe Drabowsky	6.37
57	Fernando Valenzuela	6.37
58	Earl Wilson	6.37
59	Harvey Haddix	6.34
60	Sonny Siebert	6.32
61	Chris Short	6.31
62	Greg Maddux	6.30
63	Jack McDowell	6.29
64	Bruce Hurst	6.29
65	Bill Singer	6.27
66	Todd Stottlemyre	6.27
67	Kevin Gross	6.25
68	Luis Tiant	6.24
69	Turk Farrell	6.21
70	Dazzy Vance	6.20
71	Stu Miller	6.18
72	Clay Kirby	6.17
73	Gary Bell	6.15
74	Gary Peters	6.14
75	Denny McLain	6.12
76	Greg Swindell	6.10
77	Don Sutton	6.09
78	Bret Saberhagen	6.09
79	Mike Krukow	6.07
80	Bob Feller	6.07
81	Ron Darling	6.06
82	John Smiley	6.06
83	Joe Coleman	6.05
84	Fred Norman	6.05
85	Rudy May	6.04
86	Jerry Koosman	5.99
87	John Candelaria	5.96
88	Frank Tanana	5.96
89	Dave Stewart	5.96
90	David Wells	5.95
91	Gaylord Perry	5.94
92	Woodie Fryman	5.92
93	Juan Marichal	5.91
94	Orel Hershiser	5.90
95	Steve Barber	5.89
96	John Montefusco	5.89
97	Mike Witt	5.86
98	Tom Candiotti	5.86
99	Vida Blue	5.85
100	Frank Viola	5.85

ERA

(minimum 1,500 Innings Pitched)

1	Ed Walsh	1.81
2	Addie Joss	1.89
3	Three Finger Brown	2.06
4	Monte Ward	2.10
5	Christy Mathewson	2.13
6	Rube Waddell	2.16
7	Walter Johnson	2.17
8	Orval Overall	2.23
9	Tommy Bond	2.25
10	Will White	2.28
11	Ed Reulbach	2.28
12	Jim Scott	2.30
13	Eddie Plank	2.35
14	Larry Corcoran	2.36
15	Eddie Cicotte	2.37
16	George McQuillan	2.38
17	Ed Killian	2.38
18	Doc White	2.39
19	Nap Rucker	2.42
20	Jeff Tesreau	2.43
21	Jim McCormick	2.43
22	Terry Larkin	2.43
23	Chief Bender	2.45
24	Hooks Wiltse	2.47
25	Sam Leever	2.47
26	Lefty Leifield	2.47
27	Hippo Vaughn	2.49
28	Bob Ewing	2.49
29	George Bradley	2.50
30	Hoyt Wilhelm	2.52
31	Noodles Hahn	2.55
32	Pete Alexander	2.56
33	Slim Sallee	2.56
34	Deacon Phillippe	2.59
35	Frank Smith	2.59
36	Ed Siever	2.60
37	Bob Rhoads	2.61
38	Tim Keefe	2.62
39	Barney Pelty	2.62
40	Cy Young	2.63
41	Vic Willis	2.63
42	Red Ames	2.63
43	Claude Hendrix	2.65
44	Joe McGinnity	2.66
45	Dick Rudolph	2.66
46	Jack Taylor	2.66
47	Nick Altrock	2.67
48	Carl Weilman	2.67
49	Charlie Ferguson	2.67
50	Old Hoss Radbourn	2.67
51	Cy Falkenberg	2.68
52	Jack Chesbro	2.68
53	Fred Toney	2.69
54	Wild Bill Donovan	2.69
55	Larry Cheney	2.70
56	Mickey Welch	2.71
57	Fred Goldsmith	2.73
58	Harry Howell	2.74
59	Luther Taylor	2.74
60	Whitey Ford	2.75
61	Babe Adams	2.75
62	Howie Camnitz	2.75
63	Sandy Koufax	2.76
64	Dutch Leonard	2.76
65	Jeff Pfeffer	2.77
66	Earl Moore	2.78
67	Jack Coombs	2.78
68	Jesse Tannehill	2.79
69	Tully Sparks	2.79
70	Phil Douglas	2.80
71	Greg Maddux	2.81
72	John Clarkson	2.81
73	Ed Morris	2.82
74	Ray Fisher	2.82
75	George Mullin	2.82
76	Bob Caruthers	2.83
77	Dave Foutz	2.84
78	Jim Palmer	2.86
79	Andy Messersmith	2.86
80	Tom Seaver	2.86
81	George Winter	2.87
82	Pud Galvin	2.87
83	Willie Mitchell	2.87
84	Stan Coveleski	2.88
85	Juan Marichal	2.89
86	Wilbur Cooper	2.89
87	Rollie Fingers	2.90
88	Bob Gibson	2.91
89	Harry Brecheen	2.92
90	Carl Mays	2.92
91	Doc Crandall	2.92
92	Dean Chance	2.92
93	Guy Hecker	2.92
94	Dave Davenport	2.93
95	Lefty Tyler	2.95
96	Jumbo McGinnis	2.95
97	Don Drysdale	2.95
98	Kid Nichols	2.95
99	Charlie Buffinton	2.96
100	Mort Cooper	2.97

Leaders: Career Pitching

983

Component ERA
(minimum 1,500 Innings Pitched)

#	Name	ERA
1	Addie Joss	1.73
2	Ed Walsh	1.78
3	Monte Ward	2.01
4	Walter Johnson	2.12
5	Three Finger Brown	2.13
6	Christy Mathewson	2.14
7	Rube Waddell	2.22
8	Larry Corcoran	2.23
9	Tim Keefe	2.26
10	Ed Morris	2.30
11	Terry Larkin	2.32
12	Orval Overall	2.33
13	George Bradley	2.34
14	Chief Bender	2.34
15	Charlie Ferguson	2.35
16	Ed Reulbach	2.35
17	Tommy Bond	2.35
18	Jeff Tesreau	2.35
19	Will White	2.37
20	George McQuillan	2.38
21	Eddie Plank	2.38
22	Babe Adams	2.40
23	Doc White	2.40
24	Jim McCormick	2.41
25	Frank Smith	2.44
26	Eddie Cicotte	2.44
27	Deacon Phillippe	2.44
28	Hooks Wiltse	2.47
29	Noodles Hahn	2.49
30	Nick Altrock	2.49
31	Jim Scott	2.49
32	Sam Leever	2.49
33	Jack Chesbro	2.49
34	Sandy Koufax	2.50
35	Cy Young	2.51
36	Barney Pelty	2.51
37	Old Hoss Radbourn	2.52
38	Pete Alexander	2.53
39	Hoyt Wilhelm	2.53
40	Bob Caruthers	2.56
41	Dave Foutz	2.56
42	Jim Whitney	2.58
43	Bob Ewing	2.58
44	Greg Maddux	2.58
45	Guy Hecker	2.59
46	Jumbo McGinnis	2.59
47	Fred Goldsmith	2.60
48	Nap Rucker	2.60
49	Dupee Shaw	2.60
50	Dick Rudolph	2.61
51	Claude Hendrix	2.61
52	George Winter	2.62
53	Carl Weilman	2.63
54	Jack Taylor	2.64
55	Hippo Vaughn	2.65
56	Andy Messersmith	2.66
57	Tom Seaver	2.67
58	Slim Sallee	2.68
59	Howie Camnitz	2.69
60	Wild Bill Donovan	2.71
61	Joe McGinnity	2.72
62	Cy Falkenberg	2.72
63	Ed Killian	2.72
64	Red Ames	2.72
65	Fred Toney	2.73
66	Vic Willis	2.73
67	Juan Marichal	2.73
68	Larry Cheney	2.73
69	Mickey Welch	2.74
70	John Clarkson	2.75
71	Lefty Leifield	2.76
72	Harry Howell	2.77
73	Toad Ramsey	2.77
74	Henry Boyle	2.77
75	Rollie Fingers	2.78
76	Roger Clemens	2.78
77	Jack Coombs	2.78
78	Pud Galvin	2.78
79	Tony Mullane	2.78
80	J.R. Richard	2.79
81	Phil Douglas	2.79
82	Charlie Buffinton	2.80
83	Sid Fernandez	2.81
84	Ray Fisher	2.82
85	Dave Davenport	2.83
86	Dutch Leonard	2.84
87	Tully Sparks	2.85
88	Bob Rhoads	2.85
89	Carl Mays	2.85
90	Mort Cooper	2.85
91	Jesse Tannehill	2.85
92	Gary Nolan	2.86
93	Bob Gibson	2.86
94	Bobby Mathews	2.87
95	Willie Mitchell	2.87
96	Don Sutton	2.88
97	Carl Hubbell	2.88
98	Jack Powell	2.89
99	Nolan Ryan	2.89
100	Kid Nichols	2.90

Sac Hits Allowed

#	Name	Total
1	Eppa Rixey	568
2	Walter Johnson	534
3	Red Faber	519
4	George Mullin	463
5	Pete Alexander	450
6	Burleigh Grimes	443
7	Cy Young	437
8	Christy Mathewson	397
9	Eddie Plank	393
10	Ted Lyons	391
11	Tom Zachary	389
12	Wilbur Cooper	385
13	George Uhle	382
14	Waite Hoyt	378
15	Red Ruffing	354
16	Earl Whitehill	353
17	Rube Marquard	350
18	Jesse Haines	339
19	Lee Meadows	333
20	Dolf Luque	327
21	Bill Doak	323
22	Bill Sherdel	301
23	Sad Sam Jones	298
24	Eddie Rommel	296
25	Jack Quinn	295
26	Herb Pennock	293
27	Jesse Barnes	285
	Joe McGinnity	285
29	Howard Ehmke	284
	Wild Bill Donovan	284
31	Ed Walsh	283
32	Lefty Grove	277
	Three Finger Brown	277
34	Rube Waddell	275
35	Dazzy Vance	274
36	Slim Sallee	272
37	Jimmy Ring	270
	Nap Rucker	270
39	Rube Benton	266
40	Charlie Root	265
	Ed Reulbach	265
42	Jeff Pfeffer	263
43	Mel Harder	255
	Larry Benton	255
45	Milt Gaston	254
	Jack Chesbro	254
47	Sherry Smith	253
48	Pete Donohue	252
49	Freddie Fitzsimmons	251
50	Carl Hubbell	249
	Elam Vangilder	249
52	Rube Walberg	247
53	Early Wynn	246
	Dutch Ruether	246
	Art Nehf	246
56	Fred Toney	244
	Babe Adams	244
58	Steve Carlton	235
	Stan Coveleski	235
60	Danny MacFayden	234
	Red Lucas	234
	Hal Carlson	234
63	Paul Derringer	232
64	Ray Kremer	228
	Bob Smith	228
66	Dick Rudolph	227
67	Firpo Marberry	224
68	Willis Hudlin	222
	Hippo Vaughn	222
70	Phil Niekro	219
	Tommy Thomas	219
	Guy Bush	219
73	Warren Spahn	218
	Jack Scott	218
75	Gaylord Perry	217
	Larry French	217
77	Phil Douglas	216
78	Jerry Reuss	215
	Clarence Mitchell	215
	Lefty Tyler	215
81	Ray Kolp	214
82	Slim Harriss	212
	Joe Bush	212
84	Bobo Newsom	211
85	Dutch Leonard	209
	Ed Brandt	209
87	Don Sutton	208
	Jack Russell	208
	Larry Cheney	208
90	Kid Nichols	207
91	Addie Joss	206
92	Nolan Ryan	205
93	Harry Howell	204
94	Jakie May	203
	Urban Shocker	203
96	Joe Oeschger	201
97	Bump Hadley	199
	Hugh McQuillan	199
99	Hooks Dauss	198
100	Rip Collins	197

Sac Flies Allowed

#	Name	Total
1	Nolan Ryan	146
2	Jim Kaat	141
3	Don Sutton	127
4	Charlie Hough	126
5	Fergie Jenkins	124
6	Steve Carlton	122
7	Bert Blyleven	121
8	Rick Reuschel	120
9	Frank Tanana	117
10	Jack Morris	114
11	Joe Niekro	112
12	Gaylord Perry	111
	Tom Seaver	111
14	Jerry Koosman	110
15	Danny Darwin	108
16	Dennis Martinez	106
	Jim Perry	106
18	Phil Niekro	102
	Jim Slaton	102
20	Bob Forsch	101
21	Vida Blue	97
	Doyle Alexander	97
23	Tommy John	96
24	Bob Gibson	95
25	Scott Sanderson	94
	Dave Stewart	94
27	John Candelaria	93
	Catfish Hunter	93
29	Dennis Eckersley	92
	Paul Splittorff	92
	Ray Sadecki	92
32	Mickey Lolich	91
33	Rick Sutcliffe	89
34	Larry Gura	86
35	Bill Gullickson	85
36	Jim Clancy	84
	Jim Palmer	84
	Mike Moore	84
39	Bob Welch	83
40	Mark Gubicza	82
	Bobby Witt	82
42	Jerry Reuss	81
	Mike Torrez	81
44	Rick Wise	80
45	Tom Candiotti	79
	Jim Bunning	79
47	Ed Whitson	78
	Jim Barr	78
49	Claude Osteen	77
50	Burt Hooton	76
	Mike Flanagan	76
52	Scott McGregor	75
	Mark Langston	75
54	Curt Simmons	74
	Warren Spahn	74
56	Bob Knepper	73
	Rick Honeycutt	73
	Ron Darling	73
	Jaime Navarro	73
	Pedro Ramos	73
	Vern Law	73
	Robin Roberts	73
63	Ron Reed	72
	Ray Burris	72
	Reggie Cleveland	72
	Joe Coleman	72
	Lindy McDaniel	72
68	Dick Ruthven	71
	Luis Tiant	71
	Wilbur Wood	71
	Milt Pappas	71
72	Steve Rogers	70
	Kevin Gross	70
	Bob Friend	70
75	Dock Ellis	69
	Stan Bahnsen	69
	Mike Krukow	69
	Dave Roberts	69
	Don Robinson	69
	Fernando Valenzuela	69
	Steve Renko	69
82	Dave Stieb	68
	Mike Witt	68
	Jimmy Key	68
	Danny Jackson	68
	Bob Tewksbury	68
	Todd Stottlemyre	68
88	Rudy May	67
	Goose Gossage	67
	Doc Medich	67
	Mike Cuellar	67
92	Rollie Fingers	66
	Rick Rhoden	66
	Don Drysdale	66
	Camilo Pascual	66
	Bob Buhl	66
97	7 tied with	65

Hit Batsmen

#	Name	Total
1	Walter Johnson	203
2	Eddie Plank	196
3	Joe McGinnity	182
4	Chick Fraser	177
5	Charlie Hough	174
6	Cy Young	163
7	Jim Bunning	160
8	Nolan Ryan	158
9	Vic Willis	157
10	Bert Blyleven	155
11	Don Drysdale	154
12	Howard Ehmke	137
13	Kid Nichols	133
14	Ed Doheny	132
15	George Mullin	131
16	Jesse Tannehill	130
17	Frank Tanana	129
18	Willie Sudhoff	126
19	Dave Stieb	124
20	Phil Niekro	123
21	Jim Kaat	122
22	Hooks Dauss	121
	Jack Powell	121
24	Dennis Martinez	119
	Doc White	119
26	Rube Waddell	117
27	Jack Warhop	114
28	George Uhle	113
	Jack Chesbro	113
30	Gus Weyhing	109
31	Gaylord Perry	108
32	Ed Reulbach	107
	Barney Pelty	107
34	Ed Willett	106
	Earl Moore	106
36	Jim Lonborg	105
	Jeff Pfeffer	105
38	Long Tom Hughes	104
39	Red Faber	103
40	Bob Gibson	102
	Chief Bender	102
	Clark Griffith	102
43	Earl Whitehill	101
	Red Donahue	101
45	Wilbur Cooper	100
46	Tommy John	98
	Jack Billingham	98
	Roger Clemens	98
	Don Cardwell	98
	Pink Hawley	98
51	Frank Lary	97
	Burleigh Grimes	97
	Harry Howell	97
54	Harry McIntire	96
	Tim Keefe	96
	Togie Pittinger	96
57	Rube Benton	95
	Cy Morgan	95
59	Jack Quinn	94
60	Mickey Lolich	92
	Jack Taylor	92
	Win Mercer	92
63	Kevin Brown	91
	Wild Bill Donovan	91
65	Joe Coleman	90
	Lee Meadows	90
	Sam Leever	90
68	Carl Mays	89
69	Rick Reuschel	88
	Jakie May	88
	Jack Coombs	88
	Tully Sparks	88
73	Mike Boddicker	87
74	Nixey Callahan	86
75	Tommy Byrne	85
	Hippo Vaughn	85
	Lefty Leifield	85
78	Fergie Jenkins	84
	Bill Duggleby	84
	Cy Seymour	84
81	Otto Hess	83
82	Don Sutton	82
	Orel Hershiser	82
	Frank Kitson	82
	Tony Mullane	82
86	Jim Perry	80
	Wiley Piatt	80
88	Bob Welch	79
	Kevin Gross	79
	Charlie Root	79
	Al Orth	79
92	Danny Darwin	78
	Randy Johnson	78
94	Dazzy Vance	77
	Hank O'Day	77
	Bill Dinneen	77
97	Tom Seaver	76
	Rip Collins	76
	Eppa Rixey	76
	George Mogridge	76

#	Wild Pitches	
1	Nolan Ryan	277
2	Mickey Welch	274
3	Tim Keefe	233
4	Phil Niekro	226
5	Pud Galvin	223
6	Old Hoss Radbourn	217
7	Jim Whitney	214
8	Jack Morris	206
9	Tommy John	187
10	Steve Carlton	183
	Mark Baldwin	183
12	John Clarkson	182
13	Charlie Hough	179
14	Joe Niekro	172
15	Kid Nichols	169
16	Will White	168
17	Tony Mullane	165
18	Egyptian Healy	161
19	Gaylord Perry	160
20	Jim McCormick	157
21	Red Ames	156
	Cy Young	156
23	Walter Johnson	155
24	Charlie Buffinton	154
25	Amos Rusie	153
26	Adonis Terry	148
27	Ed Crane	145
28	Monte Ward	144
29	Sam McDowell	140
30	George Bradley	139
31	Mike Moore	135
	Chick Fraser	135
33	Gus Weyhing	130
34	Jim Kaat	128
35	Tom Seaver	126
36	Mickey Lolich	124
	Jim Maloney	124
38	Jack Stivetts	122
	Bill Hutchison	122
40	Fernando Valenzuela	119
	Frank Tanana	119
	Tony Cloninger	119
	Larry Cheney	119
44	Dave Stewart	118
	Joe Coleman	118
46	David Cone	116
47	Bert Blyleven	114
	John Smoltz	114
	Christy Mathewson	114
	Jouett Meekin	114
51	Larry Corcoran	113
	John Harkins	113
53	Don Sutton	112
	Bobby Witt	112
	Lindy McDaniel	112
56	Charlie Getzien	111
57	Bob Gibson	108
58	Jerry Reuss	107
	Mark Gubicza	107
60	Silver King	105
61	Larry Dierker	104
	Matt Kilroy	104
63	Vida Blue	103
	Mike Torrez	103
65	Jim Clancy	101
	Orel Hershiser	101
	George Haddock	101
	Henry Gruber	101
69	Rick Sutcliffe	100
70	Bert Cunningham	99
71	Ken Holtzman	98
72	Jim Slaton	97
	Ron Darling	97
	Milt Pappas	97
	Johnny Klippstein	97
	Dutch Leonard	97
	Eppa Rixey	97
78	Mike Morgan	96
	Hank Gastright	96
80	Stump Wiedman	95
	Vic Willis	95
	Elton Chamberlin	95
	Ed Daily	95
84	Chuck Finley	94
	Ray Sadecki	94
	Bobby Mathews	94
	Harry Staley	94
88	Bob Forsch	93
	Tom Candiotti	93
	Jack Lynch	93
	Cy Falkenberg	93
	Red Ehret	93
93	J.R. Richard	92
	Blue Moon Odom	92
	Bob Veale	92
	Burleigh Grimes	92
	Phil Knell	92
98	Steve Barber	91
	Sadie McMahon	91
100	3 tied with	90

#	Balks	
1	Steve Carlton	90
2	Bob Welch	45
3	Bud Black	43
4	Charlie Hough	42
	Phil Niekro	42
6	Rick Sutcliffe	38
7	Kevin Gross	35
	Jim Deshaies	35
9	Joaquin Andujar	33
	Nolan Ryan	33
	Bob Walk	33
	Dwight Gooden	33
13	Charlie Leibrandt	31
	Rick Rhoden	31
	David Cone	31
16	Dennis Martinez	30
	Bob McClure	30
18	Jerry Koosman	29
19	Jack Morris	27
	Frank Tanana	27
	Tom Candiotti	27
	Jose Rijo	27
23	John Candelaria	26
	Larry Christenson	26
	Atlee Hammaker	26
	Pete Smith	26
27	Dave LaPoint	25
28	Ron Darling	24
	Mitch Williams	24
	Greg Maddux	24
31	Mike LaCoss	23
	Rick Mahler	23
	Jerry Reuss	23
	Pascual Perez	23
	Dave Stewart	23
	Rick Honeycutt	23
	Orel Hershiser	23
	Jose Guzman	23
	John Dopson	23
	Bobby Witt	23
	Eric Plunk	23
42	Mike Krukow	22
	Dick Ruthven	22
	Scott Sanderson	22
	Dave Smith	22
	Eric Show	22
	Chuck Finley	22
48	Don Sutton	21
	Andy Hawkins	21
	Neal Heaton	21
	Mark Langston	21
	Mike Jackson	21
	Joe Magrane	21
	Jack Sanford	21
55	Tom Griffin	20
	Mario Soto	20
	Lary Sorensen	20
	Juan Marichal	20
59	Juan Berenguer	19
	Bert Blyleven	19
	Bill Bonham	19
	Mike Scott	19
	Bruce Hurst	19
	Bobby Ojeda	19
	Dave Righetti	19
	Sid Fernandez	19
67	Bob Forsch	18
	Gary Lavelle	18
	Rudy May	18
	Fergie Jenkins	18
	Roger Clemens	18
72	Danny Darwin	17
	Mike Norris	17
	Oil Can Boyd	17
	Teddy Higuera	17
	Kelly Downs	17
	John Smiley	17
	Randy Johnson	17
79	Woodie Fryman	16
	Dickie Noles	16
	Bryn Smith	16
	Dennis Eckersley	16
	Tommy John	16
	Andy McGaffigan	16
	Steve Trout	16
	Ricky Horton	16
	Joe Hesketh	16
	Darryl Kile	16
89	Larry McWilliams	15
	Paul Moskau	15
	Don Robinson	15
	Roger Erickson	15
	Jim Gott	15
	Mike Bielecki	15
	Eric King	15
	Greg Mathews	15
	Melido Perez	15
	Trevor Wilson	15
	Andy Benes	15
	Tom Zachary	15

Opponent Average
(minimum 1,500 Innings Pitched)

#	Player	Avg
1	Nolan Ryan	.204
2	Sandy Koufax	.205
3	Sid Fernandez	.209
4	Randy Johnson	.211
5	J.R. Richard	.212
6	Andy Messersmith	.212
7	Sam McDowell	.215
8	Hoyt Wilhelm	.216
9	Ed Walsh	.218
10	Addie Joss	.220
11	Mario Soto	.220
12	Bob Turley	.220
13	Orval Overall	.222
14	David Cone	.223
15	Jeff Tesreau	.223
16	Jim Maloney	.224
17	Jose DeLeon	.224
18	Ed Reulbach	.224
19	Tom Seaver	.226
20	Rube Waddell	.226
21	Larry Corcoran	.226
22	Walter Johnson	.227
23	Tim Keefe	.227
24	Roger Clemens	.227
25	Don Wilson	.228
26	Bob Gibson	.228
27	Goose Gossage	.228
28	Jim Palmer	.230
29	Sam Jones	.230
30	Catfish Hunter	.231
31	Bobby Bolin	.231
32	Bob Feller	.231
33	Al Downing	.232
34	Stan Williams	.232
35	Johnny Vander Meer	.232
36	John Smoltz	.232
37	Three Finger Brown	.233
38	Charlie Hough	.233
39	Charlie Ferguson	.233
40	Ed Morris	.234
41	Larry Cheney	.234
42	Denny McLain	.234
43	Dean Chance	.234
44	Monte Ward	.235
45	Whitey Ford	.235
46	Rollie Fingers	.235
47	Ray Culp	.235
48	Moe Drabowsky	.236
49	Amos Rusie	.236
50	Bob Veale	.236
51	Dave Foutz	.236
52	Don Sutton	.236
53	Luis Tiant	.236
54	Christy Mathewson	.236
55	Toad Ramsey	.237
56	Frank Smith	.237
57	Tug McGraw	.237
58	Ramon Martinez	.237
59	Juan Marichal	.237
60	Kevin Appier	.237
61	Vida Blue	.237
62	Juan Pizarro	.237
63	Tony Mullane	.238
64	Allie Reynolds	.238
65	Greg Maddux	.238
66	Sonny Siebert	.238
67	Wild Bill Donovan	.238
68	Chief Bender	.238
69	Rudy May	.238
70	Jim Scott	.238
71	Gary Nolan	.239
72	Dave Stieb	.239
73	Hal Newhouser	.239
74	Eddie Plank	.239
75	Dwight Gooden	.239
76	Gary Bell	.239
77	Don Drysdale	.239
78	Dupee Shaw	.239
79	John Clarkson	.239
80	Barney Pelty	.240
81	Bill Singer	.240
82	Mike Scott	.240
83	Mort Cooper	.240
84	Virgil Trucks	.240
85	Billy Pierce	.240
86	Steve Carlton	.240
87	Earl Moore	.240
88	Jose Rijo	.240
89	Bob Lemon	.241
90	Will White	.241
91	Bob Caruthers	.241
92	Kirby Higbe	.241
93	Jack Coombs	.241
94	Hooks Wiltse	.241
95	George McQuillan	.241
96	Old Hoss Radbourn	.241
97	Jack Chesbro	.241
98	Jim McCormick	.242
99	Lefty Gomez	.242
100	Earl Wilson	.242

Opponent OBP
(minimum 1,500 Innings Pitched)

#	Player	OBP
1	Monte Ward	.254
2	Addie Joss	.257
3	George Bradley	.261
4	Terry Larkin	.263
5	Ed Walsh	.264
6	Larry Corcoran	.264
7	Tommy Bond	.267
8	Will White	.269
9	Charlie Ferguson	.270
10	Ed Morris	.272
11	Christy Mathewson	.273
12	Jim McCormick	.274
13	Fred Goldsmith	.275
14	Sandy Koufax	.275
15	Jim Whitney	.276
16	Tim Keefe	.276
17	Juan Marichal	.277
18	Old Hoss Radbourn	.278
19	Three Finger Brown	.279
20	Walter Johnson	.279
21	Dupee Shaw	.279
22	Guy Hecker	.279
23	Jumbo McGinnis	.282
24	Bob Caruthers	.282
25	Deacon Phillippe	.282
26	Tom Seaver	.283
27	Pud Galvin	.283
28	Babe Adams	.284
29	Bobby Mathews	.284
30	Catfish Hunter	.285
31	Gary Nolan	.285
32	Don Sutton	.286
33	Rube Waddell	.286
34	Cy Young	.286
35	Sid Fernandez	.286
36	Fergie Jenkins	.287
37	Greg Maddux	.287
38	Dave Foutz	.287
39	Andy Messersmith	.287
40	Pete Alexander	.288
41	Henry Boyle	.288
42	Noodles Hahn	.288
43	John Clarkson	.288
44	Bret Saberhagen	.288
45	Hoyt Wilhelm	.288
46	Tiny Bonham	.289
47	Dennis Eckersley	.289
48	Hooks Wiltse	.290
49	Nick Altrock	.290
50	Roger Clemens	.290
51	Charlie Buffinton	.290
52	Jack Lynch	.290
53	Chief Bender	.290
54	Denny McLain	.290
55	Carl Hubbell	.291
56	Doc White	.292
57	Robin Roberts	.292
58	Rollie Fingers	.292
59	Mickey Welch	.292
60	Ron Guidry	.292
61	Don Drysdale	.293
62	Jack Chesbro	.293
63	Eddie Plank	.293
64	Sam Leever	.293
65	Jim Palmer	.294
66	Mario Soto	.294
67	George McQuillan	.294
68	Ralph Terry	.294
69	Jeff Tesreau	.295
70	John Candelaria	.295
71	Gaylord Perry	.296
72	Warren Spahn	.296
73	John Smoltz	.297
74	Bob Gibson	.297
75	Eddie Fisher	.297
76	Jack Taylor	.297
77	Luis Tiant	.297
78	Mike Cuellar	.297
79	Tony Mullane	.297
80	George Winter	.297
81	Don Mossi	.297
82	Mike Scott	.297
83	Frank Smith	.297
84	Jim Bunning	.297
85	Toad Ramsey	.297
86	Hardie Henderson	.298
87	Dizzy Dean	.298
88	Dick Rudolph	.298
89	Don Newcombe	.298
90	Orval Overall	.298
91	Charlie Getzien	.298
92	Slim Sallee	.298
93	Lee Richmond	.298
94	Fritz Peterson	.298
95	Harry Brecheen	.298
96	Joe Horlen	.299
97	Ed Reulbach	.299
98	John Tudor	.299
99	Eddie Cicotte	.299
100	David Cone	.299

Single Season Batting Leaders

Games

	Player	Year	G
1	Maury Wills	1962	165
2	Jose Pagan	1962	164
	Ron Santo	1965	164
	Billy Williams	1965	164
	Cesar Tovar	1967	164
	Frank Taveras	1979	164
7	Brooks Robinson	1961	163
	Rocky Colavito	1961	163
	Tommy Davis	1962	163
	Leo Cardenas	1964	163
	Leon Wagner	1964	163
	Brooks Robinson	1964	163
	Ernie Banks	1965	163
	Don Buford	1966	163
	Bill Mazeroski	1967	163
	Harmon Killebrew	1967	163
	Billy Williams	1968	163
	Billy Williams	1969	163
	Pete Rose	1974	163
	Willie Montanez	1976	163
	Jim Rice	1978	163
	Pete Rose	1979	163
	Steve Garvey	1980	163
	Al Oliver	1980	163
	Greg Walker	1985	163
	Tony Fernandez	1986	163
	Jose Oquendo	1989	163
	Bobby Bonilla	1989	163
	Cal Ripken Jr.	1996	163
	Todd Zeile	1996	163
31	137 tied with		162

At-Bats

	Player	Year	AB
1	Willie Wilson	1980	705
2	Juan Samuel	1984	701
3	Dave Cash	1975	699
4	Matty Alou	1969	698
5	Woody Jensen	1936	696
6	Maury Wills	1962	695
	Omar Moreno	1979	695
8	Bobby Richardson	1962	692
9	Kirby Puckett	1985	691
10	Lou Brock	1967	689
	Sandy Alomar	1971	689
12	Dave Cash	1974	687
	Tony Fernandez	1986	687
14	Horace Clarke	1970	686
15	Nomar Garciaparra	1997	684
16	Lance Johnson	1996	682
17	Lloyd Waner	1931	681
	Jo-Jo Moore	1935	681
19	Pete Rose	1973	680
	Frank Taveras	1979	680
	Kirby Puckett	1986	680
22	Harvey Kuenn	1953	679
	Curt Flood	1964	679
	Bobby Richardson	1964	679
25	Dick Groat	1962	678
26	Matty Alou	1970	677
	Jim Rice	1978	677
	Don Mattingly	1986	677
29	Felix Millan	1975	676
	Omar Moreno	1980	676
31	Rennie Stennett	1974	673
	Bill Buckner	1985	673
33	Rabbit Maranville	1922	672
	Tony Oliva	1964	672
	Sandy Alomar	1970	672
	Garry Templeton	1979	672
37	Jack Tobin	1921	671
	Marquis Grissom	1996	671
39	Al Simmons	1932	670
	Pete Rose	1965	670
	Buddy Bell	1979	670
42	Vada Pinson	1965	669
	Larry Bowa	1974	669
44	Buddy Lewis	1937	668
	Brooks Robinson	1961	668
	Ralph Garr	1973	668
47	Carl Furillo	1951	667
48	Billy Herman	1935	666
	Zoilo Versalles	1965	666
	Felipe Alou	1966	666
	Dave Cash	1976	666
	Ron LeFlore	1978	666
	Paul Molitor	1982	666
54	Tommy Davis	1962	665
	Pete Rose	1976	665
	Paul Molitor	1991	665
57	Taylor Douthit	1930	664
	Bobby Richardson	1965	664
	Don Kessinger	1969	664
	Lou Brock	1970	664
61	Jake Wood	1961	663
	Bill Virdon	1962	663
	Bobby Bonds	1970	663
	Rick Burleson	1977	663
	Cal Ripken Jr.	1983	663
	Juan Samuel	1985	663
	Joe Carter	1986	663
68	Lloyd Waner	1929	662
	Hughie Critz	1930	662
	Richie Ashburn	1949	662
	Granny Hamner	1949	662
	Bobby Richardson	1961	662
	Curt Flood	1963	662
	Felipe Alou	1968	662
	Pete Rose	1975	662
	Kenny Lofton	1996	662
77	Doc Cramer	1933	661
	Doc Cramer	1940	661
	Ken Hubbs	1962	661
	Cecil Cooper	1983	661
	Ruben Sierra	1991	661
82	Tom Brown	1892	660
	Doc Cramer	1941	660
	Lou Brock	1968	660
	Enos Cabell	1978	660
	Paul Molitor	1996	660
87	Lloyd Waner	1928	659
	Hughie Critz	1932	659
	Red Schoendienst	1947	659
	Billy Moran	1962	659
	Zoilo Versalles	1964	659
	Luis Aparicio	1966	659
	Steve Garvey	1975	659
	Warren Cromartie	1979	659
	Travis Fryman	1992	659
96	8 tied with		658

Runs

	Player	Year	R
1	Billy Hamilton	1894	192
2	Tom Brown	1891	177
	Babe Ruth	1921	177
4	Tip O'Neill	1887	167
	Lou Gehrig	1936	167
6	Billy Hamilton	1895	166
7	Willie Keeler	1894	165
	Joe Kelley	1894	165
9	Arlie Latham	1887	163
	Babe Ruth	1928	163
	Lou Gehrig	1931	163
12	Willie Keeler	1895	162
13	Hugh Duffy	1890	161
14	Fred Dunlap	1884	160
	Hugh Duffy	1894	160
	Jesse Burkett	1896	160
17	Hughie Jennings	1895	159
18	Bobby Lowe	1894	158
	Babe Ruth	1920	158
	Babe Ruth	1927	158
	Chuck Klein	1930	158
22	John McGraw	1894	156
	Rogers Hornsby	1929	156
24	King Kelly	1886	155
	Kiki Cuyler	1930	155
26	Dan Brouthers	1887	153
	Jesse Burkett	1895	153
	Willie Keeler	1896	153
29	Arlie Latham	1886	152
	Mike Griffin	1889	152
	Harry Stovey	1889	152
	Billy Hamilton	1896	152
	Billy Hamilton	1897	152
	Lefty O'Doul	1929	152
	Woody English	1930	152
	Al Simmons	1930	152
	Chuck Klein	1932	152
38	Babe Ruth	1923	151
	Jimmie Foxx	1932	151
	Joe DiMaggio	1937	151
41	George Gore	1886	150
	Babe Ruth	1930	150
	Ted Williams	1949	150
44	Herman Long	1893	149
	Bill Dahlen	1894	149
	Ed Delahanty	1895	149
	Lou Gehrig	1927	149
	Babe Ruth	1931	149
49	Hub Collins	1890	148
	Jake Stenzel	1894	148
	Joe Kelley	1895	148
	Joe Kelley	1896	148
53	Mike Tiernan	1889	147
	Hugh Duffy	1893	147
	Ed Delahanty	1894	147
	Ty Cobb	1911	147
57	Darby O'Brien	1889	146
	Tom Brown	1890	146
	Hack Wilson	1930	146
	Rickey Henderson	1985	146
	Craig Biggio	1997	146
62	Jesse Burkett	1893	145
	Ed Delahanty	1893	145
	Cupid Childs	1893	145
	Patsy Donovan	1894	145
	Willie Keeler	1897	145
	Nap Lajoie	1901	145
	Harlond Clift	1936	145
69	Billy Hamilton	1889	144
	Hugh Duffy	1889	144
	Ty Cobb	1915	144
	Kiki Cuyler	1925	144
	Charlie Gehringer	1930	144
	Al Simmons	1932	144
	Charlie Gehringer	1936	144
	Hank Greenberg	1938	144
77	Cupid Childs	1894	143
	John McGraw	1898	143
	Babe Ruth	1924	143
	Babe Herman	1930	143
	Lou Gehrig	1930	143
	Earle Combs	1932	143
	Red Rolfe	1937	143
	Lenny Dykstra	1993	143
	Larry Walker	1997	143
86	Mike Griffin	1887	142
	Harry Stovey	1890	142
	Jesse Burkett	1901	142
	Paul Waner	1928	142
	Ted Williams	1946	142
	Ellis Burks	1996	142
92	Billy Hamilton	1891	141
	Rogers Hornsby	1922	141
	Ted Williams	1942	141
	Alex Rodriguez	1996	141
96	9 tied with		140

Hits

	Player	Year	H
1	George Sisler	1920	257
2	Lefty O'Doul	1929	254
	Bill Terry	1930	254
4	Al Simmons	1925	253
5	Rogers Hornsby	1922	250
	Chuck Klein	1930	250
7	Ty Cobb	1911	248
8	George Sisler	1922	246
9	Heinie Manush	1928	241
	Babe Herman	1930	241
11	Jesse Burkett	1896	240
	Wade Boggs	1985	240
13	Willie Keeler	1897	239
	Rod Carew	1977	239
15	Ed Delahanty	1899	238
	Don Mattingly	1986	238
17	Hugh Duffy	1894	237
	Harry Heilmann	1921	237
	Paul Waner	1927	237
	Joe Medwick	1937	237
21	Jack Tobin	1921	236
22	Rogers Hornsby	1921	235
23	Lloyd Waner	1929	234
	Kirby Puckett	1988	234
25	Joe Jackson	1911	233
26	Nap Lajoie	1901	232
	Earl Averill	1936	232
28	Earle Combs	1927	231
	Freddy Lindstrom	1928	231
	Freddy Lindstrom	1930	231
	Matty Alou	1969	231
32	Stan Musial	1948	230
	Tommy Davis	1962	230
	Joe Torre	1971	230
	Pete Rose	1973	230
	Willie Wilson	1980	230
37	Rogers Hornsby	1929	229
38	Kiki Cuyler	1930	228
	Stan Musial	1946	228
40	Nap Lajoie	1910	227
	Ty Cobb	1912	227
	Rogers Hornsby	1924	227
	Jim Bottomley	1925	227
	Sam Rice	1925	227
	Billy Herman	1935	227
	Charlie Gehringer	1936	227
	Lance Johnson	1996	227
48	Jesse Burkett	1901	226
	Joe Jackson	1912	226
	Bill Terry	1929	226
	Chuck Klein	1932	226
52	Tip O'Neill	1887	225
	Jesse Burkett	1895	225
	Ty Cobb	1917	225
	Harry Heilmann	1925	225
	Johnny Hodapp	1930	225
	Bill Terry	1932	225
	Paul Molitor	1996	225
59	Eddie Collins	1920	224
	George Sisler	1925	224
	Joe Medwick	1935	224
	Tommy Holmes	1945	224
63	Frankie Frisch	1923	223
	Lloyd Waner	1927	223
	Paul Waner	1928	223
	Chuck Klein	1933	223
	Joe Medwick	1936	223
	Hank Aaron	1959	223
	Kirby Puckett	1986	223
70	Sam Thompson	1893	222
	Tris Speaker	1912	222
	Charlie Jamieson	1923	222
73	Jesse Burkett	1899	221
	Zack Wheat	1925	221
	Lloyd Waner	1928	221
	Heinie Manush	1933	221
	Richie Ashburn	1951	221
78	Pete Browning	1887	220
	Billy Hamilton	1894	220
	Kiki Cuyler	1925	220
	Lou Gehrig	1930	220
	Stan Musial	1943	220
	Tony Gwynn	1997	220
84	Ed Delahanty	1893	219
	Willie Keeler	1894	219
	Jimmy Williams	1899	219
	Cy Seymour	1905	219
	Chuck Klein	1929	219
	Lefty O'Doul	1932	219
	Paul Waner	1937	219
	Ralph Garr	1971	219
	Cecil Cooper	1980	219
93	12 tied with		218

Doubles

	Player	Year	
1	Earl Webb	1931	67
2	George Burns	1926	64
	Joe Medwick	1936	64
4	Hank Greenberg	1934	63
5	Paul Waner	1932	62
6	Charlie Gehringer	1936	60
7	Tris Speaker	1923	59
	Chuck Klein	1930	59
9	Billy Herman	1935	57
	Billy Herman	1936	57
11	Joe Medwick	1937	56
	George Kell	1950	56
13	Ed Delahanty	1899	55
	Gee Walker	1936	55
15	Hal McRae	1977	54
	John Olerud	1993	54
	Alex Rodriguez	1996	54
	Mark Grudzielanek	1997	54
19	Tris Speaker	1912	53
	Al Simmons	1926	53
	Paul Waner	1936	53
	Stan Musial	1953	53
	Don Mattingly	1986	53
24	Tip O'Neill	1887	52
	Tris Speaker	1921	52
	Tris Speaker	1926	52
	Lou Gehrig	1927	52
	Johnny Frederick	1929	52
	Enos Slaughter	1939	52
	Edgar Martinez	1995	52
	Albert Belle	1995	52
	Edgar Martinez	1996	52
33	Hugh Duffy	1894	51
	Nap Lajoie	1910	51
	Baby Doll Jacobson	1926	51
	George Burns	1927	51
	Johnny Hodapp	1930	51
	Beau Bell	1937	51
	Joe Cronin	1938	51
	Stan Musial	1944	51
	Mickey Vernon	1946	51
	Frank Robinson	1962	51
	Pete Rose	1978	51
	Wade Boggs	1989	51
	Mark Grace	1995	51
46	Tris Speaker	1920	50
	Harry Heilmann	1927	50
	Paul Waner	1928	50
	Kiki Cuyler	1930	50
	Chuck Klein	1932	50
	Charlie Gehringer	1934	50
	Odell Hale	1936	50
	Ben Chapman	1936	50
	Hank Greenberg	1940	50
	Stan Musial	1946	50
	Stan Spence	1946	50
57	Ned Williamson	1883	49
	Ed Delahanty	1895	49
	Nap Lajoie	1904	49
	George Sisler	1920	49
	Heinie Manush	1930	49
	Riggs Stephenson	1932	49
	Hank Greenberg	1937	49
	Robin Yount	1980	49
	Rafael Palmeiro	1991	49
	Tony Gwynn	1997	49
67	Joe Kelley	1894	48
	Nap Lajoie	1901	48
	Nap Lajoie	1906	48
	Tris Speaker	1922	48
	Joe Sewell	1927	48
	Babe Herman	1930	48
	Dick Bartell	1932	48
	Earl Averill	1934	48
	Wally Moses	1937	48
	Joe Medwick	1939	48
	Stan Musial	1943	48
	Keith Hernandez	1979	48
	Don Mattingly	1985	48
	Jeff Bagwell	1996	48
81	26 tied with		47

Triples

	Player	Year	
1	Chief Wilson	1912	36
2	Dave Orr	1886	31
	Heinie Reitz	1894	31
4	Perry Werden	1893	29
5	Harry Davis	1897	28
6	George Davis	1893	27
	Sam Thompson	1894	27
	Jimmy Williams	1899	27
9	John Reilly	1890	26
	George Treadway	1894	26
	Joe Jackson	1912	26
	Sam Crawford	1914	26
	Kiki Cuyler	1925	26
14	Roger Connor	1894	25
	Buck Freeman	1899	25
	Sam Crawford	1903	25
	Larry Doyle	1911	25
	Tom Long	1915	25
19	Ed McKean	1893	24
	Ty Cobb	1911	24
	Ty Cobb	1917	24
22	Harry Stovey	1884	23
	Sam Thompson	1887	23
	Elmer Smith	1893	23
	Dan Brouthers	1894	23
	Nap Lajoie	1897	23
	Ty Cobb	1912	23
	Sam Crawford	1913	23
	Earle Combs	1927	23
	Adam Comorosky	1930	23
	Dale Mitchell	1949	23
32	Roger Connor	1887	22
	Jake Beckley	1890	22
	Joe Visner	1890	22
	Bid McPhee	1890	22
	Willie Keeler	1894	22
	Kip Selbach	1895	22
	John Anderson	1898	22
	Honus Wagner	1900	22
	Sam Crawford	1902	22
	Tommy Leach	1902	22
	Bill Bradley	1903	22
	Elmer Flick	1906	22
	Birdie Cree	1911	22
	Mike Mitchell	1911	22
	Tris Speaker	1913	22
	Hi Myers	1920	22
	Jake Daubert	1922	22
	Paul Waner	1926	22
	Earle Combs	1930	22
	Snuffy Stirnweiss	1945	22
52	Dave Orr	1885	21
	Mike Tiernan	1890	21
	Billy Shindle	1890	21
	Tom Brown	1891	21
	Ed Delahanty	1892	21
	Mike Tiernan	1895	21
	Sam Thompson	1895	21
	Tom McCreery	1896	21
	George Van Haltren	1896	21
	Bobby Wallace	1897	21
	Jimmy Williams	1901	21
	Bill Keister	1901	21
	Jimmy Williams	1902	21
	Cy Seymour	1905	21
	Wildfire Schulte	1911	21
	Home Run Baker	1912	21
	Sam Crawford	1912	21
	Vic Saier	1913	21
	Joe Jackson	1916	21
	Edd Roush	1924	21
	Earle Combs	1928	21
	Willie Wilson	1985	21
	Lance Johnson	1996	21
75	36 tied with		20

Home Runs

	Player	Year	
1	Roger Maris	1961	61
2	Babe Ruth	1927	60
3	Babe Ruth	1921	59
4	Jimmie Foxx	1932	58
	Hank Greenberg	1938	58
	Mark McGwire	1997	58
7	Hack Wilson	1930	56
	Ken Griffey Jr.	1997	56
9	Babe Ruth	1920	54
	Babe Ruth	1928	54
	Ralph Kiner	1949	54
	Mickey Mantle	1961	54
13	Mickey Mantle	1956	52
	Willie Mays	1965	52
	George Foster	1977	52
	Mark McGwire	1996	52
17	Ralph Kiner	1947	51
	Johnny Mize	1947	51
	Willie Mays	1955	51
	Cecil Fielder	1990	51
21	Jimmie Foxx	1938	50
	Albert Belle	1995	50
	Brady Anderson	1996	50
24	Babe Ruth	1930	49
	Lou Gehrig	1934	49
	Lou Gehrig	1936	49
	Ted Kluszewski	1954	49
	Willie Mays	1962	49
	Harmon Killebrew	1964	49
	Frank Robinson	1966	49
	Harmon Killebrew	1969	49
	Andre Dawson	1987	49
	Mark McGwire	1987	49
	Ken Griffey Jr.	1996	49
	Larry Walker	1997	49
36	Jimmie Foxx	1933	48
	Harmon Killebrew	1962	48
	Frank Howard	1969	48
	Willie Stargell	1971	48
	Dave Kingman	1979	48
	Mike Schmidt	1980	48
	Albert Belle	1996	48
43	Babe Ruth	1926	47
	Lou Gehrig	1927	47
	Ralph Kiner	1950	47
	Eddie Mathews	1953	47
	Ted Kluszewski	1955	47
	Ernie Banks	1958	47
	Willie Mays	1964	47
	Reggie Jackson	1969	47
	Hank Aaron	1971	47
	George Bell	1987	47
	Kevin Mitchell	1989	47
	Andres Galarraga	1996	47
	Juan Gonzalez	1996	47
56	Babe Ruth	1924	46
	Babe Ruth	1929	46
	Lou Gehrig	1931	46
	Babe Ruth	1931	46
	Joe DiMaggio	1937	46
	Eddie Mathews	1959	46
	Orlando Cepeda	1961	46
	Jim Gentile	1961	46
	Harmon Killebrew	1961	46
	Jim Rice	1978	46
	Barry Bonds	1993	46
	Juan Gonzalez	1993	46
68	Ernie Banks	1959	45
	Rocky Colavito	1961	45
	Hank Aaron	1962	45
	Harmon Killebrew	1963	45
	Willie McCovey	1969	45
	Johnny Bench	1970	45
	Mike Schmidt	1979	45
	Gorman Thomas	1979	45
	Ken Griffey Jr.	1993	45
77	Jimmie Foxx	1934	44
	Hank Greenberg	1946	44
	Ernie Banks	1955	44
	Hank Aaron	1957	44
	Willie McCovey	1963	44
	Hank Aaron	1963	44
	Hank Aaron	1966	44
	Carl Yastrzemski	1967	44
	Harmon Killebrew	1967	44
	Frank Howard	1968	44
	Hank Aaron	1969	44
	Frank Howard	1970	44
	Willie Stargell	1973	44
	Dale Murphy	1987	44
	Cecil Fielder	1991	44
	Jose Canseco	1991	44
	Jay Buhner	1996	44
	Mo Vaughn	1996	44
	Tino Martinez	1997	44
96	11 tied with		43

Home Runs (Home)

	Player	Year	
1	Hank Greenberg	1938	39
2	Jimmie Foxx	1938	35
3	Ted Kluszewski	1954	34
4	Hack Wilson	1930	33
5	Babe Ruth	1921	32
	Ken Williams	1922	32
	Jimmie Foxx	1932	32
	Andres Galarraga	1996	32
9	Jimmie Foxx	1933	31
	Ralph Kiner	1948	31
	Hank Aaron	1971	31
	Dante Bichette	1995	31
13	Lou Gehrig	1934	30
	Hal Trosky	1936	30
	Ernie Banks	1958	30
	Roger Maris	1961	30
	Johnny Bench	1970	30
	Mark McGwire	1997	30
19	Babe Ruth	1920	29
	Babe Ruth	1928	29
	Chuck Klein	1932	29
	Hank Greenberg	1946	29
	Johnny Mize	1947	29
	Ralph Kiner	1949	29
	Harmon Killebrew	1961	29
26	Babe Ruth	1927	28
	Ralph Kiner	1947	28
	Willie Mays	1962	28
	Harmon Killebrew	1969	28
	Billy Williams	1970	28
	Jim Rice	1978	28
	Fred Lynn	1979	28
33	Lou Gehrig	1936	27
	Hank Greenberg	1940	27
	Ralph Kiner	1950	27
	Mickey Mantle	1956	27
	Frank Robinson	1966	27
	Carl Yastrzemski	1967	27
	Frank Howard	1969	27
	Dick Allen	1972	27
	Jeff Burroughs	1977	27
	Jim Rice	1977	27
	Jim Rice	1979	27
	Andre Dawson	1987	27
	Cecil Fielder	1991	27
	Mo Vaughn	1996	27
	Vinny Castilla	1996	27
	Ken Griffey Jr.	1997	27
49	Tilly Walker	1922	26
	Cy Williams	1923	26
	Chuck Klein	1930	26
	Babe Ruth	1930	26
	Ralph Kiner	1951	26
	Ernie Banks	1955	26
	Roy Sievers	1957	26
	Frank Robinson	1959	26
	Willie McCovey	1963	26
	Harmon Killebrew	1963	26
	Harmon Killebrew	1964	26
	Reggie Jackson	1969	26
	Dave Johnson	1973	26
	Frank Thomas	1993	26
	Ken Griffey Jr.	1996	26
	Sammy Sosa	1996	26
65	Fred Pfeffer	1884	25
	Ned Williamson	1884	25
	Chuck Klein	1929	25
	Hack Wilson	1929	25
	Al Simmons	1930	25
	Hank Greenberg	1937	25
	Johnny Mize	1940	25
	Willard Marshall	1947	25
	Johnny Mize	1948	25
	Al Rosen	1953	25
	Gil Hodges	1954	25
	Wally Post	1955	25
	Duke Snider	1956	25
	Ernie Banks	1957	25
	Norm Cash	1962	25
	Dick Stuart	1963	25
	Willie Mays	1964	25
	George Foster	1978	25
	Dave Kingman	1979	25
	Mike Schmidt	1980	25
	Bob Horner	1982	25
	Dale Murphy	1987	25
	Ryne Sandberg	1990	25
	Cecil Fielder	1990	25
	Albert Belle	1995	25
	Sammy Sosa	1997	25
91	29 tied with		24

Home Runs (Road)

1	Babe Ruth	1927	32
2	Roger Maris	1961	31
	George Foster	1977	31
	Brady Anderson	1996	31
5	Eddie Mathews	1953	30
	Jim Gentile	1961	30
	Mickey Mantle	1961	30
8	Willie Mays	1955	29
	Mike Schmidt	1979	29
	Larry Walker	1997	29
	Ken Griffey Jr.	1997	29
12	Harmon Killebrew	1962	28
	Willie Mays	1965	28
	George Bell	1987	28
	Mark McGwire	1987	28
	Jose Canseco	1991	28
	Mark McGwire	1996	28
	Mark McGwire	1997	28
19	Babe Ruth	1921	27
	Lou Gehrig	1930	27
	Joe DiMaggio	1937	27
	Rocky Colavito	1961	27
	Hank Aaron	1962	27
	Willie Stargell	1971	27
	Jay Buhner	1997	27
26	Jimmie Foxx	1932	26
	Hank Aaron	1957	26
	Ted Williams	1957	26
	Frank Thomas	1958	26
	Eddie Mathews	1959	26
	Roger Maris	1960	26
	Frank Howard	1968	26
	Ben Oglivie	1980	26
	Jose Canseco	1988	26
	Cecil Fielder	1990	26
	Albert Belle	1996	26
	Tino Martinez	1997	26
38	Babe Ruth	1920	25
	Babe Ruth	1928	25
	Babe Ruth	1929	25
	Ralph Kiner	1949	25
	Ted Kluszewski	1955	25
	Mickey Mantle	1956	25
	Hank Aaron	1963	25
	Donn Clendenon	1966	25
	Harmon Killebrew	1970	25
	Reggie Jackson	1980	25
	Kevin Mitchell	1989	25
	Mark McGwire	1990	25
	Barry Bonds	1993	25
	Albert Belle	1995	25
	Frank Thomas	1995	25
	Matt Williams	1997	25
54	Babe Ruth	1926	24
	Joe DiMaggio	1948	24
	Gil Hodges	1951	24
	Eddie Mathews	1954	24
	Leon Wagner	1962	24
	Leon Wagner	1963	24
	Johnny Bench	1972	24
	Jesse Barfield	1986	24
	Juan Gonzalez	1992	24
	Ken Griffey Jr.	1993	24
	Mark McGwire	1995	24
	Mo Vaughn	1995	24
	Juan Gonzalez	1996	24
	Frank Thomas	1996	24
	Juan Gonzalez	1997	24
69	36 tied with		23

At-Bats/Home Run

(minimum 3.1 PA/Tm Gm)

1	Mark McGwire	1996	8.13
2	Babe Ruth	1920	8.48
3	Babe Ruth	1927	9.00
4	Babe Ruth	1921	9.15
5	Mark McGwire	1997	9.31
6	Mickey Mantle	1961	9.52
7	Hank Greenberg	1938	9.59
8	Roger Maris	1961	9.67
9	Babe Ruth	1928	9.93
10	Jimmie Foxx	1932	10.09
11	Ralph Kiner	1949	10.17
12	Mickey Mantle	1956	10.25
13	Jeff Bagwell	1994	10.26
14	Kevin Mitchell	1994	10.33
15	Matt Williams	1994	10.35
16	Hack Wilson	1930	10.45
17	Frank Thomas	1994	10.50
18	Babe Ruth	1926	10.53
	Hank Aaron	1971	10.53
20	Jim Gentile	1961	10.57
21	Barry Bonds	1994	10.57
22	Babe Ruth	1930	10.57
23	Willie Stargell	1971	10.65
24	Willie Mays	1965	10.73
25	Ken Griffey Jr.	1994	10.83
26	Babe Ruth	1929	10.85
27	Ken Griffey Jr.	1997	10.86
28	Boog Powell	1964	10.87
29	Willie McCovey	1969	10.91
30	Albert Belle	1995	10.92
31	Ted Williams	1957	11.05
32	Ralph Kiner	1947	11.08
33	Dave Kingman	1979	11.08
34	Mark McGwire	1992	11.12
35	Ken Griffey Jr.	1996	11.12
36	Babe Ruth	1932	11.15
37	Cecil Fielder	1990	11.24
38	Jimmie Foxx	1938	11.30
39	Harmon Killebrew	1969	11.33
40	Mark McGwire	1987	11.37
41	Willie Mays	1955	11.37
42	Mike Schmidt	1980	11.42
43	Mike Schmidt	1981	11.42
44	Harmon Killebrew	1963	11.44
	Albert Belle	1994	11.44
46	Johnny Mize	1947	11.49
47	Babe Ruth	1924	11.50
	Harmon Killebrew	1962	11.50
49	Juan Gonzalez	1996	11.51
50	Kevin Mitchell	1989	11.55
51	Brady Anderson	1996	11.58
52	Larry Walker	1997	11.59
53	Babe Ruth	1922	11.60
54	Babe Ruth	1931	11.61
55	Ralph Kiner	1950	11.64
56	Juan Gonzalez	1993	11.65
57	Reggie Jackson	1969	11.68
58	Ted Kluszewski	1954	11.69
59	Barry Bonds	1993	11.72
60	Jay Buhner	1995	11.75
61	Frank Robinson	1966	11.76
62	Harmon Killebrew	1961	11.76
63	Harmon Killebrew	1964	11.78
64	Lou Gehrig	1934	11.82
	Lou Gehrig	1936	11.82
66	George Foster	1977	11.83
67	Willie Stargell	1973	11.86
68	Hank Greenberg	1946	11.89
69	Eddie Mathews	1954	11.90
70	Gary Sheffield	1994	11.93
71	Rocky Colavito	1958	11.93
72	Jimmie Foxx	1933	11.94
73	Joe Adcock	1956	11.95
74	Jack Clark	1987	11.97
75	Mike Schmidt	1979	12.02
76	Eddie Mathews	1955	12.17
77	Jimmie Foxx	1934	12.25
78	Willie Mays	1964	12.30
79	Barry Bonds	1996	12.31
80	Eddie Mathews	1953	12.32
81	Ted Williams	1941	12.32
82	Frank Thomas	1995	12.33
83	Frank Howard	1969	12.33
84	Mickey Mantle	1958	12.36
	Gary Sheffield	1996	12.36
86	Gorman Thomas	1979	12.38
87	Jim Thome	1997	12.40
88	Lou Gehrig	1927	12.43
89	Harmon Killebrew	1967	12.43
	Hank Aaron	1969	12.43
91	Sammy Sosa	1996	12.45
92	Fred McGriff	1994	12.47
93	Reggie Jackson	1980	12.54
94	Albert Belle	1996	12.54
95	Greg Vaughn	1996	12.59
96	Duke Snider	1956	12.60
97	Darrell Evans	1985	12.63
98	Ralph Kiner	1951	12.64
99	Roy Campanella	1953	12.66
100	2 tied with		12.67

Extra Base Hits

1	Babe Ruth	1921	119
2	Lou Gehrig	1927	117
3	Chuck Klein	1930	107
4	Chuck Klein	1932	103
	Hank Greenberg	1937	103
	Stan Musial	1948	103
	Albert Belle	1995	103
8	Rogers Hornsby	1922	102
9	Lou Gehrig	1930	100
	Jimmie Foxx	1932	100
11	Babe Ruth	1920	99
	Babe Ruth	1923	99
	Hank Greenberg	1940	99
	Larry Walker	1997	99
15	Hank Greenberg	1935	98
16	Babe Ruth	1927	97
	Hack Wilson	1930	97
	Joe Medwick	1937	97
19	Hank Greenberg	1934	96
	Hal Trosky	1936	96
	Joe DiMaggio	1937	96
22	Lou Gehrig	1934	95
	Joe Medwick	1936	95
24	Chuck Klein	1929	94
	Rogers Hornsby	1929	94
	Babe Herman	1930	94
	Jimmie Foxx	1933	94
28	Jim Bottomley	1928	93
	Al Simmons	1930	93
	Lou Gehrig	1936	93
	Ellis Burks	1996	93
	Ken Griffey Jr.	1997	93
33	Babe Ruth	1924	92
	Lou Gehrig	1931	92
	Jimmie Foxx	1938	92
	Stan Musial	1953	92
	Hank Aaron	1959	92
	Frank Robinson	1962	92
	Brady Anderson	1996	92
40	Babe Ruth	1928	91
	Alex Rodriguez	1996	91
42	Rogers Hornsby	1925	90
	Stan Musial	1949	90
	Willie Mays	1962	90
	Willie Stargell	1973	90
46	Hal Trosky	1934	89
	Duke Snider	1954	89
	Andres Galarraga	1996	89
	Albert Belle	1996	89
50	Joe DiMaggio	1936	88
	Barry Bonds	1993	88
52	Tris Speaker	1923	87
	Kiki Cuyler	1925	87
	Lou Gehrig	1928	87
	Ripper Collins	1934	87
	Charlie Gehringer	1936	87
	Johnny Mize	1940	87
	Willie Mays	1954	87
	Robin Yount	1982	87
	Kevin Mitchell	1989	87
61	George Sisler	1920	86
	Babe Ruth	1930	86
	Wally Moses	1937	86
	Ted Williams	1939	86
	Johnny Mize	1939	86
	Stan Musial	1946	86
	Eddie Mathews	1953	86
	Reggie Jackson	1969	86
	Hal McRae	1977	86
	Jim Rice	1978	86
	Don Mattingly	1985	86
	Don Mattingly	1986	86
	Ken Griffey Jr.	1993	86
74	Tip O'Neill	1887	85
	Hugh Duffy	1894	85
	Chick Hafey	1929	85
	Goose Goslin	1930	85
	Lou Gehrig	1932	85
	Lou Gehrig	1933	85
	Earl Averill	1934	85
	Hank Greenberg	1938	85
	Rudy York	1940	85
	Ted Williams	1949	85
	Stan Musial	1954	85
	Frank Robinson	1966	85
	George Foster	1977	85
	George Brett	1979	85
	Cal Ripken Jr.	1991	85
	Mark McGwire	1997	85
	Jeff Bagwell	1997	85
	Nomar Garciaparra	1997	85
92	11 tied with		84

Total Bases

1	Babe Ruth	1921	457
2	Rogers Hornsby	1922	450
3	Lou Gehrig	1927	447
4	Chuck Klein	1930	445
5	Jimmie Foxx	1932	438
6	Stan Musial	1948	429
7	Hack Wilson	1930	423
8	Chuck Klein	1932	420
9	Lou Gehrig	1930	419
10	Joe DiMaggio	1937	418
11	Babe Ruth	1927	417
12	Babe Herman	1930	416
13	Lou Gehrig	1931	410
14	Rogers Hornsby	1929	409
	Lou Gehrig	1934	409
	Larry Walker	1997	409
17	Joe Medwick	1937	406
	Jim Rice	1978	406
19	Chuck Klein	1929	405
	Hal Trosky	1936	405
21	Jimmie Foxx	1933	403
	Lou Gehrig	1936	403
23	Hank Aaron	1959	400
24	George Sisler	1920	399
	Babe Ruth	1923	399
26	Jimmie Foxx	1938	398
27	Lefty O'Doul	1929	397
	Hank Greenberg	1937	397
29	Ken Griffey Jr.	1997	393
30	Al Simmons	1925	392
	Al Simmons	1930	392
	Bill Terry	1930	392
	Ellis Burks	1996	392
34	Babe Ruth	1924	391
35	Hank Greenberg	1935	389
36	Babe Ruth	1920	388
	George Foster	1977	388
	Don Mattingly	1986	388
39	Earl Averill	1936	385
40	Hank Greenberg	1940	384
41	Stan Musial	1949	382
	Willie Mays	1955	382
	Willie Mays	1962	382
	Jim Rice	1977	382
45	Rogers Hornsby	1925	381
46	Babe Ruth	1928	380
	Hank Greenberg	1938	380
	Frank Robinson	1962	380
49	Babe Ruth	1930	379
	Ernie Banks	1958	379
	Alex Rodriguez	1996	379
52	Rogers Hornsby	1921	378
	Duke Snider	1954	378
54	Willie Mays	1954	377
	Albert Belle	1995	377
56	Mickey Mantle	1956	376
	Andres Galarraga	1996	376
58	Albert Belle	1996	375
59	Hugh Duffy	1894	374
	Babe Ruth	1931	374
	Hal Trosky	1934	374
	Tony Oliva	1964	374
63	Rogers Hornsby	1924	373
	Al Simmons	1929	373
	Bill Terry	1932	373
	Billy Williams	1970	373
67	Lou Gehrig	1932	370
	Duke Snider	1953	370
	Hank Aaron	1963	370
	Don Mattingly	1985	370
	Mo Vaughn	1996	370
72	Kiki Cuyler	1925	369
	Ripper Collins	1934	369
	Jimmie Foxx	1936	369
	Hank Aaron	1957	369
	Jim Rice	1979	369
	George Bell	1987	369
	Brady Anderson	1996	369
79	Johnny Mize	1940	368
	Ted Williams	1949	368
	Ted Kluszewski	1954	368
	Cal Ripken Jr.	1991	368
83	Ty Cobb	1911	367
	Ken Williams	1922	367
	Heinie Manush	1928	367
	Al Simmons	1932	367
	Joe DiMaggio	1936	367
	Joe Medwick	1936	367
	Tommy Holmes	1945	367
	Al Rosen	1953	367
	Frank Robinson	1966	367
	Robin Yount	1982	367
93	Lou Gehrig	1937	366
	Stan Musial	1946	366
	Willie Mays	1957	366
	Roger Maris	1961	366
	Hank Aaron	1962	366
98	7 tied with		365

RBI

1	Hack Wilson	1930	190
2	Lou Gehrig	1931	184
3	Hank Greenberg	1937	183
4	Lou Gehrig	1927	175
	Jimmie Foxx	1938	175
6	Lou Gehrig	1930	174
7	Babe Ruth	1921	171
8	Chuck Klein	1930	170
	Hank Greenberg	1935	170
10	Jimmie Foxx	1932	169
11	Joe DiMaggio	1937	167
12	Sam Thompson	1887	166
13	Sam Thompson	1895	165
	Al Simmons	1930	165
	Lou Gehrig	1934	165
16	Babe Ruth	1927	164
17	Babe Ruth	1931	163
	Jimmie Foxx	1933	163
19	Hal Trosky	1936	162
20	Hack Wilson	1929	159
	Lou Gehrig	1937	159
	Vern Stephens	1949	159
	Ted Williams	1949	159
24	Al Simmons	1929	157
25	Jimmie Foxx	1930	156
26	Ken Williams	1922	155
	Joe DiMaggio	1948	155
28	Babe Ruth	1929	154
	Joe Medwick	1937	154
30	Babe Ruth	1930	153
	Tommy Davis	1962	153
32	Rogers Hornsby	1922	152
	Lou Gehrig	1936	152
34	Mel Ott	1929	151
	Al Simmons	1932	151
	Lou Gehrig	1932	151
37	Hank Greenberg	1940	150
	Andres Galarraga	1996	150
39	Rogers Hornsby	1929	149
	George Foster	1977	149
41	Johnny Bench	1970	148
	Albert Belle	1996	148
43	Cap Anson	1886	147
	Ken Griffey Jr.	1997	147
45	Hardy Richardson	1890	146
	Ed Delahanty	1893	146
	Babe Ruth	1926	146
	Hank Greenberg	1938	146
49	Hugh Duffy	1894	145
	Chuck Klein	1929	145
	Ted Williams	1939	145
	Al Rosen	1953	145
	Don Mattingly	1985	145
54	Walt Dropo	1950	144
	Vern Stephens	1950	144
	Juan Gonzalez	1996	144
57	Rogers Hornsby	1925	143
	Earl Averill	1931	143
	Don Hurst	1932	143
	Jimmie Foxx	1936	143
	Ernie Banks	1959	143
	Mo Vaughn	1996	143
63	Lou Gehrig	1928	142
	Babe Ruth	1928	142
	Hal Trosky	1934	142
	Roy Campanella	1953	142
	Orlando Cepeda	1961	142
	Roger Maris	1961	142
	Rafael Palmeiro	1996	142
70	Sam Thompson	1894	141
	Ted Kluszewski	1954	141
	Jim Gentile	1961	141
	Willie Mays	1962	141
	Dante Bichette	1996	141
	Tino Martinez	1997	141
76	Joe DiMaggio	1938	140
	Rocky Colavito	1961	140
	Harmon Killebrew	1969	140
	Ken Griffey Jr.	1996	140
	Andres Galarraga	1997	140
81	Harry Heilmann	1921	139
	Lou Gehrig	1933	139
	Hank Greenberg	1934	139
	Jim Rice	1978	139
	Don Baylor	1979	139
86	Bob Meusel	1925	138
	Goose Goslin	1930	138
	Zeke Bonura	1936	138
	Joe Medwick	1936	138
	Johnny Mize	1947	138
	Jay Buhner	1996	138
92	11 tied with		137

Walks

1	Babe Ruth	1923	170
2	Ted Williams	1947	162
	Ted Williams	1949	162
4	Ted Williams	1946	156
5	Eddie Yost	1956	151
	Barry Bonds	1996	151
7	Eddie Joost	1949	149
8	Babe Ruth	1920	148
	Eddie Stanky	1945	148
	Jimmy Wynn	1969	148
11	Jimmy Sheckard	1911	147
12	Mickey Mantle	1957	146
13	Ted Williams	1941	145
	Ted Williams	1942	145
	Harmon Killebrew	1969	145
	Barry Bonds	1997	145
17	Babe Ruth	1921	144
	Babe Ruth	1926	144
	Eddie Stanky	1950	144
	Ted Williams	1951	144
21	Babe Ruth	1924	142
	Gary Sheffield	1996	142
23	Eddie Yost	1950	141
24	Babe Ruth	1927	138
	Frank Thomas	1991	138
26	Eddie Stanky	1946	137
	Roy Cullenbine	1947	137
	Ralph Kiner	1951	137
	Willie McCovey	1970	137
30	Jack Crooks	1892	136
	Babe Ruth	1930	136
	Ferris Fain	1949	136
	Ted Williams	1954	136
	Jack Clark	1987	136
	Frank Thomas	1995	136
36	Babe Ruth	1928	135
	Eddie Yost	1959	135
	Jeff Bagwell	1996	135
39	Ferris Fain	1950	133
40	Lou Gehrig	1935	132
	Frank Howard	1970	132
	Joe Morgan	1975	132
	Jack Clark	1989	132
	Tony Phillips	1993	132
45	Bob Elliott	1948	131
	Eddie Yost	1954	131
	Harmon Killebrew	1967	131
48	Babe Ruth	1932	130
	Lou Gehrig	1936	130
50	Eddie Yost	1952	129
	Mickey Mantle	1958	129
	Lenny Dykstra	1993	129
53	Max Bishop	1929	128
	Max Bishop	1930	128
	Babe Ruth	1931	128
	Carl Yastrzemski	1970	128
	Harmon Killebrew	1970	128
	Mike Schmidt	1983	128
59	Lu Blue	1931	127
	Lou Gehrig	1937	127
	Eddie Stanky	1951	127
	Jimmy Wynn	1976	127
	Barry Bonds	1992	127
	Jeff Bagwell	1997	127
65	Billy Hamilton	1894	126
	Lu Blue	1929	126
	Ted Williams	1948	126
	Eddie Yost	1951	126
	Mickey Mantle	1961	126
	Darrell Evans	1974	126
	Rickey Henderson	1989	126
	Barry Bonds	1993	126
73	Richie Ashburn	1954	125
	Eddie Yost	1960	125
	Gene Tenace	1977	125
	Wade Boggs	1988	125
	Rickey Henderson	1996	125
	Tony Phillips	1996	125
79	John McGraw	1899	124
	Norm Cash	1961	124
	Eddie Mathews	1963	124
	Darrell Evans	1973	124
83	Bill Joyce	1890	123
	Eddie Yost	1953	123
	Ken Singleton	1973	123
	Edgar Martinez	1996	123
	Jim Thome	1996	123
88	Jimmy Sheckard	1912	122
	Lou Gehrig	1929	122
	Luke Appling	1935	122
	Ralph Kiner	1950	122
	Eddie Joost	1952	122
	Mickey Mantle	1962	122
	John Mayberry	1973	122
	Mickey Tettleton	1992	122
	Frank Thomas	1992	122
97	8 tied with		121

Walks/PA

(minimum 3.1 PA/Tm Gm)

1	Ted Williams	1954	.259
2	Jack Clark	1987	.243
3	Babe Ruth	1923	.243
4	Babe Ruth	1920	.241
5	Ted Williams	1941	.240
6	Mickey Mantle	1957	.234
7	Ted Williams	1947	.234
8	Ted Williams	1946	.232
9	Jimmy Wynn	1969	.227
10	Roy Cullenbine	1947	.226
11	Barry Bonds	1996	.224
12	Jack Clark	1989	.222
13	Ted Williams	1949	.222
14	Babe Ruth	1926	.221
15	Eddie Yost	1956	.221
16	Babe Ruth	1932	.221
17	Max Bishop	1926	.219
18	Eddie Joost	1949	.218
19	Mickey Tettleton	1994	.218
20	Ted Williams	1957	.218
21	Max Bishop	1930	.218
22	Jimmy Wynn	1976	.217
23	Toby Harrah	1985	.217
24	Ted Williams	1942	.216
25	Gene Tenace	1977	.215
26	Willie McCovey	1970	.215
27	Max Bishop	1927	.215
28	Eddie Stanky	1946	.213
29	Ted Williams	1951	.213
30	Mark McGwire	1996	.212
31	Frank Thomas	1994	.211
32	Max Bishop	1932	.211
33	Frank Thomas	1995	.210
34	Barry Bonds	1997	.210
35	Max Bishop	1933	.210
36	Gary Sheffield	1996	.210
37	Jimmy Sheckard	1911	.209
38	Willie Mays	1971	.209
39	Babe Ruth	1924	.209
40	Eddie Stanky	1950	.208
41	Babe Ruth	1921	.208
42	Jimmy Wynn	1975	.208
43	Gary Sheffield	1997	.208
44	Max Bishop	1929	.208
45	Rickey Henderson	1996	.208
46	Barry Bonds	1992	.208
47	Joe Morgan	1975	.207
48	Harmon Killebrew	1969	.205
49	Ralph Kiner	1951	.204
50	Elmer Valo	1952	.204
51	Hank Greenberg	1947	.204
52	Eddie Stanky	1945	.204
53	Ted Williams	1956	.203
54	Ferris Fain	1949	.202
55	Ferris Fain	1950	.202
56	Babe Ruth	1930	.201
57	Eddie Yost	1959	.200
58	Babe Ruth	1927	.199
59	Babe Ruth	1933	.198
60	Babe Ruth	1928	.198
61	Ted Williams	1948	.197
62	Mickey Mantle	1958	.197
63	Mel Ott	1943	.197
64	Frank Thomas	1991	.197
65	Mel Ott	1939	.197
66	Rickey Henderson	1993	.197
67	Eddie Yost	1960	.197
68	Lou Gehrig	1935	.196
69	Gene Tenace	1978	.196
70	Danny Tartabull	1992	.196
71	Mickey Tettleton	1995	.196
72	Mickey Cochrane	1933	.196
73	Luke Appling	1949	.195
74	Mickey Mantle	1961	.195
75	Eddie Stanky	1951	.194
76	Johnny Evers	1910	.194
77	Willie McCovey	1969	.194
78	Bob Elliott	1948	.194
79	Edgar Martinez	1996	.194
80	Eddie Yost	1955	.194
81	Mickey Mantle	1968	.194
82	Mickey Mantle	1967	.193
83	Jim Thome	1996	.193
84	Babe Ruth	1931	.193
85	Eddie Yost	1950	.193
86	Harmon Killebrew	1970	.192
87	Roy Cullenbine	1941	.192
88	George Selkirk	1939	.192
89	Ferris Fain	1953	.191
	Jeff Burroughs	1978	.191
	Rickey Henderson	1994	.191
92	Augie Galan	1947	.191
93	Jim Thome	1997	.191
94	Mike Schmidt	1983	.191
95	John Mayberry	1973	.191
96	Eddie Yost	1954	.191
97	Rickey Henderson	1997	.191
98	Joe Morgan	1976	.190
99	Harmon Killebrew	1967	.190
100	Mickey Tettleton	1990	.190

Intentional Walks

1	Willie McCovey	1969	45
2	Barry Bonds	1993	43
3	Willie McCovey	1970	40
4	Barry Bonds	1997	34
5	Ted Williams	1957	33
	John Olerud	1993	33
7	Kevin Mitchell	1989	32
	Barry Bonds	1992	32
9	George Brett	1985	31
10	Barry Bonds	1996	30
11	Adolfo Phillips	1967	29
	Frank Howard	1970	29
	Dale Murphy	1987	29
	Frank Thomas	1995	29
15	Ernie Banks	1960	28
16	Roberto Clemente	1968	27
	Will Clark	1988	27
	Jeff Bagwell	1997	27
19	Duke Snider	1956	26
	Stan Musial	1958	26
	Tim Raines	1987	26
	Tony Gwynn	1987	26
	Fred McGriff	1991	26
	Frank Thomas	1996	26
25	Ted Kluszewski	1955	25
	Leo Cardenas	1965	25
	Willie Stargell	1967	25
	Willie McCovey	1973	25
	Bill Russell	1974	25
	Ted Simmons	1977	25
	Eddie Murray	1984	25
	Mike Schmidt	1986	25
	Howard Johnson	1988	25
	Spike Owen	1989	25
	Wade Boggs	1991	25
	Barry Bonds	1991	25
	Ken Griffey Jr.	1993	25
38	Rusty Staub	1968	24
	Dave Winfield	1979	24
	Warren Cromartie	1980	24
	Garry Templeton	1985	24
	Dave Parker	1985	24
	Leon Durham	1985	24
	Eddie Murray	1989	24
45	Mickey Mantle	1957	23
	Frank Robinson	1961	23
	Orlando Cepeda	1967	23
	Hank Aaron	1968	23
	Harmon Killebrew	1970	23
	Johnny Bench	1972	23
	Dave Rader	1973	23
	Dave Parker	1978	23
	Garry Templeton	1984	23
	Chili Davis	1986	23
	Fred McGriff	1992	23
	Will Clark	1992	23
	Frank Thomas	1993	23
	Mo Vaughn	1993	23
	Ken Griffey Jr.	1997	23
60	Ted Kluszewski	1956	22
	Willie Stargell	1973	22
	Ted Simmons	1979	22
	Barry Bonds	1989	22
	Harold Baines	1991	22
	Rafael Palmeiro	1993	22
	Barry Bonds	1995	22
67	Ernie Banks	1961	21
	Rusty Staub	1967	21
	Willie McCovey	1971	21
	Hank Aaron	1971	21
	Willie Stargell	1974	21
	Ted Sizemore	1977	21
	Garry Templeton	1986	21
	Darryl Strawberry	1988	21
	Andre Dawson	1990	21
	Eddie Murray	1990	21
	Ken Griffey Jr.	1991	21
	Mike Piazza	1996	21
79	24 tied with		20

Strikeouts

Rank	Player	Year	Total
1	Bobby Bonds	1970	189
2	Bobby Bonds	1969	187
3	Rob Deer	1987	186
4	Pete Incaviglia	1986	185
5	Cecil Fielder	1990	182
6	Mike Schmidt	1975	180
7	Rob Deer	1986	179
8	Dave Nicholson	1963	175
	Gorman Thomas	1979	175
	Jose Canseco	1986	175
	Rob Deer	1991	175
	Jay Buhner	1997	175
13	Sammy Sosa	1997	174
14	Jim Presley	1986	172
	Bo Jackson	1989	172
16	Reggie Jackson	1968	171
17	Gorman Thomas	1980	170
18	Andres Galarraga	1990	169
	Rob Deer	1993	169
20	Juan Samuel	1984	168
	Pete Incaviglia	1987	168
22	Gary Alexander	1978	166
	Steve Balboni	1985	166
	Cory Snyder	1987	166
25	Donn Clendenon	1968	163
26	Butch Hobson	1977	162
	Juan Samuel	1987	162
	Ron Gant	1997	162
29	Dick Allen	1968	161
	Reggie Jackson	1971	161
31	Mickey Tettleton	1990	160
	Henry Rodriguez	1996	160
33	Jay Buhner	1996	159
	Mark McGwire	1997	159
35	Bo Jackson	1987	158
	Rob Deer	1989	158
	Andres Galarraga	1989	158
	Jose Canseco	1990	158
	Melvin Nieves	1996	158
40	Danny Tartabull	1986	157
	Jim Presley	1987	157
	Jose Canseco	1987	157
	Andres Galarraga	1996	157
	Melvin Nieves	1997	157
45	Tommie Agee	1970	156
	Reggie Jackson	1982	156
	Dave Kingman	1982	156
	Tony Armas	1984	156
	Danny Tartabull	1993	156
50	Frank Howard	1967	155
	Jeff Burroughs	1975	155
52	Willie Stargell	1971	154
	Larry Parrish	1987	154
	Dean Palmer	1992	154
	Dean Palmer	1993	154
	Mo Vaughn	1996	154
	Mo Vaughn	1997	154
58	Dave Kingman	1975	153
	Rob Deer	1988	153
	Andres Galarraga	1988	153
	Pete Incaviglia	1988	153
62	George Scott	1966	152
	Larry Hisle	1969	152
	Jose Canseco	1991	152
65	Don Lock	1963	151
	Greg Luzinski	1975	151
	Juan Samuel	1988	151
	Cecil Fielder	1991	151
	Delino DeShields	1991	151
	Cecil Fielder	1992	151
71	Dick Allen	1965	150
	Nate Colbert	1970	150
	Ron Kittle	1983	150
	Jesse Barfield	1989	150
	Jesse Barfield	1990	150
	Sammy Sosa	1990	150
	Mo Vaughn	1995	150
78	Billy Grabarkewitz	1970	149
	Mike Schmidt	1976	149
	Fred McGriff	1988	149
	Travis Fryman	1991	149
	Henry Rodriguez	1997	149
83	Bobby Bonds	1973	148
	Mike Schmidt	1983	148
	Gorman Thomas	1983	148
	Roberto Kelly	1990	148
87	Rob Deer	1990	147
	Ray Lankford	1992	147
	Cory Snyder	1993	147
	Benji Gil	1995	147
91	11 tied with		146

Hit By Pitch

Rank	Player	Year	Total
1	Hughie Jennings	1896	51
2	Ron Hunt	1971	50
3	Hughie Jennings	1897	46
	Hughie Jennings	1898	46
5	Dan McGann	1898	39
6	Dan McGann	1899	37
7	Curt Welch	1891	36
8	Don Baylor	1986	35
9	Curt Welch	1890	34
	Craig Biggio	1997	34
11	Tommy Tucker	1889	33
12	Hughie Jennings	1895	32
13	Steve Evans	1910	31
	Jason Kendall	1997	31
15	Tommy Tucker	1887	29
	Curt Welch	1888	29
	Chief Roseman	1890	29
	Tommy Tucker	1891	29
19	Pete Gilbert	1891	28
	Don Baylor	1987	28
21	Hughie Jennings	1894	27
	Craig Biggio	1996	27
23	Tommy Tucker	1892	26
	Ron Hunt	1970	26
	Ron Hunt	1972	26
26	Tommy Tucker	1890	25
	Eddie Burke	1893	25
	Kid Elberfeld	1911	25
	Ron Hunt	1968	25
	Ron Hunt	1969	25
	F.P. Santangelo	1997	25
32	Dan Brouthers	1891	24
	Fred Clarke	1897	24
	Dan McGann	1900	24
	Bill Freehan	1968	24
	Ron Hunt	1973	24
	Don Baylor	1985	24
38	Bill Dahlen	1898	23
	Steve Brodie	1899	23
	John McGraw	1900	23
	Dan McGann	1901	23
	Jake Stahl	1908	23
	Minnie Minoso	1956	23
	Don Baylor	1984	23
45	Bill Joyce	1896	22
	Dick Harley	1898	22
	Charlie Babb	1903	22
	Craig Biggio	1995	22
	Brady Anderson	1996	22
50	Jay Faatz	1888	21
	Jake Beckley	1895	21
	Bucky Harris	1920	21
	Minnie Minoso	1957	21
	Eric Young	1996	21
55	Connie Mack	1890	20
	Jake Beckley	1893	20
	Tommy Tucker	1893	20
	Joe Sullivan	1896	20
	Hughie Jennings	1900	20
	Billy Gilbert	1903	20
	Doc Gessler	1911	20
	Solly Hemus	1952	20
	Frank Robinson	1956	20
	Bill Freehan	1967	20
	Bobby Grich	1974	20
	Don Baylor	1976	20
	Chet Lemon	1983	20
	Jeff Blauser	1997	20
69	Curt Welch	1889	19
	Deacon White	1890	19
	Jake Beckley	1894	19
	Tommy Tucker	1895	19
	Dick Padden	1898	19
	John McGraw	1898	19
	Jake Stenzel	1898	19
	Tommy Tucker	1898	19
	Hughie Jennings	1899	19
	Dan McGann	1905	19
	Dan McGann	1908	19
	Steve Evans	1911	19
	Red Killefer	1915	19
	Art Fletcher	1917	19
	Dave Hollins	1992	19
	Chuck Knoblauch	1996	19
	Brady Anderson	1997	19
86	21 tied with		18

Sac Hits

Rank	Player	Year	Total
1	Ray Chapman	1917	67
2	Bill Bradley	1908	60
3	Jack Barry	1917	54
4	Bob Ganley	1908	52
	Donie Bush	1909	52
6	Ray Chapman	1919	50
7	Johnny Bates	1909	48
	Ray Chapman	1913	48
	Joe Gedeon	1920	48
	Donie Bush	1920	48
11	Ossie Vitt	1919	47
12	Bill Bradley	1907	46
	Jimmy Sheckard	1909	46
	Ralph Young	1919	46
	Bucky Harris	1924	46
16	Stuffy McInnis	1920	45
17	Buck Weaver	1916	44
18	Kid Gleason	1905	43
	Germany Schaefer	1908	43
	Roy Grover	1917	43
	Bill Wambsganss	1921	43
22	Willie Keeler	1905	42
	Otto Knabe	1908	42
	Tom Fisher	1915	42
	Buck Weaver	1915	42
	Ossie Vitt	1915	42
	Bobby Vaughn	1915	42
	Bill Wambsganss	1922	42
	Pie Traynor	1928	42
30	Bob Ganley	1909	41
	Otto Knabe	1913	41
	Everett Scott	1917	41
	Ray Chapman	1920	41
	Donie Bush	1921	41
	Bucky Harris	1925	41
	Joe Sewell	1929	41
37	George Davis	1905	40
	Tom Jones	1906	40
	Jimmy Sheckard	1906	40
	Otto Knabe	1907	40
	Shano Collins	1915	40
	Ray Chapman	1916	40
	Larry Gardner	1917	40
	Joe Gedeon	1919	40
	Eddie Collins	1919	40
	Bill Wambsganss	1920	40
	Roger Peckinpaugh	1923	40
	Ike Davis	1925	40
	Mule Haas	1929	40
	Bert Campaneris	1977	40
51	Jake Daubert	1915	39
	Max Flack	1916	39
	Eddie Collins	1916	39
	Jake Daubert	1919	39
	Topper Rigney	1922	39
	Zeb Terry	1922	39
	Eddie Collins	1923	39
	Jay Bell	1990	39
59	Wally Clement	1909	38
	Hans Lobert	1911	38
	Chick Gandil	1914	38
	Terry Turner	1914	38
63	Otto Knabe	1910	37
	Max Carey	1912	37
	George Cutshaw	1920	37
	Charlie Hollocher	1922	37
	Stuffy McInnis	1923	37
	Bill Wambsganss	1924	37
	Willie Kamm	1925	37
	Taylor Douthit	1926	37
	Freddie Maguire	1928	37
	Dick Bartell	1933	37
73	Fielder Jones	1904	36
	Hunter Hill	1905	36
	Joe Tinker	1906	36
	Jiggs Donahue	1906	36
	Bill Coughlin	1906	36
	Art Devlin	1907	36
	Harry Lord	1908	36
	Bill McKechnie	1914	36
	Dave Shean	1918	36
	Milt Stock	1921	36
	Bobby Veach	1922	36
	Harvey McClellan	1923	36
	Harry Walker	1943	36
86	18 tied with		35

Sac Flies

Rank	Player	Year	Total
1	Gil Hodges	1954	19
2	Andre Dawson	1983	18
3	Roy White	1971	17
	Bobby Bonilla	1996	17
5	Don Mattingly	1985	15
	Gary Carter	1986	15
	Bobby Bonilla	1990	15
	Howard Johnson	1991	15
9	Ron Santo	1969	14
	Jose Cardenal	1971	14
	George Hendrick	1982	14
	Dave Kingman	1984	14
	George Bell	1989	14
	Dave Parker	1990	14
	Albert Belle	1993	14
16	Johnny Temple	1959	13
	Willie Montanez	1971	13
	Sal Bando	1974	13
	Reggie Smith	1978	13
	Dan Ford	1979	13
	Darrell Porter	1979	13
	Mike Schmidt	1980	13
	Ray Knight	1982	13
	Bill Madlock	1982	13
	Gary Gaetti	1982	13
	Lance Parrish	1983	13
	Tom Herr	1985	13
	Tom Brunansky	1985	13
	Andy Van Slyke	1988	13
	Kelly Gruber	1990	13
	Will Clark	1990	13
	Barry Bonds	1991	13
	Joe Carter	1992	13
	Jeff Bagwell	1992	13
	Carlos Baerga	1993	13
	Frank Thomas	1993	13
	Joe Carter	1994	13
	Travis Fryman	1994	13
	Tino Martinez	1997	13
40	Jackie Jensen	1955	12
	Jimmy Piersall	1956	12
	Frank Thomas	1957	12
	Jackie Jensen	1959	12
	Hank Aaron	1960	12
	Del Crandall	1960	12
	Minnie Minoso	1961	12
	Leo Posada	1961	12
	Vic Power	1961	12
	Ron Santo	1967	12
	Johnny Bench	1972	12
	Jeff Burroughs	1974	12
	Barry Foote	1974	12
	Amos Otis	1974	12
	Bobby Murcer	1974	12
	Bobby Murcer	1975	12
	John Mayberry	1976	12
	Joe Morgan	1976	12
	Don Baylor	1978	12
	Don Baylor	1979	12
	Dusty Baker	1980	12
	Keith Hernandez	1982	12
	Doug DeCinces	1984	12
	Wally Joyner	1986	12
	Tom Herr	1987	12
	Ruben Sierra	1987	12
	Pedro Guerrero	1989	12
	Jeffrey Leonard	1989	12
	Johnny Ray	1989	12
	Robin Yount	1992	12
	Chuck Knoblauch	1992	12
	Darrin Fletcher	1994	12
	Frank Thomas	1995	12
	Jeff Conine	1995	12
	Roberto Alomar	1996	12
	Paul Molitor	1997	12
	Tony Gwynn	1997	12
	Ken Griffey Jr.	1997	12
	Jeff King	1997	12
	Bernard Gilkey	1997	12
80	61 tied with		11

Stolen Bases

	Player	Year	SB
1	Hugh Nicol	1887	138
2	Rickey Henderson	1982	130
3	Arlie Latham	1887	129
4	Lou Brock	1974	118
5	Charlie Comiskey	1887	117
6	Monte Ward	1887	111
	Billy Hamilton	1889	111
	Billy Hamilton	1891	111
9	Vince Coleman	1985	110
10	Arlie Latham	1888	109
	Vince Coleman	1987	109
12	Rickey Henderson	1983	108
13	Vince Coleman	1986	107
14	Tom Brown	1891	106
15	Maury Wills	1962	104
16	Pete Browning	1887	103
	Hugh Nicol	1888	103
18	Jim Fogarty	1887	102
	Billy Hamilton	1890	102
20	Rickey Henderson	1980	100
21	Jim Fogarty	1889	99
22	Billy Hamilton	1894	98
23	Harry Stovey	1890	97
	Billy Hamilton	1895	97
	Ron LeFlore	1980	97
26	Ty Cobb	1915	96
	Omar Moreno	1980	96
28	Bid McPhee	1887	95
	Curt Welch	1888	95
30	Mike Griffin	1887	94
	Maury Wills	1965	94
32	Tommy McCarthy	1888	93
	Rickey Henderson	1988	93
34	Darby O'Brien	1889	91
35	Tim Raines	1983	90
36	Curt Welch	1887	89
	Herman Long	1889	89
38	Tom Poorman	1887	88
	Blondie Purcell	1887	88
	Monte Ward	1892	88
	Clyde Milan	1912	88
42	Harry Stovey	1888	87
	Arlie Latham	1891	87
	Joe Kelley	1896	87
	Rickey Henderson	1986	87
46	Cub Stricker	1887	86
47	Tommy Tucker	1887	85
	Hub Collins	1890	85
	Hugh Duffy	1891	85
50	Chippy McGarr	1887	84
	King Kelly	1887	84
	Billy Sunday	1890	84
	Bill Lange	1896	84
54	Tommy McCarthy	1890	83
	Billy Hamilton	1896	83
	Ty Cobb	1911	83
	Willie Wilson	1979	83
58	Dummy Hoy	1888	82
	John Reilly	1888	82
60	Eddie Collins	1910	81
	Vince Coleman	1988	81
62	Emmett Seery	1888	80
	Hugh Nicol	1889	80
	Bob Bescher	1911	80
	Rickey Henderson	1985	80
	Eric Davis	1986	80
67	Tom Brown	1890	79
	Dave Collins	1980	79
	Willie Wilson	1980	79
70	Hugh Duffy	1890	78
	Tom Brown	1892	78
	John McGraw	1894	78
	Ron LeFlore	1979	78
	Tim Raines	1982	78
	Marquis Grissom	1992	78
76	Ted Scheffler	1890	77
	Jimmy Sheckard	1899	77
	Davey Lopes	1975	77
	Omar Moreno	1979	77
	Rudy Law	1983	77
	Rickey Henderson	1989	77
	Vince Coleman	1990	77
83	Ed McKean	1887	76
	Walt Wilmot	1890	76
	Dusty Miller	1896	76
	Ty Cobb	1909	76
	Marquis Grissom	1991	76
88	Yank Robinson	1887	75
	George Van Haltren	1891	75
	Clyde Milan	1913	75
	Benny Kauff	1914	75
	Bill North	1976	75
	Tim Raines	1984	75
	Kenny Lofton	1996	75
95	Frank Fennelly	1887	74
	Harry Stovey	1887	74
	Walt Wilmot	1894	74
	Fritz Maisel	1914	74
	Lou Brock	1966	74
	Brian Hunter	1997	74

Caught Stealing

	Player	Year	CS
1	Rickey Henderson	1982	42
2	Ty Cobb	1915	38
3	Miller Huggins	1914	36
4	George Burns	1913	35
5	Ty Cobb	1912	34
6	Lee Magee	1912	33
	Clyde Milan	1912	33
	Lou Brock	1974	33
	Omar Moreno	1980	33
10	Doc Cook	1914	32
	Eddie Murphy	1914	32
	Burt Shotton	1915	32
13	Duffy Lewis	1914	31
	Maury Wills	1965	31
15	Clyde Milan	1913	30
	Eddie Collins	1914	30
	Eddie Collins	1915	30
	Sam Rice	1920	30
	Steve Sax	1983	30
20	Burt Shotton	1914	29
	Tris Speaker	1914	29
	Charlie Hollocher	1922	29
	Eddie Collins	1923	29
	Bill North	1976	29
	Harold Reynolds	1988	29
26	Del Pratt	1914	28
	Burt Shotton	1916	28
	Buck Herzog	1916	28
	Pat Duncan	1922	28
	George Grantham	1923	28
	Brett Butler	1991	28
32	Dave Bancroft	1915	27
	Donie Bush	1915	27
	Tris Speaker	1916	27
	Bernie Friberg	1924	27
	Lou Brock	1965	27
	Vince Coleman	1988	27
	Gerald Young	1988	27
39	Donie Bush	1914	26
	George Sisler	1916	26
	Milt Stock	1916	26
	Benny Kauff	1916	26
	George Burns	1916	26
	Armando Marsans	1916	26
	Bill North	1974	26
	Rickey Henderson	1980	26
	Lonnie Smith	1982	26
	Omar Moreno	1982	26
49	Harry Hooper	1913	25
	Danny Moeller	1914	25
	Roy Hartzell	1914	25
	Tris Speaker	1915	25
	Lee Magee	1916	25
	Billy Southworth	1920	25
	Frank Taveras	1978	25
	Vince Coleman	1985	25
	Gerald Young	1989	25
	Eric Yelding	1990	25
59	Shano Collins	1914	24
	Tommy Griffith	1915	24
	Ty Cobb	1916	24
	Edd Roush	1920	24
	Cliff Heathcote	1924	24
	Maury Wills	1966	24
	Garry Templeton	1977	24
	Lou Brock	1977	24
	Bill North	1979	24
	Ray Lankford	1992	24
	Luis Polonia	1993	24
	Chad Curtis	1993	24
71	Jimmy Austin	1914	23
	Larry Gardner	1914	23
	George Cutshaw	1915	23
	Del Pratt	1915	23
	Amos Strunk	1916	23
	Dave Robertson	1920	23
	George Burns	1922	23
	Jigger Statz	1923	23
	Sam Rice	1926	23
	Ben Chapman	1931	23
	Jose Cruz	1977	23
	Miguel Dilone	1978	23
	Bobby Bonds	1979	23
	Alfredo Griffin	1980	23
	Brett Butler	1983	23
	Luis Polonia	1991	23
	Delino DeShields	1991	23
88	20 tied with		22

SB Percentage

(minimum 20 attempts)

	Player	Year	Pct
1	Kevin McReynolds	1988	1.000
	Paul Molitor	1994	1.000
3	Brady Anderson	1994	.969
4	Max Carey	1922	.962
5	Ken Griffey Sr.	1980	.958
6	Stan Javier	1988	.952
7	Eric Davis	1992	.950
8	Amos Otis	1970	.943
9	Jack Perconte	1985	.939
10	Miguel Dilone	1984	.931
	Bob Dernier	1986	.931
12	Kirk Gibson	1990	.929
	Barry Larkin	1994	.929
14	Don Baylor	1972	.923
	Oddibe McDowell	1987	.923
16	Davey Lopes	1985	.922
17	Eric Davis	1988	.921
18	Cesar Cedeno	1978	.920
	Henry Cotto	1992	.920
	Mike Cameron	1997	.920
21	Bobby Bonds	1969	.918
	Davey Lopes	1978	.918
23	Davey Lopes	1979	.917
	Marquis Grissom	1990	.917
25	Jimmy Wynn	1965	.915
26	Larry Bowa	1977	.914
27	Alan Trammell	1987	.913
	Ryne Sandberg	1987	.913
	Rich Amaral	1995	.913
30	Jerry Mumphrey	1980	.912
31	Tom Herr	1985	.912
32	Barry Larkin	1995	.911
33	Jack Smith	1925	.909
	Davey Lopes	1981	.909
	Tim Raines	1987	.909
	Bip Roberts	1995	.909
	Roberto Alomar	1995	.909
38	Craig Biggio	1994	.907
39	Derek Bell	1996	.906
40	Dick Howser	1962	.905
41	Willie Wilson	1984	.904
42	Bake McBride	1978	.903
43	Devon White	1992	.902
44	Jim Rivera	1957	.900
	Willie Mays	1962	.900
	Joe Morgan	1983	.900
	Henry Cotto	1988	.900
	David Hulse	1994	.900
	Larry Walker	1996	.900
50	Tony Womack	1997	.896
51	Devon White	1993	.895
52	Mitchell Page	1977	.894
53	Tommy Harper	1971	.893
	Rick Manning	1981	.893
	Eric Davis	1987	.893
	Stan Javier	1997	.893
57	Jake Wood	1962	.889
	Maury Wills	1962	.889
	Tommy Harper	1964	.889
	Enzo Hernandez	1972	.889
	Dusty Baker	1973	.889
	Lee Lacy	1981	.889
	Rickey Henderson	1985	.889
	Tony Tarasco	1995	.889
65	Willie Wilson	1980	.888
66	Tim Raines	1985	.886
	Tim Raines	1986	.886
68	Bert Campaneris	1969	.886
	Kirk Gibson	1988	.886
	Gary Redus	1988	.886
71	Willie Mays	1971	.885
	Mariano Duncan	1992	.885
	Royce Clayton	1994	.885
74	Vince Coleman	1986	.884
75	Dale Murphy	1983	.882
	Tim Raines	1984	.882
	Kirk Gibson	1985	.882
	Tim Raines	1992	.882
	Ray Durham	1996	.882
80	Willie Wilson	1983	.881
81	George Case	1942	.880
	Frank Robinson	1961	.880
	Bobby Bonds	1972	.880
	Bill Doran	1989	.880
	Rafael Palmeiro	1993	.880
86	Eric Davis	1986	.879
87	Stan Javier	1995	.878
88	Rickey Henderson	1988	.877
89	Larry Lintz	1974	.877
90	Lyn Lary	1935	.875
	Sam Jethroe	1951	.875
	Jim Rivera	1958	.875
	Mickey Mantle	1959	.875
	Hank Aaron	1966	.875
	Julio Franco	1989	.875
	Craig Biggio	1989	.875
	Henry Cotto	1990	.875
	Eric Davis	1990	.875
99	Willie Wilson	1979	.874
100	2 tied with		.872

GDP

	Player	Year	GDP
1	Jim Rice	1984	36
2	Jim Rice	1985	35
3	Jackie Jensen	1954	32
	Cal Ripken Jr.	1985	32
5	Bobby Doerr	1949	31
	Tony Armas	1983	31
	Jim Rice	1983	31
8	Ernie Lombardi	1938	30
	Billy Hitchcock	1950	30
	Carl Yastrzemski	1964	30
	Dave Winfield	1983	30
12	Jimmy Bloodworth	1943	29
	Dave Philley	1952	29
	Brooks Robinson	1960	29
	Frank Howard	1969	29
	Frank Howard	1971	29
	Ted Simmons	1973	29
	Jim Rice	1982	29
	Jim Presley	1985	29
	George Bell	1992	29
21	George Kell	1944	28
	Sid Gordon	1951	28
	Harmon Killebrew	1970	28
	Julio Franco	1986	28
	Cal Ripken Jr.	1996	28
26	Joe Vosmik	1939	27
	Bill Johnson	1943	27
	Al Rosen	1950	27
	Carl Furillo	1956	27
	Sherm Lollar	1959	27
	Carl Yastrzemski	1962	27
	John Bateman	1971	27
	Ken Singleton	1973	27
	Ron Santo	1973	27
	Rusty Staub	1977	27
	Bruce Bochte	1979	27
	Julio Franco	1989	27
	Kirby Puckett	1991	27
	Eric Karros	1996	27
40	Ernie Lombardi	1933	26
	Billy Jurges	1939	26
	Sid Gordon	1943	26
	Walt Dropo	1952	26
	Gene Green	1961	26
	Joe Torre	1964	26
	Jerry Adair	1965	26
	Cleon Jones	1970	26
	Lee May	1975	26
	Willie Montanez	1975	26
	George Scott	1975	26
	Willie Montanez	1976	26
	Lyman Bostock	1978	26
	John Wathan	1982	26
	Dave Parker	1985	26
	Julio Franco	1985	26
	Ivan Calderon	1990	26
	Albert Belle	1997	26
58	Al Todd	1938	25
	Bobby Doerr	1947	25
	Nippy Jones	1948	25
	Vern Stephens	1948	25
	Sam Dente	1950	25
	Del Ennis	1950	25
	Joe Adcock	1951	25
	Bill Tuttle	1955	25
	Ron Santo	1961	25
	Frank Bolling	1961	25
	George Scott	1966	25
	Rocky Colavito	1966	25
	Danny Cater	1969	25
	Carlos May	1970	25
	Alex Johnson	1970	25
	Lou Piniella	1972	25
	Ken Reitz	1974	25
	George Scott	1974	25
	George Hendrick	1975	25
	Bill Madlock	1977	25
	Ted Sizemore	1977	25
	Steve Garvey	1979	25
	Tony Perez	1980	25
	Steve Garvey	1984	25
	Steve Garvey	1985	25
	Bill Buckner	1986	25
	Gary Gaetti	1987	25
	Mark Grace	1993	25
	Charlie Hayes	1993	25
	Paul O'Neill	1995	25
	Frank Thomas	1996	25
89	45 tied with		24

Runs Created

1	Babe Ruth	1921	208
2	Hugh Duffy	1894	204
3	Babe Ruth	1923	193
4	Tip O'Neill	1887	192
5	Babe Ruth	1920	191
6	Jimmie Foxx	1932	189
7	Billy Hamilton	1894	187
8	Lou Gehrig	1927	182
	Lou Gehrig	1930	182
10	Lou Gehrig	1936	181
11	Rogers Hornsby	1922	179
	Babe Ruth	1924	179
	Lou Gehrig	1931	179
	Babe Ruth	1931	179
15	Rogers Hornsby	1929	178
16	Babe Ruth	1927	177
	Stan Musial	1948	177
18	Babe Ruth	1930	176
19	Ted Williams	1949	174
	Mickey Mantle	1956	174
21	Joe Kelley	1894	173
22	Ty Cobb	1911	172
	Jimmie Foxx	1938	172
24	Chuck Klein	1930	171
	Hack Wilson	1930	171
	Lou Gehrig	1934	171
27	Ted Williams	1941	170
28	Jesse Burkett	1895	169
	Nap Lajoie	1901	169
30	Babe Ruth	1926	167
	Lou Gehrig	1937	167
32	Jimmie Foxx	1933	166
33	Ed Delahanty	1899	165
	Babe Ruth	1928	165
35	Pete Browning	1887	163
	Ed Delahanty	1893	163
	Tris Speaker	1912	163
	Babe Herman	1930	163
	Lou Gehrig	1932	163
	Joe DiMaggio	1937	163
	Joe Medwick	1937	163
	Hank Greenberg	1938	163
	Ted Williams	1946	163
44	Ed Delahanty	1896	162
	Rogers Hornsby	1924	162
	Barry Bonds	1993	162
47	Ted Williams	1947	161
48	Fred Dunlap	1884	160
	Tom Brown	1891	160
	Billy Hamilton	1895	160
	Joe Kelley	1896	160
	Bill Terry	1930	160
	Hank Greenberg	1937	160
	Ted Williams	1942	160
	Ted Williams	1948	160
	Barry Bonds	1996	160
57	Ed Delahanty	1895	159
58	Tommy Tucker	1889	158
	Joe Kelley	1895	158
	Rogers Hornsby	1925	158
	Norm Cash	1961	158
	Larry Walker	1997	158
63	Lefty O'Doul	1929	157
	Mickey Mantle	1961	157
65	King Kelly	1886	156
	Billy Hamilton	1891	156
	Jesse Burkett	1896	156
	Lou Gehrig	1928	156
	Al Simmons	1930	156
	Hank Greenberg	1935	156
71	Roger Connor	1890	155
	Billy Hamilton	1896	155
	Mel Ott	1929	155
	Stan Musial	1949	155
	Mickey Mantle	1957	155
76	Denny Lyons	1887	154
	Sam Thompson	1895	154
	Ty Cobb	1915	154
	George Sisler	1920	154
	Tris Speaker	1923	154
	Rod Carew	1977	154
82	Oyster Burns	1887	153
	Hugh Duffy	1890	153
	Jake Stenzel	1894	153
	Bobby Lowe	1894	153
	Willie Keeler	1897	153
	Jesse Burkett	1901	153
	Chuck Klein	1932	153
	Ted Williams	1939	153
90	Cap Anson	1886	152
	Sam Thompson	1887	152
	Dan Brouthers	1891	152
	Rogers Hornsby	1921	152
	Jimmie Foxx	1936	152
	Hank Greenberg	1940	152
	Stan Musial	1946	152
	Frank Robinson	1962	152
98	Darby O'Brien	1889	151
	Tommy Holmes	1945	151
	Edgar Martinez	1995	151

Runs Created/27 Outs

(minimum 3.1 PA/Tm Gm)

1	Ross Barnes	1876	17.46
2	Tip O'Neill	1887	16.99
3	Hugh Duffy	1894	16.77
4	Fred Dunlap	1884	16.46
5	Babe Ruth	1920	16.44
6	Ted Williams	1941	16.09
7	Babe Ruth	1921	15.47
8	Babe Ruth	1923	14.86
9	King Kelly	1886	14.63
10	Billy Hamilton	1894	14.49
11	Ted Williams	1957	14.38
12	Ed Delahanty	1895	13.99
13	Nap Lajoie	1901	13.99
14	Babe Ruth	1931	13.93
15	John McGraw	1899	13.79
16	Ed Delahanty	1896	13.61
17	Joe Kelley	1894	13.57
18	Mickey Mantle	1957	13.54
19	Babe Ruth	1924	13.39
20	Babe Ruth	1926	13.23
21	Mickey Mantle	1956	13.20
22	Jimmie Foxx	1932	13.19
23	Billy Hamilton	1893	13.17
24	Sam Thompson	1894	13.16
25	Jesse Burkett	1895	13.08
26	Bob Caruthers	1887	13.03
27	Roger Connor	1890	12.99
28	Ted Williams	1948	12.92
29	Rogers Hornsby	1925	12.88
30	Pete Browning	1887	12.88
31	Babe Ruth	1932	12.83
32	Bill Joyce	1894	12.83
33	Deacon White	1877	12.73
34	Rogers Hornsby	1924	12.73
35	Babe Ruth	1930	12.69
36	Billy Hamilton	1895	12.65
37	Dan Brouthers	1886	12.61
38	Ted Williams	1946	12.56
39	Pete Browning	1882	12.54
40	Billy Hamilton	1898	12.54
41	George Hall	1876	12.54
42	Babe Ruth	1927	12.53
43	Ed Delahanty	1894	12.52
44	Dan Brouthers	1891	12.45
45	Ty Cobb	1911	12.42
46	Cap Anson	1886	12.41
47	Ted Williams	1942	12.40
48	Lou Gehrig	1936	12.32
49	Tommy Tucker	1889	12.32
50	John Reilly	1884	12.30
51	Bill Lange	1895	12.29
52	Cap Anson	1881	12.25
53	Joe Kelley	1896	12.24
54	Lou Gehrig	1930	12.12
55	Orator Shaffer	1884	12.08
56	Sam Thompson	1895	12.03
57	Lou Gehrig	1927	12.00
58	Ted Williams	1947	11.99
59	Roger Connor	1885	11.96
60	Ed Delahanty	1899	11.95
61	Arky Vaughan	1935	11.93
62	Lou Gehrig	1934	11.93
63	Joe Kelley	1895	11.91
64	Jimmie Foxx	1938	11.87
65	Ted Williams	1954	11.85
66	Jimmie Foxx	1933	11.85
67	Billy Hamilton	1891	11.84
68	Dan Brouthers	1889	11.80
69	Mark McGwire	1996	11.79
70	Jimmie Foxx	1939	11.78
71	Billy Hamilton	1896	11.75
72	Cap Anson	1882	11.74
73	Ted Williams	1949	11.73
74	Mickey Mantle	1961	11.73
75	Stan Musial	1948	11.72
76	Dan Brouthers	1883	11.71
77	Joe DiMaggio	1939	11.71
78	Rogers Hornsby	1922	11.70
79	Jesse Burkett	1893	11.68
80	Edgar Martinez	1995	11.67
81	George Gore	1890	11.64
82	Charley Jones	1884	11.64
83	Fred Clarke	1897	11.64
84	Dan Brouthers	1882	11.62
85	Dave Orr	1890	11.61
86	Honus Wagner	1900	11.61
87	Dan Brouthers	1887	11.60
88	Willie Keeler	1897	11.59
89	Lou Gehrig	1937	11.59
90	Rogers Hornsby	1929	11.58
91	Norm Cash	1961	11.58
92	Pete Browning	1890	11.53
93	Babe Ruth	1928	11.48
94	Jake Stenzel	1894	11.48
95	Sam Thompson	1887	11.46
96	Hughie Jennings	1896	11.43
97	Mike Griffin	1894	11.41
98	Tommy McCarthy	1893	11.41
99	Jesse Burkett	1896	11.39
100	John McGraw	1895	11.36

Batting Average

(minimum 3.1 PA/Tm Gm)

1	Hugh Duffy	1894	.440
2	Tip O'Neill	1887	.435
3	Ross Barnes	1876	.429
4	Nap Lajoie	1901	.426
5	Willie Keeler	1897	.424
6	Rogers Hornsby	1924	.424
7	George Sisler	1922	.420
8	Ty Cobb	1911	.420
9	Fred Dunlap	1884	.412
10	Ty Cobb	1912	.410
11	Ed Delahanty	1899	.410
12	Jesse Burkett	1896	.410
13	Jesse Burkett	1895	.409
14	Joe Jackson	1911	.408
15	Sam Thompson	1894	.407
16	George Sisler	1920	.407
17	Ed Delahanty	1894	.407
18	Ted Williams	1941	.406
19	Billy Hamilton	1894	.404
20	Ed Delahanty	1895	.404
21	Rogers Hornsby	1925	.403
22	Harry Heilmann	1923	.403
23	Pete Browning	1887	.402
24	Rogers Hornsby	1922	.401
25	Bill Terry	1930	.401
26	Hughie Jennings	1896	.401
27	Ty Cobb	1922	.401
28	Cap Anson	1881	.399
29	Lefty O'Doul	1929	.398
30	Harry Heilmann	1927	.398
31	Rogers Hornsby	1921	.397
32	Ed Delahanty	1896	.397
33	Jesse Burkett	1899	.396
34	Joe Jackson	1912	.395
35	Tony Gwynn	1994	.394
36	Harry Heilmann	1921	.394
37	Babe Ruth	1923	.393
38	Harry Heilmann	1925	.393
39	Babe Herman	1930	.393
40	Joe Kelley	1894	.393
41	Sam Thompson	1895	.392
42	John McGraw	1899	.391
43	Ty Cobb	1913	.390
44	Fred Clarke	1897	.390
45	Al Simmons	1931	.390
46	George Brett	1980	.390
47	Tris Speaker	1925	.389
48	Bill Lange	1895	.389
49	Billy Hamilton	1895	.389
50	Ty Cobb	1921	.389
51	Ted Williams	1957	.388
52	King Kelly	1886	.388
53	Rod Carew	1977	.388
54	Luke Appling	1936	.388
55	Tris Speaker	1920	.388
56	Deacon White	1877	.387
57	Rogers Hornsby	1928	.387
58	Tris Speaker	1916	.386
59	Willie Keeler	1896	.386
60	Chuck Klein	1930	.386
61	Lave Cross	1894	.386
	Hughie Jennings	1895	.386
63	Willie Keeler	1898	.385
64	Arky Vaughan	1935	.385
65	Al Simmons	1925	.384
66	Rogers Hornsby	1923	.384
67	Ty Cobb	1919	.384
68	Nap Lajoie	1910	.384
69	Ty Cobb	1910	.383
70	Jesse Burkett	1897	.383
71	Tris Speaker	1912	.383
72	Ty Cobb	1917	.383
73	Lefty O'Doul	1930	.383
74	Joe Jackson	1920	.382
75	Ty Cobb	1918	.382
76	Honus Wagner	1900	.381
77	Babe Herman	1929	.381
78	Joe DiMaggio	1939	.381
79	Al Simmons	1930	.381
80	Paul Waner	1927	.380
81	Rogers Hornsby	1929	.380
82	Billy Hamilton	1893	.380
83	Tris Speaker	1923	.380
84	Goose Goslin	1928	.379
85	Freddy Lindstrom	1930	.379
86	Willie Keeler	1899	.379
87	Lou Gehrig	1930	.379
88	John Cassidy	1877	.378
89	Pete Browning	1882	.378
90	Ty Cobb	1925	.378
91	Babe Ruth	1924	.378
92	Sam Crawford	1911	.378
93	Tris Speaker	1922	.378
94	Earl Averill	1936	.378
95	Babe Ruth	1921	.378
96	Heinie Manush	1928	.378
97	Heinie Manush	1926	.378
98	Ed Delahanty	1897	.377
99	Willie Keeler	1895	.377
100	Ty Cobb	1909	.377

On-Base Percentage

(minimum 3.1 PA/Tm Gm)

1	Ted Williams	1941	.551
2	John McGraw	1899	.547
3	Babe Ruth	1923	.545
4	Babe Ruth	1920	.530
5	Ted Williams	1957	.526
6	Billy Hamilton	1894	.523
7	Babe Ruth	1926	.516
8	Ted Williams	1954	.513
9	Babe Ruth	1924	.513
10	Mickey Mantle	1957	.512
11	Babe Ruth	1921	.512
12	Rogers Hornsby	1924	.507
13	John McGraw	1900	.505
14	Joe Kelley	1894	.502
15	Hugh Duffy	1894	.502
16	Ed Delahanty	1895	.500
17	Ted Williams	1942	.499
18	Ted Williams	1947	.499
19	Rogers Hornsby	1928	.498
20	Ted Williams	1946	.497
21	Ted Williams	1948	.497
22	Bill Joyce	1894	.496
23	Babe Ruth	1931	.494
24	Babe Ruth	1930	.493
25	Arky Vaughan	1935	.491
26	Ted Williams	1949	.490
27	Billy Hamilton	1895	.490
28	Billy Hamilton	1893	.490
29	Tip O'Neill	1887	.490
30	Rogers Hornsby	1925	.489
	Babe Ruth	1932	.489
32	Frank Thomas	1994	.487
33	Babe Ruth	1927	.487
34	Norm Cash	1961	.487
35	Ty Cobb	1915	.486
36	Jesse Burkett	1895	.486
37	Tris Speaker	1920	.483
38	King Kelly	1886	.483
39	Harry Heilmann	1923	.481
40	Billy Hamilton	1898	.480
41	Tris Speaker	1925	.479
	Ted Williams	1956	.479
43	Edgar Martinez	1995	.479
44	Ed Delahanty	1894	.478
45	Lou Gehrig	1936	.478
46	Billy Hamilton	1896	.477
47	Wade Boggs	1988	.476
48	Cupid Childs	1894	.475
49	John McGraw	1898	.475
50	Harry Heilmann	1927	.475
51	Tris Speaker	1922	.474
52	Lou Gehrig	1927	.474
53	Luke Appling	1936	.473
54	Lou Gehrig	1930	.473
55	Lou Gehrig	1937	.473
56	John Olerud	1993	.473
57	Hughie Jennings	1896	.472
58	Ed Delahanty	1896	.472
59	John McGraw	1897	.471
60	Dan Brouthers	1891	.471
61	Tris Speaker	1916	.470
62	Bill Joyce	1896	.470
63	Joe Kelley	1896	.469
64	Tris Speaker	1923	.469
65	Jimmie Foxx	1932	.469
66	Jesse Burkett	1897	.468
67	Ty Cobb	1925	.468
68	Joe Jackson	1911	.468
69	Lou Gehrig	1928	.467
70	Ty Cobb	1913	.467
71	Mark McGwire	1996	.467
72	George Sisler	1922	.467
73	Mike Griffin	1894	.467
74	Cupid Childs	1896	.467
75	Ty Cobb	1911	.467
76	Joe Morgan	1975	.466
77	Dan Brouthers	1890	.466
78	Lou Gehrig	1935	.466
79	Gary Sheffield	1996	.465
80	Lou Gehrig	1934	.465
81	Lefty O'Doul	1929	.465
82	Jimmie Foxx	1939	.464
83	Tris Speaker	1912	.464
84	Ed Delahanty	1899	.464
85	Pete Browning	1887	.464
86	Mickey Mantle	1956	.464
87	Edgar Martinez	1996	.464
88	Ted Williams	1951	.464
89	Willie Keeler	1897	.464
90	Bob Caruthers	1887	.463
91	Cupid Childs	1893	.463
92	Jimmie Foxx	1929	.463
93	Hughie Jennings	1897	.463
94	Nap Lajoie	1901	.463
95	Jesse Burkett	1899	.463
96	Ross Barnes	1876	.462
	Jimmie Foxx	1938	.462
98	Dan Brouthers	1889	.462
99	Fred Clarke	1897	.462
100	Ty Cobb	1922	.462

Slugging Percentage

(minimum 3.1 PA/Tm Gm)

Rank	Player	Year	SLG
1	Babe Ruth	1920	.847
2	Babe Ruth	1921	.846
3	Babe Ruth	1927	.772
4	Lou Gehrig	1927	.765
5	Babe Ruth	1923	.764
6	Rogers Hornsby	1925	.756
7	Jeff Bagwell	1994	.750
8	Jimmie Foxx	1932	.749
9	Babe Ruth	1924	.739
10	Babe Ruth	1926	.737
11	Ted Williams	1941	.735
12	Babe Ruth	1930	.732
13	Ted Williams	1957	.731
14	Mark McGwire	1996	.730
15	Frank Thomas	1994	.729
16	Hack Wilson	1930	.723
17	Rogers Hornsby	1922	.722
18	Lou Gehrig	1930	.721
19	Larry Walker	1997	.720
20	Albert Belle	1994	.714
21	Babe Ruth	1928	.709
22	Al Simmons	1930	.708
23	Lou Gehrig	1934	.706
24	Mickey Mantle	1956	.705
25	Jimmie Foxx	1938	.704
26	Jimmie Foxx	1933	.703
27	Stan Musial	1948	.702
28	Babe Ruth	1931	.700
29	Babe Ruth	1929	.697
30	Lou Gehrig	1936	.696
31	Rogers Hornsby	1924	.696
32	Hugh Duffy	1894	.694
33	Jimmie Foxx	1939	.694
34	Tip O'Neill	1887	.691
35	Albert Belle	1995	.690
36	Mickey Mantle	1961	.687
37	Chuck Klein	1930	.687
38	Sam Thompson	1894	.686
39	Hank Greenberg	1938	.683
40	Kevin Mitchell	1994	.681
41	Rogers Hornsby	1929	.679
42	Babe Herman	1930	.678
43	Barry Bonds	1993	.677
44	Ken Griffey Jr.	1994	.674
45	Joe DiMaggio	1937	.673
46	Babe Ruth	1922	.672
47	Joe DiMaggio	1939	.671
48	Hank Greenberg	1940	.670
49	Hank Aaron	1971	.669
50	Hank Greenberg	1937	.668
51	Ted Williams	1946	.667
52	Willie Mays	1954	.667
53	Mickey Mantle	1957	.665
54	George Brett	1980	.664
55	Lou Gehrig	1931	.662
56	Norm Cash	1961	.662
57	Babe Ruth	1932	.661
58	Willie Mays	1955	.659
59	Ralph Kiner	1949	.658
60	Chuck Klein	1929	.657
61	Babe Ruth	1919	.657
62	Willie McCovey	1969	.656
63	Sam Thompson	1895	.654
64	Jimmie Foxx	1934	.653
65	Chick Hafey	1930	.652
66	Ted Williams	1949	.650
67	Bill Joyce	1894	.648
68	Lou Gehrig	1928	.648
69	Ted Williams	1942	.648
70	Duke Snider	1954	.647
71	Barry Bonds	1994	.647
72	Ken Griffey Jr.	1997	.646
73	Mark McGwire	1997	.646
74	Chuck Klein	1932	.646
75	Jim Gentile	1961	.646
76	Willie Stargell	1973	.646
77	Willie Mays	1965	.645
78	Mike Schmidt	1981	.644
79	Hal Trosky	1936	.644
80	Nap Lajoie	1901	.643
81	Joe DiMaggio	1941	.643
	Juan Gonzalez	1996	.643
83	Lou Gehrig	1937	.643
84	Ted Kluszewski	1954	.642
85	Al Simmons	1929	.642
86	Joe Medwick	1937	.641
87	Al Simmons	1931	.641
88	Ellis Burks	1996	.639
89	Ralph Kiner	1947	.639
90	Rogers Hornsby	1921	.639
91	Mike Piazza	1997	.638
92	Brady Anderson	1996	.637
93	Frank Robinson	1966	.637
94	Jimmie Foxx	1930	.637
95	Fred Lynn	1979	.637
96	Hank Aaron	1959	.636
97	Johnny Mize	1940	.636
98	Jimmie Foxx	1935	.636
99	Kevin Mitchell	1989	.635
100	Mel Ott	1929	.635

OBP+Slugging

(minimum 3.1 PA/Tm Gm)

Rank	Player	Year	OPS
1	Babe Ruth	1920	1.378
2	Babe Ruth	1921	1.358
3	Babe Ruth	1923	1.309
4	Ted Williams	1941	1.286
5	Babe Ruth	1927	1.259
6	Ted Williams	1957	1.257
7	Babe Ruth	1926	1.253
8	Babe Ruth	1924	1.252
9	Rogers Hornsby	1925	1.245
10	Lou Gehrig	1927	1.240
11	Babe Ruth	1930	1.225
12	Jimmie Foxx	1932	1.218
13	Frank Thomas	1994	1.217
14	Rogers Hornsby	1924	1.203
15	Jeff Bagwell	1994	1.201
16	Mark McGwire	1996	1.198
17	Hugh Duffy	1894	1.196
18	Babe Ruth	1931	1.194
	Lou Gehrig	1930	1.194
20	Rogers Hornsby	1922	1.181
21	Tip O'Neill	1887	1.180
22	Hack Wilson	1930	1.177
	Mickey Mantle	1957	1.177
24	Lou Gehrig	1936	1.174
25	Larry Walker	1997	1.172
	Lou Gehrig	1934	1.172
27	Babe Ruth	1928	1.170
28	Mickey Mantle	1956	1.169
29	Jimmie Foxx	1938	1.166
30	Ted Williams	1946	1.164
31	Jimmie Foxx	1939	1.158
32	Jimmie Foxx	1933	1.153
33	Stan Musial	1948	1.152
	Albert Belle	1994	1.152
35	Babe Ruth	1932	1.150
36	Norm Cash	1961	1.148
	Ted Williams	1954	1.148
38	Ted Williams	1942	1.147
39	Sam Thompson	1894	1.145
40	Bill Joyce	1894	1.143
41	Ted Williams	1949	1.141
42	Rogers Hornsby	1929	1.139
43	Barry Bonds	1993	1.136
44	Mickey Mantle	1961	1.135
45	Ted Williams	1947	1.133
46	Babe Herman	1930	1.132
47	Al Simmons	1930	1.130
	Rogers Hornsby	1928	1.130
49	Babe Ruth	1929	1.128
50	Chuck Klein	1930	1.123
51	Hank Greenberg	1938	1.122
52	Joe DiMaggio	1939	1.119
53	George Brett	1980	1.118
54	Ed Delahanty	1895	1.117
55	Lou Gehrig	1937	1.116
56	Lou Gehrig	1928	1.115
57	Babe Ruth	1919	1.114
58	Harry Heilmann	1923	1.113
59	Ted Williams	1948	1.112
60	Kevin Mitchell	1994	1.110
61	Willie McCovey	1969	1.108
	Lou Gehrig	1931	1.108
63	Edgar Martinez	1995	1.107
64	Nap Lajoie	1901	1.106
	Babe Ruth	1922	1.106
66	Hank Greenberg	1937	1.105
67	Joe Kelley	1894	1.104
68	Hank Greenberg	1940	1.103
	Ed Delahanty	1896	1.103
70	Jimmie Foxx	1934	1.102
71	Arky Vaughan	1935	1.098
72	Rogers Hornsby	1921	1.097
73	Jimmie Foxx	1935	1.096
74	Albert Belle	1995	1.091
	Harry Heilmann	1927	1.091
76	Gary Sheffield	1996	1.090
77	Ralph Kiner	1949	1.089
78	Jimmie Foxx	1929	1.088
	Ty Cobb	1911	1.088
80	Lefty O'Doul	1929	1.087
81	Rogers Hornsby	1923	1.086
82	Al Simmons	1931	1.085
	Frank Thomas	1996	1.085
	Joe DiMaggio	1937	1.085
	Sam Thompson	1895	1.085
86	Ted Williams	1956	1.084
	Mel Ott	1929	1.084
88	Joe DiMaggio	1941	1.083
89	George Sisler	1920	1.082
90	Tris Speaker	1922	1.080
	Barry Bonds	1992	1.080
	Mike Schmidt	1981	1.080
93	Ralph Kiner	1951	1.079
	Tris Speaker	1923	1.079
	Hank Aaron	1971	1.079
96	Willie Mays	1954	1.078
97	Ken Griffey Jr.	1994	1.076
	Barry Bonds	1996	1.076
99	Barry Bonds	1994	1.073
100	Lou Gehrig	1932	1.072

Secondary Average

(minimum 3.1 PA/Tm Gm)

Rank	Player	Year	SecA
1	Babe Ruth	1920	.825
2	Babe Ruth	1921	.767
3	Babe Ruth	1923	.730
4	Mark McGwire	1996	.693
5	Babe Ruth	1927	.685
6	Babe Ruth	1926	.679
7	Barry Bonds	1996	.677
8	Barry Bonds	1992	.664
9	Babe Ruth	1930	.654
10	Frank Thomas	1994	.654
11	Ted Williams	1941	.651
12	Babe Ruth	1924	.647
13	Babe Ruth	1928	.646
14	Ted Williams	1954	.642
15	Mickey Mantle	1957	.641
16	Mickey Mantle	1961	.638
17	Jack Clark	1987	.637
18	Barry Bonds	1997	.635
19	Barry Bonds	1993	.629
20	Ted Williams	1946	.628
21	Ted Williams	1957	.626
22	Joe Morgan	1976	.625
23	Gary Sheffield	1996	.615
24	Babe Ruth	1932	.608
25	Willie McCovey	1970	.600
26	Ted Williams	1947	.598
27	Barry Bonds	1994	.598
28	Bill Joyce	1894	.597
29	Lou Gehrig	1927	.596
30	Ted Williams	1949	.595
31	Hank Greenberg	1938	.595
32	Jimmie Foxx	1932	.588
33	Babe Ruth	1919	.586
34	Jeff Bagwell	1997	.585
35	Jimmy Wynn	1969	.584
36	Harmon Killebrew	1969	.584
37	Rickey Henderson	1990	.583
38	Jeff Bagwell	1994	.582
39	Willie McCovey	1969	.582
40	Eric Davis	1987	.582
41	Mickey Mantle	1956	.582
42	Barry Bonds	1995	.581
43	Joe Morgan	1975	.580
44	Frank Thomas	1995	.580
45	Ralph Kiner	1951	.580
46	Babe Ruth	1931	.577
47	Jimmie Foxx	1938	.575
48	Ted Williams	1942	.575
49	Rickey Henderson	1982	.575
50	Ralph Kiner	1949	.572
51	Lou Gehrig	1936	.572
52	Eddie Mathews	1954	.571
53	Mickey Mantle	1958	.570
54	Babe Ruth	1922	.569
55	Mike Schmidt	1981	.568
56	Mark McGwire	1997	.565
57	Reggie Jackson	1969	.565
58	Norm Cash	1961	.553
59	Hack Wilson	1930	.552
60	Kevin Mitchell	1994	.552
61	Larry Walker	1997	.549
62	Mike Schmidt	1979	.549
63	John McGraw	1899	.549
	Darryl Strawberry	1987	.549
65	Joe Morgan	1974	.549
66	Jim Thome	1996	.549
67	Lou Gehrig	1934	.547
68	Jimmie Foxx	1934	.545
69	Ralph Kiner	1950	.545
70	Rickey Henderson	1993	.545
71	Barry Bonds	1990	.543
72	Jim Gentile	1961	.543
73	Harry Stovey	1890	.543
74	Rickey Henderson	1983	.540
75	Ray Lankford	1997	.540
76	Mickey Mantle	1955	.540
77	Babe Ruth	1933	.538
78	Lou Gehrig	1931	.538
79	Eddie Mathews	1955	.537
80	Lou Gehrig	1930	.537
81	Jim Thome	1997	.536
82	Billy Hamilton	1894	.535
83	Willie Mays	1971	.535
84	Jimmie Foxx	1939	.533
85	Mel Ott	1939	.530
86	Harmon Killebrew	1967	.530
87	Carl Yastrzemski	1970	.530
88	Jeff Bagwell	1996	.530
89	Duke Snider	1955	.530
90	Rickey Henderson	1985	.528
91	Rogers Hornsby	1925	.528
92	Dick Allen	1972	.528
93	Mel Ott	1929	.525
94	Hugh Nicol	1887	.524
95	Barry Larkin	1996	.524
96	Mike Schmidt	1983	.522
97	Joe Kelley	1896	.522
98	Mickey Tettleton	1995	.522
99	Lou Gehrig	1937	.522
100	Mike Schmidt	1980	.522

Isolated Power

(minimum 3.1 PA/Tm Gm)

Rank	Player	Year	ISO
1	Babe Ruth	1920	.472
2	Babe Ruth	1921	.469
3	Mark McGwire	1996	.418
4	Babe Ruth	1927	.417
5	Lou Gehrig	1927	.392
6	Babe Ruth	1928	.386
7	Jimmie Foxx	1932	.385
8	Jeff Bagwell	1994	.383
9	Frank Thomas	1994	.376
10	Albert Belle	1995	.374
11	Babe Ruth	1930	.373
12	Mark McGwire	1997	.372
13	Babe Ruth	1923	.372
14	Mickey Mantle	1961	.370
15	Hank Greenberg	1938	.369
16	Hack Wilson	1930	.368
17	Babe Ruth	1926	.366
18	Babe Ruth	1924	.361
19	Babe Ruth	1922	.357
20	Albert Belle	1994	.357
21	Jimmie Foxx	1938	.356
22	Kevin Mitchell	1994	.355
23	Larry Walker	1997	.354
24	Rogers Hornsby	1925	.353
25	Mickey Mantle	1956	.353
26	Babe Ruth	1929	.353
27	Ken Griffey Jr.	1994	.351
28	Roger Maris	1961	.351
29	Ralph Kiner	1949	.348
30	Jimmie Foxx	1933	.347
31	Willie Stargell	1973	.347
32	Kevin Mitchell	1989	.344
33	Lou Gehrig	1934	.344
34	Jim Gentile	1961	.344
35	Ted Williams	1957	.343
36	Lou Gehrig	1930	.343
37	Ken Griffey Jr.	1997	.342
38	Lou Gehrig	1936	.342
39	Hank Aaron	1971	.341
40	Barry Bonds	1993	.341
41	Brady Anderson	1996	.340
42	Willie Mays	1955	.340
43	Matt Williams	1994	.339
44	Mike Schmidt	1980	.338
45	Willie McCovey	1969	.336
46	Babe Ruth	1919	.336
47	Barry Bonds	1994	.335
48	Jimmie Foxx	1939	.334
49	Reggie Jackson	1969	.333
50	Willie Stargell	1971	.333
51	Hank Greenberg	1937	.332
52	Hank Greenberg	1940	.330
53	Juan Gonzalez	1996	.329
54	Ted Williams	1941	.329
55	Mark McGwire	1987	.329
56	Willie Mays	1965	.328
57	Babe Ruth	1931	.328
58	Mike Schmidt	1981	.328
59	Hank Greenberg	1946	.327
60	Joe DiMaggio	1937	.327
61	Al Simmons	1930	.327
62	Stan Musial	1948	.326
63	Ralph Kiner	1947	.326
64	Dave Kingman	1979	.325
65	Ted Williams	1946	.325
66	Ken Griffey Jr.	1996	.325
67	Eddie Mathews	1953	.325
68	Willie McCovey	1970	.323
69	Juan Gonzalez	1993	.323
70	Willie Mays	1954	.322
71	Lou Gehrig	1931	.321
72	Johnny Mize	1940	.321
73	Frank Robinson	1966	.321
74	Rogers Hornsby	1922	.321
75	Duke Snider	1955	.320
76	Babe Ruth	1932	.319
77	Jimmie Foxx	1934	.319
78	Ralph Kiner	1951	.318
79	Ralph Kiner	1950	.318
80	Harmon Killebrew	1961	.318
81	Bob Hamelin	1994	.317
82	Rocky Colavito	1958	.317
83	Mark McGwire	1992	.317
84	Chick Hafey	1930	.316
85	Boog Powell	1964	.316
86	Ted Kluszewski	1954	.316
87	Dick Allen	1966	.315
88	Cecil Fielder	1990	.314
89	Eddie Mathews	1954	.313
90	Duke Snider	1957	.313
91	Barry Bonds	1992	.313
92	Eddie Mathews	1955	.313
93	Albert Belle	1996	.312
94	Johnny Mize	1947	.312
95	Willie Mays	1964	.311
96	Willie Mays	1962	.311
97	George Foster	1977	.311
98	Mike Schmidt	1979	.311
99	Jack Clark	1987	.310
100	Gary Sheffield	1996	.310

Leaders: Single Season Hitting 993

Single Season Pitching Leaders

Wins

Rank	Player	Year	W
1	Old Hoss Radbourn	1884	59
2	John Clarkson	1885	53
3	Guy Hecker	1884	52
4	John Clarkson	1889	49
5	Old Hoss Radbourn	1883	48
	Charlie Buffinton	1884	48
7	Al Spalding	1876	47
	Monte Ward	1879	47
9	Pud Galvin	1883	46
	Pud Galvin	1884	46
	Matt Kilroy	1887	46
12	George Bradley	1876	45
	Jim McCormick	1880	45
	Silver King	1888	45
15	Mickey Welch	1885	44
	Bill Hutchison	1891	44
17	Will White	1879	43
	Tommy Bond	1879	43
	Larry Corcoran	1880	43
	Will White	1883	43
	Billy Taylor	1884	43
22	Lady Baldwin	1886	42
	Tim Keefe	1886	42
	Bill Hutchison	1890	42
25	Tim Keefe	1883	41
	Charlie Sweeney	1884	41
	Dave Foutz	1886	41
	Ed Morris	1886	41
	Jack Chesbro	1904	41
30	Tommy Bond	1877	40
	Tommy Bond	1878	40
	Will White	1882	40
	Bill Sweeney	1884	40
	Jim McCormick	1884	40
	Bob Caruthers	1885	40
	Bob Caruthers	1889	40
	Ed Walsh	1908	40
38	Monte Ward	1880	39
	Mickey Welch	1884	39
	Ed Morris	1885	39
41	Toad Ramsey	1886	38
	John Clarkson	1887	38
	Kid Gleason	1890	38
44	Pud Galvin	1879	37
	Jim Whitney	1883	37
	Jack Lynch	1884	37
	Tim Keefe	1884	37
	Toad Ramsey	1887	37
	Bill Hutchison	1892	37
	Christy Mathewson	1908	37
51	Jim McCormick	1882	36
	Tony Mullane	1884	36
	John Clarkson	1886	36
	Sadie McMahon	1890	36
	Cy Young	1892	36
	Frank Killen	1893	36
	Amos Rusie	1894	36
	Walter Johnson	1913	36
59	Jim Devlin	1877	35
	Tony Mullane	1883	35
	Larry Corcoran	1884	35
	Tim Keefe	1887	35
	Ed Seward	1888	35
	Tim Keefe	1888	35
	Sadie McMahon	1891	35
	Kid Nichols	1892	35
	Jack Stivetts	1892	35
	Cy Young	1895	35
	Joe McGinnity	1904	35
70	Mickey Welch	1880	34
	Larry Corcoran	1883	34
	Ed Morris	1884	34
	Will White	1884	34
	Elmer Smith	1887	34
	Silver King	1889	34
	Scott Stratton	1890	34
	Mark Baldwin	1890	34
	George Haddock	1891	34
	Cy Young	1893	34
	Kid Nichols	1893	34
	Joe Wood	1912	34
82	Old Hoss Radbourn	1882	33
	Henry Porter	1885	33
	Dave Foutz	1885	33
	Tony Mullane	1886	33
	Mickey Welch	1886	33
	John Clarkson	1888	33
	Jack Stivetts	1891	33
	Amos Rusie	1891	33
	John Clarkson	1891	33
	Amos Rusie	1893	33
	Jouett Meekin	1894	33
	Cy Young	1901	33
	Christy Mathewson	1904	33
	Walter Johnson	1912	33
	Pete Alexander	1916	33
97	9 tied with		32

Losses

Rank	Player	Year	L
1	John Coleman	1883	48
2	Will White	1880	42
3	Larry McKeon	1884	41
4	Jim McCormick	1879	40
	George Bradley	1879	40
6	Henry Porter	1888	37
	Kid Carsey	1891	37
	George Cobb	1892	37
9	Stump Wiedman	1886	36
	Bill Hutchison	1892	36
11	Jim Devlin	1876	35
	Pud Galvin	1880	35
	Fleury Sullivan	1884	35
	Adonis Terry	1884	35
	Hardie Henderson	1885	35
	Red Donahue	1897	35
17	Bobby Mathews	1876	34
	Bob Barr	1884	34
	Matt Kilroy	1886	34
	Al Mays	1887	34
	Mark Baldwin	1889	34
	Amos Rusie	1890	34
23	Harry McCormick	1879	33
	Jim Whitney	1881	33
	Lee Richmond	1882	33
	Hardie Henderson	1883	33
	Frank Mountain	1883	33
	Dupee Shaw	1884	33
	Jersey Bakely	1888	33
30	Lee Richmond	1880	32
	John Harkins	1884	32
	Jim Whitney	1885	32
	Jim Whitney	1886	32
34	Sam Weaver	1878	31
	Will White	1879	31
	Dupee Shaw	1886	31
	Old Hoss Radbourn	1886	31
	Billy Crowell	1887	31
	Amos Rusie	1892	31
40	Mickey Welch	1880	30
	Jim McCormick	1881	30
	Jim McCormick	1882	30
	Jersey Bakely	1884	30
	Jack Lynch	1886	30
	Phenomenal Smith	1887	30
	Toad Ramsey	1888	30
	John Ewing	1889	30
	Ed Beatin	1890	30
	Ted Breitenstein	1895	30
	Jim Hughey	1899	30
51	Tommy Bond	1880	29
	Pud Galvin	1883	29
	Egyptian Healy	1887	29
	Bert Cunningham	1888	29
	Hank O'Day	1888	29
	Red Ehret	1889	29
	Silver King	1891	29
	Bill Hart	1896	29
	Jack Taylor	1898	29
	Vic Willis	1905	29
61	Jim McCormick	1880	28
	Doc Landis	1882	28
	Hank O'Day	1884	28
	One Arm Daily	1884	28
	Al Mays	1886	28
	Gus Weyhing	1887	28
	Mark Baldwin	1891	28
	Duke Esper	1893	28
	Bill Hill	1896	28
70	Pud Galvin	1879	27
	Tim Keefe	1881	27
	Tim Keefe	1883	27
	Charlie Buffinton	1885	27
	Toad Ramsey	1886	27
	Tony Mullane	1886	27
	Toad Ramsey	1887	27
	Park Swartzel	1889	27
	Phil Knell	1891	27
	Mark Baldwin	1892	27
	Pink Hawley	1894	27
	Chick Fraser	1896	27
	Bill Hart	1897	27
	Willie Sudhoff	1898	27
	Bill Carrick	1899	27
	Luther Taylor	1901	27
	George Bell	1910	27
	Paul Derringer	1933	27
88	21 tied with		26

Winning Percentage
(minimum 15 decisions)

Rank	Player	Year	PCT
1	Roy Face	1959	.947
2	Johnny Allen	1937	.938
3	Phil Regan	1966	.933
4	Greg Maddux	1995	.905
5	Randy Johnson	1995	.900
6	Ron Guidry	1978	.893
7	Freddie Fitzsimmons	1940	.889
8	Lefty Grove	1931	.886
9	Bob Stanley	1978	.882
10	Preacher Roe	1951	.880
11	Fred Goldsmith	1880	.875
	Deacon Phillippe	1910	.875
	Ron Davis	1979	.875
	Tom Seaver	1981	.875
15	Joe Wood	1912	.872
16	David Cone	1988	.870
17	Roger Moret	1973	.867
18	Orel Hershiser	1985	.864
19	Wild Bill Donovan	1907	.862
	Whitey Ford	1961	.862
21	Dwight Gooden	1985	.857
	Roger Clemens	1986	.857
23	Chief Bender	1914	.850
24	Lefty Grove	1930	.848
25	Tom Hughes	1916	.842
	Emil Yde	1924	.842
	Schoolboy Rowe	1940	.842
	Sandy Consuegra	1954	.842
	Ralph Terry	1961	.842
	Ron Perranoski	1963	.842
31	Lefty Gomez	1934	.839
32	Bill Hoffer	1895	.838
	Denny McLain	1968	.838
34	Walter Johnson	1913	.837
35	Henry Boyle	1884	.833
	King Cole	1910	.833
	Spud Chandler	1943	.833
	Hoyt Wilhelm	1952	.833
	Sandy Koufax	1963	.833
	Randy Johnson	1997	.833
41	Old Hoss Radbourn	1884	.831
42	Ed Reulbach	1906	.826
	Elmer Riddle	1941	.826
	Greg Maddux	1997	.826
45	Jim Hughes	1899	.824
	Al Orth	1899	.824
	Jack Chesbro	1902	.824
	Dazzy Vance	1924	.824
	Bob Moose	1969	.824
	Wayne Simpson	1970	.824
	Roger Moret	1975	.824
	Juan Guzman	1993	.824
53	Chief Bender	1910	.821
	Bob Purkey	1962	.821
55	Sal Maglie	1950	.818
	Bob Welch	1990	.818
	Mark Portugal	1993	.818
58	Joe McGinnity	1904	.814
59	Hooks Wiltse	1904	.813
	Three Finger Brown	1906	.813
	Russ Ford	1910	.813
	Eddie Plank	1912	.813
	Carl Hubbell	1936	.813
	Atley Donald	1939	.813
	Howie Krist	1942	.813
	Rip Sewell	1948	.813
	Bob Feller	1954	.813
	Jim Coates	1960	.813
	Al McBean	1963	.813
	Tommy John	1974	.813
	Al Hrabosky	1975	.813
	Moose Haas	1983	.813
	Jamie Moyer	1996	.813
74	Dizzy Dean	1934	.811
75	Ed Reulbach	1907	.810
	Doc Crandall	1910	.810
	Johnny Allen	1932	.810
	Ted Wilks	1944	.810
	Phil Niekro	1982	.810
	Jimmy Key	1994	.810
81	General Crowder	1928	.808
	Bobo Newsom	1940	.808
	Tiny Bonham	1942	.808
	Larry Jansen	1947	.808
	Dave McNally	1971	.808
	Catfish Hunter	1973	.808
87	Howie Camnitz	1909	.806
	Christy Mathewson	1909	.806
	Boo Ferriss	1946	.806
	Juan Marichal	1966	.806
91	Eddie Cicotte	1919	.806
92	21 tied with		.800

Games

Rank	Player	Year	G
1	Mike Marshall	1974	106
2	Kent Tekulve	1979	94
3	Mike Marshall	1973	92
4	Kent Tekulve	1978	91
5	Wayne Granger	1969	90
	Mike Marshall	1979	90
	Kent Tekulve	1987	90
8	Mark Eichhorn	1987	89
	Julian Tavarez	1997	89
10	Wilbur Wood	1968	88
	Mike Myers	1997	88
12	Rob Murphy	1987	87
13	Kent Tekulve	1982	85
	Frank Williams	1987	85
	Mitch Williams	1987	85
16	Ted Abernathy	1965	84
	Enrique Romo	1979	84
	Dick Tidrow	1980	84
	Dan Quisenberry	1985	84
	Stan Belinda	1997	84
21	Ken Sanders	1971	83
	Craig Lefferts	1986	83
	Eddie Guardado	1996	83
	Mike Myers	1996	83
25	Eddie Fisher	1965	82
	Bill Campbell	1983	82
	Juan Agosto	1990	82
28	John Wyatt	1964	81
	Dale Murray	1976	81
	Jeff Robinson	1987	81
	Duane Ward	1991	81
	Joe Boever	1992	81
	Kenny Rogers	1992	81
	Mike Jackson	1993	81
	Mike Stanton	1996	81
	Brad Clontz	1996	81
37	Mudcat Grant	1970	80
	Pedro Borbon	1973	80
	Willie Hernandez	1984	80
	Mitch Williams	1986	80
	Doug Jones	1992	80
	Greg Harris	1993	80
43	Dick Radatz	1964	79
	Duane Ward	1992	79
	Bob Patterson	1996	79
46	Hal Woodeshick	1965	78
	Ted Abernathy	1968	78
	Bill Campbell	1976	78
	Rollie Fingers	1977	78
	Tom Hume	1980	78
	Kent Tekulve	1980	78
	Greg Minton	1982	78
	Ed Vande Berg	1982	78
	Ted Power	1984	78
	Tim Burke	1985	78
	Lance McCullers	1987	78
	Jeff Shaw	1996	78
	Mark Dewey	1996	78
	Jeff Shaw	1997	78
	Buddy Groom	1997	78
61	Bob Locker	1967	77
	Wilbur Wood	1970	77
	Charlie Hough	1976	77
	Butch Metzger	1976	77
	Dick Tidrow	1979	77
	Rick Camp	1980	77
	Gary Lavelle	1984	77
	Mark Davis	1985	77
	Craig Lefferts	1987	77
	Bobby Thigpen	1990	77
	Barry Jones	1991	77
	Xavier Hernandez	1992	77
	Mike Perez	1992	77
	Mark Wohlers	1996	77
	Mel Rojas	1997	77
	Jeff Nelson	1997	77
	Paul Quantrill	1997	77
78	24 tied with		76

Leaders: Single Season Pitching

Games Started

Rank	Name	Year	GS
1	Will White	1879	75
	Pud Galvin	1883	75
3	Jim McCormick	1880	74
4	Guy Hecker	1884	73
	Old Hoss Radbourn	1884	73
6	Pud Galvin	1884	72
	John Clarkson	1889	72
8	John Clarkson	1885	70
	Bill Hutchison	1892	70
10	Matt Kilroy	1887	69
11	Jim Devlin	1876	68
	Tim Keefe	1883	68
	Old Hoss Radbourn	1883	68
	Matt Kilroy	1886	68
15	Monte Ward	1880	67
	Jim McCormick	1882	67
	Charlie Buffinton	1884	67
	Toad Ramsey	1886	67
19	Pud Galvin	1879	66
	Lee Richmond	1880	66
	Dupee Shaw	1884	66
	Bill Hutchison	1890	66
23	Tony Mullane	1884	65
	Mickey Welch	1884	65
	Jim McCormick	1884	65
	Silver King	1888	65
27	George Bradley	1876	64
	Tommy Bond	1879	64
	Mickey Welch	1880	64
	Will White	1883	64
	Tim Keefe	1886	64
	Toad Ramsey	1887	64
33	Jim Whitney	1881	63
	Ed Morris	1885	63
	Ed Morris	1886	63
	Amos Rusie	1890	63
37	Will White	1880	62
38	Jim Devlin	1877	61
	John Coleman	1883	61
	Hardie Henderson	1885	61
	Jersey Bakely	1888	61
	Amos Rusie	1892	61
43	Al Spalding	1876	60
	Monte Ward	1879	60
	Jim McCormick	1879	60
	Larry Corcoran	1880	60
	Larry McKeon	1884	60
	Bill Sweeney	1884	60
49	Tommy Bond	1878	59
	Frank Mountain	1883	59
	Billy Taylor	1884	59
	Larry Corcoran	1884	59
	Mickey Welch	1886	59
	John Clarkson	1887	59
	Mark Baldwin	1889	59
56	Tommy Bond	1877	58
	Terry Larkin	1879	58
	Jim McCormick	1881	58
	One Arm Daily	1884	58
	Old Hoss Radbourn	1886	58
	Sadie McMahon	1891	58
	Bill Hutchison	1891	58
63	Tommy Bond	1880	57
	Tim Keefe	1884	57
	Dave Foutz	1886	57
	Ed Seward	1888	57
	Sadie McMahon	1890	57
	Mark Baldwin	1890	57
	Amos Rusie	1891	57
70	Bobby Mathews	1876	56
	Terry Larkin	1877	56
	Terry Larkin	1878	56
	Jim Whitney	1883	56
	Adonis Terry	1884	56
	Charlie Sweeney	1884	56
	Lady Baldwin	1886	56
	Tony Mullane	1886	56
	Tim Keefe	1887	56
	Matt Kilroy	1889	56
	Silver King	1890	56
	Jack Stivetts	1891	56
82	George Derby	1881	55
	Tony Mullane	1882	55
	Mickey Welch	1885	55
	John Clarkson	1886	55
	Gus Weyhing	1887	55
	Phenomenal Smith	1887	55
	Ed Morris	1888	55
	Kid Gleason	1890	55
90	Harry McCormick	1879	54
	George Bradley	1879	54
	Pud Galvin	1880	54
	Will White	1882	54
	Jack Lynch	1884	54
	Henry Porter	1885	54
	Henry Porter	1888	54
	John Clarkson	1888	54
	Ed Beatin	1890	54
	Bob Barr	1890	54
100	8 tied with		53

Complete Games

Rank	Name	Year	CG
1	Will White	1879	75
2	Old Hoss Radbourn	1884	73
3	Jim McCormick	1880	72
	Pud Galvin	1883	72
	Guy Hecker	1884	72
6	Pud Galvin	1884	71
7	Tim Keefe	1883	68
	John Clarkson	1885	68
	John Clarkson	1889	68
10	Bill Hutchison	1892	67
11	Jim Devlin	1876	66
	Old Hoss Radbourn	1883	66
	Matt Kilroy	1886	66
	Toad Ramsey	1886	66
	Matt Kilroy	1887	66
16	Pud Galvin	1879	65
	Jim McCormick	1882	65
	Bill Hutchison	1890	65
19	Mickey Welch	1880	64
	Will White	1883	64
	Tony Mullane	1884	64
	Silver King	1888	64
23	George Bradley	1876	63
	Charlie Buffinton	1884	63
	Jim McCormick	1884	63
	Ed Morris	1885	63
	Ed Morris	1886	63
28	Mickey Welch	1884	62
	Tim Keefe	1886	62
30	Jim Devlin	1877	61
	Toad Ramsey	1887	61
32	Dupee Shaw	1884	60
	Jersey Bakely	1888	60
34	Jim McCormick	1879	59
	Tommy Bond	1879	59
	Monte Ward	1880	59
	John Coleman	1883	59
	Larry McKeon	1884	59
	Billy Taylor	1884	59
	Hardie Henderson	1885	59
41	Tommy Bond	1877	58
	Monte Ward	1879	58
	Will White	1880	58
	Bill Sweeney	1884	58
	Amos Rusie	1892	58
46	Tommy Bond	1878	57
	Terry Larkin	1879	57
	Larry Corcoran	1880	57
	Lee Richmond	1880	57
	Jim Whitney	1881	57
	Jim McCormick	1881	57
	Frank Mountain	1883	57
	Larry Corcoran	1884	57
	Old Hoss Radbourn	1886	57
	Ed Seward	1888	57
56	Terry Larkin	1878	56
	One Arm Daily	1884	56
	Tim Keefe	1884	56
	Mickey Welch	1886	56
	John Clarkson	1887	56
	Amos Rusie	1890	56
	Bill Hutchison	1891	56
63	Bobby Mathews	1876	55
	Terry Larkin	1877	55
	George Derby	1881	55
	Adonis Terry	1884	55
	Mickey Welch	1885	55
	Lady Baldwin	1886	55
	Dave Foutz	1886	55
	Tony Mullane	1886	55
	Matt Kilroy	1889	55
	Kid Gleason	1890	55
	Mark Baldwin	1890	55
73	Jim Whitney	1883	54
	Jack Lynch	1884	54
	Phenomenal Smith	1887	54
	Tim Keefe	1887	54
	Ed Morris	1888	54
	Mark Baldwin	1889	54
	Kid Gleason	1890	54
	Mark Baldwin	1890	54
81	Al Spalding	1876	53
	George Bradley	1879	53
	Charlie Sweeney	1884	53
	Henry Porter	1885	53
	Bob Caruthers	1885	53
	Gus Weyhing	1887	53
	Henry Porter	1888	53
	John Clarkson	1888	53
	Ed Beatin	1890	53
	Sadie McMahon	1891	53
91	Will White	1878	52
	Will White	1882	52
	Will White	1884	52
	Ed Seward	1887	52
	Bob Barr	1890	52
	Amos Rusie	1891	52
97	6 tied with		51

Shutouts

Rank	Name	Year	ShO
1	George Bradley	1876	16
	Pete Alexander	1916	16
3	Jack Coombs	1910	13
	Bob Gibson	1968	13
5	Pud Galvin	1884	12
	Ed Morris	1886	12
	Pete Alexander	1915	12
8	Tommy Bond	1879	11
	Old Hoss Radbourn	1884	11
	Dave Foutz	1886	11
	Ed Walsh	1908	11
	Christy Mathewson	1908	11
	Walter Johnson	1913	11
	Sandy Koufax	1963	11
	Dean Chance	1964	11
16	Jim McCormick	1884	10
	John Clarkson	1885	10
	Cy Young	1904	10
	Ed Walsh	1906	10
	Joe Wood	1912	10
	Dave Davenport	1915	10
	Carl Hubbell	1933	10
	Mort Cooper	1942	10
	Bob Feller	1946	10
	Bob Lemon	1948	10
	Juan Marichal	1965	10
	Jim Palmer	1975	10
	John Tudor	1985	10
29	Tommy Bond	1878	9
	George Derby	1881	9
	Cy Young	1892	9
	Joe McGinnity	1904	9
	Three Finger Brown	1906	9
	Addie Joss	1906	9
	Three Finger Brown	1908	9
	Addie Joss	1908	9
	Orval Overall	1909	9
	Pete Alexander	1913	9
	Walter Johnson	1914	9
	Cy Falkenberg	1914	9
	Babe Ruth	1916	9
	Stan Coveleski	1917	9
	Pete Alexander	1919	9
	Bill Lee	1938	9
	Bob Porterfield	1953	9
	Luis Tiant	1968	9
	Denny McLain	1969	9
	Don Sutton	1972	9
	Nolan Ryan	1972	9
	Bert Blyleven	1973	9
	Ron Guidry	1978	9
52	50 tied with		8

Saves

Rank	Name	Year	Sv
1	Bobby Thigpen	1990	57
2	Randy Myers	1993	53
3	Dennis Eckersley	1992	51
4	Dennis Eckersley	1990	48
	Rod Beck	1993	48
6	Lee Smith	1991	47
7	Dave Righetti	1986	46
	Bryan Harvey	1991	46
	Lee Smith	1993	46
	Jose Mesa	1995	46
11	Dan Quisenberry	1983	45
	Bruce Sutter	1984	45
	Dennis Eckersley	1988	45
	Duane Ward	1993	45
	Bryan Harvey	1993	45
	Jeff Montgomery	1993	45
	Randy Myers	1997	45
18	Dan Quisenberry	1984	44
	Mark Davis	1989	44
	Todd Worrell	1996	44
	Jeff Brantley	1996	44
22	Doug Jones	1990	43
	Dennis Eckersley	1991	43
	Lee Smith	1992	43
	Mitch Williams	1993	43
	John Wetteland	1993	43
	John Wetteland	1996	43
	Mariano Rivera	1997	43
29	Jeff Reardon	1988	42
	Rick Aguilera	1991	42
	Trevor Hoffman	1996	42
	Jeff Shaw	1997	42
33	Jeff Reardon	1985	41
	Rick Aguilera	1992	41
35	Steve Bedrosian	1987	40
	Jeff Reardon	1991	40
	Tom Henke	1993	40
38	John Franco	1988	39
	Jeff Montgomery	1992	39
	Jose Mesa	1996	39
	Mark Wohlers	1996	39
42	John Hiller	1973	38
	Jeff Russell	1989	38
	Randy Myers	1992	38
	Roberto Hernandez	1993	38
	Randy Myers	1995	38
	Roberto Hernandez	1996	38
48	Clay Carroll	1972	37
	Rollie Fingers	1978	37
	Bruce Sutter	1979	37
	Dan Quisenberry	1985	37
	Doug Jones	1988	37
	Gregg Olson	1990	37
	John Wetteland	1992	37
	Lee Smith	1995	37
	Rod Beck	1997	37
	Trevor Hoffman	1997	37
58	Bruce Sutter	1982	36
	Bill Caudill	1984	36
	Todd Worrell	1986	36
	Lee Smith	1987	36
	Mitch Williams	1989	36
	Dave Righetti	1990	36
	Doug Jones	1992	36
	Gregg Olson	1992	36
	Dennis Eckersley	1993	36
	Tom Henke	1995	36
	Mel Rojas	1996	36
	Troy Percival	1996	36
	Dennis Eckersley	1997	36
	John Franco	1997	36
	Doug Jones	1997	36
73	Wayne Granger	1970	35
	Sparky Lyle	1972	35
	Rollie Fingers	1977	35
	Dan Quisenberry	1982	35
	Jeff Reardon	1986	35
	Rod Beck	1996	35
	Robb Nen	1996	35
	Todd Worrell	1997	35
	Robb Nen	1997	35
82	Ron Perranoski	1970	34
	Don Aase	1986	34
	Tom Henke	1987	34
	Jim Gott	1988	34
	Bobby Thigpen	1988	34
	Bobby Thigpen	1989	34
	Tom Henke	1992	34
	Rick Aguilera	1993	34
	Ricky Bottalico	1996	34
	Ricky Bottalico	1997	34
92	16 tied with		33

Games Finished

1	Mike Marshall	1979	84
2	Mike Marshall	1974	83
3	Ken Sanders	1971	77
4	Dan Quisenberry	1985	76
5	Mike Marshall	1973	73
	Bobby Thigpen	1990	73
	Doug Jones	1997	73
8	Rod Beck	1993	71
9	Doug Jones	1992	70
	Duane Ward	1993	70
11	Rollie Fingers	1977	69
	Randy Myers	1993	69
13	Bill Campbell	1976	68
	Dan Quisenberry	1980	68
	Dan Quisenberry	1982	68
	Willie Hernandez	1984	68
	Dave Righetti	1986	68
18	Dick Radatz	1964	67
	Kent Tekulve	1979	67
	Dan Quisenberry	1984	67
	Roberto Hernandez	1993	67
	Todd Worrell	1996	67
23	Tom Murphy	1974	66
	Greg Minton	1982	66
	Jeff Russell	1989	66
	Robb Nen	1996	66
	Rod Beck	1997	66
28	Kent Tekulve	1978	65
	Mark Davis	1989	65
	Dennis Eckersley	1992	65
	Robb Nen	1997	65
32	Bill Caudill	1982	64
	Kent Tekulve	1982	64
	Willie Hernandez	1985	64
	Doug Jones	1990	64
	Mel Rojas	1996	64
	Mark Wohlers	1996	64
38	Doug Corbett	1980	63
	Bruce Sutter	1984	63
	Greg Harris	1986	63
	Bryan Harvey	1991	63
	Jeff Montgomery	1993	63
43	Jim Konstanty	1950	62
	Ted Abernathy	1965	62
	Phil Regan	1968	62
	Wilbur Wood	1970	62
	Rollie Fingers	1976	62
	Butch Metzger	1976	62
	Rollie Fingers	1978	62
	Tom Hume	1980	62
	Dan Quisenberry	1983	62
	Bill Caudill	1984	62
	Tom Henke	1987	62
	Gregg Olson	1991	62
	Jeff Montgomery	1992	62
	Steve Olin	1992	62
	Trevor Hoffman	1996	62
	Jeff Shaw	1997	62
59	Roy Face	1960	61
	Ted Abernathy	1967	61
	Ron Davis	1983	61
	Al Holland	1984	61
	John Franco	1988	61
	Jeff Reardon	1989	61
	Mitch Williams	1989	61
	Dennis Eckersley	1990	61
	Lee Smith	1991	61
	Rick Aguilera	1992	61
	Rick Aguilera	1993	61
	Jeff Brantley	1996	61
	Roberto Hernandez	1996	61
	Heathcliff Slocumb	1997	61
	Ricky Bottalico	1997	61
74	Eddie Fisher	1965	60
	John Hiller	1973	60
	Dave Giusti	1973	60
	Rollie Fingers	1974	60
	Sparky Lyle	1977	60
	Bill Campbell	1977	60
	Bob James	1985	60
	Dave Righetti	1985	60
	Todd Worrell	1986	60
	John Franco	1987	60
	Steve Bedrosian	1989	60
	Mike Schooler	1989	60
	Roger McDowell	1990	60
	Rick Aguilera	1991	60
	Mitch Williams	1991	60
	Tom Henke	1993	60
	Doug Jones	1993	60
	Jose Mesa	1996	60
	Heathcliff Slocumb	1996	60
93	14 tied with		59

Batters Faced

1	Will White	1879	2,906
2	Pud Galvin	1883	2,741
3	John Clarkson	1889	2,736
4	Old Hoss Radbourn	1884	2,672
5	Jim McCormick	1880	2,669
6	Guy Hecker	1884	2,649
7	Jim Devlin	1876	2,568
8	Bill Hutchison	1892	2,565
9	Pud Galvin	1884	2,554
10	John Coleman	1883	2,546
11	Old Hoss Radbourn	1883	2,540
12	Matt Kilroy	1887	2,492
13	John Clarkson	1885	2,487
14	Toad Ramsey	1886	2,477
15	Matt Kilroy	1886	2,469
16	Bill Hutchison	1890	2,453
17	Pud Galvin	1879	2,436
18	Toad Ramsey	1887	2,430
19	Monte Ward	1879	2,425
20	Tim Keefe	1883	2,418
21	Jim McCormick	1882	2,412
22	Lee Richmond	1880	2,410
23	Mickey Welch	1880	2,387
24	Charlie Buffinton	1884	2,383
25	Mickey Welch	1884	2,370
26	Tony Mullane	1884	2,364
27	Monte Ward	1880	2,351
28	Jim Devlin	1877	2,328
29	Bobby Mathews	1876	2,327
30	Jim McCormick	1879	2,325
31	Ed Morris	1885	2,321
32	Will White	1883	2,320
33	Amos Rusie	1890	2,314
34	Bill Hutchison	1891	2,313
35	Jim Whitney	1881	2,301
36	Jim McCormick	1884	2,292
37	George Bradley	1876	2,269
38	Hardie Henderson	1885	2,268
39	Tony Mullane	1886	2,258
40	Ed Morris	1886	2,252
41	Mark Baldwin	1890	2,225
42	Mark Baldwin	1889	2,220
43	Al Spalding	1876	2,219
	Ed Daily	1890	2,219
45	Will White	1880	2,217
46	Amos Rusie	1892	2,215
47	Silver King	1888	2,210
48	Phenomenal Smith	1887	2,204
49	Tommy Bond	1879	2,189
	Jersey Bakely	1888	2,189
51	Larry McKeon	1884	2,185
52	John Clarkson	1887	2,183
53	Larry Corcoran	1884	2,180
54	Frank Mountain	1883	2,177
55	Terry Larkin	1879	2,176
	Dupee Shaw	1884	2,176
57	Tim Keefe	1886	2,173
58	George Bradley	1879	2,170
59	Tommy Bond	1877	2,165
60	Old Hoss Radbourn	1886	2,162
	Sadie McMahon	1890	2,162
62	Tommy Bond	1878	2,159
63	Bill Sweeney	1884	2,156
64	Mickey Welch	1886	2,151
65	Jim McCormick	1881	2,145
66	Billy Taylor	1884	2,140
67	Larry Corcoran	1880	2,133
68	Terry Larkin	1877	2,132
69	Kid Gleason	1890	2,113
70	Terry Larkin	1878	2,105
71	Amos Rusie	1891	2,103
72	George Derby	1881	2,101
	Jim Whitney	1883	2,101
	Sadie McMahon	1891	2,101
75	Dave Foutz	1886	2,091
76	Tommy Bond	1880	2,082
77	Ed Beatin	1890	2,079
78	Amos Rusie	1893	2,067
79	Adonis Terry	1884	2,046
80	Gus Weyhing	1887	2,042
81	Larry Corcoran	1883	2,041
82	Bob Barr	1890	2,038
83	Pud Galvin	1881	2,037
84	Henry Porter	1885	2,035
85	John Clarkson	1888	2,029
86	Henry Porter	1888	2,022
87	Ed Seward	1888	2,017
88	Matt Kilroy	1889	2,010
89	Jack Lynch	1884	2,002
	Al Mays	1887	2,002
	Ed Morris	1888	2,002
92	Guy Hecker	1883	1,993
93	Lee Richmond	1881	1,992
94	Ed Seward	1887	1,990
95	Guy Hecker	1885	1,988
96	Will White	1884	1,986
97	Ted Breitenstein	1894	1,984
98	Tim Keefe	1887	1,981
99	Harry McCormick	1879	1,975
	Silver King	1890	1,975

Innings Pitched

1	Will White	1879	680.0
2	Old Hoss Radbourn	1884	678.2
3	Guy Hecker	1884	670.2
4	Jim McCormick	1880	657.2
5	Pud Galvin	1883	656.1
6	Pud Galvin	1884	636.1
7	Old Hoss Radbourn	1883	632.1
8	John Clarkson	1885	623.0
9	Jim Devlin	1876	622.0
	Bill Hutchison	1892	622.0
11	John Clarkson	1889	620.0
12	Tim Keefe	1883	619.0
13	Bill Hutchison	1890	603.0
14	Jim McCormick	1882	595.2
15	Monte Ward	1880	595.0
16	Pud Galvin	1879	593.0
17	Lee Richmond	1880	590.2
18	Matt Kilroy	1887	589.1
19	Toad Ramsey	1886	588.2
20	Monte Ward	1879	587.0
	Charlie Buffinton	1884	587.0
22	Silver King	1888	585.2
23	Matt Kilroy	1886	583.0
24	Ed Morris	1885	581.0
25	Will White	1883	577.0
26	Mickey Welch	1880	574.0
27	George Bradley	1876	573.0
28	Jim McCormick	1884	569.0
29	Tony Mullane	1884	567.0
30	Toad Ramsey	1887	561.0
	Bill Hutchison	1891	561.0
32	Jim Devlin	1877	559.0
33	Mickey Welch	1884	557.1
34	Tommy Bond	1879	555.1
	Ed Morris	1886	555.1
36	Jim Whitney	1881	552.1
37	Amos Rusie	1890	548.2
38	Jim McCormick	1879	546.1
39	Dupee Shaw	1884	543.1
40	Tim Keefe	1886	540.0
41	Hardie Henderson	1885	539.1
42	John Coleman	1883	538.1
43	Bill Sweeney	1884	538.0
44	Larry Corcoran	1880	536.1
45	Tommy Bond	1878	532.2
	Jersey Bakely	1888	532.2
47	Amos Rusie	1892	532.0
48	Tony Mullane	1886	529.2
49	Al Spalding	1876	528.2
50	Jim McCormick	1881	526.0
51	Billy Taylor	1884	523.0
	John Clarkson	1887	523.0
53	Tommy Bond	1877	521.0
54	Ed Seward	1888	518.2
55	Will White	1880	517.1
56	Larry Corcoran	1884	516.2
57	Bobby Mathews	1876	516.0
58	Jim Whitney	1883	514.0
59	Mark Baldwin	1889	513.2
60	Terry Larkin	1879	513.1
61	Larry McKeon	1884	512.0
62	Old Hoss Radbourn	1886	509.1
63	Sadie McMahon	1890	509.0
64	Terry Larkin	1878	506.0
	Kid Gleason	1890	506.0
66	Dave Foutz	1886	504.0
67	Frank Mountain	1883	503.0
	Sadie McMahon	1891	503.0
69	Terry Larkin	1877	501.0
	Mark Baldwin	1890	501.0
71	One Arm Daily	1884	500.2
72	Amos Rusie	1891	500.1
73	Mickey Welch	1886	500.0
74	Jack Lynch	1884	496.0
75	George Derby	1881	494.2
76	Bob Barr	1890	493.1
77	Tommy Bond	1880	493.0
78	Charlie Sweeney	1884	492.0
	Mickey Welch	1885	492.0
80	Phenomenal Smith	1887	491.1
81	George Bradley	1879	487.0
	Lady Baldwin	1886	487.0
83	Adonis Terry	1884	485.0
84	John Clarkson	1888	483.1
85	Tim Keefe	1884	482.2
86	Bob Caruthers	1885	482.1
87	Amos Rusie	1893	482.0
88	Henry Porter	1885	481.2
89	Matt Kilroy	1889	480.2
90	Will White	1882	480.0
	Guy Hecker	1885	480.0
	Ed Morris	1888	480.0
93	Tim Keefe	1887	478.2
94	Ed Beatin	1890	474.1
95	Pud Galvin	1881	474.0
	Old Hoss Radbourn	1882	474.0
	Henry Porter	1888	474.0
98	Larry Corcoran	1883	473.2
99	Ed Seward	1887	470.2
100	Gus Weyhing	1892	469.2

Hits Allowed

1	John Coleman	1883	772
2	Bobby Mathews	1876	693
3	Will White	1879	676
	Pud Galvin	1883	676
5	Jim Devlin	1877	617
6	George Bradley	1879	590
7	John Clarkson	1889	589
8	Pud Galvin	1879	585
	Jim McCormick	1880	585
	Matt Kilroy	1887	585
11	Jim McCormick	1879	582
12	Mickey Welch	1880	575
13	Tommy Bond	1878	571
	Monte Ward	1879	571
	Bill Hutchison	1892	571
16	Jim Devlin	1876	566
	Pud Galvin	1884	566
18	Old Hoss Radbourn	1883	563
19	Tommy Bond	1880	559
20	Al Mays	1887	551
21	Will White	1880	550
	Jim McCormick	1882	550
23	Stump Wiedman	1886	549
24	Jim Whitney	1881	548
25	Lee Richmond	1881	547
26	Pud Galvin	1881	546
	Frank Mountain	1883	546
28	Toad Ramsey	1887	544
29	Tommy Bond	1879	543
30	Al Spalding	1876	542
31	Lee Richmond	1880	541
	Billy Crowell	1887	541
33	Hardie Henderson	1885	539
34	Tommy Bond	1877	530
35	Pud Galvin	1880	528
	Old Hoss Radbourn	1884	528
	Mickey Welch	1884	528
38	Henry Porter	1888	527
39	Guy Hecker	1884	526
	Phenomenal Smith	1887	526
41	Lee Richmond	1882	525
42	Bill Sweeney	1884	522
43	Old Hoss Radbourn	1886	521
44	Jersey Bakely	1888	518
	Ed Beatin	1890	518
46	Harry McCormick	1879	517
47	Terry Larkin	1879	514
	Mickey Welch	1886	514
49	John Clarkson	1887	513
	Kid Carsey	1891	513
51	Terry Larkin	1878	511
52	Terry Larkin	1877	510
53	Guy Hecker	1883	509
54	Jim McCormick	1884	508
	Bill Hutchison	1891	508
56	Charlie Buffinton	1884	506
57	George Derby	1881	505
	Old Hoss Radbourn	1887	505
	Bill Hutchison	1890	505
60	Jim Whitney	1885	503
61	Monte Ward	1880	501
	Tony Mullane	1886	501
63	Sadie McMahon	1890	498
	Mark Baldwin	1890	498
65	John Clarkson	1885	497
	Ted Breitenstein	1894	497
67	Fleury Sullivan	1884	496
68	George Cobb	1892	495
69	Sadie McMahon	1891	493
70	Jim Whitney	1883	492
71	Pud Galvin	1887	490
72	Larry McKeon	1884	488
	Cy Young	1894	488
	Kid Nichols	1894	488
75	Adonis Terry	1884	487
76	Tim Keefe	1883	486
77	Jack Lynch	1886	485
	Bill Carrick	1899	485
79	Jim McCormick	1881	484
	Red Donahue	1897	484
81	Larry Corcoran	1883	483
82	Tony Mullane	1884	481
	Park Swartzel	1889	481
	Pink Hawley	1894	481
85	Will White	1884	479
	Kid Gleason	1890	479
87	Tim Keefe	1886	478
88	Will White	1878	477
	Cy Young	1896	477
90	Pud Galvin	1882	476
	Matt Kilroy	1886	476
	Matt Kilroy	1889	476
	Frank Killen	1896	476
94	Will White	1883	473
	Larry Corcoran	1884	473
96	Bob Barr	1884	471
	Frank Dwyer	1894	471
98	George Bradley	1876	470
	Ed Morris	1888	470
100	Sam Weaver	1883	468

996 Leaders: Single Season Pitching

Runs Allowed

1 John Coleman	1883	510
2 Will White	1879	404
3 Bobby Mathews	1876	395
4 Phenomenal Smith	1887	369
5 Pud Galvin	1883	367
6 George Bradley	1879	361
7 Al Mays	1887	359
8 Toad Ramsey	1887	358
Mark Baldwin	1889	358
Kid Carsey	1891	358
11 Henry Gruber	1890	352
12 Larry McKeon	1884	350
Matt Kilroy	1886	350
Billy Crowell	1887	350
15 Frank Mountain	1883	345
16 Lee Richmond	1882	343
17 Gus Weyhing	1887	342
18 Mike Morrison	1887	341
19 Hardie Henderson	1883	339
20 Jersey Bakely	1884	338
21 Henry Porter	1888	336
22 Park Swartzel	1889	334
23 George Cobb	1892	333
24 Fleury Sullivan	1884	328
25 Bob Barr	1884	327
26 Matt Kilroy	1887	326
27 Will White	1880	323
Stump Wiedman	1886	323
29 Mark Baldwin	1890	322
30 Mickey Welch	1880	321
Jersey Bakely	1888	321
Ted Breitenstein	1894	321
33 Bill Hutchison	1892	316
34 Tony Mullane	1886	315
Bill Hutchison	1890	315
36 Hardie Henderson	1885	311
37 Jim Devlin	1876	309
38 Jim McCormick	1879	308
Adonis Terry	1884	308
Kid Nichols	1894	308
41 Jack Lynch	1886	307
George Haddock	1890	307
Jersey Bakely	1890	307
44 Pink Hawley	1894	306
Red Donahue	1897	306
46 Old Hoss Radbourn	1887	305
47 Lee Richmond	1881	302
48 John Harkins	1884	300
Old Hoss Radbourn	1886	300
Amos Rusie	1890	300
Ed Beatin	1890	300
52 Pud Galvin	1879	299
53 Tommy Bond	1880	298
54 Charlie Ferguson	1884	297
Toad Ramsey	1886	297
56 John Ewing	1889	296
57 Ted Breitenstein	1895	295
58 Bill Sweeney	1884	294
59 Ed Seward	1887	293
Bert Cunningham	1890	293
61 Jim Whitney	1886	292
Egyptian Healy	1887	292
Bill Hart	1897	292
64 Harry McCormick	1879	291
Brickyard Kennedy	1894	291
66 Lon Knight	1876	288
Jim Devlin	1877	288
Terry Larkin	1878	288
Al Atkinson	1886	288
Amos Rusie	1892	288
71 Guy Hecker	1883	287
Red Ehret	1889	287
Sadie McMahon	1890	287
74 Larry Corcoran	1884	286
Jim Whitney	1885	286
Frank Killen	1892	286
77 Terry Larkin	1877	285
Billy Serad	1884	285
79 Jim Whitney	1881	284
80 John Clarkson	1887	283
Matt Kilroy	1889	283
Bill Hutchison	1891	283
83 Frank Dwyer	1894	282
Chick Fraser	1896	282
Jack Taylor	1896	282
86 Pud Galvin	1880	281
Larry Corcoran	1883	281
Dupee Shaw	1884	281
89 John Clarkson	1889	280
Ed Crane	1890	280
Win Mercer	1895	280
92 Mickey Welch	1886	279
93 Lee Richmond	1880	278
Toad Ramsey	1888	278
Mark Baldwin	1891	278
Win Mercer	1894	278
Jack Stivetts	1894	278
98 Terry Larkin	1879	277
Henry Porter	1886	277
Duke Esper	1893	277

Earned Runs Allowed

1 John Coleman	1883	291
2 Ted Breitenstein	1894	238
3 Red Donahue	1897	237
4 Al Mays	1887	232
5 Kid Carsey	1891	230
6 Gus Weyhing	1887	221
7 Henry Porter	1888	219
8 Matt Kilroy	1886	218
Tony Mullane	1886	218
10 Ed Seward	1887	216
11 Old Hoss Radbourn	1887	215
Kid Nichols	1894	215
13 Stump Wiedman	1886	214
Toad Ramsey	1887	214
Pink Hawley	1894	214
16 George Cobb	1892	213
17 Ted Breitenstein	1895	212
18 Billy Crowell	1887	211
19 Phenomenal Smith	1887	207
20 Fleury Sullivan	1884	206
Mark Baldwin	1889	206
22 Bill Hart	1897	205
23 Ed Beatin	1890	202
24 Frank Mountain	1883	201
Matt Kilroy	1887	201
26 Bert Cunningham	1890	200
27 Larry McKeon	1884	199
28 Pud Galvin	1883	198
Red Ehret	1894	198
30 Park Swartzel	1889	197
Brickyard Kennedy	1894	197
32 Jim Whitney	1886	196
Egyptian Healy	1887	196
Scott Stratton	1893	196
Frank Dwyer	1894	196
36 Kid Gleason	1893	195
37 Red Ehret	1889	194
38 Tom Parrott	1894	192
39 Hardie Henderson	1885	191
Bill Hutchison	1892	191
George Hemming	1893	191
Jack Taylor	1896	191
Bill Hart	1896	191
44 Jack Lynch	1886	190
Elton Chamberlin	1891	190
46 Chick Fraser	1896	189
47 Adonis Terry	1884	188
Jersey Bakely	1884	188
John Clarkson	1889	188
50 Bill Hutchison	1894	187
Kid Carsey	1895	187
Bill Carrick	1899	187
53 George Haddock	1890	186
Bobo Newsom	1938	186
55 Sadie McMahon	1890	185
56 Mark Baldwin	1890	184
Bill Hutchison	1893	184
Jack Stivetts	1894	184
59 Henry Gruber	1890	182
Gus Weyhing	1893	182
61 Bob Barr	1884	181
Bill Hutchison	1890	181
Tony Mullane	1893	181
Ed Stein	1894	181
Gus Weyhing	1898	181
66 Ad Gumbert	1894	180
67 Hardie Henderson	1883	179
John Clarkson	1887	179
John Ewing	1889	179
Cy Young	1894	179
71 Bob Barr	1890	178
72 Jersey Bakely	1888	176
Charlie Getzien	1889	176
74 Bill Hutchison	1891	175
Duke Esper	1893	175
Al Maul	1893	175
77 Lee Richmond	1881	174
Al Atkinson	1886	174
79 Mike Morrison	1887	173
Amos Rusie	1893	173
81 Sam Weaver	1883	172
Gus Weyhing	1894	172
Red Donahue	1896	172
Jack Taylor	1898	172
Snake Wiltse	1902	172
86 Lee Richmond	1882	171
Bert Cunningham	1888	171
Kid Carsey	1894	171
89 Old Hoss Radbourn	1886	170
Wild Bill Widner	1889	170
Ed Crane	1890	170
Amos Rusie	1892	170
Mark Baldwin	1892	170
Kid Carsey	1893	170
Jim Hughey	1899	170
96 John Keefe	1890	169
Frank Killen	1892	169
Ted Breitenstein	1896	169
Gus Weyhing	1899	169
100 6 tied with		168

Home Runs Allowed

1 Bert Blyleven	1986	50
2 Robin Roberts	1956	46
Bert Blyleven	1987	46
4 Pedro Ramos	1957	43
5 Denny McLain	1966	42
6 Robin Roberts	1955	41
Phil Niekro	1979	41
8 Robin Roberts	1957	40
Ralph Terry	1962	40
Orlando Pena	1964	40
Phil Niekro	1970	40
Fergie Jenkins	1979	40
Jack Morris	1986	40
Bill Gullickson	1987	40
Shawn Boskie	1996	40
Brad Radke	1996	40
17 Murry Dickson	1948	39
Pedro Ramos	1961	39
Jim Perry	1971	39
Catfish Hunter	1973	39
Jack Morris	1987	39
22 Warren Hacker	1955	38
Pedro Ramos	1958	38
Lew Burdette	1959	38
Jim Bunning	1963	38
Don Sutton	1970	38
Mickey Lolich	1974	38
Matt Keough	1982	38
Don Sutton	1987	38
Floyd Bannister	1987	38
Curt Young	1987	38
Tim Wakefield	1996	38
33 Jim Bunning	1959	37
Earl Wilson	1964	37
Luis Tiant	1969	37
Fergie Jenkins	1975	37
Jack Morris	1982	37
Dan Petry	1983	37
Frank Viola	1986	37
Mark Leiter	1996	37
Allen Watson	1997	37
42 Larry Jansen	1949	36
Art Mahaffey	1962	36
Pete Richert	1966	36
Mickey Lolich	1971	36
Charlie Hough	1987	36
Ed Whitson	1987	36
Dennis Rasmussen	1987	36
Tom Browning	1988	36
50 Larry Corcoran	1884	35
Warren Hacker	1953	35
Robin Roberts	1954	35
Don Newcombe	1955	35
Jim Perry	1960	35
Roger Craig	1962	35
Robin Roberts	1963	35
Sammy Ellis	1966	35
Denny McLain	1967	35
Fergie Jenkins	1973	35
Mickey Lolich	1973	35
Mike Caldwell	1983	35
Mike Smithson	1984	35
Scott McGregor	1986	35
Bruce Hurst	1987	35
Scott Bankhead	1987	35
Bill Gullickson	1992	35
Mike Moore	1993	35
68 Johnny Sain	1950	34
Ken Raffensberger	1950	34
Preacher Roe	1950	34
Paul Foytack	1959	34
Robin Roberts	1959	34
Juan Marichal	1962	34
Bill Monbouquette	1964	34
Dick Ellsworth	1964	34
Bob Gibson	1965	34
Mudcat Grant	1965	34
Earl Wilson	1967	34
Catfish Hunter	1969	34
Mike Cuellar	1970	34
Gaylord Perry	1973	34
Rick Wise	1975	34
Frank Viola	1983	34
Danny Darwin	1985	34
Scott McGregor	1985	34
Ken Schrom	1986	34
Mike Witt	1987	34
Don Carman	1987	34
Kevin Tapani	1996	34
Alex Fernandez	1996	34
91 18 tied with		33

Walks

1 Amos Rusie	1890	289
2 Mark Baldwin	1889	274
3 Amos Rusie	1892	267
4 Amos Rusie	1891	262
5 Mark Baldwin	1890	249
6 Jack Stivetts	1891	232
7 Mark Baldwin	1891	227
8 Phil Knell	1891	226
9 Bob Barr	1890	219
10 Amos Rusie	1893	218
11 Cy Seymour	1898	213
12 Gus Weyhing	1889	212
13 Ed Crane	1890	210
14 Bob Feller	1938	208
15 Toad Ramsey	1886	207
16 Elton Chamberlin	1891	206
17 Mike Morrison	1887	205
18 Henry Gruber	1890	204
Nolan Ryan	1977	204
20 John Clarkson	1889	203
Ed Crane	1891	203
22 Nolan Ryan	1974	202
23 Bert Cunningham	1890	201
24 Amos Rusie	1894	200
25 Bill Hutchison	1890	199
26 Mark Baldwin	1892	194
Bob Feller	1941	194
28 Bobo Newsom	1938	192
29 Ted Breitenstein	1894	191
30 Bill Hutchison	1892	190
31 Ed Crane	1892	189
Tony Mullane	1893	189
33 Tony Mullane	1891	187
Kid Gleason	1893	187
35 Ed Beatin	1890	186
36 Sam Jones	1955	185
37 Tom Vickery	1890	184
38 Nolan Ryan	1976	183
39 Matt Kilroy	1886	182
Frank Killen	1892	182
41 Willie McGill	1893	181
Bob Harmon	1911	181
Bob Turley	1954	181
44 Jack Stivetts	1890	179
Gus Weyhing	1890	179
Tommy Byrne	1949	179
47 Bill Hutchison	1891	178
Ted Breitenstein	1895	178
49 Bob Turley	1955	177
50 Phenomenal Smith	1887	176
George Hemming	1893	176
52 Silver King	1892	174
53 Jack Stivetts	1892	171
Jouett Meekin	1894	171
Ed Stein	1894	171
Bump Hadley	1932	171
57 Elton Chamberlin	1892	170
Cy Seymour	1899	170
59 Willie McGill	1891	168
Gus Weyhing	1892	168
Brickyard Kennedy	1893	168
Elmer Myers	1916	168
63 Gus Weyhing	1887	167
Toad Ramsey	1887	167
Darby O'Brien	1889	167
Bill Daley	1890	167
Kid Gleason	1890	167
Bobo Newsom	1937	167
69 Tony Mullane	1886	166
Sadie McMahon	1890	166
Phil Knell	1890	166
Chick Fraser	1896	166
73 Elton Chamberlin	1889	165
Dan Casey	1890	165
Kid Gleason	1891	165
John Wyckoff	1915	165
77 Cy Seymour	1897	164
Earl Moore	1911	164
Phil Niekro	1977	164
80 Mickey Welch	1886	163
Silver King	1890	163
Hank O'Day	1890	163
George Haddock	1892	163
84 Johnny Vander Meer	1943	162
Nolan Ryan	1973	162
86 John Sowders	1890	161
Kid Carsey	1891	161
Gus Weyhing	1891	161
89 Tommy Byrne	1950	160
90 George Hemming	1894	159
Amos Rusie	1895	159
Marty O'Toole	1912	159
93 Joe Coleman	1974	158
94 Matt Kilroy	1887	157
Bert Cunningham	1888	157
Pink Hawley	1896	157
Grover Lowdermilk	1915	157
Nolan Ryan	1972	157
99 5 tied with		156

Leaders: Single Season Pitching 997

Intentional Walks

1	Gene Garber	1974	24
2	Mike Garman	1975	23
	Dale Murray	1978	23
	Kent Tekulve	1982	23
5	Lindy McDaniel	1965	20
	Ron Willis	1967	20
	Jim Bunning	1967	20
	Randy Jones	1978	20
	Kent Tekulve	1979	20
	Greg Minton	1984	20
	Roger McDowell	1991	20
12	Ron Perranoski	1964	19
	Don Drysdale	1967	19
	John Hiller	1974	19
15	Bob Friend	1956	18
	Mike McCormick	1967	18
	Clay Carroll	1969	18
	Tom Murphy	1974	18
	Ron Schueler	1974	18
	Gary Lavelle	1977	18
	Kent Tekulve	1978	18
	Dave Heaverlo	1979	18
	Bill Campbell	1983	18
	Greg Minton	1985	18
25	Gaylord Perry	1967	17
	Minnie Rojas	1967	17
	Phil Regan	1967	17
	Ray Sadecki	1968	17
	Tug McGraw	1970	17
	Carl Morton	1970	17
	Bill Greif	1975	17
	Dave Giusti	1975	17
	Greg Minton	1982	17
	Todd Jones	1995	17
35	Robin Roberts	1957	16
	Chuck Estrada	1962	16
	Bob Miller	1964	16
	Gaylord Perry	1965	16
	Hal Woodeshick	1965	16
	Ken Sanders	1966	16
	Ron Perranoski	1969	16
	Steve Carlton	1970	16
	Darold Knowles	1970	16
	Tommy John	1970	16
	Gaylord Perry	1972	16
	Bill Gogolewski	1973	16
	Jerry Reuss	1974	16
	Pedro Borbon	1974	16
	Danny Frisella	1975	16
	Bill Bonham	1977	16
	Charlie Williams	1977	16
	Mark Littell	1978	16
	Dale Murray	1979	16
	Mike Parrott	1979	16
	Kent Tekulve	1980	16
	Dick Tidrow	1980	16
	Shane Rawley	1980	16
	Gene Garber	1982	16
	Todd Worrell	1986	16
	Greg Maddux	1988	16
61	Roy Face	1956	15
	Larry Sherry	1960	15
	Turk Farrell	1961	15
	Don Drysdale	1961	15
	Joe Gibbon	1963	15
	Casey Cox	1966	15
	Bill Hands	1967	15
	Juan Pizarro	1967	15
	Larry Jackson	1968	15
	Ted Abernathy	1968	15
	Jim Kaat	1969	15
	Fergie Jenkins	1969	15
	Frank Linzy	1969	15
	Wilbur Wood	1969	15
	Lew Krausse	1970	15
	Steve Arlin	1972	15
	Dave McNally	1972	15
	Gene Garber	1973	15
	Pedro Borbon	1973	15
	Goose Gossage	1975	15
	Steve Foucault	1975	15
	Dave Roberts	1978	15
	Gary Lavelle	1979	15
	Dennis Kinney	1980	15
	Jeff Reardon	1980	15
	Bob Shirley	1980	15
	Dan Quisenberry	1980	15
	Dick Tidrow	1981	15
	Gary Lucas	1981	15
	Rick Rhoden	1983	15
	Greg Minton	1986	15
	Tom Niedenfuer	1986	15
	Mark Williamson	1987	15
	Tim Leary	1989	15
	Jim Clancy	1989	15
	Mike Henneman	1989	15
97	52 tied with		14

Strikeouts

1	Matt Kilroy	1886	513
2	Toad Ramsey	1886	499
3	One Arm Daily	1884	483
4	Dupee Shaw	1884	451
5	Old Hoss Radbourn	1884	441
6	Charlie Buffinton	1884	417
7	Guy Hecker	1884	385
8	Nolan Ryan	1973	383
9	Sandy Koufax	1965	382
10	Bill Sweeney	1884	374
11	Pud Galvin	1884	369
12	Mark Baldwin	1889	368
13	Nolan Ryan	1974	367
14	Tim Keefe	1883	361
15	Toad Ramsey	1887	355
16	Rube Waddell	1904	349
17	Bob Feller	1946	348
18	Hardie Henderson	1884	346
19	Jim Whitney	1883	345
	Mickey Welch	1884	345
21	Jim McCormick	1884	343
22	Amos Rusie	1890	341
	Nolan Ryan	1977	341
24	Charlie Sweeney	1884	337
	Amos Rusie	1891	337
26	Tim Keefe	1888	333
27	Nolan Ryan	1972	329
28	Nolan Ryan	1976	327
29	Ed Morris	1886	326
30	Tony Mullane	1884	325
	Sam McDowell	1965	325
32	Lady Baldwin	1886	323
33	Curt Schilling	1997	319
34	Tim Keefe	1884	317
	Sandy Koufax	1966	317
36	Old Hoss Radbourn	1883	315
37	John Clarkson	1886	313
	Walter Johnson	1910	313
	J.R. Richard	1979	313
40	Bill Hutchison	1892	312
41	Steve Carlton	1972	310
42	Larry McKeon	1884	308
	John Clarkson	1885	308
	Mickey Lolich	1971	308
	Randy Johnson	1993	308
46	Sandy Koufax	1963	306
	Mike Scott	1986	306
48	Pedro Martinez	1997	305
49	Sam McDowell	1970	304
50	Walter Johnson	1912	303
	J.R. Richard	1978	303
52	Ed Morris	1884	302
	Rube Waddell	1903	302
54	Vida Blue	1971	301
	Nolan Ryan	1989	301
56	Ed Morris	1885	298
57	Randy Johnson	1995	294
58	Jack Lynch	1884	292
	Roger Clemens	1997	292
60	Tim Keefe	1886	291
	Sadie McMahon	1890	291
	Roger Clemens	1988	291
	Randy Johnson	1997	291
64	Jack Stivetts	1890	289
	Bill Hutchison	1890	289
	Tom Seaver	1971	289
67	Amos Rusie	1892	288
68	Rube Waddell	1905	287
69	Bobby Mathews	1884	286
	Bobby Mathews	1885	286
	Steve Carlton	1980	286
	Steve Carlton	1982	286
73	Billy Taylor	1884	284
	John Clarkson	1889	284
75	Dave Foutz	1886	283
	Sam McDowell	1968	283
	Tom Seaver	1970	283
78	Denny McLain	1968	280
79	Pud Galvin	1883	279
	Sam McDowell	1969	279
81	Bob Veale	1965	276
	Dwight Gooden	1984	276
	John Smoltz	1996	276
84	Hal Newhouser	1946	275
	Steve Carlton	1983	275
86	Fergie Jenkins	1970	274
	Bob Gibson	1970	274
	Mario Soto	1982	274
89	Fergie Jenkins	1969	273
90	Larry Corcoran	1884	272
	Mickey Welch	1886	272
	Ed Seward	1888	272
93	Mickey Lolich	1969	271
94	Jim Whitney	1884	270
	Bob Gibson	1965	270
	Nolan Ryan	1987	270
97	Ed Walsh	1908	269
	Sandy Koufax	1961	269
	Bob Gibson	1969	269
	Frank Tanana	1975	269

Strikeouts/9 Innings

(minimum 1 Inning Pitched/Tm Gm)

1	Randy Johnson	1995	12.35
2	Randy Johnson	1997	12.30
3	Nolan Ryan	1987	11.48
4	Dwight Gooden	1984	11.39
5	Pedro Martinez	1997	11.37
6	Nolan Ryan	1989	11.32
7	Curt Schilling	1997	11.29
8	Hideo Nomo	1995	11.10
9	Randy Johnson	1993	10.86
10	Sam McDowell	1965	10.71
11	Randy Johnson	1994	10.67
12	Nolan Ryan	1973	10.57
13	Nolan Ryan	1991	10.56
14	Sandy Koufax	1962	10.55
15	Nolan Ryan	1972	10.43
16	Sam McDowell	1966	10.42
17	Nolan Ryan	1976	10.35
18	Randy Johnson	1992	10.31
19	Nolan Ryan	1977	10.26
20	David Cone	1997	10.25
21	Sandy Koufax	1965	10.24
22	Nolan Ryan	1990	10.24
23	Randy Johnson	1991	10.19
24	Sandy Koufax	1960	10.13
25	Hideo Nomo	1997	10.11
26	Mike Scott	1986	10.00
27	Nolan Ryan	1978	9.97
28	Roger Clemens	1997	9.95
29	Nolan Ryan	1974	9.93
30	Roger Clemens	1988	9.92
31	David Cone	1990	9.91
32	J.R. Richard	1978	9.90
33	Andy Benes	1994	9.87
34	Nolan Ryan	1986	9.81
35	John Smoltz	1996	9.79
36	Herb Score	1955	9.70
37	Nolan Ryan	1984	9.65
38	J.R. Richard	1979	9.64
39	Mario Soto	1982	9.57
40	Tom Griffin	1969	9.56
41	Roger Clemens	1996	9.53
42	Jim Maloney	1963	9.53
43	Sid Fernandez	1985	9.51
44	Herb Score	1956	9.49
45	Sandy Koufax	1961	9.47
46	Sam McDowell	1968	9.47
47	David Cone	1992	9.41
48	Frank Tanana	1975	9.41
49	Don Wilson	1969	9.40
50	Bob Veale	1965	9.34
51	Nolan Ryan	1988	9.33
52	David Cone	1991	9.32
53	Luis Tiant	1967	9.22
54	Hideo Nomo	1996	9.22
55	Pedro Martinez	1996	9.22
56	Mark Langston	1986	9.21
57	Luis Tiant	1968	9.20
58	Dave Boswell	1966	9.19
59	Sam McDowell	1964	9.19
60	Sonny Siebert	1965	9.11
61	Sid Fernandez	1988	9.10
62	Tom Seaver	1971	9.08
63	Sid Fernandez	1990	9.08
64	Dennis Eckersley	1976	9.03
65	John Smoltz	1995	9.02
66	Nolan Ryan	1979	9.01
67	Sandy Koufax	1964	9.00
	Darryl Kile	1996	9.00
69	Sam McDowell	1967	8.99
70	Sam McDowell	1970	8.97
71	Bobby Witt	1990	8.96
72	Curt Schilling	1996	8.93
73	Jose Rijo	1994	8.93
74	Jim Maloney	1964	8.92
75	Alan Benes	1997	8.91
76	Andy Benes	1997	8.90
77	Jose Rijo	1988	8.89
78	Roger Clemens	1994	8.86
79	Sandy Koufax	1963	8.86
80	Pedro Martinez	1994	8.83
81	Sandy Koufax	1966	8.83
82	Kevin Appier	1996	8.82
83	Sam McDowell	1969	8.81
84	Sid Fernandez	1986	8.81
85	Nolan Ryan	1982	8.81
86	Todd Stottlemyre	1995	8.80
87	Tom Seaver	1970	8.76
88	Al Downing	1963	8.76
89	Bob Moose	1969	8.74
90	Mike Mussina	1997	8.73
91	Steve Carlton	1983	8.73
92	Dwight Gooden	1985	8.72
93	Steve Carlton	1982	8.71
94	Juan Pizarro	1961	8.69
95	Mickey Lolich	1969	8.69
96	Vida Blue	1971	8.68
97	One Arm Daily	1884	8.68
98	Mark Langston	1987	8.67
99	Bob Johnson	1970	8.66
100	Jim Maloney	1966	8.65

ERA

(minimum 1 Inning Pitched/Tm Gm)

1	Tim Keefe	1880	0.86
2	Dutch Leonard	1914	1.00
3	Three Finger Brown	1906	1.04
4	Bob Gibson	1968	1.12
5	Christy Mathewson	1909	1.14
6	Walter Johnson	1913	1.14
7	Jack Pfiester	1907	1.15
8	Addie Joss	1908	1.16
9	Carl Lundgren	1907	1.17
10	Denny Driscoll	1882	1.21
11	Pete Alexander	1915	1.22
12	George Bradley	1876	1.23
13	Cy Young	1908	1.26
14	Ed Walsh	1910	1.27
15	Walter Johnson	1918	1.27
16	Christy Mathewson	1905	1.28
17	Guy Hecker	1882	1.30
18	Jack Coombs	1910	1.30
19	Three Finger Brown	1909	1.31
20	Jack Taylor	1902	1.33
21	Walter Johnson	1910	1.36
22	George Bradley	1880	1.38
23	Old Hoss Radbourn	1884	1.38
24	Walter Johnson	1912	1.39
25	Three Finger Brown	1907	1.39
26	Harry Krause	1909	1.39
27	Ed Walsh	1909	1.41
28	Ed Walsh	1908	1.42
29	Ed Reulbach	1905	1.42
30	Orval Overall	1909	1.42
31	Christy Mathewson	1908	1.43
32	Fred Anderson	1917	1.44
33	Three Finger Brown	1908	1.47
34	Rube Waddell	1905	1.48
35	Joe Wood	1915	1.49
36	Walter Johnson	1919	1.49
37	Jack Pfiester	1906	1.51
38	Monte Ward	1878	1.51
39	Harry McCormick	1882	1.52
40	Doc White	1906	1.52
41	George McQuillan	1908	1.53
42	Dwight Gooden	1985	1.53
43	Eddie Cicotte	1917	1.53
44	Will White	1882	1.54
45	Cy Morgan	1910	1.55
46	Pete Alexander	1916	1.55
47	Walter Johnson	1915	1.55
48	Howie Camnitz	1908	1.56
49	Greg Maddux	1994	1.56
50	Jim Devlin	1876	1.56
51	Fred Toney	1915	1.58
52	Rube Marquard	1916	1.58
53	Eddie Cicotte	1913	1.58
54	Tim Keefe	1885	1.58
55	Chief Bender	1910	1.58
56	Barney Pelty	1906	1.59
57	Addie Joss	1904	1.59
58	Ed Walsh	1907	1.60
59	Luis Tiant	1968	1.60
60	Joe McGinnity	1904	1.61
61	Ray Collins	1910	1.62
62	Rube Waddell	1904	1.62
63	Howie Camnitz	1909	1.62
64	Cy Young	1901	1.62
65	Greg Maddux	1995	1.63
66	Spud Chandler	1943	1.64
67	Ernie Shore	1915	1.64
68	Silver King	1888	1.64
69	Ed Summers	1908	1.64
70	Dean Chance	1964	1.65
71	Walter Johnson	1908	1.65
72	Ed Reulbach	1906	1.65
73	Russ Ford	1910	1.65
74	Chief Bender	1909	1.66
75	Rube Foster	1914	1.66
76	Sam Leever	1907	1.66
77	Carl Hubbell	1933	1.66
78	Mickey Welch	1885	1.66
79	Candy Cummings	1876	1.67
80	Tommy Bond	1876	1.68
81	Orval Overall	1907	1.68
82	Joe Wood	1910	1.68
83	Ed Reulbach	1907	1.69
84	Claude Hendrix	1914	1.69
85	Nolan Ryan	1981	1.69
86	Jim McCormick	1878	1.69
87	Charlie Sweeney	1884	1.70
	Bill Burns	1908	1.70
89	Addie Joss	1909	1.71
90	Ed Killian	1909	1.71
91	Walter Johnson	1914	1.72
92	Ned Garvin	1904	1.72
93	Doc White	1909	1.72
94	Bill Doak	1914	1.72
95	Addie Joss	1906	1.72
	Pete Alexander	1919	1.72
97	Sandy Koufax	1966	1.73
98	Bob Ewing	1907	1.73
99	Vic Willis	1906	1.73
100	Sandy Koufax	1964	1.74

Component ERA

(minimum 1 Inning Pitched/Tm Gm)

1	Guy Hecker	1882	1.17
2	Addie Joss	1908	1.23
3	Tim Keefe	1880	1.25
4	Walter Johnson	1913	1.27
5	Ed Walsh	1910	1.27
6	Christy Mathewson	1909	1.29
7	Three Finger Brown	1908	1.31
8	Charlie Sweeney	1884	1.32
9	Pete Alexander	1915	1.33
10	Christy Mathewson	1908	1.34
11	George Bradley	1880	1.37
12	Ed Walsh	1908	1.38
13	Greg Maddux	1995	1.41
14	Dutch Leonard	1914	1.41
15	Russ Ford	1910	1.41
16	Three Finger Brown	1909	1.42
17	Guy Hecker	1884	1.43
18	Denny Driscoll	1882	1.44
19	Silver King	1888	1.44
20	Bob Gibson	1968	1.44
21	George Bradley	1876	1.45
22	Lady Baldwin	1885	1.47
23	Henry Boyle	1884	1.47
24	Cy Young	1908	1.48
25	Eddie Cicotte	1917	1.48
26	Cy Young	1905	1.49
27	Luis Tiant	1968	1.51
28	Ed Morris	1884	1.52
29	Ed Walsh	1909	1.52
30	Doc White	1906	1.52
31	Walter Johnson	1912	1.52
32	Babe Adams	1919	1.52
33	Larry Corcoran	1880	1.52
34	Tommy Bond	1876	1.53
35	Three Finger Brown	1906	1.53
36	Walter Johnson	1910	1.54
37	Christy Mathewson	1905	1.54
38	Sandy Koufax	1963	1.55
39	Jim Whitney	1884	1.55
40	Chief Bender	1910	1.56
41	Sandy Koufax	1965	1.56
42	Monte Ward	1880	1.56
43	Jack Chesbro	1904	1.56
44	Pete Alexander	1919	1.56
45	Tim Keefe	1888	1.56
46	Larry Corcoran	1882	1.58
47	Frank Smith	1908	1.58
48	Old Hoss Radbourn	1884	1.59
49	Greg Maddux	1994	1.59
50	Tim Keefe	1883	1.59
51	Claude Hendrix	1914	1.59
52	Addie Joss	1906	1.60
53	Reb Russell	1916	1.60
54	Three Finger Brown	1904	1.60
55	Frank Smith	1909	1.60
56	Tim Keefe	1884	1.60
57	Stan Coveleski	1917	1.61
58	Charlie Getzien	1884	1.61
59	Fred Anderson	1917	1.62
60	Tony Mullane	1883	1.63
61	Jack Pfiester	1906	1.63
62	Walter Johnson	1918	1.63
63	Don Sutton	1972	1.63
64	George McQuillan	1908	1.64
65	Howie Camnitz	1909	1.64
66	Lady Baldwin	1886	1.65
67	Addie Joss	1909	1.65
68	Perry Werden	1884	1.65
69	Harry Krause	1909	1.65
70	Tom Hughes	1915	1.65
71	Dave McNally	1968	1.66
72	Sandy Koufax	1964	1.66
73	Rube Waddell	1905	1.66
74	Roger Nelson	1972	1.66
75	Jack Lynch	1884	1.66
76	Walter Johnson	1908	1.66
77	Ed Morris	1885	1.67
78	Mike Scott	1986	1.67
79	Jack Pfiester	1907	1.67
80	Walter Johnson	1915	1.67
81	Ray Caldwell	1914	1.67
82	Charlie Buffinton	1888	1.67
83	Ed Seward	1888	1.67
84	Christy Mathewson	1907	1.67
85	Jim Devlin	1876	1.67
86	Chief Bender	1909	1.68
87	Ed Reulbach	1905	1.68
88	Ed Reulbach	1906	1.68
89	Orval Overall	1909	1.68
90	Carl Lundgren	1907	1.68
91	Bill Bernhard	1902	1.69
92	Ed Walsh	1906	1.69
93	John Clarkson	1885	1.69
94	Three Finger Brown	1907	1.70
95	Addie Joss	1903	1.70
96	Frank Owen	1904	1.70
97	Catfish Hunter	1972	1.70
98	Barney Pelty	1906	1.70
99	Tim Keefe	1885	1.71
100	Ron Guidry	1978	1.71

Sac Hits Allowed

1	Nap Rucker	1908	54
	Stan Coveleski	1921	54
	Eddie Rommel	1923	54
4	Tom Zachary	1926	53
5	Roy Wilkinson	1921	52
	George Uhle	1926	52
7	George Mullin	1904	51
	Frank Smith	1909	51
	Red Faber	1920	51
	Red Faber	1922	51
11	Oscar Jones	1904	50
	Rube Vickers	1908	50
13	Eppa Rixey	1920	49
	Jack Scott	1927	49
15	Ed Walsh	1907	48
	Kaiser Wilhelm	1908	48
	Slim Sallee	1914	48
	Jesse Haines	1920	48
	Eppa Rixey	1928	48
	Red Ruffing	1929	48
21	Russ Ford	1912	47
	Jack Quinn	1922	47
	Howard Ehmke	1926	47
24	Harry Howell	1908	46
	George Bell	1910	46
	Bill Doak	1915	46
	Elam Vangilder	1923	46
	Tommy Thomas	1927	46
	Jesse Petty	1927	46
30	George Mullin	1908	45
	Pol Perritt	1914	45
	Jesse Barnes	1920	45
	Red Faber	1921	45
	Ted Wingfield	1925	45
	Paul Zahniser	1926	45
	Bob Smith	1927	45
37	Roy Patterson	1903	44
	Ed Walsh	1908	44
	Dana Fillingim	1920	44
	Charlie Robertson	1922	44
	Alex Ferguson	1924	44
	Jesse Petty	1926	44
43	Harry Howell	1905	43
	George Mullin	1909	43
	Bob Harmon	1912	43
	Wilbur Cooper	1914	43
	Elmer Jacobs	1917	43
	Dickie Kerr	1921	43
	Howard Ehmke	1922	43
	Joe Genewich	1926	43
51	Beany Jacobson	1904	42
	Jack Townsend	1904	42
	George McQuillan	1908	42
	Lew Richie	1912	42
	Al Mamaux	1916	42
	Mike Prendergast	1918	42
	Dick Rudolph	1919	42
	George Smith	1920	42
	Eddie Rommel	1921	42
	Bob Hasty	1923	42
	Ray Benge	1930	42
62	Joe McGinnity	1904	41
	George Mullin	1905	41
	Charlie Smith	1907	41
	Jack Powell	1907	41
	George Mullin	1910	41
	Rube Marquard	1914	41
	Hippo Vaughn	1916	41
	Jim Bagby	1918	41
	Tom Zachary	1920	41
	Bob Hasty	1921	41
	Allen Sothoron	1921	41
	Eppa Rixey	1921	41
	George Uhle	1923	41
	Howard Ehmke	1923	41
	Ted Wingfield	1926	41
77	Ed Killian	1904	40
	Long Tom Hughes	1904	40
	Slim Sallee	1915	40
	Pete Schneider	1917	40
	Wilbur Cooper	1919	40
	Ted Blankenship	1923	40
	Joe Bush	1923	40
	Burleigh Grimes	1926	40
	Hal Wiltse	1927	40
	Ray Kremer	1928	40
87	Harry McIntire	1905	39
	Jack Chesbro	1905	39
	Jack Chesbro	1908	39
	Nap Rucker	1909	39
	George Suggs	1912	39
	Gene Dale	1915	39
	Walter Johnson	1916	39
	Ted Lyons	1924	39
	Howard Ehmke	1925	39
	Milt Gaston	1926	39
	Slim Harriss	1927	39
	Garland Buckeye	1927	39
	Burleigh Grimes	1928	39
	Carmen Hill	1928	39

Sac Flies Allowed

1	Arnie Portocarrero	1954	17
	Larry Gura	1983	17
	Jaime Navarro	1993	17
4	Charlie Hough	1991	16
5	Doc Medich	1975	15
	Randy Lerch	1979	15
	Dave Stewart	1991	15
8	Dave Morehead	1964	14
	Jim Palmer	1976	14
	Nolan Ryan	1978	14
	Rick Reuschel	1980	14
	Charlie Hough	1987	14
	Rick Reuschel	1988	14
	Rich DeLucia	1991	14
	David Wells	1996	14
	Jaime Navarro	1997	14
17	Johnny Klippstein	1954	13
	Bob Miller	1954	13
	Bob Lemon	1954	13
	Billy O'Dell	1958	13
	Gaylord Perry	1971	13
	Bert Blyleven	1973	13
	Rick Reuschel	1976	13
	Catfish Hunter	1976	13
	Lary Sorensen	1978	13
	Mark Lemongello	1978	13
	Bob Forsch	1979	13
	Mike Krukow	1980	13
	Jack Morris	1980	13
	Fergie Jenkins	1982	13
	Bill Gullickson	1986	13
	Jim Deshaies	1988	13
	Mike Witt	1989	13
	Ron Darling	1989	13
	Randy Johnson	1989	13
	Jaime Navarro	1992	13
	Scott Erickson	1993	13
	Dennis Springer	1997	13
39	George O'Donnell	1954	12
	Bob Grim	1954	12
	Vern Law	1954	12
	Erv Palica	1955	12
	Billy Hoeft	1956	12
	Early Wynn	1956	12
	Camilo Pascual	1957	12
	Bob Rush	1957	12
	Joe McClain	1961	12
	Bob Shaw	1961	12
	Tony Cloninger	1966	12
	Casey Cox	1970	12
	Dave Roberts	1971	12
	Mickey Lolich	1971	12
	Clyde Wright	1971	12
	Denny McLain	1971	12
	Jim Perry	1971	12
	Pete Broberg	1972	12
	Vida Blue	1974	12
	Rollie Fingers	1974	12
	Gaylord Perry	1974	12
	Dick Tidrow	1974	12
	Fergie Jenkins	1974	12
	Jerry Koosman	1974	12
	Carl Morton	1974	12
	Wilbur Wood	1974	12
	Steve Carlton	1975	12
	Dennis Leonard	1976	12
	Jim Slaton	1976	12
	Bart Johnson	1976	12
	Paul Hartzell	1977	12
	Tom Seaver	1978	12
	Jack Billingham	1978	12
	Vida Blue	1979	12
	Dennis Martinez	1979	12
	Ken Kravec	1979	12
	John Candelaria	1980	12
	Mike Flanagan	1980	12
	Ron Guidry	1980	12
	Larry Gura	1980	12
	Rick Langford	1980	12
	John Montefusco	1982	12
	Rich Gale	1982	12
	Jim Clancy	1983	12
	Doyle Alexander	1984	12
	Ron Romanick	1984	12
	Joe Niekro	1985	12
	Nolan Ryan	1985	12
	Andy Hawkins	1985	12
	Ken Schrom	1986	12
	Tom Browning	1986	12
	Mike Boddicker	1988	12
	Jim Deshaies	1990	12
	Terry Mulholland	1990	12
	Cal Eldred	1993	12
	Steve Sparks	1995	12
	Dave Burba	1996	12
96	86 tied with		11

Hit Batsmen

1	Joe McGinnity	1900	41
2	Gus Weyhing	1887	37
	Ed Doheny	1899	37
4	Will White	1884	35
5	Tony Mullane	1884	32
	Tony Mullane	1887	32
	Cy Seymour	1898	32
	Chick Fraser	1901	32
9	Vic Willis	1898	30
	Vic Willis	1899	30
11	Chick Fraser	1898	29
12	Win Mercer	1897	28
	Jack Taylor	1897	28
	Joe McGinnity	1899	28
	Gus Weyhing	1899	28
16	Will White	1885	27
	Jack Easton	1890	27
	Pink Hawley	1897	27
	Willie Sudhoff	1898	27
20	Gus Shallix	1884	26
	Egyptian Healy	1890	26
	Jack Warhop	1909	26
23	Jack Taylor	1898	25
	Chief Bender	1903	25
25	Ed Seward	1887	24
	Tom Sullivan	1888	24
	Darby O'Brien	1889	24
	Frank Knauss	1890	24
	Chick Fraser	1897	24
	Wiley Piatt	1899	24
	Nixey Callahan	1899	24
	Eddie Plank	1905	24
	Otto Hess	1906	24
34	Fred Klobedanz	1897	23
	Frank Bates	1899	23
	Bill Carrick	1899	23
	Bill Magee	1899	23
	Eddie Plank	1903	23
	Jake Weimer	1907	23
	Howard Ehmke	1922	23
41	Al Atkinson	1886	22
	Mike Morrison	1887	22
	Doc McJames	1897	22
	Joe Corbett	1897	22
	Red Donahue	1897	22
	Pete Dowling	1898	22
	Pink Hawley	1898	22
	Jack Taylor	1899	22
	Willie Sudhoff	1899	22
	Chick Fraser	1899	22
	Jim Hughey	1899	22
	Ed Doheny	1900	22
	Nixey Callahan	1900	22
	Cy Morgan	1909	22
55	Jumbo McGinnis	1886	21
	Cy Seymour	1897	21
	Cy Seymour	1899	21
	Doc Newton	1901	21
	Joe McGinnity	1901	21
	Pete Dowling	1901	21
	Jack Chesbro	1902	21
	Henry Schmidt	1903	21
	Harry McIntire	1909	21
	Cy Morgan	1911	21
	Tom Murphy	1969	21
66	Fleury Sullivan	1884	20
	Bobby Mathews	1885	20
	Kid Madden	1887	20
	Billy Crowell	1887	20
	Matt Kilroy	1887	20
	Al Mays	1887	20
	Hank Gastright	1890	20
	Charlie Sprague	1890	20
	Bill Hill	1897	20
	Ed Doheny	1898	20
	Clark Griffith	1898	20
	Bert Cunningham	1898	20
	Pink Hawley	1899	20
	Win Mercer	1900	20
	Pink Hawley	1900	20
	Bill Carrick	1901	20
	Barney Pelty	1904	20
	Casey Patten	1904	20
	Harry McIntire	1905	20
	Ed Summers	1908	20
	Harry McIntire	1908	20
	Harry Coveleski	1915	20
	Howard Ehmke	1923	20
	Walter Johnson	1923	20
	Don Drysdale	1961	20
91	22 tied with		19

Wild Pitches

1	Bill Stemmeyer	1886	63
2	Hardie Henderson	1885	55
3	Tony Mullane	1886	51
	Mickey Welch	1886	51
5	Matt Kilroy	1886	50
6	Will White	1879	49
7	John Harkins	1884	48
8	Henry Gruber	1890	47
9	Jim Whitney	1881	46
10	George Bradley	1879	43
	Bob Emslie	1884	43
	John Kirby	1886	43
13	Billy Serad	1884	42
14	Mark Baldwin	1887	41
15	Will White	1878	40
	Ed Daily	1885	40
	Egyptian Healy	1886	40
	Tim Keefe	1886	40
19	George Bradley	1877	39
	Mickey Welch	1884	39
	John Harkins	1885	39
	Mickey Welch	1885	39
	Al Mays	1886	39
	Jack Lynch	1886	39
	Egyptian Healy	1887	39
	Mark Baldwin	1889	39
	Ed Crane	1890	39
28	Billy Serad	1885	38
	Frank Foreman	1889	38
30	Terry Larkin	1878	37
	Jim Whitney	1883	37
	Tim Keefe	1887	37
	Gus Weyhing	1889	37
34	Old Hoss Radbourn	1883	36
	Amos Rusie	1890	36
36	Will White	1880	35
	Tim Keefe	1885	35
	Toad Ramsey	1886	35
	Stump Wiedman	1886	35
	Park Swartzel	1889	35
41	George Bradley	1876	34
	Blondie Purcell	1879	34
	Old Hoss Radbourn	1884	34
	Ed Cushman	1885	34
	Old Hoss Radbourn	1885	34
	Cyclone Miller	1886	34
47	Tip O'Neill	1883	33
	Ed Begley	1884	33
	Charlie Ferguson	1884	33
	John Clarkson	1888	33
	Matt Kilroy	1889	33
	Jack Stivetts	1890	33
53	Monte Ward	1881	32
	Frank Mountain	1882	32
	Dupee Shaw	1885	32
	Jim Whitney	1885	32
	Adonis Terry	1886	32
	Hank Gastright	1890	32
59	Harry McCormick	1879	31
	Pud Galvin	1881	31
	Hank O'Day	1887	31
	George Haddock	1890	31
	Mark Baldwin	1890	31
	Toad Ramsey	1890	31
	Ed Crane	1892	31
66	Jim McCormick	1879	30
	Bill Hart	1886	30
	Harry Staley	1889	30
	Kid Nichols	1890	30
	Red Ames	1905	30
71	Joe Blong	1877	29
	Monte Ward	1879	29
	Lee Richmond	1880	29
	Jim Whitney	1882	29
	Sam Moffett	1884	29
	Jim Whitney	1886	29
	Red Ehret	1889	29
	Silver King	1889	29
	Bob Barr	1890	29
	Tony Mullane	1893	29
81	Pud Galvin	1883	28
	Charlie Buffinton	1885	28
	Jack Lynch	1885	28
	Jocko Flynn	1886	28
	Ed Morris	1886	28
	Tom Sullivan	1888	28
87	Larry Corcoran	1881	27
	Mickey Welch	1883	27
	Larry Corcoran	1884	27
	Pete Conway	1886	27
	Hank Gastright	1889	27
	Darby O'Brien	1889	27
	Bill Hutchison	1890	27
	Adonis Terry	1890	27
	Chick Fraser	1896	27
	Tony Cloninger	1966	27
97	11 tied with		26

Balks

1	Dave Stewart	1988	16
2	John Dopson	1989	15
3	Bob Welch	1988	13
4	John Candelaria	1988	12
	Jose Guzman	1988	12
6	Steve Carlton	1979	11
	Rod Scurry	1988	11
	Jack Morris	1988	11
	Mike Birkbeck	1988	11
10	Charlie Hough	1988	10
	Pascual Perez	1988	10
	Dennis Martinez	1988	10
	David Cone	1988	10
14	Steve Carlton	1982	9
	Steve Carlton	1983	9
	Charlie Hough	1987	9
	Bob Walk	1988	9
	Sid Fernandez	1988	9
	Gene Walter	1988	9
	Pedro Astacio	1993	9
21	Bob Shaw	1963	8
	Bill Bonham	1974	8
	Frank Tanana	1978	8
	Mike Jackson	1987	8
	Les Lancaster	1987	8
	Dennis Lamp	1988	8
	Rick Mahler	1988	8
	Mario Soto	1988	8
	Rick Honeycutt	1988	8
	Bobby Witt	1988	8
	Chuck Finley	1988	8
	Joe Magrane	1988	8
	Tom Candiotti	1989	8
34	Steve Carlton	1975	7
	Jerry Koosman	1975	7
	Steve Carlton	1977	7
	Steve Carlton	1978	7
	Larry Christenson	1978	7
	Paul Moskau	1978	7
	Steve Carlton	1980	7
	Bud Black	1982	7
	Andy McGaffigan	1983	7
	Steve Carlton	1984	7
	Dwight Gooden	1984	7
	Jim Deshaies	1986	7
	Atlee Hammaker	1987	7
	Kevin Gross	1987	7
	Greg Maddux	1987	7
	Joe Magrane	1987	7
	Nolan Ryan	1988	7
	Dave LaPoint	1988	7
	Bobby Ojeda	1988	7
	Steve Trout	1988	7
	Jerry Reed	1988	7
	Tom Candiotti	1988	7
	Jeff Russell	1988	7
	Kevin Gross	1988	7
	Roger Clemens	1988	7
	Eric Plunk	1988	7
	Jeff Sellers	1988	7
	Mike Dunne	1988	7
	Pete Smith	1988	7
	Pete Smith	1989	7
	Randy Johnson	1989	7
	Bud Black	1992	7
	Trevor Wilson	1992	7
67	42 tied with		6

Opponent Average

(minimum 1 Inning Pitched/Tm Gm)

1	Luis Tiant	1968	.168
2	Nolan Ryan	1972	.171
3	Nolan Ryan	1991	.172
4	Ed Reulbach	1906	.175
5	Dutch Leonard	1914	.179
6	Sandy Koufax	1965	.179
7	Sid Fernandez	1985	.181
8	Dave McNally	1968	.182
9	Hideo Nomo	1995	.182
10	Tommy Byrne	1949	.183
11	Pedro Martinez	1997	.184
12	Al Downing	1963	.184
13	Bob Gibson	1968	.184
14	Sam McDowell	1965	.185
15	Carl Lundgren	1907	.185
16	Herb Score	1956	.186
17	Mike Scott	1986	.186
18	Tim Keefe	1880	.187
19	Nolan Ryan	1989	.187
20	Ed Walsh	1910	.187
21	Mario Soto	1980	.187
22	Walter Johnson	1913	.187
23	Nolan Ryan	1981	.188
24	Russ Ford	1910	.188
25	Nolan Ryan	1986	.188
26	Nolan Ryan	1990	.188
27	Floyd Youmans	1986	.188
28	Sam McDowell	1966	.188
29	Guy Hecker	1882	.188
30	Sandy Koufax	1963	.189
31	Sam McDowell	1968	.189
32	Don Sutton	1972	.189
33	Catfish Hunter	1972	.189
34	Vida Blue	1971	.189
35	Nolan Ryan	1974	.190
36	Andy Messersmith	1969	.190
37	Joe Horlen	1964	.190
38	Sid Fernandez	1988	.191
39	Pete Alexander	1915	.191
40	Sandy Koufax	1964	.191
41	Adonis Terry	1888	.191
42	Bob Turley	1955	.193
43	Nolan Ryan	1977	.193
44	Fred Beebe	1908	.193
45	Charlie Sweeney	1884	.193
46	Stan Coveleski	1917	.193
47	Ron Guidry	1978	.193
48	Bob Turley	1957	.194
49	Randy Johnson	1997	.194
50	Herb Score	1955	.194
51	Three Finger Brown	1908	.195
52	Nolan Ryan	1976	.195
53	Nolan Ryan	1983	.195
54	Tim Keefe	1888	.195
55	Dean Chance	1964	.195
56	Roger Clemens	1986	.195
57	Walter Johnson	1912	.196
58	Roger Nelson	1972	.196
59	J.R. Richard	1978	.196
60	Pascual Perez	1988	.196
61	Greg Maddux	1995	.197
62	Jack Pfiester	1906	.197
63	Jeff Robinson	1988	.197
64	Lady Baldwin	1885	.197
65	Silver King	1888	.197
66	Jose DeLeon	1989	.197
67	Dave Boswell	1966	.197
68	Sandy Koufax	1962	.197
69	Addie Joss	1908	.197
70	Sonny Siebert	1968	.198
71	Rube Waddell	1905	.198
72	Sid Fernandez	1989	.198
73	Toad Ramsey	1886	.198
74	Larry Cheney	1916	.198
75	Wayne Simpson	1970	.198
76	Orval Overall	1909	.198
77	Gary Peters	1967	.199
78	Larry Corcoran	1880	.199
79	Ed Seward	1888	.199
80	Three Finger Brown	1904	.199
81	Christy Mathewson	1909	.200
82	Nolan Ryan	1987	.200
83	Denny McLain	1968	.200
84	Larry Corcoran	1882	.200
85	Bobby Bolin	1968	.200
	Jim Palmer	1969	.200
	Sid Fernandez	1990	.200
88	Christy Mathewson	1908	.200
89	Spec Shea	1947	.200
90	Art Fromme	1909	.201
91	Babe Ruth	1916	.201
92	Tony Mullane	1892	.201
93	Randy Johnson	1995	.201
94	Willie Mitchell	1913	.201
95	Dwight Gooden	1985	.201
96	Cannonball Titcomb	1888	.201
97	Hal Newhouser	1946	.201
98	Ed Reulbach	1905	.201
99	Jack Coombs	1910	.201
100	Curt Schilling	1992	.201

Opponent OBP

(minimum 1 Inning Pitched/Tm Gm)

1	Guy Hecker	1882	.199
2	Charlie Sweeney	1884	.211
3	Henry Boyle	1884	.215
4	George Bradley	1880	.217
5	Walter Johnson	1913	.217
6	Denny Driscoll	1882	.218
7	Addie Joss	1908	.218
8	Tim Keefe	1880	.222
9	Jim Whitney	1884	.223
10	Silver King	1888	.224
11	George Bradley	1876	.224
12	Greg Maddux	1995	.224
13	Christy Mathewson	1908	.225
14	Guy Hecker	1884	.226
15	Ed Walsh	1910	.226
16	Tommy Bond	1876	.227
17	Sandy Koufax	1965	.227
18	Lady Baldwin	1885	.228
19	Christy Mathewson	1909	.228
20	Juan Marichal	1966	.230
21	Sandy Koufax	1963	.230
22	Dave McNally	1968	.232
23	Monte Ward	1880	.232
24	Three Finger Brown	1908	.232
25	Ed Walsh	1908	.232
26	Bob Gibson	1968	.233
27	Luis Tiant	1968	.233
28	Pete Alexander	1915	.234
29	Larry Corcoran	1882	.234
30	Roger Nelson	1972	.234
31	Old Hoss Radbourn	1884	.234
32	Ed Morris	1884	.234
33	Jim Devlin	1876	.235
34	Perry Werden	1884	.235
35	Jack Lynch	1884	.236
36	Larry Corcoran	1880	.236
37	Charlie Getzien	1884	.237
38	John Clarkson	1885	.239
39	Juan Marichal	1965	.239
40	Three Finger Brown	1909	.239
41	Cy Young	1905	.239
42	Fred Corey	1880	.239
43	Don Sutton	1972	.240
44	Tim Keefe	1884	.240
45	Sandy Koufax	1964	.240
46	Babe Adams	1919	.241
47	Cy Young	1908	.241
48	Catfish Hunter	1972	.241
49	Tim Keefe	1883	.242
50	Mike Scott	1986	.242
51	Tony Mullane	1883	.242
52	Denny McLain	1968	.243
53	Pete Conway	1888	.243
54	Harry McCormick	1882	.243
55	Tim Keefe	1888	.243
56	Lady Baldwin	1886	.243
57	Greg Maddux	1994	.243
58	Old Hoss Radbourn	1883	.244
59	Charlie Ferguson	1886	.244
60	Charlie Buffinton	1888	.244
61	Charlie Buffinton	1884	.244
62	Russ Ford	1910	.245
63	Dutch Leonard	1914	.245
64	Pete Alexander	1919	.245
65	Christy Mathewson	1905	.245
66	Bobby Mathews	1882	.246
67	Pud Galvin	1884	.246
68	Old Hoss Radbourn	1882	.246
69	Billy Taylor	1884	.247
70	Sam Weaver	1878	.247
71	Warren Hacker	1952	.247
72	Charlie Geggus	1884	.247
73	Jim McCormick	1880	.247
74	Ed Morris	1885	.247
75	Fred Goldsmith	1880	.247
76	Dupee Shaw	1884	.247
77	Addie Joss	1906	.247
78	Bob Caruthers	1888	.248
79	Eddie Cicotte	1917	.248
80	Jack Chesbro	1904	.248
81	Ed Seward	1888	.248
82	Walter Johnson	1912	.248
83	Joe Horlen	1964	.248
84	John Tudor	1985	.249
85	Will White	1883	.249
86	Doc White	1906	.249
87	John Clarkson	1884	.249
88	Ron Guidry	1978	.249
89	Cy Young	1904	.249
90	Henry Gruber	1888	.249
91	Pedro Martinez	1997	.250
92	Will White	1882	.250
93	One Arm Daily	1884	.250
94	Terry Larkin	1879	.250
95	Monte Ward	1879	.250
96	Addie Joss	1903	.250
97	Monte Ward	1878	.251
98	Candy Cummings	1876	.251
99	Jim Whitney	1883	.251
100	Claude Hendrix	1914	.251

1000 Leaders: Single Season Pitching

Single Season Pitching Leaders—20th Century

Wins

Rank	Pitcher	Year	W
1	Jack Chesbro	1904	41
2	Ed Walsh	1908	40
3	Christy Mathewson	1908	37
4	Walter Johnson	1913	36
5	Joe McGinnity	1904	35
6	Joe Wood	1912	34
7	Cy Young	1901	33
	Christy Mathewson	1904	33
	Walter Johnson	1912	33
	Pete Alexander	1916	33
11	Cy Young	1902	32
12	Joe McGinnity	1903	31
	Christy Mathewson	1905	31
	Jack Coombs	1910	31
	Pete Alexander	1915	31
	Jim Bagby	1920	31
	Lefty Grove	1931	31
	Denny McLain	1968	31
19	Christy Mathewson	1903	30
	Pete Alexander	1917	30
	Dizzy Dean	1934	30
22	Three Finger Brown	1908	29
	George Mullin	1909	29
	Claude Hendrix	1914	29
	Eddie Cicotte	1919	29
	Hal Newhouser	1944	29
27	Joe McGinnity	1900	28
	Jack Chesbro	1902	28
	Cy Young	1903	28
	Pete Alexander	1911	28
	Jack Coombs	1911	28
	Walter Johnson	1914	28
	Eddie Cicotte	1917	28
	Dazzy Vance	1924	28
	Lefty Grove	1930	28
	Dizzy Dean	1935	28
	Robin Roberts	1952	28
38	Togie Pittinger	1902	27
	Vic Willis	1902	27
	Rube Waddell	1905	27
	Joe McGinnity	1906	27
	Al Orth	1906	27
	Addie Joss	1907	27
	Doc White	1907	27
	Three Finger Brown	1909	27
	Christy Mathewson	1910	27
	Ed Walsh	1911	27
	Ed Walsh	1912	27
	Tom Seaton	1913	27
	Pete Alexander	1914	27
	Walter Johnson	1915	27
	Pete Alexander	1920	27
	Urban Shocker	1921	27
	Carl Mays	1921	27
	Eddie Rommel	1922	27
	Dolf Luque	1923	27
	George Uhle	1926	27
	Bucky Walters	1939	27
	Bob Feller	1940	27
	Dizzy Trout	1944	27
	Don Newcombe	1956	27
	Sandy Koufax	1966	27
	Steve Carlton	1972	27
	Bob Welch	1990	27
65	Joe McGinnity	1901	26
	Eddie Plank	1904	26
	Cy Young	1904	26
	Three Finger Brown	1906	26
	Russ Ford	1910	26
	Christy Mathewson	1911	26
	Larry Cheney	1912	26
	Rube Marquard	1912	26
	Eddie Plank	1912	26
	Bill James	1914	26
	Jeff Tesreau	1914	26
	Dick Rudolph	1914	26
	Jack Quinn	1914	26
	Carl Mays	1920	26
	Joe Bush	1922	26
	George Uhle	1923	26
	Charlie Root	1927	26
	General Crowder	1932	26
	Lefty Gomez	1934	26
	Carl Hubbell	1936	26
	Hal Newhouser	1946	26
	Bob Feller	1946	26
	Sandy Koufax	1965	26
	Juan Marichal	1968	26
89	44 tied with		25

Losses

Rank	Pitcher	Year	L
1	Vic Willis	1905	29
2	Luther Taylor	1901	27
	George Bell	1910	27
	Paul Derringer	1933	27
5	Pete Dowling	1901	26
	Jack Townsend	1904	26
	Gus Dorner	1906	26
	Bob Groom	1909	26
9	Patsy Flaherty	1903	25
	Oscar Jones	1904	25
	Vic Willis	1904	25
	Harry McIntire	1905	25
	Fred Glade	1905	25
	Irv Young	1906	25
	Stoney McGlynn	1907	25
	Bugs Raymond	1908	25
	Walter Johnson	1909	25
	Scott Perry	1920	25
	Red Ruffing	1928	25
	Ben Cantwell	1935	25
21	Long Tom Hughes	1904	24
	Chick Fraser	1904	24
	Cliff Curtis	1910	24
	Joe Bush	1916	24
	Pat Caraway	1931	24
	Sam Gray	1931	24
	Roger Craig	1962	24
	Jack Fisher	1965	24
29	Long Tom Hughes	1901	23
	Beany Jacobson	1904	23
	George Mullin	1904	23
	Casey Patten	1904	23
	Jack Cronin	1904	23
	Orval Overall	1905	23
	Kaiser Wilhelm	1905	23
	Vive Lindaman	1906	23
	Irv Young	1907	23
	George Ferguson	1909	23
	Buster Brown	1910	23
	Red Ames	1914	23
	Elmer Myers	1916	23
	Lee Meadows	1916	23
	Rollie Naylor	1920	23
	Eddie Rommel	1921	23
	Dolf Luque	1922	23
46	Bill Carrick	1900	22
	Bill Carrick	1901	22
	Casey Patten	1903	22
	Togie Pittinger	1903	22
	Al Orth	1903	22
	Casey Patten	1905	22
	Harry Howell	1905	22
	Big Jeff Pfeffer	1906	22
	Joe Lake	1908	22
	Kaiser Wilhelm	1908	22
	Lefty Tyler	1912	22
	Dan Griner	1913	22
	Rube Marquard	1914	22
	John Wyckoff	1915	22
	Jack Quinn	1915	22
	Eppa Rixey	1920	22
	Red Ruffing	1929	22
	Si Johnson	1934	22
	Hugh Mulcahy	1940	22
	Art Ditmar	1956	22
	Robin Roberts	1957	22
	Roger Craig	1963	22
	Dick Ellsworth	1966	22
	Denny McLain	1971	22
	Bill Bonham	1974	22
	Randy Jones	1974	22
	Steve Rogers	1974	22
73	48 tied with		21

Games Started

Rank	Pitcher	Year	GS
1	Jack Chesbro	1904	51
2	Ed Walsh	1908	49
	Wilbur Wood	1972	49
4	Joe McGinnity	1903	48
	Wilbur Wood	1973	48
6	Vic Willis	1902	46
	Christy Mathewson	1904	46
	Rube Waddell	1904	46
	Ed Walsh	1907	46
	Dave Davenport	1915	46
11	Jack Powell	1904	45
	Pete Alexander	1916	45
	Mickey Lolich	1971	45
14	George Mullin	1904	44
	Joe McGinnity	1904	44
	Christy Mathewson	1908	44
	Pete Alexander	1917	44
	George Uhle	1923	44
	Phil Niekro	1979	44
20	Luther Taylor	1901	43
	Joe McGinnity	1901	43
	Cy Young	1902	43
	Eddie Plank	1904	43
	Vic Willis	1904	43
	Cy Falkenberg	1914	43
	Dick Rudolph	1915	43
	Wilbur Wood	1975	43
	Phil Niekro	1977	43
29	Noodles Hahn	1901	42
	Bill Dinneen	1902	42
	Christy Mathewson	1903	42
	Irv Young	1905	42
	Jack Chesbro	1906	42
	George Mullin	1907	42
	George McQuillan	1908	42
	Walter Johnson	1910	42
	Jack Quinn	1914	42
	Pete Alexander	1915	42
	Pete Schneider	1917	42
	Fred Toney	1917	42
	Bob Feller	1946	42
	Bob Friend	1956	42
	Jack Sanford	1963	42
	Don Drysdale	1963	42
	Jim Kaat	1965	42
	Don Drysdale	1965	42
	Fergie Jenkins	1969	42
	Wilbur Wood	1971	42
	Stan Bahnsen	1973	42
	Mickey Lolich	1973	42
	Wilbur Wood	1974	42
	Phil Niekro	1978	42
53	Bill Carrick	1900	41
	Cy Young	1901	41
	Oscar Jones	1904	41
	Cy Young	1904	41
	George Mullin	1905	41
	Eddie Plank	1905	41
	Vic Willis	1905	41
	Irv Young	1906	41
	Frank Smith	1909	41
	Bob Harmon	1911	41
	Ed Walsh	1912	41
	Jeff Tesreau	1914	41
	Babe Ruth	1916	41
	Bill Voiselle	1944	41
	Robin Roberts	1953	41
	Don Drysdale	1962	41
	Sandy Koufax	1965	41
	Jim Kaat	1966	41
	Jim Bunning	1966	41
	Sandy Koufax	1966	41
	Denny McLain	1968	41
	Don Sutton	1969	41
	Bill Hands	1969	41
	Denny McLain	1969	41
	Claude Osteen	1969	41
	Gaylord Perry	1970	41
	Stan Bahnsen	1972	41
	Steve Carlton	1972	41
	Mickey Lolich	1972	41
	Gaylord Perry	1973	41
	Jim Bibby	1974	41
	Nolan Ryan	1974	41
	Fergie Jenkins	1974	41
	Catfish Hunter	1974	41
	Joe Coleman	1974	41
	Mickey Lolich	1974	41
	Jim Kaat	1975	41
90	52 tied with		40

Complete Games

Rank	Pitcher	Year	CG
1	Jack Chesbro	1904	48
2	Vic Willis	1902	45
3	Joe McGinnity	1903	44
4	George Mullin	1904	42
	Ed Walsh	1908	42
6	Noodles Hahn	1901	41
	Cy Young	1902	41
	Irv Young	1905	41
9	Cy Young	1904	40
10	Joe McGinnity	1901	39
	Bill Dinneen	1902	39
	Jack Taylor	1904	39
	Vic Willis	1904	39
	Rube Waddell	1904	39
15	Cy Young	1901	38
	Oscar Jones	1904	38
	Joe McGinnity	1904	38
	Jack Powell	1904	38
	Walter Johnson	1910	38
	Pete Alexander	1916	38
21	Luther Taylor	1901	37
	Christy Mathewson	1903	37
	Eddie Plank	1904	37
	Casey Patten	1904	37
	Bill Dinneen	1904	37
	Irv Young	1906	37
	Ed Walsh	1907	37
	Frank Smith	1909	37
29	Christy Mathewson	1901	36
	Wild Bill Donovan	1901	36
	Togie Pittinger	1902	36
	Jack Powell	1902	36
	Al Orth	1902	36
	Vic Willis	1905	36
	Al Orth	1906	36
	Walter Johnson	1911	36
	Pete Alexander	1915	36
	Walter Johnson	1916	36
	Bob Feller	1946	36
40	Roscoe Miller	1901	35
	Chick Fraser	1901	35
	Joe McGinnity	1902	35
	Noodles Hahn	1902	35
	Togie Pittinger	1903	35
	Togie Pittinger	1904	35
	Bill Bernhard	1904	35
	Kid Nichols	1904	35
	George Mullin	1905	35
	Eddie Plank	1905	35
	Harry Howell	1905	35
	Chick Fraser	1905	35
	George Mullin	1906	35
	George Mullin	1907	35
	Jack Coombs	1910	35
	Joe Wood	1912	35
	Walter Johnson	1915	35
	Babe Ruth	1917	35
	Pete Alexander	1917	35
59	Pink Hawley	1900	34
	Bill Carrick	1901	34
	Doc White	1902	34
	Noodles Hahn	1903	34
	Wild Bill Donovan	1903	34
	Rube Waddell	1903	34
	Cy Young	1903	34
	Frank Owen	1904	34
	Jack Taylor	1905	34
	Addie Joss	1907	34
	Christy Mathewson	1908	34
	Walter Johnson	1912	34
	Claude Hendrix	1914	34
72	30 tied with		33

Shutouts

1	Pete Alexander	1916	16
2	Jack Coombs	1910	13
	Bob Gibson	1968	13
4	Pete Alexander	1915	12
5	Ed Walsh	1908	11
	Christy Mathewson	1908	11
	Walter Johnson	1913	11
	Sandy Koufax	1963	11
	Dean Chance	1964	11
10	Cy Young	1904	10
	Ed Walsh	1906	10
	Joe Wood	1912	10
	Dave Davenport	1915	10
	Carl Hubbell	1933	10
	Mort Cooper	1942	10
	Bob Feller	1946	10
	Bob Lemon	1948	10
	Juan Marichal	1965	10
	Jim Palmer	1975	10
	John Tudor	1985	10
21	Joe McGinnity	1904	9
	Three Finger Brown	1906	9
	Addie Joss	1906	9
	Three Finger Brown	1908	9
	Addie Joss	1908	9
	Orval Overall	1909	9
	Pete Alexander	1913	9
	Walter Johnson	1914	9
	Cy Falkenberg	1914	9
	Babe Ruth	1916	9
	Stan Coveleski	1917	9
	Pete Alexander	1919	9
	Bill Lee	1938	9
	Bob Porterfield	1953	9
	Luis Tiant	1968	9
	Denny McLain	1969	9
	Don Sutton	1972	9
	Nolan Ryan	1972	9
	Bert Blyleven	1973	9
	Ron Guidry	1978	9
41	Christy Mathewson	1902	8
	Jack Chesbro	1902	8
	Rube Waddell	1904	8
	Ed Killian	1905	8
	Christy Mathewson	1905	8
	Lefty Leifield	1906	8
	Rube Waddell	1906	8
	Orval Overall	1907	8
	Eddie Plank	1907	8
	Christy Mathewson	1907	8
	Ed Walsh	1909	8
	Three Finger Brown	1909	8
	Christy Mathewson	1909	8
	Russ Ford	1910	8
	Walter Johnson	1910	8
	Reb Russell	1913	8
	Jeff Tesreau	1914	8
	Al Mamaux	1915	8
	Jeff Tesreau	1915	8
	Joe Bush	1916	8
	Jim Bagby	1917	8
	Pete Alexander	1917	8
	Walter Johnson	1917	8
	Carl Mays	1918	8
	Lefty Tyler	1918	8
	Hippo Vaughn	1918	8
	Walter Johnson	1918	8
	Babe Adams	1920	8
	Hal Newhouser	1945	8
	Steve Barber	1961	8
	Camilo Pascual	1961	8
	Whitey Ford	1964	8
	Sandy Koufax	1965	8
	Don Drysdale	1968	8
	Juan Marichal	1969	8
	Vida Blue	1971	8
	Steve Carlton	1972	8
	Wilbur Wood	1972	8
	Fernando Valenzuela	1981	8
	Dwight Gooden	1985	8
	Orel Hershiser	1988	8
	Roger Clemens	1988	8
	Tim Belcher	1989	8
84	78 tied with		7

Batters Faced

1	Joe McGinnity	1903	1,814
2	Ed Walsh	1908	1,799
3	Jack Chesbro	1904	1,778
4	Joe McGinnity	1901	1,685
5	Vic Willis	1902	1,682
6	Ed Walsh	1907	1,663
7	Joe McGinnity	1904	1,613
8	George Mullin	1904	1,597
9	Oscar Jones	1904	1,593
10	Togie Pittinger	1902	1,592
11	Luther Taylor	1901	1,578
12	Jack Powell	1904	1,572
13	Ed Walsh	1912	1,564
14	Noodles Hahn	1901	1,550
15	Rube Waddell	1904	1,548
	George Uhle	1923	1,548
17	Mickey Lolich	1971	1,538
18	Wilbur Wood	1973	1,531
19	Wild Bill Donovan	1901	1,529
	Pete Alexander	1917	1,529
21	Cy Young	1902	1,527
	Dave Davenport	1915	1,527
23	Bill Dinneen	1902	1,524
24	Christy Mathewson	1903	1,521
25	Bob Feller	1946	1,512
26	Casey Patten	1904	1,507
27	Pete Alexander	1916	1,500
28	Christy Mathewson	1908	1,499
29	Joe McGinnity	1900	1,498
30	George Mullin	1907	1,493
31	Wilbur Wood	1972	1,490
32	Joe McGinnity	1902	1,485
33	Chick Fraser	1901	1,484
34	Ed Walsh	1911	1,480
35	Cy Young	1904	1,475
	Pete Alexander	1911	1,475
	Bobo Newsom	1938	1,475
38	George Mullin	1905	1,473
39	Jack Powell	1901	1,470
40	Cy Young	1901	1,466
	Bob Feller	1941	1,466
42	Eddie Plank	1904	1,464
	Red Faber	1922	1,464
44	Pete Alexander	1914	1,459
45	Christy Mathewson	1904	1,456
46	Walter Johnson	1916	1,449
47	Bill Carrick	1901	1,448
48	Pete Alexander	1920	1,447
49	Urban Shocker	1922	1,441
50	Walter Johnson	1914	1,438
51	Phil Niekro	1979	1,436
52	Pete Alexander	1915	1,435
53	Phil Niekro	1977	1,428
54	Frank Smith	1909	1,427
55	Walter Johnson	1912	1,426
56	Pete Schneider	1917	1,421
	Dizzy Trout	1944	1,421
58	Burleigh Grimes	1923	1,418
59	Joe McGinnity	1906	1,414
60	Al Orth	1906	1,412
	Robin Roberts	1953	1,412
62	Gaylord Perry	1973	1,410
63	George McQuillan	1908	1,409
64	George Mullin	1906	1,408
65	Walter Johnson	1910	1,402
66	Urban Shocker	1921	1,401
67	Carl Mays	1921	1,400
68	Nolan Ryan	1974	1,392
69	Jack Powell	1902	1,391
	Eddie Plank	1905	1,391
	Wes Ferrell	1935	1,391
72	Eddie Plank	1907	1,390
73	Phil Niekro	1978	1,389
74	Al Orth	1902	1,388
	Jack Coombs	1910	1,388
76	Ed Walsh	1910	1,386
77	Christy Mathewson	1901	1,383
78	Eddie Plank	1903	1,378
79	Wilbur Cooper	1921	1,377
	Howard Ehmke	1924	1,377
	Burleigh Grimes	1928	1,377
82	Fred Toney	1917	1,374
83	George Uhle	1926	1,367
84	Bump Hadley	1933	1,365
85	Ed Killian	1904	1,364
86	Jack Chesbro	1906	1,363
87	Joe Wood	1912	1,362
	Dick Rudolph	1915	1,362
	Dizzy Dean	1935	1,362
90	Kaiser Wilhelm	1908	1,360
	Dickie Kerr	1921	1,360
	Stan Coveleski	1921	1,360
93	Oscar Jones	1903	1,356
	General Crowder	1932	1,356
95	Nolan Ryan	1973	1,355
96	George Mullin	1903	1,354
	Jack Chesbro	1903	1,354
98	Harry McIntire	1905	1,353
99	George Pipgras	1928	1,352
100	Steve Carlton	1972	1,351

Innings Pitched

1	Ed Walsh	1908	464.0
2	Jack Chesbro	1904	454.2
3	Joe McGinnity	1903	434.0
4	Ed Walsh	1907	422.1
5	Vic Willis	1902	410.0
6	Joe McGinnity	1904	408.0
7	Ed Walsh	1912	393.0
8	Dave Davenport	1915	392.2
9	Christy Mathewson	1908	390.2
10	Jack Powell	1904	390.1
11	Togie Pittinger	1902	389.1
12	Pete Alexander	1916	389.0
13	Pete Alexander	1917	388.0
14	Cy Young	1902	384.2
15	Rube Waddell	1904	383.0
16	George Mullin	1904	382.1
17	Joe McGinnity	1901	382.0
18	Cy Young	1904	380.0
19	Irv Young	1905	378.0
20	Cy Falkenberg	1914	377.1
21	Oscar Jones	1904	376.2
	Wilbur Wood	1972	376.2
23	Pete Alexander	1915	376.1
24	Mickey Lolich	1971	376.0
25	Noodles Hahn	1901	375.1
26	Walter Johnson	1914	371.2
27	Cy Young	1901	371.1
	Bill Dinneen	1902	371.1
	Bob Feller	1946	371.1
30	Walter Johnson	1910	370.0
31	Ed Walsh	1910	369.2
	Walter Johnson	1916	369.2
33	Walter Johnson	1912	369.0
34	Ed Walsh	1911	368.2
35	Christy Mathewson	1904	367.2
36	Pete Alexander	1911	367.0
37	Christy Mathewson	1903	366.1
38	Frank Smith	1909	365.0
39	Pete Alexander	1920	363.1
40	Claude Hendrix	1914	362.0
41	George McQuillan	1908	359.2
42	Wilbur Wood	1973	359.1
43	Irv Young	1906	358.1
44	Casey Patten	1904	357.2
	George Uhle	1923	357.2
46	Eddie Plank	1904	357.1
	George Mullin	1907	357.1
48	Pete Alexander	1914	355.0
49	Luther Taylor	1901	353.1
50	Jack Coombs	1910	353.0
	Red Faber	1922	353.0
52	Stoney McGlynn	1907	352.1
	Dizzy Trout	1944	352.1
54	Jack Taylor	1904	352.0
55	Joe McGinnity	1902	351.2
	Togie Pittinger	1903	351.2
57	Wild Bill Donovan	1901	351.0
58	Vic Willis	1904	350.0
59	Bob Harmon	1911	348.0
	Urban Shocker	1922	348.0
61	George Mullin	1905	347.2
62	Eddie Plank	1905	346.2
	Eddie Cicotte	1917	346.2
	Robin Roberts	1953	346.2
65	Steve Carlton	1972	346.1
66	Walter Johnson	1913	346.0
67	Joe Wood	1912	344.0
	Gaylord Perry	1973	344.0
69	Eddie Plank	1907	343.2
70	Cy Young	1907	343.1
71	Joe McGinnity	1900	343.0
	Bob Feller	1941	343.0
73	Three Finger Brown	1909	342.2
	Jack Quinn	1914	342.2
	Gaylord Perry	1972	342.2
76	Vic Willis	1905	342.0
	Phil Niekro	1979	342.0
78	Bill Carrick	1900	341.2
	Cy Young	1903	341.2
	Pete Schneider	1917	341.2
81	Dick Rudolph	1915	341.1
82	Joe McGinnity	1906	339.2
	Fred Toney	1917	339.2
	Jim Bagby	1920	339.2
85	Christy Mathewson	1905	338.2
	Al Orth	1906	338.2
	Addie Joss	1907	338.2
88	Jack Powell	1901	338.1
89	Togie Pittinger	1905	337.1
90	Jack Coombs	1911	336.2
	Walter Johnson	1915	336.2
	Carl Mays	1921	336.2
	Robin Roberts	1954	336.2
94	Dick Rudolph	1914	336.1
95	Christy Mathewson	1901	336.0
	Eddie Plank	1903	336.0
	Denny McLain	1968	336.0
98	Bill Dinneen	1904	335.2
	Sandy Koufax	1965	335.2
100	Togie Pittinger	1904	335.1

Hits Allowed

1	Bill Carrick	1900	415
2	Joe McGinnity	1901	412
3	Snake Wiltse	1902	397
4	Togie Pittinger	1903	396
5	Joe McGinnity	1903	391
6	Oscar Jones	1904	387
7	Wilbur Wood	1973	381
8	George Uhle	1923	378
9	Pink Hawley	1900	377
	Luther Taylor	1901	377
11	Vic Willis	1902	372
12	Ed Scott	1900	370
	Noodles Hahn	1901	370
14	Bill Carrick	1901	367
	Al Orth	1902	367
	Casey Patten	1904	367
17	Ray Kremer	1930	366
18	Urban Shocker	1922	365
19	Bill Reidy	1901	364
	Bill Phillips	1901	364
21	Togie Pittinger	1902	360
	Jack Coombs	1911	360
23	Vic Willis	1904	357
	Dickie Kerr	1921	357
25	Burleigh Grimes	1923	356
26	Jack Powell	1901	351
	Burleigh Grimes	1924	351
28	Joe McGinnity	1900	350
	Cy Young	1902	350
30	Irv Young	1906	349
31	Bill Dinneen	1902	348
	Claude Passeau	1937	348
33	Nixey Callahan	1900	347
34	George Mullin	1907	346
35	Roy Patterson	1901	345
	George Mullin	1904	345
	Urban Shocker	1921	345
38	Chick Fraser	1901	344
	Bill Carrick	1902	344
40	Ed Walsh	1908	343
41	Jack Taylor	1901	341
	Stan Yerkes	1902	341
	Joe McGinnity	1902	341
	Ed Walsh	1907	341
	Stan Coveleski	1921	341
	Wilbur Cooper	1921	341
47	Pete Dowling	1901	340
	Jack Powell	1904	340
	Harry McIntire	1905	340
	Vic Willis	1905	340
51	Roscoe Miller	1901	339
52	Patsy Flaherty	1903	338
	Jack Chesbro	1904	338
	Jim Bagby	1920	338
55	Cy Young	1900	337
	Irv Young	1905	337
	Eppa Rixey	1922	337
58	Pete Alexander	1917	336
	Jimmy Ring	1923	336
	Sam Gray	1929	336
	Wes Ferrell	1935	336
	Mickey Lolich	1971	336
63	Jack Quinn	1914	335
	Pete Alexander	1920	335
65	Cowboy Jones	1900	334
	Ed Siever	1901	334
	Red Faber	1922	334
	Eppa Rixey	1923	334
	Bobo Newsom	1938	334
70	Harry Howell	1901	333
71	Ed Walsh	1912	332
	Cy Falkenberg	1914	332
	Red Faber	1920	332
	Carl Mays	1921	332
75	Casey Patten	1902	331
	Hooks Dauss	1923	331
	Wilbur Cooper	1923	331
	Ted Lyons	1930	331
	Paul Derringer	1936	331
80	Wilbur Cooper	1922	330
	Sloppy Thurston	1924	330
	Wes Ferrell	1936	330
83	Stoney McGlynn	1907	329
84	Watty Lee	1901	328
	Bill Bernhard	1901	328
	George Uhle	1922	328
	Dutch Leonard	1940	328
	Robin Roberts	1956	328
89	Cy Young	1904	327
	Ed Walsh	1911	327
	Pete Alexander	1914	327
92	Al Orth	1903	326
93	Jack Powell	1900	325
	Jimmy Ring	1925	325
	Larry French	1930	325
	Wes Ferrell	1937	325
	Wilbur Wood	1972	325
98	7 tied with		324

Runs Allowed

1	Snake Wiltse	1902	226
2	Bill Carrick	1900	224
3	Joe McGinnity	1901	219
4	Chick Fraser	1901	210
5	Pete Dowling	1901	209
6	Togie Pittinger	1903	205
	Bobo Newsom	1938	205
8	Pink Hawley	1900	204
9	Bill Carrick	1901	198
10	Bill Phillips	1901	196
11	Nixey Callahan	1900	195
12	Jack Powell	1900	194
	Bill Carrick	1902	194
14	Luther Taylor	1901	193
15	Ed Scott	1900	192
16	Harry Howell	1901	188
	Harry McIntire	1905	188
18	Sam Gray	1931	187
19	Casey Patten	1902	186
20	Cowboy Jones	1900	185
21	Watty Lee	1901	184
22	Bill Reidy	1901	183
23	Vic Willis	1904	182
	Dickie Kerr	1921	182
25	Al Orth	1902	181
	Ray Kremer	1930	181
27	Joe McGinnity	1900	179
28	Ray Benge	1930	178
29	Oscar Jones	1904	177
	Milt Gaston	1927	177
	Pat Caraway	1931	177
	Wes Ferrell	1937	177
33	Al Orth	1903	174
	Vic Willis	1905	174
	Chick Fraser	1905	174
	Guy Bush	1930	174
	Jack Knott	1936	174
38	Oscar Jones	1903	173
	Patsy Flaherty	1903	173
40	Ted Lewis	1901	172
41	Bill Bernhard	1901	169
	Elmer Myers	1916	169
43	Roscoe Miller	1901	168
	Jack Powell	1901	168
	Kaiser Wilhelm	1905	168
	Bump Hadley	1932	168
47	George Uhle	1923	167
	Vern Kennedy	1936	167
49	Ed Siever	1901	166
	Long Tom Hughes	1901	166
	Jack Coombs	1911	166
	George Smith	1921	166
	Jimmy Ring	1925	166
	Tommy Thomas	1931	166
	Wilbur Wood	1973	166
	Phil Niekro	1977	166
57	Jack Taylor	1901	165
	Henry Schmidt	1903	165
	Tom Fisher	1904	165
	Russ Ford	1912	165
	Burleigh Grimes	1923	165
62	Roy Patterson	1901	164
	Chick Fraser	1904	164
	Burleigh Grimes	1925	164
	Leo Sweetland	1930	164
66	Casey Patten	1901	163
	Casey Patten	1903	163
	Jack Townsend	1904	163
	Larry French	1930	163
	George Blaeholder	1932	163
	Bobo Newsom	1937	163
	Nels Potter	1939	163
73	Joe McGinnity	1903	162
	Bill Duggleby	1903	162
	Casey Patten	1904	162
	Red Ruffing	1929	162
	George Earnshaw	1930	162
	Jack Russell	1930	162
	Gordon Rhodes	1936	162
	Hugh Mulcahy	1938	162
81	Bill Dinneen	1900	161
	Buster Brown	1911	161
	Jimmy Ring	1921	161
	Burleigh Grimes	1924	161
	Jimmie DeShong	1937	161
86	Brickyard Kennedy	1900	160
	Stan Yerkes	1902	160
	Chick Fraser	1903	160
	Jimmy Ring	1922	160
	Ted Lyons	1930	160
	Chief Hogsett	1936	160
	Bobo Newsom	1936	160
	Wes Ferrell	1936	160
	George Caster	1940	160
	Joe Coleman	1974	160
	Phil Niekro	1979	160
97	6 tied with		159

Earned Runs Allowed

1	Bobo Newsom	1938	186
2	Snake Wiltse	1902	172
3	Dickie Kerr	1921	162
4	Jack Knott	1936	156
5	Guy Bush	1930	155
6	Ray Kremer	1930	154
7	Wes Ferrell	1937	153
8	Pat Caraway	1931	152
9	Joe McGinnity	1901	151
10	George Uhle	1923	150
11	Bump Hadley	1932	149
12	Phil Niekro	1977	148
13	Bobo Newsom	1937	147
	Robin Roberts	1956	147
15	George Earnshaw	1930	146
	Sam Gray	1931	146
17	Bill Phillips	1901	145
	Herm Wehmeier	1950	145
	Harry Byrd	1953	145
20	Jimmie DeShong	1937	144
	Nels Potter	1939	144
22	Al Orth	1902	143
	Leo Sweetland	1930	143
	Ray Benge	1930	143
	Rube Walberg	1932	143
26	Jack Powell	1900	142
	Mickey Lolich	1974	142
28	Pete Dowling	1901	141
	Bill Reidy	1901	141
	Milt Gaston	1927	141
	Vern Kennedy	1936	141
	Claude Passeau	1937	141
33	Chick Fraser	1901	140
	Wes Ferrell	1936	140
35	Bill Carrick	1902	139
	Ray Benge	1929	139
	Jack Russell	1930	139
	Jim Bibby	1974	139
39	Burleigh Grimes	1925	138
	Bump Hadley	1933	138
	Gordon Rhodes	1936	138
	Vern Kennedy	1940	138
	Wilbur Wood	1973	138
44	Bobo Newsom	1936	137
	Hugh Mulcahy	1938	137
	Jack Kramer	1939	137
	Vern Kennedy	1939	137
	Alex Kellner	1950	137
	Joe Coleman	1974	137
50	Togie Pittinger	1903	136
	Chief Hogsett	1936	136
	George Caster	1938	136
53	Ed Scott	1900	135
	Bill Carrick	1901	135
	Casey Patten	1902	135
	Al Orth	1903	135
	Burleigh Grimes	1922	135
	Claude Willoughby	1929	135
	George Blaeholder	1932	135
	Dick Tidrow	1973	135
	Jaime Navarro	1997	135
62	Bill Carrick	1900	134
	George Blaeholder	1933	134
	Tom Gordon	1996	134
65	Jack Powell	1901	133
	Howard Ehmke	1923	133
	Ted Blankenship	1927	133
	Larry French	1930	133
	Jack Russell	1931	133
	Lefty Stewart	1932	133
	Earl Whitehill	1935	133
	Wilbur Wood	1975	133
	Matt Keough	1982	133
74	Jack Coombs	1911	132
	Burleigh Grimes	1924	132
	Jack Scott	1927	132
	Red Ruffing	1929	132
	General Crowder	1933	132
	Eldon Auker	1941	132
	Vida Blue	1979	132
81	Dixie Davis	1921	131
	Howard Ehmke	1922	131
	Jimmy Ring	1923	131
	Jimmy Ring	1925	131
	Lew Burdette	1959	131
	Mickey Lolich	1973	131
87	Lefty Williams	1920	130
	George Uhle	1922	130
	Burleigh Grimes	1923	130
	Vic Sorrell	1929	130
	Willis Hudlin	1931	130
	George Earnshaw	1932	130
	Buck Ross	1936	130
	Wayne LaMaster	1937	130
	Bucky Walters	1937	130
	George Caster	1940	130
	Johnny Sain	1949	130
	Sammy Ellis	1966	130
	Dave Stewart	1991	130
	Mike Mussina	1996	130

Walks

1	Bob Feller	1938	208
2	Nolan Ryan	1977	204
3	Nolan Ryan	1974	202
4	Bob Feller	1941	194
5	Bobo Newsom	1938	192
6	Sam Jones	1955	185
7	Nolan Ryan	1976	183
8	Bob Harmon	1911	181
	Bob Turley	1954	181
10	Tommy Byrne	1949	179
11	Bob Turley	1955	177
12	Bump Hadley	1932	171
13	Elmer Myers	1916	168
14	Bobo Newsom	1937	167
15	John Wyckoff	1915	165
16	Earl Moore	1911	164
	Phil Niekro	1977	164
18	Johnny Vander Meer	1943	162
	Nolan Ryan	1973	162
20	Tommy Byrne	1950	160
21	Marty O'Toole	1912	159
22	Joe Coleman	1974	158
23	Grover Lowdermilk	1915	157
	Nolan Ryan	1972	157
25	Herb Score	1955	154
26	Bob Feller	1946	153
	Sam McDowell	1971	153
28	Wild Bill Donovan	1901	152
	Randy Johnson	1991	152
30	J.R. Richard	1976	151
31	Tommy Byrne	1951	150
32	Chick Fraser	1905	149
	Al Schulz	1915	149
	Dixie Davis	1920	149
	Bobo Newsom	1934	149
36	Nolan Ryan	1978	148
37	Orval Overall	1905	147
	Vern Kennedy	1936	147
39	Bobo Newsom	1936	146
	Bob Lemon	1950	146
	Bill Stoneman	1971	146
42	Togie Pittinger	1904	144
	Randy Johnson	1992	144
44	Togie Pittinger	1903	143
	Ken Chase	1940	143
	Bobby Witt	1986	143
47	Bob Feller	1939	142
	Paul Foytack	1956	142
49	Bump Hadley	1933	141
	Phil Marchildon	1947	141
	J.R. Richard	1978	141
52	Larry Cheney	1914	140
	Phil Marchildon	1942	140
	Bobby Witt	1987	140
55	George Earnshaw	1930	139
	Johnny Lindell	1953	139
57	George Mullin	1905	138
	Vic Raschi	1949	138
	Allie Reynolds	1950	138
	J.R. Richard	1975	138
61	Jim Shaw	1914	137
	Sugar Cain	1933	137
	Hal Newhouser	1941	137
	Hal Gregg	1944	137
	Bob Lemon	1949	137
	Billy Pierce	1950	137
67	Gene Krapp	1911	136
	Tom Seaton	1913	136
	Al Mamaux	1916	136
	Steve Carlton	1974	136
71	Monte Pearson	1936	135
	Bill Wight	1948	135
	Herm Wehmeier	1950	135
	Steve Renko	1971	135
75	Mel Parnell	1949	134
76	Bob Harmon	1910	133
	Mike Torrez	1975	133
78	Chick Fraser	1901	132
	Kirby Higbe	1941	132
	Early Wynn	1952	132
	Chuck Estrada	1961	132
	Sam McDowell	1965	132
	Nolan Ryan	1975	132
84	George Mullin	1904	131
	Lefty Grove	1925	131
	Phil Marchildon	1948	131
	Sam McDowell	1970	131
88	King Cole	1910	130
	Joe Bush	1916	130
	Sheriff Blake	1929	130
	Wes Ferrell	1931	130
	Monte Pearson	1934	130
	Allie Reynolds	1945	130
	Steve Barber	1961	130
	Bill Singer	1973	130
96	7 tied with		129

Strikeouts

1	Nolan Ryan	1973	383
2	Sandy Koufax	1965	382
3	Nolan Ryan	1974	367
4	Rube Waddell	1904	349
5	Bob Feller	1946	348
6	Nolan Ryan	1977	341
7	Nolan Ryan	1972	329
8	Nolan Ryan	1976	327
9	Sam McDowell	1965	325
10	Curt Schilling	1997	319
11	Sandy Koufax	1966	317
12	Walter Johnson	1910	313
	J.R. Richard	1979	313
14	Steve Carlton	1972	310
15	Mickey Lolich	1971	308
	Randy Johnson	1993	308
17	Sandy Koufax	1963	306
	Mike Scott	1986	306
19	Pedro Martinez	1997	305
20	Sam McDowell	1970	304
21	Walter Johnson	1912	303
	J.R. Richard	1978	303
23	Rube Waddell	1903	302
24	Vida Blue	1971	301
	Nolan Ryan	1989	301
26	Randy Johnson	1995	294
27	Roger Clemens	1997	292
28	Roger Clemens	1988	291
	Randy Johnson	1997	291
30	Tom Seaver	1971	289
31	Rube Waddell	1905	287
32	Steve Carlton	1980	286
	Steve Carlton	1982	286
34	Sam McDowell	1968	283
	Tom Seaver	1970	283
36	Denny McLain	1968	280
37	Sam McDowell	1969	279
38	Bob Veale	1965	276
	Dwight Gooden	1984	276
	John Smoltz	1996	276
41	Hal Newhouser	1946	275
	Steve Carlton	1983	275
43	Fergie Jenkins	1970	274
	Bob Gibson	1970	274
	Mario Soto	1982	274
46	Fergie Jenkins	1969	273
47	Mickey Lolich	1969	271
48	Bob Gibson	1965	270
	Nolan Ryan	1987	270
50	Ed Walsh	1908	269
	Sandy Koufax	1961	269
	Bob Gibson	1969	269
	Frank Tanana	1975	269
54	Jim Bunning	1965	268
	Bob Gibson	1968	268
	Dwight Gooden	1985	268
57	Christy Mathewson	1903	267
58	Jim Maloney	1963	265
59	Luis Tiant	1968	264
60	Herb Score	1956	263
	Fergie Jenkins	1971	263
62	Dazzy Vance	1924	262
	Phil Niekro	1977	262
	Mark Langston	1987	262
65	Bob Feller	1940	261
	Frank Tanana	1976	261
	David Cone	1992	261
68	Bob Feller	1941	260
	Fergie Jenkins	1968	260
	Nolan Ryan	1978	260
71	Christy Mathewson	1908	259
72	Ed Walsh	1910	258
	Joe Wood	1912	258
	Bert Blyleven	1973	258
75	Roger Clemens	1996	257
76	Roger Clemens	1987	256
77	Ed Walsh	1911	255
78	Ed Walsh	1912	254
79	Jim Bunning	1967	253
80	Jim Bunning	1966	252
81	Don Drysdale	1963	251
	Bill Stoneman	1971	251
	Tom Seaver	1973	251
84	Bob Veale	1964	250
	Mickey Lolich	1972	250
86	Tom Seaver	1972	249
	Bert Blyleven	1974	249
88	Juan Marichal	1963	248
	Phil Niekro	1978	248
	Ron Guidry	1978	248
91	Bill Singer	1969	247
92	Bob Feller	1939	246
	Don Drysdale	1960	246
	Jim Lonborg	1967	246
95	Herb Score	1955	245
	Bob Gibson	1964	245
	Nolan Ryan	1982	245
	Mark Langston	1986	245
99	Jim Maloney	1965	244
	Dennis Leonard	1977	244

Rookie Season Batting Leaders

Games

Rank	Player	Year	G
1	Jake Wood	1961	162
	Bobby Knoop	1964	162
	Dick Allen	1964	162
	George Scott	1966	162
	Johnny Ray	1982	162
	Jeff Conine	1993	162
7	Tony Oliva	1964	161
	Kevin Seitzer	1987	161
9	Ken Hubbs	1962	160
	Tommie Agee	1966	160
	Pedro Garcia	1973	160
	Phil Garner	1975	160
	Ruppert Jones	1977	160
	Eddie Murray	1977	160
	Cal Ripken Jr.	1982	160
	Juan Samuel	1984	160
17	6 tied with		159

At-Bats

Rank	Player	Year	AB
1	Juan Samuel	1984	701
2	Nomar Garciaparra	1997	684
3	Harvey Kuenn	1953	679
4	Tony Oliva	1964	672
5	Jake Wood	1961	663
6	Ken Hubbs	1962	661
7	Billy Herman	1932	656
8	Woody Williams	1944	653
9	Carl Lind	1928	650
10	Vada Pinson	1959	648
11	Johnny Ray	1982	647
12	Tom Oliver	1930	646
	Chuck Schilling	1961	646
14	Frankie Baumholtz	1947	643
15	Stan Rojek	1948	641
	Chili Davis	1982	641
	Kevin Seitzer	1987	641
	Tony Womack	1997	641
19	Roy Johnson	1929	640
	Frank McCormick	1938	640

Runs

Rank	Player	Year	R
1	Billy Hamilton	1889	144
2	Mike Griffin	1887	142
3	Herman Long	1889	137
	Roy Thomas	1899	137
5	Lloyd Waner	1927	133
6	Joe DiMaggio	1936	132
7	Ted Williams	1939	131
	Vada Pinson	1959	131
9	Jimmy Bannon	1894	130
10	Bill Everitt	1895	129
11	Roy Johnson	1929	128
12	Johnny Frederick	1929	127
13	Jimmy Williams	1899	126
	Joe Jackson	1911	126
15	Jackie Robinson	1947	125
	Jim Gilliam	1953	125
	Dick Allen	1964	125
18	Hub Collins	1887	122
	Frank Robinson	1956	122
	Nomar Garciaparra	1997	122

Hits

Rank	Player	Year	H
1	Joe Jackson	1911	233
2	Lloyd Waner	1927	223
3	Jimmy Williams	1899	219
	Ralph Garr	1971	219
5	Tony Oliva	1964	217
6	Dale Alexander	1929	215
7	Benny Kauff	1914	211
8	Frank McCormick	1938	209
	Harvey Kuenn	1953	209
	Nomar Garciaparra	1997	209
11	Kevin Seitzer	1987	207
12	Johnny Frederick	1929	206
	Billy Herman	1932	206
	Hal Trosky	1934	206
	Joe DiMaggio	1936	206
16	Johnny Pesky	1942	205
	Vada Pinson	1959	205
18	Earle Combs	1925	203
19	Roy Johnson	1929	201
	Dick Allen	1964	201

Doubles

Rank	Player	Year	2B
1	Johnny Frederick	1929	52
2	Vada Pinson	1959	47
	Fred Lynn	1975	47
4	Joe Jackson	1911	45
	Roy Johnson	1929	45
	Hal Trosky	1934	45
7	Benny Kauff	1914	44
	Bob Johnson	1933	44
	Joe DiMaggio	1936	44
	Ted Williams	1939	44
	Nomar Garciaparra	1997	44
12	Earl Averill	1929	43
	Dale Alexander	1929	43
	Tony Oliva	1964	43
15	Carl Lind	1928	42
	Billy Herman	1932	42
17	Warren Cromartie	1977	41
18	6 tied with		40

Triples

Rank	Player	Year	3B
1	Jimmy Williams	1899	27
2	Buck Freeman	1899	25
	Tom Long	1915	25
4	Paul Waner	1926	22
5	Tom McCreery	1896	21
6	Joe Cassidy	1904	19
	Home Run Baker	1909	19
	Joe Jackson	1911	19
	Juan Samuel	1984	19
10	Bill Joyce	1890	18
	Jim Canavan	1891	18
	Charlie Abbey	1894	18
	Harry Lumley	1904	18
	Glenn Wright	1924	18
	Ival Goodman	1935	18
	Jeff Heath	1938	18
17	9 tied with		17

Home Runs

Rank	Player	Year	HR
1	Mark McGwire	1987	49
2	Wally Berger	1930	38
	Frank Robinson	1956	38
4	Al Rosen	1950	37
5	Hal Trosky	1934	35
	Rudy York	1937	35
	Ron Kittle	1983	35
	Mike Piazza	1993	35
9	Walt Dropo	1950	34
10	Jimmie Hall	1963	33
	Earl Williams	1971	33
	Jose Canseco	1986	33
13	Tony Oliva	1964	32
	Matt Nokes	1987	32
15	Ted Williams	1939	31
	Jim Ray Hart	1964	31
	Tim Salmon	1993	31
18	4 tied with		30

RBI

Rank	Player	Year	RBI
1	Ted Williams	1939	145
2	Walt Dropo	1950	144
3	Hal Trosky	1934	142
4	Dale Alexander	1929	137
5	Joe DiMaggio	1936	125
6	Buck Freeman	1899	122
7	Wally Berger	1930	119
8	Mark McGwire	1987	118
9	Joe Vosmik	1931	117
	Jose Canseco	1986	117
11	Jimmy Williams	1899	116
	Maurice Van Robays	1940	116
	Al Rosen	1950	116
	Alvin Davis	1984	116
15	Jimmy Bannon	1894	114
	Tony Lazzeri	1926	114
	Smead Jolley	1930	114
18	Ken Keltner	1938	113
19	3 tied with		112

Walks

Rank	Player	Year	BB
1	Bill Joyce	1890	123
2	Roy Thomas	1899	115
3	Ted Williams	1939	107
4	Les Fleming	1942	106
5	Lu Blue	1921	103
6	Al Rosen	1950	100
	Jim Gilliam	1953	100
8	Joe Morgan	1965	97
	Alvin Davis	1984	97
10	Jack Crooks	1890	96
11	Morrie Rath	1912	95
	Ferris Fain	1947	95
	Billy Grabarkewitz	1970	95
14	Bernie Carbo	1970	94
15	Eddie Stanky	1943	92
	Dick Howser	1961	92
17	Joe Foy	1966	91
18	Don Lenhardt	1950	90
19	3 tied with		88

Strikeouts

Rank	Player	Year	SO
1	Pete Incaviglia	1986	185
2	Jose Canseco	1986	175
3	Reggie Jackson	1968	171
4	Juan Samuel	1984	168
5	Bo Jackson	1987	158
6	Danny Tartabull	1986	157
7	George Scott	1966	152
	Larry Hisle	1969	152
9	Ron Kittle	1983	150
10	Billy Grabarkewitz	1970	149
11	Benji Gil	1995	147
12	Bobby Darwin	1972	145
13	Byron Browne	1966	143
14	Jake Wood	1961	141
15	Dave Kingman	1972	140
16	Dick Allen	1964	138
	Scott Rolen	1997	138
18	Pancho Herrera	1960	136
	Mike Schmidt	1973	136
20	4 tied with		135

Stolen Bases

Rank	Player	Year	SB
1	Billy Hamilton	1889	111
2	Vince Coleman	1985	110
3	Mike Griffin	1887	94
4	Herman Long	1889	89
5	Tommy Tucker	1887	85
6	Dummy Hoy	1888	82
7	Ted Scheffler	1890	77
8	Ed McKean	1887	76
9	Benny Kauff	1914	75
10	Bill Van Dyke	1890	73
11	Juan Samuel	1984	72
12	Hub Collins	1887	71
	Tim Raines	1981	71
14	Kenny Lofton	1992	66
15	Jay Faatz	1888	64
	Eric Yelding	1990	64
17	Tim Shinnick	1890	62
18	Tony Womack	1997	60
19	Chuck Carr	1993	58
20	3 tied with		57

Runs Created

Rank	Player	Year	RC
1	Ted Williams	1939	153
2	Billy Hamilton	1889	149
3	Jimmy Williams	1899	148
4	Joe Jackson	1911	147
5	Benny Kauff	1914	142
6	Dale Alexander	1929	136
	Hal Trosky	1934	136
8	Jimmy Bannon	1894	134
9	Bug Holliday	1889	130
	Buck Freeman	1899	130
	Dick Allen	1964	130
12	Joe DiMaggio	1936	128
13	Herman Long	1889	127
	Roy Thomas	1899	127
15	Dave Orr	1884	125
	Bill Joyce	1890	125
	Mark McGwire	1987	125
18	Mike Griffin	1887	122
19	Cupid Childs	1890	121
	Wally Berger	1930	121

Batting Average

(minimum 3.1 Plate Appearances/Tm Gm)

Rank	Player	Year	AVG
1	Joe Jackson	1911	.408
2	John Cassidy	1877	.378
3	Pete Browning	1882	.378
4	Benny Kauff	1914	.370
5	Bill Everitt	1895	.358
6	Jimmy Williams	1899	.355
7	Lloyd Waner	1927	.355
8	Fielder Jones	1896	.354
9	Abner Dalrymple	1878	.354
10	Kiki Cuyler	1924	.354
11	Chick Stahl	1897	.354
12	Dave Orr	1884	.354
13	Ginger Beaumont	1899	.352
14	Hack Miller	1922	.352
15	Tom McCreery	1896	.351
16	Cupid Childs	1890	.345
17	Dale Alexander	1929	.343
18	Gene DeMontreville	1896	.343
19	Ralph Garr	1971	.343
20	Jeff Heath	1938	.343

On-Base Percentage

(minimum 3.1 Plate Appearances/Tm Gm)

Rank	Player	Year	OBP
1	Joe Jackson	1911	.468
2	Roy Thomas	1899	.457
3	Benny Kauff	1914	.447
4	Charlie Keller	1939	.447
5	Fred Snodgrass	1910	.440
6	Ted Williams	1939	.436
7	Cupid Childs	1890	.434
8	Pete Browning	1882	.430
9	Elmer Flick	1898	.430
10	Fielder Jones	1896	.427
11	Minnie Minoso	1951	.422
12	Jimmy Williams	1899	.417
13	Ginger Beaumont	1899	.416
14	Lu Blue	1921	.416
15	Jimmy Bannon	1894	.414
16	Billy Goodman	1948	.414
17	Ferris Fain	1947	.414
18	Bill Joyce	1890	.413
19	Billy Hamilton	1889	.413
20	Paul Waner	1926	.413

Slugging Percentage

(minimum 3.1 Plate Appearances/Tm Gm)

Rank	Player	Year	SLG
1	Mark McGwire	1987	.618
2	Wally Berger	1930	.614
3	Ted Williams	1939	.609
4	Jeff Heath	1938	.602
5	Bob Hamelin	1994	.599
6	Hal Trosky	1934	.598
7	Joe Jackson	1911	.590
8	Walt Dropo	1950	.583
9	Dale Alexander	1929	.580
10	Joe DiMaggio	1936	.576
11	Fred Lynn	1975	.566
12	Buck Freeman	1899	.563
13	Mike Piazza	1993	.561
14	Frank Robinson	1956	.558
15	Dick Allen	1964	.557
16	Tony Oliva	1964	.557
17	Rico Carty	1964	.554
18	Tom McCreery	1896	.546
19	Zeke Bonura	1934	.545
20	Johnny Frederick	1929	.545

Runs Created/27 Outs

(minimum 3.1 Plate Appearances/Tm Gm)

Rank	Player	Year	RC/27
1	Pete Browning	1882	12.54
2	Dave Orr	1884	11.22
3	John O'Rourke	1879	11.12
4	Joe Jackson	1911	10.92
5	Frank Fennelly	1884	10.89
6	Buster Hoover	1884	10.78
7	John Cassidy	1877	10.47
8	Ted Williams	1939	10.44
9	Billy Hamilton	1889	10.31
10	Jimmy Bannon	1894	10.29
11	Harry Moore	1884	10.12
12	Emmett Seery	1884	9.73
13	Cupid Childs	1890	9.63
14	Benny Kauff	1914	9.56
15	Ed Swartwood	1882	9.55
16	Chick Stahl	1897	9.45
17	Jimmy Williams	1899	9.23
18	Ed Crane	1884	9.23
19	Charlie Keller	1939	9.21
20	Tom McCreery	1896	9.21

Rookie Season Pitching Leaders

Wins

1 Larry Corcoran	1880	43
2 Pud Galvin	1879	37
3 Mickey Welch	1880	34
Ed Morris	1884	34
5 Lee Richmond	1880	32
Silver King	1887	32
Jesse Duryea	1889	32
8 Jim Whitney	1881	31
Bill Hoffer	1895	31
10 Will White	1878	30
Tony Mullane	1882	30
12 Terry Larkin	1877	29
George Derby	1881	29
Matt Kilroy	1886	29
15 Billy Rhines	1890	28
Nig Cuppy	1892	28
Joe McGinnity	1899	28
Pete Alexander	1911	28
19 Lee Viau	1888	27
Kid Nichols	1890	27

Losses

1 John Coleman	1883	48
2 Larry McKeon	1884	41
3 Kid Carsey	1891	37
George Cobb	1892	37
5 Fleury Sullivan	1884	35
Adonis Terry	1884	35
7 Matt Kilroy	1886	34
8 Harry McCormick	1879	33
Jim Whitney	1881	33
Hardie Henderson	1883	33
11 Lee Richmond	1880	32
John Harkins	1884	32
13 Sam Weaver	1878	31
Billy Crowell	1887	31
15 Mickey Welch	1880	30
16 Bert Cunningham	1888	29
17 Doc Landis	1882	28
Hank O'Day	1884	28
Gus Weyhing	1887	28
Bill Hill	1896	28

Winning Percentage
(minimum 15 decisions)

1 Ron Davis	1979	.875
2 Emil Yde	1924	.842
3 Bill Hoffer	1895	.838
4 Henry Boyle	1884	.833
King Cole	1910	.833
Hoyt Wilhelm	1952	.833
7 Elmer Riddle	1941	.826
8 Wayne Simpson	1970	.824
9 Hooks Wiltse	1904	.813
Russ Ford	1910	.813
Atley Donald	1939	.813
12 Johnny Allen	1932	.810
Ted Wilks	1944	.810
14 Larry Jansen	1947	.808
15 Babe Adams	1909	.800
16 Jocko Flynn	1886	.793
17 Wally Bunker	1964	.792
18 Hank Borowy	1942	.789
Joe Black	1952	.789
20 Johnny Beazley	1942	.778

Games

1 Wayne Granger	1969	90
2 Mike Myers	1996	83
3 Mitch Williams	1986	80
4 Ed Vande Berg	1982	78
Tim Burke	1985	78
6 Butch Metzger	1976	77
Mike Perez	1992	77
8 Larry Hardy	1974	76
9 Dan Quisenberry	1980	75
10 Lee Richmond	1880	74
Dan McGinn	1969	74
Todd Worrell	1986	74
Mike Stanton	1991	74
Greg McMichael	1993	74
15 Doug Corbett	1980	73
Bill Scherrer	1983	73
Kenny Rogers	1989	73
Antonio Osuna	1996	73
19 Dave Veres	1995	72
Rich Loiselle	1997	72

Games Started

1 Matt Kilroy	1886	68
2 Pud Galvin	1879	66
Lee Richmond	1880	66
4 Mickey Welch	1880	64
5 Jim Whitney	1881	63
6 John Coleman	1883	61
7 Larry Corcoran	1880	60
Larry McKeon	1884	60
9 Terry Larkin	1877	56
Adonis Terry	1884	56
11 George Derby	1881	55
Tony Mullane	1882	55
Gus Weyhing	1887	55
14 Harry McCormick	1879	54
15 Kid Carsey	1891	53
16 Will White	1878	52
Ed Morris	1884	52
Ed Seward	1887	52
19 Fleury Sullivan	1884	51
Bert Cunningham	1888	51

Complete Games

1 Matt Kilroy	1886	66
2 Pud Galvin	1879	65
3 Mickey Welch	1880	64
4 John Coleman	1883	59
Larry McKeon	1884	59
6 Larry Corcoran	1880	57
Lee Richmond	1880	57
Jim Whitney	1881	57
9 Terry Larkin	1877	55
George Derby	1881	55
Adonis Terry	1884	55
12 Gus Weyhing	1887	53
13 Will White	1878	52
Ed Seward	1887	52
15 Tony Mullane	1882	51
Fleury Sullivan	1884	51
17 Bert Cunningham	1888	50
18 Harry McCormick	1879	49
Ed Daily	1885	49
20 2 tied with		47

Shutouts

1 George Derby	1881	9
2 Ben Sanders	1888	8
Russ Ford	1910	8
Reb Russell	1913	8
Fernando Valenzuela	1981	8
6 Kid Nichols	1890	7
Irv Young	1905	7
George McQuillan	1908	7
Harry Krause	1909	7
Jerry Koosman	1968	7
12 Monte Ward	1878	6
Pud Galvin	1879	6
Jim Whitney	1881	6
Billy Rhines	1890	6
Wiley Piatt	1898	6
Fred Glade	1904	6
Ewell Blackwell	1946	6
Gene Bearden	1948	6
Harvey Haddix	1953	6

Saves

1 Todd Worrell	1986	36
2 Dan Quisenberry	1980	33
Mike Schooler	1989	33
4 Terry Forster	1972	29
Doug Henry	1992	29
Rich Loiselle	1997	29
7 Wayne Granger	1969	27
Gregg Olson	1989	27
9 Peter Ladd	1983	25
10 Dick Radatz	1962	24
11 Doug Corbett	1980	23
Ernie Camacho	1984	23
13 Ken Tatum	1969	22
Rawly Eastwick	1975	22
15 Frank Linzy	1965	21
Salome Barojas	1982	21
Danny Miceli	1995	21
18 Ryne Duren	1958	20
Doug Bird	1973	20
Frank DiPino	1983	20

Innings Pitched

1 Pud Galvin	1879	593.0
2 Lee Richmond	1880	590.2
3 Matt Kilroy	1886	583.0
4 Mickey Welch	1880	574.0
5 Jim Whitney	1881	552.1
6 John Coleman	1883	538.1
7 Larry Corcoran	1880	536.1
8 Larry McKeon	1884	512.0
9 Terry Larkin	1877	501.0
10 George Derby	1881	494.2
11 Adonis Terry	1884	485.0
12 Ed Seward	1887	470.2
13 Will White	1878	468.0
14 Gus Weyhing	1887	466.1
15 Tony Mullane	1882	460.1
16 Harry McCormick	1879	457.1
17 Bert Cunningham	1888	453.1
18 Fleury Sullivan	1884	441.0
19 Ed Daily	1885	440.0
20 Ed Morris	1884	429.2

Walks

1 Mike Morrison	1887	205
2 Sam Jones	1955	185
3 Tom Vickery	1890	184
4 Matt Kilroy	1886	182
5 Elmer Myers	1916	168
6 Gus Weyhing	1887	167
Bill Daley	1890	167
8 Phil Knell	1890	166
Chick Fraser	1896	166
10 Kid Carsey	1891	161
11 Bert Cunningham	1888	157
12 Bill Hill	1896	155
13 Herb Score	1955	154
14 Bobo Newsom	1934	149
15 John Lewis	1890	148
Ted Breitenstein	1892	148
Vic Willis	1898	148
18 Orval Overall	1905	147
19 Bill Stemmeyer	1886	144
20 Bobby Witt	1986	143

Strikeouts

1 Matt Kilroy	1886	513
2 Larry McKeon	1884	308
3 Ed Morris	1884	302
4 Dwight Gooden	1984	276
5 Larry Corcoran	1880	268
Bill Wise	1884	268
7 Walter Burke	1884	255
8 Al Atkinson	1884	247
9 Herb Score	1955	245
10 Lee Richmond	1880	243
11 Bill Stemmeyer	1886	239
12 Hideo Nomo	1995	236
13 Adonis Terry	1884	233
14 Pete Alexander	1911	227
15 Long Tom Hughes	1901	225
16 Kid Nichols	1890	222
17 Christy Mathewson	1901	221
18 John Montefusco	1975	215
19 George Derby	1881	212
20 2 tied with		209

Strikeouts/9 Innings
(minimum 1 Inning Pitched/Tm Gm)

1 Dwight Gooden	1984	11.39
2 Hideo Nomo	1995	11.10
3 Herb Score	1955	9.70
4 Tom Griffin	1969	9.56
5 Al Downing	1963	8.76
6 Bob Johnson	1970	8.66
7 Tom Gordon	1989	8.45
8 Fernando Valenzuela	1981	8.42
9 Edwin Correa	1986	8.41
10 Don Sutton	1966	8.34
11 Gary Nolan	1967	8.18
12 Mark Langston	1984	8.16
13 Shane Reynolds	1994	7.98
14 Chris Bosio	1987	7.94
15 John Montefusco	1975	7.93
16 Matt Kilroy	1886	7.92
17 Charlie Geggus	1884	7.92
18 Ray Culp	1963	7.79
19 John Clarkson	1884	7.78
20 Don Wilson	1967	7.78

ERA
(minimum 1 Inning Pitched/Tm Gm)

1 Tim Keefe	1880	0.86
2 Denny Driscoll	1882	1.21
3 Guy Hecker	1882	1.30
4 Harry Krause	1909	1.39
5 Ed Reulbach	1905	1.42
6 Jack Pfiester	1906	1.51
7 Monte Ward	1878	1.51
8 George McQuillan	1908	1.53
9 Ed Summers	1908	1.64
10 Russ Ford	1910	1.65
11 Jim McCormick	1878	1.69
12 Bill Burns	1908	1.70
13 Henry Boyle	1884	1.74
14 Will White	1878	1.79
15 King Cole	1910	1.80
16 Vean Gregg	1911	1.80
17 Hippo Vaughn	1910	1.83
18 Lady Baldwin	1885	1.86
19 Tony Mullane	1882	1.88
20 Ben Sanders	1888	1.90

Component ERA
(minimum 1 Inning Pitched/Tm Gm)

1 Guy Hecker	1882	1.17
2 Tim Keefe	1880	1.25
3 Russ Ford	1910	1.41
4 Denny Driscoll	1882	1.44
5 Lady Baldwin	1885	1.47
6 Henry Boyle	1884	1.47
7 Ed Morris	1884	1.52
8 Larry Corcoran	1880	1.52
9 Charlie Getzien	1884	1.61
10 Jack Pfiester	1906	1.63
11 George McQuillan	1908	1.64
12 Perry Werden	1884	1.65
13 Harry Krause	1909	1.65
14 Ed Reulbach	1905	1.68
15 Bill Burns	1908	1.73
16 Joe Wood	1909	1.86
17 Charlie Geggus	1884	1.86
18 Ben Sanders	1888	1.86
19 Mickey Hughes	1888	1.89
20 Fred Corey	1880	1.89

Opponent Average
(minimum 1 Inning Pitched/Tm Gm)

1 Hideo Nomo	1995	.182
2 Al Downing	1963	.184
3 Tim Keefe	1880	.187
4 Russ Ford	1910	.188
5 Guy Hecker	1882	.188
6 Herb Score	1955	.194
7 Jack Pfiester	1906	.197
8 Lady Baldwin	1885	.197
9 Wayne Simpson	1970	.198
10 Larry Corcoran	1880	.199
11 Spec Shea	1947	.200
12 Ed Reulbach	1905	.201
13 Dwight Gooden	1984	.202
14 Allie Reynolds	1943	.202
15 Henry Boyle	1884	.202
16 Jim Bibby	1973	.202
17 Dick Hughes	1967	.203
18 Charlie Getzien	1884	.204
19 Jeff Tesreau	1912	.204
20 Harry Krause	1909	.204

Opponent OBP
(minimum 1 Inning Pitched/Tm Gm)

1 Guy Hecker	1882	.199
2 Henry Boyle	1884	.215
3 Denny Driscoll	1882	.218
4 Tim Keefe	1880	.222
5 Lady Baldwin	1885	.228
6 Ed Morris	1884	.234
7 Perry Werden	1884	.235
8 Larry Corcoran	1880	.236
9 Charlie Getzien	1884	.237
10 Fred Corey	1880	.239
11 Russ Ford	1910	.245
12 Sam Weaver	1878	.247
13 Charlie Geggus	1884	.247
14 John Clarkson	1884	.249
15 Monte Ward	1878	.251
16 Dick Hughes	1967	.251
17 Pud Galvin	1879	.253
18 Ben Sanders	1888	.253
19 Dave Foutz	1884	.255
20 Bill Vinton	1884	.255

Batting Leaders—1876-1889

Games

Paul Hines	1,327
Cap Anson	1,325
Jim O'Rourke	1,282
John Morrill	1,263
Deacon White	1,177
Monte Ward	1,173
King Kelly	1,166
Jack Glasscock	1,133
Ned Williamson	1,128
Hick Carpenter	1,117

At-Bats

Paul Hines	5,653
Cap Anson	5,460
Jim O'Rourke	5,403
John Morrill	4,905
Monte Ward	4,903
Deacon White	4,896
King Kelly	4,856
Hick Carpenter	4,635
Jack Glasscock	4,589
Hardy Richardson	4,524

Runs

King Kelly	1,160
Harry Stovey	1,106
Jim O'Rourke	1,104
Cap Anson	1,103
George Gore	1,036
Paul Hines	1,006
Dan Brouthers	917
Hardy Richardson	911
Roger Connor	886
Monte Ward	851

Hits

Cap Anson	1,859
Paul Hines	1,729
Jim O'Rourke	1,674
King Kelly	1,531
Deacon White	1,505
Roger Connor	1,404
Dan Brouthers	1,389
Hardy Richardson	1,379
Jack Glasscock	1,331
Harry Stovey	1,325

Doubles

Cap Anson	355
Paul Hines	348
King Kelly	317
Jim O'Rourke	299
Dan Brouthers	283
Harry Stovey	261
Hardy Richardson	257
John Morrill	239
Roger Connor	238
Fred Dunlap	222

Triples

Roger Connor	142
Harry Stovey	125
Dan Brouthers	119
Buck Ewing	111
Jim O'Rourke	110
Hardy Richardson	103
John Reilly	100
George Wood	99
Bill Phillips	98
Charley Jones	98

Home Runs

Harry Stovey	89
Dan Brouthers	81
Fred Pfeffer	70
Jerry Denny	70
Cap Anson	69
Roger Connor	66
Ned Williamson	62
King Kelly	61
John Reilly	59
2 tied with	56

Home Runs (Home)

Fred Pfeffer	66
Ned Williamson	55
Jerry Denny	51
Cap Anson	51
Harry Stovey	47
John Reilly	43
King Kelly	43
Charley Jones	41
Dan Brouthers	40
George Wood	36

Home Runs (Road)

Harry Stovey	42
Dan Brouthers	41
Roger Connor	40
Fred Dunlap	28
Hardy Richardson	27
Paul Hines	27
Pete Browning	21
Buck Ewing	21
3 tied with	20

Extra Base Hits

Cap Anson	509
Dan Brouthers	483
Paul Hines	478
Harry Stovey	475
King Kelly	467
Roger Connor	446
Jim O'Rourke	443
Hardy Richardson	408
Ned Williamson	365
John Morrill	362

Total Bases

Cap Anson	2,591
Paul Hines	2,391
Jim O'Rourke	2,295
King Kelly	2,209
Dan Brouthers	2,153
Roger Connor	2,124
Harry Stovey	2,103
Hardy Richardson	1,986
Deacon White	1,901
John Morrill	1,802

RBI

Cap Anson	1,132
King Kelly	766
Dan Brouthers	718
Deacon White	709
Roger Connor	693
Paul Hines	663
Jim O'Rourke	649
Ned Williamson	641
John Morrill	641
Hardy Richardson	590

Walks

George Gore	499
Ned Williamson	470
Yank Robinson	457
Roger Connor	437
Cap Anson	425
Harry Stovey	396
Dan Brouthers	395
King Kelly	395
Paul Radford	357
John Morrill	356

Walks/PA
(minimum 3,000 Plate Appearances)

Yank Robinson	.149
Paul Radford	.114
Frank Fennelly	.107
George Gore	.107
Ned Williamson	.098
Roger Connor	.091
George Pinckney	.091
Charlie Bennett	.091
Dan Brouthers	.089
Hugh Nicol	.088

Strikeouts

John Morrill	655
Pud Galvin	562
Sam Wise	519
Ned Williamson	497
Jerry Denny	481
Joe Hornung	461
Silver Flint	461
George Wood	435
Charlie Bennett	396
Tom Burns	380

Hit By Pitch

Curt Welch	84
Tommy Tucker	80
John Reilly	77
Henry Larkin	57
Yank Robinson	57
Bill Gleason	52
Pop Smith	49
Fred Mann	43
Arlie Latham	41
Fred Carroll	37

Sac Hits

Statistic unavailable

Sac Flies

Statistic unavailable

Stolen Bases

Arlie Latham	367
Hugh Nicol	359
Curt Welch	309
Charlie Comiskey	295
Harry Stovey	292
Jim Fogarty	289
King Kelly	261
Bid McPhee	252
Monte Ward	247
Yank Robinson	221

Caught Stealing

Statistic unavailable

Runs Created

Cap Anson	1,346
Paul Hines	1,156
King Kelly	1,148
Jim O'Rourke	1,131
Roger Connor	1,076
Harry Stovey	1,073
Dan Brouthers	1,069
George Gore	949
Hardy Richardson	911
Deacon White	896

Runs Created/27 Outs
(minimum 3,000 Plate Appearances)

Dan Brouthers	10.72
Tip O'Neill	10.66
Cap Anson	9.99
Pete Browning	9.79
Roger Connor	9.73
King Kelly	9.18
Harry Stovey	9.03
Henry Larkin	8.75
George Gore	8.72
Charley Jones	8.71

Batting Average
(minimum 3,000 Plate Appearances)

Dan Brouthers	.345
Pete Browning	.345
Tip O'Neill	.343
Cap Anson	.340
Roger Connor	.324
King Kelly	.315
Jim O'Rourke	.310
Deacon White	.307
Paul Hines	.306
George Gore	.305

On-Base Percentage
(minimum 3,000 Plate Appearances)

Dan Brouthers	.408
Tip O'Neill	.402
Pete Browning	.393
Cap Anson	.389
Roger Connor	.388
George Gore	.382
Yank Robinson	.380
Henry Larkin	.374
King Kelly	.368
Harry Stovey	.355

Slugging Percentage
(minimum 3,000 Plate Appearances)

Dan Brouthers	.535
Roger Connor	.491
Tip O'Neill	.491
Pete Browning	.476
Cap Anson	.475
Harry Stovey	.469
King Kelly	.455
Buck Ewing	.448
John Reilly	.447
Charley Jones	.443

OBP+Slugging
(minimum 3,000 Plate Appearances)

Dan Brouthers	.942
Tip O'Neill	.892
Roger Connor	.879
Pete Browning	.870
Cap Anson	.863
Harry Stovey	.824
King Kelly	.823
Henry Larkin	.814
George Gore	.797
Charley Jones	.790

Secondary Average
(minimum 3,000 Plate Appearances)

Yank Robinson	.357
Harry Stovey	.327
Dan Brouthers	.315
Frank Fennelly	.302
Roger Connor	.292
King Kelly	.275
Tip O'Neill	.269
Ned Williamson	.262
Pete Browning	.262
Henry Larkin	.261

Isolated Power
(minimum 3,000 Plate Appearances)

Dan Brouthers	.190
Harry Stovey	.174
Roger Connor	.166
Buck Ewing	.154
John Reilly	.153
Tip O'Neill	.147
Charley Jones	.145
Charlie Bennett	.140
King Kelly	.140
Henry Larkin	.136

Pitching Leaders—1876-1889

Wins

Pud Galvin	324
Tim Keefe	291
Mickey Welch	285
Old Hoss Radbourn	271
Jim McCormick	265
Will White	229
John Clarkson	220
Tony Mullane	203
Tommy Bond	193
Jim Whitney	189

Losses

Pud Galvin	269
Jim McCormick	214
Jim Whitney	202
Mickey Welch	187
Tim Keefe	180
Old Hoss Radbourn	170
Will White	166
Stump Wiedman	156
Tony Mullane	138
Guy Hecker	137

Winning Percentage
(minimum 100 decisions)

Bob Caruthers	.732
Dave Foutz	.701
John Clarkson	.692
Silver King	.683
Larry Corcoran	.665
Lady Baldwin	.660
Tommy Bond	.627
Elton Chamberlin	.625
Fred Goldsmith	.622
Tim Keefe	.618

Games

Pud Galvin	614
Mickey Welch	504
Jim McCormick	492
Tim Keefe	489
Old Hoss Radbourn	461
Jim Whitney	407
Will White	403
Tony Mullane	368
John Clarkson	329
Bobby Mathews	323

Games Started

Pud Galvin	602
Mickey Welch	496
Tim Keefe	486
Jim McCormick	485
Old Hoss Radbourn	441
Will White	401
Jim Whitney	392
Tony Mullane	344
John Clarkson	326
Bobby Mathews	315

Complete Games

Pud Galvin	573
Mickey Welch	478
Tim Keefe	469
Jim McCormick	466
Old Hoss Radbourn	430
Will White	394
Jim Whitney	374
Tony Mullane	329
John Clarkson	309
Guy Hecker	299

Shutouts

Pud Galvin	53
Mickey Welch	39
Tim Keefe	36
Will White	36
Tommy Bond	35
Jim McCormick	33
Old Hoss Radbourn	32
Ed Morris	28
Charlie Buffinton	28
George Bradley	28

Saves

Tony Mullane	7
Jack Manning	6
Charlie Ferguson	4
Cal McVey	4
Oyster Burns	4
Adonis Terry	4
Billy Taylor	4
6 tied with	3

Games Finished

Monte Ward	32
Tony Mullane	25
George Bradley	22
Jack Manning	20
Old Hoss Radbourn	19
Curry Foley	17
Fred Corey	17
Blondie Purcell	16
3 tied with	15

Batters Faced

Pud Galvin	22,285
Mickey Welch	18,186
Jim McCormick	17,658
Tim Keefe	17,204
Old Hoss Radbourn	16,473
Will White	14,829
Jim Whitney	14,450
Tony Mullane	12,718
John Clarkson	11,954
Bobby Mathews	11,929

Innings Pitched

Pud Galvin	5,289.2
Mickey Welch	4,344.2
Jim McCormick	4,275.2
Tim Keefe	4,198.2
Old Hoss Radbourn	3,974.1
Will White	3,542.2
Jim Whitney	3,456.1
Tony Mullane	3,078.1
John Clarkson	2,858.0
Guy Hecker	2,786.1

Hits Allowed

Pud Galvin	5,615
Mickey Welch	4,132
Jim McCormick	4,092
Old Hoss Radbourn	3,747
Tim Keefe	3,593
Jim Whitney	3,537
Will White	3,440
Bobby Mathews	3,008
Tommy Bond	2,857
Tony Mullane	2,800

Runs Allowed

Pud Galvin	2,885
Mickey Welch	2,266
Jim McCormick	2,095
Jim Whitney	1,999
Tim Keefe	1,946
Old Hoss Radbourn	1,943
Will White	1,844
Bobby Mathews	1,758
Tony Mullane	1,628
Guy Hecker	1,604

Earned Runs Allowed

Pud Galvin	1,650
Mickey Welch	1,266
Jim McCormick	1,155
Tim Keefe	1,151
Jim Whitney	1,131
Old Hoss Radbourn	1,119
Tony Mullane	952
Stump Wiedman	928
Bobby Mathews	910
Will White	896

Home Runs Allowed

Pud Galvin	105
John Clarkson	103
Old Hoss Radbourn	96
Mickey Welch	94
Jim McCormick	82
Charlie Getzien	80
Jim Whitney	78
Larry Corcoran	69
Charlie Buffinton	67
Will White	65

Walks

Mickey Welch	1,074
Tim Keefe	905
Jim McCormick	749
Old Hoss Radbourn	713
Tony Mullane	709
John Clarkson	624
Pud Galvin	579
Toad Ramsey	569
Charlie Buffinton	564
Matt Kilroy	560

Intentional Walks

Statistic unavailable

Strikeouts

Tim Keefe	2,189
Mickey Welch	1,706
Jim McCormick	1,704
Old Hoss Radbourn	1,696
Pud Galvin	1,662
Jim Whitney	1,565
John Clarkson	1,470
Charlie Buffinton	1,423
Tony Mullane	1,338
Toad Ramsey	1,258

Strikeouts/9 Innings
(minimum 1,000 Innings Pitched)

Toad Ramsey	6.46
Mark Baldwin	5.64
One Arm Daily	5.38
Matt Kilroy	4.93
Dupee Shaw	4.85
Charlie Buffinton	4.81
Adonis Terry	4.71
Tim Keefe	4.69
Hardie Henderson	4.68
John Clarkson	4.63

ERA
(minimum 1,000 Innings Pitched)

Jim Devlin	1.89
Monte Ward	2.10
Tommy Bond	2.25
Will White	2.28
Larry Corcoran	2.36
Jim McCormick	2.43
Terry Larkin	2.43
Tim Keefe	2.47
George Bradley	2.50
Old Hoss Radbourn	2.53

Component ERA
(minimum 1,000 Innings Pitched)

Monte Ward	2.01
Tim Keefe	2.06
Jim Devlin	2.14
Charlie Sweeney	2.15
Ed Morris	2.19
Larry Corcoran	2.23
Bob Caruthers	2.23
Terry Larkin	2.32
George Bradley	2.34
Charlie Ferguson	2.35

Sac Hits Allowed

Statistic unavailable

Sac Flies Allowed

Statistic unavailable

Hit Batsmen

Tony Mullane	82
Will White	68
Hank O'Day	63
Ed Morris	56
Tim Keefe	56
Guy Hecker	54
Hardie Henderson	51
Kid Madden	51
Bobby Mathews	48
2 tied with	47

Wild Pitches

Mickey Welch	259
Jim Whitney	214
Pud Galvin	206
Old Hoss Radbourn	198
Tim Keefe	192
Will White	168
Jim McCormick	157
Monte Ward	144
George Bradley	139
Charlie Buffinton	135

Balks

Charlie Ferguson	3
Shorty Wetzel	2
John Henry	2
Fred Goldsmith	2
Egyptian Healy	2
John Kirby	2
Charlie Buffinton	2
Jim Whitney	2
14 tied with	1

Opponent Average
(minimum 1,000 Innings Pitched)

Tim Keefe	.223
Larry Corcoran	.226
Charlie Sweeney	.229
Ed Morris	.229
Gus Weyhing	.230
John Clarkson	.231
Dave Foutz	.231
Bob Caruthers	.233
Toad Ramsey	.233
Charlie Ferguson	.233

Opponent OBP
(minimum 1,000 Innings Pitched)

Monte Ward	.254
Jim Devlin	.258
Charlie Sweeney	.260
George Bradley	.261
Terry Larkin	.263
Larry Corcoran	.264
Tim Keefe	.266
Tommy Bond	.267
Ed Morris	.267
Will White	.269

Single Season Batting Leaders—1876-1889

Games

George Pinckney	1888	143
George Pinckney	1886	141
Bill Phillips	1886	141
Bill McClellan	1886	141
Ollie Beard	1889	141
6 tied with		140

At-Bats

Arlie Latham	1887	627
Tommy McCarthy	1889	604
Bill Gleason	1887	598
George Pinckney	1886	597
Bill McClellan	1886	595
Charlie Comiskey	1889	587
Bill Phillips	1886	585
Tom Poorman	1887	585
Dick Johnston	1888	585
Hugh Duffy	1889	584

Runs

Tip O'Neill	1887	167
Arlie Latham	1887	163
Fred Dunlap	1884	160
King Kelly	1886	155
Dan Brouthers	1887	153
Arlie Latham	1886	152
Mike Griffin	1889	152
Harry Stovey	1889	152
George Gore	1886	150
Mike Tiernan	1889	147

Hits

Tip O'Neill	1887	225
Pete Browning	1887	220
Denny Lyons	1887	209
Jack Glasscock	1889	205
Sam Thompson	1887	203
Arlie Latham	1887	198
Tommy Tucker	1889	196
Dave Orr	1886	193
Tip O'Neill	1886	190
Hardy Richardson	1886	189

Doubles

Tip O'Neill	1887	52
Ned Williamson	1883	49
Denny Lyons	1887	43
Dan Brouthers	1883	41
King Kelly	1889	41
Orator Shaffer	1884	40
Dan Brouthers	1886	40
Jack Glasscock	1889	40
3 tied with		39

Triples

Dave Orr	1886	31
Harry Stovey	1884	23
Sam Thompson	1887	23
Roger Connor	1887	22
Dave Orr	1885	21
Buck Ewing	1884	20
Roger Connor	1886	20
Dick Johnston	1887	20
Dan Brouthers	1887	20
Harry Stovey	1888	20

Home Runs

Ned Williamson	1884	27
Fred Pfeffer	1884	25
Abner Dalrymple	1884	22
Cap Anson	1884	21
Sam Thompson	1889	20
Billy O'Brien	1887	19
Bug Holliday	1889	19
Harry Stovey	1889	19
Jerry Denny	1889	18
2 tied with		17

Home Runs (Home)

Fred Pfeffer	1884	25
Ned Williamson	1884	25
Cap Anson	1884	20
Abner Dalrymple	1884	18
Jerry Denny	1889	16
Fred Pfeffer	1887	14
Bug Holliday	1889	14
Sam Thompson	1889	14
King Kelly	1884	12
Jerry Denny	1888	12

Home Runs (Road)

Harry Stovey	1889	12
Roger Connor	1888	11
Roger Connor	1887	10
Jake Beckley	1889	9
Roger Connor	1889	9
Mike Tiernan	1887	8
Billy O'Brien	1887	8
9 tied with		7

Extra Base Hits

Tip O'Neill	1887	85
Harry Stovey	1889	70
Dan Brouthers	1887	68
Dan Brouthers	1886	66
Roger Connor	1887	65
Dave Orr	1886	63
Denny Lyons	1887	63
Sam Thompson	1887	63
Jimmy Ryan	1889	62
Roger Connor	1889	62

Total Bases

Tip O'Neill	1887	357
Sam Thompson	1887	311
Dave Orr	1886	301
Pete Browning	1887	299
Denny Lyons	1887	298
Harry Stovey	1889	292
Jimmy Ryan	1889	287
Oyster Burns	1887	286
Dan Brouthers	1886	284
Jimmy Ryan	1888	283

RBI

Sam Thompson	1887	166
Cap Anson	1886	147
Roger Connor	1889	130
Tip O'Neill	1887	123
Harry Stovey	1889	119
Pete Browning	1887	118
Dan Brouthers	1889	118
Cap Anson	1889	117
Dave Foutz	1889	113
Jerry Denny	1889	112

Walks

Yank Robinson	1889	118
Yank Robinson	1888	116
Jim McTamany	1889	116
Paul Radford	1887	106
George Gore	1886	102
Mike Tiernan	1889	96
Roger Connor	1889	93
Yank Robinson	1887	92
Mike Griffin	1889	91
Paul Radford	1889	91

Walks/PA

(minimum 3.1 PA/Tm Gm)

Yank Robinson	1889	.205
Yank Robinson	1888	.199
George Gore	1886	.187
Jim McTamany	1889	.180
Paul Radford	1887	.177
Yank Robinson	1887	.171
Mike Tiernan	1889	.160
Roger Connor	1889	.157
Ned Williamson	1886	.157
Paul Radford	1889	.156

Strikeouts

Sam Wise	1884	104
Frank Meinke	1884	89
John Morrill	1884	87
John Morrill	1887	86
Charlie Bastian	1885	82
Emmett Seery	1886	82
John Morrill	1886	81
Charlie Duffee	1889	81
4 tied with		80

Hit By Pitch

Tommy Tucker	1889	33
Tommy Tucker	1887	29
Curt Welch	1888	29
Jay Faatz	1888	21
Curt Welch	1889	19
Frank Fennelly	1886	18
Tommy Tucker	1888	18
John Reilly	1889	18
Yank Robinson	1887	17

Sac Hits

Statistic unavailable

Sac Flies

Statistic unavailable

Stolen Bases

Hugh Nicol	1887	138
Arlie Latham	1887	129
Charlie Comiskey	1887	117
Monte Ward	1887	111
Billy Hamilton	1889	111
Arlie Latham	1888	109
Pete Browning	1887	103
Hugh Nicol	1888	103
Jim Fogarty	1887	102
Jim Fogarty	1889	99

Caught Stealing

Statistic unavailable

Runs Created

Tip O'Neill	1887	192
Pete Browning	1887	163
Fred Dunlap	1884	160
Tommy Tucker	1889	158
King Kelly	1886	156
Denny Lyons	1887	154
Oyster Burns	1887	153
Cap Anson	1886	152
Sam Thompson	1887	152
Darby O'Brien	1889	151

Runs Created/27 Outs

(minimum 3.1 PA/Tm Gm)

Ross Barnes	1876	17.46
Tip O'Neill	1887	16.99
Fred Dunlap	1884	16.46
King Kelly	1886	14.63
Bob Caruthers	1887	13.03
Pete Browning	1887	12.88
Deacon White	1877	12.73
Dan Brouthers	1886	12.61
Pete Browning	1882	12.54
George Hall	1876	12.54

Batting Average

(minimum 3.1 PA/Tm Gm)

Tip O'Neill	1887	.435
Ross Barnes	1876	.429
Fred Dunlap	1884	.412
Pete Browning	1887	.402
Cap Anson	1881	.399
King Kelly	1886	.388
Deacon White	1877	.387
John Cassidy	1877	.378
Pete Browning	1882	.378
Dan Brouthers	1883	.374

On-Base Percentage

(minimum 3.1 PA/Tm Gm)

Tip O'Neill	1887	.490
King Kelly	1886	.483
Pete Browning	1887	.464
Bob Caruthers	1887	.463
Ross Barnes	1876	.462
Dan Brouthers	1889	.462
Tommy Tucker	1889	.450
Fred Dunlap	1884	.448
Mike Tiernan	1889	.447
Yank Robinson	1887	.445

Slugging Percentage

(minimum 3.1 PA/Tm Gm)

Tip O'Neill	1887	.691
Fred Dunlap	1884	.621
Ross Barnes	1876	.590
Dan Brouthers	1886	.581
Dan Brouthers	1883	.572
Sam Thompson	1887	.571
Dan Brouthers	1884	.563
Dan Brouthers	1887	.562
Ned Williamson	1884	.554
John Reilly	1884	.551

OBP+Slugging

(minimum 3.1 PA/Tm Gm)

Tip O'Neill	1887	1.180
Fred Dunlap	1884	1.069
Ross Barnes	1876	1.052
Dan Brouthers	1886	1.026
King Kelly	1886	1.018
Pete Browning	1887	1.011
Bob Caruthers	1887	1.010
Dan Brouthers	1887	.988
Sam Thompson	1887	.987
Cap Anson	1886	.977

Secondary Average

(minimum 3.1 PA/Tm Gm)

Hugh Nicol	1887	.524
Jim Fogarty	1887	.521
Roger Connor	1887	.507
Bob Caruthers	1887	.505
Yank Robinson	1887	.488
Harry Stovey	1889	.469
Billy Hamilton	1889	.464
Yank Robinson	1888	.462
Harry Stovey	1888	.455
King Kelly	1887	.452

Isolated Power

(minimum 3.1 PA/Tm Gm)

Ned Williamson	1884	.276
Roger Connor	1887	.257
Tip O'Neill	1887	.255
Dan Brouthers	1884	.236
Fred Pfeffer	1884	.225
Dan Brouthers	1887	.224
Dan Brouthers	1881	.222
Harry Stovey	1884	.219
Harry Stovey	1889	.218
Billy O'Brien	1887	.214

Single Season Pitching Leaders—1876-1889

Wins

Old Hoss Radbourn	1884	59
John Clarkson	1885	53
Guy Hecker	1884	52
John Clarkson	1889	49
Old Hoss Radbourn	1883	48
Charlie Buffinton	1884	48
Al Spalding	1876	47
Monte Ward	1879	47
3 tied with		46

Losses

John Coleman	1883	48
Will White	1880	42
Larry McKeon	1884	41
Jim McCormick	1879	40
George Bradley	1879	40
Henry Porter	1888	37
Stump Wiedman	1886	36
5 tied with		35

Winning Percentage
(minimum 15 decisions)

Fred Goldsmith	1880	.875
Henry Boyle	1884	.833
Old Hoss Radbourn	1884	.831
Mickey Welch	1885	.800
Al Spalding	1876	.797
Jocko Flynn	1886	.793
Bob Caruthers	1889	.784
Jack Manning	1876	.783
Will White	1882	.769
Charlie Ferguson	1886	.769

Games

Will White	1879	76
Old Hoss Radbourn	1883	76
Pud Galvin	1883	76
Guy Hecker	1884	75
Old Hoss Radbourn	1884	75
Lee Richmond	1880	74
Jim McCormick	1880	74
John Clarkson	1889	73
Pud Galvin	1884	72
3 tied with		70

Games Started

Will White	1879	75
Pud Galvin	1883	75
Jim McCormick	1880	74
Guy Hecker	1884	73
Old Hoss Radbourn	1884	73
Pud Galvin	1884	72
John Clarkson	1889	72
John Clarkson	1885	70
Matt Kilroy	1887	69
4 tied with		68

Complete Games

Will White	1879	75
Old Hoss Radbourn	1884	73
Jim McCormick	1880	72
Pud Galvin	1883	72
Guy Hecker	1884	72
Pud Galvin	1884	71
Tim Keefe	1883	68
John Clarkson	1885	68
John Clarkson	1889	68
5 tied with		66

Shutouts

George Bradley	1876	16
Pud Galvin	1884	12
Ed Morris	1886	12
Tommy Bond	1879	11
Old Hoss Radbourn	1884	11
Dave Foutz	1886	11
Jim McCormick	1884	10
John Clarkson	1885	10
Tommy Bond	1878	9
George Derby	1881	9

Saves

Jack Manning	1876	5
Tony Mullane	1889	5
Billy Taylor	1884	4
Lee Richmond	1880	3
Oyster Burns	1885	3
Adonis Terry	1887	3
16 tied with		2

Games Finished

Jack Manning	1876	13
Amos Rusie	1889	11
Monte Ward	1879	10
Lee Richmond	1880	9
Billy Taylor	1883	9
Monte Ward	1883	9
Tony Mullane	1889	9
5 tied with		8

Batters Faced

Will White	1879	2,906
Pud Galvin	1883	2,741
John Clarkson	1889	2,736
Old Hoss Radbourn	1884	2,672
Jim McCormick	1880	2,669
Guy Hecker	1884	2,649
Jim Devlin	1876	2,568
Pud Galvin	1884	2,554
John Coleman	1883	2,546
Old Hoss Radbourn	1883	2,540

Innings Pitched

Will White	1879	680.0
Old Hoss Radbourn	1884	678.2
Guy Hecker	1884	670.2
Jim McCormick	1880	657.2
Pud Galvin	1883	656.1
Pud Galvin	1884	636.1
Old Hoss Radbourn	1883	632.1
John Clarkson	1885	623.0
Jim Devlin	1876	622.0
John Clarkson	1889	620.0

Hits Allowed

John Coleman	1883	772
Bobby Mathews	1876	693
Will White	1879	676
Pud Galvin	1883	676
Jim Devlin	1877	617
George Bradley	1879	590
John Clarkson	1889	589
Pud Galvin	1879	585
Jim McCormick	1880	585
Matt Kilroy	1887	585

Runs Allowed

John Coleman	1883	510
Will White	1879	404
Bobby Mathews	1876	395
Phenomenal Smith	1887	369
Pud Galvin	1883	367
George Bradley	1879	361
Al Mays	1887	359
Toad Ramsey	1887	358
Mark Baldwin	1889	358
3 tied with		350

Earned Runs Allowed

John Coleman	1883	291
Al Mays	1887	232
Gus Weyhing	1887	221
Henry Porter	1888	219
Matt Kilroy	1886	218
Tony Mullane	1886	218
Ed Seward	1887	216
Old Hoss Radbourn	1887	215
Stump Wiedman	1886	214
Toad Ramsey	1887	214

Home Runs Allowed

Larry Corcoran	1884	35
Charlie Getzien	1889	27
Egyptian Healy	1887	24
Charlie Getzien	1887	24
Pud Galvin	1884	23
Mark Baldwin	1887	23
Lev Shreve	1888	23
Billy Serad	1884	21
John Clarkson	1885	21
Park Swartzel	1889	21

Walks

Mark Baldwin	1889	274
Gus Weyhing	1889	212
Toad Ramsey	1886	207
Mike Morrison	1887	205
John Clarkson	1889	203
Matt Kilroy	1886	182
Phenomenal Smith	1887	176
Gus Weyhing	1887	167
Toad Ramsey	1887	167
Darby O'Brien	1889	167

Intentional Walks

Statistic unavailable

Strikeouts

Matt Kilroy	1886	513
Toad Ramsey	1886	499
One Arm Daily	1884	483
Dupee Shaw	1884	451
Old Hoss Radbourn	1884	441
Charlie Buffinton	1884	417
Guy Hecker	1884	385
Bill Sweeney	1884	374
Pud Galvin	1884	369
Mark Baldwin	1889	368

Strikeouts/9 Innings
(minimum 1 Inning Pitched/Tm Gm)

One Arm Daily	1884	8.68
Matt Kilroy	1886	7.92
Charlie Geggus	1884	7.92
John Clarkson	1884	7.78
Toad Ramsey	1886	7.63
Dupee Shaw	1884	7.47
Jim Whitney	1884	7.23
Mike Dorgan	1884	7.17
Walter Burke	1884	7.13
Hardie Henderson	1884	7.09

ERA
(minimum 1 Inning Pitched/Tm Gm)

Tim Keefe	1880	0.86
Denny Driscoll	1882	1.21
George Bradley	1876	1.23
Guy Hecker	1882	1.30
George Bradley	1880	1.38
Old Hoss Radbourn	1884	1.38
Monte Ward	1878	1.51
Harry McCormick	1882	1.52
Will White	1882	1.54
Jim Devlin	1876	1.56

Component ERA
(minimum 1 Inning Pitched/Tm Gm)

Charlie Sweeney	1884	1.32
Guy Hecker	1884	1.43
Denny Driscoll	1882	1.44
Silver King	1888	1.44
George Bradley	1876	1.45
Ed Morris	1884	1.52
Larry Corcoran	1880	1.52
Tommy Bond	1876	1.53
Jim Whitney	1884	1.55
Monte Ward	1880	1.56

Sac Hits Allowed

Statistic unavailable

Sac Flies Allowed

Statistic unavailable

Hit Batsmen

Gus Weyhing	1887	37
Will White	1884	35
Tony Mullane	1884	32
Tony Mullane	1887	32
Will White	1885	27
Gus Shallix	1884	26
Ed Seward	1887	24
Tom Sullivan	1888	24
Darby O'Brien	1889	24
2 tied with		22

Wild Pitches

Bill Stemmeyer	1886	63
Hardie Henderson	1885	55
Tony Mullane	1886	51
Mickey Welch	1886	51
Matt Kilroy	1886	50
Will White	1879	49
John Harkins	1884	48
Jim Whitney	1881	46
3 tied with		43

Balks

Charlie Ferguson	1885	3
John Henry	1884	2
Shorty Wetzel	1885	2
Charlie Buffinton	1885	2
21 tied with		1

Opponent Average
(minimum 1 Inning Pitched/Tm Gm)

Tim Keefe	1880	.187
Guy Hecker	1882	.188
Adonis Terry	1888	.191
Charlie Sweeney	1884	.193
Tim Keefe	1888	.195
Lady Baldwin	1885	.197
Silver King	1888	.197
Toad Ramsey	1886	.198
Larry Corcoran	1880	.199
Ed Seward	1888	.199

Opponent OBP
(minimum 1 Inning Pitched/Tm Gm)

Guy Hecker	1882	.199
Charlie Sweeney	1884	.211
Henry Boyle	1884	.215
George Bradley	1880	.217
Denny Driscoll	1882	.218
Tim Keefe	1880	.222
Jim Whitney	1884	.223
Silver King	1888	.224
George Bradley	1876	.224
Guy Hecker	1884	.226

Batting Leaders—1890-1899

Games

Hugh Duffy	1,362
George Van Haltren	1,340
Dummy Hoy	1,329
Tommy Corcoran	1,309
Tommy Tucker	1,281
Ed Delahanty	1,270
Ed McKean	1,268
Jake Beckley	1,267
George Davis	1,264
Herman Long	1,263

At-Bats

Hugh Duffy	5,607
George Van Haltren	5,506
Herman Long	5,334
Tommy Corcoran	5,330
Ed McKean	5,303
Dummy Hoy	5,296
Ed Delahanty	5,259
Jake Beckley	5,093
Patsy Donovan	5,092
George Davis	5,064

Runs

Billy Hamilton	1,351
Hugh Duffy	1,264
Ed Delahanty	1,209
George Van Haltren	1,185
Jesse Burkett	1,170
Cupid Childs	1,123
Herman Long	1,117
Dummy Hoy	1,091
Jimmy Ryan	1,010
Mike Tiernan	1,009

Hits

Ed Delahanty	1,863
Hugh Duffy	1,860
Jesse Burkett	1,798
George Van Haltren	1,782
Billy Hamilton	1,690
Ed McKean	1,606
George Davis	1,587
Herman Long	1,560
Jake Beckley	1,554
Patsy Donovan	1,536

Doubles

Ed Delahanty	373
Hugh Duffy	271
George Davis	265
Jimmy Ryan	264
Jake Beckley	259
Herman Long	251
Mike Griffin	239
Sam Thompson	236
Bill Dahlen	225
Jack Doyle	215

Triples

Jake Beckley	165
Ed Delahanty	139
Mike Tiernan	128
Ed McKean	122
George Van Haltren	121
Joe Kelley	120
George Davis	120
Elmer Smith	115
Bill Dahlen	113
Jesse Burkett	113

Home Runs

Hugh Duffy	83
Ed Delahanty	79
Mike Tiernan	78
Sam Thompson	75
Roger Connor	72
Herman Long	71
Bill Joyce	70
Jack Clements	66
Bobby Lowe	64
Jake Beckley	63

Home Runs (Home)

Hugh Duffy	65
Herman Long	56
Bobby Lowe	52
Sam Thompson	52
Roger Connor	48
Jack Clements	44
Ed Delahanty	40
Mike Tiernan	40
Bill Joyce	39
3 tied with	32

Home Runs (Road)

Ed Delahanty	39
Mike Tiernan	38
Jake Beckley	36
Ed McKean	35
Bill Dahlen	32
Bill Joyce	31
Joe Kelley	30
George Davis	29
Jesse Burkett	28
Jimmy Ryan	26

Extra Base Hits

Ed Delahanty	591
Jake Beckley	487
Hugh Duffy	447
George Davis	442
Jimmy Ryan	419
Sam Thompson	413
Mike Tiernan	410
Herman Long	403
Bill Dahlen	399
Ed McKean	389

Total Bases

Ed Delahanty	2,751
Hugh Duffy	2,566
Jesse Burkett	2,369
George Van Haltren	2,369
Jake Beckley	2,332
George Davis	2,263
Ed McKean	2,225
Herman Long	2,186
Jimmy Ryan	2,139
Billy Hamilton	2,121

RBI

Hugh Duffy	1,088
Ed Delahanty	1,075
Jake Beckley	953
George Davis	933
Ed McKean	927
Sam Thompson	846
Steve Brodie	817
Herman Long	785
Joe Kelley	777
Lave Cross	759

Walks

Billy Hamilton	925
Cupid Childs	904
Dummy Hoy	733
Bill Joyce	718
Bid McPhee	689
John McGraw	642
Jesse Burkett	640
Mike Griffin	608
George Van Haltren	603
Jack Crooks	600

Walks/PA

(minimum 3,000 Plate Appearances)

Jack Crooks	.176
Bill Joyce	.173
John McGraw	.163
Billy Hamilton	.161
Cupid Childs	.154
Denny Lyons	.142
Roger Connor	.139
Dan Brouthers	.138
Billy Nash	.133
Bid McPhee	.127

Strikeouts

Tom Brown	519
Tom Daly	322
Bill Joyce	280
Chief Zimmer	274
Bill Dahlen	266
Gus Weyhing	265
Bill Hutchison	245
Jimmy McAleer	241
Morgan Murphy	237
Jesse Burkett	230

Hit By Pitch

Hughie Jennings	243
Tommy Tucker	192
Jake Beckley	138
Steve Brodie	118
Bill Joyce	108
Dummy Hoy	98
Curt Welch	89
John McGraw	88
Fred Clarke	83
Bill Dahlen	83

Sac Hits

Bones Ely	111
Dummy Hoy	104
Herman Long	100
Hughie Jennings	91
Fred Tenney	90
Willie Keeler	88
Hugh Duffy	87
Bobby Lowe	83
Tommy Corcoran	83
Lave Cross	81

Sac Flies

Statistic unavailable

Stolen Bases

Billy Hamilton	730
Tom Brown	493
Hugh Duffy	483
Dummy Hoy	439
George Van Haltren	433
Jack Doyle	408
Bill Lange	399
George Davis	398
Arlie Latham	371
2 tied with	369

Caught Stealing

Statistic unavailable

Runs Created

Billy Hamilton	1,362
Hugh Duffy	1,346
Ed Delahanty	1,327
Jesse Burkett	1,230
George Van Haltren	1,203
Cupid Childs	1,109
George Davis	1,094
Dummy Hoy	1,070
Jake Beckley	1,047
Jimmy Ryan	1,035

Runs Created/27 Outs

(minimum 3,000 Plate Appearances)

Billy Hamilton	11.41
Dan Brouthers	10.65
Ed Delahanty	9.97
John McGraw	9.90
Joe Kelley	9.85
Bill Joyce	9.63
Jesse Burkett	9.60
Willie Keeler	9.57
Hugh Duffy	9.05
Sam Thompson	8.96

Batting Average

(minimum 3,000 Plate Appearances)

Willie Keeler	.384
Billy Hamilton	.357
Jesse Burkett	.356
Ed Delahanty	.354
Joe Kelley	.340
Jake Stenzel	.339
Dan Brouthers	.339
Sam Thompson	.338
John McGraw	.336
Fred Clarke	.334

On-Base Percentage

(minimum 3,000 Plate Appearances)

Billy Hamilton	.468
John McGraw	.461
Dan Brouthers	.446
Bill Joyce	.435
Jesse Burkett	.433
Joe Kelley	.432
Willie Keeler	.430
Cupid Childs	.428
Ed Delahanty	.421
Denny Lyons	.415

Slugging Percentage

(minimum 3,000 Plate Appearances)

Ed Delahanty	.523
Sam Thompson	.509
Dan Brouthers	.497
Joe Kelley	.493
Willie Keeler	.482
Roger Connor	.480
Jake Stenzel	.480
Jesse Burkett	.470
Bill Joyce	.467
Mike Tiernan	.464

OBP+Slugging

(minimum 3,000 Plate Appearances)

Ed Delahanty	.944
Dan Brouthers	.943
Joe Kelley	.925
Billy Hamilton	.916
Willie Keeler	.912
Jesse Burkett	.903
Sam Thompson	.902
Bill Joyce	.902
Jake Stenzel	.888
Roger Connor	.888

Secondary Average

(minimum 3,000 Plate Appearances)

Bill Joyce	.471
Billy Hamilton	.440
John McGraw	.394
Joe Kelley	.388
Dan Brouthers	.378
Roger Connor	.376
Jack Crooks	.375
Bill Lange	.363
Kip Selbach	.354
Mike Tiernan	.348

Isolated Power

(minimum 3,000 Plate Appearances)

Bill Joyce	.174
Roger Connor	.173
Sam Thompson	.171
Ed Delahanty	.169
Jack Clements	.158
Dan Brouthers	.158
Joe Kelley	.153
Jake Beckley	.153
Mike Tiernan	.152
Bill Dahlen	.146

Pitching Leaders—1890-1899

Wins

Kid Nichols	297
Cy Young	267
Amos Rusie	233
Jack Stivetts	191
Gus Weyhing	174
Bill Hutchison	167
Frank Killen	161
Sadie McMahon	159
Frank Dwyer	156
Brickyard Kennedy	154

Losses

Amos Rusie	163
Gus Weyhing	158
Ted Breitenstein	157
Cy Young	151
Kid Nichols	151
Pink Hawley	147
Bill Hutchison	145
Kid Carsey	138
Frank Dwyer	138
Red Ehret	136

Winning Percentage

(minimum 100 decisions)

Bill Hoffer	.701
Kid Nichols	.663
Ted Lewis	.650
Cy Young	.639
Nig Cuppy	.630
Clark Griffith	.623
Tom Lovett	.610
Jack Stivetts	.604
Al Orth	.589
Amos Rusie	.588

Games

Kid Nichols	489
Cy Young	464
Amos Rusie	426
Gus Weyhing	364
Jack Stivetts	362
Ted Breitenstein	352
Bill Hutchison	336
Frank Dwyer	329
Pink Hawley	326
Brickyard Kennedy	325

Games Started

Kid Nichols	440
Cy Young	411
Amos Rusie	403
Gus Weyhing	333
Ted Breitenstein	318
Jack Stivetts	313
Bill Hutchison	308
Jouett Meekin	306
Frank Killen	294
Brickyard Kennedy	289

Complete Games

Kid Nichols	417
Cy Young	386
Amos Rusie	371
Gus Weyhing	293
Bill Hutchison	286
Ted Breitenstein	281
Jouett Meekin	269
Jack Stivetts	260
Sadie McMahon	252
2 tied with	247

Shutouts

Kid Nichols	36
Amos Rusie	29
Cy Young	28
Gus Weyhing	19
Bill Hutchison	18
Frank Killen	13
Billy Rhines	13
Red Ehret	13
3 tied with	12

Saves

Kid Nichols	16
Brickyard Kennedy	9
Jack Taylor	9
Cy Young	8
Tony Mullane	8
Win Mercer	7
George Hemming	6
Frank Dwyer	6
4 tied with	5

Games Finished

Cy Young	50
Kid Nichols	47
Jack Stivetts	46
Frank Dwyer	45
Red Ehret	40
Pink Hawley	39
Kid Carsey	35
Duke Esper	35
Mike Sullivan	35
Brickyard Kennedy	34

Batters Faced

Kid Nichols	16,797
Cy Young	15,724
Amos Rusie	14,912
Gus Weyhing	12,738
Ted Breitenstein	11,982
Bill Hutchison	11,771
Jack Stivetts	11,648
Jouett Meekin	11,397
Frank Dwyer	10,943
Brickyard Kennedy	10,897

Innings Pitched

Kid Nichols	3,985.2
Cy Young	3,721.2
Amos Rusie	3,522.2
Gus Weyhing	2,890.0
Ted Breitenstein	2,757.0
Bill Hutchison	2,743.0
Jack Stivetts	2,696.0
Jouett Meekin	2,590.1
Pink Hawley	2,501.0
Frank Dwyer	2,501.0

Hits Allowed

Kid Nichols	3,913
Cy Young	3,855
Gus Weyhing	3,244
Amos Rusie	3,095
Frank Dwyer	2,973
Ted Breitenstein	2,862
Jouett Meekin	2,811
Bill Hutchison	2,803
Kid Carsey	2,771
Jack Stivetts	2,752

Runs Allowed

Kid Nichols	2,008
Cy Young	1,904
Gus Weyhing	1,880
Amos Rusie	1,860
Jack Stivetts	1,751
Kid Carsey	1,713
Ted Breitenstein	1,708
Bill Hutchison	1,696
Jouett Meekin	1,683
Pink Hawley	1,590

Earned Runs Allowed

Gus Weyhing	1,338
Kid Nichols	1,317
Cy Young	1,260
Ted Breitenstein	1,241
Kid Carsey	1,215
Jouett Meekin	1,167
Jack Stivetts	1,151
Amos Rusie	1,133
Brickyard Kennedy	1,108
Pink Hawley	1,104

Home Runs Allowed

Kid Nichols	132
Jack Stivetts	127
Frank Dwyer	94
Bill Hutchison	93
Cy Young	87
Brickyard Kennedy	87
Gus Weyhing	86
Kid Carsey	79
Harry Staley	75
2 tied with	74

Walks

Amos Rusie	1,585
Ted Breitenstein	1,110
Jack Stivetts	1,087
Jouett Meekin	1,050
Gus Weyhing	1,028
Bill Hutchison	1,014
Kid Nichols	997
Brickyard Kennedy	993
Pink Hawley	844
Sadie McMahon	843

Intentional Walks

Statistic unavailable

Strikeouts

Amos Rusie	1,819
Kid Nichols	1,471
Cy Young	1,124
Bill Hutchison	1,091
Jack Stivetts	1,080
Gus Weyhing	1,038
Jouett Meekin	897
Sadie McMahon	850
Ted Breitenstein	847
Pink Hawley	738

Strikeouts/9 Innings

(minimum 1,000 Innings Pitched)

Amos Rusie	4.65
Doc McJames	3.90
Elton Chamberlin	3.84
Ed Crane	3.79
Willie McGill	3.67
Jack Stivetts	3.61
Bill Hutchison	3.58
Phil Knell	3.53
Mark Baldwin	3.49
George Haddock	3.42

ERA

(minimum 1,000 Innings Pitched)

Amos Rusie	2.89
Kid Nichols	2.97
Cy Young	3.05
John Clarkson	3.27
Doc McJames	3.34
Mark Baldwin	3.37
Clark Griffith	3.47
Nig Cuppy	3.47
Billy Rhines	3.48
Sadie McMahon	3.50

Component ERA

(minimum 1,000 Innings Pitched)

Kid Nichols	2.95
Amos Rusie	2.96
Cy Young	3.00
Billy Rhines	3.30
John Clarkson	3.33
Sadie McMahon	3.52
Bill Hutchison	3.53
Silver King	3.55
Mark Baldwin	3.56
Tony Mullane	3.58

Sac Hits Allowed

Cy Young	147
Kid Nichols	122
Harley Payne	44
Bill Magee	40
Joe McGinnity	22
Jack Chesbro	12
Rube Waddell	6
Harry Howell	4
Jack Taylor	4
Wild Bill Donovan	3

Sac Flies Allowed

Statistic unavailable

Hit Batsmen

Kid Nichols	101
Cy Young	82
Chick Fraser	75
Cy Seymour	74
Pink Hawley	69
Ed Doheny	65
Jack Taylor	63
Gus Weyhing	63
Vic Willis	60
Bert Cunningham	58

Wild Pitches

Kid Nichols	142
Amos Rusie	142
Jouett Meekin	113
Jack Stivetts	106
Bill Hutchison	106
Cy Young	95
Ed Crane	95
Gus Weyhing	92
Ed Stein	90
Phil Knell	88

Balks

Cy Seymour	8
Bert Cunningham	4
Pete Dowling	3
Nixey Callahan	3
Pink Hawley	3
Frank Killen	3
Crazy Schmit	3
Al Maul	3
16 tied with	2

Opponent Average

(minimum 1,000 Innings Pitched)

Amos Rusie	.230
Tony Mullane	.245
Mark Baldwin	.248
Kid Nichols	.251
John Clarkson	.253
Elton Chamberlin	.255
Ed Crane	.257
Bill Hutchison	.257
Silver King	.257
Ed Stein	.258

Opponent OBP

(minimum 1,000 Innings Pitched)

Kid Nichols	.301
Cy Young	.302
John Clarkson	.312
Amos Rusie	.313
Billy Rhines	.318
Bill Hutchison	.320
Harry Staley	.321
Nig Cuppy	.323
Scott Stratton	.324
Silver King	.324

Single Season Batting Leaders—1890-1899

Games

George Van Haltren	1898	156
Roger Connor	1892	155
Buck Freeman	1899	155
Steve Brodie	1892	154
Bobby Wallace	1898	154
Billy Clingman	1898	154
Monte Cross	1899	154
Dummy Hoy	1899	154
3 tied with		153

At-Bats

Tom Brown	1892	660
George Van Haltren	1898	654
Lou Bierbauer	1892	649
Herman Long	1892	646
Dummy Hoy	1899	633
Duff Cooley	1898	629
Jesse Burkett	1898	624
Doggie Miller	1892	623
Arlie Latham	1892	622
2 tied with		619

Runs

Billy Hamilton	1894	192
Tom Brown	1891	177
Billy Hamilton	1895	166
Willie Keeler	1894	165
Joe Kelley	1894	165
Willie Keeler	1895	162
Hugh Duffy	1890	161
Hugh Duffy	1894	160
Jesse Burkett	1896	160
Hughie Jennings	1895	159

Hits

Jesse Burkett	1896	240
Willie Keeler	1897	239
Ed Delahanty	1899	238
Hugh Duffy	1894	237
Jesse Burkett	1895	225
Sam Thompson	1893	222
Jesse Burkett	1899	221
Billy Hamilton	1894	220
3 tied with		219

Doubles

Ed Delahanty	1899	55
Hugh Duffy	1894	51
Ed Delahanty	1895	49
Joe Kelley	1894	48
Walt Wilmot	1894	45
Sam Thompson	1895	45
Ed Delahanty	1896	44
Jake Stenzel	1897	43
Nap Lajoie	1898	43
Honus Wagner	1899	43

Triples

Heinie Reitz	1894	31
Perry Werden	1893	29
Harry Davis	1897	28
George Davis	1893	27
Sam Thompson	1894	27
Jimmy Williams	1899	27
John Reilly	1890	26
George Treadway	1894	26
Roger Connor	1894	25
Buck Freeman	1899	25

Home Runs

Buck Freeman	1899	25
Ed Delahanty	1893	19
Hugh Duffy	1894	18
Sam Thompson	1895	18
Jack Clements	1893	17
Bobby Lowe	1894	17
Bill Joyce	1894	17
Bill Joyce	1895	17
Mike Tiernan	1891	16
Harry Stovey	1891	16

Home Runs (Home)

Bobby Lowe	1894	16
Buck Freeman	1899	16
Hugh Duffy	1894	14
Sam Thompson	1895	13
Mike Tiernan	1893	12
Jack Clements	1893	12
Jimmy Collins	1898	12
Sam Thompson	1896	11
10 tied with		10

Home Runs (Road)

Charlie Duffee	1891	9
Mike Tiernan	1891	9
Ed Delahanty	1893	9
Bill Dahlen	1894	9
Buck Freeman	1899	9
8 tied with		8

Extra Base Hits

Hugh Duffy	1894	85
Sam Thompson	1895	84
Joe Kelley	1894	74
Ed Delahanty	1896	74
Ed Delahanty	1899	73
Ed Delahanty	1893	72
Jake Stenzel	1894	72
Nap Lajoie	1897	72
Dan Brouthers	1894	71
Ed Delahanty	1895	70

Total Bases

Hugh Duffy	1894	374
Sam Thompson	1895	352
Ed Delahanty	1893	347
Ed Delahanty	1899	338
Buck Freeman	1899	331
Jimmy Williams	1899	328
Bobby Lowe	1894	319
Sam Thompson	1893	318
Jesse Burkett	1896	317
Ed Delahanty	1896	315

RBI

Sam Thompson	1895	165
Hardy Richardson	1890	146
Ed Delahanty	1893	146
Hugh Duffy	1894	145
Sam Thompson	1894	141
Ed Delahanty	1899	137
George Davis	1897	136
Joe Kelley	1895	134
Steve Brodie	1895	134
Ed McKean	1893	133

Walks

Jack Crooks	1892	136
Billy Hamilton	1894	126
John McGraw	1899	124
Bill Joyce	1890	123
Jack Crooks	1893	121
Cupid Childs	1893	120
Dummy Hoy	1891	119
Cupid Childs	1892	117
Roger Connor	1892	116
Roy Thomas	1899	115

Walks/PA
(minimum 3.1 PA/Tm Gm)

Yank Robinson	1890	.242
Jack Crooks	1892	.233
John McGraw	1899	.230
Jack Crooks	1893	.209
Bill Joyce	1890	.197
Cupid Childs	1893	.197
John McGraw	1897	.195
Jim McTamany	1890	.192
Bill Joyce	1894	.190
Billy Hamilton	1894	.184

Strikeouts

Tom Brown	1891	96
Tom Brown	1892	94
Jim McTamany	1891	92
Tom Brown	1890	84
Pop Smith	1890	81
Bill Joyce	1890	77
Pete Gilbert	1891	77
Mike Lehane	1891	77
Tom Brown	1894	73
Harry Stovey	1891	69

Hit By Pitch

Hughie Jennings	1896	51
Hughie Jennings	1897	46
Hughie Jennings	1898	46
Dan McGann	1898	39
Dan McGann	1899	37
Curt Welch	1891	36
Curt Welch	1890	34
Hughie Jennings	1895	32
Chief Roseman	1890	29
Tommy Tucker	1891	29

Sac Hits

Dummy Hoy	1896	33
Claude Ritchey	1898	31
Tom McCreery	1897	30
Bones Ely	1899	29
Hughie Jennings	1895	28
Bones Ely	1896	28
Bill Dahlen	1896	27
Fred Tenney	1897	27
Jack McCarthy	1899	27
2 tied with		26

Sac Flies

Statistic unavailable

Stolen Bases

Billy Hamilton	1891	111
Tom Brown	1891	106
Billy Hamilton	1890	102
Billy Hamilton	1894	98
Harry Stovey	1890	97
Billy Hamilton	1895	97
Monte Ward	1892	88
Arlie Latham	1891	87
Joe Kelley	1896	87
2 tied with		85

Caught Stealing

Statistic unavailable

Runs Created

Hugh Duffy	1894	204
Billy Hamilton	1894	187
Joe Kelley	1894	173
Jesse Burkett	1895	169
Ed Delahanty	1899	165
Ed Delahanty	1893	163
Ed Delahanty	1896	162
Tom Brown	1891	160
Billy Hamilton	1895	160
Joe Kelley	1896	160

Runs Created/27 Outs
(minimum 3.1 PA/Tm Gm)

Hugh Duffy	1894	16.77
Billy Hamilton	1894	14.49
Ed Delahanty	1895	13.99
John McGraw	1899	13.79
Ed Delahanty	1896	13.61
Joe Kelley	1894	13.57
Billy Hamilton	1893	13.17
Sam Thompson	1894	13.16
Jesse Burkett	1895	13.08
Roger Connor	1890	12.99

Batting Average
(minimum 3.1 PA/Tm Gm)

Hugh Duffy	1894	.440
Willie Keeler	1897	.424
Ed Delahanty	1899	.410
Jesse Burkett	1896	.410
Jesse Burkett	1895	.409
Sam Thompson	1894	.407
Ed Delahanty	1894	.407
Billy Hamilton	1894	.404
Ed Delahanty	1895	.404
Hughie Jennings	1896	.401

On-Base Percentage
(minimum 3.1 PA/Tm Gm)

John McGraw	1899	.547
Billy Hamilton	1894	.523
Joe Kelley	1894	.502
Hugh Duffy	1894	.502
Ed Delahanty	1895	.500
Bill Joyce	1894	.496
Billy Hamilton	1895	.490
Billy Hamilton	1893	.490
Jesse Burkett	1895	.486
Billy Hamilton	1898	.480

Slugging Percentage
(minimum 3.1 PA/Tm Gm)

Hugh Duffy	1894	.694
Sam Thompson	1894	.686
Sam Thompson	1895	.654
Bill Joyce	1894	.648
Ed Delahanty	1896	.631
Ed Delahanty	1895	.617
Joe Kelley	1894	.602
Ed Delahanty	1894	.585
Ed Delahanty	1893	.583
Ed Delahanty	1899	.582

OBP+Slugging
(minimum 3.1 PA/Tm Gm)

Hugh Duffy	1894	1.196
Sam Thompson	1894	1.145
Bill Joyce	1894	1.143
Ed Delahanty	1895	1.117
Joe Kelley	1894	1.104
Ed Delahanty	1896	1.103
Sam Thompson	1895	1.085
Ed Delahanty	1894	1.063
Billy Hamilton	1894	1.050
Ed Delahanty	1899	1.046

Secondary Average
(minimum 3.1 PA/Tm Gm)

Bill Joyce	1894	.597
John McGraw	1899	.549
Harry Stovey	1890	.543
Billy Hamilton	1894	.535
Joe Kelley	1896	.522
Joe Kelley	1894	.511
Bill Joyce	1896	.493
Ed Delahanty	1895	.488
Jake Stenzel	1894	.487
Billy Hamilton	1891	.486

Isolated Power
(minimum 3.1 PA/Tm Gm)

Bill Joyce	1894	.293
Sam Thompson	1895	.279
Sam Thompson	1894	.262
Hugh Duffy	1894	.254
Buck Freeman	1899	.245
Roger Connor	1894	.236
Ed Delahanty	1896	.234
Jake Stenzel	1894	.226
Harry Stovey	1891	.219
Bill Joyce	1895	.215

Single Season Pitching Leaders—1890-1899

Wins

Bill Hutchison	1891	44
Bill Hutchison	1890	42
Kid Gleason	1890	38
Bill Hutchison	1892	37
Red Donahue	1890	36
Sadie McMahon	1890	36
Cy Young	1892	36
Frank Killen	1893	36
Amos Rusie	1894	36
4 tied with		35

Losses

Kid Carsey	1891	37
George Cobb	1892	37
Bill Hutchison	1892	36
Red Donahue	1897	35
Amos Rusie	1890	34
Amos Rusie	1892	31
Ed Beatin	1890	30
Ted Breitenstein	1895	30
Jim Hughey	1899	30
3 tied with		29

Winning Percentage
(minimum 15 decisions)

Bill Hoffer	1895	.838
Jim Hughes	1899	.824
Al Orth	1899	.824
Fred Klobedanz	1897	.788
Jouett Meekin	1894	.786
Bill Hoffer	1896	.781
Cy Young	1895	.778
Vic Willis	1899	.771
Jerry Nops	1897	.769
Ted Lewis	1898	.765

Games

Bill Hutchison	1892	75
Bill Hutchison	1890	71
Amos Rusie	1890	67
Bill Hutchison	1891	66
Jack Stivetts	1891	64
Amos Rusie	1892	64
Sadie McMahon	1891	61
Amos Rusie	1891	61
3 tied with		60

Games Started

Bill Hutchison	1892	70
Bill Hutchison	1890	66
Amos Rusie	1890	63
Amos Rusie	1892	61
Sadie McMahon	1891	58
Bill Hutchison	1891	58
Sadie McMahon	1890	57
Mark Baldwin	1890	57
Amos Rusie	1891	57
2 tied with		56

Complete Games

Bill Hutchison	1892	67
Bill Hutchison	1890	65
Amos Rusie	1892	58
Amos Rusie	1890	56
Bill Hutchison	1891	56
Sadie McMahon	1890	55
Kid Gleason	1890	54
Mark Baldwin	1890	54
Ed Beatin	1890	53
Sadie McMahon	1891	53

Shutouts

Cy Young	1892	9
Kid Nichols	1890	7
Billy Rhines	1890	6
Kid Gleason	1890	6
Elton Chamberlin	1890	6
Amos Rusie	1891	6
Ed Stein	1892	6
Gus Weyhing	1892	6
Wiley Piatt	1898	6
Jack Powell	1898	6

Saves

Herb Goodall	1890	4
Tony Mullane	1894	4
Kid Nichols	1898	4
13 tied with		3

Games Finished

Clark Griffith	1891	13
Bill Dammann	1898	13
John Malarkey	1895	12
Chauncey Fisher	1896	11
Red Ehret	1897	11
Sam Leever	1899	11
11 tied with		10

Batters Faced

Bill Hutchison	1892	2,565
Bill Hutchison	1890	2,453
Amos Rusie	1890	2,314
Bill Hutchison	1891	2,313
Mark Baldwin	1890	2,225
Ed Daily	1890	2,219
Amos Rusie	1892	2,215
Sadie McMahon	1890	2,162
Kid Gleason	1890	2,113
Amos Rusie	1891	2,103

Innings Pitched

Bill Hutchison	1892	622.0
Bill Hutchison	1890	603.0
Bill Hutchison	1891	561.0
Amos Rusie	1890	548.2
Amos Rusie	1892	532.0
Sadie McMahon	1890	509.0
Kid Gleason	1890	506.0
Sadie McMahon	1891	503.0
Mark Baldwin	1890	501.0
Amos Rusie	1891	500.1

Hits Allowed

Bill Hutchison	1892	571
Ed Beatin	1890	518
Kid Carsey	1891	513
Bill Hutchison	1891	508
Bill Hutchison	1890	505
Sadie McMahon	1890	498
Mark Baldwin	1890	498
Ted Breitenstein	1894	497
George Cobb	1892	495
Sadie McMahon	1891	493

Runs Allowed

Kid Carsey	1891	358
Henry Gruber	1890	352
George Cobb	1892	333
Mark Baldwin	1890	322
Ted Breitenstein	1894	321
Bill Hutchison	1892	316
Bill Hutchison	1890	315
Kid Nichols	1894	308
George Haddock	1890	307
Jersey Bakely	1890	307

Earned Runs Allowed

Ted Breitenstein	1894	238
Red Donahue	1897	237
Kid Carsey	1891	230
Kid Nichols	1894	215
Pink Hawley	1894	214
George Cobb	1892	213
Ted Breitenstein	1895	212
Bill Hart	1897	205
Ed Beatin	1890	202
Bert Cunningham	1890	200

Home Runs Allowed

Jack Stivetts	1894	27
Frank Dwyer	1894	27
Bill Hutchison	1891	26
Kid Nichols	1894	23
Harry Staley	1893	22
Kid Carsey	1894	22
George Cobb	1892	21
Ted Breitenstein	1894	21
Bill Hutchison	1890	20
Jack Stivetts	1896	20

Walks

Amos Rusie	1890	289
Amos Rusie	1892	267
Amos Rusie	1891	262
Mark Baldwin	1890	249
Jack Stivetts	1891	232
Mark Baldwin	1891	227
Phil Knell	1891	226
Bob Barr	1890	219
Amos Rusie	1893	218
Cy Seymour	1898	213

Intentional Walks

Statistic unavailable

Strikeouts

Amos Rusie	1890	341
Amos Rusie	1891	337
Bill Hutchison	1892	312
Sadie McMahon	1890	291
Jack Stivetts	1890	289
Bill Hutchison	1890	289
Amos Rusie	1892	288
Bill Hutchison	1891	261
Jack Stivetts	1891	259
Toad Ramsey	1890	257

Strikeouts/9 Innings
(minimum 1 Inning Pitched/Tm Gm)

Toad Ramsey	1890	6.63
Jack Stivetts	1890	6.20
Amos Rusie	1891	6.06
Cy Seymour	1898	6.03
George Meakim	1890	5.77
Jouett Meekin	1891	5.68
Amos Rusie	1890	5.59
Elton Chamberlin	1890	5.49
Jack Stivetts	1891	5.30
Egyptian Healy	1890	5.21

ERA
(minimum 1 Inning Pitched/Tm Gm)

Clark Griffith	1898	1.88
Cy Young	1892	1.93
Billy Rhines	1890	1.95
Al Maul	1898	2.10
Kid Nichols	1898	2.13
Kid Nichols	1890	2.23
Tony Mullane	1890	2.24
John Ewing	1891	2.27
Tim Keefe	1892	2.36
Doc McJames	1898	2.36

Component ERA
(minimum 1 Inning Pitched/Tm Gm)

Kid Nichols	1898	1.99
Cy Young	1892	2.02
Scott Stratton	1890	2.13
Al Maul	1898	2.14
Billy Rhines	1890	2.22
Charlie Buffinton	1891	2.38
Hank Gastright	1890	2.38
Tim Keefe	1892	2.39
Adonis Terry	1892	2.40
Noodles Hahn	1899	2.41

Sac Hits Allowed

Cy Young	1894	30
Kid Nichols	1896	30
Cy Young	1896	28
Cy Young	1897	26
Bill Magee	1898	26
Harley Payne	1896	23
Cy Young	1899	23
Cy Young	1895	22
Kid Nichols	1895	22
Joe McGinnity	1899	22

Sac Flies Allowed

Statistic unavailable

Hit Batsmen

Ed Doheny	1899	37
Cy Seymour	1898	32
Vic Willis	1898	30
Vic Willis	1899	30
Chick Fraser	1898	29
Win Mercer	1897	28
Jack Taylor	1897	28
Joe McGinnity	1899	28
Gus Weyhing	1899	28
3 tied with		27

Wild Pitches

Henry Gruber	1890	47
Ed Crane	1890	39
Amos Rusie	1890	36
Jack Stivetts	1890	33
Hank Gastright	1890	32
George Haddock	1890	31
Mark Baldwin	1890	31
Toad Ramsey	1890	31
Ed Crane	1892	31
Kid Nichols	1890	30

Balks

Cy Seymour	1899	4
Bert Cunningham	1899	4
Al Maul	1893	3
Crazy Schmit	1899	3
15 tied with		2

Opponent Average
(minimum 1 Inning Pitched/Tm Gm)

Tony Mullane	1892	.201
Amos Rusie	1892	.203
Adonis Terry	1892	.205
Amos Rusie	1891	.207
Jesse Duryea	1892	.212
Amos Rusie	1890	.212
Cy Young	1892	.214
Ed Stein	1892	.215
Kid Nichols	1898	.217
Jack Stivetts	1892	.217

Opponent OBP
(minimum 1 Inning Pitched/Tm Gm)

Scott Stratton	1890	.265
Kid Nichols	1898	.267
Cy Young	1892	.268
Al Maul	1898	.275
Billy Rhines	1890	.275
Cy Young	1899	.275
Jesse Duryea	1892	.281
Scott Stratton	1892	.281
Charlie Buffinton	1891	.281
Red Ehret	1892	.283

Batting Leaders—1900-1909

Games

Sam Crawford	1,410
Honus Wagner	1,391
Bobby Wallace	1,362
Bill Dahlen	1,332
Fred Tenney	1,329
Jimmy Sheckard	1,312
Jimmy Williams	1,304
Harry Steinfeldt	1,303
Bill Bradley	1,291
Fielder Jones	1,289

At-Bats

Sam Crawford	5,471
Honus Wagner	5,254
Bobby Wallace	5,072
Ginger Beaumont	5,051
Willie Keeler	5,030
Fred Tenney	4,962
Bill Bradley	4,874
Jimmy Williams	4,864
Fielder Jones	4,834
Tommy Leach	4,826

Runs

Honus Wagner	1,014
Fred Clarke	885
Roy Thomas	862
Ginger Beaumont	835
Tommy Leach	828
Sam Crawford	813
Jimmy Sheckard	807
Nap Lajoie	806
Fielder Jones	799
Willie Keeler	797

Hits

Honus Wagner	1,847
Sam Crawford	1,677
Nap Lajoie	1,660
Willie Keeler	1,566
Ginger Beaumont	1,559
Cy Seymour	1,460
Elmer Flick	1,429
Fred Clarke	1,396
Fred Tenney	1,387
Bobby Wallace	1,373

Doubles

Honus Wagner	372
Nap Lajoie	361
Harry Davis	289
Sam Crawford	263
Bill Bradley	255
Bobby Wallace	243
Jimmy Sheckard	238
Jimmy Collins	230
Elmer Flick	227
Harry Steinfeldt	225

Triples

Sam Crawford	167
Honus Wagner	148
Elmer Flick	139
Fred Clarke	134
Tommy Leach	123
Jimmy Williams	111
Buck Freeman	103
Hobe Ferris	89
Topsy Hartsel	88
2 tied with	87

Home Runs

Harry Davis	67
Charlie Hickman	58
Sam Crawford	57
Buck Freeman	54
Socks Seybold	51
Honus Wagner	51
Nap Lajoie	47
Cy Seymour	43
Hobe Ferris	40
Jimmy Williams	40

Home Runs (Home)

Harry Davis	43
Charlie Hickman	29
Buck Freeman	27
Mike Donlin	26
Socks Seybold	25
Cy Seymour	25
Nap Lajoie	24
Jimmy Collins	24
Hobe Ferris	23
Ginger Beaumont	23

Home Runs (Road)

Sam Crawford	36
Honus Wagner	33
Charlie Hickman	29
Buck Freeman	27
Socks Seybold	26
Jimmy Williams	25
Harry Davis	24
Harry Lumley	23
Elmer Flick	23
Nap Lajoie	23

Extra Base Hits

Honus Wagner	571
Nap Lajoie	495
Sam Crawford	487
Harry Davis	434
Elmer Flick	403
Bill Bradley	369
Jimmy Williams	365
Jimmy Sheckard	356
Charlie Hickman	356
Fred Clarke	349

Total Bases

Honus Wagner	2,668
Sam Crawford	2,445
Nap Lajoie	2,336
Elmer Flick	2,045
Harry Davis	1,976
Ginger Beaumont	1,969
Cy Seymour	1,968
Fred Clarke	1,931
Bill Bradley	1,862
Jimmy Sheckard	1,851

RBI

Honus Wagner	956
Sam Crawford	808
Nap Lajoie	793
Harry Davis	688
Cy Seymour	685
Jimmy Williams	680
Bobby Wallace	638
Harry Steinfeldt	610
Bill Dahlen	597
Charlie Hickman	590

Walks

Roy Thomas	912
Topsy Hartsel	749
Jimmy Sheckard	616
Fielder Jones	607
Fred Tenney	607
Jimmy Slagle	564
Bill Dahlen	525
Fred Clarke	524
Honus Wagner	518
Roger Bresnahan	500

Walks/PA
(minimum 3,000 Plate Appearances)

Roy Thomas	.159
Topsy Hartsel	.144
Sammy Strang	.132
Roger Bresnahan	.128
Miller Huggins	.128
Jimmy Barrett	.113
Jimmy Slagle	.111
Art Devlin	.109
Frank Chance	.109
Jimmy Sheckard	.109

Strikeouts

Statistic unavailable

Hit By Pitch

Dan McGann	149
Frank Chance	112
Kid Elberfeld	104
Jake Stahl	80
Elmer Flick	73
John Titus	72
Billy Gilbert	72
Bill Bradley	69
Honus Wagner	69
Willie Keeler	69

Sac Hits

Willie Keeler	277
Bill Bradley	237
Fielder Jones	214
Jimmy Sheckard	210
Frank Isbell	196
Freddy Parent	192
Harry Steinfeldt	190
Joe Tinker	175
Fred Tenney	175
Kid Gleason	175

Sac Flies

Statistic unavailable

Stolen Bases

Honus Wagner	488
Frank Chance	357
Sam Mertes	305
Jimmy Sheckard	295
Elmer Flick	275
Jimmy Slagle	251
Frank Isbell	250
Wid Conroy	239
Fielder Jones	239
Fred Clarke	239

Caught Stealing

Statistic unavailable

Runs Created

Honus Wagner	1,274
Nap Lajoie	961
Sam Crawford	955
Elmer Flick	886
Fred Clarke	868
Roy Thomas	846
Jimmy Sheckard	834
Topsy Hartsel	805
Ginger Beaumont	801
Cy Seymour	774

Runs Created/27 Outs
(minimum 3,000 Plate Appearances)

Honus Wagner	9.34
Nap Lajoie	7.68
Mike Donlin	7.63
Frank Chance	7.34
Elmer Flick	7.04
Jesse Burkett	6.83
Fred Clarke	6.59
Topsy Hartsel	6.47
Sam Crawford	6.33
Roy Thomas	6.32

Batting Average
(minimum 3,000 Plate Appearances)

Honus Wagner	.352
Nap Lajoie	.346
Mike Donlin	.338
Jesse Burkett	.312
Elmer Flick	.312
Willie Keeler	.311
Cy Seymour	.311
George Stone	.310
Jake Beckley	.309
Ginger Beaumont	.309

On-Base Percentage
(minimum 3,000 Plate Appearances)

Honus Wagner	.417
Roy Thomas	.411
Frank Chance	.397
Mike Donlin	.391
Roger Bresnahan	.389
Nap Lajoie	.388
Jesse Burkett	.388
Topsy Hartsel	.386
Elmer Flick	.383
Fred Clarke	.380

Slugging Percentage
(minimum 3,000 Plate Appearances)

Honus Wagner	.508
Nap Lajoie	.487
Mike Donlin	.474
Sam Crawford	.447
Elmer Flick	.446
Buck Freeman	.443
Charlie Hickman	.438
Socks Seybold	.427
Harry Davis	.424
Cy Seymour	.419

OBP+Slugging
(minimum 3,000 Plate Appearances)

Honus Wagner	.925
Nap Lajoie	.875
Mike Donlin	.865
Elmer Flick	.829
Sam Crawford	.802
Jesse Burkett	.800
Fred Clarke	.797
Frank Chance	.795
Buck Freeman	.785
George Stone	.781

Secondary Average
(minimum 3,000 Plate Appearances)

Honus Wagner	.348
Frank Chance	.329
Topsy Hartsel	.324
Sammy Strang	.307
Sam Mertes	.300
Roger Bresnahan	.297
Jimmy Sheckard	.296
Elmer Flick	.294
Sherry Magee	.289
Roy Thomas	.282

Isolated Power
(minimum 3,000 Plate Appearances)

Honus Wagner	.156
Buck Freeman	.156
Charlie Hickman	.144
Nap Lajoie	.141
Sam Crawford	.140
Harry Davis	.139
Mike Donlin	.136
Elmer Flick	.134
Socks Seybold	.131
Sherry Magee	.127

Pitching Leaders—1900-1909

Wins

Christy Mathewson	236
Cy Young	230
Joe McGinnity	218
Jack Chesbro	192
Vic Willis	188
Eddie Plank	186
Rube Waddell	183
Sam Leever	167
Jack Powell	160
George Mullin	156

Losses

Vic Willis	172
Jack Powell	165
Cy Young	146
Al Orth	143
Bill Dinneen	141
Rube Waddell	139
Harry Howell	138
Long Tom Hughes	135
Chick Fraser	135
George Mullin	134

Winning Percentage
(minimum 100 decisions)

Ed Reulbach	.713
Sam Leever	.699
Three Finger Brown	.689
Christy Mathewson	.678
Hooks Wiltse	.637
Ed Walsh	.636
Joe McGinnity	.634
Jack Pfiester	.634
Jesse Tannehill	.633
Deacon Phillippe	.631

Games

Joe McGinnity	417
Cy Young	403
Vic Willis	398
Christy Mathewson	388
Rube Waddell	385
Jack Powell	376
Jack Chesbro	373
Eddie Plank	334
George Mullin	330
Bill Dinneen	325

Games Started

Vic Willis	372
Cy Young	366
Christy Mathewson	344
Joe McGinnity	340
Jack Powell	334
Rube Waddell	328
Jack Chesbro	315
Eddie Plank	314
George Mullin	298
Bill Dinneen	290

Complete Games

Cy Young	337
Vic Willis	312
Christy Mathewson	281
Jack Powell	277
Joe McGinnity	276
Eddie Plank	263
George Mullin	258
Bill Dinneen	254
Rube Waddell	251
Wild Bill Donovan	246

Shutouts

Christy Mathewson	61
Rube Waddell	49
Cy Young	45
Addie Joss	44
Vic Willis	43
Three Finger Brown	41
Doc White	39
Ed Walsh	36
Eddie Plank	36
2 tied with	35

Saves

Joe McGinnity	22
Hooks Wiltse	20
Three Finger Brown	19
Christy Mathewson	15
Ed Walsh	14
Jack Powell	13
Orval Overall	11
Rube Waddell	10
Long Tom Hughes	10
Cy Young	9

Games Finished

Joe McGinnity	66
Ed Walsh	52
Hooks Wiltse	52
Clark Griffith	51
Jack Chesbro	50
Three Finger Brown	49
Harry Howell	49
George Ferguson	48
Sam Leever	48
Deacon Phillippe	46

Batters Faced

Cy Young	13,159
Vic Willis	12,937
Joe McGinnity	12,922
Jack Powell	11,900
Christy Mathewson	11,851
Rube Waddell	11,570
Jack Chesbro	11,349
George Mullin	10,941
Eddie Plank	10,858
Bill Dinneen	10,502

Innings Pitched

Cy Young	3,344.1
Vic Willis	3,130.1
Joe McGinnity	3,075.0
Christy Mathewson	2,966.2
Jack Powell	2,876.2
Rube Waddell	2,835.1
Jack Chesbro	2,747.2
Eddie Plank	2,666.0
George Mullin	2,592.1
Bill Dinneen	2,565.1

Hits Allowed

Cy Young	2,951
Joe McGinnity	2,918
Vic Willis	2,856
Jack Powell	2,720
Jack Chesbro	2,477
George Mullin	2,434
Christy Mathewson	2,434
Al Orth	2,429
Bill Dinneen	2,369
Eddie Plank	2,360

Runs Allowed

Joe McGinnity	1,274
Vic Willis	1,246
Jack Powell	1,241
Chick Fraser	1,155
Al Orth	1,134
Cy Young	1,126
George Mullin	1,116
Jack Chesbro	1,110
Bill Dinneen	1,080
Casey Patten	1,079

Earned Runs Allowed

Jack Powell	921
Joe McGinnity	907
Vic Willis	895
Al Orth	853
Bill Dinneen	805
Chick Fraser	805
Jack Chesbro	796
Cy Young	787
Casey Patten	770
George Mullin	765

Home Runs Allowed

Jack Powell	73
Bill Dinneen	67
Al Orth	51
Joe McGinnity	49
Vic Willis	49
Frank Kitson	46
Cy Young	45
Chick Fraser	42
Casey Patten	40
Togie Pittinger	40

Walks

Vic Willis	886
Wild Bill Donovan	838
Chick Fraser	836
George Mullin	833
Rube Waddell	772
Togie Pittinger	734
Joe McGinnity	719
Christy Mathewson	640
Jack Powell	638
Long Tom Hughes	637

Intentional Walks

Statistic unavailable

Strikeouts

Rube Waddell	2,251
Christy Mathewson	1,794
Cy Young	1,565
Eddie Plank	1,342
Vic Willis	1,304
Wild Bill Donovan	1,293
Jack Chesbro	1,237
Jack Powell	1,209
Long Tom Hughes	1,115
Doc White	1,105

Strikeouts/9 Innings
(minimum 1,000 Innings Pitched)

Rube Waddell	7.15
Red Ames	6.40
Orval Overall	5.53
Christy Mathewson	5.44
Chief Bender	5.43
Ed Walsh	4.94
Wild Bill Donovan	4.80
Long Tom Hughes	4.79
Eddie Plank	4.53
Frank Smith	4.40

ERA
(minimum 1,000 Innings Pitched)

Three Finger Brown	1.63
Ed Walsh	1.68
Ed Reulbach	1.72
Addie Joss	1.87
Christy Mathewson	1.98
Rube Waddell	2.11
Cy Young	2.12
Orval Overall	2.13
Frank Smith	2.19
Doc White	2.20

Component ERA
(minimum 1,000 Innings Pitched)

Ed Walsh	1.66
Addie Joss	1.70
Three Finger Brown	1.76
Ed Reulbach	1.92
Christy Mathewson	1.95
Cy Young	1.98
Frank Smith	2.05
Rube Waddell	2.19
Chief Bender	2.20
Doc White	2.25

Sac Hits Allowed

George Mullin	311
Rube Waddell	266
Joe McGinnity	263
Cy Young	261
Jack Chesbro	242
Wild Bill Donovan	237
Christy Mathewson	222
Eddie Plank	218
Harry Howell	200
Addie Joss	196

Sac Flies Allowed

Statistic unavailable

Hit Batsmen

Joe McGinnity	154
Eddie Plank	145
Rube Waddell	107
Jack Chesbro	102
Chick Fraser	102
Jesse Tannehill	97
Togie Pittinger	96
Vic Willis	96
Barney Pelty	88
2 tied with	86

Wild Pitches

Christy Mathewson	89
Red Ames	78
Rube Waddell	75
Vic Willis	71
George Mullin	67
Long Tom Hughes	66
Chick Fraser	59
Earl Moore	58
3 tied with	57

Balks

Christy Mathewson	6
Al Mattern	5
Ed Walsh	5
Fred Mitchell	5
Vic Willis	5
8 tied with	4

Opponent Average
(minimum 1,000 Innings Pitched)

Ed Reulbach	.205
Ed Walsh	.214
Three Finger Brown	.218
Addie Joss	.219
Orval Overall	.220
Frank Smith	.221
Christy Mathewson	.222
Rube Waddell	.225
Jake Weimer	.227
Red Ames	.227

Opponent OBP
(minimum 1,000 Innings Pitched)

Addie Joss	.256
Ed Walsh	.258
Three Finger Brown	.262
Cy Young	.265
Christy Mathewson	.269
Deacon Phillippe	.280
Chief Bender	.282
Ed Reulbach	.282
Frank Smith	.283
Nick Altrock	.283

Single Season Batting Leaders—1900-1909

Games

Jimmy Barrett	1904	162
Chick Stahl	1904	157
Candy LaChance	1904	157
Buck Freeman	1904	157
Elmer Flick	1906	157
Jiggs Donahue	1907	157
Art Devlin	1908	157
Joe Tinker	1908	157
Nap Lajoie	1908	157
Donie Bush	1909	157

At-Bats

Patsy Dougherty	1904	647
George Stone	1905	632
Jimmy Collins	1904	631
Eddie Grant	1909	631
Tom Jones	1904	625
Jimmy Barrett	1904	624
Elmer Flick	1906	624
Ginger Beaumont	1904	615
Ginger Beaumont	1903	613
Ed Abbaticchio	1905	610

Runs

Nap Lajoie	1901	145
Jesse Burkett	1901	142
Ginger Beaumont	1903	137
Roy Thomas	1900	132
Tommy Leach	1909	126
Mike Donlin	1905	124
Willie Keeler	1901	123
Ginger Beaumont	1901	120
Fielder Jones	1901	120
2 tied with		118

Hits

Nap Lajoie	1901	232
Jesse Burkett	1901	226
Cy Seymour	1905	219
Mike Donlin	1905	216
Ty Cobb	1909	216
Nap Lajoie	1906	214
Ty Cobb	1907	212
Ginger Beaumont	1903	209
Nap Lajoie	1904	208
George Stone	1906	208

Doubles

Nap Lajoie	1904	49
Nap Lajoie	1901	48
Nap Lajoie	1906	48
Harry Davis	1905	47
John Anderson	1901	46
Honus Wagner	1900	45
Socks Seybold	1903	45
Honus Wagner	1904	44
Harry Davis	1902	43
Ed Delahanty	1902	43

Triples

Sam Crawford	1903	25
Honus Wagner	1900	22
Sam Crawford	1902	22
Tommy Leach	1902	22
Bill Bradley	1903	22
Elmer Flick	1906	22
Jimmy Williams	1901	21
Bill Keister	1901	21
Jimmy Williams	1902	21
Cy Seymour	1905	21

Home Runs

Sam Crawford	1901	16
Socks Seybold	1902	16
Nap Lajoie	1901	14
Buck Freeman	1903	13
Herman Long	1900	12
Buck Freeman	1901	12
Charlie Hickman	1903	12
Tim Jordan	1906	12
Harry Davis	1906	12
Tim Jordan	1908	12

Home Runs (Home)

Herman Long	1900	12
Harry Davis	1906	10
Dave Brain	1907	10
Sam Crawford	1901	9
Ed Delahanty	1902	9
Socks Seybold	1902	8
Hobe Ferris	1903	8
Harry Davis	1904	8
Tim Jordan	1906	8
8 tied with		7

Home Runs (Road)

Nap Lajoie	1901	9
Bill Bradley	1902	8
Socks Seybold	1902	8
Elmer Flick	1900	7
Sam Crawford	1901	7
Jimmy Sheckard	1901	7
Buck Freeman	1901	7
Harry Lumley	1904	7
Fred Odwell	1905	7
Harry Lumley	1906	7

Extra Base Hits

Nap Lajoie	1901	76
Buck Freeman	1903	72
Honus Wagner	1900	71
Nap Lajoie	1904	69
Cy Seymour	1905	69
Buck Freeman	1902	68
Honus Wagner	1908	68
Ed Delahanty	1902	67
Jimmy Collins	1901	64
Bill Bradley	1903	64

Total Bases

Nap Lajoie	1901	350
Cy Seymour	1905	325
Honus Wagner	1908	308
Jesse Burkett	1901	306
Honus Wagner	1900	302
Nap Lajoie	1904	302
Mike Donlin	1905	300
Elmer Flick	1900	297
Jimmy Sheckard	1901	296
Ty Cobb	1909	296

RBI

Honus Wagner	1901	126
Nap Lajoie	1901	125
Buck Freeman	1902	121
Cy Seymour	1905	121
Ty Cobb	1907	119
Buck Freeman	1901	114
Elmer Flick	1900	110
Charlie Hickman	1902	110
Ed Delahanty	1900	109
Honus Wagner	1908	109

Walks

Topsy Hartsel	1905	121
Roy Thomas	1900	115
Billy Hamilton	1900	107
Roy Thomas	1902	107
Roy Thomas	1903	107
Roy Thomas	1906	107
Topsy Hartsel	1907	106
Miller Huggins	1905	103
Roy Thomas	1904	102
Roy Thomas	1901	100

Walks/PA

(minimum 3.1 PA/Tm Gm)

John McGraw	1900	.190
Topsy Hartsel	1905	.181
Roy Thomas	1903	.176
Roy Thomas	1906	.173
Roy Thomas	1902	.171
Roy Thomas	1900	.170
Topsy Hartsel	1907	.170
Billy Hamilton	1900	.169
Roy Thomas	1904	.167
Roy Thomas	1901	.166

Strikeouts

Statistic unavailable

Hit By Pitch

Dan McGann	1900	24
John McGraw	1900	23
Dan McGann	1901	23
Jake Stahl	1908	23
Charlie Babb	1903	22
Hughie Jennings	1900	20
Billy Gilbert	1903	20
Dan McGann	1905	19
Dan McGann	1908	19
2 tied with		18

Sac Hits

Bill Bradley	1908	60
Bob Ganley	1908	52
Donie Bush	1909	52
Johnny Bates	1909	48
Bill Bradley	1907	46
Jimmy Sheckard	1909	46
Kid Gleason	1905	43
Germany Schaefer	1908	43
Willie Keeler	1905	42
Otto Knabe	1908	42

Sac Flies

Statistic unavailable

Stolen Bases

Ty Cobb	1909	76
Frank Chance	1903	67
Jimmy Sheckard	1903	67
Eddie Collins	1909	67
Honus Wagner	1907	61
Art Devlin	1905	59
Billy Maloney	1905	59
Honus Wagner	1905	57
Frank Chance	1906	57
Sherry Magee	1906	55

Caught Stealing

Statistic unavailable

Runs Created

Nap Lajoie	1901	169
Jesse Burkett	1901	153
Honus Wagner	1900	150
Cy Seymour	1905	147
Elmer Flick	1900	145
Ty Cobb	1909	138
Honus Wagner	1905	136
Jimmy Sheckard	1901	135
Honus Wagner	1901	133
Ty Cobb	1907	133

Runs Created/27 Outs

(minimum 3.1 PA/Tm Gm)

Nap Lajoie	1901	13.99
Honus Wagner	1900	11.61
Ed Delahanty	1902	11.35
Jesse Burkett	1901	10.60
Elmer Flick	1900	10.55
Roger Bresnahan	1903	10.52
John McGraw	1900	10.26
Cy Seymour	1905	10.18
Honus Wagner	1904	10.11
Frank Chance	1903	9.97

Batting Average

(minimum 3.1 PA/Tm Gm)

Nap Lajoie	1901	.426
Honus Wagner	1900	.381
Ty Cobb	1909	.377
Cy Seymour	1905	.377
Ed Delahanty	1902	.376
Nap Lajoie	1904	.376
Jesse Burkett	1901	.376
Elmer Flick	1900	.367
Jesse Burkett	1900	.363
Honus Wagner	1905	.363

On-Base Percentage

(minimum 3.1 PA/Tm Gm)

John McGraw	1900	.505
Nap Lajoie	1901	.463
Roy Thomas	1903	.453
Ed Delahanty	1902	.453
Roy Thomas	1900	.451
Frank Chance	1905	.450
Billy Hamilton	1900	.449
Roger Bresnahan	1903	.443
Elmer Flick	1900	.441
Jesse Burkett	1901	.440

Slugging Percentage

(minimum 3.1 PA/Tm Gm)

Nap Lajoie	1901	.643
Ed Delahanty	1902	.590
Honus Wagner	1900	.573
Cy Seymour	1905	.559
Nap Lajoie	1904	.546
Elmer Flick	1900	.545
Honus Wagner	1908	.542
Charlie Hickman	1902	.539
Jimmy Sheckard	1901	.534
Fred Clarke	1903	.532

OBP+Slugging

(minimum 3.1 PA/Tm Gm)

Nap Lajoie	1901	1.106
Ed Delahanty	1902	1.043
Honus Wagner	1900	1.007
Cy Seymour	1905	.988
Elmer Flick	1900	.986
Nap Lajoie	1904	.959
Honus Wagner	1908	.957
Ed Delahanty	1901	.955
Jesse Burkett	1901	.949
Ty Cobb	1909	.947

Secondary Average

(minimum 3.1 PA/Tm Gm)

Frank Chance	1903	.442
Jimmy Sheckard	1903	.419
Frank Chance	1905	.413
John McGraw	1900	.413
Honus Wagner	1904	.400
Frank Chance	1906	.380
Ed Delahanty	1902	.378
Roger Bresnahan	1903	.377
Honus Wagner	1908	.377
Honus Wagner	1907	.371

Isolated Power

(minimum 3.1 PA/Tm Gm)

Nap Lajoie	1901	.217
Ed Delahanty	1902	.214
Buck Freeman	1903	.208
Sam Crawford	1901	.194
Buck Freeman	1902	.193
Honus Wagner	1900	.192
Socks Seybold	1902	.190
Honus Wagner	1908	.188
Jimmy Williams	1902	.187
Bill Bradley	1903	.183

Single Season Pitching Leaders—1900-1909

Wins

Jack Chesbro	1904	41
Ed Walsh	1908	40
Christy Mathewson	1908	37
Joe McGinnity	1904	35
Cy Young	1901	33
Christy Mathewson	1904	33
Cy Young	1902	32
Joe McGinnity	1903	31
Christy Mathewson	1905	31
Christy Mathewson	1903	30

Losses

Vic Willis	1905	29
Luther Taylor	1901	27
Pete Dowling	1901	26
Jack Townsend	1904	26
Gus Dorner	1906	26
Bob Groom	1909	26
9 tied with		25

Winning Percentage
(minimum 15 decisions)

Wild Bill Donovan	1907	.862
Ed Reulbach	1906	.826
Jack Chesbro	1902	.824
Joe McGinnity	1904	.814
Hooks Wiltse	1904	.813
Three Finger Brown	1906	.813
Ed Reulbach	1907	.810
Howie Camnitz	1909	.806
Christy Mathewson	1909	.806
3 tied with		.800

Games

Ed Walsh	1908	66
Ed Walsh	1907	56
Christy Mathewson	1908	56
Joe McGinnity	1903	55
Jack Chesbro	1904	55
Rube Vickers	1908	53
Vic Willis	1902	51
Joe McGinnity	1904	51
Frank Smith	1909	51
Three Finger Brown	1909	50

Games Started

Jack Chesbro	1904	51
Ed Walsh	1908	49
Joe McGinnity	1903	48
Vic Willis	1902	46
Christy Mathewson	1904	46
Rube Waddell	1904	46
Ed Walsh	1907	46
Jack Powell	1904	45
3 tied with		44

Complete Games

Jack Chesbro	1904	48
Vic Willis	1902	45
Joe McGinnity	1903	44
George Mullin	1904	42
Ed Walsh	1908	42
Noodles Hahn	1901	41
Cy Young	1902	41
Irv Young	1905	41
Cy Young	1904	40
5 tied with		39

Shutouts

Ed Walsh	1908	11
Christy Mathewson	1908	11
Cy Young	1904	10
Ed Walsh	1906	10
Joe McGinnity	1904	9
Three Finger Brown	1906	9
Addie Joss	1906	9
Three Finger Brown	1908	9
Addie Joss	1908	9
Orval Overall	1909	9

Saves

Frank Arellanes	1909	8
George Ferguson	1906	7
Three Finger Brown	1909	7
Claude Elliott	1905	6
Hooks Wiltse	1906	6
Ed Walsh	1908	6
Doc Crandall	1909	6
5 tied with		5

Games Finished

Doc Crandall	1909	20
George Ferguson	1906	19
Steve Melter	1909	18
Clark Griffith	1905	17
Rube Vickers	1908	17
Lew Richie	1909	17
George Ferguson	1908	16
6 tied with		15

Batters Faced

Joe McGinnity	1903	1,814
Ed Walsh	1908	1,799
Jack Chesbro	1904	1,778
Joe McGinnity	1901	1,685
Vic Willis	1902	1,682
Ed Walsh	1907	1,663
Joe McGinnity	1904	1,613
George Mullin	1904	1,597
Oscar Jones	1904	1,593
Togie Pittinger	1902	1,592

Innings Pitched

Ed Walsh	1908	464.0
Jack Chesbro	1904	454.2
Joe McGinnity	1903	434.0
Ed Walsh	1907	422.1
Vic Willis	1902	410.0
Joe McGinnity	1904	408.0
Christy Mathewson	1908	390.2
Jack Powell	1904	390.1
Togie Pittinger	1902	389.1
Cy Young	1902	384.2

Hits Allowed

Bill Carrick	1900	415
Joe McGinnity	1901	412
Snake Wiltse	1902	397
Togie Pittinger	1903	396
Joe McGinnity	1903	391
Oscar Jones	1904	387
Pink Hawley	1900	377
Luther Taylor	1901	377
Vic Willis	1902	372
2 tied with		370

Runs Allowed

Snake Wiltse	1902	226
Bill Carrick	1900	224
Joe McGinnity	1901	219
Chick Fraser	1901	210
Pete Dowling	1901	209
Togie Pittinger	1903	205
Pink Hawley	1900	204
Bill Carrick	1901	198
Bill Phillips	1901	196
Nixey Callahan	1900	195

Earned Runs Allowed

Snake Wiltse	1902	172
Joe McGinnity	1901	151
Bill Phillips	1901	145
Al Orth	1902	143
Jack Powell	1900	142
Pete Dowling	1901	141
Bill Reidy	1901	141
Chick Fraser	1901	140
Bill Carrick	1902	139
Togie Pittinger	1903	136

Home Runs Allowed

Al Orth	1902	18
Jack Powell	1904	15
Watty Lee	1901	14
Jack Powell	1901	14
Bill Reidy	1901	14
Ted Lewis	1901	14
Noodles Hahn	1901	13
5 tied with		12

Walks

Wild Bill Donovan	1901	152
Chick Fraser	1905	149
Orval Overall	1905	147
Togie Pittinger	1904	144
Togie Pittinger	1903	143
George Mullin	1905	138
Chick Fraser	1901	132
George Mullin	1904	131
Togie Pittinger	1902	128
Doc Scanlan	1906	127

Intentional Walks

Statistic unavailable

Strikeouts

+

Rube Waddell	1904	349
Rube Waddell	1903	302
Rube Waddell	1905	287
Ed Walsh	1908	269
Christy Mathewson	1903	267
Christy Mathewson	1908	259
Noodles Hahn	1901	239
Jack Chesbro	1904	239
Rube Waddell	1907	232
Rube Waddell	1908	232

Strikeouts/9 Innings
(minimum 1 Inning Pitched/Tm Gm)

Rube Waddell	1903	8.39
Rube Waddell	1904	8.20
Rube Waddell	1905	7.86
Rube Waddell	1907	7.33
Rube Waddell	1908	7.31
Red Ames	1906	6.90
Rube Waddell	1902	6.84
Red Ames	1905	6.78
Orval Overall	1908	6.68
Fred Beebe	1906	6.67

ERA
(minimum 1 Inning Pitched/Tm Gm)

Three Finger Brown	1906	1.04
Christy Mathewson	1909	1.14
Jack Pfiester	1907	1.15
Addie Joss	1908	1.16
Carl Lundgren	1907	1.17
Cy Young	1908	1.26
Christy Mathewson	1905	1.28
Three Finger Brown	1909	1.31
Jack Taylor	1902	1.33
Three Finger Brown	1907	1.39

Component ERA
(minimum 1 Inning Pitched/Tm Gm)

Addie Joss	1908	1.23
Christy Mathewson	1909	1.29
Three Finger Brown	1908	1.31
Christy Mathewson	1908	1.34
Ed Walsh	1908	1.38
Three Finger Brown	1909	1.42
Cy Young	1908	1.48
Cy Young	1905	1.49
Ed Walsh	1909	1.52
Doc White	1906	1.52

Sac Hits Allowed

Nap Rucker	1908	54
George Mullin	1904	51
Frank Smith	1909	51
Oscar Jones	1904	50
Rube Vickers	1908	50
Ed Walsh	1907	48
Kaiser Wilhelm	1908	48
Harry Howell	1908	46
George Mullin	1908	45
2 tied with		44

Sac Flies Allowed

Statistic unavailable

Hit Batsmen

Joe McGinnity	1900	41
Chick Fraser	1901	32
Jack Warhop	1909	26
Chief Bender	1903	25
Eddie Plank	1905	24
Otto Hess	1906	24
Eddie Plank	1903	23
Jake Weimer	1907	23
3 tied with		22

Wild Pitches

Red Ames	1905	30
Christy Mathewson	1901	23
Red Ames	1907	20
Jack Harper	1901	19
Jack Townsend	1904	19
Christy Mathewson	1903	18
Orval Overall	1905	18
Otto Hess	1905	18
Fred Mitchell	1903	17
2 tied with		16

Balks

Al Mattern	1909	4
Fred Mitchell	1904	3
Christy Mathewson	1905	3
Fred Burchell	1908	3
Tom McCarthy	1909	3
Bill Burns	1909	3
Ed Walsh	1909	3
23 tied with		2

Opponent Average
(minimum 1 Inning Pitched/Tm Gm)

Ed Reulbach	1906	.175
Carl Lundgren	1907	.185
Fred Beebe	1908	.193
Three Finger Brown	1908	.195
Jack Pfiester	1906	.197
Addie Joss	1908	.197
Rube Waddell	1905	.198
Orval Overall	1909	.198
Three Finger Brown	1904	.199
Christy Mathewson	1909	.200

Opponent OBP
(minimum 1 Inning Pitched/Tm Gm)

Addie Joss	1908	.218
Christy Mathewson	1908	.225
Christy Mathewson	1909	.228
Three Finger Brown	1908	.232
Ed Walsh	1908	.232
Three Finger Brown	1909	.239
Cy Young	1905	.239
Cy Young	1908	.241
Christy Mathewson	1905	.245
Addie Joss	1906	.247

Batting Leaders—1910-1919

Games

Donie Bush	1,450
Eddie Collins	1,441
Tris Speaker	1,438
Ed Konetchy	1,430
Harry Hooper	1,426
Fred Merkle	1,406
Clyde Milan	1,393
Larry Gardner	1,367
Jake Daubert	1,353
Zack Wheat	1,348

At-Bats

Harry Hooper	5,479
Donie Bush	5,462
Clyde Milan	5,305
Tris Speaker	5,290
Ed Konetchy	5,235
Eddie Collins	5,157
Fred Merkle	5,113
Jake Daubert	5,089
Zack Wheat	5,064
Ty Cobb	5,034

Runs

Ty Cobb	1,050
Eddie Collins	991
Tris Speaker	967
Donie Bush	958
Harry Hooper	868
Joe Jackson	765
Clyde Milan	758
Larry Doyle	745
Home Run Baker	733
2 tied with	727

Hits

Ty Cobb	1,949
Tris Speaker	1,821
Eddie Collins	1,682
Clyde Milan	1,556
Joe Jackson	1,548
Jake Daubert	1,535
Zack Wheat	1,516
Home Run Baker	1,502
Heinie Zimmerman	1,481
Ed Konetchy	1,475

Doubles

Tris Speaker	367
Ty Cobb	313
Duffy Lewis	277
Joe Jackson	265
Heinie Zimmerman	261
Sherry Magee	259
Home Run Baker	257
Fred Merkle	257
Fred Luderus	248
Ed Konetchy	246

Triples

Ty Cobb	161
Joe Jackson	148
Sam Crawford	135
Tris Speaker	133
Ed Konetchy	126
Eddie Collins	114
Harry Hooper	109
Zack Wheat	104
Heinie Zimmerman	102
Larry Doyle	101

Home Runs

Gavy Cravath	116
Fred Luderus	83
Home Run Baker	76
Wildfire Schulte	75
Larry Doyle	64
Sherry Magee	61
Heinie Zimmerman	58
Fred Merkle	56
Vic Saier	55
Chief Wilson	52

Home Runs (Home)

Gavy Cravath	92
Fred Luderus	62
Home Run Baker	52
Wildfire Schulte	45
Sherry Magee	39
Vic Saier	37
Zack Wheat	34
Fred Merkle	33
Heinie Zimmerman	31
Hal Chase	31

Home Runs (Road)

Babe Ruth	38
Ed Konetchy	36
Larry Doyle	35
Ty Cobb	32
Wildfire Schulte	30
Joe Jackson	29
Chief Wilson	28
Heinie Zimmerman	27
Home Run Baker	24
Gavy Cravath	24

Extra Base Hits

Tris Speaker	538
Ty Cobb	521
Joe Jackson	455
Heinie Zimmerman	421
Ed Konetchy	419
Home Run Baker	412
Sherry Magee	407
Gavy Cravath	405
Zack Wheat	399
Larry Doyle	397

Total Bases

Ty Cobb	2,725
Tris Speaker	2,568
Joe Jackson	2,235
Eddie Collins	2,163
Home Run Baker	2,145
Zack Wheat	2,121
Heinie Zimmerman	2,120
Ed Konetchy	2,114
Hal Chase	2,039
Larry Doyle	2,032

RBI

Ty Cobb	828
Home Run Baker	793
Heinie Zimmerman	765
Sherry Magee	746
Tris Speaker	728
Duffy Lewis	718
Sam Crawford	697
Ed Konetchy	687
Eddie Collins	682
Gavy Cravath	665

Walks

Donie Bush	912
Eddie Collins	829
Harry Hooper	722
Tris Speaker	702
Burt Shotton	679
Jack Graney	656
Ty Cobb	602
Dode Paskert	584
Miller Huggins	572
Bob Bescher	554

Walks/PA

(minimum 3,000 Plate Appearances)

Miller Huggins	.167
Johnny Evers	.142
Donie Bush	.139
Eddie Collins	.131
Jack Graney	.127
Burt Shotton	.126
Tommy Leach	.120
Bob Bescher	.119
Gavy Cravath	.118
Tris Speaker	.113

Strikeouts

Dode Paskert	593
Fred Merkle	550
Wildfire Schulte	512
Gavy Cravath	502
Ed Konetchy	489
Max Carey	481
Bob Bescher	451
Zack Wheat	426
Red Smith	415
Fred Luderus	415

Hit By Pitch

Art Fletcher	125
Buck Herzog	104
Steve Evans	97
Bert Daniels	72
Tris Speaker	68
Sherry Magee	68
Jack Barry	63
Fred Snodgrass	62
Wally Schang	58
Chief Meyers	57

Sac Hits

Ray Chapman	299
Eddie Collins	292
Jake Daubert	276
Jack Barry	254
Duffy Lewis	244
Jimmy Austin	228
Larry Gardner	226
Ossie Vitt	220
Stuffy McInnis	220
Buck Weaver	216

Sac Flies

Statistic unavailable

Stolen Bases

Ty Cobb	577
Eddie Collins	489
Clyde Milan	434
Max Carey	392
Bob Bescher	363
Tris Speaker	336
Donie Bush	322
George Burns	293
Burt Shotton	286
Buck Herzog	286

Caught Stealing

Clyde Milan	124
Ty Cobb	113
Max Carey	111
Burt Shotton	89
George Burns	81
Tris Speaker	81
Eddie Collins	81
Harry Hooper	70
Del Pratt	68
Amos Strunk	64

Runs Created

Ty Cobb	1,248
Tris Speaker	1,134
Eddie Collins	1,077
Joe Jackson	952
Home Run Baker	849
Larry Doyle	796
Clyde Milan	795
Harry Hooper	792
Ed Konetchy	779
Sherry Magee	758

Runs Created/27 Outs

(minimum 3,000 Plate Appearances)

Ty Cobb	9.92
Joe Jackson	8.25
Tris Speaker	7.99
Eddie Collins	7.28
Gavy Cravath	6.81
Benny Kauff	6.80
Sam Crawford	6.36
Home Run Baker	6.30
Sherry Magee	5.94
Steve Evans	5.83

Batting Average

(minimum 3,000 Plate Appearances)

Ty Cobb	.387
Joe Jackson	.354
Tris Speaker	.344
Eddie Collins	.326
Nap Lajoie	.321
Sam Crawford	.313
Benny Kauff	.313
Home Run Baker	.310
Stuffy McInnis	.309
Bobby Veach	.304

On-Base Percentage

(minimum 3,000 Plate Appearances)

Ty Cobb	.457
Tris Speaker	.428
Eddie Collins	.424
Joe Jackson	.422
Miller Huggins	.402
Benny Kauff	.389
Johnny Evers	.382
Gavy Cravath	.381
Heine Groh	.377
Steve Evans	.376

Slugging Percentage

(minimum 3,000 Plate Appearances)

Ty Cobb	.541
Joe Jackson	.511
Gavy Cravath	.490
Tris Speaker	.485
Sam Crawford	.459
Benny Kauff	.450
Home Run Baker	.442
Sherry Magee	.433
Bobby Veach	.424
Heinie Zimmerman	.424

OBP+Slugging

(minimum 3,000 Plate Appearances)

Ty Cobb	.998
Joe Jackson	.933
Tris Speaker	.913
Gavy Cravath	.871
Eddie Collins	.843
Benny Kauff	.839
Sam Crawford	.831
Home Run Baker	.810
Sherry Magee	.804
Steve Evans	.797

Secondary Average

(minimum 3,000 Plate Appearances)

Ty Cobb	.388
Gavy Cravath	.359
Eddie Collins	.349
Tris Speaker	.337
Benny Kauff	.332
Bob Bescher	.325
Miller Huggins	.321
Vic Saier	.315
Joe Jackson	.307
Sherry Magee	.297

Isolated Power

(minimum 3,000 Plate Appearances)

Gavy Cravath	.198
Joe Jackson	.157
Ty Cobb	.154
Vic Saier	.146
Sam Crawford	.146
Tris Speaker	.141
Sherry Magee	.141
Wildfire Schulte	.139
Benny Kauff	.137
Chief Wilson	.134

Pitching Leaders—1910-1919

Wins

Walter Johnson	265
Pete Alexander	208
Eddie Cicotte	162
Hippo Vaughn	156
Slim Sallee	149
Rube Marquard	144
Eddie Plank	140
Christy Mathewson	137
Claude Hendrix	135
Hooks Dauss	125

Losses

Walter Johnson	143
Bob Groom	124
Bob Harmon	122
Eddie Cicotte	121
Red Ames	117
Slim Sallee	114
Hippo Vaughn	110
Claude Hendrix	105
Ray Caldwell	104
2 tied with	103

Winning Percentage
(minimum 100 decisions)

Joe Wood	.680
Pete Alexander	.675
Chief Bender	.663
Babe Ruth	.659
Eddie Plank	.657
Walter Johnson	.650
Doc Crandall	.646
Christy Mathewson	.643
Jack Coombs	.621
Jeff Tesreau	.615

Games

Walter Johnson	454
Eddie Cicotte	396
Pete Alexander	362
Red Ames	359
Slim Sallee	356
Claude Hendrix	333
Hippo Vaughn	331
Rube Marquard	330
Bob Groom	323
Larry Cheney	313

Games Started

Walter Johnson	361
Pete Alexander	307
Eddie Cicotte	284
Hippo Vaughn	279
Bob Groom	257
Rube Marquard	254
Slim Sallee	254
Claude Hendrix	234
3 tied with	232

Complete Games

Walter Johnson	327
Pete Alexander	243
Eddie Cicotte	193
Hippo Vaughn	184
Claude Hendrix	172
Dick Rudolph	167
Slim Sallee	163
Ray Caldwell	160
Lefty Tyler	157
Hooks Dauss	156

Shutouts

Walter Johnson	74
Pete Alexander	70
Hippo Vaughn	37
Eddie Plank	33
Lefty Tyler	30
Dutch Leonard	29
Eddie Cicotte	28
Jeff Tesreau	27
Claude Hendrix	27
Babe Adams	27

Saves

Slim Sallee	32
Three Finger Brown	30
Red Ames	29
Chief Bender	25
Eddie Plank	22
Jim Bagby	21
Walter Johnson	20
Ed Walsh	20
3 tied with	19

Games Finished

Doc Crandall	117
Doc Ayers	92
Walter Johnson	90
Red Ames	89
Three Finger Brown	89
Slim Sallee	85
Claude Hendrix	80
Eddie Cicotte	80
Dave Danforth	79
Sea Lion Hall	77

Batters Faced

Walter Johnson	13,360
Pete Alexander	10,926
Eddie Cicotte	10,221
Hippo Vaughn	9,525
Slim Sallee	9,080
Claude Hendrix	8,832
Bob Groom	8,716
Rube Marquard	8,643
Red Ames	8,309
Lefty Tyler	8,217

Innings Pitched

Walter Johnson	3,427.2
Pete Alexander	2,753.0
Eddie Cicotte	2,535.0
Hippo Vaughn	2,317.1
Slim Sallee	2,244.1
Claude Hendrix	2,167.2
Rube Marquard	2,128.1
Bob Groom	2,076.0
Red Ames	2,011.1
Lefty Tyler	1,987.0

Hits Allowed

Walter Johnson	2,604
Pete Alexander	2,300
Eddie Cicotte	2,241
Slim Sallee	2,097
Hippo Vaughn	2,006
Bob Groom	1,998
Rube Marquard	1,942
Red Ames	1,914
Claude Hendrix	1,907
Dick Rudolph	1,817

Runs Allowed

Bob Groom	954
Eddie Cicotte	882
Walter Johnson	881
Bob Harmon	872
Pete Alexander	846
Lefty Tyler	842
Red Ames	838
Hippo Vaughn	835
Rube Marquard	816
Claude Hendrix	809

Earned Runs Allowed

Bob Groom	723
Bob Harmon	696
Lefty Tyler	641
Rube Marquard	641
Eddie Cicotte	641
Pete Alexander	638
Ray Caldwell	620
Claude Hendrix	617
Slim Sallee	615
Red Ames	611

Home Runs Allowed

Rube Marquard	62
Slim Sallee	53
Christy Mathewson	52
Pete Alexander	49
Bob Groom	47
Russ Ford	44
Doc Crandall	44
4 tied with	43

Walks

Lefty Tyler	758
Larry Cheney	733
Hippo Vaughn	701
Bob Harmon	697
Bob Groom	678
Walter Johnson	661
Claude Hendrix	643
Eddie Cicotte	633
Ray Caldwell	625
Pete Alexander	596

Intentional Walks

Statistic unavailable

Strikeouts

Walter Johnson	2,219
Pete Alexander	1,539
Hippo Vaughn	1,253
Rube Marquard	1,141
Eddie Cicotte	1,104
Bob Groom	1,028
Claude Hendrix	1,020
Lefty Tyler	938
Larry Cheney	926
Willie Mitchell	913

Strikeouts/9 Innings
(minimum 1,000 Innings Pitched)

Joe Wood	6.40
Walter Johnson	5.83
Ed Walsh	5.68
Willie Mitchell	5.11
Pete Alexander	5.03
Dutch Leonard	4.98
Earl Moore	4.89
Hippo Vaughn	4.87
Rube Marquard	4.82
Vean Gregg	4.79

ERA
(minimum 1,000 Innings Pitched)

Walter Johnson	1.59
Joe Wood	1.97
Ed Walsh	1.98
Pete Alexander	2.09
Carl Mays	2.15
Babe Ruth	2.19
Jeff Pfeffer	2.20
Dutch Leonard	2.22
Eddie Plank	2.25
Eddie Cicotte	2.28

Component ERA
(minimum 1,000 Innings Pitched)

Walter Johnson	1.67
Ed Walsh	1.95
Pete Alexander	2.09
Joe Wood	2.11
Reb Russell	2.14
Babe Adams	2.18
Babe Ruth	2.21
Carl Mays	2.21
Stan Coveleski	2.30
Fred Toney	2.34

Sac Hits Allowed

Walter Johnson	281
Pete Alexander	237
Slim Sallee	232
Wilbur Cooper	212
Dick Rudolph	212
Larry Cheney	208
Rube Marquard	204
Bill Doak	194
Lefty Tyler	191
Pat Ragan	189

Sac Flies Allowed

Statistic unavailable

Hit Batsmen

Walter Johnson	112
Jack Warhop	84
Hooks Dauss	82
Rube Benton	82
Jeff Pfeffer	73
Ed Willett	73
Hippo Vaughn	72
Willie Mitchell	71
Lefty Tyler	64
Jack Coombs	63

Wild Pitches

Larry Cheney	119
Walter Johnson	101
Red Ames	78
Claude Hendrix	66
Hippo Vaughn	59
Rube Marquard	56
Lefty Tyler	52
Rube Benton	52
Harry Harper	51
Eppa Rixey	50

Balks

Joe Boehling	10
Ed Walsh	9
Jim Shaw	8
George Suggs	8
Burleigh Grimes	7
Carl Weilman	7
Eppa Rixey	7
Elmer Jacobs	6
Al Mamaux	6
6 tied with	5

Opponent Average
(minimum 1,000 Innings Pitched)

Walter Johnson	.212
Babe Ruth	.219
Joe Wood	.222
Ed Walsh	.223
Jeff Tesreau	.223
Carl Mays	.229
Pete Alexander	.229
Jim Shaw	.231
Larry Cheney	.234
Dutch Leonard	.234

Opponent OBP
(minimum 1,000 Innings Pitched)

Walter Johnson	.258
Ed Walsh	.272
Pete Alexander	.276
Babe Adams	.277
Christy Mathewson	.281
Reb Russell	.281
Joe Wood	.286
Carl Mays	.289
Stan Coveleski	.291
Fred Toney	.291

Single Season Batting Leaders—1910-1919

Games

Tommy Griffith	1915	160
Heine Groh	1915	160
Nap Lajoie	1910	159
Babe Borton	1915	159
Del Pratt	1915	159
9 tied with		158

At-Bats

Jack Tobin	1915	625
Vin Campbell	1912	624
George Burns	1916	623
Doc Hoblitzell	1911	622
George Burns	1915	622
Max Carey	1913	620
Eddie Foster	1912	618
Eddie Foster	1915	618
Harry Swacina	1914	617
2 tied with		616

Runs

Ty Cobb	1911	147
Ty Cobb	1915	144
Eddie Collins	1912	137
Tris Speaker	1912	136
Donie Bush	1911	126
Joe Jackson	1911	126
Eddie Collins	1913	125
Eddie Collins	1914	122
Jimmy Sheckard	1911	121
Joe Jackson	1912	121

Hits

Ty Cobb	1911	248
Joe Jackson	1911	233
Nap Lajoie	1910	227
Ty Cobb	1912	227
Joe Jackson	1912	226
Ty Cobb	1917	225
Tris Speaker	1912	222
Sam Crawford	1911	217
Benny Kauff	1914	211
Tris Speaker	1916	211

Doubles

Tris Speaker	1912	53
Nap Lajoie	1910	51
Ty Cobb	1911	47
Tris Speaker	1914	46
Joe Jackson	1911	45
Bobby Veach	1919	45
Joe Jackson	1912	44
Benny Kauff	1914	44
Ty Cobb	1917	44
Bobby Byrne	1910	43

Triples

Chief Wilson	1912	36
Joe Jackson	1912	26
Sam Crawford	1914	26
Larry Doyle	1911	25
Tom Long	1915	25
Ty Cobb	1911	24
Ty Cobb	1917	24
Ty Cobb	1912	23
Sam Crawford	1913	23
3 tied with		22

Home Runs

Babe Ruth	1919	29
Gavy Cravath	1915	24
Wildfire Schulte	1911	21
Gavy Cravath	1913	19
Gavy Cravath	1914	19
Fred Luderus	1913	18
Vic Saier	1914	18
Hal Chase	1915	17
Fred Luderus	1911	16
Dutch Zwilling	1914	16

Home Runs (Home)

Gavy Cravath	1914	19
Gavy Cravath	1915	19
Fred Luderus	1911	15
Gavy Cravath	1913	14
Fred Luderus	1913	12
Duke Kenworthy	1914	12
Vic Saier	1914	12
Sherry Magee	1914	12
3 tied with		11

Home Runs (Road)

Babe Ruth	1919	20
Babe Ruth	1918	11
Wildfire Schulte	1911	10
Ed Lennox	1914	10
Doc Hoblitzell	1911	9
Chief Wilson	1912	9
Ed Konetchy	1915	9
Larry Doyle	1911	8
Ping Bodie	1913	8
Dave Robertson	1916	8

Extra Base Hits

Ty Cobb	1911	79
Tris Speaker	1912	75
Babe Ruth	1919	75
Ty Cobb	1917	74
Joe Jackson	1912	73
Wildfire Schulte	1911	72
Joe Jackson	1911	71
Home Run Baker	1912	71
Heinie Zimmerman	1912	69
Duke Kenworthy	1914	69

Total Bases

Ty Cobb	1911	367
Joe Jackson	1911	337
Ty Cobb	1917	335
Joe Jackson	1912	331
Tris Speaker	1912	329
Ty Cobb	1912	324
Heinie Zimmerman	1912	318
Home Run Baker	1912	312
Wildfire Schulte	1911	308
Benny Kauff	1914	305

RBI

Home Run Baker	1912	130
Gavy Cravath	1913	128
Ty Cobb	1911	127
Sherry Magee	1910	123
Sam Crawford	1910	120
Home Run Baker	1913	117
Home Run Baker	1911	115
Sam Crawford	1911	115
Gavy Cravath	1915	115
Babe Ruth	1919	114

Walks

Jimmy Sheckard	1911	147
Jimmy Sheckard	1912	122
Eddie Collins	1915	119
Burt Shotton	1915	118
Donie Bush	1915	118
Ty Cobb	1915	118
Donie Bush	1912	117
Miller Huggins	1910	116
Donie Bush	1914	112
Burt Shotton	1916	110

Walks/PA

(minimum 3.1 PA/Tm Gm)

Jimmy Sheckard	1911	.209
Johnny Evers	1910	.194
Babe Ruth	1919	.186
Miller Huggins	1913	.186
Jimmy Sheckard	1912	.185
Donie Bush	1912	.182
Jack Graney	1919	.179
Eddie Collins	1915	.175
Burt Shotton	1915	.172
Eddie Collins	1918	.172

Strikeouts

Gus Williams	1914	120
Grover Gilmore	1914	108
Danny Moeller	1913	103
Jack McCandless	1915	99
Ed McDonald	1912	91
Danny Moeller	1914	89
Gavy Cravath	1916	89
Al Boucher	1914	88
Doug Baird	1915	88
Gus Williams	1913	87

Hit By Pitch

Steve Evans	1910	31
Kid Elberfeld	1911	25
Doc Gessler	1911	20
Steve Evans	1911	19
Red Killefer	1915	19
Art Fletcher	1917	19
Bert Daniels	1911	18
Bert Daniels	1912	18
Bert Daniels	1913	18
3 tied with		17

Sac Hits

Ray Chapman	1917	67
Jack Barry	1917	54
Ray Chapman	1919	50
Ray Chapman	1913	48
Ossie Vitt	1919	47
Ralph Young	1919	46
Buck Weaver	1916	44
Roy Grover	1917	43
4 tied with		42

Sac Flies

Statistic unavailable

Stolen Bases

Ty Cobb	1915	96
Clyde Milan	1912	88
Ty Cobb	1911	83
Eddie Collins	1910	81
Bob Bescher	1911	80
Clyde Milan	1913	75
Benny Kauff	1914	75
Fritz Maisel	1914	74
Bob Bescher	1910	70
Ty Cobb	1916	68

Caught Stealing

Ty Cobb	1915	38
Miller Huggins	1914	36
George Burns	1913	35
Ty Cobb	1912	34
Lee Magee	1912	33
Clyde Milan	1912	33
Doc Cook	1914	32
Eddie Murphy	1914	32
Burt Shotton	1915	32
Duffy Lewis	1914	31

Runs Created

Ty Cobb	1911	172
Tris Speaker	1912	163
Ty Cobb	1915	154
Joe Jackson	1912	148
Ty Cobb	1912	148
Joe Jackson	1911	147
Ty Cobb	1917	144
Benny Kauff	1914	142
Ty Cobb	1910	138
2 tied with		136

Runs Created/27 Outs

(minimum 3.1 PA/Tm Gm)

Ty Cobb	1911	12.42
Tris Speaker	1912	11.36
Ty Cobb	1912	11.27
Joe Jackson	1911	10.92
Ty Cobb	1910	10.84
Babe Ruth	1919	10.53
Joe Jackson	1912	10.43
Ty Cobb	1915	10.16
Tris Speaker	1916	10.02
Ty Cobb	1917	9.87

Batting Average

(minimum 3.1 PA/Tm Gm)

Ty Cobb	1911	.420
Ty Cobb	1912	.410
Joe Jackson	1911	.408
Joe Jackson	1912	.395
Ty Cobb	1913	.390
Tris Speaker	1916	.386
Joe Jackson	1919	.384
Nap Lajoie	1910	.384
Ty Cobb	1910	.383
Tris Speaker	1912	.383

On-Base Percentage

(minimum 3.1 PA/Tm Gm)

Ty Cobb	1915	.486
Tris Speaker	1916	.470
Joe Jackson	1911	.468
Ty Cobb	1913	.467
Ty Cobb	1911	.467
Tris Speaker	1912	.464
Eddie Collins	1915	.460
Joe Jackson	1913	.460
Joe Jackson	1912	.458
Ty Cobb	1912	.458

Slugging Percentage

(minimum 3.1 PA/Tm Gm)

Babe Ruth	1919	.657
Ty Cobb	1911	.621
Joe Jackson	1911	.590
Ty Cobb	1912	.586
Joe Jackson	1912	.579
Heinie Zimmerman	1912	.571
Ty Cobb	1917	.570
Gavy Cravath	1913	.568
Tris Speaker	1912	.567
Steve Evans	1914	.556

OBP+Slugging

(minimum 3.1 PA/Tm Gm)

Babe Ruth	1919	1.114
Ty Cobb	1911	1.088
Joe Jackson	1911	1.058
Ty Cobb	1912	1.043
Joe Jackson	1912	1.036
Tris Speaker	1912	1.031
Ty Cobb	1917	1.014
Joe Jackson	1913	1.011
Ty Cobb	1910	1.008
Ty Cobb	1913	1.002

Secondary Average

(minimum 3.1 PA/Tm Gm)

Babe Ruth	1919	.586
Ty Cobb	1915	.497
Benny Kauff	1915	.458
Sherry Magee	1910	.451
Jimmy Sheckard	1911	.443
Larry Doyle	1911	.424
Ty Cobb	1910	.423
Benny Kauff	1914	.422
Eddie Collins	1915	.420
Ty Cobb	1911	.416

Isolated Power

(minimum 3.1 PA/Tm Gm)

Babe Ruth	1919	.336
Wildfire Schulte	1911	.234
Gavy Cravath	1913	.227
Gavy Cravath	1915	.224
Larry Doyle	1911	.217
Chief Wilson	1912	.213
Steve Evans	1914	.208
Duke Kenworthy	1914	.207
Ty Cobb	1911	.201
Gavy Cravath	1914	.200

Single Season Pitching Leaders—1910-1919

Wins

Walter Johnson	1913	36
Joe Wood	1912	34
Walter Johnson	1912	33
Pete Alexander	1916	33
Jack Coombs	1910	31
Pete Alexander	1915	31
Pete Alexander	1917	30
Claude Hendrix	1914	29
Eddie Cicotte	1919	29
4 tied with		28

Losses

George Bell	1910	27
Cliff Curtis	1910	24
Joe Bush	1916	24
Buster Brown	1910	23
Red Ames	1914	23
Elmer Myers	1916	23
Lee Meadows	1916	23
5 tied with		22

Winning Percentage
(minimum 15 decisions)

Deacon Phillippe	1910	.875
Joe Wood	1912	.872
Chief Bender	1914	.850
Tom Hughes	1916	.842
Walter Johnson	1913	.837
King Cole	1910	.833
Chief Bender	1910	.821
Russ Ford	1910	.813
Eddie Plank	1912	.813
Doc Crandall	1910	.810

Games

Ed Walsh	1912	62
Dave Davenport	1916	59
Ed Walsh	1911	56
Reb Russell	1916	56
Dave Davenport	1915	55
Larry Cheney	1913	54
Three Finger Brown	1911	53
Hugh Bedient	1915	53
Bob Shawkey	1916	53
Tom Seaton	1913	52

Games Started

Dave Davenport	1915	46
Pete Alexander	1916	45
Pete Alexander	1917	44
Cy Falkenberg	1914	43
Dick Rudolph	1915	43
Walter Johnson	1910	42
Jack Quinn	1914	42
Pete Alexander	1915	42
Pete Schneider	1917	42
Fred Toney	1917	42

Complete Games

Walter Johnson	1910	38
Pete Alexander	1916	38
Walter Johnson	1911	36
Pete Alexander	1915	36
Walter Johnson	1916	36
Jack Coombs	1910	35
Joe Wood	1912	35
Walter Johnson	1915	35
Babe Ruth	1917	35
Pete Alexander	1917	35

Shutouts

Pete Alexander	1916	16
Jack Coombs	1910	13
Pete Alexander	1915	12
Walter Johnson	1913	11
Joe Wood	1912	10
Dave Davenport	1915	10
6 tied with		9

Saves

Three Finger Brown	1911	13
Chief Bender	1913	13
Larry Cheney	1913	11
Ed Walsh	1912	10
Hugh Bedient	1915	10
Tom Hughes	1915	9
Jack Quinn	1914	9
Dave Danforth	1917	9
Bob Shawkey	1916	8
Red Ames	1916	8
6 tied with		7

Games Finished

Doc Crandall	1913	27
Carl Mays	1915	27
Doc Crandall	1911	26
Dave Danforth	1917	26
Doc Crandall	1912	25
Three Finger Brown	1911	24
Sad Sam Jones	1915	24
George Cunningham	1917	24
3 tied with		23

Batters Faced

Ed Walsh	1912	1,564
Pete Alexander	1917	1,529
Dave Davenport	1915	1,527
Cy Falkenberg	1914	1,519
Pete Alexander	1916	1,500
Bob Harmon	1911	1,487
Ed Walsh	1911	1,480
Pete Alexander	1911	1,475
Jack Coombs	1911	1,469
Pete Alexander	1914	1,459

Innings Pitched

Ed Walsh	1912	393.0
Dave Davenport	1915	392.2
Pete Alexander	1916	389.0
Pete Alexander	1917	388.0
Cy Falkenberg	1914	377.1
Pete Alexander	1915	376.1
Walter Johnson	1914	371.2
Walter Johnson	1910	370.0
Ed Walsh	1910	369.2
Walter Johnson	1916	369.2

Hits Allowed

Jack Coombs	1911	360
Pete Alexander	1917	336
Jack Quinn	1914	335
Ed Walsh	1912	332
Cy Falkenberg	1914	332
Ed Walsh	1911	327
Pete Alexander	1914	327
Pete Alexander	1916	323
George Suggs	1914	322
George Suggs	1912	320

Runs Allowed

Elmer Myers	1916	169
Jack Coombs	1911	166
Russ Ford	1912	165
Buster Brown	1911	161
Bob Harmon	1912	156
Bob Harmon	1911	155
Cliff Curtis	1910	154
Bill Steele	1911	153
Tom Seaton	1915	152
2 tied with		150

Earned Runs Allowed

Jack Coombs	1911	132
Elmer Myers	1916	128
Dan Griner	1913	127
Earl Moseley	1914	122
Bob Harmon	1911	121
Bill Steele	1911	119
Lefty Tyler	1912	119
Bob Harmon	1913	119
Bob Harmon	1910	117
Bob Harmon	1912	117

Home Runs Allowed

Christy Mathewson	1914	16
Al Mattern	1911	13
Phil Douglas	1917	13
Nap Rucker	1911	12
Dan Griner	1913	12
Otto Hess	1913	12
George Suggs	1915	12
8 tied with		11

Walks

Bob Harmon	1911	181
Elmer Myers	1916	168
John Wyckoff	1915	165
Earl Moore	1911	164
Marty O'Toole	1912	159
Grover Lowdermilk	1915	157
Al Schulz	1915	149
Larry Cheney	1914	140
Jim Shaw	1914	137
3 tied with		136

Intentional Walks

Statistic unavailable

Strikeouts

Walter Johnson	1910	313
Walter Johnson	1912	303
Ed Walsh	1910	258
Joe Wood	1912	258
Ed Walsh	1911	255
Ed Walsh	1912	254
Walter Johnson	1913	243
Pete Alexander	1915	241
Rube Marquard	1911	237
Cy Falkenberg	1914	236

Strikeouts/9 Innings
(minimum 1 Inning Pitched/Tm Gm)

Rube Marquard	1911	7.68
Walter Johnson	1910	7.61
Joe Wood	1911	7.51
Walter Johnson	1912	7.39
Dutch Leonard	1914	7.05
Joe Wood	1912	6.75
Joe Wood	1910	6.60
Walter Johnson	1913	6.32
Louis Drucke	1910	6.31
Ed Walsh	1910	6.28

ERA
(minimum 1 Inning Pitched/Tm Gm)

Dutch Leonard	1914	1.00
Walter Johnson	1913	1.14
Pete Alexander	1915	1.22
Ed Walsh	1910	1.27
Walter Johnson	1918	1.27
Jack Coombs	1910	1.30
Walter Johnson	1910	1.36
Walter Johnson	1912	1.39
Fred Anderson	1917	1.44
Joe Wood	1915	1.49

Component ERA
(minimum 1 Inning Pitched/Tm Gm)

Walter Johnson	1913	1.27
Ed Walsh	1910	1.27
Pete Alexander	1915	1.33
Dutch Leonard	1914	1.41
Russ Ford	1910	1.41
Eddie Cicotte	1917	1.48
Walter Johnson	1912	1.52
Babe Adams	1919	1.52
Walter Johnson	1910	1.54
Chief Bender	1910	1.56

Sac Hits Allowed

Slim Sallee	1914	48
Russ Ford	1912	47
George Bell	1910	46
Bill Doak	1915	46
Pol Perritt	1914	45
Bob Harmon	1912	43
Wilbur Cooper	1914	43
Elmer Jacobs	1917	43
4 tied with		42

Sac Flies Allowed

Statistic unavailable

Hit Batsmen

Cy Morgan	1911	21
Harry Coveleski	1915	20
Rube Benton	1915	19
Walter Johnson	1915	19
Jack Warhop	1910	18
Cy Morgan	1910	18
Rube Benton	1912	18
Hooks Dauss	1914	18
Harry Moran	1915	18
6 tied with		17

Wild Pitches

Larry Cheney	1914	26
Walter Johnson	1910	21
Larry Cheney	1913	19
Larry Cheney	1912	18
Walter Johnson	1911	17
Jean Dubuc	1912	16
Joe Bush	1916	15
Larry Cheney	1916	15
5 tied with		14

Balks

Joe Boehling	1915	6
Al Mamaux	1916	6
Ed Walsh	1912	5
Reb Russell	1913	4
Joe Engel	1913	4
12 tied with		3

Opponent Average
(minimum 1 Inning Pitched/Tm Gm)

Dutch Leonard	1914	.179
Ed Walsh	1910	.187
Walter Johnson	1913	.187
Russ Ford	1910	.188
Pete Alexander	1915	.191
Stan Coveleski	1917	.193
Walter Johnson	1912	.196
Larry Cheney	1916	.198
Babe Ruth	1916	.201
Willie Mitchell	1913	.201

Opponent OBP
(minimum 1 Inning Pitched/Tm Gm)

Walter Johnson	1913	.217
Ed Walsh	1910	.226
Pete Alexander	1915	.234
Babe Adams	1919	.241
Russ Ford	1910	.245
Dutch Leonard	1914	.245
Pete Alexander	1919	.245
Eddie Cicotte	1917	.248
Walter Johnson	1912	.248
Claude Hendrix	1914	.251

Batting Leaders—1920-1929

Games

Sam Rice	1,496
Charlie Grimm	1,458
Rogers Hornsby	1,430
Harry Heilmann	1,417
Joe Sewell	1,404
Babe Ruth	1,399
Frankie Frisch	1,378
Joe Judge	1,359
George Kelly	1,351
George Sisler	1,326

At-Bats

Sam Rice	6,184
Frankie Frisch	5,554
George Sisler	5,480
Rogers Hornsby	5,451
Charlie Grimm	5,389
Harry Heilmann	5,285
Joe Sewell	5,268
George Kelly	5,186
Charlie Jamieson	5,109
Joe Judge	5,063

Runs

Babe Ruth	1,365
Rogers Hornsby	1,195
Sam Rice	1,001
Frankie Frisch	992
Harry Heilmann	962
Lu Blue	896
George Sisler	894
Charlie Jamieson	868
Tris Speaker	830
Ty Cobb	830

Hits

Rogers Hornsby	2,085
Sam Rice	2,010
Harry Heilmann	1,924
George Sisler	1,900
Frankie Frisch	1,808
Babe Ruth	1,734
Joe Sewell	1,698
Charlie Jamieson	1,623
Charlie Grimm	1,570
George Kelly	1,569

Doubles

Rogers Hornsby	405
Harry Heilmann	397
Tris Speaker	397
Joe Sewell	358
Sam Rice	345
Bob Meusel	338
George Burns	317
Babe Ruth	314
George Kelly	304
George Sisler	297

Triples

Sam Rice	133
Rogers Hornsby	115
George Sisler	111
Edd Roush	111
Goose Goslin	110
Pie Traynor	109
Frankie Frisch	107
Curt Walker	106
Jim Bottomley	104
2 tied with	101

Home Runs

Babe Ruth	467
Rogers Hornsby	250
Cy Williams	202
Ken Williams	190
Lou Gehrig	146
Jim Bottomley	146
Bob Meusel	146
Harry Heilmann	142
Hack Wilson	137
George Kelly	134

Home Runs (Home)

Babe Ruth	230
Rogers Hornsby	140
Ken Williams	137
Cy Williams	133
Jim Bottomley	75
Harry Heilmann	75
Bob Meusel	73
Hack Wilson	72
Lou Gehrig	72
George Kelly	63

Home Runs (Road)

Babe Ruth	237
Rogers Hornsby	110
Goose Goslin	84
Lou Gehrig	74
Bob Meusel	73
Jim Bottomley	71
George Kelly	71
Jack Fournier	71
Cy Williams	69
Harry Heilmann	67

Extra Base Hits

Babe Ruth	863
Rogers Hornsby	770
Harry Heilmann	640
Bob Meusel	571
Tris Speaker	543
Ken Williams	523
Jim Bottomley	511
George Kelly	507
Sam Rice	504
George Sisler	486

Total Bases

Babe Ruth	3,613
Rogers Hornsby	3,470
Harry Heilmann	2,949
Sam Rice	2,699
George Sisler	2,653
Frankie Frisch	2,530
Bob Meusel	2,515
George Kelly	2,413
Ken Williams	2,399
Jim Bottomley	2,261

RBI

Babe Ruth	1,328
Rogers Hornsby	1,153
Harry Heilmann	1,133
Bob Meusel	1,005
George Kelly	923
Jim Bottomley	885
Ken Williams	860
George Sisler	827
Goose Goslin	821
Joe Sewell	817

Walks

Babe Ruth	1,236
Lu Blue	820
Rogers Hornsby	753
Tris Speaker	636
Harry Heilmann	615
Joe Sewell	613
Joe Judge	600
Eddie Collins	596
Max Bishop	587
Charlie Jamieson	584

Walks/PA

(minimum 3,000 Plate Appearances)

Babe Ruth	.199
Max Bishop	.193
Lu Blue	.149
Lou Gehrig	.145
Wally Schang	.136
Eddie Collins	.128
Tris Speaker	.126
Bob O'Farrell	.124
George Grantham	.122
Rogers Hornsby	.118

Strikeouts

Babe Ruth	795
George Kelly	571
Bob Meusel	556
Jimmy Dykes	497
Aaron Ward	439
Rogers Hornsby	431
Marty McManus	414
Bernie Friberg	412
Cy Williams	401
Hack Wilson	388

Hit By Pitch

Bucky Harris	98
Johnny Mostil	70
Jimmy Dykes	66
Bing Miller	61
Jack Fournier	61
Joe Sewell	60
George Burns	60
Frank O'Rourke	49
Wally Schang	48
2 tied with	46

Sac Hits

Bucky Harris	248
Joe Sewell	221
Bill Wambsganss	211
Harry Heilmann	190
Joe Judge	187
Bibb Falk	184
Wally Pipp	182
Wally Gerber	181
Eddie Collins	181
Earl Sheely	177

Sac Flies

Statistic unavailable

Stolen Bases

Max Carey	346
Frankie Frisch	310
Sam Rice	254
George Sisler	214
Kiki Cuyler	210
Eddie Collins	180
Johnny Mostil	175
Bucky Harris	166
Cliff Heathcote	145
Jack Smith	144

Caught Stealing

Sam Rice	123
Johnny Mostil	106
Charlie Jamieson	104
Bob Meusel	103
Ken Williams	102
Ty Cobb	99
Babe Ruth	94
George Burns	93
3 tied with	92

Runs Created

Babe Ruth	1,596
Rogers Hornsby	1,429
Harry Heilmann	1,209
Sam Rice	1,002
George Sisler	969
Tris Speaker	963
Frankie Frisch	960
Joe Sewell	904
Ken Williams	900
2 tied with	864

Runs Created/27 Outs

(minimum 3,000 Plate Appearances)

Babe Ruth	12.59
Rogers Hornsby	10.41
Lou Gehrig	9.33
Harry Heilmann	8.77
Tris Speaker	8.62
Al Simmons	8.02
Ty Cobb	7.87
Hack Wilson	7.68
Riggs Stephenson	7.57
Jim Bottomley	7.46

Batting Average

(minimum 3,000 Plate Appearances)

Rogers Hornsby	.382
Harry Heilmann	.364
Ty Cobb	.357
Al Simmons	.356
Babe Ruth	.355
Tris Speaker	.354
George Sisler	.347
Eddie Collins	.346
Riggs Stephenson	.340
Zack Wheat	.339

On-Base Percentage

(minimum 3,000 Plate Appearances)

Babe Ruth	.488
Rogers Hornsby	.460
Tris Speaker	.441
Eddie Collins	.436
Lou Gehrig	.436
Harry Heilmann	.433
Ty Cobb	.431
Max Bishop	.419
Riggs Stephenson	.413
Lu Blue	.405

Slugging Percentage

(minimum 3,000 Plate Appearances)

Babe Ruth	.740
Rogers Hornsby	.637
Lou Gehrig	.621
Al Simmons	.570
Harry Heilmann	.558
Hack Wilson	.557
Ken Williams	.547
Jim Bottomley	.547
Tris Speaker	.534
Cy Williams	.521

OBP+Slugging

(minimum 3,000 Plate Appearances)

Babe Ruth	1.227
Rogers Hornsby	1.096
Lou Gehrig	1.058
Harry Heilmann	.991
Tris Speaker	.976
Al Simmons	.965
Hack Wilson	.954
Ken Williams	.947
Jim Bottomley	.938
Ty Cobb	.937

Secondary Average

(minimum 3,000 Plate Appearances)

Babe Ruth	.656
Lou Gehrig	.472
Rogers Hornsby	.406
Hack Wilson	.387
Ken Williams	.373
Kiki Cuyler	.346
Tris Speaker	.345
Max Bishop	.342
George Grantham	.342
Cy Williams	.339

Isolated Power

(minimum 3,000 Plate Appearances)

Babe Ruth	.385
Lou Gehrig	.287
Rogers Hornsby	.254
Hack Wilson	.242
Ken Williams	.221
Jim Bottomley	.219
Al Simmons	.214
Cy Williams	.211
Harry Heilmann	.194
Bob Meusel	.189

Pitching Leaders—1920-1929

Wins

Burleigh Grimes	190
Eppa Rixey	166
Pete Alexander	165
Herb Pennock	163
Waite Hoyt	161
Urban Shocker	156
Eddie Rommel	154
Jesse Haines	153
George Uhle	152
Red Faber	149

Losses

Dolf Luque	146
Eppa Rixey	142
Howard Ehmke	137
Slim Harriss	135
Burleigh Grimes	130
Jimmy Ring	128
George Uhle	124
Tom Zachary	122
Jesse Haines	119
Sad Sam Jones	118

Winning Percentage
(minimum 100 decisions)

Ray Kremer	.660
Carl Mays	.636
Urban Shocker	.627
Freddie Fitzsimmons	.626
Lefty Grove	.626
Dazzy Vance	.620
Art Nehf	.615
Waite Hoyt	.612
Pete Alexander	.611
Stan Coveleski	.599

Games

Eddie Rommel	423
Eppa Rixey	386
Waite Hoyt	379
Bill Sherdel	378
Burleigh Grimes	373
Jack Quinn	367
Elam Vangilder	364
Sad Sam Jones	363
George Uhle	356
Dolf Luque	353

Games Started

Burleigh Grimes	336
Eppa Rixey	328
Dolf Luque	300
Red Faber	297
Jesse Haines	294
Pete Alexander	289
Herb Pennock	286
George Uhle	285
Waite Hoyt	279
Sad Sam Jones	278

Complete Games

Burleigh Grimes	234
Pete Alexander	195
Eppa Rixey	185
George Uhle	182
Red Faber	181
Herb Pennock	179
Dazzy Vance	171
Urban Shocker	170
Jesse Haines	169
Dolf Luque	168

Shutouts

Walter Johnson	24
Dazzy Vance	23
Urban Shocker	22
Jesse Haines	21
Sad Sam Jones	21
Dolf Luque	21
Stan Coveleski	21
Eppa Rixey	21
Herb Pennock	21
2 tied with	20

Saves

Firpo Marberry	75
Waite Hoyt	29
Sarge Connally	25
Garland Braxton	25
Allan Russell	25
Lefty Grove	24
Eddie Rommel	24
Bill Sherdel	24
Hooks Dauss	24
2 tied with	23

Games Finished

Firpo Marberry	198
Eddie Rommel	137
Elam Vangilder	118
Bill Sherdel	117
Sarge Connally	116
Jack Scott	113
Allan Russell	100
Garland Braxton	97
Jakie May	91
2 tied with	88

Batters Faced

Burleigh Grimes	12,024
Eppa Rixey	11,150
Dolf Luque	10,321
George Uhle	10,157
Red Faber	10,077
Waite Hoyt	10,054
Jesse Haines	9,897
Pete Alexander	9,893
Howard Ehmke	9,836
Herb Pennock	9,793

Innings Pitched

Burleigh Grimes	2,797.2
Eppa Rixey	2,678.1
Dolf Luque	2,479.2
Pete Alexander	2,415.1
Red Faber	2,365.0
Waite Hoyt	2,346.0
Jesse Haines	2,328.1
George Uhle	2,309.2
Herb Pennock	2,299.1
Howard Ehmke	2,265.0

Hits Allowed

Burleigh Grimes	2,988
Eppa Rixey	2,827
George Uhle	2,570
Pete Alexander	2,528
Jesse Haines	2,490
Herb Pennock	2,485
Waite Hoyt	2,464
Dolf Luque	2,446
Red Faber	2,429
Eddie Rommel	2,367

Runs Allowed

Burleigh Grimes	1,352
George Uhle	1,214
Jimmy Ring	1,169
Eppa Rixey	1,169
Howard Ehmke	1,152
Sad Sam Jones	1,137
Jesse Haines	1,132
Waite Hoyt	1,080
Dolf Luque	1,059
Eddie Rommel	1,054

Earned Runs Allowed

Burleigh Grimes	1,091
George Uhle	1,019
Eppa Rixey	964
Howard Ehmke	960
Sad Sam Jones	948
Jimmy Ring	945
Jesse Haines	935
Waite Hoyt	914
Herb Pennock	883
Red Faber	878

Home Runs Allowed

Jesse Haines	122
Eddie Rommel	116
Bill Sherdel	115
Urban Shocker	114
Pete Alexander	110
Burleigh Grimes	105
Jimmy Ring	96
Elam Vangilder	92
Art Nehf	92
2 tied with	90

Walks

Burleigh Grimes	842
Jimmy Ring	819
Howard Ehmke	805
Sad Sam Jones	791
George Uhle	719
Elam Vangilder	697
Dolf Luque	688
Joe Bush	687
Waite Hoyt	669
Red Faber	664

Intentional Walks

Statistic unavailable

Strikeouts

Dazzy Vance	1,464
Burleigh Grimes	1,018
Dolf Luque	904
Walter Johnson	895
Lefty Grove	837
Howard Ehmke	824
George Uhle	808
Red Faber	804
Bob Shawkey	788
Urban Shocker	753

Strikeouts/9 Innings
(minimum 1,000 Innings Pitched)

Dazzy Vance	6.42
Lefty Grove	6.01
Jakie May	4.69
Walter Johnson	4.42
Bob Shawkey	4.40
Charlie Root	4.27
Rube Walberg	3.96
Firpo Marberry	3.93
Red Ruffing	3.57
Earl Whitehill	3.56

ERA
(minimum 1,000 Innings Pitched)

Pete Alexander	3.04
Lefty Grove	3.09
Dolf Luque	3.09
Dazzy Vance	3.10
Stan Coveleski	3.20
Eppa Rixey	3.24
Tommy Thomas	3.24
Urban Shocker	3.32
Walter Johnson	3.33
Red Faber	3.34

Component ERA
(minimum 1,000 Innings Pitched)

Dazzy Vance	2.86
Pete Alexander	3.00
Tommy Thomas	3.03
Dolf Luque	3.05
Walter Johnson	3.12
Eppa Rixey	3.15
Lefty Grove	3.15
Red Faber	3.27
Firpo Marberry	3.28
Ray Kremer	3.28

Sac Hits Allowed

Eppa Rixey	331
George Uhle	328
Red Faber	326
Burleigh Grimes	300
Tom Zachary	288
Howard Ehmke	282
Eddie Rommel	277
Jesse Haines	271
Waite Hoyt	255
Herb Pennock	252

Sac Flies Allowed

Statistic unavailable

Hit Batsmen

Howard Ehmke	118
George Uhle	90
Rip Collins	70
Walter Johnson	63
Burleigh Grimes	62
Dazzy Vance	61
Dutch Ruether	53
Wilbur Cooper	51
Jack Quinn	50
Bill Bayne	49

Wild Pitches

Jimmy Ring	81
Burleigh Grimes	51
George Uhle	43
Milt Gaston	42
Joe Bush	41
Eppa Rixey	38
Sad Sam Jones	37
Dolf Luque	35
Rip Collins	34
Jesse Haines	33

Balks

Tom Zachary	12
Dave Danforth	9
Milt Gaston	7
Howard Ehmke	7
Tony Kaufmann	6
Jesse Haines	6
Jimmy Ring	6
Joe Oeschger	6
7 tied with	5

Opponent Average
(minimum 1,000 Innings Pitched)

Dazzy Vance	.247
Tommy Thomas	.251
Lefty Grove	.251
Walter Johnson	.256
Firpo Marberry	.261
Dolf Luque	.261
Charlie Root	.261
Bob Shawkey	.262
Dixie Davis	.265
Ray Kremer	.268

Opponent OBP
(minimum 1,000 Innings Pitched)

Pete Alexander	.299
Dazzy Vance	.305
Tommy Thomas	.309
Dolf Luque	.313
Urban Shocker	.313
Ray Kremer	.314
Jesse Petty	.316
Walter Johnson	.316
Eppa Rixey	.317
Carl Mays	.317

Single Season Batting Leaders—1920-1929

Games

Kiki Cuyler	1926	157
10 tied with		156

At-Bats

Rabbit Maranville	1922	672
Jack Tobin	1921	671
Lloyd Waner	1929	662
Lloyd Waner	1928	659
Al Simmons	1925	658
Jigger Statz	1923	655
Ivy Olson	1921	652
Dave Bancroft	1922	651
Carl Lind	1928	650
2 tied with		649

Runs

Babe Ruth	1921	177
Babe Ruth	1928	163
Babe Ruth	1920	158
Babe Ruth	1927	158
Rogers Hornsby	1929	156
Lefty O'Doul	1929	152
Babe Ruth	1923	151
Lou Gehrig	1927	149
Kiki Cuyler	1925	144
Babe Ruth	1924	143

Hits

George Sisler	1920	257
Lefty O'Doul	1929	254
Al Simmons	1925	253
Rogers Hornsby	1922	250
George Sisler	1922	246
Heinie Manush	1928	241
Harry Heilmann	1921	237
Paul Waner	1927	237
Jack Tobin	1921	236
Rogers Hornsby	1921	235

Doubles

George Burns	1926	64
Tris Speaker	1923	59
Al Simmons	1926	53
Tris Speaker	1921	52
Tris Speaker	1926	52
Lou Gehrig	1927	52
Johnny Frederick	1929	52
Baby Doll Jacobson	1926	51
George Burns	1927	51
3 tied with		50

Triples

Kiki Cuyler	1925	26
Earle Combs	1927	23
Hi Myers	1920	22
Jake Daubert	1922	22
Paul Waner	1926	22
Edd Roush	1924	21
Earle Combs	1928	21
9 tied with		20

Home Runs

Babe Ruth	1927	60
Babe Ruth	1921	59
Babe Ruth	1920	54
Babe Ruth	1928	54
Babe Ruth	1926	47
Lou Gehrig	1927	47
Babe Ruth	1924	46
Babe Ruth	1929	46
Chuck Klein	1929	43
2 tied with		42

Home Runs (Home)

Babe Ruth	1921	32
Ken Williams	1922	32
Babe Ruth	1920	29
Babe Ruth	1928	29
Babe Ruth	1927	28
Tilly Walker	1922	26
Cy Williams	1923	26
Chuck Klein	1929	25
Hack Wilson	1929	25
4 tied with		24

Home Runs (Road)

Babe Ruth	1927	32
Babe Ruth	1921	27
Babe Ruth	1920	25
Babe Ruth	1928	25
Babe Ruth	1929	25
Babe Ruth	1926	24
Lou Gehrig	1927	23
Babe Ruth	1923	22
Babe Ruth	1924	22
Mel Ott	1929	22

Extra Base Hits

Babe Ruth	1921	119
Lou Gehrig	1927	117
Rogers Hornsby	1922	102
Babe Ruth	1920	99
Babe Ruth	1923	99
Babe Ruth	1927	97
Chuck Klein	1929	94
Rogers Hornsby	1929	94
Jim Bottomley	1928	93
Babe Ruth	1924	92

Total Bases

Babe Ruth	1921	457
Rogers Hornsby	1922	450
Lou Gehrig	1927	447
Babe Ruth	1927	417
Rogers Hornsby	1929	409
Chuck Klein	1929	405
George Sisler	1920	399
Babe Ruth	1923	399
Lefty O'Doul	1929	397
Al Simmons	1925	392

RBI

Lou Gehrig	1927	175
Babe Ruth	1921	171
Babe Ruth	1927	164
Hack Wilson	1929	159
Al Simmons	1929	157
Ken Williams	1922	155
Babe Ruth	1929	154
Rogers Hornsby	1922	152
Mel Ott	1929	151
Rogers Hornsby	1929	149

Walks

Babe Ruth	1923	170
Babe Ruth	1920	148
Babe Ruth	1921	144
Babe Ruth	1926	144
Babe Ruth	1924	142
Babe Ruth	1927	138
Babe Ruth	1928	135
Max Bishop	1929	128
Lu Blue	1929	126
Lou Gehrig	1929	122

Walks/PA

(minimum 3.1 PA/Tm Gm)

Babe Ruth	1923	.243
Babe Ruth	1920	.241
Babe Ruth	1926	.221
Max Bishop	1926	.219
Max Bishop	1927	.215
Babe Ruth	1924	.209
Babe Ruth	1921	.208
Max Bishop	1929	.208
Babe Ruth	1927	.199
Babe Ruth	1928	.198

Strikeouts

Jimmy Dykes	1922	98
Tony Lazzeri	1926	96
Hack Wilson	1928	94
Frank Parkinson	1922	93
Babe Ruth	1923	93
George Kelly	1920	92
George Grantham	1923	92
Babe Ruth	1927	89
Bob Meusel	1921	88
Babe Ruth	1928	87

Hit By Pitch

Bucky Harris	1920	21
Bucky Harris	1921	18
Heinie Manush	1923	17
Heinie Manush	1924	16
George Burns	1924	15
Bucky Harris	1922	14
Johnny Mostil	1922	14
Johnny Mostil	1921	13
Bucky Harris	1923	13
Kiki Cuyler	1925	13

Sac Hits

Joe Gedeon	1920	48
Donie Bush	1920	48
Bucky Harris	1924	46
Stuffy McInnis	1920	45
Bill Wambsganss	1921	43
Bill Wambsganss	1922	42
Pie Traynor	1928	42
4 tied with		41

Sac Flies

Statistic unavailable

Stolen Bases

Sam Rice	1920	63
Max Carey	1920	52
George Sisler	1922	51
Max Carey	1922	51
Max Carey	1923	51
Frankie Frisch	1921	49
Eddie Collins	1923	49
Max Carey	1924	49
Frankie Frisch	1927	48
Max Carey	1925	46

Caught Stealing

Sam Rice	1920	30
Charlie Hollocher	1922	29
Eddie Collins	1923	29
Pat Duncan	1922	28
George Grantham	1923	28
Bernie Friberg	1924	27
Billy Southworth	1920	25
Edd Roush	1920	24
Cliff Heathcote	1924	24
4 tied with		23

Runs Created

Babe Ruth	1921	208
Babe Ruth	1923	193
Babe Ruth	1920	191
Lou Gehrig	1927	182
Rogers Hornsby	1922	179
Babe Ruth	1924	179
Rogers Hornsby	1929	178
Babe Ruth	1927	177
Babe Ruth	1926	167
Babe Ruth	1928	165

Runs Created/27 Outs

(minimum 3.1 PA/Tm Gm)

Babe Ruth	1920	16.44
Babe Ruth	1921	15.47
Babe Ruth	1923	14.86
Babe Ruth	1924	13.39
Babe Ruth	1926	13.23
Rogers Hornsby	1925	12.88
Rogers Hornsby	1924	12.73
Babe Ruth	1927	12.53
Lou Gehrig	1927	12.00
Rogers Hornsby	1922	11.70

Batting Average

(minimum 3.1 PA/Tm Gm)

Rogers Hornsby	1924	.424
George Sisler	1922	.420
George Sisler	1920	.407
Rogers Hornsby	1925	.403
Harry Heilmann	1923	.403
Rogers Hornsby	1922	.401
Ty Cobb	1922	.401
Lefty O'Doul	1929	.398
Harry Heilmann	1927	.398
Rogers Hornsby	1921	.397

On-Base Percentage

(minimum 3.1 PA/Tm Gm)

Babe Ruth	1923	.545
Babe Ruth	1920	.530
Babe Ruth	1926	.516
Babe Ruth	1924	.513
Babe Ruth	1921	.512
Rogers Hornsby	1924	.507
Rogers Hornsby	1928	.498
Rogers Hornsby	1925	.489
Babe Ruth	1927	.487
Tris Speaker	1920	.483

Slugging Percentage

(minimum 3.1 PA/Tm Gm)

Babe Ruth	1920	.847
Babe Ruth	1921	.846
Babe Ruth	1927	.772
Lou Gehrig	1927	.765
Babe Ruth	1923	.764
Rogers Hornsby	1925	.756
Babe Ruth	1924	.739
Babe Ruth	1926	.737
Rogers Hornsby	1922	.722
Babe Ruth	1928	.709

OBP+Slugging

(minimum 3.1 PA/Tm Gm)

Babe Ruth	1920	1.378
Babe Ruth	1921	1.358
Babe Ruth	1923	1.309
Babe Ruth	1927	1.259
Babe Ruth	1926	1.253
Babe Ruth	1924	1.252
Rogers Hornsby	1925	1.245
Lou Gehrig	1927	1.240
Rogers Hornsby	1924	1.203
Rogers Hornsby	1922	1.181

Secondary Average

(minimum 3.1 PA/Tm Gm)

Babe Ruth	1920	.825
Babe Ruth	1921	.767
Babe Ruth	1923	.730
Babe Ruth	1927	.685
Babe Ruth	1926	.679
Babe Ruth	1924	.647
Babe Ruth	1928	.646
Lou Gehrig	1927	.596
Babe Ruth	1922	.569
Rogers Hornsby	1925	.528

Isolated Power

(minimum 3.1 PA/Tm Gm)

Babe Ruth	1920	.472
Babe Ruth	1921	.469
Babe Ruth	1927	.417
Lou Gehrig	1927	.392
Babe Ruth	1928	.386
Babe Ruth	1923	.372
Babe Ruth	1926	.366
Babe Ruth	1924	.361
Babe Ruth	1922	.357
Rogers Hornsby	1925	.353

Single Season Pitching Leaders—1920-1929

Wins

Jim Bagby	1920	31
Dazzy Vance	1924	28
Pete Alexander	1920	27
Urban Shocker	1921	27
Carl Mays	1921	27
Eddie Rommel	1922	27
Dolf Luque	1923	27
George Uhle	1926	27
4 tied with		26

Losses

Scott Perry	1920	25
Red Ruffing	1928	25
Rollie Naylor	1920	23
Eddie Rommel	1921	23
Dolf Luque	1922	23
Eppa Rixey	1920	22
Red Ruffing	1929	22
8 tied with		21

Winning Percentage
(minimum 15 decisions)

Emil Yde	1924	.842
Dazzy Vance	1924	.824
General Crowder	1928	.808
Stan Coveleski	1925	.800
Joe Bush	1922	.788
Ray Kolp	1922	.778
Art Nehf	1924	.778
Dolf Luque	1923	.771
Ray Kremer	1926	.769
Lefty Grove	1929	.769

Games

Firpo Marberry	1926	64
Garland Braxton	1927	58
Eddie Rommel	1923	56
Firpo Marberry	1927	56
Firpo Marberry	1925	55
George Uhle	1923	54
Lou North	1922	53
Rube Walberg	1925	53
4 tied with		52

Games Started

George Uhle	1923	44
Pete Alexander	1920	40
Stan Coveleski	1921	40
George Uhle	1922	40
Red Faber	1920	39
Jim Bagby	1920	39
Urban Shocker	1921	39
Red Faber	1921	39
Howard Ehmke	1923	39
Hooks Dauss	1923	39

Complete Games

Pete Alexander	1920	33
Burleigh Grimes	1923	33
Red Faber	1921	32
George Uhle	1926	32
Urban Shocker	1921	31
Red Faber	1922	31
6 tied with		30

Shutouts

Babe Adams	1920	8
Pete Alexander	1920	7
Carl Mays	1920	6
Dolf Luque	1923	6
Walter Johnson	1924	6
Jesse Haines	1927	6
19 tied with		5

Saves

Firpo Marberry	1926	22
Firpo Marberry	1924	15
Firpo Marberry	1925	15
Wilcy Moore	1927	13
Garland Braxton	1927	13
Firpo Marberry	1929	11
Allan Russell	1923	9
Hooks Dauss	1926	9
Lefty Grove	1927	9
Firpo Marberry	1927	9

Games Finished

Firpo Marberry	1926	47
Firpo Marberry	1925	39
Jess Doyle	1925	34
Joe Pate	1926	34
Garland Braxton	1927	32
Sloppy Thurston	1923	30
Firpo Marberry	1924	30
Wilcy Moore	1927	30
Firpo Marberry	1927	30
Chick Davies	1926	29

Batters Faced

George Uhle	1923	1,548
Red Faber	1922	1,464
Pete Alexander	1920	1,447
Urban Shocker	1922	1,441
Burleigh Grimes	1923	1,418
Jim Bagby	1920	1,405
Urban Shocker	1921	1,401
Carl Mays	1921	1,400
3 tied with		1,377

Innings Pitched

Pete Alexander	1920	363.1
George Uhle	1923	357.2
Red Faber	1922	353.0
Urban Shocker	1922	348.0
Jim Bagby	1920	339.2
Carl Mays	1921	336.2
Red Faber	1921	330.2
Burleigh Grimes	1928	330.2
3 tied with		327.0

Hits Allowed

George Uhle	1923	378
Urban Shocker	1922	365
Dickie Kerr	1921	357
Burleigh Grimes	1923	356
Burleigh Grimes	1924	351
Urban Shocker	1921	345
Stan Coveleski	1921	341
Wilbur Cooper	1921	341
Jim Bagby	1920	338
Eppa Rixey	1922	337

Runs Allowed

Dickie Kerr	1921	182
Milt Gaston	1927	177
George Uhle	1923	167
George Smith	1921	166
Jimmy Ring	1925	166
Burleigh Grimes	1923	165
Burleigh Grimes	1925	164
Red Ruffing	1929	162
Jimmy Ring	1921	161
Burleigh Grimes	1924	161

Earned Runs Allowed

Dickie Kerr	1921	162
George Uhle	1923	150
Milt Gaston	1927	141
Ray Benge	1929	139
Burleigh Grimes	1925	138
Burleigh Grimes	1922	135
Claude Willoughby	1929	135
Howard Ehmke	1923	133
Ted Blankenship	1927	133
3 tied with		132

Home Runs Allowed

Joe Genewich	1928	24
Ray Benge	1929	24
Clarence Mitchell	1925	23
George Blaeholder	1928	23
Jack Ogden	1928	23
Leo Sweetland	1929	23
Urban Shocker	1922	22
Ed Brandt	1928	22
General Crowder	1929	22
Rube Walberg	1929	22

Walks

Dixie Davis	1920	149
Lefty Grove	1925	131
Sheriff Blake	1929	130
Eric Erickson	1920	128
Ferdie Schupp	1920	127
George Earnshaw	1929	125
Howard Ehmke	1920	124
Dixie Davis	1921	123
Roy Moore	1921	122
Elam Vangilder	1923	120

Intentional Walks

Statistic unavailable

Strikeouts

Dazzy Vance	1924	262
Dazzy Vance	1925	221
Dazzy Vance	1928	200
Dazzy Vance	1923	197
Lefty Grove	1926	194
Dazzy Vance	1927	184
Lefty Grove	1928	183
Lefty Grove	1927	174
Pete Alexander	1920	173
Lefty Grove	1929	170

Strikeouts/9 Innings
(minimum 1 Inning Pitched/Tm Gm)

Dazzy Vance	1924	7.65
Dazzy Vance	1925	7.50
Dazzy Vance	1926	7.46
Lefty Grove	1926	6.77
George Earnshaw	1928	6.65
Dazzy Vance	1928	6.42
Dazzy Vance	1923	6.32
Lefty Grove	1928	6.29
Dazzy Vance	1927	6.06
Lefty Grove	1927	5.97

ERA
(minimum 1 Inning Pitched/Tm Gm)

Pete Alexander	1920	1.91
Dolf Luque	1923	1.93
Dazzy Vance	1928	2.09
Babe Adams	1920	2.16
Dazzy Vance	1924	2.16
Burleigh Grimes	1920	2.22
Wilcy Moore	1927	2.28
Wilbur Cooper	1920	2.39
Bob Shawkey	1920	2.45
Sheriff Blake	1928	2.47

Component ERA
(minimum 1 Inning Pitched/Tm Gm)

Garland Braxton	1928	1.92
Babe Adams	1920	1.94
Dazzy Vance	1924	2.02
Dazzy Vance	1928	2.20
Dolf Luque	1920	2.25
Burleigh Grimes	1920	2.28
Dolf Luque	1923	2.32
Eppa Rixey	1924	2.32
Wilcy Moore	1927	2.33
Stan Coveleski	1920	2.34

Sac Hits Allowed

Stan Coveleski	1921	54
Eddie Rommel	1923	54
Tom Zachary	1926	53
Roy Wilkinson	1921	52
George Uhle	1926	52
Red Faber	1920	51
Red Faber	1922	51
Eppa Rixey	1920	49
Jack Scott	1927	49
3 tied with		48

Sac Flies Allowed

Statistic unavailable

Hit Batsmen

Howard Ehmke	1922	23
Howard Ehmke	1923	20
Walter Johnson	1923	20
Joe Oeschger	1921	15
Herman Pillette	1922	15
Leo Sweetland	1928	15
Ole Olsen	1922	14
Bill Piercy	1923	14
Jakie May	1927	14
Howard Ehmke	1927	14

Wild Pitches

Milt Gaston	1929	17
Jimmy Ring	1921	14
Jimmy Ring	1923	14
Jimmy Ring	1925	14
Jim Shaw	1920	13
Dutch Leonard	1920	13
Joe Bush	1923	12
4 tied with		11

Balks

Dave Danforth	1922	4
14 tied with		3

Opponent Average
(minimum 1 Inning Pitched/Tm Gm)

Dazzy Vance	1924	.213
Garland Braxton	1928	.217
Dazzy Vance	1928	.221
Walter Johnson	1924	.224
Dolf Luque	1920	.225
Lefty Grove	1928	.227
Hank Johnson	1928	.232
George Earnshaw	1928	.234
Wilcy Moore	1927	.234
Dolf Luque	1923	.235

Opponent OBP
(minimum 1 Inning Pitched/Tm Gm)

Babe Adams	1920	.259
Garland Braxton	1928	.261
Dazzy Vance	1924	.269
Babe Adams	1921	.272
Lefty Grove	1928	.274
Pete Alexander	1923	.277
Dazzy Vance	1928	.277
Pete Alexander	1926	.281
Burleigh Grimes	1920	.282
Stan Coveleski	1920	.283

Batting Leaders—1930-1939

Games

Mel Ott	1,473
Jimmie Foxx	1,470
Paul Waner	1,463
Earl Averill	1,445
Charlie Gehringer	1,434
Ben Chapman	1,431
Gus Suhr	1,425
Lou Gehrig	1,397
Joe Cronin	1,391
Dick Bartell	1,358

At-Bats

Paul Waner	5,834
Charlie Gehringer	5,629
Earl Averill	5,621
Ben Chapman	5,518
Jimmie Foxx	5,495
Mel Ott	5,341
Joe Cronin	5,332
Lou Gehrig	5,255
Al Simmons	5,233
Dick Bartell	5,216

Runs

Lou Gehrig	1,257
Jimmie Foxx	1,244
Charlie Gehringer	1,179
Earl Averill	1,102
Mel Ott	1,095
Ben Chapman	1,009
Paul Waner	973
Chuck Klein	955
Al Simmons	930
Joe Cronin	885

Hits

Paul Waner	1,959
Charlie Gehringer	1,865
Jimmie Foxx	1,845
Lou Gehrig	1,802
Earl Averill	1,786
Al Simmons	1,700
Ben Chapman	1,697
Chuck Klein	1,676
Mel Ott	1,673
Joe Cronin	1,650

Doubles

Charlie Gehringer	400
Joe Cronin	386
Paul Waner	372
Earl Averill	354
Joe Medwick	353
Ben Chapman	346
Lou Gehrig	328
Dick Bartell	325
Chuck Klein	323
Billy Herman	322

Triples

Gus Suhr	114
Earl Averill	114
Paul Waner	112
Ben Chapman	100
John Stone	100
Arky Vaughan	94
Buddy Myer	92
Lou Gehrig	91
Joe Cronin	90
Al Simmons	89

Home Runs

Jimmie Foxx	415
Lou Gehrig	347
Mel Ott	308
Wally Berger	241
Chuck Klein	238
Earl Averill	218
Hank Greenberg	206
Babe Ruth	198
Al Simmons	190
Bob Johnson	186

Home Runs (Home)

Jimmie Foxx	232
Mel Ott	181
Lou Gehrig	179
Chuck Klein	152
Earl Averill	134
Hank Greenberg	122
Wally Berger	120
Bill Dickey	117
Bob Johnson	112
Babe Ruth	106

Home Runs (Road)

Jimmie Foxx	183
Lou Gehrig	168
Mel Ott	127
Wally Berger	121
Babe Ruth	92
Chuck Klein	86
Al Simmons	85
Hank Greenberg	84
Earl Averill	84
Joe DiMaggio	83

Extra Base Hits

Jimmie Foxx	818
Lou Gehrig	766
Earl Averill	686
Mel Ott	649
Chuck Klein	623
Charlie Gehringer	622
Wally Berger	597
Joe Cronin	584
Joe Medwick	579
Al Simmons	571

Total Bases

Jimmie Foxx	3,580
Lou Gehrig	3,353
Earl Averill	3,022
Mel Ott	2,992
Charlie Gehringer	2,855
Chuck Klein	2,837
Paul Waner	2,765
Al Simmons	2,740
Wally Berger	2,675
Joe Cronin	2,540

RBI

Jimmie Foxx	1,403
Lou Gehrig	1,358
Mel Ott	1,135
Al Simmons	1,081
Earl Averill	1,046
Joe Cronin	1,036
Charlie Gehringer	1,003
Chuck Klein	979
Bill Dickey	937
Wally Berger	893

Walks

Lou Gehrig	1,028
Jimmie Foxx	1,015
Mel Ott	956
Charlie Gehringer	765
Joe Cronin	716
Gus Suhr	713
Ben Chapman	708
Earl Averill	705
Buddy Myer	696
Lyn Lary	677

Walks/PA
(minimum 3,000 Plate Appearances)

Babe Ruth	.206
Lou Gehrig	.162
Mickey Cochrane	.156
Harlond Clift	.155
Jimmie Foxx	.155
Mel Ott	.150
Dolph Camilli	.146
Bob Johnson	.134
Lyn Lary	.133
Hank Greenberg	.132

Strikeouts

Jimmie Foxx	876
Wally Berger	685
Dolph Camilli	592
Tony Lazzeri	591
Hank Greenberg	556
Frankie Crosetti	542
Ben Chapman	485
Bob Johnson	478
Mel Ott	474
Al Simmons	458

Hit By Pitch

Frankie Crosetti	68
Dick Bartell	64
George Watkins	44
Ival Goodman	42
Jimmy Dykes	42
Tony Piet	40
Kiki Cuyler	40
Wally Berger	38
Arky Vaughan	35
Billy Jurges	34

Sac Hits

Dick Bartell	205
Mule Haas	179
Billy Herman	129
Joe Stripp	115
Doc Cramer	112
Rabbit Warstler	105
Pinky Whitney	99
Joe Cronin	99
Billy Jurges	97
2 tied with	95

Sac Flies

Statistic unavailable

Stolen Bases

Ben Chapman	269
Bill Werber	176
Gee Walker	158
Lyn Lary	158
Pepper Martin	136
Kiki Cuyler	118
Roy Johnson	115
Charlie Gehringer	101
Pete Fox	100
Stan Hack	100

Caught Stealing

Ben Chapman	124
Lou Gehrig	70
Bill Werber	68
Buddy Myer	66
Roy Johnson	65
Gee Walker	60
Luke Appling	56
Billy Rogell	52
Charlie Gehringer	52
Pete Fox	50

Runs Created

Jimmie Foxx	1,483
Lou Gehrig	1,469
Mel Ott	1,260
Charlie Gehringer	1,204
Earl Averill	1,183
Paul Waner	1,069
Joe Cronin	1,030
Chuck Klein	1,028
Ben Chapman	1,012
Al Simmons	1,007

Runs Created/27 Outs
(minimum 3,000 Plate Appearances)

Babe Ruth	11.52
Lou Gehrig	10.82
Jimmie Foxx	10.38
Hank Greenberg	9.46
Mel Ott	8.85
Mickey Cochrane	8.46
Charlie Gehringer	8.10
Earl Averill	7.90
Arky Vaughan	7.73
Bill Dickey	7.71

Batting Average
(minimum 3,000 Plate Appearances)

Bill Terry	.352
Lou Gehrig	.343
Joe Medwick	.338
Paul Waner	.336
Jimmie Foxx	.336
Babe Ruth	.331
Charlie Gehringer	.331
Arky Vaughan	.329
Chuck Klein	.326
Al Simmons	.325

On-Base Percentage
(minimum 3,000 Plate Appearances)

Babe Ruth	.472
Lou Gehrig	.453
Jimmie Foxx	.440
Mickey Cochrane	.434
Mel Ott	.420
Arky Vaughan	.420
Hank Greenberg	.415
Charlie Gehringer	.414
Harlond Clift	.404
Bob Johnson	.401

Slugging Percentage
(minimum 3,000 Plate Appearances)

Jimmie Foxx	.652
Babe Ruth	.644
Lou Gehrig	.638
Hank Greenberg	.617
Hal Trosky	.563
Mel Ott	.560
Joe Medwick	.552
Chuck Klein	.551
Earl Averill	.538
Bob Johnson	.537

OBP+Slugging
(minimum 3,000 Plate Appearances)

Babe Ruth	1.116
Jimmie Foxx	1.091
Lou Gehrig	1.091
Hank Greenberg	1.032
Mel Ott	.980
Hal Trosky	.939
Bob Johnson	.938
Chuck Klein	.935
Earl Averill	.934
Joe Medwick	.927

Secondary Average
(minimum 3,000 Plate Appearances)

Babe Ruth	.584
Jimmie Foxx	.512
Lou Gehrig	.504
Hank Greenberg	.460
Mel Ott	.435
Bob Johnson	.402
Dolph Camilli	.401
Harlond Clift	.394
Mickey Cochrane	.367
Earl Averill	.355

Isolated Power
(minimum 3,000 Plate Appearances)

Jimmie Foxx	.316
Babe Ruth	.313
Lou Gehrig	.295
Hank Greenberg	.294
Mel Ott	.247
Hal Trosky	.246
Bob Johnson	.231
Chuck Klein	.225
Wally Berger	.222
Earl Averill	.220

Pitching Leaders—1930-1939

Wins

Lefty Grove	199
Carl Hubbell	188
Red Ruffing	175
Wes Ferrell	170
Lefty Gomez	165
Mel Harder	158
Larry French	156
Tommy Bridges	150
Paul Derringer	148
Dizzy Dean	147

Losses

Paul Derringer	137
Larry French	134
Mel Harder	123
Bump Hadley	119
Wes Ferrell	115
Ted Lyons	115
Ed Brandt	112
Danny MacFayden	111
Earl Whitehill	107
Willis Hudlin	106

Winning Percentage
(minimum 100 decisions)

Lefty Grove	.724
Johnny Allen	.706
Firpo Marberry	.686
Lefty Gomez	.650
Dizzy Dean	.648
Carl Hubbell	.644
Red Ruffing	.641
Monte Pearson	.634
Lon Warneke	.629
Bill Lee	.602

Games

Larry French	430
Jack Russell	394
Mel Harder	385
Carl Hubbell	383
Charlie Root	377
Paul Derringer	375
Bump Hadley	374
Dick Coffman	366
Lefty Grove	351
Fred Frankhouse	345

Games Started

Larry French	305
Carl Hubbell	302
Red Ruffing	298
Wes Ferrell	293
Paul Derringer	285
Mel Harder	285
Earl Whitehill	282
Lefty Gomez	278
Lefty Grove	268
Tommy Bridges	266

Complete Games

Wes Ferrell	207
Red Ruffing	201
Carl Hubbell	197
Lefty Grove	197
Ted Lyons	168
Paul Derringer	163
Lefty Gomez	163
Larry French	160
Tommy Bridges	156
Dizzy Dean	151

Shutouts

Larry French	32
Carl Hubbell	31
Red Ruffing	28
Dizzy Dean	26
Lefty Gomez	26
Lefty Grove	26
Tommy Bridges	25
Lon Warneke	25
Bill Lee	23
Paul Derringer	23

Saves

Johnny Murphy	54
Clint Brown	49
Jack Russell	37
Joe Heving	33
Chief Hogsett	33
Dick Coffman	33
Lefty Grove	31
Bob Smith	31
4 tied with	30

Games Finished

Clint Brown	177
Jack Russell	162
Chief Hogsett	158
Dick Coffman	147
Johnny Murphy	136
Joe Heving	126
Bob Smith	124
Chad Kimsey	123
Charlie Root	122
Pete Appleton	119

Batters Faced

Larry French	10,605
Carl Hubbell	10,584
Red Ruffing	10,351
Wes Ferrell	10,347
Mel Harder	10,102
Lefty Grove	10,054
Paul Derringer	9,948
Lefty Gomez	9,505
Earl Whitehill	9,482
Bump Hadley	9,372

Innings Pitched

Carl Hubbell	2,596.2
Larry French	2,481.2
Red Ruffing	2,439.0
Lefty Grove	2,399.0
Wes Ferrell	2,345.1
Paul Derringer	2,343.2
Mel Harder	2,326.0
Lefty Gomez	2,234.2
Earl Whitehill	2,129.2
Bump Hadley	2,121.2

Hits Allowed

Larry French	2,701
Paul Derringer	2,584
Mel Harder	2,557
Wes Ferrell	2,554
Carl Hubbell	2,437
Earl Whitehill	2,378
Lefty Grove	2,344
Red Ruffing	2,327
Ted Lyons	2,203
Danny MacFayden	2,200

Runs Allowed

Wes Ferrell	1,251
Earl Whitehill	1,220
Mel Harder	1,168
Bump Hadley	1,147
Larry French	1,136
Red Ruffing	1,123
Paul Derringer	1,083
Willis Hudlin	1,040
Ted Lyons	1,038
Tommy Bridges	1,021

Earned Runs Allowed

Earl Whitehill	1,072
Wes Ferrell	1,062
Bump Hadley	992
Red Ruffing	972
Mel Harder	967
Larry French	942
Paul Derringer	911
Willis Hudlin	889
Tommy Bridges	870
Danny MacFayden	858

Home Runs Allowed

Red Ruffing	150
Carl Hubbell	147
Tommy Bridges	138
Earl Whitehill	134
Bump Hadley	133
Larry French	130
Ted Lyons	130
George Blaeholder	128
George Earnshaw	127
Lon Warneke	126

Walks

Bump Hadley	1,061
Wes Ferrell	911
Lefty Gomez	904
Tommy Bridges	902
Earl Whitehill	891
Bobo Newsom	879
Red Ruffing	858
Mel Harder	692
Van Lingle Mungo	685
Monte Pearson	681

Intentional Walks

Statistic unavailable

Strikeouts

Lefty Gomez	1,337
Lefty Grove	1,313
Carl Hubbell	1,281
Red Ruffing	1,260
Tommy Bridges	1,207
Dizzy Dean	1,144
Van Lingle Mungo	1,022
Paul Derringer	1,018
Bump Hadley	1,006
Bobo Newsom	963

Strikeouts/9 Innings
(minimum 1,000 Innings Pitched)

Dizzy Dean	5.40
Lefty Gomez	5.38
Johnny Allen	5.36
Van Lingle Mungo	5.36
Tommy Bridges	5.22
Bobo Newsom	5.13
Lefty Grove	4.93
Red Ruffing	4.65
Monte Pearson	4.53
Pat Malone	4.53

ERA
(minimum 1,000 Innings Pitched)

Carl Hubbell	2.71
Lefty Grove	2.91
Dizzy Dean	2.96
Bill Lee	3.21
Lon Warneke	3.23
Lefty Gomez	3.23
Hal Schumacher	3.38
Larry French	3.42
Van Lingle Mungo	3.42
Charlie Root	3.50

Component ERA
(minimum 1,000 Innings Pitched)

Carl Hubbell	2.64
Dizzy Dean	2.88
Lefty Grove	2.98
Bill Swift	3.18
Lefty Gomez	3.19
Van Lingle Mungo	3.23
Lon Warneke	3.23
Red Ruffing	3.31
Johnny Allen	3.33
Bill Lee	3.35

Sac Hits Allowed

Earl Whitehill	171
Carl Hubbell	167
Larry French	160
Mel Harder	160
Paul Derringer	158
Ed Brandt	158
Danny MacFayden	143
Ted Lyons	138
Lefty Grove	133
Freddie Fitzsimmons	131

Sac Flies Allowed

Statistic unavailable

Hit Batsmen

Chief Hogsett	57
Roy Parmelee	54
Earl Whitehill	54
Charlie Root	47
Mel Harder	41
Danny MacFayden	41
Carl Hubbell	39
Bump Hadley	38
Tex Carleton	35
4 tied with	33

Wild Pitches

Wild Bill Hallahan	65
Roy Parmelee	53
Johnny Allen	50
Bump Hadley	50
Lon Warneke	45
Van Lingle Mungo	44
Hal Schumacher	44
Tommy Bridges	41
4 tied with	40

Balks

Bob Feller	7
Tommy Bridges	7
Carl Fischer	6
10 tied with	5

Opponent Average
(minimum 1,000 Innings Pitched)

Lefty Gomez	.240
Van Lingle Mungo	.244
Carl Hubbell	.246
Johnny Allen	.248
Red Ruffing	.249
Dizzy Dean	.251
Roy Parmelee	.251
Tommy Bridges	.252
Lefty Grove	.253
Monte Pearson	.256

Opponent OBP
(minimum 1,000 Innings Pitched)

Carl Hubbell	.283
Dizzy Dean	.295
Bill Swift	.302
Lefty Grove	.303
Lon Warneke	.307
Red Lucas	.309
Syl Johnson	.309
Watty Clark	.313
Charlie Root	.314
Red Ruffing	.314

Single Season Batting Leaders—1930-1939

Games

Player	Year	
Lou Gehrig	1937	157
Frankie Crosetti	1938	157
Lou Gehrig	1938	157
Dolph Camilli	1939	157
21 tied with		156

At-Bats

Player	Year	
Woody Jensen	1936	696
Lloyd Waner	1931	681
Jo-Jo Moore	1935	681
Al Simmons	1932	670
Buddy Lewis	1937	668
Billy Herman	1935	666
Taylor Douthit	1930	664
Hughie Critz	1930	662
Doc Cramer	1933	661
Hughie Critz	1932	659

Runs

Player	Year	
Lou Gehrig	1936	167
Lou Gehrig	1931	163
Chuck Klein	1930	158
Kiki Cuyler	1930	155
Woody English	1930	152
Al Simmons	1930	152
Chuck Klein	1932	152
Jimmie Foxx	1932	151
Joe DiMaggio	1937	151
Babe Ruth	1930	150

Hits

Player	Year	
Bill Terry	1930	254
Chuck Klein	1930	250
Babe Herman	1930	241
Joe Medwick	1937	237
Earl Averill	1936	232
Freddy Lindstrom	1930	231
Kiki Cuyler	1930	228
Billy Herman	1935	227
Charlie Gehringer	1936	227
Chuck Klein	1932	226

Doubles

Player	Year	
Earl Webb	1931	67
Joe Medwick	1936	64
Hank Greenberg	1934	63
Paul Waner	1932	62
Charlie Gehringer	1936	60
Chuck Klein	1930	59
Billy Herman	1935	57
Billy Herman	1936	57
Joe Medwick	1937	56
Gee Walker	1936	55

Triples

Player	Year	
Adam Comorosky	1930	23
Earle Combs	1930	22
Bill Terry	1931	20
Joe Vosmik	1935	20
Roy Johnson	1931	19
Babe Herman	1932	19
Arky Vaughan	1933	19
8 tied with		18

Home Runs

Player	Year	
Jimmie Foxx	1932	58
Hank Greenberg	1938	58
Hack Wilson	1930	56
Jimmie Foxx	1938	50
Babe Ruth	1930	49
Lou Gehrig	1934	49
Lou Gehrig	1936	49
Jimmie Foxx	1933	48
3 tied with		46

Home Runs (Home)

Player	Year	
Hank Greenberg	1938	39
Jimmie Foxx	1938	35
Hack Wilson	1930	33
Jimmie Foxx	1932	32
Jimmie Foxx	1933	31
Lou Gehrig	1934	30
Hal Trosky	1936	30
Chuck Klein	1932	29
Lou Gehrig	1936	27
2 tied with		26

Home Runs (Road)

Player	Year	
Lou Gehrig	1930	27
Joe DiMaggio	1937	27
Jimmie Foxx	1932	26
Hack Wilson	1930	23
Babe Ruth	1930	23
6 tied with		22

Extra Base Hits

Player	Year	
Chuck Klein	1930	107
Chuck Klein	1932	103
Hank Greenberg	1937	103
Lou Gehrig	1930	100
Jimmie Foxx	1932	100
Hank Greenberg	1935	98
Hack Wilson	1930	97
Joe Medwick	1937	97
3 tied with		96

Total Bases

Player	Year	
Chuck Klein	1930	445
Jimmie Foxx	1932	438
Hack Wilson	1930	423
Chuck Klein	1932	420
Lou Gehrig	1930	419
Joe DiMaggio	1937	418
Babe Herman	1930	416
Lou Gehrig	1931	410
Lou Gehrig	1934	409
Joe Medwick	1937	406

RBI

Player	Year	
Hack Wilson	1930	190
Lou Gehrig	1931	184
Hank Greenberg	1937	183
Jimmie Foxx	1938	175
Lou Gehrig	1930	174
Chuck Klein	1930	170
Hank Greenberg	1935	170
Jimmie Foxx	1932	169
Joe DiMaggio	1937	167
2 tied with		165

Walks

Player	Year	
Babe Ruth	1930	136
Lou Gehrig	1935	132
Babe Ruth	1932	130
Lou Gehrig	1936	130
Max Bishop	1930	128
Babe Ruth	1931	128
Lu Blue	1931	127
Lou Gehrig	1937	127
Luke Appling	1935	122
3 tied with		119

Walks/PA

(minimum 3.1 PA/Tm Gm)

Player	Year	
Babe Ruth	1932	.221
Max Bishop	1930	.218
Max Bishop	1932	.211
Max Bishop	1933	.210
Babe Ruth	1930	.201
Babe Ruth	1933	.198
Mel Ott	1939	.197
Lou Gehrig	1935	.196
Mickey Cochrane	1933	.196
Babe Ruth	1931	.193

Strikeouts

Player	Year	
Vince DiMaggio	1938	134
Jimmie Foxx	1936	119
Dolph Camilli	1935	113
Vince DiMaggio	1937	111
Dolph Camilli	1939	107
Frankie Crosetti	1937	105
Bruce Campbell	1932	104
Hank Greenberg	1937	101
Dolph Camilli	1938	101
Harlond Clift	1934	100

Hit By Pitch

Player	Year	
Ival Goodman	1938	15
Frankie Crosetti	1938	15
Frankie Crosetti	1939	13
George Watkins	1933	12
Jimmy Dykes	1933	12
Frankie Crosetti	1936	12
Frankie Crosetti	1937	12
5 tied with		10

Sac Hits

Player	Year	
Dick Bartell	1933	37
Dick Bartell	1932	35
Adam Comorosky	1930	33
Mule Haas	1930	33
Freddie Maguire	1931	31
Dick Bartell	1931	30
Mule Haas	1933	30
Ossie Bluege	1930	27
Mule Haas	1932	27
2 tied with		26

Sac Flies

Statistic unavailable

Stolen Bases

Player	Year	
Ben Chapman	1931	61
George Case	1939	51
Bill Werber	1934	40
Ben Chapman	1932	38
Kiki Cuyler	1930	37
Lyn Lary	1936	37
Bill Werber	1937	35
Ben Chapman	1937	35
Roy Johnson	1931	33
Gee Walker	1932	30

Caught Stealing

Player	Year	
Ben Chapman	1931	23
Roy Johnson	1931	21
Ben Chapman	1932	18
Ben Chapman	1933	18
George Case	1939	17
Red Kress	1931	16
Ben Chapman	1934	16
5 tied with		15

Runs Created

Player	Year	
Jimmie Foxx	1932	189
Lou Gehrig	1930	182
Lou Gehrig	1936	181
Lou Gehrig	1931	179
Babe Ruth	1931	179
Babe Ruth	1930	176
Jimmie Foxx	1938	172
Chuck Klein	1930	171
Hack Wilson	1930	171
Lou Gehrig	1934	171

Runs Created/27 Outs

(minimum 3.1 PA/Tm Gm)

Player	Year	
Babe Ruth	1931	13.93
Jimmie Foxx	1932	13.19
Babe Ruth	1932	12.83
Babe Ruth	1930	12.69
Lou Gehrig	1936	12.32
Lou Gehrig	1930	12.12
Arky Vaughan	1935	11.93
Lou Gehrig	1934	11.93
Jimmie Foxx	1938	11.87
Jimmie Foxx	1933	11.85

Batting Average

(minimum 3.1 PA/Tm Gm)

Player	Year	
Bill Terry	1930	.401
Babe Herman	1930	.393
Al Simmons	1931	.390
Luke Appling	1936	.388
Chuck Klein	1930	.386
Arky Vaughan	1935	.385
Lefty O'Doul	1930	.383
Joe DiMaggio	1939	.381
Al Simmons	1930	.381
Freddy Lindstrom	1930	.379

On-Base Percentage

(minimum 3.1 PA/Tm Gm)

Player	Year	
Babe Ruth	1931	.494
Babe Ruth	1930	.493
Arky Vaughan	1935	.491
Babe Ruth	1932	.489
Lou Gehrig	1936	.478
Luke Appling	1936	.473
Lou Gehrig	1930	.473
Lou Gehrig	1937	.473
Jimmie Foxx	1932	.469
Lou Gehrig	1935	.466

Slugging Percentage

(minimum 3.1 PA/Tm Gm)

Player	Year	
Jimmie Foxx	1932	.749
Babe Ruth	1930	.732
Hack Wilson	1930	.723
Lou Gehrig	1930	.721
Al Simmons	1930	.708
Lou Gehrig	1934	.706
Jimmie Foxx	1938	.704
Jimmie Foxx	1933	.703
Babe Ruth	1931	.700
Lou Gehrig	1936	.696

OBP+Slugging

(minimum 3.1 PA/Tm Gm)

Player	Year	
Babe Ruth	1930	1.225
Jimmie Foxx	1932	1.218
Babe Ruth	1931	1.194
Lou Gehrig	1930	1.194
Hack Wilson	1930	1.177
Lou Gehrig	1936	1.174
Lou Gehrig	1934	1.172
Jimmie Foxx	1938	1.166
Jimmie Foxx	1939	1.158
Jimmie Foxx	1933	1.153

Secondary Average

(minimum 3.1 PA/Tm Gm)

Player	Year	
Babe Ruth	1930	.654
Babe Ruth	1932	.608
Hank Greenberg	1938	.595
Jimmie Foxx	1932	.588
Babe Ruth	1931	.577
Jimmie Foxx	1938	.575
Lou Gehrig	1936	.572
Hack Wilson	1930	.552
Lou Gehrig	1934	.547
Jimmie Foxx	1934	.545

Isolated Power

(minimum 3.1 PA/Tm Gm)

Player	Year	
Jimmie Foxx	1932	.385
Babe Ruth	1930	.373
Hank Greenberg	1938	.369
Hack Wilson	1930	.368
Jimmie Foxx	1938	.356
Jimmie Foxx	1933	.347
Lou Gehrig	1934	.344
Lou Gehrig	1930	.343
Lou Gehrig	1936	.342
Jimmie Foxx	1939	.334

Single Season Pitching Leaders—1930-1939

Wins

Lefty Grove	1931	31
Dizzy Dean	1934	30
Lefty Grove	1930	28
Dizzy Dean	1935	28
Bucky Walters	1939	27
General Crowder	1932	26
Lefty Gomez	1934	26
Carl Hubbell	1936	26
4 tied with		25

Losses

Paul Derringer	1933	27
Ben Cantwell	1935	25
Pat Caraway	1931	24
Sam Gray	1931	24
Si Johnson	1934	22
Bump Hadley	1932	21
Ted Lyons	1933	21
Paul Derringer	1934	21
Bucky Walters	1936	21
Harry Kelley	1937	21

Winning Percentage
(minimum 15 decisions)

Johnny Allen	1937	.938
Lefty Grove	1931	.886
Lefty Grove	1930	.848
Lefty Gomez	1934	.839
Carl Hubbell	1936	.813
Atley Donald	1939	.813
Dizzy Dean	1934	.811
Johnny Allen	1932	.810
3 tied with		.800

Games

Clint Brown	1939	61
Russ Van Atta	1935	58
Hugh Mulcahy	1937	56
Bump Hadley	1931	55
Jim Walkup	1935	55
Firpo Marberry	1932	54
Jack Russell	1934	54
Chubby Dean	1939	54
4 tied with		53

Games Started

George Caster	1938	40
Bobo Newsom	1938	40
George Earnshaw	1930	39
General Crowder	1932	39
Ray Kremer	1930	38
Van Lingle Mungo	1934	38
Wes Ferrell	1935	38
Tommy Bridges	1936	38
Bobo Newsom	1936	38
Wes Ferrell	1936	38

Complete Games

Wes Ferrell	1935	31
Bobo Newsom	1938	31
Bucky Walters	1939	31
Ted Lyons	1930	29
Dizzy Dean	1935	29
Red Lucas	1932	28
Dizzy Dean	1936	28
Wes Ferrell	1936	28
Paul Derringer	1939	28
3 tied with		27

Shutouts

Carl Hubbell	1933	10
Bill Lee	1938	9
Hal Schumacher	1933	7
Dizzy Dean	1934	7
8 tied with		6

Saves

Johnny Murphy	1939	19
Clint Brown	1937	18
Clint Brown	1939	18
Jack Quinn	1931	15
Firpo Marberry	1932	13
Jack Russell	1933	13
Dick Coffman	1938	12
Dizzy Dean	1936	11
Johnny Murphy	1938	11
2 tied with		10

Games Finished

Clint Brown	1939	56
Clint Brown	1937	48
Chubby Dean	1939	38
Chad Kimsey	1931	35
Dick Coffman	1938	35
Chief Hogsett	1933	34
Johnny Murphy	1939	34
Mace Brown	1938	32
Jumbo Brown	1938	32
3 tied with		31

Batters Faced

Bobo Newsom	1938	1,475
Wes Ferrell	1935	1,391
Bump Hadley	1933	1,365
Dizzy Dean	1935	1,362
General Crowder	1932	1,356
Wes Ferrell	1936	1,341
Van Lingle Mungo	1934	1,329
Van Lingle Mungo	1936	1,313
Dizzy Dean	1936	1,303
George Earnshaw	1930	1,299

Innings Pitched

Bobo Newsom	1938	329.2
General Crowder	1932	327.0
Dizzy Dean	1935	325.1
Wes Ferrell	1935	322.1
Bucky Walters	1939	319.0
Bump Hadley	1933	316.2
Van Lingle Mungo	1934	315.1
Dizzy Dean	1936	315.0
Carl Hubbell	1934	313.0
2 tied with		311.2

Hits Allowed

Ray Kremer	1930	366
Claude Passeau	1937	348
Wes Ferrell	1935	336
Bobo Newsom	1938	334
Ted Lyons	1930	331
Paul Derringer	1936	331
Wes Ferrell	1936	330
Larry French	1930	325
Wes Ferrell	1937	325
Dizzy Dean	1935	324

Runs Allowed

Bobo Newsom	1938	205
Sam Gray	1931	187
Ray Kremer	1930	181
Ray Benge	1930	178
Pat Caraway	1931	177
Wes Ferrell	1937	177
Guy Bush	1930	174
Jack Knott	1936	174
Bump Hadley	1932	168
Vern Kennedy	1936	167

Earned Runs Allowed

Bobo Newsom	1938	186
Jack Knott	1936	156
Guy Bush	1930	155
Ray Kremer	1930	154
Wes Ferrell	1937	153
Pat Caraway	1931	152
Bump Hadley	1932	149
Bobo Newsom	1937	147
George Earnshaw	1930	146
Sam Gray	1931	146

Home Runs Allowed

Lon Warneke	1937	32
Phil Collins	1934	30
Bobo Newsom	1938	30
Ray Kremer	1930	29
Lynn Nelson	1938	29
George Earnshaw	1932	28
George Earnshaw	1934	28
5 tied with		27

Walks

Bob Feller	1938	208
Bobo Newsom	1938	192
Bump Hadley	1932	171
Bobo Newsom	1937	167
Bobo Newsom	1934	149
Vern Kennedy	1936	147
Bobo Newsom	1936	146
Bob Feller	1939	142
Bump Hadley	1933	141
George Earnshaw	1930	139

Intentional Walks

Statistic unavailable

Strikeouts

Bob Feller	1939	246
Bob Feller	1938	240
Van Lingle Mungo	1936	238
Bobo Newsom	1938	226
Lefty Grove	1930	209
Dizzy Dean	1933	199
Dizzy Dean	1934	195
Dizzy Dean	1936	195
Lefty Gomez	1937	194
George Earnshaw	1930	193

Strikeouts/9 Innings
(minimum 1 Inning Pitched/Tm Gm)

Bob Feller	1938	7.78
Bob Feller	1939	7.46
Van Lingle Mungo	1936	6.87
Van Lingle Mungo	1937	6.82
Wild Bill Hallahan	1930	6.71
Red Ruffing	1932	6.60
Lefty Grove	1930	6.46
Lefty Gomez	1937	6.27
Lefty Gomez	1933	6.25
Bump Hadley	1931	6.21

ERA
(minimum 1 Inning Pitched/Tm Gm)

Carl Hubbell	1933	1.66
Lon Warneke	1933	2.00
Lefty Grove	1931	2.06
Hal Schumacher	1933	2.16
Bill Walker	1931	2.26
Bucky Walters	1939	2.29
Carl Hubbell	1934	2.30
Carl Hubbell	1936	2.31
Lefty Gomez	1937	2.33
Lefty Gomez	1934	2.33

Component ERA
(minimum 1 Inning Pitched/Tm Gm)

Carl Hubbell	1933	1.84
Cy Blanton	1935	2.08
Hal Schumacher	1933	2.18
Carl Hubbell	1936	2.20
Lefty Grove	1931	2.23
Carl Hubbell	1934	2.27
Lefty Gomez	1934	2.33
Cliff Melton	1937	2.37
Jim Turner	1937	2.40
Bucky Walters	1939	2.41

Sac Hits Allowed

Ray Benge	1930	42
Ted Lyons	1930	36
Ed Brandt	1933	35
Larry French	1930	34
George Earnshaw	1930	34
Ray Kremer	1930	33
Phil Collins	1930	33
Clint Brown	1930	31
Hod Lisenbee	1930	31
7 tied with		30

Sac Flies Allowed

Statistic unavailable

Hit Batsmen

Chief Hogsett	1936	15
Earl Caldwell	1936	15
Roy Parmelee	1933	14
Ed Holley	1933	13
Carl Hubbell	1930	11
Boom-Boom Beck	1933	11
Hugh Mulcahy	1939	11
Hugh Casey	1939	11
6 tied with		10

Wild Pitches

Stu Flythe	1936	16
Monte Pearson	1934	15
Roy Parmelee	1933	14
Bob Feller	1939	14
Milt Gaston	1934	13
Johnny Allen	1936	13
Guy Bush	1930	12
Tex Carleton	1938	12
Nels Potter	1939	12
11 tied with		11

Balks

Milt Shoffner	1930	3
Carl Fischer	1931	3
Clise Dudley	1931	3
Jim Weaver	1934	3
Whitey Wilshere	1935	3
Bob Feller	1936	3
Dizzy Dean	1937	3
Bucky Walters	1939	3
47 tied with		2

Opponent Average
(minimum 1 Inning Pitched/Tm Gm)

Bob Feller	1939	.210
Johnny Vander Meer	1938	.213
Hal Schumacher	1933	.214
Lefty Gomez	1934	.215
Bump Hadley	1931	.218
Bucky Walters	1939	.220
Bob Feller	1938	.220
Steve Swetonic	1932	.221
Lefty Gomez	1937	.223
Lefty Gomez	1931	.226

Opponent OBP
(minimum 1 Inning Pitched/Tm Gm)

Carl Hubbell	1933	.260
Carl Hubbell	1934	.263
Carl Hubbell	1932	.268
Lefty Grove	1931	.271
Bill Swift	1932	.272
Cy Blanton	1935	.272
Jim Turner	1937	.274
Red Lucas	1932	.275
Carl Hubbell	1936	.276
Ted Lyons	1939	.276

Batting Leaders—1940-1949

Games

Bob Elliott	1,455
Lou Boudreau	1,425
Marty Marion	1,396
Bill Nicholson	1,389
Dixie Walker	1,363
Eddie Miller	1,328
Bobby Doerr	1,283
Rudy York	1,259
Frankie Gustine	1,230
Phil Cavarretta	1,217

At-Bats

Bob Elliott	5,361
Lou Boudreau	5,268
Marty Marion	4,941
Bill Nicholson	4,936
Bobby Doerr	4,924
Dixie Walker	4,856
Eddie Miller	4,799
Rudy York	4,718
Tommy Holmes	4,605
Frankie Gustine	4,493

Runs

Ted Williams	951
Stan Musial	815
Bob Elliott	803
Bobby Doerr	764
Lou Boudreau	758
Bill Nicholson	743
Dom DiMaggio	721
Vern Stephens	708
Dixie Walker	704
Joe DiMaggio	684

Hits

Lou Boudreau	1,578
Bob Elliott	1,563
Dixie Walker	1,512
Stan Musial	1,432
Bobby Doerr	1,407
Tommy Holmes	1,402
Luke Appling	1,376
Bill Nicholson	1,328
Marty Marion	1,310
Phil Cavarretta	1,304

Doubles

Lou Boudreau	339
Stan Musial	302
Bob Elliott	291
Dixie Walker	291
Bobby Doerr	272
Ted Williams	270
Tommy Holmes	269
Wally Moses	252
Marty Marion	251
Frank McCormick	246

Triples

Stan Musial	108
Enos Slaughter	84
Bob Elliott	80
Jeff Heath	70
Phil Cavarretta	70
Johnny Hopp	68
Joe DiMaggio	68
Snuffy Stirnweiss	66
Bobby Doerr	66
2 tied with	63

Home Runs

Ted Williams	234
Johnny Mize	217
Bill Nicholson	211
Rudy York	189
Joe Gordon	181
Joe DiMaggio	180
Vern Stephens	177
Charlie Keller	173
Ralph Kiner	168
Bobby Doerr	164

Home Runs (Home)

Johnny Mize	127
Mel Ott	112
Rudy York	111
Ted Williams	110
Bobby Doerr	108
Vern Stephens	97
Charlie Keller	97
Ralph Kiner	96
Bill Nicholson	91
Joe Gordon	85

Home Runs (Road)

Ted Williams	124
Bill Nicholson	120
Joe DiMaggio	103
Joe Gordon	96
Johnny Mize	90
Stan Musial	82
Jeff Heath	81
Vern Stephens	80
Bob Elliott	78
Rudy York	78

Extra Base Hits

Stan Musial	556
Ted Williams	549
Bill Nicholson	503
Bobby Doerr	502
Bob Elliott	480
Rudy York	465
Lou Boudreau	460
Jeff Heath	441
Joe DiMaggio	439
Johnny Mize	435

Total Bases

Stan Musial	2,388
Ted Williams	2,365
Bob Elliott	2,341
Bill Nicholson	2,304
Bobby Doerr	2,303
Lou Boudreau	2,221
Rudy York	2,155
Dixie Walker	2,119
Vern Stephens	2,088
Joe DiMaggio	2,023

RBI

Bob Elliott	903
Ted Williams	893
Bobby Doerr	887
Rudy York	854
Bill Nicholson	835
Vern Stephens	824
Joe DiMaggio	786
Dixie Walker	759
Johnny Mize	744
Joe Gordon	710

Walks

Ted Williams	992
Roy Cullenbine	806
Bob Elliott	728
Bill Nicholson	721
Lou Boudreau	706
Eddie Stanky	700
Charlie Keller	679
Luke Appling	666
Elbie Fletcher	661
2 tied with	626

Walks/PA

(minimum 3,000 Plate Appearances)

Ted Williams	.212
Roy Cullenbine	.179
Eddie Stanky	.177
Charlie Keller	.171
Eddie Lake	.171
Elbie Fletcher	.169
Augie Galan	.168
Mel Ott	.162
Eddie Joost	.148
Stan Hack	.139

Strikeouts

Bill Nicholson	708
Rudy York	688
Vince DiMaggio	582
Jeff Heath	538
Joe Gordon	529
George McQuinn	521
Eddie Joost	520
Vern Stephens	489
Pat Seerey	485
Marty Marion	465

Hit By Pitch

Bill Nicholson	48
Frankie Crosetti	46
Eddie Miller	38
Whitey Kurowski	36
Andy Pafko	33
Elbie Fletcher	32
Tommy Henrich	31
Johnny Mize	28
Danny Litwhiler	27
Lou Boudreau	27

Sac Hits

Lou Boudreau	153
Marty Marion	143
Eddie Mayo	98
George McQuinn	98
Eddie Stanky	84
Ken Keltner	84
Emil Verban	78
Harry Walker	78
Skeeter Newsome	77
George Kell	75

Sac Flies

Statistic unavailable

Stolen Bases

George Case	285
Snuffy Stirnweiss	130
Wally Moses	126
Johnny Hopp	117
Pee Wee Reese	108
Mickey Vernon	108
Joe Kuhel	93
Luke Appling	91
Bob Dillinger	90
Jackie Robinson	88

Caught Stealing

George Case	85
Mickey Vernon	57
Snuffy Stirnweiss	52
Wally Moses	52
Luke Appling	52
Oris Hockett	48
Thurman Tucker	47
Lou Boudreau	47
Don Kolloway	46
Joe Gordon	46

Runs Created

Ted Williams	1,127
Stan Musial	973
Bob Elliott	896
Bill Nicholson	861
Dixie Walker	860
Lou Boudreau	846
Bobby Doerr	826
Joe DiMaggio	806
Johnny Mize	776
Vern Stephens	767

Runs Created/27 Outs

(minimum 3,000 Plate Appearances)

Ted Williams	12.32
Stan Musial	9.24
Joe DiMaggio	8.64
Johnny Mize	8.25
Charlie Keller	8.10
Mel Ott	7.45
Enos Slaughter	7.27
Augie Galan	7.15
Tommy Henrich	7.06
Roy Cullenbine	6.83

Batting Average

(minimum 3,000 Plate Appearances)

Ted Williams	.356
Stan Musial	.346
Joe DiMaggio	.325
Barney McCosky	.321
Johnny Pesky	.316
Enos Slaughter	.312
Luke Appling	.311
Dixie Walker	.311
Taffy Wright	.308
George Kell	.305

On-Base Percentage

(minimum 3,000 Plate Appearances)

Ted Williams	.496
Stan Musial	.428
Augie Galan	.414
Roy Cullenbine	.411
Charlie Keller	.406
Joe DiMaggio	.404
Elbie Fletcher	.404
Eddie Stanky	.403
Mel Ott	.403
Luke Appling	.402

Slugging Percentage

(minimum 3,000 Plate Appearances)

Ted Williams	.647
Stan Musial	.578
Joe DiMaggio	.568
Johnny Mize	.561
Charlie Keller	.521
Jeff Heath	.499
Tommy Henrich	.492
Enos Slaughter	.484
Mel Ott	.477
Bobby Doerr	.468

OBP+Slugging

(minimum 3,000 Plate Appearances)

Ted Williams	1.143
Stan Musial	1.005
Joe DiMaggio	.972
Johnny Mize	.954
Charlie Keller	.926
Mel Ott	.879
Enos Slaughter	.876
Tommy Henrich	.871
Jeff Heath	.871
Bob Johnson	.851

Secondary Average

(minimum 3,000 Plate Appearances)

Ted Williams	.566
Charlie Keller	.459
Johnny Mize	.404
Mel Ott	.403
Roy Cullenbine	.384
Stan Musial	.379
Joe DiMaggio	.374
Tommy Henrich	.363
Jeff Heath	.355
Bob Johnson	.350

Isolated Power

(minimum 3,000 Plate Appearances)

Ted Williams	.290
Johnny Mize	.257
Joe DiMaggio	.243
Charlie Keller	.240
Stan Musial	.231
Jeff Heath	.212
Tommy Henrich	.210
Bill Nicholson	.198
Mel Ott	.197
Joe Gordon	.189

Pitching Leaders—1940-1949

Wins

Hal Newhouser	170
Bob Feller	137
Rip Sewell	133
Dizzy Trout	129
Dutch Leonard	122
Bucky Walters	122
Mort Cooper	114
Claude Passeau	111
3 tied with	105

Losses

Dutch Leonard	123
Bobo Newsom	120
Dizzy Trout	119
Hal Newhouser	118
Sid Hudson	100
Early Wynn	92
Johnny Vander Meer	92
Bucky Walters	90
Ken Raffensberger	89
Jim Tobin	88

Winning Percentage
(minimum 100 decisions)

Spud Chandler	.714
Harry Brecheen	.640
Tex Hughson	.640
Howie Pollet	.629
Mort Cooper	.626
Bob Feller	.626
Max Lanier	.621
Schoolboy Rowe	.619
Warren Spahn	.613
Rip Sewell	.605

Games

Hal Newhouser	377
Dizzy Trout	374
Kirby Higbe	354
Harry Gumbert	354
Rip Sewell	316
Clyde Shoun	315
Ace Adams	302
Bobo Newsom	302
Dutch Leonard	294
Hugh Casey	290

Games Started

Hal Newhouser	305
Dutch Leonard	274
Bobo Newsom	261
Dizzy Trout	239
Bucky Walters	238
Bob Feller	231
Rip Sewell	231
Johnny Vander Meer	219
Mort Cooper	210
Hank Borowy	208

Complete Games

Hal Newhouser	181
Bob Feller	155
Bucky Walters	153
Dutch Leonard	139
Dizzy Trout	132
Rip Sewell	132
Claude Passeau	130
Jim Tobin	127
Mort Cooper	120
Bobo Newsom	115

Shutouts

Hal Newhouser	31
Mort Cooper	30
Bob Feller	28
Bucky Walters	28
Dizzy Trout	27
Johnny Vander Meer	27
Dutch Leonard	23
Harry Brecheen	22
Spud Chandler	22
2 tied with	21

Saves

Joe Page	63
Hugh Casey	54
Johnny Murphy	53
Al Benton	50
Ace Adams	49
Harry Gumbert	47
Tom Ferrick	41
George Caster	37
Russ Christopher	35
2 tied with	33

Games Finished

Ace Adams	218
Hugh Casey	172
Harry Gumbert	164
Johnny Murphy	157
Clyde Shoun	149
Joe Page	145
George Caster	145
Tom Ferrick	141
Joe Beggs	124
Joe Haynes	119

Batters Faced

Hal Newhouser	10,360
Dizzy Trout	8,587
Dutch Leonard	8,535
Bobo Newsom	8,488
Rip Sewell	8,103
Bob Feller	7,880
Bucky Walters	7,778
Kirby Higbe	7,273
Claude Passeau	7,149
Hank Borowy	6,772

Innings Pitched

Hal Newhouser	2,453.1
Dutch Leonard	2,047.1
Dizzy Trout	2,026.1
Bobo Newsom	1,961.1
Bob Feller	1,897.0
Rip Sewell	1,894.0
Bucky Walters	1,868.1
Claude Passeau	1,693.2
Kirby Higbe	1,693.0
Hank Borowy	1,607.1

Hits Allowed

Hal Newhouser	2,127
Dutch Leonard	2,105
Bobo Newsom	1,949
Dizzy Trout	1,944
Rip Sewell	1,864
Bucky Walters	1,724
Claude Passeau	1,704
Hank Borowy	1,542
Bob Feller	1,539
Early Wynn	1,519

Runs Allowed

Hal Newhouser	927
Bobo Newsom	915
Dutch Leonard	884
Rip Sewell	848
Dizzy Trout	821
Sid Hudson	799
Kirby Higbe	759
Bucky Walters	726
Early Wynn	724
Hank Borowy	692

Earned Runs Allowed

Bobo Newsom	782
Hal Newhouser	774
Dutch Leonard	715
Rip Sewell	706
Sid Hudson	680
Dizzy Trout	678
Kirby Higbe	663
Early Wynn	617
Bucky Walters	616
Bob Feller	611

Home Runs Allowed

Tiny Bonham	117
Bill Voiselle	108
Bob Muncrief	106
Kirby Higbe	102
Rip Sewell	100
Hank Borowy	96
Bob Feller	95
Bobo Newsom	93
Bucky Walters	92
Ed Lopat	90

Walks

Hal Newhouser	1,068
Bob Feller	827
Kirby Higbe	819
Johnny Vander Meer	805
Allie Reynolds	799
Bobo Newsom	792
Dizzy Trout	746
Phil Marchildon	682
Rip Sewell	646
Bucky Walters	631

Intentional Walks

Statistic unavailable

Strikeouts

Hal Newhouser	1,579
Bob Feller	1,396
Bobo Newsom	1,070
Johnny Vander Meer	972
Dizzy Trout	930
Kirby Higbe	853
Allie Reynolds	791
Dutch Leonard	779
Mort Cooper	772
Virgil Trucks	760

Strikeouts/9 Innings
(minimum 1,000 Innings Pitched)

Bob Feller	6.62
Hal Newhouser	5.79
Johnny Vander Meer	5.50
Virgil Trucks	5.34
Max Lanier	5.13
Bobo Newsom	4.91
Allie Reynolds	4.80
Preacher Roe	4.55
Kirby Higbe	4.53
Tex Hughson	4.53

ERA
(minimum 1,000 Innings Pitched)

Spud Chandler	2.67
Max Lanier	2.68
Harry Brecheen	2.74
Hal Newhouser	2.84
Bob Feller	2.90
Mort Cooper	2.93
Claude Passeau	2.94
Tex Hughson	2.94
Bucky Walters	2.97
Howie Pollet	2.99

Component ERA
(minimum 1,000 Innings Pitched)

Spud Chandler	2.63
Whit Wyatt	2.65
Harry Brecheen	2.74
Mort Cooper	2.75
Max Lanier	2.80
Bob Feller	2.82
Tex Hughson	2.86
Tiny Bonham	2.93
Hal Newhouser	2.95
Virgil Trucks	3.04

Sac Hits Allowed

Hal Newhouser	133
Dizzy Trout	126
Bobo Newsom	120
Nels Potter	117
Kirby Higbe	112
Dutch Leonard	108
Johnny Vander Meer	106
Rip Sewell	106
Jim Tobin	100
Bill Lee	100

Sac Flies Allowed

Statistic unavailable

Hit Batsmen

Mickey Haefner	37
Johnny Niggeling	32
Bobo Newsom	32
Dutch Leonard	31
Allie Reynolds	29
Orval Grove	29
Russ Christopher	27
Harry Brecheen	27
Thornton Lee	27
2 tied with	26

Wild Pitches

Dutch Leonard	53
Hal Newhouser	52
Kirby Higbe	47
Phil Marchildon	45
Joe Dobson	40
Orval Grove	38
Allie Reynolds	36
Dizzy Trout	36
Bob Feller	36
2 tied with	35

Balks

Joe Dobson	9
Hal Newhouser	6
Dizzy Trout	6
Mort Cooper	6
Al Gettel	5
Hank Borowy	5
Charlie Fuchs	5
Phil Marchildon	5
Jack Kramer	5
14 tied with	4

Opponent Average
(minimum 1,000 Innings Pitched)

Bob Feller	.222
Hal Newhouser	.232
Spud Chandler	.233
Johnny Niggeling	.233
Johnny Vander Meer	.234
Virgil Trucks	.234
Whit Wyatt	.235
Kirby Higbe	.236
Mort Cooper	.238
Harry Brecheen	.239

Opponent OBP
(minimum 1,000 Innings Pitched)

Tiny Bonham	.289
Whit Wyatt	.289
Harry Brecheen	.295
Mort Cooper	.295
Spud Chandler	.296
Tex Hughson	.297
Paul Derringer	.300
Claude Passeau	.304
Curt Davis	.305
Dutch Leonard	.306

Single Season Batting Leaders—1940-1949

Games

Babe Dahlgren	1944	158
Eddie Lake	1947	158
Stan Musial	1943	157
Vince DiMaggio	1943	157
Stan Musial	1949	157
14 tied with		156

At-Bats

Richie Ashburn	1949	662
Granny Hamner	1949	662
Doc Cramer	1940	661
Doc Cramer	1941	660
Red Schoendienst	1947	659
George Case	1940	656
Dain Clay	1945	656
Mike Rocco	1944	653
Woody Williams	1944	653
George Case	1941	649

Runs

Ted Williams	1949	150
Ted Williams	1946	142
Ted Williams	1942	141
Tommy Henrich	1948	138
Johnny Mize	1947	137
Ted Williams	1941	135
Stan Musial	1948	135
Ted Williams	1940	134
Pee Wee Reese	1949	132
Hank Greenberg	1940	129

Hits

Stan Musial	1948	230
Stan Musial	1946	228
Tommy Holmes	1945	224
Stan Musial	1943	220
Cecil Travis	1941	218
Johnny Pesky	1946	208
Mickey Vernon	1946	207
Johnny Pesky	1947	207
Bob Dillinger	1948	207
Stan Musial	1949	207

Doubles

Stan Musial	1944	51
Mickey Vernon	1946	51
Hank Greenberg	1940	50
Stan Musial	1946	50
Stan Spence	1946	50
Stan Musial	1943	48
Tommy Holmes	1945	47
Lou Boudreau	1940	46
Rudy York	1940	46
Stan Musial	1948	46

Triples

Dale Mitchell	1949	23
Snuffy Stirnweiss	1945	22
Jeff Heath	1941	20
Stan Musial	1943	20
Stan Musial	1946	20
Barney McCosky	1940	19
Cecil Travis	1941	19
Johnny Barrett	1944	19
Stan Musial	1948	18
2 tied with		17

Home Runs

Ralph Kiner	1949	54
Ralph Kiner	1947	51
Johnny Mize	1947	51
Hank Greenberg	1946	44
Johnny Mize	1940	43
Ted Williams	1949	43
Hank Greenberg	1940	41
Ralph Kiner	1948	40
Johnny Mize	1948	40
3 tied with		39

Home Runs (Home)

Ralph Kiner	1948	31
Hank Greenberg	1946	29
Johnny Mize	1947	29
Ralph Kiner	1949	29
Ralph Kiner	1947	28
Hank Greenberg	1940	27
Johnny Mize	1940	25
Willard Marshall	1947	25
Johnny Mize	1948	25
2 tied with		23

Home Runs (Road)

Ralph Kiner	1949	25
Joe DiMaggio	1948	24
Ralph Kiner	1947	23
Walker Cooper	1947	23
Stan Musial	1948	23
Stan Musial	1949	23
Johnny Mize	1947	22
Del Ennis	1948	22
3 tied with		20

Extra Base Hits

Stan Musial	1948	103
Hank Greenberg	1940	99
Stan Musial	1949	90
Johnny Mize	1940	87
Stan Musial	1946	86
Rudy York	1940	85
Ted Williams	1949	85
Joe DiMaggio	1941	84
Ted Williams	1946	83
4 tied with		81

Total Bases

Stan Musial	1948	429
Hank Greenberg	1940	384
Stan Musial	1949	382
Johnny Mize	1940	368
Ted Williams	1949	368
Tommy Holmes	1945	367
Stan Musial	1946	366
Ralph Kiner	1947	361
Ralph Kiner	1949	361
Johnny Mize	1947	360

RBI

Vern Stephens	1949	159
Ted Williams	1949	159
Joe DiMaggio	1948	155
Hank Greenberg	1940	150
Johnny Mize	1947	138
Johnny Mize	1940	137
Ted Williams	1942	137
Vern Stephens	1948	137
Rudy York	1940	134
2 tied with		133

Walks

Ted Williams	1947	162
Ted Williams	1949	162
Ted Williams	1946	156
Eddie Joost	1949	149
Eddie Stanky	1945	148
Ted Williams	1941	145
Ted Williams	1942	145
Eddie Stanky	1946	137
Roy Cullenbine	1947	137
Ferris Fain	1949	136

Walks/PA
(minimum 3.1 PA/Tm Gm)

Ted Williams	1941	.240
Ted Williams	1947	.234
Ted Williams	1946	.232
Roy Cullenbine	1947	.226
Ted Williams	1949	.222
Eddie Joost	1949	.218
Ted Williams	1942	.216
Eddie Stanky	1946	.213
Hank Greenberg	1947	.204
Eddie Stanky	1945	.204

Strikeouts

Chet Ross	1940	127
Vince DiMaggio	1943	126
Dolph Camilli	1941	115
Eddie Joost	1947	110
Ralph Kiner	1946	109
Chet Laabs	1943	105
Jimmie Foxx	1941	103
Pat Seerey	1948	102
3 tied with		101

Hit By Pitch

Pete Reiser	1941	11
Frankie Crosetti	1940	10
Mickey Vernon	1943	10
Danny Litwhiler	1944	10
Frankie Crosetti	1945	10
Whitey Kurowski	1947	10
5 tied with		9

Sac Hits

Harry Walker	1943	36
Marty Marion	1941	28
Joe Hoover	1943	28
Eddie Mayo	1944	28
Jackie Robinson	1947	28
George Hausmann	1944	27
Phil Rizzuto	1949	25
Roy Schalk	1945	24
Eddie Joost	1947	24
Eddie Mayo	1943	23

Sac Flies

Statistic unavailable

Stolen Bases

George Case	1943	61
Wally Moses	1943	56
Snuffy Stirnweiss	1944	55
George Case	1944	49
George Case	1942	44
Jackie Robinson	1949	37
George Case	1940	35
Pete Reiser	1946	34
Bob Dillinger	1947	34
2 tied with		33

Caught Stealing

Oris Hockett	1943	18
George Case	1944	18
Dale Mitchell	1948	18
Thurman Tucker	1943	17
Snuffy Stirnweiss	1945	17
Lou Boudreau	1942	16
George Case	1945	16
Dave Philley	1947	16
5 tied with		14

Runs Created

Stan Musial	1948	177
Ted Williams	1949	174
Ted Williams	1941	170
Ted Williams	1946	163
Ted Williams	1947	161
Ted Williams	1942	160
Ted Williams	1948	160
Stan Musial	1949	155
Hank Greenberg	1940	152
Stan Musial	1946	152

Runs Created/27 Outs
(minimum 3.1 PA/Tm Gm)

Ted Williams	1941	16.09
Ted Williams	1948	12.92
Ted Williams	1946	12.56
Ted Williams	1942	12.40
Ted Williams	1947	11.99
Ted Williams	1949	11.73
Stan Musial	1948	11.72
Joe DiMaggio	1941	11.06
Hank Greenberg	1940	10.22
Ralph Kiner	1949	10.07

Batting Average
(minimum 3.1 PA/Tm Gm)

Ted Williams	1941	.406
Stan Musial	1948	.376
Ted Williams	1948	.369
Stan Musial	1946	.365
Harry Walker	1947	.363
Cecil Travis	1941	.359
Dixie Walker	1944	.357
Joe DiMaggio	1941	.357
Stan Musial	1943	.357
Ted Williams	1942	.356

On-Base Percentage
(minimum 3.1 PA/Tm Gm)

Ted Williams	1941	.551
Ted Williams	1942	.499
Ted Williams	1947	.499
Ted Williams	1946	.497
Ted Williams	1948	.497
Ted Williams	1949	.490
Lou Boudreau	1948	.453
Roy Cullenbine	1941	.452
Stan Musial	1948	.450
Phil Cavarretta	1945	.449

Slugging Percentage
(minimum 3.1 PA/Tm Gm)

Ted Williams	1941	.735
Stan Musial	1948	.702
Hank Greenberg	1940	.670
Ted Williams	1946	.667
Ralph Kiner	1949	.658
Ted Williams	1949	.650
Ted Williams	1942	.648
Joe DiMaggio	1941	.643
Ralph Kiner	1947	.639
Johnny Mize	1940	.636

OBP+Slugging

Ted Williams	1941	1.286
Ted Williams	1946	1.164
Stan Musial	1948	1.152
Ted Williams	1942	1.147
Ted Williams	1949	1.141
Ted Williams	1947	1.133
Ted Williams	1948	1.112
Hank Greenberg	1940	1.103
Ralph Kiner	1949	1.089
Joe DiMaggio	1941	1.083

Secondary Average

Ted Williams	1941	.651
Ted Williams	1946	.628
Ted Williams	1947	.598
Ted Williams	1949	.595
Ted Williams	1942	.575
Ralph Kiner	1949	.572
Hank Greenberg	1940	.503
Ted Williams	1948	.501
Ralph Kiner	1947	.501
Roy Cullenbine	1947	.500

Isolated Power
(minimum 3.1 PA/Tm Gm)

Ralph Kiner	1949	.348
Hank Greenberg	1940	.330
Ted Williams	1941	.329
Hank Greenberg	1946	.327
Stan Musial	1948	.326
Ralph Kiner	1947	.326
Ted Williams	1946	.325
Johnny Mize	1940	.321
Johnny Mize	1947	.312
Ted Williams	1949	.307

Single Season Pitching Leaders—1940-1949

Wins

Hal Newhouser	1944	29
Bob Feller	1940	27
Dizzy Trout	1944	27
Hal Newhouser	1946	26
Bob Feller	1946	26
Bob Feller	1941	25
Hal Newhouser	1945	25
Boo Ferriss	1946	25
Mel Parnell	1949	25
Johnny Sain	1948	24

Losses

Hugh Mulcahy	1940	22
Jim Tobin	1942	21
Lum Harris	1943	21
Fred Sanford	1948	21
8 tied with		20

Winning Percentage
(minimum 15 decisions)

Freddie Fitzsimmons	1940	.889
Schoolboy Rowe	1940	.842
Spud Chandler	1943	.833
Elmer Riddle	1941	.826
Howie Krist	1942	.813
Rip Sewell	1948	.813
Ted Wilks	1944	.810
Bobo Newsom	1940	.808
Tiny Bonham	1942	.808
Larry Jansen	1947	.808

Games

Ace Adams	1943	70
Andy Karl	1945	67
Ace Adams	1944	65
Ace Adams	1945	65
Joe Heving	1944	63
Ken Trinkle	1947	62
Ace Adams	1942	61
Harry Gumbert	1948	61
Joe Page	1949	60
Ted Wilks	1949	59

Games Started

Bob Feller	1946	42
Bill Voiselle	1944	41
Bob Feller	1941	40
Dizzy Trout	1944	40
Kirby Higbe	1941	39
Johnny Sain	1948	39
Bob Feller	1948	38
Warren Spahn	1949	38
Ken Raffensberger	1949	38
6 tied with		37

Complete Games

Bob Feller	1946	36
Dizzy Trout	1944	33
Bob Feller	1940	31
Thornton Lee	1941	30
Bucky Walters	1940	29
Hal Newhouser	1945	29
Hal Newhouser	1946	29
4 tied with		28

Shutouts

Mort Cooper	1942	10
Bob Feller	1946	10
Bob Lemon	1948	10
Hal Newhouser	1945	8
Whit Wyatt	1941	7
Hi Bithorn	1943	7
Dizzy Trout	1944	7
Mort Cooper	1944	7
Warren Spahn	1947	7
Harry Brecheen	1948	7

Saves

Joe Page	1949	27
Hugh Casey	1947	18
Al Benton	1940	17
Joe Page	1947	17
Ed Klieman	1947	17
Russ Christopher	1948	17
Harry Gumbert	1948	17
Joe Page	1948	16
3 tied with		15

Games Finished

Ace Adams	1943	52
Ace Adams	1945	50
Ace Adams	1942	49
Joe Page	1949	48
Joe Berry	1944	47
Harry Gumbert	1948	46
Ace Adams	1944	44
Joe Page	1947	44
3 tied with		41

Batters Faced

Bob Feller	1946	1,512
Bob Feller	1941	1,466
Dizzy Trout	1944	1,421
Bill Voiselle	1944	1,327
Johnny Sain	1948	1,313
Bob Feller	1940	1,304
Al Javery	1943	1,286
Hal Newhouser	1944	1,271
Kirby Higbe	1941	1,266
Hal Newhouser	1945	1,261

Innings Pitched

Bob Feller	1946	371.1
Dizzy Trout	1944	352.1
Bob Feller	1941	343.0
Bob Feller	1940	320.1
Johnny Sain	1948	314.2
Hal Newhouser	1945	313.1
Bill Voiselle	1944	312.2
Hal Newhouser	1944	312.1
Bucky Walters	1940	305.0
Al Javery	1943	303.0

Hits Allowed

Dutch Leonard	1940	328
Dizzy Trout	1944	314
Eldon Auker	1940	299
Johnny Sain	1948	297
Bucky Walters	1941	292
Ken Raffensberger	1949	289
Al Javery	1943	288
Red Barrett	1945	287
Johnny Sain	1949	285
2 tied with		284

Runs Allowed

George Caster	1940	160
Eldon Auker	1941	150
Johnny Sain	1949	150
Sid Hudson	1940	149
Vern Kennedy	1940	149
Bobo Newsom	1942	148
Jim Tobin	1942	145
Early Wynn	1948	144
Hal Gregg	1944	142
Hugh Mulcahy	1940	141

Earned Runs Allowed

Vern Kennedy	1940	138
Eldon Auker	1941	132
George Caster	1940	130
Johnny Sain	1949	130
Bobo Newsom	1942	129
Sid Hudson	1940	128
Bobo Newsom	1941	128
Early Wynn	1948	128
Jim Tobin	1942	127
2 tied with		120

Home Runs Allowed

Murry Dickson	1948	39
Larry Jansen	1949	36
Fred Hutchinson	1948	32
Bill Voiselle	1944	31
Warren Spahn	1949	27
Larry Jansen	1948	25
Preacher Roe	1949	25
Bob Harris	1940	24
Red Ruffing	1940	24
Ralph Branca	1948	24

Walks

Bob Feller	1941	194
Tommy Byrne	1949	179
Johnny Vander Meer	1943	162
Bob Feller	1946	153
Ken Chase	1940	143
Phil Marchildon	1947	141
Phil Marchildon	1942	140
Vic Raschi	1949	138
3 tied with		137

Intentional Walks

Statistic unavailable

Strikeouts

Bob Feller	1946	348
Hal Newhouser	1946	275
Bob Feller	1940	261
Bob Feller	1941	260
Hal Newhouser	1945	212
Johnny Vander Meer	1941	202
Bob Feller	1947	196
Ewell Blackwell	1947	193
Hal Newhouser	1944	187
Johnny Vander Meer	1942	186

Strikeouts/9 Innings
(minimum 1 Inning Pitched/Tm Gm)

Hal Newhouser	1946	8.46
Bob Feller	1946	8.43
Johnny Vander Meer	1941	8.03
Bob Feller	1940	7.33
Johnny Vander Meer	1942	6.86
Allie Reynolds	1943	6.84
Bob Feller	1941	6.82
Hal Newhouser	1943	6.62
Ewell Blackwell	1947	6.36
Bobo Newsom	1941	6.29

ERA
(minimum 1 Inning Pitched/Tm Gm)

Spud Chandler	1943	1.64
Mort Cooper	1942	1.78
Hal Newhouser	1945	1.81
Max Lanier	1943	1.90
Hal Newhouser	1946	1.94
Al Benton	1945	2.02
Ted Lyons	1942	2.10
Howie Pollet	1946	2.10
Spud Chandler	1946	2.10
Dizzy Trout	1944	2.12

Component ERA
(minimum 1 Inning Pitched/Tm Gm)

Mort Cooper	1942	1.81
Spud Chandler	1943	1.82
Roger Wolff	1945	1.87
Hal Newhouser	1946	2.00
Harry Brecheen	1948	2.01
Tex Hughson	1944	2.04
Whit Wyatt	1941	2.06
Hal Newhouser	1945	2.07
Tiny Bonham	1942	2.11
Johnny Niggeling	1943	2.20

Sac Hits Allowed

Red Barrett	1943	29
Bobo Newsom	1945	28
Tommy Hughes	1942	27
Bill Dietrich	1944	27
Hal Newhouser	1947	27
Al Javery	1942	26
Ken Raffensberger	1944	26
Kirby Higbe	1940	25
Orval Grove	1944	25
Bob Feller	1946	25

Sac Flies Allowed

Statistic unavailable

Hit Batsmen

Tommy Byrne	1949	13
Johnny Podgajny	1942	11
Johnny Niggeling	1942	11
Carl Doyle	1940	10
Thornton Lee	1945	10
Sheldon Jones	1949	10
9 tied with		9

Wild Pitches

Phil Marchildon	1942	13
Porter Vaughan	1940	12
Ken Chase	1940	12
Phil Marchildon	1941	12
Ken Chase	1941	11
Hal Newhouser	1947	11
Joe Dobson	1947	11
Gene Bearden	1949	11
10 tied with		10

Balks

Charlie Fuchs	1943	4
Yank Terry	1943	4
Phil Marchildon	1941	3
Johnny Podgajny	1942	3
Marino Pieretti	1945	3
Al Gettel	1948	3
Alex Kellner	1949	3
Adrian Zabala	1949	3
60 tied with		2

Opponent Average
(minimum 1 Inning Pitched/Tm Gm)

Tommy Byrne	1949	.183
Spec Shea	1947	.200
Hal Newhouser	1946	.201
Allie Reynolds	1943	.202
Johnny Niggeling	1943	.204
Mort Cooper	1942	.204
Hal Newhouser	1942	.207
Whit Wyatt	1943	.207
Mickey Haefner	1943	.208
Bob Feller	1946	.208

Opponent OBP
(minimum 1 Inning Pitched/Tm Gm)

Whit Wyatt	1943	.255
Ray Prim	1945	.256
Mort Cooper	1942	.258
Roger Wolff	1945	.258
Tiny Bonham	1942	.259
Spud Chandler	1943	.261
Harry Brecheen	1948	.265
Tex Hughson	1944	.267
Hal Newhouser	1946	.269
Whit Wyatt	1941	.270

Batting Leaders—1950-1959

Games

Richie Ashburn	1,523
Nellie Fox	1,512
Gil Hodges	1,477
Stan Musial	1,456
Al Dark	1,441
Eddie Yost	1,439
Puddin' Head Jones	1,419
Duke Snider	1,418
Yogi Berra	1,396
Gus Bell	1,380

At-Bats

Nellie Fox	6,115
Richie Ashburn	5,997
Al Dark	5,795
Gus Bell	5,407
Stan Musial	5,366
Gil Hodges	5,313
Duke Snider	5,219
Yogi Berra	5,214
Red Schoendienst	5,107
Eddie Yost	5,075

Runs

Mickey Mantle	994
Duke Snider	970
Richie Ashburn	952
Stan Musial	948
Nellie Fox	902
Minnie Minoso	898
Eddie Yost	898
Gil Hodges	890
Al Dark	860
Yogi Berra	848

Hits

Richie Ashburn	1,875
Nellie Fox	1,837
Stan Musial	1,771
Al Dark	1,675
Duke Snider	1,605
Gus Bell	1,551
Minnie Minoso	1,526
Red Schoendienst	1,517
Yogi Berra	1,499
Gil Hodges	1,491

Doubles

Stan Musial	356
Red Schoendienst	284
Al Dark	282
Duke Snider	274
Gus Bell	269
Minnie Minoso	259
Nellie Fox	254
Richie Ashburn	252
Mickey Vernon	251
Harvey Kuenn	244

Triples

Richie Ashburn	82
Nellie Fox	82
Willie Mays	79
Minnie Minoso	74
Bill Bruton	66
Stan Musial	61
Mickey Vernon	60
Al Dark	58
Gus Bell	57
Duke Snider	57

Home Runs

Duke Snider	326
Gil Hodges	310
Eddie Mathews	299
Mickey Mantle	280
Stan Musial	266
Yogi Berra	256
Willie Mays	250
Ted Kluszewski	239
Gus Zernial	232
Ernie Banks	228

Home Runs (Home)

Duke Snider	187
Gil Hodges	173
Yogi Berra	151
Stan Musial	149
Mickey Mantle	139
Ted Kluszewski	137
Ernie Banks	133
Eddie Mathews	129
Willie Mays	126
Gus Zernial	123

Home Runs (Road)

Eddie Mathews	170
Mickey Mantle	141
Duke Snider	139
Gil Hodges	137
Willie Mays	124
Ted Williams	118
Stan Musial	117
Roy Sievers	111
Gus Zernial	109
2 tied with	108

Extra Base Hits

Stan Musial	683
Duke Snider	657
Gil Hodges	585
Mickey Mantle	542
Willie Mays	533
Eddie Mathews	522
Gus Bell	511
Yogi Berra	511
Ted Kluszewski	482
Minnie Minoso	478

Total Bases

Stan Musial	3,047
Duke Snider	2,971
Gil Hodges	2,733
Yogi Berra	2,555
Mickey Mantle	2,548
Gus Bell	2,489
Al Dark	2,421
Willie Mays	2,403
Eddie Mathews	2,383
Minnie Minoso	2,368

RBI

Duke Snider	1,031
Gil Hodges	1,001
Yogi Berra	997
Stan Musial	972
Del Ennis	925
Jackie Jensen	863
Mickey Mantle	841
Ted Kluszewski	823
Gus Bell	817
Larry Doby	817

Walks

Eddie Yost	1,185
Mickey Mantle	892
Ted Williams	845
Stan Musial	842
Richie Ashburn	828
Earl Torgeson	772
Gil Hodges	751
Eddie Mathews	726
Larry Doby	725
Duke Snider	711

Walks/PA

(minimum 3,000 Plate Appearances)

Ted Williams	.208
Ferris Fain	.185
Eddie Yost	.184
Ralph Kiner	.166
Mickey Mantle	.165
Earl Torgeson	.161
Larry Doby	.142
Eddie Mathews	.141
Gene Woodling	.141
Solly Hemus	.140

Strikeouts

Mickey Mantle	899
Gil Hodges	882
Duke Snider	851
Larry Doby	833
Gus Zernial	729
Eddie Mathews	678
Eddie Yost	626
Wally Post	585
Bobby Thomson	581
Gil McDougald	578

Hit By Pitch

Minnie Minoso	149
Sherm Lollar	95
Nellie Fox	92
Eddie Yost	81
Solly Hemus	62
Jackie Robinson	48
Al Dark	48
Frank Robinson	47
Al Smith	47
Andy Pafko	43

Sac Hits

Bobby Avila	134
Nellie Fox	125
Phil Rizzuto	124
Johnny Logan	112
Pee Wee Reese	100
Gil McDougald	90
Richie Ashburn	90
Roy McMillan	83
Johnny Temple	79
Billy Goodman	79

Sac Flies

Frank Thomas	49
Jackie Jensen	48
Gil Hodges	43
Del Ennis	38
Gus Bell	36
Willie Mays	35
Puddin' Head Jones	34
4 tied with	33

Stolen Bases

Willie Mays	179
Minnie Minoso	167
Richie Ashburn	158
Jim Rivera	150
Luis Aparicio	134
Jackie Jensen	134
Jim Gilliam	132
Pee Wee Reese	124
Bill Bruton	121
Jackie Robinson	109

Caught Stealing

Minnie Minoso	106
Jim Gilliam	76
Richie Ashburn	75
Jim Rivera	68
Nellie Fox	65
Willie Mays	53
Dee Fondy	53
Bobby Avila	52
Bill Bruton	51
Duke Snider	48

Runs Created

Stan Musial	1,185
Mickey Mantle	1,103
Duke Snider	1,101
Gil Hodges	1,002
Richie Ashburn	979
Minnie Minoso	954
Yogi Berra	919
Eddie Yost	911
Eddie Mathews	910
Ted Williams	895

Runs Created/27 Outs

(minimum 3,000 Plate Appearances)

Ted Williams	10.87
Mickey Mantle	9.35
Stan Musial	8.39
Willie Mays	8.02
Duke Snider	7.66
Eddie Mathews	7.53
Jackie Robinson	7.44
Ralph Kiner	7.26
Hank Aaron	7.03
Larry Doby	7.01

Batting Average

(minimum 3,000 Plate Appearances)

Ted Williams	.336
Stan Musial	.330
Hank Aaron	.323
Willie Mays	.317
Harvey Kuenn	.314
Richie Ashburn	.313
Jackie Robinson	.311
Al Kaline	.311
Mickey Mantle	.311
George Kell	.308

On-Base Percentage

(minimum 3,000 Plate Appearances)

Ted Williams	.476
Ferris Fain	.431
Mickey Mantle	.425
Stan Musial	.421
Jackie Robinson	.416
Eddie Yost	.406
Minnie Minoso	.400
Richie Ashburn	.399
Ralph Kiner	.398
Willie Mays	.391

Slugging Percentage

(minimum 3,000 Plate Appearances)

Ted Williams	.622
Willie Mays	.590
Duke Snider	.569
Mickey Mantle	.569
Stan Musial	.568
Hank Aaron	.559
Ernie Banks	.558
Eddie Mathews	.548
Ralph Kiner	.533
Ted Kluszewski	.518

OBP+Slugging

(minimum 3,000 Plate Appearances)

Ted Williams	1.098
Mickey Mantle	.994
Stan Musial	.989
Willie Mays	.981
Duke Snider	.959
Eddie Mathews	.931
Ralph Kiner	.931
Hank Aaron	.931
Ernie Banks	.913
Jackie Robinson	.892

Secondary Average

(minimum 3,000 Plate Appearances)

Ted Williams	.554
Mickey Mantle	.479
Ralph Kiner	.463
Eddie Mathews	.443
Willie Mays	.441
Duke Snider	.413
Stan Musial	.400
Larry Doby	.386
Gil Hodges	.383
Al Rosen	.381

Isolated Power

(minimum 3,000 Plate Appearances)

Ted Williams	.286
Willie Mays	.273
Eddie Mathews	.267
Ernie Banks	.263
Duke Snider	.262
Ralph Kiner	.259
Mickey Mantle	.258
Stan Musial	.238
Hank Aaron	.237
Gil Hodges	.234

Leaders: By Decade

Pitching Leaders—1950-1959

Wins

Warren Spahn	202
Robin Roberts	199
Early Wynn	188
Billy Pierce	155
Bob Lemon	150
Mike Garcia	128
Lew Burdette	126
Don Newcombe	126
Whitey Ford	121
Johnny Antonelli	116

Losses

Robin Roberts	149
Warren Spahn	131
Bob Friend	127
Murry Dickson	124
Bob Rush	123
Billy Pierce	121
Early Wynn	119
Ned Garver	117
Chuck Stobbs	113
Alex Kellner	100

Winning Percentage
(minimum 100 decisions)

Whitey Ford	.708
Allie Reynolds	.669
Ed Lopat	.667
Sal Maglie	.663
Vic Raschi	.643
Don Newcombe	.633
Bob Buhl	.618
Bob Lemon	.615
Early Wynn	.612
Warren Spahn	.607

Games

Hoyt Wilhelm	432
Gerry Staley	430
Clem Labine	412
Robin Roberts	405
Johnny Klippstein	400
Warren Spahn	389
Murry Dickson	376
Early Wynn	374
Chuck Stobbs	359
Turk Lown	358

Games Started

Robin Roberts	370
Warren Spahn	350
Early Wynn	339
Billy Pierce	306
Bob Rush	278
Bob Friend	262
Mike Garcia	261
Bob Lemon	260
Ned Garver	257
Don Newcombe	246

Complete Games

Robin Roberts	237
Warren Spahn	215
Billy Pierce	162
Early Wynn	162
Bob Lemon	139
Ned Garver	125
Don Newcombe	116
Bob Rush	105
Lew Burdette	104
Mike Garcia	103

Shutouts

Billy Pierce	33
Warren Spahn	33
Early Wynn	33
Robin Roberts	30
Whitey Ford	24
Johnny Antonelli	23
Mike Garcia	22
Bob Porterfield	22
Sal Maglie	22
2 tied with	21

Saves

Ellis Kinder	96
Clem Labine	82
Jim Konstanty	65
Ray Narleski	58
Hoyt Wilhelm	58
Marv Grissom	58
Al Brazle	55
Roy Face	51
Turk Lown	51
Frank Smith	44

Games Finished

Clem Labine	236
Jim Konstanty	228
Ellis Kinder	224
Hoyt Wilhelm	204
Roy Face	187
Turk Lown	183
Frank Smith	175
Marv Grissom	172
Harry Dorish	149
2 tied with	141

Batters Faced

Robin Roberts	12,263
Warren Spahn	11,554
Early Wynn	10,756
Billy Pierce	9,940
Bob Rush	8,645
Bob Lemon	8,589
Bob Friend	8,428
Mike Garcia	8,331
Murry Dickson	8,191
Ned Garver	8,082

Innings Pitched

Robin Roberts	3,011.2
Warren Spahn	2,822.2
Early Wynn	2,562.0
Billy Pierce	2,383.0
Bob Rush	2,047.0
Bob Lemon	2,015.1
Bob Friend	1,976.0
Mike Garcia	1,960.1
Murry Dickson	1,918.0
Ned Garver	1,904.1

Hits Allowed

Robin Roberts	2,874
Warren Spahn	2,540
Early Wynn	2,217
Billy Pierce	2,107
Bob Friend	2,083
Murry Dickson	1,969
Mike Garcia	1,945
Bob Rush	1,937
Bob Lemon	1,890
Lew Burdette	1,886

Runs Allowed

Robin Roberts	1,229
Early Wynn	1,046
Warren Spahn	1,022
Bob Friend	986
Murry Dickson	945
Bob Rush	935
Billy Pierce	898
Ned Garver	891
Alex Kellner	875
Bob Lemon	872

Earned Runs Allowed

Robin Roberts	1,110
Early Wynn	934
Warren Spahn	915
Bob Friend	851
Murry Dickson	816
Bob Rush	812
Billy Pierce	809
Alex Kellner	784
Ned Garver	783
Chuck Stobbs	756

Home Runs Allowed

Robin Roberts	327
Warren Spahn	222
Early Wynn	218
Don Newcombe	217
Murry Dickson	217
Billy Pierce	189
Carl Erskine	188
Harvey Haddix	179
Bob Friend	176
Herm Wehmeier	169

Walks

Early Wynn	1,028
Billy Pierce	840
Bob Lemon	820
Bob Turley	804
Warren Spahn	790
Mickey McDermott	726
Johnny Klippstein	710
Tommy Byrne	708
Whitey Ford	664
Bob Rush	663

Intentional Walks

Bob Friend	50
Ron Kline	42
Larry Jackson	41
Vern Law	41
Harvey Haddix	39
Roy Face	38
Johnny Klippstein	38
Clem Labine	36
Warren Spahn	36
2 tied with	35

Strikeouts

Early Wynn	1,544
Robin Roberts	1,516
Billy Pierce	1,487
Warren Spahn	1,464
Harvey Haddix	1,093
Bob Rush	1,072
Johnny Antonelli	1,026
Mike Garcia	1,000
Sam Jones	994
Bob Turley	983

Strikeouts/9 Innings
(minimum 1,000 Innings Pitched)

Sam Jones	7.59
Bob Turley	6.97
Camilo Pascual	6.54
Harvey Haddix	6.26
Johnny Podres	5.89
Jack Harshman	5.78
Vinegar Bend Mizell	5.78
Hoyt Wilhelm	5.67
Allie Reynolds	5.64
Billy Pierce	5.62

ERA
(minimum 1,000 Innings Pitched)

Whitey Ford	2.66
Hoyt Wilhelm	2.79
Warren Spahn	2.92
Billy Pierce	3.06
Allie Reynolds	3.07
Ed Lopat	3.12
Bob Buhl	3.14
Johnny Antonelli	3.18
Sal Maglie	3.19
Early Wynn	3.28

Component ERA
(minimum 1,000 Innings Pitched)

Warren Spahn	2.92
Robin Roberts	3.01
Whitey Ford	3.02
Billy Pierce	3.08
Hoyt Wilhelm	3.09
Allie Reynolds	3.18
Early Wynn	3.21
Bob Rush	3.28
Johnny Antonelli	3.30
Curt Simmons	3.33

Sac Hits Allowed

Early Wynn	137
Billy Pierce	122
Robin Roberts	118
Bob Friend	115
Warren Spahn	112
Chuck Stobbs	108
Mike Garcia	98
Murry Dickson	94
Ned Garver	91
Curt Simmons	87

Sac Flies Allowed

Vern Law	44
Bob Turley	42
Harvey Haddix	41
Lew Burdette	41
Camilo Pascual	40
Johnny Klippstein	39
Robin Roberts	39
Early Wynn	39
Ruben Gomez	38
Bob Rush	38

Hit Batsmen

Tommy Byrne	59
Gerry Staley	54
Frank Lary	53
Johnny Klippstein	50
Steve Gromek	49
Sam Jones	46
Bob Lemon	44
Don Drysdale	42
Sal Maglie	42
2 tied with	41

Wild Pitches

Johnny Klippstein	57
Bob Lemon	48
Herb Score	43
Alex Kellner	43
Warren Spahn	43
Bob Rush	41
Tom Brewer	40
Carl Erskine	37
Herm Wehmeier	36
2 tied with	35

Balks

Camilo Pascual	9
Vic Raschi	7
Frank Sullivan	6
Ron Kline	6
Bob Friend	6
Bobby Shantz	6
Sal Maglie	6
Max Lanier	6
19 tied with	5

Opponent Average
(minimum 1,000 Innings Pitched)

Bob Turley	.213
Sam Jones	.224
Whitey Ford	.228
Allie Reynolds	.230
Hoyt Wilhelm	.231
Early Wynn	.233
Jack Harshman	.235
Billy Pierce	.236
Vinegar Bend Mizell	.238
Mickey McDermott	.239

Opponent OBP
(minimum 1,000 Innings Pitched)

Robin Roberts	.282
Warren Spahn	.293
Don Newcombe	.295
Warren Hacker	.298
Harvey Haddix	.299
Billy Pierce	.303
Johnny Antonelli	.306
Steve Gromek	.307
Lew Burdette	.307
Bob Rush	.307

Single Season Batting Leaders—1950-1959

Games

Carl Furillo	1951	158
Gil Hodges	1951	158
Ralph Kiner	1953	158
13 tied with		157

At-Bats

Harvey Kuenn	1953	679
Carl Furillo	1951	667
Harvey Kuenn	1954	656
Don Blasingame	1957	650
Nellie Fox	1956	649
Nellie Fox	1952	648
Red Schoendienst	1957	648
Vada Pinson	1959	648
Al Dark	1953	647
Al Dark	1951	646

Runs

Duke Snider	1953	132
Mickey Mantle	1956	132
Dom DiMaggio	1950	131
Vada Pinson	1959	131
Mickey Mantle	1954	129
Stan Musial	1953	127
Mickey Mantle	1958	127
Al Dark	1953	126
Duke Snider	1955	126
4 tied with		125

Hits

Hank Aaron	1959	223
Richie Ashburn	1951	221
George Kell	1950	218
Richie Ashburn	1958	215
Don Mueller	1954	212
Harvey Kuenn	1953	209
Willie Mays	1958	208
4 tied with		205

Doubles

George Kell	1950	56
Stan Musial	1953	53
Vada Pinson	1959	47
Hank Aaron	1959	46
Red Schoendienst	1950	43
Ferris Fain	1952	43
Mickey Vernon	1953	43
Willie Mays	1959	43
Stan Musial	1952	42
Harvey Kuenn	1959	42

Triples

Willie Mays	1957	20
Minnie Minoso	1954	18
Jim Gilliam	1953	17
Jim Rivera	1953	16
Pete Runnels	1954	15
Bill Bruton	1956	15
6 tied with		14

Home Runs

Mickey Mantle	1956	52
Willie Mays	1955	51
Ted Kluszewski	1954	49
Ralph Kiner	1950	47
Eddie Mathews	1953	47
Ted Kluszewski	1955	47
Ernie Banks	1958	47
Eddie Mathews	1959	46
Ernie Banks	1959	45
2 tied with		44

Home Runs (Home)

Ted Kluszewski	1954	34
Ernie Banks	1958	30
Ralph Kiner	1950	27
Mickey Mantle	1956	27
Ralph Kiner	1951	26
Ernie Banks	1955	26
Roy Sievers	1957	26
Frank Robinson	1959	26
5 tied with		25

Home Runs (Road)

Eddie Mathews	1953	30
Willie Mays	1955	29
Hank Aaron	1957	26
Ted Williams	1957	26
Frank Thomas	1958	26
Eddie Mathews	1959	26
Ted Kluszewski	1955	25
Mickey Mantle	1956	25
Gil Hodges	1951	24
Eddie Mathews	1954	24

Extra Base Hits

Stan Musial	1953	92
Hank Aaron	1959	92
Duke Snider	1954	89
Willie Mays	1954	87
Eddie Mathews	1953	86
Stan Musial	1954	85
Duke Snider	1953	84
Ernie Banks	1957	83
4 tied with		82

Total Bases

Hank Aaron	1959	400
Willie Mays	1955	382
Ernie Banks	1958	379
Duke Snider	1954	378
Willie Mays	1954	377
Mickey Mantle	1956	376
Duke Snider	1953	370
Hank Aaron	1957	369
Ted Kluszewski	1954	368
Al Rosen	1953	367

RBI

Al Rosen	1953	145
Walt Dropo	1950	144
Vern Stephens	1950	144
Ernie Banks	1959	143
Roy Campanella	1953	142
Ted Kluszewski	1954	141
Duke Snider	1955	136
Eddie Mathews	1953	135
Hank Aaron	1957	132
3 tied with		130

Walks

Eddie Yost	1956	151
Mickey Mantle	1957	146
Eddie Stanky	1950	144
Ted Williams	1951	144
Eddie Yost	1950	141
Ralph Kiner	1951	137
Ted Williams	1954	136
Eddie Yost	1959	135
Ferris Fain	1950	133
Eddie Yost	1954	131

Walks/PA

(minimum 3.1 PA/Tm Gm)

Ted Williams	1954	.259
Mickey Mantle	1957	.234
Eddie Yost	1956	.221
Ted Williams	1957	.218
Ted Williams	1951	.213
Eddie Stanky	1950	.208
Ralph Kiner	1951	.204
Elmer Valo	1952	.204
Ted Williams	1956	.203
Ferris Fain	1950	.202

Strikeouts

Jim Lemon	1956	138
Mickey Mantle	1959	126
Steve Bilko	1953	125
Wally Post	1956	124
Larry Doby	1953	121
Mickey Mantle	1958	120
Jim Lemon	1958	120
Woodie Held	1959	118
Harmon Killebrew	1959	116
Eddie Mathews	1952	115

Hit By Pitch

Minnie Minoso	1956	23
Minnie Minoso	1957	21
Solly Hemus	1952	20
Frank Robinson	1956	20
Minnie Minoso	1953	17
Nellie Fox	1955	17
Minnie Minoso	1959	17
4 tied with		16

Sac Hits

Roy McMillan	1954	31
Johnny Logan	1956	31
Phil Rizzuto	1951	26
Phil Rizzuto	1952	23
Charlie Neal	1959	21
Nellie Fox	1951	20
8 tied with		19

Sac Flies

Gil Hodges	1954	19
Johnny Temple	1959	13
Jackie Jensen	1955	12
Jimmy Piersall	1956	12
Frank Thomas	1957	12
Jackie Jensen	1959	12
9 tied with		11

Stolen Bases

Luis Aparicio	1959	56
Willie Mays	1956	40
Willie Mays	1957	38
Sam Jethroe	1950	35
Sam Jethroe	1951	35
Bill Bruton	1954	34
Minnie Minoso	1951	31
Willie Mays	1958	31
Pee Wee Reese	1952	30
Richie Ashburn	1958	30

Caught Stealing

Willie Mays	1957	19
Ken Boyer	1955	17
Jim Rivera	1955	17
Minnie Minoso	1952	16
Minnie Minoso	1953	16
Jim Rivera	1953	15
Jim Gilliam	1955	15
Minnie Minoso	1957	15
Don Hoak	1957	15
Don Blasingame	1959	15

Runs Created

Mickey Mantle	1956	174
Mickey Mantle	1957	155
Duke Snider	1953	148
Stan Musial	1951	147
Willie Mays	1955	146
Eddie Mathews	1953	145
Stan Musial	1953	145
Ralph Kiner	1951	144
Ted Williams	1951	144
3 tied with		143

Runs Created/27 Outs

(minimum 3.1 PA/Tm Gm)

Ted Williams	1957	14.38
Mickey Mantle	1957	13.54
Mickey Mantle	1956	13.20
Ted Williams	1954	11.85
Ted Williams	1951	10.42
Stan Musial	1951	10.30
Ted Williams	1956	10.28
Ralph Kiner	1951	10.28
Mickey Mantle	1955	9.91
Mickey Mantle	1958	9.78

Batting Average

(minimum 3.1 PA/Tm Gm)

Ted Williams	1957	.388
Mickey Mantle	1957	.365
Stan Musial	1951	.355
Hank Aaron	1959	.355
Billy Goodman	1950	.354
Harvey Kuenn	1959	.353
Mickey Mantle	1956	.353
Stan Musial	1957	.351
Richie Ashburn	1958	.350
Willie Mays	1958	.347

On-Base Percentage

(minimum 3.1 PA/Tm Gm)

Ted Williams	1957	.526
Ted Williams	1954	.513
Mickey Mantle	1957	.512
Ted Williams	1956	.479
Mickey Mantle	1956	.464
Ted Williams	1951	.464
Eddie Stanky	1950	.460
Ted Williams	1958	.458
Joe Cunningham	1959	.453
Ralph Kiner	1951	.452

Slugging Percentage

(minimum 3.1 PA/Tm Gm)

Ted Williams	1957	.731
Mickey Mantle	1956	.705
Willie Mays	1954	.667
Mickey Mantle	1957	.665
Willie Mays	1955	.659
Duke Snider	1954	.647
Ted Kluszewski	1954	.642
Hank Aaron	1959	.636
Ted Williams	1954	.635
Duke Snider	1955	.628

OBP+Slugging

(minimum 3.1 PA/Tm Gm)

Ted Williams	1957	1.257
Mickey Mantle	1957	1.177
Mickey Mantle	1956	1.169
Ted Williams	1954	1.148
Ted Williams	1956	1.084
Ralph Kiner	1951	1.079
Willie Mays	1954	1.078
Duke Snider	1954	1.071
Stan Musial	1951	1.063
Willie Mays	1955	1.059

Secondary Average

(minimum 3.1 PA/Tm Gm)

Ted Williams	1954	.642
Mickey Mantle	1957	.641
Ted Williams	1957	.626
Mickey Mantle	1956	.582
Ralph Kiner	1951	.580
Eddie Mathews	1954	.571
Mickey Mantle	1958	.570
Ralph Kiner	1950	.545
Mickey Mantle	1955	.540
Eddie Mathews	1955	.537

Isolated Power

(minimum 3.1 PA/Tm Gm)

Mickey Mantle	1956	.353
Ted Williams	1957	.343
Willie Mays	1955	.340
Eddie Mathews	1953	.325
Willie Mays	1954	.322
Duke Snider	1955	.320
Ralph Kiner	1951	.318
Ralph Kiner	1950	.318
Rocky Colavito	1958	.317
Ted Kluszewski	1954	.316

Single Season Pitching Leaders—1950-1959

Wins

Robin Roberts	1952	28
Don Newcombe	1956	27
Bobby Shantz	1952	24
10 tied with		23

Losses

Art Ditmar	1956	22
Robin Roberts	1957	22
Murry Dickson	1952	21
Don Larsen	1954	21
7 tied with		20

Winning Percentage
(minimum 15 decisions)

Roy Face	1959	.947
Preacher Roe	1951	.880
Sandy Consuegra	1954	.842
Hoyt Wilhelm	1952	.833
Sal Maglie	1950	.818
Bob Feller	1954	.813
Robin Roberts	1952	.800
Ed Lopat	1953	.800
Don Newcombe	1955	.800
Don Newcombe	1956	.794

Games

Jim Konstanty	1950	74
Hoyt Wilhelm	1952	71
Ellis Kinder	1953	69
Don Elston	1958	69
Hoyt Wilhelm	1953	68
Roy Face	1956	68
Turk Lown	1957	67
Gerry Staley	1959	67
3 tied with		65

Games Started

Bob Friend	1956	42
Robin Roberts	1953	41
Robin Roberts	1950	39
Vern Bickford	1950	39
Warren Spahn	1950	39
Robin Roberts	1951	39
Ron Kline	1956	39
Lew Burdette	1959	39
6 tied with		38

Complete Games

Robin Roberts	1953	33
Robin Roberts	1952	30
Robin Roberts	1954	29
Bob Lemon	1952	28
Vern Bickford	1950	27
Bobby Shantz	1952	27
Warren Spahn	1951	26
Robin Roberts	1955	26
Johnny Sain	1950	25
Warren Spahn	1950	25

Shutouts

Bob Porterfield	1953	9
Allie Reynolds	1951	7
Warren Spahn	1951	7
Billy Pierce	1953	7
Billy Hoeft	1955	7
Whitey Ford	1958	7
14 tied with		6

Saves

Ellis Kinder	1953	27
Jim Hughes	1954	24
Jim Konstanty	1950	22
Johnny Sain	1954	22
Frank Smith	1954	20
Ryne Duren	1958	20
Roy Face	1958	20
4 tied with		19

Games Finished

Jim Konstanty	1950	62
Ellis Kinder	1953	51
Don McMahon	1959	49
Don Elston	1959	49
Hersh Freeman	1956	47
Turk Lown	1956	47
Clem Labine	1956	47
Turk Lown	1957	47
Lindy McDaniel	1959	47
Roy Face	1959	47

Batters Faced

Robin Roberts	1953	1,412
Robin Roberts	1954	1,331
Vern Bickford	1950	1,325
Bob Friend	1956	1,315
Robin Roberts	1952	1,310
Warren Spahn	1951	1,289
Robin Roberts	1951	1,274
Frank Lary	1956	1,269
Robin Roberts	1955	1,256
Bob Lemon	1950	1,254

Innings Pitched

Robin Roberts	1953	346.2
Robin Roberts	1954	336.2
Robin Roberts	1952	330.0
Robin Roberts	1951	315.0
Bob Friend	1956	314.1
Vern Bickford	1950	311.2
Warren Spahn	1951	310.2
Bob Lemon	1952	309.2
Robin Roberts	1955	305.0
Robin Roberts	1950	304.1

Hits Allowed

Robin Roberts	1956	328
Robin Roberts	1953	324
Lew Burdette	1959	312
Bob Friend	1956	310
Bob Friend	1958	299
Johnny Sain	1950	294
Murry Dickson	1951	294
Vern Bickford	1950	293
Robin Roberts	1952	292
Robin Roberts	1955	292

Runs Allowed

Alex Kellner	1950	157
Herm Wehmeier	1950	157
Harry Byrd	1953	155
Robin Roberts	1956	155
Murry Dickson	1951	151
Bob Lemon	1950	144
Lew Burdette	1959	144
Art Ditmar	1956	141
Chuck Stobbs	1957	140
2 tied with		139

Earned Runs Allowed

Robin Roberts	1956	147
Herm Wehmeier	1950	145
Harry Byrd	1953	145
Alex Kellner	1950	137
Lew Burdette	1959	131
Murry Dickson	1951	129
Chuck Stobbs	1957	126
Early Wynn	1957	126
Art Ditmar	1956	125
Paul Foytack	1959	124

Home Runs Allowed

Robin Roberts	1956	46
Pedro Ramos	1957	43
Robin Roberts	1955	41
Robin Roberts	1957	40
Warren Hacker	1955	38
Pedro Ramos	1958	38
Lew Burdette	1959	38
Jim Bunning	1959	37
3 tied with		35

Walks

Sam Jones	1955	185
Bob Turley	1954	181
Bob Turley	1955	177
Tommy Byrne	1950	160
Herb Score	1955	154
Tommy Byrne	1951	150
Bob Lemon	1950	146
Paul Foytack	1956	142
Johnny Lindell	1953	139
Allie Reynolds	1950	138

Intentional Walks

Bob Friend	1956	18
Robin Roberts	1957	16
Roy Face	1956	15
Ron Kline	1958	14
Johnny Klippstein	1956	13
George Zuverink	1957	13
Mike McCormick	1959	13
Stu Miller	1959	13
7 tied with		12

Strikeouts

Herb Score	1956	263
Herb Score	1955	245
Don Drysdale	1959	242
Sam Jones	1958	225
Bob Turley	1955	210
Sam Jones	1959	209
Jim Bunning	1959	201
Robin Roberts	1953	198
Sam Jones	1955	198
Billy Pierce	1956	192

Strikeouts/9 Innings
(minimum 1 Inning Pitched/Tm Gm)

Herb Score	1955	9.70
Herb Score	1956	9.49
Sam Jones	1956	8.40
Herb Score	1959	8.23
Sam Jones	1958	8.10
Don Drysdale	1959	8.05
Bob Turley	1957	7.76
Camilo Pascual	1956	7.73
Bob Turley	1955	7.66
Sam Jones	1957	7.59

ERA
(minimum 1 Inning Pitched/Tm Gm)

Billy Pierce	1955	1.97
Whitey Ford	1958	2.01
Allie Reynolds	1952	2.06
Warren Spahn	1953	2.10
Hoyt Wilhelm	1959	2.19
Johnny Antonelli	1954	2.30
Mike Garcia	1952	2.37
Ed Lopat	1953	2.42
Hoyt Wilhelm	1952	2.43
Bobby Shantz	1957	2.45

Component ERA
(minimum 1 Inning Pitched/Tm Gm)

Warren Spahn	1953	2.19
Bob Lemon	1952	2.28
Mike Garcia	1954	2.30
Robin Roberts	1952	2.31
Bobby Shantz	1952	2.39
Art Ditmar	1959	2.39
Whitey Ford	1958	2.40
Joe Dobson	1952	2.42
Don Newcombe	1956	2.42
Camilo Pascual	1959	2.45

Sac Hits Allowed

Sid Hudson	1950	26
Lou Brissie	1950	24
Early Wynn	1952	22
Bob Feller	1952	22
Curt Simmons	1954	21
Early Wynn	1951	20
Max Surkont	1954	20
5 tied with		19

Sac Flies Allowed

Arnie Portocarrero	1954	17
Johnny Klippstein	1954	13
Bob Miller	1954	13
Bob Lemon	1954	13
Billy O'Dell	1958	13
8 tied with		12

Hit Batsmen

Don Drysdale	1959	18
Tommy Byrne	1950	17
Gerry Staley	1953	17
Tommy Byrne	1951	15
Bob Cain	1951	14
Ray Scarborough	1951	14
Harry Byrd	1953	14
Sam Jones	1955	14
Don Drysdale	1958	14
Danny McDevitt	1959	14

Wild Pitches

Sandy Koufax	1958	17
Milt Pappas	1959	14
Herb Score	1959	14
Johnny Klippstein	1952	12
Herb Score	1955	12
Jack Sanford	1957	12
5 tied with		11

Balks

Vic Raschi	1950	6
Max Lanier	1950	5
Mickey McDermott	1950	4
Vic Lombardi	1950	4
Ralph Branca	1950	4
Dick Starr	1951	4
Bill Wight	1952	4
20 tied with		3

Opponent Average
(minimum 1 Inning Pitched/Tm Gm)

Herb Score	1956	.186
Bob Turley	1955	.193
Bob Turley	1957	.194
Herb Score	1955	.194
Bob Turley	1954	.203
Don Larsen	1956	.204
Bob Turley	1958	.206
Sam Jones	1955	.206
Whitey Ford	1955	.208
Bob Lemon	1952	.208

Opponent OBP
(minimum 1 Inning Pitched/Tm Gm)

Warren Hacker	1952	.247
Don Newcombe	1956	.257
Robin Roberts	1952	.263
Robin Roberts	1954	.266
Art Ditmar	1959	.268
Warren Spahn	1953	.270
Harvey Haddix	1959	.271
Larry Jansen	1950	.271
Bobby Shantz	1952	.272
Johnny Podres	1957	.273

Batting Leaders—1960-1969

Games

Brooks Robinson	1,578
Hank Aaron	1,540
Ron Santo	1,536
Vada Pinson	1,516
Maury Wills	1,507
Willie Mays	1,498
Curt Flood	1,496
Ernie Banks	1,495
Luis Aparicio	1,494
Frank Robinson	1,468

At-Bats

Brooks Robinson	6,093
Maury Wills	6,091
Vada Pinson	6,086
Luis Aparicio	5,975
Hank Aaron	5,912
Roberto Clemente	5,723
Curt Flood	5,688
Billy Williams	5,662
Ron Santo	5,658
Ernie Banks	5,554

Runs

Hank Aaron	1,091
Willie Mays	1,050
Frank Robinson	1,013
Roberto Clemente	916
Vada Pinson	885
Maury Wills	874
Harmon Killebrew	864
Billy Williams	861
Ron Santo	816
Al Kaline	811

Hits

Roberto Clemente	1,877
Hank Aaron	1,819
Vada Pinson	1,776
Maury Wills	1,744
Brooks Robinson	1,692
Curt Flood	1,690
Billy Williams	1,651
Willie Mays	1,635
Frank Robinson	1,603
Ron Santo	1,592

Doubles

Carl Yastrzemski	318
Vada Pinson	310
Frank Robinson	309
Hank Aaron	309
Brooks Robinson	297
Orlando Cepeda	268
Johnny Callison	265
Billy Williams	263
Felipe Alou	260
2 tied with	259

Triples

Roberto Clemente	99
Vada Pinson	93
Lou Brock	85
Johnny Callison	84
Billy Williams	69
Willie Davis	68
Jim Fregosi	64
Zoilo Versalles	63
Maury Wills	62
Dick Allen	60

Home Runs

Harmon Killebrew	393
Hank Aaron	375
Willie Mays	350
Frank Robinson	316
Willie McCovey	300
Frank Howard	288
Norm Cash	278
Ernie Banks	269
Mickey Mantle	256
Orlando Cepeda	254

Home Runs (Home)

Harmon Killebrew	202
Hank Aaron	189
Willie Mays	178
Frank Robinson	169
Norm Cash	166
Ron Santo	160
Willie McCovey	158
Ernie Banks	148
Billy Williams	143
Frank Howard	137

Home Runs (Road)

Harmon Killebrew	191
Hank Aaron	186
Willie Mays	172
Frank Howard	151
Frank Robinson	147
Willie McCovey	142
Orlando Cepeda	133
Mickey Mantle	129
Ernie Banks	121
2 tied with	119

Extra Base Hits

Hank Aaron	729
Frank Robinson	669
Willie Mays	662
Harmon Killebrew	593
Billy Williams	581
Vada Pinson	578
Carl Yastrzemski	557
Ron Santo	554
Ernie Banks	552
Orlando Cepeda	540

Total Bases

Hank Aaron	3,343
Willie Mays	3,050
Frank Robinson	2,948
Roberto Clemente	2,865
Billy Williams	2,799
Vada Pinson	2,797
Harmon Killebrew	2,727
Ron Santo	2,706
Brooks Robinson	2,647
Ernie Banks	2,590

RBI

Hank Aaron	1,107
Harmon Killebrew	1,013
Frank Robinson	1,011
Willie Mays	1,003
Ron Santo	937
Ernie Banks	925
Orlando Cepeda	896
Roberto Clemente	862
Billy Williams	853
Brooks Robinson	836

Walks

Harmon Killebrew	970
Mickey Mantle	841
Norm Cash	778
Frank Robinson	778
Ron Santo	768
Carl Yastrzemski	751
Bob Allison	719
Eddie Mathews	718
Willie Mays	681
Rocky Colavito	676

Walks/PA
(minimum 3,000 Plate Appearances)

Mickey Mantle	.187
Harmon Killebrew	.161
Eddie Mathews	.145
Norm Siebern	.141
Bob Allison	.139
Jim Gentile	.137
Norm Cash	.136
Jimmy Wynn	.135
Willie McCovey	.130
Jim Gilliam	.127

Strikeouts

Frank Howard	1,103
Harmon Killebrew	1,029
Lou Brock	946
Donn Clendenon	934
Bob Allison	916
Ron Santo	896
Johnny Callison	854
Dick Allen	851
Leo Cardenas	824
Mickey Mantle	811

Hit By Pitch

Frank Robinson	113
Ron Hunt	101
Orlando Cepeda	81
Bill Freehan	72
Mack Jones	62
Tony Gonzalez	59
Norm Cash	58
Tony Taylor	55
Lou Johnson	53
Felipe Alou	51

Sac Hits

Maury Wills	94
Luis Aparicio	88
Jim Davenport	84
Bobby Richardson	81
Julian Javier	76
Hal Lanier	72
Nellie Fox	72
Wes Parker	68
Curt Flood	68
Jim Fregosi	67

Sac Flies

Brooks Robinson	75
Ron Santo	69
Hank Aaron	64
Ernie Banks	61
Frank Robinson	53
Bill Mazeroski	52
Vada Pinson	50
Orlando Cepeda	50
Willie Davis	47
Tommy Davis	47

Stolen Bases

Maury Wills	535
Lou Brock	387
Luis Aparicio	342
Bert Campaneris	292
Willie Davis	240
Tommy Harper	208
Hank Aaron	204
Vada Pinson	202
Don Buford	161
Tony Taylor	157

Caught Stealing

Maury Wills	183
Lou Brock	126
Luis Aparicio	94
Don Buford	87
Willie Davis	86
Vada Pinson	81
Bert Campaneris	77
Tony Taylor	73
Pete Rose	60
Hank Aaron	60

Runs Created

Hank Aaron	1,215
Frank Robinson	1,148
Willie Mays	1,142
Harmon Killebrew	1,051
Roberto Clemente	984
Ron Santo	970
Billy Williams	965
Carl Yastrzemski	927
Vada Pinson	925
Norm Cash	921

Runs Created/27 Outs
(minimum 3,000 Plate Appearances)

Mickey Mantle	8.45
Frank Robinson	7.95
Willie Mays	7.64
Dick Allen	7.58
Hank Aaron	7.54
Willie McCovey	7.49
Harmon Killebrew	7.40
Norm Cash	6.80
Al Kaline	6.79
Roberto Clemente	6.51

Batting Average
(minimum 3,000 Plate Appearances)

Roberto Clemente	.328
Matty Alou	.312
Pete Rose	.309
Tony Oliva	.308
Hank Aaron	.308
Frank Robinson	.304
Dick Allen	.300
Willie Mays	.300
Curt Flood	.297
Tommy Davis	.296

On-Base Percentage
(minimum 3,000 Plate Appearances)

Mickey Mantle	.415
Frank Robinson	.402
Harmon Killebrew	.387
Carl Yastrzemski	.383
Al Kaline	.381
Norm Cash	.380
Dick Allen	.380
Willie McCovey	.378
Willie Mays	.377
Hank Aaron	.376

Slugging Percentage
(minimum 3,000 Plate Appearances)

Hank Aaron	.565
Frank Robinson	.560
Willie Mays	.559
Dick Allen	.554
Harmon Killebrew	.546
Willie McCovey	.546
Mickey Mantle	.542
Frank Howard	.508
Orlando Cepeda	.502
Willie Stargell	.501

OBP+Slugging
(minimum 3,000 Plate Appearances)

Frank Robinson	.962
Mickey Mantle	.957
Hank Aaron	.941
Willie Mays	.935
Dick Allen	.933
Harmon Killebrew	.933
Willie McCovey	.923
Norm Cash	.878
Roberto Clemente	.875
Al Kaline	.875

Secondary Average
(minimum 3,000 Plate Appearances)

Mickey Mantle	.507
Harmon Killebrew	.476
Frank Robinson	.431
Willie McCovey	.423
Willie Mays	.407
Hank Aaron	.406
Dick Allen	.405
Bob Allison	.400
Jimmy Wynn	.396
Norm Cash	.393

Isolated Power
(minimum 3,000 Plate Appearances)

Harmon Killebrew	.280
Willie McCovey	.266
Mickey Mantle	.259
Willie Mays	.259
Hank Aaron	.258
Frank Robinson	.255
Dick Allen	.254
Frank Howard	.232
Jim Gentile	.228
Roger Maris	.228

Pitching Leaders—1960-1969

Wins

Juan Marichal	191
Bob Gibson	164
Don Drysdale	158
Jim Bunning	150
Jim Kaat	142
Larry Jackson	141
Sandy Koufax	137
Jim Maloney	134
Milt Pappas	131
Camilo Pascual	127

Losses

Jack Fisher	133
Dick Ellsworth	132
Larry Jackson	132
Don Drysdale	126
Claude Osteen	121
Jim Kaat	119
Jim Bunning	118
Don Cardwell	111
Bob Gibson	105
Ken Johnson	105

Winning Percentage
(minimum 100 decisions)

Sandy Koufax	.695
Juan Marichal	.685
Whitey Ford	.673
Denny McLain	.667
Jim Maloney	.626
Dave McNally	.621
Bob Gibson	.610
Ray Culp	.596
Bob Purkey	.593
Ralph Terry	.582

Games

Ron Perranoski	589
Lindy McDaniel	558
Hoyt Wilhelm	557
Don McMahon	547
Roy Face	524
Ron Kline	519
Eddie Fisher	468
Stu Miller	468
Bob Miller	450
2 tied with	445

Games Started

Jim Bunning	360
Don Drysdale	359
Larry Jackson	321
Juan Marichal	320
Jim Kaat	316
Dick Ellsworth	308
Bob Gibson	302
Milt Pappas	302
Claude Osteen	287
Earl Wilson	281

Complete Games

Juan Marichal	197
Bob Gibson	164
Don Drysdale	135
Sandy Koufax	122
Larry Jackson	116
Jim Bunning	108
Jim Kaat	102
Warren Spahn	95
Denny McLain	93
Camilo Pascual	93

Shutouts

Juan Marichal	45
Bob Gibson	41
Don Drysdale	40
Sandy Koufax	37
Jim Bunning	35
Dean Chance	32
Jim Maloney	30
Larry Jackson	30
Milt Pappas	28
2 tied with	26

Saves

Hoyt Wilhelm	152
Roy Face	142
Ron Perranoski	138
Stu Miller	138
Dick Radatz	122
Lindy McDaniel	112
Ted Abernathy	106
John Wyatt	103
Ron Kline	103
Al Worthington	98

Games Finished

Hoyt Wilhelm	392
Roy Face	387
Ron Perranoski	362
Lindy McDaniel	335
Stu Miller	328
Ron Kline	312
Dick Radatz	297
Ted Abernathy	292
John Wyatt	291
Don McMahon	291

Batters Faced

Don Drysdale	10,718
Jim Bunning	10,670
Juan Marichal	10,212
Bob Gibson	10,047
Larry Jackson	9,664
Jim Kaat	9,322
Dick Ellsworth	8,823
Claude Osteen	8,595
Milt Pappas	8,395
Jack Fisher	8,077

Innings Pitched

Don Drysdale	2,629.2
Jim Bunning	2,590.1
Juan Marichal	2,550.0
Bob Gibson	2,447.0
Larry Jackson	2,335.2
Jim Kaat	2,223.2
Dick Ellsworth	2,079.1
Claude Osteen	2,077.0
Milt Pappas	2,033.2
Dean Chance	1,900.2

Hits Allowed

Don Drysdale	2,341
Jim Bunning	2,338
Larry Jackson	2,264
Dick Ellsworth	2,188
Juan Marichal	2,161
Jim Kaat	2,156
Claude Osteen	2,034
Jack Fisher	1,985
Bob Gibson	1,984
Milt Pappas	1,893

Runs Allowed

Dick Ellsworth	993
Jack Fisher	988
Larry Jackson	988
Jim Bunning	984
Jim Kaat	983
Don Drysdale	961
Ray Sadecki	884
Mudcat Grant	862
Juan Marichal	861
Bob Gibson	847

Earned Runs Allowed

Jim Bunning	867
Jack Fisher	861
Dick Ellsworth	853
Larry Jackson	853
Don Drysdale	827
Jim Kaat	809
Ray Sadecki	773
Milt Pappas	759
Mudcat Grant	758
Bob Gibson	746

Home Runs Allowed

Jim Bunning	230
Mudcat Grant	228
Juan Marichal	223
Earl Wilson	214
Don Drysdale	207
Jim Kaat	204
Milt Pappas	199
Bill Monbouquette	192
Dick Ellsworth	189
Mike McCormick	187

Walks

Steve Barber	834
Bob Gibson	822
Sam McDowell	788
Jim Maloney	771
Bob Veale	714
Earl Wilson	714
Gary Bell	664
Ray Sadecki	662
Tony Cloninger	652
2 tied with	628

Intentional Walks

Ron Perranoski	108
Don Drysdale	102
Stu Miller	80
Lindy McDaniel	79
Gaylord Perry	77
Ron Kline	76
Claude Osteen	73
Mike McCormick	72
Bob Miller	69
2 tied with	68

Strikeouts

Bob Gibson	2,071
Jim Bunning	2,019
Don Drysdale	1,910
Sandy Koufax	1,910
Juan Marichal	1,840
Sam McDowell	1,663
Jim Maloney	1,585
Jim Kaat	1,435
Bob Veale	1,428
Camilo Pascual	1,391

Strikeouts/9 Innings
(minimum 1,000 Innings Pitched)

Sandy Koufax	9.51
Sam McDowell	9.41
Bob Veale	7.98
Jim Maloney	7.92
Mickey Lolich	7.87
Luis Tiant	7.81
Bob Gibson	7.62
Fergie Jenkins	7.56
Al Downing	7.49
Sonny Siebert	7.12

ERA
(minimum 1,000 Innings Pitched)

Hoyt Wilhelm	2.16
Sandy Koufax	2.36
Juan Marichal	2.57
Bob Gibson	2.74
Mike Cuellar	2.76
Dean Chance	2.77
Tommy John	2.81
Joe Horlen	2.83
Bob Veale	2.83
Don Drysdale	2.83

Component ERA
(minimum 1,000 Innings Pitched)

Hoyt Wilhelm	1.98
Sandy Koufax	2.05
Juan Marichal	2.44
Fergie Jenkins	2.64
Mike Cuellar	2.64
Bob Gibson	2.70
Dean Chance	2.72
Sonny Siebert	2.75
Denny McLain	2.79
Gaylord Perry	2.79

Sac Hits Allowed

Jim Bunning	126
Claude Osteen	108
Bob Gibson	101
Steve Barber	98
Dick Ellsworth	98
Ken Johnson	96
Turk Farrell	92
Larry Jackson	90
Ray Sadecki	88
Don Drysdale	88

Sac Flies Allowed

Ray Sadecki	62
Jim Kaat	60
Jim Perry	59
Don Drysdale	55
Earl Wilson	51
Tony Cloninger	50
Turk Farrell	50
Bob Gibson	49
Milt Pappas	49
Claude Osteen	49

Hit Batsmen

Don Drysdale	112
Jim Bunning	111
Don Cardwell	84
Jim Kaat	81
Bob Gibson	75
Mickey Lolich	60
Dave Wickersham	56
Dean Chance	55
Ken Johnson	54
Bobby Bolin	53

Wild Pitches

Jim Maloney	120
Tony Cloninger	111
Sam McDowell	84
Jim Kaat	82
Earl Wilson	78
Bob Veale	77
Ray Sadecki	75
Jack Hamilton	74
Steve Barber	72
Denny Lemaster	69

Balks

Jack Sanford	18
Juan Marichal	13
Bob Shaw	12
George Brunet	11
Jim O'Toole	10
Roger Craig	10
Tony Cloninger	9
Bob Veale	8
Phil Ortega	8
11 tied with	7

Opponent Average
(minimum 1,000 Innings Pitched)

Sandy Koufax	.198
Hoyt Wilhelm	.201
Sam McDowell	.209
Luis Tiant	.214
Sonny Siebert	.218
Bob Gibson	.220
Jim Maloney	.221
Denny McLain	.221
Al Downing	.223
Fergie Jenkins	.226

Opponent OBP
(minimum 1,000 Innings Pitched)

Sandy Koufax	.256
Hoyt Wilhelm	.261
Juan Marichal	.266
Fergie Jenkins	.276
Denny McLain	.278
Ralph Terry	.283
Eddie Fisher	.284
Sonny Siebert	.286
Mike Cuellar	.286
Luis Tiant	.287

Single Season Batting Leaders—1960-1969

Games

Maury Wills	1962	165
Jose Pagan	1962	164
Ron Santo	1965	164
Billy Williams	1965	164
Cesar Tovar	1967	164
12 tied with		163

At-Bats

Matty Alou	1969	698
Maury Wills	1962	695
Bobby Richardson	1962	692
Lou Brock	1967	689
Curt Flood	1964	679
Bobby Richardson	1964	679
Dick Groat	1962	678
Tony Oliva	1964	672
Pete Rose	1965	670
Vada Pinson	1965	669

Runs

Frank Robinson	1962	134
Roger Maris	1961	132
Mickey Mantle	1961	132
Maury Wills	1962	130
Willie Mays	1962	130
Rocky Colavito	1961	129
Willie Mays	1961	129
Hank Aaron	1962	127
Tommy Harper	1965	126
Zoilo Versalles	1965	126

Hits

Matty Alou	1969	231
Tommy Davis	1962	230
Felipe Alou	1966	218
Pete Rose	1969	218
Tony Oliva	1964	217
Curt Flood	1964	211
Roberto Clemente	1964	211
Pete Rose	1968	210
Felipe Alou	1968	210
3 tied with		209

Doubles

Frank Robinson	1962	51
Lou Brock	1968	46
Floyd Robinson	1962	45
Carl Yastrzemski	1965	45
Zoilo Versalles	1965	45
Lee Maye	1964	44
Rusty Staub	1967	44
Carl Yastrzemski	1962	43
Dick Groat	1963	43
Tony Oliva	1964	43

Triples

Johnny Callison	1965	16
Gino Cimoli	1962	15
Jake Wood	1961	14
Vada Pinson	1963	14
Dick Allen	1965	14
Donn Clendenon	1965	14
Roberto Clemente	1965	14
Lou Brock	1968	14
7 tied with		13

Home Runs

Roger Maris	1961	61
Mickey Mantle	1961	54
Willie Mays	1965	52
Willie Mays	1962	49
Harmon Killebrew	1964	49
Frank Robinson	1966	49
Harmon Killebrew	1969	49
Harmon Killebrew	1962	48
Frank Howard	1969	48
2 tied with		47

Home Runs (Home)

Roger Maris	1961	30
Harmon Killebrew	1961	29
Willie Mays	1962	28
Harmon Killebrew	1969	28
Frank Robinson	1966	27
Carl Yastrzemski	1967	27
Frank Howard	1969	27
4 tied with		26

Home Runs (Road)

Roger Maris	1961	31
Jim Gentile	1961	30
Mickey Mantle	1961	30
Harmon Killebrew	1962	28
Willie Mays	1965	28
Rocky Colavito	1961	27
Hank Aaron	1962	27
Roger Maris	1960	26
Frank Howard	1968	26
2 tied with		25

Extra Base Hits

Frank Robinson	1962	92
Willie Mays	1962	90
Reggie Jackson	1969	86
Frank Robinson	1966	85
Tony Oliva	1964	84
Hank Aaron	1961	83
Roger Maris	1961	81
Ernie Banks	1960	80
Dick Allen	1964	80
4 tied with		79

Total Bases

Willie Mays	1962	382
Frank Robinson	1962	380
Tony Oliva	1964	374
Hank Aaron	1963	370
Frank Robinson	1966	367
Roger Maris	1961	366
Hank Aaron	1962	366
Willie Mays	1965	360
Carl Yastrzemski	1967	360
Hank Aaron	1961	358

RBI

Tommy Davis	1962	153
Orlando Cepeda	1961	142
Roger Maris	1961	142
Jim Gentile	1961	141
Willie Mays	1962	141
Rocky Colavito	1961	140
Harmon Killebrew	1969	140
Frank Robinson	1962	136
Norm Cash	1961	132
2 tied with		130

Walks

Jimmy Wynn	1969	148
Harmon Killebrew	1969	145
Harmon Killebrew	1967	131
Mickey Mantle	1961	126
Eddie Yost	1960	125
Norm Cash	1961	124
Eddie Mathews	1963	124
Mickey Mantle	1962	122
Willie McCovey	1969	121
Carl Yastrzemski	1968	119

Walks/PA

(minimum 3.1 PA/Tm Gm)

Jimmy Wynn	1969	.227
Harmon Killebrew	1969	.205
Eddie Yost	1960	.197
Mickey Mantle	1961	.195
Willie McCovey	1969	.194
Mickey Mantle	1968	.194
Mickey Mantle	1967	.193
Harmon Killebrew	1967	.190
Norm Cash	1961	.185
Eddie Mathews	1963	.184

Strikeouts

Bobby Bonds	1969	187
Dave Nicholson	1963	175
Reggie Jackson	1968	171
Donn Clendenon	1968	163
Dick Allen	1968	161
Frank Howard	1967	155
George Scott	1966	152
Larry Hisle	1969	152
Don Lock	1963	151
Dick Allen	1965	150

Hit By Pitch

Ron Hunt	1968	25
Ron Hunt	1969	25
Bill Freehan	1968	24
Bill Freehan	1967	20
Frank Robinson	1965	18
Rick Reichardt	1968	18
Cesar Tovar	1968	17
Minnie Minoso	1961	16
Lou Johnson	1965	16
2 tied with		15

Sac Hits

Sonny Jackson	1966	27
Luis Aparicio	1960	20
Bobby Richardson	1962	20
Nellie Fox	1964	20
Gene Alley	1966	20
Chico Fernandez	1960	19
Wes Parker	1965	19
Mike Andrews	1967	18
Phil Niekro	1968	18
4 tied with		17

Sac Flies

Ron Santo	1969	14
Hank Aaron	1960	12
Del Crandall	1960	12
Minnie Minoso	1961	12
Leo Posada	1961	12
Vic Power	1961	12
Ron Santo	1967	12
4 tied with		11

Stolen Bases

Maury Wills	1962	104
Maury Wills	1965	94
Lou Brock	1966	74
Tommy Harper	1969	73
Lou Brock	1965	63
Bert Campaneris	1968	62
Lou Brock	1968	62
Bert Campaneris	1969	62
Luis Aparicio	1964	57
Bert Campaneris	1967	55

Caught Stealing

Maury Wills	1965	31
Lou Brock	1965	27
Maury Wills	1966	24
Don Buford	1966	22
Bert Campaneris	1968	22
Don Buford	1967	21
Maury Wills	1968	21
Maury Wills	1969	21
Maury Wills	1963	19
Bert Campaneris	1965	19

Runs Created

Norm Cash	1961	158
Mickey Mantle	1961	157
Frank Robinson	1962	152
Carl Yastrzemski	1967	148
Willie Mays	1962	146
Hank Aaron	1963	146
Frank Robinson	1966	141
Willie McCovey	1969	140
Willie Mays	1965	139
Reggie Jackson	1969	138

Runs Created/27 Outs

(minimum 3.1 PA/Tm Gm)

Mickey Mantle	1961	11.73
Norm Cash	1961	11.58
Willie McCovey	1969	10.75
Carl Yastrzemski	1967	9.84
Frank Robinson	1962	9.56
Willie Mays	1965	9.46
Jim Gentile	1961	9.34
Mickey Mantle	1964	9.27
Reggie Jackson	1969	9.05
Dick Allen	1966	8.94

Batting Average

Norm Cash	1961	.361
Roberto Clemente	1967	.357
Roberto Clemente	1961	.351
Pete Rose	1969	.348
Tommy Davis	1962	.346
Roberto Clemente	1969	.345
Vada Pinson	1961	.343
Matty Alou	1966	.342
Frank Robinson	1962	.342
Cleon Jones	1969	.340

On-Base Percentage

(minimum 3.1 PA/Tm Gm)

Norm Cash	1961	.487
Willie McCovey	1969	.453
Mickey Mantle	1961	.448
Jimmy Wynn	1969	.436
Wally Moon	1961	.434
Pete Rose	1969	.428
Harmon Killebrew	1969	.427
Carl Yastrzemski	1968	.426
Rusty Staub	1969	.426
Mickey Mantle	1964	.423

Slugging Percentage

(minimum 3.1 PA/Tm Gm)

Mickey Mantle	1961	.687
Norm Cash	1961	.662
Willie McCovey	1969	.656
Jim Gentile	1961	.646
Willie Mays	1965	.645
Frank Robinson	1966	.637
Dick Allen	1966	.632
Frank Robinson	1962	.624
Carl Yastrzemski	1967	.622
Roger Maris	1961	.620

OBP+Slugging

(minimum 3.1 PA/Tm Gm)

Norm Cash	1961	1.148
Mickey Mantle	1961	1.135
Willie McCovey	1969	1.108
Jim Gentile	1961	1.069
Frank Robinson	1966	1.047
Frank Robinson	1962	1.045
Willie Mays	1965	1.043
Carl Yastrzemski	1967	1.040
Dick Allen	1966	1.027
Reggie Jackson	1969	1.018

Secondary Average

(minimum 3.1 PA/Tm Gm)

Mickey Mantle	1961	.638
Jimmy Wynn	1969	.584
Harmon Killebrew	1969	.584
Willie McCovey	1969	.582
Reggie Jackson	1969	.565
Norm Cash	1961	.553
Jim Gentile	1961	.543
Harmon Killebrew	1967	.530
Mickey Mantle	1960	.520
Harmon Killebrew	1961	.518

Isolated Power

(minimum 3.1 PA/Tm Gm)

Mickey Mantle	1961	.370
Roger Maris	1961	.351
Jim Gentile	1961	.344
Willie McCovey	1969	.336
Reggie Jackson	1969	.333
Willie Mays	1965	.328
Frank Robinson	1966	.321
Harmon Killebrew	1961	.318
Boog Powell	1964	.316
Dick Allen	1966	.315

Single Season Pitching Leaders—1960-1969

Wins

Denny McLain	1968	31
Sandy Koufax	1966	27
Sandy Koufax	1965	26
Juan Marichal	1968	26
7 tied with		25

Losses

Roger Craig	1962	24
Jack Fisher	1965	24
Roger Craig	1963	22
Dick Ellsworth	1966	22
Larry Jackson	1965	21
11 tied with		20

Winning Percentage
(minimum 15 decisions)

Phil Regan	1966	.933
Whitey Ford	1961	.862
Ralph Terry	1961	.842
Ron Perranoski	1963	.842
Denny McLain	1968	.838
Sandy Koufax	1963	.833
Bob Moose	1969	.824
Bob Purkey	1962	.821
Jim Coates	1960	.813
Al McBean	1963	.813

Games

Wayne Granger	1969	90
Wilbur Wood	1968	88
Ted Abernathy	1965	84
Eddie Fisher	1965	82
John Wyatt	1964	81
Dick Radatz	1964	79
Hal Woodeshick	1965	78
Ted Abernathy	1968	78
Bob Locker	1967	77
Wilbur Wood	1969	76

Games Started

Jack Sanford	1963	42
Don Drysdale	1963	42
Jim Kaat	1965	42
Don Drysdale	1965	42
Fergie Jenkins	1969	42
10 tied with		41

Complete Games

Juan Marichal	1968	30
Denny McLain	1968	28
Bob Gibson	1968	28
Bob Gibson	1969	28
Sandy Koufax	1965	27
Sandy Koufax	1966	27
Juan Marichal	1969	27
Gaylord Perry	1969	26
Juan Marichal	1966	25
2 tied with		24

Shutouts

Bob Gibson	1968	13
Sandy Koufax	1963	11
Dean Chance	1964	11
Juan Marichal	1965	10
Luis Tiant	1968	9
Denny McLain	1969	9
6 tied with		8

Saves

Jack Aker	1966	32
Ted Abernathy	1965	31
Ron Perranoski	1969	31
Luis Arroyo	1961	29
Dick Radatz	1964	29
Ron Kline	1965	29
Fred Gladding	1969	29
Roy Face	1962	28
Ted Abernathy	1967	28
5 tied with		27

Games Finished

Dick Radatz	1964	67
Ted Abernathy	1965	62
Phil Regan	1968	62
Roy Face	1960	61
Ted Abernathy	1967	61
Eddie Fisher	1965	60
Stu Miller	1963	59
Dick Radatz	1963	58
Ron Kline	1965	58
3 tied with		57

Batters Faced

Gaylord Perry	1969	1,345
Juan Marichal	1968	1,307
Denny McLain	1969	1,304
Sandy Koufax	1965	1,297
Claude Osteen	1969	1,291
Don Drysdale	1962	1,289
Denny McLain	1968	1,288
Fergie Jenkins	1969	1,275
Sandy Koufax	1966	1,274
2 tied with		1,270

Innings Pitched

Denny McLain	1968	336.0
Sandy Koufax	1965	335.2
Juan Marichal	1968	326.0
Gaylord Perry	1969	325.1
Denny McLain	1969	325.0
Sandy Koufax	1966	323.0
Juan Marichal	1963	321.1
Don Drysdale	1964	321.1
Claude Osteen	1969	321.0
Bill Singer	1969	315.2

Hits Allowed

Dick Ellsworth	1966	321
Claude Osteen	1967	298
Lew Burdette	1961	295
Juan Marichal	1968	295
Claude Osteen	1969	293
Gaylord Perry	1969	290
Denny McLain	1969	288
Don Drysdale	1963	287
Fergie Jenkins	1969	284
Billy O'Dell	1962	282

Runs Allowed

Dick Ellsworth	1966	150
Jay Hook	1962	137
Sammy Ellis	1966	135
Pedro Ramos	1961	134
Tony Cloninger	1966	134
Roger Craig	1962	133
Bill Stoneman	1969	133
Jim Perry	1961	132
Al Jackson	1962	132
3 tied with		131

Earned Runs Allowed

Sammy Ellis	1966	130
Jim Merritt	1969	122
Lew Burdette	1961	121
Art Mahaffey	1962	120
Dick Ellsworth	1966	119
Dick Ellsworth	1962	118
Tony Cloninger	1966	118
4 tied with		117

Home Runs Allowed

Denny McLain	1966	42
Ralph Terry	1962	40
Orlando Pena	1964	40
Pedro Ramos	1961	39
Jim Bunning	1963	38
Earl Wilson	1964	37
Luis Tiant	1969	37
Art Mahaffey	1962	36
Pete Richert	1966	36
5 tied with		35

Walks

Chuck Estrada	1961	132
Sam McDowell	1965	132
Steve Barber	1961	130
Luis Tiant	1969	129
Bob Veale	1964	124
Sam McDowell	1967	123
Bill Stoneman	1969	123
Bo Belinsky	1962	122
Mickey Lolich	1969	122
2 tied with		121

Intentional Walks

Lindy McDaniel	1965	20
Ron Willis	1967	20
Jim Bunning	1967	20
Ron Perranoski	1964	19
Don Drysdale	1967	19
Mike McCormick	1967	18
Clay Carroll	1969	18
4 tied with		17

Strikeouts

Sandy Koufax	1965	382
Sam McDowell	1965	325
Sandy Koufax	1966	317
Sandy Koufax	1963	306
Sam McDowell	1968	283
Denny McLain	1968	280
Sam McDowell	1969	279
Bob Veale	1965	276
Fergie Jenkins	1969	273
Mickey Lolich	1969	271

Strikeouts/9 Innings
(minimum 1 Inning Pitched/Tm Gm)

Sam McDowell	1965	10.71
Sandy Koufax	1962	10.55
Sam McDowell	1966	10.42
Sandy Koufax	1965	10.24
Sandy Koufax	1960	10.13
Tom Griffin	1969	9.56
Jim Maloney	1963	9.53
Sandy Koufax	1961	9.47
Sam McDowell	1968	9.47
Don Wilson	1969	9.40

ERA
(minimum 1 Inning Pitched/Tm Gm)

Bob Gibson	1968	1.12
Luis Tiant	1968	1.60
Dean Chance	1964	1.65
Sandy Koufax	1966	1.73
Sandy Koufax	1964	1.74
Sam McDowell	1968	1.81
Phil Niekro	1967	1.87
Joe Horlen	1964	1.88
Sandy Koufax	1963	1.88
Dave McNally	1968	1.95

Component ERA
(minimum 1 Inning Pitched/Tm Gm)

Bob Gibson	1968	1.44
Luis Tiant	1968	1.51
Sandy Koufax	1963	1.55
Sandy Koufax	1965	1.56
Dave McNally	1968	1.66
Sandy Koufax	1964	1.66
Joe Horlen	1964	1.72
Dean Chance	1964	1.76
Juan Marichal	1966	1.80
Joe Horlen	1967	1.84

Sac Hits Allowed

Jim Bunning	1960	23
Dennis Bennett	1964	21
Jim Bunning	1965	21
Warren Spahn	1961	20
Buster Narum	1965	20
Tom Seaver	1969	20
Jim Bunning	1964	19
Steve Barber	1967	19
Claude Osteen	1967	19
Phil Niekro	1969	19

Sac Flies Allowed

Dave Morehead	1964	14
Joe McClain	1961	12
Bob Shaw	1961	12
Tony Cloninger	1966	12
Chuck Estrada	1960	11
Jack Kralick	1962	11
Tony Cloninger	1964	11
Earl Wilson	1964	11
Pat Jarvis	1968	11
Stan Williams	1964	11

Hit Batsmen

Tom Murphy	1969	21
Don Drysdale	1961	20
Frank Lary	1960	19
Jim Bunning	1966	19
Jim Lonborg	1967	19
Jim Kaat	1962	18
Don Drysdale	1966	17
Don Cardwell	1963	16
Ken McBride	1964	16
Chuck Estrada	1960	15

Wild Pitches

Tony Cloninger	1966	27
Jack Hamilton	1962	22
Tony Cloninger	1965	22
Earl Wilson	1963	21
Denny Lemaster	1964	20
Larry Dierker	1968	20
Jim Maloney	1963	19
Jim Maloney	1965	19
Phil Niekro	1967	19
3 tied with		18

Balks

Bob Shaw	1963	8
Roger Craig	1963	6
Bob Friend	1963	6
Don Rowe	1963	5
Jim Owens	1963	5
15 tied with		4

Opponent Average
(minimum 1 Inning Pitched/Tm Gm)

Luis Tiant	1968	.168
Sandy Koufax	1965	.179
Dave McNally	1968	.182
Al Downing	1963	.184
Bob Gibson	1968	.184
Sam McDowell	1965	.185
Sam McDowell	1966	.188
Sandy Koufax	1963	.189
Sam McDowell	1968	.189
Andy Messersmith	1969	.190

Opponent OBP
(minimum 1 Inning Pitched/Tm Gm)

Sandy Koufax	1965	.227
Juan Marichal	1966	.230
Sandy Koufax	1963	.230
Dave McNally	1968	.232
Bob Gibson	1968	.233
Luis Tiant	1968	.233
Juan Marichal	1965	.239
Sandy Koufax	1964	.240
Denny McLain	1968	.243
Joe Horlen	1964	.248

Batting Leaders—1970-1979

Games

Pete Rose	1,604
Graig Nettles	1,557
Sal Bando	1,527
Bobby Murcer	1,500
Larry Bowa	1,489
Bobby Bonds	1,479
Carl Yastrzemski	1,479
Tony Perez	1,471
Lee May	1,464
Amos Otis	1,462

At-Bats

Pete Rose	6,523
Larry Bowa	5,915
Bobby Bonds	5,720
Graig Nettles	5,683
Al Oliver	5,572
Lee May	5,558
Tony Perez	5,501
Bobby Murcer	5,483
Amos Otis	5,453
Lou Brock	5,428

Runs

Pete Rose	1,068
Bobby Bonds	1,020
Joe Morgan	1,005
Amos Otis	861
Carl Yastrzemski	845
Lou Brock	843
Rod Carew	837
Reggie Jackson	833
Bobby Murcer	816
Johnny Bench	792

Hits

Pete Rose	2,045
Rod Carew	1,787
Al Oliver	1,686
Lou Brock	1,617
Bobby Bonds	1,565
Tony Perez	1,560
Larry Bowa	1,552
Ted Simmons	1,550
Amos Otis	1,549
Bobby Murcer	1,548

Doubles

Pete Rose	394
Al Oliver	320
Tony Perez	303
Ted Simmons	299
Cesar Cedeno	292
Amos Otis	286
Hal McRae	285
Joe Morgan	275
Reggie Jackson	270
Willie Montanez	266

Triples

Rod Carew	80
Larry Bowa	74
George Brett	73
Roger Metzger	71
Willie Davis	70
Ralph Garr	64
Pete Rose	64
Al Oliver	63
Mickey Rivers	61
Lou Brock	56

Home Runs

Willie Stargell	296
Reggie Jackson	292
Johnny Bench	290
Bobby Bonds	280
Lee May	270
Dave Kingman	252
Graig Nettles	252
Mike Schmidt	235
Tony Perez	226
Reggie Smith	225

Home Runs (Home)

Reggie Jackson	146
Johnny Bench	145
Willie Stargell	143
Bobby Bonds	139
Graig Nettles	137
Lee May	131
Dave Kingman	125
Hank Aaron	118
3 tied with	115

Home Runs (Road)

Willie Stargell	153
Reggie Jackson	146
Johnny Bench	145
Bobby Bonds	141
Lee May	139
Dave Kingman	127
Mike Schmidt	121
Tony Perez	118
Graig Nettles	115
Reggie Smith	110

Extra Base Hits

Bobby Bonds	586
Reggie Jackson	586
Tony Perez	572
Johnny Bench	572
Willie Stargell	568
Pete Rose	537
Al Oliver	527
Lee May	514
Reggie Smith	511
Amos Otis	498

Total Bases

Pete Rose	2,804
Bobby Bonds	2,762
Tony Perez	2,627
Reggie Jackson	2,604
Johnny Bench	2,566
Al Oliver	2,564
Lee May	2,535
Bobby Murcer	2,455
Graig Nettles	2,441
Willie Stargell	2,440

RBI

Johnny Bench	1,013
Tony Perez	954
Lee May	936
Reggie Jackson	922
Willie Stargell	906
Rusty Staub	860
Bobby Bonds	856
Carl Yastrzemski	846
Bobby Murcer	840
Graig Nettles	831

Walks

Joe Morgan	1,071
Ken Singleton	888
Carl Yastrzemski	888
Darrell Evans	828
Sal Bando	817
Gene Tenace	805
Pete Rose	783
Bobby Murcer	744
Bobby Bonds	738
Jimmy Wynn	733

Walks/PA
(minimum 3,000 Plate Appearances)

Gene Tenace	.173
Joe Morgan	.169
Jimmy Wynn	.168
Bernie Carbo	.163
Darrell Evans	.155
Joe Ferguson	.154
Ken Singleton	.154
Mike Schmidt	.153
Willie McCovey	.152
Wayne Garrett	.150

Strikeouts

Bobby Bonds	1,368
Reggie Jackson	1,247
Lee May	1,148
Willie Stargell	1,100
Dave Kingman	1,095
Tony Perez	1,090
Greg Luzinski	998
George Scott	985
Mike Schmidt	958
Rick Monday	947

Hit By Pitch

Ron Hunt	142
Don Baylor	107
Gene Tenace	74
Richie Hebner	60
Bobby Grich	55
Greg Luzinski	55
Reggie Jackson	54
Al Oliver	54
Sal Bando	53
Hal McRae	51

Sac Hits

Bert Campaneris	159
Larry Bowa	116
Mark Belanger	114
Tito Fuentes	109
Ted Sizemore	101
Tim Foli	99
Freddie Patek	95
Felix Millan	95
Bucky Dent	90
Don Kessinger	90

Sac Flies

Al Oliver	76
Rusty Staub	70
Carl Yastrzemski	70
Amos Otis	70
Johnny Bench	68
Bobby Murcer	63
Don Baylor	61
Tony Perez	61
Joe Morgan	61
Ted Simmons	60

Stolen Bases

Lou Brock	551
Joe Morgan	488
Cesar Cedeno	427
Bobby Bonds	380
Davey Lopes	375
Freddie Patek	344
Bert Campaneris	336
Bill North	324
Ron LeFlore	294
Amos Otis	294

Caught Stealing

Lou Brock	181
Bobby Bonds	147
Bill North	135
Cesar Cedeno	127
Rod Carew	110
Freddie Patek	110
Bert Campaneris	108
Joe Morgan	105
Ron LeFlore	98
Pat Kelly	97

Runs Created

Pete Rose	1,083
Joe Morgan	1,067
Bobby Bonds	1,017
Reggie Jackson	957
Rod Carew	954
Carl Yastrzemski	933
Bobby Murcer	902
Amos Otis	894
Tony Perez	881
Willie Stargell	880

Runs Created/27 Outs
(minimum 3,000 Plate Appearances)

Joe Morgan	7.35
Willie Stargell	7.31
Fred Lynn	7.20
Rod Carew	6.85
Hank Aaron	6.78
Jim Rice	6.76
Dave Parker	6.76
Mike Schmidt	6.64
Reggie Smith	6.61
Billy Williams	6.61

Batting Average
(minimum 3,000 Plate Appearances)

Rod Carew	.343
Bill Madlock	.320
Dave Parker	.317
Pete Rose	.314
Jim Rice	.310
George Brett	.310
Ken Griffey Sr.	.310
Fred Lynn	.309
Ralph Garr	.307
Steve Garvey	.304

On-Base Percentage
(minimum 3,000 Plate Appearances)

Rod Carew	.408
Joe Morgan	.404
Mike Hargrove	.400
Ken Singleton	.398
Pete Rose	.389
Bernie Carbo	.388
Gene Tenace	.386
Carl Yastrzemski	.384
Fred Lynn	.383
Bill Madlock	.381

Slugging Percentage
(minimum 3,000 Plate Appearances)

Willie Stargell	.555
Jim Rice	.552
Hank Aaron	.527
Fred Lynn	.526
Dave Parker	.521
George Foster	.517
Dick Allen	.513
Mike Schmidt	.511
Reggie Jackson	.508
Reggie Smith	.507

OBP+Slugging
(minimum 3,000 Plate Appearances)

Willie Stargell	.928
Jim Rice	.910
Fred Lynn	.909
Hank Aaron	.899
Dave Parker	.891
Dick Allen	.889
Mike Schmidt	.885
Reggie Smith	.881
Reggie Jackson	.870
George Foster	.869

Secondary Average
(minimum 3,000 Plate Appearances)

Joe Morgan	.476
Mike Schmidt	.473
Gene Tenace	.412
Jimmy Wynn	.410
Hank Aaron	.407
Willie McCovey	.405
Bobby Bonds	.405
Willie Stargell	.405
Dick Allen	.403
Reggie Jackson	.400

Isolated Power
(minimum 3,000 Plate Appearances)

Willie Stargell	.268
Dave Kingman	.263
Mike Schmidt	.256
Hank Aaron	.248
Jim Rice	.242
Reggie Jackson	.233
George Foster	.229
Dick Allen	.229
Johnny Bench	.224
Willie McCovey	.221

Pitching Leaders—1970-1979

Wins

Jim Palmer	186
Gaylord Perry	184
Steve Carlton	178
Tom Seaver	178
Fergie Jenkins	178
Catfish Hunter	169
Don Sutton	166
Phil Niekro	164
Vida Blue	155
Nolan Ryan	155

Losses

Phil Niekro	151
Nolan Ryan	146
Gaylord Perry	133
Fergie Jenkins	130
Bert Blyleven	128
Jerry Koosman	127
Steve Carlton	126
Wilbur Wood	123
Rick Wise	117
Mickey Lolich	117

Winning Percentage
(minimum 100 decisions)

Don Gullett	.686
John Candelaria	.648
Pedro Borbon	.647
Jim Palmer	.644
Tom Seaver	.638
Catfish Hunter	.624
Tommy John	.613
Gary Nolan	.612
Clay Carroll	.610
Luis Tiant	.607

Games

Rollie Fingers	640
Mike Marshall	628
Sparky Lyle	600
Pedro Borbon	561
Darold Knowles	543
Dave LaRoche	543
Tug McGraw	542
Dave Giusti	470
Paul Lindblad	460
Tom Burgmeier	458

Games Started

Phil Niekro	376
Gaylord Perry	368
Steve Carlton	366
Fergie Jenkins	354
Jim Palmer	352
Bert Blyleven	350
Don Sutton	349
Tom Seaver	345
Nolan Ryan	333
2 tied with	327

Complete Games

Gaylord Perry	197
Fergie Jenkins	184
Jim Palmer	175
Steve Carlton	165
Nolan Ryan	164
Phil Niekro	160
Tom Seaver	147
Bert Blyleven	145
Catfish Hunter	140
Mickey Lolich	133

Shutouts

Jim Palmer	44
Nolan Ryan	42
Tom Seaver	40
Bert Blyleven	39
Don Sutton	39
Gaylord Perry	36
Fergie Jenkins	33
Vida Blue	32
Steve Carlton	32
Catfish Hunter	30

Saves

Rollie Fingers	209
Sparky Lyle	190
Mike Marshall	177
Dave Giusti	140
Tug McGraw	132
Dave LaRoche	122
John Hiller	115
Gene Garber	110
Clay Carroll	106
Bruce Sutter	105

Games Finished

Mike Marshall	505
Rollie Fingers	480
Sparky Lyle	477
Tug McGraw	374
Dave Giusti	350
Dave LaRoche	334
John Hiller	321
Darold Knowles	285
Gene Garber	281
Bill Campbell	274

Batters Faced

Phil Niekro	12,043
Gaylord Perry	11,759
Steve Carlton	11,361
Jim Palmer	11,105
Fergie Jenkins	11,009
Bert Blyleven	10,722
Tom Seaver	10,607
Nolan Ryan	10,453
Don Sutton	10,403
Vida Blue	9,827

Innings Pitched

Gaylord Perry	2,905.0
Phil Niekro	2,881.0
Steve Carlton	2,747.0
Jim Palmer	2,745.0
Fergie Jenkins	2,706.2
Tom Seaver	2,652.1
Bert Blyleven	2,624.2
Don Sutton	2,557.1
Nolan Ryan	2,465.0
Catfish Hunter	2,399.0

Hits Allowed

Phil Niekro	2,642
Gaylord Perry	2,559
Fergie Jenkins	2,507
Steve Carlton	2,413
Bert Blyleven	2,335
Jim Palmer	2,275
Don Sutton	2,174
Rick Wise	2,156
Jim Kaat	2,122
Jerry Koosman	2,119

Runs Allowed

Phil Niekro	1,228
Fergie Jenkins	1,128
Steve Carlton	1,103
Gaylord Perry	1,088
Mike Torrez	1,001
Nolan Ryan	984
Rick Wise	980
Don Sutton	975
Jack Billingham	970
Bert Blyleven	949

Earned Runs Allowed

Phil Niekro	1,045
Fergie Jenkins	1,015
Steve Carlton	971
Gaylord Perry	942
Mike Torrez	882
Don Sutton	871
Rick Wise	866
Nolan Ryan	860
Jack Billingham	857
Catfish Hunter	846

Home Runs Allowed

Fergie Jenkins	301
Phil Niekro	259
Catfish Hunter	257
Steve Carlton	238
Don Sutton	214
Gaylord Perry	207
Luis Tiant	204
Mickey Lolich	202
Tom Seaver	190
Rick Wise	188

Walks

Nolan Ryan	1,515
Mike Torrez	962
Steve Carlton	960
Phil Niekro	920
Jim Palmer	861
Joe Coleman	795
Vida Blue	780
Steve Renko	775
Gaylord Perry	758
Jerry Koosman	747

Intentional Walks

Tug McGraw	89
Steve Carlton	87
Gene Garber	82
Dave Giusti	80
Randy Jones	79
Pedro Borbon	79
Jack Billingham	76
Gaylord Perry	75
Dave LaRoche	75
3 tied with	74

Strikeouts

Nolan Ryan	2,678
Tom Seaver	2,304
Steve Carlton	2,097
Bert Blyleven	2,082
Gaylord Perry	1,907
Phil Niekro	1,866
Fergie Jenkins	1,841
Don Sutton	1,767
Vida Blue	1,600
Jerry Koosman	1,587

Strikeouts/9 Innings
(minimum 1,000 Innings Pitched)

Nolan Ryan	9.78
J.R. Richard	8.29
Tom Seaver	7.82
Rollie Fingers	7.18
Frank Tanana	7.14
Bert Blyleven	7.14
Steve Carlton	6.87
Dennis Eckersley	6.70
Wayne Twitchell	6.68
John Montefusco	6.60

ERA
(minimum 1,000 Innings Pitched)

Jim Palmer	2.58
Tom Seaver	2.61
Bert Blyleven	2.88
Rollie Fingers	2.89
Gaylord Perry	2.92
Frank Tanana	2.93
Andy Messersmith	2.93
Jon Matlack	2.97
Mike Marshall	2.98
Don Wilson	3.01

Component ERA
(minimum 1,000 Innings Pitched)

Tom Seaver	2.39
Don Sutton	2.67
Jim Palmer	2.68
Rollie Fingers	2.70
Andy Messersmith	2.77
Gaylord Perry	2.79
Catfish Hunter	2.82
Vida Blue	2.89
Bert Blyleven	2.90
Don Wilson	2.91

Sac Hits Allowed

Jerry Reuss	125
Bert Blyleven	123
Jerry Koosman	121
Phil Niekro	119
Steve Carlton	114
Don Sutton	114
Mike Marshall	110
Dave Roberts	108
Mickey Lolich	108
2 tied with	107

Sac Flies Allowed

Fergie Jenkins	82
Catfish Hunter	73
Vida Blue	71
Jerry Koosman	66
Steve Carlton	65
Jim Slaton	65
Paul Splittorff	64
Nolan Ryan	63
3 tied with	62

Hit Batsmen

Jack Billingham	87
Phil Niekro	76
Nolan Ryan	75
Bert Blyleven	70
Joe Coleman	63
Jim Lonborg	58
Pete Broberg	52
Gaylord Perry	51
Fergie Jenkins	51
Wilbur Wood	50

Wild Pitches

Phil Niekro	116
Nolan Ryan	116
J.R. Richard	90
Joe Coleman	89
Steve Carlton	81
Fred Norman	80
Clay Kirby	76
Tommy John	75
Jack Billingham	75
Mike Torrez	74

Balks

Steve Carlton	42
Phil Niekro	26
Bill Bonham	19
Jerry Koosman	18
Larry Christenson	17
Dick Ruthven	15
J.R. Richard	14
4 tied with	13

Opponent Average
(minimum 1,000 Innings Pitched)

Nolan Ryan	.199
J.R. Richard	.215
Andy Messersmith	.217
Tom Seaver	.217
Don Wilson	.225
Jim Palmer	.226
Don Sutton	.228
Catfish Hunter	.230
Rollie Fingers	.233
Don Gullett	.233

Opponent OBP
(minimum 1,000 Innings Pitched)

Tom Seaver	.273
Catfish Hunter	.279
Don Sutton	.280
Fergie Jenkins	.282
Gary Nolan	.286
Jim Palmer	.287
Gaylord Perry	.289
Andy Messersmith	.290
Frank Tanana	.291
Rollie Fingers	.291

Single Season Batting Leaders—1970-1979

Games

Frank Taveras	1979	164
Pete Rose	1974	163
Willie Montanez	1976	163
Jim Rice	1978	163
Pete Rose	1979	163
35 tied with		162

At-Bats

Dave Cash	1975	699
Omar Moreno	1979	695
Sandy Alomar	1971	689
Dave Cash	1974	687
Horace Clarke	1970	686
Pete Rose	1973	680
Frank Taveras	1979	680
Matty Alou	1970	677
Jim Rice	1978	677
Felix Millan	1975	676

Runs

Billy Williams	1970	137
Bobby Bonds	1970	134
Bobby Bonds	1973	131
Pete Rose	1976	130
Rod Carew	1977	128
Lou Brock	1971	126
Ron LeFlore	1978	126
Carl Yastrzemski	1970	125
George Foster	1977	124
Joe Morgan	1972	122

Hits

Rod Carew	1977	239
Joe Torre	1971	230
Pete Rose	1973	230
Ralph Garr	1971	219
Rod Carew	1974	218
George Brett	1976	215
Pete Rose	1976	215
Dave Parker	1977	215
Ralph Garr	1974	214
2 tied with		213

Doubles

Hal McRae	1977	54
Pete Rose	1978	51
Keith Hernandez	1979	48
Wes Parker	1970	47
Fred Lynn	1975	47
Pete Rose	1975	47
Jack Clark	1978	46
Warren Cromartie	1979	46
3 tied with		45

Triples

George Brett	1979	20
Garry Templeton	1979	19
Garry Templeton	1977	18
Ralph Garr	1974	17
Willie Davis	1970	16
Rod Carew	1977	16
Paul Molitor	1979	16
Jim Rice	1977	15
Jim Rice	1978	15
4 tied with		14

Home Runs

George Foster	1977	52
Willie Stargell	1971	48
Dave Kingman	1979	48
Hank Aaron	1971	47
Jim Rice	1978	46
Johnny Bench	1970	45
Mike Schmidt	1979	45
Gorman Thomas	1979	45
Frank Howard	1970	44
Willie Stargell	1973	44

Home Runs (Home)

Hank Aaron	1971	31
Johnny Bench	1970	30
Billy Williams	1970	28
Jim Rice	1978	28
Fred Lynn	1979	28
Dick Allen	1972	27
Jeff Burroughs	1977	27
Jim Rice	1977	27
Jim Rice	1979	27
Dave Johnson	1973	26

Home Runs (Road)

George Foster	1977	31
Mike Schmidt	1979	29
Willie Stargell	1971	27
Harmon Killebrew	1970	25
Johnny Bench	1972	24
Willie McCovey	1970	23
Bobby Bonds	1975	23
John Mayberry	1975	23
Dave Kingman	1979	23
Gorman Thomas	1979	23

Extra Base Hits

Willie Stargell	1973	90
Hal McRae	1977	86
Jim Rice	1978	86
George Foster	1977	85
George Brett	1979	85
Johnny Bench	1970	84
Jim Rice	1979	84
Jim Rice	1977	83
Fred Lynn	1979	82
2 tied with		80

Total Bases

Jim Rice	1978	406
George Foster	1977	388
Jim Rice	1977	382
Billy Williams	1970	373
Jim Rice	1979	369
George Brett	1979	363
Johnny Bench	1970	355
Joe Torre	1971	352
Rod Carew	1977	351
Billy Williams	1972	348

RBI

George Foster	1977	149
Johnny Bench	1970	148
Jim Rice	1978	139
Don Baylor	1979	139
Joe Torre	1971	137
Greg Luzinski	1977	130
Jim Rice	1979	130
Tony Perez	1970	129
Billy Williams	1970	129
Johnny Bench	1974	129

Walks

Willie McCovey	1970	137
Frank Howard	1970	132
Joe Morgan	1975	132
Carl Yastrzemski	1970	128
Harmon Killebrew	1970	128
Jimmy Wynn	1976	127
Darrell Evans	1974	126
Gene Tenace	1977	125
Darrell Evans	1973	124
Ken Singleton	1973	123

Walks/PA
(minimum 3.1 PA/Tm Gm)

Jimmy Wynn	1976	.217
Gene Tenace	1977	.215
Willie McCovey	1970	.215
Willie Mays	1971	.209
Jimmy Wynn	1975	.208
Joe Morgan	1975	.207
Gene Tenace	1978	.196
Harmon Killebrew	1970	.192
Jeff Burroughs	1978	.191
John Mayberry	1973	.191

Strikeouts

Bobby Bonds	1970	189
Mike Schmidt	1975	180
Gorman Thomas	1979	175
Gary Alexander	1978	166
Butch Hobson	1977	162
Reggie Jackson	1971	161
Tommie Agee	1970	156
Jeff Burroughs	1975	155
Willie Stargell	1971	154
Dave Kingman	1975	153

Hit By Pitch

Ron Hunt	1971	50
Ron Hunt	1970	26
Ron Hunt	1972	26
Ron Hunt	1973	24
Bobby Grich	1974	20
Don Baylor	1976	20
Don Baylor	1978	18
Ron Hunt	1974	16
3 tied with		14

Sac Hits

Bert Campaneris	1977	40
Craig Reynolds	1979	34
Ozzie Smith	1978	28
Ted Sizemore	1973	25
Roy Smalley	1976	25
Bert Campaneris	1978	25
Rob Wilfong	1979	25
Felix Millan	1974	24
Enzo Hernandez	1975	24
5 tied with		23

Sac Flies

Roy White	1971	17
Jose Cardenal	1971	14
Willie Montanez	1971	13
Sal Bando	1974	13
Reggie Smith	1978	13
Dan Ford	1979	13
Darrell Porter	1979	13
10 tied with		12

Stolen Bases

Lou Brock	1974	118
Willie Wilson	1979	83
Ron LeFlore	1979	78
Davey Lopes	1975	77
Omar Moreno	1979	77
Bill North	1976	75
Omar Moreno	1978	71
Lou Brock	1973	70
Mickey Rivers	1975	70
Frank Taveras	1977	70

Caught Stealing

Lou Brock	1974	33
Bill North	1976	29
Bill North	1974	26
Frank Taveras	1978	25
Garry Templeton	1977	24
Lou Brock	1977	24
Bill North	1979	24
Jose Cruz	1977	23
Miguel Dilone	1978	23
Bobby Bonds	1979	23

Runs Created

Rod Carew	1977	154
Carl Yastrzemski	1970	145
Billy Williams	1970	144
Jim Rice	1978	141
Joe Morgan	1975	137
Joe Torre	1971	136
Fred Lynn	1979	134
Darrell Evans	1973	131
George Brett	1979	131
Jim Rice	1979	131

Runs Created/27 Outs
(minimum 3.1 PA/Tm Gm)

Joe Morgan	1975	10.52
Rod Carew	1977	10.33
Joe Morgan	1976	9.85
Fred Lynn	1979	9.72
Carl Yastrzemski	1970	9.64
Willie McCovey	1970	9.58
Hank Aaron	1971	9.51
Rico Carty	1970	9.45
Jim Hickman	1970	9.21
Willie Stargell	1973	9.11

Batting Average
(minimum 3.1 PA/Tm Gm)

Rod Carew	1977	.388
Rico Carty	1970	.366
Rod Carew	1974	.364
Joe Torre	1971	.363
Rod Carew	1975	.359
Bill Madlock	1975	.354
Ralph Garr	1974	.353
Rod Carew	1973	.350
Keith Hernandez	1979	.344
Ralph Garr	1971	.343

On-Base Percentage
(minimum 3.1 PA/Tm Gm)

Joe Morgan	1975	.466
Rico Carty	1970	.454
Carl Yastrzemski	1970	.452
Rod Carew	1977	.449
Joe Morgan	1976	.444
Willie McCovey	1970	.444
Ken Singleton	1977	.438
Rod Carew	1974	.433
Jeff Burroughs	1978	.432
Bobby Murcer	1971	.427

Slugging Percentage
(minimum 3.1 PA/Tm Gm)

Hank Aaron	1971	.669
Willie Stargell	1973	.646
Fred Lynn	1979	.637
George Foster	1977	.631
Willie Stargell	1971	.628
Dave Kingman	1979	.613
Willie McCovey	1970	.612
Billy Williams	1972	.606
Dick Allen	1972	.603
Jim Rice	1978	.600

OBP+Slugging
(minimum 3.1 PA/Tm Gm)

Hank Aaron	1971	1.079
Fred Lynn	1979	1.059
Willie McCovey	1970	1.056
Carl Yastrzemski	1970	1.044
Willie Stargell	1973	1.038
Rico Carty	1970	1.037
Willie Stargell	1971	1.026
Dick Allen	1972	1.023
Joe Morgan	1976	1.020
Rod Carew	1977	1.019

Secondary Average
(minimum 3.1 PA/Tm Gm)

Joe Morgan	1976	.625
Willie McCovey	1970	.600
Joe Morgan	1975	.580
Mike Schmidt	1979	.549
Joe Morgan	1974	.549
Willie Mays	1971	.535
Carl Yastrzemski	1970	.530
Dick Allen	1972	.528
Mike Schmidt	1977	.518
Harmon Killebrew	1970	.518

Isolated Power
(minimum 3.1 PA/Tm Gm)

Willie Stargell	1973	.347
Hank Aaron	1971	.341
Willie Stargell	1971	.333
Dave Kingman	1979	.325
Willie McCovey	1970	.323
George Foster	1977	.311
Mike Schmidt	1979	.311
Fred Lynn	1979	.303
Mike Schmidt	1977	.300
Dick Allen	1972	.294

Single Season Pitching Leaders—1970-1979

Wins

Steve Carlton	1972	27
Mickey Lolich	1971	25
Fergie Jenkins	1974	25
Catfish Hunter	1974	25
Ron Guidry	1978	25
9 tied with		24

Losses

Denny McLain	1971	22
Bill Bonham	1974	22
Randy Jones	1974	22
Steve Rogers	1974	22
Steve Arlin	1972	21
Stan Bahnsen	1973	21
Mickey Lolich	1974	21
7 tied with		20

Winning Percentage
(minimum 15 decisions)

Ron Guidry	1978	.893
Bob Stanley	1978	.882
Ron Davis	1979	.875
Roger Moret	1973	.867
Wayne Simpson	1970	.824
Roger Moret	1975	.824
Tommy John	1974	.813
Al Hrabosky	1975	.813
Dave McNally	1971	.808
Catfish Hunter	1973	.808

Games

Mike Marshall	1974	106
Kent Tekulve	1979	94
Mike Marshall	1973	92
Kent Tekulve	1978	91
Mike Marshall	1979	90
Enrique Romo	1979	84
Ken Sanders	1971	83
Dale Murray	1976	81
Mudcat Grant	1970	80
Pedro Borbon	1973	80

Games Started

Wilbur Wood	1972	49
Wilbur Wood	1973	48
Mickey Lolich	1971	45
Phil Niekro	1979	44
Wilbur Wood	1975	43
Phil Niekro	1977	43
5 tied with		42

Complete Games

Fergie Jenkins	1971	30
Steve Carlton	1972	30
Catfish Hunter	1975	30
Mickey Lolich	1971	29
Gaylord Perry	1972	29
Gaylord Perry	1973	29
Fergie Jenkins	1974	29
Gaylord Perry	1974	28
Mickey Lolich	1974	27
2 tied with		26

Shutouts

Jim Palmer	1975	10
Don Sutton	1972	9
Nolan Ryan	1972	9
Bert Blyleven	1973	9
Ron Guidry	1978	9
Vida Blue	1971	8
Steve Carlton	1972	8
Wilbur Wood	1972	8
12 tied with		7

Saves

John Hiller	1973	38
Clay Carroll	1972	37
Rollie Fingers	1978	37
Bruce Sutter	1979	37
Wayne Granger	1970	35
Sparky Lyle	1972	35
Rollie Fingers	1977	35
Ron Perranoski	1970	34
Mike Marshall	1979	32
6 tied with		31

Games Finished

Mike Marshall	1979	84
Mike Marshall	1974	83
Ken Sanders	1971	77
Mike Marshall	1973	73
Rollie Fingers	1977	69
Bill Campbell	1976	68
Kent Tekulve	1979	67
Tom Murphy	1974	66
Kent Tekulve	1978	65
4 tied with		62

Batters Faced

Mickey Lolich	1971	1,538
Wilbur Wood	1973	1,531
Wilbur Wood	1972	1,490
Phil Niekro	1979	1,436
Phil Niekro	1977	1,428
Gaylord Perry	1973	1,410
Nolan Ryan	1974	1,392
Phil Niekro	1978	1,389
Nolan Ryan	1973	1,355
Steve Carlton	1972	1,351

Innings Pitched

Wilbur Wood	1972	376.2
Mickey Lolich	1971	376.0
Wilbur Wood	1973	359.1
Steve Carlton	1972	346.1
Gaylord Perry	1973	344.0
Gaylord Perry	1972	342.2
Phil Niekro	1979	342.0
Phil Niekro	1978	334.1
Wilbur Wood	1971	334.0
Nolan Ryan	1974	332.2

Hits Allowed

Wilbur Wood	1973	381
Mickey Lolich	1971	336
Wilbur Wood	1972	325
Jim Kaat	1975	321
Bill Lee	1974	320
Gaylord Perry	1973	315
Mickey Lolich	1973	315
Phil Niekro	1977	315
Phil Niekro	1979	311
Mickey Lolich	1974	310

Runs Allowed

Wilbur Wood	1973	166
Phil Niekro	1977	166
Joe Coleman	1974	160
Phil Niekro	1979	160
Mickey Lolich	1974	155
Dick Tidrow	1973	150
Wilbur Wood	1975	148
Steve Carlton	1973	146
Jim Bibby	1974	146
Mike Torrez	1979	144

Earned Runs Allowed

Phil Niekro	1977	148
Mickey Lolich	1974	142
Jim Bibby	1974	139
Wilbur Wood	1973	138
Joe Coleman	1974	137
Dick Tidrow	1973	135
Wilbur Wood	1975	133
Vida Blue	1979	132
Mickey Lolich	1973	131
2 tied with		129

Home Runs Allowed

Phil Niekro	1979	41
Phil Niekro	1970	40
Fergie Jenkins	1979	40
Jim Perry	1971	39
Catfish Hunter	1973	39
Don Sutton	1970	38
Mickey Lolich	1974	38
Fergie Jenkins	1975	37
Mickey Lolich	1971	36
2 tied with		35

Walks

Nolan Ryan	1977	204
Nolan Ryan	1974	202
Nolan Ryan	1976	183
Phil Niekro	1977	164
Nolan Ryan	1973	162
Joe Coleman	1974	158
Nolan Ryan	1972	157
Sam McDowell	1971	153
J.R. Richard	1976	151
Nolan Ryan	1978	148

Intentional Walks

Gene Garber	1974	24
Mike Garman	1975	23
Dale Murray	1978	23
Randy Jones	1978	20
Kent Tekulve	1979	20
John Hiller	1974	19
5 tied with		18

Strikeouts

Nolan Ryan	1973	383
Nolan Ryan	1974	367
Nolan Ryan	1977	341
Nolan Ryan	1972	329
Nolan Ryan	1976	327
Steve Carlton	1972	310
Mickey Lolich	1971	308
Sam McDowell	1970	304
J.R. Richard	1978	303

Strikeouts/9 Innings
(minimum 1 Inning Pitched/Tm Gm)

Nolan Ryan	1973	10.57
Nolan Ryan	1972	10.43
Nolan Ryan	1976	10.35
Nolan Ryan	1977	10.26
Nolan Ryan	1978	9.97
Nolan Ryan	1974	9.93
J.R. Richard	1978	9.90
J.R. Richard	1979	9.64
Frank Tanana	1975	9.41
Tom Seaver	1971	9.08

ERA
(minimum 1 Inning Pitched/Tm Gm)

Ron Guidry	1978	1.74
Tom Seaver	1971	1.76
Vida Blue	1971	1.82
Luis Tiant	1972	1.91
Wilbur Wood	1971	1.91
Gaylord Perry	1972	1.92
Steve Carlton	1972	1.97
Gary Nolan	1972	1.99
Catfish Hunter	1972	2.04
Jim Palmer	1972	2.07

Component ERA
(minimum 1 Inning Pitched/Tm Gm)

Don Sutton	1972	1.63
Catfish Hunter	1972	1.70
Ron Guidry	1978	1.71
Vida Blue	1971	1.81
Tom Seaver	1971	1.90
Steve Carlton	1972	1.92
Gaylord Perry	1972	1.93
Tom Seaver	1973	2.05
Don Sutton	1973	2.08
Don Wilson	1971	2.10

Sac Hits Allowed

Mickey Lolich	1972	23
Bill Bonham	1974	23
Randy Jones	1979	23
Mike Marshall	1974	22
Nolan Ryan	1977	22
Wilbur Wood	1972	21
Wayne Twitchell	1973	21
Steve Rogers	1979	21
4 tied with		20

Sac Flies Allowed

Doc Medich	1975	15
Randy Lerch	1979	15
Jim Palmer	1976	14
Nolan Ryan	1978	14
7 tied with		13

Hit Batsmen

Jack Billingham	1971	16
Pete Broberg	1975	16
Nolan Ryan	1971	15
Bill Stoneman	1970	14
Jim Lonborg	1971	14
Bill Greif	1974	14
Ken Kravec	1979	14
5 tied with		13

Wild Pitches

Nolan Ryan	1977	21
J.R. Richard	1975	20
Dave Lemanczyk	1977	20
Steve Renko	1974	19
Joe Niekro	1979	19
J.R. Richard	1979	19
Rich Robertson	1970	18
Ernie McAnally	1971	18
Nolan Ryan	1972	18
Phil Niekro	1979	18

Balks

Steve Carlton	1979	11
Bill Bonham	1974	8
Frank Tanana	1978	8
Steve Carlton	1975	7
Jerry Koosman	1975	7
Steve Carlton	1977	7
Steve Carlton	1978	7
Larry Christenson	1978	7
Paul Moskau	1978	7
6 tied with		6

Opponent Average
(minimum 1 Inning Pitched/Tm Gm)

Nolan Ryan	1972	.171
Don Sutton	1972	.189
Catfish Hunter	1972	.189
Vida Blue	1971	.189
Nolan Ryan	1974	.190
Nolan Ryan	1977	.193
Ron Guidry	1978	.193
Nolan Ryan	1976	.195
Roger Nelson	1972	.196
J.R. Richard	1978	.196

Opponent OBP
(minimum 1 Inning Pitched/Tm Gm)

Roger Nelson	1972	.234
Don Sutton	1972	.240
Catfish Hunter	1972	.241
Ron Guidry	1978	.249
Vida Blue	1971	.251
Tom Seaver	1971	.252
Tom Seaver	1973	.252
Don Sutton	1973	.257
Steve Carlton	1972	.257
Tom Seaver	1977	.258

Batting Leaders—1980-1989

Games

Dale Murphy	1,537
Eddie Murray	1,500
Ozzie Smith	1,468
Dwight Evans	1,466
Robin Yount	1,446
Harold Baines	1,428
Alfredo Griffin	1,419
Lou Whitaker	1,418
Frank White	1,407
Andre Dawson	1,396

At-Bats

Dale Murphy	5,694
Robin Yount	5,683
Willie Wilson	5,666
Eddie Murray	5,612
Andre Dawson	5,398
Harold Baines	5,363
Dwight Evans	5,350
Ozzie Smith	5,330
Lou Whitaker	5,282
Alan Trammell	5,192

Runs

Rickey Henderson	1,122
Robin Yount	957
Dwight Evans	956
Dale Murphy	938
Tim Raines	866
Eddie Murray	858
Willie Wilson	845
Mike Schmidt	832
Paul Molitor	828
Wade Boggs	823

Hits

Robin Yount	1,731
Eddie Murray	1,642
Willie Wilson	1,639
Wade Boggs	1,597
Dale Murphy	1,553
Harold Baines	1,547
Andre Dawson	1,539
Rickey Henderson	1,507
Alan Trammell	1,504
Dwight Evans	1,497

Doubles

Robin Yount	337
Wade Boggs	314
Dwight Evans	306
George Brett	303
Andre Dawson	290
Bill Buckner	290
Eddie Murray	289
Frank White	283
Harold Baines	276
Keith Hernandez	273

Triples

Willie Wilson	115
Robin Yount	83
Tim Raines	76
Brett Butler	74
Juan Samuel	72
Willie McGee	71
Alfredo Griffin	63
Mookie Wilson	63
Lloyd Moseby	60
Omar Moreno	58

Home Runs

Mike Schmidt	313
Dale Murphy	308
Eddie Murray	274
Dwight Evans	256
Andre Dawson	250
Darrell Evans	230
Tony Armas	225
Lance Parrish	225
Dave Winfield	223
Jack Clark	216

Home Runs (Home)

Dale Murphy	168
Mike Schmidt	151
Eddie Murray	130
Dwight Evans	127
Darrell Evans	118
Fred Lynn	112
Kent Hrbek	111
Tony Armas	108
Andre Dawson	108
3 tied with	105

Home Runs (Road)

Mike Schmidt	162
Eddie Murray	144
Andre Dawson	142
Dale Murphy	140
Dwight Evans	129
Dave Winfield	126
Jack Clark	124
Lance Parrish	120
Tom Brunansky	118
Tony Armas	117

Extra Base Hits

Dwight Evans	605
Dale Murphy	596
Robin Yount	594
Andre Dawson	593
Eddie Murray	582
Mike Schmidt	566
George Brett	543
Dave Winfield	522
Harold Baines	509
Cal Ripken Jr.	494

Total Bases

Dale Murphy	2,796
Eddie Murray	2,791
Robin Yount	2,756
Andre Dawson	2,685
Dwight Evans	2,657
Mike Schmidt	2,507
Harold Baines	2,478
Dave Winfield	2,450
George Brett	2,422
Jim Rice	2,390

RBI

Eddie Murray	996
Mike Schmidt	929
Dale Murphy	929
Dwight Evans	900
Dave Winfield	899
Andre Dawson	895
Jim Rice	868
George Brett	851
Harold Baines	835
Robin Yount	821

Walks

Rickey Henderson	962
Dwight Evans	919
Jack Clark	835
Mike Schmidt	818
Dale Murphy	784
Willie Randolph	777
Darrell Evans	776
Eddie Murray	754
Wade Boggs	754
Keith Hernandez	742

Walks/PA

(minimum 3,000 Plate Appearances)

Jack Clark	.166
Jason Thompson	.161
Rickey Henderson	.155
Mike Schmidt	.147
Darrell Evans	.145
Dwight Evans	.144
Toby Harrah	.143
Mike Hargrove	.141
Alvin Davis	.141
Wade Boggs	.140

Strikeouts

Dale Murphy	1,268
Dwight Evans	1,023
Lloyd Moseby	1,015
Reggie Jackson	991
Jesse Barfield	977
Tony Armas	971
Lance Parrish	960
Mike Schmidt	925
Larry Parrish	900
Juan Samuel	900

Hit By Pitch

Don Baylor	160
Chet Lemon	108
Brian Downing	88
Carlton Fisk	81
Lonnie Smith	68
Andre Dawson	54
Phil Bradley	54
Lloyd Moseby	50
Juan Samuel	50
Tim Wallach	47

Sac Hits

Ozzie Smith	110
Bob Boone	104
Alfredo Griffin	100
Marty Barrett	91
Alan Trammell	86
Jim Gantner	83
Scott Fletcher	75
Rick Reuschel	74
Bob Forsch	73
3 tied with	70

Sac Flies

Andre Dawson	74
Mike Schmidt	65
Keith Moreland	65
Gary Carter	64
George Brett	63
Robin Yount	63
Don Mattingly	63
Bill Buckner	61
Eddie Murray	58
Harold Baines	58

Stolen Bases

Rickey Henderson	838
Tim Raines	583
Vince Coleman	472
Willie Wilson	451
Ozzie Smith	364
Steve Sax	333
Lonnie Smith	331
Brett Butler	307
Mookie Wilson	293
Dave Collins	284

Caught Stealing

Rickey Henderson	190
Steve Sax	143
Brett Butler	141
Lonnie Smith	120
Omar Moreno	118
Alfredo Griffin	107
Vince Coleman	98
Mookie Wilson	91
Damaso Garcia	90
Tim Raines	90

Runs Created

Rickey Henderson	1,066
Eddie Murray	1,023
Robin Yount	1,020
Dwight Evans	1,018
Dale Murphy	1,010
Mike Schmidt	944
Wade Boggs	923
Tim Raines	915
George Brett	907
Keith Hernandez	855

Runs Created/27 Outs

(minimum 3,000 Plate Appearances)

Wade Boggs	7.89
Rickey Henderson	7.23
Mike Schmidt	7.20
George Brett	7.17
Pedro Guerrero	6.97
Tim Raines	6.92
Jack Clark	6.81
Don Mattingly	6.79
Dwight Evans	6.73
Alvin Davis	6.68

Batting Average

(minimum 3,000 Plate Appearances)

Wade Boggs	.352
Tony Gwynn	.332
Kirby Puckett	.323
Don Mattingly	.323
Rod Carew	.314
George Brett	.311
Pedro Guerrero	.308
Al Oliver	.307
Robin Yount	.305
Tim Raines	.303

On-Base Percentage

(minimum 3,000 Plate Appearances)

Wade Boggs	.443
Rickey Henderson	.403
George Brett	.392
Alvin Davis	.392
Tim Raines	.391
Mike Hargrove	.391
Keith Hernandez	.390
Jack Clark	.389
Tony Gwynn	.389
Rod Carew	.388

Slugging Percentage

(minimum 3,000 Plate Appearances)

Mike Schmidt	.540
Don Mattingly	.521
George Brett	.521
Darryl Strawberry	.520
Pedro Guerrero	.506
Andre Dawson	.497
Eddie Murray	.497
Dwight Evans	.497
Kent Hrbek	.496
George Bell	.495

OBP+Slugging

(minimum 3,000 Plate Appearances)

Mike Schmidt	.925
Wade Boggs	.922
George Brett	.913
Don Mattingly	.889
Pedro Guerrero	.888
Dwight Evans	.882
Darryl Strawberry	.878
Jack Clark	.873
Eddie Murray	.872
Alvin Davis	.866

Secondary Average

(minimum 3,000 Plate Appearances)

Rickey Henderson	.492
Darryl Strawberry	.464
Mike Schmidt	.452
Jack Clark	.424
Gary Redus	.412
Tim Raines	.405
Dwight Evans	.396
Dale Murphy	.380
Howard Johnson	.379
Kirk Gibson	.376

Isolated Power

(minimum 3,000 Plate Appearances)

Mike Schmidt	.263
Darryl Strawberry	.259
Steve Balboni	.223
Dale Murphy	.218
Dave Kingman	.218
Dwight Evans	.217
Gorman Thomas	.216
Tony Armas	.216
Jack Clark	.215
Glenn Davis	.214

Pitching Leaders—1980-1989

Wins

Jack Morris	162
Dave Stieb	140
Bob Welch	137
Charlie Hough	128
Fernando Valenzuela	128
Bert Blyleven	123
Nolan Ryan	122
Jim Clancy	119
Frank Viola	117
Rick Sutcliffe	116

Losses

Jim Clancy	126
Frank Tanana	122
Jack Morris	119
Bob Knepper	118
Charlie Hough	114
Floyd Bannister	109
Rich Dotson	109
Dave Stieb	109
Mike Moore	107
2 tied with	104

Winning Percentage
(minimum 100 decisions)

Dwight Gooden	.719
Roger Clemens	.679
Teddy Higuera	.639
Ron Darling	.613
John Tudor	.612
Ron Guidry	.607
Sid Fernandez	.605
Dennis Rasmussen	.605
Orel Hershiser	.605
Jimmy Key	.602

Games

Kent Tekulve	687
Dan Quisenberry	637
Jeff Reardon	629
Greg Minton	626
Lee Smith	586
Willie Hernandez	572
Dave Smith	514
Bob Stanley	504
Goose Gossage	494
Gene Garber	485

Games Started

Jack Morris	332
Dave Stieb	331
Jim Clancy	317
Nolan Ryan	314
Bob Welch	311
Bob Knepper	306
Frank Tanana	304
Floyd Bannister	294
Doyle Alexander	289
2 tied with	288

Complete Games

Jack Morris	133
Fernando Valenzuela	102
Bert Blyleven	94
Charlie Hough	93
Dave Stieb	92
Mario Soto	70
Mike Witt	70
Bruce Hurst	64
Scott McGregor	62
Mike Moore	62

Shutouts

Fernando Valenzuela	27
Dave Stieb	27
Orel Hershiser	23
Bob Welch	22
Bert Blyleven	21
Roger Clemens	21
Bob Knepper	20
Mike Witt	20
Jack Morris	20
Dwight Gooden	19

Saves

Jeff Reardon	264
Dan Quisenberry	239
Lee Smith	234
Goose Gossage	206
Bruce Sutter	195
Dave Righetti	188
Dave Smith	176
Steve Bedrosian	161
John Franco	148
Greg Minton	146

Games Finished

Dan Quisenberry	530
Jeff Reardon	507
Lee Smith	449
Kent Tekulve	424
Goose Gossage	396
Greg Minton	386
Dave Smith	358
Willie Hernandez	356
Steve Bedrosian	336
Bruce Sutter	333

Batters Faced

Jack Morris	10,208
Dave Stieb	9,654
Fernando Valenzuela	8,957
Charlie Hough	8,942
Nolan Ryan	8,704
Bob Welch	8,655
Bert Blyleven	8,623
Jim Clancy	8,582
Frank Tanana	8,493
Bob Knepper	8,484

Innings Pitched

Jack Morris	2,443.2
Dave Stieb	2,328.2
Fernando Valenzuela	2,144.2
Charlie Hough	2,121.2
Nolan Ryan	2,094.0
Bob Welch	2,082.1
Bert Blyleven	2,078.1
Jim Clancy	2,017.2
Bob Knepper	2,005.1
Doyle Alexander	2,004.1

Hits Allowed

Jack Morris	2,212
Doyle Alexander	2,065
Bob Knepper	2,045
Dave Stieb	2,019
Frank Tanana	2,014
Jim Clancy	1,996
Bert Blyleven	1,984
Rick Rhoden	1,954
Mike Witt	1,913
Bob Welch	1,885

Runs Allowed

Jack Morris	1,085
Jim Clancy	1,017
Charlie Hough	999
Frank Tanana	989
Dave Stieb	954
Bob Knepper	946
Doyle Alexander	930
Floyd Bannister	929
Rich Dotson	922
Bert Blyleven	919

Earned Runs Allowed

Jack Morris	995
Jim Clancy	918
Charlie Hough	864
Frank Tanana	861
Dave Stieb	859
Doyle Alexander	858
Bert Blyleven	841
Floyd Bannister	836
Rich Dotson	835
Bob Knepper	824

Home Runs Allowed

Jack Morris	264
Floyd Bannister	234
Doyle Alexander	223
Frank Tanana	219
Charlie Hough	218
Frank Viola	218
Bert Blyleven	212
Jim Clancy	207
Rich Dotson	191
2 tied with	190

Walks

Nolan Ryan	894
Charlie Hough	867
Jack Morris	858
Fernando Valenzuela	838
Dave Stieb	825
Rick Sutcliffe	745
Rich Dotson	720
Jim Clancy	711
Dan Petry	697
Phil Niekro	676

Intentional Walks

Kent Tekulve	120
Greg Minton	118
Gene Garber	73
Lee Smith	73
Bob Stanley	73
Mike LaCoss	67
Tom Hume	66
Jack Morris	66
Gary Lucas	65
Don Robinson	65

Strikeouts

Nolan Ryan	2,167
Fernando Valenzuela	1,644
Jack Morris	1,629
Bert Blyleven	1,480
Bob Welch	1,457
Steve Carlton	1,453
Dave Stieb	1,380
Charlie Hough	1,363
Mario Soto	1,360
Floyd Bannister	1,356

Strikeouts/9 Innings
(minimum 1,000 Innings Pitched)

Nolan Ryan	9.31
Roger Clemens	8.51
Sid Fernandez	8.47
Mark Langston	8.21
Dwight Gooden	8.14
Jose DeLeon	7.74
Mario Soto	7.58
Steve Carlton	7.55
Dave Righetti	7.46
Teddy Higuera	7.11

ERA
(minimum 1,000 Innings Pitched)

Dwight Gooden	2.64
Orel Hershiser	2.69
Roger Clemens	3.06
Dave Righetti	3.08
John Tudor	3.13
Dave Dravecky	3.13
Nolan Ryan	3.14
Fernando Valenzuela	3.19
Bob Welch	3.21
Sid Fernandez	3.22

Component ERA
(minimum 1,000 Innings Pitched)

Dwight Gooden	2.44
Orel Hershiser	2.62
Sid Fernandez	2.69
Nolan Ryan	2.73
Roger Clemens	2.76
Bret Saberhagen	2.85
Mario Soto	2.86
Mike Scott	2.95
Teddy Higuera	2.98
Jose DeLeon	3.01

Sac Hits Allowed

Fernando Valenzuela	135
Bob Knepper	103
Rick Mahler	91
Steve Carlton	89
Jerry Reuss	89
Mike Scott	89
Shane Rawley	88
Larry McWilliams	86
Bob Welch	84
Mike Krukow	80

Sac Flies Allowed

Rick Reuschel	68
Jack Morris	64
Mike Witt	62
Ed Whitson	60
Danny Darwin	60
Bob Forsch	59
Mike Krukow	58
Charlie Hough	57
Scott McGregor	57
Frank Tanana	57

Hit Batsmen

Dave Stieb	104
Charlie Hough	80
Bert Blyleven	73
Mike Smithson	73
Frank Tanana	55
Nolan Ryan	53
Mike Boddicker	52
Kevin Gross	50
Bob Welch	49
Dennis Martinez	49

Wild Pitches

Jack Morris	124
Nolan Ryan	123
Joe Niekro	110
Charlie Hough	98
Fernando Valenzuela	81
Dave Stewart	77
Steve Carlton	76
Rick Sutcliffe	74
Jim Clancy	72
2 tied with	66

Balks

Steve Carlton	47
Bob Welch	36
Charlie Hough	30
Rick Rhoden	29
Rick Sutcliffe	27
Dave LaPoint	25
Kevin Gross	25
Atlee Hammaker	24
Dwight Gooden	24
3 tied with	23

Opponent Average
(minimum 1,000 Innings Pitched)

Sid Fernandez	.205
Nolan Ryan	.210
Jose DeLeon	.217
Mario Soto	.218
Dwight Gooden	.222
Roger Clemens	.227
Orel Hershiser	.229
Charlie Hough	.234
Teddy Higuera	.234
Dave Stieb	.235

Opponent OBP
(minimum 1,000 Innings Pitched)

Dwight Gooden	.280
Bret Saberhagen	.284
Roger Clemens	.286
Sid Fernandez	.288
Orel Hershiser	.289
Mario Soto	.290
Don Sutton	.291
Teddy Higuera	.292
Dennis Eckersley	.292
Mike Scott	.294

Single Season Batting Leaders—1980-1989

Games

Steve Garvey	1980	163
Al Oliver	1980	163
Greg Walker	1985	163
Tony Fernandez	1986	163
Jose Oquendo	1989	163
Bobby Bonilla	1989	163
42 tied with		162

At-Bats

Willie Wilson	1980	705
Juan Samuel	1984	701
Kirby Puckett	1985	691
Tony Fernandez	1986	687
Kirby Puckett	1986	680
Don Mattingly	1986	677
Omar Moreno	1980	676
Bill Buckner	1985	673
Paul Molitor	1982	666
3 tied with		663

Runs

Rickey Henderson	1985	146
Paul Molitor	1982	136
Willie Wilson	1980	133
Tim Raines	1983	133
Dale Murphy	1983	131
Rickey Henderson	1986	130
Robin Yount	1982	129
Wade Boggs	1988	128
Tim Raines	1987	123
Dwight Evans	1982	122

Hits

Wade Boggs	1985	240
Don Mattingly	1986	238
Kirby Puckett	1988	234
Willie Wilson	1980	230
Kirby Puckett	1986	223
Cecil Cooper	1980	219
Tony Gwynn	1987	218
Willie McGee	1985	216
Kirby Puckett	1989	215
Wade Boggs	1988	214

Doubles

Don Mattingly	1986	53
Wade Boggs	1989	51
Robin Yount	1980	49
Don Mattingly	1985	48
Cal Ripken Jr.	1983	47
Wade Boggs	1986	47
Robin Yount	1982	46
Hal McRae	1982	46
Bill Buckner	1985	46
Von Hayes	1986	46

Triples

Willie Wilson	1985	21
Ryne Sandberg	1984	19
Juan Samuel	1984	19
Willie McGee	1985	18
8 tied with		15

Home Runs

Andre Dawson	1987	49
Mark McGwire	1987	49
Mike Schmidt	1980	48
George Bell	1987	47
Kevin Mitchell	1989	47
Dale Murphy	1987	44
Tony Armas	1984	43
Jose Canseco	1988	42
Reggie Jackson	1980	41
Ben Oglivie	1980	41

Home Runs (Home)

Andre Dawson	1987	27
Mike Schmidt	1980	25
Bob Horner	1982	25
Dale Murphy	1987	25
Dale Murphy	1982	24
Bob Horner	1980	23
5 tied with		22

Home Runs (Road)

George Bell	1987	28
Mark McGwire	1987	28
Ben Oglivie	1980	26
Jose Canseco	1988	26
Reggie Jackson	1980	25
Kevin Mitchell	1989	25
Jesse Barfield	1986	24
5 tied with		23

Extra Base Hits

Robin Yount	1982	87
Kevin Mitchell	1989	87
Don Mattingly	1985	86
Don Mattingly	1986	86
George Bell	1987	83
Robin Yount	1980	82
Mike Schmidt	1980	81
Hal McRae	1982	81
Mark McGwire	1987	81
3 tied with		80

Total Bases

Don Mattingly	1986	388
Don Mattingly	1985	370
George Bell	1987	369
Robin Yount	1982	367
Kirby Puckett	1986	365
Kirby Puckett	1988	358
Andre Dawson	1987	353
Dave Parker	1985	350
Jose Canseco	1988	347
2 tied with		345

RBI

Don Mattingly	1985	145
Andre Dawson	1987	137
George Bell	1987	134
Hal McRae	1982	133
Cecil Cooper	1983	126
Jim Rice	1983	126
Dave Parker	1985	125
Kevin Mitchell	1989	125
Eddie Murray	1985	124
Jose Canseco	1988	124

Walks

Jack Clark	1987	136
Jack Clark	1989	132
Mike Schmidt	1983	128
Rickey Henderson	1989	126
Wade Boggs	1988	125
Von Hayes	1987	121
Willie Randolph	1980	119
Fred McGriff	1989	119
Rickey Henderson	1980	117
Rickey Henderson	1982	116

Walks/PA
(minimum 3.1 PA/Tm Gm)

Jack Clark	1987	.243
Jack Clark	1989	.222
Toby Harrah	1985	.217
Mike Schmidt	1983	.191
Rickey Henderson	1989	.187
Willie Randolph	1980	.185
Jack Clark	1988	.183
Reggie Jackson	1986	.178
Von Hayes	1987	.178
Rickey Henderson	1982	.177

Strikeouts

Rob Deer	1987	186
Pete Incaviglia	1986	185
Rob Deer	1986	179
Jose Canseco	1986	175
Jim Presley	1986	172
Bo Jackson	1989	172
Gorman Thomas	1980	170
Juan Samuel	1984	168
Pete Incaviglia	1987	168
2 tied with		166

Hit By Pitch

Don Baylor	1986	35
Don Baylor	1987	28
Don Baylor	1985	24
Don Baylor	1984	23
Chet Lemon	1983	20
Carlton Fisk	1985	17
Brian Downing	1986	17
Brian Downing	1987	17
Phil Bradley	1988	16
2 tied with		15

Sac Hits

Felix Fermin	1989	32
Tim Foli	1982	26
Ozzie Smith	1980	23
Bob Boone	1982	23
Bobby Meacham	1985	23
Alvaro Espinoza	1989	23
Dwayne Murphy	1980	22
Marty Barrett	1987	22
John Castino	1980	21
3 tied with		20

Sac Flies

Andre Dawson	1983	18
Don Mattingly	1985	15
Gary Carter	1986	15
George Hendrick	1982	14
Dave Kingman	1984	14
George Bell	1989	14
8 tied with		13

Stolen Bases

Rickey Henderson	1982	130
Vince Coleman	1985	110
Vince Coleman	1987	109
Rickey Henderson	1983	108
Vince Coleman	1986	107
Rickey Henderson	1980	100
Ron LeFlore	1980	97
Omar Moreno	1980	96
Rickey Henderson	1988	93
Tim Raines	1983	90

Caught Stealing

Rickey Henderson	1982	42
Omar Moreno	1980	33
Steve Sax	1983	30
Harold Reynolds	1988	29
Vince Coleman	1988	27
Gerald Young	1988	27
Rickey Henderson	1980	26
Lonnie Smith	1982	26
Omar Moreno	1982	26
2 tied with		25

Runs Created

Will Clark	1989	141
Wade Boggs	1987	140
Jose Canseco	1988	137
Robin Yount	1982	136
Rickey Henderson	1985	135
George Brett	1985	134
Don Mattingly	1986	134
Don Mattingly	1985	133
Dale Murphy	1987	132
Wade Boggs	1985	131

Runs Created/27 Outs
(minimum 3.1 PA/Tm Gm)

Jack Clark	1987	10.84
George Brett	1980	10.72
Wade Boggs	1987	10.01
Paul Molitor	1987	9.88
Mike Schmidt	1981	9.61
Will Clark	1989	9.39
George Brett	1985	9.29
Rickey Henderson	1985	9.13
Tim Raines	1987	9.01
Eric Davis	1987	8.88

Batting Average
(minimum 3.1 PA/Tm Gm)

George Brett	1980	.390
Tony Gwynn	1987	.370
Wade Boggs	1985	.368
Wade Boggs	1988	.366
Wade Boggs	1987	.363
Wade Boggs	1983	.361
Wade Boggs	1986	.357
Kirby Puckett	1988	.356
Willie McGee	1985	.353
Paul Molitor	1987	.353

On-Base Percentage
(minimum 3.1 PA/Tm Gm)

Wade Boggs	1988	.476
Wade Boggs	1987	.461
Jack Clark	1987	.459
George Brett	1980	.454
Wade Boggs	1986	.453
Wade Boggs	1985	.450
Tony Gwynn	1987	.447
Wade Boggs	1983	.444
Paul Molitor	1987	.438
George Brett	1985	.436

Slugging Percentage
(minimum 3.1 PA/Tm Gm)

George Brett	1980	.664
Mike Schmidt	1981	.644
Kevin Mitchell	1989	.635
Mike Schmidt	1980	.624
Mark McGwire	1987	.618
George Bell	1987	.605
Reggie Jackson	1980	.597
Jack Clark	1987	.597
Eric Davis	1987	.593
Wade Boggs	1987	.588

OBP+Slugging
(minimum 3.1 PA/Tm Gm)

George Brett	1980	1.118
Mike Schmidt	1981	1.080
Jack Clark	1987	1.055
Wade Boggs	1987	1.049
Kevin Mitchell	1989	1.023
George Brett	1985	1.022
Mike Schmidt	1980	1.004
Paul Molitor	1987	1.003
Pedro Guerrero	1985	.999
Dale Murphy	1987	.997

Secondary Average
(minimum 3.1 PA/Tm Gm)

Jack Clark	1987	.637
Eric Davis	1987	.582
Rickey Henderson	1982	.575
Mike Schmidt	1981	.568
Darryl Strawberry	1987	.549
Rickey Henderson	1983	.540
Rickey Henderson	1985	.528
Mike Schmidt	1983	.522
Mike Schmidt	1980	.522
Jack Clark	1989	.521

Isolated Power
(minimum 3.1 PA/Tm Gm)

Kevin Mitchell	1989	.344
Mike Schmidt	1980	.338
Mark McGwire	1987	.329
Mike Schmidt	1981	.328
Jack Clark	1987	.310
Eric Davis	1987	.300
Darryl Strawberry	1987	.299
Reggie Jackson	1980	.298
George Bell	1987	.297
Dale Murphy	1987	.284

Single Season Pitching Leaders—1980-1989

Wins

Steve Stone	1980	25
Steve Carlton	1980	24
LaMarr Hoyt	1983	24
Dwight Gooden	1985	24
Roger Clemens	1986	24
Frank Viola	1988	24
Steve Carlton	1982	23
Orel Hershiser	1988	23
Danny Jackson	1988	23
Bret Saberhagen	1989	23

Losses

Brian Kingman	1980	20
Matt Young	1985	19
Jose DeLeon	1985	19
Mike Moore	1987	19
15 tied with		18

Winning Percentage
(minimum 15 decisions)

Tom Seaver	1981	.875
David Cone	1988	.870
Orel Hershiser	1985	.864
Dwight Gooden	1985	.857
Roger Clemens	1986	.857
Moose Haas	1983	.813
Phil Niekro	1982	.810
John Franco	1985	.800
Bret Saberhagen	1989	.793
Ron Guidry	1985	.786

Games

Kent Tekulve	1987	90
Mark Eichhorn	1987	89
Rob Murphy	1987	87
Kent Tekulve	1982	85
Frank Williams	1987	85
Mitch Williams	1987	85
Dick Tidrow	1980	84
Dan Quisenberry	1985	84
Craig Lefferts	1986	83
Bill Campbell	1983	82

Games Started

Jim Clancy	1982	40
Charlie Hough	1987	40
Dennis Martinez	1982	39
Rick Mahler	1985	39
Rick Mahler	1986	39
Tom Browning	1986	39
13 tied with		38

Complete Games

Rick Langford	1980	28
Mike Norris	1980	24
Bert Blyleven	1985	24
Ron Guidry	1983	21
Matt Keough	1980	20
Jack Morris	1983	20
Fernando Valenzuela	1986	20
Steve Carlton	1982	19
Dave Stieb	1982	19
4 tied with		18

Shutouts

John Tudor	1985	10
Fernando Valenzuela	1981	8
Dwight Gooden	1985	8
Orel Hershiser	1988	8
Roger Clemens	1988	8
Tim Belcher	1989	8
Roger Clemens	1987	7
6 tied with		6

Saves

Dave Righetti	1986	46
Dan Quisenberry	1983	45
Bruce Sutter	1984	45
Dennis Eckersley	1988	45
Dan Quisenberry	1984	44
Mark Davis	1989	44
Jeff Reardon	1988	42
Jeff Reardon	1985	41
Steve Bedrosian	1987	40
John Franco	1988	39

Games Finished

Dan Quisenberry	1985	76
Dan Quisenberry	1980	68
Dan Quisenberry	1982	68
Willie Hernandez	1984	68
Dave Righetti	1986	68
Dan Quisenberry	1984	67
Greg Minton	1982	66
Jeff Russell	1989	66
Mark Davis	1989	65
3 tied with		64

Batters Faced

Charlie Hough	1987	1,231
Steve Carlton	1980	1,228
Jack Morris	1983	1,204
Bert Blyleven	1985	1,203
Steve Carlton	1982	1,193
Dave Stieb	1982	1,187
Steve Carlton	1983	1,183
Larry Gura	1980	1,175
Dennis Leonard	1980	1,172
Rick Langford	1980	1,166

Innings Pitched

Steve Carlton	1980	304.0
Steve Carlton	1982	295.2
Jack Morris	1983	293.2
Bert Blyleven	1985	293.2
Rick Langford	1980	290.0
Dave Stieb	1982	288.1
Charlie Hough	1987	285.1
Fernando Valenzuela	1982	285.0
Mike Norris	1980	284.1
Steve Carlton	1983	283.2

Hits Allowed

Tommy John	1983	287
Rick Mahler	1986	283
Rick Reuschel	1980	281
Mike Moore	1986	279
Rick Mahler	1988	279
Mike Flanagan	1980	278
Steve Carlton	1983	277
Rick Langford	1980	276
Geoff Zahn	1980	273
Oil Can Boyd	1985	273

Runs Allowed

Charlie Hough	1987	159
Mike Moore	1987	145
Matt Keough	1982	144
Mark Langston	1986	142
Frank Viola	1983	141
Mike Moore	1986	141
Rick Mahler	1986	139
Geoff Zahn	1980	138
Frank Viola	1985	136
Frank Viola	1986	136

Earned Runs Allowed

Matt Keough	1982	133
Rick Mahler	1986	129
Mark Langston	1986	129
Frank Viola	1983	128
Mike Moore	1986	127
Jim Clancy	1984	125
Bert Blyleven	1988	125
Mike Smithson	1985	124
Frank Viola	1986	123
2 tied with		121

Home Runs Allowed

Bert Blyleven	1986	50
Bert Blyleven	1987	46
Jack Morris	1986	40
Bill Gullickson	1987	40
Jack Morris	1987	39
Matt Keough	1982	38
Don Sutton	1987	38
Floyd Bannister	1987	38
Curt Young	1987	38
3 tied with		37

Walks

Bobby Witt	1986	143
Bobby Witt	1987	140
Jim Clancy	1980	128
Edwin Correa	1986	126
Charlie Hough	1988	126
Charlie Hough	1987	124
Fernando Valenzuela	1987	124
Mark Langston	1986	123
Phil Niekro	1985	120
Mark Gubicza	1987	120

Intentional Walks

Kent Tekulve	1982	23
Greg Minton	1984	20
Bill Campbell	1983	18
Greg Minton	1985	18
Greg Minton	1982	17
6 tied with		16

Strikeouts

Mike Scott	1986	306
Nolan Ryan	1989	301
Roger Clemens	1988	291
Steve Carlton	1980	286
Steve Carlton	1982	286
Dwight Gooden	1984	276
Steve Carlton	1983	275
Mario Soto	1982	274
Nolan Ryan	1987	270
Dwight Gooden	1985	268

Strikeouts/9 Innings
(minimum 1 Inning Pitched/Tm Gm)

Nolan Ryan	1987	11.48
Dwight Gooden	1984	11.39
Nolan Ryan	1989	11.32
Mike Scott	1986	10.00
Roger Clemens	1988	9.92
Nolan Ryan	1986	9.81
Nolan Ryan	1984	9.65
Mario Soto	1982	9.57
Sid Fernandez	1985	9.51
Nolan Ryan	1988	9.33

ERA
(minimum 1 Inning Pitched/Tm Gm)

Dwight Gooden	1985	1.53
Nolan Ryan	1981	1.69
John Tudor	1985	1.93
Orel Hershiser	1985	2.03
Bret Saberhagen	1989	2.16
Joe Magrane	1988	2.18
Bob Knepper	1981	2.18
Don Sutton	1980	2.20
David Cone	1988	2.22
Mike Scott	1986	2.22

Component ERA
(minimum 1 Inning Pitched/Tm Gm)

Mike Scott	1986	1.67
Dwight Gooden	1985	1.83
John Tudor	1985	1.84
Bret Saberhagen	1989	1.89
Orel Hershiser	1985	2.01
Roger Clemens	1986	2.03
Dwight Gooden	1984	2.08
Jerry Reuss	1980	2.08
Teddy Higuera	1988	2.10
Mike Scott	1988	2.15

Sac Hits Allowed

Fernando Valenzuela	1983	27
Bob Knepper	1986	22
Mike Scott	1982	21
Steve Carlton	1983	20
Rick Reuschel	1980	19
Steve Rogers	1980	19
Fernando Valenzuela	1982	19
Rick Mahler	1988	19
Orel Hershiser	1989	19
4 tied with		18

Sac Flies Allowed

Larry Gura	1983	17
Rick Reuschel	1980	14
Charlie Hough	1987	14
Rick Reuschel	1988	14
8 tied with		13

Hit Batsmen

Charlie Hough	1987	19
Bert Blyleven	1988	16
Mike Smithson	1985	15
Dave Stieb	1986	15
Dave Stieb	1983	14
Mike Smithson	1986	14
Mike Boddicker	1988	14
Dave Stieb	1988	13
Dave Stieb	1989	13
3 tied with		12

Wild Pitches

Jack Morris	1987	24
Bobby Witt	1986	22
Joe Niekro	1985	21
Ken Howell	1989	21
Joe Niekro	1982	19
Edwin Correa	1986	19
Nolan Ryan	1989	19
Nolan Ryan	1982	18
Jack Morris	1983	18
3 tied with		17

Balks

Dave Stewart	1988	16
John Dopson	1989	15
Bob Welch	1988	13
John Candelaria	1988	12
Jose Guzman	1988	12
Rod Scurry	1988	11
Jack Morris	1988	11
Mike Birkbeck	1988	11
4 tied with		10

Opponent Average
(minimum 1 Inning Pitched/Tm Gm)

Sid Fernandez	1985	.181
Mike Scott	1986	.186
Nolan Ryan	1989	.187
Mario Soto	1980	.187
Nolan Ryan	1981	.188
Nolan Ryan	1986	.188
Floyd Youmans	1986	.188
Sid Fernandez	1988	.191
Nolan Ryan	1983	.195
Roger Clemens	1986	.195

Opponent OBP
(minimum 1 Inning Pitched/Tm Gm)

Mike Scott	1986	.242
John Tudor	1985	.249
Bret Saberhagen	1989	.251
Pascual Perez	1988	.252
Roger Clemens	1986	.252
Dennis Eckersley	1985	.254
Dwight Gooden	1985	.254
Ron Guidry	1981	.256
Don Sutton	1980	.257
Scott Garrelts	1989	.258

Batting Leaders—1990-1997

Games

Cal Ripken Jr.	1,228
Rafael Palmeiro	1,206
Joe Carter	1,201
Craig Biggio	1,195
Jay Bell	1,181
Fred McGriff	1,177
Barry Bonds	1,176
Mark Grace	1,172
Tony Phillips	1,155
Bobby Bonilla	1,145

At-Bats

Cal Ripken Jr.	4,777
Joe Carter	4,727
Rafael Palmeiro	4,664
Craig Biggio	4,538
Paul Molitor	4,505
Jay Bell	4,481
Mark Grace	4,462
Tony Phillips	4,387
Marquis Grissom	4,384
Steve Finley	4,362

Runs

Barry Bonds	880
Tony Phillips	836
Craig Biggio	796
Frank Thomas	785
Rafael Palmeiro	771
Ken Griffey Jr.	759
Rickey Henderson	742
Roberto Alomar	727
Paul Molitor	718
Chuck Knoblauch	713

Hits

Paul Molitor	1,427
Tony Gwynn	1,426
Mark Grace	1,387
Rafael Palmeiro	1,381
Roberto Alomar	1,330
Craig Biggio	1,330
Cal Ripken Jr.	1,313
Lance Johnson	1,294
Ken Griffey Jr.	1,269
Frank Thomas	1,261

Doubles

Mark Grace	281
Rafael Palmeiro	277
Edgar Martinez	277
Tony Gwynn	268
Paul Molitor	266
Albert Belle	260
Craig Biggio	255
Bobby Bonilla	254
Cal Ripken Jr.	251
Paul O'Neill	249

Triples

Lance Johnson	103
Steve Finley	67
Brett Butler	57
Delino DeShields	53
Brian McRae	51
Chuck Knoblauch	51
Brady Anderson	50
Paul Molitor	49
Kenny Lofton	48
Roberto Alomar	47

Home Runs

Barry Bonds	290
Ken Griffey Jr.	278
Cecil Fielder	271
Mark McGwire	270
Albert Belle	265
Frank Thomas	257
Juan Gonzalez	255
Fred McGriff	249
Matt Williams	245
Rafael Palmeiro	238

Home Runs (Home)

Ken Griffey Jr.	145
Cecil Fielder	142
Barry Bonds	140
Joe Carter	133
Mark McGwire	133
Frank Thomas	131
Albert Belle	126
Rafael Palmeiro	124
Fred McGriff	121
Sammy Sosa	121

Home Runs (Road)

Barry Bonds	150
Juan Gonzalez	140
Albert Belle	139
Mark McGwire	137
Ken Griffey Jr.	133
Matt Williams	131
Jay Buhner	130
Cecil Fielder	129
Fred McGriff	128
Frank Thomas	126

Extra Base Hits

Barry Bonds	558
Ken Griffey Jr.	540
Albert Belle	538
Rafael Palmeiro	536
Frank Thomas	511
Joe Carter	501
Bobby Bonilla	483
Fred McGriff	474
Larry Walker	473
Juan Gonzalez	464

Total Bases

Rafael Palmeiro	2,414
Barry Bonds	2,389
Ken Griffey Jr.	2,389
Frank Thomas	2,294
Fred McGriff	2,233
Albert Belle	2,220
Joe Carter	2,182
Bobby Bonilla	2,136
Paul Molitor	2,124
Cal Ripken Jr.	2,100

RBI

Barry Bonds	871
Cecil Fielder	856
Frank Thomas	854
Joe Carter	851
Albert Belle	830
Ken Griffey Jr.	811
Rafael Palmeiro	799
Fred McGriff	790
Juan Gonzalez	783
Bobby Bonilla	755

Walks

Barry Bonds	943
Frank Thomas	879
Tony Phillips	859
Rickey Henderson	776
Mickey Tettleton	740
Mark McGwire	656
Edgar Martinez	651
Chili Davis	629
Jeff Bagwell	627
Fred McGriff	622

Walks/PA

(minimum 3,000 Plate Appearances)

Barry Bonds	.188
Frank Thomas	.184
Rickey Henderson	.182
Mickey Tettleton	.181
Mark McGwire	.177
Tony Phillips	.161
Dave Magadan	.151
Edgar Martinez	.151
Darren Daulton	.148
Jeff Bagwell	.142

Strikeouts

Cecil Fielder	1,061
Sammy Sosa	980
Jay Buhner	974
Andres Galarraga	934
Travis Fryman	931
Mickey Tettleton	924
Jose Canseco	911
Ray Lankford	880
Greg Vaughn	879
Tony Phillips	865

Hit By Pitch

Craig Biggio	113
Brady Anderson	90
Mike Macfarlane	89
Andres Galarraga	75
Chuck Knoblauch	74
Jeff Blauser	70
Jeff Bagwell	64
Larry Walker	63
Mo Vaughn	63
Dave Hollins	58

Sac Hits

Jay Bell	121
Tom Glavine	91
Omar Vizquel	89
Brett Butler	82
Ozzie Guillen	76
Greg Maddux	70
Darren Lewis	70
John Smoltz	69
Joey Cora	67
2 tied with	64

Sac Flies

Joe Carter	73
Bobby Bonilla	66
Ruben Sierra	66
Will Clark	63
Frank Thomas	63
Travis Fryman	59
Jeff Bagwell	59
Mark Grace	56
Jeff King	56
2 tied with	55

Stolen Bases

Otis Nixon	415
Rickey Henderson	360
Delino DeShields	356
Kenny Lofton	354
Marquis Grissom	344
Barry Bonds	300
Vince Coleman	280
Chuck Knoblauch	276
Lance Johnson	274
Roberto Alomar	256

Caught Stealing

Otis Nixon	121
Brett Butler	116
Delino DeShields	116
Luis Polonia	105
Ray Lankford	96
Kenny Lofton	91
Lance Johnson	90
Rickey Henderson	87
Chad Curtis	85
Marquis Grissom	81

Runs Created

Barry Bonds	1,065
Frank Thomas	978
Ken Griffey Jr.	861
Rafael Palmeiro	858
Paul Molitor	842
Craig Biggio	805
Fred McGriff	789
Jeff Bagwell	778
Tony Phillips	774
Roberto Alomar	764

Runs Created/27 Outs

(minimum 3,000 Plate Appearances)

Barry Bonds	9.67
Frank Thomas	9.54
Mark McGwire	7.90
Edgar Martinez	7.76
Jeff Bagwell	7.67
Ken Griffey Jr.	7.62
Tim Salmon	7.41
Mo Vaughn	7.33
David Justice	7.27
Gary Sheffield	7.14

Batting Average

(minimum 3,000 Plate Appearances)

Tony Gwynn	.347
Frank Thomas	.330
Edgar Martinez	.320
Paul Molitor	.317
Kenny Lofton	.316
Kirby Puckett	.312
Mark Grace	.311
Roberto Alomar	.310
Wade Boggs	.307
Hal Morris	.307

On-Base Percentage

(minimum 3,000 Plate Appearances)

Frank Thomas	.452
Barry Bonds	.438
Edgar Martinez	.428
Rickey Henderson	.416
Jeff Bagwell	.409
Mark McGwire	.397
Gary Sheffield	.396
John Olerud	.396
Dave Magadan	.396
Tony Phillips	.396

Slugging Percentage

(minimum 3,000 Plate Appearances)

Frank Thomas	.600
Barry Bonds	.599
Ken Griffey Jr.	.577
Mark McGwire	.577
Albert Belle	.576
Juan Gonzalez	.562
Larry Walker	.547
Jeff Bagwell	.536
Mo Vaughn	.532
Tim Salmon	.527

OBP+Slugging

(minimum 3,000 Plate Appearances)

Frank Thomas	1.053
Barry Bonds	1.037
Mark McGwire	.974
Ken Griffey Jr.	.964
Edgar Martinez	.952
Jeff Bagwell	.945
Albert Belle	.944
Mo Vaughn	.925
Larry Walker	.922
Tim Salmon	.919

Secondary Average

(minimum 3,000 Plate Appearances)

Barry Bonds	.605
Mark McGwire	.540
Frank Thomas	.505
Rickey Henderson	.489
Mickey Tettleton	.450
Jeff Bagwell	.433
Ken Griffey Jr.	.426
Gary Sheffield	.421
Jose Canseco	.421
Albert Belle	.410

Isolated Power

(minimum 3,000 Plate Appearances)

Mark McGwire	.316
Barry Bonds	.294
Albert Belle	.280
Juan Gonzalez	.275
Ken Griffey Jr.	.271
Frank Thomas	.270
Jose Canseco	.256
Larry Walker	.248
Jay Buhner	.246
Matt Williams	.238

Pitching Leaders—1990-1997

Wins			Losses			Winning Percentage			Games	
						(minimum 100 decisions)				
Greg Maddux	139		Tim Belcher	93		Mike Mussina	.682		Paul Assenmacher	520
Tom Glavine	130		Andy Benes	91		Randy Johnson	.675		Mike Jackson	503
Roger Clemens	118		Bobby Witt	89		Greg Maddux	.665		Bob Patterson	485
John Smoltz	115		Mike Morgan	88		Tom Glavine	.650		Randy Myers	481
Jack McDowell	114		Tom Candiotti	88		Jose Rijo	.626		Dennis Eckersley	480
Randy Johnson	114		Chuck Finley	88		Pedro Martinez	.625		Doug Jones	479
Chuck Finley	112		Jim Abbott	88		Jimmy Key	.620		Jeff Montgomery	473
David Cone	109		Terry Mulholland	87		Jack McDowell	.620		Dan Plesac	470
Ramon Martinez	109		Doug Drabek	84		Ramon Martinez	.619		Tony Fossas	465
Kevin Brown	107		John Smoltz	84		Roger Clemens	.618		Mel Rojas	462

Games Started			Complete Games			Shutouts			Saves	
Greg Maddux	264		Greg Maddux	62		Roger Clemens	20		Dennis Eckersley	292
John Smoltz	260		Jack McDowell	61		Greg Maddux	18		Randy Myers	263
Tom Glavine	259		Roger Clemens	51		Ramon Martinez	18		Lee Smith	244
Doug Drabek	251		Kevin Brown	46		Randy Johnson	17		Jeff Montgomery	237
John Burkett	251		Chuck Finley	44		David Cone	15		Rick Aguilera	230
Chuck Finley	249		Randy Johnson	43		Doug Drabek	14		John Franco	211
Andy Benes	248		Terry Mulholland	41		Dennis Martinez	13		John Wetteland	210
Kevin Brown	244		Doug Drabek	40		Jack McDowell	13		Doug Jones	200
Tim Belcher	244		John Smoltz	39		3 tied with	12		Rod Beck	199
Roger Clemens	242		David Cone	36					Tom Henke	189

Games Finished			Batters Faced			Innings Pitched			Hits Allowed	
Dennis Eckersley	424		Greg Maddux	7,636		Greg Maddux	1,924.1		Jaime Navarro	1,711
Doug Jones	406		John Smoltz	7,376		John Smoltz	1,788.1		John Burkett	1,695
Jeff Montgomery	401		Tom Glavine	7,368		Tom Glavine	1,764.2		Kevin Brown	1,672
Randy Myers	391		Chuck Finley	7,248		Roger Clemens	1,755.1		Tom Glavine	1,640
Rick Aguilera	384		Roger Clemens	7,185		Chuck Finley	1,707.1		Chuck Finley	1,633
Lee Smith	353		Kevin Brown	7,148		Kevin Brown	1,702.0		Scott Erickson	1,626
Rod Beck	346		Doug Drabek	6,878		Doug Drabek	1,654.2		Greg Maddux	1,625
John Wetteland	341		Andy Benes	6,864		Kevin Appier	1,643.2		Bob Tewksbury	1,615
John Franco	337		Tim Belcher	6,842		Andy Benes	1,638.2		Doug Drabek	1,610
Mike Henneman	318		Jaime Navarro	6,827		David Cone	1,616.0		Tim Belcher	1,608

Runs Allowed			Earned Runs Allowed			Home Runs Allowed			Walks	
Jaime Navarro	854		Jaime Navarro	771		Chuck Finley	174		Randy Johnson	754
Tim Belcher	834		Tim Belcher	750		Alex Fernandez	173		Bobby Witt	697
Bobby Witt	797		Bobby Witt	725		David Wells	172		Chuck Finley	685
Scott Erickson	793		Scott Erickson	721		Tim Belcher	162		Tom Gordon	677
Chuck Finley	790		Todd Stottlemyre	718		Todd Stottlemyre	161		David Cone	625
John Burkett	781		John Burkett	712		Terry Mulholland	159		Tom Glavine	607
Terry Mulholland	777		Chuck Finley	707		Kevin Tapani	156		Ramon Martinez	600
Todd Stottlemyre	774		Terry Mulholland	702		Andy Benes	153		John Smoltz	585
Kevin Tapani	743		Kevin Tapani	693		Greg Swindell	152		Tim Belcher	581
Kevin Brown	741		Doug Drabek	677		Doug Drabek	149		2 tied with	562

Intentional Walks			Strikeouts			Strikeouts/9 Innings			ERA	
						(minimum 1,000 Innings Pitched)			(minimum 1,000 Innings Pitched)	
Roger McDowell	66		Randy Johnson	1,845		Randy Johnson	10.73		Greg Maddux	2.47
Joe Boever	63		Roger Clemens	1,667		David Cone	8.59		Jose Rijo	2.74
Greg Maddux	56		John Smoltz	1,564		Roger Clemens	8.55		Roger Clemens	2.90
Tom Glavine	56		David Cone	1,542		Curt Schilling	8.19		David Cone	3.14
Mike Henneman	52		Greg Maddux	1,424		John Smoltz	7.87		Tom Glavine	3.18
Mike Jackson	48		Chuck Finley	1,372		Jeff Fassero	7.79		Kevin Appier	3.22
Greg Harris	45		Kevin Appier	1,354		Jose Rijo	7.74		Randy Johnson	3.24
Orel Hershiser	45		Andy Benes	1,350		Juan Guzman	7.71		Curt Schilling	3.28
John Smoltz	45		Tom Glavine	1,170		Tom Gordon	7.61		Jeff Fassero	3.29
2 tied with	44		Tom Gordon	1,158		Andy Benes	7.41		Dennis Martinez	3.30

Component ERA			Sac Hits Allowed			Sac Flies Allowed			Hit Batsmen	
(minimum 1,000 Innings Pitched)										
Greg Maddux	2.20		Greg Maddux	98		Jaime Navarro	71		Kevin Brown	86
Roger Clemens	2.79		John Smiley	85		Bob Tewksbury	58		Randy Johnson	75
Curt Schilling	2.80		Tom Glavine	82		Todd Stottlemyre	58		Darryl Kile	72
Jose Rijo	2.80		John Smoltz	80		Bobby Witt	54		Roger Clemens	66
John Smoltz	2.97		Bob Tewksbury	77		Terry Mulholland	51		Mark Leiter	65
David Cone	3.00		Mike Morgan	76		Tom Gordon	51		Todd Stottlemyre	62
Kevin Appier	3.02		Terry Mulholland	75		Charlie Hough	49		Scott Erickson	59
Dennis Martinez	3.09		Danny Jackson	71		Tom Candiotti	49		Dennis Martinez	58
Randy Johnson	3.11		John Burkett	71		Chuck Finley	47		Orel Hershiser	51
Mike Mussina	3.17		Tom Candiotti	70		John Smoltz	47		John Burkett	51

Wild Pitches			Balks			Opponent Average			Opponent OBP	
						(minimum 1,000 Innings Pitched)			(minimum 1,000 Innings Pitched)	
John Smoltz	104		Bud Black	20		Randy Johnson	.207		Greg Maddux	.270
David Cone	87		Jim Deshaies	16		David Cone	.222		Curt Schilling	.286
Juan Guzman	82		Darryl Kile	16		Roger Clemens	.227		Jose Rijo	.290
Chuck Finley	79		Pedro Astacio	14		Greg Maddux	.229		Mike Mussina	.292
Mike Moore	76		Jose Rijo	13		Curt Schilling	.233		Roger Clemens	.293
Tom Gordon	70		David Cone	13		John Smoltz	.233		John Smoltz	.296
Jack Morris	67		Trevor Wilson	13		Kevin Appier	.235		Dennis Martinez	.298
Doug Drabek	65		5 tied with	12		Jose Rijo	.236		David Cone	.299
Erik Hanson	65					Ramon Martinez	.239		Kevin Appier	.301
Kevin Appier	62					Juan Guzman	.240		Jeff Fassero	.305

Single Season Batting Leaders—1990-1997

Games				At-Bats				Runs				Hits		
Cal Ripken Jr.	1996	163		Nomar Garciaparra	1997	684		Craig Biggio	1997	146		Lance Johnson	1996	227
Todd Zeile	1996	163		Lance Johnson	1996	682		Lenny Dykstra	1993	143		Paul Molitor	1996	225
20 tied with		162		Marquis Grissom	1996	671		Larry Walker	1997	143		Tony Gwynn	1997	220
				Paul Molitor	1991	665		Ellis Burks	1996	142		Paul Molitor	1991	216
				Kenny Lofton	1996	662		Alex Rodriguez	1996	141		Alex Rodriguez	1996	215
				Ruben Sierra	1991	661		Chuck Knoblauch	1996	140		Paul Molitor	1993	211
				Paul Molitor	1996	660		Paul Molitor	1991	133		Ellis Burks	1996	211
				Travis Fryman	1992	659		Roberto Alomar	1996	132		Cal Ripken Jr.	1991	210
				Brian Hunter	1997	658		Kenny Lofton	1996	132		Kirby Puckett	1992	210
				2 tied with		657		Barry Bonds	1993	129		Kenny Lofton	1996	210

Doubles				Triples				Home Runs				Home Runs (Home)		
John Olerud	1993	54		Lance Johnson	1996	21		Mark McGwire	1997	58		Andres Galarraga	1996	32
Alex Rodriguez	1996	54		Tony Fernandez	1990	17		Ken Griffey Jr.	1997	56		Dante Bichette	1995	31
Mark Grudzielanek	1997	54		Ray Lankford	1991	15		Mark McGwire	1996	52		Mark McGwire	1997	30
Edgar Martinez	1995	52		Deion Sanders	1992	14		Cecil Fielder	1990	51		Cecil Fielder	1991	27
Albert Belle	1995	52		Lance Johnson	1993	14		Albert Belle	1995	50		Mo Vaughn	1996	27
Edgar Martinez	1996	52		Lance Johnson	1994	14		Brady Anderson	1996	50		Vinny Castilla	1996	27
Mark Grace	1995	51		Chuck Knoblauch	1996	14		Ken Griffey Jr.	1996	49		Ken Griffey Jr.	1997	27
Rafael Palmeiro	1991	49		Delino DeShields	1997	14		Larry Walker	1997	49		Frank Thomas	1993	26
Tony Gwynn	1997	49		6 tied with		13		Albert Belle	1996	48		Ken Griffey Jr.	1996	26
Jeff Bagwell	1996	48						2 tied with		47		Sammy Sosa	1996	26

Home Runs (Road)				Extra Base Hits				Total Bases				RBI		
Brady Anderson	1996	31		Albert Belle	1995	103		Larry Walker	1997	409		Andres Galarraga	1996	150
Larry Walker	1997	29		Larry Walker	1997	99		Ken Griffey Jr.	1997	393		Albert Belle	1996	148
Ken Griffey Jr.	1997	29		Ellis Burks	1996	93		Ellis Burks	1996	392		Ken Griffey Jr.	1997	147
Jose Canseco	1991	28		Ken Griffey Jr.	1997	93		Alex Rodriguez	1996	379		Juan Gonzalez	1996	144
Mark McGwire	1996	28		Brady Anderson	1996	92		Albert Belle	1995	377		Mo Vaughn	1996	143
Mark McGwire	1997	28		Alex Rodriguez	1996	91		Andres Galarraga	1996	376		Rafael Palmeiro	1996	142
Jay Buhner	1997	27		Andres Galarraga	1996	89		Albert Belle	1996	375		Dante Bichette	1996	141
Cecil Fielder	1990	26		Albert Belle	1996	89		Mo Vaughn	1996	370		Tino Martinez	1997	141
Albert Belle	1996	26		Barry Bonds	1993	88		Brady Anderson	1996	369		Ken Griffey Jr.	1996	140
Tino Martinez	1997	26		Ken Griffey Jr.	1993	86		Cal Ripken Jr.	1991	368		Andres Galarraga	1997	140

Walks				Walks/PA (minimum 3.1 PA/Tm Gm)				Strikeouts				Hit By Pitch		
Barry Bonds	1996	151		Barry Bonds	1996	.224		Cecil Fielder	1990	182		Craig Biggio	1997	34
Barry Bonds	1997	145		Mickey Tettleton	1994	.218		Rob Deer	1991	175		Jason Kendall	1997	31
Gary Sheffield	1996	142		Mark McGwire	1996	.212		Jay Buhner	1997	175		Craig Biggio	1996	27
Frank Thomas	1991	138		Frank Thomas	1994	.211		Sammy Sosa	1997	174		F.P. Santangelo	1997	25
Frank Thomas	1995	136		Frank Thomas	1995	.210		Andres Galarraga	1990	169		Craig Biggio	1995	22
Jeff Bagwell	1996	135		Barry Bonds	1997	.210		Rob Deer	1993	169		Brady Anderson	1996	22
Tony Phillips	1993	132		Gary Sheffield	1996	.210		Ron Gant	1997	162		Eric Young	1996	21
Lenny Dykstra	1993	129		Gary Sheffield	1997	.208		Mickey Tettleton	1990	160		Jeff Blauser	1997	20
Barry Bonds	1992	127		Rickey Henderson	1996	.208		Henry Rodriguez	1996	160		3 tied with		19
Jeff Bagwell	1997	127		Barry Bonds	1992	.208		2 tied with		159				

Sac Hits				Sac Flies				Stolen Bases				Caught Stealing		
Jay Bell	1990	39		Bobby Bonilla	1996	17		Marquis Grissom	1992	78		Brett Butler	1991	28
Jay Bell	1991	30		Bobby Bonilla	1990	15		Vince Coleman	1990	77		Eric Yelding	1990	25
Jose Offerman	1993	25		Howard Johnson	1991	15		Marquis Grissom	1991	76		Ray Lankford	1992	24
Brett Butler	1992	24		Dave Parker	1990	14		Kenny Lofton	1996	75		Luis Polonia	1993	24
Tom Goodwin	1996	21		Albert Belle	1993	14		Brian Hunter	1997	74		Chad Curtis	1993	24
Luis Sojo	1991	19		10 tied with		13		Otis Nixon	1991	72		Luis Polonia	1991	23
Jay Bell	1992	19						Kenny Lofton	1993	70		Delino DeShields	1991	23
Joey Cora	1993	19						Kenny Lofton	1992	66		4 tied with		22
Edgar Renteria	1997	19						Tom Goodwin	1996	66				
Bobby Jones	1995	18						Rickey Henderson	1990	65				

Runs Created				Runs Created/27 Outs (minimum 3.1 PA/Tm Gm)				Batting Average (minimum 3.1 PA/Tm Gm)				On-Base Percentage (minimum 3.1 PA/Tm Gm)		
Barry Bonds	1993	162		Mark McGwire	1996	11.79		Tony Gwynn	1994	.394		Frank Thomas	1994	.487
Barry Bonds	1996	160		Edgar Martinez	1995	11.67		Tony Gwynn	1997	.372		Edgar Martinez	1995	.479
Larry Walker	1997	158		Barry Bonds	1996	11.33		Andres Galarraga	1993	.370		John Olerud	1993	.473
Edgar Martinez	1995	151		Barry Bonds	1993	11.27		Tony Gwynn	1995	.368		Mark McGwire	1996	.467
Andres Galarraga	1996	150		Frank Thomas	1994	11.03		Jeff Bagwell	1994	.368		Gary Sheffield	1996	.465
Frank Thomas	1997	150		Jeff Bagwell	1994	11.02		Larry Walker	1997	.366		Edgar Martinez	1996	.464
Jeff Bagwell	1996	149		Larry Walker	1997	10.99		John Olerud	1993	.363		Barry Bonds	1996	.461
Mo Vaughn	1996	149		Frank Thomas	1997	10.93		Mike Piazza	1997	.362		Paul O'Neill	1994	.460
Ken Griffey Jr.	1997	148		Albert Belle	1994	10.72		Paul O'Neill	1994	.359		Frank Thomas	1996	.459
2 tied with		147		John Olerud	1993	10.40		Tony Gwynn	1993	.358		Barry Bonds	1993	.458

Slugging Percentage (minimum 3.1 PA/Tm Gm)				OBP+Slugging (minimum 3.1 PA/Tm Gm)				Secondary Average (minimum 3.1 PA/Tm Gm)				Isolated Power (minimum 3.1 PA/Tm Gm)		
Jeff Bagwell	1994	.750		Frank Thomas	1994	1.217		Mark McGwire	1996	.693		Mark McGwire	1996	.418
Mark McGwire	1996	.730		Jeff Bagwell	1994	1.201		Barry Bonds	1996	.677		Jeff Bagwell	1994	.383
Frank Thomas	1994	.729		Mark McGwire	1996	1.198		Barry Bonds	1992	.664		Frank Thomas	1994	.376
Larry Walker	1997	.720		Larry Walker	1997	1.172		Frank Thomas	1994	.654		Albert Belle	1995	.374
Albert Belle	1994	.714		Albert Belle	1994	1.152		Barry Bonds	1997	.635		Mark McGwire	1997	.372
Albert Belle	1995	.690		Barry Bonds	1993	1.136		Barry Bonds	1993	.629		Albert Belle	1994	.357
Kevin Mitchell	1994	.681		Kevin Mitchell	1994	1.110		Gary Sheffield	1996	.615		Kevin Mitchell	1994	.355
Barry Bonds	1993	.677		Edgar Martinez	1995	1.107		Barry Bonds	1994	.598		Larry Walker	1997	.354
Ken Griffey Jr.	1994	.674		Albert Belle	1995	1.091		Jeff Bagwell	1997	.585		Ken Griffey Jr.	1994	.351
Barry Bonds	1994	.647		Gary Sheffield	1996	1.090		Rickey Henderson	1990	.583		Ken Griffey Jr.	1997	.342

Single Season Pitching Leaders—1990-1997

Wins

Bob Welch	1990	27
John Smoltz	1996	24
Dave Stewart	1990	22
Doug Drabek	1990	22
Jack McDowell	1993	22
John Burkett	1993	22
Tom Glavine	1993	22
6 tied with		21

Losses

Tim Leary	1990	19
Jose DeLeon	1990	19
Kirk McCaskill	1991	19
Scott Erickson	1993	19
Jack Morris	1990	18
Matt Young	1990	18
Allan Anderson	1990	18
Doug Drabek	1993	18
Jim Abbott	1996	18
10 tied with		17

Winning Percentage
(minimum 15 decisions)

Greg Maddux	1995	.905
Randy Johnson	1995	.900
Randy Johnson	1997	.833
Greg Maddux	1997	.826
Juan Guzman	1993	.824
Bob Welch	1990	.818
Mark Portugal	1993	.818
Jamie Moyer	1996	.813
Jimmy Key	1994	.810
2 tied with		.800

Games

Julian Tavarez	1997	89
Mike Myers	1997	88
Stan Belinda	1997	84
Eddie Guardado	1996	83
Mike Myers	1996	83
Juan Agosto	1990	82
6 tied with		81

Games Started

Greg Maddux	1991	37
14 tied with		36

Complete Games

Jack McDowell	1991	15
Roger Clemens	1991	13
Jack McDowell	1992	13
Chuck Finley	1993	13
Pedro Martinez	1997	13
Ramon Martinez	1990	12
Terry Mulholland	1992	12
Kevin Brown	1993	12
4 tied with		11

Shutouts

Dennis Martinez	1991	5
Roger Clemens	1992	5
David Cone	1992	5
Tom Glavine	1992	5
Carlos Perez	1997	5
20 tied with		4

Saves

Bobby Thigpen	1990	57
Randy Myers	1993	53
Dennis Eckersley	1992	51
Dennis Eckersley	1990	48
Rod Beck	1993	48
Lee Smith	1991	47
Bryan Harvey	1991	46
Lee Smith	1993	46
Jose Mesa	1995	46
4 tied with		45

Games Finished

Bobby Thigpen	1990	73
Doug Jones	1997	73
Rod Beck	1993	71
Doug Jones	1992	70
Duane Ward	1993	70
Randy Myers	1993	69
Roberto Hernandez	1993	67
Todd Worrell	1996	67
Robb Nen	1996	66
Rod Beck	1997	66

Batters Faced

Kevin Brown	1992	1,108
Pat Hentgen	1996	1,100
Dave Stewart	1990	1,088
Cal Eldred	1993	1,087
Pat Hentgen	1997	1,085
Bill Wegman	1992	1,079
Jack McDowell	1992	1,079
Roger Clemens	1991	1,077
Jack Morris	1990	1,073
Alex Fernandez	1996	1,071

Innings Pitched

Roger Clemens	1991	271.1
Greg Maddux	1992	268.0
Dave Stewart	1990	267.0
Greg Maddux	1993	267.0
Kevin Brown	1992	265.2
Pat Hentgen	1996	265.2
Roger Clemens	1997	264.0
Pat Hentgen	1997	264.0
Greg Maddux	1991	263.0
Bill Wegman	1992	261.2

Hits Allowed

Chris Haney	1996	267
Jaime Navarro	1997	267
Scott Erickson	1993	266
Mike Mussina	1996	264
Kevin Brown	1992	262
Tim Belcher	1996	262
Scott Erickson	1996	262
Jack McDowell	1993	261
Frank Viola	1991	259
Bob Tewksbury	1993	258

Runs Allowed

Jaime Navarro	1997	155
Tim Wakefield	1996	151
Jack Morris	1990	144
Erik Hanson	1996	143
Tom Gordon	1996	143
Scott Erickson	1993	138
Scott Erickson	1996	137
Mike Mussina	1996	137
Chris Haney	1996	136
4 tied with		135

Earned Runs Allowed

Jaime Navarro	1997	135
Tom Gordon	1996	134
Dave Stewart	1991	130
Mike Mussina	1996	130
Erik Hanson	1996	129
David Wells	1996	128
Jaime Navarro	1993	127
Scott Erickson	1993	126
Jack Morris	1990	125
Kevin Ritz	1996	125

Home Runs Allowed

Shawn Boskie	1996	40
Brad Radke	1996	40
Tim Wakefield	1996	38
Mark Leiter	1996	37
Allen Watson	1997	37
Bill Gullickson	1992	35
Mike Moore	1993	35
Kevin Tapani	1996	34
Alex Fernandez	1996	34
2 tied with		33

Walks

Randy Johnson	1991	152
Randy Johnson	1992	144
Jose DeJesus	1991	128
Wilson Alvarez	1993	122
Randy Johnson	1990	120
Charlie Hough	1990	119
Al Leiter	1996	119
Rich Robertson	1996	116
Bobby Witt	1992	114
David Cone	1993	114

Intentional Walks

Roger McDowell	1991	20
Todd Jones	1995	17
Bill Gullickson	1990	14
Scott Terry	1991	14
Greg Harris	1993	14
Paul Quantrill	1993	14
9 tied with		13

Strikeouts

Curt Schilling	1997	319
Randy Johnson	1993	308
Pedro Martinez	1997	305
Randy Johnson	1995	294
Roger Clemens	1997	292
Randy Johnson	1997	291
John Smoltz	1996	276
David Cone	1992	261
Roger Clemens	1996	257
4 tied with		241

Strikeouts/9 Innings
(minimum 1 Inning Pitched/Tm Gm)

Randy Johnson	1995	12.35
Randy Johnson	1997	12.30
Pedro Martinez	1997	11.37
Curt Schilling	1997	11.29
Hideo Nomo	1995	11.10
Randy Johnson	1993	10.86
Randy Johnson	1994	10.67
Nolan Ryan	1991	10.56
Randy Johnson	1992	10.31
David Cone	1997	10.25

ERA
(minimum 1 Inning Pitched/Tm Gm)

Greg Maddux	1994	1.56
Greg Maddux	1995	1.63
Kevin Brown	1996	1.89
Pedro Martinez	1997	1.90
Roger Clemens	1990	1.93
Roger Clemens	1997	2.05
Bill Swift	1992	2.08
Bob Tewksbury	1992	2.16
Greg Maddux	1992	2.18
Greg Maddux	1997	2.20

Component ERA
(minimum 1 Inning Pitched/Tm Gm)

Greg Maddux	1995	1.41
Greg Maddux	1994	1.59
Pedro Martinez	1997	1.79
Curt Schilling	1992	1.86
Greg Maddux	1997	1.95
Kevin Brown	1996	2.00
Greg Maddux	1992	2.01
Roger Clemens	1997	2.17
John Smoltz	1996	2.17
Randy Johnson	1995	2.18

Sac Hits Allowed

Tom Glavine	1990	21
Kent Bottenfield	1993	21
Tom Candiotti	1992	20
Charlie Leibrandt	1991	19
Andy Benes	1992	19
Jeff Fassero	1995	19
Greg Maddux	1990	18
Allen Watson	1996	18
Steve Cooke	1997	18
6 tied with		17

Sac Flies Allowed

Jaime Navarro	1993	17
Charlie Hough	1991	16
Dave Stewart	1991	15
Rich DeLucia	1991	14
David Wells	1996	14
Jaime Navarro	1997	14
Jaime Navarro	1992	13
Scott Erickson	1993	13
Dennis Springer	1997	13
5 tied with		12

Hit Batsmen

Randy Johnson	1992	18
Mark Leiter	1995	17
Randy Johnson	1993	16
Kevin Brown	1996	16
Mark Leiter	1996	16
Darryl Kile	1996	16
Tim Wakefield	1997	16
Kevin Brown	1993	15
Darryl Kile	1993	15
Aaron Sele	1997	15

Wild Pitches

Juan Guzman	1993	26
Tim Leary	1990	23
Mike Moore	1992	22
John Smoltz	1991	20
Hideo Nomo	1995	19
David Cone	1991	17
John Smoltz	1992	17
Tom Gordon	1993	17
Chuck Finley	1996	17
5 tied with		16

Balks

Pedro Astacio	1993	9
Bud Black	1992	7
Trevor Wilson	1992	7
Bud Black	1991	6
Greg Harris	1993	6
Armando Reynoso	1993	6
20 tied with		5

Opponent Average
(minimum 1 Inning Pitched/Tm Gm)

Nolan Ryan	1991	.172
Hideo Nomo	1995	.182
Pedro Martinez	1997	.184
Nolan Ryan	1990	.188
Randy Johnson	1997	.194
Greg Maddux	1995	.197
Sid Fernandez	1990	.200
Randy Johnson	1995	.201
Curt Schilling	1992	.201
Al Leiter	1996	.202

Opponent OBP
(minimum 1 Inning Pitched/Tm Gm)

Greg Maddux	1995	.224
Greg Maddux	1994	.243
Pedro Martinez	1997	.250
Curt Schilling	1992	.254
Greg Maddux	1997	.256
John Smoltz	1996	.260
Kevin Brown	1996	.262
Nolan Ryan	1991	.263
Greg Maddux	1996	.264
Bob Tewksbury	1992	.265

Batting Leaders—Through Age 18

At-Bats		Runs		Hits		Doubles	
Phil Cavarretta	610	Phil Cavarretta	90	Phil Cavarretta	170	Phil Cavarretta	28
Milt Scott	443	Mike Slattery	60	Milt Scott	110	Johnny Lush	22
Mike Slattery	413	Robin Yount	48	Johnny Lush	102	Milt Scott	17
Johnny Lush	369	Johnny Lush	39	Robin Yount	86	Robin Yount	14
Robin Yount	344	Pat Callahan	38	Mike Slattery	86	Ed Kranepool	13
Tommy Brown	342	Scott Stratton	35	Tommy Brown	72	Whitey Lockman	9
Ed Kranepool	279	Tommy Brown	30	Mel Ott	69	Mel Ott	9
Pat Callahan	258	Mel Ott	30	Pat Callahan	67	4 tied with	8
Larry McKeon	250	Milt Scott	30	Scott Stratton	64		
Scott Stratton	249	2 tied with	29	Ed Kranepool	58		

Triples		Home Runs		RBI		Stolen Bases	
Phil Cavarretta	13	Phil Cavarretta	9	Phil Cavarretta	88	Johnny Lush	12
Lew Brown	6	Robin Yount	3	Milt Scott	50	Scott Stratton	10
Robin Yount	5	Danny Murphy	3	Johnny Lush	42	Robin Yount	7
John McGraw	5	Whitey Lockman	3	Scott Stratton	29	Lew Malone	7
Pat Callahan	5	Jimmy Sheckard	3	Tommy Brown	27	Phil Cavarretta	5
Milt Scott	5	Milt Scott	3	Robin Yount	26	Merito Acosta	5
5 tied with	4	7 tied with	2	Mel Ott	23	Jack Burnett	5
				Lew Brown	21	Jimmy Sheckard	5
				Nat Hudson	20	4 tied with	4
				Whitey Lockman	18		

Runs Created		Batting Average		On-Base Percentage		Slugging Percentage	
		(minimum 300 Plate Appearances)		(minimum 300 Plate Appearances)		(minimum 300 Plate Appearances)	
Phil Cavarretta	86	Phil Cavarretta	.279	Johnny Lush	.336	Phil Cavarretta	.411
Milt Scott	59	Johnny Lush	.276	Phil Cavarretta	.326	Johnny Lush	.369
Johnny Lush	52	Robin Yount	.250	Robin Yount	.276	Robin Yount	.346
Mike Slattery	45	Milt Scott	.248	Milt Scott	.263	Milt Scott	.330
Scott Stratton	36	Tommy Brown	.211	Ed Kranepool	.254	Ed Kranepool	.290
Pat Callahan	36	Mike Slattery	.208	Tommy Brown	.242	Tommy Brown	.272
Robin Yount	32	Ed Kranepool	.208	Mike Slattery	.216	Mike Slattery	.232
Mel Ott	30						
Nat Hudson	28						
Lew Brown	28						

Single Season Batting Leaders—Age 18 or Younger

At-Bats			Runs			Hits			Doubles		
Phil Cavarretta	1935	589	Phil Cavarretta	1935	85	Phil Cavarretta	1935	162	Phil Cavarretta	1935	28
Milt Scott	1884	438	Mike Slattery	1884	60	Milt Scott	1884	108	Johnny Lush	1904	22
Mike Slattery	1884	413	Robin Yount	1974	48	Johnny Lush	1904	102	Milt Scott	1884	17
Johnny Lush	1904	369	Johnny Lush	1904	39	Mike Slattery	1884	86	Robin Yount	1974	14
Robin Yount	1974	344	Pat Callahan	1884	38	Robin Yount	1974	86	Ed Kranepool	1963	12
Ed Kranepool	1963	273	Scott Stratton	1888	35	Pat Callahan	1884	67	Whitey Lockman	1945	9
Pat Callahan	1884	258	Larry McKeon	1884	29	Scott Stratton	1888	64	Larry McKeon	1884	8
Larry McKeon	1884	250	Milt Scott	1884	29	Ed Kranepool	1963	57	Pat Callahan	1884	8
Scott Stratton	1888	249	Jim Donnelly	1884	24	Larry McKeon	1884	53	Scott Stratton	1888	8
Sibby Sisti	1939	215	2 tied with		23	2 tied with		49	Jack Burnett	1907	8

Triples			Home Runs			RBI			Stolen Bases		
Phil Cavarretta	1935	12	Phil Cavarretta	1935	8	Phil Cavarretta	1935	82	Johnny Lush	1904	12
Lew Brown	1876	6	Milt Scott	1884	3	Milt Scott	1884	50	Scott Stratton	1888	10
Pat Callahan	1884	5	Jimmy Sheckard	1897	3	Johnny Lush	1904	42	Lew Malone	1915	7
Milt Scott	1884	5	Whitey Lockman	1945	3	Scott Stratton	1888	29	Robin Yount	1974	7
John McGraw	1891	5	Robin Yount	1974	3	Robin Yount	1974	26	Jimmy Sheckard	1897	5
Robin Yount	1974	5	8 tied with		2	Lew Brown	1876	21	Jack Burnett	1907	5
5 tied with		4				Mel Ott	1927	19	5 tied with		4
						Tommy Brown	1945	19			
						Whitey Lockman	1945	18			
						2 tied with		17			

Runs Created			Batting Average			On-Base Percentage			Slugging Percentage		
			(minimum 3.1 PA/Tm Gm)			(minimum 3.1 PA/Tm Gm)			(minimum 3.1 PA/Tm Gm)		
Phil Cavarretta	1935	81	Phil Cavarretta	1935	.275	Phil Cavarretta	1935	.322	Phil Cavarretta	1935	.404
Milt Scott	1884	58	Milt Scott	1884	.247	Milt Scott	1884	.262	Milt Scott	1884	.329
Johnny Lush	1904	52	Mike Slattery	1884	.208	Mike Slattery	1884	.216	Mike Slattery	1884	.232
Mike Slattery	1884	45									
Pat Callahan	1884	36									
Scott Stratton	1888	36									
Robin Yount	1974	32									
Lew Brown	1876	28									
Jumbo McGinnis	1882	25									
Whitey Lockman	1945	25									

Pitching Leaders—Through Age 18

Wins		Losses		Winning Percentage (minimum 25 decisions)		Games	
Willie McGill	32	Larry McKeon	41	Monte Ward	.629	Willie McGill	70
Jumbo McGinnis	25	Willie McGill	25	Nat Hudson	.588	Larry McKeon	61
Monte Ward	22	Jumbo McGinnis	18	Jumbo McGinnis	.581	Bob Miller	45
Nat Hudson	20	Pete Conway	17	Willie McGill	.561	Jumbo McGinnis	45
Larry McKeon	18	Scott Stratton	17	Pete Conway	.370	Bob Feller	40
Bob Feller	14	Nat Hudson	14	Scott Stratton	.370	Nat Hudson	38
Amos Rusie	12	Pete Schneider	13	Larry McKeon	.305	Monte Ward	37
Perry Werden	12	Tony Madigan	13			Amos Rusie	33
Pete Conway	10	Monte Ward	13			Scott Stratton	33
Scott Stratton	10	5 tied with	10			Jim Brillheart	31

Complete Games		Shutouts		Saves		Innings Pitched	
Larry McKeon	59	Monte Ward	6	Bob Feller	2	Willie McGill	514.2
Willie McGill	48	Jumbo McGinnis	3	Randy Gumpert	2	Larry McKeon	512.0
Jumbo McGinnis	43	Von McDaniel	2	Herb Pennock	2	Jumbo McGinnis	388.1
Monte Ward	37	Larry McKeon	2	10 tied with	1	Monte Ward	334.0
Nat Hudson	32	Scott Stratton	2			Nat Hudson	301.1
Scott Stratton	28	Lev Shreve	2			Scott Stratton	269.2
Pete Conway	26	11 tied with	1			Amos Rusie	225.0
Amos Rusie	19					Bob Feller	210.2
Lev Shreve	18					Pete Conway	210.0
Will Sawyer	15					Lev Shreve	160.0

Strikeouts		ERA (minimum 100 Innings Pitched)		Component ERA (minimum 100 Innings Pitched)		Opponent Average (minimum 100 Innings Pitched)	
Larry McKeon	308	Monte Ward	1.51	Perry Werden	1.65	Perry Werden	.205
Willie McGill	262	Perry Werden	1.97	Monte Ward	1.92	Will Sawyer	.217
Bob Feller	226	Will Sawyer	2.36	Will Sawyer	2.24	Ed Knouff	.218
Jumbo McGinnis	134	Jumbo McGinnis	2.60	Jumbo McGinnis	2.50	Bob Feller	.222
Monte Ward	116	Pete Schneider	2.81	Larry McKeon	2.56	Monte Ward	.231
Nat Hudson	115	Bob Feller	3.38	Ed Knouff	2.94	Larry McKeon	.235
Larry Dierker	114	Larry Dierker	3.41	Larry Dierker	3.11	Larry Dierker	.239
Amos Rusie	109	Nat Hudson	3.46	Scott Stratton	3.12	Jumbo McGinnis	.245
Scott Stratton	97	Larry McKeon	3.50	Nat Hudson	3.18	Nat Hudson	.259
Pete Conway	94	Ed Knouff	3.52	Pete Schneider	3.42	Bob Miller	.261

Single Season Pitching Leaders—Age 18 or Younger

Wins			Losses			Winning Percentage (minimum 15 decisions)			Games		
Jumbo McGinnis	1882	25	Larry McKeon	1884	41	Monte Ward	1878	.629	Larry McKeon	1884	61
Monte Ward	1878	22	Jumbo McGinnis	1882	18	Nat Hudson	1886	.615	Jumbo McGinnis	1882	45
Willie McGill	1891	20	Pete Conway	1885	17	Jumbo McGinnis	1882	.581	Willie McGill	1891	43
Larry McKeon	1884	18	Scott Stratton	1888	17	Willie McGill	1891	.571	Monte Ward	1878	37
Nat Hudson	1886	16	Willie McGill	1891	15	Bob Feller	1937	.563	Scott Stratton	1888	33
Perry Werden	1884	12	Monte Ward	1878	13	Willie McGill	1890	.550	Amos Rusie	1889	33
Amos Rusie	1889	12	Tony Madigan	1886	13	Amos Rusie	1889	.545	Bob Miller	1954	32
Willie McGill	1890	11	Pete Schneider	1914	13	Larry Dierker	1965	.467	Jim Brillheart	1922	31
Pete Conway	1885	10	5 tied with		10	Lev Shreve	1887	.444	Nat Hudson	1886	29
Scott Stratton	1888	10				2 tied with		.370	Pete Schneider	1914	29

Complete Games			Shutouts			Saves			Innings Pitched		
Larry McKeon	1884	59	Monte Ward	1878	6	Herb Pennock	1912	2	Larry McKeon	1884	512.0
Jumbo McGinnis	1882	43	Jumbo McGinnis	1882	3	Randy Gumpert	1936	2	Jumbo McGinnis	1882	388.1
Monte Ward	1878	37	Larry McKeon	1884	2	12 tied with		1	Monte Ward	1878	334.0
Scott Stratton	1888	28	Lev Shreve	1887	2				Willie McGill	1891	314.0
Willie McGill	1891	28	Scott Stratton	1888	2				Scott Stratton	1888	269.2
Pete Conway	1885	26	Von McDaniel	1957	2				Nat Hudson	1886	234.1
Nat Hudson	1886	25	11 tied with		1				Amos Rusie	1889	225.0
Amos Rusie	1889	19							Pete Conway	1885	210.0
Willie McGill	1890	19							Willie McGill	1890	183.2
Lev Shreve	1887	18							Lev Shreve	1887	160.0

Strikeouts			ERA (minimum 1 Inning Pitched/Tm Gm)			Component ERA (minimum 1 Inning Pitched/Tm Gm)			Opponent Average (minimum 1 Inning Pitched/Tm Gm)		
Larry McKeon	1884	308	Monte Ward	1878	1.51	Perry Werden	1884	1.65	Perry Werden	1884	.205
Willie McGill	1891	173	Perry Werden	1884	1.97	Monte Ward	1878	1.92	Will Sawyer	1883	.217
Bob Feller	1937	150	Will Sawyer	1883	2.36	Will Sawyer	1883	2.24	Monte Ward	1878	.231
Jumbo McGinnis	1882	134	Jumbo McGinnis	1882	2.60	Jumbo McGinnis	1882	2.50	Larry McKeon	1884	.235
Monte Ward	1878	116	Nat Hudson	1886	3.03	Larry McKeon	1884	2.56	Willie McGill	1891	.240
Amos Rusie	1889	109	Willie McGill	1891	3.35	Nat Hudson	1886	2.68	Nat Hudson	1886	.243
Larry Dierker	1965	109	Larry McKeon	1884	3.50	Scott Stratton	1888	3.12	Jumbo McGinnis	1882	.245
Nat Hudson	1886	100	Scott Stratton	1888	3.64	Willie McGill	1891	3.99	Scott Stratton	1888	.263
Scott Stratton	1888	97	Willie McGill	1890	4.12	Pete Conway	1885	3.99	Lev Shreve	1887	.267
Pete Conway	1885	94	Lev Shreve	1887	4.50	Lev Shreve	1887	4.41	Pete Conway	1885	.287

Batting Leaders—Through Age 19

At-Bats		Runs		Hits		Doubles	
Phil Cavarretta	1,068	Phil Cavarretta	145	Phil Cavarretta	295	Phil Cavarretta	46
Robin Yount	902	Robin Yount	115	Robin Yount	235	Robin Yount	42
Milt Scott	801	Buddy Lewis	100	Mel Ott	209	Mel Ott	35
Ed Kranepool	699	Mel Ott	99	Milt Scott	201	Ed Kranepool	32
Sibby Sisti	674	George Davis	98	Buddy Lewis	178	Milt Scott	31
Mel Ott	658	Ed Kranepool	92	Ed Kranepool	166	Sibby Sisti	26
Buddy Lewis	629	Monte Ward	85	Sibby Sisti	164	Les Mann	24
Bob Kennedy	614	Bob Kennedy	74	Bob Kennedy	155	Ken Griffey Jr.	23
Al Kaline	532	Joe Quinn	74	Ty Cobb	149	Bob Kennedy	23
George Davis	526	2 tied with	69	Al Kaline	146	2 tied with	22

Triples		Home Runs		RBI		Stolen Bases	
Phil Cavarretta	14	Tony Conigliaro	24	Phil Cavarretta	144	Ty Cobb	25
Lew Brown	14	Mel Ott	19	Mel Ott	100	George Davis	22
Buddy Lewis	13	Phil Cavarretta	18	Milt Scott	80	Scott Stratton	20
Freddy Lindstrom	13	Ken Griffey Jr.	16	Robin Yount	78	Robin Yount	19
Sherry Magee	12	Mickey Mantle	13	Jimmy Sheckard	78	John McGraw	19
Jimmy Sheckard	11	Ed Kranepool	12	George Davis	73	Taylor Shaffer	19
George Davis	9	Robin Yount	11	Buddy Lewis	69	Cesar Cedeno	17
Billy Nash	8	Cesar Cedeno	7	Mickey Mantle	65	Ben Conroy	17
Monte Ward	8	Sibby Sisti	7	Scott Stratton	63	Ken Griffey Jr.	16
9 tied with	7	Jimmy Sheckard	7	Ken Griffey Jr.	61	Jack O'Connor	15

Runs Created		Batting Average (minimum 400 Plate Appearances)		On-Base Percentage (minimum 400 Plate Appearances)		Slugging Percentage (minimum 400 Plate Appearances)	
Phil Cavarretta	139	Mel Ott	.318	Mel Ott	.382	Tony Conigliaro	.530
Mel Ott	115	Ty Cobb	.293	John McGraw	.356	Mel Ott	.479
Milt Scott	102	Tony Conigliaro	.290	Tony Conigliaro	.354	Ken Griffey Jr.	.420
Robin Yount	97	Buddy Lewis	.283	Jimmy Sheckard	.350	Jimmy Sheckard	.416
George Davis	90	Freddy Lindstrom	.280	Johnny Lush	.338	Freddy Lindstrom	.409
Buddy Lewis	87	Johnny Lush	.278	Buddy Lewis	.337	Phil Cavarretta	.396
Jimmy Sheckard	83	Jimmy Sheckard	.278	George Davis	.336	Buddy Lewis	.386
Monte Ward	74	Phil Cavarretta	.276	Ty Cobb	.335	George Davis	.375
Scott Stratton	73	Al Kaline	.274	Ken Griffey Jr.	.329	Les Mann	.369
Ed Kranepool	71	Scott Stratton	.272	Freddy Lindstrom	.328	Johnny Lush	.366

Single Season Batting Leaders—Age 19

At-Bats			Runs			Hits			Doubles		
Bob Kennedy	1940	606	Buddy Lewis	1936	100	Buddy Lewis	1936	175	Robin Yount	1975	28
Buddy Lewis	1936	601	George Davis	1890	98	Bob Kennedy	1940	153	Mel Ott	1928	26
Robin Yount	1975	558	Joe Quinn	1884	74	Robin Yount	1975	149	Les Mann	1913	24
George Davis	1890	526	Bob Kennedy	1940	74	Mel Ott	1928	140	Bob Kennedy	1940	23
Rusty Staub	1963	513	Sibby Sisti	1940	73	George Davis	1890	139	Ken Griffey Jr.	1989	23
Al Kaline	1954	504	Monte Ward	1879	71	Al Kaline	1954	139	George Davis	1890	22
Will Smalley	1890	502	Mel Ott	1928	69	Phil Cavarretta	1936	125	5 tied with		21
Sibby Sisti	1940	459	Tony Conigliaro	1964	69	Ken Griffey Jr.	1989	120			
Phil Cavarretta	1936	458	Robin Yount	1975	67	Tony Conigliaro	1964	117			
Ken Griffey Jr.	1989	455	Will Smalley	1890	62	Joe Quinn	1884	116			

Triples			Home Runs			RBI			Stolen Bases		
Buddy Lewis	1936	13	Tony Conigliaro	1964	24	Mel Ott	1928	77	Ty Cobb	1906	23
Sherry Magee	1904	12	Mel Ott	1928	18	George Davis	1890	73	George Davis	1890	22
Freddy Lindstrom	1925	12	Ken Griffey Jr.	1989	16	Buddy Lewis	1936	67	Taylor Shaffer	1890	19
George Davis	1890	9	Mickey Mantle	1951	13	Mickey Mantle	1951	65	Ben Conroy	1890	17
Jimmy Sheckard	1898	9	Ed Kranepool	1964	10	Jimmy Sheckard	1898	64	Cesar Cedeno	1970	17
Lew Brown	1877	8	Phil Cavarretta	1936	9	Ken Griffey Jr.	1989	61	Ken Griffey Jr.	1989	16
Billy Nash	1884	8	Robin Yount	1975	8	Sherry Magee	1904	57	John McGraw	1892	15
4 tied with		7	Cesar Cedeno	1970	7	Phil Cavarretta	1936	56	Jack O'Connor	1888	12
			7 tied with		6	Cass Michaels	1945	54	Robin Yount	1975	12
						3 tied with		52	Sherry Magee	1904	11

Runs Created			Batting Average (minimum 3.1 PA/Tm Gm)			On-Base Percentage (minimum 3.1 PA/Tm Gm)			Slugging Percentage (minimum 3.1 PA/Tm Gm)		
George Davis	1890	90	Mel Ott	1928	.322	Mel Ott	1928	.397	Mel Ott	1928	.524
Buddy Lewis	1936	87	Buddy Lewis	1936	.291	Buddy Lewis	1936	.347	Ken Griffey Jr.	1989	.420
Mel Ott	1928	85	Monte Ward	1879	.286	George Davis	1890	.336	Buddy Lewis	1936	.399
Joe Quinn	1884	69	Al Kaline	1954	.276	Ken Griffey Jr.	1989	.329	Lew Brown	1877	.394
Jimmy Sheckard	1898	69	Phil Cavarretta	1936	.273	Sibby Sisti	1940	.311	Phil Cavarretta	1936	.376
Tony Conigliaro	1964	67	Joe Quinn	1884	.270	Rusty Staub	1963	.309	George Davis	1890	.375
Ken Griffey Jr.	1989	67	Robin Yount	1975	.267	Cass Michaels	1945	.307	Robin Yount	1975	.367
Robin Yount	1975	65	George Davis	1890	.264	Robin Yount	1975	.307	Sibby Sisti	1940	.353
Monte Ward	1879	59	Ken Griffey Jr.	1989	.264	Phil Cavarretta	1936	.306	Monte Ward	1879	.349
Mickey Mantle	1951	57	Milt Scott	1885	.254	Al Kaline	1954	.305	Al Kaline	1954	.347

Pitching Leaders—Through Age 19

Wins		Losses		Winning Percentage (minimum 40 decisions)		Games	
Monte Ward	69	Larry McKeon	54	Silver King	.688	Willie McGill	109
Jumbo McGinnis	53	Amos Rusie	44	Monte Ward	.683	Monte Ward	107
Willie McGill	49	Willie McGill	43	Nat Hudson	.652	Amos Rusie	100
Nat Hudson	45	Pete Conway	37	Elmer Smith	.633	Larry McKeon	94
Amos Rusie	41	Adonis Terry	35	Jumbo McGinnis	.609	Jumbo McGinnis	90
Larry McKeon	38	Lev Shreve	34	Bob Feller	.596	Bob Feller	79
Elmer Smith	38	Jumbo McGinnis	34	Willie McGill	.533	Pete Schneider	77
Silver King	33	Pete Schneider	32	Amos Rusie	.482	Nat Hudson	77
Bob Feller	31	Monte Ward	32	Larry McKeon	.413	Mike McCormick	69
2 tied with	21	2 tied with	30	Egyptian Healy	.375	Elmer Smith	62

Complete Games		Shutouts		Saves		Innings Pitched	
Monte Ward	95	Jumbo McGinnis	9	Billy McCool	7	Monte Ward	921.0
Larry McKeon	91	Monte Ward	8	George Ferguson	7	Willie McGill	817.1
Jumbo McGinnis	84	Pete Schneider	6	Don Gullett	6	Larry McKeon	802.0
Amos Rusie	75	Gary Nolan	5	Jack Bentley	5	Amos Rusie	773.2
Willie McGill	74	Joe Wood	5	Bob Feller	3	Jumbo McGinnis	771.0
Nat Hudson	68	Amos Rusie	5	Pete Schneider	3	Nat Hudson	634.1
Elmer Smith	58	Nat Hudson	5	10 tied with	2	Elmer Smith	529.0
Pete Conway	56	Larry McKeon	4			Bob Feller	488.1
Adonis Terry	55	6 tied with	3			Adonis Terry	485.0
Lev Shreve	52					Pete Conway	481.0

Strikeouts		ERA (minimum 250 Innings Pitched)		Component ERA (minimum 250 Innings Pitched)		Opponent Average (minimum 250 Innings Pitched)	
Bob Feller	466	Monte Ward	1.92	Monte Ward	1.97	Bob Feller	.221
Amos Rusie	450	Jumbo McGinnis	2.46	Jumbo McGinnis	2.16	Egyptian Healy	.227
Larry McKeon	425	Pete Schneider	2.59	Egyptian Healy	2.46	Elmer Smith	.228
Monte Ward	355	Egyptian Healy	2.90	Larry McKeon	2.53	Jumbo McGinnis	.232
Willie McGill	353	Nat Hudson	2.98	Nat Hudson	2.55	Monte Ward	.236
Dwight Gooden	276	Elmer Smith	3.06	Elmer Smith	2.57	Amos Rusie	.236
Jumbo McGinnis	262	Chief Bender	3.07	Adonis Terry	2.58	Larry McKeon	.237
Nat Hudson	245	Larry McKeon	3.27	Chief Bender	2.72	Larry Dierker	.239
Egyptian Healy	245	Larry Dierker	3.28	Larry Dierker	3.04	Nat Hudson	.240
Adonis Terry	233	Amos Rusie	3.36	Pete Schneider	3.15	Chief Bender	.245

Single Season Pitching Leaders—Age 19

Wins			Losses			Winning Percentage (minimum 15 decisions)			Games		
Monte Ward	1879	47	Adonis Terry	1884	35	Wally Bunker	1964	.792	Monte Ward	1879	70
Elmer Smith	1887	34	Amos Rusie	1890	34	Silver King	1887	.727	Amos Rusie	1890	67
Silver King	1887	32	Lev Shreve	1888	24	Nat Hudson	1888	.714	Adonis Terry	1884	57
Amos Rusie	1890	29	Egyptian Healy	1886	23	Monte Ward	1879	.712	Elmer Smith	1887	52
Jumbo McGinnis	1883	28	Pete Conway	1886	20	Elmer Smith	1887	.667	Pete Schneider	1915	48
Nat Hudson	1888	25	Monte Ward	1879	19	Dwight Gooden	1984	.654	Silver King	1887	46
Kid Madden	1887	21	Pete Schneider	1915	19	Chuck Stobbs	1949	.647	Jumbo McGinnis	1883	45
Adonis Terry	1884	20	Willie McGill	1893	18	Jumbo McGinnis	1883	.636	Terry Forster	1971	45
Larry McKeon	1885	20	Elmer Smith	1887	17	Gary Nolan	1967	.636	Don Gullett	1970	44
Wally Bunker	1964	19	2 tied with		16	Joe Wood	1909	.611	Egyptian Healy	1886	43

Complete Games			Shutouts			Saves			Innings Pitched		
Monte Ward	1879	58	Jumbo McGinnis	1883	6	George Ferguson	1906	7	Monte Ward	1879	587.0
Amos Rusie	1890	56	Nat Hudson	1888	5	Billy McCool	1964	7	Amos Rusie	1890	548.2
Adonis Terry	1884	55	Pete Schneider	1915	5	Don Gullett	1970	6	Adonis Terry	1884	485.0
Elmer Smith	1887	49	Gary Nolan	1967	5	Jack Bentley	1914	4	Elmer Smith	1887	447.1
Silver King	1887	43	Amos Rusie	1890	4	8 tied with		2	Silver King	1887	390.0
Jumbo McGinnis	1883	41	Joe Wood	1909	4				Jumbo McGinnis	1883	382.2
Egyptian Healy	1886	39	5 tied with		3				Egyptian Healy	1886	353.2
Kid Madden	1887	36							Nat Hudson	1888	333.0
Nat Hudson	1888	36							Kid Madden	1887	321.0
Elton Chamberlin	1887	35							Elton Chamberlin	1887	309.0

Strikeouts			ERA (minimum 1 Inning Pitched/Tm Gm)			Component ERA (minimum 1 Inning Pitched/Tm Gm)			Opponent Average (minimum 1 Inning Pitched/Tm Gm)		
Amos Rusie	1890	341	Monte Ward	1879	2.15	Jumbo McGinnis	1883	1.83	Dwight Gooden	1984	.202
Dwight Gooden	1984	276	Joe Wood	1909	2.18	Joe Wood	1909	1.86	Wally Bunker	1964	.207
Bob Feller	1938	240	Bill Vinton	1884	2.23	Monte Ward	1879	2.00	Joe Wood	1909	.209
Monte Ward	1879	239	Jumbo McGinnis	1883	2.33	Nat Hudson	1888	2.01	Amos Rusie	1890	.212
Adonis Terry	1884	233	Pete Schneider	1915	2.48	Dwight Gooden	1984	2.08	Jumbo McGinnis	1883	.217
Egyptian Healy	1886	213	Nat Hudson	1888	2.54	Bill Vinton	1884	2.17	Bob Feller	1938	.220
Gary Nolan	1967	206	Amos Rusie	1890	2.56	Wally Bunker	1964	2.29	Bill Vinton	1884	.220
Elmer Smith	1887	176	Gary Nolan	1967	2.58	Elmer Smith	1887	2.45	Nat Hudson	1888	.222
Bert Blyleven	1970	135	Dwight Gooden	1984	2.60	Larry McKeon	1885	2.47	Gary Nolan	1967	.228
Nat Hudson	1888	130	Frank Shellenback	1918	2.66	Egyptian Healy	1886	2.55	Egyptian Healy	1886	.230

Batting Leaders—Through Age 20

At-Bats			Runs			Hits			Doubles	
Robin Yount	1,540		Mel Ott	237		Robin Yount	396		Mel Ott	72
Phil Cavarretta	1,397		George Davis	213		Phil Cavarretta	389		Phil Cavarretta	64
Buddy Lewis	1,297		Buddy Lewis	207		Buddy Lewis	388		Cesar Cedeno	61
Milt Scott	1,285		Phil Cavarretta	188		Mel Ott	388		Robin Yount	61
Ed Kranepool	1,224		John McGraw	181		Ty Cobb	361		Alex Rodriguez	60
Sibby Sisti	1,215		Robin Yount	174		Al Kaline	346		George Davis	57
Mel Ott	1,203		Al Kaline	172		Sibby Sisti	304		Ed Kranepool	56
Al Kaline	1,120		Jimmy Sheckard	167		George Davis	304		Vada Pinson	54
Ty Cobb	1,113		Sibby Sisti	164		Ken Griffey Jr.	299		Buddy Lewis	53
George Davis	1,096		Ty Cobb	161		Ed Kranepool	299		Ken Griffey Jr.	51

Triples			Home Runs			RBI			Stolen Bases	
Sherry Magee	29		Mel Ott	61		Mel Ott	251		Jimmy Sheckard	90
Freddy Lindstrom	22		Tony Conigliaro	56		Phil Cavarretta	200		Ty Cobb	74
Sam Crawford	22		Alex Rodriguez	41		Ty Cobb	168		George Davis	64
Phil Cavarretta	21		Ken Griffey Jr.	38		George Davis	162		Sherry Magee	59
Jimmy Sheckard	21		Frank Robinson	38		Sherry Magee	155		John McGraw	57
George Davis	21		Mickey Mantle	36		Jimmy Sheckard	153		Claudell Washington	46
Ty Cobb	20		Al Kaline	32		Mickey Mantle	152		Jack O'Connor	41
Lew Brown	20		Ted Williams	31		Buddy Lewis	148		Ed Delahanty	38
Buddy Lewis	19		Orlando Cepeda	25		Al Kaline	147		Cesar Cedeno	37
Les Mann	18		Eddie Mathews	25		Ted Williams	145		Jack Doyle	36

Runs Created			Batting Average			On-Base Percentage			Slugging Percentage	
			(minimum 500 Plate Appearances)			(minimum 500 Plate Appearances)			(minimum 500 Plate Appearances)	
Mel Ott	270		Jimmie Foxx	.331		Ted Williams	.436		Ted Williams	.609
George Davis	206		Ted Williams	.327		Mel Ott	.414		Alex Rodriguez	.562
Ty Cobb	203		Alex Rodriguez	.325		John McGraw	.412		Frank Robinson	.558
John McGraw	191		Ty Cobb	.324		Jimmie Foxx	.410		Mel Ott	.549
Buddy Lewis	190		Mel Ott	.323		Frank Robinson	.379		Jimmie Foxx	.538
Phil Cavarretta	189		Arky Vaughan	.318		Alex Rodriguez	.377		Tony Conigliaro	.520
Jimmy Sheckard	186		Orlando Cepeda	.312		Mickey Mantle	.377		Orlando Cepeda	.512
Al Kaline	182		Stuffy McInnis	.312		Arky Vaughan	.375		Mickey Mantle	.497
Mickey Mantle	169		Vada Pinson	.310		Al Kaline	.369		Vada Pinson	.492
Sherry Magee	165		Al Kaline	.309		Vada Pinson	.368		Willie Mays	.472

Single Season Batting Leaders—Age 20

At-Bats				Runs				Hits				Doubles		
Buddy Lewis	1937	668		Alex Rodriguez	1996	141		Alex Rodriguez	1996	215		Alex Rodriguez	1996	54
Ken Hubbs	1962	661		Mel Ott	1929	138		Ty Cobb	1907	212		Vada Pinson	1959	47
Vada Pinson	1959	648		Ted Williams	1939	131		Buddy Lewis	1937	210		Ted Williams	1939	44
Robin Yount	1976	638		Vada Pinson	1959	131		Vada Pinson	1959	205		Johnny Bench	1968	40
Cesar Cedeno	1971	611		John McGraw	1893	123		Al Kaline	1955	200		Cesar Cedeno	1971	40
Ty Cobb	1907	605		Frank Robinson	1956	122		Orlando Cepeda	1958	188		Orlando Cepeda	1958	38
Sherry Magee	1905	603		Al Kaline	1955	121		Ted Williams	1939	185		Mel Ott	1929	37
Orlando Cepeda	1958	603		George Davis	1891	115		Claudell Washington	1975	182		Mickey Mantle	1952	37
Alex Rodriguez	1996	601		Buddy Lewis	1937	107		Sherry Magee	1905	180		George Davis	1891	35
Ken Griffey Jr.	1990	597		Jimmy Sheckard	1899	104		Travis Jackson	1924	180		2 tied with		32

Triples				Home Runs				RBI				Stolen Bases		
Sherry Magee	1905	17		Mel Ott	1929	42		Mel Ott	1929	151		Jimmy Sheckard	1899	77
Sam Crawford	1900	15		Frank Robinson	1956	38		Ted Williams	1939	145		Ty Cobb	1907	49
Ty Cobb	1907	15		Alex Rodriguez	1996	36		Alex Rodriguez	1996	123		Sherry Magee	1905	48
Whitey Witt	1916	15		Tony Conigliaro	1965	32		Ty Cobb	1907	119		George Davis	1891	42
Rogers Hornsby	1916	15		Ted Williams	1939	31		Al Kaline	1955	102		Claudell Washington	1975	40
Buttercup Dickerson	1879	14		Al Kaline	1955	27		Sherry Magee	1905	98		Ed Delahanty	1888	38
Dick Burns	1884	12		Eddie Mathews	1952	25		Orlando Cepeda	1958	96		John McGraw	1893	38
Mike Tiernan	1887	12		Orlando Cepeda	1958	25		George Davis	1891	89		Rickey Henderson	1979	33
George Davis	1891	12		Mickey Mantle	1952	23		Mickey Mantle	1952	87		Mike Tiernan	1887	28
5 tied with		11		Bob Horner	1978	23		Vada Pinson	1959	84		Jack Doyle	1890	27

Runs Created				Batting Average				On-Base Percentage				Slugging Percentage		
				(minimum 3.1 PA/Tm Gm)				(minimum 3.1 PA/Tm Gm)				(minimum 3.1 PA/Tm Gm)		
Mel Ott	1929	155		John Cassidy	1877	.378		John McGraw	1893	.454		Mel Ott	1929	.635
Ted Williams	1939	153		Alex Rodriguez	1996	.358		Mel Ott	1929	.449		Alex Rodriguez	1996	.631
Alex Rodriguez	1996	147		Abner Dalrymple	1878	.354		Ted Williams	1939	.436		Ted Williams	1939	.609
Al Kaline	1955	134		Ty Cobb	1907	.350		Al Kaline	1955	.421		Frank Robinson	1956	.558
Ty Cobb	1907	133		Al Kaline	1955	.340		Alex Rodriguez	1996	.414		Al Kaline	1955	.546
John McGraw	1893	123		Mel Ott	1929	.328		Mickey Mantle	1952	.394		Mickey Mantle	1952	.530
Vada Pinson	1959	120		Ted Williams	1939	.327		John Cassidy	1877	.386		Tony Conigliaro	1965	.512
George Davis	1891	116		John McGraw	1893	.321		Jimmy Sheckard	1899	.380		Orlando Cepeda	1958	.512
Sherry Magee	1905	115		Stuffy McInnis	1911	.321		Ty Cobb	1907	.380		Vada Pinson	1959	.509
Frank Robinson	1956	114		Arky Vaughan	1932	.318		Frank Robinson	1956	.379		Ken Griffey Jr.	1990	.481

Pitching Leaders—Through Age 20

Wins		Losses		Winning Percentage (minimum 40 decisions)		Games	
Monte Ward	108	Larry McKeon	64	Dwight Gooden	.759	Monte Ward	177
Silver King	78	Amos Rusie	64	Larry Corcoran	.754	Amos Rusie	161
Jumbo McGinnis	77	Willie McGill	62	Tommy Bond	.705	Willie McGill	136
Amos Rusie	74	Egyptian Healy	59	Silver King	.684	Jumbo McGinnis	130
Elmer Smith	60	Monte Ward	56	Wally Bunker	.674	Pete Schneider	121
Willie McGill	56	Adonis Terry	52	Monte Ward	.659	Bob Feller	118
Bob Feller	55	Pete Schneider	51	Nat Hudson	.649	Silver King	117
Nat Hudson	48	Jumbo McGinnis	50	Bob Feller	.647	Mike McCormick	116
Scott Stratton	47	John Coleman	48	Jumbo McGinnis	.606	Larry McKeon	116
Larry McKeon	46	Pete Conway	46	Elmer Smith	.606	Terry Forster	107

Complete Games		Shutouts		Saves		Innings Pitched	
Monte Ward	154	Monte Ward	16	Terry Forster	30	Monte Ward	1,516.0
Amos Rusie	127	Jumbo McGinnis	14	Billy McCool	28	Amos Rusie	1,274.0
Jumbo McGinnis	123	Dwight Gooden	11	Art Houtteman	10	Jumbo McGinnis	1,125.1
Silver King	112	Amos Rusie	11	Victor Cruz	9	Willie McGill	1,025.1
Larry McKeon	110	Pete Schneider	9	George Ferguson	8	Silver King	1,014.2
Willie McGill	96	Fernando Valenzuela	8	Don Gullett	6	Larry McKeon	979.0
Elmer Smith	95	Joe Wood	8	6 tied with	5	Elmer Smith	877.1
Egyptian Healy	87	Walter Johnson	8			Scott Stratton	834.1
Scott Stratton	85	Silver King	8			Bob Feller	785.0
Adonis Terry	78	Elmer Smith	8			Egyptian Healy	760.2

Strikeouts		ERA (minimum 300 Innings Pitched)		Component ERA (minimum 300 Innings Pitched)		Opponent Average (minimum 300 Innings Pitched)	
Amos Rusie	787	Tommy Bond	1.68	Larry Corcoran	1.52	Larry Corcoran	.199
Bob Feller	712	Walter Johnson	1.72	Tommy Bond	1.53	Dwight Gooden	.201
Monte Ward	585	Monte Ward	1.85	Monte Ward	1.79	Matt Kilroy	.210
Dwight Gooden	544	Joe Wood	1.94	Walter Johnson	1.83	Joe Wood	.213
Matt Kilroy	513	Larry Corcoran	1.95	Dwight Gooden	1.94	Gary Nolan	.215
Larry McKeon	474	Dwight Gooden	2.00	Joe Wood	2.04	Bob Feller	.217
Willie McGill	411	Kid Nichols	2.23	Silver King	2.09	Tommy Bond	.220
Silver King	409	Bill Vinton	2.46	Jumbo McGinnis	2.13	Walter Johnson	.221
Jumbo McGinnis	403	Johnny Lush	2.48	Matt Kilroy	2.20	Silver King	.224
Elmer Smith	371	Gary Nolan	2.51	Noodles Hahn	2.41	Amos Rusie	.225

Single Season Pitching Leaders—Age 20

Wins			Losses			Winning Percentage (minimum 15 decisions)			Games		
Silver King	1888	45	John Coleman	1883	48	Dwight Gooden	1985	.857	Monte Ward	1880	70
Larry Corcoran	1880	43	Kid Carsey	1891	37	Larry Corcoran	1880	.754	Matt Kilroy	1886	68
Monte Ward	1880	39	Matt Kilroy	1886	34	Noodles Hahn	1899	.742	Silver King	1888	66
Mickey Welch	1880	34	Hardie Henderson	1883	33	Herb Pennock	1914	.733	Mickey Welch	1880	65
Scott Stratton	1890	34	Mickey Welch	1880	30	Bob Feller	1939	.727	John Coleman	1883	65
Amos Rusie	1891	33	Jersey Bakely	1884	30	Don Gullett	1971	.727	Larry Corcoran	1880	63
Tommy Bond	1876	31	Egyptian Healy	1887	29	Joe Bush	1913	.714	Billy McCool	1965	62
Matt Kilroy	1886	29	Red Ehret	1889	29	Scott Stratton	1890	.708	Terry Forster	1972	62
Kid Nichols	1890	27	Gus Weyhing	1887	28	Tommy Bond	1876	.705	Amos Rusie	1891	61
Gus Weyhing	1887	26	2 tied with		25	Elton Chamberlin	1888	.694	2 tied with		55

Complete Games			Shutouts			Saves			Innings Pitched		
Matt Kilroy	1886	66	Monte Ward	1880	8	Terry Forster	1972	29	Monte Ward	1880	595.0
Mickey Welch	1880	64	Fernando Valenzuela	1981	8	Billy McCool	1965	21	Silver King	1888	585.2
Silver King	1888	64	Dwight Gooden	1985	8	Art Houtteman	1948	10	Matt Kilroy	1886	583.0
Monte Ward	1880	59	Kid Nichols	1890	7	Victor Cruz	1978	9	Mickey Welch	1880	574.0
John Coleman	1883	59	Tommy Bond	1876	6	Pedro Ramos	1955	5	John Coleman	1883	538.1
Larry Corcoran	1880	57	Silver King	1888	6	6 tied with		4	Larry Corcoran	1880	536.1
Gus Weyhing	1887	53	Amos Rusie	1891	6				Amos Rusie	1891	500.1
Ed Seward	1887	52	Walter Johnson	1908	6				Ed Seward	1887	470.2
Amos Rusie	1891	52	6 tied with		5				Gus Weyhing	1887	466.1
Kid Nichols	1890	47							Scott Stratton	1890	431.0

Strikeouts			ERA (minimum 1 Inning Pitched/Tm Gm)			Component ERA (minimum 1 Inning Pitched/Tm Gm)			Opponent Average (minimum 1 Inning Pitched/Tm Gm)		
Matt Kilroy	1886	513	Dwight Gooden	1985	1.53	Silver King	1888	1.44	Silver King	1888	.197
Amos Rusie	1891	337	Silver King	1888	1.64	Larry Corcoran	1880	1.52	Larry Corcoran	1880	.199
Larry Corcoran	1880	268	Walter Johnson	1908	1.65	Tommy Bond	1876	1.53	Dwight Gooden	1985	.201
Dwight Gooden	1985	268	Tommy Bond	1876	1.68	Monte Ward	1880	1.56	Charlie Getzien	1884	.204
Silver King	1888	258	Joe Wood	1910	1.68	Charlie Getzien	1884	1.61	Fernando Valenzuela	1981	.205
Bob Feller	1939	246	Monte Ward	1880	1.74	Walter Johnson	1908	1.66	Elton Chamberlin	1888	.207
Monte Ward	1880	230	Stump Wiedman	1881	1.80	Dwight Gooden	1985	1.83	Joe Engel	1913	.207
Jersey Bakely	1884	226	Larry Corcoran	1880	1.95	Elton Chamberlin	1888	1.88	Amos Rusie	1891	.207
Bert Blyleven	1971	224	Charlie Getzien	1884	1.95	Bob Moose	1968	1.99	Matt Kilroy	1886	.210
Kid Nichols	1890	222	Elton Chamberlin	1888	2.19	Stump Wiedman	1881	2.04	Bob Feller	1939	.210

Batting Leaders—Through Age 21

At-Bats		Runs		Hits		Doubles	
Robin Yount	2,145	Mel Ott	359	Buddy Lewis	582	Mel Ott	106
Buddy Lewis	1,953	John McGraw	337	Robin Yount	570	Cesar Cedeno	100
Al Kaline	1,737	Buddy Lewis	329	Mel Ott	570	Alex Rodriguez	100
Mel Ott	1,724	George Davis	308	Ty Cobb	549	Robin Yount	95
Ty Cobb	1,694	Al Kaline	268	Al Kaline	540	Ken Griffey Jr.	93
George Davis	1,693	Ted Williams	265	Ken Griffey Jr.	478	Vada Pinson	91
Ed Kranepool	1,688	Mickey Mantle	260	Freddy Lindstrom	458	Buddy Lewis	88
Phil Cavarretta	1,665	Alex Rodriguez	260	Phil Cavarretta	453	Ted Williams	87
Sibby Sisti	1,622	Freddy Lindstrom	259	Cesar Cedeno	450	Ty Cobb	86
Ken Griffey Jr.	1,600	Vada Pinson	258	George Davis	448	George Davis	84

Triples		Home Runs		RBI		Stolen Bases	
Ty Cobb	40	Mel Ott	86	Mel Ott	370	John McGraw	135
Sam Crawford	38	Tony Conigliaro	84	Ty Cobb	276	Rickey Henderson	133
Les Mann	37	Eddie Mathews	72	Al Kaline	275	Jimmy Sheckard	120
Sherry Magee	37	Frank Robinson	67	Ted Williams	258	Sherry Magee	114
George Davis	33	Alex Rodriguez	64	Mickey Mantle	244	Ty Cobb	113
Rogers Hornsby	32	Ken Griffey Jr.	60	George Davis	244	George Davis	100
Jimmy Sheckard	31	Al Kaline	59	Ken Griffey Jr.	241	Cesar Cedeno	92
John McGraw	31	Mickey Mantle	57	Buddy Lewis	239	Claudell Washington	83
Freddy Lindstrom	30	Bob Horner	56	Phil Cavarretta	228	Mike Tiernan	80
Arky Vaughan	29	Ted Williams	54	Alex Rodriguez	228	Denny Lyons	80

Runs Created		Batting Average (minimum 750 Plate Appearances)		On-Base Percentage (minimum 750 Plate Appearances)		Slugging Percentage (minimum 750 Plate Appearances)	
Mel Ott	403	Joe Jackson	.394	Joe Jackson	.452	Ted Williams	.601
John McGraw	330	Jimmie Foxx	.342	Ted Williams	.439	Jimmie Foxx	.579
Ty Cobb	316	Ted Williams	.336	Jimmie Foxx	.436	Joe Jackson	.567
Al Kaline	301	Denny Lyons	.334	Mel Ott	.428	Mel Ott	.558
George Davis	301	Mel Ott	.331	John McGraw	.426	Bob Horner	.547
Ted Williams	292	Ty Cobb	.324	Rickey Henderson	.392	Frank Robinson	.543
Buddy Lewis	287	Stuffy McInnis	.319	Denny Lyons	.390	Eddie Mathews	.541
Ken Griffey Jr.	273	Cecil Travis	.318	Eddie Murphy	.387	Alex Rodriguez	.534
Mickey Mantle	264	Rogers Hornsby	.316	Mickey Mantle	.384	Orlando Cepeda	.517
Jimmie Foxx	264	Arky Vaughan	.316	Arky Vaughan	.382	Tony Conigliaro	.508

Single Season Batting Leaders—Age 21

At-Bats			Runs			Hits			Doubles		
Buddy Lewis	1938	656	John McGraw	1894	156	Joe Jackson	1911	233	Joe Jackson	1911	45
Vada Pinson	1960	652	Ted Williams	1940	134	Lloyd Waner	1927	223	Hal Trosky	1934	45
Ruben Sierra	1987	643	Lloyd Waner	1927	133	Denny Lyons	1887	209	Joe DiMaggio	1936	44
Joe DiMaggio	1936	637	Joe DiMaggio	1936	132	Hal Trosky	1934	206	Denny Lyons	1887	43
Buddy Bell	1973	631	Denny Lyons	1887	128	Joe DiMaggio	1936	206	Ted Williams	1940	43
Lloyd Waner	1927	629	Joe Jackson	1911	126	Garry Templeton	1977	200	Ken Griffey Jr.	1991	42
Hal Trosky	1934	625	Jimmie Foxx	1929	123	Frank Robinson	1957	197	Dick Bartell	1929	40
Alfredo Griffin	1979	624	Mel Ott	1930	122	Buddy Lewis	1938	194	Joe Medwick	1933	40
Roberto Alomar	1989	623	Buddy Lewis	1938	122	Al Kaline	1956	194	Alex Rodriguez	1997	40
Garry Templeton	1977	621	Joe Kelley	1893	120	Ted Williams	1940	193	Cesar Cedeno	1972	39

Triples			Home Runs			RBI			Stolen Bases		
Tom McCreery	1896	21	Eddie Mathews	1953	47	Hal Trosky	1934	142	Rickey Henderson	1980	100
Ty Cobb	1908	20	Hal Trosky	1934	35	Eddie Mathews	1953	135	John McGraw	1894	78
Joe Cassidy	1904	19	Jimmie Foxx	1929	33	Al Kaline	1956	128	Denny Lyons	1887	73
Joe Jackson	1911	19	Bob Horner	1979	33	Joe DiMaggio	1936	125	Tim Raines	1981	71
Les Mann	1915	19	Jose Canseco	1986	33	Mel Ott	1930	119	Sherry Magee	1906	55
Arky Vaughan	1933	19	Ruben Sierra	1987	30	Jimmie Foxx	1929	117	Cesar Cedeno	1972	55
Garry Templeton	1977	18	Joe DiMaggio	1936	29	Joe Vosmik	1931	117	Donie Bush	1909	53
Rogers Hornsby	1917	17	Frank Robinson	1957	29	Jose Canseco	1986	117	Mike Tiernan	1888	52
Joe Kelley	1893	16	Tony Conigliaro	1966	28	Ken Keltner	1938	113	Sonny Jackson	1966	49
Sam Crawford	1901	16	Cal Ripken Jr.	1982	28	Ted Williams	1940	113	Tommy Corcoran	1890	43

Runs Created			Batting Average (minimum 3.1 PA/Tm Gm)			On-Base Percentage (minimum 3.1 PA/Tm Gm)			Slugging Percentage (minimum 3.1 PA/Tm Gm)		
Denny Lyons	1887	154	Joe Jackson	1911	.408	Joe Jackson	1911	.468	Eddie Mathews	1953	.627
Joe Jackson	1911	147	Pete Browning	1882	.378	Jimmie Foxx	1929	.463	Jimmie Foxx	1929	.625
Jimmie Foxx	1929	145	Denny Lyons	1887	.367	Mel Ott	1930	.458	Hal Trosky	1934	.598
Eddie Mathews	1953	145	Lloyd Waner	1927	.355	John McGraw	1894	.451	Ted Williams	1940	.594
John McGraw	1894	139	Jimmie Foxx	1929	.354	Ted Williams	1940	.442	Joe Jackson	1911	.590
Ted Williams	1940	139	Tom McCreery	1896	.351	Pete Browning	1882	.430	Mel Ott	1930	.578
Hal Trosky	1934	136	Mel Ott	1930	.349	Denny Lyons	1887	.421	Joe DiMaggio	1936	.576
Mel Ott	1930	133	King Kelly	1879	.348	Rickey Henderson	1980	.420	Bob Horner	1979	.552
Joe DiMaggio	1936	128	Ted Williams	1940	.344	Reddy Mack	1887	.415	Tom McCreery	1896	.546
Rickey Henderson	1980	121	Buster Hoover	1884	.341	Richie Ashburn	1948	.410	Hank Aaron	1955	.540

Pitching Leaders—Through Age 21

Wins			Losses			Winning Percentage (minimum 50 decisions)			Games	
Monte Ward	126		Amos Rusie	95		Bob Caruthers	.758		Amos Rusie	225
Silver King	112		Egyptian Healy	83		Dwight Gooden	.753		Monte Ward	216
Amos Rusie	105		Monte Ward	74		Larry Corcoran	.725		Silver King	173
Jumbo McGinnis	83		Pete Schneider	70		Tommy Bond	.703		Pete Schneider	167
Bob Feller	82		Willie McGill	70		Charlie Sweeney	.686		Bob Feller	161
Elton Chamberlin	75		Adonis Terry	68		Silver King	.683		Billy McCool	159
Matt Kilroy	75		John Coleman	65		Babe Ruth	.672		Terry Forster	158
Larry Corcoran	74		Larry McKeon	64		Bob Feller	.667		Mike McCormick	156
Tommy Bond	71		Pete Conway	60		Wally Bunker	.661		Willie McGill	156
Elmer Smith	69		Scott Stratton	59		Nat Hudson	.649		Jumbo McGinnis	143

Complete Games			Shutouts			Saves			Innings Pitched	
Monte Ward	186		Monte Ward	19		Terry Forster	46		Monte Ward	1,846.0
Amos Rusie	185		Jumbo McGinnis	17		Billy McCool	46		Amos Rusie	1,806.0
Silver King	159		Dwight Gooden	13		Victor Cruz	19		Silver King	1,472.2
Jumbo McGinnis	135		Joe Wood	13		Lloyd Allen	15		Jumbo McGinnis	1,237.1
Matt Kilroy	132		Amos Rusie	13		Bart Johnson	14		Matt Kilroy	1,172.1
Egyptian Healy	123		Fernando Valenzuela	12		Kelvim Escobar	14		Willie McGill	1,171.1
Elton Chamberlin	117		Walter Johnson	12		Jerry Walker	10		Bob Feller	1,105.1
Pete Conway	115		Kid Nichols	12		Art Houtteman	10		Egyptian Healy	1,082.0
Elmer Smith	111		Tommy Bond	12		Masanori Murakami	9		Elmer Smith	1,080.1
2 tied with	110		2 tied with	11		Erv Palica	9		Elton Chamberlin	1,070.0

Strikeouts			ERA (minimum 350 Innings Pitched)			Component ERA (minimum 350 Innings Pitched)			Opponent Average (minimum 350 Innings Pitched)	
Amos Rusie	1,075		Monte Ward	1.90		Charlie Sweeney	1.50		Toad Ramsey	.192
Bob Feller	973		Tommy Bond	1.92		Ed Morris	1.52		Vida Blue	.198
Dwight Gooden	744		Walter Johnson	1.94		Toad Ramsey	1.85		Charlie Sweeney	.204
Matt Kilroy	730		Billy Rhines	1.95		Mickey Hughes	1.89		Ed Morris	.204
Monte Ward	704		Joe Wood	1.97		Larry Corcoran	1.89		Mickey Hughes	.206
Silver King	597		Charlie Sweeney	2.03		Monte Ward	1.89		Dwight Gooden	.206
Bert Blyleven	587		Larry Corcoran	2.10		Bob Caruthers	1.89		Babe Ruth	.207
Toad Ramsey	582		Babe Ruth	2.11		Tommy Bond	1.90		Dennis Eckersley	.214
Elton Chamberlin	514		Mickey Hughes	2.13		Walter Johnson	1.98		Bob Feller	.215
Hardie Henderson	493		Bob Caruthers	2.15		Babe Ruth	2.03		Joe Wood	.217

Single Season Pitching Leaders—Age 21

Wins				Losses				Winning Percentage (minimum 15 decisions)				Games		
Matt Kilroy	1887	46		Billy Crowell	1887	31		Bob Moose	1969	.824		Mitch Williams	1986	80
Charlie Sweeney	1884	41		Amos Rusie	1892	31		Wayne Simpson	1970	.824		Matt Kilroy	1887	69
Tommy Bond	1877	40		Hank O'Day	1884	28		Bret Saberhagen	1985	.769		Toad Ramsey	1886	67
Bob Caruthers	1885	40		Al Mays	1886	28		Bob Caruthers	1885	.755		Pedro Martinez	1993	65
Toad Ramsey	1886	38		Bill Hill	1896	28		Joe Corbett	1897	.750		Amos Rusie	1892	64
Ed Seward	1888	35		Toad Ramsey	1886	27		Vida Blue	1971	.750		Victor Cruz	1979	61
Ed Morris	1884	34		Pink Hawley	1894	27		Nick Maddox	1908	.742		Charlie Sweeney	1884	60
Silver King	1889	34		John Kirby	1886	26		Dwight Gooden	1986	.739		Frank Killen	1892	60
Elton Chamberlin	1889	32		Frank Killen	1892	26		Charlie Sweeney	1884	.732		Tommy Bond	1877	58
2 tied with		31		3 tied with		25		Denny McLain	1965	.727		Larry Bearnarth	1963	58

Complete Games				Shutouts				Saves				Innings Pitched		
Toad Ramsey	1886	66		Babe Ruth	1916	9		Billy McCool	1966	18		Matt Kilroy	1887	589.1
Matt Kilroy	1887	66		Al Mamaux	1915	8		Terry Forster	1973	16		Toad Ramsey	1886	588.2
Tommy Bond	1877	58		Vida Blue	1971	8		Lloyd Allen	1971	15		Amos Rusie	1892	532.0
Amos Rusie	1892	58		Harry Krause	1909	7		Bart Johnson	1971	14		Tommy Bond	1877	521.0
Ed Seward	1888	57		7 tied with		6		Kelvim Escobar	1997	14		Ed Seward	1888	518.2
Charlie Sweeney	1884	53						Victor Cruz	1979	10		Charlie Sweeney	1884	492.0
Bob Caruthers	1885	53						Dean Chance	1962	8		Bob Caruthers	1885	482.1
Hardie Henderson	1884	50						Masanori Murakami	1965	8		Frank Killen	1892	459.2
Ed Morris	1884	47						Neil Allen	1979	8		Silver King	1889	458.0
Silver King	1889	47						Mitch Williams	1986	8		Hardie Henderson	1884	439.1

Strikeouts				ERA (minimum 1 Inning Pitched/Tm Gm)				Component ERA (minimum 1 Inning Pitched/Tm Gm)				Opponent Average (minimum 1 Inning Pitched/Tm Gm)		
Toad Ramsey	1886	499		Harry Krause	1909	1.39		Charlie Sweeney	1884	1.32		Vida Blue	1971	.189
Hardie Henderson	1884	346		Jim McCormick	1878	1.69		Ed Morris	1884	1.52		Charlie Sweeney	1884	.193
Charlie Sweeney	1884	337		Charlie Sweeney	1884	1.70		Harry Krause	1909	1.65		Dave Boswell	1966	.197
Ed Morris	1884	302		Babe Ruth	1916	1.75		Ed Seward	1888	1.67		Toad Ramsey	1886	.198
Vida Blue	1971	301		Vida Blue	1971	1.82		Pete Conway	1888	1.74		Wayne Simpson	1970	.198
Amos Rusie	1892	288		Billy Rhines	1890	1.95		Cannonball Titcomb	1888	1.75		Ed Seward	1888	.199
Ed Seward	1888	272		Pete Schneider	1917	1.98		Vida Blue	1971	1.81		Babe Ruth	1916	.201
Frank Tanana	1975	269		Ed Seward	1888	2.01		Babe Ruth	1916	1.85		Cannonball Titcomb	1888	.201
Bob Feller	1940	261		Joe Wood	1911	2.02		Mickey Hughes	1888	1.89		Amos Rusie	1892	.203
Kid Nichols	1891	240		Al Mamaux	1915	2.04		Gus Weyhing	1888	1.89		Gus Weyhing	1888	.204

Batting Leaders—Through Age 22

At-Bats		Runs		Hits		Doubles	
Robin Yount	2,647	Mel Ott	463	Ty Cobb	765	Cesar Cedeno	135
Buddy Lewis	2,489	John McGraw	447	Buddy Lewis	753	Ken Griffey Jr.	132
Al Kaline	2,314	George Davis	420	Robin Yount	717	Mel Ott	129
Ty Cobb	2,267	Buddy Lewis	416	Mel Ott	715	Vada Pinson	125
George Davis	2,242	Ted Williams	400	Al Kaline	710	Ted Williams	120
Mel Ott	2,221	Mickey Mantle	389	Freddy Lindstrom	689	Ty Cobb	119
Freddy Lindstrom	2,186	Jimmie Foxx	368	Ken Griffey Jr.	652	Robin Yount	118
Ken Griffey Jr.	2,165	Ty Cobb	365	George Davis	643	Freddy Lindstrom	112
Ed Kranepool	2,157	Vada Pinson	359	Vada Pinson	626	Buddy Lewis	111
Cesar Cedeno	2,050	Freddy Lindstrom	358	Cesar Cedeno	618	Orlando Cepeda	109

Triples		Home Runs		RBI		Stolen Bases	
Sam Crawford	60	Mel Ott	115	Mel Ott	485	John McGraw	196
George Davis	60	Eddie Mathews	112	Ty Cobb	383	Rickey Henderson	189
Joe Jackson	50	Tony Conigliaro	104	Ted Williams	378	Ty Cobb	189
Ty Cobb	50	Frank Robinson	98	Jimmie Foxx	377	Sherry Magee	160
Jimmy Sheckard	50	Bob Horner	91	Al Kaline	365	Tim Raines	156
Sherry Magee	49	Ted Williams	91	George Davis	363	Jimmy Sheckard	155
Les Mann	46	Johnny Bench	87	Mickey Mantle	346	Cesar Cedeno	148
Buddy Lewis	44	Ken Griffey Jr.	87	Ken Griffey Jr.	344	George Davis	137
Joe Kelley	44	Jimmie Foxx	86	Johnny Bench	326	Denny Lyons	119
Rogers Hornsby	43	Mickey Mantle	84	Buddy Lewis	314	Mike Tiernan	113

| Runs Created | | Batting Average | | On-Base Percentage | | Slugging Percentage | |
		(minimum 1,000 Plate Appearances)		(minimum 1,000 Plate Appearances)		(minimum 1,000 Plate Appearances)	
Mel Ott	508	Joe Jackson	.394	Ted Williams	.474	Ted Williams	.640
Ted Williams	462	Ted Williams	.356	Joe Jackson	.455	Joe DiMaggio	.624
Ty Cobb	454	Lloyd Waner	.345	Jimmie Foxx	.434	Jimmie Foxx	.599
George Davis	443	Stan Musial	.342	John McGraw	.433	Joe Jackson	.572
John McGraw	441	Jimmie Foxx	.339	Joe Kelley	.421	Eddie Mathews	.560
Jimmie Foxx	414	Ty Cobb	.337	Mel Ott	.420	Mel Ott	.555
Mickey Mantle	390	Joe DiMaggio	.335	Stan Musial	.415	Bob Horner	.540
Al Kaline	388	John McGraw	.325	Arky Vaughan	.399	Alex Rodriguez	.534
Buddy Lewis	388	Joe Kelley	.324	Rickey Henderson	.396	Stan Musial	.533
Jimmy Sheckard	387	Mel Ott	.322	Mickey Mantle	.391	Hal Trosky	.531

Single Season Batting Leaders—Age 22

At-Bats			Runs			Hits			Doubles		
Harvey Kuenn	1953	679	Willie Keeler	1894	165	Freddy Lindstrom	1928	231	Joe Kelley	1894	48
Cal Ripken Jr.	1983	663	Joe Kelley	1894	165	Joe Jackson	1912	226	Stan Musial	1943	48
Richie Ashburn	1949	662	Joe DiMaggio	1937	151	Lloyd Waner	1928	221	Cal Ripken Jr.	1983	47
Granny Hamner	1949	662	Mike Tiernan	1889	147	Stan Musial	1943	220	Lou Boudreau	1940	46
Lloyd Waner	1928	659	Hugh Duffy	1889	144	Willie Keeler	1894	219	Jack Clark	1978	46
Julio Franco	1984	658	Mike Griffin	1887	142	Jimmy Williams	1899	219	Joe Jackson	1912	44
Billy Herman	1932	656	Ted Williams	1941	135	Ty Cobb	1909	216	Carl Yastrzemski	1962	43
Carney Lansford	1979	654	Woody English	1929	131	Joe DiMaggio	1937	215	Billy Herman	1932	42
Alfredo Griffin	1980	653	Mickey Mantle	1954	129	Frankie Frisch	1921	211	Arky Vaughan	1934	41
2 tied with		647	Jimmie Foxx	1930	127	Cal Ripken Jr.	1983	211	3 tied with		40

Triples			Home Runs			RBI			Stolen Bases		
George Davis	1893	27	Joe DiMaggio	1937	46	Joe DiMaggio	1937	167	Mike Griffin	1887	94
Jimmy Williams	1899	27	Johnny Bench	1970	45	Jimmie Foxx	1930	156	Tim Raines	1982	78
Joe Jackson	1912	26	Juan Gonzalez	1992	43	Johnny Bench	1970	148	Ty Cobb	1909	76
Nap Lajoie	1897	23	Eddie Mathews	1954	40	Nap Lajoie	1897	127	Eddie Collins	1909	67
Jake Beckley	1890	22	Boog Powell	1964	39	Ben Chapman	1931	122	Tim Shinnick	1890	62
Willie Keeler	1894	22	Jimmie Foxx	1930	37	Jake Beckley	1890	120	John McGraw	1895	61
Sam Crawford	1902	22	Ted Williams	1941	37	Ted Williams	1941	120	Ben Chapman	1931	61
Vic Saier	1913	21	Bob Horner	1980	35	George Davis	1893	119	Shorty Fuller	1890	60
3 tied with		20	Earl Williams	1971	33	Jimmy Williams	1899	116	Bill Dahlen	1892	60
			4 tied with		31	Mel Ott	1931	115	Oyster Burns	1887	58

| Runs Created | | | Batting Average | | | On-Base Percentage | | | Slugging Percentage | | |
			(minimum 3.1 PA/Tm Gm)			(minimum 3.1 PA/Tm Gm)			(minimum 3.1 PA/Tm Gm)		
Joe Kelley	1894	173	Ted Williams	1941	.406	Ted Williams	1941	.551	Ted Williams	1941	.735
Ted Williams	1941	170	Joe Jackson	1912	.395	Joe Kelley	1894	.502	Joe DiMaggio	1937	.673
Joe DiMaggio	1937	163	Joe Kelley	1894	.393	John McGraw	1895	.459	Jimmie Foxx	1930	.637
Oyster Burns	1887	153	Ty Cobb	1909	.377	Joe Jackson	1912	.458	Boog Powell	1964	.606
Jimmie Foxx	1930	150	Willie Keeler	1894	.371	Charlie Keller	1939	.447	Eddie Mathews	1954	.603
Willie Keeler	1894	149	John McGraw	1895	.369	Mike Tiernan	1889	.447	Joe Kelley	1894	.602
Jimmy Williams	1899	148	Nap Lajoie	1897	.361	Fred Snodgrass	1910	.440	Johnny Bench	1970	.587
Joe Jackson	1912	148	Freddy Lindstrom	1928	.358	Cupid Childs	1890	.434	Joe Jackson	1912	.579
Mike Tiernan	1889	145	Stan Musial	1943	.357	Arky Vaughan	1934	.431	Nap Lajoie	1897	.569
George Davis	1893	142	George Davis	1893	.355	Ty Cobb	1909	.431	Stan Musial	1943	.562

Pitching Leaders—Through Age 22

Wins

Monte Ward	145
Silver King	142
Amos Rusie	138
Tommy Bond	111
Bob Feller	107
Larry Corcoran	101
Jumbo McGinnis	99
Kid Nichols	92
Matt Kilroy	92
Elton Chamberlin	90

Losses

Amos Rusie	116
Egyptian Healy	98
Hardie Henderson	91
Monte Ward	86
Pete Schneider	85
Adonis Terry	84
Pink Hawley	80
Scott Stratton	78
4 tied with	74

Winning Percentage
(minimum 60 decisions)

Dwight Gooden	.737
Bob Caruthers	.726
Larry Corcoran	.716
Tommy Bond	.694
Bob Feller	.665
Ed Morris	.664
Babe Ruth	.663
Silver King	.657
Joe Wood	.653
Al Mamaux	.653

Games

Amos Rusie	281
Monte Ward	249
Silver King	229
Terry Forster	217
Bob Feller	205
Pete Schneider	200
Mike McCormick	196
Billy McCool	190
Jumbo McGinnis	179
Matt Kilroy	177

Complete Games

Amos Rusie	235
Monte Ward	215
Silver King	207
Jumbo McGinnis	169
Matt Kilroy	167
Tommy Bond	160
Hardie Henderson	148
Gus Weyhing	148
Scott Stratton	146
Adonis Terry	145

Shutouts

Joe Wood	23
Monte Ward	23
Tommy Bond	21
Walter Johnson	20
Bert Blyleven	18
Jumbo McGinnis	18
Kid Nichols	17
Amos Rusie	17
4 tied with	16

Saves

Terry Forster	70
Billy McCool	48
Victor Cruz	31
Neil Allen	30
Gregg Olson	27
Edwin Nunez	23
Lloyd Allen	20
Steve Howe	17
Dave Beard	15
Bart Johnson	15

Innings Pitched

Amos Rusie	2,288.0
Monte Ward	2,124.0
Silver King	1,933.2
Jumbo McGinnis	1,534.1
Matt Kilroy	1,493.1
Tommy Bond	1,461.2
Bob Feller	1,448.1
Scott Stratton	1,376.1
Hardie Henderson	1,346.0
Gus Weyhing	1,319.1

Strikeouts

Amos Rusie	1,283
Bob Feller	1,233
Toad Ramsey	937
Dwight Gooden	892
Matt Kilroy	865
Bert Blyleven	845
Silver King	782
Monte Ward	776
Hardie Henderson	756
Joe Wood	733

ERA
(minimum 400 Innings Pitched)

Walter Johnson	1.73
Dutch Leonard	1.75
Joe Wood	1.95
Tommy Bond	1.97
Monte Ward	1.99
Larry Corcoran	2.06
Babe Ruth	2.07
Nick Maddox	2.10
Bill James	2.15
Ed Daily	2.21

Component ERA
(minimum 400 Innings Pitched)

Ed Morris	1.60
Charlie Sweeney	1.78
Larry Corcoran	1.79
Walter Johnson	1.80
Monte Ward	1.92
Bob Caruthers	1.92
Ed Daily	1.98
Joe Wood	2.01
Babe Ruth	2.02
Pud Galvin	2.03

Opponent Average
(minimum 400 Innings Pitched)

Dave Boswell	.202
Vida Blue	.203
Ed Morris	.207
Babe Ruth	.208
Larry Corcoran	.212
Dwight Gooden	.213
Sam McDowell	.214
Walter Johnson	.215
Toad Ramsey	.216
Ed Daily	.217

Single Season Pitching Leaders—Age 22

Wins

Tommy Bond	1878	40
Ed Morris	1885	39
Pud Galvin	1879	37
Toad Ramsey	1887	37
Sadie McMahon	1890	36
Frank Killen	1893	36
Kid Nichols	1892	35
Joe Wood	1912	34
Amos Rusie	1893	33
Pink Hawley	1895	31

Losses

Jim McCormick	1879	40
Fleury Sullivan	1884	35
Hardie Henderson	1885	35
Al Mays	1887	34
Sam Weaver	1878	31
Phenomenal Smith	1887	30
Bert Cunningham	1888	29
Pud Galvin	1879	27
Toad Ramsey	1887	27
Harry Staley	1889	26

Winning Percentage
(minimum 15 decisions)

Joe Wood	1912	.872
Doc Crandall	1910	.810
Jocko Flynn	1886	.793
Dutch Leonard	1914	.792
Bill James	1914	.788
Jack Manning	1876	.783
Jerry Nops	1897	.769
Ramon Martinez	1990	.769
Red Ames	1905	.733
Eric King	1986	.733

Games

Mitch Williams	1987	85
Edwin Nunez	1985	70
Lance McCullers	1986	70
Willie Hernandez	1977	67
Pud Galvin	1879	66
Joe Kerrigan	1977	66
Toad Ramsey	1887	65
Gregg Olson	1989	64
3 tied with		63

Complete Games

Pud Galvin	1879	65
Ed Morris	1885	63
Toad Ramsey	1887	61
Jim McCormick	1879	59
Hardie Henderson	1885	59
Tommy Bond	1878	57
Sadie McMahon	1890	55
Phenomenal Smith	1887	54
Fleury Sullivan	1884	51
4 tied with		50

Shutouts

Joe Wood	1912	10
Tommy Bond	1878	9
Bert Blyleven	1973	9
Lefty Leifield	1906	8
Walter Johnson	1910	8
Steve Barber	1961	8
Ed Morris	1885	7
Dutch Leonard	1914	7
Hal Schumacher	1933	7
7 tied with		6

Saves

Gregg Olson	1989	27
Terry Forster	1974	24
Neil Allen	1980	22
Steve Howe	1980	17
Edwin Nunez	1985	16
Rollie Fingers	1969	12
Victor Cruz	1980	12
Joe Kerrigan	1977	11
Dave Beard	1982	11
Bill Wilkinson	1987	10

Innings Pitched

Pud Galvin	1879	593.0
Ed Morris	1885	581.0
Toad Ramsey	1887	561.0
Jim McCormick	1879	546.1
Hardie Henderson	1885	539.1
Tommy Bond	1878	532.2
Sadie McMahon	1890	509.0
Phenomenal Smith	1887	491.1
Amos Rusie	1893	482.0
Silver King	1890	461.0

Strikeouts

Toad Ramsey	1887	355
Sam McDowell	1965	325
Walter Johnson	1910	313
Ed Morris	1885	298
Sadie McMahon	1890	291
Jack Stivetts	1890	289
Hardie Henderson	1885	263
Frank Tanana	1976	261
Bob Feller	1941	260
2 tied with		258

ERA
(minimum 1 Inning Pitched/Tm Gm)

Dutch Leonard	1914	1.00
Walter Johnson	1910	1.36
Ed Reulbach	1905	1.42
Hippo Vaughn	1910	1.83
Andy Coakley	1905	1.84
Lefty Leifield	1906	1.87
Bill James	1914	1.90
Joe Wood	1912	1.91
Larry Corcoran	1882	1.95
Sam Weaver	1878	1.95

Component ERA
(minimum 1 Inning Pitched/Tm Gm)

Dutch Leonard	1914	1.41
Walter Johnson	1910	1.54
Larry Corcoran	1882	1.58
Ed Morris	1885	1.67
Ed Reulbach	1905	1.68
Joe Wood	1912	1.85
Charlie Geggus	1884	1.86
Sam Weaver	1878	1.93
Charlie Ferguson	1885	1.93
Guy Morton	1915	1.95

Opponent Average
(minimum 1 Inning Pitched/Tm Gm)

Dutch Leonard	1914	.179
Sid Fernandez	1985	.181
Al Downing	1963	.184
Sam McDowell	1965	.185
Floyd Youmans	1986	.188
Herb Score	1955	.194
Larry Corcoran	1882	.200
Ed Reulbach	1905	.201
Dave Boswell	1967	.202
Frank Tanana	1976	.203

Batting Leaders—Through Age 23

At-Bats

Robin Yount	3,224
Buddy Lewis	3,089
Al Kaline	2,857
Mel Ott	2,787
Ty Cobb	2,773
Ken Griffey Jr.	2,747
Freddy Lindstrom	2,735
George Davis	2,719
Cesar Cedeno	2,660
Vada Pinson	2,622

Runs

Mel Ott	582
Ted Williams	541
George Davis	540
Buddy Lewis	517
Mickey Mantle	510
Ty Cobb	471
Joe Kelley	469
John McGraw	467
Vada Pinson	466
Jimmie Foxx	461

Hits

Ty Cobb	959
Buddy Lewis	943
Mel Ott	895
Al Kaline	880
Robin Yount	871
Freddy Lindstrom	864
Ken Griffey Jr.	832
George Davis	811
Vada Pinson	807
Cesar Cedeno	782

Doubles

Ken Griffey Jr.	170
Cesar Cedeno	164
Mel Ott	159
Vada Pinson	156
Ted Williams	154
Ty Cobb	154
Buddy Lewis	149
Robin Yount	144
Joe Medwick	138
2 tied with	137

Triples

Sam Crawford	85
George Davis	79
Joe Jackson	67
Sherry Magee	65
Ty Cobb	63
Joe Kelley	63
Jimmy Sheckard	60
Les Mann	56
Mike Tiernan	55
2 tied with	54

Home Runs

Eddie Mathews	153
Mel Ott	153
Frank Robinson	134
Ken Griffey Jr.	132
Ted Williams	127
Orlando Cepeda	122
Juan Gonzalez	121
Mickey Mantle	121
Jimmie Foxx	116
Johnny Bench	114

RBI

Mel Ott	608
Ted Williams	515
Jimmie Foxx	497
Ty Cobb	474
George Davis	454
Ken Griffey Jr.	453
Al Kaline	450
Mickey Mantle	445
Orlando Cepeda	439
Joe DiMaggio	432

Stolen Bases

Rickey Henderson	319
Ty Cobb	254
Tim Raines	246
John McGraw	209
Cesar Cedeno	205
Sherry Magee	200
Jimmy Sheckard	180
George Davis	177
Mike Tiernan	169
Eddie Collins	157

Runs Created

Mel Ott	651
Ted Williams	622
Ty Cobb	592
George Davis	575
Mickey Mantle	526
Jimmie Foxx	524
Ken Griffey Jr.	503
Buddy Lewis	491
Joe Kelley	491
Al Kaline	483

Batting Average
(minimum 1,000 Plate Appearances)

Joe Jackson	.388
Willie Keeler	.367
Ted Williams	.356
Tuck Turner	.350
Al Simmons	.348
Lloyd Waner	.348
Pete Browning	.348
Ty Cobb	.346
Stan Musial	.344
Nap Lajoie	.340

On-Base Percentage
(minimum 1,000 Plate Appearances)

Ted Williams	.481
Joe Jackson	.456
John McGraw	.433
Joe Kelley	.431
Charlie Keller	.427
Stan Musial	.423
Arky Vaughan	.422
Willie Keeler	.422
Jimmie Foxx	.421
Mel Ott	.421

Slugging Percentage
(minimum 1,000 Plate Appearances)

Ted Williams	.642
Joe DiMaggio	.610
Jimmie Foxx	.591
Eddie Mathews	.570
Hal Trosky	.568
Joe Jackson	.566
Mel Ott	.564
Willie Mays	.561
Lou Gehrig	.547
Frank Robinson	.543

Single Season Batting Leaders—Age 23

At-Bats

Juan Samuel	1984	701
Nomar Garciaparra	1997	684
Rennie Stennett	1974	673
Tony Oliva	1964	672
Garry Templeton	1979	672
Tommy Davis	1962	665
Lloyd Waner	1929	662
Travis Fryman	1992	659
Al Simmons	1925	658
Carlos Baerga	1992	657

Runs

Willie Keeler	1895	162
Hugh Duffy	1890	161
Woody English	1930	152
Joe Kelley	1895	148
Harland Clift	1936	145
Billy Hamilton	1889	144
Ted Williams	1942	141
Herman Long	1889	137
Denny Lyons	1889	135
Lou Gehrig	1926	135

Hits

Al Simmons	1925	253
Lloyd Waner	1929	234
Tommy Davis	1962	230
Joe Medwick	1935	224
Tony Oliva	1964	217
Hal Trosky	1936	216
George Brett	1976	215
Woody English	1930	214
Willie Keeler	1895	213
Garry Templeton	1979	211

Doubles

Hank Greenberg	1934	63
Enos Slaughter	1939	52
Stan Musial	1944	51
Lou Gehrig	1926	47
Eric McNair	1932	47
Fred Lynn	1975	47
Joe Medwick	1935	46
Hal Trosky	1936	45
Lou Boudreau	1941	45
3 tied with		44

Triples

Harry Davis	1897	28
Sam Crawford	1903	25
Kip Selbach	1895	22
Paul Waner	1926	22
Mike Tiernan	1890	21
Bobby Wallace	1897	21
Lou Gehrig	1926	20
Lloyd Waner	1929	20
8 tied with		19

Home Runs

Mark McGwire	1987	49
Reggie Jackson	1969	47
Orlando Cepeda	1961	46
Juan Gonzalez	1993	46
Ken Griffey Jr.	1993	45
Hank Aaron	1957	44
Hal Trosky	1936	42
Harmon Killebrew	1959	42
Jose Canseco	1988	42
2 tied with		41

RBI

Hal Trosky	1936	162
Tommy Davis	1962	153
Orlando Cepeda	1961	142
Joe DiMaggio	1938	140
Hank Greenberg	1934	139
Ted Williams	1942	137
Joe Kelley	1895	134
Hank Aaron	1957	132
Goose Goslin	1924	129
Al Simmons	1925	129

Stolen Bases

Rickey Henderson	1982	130
Billy Hamilton	1889	111
Vince Coleman	1985	110
Jim Fogarty	1887	102
Tim Raines	1983	90
Herman Long	1889	89
Tommy Tucker	1887	85
Willie Wilson	1979	83
Eddie Collins	1910	81
Hugh Duffy	1890	78

Runs Created

Ted Williams	1942	160
Joe Kelley	1895	158
Hugh Duffy	1890	153
Billy Hamilton	1889	149
Willie Keeler	1895	146
Mel Ott	1932	143
Joe Medwick	1935	143
Hank Greenberg	1934	142
Arky Vaughan	1935	142
Al Simmons	1925	140

Batting Average
(minimum 3.1 PA/Tm Gm)

Arky Vaughan	1935	.385
Al Simmons	1925	.384
Ty Cobb	1910	.383
Willie Keeler	1895	.377
Joe Jackson	1913	.373
Jim Bottomley	1923	.371
Joe Kelley	1895	.365
George Gore	1880	.360
Bob Caruthers	1887	.357
Ted Williams	1942	.356

On-Base Percentage
(minimum 3.1 PA/Tm Gm)

Ted Williams	1942	.499
Arky Vaughan	1935	.491
Bob Caruthers	1887	.463
Joe Jackson	1913	.460
Ty Cobb	1910	.456
Joe Kelley	1895	.456
Frank Thomas	1991	.453
Eddie Yost	1950	.440
Stan Musial	1944	.440
George Davis	1894	.435

Slugging Percentage
(minimum 3.1 PA/Tm Gm)

Willie Mays	1954	.667
Ted Williams	1942	.648
Hal Trosky	1936	.644
Juan Gonzalez	1993	.632
Mark McGwire	1987	.618
Ken Griffey Jr.	1993	.617
Mickey Mantle	1955	.611
Orlando Cepeda	1961	.609
Reggie Jackson	1969	.608
Arky Vaughan	1935	.607

Pitching Leaders—Through Age 23

Wins		Losses		Winning Percentage		Games	
				(minimum 70 decisions)			
Amos Rusie	174	Amos Rusie	129	John Clarkson	.753	Amos Rusie	335
Monte Ward	161	Egyptian Healy	119	Bob Caruthers	.736	Monte Ward	283
Silver King	156	Hardie Henderson	110	Dwight Gooden	.722	Silver King	277
Tommy Bond	154	Silver King	103	Vic Willis	.712	Matt Kilroy	236
Larry Corcoran	135	Scott Stratton	102	Charlie Buffinton	.694	Terry Forster	234
Kid Nichols	126	Pink Hawley	101	Tommy Bond	.694	Mitch Williams	232
Matt Kilroy	121	Monte Ward	99	Larry Corcoran	.692	Tommy Bond	226
Ed Morris	114	Matt Kilroy	99	Doc Crandall	.667	Mike McCormick	224
Gus Weyhing	114	Adonis Terry	92	Ed Morris	.667	Billy McCool	220
Elton Chamberlin	112	Toad Ramsey	90	Bob Feller	.665	Elton Chamberlin	210

Complete Games		Shutouts		Saves		Innings Pitched	
Amos Rusie	280	Tommy Bond	32	Terry Forster	74	Amos Rusie	2,732.0
Silver King	247	Walter Johnson	26	Gregg Olson	64	Monte Ward	2,401.0
Monte Ward	239	Joe Wood	24	Billy McCool	50	Silver King	2,318.0
Matt Kilroy	222	Monte Ward	24	Neil Allen	48	Tommy Bond	2,017.0
Tommy Bond	219	Ed Morris	22	Victor Cruz	32	Matt Kilroy	1,974.0
Larry Corcoran	189	Bert Blyleven	21	Mitch Williams	32	Larry Corcoran	1,762.1
Gus Weyhing	186	Amos Rusie	20	Goose Gossage	29	Kid Nichols	1,727.1
Kid Nichols	184	Frank Tanana	19	Ugueth Urbina	27	Gus Weyhing	1,709.1
Elton Chamberlin	183	Dwight Gooden	19	Lance McCullers	26	Scott Stratton	1,700.0
Egyptian Healy	182	6 tied with	18	2 tied with	25	Elton Chamberlin	1,685.2

Strikeouts		ERA		Component ERA		Opponent Average	
		(minimum 450 Innings Pitched)		(minimum 450 Innings Pitched)		(minimum 450 Innings Pitched)	
Amos Rusie	1,478	George Bradley	1.23	George Bradley	1.45	Herb Score	.190
Bob Feller	1,233	Ed Reulbach	1.52	Ed Reulbach	1.68	Ed Reulbach	.190
Toad Ramsey	1,165	Walter Johnson	1.77	Ed Reulbach	1.68	Dave Boswell	.205
Bert Blyleven	1,094	Will White	1.85	John Clarkson	1.91	Sid Fernandez	.207
Matt Kilroy	1,082	Dutch Leonard	1.92	Walter Johnson	1.94	Sam McDowell	.208
Dwight Gooden	1,067	Tommy Bond	1.97	Lee Richmond	1.96	Babe Ruth	.209
Silver King	942	John Clarkson	1.98	Addie Joss	1.96	Ed Morris	.209
Frank Tanana	937	Joe Wood	1.99	Monte Ward	1.97	Vida Blue	.210
Ed Morris	926	Monte Ward	2.07	Babe Ruth	1.99	George Bradley	.211
Walter Johnson	915	Nap Rucker	2.07	Larry Corcoran	1.99	Tom Hall	.212

Single Season Pitching Leaders—Age 23

Wins			Losses			Winning Percentage			Games		
						(minimum 15 decisions)					
John Clarkson	1885	53	Pud Galvin	1880	35	Bob Stanley	1978	.882	Ed Vande Berg	1982	78
Charlie Buffinton	1884	48	Harry McCormick	1879	33	Ron Davis	1979	.875	Lance McCullers	1987	78
George Bradley	1876	45	Jim Whitney	1881	33	Roger Moret	1973	.867	Lee Richmond	1880	74
Jim McCormick	1880	45	Frank Mountain	1883	33	Roger Clemens	1986	.857	Jim McCormick	1880	74
Tommy Bond	1879	43	Lee Richmond	1880	32	Henry Boyle	1884	.833	Scott Garrelts	1985	74
Ed Morris	1886	41	Toad Ramsey	1888	30	Ed Reulbach	1906	.826	Antonio Osuna	1996	73
Kid Gleason	1890	38	Ed Beatin	1890	30	Hooks Wiltse	1904	.813	Bill Caudill	1980	72
Amos Rusie	1894	36	Silver King	1891	29	Jim Palmer	1969	.800	Elias Sosa	1973	71
Sadie McMahon	1891	35	Jim McCormick	1880	28	Rick Rhoden	1976	.800	Chuck McElroy	1991	71
2 tied with		34	2 tied with		27	John Candelaria	1977	.800	2 tied with		70

Complete Games			Shutouts			Saves			Innings Pitched		
Jim McCormick	1880	72	George Bradley	1876	16	Gregg Olson	1990	37	Jim McCormick	1880	657.2
John Clarkson	1885	68	Ed Morris	1886	12	Ugueth Urbina	1997	27	John Clarkson	1885	623.0
George Bradley	1876	63	Tommy Bond	1879	11	Goose Gossage	1975	26	Lee Richmond	1880	590.2
Charlie Buffinton	1884	63	Dean Chance	1964	11	Doug Bird	1973	20	Charlie Buffinton	1884	587.0
Ed Morris	1886	63	John Clarkson	1885	10	Elias Sosa	1973	18	George Bradley	1876	573.0
Tommy Bond	1879	59	George Derby	1881	9	Neil Allen	1981	18	Tommy Bond	1879	555.1
Lee Richmond	1880	57	Charlie Buffinton	1884	8	Mitch Williams	1988	18	Ed Morris	1886	555.1
Jim Whitney	1881	57	Ben Sanders	1888	8	Rod Beck	1992	17	Jim Whitney	1881	552.1
Frank Mountain	1883	57	Christy Mathewson	1902	8	4 tied with		16	Kid Gleason	1890	506.0
2 tied with		55	Joe Bush	1916	8				2 tied with		503.0

Strikeouts			ERA			Component ERA			Opponent Average		
			(minimum 1 Inning Pitched/Tm Gm)			(minimum 1 Inning Pitched/Tm Gm)			(minimum 1 Inning Pitched/Tm Gm)		
Charlie Buffinton	1884	417	Tim Keefe	1880	0.86	Tim Keefe	1880	1.25	Ed Reulbach	1906	.175
Ed Morris	1886	326	George Bradley	1876	1.23	George Bradley	1876	1.45	Herb Score	1956	.186
John Clarkson	1885	308	George McQuillan	1908	1.53	Henry Boyle	1884	1.47	Tim Keefe	1880	.187
Bill Wise	1884	268	Ray Collins	1910	1.62	George McQuillan	1908	1.64	Mario Soto	1980	.187
Jim Maloney	1963	265	Ed Summers	1908	1.64	Ed Reulbach	1906	1.68	Sam McDowell	1966	.188
Herb Score	1956	263	Dean Chance	1964	1.65	John Clarkson	1885	1.69	Andy Messersmith	1969	.190
Jim McCormick	1880	260	Ed Reulbach	1906	1.65	Addie Joss	1903	1.70	Adonis Terry	1888	.191
Jack Stivetts	1891	259	Bill Doak	1914	1.72	Charlie Ferguson	1886	1.74	Dean Chance	1964	.195
Bert Blyleven	1974	249	Henry Boyle	1884	1.74	Chief Bender	1907	1.76	Roger Clemens	1986	.195
Al Atkinson	1884	247	Earl Moore	1903	1.74	Dean Chance	1964	1.76	Jim Palmer	1969	.200

Batting Leaders—Through Age 24

At-Bats		Runs		Hits		Doubles	
Robin Yount	3,835	Mel Ott	680	Ty Cobb	1,207	Joe Medwick	202
Buddy Lewis	3,658	George Davis	648	Buddy Lewis	1,112	Ty Cobb	201
Al Kaline	3,368	Mickey Mantle	642	Freddy Lindstrom	1,095	Cesar Cedeno	195
Mel Ott	3,367	Ty Cobb	618	Mel Ott	1,059	Mel Ott	195
Ty Cobb	3,364	Joe Kelley	617	Robin Yount	1,050	Ken Griffey Jr.	194
Freddy Lindstrom	3,344	Buddy Lewis	614	Al Kaline	1,047	Robin Yount	193
Vada Pinson	3,274	Jimmie Foxx	612	Vada Pinson	1,011	Vada Pinson	193
Ken Griffey Jr.	3,180	Freddy Lindstrom	584	Ken Griffey Jr.	972	Buddy Lewis	178
Cesar Cedeno	3,160	Vada Pinson	562	George Davis	957	Freddy Lindstrom	174
George Davis	3,149	John McGraw	557	Cesar Cedeno	926	Dick Bartell	171

Triples		Home Runs		RBI		Stolen Bases	
Sam Crawford	101	Eddie Mathews	190	Mel Ott	711	Rickey Henderson	427
George Davis	88	Mel Ott	176	Jimmie Foxx	666	Ty Cobb	337
Ty Cobb	87	Jimmie Foxx	174	Ty Cobb	601	Tim Raines	321
Joe Kelley	82	Mickey Mantle	173	Mickey Mantle	575	Cesar Cedeno	255
Joe Jackson	80	Ken Griffey Jr.	172	Joe DiMaggio	558	John McGraw	253
Sherry Magee	79	Frank Robinson	165	George Davis	555	Jimmy Sheckard	247
Jake Beckley	73	Orlando Cepeda	157	Orlando Cepeda	553	Sherry Magee	238
Rogers Hornsby	72	Johnny Bench	154	Hal Trosky	553	Billy Hamilton	232
Jimmy Sheckard	69	Juan Gonzalez	140	Al Kaline	544	Joe Kelley	230
John Anderson	68	Hank Aaron	140	Ken Griffey Jr.	543	Hugh Duffy	228

Runs Created		Batting Average (minimum 1,250 Plate Appearances)		On-Base Percentage (minimum 1,250 Plate Appearances)		Slugging Percentage (minimum 1,250 Plate Appearances)	
Ty Cobb	764	Joe Jackson	.378	Ted Williams	.481	Ted Williams	.642
Mel Ott	756	Willie Keeler	.373	Frank Thomas	.447	Lou Gehrig	.625
Jimmie Foxx	713	Paul Waner	.360	Joe Jackson	.445	Jimmie Foxx	.625
Mickey Mantle	700	Ty Cobb	.359	Joe Kelley	.440	Joe DiMaggio	.622
George Davis	689	Ted Williams	.356	John McGraw	.440	Willie Mays	.593
Joe Kelley	651	Pete Browning	.352	Jimmie Foxx	.432	Hank Greenberg	.575
Ted Williams	622	Lloyd Waner	.349	Arky Vaughan	.429	Babe Ruth	.568
Ken Griffey Jr.	603	Nap Lajoie	.347	Lou Gehrig	.427	Hal Trosky	.563
Jimmy Sheckard	591	Al Simmons	.346	Elmer Flick	.427	Mickey Mantle	.560
2 tied with	590	Stan Musial	.344	Paul Waner	.426	Eddie Mathews	.559

Single Season Batting Leaders—Age 24

At-Bats			Runs			Hits			Doubles		
Willie Wilson	1980	705	Willie Keeler	1896	153	Ty Cobb	1911	248	Joe Medwick	1936	64
Kirby Puckett	1985	691	Mike Griffin	1889	152	Paul Waner	1927	237	John Olerud	1993	54
Tony Fernandez	1986	687	Jimmie Foxx	1932	151	Freddy Lindstrom	1930	231	Tris Speaker	1912	53
Pete Rose	1965	670	Bill Dahlen	1894	149	Willie Wilson	1980	230	Al Simmons	1926	53
Brooks Robinson	1961	668	Lou Gehrig	1927	149	Johnny Hodapp	1930	225	Lou Gehrig	1927	52
Jake Wood	1961	663	Joe Kelley	1896	148	Frankie Frisch	1923	223	Johnny Hodapp	1930	51
Bobby Bonds	1970	663	Ty Cobb	1911	147	Joe Medwick	1936	223	Robin Yount	1980	49
Juan Samuel	1985	663	Jesse Burkett	1893	145	Tris Speaker	1912	222	Dick Bartell	1932	48
Red Schoendienst	1947	659	Cupid Childs	1892	136	Richie Ashburn	1951	221	Don Mattingly	1985	48
Zoilo Versalles	1964	659	Tris Speaker	1912	136	Chuck Klein	1929	219	3 tied with		47

Triples			Home Runs			RBI			Stolen Bases		
Larry Doyle	1911	25	Jimmie Foxx	1932	58	Lou Gehrig	1927	175	Rickey Henderson	1983	108
Ty Cobb	1911	24	Mickey Mantle	1956	52	Hank Greenberg	1935	170	Vince Coleman	1986	107
Adam Comorosky	1930	23	Ralph Kiner	1947	51	Jimmie Foxx	1932	169	Billy Hamilton	1890	102
John Anderson	1898	22	Willie Mays	1955	51	Chuck Klein	1929	145	Tommy McCarthy	1888	93
Tommy Leach	1902	22	Lou Gehrig	1927	47	Don Mattingly	1985	145	Joe Kelley	1896	87
Ed Delahanty	1892	21	Ernie Banks	1955	44	Joe Medwick	1936	138	Hugh Duffy	1891	85
Jimmy Williams	1901	21	Chuck Klein	1929	43	Bob Meusel	1921	135	Chippy McGarr	1887	84
5 tied with		20	Rocky Colavito	1958	41	Vic Wertz	1949	133	Ty Cobb	1911	83
			3 tied with		40	Paul Waner	1927	131	Eric Davis	1986	80
						Mickey Mantle	1956	130	Willie Wilson	1980	79

Runs Created			Batting Average (minimum 3.1 PA/Tm Gm)			On-Base Percentage (minimum 3.1 PA/Tm Gm)			Slugging Percentage (minimum 3.1 PA/Tm Gm)		
Jimmie Foxx	1932	189	Ty Cobb	1911	.420	Lou Gehrig	1927	.474	Lou Gehrig	1927	.765
Lou Gehrig	1927	182	Fred Clarke	1897	.390	John Olerud	1993	.473	Jimmie Foxx	1932	.749
Mickey Mantle	1956	174	Bill Lange	1895	.389	John McGraw	1897	.471	Mickey Mantle	1956	.705
Ty Cobb	1911	172	Willie Keeler	1896	.386	Joe Kelley	1896	.469	Ken Griffey Jr.	1994	.674
Tris Speaker	1912	163	Tris Speaker	1912	.383	Jimmie Foxx	1932	.469	Joe DiMaggio	1939	.671
Joe Kelley	1896	160	Joe DiMaggio	1939	.381	Ty Cobb	1911	.467	Willie Mays	1955	.659
Hank Greenberg	1935	156	Paul Waner	1927	.380	Tris Speaker	1912	.464	Chuck Klein	1929	.657
Jesse Burkett	1893	149	Freddy Lindstrom	1930	.379	Mickey Mantle	1956	.464	Babe Ruth	1919	.657
Bill Dahlen	1894	146	Heinie Manush	1926	.378	Fred Clarke	1897	.462	Ralph Kiner	1947	.639
Willie Mays	1955	146	Lou Gehrig	1927	.373	Jesse Burkett	1893	.459	Dick Allen	1966	.632

Pitching Leaders—Through Age 24

Wins		Losses		Winning Percentage (minimum 80 decisions)		Games	
Amos Rusie	197	Amos Rusie	152	Roger Clemens	.732	Amos Rusie	384
Tommy Bond	180	Egyptian Healy	129	John Clarkson	.725	Silver King	329
Silver King	179	Silver King	127	Dwight Gooden	.719	Mitch Williams	308
Larry Corcoran	170	Pink Hawley	119	Bob Caruthers	.718	Monte Ward	292
Monte Ward	164	Hardie Henderson	118	Jerry Nops	.675	Tommy Bond	289
Kid Nichols	158	Matt Kilroy	114	Larry Corcoran	.672	Billy McCool	274
Gus Weyhing	145	Scott Stratton	112	Jim Palmer	.670	Matt Kilroy	266
Bob Caruthers	135	Mickey Welch	108	Lefty Gomez	.670	Terry Forster	263
Mickey Welch	133	Toad Ramsey	107	Kid Nichols	.667	Larry Corcoran	263
Elton Chamberlin	131	Adonis Terry	107	Bob Feller	.665	Elton Chamberlin	262

Complete Games		Shutouts		Saves		Innings Pitched	
Amos Rusie	322	Tommy Bond	35	Gregg Olson	95	Amos Rusie	3,125.1
Silver King	293	Walter Johnson	33	Terry Forster	75	Silver King	2,737.1
Tommy Bond	268	Joe Wood	25	Mitch Williams	68	Tommy Bond	2,510.0
Larry Corcoran	246	Bert Blyleven	24	Neil Allen	67	Monte Ward	2,461.2
Monte Ward	244	Monte Ward	24	Rod Beck	66	Larry Corcoran	2,279.0
Mickey Welch	242	Amos Rusie	24	Bobby Thigpen	57	Mickey Welch	2,206.1
Matt Kilroy	240	Fernando Valenzuela	23	Billy McCool	57	Matt Kilroy	2,191.2
Gus Weyhing	237	Frank Tanana	23	Bruce Sutter	41	Gus Weyhing	2,159.1
Elton Chamberlin	226	Ed Morris	23	Lindy McDaniel	41	Kid Nichols	2,134.1
Kid Nichols	224	4 tied with	21	Steve Howe	38	Elton Chamberlin	2,092.0

Strikeouts		ERA (minimum 500 Innings Pitched)		Component ERA (minimum 500 Innings Pitched)		Opponent Average (minimum 500 Innings Pitched)	
Amos Rusie	1,679	Ed Reulbach	1.56	George McQuillan	1.70	Herb Score	.187
Bert Blyleven	1,327	Walter Johnson	1.69	Ed Reulbach	1.80	Andy Messersmith	.191
Toad Ramsey	1,258	George McQuillan	1.71	Walter Johnson	1.84	Ed Reulbach	.198
Bob Feller	1,233	Will White	1.93	Addie Joss	1.92	Bob Turley	.199
Walter Johnson	1,218	Ed Summers	1.93	George Bradley	1.97	Nolan Ryan	.202
Dwight Gooden	1,168	Dutch Leonard	2.05	Tony Mullane	2.00	Tom Hall	.204
Matt Kilroy	1,130	Joe Wood	2.05	Monte Ward	2.01	Dave Boswell	.211
Silver King	1,119	Jeff Tesreau	2.07	Ed Morris	2.02	Sid Fernandez	.211
Sam McDowell	1,101	George Bradley	2.08	John Clarkson	2.04	George McQuillan	.212
Larry Corcoran	1,076	Monte Ward	2.10	Bob Caruthers	2.05	Jeff Tesreau	.213

Single Season Pitching Leaders—Age 24

Wins			Losses			Winning Percentage (minimum 15 decisions)			Games		
Will White	1879	43	Red Donahue	1897	35	Fred Goldsmith	1880	.875	Julian Tavarez	1997	89
Mickey Welch	1884	39	Bobby Mathews	1876	34	Emil Yde	1924	.842	Butch Metzger	1976	77
John Clarkson	1886	36	Jersey Bakely	1888	33	Bill Hoffer	1895	.838	Mark Davis	1985	77
Tony Mullane	1883	35	Will White	1879	31	Denny McLain	1968	.838	Will White	1879	76
Larry Corcoran	1884	35	Jim McCormick	1881	30	King Cole	1910	.833	Mitch Williams	1989	76
Jack Stivetts	1892	35	Tommy Bond	1880	29	Dizzy Dean	1934	.811	Rod Beck	1993	76
George Haddock	1891	34	Duke Esper	1893	28	Ed Reulbach	1907	.810	Bob Lacey	1978	74
Walter Johnson	1912	33	Tim Keefe	1881	27	Boo Ferriss	1946	.806	Mike Stanton	1991	74
Kid Nichols	1894	32	Charlie Buffinton	1885	27	John Franco	1985	.800	Terry Adams	1997	74
3 tied with		31	2 tied with		26	Shawn Estes	1997	.792	Kenny Rogers	1989	73

Complete Games			Shutouts			Saves			Innings Pitched		
Will White	1879	75	Reb Russell	1913	8	Rod Beck	1993	48	Will White	1879	680.0
Mickey Welch	1884	62	Hal Newhouser	1945	8	Mitch Williams	1989	36	Mickey Welch	1884	557.1
Jersey Bakely	1888	60	Larry Corcoran	1884	7	Bobby Thigpen	1988	34	Jersey Bakely	1888	532.2
Jim McCormick	1881	57	Pete Alexander	1911	7	Bruce Sutter	1977	31	Jim McCormick	1881	526.0
Larry Corcoran	1884	57	Walter Johnson	1912	7	Gregg Olson	1991	31	Larry Corcoran	1884	516.2
Bobby Mathews	1876	55	Burleigh Grimes	1918	7	Lindy McDaniel	1960	26	Bobby Mathews	1876	516.0
Gus Weyhing	1891	51	Hod Eller	1919	7	Rawly Eastwick	1975	22	Tommy Bond	1880	493.0
Lee Richmond	1881	50	Dizzy Dean	1934	7	Frank Linzy	1965	21	Pud Galvin	1881	474.0
John Clarkson	1886	50	Jon Matlack	1974	7	Danny Miceli	1995	21	John Clarkson	1886	466.2
3 tied with		49	Roger Clemens	1987	7	Neil Allen	1982	19	Lee Richmond	1881	462.1

Strikeouts			ERA (minimum 1 Inning Pitched/Tm Gm)			Component ERA (minimum 1 Inning Pitched/Tm Gm)			Opponent Average (minimum 1 Inning Pitched/Tm Gm)		
Mickey Welch	1884	345	Walter Johnson	1912	1.39	Walter Johnson	1912	1.52	Bob Turley	1955	.193
John Clarkson	1886	313	Addie Joss	1904	1.59	Tony Mullane	1883	1.63	Walter Johnson	1912	.196
Walter Johnson	1912	303	Ernie Shore	1915	1.64	Frank Owen	1904	1.70	Denny McLain	1968	.200
Denny McLain	1968	280	Ed Reulbach	1907	1.69	Fred Goldsmith	1880	1.82	Andy Messersmith	1970	.205
Larry Corcoran	1884	272	Fred Goldsmith	1880	1.75	Addie Joss	1904	1.82	Sea Lion Hall	1910	.207
Christy Mathewson	1903	267	King Cole	1910	1.80	Bob Caruthers	1888	1.86	Tom Seaver	1969	.207
Fergie Jenkins	1968	260	Hal Newhouser	1945	1.81	Henry Gruber	1888	1.87	Sandy Koufax	1960	.207
Roger Clemens	1987	256	Lew Richie	1908	1.83	Frank Mountain	1884	1.89	Frank Mountain	1884	.209
Charlie Buffinton	1885	242	Wilbur Cooper	1916	1.87	Denny McLain	1968	1.91	Tony Mullane	1883	.211
Rube Marquard	1911	237	Pol Perritt	1917	1.88	Ed Karger	1907	1.91	Hal Newhouser	1945	.211

Batting Leaders—Through Age 25

At-Bats		Runs		Hits		Doubles	
Robin Yount	4,212	Mel Ott	799	Ty Cobb	1,434	Joe Medwick	258
Mel Ott	3,949	Mickey Mantle	763	Mel Ott	1,249	Ty Cobb	231
Al Kaline	3,919	George Davis	746	Al Kaline	1,200	Mel Ott	224
Ty Cobb	3,917	Jimmie Foxx	737	Freddy Lindstrom	1,186	Cesar Cedeno	221
Vada Pinson	3,899	Ty Cobb	737	Vada Pinson	1,177	Vada Pinson	216
Cesar Cedeno	3,735	Joe Kelley	730	Robin Yount	1,153	Robin Yount	208
Buddy Lewis	3,658	John McGraw	700	Hank Aaron	1,137	Hank Aaron	205
Freddy Lindstrom	3,647	Vada Pinson	661	Jimmie Foxx	1,127	Sherry Magee	205
George Davis	3,643	Willie Keeler	651	George Davis	1,115	Ken Griffey Jr.	201
Sherry Magee	3,582	Mike Tiernan	626	Buddy Lewis	1,112	Hal Trosky	200

Triples		Home Runs		RBI		Stolen Bases	
Sam Crawford	111	Eddie Mathews	222	Mel Ott	846	Rickey Henderson	493
Ty Cobb	110	Jimmie Foxx	222	Jimmie Foxx	829	Ty Cobb	398
George Davis	100	Mel Ott	211	Joe DiMaggio	691	Tim Raines	391
Sherry Magee	96	Mickey Mantle	207	Ty Cobb	684	Billy Hamilton	343
Joe Jackson	94	Frank Robinson	202	Mickey Mantle	669	Vince Coleman	326
Jake Beckley	92	Orlando Cepeda	191	Hal Trosky	663	Cesar Cedeno	313
Joe Kelley	91	Ken Griffey Jr.	189	George Davis	654	John McGraw	296
Rogers Hornsby	90	Johnny Bench	179	Orlando Cepeda	650	Jim Fogarty	289
Jimmy Williams	80	Hank Aaron	179	Joe Medwick	634	Sherry Magee	287
2 tied with	78	Joe DiMaggio	168	Hank Aaron	617	Hugh Duffy	279

| Runs Created | | Batting Average | | On-Base Percentage | | Slugging Percentage | |
		(minimum 1,500 Plate Appearances)		(minimum 1,500 Plate Appearances)		(minimum 1,500 Plate Appearances)	
Ty Cobb	912	Willie Keeler	.385	Ted Williams	.481	Chuck Klein	.657
Mel Ott	899	Chuck Klein	.369	Babe Ruth	.450	Babe Ruth	.650
Jimmie Foxx	879	Ty Cobb	.366	John McGraw	.447	Ted Williams	.642
Mickey Mantle	855	Joe Jackson	.366	Joe Kelley	.441	Jimmie Foxx	.638
George Davis	794	Paul Waner	.363	Frank Thomas	.441	Lou Gehrig	.631
Joe Kelley	778	Ted Williams	.356	Lou Gehrig	.438	Joe DiMaggio	.623
Eddie Mathews	691	Al Simmons	.355	Jimmie Foxx	.435	Johnny Mize	.597
John McGraw	691	Jim Bottomley	.350	Joe Jackson	.435	Willie Mays	.584
Joe DiMaggio	687	Stan Musial	.350	Willie Keeler	.434	Hank Greenberg	.576
Al Kaline	672	Pete Browning	.349	Cupid Childs	.433	Mickey Mantle	.574

Single Season Batting Leaders—Age 25

At-Bats			Runs			Hits			Doubles		
Lloyd Waner	1931	681	Fred Dunlap	1884	160	Chuck Klein	1930	250	Chuck Klein	1930	59
Kirby Puckett	1986	680	Bobby Lowe	1894	158	Willie Keeler	1897	239	Billy Herman	1935	57
Jim Rice	1978	677	Babe Ruth	1920	158	Don Mattingly	1986	238	Joe Medwick	1937	56
Don Mattingly	1986	677	Chuck Klein	1930	158	Joe Medwick	1937	237	Don Mattingly	1986	53
Billy Herman	1935	666	Darby O'Brien	1889	146	Rogers Hornsby	1921	235	Paul Waner	1928	50
Zoilo Versalles	1965	666	Ed Delahanty	1893	145	Stan Musial	1946	228	Stan Musial	1946	50
Paul Molitor	1982	666	Cupid Childs	1893	145	Ty Cobb	1912	227	Ned Williamson	1883	49
Bobby Richardson	1961	662	Willie Keeler	1897	145	Jim Bottomley	1925	227	Keith Hernandez	1979	48
Curt Flood	1963	662	John McGraw	1898	143	Billy Herman	1935	227	Lou Gehrig	1928	47
Ruben Sierra	1991	661	Paul Waner	1928	142	3 tied with		223	Joe Vosmik	1935	47

Triples			Home Runs			RBI			Stolen Bases		
Tom Long	1915	25	Babe Ruth	1920	54	Chuck Klein	1930	170	Billy Hamilton	1891	111
Elmer Smith	1893	23	Jimmie Foxx	1933	48	Jimmie Foxx	1933	163	Vince Coleman	1987	109
Ty Cobb	1912	23	Harmon Killebrew	1961	46	Joe Medwick	1937	154	Jim Fogarty	1889	99
Bill Bradley	1903	22	Jim Rice	1978	46	Ed Delahanty	1893	146	Darby O'Brien	1889	91
Tris Speaker	1913	22	Willie McCovey	1963	44	Lou Gehrig	1928	142	Curt Welch	1887	89
Dave Orr	1885	21	Rocky Colavito	1959	42	Jim Rice	1978	139	Clyde Milan	1912	88
Jimmy Williams	1902	21	Frank Thomas	1993	41	Babe Ruth	1920	137	Bill Lange	1896	84
4 tied with		20	Chuck Klein	1930	40	Mel Ott	1934	135	Marquis Grissom	1992	78
			Ralph Kiner	1948	40	Joe DiMaggio	1940	133	George Van Haltren	1891	75
			Wally Post	1955	40	3 tied with		128	Paul Radford	1887	73

| Runs Created | | | Batting Average | | | On-Base Percentage | | | Slugging Percentage | | |
			(minimum 3.1 PA/Tm Gm)			(minimum 3.1 PA/Tm Gm)			(minimum 3.1 PA/Tm Gm)		
Babe Ruth	1920	191	Willie Keeler	1897	.424	Babe Ruth	1920	.530	Babe Ruth	1920	.847
Chuck Klein	1930	171	Fred Dunlap	1884	.412	Mickey Mantle	1957	.512	Jimmie Foxx	1933	.703
Jimmie Foxx	1933	166	Ty Cobb	1912	.410	John McGraw	1898	.475	Chuck Klein	1930	.687
Ed Delahanty	1893	163	Rogers Hornsby	1921	.397	Lou Gehrig	1928	.467	Mickey Mantle	1957	.665
Joe Medwick	1937	163	Chuck Klein	1930	.386	Willie Keeler	1897	.464	Lou Gehrig	1928	.648
Fred Dunlap	1884	160	Babe Ruth	1920	.376	Cupid Childs	1893	.463	Joe Medwick	1937	.641
Tommy Tucker	1889	158	Joe Medwick	1937	.374	Rogers Hornsby	1921	.458	Rogers Hornsby	1921	.639
Billy Hamilton	1891	156	Dan Brouthers	1883	.374	Ty Cobb	1912	.458	Hank Aaron	1959	.636
Lou Gehrig	1928	156	Lou Gehrig	1928	.374	Roy Thomas	1899	.457	Joe DiMaggio	1940	.626
Mickey Mantle	1957	155	Tommy Tucker	1889	.372	Billy Hamilton	1891	.453	Fred Dunlap	1884	.621

Pitching Leaders—Through Age 25

Wins		Losses		Winning Percentage (minimum 90 decisions)		Games	
Amos Rusie	197	Amos Rusie	152	Bob Caruthers	.732	Amos Rusie	384
Silver King	187	Stump Wiedman	139	Ed Reulbach	.729	Mitch Williams	367
Kid Nichols	184	Silver King	137	Dwight Gooden	.721	Silver King	353
Tommy Bond	180	Egyptian Healy	136	Lefty Gomez	.712	Gus Weyhing	316
Larry Corcoran	177	Jim McCormick	136	John Clarkson	.701	Mickey Welch	313
Gus Weyhing	177	Pink Hawley	130	Roger Clemens	.696	Kid Nichols	302
Mickey Welch	177	Gus Weyhing	124	Jeff Tesreau	.684	Terry Forster	296
Bob Caruthers	175	Toad Ramsey	124	Jim Palmer	.675	Elton Chamberlin	296
Monte Ward	164	Adonis Terry	123	Joe Wood	.674	4 tied with	292
Ed Morris	157	Hardie Henderson	121	Don Gullett	.674		

Complete Games		Shutouts		Saves		Innings Pitched	
Amos Rusie	322	Walter Johnson	44	Gregg Olson	131	Amos Rusie	3,125.1
Silver King	305	Tommy Bond	35	Rod Beck	94	Silver King	2,891.1
Mickey Welch	297	Bert Blyleven	30	Bobby Thigpen	91	Mickey Welch	2,698.1
Gus Weyhing	283	Joe Wood	28	Mitch Williams	84	Gus Weyhing	2,629.0
Tommy Bond	270	Ed Morris	28	Terry Forster	76	Tommy Bond	2,535.1
Kid Nichols	266	Mickey Welch	28	Neil Allen	69	Kid Nichols	2,514.0
Jim McCormick	265	Fernando Valenzuela	26	Bruce Sutter	68	Monte Ward	2,461.2
Ed Morris	264	Denny McLain	26	Billy McCool	58	Jim McCormick	2,442.2
Larry Corcoran	254	3 tied with	24	Steve Howe	56	Ed Morris	2,363.2
Elton Chamberlin	245			Goose Gossage	56	Larry Corcoran	2,363.1

Strikeouts		ERA (minimum 550 Innings Pitched)		Component ERA (minimum 550 Innings Pitched)		Opponent Average (minimum 550 Innings Pitched)	
Amos Rusie	1,679	Walter Johnson	1.60	Walter Johnson	1.71	Herb Score	.188
Bert Blyleven	1,546	George McQuillan	1.69	George McQuillan	1.73	Nolan Ryan	.191
Toad Ramsey	1,515	Ed Reulbach	1.70	Ed Reulbach	1.92	Andy Messersmith	.200
Walter Johnson	1,461	Joe Wood	1.99	Addie Joss	1.94	Ed Reulbach	.203
Dwight Gooden	1,391	Will White	1.99	Tony Mullane	1.96	Tom Hall	.204
Sam McDowell	1,384	George Bradley	2.08	George Bradley	1.97	Sid Fernandez	.206
Fernando Valenzuela	1,274	Dutch Leonard	2.08	Monte Ward	2.01	Sam McDowell	.209
Don Drysdale	1,236	Ed Summers	2.10	Joe Wood	2.07	George McQuillan	.210
Bob Feller	1,233	Monte Ward	2.10	Ed Morris	2.10	Walter Johnson	.211
Gus Weyhing	1,208	Lew Richie	2.11	Fred Goldsmith	2.11	Jeff Tesreau	.211

Single Season Pitching Leaders—Age 25

Wins			Losses			Winning Percentage (minimum 15 decisions)			Games		
Al Spalding	1876	47	Will White	1880	42	David Cone	1988	.870	Wayne Granger	1969	90
Mickey Welch	1885	44	Stump Wiedman	1886	36	Ralph Terry	1961	.842	Eddie Guardado	1996	83
Bob Caruthers	1889	40	Mark Baldwin	1889	34	Lefty Gomez	1934	.839	Brad Clontz	1996	81
John Clarkson	1887	38	Lee Richmond	1882	33	Walter Johnson	1913	.837	Dan Spillner	1977	76
Jim Whitney	1883	37	Dupee Shaw	1884	33	Jim Hughes	1899	.824	Butch Metzger	1977	75
Jim McCormick	1882	36	John Harkins	1884	32	Roger Moret	1975	.824	Roger McDowell	1986	75
Tony Mullane	1884	36	Jim McCormick	1882	30	Al McBean	1963	.813	5 tied with		74
Cy Young	1892	36	Hank O'Day	1888	29	Al Hrabosky	1975	.813			
Walter Johnson	1913	36	Jack Taylor	1898	29	Mickey Welch	1885	.800			
Christy Mathewson	1904	33	2 tied with		27	Robin Roberts	1952	.800			

Complete Games			Shutouts			Saves			Innings Pitched		
Jim McCormick	1882	65	Walter Johnson	1913	11	John Wetteland	1992	37	Jim McCormick	1882	595.2
Tony Mullane	1884	64	Ed Walsh	1906	10	Gregg Olson	1992	36	Tony Mullane	1884	567.0
Dupee Shaw	1884	60	Dave Davenport	1915	10	Bobby Thigpen	1989	34	Dupee Shaw	1884	543.1
Will White	1880	58	Cy Young	1892	9	Jack Aker	1966	32	Al Spalding	1876	528.2
John Clarkson	1887	56	Denny McLain	1969	9	Dave Righetti	1984	31	John Clarkson	1887	523.0
Mickey Welch	1885	55	Nolan Ryan	1972	9	Lee Smith	1983	29	Will White	1880	517.1
Jim Whitney	1883	54	Al Spalding	1876	8	John Franco	1986	29	Jim Whitney	1883	514.0
Ed Morris	1888	54	Jeff Tesreau	1914	8	Rich Loiselle	1997	29	Mark Baldwin	1889	513.2
Mark Baldwin	1889	54	Roger Clemens	1988	8	Rod Beck	1994	28	Mickey Welch	1885	492.0
Al Spalding	1876	53	10 tied with		7	2 tied with		27	Ed Morris	1888	480.0

Strikeouts			ERA (minimum 1 Inning Pitched/Tm Gm)			Component ERA (minimum 1 Inning Pitched/Tm Gm)			Opponent Average (minimum 1 Inning Pitched/Tm Gm)		
Dupee Shaw	1884	451	Walter Johnson	1913	1.14	Walter Johnson	1913	1.27	Nolan Ryan	1972	.171
Mark Baldwin	1889	368	Joe Wood	1915	1.49	Claude Hendrix	1914	1.59	Dave McNally	1968	.182
Jim Whitney	1883	345	Barney Pelty	1906	1.59	Dave McNally	1968	1.66	Pedro Martinez	1997	.184
Nolan Ryan	1972	329	Chief Bender	1909	1.66	Chief Bender	1909	1.68	Walter Johnson	1913	.187
Tony Mullane	1884	325	Mickey Welch	1885	1.66	Ed Walsh	1906	1.69	Sam McDowell	1968	.189
Pedro Martinez	1997	305	Claude Hendrix	1914	1.69	Barney Pelty	1906	1.70	Sid Fernandez	1988	.191
Roger Clemens	1988	291	Carl Mays	1917	1.74	Mickey Welch	1885	1.73	Art Fromme	1909	.201
Sam McDowell	1968	283	Al Spalding	1876	1.75	Pedro Martinez	1997	1.79	Hal Newhouser	1946	.201
Tom Seaver	1970	283	Henry Boyle	1886	1.76	Art Fromme	1909	1.81	Curt Schilling	1992	.201
Hal Newhouser	1946	275	Doc White	1904	1.78	Dave Davenport	1915	1.82	Mickey Welch	1885	.203

Batting Leaders—Through Age 26

At-Bats		Runs		Hits		Doubles	
Robin Yount	4,847	Mel Ott	912	Ty Cobb	1,601	Joe Medwick	305
Vada Pinson	4,568	Mickey Mantle	890	Mel Ott	1,440	Cesar Cedeno	257
Mel Ott	4,542	George Davis	858	Al Kaline	1,390	Mel Ott	257
Al Kaline	4,505	Jimmie Foxx	857	Vada Pinson	1,381	Robin Yount	254
Ty Cobb	4,345	John McGraw	840	Robin Yount	1,363	Vada Pinson	250
Cesar Cedeno	4,265	Ty Cobb	807	Freddy Lindstrom	1,347	Ty Cobb	249
Freddy Lindstrom	4,242	Joe Kelley	801	Rogers Hornsby	1,323	Sherry Magee	237
George Davis	4,162	Willie Keeler	777	Hank Aaron	1,309	Hal Trosky	231
Ruben Sierra	4,144	Hugh Duffy	771	Jimmie Foxx	1,307	Ruben Sierra	230
Hank Aaron	4,114	Vada Pinson	758	George Davis	1,298	Frank Robinson	228

Triples		Home Runs		RBI		Stolen Bases	
Sam Crawford	127	Jimmie Foxx	266	Mel Ott	960	Rickey Henderson	573
Ty Cobb	126	Eddie Mathews	253	Jimmie Foxx	959	Tim Raines	461
Joe Jackson	115	Mickey Mantle	249	Joe DiMaggio	816	Ty Cobb	450
George Davis	110	Mel Ott	242	George Davis	790	Vince Coleman	407
Jake Beckley	110	Frank Robinson	241	Hal Trosky	767	Billy Hamilton	400
Joe Kelley	106	Ken Griffey Jr.	238	Mickey Mantle	766	Cesar Cedeno	374
Rogers Hornsby	104	Orlando Cepeda	222	Joe Medwick	756	John McGraw	369
Sherry Magee	101	Hank Aaron	219	Ty Cobb	751	George Davis	338
Tris Speaker	94	Juan Gonzalez	214	Orlando Cepeda	747	Bill Lange	336
Goose Goslin	93	Johnny Bench	212	Johnny Bench	745	Jim Fogarty	325

Runs Created		Batting Average		On-Base Percentage		Slugging Percentage	
		(minimum 1,750 Plate Appearances)		(minimum 1,750 Plate Appearances)		(minimum 1,750 Plate Appearances)	
Mel Ott	1,029	Willie Keeler	.385	Ted Williams	.481	Babe Ruth	.700
Jimmie Foxx	1,023	Ty Cobb	.368	Babe Ruth	.466	Ted Williams	.642
Ty Cobb	1,011	Nap Lajoie	.362	John McGraw	.461	Jimmie Foxx	.640
Mickey Mantle	993	Joe Jackson	.361	Frank Thomas	.449	Chuck Klein	.636
George Davis	927	Pete Browning	.361	Cupid Childs	.441	Joe DiMaggio	.626
Joe Kelley	876	Chuck Klein	.360	Jimmie Foxx	.437	Lou Gehrig	.621
Joe DiMaggio	833	Paul Waner	.356	Lou Gehrig	.436	Johnny Mize	.605
John McGraw	825	Ted Williams	.356	Joe Kelley	.435	Hank Greenberg	.600
Frank Robinson	822	Al Simmons	.354	Willie Keeler	.431	Willie Mays	.593
Mike Tiernan	789	Rogers Hornsby	.348	Paul Waner	.431	Frank Thomas	.590

Single Season Batting Leaders—Age 26

At-Bats			Runs			Hits			Doubles		
Omar Moreno	1979	695	Babe Ruth	1921	177	Rogers Hornsby	1922	250	Billy Herman	1936	57
Bobby Richardson	1962	692	Hughie Jennings	1895	159	Heinie Manush	1928	241	Frank Robinson	1962	51
Dave Cash	1974	687	Jesse Burkett	1895	153	Harry Heilmann	1921	237	Hank Greenberg	1937	49
Jo-Jo Moore	1935	681	Arlie Latham	1886	152	Nap Lajoie	1901	232	Rafael Palmeiro	1991	49
Curt Flood	1964	679	Hub Collins	1890	148	Jesse Burkett	1895	225	Nap Lajoie	1901	48
Sandy Alomar	1970	672	Hugh Duffy	1893	147	Pete Browning	1887	220	Wally Moses	1937	48
Vada Pinson	1965	669	Ed Delahanty	1894	147	Kiki Cuyler	1925	220	Heinie Manush	1928	47
Don Kessinger	1969	664	Rickey Henderson	1985	146	Babe Herman	1929	217	Chick Hafey	1929	47
Rick Burleson	1977	663	Nap Lajoie	1901	145	Willie Keeler	1898	216	Eddie Morgan	1930	47
Joe Carter	1986	663	Kiki Cuyler	1925	144	Willie McGee	1985	216	Joe Medwick	1938	47

Triples			Home Runs			RBI			Stolen Bases		
Dave Orr	1886	31	Roger Maris	1961	61	Hank Greenberg	1937	183	Pete Browning	1887	103
Kiki Cuyler	1925	26	Babe Ruth	1921	59	Babe Ruth	1921	171	Curt Welch	1888	95
Honus Wagner	1900	22	Ralph Kiner	1949	54	Rogers Hornsby	1922	152	Hub Collins	1890	85
Snuffy Stirnweiss	1945	22	Cecil Fielder	1990	51	Juan Gonzalez	1996	144	Tommy McCarthy	1890	83
Billy Shindle	1890	21	Ken Griffey Jr.	1996	49	Don Hurst	1932	143	Dummy Hoy	1888	82
Bill Keister	1901	21	Harmon Killebrew	1962	48	Roger Maris	1961	142	Vince Coleman	1988	81
Home Run Baker	1912	21	Juan Gonzalez	1996	47	Ken Griffey Jr.	1996	140	Rickey Henderson	1985	80
Joe Jackson	1916	21	Jimmie Foxx	1934	44	Harry Heilmann	1921	139	Ted Scheffler	1890	77
5 tied with		20	Jose Canseco	1991	44	Dale Alexander	1929	137	Omar Moreno	1979	77
			Ernie Banks	1957	43	3 tied with		136	Rudy Law	1983	77

Runs Created			Batting Average			On-Base Percentage			Slugging Percentage		
			(minimum 3.1 PA/Tm Gm)			(minimum 3.1 PA/Tm Gm)			(minimum 3.1 PA/Tm Gm)		
Babe Ruth	1921	208	Ross Barnes	1876	.429	John McGraw	1899	.547	Babe Ruth	1921	.846
Rogers Hornsby	1922	179	Nap Lajoie	1901	.426	Babe Ruth	1921	.512	Jeff Bagwell	1994	.750
Jesse Burkett	1895	169	Jesse Burkett	1895	.409	Frank Thomas	1994	.487	Frank Thomas	1994	.729
Nap Lajoie	1901	169	Ed Delahanty	1894	.407	Norm Cash	1961	.487	Rogers Hornsby	1922	.722
Pete Browning	1887	163	Pete Browning	1887	.402	Jesse Burkett	1895	.486	Hank Greenberg	1937	.668
Hank Greenberg	1937	160	Rogers Hornsby	1922	.401	Ed Delahanty	1894	.478	Norm Cash	1961	.662
Norm Cash	1961	158	Harry Heilmann	1921	.394	Cupid Childs	1894	.475	Ralph Kiner	1949	.658
Frank Robinson	1962	152	John McGraw	1899	.391	Ty Cobb	1913	.467	Jimmie Foxx	1934	.653
Honus Wagner	1900	150	Ty Cobb	1913	.390	Pete Browning	1887	.464	Nap Lajoie	1901	.643
2 tied with		149	Hughie Jennings	1895	.386	Nap Lajoie	1901	.463	2 tied with		.643

Pitching Leaders—Through Age 26

Wins

Amos Rusie	225
Kid Nichols	214
Mickey Welch	210
Gus Weyhing	200
Bob Caruthers	198
Silver King	187
Tommy Bond	180
Walter Johnson	179
Larry Corcoran	177
John Clarkson	171

Losses

Amos Rusie	162
Stump Wiedman	155
Jim McCormick	148
Pink Hawley	147
Mickey Welch	141
Gus Weyhing	140
Adonis Terry	139
Pud Galvin	138
Silver King	137
2 tied with	136

Winning Percentage
(minimum 100 decisions)

Bill Hoffer	.765
Bob Caruthers	.725
Dwight Gooden	.714
Ed Reulbach	.713
Mike Mussina	.703
Don Gullett	.686
John Clarkson	.684
Juan Marichal	.680
Roger Clemens	.679
Carl Erskine	.676

Games

Mitch Williams	436
Amos Rusie	422
Mickey Welch	372
Gus Weyhing	358
Silver King	353
Kid Nichols	351
Terry Forster	343
Lindy McDaniel	336
Mike Jackson	326
Pink Hawley	326

Complete Games

Amos Rusie	357
Mickey Welch	353
Gus Weyhing	316
Silver King	305
Kid Nichols	303
Jim McCormick	301
Ed Morris	282
Pud Galvin	279
Tommy Bond	270
Elton Chamberlin	263

Shutouts

Walter Johnson	53
Bert Blyleven	35
Tommy Bond	35
Mickey Welch	29
Joe Wood	28
Ed Reulbach	28
Christy Mathewson	28
Ed Morris	28
3 tied with	27

Saves

Gregg Olson	160
Bobby Thigpen	148
Rod Beck	127
Mitch Williams	114
Bruce Sutter	105
Terry Forster	98
Goose Gossage	83
John Wetteland	81
Lee Smith	80
John Franco	77

Innings Pitched

Amos Rusie	3,447.2
Mickey Welch	3,198.1
Gus Weyhing	2,974.1
Silver King	2,891.1
Kid Nichols	2,886.1
Jim McCormick	2,784.2
Pud Galvin	2,627.1
Tommy Bond	2,547.2
Ed Morris	2,533.2
Elton Chamberlin	2,510.2

Strikeouts

Amos Rusie	1,814
Bert Blyleven	1,728
Walter Johnson	1,686
Sam McDowell	1,663
Dwight Gooden	1,541
Toad Ramsey	1,515
Don Drysdale	1,487
Fernando Valenzuela	1,464
Gus Weyhing	1,309
Mickey Welch	1,299

ERA
(minimum 600 Innings Pitched)

Walter Johnson	1.62
Ed Reulbach	1.72
Ed Walsh	1.88
George McQuillan	1.95
Joe Wood	1.99
Will White	2.03
Christy Mathewson	2.08
Addie Joss	2.08
Monte Ward	2.10
Dutch Leonard	2.14

Component ERA
(minimum 600 Innings Pitched)

Walter Johnson	1.72
Addie Joss	1.86
Ed Walsh	1.89
Ed Reulbach	1.92
George McQuillan	1.96
Tony Mullane	1.96
Monte Ward	2.01
Jim Whitney	2.05
Joe Wood	2.07
Fred Goldsmith	2.07

Opponent Average
(minimum 600 Innings Pitched)

Herb Score	.193
Nolan Ryan	.195
Andy Messersmith	.202
Sid Fernandez	.205
Ed Reulbach	.205
Tom Hall	.206
Sam McDowell	.209
Bob Turley	.210
Walter Johnson	.212
Mario Soto	.212

Single Season Pitching Leaders—Age 26

Wins

Pud Galvin	1883	46
Tim Keefe	1883	41
Mark Baldwin	1890	34
Cy Young	1893	34
Henry Porter	1885	33
Mickey Welch	1886	33
John Clarkson	1888	33
Christy Mathewson	1905	31
Tom Lovett	1890	30
Kid Nichols	1896	30

Losses

George Bradley	1879	40
John Ewing	1889	30
Ted Breitenstein	1895	30
Pud Galvin	1883	29
Tim Keefe	1883	27
Phil Knell	1891	27
Luther Taylor	1901	27
Paul Derringer	1933	27
Jack Neagle	1884	26
Dupee Shaw	1885	26

Winning Percentage
(minimum 15 decisions)

Orel Hershiser	1985	.864
Elmer Riddle	1941	.826
Al Orth	1899	.824
Juan Guzman	1993	.824
Chief Bender	1910	.821
Howie Krist	1942	.813
Johnny Allen	1932	.810
Larry Jansen	1947	.808
George Stone	1973	.800
Tommy Greene	1993	.800

Games

Mark Eichhorn	1987	89
Wilbur Wood	1968	88
Dale Murray	1976	81
Jeff Robinson	1987	81
Pedro Borbon	1973	80
Tim Burke	1985	78
Bobby Thigpen	1990	77
Xavier Hernandez	1992	77
Mark Wohlers	1996	77
4 tied with		76

Complete Games

Pud Galvin	1883	72
Tim Keefe	1883	68
Mickey Welch	1886	56
Mark Baldwin	1890	54
George Bradley	1879	53
Henry Porter	1885	53
John Clarkson	1888	53
Dupee Shaw	1885	47
Phil Knell	1891	47
Ted Breitenstein	1895	46

Shutouts

Addie Joss	1906	9
Pete Alexander	1913	9
Walter Johnson	1914	9
Christy Mathewson	1905	8
Orval Overall	1907	8
Jeff Tesreau	1915	8
Carl Mays	1918	8
6 tied with		7

Saves

Bobby Thigpen	1990	57
John Wetteland	1993	43
Mark Wohlers	1996	39
Bruce Sutter	1979	37
Todd Worrell	1986	36
Troy Percival	1996	36
Wayne Granger	1970	35
Robb Nen	1996	35
Ricky Bottalico	1996	34
3 tied with		33

Innings Pitched

Pud Galvin	1883	656.1
Tim Keefe	1883	619.0
Mark Baldwin	1890	501.0
Mickey Welch	1886	500.0
George Bradley	1879	487.0
John Clarkson	1888	483.1
Henry Porter	1885	481.2
Phil Knell	1891	462.0
Ted Breitenstein	1895	429.2
Cy Young	1893	422.2

Strikeouts

Nolan Ryan	1973	383
Tim Keefe	1883	361
Rube Waddell	1903	302
Tom Seaver	1971	289
Pud Galvin	1883	279
Sam McDowell	1969	279
Fergie Jenkins	1970	274
Mickey Welch	1886	272
Jim Whitney	1884	270
Mark Langston	1987	262

ERA
(minimum 1 Inning Pitched/Tm Gm)

Denny Driscoll	1882	1.21
Christy Mathewson	1905	1.28
Guy Hecker	1882	1.30
Harry McCormick	1882	1.52
Howie Camnitz	1908	1.56
Fred Toney	1915	1.58
Chief Bender	1910	1.58
Ed Walsh	1907	1.60
Rube Foster	1914	1.66
Orval Overall	1907	1.68

Component ERA
(minimum 1 Inning Pitched/Tm Gm)

Guy Hecker	1882	1.17
Denny Driscoll	1882	1.44
Lady Baldwin	1885	1.47
Christy Mathewson	1905	1.54
Jim Whitney	1884	1.55
Chief Bender	1910	1.56
Tim Keefe	1883	1.59
Addie Joss	1906	1.60
Ray Caldwell	1914	1.67
Catfish Hunter	1972	1.70

Opponent Average
(minimum 1 Inning Pitched/Tm Gm)

Hideo Nomo	1995	.182
Guy Hecker	1882	.188
Catfish Hunter	1972	.189
Joe Horlen	1964	.190
Bob Turley	1957	.194
Jeff Robinson	1988	.197
Lady Baldwin	1885	.197
Sandy Koufax	1962	.197
Sid Fernandez	1989	.198
Spec Shea	1947	.200

Batting Leaders—Through Age 27

At-Bats

Robin Yount	5,425
Vada Pinson	5,186
Mel Ott	5,076
Al Kaline	4,903
Freddy Lindstrom	4,780
Ruben Sierra	4,774
Hank Aaron	4,717
Ty Cobb	4,690
George Davis	4,648
Bill Mazeroski	4,644

Runs

Mel Ott	1,032
Mickey Mantle	994
Jimmie Foxx	975
George Davis	938
Hugh Duffy	931
John McGraw	924
Willie Keeler	917
Joe Kelley	909
Ty Cobb	876
Rickey Henderson	862

Hits

Ty Cobb	1,728
Mel Ott	1,615
Vada Pinson	1,559
Robin Yount	1,541
Freddy Lindstrom	1,514
Al Kaline	1,511
Hank Aaron	1,506
Joe Medwick	1,492
Jimmie Foxx	1,492
Rogers Hornsby	1,486

Doubles

Joe Medwick	353
Robin Yount	296
Vada Pinson	285
Mel Ott	285
Ty Cobb	271
Hal Trosky	270
Cesar Cedeno	265
Hank Aaron	264
Sherry Magee	262
2 tied with	261

Triples

Sam Crawford	144
Ty Cobb	137
Joe Jackson	132
Jake Beckley	129
Joe Kelley	120
George Davis	115
Rogers Hornsby	114
Sherry Magee	110
Tris Speaker	106
2 tied with	103

Home Runs

Jimmie Foxx	302
Eddie Mathews	299
Ken Griffey Jr.	294
Mickey Mantle	280
Mel Ott	275
Frank Robinson	262
Juan Gonzalez	256
Hank Aaron	253
Johnny Bench	240
Jose Canseco	235

RBI

Mel Ott	1,095
Jimmie Foxx	1,074
Joe DiMaggio	930
George Davis	876
Joe Medwick	873
Ken Griffey Jr.	872
Hank Aaron	863
Hal Trosky	860
Johnny Bench	855
Mickey Mantle	841

Stolen Bases

Rickey Henderson	660
Tim Raines	511
Ty Cobb	485
Vince Coleman	472
Billy Hamilton	443
John McGraw	398
Cesar Cedeno	397
Eddie Collins	371
Hugh Duffy	371
George Davis	364

Runs Created

Mel Ott	1,169
Jimmie Foxx	1,162
Mickey Mantle	1,103
Ty Cobb	1,091
George Davis	1,012
Joe Kelley	998
Joe DiMaggio	954
Hugh Duffy	943
Ken Griffey Jr.	928
John McGraw	915

Batting Average
(minimum 2,000 Plate Appearances)

Willie Keeler	.384
Ty Cobb	.368
Nap Lajoie	.364
Paul Waner	.359
Chuck Klein	.357
Al Simmons	.356
Pete Browning	.354
Ted Williams	.353
Joe Jackson	.353
Rogers Hornsby	.351

On-Base Percentage
(minimum 2,000 Plate Appearances)

Ted Williams	.484
John McGraw	.465
Babe Ruth	.461
Frank Thomas	.450
Lou Gehrig	.443
Jimmie Foxx	.440
Cupid Childs	.434
Billy Hamilton	.433
Joe Kelley	.432
Willie Keeler	.430

Slugging Percentage
(minimum 2,000 Plate Appearances)

Babe Ruth	.696
Ted Williams	.647
Jimmie Foxx	.640
Lou Gehrig	.639
Chuck Klein	.639
Hank Greenberg	.616
Johnny Mize	.611
Joe DiMaggio	.607
Frank Thomas	.593
Willie Mays	.591

Single Season Batting Leaders—Age 27

At-Bats

Dave Cash	1975	699
Sandy Alomar	1971	689
Omar Moreno	1980	676
Buddy Bell	1979	670
Ralph Garr	1973	668
Doc Cramer	1933	661
Kirby Puckett	1988	657
Wade Boggs	1985	653
Chuck Klein	1932	650
2 tied with		649

Runs

Arlie Latham	1887	163
Hugh Duffy	1894	160
Jesse Burkett	1896	160
Chuck Klein	1932	152
Herman Long	1893	149
Ed Delahanty	1895	149
Jake Stenzel	1894	148
Charlie Gehringer	1930	144
Hank Greenberg	1938	144
2 tied with		143

Hits

George Sisler	1920	257
Babe Herman	1930	241
Jesse Burkett	1896	240
Wade Boggs	1985	240
Hugh Duffy	1894	237
Kirby Puckett	1988	234
Stan Musial	1948	230
Chuck Klein	1932	226
Lou Gehrig	1930	220
3 tied with		218

Doubles

George Kell	1950	56
Mark Grudzielanek	1997	54
Johnny Frederick	1929	52
Hugh Duffy	1894	51
Chuck Klein	1932	50
Odell Hale	1936	50
Ben Chapman	1936	50
Ed Delahanty	1895	49
George Sisler	1920	49
2 tied with		48

Triples

Heinie Reitz	1894	31
Perry Werden	1893	29
Buck Freeman	1899	25
Harry Stovey	1884	23
Sam Thompson	1887	23
Dale Mitchell	1949	23
Jake Virtue	1892	20
Jake Stenzel	1894	20
3 tied with		19

Home Runs

Hank Greenberg	1938	58
Ken Griffey Jr.	1997	56
Ralph Kiner	1950	47
Ernie Banks	1958	47
George Bell	1987	47
Kevin Mitchell	1989	47
Eddie Mathews	1959	46
Jim Gentile	1961	46
Rocky Colavito	1961	45
Harmon Killebrew	1963	45

RBI

Lou Gehrig	1930	174
Sam Thompson	1887	166
Al Simmons	1929	157
Ken Griffey Jr.	1997	147
Hank Greenberg	1938	146
Hugh Duffy	1894	145
Walt Dropo	1950	144
Jim Gentile	1961	141
Rocky Colavito	1961	140
Zeke Bonura	1936	138

Stolen Bases

Arlie Latham	1887	129
Charlie Comiskey	1887	117
Monte Ward	1887	111
Omar Moreno	1980	96
Bid McPhee	1887	95
Rickey Henderson	1986	87
Billy Sunday	1890	84
Emmett Seery	1888	80
Bob Bescher	1911	80
Dave Collins	1980	79

Runs Created

Hugh Duffy	1894	204
Lou Gehrig	1930	182
Stan Musial	1948	177
Babe Herman	1930	163
Hank Greenberg	1938	163
Ted Williams	1946	163
Ed Delahanty	1895	159
Jesse Burkett	1896	156
George Sisler	1920	154
2 tied with		153

Batting Average
(minimum 3.1 PA/Tm Gm)

Hugh Duffy	1894	.440
Jesse Burkett	1896	.410
George Sisler	1920	.407
Ed Delahanty	1895	.404
Hughie Jennings	1896	.401
Babe Herman	1930	.393
George Brett	1980	.390
Rogers Hornsby	1923	.384
Billy Hamilton	1893	.380
Goose Goslin	1928	.379

On-Base Percentage
(minimum 3.1 PA/Tm Gm)

John McGraw	1900	.505
Hugh Duffy	1894	.502
Ed Delahanty	1895	.500
Ted Williams	1946	.497
Billy Hamilton	1893	.490
Lou Gehrig	1930	.473
Hughie Jennings	1896	.472
Gary Sheffield	1996	.465
Jesse Burkett	1896	.461
Jimmie Foxx	1935	.461

Slugging Percentage
(minimum 3.1 PA/Tm Gm)

Lou Gehrig	1930	.721
Albert Belle	1994	.714
Stan Musial	1948	.702
Hugh Duffy	1894	.694
Hank Greenberg	1938	.683
Babe Herman	1930	.678
Babe Ruth	1922	.672
Ted Williams	1946	.667
George Brett	1980	.664
Chick Hafey	1930	.652

Pitching Leaders—Through Age 27

Wins

Kid Nichols	245
Amos Rusie	245
Mickey Welch	232
John Clarkson	220
Gus Weyhing	216
Bob Caruthers	216
Walter Johnson	206
Pud Galvin	205
Jim McCormick	200
Silver King	187

Losses

Amos Rusie	173
Jim McCormick	173
Pink Hawley	165
Pud Galvin	160
Stump Wiedman	156
Mickey Welch	156
Gus Weyhing	154
Red Ehret	150
Adonis Terry	147
Win Mercer	146

Winning Percentage
(minimum 110 decisions)

Bob Caruthers	.708
Ed Reulbach	.699
Roger Clemens	.695
John Clarkson	.692
Mike Mussina	.687
Don Gullett	.686
Dwight Gooden	.683
Jim Palmer	.682
Kid Nichols	.671
Joe Wood	.671

Games

Mitch Williams	502
Amos Rusie	459
Mickey Welch	412
Kid Nichols	397
Gus Weyhing	396
Mike Jackson	393
Lindy McDaniel	393
Jim McCormick	386
Pud Galvin	380
Walter Johnson	371

Complete Games

Mickey Welch	392
Amos Rusie	390
Jim McCormick	364
Pud Galvin	350
Gus Weyhing	341
Kid Nichols	340
John Clarkson	309
Silver King	305
Ed Morris	297
Bob Caruthers	288

Shutouts

Walter Johnson	60
Bert Blyleven	39
Pud Galvin	36
Tommy Bond	35
Christy Mathewson	34
Nap Rucker	33
Dean Chance	32
Addie Joss	31
Mickey Welch	31
Amos Rusie	30

Saves

Bobby Thigpen	178
Rod Beck	162
Gregg Olson	161
Mitch Williams	143
Bruce Sutter	133
John Franco	116
Lee Smith	113
Robb Nen	108
Dave Righetti	107
John Wetteland	106

Innings Pitched

Amos Rusie	3,747.2
Mickey Welch	3,544.1
Jim McCormick	3,353.2
Pud Galvin	3,263.2
Kid Nichols	3,254.1
Gus Weyhing	3,240.2
Silver King	2,891.1
John Clarkson	2,858.0
Pink Hawley	2,830.1
Walter Johnson	2,778.2

Strikeouts

Sam McDowell	1,967
Amos Rusie	1,928
Bert Blyleven	1,910
Walter Johnson	1,889
Don Drysdale	1,724
Dwight Gooden	1,686
Bob Feller	1,640
Nolan Ryan	1,572
Fernando Valenzuela	1,528
Toad Ramsey	1,515

ERA
(minimum 650 Innings Pitched)

Walter Johnson	1.61
Ed Walsh	1.73
Ed Reulbach	1.89
Howie Camnitz	1.90
Will White	1.92
George McQuillan	1.95
Joe Wood	2.00
Addie Joss	2.03
Jack Coombs	2.05
Monte Ward	2.10

Component ERA
(minimum 650 Innings Pitched)

Lady Baldwin	1.56
Ed Walsh	1.68
Walter Johnson	1.71
Addie Joss	1.85
Howie Camnitz	1.94
George McQuillan	1.96
Monte Ward	2.01
Ed Reulbach	2.02
Tim Keefe	2.02
Old Hoss Radbourn	2.03

Opponent Average
(minimum 650 Innings Pitched)

Nolan Ryan	.194
Herb Score	.198
Lady Baldwin	.199
Sid Fernandez	.204
Andy Messersmith	.204
Luis Tiant	.205
Bob Turley	.209
Tom Hall	.210
Sam McDowell	.210
Ed Reulbach	.210

Single Season Pitching Leaders—Age 27

Wins

John Clarkson	1889	49
Pud Galvin	1884	46
Lady Baldwin	1886	42
Will White	1882	40
Jim McCormick	1884	40
Ed Walsh	1908	40
Jack Lynch	1884	37
Tim Keefe	1884	37
3 tied with		33

Losses

Jim Devlin	1876	35
Bob Barr	1884	34
Jim Whitney	1885	32
Dupee Shaw	1886	31
Doc Landis	1882	28
One Arm Daily	1884	28
Mark Baldwin	1891	28
Tony Mullane	1886	27
Ted Breitenstein	1896	26
2 tied with		25

Winning Percentage
(minimum 15 decisions)

Ron Guidry	1978	.893
Ron Perranoski	1963	.842
Sandy Koufax	1963	.833
Russ Ford	1910	.813
Jim Coates	1960	.813
Moose Haas	1983	.813
Catfish Hunter	1973	.808
Howie Camnitz	1909	.806
Babe Adams	1909	.800
3 tied with		.786

Games

Rob Murphy	1987	87
Mike Myers	1996	83
Duane Ward	1991	81
Kenny Rogers	1992	81
Dick Radatz	1964	79
Bill Campbell	1976	78
Tom Hume	1980	78
Rick Camp	1980	77
Mike Perez	1992	77
4 tied with		76

Complete Games

Pud Galvin	1884	71
John Clarkson	1889	68
Jim Devlin	1876	66
Jim McCormick	1884	63
One Arm Daily	1884	56
Tim Keefe	1884	56
Lady Baldwin	1886	55
Tony Mullane	1886	55
Jack Lynch	1884	54
Will White	1882	52

Shutouts

Jack Coombs	1910	13
Pud Galvin	1884	12
Ed Walsh	1908	11
Sandy Koufax	1963	11
Jim McCormick	1884	10
Bob Feller	1946	10
Bob Lemon	1948	10
Juan Marichal	1965	10
4 tied with		9

Saves

Dave Righetti	1986	46
Mariano Rivera	1997	43
John Franco	1988	39
Jeff Russell	1989	38
Bill Caudill	1984	36
Sparky Lyle	1972	35
Rod Beck	1996	35
Robb Nen	1997	35
Ricky Bottalico	1997	34
5 tied with		33

Innings Pitched

Pud Galvin	1884	636.1
Jim Devlin	1876	622.0
John Clarkson	1889	620.0
Jim McCormick	1884	569.0
Tony Mullane	1886	529.2
One Arm Daily	1884	500.2
Jack Lynch	1884	496.0
Lady Baldwin	1886	487.0
Tim Keefe	1884	482.2
Will White	1882	480.0

Strikeouts

One Arm Daily	1884	483
Pud Galvin	1884	369
Nolan Ryan	1974	367
Rube Waddell	1904	349
Bob Feller	1946	348
Jim McCormick	1884	343
Lady Baldwin	1886	323
Tim Keefe	1884	317
Steve Carlton	1972	310
Sandy Koufax	1963	306

ERA
(minimum 1 Inning Pitched/Tm Gm)

Carl Lundgren	1907	1.17
Jack Coombs	1910	1.30
George Bradley	1880	1.38
Ed Walsh	1908	1.42
Doc White	1906	1.52
Will White	1882	1.54
Walter Johnson	1915	1.55
Jim Devlin	1876	1.56
Luis Tiant	1968	1.60
Rube Waddell	1904	1.62

Component ERA
(minimum 1 Inning Pitched/Tm Gm)

George Bradley	1880	1.37
Ed Walsh	1908	1.38
Russ Ford	1910	1.41
Luis Tiant	1968	1.51
Doc White	1906	1.52
Sandy Koufax	1963	1.55
Reb Russell	1916	1.60
Three Finger Brown	1904	1.60
Tim Keefe	1884	1.60
Stan Coveleski	1917	1.61

Opponent Average
(minimum 1 Inning Pitched/Tm Gm)

Luis Tiant	1968	.168
Carl Lundgren	1907	.185
Russ Ford	1910	.188
Sandy Koufax	1963	.189
Don Sutton	1972	.189
Nolan Ryan	1974	.190
Fred Beebe	1908	.193
Stan Coveleski	1917	.193
Ron Guidry	1978	.193
Three Finger Brown	1904	.199

Batting Leaders—Through Age 28

At-Bats		Runs		Hits		Doubles	
Robin Yount	6,049	Mel Ott	1,131	Ty Cobb	1,936	Joe Medwick	383
Vada Pinson	5,836	Mickey Mantle	1,113	Mel Ott	1,775	Robin Yount	323
Mel Ott	5,621	Jimmie Foxx	1,105	Vada Pinson	1,746	Vada Pinson	313
Al Kaline	5,454	Hugh Duffy	1,041	Robin Yount	1,727	Mel Ott	313
Hank Aaron	5,309	Willie Keeler	1,023	Rogers Hornsby	1,713	Stan Musial	302
Ty Cobb	5,253	Ty Cobb	1,020	Hank Aaron	1,697	Ty Cobb	302
Ruben Sierra	5,200	George Davis	1,006	Jimmie Foxx	1,690	Sherry Magee	298
Freddy Lindstrom	5,163	Joe Kelley	999	Al Kaline	1,683	Cesar Cedeno	292
Bill Mazeroski	5,138	John McGraw	995	Joe Medwick	1,667	Hank Aaron	292
Ron Santo	5,083	Hank Aaron	956	Freddy Lindstrom	1,625	2 tied with	290

Triples		Home Runs		RBI		Stolen Bases	
Sam Crawford	160	Jimmie Foxx	343	Jimmie Foxx	1,217	Rickey Henderson	701
Ty Cobb	150	Eddie Mathews	338	Mel Ott	1,190	Ty Cobb	581
Jake Beckley	138	Mickey Mantle	320	Lou Gehrig	995	Vince Coleman	549
Joe Kelley	137	Mel Ott	306	Hank Aaron	991	Tim Raines	544
Joe Jackson	134	Hank Aaron	298	Joe Medwick	959	Billy Hamilton	541
Rogers Hornsby	128	Ken Griffey Jr.	294	Mickey Mantle	935	Cesar Cedeno	427
Mike Tiernan	123	Frank Robinson	291	George Davis	933	John McGraw	422
George Davis	120	Harmon Killebrew	272	Joe DiMaggio	930	Eddie Collins	417
Sherry Magee	116	Ralph Kiner	257	Johnny Bench	929	Hugh Duffy	413
Tris Speaker	114	2 tied with	256	Hal Trosky	911	Bill Lange	399

| Runs Created | | Batting Average | | On-Base Percentage | | Slugging Percentage | |
		(minimum 2,250 Plate Appearances)		(minimum 2,250 Plate Appearances)		(minimum 2,250 Plate Appearances)	
Jimmie Foxx	1,314	Willie Keeler	.381	Ted Williams	.487	Babe Ruth	.708
Mel Ott	1,289	Ty Cobb	.369	Babe Ruth	.476	Ted Williams	.645
Ty Cobb	1,245	Nap Lajoie	.361	John McGraw	.468	Lou Gehrig	.642
Mickey Mantle	1,221	Al Simmons	.360	Frank Thomas	.452	Jimmie Foxx	.639
Joe Kelley	1,100	Rogers Hornsby	.359	Billy Hamilton	.449	Chuck Klein	.632
George Davis	1,094	Chuck Klein	.359	Lou Gehrig	.443	Hank Greenberg	.617
Hugh Duffy	1,082	Jesse Burkett	.353	Roy Thomas	.440	Joe DiMaggio	.607
Lou Gehrig	1,053	Joe Jackson	.353	Jimmie Foxx	.440	Johnny Mize	.600
Rogers Hornsby	1,046	Paul Waner	.353	Cupid Childs	.438	Frank Thomas	.599
Hank Aaron	1,041	Wade Boggs	.352	Wade Boggs	.435	Willie Mays	.590

Single Season Batting Leaders—Age 28

At-Bats			Runs			Hits			Doubles		
Woody Jensen	1936	696	Billy Hamilton	1894	192	Earle Combs	1927	231	Gee Walker	1936	55
Lou Brock	1967	689	Lou Gehrig	1931	163	Rogers Hornsby	1924	227	Albert Belle	1995	52
Bobby Richardson	1964	679	King Kelly	1886	155	Tommy Holmes	1945	224	Mickey Vernon	1946	51
Larry Bowa	1974	669	Al Simmons	1930	152	Chuck Klein	1933	223	Heinie Manush	1930	49
Dave Cash	1976	666	Babe Ruth	1923	151	Billy Hamilton	1894	220	Joe Sewell	1927	48
Enos Cabell	1978	660	Ty Cobb	1915	144	Pete Rose	1969	218	Jeff Bagwell	1996	48
Billy Moran	1962	659	Red Rolfe	1937	143	Rod Carew	1974	218	Dale Alexander	1931	47
Frankie Crosetti	1939	656	Dan Brouthers	1886	139	George Sisler	1921	216	Tommy Holmes	1945	47
Frank Taveras	1978	654	Earle Combs	1927	137	Kirby Puckett	1989	215	Wade Boggs	1986	47
Mike Rocco	1944	653	Herman Long	1894	136	Ralph Garr	1974	214	5 tied with		45

Triples			Home Runs			RBI			Stolen Bases		
Chief Wilson	1912	36	George Foster	1977	52	Lou Gehrig	1931	184	Arlie Latham	1888	109
Earle Combs	1927	23	Albert Belle	1995	50	Al Simmons	1930	165	Billy Hamilton	1894	98
Birdie Cree	1911	22	Harmon Killebrew	1964	49	Vern Stephens	1949	159	Ty Cobb	1915	96
Mike Tiernan	1895	21	Lou Gehrig	1931	46	George Foster	1977	149	Cub Stricker	1887	86
Wildfire Schulte	1911	21	Barry Bonds	1993	46	Jimmie Foxx	1936	143	Vince Coleman	1990	77
Roger Connor	1886	20	Ernie Banks	1959	45	Ernie Banks	1959	143	Bill North	1976	75
George Stone	1906	20	Hank Aaron	1962	45	Mo Vaughn	1996	143	Tommy Harper	1969	73
Red Murray	1912	20	Gorman Thomas	1979	45	Bob Meusel	1925	138	Charlie Comiskey	1888	72
Jim Bottomley	1928	20	Mo Vaughn	1996	44	3 tied with		136	Curt Welch	1890	72
5 tied with		19	Matt Williams	1994	43				Bob Bescher	1912	67

| Runs Created | | | Batting Average | | | On-Base Percentage | | | Slugging Percentage | | |
			(minimum 3.1 PA/Tm Gm)			(minimum 3.1 PA/Tm Gm)			(minimum 3.1 PA/Tm Gm)		
Babe Ruth	1923	193	Rogers Hornsby	1924	.424	Babe Ruth	1923	.545	Babe Ruth	1923	.764
Billy Hamilton	1894	187	Billy Hamilton	1894	.404	Billy Hamilton	1894	.523	Al Simmons	1930	.708
Lou Gehrig	1931	179	Harry Heilmann	1923	.403	Rogers Hornsby	1924	.507	Rogers Hornsby	1924	.696
Ed Delahanty	1896	162	Ed Delahanty	1896	.397	Ted Williams	1947	.499	Albert Belle	1995	.690
Rogers Hornsby	1924	162	Babe Ruth	1923	.393	Bill Joyce	1894	.496	Barry Bonds	1993	.677
Barry Bonds	1993	162	King Kelly	1886	.388	Ty Cobb	1915	.486	Lou Gehrig	1931	.662
Ted Williams	1947	161	Tris Speaker	1916	.386	King Kelly	1886	.483	Bill Joyce	1894	.648
King Kelly	1886	156	Lave Cross	1894	.386	Harry Heilmann	1923	.481	Mike Piazza	1997	.638
Al Simmons	1930	156	Jesse Burkett	1897	.383	Ed Delahanty	1896	.472	Ted Williams	1947	.634
Stan Musial	1949	155	Al Simmons	1930	.381	Tris Speaker	1916	.470	Harry Heilmann	1923	.632

Pitching Leaders—Through Age 28

Wins		Losses		Winning Percentage (minimum 120 decisions)		Games	
Kid Nichols	276	Pud Galvin	186	Whitey Ford	.734	Mitch Williams	567
Mickey Welch	258	Jim McCormick	180	Bill Hoffer	.701	Mike Jackson	474
John Clarkson	246	Pink Hawley	179	Juan Marichal	.691	Amos Rusie	459
Amos Rusie	245	Gus Weyhing	175	Ed Reulbach	.691	Mickey Welch	459
Walter Johnson	231	Mickey Welch	175	Bob Caruthers	.688	Lindy McDaniel	456
Gus Weyhing	224	Amos Rusie	173	Roger Clemens	.687	Kid Nichols	447
Pud Galvin	221	Win Mercer	164	Don Gullett	.686	Rollie Fingers	432
Jim McCormick	221	Red Ehret	160	Mike Mussina	.682	Gus Weyhing	427
Bob Caruthers	218	Stump Wiedman	156	John Clarkson	.680	Pud Galvin	424
Silver King	197	Adonis Terry	155	Kid Nichols	.676	Goose Gossage	423

Complete Games		Shutouts		Saves		Innings Pitched	
Mickey Welch	439	Walter Johnson	63	Bobby Thigpen	200	Mickey Welch	3,969.2
Jim McCormick	392	Christy Mathewson	42	Rod Beck	199	Amos Rusie	3,747.2
Pud Galvin	390	Addie Joss	40	Mitch Williams	186	Kid Nichols	3,642.1
Amos Rusie	390	Bert Blyleven	39	Gregg Olson	164	Pud Galvin	3,636.0
Kid Nichols	380	Pud Galvin	39	Bruce Sutter	158	Jim McCormick	3,605.2
Gus Weyhing	364	Pete Alexander	37	John Franco	148	Gus Weyhing	3,471.2
John Clarkson	352	Nap Rucker	37	Lee Smith	144	John Clarkson	3,241.0
Silver King	317	Ed Walsh	36	Dave Righetti	138	Walter Johnson	3,148.1
Will White	306	Mickey Welch	36	John Wetteland	137	Silver King	3,036.2
Walter Johnson	302	Tommy Bond	35	Goose Gossage	134	Pink Hawley	3,012.2

Strikeouts		ERA (minimum 700 Innings Pitched)		Component ERA (minimum 700 Innings Pitched)		Opponent Average (minimum 700 Innings Pitched)	
Sam McDowell	2,159	Walter Johnson	1.64	Ed Walsh	1.66	Nolan Ryan	.196
Walter Johnson	2,117	Ed Walsh	1.68	Addie Joss	1.71	Herb Score	.199
Bert Blyleven	2,082	Addie Joss	1.89	Walter Johnson	1.72	Sid Fernandez	.205
Don Drysdale	1,934	Jim Devlin	1.89	Guy Hecker	1.89	Andy Messersmith	.206
Amos Rusie	1,928	Will White	1.95	Old Hoss Radbourn	1.91	Sam McDowell	.210
Bob Feller	1,836	Joe Wood	2.00	Lady Baldwin	1.96	Sandy Koufax	.210
Dwight Gooden	1,835	Ed Reulbach	2.03	Tim Keefe	1.97	Tom Hall	.211
Nolan Ryan	1,758	Jeff Pfeffer	2.08	Monte Ward	2.01	Mario Soto	.212
Sandy Koufax	1,697	Monte Ward	2.10	Joe Wood	2.09	Pedro Martinez	.213
Roger Clemens	1,665	Orval Overall	2.13	Reb Russell	2.09	Walter Johnson	.213

Single Season Pitching Leaders—Age 28

Wins			Losses			Winning Percentage (minimum 15 decisions)			Games		
Guy Hecker	1884	52	Jim Whitney	1886	32	Hoyt Wilhelm	1952	.833	Mike Myers	1997	88
Old Hoss Radbourn	1883	48	Mark Baldwin	1892	27	Jack Chesbro	1902	.824	Craig Lefferts	1986	83
Will White	1883	43	Pud Galvin	1885	26	Atley Donald	1939	.813	Eddie Fisher	1965	82
Jim Devlin	1877	35	Jim Devlin	1877	25	Ted Wilks	1944	.810	Mike Jackson	1993	81
Cy Young	1895	35	Old Hoss Radbourn	1883	25	Tiny Bonham	1942	.808	Duane Ward	1992	79
Dave Foutz	1885	33	Vic Willis	1904	25	Dave McNally	1971	.808	Wilbur Wood	1970	77
Tim Keefe	1885	32	Irv Young	1906	25	Juan Marichal	1966	.806	Charlie Hough	1976	77
Tony Mullane	1887	31	Henry Porter	1887	24	Ed Doheny	1902	.800	Barry Jones	1991	77
Kid Nichols	1898	31	5 tied with		23	Denny Neagle	1997	.800	Paul Quantrill	1997	77
Pete Alexander	1915	31				Sandy Koufax	1964	.792	5 tied with		76

Complete Games			Shutouts			Saves			Innings Pitched		
Guy Hecker	1884	72	Pete Alexander	1915	12	Bryan Harvey	1991	46	Guy Hecker	1884	670.2
Old Hoss Radbourn	1883	66	Addie Joss	1908	9	Mark Davis	1989	44	Old Hoss Radbourn	1883	632.1
Will White	1883	64	Orval Overall	1909	9	Mitch Williams	1993	43	Will White	1883	577.0
Jim Devlin	1877	61	Bill Lee	1938	9	Trevor Hoffman	1996	42	Jim Devlin	1877	559.0
Tony Mullane	1887	47	Jack Chesbro	1902	8	Roberto Hernandez	1993	38	Mark Baldwin	1892	440.1
Mickey Welch	1888	47	Ed Killian	1905	8	Rod Beck	1997	37	Mickey Welch	1888	425.1
Dave Foutz	1885	46	Christy Mathewson	1907	8	Jim Gott	1988	34	Tony Mullane	1887	416.1
Tim Keefe	1885	45	Ed Walsh	1909	8	Goose Gossage	1980	33	Dave Foutz	1885	407.2
Mark Baldwin	1892	45	Lefty Tyler	1918	8	Bob Stanley	1983	33	Tim Keefe	1885	398.0
2 tied with		43	8 tied with		7	3 tied with		32	Jim Whitney	1886	393.0

Strikeouts			ERA (minimum 1 Inning Pitched/Tm Gm)			Component ERA (minimum 1 Inning Pitched/Tm Gm)			Opponent Average (minimum 1 Inning Pitched/Tm Gm)		
Guy Hecker	1884	385	Addie Joss	1908	1.16	Addie Joss	1908	1.23	Pete Alexander	1915	.191
Old Hoss Radbourn	1883	315	Pete Alexander	1915	1.22	Pete Alexander	1915	1.33	Sandy Koufax	1964	.191
J.R. Richard	1978	303	Jack Taylor	1902	1.33	Guy Hecker	1884	1.43	Roger Nelson	1972	.196
Rube Waddell	1905	287	Ed Walsh	1909	1.41	Ed Walsh	1909	1.52	J.R. Richard	1978	.196
Mickey Lolich	1969	271	Orval Overall	1909	1.42	Frank Smith	1908	1.58	Jack Pfiester	1906	.197
Tom Seaver	1973	251	Rube Waddell	1905	1.48	Greg Maddux	1994	1.59	Jose DeLeon	1989	.197
Bob Veale	1964	250	Jack Pfiester	1906	1.51	Jack Pfiester	1906	1.63	Addie Joss	1908	.197
Bob Gibson	1964	245	Greg Maddux	1994	1.56	Sandy Koufax	1964	1.66	Rube Waddell	1905	.198
4 tied with		241	Tim Keefe	1885	1.58	Rube Waddell	1905	1.66	Orval Overall	1909	.198
			Bill Burns	1908	1.70	Roger Nelson	1972	1.66	Tim Keefe	1885	.201

Batting Leaders—Through Age 29

At-Bats		Runs		Hits		Doubles	
Robin Yount	6,515	Mel Ott	1,247	Ty Cobb	2,137	Joe Medwick	416
Vada Pinson	6,335	Mickey Mantle	1,245	Mel Ott	1,939	Robin Yount	349
Mel Ott	6,148	Jimmie Foxx	1,216	Rogers Hornsby	1,916	Stan Musial	343
Al Kaline	5,979	Willie Keeler	1,146	Hank Aaron	1,898	Vada Pinson	342
Hank Aaron	5,940	Hugh Duffy	1,138	Vada Pinson	1,881	Sherry Magee	337
Ty Cobb	5,795	Ty Cobb	1,133	Robin Yount	1,856	Mel Ott	336
Bill Mazeroski	5,759	Mike Tiernan	1,083	Jimmie Foxx	1,852	Ty Cobb	333
Ruben Sierra	5,679	Hank Aaron	1,077	Joe Medwick	1,838	Rogers Hornsby	327
Ron Santo	5,658	Joe Kelley	1,076	Al Kaline	1,837	Cesar Cedeno	324
Cal Ripken Jr.	5,655	2 tied with	1,075	Willie Keeler	1,769	Tris Speaker	324

Triples		Home Runs		RBI		Stolen Bases	
Sam Crawford	174	Jimmie Foxx	379	Jimmie Foxx	1,344	Rickey Henderson	794
Ty Cobb	160	Mickey Mantle	374	Mel Ott	1,306	Ty Cobb	649
Jake Beckley	150	Eddie Mathews	370	Lou Gehrig	1,146	Billy Hamilton	638
Joe Kelley	149	Hank Aaron	342	Hank Aaron	1,121	Vince Coleman	586
Joe Jackson	148	Mel Ott	342	Mickey Mantle	1,063	Tim Raines	585
Mike Tiernan	139	Frank Robinson	324	Joe Medwick	1,047	Cesar Cedeno	475
Rogers Hornsby	138	Harmon Killebrew	297	Johnny Bench	1,038	Eddie Collins	457
Sherry Magee	127	Ken Griffey Jr.	294	Frank Robinson	1,009	Hugh Duffy	452
Ed Delahanty	126	Ralph Kiner	294	Al Simmons	1,005	Willie Wilson	436
2 tied with	125	Johnny Bench	287	Hank Greenberg	1,003	John McGraw	434

Runs Created		Batting Average		On-Base Percentage		Slugging Percentage	
		(minimum 2,500 Plate Appearances)		(minimum 2,500 Plate Appearances)		(minimum 2,500 Plate Appearances)	
Jimmie Foxx	1,433	Willie Keeler	.376	Ted Williams	.488	Babe Ruth	.712
Mel Ott	1,423	Ty Cobb	.369	Babe Ruth	.482	Ted Williams	.640
Mickey Mantle	1,378	Rogers Hornsby	.363	John McGraw	.466	Lou Gehrig	.640
Ty Cobb	1,368	Al Simmons	.363	Billy Hamilton	.455	Jimmie Foxx	.628
Lou Gehrig	1,216	Nap Lajoie	.363	Frank Thomas	.452	Hank Greenberg	.625
Rogers Hornsby	1,204	George Sisler	.361	Lou Gehrig	.444	Chuck Klein	.618
Joe Kelley	1,188	Ted Williams	.354	Roy Thomas	.443	Joe DiMaggio	.607
Hank Aaron	1,187	Wade Boggs	.354	Wade Boggs	.439	Frank Thomas	.600
Hugh Duffy	1,181	Joe Jackson	.353	Cupid Childs	.438	Al Simmons	.596
George Davis	1,174	Chuck Klein	.352	Jimmie Foxx	.435	Johnny Mize	.588

Single Season Batting Leaders—Age 29

At-Bats			Runs			Hits			Doubles		
Maury Wills	1962	695	Tip O'Neill	1887	167	George Sisler	1922	246	Paul Waner	1932	62
Frank Taveras	1979	680	Billy Hamilton	1895	166	Jack Tobin	1921	236	Tip O'Neill	1887	52
Jack Tobin	1921	671	Dan Brouthers	1887	153	Tip O'Neill	1887	225	Beau Bell	1937	51
Marquis Grissom	1996	671	George Gore	1886	150	Beau Bell	1937	218	Hank Greenberg	1940	50
Carl Furillo	1951	667	Tom Brown	1890	146	Baby Doll Jacobson	1920	216	Nap Lajoie	1904	49
Taylor Douthit	1930	664	Patsy Donovan	1894	145	Paul Waner	1932	215	Riggs Stephenson	1927	46
Bobby Richardson	1965	664	Babe Ruth	1924	143	Doc Cramer	1935	214	Lou Brock	1968	46
Hughie Critz	1930	662	Tom Poorman	1887	140	Jesse Burkett	1898	213	Edgar Martinez	1992	46
Kenny Lofton	1996	662	Earl Averill	1931	140	Gee Walker	1937	213	4 tied with		45
Lou Brock	1968	660	Lou Gehrig	1932	138	Ron LeFlore	1977	212			

Triples			Home Runs			RBI			Stolen Bases		
Ed McKean	1893	24	Mickey Mantle	1961	54	Hack Wilson	1929	159	Hugh Nicol	1887	138
Roger Connor	1887	22	Ted Kluszewski	1954	49	Lou Gehrig	1932	151	Maury Wills	1962	104
Earle Combs	1928	21	Albert Belle	1996	48	Hank Greenberg	1940	150	Billy Hamilton	1895	97
Willie Wilson	1985	21	Babe Ruth	1924	46	Albert Belle	1996	148	Rickey Henderson	1988	93
Dan Brouthers	1887	20	Mike Schmidt	1979	45	Al Rosen	1953	145	Tom Poorman	1887	88
Curt Walker	1926	20	Hank Aaron	1963	44	Vern Stephens	1950	144	King Kelly	1887	84
5 tied with		19	Tino Martinez	1997	44	Rogers Hornsby	1925	143	John Reilly	1888	82
			Al Rosen	1953	43	Earl Averill	1931	143	Tom Brown	1890	79
			Duke Snider	1956	43	Ted Kluszewski	1954	141	Kenny Lofton	1996	75
			Jeff Bagwell	1997	43	Tino Martinez	1997	141	2 tied with		69

Runs Created			Batting Average			On-Base Percentage			Slugging Percentage		
			(minimum 3.1 PA/Tm Gm)			(minimum 3.1 PA/Tm Gm)			(minimum 3.1 PA/Tm Gm)		
Tip O'Neill	1887	192	Tip O'Neill	1887	.435	Babe Ruth	1924	.513	Rogers Hornsby	1925	.756
Babe Ruth	1924	179	George Sisler	1922	.420	Ted Williams	1948	.497	Babe Ruth	1924	.739
Lou Gehrig	1932	163	Rogers Hornsby	1925	.403	Billy Hamilton	1895	.490	Tip O'Neill	1887	.691
Billy Hamilton	1895	160	Cap Anson	1881	.399	Tip O'Neill	1887	.490	Mickey Mantle	1961	.687
Ted Williams	1948	160	Al Simmons	1931	.390	Rogers Hornsby	1925	.489	Hank Greenberg	1940	.670
Rogers Hornsby	1925	158	Billy Hamilton	1895	.389	Luke Appling	1936	.473	Barry Bonds	1994	.647
Mickey Mantle	1961	157	Luke Appling	1936	.388	George Sisler	1922	.467	Ted Kluszewski	1954	.642
Hank Greenberg	1940	152	Deacon White	1877	.387	Mike Griffin	1894	.467	Al Simmons	1931	.641
Frank Thomas	1997	150	Babe Ruth	1924	.378	Wade Boggs	1987	.461	Gabby Hartnett	1930	.630
Dan Brouthers	1887	149	Ed Delahanty	1897	.377	Pete Browning	1890	.459	Albert Belle	1996	.623

Pitching Leaders—Through Age 29

Wins

Kid Nichols	297
Mickey Welch	285
John Clarkson	279
Walter Johnson	254
Jim McCormick	252
Pud Galvin	250
Amos Rusie	245
Gus Weyhing	226
Bob Caruthers	218
Christy Mathewson	211

Losses

Pud Galvin	207
Jim McCormick	191
Mickey Welch	187
Pink Hawley	179
Gus Weyhing	178
Jim Whitney	174
Amos Rusie	173
Red Ehret	167
Adonis Terry	167
Mark Baldwin	165

Winning Percentage
(minimum 130 decisions)

Whitey Ford	.724
Old Hoss Radbourn	.708
Bob Caruthers	.688
Don Gullett	.686
Ed Reulbach	.685
Mike Mussina	.682
Pete Alexander	.681
Juan Marichal	.679
Roger Clemens	.679
John Clarkson	.674

Games

Mitch Williams	592
Lindy McDaniel	527
Mike Jackson	510
Mickey Welch	504
Rollie Fingers	502
Kid Nichols	489
Pud Galvin	474
Mark Davis	469
Willie Hernandez	466
Walter Johnson	466

Complete Games

Mickey Welch	478
Pud Galvin	439
Jim McCormick	430
Kid Nichols	417
John Clarkson	399
Amos Rusie	390
Gus Weyhing	368
Will White	358
Walter Johnson	332
Jim Whitney	330

Shutouts

Walter Johnson	71
Pete Alexander	53
Christy Mathewson	53
Addie Joss	44
Ed Walsh	43
Bert Blyleven	41
Pud Galvin	41
Mickey Welch	39
Catfish Hunter	38
2 tied with	37

Saves

Bobby Thigpen	201
Rod Beck	199
Bruce Sutter	194
Mitch Williams	192
John Franco	181
Lee Smith	180
John Wetteland	180
Gregg Olson	172
Dave Righetti	163
Goose Gossage	154

Innings Pitched

Mickey Welch	4,344.2
Pud Galvin	4,070.2
Kid Nichols	3,985.2
Jim McCormick	3,953.1
Amos Rusie	3,747.2
John Clarkson	3,701.2
Gus Weyhing	3,513.2
Walter Johnson	3,474.1
Will White	3,223.1
Silver King	3,190.2

Strikeouts

Walter Johnson	2,305
Sam McDowell	2,281
Bert Blyleven	2,250
Don Drysdale	2,111
Nolan Ryan	2,085
Sandy Koufax	2,079
Bob Feller	2,000
Amos Rusie	1,928
Dwight Gooden	1,875
Roger Clemens	1,873

ERA
(minimum 750 Innings Pitched)

Ed Walsh	1.61
Walter Johnson	1.70
Three Finger Brown	1.86
Addie Joss	1.87
Ed Devlin	1.89
Old Hoss Radbourn	1.90
Joe Wood	2.00
Christy Mathewson	2.06
Monte Ward	2.10
Jeff Pfeffer	2.11

Component ERA
(minimum 750 Innings Pitched)

Ed Walsh	1.58
Addie Joss	1.70
Walter Johnson	1.72
Old Hoss Radbourn	1.80
Guy Hecker	1.97
Tim Keefe	2.00
Monte Ward	2.01
Christy Mathewson	2.03
Frank Smith	2.05
Joe Wood	2.09

Opponent Average
(minimum 750 Innings Pitched)

Nolan Ryan	.196
Herb Score	.200
Sandy Koufax	.205
Sid Fernandez	.205
Andy Messersmith	.207
Ed Walsh	.210
Tom Hall	.211
Pedro Martinez	.213
Walter Johnson	.213
Sam McDowell	.213

Single Season Pitching Leaders—Age 29

Wins

Old Hoss Radbourn	1884	59
Billy Taylor	1884	43
Tim Keefe	1886	42
Dave Foutz	1886	41
Christy Mathewson	1908	37
Will White	1884	34
John Clarkson	1891	33
Pete Alexander	1916	33
Jesse Duryea	1889	32
Jim McCormick	1886	31

Losses

Henry Porter	1888	37
Jack Lynch	1886	30
Vic Willis	1905	29
Gus Dorner	1906	26
Fred Glade	1905	25
Scott Perry	1920	25
Jim Hughey	1898	24
Guy Hecker	1885	23
Irv Young	1907	23
3 tied with		22

Winning Percentage
(minimum 15 decisions)

Phil Regan	1966	.933
Greg Maddux	1995	.905
Old Hoss Radbourn	1884	.831
Three Finger Brown	1906	.813
General Crowder	1928	.808
Joe Beggs	1940	.800
Don Newcombe	1955	.800
Joe Bush	1922	.788
Bryn Smith	1985	.783
2 tied with		.778

Games

Frank Williams	1987	85
Ken Sanders	1971	83
John Wyatt	1964	81
Mike Stanton	1996	81
Willie Hernandez	1984	80
Ted Power	1984	78
Jeff Shaw	1996	78
Bob Locker	1967	77
Craig Lefferts	1987	77
Jeff Innis	1992	76

Complete Games

Old Hoss Radbourn	1884	73
Tim Keefe	1886	62
Billy Taylor	1884	59
Dave Foutz	1886	55
Henry Porter	1888	53
Will White	1884	52
Guy Hecker	1885	51
Jack Lynch	1886	50
Pud Galvin	1886	49
John Clarkson	1891	47

Shutouts

Pete Alexander	1916	16
Old Hoss Radbourn	1884	11
Dave Foutz	1886	11
Christy Mathewson	1908	11
Mort Cooper	1942	10
Jim Palmer	1975	10
Three Finger Brown	1906	9
Bob Porterfield	1953	9
4 tied with		8

Saves

Jose Mesa	1995	46
Duane Ward	1993	45
John Wetteland	1996	43
Rick Aguilera	1991	42
Jeff Reardon	1985	41
Steve Bedrosian	1987	40
Randy Myers	1992	38
Trevor Hoffman	1997	37
3 tied with		36

Innings Pitched

Old Hoss Radbourn	1884	678.2
Tim Keefe	1886	540.0
Billy Taylor	1884	523.0
Dave Foutz	1886	504.0
Guy Hecker	1885	480.0
Henry Porter	1888	474.0
John Clarkson	1891	460.2
Will White	1884	456.0
Pud Galvin	1886	434.2
Jack Lynch	1886	432.2

Strikeouts

Old Hoss Radbourn	1884	441
Sandy Koufax	1965	382
Nolan Ryan	1976	327
J.R. Richard	1979	313
Randy Johnson	1993	308
Tim Keefe	1886	291
Billy Taylor	1884	284
Dave Foutz	1886	283
Bob Veale	1965	276
John Smoltz	1996	276

ERA
(minimum 1 Inning Pitched/Tm Gm)

Three Finger Brown	1906	1.04
Jack Pfiester	1907	1.15
Ed Walsh	1910	1.27
Old Hoss Radbourn	1884	1.38
Christy Mathewson	1908	1.43
Pete Alexander	1916	1.55
Rube Marquard	1916	1.58
Eddie Cicotte	1913	1.58
Greg Maddux	1995	1.63
Addie Joss	1909	1.71

Component ERA
(minimum 1 Inning Pitched/Tm Gm)

Ed Walsh	1910	1.27
Christy Mathewson	1908	1.34
Greg Maddux	1995	1.41
Three Finger Brown	1906	1.53
Sandy Koufax	1965	1.56
Old Hoss Radbourn	1884	1.59
Frank Smith	1909	1.60
Addie Joss	1909	1.65
Jack Pfiester	1907	1.67
Walter Johnson	1917	1.71

Opponent Average
(minimum 1 Inning Pitched/Tm Gm)

Sandy Koufax	1965	.179
Tommy Byrne	1949	.183
Ed Walsh	1910	.187
Nolan Ryan	1976	.195
Greg Maddux	1995	.197
Bobby Bolin	1968	.200
Christy Mathewson	1908	.200
Three Finger Brown	1906	.202
Randy Johnson	1993	.203
Dick Hughes	1967	.203

Batting Leaders—Through Age 30

At-Bats		Runs		Hits		Doubles	
Robin Yount	7,037	Jimmie Foxx	1,355	Ty Cobb	2,362	Joe Medwick	453
Vada Pinson	6,830	Mickey Mantle	1,341	Hank Aaron	2,085	Robin Yount	380
Mel Ott	6,544	Mel Ott	1,332	Rogers Hornsby	2,083	Ty Cobb	377
Hank Aaron	6,510	Hugh Duffy	1,268	Mel Ott	2,061	Stan Musial	373
Bill Mazeroski	6,398	Ty Cobb	1,240	Jimmie Foxx	2,049	Sherry Magee	371
Ty Cobb	6,383	Willie Keeler	1,232	Robin Yount	2,019	Vada Pinson	364
Al Kaline	6,378	Lou Gehrig	1,213	Vada Pinson	2,007	Lou Gehrig	363
Cal Ripken Jr.	6,305	Mike Tiernan	1,206	Joe Medwick	2,004	Rogers Hornsby	361
Ron Santo	6,213	Billy Hamilton	1,191	Willie Keeler	1,955	Mel Ott	359
Ruben Sierra	6,197	Hank Aaron	1,180	Al Kaline	1,949	Joe Sewell	358

Triples		Home Runs		RBI		Stolen Bases	
Sam Crawford	193	Jimmie Foxx	429	Jimmie Foxx	1,519	Rickey Henderson	871
Ty Cobb	184	Mickey Mantle	404	Mel Ott	1,386	Billy Hamilton	721
Joe Jackson	168	Eddie Mathews	399	Lou Gehrig	1,285	Ty Cobb	704
Jake Beckley	162	Frank Robinson	373	Hank Aaron	1,216	Tim Raines	634
Joe Kelley	158	Mel Ott	369	Al Simmons	1,156	Vince Coleman	610
Mike Tiernan	149	Hank Aaron	366	Mickey Mantle	1,152	Eddie Collins	510
Rogers Hornsby	143	Harmon Killebrew	336	Joe Medwick	1,143	Hugh Duffy	493
Elmer Flick	142	Ralph Kiner	329	Frank Robinson	1,131	Cesar Cedeno	487
Sherry Magee	139	Willie Mays	319	Johnny Bench	1,111	Willie Wilson	470
Tris Speaker	136	Duke Snider	316	Eddie Mathews	1,082	George Davis	454

Runs Created		Batting Average (minimum 2,750 Plate Appearances)		On-Base Percentage (minimum 2,750 Plate Appearances)		Slugging Percentage (minimum 2,750 Plate Appearances)	
Jimmie Foxx	1,605	Willie Keeler	.371	Ted Williams	.488	Babe Ruth	.697
Mel Ott	1,530	Ty Cobb	.370	Babe Ruth	.474	Ted Williams	.642
Ty Cobb	1,512	Nap Lajoie	.361	John McGraw	.466	Lou Gehrig	.636
Mickey Mantle	1,492	George Sisler	.361	Billy Hamilton	.458	Jimmie Foxx	.635
Lou Gehrig	1,365	Rogers Hornsby	.359	Frank Thomas	.452	Hank Greenberg	.622
Hugh Duffy	1,316	Al Simmons	.358	Wade Boggs	.445	Joe DiMaggio	.607
Hank Aaron	1,301	Jesse Burkett	.356	Bill Joyce	.444	Chuck Klein	.605
Rogers Hornsby	1,301	Joe Jackson	.356	Lou Gehrig	.442	Frank Thomas	.600
Frank Robinson	1,288	Wade Boggs	.356	Roy Thomas	.438	Al Simmons	.589
Ted Williams	1,280	Ted Williams	.353	Jimmie Foxx	.437	Johnny Mize	.588

Single Season Batting Leaders—Age 30

At-Bats			Runs			Hits			Doubles		
Matty Alou	1969	698	Tom Brown	1891	177	Matty Alou	1969	231	George Burns	1923	47
Horace Clarke	1970	686	Billy Hamilton	1896	152	Joe Torre	1971	230	Bob Meusel	1927	47
Rabbit Maranville	1922	672	Ted Williams	1949	150	Ty Cobb	1917	225	Wes Parker	1970	47
Al Simmons	1932	670	Hack Wilson	1930	146	Harry Heilmann	1925	225	John Valentin	1997	47
Ron LeFlore	1978	666	Al Simmons	1932	144	Charlie Jamieson	1923	222	Red Rolfe	1939	46
Dave Cash	1978	658	Lenny Dykstra	1993	143	Jesse Burkett	1899	221	Cal Ripken Jr.	1991	46
Cesar Tovar	1971	657	Larry Walker	1997	143	Cecil Cooper	1980	219	Larry Walker	1997	46
Lou Brock	1969	655	Mike Griffin	1895	140	Joe Jackson	1920	218	4 tied with		45
Cal Ripken Jr.	1991	650	Jimmie Foxx	1938	139	Al Simmons	1932	216			
2 tied with		648	Red Rolfe	1939	139	2 tied with		214			

Triples			Home Runs			RBI			Stolen Bases		
Ty Cobb	1917	24	Hack Wilson	1930	56	Hack Wilson	1930	190	Tom Brown	1891	106
Joe Visner	1890	22	Jimmie Foxx	1938	50	Jimmie Foxx	1938	175	Hugh Nicol	1888	103
Bid McPhee	1890	22	Frank Robinson	1966	49	Ted Williams	1949	159	Billy Hamilton	1896	83
Elmer Flick	1906	22	Larry Walker	1997	49	Al Simmons	1932	151	Davey Lopes	1975	77
Tom Brown	1891	21	Dave Kingman	1979	48	Lou Gehrig	1933	139	Rickey Henderson	1989	77
George Van Haltren	1896	21	Mike Schmidt	1980	48	Don Baylor	1979	139	Harry Stovey	1887	74
Joe Jackson	1920	20	Ted Kluszewski	1955	47	Joe Torre	1971	137	Walt Wilmot	1894	74
Buck Freeman	1902	19	Ted Williams	1949	43	Harry Heilmann	1925	134	Bill Greenwood	1887	71
Sam Crawford	1910	19	Dave Johnson	1973	43	Moose Solters	1936	134	Jake Stenzel	1897	69
Howard Shanks	1921	19	Tony Armas	1984	43	Bill Dickey	1937	133	Ron LeFlore	1978	68

Runs Created			Batting Average (minimum 3.1 PA/Tm Gm)			On-Base Percentage (minimum 3.1 PA/Tm Gm)			Slugging Percentage (minimum 3.1 PA/Tm Gm)		
Ted Williams	1949	174	Jesse Burkett	1899	.396	Ted Williams	1949	.490	Hack Wilson	1930	.723
Jimmie Foxx	1938	172	Harry Heilmann	1925	.393	Billy Hamilton	1896	.477	Larry Walker	1997	.720
Hack Wilson	1930	171	Ty Cobb	1917	.383	Wade Boggs	1988	.476	Jimmie Foxx	1938	.704
Tom Brown	1891	160	Joe Jackson	1920	.382	Bill Joyce	1896	.470	Ted Williams	1949	.650
Larry Walker	1997	158	Dave Orr	1890	.373	Jesse Burkett	1899	.463	Frank Robinson	1966	.637
Billy Hamilton	1896	155	Lew Fonseca	1929	.369	Jimmie Foxx	1938	.462	Mike Schmidt	1980	.624
Lou Gehrig	1933	149	Wade Boggs	1988	.366	Mickey Cochrane	1933	.459	Fred McGriff	1994	.623
Stan Musial	1951	147	Pie Traynor	1930	.366	Harry Heilmann	1925	.457	Ripper Collins	1934	.615
Carl Yastrzemski	1970	145	Larry Walker	1997	.366	Hack Wilson	1930	.454	Stan Musial	1951	.614
2 tied with		144	Rico Carty	1970	.366	Rico Carty	1970	.454	Dave Kingman	1979	.613

Pitching Leaders—Through Age 30

Wins
Kid Nichols	310
John Clarkson	304
Mickey Welch	302
Pud Galvin	278
Walter Johnson	277
Jim McCormick	265
Amos Rusie	245
Christy Mathewson	236
Charlie Buffinton	229
2 tied with	228

Losses
Pud Galvin	228
Jim McCormick	214
Mickey Welch	201
Jim Whitney	195
Adonis Terry	181
Pink Hawley	179
Gus Weyhing	178
Walter Johnson	177
Amos Rusie	174
2 tied with	167

Winning Percentage
(minimum 140 decisions)
Whitey Ford	.708
Dave Foutz	.704
Don Newcombe	.700
Juan Marichal	.688
Bob Caruthers	.688
Don Gullett	.686
Old Hoss Radbourn	.684
Pete Alexander	.683
Mike Mussina	.682
Christy Mathewson	.678

Games
Mitch Williams	612
Lindy McDaniel	591
Rollie Fingers	580
Mike Jackson	550
Mickey Welch	541
Willie Hernandez	540
Pud Galvin	523
Lee Smith	522
Kid Nichols	518
Goose Gossage	511

Complete Games
Mickey Welch	511
Pud Galvin	486
Jim McCormick	466
Kid Nichols	442
John Clarkson	441
Amos Rusie	392
Will White	391
Tim Keefe	383
Gus Weyhing	368
Jim Whitney	367

Shutouts
Walter Johnson	79
Pete Alexander	61
Christy Mathewson	61
Ed Walsh	48
Addie Joss	45
Pud Galvin	43
Bert Blyleven	42
Jim Palmer	42
Mickey Welch	41
6 tied with	40

Saves
Bruce Sutter	215
John Franco	211
John Wetteland	211
Lee Smith	209
Bobby Thigpen	201
Rod Beck	199
Mitch Williams	192
Dave Righetti	188
Goose Gossage	184
Randy Myers	184

Innings Pitched
Mickey Welch	4,637.0
Pud Galvin	4,511.1
Jim McCormick	4,275.2
Kid Nichols	4,217.0
John Clarkson	4,090.2
Walter Johnson	3,800.1
Amos Rusie	3,769.2
Will White	3,516.2
Gus Weyhing	3,513.2
Tim Keefe	3,400.1

Strikeouts
Walter Johnson	2,467
Nolan Ryan	2,426
Sandy Koufax	2,396
Sam McDowell	2,391
Bert Blyleven	2,357
Don Drysdale	2,307
Bob Feller	2,108
Tom Seaver	2,099
Fergie Jenkins	2,045
Roger Clemens	2,033

ERA
(minimum 800 Innings Pitched)
Walter Johnson	1.66
Ed Walsh	1.70
Three Finger Brown	1.77
Addie Joss	1.89
Jim Devlin	1.89
Old Hoss Radbourn	1.95
Christy Mathewson	1.98
Joe Wood	2.03
Jeff Pfeffer	2.10
Monte Ward	2.10

Component ERA
(minimum 800 Innings Pitched)
Ed Walsh	1.66
Walter Johnson	1.71
Addie Joss	1.73
Old Hoss Radbourn	1.89
Christy Mathewson	1.95
Monte Ward	2.01
Frank Smith	2.03
Three Finger Brown	2.06
Tim Keefe	2.07
Guy Hecker	2.09

Opponent Average
(minimum 800 Innings Pitched)
Nolan Ryan	.195
Herb Score	.200
Sid Fernandez	.204
Sandy Koufax	.205
Andy Messersmith	.208
Tom Hall	.211
J.R. Richard	.212
Pedro Martinez	.213
Walter Johnson	.213
Sam McDowell	.214

Single Season Pitching Leaders—Age 30

Wins
Bill Hutchison	1890	42
Jack Chesbro	1904	41
Tim Keefe	1887	35
Jim Bagby	1920	31
Pete Alexander	1917	30
Charlie Buffinton	1891	29
Old Hoss Radbourn	1885	28
Pud Galvin	1887	28
Lefty Grove	1930	28
6 tied with		27

Losses
Jim Hughey	1899	30
Bill Hart	1896	29
Bill Hutchison	1890	25
Ed Crane	1892	24
Guy Hecker	1886	23
Jim McCormick	1887	23
Jack Cronin	1904	23
Brickyard Kennedy	1898	22
Al Orth	1903	22
Robin Roberts	1957	22

Winning Percentage
(minimum 15 decisions)
Wild Bill Donovan	1907	.862
Chief Bender	1914	.850
Lefty Grove	1930	.848
Schoolboy Rowe	1940	.842
Mark Portugal	1993	.818
Christy Mathewson	1909	.806
Ed Wells	1930	.800
Larry Gura	1978	.800
Don Newcombe	1956	.794
Harry Brecheen	1945	.789

Games
Mike Marshall	1973	92
Stan Belinda	1997	84
Rollie Fingers	1977	78
Greg Minton	1982	78
Jeff Shaw	1997	78
Mel Rojas	1997	77
Jeff Nelson	1997	77
Jerry Spradlin	1997	76
3 tied with		75

Complete Games
Bill Hutchison	1890	65
Tim Keefe	1887	54
Old Hoss Radbourn	1885	49
Jack Chesbro	1904	48
Pud Galvin	1887	47
Guy Hecker	1886	45
John Clarkson	1892	42
Joe McGinnity	1901	39
Jack Taylor	1904	39
Brickyard Kennedy	1898	38

Shutouts
Carl Hubbell	1933	10
Christy Mathewson	1909	8
Pete Alexander	1917	8
Hippo Vaughn	1918	8
Walter Johnson	1918	8
Wilbur Wood	1972	8
6 tied with		7

Saves
Randy Myers	1993	53
Dan Quisenberry	1983	45
Bryan Harvey	1993	45
Jeff Shaw	1997	42
Rick Aguilera	1992	41
Jeff Montgomery	1992	39
Jose Mesa	1996	39
John Hiller	1973	38
Rollie Fingers	1977	35
Jeff Reardon	1986	35

Innings Pitched
Bill Hutchison	1890	603.0
Tim Keefe	1887	478.2
Jack Chesbro	1904	454.2
Old Hoss Radbourn	1885	445.2
Pud Galvin	1887	440.2
Guy Hecker	1886	420.2
Togie Pittinger	1902	389.1
John Clarkson	1892	389.0
Pete Alexander	1917	388.0
Joe McGinnity	1901	382.0

Strikeouts
Nolan Ryan	1977	341
Curt Schilling	1997	319
Sandy Koufax	1966	317
Mickey Lolich	1971	308
Bill Hutchison	1890	289
Ed Walsh	1911	255
Tom Seaver	1975	243
John Smoltz	1997	241
Jack Chesbro	1904	239
Gaylord Perry	1969	233

ERA
(minimum 1 Inning Pitched/Tm Gm)
Christy Mathewson	1909	1.14
Walter Johnson	1918	1.27
Three Finger Brown	1907	1.39
Carl Hubbell	1933	1.66
Ned Garvin	1904	1.72
Doc White	1909	1.72
Sandy Koufax	1966	1.73
Vic Willis	1906	1.73
Hippo Vaughn	1918	1.74
Charlie Chech	1908	1.74

Component ERA
(minimum 1 Inning Pitched/Tm Gm)
Christy Mathewson	1909	1.29
Jack Chesbro	1904	1.56
Walter Johnson	1918	1.63
Three Finger Brown	1907	1.70
Hippo Vaughn	1918	1.79
Frank Smith	1910	1.83
Carl Hubbell	1933	1.84
Jake Weimer	1904	1.90
Sandy Koufax	1966	1.92
Pete Alexander	1917	1.94

Opponent Average
(minimum 1 Inning Pitched/Tm Gm)
Nolan Ryan	1977	.193
Larry Cheney	1916	.198
Gary Peters	1967	.199
Christy Mathewson	1909	.200
Cy Morgan	1909	.202
Sonny Siebert	1967	.202
Al Leiter	1996	.202
Jake Weimer	1904	.204
Sandy Koufax	1966	.205
Jack Chesbro	1904	.205

Batting Leaders—Through Age 31

At-Bats		Runs		Hits		Doubles	
Robin Yount	7,672	Jimmie Foxx	1,485	Ty Cobb	2,523	Joe Medwick	483
Vada Pinson	7,404	Mel Ott	1,421	Rogers Hornsby	2,288	Stan Musial	415
Hank Aaron	7,080	Mickey Mantle	1,381	Hank Aaron	2,266	Robin Yount	405
Mel Ott	7,080	Hugh Duffy	1,365	Robin Yount	2,217	Lou Gehrig	403
Cal Ripken Jr.	6,942	Billy Hamilton	1,343	Jimmie Foxx	2,217	Ed Delahanty	398
Bill Mazeroski	6,904	Lou Gehrig	1,341	Mel Ott	2,216	Ty Cobb	396
Al Kaline	6,857	Willie Keeler	1,327	Vada Pinson	2,171	Joe Cronin	395
Ty Cobb	6,804	Ty Cobb	1,323	Joe Medwick	2,142	Tris Speaker	395
Ron Santo	6,768	Mike Tiernan	1,296	Willie Keeler	2,115	Rogers Hornsby	393
Sam Crawford	6,760	Rickey Henderson	1,290	Sam Crawford	2,103	Vada Pinson	392

Triples		Home Runs		RBI		Stolen Bases	
Sam Crawford	207	Jimmie Foxx	464	Jimmie Foxx	1,624	Rickey Henderson	936
Ty Cobb	198	Eddie Mathews	422	Mel Ott	1,465	Billy Hamilton	787
Jake Beckley	178	Mickey Mantle	419	Lou Gehrig	1,450	Ty Cobb	738
Joe Jackson	168	Frank Robinson	403	Hank Aaron	1,305	Tim Raines	685
Joe Kelley	162	Hank Aaron	398	Al Simmons	1,275	Vince Coleman	648
Elmer Flick	160	Mel Ott	388	Frank Robinson	1,225	Eddie Collins	532
Mike Tiernan	160	Harmon Killebrew	380	Joe Medwick	1,213	Willie Wilson	529
Rogers Hornsby	152	Willie Mays	368	Johnny Bench	1,191	Hugh Duffy	522
Tris Speaker	148	Babe Ruth	356	Mickey Mantle	1,187	Arlie Latham	506
Ed Konetchy	146	Ralph Kiner	351	Rogers Hornsby	1,176	Cesar Cedeno	503

| Runs Created | | Batting Average | | On-Base Percentage | | Slugging Percentage | |
		(minimum 3,000 Plate Appearances)		(minimum 3,000 Plate Appearances)		(minimum 3,000 Plate Appearances)	
Jimmie Foxx	1,747	Ty Cobb	.371	Ted Williams	.486	Babe Ruth	.701
Mel Ott	1,635	Willie Keeler	.366	Babe Ruth	.479	Lou Gehrig	.643
Ty Cobb	1,602	Nap Lajoie	.360	John McGraw	.466	Ted Williams	.642
Mickey Mantle	1,538	Rogers Hornsby	.359	Billy Hamilton	.458	Jimmie Foxx	.640
Lou Gehrig	1,536	Jesse Burkett	.357	Frank Thomas	.452	Hank Greenberg	.622
Rogers Hornsby	1,440	Joe Jackson	.356	Lou Gehrig	.444	Frank Thomas	.600
Hugh Duffy	1,419	Al Simmons	.355	Bill Joyce	.443	Joe DiMaggio	.596
Hank Aaron	1,418	George Sisler	.353	Wade Boggs	.443	Chuck Klein	.593
Ed Delahanty	1,405	Wade Boggs	.352	Jimmie Foxx	.439	Willie Mays	.588
Frank Robinson	1,396	Ted Williams	.350	Roy Thomas	.435	Johnny Mize	.588

Single Season Batting Leaders—Age 31

At-Bats			Runs			Hits			Doubles		
Dick Groat	1962	678	Kiki Cuyler	1930	155	Rod Carew	1977	239	Ed Delahanty	1899	55
Matty Alou	1970	677	Billy Hamilton	1897	152	Ed Delahanty	1899	238	Hal McRae	1977	54
Felix Millan	1975	676	Craig Biggio	1997	146	Kiki Cuyler	1930	228	Joe Cronin	1938	51
Felipe Alou	1966	666	Ellis Burks	1996	142	Heinie Manush	1933	221	Wade Boggs	1989	51
Lou Brock	1970	664	Babe Ruth	1926	139	Felipe Alou	1966	218	Mark Grace	1995	51
Bill Virdon	1962	663	Ed Delahanty	1899	135	Sam Crawford	1911	217	Kiki Cuyler	1930	50
Tom Brown	1892	660	Charlie Gehringer	1934	134	Paul Waner	1934	217	Charlie Gehringer	1934	50
Hughie Critz	1932	659	Rogers Hornsby	1927	133	Buddy Myer	1935	215	Stan Spence	1946	50
Heinie Manush	1933	658	Jimmy Ryan	1894	132	Richie Ashburn	1958	215	Nap Lajoie	1906	48
Steve Garvey	1980	658	Ed McKean	1895	131	2 tied with		214	Harry Davis	1905	47

Triples			Home Runs			RBI			Stolen Bases		
John Reilly	1890	26	Lou Gehrig	1934	49	Lou Gehrig	1934	165	Harry Stovey	1888	87
Mike Mitchell	1911	22	Willie Mays	1962	49	Babe Ruth	1926	146	Arlie Latham	1891	87
Hi Myers	1920	22	Willie Stargell	1971	48	Roy Campanella	1953	142	Hugh Nicol	1889	80
Earle Combs	1930	22	Babe Ruth	1926	47	Rafael Palmeiro	1996	142	Tom Brown	1892	78
Edd Roush	1924	21	Willie McCovey	1969	45	Willie Mays	1962	141	Ron LeFlore	1979	78
Harry Stovey	1888	20	Harmon Killebrew	1967	44	Jay Buhner	1996	138	Bill McClellan	1887	70
Buck Freeman	1903	20	Frank Howard	1968	44	Ed Delahanty	1899	137	King Kelly	1889	68
Chick Stahl	1904	19	Dale Murphy	1987	44	Kiki Cuyler	1930	134	Joe Morgan	1975	67
Wally Pipp	1924	19	Jay Buhner	1996	44	Roger Connor	1889	130	Billy Hamilton	1897	66
2 tied with		18	Barry Bonds	1996	42	Barry Bonds	1996	129	Rickey Henderson	1990	65

| Runs Created | | | Batting Average | | | On-Base Percentage | | | Slugging Percentage | | |
			(minimum 3.1 PA/Tm Gm)			(minimum 3.1 PA/Tm Gm)			(minimum 3.1 PA/Tm Gm)		
Lou Gehrig	1934	171	Ed Delahanty	1899	.410	Babe Ruth	1926	.516	Babe Ruth	1926	.737
Babe Ruth	1926	167	Rod Carew	1977	.388	Joe Morgan	1975	.466	Lou Gehrig	1934	.706
Ed Delahanty	1899	165	Ty Cobb	1918	.382	Lou Gehrig	1934	.465	Jimmie Foxx	1939	.694
Barry Bonds	1996	160	Sam Crawford	1911	.378	Jimmie Foxx	1939	.464	Willie McCovey	1969	.656
Rod Carew	1977	154	Dan Brouthers	1889	.373	Ed Delahanty	1899	.464	Mike Schmidt	1981	.644
Tip O'Neill	1889	147	Babe Ruth	1926	.372	Dan Brouthers	1889	.462	Ellis Burks	1996	.639
Craig Biggio	1997	147	Harry Heilmann	1926	.367	Billy Hamilton	1897	.461	Willie Stargell	1971	.628
Willie Mays	1962	146	Jesse Burkett	1900	.363	Barry Bonds	1996	.461	Dante Bichette	1995	.620
Ellis Burks	1996	146	Honus Wagner	1905	.363	Paul O'Neill	1994	.460	Willie Mays	1962	.615
Charlie Gehringer	1934	145	Lou Gehrig	1934	.363	Jack Clark	1987	.459	Barry Bonds	1996	.615

Pitching Leaders—Through Age 31

Wins

Kid Nichols	329
John Clarkson	320
Mickey Welch	309
Pud Galvin	301
Walter Johnson	297
Jim McCormick	265
Christy Mathewson	263
Tim Keefe	263
Amos Rusie	245
2 tied with	241

Losses

Pud Galvin	253
Jim McCormick	214
Mickey Welch	211
Gus Weyhing	204
Jim Whitney	202
Adonis Terry	195
Walter Johnson	191
Kid Nichols	183
Pink Hawley	179
Amos Rusie	174

Winning Percentage
(minimum 150 decisions)

Lefty Grove	.705
Dave Foutz	.696
Whitey Ford	.693
Bob Caruthers	.688
Don Gullett	.686
Christy Mathewson	.685
Juan Marichal	.685
Pete Alexander	.683
Mike Mussina	.682
Three Finger Brown	.676

Games

Rollie Fingers	647
Lindy McDaniel	632
Mike Jackson	623
Mitch Williams	612
Willie Hernandez	604
Lee Smith	586
Pud Galvin	573
Goose Gossage	568
Mickey Welch	563
Kid Nichols	556

Complete Games

Pud Galvin	535
Mickey Welch	525
Kid Nichols	475
John Clarkson	472
Jim McCormick	466
Tim Keefe	431
Gus Weyhing	407
Will White	394
Amos Rusie	392
Walter Johnson	388

Shutouts

Walter Johnson	86
Christy Mathewson	63
Pete Alexander	61
Ed Walsh	54
Pud Galvin	49
Don Drysdale	48
Jim Palmer	45
Juan Marichal	45
Addie Joss	45
Rube Waddell	45

Saves

Bruce Sutter	260
Lee Smith	234
John Franco	226
Dave Righetti	224
John Wetteland	211
Rollie Fingers	208
Goose Gossage	206
Randy Myers	205
Bobby Thigpen	201
Rod Beck	199

Innings Pitched

Pud Galvin	4,948.2
Mickey Welch	4,797.0
Kid Nichols	4,538.0
John Clarkson	4,385.2
Jim McCormick	4,275.2
Walter Johnson	4,090.2
Gus Weyhing	3,874.2
Tim Keefe	3,834.2
Amos Rusie	3,769.2
Will White	3,542.2

Strikeouts

Nolan Ryan	2,686
Walter Johnson	2,614
Don Drysdale	2,462
Sam McDowell	2,424
Sandy Koufax	2,396
Bert Blyleven	2,376
Tom Seaver	2,334
Bob Feller	2,227
Fergie Jenkins	2,202
Roger Clemens	2,201

ERA
(minimum 850 Innings Pitched)

Walter Johnson	1.65
Three Finger Brown	1.70
Ed Walsh	1.77
Addie Joss	1.89
Jim Devlin	1.89
Christy Mathewson	1.97
Jack Pfiester	1.98
Joe Wood	2.03
Monte Ward	2.10
Pete Alexander	2.12

Component ERA
(minimum 850 Innings Pitched)

Walter Johnson	1.71
Ed Walsh	1.71
Addie Joss	1.73
Three Finger Brown	1.86
Christy Mathewson	1.99
Tim Keefe	2.01
Monte Ward	2.01
Old Hoss Radbourn	2.05
Jack Pfiester	2.09
Joe Wood	2.10

Opponent Average
(minimum 850 Innings Pitched)

Nolan Ryan	.198
Herb Score	.200
Sandy Koufax	.205
Sid Fernandez	.208
Andy Messersmith	.210
Tom Hall	.211
J.R. Richard	.212
Pedro Martinez	.213
Walter Johnson	.213
Randy Johnson	.213

Single Season Pitching Leaders—Age 31

Wins

Bill Hutchison	1891	44
Tim Keefe	1888	35
Lefty Grove	1931	31
Bobby Mathews	1883	30
Three Finger Brown	1908	29
Old Hoss Radbourn	1886	27
Christy Mathewson	1910	27
Ed Walsh	1912	27
5 tied with		25

Losses

Old Hoss Radbourn	1886	31
Bill Hart	1897	27
Gus Weyhing	1898	26
Pud Galvin	1888	25
Dad Clarke	1896	24
Kaiser Wilhelm	1905	23
Red Ames	1914	23
Dolf Luque	1922	23
Togie Pittinger	1903	22
Jack Quinn	1915	22

Winning Percentage
(minimum 15 decisions)

Roy Face	1959	.947
Johnny Allen	1937	.938
Randy Johnson	1995	.900
Lefty Grove	1931	.886
Greg Maddux	1997	.826
Tommy John	1974	.813
Bill Bernhard	1902	.783
Sam Leever	1903	.781
3 tied with		.778

Games

Mike Marshall	1974	106
Kent Tekulve	1978	91
Enrique Romo	1979	84
Joe Boever	1992	81
Mark Dewey	1996	78
Buddy Groom	1997	78
Heathcliff Slocumb	1997	76
Dale Mohorcic	1987	74
3 tied with		73

Complete Games

Old Hoss Radbourn	1886	57
Bill Hutchison	1891	56
Pud Galvin	1888	49
Tim Keefe	1888	48
Bobby Mathews	1883	41
Sam Kimber	1884	40
Cy Young	1898	40
Gus Weyhing	1898	39
George Bradley	1884	36
2 tied with		35

Shutouts

John Tudor	1985	10
Three Finger Brown	1908	9
Tim Keefe	1888	8
Eddie Plank	1907	8
Don Drysdale	1968	8
Juan Marichal	1969	8
Sam Leever	1903	7
Walter Johnson	1919	7
Mort Cooper	1944	7
11 tied with		6

Saves

Bruce Sutter	1984	45
Jeff Montgomery	1993	45
Dan Quisenberry	1984	44
Roberto Hernandez	1996	38
Clay Carroll	1972	37
Rollie Fingers	1978	37
Doug Jones	1988	37
Dave Righetti	1990	36
Don Aase	1986	34
Rick Aguilera	1993	34

Innings Pitched

Bill Hutchison	1891	561.0
Old Hoss Radbourn	1886	509.1
Pud Galvin	1888	437.1
Tim Keefe	1888	434.1
Ed Walsh	1912	393.0
Bobby Mathews	1883	381.0
Cy Young	1898	377.2
Gus Weyhing	1898	361.0
Wilbur Wood	1973	359.1
Sam Kimber	1884	352.1

Strikeouts

Tim Keefe	1888	333
Mike Scott	1986	306
Randy Johnson	1995	294
Bill Hutchison	1891	261
Nolan Ryan	1978	260
Ed Walsh	1912	254
Mickey Lolich	1972	250
Tom Seaver	1976	235
Rube Waddell	1908	232
Jack Morris	1986	223

ERA
(minimum 1 Inning Pitched/Tm Gm)

Fred Anderson	1917	1.44
Three Finger Brown	1908	1.47
Walter Johnson	1919	1.49
Cy Morgan	1910	1.55
Tim Keefe	1888	1.74
Jack Powell	1906	1.77
Hippo Vaughn	1919	1.79
Russ Ford	1914	1.82
Harry Howell	1908	1.89
Rube Waddell	1908	1.89

Component ERA
(minimum 1 Inning Pitched/Tm Gm)

Three Finger Brown	1908	1.31
Tim Keefe	1888	1.56
Fred Anderson	1917	1.62
Tom Hughes	1915	1.65
Mike Scott	1986	1.67
Bill Bernhard	1902	1.69
Walter Johnson	1919	1.72
Tully Sparks	1906	1.75
Russ Ford	1914	1.83
John Tudor	1985	1.84

Opponent Average
(minimum 1 Inning Pitched/Tm Gm)

Mike Scott	1986	.186
Three Finger Brown	1908	.195
Tim Keefe	1888	.195
Pascual Perez	1988	.196
Sonny Siebert	1968	.198
Randy Johnson	1995	.201
Luis Tiant	1972	.202
Roger Clemens	1994	.204
Hank Aguirre	1962	.205
Bob Lemon	1952	.208

Batting Leaders—Through Age 32

At-Bats		Runs		Hits		Doubles	
Robin Yount	8,293	Jimmie Foxx	1,591	Ty Cobb	2,714	Joe Medwick	507
Vada Pinson	7,970	Mel Ott	1,510	Rogers Hornsby	2,476	Stan Musial	468
Hank Aaron	7,683	Mickey Mantle	1,473	Hank Aaron	2,434	Tris Speaker	445
Mel Ott	7,605	Hugh Duffy	1,468	Robin Yount	2,407	Robin Yount	443
Cal Ripken Jr.	7,583	Lou Gehrig	1,466	Jimmie Foxx	2,370	Rogers Hornsby	435
Sam Crawford	7,341	Billy Hamilton	1,453	Mel Ott	2,366	Ty Cobb	432
Al Kaline	7,315	Ty Cobb	1,415	Vada Pinson	2,320	Ed Delahanty	430
Ty Cobb	7,301	Hank Aaron	1,406	Joe Medwick	2,307	Lou Gehrig	429
Ron Santo	7,232	Willie Keeler	1,405	Willie Keeler	2,301	Joe Cronin	428
Rusty Staub	7,171	Jesse Burkett	1,400	Sam Crawford	2,292	Heinie Manush	421

Triples		Home Runs		RBI		Stolen Bases	
Sam Crawford	228	Jimmie Foxx	500	Jimmie Foxx	1,743	Rickey Henderson	994
Ty Cobb	211	Mickey Mantle	454	Lou Gehrig	1,569	Billy Hamilton	841
Jake Beckley	188	Eddie Mathews	445	Mel Ott	1,555	Ty Cobb	766
Joe Kelley	175	Hank Aaron	442	Hank Aaron	1,432	Tim Raines	730
Joe Jackson	168	Frank Robinson	418	Al Simmons	1,379	Vince Coleman	698
Mike Tiernan	162	Babe Ruth	416	Mickey Mantle	1,298	Arlie Latham	572
Elmer Flick	161	Mel Ott	415	Joe Medwick	1,298	Eddie Collins	565
Rogers Hornsby	159	Willie Mays	406	Frank Robinson	1,277	Willie Wilson	564
Tris Speaker	159	Harmon Killebrew	397	Rogers Hornsby	1,270	Hugh Duffy	548
Roger Connor	157	Lou Gehrig	378	Babe Ruth	1,262	Max Carey	532

Runs Created		Batting Average		On-Base Percentage		Slugging Percentage	
		(minimum 3,000 Plate Appearances)		(minimum 3,000 Plate Appearances)		(minimum 3,000 Plate Appearances)	
Jimmie Foxx	1,862	Ty Cobb	.372	Ted Williams	.483	Babe Ruth	.709
Mel Ott	1,745	Willie Keeler	.364	Babe Ruth	.480	Lou Gehrig	.638
Ty Cobb	1,702	Rogers Hornsby	.361	John McGraw	.466	Jimmie Foxx	.635
Lou Gehrig	1,681	Jesse Burkett	.359	Billy Hamilton	.460	Ted Williams	.633
Mickey Mantle	1,654	Joe Jackson	.356	Frank Thomas	.452	Hank Greenberg	.622
Rogers Hornsby	1,575	Nap Lajoie	.355	Lou Gehrig	.446	Frank Thomas	.600
Babe Ruth	1,552	Al Simmons	.354	Jimmie Foxx	.437	Johnny Mize	.588
Hank Aaron	1,533	George Sisler	.352	Wade Boggs	.436	Joe DiMaggio	.588
Stan Musial	1,526	Billy Hamilton	.351	Bill Joyce	.435	Willie Mays	.588
Ted Williams	1,522	Babe Ruth	.349	Rogers Hornsby	.434	Chuck Klein	.586

Single Season Batting Leaders—Age 32

At-Bats			Runs			Hits			Doubles		
Lance Johnson	1996	682	Babe Ruth	1927	158	Lefty O'Doul	1929	254	Stan Musial	1953	53
Pete Rose	1973	680	Harry Stovey	1889	152	Pete Rose	1973	230	Edgar Martinez	1995	52
Luis Aparicio	1966	659	Lefty O'Doul	1929	152	Lance Johnson	1996	227	Tris Speaker	1920	50
Doc Cramer	1938	658	Jesse Burkett	1901	142	Jesse Burkett	1901	226	Harry Heilmann	1927	50
Bill Buckner	1982	657	Max Carey	1922	140	Bill Terry	1929	226	Earl Averill	1934	48
George Van Haltren	1898	654	Tris Speaker	1920	137	George Sisler	1925	224	Socks Seybold	1903	45
Larry Bowa	1978	654	Billy Williams	1970	137	Cy Seymour	1905	219	Wade Boggs	1990	44
Cecil Cooper	1982	654	Mike Griffin	1897	136	Tris Speaker	1920	214	Earl Sheely	1925	43
Maury Wills	1965	650	Roger Connor	1890	133	Roberto Clemente	1967	209	Augie Galan	1944	43
George Sisler	1925	649	George Gore	1889	132	Max Carey	1922	207	Dick Groat	1963	43

Triples			Home Runs			RBI			Stolen Bases		
Cy Seymour	1905	21	Babe Ruth	1927	60	Babe Ruth	1927	164	Ron LeFlore	1980	97
Sam Crawford	1912	21	Mark McGwire	1996	52	Ken Williams	1922	155	Maury Wills	1965	94
Lance Johnson	1996	21	Brady Anderson	1996	50	Dante Bichette	1996	141	Monte Ward	1892	88
Rabbit Maranville	1924	20	Andre Dawson	1987	49	Andre Dawson	1987	137	Otis Nixon	1991	72
Buck Freeman	1904	19	Frank Howard	1969	48	Billy Williams	1970	129	Arlie Latham	1892	66
Hardy Richardson	1887	18	Hank Aaron	1966	44	Gavy Cravath	1913	128	Tom Brown	1893	66
Ray Powell	1921	18	Billy Williams	1970	42	Hank Aaron	1966	127	Ned Hanlon	1890	65
Sam Mertes	1905	17	Barry Bonds	1997	40	Ted Williams	1951	126	Lou Brock	1971	64
Harry Hooper	1920	17	Jay Buhner	1997	40	Willie McCovey	1970	126	Harry Stovey	1889	63
3 tied with		16	3 tied with		39	Hack Wilson	1932	123	Joe Morgan	1976	60

Runs Created			Batting Average			On-Base Percentage			Slugging Percentage		
			(minimum 3.1 PA/Tm Gm)			(minimum 3.1 PA/Tm Gm)			(minimum 3.1 PA/Tm Gm)		
Babe Ruth	1927	177	Lefty O'Doul	1929	.398	Rogers Hornsby	1928	.498	Babe Ruth	1927	.772
Lefty O'Doul	1929	157	Harry Heilmann	1927	.398	Babe Ruth	1927	.487	Mark McGwire	1996	.730
Roger Connor	1890	155	Tris Speaker	1920	.388	Tris Speaker	1920	.483	Kevin Mitchell	1994	.681
Jesse Burkett	1901	153	Rogers Hornsby	1928	.387	Billy Hamilton	1898	.480	Brady Anderson	1996	.637
Edgar Martinez	1995	151	Ty Cobb	1919	.384	Edgar Martinez	1995	.479	Rogers Hornsby	1928	.632
Cy Seymour	1905	147	Cy Seymour	1905	.377	Harry Heilmann	1927	.475	Edgar Martinez	1995	.628
Harry Stovey	1889	146	Jesse Burkett	1901	.376	Mark McGwire	1996	.467	Ken Williams	1922	.627
Tris Speaker	1920	146	Bill Terry	1929	.372	Dan Brouthers	1890	.466	Lefty O'Doul	1929	.622
Lou Gehrig	1935	145	Andres Galarraga	1993	.370	Lou Gehrig	1935	.466	Harry Heilmann	1927	.616
Stan Musial	1953	145	Billy Hamilton	1898	.369	Lefty O'Doul	1929	.465	Willie McCovey	1970	.612

Pitching Leaders—Through Age 32

Wins		Losses		Winning Percentage		Games	
				(minimum 160 decisions)			
Kid Nichols	329	Pud Galvin	269	Whitey Ford	.715	Rollie Fingers	701
John Clarkson	328	Gus Weyhing	225	Lefty Grove	.707	Mike Jackson	694
Pud Galvin	324	Jim McCormick	214	Ron Guidry	.705	Lindy McDaniel	668
Mickey Welch	309	Mickey Welch	211	Dave Foutz	.701	Lee Smith	650
Walter Johnson	305	Jim Whitney	204	Three Finger Brown	.689	Willie Hernandez	649
Tim Keefe	291	Walter Johnson	201	Bob Caruthers	.688	Goose Gossage	630
Christy Mathewson	289	Adonis Terry	196	Christy Mathewson	.683	Sparky Lyle	621
Cy Young	267	Bob Friend	188	Pete Alexander	.675	Mitch Williams	619
Jim McCormick	265	George Mullin	184	Mort Cooper	.675	Pud Galvin	614
Gus Weyhing	258	Kid Nichols	183	Juan Marichal	.674	Bruce Sutter	607

Complete Games		Shutouts		Saves		Innings Pitched	
Pud Galvin	573	Walter Johnson	90	Bruce Sutter	283	Pud Galvin	5,289.2
Mickey Welch	525	Pete Alexander	70	Lee Smith	265	Mickey Welch	4,802.0
John Clarkson	485	Christy Mathewson	68	Dave Righetti	248	Kid Nichols	4,538.0
Kid Nichols	475	Ed Walsh	55	Randy Myers	243	John Clarkson	4,536.1
Tim Keefe	469	Pud Galvin	53	John Franco	236	Jim McCormick	4,275.2
Jim McCormick	466	Jim Palmer	51	Jeff Reardon	235	Walter Johnson	4,234.1
Gus Weyhing	441	Rube Waddell	50	Goose Gossage	231	Gus Weyhing	4,209.1
Walter Johnson	400	Don Drysdale	49	Rollie Fingers	221	Tim Keefe	4,198.2
Will White	394	Don Sutton	47	Dan Quisenberry	217	Amos Rusie	3,769.2
2 tied with	392	2 tied with	46	John Wetteland	211	Cy Young	3,721.2

Strikeouts		ERA		Component ERA		Opponent Average	
		(minimum 900 Innings Pitched)		(minimum 900 Innings Pitched)		(minimum 900 Innings Pitched)	
Nolan Ryan	2,909	Three Finger Brown	1.63	Addie Joss	1.73	Nolan Ryan	.199
Walter Johnson	2,692	Walter Johnson	1.70	Walter Johnson	1.74	Sandy Koufax	.205
Tom Seaver	2,530	Ed Walsh	1.79	Ed Walsh	1.76	Sid Fernandez	.209
Bert Blyleven	2,499	Addie Joss	1.89	Three Finger Brown	1.76	Andy Messersmith	.211
Don Drysdale	2,486	Jim Devlin	1.89	Monte Ward	2.01	J.R. Richard	.212
Sam McDowell	2,453	Jack Pfiester	1.96	Christy Mathewson	2.02	Pedro Martinez	.213
Sandy Koufax	2,396	Christy Mathewson	1.97	Tim Keefe	2.06	Randy Johnson	.213
Fergie Jenkins	2,344	Joe Wood	2.03	Jack Pfiester	2.08	Walter Johnson	.214
Mickey Lolich	2,338	Pete Alexander	2.09	Pete Alexander	2.09	Sam McDowell	.215
Bob Feller	2,338	Monte Ward	2.10	Joe Wood	2.10	Tom Seaver	.216

Single Season Pitching Leaders—Age 32

Wins			Losses			Winning Percentage			Games		
						(minimum 15 decisions)					
Bill Hutchison	1892	37	Bill Hutchison	1892	36	Whitey Ford	1961	.862	Kent Tekulve	1979	94
Joe McGinnity	1903	31	Tony Mullane	1891	26	Tom Hughes	1916	.842	Ted Abernathy	1965	84
Bobby Mathews	1884	30	Roger Craig	1962	24	Bob Purkey	1962	.821	Dan Quisenberry	1985	84
Tim Keefe	1889	28	Old Hoss Radbourn	1887	23	Bobo Newsom	1940	.808	Juan Agosto	1990	82
Bert Cunningham	1898	28	Gus Weyhing	1899	21	Bert Humphries	1913	.800	Hal Woodeshick	1965	78
Three Finger Brown	1909	27	Togie Pittinger	1904	21	Firpo Marberry	1931	.800	Dick Tidrow	1979	77
Dolf Luque	1923	27	Sad Sam Jones	1925	21	Paul Derringer	1939	.781	Ron Herbel	1970	76
Cy Young	1899	26	Ted Lyons	1933	21	Steve Stone	1980	.781	Tippy Martinez	1982	76
Christy Mathewson	1911	26	Joe McGinnity	1903	20	Tom Seaver	1977	.778	Bill Hutchison	1892	75
5 tied with		25	Vern Kennedy	1939	20	Dolf Luque	1923	.771	3 tied with		74

Complete Games			Shutouts			Saves			Innings Pitched		
Bill Hutchison	1892	67	Bob Gibson	1968	13	Jeff Brantley	1996	44	Bill Hutchison	1892	622.0
Bobby Mathews	1884	48	Pete Alexander	1919	9	Jeff Reardon	1988	42	Joe McGinnity	1903	434.0
Old Hoss Radbourn	1887	48	Three Finger Brown	1909	8	Randy Myers	1995	38	Bobby Mathews	1884	430.2
Joe McGinnity	1903	44	Vic Willis	1908	7	Dan Quisenberry	1985	37	Tony Mullane	1891	426.1
Tony Mullane	1891	42	Tom Seaver	1977	7	Doug Jones	1989	32	Old Hoss Radbourn	1887	425.0
Bert Cunningham	1898	41	7 tied with		6	Tom Henke	1990	32	Cy Young	1899	369.1
Cy Young	1899	40				Ted Abernathy	1965	31	Tim Keefe	1889	364.0
Tim Keefe	1889	38				Kent Tekulve	1979	31	Bert Cunningham	1898	362.0
Pud Galvin	1889	38				Lee Smith	1990	31	Three Finger Brown	1909	342.2
Togie Pittinger	1904	35				Roberto Hernandez	1997	31	Pud Galvin	1889	341.0

Strikeouts			ERA			Component ERA			Opponent Average		
			(minimum 1 Inning Pitched/Tm Gm)			(minimum 1 Inning Pitched/Tm Gm)			(minimum 1 Inning Pitched/Tm Gm)		
Bill Hutchison	1892	312	Bob Gibson	1968	1.12	Three Finger Brown	1909	1.42	Bob Gibson	1968	.184
Bobby Mathews	1884	286	Three Finger Brown	1909	1.31	Bob Gibson	1968	1.44	Three Finger Brown	1909	.202
Bob Gibson	1968	268	Ed Killian	1909	1.71	Pete Alexander	1919	1.56	Mike Cuellar	1969	.204
Mike Scott	1987	233	Pete Alexander	1919	1.72	Vic Willis	1908	1.82	Tom Seaver	1977	.209
Sam Jones	1958	225	Eddie Cicotte	1916	1.78	Eddie Plank	1908	1.91	Virgil Trucks	1949	.211
Nolan Ryan	1979	223	Dolf Luque	1923	1.93	Tully Sparks	1907	1.97	Bob Veale	1968	.211
Jim Bunning	1964	219	Christy Mathewson	1911	1.99	Eddie Cicotte	1916	1.99	Pete Alexander	1919	.211
Mickey Lolich	1973	214	Jack Taylor	1906	1.99	Bill Bernhard	1903	2.02	Bruce Dal Canton	1974	.211
Tim Keefe	1889	209	Tully Sparks	1907	2.00	Mike Cuellar	1969	2.02	Nolan Ryan	1979	.212
Whitey Ford	1961	209	Bob Veale	1968	2.05	Tom Hughes	1916	2.03	Jesse Duryea	1892	.212

Batting Leaders—Through Age 33

At-Bats		Runs		Hits		Doubles	
Robin Yount	8,907	Jimmie Foxx	1,678	Ty Cobb	2,857	Joe Medwick	524
Vada Pinson	8,454	Lou Gehrig	1,633	Rogers Hornsby	2,705	Stan Musial	509
Hank Aaron	8,283	Mel Ott	1,628	Hank Aaron	2,618	Tris Speaker	497
Mel Ott	8,154	Hank Aaron	1,519	Robin Yount	2,602	Rogers Hornsby	482
Cal Ripken Jr.	8,027	Mickey Mantle	1,517	Mel Ott	2,528	Robin Yount	481
Sam Crawford	7,951	Billy Hamilton	1,516	Jimmie Foxx	2,516	Ed Delahanty	468
Rusty Staub	7,794	Ty Cobb	1,501	Sam Crawford	2,485	Lou Gehrig	466
Ron Santo	7,768	Jesse Burkett	1,497	Willie Keeler	2,470	Joe Cronin	463
Ty Cobb	7,729	Hugh Duffy	1,495	Vada Pinson	2,453	Ty Cobb	460
Richie Ashburn	7,669	Willie Keeler	1,486	Stan Musial	2,418	Harry Heilmann	456

Triples		Home Runs		RBI		Stolen Bases	
Sam Crawford	251	Jimmie Foxx	519	Jimmie Foxx	1,848	Rickey Henderson	1,042
Ty Cobb	219	Hank Aaron	481	Lou Gehrig	1,721	Billy Hamilton	860
Jake Beckley	201	Eddie Mathews	477	Mel Ott	1,648	Ty Cobb	780
Joe Kelley	181	Mickey Mantle	473	Hank Aaron	1,541	Tim Raines	751
Tris Speaker	173	Babe Ruth	470	Al Simmons	1,458	Vince Coleman	740
Ed Delahanty	170	Willie Mays	453	Rogers Hornsby	1,419	Arlie Latham	629
Roger Connor	170	Frank Robinson	450	Babe Ruth	1,404	Willie Wilson	588
Joe Jackson	168	Harmon Killebrew	446	Frank Robinson	1,377	Eddie Collins	584
Rogers Hornsby	167	Mel Ott	445	Ed Delahanty	1,350	Max Carey	583
Sherry Magee	165	Lou Gehrig	427	Mickey Mantle	1,344	Lou Brock	565

Runs Created		Batting Average		On-Base Percentage		Slugging Percentage	
		(minimum 3,000 Plate Appearances)		(minimum 3,000 Plate Appearances)		(minimum 3,000 Plate Appearances)	
Jimmie Foxx	1,959	Ty Cobb	.370	Ted Williams	.483	Babe Ruth	.709
Mel Ott	1,869	Rogers Hornsby	.363	Babe Ruth	.478	Lou Gehrig	.643
Lou Gehrig	1,862	Willie Keeler	.359	John McGraw	.465	Ted Williams	.634
Ty Cobb	1,783	Joe Jackson	.356	Billy Hamilton	.459	Jimmie Foxx	.627
Rogers Hornsby	1,753	Jesse Burkett	.355	Frank Thomas	.452	Hank Greenberg	.622
Mickey Mantle	1,719	Billy Hamilton	.349	Lou Gehrig	.449	Frank Thomas	.600
Babe Ruth	1,717	Nap Lajoie	.348	Rogers Hornsby	.436	Willie Mays	.589
Stan Musial	1,667	Paul Waner	.348	Jimmie Foxx	.436	Joe DiMaggio	.589
Hank Aaron	1,657	Al Simmons	.347	Bill Joyce	.435	Johnny Mize	.587
Ed Delahanty	1,636	Ted Williams	.347	Wade Boggs	.435	Stan Musial	.584

Single Season Batting Leaders—Age 33

At-Bats			Runs			Hits			Doubles		
Felipe Alou	1968	662	Lou Gehrig	1936	167	Bill Terry	1930	254	Earl Webb	1931	67
Cecil Cooper	1983	661	Babe Ruth	1928	163	Rogers Hornsby	1929	229	George Burns	1926	64
Al Oliver	1980	656	Rogers Hornsby	1929	156	Charlie Gehringer	1936	227	Charlie Gehringer	1936	60
Pete Rose	1974	652	Charlie Gehringer	1936	144	Eddie Collins	1920	224	Paul Waner	1936	53
Al Bumbry	1980	645	Earle Combs	1932	143	Sam Thompson	1893	222	Tris Speaker	1921	52
Charlie Gehringer	1936	641	Harry Stovey	1890	142	Paul Waner	1936	218	Edgar Martinez	1996	52
Dick Groat	1964	636	Bill Terry	1930	139	George Burns	1926	216	Rogers Hornsby	1929	47
Bill Terry	1930	633	George Gore	1890	132	Felipe Alou	1968	210	George Kelly	1929	45
Dave Winfield	1985	633	Dom DiMaggio	1950	131	Al Oliver	1980	209	Pete Rose	1974	45
Ken Boyer	1964	628	Sam Thompson	1893	130	Bobby Veach	1921	207	3 tied with		43

Triples			Home Runs			RBI			Stolen Bases		
Sam Crawford	1913	23	Mark McGwire	1997	58	Joe DiMaggio	1948	155	Harry Stovey	1890	97
Dan Brouthers	1891	19	Babe Ruth	1928	54	Lou Gehrig	1936	152	Blondie Purcell	1887	88
Max Carey	1923	19	Lou Gehrig	1936	49	Rogers Hornsby	1929	149	Tom Brown	1894	66
Danny Murphy	1910	18	Harmon Killebrew	1969	49	Babe Ruth	1928	142	Lou Brock	1972	63
Sam Rice	1923	18	Willie Mays	1964	47	Harmon Killebrew	1969	140	Honus Wagner	1907	61
Jimmy Collins	1903	17	Frank Howard	1970	44	Ken Caminiti	1996	130	Arlie Latham	1893	57
Ed Delahanty	1901	16	Willie Stargell	1973	44	Bill Terry	1930	129	Ozzie Smith	1988	57
John Ganzel	1907	16	Mike Schmidt	1983	40	Bobby Veach	1921	128	Ned Hanlon	1891	54
Bill Hinchman	1916	16	Ken Caminiti	1996	40	4 tied with		126	Max Carey	1923	51
4 tied with		15	3 tied with		39				Brett Butler	1990	51

Runs Created			Batting Average			On-Base Percentage			Slugging Percentage		
			(minimum 3.1 PA/Tm Gm)			(minimum 3.1 PA/Tm Gm)			(minimum 3.1 PA/Tm Gm)		
Lou Gehrig	1936	181	Bill Terry	1930	.401	Lou Gehrig	1936	.478	Babe Ruth	1928	.709
Rogers Hornsby	1929	178	Lefty O'Doul	1930	.383	Dan Brouthers	1891	.471	Lou Gehrig	1936	.696
Babe Ruth	1928	165	Rogers Hornsby	1929	.380	Edgar Martinez	1996	.464	Rogers Hornsby	1929	.679
Bill Terry	1930	160	Paul Waner	1936	.373	Babe Ruth	1928	.461	Mark McGwire	1997	.646
Dan Brouthers	1891	152	Eddie Collins	1920	.372	Eddie Stanky	1950	.460	Willie Stargell	1973	.646
Sam Thompson	1893	149	Sam Thompson	1893	.370	Rogers Hornsby	1929	.459	Ken Williams	1923	.623
Charlie Gehringer	1936	149	Tris Speaker	1921	.362	Lefty O'Doul	1930	.453	Ken Caminiti	1996	.621
Stan Musial	1954	141	George Burns	1926	.358	Bill Terry	1930	.452	Bill Terry	1930	.619
Joe DiMaggio	1948	137	Tony Gwynn	1993	.358	Max Bishop	1933	.446	Stan Musial	1954	.607
2 tied with		136	Dixie Walker	1944	.357	Paul Waner	1936	.446	Willie Mays	1964	.607

Pitching Leaders—Through Age 33

Wins

Pud Galvin	336
Kid Nichols	329
John Clarkson	328
Walter Johnson	322
Christy Mathewson	312
Mickey Welch	309
Tim Keefe	308
Cy Young	286
Jim McCormick	265
Gus Weyhing	264

Losses

Pud Galvin	282
Gus Weyhing	231
Walter Johnson	215
Jim McCormick	214
Mickey Welch	211
Bob Friend	206
Jim Whitney	204
Adonis Terry	196
George Mullin	194
2 tied with	193

Winning Percentage
(minimum 170 decisions)

Lefty Grove	.712
Whitey Ford	.711
Dave Foutz	.701
Bob Caruthers	.688
Three Finger Brown	.684
Christy Mathewson	.681
Ron Guidry	.680
Pete Alexander	.673
Joe Wood	.671
Juan Marichal	.670

Games

Rollie Fingers	767
Lindy McDaniel	719
Lee Smith	717
Willie Hernandez	712
Mike Jackson	694
Sparky Lyle	680
Goose Gossage	680
Jeff Reardon	647
Pud Galvin	640
Dave Righetti	637

Complete Games

Pud Galvin	596
Mickey Welch	525
Tim Keefe	492
John Clarkson	485
Kid Nichols	475
Jim McCormick	466
Gus Weyhing	447
Walter Johnson	425
Tony Mullane	422
Cy Young	418

Shutouts

Walter Johnson	91
Pete Alexander	77
Christy Mathewson	68
Ed Walsh	56
Pud Galvin	54
Jim Palmer	51
Juan Marichal	50
Rube Waddell	50
3 tied with	49

Saves

Lee Smith	312
Bruce Sutter	286
Randy Myers	274
Jeff Reardon	266
John Franco	266
Goose Gossage	257
Dave Righetti	251
Rollie Fingers	244
Dan Quisenberry	229
Jeff Montgomery	218

Innings Pitched

Pud Galvin	5,506.2
Mickey Welch	4,802.0
Kid Nichols	4,538.0
John Clarkson	4,536.1
Walter Johnson	4,498.1
Tim Keefe	4,427.2
Gus Weyhing	4,304.0
Jim McCormick	4,275.2
Cy Young	4,043.0
Tony Mullane	4,008.2

Strikeouts

Nolan Ryan	3,109
Walter Johnson	2,835
Tom Seaver	2,756
Bert Blyleven	2,669
Roger Clemens	2,590
Mickey Lolich	2,540
Don Drysdale	2,486
Steve Carlton	2,470
Sam McDowell	2,453
Fergie Jenkins	2,449

ERA
(minimum 950 Innings Pitched)

Three Finger Brown	1.66
Walter Johnson	1.80
Ed Walsh	1.81
Addie Joss	1.89
Jim Devlin	1.89
Christy Mathewson	1.98
Jack Pfiester	2.02
Joe Wood	2.03
Pete Alexander	2.06
Monte Ward	2.10

Component ERA
(minimum 950 Innings Pitched)

Addie Joss	1.73
Ed Walsh	1.77
Three Finger Brown	1.81
Walter Johnson	1.83
Monte Ward	2.01
Christy Mathewson	2.06
Joe Wood	2.10
Tim Keefe	2.11
Pete Alexander	2.12
Jack Pfiester	2.14

Opponent Average
(minimum 950 Innings Pitched)

Nolan Ryan	.202
Sandy Koufax	.205
Sid Fernandez	.209
Randy Johnson	.211
J.R. Richard	.212
Andy Messersmith	.212
Sam McDowell	.215
Tom Seaver	.217
Walter Johnson	.217
Ed Walsh	.218

Single Season Pitching Leaders—Age 33

Wins

Joe McGinnity	1904	35
Bobby Mathews	1885	30
Bob Barr	1890	28
Eddie Cicotte	1917	28
Dazzy Vance	1924	28
Al Orth	1906	27
Pete Alexander	1920	27
Bob Welch	1990	27
General Crowder	1932	26
Carl Hubbell	1936	26

Losses

Ben Cantwell	1935	25
Bob Barr	1890	24
Bill Hutchison	1893	24
Chick Fraser	1904	24
Sam Gray	1931	24
Roger Craig	1963	22
Ed Cushman	1885	21
Mickey Lolich	1974	21
3 tied with		20

Winning Percentage
(minimum 15 decisions)

Sandy Consuegra	1954	.842
Randy Johnson	1997	.833
Dazzy Vance	1924	.824
Sal Maglie	1950	.818
Bob Welch	1990	.818
Joe McGinnity	1904	.814
Carl Hubbell	1936	.813
Jamie Moyer	1996	.813
Jimmy Key	1994	.810
Sam Leever	1905	.800

Games

Dick Tidrow	1980	84
Kent Tekulve	1980	78
Ron Perranoski	1969	75
Doug Henry	1997	75
Jim Konstanty	1950	74
Ron Kline	1965	74
Rob Murphy	1993	73
Juan Agosto	1991	72
Norm Charlton	1996	70
5 tied with		68

Complete Games

Bob Barr	1890	52
Bobby Mathews	1885	46
Bill Hutchison	1893	38
Joe McGinnity	1904	38
Al Orth	1906	36
Bill Bernhard	1904	35
Bert Cunningham	1899	33
Cy Falkenberg	1914	33
Pete Alexander	1920	33
3 tied with		32

Shutouts

Joe McGinnity	1904	9
Cy Falkenberg	1914	9
Three Finger Brown	1910	7
Eddie Cicotte	1917	7
Pete Alexander	1920	7
Whit Wyatt	1941	7
Harry Brecheen	1948	7
Ray Herbert	1963	7
Jim Bunning	1965	7
Luis Tiant	1974	7

Saves

Lee Smith	1991	47
Dennis Eckersley	1988	45
Doug Jones	1990	43
Tom Henke	1991	32
Rick Aguilera	1995	32
Ron Perranoski	1969	31
Jeff Reardon	1989	31
Jeff Montgomery	1995	31
Randy Myers	1996	31
John Franco	1994	30

Innings Pitched

Bob Barr	1890	493.1
Bobby Mathews	1885	422.1
Joe McGinnity	1904	408.0
Cy Falkenberg	1914	377.1
Pete Alexander	1920	363.1
Red Faber	1922	353.0
Bill Hutchison	1893	348.1
Eddie Cicotte	1917	346.2
Gaylord Perry	1972	342.2
Al Orth	1906	338.2

Strikeouts

Randy Johnson	1997	291
Bobby Mathews	1885	286
Bob Gibson	1969	269
Jim Bunning	1965	268
Dazzy Vance	1924	262
Roger Clemens	1996	257
Cy Falkenberg	1914	236
Gaylord Perry	1972	234
Tom Seaver	1978	226
Jeff Fassero	1996	222

ERA
(minimum 1 Inning Pitched/Tm Gm)

Eddie Cicotte	1917	1.53
Joe McGinnity	1904	1.61
Eddie Plank	1909	1.76
Three Finger Brown	1910	1.86
Pete Alexander	1920	1.91
Gaylord Perry	1972	1.92
Jack Powell	1908	2.11
Christy Mathewson	1912	2.12
Bill Bernhard	1904	2.13
Dazzy Vance	1924	2.16

Component ERA
(minimum 1 Inning Pitched/Tm Gm)

Eddie Cicotte	1917	1.48
Joe McGinnity	1904	1.71
Jack Powell	1908	1.82
Deacon Phillippe	1905	1.93
Gaylord Perry	1972	1.93
Eddie Plank	1909	1.95
Slim Sallee	1918	2.01
Harry Brecheen	1948	2.01
Dazzy Vance	1924	2.02
Frank Miller	1919	2.06

Opponent Average
(minimum 1 Inning Pitched/Tm Gm)

Randy Johnson	1997	.194
Tony Mullane	1892	.201
Eddie Cicotte	1917	.202
Mike Scott	1988	.204
Gaylord Perry	1972	.205
Joe McGinnity	1904	.208
Whit Wyatt	1941	.212
Dazzy Vance	1924	.213
George Brunet	1968	.215
Vic Raschi	1952	.216

Batting Leaders—Through Age 34

At-Bats		Runs		Hits		Doubles	
Robin Yount	9,494	Lou Gehrig	1,771	Ty Cobb	3,054	Tris Speaker	545
Vada Pinson	8,920	Jimmie Foxx	1,721	Hank Aaron	2,792	Stan Musial	539
Hank Aaron	8,889	Mel Ott	1,693	Robin Yount	2,747	Joe Medwick	528
Cal Ripken Jr.	8,577	Ty Cobb	1,625	Rogers Hornsby	2,737	Ed Delahanty	511
Mel Ott	8,534	Billy Hamilton	1,619	Sam Crawford	2,668	Lou Gehrig	503
Sam Crawford	8,533	Hank Aaron	1,603	Willie Keeler	2,650	Joe Cronin	501
Rusty Staub	8,436	Rickey Henderson	1,586	Mel Ott	2,617	Robin Yount	498
Brooks Robinson	8,249	Willie Keeler	1,582	Stan Musial	2,597	Harry Heilmann	497
Ty Cobb	8,236	Ed Delahanty	1,577	Jimmie Foxx	2,585	Ty Cobb	497
Pete Rose	8,221	Jesse Burkett	1,570	Tris Speaker	2,576	Rogers Hornsby	487

Triples		Home Runs		RBI		Stolen Bases	
Sam Crawford	277	Jimmie Foxx	527	Jimmie Foxx	1,881	Rickey Henderson	1,095
Ty Cobb	235	Babe Ruth	516	Lou Gehrig	1,880	Billy Hamilton	892
Jake Beckley	208	Hank Aaron	510	Mel Ott	1,695	Ty Cobb	802
Joe Kelley	192	Willie Mays	505	Hank Aaron	1,627	Tim Raines	764
Ed Delahanty	184	Mickey Mantle	496	Al Simmons	1,570	Vince Coleman	752
Tris Speaker	181	Eddie Mathews	493	Babe Ruth	1,558	Arlie Latham	688
Roger Connor	181	Harmon Killebrew	487	Frank Robinson	1,455	Lou Brock	635
Paul Waner	173	Frank Robinson	475	Ed Delahanty	1,443	Max Carey	632
Ed Konetchy	172	Lou Gehrig	464	Harry Heilmann	1,442	Willie Wilson	612
Fred Clarke	172	Mel Ott	463	Goose Goslin	1,441	Tom Brown	601

Runs Created		Batting Average (minimum 3,000 Plate Appearances)		On-Base Percentage (minimum 3,000 Plate Appearances)		Slugging Percentage (minimum 3,000 Plate Appearances)	
Lou Gehrig	2,029	Ty Cobb	.371	Ted Williams	.484	Babe Ruth	.708
Jimmie Foxx	1,992	Rogers Hornsby	.362	Babe Ruth	.474	Lou Gehrig	.643
Mel Ott	1,940	Joe Jackson	.356	John McGraw	.465	Ted Williams	.638
Ty Cobb	1,903	Willie Keeler	.355	Billy Hamilton	.458	Hank Greenberg	.617
Babe Ruth	1,855	Jesse Burkett	.350	Frank Thomas	.452	Jimmie Foxx	.616
Mickey Mantle	1,788	Paul Waner	.348	Lou Gehrig	.451	Frank Thomas	.600
Stan Musial	1,787	Ted Williams	.348	Rogers Hornsby	.436	Willie Mays	.593
Rogers Hornsby	1,770	Billy Hamilton	.348	Bill Joyce	.435	Johnny Mize	.590
Ed Delahanty	1,766	Nap Lajoie	.346	Ty Cobb	.434	Joe DiMaggio	.589
Hank Aaron	1,752	Babe Ruth	.346	Jimmie Foxx	.431	Stan Musial	.583

Single Season Batting Leaders—Age 34

At-Bats			Runs			Hits			Doubles		
Paul Molitor	1991	665	Lou Gehrig	1937	138	Earl Averill	1936	232	George Burns	1927	51
Pete Rose	1975	662	Johnny Mize	1947	137	Paul Waner	1937	219	Riggs Stephenson	1932	49
Doc Cramer	1940	661	Earl Averill	1936	136	Sam Rice	1924	216	Tris Speaker	1922	48
Lou Brock	1973	650	Charlie Gehringer	1937	133	Paul Molitor	1991	216	Pete Rose	1975	47
Red Schoendienst	1957	648	Paul Molitor	1991	133	Bill Terry	1931	213	Del Pratt	1922	44
Sam Rice	1924	646	Arlie Latham	1894	129	Pete Rose	1975	210	Ed Delahanty	1902	43
Rusty Staub	1978	642	Ty Cobb	1921	124	Charlie Gehringer	1937	209	Bill Terry	1931	43
Dom DiMaggio	1951	639	Roger Connor	1892	123	Bobby Veach	1922	202	Dixie Walker	1945	42
Ivy Olson	1920	637	Hardy Richardson	1889	122	4 tied with		201	Dave Parker	1985	42
Dave Parker	1985	635	3 tied with		121				Paul O'Neill	1997	42

Triples			Home Runs			RBI			Stolen Bases		
Sam Thompson	1894	27	Willie Mays	1965	52	Lou Gehrig	1937	159	Lou Brock	1973	70
Sam Crawford	1914	26	Johnny Mize	1947	51	Babe Ruth	1929	154	Arlie Latham	1894	59
Harry Stovey	1891	20	Babe Ruth	1929	46	Cap Anson	1886	147	Harry Stovey	1891	57
Dan Brouthers	1892	20	Harmon Killebrew	1970	41	Sam Thompson	1894	141	Bert Campaneris	1976	54
Bill Terry	1931	20	Reggie Jackson	1980	41	Johnny Mize	1947	138	Honus Wagner	1908	53
Honus Wagner	1908	19	Tilly Walker	1922	37	Bobby Veach	1922	126	Rickey Henderson	1993	53
Charley Jones	1884	17	Lou Gehrig	1937	37	Earl Averill	1936	126	Dummy Hoy	1896	50
Jimmy Ryan	1897	17	Billy Williams	1972	37	Dave Parker	1985	125	Max Carey	1924	49
4 tied with		16	Mike Schmidt	1984	36	Dan Brouthers	1892	124	Dave Foutz	1891	48
			Terry Steinbach	1996	35	Dixie Walker	1945	124	3 tied with		47

Runs Created			Batting Average (minimum 3.1 PA/Tm Gm)			On-Base Percentage (minimum 3.1 PA/Tm Gm)			Slugging Percentage (minimum 3.1 PA/Tm Gm)		
Lou Gehrig	1937	167	Sam Thompson	1894	.407	Tris Speaker	1922	.474	Babe Ruth	1929	.697
Cap Anson	1886	152	Tony Gwynn	1994	.394	Lou Gehrig	1937	.473	Sam Thompson	1894	.686
Earl Averill	1936	150	Ty Cobb	1921	.389	Sam Thompson	1894	.458	Willie Mays	1965	.645
Dan Brouthers	1892	149	Tris Speaker	1922	.378	Charlie Gehringer	1937	.458	Lou Gehrig	1937	.643
Charley Jones	1884	142	Earl Averill	1936	.378	Edgar Martinez	1997	.456	Earl Averill	1936	.627
Willie Mays	1965	139	Ed Delahanty	1902	.376	Buddy Myer	1938	.454	Johnny Mize	1947	.614
Babe Ruth	1929	138	Cap Anson	1886	.371	Tony Gwynn	1994	.454	Billy Williams	1972	.606
Johnny Mize	1947	138	Charlie Gehringer	1937	.371	Ed Delahanty	1902	.453	Tris Speaker	1922	.606
Sam Thompson	1894	137	Honus Wagner	1908	.354	Ty Cobb	1921	.452	Reggie Jackson	1980	.597
Roger Connor	1892	135	Paul Waner	1937	.354	Billy Hamilton	1900	.449	Ty Cobb	1921	.596

Pitching Leaders—Through Age 34

Wins

Kid Nichols	350
Pud Galvin	350
Walter Johnson	337
Christy Mathewson	337
John Clarkson	328
Cy Young	319
Tim Keefe	312
Mickey Welch	309
Tony Mullane	277
Old Hoss Radbourn	271

Losses

Pud Galvin	296
Gus Weyhing	232
Walter Johnson	231
Bob Friend	218
Jim McCormick	214
Mickey Welch	211
Jack Powell	209
Tony Mullane	209
Vic Willis	205
Jim Whitney	204

Winning Percentage
(minimum 180 decisions)

Whitey Ford	.718
Lefty Grove	.700
Dave Foutz	.698
on Guidry	.694
Bob Caruthers	.688
Christy Mathewson	.682
Three Finger Brown	.681
Larry Corcoran	.665
Pete Alexander	.663
Sam Leever	.661

Games

Rollie Fingers	814
Lee Smith	787
Lindy McDaniel	781
Sparky Lyle	747
Willie Hernandez	744
Goose Gossage	725
Jeff Reardon	694
Mike Jackson	694
Dave Righetti	688
Roger McDowell	682

Complete Games

Pud Galvin	619
Mickey Welch	525
Kid Nichols	510
Tim Keefe	505
John Clarkson	485
Jim McCormick	466
Cy Young	456
Tony Mullane	456
Walter Johnson	448
Gus Weyhing	448

Shutouts

Walter Johnson	95
Pete Alexander	80
Christy Mathewson	72
Ed Walsh	57
Pud Galvin	56
Tom Seaver	52
Bert Blyleven	51
Jim Palmer	51
4 tied with	50

Saves

Lee Smith	355
Randy Myers	319
John Franco	295
Jeff Reardon	287
Bruce Sutter	286
Goose Gossage	278
Rollie Fingers	272
Dave Righetti	252
Jeff Montgomery	242
Dan Quisenberry	237

Innings Pitched

Pud Galvin	5,753.1
Kid Nichols	4,855.0
Mickey Welch	4,802.0
Walter Johnson	4,778.1
Tim Keefe	4,561.0
John Clarkson	4,536.1
Cy Young	4,414.1
Tony Mullane	4,375.2
Gus Weyhing	4,324.1
Jim McCormick	4,275.2

Strikeouts

Nolan Ryan	3,249
Walter Johnson	2,940
Tom Seaver	2,887
Roger Clemens	2,882
Bert Blyleven	2,875
Steve Carlton	2,683
Mickey Lolich	2,679
Fergie Jenkins	2,606
Don Sutton	2,524
Don Drysdale	2,486

ERA
(minimum 1,000 Innings Pitched)

Three Finger Brown	1.79
Ed Walsh	1.80
Walter Johnson	1.87
Addie Joss	1.89
Jim Devlin	1.89
Christy Mathewson	1.99
Jack Pfiester	2.02
Joe Wood	2.03
Monte Ward	2.10
Rube Waddell	2.16

Component ERA
(minimum 1,000 Innings Pitched)

Addie Joss	1.73
Ed Walsh	1.76
Walter Johnson	1.91
Three Finger Brown	1.92
Monte Ward	2.01
Christy Mathewson	2.06
Joe Wood	2.10
Jack Pfiester	2.14
Jim Devlin	2.14
Reb Russell	2.14

Opponent Average
(minimum 1,000 Innings Pitched)

Nolan Ryan	.201
Sandy Koufax	.205
Sid Fernandez	.209
Randy Johnson	.211
J.R. Richard	.212
Andy Messersmith	.212
Sam McDowell	.215
Ed Walsh	.217
Tom Seaver	.219
Dave Boswell	.219

Single Season Pitching Leaders—Age 34

Wins

Cy Young	1901	33
Christy Mathewson	1913	25
Burleigh Grimes	1928	25
General Crowder	1933	24
Whitey Ford	1963	24
Jim Perry	1970	24
Ellis Kinder	1949	23
Sal Maglie	1951	23
Early Wynn	1954	23
Bob Gibson	1970	23

Losses

Tony Mullane	1893	22
Kaiser Wilhelm	1908	22
Chick Fraser	1905	21
Al Orth	1907	21
Larry Jackson	1965	21
Ed Cushman	1886	20
Jack Chesbro	1908	20
Milt Gaston	1930	20
Jerry Koosman	1977	20
4 tied with		19

Winning Percentage
(minimum 15 decisions)

Ellis Kinder	1949	.793
Sal Maglie	1951	.793
Red Lucas	1936	.789
Larry French	1942	.789
Ron Guidry	1985	.786
Whitey Ford	1963	.774
Jamie Moyer	1997	.773
Cy Young	1901	.767
Bob Gibson	1970	.767
Spud Chandler	1942	.762

Games

Bill Campbell	1983	82
Mudcat Grant	1970	80
Dan Plesac	1996	73
Norm Charlton	1997	71
Rich Rodriguez	1997	71
Don McMahon	1964	70
Ted Abernathy	1967	70
Lee Smith	1992	70
Gene Garber	1982	69
Roger Mason	1993	68

Complete Games

Cy Young	1901	38
Ed Cushman	1886	37
Kid Nichols	1904	35
Chick Fraser	1905	35
Tony Mullane	1893	34
Kaiser Wilhelm	1908	33
Bob Ewing	1907	32
Thornton Lee	1941	30
George Bell	1909	29
Gaylord Perry	1973	29

Shutouts

Gaylord Perry	1973	7
Sam Leever	1906	6
Kaiser Wilhelm	1908	6
George Bell	1909	6
Ellis Kinder	1949	6
Ken Raffensberger	1952	6
Curt Simmons	1963	6
11 tied with		5

Saves

Randy Myers	1997	45
Lee Smith	1992	43
Ron Perranoski	1970	34
Tom Henke	1992	34
Dennis Eckersley	1989	33
Mike Henneman	1996	31
Gene Garber	1982	30
Luis Arroyo	1961	29
Lindy McDaniel	1970	29
John Franco	1995	29

Innings Pitched

Cy Young	1901	371.1
Tony Mullane	1893	367.0
Gaylord Perry	1973	344.0
Chick Fraser	1905	334.1
Bob Ewing	1907	332.2
Kaiser Wilhelm	1908	332.0
Burleigh Grimes	1928	330.2
Ed Cushman	1886	325.2
Joe McGinnity	1905	320.1
Kid Nichols	1904	317.0

Strikeouts

Roger Clemens	1997	292
Bob Gibson	1970	274
Jim Bunning	1966	252
Gaylord Perry	1973	238
David Cone	1997	222
Dazzy Vance	1925	221
Steve Carlton	1979	213
Bert Blyleven	1985	206
Jerry Koosman	1977	192
Sam Jones	1960	190

ERA
(minimum 1 Inning Pitched/Tm Gm)

Cy Young	1901	1.62
Nolan Ryan	1981	1.69
Bob Ewing	1907	1.73
Kaiser Wilhelm	1908	1.87
Eddie Plank	1910	2.01
Kid Nichols	1904	2.02
Al Benton	1945	2.02
Roger Clemens	1997	2.05
Slim Sallee	1919	2.06
Christy Mathewson	1913	2.06

Component ERA
(minimum 1 Inning Pitched/Tm Gm)

Kid Nichols	1904	1.83
Cy Young	1901	1.87
Roger Wolff	1945	1.87
Kaiser Wilhelm	1908	1.89
Nolan Ryan	1981	2.02
Bob Ewing	1907	2.15
Christy Mathewson	1913	2.16
Roger Clemens	1997	2.17
Sam Leever	1906	2.23
Eddie Plank	1910	2.25

Opponent Average
(minimum 1 Inning Pitched/Tm Gm)

Nolan Ryan	1981	.188
Mike Scott	1989	.212
Roger Clemens	1997	.213
Roger Wolff	1945	.215
Kaiser Wilhelm	1908	.217
David Cone	1997	.218
Steve Carlton	1979	.219
Ed Cushman	1886	.220
Jim Bunning	1966	.223
Mike Krukow	1986	.223

Batting Leaders—Through Age 35

At-Bats		Runs		Hits		Doubles	
Robin Yount	9,997	Lou Gehrig	1,886	Ty Cobb	3,265	Tris Speaker	604
Hank Aaron	9,436	Mel Ott	1,784	Hank Aaron	2,956	Stan Musial	572
Vada Pinson	9,326	Ty Cobb	1,724	Robin Yount	2,878	Joe Medwick	540
Cal Ripken Jr.	9,217	Jimmie Foxx	1,721	Rogers Hornsby	2,855	Harry Heilmann	540
Sam Crawford	9,145	Babe Ruth	1,717	Sam Crawford	2,851	Ty Cobb	539
Mel Ott	8,933	Hank Aaron	1,703	Tris Speaker	2,794	Lou Gehrig	535
Pete Rose	8,886	Billy Hamilton	1,690	Stan Musial	2,781	Nap Lajoie	526
Brooks Robinson	8,805	Rickey Henderson	1,652	Pete Rose	2,762	Rogers Hornsby	524
Rusty Staub	8,768	Jesse Burkett	1,642	Willie Keeler	2,749	Ed Delahanty	522
Ty Cobb	8,762	Willie Keeler	1,632	Mel Ott	2,732	Robin Yount	518

Triples		Home Runs		RBI		Stolen Bases	
Sam Crawford	296	Babe Ruth	565	Lou Gehrig	1,994	Rickey Henderson	1,117
Ty Cobb	251	Hank Aaron	554	Jimmie Foxx	1,881	Billy Hamilton	912
Jake Beckley	218	Willie Mays	542	Mel Ott	1,777	Ty Cobb	811
Tris Speaker	192	Jimmie Foxx	527	Hank Aaron	1,724	Tim Raines	777
Joe Kelley	192	Mickey Mantle	518	Babe Ruth	1,711	Lou Brock	753
Roger Connor	189	Harmon Killebrew	515	Al Simmons	1,654	Vince Coleman	752
Fred Clarke	187	Eddie Mathews	509	Goose Goslin	1,566	Arlie Latham	736
Ed Delahanty	185	Frank Robinson	503	Frank Robinson	1,554	Max Carey	678
Ed Konetchy	181	Lou Gehrig	493	Harry Heilmann	1,533	Willie Wilson	632
Paul Waner	179	Mel Ott	489	Rogers Hornsby	1,527	Tom Brown	629

Runs Created		Batting Average		On-Base Percentage		Slugging Percentage	
		(minimum 3,000 Plate Appearances)		(minimum 3,000 Plate Appearances)		(minimum 3,000 Plate Appearances)	
Lou Gehrig	2,160	Ty Cobb	.373	Ted Williams	.486	Babe Ruth	.710
Mel Ott	2,037	Lefty O'Doul	.361	Babe Ruth	.476	Ted Williams	.638
Babe Ruth	2,031	Rogers Hornsby	.361	John McGraw	.465	Lou Gehrig	.634
Ty Cobb	2,024	Joe Jackson	.356	Billy Hamilton	.455	Jimmie Foxx	.616
Jimmie Foxx	1,992	Nap Lajoie	.350	Frank Thomas	.452	Hank Greenberg	.616
Stan Musial	1,896	Tris Speaker	.348	Lou Gehrig	.448	Frank Thomas	.600
Hank Aaron	1,880	Willie Keeler	.348	Ty Cobb	.436	Willie Mays	.591
Mickey Mantle	1,870	Ted Williams	.348	Rogers Hornsby	.435	Joe DiMaggio	.589
Rogers Hornsby	1,851	Babe Ruth	.347	Bill Joyce	.435	Johnny Mize	.588
Ed Delahanty	1,793	Ed Delahanty	.346	Jimmie Foxx	.431	Rogers Hornsby	.581

Single Season Batting Leaders—Age 35

At-Bats			Runs			Hits			Doubles		
Bill Buckner	1985	673	Babe Ruth	1930	150	Nap Lajoie	1910	227	Tris Speaker	1923	59
Pete Rose	1976	665	Tommy Henrich	1948	138	Sam Rice	1925	227	Nap Lajoie	1910	51
Doc Cramer	1941	660	Tris Speaker	1923	133	Bill Terry	1932	225	Baby Doll Jacobson	1926	51
Ivy Olson	1921	652	Charlie Gehringer	1938	133	Lefty O'Doul	1932	219	Bill Buckner	1985	46
Sam Rice	1925	649	Sam Thompson	1895	131	Tris Speaker	1923	218	Sam Thompson	1895	45
Bill Terry	1932	643	Pete Rose	1976	130	Pete Rose	1976	215	Harry Heilmann	1930	43
Cal Ripken Jr.	1996	640	Bill Terry	1932	124	Sam Thompson	1895	211	Mickey Vernon	1953	43
Dave Parker	1986	637	Jimmy Ryan	1898	122	Ty Cobb	1922	211	Al Oliver	1982	43
Lou Brock	1974	635	Goose Goslin	1936	122	Mickey Vernon	1953	205	6 tied with		42
Cecil Cooper	1985	631				Al Oliver	1982	204			

Triples			Home Runs			RBI			Stolen Bases		
Sam Thompson	1895	21	Babe Ruth	1930	49	Sam Thompson	1895	165	Lou Brock	1974	118
Sam Crawford	1915	19	Andres Galarraga	1996	47	Babe Ruth	1930	153	Maury Wills	1968	52
Charley Jones	1885	17	Hank Greenberg	1946	44	Andres Galarraga	1996	150	Ed Cartwright	1895	50
Sam Wise	1893	17	Hank Aaron	1969	44	Hardy Richardson	1890	146	Arlie Latham	1895	48
Ed Cartwright	1895	17	Cy Williams	1923	41	Tris Speaker	1923	130	Paul Hines	1887	46
Ty Cobb	1922	16	Johnny Mize	1948	40	Jack Fournier	1925	130	Max Carey	1925	46
Jack Fournier	1925	16	Hank Sauer	1952	37	Hank Greenberg	1946	127	Patsy Donovan	1900	45
Fred Clarke	1908	15	Willie Mays	1966	37	Goose Goslin	1936	125	Hardy Richardson	1890	42
3 tied with		14	Dave Kingman	1984	35	Johnny Mize	1948	125	Otis Nixon	1994	42
			Dwight Evans	1987	34	Dwight Evans	1987	123	Brett Butler	1992	41

Runs Created			Batting Average			On-Base Percentage			Slugging Percentage		
			(minimum 3.1 PA/Tm Gm)			(minimum 3.1 PA/Tm Gm)			(minimum 3.1 PA/Tm Gm)		
Babe Ruth	1930	176	Ty Cobb	1922	.401	Ted Williams	1954	.513	Babe Ruth	1930	.732
Sam Thompson	1895	154	Sam Thompson	1895	.392	Babe Ruth	1930	.493	Sam Thompson	1895	.654
Tris Speaker	1923	154	Nap Lajoie	1910	.384	Tris Speaker	1923	.469	Ted Williams	1954	.635
Andres Galarraga	1996	150	Tris Speaker	1923	.380	Ty Cobb	1922	.462	Tris Speaker	1923	.610
Bill Terry	1932	137	Tony Gwynn	1995	.368	Augie Galan	1947	.449	Hank Aaron	1969	.607
Nap Lajoie	1910	135	Lefty O'Doul	1932	.368	Jack Fournier	1925	.446	Hank Greenberg	1946	.604
Hardy Richardson	1890	133	Babe Ruth	1930	.359	Nap Lajoie	1910	.445	Andres Galarraga	1996	.601
Johnny Mize	1948	133	Joe Start	1878	.351	George Harper	1927	.435	Joe DiMaggio	1950	.585
Jimmy Ryan	1898	131	Jack Fournier	1925	.350	Sam Thompson	1895	.430	Bill Terry	1932	.580
Lou Gehrig	1938	131	Bill Terry	1932	.350	Chili Davis	1995	.429	Harry Heilmann	1930	.577

Pitching Leaders—Through Age 35

Wins		Losses		Winning Percentage		Games	
				(minimum 190 decisions)			
Christy Mathewson	361	Pud Galvin	308	Whitey Ford	.720	Rollie Fingers	864
Kid Nichols	361	Walter Johnson	243	Lefty Grove	.693	Lee Smith	850
Pud Galvin	360	Gus Weyhing	232	Dave Foutz	.690	Lindy McDaniel	825
Walter Johnson	354	Bob Friend	230	Bob Caruthers	.688	Sparky Lyle	806
Cy Young	351	Jack Powell	220	Christy Mathewson	.680	Goose Gossage	765
Tim Keefe	331	Tony Mullane	220	Three Finger Brown	.672	Jeff Reardon	751
John Clarkson	328	Tim Keefe	218	Ron Guidry	.671	Willie Hernandez	744
Mickey Welch	309	Jim McCormick	214	Larry Corcoran	.665	Roger McDowell	723
Old Hoss Radbourn	298	Mickey Welch	211	Sam Leever	.656	John Franco	712
Tony Mullane	284	Robin Roberts	208	Pete Alexander	.655	Dave Righetti	708

Complete Games		Shutouts		Saves		Innings Pitched	
Pud Galvin	639	Walter Johnson	98	Lee Smith	401	Pud Galvin	5,941.1
Tim Keefe	536	Pete Alexander	81	Jeff Reardon	327	Kid Nichols	5,045.1
Kid Nichols	530	Christy Mathewson	77	John Franco	323	Walter Johnson	5,039.2
Mickey Welch	525	Ed Walsh	57	Randy Myers	319	Tim Keefe	4,874.1
Cy Young	497	Pud Galvin	56	Rollie Fingers	301	Mickey Welch	4,802.0
John Clarkson	485	Bert Blyleven	54	Bruce Sutter	300	Cy Young	4,799.0
Tony Mullane	468	Tom Seaver	53	Goose Gossage	289	John Clarkson	4,536.1
Walter Johnson	466	Don Sutton	52	Tom Henke	260	Tony Mullane	4,531.1
Old Hoss Radbourn	466	Juan Marichal	52	Jeff Montgomery	256	Christy Mathewson	4,520.0
Jim McCormick	466	Jim Palmer	51	Dave Righetti	252	Gus Weyhing	4,324.1

Strikeouts		ERA		Component ERA		Opponent Average	
		(minimum 1,050 Innings Pitched)		(minimum 1,050 Innings Pitched)		(minimum 1,050 Innings Pitched)	
Nolan Ryan	3,494	Ed Walsh	1.80	Addie Joss	1.73	Nolan Ryan	.202
Bert Blyleven	3,090	Three Finger Brown	1.82	Ed Walsh	1.77	Sandy Koufax	.205
Walter Johnson	3,070	Addie Joss	1.89	Three Finger Brown	1.96	Sid Fernandez	.209
Tom Seaver	2,988	Jim Devlin	1.89	Walter Johnson	1.99	Randy Johnson	.211
Steve Carlton	2,969	Walter Johnson	1.96	Monte Ward	2.01	J.R. Richard	.212
Roger Clemens	2,882	Jack Pfiester	2.02	Joe Wood	2.10	Andy Messersmith	.212
Mickey Lolich	2,799	Joe Wood	2.03	Christy Mathewson	2.10	Sam McDowell	.215
Fergie Jenkins	2,770	Christy Mathewson	2.06	Jack Pfiester	2.14	Ed Walsh	.218
Don Sutton	2,652	Monte Ward	2.10	Jim Devlin	2.14	Tom Seaver	.219
Bob Gibson	2,578	Rube Waddell	2.16	Reb Russell	2.14	Dave Boswell	.219

Single Season Pitching Leaders—Age 35

Wins			Losses			Winning Percentage			Games		
						(minimum 15 decisions)					
Cy Young	1902	32	George Bell	1910	27	Spud Chandler	1943	.833	Kent Tekulve	1982	85
Eddie Cicotte	1919	29	Stoney McGlynn	1907	25	Bob Feller	1954	.813	Doug Jones	1992	80
Old Hoss Radbourn	1890	27	Bill Hutchison	1895	21	Eddie Cicotte	1919	.806	Ted Abernathy	1968	78
Joe McGinnity	1906	27	Walt Dickson	1914	21	Stan Coveleski	1925	.800	Gary Lavelle	1984	77
Christy Mathewson	1914	24	Jack Scott	1927	21	Ed Lopat	1953	.800	Dan Plesac	1997	73
Steve Carlton	1980	24	Murry Dickson	1952	21	Tommy Byrne	1955	.762	Billy Taylor	1997	72
Eddie Plank	1911	23	Chick Fraser	1906	20	Jim Bibby	1980	.760	Stu Miller	1963	71
Bucky Walters	1944	23	Si Johnson	1942	19	Firpo Marberry	1934	.750	Aurelio Lopez	1984	71
Curt Davis	1939	22	Virgil Trucks	1952	19	Red Ruffing	1939	.750	Tony Fossas	1993	71
4 tied with		21	3 tied with		18	Rudy May	1980	.750	2 tied with		66

Complete Games			Shutouts			Saves			Innings Pitched		
Cy Young	1902	41	Whitey Ford	1964	8	Dennis Eckersley	1990	48	Cy Young	1902	384.2
Old Hoss Radbourn	1890	36	Eddie Plank	1911	6	Lee Smith	1993	46	Stoney McGlynn	1907	352.1
Stoney McGlynn	1907	33	Bucky Walters	1944	6	Jeff Reardon	1991	40	Old Hoss Radbourn	1890	343.0
Joe McGinnity	1906	32	Early Wynn	1955	6	Tom Henke	1993	40	Joe McGinnity	1906	339.2
Tim Keefe	1892	31	Jim Bunning	1967	6	Doug Jones	1992	36	Gaylord Perry	1974	322.1
Bill Hutchison	1895	30	Phil Niekro	1974	6	Todd Worrell	1995	32	Tim Keefe	1892	313.1
Eddie Cicotte	1919	30	10 tied with		5	Steve Farr	1992	30	Christy Mathewson	1914	312.0
Christy Mathewson	1914	29				Rollie Fingers	1982	29	George Bell	1910	310.0
Gaylord Perry	1974	28				John Franco	1996	28	Eddie Cicotte	1919	306.2
Bucky Walters	1944	27				Stu Miller	1963	27	Steve Carlton	1980	304.0

Strikeouts			ERA			Component ERA			Opponent Average		
			(minimum 1 Inning Pitched/Tm Gm)			(minimum 1 Inning Pitched/Tm Gm)			(minimum 1 Inning Pitched/Tm Gm)		
Steve Carlton	1980	286	Spud Chandler	1943	1.64	Whit Wyatt	1943	1.81	Gaylord Perry	1974	.204
Jim Bunning	1967	253	Sam Leever	1907	1.66	Spud Chandler	1943	1.82	Whit Wyatt	1943	.207
Nolan Ryan	1982	245	Eddie Cicotte	1919	1.82	Eddie Cicotte	1919	1.87	Don Sutton	1980	.211
Gaylord Perry	1974	216	Eddie Plank	1911	2.10	Bob Ewing	1908	2.03	Nolan Ryan	1982	.213
Bert Blyleven	1986	215	Whitey Ford	1964	2.13	Sam Leever	1907	2.13	Spud Chandler	1943	.215
Phil Niekro	1974	195	Cy Young	1902	2.15	Don Sutton	1980	2.20	Jim Bunning	1967	.217
Bob Gibson	1971	185	Vern Law	1965	2.15	Gaylord Perry	1974	2.20	Steve Carlton	1980	.218
Whitey Ford	1964	172	Hoyt Wilhelm	1959	2.19	Cy Young	1902	2.23	Bucky Walters	1944	.219
Fergie Jenkins	1979	164	Don Sutton	1980	2.20	Jim Bunning	1967	2.24	Tim Keefe	1892	.220
Jack Morris	1990	162	Bob Ewing	1908	2.21	Steve Carlton	1980	2.29	Mike Cuellar	1972	.220

Batting Leaders—Through Age 36

At-Bats		Runs		Hits		Doubles	
Robin Yount	10,554	Lou Gehrig	1,888	Ty Cobb	3,454	Tris Speaker	640
Hank Aaron	9,952	Babe Ruth	1,866	Hank Aaron	3,110	Stan Musial	610
Cal Ripken Jr.	9,832	Mel Ott	1,857	Robin Yount	3,025	Ty Cobb	579
Vada Pinson	9,645	Ty Cobb	1,827	Pete Rose	2,966	Robin Yount	558
Pete Rose	9,541	Hank Aaron	1,806	Tris Speaker	2,961	Nap Lajoie	546
Sam Crawford	9,467	Jimmie Foxx	1,721	Stan Musial	2,957	Hank Aaron	540
Mel Ott	9,384	Jesse Burkett	1,720	Sam Crawford	2,943	Joe Medwick	540
Brooks Robinson	9,354	Rickey Henderson	1,719	Roberto Clemente	2,882	Paul Waner	540
Ty Cobb	9,318	Billy Hamilton	1,690	Mel Ott	2,871	Harry Heilmann	540
Nellie Fox	9,191	Willie Mays	1,679	Rogers Hornsby	2,868	Lou Gehrig	535

Triples		Home Runs		RBI		Stolen Bases	
Sam Crawford	309	Babe Ruth	611	Lou Gehrig	1,995	Rickey Henderson	1,149
Ty Cobb	258	Hank Aaron	592	Jimmie Foxx	1,883	Billy Hamilton	912
Jake Beckley	227	Willie Mays	564	Babe Ruth	1,874	Ty Cobb	820
Roger Connor	214	Harmon Killebrew	541	Mel Ott	1,856	Lou Brock	809
Tris Speaker	201	Mickey Mantle	536	Hank Aaron	1,842	Tim Raines	787
Dan Brouthers	201	Jimmie Foxx	527	Al Simmons	1,749	Vince Coleman	752
Fred Clarke	198	Frank Robinson	522	Frank Robinson	1,613	Arlie Latham	738
Joe Kelley	194	Eddie Mathews	512	Goose Goslin	1,601	Max Carey	688
Paul Waner	185	Mel Ott	510	Willie Mays	1,575	Eddie Collins	665
Ed Delahanty	185	Mike Schmidt	495	Stan Musial	1,572	Willie Wilson	660

Runs Created		Batting Average (minimum 3,000 Plate Appearances)		On-Base Percentage (minimum 3,000 Plate Appearances)		Slugging Percentage (minimum 3,000 Plate Appearances)	
Babe Ruth	2,210	Ty Cobb	.371	Ted Williams	.487	Babe Ruth	.709
Lou Gehrig	2,161	Rogers Hornsby	.360	Babe Ruth	.477	Ted Williams	.642
Ty Cobb	2,130	Joe Jackson	.356	John McGraw	.465	Lou Gehrig	.632
Mel Ott	2,127	Lefty O'Doul	.351	Billy Hamilton	.455	Jimmie Foxx	.615
Stan Musial	2,016	Nap Lajoie	.350	Frank Thomas	.452	Hank Greenberg	.605
Jimmie Foxx	1,992	Babe Ruth	.349	Lou Gehrig	.447	Frank Thomas	.600
Hank Aaron	1,989	Ted Williams	.348	Bill Joyce	.435	Willie Mays	.583
Mickey Mantle	1,950	Tris Speaker	.348	Ty Cobb	.434	Stan Musial	.580
Willie Mays	1,864	Ed Delahanty	.346	Rogers Hornsby	.434	Rogers Hornsby	.579
Tris Speaker	1,862	Willie Keeler	.345	Tris Speaker	.431	Joe DiMaggio	.579

Single Season Batting Leaders—Age 36

At-Bats			Runs			Hits			Doubles		
Pete Rose	1977	655	Babe Ruth	1931	149	Sam Rice	1926	216	Sparky Adams	1931	46
Steve Garvey	1985	654	Dan Brouthers	1894	137	Zack Wheat	1924	212	Hal McRae	1982	46
Willie Horton	1979	646	Paul Molitor	1993	121	Paul Molitor	1993	211	Bing Miller	1931	43
Sam Rice	1926	641	Andres Galarraga	1997	120	George Sisler	1929	205	Zack Wheat	1924	41
Paul Molitor	1993	636	Tony Phillips	1995	119	Pete Rose	1977	204	Ty Cobb	1923	40
Doc Cramer	1942	630	Blondie Purcell	1890	110	Babe Ruth	1931	199	George Sisler	1929	40
George Sisler	1929	629	Brian Downing	1987	110	Luke Appling	1943	192	Robin Yount	1992	40
Bill Buckner	1986	629	Harry Hooper	1924	107	Lave Cross	1902	191	4 tied with		39
Joe Carter	1996	625	Dummy Hoy	1898	104	Andres Galarraga	1997	191			
Maury Wills	1969	623	3 tied with		103	2 tied with		189			

Triples			Home Runs			RBI			Stolen Bases		
Roger Connor	1894	25	Babe Ruth	1931	46	Babe Ruth	1931	163	Lou Brock	1975	56
Dan Brouthers	1894	23	Andres Galarraga	1997	41	Andres Galarraga	1997	140	Otis Nixon	1995	50
Dummy Hoy	1898	16	Reggie Jackson	1982	39	Hal McRae	1982	133	Eddie Collins	1923	49
Gavy Cravath	1917	16	Hank Aaron	1970	38	Dan Brouthers	1894	128	Blondie Purcell	1890	48
Earl Averill	1938	15	Mike Schmidt	1986	37	Mike Schmidt	1986	119	Bid McPhee	1896	48
Sam Rice	1926	14	Gary Gaetti	1995	35	Hank Aaron	1970	118	Jim O'Rourke	1887	46
Mickey Vernon	1954	14	Norm Cash	1971	32	Dwight Evans	1988	111	Gil Hatfield	1891	43
5 tied with		13	Luke Easter	1952	31	Paul Molitor	1993	111	Buck Ewing	1896	41
			George Crowe	1957	31	Lave Cross	1902	108	Maury Wills	1969	40
			Andre Dawson	1991	31	2 tied with		107	2 tied with		39

Runs Created			Batting Average (minimum 3.1 PA/Tm Gm)			On-Base Percentage (minimum 3.1 PA/Tm Gm)			Slugging Percentage (minimum 3.1 PA/Tm Gm)		
Babe Ruth	1931	179	Zack Wheat	1924	.375	Babe Ruth	1931	.494	Babe Ruth	1931	.700
Dan Brouthers	1894	144	Babe Ruth	1931	.373	Eddie Collins	1923	.455	Stan Musial	1957	.612
Paul Molitor	1993	134	Eddie Collins	1923	.360	Wade Boggs	1994	.433	Andres Galarraga	1997	.585
Cap Anson	1888	122	Stan Musial	1957	.351	Tris Speaker	1924	.432	Hank Aaron	1970	.574
Zack Wheat	1924	120	Dan Brouthers	1894	.347	Toby Harrah	1985	.432	Dan Brouthers	1894	.560
Stan Musial	1957	120	Cap Anson	1888	.344	Earl Averill	1938	.429	Cy Williams	1924	.552
Brian Downing	1987	118	Tris Speaker	1924	.344	Zack Wheat	1924	.428	Roger Connor	1894	.552
Andres Galarraga	1997	118	Lave Cross	1902	.342	Dan Brouthers	1894	.425	Zack Wheat	1924	.549
Dave Winfield	1988	117	Wade Boggs	1994	.342	Willie Randolph	1991	.424	Mike Schmidt	1986	.547
Mike Schmidt	1986	116	Roberto Clemente	1971	.341	Charlie Gehringer	1939	.423	Charlie Gehringer	1939	.544

Pitching Leaders—Through Age 36

Wins

Cy Young	379
Walter Johnson	377
Christy Mathewson	369
Kid Nichols	361
Pud Galvin	360
Tim Keefe	341
John Clarkson	328
Old Hoss Radbourn	309
Mickey Welch	309
Pete Alexander	288

Losses

Pud Galvin	308
Walter Johnson	250
Jack Powell	239
Gus Weyhing	232
Bob Friend	230
Tim Keefe	225
Robin Roberts	221
Tony Mullane	220
Jim McCormick	214
Mickey Welch	211

Winning Percentage
(minimum 200 decisions)

Whitey Ford	.705
Dave Foutz	.690
Bob Caruthers	.688
Lefty Grove	.684
Christy Mathewson	.667
Larry Corcoran	.665
Sam Leever	.658
Three Finger Brown	.658
Ron Guidry	.656
Sandy Koufax	.655

Games

Lee Smith	891
Rollie Fingers	864
Lindy McDaniel	862
Sparky Lyle	854
Jeff Reardon	811
Goose Gossage	811
John Franco	771
Paul Assenmacher	760
Willie Hernandez	744
Tug McGraw	731

Complete Games

Pud Galvin	639
Tim Keefe	553
Cy Young	531
Kid Nichols	531
Mickey Welch	525
Old Hoss Radbourn	489
Walter Johnson	486
John Clarkson	485
Tony Mullane	468
Jim McCormick	466

Shutouts

Walter Johnson	104
Pete Alexander	84
Christy Mathewson	78
Ed Walsh	57
Pud Galvin	56
Bert Blyleven	55
Don Sutton	55
Tom Seaver	54
Bob Gibson	54
Jim Palmer	53

Saves

Lee Smith	434
John Franco	359
Jeff Reardon	357
Randy Myers	319
Goose Gossage	302
Rollie Fingers	301
Bruce Sutter	300
Tom Henke	275
Jeff Montgomery	256
Dave Righetti	252

Innings Pitched

Pud Galvin	5,941.1
Walter Johnson	5,317.1
Cy Young	5,140.2
Kid Nichols	5,056.1
Tim Keefe	5,052.1
Mickey Welch	4,802.0
Christy Mathewson	4,706.0
John Clarkson	4,536.1
Old Hoss Radbourn	4,535.1
Tony Mullane	4,531.1

Strikeouts

Nolan Ryan	3,677
Bert Blyleven	3,286
Walter Johnson	3,228
Steve Carlton	3,148
Tom Seaver	3,075
Fergie Jenkins	2,899
Roger Clemens	2,882
Mickey Lolich	2,799
Bob Gibson	2,786
Don Sutton	2,756

ERA
(minimum 1,100 Innings Pitched)

Ed Walsh	1.81
Addie Joss	1.89
Jim Devlin	1.89
Three Finger Brown	1.89
Walter Johnson	2.00
Joe Wood	2.03
Monte Ward	2.10
Christy Mathewson	2.12
Rube Waddell	2.16
Jake Weimer	2.23

Component ERA
(minimum 1,100 Innings Pitched)

Addie Joss	1.73
Ed Walsh	1.78
Walter Johnson	2.01
Monte Ward	2.01
Three Finger Brown	2.03
Joe Wood	2.10
Christy Mathewson	2.13
Jim Devlin	2.14
Reb Russell	2.14
Rube Waddell	2.22

Opponent Average
(minimum 1,100 Innings Pitched)

Nolan Ryan	.202
Sandy Koufax	.205
Sid Fernandez	.209
Randy Johnson	.211
J.R. Richard	.212
Andy Messersmith	.212
Sam McDowell	.215
Ed Walsh	.218
Tom Seaver	.218
Addie Joss	.220

Single Season Pitching Leaders—Age 36

Wins

Cy Young	1903	28
Eddie Plank	1912	26
Walter Johnson	1924	23
Pete Alexander	1923	22
Preacher Roe	1951	22
Eddie Cicotte	1920	21
Rip Sewell	1943	21
Warren Spahn	1957	21
Tommy John	1979	21
4 tied with		20

Losses

Jack Powell	1911	19
Murry Dickson	1953	19
Joe McGinnity	1907	18
Milt Gaston	1932	17
Johnny Lindell	1953	17
Gaylord Perry	1975	17
Mike Torrez	1983	17
Ed Heusser	1945	16
Jim Perry	1972	16
7 tied with		15

Winning Percentage
(minimum 15 decisions)

Preacher Roe	1951	.880
Tom Seaver	1981	.875
Eddie Plank	1912	.813
Walter Johnson	1924	.767
Steve Carlton	1981	.765
Cy Young	1903	.757
Urban Shocker	1927	.750
Ed Lopat	1954	.750
Jim Palmer	1982	.750
John Tudor	1990	.750

Games

Mike Marshall	1979	90
Kent Tekulve	1983	76
Paul Assenmacher	1997	75
Grant Jackson	1979	72
Todd Worrell	1996	72
Doug Jones	1993	71
Greg Harris	1992	70
Gary Lavelle	1985	69
Ted Power	1991	68
Dennis Eckersley	1991	67

Complete Games

Cy Young	1903	34
Eddie Cicotte	1920	28
Pete Alexander	1923	26
Dazzy Vance	1927	25
Rip Sewell	1943	25
Gaylord Perry	1975	25
Eddie Plank	1912	24
Old Hoss Radbourn	1891	23
Joe McGinnity	1907	23
Bob Gibson	1972	23

Shutouts

Cy Young	1903	7
Allie Reynolds	1951	7
Walter Johnson	1924	6
Lefty Grove	1936	6
Eddie Plank	1912	5
Claude Passeau	1945	5
Virgil Trucks	1953	5
Gaylord Perry	1975	5
Dennis Martinez	1991	5
11 tied with		4

Saves

Todd Worrell	1996	44
Dennis Eckersley	1991	43
John Franco	1997	36
Lee Smith	1994	33
Mike Marshall	1979	32
Jeff Reardon	1992	30
Doug Jones	1993	26
Steve Farr	1993	25
Tom Burgmeier	1980	24
Stu Miller	1964	23

Innings Pitched

Cy Young	1903	341.2
Joe McGinnity	1907	310.1
Gaylord Perry	1975	305.2
Pete Alexander	1923	305.0
Jim Kaat	1975	303.2
Eddie Cicotte	1920	303.1
Bob Gibson	1972	278.0
Walter Johnson	1924	277.2
Early Wynn	1956	277.2
Ray Starr	1942	276.2

Strikeouts

Gaylord Perry	1975	233
Bob Gibson	1972	208
Bert Blyleven	1987	196
Dazzy Vance	1927	184
Nolan Ryan	1983	183
Steve Carlton	1981	179
Cy Young	1903	176
Charlie Hough	1984	164
Jack Morris	1991	163
Whitey Ford	1965	162

ERA
(minimum 1 Inning Pitched/Tm Gm)

Cy Young	1903	2.08
Sam Leever	1908	2.10
Dutch Leonard	1945	2.13
Eddie Plank	1912	2.22
Rick Reuschel	1985	2.27
Dennis Martinez	1991	2.39
Tommy Bridges	1943	2.39
Steve Carlton	1981	2.42
Bob Ewing	1909	2.43
Claude Passeau	1945	2.46

Component ERA
(minimum 1 Inning Pitched/Tm Gm)

Cy Young	1903	1.89
Don Sutton	1981	2.05
Rick Reuschel	1985	2.10
Tom Seaver	1981	2.38
Walter Johnson	1924	2.39
Steve Carlton	1981	2.45
Dennis Martinez	1991	2.46
Claude Passeau	1945	2.46
Dutch Leonard	1945	2.46
Sam Leever	1908	2.47

Opponent Average
(minimum 1 Inning Pitched/Tm Gm)

Nolan Ryan	1983	.195
Tom Seaver	1981	.205
Allie Reynolds	1951	.213
Rick Reuschel	1985	.215
Steve Carlton	1981	.222
Bob Gibson	1972	.224
Walter Johnson	1924	.224
Tommy Bridges	1943	.226
Dennis Martinez	1991	.226
Ray Starr	1942	.226

Batting Leaders—Through Age 37

At-Bats		Runs		Hits		Doubles	
Robin Yount	11,008	Babe Ruth	1,986	Ty Cobb	3,665	Tris Speaker	675
Hank Aaron	10,447	Ty Cobb	1,942	Hank Aaron	3,272	Stan Musial	645
Pete Rose	10,196	Hank Aaron	1,901	Pete Rose	3,164	Ty Cobb	617
Ty Cobb	9,943	Lou Gehrig	1,888	Robin Yount	3,142	Robin Yount	583
Brooks Robinson	9,907	Mel Ott	1,859	Tris Speaker	3,128	Nap Lajoie	580
Cal Ripken Jr.	9,832	Rickey Henderson	1,829	Stan Musial	3,116	Pete Rose	572
Eddie Murray	9,734	Willie Mays	1,763	Roberto Clemente	3,000	Hank Aaron	562
Vada Pinson	9,645	Jimmie Foxx	1,751	Sam Crawford	2,961	George Brett	559
Sam Crawford	9,571	Stan Musial	1,726	Eddie Collins	2,949	Paul Waner	556
Roberto Clemente	9,454	Frank Robinson	1,724	Willie Keeler	2,929	Charlie Gehringer	555

Triples		Home Runs		RBI		Stolen Bases	
Sam Crawford	309	Babe Ruth	652	Babe Ruth	2,011	Rickey Henderson	1,186
Ty Cobb	268	Hank Aaron	639	Lou Gehrig	1,995	Billy Hamilton	912
Jake Beckley	237	Willie Mays	587	Hank Aaron	1,960	Lou Brock	865
Roger Connor	223	Frank Robinson	552	Jimmie Foxx	1,921	Ty Cobb	843
Fred Clarke	207	Harmon Killebrew	546	Mel Ott	1,860	Tim Raines	795
Tris Speaker	206	Mickey Mantle	536	Al Simmons	1,793	Vince Coleman	752
Dan Brouthers	202	Jimmie Foxx	534	Frank Robinson	1,710	Arlie Latham	738
Joe Kelley	194	Mike Schmidt	530	Eddie Murray	1,662	Max Carey	720
Honus Wagner	192	Eddie Mathews	512	Willie Mays	1,654	Eddie Collins	707
Paul Waner	186	Mel Ott	511	Ty Cobb	1,636	Willie Wilson	667

Runs Created		Batting Average (minimum 3,000 Plate Appearances)		On-Base Percentage (minimum 3,000 Plate Appearances)		Slugging Percentage (minimum 3,000 Plate Appearances)	
Babe Ruth	2,357	Ty Cobb	.369	Ted Williams	.486	Babe Ruth	.706
Ty Cobb	2,248	Rogers Hornsby	.359	Babe Ruth	.478	Ted Williams	.639
Lou Gehrig	2,161	Joe Jackson	.356	John McGraw	.465	Lou Gehrig	.632
Mel Ott	2,127	Nap Lajoie	.351	Billy Hamilton	.455	Jimmie Foxx	.609
Hank Aaron	2,111	Tris Speaker	.350	Frank Thomas	.452	Hank Greenberg	.605
Stan Musial	2,110	Lefty O'Doul	.349	Lou Gehrig	.447	Frank Thomas	.600
Jimmie Foxx	2,025	Babe Ruth	.349	Bill Joyce	.435	Joe DiMaggio	.579
Tris Speaker	1,972	Ted Williams	.348	Rogers Hornsby	.434	Rogers Hornsby	.579
Willie Mays	1,956	Ed Delahanty	.346	Tris Speaker	.433	Willie Mays	.578
Mickey Mantle	1,950	Billy Hamilton	.344	Ty Cobb	.433	Johnny Mize	.578

Single Season Batting Leaders—Age 37

At-Bats			Runs			Hits			Doubles		
Pete Rose	1978	655	Zack Wheat	1925	125	Zack Wheat	1925	221	Pete Rose	1978	51
Dummy Hoy	1899	633	Babe Ruth	1932	120	Tony Gwynn	1997	220	Tony Gwynn	1997	49
Ty Cobb	1924	625	Tony Phillips	1996	119	Bill Terry	1934	213	George Brett	1990	45
Zack Wheat	1925	616	Dummy Hoy	1899	116	Ty Cobb	1924	211	Zack Wheat	1925	42
Joe Carter	1997	612	Ty Cobb	1924	115	Pete Rose	1978	198	Hal McRae	1983	41
Eddie Murray	1993	610	Rickey Henderson	1996	110	Dummy Hoy	1899	194	Bob Johnson	1944	40
Doc Cramer	1943	606	Bill Terry	1934	109	Eddie Collins	1924	194	Ty Cobb	1924	38
Sam Rice	1927	603	Eddie Collins	1924	108	Kiki Cuyler	1936	185	Tris Speaker	1925	35
Bill Terry	1934	602	Charlie Gehringer	1940	108	Minnie Minoso	1960	184	Stan Musial	1958	35
Tony Gwynn	1997	592	Bob Johnson	1944	106	Hal McRae	1983	183	3 tied with		34

Triples			Home Runs			RBI			Stolen Bases		
Honus Wagner	1911	16	Hank Aaron	1971	47	Babe Ruth	1932	137	Lou Brock	1976	56
Zack Wheat	1925	14	Babe Ruth	1932	41	Tony Gwynn	1997	119	Otis Nixon	1996	54
Sam Rice	1927	14	Hank Sauer	1954	41	Hank Aaron	1971	118	Nixey Callahan	1911	45
Dummy Hoy	1899	13	Carlton Fisk	1985	37	Cap Anson	1889	117	Ozzie Smith	1992	43
Jake Daubert	1921	12	Dave Kingman	1986	35	Mike Schmidt	1987	113	Eddie Collins	1924	42
Kiki Cuyler	1936	11	Mike Schmidt	1987	35	Carlton Fisk	1985	107	Rickey Henderson	1996	37
6 tied with		10	Ernie Banks	1968	32	Bob Johnson	1944	106	Paul Hines	1889	34
			Don Baylor	1986	31	Minnie Minoso	1960	105	Patsy Donovan	1902	34
			Frank Robinson	1973	30	Zack Wheat	1925	103	Dummy Hoy	1899	32
			Chili Davis	1997	30	Hank Sauer	1954	103	Max Carey	1927	32

Runs Created			Batting Average (minimum 3.1 PA/Tm Gm)			On-Base Percentage (minimum 3.1 PA/Tm Gm)			Slugging Percentage (minimum 3.1 PA/Tm Gm)		
Babe Ruth	1932	147	Tris Speaker	1925	.389	Babe Ruth	1932	.489	Hank Aaron	1971	.669
Tony Gwynn	1997	138	Tony Gwynn	1997	.372	Tris Speaker	1925	.479	Babe Ruth	1932	.661
Cap Anson	1889	127	Nap Lajoie	1912	.368	Ted Williams	1956	.479	Ted Williams	1956	.605
Zack Wheat	1925	125	Zack Wheat	1925	.359	Eddie Collins	1924	.441	Tris Speaker	1925	.578
Hank Aaron	1971	122	Bill Terry	1934	.354	Bob Johnson	1944	.431	Hank Sauer	1954	.563
Bill Terry	1934	121	Eddie Collins	1924	.349	Charlie Gehringer	1940	.428	Kirk Gibson	1994	.548
Bob Johnson	1944	120	Ted Williams	1956	.345	Roger Connor	1895	.423	Mike Schmidt	1987	.548
Eddie Collins	1924	118	Paul Molitor	1994	.341	Honus Wagner	1911	.423	Tony Gwynn	1997	.547
Ty Cobb	1924	118	Babe Ruth	1932	.341	Stan Musial	1958	.423	Zack Wheat	1925	.541
Dummy Hoy	1899	117	Rod Carew	1983	.339	Ty Cobb	1924	.418	Bob Johnson	1944	.528

Pitching Leaders—Through Age 37

Wins

Cy Young	405
Walter Johnson	397
Christy Mathewson	373
Kid Nichols	361
Pud Galvin	360
Tim Keefe	341
John Clarkson	328
Old Hoss Radbourn	309
Mickey Welch	309
Pete Alexander	300

Losses

Pud Galvin	308
Walter Johnson	257
Jack Powell	256
Gus Weyhing	232
Bob Friend	230
Robin Roberts	228
Bert Blyleven	226
Tim Keefe	225
Tony Mullane	220
Cy Young	216

Winning Percentage
(minimum 200 decisions)

Whitey Ford	.696
Dave Foutz	.690
Bob Caruthers	.688
Lefty Grove	.682
Johnny Allen	.670
Sam Leever	.665
Larry Corcoran	.665
Christy Mathewson	.665
Pete Alexander	.656
Sandy Koufax	.655

Games

Lee Smith	943
Lindy McDaniel	909
Sparky Lyle	899
Rollie Fingers	897
Jeff Reardon	869
Goose Gossage	853
Gene Garber	782
John Franco	771
Tug McGraw	765
Darold Knowles	763

Complete Games

Pud Galvin	639
Cy Young	571
Tim Keefe	553
Kid Nichols	531
Mickey Welch	525
Walter Johnson	502
Old Hoss Radbourn	489
John Clarkson	485
Tony Mullane	468
Jim McCormick	466

Shutouts

Walter Johnson	107
Pete Alexander	84
Christy Mathewson	79
Ed Walsh	57
Cy Young	57
Don Sutton	56
Pud Galvin	56
Bert Blyleven	55
Bob Gibson	55
Eddie Plank	55

Saves

Lee Smith	471
Jeff Reardon	365
John Franco	359
Rollie Fingers	324
Randy Myers	319
Tom Henke	311
Goose Gossage	307
Bruce Sutter	300
Todd Worrell	256
Jeff Montgomery	256

Innings Pitched

Pud Galvin	5,941.1
Walter Johnson	5,546.1
Cy Young	5,520.2
Kid Nichols	5,056.1
Tim Keefe	5,052.1
Mickey Welch	4,802.0
Christy Mathewson	4,780.2
John Clarkson	4,536.1
Old Hoss Radbourn	4,535.1
Tony Mullane	4,531.1

Strikeouts

Nolan Ryan	3,874
Steve Carlton	3,434
Bert Blyleven	3,431
Walter Johnson	3,336
Tom Seaver	3,137
Fergie Jenkins	2,962
Don Sutton	2,931
Bob Gibson	2,928
Roger Clemens	2,882
Mickey Lolich	2,812

ERA
(minimum 1,150 Innings Pitched)

Ed Walsh	1.81
Addie Joss	1.89
Jim Devlin	1.89
Three Finger Brown	2.02
Joe Wood	2.03
Walter Johnson	2.04
Monte Ward	2.10
Christy Mathewson	2.13
Rube Waddell	2.16
Jake Weimer	2.23

Component ERA
(minimum 1,150 Innings Pitched)

Addie Joss	1.73
Ed Walsh	1.78
Monte Ward	2.01
Walter Johnson	2.04
Joe Wood	2.10
Three Finger Brown	2.12
Christy Mathewson	2.14
Jim Devlin	2.14
Reb Russell	2.14
Babe Adams	2.17

Opponent Average
(minimum 1,150 Innings Pitched)

Nolan Ryan	.202
Sandy Koufax	.205
Sid Fernandez	.209
Randy Johnson	.211
J.R. Richard	.212
Andy Messersmith	.212
Sam McDowell	.215
Ed Walsh	.218
Addie Joss	.220
Joe Wood	.220

Single Season Pitching Leaders—Age 37

Wins

Cy Young	1904	26
George McConnell	1915	25
Steve Carlton	1982	23
Dazzy Vance	1928	22
Warren Spahn	1958	22
Mike Cuellar	1974	22
Tommy John	1980	22
Rip Sewell	1944	21
Jack Morris	1992	21
3 tied with		20

Losses

Bobo Newsom	1945	20
Murry Dickson	1954	20
Eppa Rixey	1928	18
Dick Barrett	1944	18
Jack Powell	1912	17
Early Wynn	1957	17
Larry Jackson	1968	17
Bert Blyleven	1988	17
3 tied with		16

Winning Percentage
(minimum 15 decisions)

Jesse Haines	1931	.800
Jack Morris	1992	.778
Walter Johnson	1925	.741
George McConnell	1915	.714
Red Ruffing	1941	.714
Allie Reynolds	1952	.714
Tommy John	1980	.710
Pete Alexander	1924	.706
Sal Maglie	1954	.700
3 tied with		.688

Games

Greg Harris	1993	80
Bob Patterson	1996	79
Kent Tekulve	1984	72
Dennis Eckersley	1992	69
Stu Miller	1965	67
Al Worthington	1966	65
Larry Andersen	1990	65
Todd Worrell	1997	65
Ted Power	1992	64
Don McMahon	1967	63

Complete Games

Cy Young	1904	40
Dazzy Vance	1928	24
Rip Sewell	1944	24
Allie Reynolds	1952	24
George McConnell	1915	23
Babe Adams	1919	23
Warren Spahn	1958	23
Lefty Grove	1937	21
Gaylord Perry	1976	21
2 tied with		20

Shutouts

Cy Young	1904	10
Eddie Plank	1913	7
Babe Adams	1919	6
Allie Reynolds	1952	6
Tommy John	1980	6
Steve Carlton	1982	6
6 tied with		5

Saves

Dennis Eckersley	1992	51
Lee Smith	1995	37
Tom Henke	1995	36
Todd Worrell	1997	35
Doug Jones	1994	27
Stu Miller	1965	24
Rollie Fingers	1984	23
Hoyt Wilhelm	1961	18
Al Worthington	1966	16
2 tied with		14

Innings Pitched

Cy Young	1904	380.0
George McConnell	1915	303.0
Steve Carlton	1982	295.2
Eppa Rixey	1928	291.1
Warren Spahn	1958	290.0
Rip Sewell	1944	286.0
Dazzy Vance	1928	280.1
Ray Kremer	1930	276.0
Phil Niekro	1976	270.2
Joe Niekro	1982	270.0

Strikeouts

Steve Carlton	1982	286
Cy Young	1904	200
Dazzy Vance	1928	200
Nolan Ryan	1984	197
Early Wynn	1957	184
Don Sutton	1982	175
Phil Niekro	1976	173
Allie Reynolds	1952	160
Jim Bunning	1969	157
Lefty Grove	1937	153

ERA
(minimum 1 Inning Pitched/Tm Gm)

Cy Young	1904	1.97
Babe Adams	1919	1.98
Allie Reynolds	1952	2.06
Dazzy Vance	1928	2.09
George McConnell	1915	2.20
Chick Fraser	1908	2.27
Joe McGinnity	1908	2.27
Dennis Martinez	1992	2.47
Joe Niekro	1982	2.47
Eddie Plank	1913	2.60

Component ERA
(minimum 1 Inning Pitched/Tm Gm)

Babe Adams	1919	1.52
Cy Young	1904	1.73
Dennis Martinez	1992	2.19
Dazzy Vance	1928	2.20
Eddie Plank	1913	2.26
Joe Niekro	1982	2.35
Bob Gibson	1973	2.47
George McConnell	1915	2.53
Nolan Ryan	1984	2.63
Allie Reynolds	1952	2.63

Opponent Average
(minimum 1 Inning Pitched/Tm Gm)

Nolan Ryan	1984	.211
Dennis Martinez	1992	.211
Charlie Hough	1985	.215
Allie Reynolds	1952	.218
Babe Adams	1919	.220
Dazzy Vance	1928	.221
Bob Gibson	1973	.224
Virgil Trucks	1954	.228
Joe Niekro	1982	.229
Danny Darwin	1993	.230

Batting Leaders—Through Age 38

At-Bats		Runs		Hits		Doubles	
Robin Yount	11,008	Babe Ruth	2,083	Ty Cobb	3,822	Tris Speaker	727
Hank Aaron	10,896	Ty Cobb	2,039	Hank Aaron	3,391	Stan Musial	658
Pete Rose	10,824	Hank Aaron	1,976	Pete Rose	3,372	Ty Cobb	648
Brooks Robinson	10,389	Rickey Henderson	1,913	Tris Speaker	3,292	Pete Rose	612
Ty Cobb	10,358	Lou Gehrig	1,888	Stan Musial	3,203	Nap Lajoie	605
Eddie Murray	10,167	Mel Ott	1,859	Robin Yount	3,142	George Brett	599
Carl Yastrzemski	9,929	Willie Mays	1,827	Eddie Collins	3,096	Robin Yount	583
Cal Ripken Jr.	9,832	Frank Robinson	1,805	Roberto Clemente	3,000	Charlie Gehringer	574
Frank Robinson	9,821	Tris Speaker	1,783	Sam Crawford	2,961	Hank Aaron	572
Luis Aparicio	9,731	Charlie Gehringer	1,768	Paul Waner	2,956	Paul Waner	566

Triples		Home Runs		RBI		Stolen Bases	
Sam Crawford	309	Babe Ruth	686	Babe Ruth	2,114	Rickey Henderson	1,231
Ty Cobb	280	Hank Aaron	673	Hank Aaron	2,037	Billy Hamilton	912
Jake Beckley	243	Willie Mays	600	Lou Gehrig	1,995	Lou Brock	900
Roger Connor	232	Frank Robinson	574	Jimmie Foxx	1,921	Ty Cobb	856
Fred Clarke	220	Harmon Killebrew	559	Mel Ott	1,860	Tim Raines	795
Tris Speaker	214	Mike Schmidt	542	Al Simmons	1,812	Vince Coleman	752
Honus Wagner	212	Mickey Mantle	536	Frank Robinson	1,778	Max Carey	738
Dan Brouthers	205	Jimmie Foxx	534	Eddie Murray	1,738	Arlie Latham	738
Joe Kelley	194	Eddie Mathews	512	Ty Cobb	1,738	Eddie Collins	726
Paul Waner	188	Mel Ott	511	Willie Mays	1,712	Willie Wilson	668

Runs Created		Batting Average		On-Base Percentage		Slugging Percentage	
		(minimum 3,000 Plate Appearances)		(minimum 3,000 Plate Appearances)		(minimum 3,000 Plate Appearances)	
Babe Ruth	2,479	Ty Cobb	.369	Ted Williams	.489	Babe Ruth	.699
Ty Cobb	2,359	Rogers Hornsby	.359	Babe Ruth	.476	Ted Williams	.645
Hank Aaron	2,195	Joe Jackson	.356	John McGraw	.465	Lou Gehrig	.632
Lou Gehrig	2,161	Nap Lajoie	.350	Billy Hamilton	.455	Jimmie Foxx	.609
Stan Musial	2,158	Ted Williams	.350	Frank Thomas	.452	Hank Greenberg	.605
Mel Ott	2,127	Lefty O'Doul	.349	Lou Gehrig	.447	Frank Thomas	.600
Tris Speaker	2,079	Tris Speaker	.347	Bill Joyce	.435	Joe DiMaggio	.579
Ted Williams	2,026	Ed Delahanty	.346	Ty Cobb	.435	Rogers Hornsby	.578
Jimmie Foxx	2,025	Babe Ruth	.346	Rogers Hornsby	.434	Stan Musial	.572
Willie Mays	2,022	Billy Hamilton	.344	Tris Speaker	.432	Willie Mays	.572

Single Season Batting Leaders—Age 38

At-Bats			Runs			Hits			Doubles		
Pete Rose	1979	628	Jake Daubert	1922	114	Pete Rose	1979	208	Tris Speaker	1926	52
Sam Rice	1928	616	Ty Cobb	1925	97	Jake Daubert	1922	205	Pete Rose	1979	40
Jake Daubert	1922	610	Babe Ruth	1933	97	Bill Terry	1935	203	George Brett	1991	40
Kid Gleason	1905	608	Tris Speaker	1926	96	Sam Rice	1928	202	Jim O'Rourke	1889	36
Lave Cross	1904	607	Ted Williams	1957	96	Honus Wagner	1912	181	Honus Wagner	1912	35
Maury Wills	1971	601	Tony Phillips	1997	96	Lave Cross	1904	176	Tony Phillips	1997	34
Bill Terry	1935	596	Cap Anson	1890	95	Doc Cramer	1944	169	Sam Rice	1928	32
Tony Perez	1980	585	Kid Gleason	1905	95	Maury Wills	1971	169	Bill Terry	1935	32
Doc Cramer	1944	578	Sam Rice	1928	95	Tris Speaker	1926	164	5 tied with		31
Otis Nixon	1997	576	3 tied with		91	Ted Williams	1957	163			

Triples			Home Runs			RBI			Stolen Bases		
Jake Daubert	1922	22	Darrell Evans	1985	40	Cap Anson	1890	107	Otis Nixon	1997	59
Honus Wagner	1912	20	Ted Williams	1957	38	Ernie Banks	1969	106	Rickey Henderson	1997	45
Sam Rice	1928	15	Babe Ruth	1933	34	Tony Perez	1980	105	Lou Brock	1977	35
Fred Clarke	1911	13	Hank Aaron	1972	34	Babe Ruth	1933	103	Jim O'Rourke	1889	33
Ty Cobb	1925	12	Rico Carty	1978	31	Honus Wagner	1912	102	Brett Butler	1995	32
Lave Cross	1904	10	Willie Stargell	1978	28	Ty Cobb	1925	102	Candy Nelson	1887	29
Dode Paskert	1920	10	Tony Perez	1980	25	Rico Carty	1978	99	Orator Shaffer	1890	29
4 tied with		9	Reggie Jackson	1984	25	Willie Stargell	1978	97	Cap Anson	1890	29
			Ernie Banks	1969	23	Dave Parker	1989	97	Honus Wagner	1912	26
			2 tied with		22	Darrell Evans	1985	94	Patsy Donovan	1903	25

Runs Created			Batting Average			On-Base Percentage			Slugging Percentage		
			(minimum 3.1 PA/Tm Gm)			(minimum 3.1 PA/Tm Gm)			(minimum 3.1 PA/Tm Gm)		
Ted Williams	1957	143	Ted Williams	1957	.388	Ted Williams	1957	.526	Ted Williams	1957	.731
Cap Anson	1890	127	Ty Cobb	1925	.378	Ty Cobb	1925	.468	Ty Cobb	1925	.598
Babe Ruth	1933	122	Eddie Collins	1925	.346	Eddie Collins	1925	.461	Babe Ruth	1933	.582
Jake Daubert	1922	115	Bill Terry	1935	.341	Cap Anson	1890	.443	Darrell Evans	1985	.519
Honus Wagner	1912	111	Jake Daubert	1922	.336	Babe Ruth	1933	.442	Hank Aaron	1972	.514
Ty Cobb	1925	111	Nap Lajoie	1913	.335	Pete Rose	1979	.418	Rico Carty	1978	.502
Jim O'Rourke	1889	109	Pete Rose	1979	.331	Tris Speaker	1926	.408	Honus Wagner	1912	.496
Tris Speaker	1926	107	Sam Rice	1928	.328	Joe Morgan	1982	.400	Jake Daubert	1922	.492
Pete Rose	1979	104	Joe Start	1881	.328	Rickey Henderson	1997	.400	Tris Speaker	1926	.469
Sam Rice	1928	99	Patsy Donovan	1903	.327	Nap Lajoie	1913	.398	Tony Perez	1980	.467

Pitching Leaders—Through Age 38

Wins

Cy Young	423
Walter Johnson	412
Christy Mathewson	373
Kid Nichols	361
Pud Galvin	360
Tim Keefe	341
John Clarkson	328
Pete Alexander	315
Old Hoss Radbourn	309
Mickey Welch	309

Losses

Pud Galvin	308
Walter Johnson	273
Jack Powell	256
Robin Roberts	237
Cy Young	235
Gus Weyhing	232
Bert Blyleven	231
Bob Friend	230
Tim Keefe	225
Eppa Rixey	223

Winning Percentage
(minimum 200 decisions)

Dave Foutz	.690
Whitey Ford	.690
Bob Caruthers	.688
Lefty Grove	.686
Larry Corcoran	.665
Christy Mathewson	.665
Sam Leever	.661
Sandy Koufax	.655
Johnny Allen	.654
Three Finger Brown	.653

Games

Lee Smith	997
Lindy McDaniel	947
Rollie Fingers	944
Sparky Lyle	899
Jeff Reardon	880
Goose Gossage	853
Gene Garber	843
Jesse Orosco	819
Dennis Eckersley	804
Tug McGraw	799

Complete Games

Pud Galvin	639
Cy Young	602
Tim Keefe	553
Kid Nichols	531
Mickey Welch	525
Walter Johnson	524
Old Hoss Radbourn	489
John Clarkson	485
Tony Mullane	468
Jim McCormick	466

Shutouts

Walter Johnson	109
Pete Alexander	85
Christy Mathewson	79
Cy Young	61
Bert Blyleven	60
Eddie Plank	59
Ed Walsh	57
5 tied with	56

Saves

Lee Smith	473
Jeff Reardon	367
John Franco	359
Rollie Fingers	341
Randy Myers	319
Tom Henke	311
Goose Gossage	307
Bruce Sutter	300
Dennis Eckersley	275
2 tied with	256

Innings Pitched

Pud Galvin	5,941.1
Cy Young	5,841.1
Walter Johnson	5,807.0
Kid Nichols	5,056.1
Tim Keefe	5,052.1
Mickey Welch	4,802.0
Christy Mathewson	4,780.2
Bert Blyleven	4,703.0
Robin Roberts	4,576.2
Steve Carlton	4,558.1

Strikeouts

Nolan Ryan	4,083
Steve Carlton	3,709
Bert Blyleven	3,562
Walter Johnson	3,461
Tom Seaver	3,272
Fergie Jenkins	3,096
Don Sutton	3,065
Bob Gibson	3,057
Roger Clemens	2,882
Gaylord Perry	2,847

ERA
(minimum 1,200 Innings Pitched)

Ed Walsh	1.81
Addie Joss	1.89
Three Finger Brown	2.03
Joe Wood	2.03
Monte Ward	2.10
Walter Johnson	2.11
Christy Mathewson	2.13
Rube Waddell	2.16
Jake Weimer	2.23
Orval Overall	2.23

Component ERA
(minimum 1,200 Innings Pitched)

Addie Joss	1.73
Ed Walsh	1.78
Monte Ward	2.01
Walter Johnson	2.09
Joe Wood	2.10
Three Finger Brown	2.11
Christy Mathewson	2.14
Reb Russell	2.14
Babe Adams	2.15
Rube Waddell	2.22

Opponent Average
(minimum 1,200 Innings Pitched)

Nolan Ryan	.205
Sandy Koufax	.205
Sid Fernandez	.209
Randy Johnson	.211
J.R. Richard	.212
Andy Messersmith	.212
Sam McDowell	.215
Ed Walsh	.218
Addie Joss	.220
Joe Wood	.220

Single Season Pitching Leaders—Age 38

Wins

Warren Spahn	1959	21
Spud Chandler	1946	20
Cy Young	1905	18
Ed Cushman	1890	17
Three Finger Brown	1915	17
Babe Adams	1920	17
Dutch Leonard	1947	17
Jim Perry	1974	17
Charlie Hough	1986	17
Bert Blyleven	1989	17

Losses

Ed Cushman	1890	21
Dick Barrett	1945	20
Phil Niekro	1977	20
Cy Young	1905	19
Milt Gaston	1934	19
Doyle Alexander	1989	18
5 tied with		16

Winning Percentage
(minimum 15 decisions)

Freddie Fitzsimmons	1940	.889
Deacon Phillippe	1910	.875
Lefty Grove	1938	.778
Bert Blyleven	1989	.773
Charlie Root	1937	.722
Curt Davis	1942	.714
Spud Chandler	1946	.714
Al Brazle	1952	.706
Ted Lyons	1939	.700
Orel Hershiser	1997	.700

Games

Bob Patterson	1997	76
Ellis Kinder	1953	69
Gerry Staley	1959	67
Jesse Orosco	1995	65
Tony Fossas	1996	65
Dennis Eckersley	1993	64
Ted Abernathy	1971	63
Harry Gumbert	1948	61
Kent Tekulve	1985	61
Gene Garber	1986	61

Complete Games

Ed Cushman	1890	34
Cy Young	1905	31
Walter Johnson	1926	22
Warren Spahn	1959	21
Pete Alexander	1925	20
Spud Chandler	1946	20
Phil Niekro	1977	20
4 tied with		19

Shutouts

Babe Adams	1920	8
Spud Chandler	1946	6
Curt Davis	1942	5
Mike Cuellar	1975	5
Geoff Zahn	1984	5
Bert Blyleven	1989	5
10 tied with		4

Saves

Dennis Eckersley	1993	36
Ellis Kinder	1953	27
Gene Garber	1986	24
Ted Abernathy	1971	23
Doug Jones	1995	22
Roy Face	1966	18
Stu Miller	1966	18
Harry Gumbert	1948	17
Rollie Fingers	1985	17
2 tied with		16

Innings Pitched

Phil Niekro	1977	330.1
Cy Young	1905	320.2
Ed Cushman	1890	315.2
Warren Spahn	1959	292.0
Steve Carlton	1983	283.2
Joe Niekro	1983	263.2
Babe Adams	1920	263.0
Walter Johnson	1926	260.2
Spud Chandler	1946	257.1
2 tied with		256.0

Strikeouts

Steve Carlton	1983	275
Phil Niekro	1977	262
Cy Young	1905	210
Nolan Ryan	1985	209
Early Wynn	1958	179
Gaylord Perry	1977	177
Joe Niekro	1983	152
Jim Bunning	1970	147
Charlie Hough	1986	146
Warren Spahn	1959	143

ERA
(minimum 1 Inning Pitched/Tm Gm)

Cy Young	1905	1.82
Three Finger Brown	1915	2.09
Spud Chandler	1946	2.10
Babe Adams	1920	2.16
Curt Davis	1942	2.36
Ray Prim	1945	2.40
Thornton Lee	1945	2.44
George McConnell	1916	2.57
Tommy John	1981	2.63
Johnny Niggeling	1942	2.66

Component ERA
(minimum 1 Inning Pitched/Tm Gm)

Cy Young	1905	1.49
Babe Adams	1920	1.94
Three Finger Brown	1915	2.04
George McConnell	1916	2.05
Ray Prim	1945	2.08
Spud Chandler	1946	2.25
Ted Lyons	1939	2.40
Curt Davis	1942	2.55
Robin Roberts	1965	2.57
Rick Reuschel	1987	2.64

Opponent Average
(minimum 1 Inning Pitched/Tm Gm)

Cy Young	1905	.213
Spud Chandler	1946	.218
Three Finger Brown	1915	.220
Charlie Hough	1986	.221
George McConnell	1916	.223
Johnny Niggeling	1942	.226
Ray Prim	1945	.228
Curt Davis	1942	.233
Tom Seaver	1983	.235
Robin Roberts	1965	.238

Batting Leaders—Through Age 39

At-Bats

Pete Rose	11,479
Hank Aaron	11,288
Robin Yount	11,008
Brooks Robinson	10,607
Eddie Murray	10,603
Ty Cobb	10,591
Carl Yastrzemski	10,447
Luis Aparicio	10,230
Al Kaline	10,116
Willie Mays	10,011

Runs

Babe Ruth	2,161
Ty Cobb	2,087
Hank Aaron	2,060
Willie Mays	1,921
Rickey Henderson	1,913
Lou Gehrig	1,888
Mel Ott	1,859
Tris Speaker	1,854
Pete Rose	1,842
Frank Robinson	1,824

Hits

Ty Cobb	3,901
Pete Rose	3,557
Hank Aaron	3,509
Tris Speaker	3,463
Stan Musial	3,294
Eddie Collins	3,225
Robin Yount	3,142
Eddie Murray	3,071
Willie Mays	3,065
Rod Carew	3,053

Doubles

Tris Speaker	770
Stan Musial	675
Ty Cobb	666
Pete Rose	654
George Brett	634
Nap Lajoie	619
Hank Aaron	584
Robin Yount	583
Paul Waner	583
Charlie Gehringer	574

Triples

Sam Crawford	309
Ty Cobb	285
Jake Beckley	243
Roger Connor	233
Tris Speaker	220
Fred Clarke	220
Honus Wagner	216
Dan Brouthers	205
Joe Kelley	194
Paul Waner	189

Home Runs

Hank Aaron	713
Babe Ruth	708
Willie Mays	628
Frank Robinson	583
Harmon Killebrew	573
Mike Schmidt	548
Mickey Mantle	536
Jimmie Foxx	534
Reggie Jackson	530
Eddie Mathews	512

RBI

Babe Ruth	2,198
Hank Aaron	2,133
Lou Gehrig	1,995
Jimmie Foxx	1,921
Mel Ott	1,860
Eddie Murray	1,820
Al Simmons	1,813
Frank Robinson	1,802
Ty Cobb	1,800
Willie Mays	1,795

Stolen Bases

Rickey Henderson	1,231
Lou Brock	917
Billy Hamilton	912
Ty Cobb	865
Tim Raines	795
Vince Coleman	752
Eddie Collins	739
Max Carey	738
Arlie Latham	738
Joe Morgan	681

Runs Created

Babe Ruth	2,567
Ty Cobb	2,406
Hank Aaron	2,288
Stan Musial	2,214
Tris Speaker	2,173
Lou Gehrig	2,161
Ted Williams	2,129
Mel Ott	2,127
Willie Mays	2,120
Frank Robinson	2,029

Batting Average
(minimum 3,000 Plate Appearances)

Ty Cobb	.368
Rogers Hornsby	.359
Joe Jackson	.356
Lefty O'Doul	.349
Ted Williams	.349
Tris Speaker	.346
Ed Delahanty	.346
Nap Lajoie	.346
Billy Hamilton	.344
Babe Ruth	.343

On-Base Percentage
(minimum 3,000 Plate Appearances)

Ted Williams	.487
Babe Ruth	.475
John McGraw	.465
Billy Hamilton	.455
Frank Thomas	.452
Lou Gehrig	.447
Bill Joyce	.435
Ty Cobb	.434
Rogers Hornsby	.434
Tris Speaker	.430

Slugging Percentage
(minimum 3,000 Plate Appearances)

Babe Ruth	.692
Ted Williams	.641
Lou Gehrig	.632
Jimmie Foxx	.609
Hank Greenberg	.605
Frank Thomas	.600
Joe DiMaggio	.579
Rogers Hornsby	.578
Stan Musial	.569
Hank Aaron	.569

Single Season Batting Leaders—Age 39

At-Bats

Paul Molitor	1996	660
Pete Rose	1980	655
Sam Rice	1929	616
Dave Parker	1990	610
George Brett	1992	592
Lave Cross	1905	583
Luke Appling	1946	582
Dave Winfield	1991	568
Rabbit Maranville	1931	562
Al Kaline	1974	558

Runs

Sam Rice	1929	119
Jim O'Rourke	1890	112
Dummy Hoy	1901	112
Paul Molitor	1996	99
Pete Rose	1980	95
Willie Mays	1970	94
Jimmy Ryan	1902	92
Cy Williams	1927	86
Hank Aaron	1973	84
2 tied with		81

Hits

Paul Molitor	1996	225
Sam Rice	1929	199
Pete Rose	1980	185
Luke Appling	1946	180
Dave Parker	1990	176
Jim O'Rourke	1890	172
Tris Speaker	1927	171
George Brett	1992	169
Cap Anson	1891	157
3 tied with		155

Doubles

Tris Speaker	1927	43
Pete Rose	1980	42
Paul Molitor	1996	41
Sam Rice	1929	39
Jim O'Rourke	1890	37
George Brett	1992	35
Jimmy Ryan	1902	32
Eddie Collins	1926	32
Dave Parker	1990	30
2 tied with		29

Triples

Joe Kuhel	1945	13
Deacon White	1887	11
Dummy Hoy	1901	11
Joe Start	1882	10
Chief Zimmer	1900	10
Jake Daubert	1923	10
Sam Rice	1929	10
Jimmy Austin	1919	9
4 tied with		8

Home Runs

Hank Aaron	1973	40
Willie Stargell	1979	32
Cy Williams	1927	30
Darrell Evans	1986	29
Willie Mays	1970	28
Willie McCovey	1977	28
Dave Winfield	1991	28
Reggie Jackson	1985	27
Ted Williams	1958	26
Carlton Fisk	1987	23

RBI

Cap Anson	1891	120
Jim O'Rourke	1890	115
Paul Molitor	1996	113
Cy Williams	1927	98
Hank Aaron	1973	96
Dave Parker	1990	92
Carl Yastrzemski	1979	87
Willie McCovey	1977	86
Dave Winfield	1991	86
3 tied with		85

Stolen Bases

Dummy Hoy	1901	27
Jim O'Rourke	1890	23
Honus Wagner	1913	21
Deacon White	1887	20
Bid McPhee	1899	18
Joe Morgan	1983	18
Paul Molitor	1996	18
4 tied with		17

Runs Created

Jim O'Rourke	1890	131
Dummy Hoy	1901	117
Paul Molitor	1996	117
Cap Anson	1891	112
Sam Rice	1929	104
Ted Williams	1958	103
Willie Mays	1970	98
Tris Speaker	1927	94
Hank Aaron	1973	93
Jimmy Ryan	1902	90

Batting Average
(minimum 3.1 PA/Tm Gm)

Jim O'Rourke	1890	.360
Paul Molitor	1996	.341
Joe Start	1882	.329
Ted Williams	1958	.328
Tris Speaker	1927	.327
Eddie Murray	1995	.323
Sam Rice	1929	.323
Jimmy Ryan	1902	.320
Luke Appling	1946	.309
Deacon White	1887	.303

On-Base Percentage
(minimum 3.1 PA/Tm Gm)

Ted Williams	1958	.458
Jim O'Rourke	1890	.410
Dummy Hoy	1901	.407
Tris Speaker	1927	.395
Willie Mays	1970	.390
Paul Molitor	1996	.390
Luke Appling	1946	.384
Jimmy Ryan	1902	.384
Sam Rice	1929	.381
Joe Kuhel	1945	.378

Slugging Percentage
(minimum 3.1 PA/Tm Gm)

Ted Williams	1958	.584
Eddie Murray	1995	.516
Jim O'Rourke	1890	.515
Willie Mays	1970	.506
Cy Williams	1927	.502
Willie McCovey	1977	.500
Reggie Jackson	1985	.487
Dave Winfield	1991	.472
Paul Molitor	1996	.468
Carlton Fisk	1987	.460

Pitching Leaders—Through Age 39

Wins		Losses		Winning Percentage		Games	
				(minimum 200 decisions)			
Cy Young	436	Pud Galvin	308	Lefty Grove	.691	Lee Smith	1,022
Walter Johnson	417	Walter Johnson	279	Dave Foutz	.690	Lindy McDaniel	987
Christy Mathewson	373	Cy Young	256	Whitey Ford	.690	Rollie Fingers	944
Kid Nichols	361	Jack Powell	256	Bob Caruthers	.688	Gene Garber	905
Pud Galvin	360	Robin Roberts	245	Larry Corcoran	.665	Sparky Lyle	899
Tim Keefe	341	Bert Blyleven	238	Christy Mathewson	.665	Goose Gossage	897
John Clarkson	328	Frank Tanana	236	Sam Leever	.661	Jesse Orosco	885
Pete Alexander	327	Eppa Rixey	236	Sandy Koufax	.655	Jeff Reardon	880
Steve Carlton	313	Gus Weyhing	232	Johnny Allen	.654	Kent Tekulve	853
2 tied with	309	Bob Friend	230	Ron Guidry	.651	Dennis Eckersley	849

Complete Games		Shutouts		Saves		Innings Pitched	
Pud Galvin	639	Walter Johnson	110	Lee Smith	478	Cy Young	6,129.0
Cy Young	630	Pete Alexander	87	Jeff Reardon	367	Pud Galvin	5,941.1
Tim Keefe	553	Christy Mathewson	79	John Franco	359	Walter Johnson	5,914.2
Walter Johnson	531	Eddie Plank	65	Rollie Fingers	341	Kid Nichols	5,056.1
Kid Nichols	531	Cy Young	61	Randy Myers	319	Tim Keefe	5,052.1
Mickey Welch	525	Bert Blyleven	60	Tom Henke	311	Bert Blyleven	4,837.0
Old Hoss Radbourn	489	Tom Seaver	60	Goose Gossage	308	Mickey Welch	4,802.0
John Clarkson	485	Ed Walsh	57	Bruce Sutter	300	Steve Carlton	4,787.1
Tony Mullane	468	4 tied with	56	Dennis Eckersley	294	Christy Mathewson	4,780.2
Jim McCormick	466			2 tied with	256	Robin Roberts	4,688.2

Strikeouts		ERA		Component ERA		Opponent Average	
		(minimum 1,250 Innings Pitched)		(minimum 1,250 Innings Pitched)		(minimum 1,250 Innings Pitched)	
Nolan Ryan	4,277	Ed Walsh	1.81	Addie Joss	1.73	Nolan Ryan	.204
Steve Carlton	3,872	Addie Joss	1.89	Ed Walsh	1.78	Sandy Koufax	.205
Bert Blyleven	3,631	Joe Wood	2.03	Monte Ward	2.01	Sid Fernandez	.209
Walter Johnson	3,509	Three Finger Brown	2.06	Joe Wood	2.10	Randy Johnson	.211
Tom Seaver	3,403	Monte Ward	2.10	Walter Johnson	2.12	J.R. Richard	.212
Don Sutton	3,208	Christy Mathewson	2.13	Three Finger Brown	2.13	Andy Messersmith	.212
Fergie Jenkins	3,192	Rube Waddell	2.16	Christy Mathewson	2.14	Sam McDowell	.215
Bob Gibson	3,117	Walter Johnson	2.17	Reb Russell	2.14	Ed Walsh	.218
Gaylord Perry	3,001	Jake Weimer	2.23	Babe Adams	2.16	Addie Joss	.220
Roger Clemens	2,882	Orval Overall	2.23	Rube Waddell	2.22	Joe Wood	.220

Single Season Pitching Leaders—Age 39

Wins			Losses			Winning Percentage			Games		
						(minimum 15 decisions)					
Early Wynn	1959	22	Cy Young	1906	21	Lefty Grove	1939	.789	Kent Tekulve	1986	73
Eddie Plank	1915	21	Phil Niekro	1978	18	Gaylord Perry	1978	.778	Tony Fossas	1997	71
Warren Spahn	1960	21	Jack Quinn	1923	17	Allie Reynolds	1954	.765	Jesse Orosco	1996	66
Gaylord Perry	1978	21	Dutch Leonard	1948	17	Babe Adams	1921	.737	Gerry Staley	1960	64
Phil Niekro	1978	19	Frank Tanana	1993	17	Sal Maglie	1956	.722	Mike Flanagan	1991	64
Rick Reuschel	1988	19	Dazzy Vance	1930	15	Early Wynn	1959	.688	Gene Garber	1987	62
Charlie Hough	1987	18	Sad Sam Jones	1932	15	Kent Tekulve	1986	.688	Roy Face	1967	61
Dazzy Vance	1930	17	Oscar Judd	1947	15	Warren Spahn	1960	.677	Al Brazle	1953	60
Joe Niekro	1984	16	Hal Brown	1964	15	Dick Hall	1970	.667	Ron Reed	1982	57
2 tied with		15	4 tied with		13	Eddie Plank	1915	.656	2 tied with		55

Complete Games			Shutouts			Saves			Innings Pitched		
Cy Young	1906	28	Eddie Plank	1915	6	Hoyt Wilhelm	1963	21	Phil Niekro	1978	334.1
Eddie Plank	1915	23	Early Wynn	1959	5	Dennis Eckersley	1994	19	Cy Young	1906	287.2
Phil Niekro	1978	22	Dazzy Vance	1930	4	Al Brazle	1953	18	Charlie Hough	1987	285.1
Dazzy Vance	1930	20	Ted Lyons	1940	4	Al Worthington	1968	18	Eddie Plank	1915	268.1
Warren Spahn	1960	18	Allie Reynolds	1954	4	Gene Garber	1987	18	Warren Spahn	1960	267.2
Lefty Grove	1939	17	Warren Spahn	1960	4	Roy Face	1967	17	Gaylord Perry	1978	260.2
Ted Lyons	1940	17	Phil Niekro	1978	4	Ellis Kinder	1954	15	Dazzy Vance	1930	258.2
4 tied with		16	Tom Seaver	1984	4	Marv Grissom	1957	14	Early Wynn	1959	255.2
			5 tied with		3	Ron Reed	1982	14	Joe Niekro	1984	248.1
						Don McMahon	1969	13	Rick Reuschel	1988	245.0

Strikeouts			ERA			Component ERA			Opponent Average		
			(minimum 1 Inning Pitched/Tm Gm)			(minimum 1 Inning Pitched/Tm Gm)			(minimum 1 Inning Pitched/Tm Gm)		
Phil Niekro	1978	248	Eddie Plank	1915	2.08	Eddie Plank	1915	1.74	Nolan Ryan	1986	.188
Charlie Hough	1987	223	Dutch Leonard	1948	2.51	Johnny Niggeling	1943	2.20	Johnny Niggeling	1943	.204
Nolan Ryan	1986	194	Lefty Grove	1939	2.54	Babe Adams	1921	2.32	Early Wynn	1959	.216
Early Wynn	1959	179	Johnny Niggeling	1943	2.59	Cy Young	1906	2.45	Eddie Plank	1915	.218
Dazzy Vance	1930	173	Dazzy Vance	1930	2.61	Nolan Ryan	1986	2.46	Charlie Hough	1987	.223
Steve Carlton	1984	163	Babe Adams	1921	2.64	Pete Alexander	1926	2.51	Sal Maglie	1956	.224
Warren Spahn	1960	154	Gaylord Perry	1978	2.73	Gaylord Perry	1978	2.72	Allie Reynolds	1954	.233
Gaylord Perry	1978	154	Charlie Root	1938	2.86	Dazzy Vance	1930	2.74	Phil Niekro	1978	.235
Eddie Plank	1915	147	Phil Niekro	1978	2.88	Rick Reuschel	1988	2.84	Tom Seaver	1984	.240
Don Sutton	1984	143	Sal Maglie	1956	2.89	Sal Maglie	1956	2.86	Murry Dickson	1956	.240

Batting Leaders—Through Age 40

At-Bats		Runs		Hits		Doubles	
Pete Rose	11,910	Ty Cobb	2,191	Ty Cobb	4,076	Tris Speaker	792
Hank Aaron	11,628	Babe Ruth	2,174	Pete Rose	3,697	Ty Cobb	698
Eddie Murray	11,169	Hank Aaron	2,107	Hank Aaron	3,600	Stan Musial	697
Ty Cobb	11,081	Willie Mays	2,003	Tris Speaker	3,514	Pete Rose	672
Robin Yount	11,008	Pete Rose	1,915	Stan Musial	3,401	George Brett	665
Carl Yastrzemski	10,811	Rickey Henderson	1,913	Eddie Collins	3,301	Nap Lajoie	643
Brooks Robinson	10,654	Lou Gehrig	1,888	Eddie Murray	3,218	Hank Aaron	600
Willie Mays	10,428	Tris Speaker	1,882	Paul Molitor	3,178	Paul Waner	599
George Brett	10,349	Mel Ott	1,859	Willie Mays	3,178	Carl Yastrzemski	586
Paul Molitor	10,333	Stan Musial	1,858	George Brett	3,154	Honus Wagner	586

Triples		Home Runs		RBI		Stolen Bases	
Sam Crawford	309	Hank Aaron	733	Babe Ruth	2,210	Rickey Henderson	1,231
Ty Cobb	292	Babe Ruth	714	Hank Aaron	2,202	Lou Brock	938
Jake Beckley	243	Willie Mays	646	Lou Gehrig	1,995	Billy Hamilton	912
Roger Connor	233	Frank Robinson	586	Jimmie Foxx	1,921	Ty Cobb	887
Honus Wagner	225	Harmon Killebrew	573	Eddie Murray	1,899	Tim Raines	795
Tris Speaker	222	Reggie Jackson	548	Ty Cobb	1,893	Vince Coleman	752
Fred Clarke	220	Mike Schmidt	548	Mel Ott	1,860	Eddie Collins	745
Dan Brouthers	205	Mickey Mantle	536	Willie Mays	1,856	Max Carey	738
Joe Kelley	194	Jimmie Foxx	534	Al Simmons	1,813	Arlie Latham	738
Paul Waner	189	2 tied with	512	Frank Robinson	1,812	Joe Morgan	689

Runs Created		Batting Average		On-Base Percentage		Slugging Percentage	
		(minimum 3,000 Plate Appearances)		(minimum 3,000 Plate Appearances)		(minimum 3,000 Plate Appearances)	
Babe Ruth	2,579	Ty Cobb	.368	Ted Williams	.483	Babe Ruth	.690
Ty Cobb	2,508	Rogers Hornsby	.359	Babe Ruth	.474	Ted Williams	.633
Hank Aaron	2,346	Joe Jackson	.356	John McGraw	.465	Lou Gehrig	.632
Stan Musial	2,281	Lefty O'Doul	.349	Billy Hamilton	.455	Jimmie Foxx	.609
Willie Mays	2,214	Ed Delahanty	.346	Frank Thomas	.452	Hank Greenberg	.605
Tris Speaker	2,200	Ted Williams	.346	Lou Gehrig	.447	Frank Thomas	.600
Ted Williams	2,175	Tris Speaker	.345	Bill Joyce	.435	Joe DiMaggio	.579
Lou Gehrig	2,161	Billy Hamilton	.344	Ty Cobb	.434	Rogers Hornsby	.578
Mel Ott	2,127	Dan Brouthers	.342	Rogers Hornsby	.434	Hank Aaron	.567
Frank Robinson	2,037	Nap Lajoie	.342	Jimmie Foxx	.428	Stan Musial	.566

Single Season Batting Leaders—Age 40

At-Bats			Runs			Hits			Doubles		
Sam Rice	1930	593	Sam Rice	1930	121	Sam Rice	1930	207	Sam Rice	1930	35
Dave Winfield	1992	583	Ty Cobb	1927	104	Ty Cobb	1927	175	Dave Winfield	1992	33
Rabbit Maranville	1932	571	Jim O'Rourke	1891	92	Dave Winfield	1992	169	Ty Cobb	1927	32
Eddie Murray	1996	566	Dave Winfield	1992	92	Jim O'Rourke	1891	164	Paul Molitor	1997	32
George Brett	1993	560	Darrell Evans	1987	90	Paul Molitor	1997	164	George Brett	1993	31
Cap Anson	1892	559	Willie Mays	1971	82	Deacon White	1888	157	Luke Appling	1947	29
Jim O'Rourke	1891	555	Brian Downing	1991	76	Luke Appling	1947	154	Jim O'Rourke	1891	28
Honus Wagner	1914	552	Deacon White	1888	75	Cap Anson	1892	152	Dave Parker	1991	26
Paul Molitor	1997	538	Pete Rose	1981	73	George Brett	1993	149	3 tied with		25
Deacon White	1888	527	2 tied with		69	Eddie Murray	1996	147			

Triples			Home Runs			RBI			Stolen Bases		
Sam Rice	1930	13	Darrell Evans	1987	34	Dave Winfield	1992	108	Davey Lopes	1985	47
Cap Anson	1892	9	Hank Sauer	1957	26	Darrell Evans	1987	99	Honus Wagner	1914	23
Honus Wagner	1914	9	Dave Winfield	1992	26	Jim O'Rourke	1891	95	Willie Mays	1971	23
Jake Daubert	1924	9	Eddie Murray	1996	22	Ty Cobb	1927	93	Ty Cobb	1927	22
Joe Start	1883	7	Hank Aaron	1974	20	Paul Molitor	1997	89	Lou Brock	1979	21
Jim O'Rourke	1891	7	Carlton Fisk	1988	19	Eddie Murray	1996	79	Jim O'Rourke	1891	19
Ty Cobb	1927	7	George Brett	1993	19	Hank Sauer	1957	76	Lave Cross	1906	19
Lave Cross	1906	6	Willie Mays	1971	18	George Brett	1993	75	Brett Butler	1997	15
5 tied with		5	Reggie Jackson	1986	18	Cap Anson	1892	74	Cap Anson	1892	13
			Brian Downing	1991	17	Sam Rice	1930	73	Sam Rice	1930	13

Runs Created			Batting Average			On-Base Percentage			Slugging Percentage		
			(minimum 3.1 PA/Tm Gm)			(minimum 3.1 PA/Tm Gm)			(minimum 3.1 PA/Tm Gm)		
Sam Rice	1930	114	Ty Cobb	1927	.357	Ty Cobb	1927	.440	Darrell Evans	1987	.501
Dave Winfield	1992	108	Sam Rice	1930	.349	Willie Mays	1971	.425	Dave Winfield	1992	.491
Ty Cobb	1927	102	Pete Rose	1981	.325	Sam Rice	1930	.407	Willie Mays	1971	.482
Darrell Evans	1987	99	Luke Appling	1947	.306	Pete Rose	1981	.391	Ty Cobb	1927	.482
Willie Mays	1971	94	Paul Molitor	1997	.305	Luke Appling	1947	.386	Sam Rice	1930	.457
Jim O'Rourke	1891	90	Deacon White	1888	.298	Reggie Jackson	1986	.379	Paul Molitor	1997	.435
Cap Anson	1892	88	Jim O'Rourke	1891	.295	Darrell Evans	1987	.379	George Brett	1993	.434
Deacon White	1888	84	Dave Winfield	1992	.290	Dave Winfield	1992	.377	Graig Nettles	1985	.420
Paul Molitor	1997	84	Joe Start	1883	.284	Graig Nettles	1985	.363	Eddie Murray	1996	.417
Luke Appling	1947	76	Nap Lajoie	1915	.280	Cap Anson	1892	.354	Luke Appling	1947	.412

Pitching Leaders—Through Age 40

Wins		Losses		Winning Percentage (minimum 200 decisions)		Games	
Cy Young	457	Pud Galvin	308	Dave Foutz	.690	Lee Smith	1,022
Walter Johnson	417	Walter Johnson	279	Whitey Ford	.690	Lindy McDaniel	987
Christy Mathewson	373	Cy Young	271	Bob Caruthers	.688	Jesse Orosco	956
Kid Nichols	361	Jack Powell	256	Lefty Grove	.686	Rollie Fingers	944
Pud Galvin	360	Robin Roberts	245	Larry Corcoran	.665	Kent Tekulve	943
Pete Alexander	348	Eppa Rixey	243	Christy Mathewson	.665	Gene Garber	931
Tim Keefe	341	Nolan Ryan	242	Sam Leever	.661	Goose Gossage	927
John Clarkson	328	Bert Blyleven	238	Sandy Koufax	.655	Dennis Eckersley	901
Eddie Plank	321	Frank Tanana	236	Johnny Allen	.654	Sparky Lyle	899
Steve Carlton	314	Gus Weyhing	232	Ron Guidry	.651	Jeff Reardon	880

Complete Games		Shutouts		Saves		Innings Pitched	
Cy Young	663	Walter Johnson	110	Lee Smith	478	Cy Young	6,472.1
Pud Galvin	639	Pete Alexander	89	Jeff Reardon	367	Pud Galvin	5,941.1
Tim Keefe	553	Christy Mathewson	79	John Franco	359	Walter Johnson	5,914.2
Walter Johnson	531	Eddie Plank	68	Rollie Fingers	341	Kid Nichols	5,056.1
Kid Nichols	531	Cy Young	67	Dennis Eckersley	323	Tim Keefe	5,052.1
Mickey Welch	525	Tom Seaver	61	Randy Myers	319	Steve Carlton	4,879.1
Old Hoss Radbourn	489	Bert Blyleven	60	Tom Henke	311	Bert Blyleven	4,837.0
John Clarkson	485	Don Sutton	57	Goose Gossage	308	Mickey Welch	4,802.0
Tony Mullane	468	Ed Walsh	57	Bruce Sutter	300	Don Sutton	4,796.1
Jim McCormick	466	3 tied with	56	Doug Jones	278	Pete Alexander	4,792.2

Strikeouts		ERA (minimum 1,300 Innings Pitched)		Component ERA (minimum 1,300 Innings Pitched)		Opponent Average (minimum 1,300 Innings Pitched)	
Nolan Ryan	4,547	Ed Walsh	1.81	Addie Joss	1.73	Nolan Ryan	.204
Steve Carlton	3,920	Addie Joss	1.89	Ed Walsh	1.78	Sandy Koufax	.205
Bert Blyleven	3,631	Joe Wood	2.03	Monte Ward	2.01	Sid Fernandez	.209
Tom Seaver	3,537	Three Finger Brown	2.06	Joe Wood	2.10	Randy Johnson	.211
Walter Johnson	3,509	Monte Ward	2.10	Walter Johnson	2.12	J.R. Richard	.212
Don Sutton	3,315	Christy Mathewson	2.13	Three Finger Brown	2.13	Andy Messersmith	.212
Fergie Jenkins	3,192	Rube Waddell	2.16	Christy Mathewson	2.14	Sam McDowell	.215
Gaylord Perry	3,141	Walter Johnson	2.17	Babe Adams	2.21	Ed Walsh	.218
Bob Gibson	3,117	Jake Weimer	2.23	Rube Waddell	2.22	Addie Joss	.220
Roger Clemens	2,882	Orval Overall	2.23	Larry Corcoran	2.23	Joe Wood	.220

Single Season Pitching Leaders—Age 40

Wins			Losses			Winning Percentage (minimum 15 decisions)			Games		
Cy Young	1907	21	Phil Niekro	1979	20	Dennis Martinez	1995	.706	Kent Tekulve	1987	90
Pete Alexander	1927	21	Bob Smith	1935	18	Rick Reuschel	1989	.680	Doug Jones	1997	75
Warren Spahn	1961	21	Kaiser Wilhelm	1914	17	Pete Alexander	1927	.677	Hoyt Wilhelm	1964	73
Phil Niekro	1979	21	Dutch Leonard	1949	16	Warren Spahn	1961	.618	Bob McClure	1992	71
Rick Reuschel	1989	17	Nolan Ryan	1987	16	Jerry Koosman	1983	.611	Jesse Orosco	1997	71
Eddie Plank	1916	16	Charlie Hough	1988	16	Don Sutton	1985	.600	Larry Andersen	1993	64
Tom Seaver	1985	16	Ed Green	1890	15	Tom Seaver	1985	.593	Don McMahon	1970	61
Don Sutton	1985	15	Cy Young	1907	15	Cy Young	1907	.583	Woodie Fryman	1980	61
Charlie Hough	1988	15	Eddie Plank	1916	15	Hoyt Wilhelm	1964	.571	Ron Reed	1983	61
3 tied with		13	6 tied with		13	Virgil Trucks	1957	.563	Al Brazle	1954	58

Complete Games			Shutouts			Saves			Innings Pitched		
Cy Young	1907	33	Cy Young	1907	6	Doug Jones	1997	36	Cy Young	1907	343.1
Phil Niekro	1979	23	Babe Adams	1922	4	Dennis Eckersley	1995	29	Phil Niekro	1979	342.0
Pete Alexander	1927	22	Early Wynn	1960	4	Hoyt Wilhelm	1964	27	Pete Alexander	1927	268.0
Warren Spahn	1961	21	Warren Spahn	1961	4	Don McMahon	1970	19	Warren Spahn	1961	262.2
Ed Green	1890	20	Eddie Plank	1916	3	Ellis Kinder	1955	18	Charlie Hough	1988	252.0
Ted Lyons	1941	19	11 tied with		2	Woodie Fryman	1980	17	Kaiser Wilhelm	1914	243.2
Eddie Plank	1916	17				Roy Face	1968	13	Tom Seaver	1985	238.2
Connie Marrero	1951	16				Marv Grissom	1958	10	Early Wynn	1960	237.1
Red Faber	1929	15				Art Fowler	1963	10	Eddie Plank	1916	235.2
Johnny Niggeling	1944	14				2 tied with		8	Tommy John	1983	234.2

Strikeouts			ERA (minimum 1 Inning Pitched/Tm Gm)			Component ERA (minimum 1 Inning Pitched/Tm Gm)			Opponent Average (minimum 1 Inning Pitched/Tm Gm)		
Nolan Ryan	1987	270	Cy Young	1907	1.99	Cy Young	1907	1.85	Nolan Ryan	1987	.200
Phil Niekro	1979	208	Johnny Niggeling	1944	2.32	Eddie Plank	1916	2.39	Johnny Niggeling	1944	.221
Charlie Hough	1988	174	Eddie Plank	1916	2.33	Nolan Ryan	1987	2.50	Charlie Hough	1988	.221
Early Wynn	1960	158	Pete Alexander	1927	2.52	Pete Alexander	1927	2.58	Cy Young	1907	.230
Dazzy Vance	1931	150	Nolan Ryan	1987	2.76	Johnny Niggeling	1944	2.59	Eddie Plank	1916	.237
Cy Young	1907	147	Rick Reuschel	1989	2.94	Babe Adams	1922	2.95	Phil Niekro	1979	.241
Gaylord Perry	1979	140	Warren Spahn	1961	3.02	Warren Spahn	1961	2.96	Warren Spahn	1961	.243
Tom Seaver	1985	134	Gaylord Perry	1979	3.06	Rick Reuschel	1989	3.11	Dennis Martinez	1995	.247
Johnny Niggeling	1944	121	Dennis Martinez	1995	3.08	Dazzy Vance	1931	3.14	Rick Reuschel	1989	.247
Joe Niekro	1985	121	Tom Seaver	1985	3.17	Gaylord Perry	1979	3.18	Early Wynn	1960	.247

Batting Leaders—Through Age 41

At-Bats		Runs		Hits		Doubles	
Pete Rose	12,544	Ty Cobb	2,245	Ty Cobb	4,190	Tris Speaker	792
Hank Aaron	12,093	Babe Ruth	2,174	Pete Rose	3,869	Ty Cobb	725
Ty Cobb	11,434	Hank Aaron	2,152	Hank Aaron	3,709	Stan Musial	715
Eddie Murray	11,336	Willie Mays	2,038	Stan Musial	3,544	Pete Rose	697
Carl Yastrzemski	11,149	Pete Rose	1,995	Tris Speaker	3,514	George Brett	665
Robin Yount	11,008	Stan Musial	1,915	Eddie Collins	3,311	Nap Lajoie	657
Willie Mays	10,672	Rickey Henderson	1,913	Eddie Murray	3,255	Honus Wagner	618
Brooks Robinson	10,654	Lou Gehrig	1,888	Nap Lajoie	3,242	Hank Aaron	616
Stan Musial	10,635	Tris Speaker	1,882	Willie Mays	3,239	Paul Waner	603
Dave Winfield	10,594	Mel Ott	1,859	Honus Wagner	3,230	Carl Yastrzemski	600

Triples		Home Runs		RBI		Stolen Bases	
Sam Crawford	309	Hank Aaron	745	Hank Aaron	2,262	Rickey Henderson	1,231
Ty Cobb	296	Babe Ruth	714	Babe Ruth	2,210	Lou Brock	938
Jake Beckley	243	Willie Mays	654	Lou Gehrig	1,995	Billy Hamilton	912
Honus Wagner	242	Frank Robinson	586	Ty Cobb	1,933	Ty Cobb	892
Roger Connor	233	Harmon Killebrew	573	Jimmie Foxx	1,921	Tim Raines	795
Tris Speaker	222	Reggie Jackson	563	Eddie Murray	1,917	Vince Coleman	752
Fred Clarke	220	Mike Schmidt	548	Stan Musial	1,893	Eddie Collins	745
Dan Brouthers	205	Mickey Mantle	536	Willie Mays	1,878	Max Carey	738
Joe Kelley	194	Jimmie Foxx	534	Mel Ott	1,860	Arlie Latham	738
Paul Waner	190	Ted Williams	521	Ted Williams	1,839	Honus Wagner	707

Runs Created		Batting Average (minimum 3,000 Plate Appearances)		On-Base Percentage (minimum 3,000 Plate Appearances)		Slugging Percentage (minimum 3,000 Plate Appearances)	
Babe Ruth	2,579	Ty Cobb	.366	Ted Williams	.482	Babe Ruth	.690
Ty Cobb	2,566	Rogers Hornsby	.358	Babe Ruth	.474	Ted Williams	.634
Hank Aaron	2,403	Joe Jackson	.356	John McGraw	.465	Lou Gehrig	.632
Stan Musial	2,373	Lefty O'Doul	.349	Billy Hamilton	.455	Jimmie Foxx	.609
Ted Williams	2,259	Ed Delahanty	.346	Frank Thomas	.452	Hank Greenberg	.605
Willie Mays	2,255	Tris Speaker	.345	Lou Gehrig	.447	Frank Thomas	.600
Tris Speaker	2,200	Ted Williams	.344	Bill Joyce	.435	Joe DiMaggio	.579
Lou Gehrig	2,161	Billy Hamilton	.344	Rogers Hornsby	.434	Rogers Hornsby	.577
Mel Ott	2,127	Dan Brouthers	.342	Ty Cobb	.433	Albert Belle	.566
Honus Wagner	2,071	Dave Orr	.342	Jimmie Foxx	.428	Stan Musial	.564

Single Season Batting Leaders—Age 41

At-Bats			Runs			Hits			Doubles		
Pete Rose	1982	634	Sam Rice	1931	81	Pete Rose	1982	172	Honus Wagner	1915	32
Honus Wagner	1915	566	Joe Start	1884	80	Luke Appling	1948	156	Jim O'Rourke	1892	28
Dave Winfield	1993	547	Pete Rose	1982	80	Honus Wagner	1915	155	Ty Cobb	1928	27
Luke Appling	1948	497	Dave Winfield	1993	72	Dave Winfield	1993	148	Dave Winfield	1993	27
Rabbit Maranville	1933	478	Cap Anson	1893	70	Stan Musial	1962	143	Pete Rose	1982	25
Hank Aaron	1975	465	Honus Wagner	1915	68	Jim O'Rourke	1892	136	Carlton Fisk	1989	25
Jim O'Rourke	1892	448	Luke Appling	1948	63	Sam Rice	1931	128	Cap Anson	1893	24
Darrell Evans	1988	437	Jim O'Rourke	1892	62	Cap Anson	1893	125	Sam Rice	1931	21
Stan Musial	1962	433	Stan Musial	1962	57	Ty Cobb	1928	114	Stan Musial	1962	18
Nap Lajoie	1916	426	Ted Williams	1960	56	Bob Boone	1989	111	Brian Downing	1992	18

Triples			Home Runs			RBI			Stolen Bases		
Honus Wagner	1915	17	Ted Williams	1960	29	Cap Anson	1893	91	Davey Lopes	1986	25
Sam Rice	1931	8	Darrell Evans	1988	22	Stan Musial	1962	82	Honus Wagner	1915	22
Joe Start	1884	5	Dave Winfield	1993	21	Honus Wagner	1915	78	Jim O'Rourke	1892	16
Jim O'Rourke	1892	5	Stan Musial	1962	19	Dave Winfield	1993	76	Nap Lajoie	1916	15
Nap Lajoie	1916	4	Graig Nettles	1986	16	Ted Williams	1960	72	Cap Anson	1893	13
Ty Cobb	1928	4	Willie McCovey	1979	15	Carlton Fisk	1989	68	Candy Nelson	1890	12
Rabbit Maranville	1933	4	Reggie Jackson	1987	15	Darrell Evans	1988	64	Luke Appling	1948	10
Bob Thurman	1958	4	Carlton Fisk	1989	13	Hank Aaron	1975	60	Pete Rose	1982	8
Pete Rose	1982	4	Hank Sauer	1958	12	Willie McCovey	1979	57	Ozzie Smith	1996	7
Davey Lopes	1986	3	Hank Aaron	1975	12	Jim O'Rourke	1892	56	2 tied with		6

Runs Created			Batting Average (minimum 3.1 PA/Tm Gm)			On-Base Percentage (minimum 3.1 PA/Tm Gm)			Slugging Percentage (minimum 3.1 PA/Tm Gm)		
Stan Musial	1962	92	Stan Musial	1962	.330	Luke Appling	1948	.423	Stan Musial	1962	.508
Cap Anson	1893	85	Cap Anson	1893	.314	Stan Musial	1962	.416	Dave Winfield	1993	.442
Ted Williams	1960	84	Luke Appling	1948	.314	Cap Anson	1893	.415	Honus Wagner	1915	.422
Jim O'Rourke	1892	79	Jim O'Rourke	1892	.304	Jim O'Rourke	1892	.354	Jim O'Rourke	1892	.388
Honus Wagner	1915	78	Joe Start	1884	.276	Pete Rose	1982	.345	Cap Anson	1893	.384
Luke Appling	1948	77	Honus Wagner	1915	.274	Carl Yastrzemski	1981	.338	Darrell Evans	1988	.380
Pete Rose	1982	76	Pete Rose	1982	.271	Darrell Evans	1988	.337	Carl Yastrzemski	1981	.355
Joe Start	1884	75	Dave Winfield	1993	.271	Joe Start	1884	.337	Hank Aaron	1975	.355
Dave Winfield	1993	71	Carl Yastrzemski	1981	.246	Hank Aaron	1975	.332	Luke Appling	1948	.354
Sam Rice	1931	66	Hank Aaron	1975	.234	Honus Wagner	1915	.325	Joe Start	1884	.344

Pitching Leaders—Through Age 41

Wins		Losses		Winning Percentage (minimum 200 decisions)		Games	
Cy Young	478	Pud Galvin	308	Dave Foutz	.690	Lee Smith	1,022
Walter Johnson	417	Cy Young	282	Whitey Ford	.690	Kent Tekulve	1,013
Christy Mathewson	373	Walter Johnson	279	Bob Caruthers	.688	Lindy McDaniel	987
Pete Alexander	364	Jack Powell	256	Lefty Grove	.680	Goose Gossage	966
Kid Nichols	361	Nolan Ryan	253	Larry Corcoran	.665	Dennis Eckersley	964
Pud Galvin	360	Bert Blyleven	250	Christy Mathewson	.665	Jesse Orosco	956
Tim Keefe	341	Eppa Rixey	248	Sam Leever	.661	Rollie Fingers	944
John Clarkson	328	Robin Roberts	245	Sandy Koufax	.655	Gene Garber	931
Warren Spahn	327	Don Sutton	239	Johnny Allen	.654	Sparky Lyle	899
Eddie Plank	326	Frank Tanana	236	Ron Guidry	.651	Jeff Reardon	880

Complete Games		Shutouts		Saves		Innings Pitched	
Cy Young	693	Walter Johnson	110	Lee Smith	478	Cy Young	6,771.1
Pud Galvin	639	Pete Alexander	90	Jeff Reardon	367	Pud Galvin	5,941.1
Tim Keefe	553	Christy Mathewson	79	John Franco	359	Walter Johnson	5,914.2
Walter Johnson	531	Cy Young	70	Dennis Eckersley	353	Kid Nichols	5,056.1
Kid Nichols	531	Eddie Plank	69	Rollie Fingers	341	Steve Carlton	5,055.2
Mickey Welch	525	Tom Seaver	61	Randy Myers	319	Tim Keefe	5,052.1
Old Hoss Radbourn	489	Bert Blyleven	60	Tom Henke	311	Pete Alexander	5,036.1
John Clarkson	485	Don Sutton	58	Goose Gossage	309	Don Sutton	5,003.1
Tony Mullane	468	Ed Walsh	57	Bruce Sutter	300	Bert Blyleven	4,970.0
Jim McCormick	466	3 tied with	56	Doug Jones	278	Mickey Welch	4,802.0

Strikeouts		ERA (minimum 1,350 Innings Pitched)		Component ERA (minimum 1,350 Innings Pitched)		Opponent Average (minimum 1,350 Innings Pitched)	
Nolan Ryan	4,775	Ed Walsh	1.81	Addie Joss	1.73	Nolan Ryan	.205
Steve Carlton	4,040	Addie Joss	1.89	Ed Walsh	1.78	Sandy Koufax	.205
Bert Blyleven	3,701	Joe Wood	2.03	Monte Ward	2.01	Sid Fernandez	.209
Tom Seaver	3,640	Three Finger Brown	2.06	Joe Wood	2.10	Randy Johnson	.211
Walter Johnson	3,509	Monte Ward	2.10	Walter Johnson	2.12	J.R. Richard	.212
Don Sutton	3,431	Christy Mathewson	2.13	Three Finger Brown	2.13	Andy Messersmith	.212
Gaylord Perry	3,276	Rube Waddell	2.16	Christy Mathewson	2.14	Sam McDowell	.215
Fergie Jenkins	3,192	Walter Johnson	2.17	Rube Waddell	2.22	Ed Walsh	.218
Bob Gibson	3,117	Jake Weimer	2.23	Larry Corcoran	2.23	Addie Joss	.220
Roger Clemens	2,882	Orval Overall	2.23	Tim Keefe	2.26	Joe Wood	.220

Single Season Pitching Leaders—Age 41

Wins			Losses			Winning Percentage (minimum 15 decisions)			Games		
Cy Young	1908	21	Phil Niekro	1980	18	Rip Sewell	1948	.813	Kent Tekulve	1988	70
Warren Spahn	1962	18	Jerry Koosman	1984	15	Earl Caldwell	1946	.765	Hoyt Wilhelm	1965	66
Pete Alexander	1928	16	Warren Spahn	1962	14	Ted Lyons	1942	.700	Dennis Eckersley	1996	63
Phil Niekro	1980	15	Steve Carlton	1986	14	Cy Young	1908	.656	Don McMahon	1971	61
Don Sutton	1986	15	Red Faber	1930	13	Babe Adams	1923	.650	Jim Kaat	1980	53
Ted Lyons	1942	14	Gaylord Perry	1980	13	Pete Alexander	1928	.640	Rick Honeycutt	1995	52
Jerry Koosman	1984	14	Tommy John	1984	13	Mike Ryba	1944	.632	Ellis Kinder	1956	51
4 tied with		13	Tom Seaver	1986	13	Don McMahon	1971	.625	Ron Reed	1984	51
			Charlie Hough	1989	13	Dennis Martinez	1996	.600	Roy Face	1969	44
			3 tied with		12	Murry Dickson	1958	.588	Mike Ryba	1944	42

Complete Games			Shutouts			Saves			Innings Pitched		
Cy Young	1908	30	Cy Young	1908	3	Dennis Eckersley	1996	30	Cy Young	1908	299.0
Warren Spahn	1962	22	Phil Niekro	1980	3	Hoyt Wilhelm	1965	20	Phil Niekro	1980	275.0
Ted Lyons	1942	20	Eppa Rixey	1932	2	Ron Reed	1984	12	Warren Spahn	1962	269.1
Pete Alexander	1928	18	Bob Smith	1936	2	Jim Turner	1945	10	Pete Alexander	1928	243.2
Connie Marrero	1952	16	Johnny Niggeling	1945	2	Ellis Kinder	1956	9	Jerry Koosman	1984	224.0
Jack Quinn	1925	12	Satchel Paige	1948	2	Bob Smith	1936	8	Nolan Ryan	1988	220.0
Babe Adams	1923	11	Connie Marrero	1952	2	Earl Caldwell	1946	8	Don Sutton	1986	207.0
Sad Sam Jones	1934	11	Gaylord Perry	1980	2	Woodie Fryman	1981	7	Gaylord Perry	1980	205.2
Phil Niekro	1980	11	13 tied with		1	Dutch Leonard	1950	6	Jack Quinn	1925	204.2
3 tied with		10				Al Benton	1952	6	Connie Marrero	1952	184.1

Strikeouts			ERA (minimum 1 Inning Pitched/Tm Gm)			Component ERA (minimum 1 Inning Pitched/Tm Gm)			Opponent Average (minimum 1 Inning Pitched/Tm Gm)		
Nolan Ryan	1988	228	Cy Young	1908	1.26	Cy Young	1908	1.48	Cy Young	1908	.213
Phil Niekro	1980	176	Ted Lyons	1942	2.10	Ted Lyons	1942	2.50	Nolan Ryan	1988	.227
Cy Young	1908	150	Connie Marrero	1952	2.88	Warren Spahn	1962	2.90	Johnny Niggeling	1945	.240
Jerry Koosman	1984	137	Warren Spahn	1962	3.04	Connie Marrero	1952	3.03	Don Sutton	1986	.242
Gaylord Perry	1980	135	Johnny Niggeling	1945	3.16	Nolan Ryan	1988	3.15	Ted Lyons	1942	.245
Steve Carlton	1986	120	Jerry Koosman	1984	3.25	Johnny Niggeling	1945	3.17	Charlie Hough	1989	.245
Warren Spahn	1962	118	Pete Alexander	1928	3.36	Dazzy Vance	1932	3.28	Warren Spahn	1962	.246
Don Sutton	1986	116	Nolan Ryan	1988	3.52	Pete Alexander	1928	3.30	Phil Niekro	1980	.249
Hoyt Wilhelm	1965	106	Phil Niekro	1980	3.63	Jerry Koosman	1984	3.32	Connie Marrero	1952	.249
2 tied with		103	Gaylord Perry	1980	3.68	Don Sutton	1986	3.40	Dazzy Vance	1932	.256

Batting Leaders—Through Age 42

At-Bats		Runs		Hits		Doubles	
Pete Rose	13,037	Ty Cobb	2,245	Ty Cobb	4,190	Tris Speaker	792
Hank Aaron	12,364	Hank Aaron	2,174	Pete Rose	3,990	Stan Musial	725
Carl Yastrzemski	11,608	Babe Ruth	2,174	Hank Aaron	3,771	Ty Cobb	725
Ty Cobb	11,434	Willie Mays	2,062	Stan Musial	3,630	Pete Rose	711
Eddie Murray	11,336	Pete Rose	2,047	Tris Speaker	3,514	George Brett	665
Robin Yount	11,008	Stan Musial	1,949	Honus Wagner	3,354	Nap Lajoie	657
Stan Musial	10,972	Rickey Henderson	1,913	Carl Yastrzemski	3,318	Honus Wagner	633
Dave Winfield	10,888	Lou Gehrig	1,888	Eddie Collins	3,311	Hank Aaron	624
Willie Mays	10,881	Tris Speaker	1,882	Willie Mays	3,283	Carl Yastrzemski	622
Brooks Robinson	10,654	Mel Ott	1,859	Eddie Murray	3,255	Paul Waner	603

Triples		Home Runs		RBI		Stolen Bases	
Sam Crawford	309	Hank Aaron	755	Hank Aaron	2,297	Rickey Henderson	1,231
Ty Cobb	296	Babe Ruth	714	Babe Ruth	2,210	Lou Brock	938
Honus Wagner	251	Willie Mays	660	Lou Gehrig	1,995	Billy Hamilton	912
Jake Beckley	243	Frank Robinson	586	Stan Musial	1,951	Ty Cobb	892
Roger Connor	233	Harmon Killebrew	573	Ty Cobb	1,933	Tim Raines	795
Tris Speaker	222	Reggie Jackson	563	Jimmie Foxx	1,921	Vince Coleman	752
Fred Clarke	220	Mike Schmidt	548	Eddie Murray	1,917	Eddie Collins	745
Dan Brouthers	205	Mickey Mantle	536	Willie Mays	1,903	Max Carey	738
Joe Kelley	194	Jimmie Foxx	534	Mel Ott	1,860	Arlie Latham	738
Paul Waner	190	2 tied with	521	Ted Williams	1,839	Honus Wagner	718

Runs Created		Batting Average		On-Base Percentage		Slugging Percentage	
		(minimum 3,000 Plate Appearances)		(minimum 3,000 Plate Appearances)		(minimum 3,000 Plate Appearances)	
Babe Ruth	2,579	Ty Cobb	.366	Ted Williams	.482	Babe Ruth	.690
Ty Cobb	2,566	Rogers Hornsby	.358	Babe Ruth	.474	Ted Williams	.634
Hank Aaron	2,434	Joe Jackson	.356	John McGraw	.465	Lou Gehrig	.632
Stan Musial	2,418	Lefty O'Doul	.349	Billy Hamilton	.455	Jimmie Foxx	.609
Willie Mays	2,278	Ed Delahanty	.346	Frank Thomas	.452	Hank Greenberg	.605
Ted Williams	2,259	Tris Speaker	.345	Lou Gehrig	.447	Frank Thomas	.600
Tris Speaker	2,200	Ted Williams	.344	Bill Joyce	.435	Joe DiMaggio	.579
Lou Gehrig	2,161	Billy Hamilton	.344	Rogers Hornsby	.434	Rogers Hornsby	.577
Mel Ott	2,127	Dan Brouthers	.342	Ty Cobb	.433	Albert Belle	.566
Honus Wagner	2,127	Dave Orr	.342	Jimmie Foxx	.428	Johnny Mize	.562

Single Season Batting Leaders—Age 42

At-Bats			Runs			Hits			Doubles		
Jim O'Rourke	1893	547	Cap Anson	1894	82	Jim O'Rourke	1893	157	Cap Anson	1894	28
Pete Rose	1983	493	Luke Appling	1949	82	Luke Appling	1949	148	Jim O'Rourke	1893	22
Luke Appling	1949	492	Jim O'Rourke	1893	75	Cap Anson	1894	132	Carl Yastrzemski	1982	22
Carl Yastrzemski	1982	459	Carlton Fisk	1990	65	Carlton Fisk	1990	129	Luke Appling	1949	21
Carlton Fisk	1990	452	Deacon White	1890	62	Carl Yastrzemski	1982	126	Carlton Fisk	1990	21
Deacon White	1890	439	Sam Rice	1932	58	Pete Rose	1983	121	Sam Rice	1932	16
Honus Wagner	1916	432	Carl Yastrzemski	1982	53	Honus Wagner	1916	124	Honus Wagner	1916	15
Joe Start	1885	374	Pete Rose	1983	52	Deacon White	1890	114	Dave Winfield	1994	15
Cap Anson	1894	340	Joe Start	1885	47	Joe Start	1885	103	Pete Rose	1983	14
Stan Musial	1963	337	Honus Wagner	1916	45	Sam Rice	1932	93	Deacon White	1890	13

Triples			Home Runs			RBI			Stolen Bases		
Honus Wagner	1916	9	Carlton Fisk	1990	18	Cap Anson	1894	99	Cap Anson	1894	17
Sam Rice	1932	7	Carl Yastrzemski	1982	16	Jim O'Rourke	1893	95	Jim O'Rourke	1893	15
Jim O'Rourke	1893	5	Stan Musial	1963	12	Carl Yastrzemski	1982	72	Honus Wagner	1916	11
Luke Appling	1949	5	Darrell Evans	1989	11	Carlton Fisk	1990	65	Sam Rice	1932	7
Joe Start	1885	4	Hank Aaron	1976	10	Luke Appling	1949	58	Luke Appling	1949	7
Deacon White	1890	4	Dave Winfield	1994	10	Stan Musial	1963	58	Pete Rose	1983	7
Cap Anson	1894	4	Willie Mays	1973	6	Deacon White	1890	47	Carlton Fisk	1990	7
Jack Saltzgaver	1945	3	Cap Anson	1894	5	Pete Rose	1983	45	Deacon White	1890	3
Pete Rose	1983	3	Luke Appling	1949	5	Dave Winfield	1994	43	Chief Zimmer	1903	3
Dave Winfield	1994	3	Graig Nettles	1987	5	Joe Start	1885	41	Deacon McGuire	1906	3

Runs Created			Batting Average			On-Base Percentage			Slugging Percentage		
			(minimum 3.1 PA/Tm Gm)			(minimum 3.1 PA/Tm Gm)			(minimum 3.1 PA/Tm Gm)		
Cap Anson	1894	94	Luke Appling	1949	.301	Luke Appling	1949	.439	Carlton Fisk	1990	.451
Luke Appling	1949	87	Honus Wagner	1916	.287	Deacon White	1890	.381	Carl Yastrzemski	1982	.431
Jim O'Rourke	1893	84	Jim O'Rourke	1893	.287	Carlton Fisk	1990	.378	Luke Appling	1949	.394
Deacon White	1890	76	Carlton Fisk	1990	.285	Carl Yastrzemski	1982	.358	Honus Wagner	1916	.370
Carl Yastrzemski	1982	70	Joe Start	1885	.275	Jim O'Rourke	1893	.354	Jim O'Rourke	1893	.362
Carlton Fisk	1990	65	Carl Yastrzemski	1982	.275	Honus Wagner	1916	.350	Joe Start	1885	.326
Joe Start	1885	64	Deacon White	1890	.260	Joe Start	1885	.344	Deacon White	1890	.308
Honus Wagner	1916	56	Pete Rose	1983	.245	Pete Rose	1983	.316	Pete Rose	1983	.286
Sam Rice	1932	53									
Pete Rose	1983	46									

Pitching Leaders—Through Age 42

Wins

Cy Young	497
Walter Johnson	417
Pete Alexander	373
Christy Mathewson	373
Kid Nichols	361
Pud Galvin	360
Warren Spahn	350
Tim Keefe	341
Steve Carlton	329
John Clarkson	328

Losses

Pud Galvin	308
Cy Young	297
Walter Johnson	279
Nolan Ryan	263
Jack Powell	256
Eppa Rixey	251
Bert Blyleven	250
Don Sutton	250
Robin Roberts	245
Steve Carlton	243

Winning Percentage
(minimum 200 decisions)

Dave Foutz	.690
Whitey Ford	.690
Bob Caruthers	.688
Lefty Grove	.680
Larry Corcoran	.665
Christy Mathewson	.665
Sam Leever	.661
Sandy Koufax	.655
Johnny Allen	.654
Ron Guidry	.651

Games

Kent Tekulve	1,050
Lee Smith	1,022
Dennis Eckersley	1,021
Goose Gossage	1,002
Lindy McDaniel	987
Jesse Orosco	956
Rollie Fingers	944
Gene Garber	931
Sparky Lyle	899
Jeff Reardon	880

Complete Games

Cy Young	723
Pud Galvin	639
Tim Keefe	553
Walter Johnson	531
Kid Nichols	531
Mickey Welch	525
Old Hoss Radbourn	489
John Clarkson	485
Tony Mullane	468
Jim McCormick	466

Shutouts

Walter Johnson	110
Pete Alexander	90
Christy Mathewson	79
Cy Young	73
Eddie Plank	69
Warren Spahn	62
Tom Seaver	61
Bert Blyleven	60
Don Sutton	58
2 tied with	57

Saves

Lee Smith	478
Dennis Eckersley	389
Jeff Reardon	367
John Franco	359
Rollie Fingers	341
Randy Myers	319
Tom Henke	311
Goose Gossage	310
Bruce Sutter	300
Doug Jones	278

Innings Pitched

Cy Young	7,066.0
Pud Galvin	5,941.1
Walter Johnson	5,914.2
Steve Carlton	5,207.2
Don Sutton	5,195.0
Pete Alexander	5,168.1
Kid Nichols	5,056.1
Tim Keefe	5,052.1
Bert Blyleven	4,970.0
Gaylord Perry	4,947.1

Strikeouts

Nolan Ryan	5,076
Steve Carlton	4,131
Bert Blyleven	3,701
Tom Seaver	3,640
Don Sutton	3,530
Walter Johnson	3,509
Gaylord Perry	3,336
Fergie Jenkins	3,192
Bob Gibson	3,117
Roger Clemens	2,882

ERA
(minimum 1,400 Innings Pitched)

Ed Walsh	1.81
Addie Joss	1.89
Joe Wood	2.03
Three Finger Brown	2.06
Monte Ward	2.10
Christy Mathewson	2.13
Rube Waddell	2.16
Walter Johnson	2.17
Jake Weimer	2.23
Orval Overall	2.23

Component ERA
(minimum 1,400 Innings Pitched)

Addie Joss	1.73
Ed Walsh	1.78
Monte Ward	2.01
Joe Wood	2.10
Walter Johnson	2.12
Three Finger Brown	2.13
Christy Mathewson	2.14
Rube Waddell	2.22
Larry Corcoran	2.23
Tim Keefe	2.26

Opponent Average
(minimum 1,400 Innings Pitched)

Nolan Ryan	.204
Sandy Koufax	.205
Sid Fernandez	.209
Randy Johnson	.211
J.R. Richard	.212
Andy Messersmith	.212
Sam McDowell	.215
Ed Walsh	.218
Hoyt Wilhelm	.219
Addie Joss	.220

Single Season Pitching Leaders—Age 42

Wins

Warren Spahn	1963	23
Cy Young	1909	19
Nolan Ryan	1989	16
Charlie Hough	1990	12
Don Sutton	1987	11
Jack Quinn	1926	10
Red Faber	1931	10
Dutch Leonard	1951	10
Pete Alexander	1929	9
Woodie Fryman	1982	9

Losses

Cy Young	1909	15
Early Wynn	1962	15
Red Faber	1931	14
Steve Carlton	1987	14
Joe Niekro	1987	13
Charlie Hough	1990	12
Jack Quinn	1926	11
Don Sutton	1987	11
Tommy John	1985	10
Nolan Ryan	1989	10

Winning Percentage
(minimum 15 decisions)

Warren Spahn	1963	.767
Dutch Leonard	1951	.625
Nolan Ryan	1989	.615
Cy Young	1909	.559
Sad Sam Jones	1935	.533
Charlie Root	1941	.533
Connie Marrero	1953	.533
Pete Alexander	1929	.529
Don Sutton	1987	.500
Charlie Hough	1990	.500

Games

Rick Honeycutt	1996	61
Woodie Fryman	1982	60
Dennis Eckersley	1997	57
Hoyt Wilhelm	1966	46
Red Faber	1931	44
Don McMahon	1972	44
Dutch Leonard	1951	41
Jim Kaat	1981	41
Earl Caldwell	1947	40
Murry Dickson	1959	38

Complete Games

Cy Young	1909	30
Warren Spahn	1963	22
Early Wynn	1962	11
Connie Marrero	1953	10
Jack Quinn	1926	8
Pete Alexander	1929	8
Sad Sam Jones	1935	7
Charlie Root	1941	6
Johnny Niggeling	1946	6
Nolan Ryan	1989	6

Shutouts

Warren Spahn	1963	7
Cy Young	1909	3
Jack Quinn	1926	3
Early Wynn	1962	3
Phil Niekro	1981	3
Red Ruffing	1946	2
Connie Marrero	1953	2
Nolan Ryan	1989	2
5 tied with		1

Saves

Dennis Eckersley	1997	36
Woodie Fryman	1982	12
Joe Heving	1943	9
Earl Caldwell	1947	8
Hoyt Wilhelm	1966	6
Satchel Paige	1949	5
Don McMahon	1972	5
Dolf Luque	1933	4
Jim Kaat	1981	4
Rick Honeycutt	1996	4

Innings Pitched

Cy Young	1909	294.2
Warren Spahn	1963	259.2
Nolan Ryan	1989	239.1
Charlie Hough	1990	218.2
Don Sutton	1987	191.2
Red Faber	1931	184.0
Early Wynn	1962	167.2
Jack Quinn	1926	163.2
Steve Carlton	1987	152.0
Gaylord Perry	1981	150.2

Strikeouts

Nolan Ryan	1989	301
Charlie Hough	1990	114
Cy Young	1909	109
Warren Spahn	1963	102
Don Sutton	1987	99
Early Wynn	1962	91
Steve Carlton	1987	91
Joe Niekro	1987	84
Dazzy Vance	1933	67
Connie Marrero	1953	65

ERA
(minimum 1 Inning Pitched/Tm Gm)

Cy Young	1909	2.26
Warren Spahn	1963	2.60
Phil Niekro	1981	3.10
Nolan Ryan	1989	3.20
Jack Quinn	1926	3.41
Red Faber	1931	3.82
Gaylord Perry	1981	3.94
Charlie Hough	1990	4.07
Early Wynn	1962	4.46
Don Sutton	1987	4.70

Component ERA
(minimum 1 Inning Pitched/Tm Gm)

Nolan Ryan	1989	2.31
Cy Young	1909	2.40
Warren Spahn	1963	2.84
Phil Niekro	1981	2.99
Jack Quinn	1926	3.78
Early Wynn	1962	3.91
Gaylord Perry	1981	4.12
Red Faber	1931	4.18
Charlie Hough	1990	4.19
Don Sutton	1987	4.43

Opponent Average
(minimum 1 Inning Pitched/Tm Gm)

Nolan Ryan	1989	.187
Phil Niekro	1981	.233
Charlie Hough	1990	.235
Warren Spahn	1963	.248
Cy Young	1909	.250
Early Wynn	1962	.264
Don Sutton	1987	.269
Red Faber	1931	.285
Jack Quinn	1926	.296
Gaylord Perry	1981	.304

Batting Leaders—After Age 42

At-Bats		Runs		Hits		Doubles	
Cap Anson	1,300	Cap Anson	226	Cap Anson	413	Cap Anson	58
Pete Rose	1,016	Pete Rose	118	Pete Rose	266	Pete Rose	35
Carlton Fisk	701	Sam Rice	67	Carlton Fisk	164	Carlton Fisk	29
Sam Rice	420	Carlton Fisk	56	Sam Rice	123	Carl Yastrzemski	24
Tony Perez	383	Tony Perez	39	Tony Perez	111	Sam Rice	23
Carl Yastrzemski	380	Carl Yastrzemski	38	Carl Yastrzemski	101	Tony Perez	20
Jack Quinn	275	Honus Wagner	15	Honus Wagner	61	Honus Wagner	7
Honus Wagner	230	Dave Winfield	11	Jack Quinn	43	Phil Niekro	6
Phil Niekro	153	Luke Appling	11	Luke Appling	30	Jack Quinn	6
Luke Appling	128	2 tied with	10	Phil Niekro	29	Dave Winfield	5

Triples		Home Runs		RBI		Stolen Bases	
Cap Anson	11	Carlton Fisk	22	Cap Anson	256	Cap Anson	47
Pete Rose	6	Carl Yastrzemski	10	Pete Rose	105	Pete Rose	12
Luke Appling	4	Tony Perez	8	Carlton Fisk	99	Sam Rice	5
Sam Rice	4	Cap Anson	7	Tony Perez	62	Honus Wagner	5
7 tied with	1	Enos Slaughter	6	Carl Yastrzemski	56	Carlton Fisk	4
		Dave Winfield	2	Sam Rice	45	Joe Start	4
		Pete Rose	2	Jack Quinn	30	Luke Appling	2
		Sam Rice	2	Honus Wagner	24	5 tied with	1
		7 tied with	1	Enos Slaughter	22		
				Joe Start	17		

Runs Created		Batting Average (minimum 300 Plate Appearances)		On-Base Percentage (minimum 300 Plate Appearances)		Slugging Percentage (minimum 300 Plate Appearances)	
Cap Anson	256	Cap Anson	.318	Cap Anson	.398	Tony Perez	.410
Pete Rose	127	Sam Rice	.293	Pete Rose	.364	Carl Yastrzemski	.408
Carlton Fisk	76	Tony Perez	.290	Tony Perez	.363	Cap Anson	.395
Tony Perez	58	Carl Yastrzemski	.266	Carl Yastrzemski	.359	Sam Rice	.381
Sam Rice	57	Pete Rose	.262	Sam Rice	.346	Carlton Fisk	.372
Carl Yastrzemski	53	Carlton Fisk	.234	Carlton Fisk	.298	Pete Rose	.314
Honus Wagner	25	Jack Quinn	.156	Jack Quinn	.180	Jack Quinn	.189
Joe Start	12						
Enos Slaughter	11						
Luke Appling	11						

Single Season Batting Leaders—Age 43 or Older

At-Bats			Runs			Hits			Doubles		
Cap Anson	1895	474	Cap Anson	1895	87	Cap Anson	1895	159	Carlton Fisk	1991	25
Carlton Fisk	1991	460	Cap Anson	1896	72	Cap Anson	1896	133	Carl Yastrzemski	1983	24
Cap Anson	1897	424	Cap Anson	1897	67	Cap Anson	1897	121	Cap Anson	1895	23
Pete Rose	1985	405	Pete Rose	1985	60	Carlton Fisk	1991	111	Sam Rice	1934	19
Cap Anson	1896	402	Sam Rice	1934	48	Pete Rose	1984	107	Cap Anson	1896	18
Carl Yastrzemski	1983	380	Pete Rose	1984	43	Pete Rose	1985	107	Cap Anson	1897	17
Pete Rose	1984	374	Carlton Fisk	1991	42	Carl Yastrzemski	1983	101	Pete Rose	1984	15
Sam Rice	1934	335	Carl Yastrzemski	1983	38	Sam Rice	1934	98	Pete Rose	1985	12
Pete Rose	1986	237	Tony Perez	1985	25	Honus Wagner	1917	61	Tony Perez	1986	12
Honus Wagner	1917	230	Sam Rice	1933	19	Tony Perez	1985	60	2 tied with		8

Triples			Home Runs			RBI			Stolen Bases		
Cap Anson	1895	6	Carlton Fisk	1991	18	Cap Anson	1895	91	Cap Anson	1896	24
Luke Appling	1950	4	Carl Yastrzemski	1983	10	Cap Anson	1896	90	Cap Anson	1895	12
Cap Anson	1897	3	Enos Slaughter	1959	6	Cap Anson	1897	75	Cap Anson	1897	11
Sam Rice	1933	3	Tony Perez	1985	6	Carlton Fisk	1991	74	Pete Rose	1985	8
Cap Anson	1896	2	Cap Anson	1897	3	Carl Yastrzemski	1983	56	Honus Wagner	1917	5
Pete Rose	1984	2	Carlton Fisk	1992	3	Pete Rose	1985	46	Sam Rice	1934	5
Pete Rose	1985	2	5 tied with		2	Pete Rose	1984	34	Joe Start	1886	4
Pete Rose	1986	2				Sam Rice	1934	33	Pete Rose	1986	3
8 tied with		1				Tony Perez	1985	33	Carlton Fisk	1992	3
						Tony Perez	1986	29	Luke Appling	1950	2

Runs Created			Batting Average (minimum 3.1 PA/Tm Gm)			On-Base Percentage (minimum 3.1 PA/Tm Gm)			Slugging Percentage (minimum 3.1 PA/Tm Gm)		
Cap Anson	1895	98	Cap Anson	1895	.335	Cap Anson	1895	.408	Cap Anson	1895	.422
Cap Anson	1896	83	Cap Anson	1896	.331	Cap Anson	1896	.407	Carlton Fisk	1991	.413
Cap Anson	1897	75	Cap Anson	1897	.285	Pete Rose	1985	.395	Cap Anson	1896	.400
Pete Rose	1985	61	Pete Rose	1985	.264	Cap Anson	1897	.379	Cap Anson	1897	.361
Carlton Fisk	1991	56	Carlton Fisk	1991	.241	Carlton Fisk	1991	.299	Pete Rose	1985	.319
Carl Yastrzemski	1983	53									
Sam Rice	1934	45									
Pete Rose	1984	43									
Tony Perez	1985	34									
Honus Wagner	1917	25									

Pitching Leaders—After Age 42

Wins			Losses			Winning Percentage (minimum 25 decisions)			Games	
Phil Niekro	78		Phil Niekro	58		Jack Quinn	.575		Hoyt Wilhelm	254
Jack Quinn	61		Charlie Hough	47		Phil Niekro	.574		Jack Quinn	230
Nolan Ryan	35		Jack Quinn	45		Tommy John	.547		Phil Niekro	194
Charlie Hough	30		Nolan Ryan	29		Nolan Ryan	.547		Satchel Paige	127
Tommy John	29		Warren Spahn	29		Hoyt Wilhelm	.543		Charlie Hough	113
Hoyt Wilhelm	25		Gaylord Perry	26		Satchel Paige	.439		Nolan Ryan	97
Satchel Paige	18		Tommy John	24		Cy Young	.424		Tommy John	91
Gaylord Perry	17		Satchel Paige	23		Gaylord Perry	.395		Dutch Leonard	90
Cy Young	14		Hoyt Wilhelm	21		Charlie Hough	.390		Jim Kaat	86
Warren Spahn	13		Cy Young	19		Warren Spahn	.310		Diomedes Olivo	81

Complete Games			Shutouts			Saves			Innings Pitched	
Jack Quinn	36		Jack Quinn	7		Hoyt Wilhelm	55		Phil Niekro	1,220.2
Cy Young	26		Phil Niekro	4		Jack Quinn	34		Jack Quinn	836.2
Phil Niekro	25		Nolan Ryan	4		Satchel Paige	26		Charlie Hough	693.2
Warren Spahn	12		Cy Young	3		Dutch Leonard	19		Nolan Ryan	600.2
Charlie Hough	9		Charlie Hough	2		Red Faber	11		Tommy John	498.1
Gaylord Perry	9		Satchel Paige	2		Joe Heving	10		Gaylord Perry	403.0
Nolan Ryan	9		Gaylord Perry	1		Diomedes Olivo	7		Hoyt Wilhelm	388.0
Ted Lyons	5		Tommy John	1		Dolf Luque	7		Warren Spahn	371.1
Tommy John	4		Warren Spahn	1		Don McMahon	6		Satchel Paige	320.1
Fred Johnson	4		30 tied with	0		Babe Adams	6		Cy Young	289.2

Strikeouts			ERA (minimum 250 Innings Pitched)			Component ERA (minimum 250 Innings Pitched)			Opponent Average (minimum 250 Innings Pitched)	
Phil Niekro	702		Hoyt Wilhelm	2.32		Hoyt Wilhelm	2.27		Nolan Ryan	.201
Nolan Ryan	638		Cy Young	3.08		Nolan Ryan	2.66		Hoyt Wilhelm	.202
Charlie Hough	374		Jack Quinn	3.38		Cy Young	2.80		Satchel Paige	.246
Hoyt Wilhelm	308		Nolan Ryan	3.52		Satchel Paige	3.43		Charlie Hough	.248
Jack Quinn	211		Satchel Paige	3.54		Jack Quinn	3.54		Cy Young	.264
Gaylord Perry	198		Phil Niekro	4.09		Charlie Hough	3.98		Phil Niekro	.269
Satchel Paige	191		Charlie Hough	4.26		Gaylord Perry	4.54		Warren Spahn	.284
Tommy John	190		Tommy John	4.26		Warren Spahn	4.55		Jack Quinn	.286
Warren Spahn	168		Gaylord Perry	4.51		Tommy John	4.56		Gaylord Perry	.288
Cy Young	113		Warren Spahn	4.61		Phil Niekro	4.58		Tommy John	.300

Single Season Pitching Leaders—Age 43 or Older

Wins				Losses				Winning Percentage (minimum 15 decisions)				Games		
Jack Quinn	1928	18		Warren Spahn	1965	16		Phil Niekro	1982	.810		Hoyt Wilhelm	1968	72
Phil Niekro	1982	17		Charlie Hough	1993	16		Jack Quinn	1928	.720		Joe Heving	1944	63
Phil Niekro	1984	16		Gaylord Perry	1983	14		Tommy John	1987	.684		Diomedes Olivo	1962	62
Phil Niekro	1985	16		Warren Spahn	1964	13		Phil Niekro	1984	.667		Jim Kaat	1982	62
Jack Quinn	1927	15		Phil Niekro	1987	13		Nolan Ryan	1991	.667		Satchel Paige	1953	57
Tommy John	1987	13		Gaylord Perry	1982	12		Jack Quinn	1927	.600		Hoyt Wilhelm	1970	53
Nolan Ryan	1990	13		Phil Niekro	1985	12		Nolan Ryan	1990	.591		Hoyt Wilhelm	1969	52
Satchel Paige	1952	12		Charlie Hough	1992	12		Phil Niekro	1985	.571		Hoyt Wilhelm	1967	49
Nolan Ryan	1991	12		Red Faber	1932	11		Jack Quinn	1930	.563		Satchel Paige	1952	46
3 tied with		11		Phil Niekro	1986	11		Jack Quinn	1929	.550		2 tied with		45

Complete Games				Shutouts				Saves				Innings Pitched		
Jack Quinn	1928	18		Jack Quinn	1928	4		Jack Quinn	1931	15		Phil Niekro	1982	234.1
Cy Young	1910	14		Jack Quinn	1927	3		Hoyt Wilhelm	1969	14		Phil Niekro	1985	220.0
Cy Young	1911	12		Cy Young	1911	2		Hoyt Wilhelm	1970	13		Gaylord Perry	1982	216.2
Jack Quinn	1927	11		Satchel Paige	1952	2		Hoyt Wilhelm	1967	12		Phil Niekro	1984	215.2
Warren Spahn	1965	8		Phil Niekro	1982	2		Hoyt Wilhelm	1968	12		Jack Quinn	1928	211.1
Jack Quinn	1929	7		Nolan Ryan	1990	2		Dutch Leonard	1952	11		Phil Niekro	1986	210.1
Phil Niekro	1985	7		Nolan Ryan	1991	2		Satchel Paige	1953	11		Jack Quinn	1927	207.1
Gaylord Perry	1982	6		8 tied with		1		Joe Heving	1944	10		Charlie Hough	1993	204.1
4 tied with		5						Satchel Paige	1952	10		Nolan Ryan	1990	204.0
								2 tied with		8		Phil Niekro	1983	201.2

Strikeouts				ERA (minimum 1 Inning Pitched/Tm Gm)				Component ERA (minimum 1 Inning Pitched/Tm Gm)				Opponent Average (minimum 1 Inning Pitched/Tm Gm)		
Nolan Ryan	1990	232		Cy Young	1910	2.53		Nolan Ryan	1991	1.98		Nolan Ryan	1991	.172
Nolan Ryan	1991	203		Jack Quinn	1928	2.90		Cy Young	1910	2.26		Nolan Ryan	1990	.188
Nolan Ryan	1992	157		Nolan Ryan	1991	2.91		Nolan Ryan	1990	2.28		Charlie Hough	1991	.229
Phil Niekro	1985	149		Phil Niekro	1984	3.09		Jack Quinn	1927	3.08		Charlie Hough	1992	.239
Phil Niekro	1982	144		Jack Quinn	1927	3.17		Jack Quinn	1928	3.29		Phil Niekro	1985	.245
Phil Niekro	1984	136		Nolan Ryan	1990	3.44		Phil Niekro	1982	3.61		Cy Young	1910	.252
Phil Niekro	1983	128		Phil Niekro	1982	3.61		Charlie Hough	1992	3.63		Phil Niekro	1982	.255
Charlie Hough	1993	126		Charlie Hough	1992	3.93		Charlie Hough	1991	3.69		Charlie Hough	1993	.259
Gaylord Perry	1982	116		Jack Quinn	1929	3.97		Jack Quinn	1929	3.81		Phil Niekro	1984	.267
Charlie Hough	1991	107		Phil Niekro	1983	3.97		Phil Niekro	1984	3.86		Warren Spahn	1965	.272

Batting Leaders—After Age 29

At-Bats		Runs		Hits		Doubles	
Pete Rose	9,103	Cap Anson	1,388	Pete Rose	2,724	Pete Rose	491
Sam Rice	7,898	Pete Rose	1,366	Sam Rice	2,561	Tris Speaker	468
Cap Anson	7,350	Sam Rice	1,328	Cap Anson	2,381	Sam Rice	440
Honus Wagner	6,912	Babe Ruth	1,249	Honus Wagner	2,214	Cap Anson	423
Carl Yastrzemski	6,813	Willie Mays	1,178	Ty Cobb	2,053	Honus Wagner	409
Dave Winfield	6,618	Jim O'Rourke	1,133	Stan Musial	2,006	Ty Cobb	392
Doc Cramer	6,491	Ty Cobb	1,112	Paul Molitor	1,975	Stan Musial	382
Hank Aaron	6,424	Honus Wagner	1,111	Bill Terry	1,932	Paul Molitor	376
Stan Musial	6,284	Hank Aaron	1,097	Carl Yastrzemski	1,902	George Brett	362
Carlton Fisk	6,265	Charlie Gehringer	1,035	Doc Cramer	1,888	Hal McRae	357

Triples		Home Runs		RBI		Stolen Bases	
Sam Rice	165	Babe Ruth	430	Cap Anson	1,558	Lou Brock	604
Honus Wagner	164	Hank Aaron	413	Babe Ruth	1,324	Honus Wagner	464
Ty Cobb	136	Willie Mays	381	Hank Aaron	1,176	Davey Lopes	458
Sam Crawford	135	Mike Schmidt	313	Dave Winfield	1,139	Otis Nixon	452
Roger Connor	125	Willie Stargell	310	Stan Musial	1,136	Harry Stovey	441
Jake Daubert	119	Reggie Jackson	309	Willie Mays	1,091	Rickey Henderson	437
Fred Clarke	115	Stan Musial	301	Carl Yastrzemski	1,077	Tom Brown	414
Bid McPhee	112	Ted Williams	299	Honus Wagner	1,057	Maury Wills	390
Dan Brouthers	106	Dave Winfield	298	Tony Perez	1,029	Dummy Hoy	379
Cap Anson	105	Willie McCovey	289	Eddie Murray	986	Arlie Latham	372

Runs Created		Batting Average (minimum 3,000 Plate Appearances)		On-Base Percentage (minimum 3,000 Plate Appearances)		Slugging Percentage (minimum 3,000 Plate Appearances)	
Cap Anson	1,707	Ty Cobb	.364	Ted Williams	.476	Babe Ruth	.673
Babe Ruth	1,442	Harry Heilmann	.360	Babe Ruth	.467	Ted Williams	.628
Pete Rose	1,368	Ed Delahanty	.358	Billy Hamilton	.456	Lou Gehrig	.623
Honus Wagner	1,350	Lefty O'Doul	.353	Lou Gehrig	.451	Rogers Hornsby	.570
Stan Musial	1,309	Rogers Hornsby	.349	Dan Brouthers	.441	Jimmie Foxx	.568
Sam Rice	1,292	Bill Terry	.348	Rogers Hornsby	.439	Harry Heilmann	.558
Willie Mays	1,276	Tony Gwynn	.347	Tris Speaker	.434	Ken Williams	.547
Hank Aaron	1,247	Tris Speaker	.345	Ty Cobb	.433	Willie Stargell	.547
Ty Cobb	1,198	Billy Hamilton	.338	Harry Heilmann	.432	Stan Musial	.543
Paul Molitor	1,178	Dan Brouthers	.338	Ed Delahanty	.428	Mike Schmidt	.540

Single Season Batting Leaders—Age 30 or Older

At-Bats			Runs			Hits			Doubles		
Matty Alou	1969	698	Tom Brown	1891	177	Lefty O'Doul	1929	254	Earl Webb	1931	67
Horace Clarke	1970	686	Lou Gehrig	1936	167	Bill Terry	1930	254	George Burns	1926	64
Lance Johnson	1996	682	Babe Ruth	1928	163	Rod Carew	1977	239	Charlie Gehringer	1936	60
Pete Rose	1973	680	Babe Ruth	1927	158	Ed Delahanty	1899	238	Tris Speaker	1923	59
Dick Groat	1962	678	Rogers Hornsby	1929	156	Earl Averill	1936	232	Ed Delahanty	1899	55
Matty Alou	1970	677	Kiki Cuyler	1930	155	Matty Alou	1969	231	Hal McRae	1977	54
Felix Millan	1975	676	Harry Stovey	1889	152	Joe Torre	1971	230	Paul Waner	1936	53
Bill Buckner	1985	673	Billy Hamilton	1896	152	Pete Rose	1973	230	Stan Musial	1953	53
Rabbit Maranville	1922	672	Billy Hamilton	1897	152	Rogers Hornsby	1929	229	4 tied with		52
Al Simmons	1932	670	Lefty O'Doul	1929	152	Kiki Cuyler	1930	228			

Triples			Home Runs			RBI			Stolen Bases		
Sam Thompson	1894	27	Babe Ruth	1927	60	Hack Wilson	1930	190	Lou Brock	1974	118
John Reilly	1890	26	Mark McGwire	1997	58	Jimmie Foxx	1938	175	Tom Brown	1891	106
Sam Crawford	1914	26	Hack Wilson	1930	56	Sam Thompson	1895	165	Hugh Nicol	1888	103
Roger Connor	1894	25	Babe Ruth	1928	54	Lou Gehrig	1934	165	Harry Stovey	1890	97
Ty Cobb	1917	24	Willie Mays	1965	52	Babe Ruth	1927	164	Ron LeFlore	1980	97
Dan Brouthers	1894	23	Mark McGwire	1996	52	Babe Ruth	1931	163	Maury Wills	1965	94
Sam Crawford	1913	23	Johnny Mize	1947	51	Lou Gehrig	1937	159	Blondie Purcell	1887	88
7 tied with		22	Jimmie Foxx	1938	50	Ted Williams	1949	159	Monte Ward	1892	88
			Brady Anderson	1996	50	Ken Williams	1922	155	Harry Stovey	1888	87
			8 tied with		49	Joe DiMaggio	1948	155	Arlie Latham	1891	87

Runs Created			Batting Average (minimum 3.1 PA/Tm Gm)			On-Base Percentage (minimum 3.1 PA/Tm Gm)			Slugging Percentage (minimum 3.1 PA/Tm Gm)		
Lou Gehrig	1936	181	Ed Delahanty	1899	.410	Ted Williams	1957	.526	Babe Ruth	1927	.772
Babe Ruth	1931	179	Sam Thompson	1894	.407	Babe Ruth	1926	.516	Babe Ruth	1926	.737
Rogers Hornsby	1929	178	Bill Terry	1930	.401	Ted Williams	1954	.513	Babe Ruth	1930	.732
Babe Ruth	1927	177	Ty Cobb	1922	.401	Rogers Hornsby	1928	.498	Ted Williams	1957	.731
Babe Ruth	1930	176	Lefty O'Doul	1929	.398	Babe Ruth	1931	.494	Mark McGwire	1996	.730
Ted Williams	1949	174	Harry Heilmann	1927	.398	Babe Ruth	1930	.493	Hack Wilson	1930	.723
Jimmie Foxx	1938	172	Jesse Burkett	1899	.396	Ted Williams	1949	.490	Larry Walker	1997	.720
Hack Wilson	1930	171	Tony Gwynn	1994	.394	Babe Ruth	1932	.489	Babe Ruth	1928	.709
Lou Gehrig	1934	171	Harry Heilmann	1925	.393	Babe Ruth	1927	.487	Lou Gehrig	1934	.706
2 tied with		167	Sam Thompson	1895	.392	Tris Speaker	1920	.483	Jimmie Foxx	1938	.704

Pitching Leaders—After Age 29

Wins		Losses		Winning Percentage		Games	
				(minimum 200 decisions)			
Cy Young	316	Phil Niekro	247	Sam Leever	.709	Kent Tekulve	944
Phil Niekro	287	Cy Young	213	Lefty Grove	.705	Hoyt Wilhelm	931
Warren Spahn	277	Gaylord Perry	195	Red Ruffing	.664	Don McMahon	744
Gaylord Perry	238	Warren Spahn	187	Christy Mathewson	.664	Dennis Eckersley	703
Early Wynn	217	Charlie Hough	183	Three Finger Brown	.660	Phil Niekro	702
Eddie Plank	216	Jack Quinn	181	Allie Reynolds	.648	Jesse Orosco	642
Lefty Grove	213	Nolan Ryan	176	Eddie Plank	.641	Doug Jones	638
Pete Alexander	213	Murry Dickson	170	Herb Pennock	.633	Roy Face	638
Jack Quinn	203	Red Faber	167	Carl Hubbell	.633	Jack Quinn	631
Nolan Ryan	202	Dolf Luque	163	Ray Kremer	.627	Gene Garber	618

Complete Games		Shutouts		Saves		Innings Pitched	
Cy Young	478	Cy Young	55	Dennis Eckersley	386	Phil Niekro	4,800.1
Bill Hutchison	286	Eddie Plank	53	Lee Smith	298	Cy Young	4,716.0
Warren Spahn	285	Warren Spahn	48	Doug Jones	277	Gaylord Perry	3,989.2
Old Hoss Radbourn	265	Gaylord Perry	42	Jeff Reardon	240	Warren Spahn	3,960.1
Pete Alexander	253	Early Wynn	40	Tom Henke	234	Nolan Ryan	3,451.0
Eddie Plank	246	Phil Niekro	39	Rollie Fingers	205	Charlie Hough	3,278.2
Joe McGinnity	244	Walter Johnson	39	Hoyt Wilhelm	201	Jack Quinn	3,238.1
Gaylord Perry	241	Bob Gibson	38	Randy Myers	188	Early Wynn	3,132.2
Tim Keefe	224	Three Finger Brown	38	Jeff Montgomery	180	Pete Alexander	3,086.0
Phil Niekro	220	Pete Alexander	37	John Franco	178	Red Faber	3,072.2

Strikeouts		ERA		Component ERA		Opponent Average	
		(minimum 1,500 Innings Pitched)		(minimum 1,500 Innings Pitched)		(minimum 1,500 Innings Pitched)	
Nolan Ryan	3,629	Three Finger Brown	2.14	Three Finger Brown	2.12	Nolan Ryan	.208
Phil Niekro	2,999	Eddie Plank	2.19	Cy Young	2.21	Hoyt Wilhelm	.214
Gaylord Perry	2,533	Christy Mathewson	2.22	Eddie Cicotte	2.22	Bob Gibson	.226
Steve Carlton	2,412	Sam Leever	2.26	Eddie Plank	2.25	Tim Keefe	.231
Dazzy Vance	2,027	Eddie Cicotte	2.28	Christy Mathewson	2.28	Tom Seaver	.232
Charlie Hough	1,993	Cy Young	2.36	Jack Chesbro	2.30	Three Finger Brown	.234
Cy Young	1,978	Bob Ewing	2.47	Sam Leever	2.32	Eddie Plank	.234
Warren Spahn	1,930	Hoyt Wilhelm	2.49	Deacon Phillippe	2.33	Early Wynn	.236
Bob Gibson	1,907	Deacon Phillippe	2.50	Hoyt Wilhelm	2.42	Charlie Hough	.237
Early Wynn	1,886	Jack Chesbro	2.55	Bobby Mathews	2.45	Jack Chesbro	.238

Single Season Pitching Leaders—Age 30 or Older

Wins			Losses			Winning Percentage			Games		
						(minimum 15 decisions)					
Bill Hutchison	1891	44	Bill Hutchison	1892	36	Roy Face	1959	.947	Mike Marshall	1974	106
Bill Hutchison	1890	42	Old Hoss Radbourn	1886	31	Johnny Allen	1937	.938	Kent Tekulve	1979	94
Jack Chesbro	1904	41	Jim Hughey	1899	30	Randy Johnson	1995	.900	Mike Marshall	1973	92
Bill Hutchison	1892	37	Bill Hart	1896	29	Freddie Fitzsimmons	1940	.889	Kent Tekulve	1978	91
Tim Keefe	1887	35	Bill Hart	1897	27	Lefty Grove	1931	.886	Mike Marshall	1979	90
Tim Keefe	1888	35	George Bell	1910	27	Preacher Roe	1951	.880	Kent Tekulve	1987	90
Joe McGinnity	1904	35	Tony Mullane	1891	26	Deacon Phillippe	1910	.875	Kent Tekulve	1982	85
Cy Young	1901	33	Gus Weyhing	1898	26	Tom Seaver	1981	.875	5 tied with		84
Cy Young	1902	32	4 tied with		25	Wild Bill Donovan	1907	.862			
3 tied with		31				Whitey Ford	1961	.862			

Complete Games			Shutouts			Saves			Innings Pitched		
Bill Hutchison	1892	67	Bob Gibson	1968	13	Randy Myers	1993	53	Bill Hutchison	1892	622.0
Bill Hutchison	1890	65	Cy Young	1904	10	Dennis Eckersley	1992	51	Bill Hutchison	1890	603.0
Old Hoss Radbourn	1886	57	Carl Hubbell	1933	10	Dennis Eckersley	1990	48	Bill Hutchison	1891	561.0
Bill Hutchison	1891	56	John Tudor	1985	10	Lee Smith	1991	47	Old Hoss Radbourn	1886	509.1
Tim Keefe	1887	54	Joe McGinnity	1904	9	Lee Smith	1993	46	Bob Barr	1890	493.1
Bob Barr	1890	52	Three Finger Brown	1908	9	6 tied with		45	Tim Keefe	1887	478.2
Old Hoss Radbourn	1885	49	Cy Falkenberg	1914	9				Jack Chesbro	1904	454.2
Pud Galvin	1888	49	Pete Alexander	1919	9				Old Hoss Radbourn	1885	445.2
4 tied with		48	12 tied with		8				Pud Galvin	1887	440.2
									Pud Galvin	1888	437.1

Strikeouts			ERA			Component ERA			Opponent Average		
			(minimum 1 Inning Pitched/Tm Gm)			(minimum 1 Inning Pitched/Tm Gm)			(minimum 1 Inning Pitched/Tm Gm)		
Nolan Ryan	1977	341	Bob Gibson	1968	1.12	Christy Mathewson	1909	1.29	Nolan Ryan	1991	.172
Tim Keefe	1888	333	Christy Mathewson	1909	1.14	Three Finger Brown	1908	1.31	Bob Gibson	1968	.184
Curt Schilling	1997	319	Cy Young	1908	1.26	Three Finger Brown	1909	1.42	Mike Scott	1986	.186
Sandy Koufax	1966	317	Walter Johnson	1918	1.27	Bob Gibson	1968	1.44	Nolan Ryan	1989	.187
Bill Hutchison	1892	312	Three Finger Brown	1909	1.31	Cy Young	1908	1.48	Nolan Ryan	1981	.188
Mickey Lolich	1971	308	Three Finger Brown	1907	1.39	Eddie Cicotte	1917	1.48	Nolan Ryan	1986	.188
Mike Scott	1986	306	Fred Anderson	1917	1.44	Cy Young	1905	1.49	Nolan Ryan	1990	.188
Nolan Ryan	1989	301	Three Finger Brown	1908	1.47	Babe Adams	1919	1.52	Nolan Ryan	1977	.193
Randy Johnson	1995	294	Walter Johnson	1919	1.49	Jack Chesbro	1904	1.56	Randy Johnson	1997	.194
Roger Clemens	1997	292	Eddie Cicotte	1917	1.53	Pete Alexander	1919	1.56	Three Finger Brown	1908	.195

Batting Leaders—After Age 34

At-Bats

Pete Rose	5,832
Cap Anson	5,146
Sam Rice	4,839
Honus Wagner	4,275
Carl Yastrzemski	4,229
Carlton Fisk	4,082
Jim O'Rourke	3,780
Dave Winfield	3,716
Darrell Evans	3,613
Hank Aaron	3,475

Runs

Cap Anson	924
Sam Rice	848
Pete Rose	836
Jim O'Rourke	660
Ty Cobb	620
Babe Ruth	607
Honus Wagner	599
Carl Yastrzemski	576
Hank Aaron	571
Willie Mays	565

Hits

Pete Rose	1,709
Cap Anson	1,638
Sam Rice	1,574
Honus Wagner	1,288
Carl Yastrzemski	1,152
Jim O'Rourke	1,152
Ty Cobb	1,136
Paul Molitor	1,092
Carlton Fisk	1,043
Stan Musial	1,033

Doubles

Pete Rose	305
Sam Rice	262
Cap Anson	258
Tris Speaker	247
Ty Cobb	228
George Brett	219
Honus Wagner	218
Carl Yastrzemski	210
Jim O'Rourke	208
Paul Molitor	207

Triples

Sam Rice	98
Honus Wagner	94
Jake Daubert	78
Cap Anson	71
Ty Cobb	61
Jim O'Rourke	54
Roger Connor	52
Joe Start	49
3 tied with	48

Home Runs

Hank Aaron	245
Darrell Evans	198
Babe Ruth	198
Carlton Fisk	193
Ted Williams	184
Dave Winfield	160
Willie Mays	155
Reggie Jackson	153
Hank Sauer	153
Stan Musial	150

RBI

Cap Anson	1,050
Hank Aaron	670
Carl Yastrzemski	663
Carlton Fisk	652
Babe Ruth	652
Honus Wagner	619
Jim O'Rourke	614
Dave Winfield	599
Stan Musial	590
Darrell Evans	587

Stolen Bases

Lou Brock	303
Cap Anson	218
Otis Nixon	205
Jim O'Rourke	191
Honus Wagner	187
Davey Lopes	182
Brett Butler	162
Eddie Collins	149
Patsy Donovan	149
Ozzie Smith	148

Runs Created

Cap Anson	1,132
Pete Rose	815
Sam Rice	796
Jim O'Rourke	729
Babe Ruth	724
Honus Wagner	717
Ted Williams	699
Hank Aaron	682
Ty Cobb	663
Carl Yastrzemski	661

Batting Average
(minimum 3,000 Plate Appearances)

Ty Cobb	.355
Eddie Collins	.342
Tris Speaker	.342
Ted Williams	.337
Babe Ruth	.331
Sam Rice	.325
Nap Lajoie	.321
Paul Molitor	.319
Cap Anson	.318
Stan Musial	.305

On-Base Percentage
(minimum 3,000 Plate Appearances)

Ted Williams	.477
Babe Ruth	.472
Eddie Collins	.440
Ty Cobb	.430
Tris Speaker	.428
Cap Anson	.405
Luke Appling	.397
Brett Butler	.388
Stan Musial	.387
Paul Molitor	.383

Slugging Percentage
(minimum 3,000 Plate Appearances)

Babe Ruth	.644
Ted Williams	.624
Hank Aaron	.539
Tris Speaker	.517
Stan Musial	.506
Ty Cobb	.498
Willie Mays	.474
Mickey Vernon	.472
Paul Molitor	.469
Dave Winfield	.465

Single Season Batting Leaders—Age 35 or Older

At-Bats

Bill Buckner	1985	673
Pete Rose	1976	665
Doc Cramer	1941	660
Paul Molitor	1996	660
Pete Rose	1977	655
Pete Rose	1978	655
Pete Rose	1980	655
Steve Garvey	1985	654
Ivy Olson	1921	652
Sam Rice	1925	649

Runs

Babe Ruth	1930	150
Babe Ruth	1931	149
Tommy Henrich	1948	138
Dan Brouthers	1894	137
Tris Speaker	1923	133
Charlie Gehringer	1938	133
Sam Thompson	1895	131
Pete Rose	1976	130
Hardy Richardson	1890	126
Zack Wheat	1925	125

Hits

Nap Lajoie	1910	227
Sam Rice	1925	227
Bill Terry	1932	225
Paul Molitor	1996	225
Zack Wheat	1925	221
Tony Gwynn	1997	220
Lefty O'Doul	1932	219
Tris Speaker	1923	218
Sam Rice	1926	216
Pete Rose	1976	215

Doubles

Tris Speaker	1923	59
Tris Speaker	1926	52
Nap Lajoie	1910	51
Baby Doll Jacobson	1926	51
Pete Rose	1978	51
Tony Gwynn	1997	49
Sparky Adams	1931	46
Hal McRae	1982	46
Bill Buckner	1985	46
2 tied with		45

Triples

Roger Connor	1894	25
Dan Brouthers	1894	23
Jake Daubert	1922	22
Sam Thompson	1895	21
Honus Wagner	1912	20
Sam Crawford	1915	19
Charley Jones	1885	17
Sam Wise	1893	17
Ed Cartwright	1895	17
Honus Wagner	1915	17

Home Runs

Babe Ruth	1930	49
Hank Aaron	1971	47
Andres Galarraga	1996	47
Babe Ruth	1931	46
Hank Greenberg	1946	44
Hank Aaron	1969	44
Cy Williams	1923	41
Babe Ruth	1932	41
Hank Sauer	1954	41
Andres Galarraga	1997	41

RBI

Sam Thompson	1895	165
Babe Ruth	1931	163
Babe Ruth	1930	153
Andres Galarraga	1996	150
Hardy Richardson	1890	146
Andres Galarraga	1997	140
Babe Ruth	1932	137
Hal McRae	1982	133
Tris Speaker	1923	130
Jack Fournier	1925	130

Stolen Bases

Lou Brock	1974	118
Otis Nixon	1997	59
Lou Brock	1975	56
Lou Brock	1976	56
Otis Nixon	1996	54
Maury Wills	1968	52
Ed Cartwright	1895	50
Otis Nixon	1995	50
Eddie Collins	1923	49
3 tied with		48

Runs Created

Babe Ruth	1931	179
Babe Ruth	1930	176
Sam Thompson	1895	154
Tris Speaker	1923	154
Andres Galarraga	1996	150
Babe Ruth	1932	147
Dan Brouthers	1894	144
Ted Williams	1957	143
Tony Gwynn	1997	138
Bill Terry	1932	137

Batting Average
(minimum 3.1 PA/Tm Gm)

Ty Cobb	1922	.401
Sam Thompson	1895	.392
Tris Speaker	1925	.389
Ted Williams	1957	.388
Nap Lajoie	1910	.384
Tris Speaker	1923	.380
Ty Cobb	1925	.378
Zack Wheat	1924	.375
Babe Ruth	1931	.373
Tony Gwynn	1997	.372

On-Base Percentage
(minimum 3.1 PA/Tm Gm)

Ted Williams	1957	.526
Ted Williams	1954	.513
Babe Ruth	1931	.494
Babe Ruth	1930	.493
Babe Ruth	1932	.489
Tris Speaker	1925	.479
Ted Williams	1956	.479
Tris Speaker	1923	.469
Ty Cobb	1925	.468
Ty Cobb	1922	.462

Slugging Percentage
(minimum 3.1 PA/Tm Gm)

Babe Ruth	1930	.732
Ted Williams	1957	.731
Babe Ruth	1931	.700
Hank Aaron	1971	.669
Babe Ruth	1932	.661
Sam Thompson	1895	.654
Ted Williams	1954	.635
Stan Musial	1957	.612
Tris Speaker	1923	.610
Hank Aaron	1969	.607

Pitching Leaders—After Age 34

Wins			Losses			Winning Percentage (minimum 200 decisions)			Games		
Phil Niekro		208	Phil Niekro		180	Pete Alexander		.603	Hoyt Wilhelm		670
Cy Young		192	Charlie Hough		154	Warren Spahn		.598	Kent Tekulve		564
Warren Spahn		180	Jack Quinn		144	Cy Young		.585	Jack Quinn		535
Jack Quinn		163	Cy Young		136	Tommy John		.554	Phil Niekro		506
Charlie Hough		147	Gaylord Perry		121	Early Wynn		.552	Dennis Eckersley		480
Gaylord Perry		137	Warren Spahn		121	Dazzy Vance		.541	Don McMahon		471
Nolan Ryan		135	Nolan Ryan		118	Phil Niekro		.536	Rick Honeycutt		433
Tommy John		134	Tommy John		108	Nolan Ryan		.534	Jim Kaat		407
Eddie Plank		124	Red Faber		102	Gaylord Perry		.531	Ron Reed		390
Pete Alexander		123	Joe Niekro		96	Jack Quinn		.531	Charlie Hough		386

Complete Games			Shutouts			Saves			Innings Pitched		
Cy Young		293	Cy Young		39	Dennis Eckersley		292	Phil Niekro		3,490.1
Warren Spahn		177	Eddie Plank		32	Hoyt Wilhelm		169	Cy Young		2,941.1
Phil Niekro		145	Warren Spahn		29	Doug Jones		150	Charlie Hough		2,630.1
Pete Alexander		141	Early Wynn		27	Lee Smith		123	Jack Quinn		2,571.0
Jack Quinn		141	Phil Niekro		26	Todd Worrell		111	Warren Spahn		2,565.0
Eddie Plank		125	Jack Quinn		23	Stu Miller		100	Gaylord Perry		2,369.0
Dazzy Vance		122	Gaylord Perry		20	Ellis Kinder		96	Nolan Ryan		2,312.0
Gaylord Perry		120	Allie Reynolds		20	Tom Henke		91	Tommy John		2,117.1
Ted Lyons		120	Babe Adams		20	Al Worthington		88	Early Wynn		1,836.2
Lefty Grove		114	3 tied with		17	Jeff Reardon		80	Dazzy Vance		1,834.0

Strikeouts			ERA (minimum 1,500 Innings Pitched)			Component ERA (minimum 1,500 Innings Pitched)			Opponent Average (minimum 1,500 Innings Pitched)		
Nolan Ryan		2,465	Cy Young		2.18	Cy Young		1.99	Nolan Ryan		.206
Phil Niekro		2,170	Eddie Plank		2.29	Eddie Plank		2.40	Charlie Hough		.236
Charlie Hough		1,582	Dutch Leonard		3.01	Nolan Ryan		2.72	Cy Young		.238
Gaylord Perry		1,456	Warren Spahn		3.20	Dazzy Vance		3.02	Eddie Plank		.240
Steve Carlton		1,453	Dazzy Vance		3.25	Dutch Leonard		3.10	Early Wynn		.241
Cy Young		1,405	Pete Alexander		3.29	Pete Alexander		3.13	Don Sutton		.246
Dazzy Vance		1,213	Nolan Ryan		3.31	Warren Spahn		3.17	Steve Carlton		.247
Warren Spahn		1,189	Gaylord Perry		3.38	Don Sutton		3.20	Warren Spahn		.250
Early Wynn		1,164	Jack Quinn		3.40	Gaylord Perry		3.29	Joe Niekro		.251
Hoyt Wilhelm		1,104	Steve Carlton		3.48	Steve Carlton		3.38	Phil Niekro		.253

Single Season Pitching Leaders—Age 35 or Older

Wins			Losses			Winning Percentage (minimum 15 decisions)			Games		
Cy Young	1902	32	George Bell	1910	27	Freddie Fitzsimmons	1940	.889	Mike Marshall	1979	90
Eddie Cicotte	1919	29	Stoney McGlynn	1907	25	Preacher Roe	1951	.880	Kent Tekulve	1987	90
Cy Young	1903	28	Ed Cushman	1890	21	Deacon Phillippe	1910	.875	Kent Tekulve	1982	85
Old Hoss Radbourn	1890	27	Bill Hutchison	1895	21	Tom Seaver	1981	.875	Doug Jones	1992	80
Joe McGinnity	1906	27	Cy Young	1906	21	Spud Chandler	1943	.833	Greg Harris	1993	80
Cy Young	1904	26	Walt Dickson	1914	21	Eddie Plank	1912	.813	Bob Patterson	1996	79
Eddie Plank	1912	26	Jack Scott	1927	21	Rip Sewell	1948	.813	Ted Abernathy	1968	78
George McConnell	1915	25	Murry Dickson	1952	21	Bob Feller	1954	.813	Gary Lavelle	1984	77
Christy Mathewson	1914	24	6 tied with		20	Phil Niekro	1982	.810	Kent Tekulve	1983	76
Steve Carlton	1980	24				Eddie Cicotte	1919	.806	Bob Patterson	1997	76

Complete Games			Shutouts			Saves			Innings Pitched		
Cy Young	1902	41	Cy Young	1904	10	Dennis Eckersley	1992	51	Cy Young	1902	384.2
Cy Young	1904	40	Babe Adams	1920	8	Dennis Eckersley	1990	48	Cy Young	1904	380.0
Old Hoss Radbourn	1890	36	Whitey Ford	1964	8	Lee Smith	1993	46	Stoney McGlynn	1907	352.1
Ed Cushman	1890	34	Cy Young	1903	7	Todd Worrell	1996	44	Cy Young	1907	343.1
Cy Young	1903	34	Eddie Plank	1913	7	Dennis Eckersley	1991	43	Old Hoss Radbourn	1890	343.0
Stoney McGlynn	1907	33	Allie Reynolds	1951	7	Jeff Reardon	1991	40	Phil Niekro	1979	342.0
Cy Young	1907	33	Warren Spahn	1963	7	Tom Henke	1993	40	Cy Young	1903	341.2
Joe McGinnity	1906	32	14 tied with		6	Lee Smith	1995	37	Joe McGinnity	1906	339.2
Tim Keefe	1892	31				6 tied with		36	Phil Niekro	1978	334.1
Cy Young	1905	31							Phil Niekro	1977	330.1

Strikeouts			ERA (minimum 1 Inning Pitched/Tm Gm)			Component ERA (minimum 1 Inning Pitched/Tm Gm)			Opponent Average (minimum 1 Inning Pitched/Tm Gm)		
Nolan Ryan	1989	301	Cy Young	1908	1.26	Cy Young	1908	1.48	Nolan Ryan	1991	.172
Steve Carlton	1980	286	Spud Chandler	1943	1.64	Cy Young	1905	1.49	Nolan Ryan	1989	.187
Steve Carlton	1982	286	Sam Leever	1907	1.66	Babe Adams	1919	1.52	Nolan Ryan	1986	.188
Steve Carlton	1983	275	Eddie Cicotte	1919	1.82	Cy Young	1904	1.73	Nolan Ryan	1990	.188
Nolan Ryan	1987	270	Cy Young	1905	1.82	Eddie Plank	1915	1.74	Nolan Ryan	1983	.195
Phil Niekro	1977	262	Cy Young	1904	1.97	Whit Wyatt	1943	1.81	Nolan Ryan	1987	.200
Jim Bunning	1967	253	Babe Adams	1919	1.98	Spud Chandler	1943	1.82	Johnny Niggeling	1943	.204
Phil Niekro	1978	248	Cy Young	1907	1.99	Cy Young	1907	1.85	Gaylord Perry	1974	.204
Nolan Ryan	1982	245	Allie Reynolds	1952	2.06	Eddie Cicotte	1919	1.87	Tom Seaver	1981	.205
Gaylord Perry	1975	233	Eddie Plank	1915	2.08	Cy Young	1903	1.89	Whit Wyatt	1943	.207

Batting Leaders—After Age 39

At-Bats
Cap Anson	2,597
Pete Rose	2,574
Carlton Fisk	1,781
Honus Wagner	1,780
Sam Rice	1,714
Luke Appling	1,620
Jim O'Rourke	1,554
Carl Yastrzemski	1,541
Dave Winfield	1,539
Joe Start	1,247

Runs
Cap Anson	440
Sam Rice	327
Pete Rose	323
Jim O'Rourke	230
Luke Appling	223
Dave Winfield	210
Carlton Fisk	205
Joe Start	200
Honus Wagner	188
Carl Yastrzemski	176

Hits
Cap Anson	822
Pete Rose	699
Sam Rice	551
Luke Appling	488
Honus Wagner	479
Carlton Fisk	473
Jim O'Rourke	458
Dave Winfield	413
Carl Yastrzemski	410
Joe Start	340

Doubles
Cap Anson	135
Sam Rice	95
Pete Rose	92
Carlton Fisk	83
Carl Yastrzemski	81
Dave Winfield	80
Jim O'Rourke	78
Luke Appling	69
Honus Wagner	69
Ty Cobb	59

Triples
Honus Wagner	36
Sam Rice	32
Cap Anson	26
Pete Rose	18
Jim O'Rourke	17
Joe Start	17
Luke Appling	11
Ty Cobb	11
Deacon White	10
2 tied with	9

Home Runs
Carlton Fisk	72
Darrell Evans	67
Dave Winfield	59
Carl Yastrzemski	48
Stan Musial	46
Hank Aaron	42
Hank Sauer	39
Ted Williams	39
Graig Nettles	37
Reggie Jackson	33

RBI
Cap Anson	520
Carlton Fisk	282
Jim O'Rourke	246
Pete Rose	237
Dave Winfield	231
Carl Yastrzemski	231
Stan Musial	210
Darrell Evans	202
Sam Rice	194
Honus Wagner	191

Stolen Bases
Cap Anson	90
Davey Lopes	74
Honus Wagner	61
Jim O'Rourke	50
Pete Rose	31
Sam Rice	31
Willie Mays	28
Luke Appling	27
Ty Cobb	27
Nap Lajoie	25

Runs Created
Cap Anson	523
Pete Rose	314
Sam Rice	290
Carlton Fisk	253
Jim O'Rourke	253
Luke Appling	251
Dave Winfield	223
Honus Wagner	221
Joe Start	220
Carl Yastrzemski	219

Batting Average
(minimum 1,000 Plate Appearances)
Sam Rice	.321
Cap Anson	.317
Luke Appling	.301
Jim O'Rourke	.295
Stan Musial	.294
Deacon White	.275
Joe Start	.273
Pete Rose	.272
Honus Wagner	.269
Dave Winfield	.268

On-Base Percentage
(minimum 1,000 Plate Appearances)
Luke Appling	.408
Cap Anson	.399
Willie Mays	.391
Sam Rice	.379
Stan Musial	.375
Pete Rose	.355
Carl Yastrzemski	.352
Deacon White	.350
Darrell Evans	.347
Jim O'Rourke	.347

Slugging Percentage
(minimum 1,000 Plate Appearances)
Stan Musial	.471
Dave Winfield	.446
Carlton Fisk	.438
Willie Mays	.426
Darrell Evans	.424
Sam Rice	.421
Carl Yastrzemski	.416
Cap Anson	.404
Hank Aaron	.401
Tony Perez	.397

Single Season Batting Leaders—Age 40 or Older

At-Bats
Pete Rose	1982	634
Sam Rice	1930	593
Dave Winfield	1992	583
Rabbit Maranville	1932	571
Honus Wagner	1915	566
Eddie Murray	1996	566
George Brett	1993	560
Cap Anson	1892	559
Jim O'Rourke	1891	555
Honus Wagner	1914	552

Runs
Sam Rice	1930	121
Ty Cobb	1927	104
Jim O'Rourke	1891	92
Dave Winfield	1992	92
Darrell Evans	1987	90
Cap Anson	1895	87
Cap Anson	1894	82
Luke Appling	1949	82
Willie Mays	1971	82
Sam Rice	1931	81

Hits
Sam Rice	1930	207
Ty Cobb	1927	175
Pete Rose	1982	172
Dave Winfield	1992	169
Jim O'Rourke	1891	164
Paul Molitor	1997	164
Cap Anson	1895	159
Deacon White	1888	157
Jim O'Rourke	1893	157
Luke Appling	1948	156

Doubles
Sam Rice	1930	35
Dave Winfield	1992	33
Honus Wagner	1915	32
Ty Cobb	1927	32
Paul Molitor	1997	32
George Brett	1993	31
Luke Appling	1947	29
Jim O'Rourke	1891	28
Jim O'Rourke	1892	28
Cap Anson	1894	28

Triples
Honus Wagner	1915	17
Sam Rice	1930	13
Cap Anson	1892	9
Honus Wagner	1914	9
Honus Wagner	1916	9
Jake Daubert	1924	9
Sam Rice	1931	8
4 tied with		7

Home Runs
Darrell Evans	1987	34
Ted Williams	1960	29
Hank Sauer	1957	26
Dave Winfield	1992	26
Darrell Evans	1988	22
Eddie Murray	1996	22
Dave Winfield	1993	21
Hank Aaron	1974	20
3 tied with		19

RBI
Dave Winfield	1992	108
Cap Anson	1894	99
Darrell Evans	1987	99
Jim O'Rourke	1891	95
Jim O'Rourke	1893	95
Ty Cobb	1927	93
Cap Anson	1893	91
Cap Anson	1895	91
Cap Anson	1896	90
Paul Molitor	1997	89

Stolen Bases
Davey Lopes	1985	47
Davey Lopes	1986	25
Cap Anson	1896	24
Honus Wagner	1914	23
Willie Mays	1971	23
Honus Wagner	1915	22
Ty Cobb	1927	22
Lou Brock	1979	21
Jim O'Rourke	1891	19
Lave Cross	1906	19

Runs Created
Sam Rice	1930	114
Dave Winfield	1992	108
Ty Cobb	1927	102
Darrell Evans	1987	99
Cap Anson	1895	98
Cap Anson	1894	94
Willie Mays	1971	94
Stan Musial	1962	92
Jim O'Rourke	1891	90
Cap Anson	1892	88

Batting Average
(minimum 3.1 PA/Tm Gm)
Ty Cobb	1927	.357
Sam Rice	1930	.349
Cap Anson	1895	.335
Cap Anson	1896	.331
Stan Musial	1962	.330
Pete Rose	1981	.325
Cap Anson	1893	.314
Luke Appling	1948	.314
Luke Appling	1947	.306
Paul Molitor	1997	.305

On-Base Percentage
(minimum 3.1 PA/Tm Gm)
Ty Cobb	1927	.440
Luke Appling	1949	.439
Willie Mays	1971	.425
Luke Appling	1948	.423
Stan Musial	1962	.416
Cap Anson	1893	.415
Cap Anson	1895	.408
Cap Anson	1896	.407
Sam Rice	1930	.407
Pete Rose	1985	.395

Slugging Percentage
(minimum 3.1 PA/Tm Gm)
Stan Musial	1962	.508
Darrell Evans	1987	.501
Dave Winfield	1992	.491
Willie Mays	1971	.482
Ty Cobb	1927	.482
Sam Rice	1930	.457
Carlton Fisk	1990	.451
Dave Winfield	1993	.442
Paul Molitor	1997	.435
George Brett	1993	.434

Pitching Leaders—After Age 39

Wins		Losses		Winning Percentage (minimum 50 decisions)		Games	
Phil Niekro	121	Phil Niekro	103	Pete Alexander	.605	Hoyt Wilhelm	439
Jack Quinn	96	Charlie Hough	88	Hoyt Wilhelm	.557	Jack Quinn	341
Warren Spahn	75	Jack Quinn	80	Cy Young	.556	Phil Niekro	300
Cy Young	75	Nolan Ryan	66	Jack Quinn	.545	Jim Kaat	223
Nolan Ryan	71	Warren Spahn	63	Jerry Koosman	.544	Charlie Hough	209
Charlie Hough	67	Tommy John	60	Warren Spahn	.543	Dutch Leonard	199
Tommy John	51	Cy Young	60	Babe Adams	.542	Kent Tekulve	197
Hoyt Wilhelm	49	Gaylord Perry	59	Phil Niekro	.540	Don McMahon	197
Gaylord Perry	47	Red Faber	55	Don Sutton	.537	Nolan Ryan	196
Pete Alexander	46	Hoyt Wilhelm	39	Connie Marrero	.524	Red Faber	182

Complete Games		Shutouts		Saves		Innings Pitched	
Cy Young	119	Cy Young	15	Hoyt Wilhelm	108	Phil Niekro	1,977.0
Warren Spahn	77	Warren Spahn	12	Dennis Eckersley	95	Jack Quinn	1,433.2
Jack Quinn	69	Jack Quinn	12	Jack Quinn	42	Charlie Hough	1,346.1
Phil Niekro	62	Phil Niekro	11	Woodie Fryman	36	Nolan Ryan	1,271.2
Pete Alexander	48	Nolan Ryan	7	Doug Jones	36	Cy Young	1,226.2
Ted Lyons	44	Early Wynn	7	Don McMahon	34	Warren Spahn	1,163.0
Connie Marrero	43	Connie Marrero	6	Satchel Paige	32	Tommy John	1,000.2
Early Wynn	30	5 tied with	4	Dutch Leonard	28	Gaylord Perry	992.0
Red Faber	30			Ellis Kinder	27	Red Faber	779.1
2 tied with	29			Joe Heving	27	Hoyt Wilhelm	744.2

Strikeouts		ERA (minimum 500 Innings Pitched)		Component ERA (minimum 500 Innings Pitched)		Opponent Average (minimum 500 Innings Pitched)	
Nolan Ryan	1,437	Hoyt Wilhelm	2.09	Hoyt Wilhelm	1.91	Hoyt Wilhelm	.195
Phil Niekro	1,148	Cy Young	2.14	Cy Young	2.08	Nolan Ryan	.203
Charlie Hough	756	Pete Alexander	3.31	Nolan Ryan	2.65	Cy Young	.239
Hoyt Wilhelm	570	Nolan Ryan	3.33	Pete Alexander	3.25	Charlie Hough	.241
Gaylord Perry	533	Warren Spahn	3.44	Warren Spahn	3.40	Early Wynn	.248
Cy Young	519	Connie Marrero	3.46	Dazzy Vance	3.45	Don Sutton	.256
Warren Spahn	503	Jack Quinn	3.46	Connie Marrero	3.57	Connie Marrero	.258
Dazzy Vance	390	Early Wynn	3.66	Early Wynn	3.63	Warren Spahn	.258
Jack Quinn	376	Phil Niekro	3.84	Jack Quinn	3.64	Phil Niekro	.259
Don Sutton	366	Dazzy Vance	3.87	Babe Adams	3.65	Joe Niekro	.263

Single Season Pitching Leaders—Age 40 or Older

Wins			Losses			Winning Percentage (minimum 15 decisions)			Games		
Warren Spahn	1963	23	Phil Niekro	1979	20	Rip Sewell	1948	.813	Kent Tekulve	1987	90
Cy Young	1907	21	Bob Smith	1935	18	Phil Niekro	1982	.810	Doug Jones	1997	75
Cy Young	1908	21	Phil Niekro	1980	18	Warren Spahn	1963	.767	Hoyt Wilhelm	1964	73
Pete Alexander	1927	21	Kaiser Wilhelm	1914	17	Earl Caldwell	1946	.765	Hoyt Wilhelm	1968	72
Warren Spahn	1961	21	Dutch Leonard	1949	16	Jack Quinn	1928	.720	Bob McClure	1992	71
Phil Niekro	1979	21	Warren Spahn	1965	16	Dennis Martinez	1995	.706	Jesse Orosco	1997	71
Cy Young	1909	19	Nolan Ryan	1987	16	Ted Lyons	1942	.700	Kent Tekulve	1988	70
Jack Quinn	1928	18	Charlie Hough	1988	16	Tommy John	1987	.684	Hoyt Wilhelm	1965	66
Warren Spahn	1962	18	Charlie Hough	1993	16	Rick Reuschel	1989	.680	Larry Andersen	1993	64
2 tied with		17	6 tied with		15	Pete Alexander	1927	.677	2 tied with		63

Complete Games			Shutouts			Saves			Innings Pitched		
Cy Young	1907	33	Warren Spahn	1963	7	Dennis Eckersley	1997	36	Cy Young	1907	343.1
Cy Young	1908	30	Cy Young	1907	6	Doug Jones	1997	36	Phil Niekro	1979	342.0
Cy Young	1909	30	Babe Adams	1922	4	Dennis Eckersley	1996	30	Cy Young	1908	299.0
Phil Niekro	1979	23	Jack Quinn	1928	4	Dennis Eckersley	1995	29	Cy Young	1909	294.2
Pete Alexander	1927	22	Early Wynn	1960	4	Hoyt Wilhelm	1964	27	Phil Niekro	1980	275.0
Warren Spahn	1962	22	Warren Spahn	1961	4	Hoyt Wilhelm	1965	20	Warren Spahn	1962	269.1
Warren Spahn	1963	22	8 tied with		3	Don McMahon	1970	19	Pete Alexander	1927	268.0
Warren Spahn	1961	21				Ellis Kinder	1955	18	Warren Spahn	1961	262.2
Ed Green	1890	20				Woodie Fryman	1980	17	Warren Spahn	1963	259.2
Ted Lyons	1942	20				Jack Quinn	1931	15	Charlie Hough	1988	252.0

Strikeouts			ERA (minimum 1 Inning Pitched/Tm Gm)			Component ERA (minimum 1 Inning Pitched/Tm Gm)			Opponent Average (minimum 1 Inning Pitched/Tm Gm)		
Nolan Ryan	1989	301	Cy Young	1908	1.26	Cy Young	1908	1.48	Nolan Ryan	1991	.172
Nolan Ryan	1987	270	Cy Young	1907	1.99	Cy Young	1907	1.85	Nolan Ryan	1989	.187
Nolan Ryan	1990	232	Ted Lyons	1942	2.10	Nolan Ryan	1991	1.98	Nolan Ryan	1990	.188
Nolan Ryan	1988	228	Cy Young	1909	2.26	Cy Young	1910	2.26	Nolan Ryan	1987	.200
Phil Niekro	1979	208	Johnny Niggeling	1944	2.32	Nolan Ryan	1990	2.28	Cy Young	1908	.213
Nolan Ryan	1991	203	Eddie Plank	1916	2.33	Nolan Ryan	1989	2.31	Johnny Niggeling	1944	.221
Phil Niekro	1980	176	Pete Alexander	1927	2.52	Eddie Plank	1916	2.39	Charlie Hough	1988	.221
Charlie Hough	1988	174	Cy Young	1910	2.53	Cy Young	1909	2.40	Nolan Ryan	1988	.227
Early Wynn	1960	158	Warren Spahn	1963	2.60	Nolan Ryan	1987	2.50	Charlie Hough	1991	.229
Nolan Ryan	1992	157	Nolan Ryan	1987	2.76	Ted Lyons	1942	2.50	Cy Young	1907	.230

Top Two-Year Batting Performances

Runs

Billy Hamilton	1894-1895	358
Babe Ruth	1920-1921	335
Willie Keeler	1894-1895	327
Tom Brown	1890-1891	323
Babe Ruth	1927-1928	321
Billy Hamilton	1895-1896	318
Arlie Latham	1886-1887	315
Willie Keeler	1895-1896	315
Joe Kelley	1894-1895	313
Jesse Burkett	1895-1896	313
Hugh Duffy	1893-1894	307
Lou Gehrig	1930-1931	306
Hugh Duffy	1889-1890	305
Lou Gehrig	1936-1937	305
Billy Hamilton	1896-1897	304

Hits

Rogers Hornsby	1921-1922	485
Bill Terry	1929-1930	480
Ty Cobb	1911-1912	475
George Sisler	1920-1921	473
Chuck Klein	1929-1930	469
Bill Terry	1930-1931	467
Jesse Burkett	1895-1896	465
George Sisler	1921-1922	462
Paul Waner	1927-1928	460
Joe Medwick	1936-1937	460
Joe Jackson	1911-1912	459
Babe Herman	1929-1930	458
Lefty O'Doul	1929-1930	456
Willie Keeler	1897-1898	455
Lloyd Waner	1928-1929	455

Doubles

Joe Medwick	1936-1937	120
George Burns	1926-1927	115
Billy Herman	1935-1936	114
Joe Medwick	1935-1936	110
Hank Greenberg	1934-1935	109
Tris Speaker	1922-1923	107
George Burns	1925-1926	105
Chuck Klein	1929-1930	104
Edgar Martinez	1995-1996	104
Joe Medwick	1937-1938	103
Tris Speaker	1920-1921	102
Don Mattingly	1985-1986	101
Tris Speaker	1921-1922	100
Paul Waner	1932-1933	100
Charlie Gehringer	1936-1937	100

Triples

Dave Orr	1885-1886	52
Chief Wilson	1912-1913	50
Sam Crawford	1913-1914	49
Sam Thompson	1894-1895	48
Chief Wilson	1911-1912	48
Sam Crawford	1902-1903	47
Ty Cobb	1911-1912	47
George Davis	1893-1894	46
Joe Jackson	1911-1912	45
Sam Crawford	1914-1915	45
Heinie Reitz	1893-1894	44
Harry Davis	1896-1897	44
Sam Crawford	1912-1913	44
Earle Combs	1927-1928	44
Three tied at		43

Home Runs

Babe Ruth	1927-1928	114
Babe Ruth	1920-1921	113
Mark McGwire	1996-1997	110
Babe Ruth	1926-1927	107
Jimmie Foxx	1932-1933	106
Ken Griffey Jr.	1996-1997	105
Ralph Kiner	1949-1950	101
Babe Ruth	1928-1929	100
Roger Maris	1960-1961	100
Willie Mays	1964-1965	99
Hank Greenberg	1937-1938	98
Albert Belle	1995-1996	98
Ted Kluszewski	1954-1955	96
Four tied at		95

Total Bases

Chuck Klein	1929-1930	850
Babe Ruth	1920-1921	845
Jimmie Foxx	1932-1933	841
Lou Gehrig	1930-1931	829
Rogers Hornsby	1921-1922	828
Lou Gehrig	1927-1928	811
Stan Musial	1948-1949	811
Babe Ruth	1927-1928	797
Chuck Klein	1930-1931	792
Babe Ruth	1923-1924	790
Jim Rice	1977-1978	788
Chuck Klein	1932-1933	785
Joe DiMaggio	1936-1937	785
Babe Ruth	1926-1927	782
Lou Gehrig	1931-1932	780

RBI

Lou Gehrig	1930-1931	358
Hack Wilson	1929-1930	349
Lou Gehrig	1931-1932	335
Jimmie Foxx	1932-1933	332
Hank Greenberg	1937-1938	329
Al Simmons	1929-1930	322
Lou Gehrig	1927-1928	317
Babe Ruth	1930-1931	316
Chuck Klein	1929-1930	315
Lou Gehrig	1936-1937	311
Babe Ruth	1926-1927	310
Hank Greenberg	1934-1935	309
Babe Ruth	1920-1921	308
Babe Ruth	1929-1930	307
Joe DiMaggio	1937-1938	307

Walks

Ted Williams	1946-1947	318
Babe Ruth	1923-1924	312
Barry Bonds	1996-1997	296
Babe Ruth	1920-1921	292
Ted Williams	1941-1942	290
Ted Williams	1947-1948	288
Ted Williams	1948-1949	288
Eddie Stanky	1945-1946	285
Babe Ruth	1926-1927	282
Mickey Mantle	1957-1958	275
Babe Ruth	1927-1928	273
Harmon Killebrew	1969-1970	273
Eddie Stanky	1950-1951	271
Barry Bonds	1995-1996	271
Two tied at		269

Strikeouts

Bobby Bonds	1969-1970	376
Rob Deer	1986-1987	365
Pete Incaviglia	1986-1987	353
Gorman Thomas	1979-1980	345
Rob Deer	1987-1988	339
Jay Buhner	1996-1997	334
Cecil Fielder	1990-1991	333
Jose Canseco	1986-1987	332
Mike Schmidt	1975-1976	329
Jim Presley	1986-1987	329
Andres Galarraga	1989-1990	327
Bobby Bonds	1970-1971	326
Rob Deer	1990-1991	322
Pete Incaviglia	1987-1988	321
Two tied at		318

Stolen Bases

Hugh Nicol	1887-1888	241
Arlie Latham	1887-1888	238
Rickey Henderson	1982-1983	238
Vince Coleman	1985-1986	217
Vince Coleman	1986-1987	216
Billy Hamilton	1889-1890	213
Billy Hamilton	1890-1891	213
Billy Hamilton	1894-1895	195
Vince Coleman	1987-1988	190
Arlie Latham	1886-1887	189
Charlie Comiskey	1887-1888	189
Lou Brock	1973-1974	188
Rickey Henderson	1981-1982	186
Tom Brown	1890-1891	185
Two tied at		184

Runs Created

Babe Ruth	1920-1921	399
Babe Ruth	1923-1924	372
Lou Gehrig	1930-1931	361
Babe Ruth	1930-1931	355
Jimmie Foxx	1932-1933	355
Hugh Duffy	1893-1894	351
Lou Gehrig	1936-1937	348
Billy Hamilton	1894-1895	347
Babe Ruth	1926-1927	344
Hugh Duffy	1894-1895	343
Babe Ruth	1927-1928	342
Lou Gehrig	1931-1932	342
Lou Gehrig	1927-1928	338
Ted Williams	1948-1949	334
Stan Musial	1948-1949	332

Runs Created/27 Outs
(minimum 1000 Plate Appearances)

Babe Ruth	1920-1921	15.92
Babe Ruth	1923-1924	14.12
Ted Williams	1941-1942	14.05
Billy Hamilton	1893-1894	13.95
Ed Delahanty	1895-1896	13.78
Billy Hamilton	1894-1895	13.55
Hugh Duffy	1893-1894	13.55
Babe Ruth	1919-1920	13.53
Babe Ruth	1931-1932	13.41
Mickey Mantle	1956-1957	13.36
Babe Ruth	1930-1931	13.29
Ed Delahanty	1894-1895	13.23
Hugh Duffy	1894-1895	13.08
Babe Ruth	1921-1922	12.89
Babe Ruth	1926-1927	12.86

Batting Average
(minimum 1000 Plate Appearances)

Ty Cobb	1911-1912	.415
Rogers Hornsby	1924-1925	.413
Jesse Burkett	1895-1896	.409
Rogers Hornsby	1923-1924	.406
Ed Delahanty	1894-1895	.406
Willie Keeler	1896-1897	.405
Willie Keeler	1897-1898	.404
Ty Cobb	1910-1911	.403
Ty Cobb	1912-1913	.402
Joe Jackson	1911-1912	.402
Ed Delahanty	1895-1896	.400
Hugh Duffy	1893-1894	.400
Rogers Hornsby	1921-1922	.399
Sam Thompson	1894-1895	.399
Jesse Burkett	1896-1897	.397

On-Base Percentage
(minimum 1000 Plate Appearances)

Babe Ruth	1923-1924	.529
Ted Williams	1941-1942	.524
Babe Ruth	1920-1921	.520
Billy Hamilton	1893-1894	.510
John McGraw	1898-1899	.508
Billy Hamilton	1894-1895	.507
Ted Williams	1956-1957	.503
Babe Ruth	1926-1927	.501
Babe Ruth	1922-1923	.499
Rogers Hornsby	1924-1925	.498
Ted Williams	1946-1947	.498
Ted Williams	1947-1948	.498
Babe Ruth	1919-1920	.496
Ted Williams	1940-1941	.494
Babe Ruth	1930-1931	.494

Slugging Percentage
(minimum 1000 Plate Appearances)

Babe Ruth	1920-1921	.847
Babe Ruth	1921-1922	.772
Babe Ruth	1926-1927	.756
Babe Ruth	1919-1920	.755
Babe Ruth	1923-1924	.752
Babe Ruth	1927-1928	.741
Jimmie Foxx	1932-1933	.726
Rogers Hornsby	1924-1925	.725
Babe Ruth	1922-1923	.724
Babe Ruth	1930-1931	.716
Babe Ruth	1929-1930	.715
Lou Gehrig	1927-1928	.708
Babe Ruth	1928-1929	.703
Albert Belle	1994-1995	.700
Jimmie Foxx	1938-1939	.700

OBP+Slugging
(minimum 1000 Plate Appearances)

Babe Ruth	1920-1921	1.367
Babe Ruth	1923-1924	1.280
Babe Ruth	1926-1927	1.256
Babe Ruth	1921-1922	1.251
Babe Ruth	1919-1920	1.251
Rogers Hornsby	1924-1925	1.223
Babe Ruth	1922-1923	1.223
Babe Ruth	1927-1928	1.215
Ted Williams	1941-1942	1.212
Babe Ruth	1930-1931	1.209
Jimmie Foxx	1932-1933	1.186
Babe Ruth	1929-1930	1.179
Lou Gehrig	1927-1928	1.179
Babe Ruth	1931-1932	1.174
Mickey Mantle	1956-1957	1.174

Games

Three tied at	326

At-Bats

Dave Cash	1974-1975	1,386

Home Runs (Home)

Hank Greenberg	1937-1938	64

Home Runs (Road)

Two tied at	57

AB/HR
(minimum 1000 Plate Appearances)

Mark McGwire	1996-1997	8.8

Extra-Base Hits

Babe Ruth	1920-1921	218

Walks/PA
(minimum 1000 Plate Appearances)

Ted Williams	1946-1947	0.23

Intentional Walks

Willie McCovey	1969-1970	85

Hit By Pitch

Hughie Jennings	1896-1897	97

Sacrifice Hits

Ray Chapman	1916-1917	107

Sacrifice Flies

Gil Hodges	1954-1955	29

Caught Stealing

Rickey Henderson	1981-1982	64

Stolen Base Pct.
(minimum 40 attempts)

Davey Lopes	1984-1985	.939

GDP

Jim Rice	1984-1985	71

Secondary Average
(minimum 1000 Plate Appearances)

Babe Ruth	1920-1921	.794

Isolated Power
(minimum 1000 Plate Appearances)

Babe Ruth	1920-1921	.470

Top Two-Year Pitching Performances

Wins

Old Hoss Radbourn	1883-1884	107
Pud Galvin	1883-1884	92
John Clarkson	1885-1886	89
Old Hoss Radbourn	1884-1885	87
Monte Ward	1879-1880	86
Bill Hutchison	1890-1891	86
Tommy Bond	1878-1879	83
Will White	1882-1883	83
Mickey Welch	1884-1885	83
Guy Hecker	1884-1885	82
John Clarkson	1888-1889	82
Old Hoss Radbourn	1882-1883	81
Bill Hutchison	1891-1892	81
Tommy Bond	1877-1878	80
Ed Morris	1885-1886	80

Losses

Will White	1879-1880	73
Jim McCormick	1879-1880	68
John Coleman	1883-1884	65
Jim Whitney	1885-1886	64
Pud Galvin	1879-1880	62
Al Mays	1886-1887	62
Henry Porter	1887-1888	61
Jim Devlin	1876-1877	60
Jim McCormick	1881-1882	60
Stump Wiedman	1885-1886	60
Bill Hutchison	1892-1893	60
Pud Galvin	1880-1881	59
Lee Richmond	1881-1882	59
Dupee Shaw	1884-1885	59
Red Donahue	1896-1897	59

Winning Percentage
(minimum 30 decisions)

Preacher Roe	1951-1952	.868
Lefty Grove	1930-1931	.868
Ed Reulbach	1906-1907	.818
Joe Wood	1912-1913	.818
Sandy Koufax	1963-1964	.815
Greg Maddux	1994-1995	.814
Lefty Grove	1929-1930	.814
Russ Ford	1909-1910	.813
Bill Hoffer	1895-1896	.812
Sal Maglie	1950-1951	.804
Ron Guidry	1977-1978	.804
Dwight Gooden	1985-1986	.804
57 tied at		.800

Games

Mike Marshall	1973-1974	198
Kent Tekulve	1978-1979	185
Kent Tekulve	1979-1980	172
Mike Myers	1996-1997	171
Mitch Williams	1986-1987	165
Wilbur Wood	1968-1969	164
Mike Marshall	1974-1975	163
Kent Tekulve	1977-1978	163
Kent Tekulve	1986-1987	163
Rob Murphy	1987-1988	163
Dick Tidrow	1979-1980	161
Kent Tekulve	1982-1983	161
Craig Lefferts	1986-1987	160
Kent Tekulve	1987-1988	160
Duane Ward	1991-1992	160

Games Started

Pud Galvin	1883-1884	147
Old Hoss Radbourn	1883-1884	141
Will White	1879-1880	137
Matt Kilroy	1886-1887	137
Jim McCormick	1879-1880	134
Jim McCormick	1880-1881	132
Toad Ramsey	1886-1887	131
Jim Devlin	1876-1877	129
Bill Hutchison	1891-1892	128
Will White	1878-1879	127
Monte Ward	1879-1880	127
Pud Galvin	1882-1883	126
Guy Hecker	1884-1885	126
Ed Morris	1885-1886	126
John Clarkson	1888-1889	126

Complete Games

Pud Galvin	1883-1884	143
Old Hoss Radbourn	1883-1884	139
Will White	1879-1880	133
Matt Kilroy	1886-1887	132
Jim McCormick	1879-1880	131
Jim McCormick	1880-1881	129
Jim Devlin	1876-1877	127
Will White	1878-1879	127
Toad Ramsey	1886-1887	127
Ed Morris	1885-1886	126
Old Hoss Radbourn	1883-1884	124
Guy Hecker	1884-1885	123
Bill Hutchison	1891-1892	123
Jim McCormick	1881-1882	122
Old Hoss Radbourn	1884-1885	122

Shutouts

Pete Alexander	1915-1916	28
Pete Alexander	1916-1917	24
Tommy Bond	1878-1879	20
Walter Johnson	1913-1914	20
Ed Morris	1885-1886	19
Christy Mathewson	1907-1908	19
Ed Walsh	1908-1909	19
Christy Mathewson	1908-1909	19
Jack Coombs	1909-1910	19
George Bradley	1876-1877	18
Walter Johnson	1912-1913	18
Pete Alexander	1914-1915	18
Sandy Koufax	1963-1964	18
Four tied at		17

Saves

Dennis Eckersley	1991-1992	94
Bobby Thigpen	1989-1990	91
Dennis Eckersley	1990-1991	91
Randy Myers	1992-1993	91
Lee Smith	1991-1992	90
Dan Quisenberry	1983-1984	89
Lee Smith	1992-1993	89
Bobby Thigpen	1990-1991	87
Dennis Eckersley	1992-1993	87
Jose Mesa	1995-1996	85
Jeff Montgomery	1992-1993	84
Rick Aguilera	1991-1992	83
Dan Quisenberry	1984-1985	81
Dennis Eckersley	1989-1990	81
Two tied at		80

Innings Pitched

Old Hoss Radbourn	1883-1884	1,311.0
Pud Galvin	1883-1884	1,292.2
Jim McCormick	1879-1880	1,204.0
Will White	1879-1880	1,197.1
Jim McCormick	1880-1881	1,183.2
Bill Hutchison	1891-1892	1,183.0
Monte Ward	1879-1880	1,182.0
Jim Devlin	1876-1877	1,181.0
Matt Kilroy	1886-1887	1,172.1
Bill Hutchison	1890-1891	1,164.0
Guy Hecker	1884-1885	1,150.2
Toad Ramsey	1886-1887	1,149.2
Will White	1878-1879	1,148.0
Ed Morris	1885-1886	1,136.1
Old Hoss Radbourn	1884-1885	1,124.1

Walks

Amos Rusie	1890-1891	551
Amos Rusie	1891-1892	529
Mark Baldwin	1889-1890	523
Amos Rusie	1892-1893	485
Mark Baldwin	1890-1891	476
Mark Baldwin	1891-1892	421
Amos Rusie	1893-1894	418
Ed Crane	1890-1891	413
Jack Stivetts	1890-1891	411
Amos Rusie	1889-1890	405
Jack Stivetts	1891-1892	403
Phil Knell	1890-1891	392
Ed Crane	1891-1892	392
Gus Weyhing	1889-1890	391
Nolan Ryan	1976-1977	387

Strikeouts

Toad Ramsey	1886-1887	854
Old Hoss Radbourn	1883-1884	756
Nolan Ryan	1973-1974	750
Matt Kilroy	1886-1887	730
Nolan Ryan	1972-1973	712
Sandy Koufax	1965-1966	699
Tim Keefe	1883-1884	678
Amos Rusie	1890-1891	678
Nolan Ryan	1976-1977	668
Charlie Buffinton	1884-1885	659
One Arm Daily	1883-1884	654
Rube Waddell	1903-1904	651
Pud Galvin	1883-1884	648
Dupee Shaw	1884-1885	645
Rube Waddell	1904-1905	636

Strikeouts/9 Innings
(minimum 300 Innings Pitched)

Randy Johnson	1994-1995	11.60
Nolan Ryan	1989-1990	10.82
Randy Johnson	1993-1994	10.78
Nolan Ryan	1986-1987	10.72
Randy Johnson	1992-1993	10.61
Sam McDowell	1965-1966	10.59
Nolan Ryan	1972-1973	10.50
Nolan Ryan	1990-1991	10.38
Nolan Ryan	1987-1988	10.38
Nolan Ryan	1988-1989	10.37
Pedro Martinez	1996-1997	10.36
Nolan Ryan	1976-1977	10.31
Curt Schilling	1996-1997	10.30
Randy Johnson	1991-1992	10.25
Nolan Ryan	1973-1974	10.25

ERA
(minimum 300 Innings Pitched)

Three Finger Brown	1906-1907	1.20
Walter Johnson	1912-1913	1.27
Christy Mathewson	1908-1909	1.31
Ed Walsh	1909-1910	1.32
Jack Pfiester	1906-1907	1.35
Walter Johnson	1918-1919	1.37
Pete Alexander	1915-1916	1.39
Three Finger Brown	1908-1909	1.39
Addie Joss	1908-1909	1.40
Ed Walsh	1908-1909	1.41
Three Finger Brown	1907-1908	1.44
George McQuillan	1907-1908	1.44
Walter Johnson	1913-1914	1.44
Ed Walsh	1907-1908	1.50
Addie Joss	1907-1908	1.51

Component ERA
(minimum 300 Innings Pitched)

Christy Mathewson	1908-1909	1.32
Ed Walsh	1909-1910	1.36
Three Finger Brown	1908-1909	1.37
Walter Johnson	1912-1913	1.40
Addie Joss	1908-1909	1.40
Ed Walsh	1908-1909	1.43
Three Finger Brown	1907-1908	1.47
Russ Ford	1909-1910	1.47
Christy Mathewson	1907-1908	1.48
Greg Maddux	1994-1995	1.49
Addie Joss	1907-1908	1.50
Walter Johnson	1913-1914	1.50
Charlie Sweeney	1883-1884	1.52
Pete Alexander	1915-1916	1.56
George McQuillan	1907-1908	1.58

Opponent Average
(minimum 300 Innings Pitched)

Tommy Byrne	1948-1949	.178
Nolan Ryan	1990-1991	.181
Andy Messersmith	1968-1969	.182
Sandy Koufax	1964-1965	.184
Vida Blue	1970-1971	.185
Sam McDowell	1965-1966	.186
Nolan Ryan	1989-1990	.187
Nolan Ryan	1972-1973	.188
Nolan Ryan	1971-1972	.188
Russ Ford	1909-1910	.189
Sandy Koufax	1963-1964	.190
Herb Score	1955-1956	.190
Ed Reulbach	1905-1906	.190
Sandy Koufax	1962-1963	.192
Sandy Koufax	1965-1966	.192

Opponent OBP
(minimum 300 Innings Pitched)

Charlie Sweeney	1883-1884	.226
Christy Mathewson	1908-1909	.226
Sandy Koufax	1964-1965	.233
Walter Johnson	1912-1913	.233
Greg Maddux	1994-1995	.234
Sandy Koufax	1963-1964	.234
Juan Marichal	1965-1966	.234
Addie Joss	1908-1909	.234
Three Finger Brown	1908-1909	.236
Ed Walsh	1909-1910	.236
Christy Mathewson	1907-1908	.237
Charlie Sweeney	1884-1885	.238
Old Hoss Radbourn	1883-1884	.239
Lady Baldwin	1885-1886	.239
Ed Walsh	1908-1909	.239

Games Finished

Mike Marshall	1973-1974	156

Batters Faced

Pud Galvin	1883-1884	5,295

Hits Allowed

Pud Galvin	1883-1884	1,242

Runs Allowed

Will White	1879-1880	727

Earned Runs

Ted Breitenstein	1894-1895	450

Home Runs Allowed

Bert Blyleven	1986-1987	96

Intentional Walks

Two tied at		39

Sac Hits Allowed

Two tied at		96

Sac Flies Allowed

Jaime Navarro	1992-1993	30

Hit Batsmen

Joe McGinnity	1899-1900	69

Wild Pitches

Mickey Welch	1885-1886	90

Balks

Charlie Hough	1987-1988	19

Top Three-Year Batting Performances

Runs

Billy Hamilton	1894-1896	510
Willie Keeler	1894-1896	480
Billy Hamilton	1895-1897	470
Billy Hamilton	1893-1895	468
Joe Kelley	1894-1896	461
Willie Keeler	1895-1897	460
Babe Ruth	1926-1928	460
Jesse Burkett	1894-1896	451
Lou Gehrig	1930-1932	444
Jesse Burkett	1895-1897	442
Babe Ruth	1927-1929	442
Ed Delahanty	1893-1895	441
Hugh Duffy	1889-1891	439
Lou Gehrig	1931-1933	439
Babe Ruth	1919-1921	438

Hits

George Sisler	1920-1922	719
Rogers Hornsby	1920-1922	703
Bill Terry	1929-1931	693
Bill Terry	1930-1932	692
Joe Medwick	1935-1937	684
Lloyd Waner	1927-1929	678
Chuck Klein	1930-1932	676
Willie Keeler	1897-1899	671
Ty Cobb	1910-1912	669
Chuck Klein	1929-1931	669
Willie Keeler	1896-1898	665
Bill Terry	1928-1930	665
Kirby Puckett	1986-1988	664
Jesse Burkett	1895-1897	663
Willie Keeler	1895-1897	662

Doubles

Joe Medwick	1936-1938	167
Joe Medwick	1935-1937	166
Tris Speaker	1921-1923	159
George Burns	1925-1927	156
Joe Medwick	1937-1939	151
Tris Speaker	1920-1922	150
Joe Medwick	1934-1936	150
Billy Herman	1935-1937	149
Lou Gehrig	1926-1928	146
Don Mattingly	1984-1986	145
Tris Speaker	1922-1924	143
Chuck Klein	1930-1932	143
George Burns	1924-1926	142
Hank Greenberg	1933-1935	142
Charlie Gehringer	1934-1936	142

Triples

Sam Crawford	1912-1914	70
Sam Crawford	1913-1915	68
Dave Orr	1884-1886	65
Sam Crawford	1901-1903	63
Sam Crawford	1902-1904	63
Ty Cobb	1911-1913	63
Dave Orr	1885-1887	62
Joe Jackson	1911-1913	62
Chief Wilson	1911-1913	62
Chief Wilson	1912-1914	62
Sam Thompson	1893-1895	61
Chief Wilson	1910-1912	61
Jake Beckley	1890-1892	60
Ty Cobb	1910-1912	60
Four tied at		59

Home Runs

Babe Ruth	1926-1928	161
Babe Ruth	1927-1929	160
Jimmie Foxx	1932-1934	150
Babe Ruth	1928-1930	149
Mark McGwire	1995-1997	149
Babe Ruth	1920-1922	148
Ralph Kiner	1947-1949	145
Ralph Kiner	1949-1951	143
Babe Ruth	1919-1921	142
Harmon Killebrew	1962-1964	142
Babe Ruth	1929-1931	141
Ralph Kiner	1948-1950	141
Harmon Killebrew	1961-1963	139
Willie Mays	1963-1965	137
Five tied at		136

Total Bases

Chuck Klein	1930-1932	1,212
Lou Gehrig	1930-1932	1,199
Chuck Klein	1929-1931	1,197
Jimmie Foxx	1932-1934	1,193
Babe Ruth	1926-1928	1,162
Rogers Hornsby	1920-1922	1,157
Jim Rice	1977-1979	1,157
Lou Gehrig	1929-1931	1,151
Babe Ruth	1927-1929	1,145
Stan Musial	1948-1950	1,142
Lou Gehrig	1931-1933	1,139
Lou Gehrig	1932-1934	1,138
Joe Medwick	1935-1937	1,138
Three tied at		1,133

RBI

Lou Gehrig	1930-1932	509
Lou Gehrig	1929-1931	484
Lou Gehrig	1931-1933	474
Babe Ruth	1929-1931	470
Hack Wilson	1928-1930	469
Jimmie Foxx	1932-1934	462
Babe Ruth	1927-1929	460
Jimmie Foxx	1932-1934	455
Babe Ruth	1930-1932	453
Babe Ruth	1926-1928	452
Jimmie Foxx	1931-1933	452
Al Simmons	1929-1931	450
Babe Ruth	1928-1930	449
Jimmie Foxx	1930-1932	445
Jimmie Foxx	1936-1938	445

Walks

Ted Williams	1947-1949	450
Ted Williams	1946-1948	444
Babe Ruth	1926-1928	417
Barry Bonds	1995-1997	416
Babe Ruth	1921-1923	398
Babe Ruth	1922-1924	396
Eddie Yost	1950-1952	396
Babe Ruth	1930-1932	394
Babe Ruth	1919-1921	393
Lou Gehrig	1935-1937	389
Eddie Stanky	1945-1947	388
Ted Williams	1949-1951	388
Mickey Mantle	1956-1958	387
Harmon Killebrew	1969-1971	387
Ted Williams	1940-1942	386

Strikeouts

Rob Deer	1986-1988	518
Bobby Bonds	1969-1971	513
Pete Incaviglia	1986-1988	506
Rob Deer	1987-1989	497
Cecil Fielder	1990-1992	484
Andres Galarraga	1988-1990	480
Rob Deer	1989-1991	480
Gorman Thomas	1978-1980	478
Bo Jackson	1987-1989	476
Rob Deer	1991-1993	475
Mike Schmidt	1974-1976	467
Bobby Bonds	1970-1972	463
Bobby Bonds	1968-1970	460
Jose Canseco	1986-1988	460
Two tied at		458

Stolen Bases

Vince Coleman	1985-1987	326
Billy Hamilton	1889-1891	324
Hugh Nicol	1887-1889	321
Arlie Latham	1887-1889	307
Rickey Henderson	1982-1984	304
Arlie Latham	1886-1888	298
Vince Coleman	1986-1988	297
Rickey Henderson	1981-1983	294
Rickey Henderson	1980-1982	286
Hugh Nicol	1886-1888	279
Billy Hamilton	1894-1896	278
Billy Hamilton	1890-1892	270
Tom Brown	1890-1892	263
Jim Fogarty	1887-1889	259
Vince Coleman	1987-1989	255

Runs Created

Lou Gehrig	1930-1932	524
Babe Ruth	1919-1921	520
Babe Ruth	1926-1928	509
Babe Ruth	1921-1923	508
Babe Ruth	1920-1922	506
Billy Hamilton	1894-1896	502
Babe Ruth	1930-1932	502
Jimmie Foxx	1932-1934	499
Lou Gehrig	1929-1931	498
Lou Gehrig	1934-1936	497
Ted Williams	1947-1949	495
Babe Ruth	1929-1931	493
Lou Gehrig	1935-1937	493
Joe Kelley	1894-1896	491
Lou Gehrig	1931-1933	491

Runs Created/27 Outs

(minimum 1250 Plate Appearances)

Babe Ruth	1919-1921	14.25
Babe Ruth	1920-1922	14.03
Babe Ruth	1921-1923	13.57
Billy Hamilton	1893-1895	13.46
Ed Delahanty	1894-1896	13.36
Babe Ruth	1930-1932	13.15
Billy Hamilton	1894-1896	12.94
Babe Ruth	1922-1924	12.82
Joe Kelley	1894-1896	12.55
Tip O'Neill	1885-1887	12.51
Ed Delahanty	1893-1895	12.48
Ted Williams	1946-1948	12.48
Ted Williams	1940-1942	12.39
Babe Ruth	1929-1931	12.39
Babe Ruth	1926-1928	12.38

Batting Average

(minimum 1250 Plate Appearances)

Ty Cobb	1911-1913	.408
Ty Cobb	1910-1912	.405
Rogers Hornsby	1923-1925	.405
Rogers Hornsby	1922-1924	.404
Ed Delahanty	1894-1896	.403
Jesse Burkett	1895-1897	.401
Joe Jackson	1910-1912	.401
George Sisler	1920-1922	.400
Willie Keeler	1896-1898	.398
Willie Keeler	1897-1899	.396
Willie Keeler	1895-1897	.396
Rogers Hornsby	1921-1923	.395
Ty Cobb	1909-1911	.394
Jesse Burkett	1894-1896	.393
Ty Cobb	1912-1914	.393

On-Base Percentage

(minimum 1250 Plate Appearances)

John McGraw	1899-1901	.523
John McGraw	1898-1900	.507
Babe Ruth	1922-1924	.504
Babe Ruth	1921-1923	.503
Billy Hamilton	1893-1895	.503
Babe Ruth	1919-1921	.502
Ted Williams	1955-1957	.501
Ted Williams	1946-1948	.498
Billy Hamilton	1894-1896	.497
John McGraw	1897-1899	.497
Babe Ruth	1923-1925	.497
Babe Ruth	1920-1922	.497
Ted Williams	1954-1956	.497
Ted Williams	1940-1942	.496
Ted Williams	1947-1949	.495

Slugging Percentage

(minimum 1250 Plate Appearances)

Babe Ruth	1920-1922	.796
Babe Ruth	1919-1921	.790
Babe Ruth	1921-1923	.769
Babe Ruth	1926-1928	.740
Babe Ruth	1922-1924	.730
Babe Ruth	1927-1929	.727
Babe Ruth	1928-1930	.713
Babe Ruth	1929-1931	.710
Jimmie Foxx	1932-1934	.703
Babe Ruth	1918-1920	.703
Babe Ruth	1925-1927	.701
Babe Ruth	1930-1932	.699
Babe Ruth	1923-1925	.699
Rogers Hornsby	1923-1925	.697
Rogers Hornsby	1922-1924	.688

OBP+Slugging

(minimum 1250 Plate Appearances)

Babe Ruth	1920-1922	1.293
Babe Ruth	1919-1921	1.291
Babe Ruth	1921-1923	1.273
Babe Ruth	1922-1924	1.233
Babe Ruth	1926-1928	1.227
Babe Ruth	1923-1925	1.196
Babe Ruth	1930-1932	1.191
Babe Ruth	1927-1929	1.188
Babe Ruth	1929-1931	1.184
Rogers Hornsby	1923-1925	1.184
Ted Williams	1955-1957	1.180
Babe Ruth	1918-1920	1.177
Babe Ruth	1928-1930	1.176
Babe Ruth	1925-1927	1.176
Babe Ruth	1924-1926	1.172

Games

Three tied at	488

At-Bats

Dave Cash	1974-1976	2,052

Home Runs (Home)

Ralph Kiner	1947-1949	88

Home Runs (Road)

Babe Ruth	1927-1929	82

AB/HR

(minimum 1250 Plate Appearances)

Mark McGwire	1995-1997	8.6

Extra-Base Hits

Babe Ruth	1919-1921	293

Walks/PA

(minimum 1250 Plate Appearances)

Ted Williams	1954-1956	0.23

Intentional Walks

Willie McCovey	1969-1971	106

Hit By Pitch

Hughie Jennings	1896-1898	143

Sacrifice Hits

Ray Chapman	1917-1919	152

Sacrifice Flies

Joe Carter	1992-1994	36

Caught Stealing

Rickey Henderson	1980-1982	90

Stolen Base Pct.

(minimum 60 attempts)

Barry Larkin	1993-1995	.919

GDP

Jim Rice	1983-1985	102

Secondary Average

(minimum 1250 Plate Appearances)

Babe Ruth	1919-1921	.731

Isolated Power

(minimum 1250 Plate Appearances)

Babe Ruth	1920-1922	.437

Top Three-Year Pitching Performances

Wins

Old Hoss Radbourn	1882-1884	140
Old Hoss Radbourn	1883-1885	135
John Clarkson	1885-1887	127
Tommy Bond	1877-1879	123
Bill Hutchison	1890-1892	123
Pud Galvin	1882-1884	120
John Clarkson	1887-1889	120
Will White	1882-1884	117
Mickey Welch	1884-1886	116
Ed Morris	1884-1886	114
Old Hoss Radbourn	1884-1886	114
Tim Keefe	1886-1888	112
Tommy Bond	1876-1878	111
Tim Keefe	1884-1886	111
Silver King	1887-1889	111

Losses

Jim McCormick	1879-1881	98
Will White	1878-1880	94
Lee Richmond	1880-1882	91
Hardie Henderson	1883-1885	91
Dupee Shaw	1884-1886	90
Jim McCormick	1880-1882	88
Pud Galvin	1879-1881	86
Mark Baldwin	1889-1891	86
Jim Whitney	1885-1887	85
Amos Rusie	1890-1892	85
Toad Ramsey	1886-1888	84
Pud Galvin	1880-1882	82
Stump Wiedman	1884-1886	81
Four tied at		80

Winning Percentage
(minimum 40 decisions)

Randy Johnson	1995-1997	.878
Preacher Roe	1951-1953	.846
Lefty Grove	1929-1931	.840
Randy Johnson	1994-1996	.818
Lefty Grove	1930-1932	.816
Howie Krist	1941-1943	.810
Joe Wood	1912-1914	.806
Ron Guidry	1976-1978	.804
Ed Reulbach	1906-1908	.800
Spud Chandler	1942-1944	.800
Sandy Koufax	1963-1965	.795
Lefty Grove	1928-1930	.791
Lefty Grove	1931-1933	.784
Don Gullett	1975-1977	.784
Juan Guzman	1991-1993	.784

Games

Mike Marshall	1972-1974	263
Kent Tekulve	1978-1980	263
Kent Tekulve	1977-1979	257
Mike Marshall	1973-1975	255
Wilbur Wood	1968-1970	241
Rob Murphy	1987-1989	237
Kent Tekulve	1982-1984	233
Kent Tekulve	1986-1988	233
Duane Ward	1990-1992	233
Mitch Williams	1986-1988	232
Duane Ward	1991-1993	231
Willie Hernandez	1982-1984	229
Willie Hernandez	1983-1985	228
Mitch Williams	1987-1989	228
Juan Agosto	1988-1990	228

Games Started

Jim McCormick	1880-1882	199
Pud Galvin	1882-1884	198
Bill Hutchison	1890-1892	194
Old Hoss Radbourn	1882-1884	193
Jim McCormick	1879-1881	192
Old Hoss Radbourn	1883-1885	190
Pud Galvin	1883-1885	190
Will White	1878-1880	189
John Clarkson	1887-1889	185
John Clarkson	1885-1887	184
Tommy Bond	1877-1879	181
Amos Rusie	1890-1892	181
Tommy Bond	1878-1880	180
Old Hoss Radbourn	1884-1886	180
Two tied at		179

Complete Games

Jim McCormick	1880-1882	194
Pud Galvin	1882-1884	191
Old Hoss Radbourn	1882-1884	190
Jim McCormick	1879-1881	188
Old Hoss Radbourn	1883-1885	188
Bill Hutchison	1890-1892	188
Will White	1878-1880	185
Pud Galvin	1883-1885	183
Old Hoss Radbourn	1884-1886	179
John Clarkson	1887-1889	177
Tommy Bond	1877-1879	174
John Clarkson	1885-1887	174
Ed Morris	1884-1886	173
Mickey Welch	1884-1886	173
Guy Hecker	1883-1885	172

Shutouts

Pete Alexander	1915-1917	36
Pete Alexander	1914-1916	34
Christy Mathewson	1907-1909	27
Walter Johnson	1912-1914	27
Pete Alexander	1913-1915	27
Walter Johnson	1913-1915	27
Tommy Bond	1877-1879	26
Ed Walsh	1906-1908	26
Ed Walsh	1908-1910	26
Sandy Koufax	1963-1965	26
Christy Mathewson	1906-1908	25
Six tied at		24

Saves

Dennis Eckersley	1990-1992	142
Lee Smith	1991-1993	136
Dennis Eckersley	1991-1993	130
Dan Quisenberry	1983-1985	126
Dennis Eckersley	1988-1990	126
Bobby Thigpen	1988-1990	125
Dan Quisenberry	1982-1984	124
Dennis Eckersley	1989-1991	124
Lee Smith	1992-1994	122
Bobby Thigpen	1989-1991	121
Lee Smith	1990-1992	121
Rick Aguilera	1991-1993	117
Jeff Montgomery	1991-1993	117
Lee Smith	1993-1995	116
Rick Aguilera	1990-1992	115

Innings Pitched

Bill Hutchison	1890-1892	1,786.0
Old Hoss Radbourn	1882-1884	1,785.0
Jim McCormick	1880-1882	1,779.1
Old Hoss Radbourn	1883-1885	1,756.2
Pud Galvin	1882-1884	1,738.0
Jim McCormick	1879-1881	1,730.0
Will White	1878-1880	1,665.1
Pud Galvin	1883-1885	1,665.0
Old Hoss Radbourn	1884-1886	1,633.2
John Clarkson	1887-1889	1,626.1
John Clarkson	1885-1887	1,612.2
Tommy Bond	1877-1879	1,609.0
Guy Hecker	1883-1885	1,601.2
Tommy Bond	1878-1880	1,581.0
Amos Rusie	1890-1892	1,581.0

Walks

Amos Rusie	1890-1892	818
Mark Baldwin	1889-1891	750
Amos Rusie	1891-1893	747
Amos Rusie	1892-1894	685
Mark Baldwin	1890-1892	670
Amos Rusie	1889-1891	667
Mark Baldwin	1888-1890	622
Ed Crane	1890-1892	602
Jack Stivetts	1890-1892	582
Amos Rusie	1893-1895	577
Bill Hutchison	1890-1892	567
Mark Baldwin	1891-1893	563
Gus Weyhing	1889-1891	552
Ed Crane	1889-1891	549
Cy Seymour	1897-1899	547

Strikeouts

Toad Ramsey	1886-1888	1,082
Nolan Ryan	1972-1974	1,079
Amos Rusie	1890-1892	966
Old Hoss Radbourn	1882-1884	957
Rube Waddell	1903-1905	938
Toad Ramsey	1885-1887	937
Nolan Ryan	1973-1975	936
Nolan Ryan	1976-1978	928
Ed Morris	1884-1886	926
Sandy Koufax	1964-1966	922
Sandy Koufax	1963-1965	911
Old Hoss Radbourn	1883-1885	910
Tim Keefe	1883-1885	908
Nolan Ryan	1974-1976	880
Mickey Welch	1884-1886	875

Strikeouts/9 Innings
(minimum 400 Innings Pitched)

Randy Johnson	1995-1997	12.34
Randy Johnson	1994-1996	11.72
Randy Johnson	1993-1995	11.30
Nolan Ryan	1989-1991	10.75
Nolan Ryan	1987-1989	10.72
Randy Johnson	1992-1994	10.63
Dick Radatz	1962-1964	10.59
Randy Johnson	1991-1993	10.48
Nolan Ryan	1988-1990	10.33
Nolan Ryan	1972-1974	10.30
Nolan Ryan	1986-1988	10.22
Sam McDowell	1964-1966	10.21
Nolan Ryan	1976-1978	10.21
Dick Radatz	1963-1965	10.10
Hideo Nomo	1995-1997	10.09

ERA
(minimum 400 Innings Pitched)

Three Finger Brown	1906-1908	1.30
Ed Walsh	1908-1910	1.36
Three Finger Brown	1907-1909	1.39
Walter Johnson	1912-1914	1.42
Walter Johnson	1911-1913	1.47
Walter Johnson	1913-1915	1.48
Ed Walsh	1907-1909	1.48
Christy Mathewson	1908-1910	1.50
Three Finger Brown	1905-1907	1.52
Christy Mathewson	1907-1909	1.53
Addie Joss	1908-1910	1.53
Three Finger Brown	1908-1910	1.53
Walter Johnson	1910-1912	1.53
Pete Alexander	1915-1917	1.54
Addie Joss	1907-1909	1.56

Component ERA
(minimum 400 Innings Pitched)

Ed Walsh	1908-1910	1.37
Christy Mathewson	1907-1909	1.43
Three Finger Brown	1907-1909	1.45
Three Finger Brown	1906-1908	1.49
Addie Joss	1908-1910	1.51
Walter Johnson	1912-1914	1.51
Addie Joss	1906-1908	1.53
Addie Joss	1907-1909	1.54
Walter Johnson	1913-1915	1.55
Three Finger Brown	1908-1910	1.56
Lady Baldwin	1884-1886	1.56
Ed Walsh	1907-1909	1.57
Christy Mathewson	1908-1910	1.58
Sandy Koufax	1963-1965	1.58
Ed Walsh	1906-1908	1.61

Opponent Average
(minimum 400 Innings Pitched)

Nolan Ryan	1989-1991	.183
Sandy Koufax	1963-1965	.186
Tom Hall	1970-1972	.187
Herb Score	1955-1957	.187
Nolan Ryan	1970-1972	.188
Nolan Ryan	1972-1974	.189
Andy Messersmith	1968-1970	.191
Sandy Koufax	1962-1964	.192
Sandy Koufax	1964-1966	.192
Vida Blue	1970-1972	.194
Nolan Ryan	1971-1973	.195
Bob Turley	1953-1955	.196
Sid Fernandez	1988-1990	.196
J.R. Richard	1978-1980	.197
Nolan Ryan	1974-1976	.197

Opponent OBP
(minimum 400 Innings Pitched)

Sandy Koufax	1963-1965	.232
Christy Mathewson	1907-1909	.235
Ed Walsh	1908-1910	.235
Lady Baldwin	1884-1886	.237
Sandy Koufax	1964-1966	.240
Old Hoss Radbourn	1882-1884	.241
Sandy Koufax	1962-1964	.241
Addie Joss	1908-1910	.242
Addie Joss	1906-1908	.243
Three Finger Brown	1907-1909	.243
Charlie Sweeney	1883-1885	.243
Monte Ward	1878-1880	.243
Walter Johnson	1912-1914	.244
Tim Keefe	1883-1885	.244
Addie Joss	1907-1909	.244

Games Finished

Mike Marshall	1972-1974	212

Batters Faced

Bill Hutchison	1890-1892	7,328

Hits Allowed

Pud Galvin	1882-1884	1,718

Runs Allowed

Will White	1878-1880	976

Earned Runs

Ted Breitenstein	1894-1896	619

Home Runs Allowed

Robin Roberts	1955-1957	127

Intentional Walks

Kent Tekulve	1978-1980	54

Sac Hits Allowed

Red Faber	1920-1922	147

Sac Flies Allowed

Jaime Navarro	1991-1993	38

Hit Batsmen

Joe McGinnity	1899-1901	90

Wild Pitches

Mickey Welch	1884-1886	129

Balks

Three tied at		25

Top Four-Year Batting Performances

Runs

Billy Hamilton	1894-1897	662
Willie Keeler	1894-1897	625
Billy Hamilton	1893-1896	620
Billy Hamilton	1892-1895	600
Jesse Burkett	1893-1896	596
Babe Ruth	1927-1930	592
Willie Keeler	1895-1898	586
Babe Ruth	1928-1931	583
Lou Gehrig	1930-1933	582
Joe Kelley	1893-1896	581
Babe Ruth	1926-1929	581
Jesse Burkett	1894-1897	580
Billy Hamilton	1895-1898	580
Babe Ruth	1920-1923	580
Billy Hamilton	1891-1894	575

Hits

Bill Terry	1929-1932	918
George Sisler	1919-1922	899
Chuck Klein	1930-1933	899
Chuck Klein	1929-1932	895
Ty Cobb	1909-1912	885
Joe Medwick	1934-1937	882
Willie Keeler	1894-1897	881
Willie Keeler	1896-1899	881
Kirby Puckett	1986-1989	879
Willie Keeler	1895-1898	878
Bill Terry	1928-1931	878
Paul Waner	1927-1930	877
Jesse Burkett	1895-1898	876
Willie Keeler	1897-1900	875
Rogers Hornsby	1921-1924	875

Doubles

Joe Medwick	1936-1939	215
Joe Medwick	1935-1938	213
Tris Speaker	1920-1923	209
Joe Medwick	1934-1937	206
Tris Speaker	1921-1924	195
George Burns	1924-1927	193
Joe Medwick	1933-1936	190
George Burns	1923-1926	189
Tris Speaker	1919-1922	188
Chuck Klein	1929-1932	188
Chuck Klein	1930-1933	187
Charlie Gehringer	1933-1936	184
Billy Herman	1935-1938	183
Don Mattingly	1984-1987	183
Wade Boggs	1986-1989	183

Triples

Sam Crawford	1912-1915	89
Sam Crawford	1911-1914	84
Sam Crawford	1913-1916	81
Earle Combs	1927-1930	81
Jimmy Williams	1899-1902	80
Jake Beckley	1890-1893	79
Sam Crawford	1901-1904	79
Sam Crawford	1900-1903	78
Sam Crawford	1910-1913	77
Roger Connor	1886-1889	76
Ty Cobb	1910-1913	76
Six tied at		75

Home Runs

Babe Ruth	1927-1930	209
Babe Ruth	1926-1929	207
Babe Ruth	1928-1931	195
Ralph Kiner	1947-1950	192
Babe Ruth	1920-1923	189
Harmon Killebrew	1961-1964	188
Babe Ruth	1925-1928	186
Jimmie Foxx	1932-1935	186
Willie Mays	1962-1965	186
Ralph Kiner	1948-1951	183
Babe Ruth	1929-1932	182
Babe Ruth	1921-1924	181
Jimmie Foxx	1931-1934	180
Ralph Kiner	1949-1952	180
Babe Ruth	1924-1927	178

Total Bases

Chuck Klein	1929-1932	1,617
Chuck Klein	1930-1933	1,577
Lou Gehrig	1930-1933	1,558
Lou Gehrig	1927-1930	1,552
Lou Gehrig	1931-1934	1,548
Jimmie Foxx	1932-1935	1,533
Babe Ruth	1927-1930	1,524
Lou Gehrig	1929-1932	1,521
Babe Ruth	1921-1924	1,520
Babe Ruth	1920-1923	1,517
Lou Gehrig	1928-1931	1,515
Babe Ruth	1926-1929	1,510
Stan Musial	1948-1951	1,497
Jimmie Foxx	1930-1933	1,491
Lou Gehrig	1934-1937	1,490

RBI

Lou Gehrig	1930-1933	648
Lou Gehrig	1931-1934	639
Lou Gehrig	1929-1932	635
Lou Gehrig	1928-1931	626
Lou Gehrig	1927-1930	617
Babe Ruth	1927-1930	613
Babe Ruth	1928-1931	612
Jimmie Foxx	1930-1933	608
Babe Ruth	1929-1932	607
Babe Ruth	1926-1929	606
Al Simmons	1929-1932	601
Hack Wilson	1927-1930	598
Lou Gehrig	1934-1937	595
Hank Greenberg	1937-1940	591
Jimmie Foxx	1931-1934	582

Walks

Ted Williams	1946-1949	606
Babe Ruth	1920-1923	546
Babe Ruth	1921-1924	540
Ted Williams	1947-1950	532
Eddie Yost	1950-1953	519
Babe Ruth	1923-1926	515
Ted Williams	1948-1951	514
Eddie Yost	1951-1954	509
Babe Ruth	1930-1933	508
Eddie Yost	1953-1956	500
Mickey Mantle	1955-1958	500
Lou Gehrig	1934-1937	498
Lou Gehrig	1935-1938	496
Ted Williams	1939-1942	493
Barry Bonds	1994-1997	490

Strikeouts

Rob Deer	1986-1989	676
Bobby Bonds	1969-1972	650
Rob Deer	1987-1990	644
Pete Incaviglia	1986-1989	642
Rob Deer	1988-1991	633
Rob Deer	1990-1993	622
Juan Samuel	1984-1987	613
Bobby Bonds	1970-1973	611
Rob Deer	1989-1992	611
Reggie Jackson	1968-1971	609
Cecil Fielder	1990-1993	609
Andres Galarraga	1987-1990	607
Bo Jackson	1987-1990	604
Mike Schmidt	1973-1976	603
Pete Incaviglia	1987-1990	603

Stolen Bases

Vince Coleman	1985-1988	407
Rickey Henderson	1980-1983	394
Rickey Henderson	1982-1985	384
Billy Hamilton	1889-1892	381
Arlie Latham	1886-1889	367
Vince Coleman	1986-1989	362
Rickey Henderson	1981-1984	360
Hugh Nicol	1886-1889	359
Arlie Latham	1887-1890	359
Hugh Nicol	1887-1890	345
Billy Hamilton	1894-1897	344
Billy Hamilton	1888-1891	343
Rickey Henderson	1983-1986	341
Vince Coleman	1987-1990	332
Tom Brown	1890-1893	329

Runs Created

Babe Ruth	1920-1923	699
Babe Ruth	1921-1924	687
Lou Gehrig	1930-1933	673
Lou Gehrig	1934-1937	664
Lou Gehrig	1931-1934	662
Lou Gehrig	1929-1932	661
Babe Ruth	1928-1931	658
Ted Williams	1946-1949	658
Lou Gehrig	1927-1930	657
Babe Ruth	1927-1930	656
Lou Gehrig	1928-1931	654
Babe Ruth	1926-1929	647
Lou Gehrig	1933-1936	646
Billy Hamilton	1894-1897	640
Babe Ruth	1929-1932	640

Runs Created/27 Outs
(minimum 1500 Plate Appearances)

Babe Ruth	1920-1923	14.25
Babe Ruth	1921-1924	13.53
Babe Ruth	1919-1922	13.20
Babe Ruth	1918-1921	13.15
Billy Hamilton	1893-1896	12.98
Ed Delahanty	1893-1896	12.75
Babe Ruth	1929-1932	12.49
Babe Ruth	1923-1926	12.42
Ed Delahanty	1894-1897	12.39
Babe Ruth	1930-1933	12.36
Billy Hamilton	1894-1897	12.30
Ted Williams	1946-1949	12.27
Ted Williams	1954-1957	12.22
Babe Ruth	1928-1931	12.15
Billy Hamilton	1892-1895	12.12

Batting Average
(minimum 1500 Plate Appearances)

Rogers Hornsby	1922-1925	.404
Ty Cobb	1910-1913	.402
Rogers Hornsby	1921-1924	.402
Ty Cobb	1911-1914	.401
Ty Cobb	1909-1912	.398
Ed Delahanty	1894-1897	.396
Willie Keeler	1896-1899	.393
Willie Keeler	1895-1898	.393
Ed Delahanty	1893-1896	.393
Joe Jackson	1910-1913	.392
Jesse Burkett	1894-1897	.391
Willie Keeler	1894-1897	.389
George Sisler	1919-1922	.389
Rogers Hornsby	1920-1923	.389
Willie Keeler	1897-1900	.388

On-Base Percentage
(minimum 1500 Plate Appearances)

Babe Ruth	1920-1923	.510
John McGraw	1899-1902	.508
John McGraw	1898-1901	.507
Babe Ruth	1921-1924	.506
Ted Williams	1954-1957	.505
Babe Ruth	1923-1926	.502
John McGraw	1897-1900	.499
Ted Williams	1953-1956	.497
Billy Hamilton	1893-1896	.496
Ted Williams	1946-1949	.496
John McGraw	1896-1899	.493
Ted Williams	1955-1958	.490
Billy Hamilton	1894-1897	.489
Ted Williams	1947-1950	.488
Babe Ruth	1919-1922	.487

Slugging Percentage
(minimum 1500 Plate Appearances)

Babe Ruth	1920-1923	.788
Babe Ruth	1919-1922	.764
Babe Ruth	1921-1924	.761
Babe Ruth	1918-1921	.747
Babe Ruth	1926-1929	.729
Babe Ruth	1927-1930	.728
Babe Ruth	1924-1927	.711
Babe Ruth	1925-1928	.710
Babe Ruth	1923-1926	.709
Rogers Hornsby	1922-1925	.704
Babe Ruth	1925-1928	.703
Babe Ruth	1929-1932	.699
Babe Ruth	1922-1925	.693
Jimmie Foxx	1932-1935	.687
Babe Ruth	1917-1920	.681

OBP+Slugging
(minimum 1500 Plate Appearances)

Babe Ruth	1920-1923	1.298
Babe Ruth	1921-1924	1.267
Babe Ruth	1919-1922	1.251
Babe Ruth	1918-1921	1.233
Babe Ruth	1923-1926	1.211
Babe Ruth	1926-1929	1.204
Babe Ruth	1927-1930	1.197
Babe Ruth	1924-1927	1.197
Rogers Hornsby	1922-1925	1.183
Babe Ruth	1928-1931	1.181
Babe Ruth	1929-1932	1.177
Babe Ruth	1922-1925	1.176
Babe Ruth	1925-1928	1.174
Ted Williams	1954-1957	1.172
Ted Williams	1953-1956	1.161

Games

Billy Williams	1965-1968	651

At-Bats

Dave Cash	1974-1977	2,702

Home Runs (Home)

Ralph Kiner	1947-1950	115

Home Runs(Road)

Babe Ruth	1926-1929	106

AB/HR
(minimum 1500 Plate Appearances)

Mark McGwire	1994-1997	9.0

Extra-Base Hits

Babe Ruth	1920-1923	384

Walks/PA
(minimum 1500 Plate Appearances)

Ted Williams	1954-1957	0.22

Intentional Walks

Willie McCovey	1968-1971	126

Hit By Pitch

Hughie Jennings	1895-1898	175

Sacrifice Hits

Ray Chapman	1917-1920	193

Sacrifice Flies

Joe Carter	1991-1994	45

Caught Stealing

Rickey Henderson	1980-1983	109

Stolen Base Pct.
(minimum 80 attempts)

Barry Larkin	1992-1995	.898

GDP

Jim Rice	1982-1985	131

Secondary Average
(minimum 1500 Plate Appearances)

Babe Ruth	1920-1923	.729

Isolated Power
(minimum 1500 Plate Appearances)

Babe Ruth	1920-1923	.420

Top Four-Year Pitching Performances

Wins

Old Hoss Radbourn	1882-1885	168
Old Hoss Radbourn	1881-1884	165
Old Hoss Radbourn	1883-1886	162
John Clarkson	1885-1888	160
John Clarkson	1886-1889	156
Tommy Bond	1876-1879	154
Tim Keefe	1883-1886	152
Tommy Bond	1877-1880	149
Pud Galvin	1881-1884	148
Tim Keefe	1884-1887	146
John Clarkson	1887-1890	146
Tim Keefe	1885-1888	144
Mickey Welch	1883-1886	141
Silver King	1887-1890	141
John Clarkson	1888-1891	141

Losses

Jim McCormick	1879-1882	128
Mark Baldwin	1889-1892	113
Pud Galvin	1880-1883	111
Hardie Henderson	1883-1886	110
Pud Galvin	1879-1882	109
Jim McCormick	1878-1881	106
Jim Whitney	1885-1888	106
Amos Rusie	1890-1893	106
Dupee Shaw	1883-1886	105
Stump Wiedman	1883-1886	105
Bill Hutchison	1890-1893	104
Dupee Shaw	1884-1887	103
Ted Breitenstein	1893-1896	103
Three tied at		101

Winning Percentage
(minimum 50 decisions)

Randy Johnson	1994-1997	.824
Lefty Grove	1928-1931	.817
Lefty Grove	1929-1932	.806
Lefty Grove	1930-1933	.800
Preacher Roe	1951-1954	.797
Joe Wood	1912-1915	.793
Ron Guidry	1975-1978	.788
Sandy Koufax	1963-1966	.782
Spud Chandler	1941-1944	.780
Randy Johnson	1993-1996	.775
Three Finger Brown	1906-1909	.773
Don Gullett	1975-1978	.772
Sandy Koufax	1962-1965	.771
Whitey Ford	1961-1964	.769
Preacher Roe	1950-1953	.768

Games

Kent Tekulve	1977-1980	335
Mike Marshall	1971-1974	329
Kent Tekulve	1976-1979	321
Mike Marshall	1972-1975	320
Mike Marshall	1973-1976	309
Kent Tekulve	1978-1981	308
Mitch Williams	1986-1989	308
Rob Murphy	1987-1990	305
Duane Ward	1990-1993	304
Willie Hernandez	1982-1985	303
Kent Tekulve	1979-1982	302
Juan Agosto	1988-1991	300
Rollie Fingers	1974-1977	299
Duane Ward	1989-1992	299
Dan Quisenberry	1982-1985	297

Games Started

Jim McCormick	1879-1882	259
Pud Galvin	1881-1884	251
Old Hoss Radbourn	1883-1886	248
Old Hoss Radbourn	1882-1885	242
Pud Galvin	1882-1885	241
Jim McCormick	1880-1883	240
Pud Galvin	1883-1886	240
John Clarkson	1886-1889	240
Tommy Bond	1877-1880	238
John Clarkson	1885-1888	238
Tim Keefe	1883-1886	235
Bill Hutchison	1890-1893	234
Pud Galvin	1880-1883	233
Matt Kilroy	1886-1889	233
Amos Rusie	1890-1893	233

Complete Games

Jim McCormick	1879-1882	253
Old Hoss Radbourn	1883-1886	245
Pud Galvin	1881-1884	239
Old Hoss Radbourn	1882-1885	239
Pud Galvin	1883-1886	232
Pud Galvin	1882-1885	231
Tim Keefe	1883-1886	231
Jim McCormick	1880-1883	230
Old Hoss Radbourn	1884-1887	227
John Clarkson	1885-1888	227
John Clarkson	1886-1889	227
Bill Hutchison	1890-1893	226
Old Hoss Radbourn	1881-1884	224
Tommy Bond	1877-1880	223
Matt Kilroy	1886-1889	222

Shutouts

Pete Alexander	1913-1916	43
Pete Alexander	1914-1917	42
Pete Alexander	1915-1918	36
Ed Walsh	1906-1909	34
Walter Johnson	1912-1915	34
Christy Mathewson	1905-1908	33
Christy Mathewson	1906-1909	33
Walter Johnson	1911-1914	33
Pete Alexander	1916-1919	33
Tommy Bond	1876-1879	32
Three Finger Brown	1906-1909	32
Walter Johnson	1910-1913	32
Ed Walsh	1907-1910	31
Ed Walsh	1908-1911	31
Sandy Koufax	1963-1966	31

Saves

Dennis Eckersley	1990-1993	178
Dennis Eckersley	1989-1992	175
Dennis Eckersley	1988-1991	169
Lee Smith	1991-1994	169
Lee Smith	1990-1993	167
Dan Quisenberry	1982-1985	161
Lee Smith	1992-1995	159
Bobby Thigpen	1988-1991	155
Randy Myers	1992-1995	150
Jeff Reardon	1985-1988	149
Rick Aguilera	1990-1993	149
Dennis Eckersley	1991-1994	149
Lee Smith	1989-1992	146
Jeff Montgomery	1991-1994	144
Rod Beck	1993-1996	144

Innings Pitched

Jim McCormick	1879-1882	2,325.2
Old Hoss Radbourn	1883-1886	2,266.0
Old Hoss Radbourn	1882-1885	2,230.2
Pud Galvin	1881-1884	2,212.0
Bill Hutchison	1890-1893	2,134.1
Jim McCormick	1880-1883	2,121.1
Old Hoss Radbourn	1881-1884	2,110.1
Pud Galvin	1882-1885	2,110.1
Bill Hutchison	1889-1892	2,104.0
Tommy Bond	1877-1880	2,102.0
Pud Galvin	1883-1886	2,099.2
John Clarkson	1885-1888	2,096.0
John Clarkson	1886-1889	2,093.0
Amos Rusie	1890-1893	2,063.0
Old Hoss Radbourn	1884-1887	2,058.2

Walks

Amos Rusie	1890-1893	1,036
Amos Rusie	1891-1894	947
Mark Baldwin	1889-1892	944
Amos Rusie	1889-1892	934
Mark Baldwin	1888-1891	849
Amos Rusie	1892-1895	844
Mark Baldwin	1890-1893	812
Mark Baldwin	1887-1890	744
Ed Crane	1889-1892	738
Bill Hutchison	1890-1893	723
Nolan Ryan	1974-1977	721
Gus Weyhing	1889-1892	720
Jack Stivetts	1890-1893	697
Bill Hutchison	1889-1892	684
Nolan Ryan	1973-1976	679

Strikeouts

Nolan Ryan	1972-1975	1,265
Nolan Ryan	1973-1976	1,263
Sandy Koufax	1963-1966	1,228
Nolan Ryan	1974-1977	1,221
Nolan Ryan	1971-1974	1,216
Tim Keefe	1883-1886	1,199
Toad Ramsey	1886-1889	1,175
Amos Rusie	1890-1893	1,174
Toad Ramsey	1885-1888	1,165
Nolan Ryan	1976-1979	1,151
Rube Waddell	1902-1905	1,148
Rube Waddell	1903-1906	1,134
Old Hoss Radbourn	1883-1886	1,128
Sandy Koufax	1962-1965	1,127
Nolan Ryan	1975-1978	1,114

Strikeouts/9 Innings
(minimum 500 Innings Pitched)

Randy Johnson	1994-1997	11.91
Randy Johnson	1993-1996	11.41
Randy Johnson	1992-1995	11.06
Nolan Ryan	1987-1990	10.60
Nolan Ryan	1986-1989	10.53
Randy Johnson	1991-1994	10.52
Nolan Ryan	1989-1992	10.39
Nolan Ryan	1988-1991	10.37
Dick Radatz	1962-1965	10.16
Sam McDowell	1963-1966	10.08
Sandy Koufax	1959-1962	10.02
Nolan Ryan	1971-1974	10.00
Nolan Ryan	1972-1975	9.98
Nolan Ryan	1973-1976	9.96
Nolan Ryan	1976-1979	9.95

ERA
(minimum 500 Innings Pitched)

Three Finger Brown	1906-1909	1.31
Ed Walsh	1907-1910	1.43
Walter Johnson	1910-1913	1.44
Walter Johnson	1912-1915	1.45
Three Finger Brown	1905-1908	1.50
Three Finger Brown	1907-1910	1.51
Walter Johnson	1911-1914	1.53
Pete Alexander	1915-1918	1.54
Ed Walsh	1906-1909	1.56
Ed Walsh	1908-1911	1.58
Walter Johnson	1913-1916	1.59
Three Finger Brown	1904-1907	1.59
Addie Joss	1906-1909	1.60
Christy Mathewson	1908-1911	1.62
Christy Mathewson	1907-1910	1.62

Component ERA
(minimum 500 Innings Pitched)

Three Finger Brown	1906-1909	1.47
Ed Walsh	1907-1910	1.49
Ed Walsh	1908-1911	1.54
Walter Johnson	1912-1915	1.55
Addie Joss	1906-1909	1.55
Three Finger Brown	1907-1910	1.59
Addie Joss	1907-1910	1.59
Ed Walsh	1906-1909	1.59
Three Finger Brown	1905-1908	1.60
Christy Mathewson	1907-1910	1.60
Walter Johnson	1913-1916	1.61
Addie Joss	1905-1908	1.61
Walter Johnson	1910-1913	1.61
Ed Walsh	1905-1908	1.65
Sandy Koufax	1962-1965	1.65

Opponent Average
(minimum 500 Innings Pitched)

Sandy Koufax	1962-1965	.188
Herb Score	1955-1958	.188
Nolan Ryan	1969-1972	.189
Tom Hall	1970-1973	.190
Sandy Koufax	1963-1966	.191
Nolan Ryan	1972-1975	.193
Nolan Ryan	1971-1974	.193
Nolan Ryan	1970-1973	.194
Nolan Ryan	1989-1992	.195
Nolan Ryan	1988-1991	.195
Nolan Ryan	1974-1977	.196
Hoyt Wilhelm	1962-1965	.198
Sid Fernandez	1988-1991	.198
Sam McDowell	1965-1968	.199
Nolan Ryan	1973-1976	.199

Opponent OBP
(minimum 500 Innings Pitched)

Sandy Koufax	1962-1965	.237
Sandy Koufax	1963-1966	.237
Ed Walsh	1907-1910	.245
Three Finger Brown	1906-1909	.245
Addie Joss	1906-1909	.245
Old Hoss Radbourn	1881-1884	.246
Ed Walsh	1908-1911	.247
John Clarkson	1882-1885	.247
Christy Mathewson	1907-1910	.247
Old Hoss Radbourn	1882-1885	.248
Walter Johnson	1912-1915	.248
Addie Joss	1905-1908	.248
Greg Maddux	1994-1997	.248
Addie Joss	1907-1910	.248
Monte Ward	1878-1881	.249

Games Finished

Dan Quisenberry	1982-1985	273

Batters Faced

Jim McCormick	1879-1882	9,551

Hits Allowed

Pud Galvin	1881-1884	2,264

Runs Allowed

Mark Baldwin	1889-1892	1,230

Earned Runs

Ted Breitenstein	1893-1896	754

Home Runs Allowed

Robin Roberts	1954-1957	162

Intentional Walks

Greg Minton	1982-1985	68

Sac Hits Allowed

Red Faber	1920-1923	180

Sac Flies Allowed

Larry Gura	1980-1983	45

Hit Batsmen

Joe McGinnity	1899-1902	107

Wild Pitches

Mickey Welch	1883-1886	156

Balks

Steve Carlton	1977-1980	32

Top Five-Year Batting Performances

Runs

Billy Hamilton	1893-1897	772
Billy Hamilton	1894-1898	772
Billy Hamilton	1892-1896	752
Willie Keeler	1894-1898	751
Billy Hamilton	1891-1895	741
Babe Ruth	1927-1931	741
Babe Ruth	1926-1930	731
Hugh Duffy	1890-1894	727
Willie Keeler	1895-1899	726
Jesse Burkett	1893-1897	725
Babe Ruth	1920-1924	723
Lou Gehrig	1927-1931	721
Jesse Burkett	1892-1896	715
Hugh Duffy	1889-1893	711
Two tied at		710

Hits

Chuck Klein	1929-1933	1,118
Bill Terry	1928-1932	1,103
Willie Keeler	1894-1898	1,097
Jesse Burkett	1895-1899	1,097
Willie Keeler	1895-1899	1,094
Rogers Hornsby	1920-1924	1,093
Willie Keeler	1896-1900	1,085
Rogers Hornsby	1921-1925	1,078
Kirby Puckett	1985-1989	1,078
Willie Keeler	1897-1901	1,077
Jesse Burkett	1896-1900	1,075
Joe Medwick	1935-1939	1,075
Ty Cobb	1908-1912	1,073
Joe Medwick	1934-1938	1,072
Bill Terry	1929-1933	1,071

Doubles

Joe Medwick	1935-1939	261
Joe Medwick	1934-1938	253
Tris Speaker	1919-1923	247
Joe Medwick	1933-1937	246
Tris Speaker	1920-1924	245
Joe Medwick	1936-1940	245
George Burns	1923-1927	240
Chuck Klein	1929-1933	232
Tris Speaker	1921-1925	230
Tris Speaker	1922-1926	230
Charlie Gehringer	1932-1936	228
Wade Boggs	1986-1990	227
Tris Speaker	1923-1927	225
Wade Boggs	1985-1989	225
Two tied at		224

Triples

Sam Crawford	1910-1914	103
Sam Crawford	1911-1915	103
Sam Crawford	1912-1916	102
Jake Beckley	1890-1894	97
Jake Beckley	1891-1895	94
Sam Crawford	1900-1904	94
Earle Combs	1927-1931	94
Earle Combs	1926-1930	93
Jimmy Williams	1899-1903	92
Buck Freeman	1899-1903	92
Six tied at		91

Home Runs

Babe Ruth	1926-1930	256
Babe Ruth	1927-1931	255
Babe Ruth	1928-1932	236
Babe Ruth	1920-1924	235
Ralph Kiner	1947-1951	234
Babe Ruth	1924-1928	232
Babe Ruth	1925-1929	232
Jimmie Foxx	1932-1936	227
Willie Mays	1961-1965	226
Willie Mays	1962-1966	223
Ralph Kiner	1948-1952	220
Babe Ruth	1923-1927	219
Harmon Killebrew	1960-1964	219
Babe Ruth	1919-1923	218
Jimmie Foxx	1930-1934	217

Total Bases

Chuck Klein	1929-1933	1,982
Lou Gehrig	1930-1934	1,967
Lou Gehrig	1927-1931	1,962
Babe Ruth	1920-1924	1,908
Jimmie Foxx	1932-1936	1,902
Babe Ruth	1927-1931	1,898
Babe Ruth	1926-1930	1,889
Lou Gehrig	1928-1932	1,885
Lou Gehrig	1929-1933	1,880
Lou Gehrig	1926-1930	1,866
Lou Gehrig	1931-1935	1,860
Lou Gehrig	1932-1936	1,853
Lou Gehrig	1933-1937	1,849
Rogers Hornsby	1921-1925	1,848
Jimmie Foxx	1930-1934	1,843

RBI

Lou Gehrig	1930-1934	813
Lou Gehrig	1927-1931	801
Lou Gehrig	1928-1932	777
Babe Ruth	1927-1931	776
Lou Gehrig	1929-1933	774
Babe Ruth	1926-1930	759
Lou Gehrig	1931-1935	758
Babe Ruth	1928-1932	749
Jimmie Foxx	1930-1934	738
Lou Gehrig	1933-1937	734
Lou Gehrig	1926-1930	729
Lou Gehrig	1932-1936	726
Jimmie Foxx	1929-1933	725
Al Simmons	1929-1933	720
Jimmie Foxx	1932-1936	720

Walks

Babe Ruth	1920-1924	688
Ted Williams	1946-1950	688
Ted Williams	1947-1951	676
Babe Ruth	1923-1927	653
Eddie Yost	1950-1954	650
Babe Ruth	1919-1923	647
Eddie Yost	1952-1956	629
Babe Ruth	1926-1930	625
Babe Ruth	1924-1928	618
Frank Thomas	1991-1995	617
Barry Bonds	1993-1997	616
Babe Ruth	1930-1934	611
Eddie Yost	1949-1953	610
Babe Ruth	1927-1931	609
Two tied at		605

Strikeouts

Rob Deer	1986-1990	823
Rob Deer	1987-1991	819
Bobby Bonds	1969-1973	798
Pete Incaviglia	1986-1990	788
Rob Deer	1989-1993	780
Juan Samuel	1984-1988	764
Rob Deer	1988-1992	764
Rob Deer	1985-1989	747
Bobby Bonds	1970-1974	745
Bobby Bonds	1968-1972	734
Reggie Jackson	1968-1972	734
Mike Schmidt	1973-1977	725
Gorman Thomas	1979-1983	721
Cecil Fielder	1990-1994	719
Juan Samuel	1985-1989	716

Stolen Bases

Vince Coleman	1985-1989	472
Rickey Henderson	1982-1986	471
Rickey Henderson	1980-1984	460
Arlie Latham	1887-1891	446
Rickey Henderson	1981-1985	440
Vince Coleman	1986-1990	439
Rickey Henderson	1979-1983	427
Billy Hamilton	1889-1893	424
Arlie Latham	1886-1890	419
Billy Hamilton	1890-1894	411
Billy Hamilton	1891-1895	406
Billy Hamilton	1888-1892	400
Billy Hamilton	1894-1898	398
Tom Brown	1890-1894	395
Tom Brown	1889-1893	392

Runs Created

Babe Ruth	1920-1924	878
Lou Gehrig	1930-1934	844
Lou Gehrig	1927-1931	836
Babe Ruth	1927-1931	835
Babe Ruth	1926-1930	823
Babe Ruth	1919-1923	820
Lou Gehrig	1928-1932	817
Lou Gehrig	1933-1937	813
Lou Gehrig	1929-1933	810
Lou Gehrig	1932-1936	809
Lou Gehrig	1931-1935	807
Babe Ruth	1928-1932	805
Lou Gehrig	1934-1938	795
Jimmie Foxx	1932-1936	790
Babe Ruth	1923-1927	787

Runs Created/27 Outs
(minimum 1750 Plate Appearances)

Babe Ruth	1920-1924	14.07
Babe Ruth	1919-1923	13.56
Babe Ruth	1917-1921	12.69
Babe Ruth	1918-1922	12.48
Babe Ruth	1923-1927	12.45
Babe Ruth	1921-1925	12.44
Ted Williams	1953-1957	12.44
Billy Hamilton	1893-1897	12.43
Billy Hamilton	1894-1898	12.34
Babe Ruth	1928-1932	12.27
Babe Ruth	1927-1931	12.23
Ed Delahanty	1893-1897	12.14
Babe Ruth	1926-1930	12.09
Ted Williams	1946-1950	12.07
Billy Hamilton	1891-1895	12.06

Batting Average
(minimum 1750 Plate Appearances)

Rogers Hornsby	1921-1925	.402
Ty Cobb	1910-1914	.397
Ty Cobb	1909-1913	.397
Rogers Hornsby	1920-1924	.395
Ty Cobb	1911-1915	.394
Joe Jackson	1909-1913	.391
Willie Keeler	1895-1899	.390
Ed Delahanty	1893-1897	.390
Willie Keeler	1894-1898	.388
Willie Keeler	1896-1900	.387
Jesse Burkett	1895-1899	.387
Rogers Hornsby	1922-1926	.386
Willie Keeler	1893-1897	.386
Ed Delahanty	1895-1899	.384
Ty Cobb	1908-1912	.383

On-Base Percentage
(minimum 1750 Plate Appearances)

Babe Ruth	1920-1924	.511
Ted Williams	1953-1957	.505
Babe Ruth	1919-1923	.500
John McGraw	1897-1901	.500
Babe Ruth	1923-1927	.499
John McGraw	1898-1902	.498
John McGraw	1896-1900	.495
Ted Williams	1954-1958	.495
Babe Ruth	1922-1926	.490
Babe Ruth	1921-1925	.490
Ted Williams	1946-1950	.490
Billy Hamilton	1893-1897	.489
Billy Hamilton	1894-1898	.487
John McGraw	1895-1899	.486
Ted Williams	1947-1951	.483

Slugging Percentage
(minimum 1750 Plate Appearances)

Babe Ruth	1920-1924	.777
Babe Ruth	1919-1923	.764
Babe Ruth	1918-1922	.733
Babe Ruth	1926-1930	.730
Babe Ruth	1917-1921	.729
Babe Ruth	1921-1925	.728
Babe Ruth	1923-1927	.723
Babe Ruth	1927-1931	.722
Babe Ruth	1924-1928	.711
Babe Ruth	1922-1926	.702
Babe Ruth	1925-1929	.702
Babe Ruth	1928-1932	.701
Rogers Hornsby	1921-1925	.690
Ted Williams	1953-1957	.681
Babe Ruth	1929-1933	.677

OBP+Slugging
(minimum 1750 Plate Appearances)

Babe Ruth	1920-1924	1.288
Babe Ruth	1919-1923	1.264
Babe Ruth	1923-1927	1.221
Babe Ruth	1921-1925	1.218
Babe Ruth	1918-1922	1.209
Babe Ruth	1917-1921	1.209
Babe Ruth	1926-1930	1.208
Babe Ruth	1927-1931	1.197
Babe Ruth	1922-1926	1.193
Babe Ruth	1924-1928	1.191
Ted Williams	1953-1957	1.186
Babe Ruth	1928-1932	1.175
Babe Ruth	1925-1929	1.165
Rogers Hornsby	1921-1925	1.164
Babe Ruth	1929-1933	1.148

Games

Billy Williams	1965-1969	814

At-Bats

Dave Cash	1974-1978	3,360

Home Runs (Home)

Ralph Kiner	1947-1951	141

Home Runs (Road)

Babe Ruth	1926-1930	129

AB/HR
(minimum 1750 Plate Appearances)

Mark McGwire	1993-1997	9.0

Extra-Base Hits

Babe Ruth	1920-1924	476

Walks/PA
(minimum 1750 Plate Appearances)

Ted Williams	1953-1957	0.22

Intentional Walks

Barry Bonds	1993-1997	147

Hit By Pitch

Hughie Jennings	1894-1898	202

Sacrifice Hits

Ray Chapman	1916-1920	233

Sacrifice Flies

Joe Carter	1990-1994	53

Caught Stealing

Rickey Henderson	1980-1984	127

Stolen Base Pct.
(minimum 100 attempts)

Eric Davis	1984-1988	.884

GDP

Jim Rice	1982-1986	150

Secondary Average
(minimum 1750 Plate Appearances)

Babe Ruth	1920-1924	.711

Isolated Power
(minimum 1750 Plate Appearances)

Babe Ruth	1920-1924	.407

Top Five-Year Pitching Performances

Wins

Player	Span	
John Clarkson	1885-1889	209
Old Hoss Radbourn	1882-1886	195
Old Hoss Radbourn	1881-1885	193
Tim Keefe	1883-1887	187
Old Hoss Radbourn	1883-1887	186
John Clarkson	1886-1890	182
Tim Keefe	1884-1888	181
Tommy Bond	1876-1880	180
John Clarkson	1887-1891	179
Jim McCormick	1880-1884	175
Tim Keefe	1885-1889	172
Larry Corcoran	1880-1884	170
John Clarkson	1884-1888	170
Tim Keefe	1882-1886	169
Two tied at		168

Losses

Player	Span	
Jim McCormick	1879-1883	140
Pud Galvin	1879-1883	138
Jim McCormick	1878-1882	136
Pud Galvin	1880-1884	133
Mark Baldwin	1889-1893	133
Mark Baldwin	1888-1892	128
Jim McCormick	1880-1884	125
Stump Wiedman	1882-1886	125
Pud Galvin	1881-1885	124
Ted Breitenstein	1892-1896	122
Jim Whitney	1881-1885	121
Pud Galvin	1882-1886	121
Stump Wiedman	1883-1887	121
Bill Hutchison	1889-1893	121
Four tied at		120

Winning Percentage
(minimum 60 decisions)

Player	Span	
Lefty Grove	1928-1932	.795
Lefty Grove	1929-1933	.795
Randy Johnson	1993-1997	.789
Spud Chandler	1941-1945	.774
Lefty Grove	1927-1931	.774
Lefty Grove	1930-1934	.768
Sandy Koufax	1962-1966	.766
Spud Chandler	1942-1946	.763
Preacher Roe	1949-1953	.757
Ron Guidry	1975-1979	.756
Three Finger Brown	1906-1910	.747
Chief Bender	1910-1914	.746
Preacher Roe	1950-1954	.742
Three Finger Brown	1905-1909	.741
Spud Chandler	1939-1943	.740

Games

Player	Span	
Kent Tekulve	1976-1980	399
Kent Tekulve	1978-1982	393
Mike Marshall	1971-1975	386
Kent Tekulve	1977-1981	380
Kent Tekulve	1979-1983	378
Mike Marshall	1972-1976	374
Kent Tekulve	1983-1987	372
Duane Ward	1989-1993	370
Willie Hernandez	1982-1986	367
Kent Tekulve	1982-1986	367
Mitch Williams	1986-1990	367
Rollie Fingers	1974-1978	366
Kent Tekulve	1984-1988	366
Duane Ward	1988-1992	363
Two tied at		362

Games Started

Player	Span	
John Clarkson	1885-1889	310
Jim McCormick	1880-1884	305
Pud Galvin	1880-1884	305
Jim McCormick	1879-1883	300
Old Hoss Radbourn	1882-1886	300
Pud Galvin	1879-1883	299
Old Hoss Radbourn	1883-1887	298
Pud Galvin	1881-1885	294
Pud Galvin	1882-1886	291
Tim Keefe	1883-1887	291
Pud Galvin	1883-1887	288
John Clarkson	1886-1890	284
Tommy Bond	1876-1880	283
Amos Rusie	1890-1894	283
John Clarkson	1887-1891	280

Complete Games

Player	Span	
Old Hoss Radbourn	1882-1886	296
John Clarkson	1885-1889	295
Jim McCormick	1880-1884	293
Old Hoss Radbourn	1883-1887	293
Jim McCormick	1879-1883	289
Pud Galvin	1880-1884	285
Tim Keefe	1883-1887	285
Pud Galvin	1882-1886	280
Pud Galvin	1879-1883	279
Pud Galvin	1881-1885	279
Pud Galvin	1883-1887	279
Old Hoss Radbourn	1881-1885	273
Tim Keefe	1882-1886	272
John Clarkson	1886-1890	270
Tommy Bond	1876-1880	268

Shutouts

Player	Span	
Pete Alexander	1913-1917	51
Pete Alexander	1912-1916	46
Pete Alexander	1915-1919	45
Pete Alexander	1914-1918	42
Christy Mathewson	1905-1909	41
Ed Walsh	1906-1910	41
Walter Johnson	1910-1914	41
Walter Johnson	1911-1915	40
Pete Alexander	1916-1920	40
Three Finger Brown	1906-1910	39
Walter Johnson	1913-1917	38
Christy Mathewson	1904-1908	37
Ed Walsh	1908-1912	37
Pete Alexander	1911-1915	37
Walter Johnson	1912-1916	37

Saves

Player	Span	
Dennis Eckersley	1988-1992	220
Dennis Eckersley	1989-1993	211
Lee Smith	1991-1995	206
Lee Smith	1990-1994	200
Dennis Eckersley	1990-1994	197
Lee Smith	1989-1993	192
Randy Myers	1993-1997	188
Dennis Eckersley	1987-1991	185
Randy Myers	1992-1996	181
Rod Beck	1993-1997	181
Jeff Reardon	1985-1989	180
Dan Quisenberry	1981-1985	179
John Wetteland	1992-1996	179
Dennis Eckersley	1991-1995	178
Bobby Thigpen	1988-1992	177

Innings Pitched

Player	Span	
Old Hoss Radbourn	1882-1886	2,740.0
John Clarkson	1885-1889	2,716.0
Old Hoss Radbourn	1883-1887	2,691.0
Jim McCormick	1880-1884	2,690.1
Pud Galvin	1880-1884	2,670.2
Jim McCormick	1879-1883	2,667.2
Pud Galvin	1879-1883	2,627.1
Pud Galvin	1881-1885	2,584.1
Old Hoss Radbourn	1881-1885	2,556.0
Pud Galvin	1882-1886	2,545.0
Pud Galvin	1883-1887	2,540.1
Tim Keefe	1883-1887	2,518.1
Tommy Bond	1876-1880	2,510.0
Amos Rusie	1890-1894	2,507.0
John Clarkson	1886-1890	2,476.0

Walks

Player	Span	
Amos Rusie	1890-1894	1,236
Amos Rusie	1889-1893	1,152
Amos Rusie	1891-1895	1,106
Mark Baldwin	1889-1893	1,086
Mark Baldwin	1888-1892	1,043
Mark Baldwin	1887-1891	971
Nolan Ryan	1973-1977	883
Nolan Ryan	1974-1978	869
Gus Weyhing	1889-1893	865
Bill Hutchison	1890-1894	863
Bill Hutchison	1889-1893	840
Nolan Ryan	1972-1976	836
Gus Weyhing	1888-1892	831
Gus Weyhing	1887-1891	830
Jack Stivetts	1890-1894	824

Strikeouts

Player	Span	
Nolan Ryan	1973-1977	1,604
Nolan Ryan	1972-1976	1,592
Nolan Ryan	1974-1978	1,481
Sandy Koufax	1962-1966	1,444
Toad Ramsey	1886-1890	1,432
Nolan Ryan	1971-1975	1,402
Sandy Koufax	1961-1965	1,396
Tim Keefe	1883-1887	1,385
Amos Rusie	1890-1894	1,369
Rube Waddell	1903-1907	1,366
John Clarkson	1885-1889	1,365
Tim Keefe	1884-1888	1,357
Nolan Ryan	1976-1980	1,351
Sam McDowell	1965-1969	1,348
Rube Waddell	1902-1906	1,344

Strikeouts/9 Innings
(minimum 600 Innings Pitched)

Player	Span	
Randy Johnson	1993-1997	11.61
Randy Johnson	1992-1996	11.15
Randy Johnson	1991-1995	10.89
Nolan Ryan	1987-1991	10.60
Nolan Ryan	1986-1990	10.47
Nolan Ryan	1988-1992	10.15
Nolan Ryan	1989-1993	10.06
Nolan Ryan	1972-1976	10.05
Nolan Ryan	1973-1977	10.03
Nolan Ryan	1985-1989	10.01
Randy Johnson	1990-1994	9.99
Dick Radatz	1962-1966	9.91
Nolan Ryan	1974-1978	9.88
Nolan Ryan	1970-1974	9.84
Sam McDowell	1963-1967	9.80

ERA
(minimum 600 Innings Pitched)

Player	Span	
Three Finger Brown	1906-1910	1.42
Three Finger Brown	1905-1909	1.46
Walter Johnson	1910-1914	1.50
Ed Walsh	1906-1910	1.50
Walter Johnson	1911-1915	1.54
Walter Johnson	1912-1916	1.55
Three Finger Brown	1904-1908	1.56
Pete Alexander	1915-1919	1.57
Walter Johnson	1909-1913	1.57
Ed Walsh	1907-1911	1.59
Ed Walsh	1905-1909	1.62
Addie Joss	1906-1910	1.65
Addie Joss	1904-1908	1.66
Walter Johnson	1908-1912	1.68
Addie Joss	1905-1909	1.68

Component ERA
(minimum 600 Innings Pitched)

Player	Span	
Ed Walsh	1906-1910	1.52
Three Finger Brown	1905-1909	1.55
Three Finger Brown	1906-1910	1.58
Walter Johnson	1912-1916	1.59
Addie Joss	1906-1910	1.59
Three Finger Brown	1904-1908	1.60
Ed Walsh	1907-1911	1.60
Addie Joss	1905-1909	1.62
Walter Johnson	1913-1917	1.63
Ed Walsh	1905-1909	1.63
Addie Joss	1904-1908	1.64
Christy Mathewson	1905-1909	1.64
Walter Johnson	1910-1914	1.64
Ed Walsh	1908-1912	1.64
Pete Alexander	1915-1919	1.64

Opponent Average
(minimum 600 Innings Pitched)

Player	Span	
Nolan Ryan	1968-1972	.191
Sandy Koufax	1962-1966	.192
Nolan Ryan	1970-1974	.193
Herb Score	1955-1959	.193
Nolan Ryan	1969-1973	.193
Nolan Ryan	1972-1976	.193
Sandy Koufax	1961-1965	.195
Nolan Ryan	1987-1991	.196
Nolan Ryan	1971-1975	.196
Nolan Ryan	1989-1993	.197
Nolan Ryan	1973-1977	.198
Nolan Ryan	1986-1990	.198
Herb Score	1956-1960	.199
Nolan Ryan	1974-1978	.200
Sandy Koufax	1960-1964	.201

Opponent OBP
(minimum 600 Innings Pitched)

Player	Span	
Sandy Koufax	1962-1966	.240
Ed Walsh	1906-1910	.248
Addie Joss	1906-1910	.248
Sandy Koufax	1961-1965	.249
Addie Joss	1905-1909	.249
Monte Ward	1878-1882	.250
Three Finger Brown	1905-1909	.250
Addie Joss	1904-1908	.250
Old Hoss Radbourn	1881-1885	.251
Christy Mathewson	1905-1909	.251
Monte Ward	1879-1883	.252
Three Finger Brown	1906-1910	.252
Ed Walsh	1907-1911	.252
Pete Alexander	1915-1919	.252
Walter Johnson	1912-1916	.253

Games Finished

Player	Span	
Dan Quisenberry	1982-1986	327

Batters Faced

Player	Span	
John Clarkson	1885-1889	11,349

Hits Allowed

Player	Span	
Pud Galvin	1879-1883	2,811

Runs Allowed

Player	Span	
Mark Baldwin	1889-1893	1,462

Earned Runs

Player	Span	
Bill Hutchison	1890-1894	918

Home Runs Allowed

Player	Span	
Two tied at		192

Intentional Walks

Player	Span	
Greg Minton	1982-1986	83

Sac Hits Allowed

Player	Span	
George Mullin	1904-1908	210

Sac Flies Allowed

Player	Span	
Charlie Hough	1987-1991	55

Hit Batsmen

Player	Span	
Joe McGinnity	1899-1903	126

Wild Pitches

Player	Span	
Mickey Welch	1883-1887	172

Balks

Player	Span	
Steve Carlton	1979-1983	40

Top Six-Year Batting Performances

Runs

Player	Span	Runs
Billy Hamilton	1892-1897	904
Billy Hamilton	1891-1896	893
Willie Keeler	1894-1899	891
Billy Hamilton	1893-1898	882
Babe Ruth	1926-1931	880
Billy Hamilton	1890-1895	874
Hugh Duffy	1889-1894	871
Babe Ruth	1927-1932	861
Lou Gehrig	1927-1932	859
Lou Gehrig	1931-1936	859
Lou Gehrig	1926-1931	856
Billy Hamilton	1889-1894	852
Lou Gehrig	1928-1933	848
Jesse Burkett	1892-1897	844
Jesse Burkett	1893-1898	839

Hits

Player	Span	Hits
Willie Keeler	1894-1899	1,313
Jesse Burkett	1896-1901	1,301
Jesse Burkett	1895-1900	1,300
Willie Keeler	1895-1900	1,298
Rogers Hornsby	1920-1925	1,296
Bill Terry	1927-1932	1,292
Willie Keeler	1896-1901	1,287
Ty Cobb	1907-1912	1,285
Jesse Burkett	1894-1899	1,284
Bill Terry	1929-1934	1,284
Wade Boggs	1983-1988	1,274
Joe Medwick	1934-1939	1,273
Paul Waner	1927-1932	1,272
Wade Boggs	1984-1989	1,269
Two tied at		1,263

Doubles

Player	Span	Doubles
Joe Medwick	1934-1939	301
Joe Medwick	1933-1938	293
Joe Medwick	1935-1940	291
Tris Speaker	1919-1924	283
Tris Speaker	1921-1926	282
Tris Speaker	1918-1923	280
Tris Speaker	1920-1925	280
Joe Medwick	1936-1941	278
Tris Speaker	1922-1927	273
George Burns	1922-1927	272
Wade Boggs	1985-1990	269
Wade Boggs	1986-1991	269
Charlie Gehringer	1932-1937	268
Three tied at		263

Triples

Player	Span	Triples
Sam Crawford	1910-1915	122
Sam Crawford	1909-1914	117
Jake Beckley	1890-1895	116
Sam Crawford	1911-1916	116
Buck Freeman	1899-1904	111
Joe Jackson	1911-1916	110
Joe Jackson	1912-1917	108
Jake Beckley	1889-1894	107
Sam Crawford	1908-1913	107
Roger Connor	1885-1890	106
Sam Crawford	1902-1907	106
Ty Cobb	1908-1913	106
Earle Combs	1925-1930	106
Earle Combs	1926-1931	106
Two tied at		105

Home Runs

Player	Span	HR
Babe Ruth	1926-1931	302
Babe Ruth	1927-1932	296
Babe Ruth	1925-1930	281
Babe Ruth	1924-1929	278
Babe Ruth	1923-1928	273
Ralph Kiner	1947-1952	271
Babe Ruth	1928-1933	270
Babe Ruth	1919-1924	264
Jimmie Foxx	1932-1937	263
Willie Mays	1961-1966	263
Harmon Killebrew	1959-1964	261
Babe Ruth	1920-1925	260
Jimmie Foxx	1931-1936	257
Ralph Kiner	1946-1951	257
Three tied at		255

Total Bases

Player	Span	TB
Lou Gehrig	1927-1932	2,332
Lou Gehrig	1929-1934	2,289
Lou Gehrig	1930-1935	2,279
Lou Gehrig	1926-1931	2,276
Babe Ruth	1926-1931	2,263
Lou Gehrig	1931-1936	2,263
Lou Gehrig	1928-1933	2,244
Lou Gehrig	1932-1937	2,219
Jimmie Foxx	1932-1937	2,208
Chuck Klein	1929-1934	2,204
Babe Ruth	1927-1932	2,200
Jimmie Foxx	1931-1936	2,194
Babe Ruth	1919-1924	2,192
Jimmie Foxx	1930-1935	2,183
Rogers Hornsby	1920-1925	2,177

RBI

Player	Span	RBI
Lou Gehrig	1927-1932	952
Lou Gehrig	1929-1934	939
Lou Gehrig	1930-1935	932
Babe Ruth	1926-1931	922
Lou Gehrig	1928-1933	916
Lou Gehrig	1926-1931	913
Babe Ruth	1927-1932	913
Lou Gehrig	1931-1936	910
Lou Gehrig	1932-1937	885
Jimmie Foxx	1929-1934	855
Jimmie Foxx	1930-1935	853
Jimmie Foxx	1933-1938	853
Babe Ruth	1928-1933	852
Lou Gehrig	1933-1938	848
Jimmie Foxx	1932-1937	847

Walks

Player	Span	BB
Ted Williams	1946-1951	832
Babe Ruth	1919-1924	789
Babe Ruth	1923-1928	788
Eddie Yost	1951-1956	755
Babe Ruth	1926-1931	753
Babe Ruth	1920-1925	747
Eddie Yost	1950-1955	745
Babe Ruth	1921-1926	743
Barry Bonds	1992-1997	743
Eddie Yost	1949-1954	741
Babe Ruth	1927-1932	739
Babe Ruth	1922-1927	737
Mickey Mantle	1957-1962	727
Frank Thomas	1991-1996	726
Mickey Mantle	1956-1961	717

Strikeouts

Player	Span	SO
Rob Deer	1986-1991	998
Rob Deer	1987-1992	950
Rob Deer	1988-1993	933
Bobby Bonds	1969-1974	932
Rob Deer	1985-1990	894
Juan Samuel	1984-1989	884
Bobby Bonds	1968-1973	882
Bobby Bonds	1970-1975	882
Pete Incaviglia	1986-1991	880
Gorman Thomas	1978-1983	854
Dick Allen	1964-1969	846
Reggie Jackson	1968-1973	845
Juan Samuel	1985-1990	842
Jose Canseco	1986-1991	839
Jesse Barfield	1985-1990	838

Stolen Bases

Player	Span	SB
Vince Coleman	1985-1990	549
Rickey Henderson	1980-1985	540
Rickey Henderson	1981-1986	527
Billy Hamilton	1889-1894	522
Arlie Latham	1887-1892	512
Rickey Henderson	1982-1987	512
Billy Hamilton	1890-1895	508
Arlie Latham	1886-1891	506
Rickey Henderson	1979-1984	493
Billy Hamilton	1891-1896	489
Vince Coleman	1986-1991	476
Rickey Henderson	1983-1988	475
Tom Brown	1889-1894	458
Tim Raines	1981-1986	454
Harry Stovey	1886-1891	446

Runs Created

Player	Span	RC
Babe Ruth	1926-1931	1,002
Babe Ruth	1919-1924	999
Lou Gehrig	1927-1932	999
Lou Gehrig	1930-1935	989
Lou Gehrig	1931-1936	988
Babe Ruth	1927-1932	982
Lou Gehrig	1929-1934	981
Lou Gehrig	1932-1937	976
Lou Gehrig	1928-1933	966
Lou Gehrig	1926-1931	963
Babe Ruth	1923-1928	952
Babe Ruth	1920-1925	949
Lou Gehrig	1933-1938	944
Babe Ruth	1928-1933	927
Babe Ruth	1921-1926	925

Runs Created/27 Outs
(minimum 2000 Plate Appearances)

Player	Span	RC/27
Babe Ruth	1919-1924	13.53
Babe Ruth	1920-1925	13.08
Babe Ruth	1918-1923	12.93
Babe Ruth	1921-1926	12.58
Ted Williams	1952-1957	12.47
Billy Hamilton	1893-1898	12.44
Babe Ruth	1926-1931	12.38
Babe Ruth	1927-1932	12.31
Ted Williams	1942-1947	12.31
Babe Ruth	1923-1928	12.27
Babe Ruth	1917-1922	12.14
Babe Ruth	1916-1921	12.10
Babe Ruth	1922-1927	12.04
Billy Hamilton	1891-1896	12.01
Babe Ruth	1928-1933	11.89

Batting Average
(minimum 2000 Plate Appearances)

Player	Span	AVG
Rogers Hornsby	1920-1925	.397
Ty Cobb	1909-1914	.394
Ty Cobb	1910-1915	.392
Ty Cobb	1911-1916	.390
Rogers Hornsby	1921-1926	.388
Joe Jackson	1908-1913	.388
Ed Delahanty	1894-1899	.388
Willie Keeler	1894-1899	.387
Willie Keeler	1893-1898	.386
Willie Keeler	1895-1900	.386
Willie Keeler	1892-1897	.385
Ty Cobb	1908-1913	.384
Rogers Hornsby	1919-1924	.383
Jesse Burkett	1895-1900	.383
Ty Cobb	1912-1917	.383

On-Base Percentage
(minimum 2000 Plate Appearances)

Player	Span	OBP
Ted Williams	1952-1957	.505
Babe Ruth	1919-1924	.503
Ted Williams	1942-1947	.498
John McGraw	1898-1903	.498
John McGraw	1896-1901	.497
Babe Ruth	1920-1925	.497
Ted Williams	1953-1958	.496
Babe Ruth	1921-1926	.494
John McGraw	1897-1902	.493
Babe Ruth	1923-1928	.492
Babe Ruth	1918-1923	.490
Babe Ruth	1922-1927	.490
John McGraw	1895-1900	.489
Billy Hamilton	1893-1898	.488
Ted Williams	1951-1956	.487

Slugging Percentage
(minimum 2000 Plate Appearances)

Player	Span	SLG
Babe Ruth	1919-1924	.759
Babe Ruth	1920-1925	.747
Babe Ruth	1918-1923	.739
Babe Ruth	1921-1926	.730
Babe Ruth	1926-1931	.725
Babe Ruth	1923-1928	.720
Babe Ruth	1917-1922	.719
Babe Ruth	1922-1927	.716
Babe Ruth	1927-1932	.713
Babe Ruth	1924-1929	.709
Babe Ruth	1916-1921	.708
Babe Ruth	1925-1930	.707
Babe Ruth	1928-1933	.683
Ted Williams	1952-1957	.682
Lou Gehrig	1927-1932	.667

OBP+Slugging
(minimum 2000 Plate Appearances)

Player	Span	OPS
Babe Ruth	1919-1924	1.262
Babe Ruth	1920-1925	1.244
Babe Ruth	1918-1923	1.230
Babe Ruth	1921-1926	1.224
Babe Ruth	1923-1928	1.212
Babe Ruth	1926-1931	1.206
Babe Ruth	1922-1927	1.205
Babe Ruth	1917-1922	1.191
Babe Ruth	1927-1932	1.190
Ted Williams	1952-1957	1.187
Babe Ruth	1924-1929	1.181
Babe Ruth	1916-1921	1.179
Babe Ruth	1925-1930	1.176
Ted Williams	1953-1958	1.157
Babe Ruth	1928-1933	1.152

Games
Billy Williams	1964-1969	976

At-Bats
Pete Rose	1973-1978	3,969

Home Runs (Home)
Ralph Kiner	1947-1952	163

Home Runs (Road)
Babe Ruth	1926-1931	151

AB/HR
(minimum 2000 Plate Appearances)
Mark McGwire	1992-1997	9.4

Extra-Base Hits
Lou Gehrig	1927-1932	558

Walks/PA
(minimum 2000 Plate Appearances)
Ted Williams	1942-1947	0.23

Intentional Walks
Barry Bonds	1992-1997	179

Hit By Pitch
Hughie Jennings	1894-1899	221

Sacrifice Hits
Ray Chapman	1915-1920	262

Sacrifice Flies
Don Mattingly	1984-1989	60

Caught Stealing
Rickey Henderson	1979-1984	138

Stolen Base Pct.
(minimum 120 attempts)
Eric Davis	1987-1992	.879

GDP
Jim Rice	1982-1987	172

Secondary Average
(minimum 2000 Plate Appearances)
Babe Ruth	1919-1924	.692

Isolated Power
(minimum 2000 Plate Appearances)
Babe Ruth	1919-1924	.396

Top Six-Year Pitching Performances

Wins

John Clarkson	1885-1890	235
Tim Keefe	1883-1888	222
Old Hoss Radbourn	1881-1886	220
Old Hoss Radbourn	1882-1887	219
John Clarkson	1884-1889	219
John Clarkson	1886-1891	215
Tim Keefe	1884-1889	209
Pud Galvin	1879-1884	205
Tim Keefe	1882-1887	204
John Clarkson	1887-1892	204
Jim McCormick	1880-1885	196
Jim McCormick	1879-1884	195
Pud Galvin	1881-1886	193
Pud Galvin	1882-1887	193
Old Hoss Radbourn	1883-1888	193

Losses

Jim McCormick	1879-1884	165
Pud Galvin	1879-1884	160
Pud Galvin	1880-1885	159
Jim Whitney	1881-1886	153
Jim McCormick	1878-1883	148
Mark Baldwin	1888-1893	148
Pud Galvin	1881-1886	145
Mark Baldwin	1887-1892	145
Pud Galvin	1883-1888	144
Pud Galvin	1882-1887	142
Amos Rusie	1890-1895	142
Jim Whitney	1882-1887	141
Stump Wiedman	1882-1887	141
Jim Whitney	1883-1888	141
Bill Hutchison	1890-1895	141

Winning Percentage
(minimum 70 decisions)

Lefty Grove	1928-1933	.788
Joe Wood	1912-1917	.784
Lefty Grove	1929-1934	.768
Lefty Grove	1927-1932	.763
Spud Chandler	1941-1946	.756
Spud Chandler	1942-1947	.744
Lefty Grove	1930-1935	.743
Spud Chandler	1939-1944	.740
Spud Chandler	1938-1943	.740
Johnny Allen	1932-1937	.739
Christy Mathewson	1905-1910	.738
Chief Bender	1909-1914	.736
Preacher Roe	1949-1954	.736
Lefty Grove	1926-1931	.735
Christy Mathewson	1904-1909	.735

Games

Kent Tekulve	1978-1983	469
Kent Tekulve	1977-1982	465
Kent Tekulve	1982-1987	457
Kent Tekulve	1979-1984	450
Kent Tekulve	1976-1981	444
Kent Tekulve	1983-1988	442
Mike Marshall	1971-1976	440
Mitch Williams	1986-1991	436
Duane Ward	1988-1993	434
Kent Tekulve	1975-1980	433
Rollie Fingers	1973-1978	428
Rollie Fingers	1972-1977	426
Pedro Borbon	1972-1977	424
Pedro Borbon	1973-1978	424
Mitch Williams	1987-1992	422

Games Started

Pud Galvin	1879-1884	371
Jim McCormick	1879-1884	365
John Clarkson	1885-1890	354
Old Hoss Radbourn	1882-1887	350
Pud Galvin	1880-1885	348
Pud Galvin	1881-1886	344
Tim Keefe	1883-1888	342
Pud Galvin	1882-1887	339
Pud Galvin	1883-1888	338
Old Hoss Radbourn	1881-1886	336
John Clarkson	1886-1891	335
Jim McCormick	1880-1885	333
Tim Keefe	1882-1887	333
Amos Rusie	1890-1895	330
John Clarkson	1887-1892	324

Complete Games

Jim McCormick	1879-1884	352
Pud Galvin	1879-1884	350
Old Hoss Radbourn	1882-1887	344
John Clarkson	1885-1890	338
Tim Keefe	1883-1888	333
Old Hoss Radbourn	1881-1886	330
Pud Galvin	1881-1886	328
Pud Galvin	1883-1888	328
Tim Keefe	1882-1887	326
Pud Galvin	1880-1885	325
Jim McCormick	1880-1885	321
Tim Keefe	1881-1886	317
Old Hoss Radbourn	1883-1888	317
John Clarkson	1886-1891	317

Shutouts

Pete Alexander	1912-1917	54
Pete Alexander	1911-1916	53
Pete Alexander	1915-1920	52
Pete Alexander	1913-1918	51
Pete Alexander	1914-1919	51
Walter Johnson	1910-1915	48
Ed Walsh	1906-1911	46
Walter Johnson	1913-1918	46
Christy Mathewson	1904-1909	45
Walter Johnson	1909-1914	45
Walter Johnson	1912-1917	45
Three Finger Brown	1905-1910	43
Christy Mathewson	1905-1910	43
Walter Johnson	1911-1916	43
Pete Alexander	1916-1921	43

Saves

Dennis Eckersley	1988-1993	256
Lee Smith	1990-1995	237
Dennis Eckersley	1987-1992	236
Dennis Eckersley	1989-1994	230
Dennis Eckersley	1990-1995	226
Randy Myers	1992-1997	226
Lee Smith	1989-1994	225
Lee Smith	1988-1993	221
Dan Quisenberry	1980-1985	212
Lee Smith	1987-1992	211
John Wetteland	1992-1997	210
Lee Smith	1991-1996	208
Dennis Eckersley	1991-1996	208
Rick Aguilera	1990-1995	204
Jeff Reardon	1984-1989	203

Innings Pitched

Pud Galvin	1879-1884	3,263.2
Jim McCormick	1879-1884	3,236.2
Old Hoss Radbourn	1882-1887	3,165.0
John Clarkson	1885-1890	3,099.0
Old Hoss Radbourn	1881-1886	3,065.1
Pud Galvin	1880-1885	3,043.0
Pud Galvin	1881-1886	3,019.0
Pud Galvin	1882-1887	2,985.2
Pud Galvin	1883-1888	2,977.2
Tim Keefe	1883-1888	2,952.2
Jim McCormick	1880-1885	2,942.1
John Clarkson	1886-1891	2,936.2
Amos Rusie	1890-1895	2,900.1
Old Hoss Radbourn	1883-1888	2,898.0
Tim Keefe	1882-1887	2,893.1

Walks

Amos Rusie	1890-1895	1,395
Amos Rusie	1889-1894	1,352
Mark Baldwin	1888-1893	1,185
Mark Baldwin	1887-1892	1,165
Nolan Ryan	1972-1977	1,040
Nolan Ryan	1973-1978	1,031
Gus Weyhing	1887-1892	998
Bill Hutchison	1890-1895	992
Nolan Ryan	1974-1979	983
Gus Weyhing	1889-1894	981
Bill Hutchison	1889-1894	980
Gus Weyhing	1888-1893	976
Nolan Ryan	1971-1976	952
Amos Rusie	1892-1897	931
Jack Stivetts	1890-1895	913

Strikeouts

Nolan Ryan	1972-1977	1,933
Nolan Ryan	1973-1978	1,864
Nolan Ryan	1971-1976	1,729
Tim Keefe	1883-1888	1,718
Sandy Koufax	1961-1966	1,713
Nolan Ryan	1974-1979	1,704
Sam McDowell	1965-1970	1,652
Rube Waddell	1903-1908	1,598
Sandy Koufax	1960-1965	1,593
Rube Waddell	1902-1907	1,576
Amos Rusie	1890-1895	1,570
Tim Keefe	1884-1889	1,566
Nolan Ryan	1975-1980	1,537
Nolan Ryan	1970-1975	1,527
Sam McDowell	1964-1969	1,525

Strikeouts/9 Innings
(minimum 700 Innings Pitched)

Randy Johnson	1992-1997	11.37
Randy Johnson	1991-1996	10.98
Nolan Ryan	1986-1991	10.48
Nolan Ryan	1987-1992	10.39
Randy Johnson	1990-1995	10.39
Nolan Ryan	1972-1977	10.09
Nolan Ryan	1985-1990	10.04
Nolan Ryan	1973-1978	10.02
Nolan Ryan	1984-1989	9.96
Nolan Ryan	1988-1993	9.91
Nolan Ryan	1971-1976	9.87
Nolan Ryan	1969-1974	9.80
Nolan Ryan	1974-1979	9.76
Sam McDowell	1961-1966	9.74
Sam McDowell	1963-1968	9.73

ERA
(minimum 700 Innings Pitched)

Walter Johnson	1910-1915	1.51
Three Finger Brown	1904-1909	1.51
Three Finger Brown	1905-1910	1.53
Ed Walsh	1905-1910	1.55
Walter Johnson	1908-1913	1.58
Walter Johnson	1911-1916	1.60
Walter Johnson	1909-1914	1.60
Ed Walsh	1906-1911	1.62
Three Finger Brown	1906-1911	1.63
Walter Johnson	1913-1918	1.63
Pete Alexander	1915-1920	1.64
Walter Johnson	1912-1917	1.65
Addie Joss	1904-1909	1.67
Ed Walsh	1904-1909	1.68
Ed Walsh	1907-1912	1.69

Component ERA
(minimum 700 Innings Pitched)

Three Finger Brown	1904-1909	1.56
Ed Walsh	1905-1910	1.56
Walter Johnson	1912-1917	1.61
Ed Walsh	1906-1911	1.61
Walter Johnson	1913-1918	1.63
Three Finger Brown	1905-1910	1.63
Addie Joss	1904-1909	1.64
Walter Johnson	1910-1915	1.64
Addie Joss	1903-1908	1.64
Addie Joss	1905-1910	1.65
Ed Walsh	1904-1909	1.66
Ed Walsh	1907-1912	1.67
Walter Johnson	1911-1916	1.68
Walter Johnson	1908-1913	1.68
Ed Walsh	1908-1913	1.69

Opponent Average
(minimum 700 Innings Pitched)

Nolan Ryan	1969-1974	.192
Nolan Ryan	1972-1977	.193
Nolan Ryan	1968-1973	.194
Nolan Ryan	1986-1991	.195
Nolan Ryan	1970-1975	.196
Sandy Koufax	1960-1965	.196
Nolan Ryan	1971-1976	.196
Sandy Koufax	1961-1966	.197
Herb Score	1955-1960	.198
Sid Fernandez	1988-1993	.200
Nolan Ryan	1973-1978	.201
Sid Fernandez	1985-1990	.202
Nolan Ryan	1987-1992	.202
Nolan Ryan	1974-1979	.202
Nolan Ryan	1988-1993	.203

Opponent OBP
(minimum 700 Innings Pitched)

Sandy Koufax	1961-1966	.249
Three Finger Brown	1904-1909	.250
Ed Walsh	1905-1910	.250
Addie Joss	1903-1908	.250
Addie Joss	1904-1909	.251
Addie Joss	1905-1910	.251
Monte Ward	1878-1883	.252
Ed Walsh	1906-1911	.254
Walter Johnson	1912-1917	.254
Monte Ward	1879-1884	.254
Three Finger Brown	1905-1910	.255
Christy Mathewson	1904-1909	.255
Tim Keefe	1883-1888	.255
Walter Johnson	1910-1915	.255
Walter Johnson	1913-1918	.256

Games Finished

Dan Quisenberry	1980-1985	376

Batters Faced

Pud Galvin	1879-1884	13,637

Hits Allowed

Pud Galvin	1879-1884	3,377

Runs Allowed

Pud Galvin	1879-1884	1,706

Earned Runs

Bill Hutchison	1890-1895	1,071

Home Runs Allowed

Robin Roberts	1954-1959	226

Intentional Walks

Kent Tekulve	1978-1983	94

Sac Hits Allowed

George Mullin	1904-1909	253

Sac Flies Allowed

Larry Gura	1978-1983	63

Hit Batsmen

Joe McGinnity	1899-1904	139

Wild Pitches

Jim Whitney	1881-1886	191

Balks

Two tied at		47

Top Seven-Year Batting Performances

Runs

Billy Hamilton	1891-1897	1,045
Billy Hamilton	1890-1896	1,026
Billy Hamilton	1889-1895	1,018
Billy Hamilton	1892-1898	1,014
Lou Gehrig	1930-1936	1,002
Babe Ruth	1926-1932	1,000
Willie Keeler	1894-1900	997
Lou Gehrig	1927-1933	997
Lou Gehrig	1931-1937	997
Lou Gehrig	1926-1932	994
Hugh Duffy	1889-1895	981
Lou Gehrig	1928-1934	976
Lou Gehrig	1929-1935	962
Jesse Burkett	1892-1898	958
Babe Ruth	1927-1933	958

Hits

Jesse Burkett	1895-1901	1,526
Willie Keeler	1894-1900	1,517
Willie Keeler	1895-1901	1,500
Jesse Burkett	1894-1900	1,487
Bill Terry	1929-1935	1,487
Wade Boggs	1983-1989	1,479
Willie Keeler	1896-1902	1,473
Jesse Burkett	1896-1902	1,470
Bill Terry	1928-1934	1,469
Rogers Hornsby	1920-1926	1,463
Paul Waner	1927-1933	1,463
Jesse Burkett	1893-1899	1,462
Rogers Hornsby	1919-1925	1,459
Heinie Manush	1928-1934	1,457
Wade Boggs	1984-1990	1,456

Doubles

Joe Medwick	1933-1939	341
Tris Speaker	1920-1926	332
Joe Medwick	1934-1940	331
Tris Speaker	1921-1927	325
Joe Medwick	1935-1941	324
Tris Speaker	1917-1923	322
Tris Speaker	1919-1925	318
Tris Speaker	1918-1924	316
Joe Medwick	1936-1942	315
Wade Boggs	1985-1991	311
Joe Medwick	1932-1938	305
Pete Rose	1974-1980	305
Tris Speaker	1916-1922	304
Four tied at		300

Triples

Sam Crawford	1909-1915	136
Sam Crawford	1910-1916	135
Sam Crawford	1908-1914	133
Joe Jackson	1911-1917	127
Jake Beckley	1889-1895	126
Jake Beckley	1890-1896	125
Sam Crawford	1907-1913	124
Sam Crawford	1901-1907	122
Sam Crawford	1902-1908	122
Ty Cobb	1907-1913	121
Ty Cobb	1911-1917	121
Sam Crawford	1900-1906	120
Elmer Flick	1901-1907	120
Earle Combs	1927-1933	120
Three tied at		119

Home Runs

Babe Ruth	1926-1932	343
Babe Ruth	1927-1933	330
Babe Ruth	1924-1930	327
Babe Ruth	1925-1931	327
Babe Ruth	1923-1929	319
Babe Ruth	1921-1927	313
Jimmie Foxx	1932-1938	313
Babe Ruth	1922-1928	308
Babe Ruth	1920-1926	307
Ralph Kiner	1947-1953	306
Harmon Killebrew	1961-1967	296
Jimmie Foxx	1930-1936	294
Ralph Kiner	1946-1952	294
Jimmie Foxx	1931-1937	293
Two tied at		292

Total Bases

Lou Gehrig	1927-1933	2,691
Lou Gehrig	1930-1936	2,682
Lou Gehrig	1928-1934	2,653
Lou Gehrig	1926-1932	2,646
Lou Gehrig	1931-1937	2,629
Jimmie Foxx	1932-1938	2,606
Lou Gehrig	1929-1935	2,601
Babe Ruth	1926-1932	2,565
Jimmie Foxx	1930-1936	2,552
Stan Musial	1948-1954	2,528
Hank Aaron	1957-1963	2,525
Lou Gehrig	1932-1938	2,520
Lou Gehrig	1925-1931	2,508
Jimmie Foxx	1929-1935	2,506
Jimmie Foxx	1931-1937	2,500

RBI

Lou Gehrig	1927-1933	1,091
Lou Gehrig	1930-1936	1,084
Lou Gehrig	1928-1934	1,081
Lou Gehrig	1931-1937	1,069
Lou Gehrig	1926-1932	1,064
Babe Ruth	1926-1932	1,059
Lou Gehrig	1929-1935	1,058
Jimmie Foxx	1932-1938	1,022
Babe Ruth	1927-1933	1,016
Lou Gehrig	1932-1938	999
Jimmie Foxx	1930-1936	996
Babe Ruth	1925-1931	988
Lou Gehrig	1925-1931	981
Jimmie Foxx	1929-1935	970
Jimmie Foxx	1931-1937	967

Walks

Eddie Yost	1950-1956	896
Babe Ruth	1920-1926	891
Babe Ruth	1926-1932	883
Babe Ruth	1921-1927	881
Babe Ruth	1922-1928	872
Babe Ruth	1923-1929	860
Babe Ruth	1927-1933	853
Barry Bonds	1991-1997	850
Babe Ruth	1919-1925	848
Babe Ruth	1918-1924	846
Mickey Mantle	1956-1962	839
Eddie Yost	1949-1955	836
Frank Thomas	1991-1997	835
Ted Williams	1946-1952	834
Eddie Stanky	1945-1951	833

Strikeouts

Rob Deer	1986-1992	1,129
Rob Deer	1987-1993	1,119
Bobby Bonds	1969-1975	1,069
Rob Deer	1985-1991	1,069
Bobby Bonds	1968-1974	1,016
Juan Samuel	1984-1990	1,010
Pete Incaviglia	1986-1992	979
Juan Samuel	1985-1991	975
Cecil Fielder	1990-1996	974
Bobby Bonds	1970-1976	972
Jose Canseco	1986-1992	967
Dick Allen	1964-1970	964
Reggie Jackson	1968-1974	950
Dale Murphy	1984-1990	949
Mike Schmidt	1973-1979	943

Stolen Bases

Rickey Henderson	1980-1986	627
Billy Hamilton	1889-1895	619
Rickey Henderson	1982-1988	605
Billy Hamilton	1890-1896	591
Vince Coleman	1985-1991	586
Rickey Henderson	1979-1985	573
Arlie Latham	1886-1892	572
Arlie Latham	1887-1893	569
Rickey Henderson	1981-1987	568
Billy Hamilton	1891-1897	555
Rickey Henderson	1983-1989	552
Billy Hamilton	1888-1894	541
Rickey Henderson	1984-1990	509
Arlie Latham	1885-1891	506
Two tied at		504

Runs Created

Lou Gehrig	1930-1936	1,170
Lou Gehrig	1931-1937	1,155
Babe Ruth	1926-1932	1,149
Lou Gehrig	1927-1933	1,148
Lou Gehrig	1928-1934	1,137
Lou Gehrig	1926-1932	1,126
Lou Gehrig	1929-1935	1,126
Babe Ruth	1920-1926	1,116
Lou Gehrig	1932-1938	1,107
Babe Ruth	1927-1933	1,104
Babe Ruth	1921-1927	1,102
abe Ruth	1923-1929	1,090
Jimmie Foxx	1932-1938	1,081
Three tied at		1,073

Runs Created/27 Outs
(minimum 2250 Plate Appearances)

Ted Williams	1941-1947	13.11
Babe Ruth	1920-1926	13.11
Babe Ruth	1918-1924	13.00
Babe Ruth	1919-1925	12.74
Babe Ruth	1917-1923	12.63
Babe Ruth	1921-1927	12.57
Ted Williams	1942-1948	12.46
Babe Ruth	1926-1932	12.44
Ted Williams	1940-1946	12.44
Billy Hamilton	1893-1899	12.02
Babe Ruth	1923-1929	12.02
Babe Ruth	1922-1928	11.99
Babe Ruth	1927-1933	11.95
Ted Williams	1951-1957	11.94
Babe Ruth	1915-1921	11.94

Batting Average
(minimum 2250 Plate Appearances)

Ty Cobb	1909-1915	.390
Ty Cobb	1910-1916	.389
Ty Cobb	1911-1917	.389
Rogers Hornsby	1919-1925	.386
Rogers Hornsby	1920-1926	.386
Willie Keeler	1893-1899	.385
Willie Keeler	1892-1898	.385
Ed Delahanty	1893-1899	.384
Rogers Hornsby	1921-1927	.384
Willie Keeler	1894-1900	.383
Ty Cobb	1912-1918	.383
Rogers Hornsby	1922-1928	.382
Ty Cobb	1908-1914	.382
Jesse Burkett	1895-1901	.382
Harry Heilmann	1921-1927	.380

On-Base Percentage
(minimum 2250 Plate Appearances)

Ted Williams	1941-1947	.510
Babe Ruth	1920-1926	.500
Ted Williams	1942-1948	.498
Ted Williams	1940-1946	.496
Ted Williams	1952-1958	.496
Ted Williams	1951-1957	.495
Babe Ruth	1918-1924	.494
Babe Ruth	1921-1927	.493
John McGraw	1897-1903	.493
Babe Ruth	1919-1925	.492
John McGraw	1895-1901	.491
John McGraw	1896-1902	.491
Babe Ruth	1917-1923	.486
Ted Williams	1948-1954	.485
Ted Williams	1946-1952	.485

Slugging Percentage
(minimum 2250 Plate Appearances)

Babe Ruth	1920-1926	.746
Babe Ruth	1918-1924	.739
Babe Ruth	1921-1927	.736
Babe Ruth	1919-1925	.735
Babe Ruth	1917-1923	.727
Babe Ruth	1923-1929	.717
Babe Ruth	1926-1932	.717
Babe Ruth	1922-1928	.714
Babe Ruth	1924-1930	.712
Babe Ruth	1925-1931	.706
Babe Ruth	1915-1921	.702
Babe Ruth	1916-1922	.702
Babe Ruth	1927-1933	.696
Ted Williams	1941-1947	.669
Babe Ruth	1928-1934	.667

OBP+Slugging
(minimum 2250 Plate Appearances)

Babe Ruth	1920-1926	1.245
Babe Ruth	1918-1924	1.233
Babe Ruth	1921-1927	1.230
Babe Ruth	1919-1925	1.227
Babe Ruth	1917-1923	1.214
Babe Ruth	1923-1929	1.201
Babe Ruth	1922-1928	1.200
Babe Ruth	1926-1932	1.199
Babe Ruth	1924-1930	1.187
Ted Williams	1941-1947	1.179
Babe Ruth	1925-1931	1.179
Babe Ruth	1915-1921	1.169
Babe Ruth	1927-1933	1.168
Babe Ruth	1916-1922	1.167
Ted Williams	1952-1958	1.158

Games

Two tied at		1,137

At-Bats

Pete Rose	1972-1978	4,614

Home Runs (Home)

Ralph Kiner	1947-1953	182

Home Runs (Road)

Babe Ruth	1926-1932	173

AB/HR
(minimum 2250 Plate Appearances)

Babe Ruth	1926-1932	10.4

Extra-Base Hits

Lou Gehrig	1927-1933	643

Walks/PA
(minimum 2250 Plate Appearances)

Ted Williams	1941-1947	0.23

Intentional Walks

Barry Bonds	1991-1997	204

Hit By Pitch

Hughie Jennings	1894-1900	241

Sacrifice Hits

Ray Chapman	1913-1919	287

Sacrifice Flies

Ruben Sierra	1987-1993	67

Caught Stealing

Rickey Henderson	1980-1986	155

Stolen Base Pct.
(minimum 140 attempts)

Eric Davis	1986-1992	.879

GDP

Jim Rice	1982-1988	190

Secondary Average
(minimum 2250 Plate Appearances)

Babe Ruth	1920-1926	.675

Isolated Power
(minimum 2250 Plate Appearances)

Babe Ruth	1920-1926	.384

Top Seven-Year Pitching Performances

Wins

John Clarkson	1885-1891	268
Tim Keefe	1883-1889	250
John Clarkson	1884-1890	245
Old Hoss Radbourn	1881-1887	244
John Clarkson	1886-1892	240
Tim Keefe	1882-1888	239
Jim McCormick	1880-1886	227
Old Hoss Radbourn	1882-1888	226
Tim Keefe	1884-1890	226
Tim Keefe	1881-1887	222
Pud Galvin	1879-1885	221
Pud Galvin	1881-1887	221
John Clarkson	1887-1893	220
Kid Nichols	1892-1898	219
Kid Nichols	1891-1897	218

Losses

Pud Galvin	1879-1885	186
Pud Galvin	1880-1886	180
Jim Whitney	1881-1887	174
Jim McCormick	1878-1884	173
Jim McCormick	1879-1885	172
Pud Galvin	1882-1888	167
Pud Galvin	1881-1887	166
Mark Baldwin	1887-1893	165
Jim Whitney	1882-1888	162
Pud Galvin	1883-1889	160
Bill Hutchison	1889-1895	158
Amos Rusie	1889-1895	152
Tim Keefe	1881-1887	149
Four tied at		148

Winning Percentage
(minimum 75 decisions)

Lefty Grove	1928-1934	.766
Lefty Grove	1927-1933	.761
Lefty Grove	1929-1935	.746
Whitey Ford	1950-1956	.741
Spud Chandler	1941-1947	.740
Spud Chandler	1938-1944	.740
Spud Chandler	1939-1945	.738
Christy Mathewson	1904-1910	.737
Lefty Grove	1926-1932	.732
Christy Mathewson	1903-1909	.729
Spud Chandler	1937-1943	.729
Christy Mathewson	1905-1911	.727
Bob Caruthers	1884-1890	.725
Spud Chandler	1940-1946	.724
Dwight Gooden	1985-1991	.723

Games

Kent Tekulve	1977-1983	541
Kent Tekulve	1978-1984	541
Kent Tekulve	1976-1982	529
Kent Tekulve	1982-1988	527
Kent Tekulve	1979-1985	511
Kent Tekulve	1981-1987	502
Mitch Williams	1986-1992	502
Rob Murphy	1987-1993	494
Rollie Fingers	1972-1978	493
Kent Tekulve	1980-1986	490
Mitch Williams	1987-1993	487
Pedro Borbon	1972-1978	486
Rollie Fingers	1974-1980	486
Pedro Borbon	1973-1979	484
Rollie Fingers	1973-1979	482

Games Started

Pud Galvin	1879-1885	414
John Clarkson	1885-1891	405
Pud Galvin	1880-1886	398
Jim McCormick	1879-1885	393
Pud Galvin	1881-1887	392
Pud Galvin	1882-1888	389
Tim Keefe	1883-1889	387
Old Hoss Radbourn	1881-1887	386
Tim Keefe	1882-1888	384
Jim McCormick	1878-1884	379
John Clarkson	1886-1892	379
Tim Keefe	1881-1887	378
Pud Galvin	1883-1889	378
Jim McCormick	1880-1886	375
Old Hoss Radbourn	1882-1888	374

Complete Games

Pud Galvin	1879-1885	390
John Clarkson	1885-1891	385
Jim Whitney	1879-1885	380
Old Hoss Radbourn	1881-1887	378
Pud Galvin	1882-1888	376
Pud Galvin	1881-1887	375
Pud Galvin	1880-1886	374
Tim Keefe	1882-1888	374
Tim Keefe	1881-1887	371
Tim Keefe	1883-1889	371
Old Hoss Radbourn	1882-1888	368
Pud Galvin	1883-1889	366
Jim McCormick	1878-1884	364
Jim McCormick	1880-1886	359
John Clarkson	1886-1892	359

Shutouts

Pete Alexander	1911-1917	61
Pete Alexander	1913-1919	60
Pete Alexander	1914-1920	58
Pete Alexander	1915-1921	55
Pete Alexander	1912-1918	54
Walter Johnson	1912-1918	53
Walter Johnson	1913-1919	53
Ed Walsh	1906-1912	52
Walter Johnson	1909-1915	52
Walter Johnson	1908-1914	51
Walter Johnson	1910-1916	51
Walter Johnson	1911-1917	51
Christy Mathewson	1902-1908	48
Christy Mathewson	1903-1909	48
Christy Mathewson	1905-1911	48

Saves

Dennis Eckersley	1988-1994	275
Dennis Eckersley	1987-1993	272
Lee Smith	1989-1995	262
Dennis Eckersley	1989-1995	259
Lee Smith	1987-1993	257
Dennis Eckersley	1990-1996	256
Lee Smith	1988-1994	254
Dennis Eckersley	1991-1997	244
Lee Smith	1986-1992	242
Jeff Reardon	1985-1991	241
Lee Smith	1990-1996	239
Dennis Eckersley	1986-1992	236
Lee Smith	1985-1991	232
Randy Myers	1991-1997	232
Jeff Reardon	1986-1992	230

Innings Pitched

Pud Galvin	1879-1885	3,636.0
John Clarkson	1885-1891	3,559.2
Old Hoss Radbourn	1881-1887	3,490.1
Jim McCormick	1879-1885	3,488.2
Pud Galvin	1880-1886	3,477.2
Pud Galvin	1881-1887	3,459.2
Pud Galvin	1882-1888	3,423.0
Old Hoss Radbourn	1882-1888	3,372.0
Jim McCormick	1878-1884	3,353.2
Tim Keefe	1882-1888	3,327.2
John Clarkson	1886-1892	3,325.2
Pud Galvin	1883-1889	3,318.2
Tim Keefe	1883-1889	3,316.2
Tim Keefe	1881-1887	3,295.1
Jim McCormick	1880-1886	3,290.0

Walks

Amos Rusie	1889-1895	1,511
Mark Baldwin	1887-1893	1,307
Amos Rusie	1891-1897	1,193
Nolan Ryan	1972-1978	1,188
Nolan Ryan	1971-1977	1,156
Nolan Ryan	1973-1979	1,145
Gus Weyhing	1887-1893	1,143
Bill Hutchison	1889-1895	1,109
Gus Weyhing	1888-1894	1,092
Nolan Ryan	1974-1980	1,081
Gus Weyhing	1889-1895	1,065
Nolan Ryan	1970-1976	1,049
Amos Rusie	1892-1898	1,034
Ted Breitenstein	1892-1898	1,025
Jack Stivetts	1890-1896	1,012

Strikeouts

Nolan Ryan	1972-1978	2,193
Nolan Ryan	1973-1979	2,087
Nolan Ryan	1971-1977	2,070
Tim Keefe	1883-1889	1,927
Sandy Koufax	1960-1966	1,910
Nolan Ryan	1974-1980	1,904
Nolan Ryan	1970-1976	1,854
Sam McDowell	1965-1971	1,844
Tim Keefe	1882-1888	1,834
Sam McDowell	1964-1970	1,829
Rube Waddell	1902-1908	1,808
Sandy Koufax	1959-1965	1,766
Tom Seaver	1970-1976	1,751
Rube Waddell	1901-1907	1,748
Rube Waddell	1903-1909	1,739

Strikeouts/9 Innings
(minimum 750 Innings Pitched)

Randy Johnson	1991-1997	11.19
Randy Johnson	1990-1996	10.48
Nolan Ryan	1986-1992	10.31
Nolan Ryan	1987-1993	10.17
Nolan Ryan	1985-1991	10.10
Nolan Ryan	1972-1978	10.08
Randy Johnson	1989-1995	10.04
Nolan Ryan	1984-1990	9.99
Nolan Ryan	1971-1977	9.93
Nolan Ryan	1973-1979	9.90
Nolan Ryan	1970-1976	9.77
Nolan Ryan	1983-1989	9.75
Nolan Ryan	1968-1974	9.72
Sandy Koufax	1959-1965	9.70
Nolan Ryan	1969-1975	9.63

ERA
(minimum 750 Innings Pitched)

Three Finger Brown	1904-1910	1.56
Walter Johnson	1910-1916	1.56
Walter Johnson	1909-1915	1.59
Walter Johnson	1912-1918	1.60
Walter Johnson	1907-1913	1.60
Walter Johnson	1908-1914	1.61
Ed Walsh	1904-1910	1.61
Walter Johnson	1913-1919	1.62
Three Finger Brown	1903-1909	1.63
Ed Walsh	1905-1911	1.66
Walter Johnson	1911-1917	1.68
Three Finger Brown	1906-1912	1.68
Three Finger Brown	1905-1911	1.70
Addie Joss	1904-1910	1.70
Ed Walsh	1906-1912	1.71

Component ERA
(minimum 750 Innings Pitched)

Ed Walsh	1904-1910	1.58
Walter Johnson	1912-1918	1.61
Three Finger Brown	1904-1910	1.63
Walter Johnson	1913-1919	1.64
Ed Walsh	1905-1911	1.64
Addie Joss	1903-1909	1.65
Walter Johnson	1910-1916	1.66
Addie Joss	1904-1910	1.66
Ed Walsh	1906-1912	1.67
Walter Johnson	1911-1917	1.69
Walter Johnson	1909-1915	1.69
Walter Johnson	1908-1914	1.69
Ed Walsh	1908-1914	1.71
Addie Joss	1902-1908	1.71
Walter Johnson	1907-1913	1.71

Opponent Average
(minimum 750 Innings Pitched)

Nolan Ryan	1966-1972	.191
Nolan Ryan	1968-1974	.193
Hoyt Wilhelm	1963-1969	.193
Hoyt Wilhelm	1962-1968	.195
Nolan Ryan	1969-1975	.195
Nolan Ryan	1970-1976	.195
Nolan Ryan	1971-1977	.196
Nolan Ryan	1972-1978	.197
Hoyt Wilhelm	1961-1967	.197
Sandy Koufax	1960-1966	.198
Herb Score	1955-1961	.199
Sandy Koufax	1959-1965	.200
Nolan Ryan	1986-1992	.200
Nolan Ryan	1985-1991	.202
Nolan Ryan	1973-1979	.202

Opponent OBP
(minimum 750 Innings Pitched)

Hoyt Wilhelm	1963-1969	.250
Addie Joss	1903-1909	.251
Ed Walsh	1904-1910	.252
Hoyt Wilhelm	1962-1968	.253
Addie Joss	1904-1910	.253
Monte Ward	1878-1884	.254
Three Finger Brown	1904-1910	.255
Walter Johnson	1912-1918	.255
Ed Walsh	1905-1911	.255
Addie Joss	1902-1908	.256
Sandy Koufax	1960-1966	.256
Walter Johnson	1913-1919	.256
Dennis Eckersley	1985-1991	.257
Walter Johnson	1910-1916	.257
Juan Marichal	1963-1969	.258

Games Finished

Dan Quisenberry	1980-1986	430

Batters Faced

Pud Galvin	1879-1885	15,264

Hits Allowed

Pud Galvin	1879-1885	3,830

Runs Allowed

Pud Galvin	1879-1885	1,974

Earned Runs

Bill Hutchison	1889-1895	1,196

Home Runs Allowed

Robin Roberts	1954-1960	257

Intentional Walks

Kent Tekulve	1978-1984	106

Sac Hits Allowed

George Mullin	1904-1910	294

Sac Flies Allowed

Two tied at		69

Hit Batsmen

Joe McGinnity	1899-1905	153

Wild Pitches

Mickey Welch	1880-1886	208

Balks

Two tied at		54

Top Eight-Year Batting Performances

Runs

Billy Hamilton	1890-1897	1,178
Billy Hamilton	1889-1896	1,170
Billy Hamilton	1891-1898	1,155
Lou Gehrig	1930-1937	1,140
Lou Gehrig	1926-1933	1,132
Lou Gehrig	1929-1936	1,129
Lou Gehrig	1927-1934	1,125
Willie Keeler	1894-1901	1,120
Lou Gehrig	1931-1938	1,112
Lou Gehrig	1928-1935	1,101
Babe Ruth	1926-1933	1,097
Babe Ruth	1921-1928	1,086
Babe Ruth	1923-1930	1,086
Babe Ruth	1924-1931	1,084
Babe Ruth	1920-1927	1,081

Hits

Willie Keeler	1894-1901	1,719
Jesse Burkett	1894-1901	1,713
Jesse Burkett	1895-1902	1,695
Willie Keeler	1895-1902	1,686
Paul Waner	1927-1934	1,680
Bill Terry	1928-1935	1,672
Rogers Hornsby	1920-1927	1,668
Wade Boggs	1983-1990	1,666
Jesse Burkett	1893-1900	1,665
Bill Terry	1927-1934	1,658
Pete Rose	1969-1976	1,653
Pete Rose	1968-1975	1,648
Pete Rose	1972-1979	1,648
Kirby Puckett	1985-1992	1,647
Paul Waner	1926-1933	1,643

Doubles

Tris Speaker	1920-1927	375
Joe Medwick	1933-1940	371
Tris Speaker	1919-1926	370
Joe Medwick	1934-1941	364
Tris Speaker	1916-1923	363
Joe Medwick	1935-1942	361
Tris Speaker	1917-1924	358
Joe Medwick	1932-1939	353
Tris Speaker	1918-1925	351
Tris Speaker	1921-1928	347
Joe Medwick	1936-1943	345
Charlie Gehringer	1929-1936	344
Wade Boggs	1983-1990	344
Harry Heilmann	1923-1930	342
Wade Boggs	1984-1991	342

Triples

Sam Crawford	1908-1915	152
Sam Crawford	1907-1914	150
Sam Crawford	1909-1916	149
Sam Crawford	1906-1913	140
Sam Crawford	1901-1908	138
Jake Beckley	1890-1897	137
Sam Crawford	1900-1907	137
Elmer Flick	1900-1907	136
Sam Crawford	1902-1909	136
Jake Beckley	1889-1896	135
Ty Cobb	1911-1918	135
Ty Cobb	1910-1917	134
Sam Crawford	1903-1910	133
Three tied at		132

Home Runs

Babe Ruth	1926-1933	377
Babe Ruth	1924-1931	373
Babe Ruth	1923-1930	368
Babe Ruth	1925-1932	368
Babe Ruth	1920-1927	367
Babe Ruth	1921-1928	367
Babe Ruth	1922-1929	354
Babe Ruth	1927-1934	352
Jimmie Foxx	1932-1939	348
Jimmie Foxx	1931-1938	343
Babe Ruth	1919-1926	336
Jimmie Foxx	1930-1937	330
Ralph Kiner	1946-1953	329
Ralph Kiner	1947-1954	328
Two tied at		327

Total Bases

Lou Gehrig	1927-1934	3,100
Lou Gehrig	1930-1937	3,048
Lou Gehrig	1926-1933	3,005
Lou Gehrig	1929-1936	3,004
Lou Gehrig	1928-1935	2,965
Lou Gehrig	1931-1938	2,930
Jimmie Foxx	1932-1939	2,930
Jimmie Foxx	1931-1938	2,898
Babe Ruth	1920-1927	2,885
Lou Gehrig	1925-1932	2,878
Babe Ruth	1921-1928	2,877
Jimmie Foxx	1929-1936	2,875
Babe Ruth	1923-1930	2,874
Hank Aaron	1956-1963	2,865
Jimmie Foxx	1930-1937	2,858

RBI

Lou Gehrig	1927-1934	1,256
Lou Gehrig	1930-1937	1,243
Lou Gehrig	1929-1936	1,210
Lou Gehrig	1926-1933	1,203
Lou Gehrig	1928-1935	1,200
Lou Gehrig	1931-1938	1,183
Babe Ruth	1926-1933	1,162
Jimmie Foxx	1931-1938	1,142
Lou Gehrig	1925-1932	1,132
Jimmie Foxx	1932-1939	1,127
Babe Ruth	1925-1932	1,125
Babe Ruth	1930-1937	1,123
Jimmie Foxx	1929-1936	1,113
Babe Ruth	1924-1931	1,109
Babe Ruth	1927-1934	1,100

Walks

Babe Ruth	1920-1927	1,029
Babe Ruth	1921-1928	1,016
Babe Ruth	1926-1933	997
Babe Ruth	1923-1930	996
Babe Ruth	1919-1926	992
Eddie Yost	1949-1956	987
Eddie Yost	1950-1957	969
Babe Ruth	1927-1934	956
Babe Ruth	1924-1931	954
Mickey Mantle	1955-1962	952
Babe Ruth	1922-1929	944
Barry Bonds	1990-1997	943
Babe Ruth	1925-1932	942
Mickey Mantle	1954-1961	932
Lou Gehrig	1931-1938	922

Strikeouts

Rob Deer	1986-1993	1,298
Rob Deer	1985-1992	1,200
Bobby Bonds	1969-1976	1,159
Bobby Bonds	1968-1975	1,153
Juan Samuel	1984-1991	1,143
Bobby Bonds	1970-1977	1,113
Reggie Jackson	1968-1975	1,083
Rob Deer	1984-1991	1,079
Dick Allen	1964-1971	1,077
Dick Allen	1965-1972	1,065
Dale Murphy	1982-1989	1,063
Mike Schmidt	1973-1980	1,062
Pete Incaviglia	1986-1993	1,061
Cecil Fielder	1990-1997	1,061
Dave Kingman	1972-1979	1,060

Stolen Bases

Billy Hamilton	1889-1896	702
Rickey Henderson	1982-1989	682
Rickey Henderson	1980-1987	668
Rickey Henderson	1981-1988	661
Rickey Henderson	1979-1986	660
Billy Hamilton	1890-1897	657
Billy Hamilton	1888-1895	638
Arlie Latham	1886-1893	629
Arlie Latham	1887-1894	628
Rickey Henderson	1983-1990	617
Vince Coleman	1985-1992	610
Billy Hamilton	1891-1898	609
Arlie Latham	1885-1892	572
Rickey Henderson	1984-1991	567
Rickey Henderson	1985-1992	549

Runs Created

Lou Gehrig	1930-1937	1,337
Lou Gehrig	1927-1934	1,319
Lou Gehrig	1929-1936	1,307
Babe Ruth	1920-1927	1,293
Lou Gehrig	1931-1938	1,286
Lou Gehrig	1928-1935	1,282
Lou Gehrig	1926-1933	1,275
Babe Ruth	1926-1933	1,271
Babe Ruth	1921-1928	1,267
Babe Ruth	1923-1930	1,266
Babe Ruth	1924-1931	1,252
Babe Ruth	1919-1926	1,237
Jimmie Foxx	1932-1939	1,223
Babe Ruth	1925-1932	1,220
Lou Gehrig	1925-1932	1,205

Runs Created/27 Outs

(minimum 2500 Plate Appearances)

Ted Williams	1941-1948	13.08
Babe Ruth	1920-1927	13.02
Babe Ruth	1919-1926	12.80
Babe Ruth	1917-1924	12.75
Babe Ruth	1921-1928	12.42
Babe Ruth	1918-1925	12.35
Ted Williams	1940-1947	12.34
Ted Williams	1942-1949	12.30
Babe Ruth	1916-1923	12.23
Babe Ruth	1926-1933	12.14
Babe Ruth	1923-1930	12.11
Ted Williams	1939-1946	11.99
Babe Ruth	1924-1931	11.99
Ted Williams	1946-1953	11.91
Babe Ruth	1925-1932	11.90

Batting Average

(minimum 2500 Plate Appearances)

Ty Cobb	1910-1917	.388
Ty Cobb	1911-1918	.388
Ty Cobb	1909-1916	.387
Rogers Hornsby	1921-1928	.385
Willie Keeler	1892-1899	.384
Ty Cobb	1912-1919	.383
Rogers Hornsby	1920-1927	.382
Rogers Hornsby	1922-1929	.382
Willie Keeler	1893-1900	.382
Ty Cobb	1908-1915	.380
Jesse Burkett	1894-1901	.379
Willie Keeler	1894-1901	.378
Ty Cobb	1907-1914	.378
Rogers Hornsby	1919-1926	.378
Ty Cobb	1915-1922	.377

On-Base Percentage

(minimum 2500 Plate Appearances)

Ted Williams	1941-1948	.508
Babe Ruth	1920-1927	.498
Ted Williams	1940-1947	.497
Ted Williams	1942-1949	.496
Babe Ruth	1919-1926	.495
John McGraw	1897-1904	.493
Babe Ruth	1917-1924	.491
John McGraw	1896-1903	.490
Ted Williams	1950-1957	.489
Ted Williams	1951-1958	.489
Babe Ruth	1921-1928	.489
Ted Williams	1947-1954	.488
Ted Williams	1948-1955	.487
John McGraw	1895-1902	.486
Ted Williams	1946-1953	.486

Slugging Percentage

(minimum 2500 Plate Appearances)

Babe Ruth	1920-1927	.750
Babe Ruth	1919-1926	.736
Babe Ruth	1921-1928	.733
Babe Ruth	1917-1924	.729
Babe Ruth	1918-1925	.719
Babe Ruth	1923-1930	.719
Babe Ruth	1916-1923	.713
Babe Ruth	1922-1929	.712
Babe Ruth	1924-1931	.710
Babe Ruth	1926-1933	.701
Babe Ruth	1925-1932	.701
Babe Ruth	1914-1921	.700
Babe Ruth	1915-1922	.697
Babe Ruth	1927-1934	.681
Lou Gehrig	1927-1934	.664

OBP+Slugging

(minimum 2500 Plate Appearances)

Babe Ruth	1920-1927	1.247
Babe Ruth	1919-1926	1.230
Babe Ruth	1921-1928	1.222
Babe Ruth	1917-1924	1.220
Babe Ruth	1918-1925	1.204
Babe Ruth	1923-1930	1.204
Babe Ruth	1916-1923	1.193
Babe Ruth	1922-1929	1.191
Babe Ruth	1924-1931	1.188
Babe Ruth	1926-1933	1.179
Babe Ruth	1925-1932	1.175
Babe Ruth	1914-1921	1.166
Ted Williams	1941-1948	1.166
Babe Ruth	1915-1922	1.159
Babe Ruth	1927-1934	1.151

Games

Billy Williams	1963-1970	1,298

At-Bats

Pete Rose	1973-1980	5,252

Home Runs (Home)

Two tied at		193

Home Runs (Road)

Five tied at		187

AB/HR

(minimum 2500 Plate Appearances)

Babe Ruth	1920-1927	10.5

Extra-Base Hits

Lou Gehrig	1927-1934	738

Walks/PA

(minimum 2500 Plate Appearances)

Ted Williams	1941-1948	0.22

Intentional Walks

Barry Bonds	1990-1997	219

Hit By Pitch

Hughie Jennings	1894-1901	253

Sacrifice Hits

Ray Chapman	1913-1920	328

Sacrifice Flies

Ruben Sierra	1987-1994	78

Caught Stealing

Rickey Henderson	1979-1986	166

Stolen Base Pct.

(minimum 160 attempts)

Eric Davis	1985-1992	.887

GDP

Jim Rice	1981-1988	204

Secondary Average

(minimum 2500 Plate Appearances)

Babe Ruth	1920-1927	.677

Isolated Power

(minimum 2500 Plate Appearances)

Babe Ruth	1920-1927	.389

Top Eight-Year Pitching Performances

Wins

John Clarkson	1885-1892	293
John Clarkson	1884-1891	278
Tim Keefe	1882-1889	267
Tim Keefe	1883-1890	267
Tim Keefe	1881-1888	257
John Clarkson	1886-1893	256
Id Hoss Radbourn	1881-1888	251
Pud Galvin	1879-1886	250
Kid Nichols	1891-1898	249
Jim McCormick	1879-1886	247
Old Hoss Radbourn	1882-1889	246
Kid Nichols	1890-1897	245
Pud Galvin	1881-1888	244
Pud Galvin	1880-1887	241
Three tied at		240

Losses

Pud Galvin	1879-1886	207
Pud Galvin	1880-1887	201
Jim Whitney	1881-1888	195
Pud Galvin	1881-1888	191
Jim McCormick	1879-1886	183
Pud Galvin	1882-1889	183
Jim McCormick	1878-1885	180
Pud Galvin	1883-1890	173
Jim Whitney	1882-1889	169
Jim McCormick	1880-1887	166
Will White	1878-1885	163
Tim Keefe	1881-1888	161
Old Hoss Radbourn	1881-1888	159
Old Hoss Radbourn	1882-1889	159
Pud Galvin	1884-1891	158

Winning Percentage
(minimum 80 decisions)

Joe Wood	1912-1919	.784
Lefty Grove	1928-1935	.747
Sal Maglie	1945-1952	.744
Lefty Grove	1927-1934	.744
Spud Chandler	1938-1945	.737
Lefty Grove	1926-1933	.734
Whitey Ford	1950-1957	.734
Christy Mathewson	1903-1910	.732
Spud Chandler	1939-1946	.731
Spud Chandler	1937-1944	.729
Christy Mathewson	1904-1911	.728
Lefty Grove	1929-1936	.727
Christy Mathewson	1905-1912	.719
Sam Leever	1902-1909	.719
Six tied at		.714

Games

Kent Tekulve	1977-1984	613
Kent Tekulve	1976-1983	605
Kent Tekulve	1978-1985	602
Kent Tekulve	1979-1986	584
Kent Tekulve	1980-1987	580
Kent Tekulve	1981-1988	572
Mitch Williams	1986-1993	567
Kent Tekulve	1982-1989	564
Kent Tekulve	1975-1982	563
Rollie Fingers	1973-1980	548
Rollie Fingers	1972-1979	547
Rob Murphy	1987-1994	547
Pedro Borbon	1972-1979	546
Rollie Fingers	1971-1978	541
Ron Perranoski	1962-1969	536

Games Started

Pud Galvin	1879-1886	464
John Clarkson	1885-1892	449
Pud Galvin	1880-1887	446
Pud Galvin	1881-1888	442
Jim McCormick	1879-1886	435
Tim Keefe	1881-1888	429
Tim Keefe	1882-1889	429
Pud Galvin	1882-1889	429
John Clarkson	1884-1891	418
Tim Keefe	1883-1890	417
John Clarkson	1886-1893	414
Jim McCormick	1880-1887	411
Old Hoss Radbourn	1881-1888	410
Mickey Welch	1880-1887	408
Jim McCormick	1878-1885	407

Complete Games

Pud Galvin	1879-1886	439
John Clarkson	1885-1892	427
Pud Galvin	1881-1888	424
Pud Galvin	1880-1887	421
Tim Keefe	1881-1888	419
Jim McCormick	1879-1886	418
Pud Galvin	1882-1889	414
Tim Keefe	1882-1889	412
Old Hoss Radbourn	1881-1888	402
John Clarkson	1884-1891	397
Old Hoss Radbourn	1882-1889	396
Jim McCormick	1880-1887	395
Tim Keefe	1883-1890	394
Jim McCormick	1878-1885	392
Mickey Welch	1880-1887	392

Shutouts

Pete Alexander	1913-1920	67
Pete Alexander	1912-1919	63
Pete Alexander	1911-1918	61
Pete Alexander	1914-1921	61
Walter Johnson	1912-1919	60
Walter Johnson	1910-1917	59
Walter Johnson	1911-1918	59
Walter Johnson	1908-1915	58
Walter Johnson	1913-1920	57
Christy Mathewson	1902-1909	56
Pete Alexander	1915-1922	56
Walter Johnson	1909-1916	55
Four tied at		53

Saves

Dennis Eckersley	1988-1995	304
Dennis Eckersley	1990-1997	292
Dennis Eckersley	1987-1994	291
Lee Smith	1988-1995	291
Lee Smith	1987-1994	290
Dennis Eckersley	1989-1996	289
Lee Smith	1986-1993	288
Lee Smith	1985-1992	275
Dennis Eckersley	1986-1993	272
Jeff Reardon	1985-1992	271
Lee Smith	1984-1991	265
Jeff Reardon	1984-1991	264
Lee Smith	1989-1996	264
Randy Myers	1990-1997	263
Two tied at		250

Innings Pitched

Pud Galvin	1879-1886	4,070.2
John Clarkson	1885-1892	3,948.2
Pud Galvin	1880-1887	3,918.1
Pud Galvin	1881-1888	3,897.0
Jim McCormick	1879-1886	3,836.1
Pud Galvin	1882-1889	3,764.0
Tim Keefe	1881-1888	3,729.2
Old Hoss Radbourn	1881-1888	3,697.1
Tim Keefe	1882-1889	3,691.2
John Clarkson	1884-1891	3,677.2
Old Hoss Radbourn	1882-1889	3,649.0
John Clarkson	1886-1893	3,620.2
Jim McCormick	1880-1887	3,612.1
Jim McCormick	1878-1885	3,605.2
Tim Keefe	1883-1890	3,545.2

Walks

Amos Rusie	1890-1897	1,482
Nolan Ryan	1971-1978	1,304
Nolan Ryan	1972-1979	1,302
Amos Rusie	1891-1898	1,296
Gus Weyhing	1887-1894	1,259
Nolan Ryan	1970-1977	1,253
Nolan Ryan	1973-1980	1,243
Gus Weyhing	1888-1895	1,176
Nolan Ryan	1974-1981	1,149
Nolan Ryan	1969-1976	1,102
Ted Breitenstein	1892-1899	1,096
Bobo Newsom	1934-1941	1,095
Jack Stivetts	1889-1896	1,080
Gus Weyhing	1889-1896	1,080
Bobo Newsom	1936-1943	1,068

Strikeouts

Nolan Ryan	1972-1979	2,416
Nolan Ryan	1971-1978	2,330
Nolan Ryan	1973-1980	2,287
Nolan Ryan	1970-1977	2,195
Sandy Koufax	1959-1966	2,083
Nolan Ryan	1974-1981	2,044
Tim Keefe	1882-1889	2,043
Sam McDowell	1964-1971	2,021
Tim Keefe	1883-1890	2,015
Rube Waddell	1901-1908	1,980
Sam McDowell	1965-1972	1,966
Tom Seaver	1969-1976	1,959
Rube Waddell	1902-1909	1,949
Tom Seaver	1970-1977	1,947
Nolan Ryan	1969-1976	1,946

Strikeouts/9 Innings
(minimum 800 Innings Pitched)

Randy Johnson	1990-1997	10.73
Randy Johnson	1989-1996	10.14
Nolan Ryan	1986-1993	10.13
Nolan Ryan	1984-1991	10.05
Randy Johnson	1988-1995	10.01
Nolan Ryan	1985-1992	10.00
Nolan Ryan	1972-1979	9.97
Nolan Ryan	1971-1978	9.94
Nolan Ryan	1970-1977	9.84
Nolan Ryan	1983-1990	9.81
Nolan Ryan	1969-1976	9.74
Nolan Ryan	1966-1973	9.68
Nolan Ryan	1973-1980	9.66
Nolan Ryan	1982-1989	9.61
Nolan Ryan	1968-1975	9.57

ERA
(minimum 800 Innings Pitched)

Walter Johnson	1912-1919	1.59
Walter Johnson	1908-1915	1.60
Walter Johnson	1907-1914	1.62
Walter Johnson	1911-1918	1.63
Walter Johnson	1909-1916	1.63
Walter Johnson	1910-1917	1.64
Three Finger Brown	1903-1910	1.66
Ed Walsh	1904-1911	1.70
Walter Johnson	1913-1920	1.70
Three Finger Brown	1904-1911	1.72
Ed Walsh	1905-1912	1.73
Ed Walsh	1906-1913	1.74
Three Finger Brown	1905-1912	1.74
Ed Walsh	1907-1914	1.74
Ed Walsh	1908-1915	1.77

Component ERA
(minimum 800 Innings Pitched)

Walter Johnson	1912-1919	1.62
Ed Walsh	1904-1911	1.66
Walter Johnson	1910-1917	1.67
Addie Joss	1903-1910	1.67
Walter Johnson	1913-1920	1.67
Walter Johnson	1911-1918	1.68
Walter Johnson	1908-1915	1.69
Ed Walsh	1905-1912	1.70
Ed Walsh	1908-1915	1.70
Addie Joss	1902-1909	1.70
Walter Johnson	1909-1916	1.71
Walter Johnson	1907-1914	1.72
Ed Walsh	1906-1913	1.72
Ed Walsh	1907-1914	1.73
Three Finger Brown	1904-1911	1.74

Opponent Average
(minimum 800 Innings Pitched)

Hoyt Wilhelm	1962-1969	.194
Nolan Ryan	1966-1973	.195
Nolan Ryan	1970-1977	.195
Nolan Ryan	1969-1976	.195
Nolan Ryan	1968-1975	.196
Hoyt Wilhelm	1963-1970	.198
Hoyt Wilhelm	1961-1968	.198
Nolan Ryan	1972-1979	.198
Nolan Ryan	1971-1978	.198
Herb Score	1955-1962	.200
Sandy Koufax	1959-1966	.201
Nolan Ryan	1986-1993	.201
Sandy Koufax	1958-1965	.202
Hoyt Wilhelm	1960-1967	.202
Nolan Ryan	1984-1991	.203

Opponent OBP
(minimum 800 Innings Pitched)

Addie Joss	1903-1910	.253
Hoyt Wilhelm	1962-1969	.253
Walter Johnson	1912-1919	.255
Addie Joss	1902-1909	.256
Dennis Eckersley	1985-1992	.256
Ed Walsh	1904-1911	.257
Walter Johnson	1910-1917	.258
Walter Johnson	1913-1920	.258
Walter Johnson	1911-1918	.258
Hoyt Wilhelm	1963-1970	.258
Hoyt Wilhelm	1961-1968	.259
Cy Young	1901-1908	.259
Ed Walsh	1908-1915	.259
Ed Walsh	1905-1912	.259
Walter Johnson	1908-1915	.259

Games Finished

Dan Quisenberry	1980-1987	469

Batters Faced

Pud Galvin	1879-1886	17,084

Hits Allowed

Pud Galvin	1879-1886	4,287

Runs Allowed

Pud Galvin	1879-1886	2,203

Earned Runs

Gus Weyhing	1887-1894	1,277

Home Runs Allowed

Robin Roberts	1953-1960	287

Intentional Walks

Kent Tekulve	1978-1985	116

Sac Hits Allowed

George Mullin	1904-1911	328

Sac Flies Allowed

Charlie Hough	1987-1994	77

Hit Batsmen

Two tied at		160

Wild Pitches

Mickey Welch	1880-1887	224

Balks

Steve Carlton	1977-1984	61

Top Nine-Year Batting Performances

Runs

Billy Hamilton	1889-1897	1,322
Billy Hamilton	1890-1898	1,288
Lou Gehrig	1928-1936	1,268
Lou Gehrig	1929-1937	1,267
Lou Gehrig	1926-1934	1,260
Lou Gehrig	1930-1938	1,255
Lou Gehrig	1927-1935	1,250
Babe Ruth	1920-1928	1,244
Babe Ruth	1923-1931	1,235
Billy Hamilton	1891-1899	1,218
Hugh Duffy	1889-1897	1,208
Babe Ruth	1921-1929	1,207
Willie Keeler	1894-1902	1,206
Lou Gehrig	1925-1933	1,205
Babe Ruth	1924-1932	1,204

Hits

Willie Keeler	1894-1902	1,905
Jesse Burkett	1893-1901	1,891
Jesse Burkett	1894-1902	1,882
Rogers Hornsby	1921-1929	1,867
Pete Rose	1968-1976	1,863
Bill Terry	1927-1935	1,861
Paul Waner	1926-1934	1,860
Pete Rose	1969-1977	1,857
Rogers Hornsby	1920-1928	1,856
Paul Waner	1927-1935	1,856
Wade Boggs	1983-1991	1,847
Willie Keeler	1895-1903	1,846
Jesse Burkett	1895-1903	1,846
Pete Rose	1965-1973	1,843
Pete Rose	1971-1979	1,840

Doubles

Tris Speaker	1919-1927	413
Joe Medwick	1933-1941	404
Tris Speaker	1918-1926	403
Joe Medwick	1934-1942	401
Tris Speaker	1916-1924	399
Tris Speaker	1920-1928	397
Tris Speaker	1917-1925	393
Joe Medwick	1935-1943	391
Wade Boggs	1983-1991	386
Charlie Gehringer	1929-1937	384
Joe Medwick	1932-1940	383
Ed Delahanty	1894-1902	376
Tris Speaker	1914-1922	375
Lou Gehrig	1926-1934	375

Triples

Sam Crawford	1907-1915	169
Sam Crawford	1906-1914	166
Sam Crawford	1908-1916	165
Sam Crawford	1902-1910	155
Sam Crawford	1900-1908	153
Sam Crawford	1901-1909	152
Sam Crawford	1905-1913	150
Jake Beckley	1890-1898	149
Sam Crawford	1909-1917	149
Roger Connor	1886-1894	148
Ty Cobb	1910-1918	148
Ty Cobb	1911-1919	148
Jake Beckley	1889-1897	147
Elmer Flick	1899-1907	147
Sam Crawford	1903-1911	147

Home Runs

Babe Ruth	1920-1928	421
Babe Ruth	1923-1931	414
Babe Ruth	1924-1932	414
Babe Ruth	1921-1929	413
Babe Ruth	1922-1930	403
Babe Ruth	1925-1933	402
Babe Ruth	1926-1934	399
Babe Ruth	1919-1927	396
Jimmie Foxx	1932-1940	384
Jimmie Foxx	1930-1938	380
Jimmie Foxx	1931-1939	378
Harmon Killebrew	1959-1967	369
Jimmie Foxx	1929-1937	363
Harmon Killebrew	1961-1969	362
Babe Ruth	1927-1935	358

Total Bases

Lou Gehrig	1926-1934	3,414
Lou Gehrig	1927-1935	3,412
Lou Gehrig	1929-1937	3,370
Lou Gehrig	1928-1936	3,368
Lou Gehrig	1930-1938	3,349
Babe Ruth	1920-1928	3,265
Jimmie Foxx	1930-1938	3,256
Babe Ruth	1923-1931	3,248
Lou Gehrig	1925-1933	3,237
Jimmie Foxx	1932-1940	3,229
Babe Ruth	1921-1929	3,225
Jimmie Foxx	1931-1939	3,222
Stan Musial	1946-1954	3,190
Hank Aaron	1955-1963	3,190
Jimmie Foxx	1929-1937	3,181

RBI

Lou Gehrig	1927-1935	1,375
Lou Gehrig	1929-1937	1,369
Lou Gehrig	1926-1934	1,368
Lou Gehrig	1930-1938	1,357
Lou Gehrig	1928-1936	1,352
Jimmie Foxx	1930-1938	1,298
Lou Gehrig	1925-1933	1,271
Jimmie Foxx	1931-1939	1,247
Babe Ruth	1924-1932	1,246
Babe Ruth	1926-1934	1,246
Jimmie Foxx	1932-1940	1,246
Babe Ruth	1923-1931	1,240
Jimmie Foxx	1929-1937	1,240
Babe Ruth	1925-1933	1,228
Jimmie Foxx	1928-1936	1,192

Walks

Babe Ruth	1920-1928	1,164
Babe Ruth	1919-1927	1,130
Babe Ruth	1923-1931	1,124
Babe Ruth	1926-1934	1,100
Babe Ruth	1921-1929	1,088
Babe Ruth	1924-1932	1,084
Babe Ruth	1922-1930	1,080
Eddie Yost	1948-1956	1,069
Eddie Yost	1949-1957	1,060
Eddie Yost	1953-1961	1,056
Mickey Mantle	1954-1962	1,054
Eddie Yost	1950-1958	1,050
Babe Ruth	1918-1926	1,049
Eddie Yost	1951-1959	1,044
Eddie Yost	1952-1960	1,043

Strikeouts

Rob Deer	1985-1993	1,369
Bobby Bonds	1969-1977	1,300
Bobby Bonds	1968-1976	1,243
Bobby Bonds	1970-1978	1,233
Rob Deer	1984-1992	1,210
Dick Allen	1964-1972	1,203
Dale Murphy	1982-1990	1,193
Juan Samuel	1984-1992	1,192
Reggie Jackson	1968-1976	1,191
Bobby Bonds	1971-1979	1,179
Juan Samuel	1983-1991	1,159
Dale Murphy	1983-1991	1,152
Reggie Jackson	1969-1977	1,149
Reggie Jackson	1977-1985	1,148
Jose Canseco	1986-1994	1,143

Stolen Bases

Billy Hamilton	1889-1897	768
Rickey Henderson	1980-1988	761
Rickey Henderson	1982-1990	747
Rickey Henderson	1981-1989	738
Billy Hamilton	1888-1896	721
Rickey Henderson	1979-1987	711
Billy Hamilton	1890-1898	701
Arlie Latham	1886-1894	688
Arlie Latham	1887-1895	676
Rickey Henderson	1983-1991	675
Vince Coleman	1985-1993	648
Arlie Latham	1885-1893	629
Billy Hamilton	1891-1899	628
Rickey Henderson	1984-1992	615
Lou Brock	1966-1974	607

Runs Created

Lou Gehrig	1929-1937	1,474
Lou Gehrig	1930-1938	1,468
Lou Gehrig	1927-1935	1,464
Lou Gehrig	1928-1936	1,463
Babe Ruth	1920-1928	1,458
Lou Gehrig	1926-1934	1,446
Babe Ruth	1923-1931	1,445
Babe Ruth	1919-1927	1,414
Babe Ruth	1921-1929	1,405
Babe Ruth	1924-1932	1,399
Babe Ruth	1922-1930	1,373
Babe Ruth	1926-1934	1,359
Lou Gehrig	1925-1933	1,354
Babe Ruth	1925-1933	1,342
Jimmie Foxx	1930-1938	1,341

Runs Created/27 Outs
(minimum 2750 Plate Appearances)

Babe Ruth	1920-1928	12.83
Ted Williams	1941-1949	12.82
Babe Ruth	1919-1927	12.77
Babe Ruth	1918-1926	12.45
Ted Williams	1940-1948	12.44
Babe Ruth	1916-1924	12.40
Babe Ruth	1923-1931	12.31
Babe Ruth	1921-1929	12.20
Babe Ruth	1917-1925	12.14
Ted Williams	1942-1950	12.13
Babe Ruth	1915-1923	12.11
Babe Ruth	1924-1932	12.07
Ted Williams	1939-1947	11.99
Ted Williams	1946-1954	11.90
Babe Ruth	1922-1930	11.88

Batting Average
(minimum 2750 Plate Appearances)

Ty Cobb	1911-1919	.388
Ty Cobb	1910-1918	.387
Ty Cobb	1909-1917	.387
Rogers Hornsby	1921-1929	.384
Rogers Hornsby	1920-1928	.383
Willie Keeler	1892-1900	.381
Rogers Hornsby	1922-1930	.380
Ty Cobb	1908-1916	.379
Ty Cobb	1912-1920	.378
Ty Cobb	1914-1922	.377
Ty Cobb	1907-1915	.377
Willie Keeler	1893-1901	.376
Jesse Burkett	1893-1901	.376
Rogers Hornsby	1919-1927	.376
Ed Delahanty	1894-1902	.375

On-Base Percentage
(minimum 2750 Plate Appearances)

Ted Williams	1941-1949	.505
Ted Williams	1940-1948	.497
Babe Ruth	1919-1927	.494
Babe Ruth	1920-1928	.493
Ted Williams	1942-1950	.491
John McGraw	1896-1904	.490
Ted Williams	1949-1957	.489
Ted Williams	1946-1954	.489
Ted Williams	1947-1955	.489
Babe Ruth	1918-1926	.489
Ted Williams	1939-1947	.487
Babe Ruth	1923-1931	.486
John McGraw	1895-1903	.486
Ted Williams	1948-1956	.486
Babe Ruth	1916-1924	.485

Slugging Percentage
(minimum 2750 Plate Appearances)

Babe Ruth	1920-1928	.745
Babe Ruth	1919-1927	.740
Babe Ruth	1921-1929	.729
Babe Ruth	1918-1926	.722
Babe Ruth	1916-1924	.717
Babe Ruth	1923-1931	.717
Babe Ruth	1922-1930	.715
Babe Ruth	1917-1925	.711
Babe Ruth	1915-1923	.709
Babe Ruth	1924-1932	.705
Babe Ruth	1914-1922	.696
Babe Ruth	1925-1933	.688
Babe Ruth	1926-1934	.688
Babe Ruth	1927-1935	.677
Ted Williams	1941-1949	.657

OBP+Slugging
(minimum 2750 Plate Appearances)

Babe Ruth	1920-1928	1.238
Babe Ruth	1919-1927	1.234
Babe Ruth	1921-1929	1.211
Babe Ruth	1918-1926	1.210
Babe Ruth	1923-1931	1.203
Babe Ruth	1916-1924	1.202
Babe Ruth	1922-1930	1.195
Babe Ruth	1917-1925	1.193
Babe Ruth	1915-1923	1.186
Babe Ruth	1924-1932	1.184
Babe Ruth	1926-1934	1.163
Ted Williams	1941-1949	1.161
Babe Ruth	1925-1933	1.159
Babe Ruth	1914-1922	1.157
Babe Ruth	1927-1935	1.144

Games

Billy Williams	1962-1970	1,457

At-Bats

Pete Rose	1972-1980	5,897

Home Runs (Home)

Jimmie Foxx	1930-1938	215

Home Runs (Road)

Two tied at		212

AB/HR
(minimum 2750 Plate Appearances)

Babe Ruth	1920-1928	10.4

Extra-Base Hits

Lou Gehrig	1926-1934	821

Walks/PA
(minimum 2750 Plate Appearances)

Ted Williams	1941-1949	0.22

Intentional Walks

Barry Bonds	1989-1997	241

Hit By Pitch

Hughie Jennings	1894-1902	264

Sacrifice Hits

Ray Chapman	1912-1920	340

Sacrifice Flies

Ruben Sierra	1987-1995	86

Caught Stealing

Brett Butler	1983-1991	179

Stolen Base Pct.
(minimum 180 attempts)

Three tied at		.875

GDP

Jim Rice	1980-1988	220

Secondary Average
(minimum 2750 Plate Appearances)

Babe Ruth	1920-1928	.673

Isolated Power
(minimum 2750 Plate Appearances)

Babe Ruth	1920-1928	.388

Top Nine-Year Pitching Performances

Wins

John Clarkson	1885-1893	309
John Clarkson	1884-1892	303
Tim Keefe	1881-1889	285
Tim Keefe	1882-1890	284
Pud Galvin	1879-1887	278
Kid Nichols	1890-1898	276
Old Hoss Radbourn	1882-1890	273
Old Hoss Radbourn	1881-1889	271
Tim Keefe	1883-1891	271
Kid Nichols	1891-1899	270
Pud Galvin	1881-1889	267
Pud Galvin	1880-1888	264
John Clarkson	1886-1894	264
Tim Keefe	1880-1888	263
Jim McCormick	1879-1887	260

Losses

Pud Galvin	1879-1887	228
Pud Galvin	1880-1888	226
Pud Galvin	1881-1889	207
Jim McCormick	1879-1887	206
Jim Whitney	1881-1889	202
Pud Galvin	1882-1890	196
Jim McCormick	1878-1886	191
Pud Galvin	1883-1891	187
Mickey Welch	1880-1888	175
Gus Weyhing	1887-1895	175
Tim Keefe	1881-1889	174
Jim Whitney	1882-1890	171
Old Hoss Radbourn	1882-1890	171
Old Hoss Radbourn	1881-1889	170
Pud Galvin	1884-1892	170

Winning Percentage
(minimum 90 decisions)

Spud Chandler	1938-1946	.732
Lefty Grove	1927-1935	.730
Lefty Grove	1928-1936	.730
Spud Chandler	1937-1945	.727
Christy Mathewson	1903-1911	.724
Whitey Ford	1950-1958	.724
Spud Chandler	1939-1947	.721
Christy Mathewson	1904-1912	.721
Sam Leever	1901-1909	.720
Lefty Grove	1926-1934	.720
Lefty Grove	1929-1937	.720
Joe Wood	1911-1919	.719
Lefty Grove	1930-1938	.719
Christy Mathewson	1905-1913	.716
Whitey Ford	1956-1964	.714

Games

Kent Tekulve	1976-1984	677
Kent Tekulve	1978-1986	675
Kent Tekulve	1977-1985	674
Kent Tekulve	1979-1987	674
Kent Tekulve	1980-1988	650
Kent Tekulve	1975-1983	639
Rollie Fingers	1972-1980	613
Kent Tekulve	1981-1989	609
Ron Perranoski	1962-1970	603
Mike Marshall	1971-1979	600
Rollie Fingers	1971-1979	595
Rollie Fingers	1973-1981	595
Lee Smith	1982-1990	592
Mitch Williams	1986-1994	592
Lee Smith	1984-1992	591

Games Started

Pud Galvin	1879-1887	512
Pud Galvin	1880-1888	496
John Clarkson	1885-1893	484
Pud Galvin	1881-1889	482
Tim Keefe	1881-1889	474
Jim McCormick	1879-1887	471
John Clarkson	1884-1892	462
Tim Keefe	1882-1890	459
Mickey Welch	1880-1888	455
Pud Galvin	1882-1890	454
Jim McCormick	1878-1886	449
Old Hoss Radbourn	1882-1890	443
Tim Keefe	1880-1888	441
Old Hoss Radbourn	1881-1889	441
Two tied at		434

Complete Games

Pud Galvin	1879-1887	486
Pud Galvin	1880-1888	470
Pud Galvin	1881-1889	462
John Clarkson	1885-1893	458
Tim Keefe	1881-1889	457
Jim McCormick	1879-1887	454
Mickey Welch	1880-1888	439
John Clarkson	1884-1892	439
Pud Galvin	1882-1890	437
Tim Keefe	1882-1890	435
Old Hoss Radbourn	1882-1890	432
Tim Keefe	1880-1888	431
Jim McCormick	1878-1886	430
Old Hoss Radbourn	1881-1889	430
Mickey Welch	1881-1889	414

Shutouts

Pete Alexander	1911-1919	70
Pete Alexander	1912-1920	70
Pete Alexander	1913-1921	70
Walter Johnson	1910-1918	67
Walter Johnson	1911-1919	66
Walter Johnson	1912-1920	64
Walter Johnson	1909-1917	63
Pete Alexander	1914-1922	62
Christy Mathewson	1901-1909	61
Walter Johnson	1908-1916	61
Walter Johnson	1907-1915	60
Pete Alexander	1915-1923	59
Christy Mathewson	1902-1910	58
Walter Johnson	1913-1921	58
Christy Mathewson	1903-1911	55

Saves

Dennis Eckersley	1988-1996	334
Lee Smith	1987-1995	327
Dennis Eckersley	1989-1997	325
Lee Smith	1985-1993	321
Lee Smith	1986-1994	321
Dennis Eckersley	1987-1995	320
Lee Smith	1984-1992	308
Lee Smith	1983-1991	294
Jeff Reardon	1984-1992	294
Lee Smith	1988-1996	293
Dennis Eckersley	1986-1994	291
Randy Myers	1989-1997	287
Jeff Reardon	1983-1991	285
Jeff Reardon	1985-1993	279
Bruce Sutter	1977-1985	273

Innings Pitched

Pud Galvin	1879-1887	4,511.1
Pud Galvin	1880-1888	4,355.2
John Clarkson	1885-1893	4,243.2
Pud Galvin	1881-1889	4,238.0
Jim McCormick	1879-1887	4,158.2
Tim Keefe	1881-1889	4,093.2
John Clarkson	1884-1892	4,066.2
Old Hoss Radbourn	1882-1890	3,992.0
Pud Galvin	1882-1890	3,981.0
Old Hoss Radbourn	1881-1889	3,974.1
Mickey Welch	1880-1888	3,969.2
Jim McCormick	1878-1886	3,953.1
Tim Keefe	1882-1890	3,920.2
Tim Keefe	1880-1888	3,834.2
Pud Galvin	1883-1891	3,782.1

Walks

Amos Rusie	1889-1897	1,598
Amos Rusie	1890-1898	1,585
Nolan Ryan	1971-1979	1,418
Nolan Ryan	1970-1978	1,401
Nolan Ryan	1972-1980	1,400
Gus Weyhing	1887-1895	1,343
Nolan Ryan	1973-1981	1,311
Nolan Ryan	1969-1977	1,306
Nolan Ryan	1974-1982	1,258
Bobo Newsom	1934-1942	1,201
Gus Weyhing	1888-1896	1,191
Nolan Ryan	1968-1976	1,177
Ted Breitenstein	1892-1900	1,175
Bobo Newsom	1935-1943	1,165
Nolan Ryan	1975-1983	1,157

Strikeouts

Nolan Ryan	1972-1980	2,616
Nolan Ryan	1971-1979	2,553
Nolan Ryan	1970-1978	2,455
Nolan Ryan	1973-1981	2,427
Nolan Ryan	1974-1982	2,289
Sandy Koufax	1958-1966	2,214
Tom Seaver	1970-1978	2,173
Tom Seaver	1968-1976	2,164
Tom Seaver	1969-1977	2,155
Tim Keefe	1881-1889	2,146
Sam McDowell	1964-1972	2,143
Tim Keefe	1882-1890	2,131
Rube Waddell	1901-1909	2,121
Nolan Ryan	1969-1977	2,287
Nolan Ryan	1976-1984	2,116

Strikeouts/9 Innings
(minimum 900 Innings Pitched)

Randy Johnson	1989-1997	10.41
Randy Johnson	1988-1996	10.11
Nolan Ryan	1984-1992	9.96
Nolan Ryan	1983-1991	9.88
Nolan Ryan	1970-1978	9.85
Nolan Ryan	1985-1993	9.85
Nolan Ryan	1971-1979	9.85
Nolan Ryan	1969-1977	9.82
Nolan Ryan	1972-1980	9.75
Nolan Ryan	1966-1974	9.74
Nolan Ryan	1968-1976	9.68
Nolan Ryan	1982-1990	9.68
Nolan Ryan	1973-1981	9.58
Sandy Koufax	1957-1965	9.56
Nolan Ryan	1981-1989	9.52

ERA
(minimum 900 Innings Pitched)

Walter Johnson	1910-1918	1.60
Walter Johnson	1907-1915	1.61
Walter Johnson	1911-1919	1.62
Walter Johnson	1908-1916	1.64
Walter Johnson	1912-1920	1.66
Walter Johnson	1909-1917	1.69
Ed Walsh	1907-1915	1.74
Three Finger Brown	1904-1912	1.75
Ed Walsh	1906-1914	1.76
Ed Walsh	1905-1913	1.76
Ed Walsh	1904-1912	1.77
Ed Walsh	1908-1916	1.77
Three Finger Brown	1903-1911	1.79
Three Finger Brown	1905-1913	1.83
Christy Mathewson	1905-1913	1.85

Component ERA
(minimum 900 Innings Pitched)

Walter Johnson	1912-1920	1.65
Walter Johnson	1910-1918	1.66
Walter Johnson	1911-1919	1.68
Walter Johnson	1908-1916	1.70
Walter Johnson	1909-1917	1.71
Ed Walsh	1908-1916	1.71
Walter Johnson	1907-1915	1.71
Ed Walsh	1904-1912	1.71
Addie Joss	1902-1910	1.73
Ed Walsh	1906-1914	1.73
Ed Walsh	1907-1915	1.73
Ed Walsh	1905-1913	1.74
Three Finger Brown	1904-1912	1.79
alter Johnson	1913-1921	1.82
Hoyt Wilhelm	1961-1969	1.88

Opponent Average
(minimum 900 Innings Pitched)

Nolan Ryan	1966-1974	.194
Nolan Ryan	1969-1977	.195
Nolan Ryan	1968-1976	.196
Hoyt Wilhelm	1961-1969	.197
Hoyt Wilhelm	1962-1970	.198
Nolan Ryan	1970-1978	.198
Nolan Ryan	1971-1979	.200
Nolan Ryan	1972-1980	.202
Sandy Koufax	1958-1966	.202
Nolan Ryan	1983-1991	.202
Hoyt Wilhelm	1960-1968	.202
Sandy Koufax	1957-1965	.202
Sid Fernandez	1985-1993	.203
Sid Fernandez	1983-1991	.205
Nolan Ryan	1973-1981	.205

Opponent OBP
(minimum 900 Innings Pitched)

Addie Joss	1902-1910	.257
Walter Johnson	1912-1920	.257
Walter Johnson	1910-1918	.258
Hoyt Wilhelm	1961-1969	.258
Walter Johnson	1911-1919	.258
Dennis Eckersley	1985-1993	.259
Ed Walsh	1908-1916	.259
Ed Walsh	1904-1912	.260
Walter Johnson	1907-1915	.260
Hoyt Wilhelm	1962-1970	.260
Walter Johnson	1908-1916	.261
Walter Johnson	1909-1917	.261
Ed Walsh	1907-1915	.261
George Bradley	1876-1884	.261
Ed Walsh	1906-1914	.261

Games Finished

Lee Smith	1983-1991	507

Batters Faced

Pud Galvin	1879-1887	18,981

Hits Allowed

Pud Galvin	1879-1887	4,777

Runs Allowed

Pud Galvin	1879-1887	2,462

Earned Runs

Gus Weyhing	1887-1895	1,426

Home Runs Allowed

Robin Roberts	1952-1960	309

Intentional Walks

Kent Tekulve	1978-1986	126

Sac Hits Allowed

George Mullin	1903-1911	359

Sac Flies Allowed

Larry Gura	1976-1984	81

Hit Batsmen

Joe McGinnity	1899-1907	175

Wild Pitches

Mickey Welch	1880-1888	241

Balks

Two tied at		64

Top Ten-Year Batting Performances

Runs

Billy Hamilton	1889-1898	1,432
Lou Gehrig	1927-1936	1,417
Lou Gehrig	1928-1937	1,406
Lou Gehrig	1926-1935	1,385
Lou Gehrig	1929-1938	1,382
Babe Ruth	1920-1929	1,365
Babe Ruth	1921-1930	1,357
Babe Ruth	1923-1932	1,355
Billy Hamilton	1890-1899	1,351
Babe Ruth	1919-1928	1,347
Billy Hamilton	1888-1897	1,343
Lou Gehrig	1925-1934	1,333
Babe Ruth	1922-1931	1,329
Billy Hamilton	1891-1900	1,321
Hugh Duffy	1889-1898	1,305

Hits

Rogers Hornsby	1920-1929	2,085
Paul Waner	1927-1936	2,074
Pete Rose	1968-1977	2,067
Willie Keeler	1894-1903	2,065
Jesse Burkett	1893-1902	2,060
Jesse Burkett	1892-1901	2,058
Paul Waner	1928-1937	2,056
Pete Rose	1969-1978	2,055
Pete Rose	1970-1979	2,045
Pete Rose	1967-1976	2,039
Paul Waner	1926-1935	2,036
Jesse Burkett	1894-1903	2,033
Willie Keeler	1895-1904	2,032
Pete Rose	1966-1975	2,029
Pete Rose	1965-1974	2,028

Doubles

Tris Speaker	1918-1927	446
Tris Speaker	1917-1926	445
Joe Medwick	1933-1942	441
Tris Speaker	1919-1928	435
Tris Speaker	1914-1923	434
Tris Speaker	1916-1925	434
Joe Medwick	1934-1943	431
Tris Speaker	1915-1924	424
Charlie Gehringer	1929-1938	416
Joe Medwick	1932-1941	416
Tris Speaker	1912-1921	415
Joe Medwick	1935-1944	415
Paul Waner	1927-1936	414
Charlie Gehringer	1928-1937	413
Harry Heilmann	1921-1930	412

Triples

Sam Crawford	1906-1915	185
Sam Crawford	1907-1916	182
Sam Crawford	1905-1914	176
Sam Crawford	1901-1910	171
Sam Crawford	1902-1911	169
Sam Crawford	1903-1912	168
Sam Crawford	1900-1909	167
Sam Crawford	1904-1913	166
Jake Beckley	1890-1899	165
Sam Crawford	1908-1917	165
Ty Cobb	1908-1917	164
Roger Connor	1885-1894	163
Joe Jackson	1911-1920	163
Ty Cobb	1910-1919	161
Two tied at		160

Home Runs

Babe Ruth	1920-1929	467
Babe Ruth	1921-1930	462
Babe Ruth	1923-1932	455
Babe Ruth	1919-1928	450
Babe Ruth	1922-1931	449
Babe Ruth	1924-1933	448
Babe Ruth	1925-1934	424
Jimmie Foxx	1930-1939	415
Jimmie Foxx	1931-1940	414
Jimmie Foxx	1929-1938	413
Babe Ruth	1918-1927	407
Babe Ruth	1926-1935	405
Jimmie Foxx	1932-1941	403
Harmon Killebrew	1961-1970	403
Harmon Killebrew	1960-1969	393

Total Bases

Lou Gehrig	1927-1936	3,815
Lou Gehrig	1928-1937	3,734
Lou Gehrig	1926-1935	3,726
Lou Gehrig	1929-1938	3,671
Lou Gehrig	1925-1934	3,646
Babe Ruth	1920-1929	3,613
Babe Ruth	1921-1930	3,604
Jimmie Foxx	1930-1939	3,580
Jimmie Foxx	1929-1938	3,579
Babe Ruth	1923-1932	3,550
Babe Ruth	1919-1928	3,549
Willie Mays	1954-1963	3,525
Babe Ruth	1922-1931	3,521
Jimmie Foxx	1931-1940	3,521
Stan Musial	1946-1955	3,508

RBI

Lou Gehrig	1927-1936	1,527
Lou Gehrig	1928-1937	1,511
Lou Gehrig	1926-1935	1,487
Lou Gehrig	1929-1938	1,483
Lou Gehrig	1925-1934	1,436
Jimmie Foxx	1929-1938	1,415
Jimmie Foxx	1930-1939	1,403
Babe Ruth	1923-1932	1,377
Jimmie Foxx	1931-1940	1,366
Lou Gehrig	1930-1939	1,358
Jimmie Foxx	1932-1941	1,351
Babe Ruth	1924-1933	1,349
Babe Ruth	1921-1930	1,344
Babe Ruth	1922-1931	1,336
Babe Ruth	1920-1929	1,328

Walks

Babe Ruth	1919-1928	1,265
Babe Ruth	1923-1932	1,254
Babe Ruth	1920-1929	1,236
Babe Ruth	1921-1930	1,224
Babe Ruth	1922-1931	1,208
Babe Ruth	1924-1933	1,198
Babe Ruth	1918-1927	1,187
Eddie Yost	1950-1959	1,185
Eddie Yost	1951-1960	1,169
Babe Ruth	1925-1934	1,159
Lou Gehrig	1929-1938	1,145
Eddie Yost	1948-1957	1,142
Eddie Yost	1949-1958	1,141
Lou Gehrig	1928-1937	1,133
Mickey Mantle	1953-1962	1,133

Strikeouts

Bobby Bonds	1969-1978	1,420
Bobby Bonds	1968-1977	1,384
Rob Deer	1984-1993	1,379
Bobby Bonds	1970-1979	1,368
Reggie Jackson	1968-1977	1,320
Dale Murphy	1982-1991	1,286
Reggie Jackson	1969-1978	1,282
Mike Schmidt	1974-1983	1,276
Dale Murphy	1980-1989	1,268
Dale Murphy	1981-1990	1,265
Mike Schmidt	1973-1982	1,264
Reggie Jackson	1977-1986	1,263
Reggie Jackson	1976-1985	1,256
Dick Allen	1964-1973	1,254
Mike Schmidt	1975-1984	1,254

Stolen Bases

Rickey Henderson	1980-1989	838
Billy Hamilton	1889-1898	822
Rickey Henderson	1982-1991	805
Rickey Henderson	1981-1990	803
Rickey Henderson	1979-1988	794
Billy Hamilton	1888-1897	787
Arlie Latham	1886-1895	736
Billy Hamilton	1890-1899	730
Rickey Henderson	1983-1992	723
Vince Coleman	1985-1994	698
Arlie Latham	1885-1894	688
Arlie Latham	1887-1896	678
Lou Brock	1965-1974	670
Rickey Henderson	1984-1993	668
Lou Brock	1966-1975	663

Runs Created

Lou Gehrig	1927-1936	1,645
Lou Gehrig	1928-1937	1,630
Lou Gehrig	1929-1938	1,605
Babe Ruth	1920-1929	1,596
Babe Ruth	1923-1932	1,592
Lou Gehrig	1926-1935	1,591
Babe Ruth	1921-1930	1,581
Babe Ruth	1919-1928	1,579
Babe Ruth	1922-1931	1,552
Lou Gehrig	1925-1934	1,525
Babe Ruth	1924-1933	1,521
Babe Ruth	1918-1927	1,488
Jimmie Foxx	1929-1938	1,486
Jimmie Foxx	1930-1939	1,483
Lou Gehrig	1930-1939	1,469

Runs Created/27 Outs
(minimum 3000 Plate Appearances)

Babe Ruth	1919-1928	12.62
Ted Williams	1941-1950	12.62
Babe Ruth	1920-1929	12.59
Babe Ruth	1918-1927	12.46
Babe Ruth	1923-1932	12.35
Ted Williams	1940-1949	12.32
Babe Ruth	1915-1924	12.30
Babe Ruth	1917-1926	12.27
Babe Ruth	1921-1930	12.26
Ted Williams	1939-1948	12.12
Babe Ruth	1922-1931	12.09
Babe Ruth	1914-1923	12.08
Ted Williams	1946-1955	11.95
Ted Williams	1948-1957	11.94
Babe Ruth	1924-1933	11.86

Batting Average
(minimum 3000 Plate Appearances)

Ty Cobb	1910-1919	.387
Ty Cobb	1909-1918	.386
Ty Cobb	1911-1920	.383
Rogers Hornsby	1920-1929	.382
Rogers Hornsby	1921-1930	.382
Ty Cobb	1908-1917	.380
Ty Cobb	1912-1921	.379
Ty Cobb	1913-1922	.378
Rogers Hornsby	1922-1931	.377
Rogers Hornsby	1919-1928	.377
Ty Cobb	1907-1916	.376
Willie Keeler	1892-1901	.376
Ed Delahanty	1893-1902	.374
Ed Delahanty	1894-1903	.374
Ty Cobb	1914-1923	.373

On-Base Percentage
(minimum 3000 Plate Appearances)

Ted Williams	1941-1950	.500
Ted Williams	1940-1949	.496
Ted Williams	1948-1957	.490
Babe Ruth	1919-1928	.490
Ted Williams	1946-1955	.490
Babe Ruth	1918-1927	.488
Ted Williams	1939-1948	.488
Ted Williams	1947-1956	.488
Babe Ruth	1920-1929	.488
Ted Williams	1942-1951	.487
Babe Ruth	1923-1932	.486
John McGraw	1895-1904	.486
Babe Ruth	1917-1926	.486
Ted Williams	1949-1958	.486
Babe Ruth	1921-1930	.484

Slugging Percentage
(minimum 3000 Plate Appearances)

Babe Ruth	1920-1929	.740
Babe Ruth	1919-1928	.737
Babe Ruth	1921-1930	.729
Babe Ruth	1918-1927	.727
Babe Ruth	1917-1926	.714
Babe Ruth	1915-1924	.713
Babe Ruth	1922-1931	.713
Babe Ruth	1923-1932	.712
Babe Ruth	1914-1923	.708
Babe Ruth	1916-1925	.701
Babe Ruth	1924-1933	.694
Babe Ruth	1926-1935	.684
Babe Ruth	1925-1934	.677
Lou Gehrig	1927-1936	.660
Ted Williams	1941-1950	.656

OBP+Slugging
(minimum 3000 Plate Appearances)

Babe Ruth	1920-1929	1.227
Babe Ruth	1919-1928	1.227
Babe Ruth	1918-1927	1.216
Babe Ruth	1921-1930	1.213
Babe Ruth	1917-1926	1.200
Babe Ruth	1923-1932	1.198
Babe Ruth	1915-1924	1.196
Babe Ruth	1922-1931	1.195
Babe Ruth	1914-1923	1.184
Babe Ruth	1916-1925	1.178
Babe Ruth	1924-1933	1.169
Babe Ruth	1926-1935	1.157
Ted Williams	1941-1950	1.155
Babe Ruth	1925-1934	1.146
Ted Williams	1940-1949	1.143

Games

Two tied at		1,617

At-Bats

Pete Rose	1971-1980	6,529

Home Runs (Home)

Jimmie Foxx	1929-1938	233

Home Runs (Road)

Babe Ruth	1920-1929	237

AB/HR
(minimum 3000 Plate Appearances)

Babe Ruth	1920-1929	10.5

Extra-Base Hits

Lou Gehrig	1927-1936	897

Walks/PA
(minimum 3000 Plate Appearances)

Ted Williams	1941-1950	0.22

Intentional Walks

Barry Bonds	1988-1997	255

Hit By Pitch

Hughie Jennings	1893-1902	268

Sacrifice Hits

Two tied at		310

Sacrifice Flies

Ruben Sierra	1987-1996	95

Caught Stealing

Brett Butler	1983-1992	200

Stolen Base Pct.
(minimum 200 attempts)

Eric Davis	1985-1994	.873

GDP

Jim Rice	1979-1988	236

Secondary Average
(minimum 3000 Plate Appearances)

Babe Ruth	1919-1928	.665

Isolated Power
(minimum 3000 Plate Appearances)

Babe Ruth	1920-1929	.385

Top Ten-Year Pitching Performances

Wins

John Clarkson	1884-1893	319
John Clarkson	1885-1894	317
Tim Keefe	1881-1890	302
Pud Galvin	1879-1888	301
Old Hoss Radbourn	1881-1890	298
Kid Nichols	1890-1899	297
Tim Keefe	1880-1889	291
Tim Keefe	1883-1892	290
Tim Keefe	1882-1891	288
Pud Galvin	1880-1889	287
Mickey Welch	1880-1889	285
Old Hoss Radbourn	1882-1891	284
Kid Nichols	1891-1900	283
Cy Young	1892-1901	283
Three tied at		279

Losses

Pud Galvin	1879-1888	253
Pud Galvin	1880-1889	242
Pud Galvin	1881-1890	220
Jim McCormick	1878-1887	214
Pud Galvin	1882-1891	210
Jim Whitney	1881-1890	204
Pud Galvin	1883-1892	199
Mickey Welch	1880-1889	187
Tim Keefe	1881-1890	185
Old Hoss Radbourn	1882-1891	184
Old Hoss Radbourn	1881-1890	182
Tim Keefe	1880-1889	180
Pink Hawley	1892-1901	179
Chick Fraser	1896-1905	179
Gus Weyhing	1887-1896	178

Winning Percentage
(minimum 100 decisions)

Spud Chandler	1937-1946	.725
Lefty Grove	1930-1939	.724
Lefty Grove	1929-1938	.723
Spud Chandler	1938-1947	.723
Lefty Grove	1928-1937	.723
Joe Wood	1911-1920	.719
Christy Mathewson	1904-1913	.718
Christy Mathewson	1903-1912	.718
Lefty Grove	1927-1936	.716
Whitey Ford	1955-1964	.715
Sam Leever	1901-1910	.712
Lefty Grove	1926-1935	.710
Christy Mathewson	1905-1914	.710
Whitey Ford	1954-1963	.708
Whitey Ford	1950-1959	.708

Games

Kent Tekulve	1978-1987	765
Kent Tekulve	1977-1986	747
Kent Tekulve	1979-1988	744
Kent Tekulve	1976-1985	738
Kent Tekulve	1975-1984	711
Kent Tekulve	1980-1989	687
Rollie Fingers	1971-1980	661
Rollie Fingers	1972-1981	660
Lee Smith	1982-1991	659
Lee Smith	1983-1992	657
Ron Perranoski	1961-1970	656
Lee Smith	1984-1993	654
Ron Perranoski	1962-1971	650
Kent Tekulve	1974-1983	647
Paul Assenmacher	1988-1997	647

Games Started

Pud Galvin	1879-1888	562
Pud Galvin	1880-1889	536
Pud Galvin	1881-1890	507
Tim Keefe	1881-1890	504
John Clarkson	1885-1894	502
John Clarkson	1884-1893	497
Mickey Welch	1880-1889	496
Tim Keefe	1880-1889	486
Jim McCormick	1878-1887	485
Pud Galvin	1882-1891	485
Old Hoss Radbourn	1881-1890	479
Tim Keefe	1882-1891	476
Tim Keefe	1883-1892	472
Mickey Welch	1881-1890	469
Old Hoss Radbourn	1882-1891	467

Complete Games

Pud Galvin	1879-1888	535
Pud Galvin	1880-1889	508
Pud Galvin	1881-1890	485
Tim Keefe	1881-1890	480
Mickey Welch	1880-1889	478
John Clarkson	1885-1894	471
John Clarkson	1884-1893	470
Tim Keefe	1880-1889	469
Jim McCormick	1878-1887	466
Old Hoss Radbourn	1881-1890	466
Pud Galvin	1882-1891	460
Old Hoss Radbourn	1882-1891	455
Tim Keefe	1882-1891	448
Mickey Welch	1881-1890	447
Tim Keefe	1883-1892	438

Shutouts

Pete Alexander	1911-1920	77
Walter Johnson	1910-1919	74
Pete Alexander	1912-1921	73
Walter Johnson	1909-1918	71
Pete Alexander	1913-1922	71
Walter Johnson	1911-1920	70
Walter Johnson	1908-1917	69
Walter Johnson	1912-1921	65
Pete Alexander	1914-1923	65
Christy Mathewson	1901-1910	63
Christy Mathewson	1902-1911	63
Walter Johnson	1907-1916	63
Walter Johnson	1913-1922	62
Christy Mathewson	1900-1909	61
Pete Alexander	1915-1924	59

Saves

Dennis Eckersley	1988-1997	370
Lee Smith	1986-1995	358
Lee Smith	1984-1993	354
Lee Smith	1985-1994	354
Dennis Eckersley	1987-1996	350
Lee Smith	1983-1992	337
Lee Smith	1987-1996	329
Dennis Eckersley	1986-1995	320
Jeff Reardon	1983-1992	315
Randy Myers	1988-1997	313
Jeff Reardon	1982-1991	311
Lee Smith	1982-1991	311
Jeff Reardon	1984-1993	302
Lee Smith	1988-1997	298
Tom Henke	1986-1995	295

Innings Pitched

Pud Galvin	1879-1888	4,948.2
Pud Galvin	1880-1889	4,696.2
Pud Galvin	1881-1890	4,455.0
John Clarkson	1885-1894	4,394.1
John Clarkson	1884-1893	4,361.2
Mickey Welch	1880-1889	4,344.2
Tim Keefe	1881-1890	4,322.2
Old Hoss Radbourn	1881-1890	4,317.1
Jim McCormick	1878-1887	4,275.2
Pud Galvin	1882-1891	4,227.2
Old Hoss Radbourn	1882-1891	4,210.0
Tim Keefe	1880-1889	4,198.2
Mickey Welch	1881-1890	4,063.0
Tim Keefe	1882-1891	4,054.0
Tim Keefe	1883-1892	3,992.1

Walks

Amos Rusie	1889-1898	1,701
Nolan Ryan	1971-1980	1,516
Nolan Ryan	1970-1979	1,515
Nolan Ryan	1972-1981	1,468
Nolan Ryan	1969-1978	1,454
Nolan Ryan	1973-1982	1,420
Nolan Ryan	1968-1977	1,381
Nolan Ryan	1974-1983	1,359
Gus Weyhing	1887-1896	1,358
Bobo Newsom	1934-1943	1,314
Bobo Newsom	1936-1945	1,253
Bobo Newsom	1935-1944	1,247
Nolan Ryan	1975-1984	1,226
Bobo Newsom	1937-1946	1,197
Three tied at		1,189

Strikeouts

Nolan Ryan	1972-1981	2,756
Nolan Ryan	1971-1980	2,753
Nolan Ryan	1970-1979	2,678
Nolan Ryan	1973-1982	2,672
Nolan Ryan	1969-1978	2,547
Nolan Ryan	1974-1983	2,472
Nolan Ryan	1968-1977	2,420
Tom Seaver	1969-1978	2,381
Tom Seaver	1968-1977	2,360
Sandy Koufax	1957-1966	2,336
Tom Seaver	1967-1976	2,334
Nolan Ryan	1976-1985	2,325
Tom Seaver	1970-1979	2,304
Nolan Ryan	1975-1984	2,302
Two tied at		2,295

Strikeouts/9 Innings
(minimum 1000 Innings Pitched)

Randy Johnson	1988-1997	10.38
Nolan Ryan	1969-1978	9.83
Nolan Ryan	1984-1993	9.83
Nolan Ryan	1983-1992	9.81
Nolan Ryan	1970-1979	9.78
Nolan Ryan	1968-1977	9.76
Nolan Ryan	1982-1991	9.75
Nolan Ryan	1972-1981	9.67
Nolan Ryan	1971-1980	9.65
Nolan Ryan	1981-1990	9.59
Nolan Ryan	1966-1975	9.59
Nolan Ryan	1973-1982	9.50
Sandy Koufax	1957-1966	9.45
Sandy Koufax	1956-1965	9.41
Sam McDowell	1961-1970	9.34

ERA
(minimum 1000 Innings Pitched)

Walter Johnson	1910-1919	1.59
Walter Johnson	1907-1916	1.64
Walter Johnson	1909-1918	1.65
Walter Johnson	1911-1920	1.69
Walter Johnson	1908-1917	1.69
Ed Walsh	1907-1916	1.74
Ed Walsh	1906-1915	1.75
Ed Walsh	1905-1914	1.78
Ed Walsh	1908-1917	1.78
Ed Walsh	1904-1913	1.79
Walter Johnson	1912-1921	1.82
Three Finger Brown	1903-1912	1.82
Three Finger Brown	1904-1913	1.83
Christy Mathewson	1904-1913	1.87
Christy Mathewson	1902-1911	1.89

Component ERA
(minimum 1000 Innings Pitched)

Walter Johnson	1910-1919	1.67
Walter Johnson	1909-1918	1.70
Walter Johnson	1908-1917	1.70
Walter Johnson	1911-1920	1.72
Walter Johnson	1907-1916	1.72
Ed Walsh	1906-1915	1.73
Ed Walsh	1908-1917	1.73
Ed Walsh	1907-1916	1.74
Ed Walsh	1905-1914	1.75
Ed Walsh	1904-1913	1.76
Walter Johnson	1912-1921	1.78
Three Finger Brown	1904-1913	1.88
Cy Young	1901-1910	1.92
Christy Mathewson	1904-1913	1.94
Christy Mathewson	1900-1909	1.95

Opponent Average
(minimum 1000 Innings Pitched)

Nolan Ryan	1968-1977	.195
Nolan Ryan	1966-1975	.196
Nolan Ryan	1969-1978	.197
Nolan Ryan	1970-1979	.199
Hoyt Wilhelm	1961-1970	.200
Hoyt Wilhelm	1960-1969	.201
Nolan Ryan	1972-1981	.201
Sandy Koufax	1957-1966	.203
Nolan Ryan	1971-1980	.203
Nolan Ryan	1982-1991	.204
Sid Fernandez	1984-1993	.204
Nolan Ryan	1981-1990	.205
Sandy Koufax	1956-1965	.205
Nolan Ryan	1974-1983	.205
Nolan Ryan	1983-1992	.205

Opponent OBP
(minimum 1000 Innings Pitched)

Walter Johnson	1910-1919	.258
Walter Johnson	1911-1920	.260
Walter Johnson	1909-1918	.260
Walter Johnson	1908-1917	.261
Ed Walsh	1908-1917	.261
Ed Walsh	1906-1915	.261
Hoyt Wilhelm	1960-1969	.261
Ed Walsh	1907-1916	.261
Walter Johnson	1907-1916	.261
Ed Walsh	1904-1913	.262
Ed Walsh	1905-1914	.262
Walter Johnson	1912-1921	.263
Cy Young	1901-1910	.264
Cy Young	1899-1908	.264
Hoyt Wilhelm	1961-1970	.264

Games Finished

Two tied at		562

Batters Faced

Pud Galvin	1879-1888	20,790

Hits Allowed

Pud Galvin	1879-1888	5,223

Runs Allowed

Pud Galvin	1879-1888	2,652

Earned Runs

Pud Galvin	1880-1889	1,500

Home Runs Allowed

Robin Roberts	1951-1960	329

Intentional Walks

Kent Tekulve	1978-1987	139

Sac Hits Allowed

Two tied at		386

Sac Flies Allowed

Two tied at		85

Hit Batsmen

Joe McGinnity	1899-1908	182

Wild Pitches

Mickey Welch	1880-1889	259

Balks

Steve Carlton	1975-1984	71

NL Runs Created Per 27 Outs Leaders By Position

Year	Catcher		First Baseman		Second Baseman		Third Baseman	
1876	Deacon White, ChN	10.00	Cal McVey, ChN	9.62	Ross Barnes, ChN	17.46	Cap Anson, ChN	11.14
1877	Cal McVey, ChN	10.71	Deacon White, Bos	12.73	Joe Gerhardt, Lou	6.36	Cap Anson, ChN	9.17
1878	Lew Brown, Prv	8.29	Joe Start, ChN	8.61	Joe Gerhardt, Cin	6.03	Cal McVey, Cin	7.01
1879	Deacon White, Cin	8.92	Joe Start, Prv	8.17	Mike McGeary, Prv	5.48	King Kelly, Cin	10.58
1880	John Clapp, Cin	5.93	Cap Anson, ChN	8.92	Fred Dunlap, Cle	6.40	Roger Connor, Try	8.32
1881	Charlie Bennett, Det	7.83	Cap Anson, ChN	12.25	Fred Dunlap, Cle	7.59	Jim O'Rourke, Buf	7.18
1882	Charlie Bennett, Det	8.38	Cap Anson, ChN	11.74	Fred Dunlap, Cle	6.18	Ned Williamson, ChN	8.01
1883	Buck Ewing, NYG	8.58	Dan Brouthers, Buf	11.71	Jack Burdock, Bos	9.30	Ezra Sutton, Bos	9.48
1884	Jack Rowe, Buf	8.87	Dan Brouthers, Buf	11.18	Roger Connor, NYG	9.19	Ezra Sutton, Bos	10.23
1885	Buck Ewing, NYG	8.47	Roger Connor, NYG	11.96	Hardy Richardson, Buf	7.32	Ezra Sutton, Bos	7.86
1886	John Cahill, StL	2.72	Dan Brouthers, Det	12.61	Fred Pfeffer, ChN	6.38	Billy Nash, Bos	6.13
1887	Jim O'Rourke, NYG	7.17	Dan Brouthers, Det	11.60	Hardy Richardson, Det	8.69	Billy Nash, Bos	8.23
1888	King Kelly, Bos	8.77	Cap Anson, ChN	9.49	Fred Pfeffer, ChN	5.76	Billy Nash, Bos	6.49
1889	Buck Ewing, NYG	9.21	Dan Brouthers, Bos	11.80	Hardy Richardson, Bos	8.09	Billy Nash, Bos	6.78
1890	Jack Clements, Phi	8.27	Cap Anson, ChN	9.52	Hub Collins, Bro	9.05	George Pinckney, Bro	10.02
1891	Jack Clements, Phi	7.78	Roger Connor, NYG	8.47	Cupid Childs, Cle	8.20	Arlie Latham, Cin	7.42
1892	Jim Canavan, ChN	2.80	Dan Brouthers, Bro	10.01	Cupid Childs, Cle	9.52	Billy Nash, Bos	6.28
1893	Jack Clements, Phi	7.47	Roger Connor, NYG	8.75	Cupid Childs, Cle	10.54	George Davis, NYG	10.47
1894	Wilbert Robinson, Bal	8.37	Dan Brouthers, Bal	10.23	Cupid Childs, Cle	10.78	Bill Joyce, Was	12.83
1895	Deacon McGuire, Was	7.80	Roger Connor, StL	9.08	Bid McPhee, Cin	8.04	John McGraw, Bal	11.36
1896	Deacon McGuire, Was	6.74	Jack Doyle, Bal	8.36	Cupid Childs, Cle	9.67	George Davis, NYG	7.87
1897	Klondike Douglass, StL	6.22	Nap Lajoie, Phi	8.83	Cupid Childs, Cle	8.05	Bill Joyce, NYG	9.19
1898	Ed McFarland, Phi	5.32	Bill Joyce, NYG	7.70	Gene DeMontreville, Bal	6.96	John McGraw, Bal	10.08
1899	Tommy Tucker, Cle	3.07	Fred Tenney, Bos	7.88	Tom Daly, Bro	8.21	John McGraw, Bal	13.79
1900	Monte Cross, Phi	3.17	Jake Beckley, Cin	7.39	Nap Lajoie, Phi	7.81	John McGraw, StL	10.26
1901	John Ganzel, NYG	2.31	Joe Kelley, Bro	6.68	Tom Daly, Bro	7.23	Otto Krueger, StL	5.64
1902	Johnny Kling, ChN	4.64	Fred Tenney, Bos	6.66	Claude Ritchey, Pit	5.19	Tommy Leach, Pit	6.11
1903	Johnny Kling, ChN	5.73	Frank Chance, ChN	9.97	Claude Ritchey, Pit	5.72	Harry Steinfeldt, Cin	7.26
1904	Johnny Kling, ChN	2.80	Frank Chance, ChN	7.39	Miller Huggins, Cin	5.70	Art Devlin, NYG	5.88
1905	Harry Wolverton, Bos	2.86	Frank Chance, ChN	9.54	Miller Huggins, Cin	6.20	Art Devlin, NYG	4.98
1906	Roger Bresnahan, NYG	6.53	Frank Chance, ChN	8.36	Miller Huggins, Cin	5.38	Harry Steinfeldt, ChN	6.95
1907	Bill Dahlen, NYG	2.54	Tim Jordan, Bro	5.10	Ed Abbaticchio, Pit	4.89	Art Devlin, NYG	4.53
1908	Roger Bresnahan, NYG	5.68	Frank Chance, ChN	5.17	Johnny Evers, ChN	6.85	Hans Lobert, Cin	5.65
1909	George Gibson, Pit	4.55	Ed Konetchy, StL	5.68	Johnny Evers, ChN	5.84	Art Devlin, NYG	4.68
1910	George Gibson, Pit	4.26	Ed Konetchy, StL	6.63	Johnny Evers, ChN	5.78	Bobby Byrne, Pit	5.77
1911	Eddie Grant, Cin	2.97	Ed Konetchy, StL	6.23	Larry Doyle, NYG	7.41	Hans Lobert, Phi	5.35
1912	Arnold Hauser, StL	3.60	Fred Merkle, NYG	6.64	Johnny Evers, ChN	7.62	Heinie Zimmerman, ChN	8.96
1913	Tom Fisher, Bro	3.01	Vic Saier, ChN	6.76	Jim Viox, Pit	6.86	Heinie Zimmerman, ChN	7.14
1914	Bill Sweeney, ChN	2.92	Jake Daubert, Bro	5.69	Heine Groh, Cin	5.85	Heinie Zimmerman, ChN	5.07
1915	Frank Snyder, StL	5.19	Fred Luderus, Phi	6.75	Larry Doyle, NYG	6.27	Red Smith, Bos	4.64
1916	Baldy Louden, Cin	2.84	Hal Chase, Cin	5.58	Bert Niehoff, Phi	3.59	Rogers Hornsby, StL	5.83
1917	Carson Bigbee, Pit	2.90	Fred Luderus, Phi	4.60	Larry Doyle, ChN	4.29	Heine Groh, Cin	6.12
1918	Johnny Rawlings, Bos	2.04	Sherry Magee, Cin	5.62	George Cutshaw, Pit	4.69	Heine Groh, Cin	5.97
1919	Zeb Terry, Pit	2.59	Fred Luderus, Phi	5.40	Milt Stock, StL	4.90	Heine Groh, Cin	6.63
1920	Ray Powell, Bos	2.47	Ed Konetchy, Bro	5.78	Rogers Hornsby, StL	8.37	Heine Groh, Cin	5.51
1921	Zeb Terry, ChN	3.16	Jack Fournier, StL	6.87	Rogers Hornsby, StL	10.41	Frankie Frisch, NYG	7.09
1922	Butch Henline, Phi	6.30	Ray Grimes, ChN	9.48	Rogers Hornsby, StL	11.70	Milt Stock, StL	4.97
1923	Bob O'Farrell, ChN	7.59	Jack Fournier, Bro	9.02	Rogers Hornsby, StL	10.27	Pie Traynor, Pit	6.88
1924	Cotton Tierney, Bos	3.16	Jack Fournier, Bro	8.21	Rogers Hornsby, StL	12.73	Pie Traynor, Pit	4.73
1925	Hughie Critz, Cin	3.62	Jack Fournier, Bro	9.17	Rogers Hornsby, StL	12.88	Pie Traynor, Pit	6.28
1926	Bob O'Farrell, StL	5.89	George Grantham, Pit	7.35	Rogers Hornsby, StL	6.63	Les Bell, StL	6.92
1927	Gabby Hartnett, ChN	5.72	Jim Bottomley, StL	6.92	Rogers Hornsby, NYG	9.24	Pie Traynor, Pit	5.90
1928	Heinie Sand, Phi	2.76	Jim Bottomley, StL	8.52	Rogers Hornsby, Bos	10.87	Freddy Lindstrom, NYG	7.03
1929	Hod Ford, Cin	3.90	Bill Terry, NYG	8.50	Rogers Hornsby, ChN	11.58	Pie Traynor, Pit	6.98
1930	Gabby Hartnett, ChN	8.73	Bill Terry, NYG	10.33	Frankie Frisch, StL	8.08	Freddy Lindstrom, NYG	9.04
1931	George Brickell, Phi	3.20	Bill Terry, NYG	7.86	Tony Cuccinello, Cin	5.80	Pie Traynor, Pit	5.15
1932	Shanty Hogan, NYG	4.69	Bill Terry, NYG	8.58	Billy Herman, ChN	5.39	Pie Traynor, Pit	5.98
1933	Spud Davis, Phi	6.21	Bill Terry, NYG	6.15	Frankie Frisch, StL	5.16	Pepper Martin, StL	7.06
1934	Gabby Hartnett, ChN	5.99	Ripper Collins, StL	8.94	Billy Herman, ChN	5.22	Pepper Martin, StL	5.69
1935	Gus Mancuso, NYG	4.31	Ripper Collins, StL	8.58	Billy Herman, ChN	6.87	Stan Hack, ChN	7.31
1936	Gus Mancuso, NYG	5.06	Dolph Camilli, Phi	9.43	Billy Herman, ChN	6.83	Stan Hack, ChN	6.01
1937	Al Todd, Pit	4.68	Johnny Mize, StL	10.53	Billy Herman, ChN	7.31	Pinky Whitney, Phi	6.21
1938	Ernie Lombardi, Cin	6.81	Johnny Mize, StL	9.20	Lonny Frey, Cin	4.73	Mel Ott, NYG	9.68
1939	Harry Danning, NYG	6.27	Johnny Mize, StL	9.56	Lonny Frey, Cin	6.50	Cookie Lavagetto, Bro	5.86
1940	Harry Danning, NYG	5.49	Johnny Mize, StL	9.12	Joe Orengo, StL	5.81	Stan Hack, ChN	6.92
1941	Harry Danning, NYG	3.34	Dolph Camilli, Bro	8.39	Lonny Frey, Cin	5.14	Stan Hack, ChN	7.58
1942	Mickey Owen, Bro	3.74	Johnny Mize, NYG	7.91	Lonny Frey, Cin	5.24	Stan Hack, ChN	6.42
1943	Ray Mueller, Cin	4.86	Elbie Fletcher, Pit	6.11	Billy Herman, Bro	6.35	Bob Elliott, Pit	6.15
1944	Ray Mueller, Cin	5.26	Phil Cavarretta, ChN	7.10	Don Johnson, ChN	4.06	Bob Elliott, Pit	7.03
1945	Buddy Kerr, NYG	3.13	Phil Cavarretta, ChN	9.34	Eddie Stanky, Bro	6.18	Whitey Kurowski, StL	7.36
1946	Dick Culler, Bos	3.50	Stan Musial, StL	10.01	Eddie Stanky, Bro	6.45	Whitey Kurowski, StL	6.77
1947	Walker Cooper, NYG	6.98	Johnny Mize, NYG	8.79	Bill Rigney, NYG	5.06	Whitey Kurowski, StL	8.07
1948	Eddie Miller, Phi	3.22	Johnny Mize, NYG	8.70	Jackie Robinson, Bro	6.38	Sid Gordon, NYG	7.60
1949	Roy Campanella, Bro	7.34	Gil Hodges, Bro	6.17	Jackie Robinson, Bro	8.63	Sid Gordon, NYG	6.75
1950	Roy Campanella, Bro	6.76	Earl Torgeson, Bos	7.67	Eddie Stanky, NYG	8.03	Tommy Glaviano, StL	7.21
1951	Roy Campanella, Bro	8.20	Gil Hodges, Bro	7.06	Jackie Robinson, Bro	8.86	Bob Elliott, Bos	5.98
1952	Roy Campanella, Bro	5.33	Ted Kluszewski, Cin	7.19	Jackie Robinson, Bro	8.09	Bobby Thomson, NYG	5.61
1953	Roy Campanella, Bro	8.58	Gil Hodges, Bro	8.03	Red Schoendienst, StL	6.98	Eddie Mathews, Mil	9.31
1954	Del Crandall, Mil	3.95	Ted Kluszewski, Cin	9.39	Johnny Temple, Cin	5.67	Eddie Mathews, Mil	8.77
1955	Roy Campanella, Bro	7.94	Stan Musial, StL	7.96	Johnny Temple, Cin	4.80	Eddie Mathews, Mil	8.91
1956	Stan Lopata, Phi	6.26	Ted Kluszewski, Cin	6.68	Jim Gilliam, Bro	6.18	Eddie Mathews, Mil	7.08
1957	Chico Fernandez, Phi	3.16	Stan Musial, StL	9.39	Johnny Temple, Cin	5.27	Eddie Mathews, Mil	7.68
1958	Del Crandall, Mil	5.12	Stan Musial, StL	7.55	Johnny Temple, Cin	6.30	Ken Boyer, StL	5.97

NL Runs Created Per 27 Outs Leaders By Position

Year	Shortstop		Outfielder		Outfielder		Outfielder	
1876	John Peters, ChN	9.98	George Hall, PhN	12.54	Jim O'Rourke, Bos	10.56	Lip Pike, StL	10.42
1877	Jack Manning, Cin	7.72	Jim O'Rourke, Bos	10.64	John Cassidy, Har	10.47	George Hall, Lou	7.91
1878	Bob Ferguson, ChN	8.50	Paul Hines, Prv	10.15	Orator Shaffer, Ind	10.14	Tom York, Prv	8.71
1879	George Wright, Prv	6.68	John O'Rourke, Bos	11.12	Charley Jones, Bos	10.84	Paul Hines, Prv	10.44
1880	Tom Burns, ChN	7.51	George Gore, ChN	10.74	Abner Dalrymple, ChN	8.75	Harry Stovey, Wor	7.45
1881	Tom Burns, ChN	6.41	Dan Brouthers, Buf	9.19	King Kelly, ChN	8.20	Tom York, Prv	8.17
1882	King Kelly, ChN	8.27	George Gore, ChN	9.33	Paul Hines, Prv	8.69	Abner Dalrymple, ChN	7.94
1883	Tom Burns, ChN	8.05	George Gore, ChN	10.48	Jim O'Rourke, Buf	8.23	George Wood, Det	7.92
1884	Bill McClellan, Phi	5.74	King Kelly, ChN	11.28	Jim O'Rourke, Buf	10.53	Paul Hines, Prv	9.47
1885	Tom Burns, ChN	7.20	George Gore, ChN	10.86	King Kelly, ChN	9.10	Abner Dalrymple, ChN	8.69
1886	Jack Glasscock, StL	8.37	King Kelly, ChN	14.63	Hardy Richardson, Det	10.46	George Gore, ChN	10.30
1887	Sam Wise, Bos	9.95	Sam Thompson, Det	11.46	King Kelly, Bos	10.14	Jim Fogarty, Phi	9.16
1888	Ned Williamson, ChN	6.52	Jimmy Ryan, ChN	9.46	Mike Tiernan, NYG	8.15	Dummy Hoy, WaN	7.57
1889	Jack Glasscock, Ind	9.17	Mike Tiernan, NYG	11.36	Jimmy Ryan, ChN	9.45	George Gore, NYG	9.13
1890	Jack Glasscock, NYG	8.57	Billy Hamilton, Phi	9.94	Mike Tiernan, NYG	8.79	Oyster Burns, Bro	8.39
1891	Herman Long, Bos	8.10	Billy Hamilton, Phi	11.84	Mike Tiernan, NYG	9.13	Harry Stovey, Bos	9.03
1892	Bill Dahlen, ChN	6.95	Billy Hamilton, Phi	9.00	Oyster Burns, Bro	8.57	Hugh Duffy, Bos	8.04
1893	John McGraw, Bal	9.85	Billy Hamilton, Phi	13.17	Jesse Burkett, Cle	11.68	Tommy McCarthy, Bos	11.41
1894	Bill Dahlen, ChN	11.25	Hugh Duffy, Bos	16.77	Billy Hamilton, Phi	14.49	Joe Kelley, Bal	13.57
1895	Hughie Jennings, Bal	10.70	Ed Delahanty, Phi	13.99	Jesse Burkett, Cle	13.08	Billy Hamilton, Phi	12.65
1896	Hughie Jennings, Bal	11.43	Ed Delahanty, Phi	13.61	Joe Kelley, Bal	12.24	Billy Hamilton, Bos	11.75
1897	George Davis, NYG	9.96	Fred Clarke, Lou	11.64	Willie Keeler, Bal	11.59	Billy Hamilton, Bos	10.46
1898	Hughie Jennings, Bal	9.15	Billy Hamilton, Bos	12.54	Ed Delahanty, Phi	9.49	Elmer Smith, Cin	8.94
1899	Bill Dahlen, Bro	7.46	Ed Delahanty, Phi	11.95	Jesse Burkett, StL	10.01	Chick Stahl, Bos	9.61
1900	George Davis, NYG	6.88	Honus Wagner, Pit	11.61	Elmer Flick, Phi	10.55	Billy Hamilton, Bos	9.14
1901	Honus Wagner, Pit	9.55	Jesse Burkett, StL	10.60	Jimmy Sheckard, Bro	9.80	Ed Delahanty, Phi	9.61
1902	Bill Dahlen, Bro	4.86	Honus Wagner, Pit	8.33	Fred Clarke, Pit	8.22	Ginger Beaumont, Pit	7.61
1903	Honus Wagner, Pit	9.58	Roger Bresnahan, NYG	10.52	Mike Donlin, Cin	9.34	Fred Clarke, Pit	9.12
1904	Honus Wagner, Pit	10.11	Roy Thomas, Phi	6.77	Cy Seymour, Cin	6.40	Sam Mertes, NYG	5.91
1905	Honus Wagner, Pit	9.82	Cy Seymour, Cin	10.18	Mike Donlin, NYG	8.31	John Titus, Phi	7.74
1906	Honus Wagner, Pit	8.58	Harry Lumley, Bro	6.87	Fred Clarke, Pit	5.86	Sherry Magee, Phi	5.78
1907	Honus Wagner, Pit	8.76	Sherry Magee, Phi	7.60	Fred Clarke, Pit	6.25	Ginger Beaumont, Bos	5.56
1908	Honus Wagner, Pit	8.89	Mike Donlin, NYG	6.16	Sherry Magee, Phi	5.47	Red Murray, StL	4.81
1909	Honus Wagner, Pit	8.48	Mike Mitchell, Cin	6.39	Fred Clarke, Pit	6.09	Solly Hofman, ChN	5.30
1910	Honus Wagner, Pit	6.36	Sherry Magee, Phi	9.15	Fred Snodgrass, NYG	7.44	Solly Hofman, ChN	7.05
1911	Honus Wagner, Pit	8.60	Wildfire Schulte, ChN	7.46	Jimmy Sheckard, ChN	7.26	Johnny Bates, Cin	6.42
1912	Honus Wagner, Pit	7.32	Dode Paskert, Phi	6.91	Bob Bescher, Cin	6.22	Sherry Magee, Phi	6.12
1913	Art Fletcher, NYG	4.93	Gavy Cravath, Phi	8.40	Tommy Leach, ChN	6.74	Sherry Magee, Phi	6.20
1914	Buck Herzog, Cin	4.87	Gavy Cravath, Phi	7.14	Sherry Magee, Phi	7.01	George Burns, NYG	6.63
1915	Honus Wagner, Pit	4.67	Gavy Cravath, Phi	7.76	Bill Hinchman, Pit	5.63	Tom Long, StL	5.34
1916	Art Fletcher, NYG	4.53	Gavy Cravath, Phi	6.25	Zack Wheat, Bro	6.09	Cy Williams, ChN	5.83
1917	Rogers Hornsby, StL	6.68	Edd Roush, Cin	6.54	George Burns, NYG	6.33	Gavy Cravath, Phi	6.31
1918	Charlie Hollocher, ChN	5.83	Edd Roush, Cin	5.87	Ross Youngs, NYG	5.59	George Burns, NYG	5.48
1919	Charlie Hollocher, ChN	4.10	George Burns, NYG	6.61	Edd Roush, Cin	6.36	Ross Youngs, NYG	6.36
1920	Zeb Terry, ChN	4.29	Ross Youngs, NYG	8.02	Zack Wheat, Bro	6.77	Edd Roush, Cin	6.26
1921	Dave Bancroft, NYG	6.58	Austin McHenry, StL	6.93	Ross Youngs, NYG	6.91	Zack Wheat, Bro	6.54
1922	Dave Bancroft, NYG	6.19	Max Carey, Pit	7.62	Zack Wheat, Bro	7.41	Hack Miller, ChN	7.40
1923	Dave Bancroft, NYG	6.16	Cy Williams, Phi	7.44	Edd Roush, Cin	7.37	Max Carey, Pit	6.99
1924	Travis Jackson, NYG	4.84	Ross Youngs, NYG	8.75	Zack Wheat, Bro	8.67	Kiki Cuyler, Pit	7.86
1925	Dave Bancroft, Bos	6.17	Kiki Cuyler, Pit	9.21	Zack Wheat, Bro	8.07	Ray Blades, StL	8.07
1926	Dave Bancroft, Bos	5.61	Paul Waner, Pit	8.24	Hack Wilson, ChN	7.54	Ray Blades, StL	7.15
1927	Travis Jackson, NYG	6.18	Paul Waner, Pit	8.92	Hack Wilson, ChN	7.94	George Harper, NYG	7.74
1928	Travis Jackson, NYG	4.77	Paul Waner, Pit	9.48	Chick Hafey, StL	7.79	Hack Wilson, ChN	7.64
1929	Travis Jackson, NYG	6.55	Mel Ott, NYG	10.60	Lefty O'Doul, Phi	10.17	Riggs Stephenson, ChN	9.77
1930	Travis Jackson, NYG	7.14	Hack Wilson, ChN	11.12	Babe Herman, Bro	10.79	Chuck Klein, Phi	10.69
1931	Woody English, ChN	5.90	Chick Hafey, StL	8.82	Chuck Klein, Phi	7.74	Mel Ott, NYG	7.66
1932	Dick Bartell, Phi	5.65	Mel Ott, NYG	9.65	Chuck Klein, Phi	9.47	Lefty O'Doul, Bro	8.88
1933	Arky Vaughan, Pit	6.61	Chuck Klein, Phi	9.52	Wally Berger, Bos	8.05	Mel Ott, NYG	6.57
1934	Arky Vaughan, Pit	8.87	Mel Ott, NYG	9.51	Paul Waner, Pit	8.67	Len Koenecke, Bro	7.78
1935	Arky Vaughan, Pit	11.93	Joe Medwick, StL	8.97	Mel Ott, NYG	8.47	Augie Galan, ChN	7.97
1936	Arky Vaughan, Pit	9.01	Mel Ott, NYG	10.02	Paul Waner, Pit	9.29	Joe Medwick, StL	8.59
1937	Arky Vaughan, Pit	6.77	Joe Medwick, StL	10.62	Mel Ott, NYG	8.12	Paul Waner, Pit	6.98
1938	Arky Vaughan, Pit	7.77	Ival Goodman, Cin	7.12	Joe Medwick, StL	6.72	Johnny Rizzo, Pit	6.55
1939	Arky Vaughan, Pit	6.01	Mel Ott, NYG	9.86	Ival Goodman, Cin	7.57	Augie Galan, ChN	6.53
1940	Arky Vaughan, Pit	7.41	Mel Ott, NYG	7.15	Bill Nicholson, ChN	7.01	Enos Slaughter, StL	6.89
1941	Billy Jurges, NYG	5.02	Pete Reiser, Bro	8.58	Mel Ott, NYG	7.71	Enos Slaughter, StL	7.38
1942	Pee Wee Reese, Bro	4.87	Mel Ott, NYG	8.39	Enos Slaughter, StL	8.39	Stan Musial, StL	7.97
1943	Arky Vaughan, Bro	6.03	Stan Musial, StL	8.23	Bill Nicholson, ChN	7.48	Augie Galan, Bro	7.24
1944	Buddy Kerr, NYG	4.29	Dixie Walker, Bro	9.44	Stan Musial, StL	9.42	Mel Ott, NYG	9.02
1945	Frankie Gustine, Pit	4.57	Tommy Holmes, Bos	9.51	Mel Ott, NYG	7.54	Goody Rosen, Bro	7.10
1946	Pee Wee Reese, Bro	5.44	Enos Slaughter, StL	6.64	Dixie Walker, Bro	6.62	Phil Cavarretta, ChN	6.44
1947	Pee Wee Reese, Bro	6.68	Ralph Kiner, Pit	9.36	Augie Galan, Cin	7.83	Willard Marshall, NYG	6.89
1948	Al Dark, Bos	5.41	Stan Musial, StL	11.72	Enos Slaughter, StL	7.40	Ralph Kiner, Pit	7.20
1949	Pee Wee Reese, Bro	6.95	Ralph Kiner, Pit	10.07	Stan Musial, StL	9.90	Enos Slaughter, StL	8.06
1950	Pee Wee Reese, Bro	5.39	Stan Musial, StL	9.69	Sid Gordon, Bos	8.22	Andy Pafko, ChN	8.18
1951	Al Dark, NYG	5.64	Stan Musial, StL	10.30	Ralph Kiner, Pit	10.28	Monte Irvin, NYG	7.79
1952	Solly Hemus, StL	5.90	Stan Musial, StL	8.35	Ralph Kiner, Pit	6.99	Sid Gordon, Bos	6.97
1953	Solly Hemus, StL	6.04	Duke Snider, Bro	9.50	Stan Musial, StL	9.47	Carl Furillo, Bro	8.11
1954	Pee Wee Reese, Bro	6.20	Willie Mays, NYG	9.52	Duke Snider, Bro	9.21	Stan Musial, StL	8.85
1955	Ernie Banks, ChN	7.05	Willie Mays, NYG	9.39	Duke Snider, Bro	9.25	Richie Ashburn, Phi	7.94
1956	Ernie Banks, ChN	6.35	Duke Snider, Bro	7.72	Frank Robinson, Cin	7.01	Hank Aaron, Mil	6.73
1957	Ernie Banks, ChN	7.31	Willie Mays, NYG	8.59	Hank Aaron, Mil	7.93	Duke Snider, Bro	7.31
1958	Ernie Banks, ChN	7.36	Willie Mays, SF	8.97	Richie Ashburn, Phi	7.17	Hank Aaron, Mil	6.96

NL Runs Created Per 27 Outs Leaders By Position

Year	Catcher		First Baseman		Second Baseman		Third Baseman	
1959	Del Crandall, Mil	4.06	Frank Robinson, Cin	7.84	Johnny Temple, Cin	6.22	Eddie Mathews, Mil	8.31
1960	Ed Bailey, Cin	4.81	Frank Robinson, Cin	7.81	Bill Mazeroski, Pit	4.40	Eddie Mathews, Mil	8.05
1961	Don Zimmer, ChN	3.52	Orlando Cepeda, SF	7.66	Julian Javier, StL	4.06	Ken Boyer, StL	7.72
1962	Johnny Edwards, Cin	4.58	Bill White, StL	7.02	Jim Gilliam, LA	5.09	Eddie Mathews, Mil	6.81
1963	Joe Torre, Mil	5.21	Orlando Cepeda, SF	7.18	Jim Gilliam, LA	5.36	Eddie Mathews, Mil	7.01
1964	Joe Torre, Mil	6.28	Orlando Cepeda, SF	6.70	Ron Hunt, NYN	5.26	Dick Allen, Phi	7.79
1965	Joe Torre, Mil	6.05	Willie McCovey, SF	7.61	Pete Rose, Cin	6.36	Ron Santo, ChN	7.24
1966	Joe Torre, Atl	7.23	Willie McCovey, SF	8.74	Joe Morgan, Hou	6.19	Dick Allen, Phi	8.94
1967	Tim McCarver, StL	5.91	Orlando Cepeda, StL	7.73	Joe Morgan, Hou	6.29	Dick Allen, Phi	8.43
1968	Tom Haller, LA	4.80	Willie McCovey, SF	7.69	Glenn Beckert, ChN	4.67	Ron Santo, ChN	5.24
1969	Johnny Bench, Cin	6.14	Willie McCovey, SF	10.75	Joe Morgan, Hou	5.54	Ron Santo, ChN	6.59
1970	Dick Dietz, SF	7.94	Willie McCovey, SF	9.58	Joe Morgan, Hou	5.90	Tony Perez, Cin	7.89
1971	Dick Dietz, SF	5.98	Hank Aaron, Atl	9.51	Ron Hunt, Mon	6.21	Joe Torre, StL	8.60
1972	Johnny Bench, Cin	6.99	Willie Stargell, Pit	7.32	Joe Morgan, Cin	7.72	Richie Hebner, Pit	6.95
1973	Joe Ferguson, LA	6.45	Tony Perez, Cin	7.62	Joe Morgan, Cin	7.79	Darrell Evans, Atl	7.90
1974	Johnny Bench, Cin	6.46	Steve Garvey, LA	6.06	Joe Morgan, Cin	8.45	Mike Schmidt, Phi	8.01
1975	Johnny Bench, Cin	6.73	Willie Stargell, Pit	7.08	Joe Morgan, Cin	10.52	Bill Madlock, ChN	7.25
1976	Ted Simmons, StL	5.17	Bob Watson, Hou	6.34	Joe Morgan, Cin	9.85	Mike Schmidt, Phi	7.18
1977	Ted Simmons, StL	7.33	Bob Watson, Hou	6.35	Joe Morgan, Cin	7.72	Mike Schmidt, Phi	7.71
1978	Ted Simmons, StL	6.66	Steve Garvey, LA	5.80	Bill Madlock, SF	6.26	Mike Schmidt, Phi	5.82
1979	Gene Tenace, SD	6.59	Keith Hernandez, StL	7.89	Davey Lopes, LA	6.69	Larry Parrish, Mon	7.00
1980	Ted Simmons, StL	6.79	Keith Hernandez, StL	7.50	Joe Morgan, Hou	5.03	Mike Schmidt, Phi	8.25
1981	Milt May, SF	5.03	Keith Hernandez, StL	7.00	Joe Morgan, SF	5.43	Mike Schmidt, Phi	9.61
1982	Gary Carter, Mon	6.37	Al Oliver, Mon	7.20	Joe Morgan, SF	7.12	Mike Schmidt, Phi	7.85
1983	Terry Kennedy, SD	5.53	Darrell Evans, SF	7.14	Bill Doran, Hou	4.68	Mike Schmidt, Phi	7.41
1984	Gary Carter, Mon	6.12	Keith Hernandez, NYN	7.12	Ryne Sandberg, ChN	7.50	Mike Schmidt, Phi	6.45
1985	Mike Scioscia, LA	6.20	Mike Schmidt, Phi	7.19	Ryne Sandberg, ChN	6.59	Graig Nettles, SD	5.63
1986	Bob Brenly, SF	5.31	Keith Hernandez, NYN	7.10	Steve Sax, LA	6.37	Mike Schmidt, Phi	7.67
1987	Benito Santiago, SD	4.80	Jack Clark, StL	10.84	Ryne Sandberg, ChN	5.61	Mike Schmidt, Phi	6.94
1988	Gary Carter, NYN	3.62	Will Clark, SF	7.94	Ron Gant, Atl	5.02	Bobby Bonilla, Pit	6.68
1989	Craig Biggio, Hou	5.06	Will Clark, SF	9.39	Ryne Sandberg, ChN	5.85	Howard Johnson, NYN	8.26
1990	Darren Daulton, Phi	5.47	Dave Magadan, NYN	7.87	Ryne Sandberg, ChN	7.30	Matt Williams, SF	5.91
1991	Craig Biggio, Hou	4.99	Will Clark, SF	7.79	Ryne Sandberg, ChN	7.53	Terry Pendleton, Atl	6.46
1992	Darren Daulton, Phi	7.96	Fred McGriff, SD	7.14	Ryne Sandberg, ChN	6.56	Gary Sheffield, SD	7.24
1993	Darren Daulton, Phi	7.29	Andres Galarraga, Col	9.43	Robby Thompson, SF	6.45	Matt Williams, SF	6.49
1994	Mike Piazza, LA	7.48	Jeff Bagwell, Hou	11.02	Craig Biggio, Hou	8.07	Bobby Bonilla, NYN	6.90
1995	Mike Piazza, LA	8.35	Mark Grace, ChN	7.32	Craig Biggio, Hou	7.25	Ken Caminiti, SD	6.75
1996	Mike Piazza, LA	8.27	Jeff Bagwell, Hou	9.66	Craig Biggio, Hou	6.65	Ken Caminiti, SD	9.24
1997	Mike Piazza, LA	9.71	Jeff Bagwell, Hou	8.85	Craig Biggio, Hou	8.89	Edgardo Alfonzo, NYN	7.41

NL Runs Created Per 27 Outs Leaders By Position

Year	Shortstop		Outfielder		Outfielder		Outfielder	
1959	Ernie Banks, ChN	7.35	Hank Aaron, Mil	8.86	Willie Mays, SF	7.95	Joe Cunningham, StL	7.56
1960	Ernie Banks, ChN	6.68	Willie Mays, SF	7.52	Hank Aaron, Mil	7.11	Richie Ashburn, ChN	6.43
1961	Ernie Banks, ChN	5.61	Frank Robinson, Cin	8.59	Willie Mays, SF	8.44	Wally Moon, LA	8.31
1962	Maury Wills, LA	5.98	Frank Robinson, Cin	9.56	Willie Mays, SF	8.62	Hank Aaron, Mil	8.43
1963	Dick Groat, StL	6.15	Hank Aaron, Mil	8.80	Willie Mays, SF	7.95	Willie McCovey, SF	7.07
1964	Denis Menke, Mil	6.53	Willie Mays, SF	8.06	Frank Robinson, Cin	8.03	Rico Carty, Mil	7.79
1965	Leo Cardenas, Cin	4.98	Willie Mays, SF	9.46	Hank Aaron, Mil	7.66	Billy Williams, ChN	7.60
1966	Denis Menke, Atl	4.92	Willie Mays, SF	7.65	Willie Stargell, Pit	7.57	Hank Aaron, Atl	6.79
1967	Gene Alley, Pit	4.37	Roberto Clemente, Pit	7.99	Hank Aaron, Atl	7.69	Tony Gonzalez, Phi	6.99
1968	Dal Maxvill, StL	3.51	Pete Rose, Cin	6.82	Willie Mays, SF	6.62	Dick Allen, Phi	6.57
1969	Denis Menke, Hou	5.13	Jimmy Wynn, Hou	8.79	Hank Aaron, Atl	8.43	Pete Rose, Cin	8.17
1970	Denis Menke, Hou	6.59	Rico Carty, Atl	9.45	Jim Hickman, ChN	9.21	Billy Williams, ChN	8.70
1971	Maury Wills, LA	3.89	Willie Stargell, Pit	8.95	Willie Mays, SF	7.97	Rusty Staub, Mon	6.86
1972	Chris Speier, SF	5.65	Billy Williams, ChN	8.73	Cesar Cedeno, Hou	7.58	Jimmy Wynn, Hou	7.05
1973	Chris Speier, SF	3.73	Willie Stargell, Pit	9.11	Cesar Cedeno, Hou	7.38	Ron Fairly, Mon	7.36
1974	Dave Concepcion, Cin	4.72	Willie Stargell, Pit	8.05	Ralph Garr, Atl	7.15	Reggie Smith, StL	7.01
1975	Chris Speier, SF	5.02	Greg Luzinski, Phi	6.99	Jose Cardenal, ChN	6.57	Dave Parker, Pit	6.48
1976	Dave Concepcion, Cin	4.45	Ken Griffey Sr., Cin	6.95	Greg Luzinski, Phi	6.66	George Foster, Cin	6.63
1977	Garry Templeton, StL	5.37	Reggie Smith, LA	8.86	Greg Luzinski, Phi	8.07	George Foster, Cin	7.85
1978	Dave Concepcion, Cin	4.99	Dave Parker, Pit	8.39	Jeff Burroughs, Atl	7.96	Reggie Smith, LA	7.32
1979	Garry Templeton, StL	5.37	Dave Winfield, SD	7.81	Dave Parker, Pit	7.41	George Foster, Cin	7.37
1980	Garry Templeton, StL	4.95	Jack Clark, SF	6.77	Ken Griffey Sr., Cin	6.43	Dale Murphy, Atl	6.42
1981	Dave Concepcion, Cin	4.95	Andre Dawson, Mon	7.61	Tim Raines, Mon	7.41	Gary Matthews, Phi	6.91
1982	Dickie Thon, Hou	4.91	Leon Durham, ChN	7.25	Dale Murphy, Atl	7.24	Sixto Lezcano, SD	7.13
1983	Dickie Thon, Hou	5.06	Dale Murphy, Atl	7.69	Tim Raines, Mon	6.53	Jose Cruz, Hou	6.31
1984	Craig Reynolds, Hou	3.71	Dale Murphy, Atl	7.11	Tony Gwynn, SD	7.06	Gary Matthews, ChN	7.05
1985	Ozzie Smith, StL	4.78	Pedro Guerrero, LA	8.40	Tim Raines, Mon	7.86	Willie McGee, StL	7.75
1986	Ozzie Smith, StL	5.17	Tim Raines, Mon	7.85	Darryl Strawberry, NYN	6.49	Tony Gwynn, SD	6.33
1987	Ozzie Smith, StL	6.52	Tim Raines, Mon	9.01	Eric Davis, Cin	8.88	Tony Gwynn, SD	8.60
1988	Barry Larkin, Cin	5.97	Eric Davis, Cin	7.27	Kal Daniels, Cin	7.04	Kirk Gibson, LA	6.83
1989	Shawon Dunston, ChN	4.59	Lonnie Smith, Atl	8.77	Kevin Mitchell, SF	8.47	Eric Davis, Cin	7.22
1990	Barry Larkin, Cin	5.17	Barry Bonds, Pit	8.72	Kal Daniels, LA	7.76	Lenny Dykstra, Phi	7.71
1991	Barry Larkin, Cin	6.72	Barry Bonds, Pit	8.49	Bobby Bonilla, Pit	6.95	Darryl Strawberry, LA	6.48
1992	Barry Larkin, Cin	6.57	Barry Bonds, Pit	10.08	Andy Van Slyke, Pit	7.04	Bip Roberts, Cin	6.72
1993	Jeff Blauser, Atl	6.78	Barry Bonds, SF	11.27	Lenny Dykstra, Phi	7.44	Tony Gwynn, SD	7.21
1994	Barry Larkin, Cin	5.96	Barry Bonds, SF	9.88	Kevin Mitchell, Cin	8.83	David Justice, Atl	8.36
1995	Barry Larkin, Cin	8.28	Barry Bonds, SF	8.97	Reggie Sanders, Cin	8.12	Dante Bichette, Col	8.04
1996	Barry Larkin, Cin	7.84	Barry Bonds, SF	11.33	Gary Sheffield, Fla	10.13	Ellis Burks, Col	9.14
1997	Jeff Blauser, Atl	7.24	Larry Walker, Col	10.99	Tony Gwynn, SD	9.24	Barry Bonds, SF	8.82

AL Runs Created Per 27 Outs Leaders By Position

Year	Catcher		First Baseman		Second Baseman		Third Baseman	
1901	Boileryard Clarke, Was	4.90	Buck Freeman, Bos	9.21	Nap Lajoie, Phi	13.99	Jimmy Collins, Bos	7.99
1902	Monte Cross, Phi	3.38	Harry Davis, Phi	6.70	Jimmy Williams, Bal	6.80	Lave Cross, Phi	7.35
1903	Lee Tannehill, ChA	2.43	Harry Davis, Phi	6.24	Nap Lajoie, Cle	7.88	Bill Bradley, Cle	6.67
1904	Monte Cross, Phi	2.45	Jake Stahl, Was	4.41	Nap Lajoie, Cle	9.55	Bill Bradley, Cle	5.16
1905	Lee Tannehill, ChA	2.58	Harry Davis, Phi	5.78	Danny Murphy, Phi	5.13	Jimmy Collins, Bos	4.90
1906	Bris Lord, Phi	2.72	Harry Davis, Phi	6.23	Nap Lajoie, Cle	6.72	Frank LaPorte, NYA	4.34
1907	Hobe Ferris, Bos	2.61	Hal Chase, NYA	5.05	Nap Lajoie, Cle	5.27	George Moriarty, NYA	4.88
1908	Wid Conroy, NYA	2.57	Claude Rossman, Det	5.24	Nap Lajoie, Cle	5.31	Harry Lord, Bos	3.67
1909	George McBride, Was	2.54	Jake Stahl, Bos	6.10	Eddie Collins, Phi	7.65	Home Run Baker, Phi	5.25
1910	George Stovall, Cle	3.07	Jake Stahl, Bos	4.99	Nap Lajoie, Cle	9.07	Home Run Baker, Phi	4.77
1911	Oscar Stanage, Det	3.44	Jim Delahanty, Det	7.37	Eddie Collins, Phi	9.42	Home Run Baker, Phi	7.62
1912	Ivy Olson, Cle	2.89	Stuffy McInnis, Phi	6.38	Eddie Collins, Phi	8.44	Home Run Baker, Phi	8.66
1913	Shano Collins, ChA	3.08	Stuffy McInnis, Phi	6.33	Eddie Collins, Phi	8.26	Home Run Baker, Phi	8.26
1914	Jimmy Austin, StL	2.63	Stuffy McInnis, Phi	4.86	Eddie Collins, Phi	8.43	Home Run Baker, Phi	6.83
1915	Ray Schalk, ChA	4.71	Jack Fournier, ChA	8.59	Eddie Collins, ChA	8.22	Fritz Maisel, NYA	5.22
1916	Joe Gedeon, NYA	2.39	George Sisler, StL	5.25	Eddie Collins, ChA	6.01	Larry Gardner, Bos	5.38
1917	Ray Schalk, ChA	3.92	George Sisler, StL	6.57	Eddie Collins, ChA	5.93	Home Run Baker, NYA	4.70
1918	Steve O'Neill, Cle	3.73	George Burns, Phi	6.80	Eddie Collins, ChA	5.26	Home Run Baker, NYA	5.51
1919	Steve O'Neill, Cle	5.63	George Sisler, StL	7.01	Eddie Collins, ChA	5.97	Home Run Baker, NYA	4.90
1920	Steve O'Neill, Cle	6.94	George Sisler, StL	10.01	Eddie Collins, ChA	8.19	Joe Dugan, Phi	5.57
1921	Wally Schang, NYA	7.79	George Sisler, StL	8.53	Del Pratt, Bos	6.39	Larry Gardner, Cle	6.31
1922	Wally Schang, NYA	5.97	George Sisler, StL	9.78	Eddie Collins, ChA	5.85	Jimmy Dykes, Phi	5.44
1923	Muddy Ruel, Was	5.74	Frank Brower, Cle	7.05	Eddie Collins, ChA	6.85	Willie Kamm, ChA	5.29
1924	Hank Severeid, StL	4.80	Earl Sheely, ChA	6.84	Eddie Collins, ChA	7.55	Gene Robertson, StL	5.71
1925	Mickey Cochrane, Phi	6.51	George Sisler, StL	6.58	Eddie Collins, ChA	8.34	Jimmy Dykes, Phi	6.66
1926	Fred Haney, Bos	3.05	Lou Gehrig, NYA	7.98	Max Bishop, Phi	5.80	Willie Kamm, ChA	5.59
1927	Mickey Cochrane, Phi	7.11	Lou Gehrig, NYA	12.00	Charlie Gehringer, Det	6.37	Sammy Hale, Phi	5.35
1928	Mickey Cochrane, Phi	6.27	Lou Gehrig, NYA	10.77	Max Bishop, Phi	6.96	Willie Kamm, ChA	5.93
1929	Mickey Cochrane, Phi	7.34	Jimmie Foxx, Phi	10.64	Tony Lazzeri, NYA	8.61	Marty McManus, Det	5.48
1930	Mickey Cochrane, Phi	8.86	Lou Gehrig, NYA	12.12	Charlie Gehringer, Det	7.67	Jimmy Dykes, Phi	6.97
1931	Mickey Cochrane, Phi	9.08	Lou Gehrig, NYA	11.19	Max Bishop, Phi	7.21	Joe Sewell, NYA	6.23
1932	Mickey Cochrane, Phi	8.22	Jimmie Foxx, Phi	13.19	Tony Lazzeri, NYA	7.48	Willie Kamm, Cle	5.97
1933	Mickey Cochrane, Phi	9.24	Jimmie Foxx, Phi	11.85	Max Bishop, Phi	7.26	Mike Higgins, Phi	6.80
1934	Mickey Cochrane, Det	7.50	Lou Gehrig, NYA	11.93	Charlie Gehringer, Det	9.46	Bill Werber, Bos	7.37
1935	Mickey Cochrane, Det	8.25	Lou Gehrig, NYA	10.40	Buddy Myer, Was	8.43	Harlond Clift, StL	6.51
1936	Rick Ferrell, Bos	7.03	Lou Gehrig, NYA	12.32	Charlie Gehringer, Det	9.25	Harlond Clift, StL	8.06
1937	Bill Dickey, NYA	9.04	Lou Gehrig, NYA	11.59	Charlie Gehringer, Det	9.37	Harlond Clift, StL	7.27
1938	Bill Dickey, NYA	9.05	Jimmie Foxx, Bos	11.87	Charlie Gehringer, Det	8.41	Harlond Clift, StL	8.09
1939	Bill Dickey, NYA	8.19	Jimmie Foxx, Bos	11.78	Charlie Gehringer, Det	8.66	Red Rolfe, NYA	8.16
1940	Frankie Hayes, Phi	6.79	Rudy York, Det	8.56	Charlie Gehringer, Det	7.62	Harlond Clift, StL	6.86
1941	Frankie Hayes, Phi	5.47	Jimmie Foxx, Bos	7.09	Joe Gordon, NYA	5.79	Harlond Clift, StL	5.67
1942	Pete Suder, Phi	3.01	Les Fleming, Cle	6.66	Joe Gordon, NYA	7.46	Harlond Clift, StL	6.37
1943	Jake Early, Was	4.87	Rudy York, Det	6.62	Joe Gordon, NYA	5.06	Mike Higgins, Det	4.68
1944	Frankie Hayes, Phi	3.90	Nick Etten, NYA	6.64	Bobby Doerr, Bos	8.49	Mike Higgins, Det	6.05
1945	Mike Tresh, ChA	3.70	Joe Kuhel, Was	6.02	Snuffy Stirnweiss, NYA	6.57	Oscar Grimes, NYA	5.25
1946	Mark Christman, StL	3.06	Hank Greenberg, Det	7.81	Bobby Doerr, Bos	5.18	Snuffy Stirnweiss, NYA	3.87
1947	Eddie Yost, Was	2.91	George McQuinn, NYA	6.72	Joe Gordon, Cle	5.92	George Kell, Det	5.61
1948	Yogi Berra, NYA	6.21	Ferris Fain, Phi	6.42	Bobby Doerr, Bos	7.36	Ken Keltner, Cle	6.81
1949	Jim Hegan, Cle	3.17	Ferris Fain, Phi	5.79	Bobby Doerr, Bos	6.37	George Kell, Det	7.34
1950	Yogi Berra, NYA	7.77	Walt Dropo, Bos	8.09	Bobby Doerr, Bos	6.60	Johnny Pesky, Bos	7.16
1951	Yogi Berra, NYA	6.38	Ferris Fain, Phi	8.32	Nellie Fox, ChA	5.47	Eddie Yost, Was	7.42
1952	Yogi Berra, NYA	6.10	Ferris Fain, Phi	7.30	Billy Goodman, Bos	5.72	Al Rosen, Cle	7.18
1953	Yogi Berra, NYA	7.00	Mickey Vernon, Was	7.73	Billy Goodman, Bos	6.01	Al Rosen, Cle	9.07
1954	Yogi Berra, NYA	6.94	Mickey Vernon, Was	6.25	Bobby Avila, Cle	7.05	Al Rosen, Cle	7.46
1955	Yogi Berra, NYA	5.78	Vic Power, KCA	6.28	Gil McDougald, NYA	5.50	George Kell, ChA	6.26
1956	Yogi Berra, NYA	7.68	Bill Skowron, NYA	7.20	Nellie Fox, ChA	4.70	Ray Boone, Det	7.25
1957	Yogi Berra, NYA	4.89	Vic Wertz, Cle	6.79	Nellie Fox, ChA	6.63	Eddie Yost, Was	5.00
1958	Sherm Lollar, ChA	5.72	Gail Harris, Det	5.42	Pete Runnels, Bos	6.86	Frank Malzone, Bos	4.53
1959	Yogi Berra, NYA	5.75	Vic Power, Cle	4.73	Pete Runnels, Bos	6.84	Eddie Yost, Det	7.74
1960	Earl Battey, Was	5.01	Roy Sievers, ChA	7.53	Pete Runnels, Bos	5.78	Eddie Yost, Det	6.20
1961	John Romano, Cle	6.58	Norm Cash, Det	11.58	Jerry Lumpe, KCA	5.31	Al Smith, ChA	5.85
1962	John Romano, Cle	6.09	Norm Siebern, KCA	7.69	Jerry Lumpe, KCA	5.20	Rich Rollins, Min	6.02
1963	Elston Howard, NYA	6.29	Norm Cash, Det	6.63	Jerry Lumpe, KCA	4.48	Pete Ward, ChA	6.29
1964	Elston Howard, NYA	6.48	Bob Allison, Min	7.86	Don Buford, ChA	4.25	Brooks Robinson, Bal	6.70
1965	Ken Berry, ChA	3.06	Norm Cash, Det	7.02	Don Buford, ChA	5.37	Brooks Robinson, Bal	5.80
1966	Bill Freehan, Det	3.40	Boog Powell, Bal	7.08	Cesar Tovar, Min	4.10	Harmon Killebrew, Min	7.65
1967	Bill Freehan, Det	6.41	Harmon Killebrew, Min	8.53	Dick McAuliffe, Det	5.72	Brooks Robinson, Bal	4.73
1968	Bill Freehan, Det	6.28	Mickey Mantle, NYA	6.22	Dick McAuliffe, Det	5.49	Ken McMullen, Was	4.46
1969	Bill Freehan, Det	4.99	Boog Powell, Bal	7.20	Rod Carew, Min	6.71	Harmon Killebrew, Min	8.69
1970	Thurman Munson, NYA	5.72	Carl Yastrzemski, Bos	9.64	Dave Johnson, Bal	5.11	Harmon Killebrew, Min	7.48
1971	Bill Freehan, Det	5.33	Norm Cash, Det	7.03	Dave Johnson, Bal	5.33	Paul Schaal, KC	6.14
1972	Carlton Fisk, Bos	6.98	Dick Allen, ChA	8.89	Rod Carew, Min	5.02	Sal Bando, Oak	4.51
1973	Thurman Munson, NYA	6.01	John Mayberry, KC	8.23	Rod Carew, Min	6.91	Sal Bando, Oak	6.87
1974	Fran Healy, KC	4.37	Dick Allen, ChA	6.98	Rod Carew, Min	6.92	Sal Bando, Oak	5.62
1975	Gene Tenace, Oak	7.08	John Mayberry, KC	8.06	Rod Carew, Min	8.00	George Brett, KC	5.57
1976	Thurman Munson, NYA	4.93	Rod Carew, Min	6.79	Bobby Grich, Bal	5.89	George Brett, KC	6.82
1977	Carlton Fisk, Bos	7.53	Rod Carew, Min	10.33	Don Money, Mil	5.36	Toby Harrah, Tex	6.73
1978	Carlton Fisk, Bos	6.31	Rod Carew, Min	6.37	Willie Randolph, NYA	5.51	George Brett, KC	5.85
1979	Darrell Porter, KC	7.66	John Mayberry, Tor	6.27	Bobby Grich, Cal	6.82	George Brett, KC	7.71
1980	Carlton Fisk, Bos	5.42	Cecil Cooper, Mil	7.26	Willie Randolph, NYA	7.46	George Brett, KC	10.72
1981	Jim Sundberg, Tex	5.29	Cecil Cooper, Mil	6.57	Bobby Grich, Cal	7.44	Carney Lansford, Bos	6.39
1982	Lance Parrish, Det	6.17	Eddie Murray, Bal	7.34	Bobby Grich, Cal	5.69	Toby Harrah, Cle	6.80
1983	Carlton Fisk, ChA	6.77	Eddie Murray, Bal	7.63	Lou Whitaker, Det	6.42	Wade Boggs, Bos	8.15
1984	Lance Parrish, Det	4.13	Eddie Murray, Bal	7.59	Lou Whitaker, Det	5.27	Wade Boggs, Bos	6.43
1985	Rich Gedman, Bos	5.92	Eddie Murray, Bal	7.54	Toby Harrah, Tex	6.70	George Brett, KC	9.29
1986	Rich Gedman, Bos	4.36	Don Mattingly, NYA	7.71	Tony Bernazard, Cle	6.11	Wade Boggs, Bos	8.69
1987	Matt Nokes, Det	6.18	Dwight Evans, Bos	8.35	Willie Randolph, NYA	6.60	Wade Boggs, Bos	10.01
1988	B.J. Surhoff, Mil	3.06	George Brett, KC	7.26	Johnny Ray, Cal	5.31	Wade Boggs, Bos	8.15
1989	Cory Snyder, Cle	2.79	Alvin Davis, Sea	8.47	Julio Franco, Tex	7.00	Wade Boggs, Bos	6.84
1990	Carlton Fisk, ChA	5.17	Cecil Fielder, Det	7.54	Julio Franco, Tex	6.04	Kelly Gruber, Tor	6.43
1991	Mickey Tettleton, Det	7.05	Wally Joyner, Cal	6.65	Lou Whitaker, Det	7.50	Wade Boggs, Bos	6.89
1992	Mickey Tettleton, Det	6.02	Frank Thomas, ChA	8.15	Roberto Alomar, Tor	7.54	Edgar Martinez, Sea	7.40
1993	Chris Hoiles, Bal	8.25	John Olerud, Tor	10.40	Roberto Alomar, Tor	7.31	Robin Ventura, ChA	5.56
1994	Mickey Tettleton, Det	7.36	Frank Thomas, ChA	11.03	Chuck Knoblauch, Min	7.13	Wade Boggs, NYA	7.92
1995	Mike Stanley, NYA	6.19	Frank Thomas, ChA	9.37	Chuck Knoblauch, Min	7.94	Jim Thome, Cle	8.11
1996	Terry Steinbach, Oak	6.24	Mark McGwire, Oak	11.79	Chuck Knoblauch, Min	9.53	Jim Thome, Cle	9.30
1997	Ivan Rodriguez, Tex	5.98	Frank Thomas, ChA	10.93	Chuck Knoblauch, Min	6.46	Jeff Cirillo, Mil	6.17

AL Runs Created Per 27 Outs Leaders By Position

Year	Shortstop		Outfielder		Outfielder		Outfielder	
1901	Kid Elberfeld, Det	7.75	Socks Seybold, Phi	8.92	Mike Donlin, Bal	8.61	Dummy Hoy, ChA	7.85
1902	George Davis, ChA	7.17	Ed Delahanty, Was	11.35	Socks Seybold, Phi	7.90	Topsy Hartsel, Phi	7.52
1903	Freddy Parent, Bos	5.96	Topsy Hartsel, Phi	7.74	Patsy Dougherty, Bos	6.89	Jimmy Barrett, Det	6.80
1904	Freddy Parent, Bos	4.82	Elmer Flick, Cle	6.83	Chick Stahl, Bos	5.96	Willie Keeler, NYA	5.89
1905	George Davis, ChA	5.18	Elmer Flick, Cle	7.02	Topsy Hartsel, Phi	6.83	Sam Crawford, Det	6.14
1906	George Davis, ChA	5.44	George Stone, StL	8.41	Elmer Flick, Cle	6.29	Sam Crawford, Det	5.56
1907	Kid Elberfeld, NYA	5.27	Ty Cobb, Det	8.53	Sam Crawford, Det	7.51	Elmer Flick, Cle	6.76
1908	Bobby Wallace, StL	4.09	Doc Gessler, Bos	7.31	Ty Cobb, Det	7.26	Matty McIntyre, Det	6.44
1909	Donie Bush, Det	4.96	Ty Cobb, Det	9.27	Sam Crawford, Det	6.27	Tris Speaker, Bos	6.06
1910	Donie Bush, Det	5.09	Ty Cobb, Det	10.84	Tris Speaker, Bos	7.40	Birdie Cree, NYA	5.92
1911	Jack Barry, Phi	4.57	Ty Cobb, Det	12.42	Joe Jackson, Cle	10.92	Sam Crawford, Det	9.39
1912	Heinie Wagner, Bos	5.22	Tris Speaker, Bos	11.36	Ty Cobb, Det	11.27	Joe Jackson, Cle	10.43
1913	Jack Barry, Phi	4.80	Joe Jackson, Cle	9.77	Ty Cobb, Det	9.19	Tris Speaker, Bos	8.44
1914	Donie Bush, Det	4.08	Tris Speaker, Bos	7.78	Joe Jackson, Cle	6.96	Sam Crawford, Det	6.44
1915	Ray Chapman, Cle	4.78	Ty Cobb, Det	10.16	Tris Speaker, Bos	6.87	Bobby Veach, Det	6.50
1916	Roger Peckinpaugh, NYA	4.07	Tris Speaker, Cle	10.02	Ty Cobb, Det	8.93	Joe Jackson, ChA	7.30
1917	Ray Chapman, Cle	5.20	Ty Cobb, Det	9.87	Tris Speaker, Cle	8.15	Bobby Veach, Det	6.78
1918	Ray Chapman, Cle	4.79	Ty Cobb, Det	8.66	Tris Speaker, Cle	6.39	Harry Hooper, Bos	6.16
1919	Roger Peckinpaugh, NYA	5.79	Babe Ruth, Bos	10.53	Ty Cobb, Det	8.18	Joe Jackson, ChA	8.05
1920	Ray Chapman, Cle	5.50	Babe Ruth, NYA	16.44	Joe Jackson, Cle	10.33	Joe Jackson, ChA	9.53
1921	Joe Sewell, Cle	6.94	Babe Ruth, NYA	15.47	Harry Heilmann, Det	9.59	Ty Cobb, Det	9.27
1922	Chick Galloway, Phi	5.84	Tris Speaker, Cle	10.29	Babe Ruth, NYA	9.73	Harry Heilmann, Det	9.10
1923	Joe Sewell, Cle	8.46	Babe Ruth, NYA	14.86	Harry Heilmann, Det	11.02	Tris Speaker, Cle	10.45
1924	Topper Rigney, Det	5.90	Babe Ruth, NYA	13.39	Harry Heilmann, Det	8.18	Ken Williams, StL	7.87
1925	Joe Sewell, Cle	6.16	Ty Cobb, Det	10.67	Tris Speaker, Cle	10.31	Harry Heilmann, Det	9.85
1926	Joe Sewell, Cle	6.43	Babe Ruth, NYA	13.23	Goose Goslin, Was	8.51	Harry Heilmann, Det	8.44
1927	Joe Sewell, Cle	5.42	Babe Ruth, NYA	12.53	Harry Heilmann, Det	11.35	Earle Combs, NYA	7.85
1928	Joe Sewell, Cle	5.92	Babe Ruth, NYA	11.48	Goose Goslin, Was	9.49	Heinie Manush, StL	9.24
1929	Jimmy Dykes, Phi	8.13	Babe Ruth, NYA	10.54	Al Simmons, Phi	9.54	Harry Heilmann, Det	8.34
1930	Joe Cronin, Was	8.12	Babe Ruth, NYA	12.69	Al Simmons, Phi	11.28	Carl Reynolds, ChA	8.54
1931	Joe Cronin, Was	7.37	Babe Ruth, NYA	13.93	Al Simmons, Phi	11.19	Earl Averill, Cle	8.84
1932	Joe Cronin, Was	7.63	Babe Ruth, NYA	12.83	Earl Averill, Cle	8.34	Heinie Manush, Was	7.92
1933	Joe Cronin, Was	7.16	Babe Ruth, NYA	9.91	Bob Johnson, Phi	7.30	Heinie Manush, Was	6.90
1934	Luke Appling, ChA	6.26	Earl Averill, Cle	8.55	Al Simmons, ChA	8.43	Heinie Manush, Was	7.37
1935	Luke Appling, ChA	6.97	Joe Vosmik, Cle	8.13	Pete Fox, Det	7.35	Bob Johnson, Phi	6.66
1936	Luke Appling, ChA	10.41	Earl Averill, Cle	10.06	John Stone, Was	9.18	George Selkirk, NYA	8.03
1937	Joe Cronin, Bos	7.20	Joe DiMaggio, NYA	10.32	Bob Johnson, Phi	7.95	John Stone, Was	7.09
1938	Joe Cronin, Bos	8.40	Earl Averill, Cle	8.77	Joe DiMaggio, NYA	8.63	Jeff Heath, Cle	8.48
1939	Joe Cronin, Bos	7.19	Joe DiMaggio, NYA	11.71	Ted Williams, Bos	10.44	George Selkirk, NYA	9.57
1940	Luke Appling, ChA	7.54	Hank Greenberg, Det	10.22	Joe DiMaggio, NYA	9.90	Ted Williams, Bos	9.66
1941	Cecil Travis, Was	8.42	Ted Williams, Bos	16.09	Joe DiMaggio, NYA	11.06	Charlie Keller, NYA	9.29
1942	Johnny Pesky, Bos	5.82	Ted Williams, Bos	12.40	Charlie Keller, NYA	9.04	Wally Judnich, StL	8.17
1943	Luke Appling, ChA	7.15	Charlie Keller, NYA	7.67	Jeff Heath, Cle	6.27	Roy Cullenbine, Cle	6.20
1944	Vern Stephens, StL	7.19	Bob Johnson, Bos	8.66	Stan Spence, Was	7.32	Milt Byrnes, StL	6.25
1945	Vern Stephens, StL	6.20	Wally Moses, ChA	6.51	Bobby Estalella, Phi	5.92	Johnny Dickshot, ChA	5.70
1946	Johnny Pesky, Bos	6.57	Ted Williams, Bos	12.56	Charlie Keller, NYA	7.97	Joe DiMaggio, NYA	6.58
1947	Lou Boudreau, Cle	6.28	Ted Williams, Bos	11.99	Joe DiMaggio, NYA	7.67	Tommy Henrich, NYA	6.75
1948	Lou Boudreau, Cle	8.82	Ted Williams, Bos	12.92	Joe DiMaggio, NYA	8.62	Tommy Henrich, NYA	7.98
1949	Eddie Joost, Phi	7.83	Ted Williams, Bos	11.73	Tommy Henrich, NYA	8.64	Dom DiMaggio, Bos	6.61
1950	Phil Rizzuto, NYA	7.34	Larry Doby, Cle	8.90	Joe DiMaggio, NYA	8.46	Al Zarilla, Bos	8.45
1951	Eddie Joost, Phi	7.26	Ted Williams, Bos	10.42	Larry Doby, Cle	8.28	Vic Wertz, Det	6.91
1952	Eddie Joost, Phi	6.20	Mickey Mantle, NYA	7.87	Larry Doby, Cle	7.80	Elmer Valo, Phi	6.78
1953	George Strickland, Cle	5.28	Mickey Mantle, NYA	7.72	Gene Woodling, NYA	7.16	Larry Doby, Cle	6.92
1954	Pete Runnels, Was	5.19	Ted Williams, Bos	11.85	Mickey Mantle, NYA	8.68	Minnie Minoso, ChA	7.56
1955	Harvey Kuenn, Det	5.80	Mickey Mantle, NYA	9.91	Al Kaline, Det	8.68	Al Smith, Cle	7.07
1956	Gil McDougald, NYA	6.98	Mickey Mantle, NYA	13.20	Ted Williams, Bos	10.28	Minnie Minoso, ChA	8.48
1957	Gil McDougald, NYA	5.49	Ted Williams, Bos	14.38	Mickey Mantle, NYA	13.54	Roy Sievers, Was	8.33
1958	Don Buddin, Bos	4.29	Mickey Mantle, NYA	9.78	Ted Williams, Bos	9.25	Rocky Colavito, Cle	8.60
1959	Don Buddin, Bos	5.29	Al Kaline, Det	7.88	Harvey Kuenn, Det	7.79	Mickey Mantle, NYA	7.43
1960	Ron Hansen, Bal	5.11	Mickey Mantle, NYA	7.97	Roger Maris, NYA	7.72	Gene Woodling, Bal	6.88
1961	Dick Howser, KCA	5.86	Mickey Mantle, NYA	11.73	Rocky Colavito, Det	8.13	Roger Maris, NYA	7.94
1962	Tom Tresh, NYA	5.88	Mickey Mantle, NYA	11.79	Harmon Killebrew, Min	6.87	Floyd Robinson, ChA	6.85
1963	Eddie Bressoud, Bos	5.00	Bob Allison, Min	7.31	Carl Yastrzemski, Bos	7.30	Tom Tresh, NYA	6.97
1964	Eddie Bressoud, Bos	6.01	Mickey Mantle, NYA	9.27	Boog Powell, Bal	8.55	Tony Oliva, Min	6.83
1965	Zoilo Versalles, Min	5.69	Tony Oliva, Min	7.29	Leon Wagner, Cle	6.85	Carl Yastrzemski, Bos	6.78
1966	Dick McAuliffe, Det	6.60	Frank Robinson, Bal	8.90	Al Kaline, Det	7.62	Curt Blefary, Bal	6.38
1967	Jim Fregosi, Cal	5.17	Carl Yastrzemski, Bos	9.84	Frank Robinson, Bal	8.41	Al Kaline, Det	7.85
1968	Bert Campaneris, Oak	4.41	Carl Yastrzemski, Bos	8.21	Willie Horton, Det	6.63	Frank Howard, Was	6.59
1969	Rico Petrocelli, Bos	7.95	Reggie Jackson, Oak	9.05	Frank Robinson, Bal	8.11	Frank Howard, Was	7.72
1970	Jim Fregosi, Cal	6.02	Frank Howard, Was	7.43	Frank Robinson, Bal	7.41	Roy White, NYA	6.82
1971	Leo Cardenas, Min	4.55	Bobby Murcer, NYA	8.64	Don Buford, Bal	7.56	Merv Rettenmund, Bal	7.11
1972	Bobby Grich, Bal	5.35	Carlos May, ChA	6.65	Bobby Murcer, NYA	6.49	Reggie Smith, Bos	6.36
1973	Toby Harrah, Tex	4.14	Reggie Jackson, Oak	7.39	Amos Otis, KC	6.64	Jeff Burroughs, Tex	6.17
1974	Bert Campaneris, Oak	4.97	Reggie Jackson, Oak	7.81	Jeff Burroughs, Tex	7.10	Joe Rudi, Oak	6.04
1975	Toby Harrah, Tex	7.27	Fred Lynn, Bos	8.32	Ken Singleton, Bal	7.26	Bobby Bonds, NYA	6.74
1976	Rick Burleson, Bos	5.01	Fred Lynn, Bos	6.30	Reggie Jackson, Bal	6.13	Rusty Staub, Det	5.95
1977	Freddie Patek, KC	4.38	Mitchell Page, Oak	8.47	Ken Singleton, Bal	8.40	Reggie Jackson, NYA	7.64
1978	Robin Yount, Mil	4.98	Jim Rice, Bos	7.73	Amos Otis, KC	7.19	Leon Roberts, Sea	6.74
1979	Roy Smalley, Min	5.43	Fred Lynn, Bos	9.72	Sixto Lezcano, Mil	8.02	Jim Rice, Bos	7.88
1980	Robin Yount, Mil	5.85	Reggie Jackson, NYA	8.54	Rickey Henderson, Oak	7.23	Ken Singleton, Bal	7.04
1981	Robin Yount, Mil	5.15	Dwight Evans, Bos	8.05	Rickey Henderson, Oak	7.09	Tom Paciorek, ChA	6.39
1982	Robin Yount, Mil	7.97	Dwight Evans, Bos	7.54	Reggie Jackson, Cal	6.77	Rickey Henderson, Oak	6.66
1983	Robin Yount, Mil	6.91	Rickey Henderson, Oak	7.50	Lloyd Moseby, Tor	6.73	Jim Rice, Bos	6.09
1984	Cal Ripken Jr., Bal	6.62	Dave Winfield, NYA	7.19	Rickey Henderson, Oak	7.17	Dwight Evans, Bos	7.09
1985	Cal Ripken Jr., Bal	5.28	Rickey Henderson, NYA	9.13	Kirk Gibson, Det	6.73	Jesse Barfield, Tor	6.73
1986	Cal Ripken Jr., Bal	5.69	Jesse Barfield, Tor	7.19	Phil Bradley, Sea	6.88	Jim Rice, Bos	6.73
1987	Alan Trammell, Det	8.39	George Bell, Tor	7.30	Danny Tartabull, KC	7.21	Kirby Puckett, Min	7.05
1988	Alan Trammell, Det	5.91	Jose Canseco, Oak	8.00	Mike Greenwell, Bos	8.00	Dave Winfield, NYA	7.81
1989	Kurt Stillwell, KC	4.79	Robin Yount, Mil	7.61	Ruben Sierra, Tex	7.32	Dwight Evans, Bos	6.54
1990	Alan Trammell, Det	6.86	Rickey Henderson, Oak	9.19	Jose Canseco, Oak	6.70	Jesse Barfield, NYA	6.16
1991	Cal Ripken Jr., Bal	7.22	Danny Tartabull, KC	8.64	Ken Griffey Jr., Sea	7.55	Jose Canseco, Oak	7.01
1992	Pat Listach, Mil	4.72	Danny Tartabull, NYA	7.93	Ken Griffey Jr., Sea	6.91	Kirby Puckett, Min	6.75
1993	Travis Fryman, Det	7.26	Juan Gonzalez, Tex	9.10	Ken Griffey Jr., Sea	7.71	Tim Salmon, Cal	6.98
1994	Cal Ripken Jr., Bal	6.29	Albert Belle, Cle	10.72	Paul O'Neill, NYA	9.97	Ken Griffey Jr., Sea	8.76
1995	John Valentin, Bos	8.11	Tim Salmon, Cal	9.36	Albert Belle, Cle	8.05	Manny Ramirez, Cle	7.80
1996	Alex Rodriguez, Sea	9.47	Ken Griffey Jr., Sea	8.98	Albert Belle, Cle	8.90	Bob Higginson, Det	8.81
1997	Nomar Garciaparra, Bos	6.27	David Justice, Cle	8.91	Ken Griffey Jr., Sea	8.82	Paul O'Neill, NYA	8.15

Leaders: RC/27 By Position

AL Runs Created Per 27 Outs Leaders By Position

Year	Designated Hitter		Year	Designated Hitter	
1973	Frank Robinson, Cal	6.58	1986	Larry Parrish, Tex	5.91
1974	Oscar Gamble, Cle	6.58	1987	Paul Molitor, Mil	9.88
1975	Billy Williams, Oak	5.34	1988	Jack Clark, NYA	6.17
1976	Hal McRae, KC	7.10	1989	Brian Downing, Cal	5.48
1977	Jim Rice, Bos	7.43	1990	Chris James, Cle	5.58
1978	Don Baylor, Cal	5.48	1991	Frank Thomas, ChA	9.16
1979	Carl Yastrzemski, Bos	5.35	1992	Paul Molitor, Mil	7.05
1980	Hal McRae, KC	5.71	1993	Paul Molitor, Mil	7.98
1981	Greg Luzinski, ChA	6.26	1994	Paul Molitor, Mil	8.57
1982	Hal McRae, KC	7.08	1995	Edgar Martinez, Sea	11.67
1983	Greg Luzinski, ChA	6.48	1996	Edgar Martinez, Sea	9.33
1984	Mike Easler, Bos	6.99	1997	Edgar Martinez, Sea	8.67
1985	Don Baylor, NYA	4.87			

AA Runs Created Per 27 Outs Leaders By Position

Year	Catcher		First Baseman		Second Baseman		Third Baseman	
1882	Jack O'Brien, Phi	8.80	Jumbo Latham, Phi	6.64	Pete Browning, Lou	12.54	Hick Carpenter, Cin	9.37
1883	Jack O'Brien, Phi	8.73	Harry Stovey, Phi	11.13	Cub Stricker, Phi	6.99	Hick Carpenter, Cin	7.79
1884	John Humphries, WaD	2.34	John Reilly, Cin	12.30	Sam Barkley, Tol	8.01	Dude Esterbrook, NY	8.94
1885	Frank Hankinson, NY	3.43	Harry Stovey, Phi	10.61	Sam Barkley, STL	7.26	Bill McClellan, Bro	6.53
1886	Fred Carroll, Pit	8.03	Dave Orr, NY	9.52	Yank Robinson, STL	8.19	Arlie Latham, STL	7.99
1887	Hick Carpenter, Cin	4.83	Charlie Comiskey, STL	8.66	Yank Robinson, STL	10.28	Denny Lyons, Phi	11.02
1888	Harry Lyons, STL	3.48	John Reilly, Cin	9.14	Yank Robinson, STL	7.54	Denny Lyons, Phi	8.22
1889	Jack O'Connor, CoC	5.77	Tommy Tucker, Bal	12.32	Hub Collins, Bro	7.47	Denny Lyons, Phi	9.36
1890	Jack O'Connor, CoC	7.99	Perry Werden, Tol	8.28	Cupid Childs, Syr	9.63	Jimmy Knowles, Roc	6.92
1891	Jocko Milligan, Phi	8.82	Dan Brouthers, Bos	12.45	Jack Crooks, CoC	7.00	Denny Lyons, STL	10.64

Year	Shortstop		Outfielder		Outfielder		Outfielder	
1882	Bill Gleason, STL	6.76	Ed Swartwood, Pit	9.55	Joe Sommer, Cin	7.50	Chicken Wolf, Lou	7.25
1883	Mike Moynahan, Phi	9.93	Pete Browning, Lou	10.44	Charley Jones, Cin	9.36	Jim Clinton, Bal	7.53
1884	Candy Nelson, NY	9.16	Charley Jones, Cin	11.64	Chief Roseman, NY	8.60	Fred Mann, Col	8.52
1885	Frank Fennelly, Cin	8.43	Pete Browning, Lou	11.16	Henry Larkin, Phi	11.09	Charley Jones, Cin	9.49
1886	Frank Fennelly, Cin	7.66	Henry Larkin, Phi	9.49	Tip O'Neill, STL	9.39	Pete Browning, Lou	9.02
1887	Oyster Burns, Bal	10.89	Tip O'Neill, STL	16.99	Bob Caruthers, STL	13.03	Pete Browning, Lou	12.88
1888	Ed McKean, Cle	7.49	Tip O'Neill, STL	9.37	Harry Stovey, Phi	8.94	Curt Welch, Phi	7.44
1889	Herman Long, KC	7.88	Tip O'Neill, STL	10.69	Billy Hamilton, KC	10.31	Darby O'Brien, Bro	9.82
1890	Irv Ray, Bal	9.82	Chicken Wolf, Lou	9.95	Tommy McCarthy, STL	9.82	Spud Johnson, CoC	9.49
1891	George Shoch, Mil	10.42	Hugh Duffy, Bos	10.40	Tom Brown, Bos	10.36	George Van Haltren, Bal	9.46

UA Runs Created Per 27 Outs Leaders By Position

Year	Catcher		First Baseman		Second Baseman		Third Baseman	
1884	Cal Broughton, Mil	8.05	Phil Baker, Was	7.41	Fred Dunlap, STL	16.46	Jack Gleason, STL	9.77

Year	Shortstop		Outfielder		Outfielder		Outfielder	
1884	Walter Hackett, Bos	5.54	Buster Hoover, Phi	12.11	Orator Shaffer, STL	12.08	Harry Moore, Was	10.12

PL Runs Created Per 27 Outs Leaders By Position

Year	Catcher		First Baseman		Second Baseman		Third Baseman	
1890	Fred Carroll, Pit	8.95	Roger Connor, NY	12.99	Lou Bierbauer, Bro	7.81	Bill Joyce, Bro	9.01

Year	Shortstop		Outfielder		Outfielder		Outfielder	
1890	Monte Ward, Bro	9.93	George Gore, NY	11.64	Pete Browning, Cle	11.53	Jim O'Rourke, NY	11.30

FL Runs Created Per 27 Outs Leaders By Position

Year	Catcher		First Baseman		Second Baseman		Third Baseman	
1914	Ted Easterly, KC	6.33	Joe Agler, Buf	5.19	Duke Kenworthy, KC	6.92	Ed Lennox, Pit	7.18
1915	Bill Rariden, New	4.92	Ed Konetchy, Pit	6.04	Lee Magee, Bro	5.59	Mike Mowrey, Pit	4.91

Year	Shortstop		Outfielder		Outfielder		Outfielder	
1914	Baldy Louden, Buf	6.45	Benny Kauff, Ind	9.56	Steve Evans, Bro	8.16	Vin Campbell, Ind	6.04
1915	Marty Berghammer, Pit	4.20	Benny Kauff, Bro	8.82	Dutch Zwilling, Chi	6.01	Max Flack, Chi	5.97

Relativity Leaders

Catcher

		RC/27	LRC/27	RQ
1	Roger Bresnahan	6.06	4.04	150
2	Mickey Cochrane	7.61	5.08	150
3	Gene Tenace	6.12	4.11	149
4	Buck Ewing	8.23	5.77	143
5	Bill Dickey	7.07	5.05	140
6	Joe Torre	5.62	4.06	139
7	Roy Campanella	6.17	4.48	138
8	Yogi Berra	6.13	4.45	138
9	Gabby Hartnett	6.38	4.65	137
10	Darren Daulton	5.78	4.27	135
11	Chief Meyers	5.36	3.98	135
12	Johnny Bench	5.47	4.06	135
13	Wally Schang	5.97	4.48	133
14	Fred Carroll	7.57	5.69	133
15	John Romano	5.55	4.21	132
16	Mike Grady	6.64	5.10	130
17	Smoky Burgess	5.61	4.35	129
18	Tom Haller	5.02	3.98	126
19	Bill Freehan	4.95	3.94	126
20	Ernie Lombardi	5.47	4.37	125
21	Mike Stanley	6.00	4.82	125
22	Ed Bailey	5.34	4.29	124
23	Mickey Tettleton	5.80	4.68	124
24	Carlton Fisk	5.41	4.36	124
25	Jocko Milligan	7.26	5.86	124
26	Johnny Bassler	6.04	4.89	124
27	Ted Simmons	5.15	4.21	122
28	Spud Davis	5.62	4.61	122
29	Charlie Bennett	6.56	5.40	121
30	Darrell Porter	5.16	4.25	121
31	Joe Ferguson	5.01	4.14	121
32	Duke Sims	4.70	3.90	120
33	Walker Cooper	5.18	4.32	120
34	Gary Carter	4.91	4.11	120
35	Chris Hoiles	5.78	4.87	119
36	Jim Pagliaroni	4.81	4.09	118
37	Stan Lopata	5.20	4.44	117
38	Hank Gowdy	4.78	4.10	117
39	Thurman Munson	4.82	4.15	116
40	Jack Clements	6.54	5.64	116
41	Tim McCarver	4.60	3.99	115
42	Earl Battey	4.81	4.20	115
43	Sherm Lollar	5.01	4.44	113
44	Elston Howard	4.66	4.18	112
45	Bob O'Farrell	5.21	4.67	111
46	Bob Brenly	4.58	4.14	111
47	Andy Seminick	4.81	4.43	108
48	Harry Danning	4.72	4.36	108
49	Johnny Kling	4.38	4.07	108
50	Shanty Hogan	5.07	4.78	106

First Base

		RC/27	LRC/27	RQ
1	Lou Gehrig	10.29	5.13	201
2	Frank Thomas	9.54	4.82	198
3	Johnny Mize	8.32	4.42	188
4	Dan Brouthers	10.68	5.75	186
5	Jimmie Foxx	9.35	5.07	184
6	Hank Greenberg	9.00	4.91	183
7	Dick Allen	7.07	3.98	177
8	Frank Chance	7.11	4.05	175
9	Jeff Bagwell	7.67	4.41	174
10	Willie McCovey	6.87	4.08	168
11	Dolph Camilli	7.19	4.38	164
12	Roger Connor	9.31	5.74	162
13	Harmon Killebrew	6.62	4.08	162
14	Norm Cash	6.52	4.02	162
15	Cap Anson	9.07	5.62	162
16	Mark McGwire	7.46	4.64	161
17	Will Clark	7.09	4.42	160
18	Pedro Guerrero	6.36	4.09	155
19	Bill Terry	7.35	4.77	154
20	Jack Fournier	6.75	4.39	154
21	Fred McGriff	6.64	4.42	150
22	Keith Hernandez	6.17	4.12	150
23	Rod Carew	6.20	4.16	149
24	Boog Powell	5.84	3.97	147
25	Joe Cunningham	6.35	4.33	147
26	John Kruk	6.18	4.22	146
27	Ferris Fain	6.61	4.53	146
28	Orlando Cepeda	6.00	4.15	145
29	Mark Grace	6.18	4.29	144
30	Henry Larkin	8.33	5.85	142
31	Leon Durham	5.84	4.12	142
32	Norm Siebern	5.91	4.23	140
33	Bob Watson	5.77	4.15	139
34	Hal Trosky	6.94	5.01	139
35	Bill White	5.71	4.13	138
36	Ted Kluszewski	6.18	4.48	138
37	Don Mincher	5.40	3.92	138
38	Gil Hodges	6.13	4.46	138
39	Alvin Davis	6.17	4.49	137
40	Rudy York	6.10	4.45	137
41	John Olerud	6.51	4.75	137
42	Charlie Hickman	5.70	4.16	137
43	George Sisler	6.32	4.66	136
44	Andres Galarraga	5.84	4.32	135
45	Elbie Fletcher	5.78	4.28	135
46	Jim Bottomley	6.52	4.83	135
47	Kent Hrbek	6.11	4.52	135
48	Rafael Palmeiro	6.24	4.64	135
49	Mike Hargrove	5.86	4.35	135
50	Phil Cavarretta	5.83	4.36	134

Second Base

		RC/27	LRC/27	RQ
1	Rogers Hornsby	8.95	4.42	203
2	Eddie Collins	7.14	4.25	168
3	Nap Lajoie	7.03	4.23	166
4	Joe Morgan	6.64	4.10	162
5	Jackie Robinson	7.28	4.50	162
6	Charlie Gehringer	7.38	5.10	145
7	Larry Doyle	5.50	3.84	143
8	Craig Biggio	6.13	4.34	141
9	Hardy Richardson	7.57	5.53	137
10	Ryne Sandberg	5.67	4.19	135
11	Cupid Childs	7.76	5.74	135
12	George Grantham	6.45	4.78	135
13	Danny Murphy	5.17	3.85	134
14	Chuck Knoblauch	6.47	4.85	133
15	Eddie Stanky	5.81	4.37	133
16	Miller Huggins	5.07	3.88	131
17	Roberto Alomar	5.95	4.57	130
18	Bobby Grich	5.59	4.29	130
19	Jim Delahanty	5.07	3.90	130
20	Jimmy Williams	5.33	4.17	128
21	Bobby Doerr	5.86	4.60	127
22	Tony Lazzeri	6.47	5.09	127
23	Billy Herman	5.50	4.35	126
24	Johnny Evers	4.91	3.89	126
25	Lou Whitaker	5.71	4.52	126
26	Frankie Frisch	5.89	4.67	126
27	Dick McAuliffe	5.01	3.97	126
28	Ron Hunt	4.93	3.97	124
29	Joe Gordon	5.76	4.64	124
30	Max Bishop	6.25	5.05	124
31	Davey Lopes	5.10	4.19	122
32	Dave Johnson	4.72	3.90	121
33	Frank LaPorte	4.71	3.90	121
34	Lonny Frey	5.24	4.34	121
35	Gil McDougald	5.24	4.36	120
36	Bip Roberts	5.30	4.41	120
37	Billy Goodman	5.33	4.48	119
38	Bid McPhee	6.84	5.78	118
39	Bill Doran	4.84	4.11	118
40	Tom Daly	6.54	5.56	118
41	Buddy Myer	5.94	5.09	117
42	Del Pratt	4.92	4.23	116
43	Tony Phillips	5.43	4.68	116
44	Bill Sweeney	4.51	3.99	113
45	Jim Gilliam	4.90	4.35	113
46	Willie Randolph	4.93	4.39	112
47	Bobby Avila	4.87	4.41	111
48	Juan Samuel	4.67	4.24	110
49	Johnny Temple	4.84	4.39	110
50	Claude Ritchey	4.78	4.38	109

Third Base

		RC/27	LRC/27	RQ
1	John McGraw	9.88	5.81	170
2	Mike Schmidt	6.95	4.12	169
3	Eddie Mathews	6.92	4.28	162
4	Edgar Martinez	7.57	4.76	159
5	Home Run Baker	6.08	3.99	152
6	Wade Boggs	6.97	4.62	151
7	Gary Sheffield	6.64	4.41	150
8	Al Rosen	6.59	4.52	146
9	Denny Lyons	8.71	6.01	145
10	Stan Hack	6.30	4.37	144
11	George Brett	6.28	4.41	142
12	Ron Santo	5.78	4.07	142
13	Bob Horner	5.74	4.07	141
14	Jim Ray Hart	5.55	3.98	139
15	Bob Elliott	5.98	4.32	139
16	Bobby Bonilla	6.09	4.40	138
17	Dave Magadan	5.79	4.32	134
18	H. Zimmerman	5.16	3.86	134
19	Bill Madlock	5.55	4.16	134
20	Darrell Evans	5.59	4.21	133
21	Howard Johnson	5.52	4.21	131
22	Richie Hebner	5.45	4.15	131
23	Ken Boyer	5.49	4.20	131
24	Heine Groh	5.28	4.05	130
25	Ron Cey	5.34	4.12	130
26	Harlond Clift	6.26	4.89	128
27	Deacon White	7.03	5.49	128
28	Art Devlin	4.94	3.86	128
29	Eddie Yost	5.67	4.46	127
30	Red Smith	4.85	3.83	126
31	Sal Bando	5.17	4.09	126
32	Ned Williamson	6.80	5.38	126
33	Ezra Sutton	6.71	5.35	125
34	Jimmy Collins	5.81	4.70	123
35	Toby Harrah	5.28	4.29	123
36	George Kell	5.37	4.39	122
37	Ken Caminiti	5.23	4.33	121
38	Robin Ventura	5.69	4.76	120
39	Ray Boone	5.32	4.45	119
40	Matt Williams	5.21	4.37	119
41	Hans Lobert	4.56	3.83	119
42	Kevin Seitzer	5.54	4.68	118
43	Pie Traynor	5.60	4.74	118
44	Billy Nash	6.97	5.91	118
45	Bill Melton	4.80	4.08	118
46	Freddy Lindstrom	5.59	4.76	118
47	Mike Higgins	5.62	4.84	116
48	Bob Bailey	4.64	4.01	116
49	Larry Gardner	4.82	4.18	115
50	Graig Nettles	4.75	4.19	114

Shortstop

		RC/27	LRC/27	RQ
1	Honus Wagner	7.62	4.18	182
2	Arky Vaughan	7.24	4.37	166
3	Barry Larkin	6.28	4.30	146
4	Vern Stephens	5.90	4.35	136
5	George Davis	6.72	5.00	134
6	Johnny Pesky	5.94	4.45	133
7	Joe Cronin	6.70	5.07	132
8	Hughie Jennings	7.29	5.63	129
9	Luke Appling	6.21	4.81	129
10	Kid Elberfeld	5.11	4.10	125
11	Lou Boudreau	5.53	4.44	124
12	Bill Dahlen	6.06	4.91	123
13	Jeff Blauser	5.33	4.36	122
14	Rico Petrocelli	4.75	3.93	121
15	Jim Fregosi	4.79	3.96	121
16	Robin Yount	5.33	4.42	121
17	Ed McKean	7.09	5.88	120
18	Ray Chapman	4.71	3.94	120
19	Joe Sewell	5.94	4.99	119
20	Julio Franco	5.41	4.62	117
21	Pee Wee Reese	5.13	4.38	117
22	Alan Trammell	5.26	4.54	116
23	Jack Glasscock	6.45	5.57	116
24	Jack Rowe	6.36	5.51	115
25	Sam Wise	6.58	5.73	115
26	Woodie Held	4.82	4.20	115
27	Denis Menke	4.54	3.98	114
28	Eddie Joost	4.99	4.39	114
29	Cal Ripken Jr.	5.27	4.64	114
30	Cecil Travis	5.62	4.98	113
31	Herman Long	6.08	5.52	110
32	Dave Bancroft	4.66	4.31	108
33	Dick Bartell	4.96	4.61	108
34	Bobby Wallace	4.68	4.35	108
35	Al Dark	4.78	4.45	107
36	Art Fletcher	4.21	3.93	107
37	Travis Jackson	5.10	4.79	107
38	Woody English	5.08	4.77	107
39	Roy Smalley	4.73	4.45	106
40	Glenn Wright	5.05	4.76	106
41	Tony Fernandez	4.73	4.48	106
42	Monte Ward	5.96	5.65	105
43	Phil Rizzuto	4.70	4.48	105
44	Freddy Parent	4.15	3.96	105
45	Jay Bell	4.59	4.40	104
46	Joe Tinker	4.15	3.99	104
47	Maury Wills	4.20	4.08	103
48	Donie Bush	4.14	4.05	102
49	Al Bridwell	3.90	3.85	101
50	Eddie Bressoud	4.26	4.21	101

Outfield

		RC/27	LRC/27	RQ
1	Ted Williams	11.49	4.54	253
2	Babe Ruth	11.73	4.83	243
3	Mickey Mantle	8.93	4.22	212
4	Ty Cobb	8.66	4.22	205
5	Joe Jackson	8.33	4.06	205
6	Stan Musial	8.41	4.35	193
7	Barry Bonds	8.26	4.30	192
8	Tris Speaker	8.06	4.29	188
9	Billy Hamilton	10.70	5.76	186
10	Mel Ott	8.34	4.52	184
11	Charlie Keller	8.21	4.47	184
12	Willie Mays	7.65	4.21	182
13	Joe DiMaggio	8.67	4.83	179
14	Frank Robinson	7.32	4.12	178
15	Gavy Cravath	6.68	3.78	177
16	Hank Aaron	7.21	4.18	173
17	Elmer Flick	7.23	4.25	170
18	Ralph Kiner	7.48	4.46	168
19	Pete Browning	9.60	5.77	166
20	Ed Delahanty	9.31	5.65	165
21	Harry Heilmann	7.63	4.63	165
22	Willie Stargell	6.63	4.03	165
23	Tip O'Neill	9.59	5.85	164
24	Duke Snider	7.22	4.42	163
25	Jesse Burkett	8.44	5.22	162
26	King Kelly	8.82	5.45	162
27	Sam Crawford	6.34	3.94	161
28	Topsy Hartsel	6.27	3.95	159
29	Roy Cullenbine	6.76	4.28	158
30	George Gore	8.64	5.48	158
31	Larry Walker	6.88	4.37	157
32	Hack Wilson	7.49	4.77	157
33	Harry Stovey	8.87	5.66	157
34	Reggie Smith	6.20	3.97	156
35	Ken Griffey Jr.	7.36	4.72	156
36	Chuck Klein	7.30	4.68	156
37	Paul Waner	7.15	4.58	156
38	Billy Williams	6.34	4.07	156
39	Sherry Magee	5.93	3.81	156
40	Joe Kelley	8.04	5.19	155
41	R. Henderson	7.04	4.55	155
42	Tony Gwynn	6.54	4.24	154
43	Al Kaline	6.39	4.16	154
44	Joe Medwick	6.67	4.36	153
45	Roy Thomas	6.41	4.20	153
46	Jack Clark	6.35	4.17	152
47	Larry Doby	6.84	4.49	152
48	Tommy Henrich	7.10	4.67	152
49	Darryl Strawberry	6.36	4.20	151
50	Sam Thompson	8.78	5.81	151

Starting Pitcher

		ERC	LERA	RQ
1	Addie Joss	1.73	2.72	157
2	Ed Walsh	1.78	2.75	154
3	Roger Clemens	2.78	4.27	154
4	Walter Johnson	2.12	3.24	153
5	Greg Maddux	2.58	3.87	150
6	Ed Morris	2.30	3.41	148
7	Sandy Koufax	2.50	3.70	148
8	Tim Keefe	2.26	3.34	147
9	Kevin Appier	3.08	4.41	143
10	Lefty Grove	3.12	4.42	141
11	Cy Young	2.51	3.54	141
12	Bret Saberhagen	2.94	4.08	139
13	Carl Hubbell	2.88	3.96	138
14	Charlie Ferguson	2.35	3.22	138
15	Bob Caruthers	2.55	3.51	137
16	Tom Seaver	2.67	3.65	137
17	Dave Foutz	2.56	3.50	137
18	Dazzy Vance	3.00	4.09	136
19	C. Mathewson	2.14	2.91	136
20	David Cone	2.99	4.05	136
21	T. Finger Brown	2.13	2.88	135
22	Sid Fernandez	2.81	3.79	135
23	Babe Adams	2.40	3.23	135
24	Lefty Gomez	3.35	4.50	135
25	Kid Nichols	2.90	3.89	134
26	Pete Alexander	2.53	3.39	134
27	A. Messersmith	2.66	3.55	134
28	Toad Ramsey	2.77	3.70	134
29	Randy Johnson	3.21	4.29	133
30	Dizzy Dean	2.94	3.88	132
31	Harry Brecheen	2.90	3.83	132
32	J.R. Richard	2.79	3.66	131
33	Guy Hecker	2.59	3.39	131
34	Noodles Hahn	2.48	3.25	131
35	Amos Rusie	3.10	4.06	131
36	Juan Marichal	2.73	3.56	130
37	Johnny Allen	3.37	4.39	130
38	Bob Feller	3.19	4.16	130
39	Ron Guidry	3.11	4.04	130
40	John Smoltz	3.00	3.90	130
41	Rube Waddell	2.22	2.89	130
42	O. H. Radbourn	2.52	3.26	130
43	Monte Ward	2.01	2.61	130
44	Whitey Ford	2.97	3.84	129
45	Don Sutton	2.88	3.70	129
46	John Clarkson	2.75	3.54	128
47	Nolan Ryan	2.89	3.71	128
48	Warren Spahn	3.03	3.89	128
49	Jim Palmer	2.91	3.71	128
50	Deacon Phillippe	2.44	3.10	127

Relief Pitcher

		ERC	LERA	RQ
1	Bryan Harvey	2.28	3.99	175
2	Tom Henke	2.44	4.14	170
3	Trevor Hoffman	2.48	4.16	168
4	John Wetteland	2.46	4.10	166
5	Greg McMichael	2.78	4.16	150
6	Hoyt Wilhelm	2.53	3.76	149
7	R. Hernandez	3.03	4.50	149
8	Rob Dibble	2.56	3.70	144
9	Rod Beck	2.76	3.98	144
10	Jeff Montgomery	3.02	4.25	141
11	Bruce Sutter	2.62	3.62	138
12	Dan Quisenberry	2.92	4.00	137
13	Steve Howe	2.90	3.97	137
14	Duane Ward	2.93	4.00	137
15	Mark Eichhorn	3.11	4.18	134
16	Mike Jackson	3.06	4.10	134
17	Jesse Orosco	2.96	3.94	133
18	Dave Smith	2.72	3.63	133
19	Mark Wohlers	3.08	4.08	133
20	Rollie Fingers	2.78	3.67	132
21	Dick Hall	2.81	3.71	132
22	Doug Jones	3.13	4.12	132
23	Jeff Nelson	3.50	4.54	130
24	Mel Rojas	3.08	3.99	130
25	Steve Hamilton	2.74	3.54	129
26	Kent Tekulve	2.84	3.65	129
27	Mike Henneman	3.28	4.19	128
28	Al Holland	2.87	3.65	127
29	Goose Gossage	2.98	3.79	127
30	Firpo Marberry	3.39	4.31	127
31	Johnny Murphy	3.42	4.34	127
32	Dennis Eckersley	3.11	3.94	127
33	Bob Locker	2.70	3.41	126
34	Tim Burke	2.93	3.69	126
35	Lee Smith	3.04	3.83	126
36	Eddie Watt	2.72	3.41	126
37	Todd Worrell	3.08	3.87	125
38	Stan Belinda	3.31	4.13	125
39	Doug Corbett	3.24	4.02	124
40	Dick Radatz	2.93	3.62	124
41	Joe Sambito	3.01	3.73	124
42	Alejandro Pena	3.00	3.70	123
43	Jeff Reardon	3.08	3.79	123
44	Mike Timlin	3.62	4.44	123
45	Gregg Olson	3.43	4.20	122
46	Larry Andersen	3.07	3.76	122
47	Randy Myers	3.22	3.92	122
48	Jay Howell	3.24	3.93	121
49	Gary Lucas	3.07	3.72	121
50	Ted Wilks	3.14	3.80	121

Career Fielding Leaders—Pitchers

Games

#	Player	Games
1	Hoyt Wilhelm	1,070
2	Kent Tekulve	1,050
3	Lee Smith	1,022
4	Dennis Eckersley	1,021
5	Goose Gossage	1,001
6	Lindy McDaniel	987
7	Jesse Orosco	956
8	Rollie Fingers	944
9	Gene Garber	931
10	Cy Young	906
11	Sparky Lyle	899
12	Jim Kaat	898
13	Jeff Reardon	880
14	Don McMahon	874
15	Phil Niekro	864
16	Charlie Hough	858
17	Roy Face	848
18	Tug McGraw	824
19	Nolan Ryan	807
20	Walter Johnson	803
21	Rick Honeycutt	797
22	Gaylord Perry	777
23	Don Sutton	774
24	John Franco	771
25	Darold Knowles	765
26	Paul Assenmacher	760
27	Tommy John	759
28	Jack Quinn	756
29	Ron Reed	751
30	Warren Spahn	750
31	Gary Lavelle	745
	Tom Burgmeier	745
33	Willie Hernandez	744
34	Steve Carlton	741
35	Ron Perranoski	737
36	Ron Kline	736
37	Steve Bedrosian	732
38	Clay Carroll	731
39	Mike Marshall	723
	Roger McDowell	723
41	Dave Righetti	718
42	Johnny Klippstein	711
43	Greg Minton	710
44	Stu Miller	704
45	Greg Harris	703
46	Joe Niekro	702
47	Bill Campbell	700
48	Larry Andersen	699
49	Bob McClure	698
50	Pud Galvin	697
51	Craig Lefferts	696
	Pete Alexander	696
53	Mike Jackson	694
	Bob Miller	694
55	Bert Blyleven	692
	Grant Jackson	692
57	Early Wynn	691
58	Eddie Fisher	690
59	Eppa Rixey	689
60	Danny Darwin	683
61	Ted Abernathy	681
62	Dan Plesac	680
63	Robin Roberts	676
64	Dan Quisenberry	674
65	Waite Hoyt	673
66	Red Faber	669
67	Dave Giusti	668
68	Randy Myers	666
69	Fergie Jenkins	664
70	Bruce Sutter	661
71	Tom Seaver	656
72	Paul Lindblad	655
73	Doug Jones	653
74	Wilbur Wood	651
75	Dave LaRoche	647
	Sad Sam Jones	647
77	Tom Henke	642
78	Gerry Staley	640
	Dutch Leonard	640
80	Dennis Lamp	639
	Dennis Martinez	639
	Diego Segui	639
83	Frank Tanana	638
84	Bob Stanley	637
85	Christy Mathewson	635
86	Charlie Root	632
87	Jim Perry	630
88	Jerry Reuss	628
89	Lew Burdette	626
90	Woodie Fryman	625
	Murry Dickson	625
92	Mark Davis	624
	Red Ruffing	624
	Eddie Plank	624
95	Dick Tidrow	620
	Kid Nichols	620
97	Mitch Williams	619
98	Todd Worrell	617
	Burleigh Grimes	617
	Herb Pennock	617

Putouts

#	Player	Putouts
1	Jack Morris	387
2	Phil Niekro	386
3	Fergie Jenkins	363
4	Gaylord Perry	349
5	Don Sutton	334
6	Rick Reuschel	328
	Tom Seaver	328
8	Tony Mullane	327
9	Pud Galvin	324
10	Greg Maddux	318
11	Robin Roberts	316
12	Chick Fraser	315
13	Dennis Martinez	313
14	Kid Nichols	311
15	Jim Palmer	292
16	Orel Hershiser	291
	Juan Marichal	291
	Bob Gibson	291
19	Bert Blyleven	287
20	Christy Mathewson	281
21	Mike Moore	278
	Walter Johnson	278
23	Vic Willis	271
24	Dave Stieb	267
25	Doyle Alexander	264
26	Bob Lemon	263
	Jim McCormick	263
28	Jim Kaat	262
29	Tim Keefe	260
30	Doug Drabek	258
31	Larry Jackson	257
32	Dan Petry	255
33	Joe Niekro	253
34	Mike Boddicker	245
	Milt Pappas	245
	Lew Burdette	245
	Adonis Terry	245
38	Ted Breitenstein	244
39	Bob Welch	243
40	Mel Stottlemyre	242
41	Kevin Brown	239
42	Steve Rogers	237
	Tommy John	237
	Mark Gubicza	237
	Freddie Fitzsimmons	237
46	Murry Dickson	236
47	Charlie Hough	235
48	Bob Forsch	234
49	Ed Walsh	233
50	Doc White	232
51	Old Hoss Radbourn	230
52	George Mullin	229
	Eddie Plank	229
	Cy Young	229
55	Bob Friend	228
56	Frank Tanana	226
57	Roger Clemens	225
	Catfish Hunter	225
	Burleigh Grimes	225
60	Mike Torrez	223
61	Warren Spahn	222
62	Luis Tiant	221
	John Clarkson	221
64	Nolan Ryan	219
	Ted Lyons	219
66	Mickey Welch	217
67	Guy Hecker	216
68	Tom Candiotti	213
69	Vern Law	212
70	Rick Sutcliffe	211
	Bob Buhl	211
72	Camilo Pascual	210
73	Dwight Gooden	209
	Mel Harder	209
75	Joe Bush	208
76	Rick Wise	206
	Dennis Eckersley	206
	Jim Bunning	206
79	Harry Howell	204
	Frank Dwyer	204
81	Ned Garver	203
82	Joe McGinnity	202
83	Gus Weyhing	201
84	Fernando Valenzuela	200
85	John Smoltz	198
86	Dave Stewart	197
	Bert Cunningham	197
88	Sad Sam Jones	196
	Dave Foutz	196
90	Walt Terrell	194
91	Early Wynn	193
	Dizzy Trout	193
93	Bob Caruthers	192
94	Jim Perry	191
95	Jim Lonborg	189
	Pete Alexander	189
97	Don Drysdale	188
	Dolf Luque	188
99	Mike Morgan	187
100	2 tied with	185

Assists

#	Player	Assists
1	Cy Young	2,013
2	Christy Mathewson	1,503
3	Pete Alexander	1,419
4	Pud Galvin	1,382
5	Walter Johnson	1,348
6	Burleigh Grimes	1,252
7	George Mullin	1,244
8	Jack Quinn	1,240
9	Ed Walsh	1,207
10	Eppa Rixey	1,195
11	John Clarkson	1,143
12	Carl Mays	1,138
13	Hooks Dauss	1,128
14	Vic Willis	1,124
15	Red Faber	1,108
	Eddie Plank	1,108
17	Tim Keefe	1,062
18	Kid Nichols	1,031
19	Tony Mullane	1,030
20	Tommy John	1,028
21	Red Ames	1,000
22	Warren Spahn	999
23	Eddie Cicotte	998
24	Jack Powell	968
25	Harry Howell	964
26	Doc White	962
27	Al Orth	957
28	Ted Lyons	943
29	Freddie Fitzsimmons	942
	Old Hoss Radbourn	942
31	Chick Fraser	938
32	Bill Doak	934
33	Joe McGinnity	929
34	Jim McCormick	922
35	Red Donahue	905
36	Phil Niekro	878
37	Gaylord Perry	877
38	Sad Sam Jones	876
39	Amos Rusie	872
40	Clark Griffith	863
41	Howard Ehmke	855
42	Stan Coveleski	851
	Charlie Buffinton	851
44	Lee Meadows	850
	Addie Joss	850
46	Three Finger Brown	843
47	Joe Bush	840
48	Waite Hoyt	838
49	Jesse Tannehill	837
50	Herb Pennock	834
51	Jack Chesbro	829
52	Carl Hubbell	824
53	Bill Dinneen	816
54	Ed Reulbach	814
55	Eddie Rommel	810
56	Chief Bender	808
57	Dolf Luque	786
58	Wilbur Cooper	785
59	Frank Smith	782
60	Tom Zachary	770
61	Jim Whitney	769
62	Brickyard Kennedy	767
63	Willie Sudhoff	760
64	Bucky Walters	755
65	Art Nehf	749
66	Jesse Barnes	748
67	Dennis Martinez	747
68	Gus Weyhing	746
69	Jim Kaat	744
70	Hippo Vaughn	740
	Rube Waddell	740
72	Jack Taylor	738
73	Mel Harder	734
	Willis Hudlin	734
	Adonis Terry	734
76	Cy Falkenberg	728
77	Steve Carlton	724
	Claude Hendrix	724
79	Dutch Leonard	719
80	Will White	715
81	Bob Lemon	709
82	Mickey Welch	705
83	Earl Whitehill	701
84	Claude Osteen	699
85	Bob Shawkey	697
	Rube Marquard	697
87	Ed Willett	696
88	Lefty Grove	695
89	Tom Seaver	692
90	Ted Breitenstein	690
91	Pink Hawley	688
92	Don Drysdale	686
	Sherry Smith	686
94	Red Ruffing	684
	Rube Benton	684
96	Bob Groom	682
	Bert Cunningham	682
98	Long Tom Hughes	675
99	Lefty Tyler	672
100	3 tied with	670

Errors

#	Player	Errors
1	Tim Keefe	167
2	John Clarkson	162
3	Pud Galvin	161
4	Cy Young	145
5	Mickey Welch	133
6	Gus Weyhing	128
7	Tony Mullane	123
8	Amos Rusie	121
9	Bert Cunningham	111
	Old Hoss Radbourn	111
11	Toad Ramsey	107
12	Will White	106
13	Adonis Terry	104
14	Bobby Mathews	101
15	Joe McGinnity	100
16	Jim Whitney	99
	Jim McCormick	99
18	Chick Fraser	94
	Red Ehret	94
	Charlie Buffinton	94
21	Rube Waddell	91
	Matt Kilroy	91
23	Nolan Ryan	90
24	Win Mercer	83
25	George Mullin	82
	Al Orth	82
	Frank Killen	82
28	George Bradley	78
29	Jack Taylor	77
	Mark Baldwin	77
31	Stump Wiedman	76
32	Hippo Vaughn	74
	Red Ames	74
	Bill Hutchison	74
35	Jack Powell	72
36	Burleigh Grimes	71
	Red Faber	71
	Ed Doheny	71
	Ed Morris	71
	Ed Crane	71
	Jersey Bakely	71
42	Pink Hawley	70
	Sadie McMahon	70
	Jack Lynch	70
45	Eddie Cicotte	69
	Charlie Getzien	69
47	Vic Willis	67
	Kid Carsey	67
	Kid Nichols	67
	Larry Corcoran	67
51	Cy Seymour	66
	Kid Gleason	66
53	Hardie Henderson	65
	Tommy Bond	65
55	Clark Griffith	64
	Bob Barr	64
57	Long Tom Hughes	63
58	Jack Stivetts	62
	Jumbo McGinnis	62
60	Egyptian Healy	61
	Bob Caruthers	61
62	Earl Moore	60
	Jouett Meekin	60
	Fred Goldsmith	60
65	Don Drysdale	59
	Guy Hecker	59
67	Warren Spahn	58
	Bill Lee	58
	Bill Dinneen	58
70	Willie Sudhoff	57
	Brickyard Kennedy	57
	Ted Breitenstein	57
	Silver King	57
74	Jim Kaat	56
	Ed Walsh	56
	Jack Chesbro	56
77	Ed Reulbach	55
	Chief Bender	55
79	Joaquin Andujar	54
	Allen Sothoron	54
	Casey Patten	54
	Harry Howell	54
	Frank Dwyer	54
	Elton Chamberlin	54
	Monte Ward	54
86	Walter Johnson	53
	Barney Pelty	53
	Doc Newton	53
	Noodles Hahn	53
	Wiley Piatt	53
91	Ray Sadecki	52
	Lee Meadows	52
	Sad Sam Jones	52
	Cy Falkenberg	52
	Christy Mathewson	52
	Henry Porter	52
	Frank Foreman	52
98	4 tied with	51

Leaders: Career Fielding

	Double Plays			Fielding Percentage			Assists/162 Innings	
				(minimum 500 games)			(minimum 500 games)	
1	Phil Niekro	83	1	Mark Eichhorn	.992	1	Hooks Dauss	53.89
2	Warren Spahn	82	2	Bob Patterson	.990	2	Eddie Rommel	51.33
3	Freddie Fitzsimmons	79	3	Woodie Fryman	.988	3	Jack Quinn	51.16
4	Bob Lemon	78	4	Jesse Orosco	.986	4	Christy Mathewson	50.93
5	Bucky Walters	76	5	Paul Assenmacher	.985	5	Red Ames	50.66
6	Burleigh Grimes	73	6	Pete Alexander	.985	6	Harry Gumbert	50.34
7	Tommy John	69	7	Willie Hernandez	.983	7	Eddie Cicotte	50.13
	Walter Johnson	69	8	Tom Henke	.982	8	Burleigh Grimes	48.53
9	Jim Kaat	65	9	Rick Wise	.982	9	Jack Russell	47.56
10	Dizzy Trout	63	10	Rick Aguilera	.979	10	Freddie Fitzsimmons	47.34
11	Dennis Martinez	59	11	Frank DiPino	.979	11	Frank Linzy	46.81
12	Gaylord Perry	58	12	Mike Flanagan	.979	12	Vic Willis	45.57
13	Ted Lyons	57	13	Harry Gumbert	.979	13	Cy Young	44.33
14	Carl Mays	56	14	Frank Tanana	.978	14	Pete Alexander	44.29
	Eppa Rixey	56	15	Hoyt Wilhelm	.978	15	Red Faber	43.91
16	Don Drysdale	55	16	Eppa Rixey	.978	16	Eppa Rixey	43.07
	Lew Burdette	55	17	Paul Lindblad	.978	17	Ted Abernathy	42.91
	Carl Hubbell	55	18	Wilbur Wood	.977	18	Dan Quisenberry	40.99
19	Tom Seaver	54	19	Pedro Ramos	.977	19	Darold Knowles	40.95
	Murry Dickson	54	20	Freddie Fitzsimmons	.977	20	Juan Agosto	40.87
	Willis Hudlin	54	21	Phil Regan	.976	21	John Clarkson	40.82
22	Jim Palmer	53	22	Lee Smith	.976	22	Eddie Plank	39.93
23	Red Ruffing	51	23	Bobby Shantz	.976	23	Tom Zachary	39.90
	Eddie Rommel	51	24	Charlie Root	.976	24	Bob Locker	39.81
25	Joe Bush	50	25	Ron Reed	.975	25	Dolf Luque	39.54
	Pete Alexander	50	26	Guy Bush	.974	26	Gerry Staley	39.32
27	Paul Splittorff	49	27	Charlie Hough	.974	27	Bobby Shantz	39.17
	Whitey Ford	49	28	Tom Hume	.973	28	Roger McDowell	39.03
29	Bert Blyleven	48	29	John Candelaria	.973	29	Dizzy Trout	38.34
	Bobby Shantz	48	30	Herb Pennock	.973	30	Guy Bush	38.27
	Art Nehf	48	31	Camilo Pascual	.973	31	Herb Pennock	37.97
	Sad Sam Jones	48	32	Stu Miller	.972	32	Tom Burgmeier	37.71
33	Greg Maddux	47	33	Rick Reuschel	.972	33	Pud Galvin	37.68
	Early Wynn	47	34	Christy Mathewson	.972	34	Greg Minton	37.40
35	John Denny	46	35	Phil Niekro	.972	35	Carl Hubbell	37.18
	Rick Wise	46	36	Clay Carroll	.971	36	Clay Carroll	37.11
	Bob Gibson	46	37	Eddie Plank	.971	37	Dale Murray	36.98
	Larry Jackson	46	38	Claude Osteen	.971	38	Walter Johnson	36.92
39	Fergie Jenkins	45		Gerry Staley	.971	39	Kent Tekulve	36.88
	Dave Stieb	45	40	Bill Henry	.970	40	Tony Mullane	36.82
	Ray Herbert	45	41	Gaylord Perry	.970	41	Ted Lyons	36.71
	Robin Roberts	45	42	Kent Tekulve	.970	42	Sad Sam Jones	36.55
	Stan Coveleski	45	43	Red Ruffing	.970	43	Wilbur Cooper	36.54
	Herb Pennock	45	44	Lew Burdette	.970	44	Dutch Leonard	36.19
45	Fritz Peterson	44	45	Tom Burgmeier	.970	45	Waite Hoyt	36.08
	Claude Passeau	44	46	Jim Gott	.970	46	Jack Powell	35.73
	John Clarkson	44	47	Frank Linzy	.970	47	Terry Forster	35.60
48	Johnny Schmitz	43	48	Milt Pappas	.969	48	Murry Dickson	35.45
	Three Finger Brown	43	49	Bob Friend	.969	49	Tommy John	35.36
	Pud Galvin	43	50	Rob Murphy	.969	50	Bob Miller	34.98
51	Don Sutton	42	51	Bert Blyleven	.969	51	Mel Harder	34.70
	Harry Gumbert	42	52	Joe Niekro	.969	52	Rube Walberg	34.19
	George Uhle	42	53	Paul Derringer	.969	53	Rube Marquard	34.15
54	Joe Niekro	41	54	Walter Johnson	.968	54	Tim Keefe	34.05
	Vern Law	41	55	Don Sutton	.968	55	Bob Stanley	33.88
	Ned Garver	41	56	Eddie Rommel	.968	56	Lindy McDaniel	33.85
	Sid Hudson	41	57	Murry Dickson	.968	57	Old Hoss Radbourn	33.65
	Dutch Leonard	41	58	Hooks Dauss	.968	58	Mike Marshall	33.06
	Clarence Mitchell	41	59	Early Wynn	.967	59	Kid Nichols	33.03
	Christy Mathewson	41	60	Carl Hubbell	.967	60	Mark Eichhorn	32.92
	Tony Mullane	41	61	Robin Roberts	.967	61	Jesse Haines	32.87
62	Frank Tanana	40	62	Tom Zachary	.967	62	Lew Burdette	32.84
	Orel Hershiser	40	63	Gene Garber	.967	63	Claude Osteen	32.72
	Mudcat Grant	40	64	Vida Blue	.967	64	Stu Miller	32.61
	Bob Friend	40	65	Dan Plesac	.967	65	Larry Jackson	32.57
	Hal Newhouser	40	66	Jack Quinn	.966	66	George Uhle	32.40
	Larry French	40	67	Johnny Klippstein	.966	67	Don Drysdale	32.38
	Waite Hoyt	40	68	Waite Hoyt	.966	68	Bill Sherdel	32.29
	Jack Quinn	40	69	Mudcat Grant	.966	69	Larry French	32.28
	Cy Young	40	70	Jesse Haines	.966	70	Rick Honeycutt	32.10
71	Rick Reuschel	39	71	Todd Worrell	.966	71	Earl Whitehill	31.85
	Mike Caldwell	39		Jeff Montgomery	.966	72	John Franco	31.85
	Curt Davis	39	73	Gary Bell	.965	73	Wilbur Wood	31.57
	Old Hoss Radbourn	39	74	Dutch Leonard	.965	74	Bump Hadley	31.51
75	Charlie Hough	38	75	Curt Simmons	.965	75	Dennis Lamp	31.24
	Jerry Reuss	38	76	Don Robinson	.965	76	Turk Lown	31.08
	Dan Petry	38	77	Dan Quisenberry	.965	77	Clem Labine	31.06
	Bob Stanley	38	78	Chris Short	.965	78	Dennis Martinez	30.96
	Mike Torrez	38	79	Jack Morris	.965	79	Warren Spahn	30.86
	Walt Terrell	38	80	Greg Minton	.965	80	Ron Perranoski	30.48
	Mel Stottlemyre	38	81	Syl Johnson	.965	81	Rick Reuschel	30.45
	Milt Pappas	38	82	Firpo Marberry	.965	82	Tony Fossas	30.17
	Jim Bagby Jr.	38	83	Dick Drago	.964	83	Gene Garber	30.04
	Eldon Auker	38		Don McMahon	.964	84	Al Worthington	29.76
	Mel Harder	38	85	Dennis Lamp	.964	85	Paul Derringer	29.16
	Guy Bush	38	86	Dave Giusti	.964	86	Tom Hume	29.09
87	Steve Rogers	37	87	Jeff Russell	.963	87	Firpo Marberry	28.99
	Mike Boddicker	37	88	Craig Lefferts	.963	88	Lefty Grove	28.57
	Ron Darling	37	89	Bob Feller	.963	89	Jeff Russell	28.28
	Dave McNally	37	90	John Franco	.963	90	Bob Friend	28.26
	Claude Osteen	37	91	Bruce Sutter	.963	91	Tippy Martinez	28.17
	Bill Lee	37	92	Lindy McDaniel	.963	92	Camilo Pascual	28.03
	Danny MacFayden	37	93	Mike Marshall	.963	93	Gus Weyhing	27.95
	Bob Smith	37	94	Dennis Martinez	.963	94	Eddie Fisher	27.58
	Jesse Barnes	37	95	Tommy John	.963	95	Paul Lindblad	27.36
	Ed Reulbach	37	96	Rollie Fingers	.963	96	Gary Lavelle	27.02
	Eddie Plank	37	97	Dick Tidrow	.963	97	Hoyt Wilhelm	26.80
98	8 tied with	36	98	Ted Power	.963	98	Johnny Klippstein	26.68
			99	Jim Palmer	.962	99	Jerry Reuss	26.62
			100	Bump Hadley	.962	100	Jim Kaat	26.60

Career Fielding Leaders—Catchers

	Games			Putouts			Assists			Errors	
1	Carlton Fisk	2,226	1	Gary Carter	11,785	1	Deacon McGuire	1,858	1	Deacon McGuire	578
2	Bob Boone	2,225	2	Carlton Fisk	11,369	2	Ray Schalk	1,811	2	Pop Snyder	529
3	Gary Carter	2,056	3	Bob Boone	11,260	3	Steve O'Neill	1,698	3	Silver Flint	436
4	Tony Pena	1,950	4	Tony Pena	11,212	4	Red Dooin	1,590	4	Wilbert Robinson	412
5	Jim Sundberg	1,927	5	Bill Freehan	9,941	5	Chief Zimmer	1,580	5	Doc Bushong	411
6	Al Lopez	1,918	6	Jim Sundberg	9,767	6	Johnny Kling	1,552	6	Bill Holbert	396
7	Lance Parrish	1,818	7	Lance Parrish	9,647	7	Ivy Wingo	1,487	7	Jack Clements	392
8	Rick Ferrell	1,806	8	John Roseboro	9,291	8	Wilbert Robinson	1,454	8	Charlie Bennett	379
9	Gabby Hartnett	1,793	9	Johnny Bench	9,249	9	Bill Bergen	1,444	9	King Kelly	368
10	Ted Simmons	1,771	10	Johnny Edwards	8,925	10	Wally Schang	1,420	10	Duke Farrell	365
11	Johnny Bench	1,742	11	Ted Simmons	8,906	11	Duke Farrell	1,417	11	Chief Zimmer	328
12	Ray Schalk	1,727	12	Yogi Berra	8,738	12	Oscar Stanage	1,381	12	Buck Ewing	322
13	Bill Dickey	1,708	13	Mike Scioscia	8,335	13	Malachi Kittridge	1,363	13	Red Dooin	320
14	Yogi Berra	1,699	14	Tim McCarver	8,206	14	George Gibson	1,362	14	Jocko Milligan	304
15	Rick Dempsey	1,633	15	Jerry Grote	8,081	15	Lou Criger	1,342	15	Kid Baldwin	302
16	Jim Hegan	1,629	16	Bill Dickey	7,965	16	Frank Snyder	1,332	16	Barney Gilligan	299
17	Deacon McGuire	1,611	17	Jim Hegan	7,506	17	Bill Killefer	1,319	17	Con Daily	286
18	Bill Freehan	1,581	18	Rick Dempsey	7,367	18	Billy Sullivan	1,314	18	Doggie Miller	285
19	Sherm Lollar	1,571	19	Del Crandall	7,352	19	John Warner	1,309	19	Connie Mack	281
20	Luke Sewell	1,562	20	Benito Santiago	7,315	20	Pop Snyder	1,295	20	Malachi Kittridge	264
21	Ernie Lombardi	1,544	21	Gabby Hartnett	7,292	21	Gabby Hartnett	1,254	21	Lew Brown	245
22	Steve O'Neill	1,530	22	Rick Ferrell	7,248	22	Bill Rariden	1,231		John Clapp	245
23	Darrell Porter	1,506	23	Ray Schalk	7,168	23	Gary Carter	1,203	23	Emil Gross	242
24	Rollie Hemsley	1,482	24	Alan Ashby	7,086	24	Roger Bresnahan	1,195	24	Jack Boyle	237
25	Del Crandall	1,479	25	Sherm Lollar	7,059	25	Bob Boone	1,174	25	Ivy Wingo	234
26	John Roseboro	1,476	26	Tom Haller	7,012	26	Hank Severeid	1,142	26	Pop Schriver	233
27	Mickey Cochrane	1,451	27	Deacon McGuire	6,852	27	Muddy Ruel	1,136	27	Fred Carroll	231
28	Wally Schang	1,435	28	Darrell Porter	6,755	28	Rick Ferrell	1,127	28	Oscar Stanage	229
29	Muddy Ruel	1,412	29	Al Lopez	6,644	29	Al Lopez	1,115		Charlie Ganzel	229
30	Mike Scioscia	1,395	30	Terry Kennedy	6,555	30	Heinie Peitz	1,094	30	Wally Schang	223
31	Johnny Edwards	1,392	31	Rick Cerone	6,548	31	Eddie Ainsmith	1,088		Bob Clark	223
32	Tim McCarver	1,387	32	Roy Campanella	6,520	32	Luke Sewell	1,084	32	Steve O'Neill	217
33	Terry Kennedy	1,378	33	Elston Howard	6,447	33	Jack Clements	1,079	33	Farmer Vaughn	211
34	Gus Mancuso	1,360	34	Mickey Cochrane	6,409	34	Frank Bowerman	1,055		Sam Trott	211
35	Jimmie Wilson	1,351	35	Terry Steinbach	6,301	35	Otto Miller	1,053	35	Johnny Kling	210
36	Jerry Grote	1,348	36	Butch Wynegar	6,281	36	Silver Flint	1,052	36	John Warner	205
37	Bob O'Farrell	1,338	37	Thurman Munson	6,253	37	Carlton Fisk	1,048	37	Fatty Briody	204
38	Wilbert Robinson	1,316	38	Earl Battey	6,176		Charlie Bennett	1,048	38	Dick Buckley	198
39	Frankie Hayes	1,311	39	Don Slaught	6,158	39	Tony Pena	1,045	39	Jimmy Peoples	197
40	Alan Ashby	1,299	40	Steve Yeager	6,110	40	Cy Perkins	1,044	40	George Myers	195
41	Benito Santiago	1,295	41	Ernie Whitt	6,091	41	Ed McFarland	1,024		Charlie Reipschlager	195
42	Spud Davis	1,282	42	Manny Sanguillen	5,996	42	Buck Ewing	1,017	42	Eddie Ainsmith	193
43	Rick Cerone	1,279	43	Steve O'Neill	5,967	43	Bill Holbert	1,013	43	Boileryard Clarke	190
44	Thurman Munson	1,278	44	Rollie Hemsley	5,868	44	Jim Sundberg	1,007	44	Deacon White	188
45	Del Rice	1,249	45	Randy Hundley	5,765	45	Doc Bushong	1,001	45	Heinie Peitz	187
46	Butch Wynegar	1,247	46	Ernie Lombardi	5,694	46	Hank Gowdy	1,000	46	Pat Deasley	186
	Frank Snyder	1,247	47	John Bateman	5,686	47	Chief Meyers	996	47	Jim Keenan	185
48	Ernie Whitt	1,246	48	Gus Mancuso	5,613	48	Pat Moran	990	48	Jack O'Brien	183
49	Chief Zimmer	1,239	49	Clay Dalrymple	5,557	49	Jack O'Connor	984	49	Frank Bowerman	182
50	Don Slaught	1,237	50	Jody Davis	5,520	50	Lance Parrish	980	50	Bob Boone	178
51	Steve Yeager	1,230	51	Red Dooin	5,481		Bob O'Farrell	980	51	Jack O'Connor	177
52	Hank Severeid	1,226	52	Johnny Kling	5,468	52	Jimmy Archer	979	52	Ray Schalk	175
53	Walker Cooper	1,223	53	Luke Sewell	5,450	53	Ossee Schreckengost	968	53	Morgan Murphy	174
54	Andy Seminick	1,213	54	Darren Daulton	5,417	54	Bill Dickey	954	54	Lou Criger	170
55	Ivy Wingo	1,202	55	Del Rice	5,353	55	Jimmie Wilson	932	55	Rudy Kemmler	168
56	Tom Haller	1,199	56	Muddy Ruel	5,337	56	Ted Simmons	915	56	Roger Bresnahan	167
57	Malachi Kittridge	1,196	57	Joe Azcue	5,329	57	Larry McLean	905	57	Ossee Schreckengost	166
58	Red Dooin	1,195	58	Bo Diaz	5,294	58	Rollie Hemsley	897		Paul Cook	166
59	George Gibson	1,194	59	Rich Gedman	5,274	59	Connie Mack	863	59	Joe Sugden	165
60	Roy Campanella	1,183	60	Ed Bailey	5,267	60	Joe Sugden	860	60	Tom Kinslow	163
61	Mickey Owen	1,175	61	Smoky Burgess	5,214	61	Walter Schmidt	858	61	Bill Bergen	161
62	Johnny Kling	1,168		George Gibson	5,214	62	King Kelly	857	62	John Grim	156
63	Terry Steinbach	1,166	63	Wally Schang	5,202	63	Bill Carrigan	854	63	Carlton Fisk	155
64	Smoky Burgess	1,139	64	Wilbert Robinson	5,172	64	Jeff Sweeney	852		Ed Whiting	155
65	Elston Howard	1,138	65	Walker Cooper	5,166	65	Johnny Bench	850	65	Rollie Hemsley	154
66	Billy Sullivan	1,120	66	Gus Triandos	5,123	66	Ernie Lombardi	845		Jack Ryan	154
67	Manny Sanguillen	1,114		Charlie Bennett	5,123	67	Mickey Cochrane	840	67	George Gibson	153
68	Cy Perkins	1,111	68	Malachi Kittridge	5,121	68	Mike Gonzalez	838	68	Luke Sewell	150
69	Birdie Tebbetts	1,108	69	Milt May	5,091	69	John Henry	826		Bill Rariden	150
70	Phil Masi	1,101	70	Ivan Rodriguez	5,059	70	Jocko Milligan	825	70	Gus Mancuso	148
71	Earl Battey	1,087	71	Andy Seminick	5,030	71	Boileryard Clarke	806		Bill Killefer	148
72	Mike Heath	1,083	72	Frankie Hayes	4,938	72	Gus Mancuso	803		Billy Sullivan	148
73	Oscar Stanage	1,073	73	Jimmie Wilson	4,933	73	Yogi Berra	798		Jack Rowe	148
	Jack Clements	1,073	74	Mike Heath	4,919	74	Art Wilson	796	74	Chief Meyers	146
75	Ed Bailey	1,064	75	Dave Valle	4,898	75	Admiral Schlei	792		Jim Donahue	146
76	Jody Davis	1,039	76	Andy Etchebarren	4,884	76	Sam Agnew	773	76	Tom Daly	145
77	Milt May	1,034	77	Chief Zimmer	4,883	77	Rick Dempsey	768	77	Ed McFarland	144
78	John Warner	1,032	78	Mike Macfarlane	4,878	78	Pop Schriver	761	78	Ernie Lombardi	143
79	Sammy White	1,027	79	Joe Oliver	4,853	79	Del Crandall	759		Mert Hackett	143
80	Randy Hundley	1,026	80	Joe Torre	4,850	80	Darrell Porter	754	80	Gabby Hartnett	139
81	Mike Tresh	1,019	81	Joe Girardi	4,839	81	Zack Taylor	752	81	Walker Cooper	138
82	Buck Martinez	1,008	82	Ray Fosse	4,830	82	Les Nunamaker	745		Jeff Sweeney	138
83	Bill Killefer	1,005		Bill Killefer	4,830	83	Gabby Street	744		Lave Cross	138
84	Clay Dalrymple	1,003	84	Ron Hassey	4,828	84	Thurman Munson	742	84	Jimmie Wilson	137
	Duke Farrell	1,003	85	Jack Clements	4,780	85	Mike Scioscia	737	85	Rick Ferrell	135
86	Eddie Ainsmith	993	86	Billy Sullivan	4,776	86	Val Picinich	732		Otto Miller	135
87	Gus Triandos	992	87	Ron Karkovice	4,757	87	Mike Powers	724	87	Darrell Porter	134
88	Clyde McCullough	989	88	Bob Rodgers	4,750	88	Bill Freehan	721	88	Andy Seminick	133
89	Lou Criger	984	89	Sammy White	4,738	89	Benito Santiago	711	89	Sam Agnew	132
90	Rich Gedman	980	90	Birdie Tebbetts	4,667	90	Johnny Bassler	708		Mike Grady	132
	Bob Swift	980	91	Pat Borders	4,657	91	Johnny Edwards	703	91	Hank Severeid	131
92	Roger Bresnahan	974	92	Bruce Benedict	4,651	92	Jim Hegan	695	92	Ted Simmons	130
93	Bruce Benedict	971	93	Hank Severeid	4,617	93	Doggie Miller	693		Bob O'Farrell	130
94	Bo Diaz	965	94	Mike Piazza	4,538	94	John Grim	691		Pop Tate	130
	Darren Daulton	965	95	Chief Meyers	4,537	95	Jack Ryan	690		John Kelly	130
96	Heinie Peitz	960	96	Dave Duncan	4,528	96	Sherm Lollar	688	96	Frankie Hayes	129
97	Charlie Bennett	954	97	Mickey Owen	4,527	97	Alan Ashby	684	97	Tim Donahue	128
98	John Bateman	953	98	John Warner	4,498		Spud Davis	684		Sy Sutcliffe	128
99	Bill Rariden	948	99	John Romano	4,415	99	Jack Boyle	683	99	4 tied with	127
100	Ron Hassey	946	100	Ivy Wingo	4,409	100	Tom Needham	677			

Double Plays

1	Ray Schalk	226
2	Steve O'Neill	193
3	Yogi Berra	175
4	Gabby Hartnett	163
5	Bob Boone	154
	Tony Pena	154
7	Jimmie Wilson	153
8	Gary Carter	149
	Wally Schang	149
10	Carlton Fisk	147
11	Jim Sundberg	145
12	Deacon McGuire	142
13	Rollie Hemsley	141
	Ivy Wingo	141
15	Rick Ferrell	139
16	Luke Sewell	138
17	Al Lopez	137
	Bill Dickey	137
19	Jim Hegan	136
20	Muddy Ruel	135
	Chief Zimmer	135
22	Lance Parrish	134
23	Bill Killefer	129
24	Johnny Bench	127
25	Johnny Kling	126
26	Red Dooin	122
27	Del Crandall	116
28	Charlie Bennett	114
29	George Gibson	112
	Heinie Peitz	112
31	Rick Dempsey	111
	John Roseboro	111
	Billy Sullivan	111
	Wilbert Robinson	111
35	Frank Snyder	109
36	Ernie Lombardi	107
	Oscar Stanage	107
38	Frankie Hayes	106
	Bill Bergen	106
40	Johnny Edwards	105
	Larry McLean	105
42	Darrell Porter	104
	Ted Simmons	104
	Mickey Cochrane	104
45	Frank Bowerman	103
46	Lou Criger	102
	Duke Farrell	102
48	Sherm Lollar	101
	Bob O'Farrell	101
	Hank Severeid	101
51	Gus Mancuso	100
	Cy Perkins	100
	John Warner	100
	Malachi Kittridge	100
55	Chief Meyers	99
56	Bill Freehan	98
57	Mike Scioscia	97
58	Eddie Ainsmith	96
	Roger Bresnahan	96
60	Spud Davis	95
	Mike Gonzalez	95
62	Mickey Owen	93
	Hank Gowdy	93
	Jack Clements	93
65	Terry Kennedy	92
	Buddy Rosar	92
67	Benito Santiago	90
68	Butch Wynegar	88
69	Elston Howard	87
	Birdie Tebbetts	87
	Zack Taylor	87
72	Tom Haller	86
	Walter Schmidt	86
	Jocko Milligan	86
75	Otto Miller	85
76	Joe Sugden	84
77	Sammy White	83
78	Thurman Munson	82
	Roy Campanella	82
	Wes Westrum	82
	Bill Rariden	82
82	John Bateman	81
	Doc Bushong	81
84	Andy Seminick	80
	Walker Cooper	80
86	Clay Dalrymple	79
87	Buck Ewing	78
88	Jerry Grote	76
	Jimmy Archer	76
	Pat Moran	76
91	Steve Yeager	75
	Bob Swift	75
93	Alan Ashby	74
	Tim McCarver	74
	Manny Sanguillen	74
	Bob Rodgers	74
97	6 tied with	73

Fielding Percentage
(minimum 750 games)

1	Bill Freehan	.993
2	Elston Howard	.993
3	Ron Hassey	.993
4	Jim Sundberg	.993
5	Joe Azcue	.992
6	Mike LaValliere	.992
7	Tom Pagnozzi	.992
8	Sherm Lollar	.992
9	Ron Karkovice	.992
10	Buddy Rosar	.992
11	Kirt Manwaring	.992
12	Dave Valle	.992
13	Mike Macfarlane	.992
14	Tom Haller	.992
15	Johnny Edwards	.992
16	Lance Parrish	.991
17	Jerry Grote	.991
18	Ernie Whitt	.991
19	Mickey Tettleton	.991
20	Jim Pagliaroni	.991
21	Gary Carter	.991
22	Tony Pena	.991
23	Johnny Bench	.990
24	Randy Hundley	.990
25	John Romano	.990
26	Rick Cerone	.990
27	Bruce Benedict	.990
28	Joe Girardi	.990
29	Earl Battey	.990
30	Tim McCarver	.990
31	Jim Hegan	.990
32	Joe Torre	.990
33	John Roseboro	.989
34	Joe Oliver	.989
35	Butch Wynegar	.989
36	Del Crandall	.989
37	Pat Borders	.989
38	Darren Daulton	.989
39	Ivan Rodriguez	.989
40	Yogi Berra	.989
41	Terry Steinbach	.988
42	Mike Stanley	.988
43	Ray Mueller	.988
44	Roy Campanella	.988
45	Bob Rodgers	.988
46	Bill Dickey	.988
47	Rick Dempsey	.988
48	Jeff Reed	.988
49	Carlton Fisk	.988
50	Smoky Burgess	.988
51	Mike Scioscia	.988
52	Del Rice	.987
53	Clint Courtney	.987
54	Clay Dalrymple	.987
55	Gus Triandos	.987
56	Andy Etchebarren	.987
57	Steve Yeager	.987
58	Ed Herrmann	.987
59	Joe Ferguson	.987
60	Don Slaught	.987
61	Jody Davis	.987
62	Ted Simmons	.987
63	Fred Kendall	.987
64	George Mitterwald	.987
65	Phil Roof	.986
66	Ed Bailey	.986
67	Bo Diaz	.986
68	Bob Boone	.986
69	Gene Tenace	.986
70	Manny Sanguillen	.986
71	Milt May	.986
72	Alan Ashby	.986
73	Terry Kennedy	.985
74	Ray Fosse	.985
75	Shanty Hogan	.985
76	Wes Westrum	.985
77	Mickey Cochrane	.985
78	Harry Danning	.985
79	Paul Casanova	.985
80	Bob Swift	.985
81	Al Lopez	.985
82	Buck Martinez	.984
83	Benito Santiago	.984
84	Sammy White	.984
85	Rick Ferrell	.984
86	Rich Gedman	.984
87	Dave Duncan	.984
88	Clyde McCullough	.984
89	Gabby Hartnett	.984
90	Spud Davis	.984
91	Dave Rader	.983
92	Mike Tresh	.983
93	Phil Masi	.983
94	Darrell Porter	.982
95	Muddy Ruel	.982
96	Thurman Munson	.982
97	John Bateman	.982
98	Mickey Owen	.982
99	Mike Heath	.981
100	Ray Schalk	.981

Passed Balls

1	Pop Snyder	647
2	Silver Flint	602
3	Doc Bushong	553
4	Deacon McGuire	496
5	Wilbert Robinson	491
6	Jack Clements	417
	King Kelly	417
8	Jocko Milligan	406
9	Bill Holbert	403
10	Barney Gilligan	377
11	Fred Carroll	369
12	Buck Ewing	360
13	Chief Zimmer	355
14	Charlie Bennett	352
15	Doggie Miller	346
16	Kid Baldwin	331
17	Connie Mack	310
18	Jack Boyle	303
19	John Clapp	300
20	Jack O'Connor	287
21	Duke Farrell	285
22	Jack O'Brien	279
23	Jim Keenan	275
24	Pat Deasley	274
25	Con Daily	262
26	Paul Cook	257
	Emil Gross	257
	Bill Traffley	257
29	George Myers	256
30	Ed Whiting	252
31	Sam Trott	249
32	Charlie Reipschlager	245
33	Fatty Briody	243
34	Jack Rowe	240
35	Mert Hackett	236
	Lew Brown	236
37	Dan Sullivan	226
38	Deacon White	221
39	Jackie Hayes	218
40	Farmer Vaughn	207
41	Malachi Kittridge	201
42	Jim O'Rourke	196
43	Pop Schriver	194
	John Kelly	194
45	Lance Parrish	192
46	Tom Dolan	190
47	Bob Clark	183
48	Ted Simmons	182
	Jack Ryan	182
50	Charlie Ganzel	180
	John Kerins	180
52	Ed McFarland	176
53	Jim Donahue	173
54	Rudy Kemmler	171
55	Jimmy Peoples	168
56	Frank Bowerman	165
57	Heinie Peitz	163
58	Lave Cross	157
	Mike Hines	157
60	Ernie Lombardi	152
61	John Grim	151
	Sleeper Sullivan	151
63	John Warner	147
	Tom Daly	147
65	Steve O'Neill	145
66	Chris Fulmer	144
67	Rick Ferrell	142
	Sy Sutcliffe	142
69	Billy Sullivan	140
70	Frankie Hayes	139
	Red Dooin	139
	Dick Buckley	139
73	Gus Triandos	138
74	Frank Ringo	136
75	Phil Powers	135
76	Tom Gunning	133
77	Tim McCarver	132
	Darrell Porter	132
79	Wally Schang	131
	Tom Kinslow	131
81	Jim Sundberg	130
82	Carlton Fisk	129
	Roger Bresnahan	129
84	Boileryard Clarke	128
	Pop Tate	128
86	Gabby Hartnett	126
	Johnny Kling	126
88	Ed Herrmann	125
89	Joe Crotty	123
90	Tom Haller	121
	J.C. Martin	121
92	Lou Criger	120
93	Willard Brown	119
94	Charlie Reilley	118
95	Joe Azcue	117
96	Bill Harbidge	115
97	Eddie Fusselback	114
98	Alan Ashby	113
99	Benito Santiago	112
100	2 tied with	111

Assists/162 Games
(minimum 750 games)

1	Bill Bergen	248.60
2	Duke Farrell	228.87
3	Lou Criger	220.94
4	Red Dooin	215.55
5	Johnny Kling	215.26
6	Bill Killefer	212.62
7	Bill Rariden	210.36
8	Ossee Schreckengost	208.81
9	Oscar Stanage	208.50
10	Frank Bowerman	206.91
11	Chief Zimmer	206.59
12	John Warner	205.48
13	Ed McFarland	200.83
14	Ivy Wingo	200.41
15	Roger Bresnahan	198.76
16	Larry McLean	192.65
17	Otto Miller	191.67
18	Billy Sullivan	190.06
19	Deacon McGuire	186.84
20	Jack O'Connor	185.36
21	George Gibson	184.79
22	Malachi Kittridge	184.62
23	Heinie Peitz	184.61
24	Hank Gowdy	181.41
25	Steve O'Neill	179.79
26	Wilbert Robinson	178.99
27	Charlie Bennett	177.96
28	Eddie Ainsmith	177.50
29	Chief Meyers	177.12
30	Frank Snyder	173.04
31	Ray Schalk	169.88
32	Jack Clements	162.91
33	Wally Schang	160.31
34	Mike Gonzalez	156.58
35	Cy Perkins	152.23
36	Johnny Bassler	151.92
37	Hank Severeid	150.90
38	Zack Taylor	142.32
39	Muddy Ruel	130.33
40	Val Picinich	126.96
41	Bob O'Farrell	118.65
42	Gabby Hartnett	113.30
43	Luke Sewell	112.43
44	Jimmie Wilson	111.76
45	Johnny Gooch	109.21
46	Rick Ferrell	101.09
47	Jody Davis	99.79
48	Rollie Hemsley	98.05
49	Birdie Tebbetts	97.38
50	Bruce Benedict	96.27
51	Gus Mancuso	95.65
52	Gary Carter	94.79
53	Al Lopez	94.18
54	Thurman Munson	94.06
55	Mickey Cochrane	93.78
56	Ivan Rodriguez	93.06
57	Milt May	92.28
58	Harry Danning	92.02
59	Clay Dalrymple	91.42
60	Mike Tresh	91.41
61	Bill Dickey	90.48
62	Benito Santiago	88.94
63	Ray Mueller	88.86
64	Shanty Hogan	88.84
65	Steve Yeager	88.77
66	Ernie Lombardi	88.66
67	Buddy Rosar	88.63
68	Al Todd	88.54
69	George Mitterwald	88.33
70	Bo Diaz	88.13
71	Ed Herrmann	87.64
72	Lance Parrish	87.33
73	Tony Pena	86.82
74	Spud Davis	86.43
75	Mike Scioscia	85.59
76	Bob Boone	85.48
77	Bob Rodgers	85.43
78	Alan Ashby	85.30
79	Jim Sundberg	84.66
80	Joe Azcue	84.36
81	Ted Simmons	83.70
82	John Bateman	83.46
83	Pat Borders	83.35
84	Del Crandall	83.14
85	Johnny Edwards	81.81
86	Frankie Hayes	81.68
87	Darrell Porter	81.11
88	Kirt Manwaring	80.90
89	Joe Girardi	80.90
90	Mike Heath	80.33
91	Mickey Owen	80.10
92	Gene Tenace	80.09
93	Andy Seminick	79.86
94	Sammy White	79.82
95	Ray Fosse	79.82
96	Joe Ferguson	79.52
97	Mike LaValliere	79.28
98	Johnny Bench	79.05
99	Paul Casanova	78.90
100	Bob Swift	78.85

Career Fielding Leaders—First Basemen

Rank	Games		Putouts		Assists		Errors	
1	Eddie Murray	2,413	Jake Beckley	23,709	Eddie Murray	1,865	Cap Anson	583
2	Jake Beckley	2,377	Ed Konetchy	21,360	Keith Hernandez	1,682	Dan Brouthers	512
3	Mickey Vernon	2,237	Eddie Murray	21,255	George Sisler	1,529	Jake Beckley	481
4	Lou Gehrig	2,142	Cap Anson	20,794	Mickey Vernon	1,448	Roger Connor	419
5	Charlie Grimm	2,131	Charlie Grimm	20,711	Fred Tenney	1,363	Charlie Comiskey	403
6	Joe Judge	2,084	Stuffy McInnis	19,962	Chris Chambliss	1,351	Hal Chase	402
					Bill Buckner	1,351		
7	Ed Konetchy	2,073	Mickey Vernon	19,808			Tommy Tucker	393
8	Steve Garvey	2,059	Jake Daubert	19,634	Norm Cash	1,317	Harry Davis	343
9	Cap Anson	2,058	Lou Gehrig	19,510	Jake Beckley	1,315	Fred Tenney	327
10	Joe Kuhel	2,057	Joe Kuhel	19,386	Joe Judge	1,300	Bill Phillips	324
11	Willie McCovey	2,045	Joe Judge	19,255	Ed Konetchy	1,292	John Reilly	316
12	Keith Hernandez	2,014	Steve Garvey	18,844	Gil Hodges	1,281	Joe Start	294
13	Jake Daubert	2,002	George Sisler	18,837	Wally Joyner	1,275	John Morrill	285
14	Stuffy McInnis	1,995	Wally Pipp	18,779	Stuffy McInnis	1,238	Jack Doyle	277
15	George Sisler	1,971	Jim Bottomley	18,337	Mark Grace	1,232	George Sisler	269
16	Chris Chambliss	1,962	Hal Chase	18,183	Willie McCovey	1,222	Sid Farrar	262
					Jimmie Foxx	1,222		
17	Norm Cash	1,943	Keith Hernandez	17,909			Fred Merkle	252
18	Jimmie Foxx	1,919	Fred Tenney	17,903	Charlie Grimm	1,214	George Burns	245
19	Gil Hodges	1,908	Chris Chambliss	17,771	Joe Kuhel	1,163	Harry Stovey	241
20	Jim Bottomley	1,885	Roger Connor	17,605	Wally Pipp	1,152	Kitty Bransfield	236
21	Wally Pipp	1,819	Jimmie Foxx	17,212	George Scott	1,132	Willie McCovey	233
22	Hal Chase	1,815	Willie McCovey	17,170	Jake Daubert	1,128	Dave Orr	227
23	Fred Tenney	1,810	George Burns	16,889	Andres Galarraga	1,116	Ed Konetchy	224
24	Tony Perez	1,778	Tommy Tucker	16,393	Will Clark	1,108	Jim Bottomley	223
					Bill Terry	1,108		
25	George Scott	1,773	Dan Brouthers	16,365			Mickey Vernon	211
26	Roger Connor	1,758	Bill Terry	15,972	Don Mattingly	1,104	Henry Larkin	209
27	Orlando Cepeda	1,683	Harry Davis	15,666	George Burns	1,094	Candy LaChance	207
28	Tommy Tucker	1,669	Lu Blue	15,614	Lou Gehrig	1,087	Jack Fournier	206
							Ecky Stearns	206
29	Johnny Mize	1,667	George Scott	15,435	Vic Power	1,078		
30	George Burns	1,660	Fred Merkle	15,419	George McQuinn	1,074	Fred Luderus	201
31	Don Mattingly	1,634	Gil Hodges	15,344	Pete O'Brien	1,064	Lou Gehrig	193
32	Dan Brouthers	1,633	Norm Cash	15,157	Kent Hrbek	1,049	George Stovall	192
33	Harry Davis	1,628	Johnny Mize	14,850	Hal Chase	1,048	Lu Blue	191
34	Kent Hrbek	1,609	Tony Perez	14,481	Johnny Mize	1,032	Tom Jones	183
35	Andres Galarraga	1,600	Orlando Cepeda	14,459	Steve Garvey	1,026	Jake Daubert	181
36	Wally Joyner	1,587	Andres Galarraga	14,297	Rafael Palmeiro	1,025	Doc Hoblitzell	180
37	Bill Terry	1,579	George Kelly	14,232	Mike Hargrove	1,022	Joe Kuhel	173
38	Lu Blue	1,571	Don Mattingly	14,148	Lu Blue	1,016	Dick Stuart	169
39	Will Clark	1,570	Will Clark	14,094	Orlando Cepeda	1,012	Wally Pipp	168
							Dan McGann	168
40	Bill Buckner	1,555	Bill Buckner	13,901	Fred McGriff	1,010		
41	Fred Merkle	1,547	Charlie Comiskey	13,821	Frank McCormick	1,003	Eddie Murray	167
42	George McQuinn	1,529	Frank McCormick	13,803	Cecil Cooper	1,000	George Scott	165
43	Lee May	1,507	Wally Joyner	13,742	Elbie Fletcher	975	Martin Powell	164
44	Joe Adcock	1,501	Kent Hrbek	13,725	Rudy York	961	Orlando Cepeda	162
							Charlie Grimm	162
45	Fred McGriff	1,490	Dolph Camilli	13,724	Bill White	960		
46	Ted Kluszewski	1,481	Dan McGann	13,682	Dolph Camilli	957	Jim Field	161
47	Boog Powell	1,479	George McQuinn	13,414	Cap Anson	955	Stuffy McInnis	160
48	John Mayberry	1,478	Cecil Cooper	13,361	Harry Davis	950	Perry Werden	158
49	Bill White	1,477	Elbie Fletcher	13,237	Tony Perez	936	Jimmie Foxx	155
50	Dolph Camilli	1,476	John Mayberry	13,169	Ferris Fain	927	Jake Stahl	150
51	Cecil Cooper	1,475	Fred Luderus	13,126	Bill Skowron	903	Dave Foutz	147
52	Bill Skowron	1,463	Gus Suhr	13,103	Lee May	894	Donn Clendenon	146
53	Frank McCormick	1,448	Joe Adcock	13,006	Joe Adcock	879	Earl Torgeson	143
54	Mark Grace	1,434	Mark Grace	12,889	Jeff Bagwell	874	Joe Judge	142
							Charlie Hickman	142
55	Earl Torgeson	1,416	Lee May	12,885	George Kelly	861		
56	Gus Suhr	1,406	Fred McGriff	12,849	Boog Powell	859	Dolph Camilli	141
							Guy Hecker	141
57	Elbie Fletcher	1,380	Kitty Bransfield	12,797	Roger Connor	856		
58	Mike Hargrove	1,377	Bill White	12,735	Fred Merkle	847	Ferris Fain	138
	Pete O'Brien	1,377					Bill Terry	138
59			George Stovall	12,699	George Stovall	846		
60	Dan McGann	1,376	Ted Kluszewski	12,652	Fred Luderus	843	Alex McKinnon	136
61	Dan Driessen	1,375	Doc Hoblitzell	12,584	John Mayberry	827	Frank Chance	135
62	George Kelly	1,373	Jack Fournier	12,375	Jason Thompson	819	Johnny Mize	133
					Donn Clendenon	819		
63	Charlie Comiskey	1,362	Candy LaChance	12,320			John Kerins	132
64	Rafael Palmeiro	1,356	Walter Holke	12,158	Earl Torgeson	814	Norm Cash	131
					Jim Bottomley	814		
65	Fred Luderus	1,326	Boog Powell	12,130			Chris Chambliss	130
66	Hal Trosky	1,321	Hal Trosky	12,124	Mark McGwire	809	Andres Galarraga	129
					Ernie Banks	809	Vic Saier	129
67	Jason Thompson	1,314	Earl Sheely	12,087				
68	Jack Fournier	1,313	Bill Skowron	12,043	Willie Upshaw	799	Bill Buckner	128
					Ted Kluszewski	799		
69	Ed Kranepool	1,304	Ernie Banks	12,005			Gil Hodges	126
	Vic Power	1,304						
70			Jason Thompson	11,818	Dan McGann	798	Tim Murnane	125
71	Mark McGwire	1,301	Earl Torgeson	11,680	Jim Spencer	797	Phil Cavarretta	123
							Jumbo Latham	123
72	Kitty Bransfield	1,291	Pete O'Brien	11,651	Phil Cavarretta	796		
73	Doc Hoblitzell	1,284	Phil Cavarretta	11,375	Jack Fournier	788	Rudy York	122
74	Rudy York	1,261	Rudy York	11,348	Sid Bream	786	Cecil Cooper	121
							Hal Trosky	121
							George Kelly	121
75	Ernie Banks	1,259	Rafael Palmeiro	11,295	Ed Kranepool	779		
76	Phil Cavarretta	1,254	Mike Hargrove	11,270	Rod Carew	774		
77	Jim Spencer	1,221	Chick Gandil	11,118	Gus Suhr	766	Mox McQuery	120
78	Earl Sheely	1,220	Rod Carew	10,930	Dick Stuart	758	Tony Perez	117
							John Anderson	117
79	Ron Fairly	1,218	Donn Clendenon	10,913	Chick Gandil	754		
80	George Stovall	1,216	John Reilly	10,875	Darrell Evans	752	Boog Powell	116
					Hal Trosky	752	Gus Suhr	116
81	Donn Clendenon	1,200	Tom Jones	10,872				
82	Walter Holke	1,193	Dan Driessen	10,863	Tommy Tucker	749	Mike Hargrove	115
							Keith Hernandez	115
							Ed Cartwright	115
83	Rod Carew	1,184	Mark McGwire	10,724	Eric Karros	744		
					Earl Sheely	744		
84	Candy LaChance	1,176	Hank Greenberg	10,564				
85	Walt Dropo	1,174	Bill Phillips	10,540	Dick Siebert	741	George McQuinn	113
							Earl Sheely	113
							Doc Johnston	113
86	Willie Montanez	1,164	Ed Kranepool	10,492	Kitty Bransfield	737		
87	Don Mincher	1,138	Jack Doyle	10,165	Dan Driessen	732		
	Hank Greenberg	1,138						
	Chick Gandil	1,138						
88			Vic Power	10,141	Hank Greenberg	724	Tim Jordan	112
							Jiggs Donahue	112
89			Willie Montanez	10,006	Eddie Waitkus	716		
90	Eddie Robinson	1,125	Jim Spencer	9,898	Willie Montanez	714	Will Clark	111
91	Ferris Fain	1,116	Frank Chance	9,885	Ron Fairly	704	Fred McGriff	110
							Don Hurst	110
92	Wes Parker	1,108	Eddie Robinson	9,823	Tom Jones	698		
93	Willie Upshaw	1,094	Doc Johnston	9,739	Don Mincher	696	Eddie Robinson	109
							Buddy Hassett	109
94	Bob Watson	1,088	Wes Parker	9,640	Wes Parker	695		
95	John Reilly	1,075	Babe Dahlgren	9,619	Stan Musial	688	Nick Etten	107
							Elbie Fletcher	107
96	Mike Jorgensen	1,052	Sid Farrar	9,550	Greg Brock	684		
97	Eddie Waitkus	1,049	Ferris Fain	9,530	Walt Dropo	672	Rod Carew	106
							Bill Everitt	106
98	Jack Doyle	1,043	Ron Fairly	9,294	Pete Rose	665		
					Walter Holke	665		
99	Tom Jones	1,033	Don Mincher	9,181			Bill White	105
100	Bill Phillips	1,032	Walt Dropo	9,173	Doc Hoblitzell	661	Hank Greenberg	104

Leaders: Career Fielding

Double Plays

1	Mickey Vernon	2,044
2	Eddie Murray	2,033
3	Joe Kuhel	1,769
4	Charlie Grimm	1,733
5	Chris Chambliss	1,687
6	Keith Hernandez	1,654
7	Gil Hodges	1,614
8	Jim Bottomley	1,582
9	Lou Gehrig	1,574
10	Jimmie Foxx	1,528
11	Don Mattingly	1,500
	Joe Judge	1,500
13	Steve Garvey	1,498
14	George Scott	1,480
15	George Sisler	1,468
16	Willie McCovey	1,405
17	Wally Joyner	1,367
18	Cecil Cooper	1,348
19	Norm Cash	1,347
20	Tony Perez	1,342
21	Bill Terry	1,334
22	Kent Hrbek	1,331
23	Jake Beckley	1,326
24	Johnny Mize	1,320
	Stuffy McInnis	1,320
26	Will Clark	1,313
27	John Mayberry	1,307
28	Wally Pipp	1,290
29	Ted Kluszewski	1,269
30	Bill Skowron	1,266
31	George McQuinn	1,265
32	Andres Galarraga	1,259
33	Lee May	1,235
34	Joe Adcock	1,228
35	Frank McCormick	1,221
36	Bill Buckner	1,200
37	Jake Daubert	1,199
38	Orlando Cepeda	1,192
39	Dolph Camilli	1,189
	Cap Anson	1,189
41	Lu Blue	1,187
42	Bill White	1,157
43	Hal Trosky	1,146
44	Donn Clendenon	1,136
45	Boog Powell	1,131
46	Rod Carew	1,130
47	Fred McGriff	1,129
48	Ferris Fain	1,124
49	George Burns	1,117
50	Rafael Palmeiro	1,116
51	George Kelly	1,111
52	Earl Torgeson	1,097
53	Jason Thompson	1,090
54	Pete O'Brien	1,086
	Elbie Fletcher	1,086
	Gus Suhr	1,086
	Ed Konetchy	1,086
58	Rudy York	1,072
59	Mark Grace	1,056
	Vic Power	1,056
61	Mark McGwire	1,053
62	Mike Hargrove	1,043
63	Eddie Robinson	1,018
64	Phil Cavarretta	1,012
65	Ernie Banks	1,005
66	Dan Driessen	979
67	Hank Greenberg	973
68	Walt Dropo	968
69	Willie Montanez	962
70	Jim Spencer	956
	Fred Tenney	956
72	Roger Connor	955
73	Stan Musial	935
74	Hal Chase	934
75	Tommy Tucker	925
76	Ed Kranepool	900
77	Earl Sheely	890
	Dan Brouthers	890
79	Eddie Waitkus	886
80	Walter Holke	864
81	Ron Fairly	854
82	Babe Dahlgren	848
83	Willie Upshaw	845
84	Fred Merkle	840
85	Dick Stuart	837
86	Bruce Bochte	833
87	Zeke Bonura	815
88	Nick Etten	797
89	Don Mincher	796
90	Alvin Davis	789
91	Joe Pepitone	781
92	Jack Fournier	777
93	Jack Burns	776
94	Bob Watson	771
95	Wes Parker	757
96	Roy Sievers	747
97	Jeff Bagwell	745
98	Charlie Comiskey	740
99	Dick Siebert	732
	Don Hurst	732

Fielding Percentage
(minimum 1,000 games)

1	Steve Garvey	.996
2	Don Mattingly	.996
3	Wes Parker	.996
4	Dan Driessen	.995
5	Jim Spencer	.995
6	Frank McCormick	.995
7	Mark Grace	.995
8	Wally Joyner	.994
9	Rafael Palmeiro	.994
10	Keith Hernandez	.994
11	Vic Power	.994
12	Kent Hrbek	.994
13	Joe Adcock	.994
14	Pete O'Brien	.994
15	Mike Jorgensen	.994
16	Ernie Banks	.994
17	John Mayberry	.994
18	Mark McGwire	.994
19	Lee May	.994
20	Ed Kranepool	.994
21	Chris Chambliss	.993
22	Joe Judge	.993
23	Ted Kluszewski	.993
24	Eddie Murray	.993
25	Eddie Waitkus	.993
26	Will Clark	.993
27	Charlie Grimm	.993
28	Walter Holke	.993
29	Elbie Fletcher	.993
30	Stuffy McInnis	.993
31	Gil Hodges	.992
32	Tony Perez	.992
33	Bill White	.992
34	Jason Thompson	.992
35	George McQuinn	.992
36	Bill Skowron	.992
37	Fred McGriff	.992
38	Norm Cash	.992
39	George Kelly	.992
40	Bill Terry	.992
41	Willie Montanez	.992
42	Stan Musial	.992
43	Chick Gandil	.992
44	Gus Suhr	.992
45	Andres Galarraga	.992
46	Johnny Mize	.992
47	Bill Buckner	.992
48	Jimmie Foxx	.992
49	Joe Kuhel	.992
50	Cecil Cooper	.992
51	Wally Pipp	.992
52	Bruce Bochte	.992
53	Walt Dropo	.992
54	Bob Watson	.991
55	Jake Daubert	.991
56	Earl Sheely	.991
57	Boog Powell	.991
58	Rod Carew	.991
59	Ron Fairly	.991
60	Hank Greenberg	.991
61	Mike Hargrove	.991
62	Lou Gehrig	.991
63	Hal Trosky	.991
64	Dolph Camilli	.990
65	Don Mincher	.990
66	Ed Konetchy	.990
67	Rudy York	.990
68	Mickey Vernon	.990
69	George Scott	.990
70	Babe Dahlgren	.990
71	Willie Upshaw	.990
72	Phil Cavarretta	.990
73	Eddie Robinson	.990
74	Orlando Cepeda	.990
75	Doc Johnston	.989
76	Earl Torgeson	.989
77	Lu Blue	.989
78	Dan McGann	.989
79	Jim Bottomley	.988
80	Donn Clendenon	.988
81	Willie McCovey	.987
82	Ferris Fain	.987
83	George Sisler	.987
84	Doc Hoblitzell	.987
85	George Burns	.987
86	George Stovall	.986
87	Fred Luderus	.986
88	Fred Merkle	.985
89	Jack Fournier	.985
90	Tom Jones	.984
91	Candy LaChance	.984
92	Fred Tenney	.983
93	Kitty Bransfield	.983
94	Dick Stuart	.982
95	Jake Beckley	.981
96	Harry Davis	.980
97	Hal Chase	.980
98	Roger Connor	.978
99	Tommy Tucker	.978
100	Jack Doyle	.975

Assists/162 Games
(minimum 1,000 games)

1	Bill Buckner	140.75
2	Mark Grace	139.18
3	Keith Hernandez	135.30
4	Ferris Fain	134.56
5	Vic Power	133.92
6	Wally Joyner	130.15
7	George Sisler	125.67
8	Eddie Murray	125.21
9	Pete O'Brien	125.18
10	Rudy York	123.46
11	Rafael Palmeiro	122.46
12	Fred Tenney	121.99
13	Mike Hargrove	120.24
14	Dick Stuart	119.92
15	Willie Upshaw	118.32
16	Elbie Fletcher	114.46
17	Will Clark	114.33
18	George McQuinn	113.79
19	Bill Terry	113.68
20	Andres Galarraga	113.00
21	George Stovall	112.71
22	Frank McCormick	112.21
23	Chris Chambliss	111.55
24	Eddie Waitkus	110.57
25	Donn Clendenon	110.57
26	Cecil Cooper	109.83
27	Fred McGriff	109.81
28	Norm Cash	109.81
29	Stan Musial	109.70
30	Tom Jones	109.46
31	Don Mattingly	109.45
32	Gil Hodges	108.76
33	Chick Gandil	107.34
34	George Burns	106.76
35	Rod Carew	105.90
36	Jim Spencer	105.74
37	Kent Hrbek	105.62
38	Bill White	105.29
39	Dolph Camilli	105.04
40	Mickey Vernon	104.86
41	Lu Blue	104.77
42	Ernie Banks	104.10
43	George Scott	103.43
44	Jimmie Foxx	103.16
45	Hank Greenberg	103.07
46	Fred Luderus	102.99
47	Phil Cavarretta	102.83
48	Wally Pipp	102.60
49	Wes Parker	101.62
50	George Kelly	101.59
51	Joe Judge	101.06
52	Jason Thompson	100.97
53	Ed Konetchy	100.97
54	Mark McGwire	100.74
55	Stuffy McInnis	100.53
56	Johnny Mize	100.29
57	Jack Doyle	100.18
58	Bill Skowron	99.99
59	Willie Montanez	99.37
60	Don Mincher	99.08
61	Earl Sheely	98.79
62	Bruce Bochte	98.68
63	Orlando Cepeda	97.41
64	Bob Watson	97.23
65	Jack Fournier	97.22
66	Willie McCovey	96.80
67	Ed Kranepool	96.78
68	Lee May	96.10
69	Joe Adcock	94.87
70	Harry Davis	94.53
71	Boog Powell	94.09
72	Dan McGann	93.95
73	Ron Fairly	93.64
74	Hal Chase	93.54
75	Earl Torgeson	93.13
76	Walt Dropo	92.73
77	Kitty Bransfield	92.48
78	Charlie Grimm	92.29
79	Babe Dahlgren	92.23
80	Hal Trosky	92.22
81	Joe Kuhel	91.59
82	Eddie Robinson	91.58
83	Jake Daubert	91.28
84	John Mayberry	90.65
85	Walter Holke	90.30
86	Jake Beckley	89.62
87	Fred Merkle	88.70
88	Gus Suhr	88.26
89	Ted Kluszewski	87.40
90	Dan Driessen	86.24
91	Tony Perez	85.28
92	Doc Hoblitzell	83.40
93	Mike Jorgensen	82.69
94	Lou Gehrig	82.21
95	Steve Garvey	80.72
96	Doc Johnston	80.29
97	Roger Connor	78.88
98	Cap Anson	75.17
99	Tommy Tucker	72.70
100	Jim Bottomley	69.96

Career Fielding Leaders—Second Basemen

#	Games		#	Putouts		#	Assists		#	Errors	
1	Eddie Collins	2,650	1	Bid McPhee	6,545	1	Eddie Collins	7,630	1	Fred Pfeffer	857
2	Joe Morgan	2,527	2	Eddie Collins	6,526	2	Charlie Gehringer	7,068	2	Bid McPhee	791
3	Lou Whitaker	2,308	3	Nellie Fox	6,090	3	Joe Morgan	6,967	3	Cub Stricker	701
4	Nellie Fox	2,295	4	Joe Morgan	5,742	4	Bid McPhee	6,905	4	Cupid Childs	646
5	Charlie Gehringer	2,209	5	Nap Lajoie	5,496	5	Bill Mazeroski	6,685	5	Lou Bierbauer	574
6	Willie Randolph	2,152	6	Charlie Gehringer	5,369	6	Lou Whitaker	6,653	6	Kid Gleason	572
7	Frank White	2,150	7	Bill Mazeroski	4,974	7	Nellie Fox	6,373	7	Joe Gerhardt	543
8	Bid McPhee	2,126	8	Bobby Doerr	4,928	8	Ryne Sandberg	6,363		Jack Burdock	543
9	Bill Mazeroski	2,094	9	Willie Randolph	4,858	9	Willie Randolph	6,336	9	Fred Dunlap	498
10	Nap Lajoie	2,035	10	Billy Herman	4,780	10	Frank White	6,246	10	Jack Farrell	477
11	Ryne Sandberg	1,995	11	Lou Whitaker	4,771	11	Nap Lajoie	6,202	11	Yank Robinson	471
12	Bobby Doerr	1,852	12	Frank White	4,739	12	Frankie Frisch	6,026	12	Pop Smith	469
13	Red Schoendienst	1,834	13	Fred Pfeffer	4,711	13	Bobby Doerr	5,710	13	Nap Lajoie	451
14	Billy Herman	1,813	14	Red Schoendienst	4,616	14	Billy Herman	5,681	14	Larry Doyle	443
15	Frankie Frisch	1,775	15	Frankie Frisch	4,349	15	Bobby Grich	5,381	15	Eddie Collins	435
16	Bobby Grich	1,765	16	Bobby Grich	4,217	16	Red Schoendienst	5,243	16	Bert Myers	430
17	Johnny Evers	1,735	17	Del Pratt	4,069	17	Rogers Hornsby	5,166	17	Johnny Evers	423
18	Larry Doyle	1,728	18	Kid Gleason	3,883	18	Hughie Critz	5,144	18	Tom Daly	418
19	Del Pratt	1,687	19	Cupid Childs	3,859	19	Johnny Evers	5,124	19	Joe Quinn	408
20	Steve Sax	1,679	20	Ryne Sandberg	3,807	20	Fred Pfeffer	5,104	20	Bobby Lowe	388
21	Kid Gleason	1,583	21	George Cutshaw	3,762	21	Del Pratt	5,075	21	Bill Hallman	385
22	Rogers Hornsby	1,561	22	Johnny Evers	3,758	22	Steve Sax	4,805	22	Del Pratt	381
23	Julian Javier	1,552	23	Lou Bierbauer	3,724	23	Kid Gleason	4,768	23	Miller Huggins	376
24	Fred Pfeffer	1,537	24	Larry Doyle	3,635	24	Joe Gordon	4,706	24	Joe Quest	364
25	Miller Huggins	1,530	25	Joe Gordon	3,600	25	Manny Trillo	4,699	25	Claude Ritchey	355
26	Joe Gordon	1,519	26	Steve Sax	3,574	26	Miller Huggins	4,697	26	Billy Herman	354
27	Manny Trillo	1,518	27	Felix Millan	3,495	27	Cupid Childs	4,678	27	Hardy Richardson	349
	Frank Bolling	1,518	28	Buddy Myer	3,487	28	Larry Doyle	4,655	28	Reddy Mack	330
29	Tony Taylor	1,498	29	Hughie Critz	3,447	29	Lou Bierbauer	4,555	29	George Creamer	324
30	George Cutshaw	1,486		Cub Stricker	3,447	30	Claude Ritchey	4,474	30	Charlie Gehringer	309
31	Claude Ritchey	1,478	31	Claude Ritchey	3,440	31	George Cutshaw	4,473	31	Rogers Hornsby	307
32	Cupid Childs	1,454	32	Ski Melillo	3,428	32	Ski Melillo	4,448	32	Bill McClellan	302
33	Hughie Critz	1,453	33	Miller Huggins	3,425	33	Glenn Hubbard	4,444	33	George Cutshaw	299
34	Tony Lazzeri	1,451	34	Frank Bolling	3,423	34	Tony Lazzeri	4,432	34	Bill Wambsganss	292
35	Felix Millan	1,450	35	Manny Trillo	3,403	35	Jim Gantner	4,347		Jimmy Williams	292
36	Jim Gantner	1,449	36	Bucky Harris	3,398	36	Bobby Lowe	4,162	36	Otto Knabe	287
37	Cookie Rojas	1,447	37	Julian Javier	3,380	37	Julian Javier	4,113	37	Frankie Frisch	280
38	Davey Lopes	1,418	38	Tony Lazzeri	3,341	38	Buddy Myer	4,068	38	Sam Wise	275
39	Tom Herr	1,416	39	Bobby Lowe	3,337	39	Frank Bolling	4,019	39	Bill Greenwood	273
40	Roberto Alomar	1,382	40	Joe Quinn	3,315	40	Tom Herr	3,999	40	Hobe Ferris	270
41	Lou Bierbauer	1,364	41	Tony Taylor	3,274	41	Roberto Alomar	3,974	41	Sam Crane	264
42	Bill Doran	1,359	42	Jerry Priddy	3,226	42	Harold Reynolds	3,932	42	Bucky Harris	263
43	Buddy Myer	1,340	43	Rogers Hornsby	3,206	43	Tony Cuccinello	3,891	43	Monte Ward	261
44	Harold Reynolds	1,339	44	Dave Cash	3,185	44	Max Bishop	3,850	44	Joe Gordon	260
	Bobby Richardson	1,339	45	Johnny Temple	3,172	45	Felix Millan	3,846	45	Bob Ferguson	254
46	Glenn Hubbard	1,332	46	Davey Lopes	3,142	46	Bucky Harris	3,842	46	Tony Lazzeri	252
47	Dave Cash	1,330	47	Jim Gantner	3,139	47	Dave Cash	3,841	47	George Grantham	250
48	Ski Melillo	1,316	48	Bobby Richardson	3,125	48	Johnny Ray	3,836	48	Danny Richardson	245
49	Bobby Lowe	1,313	49	Cookie Rojas	3,105	49	Davey Lopes	3,829	49	Joe Morgan	244
50	Johnny Temple	1,312	50	Don Blasingame	3,065	50	Tony Taylor	3,818	50	Sam Barkley	235
51	Don Blasingame	1,310	51	Tito Fuentes	3,046	51	Cookie Rojas	3,814	51	Willie Randolph	234
52	Joe Quinn	1,303	52	Eddie Stanky	3,030	52	Joe Quinn	3,805	52	Billy Gilbert	233
53	Ted Sizemore	1,288	53	Bill Wambsganss	2,986	53	Ted Sizemore	3,761	53	Hughie Critz	232
54	Robby Thompson	1,279	54	Tom Herr	2,932	54	Glenn Beckert	3,712		Charley Bassett	232
55	Johnny Ray	1,277	55	Ted Sizemore	2,928	55	Robby Thompson	3,704	55	Ralph Young	229
56	Tito Fuentes	1,275	56	Fred Dunlap	2,909	56	Bill Wambsganss	3,669	56	Dick Padden	224
57	Ron Hunt	1,260	57	Tony Cuccinello	2,883	57	Tito Fuentes	3,654	57	Julian Javier	219
58	Bucky Harris	1,254	58	Dave Johnson	2,837	58	Bill Doran	3,651	58	Ski Melillo	215
59	Glenn Beckert	1,242	59	Bobby Avila	2,820	59	Otto Knabe	3,583	59	Bobby Doerr	214
60	Otto Knabe	1,239	60	Glenn Hubbard	2,795	60	Jerry Priddy	3,567	60	Nellie Fox	209
61	Max Bishop	1,230	61	Roberto Alomar	2,775	61	Don Blasingame	3,550	61	Bill Mazeroski	204
62	Tony Cuccinello	1,205	62	Joe Gerhardt	2,766	62	Ron Hunt	3,512		Jack Crooks	204
63	Bill Wambsganss	1,203	63	Jimmy Williams	2,759	63	Jimmy Williams	3,509	63	Buddy Myer	200
64	Dave Johnson	1,198	64	Max Bishop	2,752	64	Bobby Richardson	3,446	64	Danny Murphy	198
65	Juan Samuel	1,188	65	Harold Reynolds	2,749	65	Julio Cruz	3,435	65	Dasher Troy	195
66	Jerry Priddy	1,179	66	Otto Knabe	2,743	66	Cub Stricker	3,387	66	Marty McManus	194
67	Jimmy Williams	1,176	67	Ron Hunt	2,734	67	Bill Hallman	3,386	67	Jerry Priddy	190
68	Ron Oester	1,171	68	Glenn Beckert	2,710	68	Johnny Temple	3,329		Tony Cuccinello	190
69	Bobby Avila	1,168	69	Jack Burdock	2,694	69	Jerry Remy	3,241	69	Lou Whitaker	189
70	Dick Green	1,158	70	Bill Hallman	2,692	70	Tommy Helms	3,237		John Farrell	189
71	Sandy Alomar	1,156	71	Tommy Helms	2,688	71	Juan Samuel	3,224	71	John O'Brien	188
72	Eddie Stanky	1,152	72	Johnny Ray	2,682	72	Bobby Knoop	3,218	72	Steve Sax	187
73	Cub Stricker	1,145		Horace Clarke	2,682	73	Eddie Stanky	3,215	73	Tommy Dowd	186
74	Bill Hallman	1,135	74	Tom Daly	2,646	74	Ron Oester	3,197	74	Jimmy Dykes	183
75	Rod Carew	1,130	75	Bill Doran	2,619	75	Jody Reed	3,187	75	Tito Fuentes	182
76	Tommy Helms	1,129	76	Robby Thompson	2,611	76	Horace Clarke	3,179	76	Frank LaPorte	180
77	Julio Cruz	1,123	77	Ron Oester	2,591	77	Fred Dunlap	3,169		Heinie Reitz	180
78	Jerry Remy	1,117	78	Juan Samuel	2,578	78	Dave Johnson	3,153	78	Glenn Beckert	179
79	Bobby Knoop	1,116	79	Rod Carew	2,573	79	Hobe Ferris	3,151	79	Frank White	178
80	Horace Clarke	1,102	80	Sandy Alomar	2,571	80	Bobby Avila	3,126		Tony Taylor	178
81	Jerry Lumpe	1,100	81	Rennie Stennett	2,568	81	Rennie Stennett	3,100	81	Johnny Temple	172
82	Tom Daly	1,056	82	Bobby Knoop	2,556	82	Jose Lind	3,094	82	Red Schoendienst	170
83	Jody Reed	1,050	83	Dick Green	2,518	83	Dick Green	3,063	83	Bill Sweeney	169
84	Rennie Stennett	1,049	84	Hobe Ferris	2,502	84	Tom Daly	3,017	84	Dots Miller	168
85	Jim Gilliam	1,046	85	Jerry Lumpe	2,469	85	Sandy Alomar	2,988	85	Juan Samuel	164
86	Jose Lind	1,038	86	Connie Ryan	2,447	86	Lonny Frey	2,986		Connie Ryan	164
87	Delino DeShields	1,035	87	Marty McManus	2,430	87	Jackie Hayes	2,983		Hub Collins	164
88	Hobe Ferris	1,017	88	Julio Cruz	2,393	88	Jack Burdock	2,968	88	Max Bishop	163
89	Tony Bernazard	1,000	89	Lonny Frey	2,369	89	Ralph Young	2,953	89	Davey Lopes	162
90	Chuck Knoblauch	999	90	Ralph Young	2,367	90	Joe Gerhardt	2,941		Eddie Stanky	162
91	Ralph Young	994	91	Jerry Remy	2,292	91	Rod Carew	2,928	91	Dick Egan	160
92	Connie Ryan	980	92	Jim Gilliam	2,279	92	Delino DeShields	2,922	92	Manny Trillo	157
93	Phil Garner	975	93	Jimmy Bloodworth	2,257	93	Tony Bernazard	2,901	93	Bobby Grich	156
94	Dick McAuliffe	971	94	Jackie Hayes	2,189	94	Marty McManus	2,853		Ron Hunt	156
95	Lonny Frey	966	95	Jose Lind	2,183	95	Jerry Lumpe	2,846		Jim Delahanty	156
96	Rich Dauer	964	96	Dick McAuliffe	2,155	96	Connie Ryan	2,818	96	Rod Carew	154
97	Fred Dunlap	963	97	Jody Reed	2,135	97	Chuck Knoblauch	2,798	97	Ray Morgan	152
98	Doug Flynn	961	98	Phil Garner	2,124	98	Damaso Garcia	2,784		Gene DeMontreville	152
99	Damaso Garcia	960	99	Tony Bernazard	2,100	99	Phil Garner	2,760	99	Felix Millan	151
100	Jack Burdock	956	100	Cass Michaels	2,073	100	Jim Gilliam	2,724		Lonny Frey	151

Leaders: Career Fielding

Double Plays

1	Bill Mazeroski	1,706
2	Nellie Fox	1,619
3	Willie Randolph	1,547
4	Lou Whitaker	1,528
5	Bobby Doerr	1,507
6	Joe Morgan	1,505
7	Charlie Gehringer	1,444
8	Frank White	1,381
9	Red Schoendienst	1,368
10	Bobby Grich	1,302
11	Eddie Collins	1,215
12	Bid McPhee	1,186
13	Billy Herman	1,177
14	Joe Gordon	1,160
15	Ryne Sandberg	1,158
16	Frankie Frisch	1,064
17	Nap Lajoie	1,050
18	Jim Gantner	1,036
19	Frank Bolling	1,003
20	Steve Sax	998
21	Tom Herr	991
22	Glenn Hubbard	975
23	Manny Trillo	973
24	Ski Melillo	965
25	Bobby Richardson	963
	Buddy Myer	963
27	Hughie Critz	960
28	Cookie Rojas	953
29	Tony Taylor	950
30	Harold Reynolds	948
31	Julian Javier	907
32	Jerry Priddy	906
33	Dave Cash	901
34	Rogers Hornsby	893
	Fred Pfeffer	893
36	Robby Thompson	873
37	Felix Millan	855
38	Ted Sizemore	835
39	Don Blasingame	834
40	Tito Fuentes	832
41	Johnny Temple	829
42	Johnny Ray	828
43	Del Pratt	825
44	Roberto Alomar	817
45	Eddie Stanky	816
46	Tony Cuccinello	812
47	Davey Lopes	811
48	Tommy Helms	807
	Tony Lazzeri	807
50	Bucky Harris	801
51	Bobby Avila	785
52	Julio Cruz	780
53	Bobby Knoop	779
54	Dave Johnson	759
55	Glenn Beckert	758
56	Jerry Remy	744
57	Bill Doran	742
58	Sandy Alomar	729
59	Dick Green	712
60	Horace Clarke	695
61	Jody Reed	690
62	Johnny Evers	689
63	Rennie Stennett	687
64	Ron Hunt	685
65	Rod Carew	664
66	Jerry Lumpe	662
67	Ron Oester	647
68	Lonny Frey	642
69	Larry Doyle	640
70	Chuck Knoblauch	639
	Jackie Hayes	639
	Max Bishop	639
73	Rich Dauer	636
74	George Cutshaw	635
75	Carlos Baerga	634
76	Cass Michaels	633
77	Juan Samuel	630
78	Jim Gilliam	628
79	Tony Bernazard	623
80	Lou Bierbauer	620
81	Pete Suder	613
82	Jackie Robinson	607
83	Phil Garner	606
84	Damaso Garcia	602
	Cupid Childs	602
86	Ray Mack	597
	Miller Huggins	597
88	Kid Gleason	584
89	Marty Barrett	580
90	Connie Ryan	573
91	Snuffy Stirnweiss	572
92	Jimmy Bloodworth	571
93	Bill Wambsganss	570
94	Delino DeShields	560
	Claude Ritchey	560
96	Billy Gardner	559
97	Marty McManus	557
	Joe Quinn	557
99	Dick McAuliffe	552
100	Duane Kuiper	551

Fielding Percentage
(minimum 1,000 games)

1	Ryne Sandberg	.989
2	Tom Herr	.989
3	Jose Lind	.988
4	Jody Reed	.988
5	Jim Gantner	.985
6	Frank White	.984
7	Bobby Grich	.984
8	Lou Whitaker	.984
9	Jerry Lumpe	.984
10	Cookie Rojas	.984
11	Dave Cash	.984
12	Nellie Fox	.984
13	Tommy Helms	.983
14	Dick Green	.983
15	Bill Doran	.983
16	Red Schoendienst	.983
17	Robby Thompson	.983
18	Bill Mazeroski	.983
19	Glenn Hubbard	.983
20	Julio Cruz	.983
21	Horace Clarke	.983
22	Roberto Alomar	.983
23	Johnny Ray	.982
24	Frank Bolling	.982
25	Joe Morgan	.981
26	Manny Trillo	.981
27	Jerry Remy	.981
28	Ron Oester	.980
29	Bobby Doerr	.980
30	Dave Johnson	.980
31	Felix Millan	.980
32	Bobby Knoop	.980
33	Willie Randolph	.980
34	Harold Reynolds	.979
35	Ted Sizemore	.979
36	Jim Gilliam	.979
37	Bobby Richardson	.979
38	Don Blasingame	.979
39	Bobby Avila	.979
40	Steve Sax	.978
41	Rennie Stennett	.978
42	Tony Bernazard	.978
43	Sandy Alomar	.977
44	Davey Lopes	.977
45	Delino DeShields	.976
46	Max Bishop	.976
47	Charlie Gehringer	.976
48	Ron Hunt	.976
49	Tony Taylor	.976
50	Eddie Stanky	.975
51	Johnny Temple	.974
52	Buddy Myer	.974
53	Frankie Frisch	.974
54	Hughie Critz	.974
55	Tito Fuentes	.974
56	Ski Melillo	.973
57	Glenn Beckert	.973
58	Jerry Priddy	.973
59	Rod Carew	.973
60	Tony Cuccinello	.973
61	Juan Samuel	.973
62	Julian Javier	.972
63	Eddie Collins	.970
64	Joe Gordon	.970
65	Tony Lazzeri	.969
66	Billy Herman	.967
67	George Cutshaw	.965
68	Bucky Harris	.965
69	Rogers Hornsby	.965
70	Nap Lajoie	.963
71	Del Pratt	.960
72	Bill Wambsganss	.958
73	Claude Ritchey	.957
74	Otto Knabe	.957
75	Miller Huggins	.956
76	Jimmy Williams	.955
77	Johnny Evers	.955
78	Hobe Ferris	.954
79	Bobby Lowe	.951
80	Larry Doyle	.949
81	Joe Quinn	.946
82	Bid McPhee	.944
83	Bill Hallman	.940
84	Kid Gleason	.938
85	Lou Bierbauer	.935
86	Tom Daly	.931
87	Cupid Childs	.930
88	Fred Pfeffer	.920
89	Cub Stricker	.907

Range
(minimum 1,000 games)

1	Fred Pfeffer	6.39
2	Bid McPhee	6.33
3	Lou Bierbauer	6.07
4	Ski Melillo	5.98
5	Cub Stricker	5.97
6	Hughie Critz	5.91
7	Cupid Childs	5.87
8	Frankie Frisch	5.85
9	Bucky Harris	5.77
10	Billy Herman	5.77
11	Jerry Priddy	5.76
12	Nap Lajoie	5.75
13	Bobby Doerr	5.74
14	Bobby Lowe	5.71
15	Buddy Myer	5.64
16	Charlie Gehringer	5.63
17	Tony Cuccinello	5.62
18	Bill Mazeroski	5.57
19	Hobe Ferris	5.56
20	George Cutshaw	5.54
21	Bill Wambsganss	5.53
22	Joe Gordon	5.47
23	Kid Gleason	5.46
24	Joe Quinn	5.46
25	Bobby Grich	5.44
26	Glenn Hubbard	5.43
27	Nellie Fox	5.43
28	Eddie Stanky	5.42
29	Del Pratt	5.42
30	Rennie Stennett	5.40
31	Red Schoendienst	5.38
32	Max Bishop	5.37
33	Rogers Hornsby	5.36
34	Tom Daly	5.36
35	Tony Lazzeri	5.36
36	Bill Hallman	5.36
37	Claude Ritchey	5.35
38	Eddie Collins	5.34
39	Manny Trillo	5.34
40	Jimmy Williams	5.33
41	Horace Clarke	5.32
42	Miller Huggins	5.31
43	Dave Cash	5.28
44	Tito Fuentes	5.25
45	Tommy Helms	5.25
46	Willie Randolph	5.20
47	Ted Sizemore	5.19
48	Julio Cruz	5.19
49	Bobby Knoop	5.17
50	Glenn Beckert	5.17
51	Jim Gantner	5.17
52	Johnny Evers	5.12
53	Frank White	5.11
54	Otto Knabe	5.11
55	Johnny Ray	5.10
56	Ryne Sandberg	5.10
57	Bobby Avila	5.09
58	Jose Lind	5.08
59	Jody Reed	5.07
60	Felix Millan	5.06
61	Don Blasingame	5.05
62	Joe Morgan	5.03
63	Tony Bernazard	5.00
64	Dave Johnson	5.00
65	Steve Sax	4.99
66	Harold Reynolds	4.99
67	Ron Hunt	4.96
68	Johnny Temple	4.96
69	Jerry Remy	4.95
70	Lou Whitaker	4.95
71	Ron Oester	4.94
72	Robby Thompson	4.94
73	Davey Lopes	4.92
74	Bobby Richardson	4.91
75	Frank Bolling	4.90
76	Tom Herr	4.89
77	Juan Samuel	4.88
78	Roberto Alomar	4.88
79	Rod Carew	4.87
80	Jerry Lumpe	4.83
81	Julian Javier	4.83
82	Dick Green	4.82
83	Sandy Alomar	4.81
84	Larry Doyle	4.80
85	Jim Gilliam	4.78
86	Cookie Rojas	4.78
87	Tony Taylor	4.73
88	Delino DeShields	4.68
89	Bill Doran	4.61

Assists/162 Games
(minimum 1,000 games)

1	Hughie Critz	573.52
2	Frankie Frisch	549.98
3	Ski Melillo	547.55
4	Lou Bierbauer	540.99
5	Glenn Hubbard	540.49
6	Fred Pfeffer	537.96
7	Rogers Hornsby	536.13
8	Bid McPhee	526.16
9	Tony Cuccinello	523.11
10	Cupid Childs	521.21
11	Charlie Gehringer	518.34
12	Bill Mazeroski	517.18
13	Ryne Sandberg	516.69
14	Bobby Lowe	513.51
15	Billy Herman	507.62
16	Max Bishop	507.07
17	Hobe Ferris	501.93
18	Joe Gordon	501.89
19	Manny Trillo	501.47
20	Bobby Doerr	499.47
21	Miller Huggins	497.33
22	Bucky Harris	496.34
23	Julio Cruz	495.52
24	Tony Lazzeri	494.82
25	Bill Wambsganss	494.08
26	Bobby Grich	493.89
27	Nap Lajoie	493.72
28	Buddy Myer	491.80
29	Jody Reed	491.71
30	Claude Ritchey	490.38
31	Jerry Priddy	490.12
32	Kid Gleason	487.94
33	George Cutshaw	487.64
34	Del Pratt	487.34
35	Johnny Ray	486.63
36	Jim Gantner	486.00
37	Glenn Beckert	484.17
38	Jimmy Williams	483.38
39	Bill Hallman	483.29
40	Jose Lind	482.88
41	Cub Stricker	479.21
42	Rennie Stennett	478.74
43	Johnny Evers	478.44
44	Willie Randolph	476.97
45	Harold Reynolds	475.72
46	Joe Quinn	473.07
47	Ted Sizemore	473.05
48	Frank White	470.63
49	Jerry Remy	470.05
50	Tony Bernazard	469.96
51	Robby Thompson	469.15
52	Otto Knabe	468.48
53	Dave Cash	467.85
54	Horace Clarke	467.33
55	Bobby Knoop	467.13
56	Lou Whitaker	466.98
57	Eddie Collins	466.44
58	Roberto Alomar	465.84
59	Tommy Helms	464.48
60	Tito Fuentes	464.27
61	Steve Sax	463.62
62	Red Schoendienst	463.12
63	Tom Daly	462.84
64	Tom Herr	457.51
65	Delino DeShields	457.36
66	Eddie Stanky	452.11
67	Ron Hunt	451.54
68	Nellie Fox	449.86
69	Joe Morgan	446.64
70	Ron Oester	442.28
71	Juan Samuel	439.64
72	Don Blasingame	439.01
73	Davey Lopes	437.45
74	Larry Doyle	436.41
75	Bill Doran	435.22
76	Bobby Avila	433.57
77	Felix Millan	429.69
78	Julian Javier	429.32
79	Frank Bolling	428.91
80	Dick Green	428.50
81	Cookie Rojas	427.00
82	Dave Johnson	426.37
83	Jim Gilliam	421.88
84	Rod Carew	419.77
85	Jerry Lumpe	419.14
86	Sandy Alomar	418.73
87	Bobby Richardson	416.92
88	Tony Taylor	412.89
89	Johnny Temple	411.05

Career Fielding Leaders—Third Basemen

	Games			Putouts			Assists			Errors	
1	Brooks Robinson	2,870	1	Brooks Robinson	2,697	1	Brooks Robinson	6,205	1	Arlie Latham	822
2	Graig Nettles	2,412	2	Jimmy Collins	2,372	2	Graig Nettles	5,299	2	Billy Nash	614
3	Mike Schmidt	2,212	3	Eddie Yost	2,356	3	Mike Schmidt	5,045	3	Hick Carpenter	591
4	Buddy Bell	2,183	4	Lave Cross	2,304	4	Buddy Bell	4,925	4	Billy Shindle	568
5	Eddie Mathews	2,181	5	Pie Traynor	2,289	5	Ron Santo	4,581	5	Jerry Denny	552
6	Ron Santo	2,130	6	Billy Nash	2,219	6	Eddie Mathews	4,322	6	Denny Lyons	507
7	Gary Gaetti	2,082	7	Home Run Baker	2,154	7	Gary Gaetti	4,170	7	Joe Mulvey	475
8	Wade Boggs	2,063	8	Willie Kamm	2,146	8	Aurelio Rodriguez	4,150	8	Jimmy Collins	465
9	Tim Wallach	2,054	9	Eddie Mathews	2,049	9	Ron Cey	4,018	9	Deacon White	444
10	Eddie Yost	2,008	10	Puddin' Head Jones	2,045	10	Wade Boggs	4,015	10	Bill Joyce	438
11	Ron Cey	1,989	11	Jimmy Austin	2,042	11	Tim Wallach	3,992	11	Ned Williamson	401
12	Aurelio Rodriguez	1,983	12	Arlie Latham	1,975	12	Terry Pendleton	3,858	12	Lave Cross	394
13	Sal Bando	1,896	13	Ron Santo	1,955	13	Sal Bando	3,720	13	George Pinckney	387
14	Pie Traynor	1,843	14	Stan Hack	1,946	14	Lave Cross	3,703	14	Bill Kuehne	373
15	Stan Hack	1,819	15	Graig Nettles	1,898	15	Jimmy Collins	3,702		Frank Hankinson	373
16	Ken Boyer	1,785	16	Mike Higgins	1,848	16	George Brett	3,674	16	Harry Steinfeldt	365
17	Mike Higgins	1,768	17	George Kell	1,825	17	Eddie Yost	3,659	17	Jimmy Austin	358
18	Terry Pendleton	1,762	18	Billy Shindle	1,815	18	Ken Boyer	3,652	18	Mike Higgins	356
19	Lave Cross	1,721	19	Buddy Bell	1,800	19	Arlie Latham	3,545	19	Tommy Leach	344
20	Carney Lansford	1,720	20	Larry Gardner	1,788	20	Pie Traynor	3,521		Art Whitney	344
21	George Brett	1,692	21	Harlond Clift	1,777	21	Stan Hack	3,458	21	Bill Bradley	336
	George Kell	1,692		Jerry Denny	1,777	22	Larry Gardner	3,406	22	Jim Donnelly	331
23	Jimmy Collins	1,683	23	Harry Steinfeldt	1,774	23	Willie Kamm	3,345	23	Tom Burns	327
24	Willie Kamm	1,672	24	Bill Bradley	1,752	24	George Kell	3,303	24	Doc Casey	325
25	Larry Gardner	1,655	25	Denny Lyons	1,672	25	Harlond Clift	3,262	25	Pie Traynor	324
26	Puddin' Head Jones	1,614	26	Tim Wallach	1,662	26	Mike Higgins	3,258	26	Home Run Baker	322
27	Arlie Latham	1,571	27	Sal Bando	1,647	27	Clete Boyer	3,218	27	Ron Santo	317
28	Harlond Clift	1,550	28	Gary Gaetti	1,593	28	Doug DeCinces	3,215		Jumbo Davis	317
29	Home Run Baker	1,548	29	Mike Schmidt	1,591	29	Home Run Baker	3,155	29	Mike Schmidt	313
30	Doug DeCinces	1,543	30	Ken Keltner	1,576	30	Darrell Evans	3,123	30	Ezra Sutton	309
31	Ken Keltner	1,500	31	Ken Boyer	1,567	31	Billy Nash	3,119	31	Graig Nettles	295
32	Ossie Bluege	1,486	32	Ossie Bluege	1,537	32	Ken Keltner	3,070	32	Eddie Mathews	293
33	Billy Nash	1,464	33	Aurelio Rodriguez	1,529	33	Ossie Bluege	3,004	33	Larry Gardner	286
34	Darrell Evans	1,442	34	Ron Cey	1,500	34	Jimmy Austin	2,949	34	John McGraw	280
35	Bill Madlock	1,440	35	Clete Boyer	1,470	35	Bill Bradley	2,942	35	Harlond Clift	279
36	Clete Boyer	1,439	36	Heine Groh	1,456	36	Puddin' Head Jones	2,934	36	Eddie Foster	278
37	Jimmy Austin	1,431	37	Pinky Whitney	1,455	37	Doug Rader	2,887	37	Jack Gleason	273
38	Bill Bradley	1,389	38	Bobby Byrne	1,454	38	Billy Shindle	2,886	38	Eddie Yost	270
39	Harry Steinfeldt	1,386	39	Wade Boggs	1,453	39	Frank Malzone	2,884	39	Ken Boyer	264
40	Frank Malzone	1,370	40	Hick Carpenter	1,450	40	Carney Lansford	2,799	40	Brooks Robinson	263
41	Bob Elliott	1,365	41	Bob Elliott	1,448		Harry Steinfeldt	2,799		Harry Wolverton	263
42	Pinky Whitney	1,358	42	Art Devlin	1,399	42	Bob Elliott	2,744		Charlie Reilly	263
43	Ken Caminiti	1,351	43	Milt Stock	1,392	43	Ken McMullen	2,731	43	George Brett	261
44	Doug Rader	1,349	44	Carney Lansford	1,382	44	Pinky Whitney	2,640	44	Bobby Byrne	258
	Milt Stock	1,349	45	Terry Pendleton	1,374	45	Ken Caminiti	2,582	45	Art Devlin	257
46	Ken Reitz	1,321	46	George Brett	1,372	46	Heine Groh	2,554	46	Buddy Bell	254
47	Ken McMullen	1,318	47	Mike Mowrey	1,363	47	Bill Madlock	2,546	47	Darrell Evans	253
48	Heine Groh	1,299	48	Jimmy Dykes	1,361	48	Milt Stock	2,508	48	Charlie Irwin	250
49	Billy Shindle	1,272	49	George Pinckney	1,343	49	Art Devlin	2,481	49	Fred Hartman	249
50	Steve Buechele	1,269	50	Tommy Leach	1,323	50	Ken Reitz	2,477	50	Stan Hack	246
51	Richie Hebner	1,262	51	Doc Casey	1,312	51	Bill Werber	2,415	51	Red Smith	244
52	Jimmy Dykes	1,249	52	Frank Malzone	1,308	52	Jimmy Dykes	2,403	52	Tim Wallach	240
53	Don Hoak	1,199	53	Hans Lobert	1,292	53	Eddie Foster	2,384	53	Terry Pendleton	236
54	Mike Mowrey	1,196	54	Eddie Foster	1,289	54	Mike Mowrey	2,363		Bob Elliott	236
55	Bob Bailey	1,194	55	Bill Coughlin	1,278	55	Richie Hebner	2,346		Heinie Zimmerman	236
56	Art Devlin	1,192	56	Darrell Evans	1,273	56	Jerry Denny	2,338	56	Bill Coughlin	231
57	Mike Pagliarulo	1,179	57	Bill Werber	1,264	57	Don Hoak	2,331	57	Sal Bando	228
58	Brook Jacoby	1,166	58	Ken McMullen	1,259	58	Steve Buechele	2,281		Milt Stock	228
59	Matt Williams	1,162	59	Doug DeCinces	1,256	59	Matt Williams	2,280		Patsy Tebeau	228
60	Eddie Foster	1,160	60	Joe Mulvey	1,235	60	Bob Bailey	2,262		Mike Muldoon	228
61	Charlie Hayes	1,157	61	Charlie Irwin	1,228	61	Charlie Hayes	2,229	61	Ron Cey	223
62	Bobby Byrne	1,147	62	Red Rolfe	1,220	62	Bobby Byrne	2,220		Joe Werrick	223
63	Bill Werber	1,143	63	Don Hoak	1,219	63	Doc Casey	2,184	63	Mike Mowrey	221
64	Jim Davenport	1,130	64	Red Smith	1,210	64	Red Smith	2,136	64	Jim Tabor	220
65	Jerry Denny	1,109	65	Doug Rader	1,138	65	Red Rolfe	2,128		Bill Werber	220
66	Doc Casey	1,103	66	Joe Dugan	1,107	66	Tommy Leach	2,127	66	Harry Lord	217
67	Toby Harrah	1,099	67	Heinie Zimmerman	1,082		Denny Lyons	2,127	67	Aurelio Rodriguez	215
68	Bob Aspromonte	1,094	68	Jim Tabor	1,077	68	Mike Pagliarulo	2,119		Wade Boggs	215
69	Red Rolfe	1,084	69	Harry Lord	1,046	69	Don Money	2,061	69	Gary Gaetti	212
70	Denny Lyons	1,083	70	Tom Burns	1,043	70	Brook Jacoby	2,058	70	George Davis	210
71	Tom Brookens	1,065	71	Bill Joyce	1,041	71	Bill Melton	2,045	71	Ossie Bluege	205
72	George Pinckney	1,061	72	Ken Caminiti	1,034	72	George Pinckney	2,042	72	Joe Battin	203
73	Robin Ventura	1,059	73	Marv Owen	1,032	73	Paul Schaal	2,038	73	George Moriarty	199
	Hick Carpenter	1,059	74	Frank Hankinson	1,029	74	Ken Oberkfell	1,996	74	Doug DeCinces	198
75	Paul Schaal	1,053	75	Art Whitney	1,026	75	Hick Carpenter	1,991	75	Frank Malzone	196
76	Kevin Seitzer	1,051	76	Bob Aspromonte	1,025	76	Don Wert	1,987	76	Bill Madlock	193
77	Red Smith	1,050		Whitey Kurowski	1,025	77	Jim Tabor	1,979	77	Ken Caminiti	192
78	Joe Dugan	1,048	78	Ken Reitz	996	78	Joe Mulvey	1,962		Puddin' Head Jones	192
79	Ken Oberkfell	1,046	79	Harry Wolverton	989	79	Robin Ventura	1,958	79	Billy Lauder	190
80	Don Wert	1,043	80	Ossie Vitt	986	80	Heinie Zimmerman	1,956	80	Chippy McGarr	189
81	Howard Johnson	1,031	81	Grady Hatton	979	81	Joe Dugan	1,943	81	Jimmy Dykes	188
82	Don Money	1,025	82	Al Rosen	970	82	Toby Harrah	1,942	82	Doug Rader	187
83	Ray Knight	1,021	83	Max Alvis	962	83	Kevin Seitzer	1,920	83	Willie Kamm	185
	Larry Parrish	1,021		Eddie Grant	962	84	Larry Parrish	1,918	84	Richie Hebner	182
85	Hans Lobert	1,000	85	Joe Stripp	956	85	Bob Aspromonte	1,879	85	Barry McCormick	176
86	Bill Coughlin	984		Charlie Deal	956	86	Bill Coughlin	1,859	86	Bob Bailey	175
87	Joe Mulvey	983	87	Deacon White	954	87	Grady Hatton	1,844	87	Hans Lobert	172
88	Jim Tabor	980	88	George Moriarty	951	88	Tom Brookens	1,833	88	Larry Parrish	171
89	Max Alvis	971	89	Bill Madlock	949		Ed Charles	1,833		Ken Keltner	171
90	Heinie Zimmerman	957	90	Bill Kuehne	932	90	Jim Davenport	1,816	90	John Irwin	169
91	Grady Hatton	956	91	Bob Jones	917	91	Ossie Vitt	1,792	91	Clete Boyer	168
92	Tommy Leach	955	92	Don Wert	914	92	Al Rosen	1,773		Jimmy Burke	168
93	Ed Charles	942	93	Tony Boeckel	912	93	Hank Majeski	1,750	93	Joe Farrell	167
94	Todd Zeile	937	94	Hank Majeski	911	94	Bill Johnson	1,728	94	Paul Schaal	166
95	Al Rosen	932	95	Don Money	897	95	George Moriarty	1,727		George Kell	166
96	Marv Owen	921	96	Matt Williams	896	96	Randy Jackson	1,725	96	Dude Esterbrook	165
97	Joe Stripp	914		Ezra Sutton	896	97	Ned Williamson	1,719	97	Bobby Bonilla	164
98	Jim Presley	911	98	Steve Buechele	895	98	Todd Zeile	1,718		Buddy Lewis	164
99	Harry Lord	907	99	Robin Ventura	893	99	Jim Presley	1,709		Pinky Whitney	164
100	Wayne Gross	903	100	Ed Charles	879	100	Charlie Deal	1,705	100	Howard Johnson	163

Double Plays

1	Brooks Robinson	618
2	Graig Nettles	470
3	Mike Schmidt	450
4	Gary Gaetti	435
5	Buddy Bell	430
6	Aurelio Rodriguez	408
7	Wade Boggs	397
8	Ron Santo	395
9	Eddie Mathews	369
10	Ken Boyer	355
11	Sal Bando	345
	Eddie Yost	345
13	Doug DeCinces	331
14	Tim Wallach	319
15	Ron Cey	315
	Clete Boyer	315
17	Terry Pendleton	310
18	Harlond Clift	309
19	George Brett	307
20	George Kell	306
	Ken Keltner	306
22	Pie Traynor	303
23	Willie Kamm	299
24	Frank Malzone	289
25	Mike Higgins	288
26	Puddin' Head Jones	273
27	Darrell Evans	270
28	Heine Groh	268
29	Ossie Bluege	266
30	Billy Nash	265
31	Home Run Baker	259
32	Ken McMullen	258
33	Carney Lansford	256
	Doug Rader	256
35	Arlie Latham	253
36	Bob Elliott	252
37	Stan Hack	247
38	Jimmy Austin	229
39	Larry Gardner	228
40	Don Hoak	227
41	Ken Caminiti	226
42	Jimmy Collins	225
43	Richie Hebner	224
	Don Money	224
45	Ken Reitz	219
	Matt Williams	219
	Pinky Whitney	219
48	Billy Shindle	215
49	Charlie Hayes	214
	Bill Werber	214
51	Eddie Foster	213
52	Lave Cross	212
53	Bob Bailey	203
54	Bill Madlock	200
	Robin Ventura	200
56	Jimmy Dykes	199
57	Milt Stock	198
58	Mike Pagliarulo	194
	Andy Carey	194
60	Hank Majeski	192
61	Kevin Seitzer	189
62	Paul Molitor	185
63	Steve Buechele	184
	Bill Melton	184
	Red Rolfe	184
66	Bill Bradley	182
67	Ken Oberkfell	180
68	Jim Tabor	178
69	Toby Harrah	177
70	Don Wert	173
71	Mike Mowrey	172
	Harry Steinfeldt	172
73	Tom Brookens	171
74	Grady Hatton	169
75	Brook Jacoby	168
	Marv Owen	168
77	Ed Charles	165
	Joe Dugan	165
	Denny Lyons	165
80	Bill Johnson	163
81	Les Bell	161
82	Roy Howell	160
	Larry Parrish	160
84	Al Rosen	159
85	Randy Jackson	157
86	Jim Davenport	155
87	Billy Cox	154
88	Todd Zeile	153
89	Jim Presley	152
	Paul Schaal	152
	Red Smith	152
92	Rico Petrocelli	150
93	Wayne Gross	149
94	Bobby Bonilla	148
	Wayne Garrett	148
96	Jerry Denny	147
97	Sammy Hale	145
98	Ray Knight	144
	Max Alvis	144
100	George Pinckney	143

Fielding Percentage
(minimum 1,000 games)

1	Brooks Robinson	.971
2	Ken Reitz	.970
3	George Kell	.969
4	Steve Buechele	.968
5	Don Money	.968
6	Don Wert	.968
7	Willie Kamm	.967
8	Heine Groh	.967
9	Carney Lansford	.966
10	Clete Boyer	.965
11	Ken Oberkfell	.965
12	Gary Gaetti	.965
13	Ken Keltner	.965
14	Jim Davenport	.964
15	Buddy Bell	.964
16	Aurelio Rodriguez	.964
17	Puddin' Head Jones	.963
18	Toby Harrah	.963
19	Wade Boggs	.962
20	Pinky Whitney	.961
21	Ron Cey	.961
22	Ken McMullen	.961
23	Matt Williams	.961
24	Graig Nettles	.961
25	Bob Aspromonte	.960
26	Tim Wallach	.959
27	Sal Bando	.959
28	Don Hoak	.959
29	Brook Jacoby	.958
30	Doug DeCinces	.958
31	Ray Knight	.957
32	Eddie Yost	.957
33	Terry Pendleton	.957
34	Ossie Bluege	.957
35	Stan Hack	.956
36	Joe Dugan	.956
37	Eddie Mathews	.956
38	Red Rolfe	.956
39	Doug Rader	.956
40	Frank Malzone	.955
41	Robin Ventura	.955
42	Mike Schmidt	.955
43	Mike Pagliarulo	.955
44	Ron Santo	.954
45	Charlie Hayes	.952
46	Jimmy Dykes	.952
47	Ken Boyer	.952
48	George Brett	.951
49	Ken Caminiti	.950
50	Kevin Seitzer	.949
51	Larry Gardner	.948
52	Bill Madlock	.948
53	Harlond Clift	.948
54	Pie Traynor	.947
55	Bob Elliott	.947
56	Richie Hebner	.946
57	Bob Bailey	.946
58	Darrell Evans	.946
59	Hans Lobert	.945
60	Milt Stock	.945
61	Mike Mowrey	.944
62	Bill Werber	.944
63	Paul Schaal	.943
64	Tom Brookens	.943
65	Home Run Baker	.943
66	Larry Parrish	.941
67	Lave Cross	.938
68	Art Devlin	.938
69	Mike Higgins	.935
70	Bobby Byrne	.934
71	Bill Bradley	.933
72	Jimmy Austin	.933
73	Red Smith	.932
74	Eddie Foster	.930
75	Howard Johnson	.929
76	Jimmy Collins	.929
77	Harry Steinfeldt	.926
78	Doc Casey	.915
79	George Pinckney	.897
80	Billy Nash	.897
81	Billy Shindle	.892
82	Denny Lyons	.882
83	Jerry Denny	.882
84	Arlie Latham	.870
85	Hick Carpenter	.853

Range
(minimum 1,000 games)

1	Jerry Denny	3.71
2	Billy Shindle	3.70
3	Billy Nash	3.65
4	Jimmy Collins	3.61
5	Arlie Latham	3.51
6	Denny Lyons	3.51
7	Lave Cross	3.49
8	Jimmy Austin	3.49
9	Home Run Baker	3.43
10	Bill Bradley	3.38
11	Harry Steinfeldt	3.30
12	Willie Kamm	3.28
13	Clete Boyer	3.26
14	Art Devlin	3.26
15	Harlond Clift	3.25
16	Hick Carpenter	3.25
17	Bill Werber	3.22
18	Bobby Byrne	3.20
19	George Pinckney	3.19
20	Red Smith	3.19
21	Doc Casey	3.17
22	Eddie Foster	3.17
23	Pie Traynor	3.15
24	Larry Gardner	3.14
25	Mike Mowrey	3.12
26	Brooks Robinson	3.10
27	Ken Keltner	3.10
28	Red Rolfe	3.09
29	Heine Groh	3.09
30	Puddin' Head Jones	3.08
31	Buddy Bell	3.08
32	Bob Elliott	3.07
33	Ron Santo	3.07
34	Frank Malzone	3.06
35	Ossie Bluege	3.06
36	Darrell Evans	3.05
37	George Kell	3.03
38	Ken McMullen	3.03
39	Pinky Whitney	3.02
40	Jimmy Dykes	3.01
41	Mike Schmidt	3.00
42	Eddie Yost	3.00
43	Graig Nettles	2.98
44	Doug Rader	2.98
45	George Brett	2.98
46	Stan Hack	2.97
47	Terry Pendleton	2.97
48	Don Hoak	2.96
49	Hans Lobert	2.95
50	Ken Boyer	2.92
51	Eddie Mathews	2.92
52	Joe Dugan	2.91
53	Doug DeCinces	2.90
54	Milt Stock	2.89
55	Mike Higgins	2.89
56	Don Money	2.89
57	Aurelio Rodriguez	2.86
58	Sal Bando	2.83
59	Don Wert	2.78
60	Ron Cey	2.77
61	Gary Gaetti	2.77
62	Tim Wallach	2.75
63	Matt Williams	2.73
64	Robin Ventura	2.69
65	Ken Caminiti	2.68
66	Larry Parrish	2.67
67	Bob Aspromonte	2.65
68	Wade Boggs	2.65
69	Ken Reitz	2.63
70	Paul Schaal	2.62
71	Charlie Hayes	2.61
72	Bob Bailey	2.56
73	Richie Hebner	2.52
74	Ken Oberkfell	2.51
75	Steve Buechele	2.50
76	Kevin Seitzer	2.49
77	Toby Harrah	2.48
78	Carney Lansford	2.43
79	Brook Jacoby	2.43
80	Bill Madlock	2.43
81	Tom Brookens	2.40
82	Mike Pagliarulo	2.39
83	Jim Davenport	2.37
84	Ray Knight	2.30
85	Howard Johnson	2.07

Assists/162 Games
(minimum 1,000 games)

1	Mike Schmidt	369.48
2	Billy Shindle	367.56
3	Arlie Latham	365.56
4	Buddy Bell	365.48
5	Clete Boyer	362.28
6	Jimmy Collins	356.34
7	Graig Nettles	355.90
8	Terry Pendleton	354.71
9	George Brett	351.77
10	Darrell Evans	350.85
11	Brooks Robinson	350.25
12	Lave Cross	348.57
13	Ron Santo	348.41
14	Doug Rader	346.70
15	Billy Nash	345.14
16	Bill Bradley	343.13
17	Bill Werber	342.28
18	Jerry Denny	341.53
19	Frank Malzone	341.03
20	Harlond Clift	340.93
21	Aurelio Rodriguez	339.03
22	Doug DeCinces	337.54
23	Art Devlin	337.18
24	Ken McMullen	335.68
25	Jimmy Austin	333.85
26	Larry Gardner	333.40
27	Eddie Foster	332.94
28	Ken Keltner	331.56
29	Ken Boyer	331.44
30	Home Run Baker	330.17
31	Red Smith	329.55
32	Ossie Bluege	327.49
33	Ron Cey	327.26
34	Harry Steinfeldt	327.16
35	Don Money	325.74
36	Bob Elliott	325.66
37	Gary Gaetti	324.47
38	Willie Kamm	324.10
39	Eddie Mathews	321.03
40	Doc Casey	320.77
41	Mike Mowrey	320.07
42	Heine Groh	318.51
43	Denny Lyons	318.17
44	Red Rolfe	318.02
45	Matt Williams	317.87
46	Sal Bando	317.85
47	George Kell	316.24
48	Wade Boggs	315.28
49	Don Hoak	314.95
50	Pinky Whitney	314.93
51	Tim Wallach	314.85
52	Bobby Byrne	313.55
53	Paul Schaal	313.54
54	Charlie Hayes	312.10
55	George Pinckney	311.79
56	Jimmy Dykes	311.68
57	Ken Caminiti	309.61
58	Pie Traynor	309.50
59	Ken Oberkfell	309.13
60	Don Wert	308.62
61	Stan Hack	307.97
62	Bob Bailey	306.90
63	Hick Carpenter	304.57
64	Larry Parrish	304.33
65	Ken Reitz	303.77
66	Milt Stock	301.18
67	Richie Hebner	301.15
68	Joe Dugan	300.35
69	Robin Ventura	299.52
70	Mike Higgins	298.53
71	Kevin Seitzer	295.95
72	Eddie Yost	295.20
73	Puddin' Head Jones	294.49
74	Steve Buechele	291.19
75	Mike Pagliarulo	291.16
76	Bill Madlock	286.43
77	Toby Harrah	286.26
78	Brook Jacoby	285.93
79	Tom Brookens	278.82
80	Bob Aspromonte	278.24
81	Hans Lobert	269.08
82	Carney Lansford	263.63
83	Ray Knight	262.28
84	Jim Davenport	260.35
85	Howard Johnson	247.64

Career Fielding Leaders—Shortstops

Games

1	Luis Aparicio	2,581
2	Ozzie Smith	2,511
3	Cal Ripken Jr.	2,302
4	Larry Bowa	2,222
5	Luke Appling	2,218
6	Dave Concepcion	2,178
7	Rabbit Maranville	2,153
8	Alan Trammell	2,139
9	Bill Dahlen	2,132
10	Bert Campaneris	2,097
11	Tommy Corcoran	2,073
12	Roy McMillan	2,028
13	Pee Wee Reese	2,014
14	Roger Peckinpaugh	1,982
15	Garry Templeton	1,964
16	Don Kessinger	1,955
17	Mark Belanger	1,942
18	Chris Speier	1,900
19	Honus Wagner	1,886
20	Dick Groat	1,877
21	Dave Bancroft	1,873
22	Donie Bush	1,866
23	Alfredo Griffin	1,861
24	Leo Cardenas	1,843
	Joe Cronin	1,843
26	Bobby Wallace	1,826
27	Ed Brinkman	1,795
28	Herman Long	1,794
29	Greg Gagne	1,765
30	Bill Russell	1,746
31	Joe Tinker	1,743
32	Ozzie Guillen	1,724
33	Dick Bartell	1,702
34	Monte Cross	1,675
35	Germany Smith	1,665
36	Phil Rizzuto	1,647
37	Everett Scott	1,643
38	Jack Glasscock	1,628
39	George McBride	1,626
40	Mickey Doolan	1,625
41	Freddie Patek	1,588
42	Tony Fernandez	1,573
43	Ed McKean	1,564
44	Maury Wills	1,555
45	Marty Marion	1,547
46	Billy Jurges	1,540
47	Lou Boudreau	1,539
48	Tim Foli	1,524
49	Frankie Crosetti	1,515
50	Leo Durocher	1,509
51	Arky Vaughan	1,485
52	Robin Yount	1,479
53	Art Fletcher	1,448
54	Wally Gerber	1,446
55	Al Dark	1,404
56	Bud Harrelson	1,400
57	Jim Fregosi	1,396
58	Eddie Miller	1,395
59	Rafael Ramirez	1,386
60	Bucky Dent	1,381
61	Johnny Logan	1,380
62	Spike Owen	1,373
63	George Davis	1,372
64	Jay Bell	1,362
65	Barry Larkin	1,353
66	Dick Schofield	1,348
67	Vern Stephens	1,330
68	Travis Jackson	1,326
69	Shawon Dunston	1,324
70	Ivan DeJesus	1,303
71	Eddie Joost	1,296
72	Zoilo Versalles	1,265
73	Chico Carrasquel	1,241
74	Craig Reynolds	1,240
75	Bones Ely	1,236
76	Billy Rogell	1,235
77	Joe Sewell	1,216
78	Dal Maxvill	1,207
79	Walt Weiss	1,195
80	Rick Burleson	1,192
81	Roger Metzger	1,173
82	Omar Vizquel	1,160
83	Dickie Thon	1,143
	Ron Hansen	1,143
85	Lyn Lary	1,138
86	Freddy Parent	1,129
87	Ernie Banks	1,125
	Doc Lavan	1,125
89	Frank Taveras	1,113
90	Al Bridwell	1,094
91	Roy Smalley	1,069
92	Bobby Wine	1,067
93	Ivy Olson	1,054
94	Glenn Wright	1,051
95	Buddy Kerr	1,038
96	Joe DeMaestri	1,029
97	Jose Uribe	1,015
98	Eddie Bressoud	1,002
99	Chick Galloway	993
100	Johnnie LeMaster	992

Putouts

1	Rabbit Maranville	5,145
2	Bill Dahlen	4,850
3	Dave Bancroft	4,623
4	Honus Wagner	4,576
5	Tommy Corcoran	4,550
6	Luis Aparicio	4,548
7	Luke Appling	4,398
8	Ozzie Smith	4,249
9	Herman Long	4,226
10	Bobby Wallace	4,142
11	Pee Wee Reese	4,040
12	Donie Bush	4,038
13	Monte Cross	3,974
14	Roger Peckinpaugh	3,919
15	Dick Bartell	3,872
16	Joe Tinker	3,758
17	Roy McMillan	3,705
18	Joe Cronin	3,696
19	Dave Concepcion	3,670
20	Cal Ripken Jr.	3,651
21	Bert Campaneris	3,608
22	George McBride	3,585
23	Mickey Doolan	3,578
24	Dick Groat	3,505
25	Garry Templeton	3,393
26	Alan Trammell	3,391
27	Everett Scott	3,351
28	Larry Bowa	3,314
29	George Davis	3,231
30	Phil Rizzuto	3,219
31	Leo Cardenas	3,218
32	Alfredo Griffin	3,207
33	Don Kessinger	3,151
34	Billy Jurges	3,133
35	Lou Boudreau	3,132
36	Leo Durocher	3,097
37	Frankie Crosetti	3,061
38	Chris Speier	3,057
39	Mark Belanger	3,005
40	Arky Vaughan	2,995
41	Marty Marion	2,986
42	Eddie Miller	2,977
43	Wally Gerber	2,963
44	Ed Brinkman	2,924
45	Travis Jackson	2,877
46	Art Fletcher	2,836
47	Jack Glasscock	2,821
48	Ed McKean	2,820
49	Germany Smith	2,813
50	Eddie Joost	2,755
51	Ozzie Guillen	2,735
52	Tony Fernandez	2,708
53	Freddie Patek	2,690
54	Tim Foli	2,687
55	Al Dark	2,672
56	Johnny Logan	2,612
57	Joe Sewell	2,591
58	Robin Yount	2,588
59	Bones Ely	2,581
60	Greg Gagne	2,559
61	Maury Wills	2,550
62	Bill Russell	2,536
63	Doc Lavan	2,451
64	Jim Fregosi	2,397
65	Hughie Jennings	2,390
66	Ivy Olson	2,389
67	Bud Harrelson	2,387
68	Vern Stephens	2,385
69	Lyn Lary	2,373
70	Billy Rogell	2,362
71	Al Bridwell	2,267
72	Shawon Dunston	2,258
73	Freddy Parent	2,253
74	Ray Chapman	2,204
75	Kid Elberfeld	2,183
76	Rafael Ramirez	2,159
77	Glenn Wright	2,157
78	Rick Burleson	2,150
79	Dick Schofield	2,140
80	Barry Larkin	2,137
81	Chico Carrasquel	2,131
82	Zoilo Versalles	2,126
83	Bucky Dent	2,116
84	Jay Bell	2,101
85	Spike Owen	2,087
	Ernie Banks	2,087
87	Chick Galloway	2,059
88	Buddy Kerr	2,045
89	Ron Hansen	2,011
90	Heinie Wagner	1,954
91	Buck Weaver	1,876
92	Roger Metzger	1,845
93	Ivan DeJesus	1,839
94	Hod Ford	1,821
95	Heinie Sand	1,811
96	Omar Vizquel	1,797
97	Walt Weiss	1,768
	Shorty Fuller	1,768
99	Red Kress	1,761
100	Dal Maxvill	1,759

Assists

1	Ozzie Smith	8,375
2	Luis Aparicio	8,016
3	Bill Dahlen	7,500
4	Rabbit Maranville	7,357
5	Luke Appling	7,218
6	Tommy Corcoran	7,106
7	Cal Ripken Jr.	6,977
8	Larry Bowa	6,857
9	Dave Concepcion	6,594
10	Dave Bancroft	6,561
11	Roger Peckinpaugh	6,334
12	Bobby Wallace	6,303
13	Don Kessinger	6,212
14	Roy McMillan	6,191
15	Alan Trammell	6,172
16	Germany Smith	6,154
17	Herman Long	6,136
18	Donie Bush	6,135
19	Bert Campaneris	6,064
20	Garry Templeton	6,041
	Honus Wagner	6,041
22	Pee Wee Reese	5,891
23	Joe Tinker	5,848
24	Joe Cronin	5,814
25	Dick Groat	5,811
26	Mark Belanger	5,786
27	Chris Speier	5,781
28	Jack Glasscock	5,630
29	Dick Bartell	5,590
30	Bill Russell	5,546
31	Ed Brinkman	5,466
32	Leo Cardenas	5,303
33	Mickey Doolan	5,290
34	George McBride	5,274
35	Monte Cross	5,269
36	Alfredo Griffin	5,186
37	Art Fletcher	5,134
38	Everett Scott	5,053
39	Ozzie Guillen	4,962
40	Billy Jurges	4,959
41	Greg Gagne	4,930
42	Ed McKean	4,853
43	Marty Marion	4,829
44	Tim Foli	4,804
	Maury Wills	4,804
46	Robin Yount	4,794
47	George Davis	4,787
48	Freddie Patek	4,786
49	Arky Vaughan	4,780
50	Lou Boudreau	4,760
51	Phil Rizzuto	4,666
52	Travis Jackson	4,635
53	Tony Fernandez	4,511
54	Eddie Miller	4,501
55	Frankie Crosetti	4,484
56	Leo Durocher	4,431
57	Johnny Logan	4,397
58	Bucky Dent	4,332
59	Bones Ely	4,323
60	Wally Gerber	4,319
61	Jay Bell	4,173
62	Jim Fregosi	4,169
63	Al Dark	4,168
64	Vern Stephens	4,150
65	Ivan DeJesus	4,036
66	Barry Larkin	3,994
67	Rafael Ramirez	3,978
68	Bud Harrelson	3,975
69	Joe Sewell	3,933
70	Billy Rogell	3,886
71	Dick Schofield	3,873
72	Rick Burleson	3,864
73	Eddie Joost	3,844
74	Spike Owen	3,814
75	Freddy Parent	3,772
76	Shawon Dunston	3,688
77	Zoilo Versalles	3,645
78	Doc Lavan	3,628
79	Chico Carrasquel	3,619
80	Roger Metzger	3,535
81	Ron Hansen	3,503
82	Craig Reynolds	3,484
83	Glenn Wright	3,473
84	Ernie Banks	3,441
85	Omar Vizquel	3,412
86	Dal Maxvill	3,405
87	Lyn Lary	3,388
88	Al Bridwell	3,351
89	Walt Weiss	3,350
90	Ivy Olson	3,313
91	Buddy Kerr	3,297
92	Roy Smalley	3,274
93	Dickie Thon	3,198
	Gene Alley	3,198
95	Hughie Jennings	3,147
96	Frank Taveras	3,099
97	Arthur Irwin	3,093
98	Kid Elberfeld	3,080
99	Shorty Fuller	3,047
100	Bobby Wine	2,974

Errors

1	Herman Long	1,070
2	Bill Dahlen	975
3	Germany Smith	971
4	Tommy Corcoran	956
5	Ed McKean	855
6	Jack Glasscock	832
7	Monte Cross	810
8	Donie Bush	689
9	Bobby Wallace	685
10	Honus Wagner	676
11	Dave Bancroft	660
12	Luke Appling	643
13	Joe Tinker	635
14	Rabbit Maranville	631
15	Arthur Irwin	594
16	Shorty Fuller	592
17	Frank Fennelly	590
18	Bones Ely	578
19	Mickey Doolan	570
20	Roger Peckinpaugh	553
21	Bill Gleason	535
22	Monte Ward	530
23	Art Fletcher	521
24	George Davis	511
25	Joe Cronin	485
26	George McBride	484
27	Freddy Parent	474
28	Dick Bartell	471
29	Hughie Jennings	470
30	Kid Elberfeld	458
31	Doc Lavan	455
32	Wally Gerber	439
33	Sam Wise	422
34	Ivy Olson	417
35	Frankie Crosetti	402
36	Arky Vaughan	397
37	Frank Shugart	391
38	Pee Wee Reese	388
39	Sadie Houck	386
40	Garry Templeton	384
41	Travis Jackson	381
42	Dick Groat	374
43	Luis Aparicio	366
	Al Bridwell	366
45	Bert Campaneris	365
46	Jack Rowe	364
47	Heinie Wagner	356
48	Tom Burns	355
49	Glenn Wright	351
50	Alfredo Griffin	340
51	Bill Russell	339
52	Ray Chapman	336
53	Don Kessinger	334
54	Joe Sewell	333
55	Bill White	331
56	Bob Allen	330
57	Candy Nelson	328
58	Dave Concepcion	311
	Buck Weaver	311
60	Leo Durocher	307
61	Everett Scott	306
62	Billy Jurges	305
63	Rafael Ramirez	301
64	Chick Galloway	296
65	Rudy Hulswitt	294
66	Freddie Patek	293
	John Peters	293
68	Eddie Joost	291
69	Roy McMillan	290
	Jack Barry	290
71	Billy Rogell	287
72	Al Dark	286
	Mark Koenig	286
74	Maury Wills	284
75	Ozzie Smith	281
76	Paul Radford	276
77	Chris Speier	275
78	Charley O'Leary	273
79	Robin Yount	272
80	Gene DeMontreville	270
81	Vern Stephens	269
82	Zoilo Versalles	268
	Lyn Lary	268
	Lou Say	268
85	Larry Kopf	266
86	Phil Rizzuto	263
87	Davy Force	262
88	Ed Brinkman	259
	Leo Cardenas	259
90	Heinie Sand	258
91	Johnny Logan	256
92	Ned Williamson	255
93	Marty Marion	252
94	Jim Fregosi	251
95	Granny Hamner	248
96	Frank Scheibeck	245
97	Red Kress	243
	Tommy Thevenow	243
99	Frank Taveras	236
100	Ivan DeJesus	228

Double Plays

1	Ozzie Smith	1,590
2	Cal Ripken Jr.	1,565
3	Luis Aparicio	1,553
4	Luke Appling	1,424
5	Alan Trammell	1,307
6	Roy McMillan	1,304
7	Dave Concepcion	1,290
8	Larry Bowa	1,265
9	Pee Wee Reese	1,246
10	Dick Groat	1,237
11	Phil Rizzuto	1,217
12	Bert Campaneris	1,186
13	Rabbit Maranville	1,183
14	Lou Boudreau	1,180
15	Don Kessinger	1,170
16	Joe Cronin	1,165
17	Garry Templeton	1,164
18	Dick Bartell	1,072
19	Mark Belanger	1,054
20	Alfredo Griffin	1,053
21	Chris Speier	1,043
22	Leo Cardenas	1,036
23	Tim Foli	1,028
24	Ozzie Guillen	1,027
25	Dave Bancroft	1,017
26	Ed Brinkman	1,005
27	Freddie Patek	1,004
28	Marty Marion	978
29	Greg Gagne	967
30	Eddie Miller	946
31	Frankie Crosetti	944
32	Tony Fernandez	943
33	Robin Yount	941
34	Al Dark	933
35	Billy Jurges	929
36	Eddie Joost	928
37	Bill Russell	909
38	Dick Schofield	900
39	Roger Peckinpaugh	898
40	Leo Durocher	895
41	Johnny Logan	894
42	Bill Dahlen	881
43	Maury Wills	859
44	Vern Stephens	853
45	Arky Vaughan	850
46	Tommy Corcoran	849
47	Rafael Ramirez	842
48	Bucky Dent	839
49	Jim Fregosi	836
50	Rick Burleson	826
	Travis Jackson	826
52	Billy Rogell	805
53	Jay Bell	794
54	Omar Vizquel	782
55	Chico Carrasquel	770
56	Honus Wagner	766
57	Herman Long	765
58	Bud Harrelson	751
59	Wally Gerber	741
60	Zoilo Versalles	727
61	Ernie Banks	724
62	Spike Owen	723
63	Ron Hansen	722
64	Everett Scott	713
65	Barry Larkin	712
	Walt Weiss	712
67	Gene Alley	709
68	Roy Smalley	702
69	Ivan DeJesus	700
	Shawon Dunston	700
71	Bobby Wine	698
72	Glenn Wright	695
73	Joe Sewell	674
74	Roger Metzger	671
75	Joe Tinker	669
76	Craig Reynolds	658
77	Dal Maxvill	649
78	Bobby Wallace	642
79	Lyn Lary	632
80	Jack Glasscock	620
81	Art Fletcher	614
82	Joe DeMaestri	612
83	George McBride	610
84	Dickie Thon	594
85	George Davis	589
86	Germany Smith	587
87	Donie Bush	585
88	Mike Bordick	578
89	Granny Hamner	571
90	Tony Kubek	569
	Mickey Doolan	569
92	Jose Uribe	565
	Hod Ford	565
94	Doc Lavan	559
95	Red Kress	558
96	Frank Taveras	555
97	Buddy Kerr	548
	Skeeter Newsome	548
99	Monte Cross	534
100	Tommy Thevenow	523

Fielding Percentage

(minimum 1,000 games)

1	Omar Vizquel	.980
2	Larry Bowa	.980
3	Tony Fernandez	.980
4	Cal Ripken Jr.	.979
5	Ozzie Smith	.978
6	Spike Owen	.977
7	Alan Trammell	.977
8	Mark Belanger	.977
9	Bucky Dent	.976
10	Dick Schofield	.976
11	Jay Bell	.976
12	Roger Metzger	.976
13	Ozzie Guillen	.974
14	Barry Larkin	.974
15	Tim Foli	.973
16	Dal Maxvill	.973
17	Lou Boudreau	.973
18	Greg Gagne	.972
19	Eddie Miller	.972
20	Luis Aparicio	.972
21	Roy McMillan	.972
22	Walt Weiss	.971
23	Rick Burleson	.971
24	Bobby Wine	.971
25	Dave Concepcion	.971
26	Leo Cardenas	.971
27	Ed Brinkman	.970
28	Chris Speier	.970
29	Ernie Banks	.969
30	Bud Harrelson	.969
31	Jose Uribe	.969
32	Chico Carrasquel	.969
33	Marty Marion	.969
34	Phil Rizzuto	.968
35	Ron Hansen	.968
36	Shawon Dunston	.967
37	Joe DeMaestri	.967
38	Buddy Kerr	.967
39	Craig Reynolds	.966
40	Roy Smalley	.966
41	Don Kessinger	.966
42	Dickie Thon	.965
43	Everett Scott	.965
44	Johnny Logan	.965
45	Robin Yount	.964
46	Billy Jurges	.964
47	Bert Campaneris	.964
48	Jim Fregosi	.963
49	Eddie Bressoud	.963
50	Maury Wills	.963
51	Ivan DeJesus	.963
52	Pee Wee Reese	.962
53	Freddie Patek	.962
54	Dick Groat	.961
55	Alfredo Griffin	.961
56	Garry Templeton	.961
57	Leo Durocher	.961
58	Vern Stephens	.960
59	Al Dark	.960
60	Bill Russell	.960
61	Eddie Joost	.958
62	Billy Rogell	.956
63	Zoilo Versalles	.956
64	Lyn Lary	.956
65	Rafael Ramirez	.953
66	Dick Bartell	.953
67	Frank Taveras	.953
68	Rabbit Maranville	.952
69	Travis Jackson	.952
70	Joe Cronin	.951
71	Joe Sewell	.951
72	Arky Vaughan	.951
73	Frankie Crosetti	.949
74	Roger Peckinpaugh	.949
75	George McBride	.948
76	Luke Appling	.948
77	Dave Bancroft	.944
78	Wally Gerber	.943
79	Glenn Wright	.941
80	Honus Wagner	.940
81	George Davis	.940
82	Mickey Doolan	.940
83	Al Bridwell	.939
84	Art Fletcher	.939
85	Bobby Wallace	.938
86	Joe Tinker	.938
87	Donie Bush	.937
88	Ivy Olson	.932
89	Doc Lavan	.930
90	Freddy Parent	.927
91	Bill Dahlen	.927
92	Tommy Corcoran	.924
93	Bones Ely	.923
94	Monte Cross	.919
95	Jack Glasscock	.910
96	Herman Long	.906
97	Germany Smith	.902
98	Ed McKean	.900

Range

(minimum 1,000 games)

1	Dave Bancroft	5.97
2	George Davis	5.84
3	Rabbit Maranville	5.81
4	Bill Dahlen	5.79
5	Herman Long	5.78
6	Bobby Wallace	5.72
7	Travis Jackson	5.67
8	Honus Wagner	5.63
9	Tommy Corcoran	5.62
10	Bones Ely	5.59
11	Dick Bartell	5.56
12	Monte Cross	5.52
13	Joe Tinker	5.51
14	Art Fletcher	5.50
15	Mickey Doolan	5.46
16	Donie Bush	5.45
17	George McBride	5.45
18	Ivy Olson	5.41
19	Doc Lavan	5.40
20	Germany Smith	5.39
21	Joe Sewell	5.37
22	Eddie Miller	5.36
23	Glenn Wright	5.36
24	Freddy Parent	5.34
25	Billy Jurges	5.25
26	Luke Appling	5.24
27	Arky Vaughan	5.24
28	Jack Glasscock	5.19
29	Roger Peckinpaugh	5.17
30	Joe Cronin	5.16
31	Buddy Kerr	5.15
32	Al Bridwell	5.14
33	Lou Boudreau	5.13
34	Everett Scott	5.12
35	Eddie Joost	5.09
36	Johnny Logan	5.08
37	Lyn Lary	5.06
38	Billy Rogell	5.06
39	Marty Marion	5.05
40	Rick Burleson	5.05
41	Wally Gerber	5.04
42	Ozzie Smith	5.03
43	Robin Yount	4.99
44	Leo Durocher	4.99
45	Frankie Crosetti	4.98
46	Dick Groat	4.96
47	Pee Wee Reese	4.93
48	Tim Foli	4.92
49	Ernie Banks	4.91
50	Vern Stephens	4.91
51	Ed McKean	4.91
52	Roy McMillan	4.88
53	Al Dark	4.87
54	Luis Aparicio	4.87
55	Ron Hansen	4.82
56	Garry Templeton	4.80
57	Don Kessinger	4.79
58	Phil Rizzuto	4.79
59	Maury Wills	4.73
60	Dave Concepcion	4.71
61	Freddie Patek	4.71
62	Jim Fregosi	4.70
63	Ed Brinkman	4.67
64	Bucky Dent	4.67
65	Chris Speier	4.65
66	Roy Smalley	4.64
67	Chico Carrasquel	4.63
68	Bill Russell	4.63
69	Leo Cardenas	4.62
70	Cal Ripken Jr.	4.62
71	Bert Campaneris	4.61
72	Jay Bell	4.61
73	Tony Fernandez	4.59
74	Roger Metzger	4.59
75	Larry Bowa	4.58
76	Zoilo Versalles	4.56
77	Bud Harrelson	4.54
78	Barry Larkin	4.53
79	Mark Belanger	4.53
80	Alfredo Griffin	4.51
81	Ivan DeJesus	4.51
82	Shawon Dunston	4.49
83	Omar Vizquel	4.49
84	Alan Trammell	4.47
85	Ozzie Guillen	4.46
86	Dick Schofield	4.46
87	Bobby Wine	4.43
88	Rafael Ramirez	4.43
89	Joe DeMaestri	4.41
90	Spike Owen	4.30
91	Walt Weiss	4.28
92	Dal Maxvill	4.28
93	Frank Taveras	4.26
94	Eddie Bressoud	4.25
95	Greg Gagne	4.24
96	Craig Reynolds	4.21
97	Dickie Thon	4.20
98	Jose Uribe	4.19

Assists/162 Games

(minimum 1,000 games)

1	Germany Smith	598.77
2	Art Fletcher	574.38
3	Bill Dahlen	569.89
4	Dave Bancroft	567.48
5	Bones Ely	566.61
6	Travis Jackson	566.27
7	George Davis	565.23
8	Jack Glasscock	560.23
9	Bobby Wallace	559.19
10	Tommy Corcoran	555.32
11	Herman Long	554.09
12	Rabbit Maranville	553.57
13	Joe Tinker	543.53
14	Freddy Parent	541.24
15	Ozzie Smith	540.32
16	Glenn Wright	535.32
17	Donie Bush	532.62
18	Dick Bartell	532.07
19	Mickey Doolan	527.37
20	Luke Appling	527.19
21	George McBride	525.45
22	Rick Burleson	525.14
23	Robin Yount	525.10
24	Joe Sewell	523.97
25	Eddie Miller	522.70
26	Doc Lavan	522.43
27	Billy Jurges	521.66
28	Arky Vaughan	521.45
29	Honus Wagner	518.90
30	Roger Peckinpaugh	517.71
31	Johnny Logan	516.17
32	Don Kessinger	514.75
33	Bill Russell	514.58
34	Buddy Kerr	514.56
35	Joe Cronin	511.05
36	Tim Foli	510.66
37	Billy Rogell	509.74
38	Monte Cross	509.60
39	Ivy Olson	509.21
40	Bucky Dent	508.17
41	Marty Marion	505.69
42	Vern Stephens	505.49
43	Luis Aparicio	503.14
44	Ed McKean	502.68
45	Ivan DeJesus	501.79
46	Dick Groat	501.54
47	Lou Boudreau	501.05
48	Maury Wills	500.48
49	Larry Bowa	499.93
50	Garry Templeton	498.29
51	Everett Scott	498.23
52	Ron Hansen	496.49
53	Jay Bell	496.35
54	Al Bridwell	496.22
55	Roy Smalley	496.15
56	Ernie Banks	495.50
57	Roy McMillan	494.55
58	Ed Brinkman	493.31
59	Chris Speier	492.91
60	Cal Ripken Jr.	491.00
61	Dave Concepcion	490.46
62	Freddie Patek	488.24
63	Roger Metzger	488.21
64	Wally Gerber	483.87
65	Jim Fregosi	483.80
66	Mark Belanger	482.66
67	Lyn Lary	482.30
68	Al Dark	480.92
69	Eddie Joost	480.50
70	Frankie Crosetti	479.48
71	Barry Larkin	478.22
72	Omar Vizquel	476.50
73	Leo Durocher	475.69
74	Pee Wee Reese	473.85
75	Chico Carrasquel	472.42
76	Bert Campaneris	468.46
77	Alan Trammell	467.44
78	Zoilo Versalles	466.79
79	Ozzie Smith	466.27
80	Leo Cardenas	466.13
81	Dick Schofield	465.45
82	Rafael Ramirez	464.96
83	Tony Fernandez	464.58
84	Bud Harrelson	459.96
85	Phil Rizzuto	458.95
86	Dal Maxvill	457.01
87	Craig Reynolds	455.17
88	Walt Weiss	454.14
89	Dickie Thon	453.26
90	Greg Gagne	452.50
91	Bobby Wine	451.54
92	Alfredo Griffin	451.44
93	Shawon Dunston	451.25
94	Frank Taveras	451.07
95	Jose Uribe	450.25
96	Spike Owen	450.01
97	Joe DeMaestri	449.00
98	Eddie Bressoud	425.69

Career Fielding Leaders—Outfielders

Games

1	Ty Cobb	2,934
2	Willie Mays	2,843
3	Hank Aaron	2,760
4	Tris Speaker	2,699
5	Lou Brock	2,507
6	Al Kaline	2,488
7	Dave Winfield	2,469
8	Max Carey	2,421
9	Vada Pinson	2,403
10	Roberto Clemente	2,370
11	Zack Wheat	2,337
12	Andre Dawson	2,323
	Willie Davis	2,323
14	Mel Ott	2,313
15	Sam Crawford	2,297
16	Paul Waner	2,288
17	Harry Hooper	2,284
18	Sam Rice	2,270
19	Rickey Henderson	2,266
20	Babe Ruth	2,240
21	Fred Clarke	2,189
22	Goose Goslin	2,187
23	Brett Butler	2,159
24	Jose Cruz	2,155
25	Ted Williams	2,151
26	Dwight Evans	2,146
27	Doc Cramer	2,142
	Al Simmons	2,142
29	Frank Robinson	2,132
30	Richie Ashburn	2,104
31	Reggie Jackson	2,102
32	Billy Williams	2,088
33	Carl Yastrzemski	2,076
34	Jimmy Sheckard	2,071
35	Enos Slaughter	2,064
36	Tony Gwynn	2,063
37	Jesse Burkett	2,054
38	Willie Keeler	2,041
39	Willie Wilson	2,031
40	Mickey Mantle	2,019
41	Tim Raines	2,002
42	Jimmy Ryan	1,943
43	Amos Otis	1,928
44	Chet Lemon	1,925
45	Duke Snider	1,918
46	Clyde Milan	1,902
47	Stan Musial	1,890
48	George Foster	1,880
49	Paul Blair	1,878
50	Gary Matthews	1,876
51	Dave Parker	1,867
52	Sherry Magee	1,861
53	Dale Murphy	1,853
54	Joe Medwick	1,852
55	Edd Roush	1,848
56	Heinie Manush	1,845
57	George Burns	1,844
58	Dusty Baker	1,842
59	Del Ennis	1,840
60	George Van Haltren	1,827
61	Fred Lynn	1,825
62	Lloyd Waner	1,818
	Cy Williams	1,818
64	George Hendrick	1,813
	Patsy Donovan	1,813
66	Jimmy Wynn	1,810
67	Kiki Cuyler	1,807
68	Willie McGee	1,802
69	Dummy Hoy	1,795
70	Wally Moses	1,792
71	Tom Brown	1,783
72	Jose Cardenal	1,778
73	Johnny Callison	1,777
74	Rocky Colavito	1,774
75	Fielder Jones	1,770
76	Bob Johnson	1,769
77	Bobby Veach	1,741
78	Carl Furillo	1,739
79	Bobby Bonds	1,736
	Dixie Walker	1,736
	Wildfire Schulte	1,736
82	Joe DiMaggio	1,721
83	Cesar Cedeno	1,718
84	Barry Bonds	1,709
85	Ken Griffey Sr.	1,703
86	Curt Flood	1,697
87	Kirby Puckett	1,696
88	Rick Monday	1,688
89	Garry Maddox	1,686
90	Claudell Washington	1,685
91	Hugh Duffy	1,681
92	Tom Brunansky	1,679
93	Rusty Staub	1,675
94	Reggie Smith	1,668
95	Minnie Minoso	1,665
96	Joe Carter	1,663
97	Bobby Murcer	1,644
98	Gus Bell	1,642
	Charlie Jamieson	1,642
100	Dode Paskert	1,633

Putouts

1	Willie Mays	7,095
2	Tris Speaker	6,792
3	Max Carey	6,363
4	Ty Cobb	6,360
5	Richie Ashburn	6,089
6	Hank Aaron	5,539
7	Rickey Henderson	5,496
8	Willie Davis	5,449
9	Doc Cramer	5,412
10	Brett Butler	5,296
11	Andre Dawson	5,158
12	Vada Pinson	5,097
13	Willie Wilson	5,060
14	Al Kaline	5,035
15	Zack Wheat	4,996
16	Chet Lemon	4,993
17	Al Simmons	4,988
18	Dave Winfield	4,975
19	Paul Waner	4,969
20	Amos Otis	4,936
21	Lloyd Waner	4,860
22	Goose Goslin	4,792
23	Fred Clarke	4,790
24	Sam Rice	4,772
25	Roberto Clemente	4,660
26	Fred Lynn	4,556
27	Edd Roush	4,537
28	Joe DiMaggio	4,516
29	Mel Ott	4,515
30	Garry Maddox	4,447
31	Babe Ruth	4,444
32	Mickey Mantle	4,438
33	Lou Brock	4,394
34	Kirby Puckett	4,392
35	Jose Cruz	4,391
36	Dwight Evans	4,371
37	Paul Blair	4,343
38	Sammy West	4,300
39	Jimmy Sheckard	4,204
40	Cy Williams	4,180
41	Tony Gwynn	4,175
42	Ted Williams	4,159
43	Cesar Cedeno	4,131
44	Duke Snider	4,099
45	Clyde Milan	4,095
46	Reggie Jackson	4,062
47	Willie McGee	4,057
48	Dale Murphy	4,053
49	Tim Raines	4,039
50	Kiki Cuyler	4,034
51	Curt Flood	4,021
52	Bob Johnson	4,003
53	Wally Moses	4,000
54	Harry Hooper	3,981
55	Frank Robinson	3,978
56	Earl Averill	3,973
57	Joe Medwick	3,967
58	Jesse Burkett	3,961
59	Dummy Hoy	3,958
60	Carl Yastrzemski	3,941
61	Enos Slaughter	3,925
62	George Burns	3,918
63	Jimmy Wynn	3,912
64	Bill Bruton	3,905
65	Dom DiMaggio	3,859
66	Jimmy Piersall	3,851
67	Heinie Manush	3,841
68	Devon White	3,837
69	Rick Manning	3,831
70	George Foster	3,809
71	Sherry Magee	3,800
72	Dave Parker	3,791
73	Bill Virdon	3,777
74	Lloyd Moseby	3,765
75	Bobby Veach	3,754
76	George Hendrick	3,751
77	Dode Paskert	3,735
78	Stan Musial	3,730
79	Jimmy Ryan	3,698
80	Reggie Smith	3,696
81	Dusty Baker	3,663
82	Gee Walker	3,661
83	Bobby Bonds	3,659
84	Sam Crawford	3,626
85	Tom Brown	3,623
86	Del Ennis	3,621
87	Larry Doby	3,616
88	Barry Bonds	3,599
89	Dwayne Murphy	3,579
	Sam Chapman	3,579
91	Fielder Jones	3,571
92	Jose Cardenal	3,565
93	Bobby Thomson	3,563
94	Billy Williams	3,562
95	Joe Carter	3,558
96	Mike Griffin	3,535
97	Rick Monday	3,534
98	Baby Doll Jacobson	3,517
99	Tom Brunansky	3,506
100	Gus Bell	3,500

Assists

1	Tris Speaker	449
2	Ty Cobb	391
3	Jimmy Ryan	375
4	George Van Haltren	348
	Tom Brown	348
6	Harry Hooper	344
7	Max Carey	339
8	Jimmy Sheckard	307
9	Clyde Milan	294
10	Orator Shaffer	289
11	King Kelly	285
12	Sam Thompson	283
13	Sam Rice	278
14	Dummy Hoy	273
15	Jesse Burkett	270
16	Sam Crawford	268
	Tommy McCarthy	268
18	Roberto Clemente	266
19	Patsy Donovan	264
20	Willie Keeler	258
21	Mel Ott	257
22	Fred Clarke	254
23	Paul Waner	247
24	Ed Delahanty	243
	Mike Griffin	243
	George Gore	243
27	Hugh Duffy	240
28	Zack Wheat	232
29	Chicken Wolf	229
30	Cy Williams	226
	Hugh Nicol	226
32	Pop Corkhill	224
33	Dode Paskert	223
	Fielder Jones	223
35	Goose Goslin	221
	Tilly Walker	221
37	Edd Roush	219
38	Paul Radford	217
	Paul Hines	217
40	Jim O'Rourke	216
41	Joe Kelley	212
42	Bobby Veach	211
43	Duffy Lewis	210
44	Bob Johnson	208
	Steve Brodie	208
	Ned Hanlon	208
47	Curt Welch	206
48	Babe Ruth	204
49	George Wood	203
50	Jack Tobin	202
51	Hank Aaron	201
	John Titus	201
53	George Burns	197
	Wildfire Schulte	197
	Elmer Flick	197
	Kip Selbach	197
57	Charlie Jamieson	196
58	Carl Yastrzemski	195
	Willie Mays	195
	Chuck Klein	195
61	Ross Youngs	192
62	Kiki Cuyler	191
63	Tommy Griffith	189
64	Roy Thomas	188
	Cy Seymour	188
66	Harry Heilmann	183
	Joe Jackson	183
68	Billy Hamilton	182
69	Max Flack	181
	Chief Wilson	181
71	Mike Mitchell	180
72	Richie Ashburn	178
73	Shano Collins	177
74	Nemo Leibold	176
	Gavy Cravath	176
	Red Murray	176
	Sherry Magee	176
	Joe Hornung	176
79	Johnny Callison	175
80	Emmett Seery	174
81	Les Mann	173
	Burt Shotton	173
83	Vada Pinson	172
	Doc Cramer	172
	Dick Johnston	172
86	Jim Fogarty	171
87	Al Kaline	170
88	Al Simmons	169
89	Jimmy Slagle	168
90	Ken Williams	167
	Ginger Beaumont	167
92	Dave Winfield	166
93	Rusty Staub	165
	Harry Stovey	165
95	Pete Hotaling	163
96	Jesse Barfield	162
	Johnny Bates	162
98	Ira Flagstead	161
	Charley Jones	161
100	3 tied with	159

Errors

1	Tom Brown	491
2	Dummy Hoy	394
3	Jesse Burkett	383
4	George Gore	368
5	Jimmy Ryan	365
6	George Van Haltren	358
7	Ned Hanlon	350
8	Paul Hines	332
9	Billy Hamilton	288
10	Abner Dalrymple	285
11	George Wood	276
12	Pete Browning	269
13	Ty Cobb	268
	Jim O'Rourke	268
15	Tommy McCarthy	263
16	King Kelly	259
17	Fred Clarke	256
18	Charley Jones	248
19	Pete Hotaling	246
20	Orator Shaffer	244
21	Blondie Purcell	241
22	Max Carey	235
23	Harry Stovey	229
24	Walt Wilmot	227
25	Tris Speaker	222
26	Hugh Duffy	220
27	Clyde Milan	216
28	Kip Selbach	214
29	Goose Goslin	209
30	Emmett Seery	203
31	Patsy Donovan	201
32	Elmer Smith	200
33	Jimmy Sheckard	197
34	Lou Brock	196
35	Dick Johnston	193
	Cliff Carroll	193
37	Mike Tiernan	187
	Ed Swartwood	187
39	Curt Welch	185
40	Sam Rice	184
	Burt Shotton	184
42	Zack Wheat	183
43	Tom York	181
44	Paul Radford	179
45	Joe Hornung	178
46	Cy Seymour	177
47	Mike Griffin	173
	Jack Manning	173
49	Sam Thompson	171
50	Tip O'Neill	169
51	Chicken Wolf	168
52	Tilly Walker	167
53	Ed Delahanty	166
54	John Cassidy	163
55	Chief Roseman	162
56	Jim McTamany	161
57	Roy Johnson	157
	Joe Sommer	157
59	Babe Ruth	155
	Mike Dorgan	155
61	Gee Walker	154
	Jimmy McAleer	154
63	Eddie Burke	153
64	Harry Hooper	151
65	Bobby Veach	150
	Jimmy Slagle	150
67	Bill Crowley	148
68	Hugh Nicol	146
69	Elmer Flick	145
	Duff Cooley	145
	Ed Daily	145
	Mike Mansell	145
73	Fielder Jones	144
	Joe Kelley	144
75	Sam Crawford	143
	Ducky Holmes	143
77	Reggie Jackson	142
	Dave Parker	142
	Steve Brodie	142
	Pete Gillespie	142
81	Willie Mays	141
	Bob Johnson	141
	Dick Harley	141
84	Roberto Clemente	140
85	Ginger Beaumont	139
86	Willie Keeler	138
87	Ken Williams	137
	Edd Roush	137
	George Browne	137
	Tommy Dowd	137
	John Coleman	137
92	Billy Sunday	136
93	Mike Donlin	135
94	Chuck Klein	134
	Paul Waner	134
	Ed Andrews	134
	Pop Corkhill	134
98	Buttercup Dickerson	133
99	Patsy Dougherty	132
100	Jake Stenzel	131

Double Plays		
1	Tris Speaker	133
2	Ty Cobb	107
3	Max Carey	86
4	Tom Brown	85
5	Harry Hooper	81
	Jimmy Sheckard	81
7	Mike Griffin	75
8	Dummy Hoy	72
9	Jimmy Ryan	71
10	Fielder Jones	70
11	Patsy Donovan	69
12	Sam Rice	67
13	George Van Haltren	64
14	Jesse Burkett	62
15	Sam Thompson	61
16	Willie Mays	60
	Mel Ott	60
	Tommy McCarthy	60
19	Sam Crawford	59
	Willie Keeler	59
21	Clyde Milan	58
22	Jimmy Slagle	57
23	Billy Hamilton	55
24	Zack Wheat	54
25	Paul Waner	53
	Jack Tobin	53
27	Ginger Beaumont	52
	Cy Seymour	52
	Steve Brodie	52
30	Burt Shotton	51
	Paul Hines	51
32	Chief Wilson	50
	Elmer Flick	50
34	Dode Paskert	49
	Curt Welch	49
36	Jesse Barfield	48
	Curt Walker	48
	Babe Ruth	48
	Kip Selbach	48
40	Goose Goslin	47
	Pop Corkhill	47
	Ned Hanlon	47
	George Gore	47
44	Ross Youngs	46
	Tilly Walker	46
	Roy Thomas	46
	Hugh Duffy	46
	George Wood	46
49	Danny Green	45
	Ed Delahanty	45
51	Kiki Cuyler	44
	Joe Kelley	44
	Paul Radford	44
54	Richie Ashburn	43
	George Burns	43
56	Dwight Evans	42
	Roberto Clemente	42
	Sammy West	42
	Cliff Heathcote	42
	Harry Heilmann	42
	Bobby Veach	42
	Shano Collins	42
	Wildfire Schulte	42
	John Titus	42
	Fred Clarke	42
	Chicken Wolf	42
67	Hank Aaron	41
	Happy Felsch	41
	Edd Roush	41
70	Bobby Bonds	40
	Jimmy Wynn	40
	Ken Williams	40
	Cy Williams	40
	Duffy Lewis	40
	Mike Mitchell	40
76	Chuck Klein	39
	Ira Flagstead	39
	Charlie Jamieson	39
	Sherry Magee	39
	Bill Lange	39
	Jim McTamany	39
82	Bibb Falk	38
	Joe Birmingham	38
	Jimmy Barrett	38
	Chick Stahl	38
	Jim Fogarty	38
	Pete Hotaling	38
88	Kirby Puckett	37
	Tommy Holmes	37
	Doc Cramer	37
	Al Simmons	37
	Jack Smith	37
	Nemo Leibold	37
	Johnny Bates	37
	Tommy Leach	37
	Cliff Carroll	37
97	8 tied with	36

Fielding Percentage		
	(minimum 1,000 games)	
1	Terry Puhl	.993
2	Brett Butler	.992
3	Pete Rose	.991
4	Amos Otis	.991
5	Joe Rudi	.991
6	Mickey Stanley	.991
7	Robin Yount	.990
8	Jimmy Piersall	.990
9	Paul O'Neill	.990
10	Otis Nixon	.990
11	Ken Berry	.989
12	Jim Landis	.989
13	Brian McRae	.989
14	Tommy Holmes	.989
15	Kirby Puckett	.989
16	Gene Woodling	.989
17	Stan Javier	.988
18	Cesar Geronimo	.988
19	Fred Lynn	.988
20	Mike Devereaux	.988
21	Jim Eisenreich	.988
22	Paul Blair	.988
23	Brady Anderson	.988
24	Tim Raines	.988
25	Andy Van Slyke	.988
26	Roy White	.988
27	Jim Busby	.988
28	Marquis Grissom	.987
29	Dwayne Murphy	.987
30	Lenny Dykstra	.987
31	Dwight Evans	.987
32	Willie Wilson	.987
33	Curt Flood	.987
34	Johnny Groth	.987
35	Kevin McReynolds	.987
36	Tony Gonzalez	.987
37	Ruppert Jones	.986
38	Jay Buhner	.986
39	Tony Gwynn	.986
40	Tommy Harper	.986
41	Ken Griffey Jr.	.986
42	Billy Hatcher	.986
43	Al Kaline	.986
44	Roberto Kelly	.986
45	Vic Davalillo	.986
46	Al Bumbry	.986
47	Gary Pettis	.986
48	Dave Collins	.986
49	Rick Miller	.986
50	George Hendrick	.985
51	Dusty Baker	.985
52	Gus Bell	.985
53	Rick Manning	.985
54	Terry Moore	.985
55	Cesar Cedeno	.985
56	Dave Martinez	.985
57	Devon White	.985
58	Steve Finley	.985
59	Eric Davis	.985
60	Al Cowens	.985
61	Duke Snider	.985
62	George Foster	.984
63	Barry Bonds	.984
64	Chet Lemon	.984
65	Dave Henderson	.984
66	Del Unser	.984
67	Lloyd Moseby	.984
68	Barney McCosky	.984
69	Johnny Callison	.984
70	Andy Pafko	.984
71	Gary Ward	.984
72	Mule Haas	.984
73	Dan Gladden	.984
74	Frank Robinson	.984
75	Tom Brunansky	.984
76	Gorman Thomas	.984
77	Stan Musial	.984
78	Milt Thompson	.984
79	Larry Doby	.983
80	Dale Murphy	.983
81	Sammy West	.983
82	Bill Tuttle	.983
83	Garry Maddox	.983
84	Hoot Evers	.983
85	Lance Johnson	.983
86	Lloyd Waner	.983
87	Ellis Burks	.983
88	Andre Dawson	.983
89	Lee Lacy	.983
90	Richie Ashburn	.983
91	Jerry Morales	.983
92	Von Hayes	.983
93	Kevin Bass	.982
94	Roger Maris	.982
95	Joe Orsulak	.982
96	Mickey Mantle	.982
97	Omar Moreno	.982
98	Al Simmons	.982
99	Steve Kemp	.982
100	Greg Gross	.982

Range		
	(minimum 1,000 games)	
1	Taylor Douthit	3.07
2	Richie Ashburn	2.98
3	Dom DiMaggio	2.92
4	Mike Kreevich	2.89
5	Dwayne Murphy	2.88
6	Sammy West	2.83
7	Sam Chapman	2.82
8	Fred Schulte	2.77
9	Max Carey	2.77
10	Lloyd Waner	2.76
11	Vince DiMaggio	2.74
12	Joe DiMaggio	2.71
13	Terry Moore	2.71
14	Bill North	2.70
15	Devon White	2.70
16	Garry Maddox	2.69
17	Tris Speaker	2.68
18	Kirby Puckett	2.67
19	Robin Yount	2.67
20	Gary Pettis	2.67
21	Chet Lemon	2.65
22	Omar Moreno	2.64
23	Baby Doll Jacobson	2.63
24	Wally Berger	2.63
25	Amos Otis	2.63
26	Jim Busby	2.62
27	Lance Johnson	2.61
28	Doc Cramer	2.61
29	Ruppert Jones	2.59
30	Mickey Rivers	2.59
31	Mickey Rivers	2.59
32	Rick Manning	2.59
33	Hi Myers	2.58
34	Jimmy McAleer	2.58
35	Edd Roush	2.57
36	Larry Doby	2.57
37	Earl Averill	2.57
38	Bill Bruton	2.57
39	Willie Mays	2.56
40	Fred Lynn	2.56
41	Mike Griffin	2.56
42	Ira Flagstead	2.55
43	Gorman Thomas	2.55
44	Earle Combs	2.54
45	Ethan Allen	2.54
46	Willie Wilson	2.53
47	Bill Virdon	2.51
48	Lloyd Moseby	2.51
49	Ron LeFlore	2.51
50	Brett Butler	2.51
51	Ken Griffey Jr.	2.51
52	Brian McRae	2.50
53	Mule Haas	2.50
54	Marquis Grissom	2.49
55	Rickey Henderson	2.48
56	Dave Henderson	2.47
57	Tommy Leach	2.47
58	Mookie Wilson	2.47
59	Cesar Cedeno	2.46
60	Al Bumbry	2.45
61	Barney McCosky	2.45
62	Jimmy Piersall	2.44
63	Bobby Thomson	2.44
64	George Case	2.44
65	Curt Flood	2.44
66	Ben Chapman	2.43
67	Tony Armas	2.43
68	Roy Thomas	2.43
69	Dode Paskert	2.42
70	Cy Williams	2.42
71	Al Simmons	2.41
72	Willie Davis	2.41
73	Ken Williams	2.41
74	Cliff Heathcote	2.40
75	Curt Welch	2.39
76	Tommy Holmes	2.39
77	Bob Johnson	2.38
78	Ed Delahanty	2.38
79	Paul Blair	2.37
80	Carson Bigbee	2.37
81	Hoot Evers	2.37
82	Jim Landis	2.37
83	Carl Reynolds	2.37
84	Mike Devereaux	2.36
85	Steve Finley	2.36
86	Dummy Hoy	2.36
87	Steve Brodie	2.36
88	Bill Tuttle	2.35
89	Roberto Kelly	2.34
90	Gee Walker	2.34
91	Kiki Cuyler	2.34
92	Burt Shotton	2.34
93	Al Oliver	2.33
94	Dave Philley	2.32
95	Willie McGee	2.32
96	Tilly Walker	2.32
97	Wally Moses	2.31
98	Hack Wilson	2.31
99	Clyde Milan	2.31
100	Fred Clarke	2.30

Assists/162 Games		
	(minimum 1,000 games)	
1	Tommy McCarthy	36.51
2	Chicken Wolf	35.57
3	Pop Corkhill	34.86
4	Sam Thompson	32.63
5	Tom Brown	31.62
6	Jimmy Ryan	31.27
7	Curt Welch	31.04
8	George Van Haltren	30.86
9	George Gore	30.35
10	Ed Delahanty	29.29
11	Paul Hines	28.37
12	Joe Hornung	27.05
13	Tris Speaker	26.95
14	Ned Hanlon	26.94
15	George Wood	26.69
16	Mike Griffin	26.63
17	Tilly Walker	26.56
18	Mike Mitchell	26.37
19	Gavy Cravath	26.16
20	Ross Youngs	25.94
21	Nemo Leibold	25.48
22	Jim O'Rourke	25.41
23	Ira Flagstead	25.20
24	Clyde Milan	25.04
25	Dummy Hoy	24.64
26	Harry Hooper	24.40
27	Red Murray	24.35
28	Johnny Bates	24.30
29	Jimmy McAleer	24.10
30	Jimmy Sheckard	24.01
31	John Titus	24.01
32	Duffy Lewis	23.76
33	Steve Brodie	23.73
34	Patsy Donovan	23.59
35	Joe Kelley	23.44
36	Hugh Duffy	23.13
37	Chief Wilson	23.11
38	Joe Jackson	23.00
39	Tommy Griffith	22.97
40	Cy Seymour	22.85
41	Max Carey	22.68
42	Carson Bigbee	22.31
43	Dode Paskert	22.12
44	Cliff Heathcote	21.96
45	Jack Tobin	21.96
46	Max Flack	21.95
47	Elmer Flick	21.93
48	Burt Shotton	21.90
49	Shano Collins	21.59
50	Ty Cobb	21.59
51	Elmer Smith	21.33
52	Jesse Burkett	21.30
53	Roy Thomas	21.24
54	Jimmy Slagle	21.10
55	Ken Williams	20.91
56	Hi Myers	20.70
57	Les Mann	20.49
58	Willie Keeler	20.48
59	Fielder Jones	20.41
60	Matty McIntyre	20.35
61	Kip Selbach	20.30
62	Cy Williams	20.14
63	Casey Stengel	20.13
64	Sam Rice	19.84
65	Jack McCarthy	19.82
66	Tommy Leach	19.82
67	Chick Stahl	19.77
68	Chuck Klein	19.76
69	Bobby Veach	19.63
70	Bob Meusel	19.50
71	Roy Johnson	19.45
72	Amos Strunk	19.41
73	George Browne	19.40
74	Charlie Jamieson	19.34
75	Ginger Beaumont	19.20
76	Edd Roush	19.20
77	Davy Jones	19.18
78	Charlie Hemphill	19.16
79	Jack Graney	19.08
80	Bob Johnson	19.05
81	Jesse Barfield	18.92
82	Sam Crawford	18.90
83	Fred Clarke	18.80
84	Jack Smith	18.74
85	Vince DiMaggio	18.73
86	Bob Bescher	18.68
87	Harry Heilmann	18.63
88	Billy Hamilton	18.61
89	Wildfire Schulte	18.38
90	Roberto Clemente	18.18
91	Mel Ott	18.00
92	Bibb Falk	17.94
93	John Anderson	17.93
94	Curt Walker	17.88
95	Willard Marshall	17.69
96	Billy Southworth	17.58
97	Paul Waner	17.49
98	Mike Tiernan	17.47
99	Dom DiMaggio	17.34
100	George Burns	17.31

Single Season Fielding Leaders—Pitchers

#	Games	Year		#	Putouts	Year		#	Assists	Year		#	Errors	Year	
1	Mike Marshall	1974	106	1	Dave Foutz	1886	57	1	Ed Walsh	1907	227	1	Jack Lynch	1884	37
2	Kent Tekulve	1979	94	2	Tony Mullane	1882	54	2	Will White	1882	223	2	Adonis Terry	1884	34
3	Mike Marshall	1973	92	3	George Bradley	1876	50	3	Ed Walsh	1908	190		Bill Sweeney	1884	34
4	Kent Tekulve	1978	91		Guy Hecker	1884	50	4	Harry Howell	1905	178	4	Bob Barr	1884	33
5	Wayne Granger	1969	90	5	Mike Boddicker	1984	49	5	Tony Mullane	1882	177	5	Al Atkinson	1884	31
	Mike Marshall	1979	90	6	Larry Corcoran	1884	47	6	John Clarkson	1885	174		Billy Taylor	1884	31
	Kent Tekulve	1987	90	7	Al Spalding	1876	45	7	John Clarkson	1889	172		Toad Ramsey	1887	31
8	Mark Eichhorn	1987	89		Ted Breitenstein	1895	45	8	Matt Kilroy	1887	167	8	Sam Kimber	1884	30
	Julian Tavarez	1997	89	9	Jim Devlin	1876	44	9	Jack Chesbro	1904	166		Tim Keefe	1884	30
10	Wilbur Wood	1968	88		Dave Foutz	1887	44	10	George Mullin	1904	163	10	Bobby Mathews	1876	28
	Mike Myers	1997	88		Bill Hutchison	1890	44	11	Ed Walsh	1911	159		Jim Whitney	1881	28
12	Rob Murphy	1987	87	12	Monte Ward	1880	43	12	Bill Hutchison	1892	156		Dupee Shaw	1884	28
13	Kent Tekulve	1982	85		Jim McCormick	1882	43	13	Pud Galvin	1884	154		Matt Kilroy	1886	28
	Frank Williams	1987	85		Nick Altrock	1904	43		Frank Smith	1909	154	14	Jersey Bakely	1884	27
	Mitch Williams	1987	85	15	Tony Mullane	1884	42		Ed Walsh	1910	154		John Clarkson	1889	27
16	Ted Abernathy	1965	84		Nat Hudson	1888	42	16	Mark Baldwin	1890	146	16	Pud Galvin	1879	26
	Enrique Romo	1979	84		Kid Gleason	1892	42	17	Guy Hecker	1884	145	17	Bobby Mathews	1884	25
	Dick Tidrow	1980	84		Ted Breitenstein	1893	42		Park Swartzel	1889	145		Bert Cunningham	1888	25
	Dan Quisenberry	1985	84		Ted Breitenstein	1894	42		Cy Young	1896	145		Chick Fraser	1896	25
	Stan Belinda	1997	84		Oil Can Boyd	1985	42	20	3 tied with		144	20	8 tied with		24

Double Plays

#	Name	Year	
1	Bob Lemon	1953	15
2	Eddie Rommel	1924	12
	Curt Davis	1934	12
	Randy Jones	1976	12
5	Art Nehf	1920	11
	Burleigh Grimes	1925	11
	Gene Bearden	1948	11
8	Addie Joss	1905	10
	Nick Altrock	1905	10
	Carl Mays	1926	10
	Willis Hudlin	1931	10
	Freddie Fitzsimmons	1932	10
	Freddie Fitzsimmons	1934	10
	Bucky Walters	1939	10
	Boo Ferriss	1945	10
	Bob Hooper	1950	10
	Don Drysdale	1958	10
	Dan Petry	1983	10
19	20 tied with		9

Fielding Percentage
(minimum 25 games)

1	3806 tied with		1.000

Assists/162 Innings
(minimum 25 games)

#	Name	Year	
1	Harry Howell	1905	89.28
2	Johnny Gorsica	1942	88.64
3	Ed Walsh	1907	87.07
4	Ed Willett	1910	81.60
5	Rube Peters	1912	77.52
6	Carl Mays	1916	77.36
	Frank Linzy	1965	77.36
8	Harry Howell	1904	77.31
9	Elmer Stricklett	1905	76.45
10	Jack Quinn	1910	76.30
11	Willie Sudhoff	1904	75.78
12	Will White	1882	75.26
13	Sherry Smith	1920	74.86
14	Bobby Shantz	1964	74.77
15	Fritz Coumbe	1916	74.04
16	Jean Dubuc	1913	73.43
17	Chet Nichols	1961	72.12
18	Hooks Dauss	1915	71.67
19	Barney Pelty	1910	71.53
20	Fritz Coumbe	1918	71.28

Single Season Fielding Leaders—Catchers

#	Games	Year		#	Putouts	Year		#	Assists	Year		#	Errors	Year	
1	Randy Hundley	1968	160	1	Johnny Edwards	1969	1,135	1	Bill Rariden	1915	238	1	Nat Hicks	1876	94
2	Ray Mueller	1944	155	2	Mike Piazza	1996	1,055	2	Bill Rariden	1914	215	2	Emil Gross	1880	86
	Frankie Hayes	1944	155	3	Dan Wilson	1997	1,051	3	Pat Moran	1903	214	3	Ed Whiting	1882	81
	Jim Sundberg	1975	155	4	Mike Piazza	1997	1,045	4	Oscar Stanage	1911	212	4	Kid Baldwin	1887	79
5	Johnny Bench	1968	154	5	Johnny Edwards	1963	1,008		Art Wilson	1914	212	5	Emil Gross	1883	74
	Ted Simmons	1975	154	6	Javy Lopez	1996	992	6	Gabby Street	1909	210	6	Jimmy Peoples	1886	73
	Carlton Fisk	1978	154	7	Darren Daulton	1993	981	7	Frank Snyder	1915	204	7	Rudy Kemmler	1883	71
8	Ted Simmons	1973	153	8	Randy Hundley	1969	978	8	George Gibson	1910	203	8	Pop Snyder	1876	67
	Gary Carter	1982	153	9	Tony Pena	1983	976	9	Bill Bergen	1909	202	9	Deacon White	1876	64
10	Jim Hegan	1949	152	10	Bill Freehan	1968	971		Claude Berry	1914	202		George Myers	1884	64
	Randy Hundley	1967	152	11	Gary Carter	1985	956	11	Red Dooin	1909	199		Ed Crane	1884	64
	Gary Carter	1978	152	12	Gary Carter	1982	954	12	Walter Blair	1914	194	12	Lew Brown	1879	63
13	Ray Schalk	1920	151	13	Jason Kendall	1997	952	13	George Gibson	1909	192		George Baker	1884	63
	Frankie Hayes	1945	151	14	Bill Freehan	1967	950	14	Red Dooin	1908	191	14	John Clapp	1880	62
	Randy Hundley	1969	151	15	Johnny Bench	1968	942	15	Oscar Stanage	1914	190		Mike Hines	1883	62
	Johnny Edwards	1969	151	16	Elston Howard	1964	939	16	Johnny Kling	1903	189	16	Silver Flint	1884	61
	Manny Sanguillen	1974	151	17	Mike Lieberthal	1997	934	17	Chief Zimmer	1890	188	17	Bill Holbert	1883	58
	Carlton Fisk	1977	151	18	Tim McCarver	1969	925	18	Boss Schmidt	1908	184		Doc Bushong	1884	58
	Jim Sundberg	1980	151		Mike Scioscia	1987	925	19	Ray Schalk	1914	183	19	4 tied with		57
	Benito Santiago	1991	151		Joe Oliver	1992	925	20	Chief Zimmer	1891	181				

Double Plays

#	Name	Year	
1	Steve O'Neill	1916	36
2	Frankie Hayes	1945	29
3	Ray Schalk	1916	25
	Yogi Berra	1951	25
5	Jack Lapp	1915	23
	Muddy Ruel	1924	23
	Tom Haller	1968	23
8	Steve O'Neill	1914	22
	Bob O'Farrell	1922	22
10	Gabby Hartnett	1927	21
	Wes Westrum	1950	21
12	Johnny Kling	1912	20
	Ray Schalk	1914	20
	Ray Schalk	1923	20
	Jason Kendall	1997	20
16	11 tied with		19

Fielding Percentage
(minimum 100 games)

#	Name	Year	
1	Buddy Rosar	1946	1.000
	Charles Johnson	1997	1.000
3	Tom Pagnozzi	1992	.999
4	Wes Westrum	1950	.999
5	Thurman Munson	1971	.998
6	Mike LaValliere	1991	.998
7	Rick Cerone	1987	.998
8	Sherm Lollar	1961	.998
9	Elston Howard	1964	.998
10	Earl Grace	1932	.998
11	Kirt Manwaring	1993	.998
12	Bill Freehan	1970	.997
13	Yogi Berra	1959	.997
14	Tony Pena	1989	.997
15	Lance Parrish	1991	.997
16	Johnny Bench	1976	.997
17	Glenn Borgmann	1974	.997
18	Dave Valle	1990	.997
19	Rick Dempsey	1983	.997
20	Jim Pagliaroni	1966	.997

Passed Balls

#	Name	Year	
1	Ed Whiting	1882	105
2	Bill Traffley	1885	104
3	Pop Snyder	1881	99
	Mike Hines	1883	99
5	Sleeper Sullivan	1882	97
6	Doc Bushong	1884	95
	Fred Carroll	1886	95
8	Jackie Hayes	1883	93
9	Charlie Reilley	1879	89
10	Wilbert Robinson	1886	87
11	John Kerins	1886	83
12	Ed Whiting	1883	82
	Silver Flint	1884	82
	Wilbert Robinson	1887	82
15	Frank Graves	1886	81
	Kid Baldwin	1887	81
17	Dan Sullivan	1882	80
18	Paul Cook	1889	77
19	Silver Flint	1883	76
	Connie Mack	1887	76

Assists/162 Games
(minimum 100 games)

#	Name	Year	
1	Pat Moran	1903	324.00
2	Bill Bergen	1909	292.18
3	Bill Rariden	1915	271.52
4	Claude Berry	1914	268.23
5	Bill Rariden	1914	267.92
6	Sam Agnew	1913	267.38
7	Jeff Sweeney	1913	260.36
8	Art Wilson	1914	260.18
9	Ivy Wingo	1916	257.38
10	Chief Zimmer	1891	252.78
11	Oscar Stanage	1914	252.30
12	Jeff Sweeney	1912	250.50
13	Wally Schang	1914	249.48
14	Gabby Street	1909	248.32
15	Steve O'Neill	1915	246.52
16	Boss Schmidt	1908	246.35
17	Walter Blair	1914	245.53
18	Chief Zimmer	1890	243.65
19	Oscar Stanage	1911	243.57
20	Sam Agnew	1915	243.00

Single Season Fielding Leaders—First Basemen

Games

1	Norm Siebern	1962	162
	Bill White	1963	162
	Ernie Banks	1965	162
	Steve Garvey	1976	162
	Steve Garvey	1979	162
	Steve Garvey	1980	162
	Pete Rose	1980	162
	Pete Rose	1982	162
	Steve Garvey	1985	162
	Bill Buckner	1985	162
	Jeff Bagwell	1996	162
	Eric Karros	1997	162
13	Wes Parker	1970	161
	Willie Montanez	1976	161
	Steve Garvey	1978	161
	Bill Buckner	1982	161
17	13 tied with		160

Putouts

1	Jiggs Donahue	1907	1,846
2	George Kelly	1920	1,759
3	Phil Todt	1926	1,755
4	Wally Pipp	1926	1,710
5	Jiggs Donahue	1906	1,697
6	Candy LaChance	1904	1,691
7	Tom Jones	1907	1,687
8	Ernie Banks	1965	1,682
9	Wally Pipp	1922	1,667
10	Lou Gehrig	1927	1,662
11	Stuffy McInnis	1917	1,658
12	Jim Bottomley	1927	1,656
13	Ed Konetchy	1911	1,652
	Jake Daubert	1922	1,652
15	Wally Pipp	1920	1,649
16	Jiggs Donahue	1905	1,645
17	George Kelly	1922	1,642
18	Earl Sheely	1921	1,637
19	Walter Holke	1917	1,635
20	2 tied with		1,626

Assists

1	Bill Buckner	1985	184
2	Mark Grace	1990	180
3	Mark Grace	1991	167
4	Sid Bream	1986	166
5	Bill Buckner	1983	161
6	Bill Buckner	1982	159
7	Bill Buckner	1986	157
8	Mickey Vernon	1949	155
9	Fred Tenney	1905	152
	Eddie Murray	1985	152
11	Ferris Fain	1952	150
12	Rudy York	1943	149
	Keith Hernandez	1986	149
	Keith Hernandez	1987	149
15	Keith Hernandez	1983	147
	Rafael Palmeiro	1993	147
	Eric Karros	1993	147
	Jeff King	1997	147
19	3 tied with		146

Errors

1	Joe Quinn	1884	62
2	Cap Anson	1884	58
3	Ecky Stearns	1883	57
	Cap Anson	1885	57
5	John Kerins	1885	56
6	Tim Murnane	1876	55
	Otto Schomberg	1887	55
8	Martin Powell	1883	54
	Ecky Stearns	1884	54
10	Alex McKinnon	1884	53
11	Jim Field	1883	52
	Jim Field	1884	52
13	Oscar Walker	1879	49
	Jumbo Schoeneck	1884	49
	Dave Orr	1884	49
	Ecky Stearns	1889	49
	Dan Brouthers	1890	49
18	Bill Phillips	1884	48
	Cap Anson	1886	48
20	2 tied with		47

Double Plays

1	Ferris Fain	1949	194
2	Ferris Fain	1950	192
3	Donn Clendenon	1966	182
4	Andres Galarraga	1997	176
5	Ron Jackson	1979	175
6	Gil Hodges	1951	171
7	Mickey Vernon	1949	168
8	Ted Kluszewski	1954	166
9	Rudy York	1944	163
10	Donn Clendenon	1965	161
	Rod Carew	1977	161
12	Cecil Cooper	1980	160
13	Jake Jones	1947	159
	Gil Hodges	1950	159
15	Mike Rocco	1944	158
	Mickey Vernon	1953	158
	Eddie Murray	1980	158
18	4 tied with		157

Fielding Percentage

(minimum 100 games)

1	Steve Garvey	1984	1.000
2	Stuffy McInnis	1921	.999
3	Frank McCormick	1946	.999
4	Steve Garvey	1981	.999
5	Jim Spencer	1973	.999
6	Wes Parker	1968	.999
7	Hal Morris	1992	.999
8	Jim Spencer	1976	.998
9	Joe Judge	1930	.998
10	Steve Garvey	1976	.998
11	Vic Power	1957	.998
12	Gil Hodges	1961	.998
13	George Brett	1989	.998
14	Darrell Evans	1986	.998
15	Dave Magadan	1990	.998
16	Don Mattingly	1993	.998
17	Dan Driessen	1982	.998
18	Mark Grace	1992	.998
19	Ed Kranepool	1971	.998
20	John Olerud	1996	.998

Assists/162 Games

(minimum 100 games)

1	Mark Grace	1990	190.59
2	Bill Buckner	1986	184.30
3	Bill Buckner	1985	184.00
4	Jeff Bagwell	1995	183.32
5	Bill Buckner	1983	181.13
6	Jeff Bagwell	1994	178.35
7	Sid Bream	1986	175.76
8	Eric Karros	1994	175.38
9	Cecil Fielder	1994	171.53
10	Tim Harkness	1963	171.17
11	Ferris Fain	1951	169.50
12	Mark Grace	1991	169.09
13	Ferris Fain	1952	168.75
14	Wally Joyner	1993	167.79
15	Eddie Murray	1988	166.72
16	Darrell Evans	1986	166.63
17	Fred Tenney	1905	166.38
18	Keith Hernandez	1983	165.38
19	Bob Robertson	1971	164.57
20	Sid Bream	1988	164.35

Single Season Fielding Leaders—Second Basemen

Games

1	Bill Mazeroski	1967	163
2	Jake Wood	1961	162
	Bill Mazeroski	1964	162
	Pete Rose	1965	162
	Bill Mazeroski	1966	162
	Felix Millan	1969	162
	Bobby Grich	1973	162
	Dave Cash	1974	162
	Dave Cash	1975	162
	Felix Millan	1975	162
	Johnny Ray	1982	162
	Bill Doran	1987	162
	Craig Biggio	1996	162
14	8 tied with		161

Putouts

1	Bid McPhee	1886	529
2	Bobby Grich	1974	484
3	Bucky Harris	1922	479
4	Nellie Fox	1956	478
5	Lou Bierbauer	1889	472
6	Billy Herman	1933	466
7	Bill Wambsganss	1924	463
8	Cub Stricker	1887	461
9	Buddy Myer	1935	460
10	Bill Sweeney	1912	459
11	Billy Herman	1936	457
12	George Cutshaw	1914	455
13	Nellie Fox	1957	453
14	Fred Pfeffer	1889	452
15	Bid McPhee	1892	451
	Nellie Fox	1953	451
17	Nap Lajoie	1908	450
	Emil Verban	1947	450
19	Eddie Collins	1920	449
20	Nellie Fox	1958	444

Assists

1	Frankie Frisch	1927	641
2	Hughie Critz	1926	588
3	Rogers Hornsby	1927	582
4	Ski Melillo	1930	572
5	Ryne Sandberg	1983	571
6	Rabbit Maranville	1924	568
7	Frank Parkinson	1922	562
8	Tony Cuccinello	1936	559
9	Johnny Hodapp	1930	557
10	Lou Bierbauer	1892	555
11	Pep Young	1938	554
12	Burgess Whitehead	1936	552
13	Sparky Adams	1925	551
14	Ryne Sandberg	1984	550
15	Rogers Hornsby	1929	547
16	Hod Ford	1924	543
	Ski Melillo	1931	543
	Bill Mazeroski	1964	543
19	4 tied with		542

Errors

1	Bill McClellan	1887	105
2	Bert Myers	1889	96
3	Yank Robinson	1886	95
4	Tom Evers	1884	94
5	Cub Stricker	1883	93
6	Tom O'Brien	1884	90
7	Pop Smith	1880	89
8	Bob Ferguson	1883	88
	Fred Pfeffer	1884	88
	Reddy Mack	1886	88
	Bill McClellan	1886	88
12	Sam Crane	1883	87
13	Fred Pfeffer	1885	86
14	Reddy Mack	1889	83
15	Cupid Childs	1891	82
16	Cub Stricker	1885	81
	Yank Robinson	1889	81
18	Cub Stricker	1884	80
	Lou Bierbauer	1886	80
	Cub Stricker	1887	80

Double Plays

1	Bill Mazeroski	1966	161
2	Jerry Priddy	1950	150
3	Bill Mazeroski	1961	144
4	Nellie Fox	1957	141
	Dave Cash	1974	141
6	Buddy Myer	1935	138
	Bill Mazeroski	1962	138
	Carlos Baerga	1992	138
9	Jerry Coleman	1950	137
	Jackie Robinson	1951	137
	Red Schoendienst	1954	137
12	Bobby Richardson	1961	136
13	Cass Michaels	1949	135
	Bobby Knoop	1966	135
15	Bobby Doerr	1949	134
16	Jackie Robinson	1950	133
	Harold Reynolds	1991	133
18	Bobby Doerr	1943	132
	Jerry Priddy	1948	132
	Bobby Grich	1974	132

Fielding Percentage

(minimum 100 games)

1	Bret Boone	1997	.997
2	Bobby Grich	1985	.997
3	Jose Oquendo	1990	.996
4	Ken Boswell	1970	.996
5	Ryne Sandberg	1991	.995
6	Jody Reed	1994	.995
7	Rob Wilfong	1980	.995
8	Bobby Grich	1973	.995
9	Frank White	1988	.994
10	Mark Lemke	1994	.994
11	Jose Oquendo	1989	.994
12	Bret Boone	1995	.994
13	Jody Reed	1995	.994
14	Jerry Adair	1964	.994
15	Ryne Sandberg	1986	.994
16	Roberto Alomar	1995	.994
17	Chuck Knoblauch	1994	.994
18	Jose Lind	1993	.994
19	Tim Cullen	1970	.994
20	Manny Trillo	1982	.994

Range Factor

(minimum 100 games)

1	Fred Pfeffer	1884	7.29
2	Pop Smith	1885	7.13
3	Bid McPhee	1886	7.09
4	Fred Pfeffer	1889	6.98
5	Bid McPhee	1884	6.96
6	Joe Gerhardt	1884	6.91
7	Joe Gerhardt	1890	6.82
8	Bid McPhee	1887	6.79
9	Frankie Frisch	1927	6.78
10	Freddie Maguire	1928	6.77
11	Lou Bierbauer	1889	6.75
12	Bid McPhee	1893	6.70
13	Fred Pfeffer	1890	6.68
14	Pop Smith	1884	6.65
15	Bid McPhee	1894	6.63
16	Bid McPhee	1888	6.61
17	Danny Richardson	1891	6.60
18	Fred Pfeffer	1891	6.59
19	Fred Pfeffer	1885	6.57
20	Sam Barkley	1884	6.56

Assists/162 Games

(minimum 100 games)

1	Frankie Frisch	1927	678.71
2	Hughie Critz	1933	658.96
3	Frank Parkinson	1922	654.99
4	Ski Melillo	1930	626.11
5	Glenn Hubbard	1985	623.70
6	Frankie Frisch	1930	622.98
7	Sparky Adams	1925	619.88
8	Freddie Maguire	1928	615.13
9	Hughie Critz	1926	614.55
10	Hughie Critz	1929	612.85
11	Fred Pfeffer	1884	610.39
12	Hughie Critz	1925	609.75
13	Danny Richardson	1891	609.63
14	John Kerr	1929	609.49
15	Frankie Frisch	1924	608.35
16	Rogers Hornsby	1927	608.28
17	Hod Ford	1924	606.66
18	Rabbit Maranville	1924	605.37
19	Charley Bassett	1887	604.44
20	Footsie Blair	1930	604.33

Single Season Fielding Leaders—Third Basemen

Games

1 Ron Santo	1965	164
2 Brooks Robinson	1961	163
Brooks Robinson	1964	163
4 Brooks Robinson	1962	162
Ron Santo	1963	162
Dick Allen	1964	162
Ken Boyer	1964	162
Sal Bando	1968	162
Ron Santo	1968	162
Brooks Robinson	1968	162
Sal Bando	1969	162
Mike Schmidt	1974	162
Ray Knight	1980	162
Cal Ripken Jr.	1997	162
15 12 tied with		161

Putouts

1 Denny Lyons	1887	255
2 Jimmy Williams	1899	251
Jimmy Collins	1900	251
4 Jimmy Collins	1898	243
Willie Kamm	1928	243
6 Willie Kamm	1927	236
7 Home Run Baker	1913	233
8 Bill Coughlin	1901	232
9 Ernie Courtney	1905	229
10 Jimmy Austin	1911	228
11 Pie Traynor	1925	226
12 Billy Shindle	1889	225
Tom Burns	1889	225
14 Charlie Irwin	1898	223
Lave Cross	1899	223
16 Ed Gremminger	1902	222
Hobe Ferris	1908	222
18 Will Smalley	1890	221
Home Run Baker	1914	221
Willie Kamm	1929	221

Assists

1 Graig Nettles	1971	412
2 Graig Nettles	1973	410
Brooks Robinson	1974	410
4 Harlond Clift	1937	405
Brooks Robinson	1967	405
6 Mike Schmidt	1974	404
7 Doug DeCinces	1982	399
8 Clete Boyer	1962	396
Mike Schmidt	1977	396
Buddy Bell	1982	396
11 Ron Santo	1967	393
12 Terry Pendleton	1989	392
13 Ron Santo	1966	391
14 Aurelio Rodriguez	1974	389
Vinny Castilla	1996	389
16 Ossie Vitt	1916	385
17 Graig Nettles	1976	383
Buddy Bell	1983	383
Tim Wallach	1985	383
20 Billy Shindle	1892	382

Errors

1 Bill Joyce	1890	107
2 Jumbo Davis	1888	91
3 Joe Werrick	1887	89
4 Arlie Latham	1886	88
Billy Shindle	1889	88
6 Ned Williamson	1883	87
John Irwin	1884	87
8 Charlie Hickman	1900	86
9 Jerry McCormick	1883	84
Pete Gilbert	1891	84
11 Jack Gleason	1882	83
12 Bill Kuehne	1890	82
13 Jack Gleason	1884	80
Denny Lyons	1889	80
15 Billy Nash	1890	78
Billy Shindle	1892	78
17 Bill Joyce	1895	77
18 Arlie Latham	1891	75
Bill Everitt	1895	75
20 4 tied with		73

Double Plays

1 Graig Nettles	1971	54
2 Harlond Clift	1937	50
3 Johnny Pesky	1949	48
Paul Molitor	1982	48
5 Sammy Hale	1927	46
Clete Boyer	1965	46
Gary Gaetti	1983	46
8 Eddie Yost	1950	45
Frank Malzone	1961	45
Darrell Evans	1974	45
11 Buddy Bell	1973	44
Brooks Robinson	1974	44
13 Hank Thompson	1950	43
Brooks Robinson	1963	43
Vinny Castilla	1996	43
16 Aurelio Rodriguez	1969	42
Don Money	1974	42
18 10 tied with		41

Fielding Percentage
(minimum 100 games)

1 Don Money	1974	.989
2 Hank Majeski	1947	.988
3 Aurelio Rodriguez	1978	.987
4 Willie Kamm	1933	.984
5 Steve Buechele	1991	.983
6 George Kell	1946	.983
7 Heine Groh	1924	.983
8 Carney Lansford	1979	.983
9 Bill Pecota	1991	.983
10 George Kell	1950	.982
11 Carney Lansford	1986	.982
12 Pinky Whitney	1937	.982
13 Wade Boggs	1995	.981
14 Buddy Bell	1980	.981
15 Brooks Robinson	1967	.980
16 Mike Schmidt	1986	.980
17 Carney Lansford	1987	.980
18 Jimmy Dykes	1932	.980
19 Ken Reitz	1977	.980
20 Floyd Baker	1947	.980

Range Factor
(minimum 100 games)

1 Billy Shindle	1892	4.34
2 Jumbo Davis	1888	4.33
3 Bill Bradley	1900	4.29
4 Billy Shindle	1888	4.13
5 Lave Cross	1899	4.12
6 Jimmy Collins	1900	4.11
7 Lave Cross	1894	4.11
8 Patsy Tebeau	1890	4.09
9 Charlie Reilly	1890	4.09
10 Billy Nash	1892	4.06
11 Arlie Latham	1891	4.05
12 Arlie Latham	1884	4.04
13 Jack Crooks	1893	4.03
14 Will Smalley	1890	4.03
15 Billy Shindle	1891	4.01
16 Tommy Leach	1904	3.99
17 Lave Cross	1895	3.99
18 Jerry Denny	1887	3.99
19 Jimmy Williams	1899	3.98
20 Billy Shindle	1889	3.97

Assists/162 Games
(minimum 100 games)

1 Jumbo Davis	1888	478.83
2 Billy Shindle	1892	461.82
3 Arlie Latham	1884	444.76
4 Bill Bradley	1900	444.74
5 Arlie Latham	1891	444.00
6 Buddy Bell	1982	442.43
7 Brooks Robinson	1974	434.12
8 Aaron Ward	1920	430.58
9 Mike Schmidt	1977	430.55
10 Harlond Clift	1937	423.29
11 Graig Nettles	1973	423.06
12 Doug DeCinces	1982	422.47
13 Graig Nettles	1971	422.43
14 Billy Nash	1892	421.20
15 Charlie Reilly	1890	418.60
16 Ron Santo	1966	416.72
17 Brooks Robinson	1967	415.25
18 Buddy Bell	1978	413.74
19 Doc Casey	1901	413.29
20 Ossie Vitt	1916	413.05

Single Season Fielding Leaders—Shortstops

Games

1 Maury Wills	1962	165
2 Jose Pagan	1962	164
Frank Taveras	1979	164
4 Leo Cardenas	1964	163
Tony Fernandez	1986	163
6 16 tied with		162

Putouts

1 Hughie Jennings	1895	425
Donie Bush	1914	425
3 Rabbit Maranville	1914	407
4 Dave Bancroft	1922	405
Eddie Miller	1940	405
6 Monte Cross	1898	404
7 Dave Bancroft	1921	396
8 Mickey Doolan	1906	395
9 Rabbit Maranville	1915	391
Buck Herzog	1915	391
11 Buck Weaver	1913	390
12 Ed Abbaticchio	1905	386
Rabbit Maranville	1916	386
14 Bobby Wallace	1905	385
15 Doc Lavan	1921	382
16 Dick Bartell	1933	381
17 Everett Scott	1921	380
18 Ray Chapman	1915	378
19 Hughie Jennings	1896	377
20 2 tied with		373

Assists

1 Ozzie Smith	1980	621
2 Glenn Wright	1924	601
3 Dave Bancroft	1920	598
4 Tommy Thevenow	1926	597
5 Ivan DeJesus	1977	595
6 Cal Ripken Jr.	1984	583
7 Whitey Wietelmann	1943	581
8 Dave Bancroft	1922	579
9 Rabbit Maranville	1914	574
10 Don Kessinger	1968	573
11 Roy Smalley	1979	572
12 Terry Turner	1906	570
Joe Tinker	1908	570
Leo Cardenas	1969	570
Ozzie Guillen	1988	570
16 Heinie Wagner	1908	569
Ed Brinkman	1970	569
18 George McBride	1908	568
19 Donie Bush	1909	567
20 Art Fletcher	1917	565

Errors

1 Billy Shindle	1890	119
2 Frank Fennelly	1886	117
Herman Long	1889	117
4 Phil Tomney	1889	114
5 Monte Ward	1890	105
6 Lou Say	1884	102
Joe Sullivan	1893	102
8 Frank Fennelly	1888	100
9 Ed McKean	1887	99
Frank Fennelly	1887	99
Frank Shugart	1892	99
Herman Long	1892	99
13 Herman Long	1893	98
John Gochnauer	1903	98
15 Gene DeMontreville	1896	97
Bill Keister	1901	97
17 Tom Burns	1885	96
Bill White	1887	96
19 Bill White	1886	95
20 2 tied with		94

Double Plays

1 Rick Burleson	1980	147
2 Roy Smalley	1979	144
3 Bobby Wine	1970	137
4 Lou Boudreau	1944	134
5 Spike Owen	1986	133
6 Rafael Ramirez	1982	130
7 Roy McMillan	1954	129
8 Hod Ford	1928	128
Vern Stephens	1949	128
Gene Alley	1966	128
11 Dick Groat	1958	127
Zoilo Versalles	1962	127
13 Eddie Joost	1949	126
Johnny Lipon	1950	126
Dick Groat	1962	126
Leo Cardenas	1969	126
Alfredo Griffin	1980	126
18 Jim Fregosi	1966	125
Dick Schofield	1988	125
20 Alfredo Griffin	1979	124

Fielding Percentage
(minimum 100 games)

1 Cal Ripken Jr.	1990	.996
2 Tony Fernandez	1989	.992
3 Larry Bowa	1979	.991
4 Ed Brinkman	1972	.990
5 Cal Ripken Jr.	1989	.990
6 Spike Owen	1990	.989
7 Omar Vizquel	1992	.989
8 Cal Ripken Jr.	1995	.989
9 Tony Fernandez	1990	.989
10 Dick Schofield	1992	.988
11 Ozzie Smith	1991	.987
12 Larry Bowa	1972	.987
13 Ozzie Smith	1987	.987
14 Larry Bowa	1971	.987
15 Manuel Lee	1992	.987
16 Larry Bowa	1978	.986
17 Cal Ripken Jr.	1991	.986
18 Frank Duffy	1973	.986
19 Greg Gagne	1993	.986
20 Roger Metzger	1976	.986

Range Factor
(minimum 100 games)

1 Danny Richardson	1894	6.80
2 Hughie Jennings	1895	6.73
3 George Davis	1899	6.69
4 Dave Bancroft	1918	6.62
5 Hughie Jennings	1896	6.56
6 Hughie Jennings	1897	6.55
7 Rabbit Maranville	1919	6.48
8 Bobby Wallace	1901	6.48
9 Monte Cross	1897	6.41
10 Dave Bancroft	1920	6.40
11 George Davis	1900	6.39
12 George Davis	1898	6.36
13 Herman Long	1889	6.36
14 Dave Bancroft	1922	6.31
15 Honus Wagner	1903	6.31
16 Bill Dahlen	1900	6.30
17 Hughie Jennings	1894	6.30
18 Lee Tannehill	1911	6.29
19 Bob Allen	1890	6.29
20 Rabbit Maranville	1914	6.29

Assists/162 Games
(minimum 100 games)

1 Germany Smith	1885	682.50
2 Art Fletcher	1919	664.58
3 Bill Dahlen	1895	661.81
4 Phil Tomney	1889	656.68
5 Bobby Wallace	1901	655.25
6 Jack Glasscock	1887	654.64
7 Germany Smith	1892	653.83
8 Henry Easterday	1888	646.59
9 Dave Bancroft	1920	645.84
10 Rogers Hornsby	1918	645.03
11 Shorty Fuller	1895	641.57
12 George Davis	1900	639.47
13 Germany Smith	1894	639.07
14 Ozzie Smith	1980	636.72
15 Glenn Wright	1924	636.35
16 Garry Templeton	1980	635.32
17 Monte Cross	1897	634.40
18 Art Fletcher	1918	632.32
19 Hughie Jennings	1894	631.55
20 Bill Dahlen	1900	629.73

Single Season Fielding Leaders—Outfielders

Games

1 Billy Williams	1965	164
2 Leon Wagner	1964	163
Billy Williams	1968	163
Pete Rose	1974	163
5 Jimmy Barrett	1904	162
Vada Pinson	1963	162
Billy Williams	1964	162
Johnny Callison	1964	162
Curt Flood	1964	162
Rocky Colavito	1965	162
Billy Williams	1966	162
Billy Williams	1967	162
Matty Alou	1969	162
Rusty Staub	1971	162
Roy White	1973	162
Ken Henderson	1974	162
Rick Bosetti	1979	162
Omar Moreno	1979	162
Omar Moreno	1980	162
Gary Matthews	1982	162
Dale Murphy	1982	162
Ruben Sierra	1989	162
Brian Hunter	1997	162
24 19 tied with		161

Putouts

1 Taylor Douthit	1928	547
2 Richie Ashburn	1951	538
3 Richie Ashburn	1949	514
4 Chet Lemon	1977	512
5 Dwayne Murphy	1980	507
6 Dom DiMaggio	1948	503
Richie Ashburn	1956	503
8 Richie Ashburn	1957	502
9 Richie Ashburn	1953	496
10 Richie Ashburn	1958	495
11 Jim Busby	1954	491
12 Omar Moreno	1979	490
13 Baby Doll Jacobson	1924	488
Bobby Thomson	1949	488
Al Bumbry	1980	488
16 Lloyd Waner	1931	484
17 Richie Ashburn	1954	483
18 Jim Busby	1953	482
Willie Wilson	1980	482
20 Omar Moreno	1980	479
21 Tom Oliver	1930	477
22 Dwayne Murphy	1984	474
23 Lloyd Moseby	1984	473
24 Jim Busby	1952	472
25 Rick Manning	1983	471
26 Lenny Dykstra	1993	469
27 Johnny Lindell	1944	468
28 Rick Bosetti	1979	466
29 Ruppert Jones	1977	465
Kirby Puckett	1985	465
31 Ken Henderson	1974	462
Gary Pettis	1986	462
33 George Wright	1983	460
34 Wally Berger	1935	458
35 Wally Berger	1931	457
Vince DiMaggio	1943	457
37 Jimmy Piersall	1956	455
Gorman Thomas	1980	455
39 Sam Rice	1920	454
40 Ruppert Jones	1979	453

Assists

1 Orator Shaffer	1879	50
2 Hugh Nicol	1884	48
3 Hardy Richardson	1881	45
4 Tommy McCarthy	1888	44
Chuck Klein	1930	44
6 Charlie Duffee	1889	43
Jimmy Bannon	1894	43
8 Jim Fogarty	1889	42
9 Orator Shaffer	1883	41
Jim Lillie	1884	41
11 Jim Fogarty	1887	39
Tom Brown	1893	39
Mike Mitchell	1907	39
14 King Kelly	1883	38
Tommy McCarthy	1889	38
Harry Stovey	1889	38
17 Jack Manning	1883	37
Tom Brown	1892	37
19 Lon Knight	1884	36
Jack McGeachey	1889	36
Jimmy Ryan	1889	36
Jimmy Sheckard	1903	36
23 Orator Shaffer	1880	35
Pop Corkhill	1885	35
Pop Corkhill	1889	35
George Davis	1890	35
George Wood	1890	35
Tris Speaker	1909	35
Tris Speaker	1912	35
30 John Cahill	1886	34
Dick Johnston	1887	34
Jimmy Ryan	1888	34
Hugh Duffy	1890	34
Charlie Duffee	1892	34
Emmett Heidrick	1899	34
Harry Niles	1906	34
Danny Murphy	1911	34
Gavy Cravath	1914	34
Chief Wilson	1914	34
Chet Chadbourne	1914	34

Errors

1 Ed Beecher	1890	55
2 Fred Clarke	1895	49
3 Pete Browning	1887	46
Jesse Burkett	1893	46
5 Jud Birchall	1883	45
George Van Haltren	1892	45
7 Henry Larkin	1886	44
Pete Browning	1886	44
9 Tom Brown	1885	43
10 Tom Brown	1883	42
Pete Hotaling	1883	42
Tom Brown	1886	42
13 Mike Slattery	1884	41
Walt Wilmot	1888	41
Ed Daily	1889	41
George Gore	1889	41
Jimmy Bannon	1894	41
Walt Wilmot	1894	41
19 Abner Dalrymple	1879	40
Jim Lillie	1884	40
Dummy Hoy	1894	40
22 Fred Treacey	1876	39
George Hall	1876	39
Ned Hanlon	1884	39
25 Buttercup Dickerson	1879	38
Fred Lewis	1883	38
John Peltz	1884	38
Emmett Seery	1884	38
Ned Hanlon	1885	38
Steve Brady	1886	38
Dummy Hoy	1892	38
George Van Haltren	1893	38
Jesse Burkett	1895	38
34 9 tied with		37

Double Plays

1 Happy Felsch	1919	15
Jack Tobin	1919	15
3 Jimmy Sheckard	1899	14
4 Fred Mann	1886	13
Tom Brown	1893	13
6 Tom Brown	1886	12
Tommy McCarthy	1888	12
Jimmy Bannon	1894	12
Mike Griffin	1895	12
Cy Seymour	1905	12
Ty Cobb	1907	12
Ginger Beaumont	1907	12
Tris Speaker	1909	12
Jimmy Sheckard	1911	12
Tris Speaker	1914	12
Mel Ott	1929	12
17 Sam Thompson	1886	11
Tommy McCarthy	1889	11
Billy Sunday	1890	11
Sam Thompson	1896	11
Danny Green	1899	11
Bill Lange	1899	11
Fielder Jones	1902	11
Jimmy Sebring	1903	11
Phil Geier	1904	11
Ben Koehler	1905	11
Burt Shotton	1913	11
Chief Wilson	1914	11
29 21 tied with		10

Fielding Percentage
(minimum 100 games)

1 Danny Litwhiler	1942	1.000
Willard Marshall	1951	1.000
Tony Gonzalez	1962	1.000
Don Demeter	1963	1.000
Russ Snyder	1965	1.000
Rocky Colavito	1965	1.000
Curt Flood	1966	1.000
Mickey Stanley	1968	1.000
Ken Harrelson	1968	1.000
Johnny Callison	1968	1.000
Ken Berry	1969	1.000
Mickey Stanley	1970	1.000
Roy White	1971	1.000
Al Kaline	1971	1.000
Ken Berry	1972	1.000
Carl Yastrzemski	1977	1.000
Terry Puhl	1979	1.000
Billy Sample	1979	1.000
Gary Roenicke	1980	1.000
Brian Downing	1982	1.000
John Lowenstein	1982	1.000
Gary Woods	1982	1.000
Bobby Clark	1982	1.000
Brian Downing	1984	1.000
Terry Puhl	1989	1.000
Willie Wilson	1990	1.000
Stan Javier	1990	1.000
Doug Dascenzo	1990	1.000
Brett Butler	1991	1.000
Darryl Hamilton	1992	1.000
Tim Raines	1993	1.000
Brett Butler	1993	1.000
Darren Lewis	1993	1.000
Lance Johnson	1994	1.000
Jim Eisenreich	1995	1.000
Stan Javier	1995	1.000
Paul O'Neill	1996	1.000
Darryl Hamilton	1996	1.000
39 Brett Butler	1985	.998
40 Devon White	1991	.998

Range Factor
(minimum 100 games)

1 Taylor Douthit	1928	3.62
2 Richie Ashburn	1951	3.59
3 Thurman Tucker	1944	3.55
4 Kirby Puckett	1984	3.55
5 Chet Lemon	1977	3.52
6 Irv Noren	1951	3.45
7 Richie Ashburn	1949	3.42
8 Carden Gillenwater	1945	3.39
9 Sammy West	1935	3.38
10 Richie Ashburn	1956	3.34
11 Richie Ashburn	1957	3.33
12 Dom DiMaggio	1948	3.33
13 Lloyd Waner	1932	3.32
14 Jim Busby	1953	3.31
15 Richie Ashburn	1958	3.31
16 Jim Busby	1952	3.31
17 Richie Ashburn	1953	3.29
18 Lloyd Waner	1931	3.29
19 Dwayne Murphy	1980	3.29
20 Taylor Douthit	1926	3.29
21 Andre Dawson	1981	3.27
22 Sammy West	1931	3.27
23 Baby Doll Jacobson	1924	3.26
24 Sammy West	1932	3.25
25 Terry Moore	1936	3.25
26 Richie Ashburn	1954	3.24
27 Taylor Douthit	1927	3.23
28 Bill North	1974	3.23
29 Dom DiMaggio	1947	3.22
30 Fred Schulte	1929	3.22
31 Rick Bosetti	1978	3.21
32 Bill North	1973	3.21
33 Max Carey	1921	3.21
34 Jim Busby	1954	3.21
35 Kiddo Davis	1932	3.20
36 Johnny Lindell	1944	3.20
37 Devon White	1988	3.20
38 Bobby Thomson	1949	3.19
39 Dwayne Murphy	1984	3.19
40 Sam Chapman	1948	3.19

Assists/162 Games
(minimum 100 games)

1 Jim Lillie	1884	58.26
2 Jimmy Ryan	1889	55.02
3 Jimmy Bannon	1894	54.42
4 Tommy McCarthy	1888	54.41
5 Lon Knight	1884	54.00
6 Jim Fogarty	1889	53.16
7 Charlie Duffee	1889	52.77
8 Ira Flagstead	1923	52.41
9 Tom Brown	1893	51.79
10 Pop Corkhill	1885	51.55
11 Jim Fogarty	1887	51.37
12 Harry Niles	1906	51.00
13 Hugh Nicol	1885	48.16
14 Mike Griffin	1890	46.49
15 Chuck Klein	1930	45.69
16 Harry Stovey	1889	44.93
17 Jack McGeachey	1889	44.52
18 John Cahill	1886	44.42
19 Charlie Duffee	1892	44.06
20 Tommy McCarthy	1889	43.97
21 Jimmy Ryan	1887	43.82
22 Dick Johnston	1887	43.37
23 Mike Mitchell	1907	43.27
24 Dick Johnston	1886	43.10
25 Jimmy Ryan	1888	43.03
26 George Wood	1890	42.95
27 Ed Delahanty	1893	42.92
28 Jimmy McAleer	1889	42.71
29 Ned Hanlon	1884	42.63
Jim Lillie	1886	42.63
George Davis	1890	42.63
32 Sam Thompson	1895	42.56
33 Ed Swartwood	1886	42.49
Harry Lyons	1888	42.49
35 Tom Brown	1886	42.26
36 Tommy McCarthy	1893	42.00
37 Jimmy Sheckard	1903	41.96
38 Charlie Duffee	1891	41.77
39 Chicken Wolf	1884	41.70
40 Billy Sunday	1890	41.54

Career Fielding Leaders—Pitchers: 19th Century Era (1876-1900)

Games			Putouts			Assists			Errors		
1	Pud Galvin	697	1	Tony Mullane	327	1	Pud Galvin	1,382	1	Tim Keefe	167
2	Tim Keefe	600	2	Pud Galvin	324	2	John Clarkson	1,143	2	John Clarkson	162
3	Mickey Welch	564	3	Kid Nichols	266	3	Cy Young	1,141	3	Pud Galvin	161
4	Tony Mullane	556	4	Jim McCormick	263	4	Tim Keefe	1,062	4	Mickey Welch	133
5	Gus Weyhing	535	5	Tim Keefe	260	5	Tony Mullane	1,030	5	Gus Weyhing	128
6	John Clarkson	531	6	Adonis Terry	245	6	Old Hoss Radbourn	942	6	Tony Mullane	123
7	Old Hoss Radbourn	528	7	Ted Breitenstein	242	7	Jim McCormick	922	7	Amos Rusie	120
8	Kid Nichols	518	8	Old Hoss Radbourn	230	8	Amos Rusie	864	8	Bert Cunningham	111
9	Cy Young	505	9	John Clarkson	221	9	Charlie Buffinton	851		Old Hoss Radbourn	111
10	Jim McCormick	492	10	Mickey Welch	217	10	Kid Nichols	845	10	Toad Ramsey	107
11	Amos Rusie	459	11	Guy Hecker	216	11	Jim Whitney	769	11	Will White	106
12	Adonis Terry	441	12	Frank Dwyer	204	12	Gus Weyhing	742	12	Adonis Terry	104
13	Charlie Buffinton	414	13	Gus Weyhing	201	13	Adonis Terry	734	13	Bobby Mathews	101
14	Jim Whitney	413	14	Dave Foutz	196	14	Will White	715	14	Jim Whitney	99
15	Will White	403	15	Bert Cunningham	195	15	Brickyard Kennedy	711		Jim McCormick	99
16	Silver King	398	16	Bob Caruthers	192	16	Mickey Welch	705	16	Red Ehret	94
17	Jack Stivetts	387	17	Larry Corcoran	182	17	Ted Breitenstein	683		Charlie Buffinton	94
18	Ted Breitenstein	376	18	Amos Rusie	176	18	Bert Cunningham	677	18	Matt Kilroy	91
19	Bill Hutchison	375	19	Mark Baldwin	175	19	Silver King	670	19	Cy Young	88
20	2 tied with	367	20	Charlie Buffinton	172	20	Tommy Bond	667	20	Frank Killen	82

Double Plays			Fielding Percentage (minimum 150 games)			Assists/162 Innings (minimum 150 games)		
1	John Clarkson	44	1	Kid Nichols	.954	1	Bill Hart	46.18
2	Pud Galvin	43	2	Nig Cuppy	.951	2	Cy Young	45.72
3	Tony Mullane	41	3	Red Donahue	.948	3	Chick Fraser	45.49
4	Old Hoss Radbourn	39	4	Duke Esper	.945	4	Jack Taylor	45.12
5	Amos Rusie	35	5	Ed Stein	.943	5	Red Donahue	43.57
6	Kid Nichols	31	6	Ted Breitenstein	.942	6	Kid Carsey	42.20
7	Charlie Buffinton	30	7	Jack Powell	.941	7	Brickyard Kennedy	41.56
8	Frank Dwyer	29	8	Brickyard Kennedy	.940	8	Scott Stratton	41.35
9	Brickyard Kennedy	28	9	Scott Stratton	.938	9	Matt Kilroy	41.17
	Tim Keefe	28	10	Cy Young	.936	10	John Clarkson	40.82
	Jim McCormick	28	11	Frank Dwyer	.935	11	Sadie McMahon	40.59
12	Gus Weyhing	27	12	Guy Hecker	.935	12	Charlie Buffinton	40.50
13	Bert Cunningham	25	13	Silver King	.935	13	Bert Cunningham	40.36
14	Sadie McMahon	24	14	Monte Ward	.932	14	Henry Gruber	40.13
15	Jim Whitney	23	15	Clark Griffith	.932	15	Al Mays	40.01
	Mickey Welch	23	16	Hank Gastright	.931	16	Clark Griffith	39.85
17	Ted Breitenstein	22	17	Billy Rhines	.930	17	Frank Killen	39.48
	Kid Carsey	22	18	George Hemming	.930	18	Nig Cuppy	39.35
	Silver King	22	19	Harry Staley	.927	19	George Haddock	39.27
	Dave Foutz	22	20	Tommy Bond	.927	20	Sam Weaver	38.91

Single Season Fielding Leaders—Pitchers: 19th Century Era (1876-1900)

Games				Putouts				Assists				Errors			
1	Will White	1879	76	1	Dave Foutz	1886	57	1	Will White	1882	223	1	Jack Lynch	1884	37
	Old Hoss Radbourn	1883	76	2	Tony Mullane	1882	54	2	Tony Mullane	1882	177	2	Adonis Terry	1884	34
	Pud Galvin	1883	76	3	George Bradley	1876	50	3	John Clarkson	1885	174		Bill Sweeney	1884	34
4	Guy Hecker	1884	75		Guy Hecker	1884	50	4	John Clarkson	1889	172	4	Bob Barr	1884	33
	Old Hoss Radbourn	1884	75	5	Larry Corcoran	1884	47	5	Matt Kilroy	1887	167	5	Al Atkinson	1884	31
	Bill Hutchison	1892	75	6	Al Spalding	1876	45	6	Bill Hutchison	1892	156		Billy Taylor	1884	31
7	Lee Richmond	1880	74		Ted Breitenstein	1895	45	7	Pud Galvin	1884	154		Toad Ramsey	1887	31
	Jim McCormick	1880	74	8	Dave Foutz	1876	44	8	Mark Baldwin	1890	146	8	Sam Kimber	1884	30
9	John Clarkson	1889	73		Dave Foutz	1887	44	9	Guy Hecker	1884	145		Tim Keefe	1884	30
10	Pud Galvin	1884	72		Bill Hutchison	1890	44		Park Swartzel	1889	145	10	Bobby Mathews	1876	28
11	Bill Hutchison	1890	71	11	Monte Ward	1880	43		Cy Young	1896	145		Jim Whitney	1881	28
12	Monte Ward	1879	70		Jim McCormick	1882	43	12	Tommy Bond	1879	144		Dupee Shaw	1884	28
	Monte Ward	1880	70	13	Tony Mullane	1884	42		Al Mays	1887	144		Matt Kilroy	1886	28
	John Clarkson	1885	70		Nat Hudson	1888	42		Jack Taylor	1898	144	14	Jersey Bakely	1884	27
15	Matt Kilroy	1887	69		Kid Gleason	1892	42	15	Tim Keefe	1883	142		John Clarkson	1889	27
16	Jim Devlin	1876	68		Ted Breitenstein	1893	42	16	Pud Galvin	1879	141	16	Pud Galvin	1879	26
	Jim McCormick	1882	68		Ted Breitenstein	1894	42		Tommy Bond	1880	141	17	Bobby Mathews	1884	25
	Tim Keefe	1883	68	18	Bobby Mathews	1876	41		Sadie McMahon	1891	141		Bert Cunningham	1888	25
	Tony Mullane	1884	68	19	4 tied with		40	19	4 tied with		139		Chick Fraser	1896	25
	Matt Kilroy	1886	68									20	8 tied with		24

Double Plays				Fielding Percentage (minimum 25 games)				Assists/162 Innings (minimum 25 games)			
1	Pud Galvin	1879	8	1	Jack Manning	1876	1.000	1	Will White	1882	75.26
	John Clarkson	1885	8		Frank Meinke	1884	1.000	2	Tony Mullane	1882	62.29
	Old Hoss Radbourn	1886	8		Jim Whitney	1884	1.000	3	Ed Scott	1900	61.71
	John Clarkson	1889	8		Kid Nichols	1896	1.000	4	Charlie Bartson	1890	60.32
	Jack Taylor	1899	8	5	Charlie Getzien	1886	.988	5	Walt Woods	1899	59.12
6	18 tied with		7	6	Bill Hill	1898	.986	6	Bill Phillips	1900	59.10
				7	Kid Nichols	1900	.985	7	Jack Taylor	1898	58.71
				8	Larry McKeon	1885	.983	8	Willie Sudhoff	1898	58.63
				9	Monte Ward	1880	.983	9	Willie Sudhoff	1899	58.18
				10	Duke Esper	1894	.983	10	Zeke Wilson	1896	57.38
				11	Ted Breitenstein	1898	.981	11	Park Swartzel	1889	57.25
				12	Frank Dwyer	1893	.980	12	Cy Seymour	1897	57.18
				13	Al Maul	1898	.978	13	Cy Young	1896	56.69
				14	Scott Stratton	1890	.977	14	Harry McCormick	1882	56.05
				15	Bill Kissinger	1895	.976	15	Sam Weaver	1882	55.89
					Dan Daub	1896	.976	16	Mike Morrison	1887	55.76
				17	Frank Kitson	1899	.976	17	Cowboy Jones	1900	55.35
				18	Red Donahue	1897	.976	18	Billy Rhines	1898	55.26
				19	Scott Stratton	1893	.975	19	Clark Griffith	1899	55.24
					Walt Woods	1899	.975	20	Joe Yeager	1898	55.05

Career Fielding Leaders—Catchers: 19th Century Era (1876-1900)

Games

1	Deacon McGuire	1,171
2	Wilbert Robinson	1,162
3	Chief Zimmer	1,095
4	Jack Clements	1,073
5	Charlie Bennett	954
6	Duke Farrell	815
7	Pop Snyder	744
8	Malachi Kittridge	739
9	Silver Flint	727
10	Doc Bushong	667
11	Doggie Miller	636
	Buck Ewing	636
13	Pop Schriver	630
14	Connie Mack	609
15	Jack O'Connor	605
16	Heinie Peitz	595
17	Jocko Milligan	585
18	King Kelly	583
19	John Grim	578
	Charlie Ganzel	578

Putouts

1	Charlie Bennett	5,123
2	Jack Clements	4,780
3	Deacon McGuire	4,776
4	Wilbert Robinson	4,675
5	Chief Zimmer	4,234
6	Pop Snyder	3,676
7	Silver Flint	3,520
8	Doc Bushong	3,477
9	Buck Ewing	3,301
10	Jocko Milligan	3,230
11	Duke Farrell	3,221
12	Malachi Kittridge	2,990
13	Bill Holbert	2,840
14	Connie Mack	2,698
15	Charlie Ganzel	2,618
16	Barney Gilligan	2,488
17	Doggie Miller	2,479
18	Pop Schriver	2,468
19	Jack Boyle	2,432
20	Con Daily	2,361

Assists

1	Chief Zimmer	1,413
2	Deacon McGuire	1,395
3	Wilbert Robinson	1,318
4	Pop Snyder	1,295
5	Duke Farrell	1,152
6	Jack Clements	1,079
7	Silver Flint	1,052
8	Charlie Bennett	1,048
9	Buck Ewing	1,017
10	Bill Holbert	1,013
11	Doc Bushong	1,001
12	Connie Mack	863
13	King Kelly	857
14	Jocko Milligan	825
15	Malachi Kittridge	780
16	Pop Schriver	718
17	Jack O'Connor	716
18	Doggie Miller	693
19	John Grim	691
20	Jack Boyle	683

Errors

1	Pop Snyder	529
2	Deacon McGuire	483
3	Silver Flint	436
4	Doc Bushong	411
5	Bill Holbert	396
6	Jack Clements	392
7	Charlie Bennett	379
8	Wilbert Robinson	378
9	King Kelly	368
10	Duke Farrell	332
11	Buck Ewing	322
12	Chief Zimmer	304
	Jocko Milligan	304
14	Kid Baldwin	302
15	Barney Gilligan	299
16	Con Daily	286
17	Doggie Miller	285
18	Connie Mack	281
19	Lew Brown	245
	John Clapp	245

Double Plays

1	Chief Zimmer	119
2	Charlie Bennett	114
3	Deacon McGuire	106
4	Wilbert Robinson	103
5	Jack Clements	93
6	Jocko Milligan	86
7	Duke Farrell	83
8	Doc Bushong	81
9	Buck Ewing	78
10	Bill Holbert	73
11	Connie Mack	71
	Charlie Ganzel	71
13	John Grim	69
14	Malachi Kittridge	68
	Farmer Vaughn	68
16	Pop Snyder	66
17	Heinie Peitz	63
18	Barney Gilligan	62
19	Jack Boyle	61
20	King Kelly	57

Fielding Percentage
(minimum 500 games)

1	Heinie Peitz	.957
2	Jack O'Connor	.952
3	Chief Zimmer	.949
4	Malachi Kittridge	.948
5	John Grim	.943
6	Charlie Bennett	.942
7	Wilbert Robinson	.941
8	Jack Clements	.937
9	Morgan Murphy	.936
10	Charlie Ganzel	.934
11	Pop Schriver	.933
12	Buck Ewing	.931
13	Jocko Milligan	.930
14	Duke Farrell	.929
15	Jack Boyle	.929
16	Deacon McGuire	.927
17	Connie Mack	.927
18	Farmer Vaughn	.926
19	Doggie Miller	.918
20	Doc Bushong	.916

Passed Balls

1	Pop Snyder	647
2	Silver Flint	602
3	Doc Bushong	553
4	Wilbert Robinson	469
5	Deacon McGuire	440
6	Jack Clements	417
	King Kelly	417
8	Jocko Milligan	406
9	Bill Holbert	403
10	Barney Gilligan	377
11	Fred Carroll	369
12	Buck Ewing	360
13	Charlie Bennett	352
14	Doggie Miller	346
15	Chief Zimmer	344
16	Kid Baldwin	331
17	Connie Mack	310
18	Jack Boyle	303
19	John Clapp	300
20	Jack O'Brien	279

Assists/162 Games
(minimum 500 games)

1	Bill Holbert	305.03
2	Pop Snyder	281.98
3	Buck Ewing	259.05
4	Doc Bushong	243.12
5	King Kelly	238.14
6	Silver Flint	234.42
7	Connie Mack	229.57
8	Duke Farrell	228.99
9	Jocko Milligan	228.46
10	Chief Zimmer	209.05
11	Jack Boyle	203.39
12	John Grim	193.67
13	Deacon McGuire	192.99
14	Jack O'Connor	191.72
15	Pop Schriver	184.63
16	Farmer Vaughn	184.26
17	Wilbert Robinson	183.75
18	Charlie Ganzel	181.06
19	Con Daily	180.56
20	Charlie Bennett	177.96

Single Season Fielding Leaders—Catchers: 19th Century Era (1876-1900)

Games

1	Deacon McGuire	1895	132
2	Chief Zimmer	1890	125
3	Tim Donahue	1898	122
4	Ed McFarland	1898	121
5	Dick Buckley	1892	119
6	Marty Bergen	1898	117
7	Chief Zimmer	1891	116
8	Connie Mack	1890	112
9	Chief Zimmer	1892	111
10	John Warner	1897	110
11	Jack Clements	1892	109
	Wilbert Robinson	1894	109
	John Warner	1898	109
14	Jack Clements	1891	107
15	Doc Bushong	1886	106
	Jack O'Connor	1890	106
17	Wilbert Robinson	1899	105
18	Morgan Murphy	1891	104
	Duke Farrell	1894	104
	Deacon McGuire	1894	104

Putouts

1	Doc Bushong	1886	647
2	Barney Gilligan	1884	605
3	Jack Clements	1892	557
4	Jack O'Connor	1890	539
5	John Warner	1898	536
6	Morgan Murphy	1891	532
7	Bill Holbert	1883	527
8	Buck Ewing	1889	524
9	Chief Zimmer	1892	514
10	Dick Buckley	1892	513
	John Warner	1897	513
12	Mert Hackett	1884	512
13	Jack Clements	1890	503
14	Marty Bergen	1898	496
15	Wilbert Robinson	1890	495
16	Jack Clements	1888	494
17	Sam Trott	1884	491
18	John Kerins	1886	487
19	Buck Ewing	1888	480
	Chief Zimmer	1890	480

Assists

1	Chief Zimmer	1890	188
2	Chief Zimmer	1891	181
3	Deacon McGuire	1895	179
4	Kid Baldwin	1887	165
5	John Kerins	1886	157
6	Harry Sage	1890	153
7	Connie Mack	1888	152
8	Buck Ewing	1889	149
9	Tom Daly	1887	148
	Jack Ryan	1890	148
11	King Kelly	1888	146
	Jack O'Connor	1890	146
13	Jimmy Peoples	1886	145
14	Pop Snyder	1887	143
	Wilbert Robinson	1888	143
	Buck Ewing	1888	143
	Connie Mack	1892	143
18	Pop Snyder	1879	142
	Bill Holbert	1884	142
20	3 tied with		140

Errors

1	Nat Hicks	1876	94
2	Emil Gross	1880	86
3	Ed Whiting	1882	81
4	Kid Baldwin	1887	79
5	Emil Gross	1883	74
6	Jimmy Peoples	1886	73
7	Rudy Kemmler	1883	71
8	Pop Snyder	1876	67
9	Deacon White	1876	64
	George Myers	1884	64
	Ed Crane	1884	64
12	Lew Brown	1879	63
	George Baker	1884	63
14	John Clapp	1880	62
	Mike Hines	1883	62
16	Silver Flint	1884	61
17	Bill Holbert	1883	58
	Doc Bushong	1884	58
19	4 tied with		57

Double Plays

1	John Warner	1897	17
2	Chief Zimmer	1894	16
	Tim Donahue	1898	16
4	Connie Mack	1887	15
	John Grim	1893	15
	Frank Bowerman	1900	15
7	Doc Bushong	1886	14
	Chief Zimmer	1890	14
	Dick Buckley	1892	14
	Deacon McGuire	1896	14
	Ed McFarland	1899	14
12	11 tied with		13

Fielding Percentage
(minimum 100 games)

1	Deacon McGuire	1899	.972
2	John Warner	1898	.968
3	Jack O'Connor	1890	.962
4	Tim Donahue	1898	.962
5	Marty Bergen	1898	.962
6	Ed McFarland	1898	.960
7	Morgan Murphy	1891	.954
8	John Warner	1897	.952
9	Jack Clements	1892	.950
10	Wilbert Robinson	1899	.949
11	Heinie Peitz	1898	.945
12	Wilbert Robinson	1894	.944
13	Doc Bushong	1886	.942
14	Bill Wilson	1897	.940
15	Chief Zimmer	1892	.938
16	Chief Zimmer	1890	.937
17	Dick Buckley	1892	.937
18	Deacon McGuire	1895	.936
19	Chief Zimmer	1891	.936
20	Jack Clements	1891	.927

Passed Balls

1	Ed Whiting	1882	105
2	Bill Traffley	1885	104
3	Pop Snyder	1881	99
	Mike Hines	1883	99
5	Sleeper Sullivan	1882	97
6	Doc Bushong	1884	95
	Fred Carroll	1886	95
8	Jackie Hayes	1883	93
9	Charlie Reilley	1879	89
10	Wilbert Robinson	1886	87
11	John Kerins	1886	83
12	Ed Whiting	1883	82
	Silver Flint	1884	82
	Wilbert Robinson	1887	82
15	Frank Graves	1886	81
	Kid Baldwin	1887	81
17	Dan Sullivan	1882	80
18	Paul Cook	1889	77
19	Silver Flint	1883	76
	Connie Mack	1887	76

Assists/162 Games
(minimum 100 games)

1	Chief Zimmer	1891	252.78
2	Chief Zimmer	1890	243.65
3	Jack O'Connor	1890	223.13
4	Deacon McGuire	1895	219.68
5	Duke Farrell	1894	218.08
6	John Warner	1898	206.59
7	Deacon McGuire	1899	204.88
8	Doc Bushong	1886	204.79
9	Connie Mack	1890	202.50
10	John Warner	1897	187.04
11	Morgan Murphy	1891	183.81
12	Ed McFarland	1898	182.08
13	Chief Zimmer	1892	178.05
14	Bill Wilson	1897	177.73
15	Deacon McGuire	1894	177.58
16	Dick Buckley	1892	167.45
17	Jack Clements	1891	163.51
18	Jack Clements	1892	159.03
19	Marty Bergen	1898	150.92
20	Heinie Peitz	1898	144.36

Career Fielding Leaders—First Basemen: 19th Century Era (1876-1900)

Games

1	Cap Anson	2,058
2	Roger Connor	1,758
3	Tommy Tucker	1,669
4	Dan Brouthers	1,632
5	Jake Beckley	1,596
6	Charlie Comiskey	1,362
7	John Reilly	1,075
8	Bill Phillips	1,032
9	Sid Farrar	943
10	John Morrill	916
11	Joe Start	797
12	Dave Orr	787
13	Henry Larkin	710
14	Jack Doyle	699
15	Perry Werden	667
16	Candy LaChance	595
	Patsy Tebeau	595
	Dave Foutz	595
19	Harry Stovey	550
20	Fred Tenney	507

Putouts

1	Cap Anson	20,794
2	Roger Connor	17,605
3	Tommy Tucker	16,393
4	Dan Brouthers	16,359
5	Jake Beckley	15,755
6	Charlie Comiskey	13,821
7	John Reilly	10,875
8	Bill Phillips	10,540
9	Sid Farrar	9,550
10	John Morrill	9,152
11	Joe Start	8,691
12	Dave Orr	7,923
13	Jack Doyle	6,815
14	Henry Larkin	6,804
15	Perry Werden	6,579
16	Candy LaChance	6,118
17	Dave Foutz	6,048
18	Patsy Tebeau	6,007
19	Harry Stovey	5,720
20	Fred Tenney	4,833

Assists

1	Cap Anson	955
2	Jake Beckley	913
3	Roger Connor	856
4	Tommy Tucker	749
5	Dan Brouthers	654
6	Charlie Comiskey	508
7	Perry Werden	416
8	Jack Doyle	405
9	John Morrill	375
10	Sid Farrar	358
11	Fred Tenney	328
12	Bill Phillips	305
13	Patsy Tebeau	290
14	Ed Cartwright	288
15	John Reilly	286
16	Dave Orr	254
17	Henry Larkin	250
18	Jack Boyle	231
19	Candy LaChance	230
20	Dave Foutz	199

Errors

1	Cap Anson	583
2	Dan Brouthers	512
3	Roger Connor	419
4	Charlie Comiskey	403
5	Tommy Tucker	393
6	Jake Beckley	329
7	Bill Phillips	324
8	John Reilly	316
9	Joe Start	294
10	John Morrill	285
11	Sid Farrar	262
12	Harry Stovey	241
13	Dave Orr	227
14	Henry Larkin	209
15	Ecky Stearns	206
16	Jack Doyle	205
17	Martin Powell	164
18	Jim Field	161
19	Perry Werden	158
20	Dave Foutz	147

Double Plays

1	Cap Anson	1,189
2	Roger Connor	955
3	Jake Beckley	931
4	Tommy Tucker	925
5	Dan Brouthers	890
6	Charlie Comiskey	740
7	John Reilly	655
8	Bill Phillips	511
9	John Morrill	450
10	Jack Doyle	439
11	Sid Farrar	431
12	Henry Larkin	388
13	Perry Werden	362
14	Joe Start	359
15	Candy LaChance	357
16	Dave Orr	356
17	Patsy Tebeau	334
18	Fred Tenney	297
19	Dave Foutz	289
20	Ed Cartwright	262

Fielding Percentage
(minimum 750 games)

1	Jake Beckley	.981
2	Roger Connor	.978
3	Tommy Tucker	.978
4	Sid Farrar	.974
5	Cap Anson	.974
6	Dave Orr	.973
7	Charlie Comiskey	.973
8	John Reilly	.972
9	Bill Phillips	.971
10	John Morrill	.971
11	Dan Brouthers	.971
12	Joe Start	.968

Assists/162 Games
(minimum 750 games)

1	Jake Beckley	92.67
2	Roger Connor	78.88
3	Cap Anson	75.17
4	Tommy Tucker	72.70
5	John Morrill	66.32
6	Dan Brouthers	64.92
7	Sid Farrar	61.50
8	Charlie Comiskey	60.42
9	Dave Orr	52.28
10	Bill Phillips	47.88
11	John Reilly	43.10
12	Joe Start	37.40

Single Season Fielding Leaders—First Basemen: 19th Century Era (1876-1900)

Games

1	Roger Connor	1892	155
2	Dan Brouthers	1892	152
3	Jake Beckley	1892	151
4	Fred Tenney	1899	150
5	Tommy Tucker	1892	149
	Perry Werden	1892	149
	Bill Everitt	1898	149
8	Jake Virtue	1892	147
9	Cap Anson	1892	146
	Klondike Douglass	1898	146
11	Dan McGann	1898	145
	Tommy Tucker	1898	145
13	Bill Phillips	1886	141
	Charlie Comiskey	1891	141
	Charlie Comiskey	1892	141
16	Mike Lehane	1890	140
	Tommy Tucker	1891	140
	Jake Beckley	1900	140
19	Jake Virtue	1891	139
	Perry Werden	1891	139

Putouts

1	Tommy Tucker	1898	1,552
2	Jake Beckley	1892	1,523
3	Bill Everitt	1898	1,519
4	Jake Virtue	1892	1,500
5	Dan Brouthers	1892	1,498
6	Cap Anson	1892	1,491
	Bill Everitt	1899	1,491
8	Tommy Tucker	1892	1,484
9	Roger Connor	1892	1,483
10	Bill Phillips	1888	1,476
11	Fred Tenney	1899	1,474
12	Charlie Comiskey	1892	1,469
13	Perry Werden	1892	1,467
14	Jake Virtue	1891	1,465
15	Dave Orr	1886	1,445
16	Charlie Comiskey	1891	1,433
17	Mike Lehane	1890	1,430
18	Roger Connor	1893	1,423
19	Perry Werden	1891	1,422
20	Dan McGann	1898	1,416

Assists

1	Jake Beckley	1892	132
2	Perry Werden	1897	116
3	Dan Brouthers	1892	105
4	Perry Werden	1892	102
5	Fred Tenney	1899	99
6	Jack Doyle	1900	96
7	Jake Beckley	1893	95
	Ed Cartwright	1895	95
	Bill Everitt	1899	95
10	Roger Connor	1896	94
11	Jake Beckley	1900	93
12	Jake Beckley	1891	87
	Bill Joyce	1898	87
14	Tommy Tucker	1898	85
15	Jake Beckley	1894	84
16	Roger Connor	1893	83
17	Roger Connor	1894	82
	Tommy Tucker	1895	82
	Fred Tenney	1900	82
20	2 tied with		81

Errors

1	Joe Quinn	1884	62
2	Cap Anson	1884	58
3	Ecky Stearns	1883	57
	Cap Anson	1885	57
5	John Kerins	1885	56
6	Tim Murnane	1876	55
	Otto Schomberg	1887	55
8	Martin Powell	1883	54
	Ecky Stearns	1884	54
10	Alex McKinnon	1884	53
11	Jim Field	1883	52
	Jim Field	1884	52
13	Oscar Walker	1879	49
	Jumbo Schoeneck	1884	49
	Dave Orr	1884	49
	Ecky Stearns	1889	49
	Dan Brouthers	1890	49
18	Bill Phillips	1884	48
	Cap Anson	1886	48
20	2 tied with		47

Double Plays

1	Bill Everitt	1898	123
2	Fred Tenney	1899	107
3	Charlie Comiskey	1892	103
	Bill Everitt	1899	103
5	Roger Connor	1892	99
6	Mike Lehane	1891	98
7	Tommy Tucker	1892	96
8	Jack Doyle	1900	92
9	Jake Beckley	1900	91
10	Tommy Tucker	1893	89
11	Henry Larkin	1889	88
	Jake Beckley	1892	88
	Patsy Tebeau	1896	88
14	Cap Anson	1884	86
	Cap Anson	1891	86
	Dan McGann	1899	86
	Ed Delahanty	1900	86
18	Cap Anson	1888	85
	Jack Doyle	1896	85
20	3 tied with		84

Fielding Percentage
(minimum 100 games)

1	Roger Connor	1887	.993
2	Dan McGann	1900	.990
3	Jay Faatz	1888	.989
4	Willard Brown	1893	.988
5	Fred Tenney	1897	.988
6	Roger Connor	1896	.988
7	Jack Boyle	1893	.988
8	Dan McGann	1899	.988
9	Scoops Carey	1895	.987
10	Roger Connor	1895	.986
11	Jake Beckley	1899	.986
12	Jake Beckley	1893	.986
13	Cap Anson	1888	.986
14	Roger Connor	1890	.985
	Patsy Tebeau	1896	.985
16	Roger Connor	1892	.985
17	Tommy Tucker	1894	.985
18	Cap Anson	1895	.985
19	Tommy Tucker	1896	.985
20	Ed Cartwright	1895	.984

Assists/162 Games
(minimum 100 games)

1	Perry Werden	1897	143.45
2	Jake Beckley	1892	141.62
3	Ed Cartwright	1895	126.15
4	Buck Ewing	1895	121.89
5	Roger Connor	1896	120.86
6	Fred Tenney	1900	119.68
7	Jake Beckley	1893	117.48
8	Jack Doyle	1900	116.93
9	Bill Everitt	1899	113.16
10	Dan Brouthers	1892	111.91
11	Perry Werden	1892	110.90
12	Roger Connor	1894	110.70
13	Hughie Jennings	1900	109.93
14	Bill Joyce	1898	108.42
15	Jake Beckley	1900	107.61
16	Jack Boyle	1893	107.04
17	Fred Tenney	1899	106.92
18	Jack Doyle	1897	106.58
19	Tommy Tucker	1895	106.27
20	Jake Beckley	1891	105.97

Career Fielding Leaders—Second Basemen: 19th Century Era (1876-1900)

Games		Putouts		Assists		Errors	
1 Bid McPhee	2,126	1 Bid McPhee	6,545	1 Bid McPhee	6,905	1 Fred Pfeffer	857
2 Fred Pfeffer	1,537	2 Fred Pfeffer	4,711	2 Fred Pfeffer	5,104	2 Bid McPhee	791
3 Cupid Childs	1,391	3 Lou Bierbauer	3,724	3 Lou Bierbauer	4,555	3 Cub Stricker	701
4 Lou Bierbauer	1,364	4 Cupid Childs	3,713	4 Cupid Childs	4,486	4 Cupid Childs	624
5 Joe Quinn	1,237	5 Cub Stricker	3,447	5 Joe Quinn	3,628	5 Lou Bierbauer	574
6 Cub Stricker	1,145	6 Joe Quinn	3,157	6 Cub Stricker	3,387	6 Joe Gerhardt	543
7 Bill Hallman	1,023	7 Fred Dunlap	2,909	7 Fred Dunlap	3,169	Jack Burdock	543
8 Bobby Lowe	993	8 Joe Gerhardt	2,766	8 Bobby Lowe	3,162	8 Fred Dunlap	498
9 Fred Dunlap	963	9 Jack Burdock	2,694	9 Bill Hallman	3,060	9 Jack Farrell	477
10 Jack Burdock	956	10 Bobby Lowe	2,521	10 Jack Burdock	2,968	10 Yank Robinson	471
11 Joe Gerhardt	880	11 Bill Hallman	2,470	11 Joe Gerhardt	2,941	11 Pop Smith	469
12 Bert Myers	806	12 Bert Myers	2,029	12 Bert Myers	2,547	12 Bert Myers	430
13 Kid Gleason	758	13 Pop Smith	2,016	13 Jack Farrell	2,480	13 Joe Quinn	392
14 Jack Farrell	740	14 Kid Gleason	1,960	14 Pop Smith	2,363	14 Bill Hallman	364
15 Pop Smith	713	15 Jack Farrell	1,778	15 Kid Gleason	2,335	Joe Quest	364
16 Yank Robinson	698	16 Hardy Richardson	1,756	16 Heinie Reitz	2,189	16 Hardy Richardson	349
17 Heinie Reitz	687	17 Jack Crooks	1,748	17 Danny Richardson	2,140	17 Reddy Mack	330
18 Tom Daly	664	18 Tom Daly	1,717	18 Yank Robinson	1,990	18 George Creamer	324
19 Danny Richardson	644	19 Danny Richardson	1,697	19 Hardy Richardson	1,986	19 Bobby Lowe	311
20 Jack Crooks	628	20 Yank Robinson	1,691	20 Tom Daly	1,966	20 Kid Gleason	310

Double Plays		Fielding Percentage (minimum 750 games)		Range Factor (minimum 750 games)		Assists/162 Games (minimum 750 games)	
1 Bid McPhee	1,186	1 Bobby Lowe	.948	1 Joe Gerhardt	6.49	1 Joe Gerhardt	541.41
2 Fred Pfeffer	893	2 Joe Quinn	.945	2 Fred Pfeffer	6.39	2 Lou Bierbauer	540.99
3 Lou Bierbauer	620	3 Bid McPhee	.944	3 Bid McPhee	6.33	3 Fred Pfeffer	537.96
4 Cupid Childs	568	4 Bill Hallman	.938	4 Fred Dunlap	6.31	4 Fred Dunlap	533.10
5 Joe Quinn	540	5 Lou Bierbauer	.935	5 Lou Bierbauer	6.07	5 Bid McPhee	526.16
6 Cub Stricker	513	6 Kid Gleason	.933	6 Cub Stricker	5.97	6 Cupid Childs	522.45
Fred Dunlap	513	7 Cupid Childs	.929	7 Jack Burdock	5.92	7 Bobby Lowe	515.86
8 Joe Gerhardt	477	8 Fred Dunlap	.924	8 Cupid Childs	5.89	8 Bert Myers	511.93
9 Bill Hallman	454	9 Fred Pfeffer	.920	9 Bobby Lowe	5.72	9 Jack Burdock	502.95
10 Bobby Lowe	407	10 Bert Myers	.914	10 Bert Myers	5.68	10 Kid Gleason	499.04
11 Jack Burdock	389	11 Joe Gerhardt	.913	11 Kid Gleason	5.67	11 Bill Hallman	484.57
12 Bert Myers	330	12 Jack Burdock	.912	12 Joe Quinn	5.49	12 Cub Stricker	479.21
13 Heinie Reitz	317	13 Cub Stricker	.907	13 Bill Hallman	5.41	13 Joe Quinn	475.13
14 Pop Smith	303						
15 Kid Gleason	281						
16 Danny Richardson	278						
Jack Farrell	278						
18 Yank Robinson	276						
19 Jack Crooks	273						
20 Tom Daly	271						

Single Season Fielding Leaders—Second Basemen: 19th Century Era (1876-1900)

Games			Putouts			Assists			Errors		
1 Lou Bierbauer	1892	152	1 Bid McPhee	1886	529	1 Lou Bierbauer	1892	555	1 Bill McClellan	1887	105
2 Monte Ward	1892	148	2 Lou Bierbauer	1889	472	2 Bid McPhee	1891	492	2 Bert Myers	1889	96
Bobby Lowe	1899	148	3 Cub Stricker	1887	461	3 Cupid Childs	1896	487	3 Yank Robinson	1886	95
4 Joe Quinn	1899	147	4 Fred Pfeffer	1889	452	4 Fred Pfeffer	1889	483	4 Tom Evers	1884	94
5 Nap Lajoie	1898	146	5 Bid McPhee	1892	451	5 Fred Pfeffer	1891	474	5 Cub Stricker	1883	93
Kid Gleason	1899	146	6 Bid McPhee	1887	442	6 Monte Ward	1892	472	6 Tom O'Brien	1884	90
7 Cupid Childs	1892	145	Nap Lajoie	1898	442	7 Bid McPhee	1892	471	7 Pop Smith	1880	89
Bobby Lowe	1898	145	8 Fred Pfeffer	1890	441	8 Lou Bierbauer	1890	468	8 Bob Ferguson	1883	88
9 Bid McPhee	1892	144	9 Cub Stricker	1889	434	Kid Gleason	1898	468	Fred Pfeffer	1884	88
Kid Gleason	1898	144	10 Joe Quinn	1890	431	10 Kid Gleason	1899	465	Reddy Mack	1886	88
11 Joe Quinn	1892	143	11 Bid McPhee	1889	429	11 Bid McPhee	1886	464	Bill McClellan	1886	88
12 Bill McClellan	1886	141	Fred Pfeffer	1891	429	Monte Ward	1893	464	12 Sam Crane	1883	87
Bill Hallman	1891	141	13 Bill McClellan	1886	423	13 Bobby Lowe	1899	461	13 Fred Pfeffer	1885	86
Cupid Childs	1891	141	14 Fred Pfeffer	1888	421	14 Fred Pfeffer	1888	457	14 Reddy Mack	1889	83
Tom Daly	1899	141	15 Bid McPhee	1884	415	Bobby Lowe	1898	457	15 Cupid Childs	1891	82
16 Bid McPhee	1886	140	16 Joe Gerhardt	1890	409	16 Cupid Childs	1891	455	16 Cub Stricker	1885	81
17 Cub Stricker	1891	139	17 Cub Stricker	1891	405	Bid McPhee	1893	455	Yank Robinson	1889	81
18 5 tied with		138	18 Bid McPhee	1890	404	18 Lou Bierbauer	1894	453	18 Cub Stricker	1884	80
			19 Kid Gleason	1899	403	Tom Daly	1899	453	Lou Bierbauer	1886	80
			20 Jack Crooks	1891	399	20 Charley Bassett	1889	451	Cub Stricker	1887	80

Double Plays			Fielding Percentage (minimum 100 games)			Range Factor (minimum 100 games)			Assists/162 Games (minimum 100 games)		
1 Bid McPhee	1893	101	1 Bid McPhee	1896	.978	1 Fred Pfeffer	1884	7.29	1 Fred Pfeffer	1884	610.39
2 Bid McPhee	1886	90	2 Joe Quinn	1899	.962	2 Pop Smith	1885	7.13	2 Danny Richardson	1891	609.63
3 Bid McPhee	1892	86	3 Heinie Reitz	1897	.962	3 Bid McPhee	1886	7.09	3 Charley Bassett	1887	604.44
4 Fred Pfeffer	1884	85	4 Heinie Reitz	1898	.959	4 Fred Pfeffer	1889	6.98	4 Cupid Childs	1896	597.68
Bid McPhee	1889	85	5 Lou Bierbauer	1893	.959	5 Bid McPhee	1884	6.96	5 Joe Gerhardt	1884	597.57
6 Lou Bierbauer	1889	80	6 Bobby Lowe	1898	.958	6 Joe Gerhardt	1884	6.91	6 Lou Bierbauer	1892	591.51
7 Fred Pfeffer	1888	78	7 Jack Crooks	1891	.957	7 Joe Gerhardt	1890	6.82	7 Pop Smith	1884	591.00
Cub Stricker	1891	78	8 Bid McPhee	1898	.956	8 Bid McPhee	1887	6.79	8 Pop Smith	1885	586.87
Fred Pfeffer	1891	78	9 Jack Crooks	1895	.956	9 Lou Bierbauer	1889	6.75	9 Fred Pfeffer	1889	583.93
10 Lou Bierbauer	1890	77	10 Bid McPhee	1899	.955	10 Bid McPhee	1893	6.70	10 Fred Pfeffer	1885	581.12
11 Bid McPhee	1887	76	11 Bid McPhee	1895	.955	11 Fred Pfeffer	1890	6.68	11 Bid McPhee	1893	580.39
12 Joe Quinn	1892	75	12 Bid McPhee	1891	.954	12 Pop Smith	1884	6.65	12 Bid McPhee	1891	577.57
Jim Connor	1898	75	13 Nap Lajoie	1900	.954	13 Bid McPhee	1894	6.63	13 Danny Richardson	1887	576.00
14 Bid McPhee	1884	74	14 Bid McPhee	1893	.954	14 Bid McPhee	1888	6.61	14 Charley Bassett	1889	575.29
Fred Pfeffer	1893	74	15 Bobby Lowe	1899	.954	15 Danny Richardson	1891	6.60	15 Bid McPhee	1894	573.43
Joe Quinn	1894	74	16 John O'Brien	1899	.953	16 Fred Pfeffer	1891	6.59	16 Fred Dunlap	1885	571.59
Bid McPhee	1898	74	17 Joe Quinn	1894	.952	17 Fred Pfeffer	1885	6.57	17 Lou Bierbauer	1890	570.05
18 Fred Pfeffer	1890	73	Claude Ritchey	1900	.952	18 Sam Barkley	1884	6.56	18 Heinie Reitz	1897	568.27
Cupid Childs	1896	73	19 Bobby Lowe	1897	.952	19 Cub Stricker	1887	6.56	19 Lou Bierbauer	1894	564.51
20 5 tied with		72	20 Danny Richardson	1891	.952	20 Cupid Childs	1896	6.53	20 Sam Barkley	1884	563.07

Career Fielding Leaders—Third Basemen: 19th Century Era (1876-1900)

Games		Putouts		Assists		Errors	
1 Arlie Latham	1,571	1 Billy Nash	2,219	1 Arlie Latham	3,545	1 Arlie Latham	822
2 Billy Nash	1,464	2 Arlie Latham	1,975	2 Billy Nash	3,119	2 Billy Nash	614
3 Billy Shindle	1,272	3 Billy Shindle	1,815	3 Billy Shindle	2,886	3 Hick Carpenter	591
4 Jerry Denny	1,109	4 Jerry Denny	1,777	4 Jerry Denny	2,338	4 Billy Shindle	568
5 Denny Lyons	1,083	5 Denny Lyons	1,672	5 Denny Lyons	2,127	5 Jerry Denny	552
6 George Pinckney	1,061	6 Hick Carpenter	1,450	6 Lave Cross	2,097	6 Denny Lyons	507
7 Hick Carpenter	1,059	7 George Pinckney	1,343	7 George Pinckney	2,042	7 Joe Mulvey	475
8 Joe Mulvey	983	8 Lave Cross	1,307	8 Hick Carpenter	1,991	8 Deacon White	444
9 Lave Cross	875	9 Joe Mulvey	1,235	9 Joe Mulvey	1,962	9 Bill Joyce	438
10 Deacon White	826	10 Jimmy Collins	1,190	10 Jimmy Collins	1,728	10 Ned Williamson	401
11 Art Whitney	802	11 Tom Burns	1,043	11 Ned Williamson	1,719	11 George Pinckney	387
12 Bill Kuehne	798	12 Bill Joyce	1,041	12 Bill Kuehne	1,691	12 Bill Kuehne	373
13 Frank Hankinson	764	13 Frank Hankinson	1,029	Art Whitney	1,691	Frank Hankinson	373
14 Jimmy Collins	735	14 Art Whitney	1,026	14 Deacon White	1,618	14 Art Whitney	344
15 Bill Joyce	733	15 Deacon White	954	15 Frank Hankinson	1,579	15 Jim Donnelly	331
16 Ned Williamson	716	16 Bill Kuehne	932	16 Tom Burns	1,494	16 Tom Burns	327
17 Tom Burns	704	17 Ezra Sutton	896	17 John McGraw	1,468	17 Jumbo Davis	317
18 John McGraw	692	18 Charlie Irwin	880	18 Bill Joyce	1,453	18 Ezra Sutton	309
19 Ezra Sutton	677	19 Ned Williamson	878	19 Charlie Reilly	1,307	19 Jack Gleason	273
20 Jim Donnelly	635	20 Charlie Reilly	814	20 Jim Donnelly	1,295	20 Charlie Reilly	263

Double Plays		Fielding Percentage (minimum 750 games)		Range Factor (minimum 750 games)		Assists/162 Games (minimum 750 games)	
1 Billy Nash	265	1 Lave Cross	.937	1 Lave Cross	3.89	1 Lave Cross	388.24
2 Arlie Latham	253	2 George Pinckney	.897	2 Jerry Denny	3.71	2 Billy Shindle	367.56
3 Billy Shindle	215	3 Billy Nash	.897	3 Billy Shindle	3.70	3 Arlie Latham	365.56
4 Denny Lyons	165	4 Billy Shindle	.892	4 Billy Nash	3.65	4 Billy Nash	345.14
5 Jerry Denny	147	5 Art Whitney	.888	5 Arlie Latham	3.51	5 Bill Kuehne	343.29
6 George Pinckney	143	6 Denny Lyons	.882	6 Denny Lyons	3.51	6 Art Whitney	341.57
7 Hick Carpenter	142	7 Jerry Denny	.882	7 Frank Hankinson	3.41	7 Jerry Denny	341.53
8 Lave Cross	141	8 Bill Kuehne	.876	8 Art Whitney	3.39	8 Frank Hankinson	334.81
9 Joe Mulvey	131	9 Frank Hankinson	.875	9 Bill Kuehne	3.29	9 Joe Mulvey	323.34
10 Bill Kuehne	128	10 Joe Mulvey	.871	10 Joe Mulvey	3.25	10 Denny Lyons	318.17
11 Ned Williamson	119	11 Arlie Latham	.870	11 Hick Carpenter	3.25	11 Deacon White	317.33
12 Tom Burns	118	12 Hick Carpenter	.853	12 George Pinckney	3.19	12 George Pinckney	311.79
Deacon White	118	13 Deacon White	.853	13 Deacon White	3.11	13 Hick Carpenter	304.57
14 Frank Hankinson	116						
15 Jimmy Collins	112						
Art Whitney	112						
17 Bill Joyce	105						
18 Charlie Irwin	98						
19 Patsy Tebeau	94						
20 John McGraw	93						

Single Season Fielding Leaders—Third Basemen: 19th Century Era (1876-1900)

Games			Putouts			Assists			Errors		
1 Jimmy Collins	1898	152	1 Denny Lyons	1887	255	1 Billy Shindle	1892	382	1 Bill Joyce	1890	107
Jimmy Williams	1899	152	2 Jimmy Williams	1899	251	2 Jimmy Collins	1899	376	2 Jumbo Davis	1888	91
3 Billy Lauder	1899	151	Jimmy Collins	1900	251	3 Arlie Latham	1891	370	3 Joe Werrick	1887	89
Jimmy Collins	1899	151	4 Jimmy Collins	1898	243	4 Lave Cross	1899	358	4 Arlie Latham	1886	88
5 Lave Cross	1898	149	5 Billy Shindle	1889	225	5 Charlie Reilly	1890	354	Billy Shindle	1889	88
6 George Pinckney	1888	143	Tom Burns	1889	225	Jimmy Williams	1899	354	6 Ned Williamson	1883	87
Doc Casey	1899	143	7 Charlie Irwin	1898	223	7 Billy Nash	1892	351	John Irwin	1884	87
8 Arlie Latham	1892	142	Lave Cross	1899	223	Lave Cross	1898	351	8 Charlie Hickman	1900	86
9 George Pinckney	1886	141	9 Will Smalley	1890	221	9 Billy Shindle	1888	340	9 Jerry McCormick	1883	84
Bobby Wallace	1898	141	10 Billy Shindle	1888	218	10 Jumbo Davis	1888	334	Pete Gilbert	1891	84
Lave Cross	1899	141	11 Jimmy Collins	1899	217	11 Jimmy Collins	1898	332	11 Jack Gleason	1882	83
Jimmy Collins	1900	141	12 Lave Cross	1898	215	12 Arlie Latham	1892	329	12 Bill Kuehne	1890	82
13 Billy Nash	1891	140	13 Denny Lyons	1893	214	Bobby Wallace	1898	329	13 Jack Gleason	1884	80
14 Tom Burns	1890	139	Jimmy Collins	1897	214	Jimmy Collins	1900	329	Denny Lyons	1889	80
Pete Gilbert	1891	139	15 Billy Nash	1891	213	15 Will Smalley	1890	327	15 Billy Nash	1890	78
16 Billy Shindle	1889	138	16 Jack Crooks	1893	210	16 Pete Gilbert	1891	324	Billy Shindle	1892	78
George Pinckney	1889	138	Billy Lauder	1899	210	17 Billy Shindle	1889	323	17 Bill Joyce	1895	77
18 4 tied with		137	18 Billy Nash	1887	207	18 Barry McCormick	1898	322	18 Arlie Latham	1891	75
			19 Harry Raymond	1889	206	19 Lave Cross	1900	321	Bill Everitt	1895	75
			Charlie Reilly	1890	206	20 Frank Hankinson	1886	316	20 4 tied with		73

Double Plays			Fielding Percentage (minimum 100 games)			Range Factor (minimum 100 games)			Assists/162 Games (minimum 100 games)		
1 Billy Nash	1890	37	1 Lave Cross	1899	.959	1 Billy Shindle	1892	4.34	1 Jumbo Davis	1888	478.83
2 Pete Gilbert	1891	34	2 Billy Clingman	1897	.947	2 Jumbo Davis	1888	4.33	2 Billy Shindle	1892	461.82
3 Lave Cross	1899	32	3 John McGraw	1899	.945	3 Bill Bradley	1900	4.29	3 Arlie Latham	1884	444.76
4 Barry McCormick	1898	31	4 Lave Cross	1898	.945	4 Billy Shindle	1888	4.13	4 Bill Bradley	1900	444.74
5 Tom Burns	1889	30	5 Lave Cross	1900	.945	5 Lave Cross	1899	4.12	5 Arlie Latham	1891	444.00
6 Denny Lyons	1887	29	6 Jimmy Collins	1899	.943	6 Jimmy Collins	1900	4.11	6 Billy Nash	1892	421.20
Denny Lyons	1889	29	7 Charlie Irwin	1897	.940	7 Lave Cross	1894	4.11	7 Charlie Reilly	1890	418.60
8 Charlie Irwin	1896	28	8 Lave Cross	1895	.940	8 Patsy Tebeau	1890	4.09	8 Lave Cross	1899	411.32
9 Jumbo Davis	1888	27	9 Charlie Irwin	1898	.940	9 Charlie Reilly	1890	4.09	9 Billy Shindle	1888	408.00
Art Whitney	1889	27	10 Suter Sullivan	1899	.938	10 Billy Nash	1892	4.06	10 Jimmy Collins	1899	403.39
Will Smalley	1890	27	11 Bobby Wallace	1898	.936	11 Arlie Latham	1891	4.05	11 Billy Shindle	1891	401.76
Billy Shindle	1892	27	12 Jimmy Collins	1900	.935	12 Arlie Latham	1884	4.04	12 Jimmy Williams	1900	399.50
George Davis	1893	27	13 Chippy McGarr	1890	.933	13 Jack Crooks	1893	4.03	13 Billy Shindle	1893	399.17
14 9 tied with		26	14 Billy Nash	1894	.933	14 Will Smalley	1890	4.03	Lave Cross	1895	399.17
			15 George Pinckney	1890	.933	15 Billy Shindle	1891	4.01	15 Jimmy Knowles	1890	399.07
			16 Jimmy Collins	1898	.932	16 Lave Cross	1895	3.99	16 Joe Farrell	1883	397.78
			17 Charlie Irwin	1896	.931	17 Jerry Denny	1887	3.99	17 Billy Clingman	1895	391.25
			18 Bobby Wallace	1897	.928	18 Jimmy Williams	1899	3.98	18 Lave Cross	1900	390.99
			19 Billy Clingman	1896	.925	19 Billy Shindle	1889	3.97	19 Bill Kuehne	1890	390.86
			20 Art Whitney	1887	.924	20 Jimmy Williams	1900	3.95	20 Will Smalley	1890	389.51

Leaders: Fielding By Era

Career Fielding Leaders—Shortstops: 19th Century Era (1876-1900)

#	Games		#	Putouts		#	Assists		#	Errors	
1	Germany Smith	1,665	1	Herman Long	3,494	1	Germany Smith	6,154	1	Germany Smith	971
2	Jack Glasscock	1,628	2	Tommy Corcoran	2,966	2	Jack Glasscock	5,630	2	Herman Long	948
3	Ed McKean	1,564	3	Jack Glasscock	2,821	3	Herman Long	5,135	3	Ed McKean	855
4	Herman Long	1,489	4	Ed McKean	2,820	4	Ed McKean	4,853	4	Jack Glasscock	832
5	Tommy Corcoran	1,373	5	Germany Smith	2,813	5	Tommy Corcoran	4,834	5	Tommy Corcoran	706
6	Bones Ely	1,022	6	Hughie Jennings	2,377	6	Bones Ely	3,602	6	Arthur Irwin	594
7	Bill Dahlen	955	7	Bill Dahlen	2,373	7	Bill Dahlen	3,516	7	Shorty Fuller	592
8	Arthur Irwin	947	8	Bones Ely	2,146	8	Hughie Jennings	3,137	8	Frank Fennelly	590
9	Shorty Fuller	924	9	Monte Cross	2,044	9	Arthur Irwin	3,093	9	Bill Dahlen	538
10	Hughie Jennings	892	10	Shorty Fuller	1,768	10	Shorty Fuller	3,047	10	Bill Gleason	535
11	Monte Ward	826	11	Monte Ward	1,522	11	Monte Cross	2,806	11	Monte Ward	530
12	Monte Cross	825	12	George Davis	1,421	12	Monte Ward	2,641	12	Monte Cross	494
13	Bill Gleason	796	13	Bob Allen	1,399	13	Frank Fennelly	2,615	13	Bones Ely	476
14	Frank Fennelly	769	14	Arthur Irwin	1,301	14	Bill Gleason	2,360	14	Hughie Jennings	465
15	Jack Rowe	657	15	Frank Fennelly	1,013	15	Bob Allen	2,169	15	Sam Wise	422
16	Bob Allen	604	16	Frank Shugart	950	16	Jack Rowe	1,944	16	Sadie Houck	386
17	Davy Force	564	17	Bill Gleason	920	17	George Davis	1,915	17	Jack Rowe	364
18	Sam Wise	563	18	Sam Wise	908	18	Davy Force	1,898	18	Tom Burns	355
19	Candy Nelson	543	19	Gene DeMontreville	872	19	Sadie Houck	1,748	19	Bill White	331
20	George Davis	539	20	Danny Richardson	813	20	Sam Wise	1,672	20	Bob Allen	330

#	Double Plays		#	Fielding Percentage (minimum 750 games)		#	Range Factor (minimum 750 games)		#	Assists/162 Games (minimum 750 games)	
1	Herman Long	646	1	Bones Ely	.924	1	Hughie Jennings	6.18	1	Germany Smith	598.77
2	Jack Glasscock	620	2	Hughie Jennings	.922	2	Bill Dahlen	6.17	2	Bill Dahlen	596.43
3	Germany Smith	587	3	Tommy Corcoran	.917	3	Monte Cross	5.88	3	Bones Ely	570.96
4	Tommy Corcoran	566	4	Bill Dahlen	.916	4	Herman Long	5.80	4	Tommy Corcoran	570.36
5	Ed McKean	497	5	Jack Glasscock	.910	5	Tommy Corcoran	5.68	5	Hughie Jennings	569.72
6	Bill Dahlen	477	6	Monte Cross	.908	6	Bones Ely	5.62	6	Jack Glasscock	560.23
7	Hughie Jennings	411	7	Germany Smith	.902	7	Germany Smith	5.39	7	Herman Long	558.68
8	Bones Ely	400	8	Herman Long	.901	8	Shorty Fuller	5.21	8	Monte Cross	551.00
9	Shorty Fuller	333	9	Ed McKean	.900	9	Jack Glasscock	5.19	9	Frank Fennelly	550.88
10	Monte Cross	317	10	Shorty Fuller	.891	10	Monte Ward	5.04	10	Shorty Fuller	534.21
11	Monte Ward	294	11	Monte Ward	.887	11	Ed McKean	4.91	11	Arthur Irwin	529.11
12	Arthur Irwin	293	12	Arthur Irwin	.881	12	Frank Fennelly	4.72	12	Monte Ward	517.97
13	Bob Allen	278	13	Frank Fennelly	.860	13	Arthur Irwin	4.64	13	Ed McKean	502.68
14	Frank Fennelly	259	14	Bill Gleason	.860	14	Bill Gleason	4.12	14	Bill Gleason	480.30
15	George Davis	254									
16	Jack Rowe	203									
17	Bill Gleason	186									
18	Frank Shugart	166									
19	Sadie Houck	165									
20	Gene DeMontreville	160									

Single Season Fielding Leaders—Shortstops: 19th Century Era (1876-1900)

#	Games			#	Putouts			#	Assists			#	Errors		
1	Monte Cross	1899	154	1	Hughie Jennings	1895	425	1	Germany Smith	1892	561	1	Billy Shindle	1890	119
2	Tommy Corcoran	1898	153	2	Monte Cross	1898	404		Tommy Corcoran	1898	561	2	Frank Fennelly	1886	117
3	Hughie Jennings	1892	152	3	Hughie Jennings	1896	377	3	Ollie Beard	1889	537		Herman Long	1889	117
	Bob Allen	1892	152	4	Monte Cross	1899	370		Hughie Jennings	1892	537	4	Phil Tomney	1889	114
5	Tommy Corcoran	1892	151	5	Bill Dahlen	1898	369		Bob Allen	1892	537	5	Monte Ward	1890	105
	Ed McKean	1898	151	6	Danny Richardson	1894	360	6	Monte Cross	1899	529	6	Lou Say	1884	102
7	Monte Cross	1898	149	7	Tommy Corcoran	1898	353	7	Bill Dahlen	1895	527		Joe Sullivan	1893	102
8	Bones Ely	1898	148	8	Herman Long	1899	351		Bones Ely	1898	527	8	Frank Fennelly	1888	100
9	Harry Lochhead	1899	146	9	George Davis	1898	349	9	Bill Dahlen	1900	517	9	Ed McKean	1887	99
10	Herman Long	1899	143	10	Herman Long	1891	345	10	Monte Cross	1897	513		Frank Fennelly	1887	99
11	Bill Dahlen	1898	142	11	Hughie Jennings	1892	343	11	Bill Dahlen	1898	511		Frank Shugart	1892	99
	Herman Long	1898	142	12	Monte Cross	1900	339	12	Germany Smith	1891	507		Herman Long	1892	99
13	Ollie Beard	1889	141	13	Bob Allen	1890	337	13	Monte Cross	1898	506	13	Herman Long	1893	98
	Ed McKean	1891	141		George Davis	1897	337	14	Bones Ely	1900	503	14	Gene DeMontreville	1896	97
	Herman Long	1892	141	15	Herman Long	1889	335	15	Germany Smith	1894	501	15	Tom Burns	1885	96
	Shorty Fuller	1892	141		Hughie Jennings	1897	335	16	Bob Allen	1890	500		Bill White	1887	96
17	Shorty Fuller	1889	140	17	Bob Allen	1892	331		Germany Smith	1893	500	17	Bill White	1886	95
18	Herman Long	1891	139	18	Monte Cross	1897	327	18	Hughie Jennings	1894	499	18	Billy Geer	1884	94
	Germany Smith	1892	139		Bobby Wallace	1900	327		Shorty Fuller	1895	499		Germany Smith	1888	94
	Jack Glasscock	1892	139	20	Herman Long	1898	326	20	Herman Long	1892	497	20	3 tied with		93

#	Double Plays			#	Fielding Percentage (minimum 100 games)			#	Range Factor (minimum 100 games)			#	Assists/162 Games (minimum 100 games)		
1	Bill Dahlen	1898	77	1	George Davis	1899	.945	1	Danny Richardson	1894	6.80	1	Germany Smith	1885	682.50
2	Tommy Corcoran	1898	76	2	George Davis	1900	.944	2	Hughie Jennings	1895	6.73	2	Bill Dahlen	1895	661.81
3	Germany Smith	1894	75	3	Bones Ely	1898	.943	3	George Davis	1899	6.69	3	Phil Tomney	1889	656.68
4	Hughie Jennings	1895	71	4	Bill Dahlen	1899	.941	4	Hughie Jennings	1896	6.56	4	Jack Glasscock	1887	654.64
5	Hughie Jennings	1895	70	5	Hughie Jennings	1895	.940	5	Hughie Jennings	1897	6.55	5	Germany Smith	1892	653.83
	Hughie Jennings	1896	70	6	Bill Dahlen	1900	.938	6	Monte Cross	1897	6.41	6	Henry Easterday	1888	646.59
7	Hughie Jennings	1894	69	7	Herman Long	1900	.937	7	George Davis	1900	6.39	7	Shorty Fuller	1895	641.57
	Tommy Corcoran	1896	69	8	Jimmy Cooney	1890	.936	8	George Davis	1898	6.36	8	George Davis	1900	639.47
9	Bob Allen	1890	68	9	Bones Ely	1900	.935	9	Herman Long	1889	6.36	9	Germany Smith	1894	639.07
	Herman Long	1899	68	10	Germany Smith	1893	.934	10	Bill Dahlen	1900	6.30	10	Monte Cross	1897	634.40
	Monte Cross	1900	68	11	Bobby Wallace	1900	.934	11	Hughie Jennings	1894	6.30	11	Hughie Jennings	1894	631.55
12	Billy Shindle	1890	67	12	George Davis	1898	.933	12	Bob Allen	1890	6.29	12	Bill Dahlen	1900	629.73
	Bob Allen	1892	67	13	Hughie Jennings	1897	.933	13	Bill Dahlen	1895	6.26	13	Bones Ely	1900	626.82
	Herman Long	1893	67	14	Ed McKean	1898	.932	14	Bobby Wallace	1899	6.24	14	Tommy Corcoran	1893	625.46
	Germany Smith	1893	67	15	Tommy Corcoran	1898	.932	15	Bill Dahlen	1898	6.20	15	Bobby Wallace	1899	625.32
	George Davis	1897	67	16	Danny Richardson	1894	.931	16	Tommy Corcoran	1895	6.15	16	Germany Smith	1893	623.08
17	Bill Dahlen	1896	66	17	Tommy Corcoran	1899	.931	17	Bobby Wallace	1900	6.14	17	Tommy Corcoran	1895	622.49
18	5 tied with		65	18	Hughie Jennings	1898	.929	18	Bill Dahlen	1896	6.13	18	Germany Smith	1887	620.73
				19	Herman Long	1899	.929	19	Monte Cross	1898	6.11	19	George Davis	1899	618.00
				20	Hughie Jennings	1896	.928	20	Shorty Fuller	1895	6.10	20	Herman Long	1893	617.71

Career Fielding Leaders—Outfielders: 19th Century Era (1876-1900)

#	Games		#	Putouts		#	Assists		#	Errors	
1	Tom Brown	1,783	1	Tom Brown	3,623	1	Jimmy Ryan	352	1	Tom Brown	491
2	Jimmy Ryan	1,709	2	Mike Griffin	3,535	2	Tom Brown	348	2	Dummy Hoy	370
3	George Van Haltren	1,593	3	Dummy Hoy	3,531	3	George Van Haltren	316	3	George Gore	368
4	Dummy Hoy	1,591	4	Hugh Duffy	3,216	4	Orator Shaffer	289	4	Ned Hanlon	350
5	Hugh Duffy	1,582	5	Billy Hamilton	3,212	5	King Kelly	285	5	Jimmy Ryan	340
6	Billy Hamilton	1,485	6	Jimmy Ryan	3,130	6	Sam Thompson	283	6	Paul Hines	332
7	Mike Griffin	1,478	7	George Van Haltren	3,048	7	Tommy McCarthy	268	7	George Van Haltren	330
8	Mike Tiernan	1,474	8	Steve Brodie	2,742	8	Dummy Hoy	253	8	Abner Dalrymple	285
9	Sam Thompson	1,397	9	Ned Hanlon	2,653	9	Mike Griffin	243	9	George Wood	276
10	Jim O'Rourke	1,377	10	Jesse Burkett	2,582		George Gore	243	10	Jesse Burkett	275
11	Jesse Burkett	1,347	11	Ed Delahanty	2,467	11	Hugh Duffy	233	11	Billy Hamilton	274
12	Patsy Donovan	1,324	12	Jimmy McAleer	2,461	12	Chicken Wolf	229	12	Pete Browning	269
13	George Gore	1,297	13	Curt Welch	2,366	13	Hugh Nicol	226	13	Jim O'Rourke	268
14	Ned Hanlon	1,251	14	Paul Hines	2,362	14	Pop Corkhill	224	14	Tommy McCarthy	263
15	Paul Hines	1,239	15	George Gore	2,359	15	Ed Delahanty	217	15	King Kelly	259
16	George Wood	1,232	16	Joe Kelley	2,215		Paul Radford	217	16	Charley Jones	248
17	Steve Brodie	1,228	17	Elmer Smith	2,181		Paul Hines	217	17	Pete Hotaling	246
18	Tommy McCarthy	1,189	18	Patsy Donovan	2,158	18	Jim O'Rourke	216	18	Orator Shaffer	244
19	Ed Delahanty	1,109	19	Pop Corkhill	2,156	19	Ned Hanlon	208	19	Blondie Purcell	241
20	Curt Welch	1,075	20	Jim O'Rourke	2,152	20	Curt Welch	206	20	Harry Stovey	229

#	Double Plays		#	Fielding Percentage (minimum 750 games)		#	Range Factor (minimum 750 games)		#	Assists/162 Games (minimum 750 games)	
1	Tom Brown	85	1	Steve Brodie	.960	1	Jimmy McAleer	2.58	1	King Kelly	61.56
2	Mike Griffin	75	2	Willie Keeler	.958	2	Mike Griffin	2.56	2	Orator Shaffer	56.27
3	Jimmy Ryan	70	3	Mike Griffin	.956	3	Kip Selbach	2.54	3	Hugh Nicol	44.49
4	Dummy Hoy	65	4	Joe Kelley	.953	4	Fred Clarke	2.46	4	Paul Radford	38.97
5	Sam Thompson	61	5	Ed Delahanty	.949	5	Ed Delahanty	2.42	5	Tommy McCarthy	36.51
6	Tommy McCarthy	60	6	Pop Corkhill	.947	6	Curt Welch	2.39	6	Chicken Wolf	35.57
7	George Van Haltren	57	7	Jimmy McAleer	.944	7	Steve Brodie	2.38	7	Pop Corkhill	34.86
8	Billy Hamilton	51	8	Hugh Duffy	.943	8	Dummy Hoy	2.38	8	Jimmy Ryan	33.37
	Paul Hines	51	9	Kip Selbach	.942	9	Ned Hanlon	2.29	9	Sam Thompson	32.82
10	Curt Welch	49	10	Bug Holliday	.935	10	Pop Corkhill	2.29	10	George Van Haltren	32.14
11	Pop Corkhill	47	11	Sam Thompson	.934	11	Billy Hamilton	2.28	11	Pete Hotaling	32.01
	Ned Hanlon	47	12	Curt Welch	.933	12	Eddie Burke	2.27	12	Ed Delahanty	31.70
	George Gore	47	13	Tommy Dowd	.933	13	Joe Kelley	2.23	13	Tom Brown	31.62
14	Patsy Donovan	46	14	Patsy Donovan	.932	14	Tom Brown	2.23	14	Curt Welch	31.04
	Hugh Duffy	46	15	Billy Hamilton	.925	15	Walt Wilmot	2.21	15	Emmett Seery	30.84
	George Wood	46	16	Mike Tiernan	.924	16	Hugh Duffy	2.18	16	George Gore	30.35
17	Jesse Burkett	45	17	Fred Clarke	.922	17	Elmer Smith	2.17	17	Jim McTamany	30.09
	Steve Brodie	45	18	Elmer Smith	.922	18	Charley Jones	2.12	18	Charley Jones	29.91
19	Paul Radford	44	19	Joe Hornung	.922	19	George Van Haltren	2.11	19	Paul Hines	28.37
20	2 tied with	42	20	Eddie Burke	.921	20	Harry Stovey	2.08	20	Harry Stovey	28.32

Single Season Fielding Leaders—Outfielders: 19th Century Era (1876-1900)

#	Games			#	Putouts			#	Assists			#	Errors		
1	George Van Haltren	1898	156	1	Jimmy Slagle	1899	407	1	Orator Shaffer	1879	50	1	Ed Beecher	1890	55
2	Buck Freeman	1899	155	2	Jimmy McAleer	1892	367	2	Hugh Nicol	1884	48	2	Fred Clarke	1895	49
3	Dummy Hoy	1899	154	3	Billy Hamilton	1894	361	3	Hardy Richardson	1881	45	3	Pete Browning	1887	46
4	Sam Thompson	1892	153	4	Dummy Hoy	1897	359	4	Tommy McCarthy	1888	44		Jesse Burkett	1893	46
	Tom Brown	1892	153	5	Kip Selbach	1899	355	5	Charlie Duffee	1889	43	5	Jud Birchall	1883	45
6	Bug Holliday	1892	152	6	Mike Griffin	1891	353		Jimmy Bannon	1894	43		George Van Haltren	1892	45
	Dummy Hoy	1892	152		Mike Griffin	1897	353	7	Jim Fogarty	1889	42	7	Henry Larkin	1886	44
	Tommy McCarthy	1892	152	8	Duff Cooley	1898	352	8	Orator Shaffer	1883	41		Pete Browning	1886	44
	Dusty Miller	1898	152	9	Tom Brown	1892	351		Jim Lillie	1884	41	9	Tom Brown	1885	43
	Hugh Duffy	1898	152	10	Mike Griffin	1895	349	10	Jim Fogarty	1887	39	10	Tom Brown	1883	42
11	George Van Haltren	1899	151	11	Dummy Hoy	1898	348		Tom Brown	1893	39		Pete Hotaling	1883	42
12	Jesse Burkett	1898	150	12	Charlie Abbey	1894	344	12	King Kelly	1883	38		Tom Brown	1886	42
13	Jimmy McAleer	1892	149		Fred Clarke	1895	344		Tommy McCarthy	1889	38	13	Mike Slattery	1884	41
	Fred Clarke	1898	149		Fred Clarke	1898	344		Harry Stovey	1889	38		Walt Wilmot	1888	41
	Duff Cooley	1898	149		Hugh Duffy	1899	344	15	Jack Manning	1883	37		Ed Daily	1889	41
16	Dummy Hoy	1898	148	16	Jimmy McAleer	1895	341		Tom Brown	1892	37		George Gore	1889	41
	Chick Stahl	1899	148		Tommy Dowd	1899	341	17	Lon Knight	1884	36		Jimmy Bannon	1894	41
18	Patsy Donovan	1898	147	18	Dick Johnston	1887	339		Jack McGeachey	1889	36		Walt Wilmot	1894	41
	Tommy Dowd	1899	147		Tom Brown	1893	339		Jimmy Ryan	1889	36	19	3 tied with		40
	Hugh Duffy	1899	147	20	Jesse Burkett	1900	337	20	5 tied with		35				

#	Double Plays			#	Fielding Percentage (minimum 100 games)			#	Range Factor (minimum 100 games)			#	Assists/162 Games (minimum 100 games)		
1	Jimmy Sheckard	1899	14	1	Mike Griffin	1892	.986	1	Tom Brown	1893	3.10	1	Jim Lillie	1884	58.26
2	Fred Mann	1886	13	2	Steve Brodie	1897	.983	2	Ed Delahanty	1893	2.98	2	Jimmy Ryan	1889	55.02
	Tom Brown	1893	13	3	Steve Brodie	1899	.979	3	Curt Welch	1887	2.97	3	Jimmy Bannon	1894	54.42
4	Tom Brown	1886	12	4	Willie Keeler	1899	.979	4	Dick Johnston	1887	2.94	4	Tommy McCarthy	1888	54.41
	Tommy McCarthy	1888	12	5	Joe Kelley	1899	.977	5	Mike Griffin	1894	2.93	5	Lon Knight	1884	54.00
	Jimmy Bannon	1894	12	6	Hugh Duffy	1897	.975	6	Jimmy Slagle	1899	2.92	6	Jim Fogarty	1889	53.16
	Mike Griffin	1895	12	7	Mike Griffin	1898	.974	7	Billy Hamilton	1894	2.91	7	Charlie Duffee	1889	52.77
8	Sam Thompson	1886	11	8	Sam Thompson	1896	.974	8	Dummy Hoy	1897	2.88	8	Tom Brown	1893	51.79
	Tommy McCarthy	1889	11	9	Mike Tiernan	1898	.973	9	Charlie Abbey	1894	2.87	9	Pop Corkhill	1885	51.55
	Billy Sunday	1890	11	10	Steve Brodie	1896	.972	10	Mike Griffin	1891	2.87	10	Jim Fogarty	1887	51.37
	Sam Thompson	1896	11	11	Willie Keeler	1897	.970	11	Mike Griffin	1895	2.84	11	Hugh Nicol	1885	48.16
	Danny Green	1899	11	12	Mike Tiernan	1896	.970	12	Hugh Duffy	1894	2.76	12	Mike Griffin	1890	46.49
	Bill Lange	1899	11	13	Ed Delahanty	1897	.970	13	Fred Clarke	1895	2.76	13	Harry Stovey	1889	44.93
14	Curt Welch	1889	10	14	Hugh Duffy	1899	.970	14	Bill Lange	1896	2.74	14	Jack McGeachey	1889	44.52
	Joe Hornung	1889	10	15	Bill Lange	1898	.970	15	Mike Griffin	1897	2.73	15	John Cahill	1886	44.42
	Mike Griffin	1890	10	16	Joe Kelley	1898	.969	16	Tom Brown	1894	2.73	16	Charlie Duffee	1892	44.06
	George Wood	1891	10	17	Mike Griffin	1894	.969	17	Kip Selbach	1899	2.73	17	Tommy McCarthy	1889	43.97
	Bill Lange	1894	10	18	Mike Griffin	1895	.969	18	Dummy Hoy	1894	2.72	18	Jimmy Ryan	1887	43.82
	Tommy McCarthy	1894	10		Chick Stahl	1899	.969	19	Duff Cooley	1895	2.72	19	Dick Johnston	1887	43.37
	Kip Selbach	1899	10		Ed Delahanty	1899	.969	20	Jimmy Ryan	1889	2.72	20	Dick Johnston	1886	43.10

Career Fielding Leaders—Pitchers: Dead Ball Era (1901-1919)

Games

1	Christy Mathewson	629
2	Eddie Plank	624
3	Walter Johnson	545
4	Red Ames	533
5	George Mullin	488
6	Three Finger Brown	481
7	Eddie Cicotte	465
8	Chief Bender	460
9	Ed Walsh	431
10	Doc White	427
11	Jack Powell	423
12	Slim Sallee	413
13	Cy Young	401
14	Ed Reulbach	399
	Vic Willis	399
16	Long Tom Hughes	396
17	Earl Moore	387
18	Joe McGinnity	373
19	Bob Groom	367
20	Rube Waddell	366

Putouts

1	Christy Mathewson	280
2	Ed Walsh	233
3	Doc White	232
4	George Mullin	229
	Eddie Plank	229
6	Vic Willis	225
7	Walter Johnson	215
8	Harry Howell	187
9	Chief Bender	173
10	Chick Fraser	172
11	Three Finger Brown	171
12	Joe McGinnity	168
13	Frank Smith	167
14	Nick Altrock	166
	Wild Bill Donovan	166
16	Rube Waddell	153
17	Jack Coombs	148
18	Addie Joss	146
	Casey Patten	146
20	Ed Reulbach	136

Assists

1	Christy Mathewson	1,494
2	George Mullin	1,244
3	Ed Walsh	1,207
4	Eddie Plank	1,108
5	Red Ames	1,000
6	Walter Johnson	999
7	Doc White	962
8	Vic Willis	927
9	Eddie Cicotte	917
10	Harry Howell	875
11	Cy Young	872
12	Addie Joss	850
13	Three Finger Brown	843
14	Ed Reulbach	814
15	Chief Bender	808
16	Frank Smith	782
17	Pete Alexander	777
18	Jack Chesbro	759
19	Joe McGinnity	758
20	Cy Falkenberg	728

Errors

1	Rube Waddell	84
2	George Mullin	82
3	Joe McGinnity	78
4	Red Ames	74
5	Eddie Cicotte	64
6	Long Tom Hughes	63
7	Hippo Vaughn	62
8	Earl Moore	60
9	Cy Young	57
10	Ed Walsh	56
11	Ed Reulbach	55
	Chief Bender	55
13	Casey Patten	54
14	Barney Pelty	53
	Jack Powell	53
16	Cy Falkenberg	52
	Christy Mathewson	52
	Al Orth	52
19	Bob Groom	51
20	Doc White	50

Double Plays

1	Walter Johnson	54
2	Three Finger Brown	43
3	Christy Mathewson	41
4	Ed Reulbach	37
	Eddie Plank	37
6	Eddie Cicotte	33
7	Ed Walsh	32
8	George Mullin	30
9	Addie Joss	29
10	Barney Pelty	26
	Cy Falkenberg	26
	Vic Willis	26
	Jack Powell	26
14	Red Ames	25
	Doc White	25
	Jack Chesbro	25
17	Chief Bender	24
18	5 tied with	23

Fielding Percentage
(minimum 150 games)

1	Hank Robinson	.990
2	Pete Alexander	.984
3	Al Demaree	.980
4	Cy Barger	.978
5	Frank Owen	.978
6	Babe Adams	.976
7	Slim Sallee	.974
8	Eppa Rixey	.973
9	George Suggs	.972
10	Christy Mathewson	.972
11	George Mogridge	.971
12	Eddie Plank	.971
13	Fred Anderson	.970
14	Joe Wood	.969
15	Bernie Boland	.969
16	Reb Russell	.968
17	Clark Griffith	.968
18	Dick Rudolph	.968
19	Erskine Mayer	.967
20	Babe Ruth	.967

Assists/162 Innings
(minimum 150 games)

1	Fritz Coumbe	67.25
2	Ed Walsh	65.94
3	Nick Altrock	65.59
4	Carl Mays	64.40
5	Ed Willett	63.59
6	Harry Howell	63.57
7	Frank Owen	62.39
8	Willie Sudhoff	61.32
9	Jean Dubuc	60.79
10	Frank Corridon	60.35
11	Joe Benz	60.06
12	Bill Doak	59.92
13	Addie Joss	59.17
14	Harry Coveleski	58.54
15	Jack Quinn	58.45
16	Patsy Flaherty	57.54
17	Hooks Dauss	57.47
18	Joe Lake	57.28
19	Cy Morgan	57.16
20	Barney Pelty	56.38

Single Season Fielding Leaders—Pitchers: Dead Ball Era (1901-1919)

Games

1	Ed Walsh	1908	66
2	Ed Walsh	1912	62
3	Dave Davenport	1916	59
4	Ed Walsh	1907	56
	Christy Mathewson	1908	56
	Ed Walsh	1911	56
	Reb Russell	1916	56
8	Joe McGinnity	1903	55
	Jack Chesbro	1904	55
	Dave Davenport	1915	55
11	Larry Cheney	1913	54
12	Rube Vickers	1908	53
	Three Finger Brown	1911	53
	Hugh Bedient	1915	53
	Bob Shawkey	1916	53
16	Tom Seaton	1913	52
17	10 tied with		51

Putouts

1	Nick Altrock	1904	43
2	Ed Walsh	1908	41
	Joe Wood	1912	41
4	Vic Willis	1904	39
5	Snake Wiltse	1902	38
	George Mullin	1903	38
7	Vic Willis	1902	37
	Jake Weimer	1904	37
	Vic Willis	1905	37
	Harry Howell	1907	37
11	Chick Fraser	1905	36
12	Chick Fraser	1901	35
	Ed Walsh	1907	35
	Three Finger Brown	1908	35
15	Irv Young	1905	33
	Eddie Plank	1907	33
	Doc White	1907	33
18	4 tied with		32

Assists

1	Ed Walsh	1907	227
2	Ed Walsh	1908	190
3	Harry Howell	1905	178
4	Jack Chesbro	1904	166
5	George Mullin	1904	163
6	Ed Walsh	1911	159
7	Frank Smith	1909	154
	Ed Walsh	1910	154
9	Harry Howell	1904	143
	Addie Joss	1907	143
11	Christy Mathewson	1908	141
12	Ed Walsh	1912	140
13	Claude Hendrix	1914	137
	Hooks Dauss	1915	137
15	George Mullin	1905	134
16	George Mullin	1907	133
17	Nick Altrock	1905	132
18	Red Donahue	1902	130
	Frank Owen	1904	130
20	Elmer Stricklett	1906	128

Errors

1	Doc Newton	1901	18
2	Joe McGinnity	1903	16
3	Togie Pittinger	1903	15
	Rube Waddell	1905	15
	Ed Walsh	1912	15
6	Vive Lindaman	1906	14
7	Wiley Piatt	1902	13
	George Mullin	1904	13
	Joe McGinnity	1904	13
	Orval Overall	1905	13
	Barney Pelty	1906	13
	Joe McGinnity	1906	13
	Hippo Vaughn	1914	13
	Jack Nabors	1916	13
15	9 tied with		12

Double Plays

1	Addie Joss	1905	10
	Nick Altrock	1905	10
3	Ed Walsh	1908	9
	George Suggs	1911	9
	Eddie Cicotte	1913	9
6	Frank Owen	1904	8
	Jack Townsend	1904	8
	Ed Summers	1909	8
	Walter Johnson	1911	8
	Joe Benz	1914	8
	Joe Bush	1916	8
12	18 tied with		7

Fielding Percentage
(minimum 25 games)

1	70 tied with		1.000

Assists/162 Innings
(minimum 25 games)

1	Harry Howell	1905	89.28
2	Ed Walsh	1907	87.07
3	Ed Willett	1910	81.60
4	Rube Peters	1912	77.52
5	Carl Mays	1916	77.36
6	Harry Howell	1904	77.31
7	Elmer Stricklett	1905	76.45
8	Jack Quinn	1910	76.30
9	Willie Sudhoff	1904	75.78
10	Fritz Coumbe	1916	74.04
11	Jean Dubuc	1913	73.43
12	Hooks Dauss	1915	71.67
13	Barney Pelty	1910	71.53
14	Fritz Coumbe	1918	71.28
15	Elmer Stricklett	1906	71.09
16	Joe Harris	1906	71.00
17	Joe Benz	1913	70.96
18	Joe Lake	1909	70.72
19	Ed Willett	1914	70.35
20	Alex Main	1914	70.27

Career Fielding Leaders—Catchers: Dead Ball Era (1901-1919)

	Games			Putouts			Assists			Errors	
1	Red Dooin	1,195	1	Red Dooin	5,481	1	Red Dooin	1,590	1	Red Dooin	320
2	George Gibson	1,194	2	Johnny Kling	5,419	2	Johnny Kling	1,537	2	Oscar Stanage	215
3	Johnny Kling	1,153	3	George Gibson	5,214	3	Bill Bergen	1,444	3	Johnny Kling	203
4	Billy Sullivan	1,032	4	Chief Meyers	4,537	4	George Gibson	1,362	4	Ivy Wingo	167
5	Oscar Stanage	993	5	Billy Sullivan	4,455	5	Oscar Stanage	1,306		Roger Bresnahan	167
6	Roger Bresnahan	973	6	Bill Killefer	4,379	6	Billy Sullivan	1,217	6	Bill Bergen	161
7	Bill Bergen	941	7	Roger Bresnahan	4,307	7	Bill Rariden	1,197	7	George Gibson	153
8	Bill Rariden	911	8	Bill Bergen	4,233	8	Bill Killefer	1,196	8	Bill Rariden	146
	Chief Meyers	911	9	Ray Schalk	4,232	9	Roger Bresnahan	1,195		Chief Meyers	146
10	Ray Schalk	905	10	Ossee Schreckengost	4,102	10	Steve O'Neill	1,131	10	Eddie Ainsmith	143
11	Bill Killefer	902	11	Bill Rariden	4,020	11	Ray Schalk	1,094	11	Jeff Sweeney	138
12	Steve O'Neill	843	12	Oscar Stanage	4,017	12	Ivy Wingo	1,057	12	Ossee Schreckengost	137
13	Ivy Wingo	771	13	Steve O'Neill	3,540	13	Lou Criger	1,004	13	Steve O'Neill	136
14	Larry McLean	761	14	Lou Criger	3,388	14	Chief Meyers	996	14	Billy Sullivan	134
15	Jimmy Archer	736	15	Pat Moran	3,383	15	Pat Moran	990	15	Sam Agnew	132
16	Art Wilson	734	16	Eddie Ainsmith	3,327	16	Jimmy Archer	979		Bill Killefer	132
17	Lou Criger	714	17	Jimmy Archer	3,293	17	Larry McLean	905	17	Jimmy Archer	127
18	Pat Moran	697	18	John Henry	3,082	18	Ossee Schreckengost	857	18	Boss Schmidt	116
19	Ossee Schreckengost	677	19	Larry McLean	3,032	19	Bill Carrigan	854	19	Bill Carrigan	115
20	Eddie Ainsmith	668	20	Bill Carrigan	2,961	20	Jeff Sweeney	852	20	Ray Schalk	113

	Double Plays			Fielding Percentage (minimum 500 games)			Passed Balls			Assists/162 Games (minimum 500 games)	
1	Steve O'Neill	136	1	Ray Schalk	.979	1	Red Dooin	139	1	Bill Bergen	248.60
2	Johnny Kling	124	2	John Henry	.978	2	Roger Bresnahan	127	2	Frank Snyder	230.16
3	Ray Schalk	122	3	George Gibson	.977	3	Johnny Kling	122	3	Pat Moran	230.10
	Red Dooin	122	4	Billy Sullivan	.977	4	Billy Sullivan	113	4	Admiral Schlei	228.71
5	Bill Killefer	117	5	Bill Killefer	.977	5	George Gibson	101	5	Sam Agnew	228.10
6	George Gibson	112	6	Lou Criger	.977	6	Pat Moran	97	6	Lou Criger	227.80
7	Bill Bergen	106	7	Frank Snyder	.977	7	Oscar Stanage	94	7	Jeff Sweeney	225.16
8	Larry McLean	105	8	John Warner	.976	8	John Henry	93	8	Ivy Wingo	222.09
9	Oscar Stanage	103	9	Pat Moran	.976	9	Chief Meyers	86	9	Steve O'Neill	217.35
10	Chief Meyers	99	10	Tommy Clarke	.975		Lou Criger	86	10	Johnny Kling	215.95
11	Billy Sullivan	98	11	Chief Meyers	.974	11	Eddie Ainsmith	85	11	Red Dooin	215.55
12	Roger Bresnahan	96	12	Les Nunamaker	.973	12	Bill Bergen	84	12	Jimmy Archer	215.49
13	Ivy Wingo	94	13	Ossee Schreckengost	.973	13	Steve O'Neill	81	13	Bill Killefer	214.80
14	Bill Rariden	79	14	Larry McLean	.973		Nig Clarke	81	14	John Henry	213.76
15	Lou Criger	78	15	Bill Rariden	.973		Frank Bowerman	81	15	John Warner	213.49
16	Jimmy Archer	76	16	Bill Bergen	.972	16	Bill Carrigan	74	16	Bill Carrigan	213.17
	Pat Moran	76	17	Otto Miller	.972	17	Ivy Wingo	72	17	Oscar Stanage	213.06
18	Eddie Ainsmith	72	18	Art Wilson	.972		Ed Phelps	72	18	Bill Rariden	212.86
19	Frank Bowerman	71	19	Steve O'Neill	.972	19	Ossee Schreckengost	71	19	Les Nunamaker	210.48
20	Les Nunamaker	68	20	Johnny Kling	.972	20	Jimmy Archer	70	20	Mike Powers	207.31

Single Season Fielding Leaders—Catchers: Dead Ball Era (1901-1919)

	Games				Putouts				Assists				Errors		
1	George Gibson	1909	150	1	Ossee Schreckengost	1905	785	1	Bill Rariden	1915	238	1	Oscar Stanage	1911	41
2	George Gibson	1910	143	2	Chief Meyers	1911	729	2	Bill Rariden	1914	215	2	Red Dooin	1909	40
3	Frank Snyder	1915	142	3	Red Dooin	1909	717	3	Pat Moran	1903	214	3	Sam Agnew	1915	39
	Bill Rariden	1915	142	4	Gabby Street	1909	714	4	Oscar Stanage	1911	212	4	Red Dooin	1904	37
5	Oscar Stanage	1911	141		Bill Rariden	1914	714		Art Wilson	1914	212		Boss Schmidt	1908	37
6	George Gibson	1908	140	6	Bill Rariden	1915	709	6	Gabby Street	1909	210	6	Boss Schmidt	1907	34
	Red Dooin	1909	140	7	Art Wilson	1914	674	7	Frank Snyder	1915	204		Jeff Sweeney	1912	34
8	Roger Bresnahan	1908	139	8	Roger Bresnahan	1908	657	8	George Gibson	1910	203	8	Red Dooin	1906	32
	Ray Schalk	1917	139	9	George Gibson	1909	655	9	Bill Bergen	1909	202		Oscar Stanage	1912	32
	Hank Severeid	1917	139		Ray Schalk	1915	655		Claude Berry	1914	202	10	Ossee Schreckengost	1901	30
11	Billy Sullivan	1908	137	11	Ray Schalk	1916	653	11	Red Dooin	1909	199		Wally Schang	1914	30
	Gabby Street	1909	137	12	Ossee Schreckengost	1907	640	12	Walter Blair	1914	194		Oscar Stanage	1914	30
13	Ray Schalk	1915	134	13	Chief Meyers	1910	638	13	George Gibson	1909	192	13	Red Dooin	1902	29
14	Johnny Kling	1903	132	14	George Gibson	1910	633	14	Red Dooin	1908	191		Bill Killefer	1910	29
	Red Dooin	1908	132	15	Ray Schalk	1917	624	15	Oscar Stanage	1914	190		Nig Clarke	1911	29
	Art Wilson	1914	132	16	Bill Killefer	1917	615	16	Johnny Kling	1903	189	16	Red Dooin	1910	28
17	Bill Rariden	1914	130	17	Ray Schalk	1914	613	17	Boss Schmidt	1908	184		Sam Agnew	1913	28
18	Ray Schalk	1919	129	18	George Gibson	1908	607	18	Ray Schalk	1914	183		Ivy Wingo	1913	28
19	5 tied with		128	19	Walter Blair	1914	604	19	Jeff Sweeney	1913	180		Ivy Wingo	1916	28
				20	2 tied with		599	20	Steve O'Neill	1915	175	20	2 tied with		27

	Double Plays				Fielding Percentage (minimum 100 games)				Passed Balls				Assists/162 Games (minimum 100 games)		
1	Steve O'Neill	1916	36	1	Fred Jacklitsch	1914	.988	1	Nig Clarke	1907	25	1	Pat Moran	1903	324.00
2	Ray Schalk	1916	25	2	Ray Schalk	1916	.988		John Henry	1911	25	2	Bill Bergen	1909	292.18
3	Jack Lapp	1915	23	3	Bill Killefer	1913	.988	3	Pat Moran	1903	24	3	Bill Rariden	1915	271.52
4	Steve O'Neill	1914	22	4	Bill Killefer	1919	.987	4	Harry Bemis	1902	22	4	Claude Berry	1914	268.23
5	Johnny Kling	1912	20	5	Roger Bresnahan	1908	.985		Pat Moran	1905	22	5	Bill Rariden	1914	267.92
	Ray Schalk	1914	20	6	Billy Sullivan	1908	.985	6	Frank Bowerman	1901	21	6	Sam Agnew	1913	267.38
7	Art Wilson	1914	19	7	Bill Killefer	1917	.984	7	Mike Powers	1901	19	7	Jeff Sweeney	1913	260.36
	Frank Owens	1915	19	8	Ray Schalk	1915	.984		Mike Kahoe	1901	19	8	Art Wilson	1914	260.18
	Hank Gowdy	1916	19	9	Walter Blair	1914	.984		Jeff Sweeney	1913	19	9	Ivy Wingo	1916	257.38
	Steve O'Neill	1917	19	10	Ossee Schreckengost	1905	.984		Hank Severeid	1917	19	10	Oscar Stanage	1914	252.30
	Walter Schmidt	1918	19	11	Malachi Kittridge	1901	.984	11	Roger Bresnahan	1905	18	11	Jeff Sweeney	1912	250.50
12	Gabby Street	1909	18	12	George Gibson	1910	.984		Sam Agnew	1914	18	12	Wally Schang	1914	249.48
	Bill Bergen	1909	18	13	Billy Sullivan	1907	.983		John Henry	1916	18	13	Gabby Street	1909	248.32
	Jim Stephens	1910	18	14	Larry McLean	1910	.983	14	16 tied with		17	14	Steve O'Neill	1915	246.52
	Larry McLean	1910	18	15	Frank Snyder	1915	.983					15	Boss Schmidt	1908	246.35
	Ray Schalk	1913	18	16	George Gibson	1909	.983					16	Walter Blair	1914	245.53
	Claude Berry	1914	18	17	Hank Severeid	1919	.983					17	Oscar Stanage	1911	243.57
	Bill Rariden	1915	18	18	Steve O'Neill	1918	.983					18	Sam Agnew	1915	243.00
	Ray Schalk	1917	18	19	Bill Killefer	1918	.982					19	Walter Schmidt	1918	238.33
20	8 tied with		17	20	Walter Schmidt	1918	.981					20	Ray Schalk	1914	237.17

Career Fielding Leaders—First Basemen: Dead Ball Era (1901-1919)

## Games		## Putouts		## Assists		## Errors	
1 Ed Konetchy	1,818	1 Ed Konetchy	18,693	1 Ed Konetchy	1,130	1 Hal Chase	402
2 Hal Chase	1,815	2 Hal Chase	18,183	2 Hal Chase	1,048	2 Harry Davis	275
3 Fred Merkle	1,456	3 Fred Merkle	14,479	3 Fred Tenney	1,035	3 Fred Merkle	237
4 Harry Davis	1,393	4 Harry Davis	13,423	4 George Stovall	846	4 Kitty Bransfield	236
5 Jake Daubert	1,347	5 Fred Luderus	13,071	5 Harry Davis	842	5 Fred Tenney	232
6 Fred Luderus	1,319	6 Fred Tenney	13,070	6 Fred Luderus	839	6 Fred Luderus	200
7 Fred Tenney	1,303	7 Jake Daubert	12,982	7 Fred Merkle	792	7 George Stovall	192
8 Kitty Bransfield	1,290	8 Kitty Bransfield	12,793	8 Jake Daubert	757	8 Ed Konetchy	190
9 Doc Hoblitzell	1,284	9 George Stovall	12,699	9 Chick Gandil	754	9 Tom Jones	183
10 George Stovall	1,216	10 Doc Hoblitzell	12,584	10 Stuffy McInnis	747	10 Doc Hoblitzell	180
11 Stuffy McInnis	1,168	11 Stuffy McInnis	11,838	11 Kitty Bransfield	737	11 Jake Beckley	152
12 Chick Gandil	1,138	12 Chick Gandil	11,118	12 Tom Jones	698	12 Jake Stahl	150
13 Tom Jones	1,033	13 Tom Jones	10,872	13 Doc Hoblitzell	661	13 Charlie Hickman	136
14 Frank Chance	992	14 Frank Chance	9,860	14 Frank Chance	614	14 Frank Chance	132
15 Dan McGann	973	15 Dan McGann	9,742	15 Dan McGann	605	15 Vic Saier	129
16 Jake Stahl	839	16 Jake Stahl	8,708	16 Jiggs Donahue	556	16 George Burns	127
17 Vic Saier	838	17 Vic Saier	8,392	17 Jake Stahl	462	17 Jake Daubert	124
18 Jake Beckley	781	18 Jiggs Donahue	8,151	18 Frank Isbell	455	18 Stuffy McInnis	116
19 Jiggs Donahue	745	19 Jake Beckley	7,954	19 Wally Pipp	452	19 3 tied with	112
20 Doc Johnston	695	20 George Burns	7,515	20 George Burns	422		

## Double Plays		## Fielding Percentage (minimum 750 games)		## Assists/162 Games (minimum 750 games)	
1 Ed Konetchy	937	1 Chick Gandil	.992	1 Fred Tenney	128.68
2 Hal Chase	934	2 Jake Daubert	.991	2 George Stovall	112.71
3 Fred Merkle	785	3 Stuffy McInnis	.991	3 Tom Jones	109.46
4 Fred Luderus	719	4 Ed Konetchy	.991	4 Chick Gandil	107.34
5 Jake Daubert	705	5 Dan McGann	.989	5 Stuffy McInnis	103.61
6 George Stovall	702	6 Frank Chance	.988	6 Fred Luderus	103.05
7 Stuffy McInnis	677	7 Doc Hoblitzell	.987	7 Dan McGann	100.73
8 Kitty Bransfield	670	8 George Stovall	.986	8 Ed Konetchy	100.69
9 Fred Tenney	659	9 Fred Luderus	.986	9 Frank Chance	100.27
10 Doc Hoblitzell	633	10 Vic Saier	.986	10 Harry Davis	97.92
11 Chick Gandil	630	11 Fred Merkle	.985	11 Hal Chase	93.54
12 Harry Davis	562	12 Tom Jones	.984	12 Kitty Bransfield	92.55
13 Dan McGann	496	13 Jake Stahl	.984	13 Jake Daubert	91.04
14 Frank Chance	470	14 Fred Tenney	.984	14 Jake Stahl	89.21
15 Tom Jones	456	15 Kitty Bransfield	.983	15 Fred Merkle	88.12
16 Wally Pipp	429	16 Jake Beckley	.982	16 Doc Hoblitzell	83.40
17 Vic Saier	422	17 Harry Davis	.981	17 Jake Beckley	83.39
18 George Burns	405	18 Hal Chase	.980	18 Vic Saier	73.07
19 Jake Beckley	395				
20 Dots Miller	390				

Single Season Fielding Leaders—First Basemen: Dead Ball Era (1901-1919)

## Games			## Putouts			## Assists			## Errors		
1 Babe Borton	1915	159	1 Jiggs Donahue	1907	1,846	1 Fred Tenney	1905	152	1 Jerry Freeman	1908	41
2 Doc Hoblitzell	1911	158	2 Jiggs Donahue	1906	1,697	2 Chick Gandil	1914	143	2 Charlie Hickman	1902	40
Ed Konetchy	1911	158	3 Candy LaChance	1904	1,691	3 Jiggs Donahue	1907	140	Charlie Hickman	1903	40
Harry Swacina	1914	158	4 Tom Jones	1907	1,687	4 Ed Konetchy	1908	122	4 Harry Davis	1907	38
Ed Konetchy	1916	158	5 Stuffy McInnis	1917	1,658	5 Charlie Carr	1904	121	5 Harry Davis	1906	37
6 Candy LaChance	1904	157	6 Ed Konetchy	1911	1,652	6 George Sisler	1919	120	6 Buck Freeman	1901	36
Jiggs Donahue	1907	157	7 Jiggs Donahue	1905	1,645	7 Jiggs Donahue	1906	118	Frank Chance	1903	36
Fred Beck	1914	157	8 Walter Holke	1917	1,635	Fred Tenney	1906	118	Hal Chase	1911	36
9 Fred Tenney	1908	156	9 Ed Konetchy	1916	1,626	9 Fred Tenney	1908	117	9 Jake Beckley	1901	34
10 Tom Jones	1907	155	10 Fred Tenney	1908	1,624	Fred Merkle	1911	117	Hal Chase	1907	34
Tom Jones	1908	155	11 Vic Saier	1916	1,622	11 Tom Jones	1906	116	11 Harry Davis	1901	33
Fred Luderus	1913	155	12 Tom Jones	1908	1,616	12 Fred Tenney	1904	115	Fred Tenney	1903	33
Wally Pipp	1917	155	Harry Swacina	1914	1,616	13 Jiggs Donahue	1905	114	Hal Chase	1906	33
14 Jim Nealon	1906	154	14 Fred Beck	1914	1,614	14 Fred Tenney	1907	113	Hal Chase	1913	33
Jiggs Donahue	1906	154	15 Ed Konetchy	1908	1,610	15 Charlie Carr	1903	111	15 Fred Tenney	1905	32
Jerry Freeman	1908	154	16 Wally Pipp	1917	1,609	16 George Stovall	1909	109	Patrick Newnam	1910	32
Ed Konetchy	1908	154	17 Fred Luderus	1917	1,597	Wally Pipp	1917	109	17 6 tied with		31
Ed Konetchy	1914	154	18 Jake Stahl	1905	1,593	18 Fred Luderus	1919	108			
Fred Luderus	1917	154	19 Jim Nealon	1906	1,592	19 Frank Chance	1904	106			
20 6 tied with		153	20 Fred Tenney	1907	1,587	20 3 tied with		105			

## Double Plays			## Fielding Percentage (minimum 100 games)			## Assists/162 Games (minimum 100 games)		
1 Butch Schmidt	1914	109	1 Chick Gandil	1919	.997	1 Fred Tenney	1905	166.38
George Burns	1918	109	2 Fritz Mollwitz	1915	.996	2 Chick Gandil	1914	159.77
3 Fritz Mollwitz	1915	107	3 Ed Konetchy	1913	.995	3 Charlie Carr	1904	158.08
4 Walter Holke	1917	104	4 Stuffy McInnis	1914	.995	4 George Sisler	1919	148.40
5 Hal Chase	1917	100	5 Ed Konetchy	1914	.995	5 Jiggs Donahue	1907	144.46
6 Frank Isbell	1902	97	6 Stuffy McInnis	1919	.995	6 Frank Chance	1904	139.61
George Sisler	1917	97	7 Chick Gandil	1917	.995	7 Jiggs Donahue	1904	136.34
Wally Pipp	1917	97	8 Chick Gandil	1916	.995	8 George Sisler	1918	135.00
9 Ed Konetchy	1916	96	9 Dan McGann	1906	.995	9 Fred Tenney	1906	133.68
10 Dots Miller	1912	93	10 Ed Konetchy	1917	.994	10 Charlie Carr	1903	133.20
11 Jake Daubert	1911	91	11 Jiggs Donahue	1907	.994	11 George Burns	1918	131.63
Jake Daubert	1913	91	12 Ed Konetchy	1915	.994	12 Tom Jones	1906	131.41
Babe Borton	1915	91	13 Frank Isbell	1909	.994	13 Fred Tenney	1904	129.38
Fred Luderus	1917	91	14 Ed Konetchy	1919	.994	14 Ed Konetchy	1908	128.34
15 Dan McGann	1902	90	15 Stuffy McInnis	1917	.993	15 Fred Merkle	1911	128.07
Jim Nealon	1906	90	16 Jake Daubert	1912	.993	16 Fred Luderus	1918	127.01
George Stovall	1907	90	17 Jake Daubert	1914	.993	17 Fred Tenney	1902	126.94
18 Chick Gandil	1913	89	18 Walter Holke	1919	.993	18 Fred Luderus	1919	126.78
Stuffy McInnis	1914	89	19 Jake Daubert	1915	.993	19 Tom Jones	1905	126.00
Wally Pipp	1916	89	20 Jake Daubert	1916	.993	20 Dan McGann	1908	124.51

Career Fielding Leaders—Second Basemen: Dead Ball Era (1901-1919)

	Games			Putouts			Assists			Errors	
1	Johnny Evers	1,733	1	Nap Lajoie	4,543	1	Nap Lajoie	5,224	1	Johnny Evers	422
2	Nap Lajoie	1,720	2	Eddie Collins	3,910	2	Johnny Evers	5,121	2	Larry Doyle	420
3	Eddie Collins	1,640	3	Johnny Evers	3,755	3	Miller Huggins	4,697	3	Miller Huggins	376
4	Larry Doyle	1,595	4	Miller Huggins	3,425	4	Eddie Collins	4,571	4	Nap Lajoie	353
5	Miller Huggins	1,530	5	Larry Doyle	3,357	5	Larry Doyle	4,266	5	Jimmy Williams	292
6	Otto Knabe	1,239	6	Del Pratt	2,829	6	Otto Knabe	3,583	6	Otto Knabe	287
7	Jimmy Williams	1,176	7	George Cutshaw	2,793	7	Jimmy Williams	3,509	7	Eddie Collins	278
8	Claude Ritchey	1,139	8	Jimmy Williams	2,759	8	Claude Ritchey	3,472	8	Hobe Ferris	270
9	Del Pratt	1,120	9	Otto Knabe	2,743	9	Del Pratt	3,336	9	Del Pratt	265
10	George Cutshaw	1,098	10	Claude Ritchey	2,561	10	George Cutshaw	3,257	10	Kid Gleason	262
11	Hobe Ferris	1,017	11	Hobe Ferris	2,502	11	Hobe Ferris	3,151	11	Claude Ritchey	245
12	Kid Gleason	825	12	Kid Gleason	1,923	12	Kid Gleason	2,433	12	Billy Gilbert	233
13	Danny Murphy	816	13	Danny Murphy	1,637	13	Danny Murphy	2,268	13	George Cutshaw	227
14	Frank LaPorte	731	14	Billy Gilbert	1,628	14	Billy Gilbert	2,172	14	John Farrell	189
15	Billy Gilbert	703	15	Frank LaPorte	1,468	15	Frank LaPorte	2,075	15	Danny Murphy	186
16	Dick Egan	686	16	Dick Egan	1,460	16	Dick Egan	2,022	16	Frank LaPorte	180
17	Ray Morgan	670	17	Bill Sweeney	1,448	17	Ralph Young	1,897	17	Bill Sweeney	169
18	Ralph Young	618	18	Germany Schaefer	1,419	18	Ray Morgan	1,802	18	Dick Egan	160
19	Dots Miller	616	19	Ralph Young	1,375	19	Dots Miller	1,761	19	Jim Delahanty	156
20	Germany Schaefer	588	20	Dave Shean	1,323	20	Bill Sweeney	1,717	20	Ray Morgan	152

	Double Plays			Fielding Percentage (minimum 750 games)			Range Factor (minimum 750 games)			Assists/162 Games (minimum 750 games)	
1	Nap Lajoie	883	1	Eddie Collins	.968	1	Nap Lajoie	5.68	1	Hobe Ferris	501.93
2	Johnny Evers	688	2	Nap Lajoie	.965	2	Hobe Ferris	5.56	2	Miller Huggins	497.33
3	Eddie Collins	664	3	George Cutshaw	.964	3	George Cutshaw	5.51	3	Claude Ritchey	493.82
4	Miller Huggins	597	4	Claude Ritchey	.961	4	Del Pratt	5.50	4	Nap Lajoie	492.03
5	Larry Doyle	579	5	Del Pratt	.959	5	Jimmy Williams	5.33	5	Jimmy Williams	483.38
6	Del Pratt	519	6	Otto Knabe	.957	6	Miller Huggins	5.31	6	Del Pratt	482.53
7	Otto Knabe	483	7	Miller Huggins	.956	7	Claude Ritchey	5.30	7	George Cutshaw	480.54
8	George Cutshaw	447	8	Jimmy Williams	.955	8	Kid Gleason	5.28	8	Johnny Evers	478.71
9	Jimmy Williams	426	9	Johnny Evers	.955	9	Eddie Collins	5.17	9	Kid Gleason	477.75
10	Claude Ritchey	423	10	Danny Murphy	.955	10	Johnny Evers	5.12	10	Otto Knabe	468.48
11	Hobe Ferris	353	11	Hobe Ferris	.954	11	Otto Knabe	5.11	11	Eddie Collins	451.53
12	Kid Gleason	303	12	Larry Doyle	.948	12	Danny Murphy	4.79	12	Danny Murphy	450.26
13	Frank LaPorte	299	13	Kid Gleason	.943	13	Larry Doyle	4.78	13	Larry Doyle	433.29
14	Dots Miller	273									
15	Ray Morgan	271									
16	Dick Egan	268									
17	Dave Shean	264									
18	Billy Gilbert	252									
19	John Farrell	222									
20	Bill Sweeney	220									

Single Season Fielding Leaders—Second Basemen: Dead Ball Era (1901-1919)

	Games				Putouts				Assists				Errors		
1	Del Pratt	1915	158	1	Bill Sweeney	1912	459	1	Nap Lajoie	1908	538	1	Kid Gleason	1901	64
	Del Pratt	1916	158	2	George Cutshaw	1914	455	2	Miller Huggins	1905	525	2	Hobe Ferris	1901	61
3	Morrie Rath	1912	157	3	Nap Lajoie	1908	450	3	Johnny Evers	1904	518	3	Erve Beck	1901	56
4	Hobe Ferris	1904	156	4	Del Pratt	1916	438	4	Johnny Evers	1907	500		Frank Truesdale	1910	56
	Claude Ritchey	1904	156	5	Duke Kenworthy	1914	437	5	Dave Shean	1910	493	5	Johnny Evers	1904	54
	Miller Huggins	1907	156	6	Hobe Ferris	1907	424	6	Del Pratt	1916	491	6	John Farrell	1903	53
	Nap Lajoie	1908	156	7	Del Pratt	1915	417		Del Pratt	1919	491		John Farrell	1904	53
	Eddie Collins	1917	156	8	Dave Shean	1910	408	8	Eddie Collins	1915	487		Larry Doyle	1910	53
9	Kid Gleason	1905	155	9	Germany Schaefer	1905	403	9	Claude Ritchey	1904	482	9	Jimmy Williams	1901	52
	Jack Farrell	1914	155	10	Eddie Collins	1910	402	10	Dick Egan	1911	480		Kid Gleason	1904	52
	Eddie Collins	1915	155		George Cutshaw	1913	402	11	Claude Ritchey	1905	478	11	Miller Huggins	1905	51
	Eddie Collins	1916	155	12	George Cutshaw	1915	397	12	Bill Sweeney	1912	475	12	Billy Gilbert	1901	49
13	George Cutshaw	1915	154	13	Nap Lajoie	1901	395	13	George Cutshaw	1915	473		Bert Niehoff	1916	49
	George Cutshaw	1916	154	14	Nap Lajoie	1910	387	14	Otto Knabe	1908	470	14	Sam Mertes	1901	47
15	8 tied with		153		Eddie Collins	1912	387	15	George Cutshaw	1916	467		Billy Gilbert	1903	47
				16	Otto Knabe	1910	383	16	Billy Gilbert	1904	466	16	6 tied with		46
				17	Johnny Evers	1904	381		Otto Knabe	1913	466				
				18	Kid Gleason	1904	379	18	Jimmy Williams	1904	465				
				19	Eddie Collins	1909	373	19	Kid Gleason	1904	463				
				20	Bill Sweeney	1911	372		Morrie Rath	1912	463				

	Double Plays				Fielding Percentage (minimum 100 games)				Range Factor (minimum 100 games)				Assists/162 Games (minimum 100 games)		
1	Dave Shean	1910	92	1	George Cutshaw	1919	.980	1	Nap Lajoie	1901	6.52	1	Nap Lajoie	1907	583.45
2	Nap Lajoie	1907	86	2	Gus Dundon	1905	.978	2	Nap Lajoie	1908	6.33	2	John Farrell	1902	579.36
3	Del Pratt	1915	82	3	Miller Huggins	1913	.977	3	Nap Lajoie	1903	6.30	3	Miller Huggins	1905	570.81
	Del Pratt	1918	82	4	Joe Gedeon	1918	.977	4	Bobby Lowe	1902	6.26	4	Del Pratt	1919	568.16
5	George Cutshaw	1913	79	5	Johnny Evers	1914	.976	5	Bill Sweeney	1912	6.10	5	Bobby Lowe	1902	562.15
	Duke Kenworthy	1914	79	6	Eddie Collins	1916	.976	6	John Farrell	1902	6.09	6	John Farrell	1904	560.77
7	Nap Lajoie	1908	78	7	Joe Gedeon	1919	.975	7	Dave Shean	1910	6.09	7	Nap Lajoie	1908	558.69
8	Nap Lajoie	1906	76	8	Jack Barry	1917	.974	8	Nap Lajoie	1907	6.05	8	Hobe Ferris	1902	557.33
	Bill Sweeney	1912	76	9	Morrie Rath	1919	.974	9	Germany Schaefer	1906	5.93	9	Luke Boone	1915	552.21
10	Eddie Collins	1916	75	10	Eddie Collins	1915	.974	10	Nap Lajoie	1906	5.92	10	Johnny Evers	1904	552.08
11	George Cutshaw	1914	74	11	Eddie Collins	1919	.974	11	Johnny Evers	1904	5.91	11	Kid Gleason	1901	548.40
	Del Pratt	1916	74	12	Nap Lajoie	1906	.973	12	Hobe Ferris	1907	5.89	12	Claude Ritchey	1903	543.94
13	Miller Huggins	1907	73	13	Dick Egan	1912	.973	13	Del Pratt	1916	5.88	13	John Farrell	1903	540.92
	Johnny Evers	1914	73	14	Nap Lajoie	1916	.973	14	Whitey Alperman	1907	5.88	14	Dave Shean	1910	539.64
	Lee Magee	1918	73	15	Amby McConnell	1911	.973	15	George Cutshaw	1914	5.88	15	Joe Gedeon	1918	538.68
16	John Farrell	1902	72	16	Gus Dundon	1904	.973	16	Hobe Ferris	1901	5.86	16	Jimmy Williams	1903	537.55
	Otto Knabe	1910	72	17	Eddie Collins	1910	.972	17	Kid Gleason	1901	5.86	17	Johnny Evers	1907	536.42
18	Johnny Evers	1912	71	18	John Hummel	1911	.972	18	Miller Huggins	1905	5.85	18	Nap Lajoie	1903	533.80
19	3 tied with		70	19	George Cutshaw	1915	.971	19	Joe Gedeon	1918	5.84	19	Whitey Alperman	1907	532.49
				20	Claude Ritchey	1907	.971	20	Duke Kenworthy	1914	5.82	20	Morrie Rath	1919	530.61

Career Fielding Leaders—Third Basemen: Dead Ball Era (1901-1919)

#	Games		#	Putouts		#	Assists		#	Errors	
1	Home Run Baker	1,405	1	Home Run Baker	2,002	1	Home Run Baker	2,874	1	Jimmy Austin	340
2	Jimmy Austin	1,342	2	Jimmy Austin	1,918	2	Jimmy Austin	2,762	2	Home Run Baker	304
3	Bill Bradley	1,253	3	Harry Steinfeldt	1,544	3	Bill Bradley	2,583	3	Harry Steinfeldt	300
4	Harry Steinfeldt	1,238	4	Bill Bradley	1,542	4	Art Devlin	2,481	4	Tommy Leach	289
5	Mike Mowrey	1,196	5	Bobby Byrne	1,454	5	Harry Steinfeldt	2,447	5	Doc Casey	261
6	Larry Gardner	1,194	6	Art Devlin	1,399	6	Larry Gardner	2,403	6	Bill Bradley	260
7	Art Devlin	1,192	7	Mike Mowrey	1,363	7	Mike Mowrey	2,363	7	Bobby Byrne	258
8	Bobby Byrne	1,147	8	Larry Gardner	1,309	8	Bobby Byrne	2,220	8	Art Devlin	257
9	Red Smith	1,050	9	Hans Lobert	1,292	9	Red Smith	2,136	9	Red Smith	244
10	Hans Lobert	1,000	10	Bill Coughlin	1,271	10	Jimmy Collins	1,974	10	Jimmy Collins	241
11	Bill Coughlin	978	11	Red Smith	1,210	11	Heinie Zimmerman	1,956	11	Heinie Zimmerman	236
12	Heinie Zimmerman	957	12	Jimmy Collins	1,182	12	Doc Casey	1,862	12	Bill Coughlin	227
13	Jimmy Collins	948	13	Tommy Leach	1,141	13	Tommy Leach	1,852	13	Eddie Foster	226
14	Doc Casey	937	14	Doc Casey	1,115	14	Bill Coughlin	1,848	14	Larry Gardner	223
15	Harry Lord	907	15	Heinie Zimmerman	1,082	15	Eddie Foster	1,828	15	Mike Mowrey	221
16	Eddie Foster	906	16	Eddie Foster	1,047	16	George Moriarty	1,727	16	Harry Lord	217
17	Lave Cross	846	17	Harry Lord	1,046	17	Hans Lobert	1,661	17	George Moriarty	199
18	Tommy Leach	841	18	Lave Cross	997	18	Lee Tannehill	1,624	18	Hans Lobert	172
19	George Moriarty	795	19	Eddie Grant	962	19	Lave Cross	1,606	19	Lave Cross	166
20	Eddie Grant	769	20	George Moriarty	951	20	Harry Lord	1,583	20	Jimmy Burke	163

#	Double Plays		#	Fielding Percentage (minimum 750 games)		#	Range Factor (minimum 750 games)		#	Assists/162 Games (minimum 750 games)	
1	Home Run Baker	236	1	Hans Lobert	.945	1	Tommy Leach	3.56	1	Tommy Leach	356.75
2	Jimmy Austin	214	2	Mike Mowrey	.944	2	Jimmy Austin	3.49	2	George Moriarty	351.92
3	Mike Mowrey	172	3	Larry Gardner	.943	3	Home Run Baker	3.47	3	Jimmy Collins	337.33
4	Bill Bradley	164	4	Eddie Grant	.942	4	George Moriarty	3.37	4	Art Devlin	337.18
5	Eddie Foster	157	5	Home Run Baker	.941	5	Jimmy Collins	3.33	5	Bill Bradley	333.96
6	Harry Steinfeldt	154	6	Bill Bradley	.941	6	Bill Bradley	3.29	6	Jimmy Austin	333.42
7	Heine Groh	153	7	Lave Cross	.940	7	Art Devlin	3.26	7	Home Run Baker	331.38
8	Red Smith	152	8	Art Devlin	.938	8	Harry Steinfeldt	3.22	8	Heinie Zimmerman	331.11
9	Larry Gardner	146	9	Bobby Byrne	.934	9	Bobby Byrne	3.20	9	Red Smith	329.55
10	Art Devlin	132	10	Jimmy Austin	.932	10	Bill Coughlin	3.19	10	Eddie Foster	326.86
11	Bobby Byrne	122	11	Bill Coughlin	.932	11	Red Smith	3.19	11	Larry Gardner	326.04
12	Heinie Zimmerman	118	12	Red Smith	.932	12	Doc Casey	3.18	12	Doc Casey	321.93
13	Ossie Vitt	117	13	George Moriarty	.931	13	Heinie Zimmerman	3.17	13	Harry Steinfeldt	320.21
14	Jimmy Collins	113	14	Harry Steinfeldt	.930	14	Eddie Foster	3.17	14	Mike Mowrey	320.07
15	Eddie Grant	105	15	Jimmy Collins	.929	15	Mike Mowrey	3.12	15	Bobby Byrne	313.55
16	Hans Lobert	96	16	Heinie Zimmerman	.928	16	Larry Gardner	3.11	16	Lave Cross	307.53
	Tommy Leach	96	17	Eddie Foster	.927	17	Eddie Grant	3.10	17	Bill Coughlin	306.11
18	Charlie Deal	95	18	Harry Lord	.924	18	Lave Cross	3.08	18	Eddie Grant	299.77
	Harry Lord	95	19	Doc Casey	.919	19	Hans Lobert	2.95	19	Harry Lord	282.74
20	Roy Hartzell	94	20	Tommy Leach	.912	20	Harry Lord	2.90	20	Hans Lobert	269.08

Single Season Fielding Leaders—Third Basemen: Dead Ball Era (1901-1919)

#	Games			#	Putouts			#	Assists			#	Errors		
1	Art Devlin	1908	157	1	Home Run Baker	1913	233	1	Ossie Vitt	1916	385	1	Tommy Leach	1903	65
	Red Smith	1915	157	2	Bill Coughlin	1901	232	2	Tommy Leach	1904	371	2	Sammy Strang	1902	63
3	Jimmy Collins	1904	156	3	Ernie Courtney	1905	229	3	Lee Tannehill	1904	369	3	Otto Krueger	1901	60
	Eddie Foster	1914	156	4	Jimmy Austin	1911	228	4	Bobby Byrne	1909	359		Tommy Leach	1904	60
5	Lave Cross	1904	155	5	Ed Gremminger	1902	222	5	Lee Tannehill	1905	358	5	Doc Casey	1901	58
	Ernie Courtney	1905	155		Hobe Ferris	1908	222	6	Art Devlin	1906	355		Hunter Hill	1904	58
7	Bill Bradley	1904	154	7	Home Run Baker	1914	221	7	Heinie Zimmerman	1917	349	7	Emil Batch	1905	57
	Eddie Grant	1909	154	8	Red Smith	1914	220	8	Bobby Byrne	1907	348	8	Doc Casey	1902	51
	Eddie Foster	1912	154	9	Jimmy Austin	1912	219		Eddie Foster	1912	348	9	Jimmy Burke	1901	50
	Heine Groh	1917	154	10	Ed Gremminger	1903	217	10	Lee Tannehill	1908	341		Jimmy Collins	1901	50
11	Lee Tannehill	1904	153		Home Run Baker	1911	217	11	Sammy Strang	1902	337		Jimmy Austin	1912	50
	Art Devlin	1905	153		Home Run Baker	1912	217		Jimmy Austin	1911	337	12	Fred Hartman	1901	49
	Larry Gardner	1914	153	13	Jimmy Austin	1913	216	13	Red Smith	1914	332		Harry Steinfeldt	1902	49
14	Eddie Grant	1910	152	14	Bobby Byrne	1909	214		Doug Baird	1917	332		Bobby Byrne	1907	49
	Bobby Byrne	1911	152	15	Tommy Leach	1904	212	15	Art Devlin	1908	331		John Knight	1907	49
16	7 tied with		151		Bobby Byrne	1907	212		Heine Groh	1917	331		Harry Lord	1908	49
				17	Home Run Baker	1909	209	17	Jimmy Collins	1901	328		Billy Purtell	1910	49
				18	Dave Brain	1906	208	18	Bill McKechnie	1914	327	18	Jim Delahanty	1904	48
					Ossie Vitt	1916	208	19	3 tied with		324		Dave Brain	1906	48
				20	2 tied with		207					20	2 tied with		47

#	Double Plays			#	Fielding Percentage (minimum 100 games)			#	Range Factor (minimum 100 games)			#	Assists/162 Games (minimum 100 games)		
1	Roy Hartzell	1912	40	1	Hans Lobert	1913	.974	1	Tommy Leach	1904	3.99	1	Doc Casey	1901	413.29
2	Heine Groh	1918	37	2	Charlie Deal	1919	.973	2	Dave Brain	1907	3.95	2	Ossie Vitt	1916	413.05
3	Home Run Baker	1910	35	3	Home Run Baker	1918	.972	3	Ossie Vitt	1916	3.93	3	Tommy Leach	1904	411.66
4	Heine Groh	1915	34	4	Heine Groh	1919	.971	4	Harry Steinfeldt	1902	3.91	4	Lee Tannehill	1905	408.42
5	Larry Gardner	1918	33	5	Bobby Byrne	1915	.969	5	Jimmy Collins	1901	3.85	5	Lee Tannehill	1908	406.19
6	Jimmy Austin	1915	32	6	Heine Groh	1915	.969	6	Jimmy Austin	1911	3.82	6	Dave Brain	1907	402.51
	Heine Groh	1916	32		Heine Groh	1918	.969	7	Dave Brain	1906	3.81	7	George Moriarty	1914	401.14
	Ossie Vitt	1916	32	8	Ossie Vitt	1919	.967	8	Bobby Byrne	1909	3.79	8	Red Smith	1918	396.15
9	Charlie Deal	1917	31	9	Harry Steinfeldt	1907	.967	9	Bobby Byrne	1907	3.78	9	Harry Steinfeldt	1902	395.58
	Eddie Foster	1918	31	10	Heine Groh	1917	.966	10	Lave Cross	1901	3.76	10	Sammy Strang	1902	392.76
11	Mike Mowrey	1910	30	11	Bill McKechnie	1918	.966	11	Bill Bradley	1902	3.74	11	Lee Tannehill	1904	390.71
	Home Run Baker	1918	30	12	Mike Mowrey	1916	.965	12	Jimmy Collins	1902	3.72	12	Art Devlin	1906	388.58
13	Harry Steinfeldt	1902	29	13	Ossie Vitt	1915	.964	13	Jimmy Austin	1909	3.71	13	George Moriarty	1909	386.66
14	Red Smith	1914	28	14	Ossie Vitt	1916	.964	14	Lee Tannehill	1905	3.70	14	Jimmy Collins	1902	386.07
	Bill McKechnie	1914	28	15	Larry Gardner	1918	.964	15	Tommy Leach	1903	3.70	15	Bobby Byrne	1909	385.15
	Heine Groh	1917	28	16	Terry Turner	1914	.963	16	Bill Coughlin	1901	3.70	16	Jimmy Collins	1901	385.04
	Home Run Baker	1919	28	17	Eddie Zimmerman	1911	.961	17	Ed Gremminger	1903	3.69	17	Bill Bradley	1902	383.12
18	6 tied with		27	18	Ed Lennox	1909	.959	18	Bill Bradley	1901	3.68	18	Lave Cross	1901	382.32
				19	Mike Mowrey	1915	.959	19	Red Smith	1914	3.68	19	Tommy Leach	1902	382.03
				20	George Perring	1915	.958	20	Jimmy Austin	1910	3.67	20	Bobby Byrne	1907	380.92

Career Fielding Leaders—Shortstops: Dead Ball Era (1901-1919)

#	Games		#	Putouts		#	Assists		#	Errors	
1	Honus Wagner	1,886	1	Honus Wagner	4,576	1	Honus Wagner	6,041	1	Honus Wagner	676
2	Joe Tinker	1,743	2	Joe Tinker	3,758	2	Joe Tinker	5,848	2	Joe Tinker	635
3	Mickey Doolan	1,625	3	Mickey Doolan	3,578	3	Bobby Wallace	5,470	3	Donie Bush	614
4	Donie Bush	1,624	4	Bobby Wallace	3,577	4	Donie Bush	5,392	4	Bobby Wallace	575
5	George McBride	1,613	5	Donie Bush	3,574	5	Mickey Doolan	5,290	5	Mickey Doolan	570
6	Bobby Wallace	1,600	6	George McBride	3,561	6	George McBride	5,242	6	George McBride	482
7	Art Fletcher	1,199	7	Bill Dahlen	2,477	7	Art Fletcher	4,233	7	Freddy Parent	474
8	Bill Dahlen	1,177	8	Art Fletcher	2,332	8	Bill Dahlen	3,984	8	Kid Elberfeld	442
9	Freddy Parent	1,129	9	Rabbit Maranville	2,283	9	Freddy Parent	3,772	9	Bill Dahlen	437
10	Al Bridwell	1,094	10	Al Bridwell	2,267	10	Al Bridwell	3,351	10	Art Fletcher	435
11	Roger Peckinpaugh	1,010	11	Freddy Parent	2,253	11	Roger Peckinpaugh	3,305	11	Al Bridwell	366
12	Kid Elberfeld	920	12	Kid Elberfeld	2,135	12	Rabbit Maranville	3,143	12	Heinie Wagner	356
13	Rabbit Maranville	913	13	Roger Peckinpaugh	2,086	13	Kid Elberfeld	3,013	13	Rabbit Maranville	328
14	Jack Barry	877	14	Ray Chapman	1,961	14	George Davis	2,872	14	Roger Peckinpaugh	322
15	Monte Cross	850	15	Heinie Wagner	1,954	15	Heinie Wagner	2,634	15	Monte Cross	316
16	Ray Chapman	846	16	Monte Cross	1,930	16	Jack Barry	2,607	16	Doc Lavan	313
17	George Davis	833	17	Buck Weaver	1,820	17	Ray Chapman	2,579	17	Ray Chapman	310
18	Heinie Wagner	824	18	George Davis	1,810	18	Buck Weaver	2,495	18	Buck Weaver	306
19	Buck Weaver	797	19	Charley O'Leary	1,709	19	Monte Cross	2,463	19	Ivy Olson	305
20	Everett Scott	785	20	Ivy Olson	1,616	20	Terry Turner	2,446	20	2 tied with	290

#	Double Plays		#	Fielding Percentage (minimum 750 games)		#	Range Factor (minimum 750 games)		#	Assists/162 Games (minimum 750 games)	
1	Honus Wagner	766	1	Everett Scott	.963	1	Rabbit Maranville	5.94	1	Art Fletcher	571.93
2	Joe Tinker	669	2	George McBride	.948	2	Bobby Wallace	5.65	2	George Davis	558.54
3	George McBride	607	3	Roger Peckinpaugh	.944	3	Honus Wagner	5.63	3	Rabbit Maranville	557.68
4	Bobby Wallace	571	4	George Davis	.944	4	George Davis	5.62	4	Bobby Wallace	553.84
5	Mickey Doolan	569	5	Rabbit Maranville	.943	5	Kid Elberfeld	5.60	5	Bill Dahlen	548.35
6	Donie Bush	500	6	Bobby Wallace	.940	6	Heinie Wagner	5.57	6	Joe Tinker	543.53
7	Art Fletcher	488	7	Honus Wagner	.940	7	Donie Bush	5.52	7	Freddy Parent	541.24
8	Rabbit Maranville	437	8	Mickey Doolan	.940	8	Joe Tinker	5.51	8	Donie Bush	537.87
9	Roger Peckinpaugh	420	9	Al Bridwell	.939	9	Bill Dahlen	5.49	9	Kid Elberfeld	530.55
10	Bill Dahlen	404	10	Joe Tinker	.938	10	Art Fletcher	5.48	10	Roger Peckinpaugh	530.11
11	Al Bridwell	391	11	Art Fletcher	.938	11	George McBride	5.46	11	Mickey Doolan	527.37
12	Freddy Parent	372	12	Bill Dahlen	.937	12	Mickey Doolan	5.46	12	George McBride	526.48
13	Jack Barry	340	13	Ray Chapman	.936	13	Buck Weaver	5.41	13	Honus Wagner	518.90
14	Kid Elberfeld	337	14	Donie Bush	.936	14	Ray Chapman	5.37	14	Heinie Wagner	517.85
15	George Davis	335	15	Jack Barry	.935	15	Roger Peckinpaugh	5.34	15	Buck Weaver	507.14
16	Doc Lavan	333	16	Buck Weaver	.934	16	Freddy Parent	5.34	16	Al Bridwell	496.22
17	Buck Weaver	321	17	Monte Cross	.933	17	Monte Cross	5.17	17	Ray Chapman	493.85
18	Terry Turner	288	18	Heinie Wagner	.928	18	Al Bridwell	5.14	18	Everett Scott	489.10
19	Tommy Corcoran	283	19	Freddy Parent	.927	19	Everett Scott	5.06	19	Jack Barry	481.57
20	Everett Scott	282	20	Kid Elberfeld	.921	20	Jack Barry	4.80	20	Monte Cross	469.42

Single Season Fielding Leaders—Shortstops: Dead Ball Era (1901-1919)

#	Games			#	Putouts			#	Assists			#	Errors		
1	Joe Tinker	1908	157	1	Donie Bush	1914	425	1	Rabbit Maranville	1914	574	1	John Gochnauer	1903	98
	Donie Bush	1909	157	2	Rabbit Maranville	1914	407	2	Terry Turner	1906	570	2	Bill Keister	1901	97
	Roger Peckinpaugh	1914	157	3	Mickey Doolan	1906	395		Joe Tinker	1908	570	3	Rudy Hulswitt	1903	81
	Donie Bush	1914	157	4	Rabbit Maranville	1915	391	4	Heinie Wagner	1908	569	4	Neal Ball	1908	80
	Doc Lavan	1915	157		Buck Herzog	1915	391	5	George McBride	1908	568	5	Billy Gilbert	1902	78
	Everett Scott	1917	157	6	Buck Weaver	1913	390	6	Donie Bush	1909	567		Ed Abbaticchio	1904	78
7	Bobby Wallace	1905	156	7	Ed Abbaticchio	1905	386	7	Art Fletcher	1917	565		Ollie O'Mara	1915	78
	George McBride	1909	156		Rabbit Maranville	1916	386	8	Donie Bush	1911	556		Whitey Witt	1916	78
	Rabbit Maranville	1914	156	9	Bobby Wallace	1905	385	9	Bill Dahlen	1908	553	9	Kid Elberfeld	1901	76
	George McBride	1914	156	10	Ray Chapman	1915	378	10	Donie Bush	1912	547		Lee Tannehill	1903	76
	Ray Chapman	1917	156	11	Monte Cross	1902	373	11	George McBride	1911	546	11	Ed Abbaticchio	1905	75
12	Freddy Parent	1904	155		Heinie Wagner	1908	373	12	Donie Bush	1914	544		Donie Bush	1911	75
	George McBride	1908	155	13	George McBride	1908	372		Art Fletcher	1915	544		Doc Lavan	1915	75
	Jimmy Esmond	1915	155		Donie Bush	1911	372	14	Bobby Wallace	1901	542	14	Harry Aubrey	1903	74
	Donie Bush	1915	155	15	Dave Bancroft	1918	371	15	Tommy Corcoran	1905	531	15	Frank Shugart	1901	73
	Rabbit Maranville	1916	155	16	Charlie Babb	1904	370	16	Ray Chapman	1917	528	16	Joe Tinker	1902	72
17	6 tied with		154		George McBride	1910	370	17	Joe Tinker	1905	527		Ivy Olson	1911	72
				18	Ed Abbaticchio	1904	367		Rogers Hornsby	1917	527	18	Donie Bush	1909	71
					Buck Weaver	1914	367	19	Donie Bush	1913	526		Buck Weaver	1912	71
					George McBride	1914	367	20	Art Fletcher	1919	521	20	Buck Weaver	1913	70

#	Double Plays			#	Fielding Percentage (minimum 100 games)			#	Range Factor (minimum 100 games)			#	Assists/162 Games (minimum 100 games)		
1	Rabbit Maranville	1914	92	1	Everett Scott	1919	.976	1	Dave Bancroft	1918	6.62	1	Art Fletcher	1919	664.58
2	Buck Herzog	1915	90	2	Everett Scott	1918	.976	2	Rabbit Maranville	1919	6.48	2	Bobby Wallace	1901	655.25
3	Roger Peckinpaugh	1917	84	3	Joe Tinker	1913	.968	3	Bobby Wallace	1901	6.48	3	Rogers Hornsby	1918	645.03
4	Rogers Hornsby	1917	82	4	George McBride	1915	.968	4	Honus Wagner	1903	6.31	4	Art Fletcher	1918	632.32
5	Doc Lavan	1915	81	5	Everett Scott	1916	.967	5	Lee Tannehill	1911	6.29	5	Terry Turner	1906	628.16
6	Rabbit Maranville	1916	79	6	Honus Wagner	1913	.962	6	Rabbit Maranville	1914	6.29	6	Bill Dahlen	1908	622.13
7	Art Fletcher	1915	76	7	Honus Wagner	1912	.962	7	Art Fletcher	1919	6.19	7	Donie Bush	1912	615.38
8	Roger Peckinpaugh	1918	75	8	Roger Peckinpaugh	1918	.961	8	Donie Bush	1911	6.19	8	Art Fletcher	1917	606.16
9	Honus Wagner	1912	74	9	Everett Scott	1915	.961	9	Donie Bush	1914	6.17	9	Art Fletcher	1916	605.37
	Rabbit Maranville	1919	74	10	Zeb Terry	1919	.960	10	Heinie Wagner	1908	6.16	10	Lee Tannehill	1911	603.53
11	Joe Tinker	1912	73	11	Terry Turner	1906	.960	11	Heinie Wagner	1907	6.15	11	Rabbit Maranville	1919	603.48
	Buck Weaver	1913	73	12	George McBride	1913	.960	12	Kid Elberfeld	1901	6.14	12	Bobby Wallace	1908	603.07
13	Billy Gilbert	1902	72	13	Art Fletcher	1918	.959	13	Monte Cross	1902	6.12	13	Heinie Wagner	1908	602.47
	George Davis	1902	72	14	George McBride	1914	.958	14	George Davis	1901	6.12	14	Donie Bush	1911	600.48
	George McBride	1914	72	15	Joe Tinker	1908	.958	15	Herman Long	1902	6.09	15	George Davis	1906	596.51
	Mickey Doolan	1915	72	16	George McBride	1916	.957	16	George McBride	1908	6.06	16	Rabbit Maranville	1914	596.08
17	Mickey Doolan	1910	71	17	Lee Tannehill	1911	.957		Art Fletcher	1918	6.06	17	George Davis	1907	595.23
	Ray Chapman	1917	71	18	Roger Peckinpaugh	1914	.956	18	Kid Elberfeld	1902	6.04	18	George McBride	1908	593.65
	Art Fletcher	1917	71	19	Art Fletcher	1917	.956	19	Buck Weaver	1913	6.03	19	Rogers Hornsby	1917	592.88
20	Lena Blackburne	1918	69	20	Donie Bush	1916	.954	20	2 tied with		6.00	20	Dave Bancroft	1917	592.65

Career Fielding Leaders—Outfielders: Dead Ball Era (1901-1919)

	Games			Putouts			Assists			Errors	
1	Sam Crawford	2,172	1	Tris Speaker	4,013	1	Tris Speaker	295	1	Clyde Milan	191
2	Ty Cobb	1,899	2	Ty Cobb	3,931	2	Ty Cobb	287	2	Ty Cobb	189
3	Sherry Magee	1,861	3	Sherry Magee	3,800	3	Clyde Milan	257	3	Burt Shotton	179
4	Jimmy Sheckard	1,740	4	Clyde Milan	3,590	4	Jimmy Sheckard	249	4	Cy Seymour	165
5	Wildfire Schulte	1,736	5	Jimmy Sheckard	3,518	5	Sam Crawford	241	5	Tris Speaker	144
6	Clyde Milan	1,669	6	Dode Paskert	3,369	6	Harry Hooper	238	6	Jimmy Sheckard	143
7	Tris Speaker	1,607	7	Sam Crawford	3,333	7	John Titus	201	7	George Browne	137
8	Harry Hooper	1,498	8	Max Carey	3,062	8	Dode Paskert	198	8	Patsy Dougherty	132
9	Dode Paskert	1,472	9	Zack Wheat	3,059	9	Wildfire Schulte	197	9	Sam Crawford	127
10	John Titus	1,356	10	Fred Clarke	2,791	10	Max Carey	193	10	Sherry Magee	123
11	Zack Wheat	1,350	11	Cy Seymour	2,784		Duffy Lewis	193	11	Jack Graney	118
12	Fred Clarke	1,327	12	Burt Shotton	2,709	12	Chief Wilson	181	12	Duffy Lewis	114
13	Duffy Lewis	1,306	13	Wildfire Schulte	2,690	13	Mike Mitchell	180		Charlie Hemphill	114
14	Cy Seymour	1,280	14	Roy Thomas	2,675	14	Cy Seymour	179	14	Tilly Walker	113
15	Chief Wilson	1,269	15	Tommy Leach	2,547	15	Gavy Cravath	176		Red Murray	113
16	Topsy Hartsel	1,250	16	Harry Hooper	2,494		Red Murray	176	16	Mike Donlin	111
17	Max Carey	1,217	17	Bob Bescher	2,493		Sherry Magee	176	17	Zack Wheat	110
18	Burt Shotton	1,215	18	Chief Wilson	2,430	18	Joe Jackson	169	18	Bob Bescher	109
19	Jack Graney	1,190	19	Duffy Lewis	2,428	19	Burt Shotton	162		Dode Paskert	109
20	Bob Bescher	1,188	20	Fielder Jones	2,424		Johnny Bates	162	20	2 tied with	108

	Double Plays			Fielding Percentage (minimum 750 games)			Range Factor (minimum 750 games)			Assists/162 Games (minimum 750 games)	
1	Tris Speaker	85	1	Amos Strunk	.980	1	Tris Speaker	2.68	1	Tris Speaker	29.74
	Ty Cobb	85	2	Roy Thomas	.975	2	Max Carey	2.67	2	Tilly Walker	27.70
3	Jimmy Sheckard	62	3	Tommy Leach	.975	3	Tommy Leach	2.47	3	Fred Snodgrass	26.54
4	Max Carey	57	4	Fred Clarke	.974	4	Roy Thomas	2.43	4	Mike Mitchell	26.37
5	Sam Crawford	55	5	Max Flack	.973	5	Dode Paskert	2.42	5	Gavy Cravath	26.28
6	Harry Hooper	54	6	Fielder Jones	.972	6	Zack Wheat	2.38	6	Harry Hooper	25.74
	Clyde Milan	54	7	Dode Paskert	.970	7	Benny Kauff	2.36	7	Max Carey	25.69
8	Chief Wilson	50	8	Max Carey	.970	8	Burt Shotton	2.36	8	Benny Kauff	25.45
	Cy Seymour	50	9	Sherry Magee	.970	9	Rebel Oakes	2.34	9	Ping Bodie	25.23
10	Burt Shotton	48	10	Chief Wilson	.968	10	Cy Seymour	2.31	10	Clyde Milan	24.95
11	Dode Paskert	44	11	Tris Speaker	.968	11	Fred Snodgrass	2.31	11	Max Flack	24.69
	Jimmy Slagle	44	12	Zack Wheat	.967	12	Tilly Walker	2.31	12	Ty Cobb	24.48
	Fielder Jones	44	13	George Burns	.967	13	Clyde Milan	2.30	13	Red Murray	24.35
14	Ginger Beaumont	43	14	Rube Oldring	.966	14	Amos Strunk	2.30	14	Johnny Bates	24.30
15	Wildfire Schulte	42	15	Sam Crawford	.966	15	Bobby Veach	2.25	15	John Titus	24.01
	John Titus	42	16	Wildfire Schulte	.966	16	Fielder Jones	2.22	16	Duffy Lewis	23.94
17	Mike Mitchell	40	17	Ping Bodie	.965	17	Ty Cobb	2.22	17	Joe Jackson	23.93
18	Duffy Lewis	39	18	Fred Snodgrass	.965	18	Bob Bescher	2.21	18	Jimmy Sheckard	23.18
	Sherry Magee	39	19	Shano Collins	.964	19	Fred Clarke	2.21	19	Chief Wilson	23.11
20	Joe Birmingham	38	20	Harry Hooper	.964	20	Jimmy Sheckard	2.16	20	Cy Seymour	22.65

Single Season Fielding Leaders—Outfielders: Dead Ball Era (1901-1919)

	Games				Putouts				Assists				Errors		
1	Jimmy Barrett	1904	162	1	Happy Felsch	1917	440	1	Mike Mitchell	1907	39	1	Cy Seymour	1903	36
2	Tommy Griffith	1915	160		Max Carey	1917	440	2	Jimmy Sheckard	1903	36	2	Dick Harley	1901	30
3	Jack Tobin	1915	158	3	Tris Speaker	1914	423	3	Tris Speaker	1909	35		George Browne	1902	30
4	Chick Stahl	1904	157	4	Max Carey	1916	419		Tris Speaker	1912	35	4	George Barclay	1902	28
	Buck Freeman	1904	157	5	Burt Shotton	1912	381	5	Harry Niles	1906	34		Red Murray	1908	28
	Al Wickland	1914	157	6	Tris Speaker	1915	378		Danny Murphy	1911	34	6	Jesse Burkett	1901	27
	Sam Crawford	1914	157	7	Ty Cobb	1911	376		Gavy Cravath	1914	34	7	Bill Hallman	1901	26
	Burt Shotton	1916	157	8	Tris Speaker	1919	375		Chief Wilson	1914	34		Jesse Burkett	1902	26
9	Spike Shannon	1906	156	9	Tris Speaker	1913	374		Chet Chadbourne	1914	34		Vern Duncan	1914	26
	Ed Hahn	1907	156	10	Roy Thomas	1905	373	10	Clyde Milan	1911	33	10	Mike Donlin	1903	25
	Ty Cobb	1909	156		Ty Cobb	1917	373	11	Joe Jackson	1911	32		Burt Shotton	1912	25
	Zack Wheat	1910	156	12	Tris Speaker	1912	372		Jimmy Sheckard	1911	32		Clyde Milan	1912	25
	Jimmy Sheckard	1911	156		Clyde Milan	1916	372		Benny Kauff	1915	32		Tris Speaker	1913	25
	Tris Speaker	1914	156	14	Max Carey	1912	369		Max Carey	1916	32	14	Danny Green	1901	24
	Bill Hinchman	1915	156	15	Tris Speaker	1917	365		Ping Bodie	1917	32		Ducky Holmes	1901	24
	Ty Cobb	1915	156	16	Rebel Oakes	1911	364		Happy Felsch	1919	32		Vin Campbell	1912	24
	Sam Crawford	1915	156	17	Max Carey	1913	363	17	5 tied with		31		Bobby Veach	1913	24
18	17 tied with		155	18	Fred Clarke	1909	362						Burt Shotton	1914	24
				19	Dode Paskert	1911	361					19	6 tied with		23
				20	Happy Felsch	1919	360								

	Double Plays				Fielding Percentage (minimum 100 games)				Range Factor (minimum 100 games)				Assists/162 Games (minimum 100 games)		
1	Happy Felsch	1919	15	1	Babe Ruth	1919	.996	1	Max Carey	1917	3.06	1	Harry Niles	1906	51.00
	Jack Tobin	1919	15	2	Wildfire Schulte	1908	.994	2	Happy Felsch	1917	3.05	2	Mike Mitchell	1907	43.27
3	Cy Seymour	1905	12	3	Max Flack	1916	.991	3	Max Carey	1918	3.05	3	Jimmy Sheckard	1903	41.96
	Ty Cobb	1907	12	4	Ed Hahn	1907	.990	4	Tris Speaker	1919	2.99	4	Danny Murphy	1911	40.50
	Ginger Beaumont	1907	12	5	George Burns	1919	.990	5	Edd Roush	1918	2.95	5	Tris Speaker	1909	39.93
	Tris Speaker	1909	12	6	Amos Strunk	1912	.990	6	Carson Bigbee	1919	2.94	6	Patsy Donovan	1902	38.57
	Jimmy Sheckard	1911	12	7	Tommy Leach	1913	.990	7	Max Carey	1916	2.93	7	Gavy Cravath	1914	38.52
	Tris Speaker	1914	12	8	Edd Roush	1919	.989	8	Dode Paskert	1913	2.91	8	Happy Felsch	1919	38.40
9	Fielder Jones	1902	11	9	Cy Williams	1916	.989	9	Hi Myers	1918	2.91	9	Benny Kauff	1915	38.12
	Jimmy Sebring	1903	11	10	Birdie Cree	1913	.988	10	Tris Speaker	1913	2.91	10	Jack Tobin	1914	38.05
	Phil Geier	1904	11	11	Sam Crawford	1905	.988	11	Happy Felsch	1919	2.90	11	Joe Birmingham	1910	37.75
	Ben Koehler	1905	11	12	Fielder Jones	1906	.988	12	Tris Speaker	1914	2.90	12	Chet Chadbourne	1914	37.73
	Burt Shotton	1913	11	13	Amos Strunk	1918	.988	13	Tris Speaker	1918	2.89	13	Gavy Cravath	1912	37.27
	Chief Wilson	1914	11	14	Fred Clarke	1907	.987	14	Hi Myers	1919	2.83	14	Jimmy Barrett	1901	37.20
15	9 tied with		10	15	Willie Keeler	1906	.987	15	Tommy Leach	1910	2.79	15	Tris Speaker	1912	37.06
				16	Fred Clarke	1909	.987	16	Ty Cobb	1911	2.74	16	Willie Hogan	1911	36.88
				17	Harry Bay	1904	.987	17	Dode Paskert	1910	2.73	17	Chief Wilson	1914	35.77
				18	Amos Strunk	1914	.987	18	Tris Speaker	1917	2.73	18	Ping Bodie	1917	35.75
				19	Amos Strunk	1917	.986	19	Roy Thomas	1905	2.72	19	Tilly Walker	1918	35.67
				20	Max Flack	1919	.986	20	Burt Shotton	1911	2.71	20	Bill Keister	1903	35.64

Career Fielding Leaders—Pitchers: Lively Ball Era (1920-1945)

Games

1	Waite Hoyt	659
2	Charlie Root	632
3	Lefty Grove	616
4	Red Ruffing	607
5	Ted Lyons	591
6	Paul Derringer	579
7	Larry French	570
8	Jack Russell	558
9	Mel Harder	554
	Jesse Haines	554
11	Firpo Marberry	551
12	Rube Walberg	544
13	Guy Bush	542
	Syl Johnson	542
15	Earl Whitehill	541
16	Carl Hubbell	535
17	Bump Hadley	528
18	Sad Sam Jones	518
19	Tom Zachary	514
20	Freddie Fitzsimmons	513

Putouts

1	Freddie Fitzsimmons	237
2	Ted Lyons	217
3	Mel Harder	204
4	Burleigh Grimes	191
5	Dolf Luque	179
6	Earl Whitehill	166
7	George Uhle	165
8	Sad Sam Jones	161
9	Eddie Rommel	159
10	Carl Hubbell	155
11	Bill Lee	153
	Waite Hoyt	153
13	Willis Hudlin	150
14	Paul Derringer	147
	Red Ruffing	147
16	Curt Davis	146
17	Tommy Bridges	143
18	Hal Schumacher	142
19	George Blaeholder	141
	Guy Bush	141

Assists

1	Burleigh Grimes	1,030
2	Freddie Fitzsimmons	942
3	Ted Lyons	933
4	Carl Hubbell	824
5	Eppa Rixey	811
6	Eddie Rommel	810
7	Waite Hoyt	805
8	Tom Zachary	753
9	Willis Hudlin	734
10	Red Faber	733
11	Dolf Luque	727
12	Mel Harder	714
13	Earl Whitehill	701
14	Lefty Grove	695
15	Sad Sam Jones	694
16	Bucky Walters	688
17	Herb Pennock	679
18	Red Ruffing	672
19	Howard Ehmke	661
20	Paul Derringer	656

Errors

1	Bill Lee	55
2	Burleigh Grimes	54
3	Ted Lyons	51
4	Earl Whitehill	47
5	Mel Harder	44
6	Dolf Luque	42
	Red Faber	42
8	Sad Sam Jones	41
9	Larry French	39
10	Willis Hudlin	38
	Lefty Grove	38
	Sam Gray	38
13	Danny MacFayden	37
	Rube Walberg	37
15	George Blaeholder	36
16	Hugh McQuillan	35
17	Thornton Lee	34
	Howard Ehmke	34
19	Carl Hubbell	33
	Waite Hoyt	33

Double Plays

1	Freddie Fitzsimmons	79
2	Bucky Walters	69
3	Burleigh Grimes	66
4	Ted Lyons	57
5	Carl Hubbell	55
6	Willis Hudlin	54
7	Eddie Rommel	51
8	Red Ruffing	50
9	George Uhle	41
10	Claude Passeau	40
	Larry French	40
12	Curt Davis	39
	Waite Hoyt	39
14	Eldon Auker	38
	Guy Bush	38
16	Mel Harder	37
	Danny MacFayden	37
	Bob Smith	37
	Carl Mays	37
	Sad Sam Jones	37

Fielding Percentage
(minimum 150 games)

1	Joe Dobson	.994
2	Joe Beggs	.993
3	Hal Newhouser	.988
4	Lon Warneke	.988
5	Walter Johnson	.988
6	Pete Alexander	.986
7	Urban Shocker	.985
8	Hooks Dauss	.985
9	General Crowder	.984
10	Bob Klinger	.982
11	Red Lucas	.981
12	Bob Smith	.981
13	Joe Bush	.981
14	Eppa Rixey	.980
15	Hugh Casey	.980
16	Jakie May	.980
17	Spud Chandler	.979
18	Herb Pennock	.979
19	Art Nehf	.979
20	Harry Gumbert	.978

Assists/162 Innings
(minimum 150 games)

1	Wilcy Moore	59.46
2	Carl Mays	58.71
3	Sherry Smith	53.92
4	Chad Kimsey	52.16
5	Johnny Gorsica	51.95
6	Eddie Rommel	51.33
7	Harry Gumbert	51.06
8	Hooks Dauss	49.50
9	Benny Frey	49.44
10	Ben Cantwell	48.90
11	Red Oldham	48.51
12	Slim Harriss	48.23
13	Leo Sweetland	47.90
14	Burleigh Grimes	47.82
15	Bill Doak	47.76
16	Jack Russell	47.56
17	Fred Heimach	47.52
18	Freddie Fitzsimmons	47.34
19	Howard Ehmke	47.07
20	Jack Quinn	46.03

Single Season Fielding Leaders—Pitchers: Lively Ball Era (1920-1945)

Games

1	Ace Adams	1943	70
2	Andy Karl	1945	67
3	Ace Adams	1944	65
	Ace Adams	1945	65
5	Firpo Marberry	1926	64
6	Joe Heving	1944	63
7	Clint Brown	1939	61
	Ace Adams	1942	61
9	Garland Braxton	1927	58
	Russ Van Atta	1935	58
11	Johnny Hutchings	1945	57
12	Eddie Rommel	1923	56
	Firpo Marberry	1927	56
	Hugh Mulcahy	1937	56
15	Firpo Marberry	1925	55
	Bump Hadley	1931	55
	Jim Walkup	1935	55
18	6 tied with		54

Putouts

1	Urban Shocker	1922	33
2	George Uhle	1926	30
3	Eldon Auker	1940	27
	Russ Christopher	1944	27
5	Russ Christopher	1945	26
6	Burleigh Grimes	1924	25
	George Blaeholder	1931	25
	Spud Chandler	1942	25
9	Joe Bush	1920	24
	Jesse Barnes	1921	24
	Joe Bush	1924	24
	Willis Hudlin	1929	24
	Freddie Fitzsimmons	1934	24
	Dizzy Trout	1942	24
	Red Barrett	1945	24
16	Stan Coveleski	1921	23
	Freddie Fitzsimmons	1928	23
	Carl Hubbell	1933	23
19	7 tied with		22

Assists

1	Carl Mays	1926	117
2	Hooks Dauss	1920	114
3	Eddie Rommel	1923	109
4	Stan Coveleski	1921	108
5	Carl Mays	1920	106
	Burleigh Grimes	1928	106
7	Pete Alexander	1920	105
8	Dana Fillingim	1920	104
	Carl Mays	1921	104
10	Eddie Rommel	1923	101
	Howard Ehmke	1923	101
12	Eppa Rixey	1921	97
	Eddie Rommel	1924	97
14	Bucky Walters	1936	96
15	Burleigh Grimes	1920	95
	Curt Davis	1934	95
17	6 tied with		94

Errors

1	Allen Sothoron	1920	14
2	Herman Pillette	1923	11
3	Red Faber	1920	10
	Hippo Vaughn	1920	10
	Burleigh Grimes	1923	10
6	Hugh McQuillan	1921	9
	Hugh McQuillan	1922	9
	Lefty Grove	1927	9
	Phil Collins	1932	9
	Dizzy Trout	1945	9
11	Pete Donohue	1923	8
	Sam Gray	1931	8
	Curt Davis	1934	8
	Van Lingle Mungo	1936	8
15	34 tied with		7

Double Plays

1	Eddie Rommel	1924	12
	Curt Davis	1934	12
3	Art Nehf	1920	11
	Burleigh Grimes	1925	11
5	Carl Mays	1926	10
	Willis Hudlin	1931	10
	Freddie Fitzsimmons	1932	10
	Freddie Fitzsimmons	1934	10
	Bucky Walters	1939	10
	Boo Ferriss	1945	10
11	11 tied with		9

Fielding Percentage
(minimum 25 games)

1	516 tied with	1.000

Assists/162 Innings
(minimum 25 games)

1	Johnny Gorsica	1942	88.64
2	Sherry Smith	1920	74.86
3	Ad Liska	1933	70.65
4	Fred Heimach	1926	70.29
5	Danny Boone	1923	69.10
6	Hooks Dauss	1920	68.32
7	Wilcy Moore	1927	67.69
8	Carl Mays	1926	67.45
9	Carl Mays	1924	67.38
10	Ed Baecht	1926	66.54
11	Joe Pate	1926	65.95
12	Bert Cole	1927	65.61
13	Fritz Coumbe	1921	65.42
14	Wilcy Moore	1929	65.32
15	Harry Gumbert	1937	64.69
16	Sherry Smith	1921	64.68
17	Jack Knight	1926	63.59
18	Carl Mays	1922	63.45
19	Slim Harriss	1924	63.22
20	Junior Thompson	1942	62.14

Career Fielding Leaders—Catchers: Lively Ball Era (1920-1945)

Games

1	Al Lopez	1,805
2	Gabby Hartnett	1,793
3	Rick Ferrell	1,769
4	Bill Dickey	1,669
5	Luke Sewell	1,562
6	Ernie Lombardi	1,457
7	Mickey Cochrane	1,451
8	Rollie Hemsley	1,435
9	Gus Mancuso	1,360
10	Jimmie Wilson	1,351
11	Muddy Ruel	1,317
12	Spud Davis	1,282
13	Bob O'Farrell	1,249
14	Frankie Hayes	1,205
15	Wally Schang	961
16	Cy Perkins	952
17	Mickey Owen	943
18	Shanty Hogan	899
19	Zack Taylor	856
20	Ray Schalk	822

Putouts

1	Bill Dickey	7,764
2	Gabby Hartnett	7,292
3	Rick Ferrell	7,114
4	Mickey Cochrane	6,409
5	Al Lopez	6,327
6	Rollie Hemsley	5,695
7	Gus Mancuso	5,613
8	Luke Sewell	5,450
9	Ernie Lombardi	5,336
10	Muddy Ruel	4,946
11	Jimmie Wilson	4,933
12	Frankie Hayes	4,417
13	Spud Davis	4,374
14	Bob O'Farrell	4,042
15	Mickey Owen	3,717
16	Wally Schang	3,313
17	Harry Danning	3,257
18	Cy Perkins	3,199
19	Shanty Hogan	3,190
20	Mike Tresh	3,148

Assists

1	Gabby Hartnett	1,254
2	Rick Ferrell	1,105
3	Luke Sewell	1,084
4	Al Lopez	1,057
5	Muddy Ruel	1,035
6	Jimmie Wilson	932
7	Bill Dickey	925
8	Bob O'Farrell	894
9	Rollie Hemsley	855
10	Mickey Cochrane	840
11	Gus Mancuso	803
12	Ernie Lombardi	798
13	Cy Perkins	785
14	Wally Schang	771
15	Zack Taylor	752
16	Ray Schalk	717
17	Spud Davis	684
18	Johnny Bassler	666
19	Mickey O'Neil	651
20	Hank Severeid	645

Errors

1	Luke Sewell	150
2	Rollie Hemsley	149
3	Gus Mancuso	148
4	Gabby Hartnett	139
5	Jimmie Wilson	137
6	Ernie Lombardi	134
	Rick Ferrell	134
8	Al Lopez	119
	Bob O'Farrell	119
10	Frankie Hayes	116
11	Wally Schang	115
12	Mickey Cochrane	111
13	Bill Dickey	105
14	Muddy Ruel	104
15	Val Picinich	92
16	Cy Perkins	87
17	Zack Taylor	86
18	Spud Davis	84
19	Al Todd	81
	Steve O'Neill	81

Double Plays

1	Gabby Hartnett	163
2	Jimmie Wilson	153
3	Luke Sewell	138
4	Rick Ferrell	134
5	Bill Dickey	133
6	Al Lopez	132
7	Rollie Hemsley	131
8	Muddy Ruel	129
9	Mickey Cochrane	104
	Ray Schalk	104
11	Gus Mancuso	100
12	Frankie Hayes	99
13	Ernie Lombardi	98
14	Spud Davis	95
15	Bob O'Farrell	92
	Wally Schang	92
17	Zack Taylor	87
18	Shanty Hogan	73
	Cy Perkins	73
20	2 tied with	70

Fielding Percentage
(minimum 500 games)

1	Frankie Pytlak	.991
2	Gene Desautels	.989
3	Ray Berres	.989
4	Bill Dickey	.988
5	Buddy Rosar	.988
6	Earl Grace	.987
7	Ray Hayworth	.987
8	Ray Mueller	.986
9	Moe Berg	.986
10	Shanty Hogan	.985
11	Mickey Cochrane	.985
12	Harry Danning	.985
13	Hank Severeid	.985
14	Frank Snyder	.984
15	Al Lopez	.984
16	Bubbles Hargrave	.984
17	Gabby Hartnett	.984
18	Rick Ferrell	.984
19	Roy Spencer	.984
20	Spud Davis	.984

Passed Balls

1	Ernie Lombardi	147
2	Rick Ferrell	141
3	Frankie Hayes	128
4	Gabby Hartnett	126
5	Luke Sewell	91
6	Mickey Cochrane	88
	Jimmie Wilson	88
8	Bill Dickey	76
	Wally Schang	76
10	Gus Mancuso	73
11	Zack Taylor	72
	Earl Smith	72
13	Rollie Hemsley	69
14	Cy Perkins	68
15	Mike Tresh	66
	Al Lopez	66
17	Val Picinich	64
	Steve O'Neill	64
19	Mickey Owen	54
	Spud Davis	54

Assists/162 Games
(minimum 500 games)

1	Mickey O'Neil	164.02
2	Johnny Bassler	148.00
3	Zack Taylor	142.32
4	Ray Schalk	141.31
5	Hank Severeid	140.26
6	Steve O'Neill	133.70
7	Cy Perkins	133.58
8	Butch Henline	131.63
9	Frank Snyder	130.82
10	Wally Schang	129.97
11	Muddy Ruel	127.31
12	Hank DeBerry	125.51
13	Bob O'Farrell	115.96
14	Gabby Hartnett	113.30
15	Earl Smith	112.90
16	Luke Sewell	112.43
17	Birdie Tebbetts	112.11
18	Val Picinich	111.95
19	Jimmie Wilson	111.76
20	Johnny Gooch	109.21

Single Season Fielding Leaders—Catchers: Lively Ball Era (1920-1945)

Games

	Player	Year	
1	Ray Mueller	1944	155
	Frankie Hayes	1944	155
3	Ray Schalk	1920	151
	Frankie Hayes	1945	151
5	Mike Tresh	1945	150
6	Steve O'Neill	1920	148
7	Muddy Ruel	1924	147
8	Cy Perkins	1920	146
	Bob O'Farrell	1926	146
10	Roy Spencer	1931	145
11	Frankie Hayes	1936	143
12	Ray Schalk	1922	142
	Gus Mancuso	1933	142
14	Cy Perkins	1921	141
	Cy Perkins	1922	141
	Luke Sewell	1933	141
	Rollie Hemsley	1935	141
18	Jimmie Wilson	1928	140
	Gabby Hartnett	1933	140
	Ray Mueller	1943	140

Putouts

	Player	Year	
1	Bill Dickey	1933	721
2	Bill Dickey	1937	692
3	Bill Dickey	1931	670
4	Mickey Cochrane	1929	659
5	Mickey Cochrane	1930	654
6	Mickey Cochrane	1932	652
7	Gabby Hartnett	1930	646
8	Mickey Cochrane	1928	645
9	Roy Spencer	1931	642
10	Bill Dickey	1932	639
	Frankie Hayes	1945	639
12	Frankie Hayes	1944	636
13	Harry Danning	1940	634
14	Mike Tresh	1940	619
15	Muddy Ruel	1924	612
16	Gabby Hartnett	1934	605
17	Al Todd	1937	603
18	Mickey Owen	1942	595
19	3 tied with		591

Assists

	Player	Year	
1	Cy Perkins	1920	179
2	Mickey O'Neil	1920	153
3	Ray Schalk	1922	150
4	Patsy Gharrity	1920	148
5	Muddy Ruel	1923	146
6	Bob O'Farrell	1922	143
7	Ray Schalk	1920	138
8	Cy Perkins	1921	137
9	Hank Severeid	1924	134
10	Johnny Bassler	1923	133
11	Cy Perkins	1922	130
12	Ray Schalk	1921	129
13	Steve O'Neill	1920	128
14	Hank Severeid	1922	123
	Zack Taylor	1926	123
16	Walter Schmidt	1921	120
17	Luke Sewell	1927	119
18	Zack Taylor	1923	118
	Bob O'Farrell	1923	118
20	4 tied with		117

Errors

	Player	Year	
1	Mickey Cochrane	1928	25
2	Buck Crouse	1924	23
	Gabby Hartnett	1925	23
4	Ivy Wingo	1920	21
5	Patsy Gharrity	1920	20
	Cy Perkins	1921	20
	Eddie Ainsmith	1922	20
	Luke Sewell	1927	20
	Al Todd	1937	20
10	Bob O'Farrell	1920	19
	Wally Schang	1921	19
	Gus Mancuso	1933	19
13	Mickey O'Neil	1920	18
	Pickles Dillhoefer	1920	18
	Ivy Wingo	1921	18
	Gabby Hartnett	1924	18
	Fred Hofmann	1927	18
	Al Spohrer	1929	18
	Luke Sewell	1929	18
20	10 tied with		17

Double Plays

	Player	Year	
1	Frankie Hayes	1945	29
2	Muddy Ruel	1924	23
3	Bob O'Farrell	1922	22
4	Gabby Hartnett	1927	21
5	Ray Schalk	1923	20
6	Ray Schalk	1920	19
	Steve O'Neill	1920	19
	Ray Schalk	1921	19
9	Ray Mueller	1925	18
10	Muddy Ruel	1922	17
	Zack Taylor	1926	17
	Jimmie Wilson	1928	17
	Merv Shea	1933	17
	Ray Mueller	1943	17
15	Cy Perkins	1921	16
	Ray Schalk	1922	16
	Jimmie Wilson	1929	16
	Gabby Hartnett	1931	16
	Rollie Hemsley	1936	16
	Bennie Warren	1941	16

Fielding Percentage
(minimum 100 games)

	Player	Year	
1	Earl Grace	1932	.998
2	Shanty Hogan	1931	.996
3	Gabby Hartnett	1937	.996
4	Bill Dickey	1931	.996
5	Gabby Hartnett	1934	.996
6	Merv Shea	1933	.996
7	Ray Berres	1941	.995
8	Bill Dickey	1935	.995
9	Mickey Owen	1941	.995
10	Spud Davis	1931	.994
11	Rollie Hemsley	1940	.994
12	Bill Dickey	1940	.994
13	Ray Hayworth	1933	.994
14	Bill Dickey	1941	.994
15	Harry Danning	1941	.993
16	Mickey Cochrane	1932	.993
17	Mickey Cochrane	1930	.993
18	Hank Severeid	1923	.993
19	Bill Dickey	1933	.993
20	Rick Ferrell	1941	.992

Passed Balls

	Player	Year	
1	Rick Ferrell	1945	21
2	Rick Ferrell	1944	20
3	Rick Ferrell	1939	19
4	Steve O'Neill	1922	17
	Ernie Lombardi	1932	17
	Frankie Hayes	1936	17
	Rick Ferrell	1940	17
	Jake Early	1941	17
9	Cy Perkins	1923	16
	Ernie Lombardi	1941	16
11	Ernie Lombardi	1939	15
	Frankie Hayes	1941	15
	Hal Wagner	1942	15
14	Cy Perkins	1922	14
	Steve O'Neill	1923	14
	Steve O'Neill	1924	14
	Frankie Hayes	1942	14
	Frankie Hayes	1945	14
19	10 tied with		13

Assists/162 Games
(minimum 100 games)

	Player	Year	
1	Mickey O'Neil	1920	236.06
2	Cy Perkins	1920	198.62
3	Patsy Gharrity	1920	198.15
4	Bob O'Farrell	1922	185.33
5	Muddy Ruel	1923	177.83
6	Walter Schmidt	1921	175.14
7	Verne Clemons	1920	174.58
8	Ivy Wingo	1920	174.11
9	Ray Schalk	1922	171.13
10	Johnny Bassler	1923	168.33
11	Gabby Hartnett	1925	167.89
12	Hank Severeid	1924	166.98
13	Ray Schalk	1921	165.86
14	Mickey O'Neil	1924	165.06
15	Zack Taylor	1926	162.00
16	Luke Sewell	1928	160.63
17	Johnny Gooch	1922	160.43
18	Johnny Bassler	1921	159.18
19	Cy Perkins	1921	157.40
20	Frank Snyder	1921	157.19

Career Fielding Leaders—First Basemen: Lively Ball Era (1920-1945)

Games

1	Lou Gehrig	2,142
2	Charlie Grimm	2,076
3	Joe Kuhel	1,989
4	Jimmie Foxx	1,919
5	Jim Bottomley	1,885
6	Joe Judge	1,608
7	Bill Terry	1,579
8	Lu Blue	1,571
9	Dolph Camilli	1,476
10	George Sisler	1,416
11	Gus Suhr	1,406
12	George Kelly	1,310
13	Hal Trosky	1,241
14	Earl Sheely	1,220
15	Frank McCormick	1,206
16	George McQuinn	1,163
17	Wally Pipp	1,143
18	Elbie Fletcher	1,062
19	Babe Dahlgren	1,007
20	Jack Fournier	993

Putouts

1	Charlie Grimm	20,208
2	Lou Gehrig	19,510
3	Joe Kuhel	18,761
4	Jim Bottomley	18,337
5	Jimmie Foxx	17,212
6	Bill Terry	15,972
7	Lu Blue	15,614
8	Joe Judge	14,837
9	Dolph Camilli	13,724
10	George Kelly	13,668
11	Gus Suhr	13,103
12	George Sisler	13,093
13	Earl Sheely	12,087
14	Wally Pipp	11,775
15	Frank McCormick	11,761
16	Hal Trosky	11,395
17	Elbie Fletcher	10,592
18	George McQuinn	10,425
19	Babe Dahlgren	9,432
20	George Burns	9,374

Assists

1	Jimmie Foxx	1,222
2	Charlie Grimm	1,198
3	Joe Kuhel	1,122
4	George Sisler	1,112
5	Bill Terry	1,108
6	Lou Gehrig	1,087
7	Lu Blue	1,016
8	Joe Judge	996
9	Dolph Camilli	957
10	George Kelly	843
11	Frank McCormick	842
12	George McQuinn	834
13	Jim Bottomley	814
14	Elbie Fletcher	773
15	Gus Suhr	766
16	Earl Sheely	744
17	Dick Siebert	741
18	Rudy York	733
19	Hal Trosky	719
20	Wally Pipp	700

Errors

1	Jim Bottomley	223
2	Lou Gehrig	193
	George Sisler	193
4	Lu Blue	191
5	Joe Kuhel	169
6	Jimmie Foxx	155
7	Charlie Grimm	146
8	Dolph Camilli	141
9	Jack Fournier	139
10	Bill Terry	138
11	George Burns	118
12	Gus Suhr	116
13	Hal Trosky	114
	George Kelly	114
15	Earl Sheely	113
16	Don Hurst	110
17	Buddy Hassett	109
18	Rudy York	106
19	Nick Etten	99
20	Babe Dahlgren	98

Double Plays

1	Charlie Grimm	1,708
2	Joe Kuhel	1,702
3	Jim Bottomley	1,582
4	Lou Gehrig	1,574
5	Jimmie Foxx	1,528
6	Bill Terry	1,334
7	Joe Judge	1,244
8	Dolph Camilli	1,189
9	Lu Blue	1,187
10	George Sisler	1,140
11	Gus Suhr	1,086
12	George Kelly	1,085
13	Hal Trosky	1,083
14	Frank McCormick	1,059
15	George McQuinn	959
16	Earl Sheely	890
17	Elbie Fletcher	865
18	Wally Pipp	861
19	Babe Dahlgren	832
20	Zeke Bonura	815

Fielding Percentage
(minimum 750 games)

1	Joe Judge	.995
2	Stuffy McInnis	.995
3	Frank McCormick	.994
4	Walter Holke	.993
5	Charlie Grimm	.993
6	Elbie Fletcher	.993
7	George McQuinn	.993
8	Zeke Bonura	.992
9	Jack Burns	.992
10	Wally Pipp	.992
11	George Kelly	.992
12	Bill Terry	.992
13	Ripper Collins	.992
14	Phil Todt	.992
15	Gus Suhr	.992
16	Jimmie Foxx	.992
17	Joe Kuhel	.992
18	Earl Sheely	.991
19	Hank Greenberg	.991
20	Johnny Mize	.991

Assists/162 Games
(minimum 750 games)

1	George Sisler	127.22
2	Dick Siebert	126.49
3	Rudy York	125.92
4	Elbie Fletcher	117.92
5	George McQuinn	116.17
6	Bill Terry	113.68
7	Frank McCormick	113.10
8	Phil Todt	111.64
9	George Burns	111.43
10	Ripper Collins	110.17
11	Don Hurst	110.00
12	Zeke Bonura	107.10
13	Dolph Camilli	105.04
14	Lu Blue	104.77
15	George Kelly	104.25
16	Jimmie Foxx	103.16
17	Hank Greenberg	101.73
18	Joe Judge	100.34
19	Wally Pipp	99.21
20	Earl Sheely	98.79

Single Season Fielding Leaders—First Basemen: Lively Ball Era (1920-1945)

Games

1	Babe Dahlgren	1944	158
2	Lou Gehrig	1937	157
	Lou Gehrig	1938	157
	Dolph Camilli	1939	157
5	Jake Daubert	1922	156
	Earl Sheely	1923	156
	Dolph Camilli	1935	156
	Buddy Hassett	1936	156
	Gus Suhr	1936	156
	Frank McCormick	1939	156
	Les Fleming	1942	156
12	18 tied with		155

Putouts

1	George Kelly	1920	1,759
2	Phil Todt	1926	1,755
3	Wally Pipp	1926	1,710
4	Wally Pipp	1922	1,667
5	Lou Gehrig	1927	1,662
6	Jim Bottomley	1927	1,656
7	Jake Daubert	1922	1,652
8	Wally Pipp	1920	1,649
9	George Kelly	1922	1,642
10	Earl Sheely	1921	1,637
11	Wally Pipp	1921	1,624
12	Bill Terry	1927	1,621
13	Jim Bottomley	1926	1,607
14	Charlie Grimm	1924	1,596
15	Bill Terry	1934	1,592
16	Elbie Fletcher	1937	1,587
	Frank McCormick	1940	1,587
18	Stuffy McInnis	1920	1,586
19	Bill Terry	1928	1,584
20	Bill Terry	1929	1,575

Assists

1	Rudy York	1943	149
2	Rudy York	1942	146
3	George Sisler	1920	140
4	Mike Rocco	1944	138
5	Bill Terry	1932	137
6	Frank McCormick	1944	135
	Dick Siebert	1945	135
8	George Sisler	1925	131
	George Sisler	1927	131
10	Dolph Camilli	1939	129
11	Bill Terry	1930	128
	Babe Dahlgren	1944	128
13	Phil Todt	1926	126
	Elbie Fletcher	1938	126
15	George Sisler	1922	125
	Jack Burns	1931	125
17	George McQuinn	1940	124
18	Charlie Grimm	1932	123
19	Buddy Hassett	1936	121
20	Hank Greenberg	1938	120

Errors

1	George Sisler	1929	28
	Red Kress	1933	28
3	George Sisler	1925	26
	Buddy Hassett	1936	26
	Mickey Vernon	1942	26
6	Jack Fournier	1920	25
7	Jim Bottomley	1924	24
	George Sisler	1927	24
	Don Hurst	1929	24
10	George Sisler	1924	23
	Jim Poole	1925	23
	Eddie Morgan	1932	23
	Don Hurst	1933	23
	Nick Etten	1941	23
15	7 tied with		22

Double Plays

1	Rudy York	1944	163
2	Mike Rocco	1944	158
3	Lou Gehrig	1938	157
	George McQuinn	1940	157
5	Jimmie Foxx	1938	153
	Frank McCormick	1939	153
7	Les Fleming	1942	152
8	Joe Kuhel	1935	150
	Zeke Bonura	1936	150
	Gus Suhr	1938	150
11	Jim Bottomley	1927	149
	Tony Lupien	1943	149
	Nick Etten	1945	149
14	Bill Terry	1928	148
	Nick Etten	1943	148
16	Charlie Grimm	1928	147
	Harvey Hendrick	1931	147
18	Bill Terry	1929	146
	Hank Greenberg	1938	146
	Frank McCormick	1940	146

Fielding Percentage
(minimum 100 games)

1	Stuffy McInnis	1921	.999
2	Joe Judge	1930	.998
3	Jimmie Foxx	1935	.997
4	Walter Holke	1921	.997
5	Phil Todt	1928	.997
6	Stuffy McInnis	1922	.997
7	Earl Sheely	1929	.996
8	Elbie Fletcher	1943	.996
9	Charlie Grimm	1933	.996
10	Zeke Bonura	1934	.996
11	Joe Judge	1921	.996
12	Joe Judge	1928	.996
13	Joe Judge	1922	.996
14	Bill Terry	1935	.996
15	Babe Dahlgren	1945	.996
16	Wally Pipp	1927	.996
17	Stuffy McInnis	1920	.996
18	Joe Judge	1929	.996
19	Frank McCormick	1939	.996
20	Joe Judge	1927	.996

Assists/162 Games
(minimum 100 games)

1	Rudy York	1943	155.73
2	Rudy York	1942	155.61
3	Dick Siebert	1945	148.78
4	Buddy Hassett	1939	147.51
5	George Sisler	1920	147.27
6	Jimmie Foxx	1941	146.32
7	Buddy Hassett	1942	144.82
8	Mike Rocco	1944	144.23
9	Bill Terry	1932	144.12
10	George Sisler	1922	143.62
11	Buddy Hassett	1937	143.45
12	Frank McCormick	1944	142.94
13	George Sisler	1927	142.43
14	Jack Burns	1931	141.61
15	George Sisler	1925	141.48
16	George McQuinn	1941	141.26
17	George Burns	1924	140.32
18	Elbie Fletcher	1938	139.81
19	Dick Siebert	1941	139.61
20	Lu Blue	1932	135.77

Career Fielding Leaders—Second Basemen: Lively Ball Era (1920-1945)

	Games			Putouts			Assists			Errors	
1	Charlie Gehringer	2,209	1	Charlie Gehringer	5,369	1	Charlie Gehringer	7,068	1	Billy Herman	345
2	Frankie Frisch	1,746	2	Billy Herman	4,629	2	Frankie Frisch	5,934	2	Charlie Gehringer	309
3	Billy Herman	1,743	3	Frankie Frisch	4,267	3	Billy Herman	5,531	3	Rogers Hornsby	301
4	Rogers Hornsby	1,535	4	Buddy Myer	3,487	4	Hughie Critz	5,144	4	Frankie Frisch	275
5	Hughie Critz	1,453	5	Hughie Critz	3,447	5	Rogers Hornsby	5,061	5	Bucky Harris	259
6	Tony Lazzeri	1,451	6	Ski Melillo	3,428	6	Ski Melillo	4,448	6	Tony Lazzeri	252
7	Buddy Myer	1,340	7	Bucky Harris	3,377	7	Tony Lazzeri	4,432	7	George Grantham	250
8	Ski Melillo	1,316	8	Tony Lazzeri	3,341	8	Buddy Myer	4,068	8	Hughie Critz	232
9	Bucky Harris	1,246	9	Rogers Hornsby	3,157	9	Tony Cuccinello	3,891	9	Ski Melillo	215
10	Max Bishop	1,230	10	Tony Cuccinello	2,883	10	Max Bishop	3,850	10	Buddy Myer	200
11	Tony Cuccinello	1,205	11	Max Bishop	2,752	11	Bucky Harris	3,814	11	Marty McManus	194
12	Bobby Doerr	1,023	12	Bobby Doerr	2,625	12	Bobby Doerr	3,150	12	Tony Cuccinello	190
13	Eddie Collins	1,010	13	Eddie Collins	2,616	13	Eddie Collins	3,059	13	Joe Gordon	171
14	Marty McManus	927	14	Marty McManus	2,430	14	Jackie Hayes	2,983	14	Bill Wambsganss	168
15	Jackie Hayes	903	15	Jackie Hayes	2,189	15	Marty McManus	2,853	15	Max Bishop	163
16	Lonny Frey	871	16	Lonny Frey	2,145	16	Lonny Frey	2,750	16	Jimmy Dykes	157
17	Joe Gordon	862	17	Joe Gordon	2,127	17	Joe Gordon	2,745		Eddie Collins	157
18	George Grantham	847	18	George Grantham	1,987	18	George Grantham	2,712	18	Fresco Thompson	145
19	Aaron Ward	804	19	Bill Wambsganss	1,952	19	Aaron Ward	2,541	19	Bobby Doerr	139
20	Bill Wambsganss	734	20	Aaron Ward	1,842	20	Burgess Whitehead	2,233	20	Bill Regan	138

	Double Plays			Fielding Percentage (minimum 750 games)			Range Factor (minimum 750 games)			Assists/162 Games (minimum 750 games)	
1	Charlie Gehringer	1,444	1	Bobby Doerr	.976	1	Ski Melillo	5.98	1	Hughie Critz	573.52
2	Billy Herman	1,148	2	Jackie Hayes	.976	2	Hughie Critz	5.91	2	Frankie Frisch	550.58
3	Frankie Frisch	1,057	3	Max Bishop	.976	3	Frankie Frisch	5.84	3	Ski Melillo	547.55
4	Ski Melillo	965	4	Charlie Gehringer	.976	4	Billy Herman	5.83	4	Jackie Hayes	535.16
5	Buddy Myer	963	5	Buddy Myer	.974	5	Bucky Harris	5.77	5	Rogers Hornsby	534.13
6	Hughie Critz	960	6	Lonny Frey	.974	6	Jackie Hayes	5.73	6	Tony Cuccinello	523.11
7	Rogers Hornsby	880	7	Frankie Frisch	.974	7	Marty McManus	5.70	7	George Grantham	518.71
8	Tony Cuccinello	812	8	Hughie Critz	.974	8	Joe Gordon	5.65	8	Charlie Gehringer	518.34
9	Tony Lazzeri	807	9	Ski Melillo	.973	9	Bobby Doerr	5.65	9	Joe Gordon	515.88
10	Bucky Harris	797	10	Eddie Collins	.973	10	Buddy Myer	5.64	10	Billy Herman	514.07
11	Bobby Doerr	778	11	Tony Cuccinello	.973	11	Charlie Gehringer	5.63	11	Aaron Ward	511.99
12	Joe Gordon	674	12	Aaron Ward	.970	12	Tony Cuccinello	5.62	12	Lonny Frey	511.48
13	Jackie Hayes	639	13	Tony Lazzeri	.969	13	Lonny Frey	5.62	13	Max Bishop	507.07
	Max Bishop	639	14	Billy Herman	.967	14	Eddie Collins	5.62	14	Bobby Doerr	498.83
15	Lonny Frey	594	15	Joe Gordon	.966	15	George Grantham	5.55	15	Marty McManus	498.58
16	Marty McManus	557	16	Bucky Harris	.965	16	Aaron Ward	5.45	16	Bucky Harris	495.88
17	Eddie Collins	551	17	Rogers Hornsby	.965	17	Max Bishop	5.37	17	Tony Lazzeri	494.82
18	Ray Mack	545	18	Marty McManus	.965	18	Tony Lazzeri	5.36	18	Buddy Myer	491.80
19	George Grantham	483	19	George Grantham	.949	19	Rogers Hornsby	5.35	19	Eddie Collins	490.65
20	Burgess Whitehead	448									

Single Season Fielding Leaders—Second Basemen: Lively Ball Era (1920-1945)

	Games				Putouts				Assists				Errors		
1	Rogers Hornsby	1929	156	1	Bucky Harris	1922	479	1	Frankie Frisch	1927	641	1	George Grantham	1923	55
	Billy Herman	1939	156	2	Billy Herman	1933	466	2	Hughie Critz	1926	588	2	Jay Partridge	1927	52
3	Jimmy Dykes	1921	155	3	Bill Wambsganss	1924	463	3	Rogers Hornsby	1927	582	3	Don Johnson	1944	47
	Bill Wambsganss	1924	155	4	Buddy Myer	1935	460	4	Ski Melillo	1930	572	4	Jimmy Dykes	1921	46
	Hughie Critz	1926	155	5	Billy Herman	1936	457	5	Rabbit Maranville	1924	568	5	Billy Herman	1933	45
	Rogers Hornsby	1927	155	6	Eddie Collins	1920	449	6	Frank Parkinson	1922	562	6	George Grantham	1924	44
	Charlie Gehringer	1933	155	7	Burgess Whitehead	1936	442	7	Tony Cuccinello	1936	559	7	Frankie Gustine	1940	43
	Joe Gordon	1940	155	8	Marty McManus	1925	440	8	Johnny Hodapp	1930	557	8	Odell Hale	1934	41
	Bobby Doerr	1943	155	9	Jimmy Dykes	1921	434	9	Pep Young	1938	554		Billy Herman	1937	41
	Woody Williams	1944	155	10	Snuffy Stirnweiss	1944	433	10	Burgess Whitehead	1936	552	10	Bama Rowell	1941	40
	Emil Verban	1945	155	11	Snuffy Stirnweiss	1945	432	11	Sparky Adams	1925	551	11	Lou Chiozza	1935	39
12	22 tied with		154	12	Eddie Stanky	1945	429	12	Rogers Hornsby	1929	547	12	Bill Wambsganss	1920	38
				13	Ski Melillo	1931	428	13	Hod Ford	1924	543		Bucky Harris	1921	38
				14	Fresco Thompson	1927	424		Ski Melillo	1931	543		Billy Herman	1932	38
				15	Irv Hall	1945	422	15	Hughie Critz	1925	542	15	Bill Wambsganss	1924	37
				16	Roy Hughes	1936	421		Charlie Gehringer	1933	542		Carl Lind	1928	37
				17	Bucky Harris	1923	418		Woody Williams	1944	542	17	Eddie Moore	1925	36
				18	Billy Herman	1935	416	18	Hughie Critz	1933	541		Ski Melillo	1927	36
				19	Bobby Doerr	1943	415	19	Frankie Frisch	1924	537		George Grantham	1930	36
				20	Bill Wambsganss	1920	414	20	Billy Herman	1932	527	20	7 tied with		35

	Double Plays				Fielding Percentage (minimum 100 games)				Range Factor (minimum 100 games)				Assists/162 Games (minimum 100 games)		
1	Buddy Myer	1935	138	1	Ski Melillo	1933	.991	1	Frankie Frisch	1927	6.78	1	Frankie Frisch	1927	678.71
2	Bobby Doerr	1943	132	2	Bobby Doerr	1943	.990	2	Freddie Maguire	1928	6.77	2	Hughie Critz	1933	658.96
3	Tony Cuccinello	1931	128	3	Max Bishop	1932	.988	3	Burgess Whitehead	1936	6.50	3	Frank Parkinson	1922	654.99
	Tony Cuccinello	1936	128	4	Max Bishop	1926	.987	4	Frankie Frisch	1924	6.49	4	Ski Melillo	1930	626.11
5	Freddie Maguire	1928	126	5	Charlie Gehringer	1937	.986	5	Odell Hale	1934	6.48	5	Frankie Frisch	1930	622.98
6	Hughie Critz	1928	124	6	Lonny Frey	1943	.985	6	Ski Melillo	1930	6.46	6	Sparky Adams	1925	619.88
7	Ray Mack	1943	123	7	Charlie Gehringer	1935	.985	7	Hughie Critz	1933	6.44	7	Freddie Maguire	1928	615.13
8	Joe Gordon	1942	121	8	Buddy Myer	1931	.984	8	Ski Melillo	1931	6.43	8	Hughie Critz	1926	614.55
9	Bucky Harris	1923	120	9	Max Bishop	1931	.984	9	Billy Herman	1933	6.39	9	Hughie Critz	1929	612.85
	Pep Young	1938	120	10	Jackie Hayes	1937	.984	10	Frank Parkinson	1922	6.37	10	Hughie Critz	1925	609.75
	Eddie Mayo	1944	120	11	Sparky Adams	1925	.983	11	Frankie Frisch	1930	6.34	11	John Kerr	1929	609.49
12	Snuffy Stirnweiss	1945	119	12	Buddy Myer	1938	.982	12	Jimmy Dykes	1920	6.31	12	Frankie Frisch	1924	608.35
13	Ski Melillo	1931	118	13	Charlie Gehringer	1941	.982	13	Hughie Critz	1934	6.30	13	Rogers Hornsby	1927	608.28
	Bobby Doerr	1938	118	14	Snuffy Stirnweiss	1944	.982	14	Sparky Adams	1925	6.28	14	Hod Ford	1924	606.66
	Bobby Doerr	1940	118	15	Hughie Critz	1933	.982	15	Tony Cuccinello	1936	6.28	15	Rabbit Maranville	1924	605.37
16	Bucky Harris	1922	116	16	Frankie Frisch	1933	.982	16	John Kerr	1929	6.28	16	Footsie Blair	1930	604.33
	Carl Lind	1928	116	17	Charlie Gehringer	1933	.981	17	Ski Melillo	1933	6.25	17	Tony Cuccinello	1936	603.72
	Charlie Gehringer	1936	116	18	Jackie Hayes	1933	.981	18	Bucky Harris	1922	6.25	18	Hughie Critz	1934	603.07
	Joe Gordon	1939	116	19	Hughie Critz	1926	.981	19	Johnny Hodapp	1930	6.23	19	Pep Young	1938	602.34
	Joe Gordon	1940	116	20	Ski Melillo	1934	.981	20	Bill Cissell	1932	6.23	20	Frankie Frisch	1926	600.80

Career Fielding Leaders—Third Basemen: Lively Ball Era (1920-1945)

	Games			Putouts			Assists			Errors	
1	Pie Traynor	1,843	1	Pie Traynor	2,289	1	Pie Traynor	3,521	1	Mike Higgins	345
2	Mike Higgins	1,692	2	Willie Kamm	2,146	2	Willie Kamm	3,345	2	Pie Traynor	324
3	Willie Kamm	1,672	3	Mike Higgins	1,784	3	Harlond Clift	3,262	3	Harlond Clift	279
4	Stan Hack	1,663	4	Stan Hack	1,780	4	Stan Hack	3,154	4	Stan Hack	229
5	Harlond Clift	1,550	5	Harlond Clift	1,777	5	Mike Higgins	3,124	5	Bill Werber	220
6	Ossie Bluege	1,486	6	Ossie Bluege	1,537	6	Ossie Bluege	3,004	6	Ossie Bluege	205
7	Pinky Whitney	1,358	7	Pinky Whitney	1,455	7	Pinky Whitney	2,640	7	Jimmy Dykes	188
8	Jimmy Dykes	1,248	8	Jimmy Dykes	1,361	8	Bill Werber	2,415	8	Jim Tabor	187
9	Bill Werber	1,143	9	Bill Werber	1,264	9	Jimmy Dykes	2,402	9	Willie Kamm	185
10	Red Rolfe	1,084	10	Red Rolfe	1,220	10	Ken Keltner	2,142	10	Buddy Lewis	164
11	Joe Dugan	1,046	11	Ken Keltner	1,126	11	Red Rolfe	2,128		Pinky Whitney	164
12	Ken Keltner	1,008	12	Joe Dugan	1,102	12	Joe Dugan	1,940	12	Red Rolfe	155
13	Marv Owen	921	13	Marv Owen	1,032	13	Marv Owen	1,695	13	Les Bell	146
14	Joe Stripp	914	14	Joe Stripp	956	14	Joe Stripp	1,666	14	Joe Dugan	139
15	Les Bell	828	15	Marty McManus	866	15	Jim Tabor	1,662	15	Marv Owen	135
16	Freddy Lindstrom	809	16	Jim Tabor	853	16	Freddy Lindstrom	1,536	16	Sammy Hale	133
17	Andy High	790	17	Freddy Lindstrom	835	17	Babe Pinelli	1,481	17	Ken Keltner	129
18	Jim Tabor	789	18	Les Bell	818	18	Marty McManus	1,450	18	Milt Stock	123
19	Milt Stock	750	19	Milt Stock	792	19	Buddy Lewis	1,445	19	Babe Pinelli	120
20	Marty McManus	725	20	Babe Pinelli	786	20	Les Bell	1,415	20	Johnny Vergez	115

	Double Plays			Fielding Percentage (minimum 750 games)			Range Factor (minimum 750 games)			Assists/162 Games (minimum 750 games)	
1	Harlond Clift	309	1	Willie Kamm	.967	1	Willie Kamm	3.28	1	Ken Keltner	344.25
2	Pie Traynor	303	2	Ken Keltner	.962	2	Harlond Clift	3.25	2	Bill Werber	342.28
3	Willie Kamm	299	3	Pinky Whitney	.961	3	Ken Keltner	3.24	3	Jim Tabor	341.25
4	Mike Higgins	272	4	Joe Stripp	.961	4	Bill Werber	3.22	4	Harlond Clift	340.93
5	Ossie Bluege	266	5	Freddy Lindstrom	.959	5	Jim Tabor	3.19	5	Ossie Bluege	327.49
6	Stan Hack	230	6	Ossie Bluege	.957	6	Pie Traynor	3.15	6	Willie Kamm	324.10
7	Ken Keltner	221	7	Joe Dugan	.956	7	Red Rolfe	3.09	7	Red Rolfe	318.02
8	Pinky Whitney	219	8	Andy High	.956	8	Ossie Bluege	3.06	8	Pinky Whitney	314.93
9	Bill Werber	214	9	Red Rolfe	.956	9	Pinky Whitney	3.02	9	Jimmy Dykes	311.80
10	Jimmy Dykes	199	10	Stan Hack	.956	10	Jimmy Dykes	3.02	10	Pie Traynor	309.50
11	Red Rolfe	184	11	Marv Owen	.953	11	Stan Hack	2.97	11	Freddy Lindstrom	307.58
12	Marv Owen	168	12	Jimmy Dykes	.952	12	Marv Owen	2.96	12	Stan Hack	307.24
13	Joe Dugan	165	13	Harlond Clift	.948	13	Freddy Lindstrom	2.93	13	Joe Dugan	300.46
14	Les Bell	161	14	Pie Traynor	.947	14	Joe Dugan	2.91	14	Mike Higgins	299.11
15	Jim Tabor	153	15	Bill Werber	.944	15	Mike Higgins	2.90	15	Marv Owen	298.14
16	Sammy Hale	145	16	Milt Stock	.943	16	Joe Stripp	2.87	16	Joe Stripp	295.29
17	Buddy Lewis	141	17	Les Bell	.939	17	Milt Stock	2.74	17	Les Bell	276.85
18	Joe Stripp	137	18	Mike Higgins	.934	18	Les Bell	2.70	18	Milt Stock	272.38
19	Freddy Lindstrom	135	19	Jim Tabor	.931	19	Andy High	2.57	19	Andy High	268.02
20	Marty McManus	131									

Single Season Fielding Leaders—Third Basemen: Lively Ball Era (1920-1945)

	Games				Putouts				Assists				Errors		
1	Babe Pinelli	1922	156	1	Willie Kamm	1928	243	1	Harlond Clift	1937	405	1	Buddy Lewis	1938	47
	Buddy Lewis	1937	156	2	Willie Kamm	1927	236	2	Ken Keltner	1944	369	2	Sibby Sisti	1941	41
	Stan Hack	1939	156	3	Pie Traynor	1925	226	3	Larry Gardner	1920	362	3	Jim Tabor	1939	40
4	Milt Stock	1920	155	4	Willie Kamm	1929	221	4	Buddy Lewis	1938	359	4	Mike Higgins	1938	39
	Les Bell	1926	155	5	Tony Boeckel	1920	219	5	Rube Lutzke	1923	358	5	Bobby Reeves	1929	38
	Willie Kamm	1928	155	6	Howard Shanks	1921	218	6	Ken Keltner	1942	353	6	Pie Traynor	1931	37
	Pie Traynor	1931	155	7	Pie Traynor	1927	212	7	Willie Kamm	1923	352		Mike Higgins	1934	37
	Harlond Clift	1937	155	8	Marty McManus	1929	206	8	Babe Pinelli	1922	350	8	Les Bell	1925	36
	Bill Johnson	1943	155	9	Babe Pinelli	1922	204	9	Ken Keltner	1941	346		Mike Higgins	1939	36
10	Larry Gardner	1920	154	10	Marv Owen	1934	202	10	George Kell	1945	345		Bob Elliott	1942	36
	Howard Shanks	1921	154	11	Gene Robertson	1925	201	11	Freddy Lindstrom	1928	340	11	Rube Lutzke	1923	35
	Gene Robertson	1925	154	12	Harlond Clift	1937	198	12	Jim Tabor	1939	338		Bert Haas	1942	35
	Pinky Whitney	1929	154	13	Red Rolfe	1937	195	13	Ossie Bluege	1927	337	13	Harlond Clift	1937	34
	Pie Traynor	1933	154		Harlond Clift	1941	195	14	Joe Sewell	1929	336		Bill Werber	1939	34
	Marv Owen	1934	154		Stan Hack	1945	195	15	Larry Gardner	1921	335	15	7 tied with		33
	Red Rolfe	1937	154	16	Bob Jones	1921	194	16	Pinky Whitney	1929	333				
	Ken Keltner	1939	154		Pinky May	1941	194	17	Howard Shanks	1921	330				
	Bob Kennedy	1940	154	18	Marv Owen	1936	190		Ossie Bluege	1928	330				
	Harlond Clift	1941	154	19	Pie Traynor	1923	189	19	Harlond Clift	1940	329				
20	5 tied with		153	20	2 tied with		188	20	3 tied with		326				

	Double Plays				Fielding Percentage (minimum 100 games)				Range Factor (minimum 100 games)				Assists/162 Games (minimum 100 games)		
1	Harlond Clift	1937	50	1	Willie Kamm	1933	.984	1	Harlond Clift	1937	3.89	1	Aaron Ward	1920	430.58
2	Sammy Hale	1927	46	2	Heine Groh	1924	.983	2	Aaron Ward	1920	3.82	2	Harlond Clift	1937	423.29
3	Pie Traynor	1925	41	3	Pinky Whitney	1937	.982	3	Rube Lutzke	1924	3.81	3	Rube Lutzke	1923	405.57
	Gene Robertson	1925	41	4	Jimmy Dykes	1932	.980	4	Rube Lutzke	1923	3.80	4	Bill Werber	1934	402.51
5	Ken Keltner	1939	40	5	Willie Kamm	1926	.978	5	Pinky May	1941	3.70	5	Ken Keltner	1944	401.19
6	Les Bell	1925	39	6	Willie Kamm	1929	.978	6	Pie Traynor	1924	3.69	6	Buddy Lewis	1939	394.12
7	Ken Keltner	1942	38	7	Willie Kamm	1934	.978	7	Bob Jones	1921	3.67	7	Babe Pinelli	1925	393.85
8	Les Bell	1928	37	8	Don Gutteridge	1937	.978	8	Frank Ellerbe	1921	3.66	8	Gil Torres	1944	391.17
	Ken Keltner	1944	37	9	Willie Kamm	1928	.977	9	Harlond Clift	1943	3.64	9	Bill Werber	1941	387.59
10	Ken Keltner	1941	36	10	Eddie Mayo	1943	.976	10	George Kell	1945	3.61	10	Buddy Lewis	1938	385.15
11	Howard Shanks	1921	35	11	Larry Gardner	1920	.976	11	Ken Keltner	1944	3.60	11	Willie Kamm	1923	382.71
	Buddy Myer	1928	35	12	Stan Hack	1945	.975	12	Bob Jones	1922	3.60	12	Harlond Clift	1943	381.86
	Oscar Grimes	1945	35	13	Heine Groh	1923	.975	13	Ossie Bluege	1927	3.58	13	Larry Gardner	1920	380.81
	Steve Mesner	1945	35	14	Joe Sewell	1929	.975	14	Bill Werber	1935	3.56	14	Fred Haney	1926	380.76
15	8 tied with		34	15	Joe Sewell	1932	.974	15	Howard Shanks	1921	3.56	15	George Kell	1945	380.20
				16	Joe Dugan	1923	.974	16	Babe Pinelli	1922	3.55	16	Cecil Travis	1940	379.91
				17	Ken Keltner	1939	.974	17	Ken Keltner	1941	3.54	17	Ken Keltner	1942	378.72
				18	Woody English	1933	.973	18	Bill Werber	1934	3.53	18	Ken Keltner	1941	376.19
				19	Charlie Deal	1921	.973	19	Frank O'Rourke	1927	3.53	19	Pinky May	1941	374.91
				20	Charlie Deal	1920	.973	20	Willie Kamm	1927	3.53	20	Rube Lutzke	1924	374.33

Career Fielding Leaders—Shortstops: Lively Ball Era (1920-1945)

	Games			Putouts			Assists			Errors	
1	Joe Cronin	1,843	1	Dick Bartell	3,872	1	Joe Cronin	5,814	1	Luke Appling	520
2	Luke Appling	1,715	2	Joe Cronin	3,696	2	Dick Bartell	5,590	2	Joe Cronin	485
3	Dick Bartell	1,702	3	Luke Appling	3,491	3	Luke Appling	5,581	3	Dick Bartell	471
4	Leo Durocher	1,509	4	Leo Durocher	3,097	4	Arky Vaughan	4,780	4	Arky Vaughan	397
5	Arky Vaughan	1,485	5	Dave Bancroft	3,074	5	Billy Jurges	4,719	5	Frankie Crosetti	396
	Frankie Crosetti	1,485	6	Frankie Crosetti	3,024	6	Travis Jackson	4,635	6	Dave Bancroft	395
7	Billy Jurges	1,453	7	Billy Jurges	3,001	7	Leo Durocher	4,431	7	Travis Jackson	381
8	Travis Jackson	1,326	8	Arky Vaughan	2,995	8	Frankie Crosetti	4,418	8	Glenn Wright	351
9	Dave Bancroft	1,245	9	Travis Jackson	2,877	9	Dave Bancroft	4,357		Wally Gerber	351
10	Rabbit Maranville	1,240	10	Rabbit Maranville	2,862	10	Rabbit Maranville	4,214	10	Joe Sewell	333
11	Billy Rogell	1,235	11	Joe Sewell	2,591	11	Joe Sewell	3,933	11	Leo Durocher	307
12	Joe Sewell	1,216	12	Wally Gerber	2,467	12	Billy Rogell	3,886	12	Rabbit Maranville	303
13	Wally Gerber	1,200	13	Lyn Lary	2,373	13	Wally Gerber	3,570	13	Billy Jurges	293
14	Lyn Lary	1,138	14	Billy Rogell	2,362	14	Glenn Wright	3,473		Chick Galloway	293
15	Glenn Wright	1,051	15	Eddie Miller	2,197	15	Lyn Lary	3,388	15	Billy Rogell	287
16	Eddie Miller	982	16	Glenn Wright	2,157	16	Eddie Miller	3,245	16	Mark Koenig	286
17	Chick Galloway	976	17	Chick Galloway	2,014	17	Roger Peckinpaugh	3,029	17	Lyn Lary	268
18	Roger Peckinpaugh	972	18	Lou Boudreau	1,841	18	Tommy Thevenow	2,818	18	Heinie Sand	258
19	Lou Boudreau	899	19	Roger Peckinpaugh	1,833	19	Lou Boudreau	2,801	19	Red Kress	243
20	Everett Scott	858	20	2 tied with	1,811	20	Chick Galloway	2,790		Tommy Thevenow	243

	Double Plays			Fielding Percentage (minimum 750 games)			Range Factor (minimum 750 games)			Assists/162 Games (minimum 750 games)	
1	Joe Cronin	1,165	1	Eddie Miller	.972	1	Dave Bancroft	5.97	1	Dave Bancroft	566.94
2	Luke Appling	1,081	2	Lou Boudreau	.970	2	Rabbit Maranville	5.71	2	Travis Jackson	566.27
3	Dick Bartell	1,072	3	Everett Scott	.966	3	Travis Jackson	5.67	3	Rabbit Maranville	550.54
4	Frankie Crosetti	926	4	Billy Jurges	.963	4	Dick Bartell	5.56	4	Tommy Thevenow	538.34
5	Leo Durocher	895	5	Marty Marion	.962	5	Eddie Miller	5.54	5	Eddie Miller	535.33
6	Billy Jurges	893	6	Leo Durocher	.961	6	Heinie Sand	5.51	6	Glenn Wright	535.32
7	Arky Vaughan	850	7	Hod Ford	.960	7	Tommy Thevenow	5.39	7	Dick Bartell	532.07
8	Travis Jackson	826	8	Rabbit Maranville	.959	8	Joe Sewell	5.37	8	Luke Appling	527.18
9	Billy Rogell	805	9	Woody English	.957	9	Glenn Wright	5.36	9	Billy Jurges	526.14
10	Rabbit Maranville	746	10	Billy Rogell	.956	10	Billy Jurges	5.31	10	Joe Sewell	523.97
11	Dave Bancroft	737	11	Lyn Lary	.956	11	Luke Appling	5.29	11	Arky Vaughan	521.45
12	Glenn Wright	695	12	Roger Peckinpaugh	.955	12	Hod Ford	5.29	12	Heinie Sand	512.65
13	Eddie Miller	687	13	Dick Bartell	.953	13	Arky Vaughan	5.24	13	Joe Cronin	511.05
14	Lou Boudreau	680	14	Travis Jackson	.952	14	Everett Scott	5.17	14	Billy Rogell	509.74
15	Joe Sewell	674	15	Joe Sewell	.951	15	Lou Boudreau	5.16	15	Everett Scott	506.58
16	Wally Gerber	661	16	Joe Cronin	.951	16	Joe Cronin	5.16	16	Hod Ford	506.30
17	Lyn Lary	632	17	Arky Vaughan	.951	17	Woody English	5.10	17	Marty Marion	505.14
18	Hod Ford	562	18	Dave Bancroft	.950	18	Lyn Lary	5.06	18	Roger Peckinpaugh	504.83
19	Red Kress	558	19	Tommy Thevenow	.950	19	Billy Rogell	5.06	19	Lou Boudreau	504.74
20	Tommy Thevenow	523	20	Frankie Crosetti	.949	20	Marty Marion	5.04	20	Woody English	494.83

Single Season Fielding Leaders—Shortstops: Lively Ball Era (1920-1945)

	Games				Putouts				Assists				Errors		
1	Frankie Crosetti	1938	157	1	Dave Bancroft	1922	405	1	Glenn Wright	1924	601	1	Dave Bancroft	1922	62
2	Dave Bancroft	1922	156		Eddie Miller	1940	405	2	Dave Bancroft	1920	598		Joe Cronin	1929	62
	Tommy Thevenow	1926	156	3	Dave Bancroft	1921	396	3	Tommy Thevenow	1926	597	3	Al Brancato	1941	61
	Jackie Tavener	1926	156	4	Doc Lavan	1921	382	4	Whitey Wietelmann	1943	581	4	Heinie Sand	1925	60
	Tommy Thevenow	1930	156	5	Dick Bartell	1933	381	5	Dave Bancroft	1922	579	5	Joe Sewell	1923	59
	Arky Vaughan	1936	156	6	Everett Scott	1921	380	6	Dick Bartell	1936	559	6	Travis Jackson	1924	58
	Lyn Lary	1937	156	7	Tommy Thevenow	1926	371	7	Luke Appling	1935	556		Jim Levey	1931	58
8	Topper Rigney	1922	155	8	Dave Bancroft	1920	362	8	Tommy Thevenow	1930	554	8	Glenn Wright	1925	56
	Chick Galloway	1922	155	9	Joe Sewell	1927	361	9	Travis Jackson	1929	552		Tommy Thevenow	1930	56
	Roger Peckinpaugh	1924	155	10	Rabbit Maranville	1922	359	10	Travis Jackson	1928	547	10	Frank O'Rourke	1921	55
	Lyn Lary	1931	155		Dick Bartell	1932	359	11	Dave Bancroft	1921	546		Heinie Sand	1926	55
	Joe Cronin	1931	155	12	Heinie Sand	1926	358	12	Eddie Miller	1944	544		Red Kress	1928	55
	Billy Rogell	1933	155	13	Bill Cissell	1929	357	13	Eddie Miller	1943	543		Bill Cissell	1929	55
	Bill Knickerbocker	1936	155		Eddie Miller	1944	357	14	Arky Vaughan	1940	542		Luke Appling	1933	55
	Lyn Lary	1936	155	15	Hod Ford	1928	355	15	Luke Appling	1937	541	15	Ike Davis	1925	53
	Lou Boudreau	1940	155	16	Rabbit Maranville	1920	354	16	Doc Lavan	1921	540	16	Wally Gerber	1920	52
	Arky Vaughan	1940	155		Travis Jackson	1928	354	17	Everett Scott	1922	538		Glenn Wright	1924	52
	Marty Marion	1941	155	18	Heinie Sand	1925	352	18	Rabbit Maranville	1929	537		Mark Koenig	1926	52
	Luke Appling	1943	155		Frankie Crosetti	1938	352	19	Travis Jackson	1924	534		Arky Vaughan	1940	52
	Eddie Miller	1944	155	20	2 tied with		350		Luke Appling	1933	534	20	3 tied with		51

	Double Plays				Fielding Percentage (minimum 100 games)				Range Factor (minimum 100 games)				Assists/162 Games (minimum 100 games)		
1	Lou Boudreau	1944	134	1	Eddie Miller	1942	.983	1	Dave Bancroft	1920	6.40	1	Dave Bancroft	1920	645.84
2	Hod Ford	1928	128	2	Eddie Miller	1943	.979	2	Dave Bancroft	1922	6.31	2	Glenn Wright	1924	636.35
3	Eddie Miller	1940	122	3	Lou Boudreau	1944	.978	3	Tommy Thevenow	1926	6.21	3	Dick Bartell	1936	628.88
	Lou Boudreau	1943	122	4	Jimmy Cooney	1927	.978	4	Dave Bancroft	1921	6.16	4	Frank Parkinson	1921	623.31
5	Eddie Miller	1943	121	5	Billy Jurges	1942	.978	5	Doc Lavan	1921	6.15	5	Travis Jackson	1930	621.23
6	Frankie Crosetti	1938	120	6	Billy Jurges	1937	.975	6	Rabbit Maranville	1920	6.14	6	Tommy Thevenow	1926	619.96
7	Luke Appling	1936	119	7	Eddie Miller	1945	.975	7	Dick Bartell	1936	6.08	7	Joe Cronin	1934	619.94
8	Frankie Crosetti	1939	118	8	Everett Scott	1920	.973	8	Ivy Olson	1921	6.08	8	Whitey Wietelmann	1943	615.18
9	Billy Rogell	1933	116	9	Everett Scott	1921	.972	9	Dave Bancroft	1925	6.07	9	Dick Bartell	1937	602.44
	Lou Boudreau	1940	116	10	Jimmy Cooney	1926	.972	10	Frank Parkinson	1921	6.07	10	Dave Bancroft	1922	601.27
11	Luke Appling	1943	115	11	Marty Marion	1944	.972	11	Dick Bartell	1930	6.05	11	Travis Jackson	1929	600.16
12	Phil Rizzuto	1942	114	12	Hod Ford	1928	.972	12	Travis Jackson	1928	6.05	12	Rabbit Maranville	1929	599.96
13	Tommy Thevenow	1930	113	13	Eddie Miller	1944	.971	13	Glenn Wright	1924	5.95	13	Dave Bancroft	1925	594.86
	Cecil Travis	1938	113	14	Billy Rogell	1935	.971	14	Rabbit Maranville	1929	5.94	14	Travis Jackson	1928	594.73
15	Travis Jackson	1928	112	15	Leo Durocher	1936	.971	15	Rabbit Maranville	1923	5.94	15	Art Fletcher	1920	591.36
	Eddie Miller	1941	112	16	Marty Marion	1943	.970	16	Jimmy Cooney	1926	5.93	16	Billy Jurges	1932	591.00
	Eddie Lake	1945	112	17	Lou Boudreau	1943	.970	17	Dick Bartell	1937	5.91	17	Dick Bartell	1930	588.86
18	Dick Bartell	1930	111	18	Joe Boley	1930	.970	18	Doc Lavan	1920	5.91	18	Luke Appling	1935	588.71
	Luke Appling	1937	111	19	Travis Jackson	1931	.970	19	Travis Jackson	1929	5.91	19	Doc Lavan	1921	583.20
20	3 tied with		110	20	Eddie Miller	1940	.970	20	Eddie Miller	1940	5.91		Tommy Thevenow	1931	583.20

Career Fielding Leaders—Outfielders: Lively Ball Era (1920-1945)

	Games			Putouts			Assists			Errors	
1	Mel Ott	2,297	1	Doc Cramer	5,242	1	Mel Ott	255	1	Goose Goslin	209
2	Paul Waner	2,288	2	Al Simmons	4,988	2	Paul Waner	247	2	Roy Johnson	157
3	Goose Goslin	2,187	3	Paul Waner	4,969	3	Sam Rice	225	3	Sam Rice	156
4	Al Simmons	2,142	4	Lloyd Waner	4,860	4	Goose Goslin	221	4	Gee Walker	154
5	Babe Ruth	2,070	5	Goose Goslin	4,792	5	Bob Johnson	208	5	Babe Ruth	147
6	Doc Cramer	2,056	6	Mel Ott	4,492	6	Chuck Klein	195	6	Bob Johnson	141
7	Sam Rice	1,922	7	Sammy West	4,300	7	Kiki Cuyler	191	7	Max Carey	135
8	Heinie Manush	1,845	8	Sam Rice	4,128	8	Babe Ruth	182	8	Chuck Klein	134
9	Lloyd Waner	1,818	9	Babe Ruth	4,101	9	Al Simmons	169		Paul Waner	134
10	Kiki Cuyler	1,807	10	Kiki Cuyler	4,034	10	Doc Cramer	167	10	Earl Averill	126
11	Joe Medwick	1,790	11	Bob Johnson	4,003	11	Charlie Jamieson	160	11	Ben Chapman	125
12	Bob Johnson	1,769	12	Earl Averill	3,973	12	Ben Chapman	159	12	Kiki Cuyler	121
13	Gee Walker	1,613	13	Joe Medwick	3,881	13	Bob Meusel	157	13	Ken Williams	117
14	Bing Miller	1,603	14	Heinie Manush	3,841	14	Tris Speaker	154	14	Doc Cramer	115
15	Chuck Klein	1,599	15	Gee Walker	3,661	15	Sammy West	151	15	Bob Meusel	114
16	Earl Averill	1,590	16	Ben Chapman	3,476		Lloyd Waner	151	16	Curt Walker	112
17	Sammy West	1,573	17	Earle Combs	3,449		Ross Youngs	151	17	Bruce Campbell	105
18	Ben Chapman	1,494	18	Wally Berger	3,324	18	Cy Williams	150		Hack Wilson	105
19	Wally Moses	1,428	19	Bing Miller	3,310	19	Ira Flagstead	146	19	Bing Miller	102
20	Charlie Jamieson	1,387	20	Mike Kreevich	3,304		Max Carey	146	20	Wally Moses	100

	Double Plays			Fielding Percentage (minimum 750 games)			Range Factor (minimum 750 games)			Assists/162 Games (minimum 750 games)	
1	Mel Ott	59	1	Johnny Cooney	.988	1	Taylor Douthit	3.07	1	Ross Youngs	25.97
2	Sam Rice	57	2	Terry Moore	.985	2	Johnny Mostil	2.93	2	Ira Flagstead	24.90
3	Paul Waner	53	3	Mule Haas	.984	3	Mike Kreevich	2.89	3	Cliff Heathcote	23.57
4	Curt Walker	48	4	Sammy West	.983	4	Max Carey	2.86	4	Tris Speaker	22.85
	Tris Speaker	48	5	Lloyd Waner	.983	5	Sammy West	2.83	5	Harry Hooper	21.85
6	Goose Goslin	47	6	Al Simmons	.982	6	Terry Moore	2.82	6	Cy Williams	21.60
7	Kiki Cuyler	44	7	Augie Galan	.982	7	Joe DiMaggio	2.78	7	Harry Rice	20.27
8	Sammy West	42	8	Mike Kreevich	.982	8	Fred Schulte	2.77	8	Ken Williams	20.13
9	Chuck Klein	39	9	Vince DiMaggio	.981	9	Lloyd Waner	2.76	9	Jack Tobin	19.85
	Cliff Heathcote	39	10	Ethan Allen	.981	10	Vince DiMaggio	2.76	10	Chuck Klein	19.76
	Babe Ruth	39	11	Mel Ott	.980	11	Baby Doll Jacobson	2.70	11	Max Carey	19.64
12	Bibb Falk	38	12	Heinie Manush	.979	12	Tris Speaker	2.69	12	Bob Meusel	19.50
13	Doc Cramer	37	13	Doc Cramer	.979	13	Wally Berger	2.63	13	Roy Johnson	19.45
	Al Simmons	37	14	Joe Vosmik	.979	14	Doc Cramer	2.63	14	Gene Moore	19.32
15	Bob Meusel	36	15	Joe Medwick	.979	15	Ira Flagstead	2.62	15	Vince DiMaggio	19.07
	Harry Heilmann	36	16	Frank Demaree	.978	16	Earl Averill	2.57	16	Bob Johnson	19.05
17	Vince DiMaggio	35	17	Riggs Stephenson	.978	17	Edd Roush	2.55	17	Sam Rice	18.96
	Bob Johnson	35	18	Pete Fox	.977	18	Earle Combs	2.54	18	Roy Cullenbine	18.71
	Ross Youngs	35	19	George Selkirk	.977	19	Ethan Allen	2.54	19	Charlie Jamieson	18.69
	Ira Flagstead	35	20	Fred Schulte	.976	20	Mule Haas	2.50	20	Edd Roush	18.30

Single Season Fielding Leaders—Outfielders: Lively Ball Era (1920-1945)

	Games				Putouts				Assists				Errors		
1	Kiki Cuyler	1926	157	1	Taylor Douthit	1928	547	1	Chuck Klein	1930	44	1	Roy Johnson	1929	31
2	George Burns	1922	156	2	Baby Doll Jacobson	1924	488	2	Ira Flagstead	1923	33	2	Ken Williams	1921	26
	Chuck Klein	1930	156	3	Lloyd Waner	1931	484	3	Gene Moore	1936	32	3	Roy Johnson	1933	25
	Kiki Cuyler	1930	156	4	Tom Oliver	1930	477	4	Harry Heilmann	1924	31	4	Chuck Klein	1936	23
	Wally Berger	1931	156	5	Johnny Lindell	1944	468	5	Cy Williams	1921	29	5	Ross Youngs	1920	22
	Ethan Allen	1935	156	6	Wally Berger	1935	458		Chuck Klein	1932	29		Tilly Walker	1920	22
	Joe Medwick	1937	156	7	Wally Berger	1931	457		Stan Spence	1944	29		Bruce Campbell	1932	22
	Earl Averill	1937	156		Vince DiMaggio	1943	457	8	Bob Meusel	1921	28	8	Irish Meusel	1920	21
	Vince DiMaggio	1943	156	9	Sam Rice	1920	454		Irish Meusel	1921	28		Sam Rice	1922	21
	Bill Nicholson	1944	156	10	Carden Gillenwater	1945	451		Jack Tobin	1921	28		Billy Southworth	1923	21
11	11 tied with		155	11	Max Carey	1923	450		Ross Youngs	1922	28		Roy Johnson	1932	21
					Lloyd Waner	1929	450		Max Carey	1923	28	12	Sam Rice	1920	20
					Sammy West	1932	450		Paul Waner	1931	28		Bob Meusel	1921	20
				14	Max Carey	1922	449	14	Carson Bigbee	1921	27		Max Carey	1921	20
					Eddie Brown	1925	449		Tommy Griffith	1921	27		Max Carey	1925	20
					Sammy West	1935	449		Ty Cobb	1921	27		Taylor Douthit	1926	20
					Buster Adams	1944	449		Carson Bigbee	1922	27		Harry Rice	1927	20
				18	Al Simmons	1925	447		Jimmy Welsh	1925	27		Bob Johnson	1935	20
				19	Johnny Mostil	1925	446		Mel Ott	1929	27	19	9 tied with		19
					Dain Clay	1945	446	20	11 tied with		26				

	Double Plays				Fielding Percentage (minimum 100 games)				Range Factor (minimum 100 games)				Assists/162 Games (minimum 100 games)		
1	Mel Ott	1929	12	1	Danny Litwhiler	1942	1.000	1	Taylor Douthit	1928	3.62	1	Ira Flagstead	1923	52.41
2	Happy Felsch	1920	10	2	Johnny Hopp	1944	.997	2	Thurman Tucker	1944	3.55	2	Chuck Klein	1930	45.69
	Freddy Leach	1927	10	3	Milt Byrnes	1943	.997	3	Carden Gillenwater	1945	3.39	3	Jimmy Welsh	1925	37.71
	Chuck Klein	1930	10	4	Harry Craft	1940	.997	4	Sammy West	1935	3.38	4	Ty Cobb	1921	36.15
	Vince DiMaggio	1938	10	5	Johnny Cooney	1941	.996	5	Lloyd Waner	1932	3.32	5	Tommy Griffith	1921	35.27
6	Nemo Leibold	1921	9	6	Dick Porter	1933	.996	6	Lloyd Waner	1931	3.29	6	Gene Moore	1936	34.33
	Baby Doll Jacobson	1925	9	7	Danny Litwhiler	1943	.996	7	Taylor Douthit	1926	3.29	7	Harry Heilmann	1924	34.16
	Tris Speaker	1925	9	8	Sammy West	1928	.996	8	Sammy West	1931	3.27	8	Paul Waner	1931	32.87
	Bibb Falk	1927	9	9	Andy Pafko	1945	.995	9	Baby Doll Jacobson	1924	3.26	9	Hi Myers	1921	32.66
	Stan Spence	1944	9	10	Vince DiMaggio	1945	.994	10	Sammy West	1932	3.25	10	Cliff Heathcote	1920	32.65
11	21 tied with		8	11	Johnny Cooney	1936	.994	11	Terry Moore	1936	3.25	11	Harry Rice	1927	32.40
				12	Charlie Keller	1943	.994	12	Taylor Douthit	1927	3.23	12	Cy Williams	1921	32.18
				13	Len Koenecke	1934	.994	13	Fred Schulte	1929	3.22	13	Bob Meusel	1922	32.13
				14	Pete Fox	1938	.994	14	Max Carey	1921	3.21	14	Charlie Jamieson	1928	32.11
				15	Mike Kreevich	1941	.994	15	Kiddo Davis	1932	3.20	15	Andy Pafko	1944	31.61
				16	Terry Moore	1939	.994	16	Johnny Lindell	1944	3.20	16	Stan Spence	1944	31.32
				17	Pat Duncan	1923	.993	17	Tom Oliver	1930	3.16	17	Irish Meusel	1921	31.07
				18	Tom Oliver	1931	.993	18	Jigger Statz	1927	3.16	18	Bob Meusel	1921	30.86
				19	Joe Medwick	1944	.993	19	Ira Flagstead	1925	3.15		Ross Youngs	1922	30.86
				20	Tommy Holmes	1943	.993	20	Johnny Mostil	1928	3.15	20	Ross Youngs	1925	30.61

Career Fielding Leaders—Pitchers: Postwar Era (1946-1960)

Games

1	Gerry Staley	588
2	Warren Spahn	567
3	Murry Dickson	556
4	Early Wynn	519
5	Robin Roberts	503
6	Ellis Kinder	484
7	Hoyt Wilhelm	473
8	Bob Lemon	460
9	Clem Labine	454
	Virgil Trucks	454
11	Johnny Klippstein	449
12	Billy Pierce	439
13	Chuck Stobbs	435
14	Al Brazle	428
15	Bob Rush	417
16	Jim Konstanty	413
17	Mike Garcia	412
18	Turk Lown	403
19	Jim Hearn	396
20	Roy Face	392

Putouts

1	Bob Lemon	263
2	Robin Roberts	232
3	Murry Dickson	220
4	Ned Garver	202
5	Lew Burdette	175
6	Bob Rush	171
7	Warren Spahn	169
8	Early Wynn	167
9	Don Newcombe	159
10	Gerry Staley	142
11	Larry Jansen	138
12	Bobby Shantz	136
13	Mike Garcia	134
14	Virgil Trucks	133
15	Vern Law	129
16	Bob Friend	128
17	Johnny Sain	126
18	Tom Brewer	123
19	Ruben Gomez	121
20	Bob Buhl	116

Assists

1	Warren Spahn	731
2	Bob Lemon	709
3	Murry Dickson	618
4	Early Wynn	506
5	Robin Roberts	470
6	Gerry Staley	467
7	Ned Garver	458
8	Johnny Schmitz	435
9	Lew Burdette	433
10	Bob Rush	428
11	Billy Pierce	403
12	Bob Friend	393
13	Ed Lopat	392
14	Bobby Shantz	375
15	Virgil Trucks	367
16	Mike Garcia	358
17	Jim Hearn	355
	Bill Wight	355
19	Whitey Ford	348
20	Johnny Sain	346

Errors

1	Warren Spahn	44
2	Bill Wight	40
3	Bob Lemon	31
4	Bob Rush	28
5	Ned Garver	27
	Murry Dickson	27
7	Herm Wehmeier	26
8	Allie Reynolds	24
	Virgil Trucks	24
10	Billy Pierce	23
	Ray Scarborough	23
12	Jim Hearn	22
	Johnny Schmitz	22
	Early Wynn	22
15	Walt Masterson	21
16	Carl Erskine	20
	Johnny Antonelli	20
18	9 tied with	19

Double Plays

1	Bob Lemon	78
2	Warren Spahn	58
3	Murry Dickson	49
4	Lew Burdette	43
5	Bobby Shantz	42
6	Ned Garver	41
7	Johnny Schmitz	40
8	Robin Roberts	35
9	Early Wynn	34
	Dizzy Trout	34
11	Jim Hearn	33
	Sid Hudson	33
13	Gerry Staley	31
	Larry Jansen	31
	Howie Pollet	31
16	Frank Sullivan	30
17	Whitey Ford	28
18	7 tied with	27

Fielding Percentage
(minimum 150 games)

1	Hersh Freeman	1.000
	Satchel Paige	1.000
3	Pedro Ramos	.993
4	Johnny Hetki	.991
5	Jim Wilson	.990
6	Bob Miller	.990
7	Don Mossi	.990
8	Harry Perkowski	.988
9	Bill Fischer	.988
10	Sam Zoldak	.987
11	Tom Acker	.986
12	Andy Hansen	.985
13	Harry Gumbert	.984
14	Vic Lombardi	.984
15	Roy Face	.983
	Ken Trinkle	.983
17	Ken Heintzelman	.983
18	Hoyt Wilhelm	.982
19	Joe Ostrowski	.981
20	Harry Brecheen	.980

Assists/162 Innings
(minimum 150 games)

1	Harry Gumbert	47.05
2	Johnny Schmitz	41.32
3	Howie Fox	40.94
4	Bill Werle	40.66
5	Dick Hyde	40.31
6	Bob Lemon	40.30
7	Ken Trinkle	39.50
8	Gerry Staley	39.40
9	Tom Morgan	39.14
10	Tom Ferrick	38.67
11	Dutch Leonard	38.59
12	Paul Minner	38.33
13	Sid Hudson	38.25
14	Jackie Collum	38.03
15	Ewell Blackwell	37.98
16	Marino Pieretti	37.55
17	Bobby Shantz	37.32
18	Dizzy Trout	37.14
19	Stu Miller	37.06
20	Gene Bearden	36.99

Single Season Fielding Leaders—Pitchers: Postwar Era (1946-1960)

Games

1	Jim Konstanty	1950	74
2	Hoyt Wilhelm	1952	71
3	Mike Fornieles	1960	70
4	Ellis Kinder	1953	69
	Don Elston	1958	69
6	Hoyt Wilhelm	1953	68
	Roy Face	1956	68
	Roy Face	1960	68
9	Turk Lown	1957	67
	Gerry Staley	1959	67
11	Ted Wilks	1951	65
	Don Elston	1959	65
	Bill Henry	1959	65
	Lindy McDaniel	1960	65
15	Hersh Freeman	1956	64
	Hoyt Wilhelm	1956	64
	Gerry Staley	1960	64
18	Ellis Kinder	1951	63
19	4 tied with		62

Putouts

1	Bob Lemon	1949	34
	Brooks Lawrence	1957	34
3	Bob Lemon	1952	32
4	Bob Lemon	1953	31
	Lew Burdette	1960	31
6	Larry Jansen	1950	30
	Bob Purkey	1960	30
8	Larry Jansen	1951	29
	Bobby Shantz	1952	29
	Murry Dickson	1952	29
11	Ned Garver	1950	28
	Tom Brewer	1956	28
	Dave Hillman	1959	28
	Vern Law	1960	28
15	Gerry Staley	1952	27
	Lew Burdette	1958	27
17	8 tied with		26

Assists

1	Bob Lemon	1948	86
2	Bob Lemon	1952	79
3	Bob Lemon	1953	74
4	Bob Lemon	1949	71
5	Ewell Blackwell	1947	70
	Murry Dickson	1951	70
7	Hal Newhouser	1949	69
8	Johnny Schmitz	1948	68
	Lew Burdette	1960	68
10	Mel Parnell	1950	67
	Warren Spahn	1958	67
	Glen Hobbie	1960	67
13	Bob Lemon	1950	66
14	Howie Fox	1949	65
	Tom Brewer	1957	65
16	Dizzy Trout	1946	64
17	Art Houtteman	1950	63
18	Murry Dickson	1952	62
19	6 tied with		61

Errors

1	Warren Spahn	1950	8
2	Gene Bearden	1950	7
	Vinegar Bend Mizell	1953	7
	Larry Jackson	1955	7
5	Joe Hatten	1946	6
	Eddie Smith	1946	6
	Walt Masterson	1947	6
	Bill Wight	1950	6
	Johnny Schmitz	1950	6
	Marlin Stuart	1952	6
	Virgil Trucks	1953	6
	Bob Lemon	1956	6
	Don Drysdale	1958	6
	Whitey Ford	1958	6
15	38 tied with		5

Double Plays

1	Bob Lemon	1953	15
2	Gene Bearden	1948	11
3	Bob Hooper	1950	10
	Don Drysdale	1958	10
5	Howie Pollet	1946	9
	Johnny Schmitz	1954	9
7	Bob Lemon	1948	8
	Johnny Schmitz	1949	8
	Murry Dickson	1949	8
	Bob Lemon	1954	8
	Bobby Shantz	1957	8
	Ray Herbert	1958	8
	Pedro Ramos	1959	8
14	25 tied with		7

Fielding Percentage
(minimum 25 games)

1	515 tied with	1.000

Assists/162 Innings
(minimum 25 games)

1	Harry Gumbert	1948	60.94
2	Andy Karl	1947	60.17
3	Dick Hyde	1959	59.63
4	Sam Zoldak	1949	58.08
5	Harry Dorish	1956	57.40
6	Harry Gumbert	1949	56.90
7	Bill Wight	1955	56.17
8	Jim McDonald	1952	56.08
9	Tom Morgan	1955	54.00
10	Gene Bearden	1949	53.57
11	Dutch Leonard	1952	53.46
12	Bobby Shantz	1957	53.38
13	Gerry Staley	1958	53.16
14	Roberto Vargas	1955	52.54
15	Hugh Casey	1946	52.01
16	Dizzy Trout	1949	51.88
17	Charlie Harris	1949	51.87
18	Bob Shaw	1958	51.82
19	Si Johnson	1947	51.76
20	Ray Herbert	1953	51.74

Career Fielding Leaders—Catchers: Postwar Era (1946-1960)

Games

1	Yogi Berra	1,616
2	Jim Hegan	1,547
3	Sherm Lollar	1,375
4	Roy Campanella	1,183
5	Del Rice	1,142
6	Del Crandall	1,135
7	Andy Seminick	1,110
8	Sammy White	967
9	Wes Westrum	902
10	Walker Cooper	826
11	Smoky Burgess	823
12	Clint Courtney	786
13	Les Moss	720
14	Stan Lopata	695
15	Clyde McCullough	685
16	Phil Masi	654
17	Ed Fitz Gerald	651
18	Ed Bailey	640
19	Joe Garagiola	614
20	Gus Triandos	613

Putouts

1	Yogi Berra	8,228
2	Jim Hegan	7,216
3	Roy Campanella	6,520
4	Sherm Lollar	6,203
5	Del Crandall	5,508
6	Del Rice	4,925
7	Andy Seminick	4,708
8	Sammy White	4,458
9	Wes Westrum	3,639
10	Smoky Burgess	3,616
11	Clint Courtney	3,485
12	Walker Cooper	3,408
13	Stan Lopata	3,406
14	Gus Triandos	2,952
15	Ed Bailey	2,903
16	Red Wilson	2,881
17	Clyde McCullough	2,771
18	Les Moss	2,612
19	Frank House	2,606
20	Hal Smith	2,536

Assists

1	Yogi Berra	760
2	Jim Hegan	653
3	Sherm Lollar	608
4	Del Crandall	596
5	Roy Campanella	550
6	Andy Seminick	547
7	Del Rice	484
8	Sammy White	482
9	Wes Westrum	415
10	Walker Cooper	394
11	Clint Courtney	362
12	Clyde McCullough	323
13	Birdie Tebbetts	311
14	Smoky Burgess	308
15	Gus Triandos	297
16	Ed Bailey	281
17	Les Moss	279
18	Joe Garagiola	271
19	Phil Masi	270
20	Ed Fitz Gerald	260

Errors

1	Andy Seminick	119
2	Yogi Berra	104
3	Walker Cooper	86
4	Roy Campanella	85
5	Jim Hegan	78
6	Sammy White	76
7	Del Crandall	75
8	Del Rice	72
9	Ed Fitz Gerald	67
10	Les Moss	64
11	Wes Westrum	62
12	Sherm Lollar	56
13	Smoky Burgess	54
14	Stan Lopata	53
15	Birdie Tebbetts	51
16	Clint Courtney	50
17	Mickey Grasso	49
18	Clyde McCullough	46
19	Hobie Landrith	44
	Joe Ginsberg	44

Double Plays

1	Yogi Berra	164
2	Jim Hegan	127
3	Del Crandall	94
4	Sherm Lollar	93
5	Roy Campanella	82
	Wes Westrum	82
7	Sammy White	79
8	Andy Seminick	75
9	Del Rice	66
10	Clint Courtney	62
11	Les Moss	52
12	Walker Cooper	51
13	Stan Lopata	50
14	Gus Triandos	49
15	Smoky Burgess	47
16	Joe Astroth	46
17	Hal Smith	45
	Clyde McCullough	45
19	Red Wilson	41
	Birdie Tebbetts	41

Fielding Percentage
(minimum 500 games)

1	Sherm Lollar	.992
2	Jim Hegan	.990
3	Red Wilson	.990
4	Aaron Robinson	.989
5	Frank House	.989
6	Yogi Berra	.989
7	Joe Astroth	.988
8	Roy Campanella	.988
9	Del Crandall	.988
10	Ed Bailey	.987
11	Clint Courtney	.987
12	Gus Triandos	.987
13	Del Rice	.987
14	Phil Masi	.987
15	Smoky Burgess	.986
16	Joe Garagiola	.986
17	Stan Lopata	.986
18	Clyde McCullough	.985
19	Wes Westrum	.985
20	Sammy White	.985

Passed Balls

1	Andy Seminick	81
2	Yogi Berra	71
3	Jim Hegan	70
4	Gus Triandos	69
5	Harry Chiti	62
	Joe Ginsberg	62
7	Wes Westrum	61
8	Hal Smith	56
	Roy Campanella	56
10	Del Rice	55
11	Clint Courtney	54
	Ed Fitz Gerald	54
	Walker Cooper	54
14	Sammy White	50
15	Del Crandall	47
	Smoky Burgess	47
17	Stan Lopata	46
18	Red Wilson	45
	Les Moss	45
20	2 tied with	44

Assists/162 Games
(minimum 500 games)

1	Del Crandall	85.07
2	Birdie Tebbetts	84.68
3	Sammy White	80.75
4	Andy Seminick	79.83
5	Gus Triandos	78.49
6	Aaron Robinson	77.65
7	Walker Cooper	77.27
8	Clyde McCullough	76.39
9	Yogi Berra	76.19
10	Roy Campanella	75.32
11	Clint Courtney	74.61
12	Wes Westrum	74.53
13	Joe Astroth	73.75
14	Frank House	73.56
15	Sherm Lollar	71.63
16	Joe Garagiola	71.50
17	Ed Bailey	71.13
18	Del Rice	68.66
19	Jim Hegan	68.38
20	Hobie Landrith	67.81

Single Season Fielding Leaders—Catchers: Postwar Era (1946-1960)

Games

1	Jim Hegan	1949	152
2	Yogi Berra	1954	149
3	Yogi Berra	1950	148
4	Del Rice	1952	147
5	Del Crandall	1959	146
6	Yogi Berra	1955	145
7	Sammy White	1955	143
8	Jim Hegan	1948	142
9	Yogi Berra	1951	141
	Hal Smith	1959	141
	Del Crandall	1960	141
12	Roy Campanella	1951	140
	Yogi Berra	1952	140
	Roy Campanella	1953	140
15	Wes Westrum	1950	139
16	Jim Hegan	1954	137
17	Del Crandall	1954	136
	Sherm Lollar	1955	136
	Earl Battey	1960	136
20	2 tied with		135

Putouts

1	John Roseboro	1959	848
2	Roy Campanella	1953	807
3	Del Crandall	1959	783
4	Yogi Berra	1950	777
5	Del Crandall	1960	764
6	Hal Smith	1959	758
7	Earl Battey	1960	749
8	Yogi Berra	1955	748
9	Yogi Berra	1956	732
10	Roy Campanella	1951	722
11	Yogi Berra	1954	717
12	Yogi Berra	1957	704
13	Cal Neeman	1957	703
14	Yogi Berra	1952	700
15	Gus Triandos	1958	698
	Yogi Berra	1959	698
17	Yogi Berra	1951	693
18	Roy Campanella	1949	684
19	Roy Campanella	1950	683
20	Clint Courtney	1958	682

Assists

1	Yogi Berra	1951	82
2	Del Rice	1952	81
3	Sammy White	1954	80
4	Del Crandall	1954	79
5	Jim Hegan	1948	76
6	Andy Seminick	1948	74
7	Buddy Rosar	1946	73
	Jim Hegan	1949	73
	Yogi Berra	1952	73
10	Roy Campanella	1951	72
11	Wes Westrum	1950	71
	Sammy White	1955	71
	Del Crandall	1959	71
14	Buddy Rosar	1947	70
	Del Crandall	1960	70
16	Harry Chiti	1955	69
17	Sammy White	1953	68
18	Del Crandall	1955	67
19	Del Rice	1951	66
	Jim Hegan	1951	66

Errors

1	Andy Seminick	1948	22
2	Mickey Grasso	1950	17
	Mickey Grasso	1952	17
4	Sammy White	1954	16
5	Ed Fitz Gerald	1948	15
	Andy Seminick	1950	15
	Toby Atwell	1953	15
	Earl Battey	1960	15
9	Andy Seminick	1946	14
	Walker Cooper	1950	14
	Hobie Landrith	1956	14
12	11 tied with		13

Double Plays

1	Yogi Berra	1951	25
2	Wes Westrum	1950	21
3	Yogi Berra	1949	18
4	Jim Hegan	1948	17
	Clint Courtney	1958	17
6	Jim Hegan	1949	16
	Yogi Berra	1950	16
8	Yogi Berra	1956	15
	Del Crandall	1959	15
10	Jim Hegan	1947	14
	Al Evans	1947	14
	Roy Campanella	1950	14
	Jim Hegan	1950	14
	Yogi Berra	1954	14
	Hal Smith	1956	14
	Sherm Lollar	1959	14
17	10 tied with		13

Fielding Percentage
(minimum 100 games)

1	Buddy Rosar	1946	1.000
2	Wes Westrum	1950	.999
3	Yogi Berra	1959	.997
4	Jim Hegan	1955	.997
5	Clint Courtney	1952	.996
6	Bill Sarni	1954	.996
7	Phil Masi	1950	.996
	Del Crandall	1956	.996
9	Buddy Rosar	1947	.996
10	Sherm Lollar	1960	.995
11	Yogi Berra	1957	.995
12	Sherm Lollar	1955	.995
13	Roy Campanella	1952	.994
14	Jim Hegan	1954	.994
15	Sherm Lollar	1953	.994
16	Del Crandall	1959	.994
17	Ray Mueller	1946	.994
18	Jim Hegan	1950	.993
19	Sherm Lollar	1956	.993
20	Sherm Lollar	1959	.993

Passed Balls

1	Gus Triandos	1959	28
2	Joe Ginsberg	1959	21
3	Al Evans	1946	18
	Harry Chiti	1958	18
	Earl Battey	1960	18
6	Andy Seminick	1947	17
	Ray Katt	1955	17
	Harry Chiti	1955	17
	Hal Smith	1957	17
10	Hal Smith	1957	16
	Dick Brown	1958	16
12	Jake Early	1946	15
	Ed Fitz Gerald	1948	15
	Walker Cooper	1949	15
	Mike Sandlock	1953	15
16	Hal Smith	1955	14
	John Roseboro	1959	14
18	7 tied with		13

Assists/162 Games
(minimum 100 games)

1	Buddy Rosar	1947	111.18
2	Ray Mueller	1946	105.30
3	Buddy Rosar	1946	101.08
4	Harry Chiti	1955	98.92
5	Sammy White	1954	97.44
6	Joe Garagiola	1952	97.20
7	Andy Seminick	1948	96.68
8	Birdie Tebbetts	1947	96.61
9	Yogi Berra	1951	94.21
10	Del Crandall	1954	94.10
11	Del Crandall	1957	93.71
12	Del Crandall	1953	93.00
13	Wes Westrum	1952	92.57
14	Ray Lamanno	1947	92.15
15	Mickey Grasso	1952	90.95
16	Del Rice	1952	89.27
17	Yogi Berra	1949	89.17
18	Del Rice	1951	89.10
19	Ed Bailey	1959	88.62
20	Sherm Lollar	1958	87.98

Career Fielding Leaders—First Basemen: Postwar Era (1946-1960)

Games

1	Gil Hodges	1,751
2	Mickey Vernon	1,732
3	Ted Kluszewski	1,415
4	Earl Torgeson	1,407
5	Walt Dropo	1,162
6	Eddie Robinson	1,124
7	Ferris Fain	1,116
8	Eddie Waitkus	1,040
9	Stan Musial	1,016
10	Joe Adcock	890
11	Dee Fondy	874
12	Whitey Lockman	771
13	Johnny Mize	721
14	Joe Collins	715
15	Vic Power	713
16	Bill Skowron	702
17	Dale Long	640
18	Vic Wertz	607
19	Dick Gernert	574
20	Ed Bouchee	485

Putouts

1	Mickey Vernon	15,180
2	Gil Hodges	14,514
3	Ted Kluszewski	12,132
4	Earl Torgeson	11,650
5	Eddie Robinson	9,816
6	Ferris Fain	9,530
7	Walt Dropo	9,111
8	Eddie Waitkus	9,079
9	Stan Musial	8,709
10	Joe Adcock	7,707
11	Dee Fondy	7,434
12	Whitey Lockman	6,716
13	Johnny Mize	6,074
14	Vic Power	5,988
15	Bill Skowron	5,774
16	Dale Long	5,421
17	Dick Gernert	5,048
18	Joe Collins	4,555
19	Vic Wertz	4,327
20	Ed Bouchee	3,920

Assists

1	Gil Hodges	1,204
2	Mickey Vernon	1,156
3	Ferris Fain	927
4	Earl Torgeson	812
5	Ted Kluszewski	771
6	Eddie Waitkus	713
7	Stan Musial	688
8	Walt Dropo	666
9	Dee Fondy	641
10	Eddie Robinson	636
11	Vic Power	635
12	Joe Adcock	546
13	Whitey Lockman	510
14	Johnny Mize	480
15	Bill Skowron	460
16	Dale Long	435
17	Dick Gernert	404
18	Joe Collins	376
19	Vic Wertz	366
20	Ed Bouchee	352

Errors

1	Mickey Vernon	150
2	Earl Torgeson	142
3	Ferris Fain	138
4	Gil Hodges	120
5	Eddie Robinson	109
6	Dee Fondy	98
7	Ted Kluszewski	91
8	Walt Dropo	84
9	Whitey Lockman	80
10	Stan Musial	78
11	Dale Long	68
	Eddie Waitkus	68
13	Dick Gernert	59
14	Vic Wertz	55
15	Bill Skowron	54
	Joe Adcock	54
17	Dick Stuart	52
	Luke Easter	52
	Dick Sisler	52
20	Joe Collins	49

Double Plays

1	Mickey Vernon	1,608
2	Gil Hodges	1,540
3	Ted Kluszewski	1,218
4	Ferris Fain	1,124
5	Earl Torgeson	1,090
6	Eddie Robinson	1,018
7	Walt Dropo	957
8	Stan Musial	935
9	Eddie Waitkus	878
10	Joe Adcock	755
11	Dee Fondy	690
12	Bill Skowron	675
13	Whitey Lockman	672
14	Vic Power	662
15	Johnny Mize	606
16	Joe Collins	580
17	Dick Gernert	566
18	Dale Long	517
19	Vic Wertz	465
20	Roy Sievers	416

Fielding Percentage
(minimum 750 games)

1	Joe Adcock	.993
2	Eddie Waitkus	.993
3	Ted Kluszewski	.993
4	Gil Hodges	.992
5	Stan Musial	.992
6	Walt Dropo	.991
7	Mickey Vernon	.991
8	Eddie Robinson	.990
9	Whitey Lockman	.989
10	Earl Torgeson	.989
11	Dee Fondy	.988
12	Ferris Fain	.987

Assists/162 Games
(minimum 750 games)

1	Ferris Fain	134.56
2	Dee Fondy	118.81
3	Gil Hodges	111.39
4	Eddie Waitkus	111.06
5	Stan Musial	109.70
6	Mickey Vernon	108.12
7	Whitey Lockman	107.16
8	Joe Adcock	99.38
9	Earl Torgeson	93.49
10	Walt Dropo	92.85
11	Eddie Robinson	91.67
12	Ted Kluszewski	88.27

Single Season Fielding Leaders—First Basemen: Postwar Era (1946-1960)

Games

1	Gil Hodges	1951	158
2	Joe Adcock	1953	157
3	Gil Hodges	1949	156
	Earl Torgeson	1950	156
5	Eddie Robinson	1950	155
	Earl Torgeson	1951	155
	Eddie Robinson	1952	155
	Eddie Robinson	1953	155
9	Rudy York	1946	154
	Mickey Vernon	1947	154
	Johnny Mize	1947	154
	Tony Lupien	1948	154
	Eddie Waitkus	1950	154
	Ted Kluszewski	1951	154
	Whitey Lockman	1952	154
	Steve Bilko	1953	154
	Gil Hodges	1954	154
	Ed Bouchee	1957	154
19	5 tied with		153

Putouts

1	Jake Jones	1947	1,462
2	Steve Bilko	1953	1,446
3	Mickey Vernon	1949	1,438
4	Tony Lupien	1948	1,436
5	Whitey Lockman	1952	1,435
6	Joe Adcock	1953	1,389
7	Ted Kluszewski	1955	1,388
8	Eddie Waitkus	1950	1,387
9	Johnny Mize	1947	1,381
	Ted Kluszewski	1951	1,381
	Gil Hodges	1954	1,381
12	Mickey Vernon	1953	1,376
13	Eddie Robinson	1953	1,366
14	Earl Torgeson	1950	1,365
	Gil Hodges	1951	1,365
	Mickey Vernon	1954	1,365
17	Stan Musial	1947	1,360
18	Johnny Mize	1948	1,359
19	Elbie Fletcher	1946	1,356
20	Bert Haas	1946	1,346

Assists

1	Mickey Vernon	1949	155
2	Ferris Fain	1952	150
3	Vic Power	1960	145
4	Roy Cullenbine	1947	139
5	Gil Hodges	1954	132
6	Vic Power	1955	130
7	Walt Dropo	1953	127
8	Gil Hodges	1951	126
9	Ed Bouchee	1957	125
10	Ferris Fain	1950	124
	Steve Bilko	1953	124
12	Ferris Fain	1949	122
13	Ferris Fain	1948	120
14	Dee Fondy	1954	119
15	Johnny Mize	1947	118
16	Rudy York	1946	116
	Gil Hodges	1952	116
18	4 tied with		115

Errors

1	Dale Long	1956	24
2	Ferris Fain	1949	22
	Ferris Fain	1952	22
	Dick Stuart	1959	22
5	Earl Torgeson	1950	21
6	Ferris Fain	1947	19
	Mickey Vernon	1947	19
	Jack Graham	1949	19
	Ferris Fain	1950	19
	Dick Gernert	1953	19
11	Earl Torgeson	1947	18
	Dick Sisler	1948	18
	Eddie Robinson	1949	18
	Luke Easter	1952	18
	Dee Fondy	1953	18
	Whitey Lockman	1954	18
17	8 tied with		17

Double Plays

1	Ferris Fain	1949	194
2	Ferris Fain	1950	192
3	Gil Hodges	1951	171
4	Mickey Vernon	1949	168
5	Ted Kluszewski	1954	166
6	Jake Jones	1947	159
	Gil Hodges	1950	159
8	Mickey Vernon	1953	158
9	Tony Lupien	1948	155
	Whitey Lockman	1952	155
11	Rudy York	1946	154
12	Ted Kluszewski	1955	153
13	Gil Hodges	1952	152
14	Rudy York	1947	151
15	Ted Kluszewski	1953	149
16	Ferris Fain	1948	148
	Billy Goodman	1949	148
18	Walt Dropo	1950	147
19	Joe Adcock	1953	146
20	3 tied with		145

Fielding Percentage
(minimum 100 games)

1	Frank McCormick	1946	.999
2	Vic Power	1957	.998
3	Ted Kluszewski	1951	.997
4	Ed Stevens	1948	.996
5	Eddie Waitkus	1946	.996
6	Ted Kluszewski	1954	.996
7	Vic Power	1960	.996
8	Johnny Mize	1947	.996
9	Frank Torre	1957	.996
10	Gil Hodges	1954	.995
11	Joe Adcock	1954	.995
12	Dale Long	1957	.995
13	Rudy York	1947	.995
14	Norm Zauchin	1955	.995
15	Gil Hodges	1949	.995
16	Walt Dropo	1955	.995
17	Joe Adcock	1956	.995
18	Ted Kluszewski	1953	.995
19	Vic Power	1959	.995
20	Eddie Robinson	1948	.995

Assists/162 Games
(minimum 100 games)

1	Ferris Fain	1951	169.50
2	Ferris Fain	1952	168.75
3	Mickey Vernon	1949	164.12
4	Roy Cullenbine	1947	163.17
5	Vic Power	1960	159.80
6	Vic Power	1959	147.27
7	Vic Power	1955	146.25
8	Vic Power	1957	141.93
9	Stan Musial	1956	141.55
10	Dee Fondy	1954	139.70
11	Gil Hodges	1954	138.86
12	Walt Dropo	1953	137.16
13	Stan Musial	1955	135.49
14	Ferris Fain	1953	135.21
15	Whitey Lockman	1953	135.00
16	Ferris Fain	1948	134.07
17	Johnny Mize	1946	133.13
18	Ferris Fain	1950	133.03
19	Dick Gernert	1958	132.16
20	Dale Long	1955	132.05

Career Fielding Leaders—Second Basemen: Postwar Era (1946-1960)

Games

1	Red Schoendienst	1,780
2	Nellie Fox	1,732
3	Bobby Avila	1,168
4	Johnny Temple	1,025
5	Jerry Priddy	1,006
6	Bobby Doerr	829
7	Eddie Stanky	807
8	Cass Michaels	799
9	Connie Ryan	789
10	Frank Bolling	779
11	Jackie Robinson	748
12	Billy Gardner	732
13	Jim Gilliam	711
14	Pete Suder	679
15	Don Blasingame	675
16	Bill Mazeroski	661
	Billy Martin	661
	Bobby Young	661
19	Joe Gordon	657
20	Danny O'Connell	630

Putouts

1	Nellie Fox	4,765
2	Red Schoendienst	4,543
3	Bobby Avila	2,820
4	Jerry Priddy	2,773
5	Johnny Temple	2,636
6	Bobby Doerr	2,303
7	Eddie Stanky	2,103
8	Cass Michaels	2,072
9	Connie Ryan	1,982
10	Jackie Robinson	1,877
11	Frank Bolling	1,863
12	Billy Gardner	1,725
13	Jim Gilliam	1,657
14	Don Blasingame	1,652
15	Bobby Young	1,610
16	Pete Suder	1,585
17	Bill Mazeroski	1,531
18	Billy Martin	1,517
19	Pete Runnels	1,513
20	Danny O'Connell	1,477

Assists

1	Red Schoendienst	5,158
2	Nellie Fox	4,877
3	Bobby Avila	3,126
4	Jerry Priddy	3,039
5	Johnny Temple	2,642
6	Bobby Doerr	2,560
7	Cass Michaels	2,341
8	Eddie Stanky	2,217
9	Connie Ryan	2,204
10	Frank Bolling	2,055
11	Jackie Robinson	2,047
12	Bill Mazeroski	2,003
13	Don Blasingame	1,976
14	Joe Gordon	1,961
15	Jim Gilliam	1,949
16	Pete Suder	1,928
17	Billy Gardner	1,925
18	Danny O'Connell	1,827
19	Bobby Young	1,754
20	Wayne Terwilliger	1,723

Errors

1	Nellie Fox	165
	Red Schoendienst	165
3	Jerry Priddy	160
4	Johnny Temple	134
5	Bobby Avila	130
6	Cass Michaels	127
7	Connie Ryan	126
8	Billy Goodman	91
9	Eddie Stanky	89
	Joe Gordon	89
11	Gene Baker	84
	Wayne Terwilliger	84
	Granny Hamner	84
14	Emil Verban	82
15	Don Blasingame	80
16	Billy Gardner	79
17	Frank Bolling	77
	Jim Gilliam	77
19	Bobby Doerr	75
20	Eddie Miksis	74

Double Plays

1	Red Schoendienst	1,348
2	Nellie Fox	1,307
3	Bobby Avila	785
4	Jerry Priddy	766
5	Bobby Doerr	729
6	Johnny Temple	685
7	Cass Michaels	633
8	Jackie Robinson	607
9	Eddie Stanky	606
10	Pete Suder	535
11	Frank Bolling	521
12	Bobby Young	503
13	Bill Mazeroski	497
14	Billy Gardner	491
15	Joe Gordon	486
16	Don Blasingame	485
17	Pete Runnels	477
	Jerry Coleman	477
19	Billy Martin	471
20	Connie Ryan	469

Fielding Percentage
(minimum 750 games)

1	Bobby Doerr	.985
2	Red Schoendienst	.983
3	Nellie Fox	.983
4	Frank Bolling	.981
5	Eddie Stanky	.980
6	Bobby Avila	.979
7	Johnny Temple	.975
8	Jerry Priddy	.973
9	Cass Michaels	.972
10	Connie Ryan	.971

Range Factor
(minimum 750 games)

1	Bobby Doerr	5.87
2	Jerry Priddy	5.78
3	Nellie Fox	5.57
4	Cass Michaels	5.52
5	Red Schoendienst	5.45
6	Eddie Stanky	5.35
7	Connie Ryan	5.31
8	Johnny Temple	5.15
9	Bobby Avila	5.09
10	Frank Bolling	5.03

Assists/162 Games
(minimum 750 games)

1	Bobby Doerr	500.27
2	Jerry Priddy	489.38
3	Cass Michaels	474.65
4	Red Schoendienst	469.44
5	Nellie Fox	456.16
6	Connie Ryan	452.53
7	Eddie Stanky	445.05
8	Bobby Avila	433.57
9	Frank Bolling	427.36
10	Johnny Temple	417.56

Single Season Fielding Leaders—Second Basemen: Postwar Era (1946-1960)

Games

1	Jerry Priddy	1950	157
2	Jackie Robinson	1949	156
	Nellie Fox	1959	156
4	Emil Verban	1947	155
	Joe Gordon	1947	155
	Nellie Fox	1954	155
	Nellie Fox	1957	155
	Nellie Fox	1958	155
9	Cass Michaels	1949	154
	Jerry Priddy	1951	154
	Connie Ryan	1952	154
	Nellie Fox	1953	154
	Gene Baker	1955	154
	Nellie Fox	1955	154
	Johnny Temple	1956	154
	Nellie Fox	1956	154
	Don Blasingame	1957	154
	Frank Bolling	1958	154
19	5 tied with		152

Putouts

1	Nellie Fox	1956	478
2	Nellie Fox	1957	453
3	Nellie Fox	1953	451
4	Emil Verban	1947	450
5	Nellie Fox	1958	444
6	Bobby Doerr	1950	443
7	Jerry Priddy	1950	440
8	Jerry Priddy	1951	437
9	Gene Baker	1955	432
10	Johnny Temple	1954	428
11	Bobby Doerr	1946	420
12	Nellie Fox	1951	413
	Bill Mazeroski	1960	413
14	Nellie Fox	1960	412
15	Cass Michaels	1950	409
16	Johnny Temple	1955	408
17	Jerry Priddy	1948	407
	Jerry Priddy	1949	407
	Eddie Stanky	1950	407
	Jim Gilliam	1957	407

Assists

1	Jerry Priddy	1950	542
2	Don Blasingame	1957	512
3	Bill Mazeroski	1958	496
4	Cass Michaels	1949	484
5	Bobby Doerr	1946	483
	Nellie Fox	1955	483
7	Red Schoendienst	1954	477
8	Jerry Priddy	1948	471
9	Joe Gordon	1947	466
	Bobby Doerr	1947	466
11	Jerry Priddy	1951	463
12	Bobby Young	1951	462
	Connie Ryan	1952	462
14	Pete Suder	1948	461
15	Tony Taylor	1959	456
16	Emil Verban	1947	453
	Nellie Fox	1957	453
	Nellie Fox	1959	453
19	Nellie Fox	1951	449
	Bill Mazeroski	1960	449

Errors

1	Jerry Priddy	1946	32
2	Gene Baker	1955	30
3	Jerry Priddy	1948	29
4	Emil Verban	1946	28
	Bobby Avila	1952	28
6	Al Kozar	1948	27
	Jerry Priddy	1949	27
8	Roy Hartsfield	1950	26
	Cass Michaels	1950	26
	Don Blasingame	1958	26
11	Gene Baker	1954	25
	Gene Baker	1956	25
	Tony Taylor	1959	25
14	Wayne Terwilliger	1950	24
	Cass Michaels	1951	24
	Curt Roberts	1954	24
	Johnny Temple	1955	24
	Nellie Fox	1955	24
	Daryl Spencer	1959	24
	Julian Javier	1960	24

Double Plays

1	Jerry Priddy	1950	150
2	Nellie Fox	1957	141
3	Jerry Coleman	1950	137
	Jackie Robinson	1951	137
	Red Schoendienst	1954	137
6	Cass Michaels	1949	135
7	Bobby Doerr	1949	134
8	Jackie Robinson	1950	133
9	Jerry Priddy	1948	132
10	Bobby Doerr	1950	130
11	Bobby Doerr	1946	129
12	Eddie Stanky	1950	128
	Don Blasingame	1957	128
14	Cass Michaels	1950	127
	Bobby Young	1952	127
	Bill Mazeroski	1960	127
17	Nellie Fox	1960	126
18	Red Schoendienst	1950	124
	Nellie Fox	1956	124
20	2 tied with		123

Fielding Percentage
(minimum 100 games)

1	Red Schoendienst	1956	.993
2	Snuffy Stirnweiss	1948	.993
3	Bobby Doerr	1948	.993
4	Jackie Robinson	1951	.992
5	Red Schoendienst	1951	.990
6	Grady Hatton	1952	.990
7	Charlie Neal	1959	.989
8	Nellie Fox	1954	.989
9	Bill Mazeroski	1960	.989
10	Nellie Fox	1959	.988
11	Pete Suder	1948	.988
12	Bobby Doerr	1950	.988
13	Frank Bolling	1959	.987
14	Red Schoendienst	1958	.987
15	Red Schoendienst	1949	.987
16	Billy Gardner	1957	.987
17	Pete Suder	1951	.987
18	Nellie Fox	1956	.986
19	Jim Gilliam	1957	.986
20	Bobby Avila	1953	.986

Range Factor
(minimum 100 games)

1	Jerry Priddy	1950	6.25
2	Billy Goodman	1952	6.06
3	Red Schoendienst	1954	6.05
4	Jerry Priddy	1948	6.01
5	Bobby Doerr	1949	6.00
6	Bobby Doerr	1946	5.98
7	Red Schoendienst	1949	5.96
8	Bobby Doerr	1950	5.87
9	Nellie Fox	1951	5.86
10	Red Schoendienst	1951	5.85
11	Nellie Fox	1957	5.85
12	Jerry Priddy	1951	5.84
13	Danny O'Connell	1955	5.84
14	Jerry Priddy	1946	5.84
15	Cass Michaels	1950	5.83
16	Emil Verban	1947	5.83
17	Joe Gordon	1946	5.81
18	Red Schoendienst	1952	5.80
19	Bobby Doerr	1951	5.79
20	Eddie Miksis	1951	5.79

Assists/162 Games
(minimum 100 games)

1	Jerry Priddy	1950	559.26
2	Don Blasingame	1957	538.60
3	Red Schoendienst	1954	536.63
4	Billy Goodman	1952	534.76
5	Bill Mazeroski	1958	528.63
6	Jerry Priddy	1948	522.62
7	Joe Gordon	1946	519.00
8	Bobby Doerr	1946	518.19
9	Jim Gilliam	1956	517.76
10	Bobby Doerr	1947	517.07
11	Bobby Avila	1953	514.93
12	Bobby Doerr	1949	511.64
13	Cass Michaels	1949	509.14
	Bobby Young	1951	509.14
15	Nellie Fox	1955	508.09
16	Danny O'Connell	1955	507.32
17	Bobby Doerr	1948	504.78
18	Pete Suder	1948	504.61
19	Red Schoendienst	1951	504.29
20	Jerry Priddy	1946	502.43

Career Fielding Leaders—Third Basemen: Postwar Era (1946-1960)

Games

1	Eddie Yost	1,910
2	Puddin' Head Jones	1,613
3	George Kell	1,405
4	Eddie Mathews	1,310
5	Grady Hatton	956
6	Al Rosen	932
7	Bob Elliott	851
8	Randy Jackson	844
9	Don Hoak	834
10	Ken Boyer	762
11	Hank Majeski	751
12	Andy Carey	747
13	Bill Johnson	742
14	Billy Cox	700
15	Bob Dillinger	692
16	Hank Thompson	655
17	Bobby Adams	652
18	Frank Malzone	643
19	Ray Jablonski	630
20	Ray Boone	510

Putouts

1	Eddie Yost	2,264
2	Puddin' Head Jones	2,045
3	George Kell	1,471
4	Eddie Mathews	1,231
5	Grady Hatton	979
6	Al Rosen	970
7	Don Hoak	901
8	Randy Jackson	868
9	Bob Elliott	863
10	Bob Dillinger	811
11	Hank Majeski	785
12	Andy Carey	761
13	Ken Boyer	725
14	Bobby Adams	711
15	Bill Johnson	677
16	Billy Cox	668
17	Frank Malzone	609
18	Hank Thompson	592
19	Ray Boone	576
20	Johnny Pesky	522

Assists

1	Eddie Yost	3,504
2	Puddin' Head Jones	2,934
3	George Kell	2,666
4	Eddie Mathews	2,626
5	Grady Hatton	1,844
6	Al Rosen	1,773
7	Randy Jackson	1,725
8	Bob Elliott	1,702
9	Don Hoak	1,639
10	Ken Boyer	1,605
11	Hank Majeski	1,528
12	Frank Malzone	1,495
	Andy Carey	1,495
14	Bill Johnson	1,402
15	Hank Thompson	1,341
16	Billy Cox	1,273
17	Bobby Adams	1,268
18	Bob Elliott	1,234
19	Ray Jablonski	1,069
20	Ray Boone	1,058

Errors

1	Eddie Yost	259
2	Puddin' Head Jones	191
3	Eddie Mathews	186
4	Grady Hatton	129
5	Bob Elliott	128
6	George Kell	126
7	Randy Jackson	123
8	Hank Thompson	122
9	Al Rosen	112
	Bob Dillinger	112
11	Don Hoak	110
12	Ken Boyer	109
13	Frank Malzone	108
14	Ray Jablonski	105
15	Hector Lopez	98
16	Andy Carey	95
17	Bobby Adams	93
	Bill Johnson	93
19	Gene Freese	74
20	Frank Thomas	73

Double Plays

1	Eddie Yost	339
2	Puddin' Head Jones	273
3	George Kell	249
4	Eddie Mathews	222
5	Ken Boyer	178
6	Andy Carey	174
7	Hank Majeski	171
8	Grady Hatton	169
9	Don Hoak	166
10	Al Rosen	159
11	Randy Jackson	157
12	Bob Elliott	156
13	Billy Cox	154
14	Frank Malzone	148
15	Hank Thompson	142
16	Bill Johnson	131
17	Gil McDougald	127
18	Bob Dillinger	125
	Bobby Adams	125
20	Johnny Pesky	121

Fielding Percentage
(minimum 750 games)

1	Hank Majeski	.972
2	George Kell	.970
3	Puddin' Head Jones	.963
4	Al Rosen	.961
5	Don Hoak	.958
6	Eddie Yost	.957
7	Grady Hatton	.956
8	Ken Boyer	.955
9	Randy Jackson	.955
10	Eddie Mathews	.954
11	Bob Elliott	.952

Range Factor
(minimum 750 games)

1	Puddin' Head Jones	3.09
2	Hank Majeski	3.08
3	Randy Jackson	3.07
4	Ken Boyer	3.06
5	Don Hoak	3.05
6	Eddie Yost	3.02
7	Bob Elliott	3.01
8	Grady Hatton	2.95
9	George Kell	2.94
10	Eddie Mathews	2.94
11	Al Rosen	2.94

Assists/162 Games
(minimum 750 games)

1	Ken Boyer	341.22
2	Randy Jackson	331.10
3	Hank Majeski	329.61
4	Eddie Mathews	324.74
5	Bob Elliott	324.00
6	Don Hoak	318.37
7	Grady Hatton	312.48
8	Al Rosen	308.18
9	George Kell	307.40
10	Eddie Yost	297.20
11	Puddin' Head Jones	294.67

Single Season Fielding Leaders—Third Basemen: Postwar Era (1946-1960)

Games

1	Puddin' Head Jones	1950	157
	George Kell	1950	157
	Eddie Yost	1952	157
	Ray Jablonski	1953	157
	Eddie Mathews	1953	157
6	Frankie Gustine	1947	156
7	Eddie Yost	1950	155
	Eddie Yost	1954	155
	Frank Malzone	1958	155
	Don Hoak	1959	155
	Don Hoak	1960	155
12	Al Rosen	1950	154
	Al Rosen	1951	154
	Bobby Adams	1952	154
	Al Rosen	1953	154
	Frank Malzone	1959	154
17	Bob Dillinger	1948	153
	Ken Keltner	1948	153
	Frank Malzone	1957	153
	Eddie Mathews	1960	153

Putouts

1	Puddin' Head Jones	1952	216
2	Eddie Yost	1952	212
3	Eddie Yost	1950	205
4	Eddie Yost	1951	203
5	Puddin' Head Jones	1955	202
	Puddin' Head Jones	1956	202
7	Frankie Gustine	1947	198
	Randy Jackson	1951	198
9	Don Hoak	1957	193
10	Puddin' Head Jones	1950	190
	Puddin' Head Jones	1951	190
	Eddie Yost	1953	190
13	Eddie Yost	1948	189
14	Bob Dillinger	1948	187
15	George Kell	1950	186
16	Johnny Pesky	1949	184
	Puddin' Head Jones	1954	184
18	Puddin' Head Jones	1949	181
19	Bobby Adams	1952	176
	Puddin' Head Jones	1953	176

Assists

1	Frank Malzone	1958	378
2	Frank Malzone	1957	370
3	Frank Malzone	1959	357
4	Eddie Mathews	1958	351
5	Ken Boyer	1958	350
6	Eddie Yost	1954	347
7	Al Rosen	1953	338
8	George Kell	1947	333
	Johnny Pesky	1949	333
10	Bill Johnson	1951	332
	Ray Boone	1954	332
12	Frankie Gustine	1947	330
13	Bobby Adams	1952	328
	Brooks Robinson	1960	328
15	Harmon Killebrew	1959	325
16	Bobby Adams	1953	324
	Don Hoak	1960	324
18	Puddin' Head Jones	1950	323
	Randy Jackson	1951	323
20	2 tied with		322

Errors

1	Ray Jablonski	1954	34
2	Frankie Gustine	1947	31
3	Eddie Yost	1950	30
	Eddie Mathews	1953	30
	Harmon Killebrew	1959	30
6	Andy Pafko	1948	29
	Frank Thomas	1958	29
8	Grady Hatton	1948	28
	Fred Marsh	1951	28
10	Puddin' Head Jones	1949	27
	Ray Jablonski	1953	27
	Frank Malzone	1958	27
13	Grady Hatton	1947	26
	Bob Elliott	1948	26
	Hank Thompson	1950	26
	Hector Lopez	1956	26
	Frank Malzone	1960	26
	Eddie Yost	1960	26
19	8 tied with		25

Double Plays

1	Johnny Pesky	1949	48
2	Eddie Yost	1950	45
3	Hank Thompson	1950	43
4	Ken Boyer	1958	41
5	Frank Malzone	1959	40
6	Bobby Adams	1953	39
7	Gil McDougald	1952	38
	Al Rosen	1953	38
9	Hank Majeski	1949	37
	Andy Carey	1955	37
	Ken Boyer	1956	37
	Ken Boyer	1960	37
13	Gil McDougald	1953	36
	Puddin' Head Jones	1953	36
	Frank Malzone	1958	36
	Frank Malzone	1960	36
17	Frankie Gustine	1947	35
	Johnny Pesky	1948	35
	Billy Cox	1950	35
20	4 tied with		34

Fielding Percentage
(minimum 100 games)

1	Hank Majeski	1947	.988
2	George Kell	1946	.983
3	George Kell	1950	.982
4	Floyd Baker	1947	.980
5	Jim Davenport	1959	.978
6	George Kell	1956	.978
7	Floyd Baker	1949	.977
8	Brooks Robinson	1960	.977
9	George Kell	1955	.976
10	Grady Hatton	1955	.976
11	Bill Johnson	1951	.976
12	Grady Hatton	1949	.975
13	Hank Majeski	1948	.975
14	Puddin' Head Jones	1953	.975
15	George Kell	1949	.975
16	Johnny Pesky	1950	.974
17	Puddin' Head Jones	1956	.973
18	Ken Keltner	1947	.972
19	George Kell	1953	.972
20	Fred Hatfield	1952	.971

Range Factor
(minimum 100 games)

1	Randy Jackson	1951	3.64
2	Andy Carey	1954	3.64
3	Johnny Pesky	1950	3.59
4	Ken Boyer	1958	3.51
5	Johnny Pesky	1949	3.49
6	Eddie Yost	1956	3.46
7	Billy Klaus	1956	3.42
8	Frank Malzone	1957	3.41
9	Gil McDougald	1952	3.39
10	Bob Elliott	1949	3.39
11	Ray Boone	1954	3.39
12	Frankie Gustine	1947	3.38
13	Puddin' Head Jones	1952	3.38
14	Tommy Glaviano	1950	3.38
15	Lee Handley	1946	3.37
16	Puddin' Head Jones	1949	3.37
17	Andy Carey	1955	3.37
18	Don Hoak	1958	3.36
19	Hector Lopez	1956	3.36
20	Jim Finigan	1954	3.35

Assists/162 Games
(minimum 100 games)

1	Floyd Baker	1947	405.80
2	Frank Malzone	1958	395.07
3	Ken Boyer	1958	393.75
4	Bill Johnson	1951	392.58
5	Frank Malzone	1957	391.76
6	Tommy Glaviano	1950	389.72
7	Andy Carey	1954	382.05
8	Eddie Mathews	1958	381.62
9	Gil McDougald	1952	378.00
10	Lee Handley	1946	376.41
11	Frank Malzone	1959	375.55
12	Bob Elliott	1949	373.85
13	Billy Klaus	1956	369.85
14	Andy Pafko	1948	365.96
15	Randy Jackson	1951	365.92
16	Johnny Pesky	1949	364.50
17	Eddie Yost	1956	363.60
18	Ray Boone	1954	363.41
19	Jim Finigan	1954	363.31
20	Eddie Yost	1954	362.67

Career Fielding Leaders—Shortstops: Postwar Era (1946-1960)

Games		Putouts		Assists		Errors	
1 Pee Wee Reese	1,629	1 Pee Wee Reese	3,167	1 Pee Wee Reese	4,698	1 Pee Wee Reese	288
2 Al Dark	1,404	2 Al Dark	2,672	2 Johnny Logan	4,257	2 Al Dark	286
3 Phil Rizzuto	1,375	3 Phil Rizzuto	2,643	3 Al Dark	4,168	3 Johnny Logan	238
4 Johnny Logan	1,328	4 Johnny Logan	2,529	4 Roy McMillan	3,948	4 Granny Hamner	228
5 Roy McMillan	1,302	5 Roy McMillan	2,478	5 Phil Rizzuto	3,822	5 Roy Smalley	207
6 Chico Carrasquel	1,241	6 Chico Carrasquel	2,131	6 Chico Carrasquel	3,619	6 Phil Rizzuto	204
7 Ernie Banks	1,021	7 Eddie Joost	2,039	7 Ernie Banks	3,083	7 Roy McMillan	193
8 Joe DeMaestri	1,011	8 Dick Groat	1,917	8 Joe DeMaestri	2,899	8 Chico Carrasquel	185
9 Dick Groat	937	9 Ernie Banks	1,914	9 Dick Groat	2,814	9 Dick Groat	184
10 Eddie Joost	927	10 Joe DeMaestri	1,674	10 Eddie Joost	2,781	10 Eddie Joost	180
11 Granny Hamner	900	11 Granny Hamner	1,514	11 Granny Hamner	2,676	11 Ernie Banks	155
12 Roy Smalley	820	12 Roy Smalley	1,435	12 Vern Stephens	2,476	Joe DeMaestri	155
13 Vern Stephens	775	13 Marty Marion	1,409	13 Luis Aparicio	2,397	13 Harvey Kuenn	129
14 Willie Miranda	768	14 Vern Stephens	1,380	14 Roy Smalley	2,291	Johnny Lipon	129
15 Harvey Kuenn	747	15 Luis Aparicio	1,372	15 Marty Marion	2,269	Vern Stephens	129
16 Luis Aparicio	744	16 Harvey Kuenn	1,343	16 Buddy Kerr	2,185	16 Don Buddin	125
17 Marty Marion	726	17 Buddy Kerr	1,324	17 Harvey Kuenn	2,114	17 Luke Appling	123
18 Buddy Kerr	714	18 Lou Boudreau	1,291	18 Johnny Lipon	2,040	18 George Strickland	120
19 Johnny Lipon	683	19 Johnny Lipon	1,265	19 Lou Boudreau	1,959	19 Willie Miranda	119
20 George Strickland	679	20 George Strickland	1,149	20 George Strickland	1,941	20 2 tied with	117

Double Plays		Fielding Percentage (minimum 750 games)		Range Factor (minimum 750 games)		Assists/162 Games (minimum 750 games)	
1 Pee Wee Reese	1,030	1 Roy McMillan	.971	1 Eddie Joost	5.20	1 Johnny Logan	519.30
2 Phil Rizzuto	994	2 Ernie Banks	.970	2 Dick Groat	5.14	2 Vern Stephens	517.56
3 Al Dark	933	3 Phil Rizzuto	.969	3 Johnny Logan	5.11	3 Dick Groat	501.21
4 Roy McMillan	868	4 Chico Carrasquel	.969	4 Vern Stephens	4.98	4 Roy McMillan	491.23
5 Johnny Logan	862	5 Vern Stephens	.968	5 Roy McMillan	4.94	5 Ernie Banks	489.17
6 Chico Carrasquel	770	6 Joe DeMaestri	.967	6 Ernie Banks	4.89	6 Eddie Joost	486.00
7 Eddie Joost	709	7 Johnny Logan	.966	7 Al Dark	4.87	7 Granny Hamner	481.68
8 Ernie Banks	656	8 Pee Wee Reese	.965	8 Pee Wee Reese	4.83	8 Al Dark	480.92
9 Dick Groat	632	9 Eddie Joost	.964	9 Phil Rizzuto	4.70	9 Chico Carrasquel	472.42
10 Joe DeMaestri	603	10 Dick Groat	.963	10 Granny Hamner	4.66	10 Pee Wee Reese	467.20
11 Vern Stephens	580	11 Willie Miranda	.962	11 Chico Carrasquel	4.63	11 Roy Smalley	452.61
12 Granny Hamner	547	12 Al Dark	.960	12 Roy Smalley	4.54	12 Joe DeMaestri	450.91
13 Lou Boudreau	500	13 Granny Hamner	.948	13 Joe DeMaestri	4.44	13 Phil Rizzuto	450.30
14 Marty Marion	477	14 Roy Smalley	.947	14 Willie Miranda	3.95	14 Willie Miranda	404.16
15 Luis Aparicio	470						
16 Roy Smalley	465						
17 Johnny Lipon	457						
18 George Strickland	456						
19 Harvey Kuenn	430						
20 Willie Miranda	412						

Single Season Fielding Leaders—Shortstops: Postwar Era (1946-1960)

Games			Putouts			Assists			Errors		
1 Eddie Lake	1947	158	1 Eddie Joost	1947	370	1 Luis Aparicio	1960	551	1 Roy Smalley	1950	51
2 Granny Hamner	1950	157	2 Eddie Joost	1949	352	2 Roy Smalley	1950	541	2 Granny Hamner	1950	48
3 Stan Rojek	1948	156	3 Roy McMillan	1954	341	3 Vern Stephens	1948	540	3 Al Dark	1951	45
Al Dark	1951	156	4 Phil Rizzuto	1947	340	4 Roy McMillan	1953	519	4 Eddie Lake	1947	43
Ernie Banks	1960	156	5 Pee Wee Reese	1948	335	Ernie Banks	1959	519	5 Maury Wills	1960	40
6 Eddie Lake	1946	155	6 Roy Smalley	1950	332	6 Granny Hamner	1950	513	6 Billy Cox	1946	39
Vern Stephens	1948	155	7 Dick Groat	1955	330	7 Billy Hunter	1953	512	Luke Appling	1946	39
Vern Stephens	1949	155	8 Marty Marion	1947	329	8 Johnny Logan	1955	511	Roy Smalley	1949	39
Pee Wee Reese	1949	155	Phil Rizzuto	1949	329	Roy McMillan	1956	511	9 Eddie Joost	1947	38
Buddy Kerr	1950	155	10 Eddie Joost	1948	325	10 Vern Stephens	1949	508	Granny Hamner	1952	38
Phil Rizzuto	1950	155	Eddie Joost	1951	325	11 Granny Hamner	1949	506	11 George Strickland	1951	37
Harvey Kuenn	1953	155	Ron Hansen	1960	325	12 Luke Appling	1946	505	12 Dick Culler	1946	36
Roy McMillan	1953	155	13 Al Dark	1952	324	13 Harvey Kuenn	1954	496	Al Dark	1954	36
Harvey Kuenn	1954	155	Johnny Logan	1954	324	14 Roy McMillan	1952	495	14 Eddie Lake	1946	35
Chico Carrasquel	1954	155	15 Roy McMillan	1956	319	Roy McMillan	1955	495	Luke Appling	1947	35
16 13 tied with		154	16 Phil Rizzuto	1951	317	16 Vern Stephens	1947	494	Sam Dente	1949	35
			17 Pee Wee Reese	1949	316	17 Chico Carrasquel	1954	492	Pee Wee Reese	1951	35
			18 Lou Boudreau	1946	315	18 Johnny Logan	1954	489	Luis Aparicio	1956	35
			19 Sam Dente	1949	314	19 Ernie Banks	1960	488	Don Buddin	1959	35
			Pete Runnels	1952	314	20 Al Dark	1954	487	20 6 tied with		34

Double Plays			Fielding Percentage (minimum 100 games)			Range Factor (minimum 100 games)			Assists/162 Games (minimum 100 games)		
1 Roy McMillan	1954	129	1 Ernie Banks	1959	.985	1 Roy Smalley	1950	5.67	1 Luis Aparicio	1960	583.41
2 Vern Stephens	1949	128	2 Lou Boudreau	1947	.982	2 Luis Aparicio	1960	5.59	2 Billy Klaus	1957	572.49
3 Dick Groat	1958	127	3 Phil Rizzuto	1950	.982	3 Don Zimmer	1958	5.59	3 Roy Smalley	1950	569.10
4 Eddie Joost	1949	126	4 Buddy Kerr	1946	.982	4 Rocky Bridges	1957	5.58	4 Rocky Bridges	1957	567.74
Johnny Lipon	1950	126	5 Vern Stephens	1950	.981	5 Marty Marion	1947	5.54	5 Vern Stephens	1948	564.39
6 Phil Rizzuto	1950	123	6 Marty Marion	1947	.981	6 Roy McMillan	1956	5.53	6 Milt Bolling	1954	560.19
7 Lou Boudreau	1947	120	7 Johnny Lipon	1952	.981	7 Eddie Joost	1949	5.51	7 Johnny Logan	1957	552.56
8 Lou Boudreau	1948	119	8 Joe DeMaestri	1958	.980	8 Johnny Logan	1957	5.45	8 Roy McMillan	1956	551.88
9 Phil Rizzuto	1949	118	9 Joe DeMaestri	1957	.980	9 Eddie Joost	1947	5.44	9 Luke Appling	1946	549.06
10 Eddie Joost	1950	117	10 Roy McMillan	1958	.980	10 Eddie Joost	1948	5.44	10 Tony Kubek	1958	547.66
Luis Aparicio	1960	117	11 Luis Aparicio	1960	.979	11 Johnny Logan	1952	5.40	11 Ernie Banks	1959	545.96
12 Al Dark	1952	116	12 Mark Christman	1947	.978	12 Dick Groat	1959	5.34	12 Billy Hunter	1953	545.68
Phil Rizzuto	1952	116	13 Marty Marion	1950	.978	13 Eddie Joost	1951	5.34	13 Roy McMillan	1953	542.44
14 Eddie Joost	1948	115	14 Buddy Kerr	1947	.977	14 Roy Smalley	1949	5.33	14 Buddy Kerr	1947	541.17
Roy Smalley	1950	115	15 Ernie Banks	1960	.977	15 Marty Marion	1946	5.31	15 Johnny Logan	1958	541.13
Vern Stephens	1950	115	16 Pee Wee Reese	1949	.977	16 Buddy Kerr	1947	5.30	16 Roy Smalley	1949	537.55
Eddie Joost	1951	115	17 Roy McMillan	1957	.977	17 Pee Wee Reese	1948	5.29	Johnny Logan	1955	537.55
18 Al Dark	1951	114	18 George Strickland	1955	.976	18 Chico Carrasquel	1951	5.29	18 Vern Stephens	1947	537.10
Roy McMillan	1953	114	19 Chico Carrasquel	1953	.976	19 Johnny Logan	1954	5.28	19 Marty Marion	1946	536.28
20 4 tied with		113	20 Phil Rizzuto	1952	.976	20 Gil McDougald	1957	5.27	20 Roy McMillan	1955	534.60

Career Fielding Leaders—Outfielders: Postwar Era (1946-1960)

#	Games		#	Putouts		#	Assists		#	Errors	
1	Richie Ashburn	1,931	1	Richie Ashburn	5,771	1	Richie Ashburn	165	1	Del Ennis	120
2	Del Ennis	1,840	2	Duke Snider	3,747	2	Carl Furillo	151	2	Richie Ashburn	102
3	Carl Furillo	1,739	3	Del Ennis	3,621	3	Del Ennis	150	3	Ralph Kiner	80
4	Duke Snider	1,664	4	Larry Doby	3,616	4	Dave Philley	137	4	Bobby Thomson	74
5	Ted Williams	1,576	5	Bobby Thomson	3,563	5	Minnie Minoso	123		Carl Furillo	74
6	Bobby Thomson	1,506	6	Willie Mays	3,328	6	Gus Bell	122	6	Minnie Minoso	72
7	Gus Bell	1,483	7	Carl Furillo	3,322	7	Willie Mays	117	7	Gus Zernial	71
8	Larry Doby	1,440	8	Gus Bell	3,273	8	Willard Marshall	112	8	Willie Mays	66
9	Enos Slaughter	1,432	9	Mickey Mantle	3,220	9	Bobby Thomson	111		Ted Williams	66
10	Dave Philley	1,423	10	Dave Philley	3,215	10	Jackie Jensen	110	10	Jackie Jensen	64
11	Hank Bauer	1,414	11	Jim Busby	3,204	11	Duke Snider	107		Hank Sauer	64
12	Minnie Minoso	1,412	12	Ted Williams	2,964	12	Hank Bauer	105		Dave Philley	64
13	Gene Woodling	1,392	13	Ralph Kiner	2,875	13	Hank Sauer	104	13	Larry Doby	63
14	Ralph Kiner	1,382	14	Minnie Minoso	2,858	14	Enos Slaughter	99	14	Dom DiMaggio	62
15	Mickey Mantle	1,363	15	Jimmy Piersall	2,810	15	Mickey Mantle	97	15	Johnny Wyrostek	61
16	Andy Pafko	1,294	16	Dom DiMaggio	2,795	16	Dom DiMaggio	96	16	Bill Bruton	60
17	Jackie Jensen	1,260	17	Enos Slaughter	2,661	17	Roberto Clemente	95	17	Mickey Mantle	59
18	Willie Mays	1,210	18	Gene Woodling	2,653		Andy Pafko	95	18	Duke Snider	58
19	Jim Busby	1,199	19	Bill Bruton	2,619		Johnny Wyrostek	95	19	Jim Lemon	55
20	Hank Sauer	1,192	20	Johnny Groth	2,566	20	Al Kaline	94		Elmer Valo	55

#	Double Plays		#	Fielding Percentage (minimum 750 games)		#	Range Factor (minimum 750 games)		#	Assists/162 Games (minimum 750 games)	
1	Richie Ashburn	42	1	Gene Woodling	.989	1	Richie Ashburn	3.07	1	Willard Marshall	17.48
2	Willie Mays	38	2	Jimmy Piersall	.989	2	Dom DiMaggio	2.94	2	Wally Post	16.96
3	Carl Furillo	34	3	Jim Busby	.988	3	Willie Mays	2.85	3	Dom DiMaggio	15.80
4	Dave Philley	33	4	Johnny Groth	.987	4	Sam Chapman	2.84	4	Willie Mays	15.66
5	Del Ennis	27	5	Sam Mele	.985	5	Bill Virdon	2.73	5	Dave Philley	15.60
6	Larry Doby	26	6	Gus Bell	.985	6	Jim Busby	2.73	6	Irv Noren	15.37
7	Mickey Mantle	25	7	Duke Snider	.985	7	Bill Tuttle	2.63	7	Bill Tuttle	15.31
	Gus Bell	25	8	Sid Gordon	.985	8	Jimmy Piersall	2.61	8	Al Kaline	14.81
9	Jim Rivera	24	9	Dale Mitchell	.985	9	Bill Bruton	2.59	9	Johnny Wyrostek	14.29
	Bobby Thomson	24	10	Al Kaline	.984	10	Larry Doby	2.57	10	Jackie Jensen	14.14
	Willard Marshall	24	11	Bill Tuttle	.984	11	Bobby Thomson	2.44	11	Hank Sauer	14.13
12	Johnny Groth	23	12	Stan Musial	.984	12	Mickey Mantle	2.43	12	Minnie Minoso	14.11
13	Bill Bruton	22	13	Irv Noren	.984	13	Hoot Evers	2.37	13	Carl Furillo	14.07
	Enos Slaughter	22	14	Larry Doby	.983	14	Dave Philley	2.36	14	Richie Ashburn	13.84
15	7 tied with	20	15	Enos Slaughter	.983	15	Al Kaline	2.34	15	Bill Virdon	13.42
			16	Richie Ashburn	.983	16	Duke Snider	2.32	16	Gus Bell	13.33
			17	Hoot Evers	.983	17	Irv Noren	2.31	17	Del Ennis	13.21
			18	Wally Westlake	.983	18	Johnny Groth	2.29	18	Vic Wertz	13.14
			19	Bill Virdon	.983	19	Gus Bell	2.29	19	Gus Zernial	13.03
			20	Mickey Mantle	.983	20	Wally Westlake	2.28	20	Sam Mele	12.94

Single Season Fielding Leaders—Outfielders: Postwar Era (1946-1960)

#	Games	Year		#	Putouts	Year		#	Assists	Year		#	Errors	Year	
1	Johnny Groth	1950	157	1	Richie Ashburn	1951	538	1	Carl Furillo	1951	24	1	Harry Walker	1947	14
	Carl Furillo	1951	157	2	Richie Ashburn	1949	514	2	Enos Slaughter	1946	23		Larry Doby	1948	14
	Ralph Kiner	1953	157	3	Dom DiMaggio	1948	503		Richie Ashburn	1952	23		Del Ennis	1948	14
	Stan Musial	1953	157		Richie Ashburn	1956	503		Willie Mays	1955	23		Gil Coan	1951	14
	Dave Philley	1953	157	5	Richie Ashburn	1957	502		Al Kaline	1958	23		Del Ennis	1954	14
6	Enos Slaughter	1946	156	6	Richie Ashburn	1953	496	6	Dave Philley	1948	22		Bill Bruton	1955	14
	Ted Williams	1947	156	7	Richie Ashburn	1958	495		Jim Rivera	1955	22	7	Johnny Blatnik	1948	13
	Bobby Thomson	1949	156	8	Jim Busby	1954	491		Roberto Clemente	1958	22		Al Zarilla	1948	13
	Stan Musial	1949	156	9	Bobby Thomson	1949	488	9	Irv Noren	1950	20		Whitey Platt	1948	13
	Jim Rivera	1953	156	10	Richie Ashburn	1954	483		Mickey Mantle	1954	20		Joe DiMaggio	1948	13
	Richie Ashburn	1953	156	11	Jim Busby	1953	482	11	Willard Marshall	1947	19		Del Ennis	1949	13
	Richie Ashburn	1957	156	12	Jim Busby	1952	472		Dom DiMaggio	1947	19		Sam Jethroe	1952	13
13	Willard Marshall	1947	155	13	Jimmy Piersall	1956	455		Dave Philley	1950	19		Roberto Clemente	1956	13
	Stan Musial	1948	155	14	Sam Chapman	1949	450		Hank Sauer	1951	19		Hank Aaron	1956	13
	Dom DiMaggio	1948	155	15	Willie Mays	1954	448		Minnie Minoso	1955	19		Bill Bruton	1956	13
	Vic Wertz	1949	155	16	Gus Bell	1953	447		Bob Skinner	1958	19		Roberto Clemente	1959	13
	Ted Williams	1949	155	17	Dave Philley	1952	442		Roberto Clemente	1960	19	17	9 tied with		12
	Jim Busby	1954	155		Bill Tuttle	1955	442	18	16 tied with		18				
	Jimmy Piersall	1956	155	19	Joe DiMaggio	1948	441								
20	17 tied with		154	20	Jim Rivera	1952	430								

#	Double Plays	Year		#	Fielding Percentage (minimum 100 games)	Year		#	Range Factor (minimum 100 games)	Year		#	Assists/162 Games (minimum 100 games)	Year	
1	Willie Mays	1954	9	1	Willard Marshall	1951	1.000	1	Richie Ashburn	1951	3.59	1	Dave Philley	1948	27.84
2	Dave Philley	1950	8	2	Hoot Evers	1950	.997	2	Irv Noren	1951	3.45	2	Irv Noren	1950	26.78
	Willie Mays	1955	8	3	Charlie Maxwell	1957	.997	3	Richie Ashburn	1949	3.42	3	Roberto Clemente	1958	26.40
4	Tommy Holmes	1946	7	4	Joe DiMaggio	1947	.997	4	Richie Ashburn	1956	3.34	4	Al Kaline	1958	25.70
	Jimmy Piersall	1953	7	5	Lloyd Merriman	1951	.997	5	Richie Ashburn	1957	3.33	5	Jim Rivera	1955	24.92
	Jim Rivera	1955	7	6	Gus Bell	1959	.996	6	Dom DiMaggio	1948	3.33	6	Carl Furillo	1951	24.76
	Richie Ashburn	1957	7	7	Ken Boyer	1957	.996	7	Jim Busby	1953	3.31	7	Roberto Clemente	1955	24.71
8	16 tied with		6	8	Sid Gordon	1952	.996	8	Richie Ashburn	1958	3.31	8	Willie Mays	1955	24.51
				9	Charlie Maxwell	1960	.996	9	Jim Busby	1952	3.31	9	Curt Flood	1958	24.30
				10	Gene Woodling	1952	.996	10	Richie Ashburn	1953	3.29	10	Richie Ashburn	1952	24.19
				11	Al Pilarcik	1957	.996	11	Richie Ashburn	1954	3.24	11	Enos Slaughter	1946	23.88
				12	Monte Irvin	1951	.996	12	Dom DiMaggio	1947	3.22	12	Frank Thomas	1953	23.34
				13	Gene Woodling	1953	.996	13	Jim Busby	1954	3.21	13	Hank Sauer	1951	23.32
				14	Gus Bell	1958	.996	14	Bobby Thomson	1949	3.19	14	Chuck Diering	1954	23.14
				15	Enos Slaughter	1953	.996	15	Sam Chapman	1948	3.19		Ken Walters	1960	23.14
				16	Sam Mele	1953	.996	16	Dave Philley	1948	3.15	16	Dom DiMaggio	1947	22.97
				17	Jim Delsing	1954	.996	17	Johnny Groth	1953	3.14	17	Bill Tuttle	1959	22.76
				18	Ted Williams	1957	.995	18	Sam Chapman	1950	3.14	18	Mickey Mantle	1954	22.50
				19	Larry Doby	1954	.995	19	Irv Noren	1950	3.12	19	Minnie Minoso	1955	22.30
				20	Gene Woodling	1955	.995	20	Jim Rivera	1952	3.11	20	Johnny Wyrostek	1952	22.15

Career Fielding Leaders—Pitchers: Expansion Era (1961-1976)

## Games		## Putouts		## Assists		## Errors	
1 Lindy McDaniel	761	1 Juan Marichal	286	1 Claude Osteen	685	1 Ray Sadecki	50
2 Ron Perranoski	737	2 Bob Gibson	278	2 Gaylord Perry	652	2 Juan Marichal	47
3 Don McMahon	696	3 Gaylord Perry	266	3 Jim Kaat	640	3 Jim Kaat	45
4 Clay Carroll	670	4 Mel Stottlemyre	242	4 Mel Stottlemyre	570	4 Don Drysdale	43
Eddie Fisher	670	5 Jim Kaat	226	5 Tommy John	569	5 Blue Moon Odom	41
6 Bob Miller	663	6 Milt Pappas	222	6 Juan Marichal	564	6 Nolan Ryan	40
7 Darold Knowles	613	7 Fergie Jenkins	217	7 Phil Niekro	474	Bob Gibson	40
8 Dave Giusti	608	8 Phil Niekro	211	8 Bob Gibson	460	8 Andy Messersmith	39
Ted Abernathy	608	9 Catfish Hunter	200	9 Mike Cuellar	453	9 Mickey Lolich	38
10 Diego Segui	599	10 Jim Palmer	187	Don Drysdale	453	10 Steve Barber	36
Wilbur Wood	599	11 Carl Morton	182	11 Fergie Jenkins	450	11 Fergie Jenkins	35
12 Jim Kaat	598	12 Tom Seaver	177	Wilbur Wood	450	12 Sam McDowell	33
13 Hoyt Wilhelm	597	13 Earl Wilson	175	Larry Jackson	450	Dean Chance	33
14 Paul Lindblad	588	14 Don Sutton	170	14 Jim Perry	442	14 Bill Singer	32
15 Jim Brewer	579	15 Larry Jackson	169	15 Mickey Lolich	433	15 Luis Tiant	31
16 Bob Locker	576	16 Jim Lonborg	167	16 Fritz Peterson	429	16 Mike Cuellar	30
17 Gaylord Perry	555	17 Luis Tiant	161	17 Ken Holtzman	428	17 Clay Kirby	29
18 Sparky Lyle	549	18 Joe Coleman	160	18 Joe Horlen	421	18 Tommy John	27
19 Jim Perry	545	19 3 tied with	159	19 Tom Seaver	419	Jim Perry	27
20 Mickey Lolich	539			20 Dave McNally	417	20 5 tied with	26

## Double Plays		## Fielding Percentage		## Assists/162 Innings	
		(minimum 150 games)		(minimum 150 games)	
1 Jim Kaat	56	1 Ron Willis	1.000	1 Dooley Womack	50.37
2 Fritz Peterson	44	Dave Baldwin	1.000	2 Bobby Shantz	48.97
3 Gaylord Perry	43	Joe Grzenda	1.000	3 Frank Linzy	46.81
4 Phil Niekro	41	4 Gary Gentry	.995	4 Larry Bearnarth	46.19
Rick Wise	41	5 Gary Nolan	.993	5 Dale Murray	44.58
Bob Gibson	41	6 Don Mossi	.992	6 Hal Woodeshick	44.43
7 Tom Seaver	40	7 Woodie Fryman	.989	7 Ted Abernathy	44.15
8 Tommy John	38	8 Mike McCormick	.987	8 Dave Tomlin	42.20
Mel Stottlemyre	38	9 Ross Grimsley	.987	9 Tom Burgmeier	41.57
10 Dave McNally	37	10 Dennis Higgins	.986	10 Darold Knowles	41.41
Claude Osteen	37	11 Bill Stafford	.986	11 Jim Todd	40.96
12 Mudcat Grant	34	12 Wes Stock	.985	12 Bob Locker	39.81
13 Mike Cuellar	33	13 Chuck Taylor	.985	13 Horacio Pina	39.21
Don Drysdale	33	14 Don Gullett	.984	14 Tommy John	38.85
15 Dean Chance	31	15 Rick Wise	.984	15 Terry Forster	38.83
Larry Jackson	31	16 Dick Hall	.984	16 Bob Purkey	38.28
17 Jim Palmer	30	17 Stu Miller	.984	17 Al McBean	38.07
Clyde Wright	30	18 Gary Waslewski	.983	18 Ron Willis	38.06
Milt Pappas	30	19 Ralph Terry	.983	19 Mike Caldwell	37.62
20 2 tied with	29	20 2 tied with	.982	20 Joe Gibbon	37.25

Single Season Fielding Leaders—Pitchers: Expansion Era (1961-1976)

## Games			## Putouts			## Assists			## Errors		
1 Mike Marshall	1974	106	1 Mel Stottlemyre	1967	36	1 Mel Stottlemyre	1969	88	1 Clay Kirby	1974	10
2 Mike Marshall	1973	92	Denny McLain	1968	36	2 Larry Jackson	1964	85	J.R. Richard	1976	10
3 Wayne Granger	1969	90	3 Earl Wilson	1966	34	3 Fred Newman	1965	83	3 Don Drysdale	1965	9
4 Wilbur Wood	1968	88	4 Juan Marichal	1968	33	4 Claude Osteen	1965	82	Andy Messersmith	1974	9
5 Ted Abernathy	1965	84	5 Frank Lary	1961	32	Wilbur Wood	1972	82	5 Roger Craig	1963	8
6 Ken Sanders	1971	83	6 Bill Monbouquette	1963	31	6 Randy Jones	1976	81	Tony Cloninger	1966	8
7 Eddie Fisher	1965	82	Ralph Terry	1963	31	7 Mel Stottlemyre	1965	74	Jim Kaat	1969	8
8 John Wyatt	1964	81	Jim Bouton	1964	31	8 Jim Kaat	1962	72	Ray Culp	1969	8
Dale Murray	1976	81	Gaylord Perry	1968	31	9 Warren Spahn	1963	71	Tommy John	1970	8
10 Mudcat Grant	1970	80	Fergie Jenkins	1971	31	10 Randy Jones	1975	70	Tom Griffin	1974	8
Pedro Borbon	1973	80	Randy Jones	1976	31	11 Bob Purkey	1961	69	Bill Lee	1974	8
12 Dick Radatz	1964	79	12 Ernie Broglio	1963	30	Claude Osteen	1969	69	Steve Busby	1974	8
13 Hal Woodeshick	1965	78	Mel Stottlemyre	1965	30	Bill Lee	1974	69	13 19 tied with		7
Ted Abernathy	1968	78	Joe Coleman	1968	30	14 Don Drysdale	1964	68			
Bill Campbell	1976	78	Gaylord Perry	1970	30	15 Gaylord Perry	1969	67			
16 Bob Locker	1967	77	Phil Niekro	1973	30	Gaylord Perry	1970	67			
Wilbur Wood	1970	77	Steve Rogers	1974	30	Clyde Wright	1971	67			
Charlie Hough	1976	77	Jim Palmer	1975	30	Wilbur Wood	1974	67			
Butch Metzger	1976	77	19 8 tied with		29	19 Tommy John	1969	66			
20 4 tied with		76				Claude Osteen	1971	66			

## Double Plays			## Fielding Percentage			## Assists/162 Innings		
			(minimum 25 games)			(minimum 25 games)		
1 Randy Jones	1976	12	1 846 tied with		1.000	1 Frank Linzy	1965	77.36
2 Dick Drago	1971	9				2 Bobby Shantz	1964	74.77
Clyde Wright	1973	9				3 Chet Nichols	1961	72.12
4 Jim Kaat	1961	8				4 Al McBean	1964	68.65
Steve Barber	1961	8				5 Don Dennis	1966	65.16
Don Mossi	1961	8				6 Dave Baldwin	1970	64.19
Ray Herbert	1961	8				7 Darold Knowles	1972	64.14
Ray Herbert	1962	8				8 Hal Woodeshick	1966	59.89
Steve Barber	1963	8				9 Ed Sprague	1969	59.44
Warren Spahn	1963	8				10 Jim Crawford	1976	59.27
Jack Aker	1969	8				11 Phil Niekro	1966	57.93
Wilbur Wood	1972	8				12 Wes Stock	1962	57.32
Terry Forster	1973	8				13 Frank Linzy	1968	56.47
14 27 tied with		7				14 Larry Bearnarth	1964	56.08
						Dan Osinski	1969	56.08
						16 Dooley Womack	1967	55.11
						17 Bob Locker	1967	54.58
						18 Dale Murray	1976	54.32
						19 Frank Linzy	1967	54.19
						20 Ted Abernathy	1964	53.50

Career Fielding Leaders—Catchers: Expansion Era (1961-1976)

Games			Putouts			Assists			Errors	
1 Bill Freehan	1,581		1 Bill Freehan	9,941		1 Bill Freehan	721		1 John Bateman	113
2 Johnny Edwards	1,392		2 Johnny Edwards	8,925		2 Johnny Edwards	703		2 Thurman Munson	95
3 Tim McCarver	1,269		3 Jerry Grote	7,698		3 Johnny Bench	622		3 Manny Sanguillen	86
4 Johnny Bench	1,256		4 Tim McCarver	7,583		4 Jerry Grote	595		4 Tim McCarver	84
5 Jerry Grote	1,249		5 John Roseboro	7,110		5 Thurman Munson	564		5 John Roseboro	83
6 Tom Haller	1,199		6 Tom Haller	7,012		6 Tim McCarver	548		6 Johnny Edwards	82
7 John Roseboro	1,149		7 Johnny Bench	6,756		7 Clay Dalrymple	541		7 Dave Duncan	79
8 Randy Hundley	1,024		8 Randy Hundley	5,755		8 John Roseboro	533		8 Jerry Grote	76
9 Manny Sanguillen	1,011		9 John Bateman	5,686		9 Tom Haller	508		9 Bill Freehan	72
10 Clay Dalrymple	955		10 Manny Sanguillen	5,540		10 Randy Hundley	493		10 Clay Dalrymple	71
11 John Bateman	953		11 Clay Dalrymple	5,385		11 John Bateman	491		11 Ray Fosse	69
12 Thurman Munson	929		12 Joe Azcue	5,263		12 Manny Sanguillen	486		Paul Casanova	69
13 Ted Simmons	911		13 Elston Howard	5,152		13 Bob Rodgers	472		13 Ted Simmons	66
14 Joe Torre	903		14 Ted Simmons	4,981		14 Ted Simmons	452		14 Andy Etchebarren	64
15 Bob Rodgers	895		15 Earl Battey	4,927		15 Joe Azcue	446		Tom Haller	64
16 Dave Duncan	885		16 Joe Torre	4,850		16 Joe Torre	428		16 Johnny Bench	63
17 Elston Howard	870		17 Bob Rodgers	4,750		17 Ed Herrmann	407		Bob Rodgers	63
18 Joe Azcue	854		18 Andy Etchebarren	4,582		18 Paul Casanova	395		Phil Roof	63
19 Andy Etchebarren	847		19 Dave Duncan	4,528		19 Ray Fosse	386		19 Chris Cannizzaro	62
20 Phil Roof	832		20 Thurman Munson	4,525		20 Earl Battey	378		20 2 tied with	61

Double Plays			Fielding Percentage (minimum 500 games)			Passed Balls			Assists/162 Games (minimum 500 games)	
1 Johnny Edwards	105		1 Bill Freehan	.993		1 Tim McCarver	127		1 Thurman Munson	98.35
2 Bill Freehan	98		2 Elston Howard	.993		2 Ted Simmons	124		2 Clay Dalrymple	91.77
3 Johnny Bench	93		3 Joe Azcue	.992		3 Tom Haller	121		3 Ed Herrmann	88.86
4 Tom Haller	86		4 Tom Haller	.992		J.C. Martin	121		4 Bob Rodgers	85.43
John Roseboro	86		5 Johnny Edwards	.992		5 Ed Herrmann	117		5 Joe Azcue	84.60
6 John Bateman	81		6 Johnny Bench	.992		6 Joe Azcue	116		6 George Mitterwald	83.95
7 Clay Dalrymple	76		7 Earl Battey	.991		7 Bill Freehan	106		7 John Bateman	83.46
8 Jerry Grote	75		8 Mike Ryan	.991		8 John Bateman	104		8 Mike Ryan	83.31
9 Bob Rodgers	74		9 John Romano	.991		9 Johnny Edwards	102		9 Johnny Edwards	81.81
10 Manny Sanguillen	71		10 Jerry Grote	.991		10 Joe Torre	87		10 Bob Boone	81.16
11 Tim McCarver	70		11 Jim Pagliaroni	.991		Clay Dalrymple	87		11 Ted Simmons	80.38
12 Thurman Munson	69		12 Ellie Hendricks	.990		12 Dick Dietz	86		12 Johnny Bench	80.23
13 Joe Azcue	67		13 Randy Hundley	.990		13 John Roseboro	83		13 Duke Sims	80.00
14 Paul Casanova	65		14 Jeff Torborg	.990		14 Manny Sanguillen	82		14 Ellie Rodriguez	79.13
Randy Hundley	65		15 Jerry May	.990		15 Dave Duncan	72		15 Ray Fosse	79.05
16 Dave Duncan	64		16 Tim McCarver	.990		16 Thurman Munson	70		16 Paul Casanova	78.90
17 Ed Herrmann	62		17 Joe Torre	.990		17 Jerry Grote	69		17 Carlton Fisk	78.41
18 Joe Torre	57		18 John Roseboro	.989		Earl Williams	69		18 Randy Hundley	77.99
Elston Howard	57		19 Ellie Rodriguez	.989		Gus Triandos	69		19 Manny Sanguillen	77.88
20 Ray Fosse	55		20 Clay Dalrymple	.988		20 Earl Battey	68		20 Jerry Grote	77.17

Single Season Fielding Leaders—Catchers: Expansion Era (1961-1976)

Games				Putouts				Assists				Errors		
1 Randy Hundley	1968	160		1 Johnny Edwards	1969	1,135		1 Johnny Bench	1968	102		1 John Bateman	1963	23
2 Jim Sundberg	1975	155		2 Johnny Edwards	1963	1,008		2 Jim Sundberg	1975	101		Thurman Munson	1975	23
3 Johnny Bench	1968	154		3 Randy Hundley	1969	978		3 Jim Sundberg	1976	96		3 Bob Boone	1974	22
Ted Simmons	1975	154		4 Bill Freehan	1968	971		4 Thurman Munson	1975	95		Thurman Munson	1974	22
5 Ted Simmons	1973	153		5 Bill Freehan	1967	950		5 Johnny Edwards	1962	92		5 Clay Dalrymple	1963	19
6 Randy Hundley	1967	152		6 Johnny Bench	1968	942		6 Clay Dalrymple	1963	90		6 Manny Sanguillen	1969	17
7 Randy Hundley	1969	151		7 Elston Howard	1964	939		7 Bob Boone	1973	89		Jim Sundberg	1975	17
Johnny Edwards	1969	151		8 Tim McCarver	1969	925		8 Johnny Edwards	1963	87		8 Jake Gibbs	1967	16
Manny Sanguillen	1974	151		9 Bill Freehan	1964	923		Bob Rodgers	1964	87		Fran Healy	1974	16
10 Bob Rodgers	1962	150		10 Bill Freehan	1971	912		10 Clay Dalrymple	1961	86		Butch Wynegar	1976	16
11 Randy Hundley	1966	149		11 John Roseboro	1963	908		Duane Josephson	1968	86		11 Choo Choo Coleman	1963	15
12 Johnny Edwards	1963	148		12 John Roseboro	1966	904		12 Randy Hundley	1966	85		John Bateman	1966	15
Tim McCarver	1966	148		13 Bill Freehan	1966	898		13 Dick Bertell	1963	84		Paul Casanova	1967	15
Dave Rader	1973	148		14 Bob Tillman	1964	897		Brian Downing	1975	84		John Bateman	1970	15
15 Earl Battey	1962	147		15 Jerry Grote	1971	892		15 Barry Foote	1974	83		Bob Barton	1971	15
Bill Freehan	1967	147		16 Johnny Edwards	1964	890		16 Earl Battey	1962	82		Carlton Fisk	1972	15
Johnny Bench	1969	147		17 Ted Simmons	1973	888		Ted Simmons	1974	82		Thurman Munson	1972	15
18 5 tied with		146		18 Randy Hundley	1968	885		Darrell Porter	1975	82		Dave Duncan	1974	15
				19 Bob Rodgers	1964	884		19 4 tied with		81		Ted Simmons	1975	15
				20 Clay Dalrymple	1963	881						John Wockenfuss	1976	15

Double Plays				Fielding Percentage (minimum 100 games)				Passed Balls				Assists/162 Games (minimum 100 games)		
1 Tom Haller	1968	23		1 Thurman Munson	1971	.998		1 J.C. Martin	1965	33		1 Thurman Munson	1975	118.38
2 Paul Casanova	1967	19		2 Sherm Lollar	1961	.998		2 Earl Williams	1972	28		2 Johnny Edwards	1962	114.65
John Bateman	1970	19		3 Elston Howard	1964	.998		Ted Simmons	1975	28		3 Clay Dalrymple	1961	114.20
4 Johnny Edwards	1964	17		4 Bill Freehan	1970	.997		4 Bob Uecker	1967	27		Duane Josephson	1968	114.20
Randy Hundley	1969	17		5 Johnny Bench	1976	.997		Bob Didier	1969	27		5 John Bateman	1963	114.10
Joe Ferguson	1973	17		6 Glenn Borgmann	1974	.997		6 Dick Dietz	1970	25		6 Clay Dalrymple	1965	111.18
7 John Roseboro	1961	16		7 Jim Pagliaroni	1966	.997		Ted Simmons	1973	25		Milt May	1975	111.18
Johnny Edwards	1963	16		8 Tim McCarver	1967	.997		8 J.C. Martin	1964	24		8 Jim Sundberg	1976	111.09
Clay Dalrymple	1963	16		9 Tom Haller	1967	.997		Ed Herrmann	1973	24		9 Barry Foote	1974	110.21
John Roseboro	1969	16		10 Joe Ferguson	1973	.996		10 Dick Bertell	1961	23		10 Steve Yeager	1976	108.47
Ray Fosse	1971	16		11 George Mitterwald	1970	.996		11 Gus Triandos	1961	21		11 Joe Azcue	1969	108.00
Bob Boone	1973	16		12 Bill Freehan	1971	.996		Jesse Gonder	1964	21		12 Johnny Bench	1968	107.30
Johnny Bench	1974	16		13 Bill Freehan	1966	.996		John Bateman	1966	21		13 Darrell Porter	1975	107.13
14 Dick Bertell	1963	15		14 Randy Hundley	1967	.996		Fran Healy	1974	21		14 Jim Sundberg	1975	105.56
Duane Josephson	1968	15		15 Bill Freehan	1965	.996		15 Bill Freehan	1965	20		15 Glenn Borgmann	1975	104.98
Bill Freehan	1968	15		16 Randy Hundley	1972	.995		Dick Dietz	1971	20		16 Thurman Munson	1976	104.43
Joe Azcue	1969	15		17 Johnny Edwards	1971	.995		Ellie Rodriguez	1974	20		17 Thurman Munson	1970	103.68
Jim Sundberg	1974	15		18 Randy Hundley	1968	.995		18 Ed Herrmann	1969	19		18 Clay Dalrymple	1963	102.68
19 5 tied with		14		19 Jerry Grote	1975	.995		Bob Boone	1973	19		19 Manny Sanguillen	1969	101.79
				20 Elston Howard	1962	.995		20 7 tied with		18		20 2 tied with		99.80

Career Fielding Leaders—First Basemen: Expansion Era (1961-1976)

	Games			Putouts			Assists			Errors	
1	Norm Cash	1,813	1	Norm Cash	14,187	1	Norm Cash	1,244	1	Willie McCovey	184
2	Willie McCovey	1,574	2	Willie McCovey	13,415	2	Willie McCovey	990	2	Donn Clendenon	146
3	Boog Powell	1,475	3	George Scott	12,200	3	George Scott	916	3	George Scott	121
4	George Scott	1,420	4	Boog Powell	12,115	4	Boog Powell	859	4	Norm Cash	120
5	Orlando Cepeda	1,351	5	Ernie Banks	12,005	5	Lee May	821		Orlando Cepeda	120
6	Lee May	1,344	6	Orlando Cepeda	11,690	6	Donn Clendenon	819	6	Dick Stuart	117
7	Ernie Banks	1,259	7	Lee May	11,628	7	Orlando Cepeda	818	7	Boog Powell	115
8	Ed Kranepool	1,231	8	Donn Clendenon	10,913	8	Ernie Banks	809	8	Don Mincher	90
9	Donn Clendenon	1,200	9	Bill White	10,064	9	Bill White	758	9	Ron Fairly	86
10	Bill White	1,142	10	Ed Kranepool	9,976	10	Ed Kranepool	726	10	Ernie Banks	80
11	Don Mincher	1,118	11	Wes Parker	9,640	11	Wes Parker	695	11	Lee May	78
12	Wes Parker	1,108	12	Don Mincher	8,972	12	Don Mincher	691	12	Bill White	77
13	Ron Fairly	1,100	13	Ron Fairly	8,500	13	Ron Fairly	643	13	Dick Allen	75
14	Tony Perez	956	14	Joe Pepitone	8,172	14	Joe Pepitone	627	14	Nate Colbert	74
15	Joe Pepitone	953	15	Nate Colbert	7,754	15	Nate Colbert	568	15	Mike Epstein	70
16	Tom McCraw	911	16	Tony Perez	7,611	16	Jim Spencer	567	16	Ed Kranepool	69
17	Harmon Killebrew	898	17	Jim Spencer	7,286	17	Dick Stuart	551	17	Tom McCraw	68
18	Nate Colbert	890	18	Chris Chambliss	7,186	18	Norm Siebern	530	18	Jim Gentile	65
19	Deron Johnson	880	19	John Mayberry	7,154	19	Chris Chambliss	524	19	Chris Chambliss	62
20	Jim Spencer	875	20	Mike Epstein	6,957	20	Harmon Killebrew	523	20	2 tied with	61

	Double Plays			Fielding Percentage (minimum 750 games)			Assists/162 Games (minimum 750 games)	
1	Norm Cash	1,260	1	Jim Spencer	.996	1	Norm Siebern	113.57
2	George Scott	1,164	2	Wes Parker	.996	2	Norm Cash	111.16
3	Donn Clendenon	1,136	3	Ernie Banks	.994	3	Donn Clendenon	110.57
4	Boog Powell	1,130	4	Lee May	.994	4	Bill White	107.53
5	Willie McCovey	1,114	5	Ed Kranepool	.994	5	Joe Pepitone	106.58
6	Lee May	1,099	6	John Mayberry	.993	6	Chris Chambliss	105.32
7	Ernie Banks	1,005	7	Joe Pepitone	.993	7	Jim Spencer	104.98
8	Orlando Cepeda	950	8	Tony Perez	.993	8	George Scott	104.50
9	Bill White	908	9	Bill White	.993	9	Ernie Banks	104.10
10	Ed Kranepool	858	10	Joe Torre	.993	10	Nate Colbert	103.39
11	Don Mincher	782	11	Bill Skowron	.993	11	Willie McCovey	101.89
12	Joe Pepitone	781	12	Deron Johnson	.993	12	Wes Parker	101.62
13	Ron Fairly	779	13	Norm Cash	.992	13	Don Mincher	100.13
14	Wes Parker	757	14	Norm Siebern	.992	14	Joe Torre	100.02
15	Jim Spencer	723	15	Chris Chambliss	.992	15	John Mayberry	100.00
16	Tony Perez	711	16	Harmon Killebrew	.992	16	Lee May	98.96
17	Chris Chambliss	690	17	Boog Powell	.991	17	Orlando Cepeda	98.09
18	Nate Colbert	686	18	Nate Colbert	.991	18	Ed Kranepool	95.54
19	John Mayberry	685	19	George Scott	.991	19	Ron Fairly	94.70
20	Mike Epstein	671	20	Don Mincher	.991	20	Harmon Killebrew	94.35

Single Season Fielding Leaders—First Basemen: Expansion Era (1961-1976)

	Games				Putouts				Assists				Errors		
1	Norm Siebern	1962	162	1	Ernie Banks	1965	1,682	1	Vic Power	1961	142	1	Dick Stuart	1963	29
	Bill White	1963	162	2	Donn Clendenon	1968	1,587	2	Vic Power	1962	134	2	Donn Clendenon	1965	28
	Ernie Banks	1965	162	3	Steve Garvey	1976	1,583		Dick Stuart	1963	134	3	Dick Stuart	1964	24
	Steve Garvey	1976	162	4	Donn Clendenon	1965	1,572		Willie McCovey	1970	134		Donn Clendenon	1966	24
5	Wes Parker	1970	161	5	Willie Montanez	1976	1,569	5	Ernie Banks	1964	132	5	Tito Francona	1962	22
	Willie Montanez	1976	161	6	Ernie Banks	1964	1,565	6	Donn Clendenon	1968	128		Willie McCovey	1966	22
7	Orlando Cepeda	1962	160	7	Steve Garvey	1974	1,536		Bob Robertson	1971	128		Willie Montanez	1976	22
	Bill White	1964	160	8	Bill White	1964	1,513	8	Norm Cash	1961	127	8	Dick Stuart	1961	21
	Harmon Killebrew	1967	160	9	Steve Garvey	1975	1,500		Norm Siebern	1962	127		Orlando Cepeda	1963	21
	Steve Garvey	1975	160	10	Wes Parker	1970	1,498		Tito Francona	1962	127		Willie McCovey	1968	21
	John Mayberry	1976	160	11	John Mayberry	1976	1,484	11	Wes Parker	1970	125		Mike Hargrove	1976	21
12	Tito Francona	1962	158	12	Joe Adcock	1961	1,471	12	Gordy Coleman	1961	121	12	Tom McCraw	1968	20
	Donn Clendenon	1965	158	13	Ernie Banks	1962	1,458		Jim Gentile	1962	121	13	George Scott	1967	19
	George Scott	1966	158	14	John Mayberry	1973	1,457		Joe Pepitone	1964	121	14	Joe Pepitone	1964	18
	Norm Cash	1966	158	15	Donn Clendenon	1966	1,452	15	Donn Clendenon	1965	119		Orlando Cepeda	1964	18
	Bill White	1966	158	16	Donn Clendenon	1963	1,450	16	Donn Clendenon	1963	118		Lee Thomas	1965	18
17	5 tied with		157	17	Chris Chambliss	1976	1,440		George Scott	1973	118		Carlos May	1971	18
				18	Chris Chambliss	1973	1,437	18	Norm Cash	1962	116		Dick Allen	1975	18
				19	Wes Parker	1965	1,434	19	3 tied with		114	19	8 tied with		17
				20	Bill White	1966	1,422								

	Double Plays				Fielding Percentage (minimum 100 games)				Assists/162 Games (minimum 100 games)		
1	Donn Clendenon	1966	182	1	Jim Spencer	1973	.999	1	Tim Harkness	1963	171.17
2	Donn Clendenon	1965	161	2	Wes Parker	1968	.999	2	Bob Robertson	1971	164.57
3	Tito Francona	1962	157	3	Jim Spencer	1976	.998	3	Vic Power	1961	163.15
4	John Mayberry	1973	156	4	Steve Garvey	1976	.998	4	Keith Hernandez	1976	157.58
5	Donn Clendenon	1963	154	5	Gil Hodges	1961	.998	5	Vic Power	1962	152.87
6	Chris Chambliss	1973	153	6	Ed Kranepool	1971	.998	6	Willie McCovey	1970	148.69
7	Rod Carew	1976	149	7	Ernie Banks	1969	.997	7	Tom McCraw	1967	144.88
8	Bill Skowron	1961	146	8	Joe Pepitone	1965	.997	8	Dick Stuart	1963	140.05
9	George Scott	1973	144	9	Boog Powell	1975	.997	9	Ernie Banks	1964	136.20
	Joe Torre	1974	144	10	Joe Adcock	1962	.997	10	Pancho Herrera	1961	135.23
11	Ernie Banks	1965	143	11	Wes Parker	1965	.997	11	Donn Clendenon	1968	133.78
	Lee May	1970	143	12	Denis Menke	1971	.997	12	Mike Hegan	1970	131.70
13	Dick Stuart	1961	141	13	Norm Cash	1964	.997	13	Norm Cash	1961	131.04
	John Mayberry	1972	141	14	Wes Parker	1972	.997	14	Lee Thomas	1963	130.85
	Willie Montanez	1976	141	15	Jim Spencer	1971	.996	15	Gordy Coleman	1961	130.68
16	Lee May	1975	138	16	Bill White	1964	.996		Jim Gentile	1962	130.68
	Steve Garvey	1976	138	17	Wes Parker	1971	.996	17	Tito Francona	1962	130.22
18	George Scott	1974	137	18	Lee Thomas	1963	.996	18	Norm Cash	1962	128.71
19	3 tied with		134	19	Bill Skowron	1964	.996	19	Norm Siebern	1962	127.00
				20	Carl Yastrzemski	1975	.996	20	Jim Spencer	1976	126.88

Career Fielding Leaders—Second Basemen: Expansion Era (1961-1976)

Games

1	Joe Morgan	1,577
2	Julian Javier	1,433
	Bill Mazeroski	1,433
4	Cookie Rojas	1,431
5	Felix Millan	1,361
6	Ron Hunt	1,260
7	Glenn Beckert	1,242
8	Dave Johnson	1,174
9	Dick Green	1,158
10	Sandy Alomar	1,132
11	Tommy Helms	1,128
12	Rod Carew	1,120
13	Bobby Knoop	1,116
14	Tito Fuentes	1,111
15	Horace Clarke	1,102
16	Tony Taylor	1,070
17	Dick McAuliffe	971
18	Bobby Richardson	934
19	Bernie Allen	914
20	Jerry Lumpe	904

Putouts

1	Joe Morgan	3,773
2	Bill Mazeroski	3,443
3	Felix Millan	3,298
4	Julian Javier	3,108
5	Cookie Rojas	3,079
6	Dave Johnson	2,804
7	Ron Hunt	2,734
8	Glenn Beckert	2,710
9	Tommy Helms	2,684
10	Horace Clarke	2,682
11	Tito Fuentes	2,650
12	Rod Carew	2,567
13	Bobby Knoop	2,556
14	Sandy Alomar	2,532
15	Dick Green	2,518
16	Tony Taylor	2,292
17	Bobby Richardson	2,220
18	Dick McAuliffe	2,155
19	Dave Cash	2,102
20	Ted Sizemore	2,049

Assists

1	Bill Mazeroski	4,682
2	Joe Morgan	4,459
3	Cookie Rojas	3,796
4	Julian Javier	3,775
5	Glenn Beckert	3,712
6	Felix Millan	3,658
7	Ron Hunt	3,512
8	Tommy Helms	3,234
9	Bobby Knoop	3,218
10	Horace Clarke	3,179
11	Tito Fuentes	3,178
12	Dave Johnson	3,111
13	Dick Green	3,063
14	Sandy Alomar	2,935
15	Rod Carew	2,925
16	Ted Sizemore	2,613
17	Tony Taylor	2,582
18	Dave Cash	2,562
19	Bobby Richardson	2,473
20	Jerry Lumpe	2,323

Errors

1	Julian Javier	195
2	Glenn Beckert	179
3	Joe Morgan	171
4	Ron Hunt	156
5	Rod Carew	154
	Tito Fuentes	154
7	Felix Millan	142
8	Bill Mazeroski	139
9	Sandy Alomar	125
10	Dave Johnson	119
	Bobby Knoop	119
12	Cookie Rojas	115
13	Mike Andrews	107
	Tony Taylor	107
15	Horace Clarke	104
	Dick McAuliffe	104
17	Ted Sizemore	101
	Tommy Helms	101
19	Dick Green	96
20	Gary Sutherland	94

Double Plays

1	Bill Mazeroski	1,209
2	Joe Morgan	959
3	Cookie Rojas	946
4	Julian Javier	836
5	Felix Millan	812
6	Tommy Helms	807
7	Bobby Knoop	779
8	Glenn Beckert	758
9	Dave Johnson	749
10	Sandy Alomar	717
11	Tito Fuentes	713
12	Dick Green	712
13	Horace Clarke	695
14	Ron Hunt	685
15	Bobby Richardson	677
16	Rod Carew	664
17	Tony Taylor	655
18	Dave Cash	647
19	Ted Sizemore	571
20	Dick McAuliffe	552

Fielding Percentage
(minimum 750 games)

1	Jerry Adair	.986
2	Jerry Lumpe	.984
3	Cookie Rojas	.984
4	Tommy Helms	.983
5	Bill Mazeroski	.983
6	Dick Green	.983
7	Dave Cash	.983
8	Horace Clarke	.983
9	Bobby Richardson	.981
10	Dave Johnson	.980
11	Felix Millan	.980
12	Bobby Knoop	.980
13	Joe Morgan	.980
14	Bernie Allen	.980
15	Ted Sizemore	.979
16	Tony Taylor	.979
17	Sandy Alomar	.978
18	Dick McAuliffe	.977
19	Denny Doyle	.977
20	Ron Hunt	.976

Range Factor
(minimum 750 games)

1	Bill Mazeroski	5.67
2	Dave Cash	5.50
3	Horace Clarke	5.32
4	Tommy Helms	5.25
5	Tito Fuentes	5.25
6	Joe Morgan	5.22
7	Ted Sizemore	5.19
8	Bobby Knoop	5.17
9	Glenn Beckert	5.17
10	Felix Millan	5.11
11	Dave Johnson	5.04
12	Bobby Richardson	5.02
13	Ron Hunt	4.96
14	Rod Carew	4.90
15	Sandy Alomar	4.83
16	Dick Green	4.82
17	Mike Andrews	4.81
18	Cookie Rojas	4.80
19	Julian Javier	4.80
20	Jerry Adair	4.80

Assists/162 Games
(minimum 750 games)

1	Bill Mazeroski	529.30
2	Dave Cash	489.44
3	Glenn Beckert	484.17
4	Ted Sizemore	470.86
5	Horace Clarke	467.33
6	Bobby Knoop	467.13
7	Tommy Helms	464.46
8	Tito Fuentes	463.40
9	Joe Morgan	458.06
10	Ron Hunt	451.54
11	Felix Millan	435.41
12	Cookie Rojas	429.74
13	Dave Johnson	429.29
14	Bobby Richardson	428.94
15	Dick Green	428.50
16	Julian Javier	426.76
17	Rod Carew	423.08
18	Sandy Alomar	420.03
19	Denny Doyle	416.90
20	Jerry Lumpe	416.29

Single Season Fielding Leaders—Second Basemen: Expansion Era (1961-1976)

Games

1	Bill Mazeroski	1967	163
2	Jake Wood	1961	162
	Bill Mazeroski	1964	162
	Pete Rose	1965	162
	Bill Mazeroski	1966	162
	Felix Millan	1969	162
	Bobby Grich	1973	162
	Dave Cash	1974	162
	Dave Cash	1975	162
	Felix Millan	1975	162
11	Bobby Richardson	1961	161
	Chuck Hiller	1962	161
	Bobby Richardson	1962	161
	Julian Javier	1963	161
	Bobby Knoop	1964	161
	Bobby Knoop	1966	161
17	5 tied with		160

Putouts

1	Bobby Grich	1974	484
2	Rennie Stennett	1974	441
3	Bobby Grich	1973	431
4	Rennie Stennett	1976	430
5	Bill Mazeroski	1962	425
6	Bobby Grich	1975	423
7	Billy Moran	1962	422
8	Bill Mazeroski	1967	417
	Joe Morgan	1973	417
10	Bobby Richardson	1961	413
	Nellie Fox	1961	413
12	Bill Mazeroski	1966	411
13	Bill Mazeroski	1961	410
	Felix Millan	1973	410
15	Dave Cash	1976	407
16	Pedro Garcia	1973	405
17	Jerry Lumpe	1961	403
18	Bobby Richardson	1964	400
	Dave Cash	1975	400
20	Chuck Schilling	1961	397

Assists

1	Bill Mazeroski	1964	543
2	Bill Mazeroski	1966	538
3	Manny Trillo	1976	527
4	Bobby Knoop	1964	522
5	Dave Cash	1974	519
6	Bill Mazeroski	1962	509
	Bobby Grich	1973	509
	Manny Trillo	1975	509
9	Bill Mazeroski	1963	506
10	Bill Mazeroski	1961	505
11	Rennie Stennett	1976	502
12	Bill Mazeroski	1967	498
13	Jerry Kindall	1962	494
	Glenn Beckert	1965	494
15	Ken Hubbs	1963	493
16	Joe Morgan	1965	492
17	Frank Bolling	1961	489
	Ken Hubbs	1962	489
19	Bobby Knoop	1966	488
20	Bobby Grich	1975	484

Errors

1	Rod Carew	1974	33
2	Dave Johnson	1973	30
3	Chuck Hiller	1962	29
	Tito Fuentes	1972	29
	Manny Trillo	1975	29
6	Julian Javier	1964	27
	Joe Morgan	1965	27
	Pedro Garcia	1973	27
9	Ron Hunt	1963	26
	Phil Garner	1975	26
	Tito Fuentes	1975	26
12	Jake Wood	1961	25
	Julian Javier	1963	25
	Glenn Beckert	1967	25
	Pete Mackanin	1975	25
16	6 tied with		24

Double Plays

1	Bill Mazeroski	1966	161
2	Bill Mazeroski	1961	144
3	Dave Cash	1974	141
4	Bill Mazeroski	1962	138
5	Bobby Richardson	1961	136
6	Bobby Knoop	1966	135
7	Bobby Grich	1974	132
8	Bill Mazeroski	1963	131
	Bill Mazeroski	1967	131
10	Tommy Helms	1971	130
	Bobby Grich	1973	130
12	Dave Cash	1975	126
13	Bob Randall	1976	124
14	Bobby Knoop	1964	123
15	Bill Mazeroski	1964	122
	Bobby Grich	1975	122
17	Chuck Schilling	1961	121
	Bobby Richardson	1965	121
19	Felix Millan	1971	120
20	Sandy Alomar	1970	119

Fielding Percentage
(minimum 100 games)

1	Ken Boswell	1970	.996
2	Bobby Grich	1973	.995
3	Jerry Adair	1964	.994
4	Tim Cullen	1970	.994
5	Tito Fuentes	1973	.993
6	Bill Mazeroski	1966	.992
7	Hal Lanier	1966	.991
8	Cookie Rojas	1971	.991
9	Bernie Allen	1968	.991
10	Chuck Schilling	1961	.991
11	Dick Green	1964	.990
12	Joe Morgan	1972	.990
13	Nellie Fox	1962	.990
14	Dave Johnson	1972	.990
15	Doug Griffin	1973	.990
16	Dave Johnson	1970	.990
17	Tommy Helms	1971	.990
18	Joe Morgan	1973	.990
19	Horace Clarke	1967	.990
20	Frank Bolling	1962	.989

Range Factor
(minimum 100 games)

1	Bill Mazeroski	1963	6.13
2	Bobby Grich	1975	6.05
3	Bill Mazeroski	1961	6.02
4	Rennie Stennett	1974	5.95
5	Rennie Stennett	1976	5.94
6	Tito Fuentes	1975	5.89
7	Bill Mazeroski	1962	5.87
8	Bill Mazeroski	1966	5.86
9	Bobby Grich	1974	5.86
10	Rennie Stennett	1975	5.85
11	Ted Sizemore	1974	5.84
12	Willie Randolph	1976	5.82
13	Bobby Grich	1973	5.80
14	Tommy Helms	1971	5.79
15	Horace Clarke	1968	5.76
16	Felix Millan	1971	5.74
17	Bill Mazeroski	1965	5.74
18	Tito Fuentes	1976	5.72
19	Tommy Helms	1972	5.71
20	Sandy Alomar	1971	5.71

Assists/162 Games
(minimum 100 games)

1	Bill Mazeroski	1963	594.00
2	Bill Mazeroski	1965	559.98
3	Manny Trillo	1976	547.27
4	Glenn Beckert	1972	543.66
5	Bill Mazeroski	1964	543.00
6	Willie Randolph	1976	542.18
7	Ted Sizemore	1973	539.61
8	Manny Trillo	1975	538.94
9	Bill Mazeroski	1961	538.22
10	Bill Mazeroski	1966	538.00
11	Rob Andrews	1976	535.96
12	Frank Bolling	1961	535.26
13	Bill Mazeroski	1968	532.77
14	Ken Hubbs	1963	525.43
15	Bobby Knoop	1964	525.24
16	Glenn Beckert	1965	523.06
17	Pete Mackanin	1975	522.99
18	Bobby Grich	1975	522.72
19	Ted Sizemore	1974	521.44
20	Rennie Stennett	1975	520.88

Career Fielding Leaders—Third Basemen: Expansion Era (1961-1976)

	Games			Putouts			Assists			Errors	
1	Brooks Robinson	2,409	1	Brooks Robinson	2,232	1	Brooks Robinson	5,288	1	Ron Santo	304
2	Ron Santo	2,036	2	Ron Santo	1,877	2	Ron Santo	4,437	2	Brooks Robinson	210
3	Sal Bando	1,446	3	Clete Boyer	1,346	3	Aurelio Rodriguez	2,985	3	Sal Bando	177
4	Aurelio Rodriguez	1,315	4	Sal Bando	1,322	4	Clete Boyer	2,941	4	Doug Rader	176
5	Ken McMullen	1,311	5	Ken McMullen	1,258	5	Sal Bando	2,760	5	Bob Bailey	175
6	Clete Boyer	1,305	6	Aurelio Rodriguez	1,143	6	Graig Nettles	2,726	6	Aurelio Rodriguez	166
7	Doug Rader	1,253	7	Doug Rader	1,057	7	Ken McMullen	2,725		Paul Schaal	166
8	Bob Bailey	1,193	8	Bob Aspromonte	1,020	8	Doug Rader	2,680	8	Ken McMullen	162
9	Graig Nettles	1,114	9	Max Alvis	962	9	Bob Bailey	2,260	9	Clete Boyer	156
10	Bob Aspromonte	1,090	10	Graig Nettles	960	10	Ken Boyer	2,047	10	Ken Boyer	155
11	Paul Schaal	1,053	11	Don Wert	914	11	Paul Schaal	2,038	11	Richie Hebner	147
12	Don Wert	1,043	12	Ed Charles	879	12	Bill Melton	2,025	12	Bill Melton	145
13	Ken Boyer	1,023	13	Ken Boyer	842	13	Don Wert	1,987	13	Dick Allen	143
14	Richie Hebner	1,002	14	Eddie Mathews	818	14	Richie Hebner	1,901	14	Graig Nettles	141
15	Max Alvis	971	15	Bob Bailey	793	15	Bob Aspromonte	1,871	15	Jim Ray Hart	134
16	Ed Charles	942	16	Don Money	756	16	Ed Charles	1,833	16	Rich Rollins	129
17	Bill Melton	888	17	Paul Schaal	726	17	Eddie Mathews	1,696	17	Darrell Evans	127
18	Eddie Mathews	871	18	Rich Rollins	716	18	Max Alvis	1,693	18	Tony Perez	123
19	Rich Rollins	830	19	Frank Malzone	699	19	Don Money	1,623		Max Alvis	123
20	Don Money	821	20	Bill Melton	692	20	Rich Rollins	1,582	20	Ed Charles	122

	Double Plays			Fielding Percentage (minimum 750 games)			Range Factor (minimum 750 games)			Assists/162 Games (minimum 750 games)	
1	Brooks Robinson	518	1	Brooks Robinson	.973	1	Graig Nettles	3.31	1	Graig Nettles	396.42
2	Ron Santo	389	2	Don Money	.969	2	Clete Boyer	3.29	2	Bill Melton	369.43
3	Aurelio Rodriguez	302	3	Don Wert	.968	3	Aurelio Rodriguez	3.14	3	Aurelio Rodriguez	367.73
4	Clete Boyer	287	4	Clete Boyer	.965	4	Brooks Robinson	3.12	4	Clete Boyer	365.09
5	Sal Bando	258	5	Graig Nettles	.963	5	Ron Santo	3.10	5	Brooks Robinson	355.61
6	Ken McMullen	257	6	Jim Davenport	.963	6	Bill Melton	3.06	6	Ron Santo	353.04
7	Graig Nettles	254	7	Aurelio Rodriguez	.961	7	Ken McMullen	3.04	7	Doug Rader	346.50
8	Doug Rader	245	8	Ken McMullen	.961	8	Doug Rader	2.98	8	Ken McMullen	336.73
9	Bob Bailey	203	9	Bob Aspromonte	.960	9	Don Money	2.90	9	Ken Boyer	324.16
10	Bill Melton	183	10	Eddie Mathews	.959	10	Eddie Mathews	2.89	10	Don Money	320.25
11	Don Money	180	11	Sal Bando	.958	11	Ed Charles	2.88	11	Tony Perez	318.88
12	Richie Hebner	179	12	Ed Charles	.957	12	Ken Boyer	2.82	12	Eddie Mathews	315.44
13	Ken Boyer	177	13	Max Alvis	.956	13	Sal Bando	2.82	13	Ed Charles	315.23
14	Don Wert	173	14	Doug Rader	.955	14	Tony Perez	2.82	14	Paul Schaal	313.54
15	Ed Charles	165	15	Ron Santo	.954	15	Don Wert	2.78	15	Sal Bando	309.21
16	Darrell Evans	154	16	Bill Melton	.949	16	Rich Rollins	2.77	16	Rich Rollins	308.78
17	Paul Schaal	152	17	Ken Boyer	.949	17	Max Alvis	2.73	17	Don Wert	308.62
18	Rico Petrocelli	150	18	Rich Rollins	.947	18	Bob Aspromonte	2.65	18	Richie Hebner	307.35
19	Eddie Mathews	147	19	Richie Hebner	.946	19	Paul Schaal	2.62	19	Bob Bailey	306.89
20	Max Alvis	144	20	Bob Bailey	.946	20	Richie Hebner	2.58	20	Max Alvis	282.46

Single Season Fielding Leaders—Third Basemen: Expansion Era (1961-1976)

	Games				Putouts				Assists				Errors		
1	Ron Santo	1965	164	1	Bubba Phillips	1961	188	1	Graig Nettles	1971	412	1	Dick Allen	1964	41
2	Brooks Robinson	1961	163		Sal Bando	1968	188	2	Graig Nettles	1973	410	2	Pete Ward	1963	38
	Brooks Robinson	1964	163	3	Clete Boyer	1962	187		Brooks Robinson	1974	410	3	Darrell Evans	1975	36
4	Brooks Robinson	1962	162		Ron Santo	1967	187	4	Brooks Robinson	1967	405	4	Dick Allen	1967	35
	Ron Santo	1963	162	5	Ken McMullen	1968	185	5	Mike Schmidt	1974	404		Tony Perez	1970	35
	Dick Allen	1964	162		Ken McMullen	1969	185	6	Clete Boyer	1962	396		Larry Parrish	1975	35
	Ken Boyer	1964	162		Darrell Evans	1974	185	7	Ron Santo	1967	393	7	Ken Boyer	1963	34
	Sal Bando	1968	162	8	Max Alvis	1966	180	8	Ron Santo	1966	391	8	Bob Bailey	1963	32
	Ron Santo	1968	162	9	Sal Bando	1969	178	9	Aurelio Rodriguez	1974	389		Jim Ray Hart	1965	32
	Brooks Robinson	1968	162	10	Bubba Phillips	1962	175	10	Graig Nettles	1976	383		Tony Perez	1969	32
	Sal Bando	1969	162	11	Brooks Robinson	1966	174	11	Darrell Evans	1975	381	11	Ron Santo	1961	31
	Mike Schmidt	1974	162	12	Max Alvis	1963	170	12	Graig Nettles	1975	379	12	Joe Foy	1968	30
13	Ron Santo	1964	161	13	Max Alvis	1965	169	13	Ron Santo	1968	378		Paul Schaal	1973	30
	Don Wert	1965	161		Max Alvis	1967	169	14	Aurelio Rodriguez	1970	377	14	Mike Shannon	1967	29
	Max Alvis	1967	161	15	Eddie Mathews	1961	168		Graig Nettles	1974	377	15	7 tied with		28
	Ron Santo	1967	161		Brooks Robinson	1968	168		Mike Schmidt	1976	377				
	Paul Schaal	1971	161	17	Clete Boyer	1967	166	17	Aurelio Rodriguez	1975	375				
	Joe Torre	1971	161	18	Clete Boyer	1963	165	18	Ron Santo	1963	374				
19	11 tied with		160	19	3 tied with		163	19	Ron Santo	1965	373				
								20	Bill Melton	1971	371				

	Double Plays				Fielding Percentage (minimum 100 games)				Range Factor (minimum 100 games)				Assists/162 Games (minimum 100 games)		
1	Graig Nettles	1971	54	1	Don Money	1974	.989	1	Clete Boyer	1962	3.71	1	Brooks Robinson	1974	434.12
2	Clete Boyer	1965	46	2	Brooks Robinson	1967	.980	2	Graig Nettles	1971	3.61	2	Graig Nettles	1973	423.06
3	Frank Malzone	1961	45	3	Brooks Robinson	1975	.979	3	Ron Santo	1967	3.60	3	Graig Nettles	1971	422.43
	Darrell Evans	1974	45	4	Brooks Robinson	1962	.979	4	Clete Boyer	1961	3.57	4	Ron Santo	1966	416.72
5	Buddy Bell	1973	44	5	Don Money	1972	.978	5	Ron Santo	1966	3.56	5	Brooks Robinson	1967	415.25
	Brooks Robinson	1974	44	6	Aurelio Rodriguez	1976	.978	6	Brooks Robinson	1967	3.49	6	Clete Boyer	1962	408.61
7	Brooks Robinson	1963	43	7	Don Wert	1967	.978	7	Darrell Evans	1975	3.47	7	Bill Melton	1971	406.09
8	Aurelio Rodriguez	1969	42	8	Brooks Robinson	1972	.977	8	Ken McMullen	1967	3.46	8	Clete Boyer	1961	405.57
	Don Money	1974	42	9	Bubba Phillips	1962	.977	9	Ken McMullen	1969	3.45	9	Mike Schmidt	1974	404.00
10	Ron Santo	1961	41	10	Don Wert	1965	.976	10	Darrell Evans	1974	3.45	10	Aurelio Rodriguez	1975	402.32
	Clete Boyer	1962	41	11	Rico Petrocelli	1971	.976	11	Brooks Robinson	1974	3.43	11	Aurelio Rodriguez	1970	399.18
	Aurelio Rodriguez	1970	41	12	Brooks Robinson	1969	.976	12	Brooks Robinson	1969	3.42	12	Charley Smith	1967	398.66
	Darrell Evans	1975	41	13	Ken McMullen	1969	.976	13	Graig Nettles	1974	3.40	13	Eric Soderholm	1975	397.12
14	Brooks Robinson	1964	40	14	Brooks Robinson	1966	.976	14	Aurelio Rodriguez	1975	3.38	14	Graig Nettles	1974	396.58
	Graig Nettles	1970	40	15	Brooks Robinson	1963	.976	15	Clete Boyer	1963	3.36	15	Aurelio Rodriguez	1974	396.34
	Aurelio Rodriguez	1974	40	16	Dave Chalk	1975	.976	16	Ken McMullen	1970	3.36	16	Darrell Evans	1975	395.65
	Mike Schmidt	1974	40	17	Ken Reitz	1974	.974	17	Graig Nettles	1973	3.36	17	Ron Santo	1967	395.44
18	4 tied with		39	18	Ken Reitz	1973	.974	18	Buddy Bell	1974	3.36	18	Mike Schmidt	1975	394.81
				19	Bob Aspromonte	1964	.973	19	Mike Schmidt	1974	3.32	19	Graig Nettles	1976	392.70
				20	Graig Nettles	1971	.973	20	Clete Boyer	1965	3.32	20	Graig Nettles	1975	391.07

Career Fielding Leaders—Shortstops: Expansion Era (1961-1976)

Games

1	Luis Aparicio	1,837
2	Leo Cardenas	1,796
3	Ed Brinkman	1,795
4	Don Kessinger	1,731
5	Bert Campaneris	1,702
6	Jim Fregosi	1,396
7	Mark Belanger	1,352
8	Maury Wills	1,328
9	Zoilo Versalles	1,221
10	Dal Maxvill	1,207
11	Bud Harrelson	1,183
12	Freddie Patek	1,109
13	Bobby Wine	1,063
14	Larry Bowa	1,025
15	Gene Alley	977
16	Ron Hansen	976
17	Dick Groat	940
18	Roger Metzger	870
19	Chris Speier	862
20	Dave Concepcion	847

Putouts

1	Luis Aparicio	3,176
2	Leo Cardenas	3,142
3	Bert Campaneris	2,932
4	Ed Brinkman	2,924
5	Don Kessinger	2,854
6	Jim Fregosi	2,397
7	Mark Belanger	2,228
8	Maury Wills	2,169
9	Bud Harrelson	2,105
10	Zoilo Versalles	2,055
11	Freddie Patek	1,916
12	Dal Maxvill	1,759
13	Bobby Wine	1,745
14	Ron Hansen	1,674
15	Gene Alley	1,609
16	Dick Groat	1,588
17	Larry Bowa	1,540
18	Dave Concepcion	1,437
19	Roger Metzger	1,422
20	Chris Speier	1,419

Assists

1	Don Kessinger	5,696
2	Luis Aparicio	5,619
3	Ed Brinkman	5,466
4	Leo Cardenas	5,175
5	Bert Campaneris	4,925
6	Mark Belanger	4,283
7	Jim Fregosi	4,169
8	Maury Wills	4,153
9	Freddie Patek	3,571
10	Zoilo Versalles	3,544
11	Bud Harrelson	3,471
12	Dal Maxvill	3,405
13	Gene Alley	3,198
14	Larry Bowa	3,190
15	Ron Hansen	3,018
16	Bobby Wine	2,964
17	Dick Groat	2,912
18	Chris Speier	2,810
19	Roger Metzger	2,750
20	Dave Concepcion	2,682

Errors

1	Don Kessinger	314
2	Bert Campaneris	291
3	Ed Brinkman	259
4	Zoilo Versalles	257
5	Jim Fregosi	251
6	Leo Cardenas	250
7	Luis Aparicio	249
8	Maury Wills	232
9	Freddie Patek	197
10	Dick Groat	190
11	Bud Harrelson	177
12	Mark Belanger	167
13	Gene Michael	155
14	Ron Hansen	153
15	Toby Harrah	149
	Sonny Jackson	149
	Gene Alley	149
18	Dal Maxvill	145
19	Bill Russell	144
	Denis Menke	144

Double Plays

1	Luis Aparicio	1,083
2	Don Kessinger	1,066
3	Ed Brinkman	1,005
4	Leo Cardenas	1,004
5	Bert Campaneris	934
6	Jim Fregosi	836
7	Mark Belanger	784
8	Freddie Patek	754
9	Maury Wills	742
10	Gene Alley	709
11	Zoilo Versalles	708
12	Bobby Wine	694
13	Dal Maxvill	649
14	Bud Harrelson	645
15	Larry Bowa	617
16	Ron Hansen	607
17	Dick Groat	605
18	Dave Concepcion	538
19	Roger Metzger	537
20	Chris Speier	500

Fielding Percentage
(minimum 750 games)

1	Larry Bowa	.979
2	Roger Metzger	.978
3	Mark Belanger	.975
4	Dal Maxvill	.973
5	Luis Aparicio	.972
6	Bobby Wine	.971
7	Leo Cardenas	.971
8	Ed Brinkman	.970
9	Gene Alley	.970
10	Rico Petrocelli	.970
11	Bud Harrelson	.969
12	Chris Speier	.969
13	Ron Hansen	.968
14	Dave Concepcion	.968
15	Freddie Patek	.965
16	Maury Wills	.965
17	Don Kessinger	.965
18	Bert Campaneris	.964
19	Jim Fregosi	.963
20	Gene Michael	.962

Range Factor
(minimum 750 games)

1	Freddie Patek	4.95
2	Don Kessinger	4.94
3	Gene Alley	4.92
4	Chris Speier	4.91
5	Dave Concepcion	4.86
6	Mark Belanger	4.82
7	Ron Hansen	4.81
8	Roger Metzger	4.80
9	Luis Aparicio	4.79
10	Dick Groat	4.79
11	Maury Wills	4.76
12	Bud Harrelson	4.71
13	Gene Michael	4.71
14	Jim Fregosi	4.70
15	Ed Brinkman	4.67
16	Rico Petrocelli	4.65
17	Leo Cardenas	4.63
18	Bert Campaneris	4.62
19	Larry Bowa	4.61
20	Zoilo Versalles	4.59

Assists/162 Games
(minimum 750 games)

1	Don Kessinger	533.07
2	Gene Alley	530.27
3	Chris Speier	528.10
4	Freddie Patek	521.64
5	Mark Belanger	513.20
6	Dave Concepcion	512.97
7	Roger Metzger	512.07
8	Maury Wills	506.62
9	Larry Bowa	504.18
10	Dick Groat	501.86
11	Ron Hansen	500.94
12	Luis Aparicio	495.52
13	Gene Michael	494.45
14	Ed Brinkman	493.31
15	Rico Petrocelli	484.12
16	Jim Fregosi	483.80
17	Bud Harrelson	475.32
18	Zoilo Versalles	470.21
19	Bert Campaneris	468.77
20	Leo Cardenas	466.79

Single Season Fielding Leaders—Shortstops: Expansion Era (1961-1976)

Games

	Player	Year	
1	Maury Wills	1962	165
2	Jose Pagan	1962	164
3	Leo Cardenas	1964	163
4	Dick Howser	1964	162
	Jim Fregosi	1966	162
	Bill Russell	1973	162
	Ed Brinkman	1973	162
	Larry Bowa	1974	162
9	Dick Groat	1962	161
	Ron Hansen	1965	161
	Robin Yount	1976	161
12	12 tied with		160

Putouts

	Player	Year	
1	Leo Cardenas	1964	336
2	Zoilo Versalles	1962	335
3	Dick Groat	1962	314
4	Jim Fregosi	1965	312
5	Leo Cardenas	1969	310
6	Jackie Hernandez	1969	306
7	Bud Harrelson	1970	305
8	Dave Concepcion	1976	304
9	Luis Aparicio	1966	303
10	Zoilo Versalles	1963	301
	Ed Brinkman	1970	301
	Freddie Patek	1971	301
13	Dick Howser	1961	299
14	Jim Fregosi	1966	297
15	Maury Wills	1962	295
16	Ron Hansen	1964	292
	Ed Brinkman	1965	292
	Leo Cardenas	1965	292
19	Eddie Bressoud	1962	291
	Dick Howser	1964	291

Assists

	Player	Year	
1	Don Kessinger	1968	573
2	Leo Cardenas	1969	570
3	Ed Brinkman	1970	569
4	Luis Aparicio	1969	563
5	Larry Bowa	1971	560
	Bill Russell	1973	560
7	Mark Belanger	1974	552
8	Mark Belanger	1976	545
9	Bucky Dent	1975	543
10	Don Kessinger	1969	542
11	Dave Concepcion	1974	536
12	Maury Wills	1965	535
	Luis Aparicio	1968	535
14	Jim Fregosi	1966	531
15	Hal Lanier	1969	530
	Mark Belanger	1973	530
17	Ron Hansen	1965	527
18	Don Kessinger	1973	526
19	Dick Groat	1962	521
20	2 tied with		517

Errors

	Player	Year	
1	Robin Yount	1975	44
2	Dick Groat	1964	40
3	Zoilo Versalles	1965	39
	Bill Russell	1974	39
5	Dick Howser	1961	38
	Dick Groat	1962	38
7	Ed Brinkman	1963	37
	Sonny Jackson	1966	37
	Darrel Chaney	1976	37
10	Maury Wills	1962	36
	Toby Harrah	1976	36
12	Andre Rodgers	1963	35
	Don Kessinger	1966	35
	Jim Fregosi	1966	35
	Zoilo Versalles	1966	35
	Sonny Jackson	1967	35
	Frank Taveras	1976	35
18	Bert Campaneris	1968	34
	Bill Russell	1972	34
	Rick Burleson	1976	34

Double Plays

	Player	Year	
1	Bobby Wine	1970	137
2	Gene Alley	1966	128
3	Zoilo Versalles	1962	127
4	Dick Groat	1962	126
	Leo Cardenas	1969	126
6	Jim Fregosi	1966	125
7	Dick Groat	1961	117
8	Freddie Patek	1973	115
9	Freddie Patek	1972	113
10	Ron Hansen	1961	110
	Roy McMillan	1961	110
12	Don Kessinger	1973	109
13	Bucky Dent	1974	108
	Freddie Patek	1974	108
	Mike Tyson	1974	108
16	Tony Kubek	1961	107
	Eddie Bressoud	1962	107
	Freddie Patek	1971	107
19	Bill Russell	1973	106
20	5 tied with		105

Fielding Percentage
(minimum 100 games)

	Player	Year	
1	Ed Brinkman	1972	.990
2	Larry Bowa	1972	.987
3	Larry Bowa	1971	.987
4	Frank Duffy	1973	.986
5	Roger Metzger	1976	.986
6	Leo Cardenas	1971	.985
7	Mark Belanger	1974	.984
8	Larry Bowa	1974	.984
9	Frank Duffy	1976	.983
10	Fred Stanley	1976	.983
11	Luis Aparicio	1963	.983
12	Ron Hansen	1963	.983
13	Mark Belanger	1976	.982
14	Chris Speier	1975	.982
15	Roger Metzger	1973	.982
16	Bobby Wine	1971	.982
17	Dal Maxvill	1970	.982
18	Rico Petrocelli	1969	.981
19	Dick Schofield	1965	.981
20	Bucky Dent	1975	.981

Range Factor
(minimum 100 games)

	Player	Year	
1	Ed Brinkman	1970	5.54
2	Freddie Patek	1973	5.52
3	Leo Cardenas	1969	5.50
4	Freddie Patek	1972	5.44
5	Gene Michael	1972	5.41
6	Dave Concepcion	1976	5.40
7	Gene Alley	1970	5.40
8	Larry Bowa	1971	5.30
9	Gene Michael	1971	5.27
10	Tim Foli	1974	5.27
11	Luis Aparicio	1969	5.27
12	Don Kessinger	1968	5.26
13	Bill Russell	1972	5.26
14	Dave Concepcion	1975	5.25
15	Bert Campaneris	1972	5.25
16	Andre Rodgers	1964	5.24
17	Bucky Dent	1975	5.24
18	Don Kessinger	1972	5.23
	Toby Harrah	1976	5.23
20	Zoilo Versalles	1962	5.23

Assists/162 Games
(minimum 100 games)

	Player	Year	
1	Freddie Patek	1972	607.50
2	Freddie Patek	1973	603.60
3	Luis Aparicio	1969	592.25
4	Bill Russell	1972	587.75
5	Ed Brinkman	1970	587.12
6	Gene Alley	1968	585.58
7	Gene Michael	1972	585.07
8	Don Kessinger	1968	583.81
9	Larry Bowa	1971	577.83
10	Leo Cardenas	1969	577.13
11	Mark Belanger	1976	577.06
12	Mark Belanger	1974	576.93
13	Hal Lanier	1969	572.40
14	Gene Alley	1970	571.50
15	Don Money	1969	569.57
16	Roger Metzger	1975	567.00
17	Gene Michael	1971	564.62
18	Luis Aparicio	1968	562.79
19	Bucky Dent	1975	560.29
20	Bill Russell	1973	560.00

Career Fielding Leaders—Outfielders: Expansion Era (1961-1976)

Games		Putouts		Assists		Errors	
1 Willie Davis	2,294	1 Willie Davis	5,389	1 Roberto Clemente	171	1 Lou Brock	177
2 Lou Brock	2,200	2 Vada Pinson	4,223	2 Carl Yastrzemski	167	2 Willie Davis	126
3 Vada Pinson	2,068	3 Paul Blair	4,000	3 Johnny Callison	163	3 Rusty Staub	100
4 Billy Williams	2,066	4 Lou Brock	3,944	4 Rusty Staub	157	Billy Williams	100
5 Carl Yastrzemski	1,787	5 Jimmy Wynn	3,862	5 Vada Pinson	146	5 Reggie Jackson	97
6 Jimmy Wynn	1,785	6 Willie Mays	3,767	6 Billy Williams	143	6 Roberto Clemente	88
7 Hank Aaron	1,758	7 Billy Williams	3,519	7 Willie Davis	142	7 Jose Cardenal	87
8 Paul Blair	1,654	8 Hank Aaron	3,514	8 Jose Cardenal	139	8 Vada Pinson	86
9 Jose Cardenal	1,653	9 Jose Cardenal	3,402	9 Jimmy Wynn	138	9 Willie Stargell	84
10 Willie Mays	1,633	10 Carl Yastrzemski	3,387	10 Lou Brock	131	Alex Johnson	84
11 Johnny Callison	1,632	11 Curt Flood	3,238	11 Hank Aaron	124	11 Jimmy Wynn	79
12 Rusty Staub	1,627	12 Johnny Callison	3,080	12 Del Unser	108	12 Carl Yastrzemski	78
13 Roberto Clemente	1,623	13 Roberto Clemente	3,074	13 Paul Blair	105	13 Willie Mays	75
14 Frank Robinson	1,615	14 Rusty Staub	2,950	14 Willie Stargell	102	14 Reggie Smith	74
15 Al Kaline	1,460	15 Reggie Smith	2,924	15 Pete Rose	97	15 Hank Aaron	66
16 Roy White	1,389	16 Roy White	2,882	16 Bobby Murcer	96	16 Bobby Bonds	64
17 Tony Gonzalez	1,349	17 Frank Robinson	2,846	Frank Robinson	96	17 Rick Monday	61
18 Curt Flood	1,337	18 Rick Monday	2,822	18 Reggie Smith	92	Tommie Agee	61
19 Ken Berry	1,311	19 Del Unser	2,821	19 Bobby Bonds	91	Tony Oliva	61
Matty Alou	1,311	20 Al Kaline	2,726	20 Reggie Jackson	90	20 Ralph Garr	58

Double Plays		Fielding Percentage (minimum 750 games)		Range Factor (minimum 750 games)		Assists/162 Games (minimum 750 games)	
1 Jimmy Wynn	40	1 Mickey Stanley	.992	1 Amos Otis	2.59	1 Roberto Clemente	17.07
2 Rusty Staub	34	2 Pete Rose	.992	2 Cesar Cedeno	2.58	2 Johnny Callison	16.18
3 Bobby Bonds	31	3 Ted Uhlaender	.991	3 Al Oliver	2.50	3 Rusty Staub	15.63
4 Johnny Callison	29	4 Joe Rudi	.990	4 Curt Flood	2.49	4 Carl Yastrzemski	15.14
5 Del Unser	28	5 Amos Otis	.989	5 Paul Blair	2.48	5 Del Unser	14.21
Roberto Clemente	28	6 Ken Berry	.989	6 Willie Davis	2.41	6 Jose Cardenal	13.62
7 Jose Cardenal	27	7 Paul Blair	.988	7 Reggie Smith	2.40	7 Bobby Murcer	13.26
8 Carl Yastrzemski	26	8 Curt Flood	.988	8 Del Unser	2.38	8 Mike Hershberger	13.12
Lou Brock	26	9 Roy White	.988	9 Willie Mays	2.35	9 Willie Stargell	12.78
Hank Aaron	26	10 Al Kaline	.988	10 Rick Monday	2.29	10 Jimmy Wynn	12.52
11 Paul Blair	25	11 Tony Gonzalez	.987	11 Mickey Stanley	2.28	11 Pete Rose	12.50
Reggie Jackson	25	12 Cesar Geronimo	.987	12 Larry Hisle	2.27	12 Lou Piniella	12.22
Amos Otis	25	13 Tommy Harper	.986	13 Dave May	2.26	13 Cesar Tovar	12.17
14 Billy Williams	24	14 Roger Maris	.986	14 Tommie Agee	2.26	14 Bobby Bonds	11.97
Curt Flood	24	15 Vic Davalillo	.986	15 Jimmy Wynn	2.24	15 Reggie Smith	11.87
16 Willie Davis	23	16 Frank Robinson	.984	16 Cesar Tovar	2.24	16 Ollie Brown	11.68
Vada Pinson	23	17 Del Unser	.984	17 Don Lock	2.22	17 Don Lock	11.50
18 Willie Mays	22	18 Johnny Callison	.984	18 Bobby Bonds	2.22	18 Jay Johnstone	11.49
19 Rick Monday	21	19 Rocky Colavito	.983	19 Bobby Tolan	2.17	19 Vada Pinson	11.44
20 Frank Robinson	20	20 Cesar Cedeno	.983	20 Bobby Murcer	2.17	20 Hank Aaron	11.43

Single Season Fielding Leaders—Outfielders: Expansion Era (1961-1976)

Games			Putouts			Assists			Errors		
1 Billy Williams	1965	164	1 Ken Henderson	1974	462	1 Roberto Clemente	1961	27	1 Lou Brock	1966	19
2 Leon Wagner	1964	163	2 Paul Blair	1974	447	2 Johnny Callison	1963	26	2 Alex Johnson	1969	18
Billy Williams	1968	163	3 Cesar Cedeno	1974	446	3 Johnny Callison	1962	24	Rusty Staub	1971	18
Pete Rose	1974	163	4 Garry Maddox	1976	441	4 Del Unser	1968	22	4 Willie Davis	1962	15
5 Vada Pinson	1963	162	5 Bill North	1974	437	5 Johnny Callison	1965	21	5 Ken Hunt	1961	14
Billy Williams	1964	162	6 Willie Mays	1962	429	Bobby Murcer	1974	21	Willie McCovey	1963	14
Johnny Callison	1964	162	Bill North	1973	429	7 Pete Rose	1968	20	Lou Brock	1964	14
Curt Flood	1964	162	8 Amos Otis	1974	425	Jimmy Wynn	1968	20	Alex Johnson	1968	14
Rocky Colavito	1965	162	9 Mickey Stanley	1973	420	Rusty Staub	1971	20	Lou Brock	1968	14
Billy Williams	1966	162	Bill North	1975	420	Ken Singleton	1973	20	Reggie Smith	1969	14
Billy Williams	1967	162	11 Bill Bruton	1961	410	11 Vada Pinson	1961	19	Jesus Alou	1969	14
Matty Alou	1969	162	Juan Beniquez	1976	410	Frank Howard	1962	19	Lou Brock	1969	14
Rusty Staub	1971	162	13 Cesar Geronimo	1975	408	Roberto Clemente	1962	19	Reggie Smith	1971	14
Roy White	1973	162	14 Paul Blair	1969	407	Carl Yastrzemski	1964	19	Lou Brock	1971	14
Ken Henderson	1974	162	Mickey Rivers	1976	407	Don Lock	1964	19	Dave Parker	1976	14
16 8 tied with		161	16 Amos Otis	1971	404	Johnny Callison	1964	19	16 8 tied with		13
			Willie Davis	1971	404	Rusty Staub	1974	19			
			Fred Lynn	1975	404	18 5 tied with		18			
			19 3 tied with		401						

Double Plays			Fielding Percentage (minimum 100 games)			Range Factor (minimum 100 games)			Assists/162 Games (minimum 100 games)		
1 Del Unser	1968	10	1 Tony Gonzalez	1962	1.000	1 Bill North	1974	3.23	1 Roberto Clemente	1961	30.38
2 Jimmy Wynn	1968	8	Don Demeter	1963	1.000	2 Bill North	1973	3.21	2 Johnny Callison	1963	26.83
Dwight Evans	1975	8	Russ Snyder	1965	1.000	3 Garry Maddox	1976	3.13	3 Johnny Callison	1962	25.58
4 Johnny Callison	1962	7	Rocky Colavito	1965	1.000	4 Bill North	1975	3.12	4 Lu Clinton	1962	24.10
Lou Brock	1963	7	Curt Flood	1966	1.000	5 Garry Maddox	1975	3.07	5 Frank Howard	1962	23.50
Mike Hershberger	1965	7	Mickey Stanley	1968	1.000	6 Mickey Rivers	1976	3.04	6 Del Unser	1968	22.85
Tommie Agee	1966	7	Ken Harrelson	1968	1.000	7 Juan Beniquez	1976	3.04	7 Pete Rose	1968	21.89
Jose Cardenal	1968	7	Johnny Callison	1968	1.000	8 Amos Otis	1974	3.03	8 Bobby Murcer	1974	21.81
Ron Fairly	1968	7	Ken Berry	1969	1.000	9 Paul Blair	1974	3.01	9 Cito Gaston	1973	21.78
Bobby Bonds	1970	7	Mickey Stanley	1970	1.000	10 Ron LeFlore	1976	2.99	10 Roberto Clemente	1962	21.68
11 Don Lock	1963	6	Roy White	1971	1.000	11 Fred Lynn	1976	2.97	11 Elliott Maddox	1974	21.60
Rick Monday	1967	6	Al Kaline	1971	1.000	12 Paul Blair	1970	2.95	12 Johnny Callison	1965	21.40
Steve Whitaker	1967	6	Ken Berry	1972	1.000	13 Ken Henderson	1975	2.93	13 Mike Hershberger	1967	21.18
Rod Gaspar	1969	6	14 Pete Rose	1974	.997	14 Cesar Cedeno	1974	2.91	14 Jimmy Wynn	1968	21.18
Wayne Comer	1969	6	15 Pete Rose	1970	.997	15 Rick Manning	1975	2.91	15 Dwight Evans	1975	21.13
Amos Otis	1970	6	16 Ken Berry	1973	.997	16 Ken Henderson	1974	2.90	16 Rusty Staub	1974	20.94
Bobby Bonds	1975	6	17 Jimmy Piersall	1962	.997	17 Fred Lynn	1975	2.88	17 Carl Yastrzemski	1964	20.80
George Hendrick	1976	6	18 Steve Brye	1974	.997	18 Al Oliver	1976	2.88	18 Willie Stargell	1970	20.74
Jerry Morales	1976	6	19 Roy White	1968	.997	19 Amos Otis	1971	2.88	19 Juan Beniquez	1976	20.68
20 28 tied with		5	20 Ted Uhlaender	1969	.997	20 Jim Landis	1961	2.86	20 Don Lock	1964	20.66

Career Fielding Leaders—Pitchers: Modern Era (1977-1997)

Games

1	Lee Smith	1,022
2	Jesse Orosco	956
3	Dennis Eckersley	951
4	Kent Tekulve	944
5	Jeff Reardon	880
6	Goose Gossage	813
7	Rick Honeycutt	797
8	John Franco	771
9	Paul Assenmacher	760
10	Willie Hernandez	744
11	Steve Bedrosian	732
12	Roger McDowell	723
13	Dave Righetti	718
14	Greg Harris	703
15	Greg Minton	696
	Larry Andersen	696
	Craig Lefferts	696
18	Mike Jackson	694
19	Danny Darwin	683
20	Gene Garber	682

Putouts

1	Jack Morris	387
2	Greg Maddux	318
3	Dennis Martinez	310
4	Orel Hershiser	291
5	Mike Moore	278
6	Dave Stieb	267
7	Doug Drabek	258
8	Dan Petry	255
9	Mike Boddicker	245
10	Bob Welch	243
11	Kevin Brown	239
12	Mark Gubicza	237
13	Roger Clemens	225
14	Rick Reuschel	221
15	Charlie Hough	220
16	Tom Candiotti	213
17	Rick Sutcliffe	211
18	Dwight Gooden	209
19	Fernando Valenzuela	200
20	John Smoltz	198

Assists

1	Dennis Martinez	743
2	Fernando Valenzuela	586
3	Greg Maddux	581
4	Charlie Hough	519
5	Frank Tanana	505
6	Orel Hershiser	492
7	Dave Stieb	488
8	Mark Langston	469
9	Charlie Leibrandt	465
10	Rick Reuschel	460
11	Tommy John	459
12	Bob Knepper	447
13	Mike Moore	444
14	Jimmy Key	441
15	Rick Honeycutt	428
16	Mike Flanagan	415
17	Joaquin Andujar	413
	Jack Morris	413
19	Phil Niekro	404
	Rick Sutcliffe	404

Errors

1	Joaquin Andujar	51
2	Nolan Ryan	50
3	Orel Hershiser	47
4	Dennis Martinez	41
5	Ron Darling	37
6	Mark Langston	36
7	Terry Mulholland	34
8	Mike Moore	33
	Dwight Gooden	33
10	Greg Harris	32
	Mike Boddicker	32
	Rick Honeycutt	32
	Frank Viola	32
14	Greg Maddux	31
15	Bob Knepper	30
	Fernando Valenzuela	30
	Danny Jackson	30
	Chuck Finley	30
19	Jack Morris	29
	Matt Young	29

Double Plays

1	Dennis Martinez	59
2	Greg Maddux	47
3	Dave Stieb	45
4	Phil Niekro	42
5	John Denny	41
6	Orel Hershiser	40
7	Dan Petry	38
	Bob Stanley	38
	Walt Terrell	38
10	Mike Boddicker	37
	Ron Darling	37
12	Charlie Hough	36
	Jack Morris	36
14	Chris Bosio	35
15	Mike Moore	34
	Zane Smith	34
17	5 tied with	32

Fielding Percentage
(minimum 150 games)

1	Doug Bird	1.000
	Roy Thomas	1.000
	Bill Landrum	1.000
	Joe Klink	1.000
	Mike Dyer	1.000
	Kevin Wickander	1.000
	Stan Belinda	1.000
	Eric Gunderson	1.000
	Jim Bullinger	1.000
	Billy Taylor	1.000
	Ricky Bottalico	1.000
	Mike James	1.000
	Terry Adams	1.000
14	Les Lancaster	.993
15	Pete Schourek	.993
16	Rick Rhoden	.992
17	Mark Eichhorn	.992
18	John Habyan	.992
19	Jim Acker	.992
20	Brian Bohanon	.990

Assists/162 Innings
(minimum 150 games)

1	Dan Quisenberry	40.99
2	Juan Agosto	40.87
3	Randy Jones	40.47
4	Jeff Dedmon	40.29
5	Ricky Horton	39.70
6	Roger McDowell	39.03
7	Darold Knowles	38.47
8	Jim Winn	38.35
9	Greg Minton	37.67
10	Greg Maddux	36.22
11	Kent Tekulve	36.14
12	Jerry Garvin	36.09
13	Craig McMurtry	35.91
14	Todd Frohwirth	35.68
15	Bob Lacey	35.23
16	John Denny	34.76
17	Mike Munoz	34.67
18	Bryan Clark	34.51
19	Russ Swan	34.02
20	Frank Williams	34.00

Single Season Fielding Leaders—Pitchers: Modern Era (1977-1997)

Games

1	Kent Tekulve	1979	94
2	Kent Tekulve	1978	91
3	Mike Marshall	1979	90
	Kent Tekulve	1987	90
5	Mark Eichhorn	1987	89
	Julian Tavarez	1997	89
7	Mike Myers	1997	88
8	Rob Murphy	1987	87
9	Kent Tekulve	1982	85
	Frank Williams	1987	85
	Mitch Williams	1987	85
12	Enrique Romo	1979	84
	Dick Tidrow	1980	84
	Dan Quisenberry	1985	84
	Stan Belinda	1997	84
16	Craig Lefferts	1986	83
	Eddie Guardado	1996	83
	Mike Myers	1996	83
19	Bill Campbell	1983	82
	Juan Agosto	1990	82

Putouts

1	Mike Boddicker	1984	49
2	Oil Can Boyd	1985	42
3	Kevin Brown	1995	40
4	Greg Maddux	1990	39
	Greg Maddux	1991	39
	Greg Maddux	1993	39
7	Dan Petry	1984	38
	Jack Morris	1990	38
9	Orel Hershiser	1987	37
	Kevin Brown	1992	37
	Greg Maddux	1996	37
12	Rick Sutcliffe	1983	36
	Dan Petry	1985	36
	Dwight Gooden	1986	36
	Kevin Brown	1997	36
16	Greg Maddux	1989	35
	Bill Wegman	1992	35
18	Dave Stieb	1985	34
	Jim Clancy	1986	34
20	3 tied with		32

Assists

1	John Denny	1978	73
2	Greg Maddux	1996	71
3	Jerry Garvin	1977	66
4	Phil Niekro	1978	65
5	Mike Caldwell	1979	64
	Fernando Valenzuela	1982	64
	Greg Maddux	1992	64
8	Steve Rogers	1977	63
	Fredie Arroyo	1977	63
10	Joaquin Andujar	1983	62
11	Randy Jones	1979	60
	Orel Hershiser	1988	60
13	Dennis Martinez	1979	59
	Greg Maddux	1993	59
15	Dave Stieb	1980	58
16	Mike Hampton	1997	57
17	Phil Niekro	1979	56
	Rick Reuschel	1980	56
	LaMarr Hoyt	1983	56
	Dwight Gooden	1988	56

Errors

1	Melido Perez	1992	10
2	Matt Young	1990	9
3	Joaquin Andujar	1977	8
	Larry Christenson	1977	8
	Jesse Jefferson	1977	8
	Nolan Ryan	1977	8
	Dick Ruthven	1978	8
	Nolan Ryan	1978	8
	John Denny	1983	8
	Danny Jackson	1992	8
	Kevin Brown	1992	8
12	12 tied with		7

Double Plays

1	Dan Petry	1983	10
2	Rick Reuschel	1979	9
	Rick Mahler	1985	9
4	John Denny	1978	8
	Bob Stanley	1980	8
	Dave Stieb	1980	8
	Rich Dotson	1983	8
	Dennis Martinez	1983	8
	Joaquin Andujar	1985	8
	Walt Terrell	1985	8
	Jose Rijo	1993	8
	Ricky Bones	1995	8
13	14 tied with		7

Fielding Percentage
(minimum 25 games)

1	1855 tied with		1.000

Assists/162 Innings
(minimum 25 games)

1	Mike Jeffcoat	1985	61.39
2	Juan Agosto	1988	60.09
3	Dan Quisenberry	1981	59.78
4	Juan Agosto	1987	59.27
5	John Franco	1992	58.91
6	Roger McDowell	1993	57.18
7	Dan Quisenberry	1982	54.53
8	Jesse Orosco	1993	54.32
9	Ricky Horton	1990	54.00
10	Tom Bolton	1988	53.41
11	Frank Williams	1984	53.32
12	Jim Mecir	1996	52.21
13	Jeff Musselman	1989	52.07
14	Greg Maddux	1987	52.03
15	Tony Arnold	1987	51.96
16	Randy Jones	1977	51.68
17	Jeff Dedmon	1985	50.86
18	Rick Camp	1980	50.84
19	Bob Lacey	1977	50.60
20	John Denny	1978	50.54

Career Fielding Leaders—Catchers: Modern Era (1977-1997)

Games

1	Tony Pena	1,950
2	Gary Carter	1,924
3	Lance Parrish	1,818
4	Bob Boone	1,720
5	Carlton Fisk	1,695
6	Jim Sundberg	1,500
7	Rick Dempsey	1,476
8	Mike Scioscia	1,395
9	Terry Kennedy	1,378
10	Benito Santiago	1,295
11	Rick Cerone	1,266
12	Ernie Whitt	1,238
13	Don Slaught	1,237
14	Terry Steinbach	1,166
15	Butch Wynegar	1,110
16	Alan Ashby	1,106
17	Mike Heath	1,083
18	Jody Davis	1,039
19	Darrell Porter	1,024
20	Rich Gedman	980

Putouts

1	Tony Pena	11,212
2	Gary Carter	11,168
3	Lance Parrish	9,647
4	Bob Boone	8,488
5	Carlton Fisk	8,447
6	Mike Scioscia	8,335
7	Jim Sundberg	7,535
8	Benito Santiago	7,315
9	Rick Dempsey	6,714
10	Terry Kennedy	6,555
11	Rick Cerone	6,505
12	Terry Steinbach	6,301
13	Don Slaught	6,158
14	Alan Ashby	6,113
15	Ernie Whitt	6,067
16	Butch Wynegar	5,631
17	Jody Davis	5,520
18	Darren Daulton	5,417
19	Bo Diaz	5,294
20	Rich Gedman	5,274

Assists

1	Gary Carter	1,126
2	Tony Pena	1,045
3	Lance Parrish	980
4	Bob Boone	921
5	Carlton Fisk	791
6	Jim Sundberg	741
7	Mike Scioscia	737
8	Benito Santiago	711
9	Rick Dempsey	690
10	Jody Davis	640
11	Terry Kennedy	623
12	Alan Ashby	590
13	Bruce Benedict	577
14	Mike Heath	537
15	Rick Cerone	534
16	Terry Steinbach	533
17	Bo Diaz	525
18	Butch Wynegar	505
19	Ernie Whitt	497
20	Ivan Rodriguez	490

Errors

1	Bob Boone	132
2	Benito Santiago	127
3	Tony Pena	117
4	Gary Carter	114
	Mike Scioscia	114
6	Terry Kennedy	106
	Mike Heath	106
8	Alan Ashby	100
9	Carlton Fisk	98
10	Lance Parrish	94
11	Rich Gedman	92
12	Alex Trevino	89
13	Don Slaught	87
14	Rick Dempsey	82
	Bo Diaz	82
16	Jody Davis	81
17	Terry Steinbach	80
18	Darrell Porter	79
19	Rick Cerone	69
20	Darren Daulton	66

Double Plays

1	Tony Pena	154
2	Gary Carter	135
3	Lance Parrish	134
4	Bob Boone	118
5	Carlton Fisk	115
6	Jim Sundberg	108
7	Rick Dempsey	103
8	Mike Scioscia	97
9	Terry Kennedy	92
10	Benito Santiago	90
11	Butch Wynegar	82
12	Mike Heath	73
13	Kirt Manwaring	72
14	Don Slaught	71
15	Darren Daulton	69
16	Ernie Whitt	67
17	Darrell Porter	65
	Jody Davis	65
	Terry Steinbach	65
20	Rich Gedman	62

Fielding Percentage
(minimum 500 games)

1	Chris Hoiles	.994
2	Jim Sundberg	.994
3	Dan Wilson	.993
4	Darrin Fletcher	.993
5	Bob Melvin	.993
6	Ron Hassey	.993
7	Mike LaValliere	.992
8	Rick Wilkins	.992
9	Tom Pagnozzi	.992
10	Ron Karkovice	.992
11	Kirt Manwaring	.992
12	Dave Valle	.992
13	Mike Macfarlane	.992
14	Lance Parrish	.991
15	Ernie Whitt	.991
16	Mickey Tettleton	.991
17	Gary Carter	.991
18	Tony Pena	.991
19	Butch Wynegar	.990
20	Charlie O'Brien	.990

Passed Balls

1	Lance Parrish	192
2	Benito Santiago	112
3	Jim Sundberg	109
4	Carlton Fisk	107
5	Tony Pena	105
6	Alan Ashby	102
7	Jody Davis	98
8	Geno Petralli	95
9	Rick Cerone	94
10	Don Slaught	92
11	Mike Stanley	90
12	Mike Macfarlane	89
13	Darrell Porter	87
14	Rich Gedman	84
15	Mike Scioscia	82
16	Gary Carter	75
	Bob Brenly	75
18	Terry Steinbach	74
19	Bo Diaz	71
	Ernie Whitt	71

Assists/162 Games
(minimum 500 games)

1	John Stearns	101.84
2	Jody Davis	99.79
3	Bruce Benedict	96.27
4	Gary Carter	94.81
5	Rick Wilkins	94.78
6	Jim Essian	94.77
7	Bob Brenly	93.75
8	Ivan Rodriguez	93.06
9	Milt May	92.78
10	Benito Santiago	88.94
11	Bo Diaz	88.13
12	Steve Yeager	87.67
13	Lance Parrish	87.33
14	Ted Simmons	87.22
15	Alex Trevino	86.89
16	Tony Pena	86.82
17	Bob Boone	86.75
18	Alan Ashby	86.42
19	Ozzie Virgil	86.14
20	Mike Scioscia	85.59

Single Season Fielding Leaders—Catchers: Modern Era (1977-1997)

Games

1	Carlton Fisk	1978	154
2	Gary Carter	1982	153
3	Gary Carter	1978	152
4	Carlton Fisk	1977	151
	Jim Sundberg	1980	151
	Benito Santiago	1991	151
7	Jim Sundberg	1979	150
	Jody Davis	1983	150
	Todd Hundley	1996	150
10	Jim Sundberg	1977	149
	Gary Carter	1980	149
	Tony Pena	1983	149
13	Jim Sundberg	1978	148
14	Rick Cerone	1980	147
	Terry Kennedy	1984	147
	Bob Boone	1985	147
17	10 tied with		146

Putouts

1	Mike Piazza	1996	1,055
2	Dan Wilson	1997	1,051
3	Mike Piazza	1997	1,045
4	Javy Lopez	1996	992
5	Darren Daulton	1993	981
6	Tony Pena	1983	976
7	Gary Carter	1985	956
8	Gary Carter	1982	954
9	Jason Kendall	1997	952
10	Mike Lieberthal	1997	934
11	Mike Scioscia	1987	925
	Joe Oliver	1992	925
13	Tony Pena	1985	922
14	Todd Hundley	1996	911
15	Bo Diaz	1983	903
16	Charles Johnson	1997	900
17	Mike Piazza	1993	899
18	Tony Pena	1984	895
	Dan Wilson	1995	895
20	Craig Biggio	1991	889

Assists

1	Gary Carter	1980	108
2	Gary Carter	1983	107
3	Jody Davis	1986	105
4	Gary Carter	1982	104
5	Jim Sundberg	1977	103
	Jason Kendall	1997	103
7	Gary Carter	1977	101
8	Tony Pena	1985	100
	Benito Santiago	1991	100
10	Tony Pena	1986	99
11	Mike Piazza	1993	98
12	Bo Diaz	1983	97
13	Tony Pena	1984	95
14	Tim Blackwell	1980	93
	Ozzie Virgil	1986	93
16	Jim Sundberg	1978	91
	Bruce Benedict	1983	91
18	Carlton Fisk	1978	90
	Tony Pena	1983	90
20	5 tied with		89

Errors

1	Benito Santiago	1987	22
2	Terry Kennedy	1981	20
	Andy Allanson	1986	20
	Benito Santiago	1989	20
5	Steve Yeager	1977	18
	Gary Alexander	1979	18
	Bob Boone	1980	18
	Rich Gedman	1984	18
	Tony Pena	1986	18
	Jason Kendall	1996	18
11	Carlton Fisk	1978	17
	Barry Foote	1979	17
	Alex Trevino	1982	17
14	Tony Pena	1982	16
	Mike Piazza	1997	16
16	6 tied with		15

Double Plays

1	Jason Kendall	1997	20
2	Darren Daulton	1993	19
3	Charles Johnson	1997	17
4	Tim Blackwell	1980	16
	Bob Boone	1986	16
	Brad Ausmus	1997	16
7	Darrell Porter	1979	15
	Jim Sundberg	1982	15
	Tony Pena	1984	15
	Bob Boone	1985	15
	Carlton Fisk	1987	15
	Lance Parrish	1990	15
	Tony Pena	1991	15
14	9 tied with		14

Fielding Percentage
(minimum 100 games)

1	Charles Johnson	1997	1.000
2	Tom Pagnozzi	1992	.999
3	Mike LaValliere	1991	.998
4	Rick Cerone	1987	.998
5	Kirt Manwaring	1993	.998
6	Tony Pena	1989	.997
7	Lance Parrish	1991	.997
8	Dave Valle	1990	.997
9	Rick Dempsey	1983	.997
10	Jim Sundberg	1978	.997
11	Joe Girardi	1996	.996
12	Rick Wilkins	1993	.996
13	Mickey Tettleton	1992	.996
14	Todd Hundley	1992	.996
15	Mike Stanley	1993	.996
16	Chris Hoiles	1995	.996
17	Dan Wilson	1996	.996
18	Charlie O'Brien	1996	.995
19	Ted Simmons	1982	.995
20	Jim Sundberg	1979	.995

Passed Balls

1	Geno Petralli	1987	35
2	Mike Macfarlane	1995	26
3	Benito Santiago	1993	23
4	Benito Santiago	1987	22
5	Lance Parrish	1979	21
	Jody Davis	1983	21
	Chad Kreuter	1989	21
8	Luis Pujols	1982	20
	Don Slaught	1987	20
	Geno Petralli	1988	20
	Geno Petralli	1990	20
12	Mark Bailey	1985	19
	Lance Parrish	1991	19
14	Donnie Scott	1984	18
	Mike Stanley	1987	18
	Brian Harper	1993	18
	Mike Stanley	1996	18
18	6 tied with		17

Assists/162 Games
(minimum 100 games)

1	Tim Blackwell	1980	146.27
2	Ozzie Virgil	1986	135.73
3	Biff Pocoroba	1977	126.36
4	Bob Brenly	1987	124.50
5	Gary Carter	1983	120.38
6	Ivan Rodriguez	1992	118.71
7	Jason Kendall	1997	117.51
8	Gary Carter	1980	117.42
9	Jody Davis	1986	117.31
10	Bo Diaz	1983	117.27
11	Steve Yeager	1977	117.22
12	George Mitterwald	1977	115.93
13	Tony Pena	1986	115.38
14	Milt May	1977	113.84
15	John Stearns	1979	113.80
16	Gary Carter	1977	112.07
17	Jim Sundberg	1977	111.99
18	Jody Davis	1982	111.77
19	Dann Bilardello	1983	111.09
20	Mike Scioscia	1992	111.00

Career Fielding Leaders—First Basemen: Modern Era (1977-1997)

	Games			Putouts			Assists			Errors	
1	Eddie Murray	2,413	1	Eddie Murray	21,255	1	Eddie Murray	1,865	1	Eddie Murray	167
2	Keith Hernandez	1,839	2	Keith Hernandez	16,508	2	Keith Hernandez	1,538	2	Andres Galarraga	129
3	Don Mattingly	1,634	3	Andres Galarraga	14,297	3	Wally Joyner	1,275	3	Bill Buckner	122
4	Kent Hrbek	1,609	4	Don Mattingly	14,148	4	Bill Buckner	1,273	4	Will Clark	111
5	Andres Galarraga	1,600	5	Will Clark	14,094	5	Mark Grace	1,232	5	Fred McGriff	110
6	Wally Joyner	1,587	6	Wally Joyner	13,742	6	Andres Galarraga	1,116	6	Keith Hernandez	101
7	Will Clark	1,570	7	Kent Hrbek	13,725	7	Will Clark	1,108	7	Cecil Cooper	99
8	Steve Garvey	1,502	8	Steve Garvey	13,474	8	Don Mattingly	1,104	8	Willie Upshaw	98
9	Fred McGriff	1,490	9	Mark Grace	12,889	9	Pete O'Brien	1,064	9	Jason Thompson	89
10	Mark Grace	1,434	10	Fred McGriff	12,849	10	Kent Hrbek	1,049	10	Rod Carew	87
11	Bill Buckner	1,408	11	Bill Buckner	12,582	11	Rafael Palmeiro	1,025		Kent Hrbek	87
12	Pete O'Brien	1,377	12	Pete O'Brien	11,651	12	Fred McGriff	1,010		Mo Vaughn	87
13	Rafael Palmeiro	1,356	13	Cecil Cooper	11,599	13	Cecil Cooper	878	13	Wally Joyner	84
14	Mark McGwire	1,301	14	Rafael Palmeiro	11,295	14	Jeff Bagwell	874	14	Mike Hargrove	79
15	Cecil Cooper	1,257	15	Mark McGwire	10,724	15	Chris Chambliss	827		Pete O'Brien	79
16	Dan Driessen	1,212	16	Jason Thompson	10,661	16	Mark McGwire	809	16	Mark Grace	76
17	Jason Thompson	1,197	17	Chris Chambliss	10,585	17	Willie Upshaw	799	17	Gerald Perry	73
18	Chris Chambliss	1,156	18	Dan Driessen	10,089	18	Mike Hargrove	797		Mark McGwire	73
19	Mike Hargrove	1,097	19	Rod Carew	9,407	19	Steve Garvey	792	19	Jeff Bagwell	71
20	Willie Upshaw	1,094	20	Mike Hargrove	9,091	20	Sid Bream	786	20	Rafael Palmeiro	70

	Double Plays			Fielding Percentage (minimum 750 games)			Assists/162 Games (minimum 750 games)	
1	Eddie Murray	2,033	1	Steve Garvey	.996	1	Bill Buckner	146.47
2	Keith Hernandez	1,525	2	Don Mattingly	.996	2	Jeff Bagwell	141.87
3	Don Mattingly	1,500	3	Tino Martinez	.995	3	Mark Grace	139.18
4	Wally Joyner	1,367	4	Dan Driessen	.995	4	Eric Karros	137.28
5	Kent Hrbek	1,331	5	John Olerud	.995	5	Keith Hernandez	135.48
6	Will Clark	1,313	6	Mark Grace	.995	6	Sid Bream	133.47
7	Andres Galarraga	1,259	7	Wally Joyner	.994	7	Wally Joyner	130.15
8	Cecil Cooper	1,180	8	Keith Hernandez	.994	8	Cecil Fielder	126.87
9	Fred McGriff	1,129	9	Rafael Palmeiro	.994	9	Eddie Murray	125.21
10	Rafael Palmeiro	1,116	10	Kent Hrbek	.994	10	Pete O'Brien	125.18
11	Steve Garvey	1,095	11	Chris Chambliss	.994	11	Rafael Palmeiro	122.46
12	Pete O'Brien	1,086	12	Pete Rose	.994	12	Willie Upshaw	118.32
13	Bill Buckner	1,073	13	Hal Morris	.994	13	Mike Hargrove	117.70
14	Mark Grace	1,056	14	Greg Brock	.994	14	Greg Brock	117.63
15	Mark McGwire	1,053	15	Pete O'Brien	.994	15	Chris Chambliss	115.89
16	Chris Chambliss	997	16	Mark McGwire	.994	16	Hal Morris	115.31
17	Jason Thompson	986	17	Paul Sorrento	.993	17	Glenn Davis	114.89
18	Rod Carew	971	18	Eddie Murray	.993	18	Pete Rose	114.85
19	Dan Driessen	883	19	Will Clark	.993	19	Will Clark	114.33
20	Mike Hargrove	859	20	Bruce Bochte	.993	20	Cecil Cooper	113.16

Single Season Fielding Leaders—First Basemen: Modern Era (1977-1997)

	Games				Putouts				Assists				Errors		
1	Steve Garvey	1979	162	1	Chris Chambliss	1980	1,626	1	Bill Buckner	1985	184	1	George Scott	1977	24
	Steve Garvey	1980	162	2	Steve Garvey	1977	1,606	2	Mark Grace	1990	180	2	Willie Upshaw	1983	21
	Pete Rose	1980	162	3	Jason Thompson	1977	1,599	3	Mark Grace	1991	167	3	Dale Murphy	1978	20
	Pete Rose	1982	162	4	Keith Hernandez	1982	1,586	4	Sid Bream	1986	166	4	Al Oliver	1982	19
	Steve Garvey	1985	162	5	Mark Grace	1992	1,580	5	Bill Buckner	1983	161		Eddie Murray	1985	19
	Bill Buckner	1985	162	6	Steve Balboni	1985	1,573	6	Bill Buckner	1982	159		Orestes Destrade	1993	19
	Jeff Bagwell	1996	162	7	Keith Hernandez	1980	1,572	7	Bill Buckner	1986	157	7	Dave Kingman	1982	18
	Eric Karros	1997	162	8	Bill Buckner	1982	1,547	8	Eddie Murray	1985	152		Steve Balboni	1986	18
9	Steve Garvey	1978	161	9	Steve Garvey	1978	1,546	9	Keith Hernandez	1986	149		Eddie Murray	1993	18
	Bill Buckner	1982	161	10	Steve Garvey	1982	1,539		Keith Hernandez	1987	149	10	12 tied with		17
11	Steve Garvey	1977	160	11	Eddie Murray	1984	1,538	11	Keith Hernandez	1983	147				
	Keith Hernandez	1979	160	12	Andres Galarraga	1996	1,528		Rafael Palmeiro	1993	147				
	Mike Hargrove	1980	160	13	Mark Grace	1991	1,520		Eric Karros	1993	147				
	Steve Balboni	1985	160	14	Eddie Murray	1978	1,504		Jeff King	1997	147				
	Don Mattingly	1986	160	15	Jason Thompson	1978	1,503	15	Keith Hernandez	1979	146				
	Pedro Guerrero	1989	160	16	Steve Garvey	1980	1,502		Pete O'Brien	1987	146				
	Mark Grace	1991	160	17	Will Clark	1988	1,492	17	Eddie Murray	1987	145				
	Rafael Palmeiro	1993	160	18	Keith Hernandez	1979	1,489		Wally Joyner	1993	145				
19	15 tied with		159	19	Wally Joyner	1989	1,487	19	3 tied with		143				
				20	Andres Galarraga	1988	1,464								

	Double Plays				Fielding Percentage (minimum 100 games)				Assists/162 Games (minimum 100 games)		
1	Andres Galarraga	1997	176	1	Steve Garvey	1984	1.000	1	Mark Grace	1990	190.59
2	Ron Jackson	1979	175	2	Steve Garvey	1981	.999	2	Bill Buckner	1986	184.30
3	Rod Carew	1977	161	3	Hal Morris	1992	.999	3	Bill Buckner	1985	184.00
4	Cecil Cooper	1980	160	4	George Brett	1989	.998	4	Jeff Bagwell	1995	183.32
5	Eddie Murray	1980	158	5	Darrell Evans	1986	.998	5	Bill Buckner	1983	181.13
6	Rafael Palmeiro	1996	157	6	Dave Magadan	1990	.998	6	Jeff Bagwell	1994	178.35
7	Cecil Cooper	1982	156	7	Don Mattingly	1993	.998	7	Sid Bream	1986	175.76
8	Eddie Murray	1985	154	8	Dan Driessen	1982	.998	8	Eric Karros	1994	175.38
	Don Mattingly	1985	154	9	Mark Grace	1992	.998	9	Cecil Fielder	1994	171.53
	Andres Galarraga	1996	154	10	John Olerud	1996	.998	10	Mark Grace	1991	169.09
11	Jason Thompson	1978	153	11	Wally Joyner	1995	.998	11	Wally Joyner	1993	167.79
12	Eddie Murray	1984	152	12	Kevin Young	1993	.998	12	Eddie Murray	1988	166.72
13	George Scott	1977	150	13	Rico Brogna	1995	.998	13	Darrell Evans	1986	166.63
	Tony Perez	1980	150	14	Wally Joyner	1989	.997	14	Keith Hernandez	1983	165.38
15	Wally Joyner	1988	148	15	John Kruk	1991	.997	15	Sid Bream	1988	164.35
	Fred McGriff	1989	148	16	Wally Joyner	1996	.997	16	Darrell Evans	1985	163.43
17	Keith Hernandez	1983	147	17	Kent Hrbek	1990	.997	17	Keith Hernandez	1986	162.00
18	4 tied with		146	18	Pete O'Brien	1991	.997	18	Bill Buckner	1982	159.99
				19	Chris Chambliss	1978	.997	19	Eddie Murray	1985	159.90
				20	Keith Hernandez	1985	.997	20	Jeff King	1997	158.76

Career Fielding Leaders—Second Basemen: Modern Era (1977-1997)

Games

1	Lou Whitaker	2,308
2	Willie Randolph	2,014
3	Ryne Sandberg	1,995
4	Frank White	1,892
5	Steve Sax	1,679
6	Jim Gantner	1,449
7	Tom Herr	1,416
8	Roberto Alomar	1,382
9	Bill Doran	1,359
10	Harold Reynolds	1,339
11	Glenn Hubbard	1,332
12	Robby Thompson	1,279
13	Johnny Ray	1,277
14	Juan Samuel	1,188
15	Manny Trillo	1,172
16	Ron Oester	1,171
17	Julio Cruz	1,123
18	Bobby Grich	1,097
19	Jody Reed	1,050
20	Jose Lind	1,038

Putouts

1	Lou Whitaker	4,771
2	Willie Randolph	4,517
3	Frank White	4,274
4	Ryne Sandberg	3,807
5	Steve Sax	3,574
6	Jim Gantner	3,139
7	Tom Herr	2,932
8	Glenn Hubbard	2,795
9	Roberto Alomar	2,775
10	Harold Reynolds	2,749
11	Johnny Ray	2,682
12	Manny Trillo	2,658
13	Bill Doran	2,619
14	Robby Thompson	2,611
15	Ron Oester	2,591
16	Juan Samuel	2,578
17	Julio Cruz	2,393
18	Bobby Grich	2,362
19	Jose Lind	2,183
20	Jody Reed	2,135

Assists

1	Lou Whitaker	6,653
2	Ryne Sandberg	6,363
3	Willie Randolph	5,879
4	Frank White	5,556
5	Steve Sax	4,805
6	Glenn Hubbard	4,444
7	Jim Gantner	4,347
8	Tom Herr	3,999
9	Roberto Alomar	3,974
10	Harold Reynolds	3,932
11	Johnny Ray	3,836
12	Robby Thompson	3,704
13	Bill Doran	3,651
14	Manny Trillo	3,603
15	Julio Cruz	3,435
16	Bobby Grich	3,384
17	Juan Samuel	3,224
18	Ron Oester	3,197
19	Jody Reed	3,187
20	Jose Lind	3,094

Errors

1	Willie Randolph	212
2	Lou Whitaker	189
3	Steve Sax	187
4	Juan Samuel	164
5	Frank White	147
6	Harold Reynolds	141
7	Glenn Hubbard	127
8	Roberto Alomar	120
9	Johnny Ray	118
	Delino DeShields	118
11	Ron Oester	116
	Carlos Baerga	116
13	Jim Gantner	115
14	Tony Bernazard	114
15	Robby Thompson	110
16	Ryne Sandberg	109
17	Bill Doran	108
18	Manny Trillo	105
19	Julio Cruz	103
	Joey Cora	103

Double Plays

1	Lou Whitaker	1,528
2	Willie Randolph	1,452
3	Frank White	1,236
4	Ryne Sandberg	1,158
5	Jim Gantner	1,036
6	Steve Sax	998
7	Tom Herr	991
8	Glenn Hubbard	975
9	Harold Reynolds	948
10	Robby Thompson	873
11	Johnny Ray	828
12	Roberto Alomar	817
13	Bobby Grich	793
14	Julio Cruz	780
15	Manny Trillo	752
16	Bill Doran	742
17	Jody Reed	690
18	Ron Oester	647
19	Chuck Knoblauch	639
20	Carlos Baerga	634

Fielding Percentage
(minimum 750 games)

1	Ryne Sandberg	.989
2	Tom Herr	.989
3	Jose Lind	.988
4	Jody Reed	.988
5	Mickey Morandini	.988
6	Rich Dauer	.987
7	Billy Ripken	.987
8	Chuck Knoblauch	.986
9	Marty Barrett	.986
10	Doug Flynn	.986
11	Frank White	.985
12	Jim Gantner	.985
13	Craig Biggio	.984
14	Joe Morgan	.984
15	Bobby Grich	.984
16	Lou Whitaker	.984
17	Mark Lemke	.984
18	Manny Trillo	.984
19	Bill Doran	.983
20	Robby Thompson	.983

Range Factor
(minimum 750 games)

1	Bump Wills	5.50
2	Glenn Hubbard	5.43
3	Manny Trillo	5.34
4	Bobby Grich	5.24
5	Frank White	5.20
6	Julio Cruz	5.19
7	Jim Gantner	5.17
8	Carlos Baerga	5.16
9	Willie Randolph	5.16
10	Johnny Ray	5.10
11	Ryne Sandberg	5.10
12	Jose Lind	5.08
13	Jody Reed	5.07
14	Tony Bernazard	5.00
15	Steve Sax	4.99
16	Harold Reynolds	4.99
17	Craig Biggio	4.97
18	Lou Whitaker	4.95
19	Ron Oester	4.94
20	Robby Thompson	4.94

Assists/162 Games
(minimum 750 games)

1	Glenn Hubbard	540.49
2	Bump Wills	522.86
3	Ryne Sandberg	516.69
4	Bobby Grich	499.73
5	Manny Trillo	498.03
6	Carlos Baerga	496.91
7	Julio Cruz	495.52
8	Jody Reed	491.71
9	Johnny Ray	486.63
10	Jim Gantner	486.00
11	Jose Lind	482.88
12	Frank White	475.73
13	Harold Reynolds	475.72
14	Willie Randolph	472.89
15	Tony Bernazard	469.96
16	Damaso Garcia	469.80
17	Marty Barrett	469.41
18	Robby Thompson	469.15
19	Lou Whitaker	466.98
20	Jerry Remy	466.06

Single Season Fielding Leaders—Second Basemen: Modern Era (1977-1997)

Games

1	Johnny Ray	1982	162
	Bill Doran	1987	162
	Craig Biggio	1996	162
4	Jim Morrison	1980	161
	Craig Biggio	1992	161
6	Lou Whitaker	1983	160
	Juan Samuel	1984	160
	Harold Reynolds	1987	160
	Juan Samuel	1987	160
	Harold Reynolds	1990	160
	Roberto Alomar	1991	160
	Carlos Baerga	1992	160
	Craig Biggio	1997	160
14	Dave Cash	1978	159
	Juan Samuel	1985	159
	Harold Reynolds	1991	159
	Mike Lansing	1996	159
18	6 tied with		158

Putouts

1	Jim Morrison	1980	422
2	Carlos Baerga	1992	400
3	Frank White	1980	395
4	Alan Wiggins	1984	391
5	Frank White	1983	390
6	Juan Samuel	1985	389
7	Juan Samuel	1984	388
8	Johnny Ray	1982	381
9	Tito Fuentes	1977	379
10	Jim Gantner	1983	374
	Juan Samuel	1987	374
12	Doug Flynn	1979	369
13	Ron Oester	1986	367
	Steve Sax	1986	367
15	Ron Oester	1985	366
16	Dave Cash	1978	362
	Jim Gantner	1984	362
18	Willie Randolph	1980	361
	Frank White	1982	361
	Craig Biggio	1996	361

Assists

1	Ryne Sandberg	1983	571
2	Ryne Sandberg	1984	550
3	Glenn Hubbard	1985	539
	Ryne Sandberg	1992	539
5	Bump Wills	1978	526
6	Ryne Sandberg	1988	522
7	Ryne Sandberg	1991	515
8	Johnny Ray	1982	512
	Jim Gantner	1983	512
10	Harold Reynolds	1987	507
11	Harold Reynolds	1989	506
12	Manny Trillo	1978	505
	Glenn Hubbard	1982	505
14	Craig Biggio	1997	504
15	Ryne Sandberg	1985	500
	Jose Oquendo	1989	500
17	Phil Garner	1980	499
	Harold Reynolds	1990	499
19	Eric Young	1997	494
20	2 tied with		492

Errors

1	Juan Samuel	1984	33
2	Alan Wiggins	1984	32
3	Steve Sax	1983	30
4	Jim Morrison	1980	29
5	Roberto Alomar	1989	28
6	Delino DeShields	1991	27
7	Tito Fuentes	1977	26
	Ron Gant	1988	26
9	Manny Trillo	1977	25
	Juan Samuel	1986	25
11	Luis Alicea	1996	24
12	Mike Edwards	1979	22
	Bobby Grich	1983	22
	Steve Sax	1985	22
	Joey Cora	1995	22
16	Phil Garner	1980	21
	Johnny Ray	1982	21
	Steve Sax	1984	21
19	10 tied with		20

Double Plays

1	Carlos Baerga	1992	138
2	Harold Reynolds	1991	133
3	Willie Randolph	1979	128
	Jim Gantner	1983	128
5	Glenn Hubbard	1985	127
6	Ryne Sandberg	1983	126
7	Frank White	1983	123
8	Tom Herr	1986	121
9	Lou Whitaker	1982	120
	Tom Herr	1985	120
	Glenn Hubbard	1986	120
12	Jim Morrison	1980	117
	Steve Sax	1989	117
14	Phil Garner	1980	116
	Tony Bernazard	1982	116
	Fernando Vina	1996	116
17	Tito Fuentes	1977	115
	Scott Fletcher	1990	115
	Mark McLemore	1996	115
20	2 tied with		114

Fielding Percentage
(minimum 100 games)

1	Bret Boone	1997	.997
2	Bobby Grich	1985	.997
3	Jose Oquendo	1990	.996
4	Ryne Sandberg	1991	.995
5	Jody Reed	1994	.995
6	Rob Wilfong	1980	.995
7	Frank White	1988	.994
8	Mark Lemke	1994	.994
9	Jose Oquendo	1989	.994
10	Bret Boone	1995	.994
11	Jody Reed	1995	.994
12	Ryne Sandberg	1986	.994
13	Roberto Alomar	1995	.994
14	Chuck Knoblauch	1994	.994
15	Jose Lind	1993	.994
16	Manny Trillo	1982	.994
17	Lou Whitaker	1991	.994
18	Johnny Ray	1986	.993
19	Tim Flannery	1986	.993
20	Ryne Sandberg	1984	.993

Range Factor
(minimum 100 games)

1	Glenn Hubbard	1985	6.27
2	Manny Trillo	1980	5.91
3	Bump Wills	1981	5.88
4	Tony Bernazard	1982	5.81
5	Bobby Grich	1983	5.81
6	Bobby Grich	1981	5.79
7	Julio Cruz	1979	5.79
8	Manny Trillo	1978	5.77
9	Paul Molitor	1979	5.75
10	Glenn Hubbard	1980	5.75
11	Ryne Sandberg	1983	5.74
12	Frank White	1983	5.74
13	Damaso Garcia	1980	5.70
14	Tom Herr	1981	5.68
15	Glenn Hubbard	1982	5.67
16	Robby Thompson	1992	5.65
17	Bump Wills	1980	5.65
18	Jim Gantner	1981	5.64
19	Phil Garner	1980	5.62
20	Bump Wills	1978	5.62

Assists/162 Games
(minimum 100 games)

1	Glenn Hubbard	1985	623.70
2	Ryne Sandberg	1983	589.18
3	Tom Herr	1981	588.23
4	Ryne Sandberg	1984	571.15
5	Bobby Grich	1983	569.75
6	Glenn Hubbard	1982	568.13
7	Bobby Grich	1981	565.38
8	Glenn Hubbard	1980	560.77
	Glenn Hubbard	1984	560.77
10	Glenn Hubbard	1987	557.09
11	Ryne Sandberg	1992	556.17
12	Glenn Hubbard	1986	555.59
13	Damaso Garcia	1980	552.91
14	Ryne Sandberg	1988	552.71
15	Manny Trillo	1978	549.06
16	Paul Molitor	1979	548.41
17	Julio Cruz	1979	546.56
18	Bump Wills	1978	546.23
19	Lou Whitaker	1978	545.56
20	Harold Reynolds	1989	542.86

Career Fielding Leaders—Third Basemen: Modern Era (1977-1997)

	Games			Putouts			Assists			Errors	
1	Gary Gaetti	2,082	1	Tim Wallach	1,662	1	Gary Gaetti	4,170	1	Tim Wallach	240
2	Wade Boggs	2,063	2	Gary Gaetti	1,593	2	Wade Boggs	4,015	2	Terry Pendleton	236
3	Tim Wallach	2,054	3	Wade Boggs	1,453	3	Tim Wallach	3,992	3	Mike Schmidt	224
4	Terry Pendleton	1,762	4	Carney Lansford	1,382	4	Terry Pendleton	3,858	4	Wade Boggs	215
5	Carney Lansford	1,720	5	Terry Pendleton	1,374	5	Mike Schmidt	3,624	5	Gary Gaetti	212
6	Mike Schmidt	1,603	6	Buddy Bell	1,284	6	Buddy Bell	3,615	6	Ken Caminiti	192
7	Buddy Bell	1,597	7	Doug DeCinces	1,138	7	Doug DeCinces	2,920	7	George Brett	187
8	Doug DeCinces	1,391	8	Mike Schmidt	1,079	8	Carney Lansford	2,799	8	Doug DeCinces	172
9	Ron Cey	1,372	9	Ken Caminiti	1,034	9	George Brett	2,677		Buddy Bell	172
10	Ken Caminiti	1,351	10	George Brett	990	10	Ron Cey	2,662	10	Bobby Bonilla	164
11	Graig Nettles	1,298	11	Ron Cey	972	11	Ken Caminiti	2,582	11	Howard Johnson	163
12	Steve Buechele	1,269	12	Graig Nettles	938	12	Graig Nettles	2,573	12	Tom Brookens	155
13	George Brett	1,231	13	Matt Williams	896	13	Steve Buechele	2,281	13	Graig Nettles	154
14	Mike Schmidt	1,179	14	Steve Buechele	895	14	Matt Williams	2,280	14	Charlie Hayes	151
15	Brook Jacoby	1,166	15	Robin Ventura	893	15	Charlie Hayes	2,229	15	Carney Lansford	148
16	Matt Williams	1,162	16	Charlie Hayes	795	16	Mike Pagliarulo	2,119	16	Ron Cey	145
17	Charlie Hayes	1,157	17	Brook Jacoby	776	17	Brook Jacoby	2,058	17	Kevin Seitzer	142
18	Tom Brookens	1,065	18	Tom Brookens	728	18	Ken Oberkfell	1,996	18	Todd Zeile	140
19	Robin Ventura	1,059	19	Wayne Gross	717	19	Robin Ventura	1,958	19	Bill Madlock	137
20	Kevin Seitzer	1,051	20	Toby Harrah	714	20	Kevin Seitzer	1,920	20	2 tied with	134

	Double Plays			Fielding Percentage (minimum 750 games)			Range Factor (minimum 750 games)			Assists/162 Games (minimum 750 games)	
1	Gary Gaetti	435	1	Steve Buechele	.968	1	Buddy Bell	3.07	1	Buddy Bell	366.71
2	Wade Boggs	397	2	Buddy Bell	.966	2	George Brett	2.98	2	Mike Schmidt	366.24
3	Tim Wallach	319	3	Carney Lansford	.966	3	Terry Pendleton	2.97	3	Terry Pendleton	354.71
4	Mike Schmidt	318	4	Travis Fryman	.966	4	Mike Schmidt	2.93	4	George Brett	352.29
5	Doug DeCinces	313	5	Ken Oberkfell	.965	5	Doug DeCinces	2.92	5	Darrell Evans	340.52
6	Terry Pendleton	310	6	Gary Gaetti	.965	6	Paul Molitor	2.88	6	Doug DeCinces	340.07
7	Buddy Bell	301	7	Toby Harrah	.964	7	Darrell Evans	2.88	7	Paul Molitor	335.67
8	Carney Lansford	256	8	Chris Sabo	.963	8	Gary Gaetti	2.77	8	Travis Fryman	326.74
9	George Brett	240	9	Wade Boggs	.962	9	Tim Wallach	2.75	9	Gary Gaetti	324.47
10	Ken Caminiti	226	10	Ron Cey	.962	10	Matt Williams	2.73	10	Graig Nettles	321.13
11	Matt Williams	219	11	Matt Williams	.961	11	Travis Fryman	2.71	11	Matt Williams	317.87
12	Graig Nettles	216	12	Doug DeCinces	.959	12	Graig Nettles	2.70	12	Kelly Gruber	316.15
13	Charlie Hayes	214	13	Tim Wallach	.959	13	Robin Ventura	2.69	13	Wade Boggs	315.28
14	Ron Cey	205	14	Brook Jacoby	.958	14	Kelly Gruber	2.68	14	Tim Wallach	314.85
15	Robin Ventura	200	15	Graig Nettles	.958	15	Ken Caminiti	2.68	15	Ron Cey	314.32
16	Mike Pagliarulo	194	16	Ray Knight	.957	16	Wade Boggs	2.65	16	Charlie Hayes	312.10
17	Kevin Seitzer	189	17	Terry Pendleton	.957	17	Ron Cey	2.65	17	Ken Caminiti	309.61
18	Paul Molitor	185	18	Robin Ventura	.955	18	Charlie Hayes	2.61	18	Ken Oberkfell	309.13
19	Steve Buechele	184	19	Kelly Gruber	.955	19	Phil Garner	2.60	19	Bobby Bonilla	304.84
20	Ken Oberkfell	180	20	Mike Pagliarulo	.955	20	Bobby Bonilla	2.59	20	Phil Garner	304.42

Single Season Fielding Leaders—Third Basemen: Modern Era (1977-1997)

	Games				Putouts				Assists				Errors		
1	Ray Knight	1980	162	1	Tim Wallach	1984	162	1	Doug DeCinces	1982	399	1	Butch Hobson	1978	43
	Cal Ripken Jr.	1997	162	2	Carney Lansford	1980	151	2	Mike Schmidt	1977	396	2	Joel Youngblood	1984	36
3	Pete Rose	1977	161		Tim Wallach	1983	151		Buddy Bell	1982	396	3	Bobby Bonilla	1989	35
	Brook Jacoby	1985	161	4	Tim Wallach	1985	148	4	Terry Pendleton	1989	392	4	Gary Sheffield	1993	34
	Wade Boggs	1985	161	5	Darrell Evans	1978	147	5	Vinny Castilla	1996	389	5	Todd Zeile	1993	33
	Terry Pendleton	1989	161	6	Bill Stein	1977	146	6	Buddy Bell	1983	383	6	Bobby Bonilla	1988	32
	Tim Wallach	1990	161		Gary Gaetti	1985	146		Tim Wallach	1985	383	7	George Brett	1979	30
	Terry Pendleton	1993	161	8	Scott Rolen	1997	144	8	George Brett	1979	373		Darrell Evans	1979	30
9	Tim Wallach	1984	160	9	Gary Gaetti	1984	142	9	Mike Schmidt	1980	372		Pedro Guerrero	1983	30
	Ken Caminiti	1989	160	10	Wade Boggs	1984	141		Robin Ventura	1992	372	10	Enos Cabell	1980	29
	Vinny Castilla	1996	160		Robin Ventura	1992	141	11	Terry Pendleton	1986	371		Tom Brookens	1980	29
	Todd Zeile	1997	160	12	Enos Cabell	1977	140	12	Darrell Evans	1979	369		Paul Molitor	1982	29
13	Butch Hobson	1977	159		Matt Williams	1990	140		Terry Pendleton	1987	369		Dean Palmer	1993	29
	Toby Harrah	1977	159	14	Jeff Hamilton	1989	139	14	Wade Boggs	1983	368		Dave Hollins	1997	29
	Graig Nettles	1978	159	15	Ron Cey	1977	138	15	Buddy Bell	1979	364	15	Keith Moreland	1987	28
	Darrell Evans	1979	159	16	Carney Lansford	1984	137	16	Mike Schmidt	1979	361	16	6 tied with		27
	Toby Harrah	1982	159	17	Enos Cabell	1978	136		Terry Pendleton	1985	361				
	Bobby Bonilla	1988	159	18	Carney Lansford	1979	135	18	Gary Gaetti	1983	360				
	Kevin Seitzer	1989	159	19	4 tied with		134	19	Buddy Bell	1978	355				
	Matt Williams	1990	159					20	2 tied with		353				

	Double Plays				Fielding Percentage (minimum 100 games)				Range Factor (minimum 100 games)				Assists/162 Games (minimum 100 games)		
1	Paul Molitor	1982	48	1	Aurelio Rodriguez	1978	.987	1	Buddy Bell	1982	3.63	1	Buddy Bell	1982	442.43
2	Gary Gaetti	1983	46	2	Steve Buechele	1991	.983	2	Buddy Bell	1978	3.45	2	Mike Schmidt	1977	430.55
3	Vinny Castilla	1996	43	3	Carney Lansford	1979	.983	3	Tim Wallach	1985	3.45	3	Doug DeCinces	1982	422.47
4	Doug DeCinces	1980	41	4	Bill Pecota	1991	.983	4	Buddy Bell	1980	3.39	4	Buddy Bell	1978	413.74
	Doug DeCinces	1982	41	5	Carney Lansford	1986	.982	5	Mike Schmidt	1977	3.37	5	George Brett	1979	405.54
	Vinny Castilla	1997	41	6	Wade Boggs	1995	.981		George Brett	1979	3.37	6	Mike Schmidt	1980	404.46
7	Wade Boggs	1983	40	7	Buddy Bell	1980	.981	7	Doug DeCinces	1982	3.34	7	Buddy Bell	1983	402.90
8	Gary Gaetti	1991	39	8	Mike Schmidt	1986	.980	8	Terry Pendleton	1985	3.29		Tim Wallach	1985	402.90
9	Travis Fryman	1995	38	9	Carney Lansford	1987	.980	9	Buddy Bell	1983	3.29	9	Buddy Bell	1979	401.14
10	Paul Molitor	1983	37	10	Ken Reitz	1977	.980	10	Robin Ventura	1992	3.27	10	Mike Schmidt	1981	399.39
	Wade Boggs	1987	37	11	Buddy Bell	1987	.979	11	George Brett	1977	3.26	11	John Castino	1980	399.13
12	Mike Schmidt	1979	36	12	Carney Lansford	1988	.979	12	Doug DeCinces	1980	3.24	12	Sal Bando	1978	397.75
	Gary Gaetti	1986	36	13	Ken Reitz	1980	.979	13	Buddy Bell	1979	3.24	13	Kelly Gruber	1989	396.15
	Terry Pendleton	1986	36	14	Ken Oberkfell	1987	.979	14	Terry Pendleton	1986	3.23	14	Terry Pendleton	1989	394.43
	Steve Lyons	1988	36	15	Travis Fryman	1996	.979	15	John Castino	1980	3.22	15	Vinny Castilla	1996	393.86
	Gary Gaetti	1990	36	16	Gary Gaetti	1997	.978	16	George Brett	1980	3.21	16	Terry Pendleton	1985	392.50
17	5 tied with		35	17	Travis Fryman	1997	.978	17	Mike Schmidt	1981	3.20	17	Ken Oberkfell	1981	390.71
				18	Eric Soderholm	1977	.978	18	Darrell Evans	1978	3.19	18	George Brett	1977	390.00
				19	Ron Cey	1979	.977	19	Gary Gaetti	1983	3.19	19	Wade Boggs	1983	389.65
				20	Scott Brosius	1997	.977	20	Wade Boggs	1983	3.18	20	Doug DeCinces	1980	387.89

Career Fielding Leaders—Shortstops: Modern Era (1977-1997)

#	Games		#	Putouts		#	Assists		#	Errors	
1	Ozzie Smith	2,511	1	Ozzie Smith	4,249	1	Ozzie Smith	8,375	1	Garry Templeton	360
2	Cal Ripken Jr.	2,302	2	Cal Ripken Jr.	3,651	2	Cal Ripken Jr.	6,977	2	Alfredo Griffin	339
3	Alan Trammell	2,139	3	Alan Trammell	3,391	3	Alan Trammell	6,172	3	Rafael Ramirez	301
4	Garry Templeton	1,911	4	Garry Templeton	3,282	4	Garry Templeton	5,869	4	Ozzie Smith	281
5	Alfredo Griffin	1,855	5	Alfredo Griffin	3,206	5	Alfredo Griffin	5,184	5	Alan Trammell	227
6	Greg Gagne	1,765	6	Ozzie Guillen	2,735	6	Ozzie Guillen	4,962	6	Cal Ripken Jr.	225
7	Ozzie Guillen	1,724	7	Tony Fernandez	2,708	7	Greg Gagne	4,930	7	Ivan DeJesus	221
8	Tony Fernandez	1,573	8	Greg Gagne	2,559	8	Tony Fernandez	4,511	8	Greg Gagne	214
9	Rafael Ramirez	1,386	9	Shawon Dunston	2,258	9	Jay Bell	4,173	9	Ozzie Guillen	203
10	Spike Owen	1,373	10	Dave Concepcion	2,233	10	Barry Larkin	3,994	10	Shawon Dunston	201
11	Jay Bell	1,362	11	Rafael Ramirez	2,159	11	Rafael Ramirez	3,978	11	Bill Russell	195
12	Barry Larkin	1,353	12	Dick Schofield	2,140	12	Dave Concepcion	3,912	12	Robin Yount	178
13	Dick Schofield	1,348	13	Barry Larkin	2,137	13	Ivan DeJesus	3,890	13	Craig Reynolds	177
14	Dave Concepcion	1,331	14	Jay Bell	2,101	14	Dick Schofield	3,873	14	Dave Concepcion	174
15	Shawon Dunston	1,324	15	Spike Owen	2,087	15	Spike Owen	3,814	15	Dickie Thon	173
16	Ivan DeJesus	1,225	16	Robin Yount	1,877	16	Shawon Dunston	3,688	16	Johnnie LeMaster	165
17	Craig Reynolds	1,206	17	Omar Vizquel	1,797	17	Larry Bowa	3,667	17	Barry Larkin	164
18	Larry Bowa	1,197	18	Ivan DeJesus	1,775	18	Robin Yount	3,555	18	Jay Bell	157
19	Walt Weiss	1,195	19	Larry Bowa	1,774	19	Omar Vizquel	3,412	19	Tony Fernandez	151
20	Omar Vizquel	1,160	20	Walt Weiss	1,768	20	Craig Reynolds	3,396		Walt Weiss	151

#	Double Plays		#	Fielding Percentage (minimum 750 games)		#	Range Factor (minimum 750 games)		#	Assists/162 Games (minimum 750 games)	
1	Ozzie Smith	1,590	1	Omar Vizquel	.980	1	Rick Burleson	5.17	1	Ozzie Smith	540.32
2	Cal Ripken Jr.	1,565	2	Larry Bowa	.980	2	Robin Yount	5.10	2	Robin Yount	540.25
3	Alan Trammell	1,307	3	Tony Fernandez	.980	3	Ozzie Smith	5.03	3	Rick Burleson	538.44
4	Garry Templeton	1,123	4	Cal Ripken Jr.	.979	4	Tim Foli	4.79	4	Ivan DeJesus	514.43
5	Alfredo Griffin	1,053	5	Ozzie Smith	.978	5	Garry Templeton	4.79	5	Bill Russell	508.99
6	Ozzie Guillen	1,027	6	Mike Bordick	.978	6	Ivan DeJesus	4.62	6	Garry Templeton	497.53
7	Greg Gagne	967	7	Spike Owen	.977	7	Roy Smalley	4.62	7	Bucky Dent	497.47
8	Tony Fernandez	943	8	Bucky Dent	.977	8	Cal Ripken Jr.	4.62	8	Jay Bell	496.35
9	Dick Schofield	900	9	Alan Trammell	.977	9	Dave Concepcion	4.62	9	Larry Bowa	496.29
10	Rafael Ramirez	842	10	Rick Burleson	.977	10	Jay Bell	4.61	10	Tim Foli	495.85
11	Jay Bell	794	11	Dick Schofield	.976	11	Bill Russell	4.60	11	Roy Smalley	494.08
12	Omar Vizquel	782	12	Tim Foli	.976	12	Tony Fernandez	4.59	12	Cal Ripken Jr.	491.00
13	Dave Concepcion	752	13	Jay Bell	.976	13	Larry Bowa	4.55	13	Gary DiSarcina	482.44
14	Spike Owen	723	14	Kevin Elster	.975	14	Barry Larkin	4.53	14	Barry Larkin	478.22
15	Barry Larkin	712	15	Ozzie Guillen	.974	15	Alfredo Griffin	4.52	15	Royce Clayton	476.89
	Walt Weiss	712	16	Gary DiSarcina	.974	16	Royce Clayton	4.52	16	Omar Vizquel	476.50
17	Robin Yount	702	17	Barry Larkin	.974	17	Bucky Dent	4.50	17	Dave Concepcion	476.14
18	Shawon Dunston	700	18	Rafael Belliard	.974	18	Shawon Dunston	4.49	18	Alan Trammell	467.44
19	Ivan DeJesus	675	19	Dave Concepcion	.972	19	Omar Vizquel	4.49	19	Ozzie Guillen	466.27
20	Larry Bowa	648	20	Greg Gagne	.972	20	Alan Trammell	4.47	20	Dick Schofield	465.45

Single Season Fielding Leaders—Shortstops: Modern Era (1977-1997)

#	Games			#	Putouts			#	Assists			#	Errors		
1	Frank Taveras	1979	164	1	Shawon Dunston	1986	320	1	Ozzie Smith	1980	621	1	Jose Offerman	1992	42
2	Tony Fernandez	1986	163	2	Alfredo Griffin	1982	319	2	Ivan DeJesus	1977	595	2	Bill Almon	1977	41
3	Alfredo Griffin	1982	162	3	Ozzie Smith	1983	304	3	Cal Ripken Jr.	1984	583	3	Alan Bannister	1977	40
	Cal Ripken Jr.	1983	162	4	Bill Almon	1977	303	4	Roy Smalley	1979	572		Garry Templeton	1978	40
	Cal Ripken Jr.	1984	162	5	Rick Burleson	1980	301	5	Ozzie Guillen	1988	570	5	Rafael Ramirez	1983	39
	Alfredo Griffin	1985	162		Rafael Santana	1985	301	6	Ivan DeJesus	1978	558	6	Frank Taveras	1978	38
	Alfredo Griffin	1986	162	7	Rafael Ramirez	1982	300	7	Ozzie Smith	1979	555		Rafael Ramirez	1982	38
	Cal Ripken Jr.	1986	162	8	Cal Ripken Jr.	1984	297	8	Ozzie Smith	1985	549	8	Alfredo Griffin	1980	37
	Cal Ripken Jr.	1987	162		Tony Fernandez	1990	297	9	Ozzie Smith	1978	548		Jose Offerman	1993	37
	Cal Ripken Jr.	1989	162	10	Roy Smalley	1979	296	10	Bill Almon	1977	538		Jose Valentin	1996	37
	Cal Ripken Jr.	1991	162	11	Alfredo Griffin	1980	295	11	Ozzie Smith	1982	535	11	Alfredo Griffin	1979	36
	Cal Ripken Jr.	1992	162	12	Tony Fernandez	1986	294	12	Cal Ripken Jr.	1983	534		U.L. Washington	1983	36
	Cal Ripken Jr.	1993	162	13	Garry Templeton	1979	292	13	Bill Russell	1978	533		Julio Franco	1984	36
14	Roy Smalley	1979	161	14	Chris Speier	1982	291		Dickie Thon	1983	533	14	Julio Franco	1985	35
	Dale Berra	1983	161	15	Ozzie Smith	1980	288	15	Cal Ripken Jr.	1989	531		Jose Offerman	1995	35
	Cal Ripken Jr.	1985	161	16	Roy Smalley	1978	287	16	Ivan DeJesus	1980	529	16	Garry Templeton	1979	34
	Cal Ripken Jr.	1988	161		Frank Taveras	1979	287	17	Rick Burleson	1980	528	17	Ivan DeJesus	1977	33
	Cal Ripken Jr.	1990	161		Cal Ripken Jr.	1992	287		Rafael Ramirez	1982	528		Roy Smalley	1977	33
	Tony Fernandez	1990	161	19	Dale Berra	1983	286		Cal Ripken Jr.	1991	528		Wil Cordero	1993	33
	Jeff Blauser	1993	161		Cal Ripken Jr.	1985	286	20	2 tied with		527	20	8 tied with		32

#	Double Plays			#	Fielding Percentage (minimum 100 games)			#	Range Factor (minimum 100 games)			#	Assists/162 Games (minimum 100 games)		
1	Rick Burleson	1980	147	1	Cal Ripken Jr.	1990	.996	1	Garry Templeton	1980	5.86	1	Ozzie Smith	1980	636.72
2	Roy Smalley	1979	144	2	Tony Fernandez	1989	.992	2	Ozzie Smith	1982	5.86	2	Garry Templeton	1980	635.32
3	Spike Owen	1986	133	3	Larry Bowa	1979	.991	3	Ozzie Smith	1981	5.84	3	Ivan DeJesus	1977	625.91
4	Rafael Ramirez	1982	130	4	Cal Ripken Jr.	1989	.990	4	Ozzie Smith	1980	5.75	4	Ozzie Smith	1982	623.53
5	Alfredo Griffin	1980	126	5	Spike Owen	1990	.989	5	Robin Yount	1978	5.59	5	Ozzie Smith	1981	621.49
6	Dick Schofield	1988	125	6	Omar Vizquel	1992	.989	6	Rick Burleson	1981	5.52	6	Ozzie Guillen	1988	591.92
7	Alfredo Griffin	1979	124	7	Cal Ripken Jr.	1995	.989	7	Garry Templeton	1979	5.45	7	Bucky Dent	1979	588.26
8	Cal Ripken Jr.	1985	123	8	Tony Fernandez	1990	.989	8	Cal Ripken Jr.	1984	5.43	8	Robin Yount	1978	587.09
9	Cal Ripken Jr.	1984	122	9	Dick Schofield	1992	.988	9	Bill Almon	1977	5.43	9	Rick Burleson	1981	585.58
	Alex Gonzalez	1996	122	10	Ozzie Smith	1991	.987	10	Ozzie Guillen	1988	5.40	10	Cal Ripken Jr.	1984	583.00
11	Roy Smalley	1978	121	11	Ozzie Smith	1987	.987	11	Ozzie Smith	1984	5.40	11	Ozzie Smith	1979	580.06
	Mike Bordick	1996	121	12	Manuel Lee	1992	.987	12	Roy Smalley	1979	5.39	12	Roy Smalley	1980	578.02
13	Cal Ripken Jr.	1988	119	13	Larry Bowa	1978	.986	13	Ivan DeJesus	1977	5.38	13	Roy Smalley	1979	575.55
	Cal Ripken Jr.	1989	119	14	Cal Ripken Jr.	1991	.986	14	Rick Burleson	1980	5.35	14	Ozzie Smith	1984	570.92
	Cal Ripken Jr.	1992	119	15	Greg Gagne	1993	.986	15	Rick Burleson	1978	5.33	15	Garry Templeton	1979	567.00
16	Roy Smalley	1977	116	16	Jay Bell	1993	.986	16	Ivan DeJesus	1981	5.32	16	Ivan DeJesus	1978	564.98
	Rafael Ramirez	1983	116	17	Spike Owen	1991	.986	17	Rafael Ramirez	1982	5.27	17	Ozzie Smith	1985	562.90
	Julio Franco	1984	116	18	Dave Concepcion	1977	.986	18	Shawon Dunston	1986	5.27	18	Bill Almon	1977	562.30
19	Rafael Ramirez	1985	115	19	Jay Bell	1996	.986	19	Dave Concepcion	1979	5.26	19	Robin Yount	1979	562.11
	Ozzie Guillen	1988	115	20	Alex Gonzalez	1997	.986	20	Robin Yount	1979	5.26	20	Bucky Dent	1980	561.83

Leaders: Fielding By Era

Career Fielding Leaders—Outfielders: Modern Era (1977-1997)

Games

1	Andre Dawson	2,299
2	Rickey Henderson	2,266
3	Brett Butler	2,159
4	Tony Gwynn	2,063
5	Dave Winfield	2,030
6	Willie Wilson	2,025
7	Tim Raines	2,002
8	Dale Murphy	1,853
9	Willie McGee	1,802
10	Chet Lemon	1,793
11	Barry Bonds	1,709
12	Kirby Puckett	1,696
13	Tom Brunansky	1,679
14	Joe Carter	1,663
15	Dwight Evans	1,634
16	Jose Cruz	1,576
17	Fred Lynn	1,541
18	Lloyd Moseby	1,529
19	Dave Parker	1,504
20	Andy Van Slyke	1,499

Putouts

1	Rickey Henderson	5,496
2	Brett Butler	5,296
3	Andre Dawson	5,097
4	Willie Wilson	5,054
5	Chet Lemon	4,640
6	Kirby Puckett	4,392
7	Tony Gwynn	4,175
8	Willie McGee	4,057
9	Dale Murphy	4,053
10	Tim Raines	4,039
11	Dave Winfield	4,029
12	Devon White	3,837
13	Fred Lynn	3,767
14	Lloyd Moseby	3,765
15	Barry Bonds	3,599
16	Dwayne Murphy	3,579
17	Joe Carter	3,558
18	Tom Brunansky	3,506
19	Andy Van Slyke	3,336
20	Dave Henderson	3,334

Assists

1	Jesse Barfield	162
2	Andre Dawson	156
3	Tony Gwynn	148
4	Kirby Puckett	142
5	Dave Winfield	130
	Tim Raines	130
7	Jim Rice	123
	Barry Bonds	123
9	Brett Butler	122
10	Willie McGee	121
11	Rickey Henderson	118
12	Tom Brunansky	117
13	Dave Parker	116
14	Dale Murphy	113
15	Dwight Evans	112
16	Glenn Wilson	109
	Vince Coleman	109
18	Joe Carter	107
	Andy Van Slyke	107
20	Joe Orsulak	105

Errors

1	Rickey Henderson	121
2	Dave Parker	112
3	Willie McGee	98
4	Lonnie Smith	92
5	Andre Dawson	91
6	Jose Cruz	90
7	George Bell	88
8	Joe Carter	85
	Ruben Sierra	85
10	Gary Matthews	82
11	Chili Davis	80
12	Chet Lemon	78
13	Sammy Sosa	76
14	Larry Herndon	72
	Claudell Washington	72
16	Dale Murphy	71
17	Vince Coleman	68
18	Willie Wilson	66
19	Dave Winfield	65
20	2 tied with	63

Double Plays

1	Jesse Barfield	48
2	Kirby Puckett	37
3	Brett Butler	32
4	Andre Dawson	29
	Tom Brunansky	29
6	Fred Lynn	28
	Dave Winfield	28
	Dwight Evans	28
	Dave Henderson	28
10	Willie McGee	27
	Andy Van Slyke	27
12	Tony Gwynn	26
	Ken Griffey Jr.	26
14	Omar Moreno	25
	Dante Bichette	25
16	Jack Clark	24
	Chet Lemon	24
	Darryl Strawberry	24
19	5 tied with	23

Fielding Percentage
(minimum 750 games)

1	Darren Lewis	.996
2	Darryl Hamilton	.994
3	Terry Puhl	.993
4	Brett Butler	.992
5	Amos Otis	.992
6	Robin Yount	.990
7	Paul O'Neill	.990
8	Otis Nixon	.990
9	Brian McRae	.989
10	Fred Lynn	.989
11	Henry Cotto	.989
12	Gary Roenicke	.989
13	Kirby Puckett	.989
14	Stan Javier	.988
15	Mike Devereaux	.988
16	Jim Eisenreich	.988
17	Phil Bradley	.988
18	Brady Anderson	.988
19	Cesar Cedeno	.988
20	Tim Raines	.988

Range Factor
(minimum 750 games)

1	Dwayne Murphy	2.88
2	Gorman Thomas	2.71
3	Devon White	2.70
4	Robin Yount	2.68
5	Amos Otis	2.67
6	Kirby Puckett	2.67
7	Gary Pettis	2.67
8	Omar Moreno	2.66
9	Chet Lemon	2.65
10	Bernie Williams	2.64
11	Garry Maddox	2.64
12	Al Bumbry	2.63
13	Kenny Lofton	2.62
14	Ruppert Jones	2.61
15	Lance Johnson	2.61
16	Lenny Dykstra	2.59
17	Ray Lankford	2.55
18	Rick Manning	2.55
19	Willie Wilson	2.53
20	Lloyd Moseby	2.51

Assists/162 Games
(minimum 750 games)

1	Jesse Barfield	18.92
2	Bernard Gilkey	17.27
3	Cory Snyder	16.44
4	Warren Cromartie	15.68
5	Glenn Wilson	15.61
6	Ellis Valentine	15.41
7	Jack Clark	14.92
8	Gene Richards	14.89
9	Sixto Lezcano	14.78
10	Jim Rice	14.74
11	Mark Whiten	14.28
12	Larry Walker	14.26
13	Sammy Sosa	13.89
14	Kenny Lofton	13.62
15	Joe Orsulak	13.58
16	Kirby Puckett	13.56
17	Vince Coleman	13.47
18	Dave Parker	12.49
19	Lee Lacy	12.49
20	Dante Bichette	12.32

Single Season Fielding Leaders—Outfielders: Modern Era (1977-1997)

Games

1	Rick Bosetti	1979	162
	Omar Moreno	1979	162
	Omar Moreno	1980	162
	Gary Matthews	1982	162
	Dale Murphy	1982	162
	Ruben Sierra	1989	162
	Brian Hunter	1997	162
8	Ruppert Jones	1979	161
	Dwight Evans	1982	161
	Harold Baines	1982	161
	George Wright	1983	161
	Dwight Evans	1984	161
	Dale Murphy	1985	161
	Kirby Puckett	1985	161
	Brett Butler	1991	161
	Ruben Sierra	1991	161
	Gary Sheffield	1996	161
	Sammy Sosa	1997	161
19	14 tied with		160

Putouts

1	Chet Lemon	1977	512
2	Dwayne Murphy	1980	507
3	Omar Moreno	1979	490
4	Al Bumbry	1980	488
5	Willie Wilson	1980	482
6	Omar Moreno	1980	479
7	Dwayne Murphy	1984	474
8	Lloyd Moseby	1984	473
9	Rick Manning	1983	471
10	Lenny Dykstra	1993	469
11	Rick Bosetti	1979	466
12	Ruppert Jones	1977	465
	Kirby Puckett	1985	465
14	Gary Pettis	1986	462
15	George Wright	1983	460
16	Gorman Thomas	1980	455
17	Ruppert Jones	1979	453
18	Dwayne Murphy	1982	452
19	Kirby Puckett	1988	450
20	Brett Butler	1984	448

Assists

1	Dave Parker	1977	26
2	Warren Cromartie	1978	24
	Ellis Valentine	1978	24
	Gary Ward	1983	24
5	Jesse Barfield	1985	22
	Joe Orsulak	1991	22
7	Gene Richards	1980	21
	Jim Rice	1983	21
	Tim Raines	1983	21
10	George Hendrick	1979	20
	Dave Winfield	1980	20
	Jesse Barfield	1986	20
	Glenn Wilson	1986	20
	Jesse Barfield	1989	20
	Bob Higginson	1997	20
16	7 tied with		19

Errors

1	Chili Davis	1988	19
2	Willie McGee	1990	17
3	Dave Parker	1977	15
	Dave Parker	1979	15
	Larry Herndon	1983	15
	Lonnie Smith	1983	15
	George Bell	1988	15
8	Mitchell Page	1977	14
	Willie Norwood	1978	14
	Jose Cruz	1979	14
	Jose Canseco	1986	14
	Pete Incaviglia	1986	14
13	10 tied with		13

Double Plays

1	Dave Parker	1977	9
	Darrin Jackson	1992	9
	Rich Becker	1996	9
4	Sixto Lezcano	1982	8
	Tom Brunansky	1983	8
	Jesse Barfield	1985	8
	Jesse Barfield	1986	8
8	Bob Bailor	1978	7
	Jack Clark	1979	7
	George Hendrick	1979	7
	Dwight Evans	1980	7
	Rob Deer	1990	7
	Dante Bichette	1991	7
	Albert Belle	1993	7
15	16 tied with		6

Fielding Percentage
(minimum 100 games)

1	23 tied with		1.000

Range Factor
(minimum 100 games)

1	Kirby Puckett	1984	3.55
2	Chet Lemon	1977	3.52
3	Dwayne Murphy	1980	3.29
4	Andre Dawson	1981	3.27
5	Rick Bosetti	1978	3.21
6	Devon White	1988	3.20
7	Dwayne Murphy	1984	3.19
8	Garry Maddox	1979	3.19
9	Dwayne Murphy	1982	3.17
10	Rickey Henderson	1985	3.16
11	Ruppert Jones	1978	3.15
12	Dwayne Murphy	1981	3.13
13	Gary Pettis	1985	3.12
14	Rickey Henderson	1981	3.12
15	Willie Wilson	1981	3.10
16	Al Bumbry	1980	3.09
17	Chet Lemon	1984	3.09
18	Omar Moreno	1979	3.09
19	Willie Wilson	1980	3.09
20	Lance Johnson	1994	3.09

Assists/162 Games
(minimum 100 games)

1	Joe Orsulak	1991	27.00
2	Dave Parker	1977	26.66
3	Ellis Valentine	1978	26.63
4	Gary Ward	1983	25.58
5	Wayne Kirby	1993	25.02
6	Warren Cromartie	1978	24.61
7	Joel Youngblood	1980	24.10
8	George Hendrick	1979	23.48
9	Cory Snyder	1989	23.33
10	Jesse Barfield	1985	23.14
	Raul Mondesi	1994	23.14
12	Bernard Gilkey	1993	22.97
13	Sixto Lezcano	1978	22.96
14	Bob Higginson	1997	22.66
15	Jim Rice	1983	22.53
16	Gene Richards	1981	22.46
	Willie Wilson	1981	22.46
18	Tim Raines	1983	22.09
19	Bob Bailor	1979	21.97
20	Mickey Rivers	1980	21.83

Teams

Yearly Finishes

For each of the 28 major league franchises that played in 1997, we show its league, record, finish and games behind by year. We also display the team's attendance and its managers, their ERA, some basic offensive stats for the team and its opponents, and its ballpark indexes for runs and home runs. At the end of each listing, we detail all of a franchise's nicknames and ballparks through its history.

Individual Leaders

For each year, we display the team's leader in six batting and six pitching categories. Minimums for the percentage categories are 3.1 plate appearances per team game for the hitters and 15 decisions (winning percentage only) or one inning per team game for the pitchers.

Franchise Records

We list each franchise's career and single-season leaders in 16 hitting and 16 pitching categories. For some franchises that had lengthy existences in more than one city, such as the St. Louis Browns/Baltimore Orioles and Brooklyn/Los Angeles Dodgers, we provide career listings for the entire franchise and each of its incarnations. Career minimums for the percentage categories vary according to the total years the franchise has existed and are explained on the leader boards. Season minimums for the percentage categories are 3.1 plate appearances

per team game for the hitters and 15 decisions (winning percentage only) or one inning per team game for the pitchers.

Team Capsules

One of the more interesting sections of this book are the Team Capsules, most of which were written by STATS' Mat Olkin. We pick each team's best and worst in a variety of serious and not-so-serious categories, ranging from best season/worst season to a franchise all-star team to its best-looking/ugliest player and best nickname. For the most part, a player mentioned with a team spent five seasons with the club as a regular or spent more time with that club than any other. Players aren't attributed to more than one team unless they made significant contributions to multiple clubs.

Major League Records

The last part of the Teams section identifies the top 20 single-season team performances in 16 batting and 16 pitching categories.

Abbreviations & Formulas

A complete list of team and statistical abbreviations are listed in the back of the book, along with an appendix explaining formulas and the availability of certain statistics.

California/Anaheim Angels (1961-1997)

Year	Lg	Pos	W-L	Pct	GB	Manager	Att.	R	OR	HR	Avg	OBP	Slg	Opponent HR	Opponent Avg	Opponent OBP	ERA	Park Index Runs	Park Index HR
1961	AL	8th	70-91	.435	38.5	Bill Rigney	603,510	744	784	189	.245	.331	.398	180	.254	.341	4.31	127	197
1962	AL	3rd	86-76	.531	10.0	Bill Rigney	1,144,063	718	706	137	.250	.325	.380	118	.253	.330	3.70	104	65
1963	AL	9th	70-91	.435	34.0	Bill Rigney	821,015	597	660	95	.250	.309	.354	120	.242	.318	3.52	82	46
1964	AL	5th	82-80	.506	17.0	Bill Rigney	760,439	544	551	102	.242	.304	.344	100	.236	.309	2.91	71	45
1965	AL	7th	75-87	.463	27.0	Bill Rigney	566,727	527	569	92	.239	.297	.341	91	.237	.312	3.17	92	65
1966	AL	6th	80-82	.494	18.0	Bill Rigney	1,400,321	604	643	122	.232	.303	.354	136	.251	.317	3.56	98	88
1967	AL	5th	84-77	.522	7.5	Bill Rigney	1,317,713	567	587	114	.238	.301	.349	118	.237	.308	3.19	90	92
1968	AL	8th	67-95	.414	36.0	Bill Rigney	1,025,956	498	615	83	.227	.291	.318	131	.233	.303	3.43	90	116
1969	AL	3rd-W	71-91	.438	26.0	Bill Rigney/Lefty Phillips	758,388	528	652	88	.230	.300	.319	126	.242	.313	3.54	97	114
1970	AL	3rd-W	86-76	.531	12.0	Lefty Phillips	1,077,741	631	630	114	.251	.309	.363	154	.237	.312	3.48	80	60
1971	AL	4th-W	76-86	.469	25.5	Lefty Phillips	926,373	511	576	96	.231	.290	.329	101	.230	.310	3.10	95	91
1972	AL	5th-W	75-80	.484	18.0	Del Rice	744,190	454	533	78	.242	.293	.330	90	.222	.310	3.06	75	53
1973	AL	4th-W	79-83	.488	15.0	Bobby Winkles	1,058,206	629	657	93	.253	.318	.348	104	.246	.324	3.53	90	84
1974	AL	6th-W	68-94	.420	22.0	B. Winkles/W. Herzog/D. Williams	917,269	618	657	95	.254	.321	.356	101	.248	.332	3.52	83	90
1975	AL	6th-W	72-89	.447	25.5	Dick Williams	1,058,163	628	723	55	.246	.322	.328	123	.253	.330	3.89	90	74
1976	AL	4th-W	76-86	.469	14.0	Dick Williams/Norm Sherry	1,006,774	550	631	63	.235	.306	.318	95	.241	.313	3.36	82	60
1977	AL	5th-W	74-88	.457	28.0	Norm Sherry/Dave Garcia	1,432,633	675	695	131	.255	.324	.386	136	.256	.330	3.72	88	101
1978	AL	2nd-W	87-75	.537	5.0	Dave Garcia/Jim Fregosi	1,755,386	691	666	108	.259	.330	.370	125	.253	.327	3.65	103	96
1979	AL	1st-W	88-74	.543	—	Jim Fregosi	2,523,575	866	768	164	.282	.351	.429	131	.267	.336	4.34	84	75
1980	AL	6th-W	65-95	.406	31.0	Jim Fregosi	2,297,327	698	797	106	.265	.332	.378	141	.278	.342	4.52	94	100
1981	AL	4th-W	31-29	.517	6.0	Jim Fregosi/Gene Mauch													
	AL	7th-W	20-30	.400	8.5	Gene Mauch	1,441,545	476	453	97	.256	.330	.380	81	.261	.321	3.70	109	99
1982	AL	1st-W	93-69	.574	—	Gene Mauch	2,807,360	814	670	186	.274	.347	.433	124	.259	.321	3.82	98	118
1983	AL	5th-W	70-92	.432	29.0	John McNamara	2,555,016	722	779	154	.260	.322	.393	130	.284	.341	4.31	93	117
1984	AL	2nd-W	81-81	.500	3.0	John McNamara	2,402,997	696	697	150	.249	.319	.381	143	.271	.328	3.96	102	124
1985	AL	2nd-W	90-72	.556	1.0	Gene Mauch	2,567,427	732	703	153	.251	.333	.386	171	.263	.326	3.91	100	113
1986	AL	1st-W	92-70	.568	—	Gene Mauch	2,655,872	786	684	167	.255	.338	.404	153	.248	.309	3.84	90	113
1987	AL	6th-W	75-87	.463	10.0	Gene Mauch	2,696,299	770	803	172	.252	.326	.401	212	.264	.327	4.38	99	113
1988	AL	4th-W	75-87	.463	29.0	Cookie Rojas/Moose Stubing	2,340,925	714	771	124	.261	.321	.385	135	.270	.338	4.32	89	99
1989	AL	3rd-W	91-71	.562	8.0	Doug Rader	2,647,291	669	578	145	.256	.311	.386	113	.253	.312	3.28	93	135
1990	AL	4th-W	80-82	.494	23.0	Doug Rader	2,555,688	690	706	147	.260	.329	.391	106	.267	.334	3.79	105	132
1991	AL	7th-W	81-81	.500	14.0	Doug Rader/Buck Rodgers	2,416,236	653	649	115	.255	.314	.374	141	.255	.321	3.69	84	108
1992	AL	5th-W	72-90	.444	24.0	B. Rodgers/J. Wathan/B. Rodgers	2,065,444	579	671	88	.243	.301	.338	130	.264	.331	3.84	109	91
1993	AL	5th-W	71-91	.438	23.0	Buck Rodgers	2,057,460	684	770	114	.260	.331	.380	153	.270	.339	4.34	110	124
1994	AL	4th-W	47-68	.409	5.5	B. Rodgers/B. Knoop/M. Lachemann	1,512,622	543	660	120	.264	.334	.409	150	.287	.360	5.42	106	134
1995	AL	2nd-W	78-67	.538	1.0	Marcel Lachemann	1,748,680	801	697	186	.277	.352	.448	163	.265	.333	4.52	96	106
1996	AL	4th-W	70-91	.435	19.5	Marcel Lachemann/John McNamara	1,820,532	762	943	192	.276	.339	.431	219	.275	.357	5.30	95	122
1997	AL	2nd-W	84-78	.519	6.0	Terry Collins	1,774,530	829	794	161	.272	.346	.416	202	.269	.343	4.52	111	134

Team Nicknames: Los Angeles Angels 1961-1965, California Angels 1966-1996, Anaheim Angels 1997.

Team Ballparks: Wrigley Field (LA) 1961, Dodger Stadium 1962-1965, Anaheim Stadium/Edison International Field 1966-1997.

Teams: Angels

California/Anaheim Angels Individual Season Batting Leaders

Year	Batting Average		On-Base Percentage		Slugging Percentage		Home Runs		RBI		Stolen Bases	
1961	Albie Pearson	.288	Albie Pearson	.420	Leon Wagner	.517	Leon Wagner	28	Ken Hunt	84	Albie Pearson	11
1962	Lee Thomas	.290	Albie Pearson	.360	Leon Wagner	.500	Leon Wagner	37	Leon Wagner	107	Albie Pearson	15
1963	Albie Pearson	.304	Albie Pearson	.402	Leon Wagner	.456	Leon Wagner	26	Leon Wagner	90	Albie Pearson	17
1964	Jim Fregosi	.277	Jim Fregosi	.369	Jim Fregosi	.463	Joe Adcock	21	Jim Fregosi	72	Jim Fregosi	8
1965	Jim Fregosi	.277	Jim Fregosi	.337	Jim Fregosi	.407	Jim Fregosi	15	Jim Fregosi	64	Jose Cardenal	37
1966	Jose Cardenal	.276	Jim Fregosi	.325	Jose Cardenal	.399	Joe Adcock	18	Bobby Knoop	72	Jose Cardenal	24
1967	Jim Fregosi	.290	Don Mincher	.367	Don Mincher	.487	Don Mincher	25	Don Mincher	76	Jose Cardenal	10
1968	Rick Reichardt	.255	Rick Reichardt	.328	Rick Reichardt	.421	Rick Reichardt	21	Rick Reichardt	73	Vic Davalillo	17
1969	Jay Johnstone	.270	Jim Fregosi	.361	Jay Johnstone	.381	Rick Reichardt	13	Rick Reichardt	68	Sandy Alomar	18
1970	Alex Johnson	.329	Alex Johnson	.370	Alex Johnson	.459	Jim Fregosi	22	Alex Johnson	86	Sandy Alomar	35
1971	Sandy Alomar	.260	Ken McMullen	.312	Ken McMullen	.395	Ken McMullen	21	Ken McMullen	68	Sandy Alomar	39
1972	Vada Pinson	.275	Ken McMullen	.335	Bob Oliver	.436	Bob Oliver	19	Bob Oliver	70	Sandy Alomar	20
1973	Frank Robinson	.266	Frank Robinson	.372	Frank Robinson	.489	Frank Robinson	30	Frank Robinson	97	Sandy Alomar	25
1974	Mickey Rivers	.285	Frank Robinson	.371	Frank Robinson	.461	Frank Robinson	20	Frank Robinson	63	Mickey Rivers	30
1975	Mickey Rivers	.284	Dave Chalk	.353	Lee Stanton	.416	Lee Stanton	14	Lee Stanton	82	Mickey Rivers	70
1976	Jerry Remy	.263	Bruce Bochte	.346	Bruce Bochte	.311	Bobby Bonds	10	Bobby Bonds	54	Jerry Remy	35
1977	Dave Chalk	.277	Dave Chalk	.345	Bobby Bonds	.520	Bobby Bonds	37	Bobby Bonds	115	Bobby Bonds / Jerry Remy	41
1978	Lyman Bostock	.296	Lyman Bostock	.362	Don Baylor	.472	Don Baylor	34	Don Baylor	99	Don Baylor	22
1979	Brian Downing	.326	Brian Downing	.418	Bobby Grich	.537	Don Baylor	36	Don Baylor	139	Don Baylor	22
1980	Rod Carew	.331	Rod Carew	.396	Rod Carew	.437	Jason Thompson	17	Carney Lansford	80	Rod Carew	23
1981	Rod Carew	.305	Rod Carew	.380	Bobby Grich	.543	Bobby Grich	22	Don Baylor	66	Rod Carew	16
1982	Rod Carew	.319	Rod Carew	.396	Doug DeCinces	.548	Reggie Jackson	39	Reggie Jackson	101	Don Baylor / Rod Carew	10
1983	Rod Carew	.339	Rod Carew	.409	Rod Carew	.411	Fred Lynn	22	Fred Lynn	74	Gary Pettis	8
1984	Brian Downing	.275	Fred Lynn	.366	Fred Lynn	.474	Reggie Jackson	25	Brian Downing	91	Gary Pettis	48
1985	Rod Carew	.280	Rod Carew	.371	Reggie Jackson	.487	Reggie Jackson	27	Brian Downing / Reggie Jackson	85	Gary Pettis	56
1986	Wally Joyner	.290	Brian Downing	.389	Doug DeCinces	.459	Doug DeCinces	26	Wally Joyner	100	Gary Pettis	50
1987	Wally Joyner	.285	Brian Downing	.400	Wally Joyner	.528	Wally Joyner	34	Wally Joyner	117	Devon White	32
1988	Johnny Ray	.306	Brian Downing	.362	Brian Downing	.442	Chili Davis	25	Chili Davis	93	Dick Schofield	20
1989	Johnny Ray	.289	Brian Downing	.354	Chili Davis	.436	Chili Davis	22	Chili Davis	90	Devon White	44
1990	Lance Parrish	.268	Lance Parrish	.338	Lance Parrish	.451	Lance Parrish	24	Dave Winfield	72	Devon White	21
1991	Wally Joyner	.301	Wally Joyner	.360	Wally Joyner	.488	Dave Winfield	28	Wally Joyner	96	Luis Polonia	48
1992	Luis Polonia	.286	Chad Curtis	.341	Chad Curtis	.372	Gary Gaetti	12	Junior Felix	72	Luis Polonia	51
1993	Chad Curtis	.285	Tim Salmon	.382	Tim Salmon	.536	Tim Salmon	31	Chili Davis	112	Luis Polonia	55
1994	Chili Davis	.311	Chili Davis	.410	Chili Davis	.561	Chili Davis	26	Chili Davis	84	Chad Curtis	25
1995	Tim Salmon	.330	Tim Salmon	.429	Tim Salmon	.594	Tim Salmon	34	Jim Edmonds	107	Rex Hudler / Tony Phillips	13
1996	Chili Davis	.292	Chili Davis	.387	Tim Salmon	.501	Tim Salmon	30	Tim Salmon	98	Rex Hudler	14
1997	Garret Anderson	.303	Tim Salmon	.394	Tim Salmon	.517	Tim Salmon	33	Tim Salmon	129	Darin Erstad	23

California/Anaheim Angels Individual Season Pitching Leaders

Year	ERA		Baserunners/9 IP		Innings Pitched		Strikeouts		Wins		Saves	
1961	Ken McBride	3.65	Ken McBride	12.6	Ken McBride	241.2	Ken McBride	180	Ken McBride	12	Art Fowler	11
1962	Dean Chance	2.96	Dean Chance	11.6	Dean Chance	206.2	Bo Belinsky	145	Dean Chance	14	Tom Morgan	9
1963	Dean Chance	3.19	Ken McBride	10.5	Ken McBride	251.0	Dean Chance	168	Dean Chance / Ken McBride	13	Julio Navarro	12
1964	Dean Chance	1.65	Dean Chance	9.1	Dean Chance	278.1	Dean Chance	207	Dean Chance	20	Bob Lee	19
1965	George Brunet	2.56	Fred Newman	10.0	Fred Newman	260.2	Dean Chance	164	Dean Chance	15	Bob Lee	23
1966	Dean Chance	3.08	Dean Chance	11.3	Dean Chance	259.2	Dean Chance	180	George Brunet / Jack Sanford	13	Bob Lee	16
1967	Rickey Clark	2.59	Jim McGlothlin	10.2	George Brunet	250.0	George Brunet	165	3 tied with	12	Minnie Rojas	27
1968	George Brunet	2.86	George Brunet	9.6	George Brunet	245.1	Jim McGlothlin	135	George Brunet	13	Minnie Rojas	6
1969	Andy Messersmith	2.52	Andy Messersmith	9.9	Andy Messersmith	250.0	Andy Messersmith	211	Andy Messersmith	16	Ken Tatum	22
1970	Clyde Wright	2.83	Andy Messersmith	10.5	Clyde Wright	260.2	Rudy May	164	Clyde Wright	22	Ken Tatum	17
1971	Andy Messersmith	2.99	Clyde Wright	10.1	Andy Messersmith / Clyde Wright	276.2	Andy Messersmith	179	Andy Messersmith	20	Lloyd Allen	15
1972	Nolan Ryan	2.28	Andy Messersmith	10.3	Nolan Ryan	284.0	Nolan Ryan	329	Nolan Ryan	19	Dave Sells	10
1973	Nolan Ryan	2.87	Nolan Ryan	11.2	Nolan Ryan	326.0	Nolan Ryan	383	Nolan Ryan	21	Dave Sells	10
1974	Nolan Ryan	2.89	Frank Tanana	11.6	Nolan Ryan	332.2	Nolan Ryan	367	Nolan Ryan	22	Orlando Pena	3
1975	Frank Tanana	2.62	Frank Tanana	10.2	Frank Tanana	257.1	Frank Tanana	269	Ed Figueroa / Frank Tanana	16	Don Kirkwood	7
1976	Frank Tanana	2.43	Frank Tanana	9.2	Frank Tanana	288.1	Nolan Ryan	327	Frank Tanana	19	Dick Drago	6
1977	Frank Tanana	2.54	Frank Tanana	10.2	Nolan Ryan	299.0	Nolan Ryan	341	Nolan Ryan	19	Dave LaRoche	13
1978	Frank Tanana	3.65	Frank Tanana	11.6	Frank Tanana	239.0	Nolan Ryan	260	Frank Tanana	18	Dave LaRoche	25
1979	Dave Frost	3.57	Dave Frost	11.6	Dave Frost	239.1	Nolan Ryan	223	Dave Frost / Nolan Ryan	16	Mark Clear	14
1980	Don Aase	4.06	Frank Tanana	12.2	Frank Tanana	204.0	Frank Tanana	113	Mark Clear / Frank Tanana	11	Andy Hassler	10
1981	Ken Forsch	2.88	Ken Forsch	10.2	Geoff Zahn	161.1	Mike Witt	75	Ken Forsch	11	Don Aase	11
1982	Mike Witt	3.51	Geoff Zahn	11.5	Geoff Zahn	229.1	Bruce Kison	86	Geoff Zahn	18	Doug Corbett	8
1983	Geoff Zahn	3.33	Geoff Zahn	11.7	Tommy John	234.2	Bruce Kison	83	3 tied with	11	Luis Sanchez	7
1984	Geoff Zahn	3.12	Geoff Zahn	11.2	Mike Witt	246.2	Mike Witt	196	Mike Witt	15	Luis Sanchez	11
1985	Mike Witt	3.56	Mike Witt	11.9	Mike Witt	250.0	Mike Witt	180	Mike Witt	15	Donnie Moore	31
1986	Mike Witt	2.84	Mike Witt	9.8	Mike Witt	269.0	Mike Witt	208	Mike Witt	18	Donnie Moore	21
1987	Willie Fraser	3.92	Don Sutton	11.6	Mike Witt	247.0	Mike Witt	192	Mike Witt	16	DeWayne Buice	17
1988	Mike Witt	4.15	Mike Witt	12.8	Mike Witt	249.2	Mike Witt	133	Mike Witt	13	Bryan Harvey	17
1989	Chuck Finley	2.57	Bert Blyleven	10.3	Bert Blyleven	241.0	Chuck Finley	156	Bert Blyleven	17	Bryan Harvey	25
1990	Chuck Finley	2.40	Chuck Finley	11.2	Chuck Finley	236.0	Mark Langston	195	Chuck Finley	18	Bryan Harvey	25
1991	Jim Abbott	2.89	Mark Langston	10.5	Mark Langston	246.1	Mark Langston	183	Mark Langston	19	Bryan Harvey	46
1992	Jim Abbott	2.77	Mark Langston	11.2	Mark Langston	229.0	Mark Langston	174	Mark Langston	13	Joe Grahe	21
1993	Chuck Finley	3.15	Mark Langston	10.7	Mark Langston	256.1	Mark Langston	196	Chuck Finley / Mark Langston	16	Steve Frey	13
1994	Chuck Finley	4.32	Chuck Finley	12.4	Chuck Finley	183.1	Chuck Finley	148	Chuck Finley	10	Joe Grahe	13
1995	Chuck Finley	4.21	Mark Langston	12.5	Chuck Finley	203.0	Chuck Finley	195	Chuck Finley / Mark Langston	15	Lee Smith	37
1996	Chuck Finley	4.16	Chuck Finley	13.1	Chuck Finley	238.0	Chuck Finley	215	Chuck Finley	15	Troy Percival	36
1997	Chuck Finley	4.23	Chuck Finley	12.2	Jason Dickson	203.2	Chuck Finley	155	Jason Dickson / Chuck Finley	13	Troy Percival	27

Teams: Angels

Angels Franchise Batting Leaders—Career

Games

1	Brian Downing	1,661
2	Jim Fregosi	1,429
3	Bobby Grich	1,222
4	Dick Schofield	1,086
5	Bob Boone	968
6	Chili Davis	950
7	Bob Rodgers	932
8	Wally Joyner	846
9	Gary DiSarcina	836
10	Rod Carew	834
11	Don Baylor	824
12	Jack Howell	822
13	Bobby Knoop	803
14	Sandy Alomar	795
15	Doug DeCinces	787
16	Dave Chalk	732
17	Tim Salmon	721
18	Albie Pearson	689
19	Reggie Jackson	687
20	Devon White	612

At-Bats

1	Brian Downing	5,854
2	Jim Fregosi	5,244
3	Bobby Grich	4,100
4	Chili Davis	3,491
5	Dick Schofield	3,434
6	Wally Joyner	3,208
7	Don Baylor	3,105
8	Rod Carew	3,080
9	Sandy Alomar	3,054
10	Bob Rodgers	3,033
	Bob Boone	3,033
12	Doug DeCinces	2,884
	Gary DiSarcina	2,884
14	Tim Salmon	2,667
15	Bobby Knoop	2,617
16	Dave Chalk	2,474
17	Jack Howell	2,408
18	Reggie Jackson	2,331
19	Albie Pearson	2,247
20	Devon White	2,231

Runs

1	Brian Downing	889
2	Jim Fregosi	691
3	Bobby Grich	601
4	Chili Davis	520
5	Don Baylor	481
6	Rod Carew	474
7	Tim Salmon	464
8	Wally Joyner	455
9	Doug DeCinces	404
	Dick Schofield	404
11	Albie Pearson	374
12	Sandy Alomar	341
13	Devon White	337
14	Gary DiSarcina	333
15	Reggie Jackson	331
16	Jack Howell	315
	Jim Edmonds	315
18	Luis Polonia	300
19	Gary Pettis	296
20	Bob Boone	286

Hits

1	Brian Downing	1,588
2	Jim Fregosi	1,408
3	Bobby Grich	1,103
4	Chili Davis	973
5	Rod Carew	968
6	Wally Joyner	925
7	Don Baylor	813
8	Dick Schofield	798
9	Tim Salmon	782
10	Doug DeCinces	765
11	Sandy Alomar	758
12	Bob Boone	742
13	Gary DiSarcina	731
14	Bob Rodgers	704
15	Dave Chalk	631
16	Bobby Knoop	629
17	Luis Polonia	628
18	Albie Pearson	618
19	Jack Howell	581
20	Reggie Jackson	557

Doubles

1	Brian Downing	282
2	Jim Fregosi	219
3	Bobby Grich	183
4	Wally Joyner	170
5	Chili Davis	167
6	Doug DeCinces	149
7	Tim Salmon	143
8	Don Baylor	140
	Rod Carew	140
10	Gary DiSarcina	138
11	Jack Howell	119
12	Bob Boone	115
13	Bob Rodgers	114
14	Dick Schofield	104
15	Jim Edmonds	102
16	Albie Pearson	98
17	Fred Lynn	94
18	Johnny Ray	92
19	Devon White	91
20	Bobby Knoop	89

Triples

1	Jim Fregosi	70
2	Mickey Rivers	32
3	Dick Schofield	27
	Luis Polonia	27
5	Bobby Knoop	25
6	Devon White	24
7	Gary Pettis	23
8	Brian Downing	22
	Rod Carew	22
10	Bobby Grich	20
11	Bob Rodgers	18
	Jerry Remy	18
13	Albie Pearson	17
	Willie Smith	17
15	Jay Johnstone	16
	Gary DiSarcina	16
17	Doug DeCinces	15
	Jack Howell	15
19	Lee Thomas	14
20	Four tied at	13

Home Runs

1	Brian Downing	222
2	Chili Davis	156
3	Bobby Grich	154
4	Tim Salmon	153
5	Don Baylor	141
6	Doug DeCinces	130
7	Reggie Jackson	123
8	Jim Fregosi	115
9	Wally Joyner	114
10	Jack Howell	100
11	Leon Wagner	91
	Jim Edmonds	91
13	Fred Lynn	71
14	Rick Reichardt	68
15	J.T. Snow	65
16	Lance Parrish	64
17	Lee Thomas	61
18	Devon White	59
19	Roger Repoz	57
	Joe Rudi	57

RBI

1	Brian Downing	846
2	Chili Davis	618
3	Bobby Grich	557
4	Jim Fregosi	546
5	Don Baylor	523
6	Wally Joyner	518
7	Tim Salmon	503
8	Doug DeCinces	481
9	Reggie Jackson	374
10	Bob Boone	318
11	Jack Howell	313
12	Jim Edmonds	294
13	Bob Rodgers	288
14	Rod Carew	282
15	Dick Schofield	280
16	Leon Wagner	276
17	Fred Lynn	270
18	Rick Reichardt	261
19	Gary DiSarcina	259
20	J.T. Snow	256

Walks

1	Brian Downing	866
2	Bobby Grich	630
3	Jim Fregosi	558
4	Chili Davis	493
5	Tim Salmon	426
6	Rod Carew	405
7	Albie Pearson	369
8	Reggie Jackson	362
9	Dick Schofield	335
10	Wally Joyner	323
11	Doug DeCinces	320
12	Don Baylor	312
13	Jack Howell	270
14	Gary Pettis	250
15	Dave Chalk	244
16	Bob Rodgers	234
17	Bob Boone	232
18	Fred Lynn	228
19	Paul Schaal	216
20	Bobby Knoop	212

Strikeouts

1	Jim Fregosi	835
2	Brian Downing	759
3	Bobby Grich	758
4	Chili Davis	713
5	Reggie Jackson	690
6	Tim Salmon	638
7	Bobby Knoop	634
8	Jack Howell	572
9	Gary Pettis	513
10	Dick Schofield	512
11	Devon White	475
12	Doug DeCinces	447
13	Lee Stanton	437
14	Bob Rodgers	409
15	Jim Edmonds	399
16	Rick Reichardt	393
17	Don Baylor	350
	Lance Parrish	350
19	Roger Repoz	333
20	Wally Joyner	331

Stolen Bases

1	Gary Pettis	186
2	Luis Polonia	174
3	Sandy Alomar	139
4	Mickey Rivers	126
5	Devon White	123
6	Chad Curtis	116
7	Jerry Remy	110
8	Dick Schofield	99
9	Don Baylor	89
10	Rod Carew	82
11	Jim Fregosi	71
	Jose Cardenal	71
	Bobby Bonds	71
14	Albie Pearson	61
15	Dave Collins	56
16	Carney Lansford	54
17	Mark McLemore	45
18	Morris Nettles	42
19	Lee Stanton	35
20	Gary DiSarcina	34

Runs Created

1	Brian Downing	994
2	Jim Fregosi	736
3	Bobby Grich	684
4	Chili Davis	602
5	Tim Salmon	545
6	Wally Joyner	531
7	Rod Carew	494
8	Don Baylor	478
9	Doug DeCinces	442
10	Dick Schofield	371
11	Reggie Jackson	358
12	Albie Pearson	349
13	Jack Howell	328
14	Jim Edmonds	310
15	Bob Boone	293
16	Fred Lynn	285
17	Luis Polonia	284
18	Sandy Alomar	276
19	Leon Wagner	273
20	Devon White	262

Runs Created/27 Outs

(minimum 2000 Plate Appearances)

1	Tim Salmon	7.41
2	Jim Edmonds	6.09
3	Chili Davis	6.01
4	Brian Downing	5.90
5	Wally Joyner	5.88
6	Rod Carew	5.72
7	Bobby Grich	5.67
8	Albie Pearson	5.50
9	Doug DeCinces	5.21
10	Don Baylor	5.21
11	Reggie Jackson	5.19
12	Jim Fregosi	4.89
13	Jack Howell	4.62
14	Luis Polonia	4.59
15	Rick Reichardt	4.50
16	Gary Pettis	4.22
17	Devon White	3.92
18	Lee Stanton	3.83
19	Dick Schofield	3.54
20	Dave Chalk	3.45

Batting Average

(minimum 2000 Plate Appearances)

1	Rod Carew	.314
2	Luis Polonia	.294
3	Tim Salmon	.293
4	Jim Edmonds	.290
5	Wally Joyner	.288
6	Chili Davis	.279
7	Albie Pearson	.275
8	Brian Downing	.271
9	Bobby Grich	.269
10	Jim Fregosi	.268
11	Doug DeCinces	.265
12	Don Baylor	.262
13	Rick Reichardt	.261
14	Dave Chalk	.255
15	Gary DiSarcina	.253
16	Sandy Alomar	.248
17	Devon White	.247
18	Lee Stanton	.247
19	Bob Boone	.245
20	Gary Pettis	.242

On-Base Percentage

(minimum 2000 Plate Appearances)

1	Rod Carew	.393
2	Tim Salmon	.392
3	Albie Pearson	.379
4	Brian Downing	.372
5	Bobby Grich	.370
6	Chili Davis	.365
7	Jim Edmonds	.358
8	Wally Joyner	.353
9	Luis Polonia	.345
10	Reggie Jackson	.343
11	Jim Fregosi	.340
12	Don Baylor	.337
13	Doug DeCinces	.336
14	Gary Pettis	.332
15	Rick Reichardt	.328
16	Dave Chalk	.327
17	Jack Howell	.319
18	Lee Stanton	.312
19	Dick Schofield	.306
20	Bobby Knoop	.298

Slugging Percentage

(minimum 2000 Plate Appearances)

1	Tim Salmon	.527
2	Jim Edmonds	.503
3	Chili Davis	.464
4	Doug DeCinces	.463
5	Wally Joyner	.455
6	Don Baylor	.448
7	Brian Downing	.441
8	Reggie Jackson	.440
9	Bobby Grich	.436
10	Jack Howell	.428
11	Rick Reichardt	.406
12	Jim Fregosi	.403
13	Rod Carew	.392
14	Devon White	.389
15	Lee Stanton	.381
16	Albie Pearson	.366
17	Luis Polonia	.358
18	Bobby Knoop	.344
19	Gary DiSarcina	.336
20	Bob Boone	.323

Teams: Angels

Angels Franchise Pitching Leaders—Career

Wins

1	Chuck Finley	142
2	Nolan Ryan	138
3	Mike Witt	109
4	Frank Tanana	102
5	Mark Langston	88
6	Clyde Wright	87
7	Kirk McCaskill	78
8	Dean Chance	74
9	Andy Messersmith	59
10	George Brunet	54
	Jim Abbott	54
12	Geoff Zahn	52
13	Rudy May	51
14	Ken McBride	40
15	Don Aase	39
16	Tom Murphy	37
17	Ken Forsch	36
18	Dave LaRoche	35
19	Bill Singer	34
20	Five tied at	33

Losses

1	Nolan Ryan	121
2	Chuck Finley	120
3	Mike Witt	107
4	Clyde Wright	85
5	Frank Tanana	78
6	Rudy May	76
7	Kirk McCaskill	74
	Jim Abbott	74
	Mark Langston	74
10	George Brunet	69
11	Dean Chance	66
12	Tom Murphy	52
13	Ken McBride	48
14	Andy Messersmith	47
15	Andy Hassler	46
16	Jim McGlothlin	43
17	Geoff Zahn	42
18	Fred Newman	39
	Don Aase	39
20	Willie Fraser	34

Winning Percentage
(minimum 75 decisions)

1	Frank Tanana	.567
2	Andy Messersmith	.557
3	Geoff Zahn	.553
4	Mark Langston	.543
5	Chuck Finley	.542
6	Nolan Ryan	.533
7	Dean Chance	.529
8	Kirk McCaskill	.513
9	Clyde Wright	.506
10	Mike Witt	.505
11	Don Aase	.500
12	Ken McBride	.455
13	George Brunet	.439
14	Jim McGlothlin	.434
15	Jim Abbott	.422
16	Tom Murphy	.416
17	Rudy May	.402

Games

1	Chuck Finley	369
2	Mike Witt	314
3	Dave LaRoche	304
4	Nolan Ryan	291
5	Clyde Wright	266
6	Andy Hassler	259
7	Bryan Harvey	250
8	Rudy May	230
9	Frank Tanana	225
10	Dean Chance	223
11	Eddie Fisher	219
12	Mark Langston	210
13	Mark Eichhorn	196
14	Bob Lee	194
	George Brunet	194
	Luis Sanchez	194
17	Don Aase	192
	Kirk McCaskill	192
19	Troy Percival	179
20	Mike James	173

Games Started

1	Chuck Finley	312
2	Nolan Ryan	288
3	Mike Witt	272
4	Frank Tanana	218
5	Mark Langston	210
6	Clyde Wright	189
	Kirk McCaskill	189
8	Rudy May	170
9	Dean Chance	168
10	Jim Abbott	161
11	George Brunet	157
12	Tom Murphy	124
13	Andy Messersmith	123
14	Geoff Zahn	121
15	Ken McBride	120
16	Jim McGlothlin	110
17	Fred Newman	93
18	Ken Forsch	88
19	Ron Romanick	82
20	Bill Singer	81

Complete Games

1	Nolan Ryan	156
2	Frank Tanana	92
3	Mike Witt	70
4	Chuck Finley	55
5	Clyde Wright	51
6	Dean Chance	48
7	Andy Messersmith	42
	Geoff Zahn	42
9	Rudy May	35
	Bill Singer	35
11	Ken Forsch	34
	Mark Langston	34
13	George Brunet	33
14	Kirk McCaskill	30
15	Ken McBride	28
16	Jim McGlothlin	22
	Jim Abbott	22
18	Ed Figueroa	21
19	Tom Murphy	19
20	Five tied at	18

Shutouts

1	Nolan Ryan	40
2	Frank Tanana	24
3	Dean Chance	21
4	George Brunet	14
5	Geoff Zahn	13
	Chuck Finley	13
7	Rudy May	12
8	Andy Messersmith	11
	Kirk McCaskill	11
10	Mike Witt	10
11	Clyde Wright	9
	Ken Forsch	9
13	Ken McBride	7
	Jim McGlothlin	7
15	Bert Blyleven	5
	Jim Abbott	5
	Mark Langston	5
18	Seven tied at	4

Saves

1	Bryan Harvey	126
2	Troy Percival	66
3	Dave LaRoche	65
4	Donnie Moore	61
5	Bob Lee	58
6	Joe Grahe	45
7	Minnie Rojas	43
8	Ken Tatum	39
9	Lee Smith	37
10	Art Fowler	27
	Don Aase	27
	Luis Sanchez	27
13	Greg Minton	25
14	Andy Hassler	24
15	Mark Clear	23
16	Doug Corbett	22
17	Lloyd Allen	21
18	Tom Morgan	20
	DeWayne Buice	20
20	Four tied at	17

Innings Pitched

1	Chuck Finley	2,238.1
2	Nolan Ryan	2,181.1
3	Mike Witt	1,965.1
4	Frank Tanana	1,615.1
5	Mark Langston	1,445.1
6	Clyde Wright	1,403.1
7	Dean Chance	1,236.2
8	Kirk McCaskill	1,221.0
9	Rudy May	1,138.2
10	Jim Abbott	1,073.2
11	George Brunet	1,047.1
12	Andy Messersmith	972.1
13	Geoff Zahn	830.0
14	Tom Murphy	795.1
15	Ken McBride	780.1
16	Don Aase	695.1
17	Jim McGlothlin	692.1
18	Andy Hassler	659.1
19	Ken Forsch	633.2
20	Fred Newman	610.0

Walks

1	Nolan Ryan	1,302
2	Chuck Finley	915
3	Mike Witt	656
4	Mark Langston	551
5	Rudy May	484
6	Dean Chance	462
7	Clyde Wright	449
8	Kirk McCaskill	448
9	Frank Tanana	422
10	Andy Messersmith	402
11	George Brunet	397
12	Jim Abbott	394
13	Ken McBride	343
14	Andy Hassler	310
15	Don Aase	289
16	Tom Murphy	268
17	Bill Singer	254
18	Geoff Zahn	221
19	Rickey Clark	213
20	Bo Belinsky	206

Strikeouts

1	Nolan Ryan	2,416
2	Chuck Finley	1,739
3	Mike Witt	1,283
4	Frank Tanana	1,233
5	Mark Langston	1,112
6	Dean Chance	857
7	Rudy May	844
8	Andy Messersmith	768
9	Kirk McCaskill	714
10	George Brunet	678
11	Jim Abbott	607
12	Clyde Wright	571
13	Ken McBride	487
14	Jim McGlothlin	418
15	Bill Singer	396
16	Dave LaRoche	386
17	Andy Hassler	383
18	Don Aase	369
19	Bryan Harvey	365
20	Tom Murphy	346

Strikeouts/9 Innings
(minimum 750 Innings Pitched)

1	Nolan Ryan	9.97
2	Andy Messersmith	7.11
3	Chuck Finley	6.99
4	Mark Langston	6.92
5	Frank Tanana	6.87
6	Rudy May	6.67
7	Dean Chance	6.24
8	Mike Witt	5.88
9	George Brunet	5.83
10	Ken McBride	5.62
11	Kirk McCaskill	5.26
12	Jim Abbott	5.09
13	Tom Murphy	3.92
14	Clyde Wright	3.66
15	Geoff Zahn	3.13

ERA
(minimum 750 Innings Pitched)

1	Andy Messersmith	2.78
2	Dean Chance	2.83
3	Nolan Ryan	3.07
4	Frank Tanana	3.08
5	George Brunet	3.13
6	Clyde Wright	3.28
7	Geoff Zahn	3.64
8	Rudy May	3.67
9	Chuck Finley	3.69
10	Mike Witt	3.76
11	Ken McBride	3.81
12	Tom Murphy	3.85
13	Kirk McCaskill	3.86
14	Mark Langston	3.97
15	Jim Abbott	4.07

Component ERA
(minimum 750 Innings Pitched)

1	Andy Messersmith	2.48
2	Dean Chance	2.92
3	George Brunet	2.96
4	Nolan Ryan	2.96
5	Frank Tanana	3.08
6	Rudy May	3.30
7	Clyde Wright	3.33
8	Tom Murphy	3.65
9	Mark Langston	3.70
10	Mike Witt	3.71
11	Geoff Zahn	3.73
12	Ken McBride	3.80
13	Kirk McCaskill	3.84
14	Chuck Finley	3.95
15	Jim Abbott	4.18

Opponent Average
(minimum 750 Innings Pitched)

1	Nolan Ryan	.198
2	Andy Messersmith	.202
3	George Brunet	.225
4	Dean Chance	.232
5	Rudy May	.232
6	Ken McBride	.239
7	Frank Tanana	.241
8	Mark Langston	.248
9	Clyde Wright	.249
10	Tom Murphy	.252
11	Chuck Finley	.255
12	Kirk McCaskill	.257
13	Mike Witt	.258
14	Geoff Zahn	.270
15	Jim Abbott	.275

Opponent OBP
(minimum 750 Innings Pitched)

1	Andy Messersmith	.286
2	Frank Tanana	.294
3	George Brunet	.298
4	Dean Chance	.306
5	Clyde Wright	.309
6	Rudy May	.313
7	Geoff Zahn	.316
8	Nolan Ryan	.317
9	Mark Langston	.318
10	Mike Witt	.319
11	Tom Murphy	.321
12	Kirk McCaskill	.323
13	Ken McBride	.328
14	Chuck Finley	.330
15	Jim Abbott	.339

Teams: Angels

Angels Franchise Batting Leaders—Single Season

Games

1	Bobby Knoop	1964	162
	Jim Fregosi	1966	162
	Sandy Alomar	1970	162
	Sandy Alomar	1971	162
	Don Baylor	1979	162
6	Jim Fregosi	1965	161
	Bobby Knoop	1966	161
	Jim Fregosi	1969	161
9	Lee Thomas	1962	160
	Leon Wagner	1962	160
	Billy Moran	1962	160
	Albie Pearson	1962	160
	Ken McMullen	1971	160
14	Bobby Knoop	1967	159
	Jim Fregosi	1968	159
	Aurelio Rodriguez	1969	159
	Devon White	1987	159
	Wally Joyner	1989	159
19	Six tied at		158

At-Bats

1	Sandy Alomar	1971	689
2	Sandy Alomar	1970	672
3	Billy Moran	1962	659
4	Carney Lansford	1979	654
5	Devon White	1987	639
6	Devon White	1989	636
7	Don Baylor	1979	628
8	Garret Anderson	1997	624
9	Brian Downing	1982	623
10	Mickey Rivers	1975	616
11	Albie Pearson	1962	614
	Jim Fregosi	1968	614
	Alex Johnson	1970	614
14	Leon Wagner	1962	612
15	Jim Fregosi	1966	611
16	Sandy Alomar	1972	610
17	Don Baylor	1982	608
18	Garret Anderson	1996	607
19	Luis Polonia	1991	604
20	Three tied at		602

Runs

1	Don Baylor	1979	120
	Jim Edmonds	1995	120
3	Tony Phillips	1995	119
4	Albie Pearson	1962	115
5	Carney Lansford	1979	114
6	Tim Salmon	1995	111
7	Brian Downing	1987	110
8	Brian Downing	1982	109
9	Bobby Bonds	1977	103
	Don Baylor	1978	103
	Devon White	1987	103
12	Dave Hollins	1997	101
13	Dan Ford	1979	100
	Wally Joyner	1987	100
15	Darin Erstad	1997	99
16	Leon Wagner	1962	96
17	Jim Fregosi	1970	95
	Tim Salmon	1997	95
19	Doug DeCinces	1982	94
	Chad Curtis	1993	94

Hits

1	Alex Johnson	1970	202
2	Garret Anderson	1997	189
3	Carney Lansford	1979	188
4	Billy Moran	1962	186
	Don Baylor	1979	186
	Johnny Ray	1988	184
7	Sandy Alomar	1971	179
	Rod Carew	1980	179
	Luis Polonia	1991	179
10	Tim Salmon	1995	177
11	Albie Pearson	1963	176
	Wally Joyner	1988	176
13	Mickey Rivers	1975	175
	Brian Downing	1982	175
15	Doug DeCinces	1982	173
	Garret Anderson	1996	173
17	Wally Joyner	1986	172
	Tim Salmon	1997	172
19	Jim Fregosi	1967	171
20	Jim Fregosi	1963	170

Doubles

1	Doug DeCinces	1982	42
	Johnny Ray	1988	42
3	Fred Lynn	1982	38
4	Brian Downing	1982	37
5	Garret Anderson	1997	36
6	Tim Salmon	1993	35
7	Bob Rodgers	1962	34
	Rod Carew	1980	34
	Wally Joyner	1991	34
	Tim Salmon	1995	34
	Darin Erstad	1997	34
12	Jim Fregosi	1970	33
	Don Baylor	1979	33
	Devon White	1987	33
	Wally Joyner	1987	33
	Garret Anderson	1996	33
17	Felix Torres	1963	32
	Jim Fregosi	1966	32
	Jack Howell	1988	32
	Chili Davis	1993	32

Triples

1	Jim Fregosi	1968	13
	Mickey Rivers	1975	13
	Devon White	1989	13
4	Jim Fregosi	1963	12
5	Bobby Knoop	1966	11
	Mickey Rivers	1974	11
7	Jerry Remy	1977	10
8	Jim Fregosi	1964	9
	Willie Smith	1965	9
	Bobby Bonds	1977	9
	Luis Polonia	1990	9
12	Gary Pettis	1985	8
	Luis Polonia	1991	8
14	Jim Fregosi	1965	7
	Paul Schaal	1966	7
	Jim Fregosi	1966	7
	Rod Carew	1980	7
	Johnny Ray	1988	7
	Luis Alicea	1997	7
20	Fifteen tied at		6

Home Runs

1	Reggie Jackson	1982	39
2	Leon Wagner	1962	37
	Bobby Bonds	1977	37
4	Don Baylor	1979	36
5	Don Baylor	1978	34
	Wally Joyner	1987	34
	Tim Salmon	1995	34
8	Jim Edmonds	1995	33
	Tim Salmon	1997	33
10	Tim Salmon	1993	31
11	Frank Robinson	1973	30
	Bobby Bonds	1979	30
	Doug DeCinces	1982	30
	Tim Salmon	1996	30
15	Brian Downing	1987	29
16	Leon Wagner	1961	28
	Brian Downing	1982	28
	Dave Winfield	1991	28
	Chili Davis	1996	28
20	Four tied at		27

RBI

1	Don Baylor	1979	139
2	Tim Salmon	1997	129
3	Wally Joyner	1987	117
4	Bobby Bonds	1977	115
5	Chili Davis	1993	112
6	Leon Wagner	1962	107
	Jim Edmonds	1995	107
8	Tim Salmon	1995	105
9	Lee Thomas	1962	104
10	J.T. Snow	1995	102
11	Dan Ford	1979	101
	Bobby Grich	1979	101
	Reggie Jackson	1982	101
14	Wally Joyner	1986	100
15	Don Baylor	1978	99
16	Tim Salmon	1996	98
17	Frank Robinson	1973	97
	Doug DeCinces	1982	97
19	Doug DeCinces	1986	96
	Wally Joyner	1991	96

Walks

1	Tony Phillips	1995	113
2	Brian Downing	1987	106
3	Albie Pearson	1961	96
4	Albie Pearson	1962	95
	Tim Salmon	1997	95
6	Jim Fregosi	1969	93
	Tim Salmon	1996	93
8	Albie Pearson	1963	92
	Reggie Jackson	1986	92
10	Tim Salmon	1995	91
11	Brian Downing	1986	90
12	Chili Davis	1995	89
13	Brian Downing	1982	86
	Chili Davis	1996	86
15	Reggie Jackson	1982	85
16	Bobby Grich	1980	84
17	Frank Robinson	1973	82
	Bobby Grich	1982	82
	Tim Salmon	1993	82
20	Two tied at		81

Strikeouts

1	Reggie Jackson	1982	156
2	Bobby Knoop	1966	144
3	Tim Salmon	1997	142
4	Bobby Bonds	1977	141
	Reggie Jackson	1984	141
6	Reggie Jackson	1983	140
7	Reggie Jackson	1985	138
8	Bobby Knoop	1967	136
9	Devon White	1987	135
	Chili Davis	1993	135
	Tim Salmon	1993	135
	Tony Phillips	1995	135
13	Gary Pettis	1986	132
14	Jack Howell	1988	130
	Jim Edmonds	1995	130
16	Devon White	1989	129
17	Bobby Knoop	1968	128
	Junior Felix	1992	128
19	Three tied at		125

Stolen Bases

1	Mickey Rivers	1975	70
2	Gary Pettis	1985	56
3	Luis Polonia	1993	55
4	Luis Polonia	1992	51
5	Gary Pettis	1986	50
6	Gary Pettis	1984	48
	Luis Polonia	1991	48
	Chad Curtis	1993	48
9	Devon White	1989	44
10	Chad Curtis	1992	43
11	Bobby Bonds	1977	41
	Jerry Remy	1977	41
13	Sandy Alomar	1971	39
14	Jose Cardenal	1965	37
15	Sandy Alomar	1970	35
	Jerry Remy	1976	35
17	Jerry Remy	1975	34
18	Dave Collins	1976	32
	Devon White	1987	32
20	Two tied at		30

Runs Created

1	Tim Salmon	1995	132
2	Tim Salmon	1997	130
3	Don Baylor	1979	128
4	Brian Downing	1987	118
5	Wally Joyner	1987	112
6	Brian Downing	1982	110
7	Doug DeCinces	1982	108
8	Tim Salmon	1996	107
9	Bobby Bonds	1977	105
10	Leon Wagner	1962	103
	Bobby Grich	1979	103
12	Reggie Jackson	1982	101
	Tim Salmon	1993	101
14	Jim Fregosi	1970	100
	Frank Robinson	1973	100
	Brian Downing	1979	100
	Darin Erstad	1997	100
18	Five tied at		99

Runs Created/27 Outs

(minimum 3.1 Plate Appearances/Tm Gm)

1	Tim Salmon	1995	9.36
2	Chili Davis	1995	8.40
3	Tim Salmon	1997	7.94
4	Chili Davis	1994	7.61
5	Bobby Grich	1981	7.44
6	Brian Downing	1987	7.32
7	Brian Downing	1979	7.29
8	Don Baylor	1979	7.22
9	Albie Pearson	1961	7.08
10	Wally Joyner	1987	6.98
11	Tim Salmon	1993	6.98
12	Tim Salmon	1994	6.85
13	Bobby Grich	1979	6.82
14	Reggie Jackson	1982	6.77
15	Tim Salmon	1996	6.73
16	Darin Erstad	1997	6.69
17	Doug DeCinces	1982	6.66
18	Wally Joyner	1991	6.65
19	Chili Davis	1996	6.63
20	Leon Wagner	1961	6.58

Batting Average

(minimum 3.1 Plate Appearances/Tm Gm)

1	Rod Carew	1983	.339
2	Rod Carew	1980	.331
3	Tim Salmon	1995	.330
4	Alex Johnson	1970	.329
5	Brian Downing	1979	.326
6	Rod Carew	1982	.319
7	Chili Davis	1995	.318
8	Chili Davis	1994	.311
9	Johnny Ray	1988	.306
10	Rod Carew	1981	.305
11	Albie Pearson	1963	.304
12	Bobby Grich	1981	.304
13	Garret Anderson	1997	.303
14	Wally Joyner	1991	.301
15	Doug DeCinces	1982	.301
16	Fred Lynn	1982	.299
17	Darin Erstad	1997	.299
18	Luis Polonia	1991	.296
19	Don Baylor	1979	.296
20	Lyman Bostock	1978	.296

On-Base Percentage

(minimum 3.1 Plate Appearances/Tm Gm)

1	Tim Salmon	1995	.429
2	Chili Davis	1995	.429
3	Albie Pearson	1961	.420
4	Brian Downing	1979	.418
5	Chili Davis	1994	.410
6	Rod Carew	1983	.409
7	Albie Pearson	1963	.402
8	Brian Downing	1987	.400
9	Rod Carew	1980	.396
10	Rod Carew	1982	.396
11	Tim Salmon	1997	.394
12	Tony Phillips	1995	.394
13	Brian Downing	1986	.389
14	Chili Davis	1996	.387
15	Tim Salmon	1996	.386
16	Tim Salmon	1993	.382
17	Tim Salmon	1994	.382
18	Rod Carew	1981	.380
19	Reggie Jackson	1986	.379
20	Bobby Grich	1981	.378

Slugging Percentage

(minimum 3.1 Plate Appearances/Tm Gm)

1	Tim Salmon	1995	.594
2	Chili Davis	1994	.561
3	Doug DeCinces	1982	.548
4	Bobby Grich	1981	.543
5	Bobby Grich	1979	.537
6	Tim Salmon	1993	.536
7	Jim Edmonds	1995	.536
8	Reggie Jackson	1982	.532
9	Tim Salmon	1994	.531
10	Don Baylor	1979	.530
11	Wally Joyner	1987	.528
12	Bobby Bonds	1977	.520
13	Tim Salmon	1997	.517
14	Fred Lynn	1982	.517
15	Leon Wagner	1961	.517
16	Chili Davis	1995	.514
17	Tim Salmon	1996	.501
18	Leon Wagner	1962	.500
	Jim Edmonds	1997	.500
20	Chili Davis	1996	.496

Angels Franchise Pitching Leaders—Single Season

Wins

1	Clyde Wright	1970	22
	Nolan Ryan	1974	22
3	Nolan Ryan	1973	21
4	Dean Chance	1964	20
	Andy Messersmith	1971	20
	Bill Singer	1973	20
7	Nolan Ryan	1972	19
	Frank Tanana	1976	19
	Nolan Ryan	1977	19
	Mark Langston	1991	19
11	Clyde Wright	1972	18
	Frank Tanana	1978	18
	Geoff Zahn	1982	18
	Mike Witt	1986	18
	Chuck Finley	1990	18
	Chuck Finley	1991	18
	Jim Abbott	1991	18
18	Nolan Ryan	1976	17
	Kirk McCaskill	1986	17
	Bert Blyleven	1989	17

Losses

1	George Brunet	1967	19
	Clyde Wright	1973	19
	Frank Tanana	1974	19
	Kirk McCaskill	1991	19
5	Dean Chance	1963	18
	Nolan Ryan	1976	18
	Jim Abbott	1996	18
8	Dean Chance	1966	17
	George Brunet	1968	17
	Tom Murphy	1971	17
	Clyde Wright	1971	17
	Rudy May	1973	17
	Mark Langston	1990	17
14	Ten tied at		16

Winning Percentage
(minimum 15 decisions)

1	Bert Blyleven	1989	.773
2	Mark Langston	1991	.704
3	Geoff Zahn	1982	.692
4	Dean Chance	1964	.690
5	Ken McBride	1962	.688
	Mark Clear	1979	.688
	Bruce Kison	1983	.688
8	Chuck Finley	1997	.684
9	Mark Langston	1995	.682
10	Bruce Kison	1982	.667
	Chuck Finley	1990	.667
	Chuck Finley	1991	.667
13	Frank Tanana	1976	.655
14	Jack Sanford	1966	.650
15	Clyde Wright	1970	.647
	Steve Renko	1982	.647
17	Mike Witt	1986	.643
18	Frank Tanana	1975	.640
	Chuck Finley	1989	.640
20	Chris Knapp	1978	.636

Games

1	Minnie Rojas	1967	72
2	Mark Eichhorn	1991	70
3	Bob Lee	1965	69
	Bill Kelso	1967	69
	Mike James	1996	69
6	Eddie Fisher	1970	67
	Bryan Harvey	1991	67
8	Mike Holtz	1997	66
9	Donnie Moore	1985	65
10	Bob Lee	1964	64
11	Ken Tatum	1970	62
	Greg Minton	1989	62
	Bob Patterson	1995	62
	Troy Percival	1995	62
	Troy Percival	1996	62
16	Bob Lee	1966	61
	Pep Harris	1997	61
18	Mark Eichhorn	1990	60
19	Tom Morgan	1961	59
	Dave LaRoche	1978	59

Games Started

1	Nolan Ryan	1974	41
2	Bill Singer	1973	40
3	Clyde Wright	1970	39
	Nolan Ryan	1972	39
	Nolan Ryan	1973	39
	Nolan Ryan	1976	39
7	Tom Murphy	1970	38
	Andy Messersmith	1971	38
9	Dean Chance	1966	37
	George Brunet	1967	37
	Clyde Wright	1971	37
	Nolan Ryan	1977	37
13	Ken McBride	1961	36
	Ken McBride	1963	36
	Fred Newman	1965	36
	George Brunet	1968	36
	Tom Murphy	1971	36
	Clyde Wright	1973	36
	Mike Witt	1987	36
20	Eleven tied at		35

Complete Games

1	Nolan Ryan	1973	26
	Nolan Ryan	1974	26
3	Frank Tanana	1976	23
4	Nolan Ryan	1977	22
5	Nolan Ryan	1976	21
6	Nolan Ryan	1972	20
	Frank Tanana	1977	20
8	Bill Singer	1973	19
9	Nolan Ryan	1979	17
10	Ed Figueroa	1975	16
	Frank Tanana	1975	16
12	Dean Chance	1964	15
	Clyde Wright	1972	15
14	Andy Messersmith	1971	14
	Nolan Ryan	1978	14
	Mike Witt	1986	14
17	Clyde Wright	1973	13
	Chuck Finley	1993	13
19	Five tied at		12

Shutouts

1	Dean Chance	1964	11
2	Nolan Ryan	1972	9
3	Nolan Ryan	1976	7
	Frank Tanana	1977	7
5	Jim McGlothlin	1967	6
6	George Brunet	1968	5
	Nolan Ryan	1975	5
	Frank Tanana	1975	5
	Nolan Ryan	1979	5
	Geoff Zahn	1984	5
	Bert Blyleven	1989	5
12	Twelve tied at		4

Saves

1	Bryan Harvey	1991	46
2	Lee Smith	1995	37
3	Troy Percival	1996	36
4	Donnie Moore	1985	31
5	Minnie Rojas	1967	27
	Troy Percival	1997	27
7	Dave LaRoche	1978	25
	Bryan Harvey	1989	25
	Bryan Harvey	1990	25
10	Bob Lee	1965	23
11	Ken Tatum	1969	22
12	Donnie Moore	1986	21
	Joe Grahe	1992	21
14	Bob Lee	1964	19
15	Ken Tatum	1970	17
	DeWayne Buice	1987	17
	Bryan Harvey	1988	17
18	Bob Lee	1966	16
19	Lloyd Allen	1971	15
20	Mark Clear	1979	14

Innings Pitched

1	Nolan Ryan	1974	332.2
2	Nolan Ryan	1973	326.0
3	Bill Singer	1973	315.2
4	Nolan Ryan	1977	299.0
5	Frank Tanana	1976	288.1
6	Nolan Ryan	1976	284.1
7	Nolan Ryan	1972	284.0
8	Dean Chance	1964	278.1
9	Andy Messersmith	1971	276.2
	Clyde Wright	1971	276.2
11	Mike Witt	1986	269.0
12	Frank Tanana	1974	268.2
13	Fred Newman	1965	260.2
	Clyde Wright	1970	260.2
15	Dean Chance	1966	259.2
16	Frank Tanana	1975	257.1
17	Clyde Wright	1973	257.0
18	Mark Langston	1993	256.1
19	Chuck Finley	1993	251.1
20	Two tied at		251.0

Walks

1	Nolan Ryan	1977	204
2	Nolan Ryan	1974	202
3	Nolan Ryan	1976	183
4	Nolan Ryan	1973	162
5	Nolan Ryan	1972	157
6	Nolan Ryan	1978	148
7	Nolan Ryan	1975	132
8	Bill Singer	1973	130
9	Bo Belinsky	1962	122
10	Andy Messersmith	1971	121
11	Eli Grba	1961	114
	Dean Chance	1966	114
	Nolan Ryan	1979	114
14	George Brunet	1966	106
15	Mark Langston	1990	104
16	Ken McBride	1961	102
17	Dean Chance	1965	101
	Chuck Finley	1991	101
19	Andy Messersmith	1969	100
20	Two tied at		98

Strikeouts

1	Nolan Ryan	1973	383
2	Nolan Ryan	1974	367
3	Nolan Ryan	1977	341
4	Nolan Ryan	1972	329
5	Nolan Ryan	1976	327
6	Frank Tanana	1975	269
7	Frank Tanana	1976	261
8	Nolan Ryan	1978	260
9	Bill Singer	1973	241
10	Nolan Ryan	1979	223
11	Chuck Finley	1996	215
12	Andy Messersmith	1969	211
13	Mike Witt	1986	208
14	Dean Chance	1964	207
15	Frank Tanana	1977	205
16	Kirk McCaskill	1986	202
17	Mike Witt	1984	196
	Mark Langston	1993	196
19	Mark Langston	1990	195
	Chuck Finley	1995	195

Strikeouts/9 Innings
(minimum 1 Inning Pitched/Tm Gm)

1	Nolan Ryan	1973	10.57
2	Nolan Ryan	1972	10.43
3	Nolan Ryan	1976	10.35
4	Nolan Ryan	1977	10.26
5	Nolan Ryan	1978	9.97
6	Nolan Ryan	1974	9.93
7	Frank Tanana	1975	9.41
8	Nolan Ryan	1979	9.01
9	Chuck Finley	1995	8.65
10	Chuck Finley	1997	8.51
11	Nolan Ryan	1975	8.45
12	Mark Langston	1994	8.22
13	Frank Tanana	1976	8.15
14	Chuck Finley	1996	8.13
15	Mark Langston	1990	7.87
16	Frank Tanana	1977	7.65
17	Andy Messersmith	1969	7.60
18	Andy Messersmith	1972	7.53
19	Andy Messersmith	1970	7.49
20	Rudy May	1972	7.41

ERA
(minimum 1 Inning Pitched/Tm Gm)

1	Dean Chance	1964	1.65
2	Nolan Ryan	1972	2.28
3	Chuck Finley	1990	2.40
4	Frank Tanana	1976	2.43
5	Andy Messersmith	1969	2.52
6	Frank Tanana	1977	2.54
7	George Brunet	1965	2.56
8	Chuck Finley	1989	2.57
9	Rickey Clark	1967	2.59
10	Frank Tanana	1975	2.62
11	Bert Blyleven	1989	2.73
12	Fred Newman	1964	2.75
13	Paul Hartzell	1976	2.77
14	Nolan Ryan	1977	2.77
15	Jim Abbott	1992	2.77
16	Andy Messersmith	1972	2.81
17	Clyde Wright	1970	2.83
18	Mike Witt	1986	2.84
19	George Brunet	1968	2.86
20	Nolan Ryan	1973	2.87

Component ERA
(minimum 1 Inning Pitched/Tm Gm)

1	Dean Chance	1964	1.76
2	Frank Tanana	1976	2.16
3	Andy Messersmith	1969	2.23
4	Andy Messersmith	1972	2.24
5	George Brunet	1965	2.28
6	Nolan Ryan	1972	2.28
7	George Brunet	1968	2.46
8	Clyde Wright	1971	2.49
9	Fred Newman	1965	2.50
10	Mike Witt	1986	2.55
11	Jim McGlothlin	1967	2.59
12	Ken Forsch	1981	2.65
13	Rudy May	1971	2.65
14	Frank Tanana	1975	2.69
15	Frank Tanana	1977	2.70
16	Fred Newman	1964	2.71
17	Rudy May	1972	2.72
18	Bert Blyleven	1989	2.77
19	George Brunet	1967	2.78
20	Nolan Ryan	1973	2.78

Opponent Average
(minimum 1 Inning Pitched/Tm Gm)

1	Nolan Ryan	1972	.171
2	Nolan Ryan	1974	.190
3	Andy Messersmith	1969	.190
4	Nolan Ryan	1977	.193
5	Nolan Ryan	1976	.195
6	Dean Chance	1964	.195
7	Nolan Ryan	1973	.203
8	Frank Tanana	1976	.203
9	Andy Messersmith	1970	.205
10	Andy Messersmith	1972	.207
11	George Brunet	1965	.209
12	Nolan Ryan	1979	.212
13	Rudy May	1971	.213
14	Nolan Ryan	1975	.213
15	Mark Langston	1991	.215
16	George Brunet	1968	.215
17	Rudy May	1972	.215
18	Bo Belinsky	1962	.216
19	Andy Messersmith	1971	.218
20	Ken McBride	1963	.218

Opponent OBP
(minimum 1 Inning Pitched/Tm Gm)

1	Dean Chance	1964	.260
2	Frank Tanana	1976	.261
3	George Brunet	1968	.270
4	Andy Messersmith	1969	.274
5	Mike Witt	1986	.275
6	George Brunet	1965	.280
7	Fred Newman	1965	.282
8	Clyde Wright	1971	.283
9	Frank Tanana	1977	.284
10	Jim McGlothlin	1967	.284
11	Ken Forsch	1981	.286
12	Frank Tanana	1975	.286
13	Bert Blyleven	1989	.287
14	Don Sutton	1986	.287
15	Andy Messersmith	1972	.288
16	Andy Messersmith	1970	.289
17	Ken McBride	1963	.291
18	Fred Newman	1964	.291
19	Nolan Ryan	1972	.291
20	Mark Langston	1991	.291

Angels Capsule

Best Season: *1979.* The Angels won the American League West with an 88-74 record, advancing to the postseason for the first time in the history of the franchise. Their loss to the Orioles in the ALCS was far less heartbreaking than their later ALCS failures in 1982 and 1986.

Worst Season: *1980.* Nolan Ryan left via free agency after the Angels were either unwilling or unable to re-sign him (GM Buzzie Bavasi, citing Ryan's 16-14 record the year before, opined that the Angels could easily replace Ryan with a couple of 8-7 pitchers), and a number of serious injuries weakened the club further. They lost 95 games and tumbled all the way to sixth place.

Best Player: *Bobby Grich.* His power, walks and defense made him one of the top second basemen in baseball over a five-year stretch. Shortstop Jim Fregosi was comparable; Grich was better, but had fewer productive seasons with the club. Brian Downing was a valuable hitter for many years.

Best Pitcher: *Nolan Ryan,* and not just for the strikeouts. He also contributed hundreds of innings year after year, and posted superior won-lost records despite a supporting cast that was generally weak.

Best Reliever: *Bryan Harvey.* Bob Lee and Troy Percival were equally dominant for slightly shorter stretches. Percival may ultimately move ahead of Harvey.

Best Defensive Player: *Devon White.* His predecessor in center field, Gary Pettis, was brilliant also.

Hall of Famers: *Nolan Ryan* spent eight years with the Angels and nine with Houston, but after all he accomplished in Anaheim, the Angels have just as much right to claim Ryan as one of their own as the Astros do. *Rod Carew* spent the final seven years of his career with California as well.

Franchise All-Star Team:

C	Bob Boone		**LF**	Brian Downing
1B	Rod Carew		**CF**	Jim Edmonds
2B	Bobby Grich		**RF**	Tim Salmon
3B	Doug DeCinces		**DH**	Don Baylor
SS	Jim Fregosi		**SP**	Nolan Ryan
			RP	Bryan Harvey

Biggest Flake: *Bo Belinsky.* A notorious partier and womanizer, Belinsky pursued starlets on the Hollywood club circuit with abandon and appeared on several TV shows. He regarded his baseball career as a convenient way to meet women.

Strangest Career: *"Wonderful Willie" Smith.* The southpaw was a remarkable two-way player in the minors, going 54-27 on the mound while batting .275 as a pinch-hitter and part-time outfielder. In the International League in 1963, he went 14-2, 2.11 while batting .380 in 79 at-bats. He was promoted to Detroit later in the year and traded to the Angels early in 1964. He began the year pitching out of the bullpen, but when he was given a few opportunities to pinch-hit, he proved so successful that he ultimately won a full-time job in the outfield. He finished the year with a .301 batting average in 359 at-bats and a 2.84 ERA in 31.2 innings—surely one of the best two-way performances since Babe Ruth. He played regularly for one more season and then spent six years as a backup outfielder, performing for several clubs. He also made three more mound appearances and didn't allow a single earned run.

What Might Have Been: *Frank Tanana.* The fireballing southpaw fanned 180 batters at age 20 in his first full season, 1974. The following season, he led the league with 269 strikeouts. He won 19 games the year after that, and led the league in ERA in 1977. In June 1978, he was pitching as well as ever with an 11-3 record when he developed a sore arm. His velocity dropped and his effectiveness fell off dramatically, but he kept taking his regular turn for the rest of the year. He never would be the same. After missing half of '79 and faring poorly in 1980, he was traded to the Red Sox, and then to the Rangers, where he struggled to succeed as a finesse pitcher. He had a breakthrough of sorts in 1984, and the Tigers acquired him in June of the following year. He remained a reliable, if unspectacular performer for many years before retiring in 1993 at age 40. It was a credit to his persistence that he was able to win 163 games after injuring his arm, but those who saw him pitch in his prime still wonder what he might of done if he hadn't gotten hurt so early on.

Best Trade: *Nolan Ryan.* It was one of the best trades of all time. In the winter of 1971, the Angels got Ryan and three players from the Mets for Jim Fregosi, who was all but finished as a shortstop.

Worst Trade: *Carney Lansford.* The Angels traded Lansford and two players to the Red Sox for shortstop Rick Burleson and change in the winter of 1980. Burleson played only one season before his career was virtually ended by a torn rotator cuff, while Lansford won the batting title in his first season in Boston and played regularly for another decade. Another unfortunate consequence of the trade was the crowding out of young shortstop Dickie Thon, who was traded to the Astros a few months later.

Best-Looking Player: *Tim Salmon.*

Ugliest Player: *Mike Witt.* Long, tall and ugly.

Best Nickname: *Leon "Daddy Wags" Wagner.*

Most Unappreciated Player: *Bobby Grich.* He never got his due, because his strengths weren't as obvious as a .320 batting average. Grich played good defense at a key defensive position, drew walks, and hit for both power and average. He had no real weaknesses. His production wasn't spectacular by normal standards, but by a second baseman's standards it was excellent. He led major league second basemen in RBI for three straight years from 1979 through 1981. His greatness also was obscured by the presence of stars like Reggie Jackson, Don Baylor, Fred Lynn and Rod Carew.

Most Overrated Player: *Garret Anderson.* A left fielder cannot live on batting average alone.

Most Admirable Star: *Nolan Ryan.*

Least Admirable Star: *Tony Phillips.* In a pennant race, the veterans must be able to teach the youngsters how not to crack under pressure.

Best Season, Player: *Tim Salmon, 1995.* He finished third in the AL with a .330 average and swatted 34 home runs while playing a solid right field. Grich had a very good year in '81, tying for the AL lead in home runs (the first second baseman since Nap Lajoie to lead the league) and topping the loop with a .543 slugging percentage. Baylor won the MVP in 1979, but he won it almost entirely on the strength of his 139 RBI, and had very little defensive value.

Best Season, Pitcher: *Nolan Ryan, 1974.* He broke the strikeout record in 1973, but the following year he won 22 games for a club that went 47-78 without him. With a contending club, he might have had a shot at winning 30 games.

Most Impressive Individual Record: *Nolan Ryan.* His ultimately successful pursuit of the modern single-season strikeout record in 1973 was one of the best sports stories of the last 30 years.

Biggest Tragedies: *Lyman Bostock, Donnie Moore.* Bostock was shot to death in 1978, only days before he was to complete his first season with the Angels. In the 1986 ALCS, the Angels were one strike away from their first World Series appearance when Moore surrendered a historic home run to Dave Henderson. The Angels ultimately lost both the game and the Championship Series, and Moore never recovered. In 1989, he shot and wounded his wife before turning the gun on himself. Shortstop Mike Miley was killed in a car accident in 1977 after playing parts of two seasons with the club. Rookie pitcher Dick Wantz died of a brain tumor in 1965.

Fan Favorite: *Wally Joyner.*

—Mat Olkin

St. Louis Browns/Baltimore Orioles (1901-1997)

														Opponent				Park Index	
Year	Lg	Pos	W-L	Pct	GB	Manager	Att.	R	OR	HR	Avg	OBP	Slg	HR	Avg	OBP	ERA	Runs	HR
1901	AL	8th	48-89	.350	35.5	Hugh Duffy	139,034	641	828	26	.261	.314	.345	32	.283	.345	4.06	93	99
1902	AL	2nd	78-58	.574	5.0	Jimmy McAleer	272,283	619	607	29	.265	.323	.353	36	.264	.319	3.34	103	81
1903	AL	6th	65-74	.468	26.5	Jimmy McAleer	380,405	500	525	12	.244	.290	.317	26	.258	.299	2.77	86	136
1904	AL	6th	65-87	.428	29.0	Jimmy McAleer	318,108	481	604	10	.239	.291	.294	25	.253	.305	2.83	94	86
1905	AL	8th	54-99	.353	40.5	Jimmy McAleer	339,112	511	608	16	.232	.288	.289	19	.244	.305	2.74	87	53
1906	AL	5th	76-73	.510	16.0	Jimmy McAleer	389,157	558	498	20	.247	.304	.312	14	.230	.285	2.23	90	212
1907	AL	6th	69-83	.454	24.0	Jimmy McAleer	419,025	542	555	10	.253	.308	.313	17	.247	.303	2.61	91	170
1908	AL	4th	83-69	.546	6.5	Jimmy McAleer	618,947	544	483	20	.245	.296	.310	7	.230	.294	2.15	102	105
1909	AL	7th	61-89	.407	36.0	Jimmy McAleer	366,274	441	575	10	.232	.287	.279	16	.258	.316	2.88	84	59
1910	AL	8th	47-107	.305	57.0	Jack O'Connor	249,889	451	743	12	.218	.281	.274	14	.265	.341	3.09	97	30
1911	AL	8th	45-107	.296	56.5	Bobby Wallace	207,984	567	812	17	.239	.307	.311	28	.278	.342	3.86	96	58
1912	AL	7th	53-101	.344	53.0	Bobby Wallace/George Stovall	214,070	552	764	19	.248	.315	.320	17	.277	.341	3.71	102	89
1913	AL	8th	57-96	.373	39.0	G. Stovall/J. Austin/B. Rickey	250,330	528	642	18	.237	.306	.312	21	.266	.332	3.06	89	158
1914	AL	5th	71-82	.464	28.5	Branch Rickey	244,714	523	615	17	.243	.306	.319	20	.251	.327	2.85	96	200
1915	AL	6th	63-91	.409	39.5	Branch Rickey	150,358	521	680	19	.246	.315	.315	21	.249	.338	3.04	95	53
1916	AL	5th	79-75	.513	12.0	Fielder Jones	335,740	588	545	14	.245	.331	.307	15	.248	.316	2.58	87	142
1917	AL	7th	57-97	.370	43.0	Fielder Jones	210,486	511	687	15	.246	.305	.315	19	.255	.329	3.20	97	113
1918	AL	5th	58-64	.475	15.0	F. Jones/J. Austin/J. Burke	122,076	426	448	5	.259	.331	.320	11	.246	.319	2.75	97	130
1919	AL	5th	67-72	.482	20.5	Jimmy Burke	349,350	533	567	31	.264	.326	.355	35	.263	.328	3.13	91	173
1920	AL	4th	76-77	.497	21.5	Jimmy Burke	419,311	797	766	50	.308	.363	.419	53	.277	.352	4.03	126	158
1921	AL	3rd	81-73	.526	17.5	Lee Fohl	355,978	835	845	67	.304	.357	.425	71	.288	.359	4.61	104	160
1922	AL	2nd	93-61	.604	1.0	Lee Fohl	712,918	867	643	98	.313	.372	.455	71	.268	.327	3.38	108	191
1923	AL	5th	74-78	.487	24.0	Lee Fohl/Jimmy Austin	430,296	688	720	82	.281	.339	.398	59	.275	.348	3.93	111	194
1924	AL	4th	74-78	.487	17.0	George Sisler	533,349	769	809	67	.295	.356	.408	68	.287	.356	4.57	120	216
1925	AL	3rd	82-71	.536	15.0	George Sisler	462,898	900	906	110	.298	.360	.439	99	.299	.381	4.92	124	229
1926	AL	7th	62-92	.403	29.0	George Sisler	283,986	682	845	72	.276	.335	.394	86	.297	.379	4.66	106	271
1927	AL	7th	59-94	.386	50.5	Dan Howley	247,879	724	904	55	.276	.337	.380	79	.297	.371	4.95	124	287
1928	AL	3rd	82-72	.532	19.0	Dan Howley	339,497	772	742	63	.274	.347	.393	93	.273	.331	4.17	108	280
1929	AL	4th	79-73	.520	26.0	Dan Howley	280,697	733	713	46	.276	.352	.381	100	.280	.340	4.08	94	118
1930	AL	6th	64-90	.416	38.0	Bill Killefer	152,088	751	886	75	.268	.333	.391	124	.300	.356	5.07	121	113
1931	AL	5th	63-91	.409	45.0	Bill Killefer	179,126	722	870	76	.271	.333	.390	84	.293	.348	4.76	109	129
1932	AL	6th	63-91	.409	44.0	Bill Killefer	112,558	736	898	67	.276	.339	.388	103	.290	.359	5.01	104	162
1933	AL	8th	55-96	.364	43.5	B. Killefer/A. Sothoron/R. Hornsby	88,113	669	820	64	.253	.322	.360	96	.289	.354	4.82	138	224
1934	AL	6th	67-85	.441	33.0	Rogers Hornsby	115,305	674	800	62	.268	.335	.373	94	.283	.361	4.49	110	160
1935	AL	7th	65-87	.428	28.5	Rogers Hornsby	80,922	718	930	73	.270	.344	.384	92	.297	.371	5.26	120	109
1936	AL	7th	57-95	.375	44.5	Rogers Hornsby	93,267	804	1064	79	.279	.356	.403	115	.314	.385	6.24	120	138
1937	AL	8th	46-108	.299	56.0	Rogers Hornsby/Jim Bottomley	123,121	715	1023	71	.285	.348	.399	143	.316	.391	6.00	110	115
1938	AL	7th	55-97	.362	44.0	Gabby Street/Oscar Melillo	130,417	755	962	92	.281	.355	.397	132	.295	.382	5.80	109	109
1939	AL	8th	43-111	.279	64.5	Fred Haney	109,159	733	1035	91	.268	.339	.381	133	.310	.393	6.01	112	131
1940	AL	6th	67-87	.435	23.0	Fred Haney	239,591	757	882	118	.263	.333	.401	113	.290	.367	5.12	119	147
1941	AL	6th	70-84	.455	31.0	Fred Haney/Luke Sewell	176,240	765	823	91	.266	.360	.390	120	.283	.351	4.72	105	113
1942	AL	3rd	82-69	.543	19.5	Luke Sewell	255,617	730	637	98	.259	.338	.385	63	.262	.330	3.59	109	128
1943	AL	6th	72-80	.474	25.0	Luke Sewell	214,392	596	604	78	.245	.322	.349	74	.263	.327	3.41	100	187
1944	AL	1st	89-65	.578	—	Luke Sewell	508,644	684	587	72	.252	.323	.352	58	.259	.320	3.17	101	113
1945	AL	3rd	81-70	.536	6.0	Luke Sewell	482,986	597	548	63	.249	.316	.341	59	.249	.316	3.14	134	119
1946	AL	7th	66-88	.429	38.0	Luke Sewell/Zack Taylor	526,435	621	710	84	.251	.313	.356	73	.272	.343	3.95	100	94
1947	AL	8th	59-95	.383	38.0	Muddy Ruel	320,474	564	744	90	.241	.320	.350	103	.272	.348	4.33	111	130
1948	AL	6th	59-94	.386	37.0	Zack Taylor	335,564	671	849	63	.271	.345	.378	103	.283	.373	5.01	117	129
1949	AL	7th	53-101	.344	44.0	Zack Taylor	270,936	667	913	117	.254	.339	.377	113	.294	.377	5.21	108	119
1950	AL	7th	58-96	.377	40.0	Zack Taylor	247,131	684	916	106	.246	.337	.370	129	.295	.372	5.20	123	115
1951	AL	8th	52-102	.338	46.0	Zack Taylor	293,790	611	882	86	.247	.317	.357	131	.282	.379	5.18	120	97
1952	AL	7th	64-90	.416	31.0	Rogers Hornsby/Marty Marion	518,796	604	733	82	.250	.321	.356	111	.260	.339	4.12	100	105
1953	AL	8th	54-100	.351	46.5	Marty Marion	297,238	555	778	112	.249	.317	.363	101	.273	.351	4.48	120	134
1954	AL	7th	54-100	.351	57.0	Jimmy Dykes	1,060,910	483	668	52	.251	.313	.338	78	.250	.338	3.88	91	48
1955	AL	7th	57-97	.370	39.0	Paul Richards	852,039	540	754	54	.240	.314	.320	103	.266	.344	4.21	82	57
1956	AL	6th	69-85	.448	28.0	Paul Richards	901,201	571	705	91	.244	.320	.350	99	.264	.334	4.20	86	64
1957	AL	5th	76-76	.500	21.0	Paul Richards	1,029,581	597	588	87	.252	.318	.353	95	.243	.310	3.46	83	58
1958	AL	6th	74-79	.484	17.5	Paul Richards	829,991	521	575	108	.241	.308	.350	106	.249	.306	3.40	84	61
1959	AL	6th	74-80	.481	20.0	Paul Richards	891,926	551	621	109	.238	.310	.345	111	.246	.311	3.56	91	88
1960	AL	2nd	89-65	.578	8.0	Paul Richards	1,187,849	682	606	123	.253	.332	.377	117	.241	.317	3.52	100	74
1961	AL	3rd	95-67	.586	14.0	Paul Richards/Lum Harris	951,089	691	588	149	.254	.326	.390	109	.227	.308	3.22	89	71
1962	AL	7th	77-85	.475	19.0	Billy Hitchcock	790,254	652	680	156	.248	.314	.387	147	.249	.318	3.69	87	74
1963	AL	4th	86-76	.531	18.5	Billy Hitchcock	774,343	644	621	146	.249	.310	.380	137	.248	.314	3.45	84	83
1964	AL	3rd	97-65	.599	2.0	Hank Bauer	1,116,215	679	567	162	.248	.316	.387	129	.239	.300	3.16	108	97
1965	AL	3rd	94-68	.580	8.0	Hank Bauer	781,649	641	578	125	.238	.307	.363	120	.233	.300	2.98	97	125
1966	AL	1st	97-63	.606	—	Hank Bauer	1,203,366	755	601	175	.258	.324	.409	127	.233	.301	3.32	100	101
1967	AL	6th	76-85	.472	15.5	Hank Bauer	955,053	654	592	138	.240	.310	.372	116	.228	.304	3.32	88	87
1968	AL	2nd	91-71	.562	12.0	Hank Bauer/Earl Weaver	943,977	579	497	133	.225	.304	.352	101	.212	.285	2.66	102	93
1969	AL	1st-E	109-53	.673	—	Earl Weaver	1,062,069	779	517	175	.265	.343	.414	117	.223	.290	2.83	102	84
1970	AL	1st-E	108-54	.667	—	Earl Weaver	1,057,069	792	574	179	.257	.344	.401	139	.240	.300	3.15	89	85
1971	AL	1st-E	101-57	.639	—	Earl Weaver	1,023,037	742	530	158	.261	.347	.398	125	.239	.295	2.99	103	111
1972	AL	3rd-E	80-74	.519	5.0	Earl Weaver	899,950	519	430	100	.229	.302	.339	85	.224	.282	2.53	91	83
1973	AL	1st-E	97-65	.599	—	Earl Weaver	958,667	754	561	119	.266	.345	.389	124	.240	.302	3.07	111	103
1974	AL	1st-E	91-71	.562	—	Earl Weaver	962,572	659	612	116	.256	.322	.370	101	.253	.314	3.27	82	76
1975	AL	2nd-E	90-69	.566	4.5	Earl Weaver	1,002,157	682	553	124	.252	.326	.373	110	.242	.306	3.17	76	68
1976	AL	2nd-E	88-74	.543	10.5	Earl Weaver	1,058,609	619	598	119	.243	.310	.358	80	.255	.315	3.32	93	93
1977	AL	2nd-E	97-64	.602	2.5	Earl Weaver	1,195,769	719	653	148	.261	.329	.393	124	.260	.322	3.74	83	99
1978	AL	4th-E	90-71	.559	9.0	Earl Weaver	1,051,724	659	633	154	.258	.326	.396	107	.251	.316	3.56	79	79
1979	AL	1st-E	102-57	.642	—	Earl Weaver	1,681,009	757	582	181	.261	.336	.419	133	.241	.301	3.26	89	72
1980	AL	2nd-E	100-62	.617	3.0	Earl Weaver	1,797,438	805	640	156	.273	.342	.413	134	.261	.323	3.64	98	116
1981	AL	2nd-E	31-23	.574	2.0	Earl Weaver													
	AL	4th-E	28-23	.549	2.0	Earl Weaver	1,024,247	429	437	88	.251	.329	.379	83	.260	.326	3.70	97	116

Year	Lg	Pos	W-L	Pct	GB	Manager	Att.	R	OR	HR	Avg	OBP	Slg	Opponent HR	Avg	OBP	ERA	Park Index Runs	HR
1982	AL	2nd-E	94-68	.580	1.0	Earl Weaver	1,613,031	774	687	179	.266	.341	.419	147	.257	.317	3.99	99	114
1983	AL	1st-E	98-64	.605	—	Joe Altobelli	2,042,071	799	652	168	.269	.340	.421	130	.261	.316	3.63	98	95
1984	AL	5th-E	85-77	.525	19.0	Joe Altobelli	2,045,784	681	667	160	.252	.328	.391	137	.256	.320	3.71	86	90
1985	AL	4th-E	83-78	.516	16.0	Joe Altobelli/Cal Ripken/Earl Weaver	2,132,387	818	764	214	.263	.336	.430	160	.270	.338	4.38	98	102
1986	AL	7th-E	73-89	.451	22.5	Earl Weaver	1,973,176	708	760	169	.258	.327	.395	177	.263	.328	4.30	98	126
1987	AL	6th-E	67-95	.414	31.0	Cal Ripken	1,835,692	729	880	211	.258	.322	.418	226	.277	.341	5.01	98	113
1988	AL	7th-E	54-107	.335	34.5	Cal Ripken/Frank Robinson	1,660,738	550	789	137	.238	.305	.359	153	.274	.340	4.54	93	104
1989	AL	2nd-E	87-75	.537	2.0	Frank Robinson	2,535,208	708	686	129	.252	.326	.379	134	.272	.331	4.00	97	92
1990	AL	5th-E	76-85	.472	11.5	Frank Robinson	2,415,189	669	698	132	.245	.330	.370	161	.264	.328	4.04	94	115
1991	AL	6th-E	67-95	.414	24.0	Frank Robinson/Johnny Oates	2,552,753	686	796	170	.254	.319	.401	147	.273	.333	4.59	93	92
1992	AL	3rd-E	89-73	.549	7.0	Johnny Oates	3,567,819	705	656	148	.259	.340	.398	124	.257	.322	3.79	98	113
1993	AL	3rd-E	85-77	.525	10.0	Johnny Oates	3,644,965	786	745	157	.267	.346	.413	153	.261	.333	4.31	111	118
1994	AL	2nd-E	63-49	.563	6.5	Johnny Oates	2,535,359	589	497	139	.272	.349	.438	131	.263	.327	4.31	113	120
1995	AL	3rd-E	71-73	.493	15.0	Phil Regan	3,098,475	704	640	173	.262	.342	.428	149	.245	.322	4.31	103	118
1996	AL	2nd-E	88-74	.543	4.0	Davey Johnson	3,646,950	949	903	257	.274	.350	.472	209	.280	.349	5.14	90	97
1997	AL	1st-E	98-64	.605	—	Davey Johnson	3,612,764	812	681	196	.268	.341	.429	164	.253	.323	3.91	98	120

Team Nicknames: Milwaukee Brewers 1901-1902, St. Louis Browns 1903-1954, Baltimore Orioles 1955-1997.

Team Ballparks: Lloyd Street Grounds 1901, Sportsman's Park II 1902-1908, Sportsman's Park III/Busch Stadium I 1909-1953, Memorial Stadium 1954-1991, Oriole Park at Camden Yards 1992-1997.

St. Louis Browns/Baltimore Orioles Individual Season Batting Leaders

Year	Batting Average		On-Base Percentage		Slugging Percentage		Home Runs		RBI		Stolen Bases	
1901	John Anderson	.330	John Anderson	.360	John Anderson	.476	John Anderson	8	John Anderson	99	John Anderson	35
1902	Charlie Hemphill	.317	Jesse Burkett	.390	Charlie Hemphill	.447	Charlie Hemphill	6	John Anderson	85	Jesse Burkett	23
											Charlie Hemphill	
1903	Jesse Burkett	.293	Jesse Burkett	.361	Emmett Heidrick	.395	Jesse Burkett	3	John Anderson	78	Emmett Heidrick	19
							Charlie Hemphill					
1904	Bobby Wallace	.275	Jesse Burkett	.363	Bobby Wallace	.355	4 tied with	2	Bobby Wallace	69	Emmett Heidrick	35
1905	George Stone	.296	George Stone	.347	George Stone	.410	George Stone	7	Bobby Wallace	59	George Stone	26
1906	George Stone	.358	George Stone	.417	George Stone	.501	George Stone	6	George Stone	71	George Stone	35
1907	George Stone	.320	George Stone	.387	George Stone	.408	George Stone	4	Bobby Wallace	70	Tom Jones	24
1908	George Stone	.281	George Stone	.345	George Stone	.369	George Stone	5	Hobe Ferris	74	Roy Hartzell	24
1909	Roy Hartzell	.271	Roy Hartzell	.312	Roy Hartzell	.308	Hobe Ferris	4	Hobe Ferris	58	Danny Hoffman	24
1910	Bobby Wallace	.258	Bobby Wallace	.324	George Stone	.329	4 tied with	2	George Stone	40	Frank Truesdale	29
1911	Frank LaPorte	.314	Frank LaPorte	.361	Frank LaPorte	.446	3 tied with	3	Frank LaPorte	82	Jimmy Austin	26
											Burt Shotton	
1912	Del Pratt	.302	Burt Shotton	.390	Del Pratt	.426	Del Pratt	5	Del Pratt	69	Burt Shotton	35
1913	Burt Shotton	.297	Burt Shotton	.405	Del Pratt	.402	Gus Williams	5	Del Pratt	87	Burt Shotton	43
1914	Tilly Walker	.298	Tilly Walker	.365	Tilly Walker	.441	Tilly Walker	6	Tilly Walker	78	Burt Shotton	40
1915	Del Pratt	.291	Burt Shotton	.409	Del Pratt	.394	Tilly Walker	5	Del Pratt	78	Burt Shotton	43
1916	George Sisler	.305	Burt Shotton	.392	George Sisler	.400	Del Pratt	5	Del Pratt	103	Armando Marsans	46
1917	George Sisler	.353	George Sisler	.390	George Sisler	.453	Baby Doll Jacobson	4	Hank Severeid	57	George Sisler	37
1918	George Sisler	.341	George Sisler	.400	George Sisler	.440	George Sisler	2	Ray Demmitt	61	George Sisler	45
1919	George Sisler	.352	George Sisler	.390	George Sisler	.530	George Sisler	10	George Sisler	83	George Sisler	28
1920	George Sisler	.407	George Sisler	.449	George Sisler	.632	George Sisler	19	Baby Doll Jacobson	122	George Sisler	42
									George Sisler			
1921	George Sisler	.371	Ken Williams	.429	Ken Williams	.561	Ken Williams	24	Ken Williams	117	George Sisler	35
1922	George Sisler	.420	George Sisler	.467	Ken Williams	.627	Ken Williams	39	Ken Williams	155	George Sisler	51
1923	Ken Williams	.357	Ken Williams	.439	Ken Williams	.623	Ken Williams	29	Marty McManus	94	Ken Williams	18
1924	Marty McManus	.333	Ken Williams	.425	Ken Williams	.533	Baby Doll Jacobson	19	Baby Doll Jacobson	97	Ken Williams	20
1925	George Sisler	.345	Baby Doll Jacobson	.392	Baby Doll Jacobson	.513	Ken Williams	25	George Sisler	105	George Sisler	11
									Ken Williams			
1926	Harry Rice	.313	Harry Rice	.384	Harry Rice	.441	Ken Williams	17	Ken Williams	74	George Sisler	12
1927	George Sisler	.327	Ken Williams	.405	Ken Williams	.527	Ken Williams	17	George Sisler	97	George Sisler	27
1928	Heinie Manush	.378	Heinie Manush	.414	Heinie Manush	.575	Lu Blue	14	Heinie Manush	108	Heinie Manush	17
1929	Heinie Manush	.355	Lu Blue	.422	Heinie Manush	.500	Red Kress	9	Red Kress	107	Frank O'Rourke	14
1930	Red Kress	.313	Red Kress	.366	Red Kress	.487	Goose Goslin	30	Red Kress	112	Ski Melillo	15
1931	Goose Goslin	.328	Goose Goslin	.412	Goose Goslin	.555	Goose Goslin	24	Red Kress	114	Jack Burns	19
1932	Rick Ferrell	.315	Rick Ferrell	.406	Goose Goslin	.469	Goose Goslin	17	Goose Goslin	104	Jack Burns	17
1933	Sammy West	.300	Sammy West	.373	Sammy West	.458	Bruce Campbell	16	Bruce Campbell	106	Ski Melillo	12
1934	Sammy West	.326	Sammy West	.403	Sammy West	.469	Harlond Clift	14	Roy Pepper	101	Jack Burns	9
1935	Moose Solters	.330	Harlond Clift	.406	Moose Solters	.520	Moose Solters	18	Moose Solters	104	Lyn Lary	25
1936	Beau Bell	.344	Harlond Clift	.424	Harlond Clift	.514	Harlond Clift	20	Moose Solters	134	Lyn Lary	37
1937	Beau Bell	.340	Harlond Clift	.413	Harlond Clift	.546	Harlond Clift	29	Harlond Clift	118	Harlond Clift	8
1938	George McQuinn	.324	Harlond Clift	.423	Harlond Clift	.554	Harlond Clift	34	Harlond Clift	118	Harlond Clift	10
1939	George McQuinn	.316	Harlond Clift	.402	George McQuinn	.515	Harlond Clift	20	George McQuinn	94	Myril Hoag	9
1940	Rip Radcliff	.342	Harlond Clift	.396	Wally Judnich	.520	Wally Judnich	24	Wally Judnich	89	Harlond Clift	9
1941	Roy Cullenbine	.317	Roy Cullenbine	.452	George McQuinn	.479	George McQuinn	18	Roy Cullenbine	98	Harlond Clift	6
											Roy Cullenbine	
1942	Wally Judnich	.313	Wally Judnich	.413	Wally Judnich	.499	Chet Laabs	27	Chet Laabs	99	Don Gutteridge	16
1943	Vern Stephens	.289	Milt Byrnes	.362	Vern Stephens	.482	Vern Stephens	22	Vern Stephens	91	Don Gutteridge	10
1944	Milt Byrnes	.295	Milt Byrnes	.396	Vern Stephens	.462	Vern Stephens	20	Vern Stephens	109	Don Gutteridge	20
1945	Vern Stephens	.289	George McQuinn	.364	Vern Stephens	.473	Vern Stephens	24	Vern Stephens	89	Don Gutteridge	9
1946	Vern Stephens	.307	Vern Stephens	.357	Vern Stephens	.460	Chet Laabs	16	Wally Judnich	72	Bob Dillinger	8
1947	Bob Dillinger	.294	Jeff Heath	.366	Jeff Heath	.485	Jeff Heath	27	Jeff Heath	85	Bob Dillinger	34
1948	Al Zarilla	.329	Jerry Priddy	.391	Al Zarilla	.482	Les Moss	14	Whitey Platt	82	Bob Dillinger	28
1949	Bob Dillinger	.324	Roy Sievers	.398	Roy Sievers	.471	Jack Graham	24	Roy Sievers	91	Bob Dillinger	20
1950	Don Lenhardt	.273	Don Lenhardt	.390	Don Lenhardt	.481	Don Lenhardt	22	Don Lenhardt	81	Dick Kokos	8
1951	Bobby Young	.260	Jim Delsing	.338	Jim Delsing	.356	Ken Wood	15	Ray Coleman	55	Bobby Young	8
1952	Bob Nieman	.289	Bob Nieman	.352	Bob Nieman	.456	Bob Nieman	18	Bob Nieman	74	Jim Rivera	8
1953	Vic Wertz	.268	Vic Wertz	.376	Vic Wertz	.466	Vic Wertz	19	Vic Wertz	70	Johnny Groth	5
1954	Cal Abrams	.293	Cal Abrams	.400	Cal Abrams	.421	Vern Stephens	8	Vern Stephens	46	Gil Coan	9
1955	Gus Triandos	.277	Gus Triandos	.333	Gus Triandos	.399	Gus Triandos	12	Gus Triandos	65	Chuck Diering	5
											Dave Pope	
1956	Bob Nieman	.322	Bob Nieman	.442	Bob Nieman	.497	Gus Triandos	21	Gus Triandos	88	Tito Francona	11
1957	Bob Boyd	.318	Bob Boyd	.388	Bob Nieman	.429	Gus Triandos	19	Gus Triandos	72	Al Pilarcik	14
1958	Gene Woodling	.276	Gene Woodling	.378	Gus Triandos	.456	Gus Triandos	30	Gus Triandos	79	Al Pilarcik	7
1959	Gene Woodling	.300	Gene Woodling	.402	Gene Woodling	.455	Gus Triandos	25	Gene Woodling	77	Al Pilarcik	9
1960	Brooks Robinson	.294	Brooks Robinson	.401	Brooks Robinson	.440	Ron Hansen	22	Jim Gentile	98	Marv Breeding	10
1961	Jim Gentile	.302	Jim Gentile	.423	Jim Gentile	.646	Jim Gentile	46	Jim Gentile	141	Jackie Brandt	10
1962	Brooks Robinson	.303	Jim Gentile	.346	Brooks Robinson	.486	Jim Gentile	33	Jim Gentile	87	Jackie Brandt	9
1963	Boog Powell	.265	Jim Gentile	.353	Boog Powell	.470	Boog Powell	25	Boog Powell	82	Luis Aparicio	40
1964	Brooks Robinson	.317	Boog Powell	.399	Boog Powell	.606	Boog Powell	39	Brooks Robinson	118	Luis Aparicio	57
1965	Brooks Robinson	.297	Curt Blefary	.381	Curt Blefary	.470	Curt Blefary	22	Brooks Robinson	80	Luis Aparicio	26
1966	Frank Robinson	.316	Frank Robinson	.410	Frank Robinson	.637	Frank Robinson	49	Frank Robinson	122	Luis Aparicio	25
1967	Frank Robinson	.311	Frank Robinson	.403	Frank Robinson	.576	Frank Robinson	30	Frank Robinson	94	Luis Aparicio	18
1968	Frank Robinson	.268	Frank Robinson	.390	Frank Robinson	.444	Boog Powell	22	Boog Powell	85	Don Buford	27
1969	Frank Robinson	.308	Frank Robinson	.415	Boog Powell	.559	Boog Powell	37	Boog Powell	121	Paul Blair	20
1970	Frank Robinson	.306	Boog Powell	.412	Boog Powell	.549	Boog Powell	35	Boog Powell	114	Paul Blair	24
1971	Merv Rettenmund	.318	Merv Rettenmund	.422	Frank Robinson	.510	Frank Robinson	28	Frank Robinson	99	Don Buford	15
											Merv Rettenmund	
1972	Bobby Grich	.278	Bobby Grich	.358	Boog Powell	.434	Boog Powell	21	Boog Powell	81	Don Baylor	24
1973	Tommy Davis	.306	Bobby Grich	.373	Earl Williams	.425	Earl Williams	22	Tommy Davis	89	Don Baylor	32
1974	Tommy Davis	.289	Bobby Grich	.376	Bobby Grich	.431	Bobby Grich	19	Tommy Davis	84	Don Baylor	29
1975	Ken Singleton	.300	Ken Singleton	.415	Don Baylor	.489	Don Baylor	25	Lee May	99	Don Baylor	32
1976	Ken Singleton	.278	Bobby Grich	.373	Reggie Jackson	.502	Reggie Jackson	27	Lee May	109	Al Bumbry	42

1210

Year	Batting Average		On-Base Percentage		Slugging Percentage		Home Runs		RBI		Stolen Bases	
1977	Ken Singleton	.328	Ken Singleton	.438	Ken Singleton	.507	Lee May / Eddie Murray	27	Lee May / Ken Singleton	99	Pat Kelly	25
1978	Ken Singleton	.293	Ken Singleton	.409	Doug DeCinces	.526	Doug DeCinces	28	Eddie Murray	95	Larry Harlow	14
1979	Eddie Murray	.295	Ken Singleton	.405	Ken Singleton	.533	Ken Singleton	35	Ken Singleton	111	Al Bumbry	37
1980	Al Bumbry	.318	Ken Singleton	.397	Eddie Murray	.519	Eddie Murray	32	Eddie Murray	116	Al Bumbry	44
1981	Eddie Murray	.294	Ken Singleton	.380	Eddie Murray	.534	Eddie Murray	22	Eddie Murray	78	Al Bumbry	22
1982	Eddie Murray	.316	Eddie Murray	.391	Eddie Murray	.549	Eddie Murray	32	Eddie Murray	110	Al Bumbry	10
1983	Cal Ripken Jr.	.318	Ken Singleton	.393	Eddie Murray	.538	Eddie Murray	33	Eddie Murray	111	John Shelby	15
1984	Eddie Murray	.306	Eddie Murray	.410	Cal Ripken Jr.	.510	Eddie Murray	29	Eddie Murray	110	John Shelby	12
1985	Eddie Murray	.297	Eddie Murray	.383	Eddie Murray	.523	Eddie Murray	31	Eddie Murray	124	Alan Wiggins	30
1986	Eddie Murray	.305	Eddie Murray	.396	Eddie Murray	.463	Cal Ripken Jr.	25	Eddie Murray	84	Alan Wiggins	21
1987	Larry Sheets	.316	Larry Sheets	.358	Larry Sheets	.563	Larry Sheets	31	Cal Ripken Jr.	98	Alan Wiggins	20
1988	Eddie Murray	.284	Cal Ripken Jr.	.372	Eddie Murray	.474	Eddie Murray	28	Eddie Murray	84	Pete Stanicek	12
1989	Phil Bradley	.277	Phil Bradley	.364	Phil Bradley	.417	Mickey Tettleton	26	Cal Ripken Jr.	93	Mike Devereaux	22
1990	Steve Finley	.256	Mickey Tettleton	.376	Cal Ripken Jr.	.415	Cal Ripken Jr.	21	Cal Ripken Jr.	84	Steve Finley	22
1991	Cal Ripken Jr.	.323	Cal Ripken Jr.	.374	Cal Ripken Jr.	.566	Cal Ripken Jr.	34	Cal Ripken Jr.	114	Mike Devereaux	16
1992	Mike Devereaux	.276	Randy Milligan	.383	Mike Devereaux	.464	Mike Devereaux	24	Mike Devereaux	107	Brady Anderson	53
1993	Chris Hoiles	.310	Chris Hoiles	.416	Chris Hoiles	.585	Chris Hoiles	29	Cal Ripken Jr.	90	Brady Anderson	24
1994	Rafael Palmeiro	.319	Rafael Palmeiro	.392	Rafael Palmeiro	.550	Rafael Palmeiro	23	Rafael Palmeiro	76	Brady Anderson	31
1995	Rafael Palmeiro	.310	Harold Baines	.403	Rafael Palmeiro	.583	Rafael Palmeiro	39	Rafael Palmeiro	104	Brady Anderson	26
1996	Roberto Alomar	.328	Roberto Alomar	.411	Brady Anderson	.637	Brady Anderson	50	Rafael Palmeiro	142	Brady Anderson	21
1997	Brady Anderson	.288	Brady Anderson	.393	Rafael Palmeiro	.485	Rafael Palmeiro	38	Rafael Palmeiro	110	Brady Anderson	18

St. Louis Browns/Baltimore Orioles Individual Season Pitching Leaders

Year	ERA		Baserunners/9 IP		Innings Pitched		Strikeouts		Wins		Saves	
1901	Ned Garvin	3.46	Ned Garvin	12.7	Bill Reidy	301.1	Ned Garvin	122	Bill Reidy	16	Ned Garvin	2
1902	Red Donahue	2.76	Red Donahue	11.2	Jack Powell	328.1	Jack Powell	137	Red Donahue	22	Jack Powell	3
									Jack Powell			
1903	Willie Sudhoff	2.27	Willie Sudhoff	10.0	Jack Powell	306.1	Jack Powell	169	Willie Sudhoff	21	Jack Powell	2
1904	Harry Howell	2.19	Harry Howell	9.8	Barney Pelty	301.0	Fred Glade	156	Fred Glade	18	Fred Glade	1
1905	Harry Howell	1.98	Harry Howell	10.2	Harry Howell	323.0	Harry Howell	198	Harry Howell	15	Jim Buchanan	2
1906	Barney Pelty	1.59	Barney Pelty	9.2	Harry Howell	276.2	Harry Howell	140	Barney Pelty	16	Barney Pelty	2
1907	Harry Howell	1.93	Harry Howell	10.1	Harry Howell	316.1	Harry Howell	118	Harry Howell	16	Bill Dinneen	4
1908	Harry Howell	1.89	Jack Powell	9.2	Harry Howell	324.1	Rube Waddell	232	Rube Waddell	19	Rube Waddell	3
1909	Jack Powell	2.11	Barney Pelty	9.8	Jack Powell	239.0	Rube Waddell	141	Jack Powell	12	Jack Powell	2
1910	Joe Lake	2.20	Joe Lake	11.1	Joe Lake	261.1	Joe Lake	141	Joe Lake	11	Joe Lake	2
1911	Barney Pelty	2.97	Jack Powell	11.9	Joe Lake	215.1	Joe Lake	69	Joe Lake	10	Earl Hamilton	1
											Jack Powell	
1912	Jack Powell	3.10	Jack Powell	11.6	Earl Hamilton	249.2	Earl Hamilton	139	G. Baumgardner	11	Earl Hamilton	2
									Earl Hamilton			
1913	Earl Hamilton	2.36	Walt Leverenz	11.5	George Baumgardner	253.1	Earl Hamilton	101	Earl Hamilton	13	4 tied with	1
									Roy Mitchell			
1914	Carl Weilman	2.08	Carl Weilman	10.7	Earl Hamilton	302.1	Carl Weilman	119	Carl Weilman	18	Roy Mitchell	4
1915	Carl Weilman	2.34	Carl Weilman	9.9	Carl Weilman	295.2	Grover Lowdermilk	130	Carl Weilman	18	Carl Weilman	4
1916	Carl Weilman	2.15	Carl Weilman	10.5	Dave Davenport	290.2	Dave Davenport	129	Carl Weilman	17	Bob Groom	4
1917	Allen Sothoron	2.83	Bob Groom	11.3	Dave Davenport	280.2	Dave Davenport	100	Dave Davenport	17	Allen Sothoron	4
1918	Allen Sothoron	1.94	Allen Sothoron	9.6	Allen Sothoron	209.0	Allen Sothoron	71	Allen Sothoron	12	3 tied with	2
1919	Carl Weilman	2.07	Urban Shocker	10.7	Allen Sothoron	270.0	Allen Sothoron	106	Allen Sothoron	20	Allen Sothoron	3
1920	Urban Shocker	2.71	Urban Shocker	10.9	Dixie Davis	269.1	Urban Shocker	107	Urban Shocker	20	Urban Shocker	5
1921	Urban Shocker	3.55	Urban Shocker	12.0	Urban Shocker	326.2	Urban Shocker	132	Urban Shocker	27	Urban Shocker	4
1922	Rasty Wright	2.92	Urban Shocker	11.0	Urban Shocker	348.0	Urban Shocker	149	Urban Shocker	24	Hub Pruett	7
1923	Elam Vangilder	3.06	Urban Shocker	11.2	Elam Vangilder	282.1	Urban Shocker	109	Urban Shocker	20	Urban Shocker	5
1924	Ernie Wingard	3.51	Urban Shocker	11.9	Urban Shocker	246.1	Urban Shocker	88	Urban Shocker	16	Dave Danforth	4
1925	Dave Danforth	4.36	Dave Danforth	13.4	Milt Gaston	238.2	Milt Gaston	84	Milt Gaston	15	Elam Vangilder	6
1926	Ernie Wingard	3.57	Tom Zachary	13.4	Tom Zachary	247.1	Win Ballou	59	Tom Zachary	14	Ernie Wingard	3
1927	Lefty Stewart	4.28	Milt Gaston	13.4	Milt Gaston	254.0	Milt Gaston	77	Milt Gaston	13	General Crowder	3
1928	Sam Gray	3.19	Sam Gray	11.8	Sam Gray	262.2	Sam Gray	102	General Crowder	21	3 tied with	3
1929	Sam Gray	3.72	George Blaeholder	12.1	Sam Gray	305.0	Sam Gray	109	Sam Gray	18	General Crowder	4
1930	Lefty Stewart	3.45	Lefty Stewart	11.7	Lefty Stewart	271.0	Lefty Stewart	79	Lefty Stewart	20	George Blaeholder	4
1931	Dick Coffman	3.88	Dick Coffman	11.3	Sam Gray	258.0	Lefty Stewart	89	Lefty Stewart	14	Chad Kimsey	7
					Lefty Stewart							
1932	Sam Gray	4.53	Lefty Stewart	12.9	Lefty Stewart	259.2	Bump Hadley	132	Lefty Stewart	15	Sam Gray	4
1933	Bump Hadley	3.92	George Blaeholder	12.4	Bump Hadley	316.2	Bump Hadley	149	George Blaeholder	15	Sam Gray	4
									Bump Hadley			
1934	Bobo Newsom	4.01	George Blaeholder	13.2	Bobo Newsom	262.1	Bobo Newsom	135	Bobo Newsom	16	Bobo Newsom	5
1935	Ivy Andrews	3.54	Ivy Andrews	12.0	Ivy Andrews	213.1	Russ Van Atta	87	Ivy Andrews	13	Jack Knott	7
1936	Ivy Andrews	4.84	Ivy Andrews	12.7	Chief Hogsett	215.1	Chief Hogsett	67	Chief Hogsett	13	Jack Knott	6
1937	Jack Knott	4.89	Oral Hildebrand	14.2	Oral Hildebrand	201.1	Oral Hildebrand	75	Jim Walkup	9	Chief Hogsett	2
											Jack Knott	
1938	Bobo Newsom	5.08	Bobo Newsom	14.5	Bobo Newsom	329.2	Bobo Newsom	226	Bobo Newsom	20	Ed Cole	3
											Fred Johnson	
1939	Bill Trotter	5.34	Bill Trotter	15.2	Jack Kramer	211.2	Lefty Mills	103	Vern Kennedy	9	Lefty Mills	2
									Jack Kramer			
1940	Eldon Auker	3.96	Eldon Auker	13.6	Eldon Auker	263.2	Johnny Niggeling	82	Eldon Auker	16	Roxie Lawson	4
1941	Denny Galehouse	3.64	Bob Muncrief	11.7	Eldon Auker	216.0	Johnny Niggeling	68	Eldon Auker	14	George Caster	3
1942	Johnny Niggeling	2.66	Johnny Niggeling	12.1	Eldon Auker	249.0	Johnny Niggeling	107	Johnny Niggeling	15	George Caster	5
1943	Denny Galehouse	2.77	Nels Potter	10.9	Denny Galehouse	224.0	Denny Galehouse	114	Steve Sundra	15	George Caster	8
1944	Jack Kramer	2.49	Jack Kramer	10.8	Jack Kramer	257.0	Jack Kramer	124	Nels Potter	19	George Caster	12
1945	Nels Potter	2.47	Nels Potter	9.9	Nels Potter	255.1	Nels Potter	129	Nels Potter	15	Sig Jakucki	2
											Jack Kramer	
1946	Jack Kramer	3.19	Sam Zoldak	11.8	Jack Kramer	194.2	Denny Galehouse	90	Jack Kramer	13	Tom Ferrick	5
1947	Sam Zoldak	3.47	Sam Zoldak	12.5	Jack Kramer	199.1	Ellis Kinder	110	Jack Kramer	11	Fred Sanford	4
1948	Ned Garver	3.41	Cliff Fannin	12.8	Fred Sanford	227.0	Cliff Fannin	102	Fred Sanford	12	Ned Garver	5
1949	Ned Garver	3.98	Ned Garver	14.1	Ned Garver	223.2	Ned Garver	70	Ned Garver	12	Tom Ferrick	6
1950	Ned Garver	3.39	Ned Garver	13.0	Ned Garver	260.0	Ned Garver	85	Ned Garver	13	Al Widmar	4
1951	Ned Garver	3.73	Ned Garver	12.4	Ned Garver	246.0	Ned Garver	84	Ned Garver	20	Satchel Paige	5
1952	Duane Pillette	3.59	Bob Cain	12.3	Duane Pillette	205.1	Tommy Byrne	91	Bob Cain	12	Satchel Paige	10
							Satchel Paige		Satchel Paige			
1953	Don Larsen	4.16	Don Larsen	12.6	Don Larsen	192.2	Dick Littlefield	104	Marlin Stuart	8	Satchel Paige	11
1954	Duane Pillette	3.12	Duane Pillette	11.4	Bob Turley	247.1	Bob Turley	185	Bob Turley	14	Bob Chakales	3
1955	Jim Wilson	3.44	Jim Wilson	11.1	Jim Wilson	235.1	Jim Wilson	96	Jim Wilson	12	Harry Dorish	6
											Ray Moore	
1956	Connie Johnson	3.43	Connie Johnson	11.2	Ray Moore	185.0	Connie Johnson	130	Ray Moore	12	George Zuverink	16
1957	Connie Johnson	3.20	Connie Johnson	10.5	Connie Johnson	242.0	Connie Johnson	177	Connie Johnson	14	George Zuverink	9
1958	Jack Harshman	2.89	Arnie Portocarrero	10.2	Jack Harshman	236.1	Jack Harshman	161	Arnie Portocarrero	15	Billy O'Dell	8
1959	Hoyt Wilhelm	2.19	Billy O'Dell	10.4	Hoyt Wilhelm	226.0	Hoyt Wilhelm	139	Milt Pappas	15	Billy Loes	14
									Hoyt Wilhelm			
1960	Hal Brown	3.06	Hal Brown	10.1	Chuck Estrada	208.2	Chuck Estrada	144	Chuck Estrada	18	Hoyt Wilhelm	7
1961	Milt Pappas	3.04	Hal Brown	10.1	Steve Barber	248.1	Chuck Estrada	160	Steve Barber	18	Hoyt Wilhelm	18
1962	Robin Roberts	2.78	Robin Roberts	10.4	Chuck Estrada	223.1	Chuck Estrada	165	Milt Pappas	12	Hoyt Wilhelm	15
1963	Steve Barber	2.75	Robin Roberts	9.8	Steve Barber	258.2	Steve Barber	180	Steve Barber	20	Stu Miller	27
1964	Wally Bunker	2.69	Wally Bunker	9.5	Milt Pappas	251.2	Milt Pappas	157	Wally Bunker	19	Stu Miller	23
1965	Milt Pappas	2.60	Milt Pappas	10.0	Milt Pappas	221.1	Steve Barber	130	Steve Barber	15	Stu Miller	24
1966	Dave McNally	3.17	Jim Palmer	11.5	Dave McNally	213.0	Dave McNally	158	Jim Palmer	15	Stu Miller	18
1967	Tom Phoebus	3.33	Tom Phoebus	12.6	Tom Phoebus	208.0	Tom Phoebus	179	Tom Phoebus	14	Moe Drabowsky	12
1968	Dave McNally	1.95	Dave McNally	7.9	Dave McNally	273.0	Dave McNally	202	Dave McNally	22	Eddie Watt	11
1969	Jim Palmer	2.34	Mike Cuellar	9.1	Mike Cuellar	290.2	Mike Cuellar	182	Mike Cuellar	23	Eddie Watt	16
1970	Jim Palmer	2.71	Mike Cuellar	10.4	Jim Palmer	305.0	Jim Palmer	199	Mike Cuellar	24	Pete Richert	13
									Dave McNally			
1971	Jim Palmer	2.68	Pat Dobson	10.0	Mike Cuellar	292.1	Pat Dobson	187	Dave McNally	21	Eddie Watt	11

Year	ERA			Baserunners/9 IP			Innings Pitched			Strikeouts			Wins			Saves		
1972	Jim Palmer	2.07		Jim Palmer	9.5		Jim Palmer	274.1		Jim Palmer	184		Jim Palmer	21		Grant Jackson	8
1973	Jim Palmer	2.40		Jim Palmer	10.4		Jim Palmer	296.1		Jim Palmer	158		Jim Palmer	22		Grant Jackson	9
																Bob Reynolds	
1974	Ross Grimsley	3.07		Ross Grimsley	10.5		Ross Grimsley	295.2		Ross Grimsley	158		Mike Cuellar	22		Grant Jackson	12
1975	Jim Palmer	2.09		Jim Palmer	9.3		Jim Palmer	323.0		Jim Palmer	193		Jim Palmer	23		Dyar Miller	8
1976	Jim Palmer	2.51		Jim Palmer	9.9		Jim Palmer	315.0		Jim Palmer	159		Jim Palmer	22		Tippy Martinez	8
1977	Jim Palmer	2.91		Jim Palmer	10.3		Jim Palmer	319.0		Jim Palmer	193		Jim Palmer	20		Tippy Martinez	9
1978	Jim Palmer	2.46		Scott McGregor	10.2		Jim Palmer	296.0		Mike Flanagan	167		Jim Palmer	21		Don Stanhouse	24
1979	Mike Flanagan	3.08		Scott McGregor	9.8		Dennis Martinez	292.1		Mike Flanagan	190		Mike Flanagan	23		Don Stanhouse	21
1980	Steve Stone	3.23		Scott McGregor	11.2		Scott McGregor	252.0		Steve Stone	149		Steve Stone	25		Tim Stoddard	26
1981	Sammy Stewart	2.32		Mike Flanagan	11.4		Dennis Martinez	179.0		Dennis Martinez	88		Dennis Martinez	14		Tippy Martinez	11
1982	Jim Palmer	3.13		Jim Palmer	10.4		Dennis Martinez	252.0		Dennis Martinez	111		Dennis Martinez	16		Tippy Martinez	16
1983	Mike Boddicker	2.77		Mike Boddicker	9.7		Scott McGregor	260.0		Storm Davis	125		Scott McGregor	18		Tippy Martinez	21
1984	Mike Boddicker	2.79		Mike Boddicker	10.5		Mike Boddicker	261.1		Mike Boddicker	128		Mike Boddicker	20		Tippy Martinez	17
1985	Ken Dixon	3.67		Ken Dixon	11.7		Scott McGregor	204.0		Mike Boddicker	135		Scott McGregor	14		Don Aase	14
1986	Mike Flanagan	4.24		Scott McGregor	12.2		Mike Boddicker	218.1		Mike Boddicker	175		Mike Boddicker	14		Don Aase	34
1987	Mike Boddicker	4.18		Mike Boddicker	11.8		Mike Boddicker	226.0		Mike Boddicker	152		3 tied with	10		Tom Niedenfuer	13
1988	Jose Bautista	4.30		Jose Bautista	11.7		Jose Bautista	171.2		Mike Boddicker	100		Jeff Ballard	8		Tom Niedenfuer	18
													Dave Schmidt				
1989	Jeff Ballard	3.43		Bob Milacki	12.0		Bob Milacki	243.0		Bob Milacki	113		Jeff Ballard	18		Gregg Olson	27
1990	Dave Johnson	4.10		Dave Johnson	12.1		Pete Harnisch	188.2		Pete Harnisch	122		Dave Johnson	13		Gregg Olson	37
1991	Bob Milacki	4.01		Bob Milacki	11.2		Bob Milacki	184.0		Bob Milacki	108		Bob Milacki	10		Gregg Olson	31
1992	Mike Mussina	2.54		Mike Mussina	9.8		Mike Mussina	241.0		Ben McDonald	158		Mike Mussina	18		Gregg Olson	36
1993	Ben McDonald	3.39		Mike Mussina	11.3		Ben McDonald	220.1		Ben McDonald	171		Mike Mussina	14		Gregg Olson	29
1994	Mike Mussina	3.06		Mike Mussina	10.5		Mike Mussina	176.1		Mike Mussina	99		Mike Mussina	16		Lee Smith	33
1995	Mike Mussina	3.29		Mike Mussina	9.7		Mike Mussina	221.2		Mike Mussina	158		Mike Mussina	19		Doug Jones	22
1996	Mike Mussina	4.81		David Wells	12.2		Mike Mussina	243.1		Mike Mussina	204		Mike Mussina	19		Randy Myers	31
1997	Mike Mussina	3.20		Mike Mussina	10.2		Mike Mussina	224.2		Mike Mussina	218		Scott Erickson	16		Randy Myers	45
													Jimmy Key				

Teams: Orioles

Browns/Orioles Franchise Batting Leaders—Career

Games

1	Brooks Robinson	2,896
2	Cal Ripken Jr.	2,543
3	Mark Belanger	1,962
4	Eddie Murray	1,884
5	Boog Powell	1,763
6	Paul Blair	1,700
7	George Sisler	1,647
8	Bobby Wallace	1,569
9	Ken Singleton	1,446
10	Harlond Clift	1,443
11	Al Bumbry	1,428
12	Jimmy Austin	1,311
13	Wally Gerber	1,284
14	Rick Dempsey	1,245
15	Baby Doll Jacobson	1,243
16	Brady Anderson	1,204
17	Hank Severeid	1,182
18	Ski Melillo	1,147
19	Rich Dauer	1,140
20	George McQuinn	1,138

At-Bats

1	Brooks Robinson	10,654
2	Cal Ripken Jr.	9,832
3	Eddie Murray	7,075
4	George Sisler	6,667
5	Boog Powell	5,912
6	Mark Belanger	5,734
7	Paul Blair	5,606
8	Bobby Wallace	5,529
9	Harlond Clift	5,281
10	Ken Singleton	5,115
11	Al Bumbry	4,958
12	Baby Doll Jacobson	4,755
13	Jimmy Austin	4,519
14	Wally Gerber	4,510
15	Jack Tobin	4,404
16	George McQuinn	4,310
17	Brady Anderson	4,292
18	Ski Melillo	4,281
19	Ken Williams	4,013
20	Burt Shotton	3,912

Runs

1	Cal Ripken Jr.	1,445
2	Brooks Robinson	1,232
3	George Sisler	1,091
4	Eddie Murray	1,084
5	Harlond Clift	1,013
6	Boog Powell	796
7	Al Bumbry	772
8	Ken Williams	757
9	Paul Blair	737
10	Brady Anderson	712
11	Baby Doll Jacobson	711
12	Ken Singleton	684
13	Jack Tobin	680
14	Mark Belanger	670
15	George McQuinn	663
16	Bobby Wallace	609
17	Burt Shotton	601
18	Jimmy Austin	578
19	Frank Robinson	555
20	Vern Stephens	528

Hits

1	Brooks Robinson	2,848
2	Cal Ripken Jr.	2,715
3	George Sisler	2,295
4	Eddie Murray	2,080
5	Boog Powell	1,574
6	Baby Doll Jacobson	1,508
7	Harlond Clift	1,463
8	Ken Singleton	1,455
9	Paul Blair	1,426
10	Bobby Wallace	1,424
11	Al Bumbry	1,403
12	Jack Tobin	1,399
13	Ken Williams	1,308
14	Mark Belanger	1,304
15	George McQuinn	1,220
16	Wally Gerber	1,189
17	Jimmy Austin	1,133
18	Brady Anderson	1,125
19	Ski Melillo	1,124
20	Hank Severeid	1,121

Doubles

1	Cal Ripken Jr.	517
2	Brooks Robinson	482
3	Eddie Murray	363
4	George Sisler	343
5	Harlond Clift	294
6	Baby Doll Jacobson	269
	Paul Blair	269
8	George McQuinn	254
9	Boog Powell	243
10	Bobby Wallace	236
	Ken Williams	236
12	Ken Singleton	235
	Brady Anderson	235
14	Jack Tobin	217
	Al Bumbry	217
16	Rich Dauer	193
17	Red Kress	189
18	Dave Johnson	186
19	Marty McManus	185
20	Ski Melillo	183

Triples

1	George Sisler	145
2	Baby Doll Jacobson	88
3	Del Pratt	72
	Jack Tobin	72
5	George Stone	70
	Ken Williams	70
7	Brooks Robinson	68
8	Jimmy Austin	67
9	Bobby Wallace	65
10	Harlond Clift	62
11	Ski Melillo	58
12	Marty McManus	53
	Brady Anderson	53
14	Burt Shotton	52
	Al Bumbry	52
16	Paul Blair	51
17	George McQuinn	47
18	Wally Gerber	43
	Cal Ripken Jr.	43
20	Four tied at	37

Home Runs

1	Cal Ripken Jr.	370
2	Eddie Murray	343
3	Boog Powell	303
4	Brooks Robinson	268
5	Ken Williams	185
6	Ken Singleton	182
7	Frank Robinson	179
8	Harlond Clift	170
9	Gus Triandos	142
10	Brady Anderson	140
11	Rafael Palmeiro	139
12	Chris Hoiles	136
13	Paul Blair	126
14	Jim Gentile	124
15	Lee May	123
16	Vern Stephens	121
17	George McQuinn	108
18	Doug DeCinces	107
19	Gary Roenicke	106
20	Chet Laabs	101

RBI

1	Cal Ripken Jr.	1,453
2	Brooks Robinson	1,357
3	Eddie Murray	1,224
4	Boog Powell	1,063
5	George Sisler	959
6	Ken Williams	808
7	Harlond Clift	769
8	Ken Singleton	766
9	Baby Doll Jacobson	704
10	George McQuinn	625
11	Bobby Wallace	607
12	Vern Stephens	591
13	Paul Blair	567
14	Frank Robinson	545
15	Gus Triandos	517
	Brady Anderson	517
17	Red Kress	513
18	Marty McManus	506
19	Lee May	487
20	Hank Severeid	485

Walks

1	Cal Ripken Jr.	1,016
2	Harlond Clift	986
3	Boog Powell	889
4	Ken Singleton	886
5	Eddie Murray	884
6	Brooks Robinson	860
7	Brady Anderson	604
8	Burt Shotton	595
9	Mark Belanger	571
10	Bobby Wallace	526
11	George McQuinn	520
12	Jimmy Austin	513
13	Ken Williams	497
14	Al Bumbry	464
15	Frank Robinson	460
16	Bobby Grich	457
17	Rick Dempsey	424
18	Paul Blair	420
	Don Buford	420
20	Wally Gerber	414

Strikeouts

1	Cal Ripken Jr.	1,106
2	Boog Powell	1,102
3	Brooks Robinson	990
4	Eddie Murray	969
5	Ken Singleton	860
6	Mark Belanger	829
7	Paul Blair	816
8	Brady Anderson	769
9	Al Bumbry	700
10	Harlond Clift	649
11	Lee May	577
12	Chris Hoiles	566
13	Mike Devereaux	541
14	Rick Dempsey	538
15	Bobby Grich	520
16	Gus Triandos	487
17	Dave Johnson	475
18	Chet Laabs	473
19	Doug DeCinces	455
20	Four tied at	452

Stolen Bases

1	George Sisler	351
2	Al Bumbry	252
3	Burt Shotton	247
4	Brady Anderson	222
5	Jimmy Austin	192
6	Del Pratt	174
7	Paul Blair	167
8	Luis Aparicio	166
	Mark Belanger	166
10	Ken Williams	144
11	Bobby Wallace	138
12	George Stone	132
13	Don Baylor	118
14	Charlie Hemphill	109
15	Tom Jones	103
16	Gus Williams	95
17	Bob Dillinger	90
18	Jack Tobin	85
	Don Buford	85
20	Roy Hartzell	84

Runs Created

1	Cal Ripken Jr.	1,481
2	Brooks Robinson	1,337
3	Eddie Murray	1,259
4	George Sisler	1,173
5	Boog Powell	993
6	Harlond Clift	968
7	Ken Singleton	881
8	Ken Williams	846
9	Baby Doll Jacobson	762
10	Brady Anderson	722
11	George McQuinn	711
12	Al Bumbry	681
13	Bobby Wallace	674
14	Jack Tobin	670
15	Paul Blair	663
16	Frank Robinson	622
17	Vern Stephens	596
18	Burt Shotton	557
19	Jimmy Austin	526
20	George Stone	521

Runs Created/27 Outs

(minimum 2000 Plate Appearances)

1	Frank Robinson	7.66
2	Ken Williams	7.57
3	Rafael Palmeiro	7.00
4	Jim Gentile	6.82
5	George Sisler	6.58
6	Harlond Clift	6.46
7	Eddie Murray	6.42
8	Bob Nieman	6.25
9	Wally Judnich	6.21
10	Sammy West	6.16
11	Ken Singleton	6.09
12	Beau Bell	6.06
13	Merv Rettenmund	5.99
14	Don Buford	5.97
15	Boog Powell	5.86
16	George McQuinn	5.82
17	Chet Laabs	5.80
18	Baby Doll Jacobson	5.79
19	Vern Stephens	5.79
20	Chris Hoiles	5.78

Batting Average

(minimum 2000 Plate Appearances)

1	George Sisler	.344
2	Ken Williams	.326
3	Jack Tobin	.318
4	Baby Doll Jacobson	.317
5	Bob Dillinger	.309
6	Beau Bell	.309
7	Sammy West	.305
8	George Stone	.301
9	Bob Nieman	.301
10	Frank Robinson	.300
11	Red Kress	.299
12	Marty McManus	.298
13	Fred Schulte	.296
14	Eddie Murray	.294
15	Vern Stephens	.292
16	Rafael Palmeiro	.291
17	Hank Severeid	.290
18	Merv Rettenmund	.284
	Ken Singleton	.284
20	Wally Judnich	.283

On-Base Percentage

(minimum 2000 Plate Appearances)

1	Ken Williams	.404
2	Frank Robinson	.401
3	Harlond Clift	.394
4	Ken Singleton	.388
5	Randy Milligan	.388
6	Sammy West	.386
7	Don Buford	.385
8	Bob Nieman	.384
9	George Sisler	.384
10	Merv Rettenmund	.383
11	Jim Gentile	.379
12	Beau Bell	.373
13	Bob Dillinger	.373
14	Burt Shotton	.372
15	Bobby Grich	.372
16	Eddie Murray	.370
17	Rafael Palmeiro	.369
18	Rick Ferrell	.368
19	Jack Tobin	.368
20	Chris Hoiles	.367

Slugging Percentage

(minimum 2000 Plate Appearances)

1	Ken Williams	.558
2	Frank Robinson	.543
3	Rafael Palmeiro	.539
4	Jim Gentile	.512
5	Eddie Murray	.498
6	Bob Nieman	.486
7	George Sisler	.481
8	Chris Hoiles	.467
9	Boog Powell	.465
10	Beau Bell	.462
11	Wally Judnich	.462
12	Chet Laabs	.459
13	Baby Doll Jacobson	.459
14	Harlond Clift	.453
15	Cal Ripken Jr.	.450
16	Gary Roenicke	.448
17	Vern Stephens	.446
18	Larry Sheets	.445
19	Ken Singleton	.445
20	Marty McManus	.443

Teams: Orioles

Browns/Orioles Franchise Pitching Leaders—Career

Wins

1	Jim Palmer	268
2	Dave McNally	181
3	Mike Cuellar	143
4	Mike Flanagan	141
5	Scott McGregor	138
6	Urban Shocker	126
7	Jack Powell	117
8	Milt Pappas	110
9	Dennis Martinez	108
10	Mike Mussina	105
11	Steve Barber	95
12	Barney Pelty	91
13	George Blaeholder	90
14	Elam Vangilder	88
15	Carl Weilman	85
16	Mike Boddicker	79
17	Harry Howell	78
18	Dixie Davis	75
19	Lefty Stewart	73
20	Bob Muncrief	69

Losses

1	Jim Palmer	152
2	Jack Powell	143
3	Mike Flanagan	116
4	Barney Pelty	113
	Dave McNally	113
6	George Blaeholder	111
7	Scott McGregor	108
8	Carl Weilman	95
9	Dennis Martinez	93
10	Harry Howell	91
	Elam Vangilder	91
12	Earl Hamilton	89
13	Mike Cuellar	88
14	Sam Gray	82
15	Jack Kramer	81
16	Urban Shocker	80
17	Steve Barber	75
18	Lefty Stewart	74
	Milt Pappas	74
20	Mike Boddicker	73

Winning Percentage
(minimum 100 decisions)

1	Mike Mussina	.682
2	Jim Palmer	.638
3	Dick Hall	.619
	Mike Cuellar	.619
5	Dave McNally	.616
6	Urban Shocker	.612
7	Milt Pappas	.598
8	Storm Davis	.587
9	Nels Potter	.570
10	Hal Brown	.564
11	Scott McGregor	.561
12	Steve Barber	.559
13	Mike Flanagan	.549
14	Dennis Martinez	.537
15	Dixie Davis	.524
16	Ben McDonald	.523
17	Mike Boddicker	.520
18	Bob Muncrief	.507
19	Lefty Stewart	.497
20	Elam Vangilder	.492

Games

1	Jim Palmer	558
2	Tippy Martinez	499
3	Mike Flanagan	450
4	Dave McNally	412
5	Mark Williamson	365
6	Eddie Watt	363
7	Scott McGregor	356
8	Dick Hall	342
9	Elam Vangilder	323
10	Gregg Olson	320
11	Dennis Martinez	319
12	Sammy Stewart	307
13	Stu Miller	297
14	Jack Powell	294
15	Mike Cuellar	290
16	George Blaeholder	280
17	Milt Pappas	264
18	Urban Shocker	259
19	Barney Pelty	255
20	Steve Barber	253

Games Started

1	Jim Palmer	521
2	Dave McNally	384
3	Mike Flanagan	328
4	Scott McGregor	309
5	Mike Cuellar	283
6	Jack Powell	264
7	Dennis Martinez	243
8	Milt Pappas	232
9	George Blaeholder	213
10	Barney Pelty	212
11	Steve Barber	211
12	Urban Shocker	207
13	Mike Mussina	194
14	Mike Boddicker	180
15	Carl Weilman	179
16	Elam Vangilder	176
17	Harry Howell	173
18	Dixie Davis	163
19	Jack Kramer	155
20	Sam Gray	153

Complete Games

1	Jim Palmer	211
2	Jack Powell	210
3	Barney Pelty	173
4	Harry Howell	150
5	Urban Shocker	144
6	Mike Cuellar	133
7	Dave McNally	120
8	Carl Weilman	105
9	Fred Glade	104
10	Mike Flanagan	98
11	Willie Sudhoff	93
12	George Blaeholder	90
13	Lefty Stewart	87
14	Earl Hamilton	83
	Elam Vangilder	83
	Scott McGregor	83
17	Milt Pappas	82
18	Dixie Davis	76
	Ned Garver	76
20	Sam Gray	71

Shutouts

1	Jim Palmer	53
2	Dave McNally	33
3	Mike Cuellar	30
4	Jack Powell	28
5	Milt Pappas	26
6	Barney Pelty	23
	Urban Shocker	23
	Scott McGregor	23
9	Steve Barber	19
10	Mike Flanagan	17
11	Harry Howell	16
12	Carl Weilman	15
13	Fred Glade	14
14	Elam Vangilder	13
	Mike Boddicker	13
16	George Blaeholder	12
	Mike Mussina	12
18	Denny Galehouse	11
	Tom Phoebus	11
20	Twelve tied at	10

Saves

1	Gregg Olson	160
2	Tippy Martinez	105
3	Stu Miller	100
4	Randy Myers	76
5	Eddie Watt	74
6	Dick Hall	58
7	Tim Stoddard	57
8	Don Aase	50
9	Don Stanhouse	45
10	Sammy Stewart	42
11	Hoyt Wilhelm	40
12	Grant Jackson	39
13	Pete Richert	37
14	George Zuverink	36
15	Lee Smith	33
16	Tom Niedenfuer	31
17	George Caster	29
18	Moe Drabowsky	27
19	Satchel Paige	26
	Billy Loes	26

Innings Pitched

1	Jim Palmer	3,948.0
2	Dave McNally	2,652.2
3	Mike Flanagan	2,317.2
4	Jack Powell	2,229.2
5	Scott McGregor	2,140.2
6	Mike Cuellar	2,028.1
7	Barney Pelty	1,864.1
8	Dennis Martinez	1,775.0
9	Urban Shocker	1,749.2
10	Milt Pappas	1,632.0
11	George Blaeholder	1,631.0
12	Harry Howell	1,580.2
13	Elam Vangilder	1,548.0
14	Carl Weilman	1,521.0
15	Steve Barber	1,414.2
16	Mike Mussina	1,362.1
17	Earl Hamilton	1,328.2
18	Sam Gray	1,312.0
19	Mike Boddicker	1,273.2
20	Dixie Davis	1,242.0

Walks

1	Jim Palmer	1,311
2	Dave McNally	790
3	Mike Flanagan	740
4	Steve Barber	668
5	Dixie Davis	640
6	Elam Vangilder	625
7	Mike Cuellar	601
8	Dennis Martinez	583
9	Milt Pappas	531
10	Barney Pelty	522
11	Scott McGregor	518
12	Jack Kramer	506
13	Jack Powell	486
14	Earl Hamilton	478
15	Ned Garver	456
16	Mike Boddicker	444
17	George Blaeholder	439
18	Sammy Stewart	433
19	Bump Hadley	431
20	Carl Weilman	418

Strikeouts

1	Jim Palmer	2,212
2	Dave McNally	1,476
3	Mike Flanagan	1,297
4	Mike Cuellar	1,011
5	Mike Mussina	978
6	Milt Pappas	944
7	Steve Barber	918
8	Scott McGregor	904
9	Jack Powell	884
10	Dennis Martinez	858
11	Mike Boddicker	836
12	Harry Howell	712
13	Urban Shocker	704
14	Barney Pelty	678
15	Ben McDonald	638
16	Tippy Martinez	585
17	Tom Phoebus	578
18	Storm Davis	539
19	Carl Weilman	536
20	George Blaeholder	520

Strikeouts/9 Innings
(minimum 1000 Innings Pitched)

1	Mike Mussina	6.46
2	Mike Boddicker	5.91
3	Steve Barber	5.84
4	Milt Pappas	5.21
5	Jim Palmer	5.04
6	Mike Flanagan	5.04
7	Dave McNally	5.01
8	Mike Cuellar	4.49
9	Dennis Martinez	4.35
10	Harry Howell	4.05
11	Fred Glade	3.92
12	Scott McGregor	3.80
13	Hal Brown	3.68
14	Urban Shocker	3.62
15	Jack Kramer	3.58
16	Jack Powell	3.57
17	Earl Hamilton	3.47
18	Bob Muncrief	3.35
19	Barney Pelty	3.27
20	Sam Gray	3.19

ERA
(minimum 1000 Innings Pitched)

1	Harry Howell	2.06
2	Fred Glade	2.52
3	Barney Pelty	2.61
4	Jack Powell	2.63
5	Carl Weilman	2.67
6	Jim Palmer	2.86
7	Earl Hamilton	2.94
8	Allen Sothoron	2.98
9	Steve Barber	3.12
10	Urban Shocker	3.17
11	Mike Cuellar	3.18
12	Dave McNally	3.18
13	Milt Pappas	3.24
14	Mike Mussina	3.50
15	Hal Brown	3.61
16	Ned Garver	3.64
17	Bob Muncrief	3.66
18	Mike Boddicker	3.73
19	Mike Flanagan	3.89
20	Scott McGregor	3.99

Component ERA
(minimum 1000 Innings Pitched)

1	Harry Howell	2.18
2	Fred Glade	2.29
3	Barney Pelty	2.51
4	Jack Powell	2.55
5	Carl Weilman	2.63
6	Jim Palmer	2.91
7	Mike Cuellar	3.03
8	Urban Shocker	3.10
9	Hal Brown	3.11
10	Milt Pappas	3.14
11	Allen Sothoron	3.14
12	Earl Hamilton	3.15
13	Mike Mussina	3.17
14	Dave McNally	3.18
15	Steve Barber	3.36
16	Bob Muncrief	3.66
17	Mike Boddicker	3.67
18	Mike Flanagan	3.79
19	Scott McGregor	3.84
20	Lefty Stewart	3.88

Opponent Average
(minimum 1000 Innings Pitched)

1	Jim Palmer	.230
2	Harry Howell	.233
3	Steve Barber	.234
4	Milt Pappas	.237
5	Fred Glade	.239
6	Barney Pelty	.239
7	Mike Cuellar	.241
8	Dave McNally	.244
9	Mike Mussina	.246
10	Jack Powell	.248
11	Mike Boddicker	.249
12	Carl Weilman	.250
13	Hal Brown	.251
14	Allen Sothoron	.254
15	Earl Hamilton	.258
16	Ned Garver	.262
17	Urban Shocker	.263
18	Mike Flanagan	.264
19	Dixie Davis	.265
20	Dennis Martinez	.267

Opponent OBP
(minimum 1000 Innings Pitched)

1	Fred Glade	.288
2	Harry Howell	.289
3	Mike Mussina	.292
4	Hal Brown	.292
5	Jack Powell	.293
6	Jim Palmer	.294
7	Mike Cuellar	.296
8	Milt Pappas	.301
9	Dave McNally	.303
10	Barney Pelty	.304
11	Carl Weilman	.306
12	Urban Shocker	.307
13	Scott McGregor	.313
14	Mike Boddicker	.316
15	Bob Muncrief	.320
16	Mike Flanagan	.321
17	Allen Sothoron	.322
18	Steve Barber	.323
19	Dennis Martinez	.326
20	Earl Hamilton	.329

Teams: Orioles

St. Louis Browns Team Batting Leaders—Career

Games

1	George Sisler	1,647
2	Bobby Wallace	1,569
3	Harlond Clift	1,443
4	Jimmy Austin	1,311
5	Wally Gerber	1,284
6	Baby Doll Jacobson	1,243
7	Hank Severeid	1,182
8	Ski Melillo	1,147
9	George McQuinn	1,138
10	Jack Tobin	1,133
11	Ken Williams	1,109
12	Burt Shotton	1,041
13	Del Pratt	904
14	Vern Stephens	890
15	Marty McManus	856
16	George Stone	846
17	Tom Jones	842
18	Chet Laabs	794
19	Red Kress	785
20	Jack Burns	752

At-Bats

1	George Sisler	6,667
2	Bobby Wallace	5,529
3	Harlond Clift	5,281
4	Baby Doll Jacobson	4,755
5	Jimmy Austin	4,519
6	Wally Gerber	4,510
7	Jack Tobin	4,404
8	George McQuinn	4,310
9	Ski Melillo	4,281
10	Ken Williams	4,013
11	Burt Shotton	3,912
12	Hank Severeid	3,865
13	Vern Stephens	3,396
14	Del Pratt	3,394
15	George Stone	3,269
16	Marty McManus	3,181
17	Tom Jones	3,103
18	Red Kress	3,020
19	Jack Burns	2,948
20	Fred Schulte	2,701

Runs

1	George Sisler	1,091
2	Harlond Clift	1,013
3	Ken Williams	757
4	Baby Doll Jacobson	711
5	Jack Tobin	680
6	George McQuinn	663
7	Bobby Wallace	609
8	Burt Shotton	601
9	Jimmy Austin	578
10	Wally Gerber	518
11	Marty McManus	504
12	Ski Melillo	498
13	Vern Stephens	497
14	Fred Schulte	450
15	Jack Burns	445
16	Sammy West	439
17	George Stone	426
18	Red Kress	425
19	Chet Laabs	404
20	Del Pratt	386

Hits

1	George Sisler	2,295
2	Baby Doll Jacobson	1,508
3	Harlond Clift	1,463
4	Bobby Wallace	1,424
5	Jack Tobin	1,399
6	Ken Williams	1,308
7	George McQuinn	1,220
8	Wally Gerber	1,189
9	Jimmy Austin	1,133
10	Ski Melillo	1,124
11	Hank Severeid	1,121
12	Burt Shotton	1,070
13	Vern Stephens	995
14	George Stone	984
15	Del Pratt	957
16	Marty McManus	949
17	Red Kress	902
18	Jack Burns	822
19	Sammy West	819
20	Fred Schulte	799

Doubles

1	George Sisler	343
2	Harlond Clift	294
3	Baby Doll Jacobson	269
4	George McQuinn	254
5	Bobby Wallace	236
	Ken Williams	236
7	Jack Tobin	217
8	Red Kress	189
9	Marty McManus	185
10	Ski Melillo	183
11	Hank Severeid	181
12	Del Pratt	179
13	Fred Schulte	174
14	Jack Burns	163
15	Wally Gerber	160
16	Vern Stephens	157
17	Sammy West	155
18	Jimmy Austin	152
19	Johnny Berardino	149
20	Wally Judnich	136

Triples

1	George Sisler	145
2	Baby Doll Jacobson	88
3	Del Pratt	72
	Jack Tobin	72
5	George Stone	70
	Ken Williams	70
7	Jimmy Austin	67
8	Bobby Wallace	65
9	Harlond Clift	62
10	Ski Melillo	58
11	Marty McManus	53
12	Burt Shotton	52
13	George McQuinn	47
14	Wally Gerber	43
15	Charlie Hemphill	37
	Emmett Heidrick	37
17	Hank Severeid	36
	Sammy West	36
19	Red Kress	35
	Chet Laabs	35

Home Runs

1	Ken Williams	185
2	Harlond Clift	170
3	Vern Stephens	113
4	George McQuinn	108
5	Chet Laabs	101
6	George Sisler	93
7	Wally Judnich	88
8	Baby Doll Jacobson	76
9	Goose Goslin	71
10	Dick Kokos	58
11	Marty McManus	56
12	Red Kress	54
13	Jack Tobin	48
14	Sammy West	45
15	Les Moss	44
16	Beau Bell	42
17	Jack Burns	40
18	Bruce Campbell	39
	Jeff Heath	39
20	Don Lenhardt	38

RBI

1	George Sisler	959
2	Ken Williams	808
3	Harlond Clift	769
4	Baby Doll Jacobson	704
5	George McQuinn	625
6	Bobby Wallace	607
7	Vern Stephens	545
8	Red Kress	513
9	Marty McManus	506
10	Hank Severeid	485
11	Ski Melillo	471
12	Del Pratt	455
13	Jack Tobin	438
14	Wally Gerber	431
15	Chet Laabs	428
16	Fred Schulte	390
	Wally Judnich	390
18	Jack Burns	354
19	Beau Bell	346
20	Johnny Berardino	343

Walks

1	Harlond Clift	986
2	Burt Shotton	595
3	Bobby Wallace	526
4	George McQuinn	520
5	Jimmy Austin	513
6	Ken Williams	497
7	Wally Gerber	414
8	George Sisler	385
9	Sammy West	350
10	Chet Laabs	344
11	Vern Stephens	335
12	Rick Ferrell	331
13	Wally Judnich	328
14	Jack Tobin	327
15	Baby Doll Jacobson	317
16	Lu Blue	312
17	Fred Schulte	298
18	Marty McManus	297
	Jack Burns	297
20	Hank Severeid	290

Strikeouts

1	Harlond Clift	649
2	Chet Laabs	473
3	George McQuinn	446
4	Vern Stephens	384
5	Jimmy Austin	363
6	Baby Doll Jacobson	355
7	Burt Shotton	303
8	Marty McManus	292
9	Wally Gerber	290
10	Red Kress	286
11	George Sisler	278
12	Wally Judnich	273
13	Ski Melillo	264
14	Sammy West	257
15	Fred Schulte	255
16	Jack Burns	254
17	Dick Kokos	249
18	Bruce Campbell	241
19	Doc Lavan	240
	Ken Williams	240

Stolen Bases

1	George Sisler	351
2	Burt Shotton	247
3	Jimmy Austin	192
4	Del Pratt	174
5	Ken Williams	144
6	Bobby Wallace	138
7	George Stone	132
8	Charlie Hemphill	109
9	Tom Jones	103
10	Gus Williams	95
11	Bob Dillinger	90
12	Jack Tobin	85
13	Roy Hartzell	84
14	Baby Doll Jacobson	81
15	Emmett Heidrick	74
16	Harlond Clift	67
17	Ski Melillo	66
18	Lyn Lary	62
19	Danny Hoffman	60
20	Jack Burns	59

Runs Created

1	George Sisler	1,173
2	Harlond Clift	968
3	Ken Williams	846
4	Baby Doll Jacobson	762
5	George McQuinn	711
6	Bobby Wallace	674
7	Jack Tobin	670
8	Burt Shotton	557
	Vern Stephens	557
10	Jimmy Austin	526
11	George Stone	521
12	Marty McManus	498
13	Hank Severeid	492
14	Wally Gerber	489
15	Red Kress	476
16	Ski Melillo	462
17	Del Pratt	457
18	Sammy West	454
19	Wally Judnich	438
20	Fred Schulte	437

Runs Created/27 Outs

(minimum 2000 Plate Appearances)

1	Ken Williams	7.57
2	George Sisler	6.58
3	Harlond Clift	6.46
4	Wally Judnich	6.21
5	Sammy West	6.16
6	Beau Bell	6.06
7	Vern Stephens	6.02
8	George McQuinn	5.82
9	Chet Laabs	5.80
10	Baby Doll Jacobson	5.79
11	Fred Schulte	5.76
12	George Stone	5.69
13	Red Kress	5.56
14	Jack Tobin	5.52
15	Marty McManus	5.44
16	Bob Dillinger	5.14
17	Rick Ferrell	4.98
18	Jack Burns	4.91
19	Burt Shotton	4.87
20	Al Zarilla	4.85

Batting Average

(minimum 2000 Plate Appearances)

1	George Sisler	.344
2	Ken Williams	.326
3	Jack Tobin	.318
4	Baby Doll Jacobson	.317
5	Bob Dillinger	.309
6	Beau Bell	.309
7	Sammy West	.305
8	George Stone	.301
9	Red Kress	.299
10	Marty McManus	.298
11	Fred Schulte	.296
12	Vern Stephens	.293
13	Hank Severeid	.290
14	Wally Judnich	.283
15	George McQuinn	.283
16	Del Pratt	.282
17	Jack Burns	.279
18	Harlond Clift	.277
19	Al Zarilla	.274
20	Burt Shotton	.274

On-Base Percentage

(minimum 2000 Plate Appearances)

1	Ken Williams	.404
2	Harlond Clift	.394
3	Sammy West	.386
4	George Sisler	.384
5	Beau Bell	.373
6	Bob Dillinger	.373
7	Burt Shotton	.372
8	Rick Ferrell	.368
9	Jack Tobin	.368
10	Wally Judnich	.367
11	Fred Schulte	.367
12	Baby Doll Jacobson	.364
13	Marty McManus	.362
14	George McQuinn	.361
15	George Stone	.360
16	Red Kress	.359
17	Vern Stephens	.357
18	Chet Laabs	.354
19	Jack Burns	.346
20	Al Zarilla	.345

Slugging Percentage

(minimum 2000 Plate Appearances)

1	Ken Williams	.558
2	George Sisler	.481
3	Beau Bell	.462
4	Wally Judnich	.462
5	Chet Laabs	.459
6	Baby Doll Jacobson	.459
7	Harlond Clift	.453
8	Vern Stephens	.451
9	Marty McManus	.443
10	Sammy West	.441
11	George McQuinn	.439
12	Red Kress	.438
13	Jack Tobin	.432
14	Fred Schulte	.425
15	George Stone	.398
16	Del Pratt	.396
17	Jack Burns	.394
18	Bob Dillinger	.394
19	Al Zarilla	.392
20	Johnny Berardino	.375

St. Louis Browns Team Pitching Leaders—Career

Wins

1	Urban Shocker	126
2	Jack Powell	117
3	Barney Pelty	91
4	George Blaeholder	90
5	Elam Vangilder	88
6	Carl Weilman	85
7	Harry Howell	78
8	Dixie Davis	75
9	Lefty Stewart	73
10	Bob Muncrief	69
11	Sam Gray	67
	Jack Kramer	67
13	Earl Hamilton	60
14	Ned Garver	59
15	Nels Potter	57
16	Allen Sothoron	55
17	Fred Glade	52
18	Willie Sudhoff	51
19	Denny Galehouse	50
20	Three tied at	44

Losses

1	Jack Powell	143
2	Barney Pelty	113
3	George Blaeholder	111
4	Carl Weilman	95
5	Harry Howell	91
	Elam Vangilder	91
7	Earl Hamilton	89
8	Sam Gray	82
9	Jack Kramer	81
10	Urban Shocker	80
11	Lefty Stewart	74
12	Dixie Davis	68
	Dick Coffman	68
	Ned Garver	68
15	Bob Muncrief	67
16	Fred Glade	63
17	Willie Sudhoff	62
	Allen Sothoron	62
19	Denny Galehouse	58
20	Two tied at	56

Winning Percentage
(minimum 100 decisions)

1	Urban Shocker	.612
2	Nels Potter	.570
3	Dixie Davis	.524
4	Bob Muncrief	.507
5	Lefty Stewart	.497
6	Elam Vangilder	.492
7	Carl Weilman	.472
8	Allen Sothoron	.470
9	Ned Garver	.465
10	Denny Galehouse	.463
11	Harry Howell	.462
12	Jack Kramer	.453
13	Fred Glade	.452
14	Willie Sudhoff	.451
15	Jack Powell	.450
16	Sam Gray	.450
17	George Blaeholder	.448
18	Barney Pelty	.446
19	Earl Hamilton	.403
20	Dick Coffman	.393

Games

1	Elam Vangilder	323
2	Jack Powell	294
3	George Blaeholder	280
4	Urban Shocker	259
5	Barney Pelty	255
6	Carl Weilman	240
7	Sam Gray	238
8	Dick Coffman	237
9	Earl Hamilton	233
10	Bob Muncrief	218
11	Jack Kramer	214
12	Dixie Davis	213
13	Jack Knott	205
14	Harry Howell	201
15	Lefty Stewart	191
16	Ned Garver	170
17	Cliff Fannin	164
18	Allen Sothoron	162
19	Dave Davenport	161
20	George Caster	158

Games Started

1	Jack Powell	264
2	George Blaeholder	213
3	Barney Pelty	212
4	Urban Shocker	207
5	Carl Weilman	179
6	Elam Vangilder	176
7	Harry Howell	173
8	Dixie Davis	163
9	Jack Kramer	155
10	Sam Gray	153
11	Lefty Stewart	152
12	Earl Hamilton	149
	Bob Muncrief	149
14	Ned Garver	138
15	Denny Galehouse	127
16	Fred Glade	120
17	Allen Sothoron	117
18	Dick Coffman	115
19	Willie Sudhoff	114
20	Dave Davenport	108

Complete Games

1	Jack Powell	210
2	Barney Pelty	173
3	Harry Howell	150
4	Urban Shocker	144
5	Carl Weilman	105
6	Fred Glade	104
7	Willie Sudhoff	93
8	George Blaeholder	90
9	Lefty Stewart	87
10	Earl Hamilton	83
	Elam Vangilder	83
12	Dixie Davis	76
	Ned Garver	76
14	Sam Gray	71
15	Jack Kramer	66
16	Allen Sothoron	65
17	Bob Muncrief	64
18	Nels Potter	58
19	Denny Galehouse	54
20	Two tied at	51

Shutouts

1	Jack Powell	28
2	Barney Pelty	23
	Urban Shocker	23
4	Harry Howell	16
5	Carl Weilman	15
6	Fred Glade	14
7	Elam Vangilder	13
8	George Blaeholder	12
9	Denny Galehouse	11
10	Rube Waddell	10
	Earl Hamilton	10
	Dixie Davis	10
	Bob Muncrief	10
	Jack Kramer	10
15	Allen Sothoron	9
	Sam Gray	9
17	Willie Sudhoff	7
	George Baumgardner	7
	General Crowder	7
	Dick Coffman	7

Saves

1	George Caster	29
2	Satchel Paige	26
3	Urban Shocker	20
4	Jack Knott	19
5	Elam Vangilder	14
	Sam Gray	14
7	Tom Ferrick	13
8	George Blaeholder	12
	Chad Kimsey	12
10	Jack Powell	10
	Carl Weilman	10
	General Crowder	10
	Dick Coffman	10
14	Allen Sothoron	9
	Hub Pruett	9
	Al Hollingsworth	9
17	Dave Danforth	8
	Ned Garver	8
	Marlin Stuart	8
20	Two tied at	7

Innings Pitched

1	Jack Powell	2,229.2
2	Barney Pelty	1,864.1
3	Urban Shocker	1,749.2
4	George Blaeholder	1,631.0
5	Harry Howell	1,580.2
6	Elam Vangilder	1,548.0
7	Carl Weilman	1,521.0
8	Earl Hamilton	1,328.2
9	Sam Gray	1,312.0
10	Dixie Davis	1,242.0
11	Lefty Stewart	1,236.2
12	Bob Muncrief	1,215.1
13	Jack Kramer	1,188.2
14	Ned Garver	1,076.1
15	Fred Glade	1,032.2
16	Allen Sothoron	1,011.1
17	Willie Sudhoff	980.0
18	Denny Galehouse	972.0
19	Dick Coffman	962.1
20	Nels Potter	933.2

Walks

1	Dixie Davis	640
2	Elam Vangilder	625
3	Barney Pelty	522
4	Jack Kramer	506
5	Jack Powell	486
6	Earl Hamilton	478
7	Ned Garver	456
8	George Blaeholder	439
9	Bump Hadley	431
10	Carl Weilman	418
11	Bobo Newsom	411
12	Urban Shocker	409
13	Cliff Fannin	393
14	Harry Howell	390
15	Sam Gray	386
16	Lefty Stewart	378
17	Jack Knott	377
18	Allen Sothoron	356
19	Dick Coffman	336
20	Denny Galehouse	333

Strikeouts

1	Jack Powell	884
2	Harry Howell	712
3	Urban Shocker	704
4	Barney Pelty	678
5	Carl Weilman	536
6	George Blaeholder	520
7	Earl Hamilton	513
8	Jack Kramer	473
9	Sam Gray	465
10	Bob Muncrief	452
11	Fred Glade	450
12	Bobo Newsom	448
13	Nels Potter	441
14	Denny Galehouse	431
15	Elam Vangilder	428
	Dixie Davis	428
17	Rube Waddell	389
18	Ned Garver	374
19	Lefty Stewart	369
20	Bump Hadley	360

Strikeouts/9 Innings
(minimum 1000 Innings Pitched)

1	Harry Howell	4.05
2	Fred Glade	3.92
3	Urban Shocker	3.62
4	Jack Kramer	3.58
5	Jack Powell	3.57
6	Earl Hamilton	3.47
7	Bob Muncrief	3.35
8	Barney Pelty	3.27
9	Sam Gray	3.19
10	Allen Sothoron	3.18
11	Carl Weilman	3.17
12	Ned Garver	3.13
13	Dixie Davis	3.10
14	George Blaeholder	2.87
15	Lefty Stewart	2.69
16	Elam Vangilder	2.49

ERA
(minimum 1000 Innings Pitched)

1	Harry Howell	2.06
2	Fred Glade	2.52
3	Barney Pelty	2.61
4	Jack Powell	2.63
5	Carl Weilman	2.67
6	Earl Hamilton	2.94
7	Allen Sothoron	2.98
8	Urban Shocker	3.17
9	Ned Garver	3.64
10	Bob Muncrief	3.66
11	Dixie Davis	4.04
12	Lefty Stewart	4.11
13	Jack Kramer	4.13
14	Elam Vangilder	4.31
15	Sam Gray	4.37
16	George Blaeholder	4.55

Component ERA
(minimum 1000 Innings Pitched)

1	Harry Howell	2.18
2	Fred Glade	2.29
3	Barney Pelty	2.51
4	Jack Powell	2.55
5	Carl Weilman	2.63
6	Urban Shocker	3.10
7	Allen Sothoron	3.14
8	Earl Hamilton	3.15
9	Bob Muncrief	3.66
10	Lefty Stewart	3.88
11	Ned Garver	3.95
12	Jack Kramer	4.08
13	Dixie Davis	4.14
14	Sam Gray	4.16
15	George Blaeholder	4.26
16	Elam Vangilder	4.30

Opponent Average
(minimum 1000 Innings Pitched)

1	Harry Howell	.233
2	Fred Glade	.239
3	Barney Pelty	.239
4	Jack Powell	.248
5	Carl Weilman	.250
6	Allen Sothoron	.254
7	Earl Hamilton	.258
8	Ned Garver	.262
9	Urban Shocker	.263
10	Dixie Davis	.265
11	Jack Kramer	.273
12	Bob Muncrief	.273
13	Lefty Stewart	.277
14	Elam Vangilder	.284
15	George Blaeholder	.288
16	Sam Gray	.288

Opponent OBP
(minimum 1000 Innings Pitched)

1	Fred Glade	.288
2	Harry Howell	.289
3	Jack Powell	.293
4	Barney Pelty	.304
5	Carl Weilman	.306
6	Urban Shocker	.307
7	Bob Muncrief	.320
8	Allen Sothoron	.322
9	Earl Hamilton	.329
10	Lefty Stewart	.332
11	George Blaeholder	.334
12	Ned Garver	.338
13	Sam Gray	.338
14	Jack Kramer	.346
15	Elam Vangilder	.355
16	Dixie Davis	.359

Teams: Orioles

1217

Baltimore Orioles Team Batting Leaders—Career

Games

1	Brooks Robinson	2,896
2	Cal Ripken Jr.	2,543
3	Mark Belanger	1,962
4	Eddie Murray	1,884
5	Boog Powell	1,763
6	Paul Blair	1,700
7	Ken Singleton	1,446
8	Al Bumbry	1,428
9	Rick Dempsey	1,245
10	Brady Anderson	1,204
11	Rich Dauer	1,140
12	Dave Johnson	995
13	Gus Triandos	953
14	Mike Devereaux	878
15	Doug DeCinces	858
16	Gary Roenicke	850
17	Frank Robinson	827
18	Russ Snyder	815
19	Jackie Brandt	802
20	Chris Hoiles	797

At-Bats

1	Brooks Robinson	10,654
2	Cal Ripken Jr.	9,832
3	Eddie Murray	7,075
4	Boog Powell	5,912
5	Mark Belanger	5,734
6	Paul Blair	5,606
7	Ken Singleton	5,115
8	Al Bumbry	4,958
9	Brady Anderson	4,292
10	Rich Dauer	3,829
11	Rick Dempsey	3,585
12	Dave Johnson	3,489
13	Gus Triandos	3,186
14	Mike Devereaux	3,170
15	Luis Aparicio	2,948
16	Frank Robinson	2,941
17	Lee May	2,929
18	Doug DeCinces	2,916
19	Bobby Grich	2,790
20	Jackie Brandt	2,749

Runs

1	Cal Ripken Jr.	1,445
2	Brooks Robinson	1,232
3	Eddie Murray	1,084
4	Boog Powell	796
5	Al Bumbry	772
6	Paul Blair	737
7	Brady Anderson	712
8	Ken Singleton	684
9	Mark Belanger	670
10	Frank Robinson	555
11	Rich Dauer	448
12	Bobby Grich	432
13	Mike Devereaux	417
14	Don Buford	408
15	Rick Dempsey	405
16	Jackie Brandt	392
17	Luis Aparicio	385
18	Dave Johnson	382
19	Chris Hoiles	379
20	Rafael Palmeiro	376

Hits

1	Brooks Robinson	2,848
2	Cal Ripken Jr.	2,715
3	Eddie Murray	2,080
4	Boog Powell	1,574
5	Ken Singleton	1,455
6	Paul Blair	1,426
7	Al Bumbry	1,403
8	Mark Belanger	1,304
9	Brady Anderson	1,125
10	Rich Dauer	984
11	Dave Johnson	904
12	Frank Robinson	882
13	Rick Dempsey	854
14	Mike Devereaux	797
15	Gus Triandos	794
16	Lee May	744
17	Luis Aparicio	740
18	Doug DeCinces	738
19	Bobby Grich	730
20	Jackie Brandt	710

Doubles

1	Cal Ripken Jr.	517
2	Brooks Robinson	482
3	Eddie Murray	363
4	Paul Blair	269
5	Boog Powell	243
6	Ken Singleton	235
	Brady Anderson	235
8	Al Bumbry	217
9	Rich Dauer	193
10	Dave Johnson	186
11	Mark Belanger	174
12	Rick Dempsey	169
13	Doug DeCinces	161
14	Frank Robinson	143
15	Mike Devereaux	138
16	Bobby Grich	137
17	Jackie Brandt	128
18	Rafael Palmeiro	126
19	Gus Triandos	119
20	Jerry Adair	118

Triples

1	Brooks Robinson	68
2	Brady Anderson	53
3	Al Bumbry	52
4	Paul Blair	51
5	Cal Ripken Jr.	43
6	Luis Aparicio	34
7	Mark Belanger	33
8	Mike Devereaux	32
9	Bobby Grich	27
10	Eddie Murray	25
11	Jackie Brandt	22
12	Bob Boyd	20
	Russ Snyder	20
14	Ken Singleton	19
15	Frank Robinson	18
16	Bob Nieman	16
	Dave Johnson	16
18	Jerry Adair	15
	Don Buford	15
	Joe Orsulak	15

Home Runs

1	Cal Ripken Jr.	370
2	Eddie Murray	343
3	Boog Powell	303
4	Brooks Robinson	268
5	Ken Singleton	182
6	Frank Robinson	179
7	Gus Triandos	142
8	Brady Anderson	140
9	Rafael Palmeiro	139
10	Chris Hoiles	136
11	Paul Blair	126
12	Jim Gentile	124
13	Lee May	123
14	Doug DeCinces	107
15	Gary Roenicke	106
16	Mike Devereaux	94
17	Fred Lynn	87
18	Jackie Brandt	86
19	Larry Sheets	84
20	Curt Blefary	82

RBI

1	Cal Ripken Jr.	1,453
2	Brooks Robinson	1,357
3	Eddie Murray	1,224
4	Boog Powell	1,063
5	Ken Singleton	766
6	Paul Blair	567
7	Frank Robinson	545
8	Gus Triandos	517
	Brady Anderson	517
10	Lee May	487
11	Rafael Palmeiro	432
12	Mike Devereaux	403
13	Jim Gentile	398
14	Doug DeCinces	397
15	Chris Hoiles	393
16	Al Bumbry	392
17	Dave Johnson	391
18	Mark Belanger	385
19	Rich Dauer	372
20	Rick Dempsey	355

Walks

1	Cal Ripken Jr.	1,016
2	Boog Powell	889
3	Ken Singleton	886
4	Eddie Murray	884
5	Brooks Robinson	860
6	Brady Anderson	604
7	Mark Belanger	571
8	Al Bumbry	464
9	Frank Robinson	460
10	Bobby Grich	457
11	Rick Dempsey	424
12	Paul Blair	420
	Don Buford	420
14	Chris Hoiles	397
15	Gus Triandos	365
	Dave Johnson	365
17	Randy Milligan	352
18	Gary Roenicke	335
19	Jim Gentile	317
20	Curt Blefary	299

Strikeouts

1	Cal Ripken Jr.	1,106
2	Boog Powell	1,102
3	Brooks Robinson	990
4	Eddie Murray	969
5	Ken Singleton	860
6	Mark Belanger	829
7	Paul Blair	816
8	Brady Anderson	769
9	Al Bumbry	700
10	Lee May	577
11	Chris Hoiles	566
12	Mike Devereaux	541
13	Rick Dempsey	538
14	Bobby Grich	520
15	Gus Triandos	487
16	Dave Johnson	475
17	Doug DeCinces	455
18	Andy Etchebarren	452
	Frank Robinson	452
20	Jackie Brandt	413

Stolen Bases

1	Al Bumbry	252
2	Brady Anderson	222
3	Paul Blair	167
4	Luis Aparicio	166
	Mark Belanger	166
6	Don Baylor	118
7	Don Buford	85
8	Bobby Grich	77
9	Mike Devereaux	73
10	Alan Wiggins	71
11	Eddie Murray	62
12	Pat Kelly	55
13	Merv Rettenmund	52
	John Shelby	52
	Mark McLemore	52
16	Rich Coggins	43
17	Russ Snyder	40
	John Lowenstein	40
19	Doug DeCinces	39
	Steve Finley	39

Runs Created

1	Cal Ripken Jr.	1,481
2	Brooks Robinson	1,337
3	Eddie Murray	1,259
4	Boog Powell	993
5	Ken Singleton	881
6	Brady Anderson	722
7	Al Bumbry	681
8	Paul Blair	663
9	Frank Robinson	622
10	Mark Belanger	507
11	Bobby Grich	446
12	Dave Johnson	432
	Rafael Palmeiro	432
14	Gus Triandos	426
15	Chris Hoiles	425
16	Rick Dempsey	413
17	Don Buford	398
18	Doug DeCinces	389
19	Rich Dauer	385
20	Mike Devereaux	382

Runs Created/27 Outs

(minimum 2000 Plate Appearances)

1	Frank Robinson	7.66
2	Rafael Palmeiro	7.00
3	Jim Gentile	6.82
4	Eddie Murray	6.42
5	Ken Singleton	6.09
6	Merv Rettenmund	5.99
7	Don Buford	5.97
8	Boog Powell	5.86
9	Chris Hoiles	5.78
10	Brady Anderson	5.77
11	Randy Milligan	5.56
12	Bobby Grich	5.48
13	Gary Roenicke	5.33
14	Curt Blefary	5.32
15	Cal Ripken Jr.	5.27
16	Al Bumbry	4.85
17	Larry Sheets	4.74
18	Jackie Brandt	4.62
19	Joe Orsulak	4.62
20	Russ Snyder	4.53

Batting Average

(minimum 2000 Plate Appearances)

1	Frank Robinson	.300
2	Eddie Murray	.294
3	Rafael Palmeiro	.291
4	Merv Rettenmund	.284
	Ken Singleton	.284
6	Al Bumbry	.283
7	Joe Orsulak	.281
8	Russ Snyder	.280
9	Cal Ripken Jr.	.276
10	Jim Gentile	.272
11	Don Buford	.270
12	Larry Sheets	.268
13	Brooks Robinson	.267
14	Boog Powell	.266
15	Brady Anderson	.262
16	Chris Hoiles	.262
17	Bobby Grich	.262
18	Dave Johnson	.259
19	Randy Milligan	.258
20	Jackie Brandt	.258

On-Base Percentage

(minimum 2000 Plate Appearances)

1	Frank Robinson	.401
2	Ken Singleton	.388
3	Randy Milligan	.388
4	Don Buford	.385
5	Merv Rettenmund	.383
6	Jim Gentile	.379
7	Bobby Grich	.372
8	Eddie Murray	.370
9	Rafael Palmeiro	.369
10	Chris Hoiles	.367
11	Brady Anderson	.363
12	Boog Powell	.362
13	Gary Roenicke	.355
14	Curt Blefary	.347
15	Al Bumbry	.345
16	Cal Ripken Jr.	.344
17	Joe Orsulak	.337
18	Russ Snyder	.334
19	Dave Johnson	.330
20	Gus Triandos	.326

Slugging Percentage

(minimum 2000 Plate Appearances)

1	Frank Robinson	.543
2	Rafael Palmeiro	.539
3	Jim Gentile	.512
4	Eddie Murray	.498
5	Chris Hoiles	.467
6	Boog Powell	.465
7	Cal Ripken Jr.	.450
8	Gary Roenicke	.448
9	Larry Sheets	.445
10	Ken Singleton	.445
11	Brady Anderson	.439
12	Merv Rettenmund	.436
13	Doug DeCinces	.428
14	Gus Triandos	.424
15	Randy Milligan	.423
16	Lee May	.423
17	Curt Blefary	.417
18	Jackie Brandt	.415
19	Bobby Grich	.405
20	Don Buford	.405

Baltimore Orioles Team Pitching Leaders—Career

Wins

1	Jim Palmer	268
2	Dave McNally	181
3	Mike Cuellar	143
4	Mike Flanagan	141
5	Scott McGregor	138
6	Milt Pappas	110
7	Dennis Martinez	108
8	Mike Mussina	105
9	Steve Barber	95
10	Mike Boddicker	79
11	Dick Hall	65
12	Hal Brown	62
13	Storm Davis	61
14	Ben McDonald	58
15	Tippy Martinez	52
16	Ross Grimsley	51
	Sammy Stewart	51
18	Tom Phoebus	50
19	Chuck Estrada	48
20	Mark Williamson	46

Losses

1	Jim Palmer	152
2	Mike Flanagan	116
3	Dave McNally	113
4	Scott McGregor	108
5	Dennis Martinez	93
6	Mike Cuellar	88
7	Steve Barber	75
8	Milt Pappas	74
9	Mike Boddicker	73
10	Ben McDonald	53
11	Jeff Ballard	51
12	Mike Mussina	49
13	Hal Brown	48
14	Ross Grimsley	45
	Sammy Stewart	45
16	Storm Davis	43
17	Chuck Estrada	41
18	Dick Hall	40
	Tippy Martinez	40
20	Two tied at	39

Winning Percentage
(minimum 75 decisions)

1	Mike Mussina	.682
2	Jim Palmer	.638
3	Dick Hall	.619
	Mike Cuellar	.619
5	Dave McNally	.616
6	Milt Pappas	.598
7	Storm Davis	.587
8	Tom Phoebus	.575
9	Mark Williamson	.568
10	Tippy Martinez	.565
11	Hal Brown	.564
12	Scott McGregor	.561
13	Steve Barber	.559
14	Mike Flanagan	.549
15	Chuck Estrada	.539
16	Robin Roberts	.538
17	Dennis Martinez	.537
18	Ross Grimsley	.531
	Sammy Stewart	.531
20	Hoyt Wilhelm	.524

Games

1	Jim Palmer	558
2	Tippy Martinez	499
3	Mike Flanagan	450
4	Dave McNally	412
5	Mark Williamson	365
6	Eddie Watt	363
7	Scott McGregor	356
8	Dick Hall	342
9	Gregg Olson	320
10	Dennis Martinez	319
11	Sammy Stewart	307
12	Stu Miller	297
13	Mike Cuellar	290
14	Milt Pappas	264
15	Steve Barber	253
16	Alan Mills	236
17	Tim Stoddard	229
18	Grant Jackson	209
19	Hal Brown	204
20	Two tied at	202

Games Started

1	Jim Palmer	521
2	Dave McNally	384
3	Mike Flanagan	328
4	Scott McGregor	309
5	Mike Cuellar	283
6	Dennis Martinez	243
7	Milt Pappas	232
8	Steve Barber	211
9	Mike Mussina	194
10	Mike Boddicker	180
11	Ben McDonald	142
12	Hal Brown	131
13	Tom Phoebus	126
14	Ross Grimsley	124
15	Storm Davis	123
16	Jeff Ballard	113
17	Bob Milacki	109
18	Robin Roberts	106
19	Chuck Estrada	102
20	Wally Bunker	100

Complete Games

1	Jim Palmer	211
2	Mike Cuellar	133
3	Dave McNally	120
4	Mike Flanagan	98
5	Scott McGregor	83
6	Milt Pappas	82
7	Dennis Martinez	69
8	Steve Barber	53
	Mike Boddicker	53
10	Ross Grimsley	38
11	Pat Dobson	31
	Mike Mussina	31
13	Hal Brown	30
14	Robin Roberts	28
15	Connie Johnson	27
	Tom Phoebus	27
	Jim Hardin	27
	Storm Davis	27
19	Chuck Estrada	24
20	Jack Fisher	23

Shutouts

1	Jim Palmer	53
2	Dave McNally	33
3	Mike Cuellar	30
4	Milt Pappas	26
5	Scott McGregor	23
6	Steve Barber	19
7	Mike Flanagan	17
8	Mike Boddicker	13
9	Mike Mussina	12
10	Tom Phoebus	11
11	Dennis Martinez	10
12	Hal Brown	9
13	Robin Roberts	7
	Jim Hardin	7
	Pat Dobson	7
	Ross Grimsley	7
17	Billy O'Dell	6
	Ben McDonald	6
19	Five tied at	5

Saves

1	Gregg Olson	160
2	Tippy Martinez	105
3	Stu Miller	100
4	Randy Myers	76
5	Eddie Watt	74
6	Dick Hall	58
7	Tim Stoddard	57
8	Don Aase	50
9	Don Stanhouse	45
10	Sammy Stewart	42
11	Hoyt Wilhelm	40
12	Grant Jackson	39
13	Pete Richert	37
14	George Zuverink	36
15	Lee Smith	33
16	Tom Niedenfuer	31
17	Moe Drabowsky	27
18	Billy Loes	26
19	Doug Jones	22
20	Mark Williamson	21

Innings Pitched

1	Jim Palmer	3,948.0
2	Dave McNally	2,652.2
3	Mike Flanagan	2,317.2
4	Scott McGregor	2,140.2
5	Mike Cuellar	2,028.1
6	Dennis Martinez	1,775.0
7	Milt Pappas	1,632.0
8	Steve Barber	1,414.2
9	Mike Mussina	1,362.1
10	Mike Boddicker	1,273.2
11	Hal Brown	1,030.2
12	Storm Davis	944.1
13	Ben McDonald	937.0
14	Ross Grimsley	907.2
15	Sammy Stewart	866.0
16	Tom Phoebus	807.2
17	Dick Hall	770.0
18	Robin Roberts	761.1
19	Tippy Martinez	752.1
20	Chuck Estrada	730.0

Walks

1	Jim Palmer	1,311
2	Dave McNally	790
3	Mike Flanagan	740
4	Steve Barber	668
5	Mike Cuellar	601
6	Dennis Martinez	583
7	Milt Pappas	531
8	Scott McGregor	518
9	Mike Boddicker	444
10	Sammy Stewart	433
11	Chuck Estrada	394
12	Tom Phoebus	374
13	Tippy Martinez	366
14	Ben McDonald	334
15	Mike Mussina	328
16	Storm Davis	318
17	Ray Moore	291
18	Bob Milacki	255
19	Ross Grimsley	254
20	Jack Fisher	247

Strikeouts

1	Jim Palmer	2,212
2	Dave McNally	1,476
3	Mike Flanagan	1,297
4	Mike Cuellar	1,011
5	Mike Mussina	978
6	Milt Pappas	944
7	Steve Barber	918
8	Scott McGregor	904
9	Dennis Martinez	858
10	Mike Boddicker	836
11	Ben McDonald	638
12	Tippy Martinez	585
13	Tom Phoebus	578
14	Storm Davis	539
15	Chuck Estrada	517
16	Sammy Stewart	514
17	Dick Hall	499
18	Hoyt Wilhelm	458
19	Arthur Rhodes	437
20	Eddie Watt	433

Strikeouts/9 Innings
(minimum 750 Innings Pitched)

1	Tippy Martinez	7.00
2	Mike Mussina	6.46
3	Tom Phoebus	6.44
4	Ben McDonald	6.13
5	Mike Boddicker	5.91
6	Steve Barber	5.84
7	Dick Hall	5.83
8	Sammy Stewart	5.34
9	Milt Pappas	5.21
10	Storm Davis	5.14
11	Jim Palmer	5.04
12	Mike Flanagan	5.04
13	Dave McNally	5.01
14	Robin Roberts	4.70
15	Mike Cuellar	4.49
16	Dennis Martinez	4.35
17	Scott McGregor	3.80
18	Hal Brown	3.68
19	Ross Grimsley	3.56

ERA
(minimum 750 Innings Pitched)

1	Jim Palmer	2.86
2	Dick Hall	2.89
3	Tom Phoebus	3.06
4	Robin Roberts	3.09
5	Steve Barber	3.12
6	Mike Cuellar	3.18
7	Dave McNally	3.18
8	Milt Pappas	3.24
9	Tippy Martinez	3.46
10	Sammy Stewart	3.47
11	Mike Mussina	3.50
12	Hal Brown	3.61
13	Storm Davis	3.63
14	Mike Boddicker	3.73
15	Ross Grimsley	3.78
16	Mike Flanagan	3.89
17	Ben McDonald	3.89
18	Scott McGregor	3.99
19	Dennis Martinez	4.16

Component ERA
(minimum 750 Innings Pitched)

1	Dick Hall	2.34
2	Jim Palmer	2.91
3	Mike Cuellar	3.03
4	Hal Brown	3.11
5	Robin Roberts	3.12
6	Milt Pappas	3.14
7	Mike Mussina	3.17
8	Dave McNally	3.18
9	Tom Phoebus	3.24
10	Storm Davis	3.35
11	Steve Barber	3.36
12	Ben McDonald	3.45
13	Tippy Martinez	3.49
14	Mike Boddicker	3.67
15	Ross Grimsley	3.72
16	Sammy Stewart	3.75
17	Mike Flanagan	3.79
18	Scott McGregor	3.84
19	Dennis Martinez	4.08

Opponent Average
(minimum 750 Innings Pitched)

1	Tom Phoebus	.225
2	Dick Hall	.229
3	Jim Palmer	.230
4	Steve Barber	.234
5	Milt Pappas	.237
6	Ben McDonald	.239
7	Mike Cuellar	.241
8	Tippy Martinez	.243
9	Sammy Stewart	.243
10	Dave McNally	.244
11	Mike Mussina	.246
12	Robin Roberts	.248
13	Mike Boddicker	.249
14	Hal Brown	.251
15	Storm Davis	.252
16	Mike Flanagan	.264
17	Ross Grimsley	.266
18	Dennis Martinez	.267
19	Scott McGregor	.271

Opponent OBP
(minimum 750 Innings Pitched)

1	Dick Hall	.262
2	Robin Roberts	.287
3	Mike Mussina	.292
4	Hal Brown	.292
5	Jim Palmer	.294
6	Mike Cuellar	.296
7	Milt Pappas	.301
8	Dave McNally	.303
9	Ben McDonald	.307
10	Storm Davis	.313
11	Scott McGregor	.313
12	Tom Phoebus	.313
13	Ross Grimsley	.315
14	Mike Boddicker	.316
15	Mike Flanagan	.321
16	Steve Barber	.323
17	Dennis Martinez	.326
18	Tippy Martinez	.330
19	Sammy Stewart	.334

Browns/Orioles Franchise Batting Leaders—Single Season

Games

1	Brooks Robinson	1961	163
	Brooks Robinson	1964	163
	Cal Ripken Jr.	1996	163
4	Brooks Robinson	1962	162
	Brooks Robinson	1968	162
	Bobby Grich	1973	162
	Cal Ripken Jr.	1983	162
	Eddie Murray	1984	162
	Cal Ripken Jr.	1984	162
	Cal Ripken Jr.	1986	162
	Cal Ripken Jr.	1987	162
	Cal Ripken Jr.	1989	162
	Cal Ripken Jr.	1991	162
	Cal Ripken Jr.	1992	162
	Cal Ripken Jr.	1993	162
	Rafael Palmeiro	1996	162
	Cal Ripken Jr.	1997	162
18	Six tied at		161

At-Bats

1	Jack Tobin	1921	671
2	Brooks Robinson	1961	668
3	Cal Ripken Jr.	1983	663
4	Luis Aparicio	1966	659
5	Mike Devereaux	1992	653
6	Cal Ripken Jr.	1991	650
7	George Sisler	1925	649
8	Cal Ripken Jr.	1989	646
9	Al Bumbry	1980	645
10	Bob Dillinger	1948	644
	Billy Gardner	1957	644
12	Beau Bell	1937	642
	Cal Ripken Jr.	1985	642
14	Cal Ripken Jr.	1984	641
	Cal Ripken Jr.	1993	641
16	Cal Ripken Jr.	1996	640
17	Heinie Manush	1928	638
18	Jack Tobin	1923	637
	Cal Ripken Jr.	1992	637
20	George Sisler	1924	636

Runs

1	Harlond Clift	1936	145
2	George Sisler	1920	137
3	George Sisler	1922	134
4	Jack Tobin	1921	132
	Roberto Alomar	1996	132
6	Ken Williams	1922	128
7	George Sisler	1921	125
8	Jack Tobin	1922	122
	Frank Robinson	1966	122
10	Cal Ripken Jr.	1983	121
11	Harlond Clift	1938	119
12	Al Bumbry	1980	118
13	Brady Anderson	1996	117
14	Lu Blue	1928	116
	Cal Ripken Jr.	1985	116
16	Ken Williams	1921	115
	Eddie Murray	1983	115
18	Goose Goslin	1931	114
19	Lyn Lary	1936	112
20	Four tied at		111

Hits

1	George Sisler	1920	257
2	George Sisler	1922	246
3	Heinie Manush	1928	241
4	Jack Tobin	1921	236
5	George Sisler	1925	224
6	Beau Bell	1937	218
7	Baby Doll Jacobson	1920	216
	George Sisler	1921	216
9	Beau Bell	1936	212
10	Baby Doll Jacobson	1921	211
	Cal Ripken Jr.	1983	211
12	Cal Ripken Jr.	1991	210
13	George Stone	1906	208
14	Jack Tobin	1922	207
	Bob Dillinger	1948	207
16	Al Bumbry	1980	205
17	Heinie Manush	1929	204
18	Jack Tobin	1920	202
	Jack Tobin	1923	202
20	George Sisler	1927	201

Doubles

1	Beau Bell	1937	51
2	George Sisler	1920	49
3	Heinie Manush	1928	47
	Joe Vosmik	1937	47
	Cal Ripken Jr.	1983	47
6	John Anderson	1901	46
	Red Kress	1931	46
	Cal Ripken Jr.	1991	46
9	Heinie Manush	1929	45
	Moose Solters	1936	45
11	Marty McManus	1925	44
	Fred Schulte	1928	44
13	Red Kress	1930	43
	Jack Burns	1933	43
	Roberto Alomar	1996	43
16	George Sisler	1922	42
	Goose Goslin	1931	42
	George McQuinn	1938	42
19	Baby Doll Jacobson	1924	41
20	Seven tied at		40

Triples

1	George Stone	1906	20
	Heinie Manush	1928	20
3	George Sisler	1920	18
	George Sisler	1921	18
	Jack Tobin	1921	18
	George Sisler	1922	18
7	Gus Williams	1913	16
	Tilly Walker	1914	16
	Baby Doll Jacobson	1922	16
10	Emmett Heidrick	1903	15
	Del Pratt	1912	15
	George Sisler	1919	15
	Jack Tobin	1923	15
	George Sisler	1925	15
15	Baby Doll Jacobson	1920	14
	Baby Doll Jacobson	1921	14
	Carl Reynolds	1933	14
18	Seven tied at		13

Home Runs

1	Brady Anderson	1996	50
2	Frank Robinson	1966	49
3	Jim Gentile	1961	46
4	Ken Williams	1922	39
	Boog Powell	1964	39
	Rafael Palmeiro	1995	39
	Rafael Palmeiro	1996	39
8	Rafael Palmeiro	1997	38
9	Boog Powell	1969	37
10	Boog Powell	1970	35
	Ken Singleton	1979	35
12	Harlond Clift	1938	34
	Boog Powell	1966	34
	Cal Ripken Jr.	1991	34
15	Jim Gentile	1962	33
	Eddie Murray	1983	33
17	Frank Robinson	1969	32
	Eddie Murray	1980	32
	Eddie Murray	1982	32
20	Two tied at		31

RBI

1	Ken Williams	1922	155
2	Rafael Palmeiro	1996	142
3	Jim Gentile	1961	141
4	Moose Solters	1936	134
5	Eddie Murray	1985	124
6	Beau Bell	1936	123
7	George Sisler	1920	122
	Baby Doll Jacobson	1920	122
	Frank Robinson	1966	122
10	Boog Powell	1969	121
11	Harlond Clift	1937	118
	Harlond Clift	1938	118
	Brooks Robinson	1964	118
14	Ken Williams	1921	117
	Beau Bell	1937	117
16	Eddie Murray	1980	116
	Bobby Bonilla	1996	116
18	Red Kress	1931	114
	Boog Powell	1970	114
	Cal Ripken Jr.	1991	114

Walks

1	Lu Blue	1929	126
2	Roy Cullenbine	1941	121
3	Burt Shotton	1915	118
	Harlond Clift	1938	118
	Ken Singleton	1975	118
6	Lyn Lary	1936	117
7	Harlond Clift	1936	115
8	Harlond Clift	1941	113
9	Harlond Clift	1939	111
10	Burt Shotton	1916	110
11	Don Buford	1970	109
	Ken Singleton	1979	109
13	Bobby Grich	1973	107
	Bobby Grich	1975	107
	Ken Singleton	1977	107
	Eddie Murray	1984	107
17	Harlond Clift	1942	106
	Norm Siebern	1964	106
	Mickey Tettleton	1990	106
	Randy Milligan	1992	106

Strikeouts

1	Mickey Tettleton	1990	160
2	Boog Powell	1966	125
3	Gus Williams	1914	120
4	Lee May	1977	119
5	Ken Singleton	1979	118
6	Bobby Grich	1974	117
	Mickey Tettleton	1989	117
8	Mike Devereaux	1991	115
9	Mark Belanger	1968	114
	Craig Worthington	1989	114
11	Terry Kennedy	1987	112
12	Brady Anderson	1995	111
13	Lee May	1978	110
	Mike Young	1984	110
15	Rafael Palmeiro	1997	109
16	Reggie Jackson	1976	108
	Randy Milligan	1991	108
18	Earl Williams	1973	107
19	Three tied at		106

Stolen Bases

1	Luis Aparicio	1964	57
2	Brady Anderson	1992	53
3	George Sisler	1922	51
4	Armando Marsans	1916	46
5	George Sisler	1918	45
6	Al Bumbry	1980	44
7	Burt Shotton	1913	43
	Burt Shotton	1915	43
9	George Sisler	1920	42
	Al Bumbry	1976	42
11	Burt Shotton	1916	41
12	Burt Shotton	1914	40
	Luis Aparicio	1963	40
14	Del Pratt	1913	37
	Jimmy Austin	1913	37
	Del Pratt	1914	37
	George Sisler	1917	37
	Ken Williams	1922	37
	Lyn Lary	1936	37
	Al Bumbry	1979	37

Runs Created

1	George Sisler	1920	154
2	Heinie Manush	1928	149
3	Frank Robinson	1966	141
	Rafael Palmeiro	1996	141
5	George Sisler	1922	140
6	Ken Williams	1922	134
	Goose Goslin	1931	134
8	Brady Anderson	1996	130
9	Ken Williams	1923	129
10	Roberto Alomar	1996	128
11	George Stone	1906	127
	George Sisler	1921	127
	Harlond Clift	1936	127
14	Jim Gentile	1961	125
	Cal Ripken Jr.	1991	125
16	Ken Williams	1921	124
17	George McQuinn	1939	122
18	Harlond Clift	1938	121
	Eddie Murray	1983	121
20	Four tied at		120

Runs Created/27 Outs

(minimum 3.1 Plate Appearances/Tm Gm)

1	George Sisler	1920	10.01
2	George Sisler	1922	9.78
3	Jim Gentile	1961	9.34
4	Heinie Manush	1928	9.24
5	Frank Robinson	1966	8.90
6	Ken Williams	1923	8.82
7	Goose Goslin	1931	8.77
8	Boog Powell	1964	8.55
9	George Sisler	1921	8.53
10	Ken Singleton	1977	8.41
11	Frank Robinson	1967	8.41
12	Ken Singleton	1977	8.40
13	Roy Cullenbine	1941	8.36
14	Ken Williams	1922	8.32
15	Chris Hoiles	1993	8.25
16	Ken Williams	1921	8.24
17	Rafael Palmeiro	1996	8.22
18	Wally Judnich	1942	8.17
19	Bob Nieman	1956	8.12
20	Frank Robinson	1969	8.11

Batting Average

(minimum 3.1 Plate Appearances/Tm Gm)

1	George Sisler	1922	.420
2	George Sisler	1920	.407
3	Heinie Manush	1928	.378
4	George Sisler	1921	.371
5	George Stone	1906	.358
6	Ken Williams	1923	.357
7	Heinie Manush	1929	.355
8	Baby Doll Jacobson	1920	.355
9	George Sisler	1917	.353
10	Baby Doll Jacobson	1921	.352
11	George Sisler	1919	.352
12	Jack Tobin	1921	.352
13	Ken Williams	1921	.347
14	George Sisler	1925	.345
15	Beau Bell	1936	.344
16	Rip Radcliff	1940	.342
17	Baby Doll Jacobson	1925	.341
18	George Sisler	1918	.341
19	Jack Tobin	1920	.341
20	Beau Bell	1937	.340

On-Base Percentage

(minimum 3.1 Plate Appearances/Tm Gm)

1	George Sisler	1922	.467
2	Roy Cullenbine	1941	.452
3	George Sisler	1920	.449
4	Bob Nieman	1956	.442
5	Ken Williams	1923	.439
6	Ken Singleton	1977	.438
7	Ken Williams	1921	.429
8	Ken Williams	1924	.425
9	Harlond Clift	1936	.424
10	Harlond Clift	1938	.423
11	Jim Gentile	1961	.423
12	Lu Blue	1929	.422
13	Merv Rettenmund	1971	.422
14	George Stone	1906	.417
15	Chris Hoiles	1993	.416
16	Frank Robinson	1969	.415
17	Ken Singleton	1975	.415
18	Heinie Manush	1928	.414
19	Harlond Clift	1937	.413
20	Don Buford	1971	.413

Slugging Percentage

(minimum 3.1 Plate Appearances/Tm Gm)

1	Jim Gentile	1961	.646
2	Brady Anderson	1996	.637
3	Frank Robinson	1966	.637
4	George Sisler	1920	.632
5	Ken Williams	1922	.627
6	Ken Williams	1923	.623
7	Boog Powell	1964	.606
8	George Sisler	1922	.594
9	Chris Hoiles	1993	.585
10	Rafael Palmeiro	1995	.583
11	Frank Robinson	1967	.576
12	Heinie Manush	1928	.575
13	Cal Ripken Jr.	1991	.566
14	Larry Sheets	1987	.563
15	Ken Williams	1921	.561
16	George Sisler	1921	.560
17	Boog Powell	1969	.559
18	Goose Goslin	1931	.555
19	Harlond Clift	1938	.554
20	Rafael Palmeiro	1994	.550

Teams: Orioles

Browns/Orioles Franchise Pitching Leaders—Single Season

Wins

1	Urban Shocker	1921	27
2	Steve Stone	1980	25
3	Urban Shocker	1922	24
	Dave McNally	1970	24
	Mike Cuellar	1970	24
6	Mike Cuellar	1969	23
	Jim Palmer	1975	23
	Mike Flanagan	1979	23
9	Jack Powell	1902	22
	Red Donahue	1902	22
	Dave McNally	1968	22
	Jim Palmer	1973	22
	Mike Cuellar	1974	22
	Jim Palmer	1976	22
15	Willie Sudhoff	1903	21
	General Crowder	1928	21
	Dave McNally	1971	21
	Jim Palmer	1972	21
	Jim Palmer	1978	21
20	Eighteen tied at		20

Losses

1	Fred Glade	1905	25
2	Sam Gray	1931	24
3	Harry Howell	1905	22
4	Harry Howell	1904	21
	Barney Pelty	1907	21
	Fred Sanford	1948	21
	Don Larsen	1954	21
8	Bill Reidy	1901	20
	Ned Garvin	1901	20
	Willie Sudhoff	1905	20
	Carl Weilman	1913	20
	Bump Hadley	1932	20
	Bump Hadley	1933	20
	Bobo Newsom	1934	20
15	Nine tied at		19

Winning Percentage
(minimum 15 decisions)

1	General Crowder	1928	.808
	Dave McNally	1971	.808
3	Jim Palmer	1969	.800
4	Wally Bunker	1964	.792
5	Mike Mussina	1992	.783
6	Steve Stone	1980	.781
7	Ray Kolp	1922	.778
8	Bob Muncrief	1945	.765
9	Mike Mussina	1994	.762
10	Mike Cuellar	1970	.750
	Jim Palmer	1982	.750
	Mike Flanagan	1983	.750
13	Dave McNally	1969	.741
	Wayne Garland	1976	.741
15	Dennis Martinez	1981	.737
16	Nels Potter	1944	.731
17	Dave McNally	1970	.727
18	Scott McGregor	1981	.722
19	Scott McGregor	1983	.720
20	Mike Flanagan	1979	.719

Games

1	Tippy Martinez	1982	76
2	Gregg Olson	1991	72
3	Stu Miller	1963	71
	Jesse Orosco	1997	71
	Armando Benitez	1997	71
6	Todd Frohwirth	1993	70
7	Stu Miller	1965	67
8	Stu Miller	1964	66
	Don Aase	1986	66
	Jesse Orosco	1996	66
11	Tippy Martinez	1983	65
	Mark Williamson	1989	65
	Mark Williamson	1991	65
	Todd Frohwirth	1992	65
	Jesse Orosco	1995	65
16	Tim Stoddard	1980	64
	Gregg Olson	1989	64
	Gregg Olson	1990	64
	Mike Flanagan	1991	64
20	Two tied at		62

Games Started

1	Bobo Newsom	1938	40
	Dave McNally	1969	40
	Dave McNally	1970	40
	Mike Cuellar	1970	40
	Jim Palmer	1976	40
	Mike Flanagan	1978	40
7	Jack Powell	1902	39
	Dave Davenport	1917	39
	Urban Shocker	1921	39
	Mike Cuellar	1969	39
	Jim Palmer	1970	39
	Ross Grimsley	1974	39
	Jim Palmer	1977	39
	Dennis Martinez	1979	39
	Dennis Martinez	1982	39
16	Nine tied at		38

Complete Games

1	Jack Powell	1902	36
2	Harry Howell	1905	35
3	Red Donahue	1902	33
	Jack Powell	1903	33
5	Harry Howell	1904	32
6	Barney Pelty	1904	31
	Urban Shocker	1921	31
	Bobo Newsom	1938	31
9	Willie Sudhoff	1903	30
	Fred Glade	1904	30
	Harry Howell	1906	30
12	Barney Pelty	1907	29
	Urban Shocker	1922	29
14	Bill Reidy	1901	28
	Fred Glade	1905	28
	Fred Glade	1906	28
17	Barney Pelty	1905	27
	Jack Powell	1907	27
	Harry Howell	1908	27
20	Harry Howell	1907	26

Shutouts

1	Jim Palmer	1975	10
2	Steve Barber	1961	8
3	Milt Pappas	1964	7
4	Fred Glade	1904	6
	Harry Howell	1906	6
	Jack Powell	1908	6
	Jim Palmer	1969	6
	Dave McNally	1972	6
	Jim Palmer	1973	6
	Jim Palmer	1976	6
	Jim Palmer	1978	6
12	Sixteen tied at		5

Saves

1	Randy Myers	1997	45
2	Gregg Olson	1990	37
3	Gregg Olson	1992	36
4	Don Aase	1986	34
5	Lee Smith	1994	33
6	Gregg Olson	1991	31
	Randy Myers	1996	31
8	Gregg Olson	1993	29
9	Stu Miller	1963	27
	Gregg Olson	1989	27
11	Tim Stoddard	1980	26
12	Stu Miller	1965	24
	Don Stanhouse	1978	24
14	Stu Miller	1964	23
15	Doug Jones	1995	22
16	Don Stanhouse	1979	21
	Tippy Martinez	1983	21
18	Hoyt Wilhelm	1961	18
	Stu Miller	1966	18
	Tom Niedenfuer	1988	18

Innings Pitched

1	Urban Shocker	1922	348.0
2	Bobo Newsom	1938	329.2
3	Jack Powell	1902	328.1
4	Urban Shocker	1921	326.2
5	Harry Howell	1908	324.1
6	Harry Howell	1905	323.0
	Jim Palmer	1975	323.0
8	Jim Palmer	1977	319.0
9	Bump Hadley	1933	316.2
10	Red Donahue	1902	316.1
	Harry Howell	1907	316.1
12	Jim Palmer	1976	315.0
13	Jack Powell	1903	306.1
14	Sam Gray	1929	305.0
	Jim Palmer	1970	305.0
16	Earl Hamilton	1914	302.1
17	Bill Reidy	1901	301.1
18	Barney Pelty	1904	301.0
19	Harry Howell	1904	299.2
20	Carl Weilman	1914	299.0

Walks

1	Bobo Newsom	1938	192
2	Bob Turley	1954	181
3	Bump Hadley	1932	163
4	Dixie Davis	1920	149
	Bobo Newsom	1934	149
6	Bump Hadley	1933	141
7	Grover Lowdermilk	1915	133
	Mike Torrez	1975	133
9	Chuck Estrada	1961	132
10	Steve Barber	1961	130
11	Bump Hadley	1934	127
	Jack Kramer	1939	127
13	Dixie Davis	1921	123
14	Vern Kennedy	1940	122
15	Chuck Estrada	1962	121
16	Elam Vangilder	1923	120
17	Lefty Mills	1938	116
18	Vern Kennedy	1939	115
	Duane Pillette	1951	115
20	Two tied at		114

Strikeouts

1	Rube Waddell	1908	232
2	Bobo Newsom	1938	226
3	Mike Mussina	1997	218
4	Mike Mussina	1996	204
5	Dave McNally	1968	202
6	Jim Palmer	1970	199
7	Harry Howell	1905	198
8	Tom Phoebus	1968	193
	Jim Palmer	1975	193
	Jim Palmer	1977	193
11	Mike Cuellar	1970	190
	Mike Flanagan	1979	190
13	Pat Dobson	1971	187
14	Bob Turley	1954	185
	Dave McNally	1970	185
16	Jim Palmer	1971	184
	Jim Palmer	1972	184
18	Mike Cuellar	1969	182
19	Steve Barber	1963	180
20	Tom Phoebus	1967	179

Strikeouts/9 Innings
(minimum 1 Inning Pitched/Tm Gm)

1	Mike Mussina	1997	8.73
2	Tom Phoebus	1967	7.75
3	Ken Dixon	1986	7.56
4	Mike Mussina	1996	7.55
5	Sid Fernandez	1994	7.41
6	Rube Waddell	1908	7.31
7	Tom Phoebus	1968	7.22
8	Mike Boddicker	1986	7.21
9	Ben McDonald	1993	6.98
10	Chuck Estrada	1961	6.79
11	Bob Turley	1954	6.73
12	Dave McNally	1966	6.68
13	Dave McNally	1968	6.66
14	Chuck Estrada	1962	6.65
15	Connie Johnson	1957	6.58
16	Mike Flanagan	1979	6.44
17	Mike Mussina	1995	6.42
18	Connie Johnson	1956	6.37
19	Jim Palmer	1966	6.35
20	Mike Mussina	1993	6.28

ERA
(minimum 1 Inning Pitched/Tm Gm)

1	Barney Pelty	1906	1.59
2	Jack Powell	1906	1.77
3	Harry Howell	1908	1.89
4	Rube Waddell	1908	1.89
5	Harry Howell	1907	1.93
6	Allen Sothoron	1918	1.94
7	Dave McNally	1968	1.95
8	Harry Howell	1905	1.98
9	Jim Palmer	1972	2.07
10	Carl Weilman	1919	2.07
11	Carl Weilman	1914	2.08
12	Jim Palmer	1975	2.09
13	Bill Dinneen	1908	2.10
14	Jack Powell	1909	2.11
15	Jack Powell	1908	2.11
16	Harry Howell	1906	2.11
17	Carl Weilman	1916	2.15
18	Hoyt Wilhelm	1959	2.19
19	Harry Howell	1904	2.19
20	Allen Sothoron	1919	2.20

Component ERA
(minimum 1 Inning Pitched/Tm Gm)

1	Dave McNally	1968	1.66
2	Barney Pelty	1906	1.70
3	Jack Powell	1908	1.82
4	Allen Sothoron	1918	1.86
5	Jack Powell	1906	1.95
6	Rube Waddell	1908	1.98
7	Fred Glade	1906	2.01
8	Barney Pelty	1909	2.01
9	Mike Cuellar	1969	2.02
10	Harry Howell	1904	2.09
11	Harry Howell	1906	2.10
12	Harry Howell	1905	2.11
13	Fred Glade	1904	2.13
14	Harry Howell	1907	2.15
15	Carl Weilman	1915	2.16
16	Bill Dinneen	1908	2.18
17	Jim Palmer	1975	2.20
18	Willie Sudhoff	1903	2.21
19	Harry Howell	1908	2.22
20	Jim Palmer	1969	2.26

Opponent Average
(minimum 1 Inning Pitched/Tm Gm)

1	Dave McNally	1968	.182
2	Jim Palmer	1969	.200
3	Bob Turley	1954	.203
4	Mike Cuellar	1969	.204
5	Allen Sothoron	1918	.205
6	Barney Pelty	1906	.206
7	Chuck Estrada	1961	.207
8	Wally Bunker	1964	.207
9	Milt Pappas	1961	.208
10	Jim Palmer	1973	.211
11	Jim Hardin	1968	.212
12	Tom Phoebus	1968	.212
13	Rube Waddell	1908	.213
14	Jim Palmer	1975	.216
15	Mike Boddicker	1983	.216
16	Jim Palmer	1972	.217
17	Steve Barber	1961	.218
18	Chuck Estrada	1960	.218
19	Mike Cuellar	1972	.220
20	Billy O'Dell	1959	.220

Opponent OBP
(minimum 1 Inning Pitched/Tm Gm)

1	Dave McNally	1968	.232
2	Mike Cuellar	1969	.260
3	Jim Palmer	1975	.266
4	Wally Bunker	1964	.267
5	Jim Palmer	1972	.268
6	Barney Pelty	1906	.268
7	Mike Mussina	1995	.270
8	Robin Roberts	1963	.272
9	Jim Palmer	1969	.272
10	Mike Boddicker	1983	.273
11	Scott McGregor	1979	.273
12	Jack Powell	1908	.274
13	Allen Sothoron	1918	.274
14	Jack Powell	1906	.276
15	Willie Sudhoff	1903	.276
16	Fred Glade	1906	.276
17	Mike Cuellar	1972	.276
18	Jim Hardin	1968	.277
19	Pat Dobson	1972	.277
20	Mike Mussina	1992	.278

Teams: Orioles

Orioles Capsule

Best Season: *1970.* The Orioles won 108 games and took the American League East by 15 games, before sweeping the Minnesota Twins in the ALCS and downing the Cincinnati Reds in a five-game World Series.

Worst Season: *1988.* They began the season with an AL-record 21-game losing streak, and things didn't get much better after that. They finished the year with 107 losses, a total that the old St. Louis Browns exceeded only two times this century before moving to Baltimore.

Best Player: *Cal Ripken Jr.*

Best Pitcher: *Jim Palmer.*

Best Reliever: *Stu Miller.* Gregg Olson was terrific, but Miller attracted support in the MVP voting three times in four years.

Best Defensive Player: *Brooks Robinson* won 16 Gold Gloves and set the standard by which third basemen are measured. Shortstop Mark Belanger and center fielder Paul Blair each won eight Gold Gloves.

Hall of Famers: *Jim Palmer, Brooks Robinson* and *Frank Robinson* as players; *Earl Weaver* as a manager.

Franchise All-Star Team:

C	Chris Hoiles	**LF**	Ken Singleton
1B	Eddie Murray	**CF**	Brady Anderson
2B	Bobby Grich	**RF**	Frank Robinson
3B	Brooks Robinson	**DH**	Lee May
SS	Cal Ripken	**SP**	Jim Palmer
		RP	Stu Miller

Biggest Flakes: The Orioles have had their share of characters. Some of the most unforgettable were *Don Stanhouse, Jackie Brandt, John Lowenstein* and *Moe Drabowsky.*

Strangest Career: *Steve Stone* never won more than 15 games in a season until 1980, when he went 25-7 and won the AL Cy Young Award. An elbow injury finished his career the following year.

What Might Have Been: *Steve Dalkowski* was quite possibly the hardest throwing pitcher of all time, but his wildness was equally legendary. Countless coaches and managers tried to solve his control problems, and he was made the guinea pig of increasingly bizarre experiments. Pitching in the Eastern League in 1962, he found himself playing for a manager—Earl Weaver—who simply left him alone and let him pitch. Relying on only his fastball and slider, Dalkowski finally harnessed his control, and was nearly untouchable over the second half of the season. In the spring of '63, he was the talk of the Orioles' camp, but he hurt his arm just before the start of the season. After drifting through the minors for a few more years, he retired without ever having thrown a major league pitch.

Best Trade: *Frank Robinson.* They got him from the Reds after the 1965 season for Milt Pappas and a couple of bodies. Robinson won the Triple Crown and led the O's to a World Series championship in 1966. Another winner was the December 1974 deal that sent a washed-up Dave McNally and Rich Coggins to the Montreal Expos for Ken Singleton and Mike Torrez.

Worst Trades: First baseman *Glenn Davis* came over from the Astros in January of 1991 for Steve Finley, Curt Schilling and Pete Harnisch. Davis was a bust, while all three of the ex-Orioles became quality players.

Best-Looking Player: *Jim Palmer.* He sold underwear in his spare time.

Ugliest Player: *Andy Etchebarren.* Even his biography in *The Ballplayers* notes that Etchebarren "was known for his bushy eyebrows."

Best Nickname: *"Stan the Man Unusual" Stanhouse.*

Best Real Name: *Drungo Larue Hazewood.*

Most Unappreciated Player: *Scott McGregor.* He wasn't nearly as well-known as fellow lefthander Mike Flanagan, even though the two of them were in the rotation together for seven years and posted nearly identical overall numbers.

Most Overrated Player: Shortstop *Manny Alexander.* While he was in the minors, Alexander was touted as a prospect despite consistently high error totals and low batting averages. With Cal Ripken firmly entrenched at short, the Orioles fretted over finding a way to get Alexander into the lineup. They ultimately shifted Ripken to third for Alexander in 1996, but Alexander was such a brutal failure that the experiment was scrapped within a matter of days. After the season, Alexander was traded away for next to nothing.

Most Admirable Star: *Brooks Robinson.* He handled his status as a living legend with grace and class. As an Orioles broadcaster, his popularity endures.

Least Admirable Star: *Earl Williams.* The Orioles traded pitcher Pat Dobson, second baseman Davey Johnson and a couple of other players to the Braves for the powerful catcher after the 1972 season. He had a couple of decent seasons in Baltimore, but Earl Weaver was so exasperated with Williams' indifference behind the plate that the Orioles sent him back to the Braves in '75 for a body and some cash.

Best Season, Player: *Frank Robinson, 1966,* by a hair over Cal Ripken Jr., 1983 or 1991. All three were MVP seasons, but Robinson won the Triple Crown.

Best Season, Pitcher: *Jim Palmer, 1975.* He won 23 games and his 2.09 ERA was almost a half-run lower than the next-best mark in the AL.

Most Impressive Individual Record: *Cal Ripken Jr.* Lou Gehrig's consecutive-games record seemed unbreakable until Ripken broke it.

Biggest Tragedy: *Dick Brown.* Surgery for a brain tumor ended his career in 1965, and he died five years later at the age of 35.

Fan Favorite: *Cal Ripken Jr.*

—Mat Olkin

Boston Red Sox (1901-1997)

Year	Lg	Pos	W-L	Pct	GB	Manager	Att.	R	OR	HR	Avg	OBP	Slg	Opponent HR	Opponent Avg	Opponent OBP	ERA	Park Index Runs	Park Index HR
1901	AL	2nd	79-57	.581	4.0	Jimmy Collins	289,448	759	608	37	.278	.330	.381	33	.250	.300	3.04	84	109
1902	AL	3rd	77-60	.562	6.5	Jimmy Collins	348,567	664	600	42	.278	.322	.383	27	.259	.312	3.02	96	104
1903	AL	1st	91-47	.659	—	Jimmy Collins	379,338	708	504	48	.272	.313	.392	23	.244	.290	2.57	120	196
1904	AL	1st	95-59	.617	—	Jimmy Collins	623,295	608	466	26	.247	.301	.340	31	.232	.269	2.12	105	151
1905	AL	4th	78-74	.513	16.0	Jimmy Collins	468,828	579	564	29	.234	.305	.311	33	.239	.287	2.84	102	195
1906	AL	8th	49-105	.318	45.5	Jimmy Collins/Chick Stahl	410,209	463	706	13	.237	.284	.304	37	.261	.305	3.41	106	182
1907	AL	7th	59-90	.396	32.5	Young/Huff/Unglaub/McGuire	436,777	464	558	18	.234	.281	.292	22	.237	.289	2.45	102	133
1908	AL	5th	75-79	.487	15.5	Deacon McGuire/Fred Lake	473,048	564	513	14	.245	.295	.312	18	.248	.307	2.28	94	129
1909	AL	3rd	88-63	.583	9.5	Fred Lake	668,965	597	550	20	.263	.321	.333	18	.243	.303	2.59	121	380
1910	AL	4th	81-72	.529	22.5	Patsy Donovan	584,619	638	564	43	.259	.323	.351	30	.235	.297	2.45	93	248
1911	AL	5th	78-75	.510	24.0	Patsy Donovan	503,961	680	643	35	.275	.350	.363	21	.262	.332	2.74	96	132
1912	AL	1st	105-47	.691	—	Jake Stahl	597,096	799	544	29	.277	.355	.380	18	.248	.306	2.76	107	72
1913	AL	4th	79-71	.527	15.5	Jake Stahl/Bill Carrigan	437,194	631	610	17	.269	.336	.364	6	.262	.325	2.94	106	15
1914	AL	2nd	91-62	.595	8.5	Bill Carrigan	481,359	589	510	18	.250	.320	.338	18	.236	.295	2.36	92	25
1915	AL	1st	101-50	.669	—	Bill Carrigan	539,885	669	499	14	.260	.336	.339	18	.231	.300	2.39	88	40
1916	AL	1st	91-63	.591	—	Bill Carrigan	496,397	550	480	14	.248	.317	.318	10	.239	.307	2.48	80	9
1917	AL	2nd	90-62	.592	9.0	Jack Barry	387,856	555	454	14	.246	.314	.319	12	.231	.294	2.20	108	35
1918	AL	1st	75-51	.595	—	Ed Barrow	249,513	474	380	15	.249	.322	.327	9	.231	.302	2.31	84	21
1919	AL	6th	66-71	.482	20.5	Ed Barrow	417,291	564	552	33	.261	.336	.344	16	.275	.341	3.31	82	40
1920	AL	5th	72-81	.471	25.5	Ed Barrow	402,445	650	698	22	.269	.342	.350	39	.272	.332	3.82	88	36
1921	AL	5th	75-79	.487	23.5	Hugh Duffy	279,273	668	696	17	.277	.335	.361	53	.291	.352	3.98	95	37
1922	AL	8th	61-93	.396	33.0	Hugh Duffy	259,184	598	769	45	.263	.316	.357	48	.287	.354	4.30	93	36
1923	AL	8th	61-91	.401	37.0	Frank Chance	229,688	584	809	34	.261	.318	.351	48	.295	.367	4.20	107	45
1924	AL	7th	67-87	.435	25.0	Lee Fohl	448,556	737	806	30	.277	.356	.374	43	.285	.354	4.35	106	52
1925	AL	8th	47-105	.309	49.5	Lee Fohl	267,782	639	922	41	.266	.336	.364	67	.308	.374	4.97	95	56
1926	AL	8th	46-107	.301	44.5	Lee Fohl	285,155	562	835	32	.256	.321	.343	45	.294	.365	4.72	110	49
1927	AL	8th	51-103	.331	59.0	Bill Carrigan	305,275	597	856	28	.259	.320	.357	56	.305	.376	4.72	93	66
1928	AL	8th	57-96	.373	43.5	Bill Carrigan	396,920	589	770	38	.264	.319	.361	49	.281	.342	4.39	99	44
1929	AL	8th	58-96	.377	48.0	Bill Carrigan	394,620	605	803	28	.267	.325	.365	78	.291	.355	4.43	107	80
1930	AL	8th	52-102	.338	50.0	Heinie Wagner	444,045	612	814	47	.264	.313	.364	75	.286	.348	4.68	84	62
1931	AL	6th	62-90	.408	45.0	Shano Collins	350,975	625	800	37	.262	.315	.349	54	.285	.344	4.60	88	72
1932	AL	8th	43-111	.279	64.0	Shano Collins/Marty McManus	182,150	566	915	53	.251	.314	.351	79	.289	.364	5.02	98	59
1933	AL	7th	63-86	.423	34.5	Marty McManus	268,715	700	758	50	.271	.339	.377	75	.271	.348	4.35	104	93
1934	AL	4th	76-76	.500	24.0	Bucky Harris	610,640	820	775	51	.274	.350	.383	70	.283	.351	4.32	112	62
1935	AL	4th	78-75	.510	16.0	Joe Cronin	558,568	718	732	69	.276	.353	.392	67	.280	.346	4.05	117	65
1936	AL	6th	74-80	.481	28.5	Joe Cronin	626,895	775	764	86	.276	.349	.400	78	.277	.346	4.39	110	75
1937	AL	5th	80-72	.526	21.0	Joe Cronin	559,659	821	775	100	.281	.357	.411	92	.279	.352	4.48	106	108
1938	AL	2nd	88-61	.591	9.5	Joe Cronin	646,459	902	751	98	.299	.378	.434	102	.281	.349	4.46	101	145
1939	AL	2nd	89-62	.589	17.0	Joe Cronin	573,070	890	795	124	.291	.363	.436	77	.287	.355	4.56	120	95
1940	AL	4th	82-72	.532	8.0	Joe Cronin	716,234	872	825	145	.286	.356	.449	124	.284	.359	4.89	104	99
1941	AL	2nd	84-70	.545	17.0	Joe Cronin	718,497	865	750	124	.283	.366	.430	88	.270	.347	4.19	106	133
1942	AL	2nd	93-59	.612	9.0	Joe Cronin	730,340	761	594	103	.276	.352	.403	65	.247	.322	3.44	105	105
1943	AL	7th	68-84	.447	29.0	Joe Cronin	358,275	563	607	57	.244	.308	.332	61	.257	.335	3.45	110	87
1944	AL	4th	77-77	.500	12.0	Joe Cronin	506,975	739	676	69	.270	.336	.380	66	.263	.339	3.82	98	155
1945	AL	7th	71-83	.461	17.5	Joe Cronin	603,794	599	674	50	.260	.330	.346	58	.264	.348	3.80	91	86
1946	AL	1st	104-50	.675	—	Joe Cronin	1,416,944	792	594	109	.271	.356	.402	89	.254	.319	3.38	130	122
1947	AL	3rd	83-71	.539	14.0	Joe Cronin	1,427,315	720	669	103	.265	.349	.382	84	.261	.335	3.81	120	109
1948	AL	2nd	96-59	.619	1.0	Joe McCarthy	1,558,798	907	720	121	.274	.374	.409	83	.270	.345	4.26	100	101
1949	AL	2nd	96-58	.623	1.0	Joe McCarthy	1,596,650	896	667	131	.282	.381	.420	82	.262	.347	3.97	112	115
1950	AL	3rd	94-60	.610	4.0	Joe McCarthy/Steve O'Neill	1,344,080	1027	804	161	.302	.385	.464	121	.270	.364	4.88	135	145
1951	AL	3rd	87-67	.565	11.0	Steve O'Neill	1,312,282	804	725	127	.266	.358	.392	100	.264	.342	4.14	118	186
1952	AL	6th	76-78	.494	19.0	Lou Boudreau	1,115,750	668	658	113	.255	.329	.377	107	.256	.340	3.80	117	114
1953	AL	4th	84-69	.549	16.0	Lou Boudreau	1,026,133	656	632	101	.264	.332	.384	92	.254	.331	3.58	117	153
1954	AL	4th	69-85	.448	42.0	Lou Boudreau	931,127	700	728	123	.266	.345	.395	118	.265	.341	4.01	108	136
1955	AL	4th	84-70	.545	12.0	Pinky Higgins	1,203,200	755	652	137	.264	.351	.402	128	.253	.328	3.72	156	156
1956	AL	4th	84-70	.545	13.0	Pinky Higgins	1,137,158	780	751	139	.275	.362	.419	130	.254	.340	4.17	108	96
1957	AL	3rd	82-72	.532	16.0	Pinky Higgins	1,181,087	721	668	153	.262	.341	.405	116	.264	.329	3.88	124	107
1958	AL	3rd	79-75	.513	13.0	Pinky Higgins	1,077,047	697	691	155	.256	.338	.400	121	.264	.332	3.92	112	100
1959	AL	5th	75-79	.487	19.0	Pinky Higgins/Rudy York/Billy Jurges	984,102	726	696	125	.256	.335	.385	135	.266	.341	4.17	115	97
1960	AL	7th	65-89	.422	32.0	Billy Jurges/Del Baker/Pinky Higgins	1,129,866	658	775	124	.261	.333	.389	127	.273	.346	4.62	113	115
1961	AL	6th	76-86	.469	33.0	Pinky Higgins	850,589	729	792	112	.254	.334	.374	167	.266	.345	4.29	107	123
1962	AL	8th	76-84	.475	19.0	Pinky Higgins	733,080	707	756	146	.258	.324	.403	159	.258	.337	4.22	107	97
1963	AL	7th	76-85	.472	28.0	Johnny Pesky	942,642	666	704	171	.252	.312	.400	152	.248	.316	3.97	115	110
1964	AL	8th	72-90	.444	27.0	Johnny Pesky/Billy Herman	883,276	688	793	186	.258	.322	.416	178	.266	.336	4.50	110	106
1965	AL	9th	62-100	.383	40.0	Billy Herman	652,201	669	791	165	.251	.327	.400	158	.260	.327	4.24	124	129
1966	AL	9th	72-90	.444	26.0	Billy Herman/Pete Runnels	811,172	655	731	145	.240	.310	.376	164	.253	.325	3.92	125	134
1967	AL	1st	92-70	.568	—	Dick Williams	1,727,832	722	614	158	.255	.321	.395	142	.239	.304	3.36	133	146
1968	AL	4th	86-76	.531	17.0	Dick Williams	1,940,788	614	611	125	.236	.313	.352	115	.241	.312	3.33	104	98
1969	AL	3rd-E	87-75	.537	22.0	Dick Williams/Eddie Popowski	1,833,246	743	736	197	.251	.333	.415	155	.256	.341	3.92	113	108
1970	AL	3rd-E	87-75	.537	21.0	Eddie Kasko	1,595,278	786	722	203	.262	.335	.428	156	.251	.327	3.87	125	115
1971	AL	3rd-E	85-77	.525	18.0	Eddie Kasko	1,678,732	691	667	161	.252	.322	.397	136	.259	.327	3.80	113	125
1972	AL	2nd-E	85-70	.548	0.5	Eddie Kasko	1,441,718	640	620	124	.248	.318	.376	101	.251	.321	3.47	114	113
1973	AL	2nd-E	89-73	.549	8.0	Eddie Kasko/Eddie Popowski	1,481,002	738	647	147	.267	.338	.401	158	.259	.323	3.65	111	119
1974	AL	3rd-E	84-78	.519	7.0	Darrell Johnson	1,556,411	696	661	109	.264	.333	.377	126	.262	.320	3.72	114	112
1975	AL	1st-E	95-65	.594	—	Darrell Johnson	1,748,587	796	709	134	.275	.344	.417	145	.265	.325	3.98	119	126
1976	AL	3rd-E	83-79	.512	15.5	Darrell Johnson/Don Zimmer	1,895,846	716	660	134	.263	.324	.402	109	.267	.318	3.52	123	119
1977	AL	2nd-E	97-64	.602	2.5	Don Zimmer	2,074,549	859	712	213	.281	.345	.465	158	.278	.325	4.11	137	146
1978	AL	2nd-E	99-64	.607	1.0	Don Zimmer	2,320,643	796	657	172	.267	.336	.424	137	.270	.327	3.54	114	115
1979	AL	3rd-E	91-69	.569	11.5	Don Zimmer	2,353,114	841	711	194	.283	.344	.456	133	.270	.328	4.03	114	122
1980	AL	4th-E	83-77	.519	19.0	Don Zimmer/Johnny Pesky	1,956,092	757	767	162	.283	.340	.436	129	.279	.337	4.38	105	108
1981	AL	5th-E	30-26	.536	4.0	Ralph Houk													
	AL	2nd-E	29-93	.558	1.5	Ralph Houk	1,060,379	519	481	90	.275	.340	.399	90	.262	.328	3.81	115	127

Year	Lg	Pos	W-L	Pct	GB	Manager	Att.	R	OR	HR	Avg	OBP	Slg	Opponent HR	Opponent Avg	Opponent OBP	ERA	Park Index Runs	Park Index HR
1982	AL	3rd-E	89-73	.549	6.0	Ralph Houk	1,950,124	753	713	136	.274	.340	.407	155	.276	.334	4.03	121	105
1983	AL	6th-E	78-84	.481	20.0	Ralph Houk	1,782,285	724	775	142	.270	.335	.409	158	.279	.337	4.34	104	89
1984	AL	4th-E	86-76	.531	18.0	Ralph Houk	1,661,618	810	764	181	.283	.341	.441	141	.270	.332	4.18	123	121
1985	AL	5th-E	81-81	.500	18.5	John McNamara	1,786,633	800	720	162	.282	.347	.429	130	.265	.331	4.06	106	91
1986	AL	1st-E	95-66	.590	—	John McNamara	2,147,641	794	696	144	.271	.346	.415	167	.266	.325	3.93	97	81
1987	AL	5th-E	78-84	.481	20.0	John McNamara	2,231,551	842	825	174	.278	.352	.430	190	.282	.344	4.77	99	81
1988	AL	1st-E	89-73	.549	—	John McNamara/Joe Morgan	2,464,851	813	689	124	.283	.357	.420	143	.259	.322	3.97	119	112
1989	AL	3rd-E	83-79	.512	6.0	Joe Morgan	2,510,012	774	735	108	.277	.351	.403	131	.261	.328	4.01	111	104
1990	AL	1st-E	88-74	.543	—	Joe Morgan	2,528,986	699	664	106	.272	.344	.395	92	.261	.327	3.72	109	113
1991	AL	2nd-E	84-78	.519	7.0	Joe Morgan	2,562,435	731	712	126	.269	.340	.401	147	.257	.323	4.01	109	113
1992	AL	7th-E	73-89	.451	23.0	Butch Hobson	2,468,574	599	669	84	.246	.321	.347	107	.255	.323	3.63	112	91
1993	AL	5th-E	80-82	.494	15.0	Butch Hobson	2,422,021	686	698	114	.264	.330	.395	127	.252	.322	3.77	120	80
1994	AL	4th-E	54-61	.470	17.0	Butch Hobson	1,775,826	552	621	120	.263	.334	.421	120	.276	.351	4.93	107	102
1995	AL	1st-E	86-58	.597	—	Kevin Kennedy	2,164,378	791	698	175	.280	.357	.455	127	.268	.334	4.39	101	79
1996	AL	3rd-E	85-77	.525	7.0	Kevin Kennedy	2,315,233	928	921	209	.283	.359	.457	185	.279	.360	4.98	113	119
1997	AL	4th-E	78-84	.481	20.0	Jimy Williams	2,206,145	851	857	185	.291	.352	.463	149	.277	.351	4.85	99	84

Team Nicknames: Boston Americans 1901-1902, Boston Pilgrims 1903-1909, Boston Red Sox 1910-1997.

Team Ballparks: Huntington Avenue Grounds 1901-1911, Fenway Park I 1912-1933, Fenway Park II 1934-1997.

Teams: Red Sox

Boston Red Sox Individual Season Batting Leaders

Year	Batting Average		On-Base Percentage		Slugging Percentage		Home Runs		RBI		Stolen Bases	
1901	Buck Freeman	.339	Buck Freeman	.400	Buck Freeman	.520	Buck Freeman	12	Buck Freeman	114	Tommy Dowd	33
1902	Patsy Dougherty	.342	Patsy Dougherty	.407	Buck Freeman	.502	Buck Freeman	11	Buck Freeman	121	Chick Stahl	24
1903	Patsy Dougherty	.331	Patsy Dougherty	.372	Buck Freeman	.496	Buck Freeman	13	Buck Freeman	104	Patsy Dougherty	35
1904	Freddy Parent	.291	Chick Stahl	.366	Buck Freeman	.416	Buck Freeman	7	Buck Freeman	84	Freddy Parent	20
1905	Jimmy Collins	.276	Kip Selbach	.355	Jimmy Collins	.368	Hobe Ferris	6	Jimmy Collins	65	Freddy Parent	25
1906	Chick Stahl	.286	Chick Stahl	.346	Chick Stahl	.366	Chick Stahl	4	Chick Stahl	51	Freddy Parent	16
1907	Bunk Congalton	.286	Bunk Congalton	.318	Bunk Congalton	.353	Hobe Ferris	4	Bob Unglaub	62	Heinie Wagner	20
1908	Doc Gessler	.308	Doc Gessler	.394	Doc Gessler	.423	Doc Gessler	3	Doc Gessler	63	Amby McConnell	31
1909	Harry Lord	.311	Jake Stahl	.377	Tris Speaker	.443	Tris Speaker	7	Tris Speaker	77	Harry Lord	36
1910	Tris Speaker	.340	Tris Speaker	.404	Tris Speaker	.468	Jake Stahl	10	Jake Stahl	77	Harry Hooper	40
1911	Tris Speaker	.334	Tris Speaker	.418	Tris Speaker	.502	Tris Speaker	8	Duffy Lewis	86	Harry Hooper	38
1912	Tris Speaker	.383	Tris Speaker	.464	Tris Speaker	.567	Tris Speaker	10	Duffy Lewis	109	Tris Speaker	52
1913	Tris Speaker	.363	Tris Speaker	.441	Tris Speaker	.533	Harry Hooper	4	Duffy Lewis	90	Tris Speaker	46
1914	Tris Speaker	.338	Tris Speaker	.423	Tris Speaker	.503	Tris Speaker	4	Tris Speaker	90	Tris Speaker	42
1915	Tris Speaker	.322	Tris Speaker	.416	Tris Speaker	.411	Babe Ruth	4	Duffy Lewis	76	Tris Speaker	29
1916	Larry Gardner	.308	Larry Gardner	.372	Tilly Walker	.394	3 tied with	3	Larry Gardner	62	Harry Hooper	27
1917	Duffy Lewis	.302	Harry Hooper	.355	Duffy Lewis	.392	Harry Hooper	3	Duffy Lewis	65	Harry Hooper	21
1918	Harry Hooper	.289	Harry Hooper	.391	Harry Hooper	.405	Babe Ruth	11	Babe Ruth	66	Harry Hooper	24
1919	Babe Ruth	.322	Babe Ruth	.456	Babe Ruth	.657	Babe Ruth	29	Babe Ruth	114	Harry Hooper	23
1920	Harry Hooper	.312	Harry Hooper	.411	Harry Hooper	.470	Harry Hooper	7	Tim Hendryx	73	Mike Menosky	23
1921	Del Pratt	.324	Mike Menosky	.388	Del Pratt	.461	Del Pratt	5	Del Pratt	100	Shano Collins	15
1922	George Burns	.306	Del Pratt	.361	George Burns	.446	George Burns	12	Del Pratt	86	Mike Menosky	9
1923	Joe Harris	.335	Joe Harris	.406	Joe Harris	.520	Joe Harris	13	George Burns	82	Norm McMillan	13
1924	Ike Boone	.333	Joe Harris	.406	Ike Boone	.492	Ike Boone	13	Bobby Veach	99	Bill Wambsganss	14
1925	Ike Boone	.330	Ike Boone	.406	Ike Boone	.479	Phil Todt	11	Phil Todt	75	Homer Ezzell / Doc Prothro	9
1926	Topper Rigney	.270	Topper Rigney	.395	Topper Rigney	.377	Phil Todt	7	Baby Doll Jacobson / Phil Todt	69	Fred Haney	13
1927	Buddy Myer	.288	Ira Flagstead	.374	Bill Regan	.408	Phil Todt	6	Ira Flagstead	69	Ira Flagstead	12
1928	Buddy Myer	.313	Buddy Myer	.379	Doug Taitt	.434	Phil Todt	12	Bill Regan	75	Buddy Myer	30
1929	Jack Rothrock	.300	Jack Rothrock	.361	Russ Scarritt	.411	Jack Rothrock	6	Russ Scarritt	71	Jack Rothrock	23
1930	Earl Webb	.323	Earl Webb	.385	Earl Webb	.523	Earl Webb	16	Earl Webb	66	Tom Oliver / Bobby Reeves	6
1931	Earl Webb	.333	Earl Webb	.404	Earl Webb	.528	Earl Webb	14	Earl Webb	103	Jack Rothrock	13
1932	Smead Jolley	.309	Smead Jolley	.345	Smead Jolley	.480	Smead Jolley	18	Smead Jolley	99	Roy Johnson	13
1933	Roy Johnson	.313	Roy Johnson	.387	Roy Johnson	.466	Roy Johnson	10	Roy Johnson	95	Bill Werber	15
1934	Bill Werber	.321	Bill Werber	.397	Bill Werber	.472	Bill Werber	11	Roy Johnson	119	Bill Werber	40
1935	Roy Johnson	.315	Roy Johnson	.398	Joe Cronin	.460	Joe Cronin	14	Joe Cronin	95	Bill Werber	29
1936	Jimmie Foxx	.338	Jimmie Foxx	.440	Jimmie Foxx	.631	Jimmie Foxx	41	Jimmie Foxx	143	Bill Werber	23
1937	Ben Chapman	.307	Joe Cronin	.402	Jimmie Foxx	.538	Jimmie Foxx	36	Jimmie Foxx	127	Ben Chapman	27
1938	Jimmie Foxx	.349	Jimmie Foxx	.462	Jimmie Foxx	.704	Jimmie Foxx	50	Jimmie Foxx	175	Ben Chapman	13
1939	Jimmie Foxx	.360	Jimmie Foxx	.464	Jimmie Foxx	.694	Jimmie Foxx	35	Ted Williams	145	Jim Tabor	16
1940	Ted Williams	.344	Ted Williams	.442	Ted Williams	.594	Jimmie Foxx	36	Jimmie Foxx	119	Jim Tabor	14
1941	Ted Williams	.406	Ted Williams	.551	Ted Williams	.735	Ted Williams	37	Ted Williams	120	Jim Tabor	17
1942	Ted Williams	.356	Ted Williams	.499	Ted Williams	.648	Ted Williams	36	Ted Williams	137	Dom DiMaggio	16
1943	Pete Fox	.288	Bobby Doerr	.339	Bobby Doerr	.412	Bobby Doerr	16	Jim Tabor	85	Pete Fox	22
1944	Bobby Doerr	.325	Bob Johnson	.431	Bobby Doerr	.528	Bob Johnson	17	Bob Johnson	106	Catfish Metkovich	13
1945	Bob Johnson	.280	Eddie Lake	.412	Bob Johnson	.425	Bob Johnson	12	Bob Johnson	74	Catfish Metkovich	19
1946	Ted Williams	.342	Ted Williams	.497	Ted Williams	.667	Ted Williams	38	Ted Williams	123	Dom DiMaggio	10
1947	Ted Williams	.343	Ted Williams	.499	Ted Williams	.634	Ted Williams	32	Ted Williams	114	Johnny Pesky	12
1948	Ted Williams	.369	Ted Williams	.497	Ted Williams	.615	Vern Stephens	29	Vern Stephens	137	Dom DiMaggio	10
1949	Ted Williams	.343	Ted Williams	.490	Ted Williams	.650	Ted Williams	43	Vern Stephens / Ted Williams	159	Dom DiMaggio	9
1950	Billy Goodman	.354	Johnny Pesky	.437	Walt Dropo	.583	Walt Dropo	34	Walt Dropo / Vern Stephens	144	Dom DiMaggio	15
1951	Ted Williams	.318	Ted Williams	.464	Ted Williams	.556	Ted Williams	30	Ted Williams	126	Billy Goodman	7
1952	Billy Goodman	.306	Dom DiMaggio	.371	Billy Goodman	.394	Dick Gernert	19	Dick Gernert	67	Faye Throneberry	16
1953	Billy Goodman	.313	Billy Goodman	.384	George Kell	.483	Dick Gernert	21	George Kell	73	Jimmy Piersall	11
1954	Ted Williams	.345	Ted Williams	.513	Ted Williams	.635	Ted Williams	29	Jackie Jensen	117	Jackie Jensen	22
1955	Billy Goodman	.294	Billy Goodman	.394	Jackie Jensen	.479	Ted Williams	28	Jackie Jensen	116	Jackie Jensen	16
1956	Ted Williams	.345	Ted Williams	.479	Ted Williams	.605	Ted Williams	24	Jackie Jensen	97	Jackie Jensen	11
1957	Ted Williams	.388	Ted Williams	.526	Ted Williams	.731	Ted Williams	38	Jackie Jensen / Frank Malzone	103	Jimmy Piersall	14
1958	Ted Williams	.328	Ted Williams	.458	Ted Williams	.584	Jackie Jensen	35	Jackie Jensen	122	Jimmy Piersall	12
1959	Pete Runnels	.314	Pete Runnels	.415	Jackie Jensen	.492	Jackie Jensen	28	Jackie Jensen	112	Jackie Jensen	20
1960	Pete Runnels	.320	Pete Runnels	.401	Vic Wertz	.460	Ted Williams	29	Vic Wertz	103	Pete Runnels / Gene Stephens	5
1961	Frank Malzone	.266	Jackie Jensen	.350	Gary Geiger	.407	Gary Geiger	18	Frank Malzone	87	Gary Geiger	16
1962	Pete Runnels	.326	Pete Runnels	.408	Carl Yastrzemski	.469	Frank Malzone	21	Frank Malzone	95	Gary Geiger	18
1963	Carl Yastrzemski	.321	Carl Yastrzemski	.418	Dick Stuart	.521	Dick Stuart	42	Dick Stuart	118	Gary Geiger	9
1964	Eddie Bressoud	.293	Carl Yastrzemski	.374	Dick Stuart	.491	Dick Stuart	33	Dick Stuart	114	Dalton Jones / Carl Yastrzemski	6
1965	Carl Yastrzemski	.312	Carl Yastrzemski	.395	Carl Yastrzemski	.536	Tony Conigliaro	32	Felix Mantilla	92	Lenny Green / Dalton Jones	8
1966	Carl Yastrzemski	.278	Carl Yastrzemski	.368	Tony Conigliaro	.487	Tony Conigliaro	28	Tony Conigliaro	93	Jose Tartabull	11
1967	Carl Yastrzemski	.326	Carl Yastrzemski	.418	Carl Yastrzemski	.622	Carl Yastrzemski	44	Carl Yastrzemski	121	Reggie Smith	16
1968	Carl Yastrzemski	.301	Carl Yastrzemski	.426	Ken Harrelson	.518	Ken Harrelson	35	Ken Harrelson	109	Joe Foy	26
1969	Reggie Smith	.309	Rico Petrocelli	.403	Rico Petrocelli	.589	Rico Petrocelli / Carl Yastrzemski	40	Carl Yastrzemski	111	Carl Yastrzemski	15
1970	Carl Yastrzemski	.329	Carl Yastrzemski	.452	Carl Yastrzemski	.592	Carl Yastrzemski	40	Tony Conigliaro	116	Carl Yastrzemski	23
1971	Reggie Smith	.283	Carl Yastrzemski	.381	Reggie Smith	.489	Reggie Smith	30	Reggie Smith	96	Doug Griffin / Reggie Smith	11
1972	Carlton Fisk	.293	Carlton Fisk	.370	Carlton Fisk	.538	Carlton Fisk	22	Rico Petrocelli	75	Tommy Harper	25
1973	Carl Yastrzemski	.296	Carl Yastrzemski	.407	Carl Yastrzemski	.463	Carlton Fisk	26	Carl Yastrzemski	95	Tommy Harper	54

1226

Teams: Red Sox

Year	Batting Average		On-Base Percentage		Slugging Percentage		Home Runs		RBI		Stolen Bases	
1974	Carl Yastrzemski	.301	Carl Yastrzemski	.414	Carl Yastrzemski	.445	Rico Petrocelli	15	Carl Yastrzemski	79	Tommy Harper	28
							Carl Yastrzemski					
1975	Fred Lynn	.331	Fred Lynn	.401	Fred Lynn	.566	Jim Rice	22	Fred Lynn	105	Fred Lynn	10
											Jim Rice	
1976	Fred Lynn	.314	Fred Lynn	.367	Jim Rice	.482	Jim Rice	25	Carl Yastrzemski	102	Rick Burleson	14
											Fred Lynn	
1977	Jim Rice	.320	Carlton Fisk	.402	Jim Rice	.593	Jim Rice	39	Jim Rice	114	Rick Burleson	13
1978	Jim Rice	.315	Fred Lynn	.380	Jim Rice	.600	Jim Rice	46	Jim Rice	139	Jerry Remy	30
1979	Fred Lynn	.333	Fred Lynn	.423	Fred Lynn	.637	Fred Lynn	39	Jim Rice	130	Jerry Remy	14
							Jim Rice					
1980	Jim Rice	.294	Dwight Evans	.358	Jim Rice	.504	Tony Perez	25	Tony Perez	105	Jerry Remy	14
1981	Carney Lansford	.336	Dwight Evans	.415	Dwight Evans	.522	Dwight Evans	22	Dwight Evans	71	Carney Lansford	15
1982	Jim Rice	.309	Dwight Evans	.402	Dwight Evans	.534	Dwight Evans	32	Dwight Evans	98	Jerry Remy	16
1983	Wade Boggs	.361	Wade Boggs	.444	Jim Rice	.550	Jim Rice	39	Jim Rice	126	Jerry Remy	11
1984	Wade Boggs	.325	Wade Boggs	.407	Dwight Evans	.532	Tony Armas	43	Tony Armas	123	Jackie Gutierrez	12
1985	Wade Boggs	.368	Wade Boggs	.450	Jim Rice	.487	Dwight Evans	29	Bill Buckner	110	Bill Buckner	18
1986	Wade Boggs	.357	Wade Boggs	.453	Jim Rice	.490	Don Baylor	31	Jim Rice	110	Marty Barrett	15
1987	Wade Boggs	.363	Wade Boggs	.461	Wade Boggs	.588	Dwight Evans	34	Dwight Evans	123	Ellis Burks	27
1988	Wade Boggs	.366	Wade Boggs	.476	Mike Greenwell	.531	Mike Greenwell	22	Mike Greenwell	119	Ellis Burks	25
1989	Wade Boggs	.330	Wade Boggs	.430	Nick Esasky	.500	Nick Esasky	30	Nick Esasky	108	Ellis Burks	21
1990	Wade Boggs	.302	Wade Boggs	.386	Ellis Burks	.486	Ellis Burks	21	Ellis Burks	89	Ellis Burks	9
1991	Wade Boggs	.332	Wade Boggs	.421	Jack Clark	.466	Jack Clark	28	Jack Clark	87	Mike Greenwell	15
1992	Tom Brunansky	.266	Tom Brunansky	.354	Tom Brunansky	.445	Tom Brunansky	15	Tom Brunansky	74	Jody Reed	7
1993	Mike Greenwell	.315	Mo Vaughn	.390	Mo Vaughn	.525	Mo Vaughn	29	Mo Vaughn	101	Scott Fletcher	16
1994	Mo Vaughn	.310	Mo Vaughn	.408	Mo Vaughn	.576	Mo Vaughn	26	Mo Vaughn	82	Otis Nixon	42
1995	Tim Naehring	.307	Tim Naehring	.415	Mo Vaughn	.575	Mo Vaughn	39	Mo Vaughn	126	John Valentin	20
1996	Mo Vaughn	.326	Mo Vaughn	.420	Mo Vaughn	.583	Mo Vaughn	44	Mo Vaughn	143	Jeff Frye	18
1997	Reggie Jefferson	.319	Mo Vaughn	.420	Mo Vaughn	.560	Mo Vaughn	35	Nomar Garciaparra	98	Nomar Garciaparra	22

Teams: Red Sox

Boston Red Sox Individual Season Pitching Leaders

Year	ERA		Baserunners/9 IP		Innings Pitched		Strikeouts		Wins		Saves	
1901	Cy Young	1.62	Cy Young	8.9	Cy Young	371.1	Cy Young	158	Cy Young	33	Ted Lewis	1
1902	Cy Young	2.15	Cy Young	9.7	Cy Young	384.2	Cy Young	160	Cy Young	32	Nick Altrock	1
1903	Cy Young	2.08	Cy Young	9.0	Cy Young	341.2	Cy Young	176	Cy Young	28	Bill Dinneen Cy Young	2
1904	Cy Young	1.97	Cy Young	8.5	Cy Young	380.0	Cy Young	200	Cy Young	26	Cy Young	1
1905	Cy Young	1.82	Cy Young	8.1	Cy Young	320.2	Cy Young	210	Jesse Tannehill	22	Bill Dinneen	1
1906	Bill Dinneen	2.92	Cy Young	10.0	Cy Young	287.2	Cy Young	140	Jesse Tannehill Cy Young	13	3 tied with	2
1907	Cy Young	1.99	Cy Young	9.0	Cy Young	343.1	Cy Young	147	Cy Young	21	Tex Pruiett	3
1908	Cy Young	1.26	Cy Young	8.1	Cy Young	299.0	Cy Young	150	Cy Young	21	3 tied with	2
1909	Eddie Cicotte	1.95	Frank Arellanes	9.4	Frank Arellanes	230.2	Joe Wood	88	Frank Arellanes	16	Frank Arellanes	8
1910	Ray Collins	1.62	Ray Collins	9.1	Eddie Cicotte	250.0	Joe Wood	145	Eddie Cicotte	15	Sea Lion Hall	5
1911	Joe Wood	2.02	Joe Wood	10.2	Joe Wood	276.2	Joe Wood	231	Joe Wood	23	Sea Lion Hall	5
1912	Joe Wood	1.91	Joe Wood	9.4	Joe Wood	344.0	Joe Wood	258	Joe Wood	34	Hugh Bedient Sea Lion Hall	2
1913	Dutch Leonard	2.39	Ray Collins	10.3	Hugh Bedient	259.2	Dutch Leonard	144	Ray Collins	19	Hugh Bedient	5
1914	Dutch Leonard	1.00	Dutch Leonard	8.3	Ray Collins	272.1	Dutch Leonard	176	Ray Collins	20	Dutch Leonard	3
1915	Joe Wood	1.49	Joe Wood	9.4	Rube Foster	255.1	Dutch Leonard	116	Rube Foster Ernie Shore	19	Carl Mays	7
1916	Babe Ruth	1.75	Babe Ruth	9.9	Babe Ruth	323.2	Babe Ruth	170	Babe Ruth	23	Dutch Leonard	6
1917	Carl Mays	1.74	Carl Mays	9.9	Babe Ruth	326.1	Dutch Leonard	144	Babe Ruth	24	Babe Ruth	2
1918	Joe Bush	2.11	Babe Ruth	9.5	Carl Mays	293.1	Joe Bush	125	Carl Mays	21	Joe Bush	2
1919	Carl Mays	2.47	Carl Mays	10.8	Sad Sam Jones	245.0	Herb Pennock	70	Herb Pennock	16	Allan Russell	4
1920	Harry Harper	3.04	Herb Pennock	11.5	Sad Sam Jones	274.0	Joe Bush	88	Herb Pennock	16	Herb Pennock	2
1921	Sad Sam Jones	3.22	Sad Sam Jones	12.1	Sad Sam Jones	298.2	Sad Sam Jones	98	Sad Sam Jones	23	Allan Russell	3
1922	Jack Quinn	3.48	Jack Quinn	11.4	Jack Quinn	256.0	Rip Collins	69	Rip Collins	14	Alex Ferguson Allan Russell	2
1923	Bill Piercy	3.41	Howard Ehmke	13.0	Howard Ehmke	316.2	Howard Ehmke	121	Howard Ehmke	20	Jack Quinn	7
1924	Jack Quinn	3.19	Howard Ehmke	11.9	Howard Ehmke	315.0	Howard Ehmke	119	Howard Ehmke	19	Jack Quinn	7
1925	Howard Ehmke	3.73	Ted Wingfield	13.0	Howard Ehmke	260.2	Howard Ehmke	95	Ted Wingfield	12	Ted Wingfield	2
1926	Hal Wiltse	4.22	Ted Wingfield	12.8	Hal Wiltse	196.1	Hal Wiltse	59	Ted Wingfield	11	Ted Wingfield	3
1927	Slim Harriss	4.18	Danny MacFayden	13.5	Hal Wiltse	219.0	Slim Harriss Red Ruffing	77	Slim Harriss	14	Danny MacFayden Red Ruffing	2
1928	Ed Morris	3.53	Ed Morris	11.9	Red Ruffing	289.1	Red Ruffing	118	Ed Morris	19	Ed Morris	5
1929	Danny MacFayden	3.62	Jack Russell	12.1	Red Ruffing	244.1	Red Ruffing	109	Ed Morris	14	Milt Gaston	2
1930	Milt Gaston	3.92	Milt Gaston	12.2	Milt Gaston	273.0	Milt Gaston	99	Milt Gaston	13	Milt Gaston Danny MacFayden	2
1931	Wilcy Moore	3.88	Wilcy Moore	12.2	Jack Russell	232.0	Danny MacFayden	74	Danny MacFayden	16	Wilcy Moore	10
1932	Ed Durham	3.80	Ed Durham	12.3	Bob Weiland	195.2	Bob Weiland	63	Bob Kline	11	Wilcy Moore	4
1933	Bob Weiland	3.87	Bob Weiland	12.6	Gordon Rhodes	232.0	Bob Weiland	97	Gordon Rhodes	12	Bob Kline	4
1934	Fritz Ostermueller	3.49	Wes Ferrell	12.6	Gordon Rhodes	219.0	Johnny Welch	91	Wes Ferrell	14	Fritz Ostermueller	3
1935	Lefty Grove	2.70	Lefty Grove	11.1	Wes Ferrell	322.1	Lefty Grove	121	Wes Ferrell	25	Rube Walberg	3
1936	Lefty Grove	2.81	Lefty Grove	10.9	Wes Ferrell	301.0	Lefty Grove	130	Wes Ferrell	20	Jack Wilson	3
1937	Lefty Grove	3.02	Lefty Grove	12.1	Lefty Grove	262.0	Lefty Grove	153	Lefty Grove	17	Jack Wilson	7
1938	Lefty Grove	3.08	Lefty Grove	12.2	Jim Bagby Jr.	198.2	Lefty Grove	99	Jim Bagby Jr. Jack Wilson	15	Archie McKain	6
1939	Lefty Grove	2.54	Lefty Grove	11.3	Lefty Grove	191.0	Lefty Grove	81	Lefty Grove	15	Joe Heving	7
1940	Jim Bagby Jr.	4.73	Jim Bagby Jr.	14.8	Jim Bagby Jr.	182.2	Jack Wilson	102	Joe Heving Jack Wilson	12	Jack Wilson	5
1941	Charlie Wagner	3.07	Charlie Wagner	12.5	Dick Newsome	213.2	Mickey Harris	111	Dick Newsome	19	Mike Ryba	6
1942	Tex Hughson	2.59	Tex Hughson	10.7	Tex Hughson	281.0	Tex Hughson	113	Tex Hughson	22	Mace Brown	6
1943	Tex Hughson	2.64	Tex Hughson	10.7	Tex Hughson	266.0	Tex Hughson	114	Tex Hughson	12	Mace Brown	9
1944	Tex Hughson	2.26	Tex Hughson	9.5	Tex Hughson	203.1	Tex Hughson	112	Tex Hughson	18	Frank Barrett	8
1945	Boo Ferriss	2.96	Boo Ferriss	12.1	Boo Ferriss	264.2	Boo Ferriss	94	Boo Ferriss	21	Frank Barrett	3
1946	Tex Hughson	2.75	Tex Hughson	9.9	Tex Hughson	278.0	Tex Hughson	172	Boo Ferriss	25	Bob Klinger	9
1947	Joe Dobson	2.95	Joe Dobson	10.9	Joe Dobson	228.2	Tex Hughson	119	Joe Dobson	18	Earl Johnson	8
1948	Mel Parnell	3.14	Joe Dobson	12.1	Joe Dobson	245.1	Joe Dobson	116	Jack Kramer	18	Earl Johnson	5
1949	Mel Parnell	2.77	Mel Parnell	12.1	Mel Parnell	295.1	Ellis Kinder	138	Mel Parnell	25	Ellis Kinder Walt Masterson	4
1950	Mel Parnell	3.61	Ellis Kinder	12.7	Mel Parnell	249.0	Mickey McDermott	96	Mel Parnell	18	Ellis Kinder	9
1951	Mel Parnell	3.26	Mickey McDermott	12.5	Mel Parnell	221.0	Mickey McDermott	127	Mel Parnell	18	Ellis Kinder	14
1952	Mel Parnell	3.62	Mel Parnell	12.7	Mel Parnell	214.0	Mickey McDermott	117	Mel Parnell	12	Al Benton	6
1953	Mickey McDermott	3.01	Mickey McDermott	12.2	Mel Parnell	241.0	Mel Parnell	136	Mel Parnell	21	Ellis Kinder	27
1954	Frank Sullivan	3.14	Frank Sullivan	11.2	Frank Sullivan	206.1	Frank Sullivan	124	Frank Sullivan	15	Ellis Kinder	15
1955	Frank Sullivan	2.91	Frank Sullivan	11.7	Frank Sullivan	260.0	Frank Sullivan	129	Frank Sullivan	18	Ellis Kinder	18
1956	Frank Sullivan	3.42	Tom Brewer	11.7	Tom Brewer	244.1	Tom Brewer	127	Tom Brewer	19	Ike Delock	9
1957	Frank Sullivan	2.73	Frank Sullivan	9.8	Frank Sullivan	240.2	Tom Brewer	128	Tom Brewer	16	Ike Delock	11
1958	Ike Delock	3.38	Ike Delock	11.9	Tom Brewer	227.1	Tom Brewer	124	Ike Delock	14	Leo Kiely	12
1959	Tom Brewer	3.76	Frank Sullivan	12.5	Tom Brewer	215.1	Tom Brewer	121	Jerry Casale	13	Mike Fornieles	11
1960	Bill Monbouquette	3.64	Bill Monbouquette	12.0	Bill Monbouquette	215.0	Bill Monbouquette	134	Bill Monbouquette	14	Mike Fornieles	14
1961	Don Schwall	3.22	Bill Monbouquette	12.7	Bill Monbouquette	236.1	Bill Monbouquette	161	Don Schwall	15	Mike Fornieles	15
1962	Bill Monbouquette	3.33	Bill Monbouquette	11.3	Gene Conley	241.2	Bill Monbouquette	153	Gene Conley Bill Monbouquette	15	Dick Radatz	24
1963	Earl Wilson	3.76	Bill Monbouquette	10.1	Bill Monbouquette	266.2	Bill Monbouquette	174	Bill Monbouquette	20	Dick Radatz	25
1964	Bill Monbouquette	4.04	Bill Monbouquette	11.5	Bill Monbouquette	234.0	Dick Radatz	181	Dick Radatz	16	Dick Radatz	29
1965	Bill Monbouquette	3.70	Bill Monbouquette	11.0	Earl Wilson	230.2	Earl Wilson	164	Earl Wilson	13	Dick Radatz	22
1966	Jose Santiago	3.66	Jose Santiago	11.3	Jim Lonborg	181.2	Jim Lonborg	131	Jose Santiago	12	Don McMahon	9
1967	Lee Stange	2.77	Lee Stange	10.2	Jim Lonborg	273.1	Jim Lonborg	246	Jim Lonborg	22	John Wyatt	20
1968	Ray Culp	2.91	Ray Culp	10.7	Ray Culp	216.1	Ray Culp	190	Ray Culp Dick Ellsworth	16	Lee Stange	12
1969	Mike Nagy	3.11	Ray Culp	11.1	Ray Culp	227.0	Ray Culp	172	Ray Culp	17	Sparky Lyle	17
1970	Ray Culp	3.04	Sonny Siebert	11.0	Ray Culp	251.1	Ray Culp	197	Ray Culp	17	Sparky Lyle	20
1971	Sonny Siebert	2.91	Sonny Siebert	10.8	Ray Culp	242.1	Ray Culp	151	Sonny Siebert	16	Sparky Lyle	16
1972	Luis Tiant	1.91	Luis Tiant	9.7	Marty Pattin	253.0	Marty Pattin	168	Marty Pattin	17	Bobby Bolin Bill Lee	5

Teams: Red Sox

Year	ERA		Baserunners/9 IP		Innings Pitched		Strikeouts		Wins		Saves	
1973	Bill Lee	2.75	Luis Tiant	10.0	Bill Lee	284.2	Luis Tiant	206	Luis Tiant	20	Bobby Bolin	15
1974	Luis Tiant	2.92	Luis Tiant	10.6	Luis Tiant	311.1	Luis Tiant	176	Luis Tiant	22	Diego Segui	10
1975	Bill Lee	3.95	Luis Tiant	11.7	Bill Lee	260.0	Luis Tiant	142	Rick Wise	19	Dick Drago	15
					Luis Tiant							
1976	Luis Tiant	3.06	Fergie Jenkins	10.7	Luis Tiant	279.0	Fergie Jenkins	142	Luis Tiant	21	Jim Willoughby	10
1977	Fergie Jenkins	3.68	Fergie Jenkins	10.5	Fergie Jenkins	193.0	Luis Tiant	124	Bill Campbell	13	Bill Campbell	31
1978	Dennis Eckersley	2.99	Luis Tiant	10.5	Dennis Eckersley	268.1	Dennis Eckersley	162	Dennis Eckersley	20	Bob Stanley	10
1979	Dennis Eckersley	2.99	Dennis Eckersley	10.9	Mike Torrez	252.1	Dennis Eckersley	150	Dennis Eckersley	17	Dick Drago	13
1980	Bob Stanley	3.39	Dennis Eckersley	10.7	Mike Torrez	207.1	Dennis Eckersley	121	Dennis Eckersley	12	Tom Burgmeier	24
1981	Mike Torrez	3.68	Dennis Eckersley	11.6	Dennis Eckersley	154.0	Mark Clear	82	Bob Stanley	10	Mark Clear	9
									Mike Torrez			
1982	Bob Stanley	3.10	Dennis Eckersley	11.0	Dennis Eckersley	224.1	John Tudor	146	Mark Clear	14	Mark Clear	14
											Bob Stanley	
1983	Bobby Ojeda	4.04	John Tudor	11.9	John Tudor	242.0	John Tudor	136	John Tudor	13	Bob Stanley	33
1984	Al Nipper	3.89	Oil Can Boyd	11.9	Bruce Hurst	218.0	Bobby Ojeda	137	3 tied with	12	Bob Stanley	22
1985	Oil Can Boyd	3.70	Oil Can Boyd	11.4	Oil Can Boyd	272.1	Bruce Hurst	189	Oil Can Boyd	15	Steve Crawford	12
1986	Roger Clemens	2.48	Roger Clemens	8.9	Roger Clemens	254.0	Roger Clemens	238	Roger Clemens	24	Bob Stanley	16
1987	Roger Clemens	2.97	Roger Clemens	10.9	Roger Clemens	281.2	Roger Clemens	256	Roger Clemens	20	Wes Gardner	10
1988	Roger Clemens	2.93	Roger Clemens	9.7	Roger Clemens	264.0	Roger Clemens	291	Roger Clemens	18	Lee Smith	29
									Bruce Hurst			
1989	Roger Clemens	3.13	Roger Clemens	11.2	Roger Clemens	253.1	Roger Clemens	230	Roger Clemens	17	Lee Smith	25
1990	Roger Clemens	1.93	Roger Clemens	10.0	Roger Clemens	228.1	Roger Clemens	209	Roger Clemens	21	Jeff Reardon	21
1991	Roger Clemens	2.62	Roger Clemens	9.6	Roger Clemens	271.1	Roger Clemens	241	Roger Clemens	18	Jeff Reardon	40
1992	Roger Clemens	2.41	Roger Clemens	10.0	Roger Clemens	246.2	Roger Clemens	208	Roger Clemens	18	Jeff Reardon	27
1993	Frank Viola	3.14	Danny Darwin	9.7	Danny Darwin	229.1	Roger Clemens	160	Danny Darwin	15	Jeff Russell	33
1994	Roger Clemens	2.85	Roger Clemens	10.5	Roger Clemens	170.2	Roger Clemens	168	Roger Clemens	9	Ken Ryan	13
1995	Tim Wakefield	2.95	Tim Wakefield	11.1	Tim Wakefield	195.1	Erik Hanson	139	Tim Wakefield	16	Rick Aguilera	20
1996	Roger Clemens	3.63	Roger Clemens	12.1	Roger Clemens	242.2	Roger Clemens	257	Tim Wakefield	14	Heathcliff Slocumb	31
1997	Tom Gordon	3.74	Tom Gordon	11.6	Tim Wakefield	201.1	Tom Gordon	159	Aaron Sele	13	Heathcliff Slocumb	17

Red Sox Franchise Batting Leaders—Career

Games

1	Carl Yastrzemski	3,308
2	Dwight Evans	2,505
3	Ted Williams	2,292
4	Jim Rice	2,089
5	Bobby Doerr	1,865
6	Harry Hooper	1,646
7	Wade Boggs	1,625
8	Rico Petrocelli	1,553
9	Dom DiMaggio	1,399
10	Frank Malzone	1,359
11	Mike Greenwell	1,269
12	George Scott	1,192
13	Duffy Lewis	1,184
14	Billy Goodman	1,177
15	Joe Cronin	1,134
16	Larry Gardner	1,122
17	Rick Miller	1,101
18	Everett Scott	1,096
19	Carlton Fisk	1,078
20	Tris Speaker	1,065

At-Bats

1	Carl Yastrzemski	11,988
2	Dwight Evans	8,726
3	Jim Rice	8,225
4	Ted Williams	7,706
5	Bobby Doerr	7,093
6	Harry Hooper	6,270
7	Wade Boggs	6,213
8	Dom DiMaggio	5,640
9	Rico Petrocelli	5,390
10	Frank Malzone	5,273
11	Mike Greenwell	4,623
12	Billy Goodman	4,399
13	Duffy Lewis	4,325
14	George Scott	4,234
15	Johnny Pesky	4,085
16	Rick Burleson	4,064
17	Tris Speaker	3,935
18	Larry Gardner	3,915
19	Joe Cronin	3,892
20	Everett Scott	3,887

Runs

1	Carl Yastrzemski	1,816
2	Ted Williams	1,798
3	Dwight Evans	1,435
4	Jim Rice	1,249
5	Bobby Doerr	1,094
6	Wade Boggs	1,067
7	Dom DiMaggio	1,046
8	Harry Hooper	988
9	Johnny Pesky	776
10	Jimmie Foxx	721
11	Tris Speaker	704
12	Billy Goodman	688
13	Mike Greenwell	657
14	Rico Petrocelli	653
15	Joe Cronin	645
16	Frank Malzone	641
17	Carlton Fisk	627
18	Jackie Jensen	597
19	Reggie Smith	592
20	George Scott	527

Hits

1	Carl Yastrzemski	3,419
2	Ted Williams	2,654
3	Jim Rice	2,452
4	Dwight Evans	2,373
5	Wade Boggs	2,098
6	Bobby Doerr	2,042
7	Harry Hooper	1,707
8	Dom DiMaggio	1,680
9	Frank Malzone	1,454
10	Mike Greenwell	1,400
11	Rico Petrocelli	1,352
12	Billy Goodman	1,344
13	Tris Speaker	1,327
14	Johnny Pesky	1,277
15	Duffy Lewis	1,248
16	Joe Cronin	1,168
17	Rick Burleson	1,114
18	Larry Gardner	1,106
19	Carlton Fisk	1,097
20	Jackie Jensen	1,089

Doubles

1	Carl Yastrzemski	646
2	Ted Williams	525
3	Dwight Evans	474
4	Wade Boggs	422
5	Bobby Doerr	381
6	Jim Rice	373
7	Dom DiMaggio	308
8	Mike Greenwell	275
9	Joe Cronin	270
10	Duffy Lewis	254
11	Billy Goodman	248
12	Harry Hooper	246
13	Tris Speaker	241
14	Rico Petrocelli	237
15	Frank Malzone	234
16	Fred Lynn	217
17	Carlton Fisk	207
18	Reggie Smith	204
19	Rick Burleson	203
20	Four tied at	196

Triples

1	Harry Hooper	130
2	Tris Speaker	106
3	Buck Freeman	90
4	Bobby Doerr	89
5	Larry Gardner	87
6	Jim Rice	79
7	Hobe Ferris	77
8	Dwight Evans	72
9	Ted Williams	71
10	Jimmy Collins	65
11	Freddy Parent	63
12	Chick Stahl	62
	Duffy Lewis	62
14	Carl Yastrzemski	59
15	Dom DiMaggio	57
16	Phil Todt	56
17	Jake Stahl	50
18	Heinie Wagner	47
	Wade Boggs	47
20	Johnny Pesky	46

Home Runs

1	Ted Williams	521
2	Carl Yastrzemski	452
3	Jim Rice	382
4	Dwight Evans	379
5	Bobby Doerr	223
6	Jimmie Foxx	222
7	Rico Petrocelli	210
8	Mo Vaughn	190
9	Jackie Jensen	170
10	Tony Conigliaro	162
	Carlton Fisk	162
12	George Scott	154
13	Reggie Smith	149
14	Frank Malzone	131
15	Mike Greenwell	130
16	Fred Lynn	124
17	Vern Stephens	122
18	Joe Cronin	119
19	Tony Armas	113
20	Dick Gernert	101

RBI

1	Carl Yastrzemski	1,844
2	Ted Williams	1,839
3	Jim Rice	1,451
4	Dwight Evans	1,346
5	Bobby Doerr	1,247
6	Jimmie Foxx	788
7	Rico Petrocelli	773
8	Joe Cronin	737
9	Jackie Jensen	733
10	Mike Greenwell	726
11	Frank Malzone	716
12	Wade Boggs	687
13	Mo Vaughn	637
14	Duffy Lewis	629
15	Dom DiMaggio	618
16	Carlton Fisk	568
17	Vern Stephens	562
	George Scott	562
19	Tris Speaker	552
20	Reggie Smith	536

Walks

1	Ted Williams	2,019
2	Carl Yastrzemski	1,845
3	Dwight Evans	1,337
4	Wade Boggs	1,004
5	Harry Hooper	826
6	Bobby Doerr	809
7	Dom DiMaggio	750
8	Jim Rice	670
9	Rico Petrocelli	661
10	Jimmie Foxx	624
11	Joe Cronin	585
	Jackie Jensen	585
13	Johnny Pesky	581
14	Billy Goodman	561
15	Mike Greenwell	460
16	Tris Speaker	459
17	Mo Vaughn	458
18	Reggie Smith	425
19	George Scott	418
20	Carlton Fisk	389

Strikeouts

1	Dwight Evans	1,643
2	Jim Rice	1,423
3	Carl Yastrzemski	1,393
4	Rico Petrocelli	926
5	George Scott	850
6	Mo Vaughn	810
7	Ted Williams	709
8	Bobby Doerr	608
9	Carlton Fisk	588
10	Tony Conigliaro	577
11	Dom DiMaggio	571
12	Jimmie Foxx	568
13	Reggie Smith	498
14	Butch Hobson	495
15	Wade Boggs	470
16	Tony Armas	454
17	Ellis Burks	450
18	Rich Gedman	448
19	Jackie Jensen	425
20	Frank Malzone	423

Stolen Bases

1	Harry Hooper	300
2	Tris Speaker	267
3	Carl Yastrzemski	168
4	Heinie Wagner	141
5	Larry Gardner	134
6	Freddy Parent	129
7	Bill Werber	107
	Tommy Harper	107
9	Chick Stahl	105
10	Jimmy Collins	102
	Duffy Lewis	102
12	Dom DiMaggio	100
13	Jerry Remy	98
14	Jackie Jensen	95
15	Ellis Burks	93
16	Reggie Smith	84
17	Clyde Engle	80
	Mike Greenwell	80
19	Harry Lord	77
20	Dwight Evans	76

Runs Created

1	Ted Williams	2,259
2	Carl Yastrzemski	2,079
3	Dwight Evans	1,515
4	Jim Rice	1,341
5	Wade Boggs	1,196
6	Bobby Doerr	1,182
7	Dom DiMaggio	950
8	Harry Hooper	927
9	Tris Speaker	821
10	Jimmie Foxx	816
11	Rico Petrocelli	751
12	Joe Cronin	745
13	Mike Greenwell	732
14	Johnny Pesky	694
15	Billy Goodman	691
16	Jackie Jensen	667
17	Carlton Fisk	650
	Mo Vaughn	650
19	Frank Malzone	633
20	Reggie Smith	623

Runs Created/27 Outs

(minimum 2000 Plate Appearances)

1	Ted Williams	11.49
2	Jimmie Foxx	9.18
3	Tris Speaker	7.67
4	Wade Boggs	7.34
5	Mo Vaughn	7.33
6	Fred Lynn	7.12
7	Joe Cronin	6.78
8	Pete Runnels	6.61
9	Roy Johnson	6.54
10	Vern Stephens	6.31
11	Johnny Pesky	6.23
12	Rick Ferrell	6.17
13	John Valentin	6.17
14	Carl Yastrzemski	6.16
15	Dom DiMaggio	6.10
16	Dwight Evans	6.05
17	Carlton Fisk	6.01
18	Jackie Jensen	5.96
19	Buck Freeman	5.94
20	Bobby Doerr	5.86

Batting Average

(minimum 2000 Plate Appearances)

1	Ted Williams	.344
2	Wade Boggs	.338
3	Tris Speaker	.337
4	Pete Runnels	.320
5	Jimmie Foxx	.320
6	Roy Johnson	.313
7	Johnny Pesky	.313
8	Fred Lynn	.308
9	Billy Goodman	.306
10	Mike Greenwell	.303
11	Doc Cramer	.302
12	Rick Ferrell	.302
13	Lou Finney	.301
14	Joe Cronin	.300
15	Mo Vaughn	.298
16	Jim Rice	.298
17	Dom DiMaggio	.298
18	Jimmy Collins	.296
19	John Valentin	.296
20	Stuffy McInnis	.296

On-Base Percentage

(minimum 2000 Plate Appearances)

1	Ted Williams	.482
2	Jimmie Foxx	.429
3	Wade Boggs	.428
4	Tris Speaker	.414
5	Pete Runnels	.408
6	Johnny Pesky	.401
7	Joe Cronin	.394
8	Rick Ferrell	.394
9	Mo Vaughn	.393
10	Roy Johnson	.387
11	Billy Goodman	.386
12	Dom DiMaggio	.383
13	Fred Lynn	.383
14	Carl Yastrzemski	.379
15	John Valentin	.375
16	Jackie Jensen	.374
17	Ira Flagstead	.374
18	Dwight Evans	.369
19	Mike Greenwell	.368
20	Bill Werber	.367

Slugging Percentage

(minimum 2000 Plate Appearances)

1	Ted Williams	.634
2	Jimmie Foxx	.605
3	Mo Vaughn	.532
4	Fred Lynn	.520
5	Jim Rice	.502
6	Vern Stephens	.492
7	Tony Conigliaro	.488
8	Joe Cronin	.484
9	Tris Speaker	.482
10	Carlton Fisk	.481
11	Tony Armas	.480
12	John Valentin	.479
13	Jackie Jensen	.478
14	Dwight Evans	.473
15	Reggie Smith	.471
16	Mike Greenwell	.463
17	Carl Yastrzemski	.462
18	Wade Boggs	.462
19	Bobby Doerr	.461
20	Roy Johnson	.458

Teams: Red Sox

Red Sox Franchise Pitching Leaders—Career

Wins

1	Cy Young	192
	Roger Clemens	192
3	Mel Parnell	123
4	Luis Tiant	122
5	Joe Wood	116
6	Bob Stanley	115
7	Joe Dobson	106
8	Lefty Grove	105
9	Tex Hughson	96
	Bill Monbouquette	96
11	Bill Lee	94
12	Tom Brewer	91
13	Dutch Leonard	90
	Frank Sullivan	90
15	Babe Ruth	89
16	Bruce Hurst	88
17	Ellis Kinder	86
18	Bill Dinneen	85
19	Ray Collins	84
	Dennis Eckersley	84

Losses

1	Cy Young	112
2	Roger Clemens	111
3	George Winter	97
	Bob Stanley	97
5	Red Ruffing	96
6	Jack Russell	94
7	Bill Monbouquette	91
8	Bill Dinneen	85
9	Tom Brewer	82
10	Luis Tiant	81
11	Frank Sullivan	80
12	Danny MacFayden	78
13	Mel Parnell	75
14	Bruce Hurst	73
15	Joe Dobson	72
	Willard Nixon	72
	Ike Delock	72
18	Dennis Eckersley	70
19	Bill Lee	68
20	Jack Wilson	67

Winning Percentage
(minimum 100 decisions)

1	Joe Wood	.674
2	Babe Ruth	.659
3	Tex Hughson	.640
4	Roger Clemens	.634
5	Cy Young	.632
6	Lefty Grove	.629
7	Ellis Kinder	.623
8	Mel Parnell	.621
9	Jesse Tannehill	.620
10	Wes Ferrell	.608
11	Luis Tiant	.601
12	Joe Dobson	.596
13	Dutch Leonard	.588
14	Carl Mays	.585
15	Bill Lee	.580
16	Ray Collins	.575
17	Ray Culp	.550
18	Bruce Hurst	.547
19	Dennis Eckersley	.545
20	Bob Stanley	.542

Games

1	Bob Stanley	637
2	Roger Clemens	383
3	Ellis Kinder	365
4	Cy Young	327
5	Ike Delock	322
6	Bill Lee	321
7	Mel Parnell	289
8	Greg Harris	287
9	Mike Fornieles	286
	Dick Radatz	286
11	Luis Tiant	274
12	Sparky Lyle	260
13	Joe Dobson	259
14	Jack Wilson	258
15	Bill Monbouquette	254
16	Frank Sullivan	252
17	Jack Russell	242
18	Tom Brewer	241
19	Tony Fossas	239
20	Bruce Hurst	237

Games Started

1	Roger Clemens	382
2	Cy Young	297
3	Luis Tiant	238
4	Mel Parnell	232
5	Bill Monbouquette	228
6	Tom Brewer	217
	Bruce Hurst	217
8	Joe Dobson	202
9	Frank Sullivan	201
10	Dennis Eckersley	191
11	Lefty Grove	190
12	Willard Nixon	177
13	George Winter	176
14	Bill Dinneen	174
15	Bill Lee	167
16	Jim Lonborg	163
17	Dutch Leonard	160
18	Joe Wood	157
	Mike Torrez	157
20	Four tied at	156

Complete Games

1	Cy Young	275
2	Bill Dinneen	156
3	George Winter	141
4	Joe Wood	121
5	Lefty Grove	119
6	Mel Parnell	113
	Luis Tiant	113
8	Babe Ruth	105
9	Roger Clemens	100
10	Tex Hughson	99
11	Dutch Leonard	96
12	Ray Collins	90
	Joe Dobson	90
14	Carl Mays	87
15	Jesse Tannehill	85
16	Howard Ehmke	83
17	Sad Sam Jones	82
18	Wes Ferrell	81
19	Tom Brewer	75
20	Red Ruffing	73

Shutouts

1	Cy Young	38
	Roger Clemens	38
3	Joe Wood	28
4	Luis Tiant	26
5	Dutch Leonard	25
6	Mel Parnell	20
7	Ray Collins	19
	Tex Hughson	19
9	Sad Sam Jones	18
10	Babe Ruth	17
	Joe Dobson	17
12	Bill Dinneen	16
	Bill Monbouquette	16
14	Rube Foster	15
	Lefty Grove	15
16	Jesse Tannehill	14
	Carl Mays	14
	Frank Sullivan	14
19	Six tied at	13

Saves

1	Bob Stanley	132
2	Dick Radatz	104
3	Ellis Kinder	91
4	Jeff Reardon	88
5	Sparky Lyle	69
6	Lee Smith	58
7	Bill Campbell	51
8	Mike Fornieles	48
	Heathcliff Slocumb	48
10	Jeff Russell	45
11	Dick Drago	41
12	Tom Burgmeier	40
13	Mark Clear	38
14	Ike Delock	31
15	Leo Kiely	28
	John Wyatt	28
	Bobby Bolin	28
18	Ken Ryan	22
19	Six tied at	20

Innings Pitched

1	Roger Clemens	2,776.0
2	Cy Young	2,728.1
3	Luis Tiant	1,774.2
4	Mel Parnell	1,752.2
5	Bob Stanley	1,707.0
6	Bill Monbouquette	1,622.0
7	George Winter	1,599.2
8	Joe Dobson	1,544.0
9	Lefty Grove	1,539.2
10	Tom Brewer	1,509.1
11	Frank Sullivan	1,505.1
12	Bill Lee	1,503.1
13	Bill Dinneen	1,501.0
14	Bruce Hurst	1,459.0
15	Joe Wood	1,418.0
16	Tex Hughson	1,375.2
17	Dutch Leonard	1,361.1
18	Ray Collins	1,336.0
19	Dennis Eckersley	1,332.0
20	Willard Nixon	1,234.0

Walks

1	Roger Clemens	856
2	Mel Parnell	758
3	Tom Brewer	669
4	Joe Dobson	604
5	Jack Wilson	564
6	Willard Nixon	530
7	Ike Delock	514
8	Mickey McDermott	504
9	Luis Tiant	501
10	Fritz Ostermueller	491
11	Earl Wilson	481
12	Bruce Hurst	479
13	Frank Sullivan	475
14	Bob Stanley	471
15	Red Ruffing	459
16	Bill Lee	448
17	Lefty Grove	447
18	Danny MacFayden	430
19	Babe Ruth	425
20	Mike Torrez	420

Strikeouts

1	Roger Clemens	2,590
2	Cy Young	1,341
3	Luis Tiant	1,075
4	Bruce Hurst	1,043
5	Joe Wood	986
6	Bill Monbouquette	969
7	Frank Sullivan	821
8	Ray Culp	794
9	Jim Lonborg	784
10	Dutch Leonard	771
11	Dennis Eckersley	749
12	Lefty Grove	743
13	Tom Brewer	733
14	Mel Parnell	732
15	Earl Wilson	714
16	Tex Hughson	693
	Bob Stanley	693
18	Joe Dobson	690
19	Ike Delock	661
20	Dick Radatz	627

Strikeouts/9 Innings
(minimum 1000 Innings Pitched)

1	Roger Clemens	8.40
2	Ray Culp	6.54
3	Bruce Hurst	6.43
4	Jim Lonborg	6.42
5	Earl Wilson	6.27
6	Joe Wood	6.26
7	Luis Tiant	5.45
8	Bill Monbouquette	5.38
9	Dutch Leonard	5.10
10	Dennis Eckersley	5.06
11	Oil Can Boyd	5.05
12	Ike Delock	4.93
13	Frank Sullivan	4.91
14	Jack Wilson	4.75
15	Tex Hughson	4.53
16	Willard Nixon	4.49
17	Cy Young	4.42
18	Ellis Kinder	4.39
19	Tom Brewer	4.37
20	Lefty Grove	4.34

ERA
(minimum 1000 Innings Pitched)

1	Joe Wood	1.99
2	Cy Young	2.00
3	Dutch Leonard	2.14
4	Babe Ruth	2.19
5	Carl Mays	2.21
6	Ray Collins	2.53
7	Bill Dinneen	2.81
8	George Winter	2.91
9	Tex Hughson	2.94
10	Roger Clemens	3.06
11	Ellis Kinder	3.28
12	Lefty Grove	3.34
13	Luis Tiant	3.36
14	Sad Sam Jones	3.39
15	Frank Sullivan	3.47
16	Ray Culp	3.50
17	Mel Parnell	3.50
18	Joe Dobson	3.57
19	Bob Stanley	3.64
20	Bill Lee	3.64

Component ERA
(minimum 1000 Innings Pitched)

1	Cy Young	1.85
2	Joe Wood	2.07
3	Carl Mays	2.20
4	Babe Ruth	2.21
5	Dutch Leonard	2.32
6	Ray Collins	2.42
7	Bill Dinneen	2.53
8	George Winter	2.64
9	Roger Clemens	2.84
10	Tex Hughson	2.86
11	Luis Tiant	3.22
12	Ray Culp	3.33
13	Sad Sam Jones	3.35
14	Joe Dobson	3.41
15	Lefty Grove	3.41
16	Ellis Kinder	3.43
17	Frank Sullivan	3.48
18	Herb Pennock	3.48
19	Bill Monbouquette	3.65
20	Dennis Eckersley	3.70

Opponent Average
(minimum 1000 Innings Pitched)

1	Babe Ruth	.219
2	Joe Wood	.219
3	Roger Clemens	.229
4	Carl Mays	.230
5	Dutch Leonard	.230
6	Cy Young	.232
7	Ray Culp	.234
8	Luis Tiant	.245
9	Tex Hughson	.245
10	Earl Wilson	.245
11	Bill Dinneen	.246
12	Jim Lonborg	.247
13	George Winter	.250
14	Ellis Kinder	.250
15	Joe Dobson	.251
16	Ray Collins	.254
17	Frank Sullivan	.254
18	Tom Brewer	.257
19	Mel Parnell	.257
20	Ike Delock	.260

Opponent OBP
(minimum 1000 Innings Pitched)

1	Cy Young	.259
2	Joe Wood	.284
3	Carl Mays	.289
4	Roger Clemens	.292
5	Bill Dinneen	.292
6	Babe Ruth	.294
7	Ray Collins	.294
8	Dutch Leonard	.295
9	Tex Hughson	.297
10	George Winter	.298
11	Luis Tiant	.298
12	Dennis Eckersley	.305
13	Bill Monbouquette	.307
14	Ray Culp	.307
15	Frank Sullivan	.314
16	Oil Can Boyd	.314
17	Ellis Kinder	.315
18	Lefty Grove	.317
19	Jim Lonborg	.320
20	Joe Dobson	.322

Red Sox Franchise Batting Leaders—Single Season

Games

1	Jim Rice	1978	163
2	George Scott	1966	162
	Carl Yastrzemski	1969	162
	Dwight Evans	1982	162
	Dwight Evans	1984	162
	Bill Buckner	1985	162
7	Carl Yastrzemski	1967	161
	Carl Yastrzemski	1970	161
	Wade Boggs	1985	161
	Mo Vaughn	1996	161
11	Carl Yastrzemski	1962	160
	Carl Yastrzemski	1966	160
	Jim Rice	1977	160
	Don Baylor	1986	160
15	George Scott	1967	159
	Reggie Smith	1971	159
	Butch Hobson	1977	159
	Jim Rice	1984	159
	Dwight Evans	1985	159
	Mike Greenwell	1990	159

At-Bats

1	Nomar Garciaparra	1997	684
2	Jim Rice	1978	677
3	Bill Buckner	1985	673
4	Rick Burleson	1977	663
5	Doc Cramer	1940	661
6	Doc Cramer	1938	658
7	Jim Rice	1984	657
8	Wade Boggs	1985	653
9	Dom DiMaggio	1948	648
10	Tom Oliver	1930	646
	Chuck Schilling	1961	646
	Carl Yastrzemski	1962	646
13	Jim Rice	1977	644
	Rick Burleson	1980	644
15	Doc Cramer	1936	643
16	Dom DiMaggio	1951	639
	Tony Armas	1984	639
18	Johnny Pesky	1947	638
19	Bill Wambsganss	1924	636
	Jerry Remy	1982	636

Runs

1	Ted Williams	1949	150
2	Ted Williams	1946	142
3	Ted Williams	1942	141
4	Jimmie Foxx	1938	139
5	Tris Speaker	1912	136
6	Ted Williams	1941	135
7	Ted Williams	1940	134
8	Ted Williams	1939	131
	Dom DiMaggio	1950	131
10	Jimmie Foxx	1936	130
	Jimmie Foxx	1939	130
12	Bill Werber	1934	129
13	Wade Boggs	1988	128
14	Dom DiMaggio	1948	127
15	Dom DiMaggio	1949	126
16	Ted Williams	1947	125
	Vern Stephens	1950	125
	Carl Yastrzemski	1970	125
19	Johnny Pesky	1948	124
	Ted Williams	1948	124

Hits

1	Wade Boggs	1985	240
2	Tris Speaker	1912	222
3	Wade Boggs	1988	214
4	Jim Rice	1978	213
5	Wade Boggs	1983	210
6	Nomar Garciaparra	1997	209
7	Johnny Pesky	1946	208
8	Johnny Pesky	1947	207
	Wade Boggs	1986	207
	Mo Vaughn	1996	207
11	Jim Rice	1977	206
12	Johnny Pesky	1942	205
	Wade Boggs	1989	205
14	Wade Boggs	1984	203
15	Joe Vosmik	1938	201
	Jim Rice	1979	201
	Bill Buckner	1985	201
18	Four tied at		200

Doubles

1	Earl Webb	1931	67
2	Tris Speaker	1912	53
3	Joe Cronin	1938	51
	Wade Boggs	1989	51
5	George Burns	1923	47
	Fred Lynn	1975	47
	Wade Boggs	1986	47
	John Valentin	1997	47
9	Tris Speaker	1914	46
	Bill Buckner	1985	46
11	Carl Yastrzemski	1965	45
	Wade Boggs	1988	45
	Jody Reed	1990	45
14	Del Pratt	1922	44
	Ted Williams	1939	44
	Ted Williams	1948	44
	Wade Boggs	1983	44
	Wade Boggs	1990	44
	Nomar Garciaparra	1997	44
20	Four tied at		43

Triples

1	Tris Speaker	1913	22
2	Buck Freeman	1903	20
3	Buck Freeman	1902	19
	Chick Stahl	1904	19
	Buck Freeman	1904	19
	Larry Gardner	1914	19
7	Larry Gardner	1912	18
	Tris Speaker	1914	18
9	Freddy Parent	1903	17
	Jimmy Collins	1903	17
	Harry Hooper	1920	17
	Russ Scarritt	1929	17
13	Chick Stahl	1901	16
	Jimmy Collins	1901	16
	Hobe Ferris	1905	16
	Jake Stahl	1910	16
17	Six tied at		15

Home Runs

1	Jimmie Foxx	1938	50
2	Jim Rice	1978	46
3	Carl Yastrzemski	1967	44
	Mo Vaughn	1996	44
5	Ted Williams	1949	43
	Tony Armas	1984	43
7	Dick Stuart	1963	42
8	Jimmie Foxx	1936	41
9	Carl Yastrzemski	1969	40
	Rico Petrocelli	1969	40
	Carl Yastrzemski	1970	40
12	Vern Stephens	1949	39
	Jim Rice	1977	39
	Fred Lynn	1979	39
	Jim Rice	1979	39
	Jim Rice	1983	39
	Mo Vaughn	1995	39
18	Ted Williams	1946	38
	Ted Williams	1957	38
20	Ted Williams	1941	37

RBI

1	Jimmie Foxx	1938	175
2	Vern Stephens	1949	159
	Ted Williams	1949	159
4	Ted Williams	1939	145
5	Walt Dropo	1950	144
	Vern Stephens	1950	144
7	Jimmie Foxx	1936	143
	Mo Vaughn	1996	143
9	Jim Rice	1978	139
10	Ted Williams	1942	137
	Vern Stephens	1948	137
12	Jim Rice	1979	130
13	Jimmie Foxx	1937	127
	Ted Williams	1948	127
15	Ted Williams	1951	126
	Jim Rice	1983	126
	Mo Vaughn	1995	126
18	Ted Williams	1946	123
	Tony Armas	1984	123
	Dwight Evans	1987	123

Walks

1	Ted Williams	1947	162
	Ted Williams	1949	162
3	Ted Williams	1946	156
4	Ted Williams	1941	145
	Ted Williams	1942	145
6	Ted Williams	1951	144
7	Ted Williams	1954	136
8	Carl Yastrzemski	1970	128
9	Ted Williams	1948	126
10	Wade Boggs	1988	125
11	Jimmie Foxx	1938	119
	Ted Williams	1957	119
	Carl Yastrzemski	1968	119
14	Dwight Evans	1985	114
15	Dwight Evans	1982	112
16	Topper Rigney	1926	108
17	Ted Williams	1939	107
	Wade Boggs	1989	107
19	Three tied at		106

Strikeouts

1	Butch Hobson	1977	162
2	Tony Armas	1984	156
3	Mo Vaughn	1996	154
	Mo Vaughn	1997	154
5	George Scott	1966	152
6	Mo Vaughn	1995	150
7	Dick Stuart	1963	144
8	Mike Easler	1984	134
9	Jack Clark	1991	133
10	Tony Armas	1983	131
11	Dick Stuart	1964	130
	Mo Vaughn	1993	130
13	Mike Easler	1985	129
14	Jim Rice	1978	126
15	Dwight Evans	1982	125
16	Jim Rice	1976	123
17	Jim Rice	1975	122
	Butch Hobson	1978	122
	Wil Cordero	1997	122
20	Jim Rice	1977	120

Stolen Bases

1	Tommy Harper	1973	54
2	Tris Speaker	1912	52
3	Tris Speaker	1913	46
4	Tris Speaker	1914	42
	Otis Nixon	1994	42
6	Harry Hooper	1910	40
	Bill Werber	1934	40
8	Harry Hooper	1911	38
9	Harry Lord	1909	36
10	Patsy Dougherty	1903	35
	Tris Speaker	1909	35
	Tris Speaker	1910	35
13	Tommy Dowd	1901	33
14	Amby McConnell	1908	31
15	Buddy Myer	1928	30
	Jerry Remy	1978	30
17	Five tied at		29

Runs Created

1	Ted Williams	1949	174
2	Jimmie Foxx	1938	172
3	Ted Williams	1941	170
4	Tris Speaker	1912	163
	Ted Williams	1946	163
6	Ted Williams	1947	161
7	Ted Williams	1942	160
	Ted Williams	1948	160
9	Ted Williams	1939	153
10	Jimmie Foxx	1936	152
11	Mo Vaughn	1996	149
12	Carl Yastrzemski	1967	148
13	Carl Yastrzemski	1970	145
14	Ted Williams	1951	144
15	Ted Williams	1957	143
16	Jimmie Foxx	1939	142
17	Jim Rice	1978	141
18	Wade Boggs	1987	140
19	Ted Williams	1940	139
20	Fred Lynn	1979	134

Runs Created/27 Outs

(minimum 3.1 Plate Appearances/Tm Gm)

1	Ted Williams	1941	16.09
2	Ted Williams	1957	14.38
3	Ted Williams	1948	12.92
4	Ted Williams	1946	12.56
5	Ted Williams	1942	12.40
6	Ted Williams	1947	11.99
7	Jimmie Foxx	1938	11.87
8	Ted Williams	1954	11.85
9	Jimmie Foxx	1939	11.78
10	Ted Williams	1949	11.73
11	Tris Speaker	1912	11.36
12	Babe Ruth	1919	10.53
13	Ted Williams	1939	10.44
14	Ted Williams	1951	10.42
15	Ted Williams	1956	10.28
16	Jimmie Foxx	1936	10.03
17	Wade Boggs	1987	10.01
18	Carl Yastrzemski	1967	9.84
19	Fred Lynn	1979	9.72
20	Ted Williams	1940	9.66

Batting Average

(minimum 3.1 Plate Appearances/Tm Gm)

1	Ted Williams	1941	.406
2	Ted Williams	1957	.388
3	Tris Speaker	1912	.383
4	Ted Williams	1948	.369
5	Wade Boggs	1985	.368
6	Wade Boggs	1988	.366
7	Tris Speaker	1913	.363
8	Wade Boggs	1987	.363
9	Wade Boggs	1983	.361
10	Jimmie Foxx	1939	.360
11	Wade Boggs	1986	.357
12	Ted Williams	1942	.356
13	Billy Goodman	1950	.354
14	Jimmie Foxx	1938	.349
15	Ted Williams	1956	.345
16	Ted Williams	1954	.345
17	Ted Williams	1940	.344
18	Ted Williams	1947	.343
19	Ted Williams	1949	.343
20	Patsy Dougherty	1902	.342

On-Base Percentage

(minimum 3.1 Plate Appearances/Tm Gm)

1	Ted Williams	1941	.551
2	Ted Williams	1957	.526
3	Ted Williams	1954	.513
4	Ted Williams	1942	.499
5	Ted Williams	1947	.499
6	Ted Williams	1946	.497
7	Ted Williams	1948	.497
8	Ted Williams	1949	.490
9	Ted Williams	1956	.479
10	Wade Boggs	1988	.476
11	Jimmie Foxx	1939	.464
12	Tris Speaker	1912	.464
13	Ted Williams	1951	.464
14	Jimmie Foxx	1938	.462
15	Wade Boggs	1987	.461
16	Ted Williams	1958	.458
17	Babe Ruth	1919	.456
18	Wade Boggs	1986	.453
19	Carl Yastrzemski	1970	.452
20	Wade Boggs	1985	.450

Slugging Percentage

(minimum 3.1 Plate Appearances/Tm Gm)

1	Ted Williams	1941	.735
2	Ted Williams	1957	.731
3	Jimmie Foxx	1938	.704
4	Jimmie Foxx	1939	.694
5	Ted Williams	1946	.667
6	Babe Ruth	1919	.657
7	Ted Williams	1949	.650
8	Ted Williams	1942	.648
9	Fred Lynn	1979	.637
10	Ted Williams	1954	.635
11	Ted Williams	1947	.634
12	Jimmie Foxx	1936	.631
13	Carl Yastrzemski	1967	.622
14	Ted Williams	1948	.615
15	Ted Williams	1939	.609
16	Ted Williams	1956	.605
17	Jim Rice	1978	.600
18	Jim Rice	1979	.596
19	Ted Williams	1940	.594
20	Jim Rice	1977	.593

Teams: Red Sox

Red Sox Franchise Pitching Leaders—Single Season

Wins

1	Joe Wood	1912	34
2	Cy Young	1901	33
3	Cy Young	1902	32
4	Cy Young	1903	28
5	Cy Young	1904	26
6	Wes Ferrell	1935	25
	Boo Ferriss	1946	25
	Mel Parnell	1949	25
9	Babe Ruth	1917	24
	Roger Clemens	1986	24
11	Bill Dinneen	1904	23
	Joe Wood	1911	23
	Babe Ruth	1916	23
	Sad Sam Jones	1921	23
	Ellis Kinder	1949	23
16	Jesse Tannehill	1905	22
	Carl Mays	1917	22
	Tex Hughson	1942	22
	Jim Lonborg	1967	22
	Luis Tiant	1974	22

Losses

1	Red Ruffing	1928	25
2	Red Ruffing	1929	22
3	Bill Dinneen	1902	21
	Joe Harris	1906	21
	Cy Young	1906	21
	Slim Harriss	1927	21
7	Sad Sam Jones	1919	20
	Howard Ehmke	1925	20
	Jack Russell	1930	20
	Milt Gaston	1930	20
11	Cy Young	1905	19
	Bill Dinneen	1906	19
	Ted Wingfield	1925	19
	Milt Gaston	1929	19
15	Nine tied at		18

Winning Percentage
(minimum 15 decisions)

1	Bob Stanley	1978	.882
2	Joe Wood	1912	.872
3	Roger Moret	1973	.867
4	Roger Clemens	1986	.857
5	Roger Moret	1975	.824
6	Boo Ferriss	1946	.806
7	Ellis Kinder	1949	.793
8	Dutch Leonard	1914	.792
9	Lefty Grove	1939	.789
10	Tex Hughson	1942	.786
11	Tex Hughson	1944	.783
	Jack Kramer	1948	.783
13	Mel Parnell	1949	.781
14	Lefty Grove	1938	.778
	Roger Clemens	1990	.778
16	Cy Young	1901	.767
17	Sad Sam Jones	1918	.762
18	Cy Young	1903	.757
19	Five tied at		.750

Games

1	Greg Harris	1993	80
2	Dick Radatz	1964	79
3	Heathcliff Slocumb	1996	75
4	Rob Murphy	1989	74
5	Sparky Lyle	1969	71
	Tony Fossas	1993	71
7	Mike Fornieles	1960	70
	Greg Harris	1992	70
9	Ellis Kinder	1953	69
	Bill Campbell	1977	69
11	Rob Murphy	1990	68
12	Dick Radatz	1963	66
	Bob Stanley	1986	66
14	Jack Lamabe	1963	65
15	Bob Stanley	1983	64
	Lee Smith	1988	64
	Lee Smith	1989	64
	Tony Fossas	1991	64
19	Four tied at		63

Games Started

1	Cy Young	1902	43
2	Bill Dinneen	1902	42
3	Cy Young	1901	41
	Cy Young	1904	41
	Babe Ruth	1916	41
6	Howard Ehmke	1923	39
	Jim Lonborg	1967	39
8	Joe Wood	1912	38
	Babe Ruth	1917	38
	Sad Sam Jones	1921	38
	Wes Ferrell	1935	38
	Wes Ferrell	1936	38
	Luis Tiant	1974	38
	Luis Tiant	1976	38
15	Bill Dinneen	1904	37
	Cy Young	1907	37
	Bill Lee	1974	37
18	Seven tied at		36

Complete Games

1	Cy Young	1902	41
2	Cy Young	1904	40
3	Bill Dinneen	1902	39
4	Cy Young	1901	38
5	Bill Dinneen	1904	37
6	Joe Wood	1912	35
	Babe Ruth	1917	35
8	Cy Young	1903	34
9	Cy Young	1907	33
10	Bill Dinneen	1903	32
11	Ted Lewis	1901	31
	Cy Young	1905	31
	Wes Ferrell	1935	31
14	Jesse Tannehill	1904	30
	Cy Young	1908	30
	Carl Mays	1918	30
17	Norwood Gibson	1904	29
18	Cy Young	1906	28
	Howard Ehmke	1923	28
	Wes Ferrell	1936	28

Shutouts

1	Cy Young	1904	10
	Joe Wood	1912	10
3	Babe Ruth	1916	9
4	Carl Mays	1918	8
	Roger Clemens	1988	8
6	Cy Young	1903	7
	Dutch Leonard	1914	7
	Joe Bush	1918	7
	Luis Tiant	1974	7
	Roger Clemens	1987	7
11	Twelve tied at		6

Saves

1	Jeff Reardon	1991	40
2	Bob Stanley	1983	33
	Jeff Russell	1993	33
4	Bill Campbell	1977	31
	Heathcliff Slocumb	1996	31
6	Dick Radatz	1964	29
	Lee Smith	1988	29
8	Ellis Kinder	1953	27
	Jeff Reardon	1992	27
10	Dick Radatz	1963	25
	Lee Smith	1989	25
12	Dick Radatz	1962	24
	Tom Burgmeier	1980	24
14	Dick Radatz	1965	22
	Bob Stanley	1984	22
16	Jeff Reardon	1990	21
17	John Wyatt	1967	20
	Sparky Lyle	1970	20
	Rick Aguilera	1995	20
20	Ellis Kinder	1955	18

Innings Pitched

1	Cy Young	1902	384.2
2	Cy Young	1904	380.0
3	Cy Young	1901	371.1
	Bill Dinneen	1902	371.1
5	Joe Wood	1912	344.0
6	Cy Young	1907	343.1
7	Cy Young	1903	341.2
8	Bill Dinneen	1904	335.2
9	Babe Ruth	1917	326.1
10	Babe Ruth	1916	323.2
11	Wes Ferrell	1935	322.1
12	Cy Young	1905	320.2
13	Howard Ehmke	1923	316.2
14	Ted Lewis	1901	316.1
15	Howard Ehmke	1924	315.0
16	Luis Tiant	1974	311.1
17	Wes Ferrell	1936	301.0
18	Bill Dinneen	1903	299.0
	Cy Young	1908	299.0
20	Sad Sam Jones	1921	298.2

Walks

1	Mel Parnell	1949	134
2	Mickey McDermott	1950	124
3	Don Schwall	1962	121
	Mike Torrez	1979	121
5	Howard Ehmke	1923	119
	Wes Ferrell	1936	119
	Jack Wilson	1937	119
	Bobo Newsom	1937	119
9	Babe Ruth	1916	118
	Red Ruffing	1929	118
11	Emmett O'Neill	1945	117
12	Mel Parnell	1953	116
13	Dave Morehead	1965	113
14	Tom Brewer	1956	112
	Dave Morehead	1964	112
16	Earl Wilson	1962	111
17	Don Schwall	1961	110
18	Mickey McDermott	1953	109
19	Three tied at		108

Strikeouts

1	Roger Clemens	1988	291
2	Joe Wood	1912	258
3	Roger Clemens	1996	257
4	Roger Clemens	1987	256
5	Jim Lonborg	1967	246
6	Roger Clemens	1991	241
7	Roger Clemens	1986	238
8	Joe Wood	1911	231
9	Roger Clemens	1989	230
10	Cy Young	1905	210
11	Roger Clemens	1990	209
12	Roger Clemens	1992	208
13	Luis Tiant	1973	206
14	Cy Young	1904	200
15	Ray Culp	1970	197
16	Ray Culp	1968	190
	Bruce Hurst	1987	190
18	Bruce Hurst	1985	189
19	Dick Radatz	1964	181
20	Three tied at		176

Strikeouts/9 Innings
(minimum 1 Inning Pitched/Tm Gm)

1	Roger Clemens	1988	9.92
2	Roger Clemens	1996	9.53
3	Roger Clemens	1994	8.86
4	Bruce Hurst	1986	8.62
5	Roger Clemens	1986	8.43
6	Roger Clemens	1990	8.24
7	Roger Clemens	1987	8.18
8	Roger Clemens	1989	8.17
9	Jim Lonborg	1967	8.10
10	Roger Clemens	1991	7.99
11	Ray Culp	1968	7.90
12	Tom Gordon	1997	7.83
13	Dave Morehead	1965	7.61
14	Roger Clemens	1992	7.59
15	Joe Wood	1911	7.51
16	Roger Clemens	1993	7.51
17	Dave Morehead	1964	7.51
18	Bruce Hurst	1985	7.42
19	Earl Wilson	1964	7.38
20	Bruce Hurst	1987	7.16

ERA
(minimum 1 Inning Pitched/Tm Gm)

1	Dutch Leonard	1914	1.00
2	Cy Young	1908	1.26
3	Joe Wood	1915	1.49
4	Ray Collins	1910	1.62
5	Cy Young	1901	1.62
6	Ernie Shore	1915	1.64
7	Rube Foster	1914	1.66
8	Joe Wood	1910	1.68
9	Carl Mays	1917	1.74
10	Babe Ruth	1916	1.75
11	Cy Young	1905	1.82
12	Sea Lion Hall	1910	1.91
13	Joe Wood	1912	1.91
14	Luis Tiant	1972	1.91
15	Roger Clemens	1990	1.93
16	Eddie Cicotte	1909	1.95
17	Cy Young	1904	1.97
18	Cy Young	1907	1.99
19	Babe Ruth	1917	2.01
20	Joe Wood	1911	2.02

Component ERA
(minimum 1 Inning Pitched/Tm Gm)

1	Dutch Leonard	1914	1.41
2	Cy Young	1908	1.48
3	Cy Young	1905	1.49
4	Cy Young	1904	1.73
5	George Winter	1907	1.75
6	Ray Collins	1910	1.83
7	Babe Ruth	1918	1.84
8	Joe Wood	1915	1.84
9	Cy Young	1907	1.85
10	Joe Wood	1912	1.85
11	Babe Ruth	1916	1.85
12	Joe Wood	1909	1.86
13	Cy Young	1901	1.87
14	Cy Young	1903	1.89
15	Rube Foster	1914	1.89
16	Eddie Cicotte	1909	1.93
17	Frank Arellanes	1909	1.97
18	Babe Ruth	1917	1.99
19	Bill Dinneen	1904	2.02
20	Carl Mays	1917	2.02

Opponent Average
(minimum 1 Inning Pitched/Tm Gm)

1	Dutch Leonard	1914	.179
2	Roger Clemens	1986	.195
3	Babe Ruth	1916	.201
4	Luis Tiant	1972	.202
5	Roger Clemens	1994	.204
6	Sea Lion Hall	1910	.207
7	Dutch Leonard	1915	.208
8	Joe Wood	1909	.209
9	Babe Ruth	1917	.210
10	Ray Culp	1968	.210
11	Dave Morehead	1963	.211
12	Babe Ruth	1915	.212
13	Cy Young	1905	.213
14	Cy Young	1908	.213
15	Babe Ruth	1918	.214
16	George Winter	1907	.215
17	Joe Wood	1915	.216
18	Joe Wood	1912	.216
19	Norwood Gibson	1904	.216
20	Eddie Cicotte	1909	.217

Opponent OBP
(minimum 1 Inning Pitched/Tm Gm)

1	Cy Young	1905	.239
2	Cy Young	1908	.241
3	Dutch Leonard	1914	.245
4	Cy Young	1904	.249
5	Roger Clemens	1986	.252
6	Cy Young	1901	.254
7	Cy Young	1903	.257
8	Ray Collins	1910	.264
9	Cy Young	1907	.264
10	George Winter	1907	.266
11	Tex Hughson	1944	.267
12	Roger Clemens	1988	.270
13	Bill Dinneen	1904	.270
14	Roger Clemens	1991	.270
15	Joe Wood	1909	.270
	Frank Arellanes	1909	.270
17	Danny Darwin	1993	.272
18	Joe Wood	1912	.272
19	Frank Sullivan	1957	.273
20	Rube Foster	1914	.274

Red Sox Capsule

Best Season: *1967.* Boston was coming off a 72-90 season, a half-game out of last place, and hadn't seriously contended since 1950. The Red Sox hadn't even posted a winning record in the previous eight years. All that would change dramatically under new manager Dick Williams. Carl Yastrzemski captured the Triple Crown and the MVP Award, while Jim Lonborg won 22 games and the Cy Young Award. Boston clinched a tight four-team race on the final day of the season, as Yastrzemski went 4-for-4 and Lonborg beat the Twins. Bob Gibson and the Cardinals edged Boston in seven games to win the World Series, but that couldn't dampen the Impossible Dream.

Worst Season: For a franchise with six 100-loss seasons, it may seem odd to choose a 99-win year as its worst. But *1978* will live in infamy. Boston raced to a 62-28 record and opened a 14-game lead on the defending World Series champion Yankees in mid-July. Then injuries to Rick Burleson, Jerry Remy and Dwight Evans began to take their toll, as did manager Don Zimmer's insistence on playing his regulars every day and exiling Bill Lee. The Red Sox lost 14 out of 17 in late August and early September, including a four-game sweep at the hands of the Yankees that became known as the Boston Massacre. New York took a three-and-a-half game lead with 14 to play, before Boston gamely rallied. The Red Sox won their final eight scheduled games to force a one-game playoff, then took a 2-0 lead against New York. It was just a tease. Bucky Dent hit a three-run homer into the screen on top of the Green Monster, and Carl Yastrzemski fouled out to end Boston's most heartbreaking season.

Best Player: *Ted Williams* once said, "I want to walk down the street after I'm through and have people say, 'There goes the greatest hitter who ever lived.' " He accomplished his goal.

Best Pitcher: Some might argue for Cy Young, but we'll take *Roger Clemens.* The Rocket was more dominant in his era and holds virtually every significant Red Sox pitching record.

Best Reliever: *Dick Radatz.* In his first three seasons, The Monster was as good as any closer ever: 40-21, 2.17 with 78 saves in 207 games, 487 strikeouts and 292 hits allowed in 414 innings. He had a hand in more than half of Boston's victories from 1962-64.

Best Defensive Player: John McGraw said that *Jimmy Collins* unquestionably was the best defensive third baseman he ever saw. Collins was a master at fielding bunts, a prized skill in the dead-ball era, and he was an integral part of the 1903 World Series champions. Other stalwarts included outfielders Jimmy Piersall and Harry Hooper.

Hall of Famers: Thirty-three Cooperstown immortals have been with Boston as players, managers or executives, and seven were primarily associated with the Red Sox—*Jimmy Collins, Joe Cronin, Bobby Doerr, Harry Hooper, Ted Williams, Tom Yawkey* and *Carl Yastrzemski.*

Franchise All-Star Team:

C	Carlton Fisk	LF	Ted Williams
1B	Carl Yastrzemski	CF	Tris Speaker
2B	Bobby Doerr	RF	Dwight Evans
3B	Wade Boggs	DH	Jim Rice
SS	Joe Cronin	SP	Roger Clemens
		RP	Dick Radatz

Biggest Flake: *Bill Lee* was nicknamed Spaceman for good reason. Boiling down his antics into a single paragraph is all but impossible, but we'll try. In a decade in Boston, Lee: kept ginseng in his locker; admitted to throwing spitballs and smoking marijuana; liked to toss a blooper pitch he called the Leephus; was a founding member of the Buffalo Head Gang; punted bubble gum from the bullpen to the bleachers; and repeatedly challenged authority, including his memorable comparison of manager Don Zimmer to a gerbil. "I'm a southpaw in a northpaw world," said Lee, who was a beat writer's dream. He also won 94 games for the Red Sox.

Strangest Career: Few pitchers have been more valuable than a healthy *Smokey Joe Wood.* And according to Walter Johnson, no one in their era threw faster than Wood. Wood posted 2.18 and 1.69 ERAs in his first two seasons, then went 23-17, 2.02 in 1911. He was even better in 1912, going 34-5, 1.91 (including a record-tying 16-game winning streak) and picking up three more victories as the Red Sox won the World Series. In spring training the following season, Wood slipped on some wet grass while fielding a grounder and broke his thumb. When he returned to the mound, he had lost velocity and pitched in a great deal of pain. Wood went 35-13, 2.08 over the next three seasons, sat out all of 1916 and pitched in five games for the 1917 Indians. A lifetime .241 hitter to that point, Wood convinced Cleveland to try him as an outfielder. He spent five more years with the Tribe and batted .298, including .366 as a part-timer in 1921. After hitting .297-8-92, Wood retired to become the baseball coach at Yale University.

What Might Have Been: *Tony Conigliaro* had a lot going for him on August 18, 1967. He was 22, good-looking, a local hero from Revere, Mass., and the proud owner of 104 home runs in 494 big-league games. Two years earlier, he had hit 32 longballs at age 20 to become the youngest home-run champion in American League history. The Red Sox were dreaming the Impossible Dream. That night, a Jack Hamilton pitch (which may have been a spitball) shattered Conigliaro's cheekbone and his life. Conigliaro missed the rest of the season and all of 1968 before making a brief comeback. He was named AL Comeback Player of the Year in 1969 and hit 36 homers in 1970, then was sent to the Angels in a controversial trade. Conigliaro played only 74 games in 1971 for the Angels and 21 more in an aborted last hurrah with Boston in 1975. Tragedy struck again in 1982, when he suffered a heart attack while en route to an interview for a broadcasting job. He was in a coma for four months and had severe brain damage. Conigliaro died on February 24, 1990, of pneumonia and kidney failure at age 45.

Best Trade: *Jackie Jensen* never had hit more than 10 homers or driven in more than 84 runs in a season when Boston acquired him from the Senators for Mickey McDermott and Tommy Umphlett after the 1953 season. Jensen averaged .285-26-111 for the Red Sox over the next six years, winning three RBI titles and the 1958 American League MVP Award. Even his premature retirement because of a fear of flying couldn't sour this deal for Boston.

Worst Trade: The Red Sox have made more then their share of awful deals. None was worse than the sale of *Babe Ruth* to the Yankees in 1920 for $125,000 and a $300,000 mortgage on Fenway Park. As for non-cash transactions, Danny Cater for Sparky Lyle (Yankees, 1972) and Jeff Bagwell for Larry Andersen (Astros, 1990) are infamous..

Best-Looking Player: *Carlton Fisk*.

Ugliest Player: *George Scott*, during his second tour of duty with the Red Sox.

Best Nickname: *"The Splendid Splinter,"* Ted Williams.

Most Unappreciated Player: *Carl Mays* might be in the Hall of Fame if he hadn't killed Ray Chapman with a pitch in 1920. He went 208-126, 2.92 in 15 seasons, and was part of three World Series champions with Boston.

Most Overrated Player: On the surface, his .296 batting average and 2,705 career hits seem to make a case for *Doc Cramer's* induction into the Hall of Fame. But that, and good center-field defense, was the extent of his contributions. Cramer's on-base (.340) and slugging (.375) percentages were laughable for an outfielder in a hitter's era. *Total Baseball* estimates that Cramer cost his teams 28 victories over the course of his career, making him arguably the worst player ever. Yet he made four consecutive All-Star teams with the Red Sox.

Most Admirable Star: *Harry Hooper* was popular with teammates, fans and opponents. He was an intelligent man who graduated from St. Mary's College in California and planned to make a career as a surveyor before realizing his considerable baseball talents. An extremely gifted outfielder, he never complained about taking a back seat to Tris Speaker and was a major factor in Boston's four World Series championships in the 1910s.

Least Admirable Star: *Wade Boggs*. Two words: Margo Adams.

Best Season, Player: It's difficult to overlook Ted Williams' brilliant 1941, but *Carl Yastrzemski's 1967* meant more to the Red Sox. No one has won the Triple Crown since Yaz hit .326-44-121, and he also led the American League in seven other major categories. He batted .522 with five homers and 16 RBI over the final two weeks, and went 7-for-8 with six RBI in the final two contests, both must-wins against the Twins. In the World Series against the Cardinals, he hit .400 with three homers and five RBI.

Best Season, Pitcher: *Smokey Joe Wood, 1912.* Wood led the American League with 34 victories, including a still-standing record of 16 consecutively. The 14th in that streak was a 1-0 duel with Walter Johnson, who established the mark earlier in the year. Wood added three more wins in the World Series, including the decisive victory.

Most Impressive Individual Record: *Ted Williams.* The Splendid Splinter's .406 average in 1941 hasn't been topped since and is one of the Holy Grails of sports milestones. Williams entered the final day of the season with a .3996 average, refused to sit out and went 6-for-8 to establish himself in baseball lore.

Biggest Tragedy: Cleveland Browns coach Paul Brown wanted *Harry Agganis* to succeed Otto Graham at quarterback, but the Golden Greek signed with his hometown Red Sox for $35,000. A bout with pneumonia hospitalized him in 1955, his second season in Boston, but he returned to the lineup and was hitting .313 before taking ill again. He appeared to be recovering before dying suddenly on June 27 at age 26, the result of a massive blood clot. His body lay in state in his hometown of Lynn, Mass., drawing 10,000 mourners.

Fan Favorite: *Luis Tiant*, for his clutch pitching ability, oddly shaped body and unique gyrations on the mound.

—Jim Callis

Chicago White Sox (1901-1997)

Year	Lg	Pos	W-L	Pct	GB	Manager	Att.	R	OR	HR	Avg	OBP	Slg	Opponent HR	Opponent Avg	Opponent OBP	ERA	Park Index Runs	Park Index HR
1901	AL	1st	83-53	.610	—	Clark Griffith	354,350	819	631	32	.276	.350	.370	27	.263	.316	2.98	95	69
1902	AL	4th	74-60	.552	8.0	Clark Griffith	337,898	675	602	14	.268	.332	.335	30	.269	.324	3.41	91	19
1903	AL	7th	60-77	.438	30.5	Nixey Callahan	286,183	516	613	14	.247	.301	.314	23	.260	.309	3.02	87	23
1904	AL	3rd	89-65	.578	6.0	Nixey Callahan/Fielder Jones	557,123	600	482	14	.242	.300	.316	13	.226	.275	2.30	94	8
1905	AL	2nd	92-60	.605	2.0	Fielder Jones	687,419	612	451	11	.237	.305	.304	11	.225	.276	1.99	84	27
1906	AL	1st	93-58	.616	—	Fielder Jones	585,202	570	460	7	.230	.302	.286	11	.240	.281	2.13	76	19
1907	AL	3rd	87-64	.576	5.5	Fielder Jones	666,307	588	474	5	.238	.302	.283	13	.245	.289	2.22	99	37
1908	AL	3rd	88-64	.579	1.5	Fielder Jones	636,096	537	470	3	.224	.298	.271	11	.225	.269	2.22	82	56
1909	AL	4th	78-74	.513	20.0	Billy Sullivan	478,400	492	463	4	.221	.291	.275	8	.235	.290	2.05	92	50
1910	AL	6th	68-85	.444	35.5	Hugh Duffy	552,084	457	479	7	.211	.275	.261	16	.222	.281	2.03	82	20
1911	AL	4th	77-74	.510	24.0	Hugh Duffy	583,208	719	624	20	.269	.325	.350	22	.255	.310	2.97	90	119
1912	AL	4th	78-76	.506	28.0	Nixey Callahan	602,241	639	648	17	.255	.317	.329	26	.263	.322	3.06	92	105
1913	AL	5th	78-74	.513	17.5	Nixey Callahan	644,501	488	498	24	.236	.299	.311	10	.239	.305	2.33	81	35
1914	AL	6th	70-84	.455	30.0	Nixey Callahan	469,290	487	560	19	.239	.302	.311	15	.239	.298	2.48	105	44
1915	AL	3rd	93-61	.604	9.5	Pants Rowland	539,461	717	509	25	.258	.345	.348	14	.242	.295	2.43	90	49
1916	AL	2nd	89-65	.578	2.0	Pants Rowland	679,923	601	497	17	.251	.319	.339	14	.236	.296	2.36	112	82
1917	AL	1st	100-54	.649	—	Pants Rowland	684,521	656	464	18	.253	.329	.326	10	.237	.297	2.16	90	56
1918	AL	6th	57-67	.460	17.0	Pants Rowland	195,081	457	446	8	.256	.322	.321	9	.265	.318	2.73	101	108
1919	AL	1st	88-52	.629	—	Kid Gleason	627,186	667	534	25	.287	.351	.380	24	.262	.315	3.04	108	48
1920	AL	2nd	96-58	.623	2.0	Kid Gleason	833,492	794	665	37	.295	.357	.402	45	.278	.332	3.59	87	52
1921	AL	7th	62-92	.403	36.5	Kid Gleason	543,650	683	858	35	.283	.343	.379	52	.303	.372	4.94	102	58
1922	AL	5th	77-77	.500	17.0	Kid Gleason	602,860	691	691	45	.278	.343	.373	57	.277	.345	3.94	99	44
1923	AL	7th	69-85	.448	30.0	Kid Gleason	573,778	692	741	42	.279	.350	.373	49	.282	.351	4.05	94	72
1924	AL	8th	66-87	.431	25.5	J. Evers/E. Walsh/E. Collins/J. Evers	606,658	793	858	41	.288	.365	.382	52	.300	.363	4.74	99	64
1925	AL	5th	79-75	.513	18.5	Eddie Collins	832,231	811	770	38	.284	.369	.385	69	.294	.356	4.29	89	73
1926	AL	5th	81-72	.529	9.5	Eddie Collins	710,339	730	665	32	.289	.361	.390	47	.271	.336	3.74	78	50
1927	AL	5th	70-83	.458	39.5	Ray Schalk	614,423	662	708	36	.278	.344	.378	55	.283	.342	3.91	102	46
1928	AL	5th	72-82	.468	29.0	Ray Schalk/Lena Blackburne	494,152	656	725	24	.270	.334	.358	66	.274	.338	3.98	98	76
1929	AL	7th	59-93	.388	46.0	Lena Blackburne	426,795	627	792	37	.268	.325	.363	84	.284	.351	4.41	90	98
1930	AL	7th	62-92	.403	40.0	Donie Bush	406,123	729	884	63	.276	.328	.391	74	.300	.352	4.71	109	93
1931	AL	8th	56-97	.366	51.5	Donie Bush	403,550	704	939	27	.260	.323	.343	82	.288	.359	5.04	88	107
1932	AL	7th	49-102	.325	56.5	Lew Fonseca	233,198	667	897	36	.267	.327	.360	88	.287	.359	4.82	76	57
1933	AL	6th	67-83	.447	31.0	Lew Fonseca	397,789	683	814	43	.272	.342	.360	85	.277	.343	4.45	106	91
1934	AL	8th	53-99	.349	47.0	Lew Fonseca/Jimmy Dykes	236,559	704	946	71	.263	.336	.363	139	.292	.367	5.41	105	164
1935	AL	5th	74-78	.487	19.5	Jimmy Dykes	470,281	738	750	74	.275	.348	.382	105	.272	.346	4.38	121	163
1936	AL	3rd	81-70	.536	20.0	Jimmy Dykes	440,810	920	873	60	.292	.373	.397	104	.293	.363	5.06	96	92
1937	AL	3rd	86-68	.558	16.0	Jimmy Dykes	589,245	780	730	67	.280	.350	.400	115	.273	.341	4.17	102	125
1938	AL	6th	65-83	.439	32.0	Jimmy Dykes	338,278	709	752	67	.277	.343	.383	101	.279	.350	4.36	94	67
1939	AL	4th	85-69	.552	22.5	Jimmy Dykes	594,104	755	737	64	.275	.349	.374	99	.275	.333	4.31	110	120
1940	AL	4th	82-72	.532	8.0	Jimmy Dykes	660,336	735	672	73	.278	.340	.387	111	.250	.313	3.74	105	122
1941	AL	3rd	77-77	.500	24.0	Jimmy Dykes	677,077	638	649	47	.255	.322	.343	89	.252	.320	3.52	83	72
1942	AL	6th	66-82	.446	34.0	Jimmy Dykes	425,734	538	609	25	.246	.316	.318	74	.258	.325	3.58	96	66
1943	AL	4th	82-72	.532	16.0	Jimmy Dykes	508,962	573	594	33	.247	.322	.320	54	.255	.324	3.20	100	110
1944	AL	7th	71-83	.461	18.0	Jimmy Dykes	563,539	543	662	23	.247	.307	.320	68	.264	.320	3.58	101	63
1945	AL	6th	71-78	.477	15.0	Jimmy Dykes	657,981	596	633	22	.262	.326	.337	63	.270	.332	3.69	94	102
1946	AL	5th	74-80	.481	30.0	Jimmy Dykes/Ted Lyons	983,403	562	595	37	.257	.323	.333	80	.255	.323	3.10	92	114
1947	AL	6th	70-84	.455	27.0	Ted Lyons	876,948	553	661	53	.256	.321	.342	76	.261	.339	3.64	92	69
1948	AL	8th	51-101	.336	44.5	Ted Lyons	777,844	559	814	55	.251	.329	.331	89	.280	.365	4.89	94	67
1949	AL	6th	63-91	.409	34.0	Jack Onslow	937,151	648	737	43	.257	.347	.347	108	.264	.353	4.30	96	80
1950	AL	6th	60-94	.390	38.0	Jack Onslow/Red Corriden	781,330	625	749	93	.260	.333	.364	107	.263	.356	4.41	95	115
1951	AL	4th	81-73	.526	17.0	Paul Richards	1,328,234	714	644	86	.270	.349	.385	109	.252	.323	3.50	90	63
1952	AL	3rd	81-73	.526	14.0	Paul Richards	1,231,675	610	568	80	.252	.327	.348	86	.238	.316	3.25	97	95
1953	AL	3rd	89-65	.578	11.5	Paul Richards	1,191,353	716	592	74	.258	.341	.364	113	.246	.324	3.41	107	85
1954	AL	3rd	94-60	.610	17.0	Paul Richards/Marty Marion	1,231,629	711	521	94	.267	.347	.379	94	.244	.313	3.05	102	92
1955	AL	3rd	91-63	.591	5.0	Marty Marion	1,175,684	725	557	116	.268	.344	.388	111	.251	.317	3.37	93	80
1956	AL	3rd	85-69	.552	12.0	Marty Marion	1,000,090	776	634	128	.267	.349	.397	118	.255	.324	3.73	105	89
1957	AL	2nd	90-64	.584	8.0	Al Lopez	1,135,668	707	566	106	.260	.345	.375	124	.248	.311	3.35	92	76
1958	AL	2nd	82-72	.532	10.0	Al Lopez	797,451	634	615	101	.257	.327	.367	152	.250	.317	3.61	92	83
1959	AL	1st	94-60	.610	—	Al Lopez	1,423,144	669	588	97	.250	.327	.364	129	.242	.311	3.29	87	87
1960	AL	3rd	87-67	.565	10.0	Al Lopez	1,644,460	741	617	112	.270	.345	.396	127	.258	.326	3.60	99	87
1961	AL	4th	86-76	.531	23.0	Al Lopez	1,146,019	765	726	138	.265	.335	.395	158	.268	.326	4.06	96	84
1962	AL	5th	85-77	.525	11.0	Al Lopez	1,131,562	707	658	92	.257	.334	.372	123	.251	.317	3.73	87	78
1963	AL	2nd	94-68	.580	10.5	Al Lopez	1,158,848	683	544	114	.250	.323	.365	100	.239	.297	2.97	104	101
1964	AL	2nd	98-64	.605	1.0	Al Lopez	1,250,053	642	501	106	.247	.320	.353	124	.226	.282	2.72	83	59
1965	AL	2nd	95-67	.586	7.0	Al Lopez	1,130,519	647	555	125	.246	.315	.364	122	.231	.292	2.99	79	64
1966	AL	4th	83-79	.512	15.0	Eddie Stanky	990,016	574	517	87	.231	.297	.331	101	.226	.282	2.68	82	55
1967	AL	4th	89-73	.549	3.0	Eddie Stanky	985,634	531	491	89	.225	.291	.320	87	.219	.287	2.45	81	74
1968	AL	8th	67-95	.414	36.0	Stanky/Moss/Lopez/Moss/Lopez	803,775	463	527	71	.228	.284	.311	97	.236	.301	2.75	101	83
1969	AL	5th-W	68-94	.420	29.0	Al Lopez/Don Gutteridge	589,546	625	723	112	.247	.320	.357	146	.267	.337	4.21	121	121
1970	AL	6th-W	56-106	.346	42.0	Don Gutteridge/Bill Adair/Chuck Tanner	495,355	633	822	123	.253	.315	.362	164	.280	.347	4.54	118	145
1971	AL	3rd-W	79-83	.488	22.5	Chuck Tanner	833,891	617	597	138	.250	.325	.373	100	.247	.307	3.12	94	90
1972	AL	2nd-W	87-67	.565	5.5	Chuck Tanner	1,177,318	566	538	108	.238	.310	.346	94	.245	.305	3.12	113	114
1973	AL	5th-W	77-85	.475	17.0	Chuck Tanner	1,302,527	652	705	111	.256	.324	.372	110	.266	.336	3.86	106	107
1974	AL	4th-W	80-80	.500	9.0	Chuck Tanner	1,149,596	684	721	135	.268	.330	.389	103	.263	.332	3.94	107	84
1975	AL	5th-W	75-86	.466	22.5	Chuck Tanner	750,802	655	703	94	.255	.331	.358	107	.268	.347	3.93	108	90
1976	AL	6th-W	64-97	.398	25.5	Paul Richards	914,945	586	745	73	.255	.314	.349	87	.266	.338	4.25	102	69
1977	AL	3rd-W	90-72	.556	12.0	Bob Lemon	1,657,135	844	771	192	.278	.344	.444	136	.277	.339	4.25	99	77
1978	AL	5th-W	71-90	.441	20.5	Bob Lemon/Larry Doby	1,491,100	634	731	106	.264	.317	.379	128	.259	.334	4.21	104	96
1979	AL	5th-W	73-87	.456	14.0	Don Kessinger/Tony La Russa	1,280,702	730	748	127	.275	.333	.410	114	.256	.334	4.10	106	95
1980	AL	5th-W	70-90	.438	26.0	Tony La Russa	1,200,365	587	722	91	.259	.311	.370	108	.263	.333	3.92	95	66
1981	AL	3rd-W	31-22	.585	2.5	Tony La Russa													
	AL	6th-W	23-30	.434	7.0	Tony La Russa	946,651	476	423	76	.272	.335	.387	73	.252	.319	3.47	99	88

Year	Lg	Pos	W-L	Pct	GB	Manager	Att.	R	OR	HR	Avg	OBP	Slg	Opponent HR	Avg	OBP	ERA	Park Index Runs	HR
1982	AL	3rd-W	87-75	.537	6.0	Tony La Russa	1,567,787	786	710	136	.273	.337	.413	99	.270	.326	3.87	94	68
1983	AL	1st-W	99-63	.611	—	Tony La Russa	2,312,821	800	650	157	.262	.329	.413	128	.248	.307	3.67	104	108
1984	AL	5th-W	74-88	.457	10.0	Tony La Russa	2,136,988	679	736	172	.247	.314	.395	155	.256	.317	4.13	124	122
1985	AL	3rd-W	85-77	.525	6.0	Tony La Russa	1,669,888	736	720	146	.253	.315	.392	161	.256	.327	4.07	98	105
1986	AL	5th-W	72-90	.444	20.0	Tony La Russa/Doug Rader/Jim Fregosi	1,424,313	644	699	121	.247	.310	.363	143	.251	.323	3.93	101	76
1987	AL	5th-W	77-85	.475	8.0	Jim Fregosi	1,208,060	748	746	173	.258	.319	.415	189	.259	.327	4.30	118	81
1988	AL	5th-W	71-90	.441	32.5	Jim Fregosi	1,115,749	631	757	132	.244	.303	.370	138	.266	.331	4.12	96	78
1989	AL	7th-W	69-92	.429	29.5	Jeff Torborg	1,045,651	693	750	94	.271	.328	.383	144	.269	.335	4.23	87	66
1990	AL	2nd-W	94-68	.580	9.0	Jeff Torborg	2,002,357	682	633	106	.258	.320	.379	106	.244	.316	3.61	103	82
1991	AL	2nd-W	87-75	.537	8.0	Jeff Torborg	2,934,154	758	681	139	.262	.336	.391	154	.239	.315	3.79	99	109
1992	AL	3rd-W	86-76	.531	10.0	Gene Lamont	2,681,156	738	690	110	.261	.336	.383	123	.252	.323	3.84	89	97
1993	AL	1st-W	94-68	.580	—	Gene Lamont	2,581,091	776	664	162	.265	.338	.411	125	.255	.328	3.70	99	113
1994	AL	1st-C	67-46	.593	—	Gene Lamont	1,697,398	633	498	121	.287	.366	.444	115	.250	.317	3.96	90	91
1995	AL	3rd-C	68-76	.472	32.0	Gene Lamont/Terry Bevington	1,609,773	755	758	146	.280	.354	.431	164	.275	.356	4.85	91	74
1996	AL	2nd-C	85-77	.525	14.5	Terry Bevington	1,676,416	898	794	195	.281	.360	.447	174	.270	.343	4.52	83	82
1997	AL	2nd-C	80-81	.497	6.0	Terry Bevington	1,824,999	779	833	158	.273	.341	.417	175	.271	.340	4.74	93	82

Team Nicknames: Chicago White Stockings 1901-1902, Chicago White Sox 1903-1997.

Team Ballparks: South Side Park III 1901-1909, White Sox Park/Comiskey Park I 1910-1990, Comiskey Park II 1991-1997.

Teams: White Sox

Chicago White Sox Individual Season Batting Leaders

Year	Batting Average		On-Base Percentage		Slugging Percentage		Home Runs		RBI		Stolen Bases	
1901	Fielder Jones	.311	Fielder Jones	.412	Fred Hartman	.431	Sam Mertes	5	Sam Mertes	98	Frank Isbell	52
1902	Fielder Jones	.321	Fielder Jones	.390	George Davis	.402	Frank Isbell	4	George Davis	93	Sam Mertes	46
1903	Danny Green	.309	Danny Green	.375	Danny Green	.425	Danny Green	6	Danny Green	62	Danny Green	29
1904	Danny Green	.265	Danny Green	.352	George Davis	.359	Fielder Jones	3	George Davis	69	George Davis	32
1905	Jiggs Donahue	.287	George Davis	.353	Jiggs Donahue	.349	3 tied with	2	Jiggs Donahue	76	Jiggs Donahue	32
1906	Frank Isbell	.279	Fielder Jones	.346	George Davis	.355	Fielder Jones Billy Sullivan	2	George Davis	80	Frank Isbell	37
1907	Patsy Dougherty	.270	Ed Hahn	.359	Patsy Dougherty	.315	George Rohe	2	Jiggs Donahue	68	Patsy Dougherty	33
1908	Patsy Dougherty	.278	Patsy Dougherty	.367	Patsy Dougherty	.326	3 tied with	1	Fielder Jones	50	Patsy Dougherty	47
1909	Patsy Dougherty	.285	Patsy Dougherty	.359	Patsy Dougherty	.391	4 tied with	1	Patsy Dougherty	55	Patsy Dougherty	36
1910	Patsy Dougherty	.248	Patsy Dougherty	.318	Patsy Dougherty	.300	Chick Gandil	2	Patsy Dougherty	43	Rollie Zeider	49
1911	Matty McIntyre	.323	Matty McIntyre	.397	Harry Lord	.433	Ping Bodie Shano Collins	4	Ping Bodie	97	Nixey Callahan	45
1912	Ping Bodie	.294	Morrie Rath	.380	Ping Bodie	.407	Ping Bodie Harry Lord	5	Shano Collins	81	Rollie Zeider	47
1913	Buck Weaver	.272	Harry Lord	.327	Buck Weaver	.356	Ping Bodie	8	Buck Weaver	52	Harry Lord	24
1914	Shano Collins	.274	Ray Demmitt	.344	Shano Collins	.376	Jack Fournier	6	Shano Collins	65	Shano Collins	30
1915	Eddie Collins	.332	Eddie Collins	.460	Jack Fournier	.491	Jack Fournier	5	Shano Collins	85	Eddie Collins	46
1916	Joe Jackson	.341	Eddie Collins	.405	Joe Jackson	.495	Happy Felsch	7	Joe Jackson	78	Eddie Collins	40
1917	Happy Felsch	.308	Eddie Collins	.389	Joe Jackson	.429	Happy Felsch	6	Happy Felsch	102	Eddie Collins	53
1918	Buck Weaver	.300	Eddie Collins	.407	Shano Collins	.392	Eddie Collins	2	Shano Collins	56	Eddie Collins	22
1919	Joe Jackson	.351	Joe Jackson	.422	Joe Jackson	.506	Happy Felsch Joe Jackson	7	Joe Jackson	96	Eddie Collins	33
1920	Joe Jackson	.382	Joe Jackson	.444	Joe Jackson	.589	Happy Felsch	14	Joe Jackson	121	Eddie Collins Buck Weaver	19
1921	Eddie Collins	.337	Eddie Collins	.412	Harry Hooper	.470	Earl Sheely	11	Earl Sheely	95	Ernie Johnson	22
1922	Eddie Collins	.324	Eddie Collins	.401	Johnny Mostil	.472	Bibb Falk	12	Harry Hooper Earl Sheely	80	Ernie Johnson	21
1923	Eddie Collins	.360	Eddie Collins	.455	Eddie Collins	.453	Harry Hooper	10	Earl Sheely	88	Eddie Collins	49
1924	Bibb Falk	.352	Eddie Collins	.441	Bibb Falk	.487	Harry Hooper	10	Earl Sheely	103	Eddie Collins	42
1925	Eddie Collins	.346	Eddie Collins	.461	Eddie Collins	.442	Earl Sheely	9	Earl Sheely	111	Johnny Mostil	43
1926	Bibb Falk	.345	Johnny Mostil	.415	Bibb Falk	.477	Bibb Falk	8	Bibb Falk	108	Johnny Mostil	35
1927	Bibb Falk	.327	Alex Metzler	.396	Bibb Falk	.465	Bibb Falk	9	Bill Barrett Bibb Falk	83	Bill Barrett	20
1928	Willie Kamm	.308	Alex Metzler	.410	Alex Metzler	.422	Bill Barrett Alex Metzler	3	Willie Kamm	84	Johnny Mostil	23
1929	Carl Reynolds	.317	Alex Metzler	.367	Carl Reynolds	.474	Carl Reynolds	11	Carl Reynolds	67	Bill Cissell	26
1930	Carl Reynolds	.359	Carl Reynolds	.388	Carl Reynolds	.584	Carl Reynolds	22	Smead Jolley	114	Bill Cissell Carl Reynolds	16
1931	Lu Blue	.304	Lu Blue	.430	Carl Reynolds	.442	Carl Reynolds	6	Carl Reynolds	77	Bill Cissell	18
1932	Bob Seeds	.290	Red Kress	.346	Red Kress	.435	Red Kress	9	Luke Appling	63	Lu Blue Liz Funk	17
1933	Al Simmons	.331	Evar Swanson	.411	Al Simmons	.481	Al Simmons	14	Al Simmons	119	Evar Swanson	19
1934	Al Simmons	.344	Al Simmons	.403	Zeke Bonura	.545	Zeke Bonura	27	Zeke Bonura	110	Evar Swanson	10
1935	Luke Appling	.307	Luke Appling	.437	Zeke Bonura	.485	Zeke Bonura	21	Zeke Bonura	92	Luke Appling	12
1936	Luke Appling	.388	Luke Appling	.473	Luke Appling	.508	Zeke Bonura	12	Zeke Bonura	138	Tony Piet	15
1937	Zeke Bonura	.345	Zeke Bonura	.412	Zeke Bonura	.573	Zeke Bonura	19	Zeke Bonura	100	Luke Appling	18
1938	Rip Radcliff	.330	Joe Kuhel	.376	Gee Walker	.493	Gee Walker	16	Gee Walker	87	Mike Kreevich	13
1939	Eric McNair	.324	Luke Appling	.430	Joe Kuhel	.460	Joe Kuhel	15	Gee Walker	111	Mike Kreevich	23
1940	Luke Appling	.348	Luke Appling	.420	Joe Kuhel	.488	Joe Kuhel	27	Joe Kuhel	94	Mike Kreevich	15
1941	Taffy Wright	.322	Taffy Wright	.399	Taffy Wright	.468	Joe Kuhel	12	Taffy Wright	97	Joe Kuhel	20
1942	Don Kolloway	.273	Wally Moses	.353	Wally Moses	.369	Wally Moses	7	Don Kolloway	60	Joe Kuhel	22
1943	Luke Appling	.328	Luke Appling	.419	Luke Appling	.407	Joe Kuhel	5	Luke Appling	80	Wally Moses	56
1944	Ralph Hodgin	.295	Thurman Tucker	.368	Ralph Hodgin	.385	Hal Trosky	10	Hal Trosky	70	Wally Moses	21
1945	Johnny Dickshot	.302	Wally Moses	.373	Wally Moses	.420	Guy Curtright Johnny Dickshot	4	Roy Schalk	65	Johnny Dickshot	18
1946	Luke Appling	.309	Luke Appling	.384	Luke Appling	.378	Taffy Wright	7	Luke Appling	55	Don Kolloway	14
1947	Luke Appling	.306	Luke Appling	.386	Luke Appling	.412	Rudy York	15	Rudy York	64	Dave Philley	21
1948	Luke Appling	.314	Luke Appling	.423	Dave Philley	.387	Pat Seerey	18	Pat Seerey	64	Tony Lupien	11
1949	Cass Michaels	.308	Luke Appling	.439	Cass Michaels	.421	Steve Souchock	7	Cass Michaels	83	Dave Philley	13
1950	Eddie Robinson	.311	Eddie Robinson	.402	Eddie Robinson	.486	Gus Zernial	29	Gus Zernial	93	Dave Philley	6
1951	Minnie Minoso	.324	Minnie Minoso	.419	Minnie Minoso	.498	Eddie Robinson	29	Eddie Robinson	117	Minnie Minoso	31
1952	Nellie Fox	.296	Eddie Robinson	.382	Eddie Robinson	.466	Eddie Robinson	22	Eddie Robinson	104	Minnie Minoso	22
1953	Minnie Minoso	.313	Minnie Minoso	.410	Minnie Minoso	.466	Minnie Minoso	15	Minnie Minoso	104	Minnie Minoso	25
1954	Minnie Minoso	.320	Minnie Minoso	.411	Minnie Minoso	.535	Minnie Minoso	19	Minnie Minoso	116	Minnie Minoso Jim Rivera	18
1955	George Kell	.312	George Kell	.389	Walt Dropo	.448	Walt Dropo	19	George Kell	81	Jim Rivera	25
1956	Minnie Minoso	.316	Minnie Minoso	.425	Minnie Minoso	.525	Larry Doby	24	Larry Doby	102	Luis Aparicio	21
1957	Nellie Fox	.317	Minnie Minoso	.408	Minnie Minoso	.454	Larry Doby Jim Rivera	14	Minnie Minoso	103	Luis Aparicio	28
1958	Nellie Fox	.300	Sherm Lollar	.367	Sherm Lollar	.454	Sherm Lollar	20	Sherm Lollar	84	Luis Aparicio	29
1959	Nellie Fox	.306	Nellie Fox	.380	Sherm Lollar	.451	Sherm Lollar	22	Sherm Lollar	84	Luis Aparicio	56
1960	Al Smith	.315	Roy Sievers	.396	Roy Sievers	.534	Roy Sievers	28	Minnie Minoso	105	Luis Aparicio	51
1961	Roy Sievers	.295	Roy Sievers	.377	Roy Sievers	.537	Al Smith	28	Al Smith	93	Luis Aparicio	53
1962	Floyd Robinson	.312	Joe Cunningham	.410	Floyd Robinson	.475	Al Smith	16	Floyd Robinson	109	Luis Aparicio	31
1963	Pete Ward	.295	Floyd Robinson	.361	Pete Ward	.482	Dave Nicholson Pete Ward	22	Pete Ward	84	Tom McCraw Al Weis	15
1964	Floyd Robinson	.301	Floyd Robinson	.388	Pete Ward	.473	Pete Ward	23	Pete Ward	94	Al Weis	22
1965	Don Buford	.283	Don Buford	.358	Bill Skowron	.424	John Romano Bill Skowron	18	Bill Skowron	78	Don Buford	17
1966	Tommie Agee	.273	Tommie Agee	.326	Tommie Agee	.447	Tommie Agee	22	Tommie Agee	86	Don Buford	51
1967	Ken Berry	.241	Pete Ward	.334	Pete Ward	.392	Pete Ward	18	Pete Ward	62	Don Buford	34
1968	Luis Aparicio	.264	Luis Aparicio	.302	Tom McCraw	.375	Pete Ward	15	Tommy Davis Pete Ward	50	Sandy Alomar	21
1969	Walt Williams	.304	Luis Aparicio	.352	Bill Melton	.433	Bill Melton	23	Bill Melton	87	Luis Aparicio	24

Year	Batting Average		On-Base Percentage		Slugging Percentage		Home Runs		RBI		Stolen Bases	
1970	Luis Aparicio	.313	Carlos May	.373	Bill Melton	.488	Bill Melton	33	Bill Melton	96	Carlos May	12
											Tom McCraw	
1971	Carlos May	.294	Carlos May	.375	Bill Melton	.492	Bill Melton	33	Bill Melton	86	Carlos May	16
1972	Dick Allen	.308	Dick Allen	.420	Dick Allen	.603	Dick Allen	37	Dick Allen	113	Pat Kelly	32
1973	Pat Kelly	.280	Bill Melton	.363	Bill Melton	.439	Carlos May	20	Carlos May	96	Pat Kelly	22
							Bill Melton					
1974	Jorge Orta	.316	Dick Allen	.375	Dick Allen	.563	Dick Allen	32	Ken Henderson	95	Pat Kelly	18
1975	Jorge Orta	.304	Carlos May	.373	Jorge Orta	.450	Deron Johnson	18	Jorge Orta	83	Pat Kelly	18
1976	Ralph Garr	.300	Ralph Garr	.322	Jorge Orta	.410	Jorge Orta	14	Jorge Orta	72	Jorge Orta	24
							Jim Spencer					
1977	Ralph Garr	.300	Richie Zisk	.355	Richie Zisk	.514	Oscar Gamble	31	Richie Zisk	101	Ralph Garr	12
1978	Lamar Johnson	.273	Lamar Johnson	.329	Eric Soderholm	.431	Eric Soderholm	20	Lamar Johnson	72	Bob Molinaro	22
1979	Chet Lemon	.318	Chet Lemon	.391	Chet Lemon	.496	Chet Lemon	17	Chet Lemon	86	Alan Bannister	22
1980	Chet Lemon	.292	Chet Lemon	.388	Chet Lemon	.442	Jim Morrison	15	Lamar Johnson	81	Bob Molinaro	18
							Wayne Nordhagen					
1981	Chet Lemon	.302	Chet Lemon	.384	Chet Lemon	.491	Greg Luzinski	21	Greg Luzinski	62	Ron LeFlore	36
1982	Greg Luzinski	.292	Greg Luzinski	.386	Harold Baines	.469	Harold Baines	25	Harold Baines	105	Rudy Law	36
1983	Carlton Fisk	.289	Carlton Fisk	.355	Carlton Fisk	.518	Ron Kittle	35	Ron Kittle	100	Rudy Law	77
1984	Harold Baines	.304	Harold Baines	.361	Harold Baines	.541	Ron Kittle	32	Harold Baines	94	Rudy Law	29
1985	Harold Baines	.309	Harold Baines	.348	Carlton Fisk	.488	Carlton Fisk	37	Harold Baines	113	Rudy Law	29
1986	Harold Baines	.296	John Cangelosi	.349	Harold Baines	.465	Harold Baines	21	Harold Baines	88	John Cangelosi	50
1987	Ivan Calderon	.293	Ivan Calderon	.362	Ivan Calderon	.526	Ivan Calderon	28	Greg Walker	94	Gary Redus	52
1988	Harold Baines	.277	Harold Baines	.347	Harold Baines	.411	Dan Pasqua	20	Harold Baines	81	Gary Redus	26
1989	Ivan Calderon	.286	Ivan Calderon	.332	Ivan Calderon	.437	Ivan Calderon	14	Ivan Calderon	87	Ozzie Guillen	36
1990	Carlton Fisk	.285	Carlton Fisk	.378	Carlton Fisk	.451	Carlton Fisk	18	Ivan Calderon	74	Lance Johnson	36
1991	Frank Thomas	.318	Frank Thomas	.453	Frank Thomas	.553	Frank Thomas	32	Frank Thomas	109	Tim Raines	51
1992	Frank Thomas	.323	Frank Thomas	.439	Frank Thomas	.536	George Bell	25	Frank Thomas	115	Tim Raines	45
1993	Frank Thomas	.317	Frank Thomas	.426	Frank Thomas	.607	Frank Thomas	41	Frank Thomas	128	Lance Johnson	35
1994	Frank Thomas	.353	Frank Thomas	.487	Frank Thomas	.729	Frank Thomas	38	Frank Thomas	101	Lance Johnson	26
1995	Frank Thomas	.308	Frank Thomas	.454	Frank Thomas	.606	Frank Thomas	40	Frank Thomas	111	Lance Johnson	40
1996	Frank Thomas	.349	Frank Thomas	.459	Frank Thomas	.626	Frank Thomas	40	Frank Thomas	134	Ray Durham	30
1997	Frank Thomas	.347	Frank Thomas	.456	Frank Thomas	.611	Frank Thomas	35	Frank Thomas	125	Ray Durham	33

Teams: White Sox

Chicago White Sox Individual Season Pitching Leaders

Year	ERA		Baserunners/9 IP		Innings Pitched		Strikeouts		Wins		Saves	
1901	Nixey Callahan	2.42	Nixey Callahan	10.6	Roy Patterson	312.1	Roy Patterson	127	Clark Griffith	24	Clark Griffith	1
											Erwin Harvey	
1902	Ned Garvin	2.21	Roy Patterson	11.1	Nixey Callahan	282.1	Wiley Piatt	96	Roy Patterson	19	11 tied with	0
1903	Doc White	2.13	Doc White	10.2	Doc White	300.0	Doc White	114	Doc White	17	4 tied with	1
1904	Doc White	1.78	Frank Owen	9.0	Frank Owen	315.0	Doc White	115	Frank Owen	21	Frank Owen	1
											Ed Walsh	
1905	Doc White	1.76	Frank Owen	9.2	Frank Owen	334.0	Frank Smith	171	Nick Altrock	23	6 tied with	0
1906	Doc White	1.52	Doc White	8.3	Frank Owen	293.0	Ed Walsh	171	Frank Owen	22	Frank Owen	2
1907	Ed Walsh	1.60	Ed Walsh	9.3	Ed Walsh	422.1	Ed Walsh	206	Doc White	27	Ed Walsh	4
1908	Ed Walsh	1.42	Ed Walsh	7.9	Ed Walsh	464.0	Ed Walsh	269	Ed Walsh	40	Ed Walsh	6
1909	Ed Walsh	1.41	Ed Walsh	8.6	Frank Smith	365.0	Frank Smith	177	Frank Smith	25	Ed Walsh	2
1910	Ed Walsh	1.27	Ed Walsh	7.5	Ed Walsh	369.2	Ed Walsh	258	Ed Walsh	18	Ed Walsh	5
1911	Ed Walsh	2.22	Ed Walsh	9.9	Ed Walsh	368.2	Ed Walsh	255	Ed Walsh	27	Ed Walsh	4
1912	Ed Walsh	2.15	Ed Walsh	9.8	Ed Walsh	393.0	Ed Walsh	254	Ed Walsh	27	Ed Walsh	10
1913	Eddie Cicotte	1.58	Reb Russell	9.6	Reb Russell	316.1	Jim Scott	158	Reb Russell	22	Reb Russell	4
1914	Eddie Cicotte	2.04	Eddie Cicotte	9.9	Joe Benz	283.1	Joe Benz	142	Joe Benz	14	Red Faber	4
									Jim Scott			
1915	Jim Scott	2.03	Joe Benz	9.6	Red Faber	299.2	Red Faber	182	Red Faber	24	Eddie Cicotte	3
									Jim Scott			
1916	Eddie Cicotte	1.78	Reb Russell	8.5	Reb Russell	264.1	Lefty Williams	138	Reb Russell	18	Eddie Cicotte	5
1917	Eddie Cicotte	1.53	Eddie Cicotte	8.3	Eddie Cicotte	346.2	Eddie Cicotte	150	Eddie Cicotte	28	Dave Danforth	9
1918	Joe Benz	2.51	Eddie Cicotte	10.7	Eddie Cicotte	266.0	Eddie Cicotte	104	Eddie Cicotte	12	3 tied with	2
1919	Eddie Cicotte	1.82	Eddie Cicotte	9.0	Eddie Cicotte	306.2	Lefty Williams	125	Eddie Cicotte	29	3 tied with	1
1920	Red Faber	2.99	Eddie Cicotte	11.6	Red Faber	319.0	Lefty Williams	128	Red Faber	23	Dickie Kerr	5
1921	Red Faber	2.48	Red Faber	10.5	Red Faber	330.2	Red Faber	124	Red Faber	25	Roy Wilkinson	3
1922	Red Faber	2.80	Red Faber	10.8	Red Faber	353.0	Red Faber	148	Red Faber	21	Red Faber	2
											Dixie Leverett	
1923	Sloppy Thurston	3.05	Red Faber	11.7	Charlie Robertson	255.0	Red Faber	91	Red Faber	14	Sloppy Thurston	4
								Charlie Robertson				
1924	Sloppy Thurston	3.80	Sloppy Thurston	12.2	Sloppy Thurston	291.0	Sarge Connally	55	Sloppy Thurston	20	Sarge Connally	6
1925	Ted Blankenship	3.16	Ted Blankenship	11.6	Ted Lyons	262.2	Ted Blankenship	81	Ted Lyons	21	Sarge Connally	8
1926	Ted Lyons	3.01	Ted Lyons	11.9	Ted Lyons	283.2	Tommy Thomas	127	Ted Lyons	18	Sarge Connally	3
											Sloppy Thurston	
1927	Ted Lyons	2.84	Ted Lyons	10.5	Ted Lyons	307.2	Tommy Thomas	107	Ted Lyons	22	Sarge Connally	5
						Tommy Thomas						
1928	Tommy Thomas	3.08	Tommy Thomas	11.4	Tommy Thomas	283.0	Tommy Thomas	129	Tommy Thomas	17	Ted Lyons	6
1929	Tommy Thomas	3.19	Tommy Thomas	11.4	Tommy Thomas	259.2	Red Faber	68	Ted Lyons	14	Ted Lyons	2
									Tommy Thomas			
1930	Ted Lyons	3.78	Ted Lyons	11.8	Ted Lyons	297.2	Pat Caraway	83	Ted Lyons	22	Hal McKain	5
1931	Red Faber	3.82	Red Faber	13.2	Vic Frasier	254.0	Vic Frasier	87	Vic Frasier	13	Vic Frasier	4
1932	Ted Lyons	3.28	Ted Lyons	12.4	Ted Lyons	230.2	Sad Sam Jones	64	Sad Sam Jones	10	Red Faber	6
									Ted Lyons			
1933	Sad Sam Jones	3.36	Sad Sam Jones	12.7	Ted Lyons	228.0	Ted Lyons	74	3 tied with	10	Joe Heving	6
1934	George Earnshaw	4.52	Sad Sam Jones	13.7	George Earnshaw	227.0	George Earnshaw	97	George Earnshaw	14	Joe Heving	4
1935	Ted Lyons	3.02	Ted Lyons	11.9	John Whitehead	222.1	John Whitehead	72	Ted Lyons	15	Whit Wyatt	5
1936	Vern Kennedy	4.63	Ted Lyons	13.6	Vern Kennedy	274.1	Vern Kennedy	99	Vern Kennedy	21	Clint Brown	5
1937	Monty Stratton	2.40	Monty Stratton	9.9	Vern Kennedy	221.0	Vern Kennedy	114	Monty Stratton	15	Clint Brown	18
1938	Thornton Lee	3.49	Monty Stratton	12.0	Thornton Lee	245.1	Johnny Rigney	84	Monty Stratton	15	3 tied with	2
1939	Ted Lyons	2.76	Ted Lyons	9.9	Thornton Lee	235.0	Johnny Rigney	119	Thornton Lee	15	Clint Brown	18
											Johnny Rigney	
1940	Johnny Rigney	3.11	Johnny Rigney	10.6	Johnny Rigney	280.2	Johnny Rigney	141	Johnny Rigney	14	Clint Brown	10
									Eddie Smith			
1941	Thornton Lee	2.37	Thornton Lee	10.6	Thornton Lee	300.1	Thornton Lee	130	Thornton Lee	22	4 tied with	1
1942	Ted Lyons	2.10	Ted Lyons	9.7	Johnny Humphries	228.0	Eddie Smith	78	Ted Lyons	14	Joe Haynes	6
1943	Orval Grove	2.75	Orval Grove	11.1	Orval Grove	216.1	Orval Grove	76	Orval Grove	15	Gordon Maltzberger	14
1944	Joe Haynes	2.57	Joe Haynes	11.1	Bill Dietrich	246.0	Orval Grove	105	Bill Dietrich	16	Gordon Maltzberger	12
1945	Thornton Lee	2.44	Thornton Lee	11.6	Thornton Lee	228.1	Thornton Lee	108	Thornton Lee	15	Earl Caldwell	4
											Johnny Johnson	
1946	Ed Lopat	2.73	Ed Lopat	10.3	Ed Lopat	231.0	Ed Lopat	89	Earl Caldwell	13	Earl Caldwell	8
									Ed Lopat			
1947	Joe Haynes	2.42	Ed Lopat	11.3	Ed Lopat	252.2	Ed Lopat	109	Ed Lopat	16	Earl Caldwell	8
1948	Bill Wight	4.80	Bill Wight	15.1	Bill Wight	223.1	Bill Wight	68	Joe Haynes	9	Howie Judson	8
									Bill Wight			
1949	Bill Wight	3.31	Randy Gumpert	11.8	Bill Wight	245.0	Billy Pierce	95	Bill Wight	15	Marino Pieretti	4
											Max Surkont	
1950	Bill Wight	3.58	Bill Wight	12.8	Billy Pierce	219.1	Billy Pierce	118	Billy Pierce	12	Luis Aloma	4
1951	Saul Rogovin	2.48	Saul Rogovin	10.9	Billy Pierce	240.1	Billy Pierce	113	Billy Pierce	15	Luis Aloma	3
											Joe Dobson	
1952	Joe Dobson	2.51	Joe Dobson	10.0	Billy Pierce	255.1	Billy Pierce	144	Billy Pierce	15	Harry Dorish	11
1953	Billy Pierce	2.72	Billy Pierce	10.6	Billy Pierce	271.1	Billy Pierce	186	Billy Pierce	18	Harry Dorish	18
1954	Virgil Trucks	2.79	Virgil Trucks	10.9	Virgil Trucks	264.2	Virgil Trucks	152	Virgil Trucks	19	Don Johnson	7
1955	Billy Pierce	1.97	Billy Pierce	10.0	Billy Pierce	205.2	Billy Pierce	157	Dick Donovan	15	Dixie Howell	9
									Billy Pierce			
1956	Jack Harshman	3.10	Dick Donovan	10.6	Billy Pierce	276.1	Billy Pierce	192	Billy Pierce	20	Dixie Howell	4
1957	Dick Donovan	2.77	Dick Donovan	10.4	Billy Pierce	257.0	Billy Pierce	171	Billy Pierce	20	Paul LaPalme	7
											Gerry Staley	
1958	Billy Pierce	2.68	Billy Pierce	10.0	Dick Donovan	248.0	Early Wynn	179	Billy Pierce	17	Turk Lown	8
											Gerry Staley	
1959	Bob Shaw	2.69	Bob Shaw	10.8	Early Wynn	255.2	Early Wynn	179	Early Wynn	22	Turk Lown	15
1960	Frank Baumann	2.67	Frank Baumann	10.8	Early Wynn	237.1	Early Wynn	158	Billy Pierce	14	Gerry Staley	10
1961	Juan Pizarro	3.05	Juan Pizarro	11.9	Juan Pizarro	194.2	Juan Pizarro	188	Juan Pizarro	14	Turk Lown	11
1962	Eddie Fisher	3.10	Eddie Fisher	10.6	Ray Herbert	236.2	Juan Pizarro	173	Ray Herbert	20	Turk Lown	6
1963	Gary Peters	2.33	Gary Peters	9.9	Gary Peters	243.0	Gary Peters	189	Gary Peters	19	Hoyt Wilhelm	21
1964	Joe Horlen	1.88	Joe Horlen	8.6	Gary Peters	273.2	Gary Peters	205	Gary Peters	20	Hoyt Wilhelm	27
1965	Eddie Fisher	2.40	Eddie Fisher	8.9	Joe Horlen	219.0	Tommy John	126	Eddie Fisher	15	Eddie Fisher	24

Year	ERA		Baserunners/9 IP		Innings Pitched		Strikeouts		Wins		Saves	
1966	Gary Peters	1.98	Gary Peters	9.0	Tommy John	223.0	Tommy John	138	Tommy John	14	Bob Locker	12
1967	Joe Horlen	2.06	Joe Horlen	8.7	Gary Peters	260.0	Gary Peters	215	Joe Horlen	19	Bob Locker	20
1968	Tommy John	1.98	Tommy John	9.9	Joe Horlen	223.2	Tommy John	117	Wilbur Wood	13	Wilbur Wood	16
1969	Tommy John	3.25	Joe Horlen	12.2	Joe Horlen	235.2	Gary Peters	140	Joe Horlen	13	Wilbur Wood	15
1970	Tommy John	3.27	Tommy John	12.1	Tommy John	269.1	Tommy John	138	Tommy John	12	Wilbur Wood	21
1971	Wilbur Wood	1.91	Wilbur Wood	9.2	Wilbur Wood	334.0	Wilbur Wood	210	Wilbur Wood	22	Bart Johnson	14
1972	Wilbur Wood	2.51	Wilbur Wood	9.7	Wilbur Wood	376.2	Tom Bradley	209	Wilbur Wood	24	Terry Forster	29
1973	Terry Forster	3.23	Wilbur Wood	12.0	Wilbur Wood	359.1	Wilbur Wood	199	Wilbur Wood	24	Cy Acosta	18
1974	Jim Kaat	2.92	Jim Kaat	10.8	Wilbur Wood	320.1	Wilbur Wood	169	Jim Kaat	21	Terry Forster	24
1975	Jim Kaat	3.11	Jim Kaat	12.1	Jim Kaat	303.2	Jim Kaat	142	Jim Kaat	20	Goose Gossage	26
1976	Ken Brett	3.32	Ken Brett	11.2	Goose Gossage	224.0	Goose Gossage	135	Ken Brett	10	Dave Hamilton	10
1977	Ken Kravec	4.10	Francisco Barrios	11.8	Francisco Barrios	231.1	Ken Kravec	125	Steve Stone	15	Lerrin LaGrow	25
1978	Francisco Barrios	4.05	Steve Stone	12.0	Steve Stone	212.0	Ken Kravec	154	Steve Stone	12	Lerrin LaGrow	16
1979	Ross Baumgarten	3.54	Ken Kravec	12.0	Ken Kravec	250.0	Ken Kravec	132	Ken Kravec	15	Ed Farmer	14
1980	Britt Burns	2.84	Britt Burns	10.6	Britt Burns	238.0	Britt Burns	133	Britt Burns	15	Ed Farmer	30
1981	Dennis Lamp	2.41	Dennis Lamp	10.4	Britt Burns	156.2	Britt Burns	108	Britt Burns	10	Ed Farmer	10
											LaMarr Hoyt	
1982	LaMarr Hoyt	3.53	LaMarr Hoyt	11.2	LaMarr Hoyt	239.2	LaMarr Hoyt	124	LaMarr Hoyt	19	Salome Barojas	21
1983	Rich Dotson	3.23	LaMarr Hoyt	9.3	LaMarr Hoyt	260.2	Floyd Bannister	193	LaMarr Hoyt	24	Dennis Lamp	15
1984	Rich Dotson	3.59	Tom Seaver	10.6	Rich Dotson	245.2	Floyd Bannister	152	Tom Seaver	15	Ron Reed	12
1985	Tom Seaver	3.17	Tom Seaver	11.3	Tom Seaver	238.2	Floyd Bannister	198	Britt Burns	18	Bob James	32
1986	Floyd Bannister	3.54	Floyd Bannister	11.5	Rich Dotson	197.0	Joe Cowley	132	Joe Cowley	11	Bob James	14
1987	Floyd Bannister	3.58	Floyd Bannister	10.4	Floyd Bannister	228.2	Jose DeLeon	153	Floyd Bannister	16	Bobby Thigpen	16
1988	Dave LaPoint	3.40	Dave LaPoint	11.2	Melido Perez	197.0	Melido Perez	138	Jerry Reuss	13	Bobby Thigpen	34
1989	Melido Perez	5.01	Melido Perez	13.7	Melido Perez	183.1	Melido Perez	141	Melido Perez	11	Bobby Thigpen	34
1990	Greg Hibbard	3.16	Greg Hibbard	11.2	Greg Hibbard	211.0	Jack McDowell	165	Greg Hibbard	14	Bobby Thigpen	57
									Jack McDowell			
1991	Jack McDowell	3.41	Jack McDowell	10.6	Jack McDowell	253.2	Jack McDowell	191	Jack McDowell	17	Bobby Thigpen	30
1992	Jack McDowell	3.18	Jack McDowell	11.4	Jack McDowell	260.2	Jack McDowell	178	Jack McDowell	20	Bobby Thigpen	22
1993	Wilson Alvarez	2.95	Alex Fernandez	10.7	Jack McDowell	256.2	Alex Fernandez	169	Jack McDowell	22	Roberto Hernandez	38
1994	Wilson Alvarez	3.45	Alex Fernandez	11.3	Jack McDowell	181.0	Jason Bere	127	Wilson Alvarez	12	Roberto Hernandez	14
							Jack McDowell		Jason Bere			
1995	Alex Fernandez	3.80	Alex Fernandez	11.7	Alex Fernandez	203.2	Alex Fernandez	159	Alex Fernandez	12	Roberto Hernandez	32
1996	Alex Fernandez	3.45	Alex Fernandez	11.4	Alex Fernandez	258.0	Alex Fernandez	200	Alex Fernandez	16	Roberto Hernandez	38
1997	James Baldwin	5.27	Doug Drabek	12.9	Jaime Navarro	209.2	Jaime Navarro	142	James Baldwin	12	Roberto Hernandez	27
									Doug Drabek			

White Sox Franchise Batting Leaders—Career

Games

1	Luke Appling	2,422
2	Nellie Fox	2,115
3	Ray Schalk	1,755
4	Ozzie Guillen	1,743
5	Eddie Collins	1,670
6	Harold Baines	1,614
7	Luis Aparicio	1,511
8	Carlton Fisk	1,421
9	Minnie Minoso	1,373
10	Sherm Lollar	1,358
11	Shano Collins	1,335
12	Buck Weaver	1,254
13	Willie Kamm	1,170
14	Fielder Jones	1,153
15	Robin Ventura	1,093
16	Lee Tannehill	1,090
17	Frank Thomas	1,076
18	Frank Isbell	1,074
19	Bibb Falk	1,067
20	Jim Landis	1,063

At-Bats

1	Luke Appling	8,857
2	Nellie Fox	8,486
3	Ozzie Guillen	6,067
4	Eddie Collins	6,065
5	Harold Baines	6,004
6	Luis Aparicio	5,856
7	Ray Schalk	5,304
8	Minnie Minoso	5,011
9	Carlton Fisk	4,896
10	Buck Weaver	4,809
11	Shano Collins	4,791
12	Fielder Jones	4,282
13	Sherm Lollar	4,229
14	Willie Kamm	4,066
15	Frank Isbell	4,060
16	Robin Ventura	3,952
17	Bibb Falk	3,874
18	Frank Thomas	3,821
19	Lee Tannehill	3,778
20	Carlos May	3,633

Runs

1	Luke Appling	1,319
2	Nellie Fox	1,187
3	Eddie Collins	1,065
4	Minnie Minoso	893
5	Luis Aparicio	791
6	Frank Thomas	785
7	Harold Baines	781
8	Fielder Jones	693
	Ozzie Guillen	693
10	Carlton Fisk	649
11	Buck Weaver	623
12	Johnny Mostil	618
13	Ray Schalk	579
14	Robin Ventura	574
15	Shano Collins	572
16	Willie Kamm	545
17	Jim Landis	532
18	Bibb Falk	526
19	Joe Kuhel	523
20	Carlos May	486

Hits

1	Luke Appling	2,749
2	Nellie Fox	2,470
3	Eddie Collins	2,007
4	Harold Baines	1,749
5	Ozzie Guillen	1,608
6	Luis Aparicio	1,576
7	Minnie Minoso	1,523
8	Ray Schalk	1,345
9	Buck Weaver	1,308
10	Frank Thomas	1,261
11	Carlton Fisk	1,259
12	Shano Collins	1,254
13	Bibb Falk	1,219
14	Fielder Jones	1,151
15	Willie Kamm	1,136
16	Sherm Lollar	1,122
17	Robin Ventura	1,089
18	Johnny Mostil	1,054
19	Earl Sheely	1,051
20	Frank Isbell	1,019

Doubles

1	Luke Appling	440
2	Nellie Fox	335
3	Harold Baines	314
4	Eddie Collins	266
5	Minnie Minoso	260
6	Frank Thomas	246
7	Bibb Falk	245
8	Willie Kamm	243
9	Ozzie Guillen	240
10	Shano Collins	230
11	Luis Aparicio	223
12	Carlton Fisk	214
13	Johnny Mostil	209
14	Earl Sheely	207
15	Ray Schalk	199
16	Buck Weaver	198
17	Robin Ventura	188
18	Sherm Lollar	186
19	Chet Lemon	178
20	Greg Walker	164

Triples

1	Shano Collins	104
	Nellie Fox	104
3	Eddie Collins	102
	Luke Appling	102
5	Johnny Mostil	82
6	Joe Jackson	79
	Minnie Minoso	79
8	Lance Johnson	77
9	Buck Weaver	69
10	Ozzie Guillen	68
11	Willie Kamm	67
12	Mike Kreevich	65
13	Happy Felsch	64
14	Frank Isbell	62
15	Carl Reynolds	55
16	Luis Aparicio	54
17	Bibb Falk	50
	Jim Rivera	50
19	Ray Schalk	49
20	Jim Landis	47

Home Runs

1	Frank Thomas	257
2	Harold Baines	220
3	Carlton Fisk	214
4	Bill Melton	154
5	Robin Ventura	150
6	Ron Kittle	140
7	Minnie Minoso	135
8	Sherm Lollar	124
9	Greg Walker	113
10	Pete Ward	97
11	Ron Karkovice	96
12	Al Smith	85
	Carlos May	85
	Dick Allen	85
15	Greg Luzinski	84
16	Jim Landis	83
17	Zeke Bonura	79
	Jorge Orta	79
19	Jim Rivera	77
20	Four tied at	75

RBI

1	Luke Appling	1,116
2	Harold Baines	966
3	Frank Thomas	854
4	Minnie Minoso	808
5	Eddie Collins	804
6	Carlton Fisk	762
7	Nellie Fox	740
8	Robin Ventura	650
9	Sherm Lollar	631
10	Bibb Falk	627
11	Ray Schalk	594
12	Willie Kamm	587
13	Earl Sheely	582
14	Ozzie Guillen	565
15	Shano Collins	541
16	Bill Melton	535
17	Carlos May	479
18	Luis Aparicio	464
19	Jorge Orta	456
20	Frank Isbell	447

Walks

1	Luke Appling	1,302
2	Eddie Collins	965
3	Frank Thomas	879
4	Nellie Fox	658
	Minnie Minoso	658
6	Ray Schalk	638
7	Robin Ventura	589
8	Willie Kamm	569
9	Fielder Jones	550
	Harold Baines	550
11	Sherm Lollar	525
12	Jim Landis	483
13	Carlton Fisk	460
14	Carlos May	456
15	Earl Sheely	454
16	Joe Kuhel	450
17	Luis Aparicio	439
18	Bill Melton	418
19	Johnny Mostil	415
20	Mike Tresh	397

Strikeouts

1	Harold Baines	891
2	Carlton Fisk	798
3	Ron Karkovice	749
4	Jim Landis	608
5	Ron Kittle	606
6	Bill Melton	595
7	Frank Thomas	582
8	Robin Ventura	548
9	Luke Appling	528
10	Pete Ward	517
11	Greg Walker	511
12	Carlos May	508
13	Red Faber	477
	Jorge Orta	477
15	Ozzie Guillen	460
16	Jim Rivera	450
17	Minnie Minoso	427
	Dan Pasqua	427
19	Luis Aparicio	410
20	Ken Berry	406

Stolen Bases

1	Eddie Collins	368
2	Luis Aparicio	318
3	Frank Isbell	250
4	Lance Johnson	226
5	Fielder Jones	206
6	Shano Collins	192
7	Luke Appling	179
8	Ray Schalk	176
	Johnny Mostil	176
10	Buck Weaver	172
11	Minnie Minoso	171
	Rudy Law	171
13	Patsy Dougherty	168
14	Ozzie Guillen	163
15	George Davis	162
16	Nixey Callahan	157
17	Jim Rivera	146
18	Tim Raines	143
19	Six tied at	127

Runs Created

1	Luke Appling	1,499
2	Eddie Collins	1,177
3	Nellie Fox	1,114
4	Frank Thomas	978
5	Harold Baines	950
6	Minnie Minoso	940
7	Carlton Fisk	706
8	Luis Aparicio	689
9	Fielder Jones	669
10	Robin Ventura	648
11	Ray Schalk	642
12	Bibb Falk	625
13	Sherm Lollar	623
14	Willie Kamm	619
15	Ozzie Guillen	598
16	Shano Collins	585
17	Johnny Mostil	580
18	Earl Sheely	575
19	Buck Weaver	550
20	Four tied at	516

Runs Created/27 Outs
(minimum 2000 Plate Appearances)

1	Frank Thomas	9.54
2	Zeke Bonura	7.86
3	Joe Jackson	7.60
4	Eddie Collins	6.80
5	Carl Reynolds	6.65
6	Minnie Minoso	6.62
7	Luke Appling	6.21
8	Tim Raines	6.07
9	Danny Green	5.93
10	Taffy Wright	5.91
11	Harry Hooper	5.87
12	Floyd Robinson	5.85
13	Earl Sheely	5.82
14	Greg Luzinski	5.81
15	Rip Radcliff	5.76
16	Bibb Falk	5.71
17	Johnny Mostil	5.70
18	Robin Ventura	5.69
19	Harold Baines	5.67
20	Chet Lemon	5.57

Batting Average
(minimum 2000 Plate Appearances)

1	Joe Jackson	.339
2	Eddie Collins	.331
3	Frank Thomas	.330
4	Carl Reynolds	.322
5	Zeke Bonura	.317
6	Bibb Falk	.315
7	Taffy Wright	.312
8	Luke Appling	.310
9	Rip Radcliff	.310
10	Earl Sheely	.305
11	Minnie Minoso	.304
12	Harry Hooper	.302
13	Johnny Mostil	.301
14	Bill Barrett	.294
15	Happy Felsch	.293
16	Harold Baines	.291
17	Nellie Fox	.291
18	Lamar Johnson	.291
19	Mike Kreevich	.290
20	Chet Lemon	.288

On-Base Percentage
(minimum 2000 Plate Appearances)

1	Frank Thomas	.452
2	Eddie Collins	.426
3	Joe Jackson	.407
4	Luke Appling	.399
5	Minnie Minoso	.397
6	Zeke Bonura	.396
7	Earl Sheely	.391
8	Johnny Mostil	.386
9	Harry Hooper	.383
10	Taffy Wright	.381
11	Tim Raines	.375
12	Bibb Falk	.370
13	Willie Kamm	.370
14	Floyd Robinson	.370
15	Robin Ventura	.367
16	Danny Green	.366
17	Jimmy Dykes	.365
18	Chet Lemon	.363
19	Mule Haas	.362
20	Rip Radcliff	.361

Slugging Percentage
(minimum 2000 Plate Appearances)

1	Frank Thomas	.600
2	Zeke Bonura	.518
3	Carl Reynolds	.499
4	Joe Jackson	.498
5	Ron Kittle	.470
6	Harold Baines	.468
7	Minnie Minoso	.468
8	Greg Walker	.453
9	Ivan Calderon	.451
10	Greg Luzinski	.451
11	Chet Lemon	.451
12	Al Smith	.444
13	Bibb Falk	.442
14	Robin Ventura	.441
15	Carlton Fisk	.438
16	Harry Hooper	.436
17	Bill Melton	.432
18	Dan Pasqua	.429
19	Happy Felsch	.427
20	Johnny Mostil	.427

Teams: White Sox

White Sox Franchise Pitching Leaders—Career

Wins

1	Ted Lyons	260
2	Red Faber	254
3	Ed Walsh	195
4	Billy Pierce	186
5	Wilbur Wood	163
6	Doc White	159
7	Eddie Cicotte	156
8	Joe Horlen	113
9	Frank Smith	107
	Jim Scott	107
11	Thornton Lee	104
12	Rich Dotson	97
13	Gary Peters	91
	Jack McDowell	91
15	Tommy Thomas	83
16	Tommy John	82
17	Roy Patterson	81
	Frank Owen	81
	Reb Russell	81
	Lefty Williams	81

Losses

1	Ted Lyons	230
2	Red Faber	213
3	Billy Pierce	152
4	Wilbur Wood	148
5	Ed Walsh	125
6	Doc White	123
7	Jim Scott	113
	Joe Horlen	113
9	Thornton Lee	104
10	Eddie Cicotte	102
11	Rich Dotson	95
12	Tommy Thomas	92
13	Bill Dietrich	91
14	Eddie Smith	82
15	Frank Smith	81
16	Tommy John	80
17	Ted Blankenship	79
18	Gary Peters	78
19	Joe Benz	75
20	Four tied at	73

Winning Percentage
(minimum 100 decisions)

1	Lefty Williams	.648
2	Juan Pizarro	.615
3	Jack McDowell	.611
4	Ed Walsh	.609
5	Eddie Cicotte	.605
6	LaMarr Hoyt	.602
7	Dick Donovan	.593
8	Reb Russell	.579
9	Wilson Alvarez	.573
10	Frank Smith	.569
11	Doc White	.564
12	Nick Altrock	.560
13	Frank Owen	.559
14	Alex Fernandez	.556
15	Billy Pierce	.550
16	Red Faber	.544
17	Gary Peters	.538
	Britt Burns	.538
19	Early Wynn	.538
20	Ted Lyons	.531

Games

1	Red Faber	669
2	Ted Lyons	594
3	Wilbur Wood	578
4	Billy Pierce	456
5	Ed Walsh	427
6	Bobby Thigpen	424
7	Hoyt Wilhelm	361
8	Doc White	360
9	Eddie Cicotte	353
10	Roberto Hernandez	345
11	Joe Horlen	329
12	Jim Scott	317
13	Scott Radinsky	316
14	Eddie Fisher	286
15	Bob Locker	271
16	Gerry Staley	270
17	Terry Forster	263
18	Thornton Lee	261
19	Gary Peters	258
20	Donn Pall	255

Games Started

1	Ted Lyons	484
2	Red Faber	483
3	Billy Pierce	390
4	Ed Walsh	312
5	Doc White	301
6	Wilbur Wood	286
7	Joe Horlen	284
8	Eddie Cicotte	258
9	Rich Dotson	250
10	Thornton Lee	232
11	Jim Scott	225
12	Tommy John	219
13	Gary Peters	216
14	Bill Dietrich	199
15	Tommy Thomas	197
	Alex Fernandez	197
17	Frank Smith	195
18	Jack McDowell	191
19	Joe Benz	163
20	Four tied at	162

Complete Games

1	Ted Lyons	356
2	Red Faber	274
3	Ed Walsh	249
4	Doc White	206
5	Eddie Cicotte	183
	Billy Pierce	183
7	Frank Smith	156
8	Thornton Lee	142
9	Jim Scott	125
10	Roy Patterson	119
11	Nick Altrock	117
12	Frank Owen	116
13	Wilbur Wood	113
14	Tommy Thomas	104
15	Reb Russell	81
16	Lefty Williams	78
17	Joe Benz	76
18	Eddie Smith	75
19	Ted Blankenship	73
20	Ed Lopat	72

Shutouts

1	Ed Walsh	57
2	Doc White	43
3	Billy Pierce	35
4	Red Faber	30
5	Eddie Cicotte	28
6	Ted Lyons	27
7	Jim Scott	26
8	Frank Smith	25
9	Reb Russell	24
	Wilbur Wood	24
11	Tommy John	21
12	Gary Peters	18
	Joe Horlen	18
14	Joe Benz	17
15	Roy Patterson	16
	Frank Owen	16
	Nick Altrock	16
	Early Wynn	16
19	Dick Donovan	15
20	Six tied at	13

Saves

1	Bobby Thigpen	201
2	Roberto Hernandez	161
3	Hoyt Wilhelm	98
4	Terry Forster	75
5	Wilbur Wood	57
6	Bob James	56
7	Ed Farmer	54
8	Clint Brown	53
9	Bob Locker	48
10	Turk Lown	45
11	Eddie Fisher	44
12	Lerrin LaGrow	42
13	Gerry Staley	39
14	Harry Dorish	36
15	Ed Walsh	34
	Salome Barojas	34
17	Gordon Maltzberger	33
18	Scott Radinsky	32
19	Goose Gossage	30
20	Red Faber	28

Innings Pitched

1	Ted Lyons	4,161.0
2	Red Faber	4,087.2
3	Ed Walsh	2,947.1
4	Billy Pierce	2,931.0
5	Wilbur Wood	2,524.1
6	Doc White	2,498.1
7	Eddie Cicotte	2,321.2
8	Joe Horlen	1,918.0
9	Jim Scott	1,892.0
10	Thornton Lee	1,888.0
11	Frank Smith	1,717.1
12	Rich Dotson	1,606.0
13	Gary Peters	1,560.0
14	Tommy Thomas	1,557.1
15	Tommy John	1,493.1
16	Bill Dietrich	1,437.2
17	Roy Patterson	1,365.0
18	Joe Benz	1,359.1
19	Alex Fernandez	1,346.1
20	Jack McDowell	1,343.2

Walks

1	Red Faber	1,213
2	Ted Lyons	1,121
3	Billy Pierce	1,052
4	Wilbur Wood	671
5	Rich Dotson	637
6	Thornton Lee	633
7	Jim Scott	609
8	Ed Walsh	608
9	Bill Dietrich	561
10	Eddie Smith	545
11	Doc White	542
12	Joe Horlen	534
13	Eddie Cicotte	533
14	Wilson Alvarez	523
15	Gary Peters	515
16	Frank Smith	496
17	Ted Blankenship	489
18	Tommy Thomas	468
19	Tommy John	460
20	Johnny Rigney	450

Strikeouts

1	Billy Pierce	1,796
2	Ed Walsh	1,732
3	Red Faber	1,471
4	Wilbur Wood	1,332
5	Gary Peters	1,098
6	Ted Lyons	1,073
7	Doc White	1,067
8	Joe Horlen	1,007
9	Eddie Cicotte	961
10	Alex Fernandez	951
11	Jim Scott	945
12	Jack McDowell	918
13	Tommy John	888
14	Rich Dotson	873
15	Frank Smith	826
16	Juan Pizarro	793
17	Wilson Alvarez	770
18	Floyd Bannister	759
19	Thornton Lee	742
20	Britt Burns	734

Strikeouts/9 Innings
(minimum 1000 Innings Pitched)

1	Juan Pizarro	6.88
2	Floyd Bannister	6.57
3	Wilson Alvarez	6.51
4	Alex Fernandez	6.36
5	Gary Peters	6.33
6	Jack McDowell	6.15
7	Britt Burns	6.04
8	Early Wynn	5.98
9	Billy Pierce	5.51
10	Tommy John	5.35
11	Ed Walsh	5.29
12	Rich Dotson	4.89
13	Wilbur Wood	4.75
14	Joe Horlen	4.73
15	Johnny Rigney	4.59
16	Jim Scott	4.50
17	Frank Smith	4.33
18	Dick Donovan	4.11
19	Lefty Williams	3.94
20	Doc White	3.84

ERA
(minimum 1000 Innings Pitched)

1	Ed Walsh	1.80
2	Frank Smith	2.18
3	Eddie Cicotte	2.24
4	Jim Scott	2.30
5	Doc White	2.30
6	Reb Russell	2.33
7	Nick Altrock	2.40
8	Joe Benz	2.42
9	Frank Owen	2.48
10	Roy Patterson	2.75
11	Gary Peters	2.92
12	Tommy John	2.95
13	Juan Pizarro	3.05
14	Lefty Williams	3.09
15	Joe Horlen	3.11
16	Joe Haynes	3.14
17	Red Faber	3.15
18	Wilbur Wood	3.18
19	Billy Pierce	3.19
20	Thornton Lee	3.33

Component ERA
(minimum 1000 Innings Pitched)

1	Ed Walsh	1.77
2	Frank Smith	2.02
3	Reb Russell	2.14
4	Nick Altrock	2.23
5	Eddie Cicotte	2.27
6	Frank Owen	2.31
7	Doc White	2.33
8	Joe Benz	2.45
9	Jim Scott	2.49
10	Roy Patterson	2.69
11	Gary Peters	2.91
12	Lefty Williams	2.93
13	Joe Horlen	3.05
14	Tommy John	3.11
15	Juan Pizarro	3.14
16	Billy Pierce	3.21
17	Red Faber	3.21
18	Wilbur Wood	3.25
19	Dick Donovan	3.25
20	Jack McDowell	3.35

Opponent Average
(minimum 1000 Innings Pitched)

1	Ed Walsh	.218
2	Frank Smith	.220
3	Juan Pizarro	.232
4	Gary Peters	.233
5	Reb Russell	.238
6	Early Wynn	.238
7	Jim Scott	.238
8	Billy Pierce	.240
9	Doc White	.240
10	Frank Owen	.240
11	Eddie Cicotte	.243
12	Joe Horlen	.244
13	Tommy John	.244
14	Johnny Rigney	.244
15	Nick Altrock	.245
16	Joe Benz	.245
17	Wilson Alvarez	.246
18	Jack McDowell	.248
19	Floyd Bannister	.250
20	Britt Burns	.251

Opponent OBP
(minimum 1000 Innings Pitched)

1	Ed Walsh	.263
2	Nick Altrock	.279
3	Reb Russell	.281
4	Frank Smith	.282
5	Frank Owen	.285
6	Doc White	.289
7	Eddie Cicotte	.289
8	Joe Benz	.296
9	Roy Patterson	.299
10	Joe Horlen	.299
11	Gary Peters	.299
12	Dick Donovan	.301
13	Juan Pizarro	.301
14	Tommy John	.305
15	Wilbur Wood	.305
16	Jim Scott	.306
17	Billy Pierce	.307
18	Jack McDowell	.308
19	Floyd Bannister	.310
20	Britt Burns	.313

Teams: White Sox

White Sox Franchise Batting Leaders—Single Season

Games

1	Don Buford	1966	163
	Greg Walker	1985	163
3	Ron Hansen	1965	162
	Ken Henderson	1974	162
	Jim Morrison	1980	162
6	Harold Baines	1982	161
	Dave Gallagher	1989	161
	Albert Belle	1997	161
9	Tommie Agee	1966	160
	Steve Kemp	1982	160
	Harold Baines	1985	160
	Ozzie Guillen	1990	160
	Lance Johnson	1991	160
	Frank Thomas	1992	160
15	Nellie Fox	1961	159
	Greg Luzinski	1982	159
	Ozzie Guillen	1986	159
18	Eight tied at		158

At-Bats

1	Nellie Fox	1956	649
2	Nellie Fox	1952	648
3	Harold Baines	1985	640
4	Nellie Fox	1955	636
	Jorge Orta	1976	636
6	Albert Belle	1997	634
	Ray Durham	1997	634
8	Nellie Fox	1954	631
9	Buck Weaver	1920	629
	Tommie Agee	1966	629
11	George Bell	1992	627
12	Luis Aparicio	1961	625
13	Nellie Fox	1953	624
	Nellie Fox	1959	624
15	Rip Radcliff	1935	623
	Nellie Fox	1958	623
17	Luis Aparicio	1968	622
	Ivan Calderon	1989	622
19	Nellie Fox	1962	621
20	Chico Carrasquel	1954	620

Runs

1	Johnny Mostil	1925	135
2	Fielder Jones	1901	120
	Johnny Mostil	1926	120
	Rip Radcliff	1936	120
	Zeke Bonura	1936	120
6	Lu Blue	1931	119
	Minnie Minoso	1954	119
	Tony Phillips	1996	119
9	Eddie Collins	1915	118
10	Eddie Collins	1920	117
11	Dummy Hoy	1901	112
12	Harry Hooper	1922	111
	Luke Appling	1936	111
	Joe Kuhel	1940	111
	Nellie Fox	1954	111
16	Nellie Fox	1957	110
	Frank Thomas	1996	110
	Frank Thomas	1997	110
19	Minnie Minoso	1951	109
	Nellie Fox	1956	109

Hits

1	Eddie Collins	1920	224
2	Joe Jackson	1920	218
3	Buck Weaver	1920	208
4	Rip Radcliff	1936	207
5	Luke Appling	1936	204
6	Joe Jackson	1916	202
	Carl Reynolds	1930	202
8	Nellie Fox	1954	201
9	Al Simmons	1933	200
10	Nellie Fox	1955	198
	Harold Baines	1985	198
12	Johnny Mostil	1926	197
	Luke Appling	1933	197
	Luke Appling	1940	197
15	Taffy Wright	1940	196
	Nellie Fox	1957	196
17	Bibb Falk	1926	195
18	Eddie Collins	1922	194
	Eddie Collins	1924	194
	Zeke Bonura	1936	194

Doubles

1	Frank Thomas	1992	46
2	Floyd Robinson	1962	45
	Albert Belle	1997	45
4	Chet Lemon	1979	44
	Ivan Calderon	1990	44
6	Earl Sheely	1925	43
	Bibb Falk	1926	43
8	Joe Jackson	1920	42
	Red Kress	1932	42
	Luke Appling	1937	42
11	Johnny Mostil	1926	41
	Zeke Bonura	1937	41
13	Joe Jackson	1916	40
	Happy Felsch	1920	40
	Earl Sheely	1926	40
	Don Kolloway	1942	40
	Jim Morrison	1980	40
18	Four tied at		39

Triples

1	Joe Jackson	1916	21
2	Joe Jackson	1920	20
3	Harry Lord	1911	18
	Jack Fournier	1915	18
	Carl Reynolds	1930	18
	Minnie Minoso	1954	18
7	Sam Mertes	1901	17
	Shano Collins	1915	17
	Eddie Collins	1916	17
	Joe Jackson	1917	17
11	Johnny Mostil	1925	16
	Mike Kreevich	1937	16
	Dixie Walker	1937	16
	Jim Rivera	1953	16
15	George Davis	1904	15
	Happy Felsch	1920	15
	Johnny Mostil	1923	15
	Johnny Mostil	1926	15
	Lu Blue	1931	15
	Wally Moses	1945	15

Home Runs

1	Frank Thomas	1993	41
2	Frank Thomas	1995	40
	Frank Thomas	1996	40
4	Frank Thomas	1994	38
5	Dick Allen	1972	37
	Carlton Fisk	1985	37
7	Ron Kittle	1983	35
	Frank Thomas	1997	35
9	Robin Ventura	1996	34
10	Bill Melton	1970	33
	Bill Melton	1971	33
12	Dick Allen	1974	32
	Greg Luzinski	1983	32
	Ron Kittle	1984	32
	Frank Thomas	1991	32
16	Oscar Gamble	1977	31
17	Richie Zisk	1977	30
	Albert Belle	1997	30
19	Three tied at		29

RBI

1	Zeke Bonura	1936	138
2	Frank Thomas	1996	134
3	Luke Appling	1936	128
	Frank Thomas	1993	128
5	Frank Thomas	1997	125
6	Joe Jackson	1920	121
7	Al Simmons	1933	119
8	Eddie Robinson	1951	117
9	Minnie Minoso	1954	116
	Albert Belle	1997	116
11	Happy Felsch	1920	115
	Frank Thomas	1992	115
13	Smead Jolley	1930	114
14	Dick Allen	1972	113
	Harold Baines	1985	113
16	George Bell	1992	112
17	Earl Sheely	1925	111
	Gee Walker	1939	111
	Frank Thomas	1995	111
20	Zeke Bonura	1934	110

Walks

1	Frank Thomas	1991	138
2	Frank Thomas	1995	136
3	Lu Blue	1931	127
4	Tony Phillips	1996	125
5	Luke Appling	1935	122
	Frank Thomas	1992	122
7	Luke Appling	1949	121
8	Eddie Collins	1915	119
9	Frank Thomas	1993	112
10	Frank Thomas	1994	109
	Frank Thomas	1996	109
	Frank Thomas	1997	109
13	Ferris Fain	1953	108
14	Luke Appling	1939	105
	Robin Ventura	1993	105
16	Larry Doby	1956	102
17	Cass Michaels	1949	101
	Joe Cunningham	1962	101
19	Dick Allen	1972	99
20	Two tied at		95

Strikeouts

1	Dave Nicholson	1963	175
2	Ron Kittle	1983	150
	Sammy Sosa	1990	150
4	Ron Kittle	1984	137
5	Tony Phillips	1996	132
6	Tommie Agee	1967	129
7	Danny Tartabull	1996	128
8	Tommie Agee	1966	127
9	Dave Nicholson	1964	126
	Dick Allen	1972	126
	Ron Karkovice	1993	126
12	Greg Luzinski	1982	120
13	Deron Johnson	1975	117
	Greg Luzinski	1983	117
15	Ken Henderson	1974	112
	Greg Walker	1987	112
	Frank Thomas	1991	112
18	Gus Zernial	1950	110
19	Three tied at		109

Stolen Bases

1	Rudy Law	1983	77
2	Wally Moses	1943	56
	Luis Aparicio	1959	56
4	Eddie Collins	1917	53
	Luis Aparicio	1961	53
6	Frank Isbell	1901	52
	Gary Redus	1987	52
8	Luis Aparicio	1960	51
	Don Buford	1966	51
	Tim Raines	1991	51
11	John Cangelosi	1986	50
12	Rollie Zeider	1910	49
	Eddie Collins	1923	49
14	Patsy Dougherty	1908	47
	Rollie Zeider	1912	47
16	Sam Mertes	1901	46
	Sam Mertes	1902	46
	Eddie Collins	1915	46
19	Nixey Callahan	1911	45
	Tim Raines	1992	45

Runs Created

1	Frank Thomas	1997	150
2	Joe Jackson	1920	138
3	Frank Thomas	1991	137
4	Frank Thomas	1993	136
	Frank Thomas	1996	136
6	Luke Appling	1936	134
7	Eddie Collins	1920	131
	Zeke Bonura	1936	131
9	Frank Thomas	1995	129
10	Eddie Collins	1915	128
11	Frank Thomas	1992	127
12	Minnie Minoso	1956	126
13	Carl Reynolds	1930	123
	Lu Blue	1931	123
	Dick Allen	1972	123
16	Minnie Minoso	1954	121
17	Al Simmons	1934	119
18	Eddie Collins	1924	118
19	Dummy Hoy	1901	117
20	Two tied at		116

Runs Created/27 Outs
(minimum 3.1 Plate Appearances/Tm Gm)

1	Frank Thomas	1994	11.03
2	Frank Thomas	1997	10.93
3	Luke Appling	1936	10.41
4	Frank Thomas	1996	9.72
5	Joe Jackson	1920	9.53
6	Frank Thomas	1995	9.37
7	Frank Thomas	1991	9.16
8	Frank Thomas	1993	9.14
9	Dick Allen	1972	8.89
10	Zeke Bonura	1937	8.84
11	Jack Fournier	1915	8.59
12	Zeke Bonura	1936	8.56
13	Carl Reynolds	1930	8.54
14	Minnie Minoso	1956	8.48
15	Al Simmons	1934	8.43
16	Eddie Collins	1925	8.34
17	Eddie Collins	1915	8.22
18	Eddie Collins	1920	8.19
19	Frank Thomas	1992	8.15
20	Joe Jackson	1919	8.05

Batting Average
(minimum 3.1 Plate Appearances/Tm Gm)

1	Luke Appling	1936	.388
2	Joe Jackson	1920	.382
3	Eddie Collins	1920	.372
4	Eddie Collins	1923	.360
5	Carl Reynolds	1930	.359
6	Frank Thomas	1994	.353
7	Bibb Falk	1924	.352
8	Joe Jackson	1919	.351
9	Frank Thomas	1996	.349
10	Eddie Collins	1924	.349
11	Luke Appling	1940	.348
12	Frank Thomas	1997	.347
13	Eddie Collins	1925	.346
14	Bibb Falk	1926	.345
15	Zeke Bonura	1937	.345
16	Al Simmons	1934	.344
17	Joe Jackson	1916	.341
18	Happy Felsch	1920	.338
19	Taffy Wright	1940	.337
20	Eddie Collins	1921	.337

On-Base Percentage
(minimum 3.1 Plate Appearances/Tm Gm)

1	Frank Thomas	1994	.487
2	Luke Appling	1936	.473
3	Eddie Collins	1925	.461
4	Eddie Collins	1915	.460
5	Frank Thomas	1996	.459
6	Frank Thomas	1997	.456
7	Eddie Collins	1923	.455
8	Frank Thomas	1995	.454
9	Frank Thomas	1991	.453
10	Joe Jackson	1920	.444
11	Eddie Collins	1924	.441
12	Luke Appling	1949	.439
13	Frank Thomas	1992	.439
14	Eddie Collins	1920	.438
15	Luke Appling	1935	.437
16	Luke Appling	1939	.430
17	Lu Blue	1931	.430
18	Jack Fournier	1915	.429
19	Zeke Bonura	1936	.426
20	Frank Thomas	1993	.426

Slugging Percentage
(minimum 3.1 Plate Appearances/Tm Gm)

1	Frank Thomas	1994	.729
2	Frank Thomas	1996	.626
3	Frank Thomas	1997	.611
4	Frank Thomas	1993	.607
5	Frank Thomas	1995	.606
6	Dick Allen	1972	.603
7	Joe Jackson	1920	.589
8	Carl Reynolds	1930	.584
9	Zeke Bonura	1937	.573
10	Dick Allen	1974	.563
11	Frank Thomas	1991	.553
12	Zeke Bonura	1934	.545
13	Harold Baines	1984	.541
14	Happy Felsch	1920	.540
15	Roy Sievers	1961	.537
16	Frank Thomas	1992	.536
17	Minnie Minoso	1954	.535
18	Roy Sievers	1960	.534
19	Al Simmons	1934	.530
20	Ivan Calderon	1987	.526

Teams: White Sox

White Sox Franchise Pitching Leaders—Single Season

Wins

1	Ed Walsh	1908	40
2	Eddie Cicotte	1919	29
3	Eddie Cicotte	1917	28
4	Doc White	1907	27
	Ed Walsh	1911	27
	Ed Walsh	1912	27
7	Frank Smith	1909	25
	Red Faber	1921	25
9	Clark Griffith	1901	24
	Ed Walsh	1907	24
	Red Faber	1915	24
	Jim Scott	1915	24
	Wilbur Wood	1972	24
	Wilbur Wood	1973	24
	LaMarr Hoyt	1983	24
16	Nick Altrock	1905	23
	Lefty Williams	1919	23
	Red Faber	1920	23
19	Eleven tied at		22

Losses

1	Patsy Flaherty	1903	25
2	Pat Caraway	1931	24
3	Ted Lyons	1933	21
	Stan Bahnsen	1973	21
5	Ed Walsh	1910	20
	Jim Scott	1913	20
	Roy Wilkinson	1921	20
	Ted Lyons	1929	20
	Eddie Smith	1942	20
	Bill Wight	1948	20
	Wilbur Wood	1973	20
	Wilbur Wood	1975	20
13	Joe Benz	1914	19
	Eddie Cicotte	1918	19
	Milt Gaston	1934	19
	Wilbur Wood	1974	19
17	Eight tied at		18

Winning Percentage
(minimum 15 decisions)

1	Sandy Consuegra	1954	.842
2	Eddie Cicotte	1919	.806
3	Clark Griffith	1901	.774
4	Earl Caldwell	1946	.765
5	Rich Dotson	1983	.759
6	Doc White	1906	.750
	Reb Russell	1917	.750
	Monty Stratton	1937	.750
	Bob Shaw	1959	.750
	Eric King	1990	.750
11	Barry Jones	1990	.733
12	Joe Horlen	1967	.731
13	Ed Walsh	1908	.727
	Dick Donovan	1957	.727
15	Britt Burns	1982	.722
16	Virgil Trucks	1953	.714
	Gary Peters	1964	.714
18	LaMarr Hoyt	1983	.706
	Jason Bere	1993	.706
20	Gary Peters	1963	.704

Games

1	Wilbur Wood	1968	88
2	Eddie Fisher	1965	82
3	Bob Locker	1967	77
	Wilbur Wood	1970	77
	Bobby Thigpen	1990	77
6	Wilbur Wood	1969	76
7	Hoyt Wilhelm	1964	73
	Scott Radinsky	1993	73
9	Hoyt Wilhelm	1968	72
	Roberto Hernandez	1996	72
11	Bob Locker	1968	70
	Roberto Hernandez	1993	70
13	Bob James	1985	69
14	Bobby Thigpen	1988	68
	Scott Radinsky	1992	68
16	Gerry Staley	1959	67
	Bobby Thigpen	1991	67
	Scott Radinsky	1991	67
19	Three tied at		66

Games Started

1	Ed Walsh	1908	49
	Wilbur Wood	1972	49
3	Wilbur Wood	1973	48
4	Ed Walsh	1907	46
5	Wilbur Wood	1975	43
6	Wilbur Wood	1971	42
	Stan Bahnsen	1973	42
	Wilbur Wood	1974	42
9	Frank Smith	1909	41
	Ed Walsh	1912	41
	Stan Bahnsen	1972	41
	Jim Kaat	1975	41
13	Lefty Williams	1919	40
	Tom Bradley	1972	40
15	Red Faber	1920	39
	Red Faber	1921	39
	Tom Bradley	1971	39
	Jim Kaat	1974	39
19	Four tied at		38

Complete Games

1	Ed Walsh	1908	42
2	Ed Walsh	1907	37
	Frank Smith	1909	37
4	Frank Owen	1904	34
5	Ed Walsh	1910	33
	Ed Walsh	1911	33
7	Frank Owen	1905	32
	Ed Walsh	1912	32
	Red Faber	1921	32
10	Nick Altrock	1904	31
	Nick Altrock	1905	31
	Red Faber	1922	31
13	Roy Patterson	1901	30
	Eddie Cicotte	1919	30
	Ted Lyons	1927	30
	Thornton Lee	1941	30
17	Six tied at		29

Shutouts

1	Ed Walsh	1908	11
2	Ed Walsh	1906	10
3	Ed Walsh	1909	8
	Reb Russell	1913	8
	Wilbur Wood	1972	8
6	Doc White	1904	7
	Frank Owen	1906	7
	Doc White	1906	7
	Doc White	1907	7
	Frank Smith	1909	7
	Ed Walsh	1910	7
	Jim Scott	1915	7
	Eddie Cicotte	1917	7
	Billy Pierce	1953	7
	Ray Herbert	1963	7
	Wilbur Wood	1971	7
17	Six tied at		6

Saves

1	Bobby Thigpen	1990	57
2	Roberto Hernandez	1993	38
	Roberto Hernandez	1996	38
4	Bobby Thigpen	1988	34
	Bobby Thigpen	1989	34
6	Bob James	1985	32
	Roberto Hernandez	1995	32
8	Ed Farmer	1980	30
	Bobby Thigpen	1991	30
10	Terry Forster	1972	29
11	Hoyt Wilhelm	1964	27
	Roberto Hernandez	1997	27
13	Goose Gossage	1975	26
14	Lerrin LaGrow	1977	25
15	Eddie Fisher	1965	24
	Terry Forster	1974	24
17	Bobby Thigpen	1992	22
18	Hoyt Wilhelm	1963	21
	Wilbur Wood	1970	21
	Salome Barojas	1982	21

Innings Pitched

1	Ed Walsh	1908	464.0
2	Ed Walsh	1907	422.1
3	Ed Walsh	1912	393.0
4	Wilbur Wood	1972	376.2
5	Ed Walsh	1910	369.2
6	Ed Walsh	1911	368.2
7	Frank Smith	1909	365.0
8	Wilbur Wood	1973	359.1
9	Red Faber	1922	353.0
10	Eddie Cicotte	1917	346.2
11	Frank Owen	1905	334.0
	Wilbur Wood	1971	334.0
13	Red Faber	1921	330.2
14	Wilbur Wood	1974	320.1
15	Red Faber	1920	319.0
16	Reb Russell	1913	316.1
17	Nick Altrock	1905	315.2
18	Frank Owen	1904	315.0
19	Roy Patterson	1901	312.1
	Jim Scott	1913	312.1

Walks

1	Vern Kennedy	1936	147
2	Billy Pierce	1950	137
3	Bill Wight	1948	135
4	Vic Frasier	1931	127
5	Vern Kennedy	1937	124
6	Wilson Alvarez	1993	122
7	Early Wynn	1959	119
8	Stan Bahnsen	1973	117
9	Eddie Smith	1941	114
10	Billy Pierce	1949	112
	Early Wynn	1960	112
12	Frank Smith	1907	111
	Bart Johnson	1971	111
	Ken Kravec	1979	111
15	Tommy Thomas	1926	110
	Stan Bahnsen	1974	110
17	Bob Cain	1950	109
18	Frank Smith	1905	107
	Mike Cvengros	1923	107
20	Three tied at		106

Strikeouts

1	Ed Walsh	1908	269
2	Ed Walsh	1910	258
3	Ed Walsh	1911	255
4	Ed Walsh	1912	254
5	Gary Peters	1967	215
6	Wilbur Wood	1971	210
7	Tom Bradley	1972	209
8	Ed Walsh	1907	206
	Tom Bradley	1971	206
10	Gary Peters	1964	205
11	Alex Fernandez	1996	200
12	Wilbur Wood	1973	199
13	Floyd Bannister	1985	198
14	Wilbur Wood	1972	193
	Floyd Bannister	1983	193
16	Billy Pierce	1956	192
17	Jack McDowell	1991	191
18	Gary Peters	1963	189
19	Juan Pizarro	1961	188
20	Billy Pierce	1953	186

Strikeouts/9 Innings
(minimum 1 Inning Pitched/Tm Gm)

1	Juan Pizarro	1961	8.69
2	Floyd Bannister	1985	8.46
3	Jason Bere	1994	8.07
4	Floyd Bannister	1983	7.99
5	Bart Johnson	1971	7.74
6	Juan Pizarro	1962	7.66
7	Wilson Alvarez	1996	7.50
8	Gary Peters	1967	7.44
9	Melido Perez	1990	7.36
10	Joe Cowley	1986	7.32
11	Jack McDowell	1990	7.24
12	Tom Bradley	1972	7.23
13	Billy Pierce	1954	7.06
14	Steve Stone	1973	7.04
15	Alex Fernandez	1995	7.03
16	Gary Peters	1963	7.00
17	Alex Fernandez	1996	6.98
18	Melido Perez	1989	6.92
19	Billy Pierce	1955	6.87
20	Juan Pizarro	1963	6.83

ERA
(minimum 1 Inning Pitched/Tm Gm)

1	Ed Walsh	1910	1.27
2	Ed Walsh	1909	1.41
3	Ed Walsh	1908	1.42
4	Doc White	1906	1.52
5	Eddie Cicotte	1917	1.53
6	Eddie Cicotte	1913	1.58
7	Ed Walsh	1907	1.60
8	Doc White	1909	1.72
9	Doc White	1905	1.76
10	Doc White	1904	1.78
11	Eddie Cicotte	1916	1.78
12	Frank Smith	1909	1.80
13	Eddie Cicotte	1919	1.82
14	Ed Walsh	1906	1.88
15	Joe Horlen	1964	1.88
16	Nick Altrock	1905	1.88
17	Jim Scott	1913	1.90
18	Reb Russell	1913	1.91
19	Wilbur Wood	1971	1.91
20	Red Faber	1917	1.92

Component ERA
(minimum 1 Inning Pitched/Tm Gm)

1	Ed Walsh	1910	1.27
2	Ed Walsh	1908	1.38
3	Eddie Cicotte	1917	1.48
4	Ed Walsh	1909	1.52
5	Doc White	1906	1.52
6	Frank Smith	1908	1.58
7	Reb Russell	1916	1.60
8	Frank Smith	1909	1.60
9	Ed Walsh	1906	1.69
10	Frank Owen	1904	1.70
11	Joe Horlen	1964	1.72
12	Joe Horlen	1967	1.84
13	Doc White	1905	1.86
14	Ed Walsh	1907	1.86
15	Eddie Cicotte	1919	1.87
16	Reb Russell	1913	1.92
17	Frank Owen	1905	1.92
18	Gary Peters	1966	1.96
19	Eddie Fisher	1965	1.97
20	Doc White	1909	1.97

Opponent Average
(minimum 1 Inning Pitched/Tm Gm)

1	Ed Walsh	1910	.187
2	Joe Horlen	1964	.190
3	Gary Peters	1967	.199
4	Eddie Cicotte	1917	.202
5	Frank Smith	1908	.203
6	Ed Walsh	1908	.203
7	Ed Walsh	1909	.203
8	Joe Horlen	1967	.203
9	Eddie Fisher	1965	.205
10	Doc White	1906	.207
11	Frank Smith	1905	.208
12	Tommy John	1968	.212
13	Gary Peters	1966	.212
14	Billy Pierce	1955	.213
15	Frank Smith	1909	.214
16	Frank Owen	1904	.214
17	Ed Walsh	1906	.215
18	Early Wynn	1959	.216
19	Frank Smith	1904	.216
20	Gary Peters	1963	.216

Opponent OBP
(minimum 1 Inning Pitched/Tm Gm)

1	Ed Walsh	1910	.226
2	Ed Walsh	1908	.232
3	Eddie Cicotte	1917	.248
4	Joe Horlen	1964	.248
5	Doc White	1906	.249
6	Ed Walsh	1909	.253
7	Joe Horlen	1967	.253
8	Reb Russell	1916	.254
9	Frank Smith	1908	.256
10	Frank Smith	1909	.257
11	Eddie Fisher	1965	.259
12	Gary Peters	1966	.260
13	LaMarr Hoyt	1983	.260
14	Frank Owen	1904	.261
15	Eddie Cicotte	1919	.261
16	Wilbur Wood	1971	.263
17	Ed Walsh	1906	.263
18	Frank Owen	1905	.267
19	Juan Pizarro	1964	.267
20	Ed Walsh	1907	.270

White Sox Team Capsule

Best Season: *1917*. Two years before they sold out the World Series and became the "Black Sox," the White Sox won a franchise-record 100 games, then went on to beat John McGraw's Giants in a six-game World Series.

Most Fun Season: *1977*. After finishing last in 1976, the Sox weren't expected to do much in '77. Instead they held first place for most of the season with a colorful group of sluggers known as the "South Side Hit Men." The combination of a rare Sox team that won with hitting, plus Bill Veeck's wild promotions and the peerless announcing duo of Harry Caray and Jimmy Piersall, kept Comiskey jumping even after the Sox faded from first in August.

Worst Season: We're tempted to pick 1919, but no one knew about the scandal until a year later. So we'll go with *1932*, when the Sox went 49-102 for a franchise-worst .325 winning percentage. Surprisingly, the '32 club avoided last place, as the Boston Red Sox (43-111) were even worse, but it was still the bleakest period in club history. Despite the presence of Hall of Famers Ted Lyons and Luke Appling, the Sox lost 90 or more games in every season from 1929 to 1932.

Best Player: *Frank Thomas*. Eddie Collins had 12 great years with the Sox, and you can't dismiss Luke Appling, Ted Lyons and Nellie Fox, but Thomas is already the greatest slugger in team history and only needs to avoid injury to rank among the best hitters of all time.

Best Pitcher: Ed Walsh was more spectacular, but the choice is *Ted Lyons*, who won a club-record 260 games while pitching for mostly indifferent teams from 1923 to 1946.

Best Reliever: Others had more saves, but knuckleballer *Hoyt Wilhelm* was all but unhittable in his six seasons with the Sox (1963-68). Averaging 60 appearances a season, Wilhelm posted a 1.92 ERA for the Sox, with a sub-2.00 ERA in five of the six years.

Best Defensive Player: For much of their history, Sox teams were known for their defensive artistry, and there was none greater than Hall of Fame shortstop *Luis Aparicio*. The slick Venezuelan won nine Gold Gloves in his career, seven of them with the Sox.

Hall of Famers: Fourteen men who saw extensive duty with the White Sox are enshrined in Cooperstown. *Luis Aparicio, Luke Appling, Eddie Collins, Red Faber, Nellie Fox, Harry Hooper, Ted Lyons, Ray Schalk, Ed Walsh, Hoyt Wilhelm* and *Early Wynn* made it as players; *Al Lopez* gained entry as a manager; and *Charlie Comiskey* and *Bill Veeck* got in as owners.

Franchise All-Star Team:

C	*Carlton Fisk*		LF	*Minnie Minoso*
1B	*Dick Allen*		CF	*Johnny Mostil*
2B	*Eddie Collins*		RF	*Harold Baines*
3B	*Robin Ventura*		DH	*Frank Thomas*
SS	*Luke Appling*		SP	*Ted Lyons*
			RP	*Hoyt Wilhelm*

Strangest Career: Lefthanded pitcher *Reb Russell* had a remarkable debut with the Sox, going 22-16, 1.91 as a rookie in 1913. Russell never duplicated those figures, but he had seasons of 18 and 15 wins with the Sox before his arm went dead. Four years later, Russell resurfaced as an outfielder with the Pirates, and had one of the most wicked seasons ever for a part-time player: he batted .368, slugged .668 and drove in 75 runs in only 60 games and 220 at-bats. After one more good year as a part-time outfielder, he disappeared for good.

Most Unique Individual Season: *Ted Lyons, 1942*. Toward the end of his lengthy career, Lyons was a once-a-week pitcher, usually working in one of the games of a Sunday doubleheader. In 1942, at the age of 41, he produced this amazing set of statistics: 20 games, 20 starts, 20 complete games, 180.1 innings, a 14-6 record and a league-leading 2.10 ERA. Lyons might have kept that up for a couple of more years, but he spent the next three years in the military.

Biggest Tragedy: The Sox have had their share of tragic careers. The eight banished members of the Black Sox team included Joe Jackson, who was one of the greatest hitters in history, and third sacker Buck Weaver, whose only crime was that he didn't turn in his teammates. Jackie Hayes, Luke Appling's double-play partner in the 1930s, went blind. Infielder Cass Michaels suffered a double skull fracture when beaned in 1954, ending his career at the age of 28. But our choice is pitcher *Monty Stratton*, whose major league career was cut short when he accidentally shot himself in the leg in a hunting accident following the 1938 season. Only 26 years old, Stratton was coming off back-to-back 15-win seasons.

Best Nickname: *"Old Aches and Pains," Luke Appling.*

Best Trade: Frank Lane pulled off some spectacular heists during his career as the White Sox general manager from 1948 to 1955. Probably his best deal was the 1949 trade in which he obtained future Hall of Famer *Nellie Fox* from the A's for backup catcher Joe Tipton.

Worst Trades: In 1959 the White Sox won their first American League pennant in 40 years. Better yet, their farm system had some of the best young talent in baseball. But owner Bill Veeck was convinced the Sox needed more veteran sluggers to stay ahead of the New York Yankees, so in the 1959-60 offseason he traded catcher *Johnny Romano* and first baseman *Norm Cash* to get Minoso back from the Indians; outfielder *Johnny Callison* to the Phillies for journeyman third baseman Gene Freese; and catcher *Earl Battey* and first baseman *Don Mincher* to the Senators for aging slugger Roy Sievers. All the young players Veeck dealt away went on to have excellent major league careers, while Minoso, Freese and Sievers failed to help the Sox come close to another pennant.

Best-Looking Player: *Bob Kennedy*, a strong-armed outfielder and third baseman of the 1930s, '40s and '50s, gets the nod. Kennedy was later a big-league manager and general manager, as well as the father of Terry Kennedy, who caught in the major leagues for 14 seasons.

Ugliest Player: Ever see portly knuckleballer *Wilbur Wood* in the short pants Bill Veeck had the Sox wear on occasion in the late 1970s?

Best Season, Hitter: *Frank Thomas, 1994.* Although limited to 113 games by the strike, Thomas still hit 38 homers, drove in 101 runs, drew 109 walks and led the American League in both on-base (.487) and slugging percentage (.729). He also batted .353. If only they'd played 162 games. . .

Best Season, Pitcher: How can you pick anything but *Ed Walsh, 1908*? Working 66 games and 464 innings—a staggering workload even in 1908—Walsh became the last pitcher to win 40 games, while posting a 1.42 ERA.

Most Overrated Player: *Buck Weaver* may have gotten a raw deal from Judge Landis, but there's little evidence that he was anything more than a slightly above-average player, if that. He has a reputation as a great defensive player, but the stats don't show it: his range figures at third base are nothing to brag about, and he led the American League in errors four times (three of them as a shortstop). As a hitter he's remembered for his .331 average in 1920, his last season, but he batted .300 only one other time, and his lifetime OBP was .307.

Most Underrated Player: After a two-year gap following Weaver's banishment, *Willie Kamm* took over as the Sox third baseman. Did he ever. Kamm was the Brooks Robinson of his day. In one nine-year stretch, he led AL third sackers in range factor eight times. He also topped the AL in fielding average eight times, in putouts seven times, in assists four times, in double plays three times. And he wasn't a bad offensive player either, with a lifetime OBP of .372.

Fan Favorite: No player in franchise history was more popular than *Minnie Minoso,* who was also the first black player in club history.

—Don Zminda

Cleveland Indians (1901-1997)

														Opponent				Park Index	
Year	Lg	Pos	W-L	Pct	GB	Manager	Att.	R	OR	HR	Avg	OBP	Slg	HR	Avg	OBP	ERA	Runs	HR
1901	AL	7th	54-82	.397	29.0	Jimmy McAleer	131,380	667	831	12	.271	.313	.348	22	.288	.361	4.12	95	64
1902	AL	5th	69-67	.507	14.0	Bill Armour	275,395	686	667	33	.289	.336	.389	26	.259	.326	3.28	91	65
1903	AL	3rd	77-63	.550	15.0	Bill Armour	311,280	639	579	31	.265	.308	.373	16	.245	.291	2.73	92	51
1904	AL	4th	86-65	.570	7.5	Bill Armour	264,749	647	482	27	.260	.308	.354	10	.246	.290	2.22	104	77
1905	AL	5th	76-78	.494	19.0	Nap Lajoie/Bill Bradley/Nap Lajoie	316,306	567	587	18	.255	.301	.334	23	.245	.300	2.85	99	78
1906	AL	3rd	89-64	.582	5.0	Nap Lajoie	325,733	663	482	12	.279	.325	.357	16	.232	.289	2.09	101	64
1907	AL	4th	85-67	.559	8.0	Nap Lajoie	382,046	530	525	11	.241	.295	.310	8	.243	.301	2.26	85	88
1908	AL	2nd	90-64	.584	0.5	Nap Lajoie	422,262	568	457	18	.239	.297	.309	16	.228	.279	2.02	106	70
1909	AL	6th	71-82	.464	27.5	Nap Lajoie/Deacon McGuire	354,627	493	532	10	.241	.288	.313	9	.237	.291	2.40	105	12
1910	AL	5th	71-81	.467	32.0	Deacon McGuire	293,456	548	657	9	.244	.297	.308	10	.262	.331	2.88	105	47
1911	AL	3rd	80-73	.523	22.0	Deacon McGuire/George Stovall	406,296	691	712	20	.282	.333	.369	17	.268	.347	3.36	104	119
1912	AL	5th	75-78	.490	30.5	Harry Davis/Joe Birmingham	336,844	677	681	12	.273	.333	.353	15	.272	.346	3.30	102	63
1913	AL	3rd	86-66	.566	9.5	Joe Birmingham	541,000	633	536	16	.268	.331	.348	19	.244	.315	2.54	113	59
1914	AL	8th	51-102	.333	48.5	Joe Birmingham	185,997	538	709	10	.245	.310	.312	10	.268	.357	3.21	108	50
1915	AL	7th	57-95	.375	44.5	Joe Birmingham/Lee Fohl	159,285	539	670	20	.240	.312	.317	18	.256	.329	3.13	109	71
1916	AL	6th	77-77	.500	14.0	Lee Fohl	492,106	630	602	16	.250	.324	.331	16	.264	.328	2.90	100	68
1917	AL	3rd	88-66	.571	12.0	Lee Fohl	477,298	584	543	13	.245	.324	.322	17	.246	.309	2.52	127	76
1918	AL	2nd	73-54	.575	2.5	Lee Fohl	295,515	504	447	9	.260	.344	.341	9	.262	.319	2.64	120	43
1919	AL	2nd	84-55	.604	3.5	Lee Fohl/Tris Speaker	538,135	636	537	24	.278	.354	.381	19	.266	.323	2.94	112	60
1920	AL	1st	98-56	.636	—	Tris Speaker	912,832	857	642	35	.303	.376	.417	31	.275	.329	3.41	103	81
1921	AL	2nd	94-60	.610	4.5	Tris Speaker	748,705	925	712	42	.308	.383	.430	43	.288	.344	3.90	95	42
1922	AL	4th	78-76	.506	16.0	Tris Speaker	528,145	768	817	32	.292	.364	.398	58	.296	.356	4.59	109	52
1923	AL	3rd	82-71	.536	16.5	Tris Speaker	558,856	888	746	59	.301	.381	.420	36	.284	.346	3.91	104	64
1924	AL	6th	67-86	.438	24.5	Tris Speaker	481,905	755	814	41	.296	.361	.399	43	.299	.363	4.40	95	61
1925	AL	6th	70-84	.455	27.5	Tris Speaker	419,005	782	817	52	.297	.361	.399	41	.296	.359	4.49	117	85
1926	AL	2nd	88-66	.571	3.0	Tris Speaker	627,426	738	612	27	.289	.349	.386	49	.271	.334	3.40	93	60
1927	AL	6th	66-87	.431	43.5	Jack McCallister	373,138	668	766	26	.283	.337	.379	37	.295	.361	4.27	94	49
1928	AL	7th	62-92	.403	39.0	Roger Peckinpaugh	375,907	674	830	34	.285	.336	.382	52	.296	.361	4.47	116	41
1929	AL	3rd	81-71	.533	24.0	Roger Peckinpaugh	536,210	717	736	62	.294	.353	.417	56	.295	.357	4.05	99	69
1930	AL	4th	81-73	.526	21.0	Roger Peckinpaugh	528,657	890	915	72	.304	.364	.431	85	.305	.368	4.88	114	104
1931	AL	4th	78-76	.506	30.0	Roger Peckinpaugh	483,027	885	833	71	.296	.363	.419	64	.286	.355	4.63	115	111
1932	AL	4th	87-65	.572	19.0	Roger Peckinpaugh	468,953	845	747	78	.285	.356	.413	70	.273	.329	4.12	118	87
1933	AL	4th	75-76	.497	23.5	R. Peckinpaugh/B. Falk/W. Johnson	387,936	654	669	50	.261	.321	.360	60	.264	.325	3.71	106	69
1934	AL	3rd	85-69	.552	16.0	Walter Johnson	391,338	814	763	100	.287	.353	.423	70	.275	.349	4.28	100	85
1935	AL	3rd	82-71	.536	12.0	Walter Johnson/Steve O'Neill	397,615	776	739	93	.284	.341	.421	68	.278	.335	4.15	92	105
1936	AL	5th	80-74	.519	22.5	Steve O'Neill	500,391	921	862	123	.304	.364	.461	73	.289	.362	4.83	113	112
1937	AL	4th	83-71	.539	19.0	Steve O'Neill	564,849	817	768	103	.280	.352	.423	61	.285	.356	4.39	90	73
1938	AL	3rd	86-66	.566	13.0	Ossie Vitt	652,006	847	782	113	.281	.350	.434	100	.268	.355	4.60	94	72
1939	AL	3rd	87-67	.565	20.5	Ossie Vitt	563,926	797	700	85	.280	.350	.413	75	.267	.344	4.08	90	65
1940	AL	2nd	89-65	.578	1.0	Ossie Vitt	902,576	710	637	101	.265	.332	.398	86	.254	.324	3.63	79	47
1941	AL	4th	75-79	.487	26.0	Roger Peckinpaugh	745,948	677	668	103	.256	.323	.393	71	.259	.344	3.90	97	85
1942	AL	4th	75-79	.487	28.0	Lou Boudreau	459,447	590	659	50	.253	.320	.345	61	.254	.327	3.59	83	64
1943	AL	3rd	82-71	.536	15.5	Lou Boudreau	438,894	600	577	55	.255	.329	.350	52	.239	.322	3.15	77	52
1944	AL	5th	72-82	.468	17.0	Lou Boudreau	475,272	643	677	70	.266	.331	.372	40	.265	.344	3.65	104	64
1945	AL	5th	73-72	.503	11.0	Lou Boudreau	558,182	557	548	65	.255	.326	.359	39	.257	.328	3.31	92	60
1946	AL	6th	68-86	.442	36.0	Lou Boudreau	1,057,289	537	638	79	.245	.313	.356	84	.245	.331	3.62	73	60
1947	AL	4th	80-74	.519	17.0	Lou Boudreau	1,521,978	687	588	112	.259	.324	.385	94	.240	.325	3.44	87	100
1948	AL	1st	97-58	.626	—	Lou Boudreau	2,620,627	840	568	155	.282	.360	.431	82	.239	.323	3.22	90	98
1949	AL	3rd	89-65	.578	8.0	Lou Boudreau	2,233,771	675	574	112	.260	.339	.384	82	.247	.329	3.36	87	113
1950	AL	4th	92-62	.597	6.0	Lou Boudreau	1,727,464	806	654	164	.269	.358	.422	120	.248	.333	3.75	88	127
1951	AL	2nd	93-61	.604	5.0	Al Lopez	1,704,984	696	594	140	.256	.336	.389	86	.245	.323	3.38	80	109
1952	AL	2nd	93-61	.604	2.0	Al Lopez	1,444,607	763	606	148	.262	.342	.404	94	.241	.316	3.32	76	91
1953	AL	2nd	92-62	.597	8.5	Al Lopez	1,069,176	770	627	160	.270	.349	.410	92	.253	.325	3.64	87	114
1954	AL	1st	111-43	.721	—	Al Lopez	1,335,472	746	504	156	.262	.341	.403	89	.232	.297	2.78	101	123
1955	AL	2nd	93-61	.604	3.0	Al Lopez	1,221,780	698	601	148	.257	.349	.394	111	.245	.319	3.39	104	121
1956	AL	2nd	88-66	.571	9.0	Al Lopez	865,467	712	581	153	.244	.335	.381	116	.238	.314	3.32	94	96
1957	AL	6th	76-77	.497	21.5	Kerby Farrell	722,256	682	722	140	.252	.329	.382	130	.261	.340	4.06	108	114
1958	AL	4th	77-76	.503	14.5	Bobby Bragan/Joe Gordon	663,805	694	635	161	.258	.325	.403	123	.249	.328	3.73	88	87
1959	AL	2nd	89-65	.578	5.0	Joe Gordon	1,497,976	745	646	167	.263	.321	.408	148	.239	.323	3.75	91	101
1960	AL	4th	76-78	.494	21.0	Joe Gordon/Jo-Jo White/Jimmy Dykes	950,985	667	693	127	.267	.325	.388	161	.252	.334	3.95	96	103
1961	AL	5th	78-83	.484	30.5	Jimmy Dykes/Mel Harder	725,547	737	752	150	.266	.326	.406	178	.258	.331	4.15	93	109
1962	AL	6th	80-82	.494	16.0	Mel McGaha/Mel Harder	716,076	682	745	180	.245	.312	.388	174	.258	.331	4.14	96	119
1963	AL	5th	79-83	.488	25.5	Birdie Tebbetts	562,507	635	702	169	.239	.301	.381	176	.249	.309	3.79	94	103
1964	AL	6th	79-83	.488	20.0	George Strickland/Birdie Tebbetts	653,293	689	693	164	.247	.312	.380	154	.255	.324	3.75	108	109
1965	AL	5th	87-75	.537	15.0	Birdie Tebbetts	934,786	663	613	156	.250	.315	.379	129	.232	.298	3.30	95	105
1966	AL	5th	81-81	.500	17.0	Birdie Tebbetts/George Strickland	903,359	574	586	155	.237	.297	.360	129	.232	.297	3.23	101	107
1967	AL	8th	75-87	.463	17.0	Joe Adcock	662,980	559	613	131	.235	.293	.359	120	.231	.305	3.25	101	137
1968	AL	3rd	86-75	.534	16.5	Alvin Dark	857,994	516	504	75	.234	.293	.327	98	.206	.285	2.66	100	115
1969	AL	6th-E	62-99	.385	46.5	Alvin Dark	619,970	573	717	119	.237	.307	.345	134	.248	.335	3.94	91	84
1970	AL	5th-E	76-86	.469	32.0	Alvin Dark	729,752	649	675	183	.249	.314	.394	163	.247	.335	3.91	133	215
1971	AL	6th-E	60-102	.370	43.0	Alvin Dark/Johnny Lipon	591,361	543	747	109	.238	.300	.342	154	.252	.348	4.28	118	158
1972	AL	5th-E	72-84	.462	14.0	Ken Aspromonte	626,354	472	519	91	.234	.293	.330	123	.237	.311	2.92	115	186
1973	AL	6th-E	71-91	.438	26.0	Ken Aspromonte	615,107	680	826	158	.256	.315	.387	172	.271	.343	4.58	98	139
1974	AL	4th-E	77-85	.475	14.0	Ken Aspromonte	1,114,262	662	694	131	.255	.311	.370	138	.260	.320	3.80	103	156
1975	AL	4th-E	79-80	.497	15.5	Frank Robinson	977,039	688	703	153	.261	.327	.392	136	.258	.333	3.84	99	130
1976	AL	4th-E	81-78	.509	16.0	Frank Robinson	948,776	615	615	85	.263	.321	.359	80	.255	.324	3.47	98	103
1977	AL	5th-E	71-90	.441	28.5	Frank Robinson/Jeff Torborg	900,365	676	739	100	.269	.334	.380	136	.261	.329	4.10	96	102
1978	AL	6th-E	69-90	.434	29.0	Jeff Torborg	800,584	639	694	106	.261	.323	.379	100	.261	.332	3.97	87	76
1979	AL	6th-E	81-80	.503	22.0	Jeff Torborg/Dave Garcia	1,011,644	760	805	138	.258	.340	.384	138	.272	.339	4.57	114	134
1980	AL	6th-E	79-81	.494	23.0	Dave Garcia	1,033,827	738	807	89	.277	.350	.381	137	.275	.341	4.68	107	118
1981	AL	6th-E	26-24	.520	5.0	Dave Garcia													
	AL	5th-E	26-27	.491	5.0	Dave Garcia	661,395	431	442	39	.263	.327	.351	67	.274	.330	3.88	86	87

Year	Lg	Pos	W-L	Pct	GB	Manager	Att.	R	OR	HR	Avg	OBP	Slg	Opponent HR	Opponent Avg	Opponent OBP	ERA	Park Index Runs	Park Index HR
1982	AL	6th-E	78-84	.481	17.0	Dave Garcia	1,044,021	683	748	109	.262	.341	.373	122	.257	.327	4.12	101	96
1983	AL	7th-E	70-92	.432	28.0	Mike Ferraro/Pat Corrales	768,941	704	785	86	.265	.338	.369	120	.275	.339	4.43	113	137
1984	AL	6th-E	75-87	.463	29.0	Pat Corrales	734,079	761	766	123	.265	.335	.384	141	.269	.332	4.26	116	112
1985	AL	7th-E	60-102	.370	39.5	Pat Corrales	655,181	729	861	116	.265	.324	.385	170	.281	.346	4.91	91	81
1986	AL	5th-E	84-78	.519	11.5	Pat Corrales	1,471,805	831	841	157	.284	.337	.430	167	.273	.346	4.58	98	100
1987	AL	7th-E	61-101	.377	37.0	Pat Corrales/Doc Edwards	1,077,898	742	957	187	.263	.324	.422	219	.279	.351	5.28	111	109
1988	AL	6th-E	78-84	.481	11.0	Doc Edwards	1,411,610	666	731	134	.261	.314	.387	120	.270	.326	4.16	104	81
1989	AL	6th-E	73-89	.451	16.0	Doc Edwards/John Hart	1,285,542	604	654	127	.245	.310	.365	107	.257	.313	3.65	107	84
1990	AL	4th-E	77-85	.475	11.0	John McNamara	1,225,240	732	737	110	.267	.324	.391	163	.270	.334	4.26	100	102
1991	AL	7th-E	57-105	.352	34.0	John McNamara/Mike Hargrove	1,051,863	576	759	79	.254	.313	.350	110	.276	.329	4.23	92	49
1992	AL	4th-E	76-86	.469	20.0	Mike Hargrove	1,224,094	674	746	127	.266	.323	.383	159	.268	.336	4.11	116	120
1993	AL	6th-E	76-86	.469	19.0	Mike Hargrove	2,177,908	790	813	141	.275	.335	.409	182	.281	.351	4.58	85	89
1994	AL	2nd-C	66-47	.584	1.0	Mike Hargrove	1,995,174	679	562	167	.290	.351	.484	94	.275	.346	4.36	108	123
1995	AL	1st-C	100-44	.694	—	Mike Hargrove	2,842,725	840	607	207	.291	.361	.479	135	.255	.320	3.83	87	87
1996	AL	1st-C	99-62	.615	—	Mike Hargrove	3,318,174	952	769	218	.293	.369	.475	173	.271	.331	4.34	105	84
1997	AL	1st-C	86-75	.534	—	Mike Hargrove	3,275,899	868	815	220	.286	.358	.467	181	.276	.347	4.73	97	85

Team Nicknames: Cleveland Blues 1901-1902, Cleveland Bronchos 1903-1915, Cleveland Indians 1916-1997.

Team Ballparks: League Park I (Cle) 1901-1909, League Park II (Cle) 1910-1931, League Park II (Cle) & Municipal Stadium (Cle)/Cleveland Stadium (shared) 1932-1946, Municipal Stadium (Cle)/Cleveland Stadium 1947-1993, Jacobs Field 1994-1997.

Cleveland Indians Individual Season Batting Leaders

Year	Batting Average		On-Base Percentage		Slugging Percentage		Home Runs		RBI		Stolen Bases	
1901	Ollie Pickering	.309	Ollie Pickering	.383	Bill Bradley	.403	Erve Beck	6	Erve Beck	79	Ollie Pickering	36
1902	Charlie Hickman	.378	Charlie Hickman	.399	Charlie Hickman	.559	Bill Bradley	11	Charlie Hickman	94	Harry Bay	22
											Ollie Pickering	
1903	Nap Lajoie	.344	Nap Lajoie	.379	Nap Lajoie	.518	Charlie Hickman	12	Charlie Hickman	97	Harry Bay	45
1904	Nap Lajoie	.376	Nap Lajoie	.413	Nap Lajoie	.546	Bill Bradley	6	Nap Lajoie	102	Harry Bay	38
							Elmer Flick				Elmer Flick	
1905	Elmer Flick	.306	Elmer Flick	.382	Elmer Flick	.462	Elmer Flick	4	Terry Turner	72	Harry Bay	36
							Terry Turner					
1906	Nap Lajoie	.355	Nap Lajoie	.392	Nap Lajoie	.465	Bunk Congalton	3	Nap Lajoie	91	Elmer Flick	39
1907	Elmer Flick	.302	Elmer Flick	.386	Elmer Flick	.412	Nig Clarke	3	Nap Lajoie	63	Elmer Flick	41
							Elmer Flick					
1908	George Stovall	.292	Nap Lajoie	.352	George Stovall	.380	Bill Hinchman	6	Nap Lajoie	74	Josh Clarke	37
1909	Nap Lajoie	.324	Nap Lajoie	.378	Nap Lajoie	.431	Bill Hinchman	2	Bill Hinchman	53	George Stovall	25
							George Stovall					
1910	Nap Lajoie	.384	Nap Lajoie	.445	Nap Lajoie	.514	Nap Lajoie	4	Nap Lajoie	76	Terry Turner	31
1911	Joe Jackson	.408	Joe Jackson	.468	Joe Jackson	.590	Joe Jackson	7	Joe Jackson	83	Joe Jackson	41
1912	Joe Jackson	.395	Joe Jackson	.458	Joe Jackson	.579	Joe Jackson	3	Joe Jackson	90	Joe Jackson	35
									Nap Lajoie			
1913	Joe Jackson	.373	Joe Jackson	.460	Joe Jackson	.551	Joe Jackson	7	Joe Jackson	71	Ray Chapman	29
1914	Joe Jackson	.338	Joe Jackson	.399	Joe Jackson	.464	Joe Jackson	3	Joe Jackson	53	Ray Chapman	24
1915	Ray Chapman	.270	Ray Chapman	.353	Ray Chapman	.370	Braggo Roth	4	Ray Chapman	67	Ray Chapman	36
									Elmer Smith			
1916	Tris Speaker	.386	Tris Speaker	.470	Tris Speaker	.502	Jack Graney	5	Tris Speaker	79	Tris Speaker	35
1917	Tris Speaker	.352	Tris Speaker	.432	Tris Speaker	.486	Jack Graney	3	Braggo Roth	72	Ray Chapman	52
							Elmer Smith					
1918	Tris Speaker	.318	Tris Speaker	.403	Tris Speaker	.435	Joe Wood	5	Joe Wood	66	Braggo Roth	35
1919	Ray Chapman	.300	Tris Speaker	.395	Elmer Smith	.438	Elmer Smith	9	Larry Gardner	79	Doc Johnston	21
1920	Tris Speaker	.388	Tris Speaker	.483	Tris Speaker	.562	Elmer Smith	12	Larry Gardner	118	Ray Chapman	13
											Doc Johnston	
1921	Tris Speaker	.362	Tris Speaker	.439	Tris Speaker	.538	Elmer Smith	16	Larry Gardner	115	Bill Wambsganss	13
1922	Tris Speaker	.378	Tris Speaker	.474	Tris Speaker	.606	Tris Speaker	11	Joe Wood	92	Bill Wambsganss	17
1923	Tris Speaker	.380	Tris Speaker	.469	Tris Speaker	.610	Tris Speaker	17	Tris Speaker	130	Charlie Jamieson	19
1924	Charlie Jamieson	.359	Tris Speaker	.432	Tris Speaker	.510	Tris Speaker	9	Joe Sewell	104	Charlie Jamieson	21
1925	Tris Speaker	.389	Tris Speaker	.479	Tris Speaker	.578	Tris Speaker	12	Joe Sewell	98	George Burns	16
1926	George Burns	.358	Tris Speaker	.408	George Burns	.494	Tris Speaker	7	George Burns	114	Joe Sewell	17
1927	George Burns	.319	Charlie Jamieson	.394	George Burns	.435	Johnny Hodapp	5	Joe Sewell	92	George Burns	13
1928	Joe Sewell	.323	Joe Sewell	.391	Johnny Hodapp	.432	George Burns	5	Johnny Hodapp	73	Carl Lind	8
1929	Lew Fonseca	.369	Lew Fonseca	.426	Earl Averill	.534	Earl Averill	18	Lew Fonseca	103	Lew Fonseca	19
1930	Johnny Hodapp	.354	Dick Porter	.420	Eddie Morgan	.601	Eddie Morgan	26	Eddie Morgan	136	Earl Averill	10
1931	Eddie Morgan	.351	Eddie Morgan	.451	Earl Averill	.576	Earl Averill	32	Earl Averill	143	Willie Kamm	13
1932	Bill Cissell	.320	Eddie Morgan	.402	Earl Averill	.569	Earl Averill	32	Earl Averill	124	Bill Cissell	18
1933	Earl Averill	.301	Earl Averill	.363	Earl Averill	.474	Earl Averill	11	Earl Averill	92	Willie Kamm	7
1934	Hal Trosky	.330	Earl Averill	.414	Hal Trosky	.598	Hal Trosky	35	Hal Trosky	142	Frankie Pytlak	11
1935	Joe Vosmik	.348	Joe Vosmik	.408	Joe Vosmik	.537	Hal Trosky	26	Hal Trosky	113	Odell Hale	15
1936	Earl Averill	.378	Earl Averill	.438	Hal Trosky	.644	Hal Trosky	42	Hal Trosky	162	Roy Hughes	20
1937	Moose Solters	.323	Bruce Campbell	.392	Hal Trosky	.547	Hal Trosky	32	Hal Trosky	128	Lyn Lary	18
1938	Jeff Heath	.343	Earl Averill	.429	Jeff Heath	.602	Ken Keltner	26	Ken Keltner	113	Lyn Lary	23
1939	Hal Trosky	.335	Hal Trosky	.405	Hal Trosky	.589	Hal Trosky	25	Hal Trosky	104	Ben Chapman	18
1940	Roy Weatherly	.303	Hal Trosky	.392	Hal Trosky	.529	Hal Trosky	25	Lou Boudreau	101	Ben Chapman	13
1941	Jeff Heath	.340	Jeff Heath	.396	Jeff Heath	.586	Jeff Heath	24	Jeff Heath	123	Jeff Heath	18
1942	Les Fleming	.292	Les Fleming	.412	Jeff Heath	.442	Les Fleming	14	Les Fleming	82	Oris Hockett	12
1943	Roy Cullenbine	.289	Roy Cullenbine	.407	Jeff Heath	.481	Jeff Heath	18	Jeff Heath	79	Oris Hockett	13
1944	Lou Boudreau	.327	Lou Boudreau	.406	Ken Keltner	.466	Roy Cullenbine	16	Ken Keltner	91	Lou Boudreau	11
1945	Dutch Meyer	.292	Dutch Meyer	.342	Dutch Meyer	.418	Jeff Heath	15	Jeff Heath	61	Felix Mackiewicz	5
1946	Hank Edwards	.301	Hank Edwards	.361	Hank Edwards	.509	Pat Seerey	26	Lou Boudreau	62	George Case	28
									Pat Seerey			
1947	Dale Mitchell	.316	Lou Boudreau	.388	Joe Gordon	.496	Joe Gordon	29	Joe Gordon	93	Joe Gordon	7
1948	Lou Boudreau	.355	Lou Boudreau	.453	Lou Boudreau	.534	Joe Gordon	32	Joe Gordon	124	Dale Mitchell	13
1949	Dale Mitchell	.317	Larry Doby	.389	Larry Doby	.468	Larry Doby	24	Larry Doby	85	Larry Doby	10
											Dale Mitchell	
1950	Larry Doby	.326	Larry Doby	.442	Larry Doby	.545	Al Rosen	37	Al Rosen	116	Larry Doby	8
1951	Bobby Avila	.304	Larry Doby	.428	Larry Doby	.512	Luke Easter	27	Luke Easter	103	Bobby Avila	14
1952	Dale Mitchell	.323	Al Rosen	.387	Larry Doby	.541	Larry Doby	32	Al Rosen	105	Bobby Avila	12
1953	Al Rosen	.336	Al Rosen	.422	Al Rosen	.613	Al Rosen	43	Al Rosen	145	Bobby Avila	10
1954	Bobby Avila	.341	Al Rosen	.404	Larry Doby	.506	Larry Doby	32	Larry Doby	126	Bobby Avila	9
1955	Al Smith	.306	Al Smith	.407	Larry Doby	.505	Larry Doby	26	Al Rosen	81	Al Smith	11
1956	Al Smith	.274	Al Smith	.378	Vic Wertz	.509	Vic Wertz	32	Vic Wertz	106	Bobby Avila	17
1957	Gene Woodling	.321	Gene Woodling	.408	Gene Woodling	.521	Vic Wertz	28	Vic Wertz	105	Al Smith	12
1958	Rocky Colavito	.303	Rocky Colavito	.405	Rocky Colavito	.620	Rocky Colavito	41	Rocky Colavito	113	Minnie Minoso	14
1959	Minnie Minoso	.302	Minnie Minoso	.377	Rocky Colavito	.512	Rocky Colavito	42	Rocky Colavito	111	Vic Power	9
1960	Harvey Kuenn	.308	Harvey Kuenn	.379	Tito Francona	.460	Woodie Held	21	Vic Power	84	Jimmy Piersall	18
1961	Jimmy Piersall	.322	Jimmy Piersall	.378	John Romano	.483	Willie Kirkland	27	Willie Kirkland	95	Johnny Temple	9
1962	Tito Francona	.272	John Romano	.363	John Romano	.479	John Romano	25	John Romano	81	Willie Kirkland	9
1963	Max Alvis	.274	Max Alvis	.324	Max Alvis	.460	Max Alvis	22	Max Alvis	67	3 tied with	9
1964	Vic Davalillo	.270	Dick Howser	.335	Leon Wagner	.434	Leon Wagner	31	Leon Wagner	100	Vic Davalillo	21
1965	Vic Davalillo	.301	Rocky Colavito	.383	Leon Wagner	.495	Leon Wagner	28	Rocky Colavito	108	Vic Davalillo	26
1966	Leon Wagner	.279	Rocky Colavito	.336	Leon Wagner	.441	Rocky Colavito	30	Fred Whitfield	78	Chuck Hinton	10
											Chico Salmon	
1967	Max Alvis	.256	Larry Brown	.308	Max Alvis	.403	Max Alvis	21	Max Alvis	70	Chico Salmon	10
1968	Jose Cardenal	.257	Jose Cardenal	.305	Tony Horton	.411	Tony Horton	14	Tony Horton	59	Jose Cardenal	40
1969	Tony Horton	.278	Ken Harrelson	.341	Tony Horton	.461	Ken Harrelson	27	Tony Horton	93	Jose Cardenal	36
							Tony Horton					
1970	Vada Pinson	.286	Roy Foster	.357	Vada Pinson	.481	Graig Nettles	26	Vada Pinson	82	Vada Pinson	7
1971	Ted Uhlaender	.288	Graig Nettles	.350	Graig Nettles	.435	Graig Nettles	28	Graig Nettles	86	Vada Pinson	25
1972	Chris Chambliss	.292	Chris Chambliss	.327	Chris Chambliss	.397	Graig Nettles	17	Graig Nettles	70	Tom McCraw	12

Year	Batting Average		On-Base Percentage		Slugging Percentage		Home Runs		RBI		Stolen Bases	
1973	Chris Chambliss	.273	Chris Chambliss	.342	Charlie Spikes	.409	Charlie Spikes	23	Charlie Spikes	73	Walt Williams	9
1974	Oscar Gamble	.291	Oscar Gamble	.363	Oscar Gamble	.469	Charlie Spikes	22	Charlie Spikes	80	John Lowenstein	36
1975	Boog Powell	.297	Boog Powell	.377	Boog Powell	.524	Boog Powell	27	George Hendrick Boog Powell	86	Duane Kuiper Rick Manning	19
1976	Rico Carty	.310	Rico Carty	.379	George Hendrick	.448	George Hendrick	25	Rico Carty	83	Rick Manning	16
1977	Buddy Bell	.292	Andre Thornton	.378	Andre Thornton	.527	Andre Thornton	28	Rico Carty	80	Jim Norris	26
1978	Duane Kuiper	.283	Andre Thornton	.377	Andre Thornton	.516	Andre Thornton	33	Andre Thornton	105	Jim Norris	12
1979	Toby Harrah	.279	Toby Harrah	.389	Bobby Bonds	.463	Andre Thornton	26	Andre Thornton	93	Bobby Bonds	34
1980	Miguel Dilone	.341	Mike Hargrove	.415	Joe Charboneau	.488	Joe Charboneau	23	Joe Charboneau	87	Miguel Dilone	61
1981	Mike Hargrove	.317	Mike Hargrove	.424	Mike Hargrove	.401	Bo Diaz	7	Mike Hargrove	49	Miguel Dilone	29
1982	Toby Harrah	.304	Toby Harrah	.398	Toby Harrah	.490	Andre Thornton	32	Andre Thornton	116	Miguel Dilone	33
1983	Mike Hargrove	.286	Mike Hargrove	.388	Andre Thornton	.439	Gorman Thomas Andre Thornton	17	Julio Franco	80	Julio Franco	32
1984	Pat Tabler	.290	Andre Thornton	.366	Andre Thornton	.484	Andre Thornton	33	Andre Thornton	99	Brett Butler	52
1985	Brett Butler	.311	Brett Butler	.377	Brett Butler	.431	Andre Thornton	22	Julio Franco	90	Brett Butler	47
1986	Pat Tabler	.326	Pat Tabler	.368	Joe Carter	.514	Joe Carter	29	Joe Carter	121	Brett Butler	32
1987	Julio Franco	.319	Brett Butler	.399	Brook Jacoby	.541	Cory Snyder	33	Joe Carter	106	Brett Butler	33
1988	Julio Franco	.303	Julio Franco	.361	Cory Snyder	.483	Joe Carter	27	Joe Carter	98	Joe Carter	27
1989	Jerry Browne	.299	Jerry Browne	.370	Joe Carter	.465	Joe Carter	35	Joe Carter	105	Jerry Browne	14
1990	Chris James	.299	Brook Jacoby	.365	Candy Maldonado	.446	Candy Maldonado	22	Candy Maldonado	95	Alex Cole	40
1991	Carlos Baerga	.288	Carlos Baerga	.346	Carlos Baerga	.398	Albert Belle	28	Albert Belle	95	Alex Cole	27
1992	Carlos Baerga	.312	Kenny Lofton	.362	Albert Belle	.477	Albert Belle	34	Albert Belle	112	Kenny Lofton	66
1993	Kenny Lofton	.325	Kenny Lofton	.408	Albert Belle	.552	Albert Belle	38	Albert Belle	129	Kenny Lofton	70
1994	Albert Belle	.357	Albert Belle	.438	Albert Belle	.714	Albert Belle	36	Albert Belle	101	Kenny Lofton	60
1995	Eddie Murray	.323	Jim Thome	.438	Albert Belle	.690	Albert Belle	50	Albert Belle	126	Kenny Lofton	54
1996	Julio Franco	.322	Jim Thome	.450	Albert Belle	.623	Albert Belle	48	Albert Belle	148	Kenny Lofton	75
1997	David Justice	.329	Jim Thome	.423	David Justice	.596	Jim Thome	40	Matt Williams	105	Omar Vizquel	43

Cleveland Indians Individual Season Pitching Leaders

Year	ERA		Baserunners/9 IP		Innings Pitched		Strikeouts		Wins		Saves	
1901	Earl Moore	2.90	Earl Moore	12.5	Pete Dowling	256.1	Pete Dowling / Earl Moore	99	Earl Moore	16	Bill Hoffer	3
1902	Bill Bernhard	2.20	Bill Bernhard	8.6	Earl Moore	293.0	Addie Joss	106	3 tied with	17	3 tied with	1
1903	Earl Moore	1.74	Addie Joss	8.9	Addie Joss	283.2	Earl Moore	148	Earl Moore	19	Earl Moore	1
1904	Addie Joss	1.59	Addie Joss	9.2	Bill Bernhard	320.2	Earl Moore	139	Bill Bernhard	23	7 tied with	0
1905	Addie Joss	2.01	Addie Joss	9.6	Addie Joss	286.0	Addie Joss	132	Addie Joss	20	9 tied with	0
1906	Addie Joss	1.72	Addie Joss	8.5	Otto Hess	333.2	Otto Hess	167	Bob Rhoads	22	Otto Hess	3
1907	Addie Joss	1.83	Addie Joss	9.0	Addie Joss	338.2	Addie Joss	127	Addie Joss	27	Addie Joss	2
1908	Addie Joss	1.16	Addie Joss	7.3	Addie Joss	325.0	Glenn Liebhardt	146	Addie Joss	24	Slim Foster / Addie Joss	2
1909	Addie Joss	1.71	Addie Joss	8.6	Cy Young	294.2	Heinie Berger	162	Cy Young	19	Heinie Berger / Fred Winchell	1
1910	Cy Young	2.53	Cy Young	9.9	Cy Falkenberg	256.2	Cy Falkenberg	107	Cy Falkenberg	14	Elmer Koestner	2
1911	Vean Gregg	1.80	Vean Gregg	9.9	Vean Gregg	244.1	Gene Krapp	130	Vean Gregg	23	Fred Blanding	2
1912	Vean Gregg	2.59	Vean Gregg	11.3	Vean Gregg	271.1	Vean Gregg	184	Vean Gregg	20	Vean Gregg	2
1913	Willie Mitchell	1.87	Willie Mitchell	10.3	Vean Gregg	285.1	Cy Falkenberg	166	Cy Falkenberg / Vean Gregg	23	Vean Gregg	3
1914	Bill Steen	2.60	Bill Steen	12.2	Willie Mitchell	257.0	Willie Mitchell	179	Willie Mitchell	12	3 tied with	1
1915	Guy Morton	2.14	Guy Morton	9.4	Guy Morton	240.0	Willie Mitchell	149	Guy Morton	16	Sad Sam Jones	5
1916	Jim Bagby	2.61	Jim Bagby	10.8	Jim Bagby	272.2	Jim Bagby / Guy Morton	88	Jim Bagby	16	Jim Bagby	5
1917	Stan Coveleski	1.81	Stan Coveleski	8.9	Jim Bagby	320.2	Stan Coveleski	133	Jim Bagby	23	Jim Bagby	7
1918	Stan Coveleski	1.82	Stan Coveleski	9.9	Stan Coveleski	311.0	Guy Morton	123	Stan Coveleski	22	Jim Bagby	6
1919	Stan Coveleski	2.52	Stan Coveleski	10.7	Stan Coveleski	296.0	Stan Coveleski	118	Stan Coveleski	24	Stan Coveleski	4
1920	Stan Coveleski	2.49	Stan Coveleski	10.1	Jim Bagby	339.2	Stan Coveleski	133	Jim Bagby	31	Stan Coveleski / Dick Niehaus	2
1921	Stan Coveleski	3.36	Stan Coveleski	12.2	Stan Coveleski	316.0	Stan Coveleski	99	Stan Coveleski	23	Jim Bagby / Ray Caldwell	4
1922	Stan Coveleski	3.32	Stan Coveleski	11.6	George Uhle	287.1	Guy Morton	102	George Uhle	22	George Uhle	3
1923	Stan Coveleski	2.76	Stan Coveleski	11.6	George Uhle	357.2	George Uhle	109	George Uhle	26	George Uhle	5
1924	Sherry Smith	3.02	Sherry Smith	11.5	Joe Shaute	283.0	Joe Shaute	68	Joe Shaute	20	Dewey Metivier	3
1925	Jake Miller	3.31	George Uhle	13.0	Sherry Smith	237.0	George Uhle	68	Garland Buckeye / George Uhle	13	Joe Shaute	4
1926	George Uhle	2.83	Sherry Smith	11.9	George Uhle	318.1	George Uhle	159	George Uhle	27	4 tied with	1
1927	Jake Miller	3.21	Jake Miller	11.8	Willis Hudlin	264.2	George Uhle	69	Willis Hudlin	18	Benn Karr / Joe Shaute	2
1928	Willis Hudlin	4.04	George Uhle	12.9	Joe Shaute	253.2	Joe Shaute	81	Willis Hudlin	14	Willis Hudlin	7
1929	Willis Hudlin	3.34	Willis Hudlin	12.0	Willis Hudlin	280.1	Wes Ferrell	100	Wes Ferrell	21	Wes Ferrell	5
1930	Wes Ferrell	3.31	Wes Ferrell	12.3	Wes Ferrell	296.2	Wes Ferrell	143	Wes Ferrell	25	Wes Ferrell	3
1931	Wes Ferrell	3.75	Clint Brown	13.1	Wes Ferrell	276.1	Wes Ferrell	123	Wes Ferrell	22	Willis Hudlin	4
1932	Wes Ferrell	3.66	Clint Brown	12.1	Wes Ferrell	287.2	Wes Ferrell	105	Wes Ferrell	23	Sarge Connally	3
1933	Mel Harder	2.95	Mel Harder	11.5	Mel Harder	253.0	Oral Hildebrand	90	Oral Hildebrand	16	Mel Harder	4
1934	Mel Harder	2.61	Mel Harder	11.8	Mel Harder	255.1	Monte Pearson	140	Mel Harder	20	Lloyd Brown	6
1935	Mel Harder	3.29	Mel Harder	11.5	Mel Harder	287.1	Mel Harder	95	Mel Harder	22	Oral Hildebrand / Willis Hudlin	5
1936	Johnny Allen	3.44	Johnny Allen	12.3	Johnny Allen	243.0	Johnny Allen	165	Johnny Allen	20	Oral Hildebrand	4
1937	Johnny Allen	2.55	Johnny Allen	11.5	Mel Harder	233.2	Bob Feller	150	Johnny Allen / Mel Harder	15	Joe Heving	5
1938	Mel Harder	3.83	Mel Harder	12.2	Bob Feller	277.2	Bob Feller	240	Bob Feller / Mel Harder	17	Johnny Humphries	6
1939	Bob Feller	2.85	Bob Feller	11.3	Bob Feller	296.2	Bob Feller	246	Bob Feller	24	Willis Hudlin / Al Milnar	3
1940	Bob Feller	2.61	Bob Feller	10.3	Bob Feller	320.1	Bob Feller	261	Bob Feller	27	Johnny Allen	5
1941	Bob Feller	3.15	Al Smith	12.2	Bob Feller	343.0	Bob Feller	260	Bob Feller	25	Clint Brown / Joe Heving	5
1942	Jim Bagby Jr.	2.96	Jim Bagby Jr.	11.0	Jim Bagby Jr.	270.2	Mel Harder	74	Jim Bagby Jr.	17	Tom Ferrick / Joe Heving	3
1943	Al Smith	2.55	Jim Bagby Jr.	10.9	Jim Bagby Jr.	273.0	Allie Reynolds	151	Jim Bagby Jr. / Al Smith	17	Joe Heving	9
1944	Steve Gromek	2.56	Steve Gromek	10.3	Steve Gromek	203.2	Steve Gromek	115	Mel Harder	12	Joe Heving	10
1945	Steve Gromek	2.55	Steve Gromek	10.7	Steve Gromek	251.0	Allie Reynolds	112	Steve Gromek	19	Ed Klieman / Allie Reynolds	4
1946	Bob Feller	2.18	Bob Feller	10.5	Bob Feller	371.1	Bob Feller	348	Bob Feller	26	Bob Feller / Steve Gromek	4
1947	Bob Feller	2.68	Bob Feller	10.9	Bob Feller	299.0	Bob Feller	196	Bob Feller	20	Ed Klieman	17
1948	Gene Bearden	2.43	Bob Lemon	11.1	Bob Lemon	293.2	Bob Feller	164	Gene Bearden / Bob Lemon	20	Russ Christopher	17
1949	Mike Garcia	2.36	Mike Garcia	11.1	Bob Lemon	279.2	Bob Lemon	138	Bob Lemon	22	Al Benton	10
1950	Early Wynn	3.20	Early Wynn	11.4	Bob Lemon	288.0	Bob Lemon	170	Bob Lemon	23	3 tied with	4
1951	Early Wynn	3.02	Early Wynn	11.1	Early Wynn	274.1	Early Wynn	133	Bob Feller	22	Lou Brissie	9
1952	Mike Garcia	2.37	Bob Lemon	10.1	Bob Lemon	309.2	Early Wynn	153	Early Wynn	23	Mike Garcia / Bob Lemon	4
1953	Mike Garcia	3.25	Mike Garcia	11.4	Bob Lemon	286.2	Early Wynn	138	Bob Lemon	21	Bob Hooper	7
1954	Mike Garcia	2.64	Mike Garcia	10.2	Early Wynn	270.2	Early Wynn	155	Bob Lemon / Early Wynn	23	Ray Narleski	13
1955	Early Wynn	2.82	Early Wynn	11.3	Early Wynn	230.0	Herb Score	245	Bob Lemon	18	Ray Narleski	19
1956	Herb Score	2.53	Herb Score	10.6	Early Wynn	277.2	Herb Score	263	3 tied with	20	Don Mossi	11
1957	Ray Narleski	3.09	Ray Narleski	12.2	Early Wynn	263.0	Early Wynn	184	Early Wynn	14	Ray Narleski	16
1958	Cal McLish	2.99	Gary Bell	10.8	Cal McLish	225.2	Mudcat Grant	111	Cal McLish	16	Hoyt Wilhelm	5
1959	Cal McLish	3.63	Mudcat Grant	12.1	Cal McLish	235.1	Herb Score	147	Cal McLish	19	Gary Bell / Dick Brodowski	5
1960	Jim Perry	3.62	Jim Perry	12.1	Jim Perry	261.1	Jim Perry	120	Jim Perry	18	Johnny Klippstein	14
1961	Mudcat Grant	3.86	Barry Latman	11.3	Mudcat Grant	244.2	Gary Bell	163	Mudcat Grant	15	Frank Funk	11
1962	Dick Donovan	3.59	Dick Donovan	10.9	Dick Donovan	250.2	Barry Latman	117	Dick Donovan	20	Gary Bell	12
1963	Jack Kralick	2.92	Pedro Ramos	9.8	Mudcat Grant	229.1	Pedro Ramos	169	Mudcat Grant / Jack Kralick	13	Ted Abernathy	12

Year	ERA		Baserunners/9 IP		Innings Pitched		Strikeouts		Wins		Saves	
1964	Sam McDowell	2.70	Jack Kralick	12.1	Jack Kralick	190.2	Sam McDowell	177	Jack Kralick	12	Don McMahon	16
1965	Sam McDowell	2.18	Sonny Siebert	9.1	Sam McDowell	273.0	Sam McDowell	325	Sam McDowell	17	Gary Bell	17
1966	Steve Hargan	2.48	Sonny Siebert	9.7	Gary Bell	254.1	Sam McDowell	225	Sonny Siebert	16	Dick Radatz	10
1967	Sonny Siebert	2.38	Sonny Siebert	9.5	Sam McDowell	236.1	Sam McDowell	236	Steve Hargan	14	Orlando Pena	8
1968	Luis Tiant	1.60	Luis Tiant	8.0	Sam McDowell	269.0	Sam McDowell	283	Luis Tiant	21	Vicente Romo	12
1969	Sam McDowell	2.94	Sam McDowell	10.5	Sam McDowell	285.0	Sam McDowell	279	Sam McDowell	18	Stan Williams	12
1970	Sam McDowell	2.92	Sam McDowell	11.0	Sam McDowell	305.0	Sam McDowell	304	Sam McDowell	20	Dennis Higgins	11
1971	Sam McDowell	3.40	Alan Foster	12.1	Sam McDowell	214.2	Sam McDowell	192	Sam McDowell	13	Phil Hennigan	14
1972	Gaylord Perry	1.92	Gaylord Perry	9.1	Gaylord Perry	342.2	Gaylord Perry	234	Gaylord Perry	24	Steve Mingori	10
1973	Gaylord Perry	3.38	Gaylord Perry	11.4	Gaylord Perry	344.0	Gaylord Perry	238	Gaylord Perry	19	Tom Hilgendorf	6
1974	Gaylord Perry	2.51	Gaylord Perry	9.4	Gaylord Perry	322.1	Gaylord Perry	216	Gaylord Perry	21	Tom Buskey	17
1975	Dennis Eckersley	2.60	Dennis Eckersley	11.8	Dennis Eckersley	186.2	Dennis Eckersley	152	Fritz Peterson	14	Dave LaRoche	17
1976	Jim Bibby	3.20	Dennis Eckersley	10.7	Pat Dobson	217.1	Dennis Eckersley	200	Pat Dobson	16	Dave LaRoche	21
1977	Dennis Eckersley	3.53	Dennis Eckersley	10.0	Wayne Garland	282.2	Dennis Eckersley	191	Dennis Eckersley	14	Jim Kern	18
1978	Rick Waits	3.20	Rick Waits	11.5	Rick Waits	230.1	Rick Wise	106	Rick Waits	13	Jim Kern	13
1979	Rick Wise	3.73	Rick Wise	11.6	Rick Wise	231.2	Sid Monge / Rick Wise	108	Rick Waits	16	Sid Monge	19
1980	Len Barker	4.17	Len Barker	12.1	Len Barker	246.1	Len Barker	187	Len Barker	19	Sid Monge	14
1981	Bert Blyleven	2.88	Bert Blyleven	10.7	Bert Blyleven	159.1	Len Barker	127	Bert Blyleven	11	Dan Spillner	7
1982	Rick Sutcliffe	2.96	Len Barker	11.1	Len Barker	244.2	Len Barker	187	Len Barker	15	Dan Spillner	21
1983	Lary Sorensen	4.24	Lary Sorensen	12.3	Rick Sutcliffe	243.1	Rick Sutcliffe	160	Rick Sutcliffe	17	Dan Spillner	8
1984	Bert Blyleven	2.87	Bert Blyleven	10.4	Bert Blyleven	245.0	Bert Blyleven	170	Bert Blyleven	19	Ernie Camacho	23
1985	Bert Blyleven	3.26	Bert Blyleven	11.0	Neal Heaton	207.2	Bert Blyleven	129	Bert Blyleven / Neal Heaton	9	Tom Waddell	9
1986	Tom Candiotti	3.57	Ken Schrom	12.1	Tom Candiotti	252.1	Tom Candiotti	167	Tom Candiotti	16	Ernie Camacho	20
1987	Tom Candiotti	4.78	Tom Candiotti	12.9	Tom Candiotti	201.2	Tom Candiotti	111	3 tied with	7	Doug Jones	8
1988	Greg Swindell	3.20	Greg Swindell	10.4	Greg Swindell	242.0	Greg Swindell	180	Greg Swindell	18	Doug Jones	37
1989	Tom Candiotti	3.10	Bud Black	10.8	Bud Black	222.1	John Farrell	132	Tom Candiotti / Greg Swindell	13	Doug Jones	32
1990	Bud Black	3.53	Bud Black	11.0	Greg Swindell	214.2	Greg Swindell	135	Tom Candiotti	15	Doug Jones	43
1991	Greg Swindell	3.48	Greg Swindell	10.4	Greg Swindell	238.0	Greg Swindell	169	Charles Nagy	10	Steve Olin	17
1992	Charles Nagy	2.96	Charles Nagy	10.9	Charles Nagy	252.0	Charles Nagy	169	Charles Nagy	17	Steve Olin	29
1993	Jose Mesa	4.92	Jose Mesa	13.0	Jose Mesa	208.2	Jose Mesa	118	Jose Mesa	10	Eric Plunk	15
1994	Charles Nagy	3.45	Dennis Martinez	11.1	Dennis Martinez	176.2	Charles Nagy	108	Mark Clark / Dennis Martinez	11	Jeff Russell / Paul Shuey	5
1995	Dennis Martinez	3.08	Orel Hershiser	11.1	Dennis Martinez	187.0	Charles Nagy	139	Orel Hershiser / Charles Nagy	16	Jose Mesa	46
1996	Charles Nagy	3.41	Charles Nagy	11.4	Charles Nagy	222.0	Charles Nagy	167	Charles Nagy	17	Jose Mesa	39
1997	Charles Nagy	4.28	Orel Hershiser	12.9	Charles Nagy	227.0	Charles Nagy	149	Charles Nagy	15	Jose Mesa	16

Indians Franchise Batting Leaders—Career

	Games			At-Bats			Runs			Hits	
1	Terry Turner	1,625	1	Nap Lajoie	6,034	1	Earl Averill	1,154	1	Nap Lajoie	2,046
2	Nap Lajoie	1,614	2	Earl Averill	5,915	2	Tris Speaker	1,079	2	Tris Speaker	1,965
3	Lou Boudreau	1,560	3	Terry Turner	5,783	3	Charlie Jamieson	942	3	Earl Averill	1,904
4	Jim Hegan	1,526	4	Lou Boudreau	5,754	4	Nap Lajoie	865	4	Joe Sewell	1,800
5	Tris Speaker	1,519	5	Ken Keltner	5,655	5	Joe Sewell	857	5	Charlie Jamieson	1,753
6	Joe Sewell	1,513	6	Joe Sewell	5,621	6	Lou Boudreau	823	6	Lou Boudreau	1,706
	Ken Keltner	1,513	7	Charlie Jamieson	5,551	7	Larry Doby	808	7	Ken Keltner	1,561
8	Earl Averill	1,510	8	Tris Speaker	5,546	8	Hal Trosky	758	8	Terry Turner	1,470
9	Charlie Jamieson	1,483	9	Jack Graney	4,705	9	Ken Keltner	735	9	Hal Trosky	1,365
10	Jack Graney	1,402	10	Bill Bradley	4,644	10	Jack Graney	706	10	Julio Franco	1,272
11	Steve O'Neill	1,361	11	Jim Hegan	4,459	11	Terry Turner	692	11	Bill Bradley	1,264
12	Brook Jacoby	1,240	12	Hal Trosky	4,365	12	Bobby Avila	688	12	Dale Mitchell	1,237
13	Larry Doby	1,235	13	Bobby Avila	4,356	13	Ray Chapman	671	13	Bobby Avila	1,236
14	Bill Bradley	1,230	14	Larry Doby	4,315	14	Andre Thornton	650	14	Larry Doby	1,234
15	Andre Thornton	1,225	15	Brook Jacoby	4,314	15	Bill Bradley	649	15	Jack Graney	1,178
16	Bobby Avila	1,207	16	Andre Thornton	4,313	16	Julio Franco	619		Brook Jacoby	1,178
17	Bill Wambsganss	1,171	17	Julio Franco	4,282	17	Al Rosen	603	17	Steve O'Neill	1,109
18	Hal Trosky	1,124	18	Bill Wambsganss	4,191	18	Albert Belle	592	18	Andre Thornton	1,095
19	Dale Mitchell	1,108	19	Steve O'Neill	4,182	19	Bill Wambsganss	556	19	Carlos Baerga	1,084
20	Julio Franco	1,088	20	Rick Manning	3,997	20	Dale Mitchell	552	20	Bill Wambsganss	1,083

	Doubles			Triples			Home Runs			RBI	
1	Tris Speaker	486	1	Earl Averill	121	1	Albert Belle	242	1	Earl Averill	1,085
2	Nap Lajoie	424	2	Tris Speaker	108	2	Earl Averill	226	2	Nap Lajoie	919
3	Earl Averill	377	3	Elmer Flick	106	3	Hal Trosky	216	3	Hal Trosky	911
4	Joe Sewell	375	4	Joe Jackson	89	4	Larry Doby	215	4	Tris Speaker	883
5	Lou Boudreau	367	5	Jeff Heath	83	5	Andre Thornton	214	5	Joe Sewell	865
6	Ken Keltner	306	6	Ray Chapman	81	6	Al Rosen	192	6	Ken Keltner	850
7	Charlie Jamieson	296	7	Jack Graney	79	7	Rocky Colavito	190	7	Larry Doby	776
8	Hal Trosky	287	8	Nap Lajoie	78	8	Ken Keltner	163	8	Albert Belle	751
9	Bill Bradley	237	9	Terry Turner	77	9	Joe Carter	151	9	Andre Thornton	749
10	Odell Hale	235	10	Bill Bradley	74	10	Jim Thome	133	10	Lou Boudreau	740
11	George Burns	230		Charlie Jamieson	74	11	Woodie Held	130	11	Al Rosen	717
12	Albert Belle	223	12	Ken Keltner	69	12	Jeff Heath	122	12	Jeff Heath	619
13	Steve O'Neill	220	13	Joe Vosmik	65	13	Brook Jacoby	120	13	Rocky Colavito	574
14	Jack Graney	219		Lou Boudreau	65	14	Cory Snyder	115	14	Odell Hale	563
15	Joe Vosmik	206	15	Joe Sewell	63	15	Manny Ramirez	109	15	Carlos Baerga	560
16	Terry Turner	204	16	Dale Mitchell	61	16	Max Alvis	108	16	Joe Vosmik	556
17	Jeff Heath	194	17	Hal Trosky	53	17	Carlos Baerga	103	17	Julio Franco	530
18	Andre Thornton	193	18	Odell Hale	51	18	Joe Gordon	100		Joe Carter	530
19	Brook Jacoby	192	19	Bill Wambsganss	50	19	Leon Wagner	97	19	Brook Jacoby	524
20	Four tied at	190	20	Six tied at	45	20	Four tied at	93	20	Terry Turner	521

	Walks			Strikeouts			Stolen Bases			Runs Created	
1	Tris Speaker	857	1	Larry Doby	805	1	Kenny Lofton	325	1	Tris Speaker	1,258
2	Lou Boudreau	766	2	Brook Jacoby	738	2	Terry Turner	254	2	Earl Averill	1,244
3	Earl Averill	726	3	Andre Thornton	683	3	Nap Lajoie	240	3	Nap Lajoie	1,103
4	Jack Graney	712	4	Jim Hegan	664	4	Ray Chapman	233	4	Joe Sewell	957
5	Larry Doby	703	5	Max Alvis	642	5	Elmer Flick	207	5	Lou Boudreau	907
6	Andre Thornton	685		Cory Snyder	642	6	Harry Bay	165	6	Hal Trosky	879
7	Joe Sewell	655	7	Woodie Held	629	7	Brett Butler	164	7	Charlie Jamieson	874
8	Charlie Jamieson	627	8	Albert Belle	622	8	Bill Bradley	157	8	Larry Doby	841
9	Al Rosen	587	9	Jim Thome	570	9	Tris Speaker	153	9	Ken Keltner	814
10	Bobby Avila	527	10	Julio Franco	543	10	Jack Graney	148	10	Andre Thornton	709
11	Ken Keltner	511	11	Joe Carter	516	11	Julio Franco	147	11	Al Rosen	698
12	Mike Hargrove	505	12	Bob Feller	505	12	Rick Manning	142	12	Albert Belle	690
13	Steve O'Neill	491	13	Rick Manning	487	13	Joe Jackson	138	13	Jack Graney	643
14	Rocky Colavito	468	14	Rocky Colavito	478	14	Braggo Roth	129	14	Jeff Heath	632
15	Ray Chapman	452	15	Ken Keltner	474	15	Miguel Dilone	128	15	Terry Turner	631
16	Hal Trosky	449	16	Earl Averill	470	16	Joe Carter	126		Bobby Avila	631
17	Jim Hegan	437	17	Jeff Heath	438	17	Bill Wambsganss	124	17	Elmer Flick	624
18	Terry Turner	430	18	Ray Chapman	414	18	Omar Vizquel	120	18	Bill Bradley	612
	Jim Thome	430	19	Manny Ramirez	411	19	George Stovall	111	19	Dale Mitchell	606
20	Brook Jacoby	428	20	Pat Seerey	390	20	Four tied at	108	20	Joe Jackson	588

	Runs Created/27 Outs (minimum 2000 Plate Appearances)			Batting Average (minimum 2000 Plate Appearances)			On-Base Percentage (minimum 2000 Plate Appearances)			Slugging Percentage (minimum 2000 Plate Appearances)	
1	Joe Jackson	9.24	1	Joe Jackson	.375	1	Tris Speaker	.444	1	Albert Belle	.580
2	Tris Speaker	8.63	2	Tris Speaker	.354	2	Joe Jackson	.442	2	Hal Trosky	.551
3	Earl Averill	7.92	3	Nap Lajoie	.339	3	Jim Thome	.408	3	Manny Ramirez	.546
4	Hal Trosky	7.54	4	George Burns	.327	4	Eddie Morgan	.405	4	Joe Jackson	.542
5	Eddie Morgan	7.46	5	Eddie Morgan	.323	5	Earl Averill	.399	5	Jim Thome	.541
6	Jim Thome	7.23	6	Earl Averill	.322	6	Joe Sewell	.398	6	Earl Averill	.541
7	Albert Belle	7.11	7	Joe Sewell	.320	7	Mike Hargrove	.396	7	Tris Speaker	.520
8	Manny Ramirez	7.02	8	Johnny Hodapp	.318	8	Manny Ramirez	.393	8	Jeff Heath	.506
9	Larry Doby	7.01	9	Kenny Lofton	.316	9	Larry Doby	.389	9	Larry Doby	.500
10	Nap Lajoie	6.83	10	Charlie Jamieson	.316	10	Nap Lajoie	.388	10	Al Rosen	.495
11	Jeff Heath	6.68	11	Joe Vosmik	.313	11	Charlie Jamieson	.388	11	Rocky Colavito	.495
12	Bruce Campbell	6.66	12	Hal Trosky	.313	12	Bruce Campbell	.385	12	Eddie Morgan	.493
13	Kenny Lofton	6.65	13	Dale Mitchell	.312	13	Al Rosen	.384	13	Bruce Campbell	.478
14	Al Rosen	6.59	14	Dick Porter	.308	14	Toby Harrah	.383	14	Joe Carter	.472
15	Joe Vosmik	6.52	15	Bruce Campbell	.305	15	Kenny Lofton	.382	15	Joe Gordon	.463
16	Elmer Flick	6.33	16	Manny Ramirez	.304	16	Lou Boudreau	.382	16	John Romano	.461
17	Rocky Colavito	6.24	17	Homer Summa	.303	17	Hal Trosky	.379	17	Joe Vosmik	.459
18	Joe Sewell	6.08	18	Larry Gardner	.301	18	Dick Porter	.378	18	Fred Whitfield	.456
19	George Burns	6.03	19	Carlos Baerga	.300	19	Joe Vosmik	.376	19	George Burns	.455
20	Toby Harrah	5.99	20	Elmer Flick	.299	20	Willie Kamm	.375	20	Andre Thornton	.453

Teams: Indians

Indians Franchise Pitching Leaders—Career

Wins

1	Bob Feller	266
2	Mel Harder	223
3	Bob Lemon	207
4	Stan Coveleski	172
5	Early Wynn	164
6	Addie Joss	160
7	Willis Hudlin	157
8	George Uhle	147
9	Mike Garcia	142
10	Jim Bagby	122
	Sam McDowell	122
12	Wes Ferrell	102
13	Guy Morton	98
14	Gary Bell	96
15	Charles Nagy	89
16	Bob Rhoads	88
17	Earl Moore	81
18	Joe Shaute	78
	Steve Gromek	78
20	Bill Bernhard	77

Losses

1	Mel Harder	186
2	Bob Feller	162
3	Willis Hudlin	151
4	Bob Lemon	128
5	Stan Coveleski	123
6	George Uhle	119
7	Sam McDowell	109
8	Early Wynn	102
9	Addie Joss	97
10	Mike Garcia	96
11	Gary Bell	92
12	Guy Morton	88
	Joe Shaute	88
14	Jim Bagby	85
15	Rick Waits	84
16	Willie Mitchell	76
17	Steve Hargan	74
18	Earl Moore	68
19	Six tied at	67

Winning Percentage
(minimum 100 decisions)

1	Vean Gregg	.667
2	Johnny Allen	.663
3	Addie Joss	.623
4	Wes Ferrell	.622
5	Bob Feller	.621
6	Bob Lemon	.618
7	Early Wynn	.617
8	Mike Garcia	.597
9	Jim Bagby	.589
10	Stan Coveleski	.583
11	Bill Bernhard	.579
12	Charles Nagy	.578
13	Bob Rhoads	.571
14	Sonny Siebert	.560
15	George Uhle	.553
16	Gaylord Perry	.551
17	Oral Hildebrand	.549
18	Mel Harder	.545
19	Earl Moore	.544
20	Luis Tiant	.540

Games

1	Mel Harder	582
2	Bob Feller	570
3	Willis Hudlin	475
4	Bob Lemon	460
5	Gary Bell	419
6	Mike Garcia	397
7	Stan Coveleski	360
8	George Uhle	357
9	Early Wynn	343
10	Sam McDowell	336
	Eric Plunk	336
12	Guy Morton	317
13	Steve Gromek	309
14	Jose Mesa	297
15	Jim Bagby	290
	Dan Spillner	290
17	Addie Joss	286
18	Doug Jones	272
19	Sid Monge	255
20	Joe Shaute	252

Games Started

1	Bob Feller	484
2	Mel Harder	433
3	Bob Lemon	350
4	Willis Hudlin	320
5	Stan Coveleski	304
6	Early Wynn	296
7	Sam McDowell	295
8	Mike Garcia	281
9	George Uhle	267
10	Addie Joss	260
11	Jim Bagby	202
12	Charles Nagy	201
13	Rick Waits	187
14	Guy Morton	184
15	Joe Shaute	176
16	Tom Candiotti	172
17	Gary Bell	169
18	Mudcat Grant	165
19	Bob Rhoads	160
	Luis Tiant	160

Complete Games

1	Bob Feller	279
2	Addie Joss	234
3	Stan Coveleski	195
4	Bob Lemon	188
5	Mel Harder	181
6	George Uhle	166
7	Willis Hudlin	154
8	Early Wynn	144
9	Earl Moore	137
10	Bob Rhoads	130
	Jim Bagby	130
12	Bill Bernhard	118
13	Wes Ferrell	113
14	Mike Garcia	111
15	Sam McDowell	97
16	Joe Shaute	96
	Gaylord Perry	96
18	Otto Hess	81
19	Guy Morton	80
20	Vean Gregg	77

Shutouts

1	Addie Joss	45
2	Bob Feller	44
3	Stan Coveleski	31
	Bob Lemon	31
5	Mike Garcia	27
6	Mel Harder	25
7	Early Wynn	24
8	Sam McDowell	22
9	Luis Tiant	21
10	Bob Rhoads	19
	Guy Morton	19
12	Gaylord Perry	17
13	Jim Bagby	16
	George Uhle	16
15	Earl Moore	15
	Otto Hess	15
17	Jim Perry	13
	Steve Hargan	13
19	Bill Bernhard	12
20	Eight tied at	11

Saves

1	Doug Jones	128
2	Jose Mesa	103
3	Ray Narleski	53
4	Steve Olin	48
5	Jim Kern	46
	Sid Monge	46
7	Gary Bell	45
8	Ernie Camacho	44
9	Dave LaRoche	42
10	Dan Spillner	41
11	Joe Heving	32
	Don Mossi	32
13	Willis Hudlin	31
14	Ed Klieman	30
15	Don McMahon	28
16	Jim Bagby	26
	Eric Plunk	26
18	Tom Buskey	25
19	Mel Harder	23
	Ted Abernathy	23

Innings Pitched

1	Bob Feller	3,827.0
2	Mel Harder	3,426.1
3	Bob Lemon	2,850.0
4	Willis Hudlin	2,557.2
5	Stan Coveleski	2,513.2
6	Addie Joss	2,327.0
7	Early Wynn	2,286.2
8	George Uhle	2,200.1
9	Mike Garcia	2,138.0
10	Sam McDowell	2,109.2
11	Jim Bagby	1,735.2
12	Guy Morton	1,628.2
13	Gary Bell	1,550.1
14	Joe Shaute	1,447.0
15	Bob Rhoads	1,444.2
16	Charles Nagy	1,354.0
17	Steve Gromek	1,340.2
18	Earl Moore	1,337.2
19	Wes Ferrell	1,321.1
20	Willie Mitchell	1,301.1

Walks

1	Bob Feller	1,764
2	Bob Lemon	1,251
3	Mel Harder	1,118
4	Sam McDowell	1,072
5	Early Wynn	877
6	Willis Hudlin	832
7	George Uhle	709
8	Mike Garcia	696
9	Gary Bell	670
10	Stan Coveleski	616
11	Guy Morton	583
12	Mudcat Grant	565
13	Wes Ferrell	526
14	Rick Waits	512
15	Willie Mitchell	496
16	Al Milnar	478
17	Herb Score	458
18	Earl Moore	449
19	Joe Shaute	447
20	Allie Reynolds	442

Strikeouts

1	Bob Feller	2,581
2	Sam McDowell	2,159
3	Bob Lemon	1,277
	Early Wynn	1,277
5	Mel Harder	1,160
6	Gary Bell	1,104
7	Mike Garcia	1,095
8	Luis Tiant	1,041
9	Addie Joss	920
10	Charles Nagy	897
11	Stan Coveleski	856
12	Guy Morton	830
13	Sonny Siebert	786
14	Greg Swindell	777
15	Willie Mitchell	775
16	Gaylord Perry	773
17	George Uhle	763
18	Tom Candiotti	753
19	Herb Score	742
20	Mudcat Grant	707

Strikeouts/9 Innings
(minimum 1000 Innings Pitched)

1	Sam McDowell	9.21
2	Luis Tiant	7.81
3	Greg Swindell	6.53
4	Gary Bell	6.41
5	Gaylord Perry	6.15
6	Bob Feller	6.07
7	Charles Nagy	5.96
8	Tom Candiotti	5.71
9	Willie Mitchell	5.36
10	Mudcat Grant	5.24
11	Steve Hargan	5.11
12	Early Wynn	5.03
13	Mike Garcia	4.61
14	Guy Morton	4.59
15	Earl Moore	4.14
16	Bob Lemon	4.03
17	Steve Gromek	3.99
18	Rick Waits	3.99
19	Jim Perry	3.59
20	Addie Joss	3.56

ERA
(minimum 1000 Innings Pitched)

1	Addie Joss	1.89
2	Bob Rhoads	2.39
3	Bill Bernhard	2.45
4	Earl Moore	2.58
5	Gaylord Perry	2.71
6	Stan Coveleski	2.79
7	Luis Tiant	2.84
8	Willie Mitchell	2.88
9	Sam McDowell	2.99
10	Jim Bagby	3.03
11	Guy Morton	3.13
12	Steve Gromek	3.22
13	Bob Lemon	3.23
14	Mike Garcia	3.24
15	Early Wynn	3.24
16	Bob Feller	3.25
17	Al Smith	3.47
18	Tom Candiotti	3.53
19	Wes Ferrell	3.67
20	Gary Bell	3.71

Component ERA
(minimum 1000 Innings Pitched)

1	Addie Joss	1.73
2	Bill Bernhard	2.42
3	Bob Rhoads	2.63
4	Gaylord Perry	2.63
5	Earl Moore	2.75
6	Stan Coveleski	2.81
7	Luis Tiant	2.83
8	Willie Mitchell	2.85
9	Guy Morton	2.95
10	Sam McDowell	3.01
11	Steve Gromek	3.05
12	Jim Bagby	3.09
13	Bob Feller	3.19
14	Early Wynn	3.23
15	Mike Garcia	3.36
16	Bob Lemon	3.40
17	Steve Hargan	3.46
18	Al Smith	3.53
19	Tom Candiotti	3.53
20	Greg Swindell	3.56

Opponent Average
(minimum 1000 Innings Pitched)

1	Sam McDowell	.210
2	Luis Tiant	.214
3	Addie Joss	.220
4	Gaylord Perry	.223
5	Bob Feller	.231
6	Gary Bell	.235
7	Early Wynn	.238
8	Earl Moore	.239
9	Mudcat Grant	.239
10	Steve Gromek	.240
11	Bob Lemon	.241
12	Willie Mitchell	.241
13	Steve Hargan	.244
14	Bob Rhoads	.250
15	Guy Morton	.251
16	Tom Candiotti	.251
17	Bill Bernhard	.253
18	Mike Garcia	.256
19	Stan Coveleski	.259
20	Al Smith	.261

Opponent OBP
(minimum 1000 Innings Pitched)

1	Addie Joss	.257
2	Gaylord Perry	.284
3	Luis Tiant	.287
4	Bill Bernhard	.287
5	Greg Swindell	.303
6	Steve Gromek	.304
7	Stan Coveleski	.306
8	Earl Moore	.308
9	Bob Rhoads	.309
10	Sam McDowell	.310
11	Early Wynn	.310
12	Tom Candiotti	.312
13	Jim Bagby	.315
14	Mike Garcia	.316
15	Gary Bell	.317
16	Bob Feller	.319
17	Guy Morton	.319
18	Willie Mitchell	.320
19	Steve Hargan	.321
20	Mudcat Grant	.322

Teams: Indians

Indians Franchise Batting Leaders—Single Season

Games

1	Leon Wagner	1964	163
2	Dick Howser	1964	162
	Rocky Colavito	1965	162
	Toby Harrah	1982	162
	Joe Carter	1986	162
	Joe Carter	1989	162
7	Max Alvis	1967	161
	Andre Thornton	1982	161
	Brook Jacoby	1985	161
	Brett Butler	1986	161
	Carlos Baerga	1992	161
12	Mike Hargrove	1980	160
	Toby Harrah	1980	160
	Mike Hargrove	1982	160
	Julio Franco	1984	160
	Julio Franco	1985	160
17	Six tied at		159

At-Bats

1	Joe Carter	1986	663
2	Kenny Lofton	1996	662
3	Julio Franco	1984	658
4	Carlos Baerga	1992	657
5	Mike Rocco	1944	653
6	Joe Carter	1989	651
7	Carl Lind	1928	650
8	Charlie Jamieson	1923	644
	Lyn Lary	1937	644
10	Leon Wagner	1964	641
11	Dale Mitchell	1949	640
12	Roy Hughes	1936	638
13	Dick Howser	1964	637
	Max Alvis	1967	637
15	Julio Franco	1985	636
16	Johnny Hodapp	1930	635
17	Hal Trosky	1935	632
18	Earl Averill	1932	631
	Buddy Bell	1973	631
20	Hal Trosky	1936	629

Runs

1	Earl Averill	1931	140
2	Tris Speaker	1920	137
3	Earl Averill	1936	136
4	Tris Speaker	1923	133
5	Kenny Lofton	1996	132
6	Charlie Jamieson	1923	130
7	Earl Averill	1934	128
8	Joe Jackson	1911	126
	Odell Hale	1936	126
10	Hal Trosky	1936	124
	Albert Belle	1996	124
12	Al Smith	1955	123
13	Eddie Morgan	1930	122
	Jim Thome	1996	122
15	Joe Jackson	1912	121
	Earl Averill	1937	121
	Albert Belle	1995	121
18	Hal Trosky	1934	117
19	Three tied at		116

Hits

1	Joe Jackson	1911	233
2	Earl Averill	1936	232
3	Nap Lajoie	1910	227
4	Joe Jackson	1912	226
5	Johnny Hodapp	1930	225
6	Charlie Jamieson	1923	222
7	Tris Speaker	1923	218
8	George Burns	1926	216
	Joe Vosmik	1935	216
	Hal Trosky	1936	216
11	Nap Lajoie	1906	214
	Tris Speaker	1920	214
13	Charlie Jamieson	1924	213
14	Tris Speaker	1916	211
15	Kenny Lofton	1996	210
16	Lew Fonseca	1929	209
	Earl Averill	1931	209
18	Nap Lajoie	1904	208
19	Hal Trosky	1934	206
20	Carlos Baerga	1992	205

Doubles

1	George Burns	1926	64
2	Tris Speaker	1923	59
3	Tris Speaker	1921	52
	Tris Speaker	1926	52
	Albert Belle	1995	52
6	Nap Lajoie	1910	51
	George Burns	1927	51
	Johnny Hodapp	1930	51
9	Tris Speaker	1920	50
	Odell Hale	1936	50
11	Nap Lajoie	1904	49
12	Nap Lajoie	1906	48
	Tris Speaker	1922	48
	Joe Sewell	1927	48
	Earl Averill	1934	48
16	Eddie Morgan	1930	47
	Joe Vosmik	1935	47
18	Lyn Lary	1937	46
	Lou Boudreau	1940	46
20	Eight tied at		45

Triples

1	Joe Jackson	1912	26
2	Dale Mitchell	1949	23
3	Bill Bradley	1903	22
	Elmer Flick	1906	22
5	Joe Vosmik	1935	20
	Jeff Heath	1941	20
7	Joe Jackson	1911	19
8	Elmer Flick	1905	18
	Elmer Flick	1907	18
	Jeff Heath	1938	18
11	Elmer Flick	1904	17
	Joe Jackson	1913	17
	Ray Chapman	1915	17
14	Elmer Flick	1903	16
	Earl Averill	1933	16
	Hank Edwards	1946	16
17	Nap Lajoie	1904	15
	Lew Fonseca	1929	15
	Earl Averill	1936	15
	Earl Averill	1938	15

Home Runs

1	Albert Belle	1995	50
2	Albert Belle	1996	48
3	Al Rosen	1953	43
4	Hal Trosky	1936	42
	Rocky Colavito	1959	42
6	Rocky Colavito	1958	41
7	Jim Thome	1997	40
8	Albert Belle	1993	38
	Jim Thome	1996	38
10	Al Rosen	1950	37
11	Albert Belle	1994	36
12	Hal Trosky	1934	35
	Joe Carter	1989	35
14	Albert Belle	1992	34
15	Andre Thornton	1978	33
	Andre Thornton	1984	33
	Cory Snyder	1987	33
	Manny Ramirez	1996	33
	David Justice	1997	33
20	Eleven tied at		32

RBI

1	Hal Trosky	1936	162
2	Albert Belle	1996	148
3	Al Rosen	1953	145
4	Earl Averill	1931	143
5	Hal Trosky	1934	142
6	Eddie Morgan	1930	136
7	Tris Speaker	1923	130
8	Albert Belle	1993	129
9	Hal Trosky	1937	128
10	Earl Averill	1936	126
	Larry Doby	1954	126
	Albert Belle	1995	126
13	Earl Averill	1932	124
	Joe Gordon	1948	124
15	Jeff Heath	1941	123
16	Johnny Hodapp	1930	121
	Joe Carter	1986	121
18	Earl Averill	1930	119
	Ken Keltner	1948	119
20	Larry Gardner	1920	118

Walks

1	Jim Thome	1996	123
2	Jim Thome	1997	120
3	Mike Hargrove	1980	111
4	Andre Thornton	1982	109
5	Les Fleming	1942	106
6	Jack Graney	1919	105
7	Jack Graney	1916	102
8	Larry Doby	1951	101
	Mike Hargrove	1982	101
10	Al Rosen	1950	100
11	Earl Averill	1934	99
	Albert Belle	1996	99
13	Joe Sewell	1923	98
	Lou Boudreau	1948	98
	Larry Doby	1950	98
	Toby Harrah	1980	98
17	Tris Speaker	1920	97
	Jim Thome	1995	97
19	Roy Cullenbine	1943	96
	Larry Doby	1953	96

Strikeouts

1	Cory Snyder	1987	166
2	Jim Thome	1997	146
3	Jim Thome	1996	141
4	Brook Jacoby	1986	137
5	Bobby Bonds	1979	135
6	Cory Snyder	1989	134
	Candy Maldonado	1990	134
8	Albert Belle	1992	128
9	Cory Snyder	1986	123
10	Larry Doby	1953	121
	Leon Wagner	1964	121
	Max Alvis	1965	121
	Paul Sorrento	1993	121
14	Brook Jacoby	1985	120
15	Woodie Held	1959	118
	Cory Snyder	1990	118
17	Manny Ramirez	1997	115
18	Jim Thome	1995	113
19	Joe Carter	1989	112
	Manny Ramirez	1995	112

Stolen Bases

1	Kenny Lofton	1996	75
2	Kenny Lofton	1993	70
3	Kenny Lofton	1992	66
4	Miguel Dilone	1980	61
5	Kenny Lofton	1994	60
6	Kenny Lofton	1995	54
7	Ray Chapman	1917	52
	Brett Butler	1984	52
9	Braggo Roth	1917	51
10	Brett Butler	1985	47
11	Harry Bay	1903	45
12	Omar Vizquel	1997	43
13	Elmer Flick	1907	41
	Joe Jackson	1911	41
15	Jose Cardenal	1968	40
	Alex Cole	1990	40
17	Elmer Flick	1906	39
18	Harry Bay	1904	38
	Elmer Flick	1904	38
20	Josh Clarke	1908	37

Runs Created

1	Tris Speaker	1923	154
2	Earl Averill	1936	150
3	Joe Jackson	1912	148
4	Joe Jackson	1911	147
5	Tris Speaker	1920	146
	Albert Belle	1996	146
7	Earl Averill	1931	143
	Al Rosen	1953	143
9	Eddie Morgan	1930	140
10	Earl Averill	1932	139
	Hal Trosky	1936	139
12	Tris Speaker	1916	136
	Hal Trosky	1934	136
	Earl Averill	1934	136
15	Nap Lajoie	1910	135
16	Joe Jackson	1913	132
17	Lou Boudreau	1948	130
18	Nap Lajoie	1904	129
19	Joe Vosmik	1935	127
	Jeff Heath	1941	127

Runs Created/27 Outs

(minimum 3.1 Plate Appearances/Tm Gm)

1	Joe Jackson	1911	10.92
2	Albert Belle	1994	10.72
3	Tris Speaker	1923	10.45
4	Joe Jackson	1912	10.43
5	Tris Speaker	1920	10.33
6	Tris Speaker	1925	10.31
7	Tris Speaker	1922	10.29
8	Earl Averill	1936	10.06
9	Tris Speaker	1916	10.02
10	Joe Jackson	1913	9.77
11	Nap Lajoie	1904	9.55
12	Jim Thome	1996	9.30
13	Eddie Morgan	1931	9.25
14	Eddie Morgan	1930	9.09
15	Al Rosen	1953	9.07
16	Nap Lajoie	1910	9.07
17	Tris Speaker	1921	8.98
18	David Justice	1997	8.91
19	Larry Doby	1950	8.90
20	Albert Belle	1996	8.90

Batting Average

(minimum 3.1 Plate Appearances/Tm Gm)

1	Joe Jackson	1911	.408
2	Joe Jackson	1912	.395
3	Tris Speaker	1925	.389
4	Tris Speaker	1920	.388
5	Tris Speaker	1916	.386
6	Nap Lajoie	1910	.384
7	Tris Speaker	1923	.380
8	Charlie Hickman	1902	.378
	Tris Speaker	1922	.378
10	Earl Averill	1936	.378
11	Nap Lajoie	1904	.376
12	Joe Jackson	1913	.373
13	Lew Fonseca	1929	.369
14	Nap Lajoie	1912	.368
15	Tris Speaker	1921	.362
16	Charlie Jamieson	1924	.359
17	George Burns	1926	.358
18	Albert Belle	1994	.357
19	Nap Lajoie	1906	.355
20	Lou Boudreau	1948	.355

On-Base Percentage

(minimum 3.1 Plate Appearances/Tm Gm)

1	Tris Speaker	1920	.483
2	Tris Speaker	1925	.479
3	Tris Speaker	1922	.474
4	Tris Speaker	1916	.470
5	Tris Speaker	1923	.469
6	Joe Jackson	1911	.468
7	Joe Jackson	1913	.460
8	Joe Jackson	1912	.458
9	Joe Sewell	1923	.456
10	Lou Boudreau	1948	.453
11	Eddie Morgan	1931	.451
12	Jim Thome	1996	.450
13	Nap Lajoie	1910	.445
14	Larry Doby	1950	.442
15	Tris Speaker	1921	.439
16	Albert Belle	1994	.438
17	Earl Averill	1936	.438
18	Jim Thome	1995	.438
19	Tris Speaker	1924	.432
20	Tris Speaker	1917	.432

Slugging Percentage

(minimum 3.1 Plate Appearances/Tm Gm)

1	Albert Belle	1994	.714
2	Albert Belle	1995	.690
3	Hal Trosky	1936	.644
4	Earl Averill	1936	.627
5	Albert Belle	1996	.623
6	Rocky Colavito	1958	.620
7	Al Rosen	1953	.613
8	Jim Thome	1996	.612
9	Tris Speaker	1923	.610
10	Tris Speaker	1922	.606
11	Jeff Heath	1938	.602
12	Eddie Morgan	1930	.601
13	Hal Trosky	1934	.598
14	David Justice	1997	.596
15	Joe Jackson	1911	.590
16	Hal Trosky	1939	.589
17	Jeff Heath	1941	.586
18	Manny Ramirez	1996	.582
19	Joe Jackson	1912	.579
20	Jim Thome	1997	.579

Teams: Indians

Indians Franchise Pitching Leaders—Single Season

Wins

1	Jim Bagby	1920	31
2	Addie Joss	1907	27
	George Uhle	1926	27
	Bob Feller	1940	27
5	George Uhle	1923	26
	Bob Feller	1946	26
7	Wes Ferrell	1930	25
	Bob Feller	1941	25
9	Addie Joss	1908	24
	Stan Coveleski	1919	24
	Stan Coveleski	1920	24
	Bob Feller	1939	24
	Gaylord Perry	1972	24
14	Ten tied at		23

Losses

1	Pete Dowling	1901	22
2	Luis Tiant	1969	20
3	George Kahler	1912	19
	Al Milnar	1941	19
	Gaylord Perry	1973	19
	Wayne Garland	1977	19
	Rick Wise	1978	19
8	Tom Candiotti	1987	18
9	Earl Moore	1902	17
	Otto Hess	1906	17
	Willie Mitchell	1914	17
	Joe Shaute	1924	17
	Garland Buckeye	1927	17
	Joe Shaute	1928	17
	George Uhle	1928	17
	Mel Harder	1933	17
	Early Wynn	1957	17
	Jim Perry	1961	17
	Sam McDowell	1971	17
	Neal Heaton	1985	17

Winning Percentage
(minimum 15 decisions)

1	Johnny Allen	1937	.938
2	Bob Feller	1954	.813
3	Ed Klepfer	1917	.778
4	Bill Bernhard	1902	.773
	Charles Nagy	1996	.773
6	Vean Gregg	1911	.767
	Bob Lemon	1954	.767
8	Allen Sothoron	1921	.750
9	Gene Bearden	1948	.741
10	Mike Garcia	1949	.737
11	Bob Feller	1951	.733
12	Bert Blyleven	1984	.731
13	Bob Feller	1939	.727
	Orel Hershiser	1995	.727
	Charles Nagy	1995	.727
16	Barry Latman	1961	.722
17	Jim Bagby	1920	.721
18	Addie Joss	1907	.711
	George Uhle	1926	.711
	Bob Feller	1940	.711

Games

1	Sid Monge	1979	76
2	Paul Assenmacher	1997	75
3	Steve Olin	1992	72
4	Derek Lilliquist	1992	71
	Mike Jackson	1997	71
6	Don McMahon	1964	70
	Eric Plunk	1993	70
8	Ernie Camacho	1984	69
	Jesse Orosco	1989	69
	Jose Mesa	1996	69
11	Sid Monge	1980	67
12	Doug Jones	1990	66
	Jose Mesa	1997	66
14	Dan Spillner	1982	65
15	Ted Power	1992	64
16	Joe Heving	1944	63
	Mike Jeffcoat	1984	63
	Paul Assenmacher	1996	63
19	Scott Bailes	1986	62
	Jose Mesa	1995	62

Games Started

1	George Uhle	1923	44
2	Bob Feller	1946	42
3	Gaylord Perry	1973	41
4	Stan Coveleski	1921	40
	George Uhle	1922	40
	Bob Feller	1941	40
	Gaylord Perry	1972	40
	Dick Tidrow	1973	40
9	Jim Bagby	1920	39
	Sam McDowell	1970	39
11	Addie Joss	1907	38
	Bob Feller	1948	38
	Sam McDowell	1969	38
	Wayne Garland	1977	38
15	Thirteen tied at		37

Complete Games

1	Bob Feller	1946	36
2	Bill Bernhard	1904	35
3	Addie Joss	1907	34
4	Otto Hess	1906	33
5	George Uhle	1926	32
6	Addie Joss	1903	31
	Addie Joss	1905	31
	Bob Rhoads	1906	31
	Bob Feller	1940	31
10	Red Donahue	1904	30
	Cy Young	1909	30
	Jim Bagby	1920	30
13	Earl Moore	1902	29
	Addie Joss	1908	29
	Stan Coveleski	1921	29
	George Uhle	1923	29
	Gaylord Perry	1972	29
	Gaylord Perry	1973	29
19	Eight tied at		28

Shutouts

1	Bob Feller	1946	10
	Bob Lemon	1948	10
3	Addie Joss	1906	9
	Addie Joss	1908	9
	Stan Coveleski	1917	9
	Luis Tiant	1968	9
7	Jim Bagby	1917	8
8	Otto Hess	1906	7
	Bob Rhoads	1906	7
	Gaylord Perry	1973	7
11	Eleven tied at		6

Saves

1	Jose Mesa	1995	46
2	Doug Jones	1990	43
3	Jose Mesa	1996	39
4	Doug Jones	1988	37
5	Doug Jones	1989	32
6	Steve Olin	1992	29
7	Ernie Camacho	1984	23
8	Dave LaRoche	1976	21
	Dan Spillner	1982	21
10	Ernie Camacho	1986	20
11	Ray Narleski	1955	19
	Sid Monge	1979	19
13	Jim Kern	1977	18
14	Ed Klieman	1947	17
	Russ Christopher	1948	17
	Gary Bell	1965	17
	Tom Buskey	1974	17
	Dave LaRoche	1975	17
	Steve Olin	1991	17
20	Three tied at		16

Innings Pitched

1	Bob Feller	1946	371.1
2	George Uhle	1923	357.2
3	Gaylord Perry	1973	344.0
4	Bob Feller	1941	343.0
5	Gaylord Perry	1972	342.2
6	Jim Bagby	1920	339.2
7	Addie Joss	1907	338.2
8	Otto Hess	1906	333.2
9	Addie Joss	1908	325.0
10	Gaylord Perry	1974	322.1
11	Bill Bernhard	1904	320.2
	Jim Bagby	1917	320.2
13	Bob Feller	1940	320.1
14	George Uhle	1926	318.1
15	Stan Coveleski	1921	316.0
16	Bob Rhoads	1906	315.0
	Stan Coveleski	1920	315.0
18	Stan Coveleski	1918	311.0
19	Bob Lemon	1952	309.2
20	Sam McDowell	1970	305.0

Walks

1	Bob Feller	1938	208
2	Bob Feller	1941	194
3	Herb Score	1955	154
4	Bob Feller	1946	153
	Sam McDowell	1971	153
6	Bob Lemon	1950	146
7	Bob Feller	1939	142
8	Bob Lemon	1949	137
9	Gene Krapp	1911	136
10	Early Wynn	1952	132
	Sam McDowell	1965	132
12	Sam McDowell	1970	131
13	Wes Ferrell	1931	130
	Monte Pearson	1934	130
	Allie Reynolds	1945	130
16	Bob Lemon	1948	129
	Herb Score	1956	129
	Luis Tiant	1969	129
19	Bob Feller	1947	127
20	Three tied at		124

Strikeouts

1	Bob Feller	1946	348
2	Sam McDowell	1965	325
3	Sam McDowell	1970	304
4	Sam McDowell	1968	283
5	Sam McDowell	1969	279
6	Luis Tiant	1968	264
7	Herb Score	1956	263
8	Bob Feller	1940	261
9	Bob Feller	1941	260
10	Bob Feller	1939	246
11	Herb Score	1955	245
12	Bob Feller	1938	240
13	Gaylord Perry	1973	238
14	Sam McDowell	1967	236
15	Gaylord Perry	1972	234
16	Sam McDowell	1966	225
17	Luis Tiant	1967	219
18	Gaylord Perry	1974	216
19	Dennis Eckersley	1976	200
20	Bob Feller	1947	196

Strikeouts/9 Innings
(minimum 1 Inning Pitched/Tm Gm)

1	Sam McDowell	1965	10.71
2	Sam McDowell	1966	10.42
3	Herb Score	1955	9.70
4	Herb Score	1956	9.49
5	Sam McDowell	1968	9.47
6	Luis Tiant	1967	9.22
7	Luis Tiant	1968	9.20
8	Sam McDowell	1964	9.19
9	Sonny Siebert	1965	9.11
10	Dennis Eckersley	1976	9.03
11	Sam McDowell	1967	8.99
12	Sam McDowell	1970	8.97
13	Sam McDowell	1969	8.81
14	Bob Feller	1946	8.43
15	Pedro Ramos	1963	8.24
16	Herb Score	1959	8.23
17	Sam McDowell	1971	8.05
18	Bob Feller	1938	7.78
19	Bob Feller	1939	7.46
20	Len Barker	1981	7.41

ERA
(minimum 1 Inning Pitched/Tm Gm)

1	Addie Joss	1908	1.16
2	Addie Joss	1904	1.59
3	Luis Tiant	1968	1.60
4	Addie Joss	1909	1.71
5	Addie Joss	1906	1.72
6	Charlie Chech	1908	1.74
7	Earl Moore	1903	1.74
8	Bob Rhoads	1908	1.77
9	Bob Rhoads	1906	1.80
10	Vean Gregg	1911	1.80
11	Sam McDowell	1968	1.81
12	Stan Coveleski	1917	1.81
13	Stan Coveleski	1918	1.82
14	Addie Joss	1907	1.83
15	Otto Hess	1906	1.83
16	Willie Mitchell	1913	1.87
17	Gaylord Perry	1972	1.92
18	Jim Bagby	1917	1.96
19	Addie Joss	1905	2.01
20	Glenn Liebhardt	1907	2.09

Component ERA
(minimum 1 Inning Pitched/Tm Gm)

1	Addie Joss	1908	1.23
2	Luis Tiant	1968	1.51
3	Addie Joss	1906	1.60
4	Stan Coveleski	1917	1.61
5	Addie Joss	1909	1.65
6	Bill Bernhard	1902	1.68
7	Addie Joss	1903	1.70
8	Addie Joss	1907	1.80
9	Addie Joss	1904	1.82
10	Earl Moore	1903	1.83
11	Vean Gregg	1911	1.89
12	Gaylord Perry	1972	1.93
13	Guy Morton	1915	1.95
14	Addie Joss	1905	1.98
15	Willie Mitchell	1913	2.02
16	Bill Bernhard	1903	2.02
17	Heinie Berger	1908	2.02
18	Charlie Chech	1908	2.02
19	Stan Coveleski	1918	2.07
20	Sonny Siebert	1965	2.09

Opponent Average
(minimum 1 Inning Pitched/Tm Gm)

1	Luis Tiant	1968	.168
2	Sam McDowell	1965	.185
3	Herb Score	1956	.186
4	Sam McDowell	1966	.188
5	Sam McDowell	1968	.189
6	Stan Coveleski	1917	.193
7	Herb Score	1955	.194
8	Addie Joss	1908	.197
9	Sonny Siebert	1968	.198
10	Willie Mitchell	1913	.201
11	Allie Reynolds	1943	.202
12	Sonny Siebert	1967	.202
13	Gaylord Perry	1974	.204
14	Vean Gregg	1911	.205
15	Gaylord Perry	1972	.205
16	Sonny Siebert	1965	.206
17	Sam McDowell	1971	.207
18	Bob Feller	1946	.208
19	Bob Lemon	1952	.208
20	Bob Feller	1940	.210

Opponent OBP
(minimum 1 Inning Pitched/Tm Gm)

1	Addie Joss	1908	.218
2	Luis Tiant	1968	.233
3	Addie Joss	1906	.247
4	Addie Joss	1903	.250
5	Bill Bernhard	1902	.253
6	Addie Joss	1909	.255
7	Sonny Siebert	1965	.259
8	Stan Coveleski	1917	.260
9	Gaylord Perry	1972	.261
10	Addie Joss	1907	.261
11	Addie Joss	1904	.265
12	Addie Joss	1905	.266
13	Sonny Siebert	1967	.266
14	Earl Moore	1903	.267
15	Ralph Terry	1965	.268
16	Gaylord Perry	1974	.270
17	Guy Morton	1915	.270
18	Pedro Ramos	1963	.272
19	Bill Bernhard	1903	.272
20	Sonny Siebert	1966	.276

Indians Capsule

Best Season: *1948.* An exciting three-team pennant race ended with the Indians and the Boston Red Sox tied for first. Cleveland traveled to Fenway Park to play a one-game playoff for the American League pennant. MVP Lou Boudreau hit two home runs while rookie Gene Bearden won his 20th game to put Cleveland in the World Series. The Indians beat the Boston Braves in six games for the championship, and set a season attendance record than stood for 14 years.

Worst Season: Hard to say. The bleak seasons all run together after a certain point. Pick any season from 1960 to 1993, and chances are that you can make an argument that it was their worst. The embarrassments and misfortunes never hit all at once. They just kept coming, with jarring regularity, for 30-odd seasons.

Best Player: *Nap Lajoie.*

Best Pitcher: *Bob Feller.*

Best Reliever: *Doug Jones.*

Best Defensive Player: *Tris Speaker.*

Hall of Famers: Twenty-four Hall of Famers have played for the Indians. Those best remembered as Cleveland players or managers are *Earl Averill, Lou Boudreau, Stan Coveleski, Larry Doby, Bob Feller, Elmer Flick, Addie Joss, Nap Lajoie, Bob Lemon, Al Lopez, Gaylord Perry, Joe Sewell, Tris Speaker* and *Early Wynn.*

Franchise All-Star Team:

C	*Steve O'Neill*	LF	*Joe Jackson*
1B	*Hal Trosky*	CF	*Tris Speaker*
2B	*Nap Lajoie*	RF	*Earl Averill*
3B	*Al Rosen*	DH	*Albert Belle*
SS	*Lou Boudreau*	SP	*Bob Feller*
		RP	*Doug Jones*

Biggest Flakes: *Jim Kern, Dave LaRoche, Jay Kirke, Kevin Rhomberg, Joe Charboneau.*

Strangest Career: *Miguel Dilone.* In 1980, his first season with the Indians, he finished third in the AL with a .341 batting average and stole 61 bases. He never played regularly again. He batted .290, .235 and .191 over the next three years as his playing time steadily evaporated.

What Might Have Been: *Joe Charboneau.* The oddball outfielder won AL Rookie of the Year honors and became a cult hero in 1980, but he ruptured a disk in his back the following spring and never hit well again.

Best Trade: The Tribe acquired *Tris Speaker* from the Red Sox on April 12, 1916 for Sad Sam Jones, Fred Thomas and $55,000. Jones had a long and successful career, but Cleveland got 11 Hall of Fame seasons out of Speaker. "Spoke" managed the club for his last eight seasons in Cleveland, leading the Indians to the 1920 World Championship and their only pre-World War II pennant while compiling the second-most victories of any manager in club history.

Worst Trade: Just before the start of the 1960 season, GM Frank Lane traded AL home-run champ and Cleveland icon *Rocky Colavito* to the Detroit Tigers for AL batting champion Harvey Kuenn. The trade was a complete disaster from every possible standpoint. In one fell swoop, Lane had cut the heart out of the team and alienated fans. The Indians declined by 13 games and attendance fell off by over 50 percent. For the next 33 years, the Indians never finished higher than third place and Cleveland's home attendance remained below 1959 levels. Many trace the Indians' perpetual futility in the '60s, '70s and '80s to the Colavito trade.

Best-Looking Player: *Rocky Colavito.*

Ugliest Player: *Addie Joss.*

Best Nicknames: *"Sudden Sam" McDowell, Walter "The Great" Mails.*

Most Unappreciated Player: *Willis Hudlin.*

Most Overrated Player: *Rick Manning.*

Most Admirable Star: *Andre Thornton.*

Least Admirable Star: *Albert Belle.*

Best Season, Player: In *1995, Albert Belle* became the first batter in history to notch 50 homers and 50 doubles in the same season. Ford Frick would hasten to add that Belle accomplished the feat in a 144-game season.

Best Season, Pitcher: *Bob Feller, 1946.* Feller returned from the service to fan 348 batters, which was thought to be a record at the time. In addition to a career-low 2.18 ERA, he posted a 26-15 record while the rest of the staff went 42-71 combined.

Most Impressive Individual Record: *Johnny Allen's* 15-1 won-lost mark in 1937, the best single-season winning percentage ever for a starting pitcher with 15 or more victories. Allen was 15-0 going into the last day of the season, but lost to Detroit's Jake Wade, 1-0.

Biggest Tragedies: Few teams' histories are as rife with tragedy as the Indians'. Lefthander *Herb Score* was one of the league's rising stars until Gil McDougald's line drive struck him in the eye in 1957. He was never the same again (although Score himself blames his loss of effectiveness on a subsequent arm injury rather than the line drive). First baseman *Tony Horton's* career was ended in 1970 by mental problems. *Steve Olin* and *Tim Crews* were killed and *Bobby Ojeda* was badly injured in a boating accident in the spring of 1993. That winter, *Cliff Young* was killed in a car accident. *Addie Joss* died of tubercular meningitis in 1911. Indians shortstop *Ray Chapman* was killed when he was hit in the head by a pitch in 1920. That was major league baseball's only on-field death and one of its most tragic episodes. It's no small irony that the team's nickname is in honor of *Lou Sockalexis,* a tragic case in his own right. Sockalexis, the majors' first Native American, played for the Cleveland Spiders in the late 1890s before losing his career and, ultimately, his life, to alcoholism.

Fan Favorite: *Rocky Colavito.*

—Mat Olkin

Detroit Tigers (1901-1997)

														Opponent				Park Index	
Year	Lg	Pos	W-L	Pct	GB	Manager	Att.	R	OR	HR	Avg	OBP	Slg	HR	Avg	OBP	ERA	Runs	HR
1901	AL	3rd	74-61	.548	8.5	George Stallings	259,430	741	694	29	.279	.340	.370	22	.280	.330	3.30	123	92
1902	AL	7th	52-83	.385	30.5	Frank Dwyer	189,469	566	657	22	.251	.312	.320	20	.274	.333	3.56	94	99
1903	AL	5th	65-71	.478	25.0	Ed Barrow	224,523	567	539	12	.268	.318	.351	19	.256	.311	2.75	90	69
1904	AL	7th	62-90	.408	32.0	Ed Barrow/Bobby Lowe	177,796	505	627	11	.231	.282	.292	16	.252	.316	2.77	93	37
1905	AL	3rd	79-74	.516	15.5	Bill Armour	193,384	512	602	13	.243	.302	.311	11	.245	.316	2.83	99	74
1906	AL	6th	71-78	.477	21.0	Bill Armour	174,043	518	599	10	.242	.295	.306	14	.273	.331	3.06	125	58
1907	AL	1st	92-58	.613	—	Hughie Jennings	297,079	694	532	11	.266	.313	.335	8	.250	.308	2.33	103	69
1908	AL	1st	90-63	.588	—	Hughie Jennings	436,199	647	547	19	.263	.312	.347	12	.255	.306	2.40	105	62
1909	AL	1st	98-54	.645	—	Hughie Jennings	490,490	666	493	19	.267	.325	.342	16	.238	.293	2.26	116	218
1910	AL	3rd	86-68	.558	18.0	Hughie Jennings	391,288	679	582	28	.261	.329	.344	34	.248	.319	2.82	107	195
1911	AL	2nd	89-65	.578	13.5	Hughie Jennings	484,988	831	776	30	.292	.355	.388	28	.283	.348	3.73	121	110
1912	AL	6th	69-84	.451	36.5	Hughie Jennings	402,870	720	777	19	.268	.343	.349	16	.279	.352	3.77	92	68
1913	AL	6th	66-87	.431	30.0	Hughie Jennings	398,502	624	716	24	.265	.336	.355	13	.266	.338	3.38	104	55
1914	AL	4th	80-73	.523	19.5	Hughie Jennings	416,225	615	618	25	.258	.336	.344	17	.249	.322	2.86	104	90
1915	AL	2nd	100-54	.649	2.5	Hughie Jennings	476,105	778	597	23	.268	.357	.358	14	.243	.316	2.86	114	97
1916	AL	3rd	87-67	.565	4.0	Hughie Jennings	616,772	670	595	17	.264	.337	.350	12	.248	.333	2.97	110	107
1917	AL	4th	78-75	.510	21.5	Hughie Jennings	457,289	639	577	25	.259	.328	.344	12	.239	.314	2.56	97	39
1918	AL	7th	55-71	.437	20.0	Hughie Jennings	203,719	476	557	13	.249	.325	.318	10	.263	.335	3.40	100	78
1919	AL	4th	80-60	.571	8.0	Hughie Jennings	643,805	618	578	23	.283	.346	.381	35	.266	.333	3.30	85	71
1920	AL	7th	61-93	.396	37.0	Hughie Jennings	579,650	652	833	30	.270	.334	.359	46	.280	.355	4.04	110	88
1921	AL	6th	71-82	.464	27.0	Ty Cobb	661,527	883	852	58	.316	.385	.433	71	.297	.361	4.40	94	57
1922	AL	3rd	79-75	.513	15.0	Ty Cobb	861,206	828	791	54	.306	.372	.415	62	.288	.354	4.27	97	68
1923	AL	2nd	83-71	.539	16.0	Ty Cobb	911,377	831	741	41	.300	.377	.401	58	.283	.345	4.09	91	111
1924	AL	3rd	86-68	.558	6.0	Ty Cobb	1,015,136	849	796	35	.298	.373	.404	55	.291	.352	4.19	97	97
1925	AL	4th	81-73	.526	16.5	Ty Cobb	820,766	903	829	50	.302	.379	.413	70	.296	.366	4.61	96	82
1926	AL	6th	79-75	.513	12.0	Ty Cobb	711,914	793	830	36	.291	.366	.398	58	.292	.363	4.41	96	125
1927	AL	4th	82-71	.536	27.5	George Moriarty	773,716	845	805	51	.289	.363	.409	52	.290	.364	4.14	122	107
1928	AL	6th	68-86	.442	33.0	George Moriarty	474,323	744	804	62	.279	.340	.401	58	.276	.350	4.32	102	97
1929	AL	6th	70-84	.455	36.0	Bucky Harris	869,318	926	928	110	.299	.361	.453	73	.301	.377	4.96	100	97
1930	AL	5th	75-79	.487	27.0	Bucky Harris	649,450	783	833	82	.284	.344	.421	86	.286	.359	4.70	111	121
1931	AL	7th	61-93	.396	47.0	Bucky Harris	434,056	651	836	43	.268	.330	.371	79	.282	.355	4.56	111	103
1932	AL	5th	76-75	.503	29.5	Bucky Harris	397,157	799	787	80	.273	.335	.401	89	.269	.346	4.30	106	87
1933	AL	5th	75-79	.487	25.0	Bucky Harris/Del Baker	320,972	722	733	57	.269	.329	.380	84	.263	.335	3.95	111	79
1934	AL	1st	101-53	.656	—	Mickey Cochrane	919,161	958	708	74	.300	.376	.424	86	.273	.335	4.06	91	56
1935	AL	1st	93-58	.616	—	Mickey Cochrane	1,034,929	919	665	106	.290	.366	.435	78	.271	.339	3.82	89	77
1936	AL	2nd	83-71	.539	19.5	M. Cochrane/D. Baker/M. Cochrane	875,948	921	871	94	.300	.377	.431	100	.289	.358	5.00	90	128
1937	AL	2nd	89-65	.578	13.0	M. Cochrane/D. Baker/M. Cochrane	1,072,276	935	841	150	.292	.370	.452	102	.279	.357	4.87	120	145
1938	AL	4th	84-70	.545	16.0	Mickey Cochrane/Del Baker	799,557	862	795	137	.272	.359	.411	110	.287	.361	4.79	97	131
1939	AL	5th	81-73	.526	26.5	Del Baker	836,279	849	762	124	.279	.356	.426	104	.268	.341	4.29	125	135
1940	AL	1st	90-64	.584	—	Del Baker	1,112,693	888	717	134	.286	.366	.442	102	.266	.338	4.01	122	154
1941	AL	4th	75-79	.487	26.0	Del Baker	684,915	686	743	81	.263	.340	.375	80	.260	.341	4.18	113	137
1942	AL	5th	73-81	.474	30.0	Del Baker	580,087	589	587	76	.246	.314	.344	60	.248	.326	3.13	122	196
1943	AL	5th	78-76	.506	20.0	Steve O'Neill	606,287	632	560	77	.261	.324	.359	51	.234	.308	3.00	112	125
1944	AL	2nd	88-66	.571	1.0	Steve O'Neill	923,176	658	581	60	.263	.332	.354	39	.257	.318	3.09	108	147
1945	AL	1st	88-65	.575	—	Steve O'Neill	1,280,341	633	565	77	.256	.324	.361	48	.250	.322	2.99	108	133
1946	AL	2nd	92-62	.597	12.0	Steve O'Neill	1,722,590	704	567	108	.258	.337	.374	97	.241	.307	3.22	116	225
1947	AL	2nd	85-69	.552	12.0	Steve O'Neill	1,398,093	714	642	103	.258	.353	.377	79	.258	.326	3.57	112	149
1948	AL	5th	78-76	.506	18.5	Steve O'Neill	1,743,035	700	726	78	.267	.353	.375	92	.259	.335	4.15	92	143
1949	AL	4th	87-67	.565	10.0	Red Rolfe	1,821,204	751	655	88	.267	.361	.378	102	.254	.335	3.77	115	160
1950	AL	2nd	95-59	.617	3.0	Red Rolfe	1,951,474	837	713	114	.282	.369	.417	141	.267	.339	4.12	87	99
1951	AL	5th	73-81	.474	25.0	Red Rolfe	1,132,641	685	741	104	.265	.338	.380	102	.262	.342	4.29	114	134
1952	AL	8th	50-104	.325	45.0	Red Rolfe/Fred Hutchinson	1,026,846	557	738	103	.243	.318	.352	111	.262	.338	4.25	101	138
1953	AL	6th	60-94	.390	40.5	Fred Hutchinson	884,658	695	923	108	.266	.331	.387	154	.291	.363	5.25	106	138
1954	AL	5th	68-86	.442	43.0	Fred Hutchinson	1,079,847	584	664	90	.258	.322	.367	138	.261	.328	3.81	99	119
1955	AL	5th	79-75	.513	17.0	Bucky Harris	1,181,838	775	658	130	.266	.345	.394	126	.261	.328	3.79	92	121
1956	AL	5th	82-72	.532	15.0	Bucky Harris	1,051,182	789	699	150	.279	.356	.420	140	.264	.348	4.06	93	110
1957	AL	4th	78-76	.506	20.0	Jack Tighe	1,272,346	614	614	116	.257	.323	.378	147	.250	.318	3.56	114	148
1958	AL	5th	77-77	.500	15.0	Jack Tighe/Bill Norman	1,098,924	659	606	109	.266	.326	.389	133	.252	.314	3.59	107	133
1959	AL	4th	76-78	.494	18.0	Bill Norman/Jimmy Dykes	1,221,221	713	732	160	.258	.335	.400	177	.254	.315	4.20	128	146
1960	AL	6th	71-83	.461	26.0	J. Dykes/B. Hitchcock/J. Gordon	1,167,669	633	644	150	.239	.324	.375	141	.251	.316	3.64	102	127
1961	AL	2nd	101-61	.623	8.0	Bob Scheffing	1,600,710	841	671	180	.266	.347	.421	170	.252	.311	3.55	89	112
1962	AL	4th	85-76	.528	10.5	Bob Scheffing	1,207,881	758	692	209	.248	.330	.411	169	.259	.321	3.81	124	118
1963	AL	5th	79-83	.488	25.5	Bob Scheffing/Chuck Dressen	821,952	700	703	148	.252	.327	.382	195	.253	.315	3.90	110	145
1964	AL	4th	85-77	.525	14.0	Chuck Dressen	816,139	699	678	157	.253	.319	.395	164	.244	.316	3.84	92	118
1965	AL	4th	89-73	.549	13.0	Bob Swift/Chuck Dressen	1,029,645	680	602	162	.238	.312	.374	137	.237	.306	3.35	110	153
1966	AL	3rd	88-74	.543	10.0	Chuck Dressen/Bob Swift/Frank Skaff	1,124,293	719	698	179	.251	.321	.406	185	.247	.315	3.85	107	119
1967	AL	2nd	91-71	.562	1.0	Mayo Smith	1,447,143	683	587	152	.243	.325	.376	151	.230	.295	3.32	99	115
1968	AL	1st	103-59	.636	—	Mayo Smith	2,031,847	671	492	185	.235	.307	.385	129	.217	.284	2.71	107	138
1969	AL	2nd-E	90-72	.556	19.0	Mayo Smith	1,577,481	701	601	182	.242	.316	.387	128	.232	.310	3.31	105	131
1970	AL	4th-E	79-83	.488	29.0	Mayo Smith	1,501,293	666	731	148	.238	.322	.374	153	.260	.336	4.09	109	133
1971	AL	2nd-E	91-71	.562	12.0	Billy Martin	1,591,073	701	645	179	.254	.325	.405	126	.247	.325	3.63	91	110
1972	AL	1st-E	86-70	.551	—	Billy Martin	1,892,386	558	514	122	.237	.305	.356	101	.236	.304	2.96	127	153
1973	AL	3rd-E	85-77	.525	12.0	Billy Martin/Joe Schultz	1,724,146	642	674	157	.254	.320	.390	154	.265	.326	3.90	101	102
1974	AL	6th-E	72-90	.444	19.0	Ralph Houk	1,243,080	620	768	131	.247	.303	.366	148	.262	.338	4.16	117	131
1975	AL	6th-E	57-102	.358	37.5	Ralph Houk	1,058,836	570	786	125	.249	.301	.366	137	.275	.340	4.27	112	124
1976	AL	5th-E	74-87	.460	24.0	Ralph Houk	1,467,020	609	709	101	.257	.315	.365	101	.263	.331	3.87	110	129
1977	AL	4th-E	74-88	.457	26.0	Ralph Houk	1,359,856	714	751	166	.264	.318	.410	162	.271	.327	4.13	111	123
1978	AL	5th-E	86-76	.531	13.5	Ralph Houk	1,714,893	714	653	129	.271	.339	.392	135	.263	.325	3.64	116	136
1979	AL	5th-E	85-76	.528	18.0	L. Moss/D. Tracewski/S. Anderson	1,630,929	770	738	164	.269	.339	.415	167	.265	.335	4.27	92	114
1980	AL	5th-E	84-78	.519	19.0	Sparky Anderson	1,785,293	830	757	143	.273	.348	.409	152	.267	.334	4.25	114	140
1981	AL	4th-E	31-26	.544	3.5	Sparky Anderson													
	AL	2nd-E	29-23	.558	1.5	Sparky Anderson	1,149,144	427	404	65	.256	.331	.368	83	.236	.310	3.53	109	140

Year	Lg	Pos	W-L	Pct	GB	Manager	Att.	R	OR	HR	Avg	OBP	Slg	Opponent HR	Opponent Avg	Opponent OBP	ERA	Park Index Runs	Park Index HR
1982	AL	4th-E	83-79	.512	12.0	Sparky Anderson	1,636,058	729	685	177	.266	.324	.418	172	.251	.321	3.80	100	148
1983	AL	2nd-E	92-70	.568	6.0	Sparky Anderson	1,829,636	789	679	156	.274	.335	.427	170	.242	.309	3.80	89	109
1984	AL	1st-E	104-58	.642	—	Sparky Anderson	2,704,794	829	643	187	.271	.342	.432	130	.246	.308	3.49	89	92
1985	AL	3rd-E	84-77	.522	15.0	Sparky Anderson	2,286,609	729	688	202	.253	.318	.424	141	.240	.311	3.78	112	140
1986	AL	3rd-E	87-75	.537	8.5	Sparky Anderson	1,899,437	798	714	198	.263	.338	.424	183	.251	.323	4.02	89	89
1987	AL	1st-E	98-64	.605	—	Sparky Anderson	2,061,830	896	735	225	.272	.349	.451	180	.256	.325	4.02	92	126
1988	AL	2nd-E	88-74	.543	1.0	Sparky Anderson	2,081,162	703	658	143	.250	.324	.378	150	.248	.312	3.71	86	119
1989	AL	7th-E	59-103	.364	30.0	Sparky Anderson	1,543,656	617	816	116	.242	.318	.351	150	.274	.352	4.53	98	131
1990	AL	3rd-E	79-83	.488	9.0	Sparky Anderson	1,495,785	750	754	172	.259	.337	.409	154	.259	.341	4.39	105	105
1991	AL	2nd-E	84-78	.519	7.0	Sparky Anderson	1,641,661	817	794	209	.247	.333	.416	148	.281	.348	4.51	109	125
1992	AL	6th-E	75-87	.463	21.0	Sparky Anderson	1,423,963	791	794	182	.256	.337	.407	155	.277	.343	4.61	101	119
1993	AL	3rd-E	85-77	.525	10.0	Sparky Anderson	1,971,421	899	837	178	.275	.362	.434	188	.276	.342	4.65	99	123
1994	AL	5th-E	53-62	.461	18.0	Sparky Anderson	1,184,783	652	671	161	.265	.352	.454	148	.282	.356	5.38	102	107
1995	AL	4th-E	60-84	.417	26.0	Sparky Anderson	1,180,979	654	844	159	.247	.327	.404	170	.296	.365	5.49	109	128
1996	AL	5th-E	53-109	.327	39.0	Buddy Bell	1,168,610	783	1103	204	.256	.323	.420	241	.296	.384	6.38	97	107
1997	AL	3rd-E	79-83	.488	19.0	Buddy Bell	1,365,157	784	790	176	.258	.332	.415	178	.266	.334	4.56	102	115

Team Nicknames: Detroit Tigers 1901-1997.

Team Ballparks: Bennett Park 1901-1911, Navin Field 1912-1937, Briggs Stadium/Tiger Stadium 1938-1997.

Teams: Tigers

1261

Detroit Tigers Individual Season Batting Leaders

Year	Batting Average		On-Base Percentage		Slugging Percentage		Home Runs		RBI		Stolen Bases	
1901	Kid Elberfeld	.308	Kid Elberfeld	.397	Kid Elberfeld	.428	Jimmy Barrett Ducky Holmes	4	Kid Elberfeld	76	Ducky Holmes	35
1902	Jimmy Barrett	.303	Jimmy Barrett	.397	Jimmy Barrett	.387	Jimmy Barrett	4	Kid Elberfeld	64	Jimmy Barrett	24
1903	Sam Crawford	.335	Jimmy Barrett	.407	Sam Crawford	.489	Sam Crawford	4	Sam Crawford	89	Sam Crawford	27
1904	Jimmy Barrett	.268	Jimmy Barrett	.353	Sam Crawford	.361	3 tied with	2	Sam Crawford	73	Sam Crawford	20
1905	Sam Crawford	.297	Sam Crawford	.357	Sam Crawford	.430	Sam Crawford	6	Sam Crawford	75	Sam Crawford	22
1906	Sam Crawford	.295	Sam Crawford	.341	Sam Crawford	.407	4 tied with	2	Sam Crawford	72	Bill Coughlin Germany Schaefer	31
1907	Ty Cobb	.350	Ty Cobb	.380	Ty Cobb	.473	Ty Cobb	5	Ty Cobb	119	Ty Cobb	49
1908	Ty Cobb	.324	Matty McIntyre	.392	Ty Cobb	.475	Sam Crawford	7	Ty Cobb	108	Germany Schaefer	40
1909	Ty Cobb	.377	Ty Cobb	.431	Ty Cobb	.517	Ty Cobb	9	Ty Cobb	107	Ty Cobb	76
1910	Ty Cobb	.383	Ty Cobb	.456	Ty Cobb	.551	Ty Cobb	8	Sam Crawford	120	Ty Cobb	65
1911	Ty Cobb	.420	Ty Cobb	.467	Ty Cobb	.621	Ty Cobb	8	Ty Cobb	127	Ty Cobb	83
1912	Ty Cobb	.410	Ty Cobb	.458	Ty Cobb	.586	Ty Cobb	7	Sam Crawford	109	Ty Cobb	61
1913	Ty Cobb	.390	Ty Cobb	.467	Ty Cobb	.535	Sam Crawford	9	Sam Crawford	83	Ty Cobb	52
1914	Sam Crawford	.314	Sam Crawford	.388	Sam Crawford	.483	Sam Crawford	8	Sam Crawford	104	Donie Bush Ty Cobb	35
1915	Ty Cobb	.369	Ty Cobb	.486	Ty Cobb	.487	George Burns	5	Sam Crawford Bobby Veach	112	Ty Cobb	96
1916	Ty Cobb	.371	Ty Cobb	.452	Ty Cobb	.493	Ty Cobb	5	Bobby Veach	91	Ty Cobb	68
1917	Ty Cobb	.383	Ty Cobb	.444	Ty Cobb	.570	Bobby Veach	8	Bobby Veach	103	Ty Cobb	55
1918	Ty Cobb	.382	Ty Cobb	.440	Ty Cobb	.515	Harry Heilmann	5	Bobby Veach	78	Ty Cobb	34
1919	Ty Cobb	.384	Ty Cobb	.429	Bobby Veach	.519	Harry Heilmann	8	Bobby Veach	101	Ty Cobb	28
1920	Ty Cobb	.334	Ty Cobb	.416	Bobby Veach	.474	Bobby Veach	11	Bobby Veach	113	Donie Bush	15
1921	Harry Heilmann	.394	Ty Cobb	.452	Harry Heilmann	.606	Harry Heilmann	19	Harry Heilmann	139	Ty Cobb	22
1922	Ty Cobb	.401	Ty Cobb	.462	Harry Heilmann	.598	Harry Heilmann	21	Bobby Veach	126	Topper Rigney	17
1923	Harry Heilmann	.403	Harry Heilmann	.481	Harry Heilmann	.632	Harry Heilmann	18	Harry Heilmann	115	Fred Haney	12
1924	Harry Heilmann	.346	Harry Heilmann	.428	Harry Heilmann	.533	Harry Heilmann	10	Harry Heilmann	114	Ty Cobb	23
1925	Harry Heilmann	.393	Ty Cobb	.468	Ty Cobb	.598	Harry Heilmann	13	Harry Heilmann	134	Lu Blue	19
1926	Heinie Manush	.378	Harry Heilmann	.445	Heinie Manush	.564	Heinie Manush	14	Harry Heilmann	103	Lu Blue	13
1927	Harry Heilmann	.398	Harry Heilmann	.475	Harry Heilmann	.616	Harry Heilmann	14	Harry Heilmann	120	Johnny Neun	22
1928	Harry Heilmann	.328	Charlie Gehringer	.395	Harry Heilmann	.507	Harry Heilmann	14	Harry Heilmann	107	Harry Rice	20
1929	Harry Heilmann	.344	Harry Heilmann	.412	Dale Alexander	.580	Dale Alexander	25	Dale Alexander	137	Charlie Gehringer	27
1930	Charlie Gehringer	.330	Charlie Gehringer	.404	Charlie Gehringer	.534	Dale Alexander	20	Dale Alexander	135	Marty McManus	23
1931	John Stone	.327	Dale Alexander	.401	John Stone	.464	John Stone	10	Dale Alexander	87	Roy Johnson	33
1932	Gee Walker	.323	Charlie Gehringer	.370	Charlie Gehringer	.497	Charlie Gehringer	19	John Stone	108	Gee Walker	30
1933	Charlie Gehringer	.325	Charlie Gehringer	.393	Charlie Gehringer	.468	Charlie Gehringer Hank Greenberg	12	Charlie Gehringer	105	Gee Walker	26
1934	Charlie Gehringer	.356	Charlie Gehringer	.450	Hank Greenberg	.600	Hank Greenberg	26	Hank Greenberg	139	Jo-Jo White	28
1935	Charlie Gehringer	.330	Mickey Cochrane	.452	Hank Greenberg	.628	Hank Greenberg	36	Hank Greenberg	170	Jo-Jo White	19
1936	Charlie Gehringer	.354	Charlie Gehringer	.431	Charlie Gehringer	.555	Goose Goslin	24	Goose Goslin	125	Gee Walker	17
1937	Charlie Gehringer	.371	Charlie Gehringer	.458	Hank Greenberg	.668	Hank Greenberg	40	Hank Greenberg	183	Gee Walker	23
1938	Hank Greenberg	.315	Hank Greenberg	.438	Hank Greenberg	.683	Hank Greenberg	58	Hank Greenberg	146	Pete Fox	16
1939	Charlie Gehringer	.325	Charlie Gehringer	.423	Hank Greenberg	.622	Hank Greenberg	33	Hank Greenberg	112	Pete Fox	23
1940	Hank Greenberg	.340	Hank Greenberg	.433	Hank Greenberg	.670	Hank Greenberg	41	Hank Greenberg	150	Barney McCosky	13
1941	Barney McCosky	.324	Barney McCosky	.401	Bruce Campbell	.457	Rudy York	27	Rudy York	111	Barney McCosky	8
1942	Barney McCosky	.293	Barney McCosky	.365	Rudy York	.428	Rudy York	21	Rudy York	90	Barney McCosky	11
1943	Dick Wakefield	.316	Dick Wakefield	.377	Rudy York	.527	Rudy York	34	Rudy York	118	Ned Harris Joe Hoover	6
1944	Mike Higgins	.297	Mike Higgins	.392	Rudy York	.439	Rudy York	18	Rudy York	98	Eddie Mayo	9
1945	Eddie Mayo	.285	Roy Cullenbine	.397	Roy Cullenbine	.451	Roy Cullenbine Rudy York	18	Roy Cullenbine	93	Skeeter Webb	8
1946	Hank Greenberg	.277	Hank Greenberg	.373	Hank Greenberg	.604	Hank Greenberg	44	Hank Greenberg	127	Eddie Lake	15
1947	George Kell	.320	Roy Cullenbine	.401	Hoot Evers	.435	Roy Cullenbine	24	George Kell	93	Eddie Lake	11
1948	Hoot Evers	.314	Pat Mullin	.385	Pat Mullin	.504	Pat Mullin	23	Hoot Evers	103	Johnny Lipon	4
1949	George Kell	.343	George Kell	.424	George Kell	.467	Vic Wertz	20	Vic Wertz	133	George Kell Don Kolloway	7
1950	George Kell	.340	Vic Wertz	.408	Hoot Evers	.551	Vic Wertz	27	Vic Wertz	123	Johnny Lipon	9
1951	George Kell	.319	George Kell	.386	Vic Wertz	.511	Vic Wertz	27	Vic Wertz	94	George Kell	10
1952	Johnny Groth	.284	Johnny Groth	.348	Walt Dropo	.479	Walt Dropo	23	Walt Dropo	70	Pat Mullin	4
1953	Harvey Kuenn	.308	Jim Delsing	.380	Bob Nieman	.453	Ray Boone	22	Walt Dropo	96	Harvey Kuenn	6
1954	Harvey Kuenn	.306	Ray Boone	.376	Ray Boone	.466	Ray Boone	20	Ray Boone	85	Al Kaline Harvey Kuenn	9
1955	Al Kaline	.340	Al Kaline	.421	Al Kaline	.546	Al Kaline	27	Ray Boone	116	Earl Torgeson	9
1956	Harvey Kuenn	.332	Charlie Maxwell	.414	Charlie Maxwell	.534	Charlie Maxwell	28	Al Kaline	128	Harvey Kuenn	9
1957	Al Kaline	.295	Charlie Maxwell	.377	Charlie Maxwell	.482	Charlie Maxwell	24	Al Kaline	90	Al Kaline	11
1958	Harvey Kuenn	.319	Al Kaline	.374	Al Kaline	.490	Gail Harris	20	Al Kaline	85	Red Wilson	10
1959	Harvey Kuenn	.353	Eddie Yost	.435	Al Kaline	.530	Charlie Maxwell	31	Charlie Maxwell	95	Al Kaline	10
1960	Al Kaline	.278	Eddie Yost	.414	Rocky Colavito	.474	Rocky Colavito	35	Rocky Colavito	87	Al Kaline	19
1961	Norm Cash	.361	Norm Cash	.487	Norm Cash	.662	Rocky Colavito	45	Rocky Colavito	140	Jake Wood	30
1962	Bill Bruton	.278	Norm Cash	.382	Rocky Colavito	.514	Norm Cash	39	Rocky Colavito	112	Jake Wood	24
1963	Al Kaline	.312	Norm Cash	.386	Al Kaline	.514	Al Kaline	27	Al Kaline	101	Jake Wood	18
1964	Bill Freehan	.300	Al Kaline	.383	Al Kaline	.469	Dick McAuliffe	24	Norm Cash	83	Bill Bruton	14
1965	Willie Horton	.273	Norm Cash	.371	Norm Cash	.512	Norm Cash	30	Willie Horton	104	Jerry Lumpe	7
1966	Al Kaline	.288	Al Kaline	.392	Al Kaline	.534	Norm Cash	32	Willie Horton	100	Don Wert	6
1967	Al Kaline	.308	Al Kaline	.411	Al Kaline	.541	Al Kaline	25	Al Kaline	78	Mickey Stanley	9
1968	Willie Horton	.285	Bill Freehan	.366	Willie Horton	.543	Willie Horton	36	Jim Northrup	90	Dick McAuliffe	8
1969	Jim Northrup	.295	Norm Cash	.368	Jim Northrup	.508	Willie Horton	28	Willie Horton	91	Mickey Stanley	8
1970	Al Kaline	.278	Al Kaline	.377	Jim Northrup	.458	Jim Northrup	24	Jim Northrup	80	Mickey Stanley	10
1971	Norm Cash	.283	Norm Cash	.372	Norm Cash	.531	Norm Cash	32	Norm Cash	91	Jim Northrup	7
1972	Norm Cash	.259	Norm Cash	.338	Norm Cash	.445	Norm Cash	22	Norm Cash	61	Tony Taylor	5
1973	Mickey Stanley	.244	Mickey Stanley	.297	Mickey Stanley	.384	Norm Cash	19	Aurelio Rodriguez	58	Tony Taylor	9
1974	Bill Freehan	.297	Bill Freehan	.361	Bill Freehan	.479	Bill Freehan	18	Al Kaline	64	Ron LeFlore	23
1975	Willie Horton	.275	Gary Sutherland	.321	Willie Horton	.421	Willie Horton	25	Willie Horton	92	Ron LeFlore	28

1262   Teams: Tigers

Year	Batting Average		On-Base Percentage		Slugging Percentage		Home Runs		RBI		Stolen Bases	
1976	Ron LeFlore	.316	Rusty Staub	.386	Rusty Staub	.433	Jason Thompson	17	Rusty Staub	96	Ron LeFlore	58
1977	Ron LeFlore	.325	Ron LeFlore	.363	Jason Thompson	.487	Jason Thompson	31	Jason Thompson	105	Ron LeFlore	39
1978	Ron LeFlore	.297	Steve Kemp	.379	Jason Thompson	.472	Jason Thompson	26	Rusty Staub	121	Ron LeFlore	68
1979	Steve Kemp	.318	Steve Kemp	.398	Steve Kemp	.543	Steve Kemp	26	Steve Kemp	105	Ron LeFlore	78
1980	Alan Trammell	.300	Steve Kemp	.376	Lance Parrish	.499	Lance Parrish	24	Steve Kemp	101	Tom Brookens / Ricky Peters	13
1981	Steve Kemp	.277	Steve Kemp	.389	Steve Kemp	.419	Lance Parrish	10	Steve Kemp	49	Alan Trammell	17
1982	Larry Herndon	.292	Chet Lemon	.368	Lance Parrish	.529	Lance Parrish	32	Larry Herndon	88	Alan Trammell	19
1983	Lou Whitaker	.320	Alan Trammell	.385	Lance Parrish	.483	Lance Parrish	27	Lance Parrish	114	Alan Trammell	30
1984	Alan Trammell	.314	Alan Trammell	.382	Kirk Gibson	.516	Lance Parrish	33	Lance Parrish	98	Kirk Gibson	29
1985	Kirk Gibson	.287	Kirk Gibson	.364	Darrell Evans	.519	Darrell Evans	40	Lance Parrish	98	Kirk Gibson	30
1986	Alan Trammell	.277	Kirk Gibson	.371	Kirk Gibson	.492	Darrell Evans	29	Darnell Coles / Kirk Gibson	86	Kirk Gibson	34
1987	Alan Trammell	.343	Alan Trammell	.402	Alan Trammell	.551	Darrell Evans	34	Alan Trammell	105	Kirk Gibson	26
1988	Alan Trammell	.311	Alan Trammell	.373	Alan Trammell	.464	Darrell Evans	22	Alan Trammell	69	Gary Pettis	44
1989	Gary Pettis	.257	Gary Pettis	.375	Lou Whitaker	.462	Lou Whitaker	28	Lou Whitaker	85	Gary Pettis	43
1990	Alan Trammell	.304	Cecil Fielder	.377	Cecil Fielder	.592	Cecil Fielder	51	Cecil Fielder	132	Tony Phillips	19
1991	Tony Phillips	.284	Lou Whitaker	.391	Cecil Fielder	.513	Cecil Fielder	44	Cecil Fielder	133	Milt Cuyler	41
1992	Lou Whitaker	.278	Tony Phillips	.387	Mickey Tettleton	.469	Cecil Fielder	35	Cecil Fielder	124	Gary Pettis	13
1993	Tony Phillips	.313	Tony Phillips	.443	Mickey Tettleton	.492	Mickey Tettleton	32	Cecil Fielder	117	Tony Phillips	16
1994	Lou Whitaker	.301	Mickey Tettleton	.419	Kirk Gibson	.548	Cecil Fielder	28	Cecil Fielder	90	Tony Phillips	13
1995	Travis Fryman	.275	Chad Curtis	.349	Cecil Fielder	.472	Cecil Fielder	31	Cecil Fielder	82	Chad Curtis	27
1996	Bob Higginson	.320	Bob Higginson	.404	Bob Higginson	.577	Tony Clark	27	Travis Fryman	100	Kimera Bartee	20
1997	Bob Higginson	.299	Bob Higginson	.379	Bob Higginson	.520	Tony Clark	32	Tony Clark	117	Brian Hunter	74

Teams: Tigers

Detroit Tigers Individual Season Pitching Leaders

Year	ERA		Baserunners/9 IP		Innings Pitched		Strikeouts		Wins		Saves	
1901	Joe Yeager	2.61	Joe Yeager	11.9	Roscoe Miller	332.0	Ed Siever	85	Roscoe Miller	23	Roscoe Miller / Joe Yeager	1
1902	Ed Siever	1.91	Ed Siever	9.6	Win Mercer	281.2	George Mullin	78	Win Mercer	15	3 tied with	1
1903	George Mullin	2.25	Wild Bill Donovan	10.2	George Mullin	320.2	Wild Bill Donovan	187	George Mullin	18	George Mullin	2
1904	George Mullin	2.40	Wild Bill Donovan	10.9	George Mullin	382.1	George Mullin	161	Wild Bill Donovan / George Mullin	17	Ed Killian / Frank Kitson	1
1905	Ed Killian	2.27	Ed Killian	10.9	George Mullin	347.2	George Mullin	168	Ed Killian	23	Ed Killian / Frank Kitson	1
1906	Ed Siever	2.71	Ed Siever	11.9	George Mullin	330.0	George Mullin	123	George Mullin	21	John Eubank / Ed Killian	2
1907	Ed Killian	1.78	Wild Bill Donovan	10.4	George Mullin	357.1	George Mullin	146	Wild Bill Donovan / Ed Killian	25	George Mullin	3
1908	Ed Summers	1.64	Wild Bill Donovan	10.0	Ed Summers	301.0	Wild Bill Donovan	141	Ed Summers	24	5 tied with	1
1909	Ed Killian	1.71	Ed Summers	9.7	George Mullin	303.2	George Mullin	124	George Mullin	29	Wild Bill Donovan / Ralph Works	2
1910	Ed Willett	2.37	Ed Willett	10.7	George Mullin	289.0	Wild Bill Donovan	107	George Mullin	21	Frank Browning	3
1911	George Mullin	3.07	Wild Bill Donovan	12.1	George Mullin	234.1	George Mullin	87	George Mullin	18	5 tied with	1
1912	Jean Dubuc	2.77	Jean Dubuc	12.0	Ed Willett	284.1	Jean Dubuc	97	Jean Dubuc / Ed Willett	17	Jean Dubuc	3
1913	Hooks Dauss	2.68	Hooks Dauss	11.3	Jean Dubuc	242.2	Hooks Dauss	107	Jean Dubuc	15	Jean Dubuc	2
1914	Harry Coveleski	2.49	Harry Coveleski	10.8	Harry Coveleski	303.1	Hooks Dauss	150	Harry Coveleski	22	Hooks Dauss	4
1915	Harry Coveleski	2.45	Harry Coveleski	10.9	Harry Coveleski	312.2	Harry Coveleski	150	Hooks Dauss	24	3 tied with	4
1916	Harry Coveleski	1.97	Harry Coveleski	9.8	Harry Coveleski	324.1	Harry Coveleski	108	Harry Coveleski	21	Hooks Dauss	4
1917	Bill James	2.09	Bernie Boland	11.1	Hooks Dauss	270.2	Hooks Dauss	102	Hooks Dauss	17	Bernie Boland	6
1918	Bernie Boland	2.65	Bernie Boland	11.0	Hooks Dauss	249.2	Hooks Dauss	73	Bernie Boland	14	Hooks Dauss	3
1919	Dutch Leonard	2.77	Bernie Boland	11.3	Hooks Dauss	256.1	Dutch Leonard	102	Hooks Dauss	21	4 tied with	1
1920	Howard Ehmke	3.29	Dutch Leonard	12.4	Hooks Dauss	270.1	Doc Ayers	103	Howard Ehmke	15	Howard Ehmke	3
1921	Dutch Leonard	3.75	Dutch Leonard	12.7	Dutch Leonard	245.0	Dutch Leonard	120	Howard Ehmke	13	Jim Middleton	7
1922	Herman Pillette	2.85	Dutch Leonard	12.5	Howard Ehmke	279.2	Howard Ehmke	108	Herman Pillette	19	Hooks Dauss	4
1923	Hooks Dauss	3.62	Syl Johnson	11.8	Hooks Dauss	316.0	Hooks Dauss	105	Hooks Dauss	21	Bert Cole	5
1924	Rip Collins	3.21	Rip Collins	11.1	Earl Whitehill	233.0	Rip Collins	75	Earl Whitehill	17	Hooks Dauss	6
1925	Hooks Dauss	3.16	Hooks Dauss	12.9	Earl Whitehill	239.1	Earl Whitehill	83	Hooks Dauss	16	Jess Doyle	8
1926	Sam Gibson	3.48	Earl Whitehill	12.8	Earl Whitehill	252.1	Earl Whitehill	109	Earl Whitehill	16	Hooks Dauss	9
1927	Earl Whitehill	3.36	Earl Whitehill	13.4	Earl Whitehill	236.0	Earl Whitehill	95	Earl Whitehill	16	Ken Holloway	6
1928	Ownie Carroll	3.27	Ownie Carroll	12.2	Ownie Carroll	231.0	Earl Whitehill	93	Ownie Carroll	16	Elam Vangilder	5
1929	George Uhle	4.08	George Uhle	12.4	George Uhle	249.0	Earl Whitehill	103	George Uhle	15	Lil Stoner	4
1930	George Uhle	3.65	George Uhle	12.0	George Uhle	239.0	George Uhle	117	Earl Whitehill	17	Charlie Sullivan	5
1931	George Uhle	3.50	George Uhle	11.3	Earl Whitehill	271.2	Tommy Bridges	105	Vic Sorrell / Earl Whitehill	13	Chief Hogsett / George Uhle	2
1932	Tommy Bridges	3.36	Vic Sorrell	12.1	Earl Whitehill	244.0	Tommy Bridges	108	Earl Whitehill	16	Chief Hogsett	7
1933	Tommy Bridges	3.09	Firpo Marberry	11.1	Firpo Marberry	238.1	Tommy Bridges	120	Firpo Marberry	16	Chief Hogsett	9
1934	Eldon Auker	3.42	Schoolboy Rowe	11.5	Tommy Bridges	275.0	Tommy Bridges	151	Schoolboy Rowe	24	Chief Hogsett / Firpo Marberry	3
1935	Tommy Bridges	3.51	Schoolboy Rowe	11.2	Schoolboy Rowe	275.2	Tommy Bridges	163	Tommy Bridges	21	Chief Hogsett	5
1936	Tommy Bridges	3.60	Schoolboy Rowe	12.2	Tommy Bridges	294.2	Tommy Bridges	175	Tommy Bridges	23	4 tied with	3
1937	Eldon Auker	3.88	Eldon Auker	12.6	Eldon Auker	252.2	Tommy Bridges	138	Roxie Lawson	18	Jack Russell	4
1938	George Gill	4.12	George Gill	13.6	Vern Kennedy	190.1	Tommy Bridges	101	Tommy Bridges	13	Harry Eisenstat	4
1939	Bobo Newsom	3.37	Tommy Bridges	11.5	Bobo Newsom	246.0	Bobo Newsom	164	Tommy Bridges / Bobo Newsom	17	Al Benton	5
1940	Bobo Newsom	2.83	Schoolboy Rowe	11.4	Bobo Newsom	264.0	Bobo Newsom	164	Bobo Newsom	21	Al Benton	17
1941	Al Benton	2.97	Al Benton	11.3	Bobo Newsom	250.1	Bobo Newsom	175	Al Benton	15	Al Benton	7
1942	Hal Newhouser	2.45	Al Benton	11.7	Al Benton	226.2	Al Benton	110	Virgil Trucks	14	Hal Newhouser	5
1943	Tommy Bridges	2.39	Virgil Trucks	9.9	Dizzy Trout	246.2	Hal Newhouser	144	Dizzy Trout	20	Dizzy Trout	6
1944	Dizzy Trout	2.12	Dizzy Trout	10.2	Dizzy Trout	352.1	Hal Newhouser	187	Hal Newhouser	29	Johnny Gorsica	4
1945	Hal Newhouser	1.81	Hal Newhouser	10.0	Hal Newhouser	313.1	Hal Newhouser	212	Hal Newhouser	25	Stubby Overmire	4
1946	Hal Newhouser	1.94	Hal Newhouser	9.7	Hal Newhouser	292.2	Hal Newhouser	275	Hal Newhouser	26	George Caster	4
1947	Hal Newhouser	2.87	Fred Hutchinson	11.2	Hal Newhouser	285.0	Hal Newhouser	176	Fred Hutchinson	18	Al Benton	7
1948	Hal Newhouser	3.01	Fred Hutchinson	11.1	Hal Newhouser	272.1	Hal Newhouser	143	Hal Newhouser	21	Art Houtteman	10
1949	Virgil Trucks	2.81	Fred Hutchinson	10.5	Hal Newhouser	292.0	Virgil Trucks	153	Virgil Trucks	19	Virgil Trucks	4
1950	Art Houtteman	3.54	Art Houtteman	11.9	Art Houtteman	274.2	Ted Gray	102	Art Houtteman	19	3 tied with	4
1951	Fred Hutchinson	3.68	Fred Hutchinson	11.1	Ted Gray	197.1	Ted Gray	131	Virgil Trucks	13	Dizzy Trout	5
1952	Virgil Trucks	3.97	Art Houtteman	11.7	Ted Gray	224.0	Ted Gray	138	Ted Gray	12	Hal White	5
1953	Ned Garver	4.45	Ted Gray	12.7	Ted Gray	198.1	Ted Gray	115	Ned Garver	11	Ray Herbert	6
1954	Steve Gromek	2.74	Ned Garver	10.3	Steve Gromek	252.2	Billy Hoeft	114	Steve Gromek	18	George Zuverink	4
1955	Billy Hoeft	2.99	Billy Hoeft	10.8	Frank Lary	235.0	Billy Hoeft	133	Billy Hoeft	16	3 tied with	3
1956	Frank Lary	3.15	Paul Foytack	12.5	Frank Lary	294.0	Paul Foytack	184	Frank Lary	21	Al Aber	7
1957	Jim Bunning	2.69	Jim Bunning	10.0	Jim Bunning	267.1	Jim Bunning	182	Jim Bunning	20	Duke Maas	6
1958	Frank Lary	2.90	Paul Foytack	10.9	Frank Lary	260.1	Jim Bunning	177	Frank Lary	16	Hank Aguirre	5
1959	Don Mossi	3.36	Don Mossi	10.3	Jim Bunning	249.2	Jim Bunning	201	3 tied with	17	Tom Morgan	9
1960	Jim Bunning	2.79	Jim Bunning	10.4	Frank Lary	274.1	Jim Bunning	201	Frank Lary	15	Hank Aguirre	10
1961	Don Mossi	2.96	Jim Bunning	10.5	Frank Lary	275.1	Jim Bunning	194	Frank Lary	23	Terry Fox	12
1962	Hank Aguirre	2.21	Hank Aguirre	9.7	Jim Bunning	258.0	Jim Bunning	184	Jim Bunning	19	Terry Fox	16
1963	Hank Aguirre	3.67	Jim Bunning	11.6	Jim Bunning	248.1	Jim Bunning	196	Phil Regan	15	Terry Fox	11
1964	Mickey Lolich	3.26	Mickey Lolich	10.3	Dave Wickersham	254.0	Mickey Lolich	192	Dave Wickersham	19	Larry Sherry	11
1965	Denny McLain	2.61	Denny McLain	9.7	Mickey Lolich	243.2	Mickey Lolich	226	Denny McLain	16	Terry Fox	10
1966	Earl Wilson	2.59	Earl Wilson	9.3	Denny McLain	264.1	Denny McLain	192	Denny McLain	20	Larry Sherry	20
1967	Mickey Lolich	3.04	Mickey Lolich	10.1	Earl Wilson	264.0	Earl Wilson	184	Earl Wilson	22	Fred Gladding	12
1968	Denny McLain	1.96	Denny McLain	8.3	Denny McLain	336.0	Denny McLain	280	Denny McLain	31	Pat Dobson / Daryl Patterson	7
1969	Denny McLain	2.80	Denny McLain	9.9	Denny McLain	325.0	Mickey Lolich	271	Denny McLain	24	Don McMahon	11
1970	Mickey Lolich	3.80	Joe Niekro	12.5	Mickey Lolich	272.2	Mickey Lolich	230	Mickey Lolich	14	Tom Timmermann	27
1971	Mickey Lolich	2.92	Mickey Lolich	10.4	Mickey Lolich	376.0	Mickey Lolich	308	Mickey Lolich	25	Fred Scherman	20
1972	Mickey Lolich	2.50	Mickey Lolich	10.1	Mickey Lolich	327.1	Mickey Lolich	250	Mickey Lolich	22	Chuck Seelbach	14
1973	Joe Coleman	3.53	Mickey Lolich	11.6	Mickey Lolich	308.2	Mickey Lolich	214	Joe Coleman	23	John Hiller	38

Teams: Tigers

Year	ERA		Baserunners/9 IP		Innings Pitched		Strikeouts		Wins		Saves	
1974	Mickey Lolich	4.15	Mickey Lolich	11.4	Mickey Lolich	308.0	Mickey Lolich	202	John Hiller	17	John Hiller	13
1975	Mickey Lolich	3.78	Mickey Lolich	12.1	Mickey Lolich	240.2	Mickey Lolich	139	Mickey Lolich	12	John Hiller	14
1976	Mark Fidrych	2.34	Mark Fidrych	9.8	Dave Roberts	252.0	John Hiller	117	Mark Fidrych	19	John Hiller	13
1977	Dave Rozema	3.09	Dave Rozema	10.8	Dave Rozema	218.1	John Hiller	115	Dave Rozema	15	Steve Foucault	13
1978	Dave Rozema	3.14	Dave Rozema	10.7	Jim Slaton	233.2	Milt Wilcox	132	Jim Slaton	17	John Hiller	15
1979	Jack Morris	3.28	Jack Morris	11.0	Jack Morris	197.2	Jack Morris	113	Jack Morris	17	Aurelio Lopez	21
1980	Dan Petry	3.94	Dan Schatzeder	11.2	Jack Morris	250.0	Jack Morris	112	Jack Morris	16	Aurelio Lopez	21
1981	Dan Petry	3.00	Jack Morris	10.6	Jack Morris	198.0	Jack Morris	97	Jack Morris	14	Kevin Saucier	13
1982	Dan Petry	3.22	Jerry Ujdur	11.2	Jack Morris	266.1	Jack Morris	135	Jack Morris	17	Dave Tobik	9
1983	Jack Morris	3.34	Jack Morris	10.5	Jack Morris	293.2	Jack Morris	232	Jack Morris	20	Aurelio Lopez	18
1984	Dan Petry	3.24	Dan Petry	11.6	Jack Morris	240.1	Jack Morris	148	Jack Morris	19	Willie Hernandez	32
1985	Jack Morris	3.33	Dan Petry	10.3	Jack Morris	257.0	Jack Morris	191	Jack Morris	16	Willie Hernandez	31
1986	Jack Morris	3.27	Jack Morris	10.5	Jack Morris	267.0	Jack Morris	223	Jack Morris	21	Willie Hernandez	24
1987	Jack Morris	3.38	Jack Morris	10.9	Jack Morris	266.0	Jack Morris	208	Jack Morris	18	Eric King	9
1988	Jeff Robinson	2.98	Jeff Robinson	10.3	Jack Morris	235.0	Jack Morris	168	Jack Morris	15	Mike Henneman	22
1989	Frank Tanana	3.58	Frank Tanana	12.4	Frank Tanana	223.2	Frank Tanana	147	Mike Henneman	11	Willie Hernandez	15
1990	Jack Morris	4.51	Jack Morris	12.0	Jack Morris	249.2	Jack Morris	162	Jack Morris	15	Mike Henneman	22
1991	Frank Tanana	3.69	Bill Gullickson	12.1	Bill Gullickson	226.1	Frank Tanana	107	Bill Gullickson	20	Mike Henneman	21
1992	Bill Gullickson	4.34	Bill Gullickson	11.3	Bill Gullickson	221.2	Frank Tanana	91	Bill Gullickson	14	Mike Henneman	24
1993	David Wells	4.19	David Wells	11.2	Mike Moore	213.2	David Wells	139	John Doherty	14	Mike Henneman	24
1994	Mike Moore	5.42	Mike Moore	14.2	Tim Belcher	162.0	Tim Belcher	76	Mike Moore	11	Mike Henneman	8
1995	Felipe Lira	4.31	Felipe Lira	13.2	Felipe Lira	146.1	Felipe Lira	89	David Wells	10	Mike Henneman	18
1996	Felipe Lira	5.22	Felipe Lira	12.9	Felipe Lira	194.2	Felipe Lira	113	Omar Olivares	7	Gregg Olson	8
1997	Justin Thompson	3.02	Justin Thompson	10.3	Justin Thompson	223.1	Justin Thompson	151	Willie Blair	16	Todd Jones	31

Teams: Tigers

Tigers Franchise Batting Leaders—Career

Games

1	Al Kaline	2,834
2	Ty Cobb	2,805
3	Lou Whitaker	2,390
4	Charlie Gehringer	2,323
5	Alan Trammell	2,293
6	Sam Crawford	2,114
7	Norm Cash	2,018
8	Harry Heilmann	1,991
9	Donie Bush	1,872
10	Bill Freehan	1,774
11	Dick McAuliffe	1,656
12	Bobby Veach	1,605
13	Mickey Stanley	1,516
14	Willie Horton	1,515
15	Jim Northrup	1,279
16	Hank Greenberg	1,269
17	Rudy York	1,268
18	Aurelio Rodriguez	1,241
19	Billy Rogell	1,207
20	Tom Brookens	1,206

At-Bats

1	Ty Cobb	10,591
2	Al Kaline	10,116
3	Charlie Gehringer	8,860
4	Lou Whitaker	8,570
5	Alan Trammell	8,288
6	Sam Crawford	7,985
7	Harry Heilmann	7,297
8	Donie Bush	6,970
9	Norm Cash	6,593
10	Bill Freehan	6,073
11	Bobby Veach	5,982
12	Dick McAuliffe	5,898
13	Willie Horton	5,405
14	Mickey Stanley	5,022
15	Hank Greenberg	4,791
16	Rudy York	4,677
17	Jim Northrup	4,437
18	Billy Rogell	4,418
19	Harvey Kuenn	4,372
20	Aurelio Rodriguez	4,352

Runs

1	Ty Cobb	2,087
2	Charlie Gehringer	1,774
3	Al Kaline	1,622
4	Lou Whitaker	1,386
5	Donie Bush	1,242
6	Alan Trammell	1,231
7	Harry Heilmann	1,209
8	Sam Crawford	1,115
9	Norm Cash	1,028
10	Hank Greenberg	980
11	Bobby Veach	859
12	Dick McAuliffe	856
13	Rudy York	738
14	Bill Freehan	706
15	Kirk Gibson	698
16	Willie Horton	671
17	Pete Fox	670
18	Lu Blue	669
19	Billy Rogell	668
20	Mickey Stanley	641

Hits

1	Ty Cobb	3,901
2	Al Kaline	3,007
3	Charlie Gehringer	2,839
4	Harry Heilmann	2,499
5	Sam Crawford	2,466
6	Lou Whitaker	2,369
7	Alan Trammell	2,365
8	Bobby Veach	1,860
9	Norm Cash	1,793
10	Donie Bush	1,745
11	Bill Freehan	1,591
12	Hank Greenberg	1,528
13	Willie Horton	1,490
14	Dick McAuliffe	1,471
15	Harvey Kuenn	1,372
16	Rudy York	1,317
17	Mickey Stanley	1,243
18	Billy Rogell	1,210
19	Jim Northrup	1,184
20	Pete Fox	1,182

Doubles

1	Ty Cobb	666
2	Charlie Gehringer	574
3	Al Kaline	498
4	Harry Heilmann	497
5	Lou Whitaker	420
6	Alan Trammell	412
7	Sam Crawford	402
8	Hank Greenberg	366
9	Bobby Veach	345
10	Harvey Kuenn	244
11	Norm Cash	241
	Bill Freehan	241
13	Rudy York	236
14	Travis Fryman	229
15	Billy Rogell	227
16	Pete Fox	222
17	Dick McAuliffe	218
	Chet Lemon	218
19	Gee Walker	216
20	Willie Horton	211

Triples

1	Ty Cobb	285
2	Sam Crawford	249
3	Charlie Gehringer	146
4	Harry Heilmann	145
5	Bobby Veach	136
6	Al Kaline	75
7	Donie Bush	73
8	Dick McAuliffe	70
9	Hank Greenberg	69
10	Lu Blue	66
11	Lou Whitaker	65
12	Billy Rogell	64
13	Alan Trammell	55
14	Matty McIntyre	54
15	Pete Fox	52
	Barney McCosky	52
17	John Stone	50
18	Jackie Tavener	49
19	Roy Johnson	48
	Mickey Stanley	48

Home Runs

1	Al Kaline	399
2	Norm Cash	373
3	Hank Greenberg	306
4	Willie Horton	262
5	Cecil Fielder	245
6	Lou Whitaker	244
7	Rudy York	239
8	Lance Parrish	212
9	Bill Freehan	200
10	Kirk Gibson	195
11	Dick McAuliffe	192
12	Alan Trammell	185
13	Charlie Gehringer	184
14	Harry Heilmann	164
15	Travis Fryman	149
16	Jim Northrup	145
17	Chet Lemon	142
18	Darrell Evans	141
19	Rocky Colavito	139
20	Charlie Maxwell	133

RBI

1	Ty Cobb	1,800
2	Al Kaline	1,583
3	Harry Heilmann	1,442
4	Charlie Gehringer	1,427
5	Sam Crawford	1,264
6	Hank Greenberg	1,202
7	Norm Cash	1,087
8	Lou Whitaker	1,084
9	Bobby Veach	1,042
10	Alan Trammell	1,003
11	Rudy York	936
12	Willie Horton	886
13	Bill Freehan	758
	Cecil Fielder	758
15	Lance Parrish	700
16	Travis Fryman	679
17	Dick McAuliffe	672
18	Kirk Gibson	668
19	Jim Northrup	570
20	Chet Lemon	536

Walks

1	Al Kaline	1,277
2	Lou Whitaker	1,197
3	Charlie Gehringer	1,185
4	Ty Cobb	1,148
5	Donie Bush	1,125
6	Norm Cash	1,025
7	Alan Trammell	850
8	Dick McAuliffe	842
9	Harry Heilmann	792
10	Hank Greenberg	748
11	Sam Crawford	646
12	Rudy York	640
13	Bill Freehan	626
14	Billy Rogell	590
15	Lu Blue	589
16	Tony Phillips	519
	Cecil Fielder	519
18	Bobby Veach	512
19	Kirk Gibson	499
20	Willie Horton	469

Strikeouts

1	Lou Whitaker	1,099
2	Norm Cash	1,081
3	Al Kaline	1,020
4	Willie Horton	945
5	Dick McAuliffe	932
6	Travis Fryman	931
7	Kirk Gibson	930
8	Cecil Fielder	926
9	Alan Trammell	874
10	Lance Parrish	847
11	Hank Greenberg	771
12	Bill Freehan	753
13	Rudy York	672
14	Chet Lemon	647
15	Ron LeFlore	628
16	Jim Northrup	603
17	Aurelio Rodriguez	589
18	Mickey Stanley	564
19	Tom Brookens	553
20	Don Wert	519

Stolen Bases

1	Ty Cobb	865
2	Donie Bush	400
3	Sam Crawford	317
4	Ron LeFlore	294
5	Alan Trammell	236
6	Kirk Gibson	194
7	George Moriarty	190
8	Bobby Veach	189
9	Charlie Gehringer	181
10	Lou Whitaker	143
11	Davy Jones	140
12	Al Kaline	137
13	Gee Walker	132
14	Germany Schaefer	123
15	Harry Heilmann	110
16	Pete Fox	107
17	Gary Pettis	100
18	Ossie Vitt	99
19	Jimmy Barrett	92
20	Matty McIntyre	89

Runs Created

1	Ty Cobb	2,406
2	Al Kaline	1,794
3	Charlie Gehringer	1,766
4	Harry Heilmann	1,502
5	Lou Whitaker	1,398
6	Sam Crawford	1,392
7	Alan Trammell	1,248
8	Norm Cash	1,218
9	Hank Greenberg	1,180
10	Bobby Veach	986
11	Donie Bush	903
12	Dick McAuliffe	869
13	Bill Freehan	864
14	Rudy York	859
15	Willie Horton	828
16	Kirk Gibson	725
17	Billy Rogell	662
	Cecil Fielder	662
19	Travis Fryman	648
20	Harvey Kuenn	646

Runs Created/27 Outs

(minimum 2000 Plate Appearances)

1	Hank Greenberg	9.22
2	Ty Cobb	8.79
3	Harry Heilmann	7.65
4	Charlie Gehringer	7.38
5	Mickey Tettleton	6.81
6	Dick Wakefield	6.63
7	Goose Goslin	6.55
8	Norm Cash	6.55
9	Rudy York	6.54
10	Bob Fothergill	6.46
11	Barney McCosky	6.44
12	Heinie Manush	6.42
13	Al Kaline	6.39
14	Vic Wertz	6.38
15	Sam Crawford	6.25
16	Rocky Colavito	6.22
17	Jimmy Barrett	6.21
18	Cecil Fielder	6.20
19	Johnny Bassler	6.17
20	Ray Boone	6.14

Batting Average

(minimum 2000 Plate Appearances)

1	Ty Cobb	.368
2	Harry Heilmann	.342
3	Bob Fothergill	.337
4	George Kell	.325
5	Heinie Manush	.321
6	Charlie Gehringer	.320
7	Hank Greenberg	.319
8	Gee Walker	.317
9	Harvey Kuenn	.314
10	Barney McCosky	.312
11	Bobby Veach	.311
12	Sam Crawford	.309
13	Johnny Bassler	.308
14	John Stone	.304
15	Pete Fox	.302
16	Goose Goslin	.297
17	Al Kaline	.297
18	Ron LeFlore	.297
19	Topper Rigney	.296
20	Lu Blue	.295

On-Base Percentage

(minimum 2000 Plate Appearances)

1	Ty Cobb	.434
2	Johnny Bassler	.420
3	Hank Greenberg	.412
4	Harry Heilmann	.410
5	Charlie Gehringer	.404
6	Lu Blue	.403
7	Dick Wakefield	.396
8	Tony Phillips	.395
9	George Kell	.391
10	Topper Rigney	.389
11	Mickey Tettleton	.387
12	Barney McCosky	.386
13	Jimmy Barrett	.382
14	Bob Fothergill	.379
15	Heinie Manush	.379
16	Goose Goslin	.376
17	Vic Wertz	.376
18	Steve Kemp	.376
19	Al Kaline	.376
20	Norm Cash	.374

Slugging Percentage

(minimum 2000 Plate Appearances)

1	Hank Greenberg	.616
2	Harry Heilmann	.518
3	Ty Cobb	.516
4	Rudy York	.503
5	Rocky Colavito	.501
6	Cecil Fielder	.498
7	Norm Cash	.490
8	Ray Boone	.482
9	Bob Fothergill	.482
10	Charlie Gehringer	.480
11	Mickey Tettleton	.480
12	Kirk Gibson	.480
13	Al Kaline	.480
14	Vic Wertz	.476
15	Heinie Manush	.475
16	Willie Horton	.472
17	Lance Parrish	.469
18	Gee Walker	.469
19	Charlie Maxwell	.465
20	John Stone	.461

Teams: Tigers

Tigers Franchise Pitching Leaders—Career

Wins

1	Hooks Dauss	222
2	George Mullin	208
3	Mickey Lolich	207
4	Hal Newhouser	200
5	Jack Morris	198
6	Tommy Bridges	194
7	Dizzy Trout	161
8	Wild Bill Donovan	141
9	Earl Whitehill	133
10	Frank Lary	123
11	Dan Petry	119
12	Jim Bunning	118
13	Denny McLain	117
14	Virgil Trucks	114
15	Schoolboy Rowe	105
16	Ed Killian	99
17	Milt Wilcox	97
18	Ed Willett	96
	Frank Tanana	96
20	Fred Hutchinson	95

Losses

1	Hooks Dauss	182
2	George Mullin	179
3	Mickey Lolich	175
4	Dizzy Trout	153
5	Jack Morris	150
6	Hal Newhouser	148
7	Tommy Bridges	138
8	Earl Whitehill	119
9	Frank Lary	110
10	Vic Sorrell	101
11	Wild Bill Donovan	96
	Virgil Trucks	96
13	Dan Petry	93
14	Jim Bunning	87
15	Frank Tanana	82
16	Paul Foytack	81
17	Ed Willett	80
18	Billy Hoeft	78
19	John Hiller	76
	Walt Terrell	76

Winning Percentage
(minimum 100 decisions)

1	Denny McLain	.654
2	Schoolboy Rowe	.629
3	Harry Coveleski	.616
4	Ed Summers	.602
5	Eldon Auker	.597
6	Wild Bill Donovan	.595
7	Earl Wilson	.587
8	Tommy Bridges	.584
9	Bernie Boland	.578
10	Jim Bunning	.576
11	Hal Newhouser	.575
12	Don Mossi	.573
13	Fred Hutchinson	.572
14	Ed Killian	.572
15	Jack Morris	.569
16	Milt Wilcox	.564
17	Dan Petry	.561
18	Ken Holloway	.553
	Dave Rozema	.553
20	Hooks Dauss	.550

Games

1	John Hiller	545
2	Hooks Dauss	538
3	Mickey Lolich	508
4	Dizzy Trout	493
5	Mike Henneman	491
6	Hal Newhouser	460
7	George Mullin	435
8	Jack Morris	430
9	Tommy Bridges	424
10	Willie Hernandez	358
11	Aurelio Lopez	355
12	Hank Aguirre	334
13	Earl Whitehill	325
14	Virgil Trucks	316
15	Dan Petry	306
16	Frank Lary	304
	Jim Bunning	304
18	Al Benton	296
19	Paul Foytack	285
20	Vic Sorrell	280

Games Started

1	Mickey Lolich	459
2	Jack Morris	408
3	George Mullin	395
4	Hooks Dauss	388
5	Hal Newhouser	373
6	Tommy Bridges	362
7	Dizzy Trout	305
8	Earl Whitehill	287
9	Frank Lary	274
	Dan Petry	274
11	Jim Bunning	251
12	Frank Tanana	243
13	Wild Bill Donovan	242
14	Virgil Trucks	229
15	Milt Wilcox	220
16	Denny McLain	219
17	Vic Sorrell	216
18	Joe Coleman	201
19	Walt Terrell	190
20	Paul Foytack	185

Complete Games

1	George Mullin	336
2	Hooks Dauss	245
3	Wild Bill Donovan	213
4	Hal Newhouser	212
5	Tommy Bridges	200
6	Mickey Lolich	190
7	Dizzy Trout	156
8	Jack Morris	154
9	Earl Whitehill	148
10	Ed Killian	142
11	Ed Willett	127
12	Frank Lary	123
13	Vic Sorrell	95
14	Denny McLain	94
15	Ed Siever	93
16	Schoolboy Rowe	92
17	Jean Dubuc	90
18	Howard Ehmke	89
19	Virgil Trucks	84
20	Fred Hutchinson	81

Shutouts

1	Mickey Lolich	39
2	George Mullin	34
3	Tommy Bridges	33
	Hal Newhouser	33
5	Wild Bill Donovan	29
6	Dizzy Trout	28
7	Denny McLain	26
8	Jack Morris	24
9	Hooks Dauss	22
10	Virgil Trucks	20
	Frank Lary	20
12	Ed Killian	19
13	Schoolboy Rowe	16
	Billy Hoeft	16
	Jim Bunning	16
16	Fred Hutchinson	13
17	Ed Willett	12
	Earl Whitehill	12
19	Jean Dubuc	11
	Joe Coleman	11

Saves

1	Mike Henneman	154
2	John Hiller	125
3	Willie Hernandez	120
4	Aurelio Lopez	85
5	Terry Fox	55
6	Al Benton	45
7	Hooks Dauss	41
8	Larry Sherry	37
9	Dizzy Trout	34
	Fred Scherman	34
11	Fred Gladding	33
	Tom Timmermann	33
13	Todd Jones	31
14	Chief Hogsett	27
	Hank Aguirre	27
16	Hal Newhouser	19
17	Hal White	18
	Kevin Saucier	18
19	Six tied at	17

Innings Pitched

1	George Mullin	3,394.0
2	Hooks Dauss	3,390.2
3	Mickey Lolich	3,361.2
4	Jack Morris	3,042.2
5	Hal Newhouser	2,944.0
6	Tommy Bridges	2,826.1
7	Dizzy Trout	2,591.2
8	Earl Whitehill	2,171.2
9	Wild Bill Donovan	2,137.1
10	Frank Lary	2,008.2
11	Jim Bunning	1,867.1
12	Dan Petry	1,843.0
13	Virgil Trucks	1,800.2
14	Vic Sorrell	1,671.2
15	Denny McLain	1,593.0
16	Frank Tanana	1,551.1
17	Ed Willett	1,545.1
18	Ed Killian	1,536.2
19	Milt Wilcox	1,495.1
20	Fred Hutchinson	1,464.0

Walks

1	Hal Newhouser	1,227
2	Tommy Bridges	1,192
3	George Mullin	1,106
4	Jack Morris	1,086
5	Hooks Dauss	1,064
6	Mickey Lolich	1,014
7	Dizzy Trout	978
8	Earl Whitehill	831
9	Dan Petry	744
10	Virgil Trucks	732
11	Vic Sorrell	706
12	Wild Bill Donovan	685
13	Paul Foytack	631
14	Ted Gray	580
15	Frank Lary	579
16	Joe Coleman	576
17	Jim Bunning	564
18	Milt Wilcox	537
19	John Hiller	535
20	Frank Tanana	527

Strikeouts

1	Mickey Lolich	2,679
2	Jack Morris	1,980
3	Hal Newhouser	1,770
4	Tommy Bridges	1,674
5	Jim Bunning	1,406
6	George Mullin	1,380
7	Hooks Dauss	1,201
8	Dizzy Trout	1,199
9	Denny McLain	1,150
10	Wild Bill Donovan	1,079
11	Virgil Trucks	1,046
12	John Hiller	1,036
13	Frank Lary	1,031
14	Joe Coleman	1,000
15	Frank Tanana	958
16	Dan Petry	957
17	Milt Wilcox	851
18	Earl Whitehill	838
19	Paul Foytack	789
20	Billy Hoeft	783

Strikeouts/9 Innings
(minimum 1000 Innings Pitched)

1	John Hiller	7.51
2	Mickey Lolich	7.17
3	Jim Bunning	6.78
4	Denny McLain	6.50
5	Joe Coleman	6.39
6	Jack Morris	5.86
7	Hank Aguirre	5.76
8	Frank Tanana	5.56
9	Ted Gray	5.48
10	Hal Newhouser	5.41
11	Tommy Bridges	5.33
12	Billy Hoeft	5.32
13	Virgil Trucks	5.23
14	Milt Wilcox	5.12
15	Paul Foytack	4.98
16	Dan Petry	4.67
17	Frank Lary	4.62
18	Wild Bill Donovan	4.54
19	Walt Terrell	4.21
20	Dizzy Trout	4.16

ERA
(minimum 1000 Innings Pitched)

1	Harry Coveleski	2.34
2	Ed Killian	2.38
3	Wild Bill Donovan	2.49
4	Ed Siever	2.61
5	George Mullin	2.76
6	John Hiller	2.83
7	Ed Willett	2.89
8	Jean Dubuc	3.06
9	Hal Newhouser	3.07
10	Bernie Boland	3.09
11	Denny McLain	3.13
12	Dizzy Trout	3.20
13	Hank Aguirre	3.29
14	Hooks Dauss	3.32
15	Dave Rozema	3.38
16	Jim Bunning	3.45
17	Mickey Lolich	3.45
18	Al Benton	3.46
19	Frank Lary	3.46
20	Virgil Trucks	3.50

Component ERA
(minimum 1000 Innings Pitched)

1	Harry Coveleski	2.41
2	Wild Bill Donovan	2.55
3	Ed Killian	2.71
4	Bernie Boland	2.71
5	Jean Dubuc	2.89
6	Denny McLain	2.91
7	George Mullin	2.93
8	Ed Willett	2.97
9	Ed Siever	2.98
10	Hal Newhouser	3.13
11	Hank Aguirre	3.18
12	John Hiller	3.19
13	Virgil Trucks	3.29
14	Hooks Dauss	3.31
15	Mickey Lolich	3.33
16	Dizzy Trout	3.36
17	Jim Bunning	3.42
18	Jack Morris	3.46
19	Dave Rozema	3.50
20	Fred Hutchinson	3.52

Opponent Average
(minimum 1000 Innings Pitched)

1	Denny McLain	.225
2	John Hiller	.229
3	Hank Aguirre	.234
4	Wild Bill Donovan	.236
5	Harry Coveleski	.236
6	Bernie Boland	.239
7	Virgil Trucks	.239
8	Hal Newhouser	.239
9	Jim Bunning	.240
10	Jean Dubuc	.240
11	Jack Morris	.242
12	Mickey Lolich	.245
13	Paul Foytack	.245
14	Ed Killian	.246
15	Tommy Bridges	.248
16	Ted Gray	.248
17	Joe Coleman	.251
18	Dan Petry	.251
19	George Mullin	.253
20	Dizzy Trout	.254

Opponent OBP
(minimum 1000 Innings Pitched)

1	Denny McLain	.281
2	Harry Coveleski	.295
3	Hank Aguirre	.300
4	Jim Bunning	.301
5	Wild Bill Donovan	.302
6	Mickey Lolich	.304
7	Dave Rozema	.307
8	Jack Morris	.308
9	Ed Siever	.308
10	John Hiller	.309
11	Fred Hutchinson	.311
12	Ed Killian	.311
13	Frank Lary	.315
14	Virgil Trucks	.316
15	Hal Newhouser	.316
16	Jean Dubuc	.317
17	Bernie Boland	.318
18	Schoolboy Rowe	.319
19	George Mullin	.319
20	Milt Wilcox	.323

Tigers Franchise Batting Leaders—Single Season

Games

#	Player	Year	
1	Rocky Colavito	1961	163
2	Jimmy Barrett	1904	162
	Jake Wood	1961	162
	Dick McAuliffe	1964	162
	Don Wert	1965	162
	Ed Brinkman	1973	162
	Rusty Staub	1978	162
	Cecil Fielder	1991	162
	Brian Hunter	1997	162
10	Rocky Colavito	1962	161
	Rusty Staub	1976	161
	Lou Whitaker	1983	161
	Travis Fryman	1992	161
14	Bill Bruton	1961	160
	Rocky Colavito	1963	160
	Norm Cash	1966	160
	Aurelio Rodriguez	1973	160
18	Eight tied at		159

At-Bats

#	Player	Year	
1	Harvey Kuenn	1953	679
2	Ron LeFlore	1978	666
3	Jake Wood	1961	663
4	Travis Fryman	1992	659
5	Brian Hunter	1997	658
6	Harvey Kuenn	1954	656
7	Ron LeFlore	1977	652
8	Lou Whitaker	1983	643
9	Rusty Staub	1978	642
10	Charlie Gehringer	1936	641
	George Kell	1950	641
12	Roy Johnson	1929	640
13	Gee Walker	1937	635
14	Charlie Gehringer	1929	634
	Pete Fox	1938	634
16	Dick Wakefield	1943	633
17	Doc Cramer	1942	630
18	Charlie Gehringer	1933	628
	Pete Fox	1937	628
20	Dale Alexander	1929	626

Runs

#	Player	Year	
1	Ty Cobb	1911	147
2	Ty Cobb	1915	144
	Charlie Gehringer	1930	144
	Charlie Gehringer	1936	144
	Hank Greenberg	1938	144
6	Hank Greenberg	1937	137
7	Charlie Gehringer	1934	134
8	Charlie Gehringer	1937	133
	Charlie Gehringer	1938	133
10	Lu Blue	1922	131
	Charlie Gehringer	1929	131
12	Hank Greenberg	1940	129
	Rocky Colavito	1961	129
14	Roy Johnson	1929	128
15	Donie Bush	1911	126
	Ron LeFlore	1978	126
17	Ty Cobb	1921	124
18	Charlie Gehringer	1935	123
	Barney McCosky	1940	123
20	Goose Goslin	1936	122

Hits

#	Player	Year	
1	Ty Cobb	1911	248
2	Harry Heilmann	1921	237
3	Ty Cobb	1912	227
	Charlie Gehringer	1936	227
5	Ty Cobb	1917	225
	Harry Heilmann	1925	225
7	George Kell	1950	218
8	Sam Crawford	1911	217
9	Ty Cobb	1909	216
10	Dale Alexander	1929	215
	Charlie Gehringer	1929	215
12	Charlie Gehringer	1934	214
13	Gee Walker	1937	213
14	Ty Cobb	1907	212
	Ron LeFlore	1977	212
16	Ty Cobb	1922	211
	Harry Heilmann	1923	211
	Ty Cobb	1924	211
19	Charlie Gehringer	1937	209
	Harvey Kuenn	1953	209

Doubles

#	Player	Year	
1	Hank Greenberg	1934	63
2	Charlie Gehringer	1936	60
3	George Kell	1950	56
4	Gee Walker	1936	55
5	Harry Heilmann	1927	50
	Charlie Gehringer	1934	50
	Hank Greenberg	1940	50
8	Hank Greenberg	1937	49
9	Ty Cobb	1911	47
	Charlie Gehringer	1930	47
	Dale Alexander	1931	47
12	Hank Greenberg	1935	46
	Rudy York	1940	46
14	Bobby Veach	1919	45
	Harry Heilmann	1924	45
	Roy Johnson	1929	45
	Charlie Gehringer	1929	45
18	Ty Cobb	1917	44
	Harry Heilmann	1923	44
	Charlie Gehringer	1932	44

Triples

#	Player	Year	
1	Sam Crawford	1914	26
2	Sam Crawford	1903	25
3	Ty Cobb	1911	24
	Ty Cobb	1917	24
5	Ty Cobb	1912	23
	Sam Crawford	1913	23
7	Sam Crawford	1912	21
8	Ty Cobb	1908	20
9	Sam Crawford	1910	19
	Sam Crawford	1915	19
	Charlie Gehringer	1929	19
	Roy Johnson	1931	19
	Barney McCosky	1940	19
14	Heinie Manush	1927	18
15	Sam Crawford	1907	17
	Bobby Veach	1919	17
	Charlie Gehringer	1926	17
18	Nine tied at		16

Home Runs

#	Player	Year	
1	Hank Greenberg	1938	58
2	Cecil Fielder	1990	51
3	Rocky Colavito	1961	45
4	Hank Greenberg	1946	44
	Cecil Fielder	1991	44
6	Hank Greenberg	1940	41
	Norm Cash	1961	41
8	Hank Greenberg	1937	40
	Darrell Evans	1985	40
10	Norm Cash	1962	39
11	Rocky Colavito	1962	37
12	Hank Greenberg	1935	36
	Willie Horton	1968	36
14	Rudy York	1937	35
	Rocky Colavito	1960	35
	Cecil Fielder	1992	35
17	Rudy York	1943	34
	Darrell Evans	1987	34
19	Four tied at		33

RBI

#	Player	Year	
1	Hank Greenberg	1937	183
2	Hank Greenberg	1935	170
3	Hank Greenberg	1940	150
4	Hank Greenberg	1938	146
5	Rocky Colavito	1961	140
6	Harry Heilmann	1921	139
	Hank Greenberg	1934	139
8	Dale Alexander	1929	137
9	Dale Alexander	1930	135
10	Harry Heilmann	1925	134
	Rudy York	1940	134
12	Vic Wertz	1949	133
	Cecil Fielder	1991	133
14	Norm Cash	1961	132
	Cecil Fielder	1990	132
16	Bobby Veach	1921	128
	Al Kaline	1956	128
18	Four tied at		127

Walks

#	Player	Year	
1	Roy Cullenbine	1947	137
2	Eddie Yost	1959	135
3	Tony Phillips	1993	132
4	Eddie Yost	1960	125
5	Norm Cash	1961	124
6	Mickey Tettleton	1992	122
7	Eddie Lake	1947	120
8	Hank Greenberg	1938	119
9	Donie Bush	1915	118
	Ty Cobb	1915	118
11	Donie Bush	1912	117
12	Tony Phillips	1992	114
13	Rocky Colavito	1961	113
14	Donie Bush	1914	112
	Charlie Gehringer	1938	112
16	Mickey Tettleton	1993	109
17	Dick McAuliffe	1967	105
18	Norm Cash	1962	104
19	Lu Blue	1921	103
	Eddie Lake	1946	103

Strikeouts

#	Player	Year	
1	Cecil Fielder	1990	182
2	Rob Deer	1991	175
3	Melvin Nieves	1996	158
4	Melvin Nieves	1997	157
5	Cecil Fielder	1991	151
	Cecil Fielder	1992	151
7	Travis Fryman	1991	149
8	Travis Fryman	1992	144
	Tony Clark	1997	144
10	Jake Wood	1961	141
11	Ron LeFlore	1975	139
	Mickey Tettleton	1993	139
13	Kirk Gibson	1985	137
	Mickey Tettleton	1992	137
15	Mickey Tettleton	1991	131
	Rob Deer	1992	131
17	Travis Fryman	1993	128
	Travis Fryman	1994	128
19	Tony Clark	1996	127
20	Cecil Fielder	1993	125

Stolen Bases

#	Player	Year	
1	Ty Cobb	1915	96
2	Ty Cobb	1911	83
3	Ron LeFlore	1979	78
4	Ty Cobb	1909	76
5	Brian Hunter	1997	74
6	Ty Cobb	1916	68
	Ron LeFlore	1978	68
8	Ty Cobb	1910	65
9	Ty Cobb	1912	61
10	Ron LeFlore	1976	58
11	Ty Cobb	1917	55
12	Donie Bush	1909	53
13	Ty Cobb	1913	52
14	Ty Cobb	1907	49
	Donie Bush	1910	49
16	Donie Bush	1913	44
	Gary Pettis	1988	44
18	Gary Pettis	1989	43
19	Sam Crawford	1912	41
	Milt Cuyler	1991	41

Runs Created

#	Player	Year	
1	Ty Cobb	1911	172
2	Hank Greenberg	1938	163
3	Hank Greenberg	1937	160
4	Norm Cash	1961	158
5	Hank Greenberg	1935	156
6	Ty Cobb	1915	154
7	Hank Greenberg	1940	152
8	Charlie Gehringer	1936	149
9	Ty Cobb	1912	148
10	Charlie Gehringer	1934	145
11	Ty Cobb	1917	144
	Harry Heilmann	1923	144
13	Harry Heilmann	1925	142
	Harry Heilmann	1927	142
	Hank Greenberg	1934	142
16	Harry Heilmann	1921	141
17	Ty Cobb	1909	138
	Ty Cobb	1910	138
19	Three tied at		136

Runs Created/27 Outs

(minimum 3.1 Plate Appearances/Tm Gm)

#	Player	Year	
1	Ty Cobb	1911	12.42
2	Norm Cash	1961	11.58
3	Harry Heilmann	1927	11.35
4	Ty Cobb	1912	11.27
5	Harry Heilmann	1923	11.02
6	Ty Cobb	1910	10.84
7	Hank Greenberg	1938	10.79
8	Ty Cobb	1925	10.67
9	Hank Greenberg	1937	10.36
10	Hank Greenberg	1940	10.22
11	Ty Cobb	1915	10.16
12	Ty Cobb	1917	9.87
13	Harry Heilmann	1925	9.85
14	Hank Greenberg	1935	9.68
15	Harry Heilmann	1921	9.59
16	Hank Greenberg	1939	9.55
17	Charlie Gehringer	1934	9.46
18	Sam Crawford	1911	9.39
19	Charlie Gehringer	1937	9.37
20	Ty Cobb	1909	9.27

Batting Average

(minimum 3.1 Plate Appearances/Tm Gm)

#	Player	Year	
1	Ty Cobb	1911	.420
2	Ty Cobb	1912	.410
3	Harry Heilmann	1923	.403
4	Ty Cobb	1922	.401
5	Harry Heilmann	1927	.398
6	Harry Heilmann	1921	.394
7	Harry Heilmann	1925	.393
8	Ty Cobb	1913	.390
9	Ty Cobb	1921	.389
10	Ty Cobb	1919	.384
11	Ty Cobb	1910	.383
12	Ty Cobb	1917	.383
13	Ty Cobb	1918	.382
14	Ty Cobb	1925	.378
15	Sam Crawford	1911	.378
16	Heinie Manush	1926	.378
17	Ty Cobb	1909	.377
18	Ty Cobb	1916	.371
19	Charlie Gehringer	1937	.371
20	Al Wingo	1925	.370

On-Base Percentage

(minimum 3.1 Plate Appearances/Tm Gm)

#	Player	Year	
1	Norm Cash	1961	.487
2	Ty Cobb	1915	.486
3	Harry Heilmann	1923	.481
4	Harry Heilmann	1927	.475
5	Ty Cobb	1925	.468
6	Ty Cobb	1913	.467
7	Ty Cobb	1911	.467
8	Ty Cobb	1922	.462
9	Charlie Gehringer	1937	.458
10	Ty Cobb	1912	.458
11	Harry Heilmann	1925	.457
12	Ty Cobb	1910	.456
13	Al Wingo	1925	.456
14	Ty Cobb	1921	.452
15	Mickey Cochrane	1935	.452
16	Ty Cobb	1916	.452
17	Charlie Gehringer	1934	.450
18	Harry Heilmann	1926	.445
19	Harry Heilmann	1921	.444
20	Ty Cobb	1917	.444

Slugging Percentage

(minimum 3.1 Plate Appearances/Tm Gm)

#	Player	Year	
1	Hank Greenberg	1938	.683
2	Hank Greenberg	1940	.670
3	Hank Greenberg	1937	.668
4	Norm Cash	1961	.662
5	Harry Heilmann	1923	.632
6	Hank Greenberg	1935	.628
7	Hank Greenberg	1939	.622
8	Ty Cobb	1911	.621
9	Harry Heilmann	1927	.616
10	Harry Heilmann	1921	.606
11	Hank Greenberg	1946	.604
12	Hank Greenberg	1934	.600
13	Harry Heilmann	1922	.598
14	Ty Cobb	1925	.598
15	Ty Cobb	1921	.596
16	Cecil Fielder	1990	.592
17	Ty Cobb	1912	.586
18	Rudy York	1940	.583
19	Dale Alexander	1929	.580
20	Rocky Colavito	1961	.580

Teams: Tigers

Tigers Franchise Pitching Leaders—Single Season

Wins

1	Denny McLain	1968	31
2	George Mullin	1909	29
	Hal Newhouser	1944	29
4	Dizzy Trout	1944	27
5	Hal Newhouser	1946	26
6	Ed Killian	1907	25
	Wild Bill Donovan	1907	25
	Hal Newhouser	1945	25
	Mickey Lolich	1971	25
10	Ed Summers	1908	24
	Hooks Dauss	1915	24
	Schoolboy Rowe	1934	24
	Denny McLain	1969	24
14	Roscoe Miller	1901	23
	Ed Killian	1905	23
	Tommy Bridges	1936	23
	Frank Lary	1961	23
	Joe Coleman	1973	23
19	Five tied at		22

Losses

1	George Mullin	1904	23
2	George Mullin	1905	21
	Hooks Dauss	1920	21
	Mickey Lolich	1974	21
5	Ed Killian	1904	20
	George Mullin	1907	20
	Bobo Newsom	1941	20
	Art Houtteman	1952	20
9	Herman Pillette	1923	19
	Virgil Trucks	1952	19
	Mickey Lolich	1970	19
	Lerrin LaGrow	1974	19
13	Nine tied at		18

Winning Percentage
(minimum 15 decisions)

1	Wild Bill Donovan	1907	.862
2	Schoolboy Rowe	1940	.842
3	Denny McLain	1968	.838
4	Bobo Newsom	1940	.808
5	George Mullin	1909	.784
6	Ken Holloway	1925	.765
7	Hal Newhouser	1944	.763
8	Schoolboy Rowe	1934	.750
	Firpo Marberry	1934	.750
10	Hal Newhouser	1946	.743
11	Hal Newhouser	1945	.735
12	Dutch Leonard	1925	.733
	George Gill	1937	.733
	Eric King	1986	.733
	Mike Henneman	1989	.733
16	Denny McLain	1965	.727
	Denny McLain	1969	.727
18	Jack Morris	1986	.724
19	Bert Cole	1923	.722
	Dizzy Trout	1950	.722

Games

1	Mike Myers	1997	88
2	Mike Myers	1996	83
3	Willie Hernandez	1984	80
4	Willie Hernandez	1985	74
5	Richie Lewis	1996	72
6	Aurelio Lopez	1984	71
	Danny Miceli	1997	71
8	Fred Scherman	1971	69
	Mike Henneman	1990	69
10	Paul Gibson	1991	68
	Bob MacDonald	1993	68
	Todd Jones	1997	68
13	Aurelio Lopez	1980	67
14	John Hiller	1973	65
	Mike Henneman	1988	65
	Mike Munoz	1992	65
17	Willie Hernandez	1986	64
18	Willie Hernandez	1988	63
	Mike Henneman	1993	63
20	Five tied at		61

Games Started

1	Mickey Lolich	1971	45
2	George Mullin	1904	44
3	George Mullin	1907	42
	Mickey Lolich	1973	42
5	George Mullin	1905	41
	Denny McLain	1968	41
	Denny McLain	1969	41
	Mickey Lolich	1972	41
	Joe Coleman	1974	41
	Mickey Lolich	1974	41
11	George Mullin	1906	40
	Dizzy Trout	1944	40
	Joe Coleman	1973	40
14	Harry Coveleski	1916	39
	Hooks Dauss	1923	39
	Mickey Lolich	1970	39
	Joe Coleman	1972	39
18	Seven tied at		38

Complete Games

1	George Mullin	1904	42
2	Roscoe Miller	1901	35
	George Mullin	1905	35
	George Mullin	1906	35
	George Mullin	1907	35
6	Wild Bill Donovan	1903	34
7	Ed Killian	1905	33
	Dizzy Trout	1944	33
9	Ed Killian	1904	32
10	George Mullin	1903	31
11	Ed Siever	1901	30
	Wild Bill Donovan	1904	30
13	Ed Killian	1907	29
	George Mullin	1909	29
	Hal Newhouser	1945	29
	Hal Newhouser	1946	29
	Mickey Lolich	1971	29
18	Four tied at		28

Shutouts

1	Denny McLain	1969	9
2	Ed Killian	1905	8
	Hal Newhouser	1945	8
4	George Mullin	1904	7
	Dizzy Trout	1944	7
	Billy Hoeft	1955	7
7	George Mullin	1903	6
	Wild Bill Donovan	1908	6
	Hooks Dauss	1917	6
	Schoolboy Rowe	1935	6
	Hal Newhouser	1944	6
	Hal Newhouser	1946	6
	Virgil Trucks	1949	6
	Mickey Lolich	1964	6
	Mickey Lolich	1967	6
	Denny McLain	1968	6
	Jack Morris	1986	6
18	Twelve tied at		5

Saves

1	John Hiller	1973	38
2	Willie Hernandez	1984	32
3	Willie Hernandez	1985	31
	Todd Jones	1997	31
5	Tom Timmermann	1970	27
6	Willie Hernandez	1986	24
	Mike Henneman	1992	24
	Mike Henneman	1993	24
9	Mike Henneman	1988	22
	Mike Henneman	1990	22
11	Aurelio Lopez	1979	21
	Aurelio Lopez	1980	21
	Mike Henneman	1991	21
14	Larry Sherry	1966	20
	Fred Scherman	1971	20
16	Aurelio Lopez	1983	18
	Mike Henneman	1995	18
18	Al Benton	1940	17
19	Terry Fox	1962	16
20	Two tied at		15

Innings Pitched

1	George Mullin	1904	382.1
2	Mickey Lolich	1971	376.0
3	George Mullin	1907	357.1
4	Dizzy Trout	1944	352.1
5	George Mullin	1905	347.2
6	Denny McLain	1968	336.0
7	Roscoe Miller	1901	332.0
8	Ed Killian	1904	331.2
9	George Mullin	1906	330.0
10	Mickey Lolich	1972	327.1
11	Denny McLain	1969	325.0
12	Harry Coveleski	1916	324.1
13	George Mullin	1903	320.2
14	Hooks Dauss	1923	316.0
15	Ed Killian	1907	314.0
16	Ed Killian	1905	313.1
	Hal Newhouser	1945	313.1
18	Harry Coveleski	1915	312.2
19	Hal Newhouser	1944	312.1
20	Hooks Dauss	1915	309.2

Walks

1	Joe Coleman	1974	158
2	Paul Foytack	1956	142
3	George Mullin	1905	138
4	Hal Newhouser	1941	137
5	George Mullin	1904	131
6	Howard Ehmke	1920	124
	Virgil Trucks	1949	124
8	Mickey Lolich	1969	122
9	Tommy Bridges	1932	119
10	Earl Whitehill	1931	118
	Bobo Newsom	1941	118
12	Frank Lary	1956	116
13	Tommy Bridges	1936	115
	Roxie Lawson	1937	115
15	Vic Sorrell	1931	114
	Hal Newhouser	1942	114
17	Tommy Bridges	1935	113
	Vern Kennedy	1938	113
19	Hooks Dauss	1915	112
20	Two tied at		111

Strikeouts

1	Mickey Lolich	1971	308
2	Denny McLain	1968	280
3	Hal Newhouser	1946	275
4	Mickey Lolich	1969	271
5	Mickey Lolich	1972	250
6	Joe Coleman	1971	236
7	Jack Morris	1983	232
8	Mickey Lolich	1970	230
9	Mickey Lolich	1965	226
10	Jack Morris	1986	223
11	Joe Coleman	1972	222
12	Mickey Lolich	1973	214
13	Hal Newhouser	1945	212
14	Jack Morris	1987	208
15	Joe Coleman	1973	202
	Mickey Lolich	1974	202
17	Jim Bunning	1959	201
	Jim Bunning	1960	201
19	Mickey Lolich	1968	197
20	Jim Bunning	1963	196

Strikeouts/9 Innings
(minimum 1 Inning Pitched/Tm Gm)

1	Mickey Lolich	1969	8.69
2	Hal Newhouser	1946	8.46
3	Mickey Lolich	1965	8.35
4	Mickey Lolich	1968	8.06
5	Denny McLain	1965	7.84
6	Les Cain	1970	7.77
7	Mickey Lolich	1967	7.68
8	Mickey Lolich	1966	7.64
9	Mickey Lolich	1970	7.59
10	Jack Morris	1986	7.52
11	Denny McLain	1968	7.50
12	Mickey Lolich	1964	7.45
13	Joe Coleman	1971	7.43
14	Mickey Lolich	1971	7.37
15	Earl Wilson	1966	7.33
16	Jim Bunning	1958	7.25
17	Jim Bunning	1959	7.25
18	Jim Bunning	1960	7.18
19	Joe Coleman	1972	7.14
20	Jack Morris	1983	7.11

ERA
(minimum 1 Inning Pitched/Tm Gm)

1	Ed Summers	1908	1.64
2	Ed Killian	1909	1.71
3	Ed Killian	1907	1.78
4	Hal Newhouser	1945	1.81
5	Ed Siever	1902	1.91
6	Hal Newhouser	1946	1.94
7	Denny McLain	1968	1.96
8	Harry Coveleski	1916	1.97
9	Al Benton	1945	2.02
10	Wild Bill Donovan	1908	2.08
11	Bill James	1917	2.09
12	Dizzy Trout	1944	2.12
13	Ed Siever	1907	2.16
14	Willie Mitchell	1917	2.19
15	Wild Bill Donovan	1907	2.19
16	Hank Aguirre	1962	2.21
17	Hal Newhouser	1944	2.22
18	George Mullin	1909	2.22
19	Ed Summers	1909	2.24
20	George Mullin	1903	2.25

Component ERA
(minimum 1 Inning Pitched/Tm Gm)

1	Denny McLain	1968	1.91
2	Hal Newhouser	1946	2.00
3	Ed Siever	1902	2.03
4	Hal Newhouser	1945	2.07
5	Wild Bill Donovan	1908	2.12
6	Ed Summers	1909	2.14
7	Harry Coveleski	1916	2.16
8	Wild Bill Donovan	1903	2.17
9	George Mullin	1909	2.18
10	Hank Aguirre	1962	2.20
11	Ed Willett	1909	2.22
12	Wild Bill Donovan	1907	2.24
13	Ed Willett	1910	2.28
14	Earl Wilson	1966	2.37
15	Virgil Trucks	1943	2.37
16	Ed Summers	1908	2.37
17	Ed Killian	1905	2.38
18	Ed Siever	1907	2.39
19	Ed Killian	1909	2.39
20	Bernie Boland	1917	2.40

Opponent Average
(minimum 1 Inning Pitched/Tm Gm)

1	Jeff Robinson	1988	.197
2	Denny McLain	1968	.200
3	Hal Newhouser	1946	.201
4	Hank Aguirre	1962	.205
5	Hal Newhouser	1942	.207
6	Mickey Lolich	1969	.210
7	Virgil Trucks	1949	.211
8	Hal Newhouser	1945	.211
9	Earl Wilson	1966	.213
10	Joe Coleman	1972	.214
11	Denny McLain	1966	.214
12	Denny McLain	1965	.216
13	Ed Willett	1910	.217
14	Dan Petry	1985	.217
15	Jack Morris	1981	.218
16	Jim Bunning	1957	.218
17	Mickey Lolich	1968	.219
18	Ed Willett	1909	.221
19	Mickey Lolich	1967	.221
20	Al Benton	1941	.221

Opponent OBP
(minimum 1 Inning Pitched/Tm Gm)

1	Denny McLain	1968	.243
2	Earl Wilson	1966	.265
3	Hank Aguirre	1962	.267
4	Hal Newhouser	1946	.269
5	Ed Summers	1909	.269
6	Ed Siever	1902	.273
7	Denny McLain	1965	.273
8	Virgil Trucks	1943	.276
9	Jim Bunning	1957	.277
10	Mark Fidrych	1976	.277
11	Denny McLain	1969	.278
12	Wild Bill Donovan	1908	.278
13	Hal Newhouser	1945	.281
14	Ed Willett	1909	.281
15	Mickey Lolich	1967	.281
16	Jeff Robinson	1988	.282
17	Mickey Lolich	1964	.282
18	Harry Coveleski	1916	.282
19	Mickey Lolich	1972	.283
20	Jim Bunning	1961	.284

Tigers Capsule

Best Season: The *1984* Tigers got off to one of the best starts in baseball history, winning 35 of their first 40 games. They won the American League East by 15 games with a franchise-best 104-58 record, and swept the Kansas City Royals in the ALCS before defeating the San Diego Padres in a five-game World Series.

Worst Season: *1996.* They lost 109 games, and their 6.38 team ERA was the worst in AL history.

Best Player: *Ty Cobb.*

Best Pitcher: *Hal Newhouser.* The battle for second place is close. Jack Morris edges Tommy Bridges, with George Mullin placing fourth.

Best Reliever: *John Hiller.*

Best Defensive Player: *Charlie Gehringer.* Honorable mention to both right fielder Al Kaline, who won 10 Gold Gloves, and third baseman Aurelio Rodriguez, who won one and who would have won several more if his career hadn't run concurrently with Brooks Robinson's.

Hall of Famers: *Ty Cobb, Sam Crawford, Charlie Gehringer, Hank Greenberg, Harry Heilmann, Al Kaline, George Kell* and *Hal Newhouser.*

Franchise All-Star Team:

C	*Lance Parrish*	LF	*Harry Heilmann*
1B	*Hank Greenberg*	CF	*Ty Cobb*
2B	*Charlie Gehringer*	RF	*Al Kaline*
3B	*George Kell*	DH	*Cecil Fielder*
SS	*Alan Trammell*	SP	*Hal Newhouser*
		RP	*John Hiller*

Biggest Flake: *Mark "The Bird" Fidrych.* He won 19 games in 1976 while talking to the baseball and manicuring the mound on his hands and knees between pitches.

Strangest Career: *Norm Cash.* In 1961, in his first year as the Tigers' full-time first baseman, he hit 41 homers, drove in 132 runs, and won the AL batting title with a .361 average. Although he spent another 13 years in the majors and retired with 377 career home runs, he never came close to driving in 100 runs or batting .300 again.

What Might Have Been: Bonus baby *Dick Wakefield* came up in 1943 and led the AL with 200 hits and 38 doubles, and finished second in the batting race with a .316 average. He spent the first half of '44 in the Navy, but came back to hit .355 with 12 home runs in the second half. After spending all of '45 in the military, he suffered two broken bones in 1946 and had an off year. He played semi-regularly for the next few years, never reaching his wartime heights. His career virtually ended in 1950, and Wakefield felt he'd been blacklisted for offenses such as holding out for a raise and supporting the creation of the players' pension fund. He probably wasn't quite the hitter he seemed to be against weakened wartime pitching, but he probably would have been a productive regular under better circumstances.

Best Trade: *Norm Cash* came over from Indians in exchange for third baseman Steve Demeter in April 1960. After the trade, Cash outhomered Demeter 374 to nothing.

Worst Trades: *Heinie Manush, Billy Pierce.* The Tigers traded away outfielder and future Hall of Famer Heinie Manush after the 1927 season, when he still had another 10 years in front of him. They also gave up first baseman Lu Blue in the deal, receiving three players in return. Blue went on to have more good years afterward (four) than the three players combined. Over the winter of '58, the Tigers sent lefty Billy Pierce and cash to the White Sox for Aaron Robinson. Pierce won over 200 games in the years following the trade.

The All-Nickname Team:

C	*Squanto Wilson*	LF	*Charlie "Paw Paw" Maxwell*
1B	*"Hammerin' Hank" Greenberg*	CF	*Ty Cobb, "The Georgia Peach"*
2B	*Charlie Gehringer,*	RF	*"Wahoo Sam" Crawford*
	"The Mechanical Man"	DH	*Cecil "Big Daddy" Fielder*
3B	*Skeeter Barnes*	SP	*General Crowder*
SS	*Yats Wuestling*	RP	*Firpo Marberry*

Best-Looking Player: *Al Kaline.*

Ugliest Player: *Don Mossi.*

Most Unappreciated Player: *Bobby Veach.* He led the AL in RBI three times in four years, but had poor timing, reaching his peak just before the dawn of the lively-ball era.

Most Overrated Player: *Tom Brookens.* He remained the Tigers' regular third baseman for the better part of a decade without doing anything to justify his full-time status.

Most Admirable Star: *Al Kaline.*

Least Admirable Stars: *Ty Cobb, Denny McLain.*

Best Season, Player: *Ty Cobb, 1911.* It was the best season of Ty Cobb's career; that should say enough. He batted a career-high .420 and led the league in runs, hits, doubles, triples, RBI, and of course, batting average.

Best Season, Pitcher: *Denny McLain, 1968.* So far, his 31-6 record has been the only 30-win season in the post-World War II era. He barely edges Hal Newhouser, who had three brilliant years in a row. Newhouser won back-to-back MVP Awards in 1944 and 1945, and followed with a 26-win season after the real players returned from the war.

Most Impressive Individual Record: *Ty Cobb's* .366 lifetime batting average.

Biggest Tragedy: *Mickey Cochrane's* career was ended when the Yankees' Bump Hadley beaned him in 1937. It could have been worse, though. Cochrane was lucky to have survived.

Biggest Travesty: *The 1987 MVP voting.* Compare the 1987 seasons of Toronto left fielder George Bell and Detroit shortstop Alan Trammell. Bell batted cleanup for the Blue Jays, notching 47 homers and driving in a league-high 134 runs. Trammell batted cleanup also; Detroit manager Sparky Anderson moved him into the No. 4 spot after free agent Lance Parrish departed over the winter. Taking over the most important offensive position on the team while continuing to man the most critical defensive position, Trammell rose to the challenge and enjoyed the best year of his career. He went deep 28 times, drove in a team-high 105 runs, and finished third in the batting race at .343. Trammell also played his usual strong defense at shortstop. Meanwhile, Bell played left field so poorly that the following spring, Toronto manager Jimy Williams tried to make him a DH, even when he refused to go along with it. In September and October, Bell hit .308 with six home runs, but Trammell hit .417 with seven home runs. Bell and Trammell's respective teams met for a season-ending, three-game series that was to decide the AL East race. Bell went 1-for-10 without a single RBI; Trammell went 3-for-9 with a home run and two RBI. Trammell's team swept the series and won the division. The only way to conclude that Bell had a better year is to focus on the RBI category to the exclusion of everything else.

Fan Favorites: *Gee Walker, Charlie Maxwell, Al Kaline.*

—Mat Olkin

Kansas City Royals (1969-1997)

Year	Lg	Pos	W-L	Pct	GB	Manager	Att.	R	OR	HR	Avg	OBP	Slg	Opponent HR	Avg	OBP	ERA	Park Index Runs	HR
1969	AL	4th-W	69-93	.426	28.0	Joe Gordon	902,414	586	688	98	.240	.309	.338	136	.246	.316	3.72	109	77
1970	AL	4th-W	65-97	.401	33.0	Charlie Metro/Bob Lemon	693,047	611	705	97	.244	.309	.348	138	.247	.328	3.78	98	70
1971	AL	2nd-W	85-76	.528	16.0	Bob Lemon	910,784	603	566	80	.250	.313	.353	84	.247	.314	3.25	95	55
1972	AL	4th-W	76-78	.494	16.5	Bob Lemon	707,656	580	545	78	.255	.327	.353	85	.251	.307	3.24	101	54
1973	AL	2nd-W	88-74	.543	6.0	Jack McKeon	1,345,341	755	752	114	.261	.339	.381	114	.273	.346	4.19	121	102
1974	AL	5th-W	77-85	.475	13.0	Jack McKeon	1,173,292	667	662	89	.259	.327	.364	91	.263	.322	3.51	114	80
1975	AL	2nd-W	91-71	.562	7.0	Jack McKeon/Whitey Herzog	1,151,836	710	649	118	.261	.333	.394	108	.258	.320	3.47	102	67
1976	AL	1st-W	90-72	.556	—	Whitey Herzog	1,680,265	713	611	65	.269	.327	.371	83	.247	.309	3.21	98	95
1977	AL	1st-W	102-60	.630	—	Whitey Herzog	1,852,603	822	651	146	.277	.340	.436	110	.251	.315	3.52	98	71
1978	AL	1st-W	92-70	.568	—	Whitey Herzog	2,255,493	743	634	98	.268	.329	.399	108	.251	.313	3.44	103	73
1979	AL	2nd-W	85-77	.525	3.0	Whitey Herzog	2,261,845	851	816	116	.282	.343	.422	165	.267	.331	4.45	113	91
1980	AL	1st-W	97-65	.599	—	Jim Frey	2,288,714	809	694	115	.286	.345	.413	129	.267	.323	3.83	95	67
1981	AL	5th-W	20-30	.400	12.0	Jim Frey													
	AL	1st-W	30-23	.566	—	Jim Frey/Dick Howser	1,279,403	397	405	61	.267	.325	.383	75	.260	.313	3.56	97	57
1982	AL	2nd-W	90-72	.556	3.0	Dick Howser	2,284,464	784	717	132	.285	.337	.428	163	.262	.320	4.08	100	74
1983	AL	2nd-W	79-83	.488	20.0	Dick Howser	1,963,875	696	767	109	.271	.320	.397	133	.274	.330	4.25	105	92
1984	AL	1st-W	84-78	.519	—	Dick Howser	1,810,018	673	686	117	.268	.317	.399	136	.258	.312	3.92	97	73
1985	AL	1st-W	91-71	.562	—	Dick Howser	2,162,717	687	639	154	.252	.313	.401	103	.257	.315	3.49	101	73
1986	AL	3rd-W	76-86	.469	16.0	Dick Howser/Mike Ferraro	2,320,794	654	673	137	.252	.313	.390	121	.258	.319	3.82	99	70
1987	AL	2nd-W	83-79	.512	2.0	Billy Gardner/John Wathan	2,392,471	715	691	168	.262	.328	.412	128	.261	.330	3.86	106	78
1988	AL	3rd-W	84-77	.522	19.5	John Wathan	2,350,181	704	648	121	.259	.321	.391	102	.258	.318	3.65	105	71
1989	AL	2nd-W	92-70	.568	7.0	John Wathan	2,477,700	690	635	101	.261	.329	.373	86	.257	.314	3.55	89	52
1990	AL	6th-W	75-86	.466	27.5	John Wathan	2,244,956	707	709	100	.267	.328	.395	116	.264	.335	3.93	100	68
1991	AL	6th-W	82-80	.506	13.0	John Wathan/Bob Schaefer/Hal McRae	2,161,537	727	722	117	.264	.328	.394	105	.261	.327	3.92	99	64
1992	AL	5th-W	72-90	.444	24.0	Hal McRae	1,867,689	610	667	75	.256	.315	.364	106	.259	.323	3.81	104	56
1993	AL	3rd-W	84-78	.519	10.0	Hal McRae	1,934,578	675	694	125	.263	.320	.397	105	.254	.327	4.04	112	76
1994	AL	3rd-C	64-51	.557	4.0	Hal McRae	1,400,494	574	532	100	.269	.335	.419	95	.260	.328	4.23	118	80
1995	AL	2nd-C	70-74	.486	30.0	Bob Boone	1,232,969	629	691	119	.260	.328	.396	142	.268	.338	4.49	92	81
1996	AL	5th-C	75-86	.466	24.0	Bob Boone	1,436,007	746	786	123	.267	.332	.398	176	.277	.335	4.55	95	89
1997	AL	5th-C	67-94	.416	19.0	Bob Boone/Tony Muser	1,517,638	747	820	158	.264	.333	.407	186	.274	.340	4.71	111	114

Team Nicknames: Kansas City Royals 1969-1997.

Team Ballparks: Municipal Stadium (KC) 1969-1972, Royals Stadium/Kauffman Stadium 1973-1997.

Teams: Royals

Kansas City Royals Individual Season Batting Leaders

Year	Batting Average		On-Base Percentage		Slugging Percentage		Home Runs		RBI		Stolen Bases	
1969	Lou Piniella	.282	Joe Foy	.354	Lou Piniella	.416	Ed Kirkpatrick	14	Joe Foy	71	Pat Kelly	40
1970	Lou Piniella	.301	Amos Otis	.353	Bob Oliver	.451	Bob Oliver	27	Bob Oliver	99	Pat Kelly	34
1971	Amos Otis	.301	Paul Schaal	.387	Amos Otis	.443	Amos Otis	15	Amos Otis	79	Amos Otis	52
1972	Lou Piniella	.312	John Mayberry	.394	John Mayberry	.507	John Mayberry	25	John Mayberry	100	Freddie Patek	33
1973	Amos Otis	.300	John Mayberry	.417	Amos Otis	.484	John Mayberry / Amos Otis	26	John Mayberry	100	Freddie Patek	36
1974	Hal McRae	.310	Hal McRae	.375	Hal McRae	.475	John Mayberry	22	Hal McRae	88	Freddie Patek	33
1975	George Brett	.308	John Mayberry	.416	John Mayberry	.547	John Mayberry	34	John Mayberry	106	Amos Otis	39
1976	George Brett	.333	Hal McRae	.407	George Brett	.462	Amos Otis	18	John Mayberry	95	Freddie Patek	51
1977	George Brett	.312	George Brett	.373	George Brett	.532	Al Cowens / John Mayberry	23	Al Cowens	112	Freddie Patek	53
1978	Amos Otis	.298	Amos Otis	.380	Amos Otis	.525	Amos Otis	22	Amos Otis	96	Willie Wilson	46
1979	George Brett	.329	Darrell Porter	.421	George Brett	.563	George Brett	23	Darrell Porter	112	Willie Wilson	83
1980	George Brett	.390	George Brett	.454	George Brett	.664	George Brett	24	George Brett	118	Willie Wilson	79
1981	George Brett	.314	Willie Aikens	.377	George Brett	.484	Amos Otis	17	Amos Otis	57	Willie Wilson	34
1982	Willie Wilson	.332	George Brett	.378	Hal McRae	.542	Hal McRae	27	Hal McRae	133	Willie Wilson	37
1983	Hal McRae	.311	George Brett	.385	George Brett	.563	George Brett	25	George Brett	93	Willie Wilson	59
1984	Willie Wilson	.301	Willie Wilson	.350	Frank White	.445	Steve Balboni	28	Steve Balboni	77	Willie Wilson	47
1985	George Brett	.335	George Brett	.436	George Brett	.585	Steve Balboni	36	George Brett	112	Willie Wilson	43
1986	George Brett	.290	George Brett	.401	George Brett	.481	Steve Balboni	29	Steve Balboni	88	Willie Wilson	34
1987	Kevin Seitzer	.323	Kevin Seitzer	.399	Danny Tartabull	.541	Danny Tartabull	34	Danny Tartabull	101	Willie Wilson	59
1988	George Brett	.306	George Brett	.389	Danny Tartabull	.515	Danny Tartabull	26	George Brett	103	Willie Wilson	35
1989	Jim Eisenreich	.293	Kevin Seitzer	.387	Bo Jackson	.495	Bo Jackson	32	Bo Jackson	105	Jim Eisenreich	27
1990	George Brett	.329	George Brett	.387	George Brett	.515	Bo Jackson	28	George Brett	87	Willie Wilson	24
1991	Danny Tartabull	.316	Danny Tartabull	.397	Danny Tartabull	.593	Danny Tartabull	31	Danny Tartabull	100	Brian McRae	20
1992	George Brett	.285	Wally Joyner	.336	Gregg Jefferies	.404	Mike Macfarlane	17	Gregg Jefferies	75	Gregg Jefferies	19
1993	Wally Joyner	.292	Wally Joyner	.375	Wally Joyner	.467	Mike Macfarlane	20	George Brett	75	Felix Jose	31
1994	Wally Joyner	.311	Bob Hamelin	.388	Bob Hamelin	.599	Bob Hamelin	24	Bob Hamelin	65	Vince Coleman	50
1995	Wally Joyner	.310	Wally Joyner	.394	Gary Gaetti	.518	Gary Gaetti	35	Gary Gaetti	96	Tom Goodwin	50
1996	Jose Offerman	.303	Jose Offerman	.384	Jose Offerman	.417	Craig Paquette	22	Craig Paquette	67	Tom Goodwin	66
1997	Jay Bell	.291	Chili Davis	.386	Chili Davis	.509	Chili Davis	30	Jeff King	112	Tom Goodwin	34

Kansas City Royals Individual Season Pitching Leaders

Year	ERA		Baserunners/9 IP		Innings Pitched		Strikeouts		Wins		Saves	
1969	Wally Bunker	3.23	Wally Bunker	10.7	Wally Bunker	222.2	Bill Butler	156	Wally Bunker	12	Moe Drabowsky	11
1970	Bob Johnson	3.07	Bob Johnson	11.4	Dick Drago	240.0	Bob Johnson	206	Jim Rooker	10	Ted Abernathy	12
1971	Mike Hedlund	2.71	Mike Hedlund	10.5	Dick Drago	241.1	Dick Drago	109	Dick Drago	17	Ted Abernathy	23
1972	Roger Nelson	2.08	Roger Nelson	7.9	Dick Drago	239.1	Paul Splittorff	140	Dick Drago / Paul Splittorff	12	Tom Burgmeier	9
1973	Paul Splittorff	3.98	Paul Splittorff	12.4	Paul Splittorff	262.0	Steve Busby	174	Paul Splittorff	20	Doug Bird	20
1974	Al Fitzmorris	2.79	Bruce Dal Canton	11.4	Steve Busby	292.1	Steve Busby	198	Steve Busby	22	Doug Bird	10
1975	Steve Busby	3.08	Steve Busby	11.0	Steve Busby	260.1	Steve Busby	160	Steve Busby	18	Doug Bird	11
1976	Al Fitzmorris	3.06	Doug Bird	10.2	Dennis Leonard	259.0	Dennis Leonard	150	Dennis Leonard	17	Mark Littell	16
1977	Dennis Leonard	3.04	Dennis Leonard	10.2	Dennis Leonard	292.2	Dennis Leonard	244	Dennis Leonard	20	Doug Bird	14
1978	Larry Gura	2.72	Larry Gura	10.0	Dennis Leonard	294.2	Dennis Leonard	183	Dennis Leonard	21	Al Hrabosky	20
1979	Dennis Leonard	4.08	Dennis Leonard	10.8	Paul Splittorff	240.0	Dennis Leonard	126	Paul Splittorff	15	Al Hrabosky	11
1980	Larry Gura	2.95	Larry Gura	11.2	Larry Gura	283.1	Dennis Leonard	155	Dennis Leonard	20	Dan Quisenberry	33
1981	Larry Gura	2.72	Larry Gura	9.3	Dennis Leonard	201.2	Dennis Leonard	107	Dennis Leonard	13	Dan Quisenberry	18
1982	Vida Blue	3.78	Larry Gura	11.6	Larry Gura	248.0	Vida Blue	103	Larry Gura	18	Dan Quisenberry	35
1983	Larry Gura	4.90	Larry Gura	13.7	Larry Gura	200.1	Paul Splittorff	61	Paul Splittorff	13	Dan Quisenberry	45
1984	Bud Black	3.12	Bud Black	10.3	Bud Black	257.0	Bud Black	140	Bud Black	17	Dan Quisenberry	44
1985	Charlie Leibrandt	2.69	Bret Saberhagen	9.6	Charlie Leibrandt	237.2	Bret Saberhagen	158	Bret Saberhagen	20	Dan Quisenberry	37
1986	Danny Jackson	3.20	Charlie Leibrandt	11.9	Charlie Leibrandt	231.1	Mark Gubicza	118	Charlie Leibrandt	14	Dan Quisenberry	12
1987	Bret Saberhagen	3.36	Bret Saberhagen	10.7	Bret Saberhagen	257.0	Mark Gubicza	166	Bret Saberhagen	18	Gene Garber / Dan Quisenberry	8
1988	Mark Gubicza	2.70	Mark Gubicza	10.9	Mark Gubicza	269.2	Mark Gubicza	183	Mark Gubicza	20	Steve Farr	20
1989	Bret Saberhagen	2.16	Bret Saberhagen	8.7	Bret Saberhagen	262.1	Bret Saberhagen	193	Bret Saberhagen	23	Steve Farr / Jeff Montgomery	18
1990	Kevin Appier	2.76	Kevin Appier	11.6	Tom Gordon	195.1	Tom Gordon	175	Steve Farr	13	Jeff Montgomery	24
1991	Bret Saberhagen	3.07	Bret Saberhagen	10.0	Kevin Appier	207.2	Tom Gordon	167	Kevin Appier / Bret Saberhagen	13	Jeff Montgomery	33
1992	Kevin Appier	2.46	Kevin Appier	10.2	Kevin Appier	208.1	Kevin Appier	150	Kevin Appier	15	Jeff Montgomery	39
1993	Kevin Appier	2.56	Kevin Appier	10.0	David Cone	254.0	David Cone	191	Kevin Appier	18	Jeff Montgomery	45
1994	David Cone	2.94	David Cone	10.0	David Cone	171.2	Kevin Appier	145	David Cone	16	Jeff Montgomery	27
1995	Mark Gubicza	3.75	Kevin Appier	11.2	Mark Gubicza	213.1	Kevin Appier	185	Kevin Appier	15	Jeff Montgomery	31
1996	Kevin Appier	3.62	Kevin Appier	11.6	Tim Belcher	238.2	Kevin Appier	207	Tim Belcher	15	Jeff Montgomery	24
1997	Kevin Appier	3.40	Kevin Appier	11.2	Kevin Appier	235.2	Kevin Appier	196	Tim Belcher	13	Jeff Montgomery	14

Teams: Royals

Royals Franchise Batting Leaders—Career

Games

1	George Brett	2,707
2	Frank White	2,324
3	Amos Otis	1,891
4	Hal McRae	1,837
5	Willie Wilson	1,787
6	Freddie Patek	1,245
7	John Mayberry	897
8	Mike Macfarlane	887
9	Cookie Rojas	880
10	John Wathan	860
11	Al Cowens	812
12	U.L. Washington	757
13	Kevin Seitzer	741
14	Lou Piniella	700
15	Danny Tartabull	657
16	Jim Eisenreich	650
17	Brian McRae	614
18	Ed Kirkpatrick	613
19	Paul Schaal	606
20	Jamie Quirk	582

At-Bats

1	George Brett	10,349
2	Frank White	7,859
3	Amos Otis	7,050
4	Willie Wilson	6,799
5	Hal McRae	6,568
6	Freddie Patek	4,305
7	John Mayberry	3,131
8	Cookie Rojas	3,072
9	Mike Macfarlane	2,794
10	Al Cowens	2,785
11	Kevin Seitzer	2,749
12	Lou Piniella	2,570
13	John Wathan	2,505
14	U.L. Washington	2,459
15	Brian McRae	2,393
16	Danny Tartabull	2,327
17	Jim Eisenreich	2,006
18	Steve Balboni	1,999
19	Paul Schaal	1,998
20	Four tied at	1,897

Runs

1	George Brett	1,583
2	Amos Otis	1,074
3	Willie Wilson	1,060
4	Frank White	912
5	Hal McRae	873
6	Freddie Patek	571
7	John Mayberry	459
8	Kevin Seitzer	408
9	Al Cowens	373
10	Mike Macfarlane	360
11	Danny Tartabull	348
12	Cookie Rojas	324
13	U.L. Washington	319
	Brian McRae	319
15	John Wathan	305
16	Darrell Porter	290
17	Bo Jackson	278
18	Wally Joyner	270
19	Paul Schaal	263
20	Lou Piniella	258

Hits

1	George Brett	3,154
2	Frank White	2,006
3	Amos Otis	1,977
4	Willie Wilson	1,968
5	Hal McRae	1,924
6	Freddie Patek	1,036
7	Cookie Rojas	824
8	John Mayberry	816
9	Kevin Seitzer	809
10	Al Cowens	784
11	Lou Piniella	734
12	Mike Macfarlane	716
13	Danny Tartabull	674
14	John Wathan	656
15	Brian McRae	627
16	U.L. Washington	625
17	Wally Joyner	556
18	Jim Eisenreich	555
19	Paul Schaal	525
20	Darrell Porter	514

Doubles

1	George Brett	665
2	Hal McRae	449
3	Frank White	407
4	Amos Otis	365
5	Willie Wilson	241
6	Freddie Patek	182
7	Mike Macfarlane	174
8	Danny Tartabull	141
9	Cookie Rojas	139
	John Mayberry	139
11	Kevin Seitzer	128
12	Lou Piniella	127
13	Wally Joyner	120
14	Al Cowens	117
15	Jim Eisenreich	113
16	Brian McRae	109
17	Kurt Stillwell	100
18	Willie Aikens	95
19	U.L. Washington	94
20	John Wathan	90

Triples

1	George Brett	137
2	Willie Wilson	133
3	Amos Otis	65
4	Hal McRae	63
5	Frank White	58
6	Al Cowens	44
7	Freddie Patek	41
8	Brian McRae	32
9	U.L. Washington	28
10	John Wathan	25
11	Kevin Seitzer	24
12	Jim Eisenreich	23
13	Lou Piniella	21
	Darrell Porter	21
15	Tom Poquette	18
	Johnny Damon	18
17	Jim Wohlford	17
	Kurt Stillwell	17
19	Mike Macfarlane	16
	Vince Coleman	16

Home Runs

1	George Brett	317
2	Amos Otis	193
3	Hal McRae	169
4	Frank White	160
5	John Mayberry	143
6	Danny Tartabull	124
7	Steve Balboni	119
8	Bo Jackson	109
9	Mike Macfarlane	103
10	Willie Aikens	77
11	Darrell Porter	61
	Gary Gaetti	61
13	Ed Kirkpatrick	56
14	Bob Oliver	49
15	Lou Piniella	45
	Al Cowens	45
17	Darryl Motley	44
	Wally Joyner	44
19	Bob Hamelin	42
20	Willie Wilson	40

RBI

1	George Brett	1,595
2	Hal McRae	1,012
3	Amos Otis	992
4	Frank White	886
5	John Mayberry	552
6	Willie Wilson	509
7	Danny Tartabull	425
8	Mike Macfarlane	398
9	Freddie Patek	382
10	Al Cowens	374
11	Lou Piniella	348
12	Cookie Rojas	332
13	Steve Balboni	318
14	Bo Jackson	313
15	Darrell Porter	301
16	Willie Aikens	297
17	Wally Joyner	271
18	Kevin Seitzer	265
19	John Wathan	261
20	Brian McRae	248

Walks

1	George Brett	1,096
2	Amos Otis	739
3	Hal McRae	616
4	John Mayberry	561
5	Freddie Patek	413
6	Frank White	412
7	Kevin Seitzer	369
8	Willie Wilson	360
9	Danny Tartabull	325
10	Darrell Porter	318
11	Paul Schaal	300
12	Ed Kirkpatrick	243
13	Wally Joyner	237
14	Mike Macfarlane	232
15	U.L. Washington	229
16	Willie Aikens	216
17	Cookie Rojas	213
18	John Wathan	199
19	Al Cowens	189
20	Steve Balboni	175

Strikeouts

1	Frank White	1,035
2	Willie Wilson	990
3	Amos Otis	953
4	George Brett	908
5	Hal McRae	697
6	Bo Jackson	638
7	Danny Tartabull	592
8	Freddie Patek	586
9	Steve Balboni	568
10	Mike Macfarlane	534
11	John Mayberry	457
12	Brian McRae	388
13	U.L. Washington	346
14	Kevin Seitzer	326
15	Bob Oliver	300
16	Al Cowens	286
17	Willie Aikens	280
18	Lou Piniella	265
	Ed Kirkpatrick	265
	John Wathan	265

Stolen Bases

1	Willie Wilson	612
2	Amos Otis	340
3	Freddie Patek	336
4	George Brett	201
5	Frank White	178
6	Tom Goodwin	150
7	U.L. Washington	120
8	Hal McRae	105
	John Wathan	105
10	Brian McRae	93
11	Bo Jackson	81
12	Al Cowens	80
13	Vince Coleman	76
14	Lonnie Smith	75
15	Pat Kelly	74
16	Jim Eisenreich	65
17	Gary Thurman	53
18	Jim Wohlford	51
19	Kevin Seitzer	50
20	Johnny Damon	48

Runs Created

1	George Brett	1,787
2	Amos Otis	1,090
3	Hal McRae	1,034
4	Willie Wilson	919
5	Frank White	844
6	John Mayberry	545
7	Freddie Patek	469
8	Danny Tartabull	433
9	Kevin Seitzer	415
10	Mike Macfarlane	386
11	Al Cowens	363
12	Darrell Porter	319
13	Lou Piniella	318
14	Cookie Rojas	315
15	Wally Joyner	301
16	Paul Schaal	281
	Brian McRae	281
18	U.L. Washington	276
	Willie Aikens	276
20	Bo Jackson	270

Runs Created/27 Outs

(minimum 2000 Plate Appearances)

1	Danny Tartabull	6.69
2	George Brett	6.28
3	John Mayberry	6.10
4	Darrell Porter	5.85
5	Wally Joyner	5.64
6	Hal McRae	5.60
7	Willie Aikens	5.49
8	Kevin Seitzer	5.42
9	Amos Otis	5.39
10	Bo Jackson	5.00
11	Willie Wilson	4.85
12	Paul Schaal	4.83
13	Mike Macfarlane	4.75
14	Al Cowens	4.55
15	Ed Kirkpatrick	4.46
16	Steve Balboni	4.38
17	Lou Piniella	4.34
18	Kurt Stillwell	4.33
19	Jim Eisenreich	4.17
20	Brian McRae	4.00

Batting Average

(minimum 2000 Plate Appearances)

1	George Brett	.305
2	Kevin Seitzer	.294
3	Wally Joyner	.293
4	Hal McRae	.293
5	Danny Tartabull	.290
6	Willie Wilson	.289
7	Lou Piniella	.286
8	Willie Aikens	.282
9	Al Cowens	.282
10	Amos Otis	.280
11	Jim Eisenreich	.277
12	Darrell Porter	.271
13	Cookie Rojas	.268
14	Paul Schaal	.263
15	Brian McRae	.262
16	John Wathan	.262
17	John Mayberry	.261
18	Mike Macfarlane	.256
19	Kurt Stillwell	.256
20	Frank White	.255

On-Base Percentage

(minimum 2000 Plate Appearances)

1	Kevin Seitzer	.380
2	Danny Tartabull	.376
3	Darrell Porter	.375
4	John Mayberry	.374
5	Wally Joyner	.371
6	George Brett	.369
7	Willie Aikens	.362
8	Paul Schaal	.360
9	Hal McRae	.356
10	Amos Otis	.347
11	Ed Kirkpatrick	.334
12	Al Cowens	.329
13	Willie Wilson	.329
14	Mike Macfarlane	.328
15	Lou Piniella	.327
16	Jim Eisenreich	.320
17	Kurt Stillwell	.318
18	John Wathan	.318
19	U.L. Washington	.316
20	Cookie Rojas	.314

Slugging Percentage

(minimum 2000 Plate Appearances)

1	Danny Tartabull	.518
2	George Brett	.487
3	Bo Jackson	.480
4	Willie Aikens	.469
5	Steve Balboni	.459
6	Hal McRae	.458
7	John Mayberry	.448
8	Mike Macfarlane	.441
9	Darrell Porter	.435
10	Wally Joyner	.434
11	Amos Otis	.433
12	Lou Piniella	.404
13	Al Cowens	.404
14	Kevin Seitzer	.394
15	Jim Eisenreich	.390
16	Ed Kirkpatrick	.390
17	Frank White	.383
18	Willie Wilson	.382
19	Kurt Stillwell	.373
20	Brian McRae	.372

Teams: Royals

Royals Franchise Pitching Leaders—Career

Wins

1	Paul Splittorff	166
2	Dennis Leonard	144
3	Mark Gubicza	132
4	Larry Gura	111
5	Bret Saberhagen	110
6	Kevin Appier	104
7	Tom Gordon	79
8	Charlie Leibrandt	76
9	Al Fitzmorris	70
	Steve Busby	70
11	Dick Drago	61
12	Bud Black	56
13	Dan Quisenberry	51
14	Doug Bird	49
15	Marty Pattin	43
16	Rich Gale	42
17	Jeff Montgomery	41
18	Danny Jackson	37
19	Hipolito Pichardo	35
20	Steve Farr	34

Losses

1	Paul Splittorff	143
2	Mark Gubicza	135
3	Dennis Leonard	106
4	Larry Gura	78
	Bret Saberhagen	78
	Kevin Appier	78
7	Tom Gordon	71
8	Dick Drago	70
9	Charlie Leibrandt	61
10	Bud Black	57
11	Steve Busby	54
12	Danny Jackson	49
13	Al Fitzmorris	48
14	Jim Rooker	44
	Dan Quisenberry	44
16	Jeff Montgomery	41
17	Marty Pattin	39
18	Doug Bird	36
19	Chris Haney	34
20	Rich Gale	33

Winning Percentage
(minimum 75 decisions)

1	Al Fitzmorris	.593
2	Larry Gura	.587
3	Bret Saberhagen	.585
4	Doug Bird	.576
5	Dennis Leonard	.576
6	Kevin Appier	.571
7	Steve Busby	.565
8	Rich Gale	.560
9	Charlie Leibrandt	.555
10	Paul Splittorff	.537
11	Dan Quisenberry	.537
12	Tom Gordon	.527
13	Marty Pattin	.524
14	Jeff Montgomery	.500
15	Bud Black	.496
16	Mark Gubicza	.494
17	Dick Drago	.466
18	Danny Jackson	.430

Games

1	Jeff Montgomery	581
2	Dan Quisenberry	573
3	Paul Splittorff	429
4	Mark Gubicza	382
5	Dennis Leonard	312
6	Larry Gura	310
7	Doug Bird	292
8	Steve Farr	289
9	Tom Gordon	274
10	Steve Mingori	264
11	Kevin Appier	256
12	Hipolito Pichardo	254
13	Bret Saberhagen	252
14	Marty Pattin	244
15	Al Fitzmorris	243
16	Bud Black	216
17	Tom Burgmeier	196
18	Charlie Leibrandt	194
19	Mike Magnante	191
20	Dick Drago	182

Games Started

1	Paul Splittorff	392
2	Mark Gubicza	327
3	Dennis Leonard	302
4	Kevin Appier	244
5	Bret Saberhagen	226
6	Larry Gura	219
7	Charlie Leibrandt	187
8	Dick Drago	160
9	Steve Busby	150
10	Tom Gordon	144
11	Al Fitzmorris	136
12	Bud Black	128
13	Danny Jackson	107
14	Rich Gale	104
15	Chris Haney	87
16	Jim Rooker	68
17	Tim Belcher	67
18	Bruce Dal Canton	65
19	Marty Pattin	63
20	Mike Hedlund	62

Complete Games

1	Dennis Leonard	103
2	Paul Splittorff	88
3	Bret Saberhagen	64
4	Larry Gura	61
5	Dick Drago	53
	Steve Busby	53
7	Mark Gubicza	42
8	Al Fitzmorris	35
9	Charlie Leibrandt	34
10	Kevin Appier	31
11	Danny Jackson	20
12	Jim Rooker	19
	Rich Gale	19
14	Roger Nelson	18
	Marty Pattin	18
16	Bud Black	16
17	Bruce Dal Canton	13
18	Wally Bunker	12
	Tom Gordon	12
20	Four tied at	10

Shutouts

1	Dennis Leonard	23
2	Paul Splittorff	17
3	Mark Gubicza	16
4	Larry Gura	14
	Bret Saberhagen	14
6	Al Fitzmorris	11
7	Dick Drago	10
	Charlie Leibrandt	10
	Kevin Appier	10
10	Jim Rooker	7
	Roger Nelson	7
	Steve Busby	7
13	Danny Jackson	6
14	Bill Butler	5
	Rich Gale	5
16	David Cone	4
17	Bud Black	3
	Luis Aquino	3
	Chris Haney	3
20	Sixteen tied at	2

Saves

1	Jeff Montgomery	256
2	Dan Quisenberry	238
3	Doug Bird	58
4	Steve Farr	49
5	Ted Abernathy	40
6	Al Hrabosky	31
7	Tom Burgmeier	28
	Mark Littell	28
9	Steve Mingori	27
10	Gene Garber	26
11	Marty Pattin	21
12	Hipolito Pichardo	18
13	Moe Drabowsky	13
14	Larry Gura	12
15	Renie Martin	11
16	Bud Black	10
17	Mike Armstrong	9
18	Ken Wright	8
	Jerry Don Gleaton	8
	Rusty Meacham	8

Innings Pitched

1	Paul Splittorff	2,554.2
2	Mark Gubicza	2,218.2
3	Dennis Leonard	2,187.0
4	Larry Gura	1,701.1
5	Kevin Appier	1,665.1
6	Bret Saberhagen	1,660.1
7	Charlie Leibrandt	1,257.0
8	Tom Gordon	1,149.2
9	Dick Drago	1,133.2
10	Al Fitzmorris	1,098.0
11	Steve Busby	1,060.2
12	Bud Black	977.2
13	Dan Quisenberry	920.1
14	Marty Pattin	825.2
15	Jeff Montgomery	742.0
16	Doug Bird	714.2
17	Danny Jackson	712.2
18	Rich Gale	666.1
19	Hipolito Pichardo	557.1
20	Bruce Dal Canton	555.0

Walks

1	Mark Gubicza	783
2	Paul Splittorff	780
3	Dennis Leonard	622
4	Tom Gordon	587
5	Kevin Appier	568
6	Larry Gura	503
7	Steve Busby	433
8	Al Fitzmorris	359
	Charlie Leibrandt	359
10	Bret Saberhagen	331
11	Rich Gale	315
12	Dick Drago	310
13	Danny Jackson	305
14	Bud Black	289
15	Jeff Montgomery	244
16	Jim Rooker	223
17	Marty Pattin	217
18	Bruce Dal Canton	208
19	Hipolito Pichardo	206
20	Steve Farr	203

Strikeouts

1	Mark Gubicza	1,366
2	Kevin Appier	1,364
3	Dennis Leonard	1,323
4	Bret Saberhagen	1,093
5	Paul Splittorff	1,057
6	Tom Gordon	999
7	Steve Busby	659
8	Jeff Montgomery	639
9	Larry Gura	633
10	Charlie Leibrandt	618
11	Dick Drago	577
12	Bud Black	508
13	Doug Bird	464
14	Danny Jackson	430
15	Steve Farr	429
16	Al Fitzmorris	391
17	Marty Pattin	370
18	David Cone	344
19	Rich Gale	335
20	Dan Quisenberry	321

Strikeouts/9 Innings
(minimum 750 Innings Pitched)

1	Tom Gordon	7.82
2	Kevin Appier	7.37
3	Bret Saberhagen	5.92
4	Steve Busby	5.59
5	Mark Gubicza	5.54
6	Dennis Leonard	5.44
7	Bud Black	4.68
8	Dick Drago	4.58
9	Charlie Leibrandt	4.42
10	Marty Pattin	4.03
11	Paul Splittorff	3.72
12	Larry Gura	3.35
13	Al Fitzmorris	3.20
14	Dan Quisenberry	3.14

ERA
(minimum 750 Innings Pitched)

1	Dan Quisenberry	2.55
2	Bret Saberhagen	3.21
3	Kevin Appier	3.30
4	Al Fitzmorris	3.46
5	Marty Pattin	3.48
6	Dick Drago	3.52
7	Charlie Leibrandt	3.60
8	Dennis Leonard	3.70
9	Steve Busby	3.72
10	Larry Gura	3.72
11	Bud Black	3.73
12	Paul Splittorff	3.81
13	Mark Gubicza	3.91
14	Tom Gordon	4.02

Component ERA
(minimum 750 Innings Pitched)

1	Dan Quisenberry	2.80
2	Bret Saberhagen	2.87
3	Kevin Appier	3.08
4	Marty Pattin	3.31
5	Al Fitzmorris	3.42
6	Larry Gura	3.50
7	Dennis Leonard	3.53
8	Bud Black	3.57
9	Steve Busby	3.69
10	Charlie Leibrandt	3.71
11	Dick Drago	3.71
12	Paul Splittorff	3.78
13	Mark Gubicza	3.79
14	Tom Gordon	3.87

Opponent Average
(minimum 750 Innings Pitched)

1	Kevin Appier	.237
2	Tom Gordon	.243
3	Bret Saberhagen	.248
4	Bud Black	.252
5	Steve Busby	.253
6	Marty Pattin	.254
7	Larry Gura	.254
8	Dennis Leonard	.257
9	Al Fitzmorris	.260
10	Dan Quisenberry	.262
11	Mark Gubicza	.263
12	Charlie Leibrandt	.266
13	Dick Drago	.269
14	Paul Splittorff	.270

Opponent OBP
(minimum 750 Innings Pitched)

1	Bret Saberhagen	.286
2	Dan Quisenberry	.289
3	Marty Pattin	.302
4	Kevin Appier	.303
5	Larry Gura	.308
6	Bud Black	.309
7	Dennis Leonard	.310
8	Charlie Leibrandt	.317
9	Al Fitzmorris	.318
10	Dick Drago	.320
11	Paul Splittorff	.323
12	Mark Gubicza	.327
13	Steve Busby	.328
14	Tom Gordon	.334

Royals Franchise Batting Leaders—Single Season

Games

1	Al Cowens	1977	162
	Hal McRae	1977	162
3	Paul Schaal	1971	161
	John Mayberry	1976	161
	Willie Wilson	1980	161
	Kevin Seitzer	1987	161
7	Bob Oliver	1970	160
	Steve Balboni	1985	160
	Kevin Seitzer	1989	160
10	Amos Otis	1970	159
	George Brett	1975	159
	George Brett	1976	159
	Hal McRae	1982	159
	Greg Gagne	1993	159
15	Danny Tartabull	1987	158
	Kevin Seitzer	1990	158
17	Darrell Porter	1979	157
	Hal McRae	1983	157
	George Brett	1988	157
20	Three tied at		156

At-Bats

1	Willie Wilson	1980	705
2	George Brett	1976	645
	George Brett	1979	645
4	Hal McRae	1977	641
	Kevin Seitzer	1987	641
6	George Brett	1975	634
7	Willie Wilson	1986	631
8	Brian McRae	1991	629
9	Brian McRae	1993	627
10	Hal McRae	1978	623
11	Kevin Seitzer	1990	622
12	Amos Otis	1970	620
13	Hal McRae	1982	613
14	Bob Oliver	1970	612
15	Willie Wilson	1987	610
16	Al Cowens	1977	606
17	Willie Wilson	1985	605
18	Gregg Jefferies	1992	604
19	Steve Balboni	1985	600
20	Kevin Seitzer	1989	597

Runs

1	Willie Wilson	1980	133
2	George Brett	1979	119
3	Willie Wilson	1979	113
4	George Brett	1985	108
5	George Brett	1977	105
	Kevin Seitzer	1987	105
7	Hal McRae	1977	104
8	Darrell Porter	1979	101
	George Brett	1982	101
10	Amos Otis	1979	100
11	Al Cowens	1977	98
12	Willie Wilson	1987	97
13	John Mayberry	1975	95
	Danny Tartabull	1987	95
15	George Brett	1976	94
16	Amos Otis	1976	93
17	Amos Otis	1970	91
	Hal McRae	1982	91
	Kevin Seitzer	1990	91
20	Five tied at		90

Hits

1	Willie Wilson	1980	230
2	George Brett	1976	215
3	George Brett	1979	212
4	Kevin Seitzer	1987	207
5	George Brett	1975	195
6	Willie Wilson	1982	194
7	Hal McRae	1977	191
8	Al Cowens	1977	189
	Hal McRae	1982	189
10	Willie Wilson	1979	185
11	George Brett	1985	184
12	Hal McRae	1983	183
13	Danny Tartabull	1987	180
	George Brett	1988	180
15	Lou Piniella	1972	179
	George Brett	1990	179
17	Brian McRae	1993	177
18	Amos Otis	1970	176
	George Brett	1977	176
20	Three tied at		175

Doubles

1	Hal McRae	1977	54
2	Hal McRae	1982	46
3	George Brett	1978	45
	Frank White	1982	45
	George Brett	1990	45
6	George Brett	1979	42
	George Brett	1988	42
8	Hal McRae	1983	41
9	Amos Otis	1976	40
	George Brett	1991	40
11	Hal McRae	1978	39
	Hal McRae	1980	39
13	John Mayberry	1975	38
	Hal McRae	1975	38
	George Brett	1983	38
	George Brett	1985	38
	Danny Tartabull	1988	38
18	Frank White	1986	37
19	Five tied at		36

Triples

1	Willie Wilson	1985	21
2	George Brett	1979	20
3	Willie Wilson	1980	15
	Willie Wilson	1982	15
	Willie Wilson	1987	15
6	George Brett	1976	14
	Al Cowens	1977	14
8	George Brett	1975	13
	George Brett	1977	13
	Willie Wilson	1979	13
11	Vince Coleman	1994	12
12	Freddie Patek	1971	11
	Hal McRae	1977	11
	U.L. Washington	1980	11
	Willie Wilson	1988	11
16	Tom Poquette	1976	10
	Darrell Porter	1979	10
18	Seven tied at		9

Home Runs

1	Steve Balboni	1985	36
2	Gary Gaetti	1995	35
3	John Mayberry	1975	34
	Danny Tartabull	1987	34
5	Bo Jackson	1989	32
6	Danny Tartabull	1991	31
7	George Brett	1985	30
	Chili Davis	1997	30
9	Steve Balboni	1986	29
10	Steve Balboni	1984	28
	Bo Jackson	1990	28
	Jeff King	1997	28
13	Bob Oliver	1970	27
	Hal McRae	1982	27
15	John Mayberry	1973	26
	Amos Otis	1973	26
	Danny Tartabull	1988	26
18	John Mayberry	1972	25
	George Brett	1983	25
	Bo Jackson	1988	25

RBI

1	Hal McRae	1982	133
2	George Brett	1980	118
3	Al Cowens	1977	112
	Darrell Porter	1979	112
	George Brett	1985	112
	Jeff King	1997	112
7	George Brett	1979	107
8	John Mayberry	1975	106
9	Bo Jackson	1989	105
10	George Brett	1988	103
11	Danny Tartabull	1988	102
12	Danny Tartabull	1987	101
13	John Mayberry	1972	100
	John Mayberry	1973	100
	Danny Tartabull	1991	100
16	Bob Oliver	1970	99
17	Willie Aikens	1980	98
18	Amos Otis	1978	96
	Gary Gaetti	1995	96
20	John Mayberry	1976	95

Walks

1	John Mayberry	1973	122
2	Darrell Porter	1979	121
3	John Mayberry	1975	119
4	Paul Schaal	1971	103
	George Brett	1985	103
6	Kevin Seitzer	1989	102
7	Jeff King	1997	89
8	Chili Davis	1997	85
9	Mike Fiore	1969	84
10	John Mayberry	1977	83
11	John Mayberry	1976	82
	George Brett	1988	82
13	George Brett	1986	80
	Kevin Seitzer	1987	80
15	Danny Tartabull	1987	79
16	John Mayberry	1972	78
17	John Mayberry	1974	77
	Freddie Patek	1974	77
19	Pat Kelly	1970	76
	Danny Tartabull	1988	76

Strikeouts

1	Bo Jackson	1989	172
2	Steve Balboni	1985	166
3	Bo Jackson	1987	158
4	Steve Balboni	1986	146
	Bo Jackson	1988	146
6	Steve Balboni	1984	139
7	Jerry Martin	1982	138
8	Danny Tartabull	1987	136
9	Bo Jackson	1990	128
10	Bob Oliver	1970	126
11	Danny Tartabull	1989	123
12	Danny Tartabull	1991	121
13	Danny Tartabull	1988	119
14	Jackie Hernandez	1969	111
15	Willie Wilson	1988	106
16	Pat Kelly	1970	105
	Brian McRae	1993	105
18	Kirk Gibson	1991	103
19	Craig Paquette	1996	101
	Jay Bell	1997	101

Stolen Bases

1	Willie Wilson	1979	83
2	Willie Wilson	1980	79
3	Tom Goodwin	1996	66
4	Willie Wilson	1983	59
	Willie Wilson	1987	59
6	Freddie Patek	1977	53
7	Amos Otis	1971	52
8	Freddie Patek	1976	51
9	Vince Coleman	1994	50
	Tom Goodwin	1995	50
11	Freddie Patek	1971	49
12	Willie Wilson	1984	47
13	Willie Wilson	1978	46
14	Willie Wilson	1985	43
15	Pat Kelly	1969	40
	U.L. Washington	1983	40
	Lonnie Smith	1985	40
18	Amos Otis	1975	39
19	Freddie Patek	1978	38
20	Two tied at		37

Runs Created

1	George Brett	1985	134
2	George Brett	1979	131
3	John Mayberry	1975	122
4	George Brett	1980	118
5	Darrell Porter	1979	117
	George Brett	1988	117
7	John Mayberry	1973	115
	George Brett	1976	115
	Hal McRae	1982	115
10	Hal McRae	1977	114
	Danny Tartabull	1987	114
12	Willie Wilson	1980	113
13	Kevin Seitzer	1987	112
14	Danny Tartabull	1991	111
15	George Brett	1990	108
16	Amos Otis	1973	106
	Al Cowens	1977	106
18	Amos Otis	1970	104
	George Brett	1977	104
20	Willie Wilson	1979	102

Runs Created/27 Outs

(minimum 3.1 Plate Appearances/Tm Gm)

1	George Brett	1980	10.72
2	George Brett	1985	9.29
3	Danny Tartabull	1991	8.64
4	John Mayberry	1973	8.23
5	John Mayberry	1975	8.06
6	George Brett	1979	7.71
7	Darrell Porter	1979	7.66
8	Bob Hamelin	1994	7.64
9	George Brett	1983	7.52
10	George Brett	1990	7.41
11	George Brett	1988	7.26
12	Danny Tartabull	1987	7.21
13	Amos Otis	1978	7.19
14	Hal McRae	1976	7.10
15	Hal McRae	1982	7.08
16	George Brett	1986	6.86
17	George Brett	1976	6.82
18	John Mayberry	1972	6.78
19	Chili Davis	1997	6.76
20	George Brett	1982	6.75

Batting Average

(minimum 3.1 Plate Appearances/Tm Gm)

1	George Brett	1980	.390
2	George Brett	1985	.335
3	George Brett	1976	.333
4	Hal McRae	1976	.332
5	Willie Wilson	1982	.332
6	George Brett	1990	.329
7	George Brett	1979	.329
8	Willie Wilson	1980	.326
9	Kevin Seitzer	1987	.323
10	Danny Tartabull	1991	.316
11	Willie Wilson	1979	.315
12	George Brett	1981	.314
13	George Brett	1977	.312
14	Al Cowens	1977	.312
15	Lou Piniella	1972	.312
16	Wally Joyner	1994	.311
17	Hal McRae	1983	.311
18	George Brett	1983	.310
19	Hal McRae	1974	.310
20	Wally Joyner	1995	.310

On-Base Percentage

(minimum 3.1 Plate Appearances/Tm Gm)

1	George Brett	1980	.454
2	George Brett	1985	.436
3	Darrell Porter	1979	.421
4	John Mayberry	1973	.417
5	John Mayberry	1975	.416
6	Hal McRae	1976	.407
7	George Brett	1986	.401
8	Kevin Seitzer	1987	.399
9	Danny Tartabull	1991	.397
10	Wally Joyner	1995	.394
11	John Mayberry	1972	.394
12	Danny Tartabull	1987	.390
13	George Brett	1988	.389
14	George Brett	1987	.388
15	Bob Hamelin	1994	.388
16	Kevin Seitzer	1988	.388
17	George Brett	1990	.387
18	Paul Schaal	1971	.387
19	Kevin Seitzer	1989	.387
20	Chili Davis	1997	.386

Slugging Percentage

(minimum 3.1 Plate Appearances/Tm Gm)

1	George Brett	1980	.664
2	Bob Hamelin	1994	.599
3	Danny Tartabull	1991	.593
4	George Brett	1985	.585
5	George Brett	1979	.563
6	George Brett	1983	.563
7	John Mayberry	1975	.547
8	Hal McRae	1982	.542
9	Danny Tartabull	1987	.541
10	George Brett	1977	.532
11	Al Cowens	1977	.525
12	Amos Otis	1978	.525
13	Gary Gaetti	1995	.518
14	Hal McRae	1977	.515
15	Danny Tartabull	1988	.515
16	George Brett	1990	.515
17	Chili Davis	1997	.509
18	George Brett	1988	.509
19	John Mayberry	1972	.507
20	George Brett	1982	.505

Royals Franchise Pitching Leaders—Single Season

Wins

1	Bret Saberhagen	1989	23
2	Steve Busby	1974	22
3	Dennis Leonard	1978	21
4	Paul Splittorff	1973	20
	Dennis Leonard	1977	20
	Dennis Leonard	1980	20
	Bret Saberhagen	1985	20
	Mark Gubicza	1988	20
9	Paul Splittorff	1978	19
10	Steve Busby	1975	18
	Jim Colborn	1977	18
	Larry Gura	1980	18
	Larry Gura	1982	18
	Bret Saberhagen	1987	18
	Kevin Appier	1993	18
16	Dick Drago	1971	17
	Dennis Leonard	1976	17
	Bud Black	1984	17
	Charlie Leibrandt	1985	17
	Tom Gordon	1989	17

Losses

1	Paul Splittorff	1974	19
2	Larry Gura	1983	18
	Mark Gubicza	1987	18
	Danny Jackson	1987	18
5	Dick Drago	1972	17
	Dennis Leonard	1978	17
	Paul Splittorff	1979	17
8	Jim Rooker	1969	16
	Bret Saberhagen	1988	16
10	Dick Drago	1970	15
	Jim Rooker	1970	15
	Steve Busby	1973	15
	Bud Black	1985	15
14	Nine tied at		14

Winning Percentage
(minimum 15 decisions)

1	Larry Gura	1978	.800
2	Bret Saberhagen	1989	.793
3	Bret Saberhagen	1985	.769
4	David Cone	1994	.762
5	Doug Bird	1977	.733
6	Paul Splittorff	1977	.727
7	Mark Gubicza	1988	.714
8	Kevin Appier	1993	.692
9	Al Fitzmorris	1974	.684
10	Dennis Leonard	1975	.682
11	Mark Gubicza	1986	.667
	Tom Gordon	1993	.667
13	Charlie Leibrandt	1985	.654
	Tom Gordon	1989	.654
15	Mike Hedlund	1971	.652
	Kevin Appier	1992	.652
17	Steve Farr	1990	.650
18	Roger Nelson	1972	.647
19	Paul Splittorff	1973	.645
	Dennis Leonard	1980	.645

Games

1	Dan Quisenberry	1985	84
2	Dan Quisenberry	1980	75
3	Jeff Montgomery	1990	73
4	Dan Quisenberry	1982	72
	Dan Quisenberry	1984	72
6	Dan Quisenberry	1983	69
	Jeff Montgomery	1993	69
8	Tom Burgmeier	1971	67
	Jeff Montgomery	1991	67
10	Jeff Montgomery	1992	65
11	Rusty Meacham	1992	64
12	Ted Abernathy	1971	63
	Jeff Montgomery	1989	63
14	Dan Quisenberry	1986	62
	Steve Farr	1988	62
16	Mark Littell	1976	60
17	Al Hrabosky	1978	58
	Al Hrabosky	1979	58
	Mike Armstrong	1983	58
20	Two tied at		57

Games Started

1	Dennis Leonard	1978	40
2	Paul Splittorff	1973	38
	Steve Busby	1974	38
	Paul Splittorff	1978	38
	Dennis Leonard	1980	38
6	Steve Busby	1973	37
	Dennis Leonard	1977	37
	Paul Splittorff	1977	37
	Larry Gura	1982	37
10	Paul Splittorff	1974	36
	Larry Gura	1980	36
	Mark Gubicza	1989	36
13	Twelve tied at		35

Complete Games

1	Dennis Leonard	1977	21
2	Steve Busby	1974	20
	Dennis Leonard	1978	20
4	Steve Busby	1975	18
5	Dennis Leonard	1976	16
	Larry Gura	1980	16
7	Dick Drago	1971	15
	Bret Saberhagen	1987	15
9	Paul Splittorff	1978	13
10	Paul Splittorff	1972	12
	Paul Splittorff	1973	12
	Dennis Leonard	1979	12
	Larry Gura	1981	12
	Bret Saberhagen	1989	12
15	Dick Drago	1972	11
	Al Fitzmorris	1975	11
	Paul Splittorff	1979	11
	Danny Jackson	1987	11
19	Seven tied at		10

Shutouts

1	Roger Nelson	1972	6
2	Dennis Leonard	1977	5
	Dennis Leonard	1979	5
4	Bill Butler	1969	4
	Dick Drago	1971	4
	Al Fitzmorris	1974	4
	Dennis Leonard	1978	4
	Larry Gura	1980	4
	Bret Saberhagen	1987	4
	Mark Gubicza	1988	4
	Bret Saberhagen	1989	4
12	Sixteen tied at		3

Saves

1	Dan Quisenberry	1983	45
	Jeff Montgomery	1993	45
3	Dan Quisenberry	1984	44
4	Jeff Montgomery	1992	39
5	Dan Quisenberry	1985	37
6	Dan Quisenberry	1982	35
7	Dan Quisenberry	1980	33
	Jeff Montgomery	1991	33
9	Jeff Montgomery	1995	31
10	Jeff Montgomery	1994	27
11	Jeff Montgomery	1990	24
	Jeff Montgomery	1996	24
13	Ted Abernathy	1971	23
14	Doug Bird	1973	20
	Al Hrabosky	1978	20
	Steve Farr	1988	20
17	Dan Quisenberry	1981	18
	Steve Farr	1989	18
	Jeff Montgomery	1989	18
20	Tom Burgmeier	1971	17

Innings Pitched

1	Dennis Leonard	1978	294.2
2	Dennis Leonard	1977	292.2
3	Steve Busby	1974	292.1
4	Larry Gura	1980	283.1
5	Dennis Leonard	1980	280.1
6	Mark Gubicza	1988	269.2
7	Bret Saberhagen	1989	262.1
8	Paul Splittorff	1973	262.0
	Paul Splittorff	1978	262.0
10	Bret Saberhagen	1988	260.2
11	Steve Busby	1975	260.1
12	Dennis Leonard	1976	259.0
13	Bud Black	1984	257.0
	Bret Saberhagen	1987	257.0
15	Mark Gubicza	1989	255.0
16	David Cone	1993	254.0
17	Larry Gura	1982	248.0
18	Charlie Leibrandt	1988	243.0
19	Al Fitzmorris	1975	242.0
20	Mark Gubicza	1987	241.2

Walks

1	Mark Gubicza	1987	120
2	David Cone	1993	114
3	Danny Jackson	1987	109
4	Steve Busby	1973	105
5	Jim Rooker	1970	102
6	Rich Gale	1978	100
7	Rich Gale	1979	99
	Tom Gordon	1990	99
9	Steve Busby	1974	92
10	Bill Butler	1969	91
11	Dennis Leonard	1975	90
12	Tom Gordon	1995	89
13	Bill Butler	1970	87
	Tom Gordon	1991	87
	Tom Gordon	1994	87
16	Tom Gordon	1989	86
17	Mark Gubicza	1986	84
18	Paul Splittorff	1977	83
	Mark Gubicza	1988	83
20	Three tied at		82

Strikeouts

1	Dennis Leonard	1977	244
2	Kevin Appier	1996	207
3	Bob Johnson	1970	206
4	Steve Busby	1974	198
5	Kevin Appier	1997	196
6	Bret Saberhagen	1989	193
7	David Cone	1993	191
8	Kevin Appier	1993	186
9	Kevin Appier	1995	185
10	Dennis Leonard	1978	183
	Mark Gubicza	1988	183
12	Tom Gordon	1990	175
13	Steve Busby	1973	174
14	Mark Gubicza	1989	173
15	Bret Saberhagen	1988	171
16	Tom Gordon	1991	167
17	Mark Gubicza	1987	166
18	Bret Saberhagen	1987	163
19	Steve Busby	1975	160
20	Two tied at		158

Strikeouts/9 Innings
(minimum 1 Inning Pitched/Tm Gm)

1	Kevin Appier	1996	8.82
2	Bob Johnson	1970	8.66
3	Tom Gordon	1989	8.45
4	Kevin Appier	1994	8.42
5	Kevin Appier	1995	8.27
6	Tom Gordon	1990	8.06
7	Dennis Leonard	1977	7.50
8	Kevin Appier	1997	7.49
9	Tom Gordon	1994	7.30
10	Bill Butler	1969	7.25
11	Kevin Appier	1993	7.01
12	David Cone	1994	6.92
13	Kevin Appier	1991	6.85
14	David Cone	1993	6.77
15	Bret Saberhagen	1989	6.62
16	Steve Busby	1973	6.57
17	Kevin Appier	1992	6.48
18	Bret Saberhagen	1991	6.23
19	Roger Nelson	1972	6.23
20	Dennis Leonard	1975	6.19

ERA
(minimum 1 Inning Pitched/Tm Gm)

1	Roger Nelson	1972	2.08
2	Bret Saberhagen	1989	2.16
3	Kevin Appier	1992	2.46
4	Kevin Appier	1993	2.56
5	Charlie Leibrandt	1985	2.69
6	Mark Gubicza	1988	2.70
7	Mike Hedlund	1971	2.71
8	Larry Gura	1981	2.72
9	Larry Gura	1978	2.72
10	Kevin Appier	1990	2.76
11	Al Fitzmorris	1974	2.79
12	Bret Saberhagen	1985	2.87
13	David Cone	1994	2.94
14	Larry Gura	1980	2.95
15	Dick Drago	1971	2.98
16	Dennis Leonard	1981	2.99
17	Dick Drago	1972	3.01
18	Mark Gubicza	1989	3.04
19	Dennis Leonard	1977	3.04
20	Al Fitzmorris	1976	3.06

Component ERA
(minimum 1 Inning Pitched/Tm Gm)

1	Roger Nelson	1972	1.66
2	Bret Saberhagen	1989	1.89
3	Larry Gura	1981	2.23
4	Kevin Appier	1993	2.25
5	Kevin Appier	1992	2.41
6	Larry Gura	1978	2.49
7	Bret Saberhagen	1991	2.51
8	Bret Saberhagen	1985	2.56
9	David Cone	1994	2.57
10	Dennis Leonard	1977	2.61
11	Bruce Dal Canton	1974	2.69
12	Mark Gubicza	1988	2.77
13	Mike Hedlund	1971	2.79
14	Bud Black	1984	2.82
15	Paul Splittorff	1972	2.86
16	Doug Bird	1976	2.89
17	Tom Gordon	1989	2.97
18	Paul Splittorff	1978	3.00
19	Kevin Appier	1995	3.01
20	Steve Busby	1975	3.03

Opponent Average
(minimum 1 Inning Pitched/Tm Gm)

1	Roger Nelson	1972	.196
2	David Cone	1994	.209
3	Tom Gordon	1989	.210
4	Bruce Dal Canton	1974	.211
5	Kevin Appier	1993	.212
6	Kevin Appier	1992	.217
7	Bret Saberhagen	1989	.217
8	Kevin Appier	1995	.221
9	David Cone	1993	.223
10	Larry Gura	1981	.223
11	Mike Hedlund	1971	.227
12	Dennis Leonard	1977	.227
13	Bob Johnson	1970	.228
14	Bret Saberhagen	1991	.228
15	Larry Gura	1978	.229
16	Bud Black	1984	.233
17	Mark Gubicza	1986	.233
18	Mark Gubicza	1988	.234
19	Tom Gordon	1994	.237
20	Vida Blue	1982	.238

Opponent OBP
(minimum 1 Inning Pitched/Tm Gm)

1	Roger Nelson	1972	.234
2	Bret Saberhagen	1989	.251
3	Larry Gura	1981	.265
4	Bret Saberhagen	1985	.271
5	David Cone	1994	.277
6	Kevin Appier	1993	.279
7	Doug Bird	1976	.279
8	Bret Saberhagen	1991	.280
9	Kevin Appier	1992	.281
10	Dennis Leonard	1977	.283
11	Bud Black	1984	.283
12	Larry Gura	1978	.283
13	Paul Splittorff	1978	.290
14	Wally Bunker	1969	.293
15	Bret Saberhagen	1987	.294
16	Mark Gubicza	1988	.294
17	Mike Hedlund	1971	.295
18	Dennis Leonard	1981	.296
19	Dick Drago	1972	.297
20	Dennis Leonard	1979	.297

Teams: Royals

Royals Capsule

Best Season: *1985.* The underdog Royals lost three out of the first four games of both the American League Championship Series and the World Series, but overcame both obstacles to win the World Championship.

Worst Season: *1983.* Many key players suffered injuries and a cloud hung over the club due to an ongoing drug investigation. In October, Willie Aikens, Vida Blue, Jerry Martin and Willie Wilson pled guilty to attempting to possess cocaine. All four served jail time.

Best Player: *George Brett.*

Best Pitcher: *Kevin Appier.* Dennis Leonard has comparable numbers, but they were compiled for much better teams in a less batter-friendly era.

Best Reliever: *Dan Quisenberry.*

Best Defensive Player: *Frank White.*

Hall of Famers: *Harmon Killebrew and Gaylord Perry* stopped through at the tail end of their careers. George Brett will be the first true Royal to get a plaque.

Franchise All-Star Team:

C	*Darrell Porter*	LF	*Willie Wilson*
1B	*John Mayberry*	CF	*Amos Otis*
2B	*Frank White*	RF	*Danny Tartabull*
3B	*George Brett*	DH	*Hal McRae*
SS	*Fred Patek*	SP	*Kevin Appier*
		RP	*Dan Quisenberry*

Biggest Flake: *Dan Quisenberry.* "Quiz" was articulate, intelligent, and very funny, but he gave so many unique quotes that writers couldn't resist painting him as a flake.

Strangest Career: *Kevin Seitzer.* Seitzer's career was just all wrong. Most players have their best years in the middle of their careers, but Seitzer's top seasons came right at the beginning and the end. He had a tremendous rookie year in 1987, but lost out in the Rookie of the Year balloting to Mark McGwire, who had one of the most spectacular rookie seasons of all time. Seitzer didn't even get the attention he deserved in his home city that year, since another rookie named Bo Jackson garnered most of the ink. Seitzer's batting average dropped steadily for the next four years, though, and after playing part-time in 1992, he was released. Playing mostly with the Brewers over the next five years, he steadily regained what he'd lost, and peaked in 1996 when he virtually duplicated the career-best numbers from his rookie season. Then it was over. He spent 1997 as a bench player in Cleveland, and retired when the season ended. One last note: he made one mound appearance in his career, facing only one batter. It came while he was playing for Oakland in 1993. He entered with a 2-2 count on Glenallen Hill, amd threw one pitch, which Hill watched for strike three. One batter, one pitch, one strikeout.

What Might Have Been: *Clint Hurdle.* He was one of the most super-hyped prospects of his time, and he seemed on track to stardom when he became a major league regular at age 20 and batted .294 at age 22. Back problems rendered him a fringe player from that point on, however.

Best Trade: *Amos Otis.* Over the winter of 1969, the Royals obtained outfielder Amos Otis and pitcher Bob Johnson from the Mets for third baseman Joe Foy. Otis starred for the Royals for over a decade. Johnson had a very good year in 1970, which enabled the Royals to deal him to Pittsburgh for a package that included shortstop Freddie Patek. The Royals have pulled off many other stunningly one-sided deals, acquiring players like Hal McRae, John Mayberry, Darrell Porter, Larry Gura and Jeff Montgomery at a minimal cost.

Worst Trade: *David Cone.* Just before the start of the 1987 season, they dealt Cone to the Mets for catcher Ed Hearn and a couple of nondescript pitchers, Rick Anderson and Mauro Gozzo. It was one of the few trades where the Royals clearly got taken.

Best-Looking Player: *Jamie Quirk.*

Ugliest Player: *Steve Balboni.*

Best Nickname: *U.L. Washington*—because it wasn't just a nickname. His given name really was "U.L."

Most Unappreciated Player: *Amos Otis.*

Most Overrated Player: *Willie Wilson.* Wilson was one of the fastest baserunners in the game and covered two-thirds of the outfield by himself, but he simply didn't get on base enough to be an effective leadoff man. In 11 years as a regular, he scored over 100 runs only twice.

Most Admirable Star: *Jim Eisenreich.* Virtually driven out of the majors by Tourette's Syndrome, Eisenreich got his condition under control with medication and returned to the big leagues with the Royals in 1987.

Least Admirable Stars: *Willie Wilson, Al Cowens.*

Best Season, Player: *George Brett, 1980.* Brett flirted with .400 so seriously that he nearly succeeded in seducing it.

Best Season, Pitcher: *Bret Saberhagen, 1989.* He led the majors with 23 wins and a 2.16 ERA.

Most Impressive Individual Record: *George Brett's* .390 batting average in 1980 was the closest anyone had come to the .400 mark since Ted Williams hit .406 in 1941.

Biggest Tragedy: *Dick Howser.* He led the Royals to the World Championship in 1985, but was diagnosed with brain cancer the following year. Many recall his attempt to return to managing in the spring of 1987 after undergoing brain surgery. It proved to be too much for him, and he passed away a couple of months later. In 1997, Royals fans were shocked to learn that Dan Quisenberry had been diagnosed with the same type of brain tumor.

Fan Favorite: *Frank White.*

—Mat Olkin

Milwaukee Brewers (1969-1997)

Year	Lg	Pos	W-L	Pct	GB	Manager	Att.	R	OR	HR	Avg	OBP	Slg	Opponent HR	Opponent Avg	Opponent OBP	ERA	Park Index Runs	Park Index HR
1969	AL	6th-W	64-98	.395	33.0	Joe Schultz	677,944	639	799	125	.234	.316	.346	172	.264	.343	4.35	103	128
1970	AL	4th-W	65-97	.401	33.0	Dave Bristol	933,690	613	751	126	.242	.319	.358	146	.255	.330	4.21	100	109
1971	AL	6th-W	69-92	.429	32.0	Dave Bristol	731,531	534	609	104	.229	.304	.329	130	.247	.321	3.38	107	85
1972	AL	6th-E	65-91	.417	21.0	Dave Bristol/Roy McMillan/Del Crandall	600,440	493	595	88	.235	.302	.328	116	.247	.312	3.45	92	64
1973	AL	5th-E	74-88	.457	23.0	Del Crandall	1,092,158	708	731	145	.253	.325	.388	119	.265	.340	3.98	93	90
1974	AL	5th-E	76-86	.469	15.0	Del Crandall	955,741	647	660	120	.244	.309	.369	126	.266	.326	3.76	106	107
1975	AL	5th-E	68-94	.420	28.0	Del Crandall/Harvey Kuenn	1,213,357	675	792	146	.250	.320	.389	133	.271	.348	4.34	103	94
1976	AL	6th-E	66-95	.410	32.0	Alex Grammas	1,012,164	570	655	88	.246	.311	.340	99	.260	.331	3.64	99	88
1977	AL	6th-E	67-95	.414	33.0	Alex Grammas	1,114,938	639	765	125	.258	.314	.389	136	.268	.337	4.32	91	65
1978	AL	3rd-E	93-69	.574	6.5	George Bamberger	1,601,406	804	650	173	.276	.339	.432	109	.262	.313	3.65	111	104
1979	AL	2nd-E	95-66	.590	8.0	George Bamberger	1,918,343	807	722	185	.280	.345	.448	162	.279	.324	4.03	98	97
1980	AL	3rd-E	86-76	.531	17.0	B. Rodgers/G. Bamberger/B. Rodgers	1,857,408	811	682	203	.275	.329	.448	137	.273	.323	3.71	87	82
1981	AL	3rd-E	31-25	.554	3.0	Buck Rodgers													
	AL	1st-E	31-22	.585	—	Buck Rodgers	874,292	493	459	96	.257	.313	.391	72	.266	.328	3.91	91	72
1982	AL	1st-E	95-67	.586	—	Buck Rodgers/Harvey Kuenn	1,978,896	891	717	216	.279	.335	.455	152	.270	.330	3.98	85	69
1983	AL	5th-E	87-75	.537	11.0	Harvey Kuenn	2,397,131	764	708	132	.277	.333	.418	133	.270	.329	4.02	82	84
1984	AL	7th-E	67-94	.416	36.5	Rene Lachemann	1,608,509	641	734	96	.262	.317	.370	137	.274	.331	4.06	84	88
1985	AL	6th-E	71-90	.441	28.0	George Bamberger	1,360,265	690	802	101	.263	.319	.379	175	.271	.331	4.39	112	98
1986	AL	6th-E	77-84	.478	18.0	George Bamberger/Tom Trebelhorn	1,265,041	667	734	127	.255	.321	.385	158	.267	.328	4.01	105	101
1987	AL	3rd-E	91-71	.562	7.0	Tom Trebelhorn	1,909,244	862	817	163	.276	.346	.428	169	.271	.333	4.62	105	83
1988	AL	3rd-E	87-75	.537	2.0	Tom Trebelhorn	1,923,238	682	616	113	.257	.314	.375	125	.248	.303	3.45	105	111
1989	AL	4th-E	81-81	.500	8.0	Tom Trebelhorn	1,970,735	707	679	126	.259	.318	.382	129	.265	.321	3.80	92	93
1990	AL	6th-E	74-88	.457	14.0	Tom Trebelhorn	1,752,900	732	760	128	.256	.320	.384	121	.275	.331	4.08	96	92
1991	AL	4th-E	83-79	.512	8.0	Tom Trebelhorn	1,478,729	799	744	116	.271	.336	.396	147	.266	.332	4.14	109	108
1992	AL	2nd-E	92-70	.568	4.0	Phil Garner	1,857,351	740	604	82	.268	.330	.375	127	.246	.305	3.43	79	70
1993	AL	7th-E	69-93	.426	26.0	Phil Garner	1,688,080	733	792	125	.258	.328	.378	153	.271	.336	4.45	97	74
1994	AL	5th-C	53-62	.461	15.0	Phil Garner	1,268,397	547	586	99	.263	.335	.408	127	.269	.340	4.62	113	102
1995	AL	4th-C	65-79	.451	35.0	Phil Garner	1,087,560	740	747	128	.266	.336	.409	146	.280	.360	4.82	122	86
1996	AL	3rd-C	80-82	.494	19.5	Phil Garner	1,327,155	894	899	178	.279	.353	.441	213	.278	.354	5.14	103	91
1997	AL	3rd-C	78-83	.484	8.0	Phil Garner	1,421,478	681	742	135	.260	.325	.398	177	.261	.333	4.23	99	91

Team Nicknames: Seattle Pilots 1969-1970, Milwaukee Brewers 1971-1997.

Team Ballparks: Sicks Stadium 1969, County Stadium 1970-1997.

Teams: Brewers

Milwaukee Brewers Individual Season Batting Leaders

Year	Batting Average		On-Base Percentage		Slugging Percentage		Home Runs		RBI		Stolen Bases	
1969	Don Mincher	.246	Don Mincher	.366	Don Mincher	.454	Don Mincher	25	Tommy Davis	80	Tommy Harper	73
1970	Tommy Harper	.296	Tommy Harper	.377	Tommy Harper	.522	Tommy Harper	31	Tommy Harper	82	Tommy Harper	38
1971	Dave May	.277	Dave May	.343	Dave May	.425	John Briggs	21	Dave May	65	Tommy Harper	25
1972	George Scott	.266	George Scott	.321	George Scott	.426	John Briggs	21	George Scott	88	Rick Auerbach	24
1973	George Scott	.306	George Scott	.370	George Scott	.488	Dave May	25	George Scott	107	Don Money	22
1974	Don Money	.283	Don Money	.346	George Scott	.432	John Briggs / George Scott	17	George Scott	82	Don Money	19
1975	George Scott	.285	Darrell Porter	.371	George Scott	.515	George Scott	36	George Scott	109	Pedro Garcia / Robin Yount	12
1976	Sixto Lezcano	.285	Sixto Lezcano	.348	George Scott	.414	George Scott	18	George Scott	77	Robin Yount	16
1977	Cecil Cooper	.300	Don Money	.348	Don Money	.470	Cecil Cooper	25	Don Money	83	Jim Wohlford	17
1978	Ben Oglivie	.303	Sixto Lezcano	.377	Larry Hisle	.533	Larry Hisle	34	Larry Hisle	115	Paul Molitor	30
1979	Paul Molitor	.322	Sixto Lezcano	.414	Sixto Lezcano	.573	Gorman Thomas	45	Gorman Thomas	123	Paul Molitor	33
1980	Cecil Cooper	.352	Cecil Cooper	.387	Ben Oglivie	.563	Ben Oglivie	41	Cecil Cooper	122	Paul Molitor	34
1981	Cecil Cooper	.320	Cecil Cooper	.363	Cecil Cooper	.495	Gorman Thomas	21	Ben Oglivie	72	Paul Molitor	10
1982	Robin Yount	.331	Robin Yount	.379	Robin Yount	.578	Gorman Thomas	39	Cecil Cooper	121	Paul Molitor	41
1983	Ted Simmons	.308	Robin Yount	.383	Cecil Cooper	.508	Cecil Cooper	30	Cecil Cooper	126	Paul Molitor	41
1984	Robin Yount	.298	Robin Yount	.362	Robin Yount	.441	Robin Yount	16	Robin Yount	80	Robin Yount	14
1985	Paul Molitor	.297	Paul Molitor	.356	Cecil Cooper	.456	Cecil Cooper	16	Cecil Cooper	99	Paul Molitor	21
1986	Robin Yount	.312	Robin Yount	.388	Rob Deer	.494	Rob Deer	33	Rob Deer	86	Paul Molitor	20
1987	Paul Molitor	.353	Paul Molitor	.438	Paul Molitor	.566	Rob Deer	28	Robin Yount	103	Paul Molitor	45
1988	Paul Molitor	.312	Paul Molitor	.384	Robin Yount	.465	Rob Deer	23	Robin Yount	91	Paul Molitor	41
1989	Robin Yount	.318	Robin Yount	.384	Robin Yount	.511	Rob Deer	26	Robin Yount	103	Paul Molitor	27
1990	Gary Sheffield	.294	Gary Sheffield	.350	Dave Parker	.451	Rob Deer	27	Dave Parker	92	Gary Sheffield	25
1991	Willie Randolph	.327	Willie Randolph	.424	Paul Molitor	.489	Greg Vaughn	27	Greg Vaughn	98	Paul Molitor	19
1992	Paul Molitor	.320	Paul Molitor	.389	Paul Molitor	.461	Greg Vaughn	23	Paul Molitor	89	Pat Listach	54
1993	Darryl Hamilton	.310	Greg Vaughn	.369	Greg Vaughn	.482	Greg Vaughn	30	Greg Vaughn	97	Darryl Hamilton	21
1994	Dave Nilsson	.275	Jody Reed	.362	Greg Vaughn	.478	Greg Vaughn	19	Dave Nilsson	69	Jose Valentin	12
1995	B.J. Surhoff	.320	Kevin Seitzer	.395	B.J. Surhoff	.492	John Jaha	20	B.J. Surhoff	73	Jose Valentin	16
1996	Dave Nilsson	.331	Dave Nilsson	.407	John Jaha	.543	John Jaha	34	John Jaha	118	Pat Listach	25
1997	Jeff Cirillo	.288	Jeromy Burnitz	.382	Jeromy Burnitz	.553	Jeromy Burnitz	27	Jeromy Burnitz	85	Gerald Williams	23

Milwaukee Brewers Individual Season Pitching Leaders

Year	ERA		Baserunners/9 IP		Innings Pitched		Strikeouts		Wins		Saves	
1969	Gene Brabender	4.36	Gene Brabender	13.7	Gene Brabender	202.1	Gene Brabender	139	Gene Brabender	13	Diego Segui	12
1970	Marty Pattin	3.39	Marty Pattin	10.8	Marty Pattin	233.1	Marty Pattin	161	Marty Pattin	14	Ken Sanders	13
1971	Lew Krausse	2.94	Marty Pattin	10.3	Marty Pattin	264.2	Marty Pattin	169	Marty Pattin	14	Ken Sanders	31
1972	Jim Lonborg	2.83	Bill Parsons	11.1	Jim Lonborg	223.0	Jim Lonborg	143	Jim Lonborg	14	Ken Sanders	17
1973	Jim Colborn	3.18	Jim Colborn	11.1	Jim Colborn	314.1	Jim Colborn	135	Jim Colborn	20	Frank Linzy	13
1974	Jim Slaton	3.92	Kevin Kobel	11.8	Jim Slaton	250.0	Jim Slaton	126	Jim Slaton	13	Tom Murphy	20
1975	Pete Broberg	4.13	Jim Colborn	12.4	Pete Broberg	220.1	Jim Colborn	119	Pete Broberg	14	Tom Murphy	20
1976	Bill Travers	2.81	Jim Colborn	11.5	Jim Slaton	292.2	Jim Slaton	138	Bill Travers	15	Danny Frisella	9
1977	Jim Slaton	3.58	Jim Slaton	12.7	Jim Slaton	221.0	Moose Haas	113	Jerry Augustine	12	Bill Castro	13
1978	Mike Caldwell	2.36	Mike Caldwell	9.8	Mike Caldwell	293.1	Mike Caldwell	131	Mike Caldwell	22	Bob McClure	9
1979	Mike Caldwell	3.29	Mike Caldwell	11.3	Lary Sorensen	235.1	Moose Haas	95	Mike Caldwell	16	Bill Castro	6
1980	Moose Haas	3.10	Moose Haas	10.8	Moose Haas	252.1	Moose Haas	146	Moose Haas	16	Bob McClure	10
1981	Pete Vuckovich	3.55	Mike Caldwell	11.8	Pete Vuckovich	149.2	Pete Vuckovich	84	Pete Vuckovich	14	Rollie Fingers	28
1982	Pete Vuckovich	3.34	Mike Caldwell	11.4	Mike Caldwell	258.0	Pete Vuckovich	105	Pete Vuckovich	18	Rollie Fingers	29
1983	Moose Haas	3.27	Moose Haas	10.7	Mike Caldwell	228.1	Don Sutton	134	Jim Slaton	14	Peter Ladd	25
1984	Don Sutton	3.77	Don Sutton	11.8	Don Sutton	212.2	Don Sutton	143	Don Sutton	14	Rollie Fingers	23
1985	Danny Darwin	3.80	Moose Haas	10.6	Danny Darwin	217.2	Teddy Higuera	127	Teddy Higuera	15	Rollie Fingers	17
1986	Teddy Higuera	2.79	Teddy Higuera	11.0	Teddy Higuera	248.1	Teddy Higuera	207	Teddy Higuera	20	Mark Clear	16
1987	Teddy Higuera	3.85	Teddy Higuera	11.2	Teddy Higuera	261.2	Teddy Higuera	240	Teddy Higuera	18	Dan Plesac	23
1988	Teddy Higuera	2.45	Teddy Higuera	9.2	Teddy Higuera	227.1	Teddy Higuera	192	Teddy Higuera	16	Dan Plesac	30
1989	Chris Bosio	2.95	Chris Bosio	10.7	Chris Bosio	234.2	Chris Bosio	173	Chris Bosio	15	Dan Plesac	33
1990	Teddy Higuera	3.76	Teddy Higuera	11.6	Teddy Higuera	170.0	Teddy Higuera	129	Ron Robinson	12	Dan Plesac	24
1991	Bill Wegman	2.84	Bill Wegman	10.4	Jaime Navarro	234.0	Chris Bosio	117	Jaime Navarro / Bill Wegman	15	Doug Henry	15
1992	Bill Wegman	3.20	Chris Bosio	10.5	Bill Wegman	261.2	Bill Wegman	127	Jaime Navarro	17	Doug Henry	29
1993	Cal Eldred	4.01	Cal Eldred	11.6	Cal Eldred	258.0	Cal Eldred	180	Cal Eldred	16	Doug Henry	17
1994	Ricky Bones	3.43	Ricky Bones	11.3	Cal Eldred	179.0	Cal Eldred	98	Cal Eldred	11	Mike Fetters	17
1995	Ricky Bones	4.63	Steve Sparks	13.4	Steve Sparks	202.0	Steve Sparks	96	Ricky Bones	10	Mike Fetters	22
1996	Ben McDonald	3.90	Ben McDonald	12.2	Ben McDonald	221.1	Ben McDonald	146	Scott Karl	13	Mike Fetters	32
1997	Scott Karl	4.47	Scott Karl	13.2	Cal Eldred	202.0	Cal Eldred	122	Cal Eldred	13	Doug Jones	36

Teams: Brewers

Brewers Franchise Batting Leaders—Career

Games

1	Robin Yount	2,856
2	Paul Molitor	1,856
3	Jim Gantner	1,801
4	Cecil Cooper	1,490
5	Charlie Moore	1,283
6	Don Money	1,196
7	Ben Oglivie	1,149
8	Gorman Thomas	1,102
	B.J. Surhoff	1,102
10	Greg Vaughn	903
11	Sixto Lezcano	785
12	George Scott	782
13	Dave May	718
14	Rob Deer	667
15	Darryl Hamilton	666
16	Ted Simmons	665
17	Dave Nilsson	620
18	Mike Hegan	586
19	John Briggs	584
20	John Jaha	566

At-Bats

1	Robin Yount	11,008
2	Paul Molitor	7,520
3	Jim Gantner	6,189
4	Cecil Cooper	6,019
5	Don Money	4,330
6	Ben Oglivie	4,136
7	Charlie Moore	3,926
8	B.J. Surhoff	3,884
9	Gorman Thomas	3,544
0	Greg Vaughn	3,244
11	George Scott	3,009
12	Sixto Lezcano	2,722
13	Ted Simmons	2,544
14	Dave May	2,521
15	Rob Deer	2,338
16	Darryl Hamilton	2,193
17	Dave Nilsson	2,127
18	Kevin Seitzer	1,993
19	John Jaha	1,960
20	Sal Bando	1,915

Runs

1	Robin Yount	1,632
2	Paul Molitor	1,275
3	Cecil Cooper	821
4	Jim Gantner	726
5	Don Money	596
6	Ben Oglivie	567
7	Greg Vaughn	528
8	Gorman Thomas	524
9	B.J. Surhoff	472
10	Charlie Moore	441
11	George Scott	402
12	Sixto Lezcano	360
13	Rob Deer	346
14	John Jaha	332
15	Darryl Hamilton	323
16	Dave May	320
17	Ted Simmons	298
18	Dave Nilsson	294
19	John Briggs	271
20	Kevin Seitzer	269

Hits

1	Robin Yount	3,142
2	Paul Molitor	2,281
3	Cecil Cooper	1,815
4	Jim Gantner	1,696
5	Don Money	1,168
6	Ben Oglivie	1,144
7	B.J. Surhoff	1,064
8	Charlie Moore	1,029
9	George Scott	851
10	Gorman Thomas	815
11	Greg Vaughn	799
12	Sixto Lezcano	749
13	Ted Simmons	666
14	Dave May	652
15	Darryl Hamilton	637
16	Dave Nilsson	600
17	Kevin Seitzer	598
18	John Jaha	538
19	Rob Deer	535
20	John Briggs	492

Doubles

1	Robin Yount	583
2	Paul Molitor	405
3	Cecil Cooper	345
4	Jim Gantner	262
5	Don Money	215
6	Ben Oglivie	194
	B.J. Surhoff	194
8	Charlie Moore	177
9	Gorman Thomas	172
10	Greg Vaughn	158
11	George Scott	137
12	Ted Simmons	132
13	Sixto Lezcano	130
14	Dave Nilsson	124
15	Kevin Seitzer	123
16	Jeff Cirillo	120
17	Jose Valentin	99
18	Darryl Hamilton	94
19	John Jaha	93
20	Dave May	90

Triples

1	Robin Yount	126
2	Paul Molitor	86
3	Charlie Moore	42
4	Jim Gantner	38
5	Cecil Cooper	33
6	B.J. Surhoff	24
7	Sixto Lezcano	22
8	Ben Oglivie	21
	Darryl Hamilton	21
10	Don Money	20
11	George Scott	19
	Fernando Vina	19
13	John Briggs	17
	Bill Spiers	17
15	Mike Felder	16
16	Rick Manning	14
17	Nine tied at	13

Home Runs

1	Robin Yount	251
2	Gorman Thomas	208
3	Cecil Cooper	201
4	Ben Oglivie	176
5	Greg Vaughn	169
6	Paul Molitor	160
7	Rob Deer	137
8	Don Money	134
9	George Scott	115
10	Sixto Lezcano	102
11	John Jaha	98
12	John Briggs	80
13	Dave May	72
14	Dave May	69
15	Ted Simmons	66
16	Jose Valentin	64
17	B.J. Surhoff	57
18	Tommy Harper	54
	Darrell Porter	54
20	Bill Schroeder	51

RBI

1	Robin Yount	1,406
2	Cecil Cooper	944
3	Paul Molitor	790
4	Ben Oglivie	685
5	Gorman Thomas	605
6	Jim Gantner	568
7	Greg Vaughn	566
8	Don Money	529
9	B.J. Surhoff	524
10	George Scott	463
11	Charlie Moore	401
12	Ted Simmons	394
13	Rob Deer	385
14	Sixto Lezcano	374
15	Dave Nilsson	352
16	John Jaha	328
17	Dave May	287
18	Kevin Seitzer	281
19	John Briggs	259
20	Jose Valentin	256

Walks

1	Robin Yount	966
2	Paul Molitor	755
3	Gorman Thomas	501
4	Don Money	440
5	Ben Oglivie	432
6	Greg Vaughn	421
7	Jim Gantner	383
8	Cecil Cooper	367
9	Charlie Moore	333
	Sixto Lezcano	333
	Rob Deer	333
12	John Briggs	303
13	B.J. Surhoff	294
14	George Scott	267
15	Darrell Porter	261
16	Mike Hegan	254
17	Kevin Seitzer	241
	John Jaha	241
19	Sal Bando	239
20	Tommy Harper	237

Strikeouts

1	Robin Yount	1,350
2	Gorman Thomas	1,033
3	Paul Molitor	882
4	Rob Deer	823
5	Greg Vaughn	761
6	Cecil Cooper	721
7	Don Money	539
8	Ben Oglivie	530
9	George Scott	529
10	Sixto Lezcano	524
11	Jim Gantner	501
12	Charlie Moore	458
13	John Jaha	438
14	Jose Valentin	428
15	Dale Sveum	426
16	Darrell Porter	352
17	John Briggs	344
18	Mike Hegan	343
19	Glenn Braggs	335
20	Dave May	332

Stolen Bases

1	Paul Molitor	412
2	Robin Yount	271
3	Jim Gantner	137
4	Tommy Harper	136
5	Pat Listach	112
6	Darryl Hamilton	109
7	Mike Felder	108
8	B.J. Surhoff	102
9	Cecil Cooper	77
10	Don Money	66
11	Jose Valentin	65
12	Greg Vaughn	62
13	Bill Spiers	52
14	Charlie Moore	51
15	Dave May	44
	Ben Oglivie	44
17	Gary Sheffield	43
18	Glenn Braggs	41
19	George Scott	40
20	Gorman Thomas	38

Runs Created

1	Robin Yount	1,665
2	Paul Molitor	1,284
3	Cecil Cooper	925
4	Jim Gantner	689
5	Ben Oglivie	649
6	Don Money	628
7	Gorman Thomas	538
8	Greg Vaughn	535
9	B.J. Surhoff	508
10	George Scott	449
11	Charlie Moore	431
12	Sixto Lezcano	428
13	Rob Deer	370
14	Kevin Seitzer	340
15	John Jaha	339
16	Dave Nilsson	325
17	Darryl Hamilton	323
18	John Briggs	316
19	Ted Simmons	304
20	Dave May	302

Runs Created/27 Outs

(minimum 2000 Plate Appearances)

1	Paul Molitor	6.17
2	Kevin Seitzer	6.08
3	John Jaha	6.06
4	John Briggs	5.74
5	Greg Vaughn	5.58
6	Cecil Cooper	5.57
7	Ben Oglivie	5.50
8	Sixto Lezcano	5.45
9	Dave Nilsson	5.42
10	Rob Deer	5.35
11	Robin Yount	5.33
12	George Scott	5.25
13	Darryl Hamilton	5.17
14	Don Money	5.02
15	Gorman Thomas	5.00
16	Darrell Porter	4.50
17	B.J. Surhoff	4.43
18	Sal Bando	4.34
19	Ted Simmons	4.09
20	Dave May	4.06

Batting Average

(minimum 2000 Plate Appearances)

1	Paul Molitor	.303
2	Cecil Cooper	.302
3	Kevin Seitzer	.300
4	Darryl Hamilton	.290
5	Robin Yount	.285
6	George Scott	.283
7	Dave Nilsson	.282
8	Ben Oglivie	.277
9	Sixto Lezcano	.275
10	John Jaha	.274
11	Jim Gantner	.274
12	B.J. Surhoff	.274
13	Don Money	.270
14	Charlie Moore	.262
15	Ted Simmons	.262
16	Dave May	.259
17	John Briggs	.258
18	Sal Bando	.250
19	Greg Vaughn	.246
20	Gorman Thomas	.230

On-Base Percentage

(minimum 2000 Plate Appearances)

1	Kevin Seitzer	.376
2	Paul Molitor	.367
3	John Jaha	.360
4	John Briggs	.358
5	Sixto Lezcano	.354
6	Dave Nilsson	.351
7	Darryl Hamilton	.351
8	Ben Oglivie	.345
9	George Scott	.342
10	Robin Yount	.342
11	Cecil Cooper	.339
12	Don Money	.338
13	Sal Bando	.335
14	Darrell Porter	.334
15	Greg Vaughn	.333
16	Rob Deer	.329
17	Gorman Thomas	.325
18	B.J. Surhoff	.323
19	Dave May	.322
20	Charlie Moore	.320

Slugging Percentage

(minimum 2000 Plate Appearances)

1	John Jaha	.476
2	Cecil Cooper	.470
3	Gorman Thomas	.461
4	Ben Oglivie	.461
5	Greg Vaughn	.459
6	George Scott	.456
7	Sixto Lezcano	.452
8	Rob Deer	.450
9	Dave Nilsson	.449
10	Paul Molitor	.444
11	John Briggs	.441
12	Robin Yount	.430
13	Kevin Seitzer	.422
14	Don Money	.421
15	Ted Simmons	.399
16	Dave May	.385
17	Darryl Hamilton	.384
18	Sal Bando	.382
19	B.J. Surhoff	.380
20	Darrell Porter	.375

Teams: Brewers

Brewers Franchise Pitching Leaders—Career

Wins

1	Jim Slaton	117
2	Mike Caldwell	102
3	Teddy Higuera	94
4	Moose Haas	91
5	Bill Wegman	81
6	Chris Bosio	67
7	Bill Travers	65
8	Jaime Navarro	62
9	Cal Eldred	58
10	Jim Colborn	57
11	Jerry Augustine	55
12	Lary Sorensen	52
13	Ricky Bones	47
14	Bob McClure	45
15	Pete Vuckovich	40
16	Ed Rodriguez	38
17	Marty Pattin	35
18	Don August	34
19	Chuck Crim	33
20	Juan Nieves	32

Losses

1	Jim Slaton	121
2	Bill Wegman	90
3	Mike Caldwell	80
4	Moose Haas	79
5	Bill Travers	67
6	Teddy Higuera	64
7	Chris Bosio	62
8	Jim Colborn	60
9	Jerry Augustine	59
	Jaime Navarro	59
11	Ricky Bones	56
12	Skip Lockwood	55
13	Cal Eldred	49
14	Lary Sorensen	46
15	Bob McClure	43
16	Marty Pattin	38
17	Dan Plesac	37
18	Bill Parsons	36
19	Ed Rodriguez	35
20	Chuck Crim	31

Winning Percentage

(minimum 75 decisions)

1	Teddy Higuera	.595
2	Mike Caldwell	.560
3	Cal Eldred	.542
4	Moose Haas	.535
5	Lary Sorensen	.531
6	Chris Bosio	.519
7	Jaime Navarro	.512
8	Bob McClure	.511
9	Bill Travers	.492
10	Jim Slaton	.492
11	Jim Colborn	.487
12	Jerry Augustine	.482
13	Bill Wegman	.474
14	Ricky Bones	.456
15	Skip Lockwood	.337

Games

1	Dan Plesac	365
2	Jim Slaton	364
3	Bob McClure	352
4	Chuck Crim	332
5	Mike Fetters	289
6	Jerry Augustine	279
7	Bill Wegman	262
8	Bill Castro	253
9	Moose Haas	245
10	Mike Caldwell	239
11	Ed Rodriguez	235
12	Teddy Higuera	213
13	Chris Bosio	212
14	Ken Sanders	195
15	Bill Travers	191
16	Jim Colborn	183
	Jaime Navarro	183
	Graeme Lloyd	183
19	Doug Henry	179
20	Rollie Fingers	177

Games Started

1	Jim Slaton	268
2	Moose Haas	231
3	Mike Caldwell	217
4	Bill Wegman	216
5	Teddy Higuera	205
6	Chris Bosio	163
7	Bill Travers	157
8	Jaime Navarro	151
9	Jim Colborn	140
10	Ricky Bones	137
11	Cal Eldred	131
12	Lary Sorensen	119
13	Jerry Augustine	104
14	Skip Lockwood	103
15	Marty Pattin	92
16	Pete Vuckovich	84
17	Bill Parsons	82
	Scott Karl	82
19	Juan Nieves	81
20	Bob McClure	73

Complete Games

1	Mike Caldwell	81
2	Jim Slaton	69
3	Moose Haas	55
4	Jim Colborn	51
5	Lary Sorensen	50
	Teddy Higuera	50
7	Bill Travers	46
8	Bill Wegman	33
9	Chris Bosio	32
10	Jerry Augustine	27
11	Jaime Navarro	24
12	Marty Pattin	22
	Bill Parsons	22
14	Cal Eldred	17
15	Skip Lockwood	16
	Danny Darwin	16
17	Clyde Wright	15
18	Bob McClure	12
	Pete Vuckovich	12
20	Jim Lonborg	11

Shutouts

1	Jim Slaton	19
2	Mike Caldwell	18
3	Teddy Higuera	12
4	Bill Travers	10
5	Moose Haas	8
	Chris Bosio	8
7	Jim Colborn	7
	Lary Sorensen	7
9	Marty Pattin	6
	Bill Parsons	6
	Jerry Augustine	6
	Jaime Navarro	6
13	Skip Lockwood	5
	Juan Nieves	5
15	Bill Wegman	4
16	Don August	3
	Cal Eldred	3
18	Twenty tied at	2

Saves

1	Dan Plesac	133
2	Rollie Fingers	97
3	Mike Fetters	79
4	Ken Sanders	61
	Doug Henry	61
6	Bill Castro	44
7	Chuck Crim	42
8	Tom Murphy	41
9	Doug Jones	37
10	Bob McClure	34
11	Peter Ladd	33
12	Ed Rodriguez	30
13	Frank Linzy	25
14	Mark Clear	22
15	Bob Gibson	13
16	Diego Segui	12
	Tom Tellmann	12
18	Jim Slaton	11
	Jerry Augustine	11
20	Nine tied at	9

Innings Pitched

1	Jim Slaton	2,025.1
2	Mike Caldwell	1,604.2
3	Moose Haas	1,542.0
4	Bill Wegman	1,482.2
5	Teddy Higuera	1,380.0
6	Chris Bosio	1,190.0
7	Jim Colborn	1,118.0
8	Bill Travers	1,068.1
9	Jaime Navarro	1,043.0
10	Jerry Augustine	944.0
11	Ricky Bones	883.0
12	Cal Eldred	863.2
13	Lary Sorensen	854.0
14	Bob McClure	842.0
15	Skip Lockwood	729.1
16	Ed Rodriguez	659.2
17	Marty Pattin	656.2
18	Pete Vuckovich	533.0
19	Chuck Crim	529.2
20	Scott Karl	524.2

Walks

1	Jim Slaton	760
2	Teddy Higuera	443
3	Moose Haas	408
4	Bill Travers	392
5	Bob McClure	363
6	Mike Caldwell	353
7	Bill Wegman	352
8	Cal Eldred	341
9	Jerry Augustine	340
10	Jaime Navarro	318
11	Jim Colborn	309
12	Skip Lockwood	306
13	Ricky Bones	301
14	Ed Rodriguez	289
	Chris Bosio	289
16	Bill Parsons	228
	Pete Vuckovich	228
18	Juan Nieves	227
19	Marty Pattin	215
20	Angel Miranda	206

Strikeouts

1	Teddy Higuera	1,081
2	Jim Slaton	929
3	Moose Haas	800
4	Chris Bosio	749
5	Bill Wegman	696
6	Mike Caldwell	540
	Cal Eldred	540
8	Jaime Navarro	524
9	Bob McClure	497
10	Jim Colborn	495
11	Bill Travers	459
12	Marty Pattin	456
13	Dan Plesac	448
14	Skip Lockwood	411
15	Ed Rodriguez	404
16	Juan Nieves	352
17	Jerry Augustine	348
18	Ricky Bones	321
19	Don Sutton	313
20	Scott Karl	299

Strikeouts/9 Innings

(minimum 750 Innings Pitched)

1	Teddy Higuera	7.05
2	Chris Bosio	5.66
3	Cal Eldred	5.63
4	Bob McClure	5.31
5	Moose Haas	4.67
6	Jaime Navarro	4.52
7	Bill Wegman	4.22
8	Jim Slaton	4.13
9	Jim Colborn	3.98
10	Bill Travers	3.87
11	Jerry Augustine	3.32
12	Ricky Bones	3.27
13	Mike Caldwell	3.03
14	Lary Sorensen	2.66

ERA

(minimum 750 Innings Pitched)

1	Teddy Higuera	3.61
2	Jim Colborn	3.65
3	Lary Sorensen	3.72
4	Mike Caldwell	3.74
5	Chris Bosio	3.76
6	Jim Slaton	3.86
7	Bob McClure	3.97
8	Bill Travers	3.99
9	Moose Haas	4.03
10	Cal Eldred	4.16
11	Bill Wegman	4.16
12	Jerry Augustine	4.23
13	Jaime Navarro	4.30
14	Ricky Bones	4.64

Component ERA

(minimum 750 Innings Pitched)

1	Teddy Higuera	3.33
2	Chris Bosio	3.44
3	Jim Colborn	3.54
4	Lary Sorensen	3.63
5	Moose Haas	3.77
6	Mike Caldwell	3.79
7	Cal Eldred	3.92
8	Bill Wegman	4.03
9	Jaime Navarro	4.07
10	Jim Slaton	4.08
11	Bob McClure	4.17
12	Bill Travers	4.22
13	Jerry Augustine	4.43
14	Ricky Bones	4.70

Opponent Average

(minimum 750 Innings Pitched)

1	Teddy Higuera	.243
2	Cal Eldred	.245
3	Chris Bosio	.258
4	Jim Colborn	.261
5	Bob McClure	.261
6	Bill Travers	.261
7	Jim Slaton	.266
8	Moose Haas	.270
9	Bill Wegman	.271
10	Ricky Bones	.274
11	Mike Caldwell	.275
12	Jaime Navarro	.277
13	Lary Sorensen	.277
14	Jerry Augustine	.281

Opponent OBP

(minimum 750 Innings Pitched)

1	Teddy Higuera	.303
2	Chris Bosio	.304
3	Jim Colborn	.311
4	Lary Sorensen	.313
5	Mike Caldwell	.314
6	Moose Haas	.314
7	Bill Wegman	.315
8	Cal Eldred	.320
9	Bill Travers	.329
10	Jaime Navarro	.330
11	Jim Slaton	.331
12	Ricky Bones	.335
13	Bob McClure	.338
14	Jerry Augustine	.342

Teams: Brewers

Brewers Franchise Batting Leaders—Single Season

Games

1	Gorman Thomas	1980	162
	Robin Yount	1988	162
3	Robin Yount	1976	161
	Jim Gantner	1983	161
5	Pedro Garcia	1973	160
	Cecil Cooper	1977	160
	Paul Molitor	1982	160
	Cecil Cooper	1983	160
	Robin Yount	1984	160
	Robin Yount	1989	160
11	Don Money	1974	159
	Sal Bando	1977	159
	Ben Oglivie	1982	159
14	Ten tied at		158

At-Bats

1	Paul Molitor	1982	666
2	Paul Molitor	1991	665
3	Cecil Cooper	1983	661
4	Cecil Cooper	1982	654
5	Cecil Cooper	1977	643
6	Robin Yount	1976	638
7	Robin Yount	1982	635
	Robin Yount	1987	635
9	Cecil Cooper	1985	631
10	Don Money	1974	629
11	Gorman Thomas	1980	628
12	Dave May	1973	624
	Robin Yount	1984	624
14	Cecil Cooper	1980	622
15	Robin Yount	1988	621
16	George Scott	1975	617
17	Paul Molitor	1989	615
18	Robin Yount	1989	614
19	Jim Gantner	1984	613
20	Robin Yount	1980	611

Runs

1	Paul Molitor	1982	136
2	Paul Molitor	1991	133
3	Robin Yount	1982	129
4	Robin Yount	1980	121
5	Paul Molitor	1988	115
6	Paul Molitor	1987	114
7	John Jaha	1996	108
8	Cecil Cooper	1983	106
9	Robin Yount	1984	105
10	Tommy Harper	1970	104
	Cecil Cooper	1982	104
12	Robin Yount	1983	102
13	Robin Yount	1989	101
	Jeff Cirillo	1996	101
15	Robin Yount	1987	99
16	George Scott	1973	98
	Robin Yount	1990	98
18	Gorman Thomas	1979	97
	Greg Vaughn	1993	97
20	Four tied at		96

Hits

1	Cecil Cooper	1980	219
2	Paul Molitor	1991	216
3	Robin Yount	1982	210
4	Cecil Cooper	1982	205
5	Cecil Cooper	1983	203
6	Paul Molitor	1982	201
7	Robin Yount	1987	198
8	Robin Yount	1989	195
	Paul Molitor	1992	195
10	Paul Molitor	1989	194
11	Cecil Cooper	1977	193
12	Robin Yount	1988	190
	Paul Molitor	1988	190
14	Dave May	1973	189
15	Paul Molitor	1979	188
16	Robin Yount	1984	186
17	George Scott	1973	185
	Ted Simmons	1983	185
	Cecil Cooper	1985	185
20	Jeff Cirillo	1996	184

Doubles

1	Robin Yount	1980	49
2	Robin Yount	1982	46
	Jeff Cirillo	1996	46
	Jeff Cirillo	1997	46
5	Cecil Cooper	1979	44
6	Robin Yount	1983	42
7	Paul Molitor	1987	41
8	Robin Yount	1992	40
9	Ted Simmons	1983	39
	Cecil Cooper	1985	39
11	Cecil Cooper	1982	38
	Robin Yount	1988	38
	Robin Yount	1989	38
	B.J. Surhoff	1993	38
15	Cecil Cooper	1983	37
	Jeromy Burnitz	1997	37
17	George Scott	1974	36
	Paul Molitor	1992	36
19	Four tied at		35

Triples

1	Paul Molitor	1979	16
2	Paul Molitor	1991	13
3	Robin Yount	1982	12
4	Robin Yount	1988	11
5	Robin Yount	1980	10
	Robin Yount	1983	10
	Fernando Vina	1996	10
8	Robin Yount	1978	9
	Robin Yount	1987	9
	Robin Yount	1989	9
11	Bob Coluccio	1973	8
	John Briggs	1974	8
	Paul Molitor	1982	8
	Jim Gantner	1983	8
	Cecil Cooper	1985	8
	Jeromy Burnitz	1997	8
17	Fourteen tied at		7

Home Runs

1	Gorman Thomas	1979	45
2	Ben Oglivie	1980	41
3	Gorman Thomas	1982	39
4	Gorman Thomas	1980	38
5	George Scott	1975	36
6	Larry Hisle	1978	34
	Ben Oglivie	1982	34
	John Jaha	1996	34
9	Rob Deer	1986	33
10	Gorman Thomas	1978	32
	Cecil Cooper	1982	32
12	Tommy Harper	1970	31
	Greg Vaughn	1996	31
14	Cecil Cooper	1983	30
	Greg Vaughn	1993	30
16	Ben Oglivie	1979	29
	Robin Yount	1982	29
18	Sixto Lezcano	1979	28
	Rob Deer	1987	28
20	Three tied at		27

RBI

1	Cecil Cooper	1983	126
2	Gorman Thomas	1979	123
3	Cecil Cooper	1980	122
4	Cecil Cooper	1982	121
5	Ben Oglivie	1980	118
	John Jaha	1996	118
7	Larry Hisle	1978	115
8	Robin Yount	1982	114
9	Gorman Thomas	1982	112
10	George Scott	1975	109
11	Ted Simmons	1983	108
12	George Scott	1973	107
13	Cecil Cooper	1979	106
14	Gorman Thomas	1980	105
15	Robin Yount	1987	103
	Robin Yount	1989	103
17	Ben Oglivie	1982	102
18	Sixto Lezcano	1979	101
19	Cecil Cooper	1985	99
20	Greg Vaughn	1991	98

Walks

1	Gorman Thomas	1979	98
2	Tommy Harper	1969	95
3	Darrell Porter	1975	89
	Greg Vaughn	1993	89
5	John Briggs	1973	87
6	Rob Deer	1987	86
7	John Jaha	1996	85
8	Gorman Thomas	1982	84
9	Wayne Comer	1969	82
10	Don Mincher	1969	78
	Robin Yount	1990	78
12	Tommy Harper	1970	77
	Sixto Lezcano	1979	77
	Paul Molitor	1991	77
15	Robin Yount	1987	76
16	Sal Bando	1977	75
	Willie Randolph	1991	75
	Jeromy Burnitz	1997	75
19	Three tied at		73

Strikeouts

1	Rob Deer	1987	186
2	Rob Deer	1986	179
3	Gorman Thomas	1979	175
4	Gorman Thomas	1980	170
5	Rob Deer	1989	158
6	Rob Deer	1988	153
7	Rob Deer	1990	147
8	Jose Valentin	1996	145
9	Gorman Thomas	1982	143
10	Gorman Thomas	1978	133
	Dale Sveum	1987	133
12	George Scott	1972	130
13	Danny Walton	1970	126
14	Greg Vaughn	1991	125
15	Pat Listach	1992	124
16	Greg Vaughn	1992	123
17	Dale Sveum	1988	122
18	Pedro Garcia	1973	119
19	Three tied at		118

Stolen Bases

1	Tommy Harper	1969	73
2	Pat Listach	1992	54
3	Paul Molitor	1987	45
4	Paul Molitor	1982	41
	Paul Molitor	1983	41
	Paul Molitor	1988	41
	Darryl Hamilton	1992	41
8	Tommy Harper	1970	38
9	Paul Molitor	1980	34
	Mike Felder	1987	34
11	Paul Molitor	1979	33
12	Paul Molitor	1992	31
13	Paul Molitor	1978	30
14	Paul Molitor	1989	27
15	Mike Felder	1989	26
16	Tommy Harper	1971	25
	Gary Sheffield	1990	25
	Pat Listach	1996	25
19	Rick Auerbach	1972	24
20	Gerald Williams	1997	23

Runs Created

1	Robin Yount	1982	136
2	Paul Molitor	1991	132
3	Robin Yount	1989	124
4	Paul Molitor	1982	119
5	Tommy Harper	1970	118
	Cecil Cooper	1980	118
	Cecil Cooper	1982	118
	Robin Yount	1987	118
	Paul Molitor	1987	118
10	Paul Molitor	1992	117
11	Paul Molitor	1988	115
12	Ben Oglivie	1980	113
	Robin Yount	1988	113
14	John Jaha	1996	112
15	Robin Yount	1983	109
	Greg Vaughn	1993	109
	Jeff Cirillo	1996	109
18	Cecil Cooper	1983	107
19	George Scott	1973	104
	Sixto Lezcano	1979	104

Runs Created/27 Outs

(minimum 3.1 Plate Appearances/Tm Gm)

1	Paul Molitor	1987	9.88
2	Sixto Lezcano	1979	8.02
3	Dave Nilsson	1996	8.00
4	Robin Yount	1982	7.97
5	Paul Molitor	1991	7.62
6	Robin Yount	1989	7.61
7	B.J. Surhoff	1995	7.56
8	John Jaha	1996	7.54
9	Cecil Cooper	1980	7.26
10	Paul Molitor	1992	7.05
11	Jeff Cirillo	1996	7.04
12	Ben Oglivie	1980	7.03
13	Willie Randolph	1991	7.03
14	Tommy Harper	1970	7.00
15	Paul Molitor	1988	6.92
16	Robin Yount	1983	6.91
17	Cecil Cooper	1982	6.84
18	Robin Yount	1987	6.80
19	Kevin Seitzer	1996	6.79
20	Kevin Seitzer	1995	6.78

Batting Average

(minimum 3.1 Plate Appearances/Tm Gm)

1	Paul Molitor	1987	.353
2	Cecil Cooper	1980	.352
3	Dave Nilsson	1996	.331
4	Robin Yount	1982	.331
5	Willie Randolph	1991	.327
6	Jeff Cirillo	1996	.325
7	Paul Molitor	1991	.325
8	Paul Molitor	1979	.322
9	Sixto Lezcano	1979	.321
10	B.J. Surhoff	1995	.320
	Paul Molitor	1992	.320
12	Cecil Cooper	1981	.320
13	Robin Yount	1989	.318
14	Kevin Seitzer	1996	.316
15	Paul Molitor	1989	.315
16	Cecil Cooper	1982	.313
17	Robin Yount	1986	.312
18	Paul Molitor	1988	.312
19	Robin Yount	1987	.312
20	Kevin Seitzer	1995	.311

On-Base Percentage

(minimum 3.1 Plate Appearances/Tm Gm)

1	Paul Molitor	1987	.438
2	Willie Randolph	1991	.424
3	Sixto Lezcano	1979	.414
4	Dave Nilsson	1996	.407
5	Kevin Seitzer	1996	.406
6	Paul Molitor	1991	.399
7	John Jaha	1996	.398
8	Kevin Seitzer	1995	.395
9	Jeff Cirillo	1996	.391
10	Paul Molitor	1992	.389
11	Robin Yount	1986	.388
12	Cecil Cooper	1980	.387
13	Robin Yount	1989	.384
14	Paul Molitor	1988	.384
15	Robin Yount	1987	.384
16	Robin Yount	1983	.383
17	Jeromy Burnitz	1997	.382
18	Paul Molitor	1989	.379
19	Robin Yount	1982	.379
20	B.J. Surhoff	1995	.378

Slugging Percentage

(minimum 3.1 Plate Appearances/Tm Gm)

1	Robin Yount	1982	.578
2	Sixto Lezcano	1979	.573
3	Paul Molitor	1987	.566
4	Ben Oglivie	1980	.563
5	Jeromy Burnitz	1997	.553
6	John Jaha	1996	.543
7	Gorman Thomas	1979	.539
8	Cecil Cooper	1980	.539
9	Larry Hisle	1978	.533
10	Cecil Cooper	1982	.528
11	Dave Nilsson	1996	.525
12	Ben Oglivie	1979	.525
13	Tommy Harper	1970	.522
14	Robin Yount	1980	.519
15	Gorman Thomas	1978	.515
16	George Scott	1975	.515
17	Robin Yount	1989	.511
18	Cecil Cooper	1979	.508
19	Cecil Cooper	1983	.508
20	Gorman Thomas	1982	.506

Teams: Brewers

Brewers Franchise Pitching Leaders—Single Season

Wins

1	Mike Caldwell	1978	22
2	Jim Colborn	1973	20
	Teddy Higuera	1986	20
4	Lary Sorensen	1978	18
	Pete Vuckovich	1982	18
	Teddy Higuera	1987	18
7	Mike Caldwell	1982	17
	Jaime Navarro	1992	17
9	Mike Caldwell	1979	16
	Moose Haas	1980	16
	Teddy Higuera	1988	16
	Chris Bosio	1992	16
	Cal Eldred	1993	16
14	Bill Travers	1976	15
	Lary Sorensen	1979	15
	Jim Slaton	1979	15
	Teddy Higuera	1985	15
	Chris Bosio	1989	15
	Bill Wegman	1991	15
	Jaime Navarro	1991	15

Losses

1	Clyde Wright	1974	20
2	Lew Krausse	1970	18
	Jim Slaton	1975	18
	Jerry Augustine	1977	18
	Danny Darwin	1985	18
6	Bill Parsons	1971	17
7	Jim Slaton	1974	16
	Pete Broberg	1975	16
	Bill Travers	1976	16
	Jamie Cocanower	1984	16
	Cal Eldred	1993	16
12	Gene Brabender	1970	15
	Skip Lockwood	1971	15
	Skip Lockwood	1972	15
	Jim Slaton	1973	15
	Jim Slaton	1976	15
	Jim Colborn	1976	15
	Moose Haas	1980	15
	Chris Bosio	1988	15
	Cal Eldred	1997	15

Winning Percentage
(minimum 15 decisions)

1	Moose Haas	1983	.813
2	Pete Vuckovich	1981	.778
3	Pete Vuckovich	1982	.750
4	Billy Champion	1974	.733
5	Mike Caldwell	1979	.727
	Chris Bosio	1992	.727
7	Mike Caldwell	1978	.710
8	Ron Robinson	1990	.706
9	Jim Slaton	1983	.700
10	Bill Wegman	1991	.682
11	Diego Segui	1969	.667
	Bill Travers	1980	.667
13	Teddy Higuera	1985	.652
14	Don August	1988	.650
15	Teddy Higuera	1986	.645
16	Teddy Higuera	1987	.643
17	Teddy Higuera	1988	.640
18	Bill Travers	1979	.636
	Juan Nieves	1987	.636
20	Bob McClure	1982	.632

Games

1	Ken Sanders	1971	83
2	Chuck Crim	1989	76
3	Doug Jones	1997	75
4	Bob Wickman	1997	74
5	Tom Murphy	1974	70
	Chuck Crim	1988	70
7	Bob McClure	1977	68
	Doug Henry	1992	68
9	Chuck Crim	1990	67
10	Diego Segui	1969	66
	Dan Plesac	1990	66
	Chuck Crim	1991	66
13	Ken Sanders	1972	62
	Mark Lee	1991	62
15	Mike Fetters	1996	61
16	Mark Clear	1986	59
	Jesse Orosco	1992	59
18	Mark Clear	1987	58
19	Three tied at		57

Games Started

1	Jim Slaton	1973	38
	Jim Slaton	1976	38
3	Marty Pattin	1971	36
	Jim Colborn	1973	36
	Lary Sorensen	1978	36
	Cal Eldred	1993	36
7	Lew Krausse	1970	35
	Bill Parsons	1971	35
	Jim Slaton	1974	35
	Teddy Higuera	1987	35
	Bill Wegman	1992	35
	Ben McDonald	1996	35
13	Nine tied at		34

Complete Games

1	Mike Caldwell	1978	23
2	Jim Colborn	1973	22
3	Lary Sorensen	1978	17
4	Lary Sorensen	1979	16
	Mike Caldwell	1979	16
6	Clyde Wright	1974	15
	Bill Travers	1976	15
	Teddy Higuera	1986	15
9	Moose Haas	1980	14
	Teddy Higuera	1987	14
11	Jim Slaton	1973	13
12	Bill Parsons	1971	12
	Jim Slaton	1976	12
	Jim Slaton	1979	12
	Mike Caldwell	1982	12
16	Marty Pattin	1970	11
	Jim Lonborg	1972	11
	Mike Caldwell	1980	11
	Danny Darwin	1985	11
20	Seven tied at		10

Shutouts

1	Mike Caldwell	1978	6
2	Marty Pattin	1971	5
3	Jim Slaton	1971	4
	Bill Parsons	1971	4
	Jim Colborn	1973	4
	Mike Caldwell	1979	4
	Teddy Higuera	1986	4
8	Fifteen tied at		3

Saves

1	Doug Jones	1997	36
2	Dan Plesac	1989	33
3	Mike Fetters	1996	32
4	Ken Sanders	1971	31
5	Dan Plesac	1988	30
6	Rollie Fingers	1982	29
	Doug Henry	1992	29
8	Rollie Fingers	1981	28
9	Peter Ladd	1983	25
10	Dan Plesac	1990	24
11	Rollie Fingers	1984	23
	Dan Plesac	1987	23
13	Mike Fetters	1995	22
14	Tom Murphy	1974	20
	Tom Murphy	1975	20
16	Ken Sanders	1972	17
	Rollie Fingers	1985	17
	Doug Henry	1993	17
	Mike Fetters	1994	17
20	Mark Clear	1986	16

Innings Pitched

1	Jim Colborn	1973	314.1
2	Mike Caldwell	1978	293.1
3	Jim Slaton	1976	292.2
4	Lary Sorensen	1978	280.2
5	Jim Slaton	1973	276.1
6	Marty Pattin	1971	264.2
7	Teddy Higuera	1987	261.2
	Bill Wegman	1992	261.2
9	Mike Caldwell	1982	258.0
	Cal Eldred	1993	258.0
11	Moose Haas	1980	252.1
12	Jim Slaton	1974	250.0
13	Teddy Higuera	1986	248.1
14	Jaime Navarro	1992	246.0
15	Bill Parsons	1971	244.2
16	Bill Travers	1976	240.0
17	Lary Sorensen	1979	235.1
18	Mike Caldwell	1979	235.0
19	Chris Bosio	1989	234.2
20	Jaime Navarro	1991	234.0

Walks

1	Pete Broberg	1975	106
2	Gene Brabender	1969	103
3	Jim Slaton	1974	102
	Pete Vuckovich	1982	102
5	Juan Nieves	1987	100
6	Jim Slaton	1973	99
7	Bill Travers	1976	95
8	Jim Slaton	1976	94
9	Bill Parsons	1971	93
10	Skip Lockwood	1971	91
	Cal Eldred	1993	91
12	Jim Slaton	1975	90
13	Cal Eldred	1997	89
14	Jim Colborn	1973	87
	Teddy Higuera	1987	87
16	Steve Sparks	1995	86
17	Moose Haas	1977	84
	Cal Eldred	1994	84
19	Ricky Bones	1995	83
20	Two tied at		79

Strikeouts

1	Teddy Higuera	1987	240
2	Teddy Higuera	1986	207
3	Teddy Higuera	1988	192
4	Cal Eldred	1993	180
5	Chris Bosio	1989	173
6	Marty Pattin	1971	169
7	Juan Nieves	1987	163
8	Marty Pattin	1970	161
9	Chris Bosio	1987	150
10	Moose Haas	1980	146
	Ben McDonald	1996	146
12	Jim Lonborg	1972	143
	Don Sutton	1984	143
14	Gene Brabender	1969	139
	Bill Parsons	1971	139
16	Jim Slaton	1976	138
17	Jim Colborn	1973	135
18	Jim Slaton	1973	134
	Don Sutton	1983	134
20	Mike Caldwell	1978	131

Strikeouts/9 Innings
(minimum 1 Inning Pitched/Tm Gm)

1	Teddy Higuera	1987	8.25
2	Chris Bosio	1987	7.94
3	Teddy Higuera	1988	7.60
4	Teddy Higuera	1986	7.50
5	Juan Nieves	1987	7.50
6	Teddy Higuera	1990	6.83
7	Chris Bosio	1989	6.63
8	Cal Eldred	1993	6.28
9	Marty Pattin	1970	6.21
10	Gene Brabender	1969	6.18
11	Don Sutton	1984	6.05
12	Ben McDonald	1996	5.94
13	Jim Lonborg	1972	5.77
14	Marty Pattin	1971	5.75
15	Juan Nieves	1986	5.65
16	Skip Lockwood	1972	5.61
17	Scott Karl	1997	5.54
18	Don Sutton	1983	5.47
19	Cal Eldred	1997	5.44
20	Lew Krausse	1970	5.42

ERA
(minimum 1 Inning Pitched/Tm Gm)

1	Mike Caldwell	1978	2.36
2	Teddy Higuera	1988	2.45
3	Teddy Higuera	1986	2.79
4	Bill Travers	1976	2.81
5	Jim Lonborg	1972	2.83
6	Bill Wegman	1991	2.84
7	Lew Krausse	1971	2.94
8	Chris Bosio	1989	2.95
9	Moose Haas	1980	3.10
10	Marty Pattin	1971	3.13
11	Jim Colborn	1973	3.18
12	Bill Wegman	1992	3.20
13	Bill Parsons	1971	3.20
14	Lary Sorensen	1978	3.21
15	Chris Bosio	1991	3.25
16	Moose Haas	1983	3.27
17	Mike Caldwell	1979	3.29
18	Jerry Augustine	1976	3.30
19	Jaime Navarro	1992	3.33
20	Skip Lockwood	1971	3.33

Component ERA
(minimum 1 Inning Pitched/Tm Gm)

1	Teddy Higuera	1988	2.10
2	Mike Caldwell	1978	2.39
3	Jaime Navarro	1992	2.88
4	Lary Sorensen	1978	2.89
5	Bill Wegman	1991	2.90
6	Marty Pattin	1971	2.93
7	Moose Haas	1983	2.97
8	Chris Bosio	1989	2.97
9	Marty Pattin	1970	3.01
10	Teddy Higuera	1985	3.09
11	Chris Bosio	1992	3.12
12	Jim Colborn	1973	3.15
13	Chris Bosio	1991	3.18
14	Don Sutton	1983	3.19
15	Jim Lonborg	1972	3.19
16	Skip Lockwood	1972	3.21
17	Teddy Higuera	1986	3.23
18	Teddy Higuera	1987	3.27
19	Bill Wegman	1992	3.28
20	Moose Haas	1980	3.29

Opponent Average
(minimum 1 Inning Pitched/Tm Gm)

1	Teddy Higuera	1988	.207
2	Skip Lockwood	1972	.232
3	Mike Caldwell	1978	.234
4	Teddy Higuera	1985	.235
5	Marty Pattin	1971	.235
6	Marty Pattin	1970	.235
7	Cal Eldred	1994	.236
8	Bill Travers	1976	.237
9	Jim Lonborg	1972	.238
10	Lew Krausse	1971	.239
11	Cal Eldred	1993	.239
12	Bill Parsons	1972	.240
13	Teddy Higuera	1987	.241
14	Teddy Higuera	1986	.241
15	Bill Parsons	1971	.241
16	Bill Wegman	1991	.242
17	Chris Bosio	1991	.244
18	Don Sutton	1983	.246
19	Jaime Navarro	1992	.246
20	Skip Lockwood	1971	.246

Opponent OBP
(minimum 1 Inning Pitched/Tm Gm)

1	Teddy Higuera	1988	.263
2	Mike Caldwell	1978	.273
3	Bill Wegman	1991	.286
4	Moose Haas	1985	.287
5	Marty Pattin	1971	.289
6	Chris Bosio	1989	.289
7	Teddy Higuera	1985	.290
8	Chris Bosio	1992	.291
9	Lary Sorensen	1978	.291
10	Don Sutton	1983	.292
11	Moose Haas	1983	.294
12	Bill Wegman	1992	.294
13	Jaime Navarro	1992	.295
14	Teddy Higuera	1986	.296
15	Marty Pattin	1970	.296
16	Moose Haas	1980	.297
17	Bill Parsons	1972	.299
18	Teddy Higuera	1987	.301
19	Chris Bosio	1991	.302
20	Jim Colborn	1973	.302

Brewers Capsule

Best Season: The Brewers came within a game of winning it all during the magical season of *1982*. Milwaukee beat Baltimore's Jim Palmer on the last day of the season to claim the American League East crown. They fell behind the California Angels two games to none in the five-game ALCS, but rallied to win the next two games. In Game 5, Cecil Cooper's seventh-inning, two-run single off Luis Sanchez gave them a 4-3 victory and sent them to the World Series. They blew out the Cardinals 10-0 in the opener and went on to take a three-games-to-two advantage, but lost the next two games.

Worst Season: Laden with veterans, the Brewers contended in 1983 before collapsing in *1984*. Leadoff man Paul Molitor tore an elbow ligament and missed virtually the entire season. In addition, Cecil Cooper, Ben Oglivie and Ted Simmons began to show their age, and the Brewers plunged into the AL East cellar with a league-worst 67-94 record.

Best Players: *Paul Molitor* and *Robin Yount*. During the 15 years they spent together in Milwaukee, Molitor and Yount were the nucleus of every contending team the Brewers ever fielded. When Molitor joined Yount in '78, the Brewers rocketed into contention for the first time in the history of the franchise. The two of them batted first and second in the batting order when the Brewers reached the postseason in '81 and '82. Later, they formed the heart of the strong Brewers teams of '87, '88 and '92.

Best Pitcher: *Teddy Higuera.* Like Fernando Valenzuela, Teddy Higuera was a lefthanded Mexican screwball artist who seemingly came out of nowhere. He was the ace of the staff and one of the best southpaws in baseball for four years in the mid-'80s before arm trouble ended his career prematurely.

Best Reliever: *Rollie Fingers.* He may have been at his best for them for only two seasons, but he did just about everything a pitcher could do in that short time. In 1981, he won the AL MVP Award and the Cy Young, while leading the Brewers to their first-ever postseason appearance. The following season, he propelled the Brewers to the AL East title before going down with an arm injury late in the year, which may have cost Milwaukee the World Series.

Best Defensive Player: *Jim Gantner.* The Brewers' quiet, reliable second baseman manned the keystone for 12 years. He was known for his lightning-quick double-play pivot and his sure hands. In 1981, his fielding prowess prompted the Brewers to move Paul Molitor from second base to the outfield.

Hall of Famers: All-time home-run champ *Hank Aaron* returned to Milwaukee for the final two seasons of his career. He starred for the Braves at Milwaukee County Stadium for 12 years before the Braves moved to Atlanta after the 1965 season. *Rollie Fingers* spent the last five seasons of his career with the Brewers. Robin Yount and Paul Molitor are expected to be the first two players who spent the bulk of their careers with the Brewers to be enshrined.

Franchise All-Star Team:

C	Darrell Porter		LF	Ben Oglivie
1B	Cecil Cooper		CF	Gorman Thomas
2B	Jim Gantner		RF	Sixto Lezcano
3B	Don Money		DH	Paul Molitor
SS	Robin Yount		SP	Teddy Higuera
			RP	Rollie Fingers

Biggest Flake: *Pete Vuckovich.* The righthander won the AL Cy Young Award in 1982 despite chronic shoulder pain; his numbers that year were possibly the worst of any Cy Young winner ever. Long-haired, unshaven and hardly a model of physical fitness, he cultivated his flaky reputation with various antics on the mound. To look back a runner, he'd sometimes jerk his head violently toward first base, then back to the plate, back to first, back, back, and back. If his intention was to get the hitter to wonder about Vuke's sanity rather than his next offering, it seemed to work.

Strangest Career: *Dale Sveum.* He came up as a third baseman in 1986 and debuted with one of the poorest defensive seasons of all time, commiting 26 errors in 65 games at third base for an abominable .865 fielding percentage (he also committed three errors at shortstop and one at second base for a total of 30 in 91 games). The next spring, a rash of injuries hit the infield, and Sveum was pressed into service at the diamond's most demanding position: *shortstop.* Incredibly, he held his own, booting only 21 balls in 142 games, while contributing with the bat, slugging 25 homers and driving in 95 runs. He slumped the next year before breaking his leg in a late-season collision. The injuries kept him out for an entire year, and when he finally returned, he spent two seasons on the bench before leaving for Philadelphia. All in all, most of the time he was awful, but for one season he was amazingly good.

What Might Have Been: *Ill fortune befell virtually every Brewers' prospect between 1983 and 1991.* The Brewers' farm system was one of the most productive in baseball during the 1980s, but the young players' inability to develop upon reaching the majors prevented the team from building the core of a contending club.

Best Trade: On December 6, 1976, new GM Harry Dalton sent first baseman George Scott and outfielder Bernie Carbo to the Boston Red Sox for first baseman *Cecil Cooper.* Cooper took over as the Brewers' first baseman and batted .300 or higher for seven straight seasons, reaching a high of .352 in 1980. He led the AL in RBI in 1980 and tied for the league lead in 1983. Scott, meanwhile, had only one more productive season for the Red Sox.

Worst Trade: After the 1976 season, the Brewers dealt catcher *Darrell Porter* and pitcher Jim Colborn to the Kansas City Royals for pitcher Bob McClure, catcher Jamie Quirk and outfielder Jim Wohlford. Only 24, Porter developed into one of the top catchers in the league. Quirk, his replacement, batted .217 with three homers and was returned to the Royals the following year. Colborn won 18 games for the Royals, although it was his last good year. All the Brewers got out of the Porter trade was a serviceable lefthander, McClure.

Best-Looking Player: *Paul Molitor,* who fit the stereotype of the All-American baseball hero both in looks and personality.

Ugliest Player: *Gorman Thomas,* who looked like he was born on a motorcycle. Thomas was a big, power-hitting center fielder who did everything hard, whether he was swinging the bat, charging after a ball in the gap, or slamming into the outfield wall. Always unshaven, with long hair poking out of the back of his cap, his all-out hustle won him the everlasting affection of Milwaukee's blue-collar fans. Honorable mention goes to Pete Vuckovich, who was as ugly as he was flaky.

Best Nickname: Righthander *Moose Haas,* who might have been the smallest "Moose" in baseball history at six feet even and 180 pounds. Honorable mention goes to "Mr. Warmth," irascible southpaw Mike Caldwell.

Most Unappreciated Player: *Darrell Porter.* Although he didn't hit for a high average, the lefthanded-hitting catcher had three good years as the Brewers' starting catcher before suffering through an unproductive 1976 season. Although he was just 24, the Brewers shipped him to Kansas City in one of their worst trades ever. Porter remained underappreciated (except by Whitey Herzog) but had many quality seasons and made it to the postseason five times with the Kansas City Royals and St. Louis Cardinals.

Most Overrated Player: *Ted Simmons.* During his best two seasons with the Brewers (1982-1983) he was a fairly productive hitter and an average defensive catcher. After that, he got too old to catch, and stopped hitting too. During his last two years with the team, he was one of the worst designated hitters in baseball.

Most Admirable Star: *Paul Molitor.* The golden boy's image was temporarily tarnished by a brush with drugs, but he overcame his cocaine addiction and went on to give many talks to youth groups about the dangers of drugs and alcohol. Honorable mention goes to lefthanded reliever Dan Plesac, who always was good-natured and approachable, even after his effectiveness declined and he slipped into middle relief.

Least Admirable Star: *Gary Sheffield.* Maybe it was culture shock, the pressure of big expectations, or sheer immaturity, but Sheffield sure packed a lot of complaining into his three-plus years in Milwaukee. After receiving a September callup in 1988, he began 1989 as the Brewers' starting shortstop. When his defensive deficiencies became apparent, shortstop Bill Spiers was called up and Sheffield was moved to third base. He did not take the move quietly. He was cited as a "cancer" in the clubhouse, and he criticized the veterans when they failed to "reach out" to him. Later, he accused the pitching staff of failing to "protect" him when other teams threw at him. Sal Bando took over as the team's GM after the '91 season, and his first priority was to find a way to unload Sheffield. He found a taker in San Diego, and the Brewers improved by nine games that year. Sheffield later admitted he intentionally made throwing errors to provoke Milwaukee fans.

Best Season, Player: *Robin Yount, 1982.* Yount did it all that year, missing the batting title by a single point while crashing 29 homers—with two of them coming in Milwaukee's division-clinching win over Baltimore. He led the AL in slugging percentage, won a Gold Glove at shortstop and batted .414 in the World Series.

Best Season, Pitcher: *Rollie Fingers, 1981.* In the strike-shortened '81 season, Fingers led the majors with 28 saves, eight more than anyone else in the American League. He allowed only nine runs all year for a stellar 1.04 ERA, and captured both the AL MVP and Cy Young Award.

Most Impressive Individual Record: *Paul Molitor's* 39-game hitting streak in 1987, the seventh-longest ever.

Biggest Tragedy: It all ended in despair for the "Sundown Kid," *Danny Thomas.* The Brewers took him with the sixth overall pick in the 1972 draft, and in 1976 he looked like a potential star after winning the Eastern League Triple Crown and hitting well in a late-season call-up. His behavior grew increasingly erratic, however, and the Brewers sent him back down early in the following season. Plagued by depression, he hung himself in a jail cell in 1980.

Fan Favorite: *Gorman Thomas.*

—Mat Olkin

Teams: Brewers

Washington Senators/Minnesota Twins (1901-1997)

														Opponent				Park Index	
Year	Lg	Pos	W-L	Pct	GB	Manager	Att.	R	OR	HR	Avg	OBP	Slg	HR	Avg	OBP	ERA	Runs	HR
1901	AL	6th	61-72	.459	20.5	Jimmy Manning	161,661	682	771	33	.269	.326	.364	51	.290	.338	4.09	96	174
1902	AL	6th	61-75	.449	22.0	Tom Loftus	188,158	707	790	47	.283	.335	.395	56	.288	.337	4.36	100	255
1903	AL	8th	43-94	.314	47.5	Tom Loftus	128,878	437	691	17	.231	.277	.311	38	.277	.326	3.82	122	240
1904	AL	8th	38-113	.252	55.5	Mal Kittridge/Patsy Donovan	131,744	437	743	10	.227	.275	.288	19	.281	.333	3.62	95	21
1905	AL	7th	64-87	.424	29.5	Jake Stahl	252,027	559	623	22	.224	.274	.302	12	.247	.308	2.87	115	71
1906	AL	7th	55-95	.367	37.5	Jake Stahl	129,903	518	664	26	.238	.289	.309	15	.265	.331	3.25	89	42
1907	AL	8th	49-102	.325	43.5	Joe Cantillon	221,929	506	691	12	.243	.304	.299	10	.263	.315	3.11	85	31
1908	AL	7th	67-85	.441	22.5	Joe Cantillon	264,252	479	539	8	.235	.293	.296	16	.240	.293	2.34	94	73
1909	AL	8th	42-110	.276	56.0	Joe Cantillon	205,199	380	656	9	.223	.276	.275	12	.248	.312	3.04	85	63
1910	AL	7th	66-85	.437	36.5	Jimmy McAleer	254,591	501	550	9	.236	.309	.289	19	.244	.304	2.46	103	51
1911	AL	7th	64-90	.416	38.5	Jimmy McAleer	244,884	625	766	16	.258	.330	.320	39	.277	.334	3.52	95	45
1912	AL	2nd	91-61	.599	14.0	Clark Griffith	350,663	699	581	20	.256	.324	.341	24	.242	.320	2.69	92	125
1913	AL	2nd	90-64	.584	6.5	Clark Griffith	325,831	596	561	19	.252	.317	.326	35	.226	.297	2.73	111	231
1914	AL	3rd	81-73	.526	19.0	Clark Griffith	243,888	572	519	18	.244	.313	.320	20	.233	.311	2.54	104	81
1915	AL	4th	85-68	.556	17.0	Clark Griffith	167,332	569	491	12	.244	.312	.312	12	.232	.302	2.31	95	27
1916	AL	7th	76-77	.497	14.5	Clark Griffith	177,265	536	543	12	.242	.320	.306	14	.244	.314	2.67	100	36
1917	AL	5th	74-79	.484	25.5	Clark Griffith	89,682	543	566	4	.241	.313	.304	12	.238	.315	2.75	85	32
1918	AL	3rd	72-56	.563	4.0	Clark Griffith	182,122	461	412	4	.256	.318	.315	10	.231	.299	2.14	104	75
1919	AL	7th	56-84	.400	32.0	Clark Griffith	234,096	533	570	24	.260	.325	.339	20	.259	.328	3.01	93	18
1920	AL	6th	68-84	.447	29.0	Clark Griffith	359,260	723	802	36	.291	.351	.386	51	.286	.355	4.17	94	16
1921	AL	4th	80-73	.523	18.0	George McBride	456,069	704	738	42	.277	.342	.383	51	.291	.349	3.97	93	41
1922	AL	6th	69-85	.448	25.0	Clyde Milan	458,552	650	706	45	.268	.334	.367	49	.281	.349	3.81	81	22
1923	AL	4th	75-78	.490	23.5	Donie Bush	357,406	720	747	26	.274	.346	.367	56	.291	.364	3.98	91	38
1924	AL	1st	92-62	.597	—	Bucky Harris	584,310	755	613	22	.294	.362	.387	34	.258	.329	3.34	91	17
1925	AL	1st	96-55	.636	—	Bucky Harris	817,199	829	670	56	.303	.372	.411	49	.278	.351	3.70	90	33
1926	AL	4th	81-69	.540	8.0	Bucky Harris	551,580	802	761	43	.292	.364	.401	45	.287	.361	4.34	100	30
1927	AL	3rd	85-69	.552	25.0	Bucky Harris	528,976	782	730	29	.287	.351	.386	53	.269	.336	3.97	87	52
1928	AL	4th	75-79	.487	26.0	Bucky Harris	378,501	718	705	40	.284	.347	.393	40	.268	.331	3.88	101	50
1929	AL	5th	71-81	.467	34.0	Walter Johnson	355,506	730	776	48	.276	.347	.375	48	.276	.342	4.34	101	38
1930	AL	2nd	94-60	.610	8.0	Walter Johnson	614,474	892	689	57	.302	.369	.426	52	.264	.332	3.96	96	42
1931	AL	3rd	92-62	.597	16.0	Walter Johnson	492,657	843	691	49	.285	.345	.400	73	.264	.327	3.76	98	44
1932	AL	3rd	93-61	.604	14.0	Walter Johnson	371,396	840	716	61	.284	.346	.408	73	.271	.337	4.16	95	54
1933	AL	1st	99-53	.651	—	Joe Cronin	437,533	850	665	60	.287	.353	.402	64	.263	.322	3.82	85	32
1934	AL	7th	66-86	.434	34.0	Joe Cronin	330,074	729	806	51	.278	.348	.382	74	.295	.355	4.68	105	50
1935	AL	6th	67-86	.438	27.0	Bucky Harris	255,011	823	903	32	.285	.357	.381	89	.302	.374	5.25	88	38
1936	AL	4th	82-71	.536	20.0	Bucky Harris	379,525	889	799	62	.295	.365	.414	73	.279	.353	4.58	92	46
1937	AL	6th	73-80	.477	28.5	Bucky Harris	397,799	757	841	47	.279	.351	.379	96	.275	.357	4.58	87	43
1938	AL	5th	75-76	.497	23.5	Bucky Harris	522,694	814	873	85	.293	.362	.416	92	.276	.358	4.94	92	49
1939	AL	6th	65-87	.428	41.5	Bucky Harris	339,257	702	797	44	.278	.347	.379	75	.271	.348	4.60	79	34
1940	AL	7th	64-90	.416	26.0	Bucky Harris	381,241	665	811	52	.271	.331	.374	93	.281	.359	4.59	86	48
1941	AL	6th	70-84	.455	31.0	Bucky Harris	415,663	728	798	52	.272	.331	.376	69	.279	.353	4.35	98	36
1942	AL	7th	62-89	.411	39.5	Bucky Harris	403,493	653	817	40	.258	.333	.341	50	.279	.349	4.58	100	35
1943	AL	2nd	84-69	.549	13.5	Ossie Bluege	574,694	666	595	47	.254	.336	.347	48	.246	.318	3.18	108	32
1944	AL	8th	64-90	.416	25.0	Ossie Bluege	525,235	592	664	33	.261	.324	.330	48	.264	.327	3.49	79	37
1945	AL	2nd	87-67	.565	1.5	Ossie Bluege	652,660	622	562	27	.258	.330	.334	42	.242	.301	2.92	82	11
1946	AL	4th	76-78	.494	28.0	Ossie Bluege	1,027,216	608	706	60	.260	.327	.366	81	.269	.339	3.74	85	42
1947	AL	7th	64-90	.416	33.0	Ossie Bluege	850,758	496	675	42	.241	.313	.321	63	.267	.342	3.97	95	40
1948	AL	7th	56-97	.366	40.0	Joe Kuhel	795,254	578	796	31	.244	.322	.331	81	.273	.364	4.65	112	45
1949	AL	8th	50-104	.325	47.0	Joe Kuhel	770,745	584	868	81	.254	.333	.356	79	.276	.373	5.10	88	27
1950	AL	5th	67-87	.435	31.0	Bucky Harris	699,697	690	813	76	.260	.347	.360	99	.278	.359	4.66	101	36
1951	AL	7th	62-92	.403	36.0	Bucky Harris	695,167	672	764	54	.263	.336	.355	110	.269	.348	4.49	93	42
1952	AL	5th	78-76	.506	17.0	Bucky Harris	699,457	598	608	50	.239	.317	.326	78	.258	.332	3.37	96	32
1953	AL	5th	76-76	.500	23.5	Bucky Harris	595,594	687	614	69	.263	.343	.368	112	.258	.324	3.66	85	30
1954	AL	6th	66-88	.429	45.0	Bucky Harris	503,542	632	680	81	.246	.325	.355	79	.265	.338	3.84	97	50
1955	AL	8th	53-101	.344	43.0	Chuck Dressen	425,238	598	789	80	.248	.322	.351	99	.279	.359	4.62	85	34
1956	AL	7th	59-95	.383	38.0	Chuck Dressen	431,647	652	924	112	.250	.341	.377	171	.287	.373	5.33	113	126
1957	AL	8th	55-99	.357	43.0	Chuck Dressen/Cookie Lavagetto	457,079	603	808	111	.244	.316	.363	149	.278	.349	4.85	104	115
1958	AL	8th	61-93	.396	31.0	Cookie Lavagetto	475,288	553	747	121	.240	.307	.357	156	.272	.341	4.53	98	87
1959	AL	8th	63-91	.409	31.0	Cookie Lavagetto	615,372	619	701	163	.237	.308	.379	123	.259	.321	4.01	102	112
1960	AL	5th	73-81	.474	24.0	Cookie Lavagetto	743,404	672	696	147	.244	.324	.384	130	.260	.329	3.77	105	116
1961	AL	7th	70-90	.438	38.0	Lavagetto/Mele/Lavagetto/Mele	1,256,723	707	778	167	.250	.326	.397	163	.256	.329	4.28	118	121
1962	AL	2nd	91-71	.562	5.0	Sam Mele	1,433,116	798	713	185	.260	.338	.412	166	.253	.317	3.89	111	124
1963	AL	3rd	91-70	.565	13.0	Sam Mele	1,406,652	767	602	225	.255	.325	.430	162	.242	.302	3.28	98	118
1964	AL	6th	79-83	.488	20.0	Sam Mele	1,207,514	737	678	221	.252	.322	.427	181	.243	.312	3.58	104	102
1965	AL	1st	102-60	.630	—	Sam Mele	1,463,258	774	600	150	.254	.324	.399	166	.235	.301	3.14	100	98
1966	AL	2nd	89-73	.549	9.0	Sam Mele	1,259,374	663	581	144	.249	.316	.382	139	.232	.286	3.13	123	167
1967	AL	2nd	91-71	.562	1.0	Sam Mele/Cal Ermer	1,483,547	671	590	131	.240	.309	.369	115	.243	.296	3.14	111	118
1968	AL	7th	79-83	.488	24.0	Cal Ermer	1,143,257	562	546	105	.237	.299	.350	92	.229	.288	2.89	113	105
1969	AL	1st-W	97-65	.599	—	Billy Martin	1,349,328	790	618	163	.268	.340	.408	119	.246	.313	3.24	102	99
1970	AL	1st-W	98-64	.605	—	Bill Rigney	1,261,887	744	605	153	.262	.327	.403	130	.244	.308	3.23	93	73
1971	AL	5th-W	74-86	.463	26.5	Bill Rigney	940,858	654	670	116	.260	.323	.372	139	.257	.326	3.81	111	103
1972	AL	3rd-W	77-77	.500	15.5	Bill Rigney/Frank Quilici	797,901	537	535	93	.244	.310	.344	105	.230	.294	2.84	116	125
1973	AL	3rd-W	81-81	.500	13.0	Frank Quilici	907,499	738	692	120	.270	.342	.393	115	.259	.324	3.77	108	97
1974	AL	3rd-W	82-80	.506	8.0	Frank Quilici	662,401	673	669	111	.272	.336	.378	115	.260	.325	3.64	103	105
1975	AL	4th-W	76-83	.478	20.5	Frank Quilici	737,156	724	736	121	.271	.341	.386	137	.257	.335	4.05	117	161
1976	AL	3rd-W	85-77	.525	5.0	Gene Mauch	715,394	743	704	81	.274	.341	.375	89	.259	.335	3.69	98	102
1977	AL	4th-W	84-77	.522	17.5	Gene Mauch	1,162,727	867	776	123	.282	.348	.417	151	.278	.340	4.36	107	106
1978	AL	4th-W	73-89	.451	19.0	Gene Mauch	787,878	666	678	82	.267	.339	.375	102	.266	.330	3.69	88	82
1979	AL	4th-W	82-80	.506	6.0	Gene Mauch	1,070,521	764	725	112	.278	.341	.402	128	.285	.338	4.13	118	114
1980	AL	3rd-W	77-84	.478	19.5	Gene Mauch/John Goryl	769,206	670	724	99	.265	.319	.381	120	.272	.328	3.93	119	110
1981	AL	7th-W	17-39	.304	18.0	John Goryl/Billy Gardner													
	AL	4th-W	24-29	.453	6.0	Billy Gardner	469,090	378	486	47	.240	.293	.338	79	.272	.338	3.98	115	109

1288 Teams: Twins

Year	Lg	Pos	W-L	Pct	GB	Manager	Att.	R	OR	HR	Avg	OBP	Slg	Opponent HR	Opponent Avg	Opponent OBP	ERA	Park Index Runs	Park Index HR
1982	AL	7th-W	60-102	.370	33.0	Billy Gardner	921,186	657	819	148	.257	.316	.396	208	.269	.344	4.72	104	116
1983	AL	5th-W	70-92	.432	29.0	Billy Gardner	858,939	709	822	141	.261	.319	.401	163	.280	.348	4.66	114	94
1984	AL	2nd-W	81-81	.500	3.0	Billy Gardner	1,598,692	673	675	114	.265	.318	.385	159	.260	.319	3.85	111	105
1985	AL	4th-W	77-85	.475	14.0	Billy Gardner/Ray Miller	1,651,814	705	782	141	.264	.326	.407	164	.268	.326	4.48	108	95
1986	AL	6th-W	71-91	.438	21.0	Ray Miller/Tom Kelly	1,255,453	741	839	196	.261	.325	.428	200	.281	.342	4.77	121	129
1987	AL	1st-W	85-77	.525	—	Tom Kelly	2,081,976	786	806	196	.261	.328	.430	210	.266	.337	4.63	91	95
1988	AL	2nd-W	91-71	.562	13.0	Tom Kelly	3,030,672	759	672	151	.274	.340	.421	146	.266	.325	3.93	112	109
1989	AL	5th-W	80-82	.494	19.0	Tom Kelly	2,277,438	740	738	117	.276	.334	.402	139	.269	.332	4.28	115	100
1990	AL	7th-W	74-88	.457	29.0	Tom Kelly	1,751,584	666	729	100	.265	.324	.385	134	.273	.332	4.12	117	97
1991	AL	1st-W	95-67	.586	—	Tom Kelly	2,293,842	776	652	140	.280	.344	.420	139	.255	.317	3.69	109	96
1992	AL	2nd-W	90-72	.556	6.0	Tom Kelly	2,482,428	747	653	104	.277	.341	.391	121	.254	.316	3.72	100	99
1993	AL	5th-W	71-91	.438	23.0	Tom Kelly	2,048,673	693	830	121	.264	.327	.385	148	.283	.344	4.71	109	88
1994	AL	4th-C	53-60	.469	14.0	Tom Kelly	1,398,565	594	688	103	.276	.340	.427	153	.299	.361	5.68	97	104
1995	AL	5th-C	56-88	.389	44.0	Tom Kelly	1,057,667	703	889	120	.279	.346	.419	210	.287	.356	5.76	105	119
1996	AL	4th-C	78-84	.481	21.5	Tom Kelly	1,437,352	877	900	118	.288	.357	.425	233	.277	.346	5.28	108	105
1997	AL	4th-C	68-94	.420	18.5	Tom Kelly	1,411,064	772	861	132	.270	.333	.409	187	.283	.342	5.02	104	90

Team Nicknames: Washington Senators 1901-1961, Minnesota Twins 1962-1997.

Team Ballparks: American League Park I 1901-1903, American League Park II 1904-1910, Griffith Stadium 1911-1960, Metropolitan Stadium 1961-1981, Hubert H. Humphrey Metrodome 1982-1997.

Teams: Twins

Washington Senators/Minnesota Twins
Individual Season Batting Leaders

Year	Batting Average		On-Base Percentage		Slugging Percentage		Home Runs		RBI		Stolen Bases	
1901	Sam Dungan	.320	Sam Dungan	.368	Sam Dungan	.415	Mike Grady	9	Sam Dungan	72	John Farrell	25
1902	Ed Delahanty	.376	Ed Delahanty	.453	Ed Delahanty	.590	Ed Delahanty	10	Ed Delahanty	93	Bill Coughlin	29
1903	Kip Selbach	.251	Kip Selbach	.305	Jimmy Ryan	.373	Jimmy Ryan	7	Kip Selbach	49	Bill Coughlin	30
1904	Jake Stahl	.262	Jake Stahl	.309	Jake Stahl	.381	Jake Stahl	3	Jake Stahl	50	Jake Stahl	25
1905	Jake Stahl	.244	Jake Stahl	.306	Jake Stahl	.365	Jake Stahl	5	Jake Stahl	66	Jake Stahl	41
1906	Charlie Hickman	.284	Harry Schlafly	.345	Charlie Hickman	.421	Charlie Hickman	9	John Anderson	70	John Anderson	39
1907	Bob Ganley	.276	Bob Ganley	.337	Charlie Jones	.343	Dave Altizer	2	Jim Delahanty	54	Bob Ganley	40
							Jim Delahanty					
1908	Jerry Freeman	.252	Clyde Milan	.304	Clyde Milan	.315	Ollie Pickering	2	Jerry Freeman	45	Bob Ganley	30
1909	Bob Unglaub	.265	Bob Unglaub	.301	Bob Unglaub	.350	Bob Unglaub	3	Bob Unglaub	41	Wid Conroy	24
1910	Clyde Milan	.279	Clyde Milan	.379	Doc Gessler	.351	3 tied with	2	George McBride	55	Clyde Milan	44
1911	Germany Schaefer	.334	Germany Schaefer	.412	Germany Schaefer	.398	Doc Gessler	4	Doc Gessler	78	Clyde Milan	58
1912	Clyde Milan	.306	Clyde Milan	.377	Chick Gandil	.431	Danny Moeller	6	Chick Gandil	81	Clyde Milan	88
1913	Chick Gandil	.318	Ray Morgan	.369	Chick Gandil	.398	Danny Moeller	6	Chick Gandil	72	Clyde Milan	75
1914	Eddie Foster	.282	Ray Morgan	.352	Chick Gandil	.359	Howard Shanks	4	Chick Gandil	75	Clyde Milan	38
1915	Chick Gandil	.291	Clyde Milan	.353	Chick Gandil	.406	4 tied with	2	Clyde Milan	66	Clyde Milan	40
1916	Clyde Milan	.273	Clyde Milan	.343	Howard Shanks	.321	Elmer Smith	2	Howard Shanks	48	Clyde Milan	34
1917	Sam Rice	.302	Clyde Milan	.364	Sam Rice	.369	Joe Judge	2	Clyde Milan	69	Sam Rice	35
1918	Clyde Milan	.290	Burt Shotton	.349	Clyde Milan	.346	4 tied with	1	Clyde Milan	56	Clyde Milan	26
									Howard Shanks			
1919	Sam Rice	.321	Joe Judge	.386	Sam Rice	.411	Mike Menosky	6	Sam Rice	71	Sam Rice	26
1920	Sam Rice	.338	Joe Judge	.416	Joe Judge	.462	Braggo Roth	9	Braggo Roth	92	Sam Rice	63
1921	Sam Rice	.330	Sam Rice	.382	Sam Rice	.467	Bing Miller	9	Sam Rice	79	Bucky Harris	29
1922	Sam Rice	.295	Frank Brower	.375	Joe Judge	.450	Joe Judge	10	Joe Judge	81	Bucky Harris	25
1923	Muddy Ruel	.316	Joe Judge	.406	Goose Goslin	.453	Goose Goslin	9	Goose Goslin	99	Bucky Harris	23
1924	Goose Goslin	.344	Goose Goslin	.421	Goose Goslin	.516	Goose Goslin	12	Goose Goslin	129	Sam Rice	24
1925	Sam Rice	.350	Muddy Ruel	.411	Goose Goslin	.547	Goose Goslin	18	Goose Goslin	113	Goose Goslin	26
											Sam Rice	
1926	Goose Goslin	.354	Goose Goslin	.425	Goose Goslin	.542	Goose Goslin	17	Goose Goslin	108	Sam Rice	25
1927	Goose Goslin	.334	Muddy Ruel	.403	Goose Goslin	.516	Goose Goslin	13	Goose Goslin	120	Goose Goslin	21
1928	Goose Goslin	.379	Goose Goslin	.443	Goose Goslin	.614	Goose Goslin	17	Goose Goslin	102	Ossie Bluege	18
1929	Sam Rice	.323	Joe Judge	.396	Goose Goslin	.461	Goose Goslin	18	Goose Goslin	91	Buddy Myer	18
1930	Sam Rice	.349	Joe Cronin	.422	Joe Cronin	.513	Joe Cronin	13	Joe Cronin	126	Joe Cronin	17
1931	Sammy West	.333	Joe Cronin	.391	Sammy West	.481	Joe Cronin	12	Joe Cronin	126	Ossie Bluege	16
1932	Heinie Manush	.342	Joe Cronin	.393	Heinie Manush	.520	Heinie Manush	14	Joe Cronin	116	Buddy Myer	12
									Heinie Manush			
1933	Heinie Manush	.336	Joe Cronin	.398	Joe Kuhel	.467	Joe Kuhel	11	Joe Cronin	118	Joe Kuhel	17
1934	Heinie Manush	.349	Buddy Myer	.419	Heinie Manush	.523	Heinie Manush	11	Joe Cronin	101	Joe Cronin	8
1935	Buddy Myer	.349	Buddy Myer	.440	Buddy Myer	.468	Jake Powell	6	Buddy Myer	100	Jake Powell	15
1936	John Stone	.341	John Stone	.421	John Stone	.545	Joe Kuhel	16	Joe Kuhel	118	Ben Chapman	19
1937	Cecil Travis	.344	Buddy Myer	.407	John Stone	.480	Buddy Lewis	10	John Stone	88	Mel Almada	12
1938	Buddy Myer	.336	Buddy Myer	.454	Al Simmons	.511	Zeke Bonura	22	Zeke Bonura	114	Buddy Lewis	17
1939	Buddy Lewis	.319	Buddy Lewis	.402	Buddy Lewis	.478	Buddy Lewis	10	Taffy Wright	93	George Case	51
1940	Cecil Travis	.322	Buddy Lewis	.393	Cecil Travis	.445	Gee Walker	13	Gee Walker	96	George Case	35
1941	Cecil Travis	.359	Cecil Travis	.410	Cecil Travis	.520	Jake Early	10	Cecil Travis	101	George Case	33
1942	Stan Spence	.323	Bobby Estalella	.400	Stan Spence	.432	Mickey Vernon	9	Mickey Vernon	86	George Case	44
1943	George Case	.294	Stan Spence	.366	Stan Spence	.405	Stan Spence	12	Stan Spence	88	George Case	61
1944	Stan Spence	.316	Stan Spence	.391	Stan Spence	.486	Stan Spence	18	Stan Spence	100	George Case	49
1945	George Myatt	.296	Joe Kuhel	.378	Joe Kuhel	.400	Harlond Clift	8	George Binks	81	George Case	30
											George Myatt	
1946	Mickey Vernon	.353	Mickey Vernon	.403	Mickey Vernon	.508	Stan Spence	16	Stan Spence	87	Mickey Vernon	14
1947	Stan Spence	.279	Stan Spence	.378	Stan Spence	.441	Stan Spence	16	Mickey Vernon	85	Mickey Vernon	12
1948	Al Kozar	.250	Eddie Yost	.349	Eddie Yost	.357	Gil Coan	7	Bud Stewart	69	Gil Coan	23
							Bud Stewart					
1949	Eddie Robinson	.294	Eddie Yost	.383	Eddie Robinson	.459	Eddie Robinson	18	Eddie Robinson	78	Sherry Robertson	10
1950	Irv Noren	.295	Eddie Yost	.440	Irv Noren	.459	Irv Noren	14	Irv Noren	98	Gil Coan	10
1951	Gil Coan	.303	Eddie Yost	.423	Gil Coan	.426	Eddie Yost	12	Sam Mele	94	Irv Noren	10
1952	Jackie Jensen	.286	Eddie Yost	.378	Jackie Jensen	.407	Eddie Yost	12	Jackie Jensen	80	Jackie Jensen	17
									Mickey Vernon			
1953	Mickey Vernon	.337	Eddie Yost	.403	Mickey Vernon	.518	Mickey Vernon	15	Mickey Vernon	115	Jackie Jensen	18
1954	Jim Busby	.298	Eddie Yost	.405	Mickey Vernon	.492	Roy Sievers	24	Roy Sievers	102	Jim Busby	17
1955	Mickey Vernon	.301	Eddie Yost	.407	Roy Sievers	.489	Roy Sievers	25	Roy Sievers	106	Jim Busby	5
1956	Pete Runnels	.310	Eddie Yost	.412	Jim Lemon	.502	Roy Sievers	29	Jim Lemon	96	Whitey Herzog	8
											Eddie Yost	
1957	Roy Sievers	.301	Roy Sievers	.388	Roy Sievers	.579	Roy Sievers	42	Roy Sievers	114	Julio Becquer	3
1958	Roy Sievers	.295	Eddie Yost	.361	Roy Sievers	.544	Roy Sievers	39	Roy Sievers	108	Albie Pearson	7
1959	Jim Lemon	.279	Harmon Killebrew	.354	Harmon Killebrew	.516	Harmon Killebrew	42	Harmon Killebrew	105	Bob Allison	13
1960	Harmon Killebrew	.276	Harmon Killebrew	.375	Harmon Killebrew	.534	Jim Lemon	38	Jim Lemon	100	Lenny Green	21
1961	Earl Battey	.302	Harmon Killebrew	.405	Harmon Killebrew	.606	Harmon Killebrew	46	Harmon Killebrew	122	Lenny Green	17
1962	Rich Rollins	.298	Rich Rollins	.374	Harmon Killebrew	.545	Harmon Killebrew	48	Harmon Killebrew	126	Bob Allison	8
											Lenny Green	
1963	Rich Rollins	.307	Bob Allison	.378	Harmon Killebrew	.555	Harmon Killebrew	45	Harmon Killebrew	96	Lenny Green	11
1964	Tony Oliva	.323	Bob Allison	.404	Tony Oliva	.557	Harmon Killebrew	49	Harmon Killebrew	111	Zoilo Versalles	14
1965	Tony Oliva	.321	Tony Oliva	.378	Tony Oliva	.491	Harmon Killebrew	25	Tony Oliva	98	Zoilo Versalles	27
1966	Tony Oliva	.307	Harmon Killebrew	.391	Harmon Killebrew	.538	Harmon Killebrew	39	Harmon Killebrew	110	Cesar Tovar	16
1967	Rod Carew	.292	Harmon Killebrew	.408	Harmon Killebrew	.558	Harmon Killebrew	44	Harmon Killebrew	113	Cesar Tovar	19
1968	Tony Oliva	.289	Tony Oliva	.357	Tony Oliva	.477	Bob Allison	22	Tony Oliva	68	Cesar Tovar	35
1969	Rod Carew	.332	Harmon Killebrew	.427	Harmon Killebrew	.584	Harmon Killebrew	49	Harmon Killebrew	140	Cesar Tovar	45
1970	Tony Oliva	.325	Harmon Killebrew	.411	Harmon Killebrew	.546	Harmon Killebrew	41	Harmon Killebrew	113	Cesar Tovar	30
1971	Tony Oliva	.337	Harmon Killebrew	.386	Tony Oliva	.546	Harmon Killebrew	28	Harmon Killebrew	119	Cesar Tovar	18
1972	Rod Carew	.318	Rod Carew	.369	Harmon Killebrew	.450	Harmon Killebrew	26	Bobby Darwin	80	Cesar Tovar	21
1973	Rod Carew	.350	Rod Carew	.411	Rod Carew	.471	Bobby Darwin	18	Tony Oliva	92	Rod Carew	41

Year	Batting Average		On-Base Percentage		Slugging Percentage		Home Runs		RBI		Stolen Bases	
1974	Rod Carew	.364	Rod Carew	.433	Larry Hisle	.465	Bobby Darwin	25	Bobby Darwin	94	Rod Carew	38
1975	Rod Carew	.359	Rod Carew	.421	Rod Carew	.497	Dan Ford	15	Rod Carew	80	Rod Carew	35
1976	Rod Carew	.331	Rod Carew	.395	Rod Carew	.463	Dan Ford	20	Larry Hisle	96	Rod Carew	49
1977	Rod Carew	.388	Rod Carew	.449	Rod Carew	.570	Larry Hisle	28	Larry Hisle	119	Rod Carew	23
1978	Rod Carew	.333	Rod Carew	.411	Rod Carew	.441	Roy Smalley	19	Dan Ford	82	Rod Carew	27
1979	Ken Landreaux	.305	Butch Wynegar	.363	Ken Landreaux	.450	Roy Smalley	24	Roy Smalley	95	Rob Wilfong	11
1980	John Castino	.302	Roy Smalley	.359	John Castino	.430	John Castino	13	John Castino	64	Hosken Powell	14
1981	John Castino	.268	John Castino	.301	John Castino	.396	Roy Smalley	7	Mickey Hatcher	37	Hosken Powell	7
1982	Kent Hrbek	.301	Tom Brunansky	.377	Gary Ward	.519	Gary Ward	28	Kent Hrbek	92	Gary Ward	13
1983	Kent Hrbek	.297	Kent Hrbek	.366	Kent Hrbek	.489	Tom Brunansky	28	Gary Ward	88	Ron Washington	10
1984	Kent Hrbek	.311	Kent Hrbek	.383	Kent Hrbek	.522	Tom Brunansky	32	Kent Hrbek	107	Kirby Puckett	14
1985	Kirby Puckett	.288	Kent Hrbek	.351	Tom Brunansky	.448	Tom Brunansky	27	Kent Hrbek	93	Kirby Puckett	21
1986	Kirby Puckett	.328	Kirby Puckett	.366	Kirby Puckett	.537	Gary Gaetti	34	Gary Gaetti	108	Kirby Puckett	20
1987	Kirby Puckett	.332	Kent Hrbek	.389	Kent Hrbek	.545	Kent Hrbek	34	Gary Gaetti	109	Dan Gladden	25
1988	Kirby Puckett	.356	Kent Hrbek	.387	Gary Gaetti	.551	Gary Gaetti	28	Kirby Puckett	121	Dan Gladden	28
1989	Kirby Puckett	.339	Kirby Puckett	.379	Kirby Puckett	.465	Kent Hrbek	25	Kirby Puckett	85	Al Newman	25
1990	Kirby Puckett	.298	Kent Hrbek	.377	Kent Hrbek	.474	Kent Hrbek	22	Gary Gaetti	85	Dan Gladden	25
1991	Kirby Puckett	.319	Chili Davis	.385	Chili Davis	.507	Chili Davis	29	Chili Davis	93	Chuck Knoblauch	25
1992	Kirby Puckett	.329	Shane Mack	.394	Kirby Puckett	.490	Kirby Puckett	19	Kirby Puckett	110	Chuck Knoblauch	34
1993	Brian Harper	.304	Chuck Knoblauch	.354	Kirby Puckett	.474	Kent Hrbek	25	Kirby Puckett	89	Chuck Knoblauch	29
1994	Kirby Puckett	.317	Chuck Knoblauch	.381	Kirby Puckett	.540	Kirby Puckett	20	Kirby Puckett	112	Chuck Knoblauch	35
1995	Chuck Knoblauch	.333	Chuck Knoblauch	.424	Kirby Puckett	.515	Marty Cordova	24	Kirby Puckett	99	Chuck Knoblauch	46
1996	Paul Molitor	.341	Chuck Knoblauch	.448	Chuck Knoblauch	.517	Marty Cordova	16	Paul Molitor	113	Chuck Knoblauch	45
1997	Paul Molitor	.305	Chuck Knoblauch	.390	Ron Coomer	.438	Marty Cordova	15	Paul Molitor	89	Chuck Knoblauch	62

Teams: Twins

Washington Senators/Minnesota Twins
Individual Season Pitching Leaders

Year	ERA		Baserunners/9 IP		Innings Pitched		Strikeouts		Wins		Saves	
1901	Bill Carrick	3.75	Dale Gear	12.4	Bill Carrick	324.0	Casey Patten	109	Casey Patten	18	Win Mercer	1
1902	Al Orth	3.97	Al Orth	11.6	Al Orth	324.0	Casey Patten	92	Al Orth	19	Watty Lee	1
											Casey Patten	
1903	Watty Lee	3.08	Watty Lee	11.7	Casey Patten	300.0	Casey Patten	133	Al Orth	11	Al Orth	2
									Casey Patten			
1904	Casey Patten	3.07	Casey Patten	11.7	Casey Patten	357.2	Casey Patten	150	Casey Patten	14	Casey Patten	3
1905	Long Tom Hughes	2.35	Long Tom Hughes	10.2	Casey Patten	309.2	Long Tom Hughes	149	Long Tom Hughes	17	Bill Wolfe	2
1906	Casey Patten	2.17	Casey Patten	10.8	Cy Falkenberg	298.2	Cy Falkenberg	178	Casey Patten	19	Cy Falkenberg	1
1907	Cy Falkenberg	2.35	Charlie Smith	10.6	Charlie Smith	258.2	Charlie Smith	119	Casey Patten	12	Long Tom Hughes	3
1908	Walter Johnson	1.65	Bill Burns	8.6	Long Tom Hughes	276.1	Long Tom Hughes	165	Long Tom Hughes	18	Long Tom Hughes	4
1909	Walter Johnson	2.22	Walter Johnson	10.5	Walter Johnson	296.1	Walter Johnson	164	Walter Johnson	13	Long Tom Hughes	1
											Walter Johnson	
1910	Walter Johnson	1.36	Walter Johnson	8.5	Walter Johnson	370.0	Walter Johnson	313	Walter Johnson	25	3 tied with	1
1911	Walter Johnson	1.90	Walter Johnson	10.3	Walter Johnson	322.1	Walter Johnson	207	Walter Johnson	25	Bob Groom	2
											Long Tom Hughes	
1912	Walter Johnson	1.39	Walter Johnson	8.6	Walter Johnson	369.0	Walter Johnson	303	Walter Johnson	33	Walter Johnson	2
1913	Walter Johnson	1.14	Walter Johnson	7.3	Walter Johnson	346.0	Walter Johnson	243	Walter Johnson	36	Long Tom Hughes	7
1914	Walter Johnson	1.72	Walter Johnson	9.0	Walter Johnson	371.2	Walter Johnson	225	Walter Johnson	28	Jack Bentley	4
											Jim Shaw	
1915	Walter Johnson	1.55	Walter Johnson	8.9	Walter Johnson	336.2	Walter Johnson	203	Walter Johnson	27	Walter Johnson	4
1916	Walter Johnson	1.90	Walter Johnson	9.3	Walter Johnson	369.2	Walter Johnson	228	Walter Johnson	25	Doc Ayers	2
											Bert Gallia	
1917	Doc Ayers	2.17	Walter Johnson	9.1	Walter Johnson	326.0	Walter Johnson	188	Walter Johnson	23	Walter Johnson	3
1918	Walter Johnson	1.27	Walter Johnson	8.8	Walter Johnson	326.0	Walter Johnson	162	Walter Johnson	23	Doc Ayers	3
											Walter Johnson	
1919	Walter Johnson	1.49	Walter Johnson	9.1	Jim Shaw	306.2	Walter Johnson	147	Walter Johnson	20	Jim Shaw	4
1920	Tom Zachary	3.77	Tom Zachary	12.7	Tom Zachary	262.2	Jim Shaw	88	Tom Zachary	15	Walter Johnson	3
1921	George Mogridge	3.00	George Mogridge	11.7	George Mogridge	288.0	Walter Johnson	143	George Mogridge	18	Jose Acosta	3
									Tom Zachary		Jim Shaw	
1922	Walter Johnson	2.99	Tom Zachary	11.5	Walter Johnson	280.0	Walter Johnson	105	George Mogridge	18	Walter Johnson	4
1923	Allan Russell	3.03	George Mogridge	12.2	Walter Johnson	261.1	Walter Johnson	130	Walter Johnson	17	Allan Russell	9
1924	Walter Johnson	2.72	Walter Johnson	10.4	Walter Johnson	277.2	Walter Johnson	158	Walter Johnson	23	Firpo Marberry	15
1925	Stan Coveleski	2.84	Stan Coveleski	11.4	Stan Coveleski	241.0	Walter Johnson	108	Stan Coveleski	20	Firpo Marberry	15
									Walter Johnson			
1926	Stan Coveleski	3.12	Walter Johnson	11.6	Walter Johnson	260.2	Walter Johnson	125	Walter Johnson	15	Firpo Marberry	22
1927	Bump Hadley	2.85	Hod Lisenbee	11.2	Hod Lisenbee	242.0	Hod Lisenbee	105	Hod Lisenbee	18	Garland Braxton	13
1928	Garland Braxton	2.51	Garland Braxton	9.3	Bump Hadley	231.2	Garland Braxton	94	Sad Sam Jones	17	Garland Braxton	6
1929	Firpo Marberry	3.06	Firpo Marberry	11.1	Firpo Marberry	250.1	Firpo Marberry	121	Firpo Marberry	19	Firpo Marberry	11
1930	General Crowder	3.60	General Crowder	11.6	Bump Hadley	260.1	Bump Hadley	162	Lloyd Brown	16	Garland Braxton	5
1931	Bump Hadley	3.06	Firpo Marberry	11.4	Lloyd Brown	258.2	Bump Hadley	124	General Crowder	18	Bump Hadley	8
1932	General Crowder	3.33	General Crowder	10.9	General Crowder	327.0	General Crowder	103	General Crowder	26	Firpo Marberry	13
1933	Earl Whitehill	3.33	Lefty Stewart	11.2	General Crowder	299.1	General Crowder	110	General Crowder	24	Jack Russell	13
1934	Bobby Burke	3.21	Bobby Burke	12.2	Earl Whitehill	235.0	Earl Whitehill	96	Earl Whitehill	14	Jack Russell	7
1935	Earl Whitehill	4.29	Earl Whitehill	13.8	Earl Whitehill	279.1	Earl Whitehill	102	Earl Whitehill	14	3 tied with	3
1936	Pete Appleton	3.53	Pete Appleton	12.5	Bobo Newsom	285.1	Bobo Newsom	156	Jimmie DeShong	18	Pete Appleton	3
											Jack Russell	
1937	Wes Ferrell	3.94	Montie Weaver	12.7	Jimmie DeShong	264.1	Wes Ferrell	92	Jimmie DeShong	14	Syd Cohen	4
1938	Dutch Leonard	3.43	Dutch Leonard	11.3	Dutch Leonard	223.1	Joe Krakauskas	104	Wes Ferrell	13	Pete Appleton	5
1939	Dutch Leonard	3.54	Dutch Leonard	11.3	Dutch Leonard	269.1	Ken Chase	118	Dutch Leonard	20	Pete Appleton	6
1940	Ken Chase	3.23	Dutch Leonard	12.7	Dutch Leonard	289.0	Ken Chase	129	Sid Hudson	17	3 tied with	2
1941	Dutch Leonard	3.45	Dutch Leonard	11.5	Dutch Leonard	256.0	Sid Hudson	108	Dutch Leonard	18	Walt Masterson	3
1942	Alex Carrasquel	3.43	Alex Carrasquel	12.7	Sid Hudson	239.1	Bobo Newsom	113	Bobo Newsom	11	Alex Carrasquel	4
1943	Mickey Haefner	2.29	Mickey Haefner	10.3	Early Wynn	256.2	Early Wynn	89	Early Wynn	18	Mickey Haefner	6
1944	Johnny Niggeling	2.32	Dutch Leonard	10.3	Dutch Leonard	229.1	Johnny Niggeling	121	Dutch Leonard	14	Bill LeFebvre	3
1945	Roger Wolff	2.12	Roger Wolff	9.1	Roger Wolff	250.0	Roger Wolff	108	Roger Wolff	20	Mickey Haefner	3
1946	Bobo Newsom	2.78	Bobo Newsom	11.4	Mickey Haefner	227.2	Mickey Haefner	85	Mickey Haefner	14	Bill Kennedy	3
1947	Walt Masterson	3.13	Walt Masterson	11.2	Walt Masterson	253.0	Walt Masterson	135	Early Wynn	17	Tom Ferrick	9
1948	Ray Scarborough	2.82	Ray Scarborough	11.7	Early Wynn	198.0	Ray Scarborough	76	Ray Scarborough	15	Tom Ferrick	10
1949	Sid Hudson	4.22	Ray Scarborough	13.5	Sid Hudson	209.0	Ray Scarborough	81	Ray Scarborough	13	Joe Haynes	2
											Dick Welteroth	
1950	Bob Kuzava	3.95	Bob Kuzava	13.5	Sid Hudson	237.2	Bob Kuzava	84	Sid Hudson	14	Mickey Harris	15
1951	Connie Marrero	3.90	Connie Marrero	13.1	Connie Marrero	187.0	Connie Marrero	66	Connie Marrero	11	Mickey Harris	4
1952	Bob Porterfield	2.72	Connie Marrero	11.3	Bob Porterfield	231.1	Walt Masterson	89	Bob Porterfield	13	Sandy Consuegra	5
1953	Chuck Stobbs	3.29	Bob Porterfield	11.2	Bob Porterfield	255.0	Walt Masterson	95	Bob Porterfield	22	Johnny Schmitz	4
1954	Johnny Schmitz	2.91	Dean Stone	11.6	Bob Porterfield	244.0	Mickey McDermott	95	Bob Porterfield	13	Camilo Pascual	3
1955	Johnny Schmitz	3.71	Bob Porterfield	12.8	Dean Stone	180.0	Dean Stone	84	Mickey McDermott	10	Pedro Ramos	5
									Bob Porterfield			
1956	Chuck Stobbs	3.60	Chuck Stobbs	12.0	Chuck Stobbs	240.0	Camilo Pascual	162	Chuck Stobbs	15	Bud Byerly	4
											Bob Chakales	
1957	Camilo Pascual	4.10	Camilo Pascual	12.7	Pedro Ramos	231.0	Chuck Stobbs	114	Pedro Ramos	12	Tex Clevenger	8
1958	Camilo Pascual	3.15	Camilo Pascual	11.6	Pedro Ramos	259.1	Camilo Pascual	146	Pedro Ramos	14	Dick Hyde	18
1959	Camilo Pascual	2.64	Camilo Pascual	10.3	Camilo Pascual	238.2	Camilo Pascual	185	Camilo Pascual	17	Tex Clevenger	8
1960	Don Lee	3.44	Pedro Ramos	11.8	Pedro Ramos	274.0	Pedro Ramos	160	Camilo Pascual	12	Ray Moore	13
									Chuck Stobbs			
1961	Camilo Pascual	3.46	Camilo Pascual	11.0	Pedro Ramos	264.1	Camilo Pascual	221	Camilo Pascual	15	Ray Moore	14
1962	Jim Kaat	3.14	Camilo Pascual	10.4	Jim Kaat	269.0	Camilo Pascual	206	Camilo Pascual	20	Ray Moore	9
1963	Camilo Pascual	2.46	Lee Stange	10.3	Camilo Pascual	248.1	Camilo Pascual	202	Camilo Pascual	21	Bill Dailey	21
1964	Mudcat Grant	2.82	Mudcat Grant	10.7	Camilo Pascual	267.1	Camilo Pascual	213	Jim Kaat	17	Al Worthington	14
1965	Jim Perry	2.63	Jim Perry	10.3	Mudcat Grant	270.1	Jim Kaat	154	Mudcat Grant	21	Al Worthington	21
1966	Jim Perry	2.54	Jim Kaat	9.7	Jim Kaat	304.2	Jim Kaat	205	Jim Kaat	25	Al Worthington	16
1967	Jim Merritt	2.53	Jim Merritt	9.2	Dean Chance	283.2	Dean Chance	220	Dean Chance	20	Al Worthington	16
1968	Dean Chance	2.53	Dean Chance	9.2	Dean Chance	292.0	Dean Chance	234	Dean Chance	16	Al Worthington	18

Teams: Twins

Year	ERA		Baserunners/9 IP		Innings Pitched		Strikeouts		Wins		Saves	
1969	Jim Perry	2.82	Jim Perry	11.0	Jim Perry	261.2	Dave Boswell	190	Dave Boswell	20	Ron Perranoski	31
									Jim Perry			
1970	Jim Perry	3.04	Jim Perry	10.5	Jim Perry	278.2	Tom Hall	184	Jim Perry	24	Ron Perranoski	34
1971	Bert Blyleven	2.81	Bert Blyleven	10.7	Bert Blyleven	278.1	Bert Blyleven	224	Jim Perry	17	Tom Hall	9
1972	Ray Corbin	2.62	Bert Blyleven	10.2	Bert Blyleven	287.1	Bert Blyleven	228	Bert Blyleven	17	Wayne Granger	19
1973	Bert Blyleven	2.52	Bert Blyleven	10.3	Bert Blyleven	325.0	Bert Blyleven	258	Bert Blyleven	20	Ray Corbin	14
1974	Bert Blyleven	2.66	Bert Blyleven	10.6	Bert Blyleven	281.0	Bert Blyleven	249	Bert Blyleven	17	Bill Campbell	19
1975	Bert Blyleven	3.00	Bert Blyleven	10.0	Bert Blyleven	275.2	Bert Blyleven	233	Jim Hughes	16	Tom Burgmeier	11
1976	Bill Campbell	3.01	Bill Campbell	11.4	Dave Goltz	249.1	Dave Goltz	133	Bill Campbell	17	Bill Campbell	20
1977	Dave Goltz	3.36	Dave Goltz	11.2	Dave Goltz	303.0	Dave Goltz	186	Dave Goltz	20	Tom Johnson	15
1978	Dave Goltz	2.49	Dave Goltz	11.3	Roger Erickson	265.2	Roger Erickson	121	Dave Goltz	15	Mike Marshall	21
1979	Jerry Koosman	3.38	Geoff Zahn	11.8	Jerry Koosman	263.2	Jerry Koosman	157	Jerry Koosman	20	Mike Marshall	32
1980	Roger Erickson	3.25	Jerry Koosman	12.1	Jerry Koosman	243.1	Jerry Koosman	149	Jerry Koosman	16	Doug Corbett	23
1981	Fredie Arroyo	3.93	Pete Redfern	12.3	Pete Redfern	150.0	Pete Redfern	77	Pete Redfern	9	Doug Corbett	17
1982	Bobby Castillo	3.66	Bobby Castillo	11.5	Bobby Castillo	218.2	Brad Havens	129	Bobby Castillo	13	Ron Davis	22
1983	Ken Schrom	3.71	Al Williams	12.5	Frank Viola	210.0	Frank Viola	127	Ken Schrom	15	Ron Davis	30
1984	Frank Viola	3.21	Frank Viola	10.5	Frank Viola	257.2	Frank Viola	149	Frank Viola	18	Ron Davis	29
1985	Frank Viola	4.09	Frank Viola	11.9	Mike Smithson	257.0	Frank Viola	135	Frank Viola	18	Ron Davis	25
1986	Bert Blyleven	4.01	Bert Blyleven	10.9	Bert Blyleven	271.2	Bert Blyleven	215	Bert Blyleven	17	Keith Atherton	10
1987	Frank Viola	2.90	Frank Viola	10.8	Bert Blyleven	267.0	Frank Viola	197	Frank Viola	17	Jeff Reardon	31
1988	Allan Anderson	2.45	Frank Viola	10.3	Frank Viola	255.1	Frank Viola	193	Frank Viola	24	Jeff Reardon	42
1989	Frank Viola	3.79	Frank Viola	11.3	Allan Anderson	196.2	Frank Viola	138	Allan Anderson	17	Jeff Reardon	31
1990	Allan Anderson	4.53	Allan Anderson	12.3	Allan Anderson	188.2	Mark Guthrie	101	Kevin Tapani	12	Rick Aguilera	32
							Kevin Tapani					
1991	Kevin Tapani	2.99	Kevin Tapani	9.8	Jack Morris	246.2	Jack Morris	163	Scott Erickson	20	Rick Aguilera	42
1992	John Smiley	3.21	John Smiley	10.3	John Smiley	241.0	John Smiley	163	John Smiley	16	Rick Aguilera	41
									Kevin Tapani			
1993	Willie Banks	4.04	Jim Deshaies	11.6	Kevin Tapani	225.2	Kevin Tapani	150	Kevin Tapani	12	Rick Aguilera	34
1994	Kevin Tapani	4.62	Kevin Tapani	12.9	Kevin Tapani	156.0	Scott Erickson	104	Kevin Tapani	11	Rick Aguilera	23
1995	Brad Radke	5.32	Brad Radke	12.2	Brad Radke	181.0	Kevin Tapani	88	Brad Radke	11	Rick Aguilera	12
1996	Brad Radke	4.46	Brad Radke	11.3	Brad Radke	232.0	Brad Radke	148	Frank Rodriguez	13	Dave Stevens	11
1997	Brad Radke	3.87	Brad Radke	10.9	Brad Radke	239.2	Brad Radke	174	Brad Radke	20	Rick Aguilera	26

Senators/Twins Franchise Batting Leaders—Career

Games

1	Harmon Killebrew	2,329
2	Sam Rice	2,307
3	Joe Judge	2,084
4	Clyde Milan	1,981
5	Ossie Bluege	1,867
6	Mickey Vernon	1,805
7	Kirby Puckett	1,783
8	Kent Hrbek	1,747
9	Eddie Yost	1,690
10	Tony Oliva	1,676
11	Buddy Myer	1,643
12	Rod Carew	1,635
13	Bob Allison	1,541
14	George McBride	1,458
15	Howard Shanks	1,396
16	Goose Goslin	1,361
	Gary Gaetti	1,361
18	Buddy Lewis	1,349
19	Cecil Travis	1,328
20	Bucky Harris	1,253

At-Bats

1	Sam Rice	8,934
2	Harmon Killebrew	7,835
3	Joe Judge	7,663
4	Clyde Milan	7,359
5	Kirby Puckett	7,244
6	Mickey Vernon	6,930
7	Ossie Bluege	6,440
8	Tony Oliva	6,301
9	Rod Carew	6,235
10	Kent Hrbek	6,192
11	Buddy Myer	6,033
12	Eddie Yost	6,011
13	Buddy Lewis	5,261
14	Goose Goslin	5,140
15	Bob Allison	5,032
16	Gary Gaetti	4,989
17	Cecil Travis	4,914
18	Howard Shanks	4,887
19	George McBride	4,833
20	Bucky Harris	4,717

Runs

1	Sam Rice	1,466
2	Harmon Killebrew	1,258
3	Joe Judge	1,154
4	Kirby Puckett	1,071
5	Buddy Myer	1,037
6	Clyde Milan	1,004
7	Eddie Yost	971
8	Mickey Vernon	956
9	Rod Carew	950
10	Kent Hrbek	903
11	Ossie Bluege	883
12	Tony Oliva	870
13	Goose Goslin	854
14	Buddy Lewis	830
15	Bob Allison	811
16	George Case	739
17	Bucky Harris	718
18	Joe Kuhel	713
	Chuck Knoblauch	713
20	Cecil Travis	665

Hits

1	Sam Rice	2,889
2	Kirby Puckett	2,304
3	Joe Judge	2,291
4	Clyde Milan	2,100
5	Rod Carew	2,085
6	Harmon Killebrew	2,024
7	Mickey Vernon	1,993
8	Tony Oliva	1,917
9	Buddy Myer	1,828
10	Ossie Bluege	1,751
11	Kent Hrbek	1,749
12	Goose Goslin	1,659
13	Buddy Lewis	1,563
14	Cecil Travis	1,544
15	Eddie Yost	1,521
16	Joe Kuhel	1,338
17	George Case	1,306
18	Bucky Harris	1,295
19	Bob Allison	1,281
20	Gary Gaetti	1,276

Doubles

1	Sam Rice	478
2	Joe Judge	421
3	Kirby Puckett	414
4	Mickey Vernon	391
5	Tony Oliva	329
6	Kent Hrbek	312
7	Buddy Myer	305
	Rod Carew	305
9	Goose Goslin	289
10	Eddie Yost	282
11	Harmon Killebrew	277
12	Ossie Bluege	276
13	Cecil Travis	265
14	Gary Gaetti	252
15	Joe Kuhel	250
16	Buddy Lewis	249
17	Joe Cronin	242
18	Clyde Milan	240
19	Bucky Harris	223
20	Bob Allison	216

Triples

1	Sam Rice	183
2	Joe Judge	157
3	Goose Goslin	125
4	Buddy Myer	113
5	Mickey Vernon	108
6	Clyde Milan	105
7	Buddy Lewis	93
8	Rod Carew	90
9	Howard Shanks	88
10	Cecil Travis	78
11	Joe Kuhel	77
12	Joe Cronin	72
13	Heinie Manush	70
14	Ossie Bluege	67
15	Sammy West	65
16	Bucky Harris	64
17	Eddie Foster	59
18	Zoilo Versalles	58
19	Kirby Puckett	57
20	John Stone	55

Home Runs

1	Harmon Killebrew	559
2	Kent Hrbek	293
3	Bob Allison	256
4	Tony Oliva	220
5	Kirby Puckett	207
6	Gary Gaetti	201
7	Roy Sievers	180
8	Tom Brunansky	163
9	Jim Lemon	159
10	Goose Goslin	127
11	Mickey Vernon	121
12	Roy Smalley	110
13	Eddie Yost	101
14	Jimmie Hall	98
15	Randy Bush	96
16	Don Mincher	92
17	Earl Battey	91
18	Zoilo Versalles	87
	Larry Hisle	87
20	Tim Laudner	77

RBI

1	Harmon Killebrew	1,540
2	Kent Hrbek	1,086
3	Kirby Puckett	1,085
4	Sam Rice	1,045
5	Mickey Vernon	1,026
6	Joe Judge	1,001
7	Tony Oliva	947
8	Goose Goslin	931
9	Ossie Bluege	848
10	Bob Allison	796
11	Buddy Myer	759
12	Gary Gaetti	758
13	Rod Carew	733
14	Joe Cronin	673
15	Joe Kuhel	667
16	Cecil Travis	657
17	Clyde Milan	617
18	Buddy Lewis	607
19	Roy Sievers	574
20	Eddie Yost	550

Walks

1	Harmon Killebrew	1,505
2	Eddie Yost	1,274
3	Joe Judge	943
4	Buddy Myer	864
5	Kent Hrbek	838
6	Bob Allison	795
7	Mickey Vernon	735
8	Ossie Bluege	724
9	Clyde Milan	685
10	Sam Rice	681
11	Rod Carew	613
12	Buddy Lewis	573
13	Roy Smalley	549
14	Joe Kuhel	530
15	Chuck Knoblauch	513
16	Goose Goslin	488
17	Bucky Harris	469
18	Joe Cronin	466
19	Kirby Puckett	450
20	Tony Oliva	448

Strikeouts

1	Harmon Killebrew	1,629
2	Bob Allison	1,033
3	Kirby Puckett	965
4	Gary Gaetti	877
5	Kent Hrbek	798
6	Rod Carew	716
7	Jim Lemon	710
8	Eddie Yost	705
9	Greg Gagne	676
10	Mickey Vernon	657
11	Tony Oliva	645
12	Zoilo Versalles	626
13	Roy Smalley	606
14	Tom Brunansky	589
15	Tim Laudner	553
16	Ossie Bluege	525
17	Randy Bush	505
18	Larry Hisle	478
19	Joe Judge	463
20	Four tied at	453

Stolen Bases

1	Clyde Milan	495
2	Sam Rice	346
3	George Case	321
4	Chuck Knoblauch	276
5	Rod Carew	271
6	Joe Judge	210
7	Cesar Tovar	186
8	Howard Shanks	176
9	Eddie Foster	166
10	Bucky Harris	165
11	Danny Moeller	163
12	Ossie Bluege	140
13	Kirby Puckett	134
14	Mickey Vernon	125
15	Buddy Myer	117
16	George McBride	116
	Goose Goslin	116
	Dan Gladden	116
19	Jake Stahl	96
20	Chick Gandil	93

Runs Created

1	Harmon Killebrew	1,527
2	Sam Rice	1,447
3	Joe Judge	1,264
4	Kirby Puckett	1,194
5	Rod Carew	1,080
6	Mickey Vernon	1,077
7	Kent Hrbek	1,069
8	Clyde Milan	1,030
9	Buddy Myer	1,026
10	Tony Oliva	1,023
11	Goose Goslin	989
12	Eddie Yost	977
13	Ossie Bluege	874
14	Bob Allison	868
15	Buddy Lewis	813
16	Cecil Travis	750
17	Joe Kuhel	736
18	Chuck Knoblauch	706
19	Joe Cronin	663
20	Gary Gaetti	649

Runs Created/27 Outs
(minimum 2000 Plate Appearances)

1	Goose Goslin	7.05
2	John Stone	6.98
3	Heinie Manush	6.89
4	Harmon Killebrew	6.73
5	Joe Cronin	6.70
6	Shane Mack	6.53
7	Chuck Knoblauch	6.47
8	Rod Carew	6.45
9	Stan Spence	6.34
10	Roy Sievers	6.24
11	Kent Hrbek	6.11
12	Buddy Myer	6.10
13	Kirby Puckett	6.08
14	Tony Oliva	5.96
15	Sam Rice	5.91
16	Bob Allison	5.91
17	Joe Judge	5.78
18	Joe Kuhel	5.70
19	Larry Hisle	5.65
20	Cecil Travis	5.62

Batting Average
(minimum 2000 Plate Appearances)

1	Rod Carew	.334
2	Heinie Manush	.328
3	Sam Rice	.323
4	Goose Goslin	.323
5	Kirby Puckett	.318
6	John Stone	.317
7	Cecil Travis	.314
8	Shane Mack	.309
9	Brian Harper	.306
10	Joe Cronin	.304
11	Tony Oliva	.304
12	Chuck Knoblauch	.304
13	Buddy Myer	.303
14	Joe Judge	.299
15	Buddy Lewis	.297
16	Sammy West	.297
17	Stan Spence	.296
18	Chick Gandil	.293
19	Muddy Ruel	.290
20	Joe Kuhel	.288

On-Base Percentage
(minimum 2000 Plate Appearances)

1	Rod Carew	.393
2	Buddy Myer	.392
3	John Stone	.392
4	Chuck Knoblauch	.391
5	Eddie Yost	.389
6	Joe Cronin	.387
7	Goose Goslin	.386
8	Muddy Ruel	.382
9	Joe Judge	.379
10	Harmon Killebrew	.378
11	Stan Spence	.377
12	Steve Braun	.376
13	Shane Mack	.375
14	Sam Rice	.375
15	Rick Ferrell	.374
16	Heinie Manush	.371
17	Cecil Travis	.370
18	Buddy Lewis	.368
19	Kent Hrbek	.367
20	Joe Kuhel	.364

Slugging Percentage
(minimum 2000 Plate Appearances)

1	Harmon Killebrew	.514
2	Goose Goslin	.502
3	Roy Sievers	.500
4	Jimmie Hall	.481
5	Kent Hrbek	.481
6	Shane Mack	.479
7	Heinie Manush	.478
8	Kirby Puckett	.477
9	Tony Oliva	.476
10	John Stone	.476
11	Bob Allison	.471
12	Jim Lemon	.470
13	Larry Hisle	.457
14	Joe Cronin	.455
15	Stan Spence	.453
16	Tom Brunansky	.452
17	Rod Carew	.448
18	Gary Gaetti	.437
19	Dan Ford	.435
20	Brian Harper	.431

Teams: Twins

Senators/Twins Franchise Pitching Leaders—Career

Wins

1	Walter Johnson	417
2	Jim Kaat	190
3	Bert Blyleven	149
4	Camilo Pascual	145
5	Jim Perry	128
6	Dutch Leonard	118
7	Firpo Marberry	116
8	Frank Viola	112
9	Casey Patten	105
10	General Crowder	98
11	Tom Zachary	96
	Dave Goltz	96
13	Sid Hudson	88
14	Long Tom Hughes	84
15	Jim Shaw	83
16	Pedro Ramos	78
17	Kevin Tapani	75
18	Mickey Haefner	73
19	Bob Groom	72
	Early Wynn	72

Losses

1	Walter Johnson	279
2	Jim Kaat	159
3	Camilo Pascual	141
4	Bert Blyleven	138
5	Sid Hudson	130
6	Casey Patten	127
7	Long Tom Hughes	124
8	Pedro Ramos	112
9	Tom Zachary	103
10	Dutch Leonard	101
11	Jim Shaw	98
12	Frank Viola	93
13	Chuck Stobbs	92
14	Jim Perry	90
15	Bob Groom	89
16	Walt Masterson	88
17	Early Wynn	87
18	Dave Goltz	79
19	Mickey Haefner	77
20	Firpo Marberry	72

Winning Percentage

(minimum 100 decisions)

1	Firpo Marberry	.617
2	Walter Johnson	.599
3	Earl Whitehill	.598
4	Jim Perry	.587
5	General Crowder	.587
6	Montie Weaver	.583
7	George Mogridge	.561
8	Dave Boswell	.554
9	Dave Goltz	.549
10	Frank Viola	.546
11	Jim Kaat	.544
12	Kevin Tapani	.543
13	Lloyd Brown	.542
14	Dutch Leonard	.539
15	Bert Blyleven	.519
16	Bob Porterfield	.511
17	Camilo Pascual	.507
18	Scott Erickson	.504
19	Geoff Zahn	.500
20	Bump Hadley	.489

Games

1	Walter Johnson	802
2	Jim Kaat	484
3	Firpo Marberry	470
4	Camilo Pascual	432
5	Rick Aguilera	405
6	Jim Perry	376
7	Bert Blyleven	348
8	Al Worthington	327
9	Chuck Stobbs	302
10	Sid Hudson	296
11	Pedro Ramos	290
12	Jim Shaw	287
13	Ron Davis	286
14	Long Tom Hughes	285
15	Walt Masterson	278
16	Tom Zachary	273
17	Casey Patten	269
18	Dutch Leonard	262
19	Frank Viola	260
20	Alex Carrasquel	255

Games Started

1	Walter Johnson	666
2	Jim Kaat	433
3	Bert Blyleven	345
4	Camilo Pascual	331
5	Frank Viola	259
6	Dutch Leonard	251
7	Jim Perry	249
8	Sid Hudson	239
9	Casey Patten	237
10	Dave Goltz	215
11	Tom Zachary	210
12	Long Tom Hughes	206
13	Pedro Ramos	199
14	Jim Shaw	194
15	Kevin Tapani	180
16	Bob Groom	169
17	Early Wynn	168
18	Bump Hadley	162
	Walt Masterson	162
20	General Crowder	161

Complete Games

1	Walter Johnson	531
2	Casey Patten	206
3	Bert Blyleven	141
4	Long Tom Hughes	139
5	Jim Kaat	133
6	Dutch Leonard	130
7	Camilo Pascual	119
8	Sid Hudson	112
9	Bob Groom	106
10	Jim Shaw	96
11	Tom Zachary	92
	Early Wynn	92
13	Jack Townsend	85
	General Crowder	85
15	Mickey Haefner	84
16	Dave Goltz	80
17	Bob Porterfield	78
18	Bobo Newsom	76
19	Al Orth	73
20	George Mogridge	72

Shutouts

1	Walter Johnson	110
2	Camilo Pascual	31
3	Bert Blyleven	29
4	Dutch Leonard	23
	Jim Kaat	23
6	Bob Porterfield	19
7	Jim Shaw	17
	Jim Perry	17
9	Casey Patten	16
	Long Tom Hughes	16
11	Walt Masterson	15
12	Doc Ayers	13
13	Bob Groom	12
	George Mogridge	12
	Mickey Haefner	12
16	Harry Harper	11
	Sid Hudson	11
	Dean Chance	11
	Dave Goltz	11
20	Nine tied at	10

Saves

1	Rick Aguilera	210
2	Ron Davis	108
3	Jeff Reardon	104
4	Firpo Marberry	96
5	Al Worthington	88
6	Ron Perranoski	76
7	Mike Marshall	54
8	Bill Campbell	51
9	Doug Corbett	43
10	Ray Moore	38
11	Walter Johnson	34
12	Tex Clevenger	29
13	Garland Braxton	28
14	Jack Russell	26
15	Dick Hyde	23
	Tom Burgmeier	23
17	Tom Ferrick	22
	Tom Johnson	22
19	Bill Dailey	21
	Dave Stevens	21

Innings Pitched

1	Walter Johnson	5,914.2
2	Jim Kaat	3,014.1
3	Bert Blyleven	2,566.2
4	Camilo Pascual	2,465.0
5	Casey Patten	2,059.1
6	Dutch Leonard	1,899.1
7	Jim Perry	1,883.1
8	Sid Hudson	1,819.1
9	Long Tom Hughes	1,776.0
10	Frank Viola	1,772.2
11	Firpo Marberry	1,654.0
12	Dave Goltz	1,638.0
13	Jim Shaw	1,600.1
14	Tom Zachary	1,589.0
15	Pedro Ramos	1,544.1
16	Bob Groom	1,353.2
17	Walt Masterson	1,347.0
18	General Crowder	1,331.0
19	Bump Hadley	1,299.0
20	Mickey Haefner	1,291.2

Walks

1	Walter Johnson	1,363
2	Camilo Pascual	909
3	Jim Kaat	729
4	Sid Hudson	720
5	Walt Masterson	694
6	Jim Shaw	688
7	Bert Blyleven	674
8	Bump Hadley	572
9	Firpo Marberry	568
10	Long Tom Hughes	567
11	Casey Patten	556
12	Ken Chase	549
13	Jim Perry	541
14	Frank Viola	521
15	Bobo Newsom	497
16	Dave Goltz	493
17	Pedro Ramos	491
18	Harry Harper	488
19	Mickey Haefner	479
20	Six tied at	460

Strikeouts

1	Walter Johnson	3,509
2	Bert Blyleven	2,035
3	Camilo Pascual	1,885
4	Jim Kaat	1,851
5	Frank Viola	1,214
6	Jim Perry	1,025
7	Dave Goltz	887
8	Long Tom Hughes	884
9	Dave Boswell	865
10	Jim Shaw	767
11	Casey Patten	757
12	Pedro Ramos	740
13	Kevin Tapani	724
14	Bob Groom	699
15	Firpo Marberry	667
16	Walt Masterson	666
17	Dutch Leonard	657
18	Bump Hadley	601
19	Sid Hudson	597
20	Chuck Stobbs	567

Strikeouts/9 Innings

(minimum 1000 Innings Pitched)

1	Dave Boswell	7.51
2	Bert Blyleven	7.14
3	Camilo Pascual	6.88
4	Frank Viola	6.16
5	Kevin Tapani	5.56
6	Jim Kaat	5.53
7	Walter Johnson	5.34
8	Jim Perry	4.90
9	Dave Goltz	4.87
10	Bob Groom	4.65
11	Harry Harper	4.57
12	Long Tom Hughes	4.48
13	Walt Masterson	4.45
14	Jim Shaw	4.31
15	Pedro Ramos	4.31
16	Bobo Newsom	4.26
17	Bump Hadley	4.16
18	Chuck Stobbs	4.12
19	Doc Ayers	3.91
20	Firpo Marberry	3.63

ERA

(minimum 1000 Innings Pitched)

1	Walter Johnson	2.17
2	Doc Ayers	2.66
3	Harry Harper	2.75
4	Long Tom Hughes	2.99
5	Bob Groom	3.04
6	Jim Shaw	3.06
7	Jim Perry	3.15
8	Dutch Leonard	3.27
9	Bert Blyleven	3.28
10	Mickey Haefner	3.29
11	Jim Kaat	3.34
12	Casey Patten	3.34
13	George Mogridge	3.35
14	Bob Porterfield	3.38
15	Dave Goltz	3.48
16	Dave Boswell	3.49
17	Firpo Marberry	3.59
18	Camilo Pascual	3.66
19	Tom Zachary	3.78
20	Frank Viola	3.86

Component ERA

(minimum 1000 Innings Pitched)

1	Walter Johnson	2.12
2	Doc Ayers	2.68
3	Harry Harper	2.92
4	Bob Groom	3.04
5	Jim Shaw	3.06
6	Dutch Leonard	3.12
7	Long Tom Hughes	3.12
8	Jim Perry	3.13
9	Bert Blyleven	3.22
10	Mickey Haefner	3.24
11	Dave Boswell	3.25
12	Casey Patten	3.28
13	Firpo Marberry	3.36
14	Bob Porterfield	3.41
15	Camilo Pascual	3.42
16	Jim Kaat	3.43
17	General Crowder	3.55
18	George Mogridge	3.56
19	Bump Hadley	3.61
20	Dave Goltz	3.63

Opponent Average

(minimum 1000 Innings Pitched)

1	Dave Boswell	.217
2	Walter Johnson	.227
3	Harry Harper	.236
4	Jim Perry	.242
5	Camilo Pascual	.244
6	Bert Blyleven	.246
7	Jim Shaw	.247
8	Mickey Haefner	.248
9	Walt Masterson	.253
10	Doc Ayers	.255
11	Long Tom Hughes	.256
12	Bob Groom	.256
13	Jim Kaat	.256
14	Bump Hadley	.257
15	Bob Porterfield	.259
16	Frank Viola	.260
17	Firpo Marberry	.261
18	Dutch Leonard	.263
19	Pedro Ramos	.264
20	Dave Goltz	.264

Opponent OBP

(minimum 1000 Innings Pitched)

1	Walter Johnson	.279
2	Jim Perry	.298
3	Bert Blyleven	.299
4	Jim Kaat	.304
5	Dutch Leonard	.304
6	Dave Boswell	.306
7	Kevin Tapani	.309
8	Doc Ayers	.310
9	Camilo Pascual	.313
10	Frank Viola	.314
11	Dave Goltz	.318
12	Bob Groom	.319
13	Mickey Haefner	.319
14	Bob Porterfield	.319
15	Long Tom Hughes	.320
16	Casey Patten	.320
17	Pedro Ramos	.322
18	General Crowder	.324
19	George Mogridge	.326
20	Firpo Marberry	.327

Teams: Twins

Washington Senators I Team Batting Leaders—Career

Games

1	Sam Rice	2,307
2	Joe Judge	2,084
3	Clyde Milan	1,981
4	Ossie Bluege	1,867
5	Mickey Vernon	1,805
6	Eddie Yost	1,690
7	Buddy Myer	1,643
8	George McBride	1,458
9	Howard Shanks	1,396
10	Goose Goslin	1,361
11	Buddy Lewis	1,349
12	Cecil Travis	1,328
13	Bucky Harris	1,253
14	Joe Kuhel	1,205
15	Eddie Foster	1,121
16	George Case	1,108
17	Sammy West	993
18	Joe Cronin	940
19	Walter Johnson	928
20	Pete Runnels	921

At-Bats

1	Sam Rice	8,934
2	Joe Judge	7,663
3	Clyde Milan	7,359
4	Mickey Vernon	6,930
5	Ossie Bluege	6,440
6	Buddy Myer	6,033
7	Eddie Yost	6,011
8	Buddy Lewis	5,261
9	Goose Goslin	5,140
10	Cecil Travis	4,914
11	Howard Shanks	4,887
12	George McBride	4,833
13	Bucky Harris	4,717
14	Joe Kuhel	4,638
15	George Case	4,533
16	Eddie Foster	4,418
17	Joe Cronin	3,582
18	Pete Runnels	3,356
19	Sammy West	3,316
20	Heinie Manush	3,290

Runs

1	Sam Rice	1,466
2	Joe Judge	1,154
3	Buddy Myer	1,037
4	Clyde Milan	1,004
5	Eddie Yost	971
6	Mickey Vernon	956
7	Ossie Bluege	883
8	Goose Goslin	854
9	Buddy Lewis	830
10	George Case	739
11	Bucky Harris	718
12	Joe Kuhel	713
13	Cecil Travis	665
14	Eddie Foster	579
15	Joe Cronin	577
16	Heinie Manush	576
17	Howard Shanks	529
18	Sammy West	481
19	Roy Sievers	480
20	George McBride	461

Hits

1	Sam Rice	2,889
2	Joe Judge	2,291
3	Clyde Milan	2,100
4	Mickey Vernon	1,993
5	Buddy Myer	1,828
6	Ossie Bluege	1,751
7	Goose Goslin	1,659
8	Buddy Lewis	1,563
9	Cecil Travis	1,544
10	Eddie Yost	1,521
11	Joe Kuhel	1,338
12	George Case	1,306
13	Bucky Harris	1,295
14	Howard Shanks	1,232
15	Eddie Foster	1,177
16	Joe Cronin	1,090
17	Heinie Manush	1,078
18	George McBride	1,068
19	Sammy West	984
20	Pete Runnels	921

Doubles

1	Sam Rice	478
2	Joe Judge	421
3	Mickey Vernon	391
4	Buddy Myer	305
5	Goose Goslin	289
6	Eddie Yost	282
7	Ossie Bluege	276
8	Cecil Travis	265
9	Joe Kuhel	250
10	Buddy Lewis	249
11	Joe Cronin	242
12	Clyde Milan	240
13	Bucky Harris	223
14	Heinie Manush	215
15	George Case	210
16	Sammy West	187
17	Howard Shanks	174
18	Stan Spence	153
19	Eddie Foster	145
20	Roy Sievers	133

Triples

1	Sam Rice	183
2	Joe Judge	157
3	Goose Goslin	125
4	Buddy Myer	113
5	Mickey Vernon	108
6	Clyde Milan	105
7	Buddy Lewis	93
8	Howard Shanks	88
9	Cecil Travis	78
10	Joe Kuhel	77
11	Joe Cronin	72
12	Heinie Manush	70
13	Ossie Bluege	67
14	Sammy West	65
15	Bucky Harris	64
16	Eddie Foster	59
17	John Stone	55
18	Eddie Yost	53
19	Stan Spence	49
20	Chick Gandil	48

Home Runs

1	Roy Sievers	180
2	Jim Lemon	144
3	Goose Goslin	127
4	Mickey Vernon	121
5	Eddie Yost	101
6	Harmon Killebrew	84
7	Joe Judge	71
	Buddy Lewis	71
9	Stan Spence	66
10	Joe Kuhel	56
11	Joe Cronin	51
12	Heinie Manush	47
13	Bob Allison	45
14	Ossie Bluege	43
15	Gil Coan	36
16	Buddy Myer	35
17	Sam Rice	33
18	John Stone	32
19	Sammy West	30
20	Two tied at	29

RBI

1	Sam Rice	1,045
2	Mickey Vernon	1,026
3	Joe Judge	1,001
4	Goose Goslin	931
5	Ossie Bluege	848
6	Buddy Myer	759
7	Joe Cronin	673
8	Joe Kuhel	667
9	Cecil Travis	657
10	Clyde Milan	617
11	Buddy Lewis	607
12	Roy Sievers	574
13	Eddie Yost	550
14	Howard Shanks	520
15	Bucky Harris	506
16	Heinie Manush	491
17	Sammy West	485
18	Jim Lemon	451
19	Stan Spence	427
20	George McBride	393

Walks

1	Eddie Yost	1,274
2	Joe Judge	943
3	Buddy Myer	864
4	Mickey Vernon	735
5	Ossie Bluege	724
6	Clyde Milan	685
7	Sam Rice	681
8	Buddy Lewis	573
9	Joe Kuhel	530
10	Goose Goslin	488
11	Bucky Harris	469
12	Joe Cronin	466
13	Roy Sievers	435
14	Pete Runnels	413
15	Muddy Ruel	403
16	Cecil Travis	402
17	George Case	392
18	Eddie Foster	385
19	George McBride	381
20	Stan Spence	358

Strikeouts

1	Eddie Yost	705
2	Mickey Vernon	657
3	Jim Lemon	603
4	Ossie Bluege	525
5	Joe Judge	463
6	Roy Sievers	411
7	Buddy Myer	385
8	Howard Shanks	379
9	Gil Coan	345
10	Pete Runnels	341
11	Goose Goslin	337
12	Joe Kuhel	318
13	Harmon Killebrew	315
14	Bucky Harris	307
15	Buddy Lewis	303
16	Cecil Travis	291
17	Danny Moeller	290
18	Joe Cronin	274
19	George McBride	271
20	Sam Rice	266

Stolen Bases

1	Clyde Milan	495
2	Sam Rice	346
3	George Case	321
4	Joe Judge	210
5	Howard Shanks	176
6	Eddie Foster	166
7	Bucky Harris	165
8	Danny Moeller	163
9	Ossie Bluege	140
10	Mickey Vernon	125
11	Buddy Myer	117
12	George McBride	116
	Goose Goslin	116
14	Jake Stahl	96
15	Chick Gandil	93
16	Ray Morgan	87
17	Bill Coughlin	85
18	Charlie Jones	84
19	Dave Altizer	83
	Buddy Lewis	83

Runs Created

1	Sam Rice	1,447
2	Joe Judge	1,264
3	Mickey Vernon	1,077
4	Clyde Milan	1,030
5	Buddy Myer	1,026
6	Goose Goslin	989
7	Eddie Yost	977
8	Ossie Bluege	874
9	Buddy Lewis	813
10	Cecil Travis	750
11	Joe Kuhel	736
12	Joe Cronin	663
13	Bucky Harris	627
	George Case	627
15	Heinie Manush	596
16	Roy Sievers	549
17	Howard Shanks	533
18	Eddie Foster	532
19	Sammy West	511
20	Stan Spence	493

Runs Created/27 Outs

(minimum 2000 Plate Appearances)

1	Goose Goslin	7.05
2	John Stone	6.98
3	Heinie Manush	6.89
4	Joe Cronin	6.70
5	Stan Spence	6.34
6	Roy Sievers	6.24
7	Buddy Myer	6.10
8	Sam Rice	5.91
9	Joe Judge	5.78
10	Joe Kuhel	5.70
11	Cecil Travis	5.62
12	Jim Lemon	5.56
13	Mickey Vernon	5.55
14	Eddie Yost	5.52
15	Buddy Lewis	5.51
16	Sammy West	5.50
17	Chick Gandil	5.15
18	Muddy Ruel	4.99
19	George Case	4.95
20	Clyde Milan	4.85

Batting Average

(minimum 2000 Plate Appearances)

1	Heinie Manush	.328
2	Sam Rice	.323
3	Goose Goslin	.323
4	John Stone	.317
5	Cecil Travis	.314
6	Joe Cronin	.304
7	Buddy Myer	.303
8	Joe Judge	.299
9	Buddy Lewis	.297
10	Sammy West	.297
11	Stan Spence	.296
12	Chick Gandil	.293
13	Muddy Ruel	.290
14	Joe Kuhel	.288
15	George Case	.288
16	Mickey Vernon	.288
17	Clyde Milan	.285
18	Jim Busby	.281
19	Bucky Harris	.275
20	Pete Runnels	.274

On-Base Percentage

(minimum 2000 Plate Appearances)

1	Buddy Myer	.392
2	John Stone	.392
3	Eddie Yost	.389
4	Joe Cronin	.387
5	Goose Goslin	.386
6	Muddy Ruel	.382
7	Joe Judge	.379
8	Stan Spence	.377
9	Sam Rice	.375
10	Rick Ferrell	.374
11	Heinie Manush	.371
12	Cecil Travis	.370
13	Buddy Lewis	.368
14	Joe Kuhel	.364
15	Roy Sievers	.359
16	Sammy West	.358
17	Mickey Vernon	.358
18	Pete Runnels	.354
19	Clyde Milan	.353
20	Bucky Harris	.353

Slugging Percentage

(minimum 2000 Plate Appearances)

1	Goose Goslin	.502
2	Roy Sievers	.500
3	Jim Lemon	.480
4	Heinie Manush	.478
5	John Stone	.476
6	Joe Cronin	.455
7	Stan Spence	.453
8	Sam Rice	.429
9	Mickey Vernon	.428
10	Joe Judge	.423
11	Buddy Lewis	.420
12	Sammy West	.419
13	Cecil Travis	.416
14	Joe Kuhel	.412
15	Buddy Myer	.408
16	Chick Gandil	.397
17	Jim Busby	.377
18	Eddie Yost	.368
19	Patsy Gharrity	.366
20	George Case	.365

Teams: Twins

Washington Senators I Team Pitching Leaders—Career

Wins

1	Walter Johnson	417
2	Dutch Leonard	118
3	Firpo Marberry	116
4	Casey Patten	105
5	General Crowder	98
6	Tom Zachary	96
7	Sid Hudson	88
8	Long Tom Hughes	84
9	Jim Shaw	83
10	Mickey Haefner	73
11	Bob Groom	72
	Early Wynn	72
13	Montie Weaver	70
14	George Mogridge	69
15	Bump Hadley	68
16	Bob Porterfield	67
	Pedro Ramos	67
18	Earl Whitehill	64
	Chuck Stobbs	64
20	Walt Masterson	62

Losses

1	Walter Johnson	279
2	Sid Hudson	130
3	Casey Patten	127
4	Long Tom Hughes	124
5	Tom Zachary	103
6	Dutch Leonard	101
7	Jim Shaw	98
8	Pedro Ramos	92
9	Bob Groom	89
	Chuck Stobbs	89
11	Walt Masterson	88
12	Early Wynn	87
13	Camilo Pascual	84
14	Mickey Haefner	77
15	Firpo Marberry	72
16	Bump Hadley	71
17	Jack Townsend	69
	General Crowder	69
19	Ken Chase	67
20	Bobo Newsom	66

Winning Percentage
(minimum 100 decisions)

1	Firpo Marberry	.617
2	Walter Johnson	.599
3	Earl Whitehill	.598
4	General Crowder	.587
5	Montie Weaver	.583
6	George Mogridge	.561
7	Lloyd Brown	.542
8	Dutch Leonard	.539
9	Bob Porterfield	.511
10	Bump Hadley	.489
11	Mickey Haefner	.487
12	Ray Scarborough	.485
13	Tom Zachary	.482
14	Bobo Newsom	.480
15	Doc Ayers	.466
16	Jim Shaw	.459
17	Harry Harper	.453
	Early Wynn	.453
19	Casey Patten	.453
20	Bob Groom	.447

Games

1	Walter Johnson	802
2	Firpo Marberry	470
3	Sid Hudson	296
4	Jim Shaw	287
5	Long Tom Hughes	285
6	Walt Masterson	278
	Chuck Stobbs	278
8	Tom Zachary	273
9	Casey Patten	269
10	Dutch Leonard	262
11	Alex Carrasquel	255
12	Bobby Burke	252
13	Camilo Pascual	248
	Pedro Ramos	248
15	General Crowder	236
16	Bump Hadley	233
17	Tex Clevenger	230
18	Doc Ayers	227
19	Mickey Haefner	215
20	Bob Groom	195

Games Started

1	Walter Johnson	666
2	Dutch Leonard	251
3	Sid Hudson	239
4	Casey Patten	237
5	Tom Zachary	210
6	Long Tom Hughes	206
7	Jim Shaw	194
8	Bob Groom	169
9	Early Wynn	168
10	Pedro Ramos	165
11	Bump Hadley	162
	Walt Masterson	162
13	General Crowder	161
14	Mickey Haefner	156
15	Chuck Stobbs	152
	Camilo Pascual	152
17	Bobo Newsom	141
18	Harry Harper	140
19	Bob Porterfield	138
20	George Mogridge	136

Complete Games

1	Walter Johnson	531
2	Casey Patten	206
3	Long Tom Hughes	139
4	Dutch Leonard	130
5	Sid Hudson	112
6	Bob Groom	106
7	Jim Shaw	96
8	Tom Zachary	92
	Early Wynn	92
10	Jack Townsend	85
	General Crowder	85
12	Mickey Haefner	84
13	Bob Porterfield	78
14	Bobo Newsom	76
15	Al Orth	73
16	George Mogridge	72
17	Earl Whitehill	67
18	Bump Hadley	66
19	Firpo Marberry	64
20	Walt Masterson	63

Shutouts

1	Walter Johnson	110
2	Dutch Leonard	23
3	Bob Porterfield	19
4	Jim Shaw	17
5	Casey Patten	16
	Long Tom Hughes	16
7	Walt Masterson	15
8	Doc Ayers	13
	Camilo Pascual	13
10	Bob Groom	12
	George Mogridge	12
	Mickey Haefner	12
13	Harry Harper	11
	Sid Hudson	11
15	Tom Zachary	10
	Bobo Newsom	10
17	Joe Boehling	9
	Early Wynn	9
19	Seven tied at	7

Saves

1	Firpo Marberry	96
2	Walter Johnson	34
3	Tex Clevenger	29
4	Garland Braxton	28
5	Jack Russell	26
6	Dick Hyde	23
7	Tom Ferrick	22
8	Long Tom Hughes	20
9	Allan Russell	19
	Mickey Harris	19
11	Jim Shaw	17
	Pete Appleton	17
13	Alex Carrasquel	16
14	Chuck Stobbs	14
15	Doc Ayers	13
	Walt Masterson	13
	Ray Moore	13
18	General Crowder	12
	Mickey Haefner	12
20	Bud Byerly	11

Innings Pitched

1	Walter Johnson	5,914.2
2	Casey Patten	2,059.1
3	Dutch Leonard	1,899.1
4	Sid Hudson	1,819.1
5	Long Tom Hughes	1,776.0
6	Firpo Marberry	1,654.0
7	Jim Shaw	1,600.1
8	Tom Zachary	1,589.0
9	Bob Groom	1,353.2
10	Walt Masterson	1,347.0
11	General Crowder	1,331.0
12	Bump Hadley	1,299.0
13	Mickey Haefner	1,291.2
14	Pedro Ramos	1,280.0
15	Early Wynn	1,266.2
16	Chuck Stobbs	1,193.2
17	Camilo Pascual	1,180.1
18	Doc Ayers	1,122.1
19	Bobo Newsom	1,079.1
20	Bob Porterfield	1,041.2

Walks

1	Walter Johnson	1,363
2	Sid Hudson	720
3	Walt Masterson	694
4	Jim Shaw	688
5	Bump Hadley	572
6	Firpo Marberry	568
7	Long Tom Hughes	567
8	Casey Patten	556
9	Ken Chase	549
10	Bobo Newsom	497
11	Harry Harper	488
12	Mickey Haefner	479
13	Camilo Pascual	478
14	Tom Zachary	460
	Early Wynn	460
16	General Crowder	439
17	Bob Groom	424
18	Montie Weaver	422
19	Pedro Ramos	412
20	Dutch Leonard	403

Strikeouts

1	Walter Johnson	3,509
2	Camilo Pascual	891
3	Long Tom Hughes	884
4	Jim Shaw	767
5	Casey Patten	757
6	Bob Groom	699
7	Firpo Marberry	667
8	Walt Masterson	666
9	Dutch Leonard	657
10	Bump Hadley	601
11	Sid Hudson	597
12	Pedro Ramos	566
13	Chuck Stobbs	550
14	Harry Harper	526
15	Bobo Newsom	511
16	Doc Ayers	487
17	Mickey Haefner	464
18	Ken Chase	453
19	General Crowder	450
20	Early Wynn	386

Strikeouts/9 Innings
(minimum 1000 Innings Pitched)

1	Camilo Pascual	6.79
2	Walter Johnson	5.34
3	Bob Groom	4.65
4	Harry Harper	4.57
5	Long Tom Hughes	4.48
6	Walt Masterson	4.45
7	Jim Shaw	4.31
8	Bobo Newsom	4.26
9	Bump Hadley	4.16
10	Chuck Stobbs	4.15
11	Pedro Ramos	3.98
12	Doc Ayers	3.91
13	Firpo Marberry	3.63
14	Casey Patten	3.31
15	Mickey Haefner	3.23
16	Bob Porterfield	3.16
17	Dutch Leonard	3.11
18	General Crowder	3.04
19	Sid Hudson	2.95
20	Early Wynn	2.74

ERA
(minimum 1000 Innings Pitched)

1	Walter Johnson	2.17
2	Doc Ayers	2.66
3	Harry Harper	2.75
4	Long Tom Hughes	2.99
5	Bob Groom	3.04
6	Jim Shaw	3.06
7	Dutch Leonard	3.27
8	Mickey Haefner	3.29
9	Casey Patten	3.34
10	George Mogridge	3.35
11	Bob Porterfield	3.38
12	Firpo Marberry	3.59
13	Tom Zachary	3.78
14	Early Wynn	3.94
15	Walt Masterson	3.98
16	General Crowder	3.98
17	Bump Hadley	3.98
18	Camilo Pascual	4.04
19	Chuck Stobbs	4.15
20	Pedro Ramos	4.24

Component ERA
(minimum 1000 Innings Pitched)

1	Walter Johnson	2.12
2	Doc Ayers	2.68
3	Harry Harper	2.92
4	Bob Groom	3.04
5	Jim Shaw	3.06
6	Dutch Leonard	3.12
7	Long Tom Hughes	3.12
8	Mickey Haefner	3.24
9	Casey Patten	3.28
10	Firpo Marberry	3.36
11	Bob Porterfield	3.41
12	General Crowder	3.55
13	George Mogridge	3.56
14	Bump Hadley	3.61
15	Camilo Pascual	3.78
16	Walt Masterson	3.93
17	Early Wynn	3.93
18	Tom Zachary	4.01
19	Chuck Stobbs	4.13
20	Bobo Newsom	4.14

Opponent Average
(minimum 1000 Innings Pitched)

1	Walter Johnson	.227
2	Harry Harper	.236
3	Jim Shaw	.247
4	Mickey Haefner	.248
5	Walt Masterson	.253
6	Doc Ayers	.255
7	Long Tom Hughes	.256
8	Bob Groom	.256
9	Camilo Pascual	.256
10	Bump Hadley	.257
11	Bob Porterfield	.259
12	Firpo Marberry	.261
13	Dutch Leonard	.263
14	Pedro Ramos	.265
15	General Crowder	.266
16	Casey Patten	.267
17	Bobo Newsom	.273
18	Early Wynn	.274
19	Montie Weaver	.275
20	George Mogridge	.275

Opponent OBP
(minimum 1000 Innings Pitched)

1	Walter Johnson	.279
2	Dutch Leonard	.304
3	Doc Ayers	.310
4	Bob Groom	.319
5	Mickey Haefner	.319
6	Bob Porterfield	.319
7	Long Tom Hughes	.320
8	Casey Patten	.320
9	General Crowder	.324
10	Pedro Ramos	.324
11	George Mogridge	.326
12	Firpo Marberry	.327
13	Jim Shaw	.329
14	Camilo Pascual	.329
15	Chuck Stobbs	.329
16	Harry Harper	.330
17	Early Wynn	.337
18	Bump Hadley	.338
19	Montie Weaver	.344
20	Walt Masterson	.346

Teams: Twins

Minnesota Twins Team Batting Leaders—Career

	Games			At-Bats			Runs			Hits	
1	Harmon Killebrew	1,939	1	Kirby Puckett	7,244	1	Kirby Puckett	1,071	1	Kirby Puckett	2,304
2	Kirby Puckett	1,783	2	Harmon Killebrew	6,593	2	Harmon Killebrew	1,047	2	Rod Carew	2,085
3	Kent Hrbek	1,747	3	Tony Oliva	6,301	3	Rod Carew	950	3	Tony Oliva	1,917
4	Tony Oliva	1,676	4	Rod Carew	6,235	4	Kent Hrbek	903	4	Kent Hrbek	1,749
5	Rod Carew	1,635	5	Kent Hrbek	6,192	5	Tony Oliva	870	5	Harmon Killebrew	1,713
6	Gary Gaetti	1,361	6	Gary Gaetti	4,989	6	Chuck Knoblauch	713	6	Gary Gaetti	1,276
7	Bob Allison	1,236	7	Zoilo Versalles	4,148	7	Bob Allison	648	7	Chuck Knoblauch	1,197
8	Randy Bush	1,219	8	Cesar Tovar	4,142	8	Cesar Tovar	646	8	Cesar Tovar	1,164
9	Roy Smalley	1,148	9	Roy Smalley	3,997		Gary Gaetti	646	9	Zoilo Versalles	1,046
10	Greg Gagne	1,140	10	Chuck Knoblauch	3,939	10	Zoilo Versalles	564		Roy Smalley	1,046
11	Cesar Tovar	1,090	11	Bob Allison	3,926	11	Roy Smalley	551	11	Bob Allison	999
12	Zoilo Versalles	1,065	12	Greg Gagne	3,386	12	Greg Gagne	452	12	Greg Gagne	844
13	Chuck Knoblauch	1,013	13	Tom Brunansky	3,313	13	Tom Brunansky	450	13	Rich Rollins	830
14	Tom Brunansky	916	14	Rich Rollins	3,048	14	Rich Rollins	395	14	Tom Brunansky	829
15	Rich Rollins	888	15	Randy Bush	3,045	15	Randy Bush	388	15	Earl Battey	768
16	Earl Battey	853	16	Earl Battey	2,762	16	Larry Hisle	369	16	Brian Harper	767
17	Rich Reese	807	17	Butch Wynegar	2,746	17	Dan Gladden	358	17	Randy Bush	763
18	Butch Wynegar	794	18	Brian Harper	2,503	18	Shane Mack	351		Butch Wynegar	697
19	Gene Larkin	758	19	Dan Gladden	2,470	19	Steve Braun	333		Larry Hisle	697
20	Steve Braun	751	20	Larry Hisle	2,437	20	Butch Wynegar	325	20	Steve Braun	689

	Doubles			Triples			Home Runs			RBI	
1	Kirby Puckett	414	1	Rod Carew	90	1	Harmon Killebrew	475	1	Harmon Killebrew	1,325
2	Tony Oliva	329	2	Kirby Puckett	57	2	Kent Hrbek	293	2	Kent Hrbek	1,086
3	Kent Hrbek	312	3	Zoilo Versalles	56	3	Tony Oliva	220	3	Kirby Puckett	1,085
4	Rod Carew	305	4	Chuck Knoblauch	51	4	Bob Allison	211	4	Tony Oliva	947
5	Gary Gaetti	252	5	Tony Oliva	48	5	Kirby Puckett	207	5	Gary Gaetti	758
6	Harmon Killebrew	232	6	Cesar Tovar	45	6	Gary Gaetti	201	6	Rod Carew	733
7	Chuck Knoblauch	210	7	Bob Allison	41	7	Tom Brunansky	163	7	Bob Allison	642
8	Cesar Tovar	193	8	Greg Gagne	35	8	Roy Smalley	110	8	Roy Smalley	485
9	Zoilo Versalles	188	9	John Castino	34	9	Jimmie Hall	98	9	Tom Brunansky	469
10	Roy Smalley	184	10	Lyman Bostock	26	10	Randy Bush	96	10	Larry Hisle	409
11	Greg Gagne	183		Randy Bush	26	11	Don Mincher	90		Randy Bush	409
12	Bob Allison	167		Dan Gladden	26	12	Larry Hisle	87	12	Zoilo Versalles	401
13	Brian Harper	156	13	Dan Ford	25	13	Zoilo Versalles	86	13	Chuck Knoblauch	391
14	Tom Brunansky	154		Gary Gaetti	25	14	Tim Laudner	77	14	Rich Rollins	369
	Randy Bush	154	15	Shane Mack	24	15	Earl Battey	76	15	Earl Battey	350
16	Gene Larkin	131	16	Larry Hisle	23	16	Rod Carew	74	16	Brian Harper	346
17	Mickey Hatcher	127	17	Harmon Killebrew	21	17	Rich Rollins	71	17	Greg Gagne	335
18	Shane Mack	119		Roy Smalley	21	18	Bobby Darwin	70	18	Butch Wynegar	325
19	Rich Rollins	117	19	Rich Rollins	20	19	Greg Gagne	69	19	Cesar Tovar	319
	Dan Gladden	117		Gary Ward	20	20	Shane Mack	67	20	Shane Mack	315

	Walks			Strikeouts			Stolen Bases			Runs Created	
1	Harmon Killebrew	1,321	1	Harmon Killebrew	1,314	1	Chuck Knoblauch	276	1	Harmon Killebrew	1,307
2	Kent Hrbek	838	2	Kirby Puckett	965	2	Rod Carew	271	2	Kirby Puckett	1,194
3	Bob Allison	641	3	Gary Gaetti	877	3	Cesar Tovar	186	3	Rod Carew	1,080
4	Rod Carew	613	4	Bob Allison	842	4	Kirby Puckett	134	4	Kent Hrbek	1,069
5	Roy Smalley	549	5	Kent Hrbek	798	5	Dan Gladden	116	5	Tony Oliva	1,023
6	Chuck Knoblauch	513	6	Rod Carew	716	6	Larry Hisle	92	6	Chuck Knoblauch	706
7	Kirby Puckett	450	7	Greg Gagne	676	7	Tony Oliva	86	7	Bob Allison	698
8	Tony Oliva	448	8	Tony Oliva	645	8	Zoilo Versalles	84	8	Gary Gaetti	649
9	Tom Brunansky	394	9	Zoilo Versalles	606	9	Greg Gagne	79	9	Roy Smalley	572
10	Butch Wynegar	358		Roy Smalley	606	10	Gary Gaetti	74	10	Cesar Tovar	563
	Gary Gaetti	358	11	Tom Brunansky	589	11	Shane Mack	71	11	Tom Brunansky	488
12	Steve Braun	356	12	Tim Laudner	553	12	Al Newman	69	12	Zoilo Versalles	478
13	Randy Bush	348	13	Randy Bush	505	13	Bob Allison	60	13	Randy Bush	426
14	Earl Battey	328	14	Larry Hisle	478	14	Rich Becker	51	14	Rich Rollins	399
15	Cesar Tovar	299	15	Bobby Darwin	453	15	Ted Uhlaender	46	15	Earl Battey	395
16	Gene Larkin	268		Chuck Knoblauch	453	16	Jerry Terrell	41	16	Larry Hisle	394
17	Rich Rollins	253	17	George Mitterwald	391		Rob Wilfong	41	17	Shane Mack	391
18	Zoilo Versalles	251	18	Pedro Munoz	387		Willie Norwood	41	18	Steve Braun	363
	Larry Hisle	251	19	Rich Rollins	383	19	Hosken Powell	37	19	Greg Gagne	356
20	Don Mincher	220	20	Shane Mack	381		Kent Hrbek	37	20	Brian Harper	349

	Runs Created/27 Outs			Batting Average			On-Base Percentage			Slugging Percentage	
	(minimum 2000 Plate Appearances)			(minimum 2000 Plate Appearances)			(minimum 2000 Plate Appearances)			(minimum 2000 Plate Appearances)	
1	Harmon Killebrew	6.85	1	Rod Carew	.334	1	Rod Carew	.393	1	Harmon Killebrew	.518
2	Shane Mack	6.53	2	Kirby Puckett	.318	2	Chuck Knoblauch	.391	2	Jimmie Hall	.481
3	Chuck Knoblauch	6.47	3	Shane Mack	.309	3	Harmon Killebrew	.383	3	Kent Hrbek	.481
4	Rod Carew	6.45	4	Brian Harper	.306	4	Steve Braun	.376	4	Shane Mack	.479
5	Bob Allison	6.14	5	Tony Oliva	.304	5	Shane Mack	.375	5	Bob Allison	.479
6	Kent Hrbek	6.11	6	Chuck Knoblauch	.304	6	Kent Hrbek	.367	6	Kirby Puckett	.477
7	Kirby Puckett	6.08	7	Larry Hisle	.286	7	Bob Allison	.361	7	Tony Oliva	.476
8	Tony Oliva	5.96	8	Steve Braun	.284	8	Kirby Puckett	.360	8	Larry Hisle	.457
9	Larry Hisle	5.65	9	Mickey Hatcher	.284	9	Earl Battey	.356	9	Tom Brunansky	.452
10	Jimmie Hall	5.55	10	Kent Hrbek	.282	10	Larry Hisle	.354	10	Rod Carew	.448
11	Steve Braun	5.33	11	Cesar Tovar	.281	11	Tony Oliva	.353	11	Gary Gaetti	.437
12	Brian Harper	5.01	12	John Castino	.278	12	Roy Smalley	.350	12	Dan Ford	.435
13	Tom Brunansky	5.00	13	Earl Battey	.278	13	Gene Larkin	.348	13	Brian Harper	.431
14	Earl Battey	4.96	14	Rich Rollins	.272	14	Brian Harper	.342	14	Chuck Knoblauch	.416
15	Roy Smalley	4.83	15	Dan Ford	.272	15	Butch Wynegar	.340	15	Randy Bush	.413
16	Dan Ford	4.82	16	Jimmie Hall	.269	16	Cesar Tovar	.337	16	Earl Battey	.409
17	Cesar Tovar	4.78	17	Dan Gladden	.268	17	Jimmie Hall	.334	17	Roy Smalley	.401
18	Randy Bush	4.75	18	Pat Meares	.267	18	Randy Bush	.334	18	John Castino	.398
19	Rich Rollins	4.57	19	Gene Larkin	.266	19	Rich Rollins	.333	19	Rich Rollins	.394
20	John Castino	4.54	20	Roy Smalley	.262	20	Dan Ford	.331	20	Rich Reese	.393

Minnesota Twins Team Pitching Leaders—Career

Wins

1	Jim Kaat	189
2	Bert Blyleven	149
3	Jim Perry	128
4	Frank Viola	112
5	Dave Goltz	96
6	Camilo Pascual	88
7	Kevin Tapani	75
8	Dave Boswell	67
9	Scott Erickson	61
10	Geoff Zahn	53
11	Mudcat Grant	50
12	Allan Anderson	49
13	Mike Smithson	47
14	Pete Redfern	42
	Brad Radke	42
16	Dean Chance	41
17	Jerry Koosman	39
18	Dick Stigman	37
	Al Worthington	37
	Jim Merritt	37

Losses

1	Jim Kaat	152
2	Bert Blyleven	138
3	Frank Viola	93
4	Jim Perry	90
5	Dave Goltz	79
6	Kevin Tapani	63
7	Scott Erickson	60
8	Camilo Pascual	57
9	Dave Boswell	54
	Allan Anderson	54
11	Geoff Zahn	53
12	Pete Redfern	48
	Mike Smithson	48
14	Roger Erickson	47
15	Jim Merritt	41
16	Ron Davis	40
	Brad Radke	40
18	Ray Corbin	38
	Al Williams	38
20	Two tied at	37

Winning Percentage
(minimum 75 decisions)

1	Camilo Pascual	.607
2	Mudcat Grant	.588
3	Jim Perry	.587
4	Jim Kaat	.554
5	Dave Boswell	.554
6	Dave Goltz	.549
7	Dean Chance	.547
8	Frank Viola	.546
9	Kevin Tapani	.543
10	Bert Blyleven	.519
11	Brad Radke	.512
12	Scott Erickson	.504
13	Geoff Zahn	.500
14	Mike Smithson	.495
15	Allan Anderson	.476
16	Jim Merritt	.474
17	Pete Redfern	.467
18	Roger Erickson	.397

Games

1	Jim Kaat	468
2	Rick Aguilera	405
3	Jim Perry	376
4	Bert Blyleven	348
5	Al Worthington	327
6	Ron Davis	286
7	Frank Viola	260
8	Dave Goltz	247
9	Ron Perranoski	244
10	Mark Guthrie	240
11	Eddie Guardado	226
12	Bill Campbell	216
13	Tom Burgmeier	214
14	Juan Berenguer	211
15	Mike Trombley	208
16	Carl Willis	204
17	Jeff Reardon	191
18	Bill Pleis	190
19	Dave Boswell	187
20	Camilo Pascual	184

Games Started

1	Jim Kaat	422
2	Bert Blyleven	345
3	Frank Viola	259
4	Jim Perry	249
5	Dave Goltz	215
6	Kevin Tapani	180
7	Camilo Pascual	179
8	Scott Erickson	153
9	Dave Boswell	150
10	Allan Anderson	128
11	Geoff Zahn	126
	Mike Smithson	126
13	Mudcat Grant	111
	Pete Redfern	111
15	Roger Erickson	106
16	Brad Radke	98
17	Al Williams	97
18	Dean Chance	93
19	Jim Merritt	89
20	Dick Stigman	85

Complete Games

1	Bert Blyleven	141
2	Jim Kaat	133
3	Dave Goltz	80
4	Camilo Pascual	72
5	Jim Perry	61
6	Frank Viola	54
7	Dave Boswell	37
8	Mudcat Grant	36
	Geoff Zahn	36
10	Dean Chance	34
11	Jim Merritt	28
12	Dick Stigman	26
	Mike Smithson	26
14	Roger Erickson	24
15	Jerry Koosman	20
16	Jack Kralick	19
	Kevin Tapani	19
18	Joe Decker	18
19	John Butcher	17
20	Jim Hughes	16

Shutouts

1	Bert Blyleven	29
2	Jim Kaat	23
3	Camilo Pascual	18
4	Jim Perry	17
5	Dean Chance	11
	Dave Goltz	11
7	Mudcat Grant	10
	Frank Viola	10
9	Geoff Zahn	7
	Scott Erickson	7
11	Dave Boswell	6
	Jim Merritt	6
	Kevin Tapani	6
14	Dick Woodson	5
	Mike Smithson	5
16	Jack Kralick	4
	Dick Stigman	4
	Joe Decker	4
19	Seven tied at	3

Saves

1	Rick Aguilera	210
2	Ron Davis	108
3	Jeff Reardon	104
4	Al Worthington	88
5	Ron Perranoski	76
6	Mike Marshall	54
7	Bill Campbell	51
8	Doug Corbett	43
9	Ray Moore	25
10	Tom Burgmeier	23
11	Tom Johnson	22
12	Bill Dailey	21
	Dave Stevens	21
14	Stan Williams	19
	Wayne Granger	19
16	Ray Corbin	17
17	Keith Atherton	15
18	Bill Pleis	13
	Tom Hall	13
20	Two tied at	11

Innings Pitched

1	Jim Kaat	2,959.1
2	Bert Blyleven	2,566.2
3	Jim Perry	1,883.1
4	Frank Viola	1,772.2
5	Dave Goltz	1,638.0
6	Camilo Pascual	1,284.2
7	Kevin Tapani	1,171.1
8	Dave Boswell	1,036.1
9	Scott Erickson	979.1
10	Geoff Zahn	852.0
11	Allan Anderson	818.2
12	Mike Smithson	816.0
13	Mudcat Grant	780.2
14	Pete Redfern	714.0
15	Roger Erickson	712.0
16	Jim Merritt	686.2
17	Dean Chance	664.0
18	Brad Radke	652.2
19	Ray Corbin	652.1
20	Dick Stigman	643.2

Walks

1	Jim Kaat	694
2	Bert Blyleven	674
3	Jim Perry	541
4	Frank Viola	521
5	Dave Goltz	493
6	Dave Boswell	460
7	Camilo Pascual	431
8	Scott Erickson	367
9	Pete Redfern	306
10	Joe Decker	272
11	Ray Corbin	261
12	Kevin Tapani	255
13	Geoff Zahn	254
14	Dick Stigman	248
15	Dick Woodson	241
16	Al Williams	227
	Mike Smithson	227
18	Roger Erickson	226
19	Vic Albury	220
20	Rich Robertson	217

Strikeouts

1	Bert Blyleven	2,035
2	Jim Kaat	1,824
3	Frank Viola	1,214
4	Jim Perry	1,025
5	Camilo Pascual	994
6	Dave Goltz	887
7	Dave Boswell	865
8	Kevin Tapani	724
9	Dick Stigman	538
10	Jim Merritt	527
	Scott Erickson	527
12	Rick Aguilera	516
13	Dean Chance	504
14	Mike Smithson	438
15	Tom Hall	431
16	Pete Redfern	426
17	Al Worthington	399
18	Brad Radke	397
19	Mark Guthrie	388
20	Juan Berenguer	379

Strikeouts/9 Innings
(minimum 750 Innings Pitched)

1	Dave Boswell	7.51
2	Bert Blyleven	7.14
3	Camilo Pascual	6.96
4	Frank Viola	6.16
5	Kevin Tapani	5.56
6	Jim Kaat	5.55
7	Jim Perry	4.90
8	Dave Goltz	4.87
9	Scott Erickson	4.84
10	Mike Smithson	4.83
11	Mudcat Grant	4.35
12	Allan Anderson	3.73
13	Geoff Zahn	3.68

ERA
(minimum 750 Innings Pitched)

1	Jim Perry	3.15
2	Bert Blyleven	3.28
3	Jim Kaat	3.28
4	Camilo Pascual	3.31
5	Mudcat Grant	3.35
6	Dave Goltz	3.48
7	Dave Boswell	3.49
8	Frank Viola	3.86
9	Geoff Zahn	3.90
10	Kevin Tapani	4.06
11	Allan Anderson	4.11
12	Scott Erickson	4.22
13	Mike Smithson	4.46

Component ERA
(minimum 750 Innings Pitched)

1	Camilo Pascual	3.10
2	Jim Perry	3.13
3	Bert Blyleven	3.22
4	Dave Boswell	3.25
5	Jim Kaat	3.39
6	Mudcat Grant	3.46
7	Dave Goltz	3.63
8	Kevin Tapani	3.67
9	Frank Viola	3.88
10	Allan Anderson	4.28
11	Geoff Zahn	4.28
12	Mike Smithson	4.35
13	Scott Erickson	4.39

Opponent Average
(minimum 750 Innings Pitched)

1	Dave Boswell	.217
2	Camilo Pascual	.233
3	Jim Perry	.242
4	Bert Blyleven	.246
5	Jim Kaat	.256
6	Frank Viola	.260
7	Mudcat Grant	.260
8	Dave Goltz	.264
9	Kevin Tapani	.270
10	Mike Smithson	.273
11	Scott Erickson	.275
12	Allan Anderson	.282
13	Geoff Zahn	.289

Opponent OBP
(minimum 750 Innings Pitched)

1	Camilo Pascual	.297
2	Mudcat Grant	.298
3	Jim Perry	.298
4	Bert Blyleven	.299
5	Jim Kaat	.302
6	Dave Boswell	.306
7	Kevin Tapani	.309
8	Frank Viola	.314
9	Dave Goltz	.318
10	Mike Smithson	.328
11	Allan Anderson	.329
12	Geoff Zahn	.339
13	Scott Erickson	.343

Senators/Twins Franchise Batting Leaders—Single Season

Games

#	Player	Year	G
1	Cesar Tovar	1967	164
2	Harmon Killebrew	1967	163
3	Harmon Killebrew	1966	162
	Harmon Killebrew	1969	162
	Roy Smalley	1979	162
	Gary Gaetti	1984	162
7	Tony Oliva	1964	161
	Cesar Tovar	1970	161
	Kirby Puckett	1985	161
	Kirby Puckett	1986	161
	Paul Molitor	1996	161
12	Zoilo Versalles	1962	160
	Zoilo Versalles	1964	160
	Zoilo Versalles	1965	160
	Zoilo Versalles	1967	160
	Leo Cardenas	1969	160
	Leo Cardenas	1970	160
	Gary Gaetti	1985	160
	Kirby Puckett	1992	160
20	Seven tied at		159

At-Bats

#	Player	Year	AB
1	Kirby Puckett	1985	691
2	Kirby Puckett	1986	680
3	Tony Oliva	1964	672
4	Buddy Lewis	1937	668
5	Zoilo Versalles	1965	666
6	Doc Cramer	1941	660
	Paul Molitor	1996	660
8	Zoilo Versalles	1964	659
9	Heinie Manush	1933	658
10	Cesar Tovar	1971	657
	Kirby Puckett	1988	657
12	Buddy Lewis	1938	656
	George Case	1940	656
14	Cesar Tovar	1970	650
15	Sam Rice	1925	649
	George Case	1941	649
	Cesar Tovar	1967	649
18	Sam Rice	1924	646
19	Sam Rice	1926	641
20	Kirby Puckett	1992	639

Runs

#	Player	Year	R
1	Chuck Knoblauch	1996	140
2	Rod Carew	1977	128
3	Joe Cronin	1930	127
4	Zoilo Versalles	1965	126
5	Buddy Lewis	1938	122
6	Sam Rice	1930	121
	Heinie Manush	1932	121
8	Buddy Myer	1932	120
	Cesar Tovar	1970	120
10	Sam Rice	1929	119
	Kirby Puckett	1986	119
12	Sam Rice	1923	117
	Chuck Knoblauch	1997	117
14	Goose Goslin	1925	116
15	Heinie Manush	1933	115
	Buddy Myer	1935	115
17	Buddy Myer	1931	114
	Eddie Yost	1950	114
19	Sam Rice	1925	111
20	Heinie Manush	1931	110

Hits

#	Player	Year	H
1	Rod Carew	1977	239
2	Kirby Puckett	1988	234
3	Sam Rice	1925	227
4	Paul Molitor	1996	225
5	Kirby Puckett	1986	223
6	Heinie Manush	1933	221
7	Cecil Travis	1941	218
	Rod Carew	1974	218
9	Tony Oliva	1964	217
10	Sam Rice	1924	216
	Sam Rice	1926	216
12	Buddy Myer	1935	215
	Kirby Puckett	1989	215
14	Heinie Manush	1932	214
15	Sam Rice	1920	211
16	Buddy Lewis	1937	210
	Kirby Puckett	1992	210
18	Sam Rice	1930	207
	Mickey Vernon	1946	207
	Kirby Puckett	1987	207

Doubles

#	Player	Year	2B
1	Mickey Vernon	1946	51
2	Stan Spence	1946	50
3	Marty Cordova	1996	46
4	Joe Cronin	1933	45
	Zoilo Versalles	1965	45
	Kirby Puckett	1989	45
	Chuck Knoblauch	1994	45
8	Joe Cronin	1931	44
9	Ed Delahanty	1902	43
	Tris Speaker	1927	43
	Sammy West	1931	43
	Joe Cronin	1932	43
	Mickey Vernon	1953	43
	Tony Oliva	1964	43
15	Heinie Manush	1934	42
	Joe Kuhel	1936	42
	Kirby Puckett	1988	42
	Brian Harper	1990	42
19	Five tied at		41

Triples

#	Player	Year	3B
1	Goose Goslin	1925	20
2	Joe Cassidy	1904	19
	Howard Shanks	1921	19
	Cecil Travis	1941	19
5	Goose Goslin	1923	18
	Sam Rice	1923	18
	Joe Cronin	1932	18
	John Stone	1935	18
9	Goose Goslin	1924	17
	Heinie Manush	1933	17
11	Buddy Myer	1932	16
	Buddy Lewis	1939	16
	Rod Carew	1977	16
14	Thirteen tied at		15

Home Runs

#	Player	Year	HR
1	Harmon Killebrew	1964	49
	Harmon Killebrew	1969	49
3	Harmon Killebrew	1962	48
4	Harmon Killebrew	1961	46
5	Harmon Killebrew	1963	45
6	Harmon Killebrew	1967	44
7	Roy Sievers	1957	42
	Harmon Killebrew	1959	42
9	Harmon Killebrew	1970	41
10	Roy Sievers	1958	39
	Harmon Killebrew	1966	39
12	Jim Lemon	1960	38
13	Bob Allison	1963	35
14	Gary Gaetti	1986	34
	Kent Hrbek	1987	34
16	Jim Lemon	1959	33
	Jimmie Hall	1963	33
18	Four tied at		32

RBI

#	Player	Year	RBI
1	Harmon Killebrew	1969	140
2	Goose Goslin	1924	129
3	Joe Cronin	1930	126
	Joe Cronin	1931	126
	Harmon Killebrew	1962	126
6	Harmon Killebrew	1961	122
7	Kirby Puckett	1988	121
8	Goose Goslin	1927	120
9	Harmon Killebrew	1971	119
	Larry Hisle	1977	119
11	Joe Cronin	1933	118
	Joe Kuhel	1936	118
13	Joe Cronin	1932	116
	Heinie Manush	1932	116
15	Mickey Vernon	1953	115
16	Zeke Bonura	1938	114
	Roy Sievers	1957	114
18	Four tied at		113

Walks

#	Player	Year	BB
1	Eddie Yost	1956	151
2	Harmon Killebrew	1969	145
3	Eddie Yost	1950	141
4	Eddie Yost	1954	131
	Harmon Killebrew	1967	131
6	Eddie Yost	1952	129
7	Harmon Killebrew	1970	128
8	Eddie Yost	1951	126
9	Eddie Yost	1953	123
10	Harmon Killebrew	1971	114
11	Harmon Killebrew	1961	107
12	Harmon Killebrew	1962	106
13	Bob Allison	1961	103
	Harmon Killebrew	1966	103
15	Buddy Myer	1934	102
16	Roy Sievers	1956	100
17	Chuck Knoblauch	1996	98
18	Buddy Myer	1935	96
19	Eddie Yost	1955	95
	Chili Davis	1991	95

Strikeouts

#	Player	Year	SO
1	Bobby Darwin	1972	145
2	Harmon Killebrew	1962	142
3	Jim Lemon	1956	138
4	Bobby Darwin	1973	137
5	Harmon Killebrew	1964	135
6	Rich Becker	1997	130
7	Larry Hisle	1973	128
8	Bobby Darwin	1974	127
9	Zoilo Versalles	1965	122
10	Gary Gaetti	1983	121
11	Jim Lemon	1958	120
12	Dan Ford	1976	118
	Rich Becker	1996	118
14	Chili Davis	1991	117
15	Harmon Killebrew	1959	116
16	Bob Allison	1962	115
17	Jim Lemon	1960	114
	Bob Allison	1965	114
	Bob Allison	1967	114
	Scott Stahoviak	1996	114

Stolen Bases

#	Player	Year	SB
1	Clyde Milan	1912	88
2	Clyde Milan	1913	75
3	Sam Rice	1920	63
4	Danny Moeller	1913	62
	Chuck Knoblauch	1997	62
6	George Case	1943	61
7	Clyde Milan	1911	58
8	George Case	1939	51
9	George Case	1944	49
	Rod Carew	1976	49
11	Chuck Knoblauch	1995	46
12	Cesar Tovar	1969	45
	Chuck Knoblauch	1996	45
14	Clyde Milan	1910	44
	George Case	1942	44
16	Jake Stahl	1905	41
	Rod Carew	1973	41
18	Bob Ganley	1907	40
	Clyde Milan	1915	40
20	John Anderson	1906	39

Runs Created

#	Player	Year	RC
1	Rod Carew	1977	154
2	Chuck Knoblauch	1996	145
3	Harmon Killebrew	1969	136
4	Harmon Killebrew	1967	133
5	Buddy Myer	1935	132
6	Ed Delahanty	1902	130
	Harmon Killebrew	1961	130
8	Joe Cronin	1930	129
9	Goose Goslin	1926	128
10	Heinie Manush	1932	127
	Cecil Travis	1941	127
12	Goose Goslin	1925	126
	Roy Sievers	1957	126
14	Mickey Vernon	1953	123
15	Joe Cronin	1931	122
16	Kirby Puckett	1986	121
17	Tony Oliva	1964	120
	Harmon Killebrew	1966	120
	Kirby Puckett	1988	120
20	Joe Kuhel	1936	119

Runs Created/27 Outs

(minimum 3.1 Plate Appearances/Tm Gm)

#	Player	Year	RC/27
1	Ed Delahanty	1902	11.35
2	Rod Carew	1977	10.33
3	Chuck Knoblauch	1996	9.53
4	Goose Goslin	1928	9.49
5	John Stone	1936	9.18
6	Harmon Killebrew	1969	8.69
7	Harmon Killebrew	1961	8.67
8	Harmon Killebrew	1967	8.53
9	Goose Goslin	1926	8.51
10	Buddy Myer	1935	8.43
11	Cecil Travis	1941	8.42
12	Roy Sievers	1957	8.33
13	Joe Cronin	1930	8.12
14	Rod Carew	1975	8.00
15	Buddy Myer	1938	7.95
16	Chuck Knoblauch	1995	7.94
17	Kirby Puckett	1994	7.94
18	Heinie Manush	1932	7.92
19	Joe Judge	1930	7.92
20	Goose Goslin	1925	7.88

Batting Average

(minimum 3.1 Plate Appearances/Tm Gm)

#	Player	Year	AVG
1	Rod Carew	1977	.388
2	Goose Goslin	1928	.379
3	Ed Delahanty	1902	.376
4	Rod Carew	1974	.364
5	Rod Carew	1975	.359
6	Cecil Travis	1941	.359
7	Kirby Puckett	1988	.356
8	Goose Goslin	1926	.354
9	Mickey Vernon	1946	.353
10	Rod Carew	1973	.350
11	Sam Rice	1925	.350
12	Sam Rice	1930	.349
13	Buddy Myer	1935	.349
14	Heinie Manush	1934	.349
15	Joe Cronin	1930	.346
16	Cecil Travis	1937	.344
17	Goose Goslin	1924	.344
18	Heinie Manush	1932	.342
19	John Stone	1936	.341
20	Paul Molitor	1996	.341

On-Base Percentage

(minimum 3.1 Plate Appearances/Tm Gm)

#	Player	Year	OBP
1	Buddy Myer	1938	.454
2	Ed Delahanty	1902	.453
3	Rod Carew	1977	.449
4	Chuck Knoblauch	1996	.448
5	Goose Goslin	1928	.443
6	Eddie Yost	1950	.440
7	Buddy Myer	1935	.440
8	Rod Carew	1974	.433
9	Harmon Killebrew	1969	.427
10	Goose Goslin	1926	.425
11	Chuck Knoblauch	1995	.424
12	Eddie Yost	1951	.423
13	Joe Cronin	1930	.422
14	Rod Carew	1975	.421
15	Goose Goslin	1924	.421
16	John Stone	1936	.421
17	Buddy Myer	1934	.419
18	Joe Judge	1920	.416
19	Eddie Yost	1956	.412
20	Germany Schaefer	1911	.412

Slugging Percentage

(minimum 3.1 Plate Appearances/Tm Gm)

#	Player	Year	SLG
1	Goose Goslin	1928	.614
2	Harmon Killebrew	1961	.606
3	Ed Delahanty	1902	.590
4	Harmon Killebrew	1969	.584
5	Roy Sievers	1957	.579
6	Rod Carew	1977	.570
7	Harmon Killebrew	1967	.558
8	Tony Oliva	1964	.557
9	Harmon Killebrew	1963	.555
10	Bob Allison	1964	.553
11	Gary Gaetti	1988	.551
12	Harmon Killebrew	1964	.548
13	Goose Goslin	1925	.547
14	Harmon Killebrew	1970	.546
15	Tony Oliva	1971	.546
16	Harmon Killebrew	1962	.545
17	Kent Hrbek	1987	.545
18	Kirby Puckett	1988	.545
19	John Stone	1936	.545
20	Roy Sievers	1958	.544

Senators/Twins Franchise Pitching Leaders—Single Season

Wins

1	Walter Johnson	1913	36
2	Walter Johnson	1912	33
3	Walter Johnson	1914	28
4	Walter Johnson	1915	27
5	General Crowder	1932	26
6	Walter Johnson	1910	25
	Walter Johnson	1911	25
	Walter Johnson	1916	25
	Jim Kaat	1966	25
10	Bob Groom	1912	24
	General Crowder	1933	24
	Jim Perry	1970	24
	Frank Viola	1988	24
14	Walter Johnson	1917	23
	Walter Johnson	1918	23
	Walter Johnson	1924	23
17	Montie Weaver	1932	22
	Earl Whitehill	1933	22
	Bob Porterfield	1953	22
20	Two tied at		21

Losses

1	Jack Townsend	1904	26
	Bob Groom	1909	26
3	Walter Johnson	1909	25
4	Beany Jacobson	1904	23
	Casey Patten	1904	23
6	Bill Carrick	1901	22
	Casey Patten	1903	22
	Al Orth	1903	22
	Casey Patten	1905	22
10	Harry Harper	1919	21
11	Long Tom Hughes	1905	20
	Cy Falkenberg	1906	20
	Charlie Smith	1907	20
	Walter Johnson	1916	20
	Chuck Stobbs	1957	20
	Pedro Ramos	1961	20
17	Seven tied at		19

Winning Percentage
(minimum 15 decisions)

1	Walter Johnson	1913	.837
2	Stan Coveleski	1925	.800
	Firpo Marberry	1931	.800
4	Frank Viola	1988	.774
5	Bill Campbell	1976	.773
6	Jim Perry	1969	.769
7	Walter Johnson	1924	.767
8	Firpo Marberry	1930	.750
	Mudcat Grant	1965	.750
10	Walter Johnson	1925	.741
11	Walter Johnson	1912	.733
	Earl Whitehill	1933	.733
13	Dutch Ruether	1925	.720
14	Lefty Stewart	1933	.714
	Dutch Leonard	1939	.714
	Scott Erickson	1991	.714
17	Joe Boehling	1913	.708
	Sad Sam Jones	1928	.708
	Dutch Leonard	1945	.708
20	Three tied at		.706

Games

1	Mike Marshall	1979	90
2	Eddie Guardado	1996	83
3	Bill Campbell	1976	78
4	Ron Perranoski	1969	75
5	Doug Corbett	1980	73
6	Tom Johnson	1977	71
7	Eddie Guardado	1997	69
8	Stan Williams	1970	68
9	Ron Perranoski	1970	67
	Mike Trombley	1997	67
11	Bill Dailey	1963	66
	Ron Perranoski	1968	66
	Ron Davis	1983	66
14	Al Worthington	1966	65
	Jeff Reardon	1989	65
	Rick Aguilera	1993	65
	Greg Swindell	1997	65
18	Firpo Marberry	1926	64
	Ron Davis	1984	64
	Rick Aguilera	1992	64

Games Started

1	Walter Johnson	1910	42
	Jim Kaat	1965	42
3	Jim Kaat	1966	41
4	Bob Groom	1912	40
	Walter Johnson	1914	40
	Jim Perry	1970	40
	Bert Blyleven	1973	40
8	Casey Patten	1904	39
	Walter Johnson	1915	39
	General Crowder	1932	39
	Mudcat Grant	1965	39
	Dean Chance	1967	39
	Dean Chance	1968	39
	Jim Perry	1971	39
	Dave Goltz	1977	39
16	Nine tied at		38

Complete Games

1	Walter Johnson	1910	38
2	Casey Patten	1904	37
3	Al Orth	1902	36
	Walter Johnson	1911	36
	Walter Johnson	1916	36
6	Walter Johnson	1915	35
7	Bill Carrick	1901	34
	Walter Johnson	1912	34
9	Casey Patten	1902	33
	Walter Johnson	1914	33
11	Casey Patten	1903	32
12	Jack Townsend	1904	31
13	Al Orth	1903	30
	Cy Falkenberg	1906	30
	Walter Johnson	1917	30
16	Casey Patten	1905	29
	Bob Groom	1912	29
	Walter Johnson	1913	29
	Walter Johnson	1918	29
20	Two tied at		28

Shutouts

1	Walter Johnson	1913	11
2	Walter Johnson	1914	9
	Bob Porterfield	1953	9
	Bert Blyleven	1973	9
5	Walter Johnson	1910	8
	Walter Johnson	1917	8
	Walter Johnson	1918	8
	Camilo Pascual	1961	8
9	Walter Johnson	1912	7
	Walter Johnson	1915	7
	Walter Johnson	1919	7
12	Casey Patten	1906	6
	Walter Johnson	1908	6
	Walter Johnson	1911	6
	Walter Johnson	1924	6
	Camilo Pascual	1959	6
	Mudcat Grant	1965	6
	Dean Chance	1968	6
19	Seven tied at		5

Saves

1	Jeff Reardon	1988	42
	Rick Aguilera	1991	42
3	Rick Aguilera	1992	41
4	Ron Perranoski	1970	34
	Rick Aguilera	1993	34
6	Mike Marshall	1979	32
	Rick Aguilera	1990	32
8	Ron Perranoski	1969	31
	Jeff Reardon	1987	31
	Jeff Reardon	1989	31
11	Ron Davis	1983	30
12	Ron Davis	1984	29
13	Rick Aguilera	1997	26
14	Ron Davis	1985	25
15	Doug Corbett	1980	23
	Rick Aguilera	1994	23
17	Firpo Marberry	1926	22
	Ron Davis	1982	22
19	Three tied at		21

Innings Pitched

1	Walter Johnson	1914	371.2
2	Walter Johnson	1910	370.0
3	Walter Johnson	1916	369.2
4	Walter Johnson	1912	369.0
5	Casey Patten	1904	357.2
6	Walter Johnson	1913	346.0
7	Walter Johnson	1915	336.2
8	General Crowder	1932	327.0
9	Walter Johnson	1917	326.0
	Walter Johnson	1918	326.0
11	Bert Blyleven	1973	325.0
12	Bill Carrick	1901	324.0
	Al Orth	1902	324.0
14	Walter Johnson	1911	322.1
15	Bob Groom	1912	316.0
16	Casey Patten	1905	309.2
17	Jim Shaw	1919	306.2
18	Jim Kaat	1966	304.2
19	Dave Goltz	1977	303.0
20	Casey Patten	1903	300.0

Walks

1	Bobo Newsom	1936	146
2	Ken Chase	1940	143
3	Jim Shaw	1914	137
4	Eric Erickson	1920	128
5	Jim Hughes	1975	127
6	Jimmie DeShong	1937	124
7	Jim Shaw	1917	123
8	Walt Masterson	1948	122
9	Joe Boehling	1915	119
10	Rich Robertson	1996	116
11	Ken Chase	1941	115
12	Joe Krakauskas	1939	114
	Ken Chase	1939	114
	Dean Stone	1955	114
15	Ken Chase	1938	113
16	Montie Weaver	1932	112
	Bob Wiesler	1956	112
18	Mickey McDermott	1954	110
19	Cy Falkenberg	1906	108
20	Two tied at		107

Strikeouts

1	Walter Johnson	1910	313
2	Walter Johnson	1912	303
3	Bert Blyleven	1973	258
4	Bert Blyleven	1974	249
5	Walter Johnson	1913	243
6	Dean Chance	1968	234
7	Bert Blyleven	1975	233
8	Walter Johnson	1916	228
	Bert Blyleven	1972	228
10	Walter Johnson	1914	225
11	Bert Blyleven	1971	224
12	Camilo Pascual	1961	221
13	Dean Chance	1967	220
14	Bert Blyleven	1986	215
15	Camilo Pascual	1964	213
16	Jim Kaat	1967	211
17	Walter Johnson	1911	207
18	Camilo Pascual	1962	206
19	Jim Kaat	1966	205
20	Dave Boswell	1967	204

Strikeouts/9 Innings
(minimum 1 Inning Pitched/Tm Gm)

1	Dave Boswell	1966	9.19
2	Dave Boswell	1967	8.25
3	Bert Blyleven	1974	7.98
4	Camilo Pascual	1961	7.88
5	Camilo Pascual	1956	7.73
6	Walter Johnson	1910	7.61
7	Bert Blyleven	1975	7.61
8	Dick Stigman	1964	7.53
9	Camilo Pascual	1958	7.41
10	Bert Blyleven	1970	7.41
11	Walter Johnson	1912	7.39
12	Camilo Pascual	1963	7.32
13	Willie Banks	1993	7.25
14	Bert Blyleven	1971	7.24
15	Dean Chance	1968	7.21
16	Jim Kaat	1967	7.21
17	Dick Stigman	1963	7.21
18	Camilo Pascual	1962	7.20
19	Camilo Pascual	1964	7.17
20	Bert Blyleven	1973	7.14

ERA
(minimum 1 Inning Pitched/Tm Gm)

1	Walter Johnson	1913	1.14
2	Walter Johnson	1918	1.27
3	Walter Johnson	1910	1.36
4	Walter Johnson	1912	1.39
5	Walter Johnson	1919	1.49
6	Walter Johnson	1915	1.55
7	Walter Johnson	1908	1.65
8	Bill Burns	1908	1.70
9	Walter Johnson	1914	1.72
10	Walter Johnson	1911	1.90
11	Walter Johnson	1916	1.90
12	Joe Boehling	1913	2.07
13	Roger Wolff	1945	2.12
14	Dutch Leonard	1945	2.13
15	Casey Patten	1906	2.17
16	Doc Ayers	1917	2.17
17	Harry Harper	1918	2.18
18	Walter Johnson	1917	2.21
19	Doc Ayers	1915	2.21
20	Long Tom Hughes	1908	2.21

Component ERA
(minimum 1 Inning Pitched/Tm Gm)

1	Walter Johnson	1913	1.27
2	Walter Johnson	1912	1.52
3	Walter Johnson	1910	1.54
4	Walter Johnson	1918	1.63
5	Walter Johnson	1908	1.66
6	Walter Johnson	1915	1.67
7	Walter Johnson	1917	1.71
8	Walter Johnson	1919	1.72
9	Bill Burns	1908	1.73
10	Walter Johnson	1914	1.75
11	Walter Johnson	1916	1.79
12	Roger Wolff	1945	1.87
13	Garland Braxton	1928	1.92
14	Doc Ayers	1915	1.97
15	Dean Chance	1968	1.99
16	Doc Ayers	1914	2.07
17	Long Tom Hughes	1908	2.12
18	Bert Gallia	1915	2.16
19	Walter Johnson	1909	2.16
20	Long Tom Hughes	1905	2.19

Opponent Average
(minimum 1 Inning Pitched/Tm Gm)

1	Walter Johnson	1913	.187
2	Walter Johnson	1912	.196
3	Dave Boswell	1966	.197
4	Dave Boswell	1967	.202
5	Walter Johnson	1910	.205
6	Joe Engel	1913	.207
7	Mickey Haefner	1943	.208
8	Walter Johnson	1918	.210
9	Dean Chance	1968	.211
10	Walter Johnson	1908	.211
11	Dick Woodson	1972	.211
12	Walter Johnson	1917	.211
13	Harry Harper	1918	.212
14	Dave Boswell	1968	.213
15	Walter Johnson	1915	.214
16	Roger Wolff	1945	.215
17	Jim Shaw	1914	.216
18	Garland Braxton	1928	.217
19	Camilo Pascual	1961	.217
20	Walter Johnson	1914	.217

Opponent OBP
(minimum 1 Inning Pitched/Tm Gm)

1	Walter Johnson	1913	.217
2	Walter Johnson	1912	.248
3	Bill Burns	1908	.257
4	Walter Johnson	1910	.257
5	Roger Wolff	1945	.258
6	Walter Johnson	1919	.259
7	Dean Chance	1968	.260
8	Walter Johnson	1918	.260
9	Jim Merritt	1967	.260
10	Walter Johnson	1915	.260
11	Garland Braxton	1928	.261
12	Walter Johnson	1917	.262
13	Walter Johnson	1908	.262
14	Walter Johnson	1914	.265
15	Jim Kaat	1966	.270
16	Walter Johnson	1916	.270
17	Doc Ayers	1915	.276
18	Kevin Tapani	1991	.277
19	Jim Merritt	1968	.277
20	Dean Chance	1967	.278

Twins Capsule

Best Season: In *1991*, the Twins went from last place to World Champions in one year. They captured the American League West crown and toppled the Blue Jays in the ALCS. In one of the most thrilling World Series of modern times, they edged the Atlanta Braves 4-3 by winning each of the last two games in their final at-bat.

Worst Season: *1982.* Calvin Griffith's cost-cutting stripped the club of virtually all of its veteran talent, leaving the team with a roster comprised almost entirely of rookies. Some of the kids (Gary Gaetti, Kent Hrbek and Tom Brunansky) panned out, but on the whole, the team would have had a hard time staying competitive in the Texas League. Forced to compete in the AL, they lost 102 games.

Best Players: *Harmon Killebrew, Rod Carew.* Killebrew won six home-run crowns; Carew won seven batting titles.

Best Pitcher: *Jim Kaat.* Camilo Pascual, Jim Perry, Bert Blyleven and Frank Viola were just as good for shorter stretches.

Best Reliever: *Rick Aguilera.*

Best Defensive Player: *Jim Kaat* was the consensus pick as the majors' best-fielding pitcher for nearly two decades. Gary Gaetti and Kirby Puckett deserve mention for their stellar work at third base and center field, respectively.

Hall of Famers: *Harmon Killebrew, Rod Carew.*

Franchise All-Star Team:

C	Earl Battey	**LF**	Larry Hisle
1B	Harmon Killebrew	**CF**	Kirby Puckett
2B	Rod Carew	**RF**	Bob Allison
3B	Gary Gaetti	**DH**	Tony Oliva
SS	Roy Smalley	**SP**	Jim Kaat
		RP	Rick Aguilera

Biggest Flake: *Mickey Hatcher.*

Strangest Career: *Brian Harper* made the majors at age 19, but it took him another decade to nail down a starting job. His offensive talent was obvious right from the start, but defensive limitations held him back. As a teenager, he batted .315 with 37 doubles and 90 RBI in Triple-A, but committed almost 30 errors in less than 100 games behind the plate. Two years later, he hit .350 with 82 extra-base hits and 122 RBI in Triple-A. Two years after that, he landed a job as the 25th man on the Pirates' roster, which he held for two seasons. Over the next four years, he was traded to St. Louis, released by St. Louis, signed by Detroit, released by Detroit, signed by the independent San Jose Bees of the California League, sold to the A's, released by the A's, and signed by the Twins. When he batted .353 with 42 RBI in 46 games for the Twins' Triple-A team in 1988, the Twins called him up and gave him something he'd never received before: a chance to catch every day in the major leagues. Having made himself into an adequate receiver, Harper held the job for the next five seasons and batted .307 over that span. He also got a World Series ring in 1991.

What Might Have Been: *Tony Oliva.* In 1964, Oliva enjoyed one of the finest rookie seasons of all time, slugging 32 home runs while winning the batting title with a .323 average. The following year, he became the only player to lead the league in hitting during his first two full seasons in the big leagues. He finished in the top three in the league in batting in seven of his first eight years, but his career was irreparably damaged when he tore cartilage in his right knee midway through the 1971 season. He played out the year in pain and even managed to win the batting title, but underwent surgery over the winter and missed almost all of 1972. He had been a strong defensive right fielder, but when he finally made it all the way back in 1973, his speed was gone and he was forced to DH. He played for four more years, but never approached the level of stardom he reached during his first eight years in the bigs. When he hurt his knee, he was only 30 years old and well on his way to a Hall of Fame career.

Best Trade: *Larry Hisle.* The future AL RBI champ was stolen from the Cardinals in 1972 for the washed-up Wayne Granger.

Worst Trade: *Graig Nettles.* The Twins sent Nettles to the Indians in an otherwise inconsequential six-player trade after the 1969 season. The Twins acquired Luis Tiant in the deal, but released him after one season. Nettles played regularly for the next 17 years.

Best-Looking Player: *Tom Brunansky.*

Ugliest Player: *Juan Berenguer.*

Best Nickname: *Frank "Sweet Music" Viola.*

Most Unappreciated Player: *Shane Mack.* He batted well over .300 for four of his five seasons in Minnesota, with respectable power and speed.

Most Overrated Player: *Dan Gladden.* As both a left fielder and a leadoff man, Gladden was woefully inadequate. Still, he was allowed to hold both titles for five full seasons. During that time, he scored more than 69 runs only once.

Most Admirable Star: *Kirby Puckett.*

Least Admirable Star: *None.* The Twins have been fan friendly to a man during their stay in Minnesota.

Best Season, Player: *Rod Carew, 1977.* Carew rapped out 239 hits and batted .388, the second-closest approach to .400 since the retirement of Ted Williams.

Best Season, Pitcher: *Frank Viola, 1988.* He led the majors with 24 victories against only seven defeats.

Most Impressive Individual Record: *Jim Kaat's* record 16 straight Gold Gloves. The first 11 came while he was with Minnesota.

Biggest Tragedy: *Kirby Puckett.* He was still at his peak in the spring of 1996 when his career was suddenly ended by vision problems. Glaucoma in his right eye caused irreversible damage to his retina, forcing one of the game's most popular players to retire prematurely at age 34.

Fan Favorites: *Kirby Puckett, Kent Hrbek.*

—Mat Olkin

New York Yankees (1901-1997)

Year	Lg	Pos	W-L	Pct	GB	Manager	Att.	R	OR	HR	Avg	OBP	Slg	Opponent HR	Opponent Avg	Opponent OBP	ERA	Park Index Runs	Park Index HR
1901	AL	5th	68-65	.511	13.5	John McGraw	141,952	760	750	24	.294	.353	.397	21	.280	.336	3.73	117	92
1902	AL	8th	50-88	.362	34.0	John McGraw/Wilbert Robinson	174,606	715	848	33	.277	.342	.385	30	.309	.359	4.33	113	140
1903	AL	4th	72-62	.537	17.0	Clark Griffith	211,808	579	573	18	.249	.309	.330	19	.253	.297	3.08	98	76
1904	AL	2nd	92-59	.609	1.5	Clark Griffith	438,919	598	526	27	.259	.308	.347	29	.232	.282	2.57	120	529
1905	AL	6th	71-78	.477	21.5	Clark Griffith	309,100	586	622	23	.248	.307	.319	26	.245	.306	2.93	104	156
1906	AL	2nd	90-61	.596	3.0	Clark Griffith	434,700	644	543	17	.266	.316	.339	21	.243	.298	2.78	138	136
1907	AL	5th	70-78	.473	21.0	Clark Griffith	350,020	605	665	15	.249	.299	.315	13	.257	.319	3.03	127	159
1908	AL	8th	51-103	.331	39.5	Clark Griffith/Kid Elberfeld	305,500	459	713	13	.236	.283	.291	26	.252	.314	3.16	100	225
1909	AL	5th	74-77	.490	23.5	George Stallings	501,700	590	587	16	.248	.313	.311	21	.246	.314	2.65	103	84
1910	AL	2nd	88-63	.583	14.5	George Stallings/Hal Chase	355,857	626	557	20	.248	.320	.322	16	.243	.300	2.61	117	116
1911	AL	6th	76-76	.500	25.5	Hal Chase	302,444	684	724	25	.272	.344	.362	26	.270	.329	3.54	127	96
1912	AL	8th	50-102	.329	55.0	Harry Wolverton	242,194	630	842	18	.259	.329	.334	28	.281	.343	4.13	114	193
1913	AL	7th	57-94	.377	38.0	Frank Chance	357,551	529	668	8	.237	.320	.292	31	.255	.322	3.27	106	186
1914	AL	6th	70-84	.455	30.0	Frank Chance/Roger Peckinpaugh	359,477	537	550	12	.229	.315	.287	30	.250	.308	2.81	100	328
1915	AL	5th	69-83	.454	32.5	Wild Bill Donovan	256,035	584	588	31	.233	.317	.305	41	.254	.329	3.06	97	438
1916	AL	4th	80-74	.519	11.0	Wild Bill Donovan	469,211	577	561	35	.246	.318	.326	37	.244	.314	2.77	105	157
1917	AL	6th	71-82	.464	28.5	Wild Bill Donovan	330,294	524	558	27	.239	.310	.308	28	.251	.313	2.66	112	416
1918	AL	4th	60-63	.488	13.5	Miller Huggins	282,047	493	475	20	.257	.320	.330	25	.264	.343	3.00	88	213
1919	AL	3rd	80-59	.576	7.5	Miller Huggins	619,164	578	506	45	.267	.326	.356	47	.239	.307	2.82	111	208
1920	AL	3rd	95-59	.617	3.0	Miller Huggins	1,289,422	838	629	115	.280	.350	.426	48	.259	.316	3.32	100	191
1921	AL	1st	98-55	.641	—	Miller Huggins	1,230,696	948	708	134	.300	.375	.464	51	.277	.342	3.82	103	165
1922	AL	1st	94-60	.610	—	Miller Huggins	1,026,134	758	618	95	.287	.353	.412	73	.267	.325	3.39	97	151
1923	AL	1st	98-54	.645	—	Miller Huggins	1,007,066	823	622	105	.291	.357	.422	68	.263	.330	3.62	104	184
1924	AL	2nd	89-63	.586	2.0	Miller Huggins	1,053,533	798	667	98	.289	.352	.426	59	.281	.349	3.86	94	186
1925	AL	7th	69-85	.448	28.5	Miller Huggins	697,267	706	774	110	.275	.336	.410	78	.289	.353	4.33	90	137
1926	AL	1st	91-63	.591	—	Miller Huggins	1,027,675	847	713	121	.289	.369	.437	56	.274	.337	3.86	96	111
1927	AL	1st	110-44	.714	—	Miller Huggins	1,164,015	975	599	158	.307	.383	.489	42	.267	.323	3.20	92	133
1928	AL	1st	101-53	.656	—	Miller Huggins	1,072,132	894	685	133	.296	.365	.450	59	.264	.322	3.74	80	121
1929	AL	2nd	88-66	.571	18.0	Miller Huggins/Art Fletcher	960,148	899	775	142	.295	.363	.450	83	.278	.341	4.19	97	123
1930	AL	3rd	86-68	.558	16.0	Bob Shawkey	1,169,230	1062	898	152	.309	.384	.488	93	.287	.352	4.88	80	103
1931	AL	2nd	94-59	.614	13.5	Joe McCarthy	912,437	1067	760	155	.297	.383	.457	67	.263	.332	4.20	95	128
1932	AL	1st	107-47	.695	—	Joe McCarthy	962,320	1002	724	160	.286	.376	.454	93	.260	.331	3.98	83	98
1933	AL	2nd	91-59	.607	7.0	Joe McCarthy	728,014	927	768	144	.283	.369	.440	66	.267	.344	4.36	81	103
1934	AL	2nd	94-60	.610	7.0	Joe McCarthy	854,682	842	669	135	.278	.364	.419	71	.254	.324	3.76	84	112
1935	AL	2nd	89-60	.597	3.0	Joe McCarthy	657,508	818	632	104	.280	.358	.416	91	.251	.321	3.60	79	134
1936	AL	1st	102-51	.667	—	Joe McCarthy	976,913	1065	731	182	.300	.381	.483	84	.271	.351	4.17	80	85
1937	AL	1st	102-52	.662	—	Joe McCarthy	998,148	979	671	174	.283	.369	.456	92	.261	.325	3.65	98	103
1938	AL	1st	99-53	.651	—	Joe McCarthy	970,916	966	710	174	.274	.366	.446	85	.268	.339	3.91	104	145
1939	AL	1st	106-45	.702	—	Joe McCarthy	859,785	967	556	166	.287	.374	.451	85	.241	.319	3.31	70	107
1940	AL	3rd	88-66	.571	2.0	Joe McCarthy	988,975	817	671	155	.259	.344	.418	119	.261	.328	3.89	91	117
1941	AL	1st	101-53	.656	—	Joe McCarthy	964,722	830	631	151	.269	.346	.419	81	.248	.325	3.53	90	107
1942	AL	1st	103-51	.669	—	Joe McCarthy	922,011	801	507	108	.269	.346	.394	71	.244	.304	2.91	90	129
1943	AL	1st	98-56	.636	—	Joe McCarthy	618,330	669	542	100	.256	.337	.376	60	.234	.301	2.93	87	139
1944	AL	3rd	83-71	.539	6.0	Joe McCarthy	789,995	674	617	96	.264	.333	.387	82	.257	.326	3.39	114	134
1945	AL	4th	81-71	.533	6.5	Joe McCarthy	881,845	676	606	93	.259	.343	.373	66	.250	.316	3.45	117	270
1946	AL	3rd	87-67	.565	17.0	Joe McCarthy/Bill Dickey/Johnny Neun	2,265,512	684	547	136	.248	.334	.387	66	.243	.319	3.13	96	102
1947	AL	1st	97-57	.630	—	Bucky Harris	2,178,937	794	568	115	.271	.349	.407	95	.238	.323	3.39	87	96
1948	AL	3rd	94-60	.610	2.5	Bucky Harris	2,373,901	857	633	139	.278	.356	.432	94	.250	.336	3.75	96	114
1949	AL	1st	97-57	.630	—	Casey Stengel	2,283,676	829	637	115	.269	.362	.400	98	.242	.351	3.69	97	142
1950	AL	1st	98-56	.636	—	Casey Stengel	2,081,380	914	691	159	.282	.366	.441	118	.255	.348	4.15	93	87
1951	AL	1st	98-56	.636	—	Casey Stengel	1,950,107	798	621	140	.269	.349	.408	92	.250	.328	3.56	76	96
1952	AL	1st	95-59	.617	—	Casey Stengel	1,629,665	727	557	129	.267	.341	.403	94	.243	.324	3.14	90	101
1953	AL	1st	99-52	.656	—	Casey Stengel	1,537,811	801	547	139	.273	.359	.417	94	.251	.321	3.20	78	76
1954	AL	2nd	103-51	.669	8.0	Casey Stengel	1,475,171	805	563	133	.268	.348	.408	86	.251	.325	3.26	94	101
1955	AL	1st	96-58	.623	—	Casey Stengel	1,490,138	762	569	175	.260	.340	.418	108	.232	.326	3.23	89	89
1956	AL	1st	97-57	.630	—	Casey Stengel	1,491,784	857	631	190	.270	.347	.434	114	.249	.335	3.63	92	81
1957	AL	1st	98-56	.636	—	Casey Stengel	1,497,134	723	534	145	.268	.339	.409	110	.234	.315	3.00	80	77
1958	AL	1st	92-62	.597	—	Casey Stengel	1,428,438	759	577	164	.268	.336	.416	116	.235	.313	3.22	104	100
1959	AL	3rd	79-75	.513	15.0	Casey Stengel	1,552,030	687	647	153	.260	.319	.402	120	.244	.322	3.60	81	65
1960	AL	1st	97-57	.630	—	Casey Stengel	1,627,349	746	627	193	.260	.329	.426	123	.238	.320	3.52	83	84
1961	AL	1st	109-53	.673	—	Ralph Houk	1,747,725	827	612	240	.263	.330	.442	137	.239	.311	3.46	85	83
1962	AL	1st	96-66	.593	—	Ralph Houk	1,493,574	817	680	199	.267	.337	.426	146	.247	.310	3.70	84	88
1963	AL	1st	104-57	.646	—	Ralph Houk	1,308,920	714	547	188	.252	.309	.403	115	.232	.295	3.07	96	90
1964	AL	1st	99-63	.611	—	Yogi Berra	1,305,638	730	577	162	.253	.317	.387	129	.234	.299	3.15	100	75
1965	AL	6th	77-85	.475	25.0	Johnny Keane	1,213,552	611	604	149	.235	.299	.364	126	.245	.311	3.28	101	99
1966	AL	10th	70-89	.440	26.5	Johnny Keane/Ralph Houk	1,124,648	611	612	162	.235	.299	.374	124	.248	.306	3.41	87	89
1967	AL	9th	72-90	.444	20.0	Ralph Houk	1,259,514	522	621	100	.225	.296	.317	110	.249	.310	3.24	89	104
1968	AL	5th	83-79	.512	20.0	Ralph Houk	1,185,666	536	531	109	.214	.292	.318	99	.240	.297	2.79	101	104
1969	AL	5th-E	80-81	.497	28.5	Ralph Houk	1,067,996	562	587	94	.235	.308	.344	118	.236	.304	3.23	86	82
1970	AL	2nd-E	93-69	.574	15.0	Ralph Houk	1,136,879	680	612	111	.251	.324	.365	130	.249	.306	3.24	80	71
1971	AL	4th-E	82-80	.506	21.0	Ralph Houk	1,070,771	648	641	97	.254	.328	.360	126	.252	.306	3.43	94	81
1972	AL	4th-E	79-76	.510	6.5	Ralph Houk	966,328	557	527	103	.249	.316	.357	87	.252	.310	3.05	83	91
1973	AL	4th-E	80-82	.494	17.0	Ralph Houk	1,262,103	641	610	131	.261	.322	.378	109	.254	.313	3.34	99	94
1974	AL	2nd-E	89-73	.549	2.0	Bill Virdon	1,273,075	671	623	101	.263	.324	.368	104	.256	.323	3.31	89	81
1975	AL	3rd-E	83-77	.519	12.0	Bill Virdon/Billy Martin	1,288,048	681	588	110	.264	.325	.382	104	.249	.314	3.29	94	103
1976	AL	1st-E	97-62	.610	—	Billy Martin	2,012,434	730	575	120	.269	.328	.389	97	.241	.298	3.19	96	118
1977	AL	1st-E	100-62	.617	—	Billy Martin	2,103,092	831	651	184	.281	.344	.444	139	.254	.315	3.61	94	84
1978	AL	1st-E	100-63	.613	—	Billy Martin/Dick Howser/Bob Lemon	2,335,871	735	582	125	.267	.329	.388	111	.243	.306	3.18	94	118
1979	AL	4th-E	89-71	.556	13.5	Bob Lemon/Billy Martin	2,537,765	734	672	150	.266	.328	.406	123	.268	.323	3.83	88	97
1980	AL	1st-E	103-59	.636	—	Dick Howser	2,627,417	820	662	189	.267	.343	.425	102	.259	.316	3.58	96	90
1981	AL	1st-E	34-22	.607	—	Gene Michael													
	AL	6th-E	25-26	.490	5.0	Gene Michael/Bob Lemon	1,614,353	421	343	100	.252	.325	.391	64	.235	.293	2.90	96	84

Year	Lg	Pos	W-L	Pct	GB	Manager	Att.	R	OR	HR	Avg	OBP	Slg	Opponent HR	Avg	OBP	ERA	Park Index Runs	HR
1982	AL	5th-E	79-83	.488	16.0	Bob Lemon/Gene Michael/Clyde King	2,041,219	709	716	161	.256	.328	.398	113	.264	.323	3.99	92	88
1983	AL	3rd-E	91-71	.562	7.0	Billy Martin	2,257,976	770	703	153	.273	.337	.416	116	.260	.315	3.86	96	83
1984	AL	3rd-E	87-75	.537	17.0	Yogi Berra	1,821,815	758	679	130	.276	.339	.404	120	.264	.325	3.78	86	80
1985	AL	2nd-E	97-64	.602	2.0	Yogi Berra/Billy Martin	2,214,587	839	660	176	.267	.344	.425	157	.251	.316	3.69	88	93
1986	AL	2nd-E	90-72	.556	5.5	Lou Piniella	2,268,030	797	738	188	.271	.347	.430	175	.263	.323	4.11	106	111
1987	AL	4th-E	89-73	.549	9.0	Lou Piniella	2,427,672	788	758	196	.262	.336	.418	179	.266	.332	4.36	93	98
1988	AL	5th-E	85-76	.528	3.5	Billy Martin/Lou Piniella	2,633,701	772	748	148	.263	.333	.395	157	.267	.328	4.26	92	101
1989	AL	5th-E	74-87	.460	14.5	Dallas Green/Bucky Dent	2,170,485	698	792	130	.269	.331	.391	150	.281	.344	4.50	112	117
1990	AL	7th-E	67-95	.414	21.0	Bucky Dent/Stump Merrill	2,006,436	603	749	147	.241	.300	.366	144	.261	.336	4.21	95	95
1991	AL	5th-E	71-91	.438	20.0	Stump Merrill	1,863,733	674	777	147	.256	.316	.387	152	.271	.334	4.42	103	125
1992	AL	4th-E	76-86	.469	20.0	Buck Showalter	1,748,737	733	746	163	.261	.328	.406	129	.263	.338	4.22	109	118
1993	AL	2nd-E	88-74	.543	7.0	Buck Showalter	2,416,942	821	761	178	.279	.353	.435	170	.266	.333	4.35	86	99
1994	AL	1st-E	70-43	.619	—	Buck Showalter	1,675,557	670	534	139	.290	.374	.462	120	.267	.335	4.34	83	92
1995	AL	2nd-E	79-65	.549	7.0	Buck Showalter	1,705,257	749	688	122	.276	.357	.420	159	.261	.334	4.56	104	107
1996	AL	1st-E	92-70	.568	—	Joe Torre	2,250,839	871	787	162	.288	.360	.436	143	.265	.341	4.65	101	102
1997	AL	2nd-E	96-66	.593	2.0	Joe Torre	2,580,443	891	688	161	.287	.362	.436	144	.260	.327	3.84	89	94

Team Nicknames: Baltimore Orioles 1901-1903, New York Highlanders 1904-1913, New York Yankees 1914-1997.

Team Ballparks: Oriole Park IV 1901-1902, Hilltop Park 1903-1912, Polo Grounds V 1913-1922, Yankee Stadium I 1923-1973, Shea Stadium 1974-1975, Yankee Stadium II 1976-1997.

New York Yankees Individual Season Batting Leaders

Year	Batting Average		On-Base Percentage		Slugging Percentage		Home Runs		RBI		Stolen Bases	
1901	Mike Donlin	.340	Mike Donlin	.409	Jimmy Williams	.495	Jimmy Williams	7	Jimmy Williams	96	Cy Seymour	38
1902	Kip Selbach	.320	Kip Selbach	.393	Jimmy Williams	.500	Jimmy Williams	8	Jimmy Williams	83	Billy Gilbert	38
1903	Willie Keeler	.313	Willie Keeler	.368	Jimmy Williams	.392	Herm McFarland	5	Jimmy Williams	82	Wid Conroy	33
1904	Willie Keeler	.343	Willie Keeler	.390	Willie Keeler	.409	Patsy Dougherty / John Ganzel	6	John Anderson	82	Wid Conroy	30
1905	Willie Keeler	.302	Willie Keeler	.357	Willie Keeler	.363	Jimmy Williams	6	Jimmy Williams	62	Dave Fultz	44
1906	Hal Chase	.323	Willie Keeler	.353	Hal Chase	.395	Wid Conroy	4	Jimmy Williams	77	Wid Conroy / Danny Hoffman	32
1907	Hal Chase	.287	Kid Elberfeld	.343	Frank LaPorte	.360	Danny Hoffman	5	Hal Chase	68	Wid Conroy	41
1908	Charlie Hemphill	.297	Charlie Hemphill	.374	Charlie Hemphill	.356	Harry Niles	4	Charlie Hemphill	44	Charlie Hemphill	42
1909	Hal Chase	.283	Clyde Engle	.347	Ray Demmitt	.358	Hal Chase / Ray Demmitt	4	Clyde Engle	71	Jimmy Austin	30
1910	Hal Chase	.290	Harry Wolter	.364	Birdie Cree	.422	Birdie Cree / Harry Wolter	4	Hal Chase / Birdie Cree	73	Bert Daniels	41
1911	Birdie Cree	.348	Birdie Cree	.415	Birdie Cree	.513	Birdie Cree / Harry Wolter	4	Roy Hartzell	91	Birdie Cree	48
1912	Bert Daniels	.274	Roy Hartzell	.370	Bert Daniels	.381	Guy Zinn	6	Hal Chase	58	Bert Daniels	37
1913	Birdie Cree	.272	Harry Wolter	.377	Birdie Cree	.346	Jeff Sweeney / Harry Wolter	2	Birdie Cree	63	Bert Daniels	27
1914	Doc Cook	.283	Doc Cook	.356	Doc Cook	.326	Roger Peckinpaugh	3	Roger Peckinpaugh	51	Fritz Maisel	74
1915	Fritz Maisel	.281	Doc Cook	.364	Wally Pipp	.367	Luke Boone / Roger Peckinpaugh	5	Roy Hartzell / Wally Pipp	60	Fritz Maisel	51
1916	Wally Pipp	.262	Roger Peckinpaugh	.332	Wally Pipp	.417	Wally Pipp	12	Wally Pipp	93	Lee Magee	29
1917	Home Run Baker	.282	Home Run Baker	.345	Wally Pipp	.380	Wally Pipp	9	Home Run Baker	71	Fritz Maisel	29
1918	Home Run Baker	.306	Frank Gilhooley	.358	Home Run Baker	.409	Home Run Baker	6	Home Run Baker	62	Roger Peckinpaugh / Del Pratt	12
1919	Roger Peckinpaugh	.305	Roger Peckinpaugh	.390	Ping Bodie	.406	Home Run Baker	10	Duffy Lewis	89	Del Pratt	22
1920	Babe Ruth	.376	Babe Ruth	.530	Babe Ruth	.847	Babe Ruth	54	Babe Ruth	137	Babe Ruth	14
1921	Babe Ruth	.378	Babe Ruth	.512	Babe Ruth	.846	Babe Ruth	59	Babe Ruth	171	3 tied with	17
1922	Wally Pipp	.329	Babe Ruth	.434	Babe Ruth	.672	Babe Ruth	35	Babe Ruth	96	Bob Meusel	13
1923	Babe Ruth	.393	Babe Ruth	.545	Babe Ruth	.764	Babe Ruth	41	Babe Ruth	131	Babe Ruth	17
1924	Babe Ruth	.378	Babe Ruth	.513	Babe Ruth	.739	Babe Ruth	46	Babe Ruth	121	Bob Meusel	26
1925	Earle Combs	.342	Earle Combs	.411	Bob Meusel	.542	Bob Meusel	33	Bob Meusel	138	Ben Paschal	14
1926	Babe Ruth	.372	Babe Ruth	.516	Babe Ruth	.737	Babe Ruth	47	Babe Ruth	146	Tony Lazzeri / Bob Meusel	16
1927	Lou Gehrig	.373	Babe Ruth	.487	Babe Ruth	.772	Babe Ruth	60	Lou Gehrig	175	Bob Meusel	24
1928	Lou Gehrig	.374	Lou Gehrig	.467	Babe Ruth	.709	Babe Ruth	54	Lou Gehrig / Babe Ruth	142	Tony Lazzeri	15
1929	Tony Lazzeri	.354	Lou Gehrig	.431	Babe Ruth	.697	Babe Ruth	46	Babe Ruth	154	Earle Combs	11
1930	Lou Gehrig	.379	Babe Ruth	.493	Babe Ruth	.732	Babe Ruth	49	Lou Gehrig	174	Earle Combs	16
1931	Babe Ruth	.373	Babe Ruth	.494	Babe Ruth	.700	Lou Gehrig / Babe Ruth	46	Lou Gehrig	184	Ben Chapman	61
1932	Lou Gehrig	.349	Babe Ruth	.489	Babe Ruth	.661	Babe Ruth	41	Lou Gehrig	151	Ben Chapman	38
1933	Lou Gehrig	.334	Babe Ruth	.442	Lou Gehrig	.605	Babe Ruth	34	Lou Gehrig	139	Ben Chapman	27
1934	Lou Gehrig	.363	Lou Gehrig	.465	Lou Gehrig	.706	Lou Gehrig	49	Lou Gehrig	165	Ben Chapman	26
1935	Lou Gehrig	.329	Lou Gehrig	.466	Lou Gehrig	.583	Lou Gehrig	30	Lou Gehrig	119	Ben Chapman	17
1936	Lou Gehrig	.354	Lou Gehrig	.478	Lou Gehrig	.696	Lou Gehrig	49	Lou Gehrig	152	Frankie Crosetti	18
1937	Lou Gehrig	.351	Lou Gehrig	.473	Joe DiMaggio	.673	Joe DiMaggio	46	Joe DiMaggio	167	Frankie Crosetti	13
1938	Joe DiMaggio	.324	Bill Dickey	.412	Joe DiMaggio	.581	Joe DiMaggio	32	Joe DiMaggio	140	Frankie Crosetti	27
1939	Joe DiMaggio	.381	George Selkirk	.452	Joe DiMaggio	.671	Joe DiMaggio	30	Joe DiMaggio	126	George Selkirk	12
1940	Joe DiMaggio	.352	Joe DiMaggio	.425	Joe DiMaggio	.626	Joe DiMaggio	31	Joe DiMaggio	133	Joe Gordon	18
1941	Joe DiMaggio	.357	Joe DiMaggio	.440	Joe DiMaggio	.643	Charlie Keller	33	Joe DiMaggio	125	Phil Rizzuto	14
1942	Joe Gordon	.322	Charlie Keller	.417	Charlie Keller	.513	Charlie Keller	26	Joe DiMaggio	114	Phil Rizzuto	22
1943	Bill Johnson	.280	Charlie Keller	.396	Charlie Keller	.525	Charlie Keller	31	Nick Etten	107	Snuffy Stirnweiss	11
1944	Snuffy Stirnweiss	.319	Nick Etten	.399	Johnny Lindell	.500	Nick Etten	22	Johnny Lindell	103	Snuffy Stirnweiss	55
1945	Snuffy Stirnweiss	.309	Oscar Grimes	.395	Snuffy Stirnweiss	.476	Nick Etten	18	Nick Etten	111	Snuffy Stirnweiss	33
1946	Joe DiMaggio	.290	Charlie Keller	.405	Charlie Keller	.533	Charlie Keller	30	Charlie Keller	101	Snuffy Stirnweiss	18
1947	Joe DiMaggio	.315	George McQuinn	.395	Joe DiMaggio	.522	Joe DiMaggio	20	Tommy Henrich	98	Phil Rizzuto	11
1948	Joe DiMaggio	.320	Joe DiMaggio	.396	Joe DiMaggio	.598	Joe DiMaggio	39	Joe DiMaggio	155	Phil Rizzuto	6
1949	Tommy Henrich	.287	Tommy Henrich	.416	Tommy Henrich	.526	Tommy Henrich	24	Yogi Berra	91	Phil Rizzuto	18
1950	Phil Rizzuto	.324	Phil Rizzuto	.417	Joe DiMaggio	.585	Joe DiMaggio	32	Yogi Berra	124	Phil Rizzuto	12
1951	Yogi Berra	.294	Gene Woodling	.373	Yogi Berra	.492	Yogi Berra	27	Yogi Berra	88	Phil Rizzuto	18
1952	Mickey Mantle	.311	Mickey Mantle	.394	Mickey Mantle	.530	Yogi Berra	30	Yogi Berra	98	Phil Rizzuto	17
1953	Gene Woodling	.306	Gene Woodling	.429	Yogi Berra	.523	Yogi Berra	27	Yogi Berra	108	Mickey Mantle	8
1954	Irv Noren	.319	Mickey Mantle	.408	Mickey Mantle	.525	Mickey Mantle	27	Yogi Berra	125	Andy Carey / Mickey Mantle	5
1955	Mickey Mantle	.306	Mickey Mantle	.431	Mickey Mantle	.611	Mickey Mantle	37	Yogi Berra	108	Billy Hunter	9
1956	Mickey Mantle	.353	Mickey Mantle	.464	Mickey Mantle	.705	Mickey Mantle	52	Mickey Mantle	130	Mickey Mantle	10
1957	Mickey Mantle	.365	Mickey Mantle	.512	Mickey Mantle	.665	Mickey Mantle	34	Mickey Mantle	94	Mickey Mantle	16
1958	Mickey Mantle	.304	Mickey Mantle	.443	Mickey Mantle	.592	Mickey Mantle	42	Mickey Mantle	97	Mickey Mantle	18
1959	Bobby Richardson	.301	Mickey Mantle	.390	Mickey Mantle	.514	Mickey Mantle	31	Mickey Mantle	75	Mickey Mantle	21
1960	Bill Skowron	.309	Mickey Mantle	.399	Roger Maris	.581	Mickey Mantle	40	Roger Maris	112	Mickey Mantle	14
1961	Mickey Mantle	.317	Mickey Mantle	.448	Mickey Mantle	.687	Roger Maris	61	Roger Maris	142	Mickey Mantle	12
1962	Mickey Mantle	.321	Mickey Mantle	.486	Mickey Mantle	.605	Roger Maris	33	Roger Maris	100	Bobby Richardson	11
1963	Elston Howard	.287	Tom Tresh	.371	Elston Howard	.528	Elston Howard	28	Joe Pepitone	89	Bobby Richardson	15
1964	Elston Howard	.313	Mickey Mantle	.423	Mickey Mantle	.591	Mickey Mantle	35	Mickey Mantle	111	Tom Tresh	13
1965	Tom Tresh	.279	Tom Tresh	.348	Tom Tresh	.477	Tom Tresh	26	Tom Tresh	74	Bobby Richardson	7
1966	Joe Pepitone	.255	Tom Tresh	.341	Joe Pepitone	.463	Joe Pepitone	31	Joe Pepitone	83	Roy White	14
1967	Horace Clarke	.272	Mickey Mantle	.391	Mickey Mantle	.434	Mickey Mantle	22	Joe Pepitone	64	Horace Clarke	21
1968	Roy White	.267	Mickey Mantle	.385	Roy White	.414	Mickey Mantle	18	Roy White	62	Horace Clarke / Roy White	20
1969	Roy White	.290	Roy White	.392	Bobby Murcer	.454	Joe Pepitone	27	Bobby Murcer	82	Horace Clarke	33
1970	Thurman Munson	.302	Roy White	.387	Roy White	.473	Bobby Murcer	23	Roy White	94	Roy White	24
1971	Bobby Murcer	.331	Bobby Murcer	.427	Bobby Murcer	.543	Bobby Murcer	25	Bobby Murcer	94	Horace Clarke	17
1972	Bobby Murcer	.292	Roy White	.384	Bobby Murcer	.537	Bobby Murcer	33	Bobby Murcer	96	Roy White	23

1306

Teams: Yankees

Year	Batting Average		On-Base Percentage		Slugging Percentage		Home Runs		RBI		Stolen Bases	
1973	Bobby Murcer	.304	Thurman Munson	.362	Thurman Munson	.487	Bobby Murcer / Graig Nettles	22	Bobby Murcer	95	Roy White	16
1974	Lou Piniella	.305	Elliott Maddox	.395	Lou Piniella	.407	Graig Nettles	22	Bobby Murcer	88	Roy White	15
1975	Thurman Munson	.318	Bobby Bonds	.375	Bobby Bonds	.512	Bobby Bonds	32	Thurman Munson	102	Bobby Bonds	30
1976	Mickey Rivers	.312	Roy White	.365	Graig Nettles	.475	Graig Nettles	32	Thurman Munson	105	Mickey Rivers	43
1977	Mickey Rivers	.326	Reggie Jackson	.375	Reggie Jackson	.550	Graig Nettles	37	Reggie Jackson	110	Mickey Rivers	22
1978	Lou Piniella	.314	Willie Randolph	.381	Reggie Jackson	.477	Reggie Jackson / Graig Nettles	27	Reggie Jackson	97	Willie Randolph	36
1979	Reggie Jackson	.297	Reggie Jackson	.382	Reggie Jackson	.544	Reggie Jackson	29	Reggie Jackson	89	Willie Randolph	33
1980	Bob Watson	.307	Willie Randolph	.427	Reggie Jackson	.597	Reggie Jackson	41	Reggie Jackson	111	Willie Randolph	30
1981	Jerry Mumphrey	.307	Dave Winfield	.360	Dave Winfield	.464	Reggie Jackson	15	Dave Winfield	68	Jerry Mumphrey / Willie Randolph	14
1982	Jerry Mumphrey	.300	Willie Randolph	.368	Dave Winfield	.560	Dave Winfield	37	Dave Winfield	106	Willie Randolph	16
1983	Don Baylor	.303	Don Baylor	.361	Dave Winfield	.513	Dave Winfield	32	Dave Winfield	116	Don Baylor	17
1984	Don Mattingly	.343	Dave Winfield	.393	Don Mattingly	.537	Don Baylor	27	Don Mattingly	110	Omar Moreno	20
1985	Don Mattingly	.324	Rickey Henderson	.419	Don Mattingly	.567	Don Mattingly	35	Don Mattingly	145	Rickey Henderson	80
1986	Don Mattingly	.352	Don Mattingly	.394	Don Mattingly	.573	Don Mattingly	31	Don Mattingly	113	Rickey Henderson	87
1987	Don Mattingly	.327	Willie Randolph	.411	Don Mattingly	.559	Don Mattingly	32	Don Mattingly	115	Rickey Henderson	41
1988	Dave Winfield	.322	Dave Winfield	.398	Dave Winfield	.530	Jack Clark	27	Dave Winfield	107	Rickey Henderson	93
1989	Steve Sax	.315	Steve Sax	.364	Don Mattingly	.477	Don Mattingly	23	Don Mattingly	113	Steve Sax	43
1990	Roberto Kelly	.285	Jesse Barfield	.359	Jesse Barfield	.456	Jesse Barfield	25	Jesse Barfield	78	Steve Sax	43
1991	Steve Sax	.304	Steve Sax	.345	Mel Hall	.455	Matt Nokes	24	Mel Hall	80	Roberto Kelly	32
1992	Don Mattingly	.288	Danny Tartabull	.409	Danny Tartabull	.489	Danny Tartabull	25	Don Mattingly	86	Roberto Kelly	28
1993	Paul O'Neill	.311	Wade Boggs	.378	Paul O'Neill	.504	Danny Tartabull	31	Danny Tartabull	102	Pat Kelly	14
1994	Paul O'Neill	.359	Paul O'Neill	.460	Paul O'Neill	.603	Paul O'Neill	21	Paul O'Neill	83	Luis Polonia	20
1995	Wade Boggs	.324	Wade Boggs	.412	Paul O'Neill	.526	Paul O'Neill	22	Paul O'Neill	96	Luis Polonia	10
1996	Derek Jeter	.314	Paul O'Neill	.411	Bernie Williams	.535	Bernie Williams	29	Tino Martinez	117	Bernie Williams	17
1997	Bernie Williams	.328	Bernie Williams	.408	Tino Martinez	.577	Tino Martinez	44	Tino Martinez	141	Derek Jeter	23

Teams: Yankees

New York Yankees Individual Season Pitching Leaders

Year	ERA		Baserunners/9 IP		Innings Pitched		Strikeouts		Wins		Saves	
1901	Joe McGinnity	3.56	Joe McGinnity	12.5	Joe McGinnity	382.0	Harry Howell	93	Joe McGinnity	26	3 tied with	1
1902	Joe McGinnity	3.44	Joe McGinnity	12.4	Harry Howell	199.0	Long Tom Hughes	45	Joe McGinnity	13	14 tied with	0
1903	Clark Griffith	2.70	Clark Griffith	10.1	Jack Chesbro	324.2	Jack Chesbro	147	Jack Chesbro	21	Doc Adkins	1
											Snake Wiltse	
1904	Jack Chesbro	1.82	Jack Chesbro	8.6	Jack Chesbro	454.2	Jack Chesbro	239	Jack Chesbro	41	Walter Clarkson	1
											Clark Griffith	
1905	Jack Chesbro	2.20	Jack Chesbro	10.1	Al Orth	305.1	Jack Chesbro	156	Jack Chesbro	19	Clark Griffith	3
1906	Al Orth	2.34	Al Orth	10.2	Al Orth	338.2	Jack Chesbro	152	Al Orth	27	Clark Griffith	2
1907	Jack Chesbro	2.53	Jack Chesbro	10.7	Al Orth	248.2	Slow Joe Doyle	94	Al Orth	14	Bobby Keefe	3
1908	Jack Chesbro	2.93	Jack Chesbro	11.0	Jack Chesbro	288.2	Jack Chesbro	124	Jack Chesbro	14	3 tied with	1
1909	Joe Lake	1.88	Joe Lake	10.2	Jack Warhop	243.1	Joe Lake	117	Joe Lake	14	Jack Warhop	2
1910	Russ Ford	1.65	Russ Ford	8.2	Russ Ford	299.2	Russ Ford	209	Russ Ford	26	Jack Warhop	2
1911	Russ Ford	2.27	Russ Ford	10.6	Russ Ford	281.1	Russ Ford	158	Russ Ford	22	Jack Quinn	2
1912	George McConnell	2.75	Jack Warhop	11.5	Russ Ford	291.2	Russ Ford	112	Russ Ford	13	Jack Warhop	3
1913	Ray Caldwell	2.41	Ray Caldwell	11.0	Ray Fisher	246.1	Ray Fisher	92	Ray Fisher	12	George McConnell	3
									Russ Ford			
1914	Ray Caldwell	1.94	Ray Caldwell	8.8	Jack Warhop	216.2	Ray Keating	109	Ray Caldwell	17	5 tied with	1
1915	Ray Fisher	2.11	Ray Fisher	10.4	Ray Caldwell	305.0	Ray Caldwell	130	Ray Caldwell	19	King Cole	1
											Cy Pieh	
1916	Nick Cullop	2.05	Bob Shawkey	9.5	Bob Shawkey	276.2	Bob Shawkey	122	Bob Shawkey	24	Bob Shawkey	8
1917	Bob Shawkey	2.44	George Mogridge	10.7	Bob Shawkey	236.1	Ray Caldwell	102	Ray Caldwell	13	Allan Russell	2
									Bob Shawkey			
1918	George Mogridge	2.18	George Mogridge	10.6	George Mogridge	239.1	Slim Love	95	George Mogridge	16	George Mogridge	7
1919	Jack Quinn	2.61	Hank Thormahlen	10.5	Jack Quinn	266.0	Bob Shawkey	122	Bob Shawkey	20	Bob Shawkey	4
1920	Bob Shawkey	2.45	Bob Shawkey	11.2	Carl Mays	312.0	Bob Shawkey	126	Carl Mays	26	Jack Quinn	3
1921	Carl Mays	3.05	Carl Mays	11.1	Carl Mays	336.2	Bob Shawkey	126	Carl Mays	27	Carl Mays	7
1922	Bob Shawkey	2.91	Joe Bush	11.5	Bob Shawkey	299.2	Bob Shawkey	130	Joe Bush	26	Sad Sam Jones	8
1923	Waite Hoyt	3.02	Waite Hoyt	11.2	Joe Bush	275.2	Joe Bush	125	Sad Sam Jones	21	Sad Sam Jones	4
							Bob Shawkey					
1924	Herb Pennock	2.83	Herb Pennock	11.5	Herb Pennock	286.1	Bob Shawkey	114	Herb Pennock	21	Waite Hoyt	4
1925	Herb Pennock	2.96	Herb Pennock	11.0	Herb Pennock	277.0	Sad Sam Jones	92	Herb Pennock	16	Waite Hoyt	6
1926	Urban Shocker	3.38	Herb Pennock	11.5	Herb Pennock	266.1	Waite Hoyt	79	Herb Pennock	23	Sad Sam Jones	5
1927	Wilcy Moore	2.28	Wilcy Moore	10.4	Waite Hoyt	256.1	Waite Hoyt	86	Waite Hoyt	22	Wilcy Moore	13
1928	Herb Pennock	2.56	Herb Pennock	10.9	George Pipgras	300.2	George Pipgras	139	George Pipgras	24	Waite Hoyt	8
1929	Roy Sherid	3.61	Ed Wells	12.2	George Pipgras	225.1	George Pipgras	125	George Pipgras	18	Wilcy Moore	8
1930	George Pipgras	4.11	Red Ruffing	12.0	George Pipgras	221.0	Red Ruffing	117	George Pipgras	15	George Pipgras	4
									Red Ruffing		Roy Sherid	
1931	Lefty Gomez	2.63	Lefty Gomez	10.9	Lefty Gomez	243.0	Lefty Gomez	150	Lefty Gomez	21	Hank Johnson	4
1932	Red Ruffing	3.09	Johnny Allen	11.4	Lefty Gomez	265.1	Red Ruffing	190	Lefty Gomez	24	Johnny Allen	4
											Wilcy Moore	
1933	Lefty Gomez	3.18	Lefty Gomez	12.4	Red Ruffing	235.0	Lefty Gomez	163	Lefty Gomez	16	Wilcy Moore	8
1934	Lefty Gomez	2.33	Lefty Gomez	10.2	Lefty Gomez	281.2	Lefty Gomez	158	Lefty Gomez	26	Johnny Murphy	4
1935	Red Ruffing	3.12	Red Ruffing	11.3	Lefty Gomez	246.0	Lefty Gomez	138	Red Ruffing	16	Johnny Murphy	5
1936	Monte Pearson	3.71	Red Ruffing	12.2	Red Ruffing	271.0	Monte Pearson	118	Red Ruffing	20	Pat Malone	9
1937	Lefty Gomez	2.33	Lefty Gomez	10.6	Lefty Gomez	278.1	Lefty Gomez	194	Lefty Gomez	21	Johnny Murphy	10
1938	Red Ruffing	3.31	Red Ruffing	11.9	Red Ruffing	247.1	Lefty Gomez	129	Red Ruffing	21	Johnny Murphy	11
1939	Red Ruffing	2.93	Red Ruffing	11.1	Red Ruffing	233.1	Lefty Gomez	102	Red Ruffing	21	Johnny Murphy	19
1940	Marius Russo	3.28	Marius Russo	11.3	Red Ruffing	226.0	Red Ruffing	97	Red Ruffing	15	Johnny Murphy	9
1941	Marius Russo	3.09	Red Ruffing	11.2	Marius Russo	209.2	Marius Russo	105	Lefty Gomez	15	Johnny Murphy	15
									Red Ruffing			
1942	Tiny Bonham	2.27	Tiny Bonham	8.9	Tiny Bonham	226.0	Hank Borowy	85	Tiny Bonham	21	Johnny Murphy	11
1943	Spud Chandler	1.64	Spud Chandler	9.1	Spud Chandler	253.0	Spud Chandler	134	Spud Chandler	20	Johnny Murphy	8
1944	Hank Borowy	2.64	Hank Borowy	11.1	Hank Borowy	252.2	Hank Borowy	107	Hank Borowy	17	Jim Turner	7
1945	Tiny Bonham	3.29	Tiny Bonham	10.4	Bill Bevens	184.0	Bill Bevens	76	Bill Bevens	13	Jim Turner	10
1946	Spud Chandler	2.10	Spud Chandler	10.2	Spud Chandler	257.1	Spud Chandler	138	Spud Chandler	20	Johnny Murphy	7
1947	Spec Shea	3.07	Spec Shea	11.1	Allie Reynolds	241.2	Allie Reynolds	129	Allie Reynolds	19	Joe Page	17
1948	Spec Shea	3.41	Vic Raschi	11.5	Allie Reynolds	236.1	Vic Raschi	124	Vic Raschi	19	Joe Page	16
1949	Ed Lopat	3.26	Ed Lopat	12.4	Vic Raschi	274.2	Tommy Byrne	129	Vic Raschi	21	Joe Page	27
1950	Ed Lopat	3.47	Ed Lopat	11.9	Vic Raschi	256.2	Allie Reynolds	160	Vic Raschi	21	Joe Page	13
1951	Ed Lopat	2.91	Ed Lopat	10.9	Vic Raschi	258.1	Vic Raschi	164	Ed Lopat	21	Allie Reynolds	7
									Vic Raschi			
1952	Allie Reynolds	2.06	Vic Raschi	10.9	Allie Reynolds	244.1	Allie Reynolds	160	Allie Reynolds	20	Johnny Sain	7
1953	Ed Lopat	2.42	Vic Raschi	10.2	Whitey Ford	207.0	Whitey Ford	110	Whitey Ford	18	Allie Reynolds	13
1954	Whitey Ford	2.82	Allie Reynolds	11.6	Whitey Ford	210.2	Whitey Ford	125	Bob Grim	20	Johnny Sain	22
1955	Whitey Ford	2.63	Whitey Ford	10.7	Whitey Ford	253.2	Bob Turley	210	Whitey Ford	18	Jim Konstanty	11
1956	Whitey Ford	2.47	Tom Sturdivant	10.8	Whitey Ford	225.2	Whitey Ford	141	Whitey Ford	19	Tom Morgan	11
1957	Bobby Shantz	2.45	Bobby Shantz	10.6	Tom Sturdivant	201.2	Tom Sturdivant	152	Tom Sturdivant	16	Bob Grim	19
1958	Whitey Ford	2.01	Whitey Ford	9.8	Bob Turley	245.1	Bob Turley	168	Bob Turley	21	Ryne Duren	20
1959	Art Ditmar	2.90	Art Ditmar	9.6	Whitey Ford	204.0	Whitey Ford	114	Whitey Ford	16	Ryne Duren	14
1960	Art Ditmar	3.06	Whitey Ford	10.9	Art Ditmar	200.0	Ralph Terry	92	Art Ditmar	15	Bobby Shantz	11
1961	Bill Stafford	2.68	Ralph Terry	9.8	Whitey Ford	283.0	Whitey Ford	209	Whitey Ford	25	Luis Arroyo	29
1962	Whitey Ford	2.90	Ralph Terry	9.6	Ralph Terry	298.2	Ralph Terry	176	Ralph Terry	23	Marshall Bridges	18
1963	Jim Bouton	2.53	Ralph Terry	9.7	Whitey Ford	269.1	Whitey Ford	189	Whitey Ford	24	Hal Reniff	18
1964	Whitey Ford	2.13	Jim Bouton	9.7	Jim Bouton	271.1	Al Downing	217	Jim Bouton	18	Pete Mikkelsen	12
1965	Mel Stottlemyre	2.63	Mel Stottlemyre	10.7	Mel Stottlemyre	291.0	Al Downing	179	Mel Stottlemyre	20	Pedro Ramos	19
1966	Fritz Peterson	3.31	Fritz Peterson	10.0	Mel Stottlemyre	251.0	Al Downing	152	Fritz Peterson	12	Pedro Ramos	13
									Mel Stottlemyre			
1967	Al Downing	2.63	Al Downing	10.0	Mel Stottlemyre	255.0	Al Downing	171	Mel Stottlemyre	15	Dooley Womack	18
1968	Stan Bahnsen	2.05	Fritz Peterson	9.3	Mel Stottlemyre	278.2	Stan Bahnsen	162	Mel Stottlemyre	21	Steve Hamilton	11
1969	Fritz Peterson	2.55	Fritz Peterson	9.1	Mel Stottlemyre	303.0	Fritz Peterson	150	Mel Stottlemyre	20	Jack Aker	11
1970	Fritz Peterson	2.90	Fritz Peterson	10.0	Mel Stottlemyre	271.0	Fritz Peterson	127	Fritz Peterson	20	Lindy McDaniel	29
1971	Mel Stottlemyre	2.87	Steve Kline	9.8	Fritz Peterson	274.0	Fritz Peterson	139	Mel Stottlemyre	16	Jack Aker	4
											Lindy McDaniel	
1972	Steve Kline	2.40	Steve Kline	10.1	Mel Stottlemyre	260.0	Mel Stottlemyre	110	Fritz Peterson	17	Sparky Lyle	35
1973	Doc Medich	2.95	Doc Medich	11.3	Mel Stottlemyre	273.0	Doc Medich	145	Mel Stottlemyre	16	Sparky Lyle	27

Teams: Yankees

Year	ERA		Baserunners/9 IP		Innings Pitched		Strikeouts		Wins		Saves	
1974	Pat Dobson	3.07	Pat Dobson	11.6	Pat Dobson	281.0	Pat Dobson	157	Pat Dobson	19	Sparky Lyle	15
									Doc Medich			
1975	Catfish Hunter	2.58	Catfish Hunter	9.2	Catfish Hunter	328.0	Catfish Hunter	177	Catfish Hunter	23	Tippy Martinez	8
1976	Ed Figueroa	3.02	Catfish Hunter	10.2	Catfish Hunter	298.2	Catfish Hunter	173	Ed Figueroa	19	Sparky Lyle	23
1977	Ron Guidry	2.82	Ron Guidry	10.2	Ed Figueroa	239.1	Ron Guidry	176	Ed Figueroa	16	Sparky Lyle	26
									Ron Guidry			
1978	Ron Guidry	1.74	Ron Guidry	8.6	Ron Guidry	273.2	Ron Guidry	248	Ron Guidry	25	Goose Gossage	27
1979	Ron Guidry	2.78	Ron Guidry	10.4	Tommy John	276.1	Ron Guidry	201	Tommy John	21	Goose Gossage	18
1980	Rudy May	2.46	Rudy May	9.4	Tommy John	265.1	Ron Guidry	166	Tommy John	22	Goose Gossage	33
1981	Tommy John	2.63	Ron Guidry	9.0	Rudy May	147.2	Ron Guidry	104	Ron Guidry	11	Goose Gossage	20
1982	Tommy John	3.66	Tommy John	10.9	Ron Guidry	222.0	Dave Righetti	163	Ron Guidry	14	Goose Gossage	30
1983	Ron Guidry	3.42	Ron Guidry	10.6	Ron Guidry	250.1	Dave Righetti	169	Ron Guidry	21	Goose Gossage	22
1984	Phil Niekro	3.09	Ron Guidry	12.4	Phil Niekro	215.2	Phil Niekro	136	Phil Niekro	16	Dave Righetti	31
1985	Ron Guidry	3.27	Ron Guidry	9.9	Ron Guidry	259.0	Phil Niekro	149	Ron Guidry	22	Dave Righetti	29
1986	Dennis Rasmussen	3.88	Dennis Rasmussen	10.5	Dennis Rasmussen	202.0	Ron Guidry	140	Dennis Rasmussen	18	Dave Righetti	46
1987	Rick Rhoden	3.86	Rick Rhoden	12.3	Tommy John	187.2	Rick Rhoden	107	Rick Rhoden	16	Dave Righetti	31
1988	Rick Rhoden	4.29	Rick Rhoden	12.3	Rick Rhoden	197.0	John Candelaria	121	John Candelaria	13	Dave Righetti	25
1989	Andy Hawkins	4.80	Andy Hawkins	13.8	Andy Hawkins	208.1	Andy Hawkins	98	Andy Hawkins	15	Dave Righetti	25
1990	Tim Leary	4.11	Tim Leary	12.4	Tim Leary	208.0	Tim Leary	138	Lee Guetterman	11	Dave Righetti	36
1991	Scott Sanderson	3.81	Scott Sanderson	10.0	Scott Sanderson	208.0	Scott Sanderson	130	Scott Sanderson	16	Steve Farr	23
1992	Melido Perez	2.87	Melido Perez	11.3	Melido Perez	247.2	Melido Perez	218	Melido Perez	13	Steve Farr	30
1993	Jimmy Key	3.00	Jimmy Key	10.0	Jimmy Key	236.2	Jimmy Key	173	Jimmy Key	18	Steve Farr	25
1994	Jimmy Key	3.27	Melido Perez	11.6	Jimmy Key	168.0	Melido Perez	109	Jimmy Key	17	Steve Howe	15
1995	Jack McDowell	3.93	Jack McDowell	12.2	Jack McDowell	217.2	Jack McDowell	157	Jack McDowell	15	John Wetteland	31
1996	Andy Pettitte	3.87	Jimmy Key	12.3	Andy Pettitte	221.0	Andy Pettitte	162	Andy Pettitte	21	John Wetteland	43
1997	David Cone	2.82	Andy Pettitte	11.3	Andy Pettitte	240.1	David Cone	222	Andy Pettitte	18	Mariano Rivera	43

Teams: Yankees

Yankees Franchise Batting Leaders—Career

Games

1	Mickey Mantle	2,401
2	Lou Gehrig	2,164
3	Yogi Berra	2,116
4	Babe Ruth	2,084
5	Roy White	1,881
6	Bill Dickey	1,789
7	Don Mattingly	1,785
8	Joe DiMaggio	1,736
9	Willie Randolph	1,694
10	Frankie Crosetti	1,683
11	Phil Rizzuto	1,661
12	Tony Lazzeri	1,659
13	Graig Nettles	1,535
14	Elston Howard	1,492
15	Wally Pipp	1,488
16	Earle Combs	1,455
17	Thurman Munson	1,423
18	Bobby Richardson	1,412
19	Hank Bauer	1,406
20	Gil McDougald	1,336

At-Bats

1	Mickey Mantle	8,102
2	Lou Gehrig	8,001
3	Yogi Berra	7,546
4	Babe Ruth	7,217
5	Don Mattingly	7,003
6	Joe DiMaggio	6,821
7	Roy White	6,650
8	Willie Randolph	6,303
9	Bill Dickey	6,300
10	Frankie Crosetti	6,277
11	Tony Lazzeri	6,094
12	Phil Rizzuto	5,816
13	Earle Combs	5,748
14	Wally Pipp	5,594
15	Graig Nettles	5,519
16	Bobby Richardson	5,386
17	Thurman Munson	5,344
18	Elston Howard	5,044
19	Bob Meusel	5,032
20	Red Rolfe	4,827

Runs

1	Babe Ruth	1,959
2	Lou Gehrig	1,888
3	Mickey Mantle	1,677
4	Joe DiMaggio	1,390
5	Earle Combs	1,186
6	Yogi Berra	1,174
7	Willie Randolph	1,027
8	Don Mattingly	1,007
9	Frankie Crosetti	1,006
10	Roy White	964
11	Tony Lazzeri	952
12	Red Rolfe	942
13	Bill Dickey	930
14	Tommy Henrich	901
15	Phil Rizzuto	877
16	Wally Pipp	820
17	Hank Bauer	792
18	Bob Meusel	764
19	Graig Nettles	750
20	Dave Winfield	722

Hits

1	Lou Gehrig	2,721
2	Babe Ruth	2,518
3	Mickey Mantle	2,415
4	Joe DiMaggio	2,214
5	Don Mattingly	2,153
6	Yogi Berra	2,148
7	Bill Dickey	1,969
8	Earle Combs	1,866
9	Roy White	1,803
10	Tony Lazzeri	1,784
11	Willie Randolph	1,731
12	Phil Rizzuto	1,588
13	Wally Pipp	1,577
14	Bob Meusel	1,565
15	Thurman Munson	1,558
16	Frankie Crosetti	1,541
17	Bobby Richardson	1,432
18	Elston Howard	1,405
19	Graig Nettles	1,396
20	Red Rolfe	1,394

Doubles

1	Lou Gehrig	535
2	Don Mattingly	442
3	Babe Ruth	424
4	Joe DiMaggio	389
5	Mickey Mantle	344
6	Bill Dickey	343
7	Bob Meusel	338
8	Tony Lazzeri	327
9	Yogi Berra	321
10	Earle Combs	309
11	Roy White	300
12	Tommy Henrich	269
13	Frankie Crosetti	260
14	Wally Pipp	259
	Willie Randolph	259
16	Red Rolfe	257
17	Phil Rizzuto	239
18	Dave Winfield	236
19	Thurman Munson	229
20	Four tied at	211

Triples

1	Lou Gehrig	162
2	Earle Combs	154
3	Joe DiMaggio	131
4	Wally Pipp	121
5	Tony Lazzeri	115
6	Babe Ruth	106
7	Jimmy Williams	87
	Bob Meusel	87
9	Tommy Henrich	73
10	Bill Dickey	72
	Mickey Mantle	72
12	Charlie Keller	69
13	Red Rolfe	67
14	Snuffy Stirnweiss	66
15	Frankie Crosetti	65
16	Ben Chapman	64
17	Birdie Cree	62
	Phil Rizzuto	62
19	Wid Conroy	59
20	Willie Randolph	58

Home Runs

1	Babe Ruth	659
2	Mickey Mantle	536
3	Lou Gehrig	493
4	Joe DiMaggio	361
5	Yogi Berra	358
6	Graig Nettles	250
7	Don Mattingly	222
8	Dave Winfield	205
9	Roger Maris	203
10	Bill Dickey	202
11	Charlie Keller	184
12	Tommy Henrich	183
13	Bobby Murcer	175
14	Tony Lazzeri	169
15	Joe Pepitone	166
16	Bill Skowron	165
17	Elston Howard	161
18	Roy White	160
19	Hank Bauer	158
20	Joe Gordon	153

RBI

1	Lou Gehrig	1,995
2	Babe Ruth	1,968
3	Joe DiMaggio	1,537
4	Mickey Mantle	1,509
5	Yogi Berra	1,430
6	Bill Dickey	1,209
7	Tony Lazzeri	1,154
8	Don Mattingly	1,099
9	Bob Meusel	1,005
10	Graig Nettles	834
11	Wally Pipp	825
12	Dave Winfield	818
13	Tommy Henrich	795
14	Roy White	758
15	Elston Howard	733
16	Charlie Keller	723
17	Thurman Munson	701
18	Bobby Murcer	687
19	Bill Skowron	672
20	Hank Bauer	654

Walks

1	Babe Ruth	1,847
2	Mickey Mantle	1,733
3	Lou Gehrig	1,508
4	Willie Randolph	1,005
5	Roy White	934
6	Tony Lazzeri	831
7	Frankie Crosetti	792
8	Joe DiMaggio	790
9	Charlie Keller	760
10	Tommy Henrich	712
11	Yogi Berra	704
12	Bill Dickey	678
13	Earle Combs	670
14	Phil Rizzuto	650
15	Graig Nettles	627
16	Don Mattingly	588
17	Gil McDougald	559
18	Red Rolfe	526
19	Tom Tresh	511
20	Roger Peckinpaugh	508

Strikeouts

1	Mickey Mantle	1,710
2	Babe Ruth	1,122
3	Tony Lazzeri	821
4	Frankie Crosetti	799
5	Lou Gehrig	790
6	Graig Nettles	739
7	Elston Howard	717
8	Roy White	708
9	Dave Winfield	652
10	Tom Tresh	651
11	Gil McDougald	623
12	Clete Boyer	608
13	Hank Bauer	594
14	Bill Skowron	588
15	Reggie Jackson	573
16	Thurman Munson	571
17	Bobby Murcer	564
18	Bob Meusel	556
19	Willie Randolph	512
20	Mike Pagliarulo	510

Stolen Bases

1	Rickey Henderson	326
2	Willie Randolph	251
3	Hal Chase	248
4	Roy White	233
5	Wid Conroy	184
	Ben Chapman	184
7	Fritz Maisel	183
8	Mickey Mantle	153
9	Horace Clarke	151
	Roberto Kelly	151
11	Phil Rizzuto	149
12	Tony Lazzeri	147
13	Bert Daniels	145
14	Roger Peckinpaugh	143
15	Birdie Cree	132
16	Bob Meusel	130
	Snuffy Stirnweiss	130
18	Willie Keeler	118
19	Kid Elberfeld	117
	Steve Sax	117

Runs Created

1	Babe Ruth	2,308
2	Lou Gehrig	2,161
3	Mickey Mantle	1,950
4	Joe DiMaggio	1,554
5	Yogi Berra	1,283
6	Bill Dickey	1,196
7	Don Mattingly	1,157
8	Tony Lazzeri	1,113
9	Earle Combs	1,067
10	Roy White	1,018
11	Willie Randolph	927
12	Tommy Henrich	918
13	Bob Meusel	863
14	Frankie Crosetti	827
15	Charlie Keller	826
16	Wally Pipp	820
17	Phil Rizzuto	802
18	Graig Nettles	787
19	Red Rolfe	772
20	Hank Bauer	756

Runs Created/27 Outs

(minimum 2000 Plate Appearances)

1	Babe Ruth	12.32
2	Lou Gehrig	10.29
3	Mickey Mantle	8.93
4	Joe DiMaggio	8.67
5	Charlie Keller	8.21
6	George Selkirk	7.35
7	Rickey Henderson	7.31
8	Paul O'Neill	7.23
9	Tommy Henrich	7.10
10	Bill Dickey	7.07
11	Earle Combs	6.95
12	Reggie Jackson	6.83
13	Roger Maris	6.66
14	Tony Lazzeri	6.47
15	Ben Chapman	6.35
16	Gene Woodling	6.33
17	Yogi Berra	6.14
18	Bob Meusel	6.08
19	Bernie Williams	6.08
20	Don Mattingly	6.04

Batting Average

(minimum 2000 Plate Appearances)

1	Babe Ruth	.349
2	Lou Gehrig	.340
3	Earle Combs	.325
4	Joe DiMaggio	.325
5	Paul O'Neill	.317
6	Wade Boggs	.313
7	Bill Dickey	.313
8	Bob Meusel	.311
9	Don Mattingly	.307
10	Ben Chapman	.305
11	Whitey Witt	.300
12	Mickey Rivers	.299
13	Mickey Mantle	.298
14	Lou Piniella	.295
15	Bill Skowron	.294
16	Willie Keeler	.294
17	Steve Sax	.294
18	Tony Lazzeri	.293
19	Birdie Cree	.292
20	Bernie Williams	.292

On-Base Percentage

(minimum 2000 Plate Appearances)

1	Babe Ruth	.484
2	Lou Gehrig	.447
3	Mickey Mantle	.421
4	Charlie Keller	.410
5	Paul O'Neill	.403
6	George Selkirk	.400
7	Joe DiMaggio	.398
8	Earle Combs	.397
9	Wade Boggs	.396
10	Rickey Henderson	.395
11	Gene Woodling	.388
12	Bill Dickey	.382
13	Tommy Henrich	.382
14	Tony Lazzeri	.379
15	Ben Chapman	.379
16	Whitey Witt	.375
17	Bernie Williams	.374
18	Willie Randolph	.374
19	Reggie Jackson	.371
20	Nick Etten	.370

Slugging Percentage

(minimum 2000 Plate Appearances)

1	Babe Ruth	.711
2	Lou Gehrig	.632
3	Joe DiMaggio	.579
4	Mickey Mantle	.557
5	Reggie Jackson	.526
6	Paul O'Neill	.519
7	Charlie Keller	.518
8	Roger Maris	.515
9	Bob Meusel	.500
10	Bill Skowron	.496
11	Dave Winfield	.495
12	Tommy Henrich	.491
13	Bill Dickey	.486
14	George Selkirk	.483
15	Yogi Berra	.483
16	Don Mattingly	.471
17	Tony Lazzeri	.467
18	Joe Gordon	.467
19	Bernie Williams	.464
20	Earle Combs	.462

Teams: Yankees

Yankees Franchise Pitching Leaders—Career

Wins

1	Whitey Ford	236
2	Red Ruffing	231
3	Lefty Gomez	189
4	Ron Guidry	170
5	Bob Shawkey	168
6	Mel Stottlemyre	164
7	Herb Pennock	162
8	Waite Hoyt	157
9	Allie Reynolds	131
10	Jack Chesbro	128
11	Vic Raschi	120
12	Ed Lopat	113
13	Spud Chandler	109
	Fritz Peterson	109
15	Ray Caldwell	95
16	George Pipgras	93
	Johnny Murphy	93
18	Tommy John	91
19	Bob Turley	82
20	Jack Quinn	81

Losses

1	Mel Stottlemyre	139
2	Bob Shawkey	131
3	Red Ruffing	124
4	Whitey Ford	106
	Fritz Peterson	106
6	Lefty Gomez	101
7	Ray Caldwell	99
8	Waite Hoyt	98
9	Jack Chesbro	93
	Jack Warhop	93
11	Ron Guidry	91
12	Herb Pennock	90
13	Ray Fisher	78
14	Al Orth	73
15	Jack Quinn	65
16	George Pipgras	64
17	Dave Righetti	61
18	Allie Reynolds	60
	Tommy John	60
20	Four tied at	59

Winning Percentage
(minimum 100 decisions)

1	Spud Chandler	.717
2	Vic Raschi	.706
3	Whitey Ford	.690
4	Allie Reynolds	.686
5	Carl Mays	.669
6	Ed Lopat	.657
7	Lefty Gomez	.652
8	Ron Guidry	.651
9	Red Ruffing	.651
10	Herb Pennock	.643
	Tommy Byrne	.643
12	Johnny Murphy	.637
13	Joe Bush	.620
14	Waite Hoyt	.616
15	Ed Figueroa	.614
16	Tiny Bonham	.612
	Bob Turley	.612
18	Tommy John	.603
19	George Pipgras	.592
20	Jack Chesbro	.579

Games

1	Dave Righetti	522
2	Whitey Ford	498
3	Red Ruffing	426
4	Sparky Lyle	420
5	Bob Shawkey	415
6	Johnny Murphy	383
7	Ron Guidry	368
8	Lefty Gomez	367
9	Waite Hoyt	365
10	Mel Stottlemyre	360
11	Herb Pennock	346
12	Goose Gossage	319
13	Steve Hamilton	311
14	Allie Reynolds	295
15	Fritz Peterson	288
16	Joe Page	278
17	Jack Chesbro	269
18	Lindy McDaniel	265
19	Ray Caldwell	248
20	Four tied at	247

Games Started

1	Whitey Ford	438
2	Red Ruffing	391
3	Mel Stottlemyre	356
4	Ron Guidry	323
5	Lefty Gomez	319
6	Waite Hoyt	275
7	Bob Shawkey	274
8	Herb Pennock	268
9	Fritz Peterson	265
10	Jack Chesbro	227
11	Allie Reynolds	209
12	Vic Raschi	207
13	Tommy John	203
14	Ed Lopat	202
15	Ray Caldwell	197
16	Spud Chandler	184
17	Bob Turley	175
	Al Downing	175
19	George Pipgras	170
20	Ray Fisher	166

Complete Games

1	Red Ruffing	261
2	Lefty Gomez	173
3	Jack Chesbro	168
4	Herb Pennock	164
5	Bob Shawkey	161
6	Waite Hoyt	156
	Whitey Ford	156
8	Mel Stottlemyre	152
9	Ray Caldwell	150
10	Spud Chandler	109
11	Jack Warhop	105
12	Al Orth	102
13	Russ Ford	100
14	Vic Raschi	99
15	Allie Reynolds	96
16	Ron Guidry	95
17	Carl Mays	91
	Tiny Bonham	91
	Ed Lopat	91
20	Ray Fisher	88

Shutouts

1	Whitey Ford	45
2	Red Ruffing	40
	Mel Stottlemyre	40
4	Lefty Gomez	28
5	Allie Reynolds	27
6	Bob Shawkey	26
	Spud Chandler	26
	Ron Guidry	26
9	Vic Raschi	24
10	Bob Turley	21
11	Ed Lopat	20
12	Herb Pennock	19
13	Jack Chesbro	18
	Fritz Peterson	18
15	Ray Caldwell	17
	Tiny Bonham	17
17	Waite Hoyt	15
18	Al Orth	14
	George Pipgras	14
	Ralph Terry	14

Saves

1	Dave Righetti	224
2	Goose Gossage	151
3	Sparky Lyle	141
4	Johnny Murphy	104
5	Steve Farr	78
6	Joe Page	76
7	John Wetteland	74
8	Lindy McDaniel	58
9	Mariano Rivera	48
10	Ryne Duren	43
	Luis Arroyo	43
12	Allie Reynolds	41
	Hal Reniff	41
14	Pedro Ramos	40
15	Johnny Sain	39
16	Steve Hamilton	36
17	Wilcy Moore	35
18	Jack Aker	31
	Steve Howe	31
20	Four tied at	28

Innings Pitched

1	Whitey Ford	3,170.1
2	Red Ruffing	3,168.2
3	Mel Stottlemyre	2,661.1
4	Lefty Gomez	2,498.1
5	Bob Shawkey	2,488.2
6	Ron Guidry	2,392.0
7	Waite Hoyt	2,272.1
8	Herb Pennock	2,189.2
9	Jack Chesbro	1,952.0
10	Fritz Peterson	1,857.1
11	Ray Caldwell	1,718.1
12	Allie Reynolds	1,700.0
13	Vic Raschi	1,537.0
14	Ed Lopat	1,497.1
15	Spud Chandler	1,485.0
16	Jack Warhop	1,412.2
17	Ray Fisher	1,380.1
18	Tommy John	1,367.0
19	George Pipgras	1,351.2
20	Jack Quinn	1,270.0

Walks

1	Lefty Gomez	1,090
2	Whitey Ford	1,086
3	Red Ruffing	1,066
4	Bob Shawkey	855
5	Allie Reynolds	819
6	Mel Stottlemyre	809
7	Tommy Byrne	763
8	Bob Turley	761
9	Ron Guidry	633
10	Waite Hoyt	631
11	Vic Raschi	620
12	Ray Caldwell	576
13	George Pipgras	545
14	Al Downing	526
15	Dave Righetti	473
16	Herb Pennock	471
17	Spud Chandler	463
18	Jack Chesbro	434
19	Monte Pearson	426
20	Johnny Murphy	416

Strikeouts

1	Whitey Ford	1,956
2	Ron Guidry	1,778
3	Red Ruffing	1,526
4	Lefty Gomez	1,468
5	Mel Stottlemyre	1,257
6	Bob Shawkey	1,163
7	Al Downing	1,028
8	Allie Reynolds	967
9	Dave Righetti	940
10	Jack Chesbro	913
11	Bob Turley	909
12	Fritz Peterson	893
13	Vic Raschi	832
14	Ray Caldwell	803
15	Waite Hoyt	713
16	Herb Pennock	700
17	George Pipgras	656
18	Ralph Terry	615
19	Spud Chandler	614
20	Tommy Byrne	592

Strikeouts/9 Innings
(minimum 1000 Innings Pitched)

1	Al Downing	7.49
2	Dave Righetti	7.44
3	Ron Guidry	6.69
4	Bob Turley	6.45
5	Whitey Ford	5.55
6	Lefty Gomez	5.29
7	Allie Reynolds	5.12
8	Jim Bouton	4.98
9	Vic Raschi	4.87
10	Ralph Terry	4.62
11	Russ Ford	4.47
12	George Pipgras	4.37
13	Red Ruffing	4.33
14	Fritz Peterson	4.33
15	Mel Stottlemyre	4.25
16	Jack Chesbro	4.21
17	Bob Shawkey	4.21
18	Ray Caldwell	4.21
19	Ray Fisher	3.80
20	Spud Chandler	3.72

ERA
(minimum 1000 Innings Pitched)

1	Russ Ford	2.54
2	Jack Chesbro	2.58
3	Al Orth	2.72
4	Tiny Bonham	2.73
5	Whitey Ford	2.75
6	Spud Chandler	2.84
7	Ray Fisher	2.91
8	Mel Stottlemyre	2.97
9	Ray Caldwell	3.00
10	Fritz Peterson	3.10
11	Dave Righetti	3.11
12	Jack Warhop	3.12
13	Bob Shawkey	3.12
14	Jack Quinn	3.16
15	Ed Lopat	3.19
16	Al Downing	3.23
17	Carl Mays	3.25
18	Ron Guidry	3.29
19	Allie Reynolds	3.30
20	Lefty Gomez	3.34

Component ERA
(minimum 1000 Innings Pitched)

1	Jack Chesbro	2.33
2	Al Orth	2.42
3	Russ Ford	2.58
4	Tiny Bonham	2.66
5	Ray Caldwell	2.75
6	Spud Chandler	2.80
7	Fritz Peterson	2.92
8	Ray Fisher	2.94
9	Whitey Ford	2.97
10	Mel Stottlemyre	3.06
11	Al Downing	3.07
12	Bob Shawkey	3.07
13	Ron Guidry	3.11
14	Ralph Terry	3.12
15	Jack Warhop	3.13
16	Dave Righetti	3.18
17	Vic Raschi	3.19
18	Jack Quinn	3.21
19	Red Ruffing	3.23
20	Carl Mays	3.33

Opponent Average
(minimum 1000 Innings Pitched)

1	Bob Turley	.223
2	Al Downing	.223
3	Whitey Ford	.235
4	Vic Raschi	.236
5	Dave Righetti	.236
6	Allie Reynolds	.238
7	Jack Chesbro	.238
8	Spud Chandler	.240
9	Jim Bouton	.241
10	Lefty Gomez	.242
11	Ray Caldwell	.244
12	Ron Guidry	.244
13	Mel Stottlemyre	.245
14	Russ Ford	.245
15	Ralph Terry	.245
16	Al Orth	.247
17	Red Ruffing	.247
18	Tiny Bonham	.248
19	Bob Shawkey	.251
20	Fritz Peterson	.254

Opponent OBP
(minimum 1000 Innings Pitched)

1	Tiny Bonham	.282
2	Jack Chesbro	.286
3	Al Orth	.288
4	Ralph Terry	.288
5	Fritz Peterson	.289
6	Ron Guidry	.292
7	Russ Ford	.298
8	Whitey Ford	.300
9	Spud Chandler	.301
10	Mel Stottlemyre	.303
11	Jim Bouton	.304
12	Al Downing	.304
13	Red Ruffing	.310
14	Ray Fisher	.312
15	Dave Righetti	.313
16	Vic Raschi	.313
17	Ray Caldwell	.313
18	Ed Lopat	.316
19	Carl Mays	.317
20	Bob Shawkey	.317

Teams: Yankees

Yankees Franchise Batting Leaders—Single Season

Games

#	Player	Year	G
1	Bobby Richardson	1961	162
	Roy White	1970	162
	Roy White	1973	162
	Chris Chambliss	1978	162
	Don Mattingly	1986	162
	Roberto Kelly	1990	162
7	Roger Maris	1961	161
	Bobby Richardson	1962	161
9	Joe Pepitone	1964	160
	Bobby Richardson	1965	160
	Graig Nettles	1973	160
	Bobby Murcer	1973	160
13	Bobby Richardson	1964	159
	Roy White	1968	159
	Bobby Murcer	1970	159
	Horace Clarke	1971	159
	Graig Nettles	1978	159
	Don Mattingly	1985	159
	Derek Jeter	1997	159
20	Nine tied at		158

At-Bats

#	Player	Year	AB
1	Bobby Richardson	1962	692
2	Horace Clarke	1970	686
3	Bobby Richardson	1964	679
4	Don Mattingly	1986	677
5	Bobby Richardson	1965	664
6	Bobby Richardson	1961	662
7	Frankie Crosetti	1939	656
8	Derek Jeter	1997	654
9	Don Mattingly	1985	652
	Steve Sax	1991	652
11	Steve Sax	1989	651
12	Earle Combs	1927	648
	Red Rolfe	1937	648
	Red Rolfe	1939	648
15	Joe Dugan	1923	644
16	Snuffy Stirnweiss	1944	643
17	Horace Clarke	1969	641
	Chris Chambliss	1976	641
	Roberto Kelly	1990	641
20	Don Mattingly	1992	640

Runs

#	Player	Year	R
1	Babe Ruth	1921	177
2	Lou Gehrig	1936	167
3	Babe Ruth	1928	163
	Lou Gehrig	1931	163
5	Babe Ruth	1920	158
	Babe Ruth	1927	158
7	Babe Ruth	1923	151
	Joe DiMaggio	1937	151
9	Babe Ruth	1930	150
10	Lou Gehrig	1927	149
	Babe Ruth	1931	149
12	Rickey Henderson	1985	146
13	Babe Ruth	1924	143
	Lou Gehrig	1930	143
	Earle Combs	1932	143
	Red Rolfe	1937	143
17	Babe Ruth	1926	139
	Lou Gehrig	1928	139
	Red Rolfe	1939	139
20	Four tied at		138

Hits

#	Player	Year	H
1	Don Mattingly	1986	238
2	Earle Combs	1927	231
3	Lou Gehrig	1930	220
4	Lou Gehrig	1927	218
5	Joe DiMaggio	1937	215
6	Red Rolfe	1939	213
7	Lou Gehrig	1931	211
	Don Mattingly	1985	211
9	Lou Gehrig	1928	210
	Lou Gehrig	1934	210
11	Bobby Richardson	1962	209
12	Lou Gehrig	1932	208
13	Don Mattingly	1984	207
14	Joe DiMaggio	1936	206
15	Babe Ruth	1923	205
	Lou Gehrig	1936	205
	Snuffy Stirnweiss	1944	205
	Steve Sax	1989	205
19	Babe Ruth	1921	204
20	Earle Combs	1925	203

Doubles

#	Player	Year	2B
1	Don Mattingly	1986	53
2	Lou Gehrig	1927	52
3	Don Mattingly	1985	48
4	Lou Gehrig	1926	47
	Bob Meusel	1927	47
	Lou Gehrig	1928	47
7	Red Rolfe	1939	46
8	Babe Ruth	1923	45
	Bob Meusel	1928	45
10	Babe Ruth	1921	44
	Joe DiMaggio	1936	44
	Don Mattingly	1984	44
13	Joe DiMaggio	1941	43
14	Lou Gehrig	1930	42
	Lou Gehrig	1932	42
	Tommy Henrich	1948	42
	Paul O'Neill	1997	42
18	Ben Chapman	1932	41
	Lou Gehrig	1933	41
20	Five tied at		40

Triples

#	Player	Year	3B
1	Earle Combs	1927	23
2	Birdie Cree	1911	22
	Earle Combs	1930	22
	Snuffy Stirnweiss	1945	22
5	Jimmy Williams	1901	21
	Bill Keister	1901	21
	Jimmy Williams	1902	21
	Earle Combs	1928	21
9	Lou Gehrig	1926	20
10	Wally Pipp	1924	19
11	Lou Gehrig	1927	18
12	Lou Gehrig	1930	17
13	Birdie Cree	1910	16
	Bob Meusel	1921	16
	Babe Ruth	1921	16
	Tony Lazzeri	1932	16
	Earle Combs	1933	16
	Snuffy Stirnweiss	1944	16
	Johnny Lindell	1944	16
20	Nine tied at		15

Home Runs

#	Player	Year	HR
1	Roger Maris	1961	61
2	Babe Ruth	1927	60
3	Babe Ruth	1921	59
4	Babe Ruth	1920	54
	Babe Ruth	1928	54
	Mickey Mantle	1961	54
7	Mickey Mantle	1956	52
8	Babe Ruth	1930	49
	Lou Gehrig	1934	49
	Lou Gehrig	1936	49
11	Babe Ruth	1926	47
	Lou Gehrig	1927	47
13	Babe Ruth	1924	46
	Babe Ruth	1929	46
	Lou Gehrig	1931	46
	Babe Ruth	1931	46
	Joe DiMaggio	1937	46
18	Tino Martinez	1997	44
19	Mickey Mantle	1958	42
20	Four tied at		41

RBI

#	Player	Year	RBI
1	Lou Gehrig	1931	184
2	Lou Gehrig	1927	175
3	Lou Gehrig	1930	174
4	Babe Ruth	1921	171
5	Joe DiMaggio	1937	167
6	Lou Gehrig	1934	165
7	Babe Ruth	1927	164
8	Babe Ruth	1931	163
9	Lou Gehrig	1937	159
10	Joe DiMaggio	1948	155
11	Babe Ruth	1929	154
12	Babe Ruth	1930	153
13	Lou Gehrig	1936	152
14	Lou Gehrig	1932	151
15	Babe Ruth	1926	146
16	Don Mattingly	1985	145
17	Lou Gehrig	1928	142
	Babe Ruth	1928	142
	Roger Maris	1961	142
20	Tino Martinez	1997	141

Walks

#	Player	Year	BB
1	Babe Ruth	1923	170
2	Babe Ruth	1920	148
3	Mickey Mantle	1957	146
4	Babe Ruth	1921	144
	Babe Ruth	1926	144
6	Babe Ruth	1924	142
7	Babe Ruth	1927	138
8	Babe Ruth	1930	136
9	Babe Ruth	1928	135
10	Lou Gehrig	1935	132
11	Babe Ruth	1932	130
	Lou Gehrig	1936	130
13	Mickey Mantle	1958	129
14	Babe Ruth	1931	128
15	Lou Gehrig	1937	127
16	Mickey Mantle	1961	126
17	Lou Gehrig	1929	122
	Mickey Mantle	1962	122
19	Willie Randolph	1980	119
20	Lou Gehrig	1931	117

Strikeouts

#	Player	Year	SO
1	Danny Tartabull	1993	156
2	Jesse Barfield	1990	150
3	Roberto Kelly	1990	148
4	Jack Clark	1988	141
5	Bobby Bonds	1975	137
6	Reggie Jackson	1978	133
7	Reggie Jackson	1977	129
8	Kevin Maas	1991	128
9	Mickey Mantle	1959	126
10	Mickey Mantle	1960	125
	Derek Jeter	1997	125
12	Reggie Jackson	1980	122
	Jesse Barfield	1989	122
14	Mickey Mantle	1958	120
	Mike Pagliarulo	1986	120
16	Danny Tartabull	1992	115
17	Mickey Mantle	1967	113
18	Mickey Mantle	1961	112
19	Three tied at		111

Stolen Bases

#	Player	Year	SB
1	Rickey Henderson	1988	93
2	Rickey Henderson	1986	87
3	Rickey Henderson	1985	80
4	Fritz Maisel	1914	74
5	Ben Chapman	1931	61
6	Snuffy Stirnweiss	1944	55
7	Fritz Maisel	1915	51
8	Birdie Cree	1911	48
9	Dave Fultz	1905	44
10	Mickey Rivers	1976	43
	Steve Sax	1989	43
	Steve Sax	1990	43
13	Charlie Hemphill	1908	42
	Roberto Kelly	1990	42
15	Wid Conroy	1907	41
	Bert Daniels	1910	41
	Rickey Henderson	1987	41
18	Hal Chase	1910	40
	Bert Daniels	1911	40
20	Harry Wolter	1910	39

Runs Created

#	Player	Year	RC
1	Babe Ruth	1921	208
2	Babe Ruth	1923	193
3	Babe Ruth	1920	191
4	Lou Gehrig	1927	182
	Lou Gehrig	1930	182
6	Lou Gehrig	1936	181
7	Babe Ruth	1924	179
	Lou Gehrig	1931	179
	Babe Ruth	1931	179
10	Babe Ruth	1927	177
11	Babe Ruth	1930	176
12	Mickey Mantle	1956	174
13	Lou Gehrig	1934	171
14	Babe Ruth	1926	167
	Lou Gehrig	1937	167
16	Babe Ruth	1928	165
17	Lou Gehrig	1932	163
	Joe DiMaggio	1937	163
19	Mickey Mantle	1961	157
20	Lou Gehrig	1928	156

Runs Created/27 Outs

(minimum 3.1 Plate Appearances/Tm Gm)

#	Player	Year	RC/27
1	Babe Ruth	1920	16.44
2	Babe Ruth	1921	15.47
3	Babe Ruth	1923	14.86
4	Babe Ruth	1931	13.93
5	Mickey Mantle	1957	13.54
6	Babe Ruth	1924	13.39
7	Babe Ruth	1926	13.23
8	Mickey Mantle	1956	13.20
9	Babe Ruth	1932	12.83
10	Babe Ruth	1930	12.69
11	Babe Ruth	1927	12.53
12	Lou Gehrig	1936	12.32
13	Lou Gehrig	1930	12.12
14	Lou Gehrig	1927	12.00
15	Lou Gehrig	1934	11.93
16	Mickey Mantle	1962	11.79
17	Mickey Mantle	1961	11.73
18	Joe DiMaggio	1939	11.71
19	Lou Gehrig	1937	11.59
20	Babe Ruth	1928	11.48

Batting Average

(minimum 3.1 Plate Appearances/Tm Gm)

#	Player	Year	AVG
1	Babe Ruth	1923	.393
2	Joe DiMaggio	1939	.381
3	Lou Gehrig	1930	.379
4	Babe Ruth	1924	.378
5	Babe Ruth	1921	.378
6	Babe Ruth	1920	.376
7	Lou Gehrig	1928	.374
8	Lou Gehrig	1927	.373
9	Babe Ruth	1931	.373
10	Babe Ruth	1926	.372
11	Mickey Mantle	1957	.365
12	Lou Gehrig	1934	.363
13	Babe Ruth	1930	.359
14	Paul O'Neill	1994	.359
15	Joe DiMaggio	1941	.357
16	Earle Combs	1927	.356
17	Babe Ruth	1927	.356
18	Tony Lazzeri	1929	.354
19	Lou Gehrig	1936	.354
20	Mickey Mantle	1956	.353

On-Base Percentage

(minimum 3.1 Plate Appearances/Tm Gm)

#	Player	Year	OBP
1	Babe Ruth	1923	.545
2	Babe Ruth	1920	.530
3	Babe Ruth	1926	.516
4	Babe Ruth	1924	.513
5	Mickey Mantle	1957	.512
6	Babe Ruth	1921	.512
7	Babe Ruth	1931	.494
8	Lou Gehrig	1930	.493
9	Lou Gehrig	1932	.489
10	Babe Ruth	1927	.487
11	Mickey Mantle	1962	.486
12	Lou Gehrig	1936	.478
13	Lou Gehrig	1927	.474
14	Lou Gehrig	1930	.473
15	Lou Gehrig	1937	.473
16	Lou Gehrig	1928	.467
17	Lou Gehrig	1935	.466
18	Lou Gehrig	1934	.465
19	Mickey Mantle	1956	.464
20	Babe Ruth	1928	.461

Slugging Percentage

(minimum 3.1 Plate Appearances/Tm Gm)

#	Player	Year	SLG
1	Babe Ruth	1920	.847
2	Babe Ruth	1921	.846
3	Babe Ruth	1927	.772
4	Lou Gehrig	1927	.765
5	Babe Ruth	1923	.764
6	Babe Ruth	1924	.739
7	Babe Ruth	1926	.737
8	Babe Ruth	1930	.732
9	Lou Gehrig	1930	.721
10	Babe Ruth	1928	.709
11	Lou Gehrig	1934	.706
12	Mickey Mantle	1956	.705
13	Babe Ruth	1931	.700
14	Babe Ruth	1929	.697
15	Lou Gehrig	1936	.696
16	Mickey Mantle	1961	.687
17	Joe DiMaggio	1937	.673
18	Babe Ruth	1922	.672
19	Joe DiMaggio	1939	.671
20	Mickey Mantle	1957	.665

Teams: Yankees

Yankees Franchise Pitching Leaders—Single Season

Wins

1	Jack Chesbro	1904	41
2	Al Orth	1906	27
	Carl Mays	1921	27
4	Joe McGinnity	1901	26
	Russ Ford	1910	26
	Carl Mays	1920	26
	Joe Bush	1922	26
	Lefty Gomez	1934	26
9	Whitey Ford	1961	25
	Ron Guidry	1978	25
11	Bob Shawkey	1916	24
	George Pipgras	1928	24
	Lefty Gomez	1932	24
	Whitey Ford	1963	24
15	Jack Powell	1904	23
	Jack Chesbro	1906	23
	Herb Pennock	1926	23
	Waite Hoyt	1928	23
	Ralph Terry	1962	23
	Catfish Hunter	1975	23

Losses

1	Joe Lake	1908	22
2	Harry Howell	1901	21
	Al Orth	1907	21
	Russ Ford	1912	21
	Sad Sam Jones	1925	21
6	Joe McGinnity	1901	20
	Jack Chesbro	1908	20
	Mel Stottlemyre	1966	20
9	Jack Powell	1904	19
	Jack Warhop	1912	19
	Tim Leary	1990	19
12	Russ Ford	1913	18
	Mel Stottlemyre	1972	18
14	Jack Chesbro	1906	17
	Al Orth	1906	17
	Herb Pennock	1925	17
17	Thirteen tied at		16

Winning Percentage
(minimum 15 decisions)

1	Ron Guidry	1978	.893
2	Ron Davis	1979	.875
3	Whitey Ford	1961	.862
4	Ralph Terry	1961	.842
5	Lefty Gomez	1934	.839
6	Spud Chandler	1943	.833
7	Russ Ford	1910	.813
	Atley Donald	1939	.813
	Jim Coates	1960	.813
10	Johnny Allen	1932	.810
	Jimmy Key	1994	.810
12	Tiny Bonham	1942	.808
13	Ed Wells	1930	.800
	Ed Lopat	1953	.800
15	Hank Borowy	1942	.789
16	Joe Bush	1922	.788
17	Ron Guidry	1985	.786
18	Bump Hadley	1936	.778
	Don Gullett	1977	.778
	Bob Wickman	1993	.778

Games

1	Jeff Nelson	1997	77
2	Dave Righetti	1985	74
	Dave Righetti	1986	74
4	Jeff Nelson	1996	73
5	Sparky Lyle	1977	72
6	Lee Guetterman	1989	70
7	Greg Cadaret	1991	68
8	Sparky Lyle	1974	66
	John Habyan	1991	66
	Mariano Rivera	1997	66
11	Luis Arroyo	1961	65
	Pedro Ramos	1965	65
	Dooley Womack	1967	65
14	Sparky Lyle	1976	64
	Goose Gossage	1980	64
	Dave Righetti	1984	64
	Lee Guetterman	1990	64
	Lee Guetterman	1991	64
	Mike Stanton	1997	64
20	Three tied at		63

Games Started

1	Jack Chesbro	1904	51
2	Jack Powell	1904	45
3	Joe McGinnity	1901	43
4	Jack Chesbro	1906	42
5	Al Orth	1906	39
	Whitey Ford	1961	39
	Ralph Terry	1962	39
	Mel Stottlemyre	1969	39
	Pat Dobson	1974	39
	Catfish Hunter	1975	39
11	Jack Chesbro	1905	38
	Carl Mays	1921	38
	George Pipgras	1928	38
	Mel Stottlemyre	1973	38
	Doc Medich	1974	38
16	Twelve tied at		37

Complete Games

1	Jack Chesbro	1904	48
2	Joe McGinnity	1901	39
3	Jack Powell	1904	38
4	Al Orth	1906	36
5	Jack Chesbro	1903	33
6	Harry Howell	1901	32
7	Ray Caldwell	1915	31
8	Russ Ford	1912	30
	Carl Mays	1921	30
	Catfish Hunter	1975	30
11	Russ Ford	1910	29
12	Al Orth	1905	26
	Russ Ford	1911	26
	Carl Mays	1920	26
15	Herb Pennock	1924	25
	Lefty Gomez	1934	25
	Red Ruffing	1936	25
	Lefty Gomez	1937	25
19	Four tied at		24

Shutouts

1	Ron Guidry	1978	9
2	Russ Ford	1910	8
	Whitey Ford	1964	8
4	Allie Reynolds	1951	7
	Whitey Ford	1958	7
	Mel Stottlemyre	1971	7
	Mel Stottlemyre	1972	7
	Catfish Hunter	1975	7
9	Fourteen tied at		6

Saves

1	Dave Righetti	1986	46
2	John Wetteland	1996	43
	Mariano Rivera	1997	43
4	Dave Righetti	1990	36
5	Sparky Lyle	1972	35
6	Goose Gossage	1980	33
7	Dave Righetti	1984	31
	Dave Righetti	1987	31
	John Wetteland	1995	31
10	Goose Gossage	1982	30
	Steve Farr	1992	30
12	Luis Arroyo	1961	29
	Lindy McDaniel	1970	29
	Dave Righetti	1985	29
15	Joe Page	1949	27
	Sparky Lyle	1973	27
	Goose Gossage	1978	27
18	Sparky Lyle	1977	26
19	Three tied at		25

Innings Pitched

1	Jack Chesbro	1904	454.2
2	Jack Powell	1904	390.1
3	Joe McGinnity	1901	382.0
4	Al Orth	1906	338.2
5	Carl Mays	1921	336.2
6	Catfish Hunter	1975	328.0
7	Jack Chesbro	1906	325.0
8	Jack Chesbro	1903	324.2
9	Carl Mays	1920	312.0
10	Al Orth	1905	305.1
11	Ray Caldwell	1915	305.0
12	Jack Chesbro	1905	303.1
13	Mel Stottlemyre	1969	303.0
14	George Pipgras	1928	300.2
15	Russ Ford	1910	299.2
	Bob Shawkey	1922	299.2
17	Ralph Terry	1962	298.2
	Catfish Hunter	1976	298.2
19	Harry Howell	1901	294.2
20	Russ Ford	1912	291.2

Walks

1	Tommy Byrne	1949	179
2	Bob Turley	1955	177
3	Tommy Byrne	1950	160
4	Vic Raschi	1949	138
	Allie Reynolds	1950	138
6	Monte Pearson	1936	135
7	Bob Turley	1958	128
8	Allie Reynolds	1947	123
	Allie Reynolds	1949	123
10	Lefty Gomez	1936	122
11	Al Downing	1964	120
	Phil Niekro	1985	120
13	Joe Bush	1923	117
14	Slim Love	1918	116
	Vic Raschi	1950	116
16	Red Ruffing	1932	115
17	Monte Pearson	1938	113
	Whitey Ford	1955	113
19	Allie Reynolds	1948	111
20	Whitey Ford	1953	110

Strikeouts

1	Ron Guidry	1978	248
2	Jack Chesbro	1904	239
3	David Cone	1997	222
4	Melido Perez	1992	218
5	Al Downing	1964	217
6	Bob Turley	1955	210
7	Russ Ford	1910	209
	Whitey Ford	1961	209
9	Jack Powell	1904	202
10	Ron Guidry	1979	201
11	Lefty Gomez	1937	194
12	Red Ruffing	1932	190
13	Whitey Ford	1963	189
14	Al Downing	1965	179
15	Catfish Hunter	1975	177
16	Lefty Gomez	1932	176
	Ralph Terry	1962	176
	Ron Guidry	1977	176
19	Catfish Hunter	1976	173
	Jimmy Key	1993	173

Strikeouts/9 Innings
(minimum 1 Inning Pitched/Tm Gm)

1	David Cone	1997	10.25
2	Al Downing	1963	8.76
3	Melido Perez	1993	8.17
4	Ron Guidry	1978	8.16
5	Dave Righetti	1982	8.02
6	Al Downing	1964	8.00
7	Melido Perez	1992	7.92
8	Bob Turley	1957	7.76
9	Bob Turley	1955	7.66
10	Ron Guidry	1979	7.65
11	Al Downing	1967	7.63
12	Al Downing	1965	7.60
13	Ron Guidry	1977	7.52
14	Ron Guidry	1981	7.37
15	Dave Righetti	1983	7.01
16	Al Downing	1966	6.84
17	Rudy May	1980	6.83
18	Ron Guidry	1980	6.80
19	Whitey Ford	1961	6.65
20	Dwight Gooden	1996	6.64

ERA
(minimum 1 Inning Pitched/Tm Gm)

1	Spud Chandler	1943	1.64
2	Russ Ford	1910	1.65
3	Ron Guidry	1978	1.74
4	Jack Chesbro	1904	1.82
5	Hippo Vaughn	1910	1.83
6	Joe Lake	1909	1.88
7	Ray Caldwell	1914	1.94
8	Whitey Ford	1958	2.01
9	Nick Cullop	1916	2.05
10	Stan Bahnsen	1968	2.05
11	Allie Reynolds	1952	2.06
12	Spud Chandler	1946	2.10
13	Ray Fisher	1915	2.11
14	Lew Brockett	1909	2.12
15	Whitey Ford	1964	2.13
16	George Mogridge	1918	2.18
17	Jack Chesbro	1905	2.20
18	Bob Shawkey	1916	2.21
19	Bill Bevens	1946	2.23
20	Tiny Bonham	1942	2.27

Component ERA
(minimum 1 Inning Pitched/Tm Gm)

1	Russ Ford	1910	1.41
2	Jack Chesbro	1904	1.56
3	Ray Caldwell	1914	1.67
4	Ron Guidry	1978	1.71
5	Spud Chandler	1943	1.82
6	Bob Shawkey	1916	1.86
7	Fritz Peterson	1969	2.08
8	Al Downing	1963	2.09
9	Tiny Bonham	1942	2.11
10	Catfish Hunter	1975	2.18
11	Jack Chesbro	1905	2.21
12	Joe Lake	1909	2.22
13	Butch Wensloff	1943	2.23
14	Stan Bahnsen	1968	2.24
15	Spud Chandler	1946	2.25
16	Al Orth	1906	2.26
17	Ron Guidry	1981	2.27
18	Jack Warhop	1914	2.28
19	Fritz Peterson	1968	2.28
20	Ray Fisher	1914	2.31

Opponent Average
(minimum 1 Inning Pitched/Tm Gm)

1	Tommy Byrne	1949	.183
2	Al Downing	1963	.184
3	Russ Ford	1910	.188
4	Bob Turley	1955	.193
5	Ron Guidry	1978	.193
6	Bob Turley	1957	.194
7	Spec Shea	1947	.200
8	Don Larsen	1956	.204
9	Jack Chesbro	1904	.205
10	Ray Caldwell	1914	.205
11	Bob Turley	1958	.206
12	Whitey Ford	1955	.208
13	Spec Shea	1948	.208
14	Catfish Hunter	1975	.208
15	Bob Shawkey	1916	.209
16	Art Ditmar	1959	.211
17	Jim Bouton	1963	.212
18	Allie Reynolds	1951	.213
19	Ron Guidry	1981	.214
20	Spud Chandler	1943	.215

Opponent OBP
(minimum 1 Inning Pitched/Tm Gm)

1	Russ Ford	1910	.245
2	Jack Chesbro	1904	.248
3	Ron Guidry	1978	.249
4	Ron Guidry	1981	.256
5	Tiny Bonham	1942	.259
6	Ray Caldwell	1914	.260
7	Catfish Hunter	1975	.261
8	Fritz Peterson	1969	.261
9	Spud Chandler	1943	.261
10	Rudy May	1980	.268
11	Ralph Terry	1962	.268
12	Art Ditmar	1959	.268
13	Fritz Peterson	1968	.270
14	Stan Bahnsen	1968	.271
15	Ralph Terry	1963	.271
16	Jim Bouton	1964	.272
17	Bob Shawkey	1916	.273
18	Steve Kline	1971	.275
19	Ralph Terry	1961	.275
20	Whitey Ford	1958	.276

Yankees Capsule

Best Season: The *1927* Yankees won the pennant by 19 games and swept the Pittsburgh Pirates in the World Series, setting the standard by which all other great teams have been judged ever since.

Worst Season: *1965.* Johnny Keane took the reins of a club that had won five straight pennants, and arrived just in time to witness the end of the Yankees' 45-year dynasty. Hit hard by injuries, the aging Yankees fell to sixth place, and tumbled into the cellar the following year.

Best Player: *Babe Ruth.*

Best Pitcher: *Whitey Ford.* This is a surprisingly difficult choice. Red Ruffing's record with the Yankees was nearly as impressive, and Ruffing was one of the best-hitting pitchers of all time. Spud Chandler almost never lost, but he came up late and lost several years to World War II. In the final analysis, Ford's relentless brilliance wins out.

Best Reliever: *Goose Gossage.* Few relievers inspired more fear.

Best Defensive Players: *Clete Boyer, Graig Nettles, Joe DiMaggio, Mickey Mantle.* Brooks Robinson kept Boyer and Nettles from winning more Gold Gloves.

Hall of Famers: *Yogi Berra, Jack Chesbro, Earle Combs, Bill Dickey, Joe DiMaggio, Whitey Ford, Lou Gehrig, Waite Hoyt, Tony Lazzeri, Mickey Mantle, Herb Pennock, Phil Rizzuto, Red Ruffing, Babe Ruth.* The Yankees also put three managers in Cooperstown—*Miller Huggins, Joe McCarthy* and *Casey Stengel.* Executive *Lee MacPhail* also made it.

Franchise All-Star Team:

C	Yogi Berra	**LF**	Charlie Keller
1B	Lou Gehrig	**CF**	Mickey Mantle
2B	Joe Gordon	**RF**	Babe Ruth
3B	Graig Nettles	**DH**	Don Baylor
SS	Phil Rizzuto	**SP**	Whitey Ford
		RP	Goose Gossage

Biggest Flakes: *Joe Pepitone, Sparky Lyle, Mickey Rivers.*

Strangest Career: *Johnny Lindell* came up as a pitcher in 1942, but he moved to the outfield when Joe DiMaggio and Tommy Henrich went into the service in 1943. He batted .300 with 103 RBI in 1944, and remained a semi-regular after the war. In 1951, he went back to the minors to take up pitching once more as a knuckleballer. The following year, he won 24 games to earn a return trip to the majors. He pitched 32 games for two different clubs in 1953, going 6-17 before retiring for good in early 1954.

What Might Have Been: *Tom Tresh* won the AL Rookie of the Year Award in 1962. Over the next several years, he proved to be a strong all-around performer, hitting for good power while proving adept both as an infielder and outfielder. A knee injury in spring training of 1967 suddenly ended his days as a useful player, although he hung on for three more years.

Best Trade: The acquistion of *Babe Ruth* from the Red Sox for $125,000 in cash and $300,000 in loans sent the franchise on the path to greatness.

Worst Trade: Future Cy Young Award winner *Doug Drabek* was dealt to the Pirates in a six-player trade in 1986 that netted starter Rick Rhoden and a couple of relievers.

Best-Looking Players: *Mickey Mantle, Bucky Dent.*

Ugliest Player: *Hank Bauer.*

Best Nicknames: *"Babe Ruth's Legs," Sammy Byrd; George "Twinkletoes" Selkirk; Cuddles Marshall; Yogi Berra; "The Scooter," Phil Rizzuto.*

Most Unappreciated Player: *Roy White* was easily underestimated because he didn't excel in any particular area. He had virtually no weaknesses, however, and performed admirably for over a decade. He had good power and speed, he drew walks and he played solid defense in Yankee Stadium's spacious left field.

Most Overrated Player: *Bucky Dent.* Good looks and a timely wind-blown fly ball were all that distinguished him from the likes of Alvaro Espinoza.

Most Admirable Stars: *Lou Gehrig, Don Mattingly.*

Least Admirable Stars: *Carl Mays, Joe Bush, Hal Chase, Ben Chapman.* Miller Huggins wasn't the only one who suspected that Mays and Bush had thrown World Series games in the early '20s. Chase was corruption personified. Chapman was a virulent racist; as the Phillies' manager in 1947, he baited Jackie Robinson so viciously that the National League ordered him to cease and desist.

Best Season, Player: *Babe Ruth, 1921.* He batted .378 with 59 home runs, and set a personal high with 171 RBI. He also pitched twice, winning both games.

Best Season, Pitcher: *Ron Guidry, 1978.* Guidry went 25-3 with a 1.74 ERA. His presence kept the staff from completely disintegrating when a string of injuries hit in midsummer, and he won the crucial playoff game against the Red Sox to give the Yankees the AL East crown.

Most Impressive Individual Record: *Roger Maris.* He earned the single-season home-run record. Honorable mention goes to Lou Gehrig, who used to hold a notable consecutive-games record.

Biggest Tragedies: *Lou Gehrig, Thurman Munson.* Gehrig died of amyotrophic lateral sclerosis in 1941. Munson died in a plane crash in August 1979.

Fan Favorites: *Babe Ruth, Bucky Dent, Don Mattingly.*

—Mat Olkin

Philadelphia/Kansas City/Oakland Athletics (1901-1997)

														Opponent				Park Index	
Year	Lg	Pos	W-L	Pct	GB	Manager	Att.	R	OR	HR	Avg	OBP	Slg	HR	Avg	OBP	ERA	Runs	HR
1901	AL	4th	74-62	.544	9.0	Connie Mack	206,329	805	761	35	.289	.337	.395	20	.281	.340	4.00	101	82
1902	AL	1st	83-53	.610	—	Connie Mack	420,078	775	636	38	.287	.340	.389	33	.274	.335	3.29	115	67
1903	AL	2nd	75-60	.556	14.5	Connie Mack	422,473	597	519	32	.264	.309	.363	20	.249	.309	2.98	109	100
1904	AL	5th	81-70	.536	12.5	Connie Mack	512,294	557	503	31	.249	.298	.336	13	.227	.287	2.35	98	149
1905	AL	1st	92-56	.622	—	Connie Mack	554,576	623	492	24	.255	.310	.338	21	.225	.292	2.19	113	117
1906	AL	4th	78-67	.538	12.0	Connie Mack	489,129	561	543	32	.247	.308	.330	9	.234	.303	2.60	85	163
1907	AL	2nd	88-57	.607	1.5	Connie Mack	625,581	582	511	22	.255	.311	.329	13	.222	.286	2.35	112	143
1908	AL	6th	68-85	.444	22.0	Connie Mack	455,062	486	562	21	.223	.281	.292	10	.235	.298	2.56	119	108
1909	AL	2nd	95-58	.621	3.5	Connie Mack	674,915	605	408	21	.256	.321	.343	9	.218	.283	1.93	96	77
1910	AL	1st	102-48	.680	—	Connie Mack	588,905	673	441	19	.266	.326	.355	8	.221	.292	1.79	95	49
1911	AL	1st	101-50	.669	—	Connie Mack	605,749	861	601	35	.296	.357	.398	17	.265	.339	3.01	80	46
1912	AL	3rd	90-62	.592	15.0	Connie Mack	517,653	779	658	22	.282	.349	.377	12	.258	.336	3.32	99	97
1913	AL	1st	96-57	.627	—	Connie Mack	571,896	794	592	33	.280	.356	.375	24	.229	.304	3.19	92	139
1914	AL	1st	99-53	.651	—	Connie Mack	346,641	749	529	29	.272	.348	.352	18	.249	.322	2.78	91	181
1915	AL	8th	43-109	.283	58.5	Connie Mack	146,223	545	888	16	.237	.304	.311	22	.278	.388	4.29	110	222
1916	AL	8th	36-117	.235	54.5	Connie Mack	184,471	447	776	19	.242	.303	.313	26	.267	.364	3.92	108	249
1917	AL	8th	55-98	.359	44.5	Connie Mack	221,432	529	691	17	.254	.316	.323	23	.250	.326	3.27	93	236
1918	AL	8th	52-76	.406	24.0	Connie Mack	177,926	412	538	22	.243	.303	.308	13	.264	.346	3.22	114	175
1919	AL	8th	36-104	.257	52.0	Connie Mack	225,209	457	742	35	.244	.300	.334	44	.290	.362	4.26	125	316
1920	AL	8th	48-106	.312	50.0	Connie Mack	287,888	558	834	44	.252	.304	.338	56	.300	.360	3.93	94	316
1921	AL	8th	53-100	.346	45.0	Connie Mack	344,430	657	894	82	.274	.330	.389	85	.300	.367	4.61	116	300
1922	AL	7th	65-89	.422	29.0	Connie Mack	425,356	705	830	111	.270	.331	.402	107	.297	.357	4.59	116	289
1923	AL	6th	69-83	.454	29.0	Connie Mack	534,122	661	761	53	.271	.334	.370	68	.280	.351	4.08	101	101
1924	AL	5th	71-81	.467	20.0	Connie Mack	531,992	685	778	63	.281	.334	.389	43	.292	.367	4.39	99	111
1925	AL	2nd	88-64	.579	8.5	Connie Mack	869,703	831	713	76	.307	.364	.434	60	.276	.347	3.87	101	110
1926	AL	3rd	83-67	.553	6.0	Connie Mack	714,508	677	570	61	.269	.341	.383	38	.268	.332	3.00	133	179
1927	AL	2nd	91-63	.591	19.0	Connie Mack	605,529	841	726	56	.303	.372	.414	65	.278	.338	3.97	89	105
1928	AL	2nd	98-55	.641	2.5	Connie Mack	689,756	829	615	89	.295	.364	.436	66	.256	.314	3.36	100	126
1929	AL	1st	104-46	.693	—	Connie Mack	839,176	901	615	122	.296	.365	.451	73	.264	.329	3.44	114	165
1930	AL	1st	102-52	.662	—	Connie Mack	721,663	951	751	125	.294	.369	.452	84	.274	.337	4.28	94	153
1931	AL	1st	107-45	.704	—	Connie Mack	627,464	858	626	118	.287	.355	.435	73	.258	.319	3.47	101	104
1932	AL	2nd	94-60	.610	13.0	Connie Mack	405,500	981	752	172	.290	.366	.457	112	.271	.336	4.45	130	199
1933	AL	3rd	79-72	.523	19.5	Connie Mack	297,138	875	853	139	.285	.362	.440	77	.283	.361	4.81	88	159
1934	AL	5th	68-82	.453	31.0	Connie Mack	305,847	764	838	144	.280	.343	.425	84	.275	.363	5.01	98	134
1935	AL	8th	58-91	.389	34.0	Connie Mack	233,173	710	869	112	.279	.341	.406	73	.285	.372	5.12	105	131
1936	AL	8th	53-100	.346	49.0	Connie Mack	285,173	714	1045	72	.269	.336	.376	131	.300	.381	6.08	107	143
1937	AL	7th	54-97	.358	46.5	Connie Mack/Earle Mack	430,738	699	854	94	.267	.341	.397	105	.281	.357	4.85	90	93
1938	AL	8th	53-99	.349	46.0	Connie Mack	385,357	726	956	98	.270	.348	.396	142	.292	.365	5.48	108	101
1939	AL	7th	55-97	.362	51.5	Connie Mack/Earle Mack	395,022	711	1022	98	.271	.336	.400	148	.307	.375	5.79	102	108
1940	AL	8th	54-100	.351	36.0	Connie Mack	432,145	703	932	105	.262	.334	.387	135	.283	.348	5.22	98	92
1941	AL	8th	64-90	.416	37.0	Connie Mack	528,894	713	840	85	.268	.340	.387	136	.279	.348	4.83	108	115
1942	AL	8th	55-99	.357	48.0	Connie Mack	423,487	549	801	33	.249	.309	.325	89	.263	.344	4.45	99	93
1943	AL	8th	49-105	.318	49.0	Connie Mack	376,735	497	717	26	.232	.294	.297	73	.265	.336	4.05	112	99
1944	AL	5th	72-82	.468	17.0	Connie Mack	505,322	525	594	36	.257	.314	.327	58	.252	.307	3.26	98	98
1945	AL	8th	52-98	.347	34.5	Connie Mack	462,631	494	638	33	.245	.306	.316	55	.262	.337	3.62	92	75
1946	AL	8th	49-105	.318	55.0	Connie Mack	621,793	529	680	40	.253	.318	.338	83	.264	.340	3.90	116	92
1947	AL	5th	78-76	.506	19.0	Connie Mack	911,566	633	614	61	.252	.333	.349	85	.247	.326	3.51	99	103
1948	AL	4th	84-70	.545	12.5	Connie Mack	945,076	729	735	68	.260	.353	.362	86	.275	.355	4.43	103	108
1949	AL	5th	81-73	.526	16.0	Connie Mack	816,514	726	725	82	.260	.361	.369	105	.263	.360	4.23	97	82
1950	AL	8th	52-102	.338	46.0	Connie Mack	309,805	670	913	100	.261	.349	.378	138	.287	.376	5.49	83	89
1951	AL	6th	70-84	.455	28.0	Jimmy Dykes	465,469	736	745	102	.262	.349	.386	109	.272	.347	4.47	116	109
1952	AL	4th	79-75	.513	16.0	Jimmy Dykes	627,100	664	723	89	.253	.343	.359	113	.263	.333	4.15	130	132
1953	AL	7th	59-95	.383	41.5	Jimmy Dykes	362,113	632	799	116	.256	.321	.372	121	.271	.349	4.67	109	108
1954	AL	8th	51-103	.331	60.0	Eddie Joost	304,666	542	875	94	.236	.305	.342	141	.285	.366	5.18	108	125
1955	AL	6th	63-91	.409	33.0	Lou Boudreau	1,393,054	638	911	121	.261	.322	.382	175	.278	.363	5.35	104	159
1956	AL	8th	52-102	.338	45.0	Lou Boudreau	1,015,154	619	831	112	.252	.315	.370	187	.271	.357	4.86	108	141
1957	AL	7th	59-94	.386	38.5	Lou Boudreau/Harry Craft	901,067	563	710	166	.244	.295	.394	153	.260	.333	4.19	99	110
1958	AL	7th	73-81	.474	19.0	Harry Craft	925,090	642	713	138	.247	.307	.381	150	.262	.323	4.15	116	177
1959	AL	7th	66-88	.429	28.0	Harry Craft	963,683	681	760	117	.263	.326	.390	148	.274	.338	4.35	108	109
1960	AL	8th	58-96	.377	39.0	Bob Elliott	774,944	615	756	110	.249	.316	.366	160	.271	.339	4.38	103	103
1961	AL	9th	61-100	.379	47.5	Joe Gordon/Hank Bauer	683,817	683	863	90	.247	.320	.354	141	.275	.351	4.74	108	69
1962	AL	9th	72-90	.444	24.0	Hank Bauer	635,675	745	837	116	.263	.332	.386	199	.263	.343	4.79	105	137
1963	AL	8th	73-89	.451	31.5	Ed Lopat	762,364	615	704	95	.247	.313	.353	156	.256	.324	3.92	119	124
1964	AL	10th	57-105	.352	42.0	Ed Lopat/Mel McGaha	642,478	621	836	166	.239	.311	.379	220	.269	.344	4.71	117	163
1965	AL	10th	59-103	.364	43.0	Mel McGaha/Haywood Sullivan	528,344	585	755	110	.240	.309	.358	161	.256	.329	4.24	99	74
1966	AL	7th	74-86	.463	23.0	Alvin Dark	773,929	564	648	70	.236	.294	.337	106	.241	.323	3.56	88	34
1967	AL	10th	62-99	.385	29.5	Alvin Dark/Luke Appling	726,639	533	660	69	.233	.296	.330	125	.238	.313	3.68	103	41
1968	AL	6th	82-80	.506	21.0	Bob Kennedy	837,466	569	544	94	.240	.304	.343	124	.227	.295	2.94	97	77
1969	AL	2nd-W	88-74	.543	9.0	Hank Bauer/John McNamara	778,232	740	678	148	.249	.329	.376	163	.245	.320	3.71	83	85
1970	AL	2nd-W	89-73	.549	9.0	John McNamara	778,355	678	593	171	.249	.325	.392	134	.234	.307	3.30	90	84
1971	AL	1st-W	101-60	.627	—	Dick Williams	914,993	691	564	160	.252	.321	.384	131	.228	.296	3.05	98	117
1972	AL	1st-W	93-62	.600	—	Dick Williams	921,323	604	457	134	.240	.306	.366	96	.226	.284	2.58	89	111
1973	AL	1st-W	94-68	.580	—	Dick Williams	1,000,763	758	615	147	.260	.333	.389	143	.241	.305	3.29	70	93
1974	AL	1st-W	90-72	.556	—	Alvin Dark	845,693	689	551	132	.247	.321	.373	90	.246	.302	2.95	97	102
1975	AL	1st-W	98-64	.605	—	Alvin Dark	1,075,518	758	606	151	.254	.333	.391	102	.236	.306	3.27	82	87
1976	AL	2nd-W	87-74	.540	2.5	Chuck Tanner	780,593	686	598	113	.246	.323	.361	96	.255	.308	3.26	97	116
1977	AL	7th-W	63-98	.391	38.5	Jack McKeon/Bobby Winkles	495,599	605	749	117	.240	.308	.352	145	.265	.333	4.04	91	93
1978	AL	6th-W	69-93	.426	23.0	Bobby Winkles/Jack McKeon	526,999	532	690	100	.245	.303	.351	106	.259	.330	3.62	103	103
1979	AL	7th-W	54-108	.333	34.0	Jim Marshall	306,763	573	860	108	.239	.302	.346	147	.288	.363	4.75	79	77
1980	AL	2nd-W	83-79	.512	14.0	Billy Martin	842,259	686	642	137	.259	.322	.385	142	.244	.310	3.46	86	70
1981	AL	1st-W	37-23	.617	—	Billy Martin													
	AL	2nd-W	27-22	.551	1.0	Billy Martin	1,304,052	458	403	104	.247	.312	.379	80	.240	.311	3.30	89	120

Year	Lg	Pos	W-L	Pct	GB	Manager	Att.	R	OR	HR	Avg	OBP	Slg	HR	Avg	OBP	ERA	Runs	HR
														Opponent				**Park Index**	
1982	AL	5th-W	68-94	.420	25.0	Billy Martin	1,735,489	691	819	149	.236	.309	.367	177	.268	.343	4.54	93	90
1983	AL	4th-W	74-88	.457	25.0	Steve Boros	1,294,941	708	782	121	.262	.326	.381	135	.263	.337	4.34	92	80
1984	AL	4th-W	77-85	.475	7.0	Steve Boros/Jackie Moore	1,353,281	738	796	158	.259	.327	.404	155	.278	.348	4.48	84	91
1985	AL	4th-W	77-85	.475	14.0	Jackie Moore	1,334,599	757	787	155	.264	.325	.401	172	.259	.331	4.41	86	76
1986	AL	3rd-W	76-86	.469	16.0	J. Moore/J. Newman/T. La Russa	1,314,646	731	760	163	.252	.322	.390	166	.247	.330	4.31	87	86
1987	AL	3rd-W	81-81	.500	4.0	Tony La Russa	1,678,921	806	789	199	.260	.333	.428	176	.258	.324	4.32	81	77
1988	AL	1st-W	104-58	.642	—	Tony La Russa	2,287,335	800	620	156	.263	.336	.399	116	.247	.316	3.44	86	72
1989	AL	1st-W	99-63	.611	—	Tony La Russa	2,667,225	712	576	127	.261	.331	.381	103	.239	.305	3.09	103	102
1990	AL	1st-W	103-59	.636	—	Tony La Russa	2,900,217	733	570	164	.254	.336	.391	123	.238	.302	3.18	77	73
1991	AL	4th-W	84-78	.519	11.0	Tony La Russa	2,713,493	760	776	159	.248	.331	.389	155	.260	.342	4.57	86	84
1992	AL	1st-W	96-66	.593	—	Tony La Russa	2,494,160	745	672	142	.258	.346	.386	129	.256	.332	3.73	95	122
1993	AL	7th-W	68-94	.420	26.0	Tony La Russa	2,035,025	715	846	158	.254	.330	.394	157	.276	.356	4.90	86	98
1994	AL	2nd-W	51-63	.447	1.0	Tony La Russa	1,242,692	549	589	113	.260	.330	.399	128	.257	.347	4.80	82	80
1995	AL	4th-W	67-77	.465	11.5	Tony La Russa	1,174,310	730	761	169	.264	.341	.420	153	.269	.347	4.93	82	93
1996	AL	3rd-W	78-84	.481	12.0	Art Howe	1,148,380	861	900	243	.265	.344	.452	205	.287	.362	5.20	103	92
1997	AL	4th-W	65-97	.401	25.0	Art Howe	1,264,621	764	946	197	.260	.339	.423	197	.301	.372	5.49	108	106

Team Nicknames: Philadelphia Athletics 1901-1955, Kansas City Athletics 1956-1968, Oakland Athletics 1969-1997.

Team Ballparks: Columbia Park 1901-1908, Shibe Park/Connie Mack Stadium 1909-1954, Municipal Stadium (KC) 1955-1967, Oakland-Alameda Coliseum 1968-1997.

Teams: Athletics

Philadelphia/Kansas City/Oakland Athletics
Individual Season Batting Leaders

Year	Batting Average		On-Base Percentage		Slugging Percentage		Home Runs		RBI		Stolen Bases	
1901	Nap Lajoie	.426	Nap Lajoie	.463	Nap Lajoie	.643	Nap Lajoie	14	Nap Lajoie	125	Dave Fultz	36
1902	Lave Cross	.342	Topsy Hartsel	.383	Socks Seybold	.506	Socks Seybold	16	Lave Cross	108	Topsy Hartsel	47
1903	Topsy Hartsel	.311	Topsy Hartsel	.391	Topsy Hartsel	.477	Socks Seybold	8	Lave Cross	90	Ollie Pickering	40
1904	Socks Seybold	.292	Socks Seybold	.351	Danny Murphy	.440	Harry Davis	10	Danny Murphy	77	Danny Murphy	22
1905	Harry Davis	.282	Topsy Hartsel	.411	Harry Davis	.418	Harry Davis	8	Harry Davis	83	Danny Hoffman	46
1906	Danny Murphy	.301	Topsy Hartsel	.363	Harry Davis	.459	Harry Davis	12	Harry Davis	96	Topsy Hartsel	31
1907	Simon Nicholls	.302	Topsy Hartsel	.405	Harry Davis	.399	Harry Davis	8	Socks Seybold	92	Rube Oldring	29
1908	Danny Murphy	.265	Topsy Hartsel	.371	Danny Murphy	.364	Harry Davis	5	Danny Murphy	66	Harry Davis	20
1909	Eddie Collins	.346	Eddie Collins	.416	Eddie Collins	.449	Danny Murphy	5	Home Run Baker	85	Eddie Collins	67
1910	Eddie Collins	.322	Eddie Collins	.381	Danny Murphy	.436	Danny Murphy	4	Eddie Collins	81	Eddie Collins	81
							Rube Oldring					
1911	Eddie Collins	.365	Eddie Collins	.451	Home Run Baker	.508	Home Run Baker	11	Home Run Baker	115	Home Run Baker	38
											Eddie Collins	
1912	Eddie Collins	.348	Eddie Collins	.450	Home Run Baker	.541	Home Run Baker	10	Home Run Baker	130	Eddie Collins	63
1913	Eddie Collins	.345	Eddie Collins	.441	Home Run Baker	.492	Home Run Baker	12	Home Run Baker	117	Eddie Collins	55
1914	Eddie Collins	.344	Eddie Collins	.452	Eddie Collins	.452	Home Run Baker	9	Stuffy McInnis	95	Eddie Collins	58
1915	Stuffy McInnis	.314	Amos Strunk	.371	Amos Strunk	.427	Rube Oldring	6	Nap Lajoie	61	Jimmy Walsh	22
1916	Amos Strunk	.316	Amos Strunk	.393	Amos Strunk	.421	Wally Schang	7	Stuffy McInnis	60	Jimmy Walsh	27
1917	Stuffy McInnis	.303	Amos Strunk	.363	Ping Bodie	.418	Ping Bodie	7	Ping Bodie	74	Stuffy McInnis	18
1918	George Burns	.352	George Burns	.390	George Burns	.467	Tilly Walker	11	George Burns	70	Merlin Kopp	22
1919	George Burns	.296	George Burns	.339	Tilly Walker	.450	Tilly Walker	10	Tilly Walker	64	Merlin Kopp	16
1920	Joe Dugan	.322	Joe Dugan	.351	Joe Dugan	.442	Tilly Walker	17	Tilly Walker	82	Tilly Walker	9
1921	Whitey Witt	.315	Whitey Witt	.390	Tilly Walker	.504	Tilly Walker	23	Tilly Walker	101	Whitey Witt	16
1922	Bing Miller	.336	Bing Miller	.373	Bing Miller	.553	Tilly Walker	37	Tilly Walker	99	Chick Galloway	10
											Bing Miller	
1923	Joe Hauser	.307	Joe Hauser	.398	Joe Hauser	.475	Joe Hauser	17	Joe Hauser	94	Wid Matthews	16
1924	Al Simmons	.308	Joe Hauser	.358	Joe Hauser	.516	Joe Hauser	27	Joe Hauser	115	Al Simmons	16
1925	Al Simmons	.384	Al Simmons	.416	Al Simmons	.596	Al Simmons	24	Al Simmons	129	Chick Galloway	16
1926	Al Simmons	.343	Max Bishop	.431	Al Simmons	.566	Al Simmons	19	Al Simmons	109	Al Simmons	10
1927	Ty Cobb	.357	Max Bishop	.442	Mickey Cochrane	.495	Al Simmons	15	Al Simmons	108	Ty Cobb	22
1928	Al Simmons	.351	Max Bishop	.435	Al Simmons	.558	Joe Hauser	16	Al Simmons	107	Bing Miller	10
1929	Al Simmons	.365	Jimmie Foxx	.463	Al Simmons	.642	Al Simmons	34	Al Simmons	157	Bing Miller	24
1930	Al Simmons	.381	Al Simmons	.429	Al Simmons	.708	Jimmie Foxx	37	Al Simmons	165	Bing Miller	13
1931	Al Simmons	.390	Al Simmons	.444	Al Simmons	.641	Jimmie Foxx	30	Al Simmons	128	Bing Miller	5
1932	Jimmie Foxx	.364	Jimmie Foxx	.469	Jimmie Foxx	.749	Jimmie Foxx	58	Jimmie Foxx	169	Jimmy Dykes	8
											Eric McNair	
1933	Jimmie Foxx	.356	Mickey Cochrane	.459	Jimmie Foxx	.703	Jimmie Foxx	48	Jimmie Foxx	163	Mickey Cochrane	8
											Bob Johnson	
1934	Jimmie Foxx	.334	Jimmie Foxx	.449	Jimmie Foxx	.653	Jimmie Foxx	44	Jimmie Foxx	130	Bob Johnson	12
1935	Jimmie Foxx	.346	Jimmie Foxx	.461	Jimmie Foxx	.636	Jimmie Foxx	36	Jimmie Foxx	115	Rabbit Warstler	8
1936	Wally Moses	.345	Wally Moses	.410	Bob Johnson	.525	Bob Johnson	25	Bob Johnson	121	Skeeter Newsome	13
1937	Wally Moses	.320	Bob Johnson	.425	Bob Johnson	.556	Bob Johnson	25	Bob Johnson	108	Bill Werber	35
							Wally Moses					
1938	Bob Johnson	.313	Bob Johnson	.406	Bob Johnson	.552	Bob Johnson	30	Bob Johnson	113	Bill Werber	19
1939	Bob Johnson	.338	Bob Johnson	.440	Bob Johnson	.553	Bob Johnson	23	Bob Johnson	114	Bob Johnson	15
1940	Wally Moses	.309	Wally Moses	.396	Bob Johnson	.514	Bob Johnson	31	Bob Johnson	103	Frankie Hayes	9
1941	Dick Siebert	.334	Wally Moses	.388	Sam Chapman	.543	Sam Chapman	25	Bob Johnson	107	Sam Chapman	6
											Bob Johnson	
1942	Bob Johnson	.291	Bob Johnson	.384	Bob Johnson	.451	Bob Johnson	13	Bob Johnson	80	Elmer Valo	13
1943	Irv Hall	.256	Jo-Jo White	.335	Dick Siebert	.328	Bobby Estalella	11	Dick Siebert	72	Johnny Welaj	12
											Jo-Jo White	
1944	Dick Siebert	.306	Dick Siebert	.387	Dick Siebert	.423	Frankie Hayes	13	Frankie Hayes	78	Ford Garrison	10
1945	Bobby Estalella	.299	Bobby Estalella	.399	Bobby Estalella	.435	Bobby Estalella	8	George Kell	56	Hal Peck	5
1946	Pete Suder	.281	Sam Chapman	.327	Sam Chapman	.429	Sam Chapman	20	Sam Chapman	67	Elmer Valo	9
1947	Barney McCosky	.328	Ferris Fain	.414	Ferris Fain	.423	Sam Chapman	14	Sam Chapman	83	Elmer Valo	11
1948	Barney McCosky	.326	Ferris Fain	.412	Hank Majeski	.454	Eddie Joost	16	Hank Majeski	120	Ferris Fain	10
											Elmer Valo	
1949	Elmer Valo	.283	Eddie Joost	.429	Sam Chapman	.455	Sam Chapman	24	Sam Chapman	108	Elmer Valo	14
1950	Ferris Fain	.282	Ferris Fain	.430	Sam Chapman	.434	Sam Chapman	23	Sam Chapman	95	Elmer Valo	12
1951	Ferris Fain	.344	Ferris Fain	.451	Gus Zernial	.525	Gus Zernial	33	Gus Zernial	125	Elmer Valo	11
1952	Ferris Fain	.327	Ferris Fain	.438	Gus Zernial	.452	Gus Zernial	29	Gus Zernial	100	Elmer Valo	12
1953	Dave Philley	.303	Dave Philley	.358	Gus Zernial	.559	Gus Zernial	42	Gus Zernial	108	Dave Philley	13
1954	Jim Finigan	.302	Jim Finigan	.381	Jim Finigan	.421	Bill Wilson	15	Gus Zernial	62	Spook Jacobs	17
1955	Vic Power	.319	Vic Power	.354	Vic Power	.505	Gus Zernial	30	Gus Zernial	84	Elmer Valo	5
1956	Vic Power	.309	Harry Simpson	.347	Harry Simpson	.490	Harry Simpson	21	Harry Simpson	105	Al Pilarcik	9
1957	Vic Power	.259	Vic Power	.291	Gus Zernial	.471	Gus Zernial	27	Gus Zernial	69	Billy Martin	7
1958	Bob Cerv	.305	Bob Cerv	.371	Bob Cerv	.592	Bob Cerv	38	Bob Cerv	104	Bill Tuttle	7
1959	Bill Tuttle	.300	Bill Tuttle	.369	Bob Cerv	.479	Bob Cerv	20	Bob Cerv	87	Bill Tuttle	10
1960	Norm Siebern	.279	Norm Siebern	.366	Norm Siebern	.471	Norm Siebern	19	Norm Siebern	69	Russ Snyder	7
1961	Norm Siebern	.296	Norm Siebern	.384	Norm Siebern	.475	Norm Siebern	18	Norm Siebern	98	Dick Howser	37
1962	Norm Siebern	.308	Norm Siebern	.412	Norm Siebern	.495	Norm Siebern	25	Norm Siebern	117	Ed Charles	20
1963	Wayne Causey	.280	Norm Siebern	.358	Norm Siebern	.410	Norm Siebern	16	Norm Siebern	83	Jose Tartabull	16
1964	Wayne Causey	.281	Wayne Causey	.377	Rocky Colavito	.507	Rocky Colavito	34	Rocky Colavito	102	Ed Charles	12
1965	Bert Campaneris	.270	Wayne Causey	.341	Ken Harrelson	.429	Ken Harrelson	23	Ken Harrelson	66	Bert Campaneris	51
1966	Bert Campaneris	.267	Mike Hershberger	.313	Bert Campaneris	.379	Roger Repoz	11	Dick Green	62	Bert Campaneris	52
1967	Danny Cater	.270	Danny Cater	.317	Danny Cater	.340	Rick Monday	14	Rick Monday	58	Bert Campaneris	55
1968	Danny Cater	.290	Rick Monday	.371	Reggie Jackson	.452	Reggie Jackson	29	Reggie Jackson	74	Bert Campaneris	62
1969	Sal Bando	.281	Reggie Jackson	.410	Reggie Jackson	.608	Reggie Jackson	47	Reggie Jackson	118	Bert Campaneris	62
1970	Bert Campaneris	.279	Sal Bando	.407	Don Mincher	.460	Don Mincher	27	Sal Bando	75	Bert Campaneris	42
1971	Reggie Jackson	.277	Sal Bando	.377	Reggie Jackson	.508	Reggie Jackson	32	Sal Bando	94	Bert Campaneris	34
1972	Joe Rudi	.305	Mike Epstein	.376	Mike Epstein	.490	Mike Epstein	26	Sal Bando	77	Bert Campaneris	52
1973	Reggie Jackson	.293	Gene Tenace	.387	Reggie Jackson	.531	Reggie Jackson	32	Reggie Jackson	117	Bill North	53

Teams: Athletics

Year	Batting Average		On-Base Percentage		Slugging Percentage		Home Runs		RBI		Stolen Bases	
1974	Joe Rudi	.293	Reggie Jackson	.391	Reggie Jackson	.514	Reggie Jackson	29	Sal Bando	103	Bill North	54
1975	Claudell Washington	.308	Gene Tenace	.395	Reggie Jackson	.511	Reggie Jackson	36	Reggie Jackson	104	Claudell Washington	40
1976	Bill North	.276	Gene Tenace	.373	Gene Tenace	.458	Sal Bando	27	Joe Rudi	94	Bill North	75
1977	Mitchell Page	.307	Mitchell Page	.405	Mitchell Page	.521	Wayne Gross	22	Mitchell Page	75	Mitchell Page	42
1978	Mitchell Page	.285	Mitchell Page	.355	Mitchell Page	.459	Mitchell Page	17	Mitchell Page	70	Miguel Dilone	50
1979	Dave Revering	.288	Dave Revering	.334	Dave Revering	.483	Jeff Newman	22	Dave Revering	77	Rickey Henderson	33
1980	Rickey Henderson	.303	Rickey Henderson	.420	Tony Armas	.500	Tony Armas	35	Tony Armas	109	Rickey Henderson	100
1981	Rickey Henderson	.319	Rickey Henderson	.408	Tony Armas	.480	Tony Armas	22	Tony Armas	76	Rickey Henderson	56
1982	Rickey Henderson	.267	Rickey Henderson	.398	Tony Armas	.433	Tony Armas	28	Dwayne Murphy	94	Rickey Henderson	130
1983	Rickey Henderson	.292	Rickey Henderson	.414	Davey Lopes	.423	Davey Lopes Dwayne Murphy	17	Dwayne Murphy	75	Rickey Henderson	108
1984	Carney Lansford	.300	Rickey Henderson	.399	Dave Kingman	.505	Dave Kingman	35	Dave Kingman	118	Rickey Henderson	66
1985	Mike Davis	.287	Mike Davis	.348	Mike Davis	.484	Dave Kingman	30	Dave Kingman	91	Dave Collins	29
1986	Alfredo Griffin	.285	Tony Phillips	.367	Jose Canseco	.457	Dave Kingman	35	Jose Canseco	117	Alfredo Griffin	33
1987	Mark McGwire	.289	Mark McGwire	.370	Mark McGwire	.618	Mark McGwire	49	Mark McGwire	118	Alfredo Griffin	29
1988	Jose Canseco	.307	Jose Canseco	.391	Jose Canseco	.569	Jose Canseco	42	Jose Canseco	124	Jose Canseco	40
1989	Carney Lansford	.336	Carney Lansford	.398	Mark McGwire	.467	Mark McGwire	33	Dave Parker	97	Rickey Henderson	52
1990	Rickey Henderson	.325	Rickey Henderson	.439	Rickey Henderson	.577	Mark McGwire	39	Mark McGwire	108	Rickey Henderson	65
1991	Harold Baines	.295	Rickey Henderson	.400	Jose Canseco	.556	Jose Canseco	44	Jose Canseco	122	Rickey Henderson	58
1992	Mike Bordick	.300	Mark McGwire	.385	Mark McGwire	.585	Mark McGwire	42	Mark McGwire	104	Rickey Henderson	48
1993	Brent Gates	.290	Brent Gates	.357	Brent Gates	.391	Ruben Sierra	22	Ruben Sierra	101	Rickey Henderson	31
1994	Geronimo Berroa	.306	Rickey Henderson	.411	Geronimo Berroa	.485	Ruben Sierra	23	Ruben Sierra	92	Stan Javier	24
1995	Rickey Henderson	.300	Rickey Henderson	.407	Geronimo Berroa	.451	Mark McGwire	39	Mark McGwire	90	Stan Javier	36
1996	Mark McGwire	.312	Mark McGwire	.467	Mark McGwire	.730	Mark McGwire	52	Mark McGwire	113	Allen Battle	10
1997	Jason Giambi	.293	Jason Giambi	.362	Jason Giambi	.495	Mark McGwire	34	Jason Giambi Mark McGwire	81	Jason McDonald	13

Teams: Athletics

1319

Philadelphia/Kansas City/Oakland Athletics
Individual Season Pitching Leaders

Year	ERA		Baserunners/9 IP		Innings Pitched		Strikeouts		Wins		Saves	
1901	Eddie Plank	3.31	Eddie Plank	11.5	Chick Fraser	331.0	Chick Fraser	110	Chick Fraser	22	Wiley Piatt	1
1902	Rube Waddell	2.05	Rube Waddell	9.7	Eddie Plank	300.0	Rube Waddell	210	Rube Waddell	24	3 tied with	1
1903	Eddie Plank	2.38	Rube Waddell	10.2	Eddie Plank	336.0	Rube Waddell	302	Eddie Plank	23	Ed Pinnance	1
1904	Rube Waddell	1.62	Rube Waddell	9.7	Rube Waddell	383.0	Rube Waddell	349	Eddie Plank	26	9 tied with	0
1905	Rube Waddell	1.48	Rube Waddell	9.1	Eddie Plank	346.2	Rube Waddell	287	Rube Waddell	27	Rube Waddell	4
1906	Rube Waddell	2.21	Chief Bender	10.0	Rube Waddell	272.2	Rube Waddell	196	Eddie Plank	19	Chief Bender	3
1907	Chief Bender	2.05	Chief Bender	9.1	Eddie Plank	343.2	Rube Waddell	232	Eddie Plank	24	Chief Bender	3
1908	Eddie Plank	2.17	Eddie Plank	9.5	Rube Vickers	317.0	Jimmy Dygert	164	Rube Vickers	18	Rube Vickers	2
1909	Harry Krause	1.39	Chief Bender	8.9	Eddie Plank	265.1	Chief Bender	161	Eddie Plank	19	3 tied with	1
1910	Jack Coombs	1.30	Chief Bender	8.6	Jack Coombs	353.0	Jack Coombs	224	Jack Coombs	31	Tommy Atkins	2
											Eddie Plank	
1911	Eddie Plank	2.10	Chief Bender	10.8	Jack Coombs	336.2	Jack Coombs	185	Jack Coombs	28	Eddie Plank	4
1912	Eddie Plank	2.22	Chief Bender	10.7	Jack Coombs	262.1	Jack Coombs	120	Eddie Plank	26	Jack Coombs	3
1913	Chief Bender	2.20	Eddie Plank	10.2	Eddie Plank	242.2	Eddie Plank	151	Chief Bender	21	Chief Bender	13
1914	Chief Bender	2.26	Chief Bender	10.8	Bob Shawkey	237.0	Eddie Plank	110	Chief Bender	17	3 tied with	3
									Joe Bush			
1915	John Wyckoff	3.52	John Wyckoff	13.3	John Wyckoff	276.0	John Wyckoff	157	John Wyckoff	10	Harry Eccles	1
											Herb Pennock	
1916	Joe Bush	2.57	Joe Bush	11.1	Elmer Myers	315.0	Elmer Myers	182	Joe Bush	15	3 tied with	1
1917	Joe Bush	2.47	Jing Johnson	11.5	Joe Bush	233.1	Joe Bush	121	Joe Bush	11	Elmer Myers	3
1918	Scott Perry	1.98	Scott Perry	11.0	Scott Perry	332.1	Scott Perry	81	Scott Perry	20	Bob Geary	4
1919	Rollie Naylor	3.34	Rollie Naylor	12.2	Rollie Naylor	204.2	Walt Kinney	97	Jing Johnson	9	Walt Kinney	2
									Walt Kinney			
1920	Eddie Rommel	2.85	Eddie Rommel	11.0	Scott Perry	263.2	Rollie Naylor	90	Scott Perry	11	Scott Perry	1
											Eddie Rommel	
1921	Eddie Rommel	3.94	Eddie Rommel	12.6	Eddie Rommel	285.1	Slim Harriss	92	Eddie Rommel	16	Eddie Rommel	3
1922	Eddie Rommel	3.28	Eddie Rommel	11.1	Eddie Rommel	294.0	Slim Harriss	102	Eddie Rommel	27	Slim Harriss	3
1923	Eddie Rommel	3.27	Eddie Rommel	12.5	Eddie Rommel	297.2	Slim Harriss	89	Eddie Rommel	18	Slim Harriss	6
1924	Stan Baumgartner	2.88	Stan Baumgartner	12.8	Eddie Rommel	278.0	Eddie Rommel	72	Eddie Rommel	18	Stan Baumgartner	4
1925	Sam Gray	3.27	Sam Gray	11.7	Eddie Rommel	261.0	Lefty Grove	116	Eddie Rommel	21	Rube Walberg	7
1926	Lefty Grove	2.51	Eddie Rommel	11.5	Lefty Grove	258.0	Lefty Grove	194	Lefty Grove	13	Lefty Grove	6
											Joe Pate	
1927	Jack Quinn	3.17	Jack Quinn	10.9	Lefty Grove	262.1	Lefty Grove	174	Lefty Grove	20	Lefty Grove	9
1928	Lefty Grove	2.58	Lefty Grove	10.1	Lefty Grove	261.2	Lefty Grove	183	Lefty Grove	24	Lefty Grove	4
											Eddie Rommel	
1929	Lefty Grove	2.81	Lefty Grove	11.8	Lefty Grove	275.0	Lefty Grove	170	George Earnshaw	24	Bill Shores	7
1930	Lefty Grove	2.54	Lefty Grove	10.5	George Earnshaw	296.0	Lefty Grove	209	Lefty Grove	28	Lefty Grove	9
1931	Lefty Grove	2.06	Lefty Grove	9.7	Rube Walberg	291.0	Lefty Grove	175	Lefty Grove	31	George Earnshaw	6
1932	Lefty Grove	2.84	Lefty Grove	10.8	Lefty Grove	291.2	Lefty Grove	188	Lefty Grove	25	Lefty Grove	7
1933	Lefty Grove	3.20	Lefty Grove	12.0	Lefty Grove	275.1	Lefty Grove	114	Lefty Grove	24	Lefty Grove	6
1934	Sugar Cain	4.41	Johnny Marcum	13.5	Johnny Marcum	232.0	Johnny Marcum	92	Johnny Marcum	14	Bill Dietrich	3
1935	George Blaeholder	3.99	Johnny Marcum	12.6	Johnny Marcum	242.2	Johnny Marcum	99	Johnny Marcum	17	Bill Dietrich	3
											Johnny Marcum	
1936	Harry Kelley	3.86	Harry Kelley	12.5	Harry Kelley	235.1	Harry Kelley	82	Harry Kelley	15	3 tied with	3
1937	Eddie Smith	3.94	Eddie Smith	12.4	George Caster	231.2	George Caster	100	Harry Kelley	13	Eddie Smith	5
1938	George Caster	4.35	Bud Thomas	13.7	George Caster	281.1	George Caster	112	George Caster	16	Nels Potter	5
1939	Lynn Nelson	4.78	Lynn Nelson	13.7	Lynn Nelson	197.2	Lynn Nelson	75	Lynn Nelson	10	Chubby Dean	7
1940	Johnny Babich	3.73	Johnny Babich	11.9	Johnny Babich	229.1	Johnny Babich	94	Johnny Babich	14	Ed Heusser	5
1941	Phil Marchildon	3.57	Phil Marchildon	13.6	Phil Marchildon	204.1	Phil Marchildon	74	Jack Knott	13	Tom Ferrick	7
1942	Roger Wolff	3.32	Roger Wolff	11.7	Phil Marchildon	244.0	Phil Marchildon	110	Phil Marchildon	17	Roger Wolff	3
1943	Jesse Flores	3.11	Jesse Flores	11.0	Jesse Flores	231.1	Jesse Flores	113	Jesse Flores	12	Roger Wolff	6
1944	Bobo Newsom	2.82	Jesse Flores	10.9	Bobo Newsom	265.0	Bobo Newsom	142	Russ Christopher	14	Joe Berry	12
1945	Russ Christopher	3.17	Jesse Flores	11.6	Bobo Newsom	257.1	Bobo Newsom	127	Russ Christopher	13	Joe Berry	5
1946	Jesse Flores	2.32	Jesse Flores	10.8	Phil Marchildon	226.2	Phil Marchildon	95	Phil Marchildon	13	Bob Savage	2
1947	Dick Fowler	2.81	Dick Fowler	11.8	Phil Marchildon	276.2	Phil Marchildon	128	Phil Marchildon	19	Russ Christopher	12
1948	Dick Fowler	3.78	Joe Coleman	13.1	Phil Marchildon	226.1	Lou Brissie	127	Dick Fowler	15	3 tied with	5
1949	Alex Kellner	3.75	Lou Brissie	13.5	Alex Kellner	245.0	Lou Brissie	118	Alex Kellner	20	Lou Brissie	3
											Charlie Harris	
1950	Lou Brissie	4.02	Lou Brissie	13.1	Lou Brissie	246.0	Lou Brissie	101	Bob Hooper	15	Lou Brissie	8
1951	Bobby Shantz	3.94	Bob Hooper	12.2	Alex Kellner	209.2	Alex Kellner	94	Bobby Shantz	18	Carl Scheib	10
1952	Bobby Shantz	2.48	Bobby Shantz	9.6	Bobby Shantz	279.2	Bobby Shantz	152	Bobby Shantz	24	Bob Hooper	6
1953	Marion Fricano	3.88	Alex Kellner	11.8	Harry Byrd	236.2	Harry Byrd	122	Harry Byrd	11	Morrie Martin	7
									Alex Kellner			
1954	Arnie Portocarrero	4.06	Arnie Portocarrero	12.8	Arnie Portocarrero	248.0	Arnie Portocarrero	132	Arnie Portocarrero	9	Moe Burtschy	4
											Sonny Dixon	
1955	Alex Kellner	4.20	Alex Kellner	12.7	Art Ditmar	175.1	Art Ditmar	79	Art Ditmar	12	Tom Gorman	18
1956	Tom Gorman	3.83	Tom Gorman	12.5	Art Ditmar	254.1	Art Ditmar	126	Art Ditmar	12	Bobby Shantz	9
1957	No qualifier		No qualifier		Ned Garver	145.1	Ralph Terry	80	Tom Morgan	9	Tom Morgan	7
									Virgil Trucks		Virgil Trucks	
1958	Ray Herbert	3.50	Ray Herbert	11.3	Ralph Terry	216.2	Ralph Terry	134	Ned Garver	12	Tom Gorman	8
1959	Bud Daley	3.16	Ned Garver	11.6	Bud Daley	216.1	Bud Daley	125	Bud Daley	16	Tom Sturdivant	5
1960	Ray Herbert	3.28	Dick Hall	11.1	Ray Herbert	252.2	Bud Daley	126	Bud Daley	16	Marty Kutyna	4
1961	Jim Archer	3.20	Jim Archer	11.8	Jim Archer	205.1	Jim Archer	110	Norm Bass	11	Jim Archer	5
1962	Ed Rakow	4.25	Ed Rakow	12.8	Ed Rakow	235.1	Ed Rakow	159	Ed Rakow	14	John Wyatt	11
1963	Moe Drabowsky	3.05	Moe Drabowsky	10.7	Dave Wickersham	237.2	Orlando Pena	128	Orlando Pena	12	John Wyatt	21
									Dave Wickersham			
1964	Orlando Pena	4.43	Orlando Pena	12.8	Orlando Pena	219.1	Orlando Pena	184	Orlando Pena	12	John Wyatt	20
1965	John O'Donoghue	3.95	Rollie Sheldon	11.7	Fred Talbot	198.0	Diego Segui	119	Rollie Sheldon	10	John Wyatt	18
									Fred Talbot			
1966	Lew Krausse	2.99	Lew Krausse	10.8	Lew Krausse	177.2	Catfish Hunter	103	Lew Krausse	14	Jack Aker	32
1967	Catfish Hunter	2.81	Catfish Hunter	10.2	Catfish Hunter	259.2	Catfish Hunter	196	Catfish Hunter	13	Jack Aker	12
1968	Jim Nash	2.28	Jim Nash	9.6	Catfish Hunter	234.0	Catfish Hunter	172	Blue Moon Odom	16	Jack Aker	11

Teams: Athletics

Year	ERA		Baserunners/9 IP		Innings Pitched		Strikeouts		Wins		Saves	
1969	Blue Moon Odom	2.92	Catfish Hunter	10.9	Catfish Hunter	247.0	Catfish Hunter	150	Chuck Dobson	15	Rollie Fingers	12
							Blue Moon Odom		Blue Moon Odom			
1970	Diego Segui	2.56	Chuck Dobson	11.0	Chuck Dobson	267.0	Catfish Hunter	178	Catfish Hunter	18	Mudcat Grant	24
1971	Vida Blue	1.82	Vida Blue	8.7	Vida Blue	312.0	Vida Blue	301	Vida Blue	24	Rollie Fingers	17
1972	Catfish Hunter	2.04	Catfish Hunter	8.3	Catfish Hunter	295.1	Catfish Hunter	191	Catfish Hunter	21	Rollie Fingers	21
1973	Ken Holtzman	2.97	Catfish Hunter	10.3	Ken Holtzman	297.1	Vida Blue	158	Ken Holtzman	21	Rollie Fingers	22
									Catfish Hunter			
1974	Catfish Hunter	2.49	Catfish Hunter	9.0	Catfish Hunter	318.1	Vida Blue	174	Catfish Hunter	25	Rollie Fingers	18
1975	Vida Blue	3.01	Ken Holtzman	11.2	Vida Blue	278.0	Vida Blue	189	Vida Blue	22	Rollie Fingers	24
1976	Vida Blue	2.35	Vida Blue	10.0	Vida Blue	298.1	Vida Blue	166	Vida Blue	18	Rollie Fingers	20
1977	Vida Blue	3.83	Vida Blue	11.9	Vida Blue	279.2	Vida Blue	157	Vida Blue	14	Doug Bair	8
1978	Matt Keough	3.24	Rick Langford	11.7	Matt Keough	197.1	Matt Keough	108	John Henry Johnson	11	Elias Sosa	14
1979	Steve McCatty	4.22	Rick Langford	12.1	Rick Langford	218.2	Rick Langford	101	Rick Langford	12	Dave Heaverlo	9
1980	Mike Norris	2.53	Mike Norris	9.6	Rick Langford	290.0	Mike Norris	180	Mike Norris	22	Bob Lacey	6
1981	Steve McCatty	2.33	Steve McCatty	9.8	Rick Langford	195.1	Steve McCatty	91	Steve McCatty	14	Dave Beard	3
											Jeff Jones	
1982	Rick Langford	4.21	Rick Langford	12.0	Rick Langford	237.1	Mike Norris	83	Matt Keough	11	Dave Beard	11
									Rick Langford			
1983	Tim Conroy	3.94	Chris Codiroli	12.6	Chris Codiroli	205.2	Tim Conroy	112	Chris Codiroli	12	Dave Beard	10
1984	Ray Burris	3.15	Ray Burris	12.4	Ray Burris	211.2	Ray Burris	93	Ray Burris	13	Bill Caudill	36
1985	Don Sutton	3.89	Don Sutton	11.3	Chris Codiroli	226.0	Chris Codiroli	111	Chris Codiroli	14	Jay Howell	29
1986	Curt Young	3.45	Curt Young	10.9	Curt Young	198.0	Jose Rijo	176	Curt Young	13	Jay Howell	16
1987	Dave Stewart	3.68	Curt Young	10.7	Dave Stewart	261.1	Dave Stewart	205	Dave Stewart	20	Dennis Eckersley	16
											Jay Howell	
1988	Dave Stewart	3.23	Dave Stewart	11.5	Dave Stewart	275.2	Dave Stewart	192	Dave Stewart	21	Dennis Eckersley	45
1989	Mike Moore	2.61	Mike Moore	10.4	Dave Stewart	257.2	Mike Moore	172	Dave Stewart	21	Dennis Eckersley	33
1990	Dave Stewart	2.56	Dave Stewart	10.6	Dave Stewart	267.0	Dave Stewart	166	Bob Welch	27	Dennis Eckersley	48
1991	Mike Moore	2.96	Mike Moore	12.3	Dave Stewart	226.0	Mike Moore	153	Mike Moore	17	Dennis Eckersley	43
1992	Dave Stewart	3.66	Dave Stewart	11.8	Mike Moore	223.0	Dave Stewart	130	Mike Moore	17	Dennis Eckersley	51
1993	Bobby Witt	4.21	Bobby Witt	13.1	Bobby Witt	220.0	Bobby Witt	131	Bobby Witt	14	Dennis Eckersley	36
1994	Steve Ontiveros	2.65	Steve Ontiveros	9.8	Ron Darling	160.0	Bobby Witt	111	Ron Darling	10	Dennis Eckersley	19
1995	Todd Stottlemyre	4.55	Todd Stottlemyre	13.5	Todd Stottlemyre	209.2	Todd Stottlemyre	205	Todd Stottlemyre	14	Dennis Eckersley	29
1996	No qualifier		No qualifier		Don Wengert	161.1	Carlos Reyes	78	John Wasdin	8	Billy Taylor	17
1997	No qualifier		No qualifier		Don Wengert	134.0	Steve Karsay	92	Aaron Small	9	Billy Taylor	23

Teams: Athletics

Athletics Franchise Batting Leaders—Career

Games

1	Bert Campaneris	1,795
2	Jimmy Dykes	1,702
3	Rickey Henderson	1,552
4	Sal Bando	1,468
5	Bob Johnson	1,459
6	Pete Suder	1,421
7	Harry Davis	1,413
8	Danny Murphy	1,411
9	Bing Miller	1,361
	Elmer Valo	1,361
11	Reggie Jackson	1,346
12	Mark McGwire	1,329
13	Al Simmons	1,290
14	Dick Green	1,288
15	Sam Chapman	1,274
16	Jimmie Foxx	1,256
17	Dwayne Murphy	1,213
18	Carney Lansford	1,203
19	Terry Steinbach	1,199
20	Rube Oldring	1,187

At-Bats

1	Bert Campaneris	7,180
2	Jimmy Dykes	6,023
3	Rickey Henderson	5,598
4	Bob Johnson	5,428
5	Harry Davis	5,367
6	Sal Bando	5,145
7	Danny Murphy	5,134
8	Al Simmons	5,132
9	Pete Suder	5,085
10	Bing Miller	4,762
11	Sam Chapman	4,742
12	Reggie Jackson	4,686
13	Carney Lansford	4,568
14	Rube Oldring	4,502
15	Mark McGwire	4,448
16	Jimmie Foxx	4,397
17	Elmer Valo	4,308
18	Wally Moses	4,289
19	Terry Steinbach	4,162
20	Max Bishop	4,119

Runs

1	Rickey Henderson	1,169
2	Bob Johnson	997
3	Bert Campaneris	983
4	Jimmie Foxx	975
5	Al Simmons	969
6	Max Bishop	882
7	Jimmy Dykes	881
8	Mickey Cochrane	823
9	Harry Davis	811
10	Mark McGwire	773
11	Eddie Collins	756
	Reggie Jackson	756
13	Sal Bando	737
14	Sam Chapman	730
15	Bing Miller	720
16	Wally Moses	707
17	Elmer Valo	691
18	Topsy Hartsel	686
19	Danny Murphy	678
20	Jose Canseco	662

Hits

1	Bert Campaneris	1,882
2	Al Simmons	1,827
3	Jimmy Dykes	1,705
4	Rickey Henderson	1,640
5	Bob Johnson	1,617
6	Harry Davis	1,498
7	Jimmie Foxx	1,492
8	Danny Murphy	1,488
9	Bing Miller	1,483
10	Mickey Cochrane	1,317
	Carney Lansford	1,317
12	Wally Moses	1,316
13	Sal Bando	1,311
14	Eddie Collins	1,305
15	Sam Chapman	1,273
16	Pete Suder	1,268
17	Elmer Valo	1,229
18	Reggie Jackson	1,228
19	Rube Oldring	1,222
20	Stuffy McInnis	1,193

Doubles

1	Jimmy Dykes	365
2	Al Simmons	348
3	Harry Davis	319
4	Bob Johnson	307
5	Bing Miller	292
6	Danny Murphy	275
7	Wally Moses	274
8	Rickey Henderson	273
9	Bert Campaneris	270
10	Jimmie Foxx	257
11	Mickey Cochrane	250
12	Reggie Jackson	234
13	Max Bishop	220
14	Joe Rudi	216
15	Socks Seybold	213
16	Sal Bando	212
17	Pete Suder	210
18	Terry Steinbach	205
19	Dick Siebert	202
20	Four tied at	201

Triples

1	Danny Murphy	102
2	Al Simmons	98
3	Home Run Baker	88
4	Eddie Collins	84
5	Harry Davis	83
6	Jimmie Foxx	79
7	Rube Oldring	75
8	Topsy Hartsel	74
9	Jimmy Dykes	73
	Bing Miller	73
11	Bob Johnson	72
12	Bert Campaneris	70
13	Amos Strunk	69
14	Elmer Valo	68
15	Wally Moses	63
16	Mickey Cochrane	59
17	Socks Seybold	53
18	Sam Chapman	51
19	Stuffy McInnis	50
	Sammy Hale	50

Home Runs

1	Mark McGwire	363
2	Jimmie Foxx	302
3	Reggie Jackson	269
4	Jose Canseco	254
5	Bob Johnson	252
6	Al Simmons	209
7	Sal Bando	192
8	Gus Zernial	191
9	Sam Chapman	174
10	Dwayne Murphy	153
	Rickey Henderson	153
12	Terry Steinbach	132
13	Gene Tenace	121
14	Eddie Joost	116
	Joe Rudi	116
16	Tony Armas	111
17	Mickey Cochrane	108
18	Dave Henderson	104
19	Frankie Hayes	101
20	Four tied at	100

RBI

1	Al Simmons	1,178
2	Jimmie Foxx	1,074
3	Bob Johnson	1,040
4	Mark McGwire	941
5	Sal Bando	796
6	Jose Canseco	793
7	Reggie Jackson	776
8	Jimmy Dykes	764
9	Harry Davis	762
	Bing Miller	762
11	Sam Chapman	737
12	Mickey Cochrane	680
13	Danny Murphy	664
14	Home Run Baker	612
15	Terry Steinbach	595
16	Gus Zernial	592
17	Rickey Henderson	591
18	Dwayne Murphy	563
19	Socks Seybold	548
	Carney Lansford	548

Walks

1	Rickey Henderson	1,109
2	Max Bishop	1,043
3	Bob Johnson	853
4	Mark McGwire	847
5	Elmer Valo	821
6	Sal Bando	792
7	Jimmie Foxx	781
8	Eddie Joost	768
9	Topsy Hartsel	733
10	Dwayne Murphy	694
11	Jimmy Dykes	686
12	Ferris Fain	662
13	Reggie Jackson	633
14	Mickey Cochrane	612
15	Eddie Collins	538
16	Sam Chapman	534
17	Bert Campaneris	504
18	Wally Moses	492
19	Gene Tenace	475
20	Jose Canseco	469

Strikeouts

1	Reggie Jackson	1,226
2	Jose Canseco	1,096
3	Mark McGwire	1,043
4	Bert Campaneris	933
5	Dwayne Murphy	883
6	Rickey Henderson	801
7	Dick Green	785
8	Jimmy Dykes	705
9	Sal Bando	702
10	Terry Steinbach	689
11	Bob Johnson	678
12	Sam Chapman	650
13	Jimmie Foxx	644
14	Tony Armas	599
15	Dave Henderson	570
16	Joe Rudi	566
17	Gus Zernial	565
18	Rick Monday	558
19	Eddie Joost	543
20	Gene Tenace	538

Stolen Bases

1	Rickey Henderson	801
2	Bert Campaneris	566
3	Eddie Collins	377
4	Bill North	232
5	Harry Davis	223
6	Topsy Hartsel	195
7	Rube Oldring	187
8	Danny Murphy	185
9	Home Run Baker	172
10	Carney Lansford	146
11	Reggie Jackson	145
12	Amos Strunk	144
13	Jose Canseco	135
14	Jack Barry	131
15	Stuffy McInnis	127
16	Mike Davis	121
17	Monte Cross	114
18	Bing Miller	109
19	Mitchell Page	104
20	Three tied at	103

Runs Created

1	Jimmie Foxx	1,162
2	Rickey Henderson	1,157
3	Al Simmons	1,122
4	Bob Johnson	1,082
5	Mark McGwire	954
6	Jimmy Dykes	935
7	Bert Campaneris	873
8	Reggie Jackson	850
9	Mickey Cochrane	845
10	Harry Davis	843
11	Eddie Collins	829
12	Sal Bando	823
13	Bing Miller	785
14	Danny Murphy	770
15	Max Bishop	749
16	Elmer Valo	746
17	Wally Moses	725
18	Topsy Hartsel	706
19	Sam Chapman	703
	Jose Canseco	703

Runs Created/27 Outs

(minimum 2000 Plate Appearances)

1	Jimmie Foxx	10.18
2	Al Simmons	8.51
3	Eddie Collins	7.69
4	Mickey Cochrane	7.54
5	Mark McGwire	7.39
6	Rickey Henderson	7.24
7	Bob Johnson	7.23
8	Home Run Baker	6.83
9	Norm Siebern	6.68
10	Ferris Fain	6.68
11	Mike Higgins	6.41
12	Reggie Jackson	6.31
13	Max Bishop	6.29
14	Wally Moses	6.19
15	Joe Hauser	6.11
16	Eddie Joost	6.11
17	Elmer Valo	6.06
18	Jose Canseco	6.05
19	Gene Tenace	6.03
20	Topsy Hartsel	5.96

Batting Average

(minimum 2000 Plate Appearances)

1	Al Simmons	.356
2	Jimmie Foxx	.339
3	Eddie Collins	.336
4	Mickey Cochrane	.321
5	Home Run Baker	.321
6	Stuffy McInnis	.313
7	Bing Miller	.311
8	Doc Cramer	.308
9	Wally Moses	.307
10	Mike Higgins	.307
11	Sammy Hale	.305
12	Mule Haas	.302
13	Lave Cross	.302
14	Bob Johnson	.298
15	Ferris Fain	.297
16	Socks Seybold	.296
17	Rickey Henderson	.293
18	Danny Murphy	.290
19	Vic Power	.290
20	Norm Siebern	.289

On-Base Percentage

(minimum 2000 Plate Appearances)

1	Jimmie Foxx	.440
2	Ferris Fain	.426
3	Max Bishop	.423
4	Eddie Collins	.422
5	Rickey Henderson	.412
6	Mickey Cochrane	.412
7	Elmer Valo	.403
8	Al Simmons	.398
9	Bob Johnson	.395
10	Eddie Joost	.392
11	Norm Siebern	.381
12	Mark McGwire	.380
13	Wally Moses	.380
14	Topsy Hartsel	.379
15	Home Run Baker	.375
16	Gene Tenace	.374
17	Mike Higgins	.373
18	Joe Hauser	.369
19	Jimmy Dykes	.365
20	Bill North	.364

Slugging Percentage

(minimum 2000 Plate Appearances)

1	Jimmie Foxx	.640
2	Al Simmons	.584
3	Mark McGwire	.551
4	Bob Johnson	.520
5	Jose Canseco	.507
6	Reggie Jackson	.496
7	Mickey Cochrane	.490
8	Gus Zernial	.489
9	Joe Hauser	.478
10	Mike Higgins	.477
11	Home Run Baker	.470
12	Tilly Walker	.469
13	Norm Siebern	.463
14	Bing Miller	.463
15	Wally Moses	.445
16	Dave Henderson	.445
17	Sam Chapman	.442
18	Rickey Henderson	.438
19	Eddie Collins	.436
20	Gene Tenace	.435

Teams: Athletics

Athletics Franchise Pitching Leaders—Career

Wins

1	Eddie Plank	284
2	Lefty Grove	195
3	Chief Bender	193
4	Eddie Rommel	171
5	Catfish Hunter	161
6	Rube Walberg	134
7	Rube Waddell	131
8	Vida Blue	124
9	Dave Stewart	119
10	Jack Coombs	115
11	George Earnshaw	98
12	Bob Welch	96
13	Alex Kellner	92
14	Blue Moon Odom	80
15	Ken Holtzman	77
16	Rick Langford	73
17	Chuck Dobson	72
18	Jack Quinn	69
	Bobby Shantz	69
20	Phil Marchildon	68

Losses

1	Eddie Plank	162
2	Eddie Rommel	119
3	Rube Walberg	114
4	Catfish Hunter	113
5	Alex Kellner	108
6	Rick Langford	105
7	Chief Bender	102
8	Slim Harriss	93
9	Vida Blue	86
10	Rollie Naylor	83
11	Rube Waddell	82
12	Lefty Grove	79
	Dick Fowler	79
14	Dave Stewart	78
15	Blue Moon Odom	76
16	Joe Bush	75
	Phil Marchildon	75
	Matt Keough	75
19	George Caster	73
20	Diego Segui	71

Winning Percentage
(minimum 100 decisions)

1	Lefty Grove	.712
2	Chief Bender	.654
3	Eddie Plank	.637
4	Jack Coombs	.632
5	George Earnshaw	.628
6	Bob Welch	.615
7	Rube Waddell	.615
8	Dave Stewart	.604
9	Roy Mahaffey	.598
10	Jack Quinn	.595
11	Vida Blue	.590
12	Eddie Rommel	.590
13	Mike Moore	.589
14	Catfish Hunter	.588
15	Ken Holtzman	.583
16	Curt Young	.560
17	Rube Walberg	.540
18	Jimmy Dygert	.533
19	Chuck Dobson	.529
20	Rollie Fingers	.523

Games

1	Dennis Eckersley	525
2	Eddie Plank	524
3	Rollie Fingers	502
4	Eddie Rommel	500
5	Paul Lindblad	479
6	Rube Walberg	412
7	Lefty Grove	402
8	Rick Honeycutt	387
9	Chief Bender	385
10	Catfish Hunter	363
11	Diego Segui	323
12	John Wyatt	296
13	Alex Kellner	291
14	Gene Nelson	281
15	Vida Blue	273
16	Blue Moon Odom	269
17	Carl Scheib	264
18	Slim Harriss	257
	Dave Stewart	257
20	Rube Waddell	251

Games Started

1	Eddie Plank	459
2	Catfish Hunter	340
3	Chief Bender	288
4	Rube Walberg	267
	Lefty Grove	267
6	Vida Blue	262
7	Eddie Rommel	249
8	Dave Stewart	245
9	Alex Kellner	239
10	Blue Moon Odom	214
11	Rube Waddell	212
12	Rick Langford	195
	Bob Welch	195
14	Jack Coombs	192
15	Chuck Dobson	183
16	George Earnshaw	175
17	Dick Fowler	170
18	Slim Harriss	168
19	Phil Marchildon	162
20	Steve McCatty	161

Complete Games

1	Eddie Plank	362
2	Chief Bender	230
3	Lefty Grove	181
4	Rube Waddell	168
5	Eddie Rommel	147
6	Jack Coombs	136
7	Rube Walberg	126
8	Catfish Hunter	116
9	Vida Blue	105
10	Alex Kellner	95
11	George Earnshaw	88
12	Rick Langford	85
13	Phil Marchildon	82
14	Dick Fowler	75
15	Joe Bush	70
16	Slim Harriss	68
17	Rollie Naylor	67
	Scott Perry	67
19	Cy Morgan	64
20	Jimmy Dygert	62

Shutouts

1	Eddie Plank	59
2	Rube Waddell	37
	Chief Bender	37
4	Catfish Hunter	31
5	Jack Coombs	28
	Vida Blue	28
7	Lefty Grove	20
8	Eddie Rommel	18
9	Jimmy Dygert	16
10	Joe Bush	15
	Rube Walberg	15
12	Blue Moon Odom	14
13	George Earnshaw	13
	Ken Holtzman	13
15	Dick Fowler	11
	Bobby Shantz	11
	Chuck Dobson	11
18	Twelve tied at	10

Saves

1	Dennis Eckersley	320
2	Rollie Fingers	136
3	John Wyatt	73
4	Jay Howell	61
5	Jack Aker	58
6	Lefty Grove	51
7	Paul Lindblad	41
	Billy Taylor	41
9	Bill Caudill	37
10	Tom Gorman	33
11	Rick Honeycutt	32
12	Darold Knowles	30
13	Eddie Rommel	29
14	Chief Bender	27
	Rube Walberg	27
	Mudcat Grant	27
17	Dave Beard	25
18	Bob Lacey	22
19	Lew Krausse	20
	Bob Locker	20

Innings Pitched

1	Eddie Plank	3,860.2
2	Chief Bender	2,603.0
3	Eddie Rommel	2,556.1
4	Catfish Hunter	2,456.1
5	Lefty Grove	2,400.2
6	Rube Walberg	2,186.2
7	Vida Blue	1,945.2
8	Rube Waddell	1,869.1
9	Alex Kellner	1,730.1
10	Dave Stewart	1,717.1
11	Jack Coombs	1,629.2
12	Rick Langford	1,468.0
13	Blue Moon Odom	1,414.2
14	George Earnshaw	1,353.2
15	Dick Fowler	1,303.0
16	Slim Harriss	1,291.0
17	Bob Welch	1,271.1
18	Phil Marchildon	1,213.0
19	Chuck Dobson	1,200.1
20	Steve McCatty	1,188.1

Walks

1	Eddie Plank	913
2	Rube Walberg	853
3	Lefty Grove	740
4	Blue Moon Odom	732
5	Eddie Rommel	724
6	Alex Kellner	717
7	Catfish Hunter	687
8	Phil Marchildon	682
9	Dave Stewart	655
10	Vida Blue	617
11	Chief Bender	614
12	Jack Coombs	606
13	George Earnshaw	591
14	Dick Fowler	578
15	Steve McCatty	520
16	Joe Bush	499
	Mike Norris	499
18	Slim Harriss	498
19	Rube Waddell	495
20	Carl Scheib	488

Strikeouts

1	Eddie Plank	1,985
2	Rube Waddell	1,576
3	Chief Bender	1,536
4	Lefty Grove	1,523
5	Catfish Hunter	1,520
6	Vida Blue	1,315
7	Dave Stewart	1,152
8	Rube Walberg	907
9	Jack Coombs	870
10	Blue Moon Odom	799
11	Rollie Fingers	784
12	Diego Segui	772
13	George Earnshaw	757
14	Alex Kellner	755
15	Chuck Dobson	728
16	Bob Welch	677
17	Dennis Eckersley	658
18	Rick Langford	654
19	Mike Norris	636
20	Eddie Rommel	599

Strikeouts/9 Innings
(minimum 1000 Innings Pitched)

1	Rube Waddell	7.59
2	Rollie Fingers	6.94
3	Vida Blue	6.08
4	Diego Segui	6.05
5	Dave Stewart	6.04
6	Lefty Grove	5.71
7	Catfish Hunter	5.57
8	Chuck Dobson	5.46
9	Chief Bender	5.31
10	Mike Norris	5.09
11	Blue Moon Odom	5.08
12	George Earnshaw	5.03
13	Jack Coombs	4.80
14	Bob Welch	4.79
15	Joe Bush	4.64
16	Eddie Plank	4.63
17	Curt Young	4.47
18	Ken Holtzman	4.40
19	Bobby Shantz	4.37
20	Matt Keough	4.33

ERA
(minimum 1000 Innings Pitched)

1	Rube Waddell	1.97
2	Chief Bender	2.32
3	Eddie Plank	2.39
4	Jack Coombs	2.60
5	Lefty Grove	2.88
6	Rollie Fingers	2.91
7	Ken Holtzman	2.92
8	Vida Blue	2.94
9	Catfish Hunter	3.13
10	Joe Bush	3.19
11	Blue Moon Odom	3.53
12	Eddie Rommel	3.54
13	Diego Segui	3.65
14	Chuck Dobson	3.66
15	Dave Stewart	3.73
16	Bobby Shantz	3.80
17	Mike Norris	3.89
18	Phil Marchildon	3.92
19	Rollie Naylor	3.93
20	Bob Welch	3.94

Component ERA
(minimum 1000 Innings Pitched)

1	Rube Waddell	2.05
2	Chief Bender	2.22
3	Eddie Plank	2.44
4	Jack Coombs	2.63
5	Rollie Fingers	2.76
6	Vida Blue	2.80
7	Catfish Hunter	2.87
8	Lefty Grove	2.94
9	Ken Holtzman	2.94
10	Joe Bush	3.06
11	Chuck Dobson	3.56
12	Mike Norris	3.60
13	Diego Segui	3.62
14	Dave Stewart	3.66
15	Eddie Rommel	3.66
16	Bobby Shantz	3.68
17	Blue Moon Odom	3.72
18	Phil Marchildon	3.80
19	George Earnshaw	3.80
20	Rube Walberg	3.92

Opponent Average
(minimum 1000 Innings Pitched)

1	Rube Waddell	.219
2	Catfish Hunter	.228
3	Vida Blue	.230
4	Rollie Fingers	.232
5	Chief Bender	.233
6	Mike Norris	.233
7	Jack Coombs	.235
8	Blue Moon Odom	.240
9	Phil Marchildon	.240
10	Joe Bush	.240
11	Eddie Plank	.241
12	Diego Segui	.241
13	Ken Holtzman	.243
14	Chuck Dobson	.244
15	Dave Stewart	.248
16	Lefty Grove	.248
17	George Earnshaw	.256
18	Bobby Shantz	.257
19	Steve McCatty	.258
20	Bob Welch	.261

Opponent OBP
(minimum 1000 Innings Pitched)

1	Rube Waddell	.278
2	Catfish Hunter	.283
3	Chief Bender	.285
4	Vida Blue	.291
5	Rollie Fingers	.292
6	Ken Holtzman	.293
7	Eddie Plank	.295
8	Lefty Grove	.306
9	Jack Coombs	.312
10	Chuck Dobson	.314
11	Diego Segui	.317
12	Rick Langford	.318
13	Dave Stewart	.318
14	Mike Norris	.319
15	Joe Bush	.324
16	Bobby Shantz	.325
17	Curt Young	.325
18	Eddie Rommel	.329
19	Bob Welch	.330
20	George Earnshaw	.333

Philadelphia Athletics Team Batting Leaders—Career

#	Games		#	At-Bats		#	Runs		#	Hits	
1	Jimmy Dykes	1,702	1	Jimmy Dykes	6,023	1	Bob Johnson	997	1	Al Simmons	1,827
2	Bob Johnson	1,459	2	Bob Johnson	5,428	2	Jimmie Foxx	975	2	Jimmy Dykes	1,705
3	Harry Davis	1,413	3	Harry Davis	5,367	3	Al Simmons	969	3	Bob Johnson	1,617
4	Danny Murphy	1,411	4	Danny Murphy	5,134	4	Max Bishop	882	4	Harry Davis	1,498
5	Pete Suder	1,395	5	Al Simmons	5,132	5	Jimmy Dykes	881	5	Jimmie Foxx	1,492
6	Bing Miller	1,361	6	Pete Suder	5,004	6	Mickey Cochrane	823	6	Danny Murphy	1,488
7	Al Simmons	1,290	7	Bing Miller	4,762	7	Harry Davis	811	7	Bing Miller	1,483
8	Sam Chapman	1,274	8	Sam Chapman	4,742	8	Eddie Collins	756	8	Mickey Cochrane	1,317
9	Jimmie Foxx	1,256	9	Rube Oldring	4,502	9	Sam Chapman	730	9	Wally Moses	1,316
10	Elmer Valo	1,240	10	Jimmie Foxx	4,397	10	Bing Miller	720	10	Eddie Collins	1,305
11	Rube Oldring	1,187	11	Wally Moses	4,289	11	Wally Moses	707	11	Sam Chapman	1,273
12	Max Bishop	1,181	12	Max Bishop	4,119	12	Topsy Hartsel	686	12	Pete Suder	1,251
13	Wally Moses	1,168	13	Mickey Cochrane	4,097	13	Danny Murphy	678	13	Rube Oldring	1,222
14	Mickey Cochrane	1,167	14	Topsy Hartsel	4,075	14	Elmer Valo	640	14	Stuffy McInnis	1,193
15	Eddie Collins	1,156	15	Elmer Valo	4,016	15	Eddie Joost	629	15	Elmer Valo	1,124
16	Cy Perkins	1,154	16	Eddie Collins	3,883	16	Rube Oldring	597	16	Max Bishop	1,122
17	Topsy Hartsel	1,144	17	Dick Siebert	3,869	17	Home Run Baker	573	17	Home Run Baker	1,103
18	Stuffy McInnis	1,042	18	Stuffy McInnis	3,809	18	Amos Strunk	475	18	Dick Siebert	1,094
19	Amos Strunk	1,026	19	Socks Seybold	3,596	19	Pete Suder	466	19	Topsy Hartsel	1,086
20	Chick Galloway	1,023	20	Cy Perkins	3,556	20	Socks Seybold	465	20	Socks Seybold	1,063

#	Doubles		#	Triples		#	Home Runs		#	RBI	
1	Jimmy Dykes	365	1	Danny Murphy	102	1	Jimmie Foxx	302	1	Al Simmons	1,178
2	Al Simmons	348	2	Al Simmons	98	2	Bob Johnson	252	2	Jimmie Foxx	1,074
3	Harry Davis	319	3	Home Run Baker	88	3	Al Simmons	209	3	Bob Johnson	1,040
4	Bob Johnson	307	4	Eddie Collins	84	4	Sam Chapman	174	4	Jimmy Dykes	764
5	Bing Miller	292	5	Harry Davis	83	5	Gus Zernial	118	5	Harry Davis	762
6	Danny Murphy	275	6	Jimmie Foxx	79	6	Eddie Joost	116		Bing Miller	762
7	Wally Moses	274	7	Rube Oldring	75	7	Mickey Cochrane	108	7	Sam Chapman	737
8	Jimmie Foxx	257	8	Topsy Hartsel	74	8	Frankie Hayes	101	8	Mickey Cochrane	680
9	Mickey Cochrane	250	9	Jimmy Dykes	73	9	Tilly Walker	100	9	Danny Murphy	664
10	Max Bishop	220		Bing Miller	73	10	Bing Miller	95	10	Home Run Baker	612
11	Socks Seybold	213	11	Bob Johnson	72	11	Jimmy Dykes	86	11	Socks Seybold	548
12	Pete Suder	206	12	Amos Strunk	69	12	Joe Hauser	77	12	Pete Suder	540
13	Dick Siebert	202	13	Elmer Valo	64	13	Harry Davis	69	13	Stuffy McInnis	532
14	Sam Chapman	201	14	Wally Moses	63	14	Mike Higgins	64	14	Frankie Hayes	503
15	Rube Oldring	197	15	Mickey Cochrane	59		Wally Moses	64	15	Eddie Collins	496
16	Home Run Baker	194	16	Socks Seybold	53	16	Socks Seybold	51	16	Dick Siebert	480
17	Elmer Valo	179	17	Sam Chapman	51		Eric McNair	51	17	Rube Oldring	453
18	Cy Perkins	174	18	Stuffy McInnis	50	18	Pete Suder	49	18	Elmer Valo	452
	Ferris Fain	174		Sammy Hale	50	19	Home Run Baker	48	19	Ferris Fain	436
20	Eddie Collins	172	20	Two tied at	44	20	Elmer Valo	44	20	Eddie Joost	435

#	Walks		#	Strikeouts		#	Stolen Bases		#	Runs Created	
1	Max Bishop	1,043	1	Jimmy Dykes	705	1	Eddie Collins	377	1	Jimmie Foxx	1,162
2	Bob Johnson	853	2	Bob Johnson	678	2	Harry Davis	223	2	Al Simmons	1,122
3	Jimmie Foxx	781	3	Sam Chapman	650	3	Topsy Hartsel	195	3	Bob Johnson	1,082
4	Elmer Valo	768	4	Jimmie Foxx	644	4	Rube Oldring	187	4	Jimmy Dykes	935
	Eddie Joost	768	5	Eddie Joost	543	5	Danny Murphy	185	5	Mickey Cochrane	845
6	Topsy Hartsel	733	6	Pete Suder	443	6	Home Run Baker	172	6	Harry Davis	843
7	Jimmy Dykes	686	7	Frankie Hayes	440	7	Amos Strunk	144	7	Eddie Collins	829
8	Ferris Fain	662	8	Max Bishop	416	8	Jack Barry	131	8	Bing Miller	785
9	Mickey Cochrane	612	9	Al Simmons	413	9	Stuffy McInnis	127	9	Danny Murphy	770
10	Eddie Collins	538	10	Lefty Grove	360	10	Monte Cross	114	10	Max Bishop	749
11	Sam Chapman	534	11	Gus Zernial	325	11	Bing Miller	109	11	Wally Moses	725
12	Wally Moses	492	12	Tilly Walker	260	12	Elmer Valo	98	12	Topsy Hartsel	706
13	Harry Davis	426	13	Wally Moses	258	13	Dave Fultz	80	13	Sam Chapman	703
14	Amos Strunk	417	14	Mike Higgins	251		Lave Cross	80	14	Elmer Valo	682
15	Frankie Hayes	396	15	Bing Miller	239	15	Bob Johnson	78	15	Home Run Baker	654
16	Al Simmons	344	16	Amos Strunk	230	16	Jimmy Walsh	77	16	Eddie Joost	604
17	Danny Murphy	309	17	Frank Welch	224		Eddie Murphy	77	17	Socks Seybold	603
18	Jack Barry	303	18	Chick Galloway	221	18	Chick Galloway	72	18	Stuffy McInnis	563
19	Cy Perkins	300	19	Joe Hauser	220	19	Socks Seybold	64	19	Ferris Fain	562
20	Bing Miller	291	20	Cy Perkins	217		Al Simmons	64	20	Rube Oldring	560

#	Runs Created/27 Outs (minimum 2000 Plate Appearances)		#	Batting Average (minimum 2000 Plate Appearances)		#	On-Base Percentage (minimum 2000 Plate Appearances)		#	Slugging Percentage (minimum 2000 Plate Appearances)	
1	Jimmie Foxx	10.18	1	Al Simmons	.356	1	Jimmie Foxx	.440	1	Jimmie Foxx	.640
2	Al Simmons	8.51	2	Jimmie Foxx	.339	2	Ferris Fain	.426	2	Al Simmons	.584
3	Eddie Collins	7.69	3	Eddie Collins	.336	3	Max Bishop	.423	3	Bob Johnson	.520
4	Mickey Cochrane	7.54	4	Mickey Cochrane	.321	4	Eddie Collins	.422	4	Gus Zernial	.495
5	Bob Johnson	7.23	5	Home Run Baker	.321	5	Mickey Cochrane	.412	5	Mickey Cochrane	.490
6	Home Run Baker	6.83	6	Stuffy McInnis	.313	6	Elmer Valo	.399	6	Joe Hauser	.478
7	Ferris Fain	6.68	7	Bing Miller	.311	7	Al Simmons	.398	7	Mike Higgins	.477
8	Mike Higgins	6.41	8	Doc Cramer	.308	8	Bob Johnson	.395	8	Home Run Baker	.470
9	Max Bishop	6.29	9	Wally Moses	.307	9	Eddie Joost	.392	9	Tilly Walker	.469
10	Wally Moses	6.19	10	Mike Higgins	.307	10	Wally Moses	.380	10	Bing Miller	.463
11	Joe Hauser	6.11	11	Sammy Hale	.305	11	Topsy Hartsel	.379	11	Wally Moses	.445
12	Eddie Joost	6.11	12	Mule Haas	.302	12	Home Run Baker	.375	12	Sam Chapman	.442
13	Topsy Hartsel	5.96	13	Lave Cross	.302	13	Mike Higgins	.373	13	Eddie Collins	.436
14	Socks Seybold	5.95	14	Bob Johnson	.298	14	Joe Hauser	.369	14	Mule Haas	.434
15	Gus Zernial	5.95	15	Ferris Fain	.297	15	Jimmy Dykes	.365	15	Sammy Hale	.430
16	Bing Miller	5.90	16	Socks Seybold	.296	16	Amos Strunk	.362	16	Socks Seybold	.427
17	Elmer Valo	5.90	17	Danny Murphy	.290	17	Bing Miller	.358	17	Frankie Hayes	.426
18	Mule Haas	5.63	18	Tilly Walker	.287	18	Mule Haas	.357	18	Hank Majeski	.412
19	Tilly Walker	5.61	19	Joe Hauser	.285	19	Stuffy McInnis	.354	19	Jimmy Dykes	.411
20	Harry Davis	5.48	20	Amos Strunk	.283	20	Socks Seybold	.354	20	Harry Davis	.408

Teams: Athletics

Philadelphia Athletics Team Pitching Leaders—Career

Wins

1	Eddie Plank	284
2	Lefty Grove	195
3	Chief Bender	193
4	Eddie Rommel	171
5	Rube Walberg	134
6	Rube Waddell	131
7	Jack Coombs	115
8	George Earnshaw	98
9	Jack Quinn	69
10	Phil Marchildon	68
	Alex Kellner	68
12	Slim Harriss	67
13	Dick Fowler	66
14	Joe Bush	65
15	Roy Mahaffey	64
16	Bobby Shantz	62
17	Jimmy Dygert	56
18	Cy Morgan	52
19	Russ Christopher	51
20	Two tied at	45

Losses

1	Eddie Plank	162
2	Eddie Rommel	119
3	Rube Walberg	114
4	Chief Bender	102
5	Slim Harriss	93
6	Alex Kellner	89
7	Rollie Naylor	83
8	Rube Waddell	82
9	Lefty Grove	79
	Dick Fowler	79
11	Joe Bush	75
	Phil Marchildon	75
13	George Caster	73
14	Jack Coombs	67
	Scott Perry	67
16	Buck Ross	65
17	Carl Scheib	64
18	Lum Harris	63
19	Russ Christopher	62
20	George Earnshaw	58

Winning Percentage
(minimum 100 decisions)

1	Lefty Grove	.712
2	Chief Bender	.654
3	Eddie Plank	.637
4	Jack Coombs	.632
5	George Earnshaw	.628
6	Rube Waddell	.615
7	Roy Mahaffey	.598
8	Jack Quinn	.595
9	Eddie Rommel	.590
10	Bobby Shantz	.564
11	Rube Walberg	.540
12	Jimmy Dygert	.533
13	Phil Marchildon	.476
14	Joe Bush	.464
15	Dick Fowler	.455
16	Russ Christopher	.451
17	Alex Kellner	.433
18	Slim Harriss	.419
19	Carl Scheib	.413
20	George Caster	.381

Games

1	Eddie Plank	524
2	Eddie Rommel	500
3	Rube Walberg	412
4	Lefty Grove	402
5	Chief Bender	385
6	Carl Scheib	264
7	Slim Harriss	257
8	Rube Waddell	251
9	Jack Coombs	239
10	Dick Fowler	221
11	George Earnshaw	219
12	Alex Kellner	206
13	Roy Mahaffey	197
14	Russ Christopher	196
15	Joe Bush	191
16	Jack Quinn	184
	Phil Marchildon	184
18	Rollie Naylor	181
19	Jimmy Dygert	175
20	George Caster	170

Games Started

1	Eddie Plank	459
2	Chief Bender	288
3	Rube Walberg	267
	Lefty Grove	267
5	Eddie Rommel	249
6	Rube Waddell	212
7	Jack Coombs	192
8	George Earnshaw	175
9	Alex Kellner	171
10	Dick Fowler	170
11	Slim Harriss	168
12	Phil Marchildon	162
13	Rollie Naylor	136
14	Buck Ross	125
15	Joe Bush	123
16	Roy Mahaffey	118
	George Caster	118
18	Jack Quinn	113
19	Jesse Flores	111
20	Four tied at	106

Complete Games

1	Eddie Plank	362
2	Chief Bender	230
3	Lefty Grove	181
4	Rube Waddell	168
5	Eddie Rommel	147
6	Jack Coombs	136
7	Rube Walberg	126
8	George Earnshaw	88
9	Phil Marchildon	82
10	Alex Kellner	81
11	Dick Fowler	75
12	Joe Bush	70
13	Slim Harriss	68
14	Rollie Naylor	67
	Scott Perry	67
16	Cy Morgan	64
17	Jimmy Dygert	62
18	George Caster	59
19	Weldon Henley	57
20	Bobby Shantz	56

Shutouts

1	Eddie Plank	59
2	Rube Waddell	37
	Chief Bender	37
4	Jack Coombs	28
5	Lefty Grove	20
6	Eddie Rommel	18
7	Jimmy Dygert	16
8	Joe Bush	15
	Rube Walberg	15
10	George Earnshaw	13
11	Dick Fowler	11
12	Harry Krause	10
	Cy Morgan	10
	Jack Quinn	10
	Jesse Flores	10
	Bobby Shantz	10
17	Five tied at	7

Saves

1	Lefty Grove	51
2	Eddie Rommel	29
3	Chief Bender	27
	Rube Walberg	27
5	Russ Christopher	18
6	Carl Scheib	17
	Joe Berry	17
8	Eddie Plank	16
	Lou Brissie	16
	Bob Hooper	16
11	Slim Harriss	14
12	Joe Pate	12
13	Jack Quinn	11
14	Jack Coombs	10
	George Earnshaw	10
	Nels Potter	10
17	Five tied at	9

Innings Pitched

1	Eddie Plank	3,860.2
2	Chief Bender	2,603.0
3	Eddie Rommel	2,556.1
4	Lefty Grove	2,400.2
5	Rube Walberg	2,186.2
6	Rube Waddell	1,869.1
7	Jack Coombs	1,629.2
8	George Earnshaw	1,353.2
9	Alex Kellner	1,309.2
10	Dick Fowler	1,303.0
11	Slim Harriss	1,291.0
12	Phil Marchildon	1,213.0
13	Joe Bush	1,115.1
14	Carl Scheib	1,066.0
15	Rollie Naylor	1,011.0
16	Jimmy Dygert	986.0
17	Roy Mahaffey	982.0
18	Russ Christopher	940.2
19	Bobby Shantz	940.1
20	Jack Quinn	932.2

Walks

1	Eddie Plank	913
2	Rube Walberg	853
3	Lefty Grove	740
4	Eddie Rommel	724
5	Phil Marchildon	682
6	Chief Bender	614
7	Jack Coombs	606
8	George Earnshaw	591
9	Dick Fowler	578
10	Alex Kellner	575
11	Joe Bush	499
12	Slim Harriss	498
13	Rube Waddell	495
14	Carl Scheib	488
15	Joe Coleman	446
16	Roy Mahaffey	402
17	George Caster	389
18	Jimmy Dygert	383
	Buck Ross	383
20	Russ Christopher	372

Strikeouts

1	Eddie Plank	1,985
2	Rube Waddell	1,576
3	Chief Bender	1,536
4	Lefty Grove	1,523
5	Rube Walberg	907
6	Jack Coombs	870
7	George Earnshaw	757
8	Eddie Rommel	599
9	Jimmy Dygert	583
10	Joe Bush	575
11	Alex Kellner	542
12	Slim Harriss	496
13	Phil Marchildon	481
14	Bobby Shantz	441
15	Russ Christopher	410
16	Cy Morgan	398
17	George Caster	385
18	Dick Fowler	382
19	Lou Brissie	353
20	Roy Mahaffey	345

Strikeouts/9 Innings
(minimum 1000 Innings Pitched)

1	Rube Waddell	7.59
2	Lefty Grove	5.71
3	Chief Bender	5.31
4	George Earnshaw	5.03
5	Jack Coombs	4.80
6	Joe Bush	4.64
7	Eddie Plank	4.63
8	Rube Walberg	3.73
9	Alex Kellner	3.72
10	Phil Marchildon	3.57
11	Slim Harriss	3.46
12	Dick Fowler	2.64
13	Rollie Naylor	2.51
14	Carl Scheib	2.41
15	Eddie Rommel	2.11

ERA
(minimum 1000 Innings Pitched)

1	Rube Waddell	1.97
2	Chief Bender	2.32
3	Eddie Plank	2.39
4	Jack Coombs	2.60
5	Lefty Grove	2.88
6	Joe Bush	3.19
7	Eddie Rommel	3.54
8	Phil Marchildon	3.92
9	Rollie Naylor	3.93
10	Dick Fowler	4.11
11	Rube Walberg	4.12
12	George Earnshaw	4.18
13	Slim Harriss	4.21
14	Alex Kellner	4.58
15	Carl Scheib	4.85

Component ERA
(minimum 1000 Innings Pitched)

1	Rube Waddell	2.05
2	Chief Bender	2.22
3	Eddie Plank	2.44
4	Jack Coombs	2.63
5	Lefty Grove	2.94
6	Joe Bush	3.06
7	Eddie Rommel	3.66
8	Phil Marchildon	3.80
9	George Earnshaw	3.80
10	Rube Walberg	3.92
11	Rollie Naylor	4.22
12	Slim Harriss	4.24
13	Dick Fowler	4.32
14	Alex Kellner	4.37
15	Carl Scheib	4.57

Opponent Average
(minimum 1000 Innings Pitched)

1	Rube Waddell	.219
2	Chief Bender	.233
3	Jack Coombs	.235
4	Phil Marchildon	.240
5	Joe Bush	.240
6	Eddie Plank	.241
7	Lefty Grove	.248
8	George Earnshaw	.256
9	Rube Walberg	.270
10	Alex Kellner	.271
11	Dick Fowler	.273
12	Carl Scheib	.274
13	Eddie Rommel	.278
14	Slim Harriss	.285
15	Rollie Naylor	.299

Opponent OBP
(minimum 1000 Innings Pitched)

1	Rube Waddell	.278
2	Chief Bender	.285
3	Eddie Plank	.295
4	Lefty Grove	.306
5	Jack Coombs	.312
6	Joe Bush	.324
7	Eddie Rommel	.329
8	George Earnshaw	.333
9	Rube Walberg	.339
10	Phil Marchildon	.342
11	Alex Kellner	.347
12	Dick Fowler	.351
13	Slim Harriss	.353
14	Carl Scheib	.355
15	Rollie Naylor	.358

Teams: Athletics

Kansas City Athletics Team Batting Leaders—Career

Games

1	Ed Charles	726
2	Jerry Lumpe	715
3	Wayne Causey	689
4	Joe DeMaestri	648
5	Norm Siebern	611
6	Hector Lopez	586
7	Dick Green	538
8	Bert Campaneris	500
9	Vic Power	455
10	Bill Tuttle	450
11	Mike Hershberger	438
12	Bob Cerv	413
13	Ken Harrelson	402
14	Jose Tartabull	395
15	Harry Simpson	389
16	Gus Zernial	360
17	Hal Smith	350
18	Bobby Del Greco	327
19	Manny Jimenez	307
20	Gino Cimoli	301

At-Bats

1	Jerry Lumpe	2,782
2	Ed Charles	2,621
3	Wayne Causey	2,367
4	Norm Siebern	2,236
5	Joe DeMaestri	2,146
6	Hector Lopez	2,134
7	Bert Campaneris	2,021
8	Dick Green	1,802
9	Vic Power	1,798
10	Bill Tuttle	1,617
11	Mike Hershberger	1,512
12	Bob Cerv	1,401
13	Harry Simpson	1,344
14	Ken Harrelson	1,232
15	Gus Zernial	1,122
16	Hal Smith	1,109
17	Gino Cimoli	1,088
18	Jose Tartabull	997
19	Danny Cater	954
20	Dick Howser	938

Runs

1	Jerry Lumpe	361
2	Ed Charles	344
3	Norm Siebern	331
4	Hector Lopez	298
5	Wayne Causey	280
6	Bert Campaneris	261
7	Vic Power	251
8	Bill Tuttle	241
9	Bob Cerv	203
10	Dick Green	201
11	Joe DeMaestri	190
12	Dick Howser	165
13	Harry Simpson	164
14	Gus Zernial	154
15	Mike Hershberger	153
16	Ken Harrelson	139
17	Bobby Del Greco	135
18	Roger Maris	130
19	Jose Tartabull	126
20	Two tied at	124

Hits

1	Jerry Lumpe	775
2	Ed Charles	703
3	Norm Siebern	647
4	Wayne Causey	640
5	Hector Lopez	593
6	Vic Power	537
7	Bert Campaneris	527
8	Joe DeMaestri	511
9	Dick Green	431
10	Bill Tuttle	422
11	Bob Cerv	403
12	Harry Simpson	391
13	Mike Hershberger	372
14	Hal Smith	318
15	Ken Harrelson	294
16	Gino Cimoli	290
17	Gus Zernial	269
18	Danny Cater	267
19	Jose Tartabull	262
20	Dick Williams	251

Doubles

1	Jerry Lumpe	119
2	Norm Siebern	117
3	Ed Charles	115
4	Wayne Causey	108
5	Hector Lopez	99
6	Bert Campaneris	95
7	Vic Power	83
8	Joe DeMaestri	71
9	Dick Green	67
	Mike Hershberger	67
11	Hal Smith	66
12	Dick Williams	64
13	Bob Cerv	57
14	Bill Tuttle	56
15	Harry Simpson	54
16	Ken Harrelson	48
17	Bobby Del Greco	42
18	Gus Zernial	41
19	Manny Jimenez	40
20	Gino Cimoli	39

Triples

1	Jerry Lumpe	34
2	Bert Campaneris	31
3	Ed Charles	26
	Gino Cimoli	26
5	Harry Simpson	25
6	Vic Power	20
	Bill Tuttle	20
8	Norm Siebern	19
9	Wayne Causey	18
10	Jose Tartabull	17
11	Hector Lopez	16
12	Joe DeMaestri	14
	Bob Cerv	14
14	Dick Green	13
	Mike Hershberger	13
16	Nelson Mathews	12
17	Bob Martyn	11
18	Roger Maris	10
19	Three tied at	9

Home Runs

1	Norm Siebern	78
2	Bob Cerv	75
3	Gus Zernial	73
4	Hector Lopez	67
5	Ed Charles	65
6	Vic Power	51
7	Ken Harrelson	47
8	Dick Green	41
9	Harry Simpson	40
10	Jim Gentile	38
11	Roger Maris	35
12	Rocky Colavito	34
	Joe DeMaestri	33
	Billy Bryan	33
15	Wayne Causey	31
16	Lou Skizas	29
	Jerry Lumpe	29
18	Dick Williams	28
19	Bill Tuttle	26
20	Hal Smith	25

RBI

1	Norm Siebern	367
2	Ed Charles	319
3	Jerry Lumpe	277
4	Hector Lopez	269
5	Bob Cerv	247
6	Wayne Causey	219
7	Harry Simpson	210
8	Vic Power	208
9	Gus Zernial	197
10	Dick Green	195
11	Joe DeMaestri	181
12	Mike Hershberger	154
13	Ken Harrelson	153
14	Hal Smith	142
	Bill Tuttle	142
16	Dick Williams	140
17	Bert Campaneris	138
18	Roger Maris	125
19	Manny Jimenez	123
20	Gino Cimoli	119

Walks

1	Norm Siebern	343
2	Wayne Causey	290
3	Ed Charles	262
4	Jerry Lumpe	239
5	Bill Tuttle	197
6	Hector Lopez	194
7	Ken Harrelson	146
8	Dick Howser	137
9	Dick Green	136
10	Mike Hershberger	122
11	Harry Simpson	121
12	Bobby Del Greco	119
13	Bert Campaneris	117
14	Bob Cerv	115
15	Joe DeMaestri	111
16	Gus Zernial	97
17	Jim Gentile	93
18	Haywood Sullivan	92
19	Jim Finigan	91
20	Two tied at	90

Strikeouts

1	Ed Charles	379
2	Dick Green	376
3	Joe DeMaestri	351
4	Norm Siebern	329
5	Hector Lopez	281
6	Ken Harrelson	280
7	Bert Campaneris	266
8	Bob Cerv	243
9	Gus Zernial	240
10	Billy Bryan	234
11	Wayne Causey	231
12	Harry Simpson	208
13	Jerry Lumpe	202
14	Nelson Mathews	192
15	Phil Roof	180
16	Gino Cimoli	162
17	Bill Tuttle	157
18	Jim Gentile	148
19	Bobby Del Greco	145
20	Hal Smith	142

Stolen Bases

1	Bert Campaneris	168
2	Ed Charles	73
3	Jose Tartabull	58
4	Dick Howser	56
5	Mike Hershberger	30
6	Ken Harrelson	27
7	Bill Tuttle	18
8	Dick Green	15
9	Joe DeMaestri	14
	Allan Lewis	14
11	Russ Snyder	13
12	Al Pilarcik	10
	Jim Gosger	10
14	Hector Lopez	9
	Tommie Reynolds	9
16	Lou Skizas	8
	Wayne Causey	8
	Jim Landis	8
19	Five tied at	7

Runs Created

1	Norm Siebern	411
2	Jerry Lumpe	359
3	Ed Charles	355
4	Wayne Causey	315
5	Hector Lopez	304
6	Vic Power	257
7	Bert Campaneris	248
8	Bob Cerv	236
9	Bill Tuttle	211
10	Harry Simpson	203
11	Dick Green	188
12	Joe DeMaestri	181
13	Gus Zernial	155
14	Hal Smith	152
15	Ken Harrelson	150
16	Mike Hershberger	149
17	Dick Howser	143
18	Roger Maris	133
	Gino Cimoli	133
20	Dick Williams	130

Runs Created/27 Outs

(minimum 1000 Plate Appearances)

1	Norm Siebern	6.68
2	Bob Cerv	5.95
3	Harry Simpson	5.38
4	Vic Power	5.23
5	Dick Howser	5.22
6	Dick Williams	4.95
7	Hector Lopez	4.92
8	Hal Smith	4.86
9	Ed Charles	4.67
10	Wayne Causey	4.66
11	Gus Zernial	4.63
12	Jerry Lumpe	4.59
13	Bobby Del Greco	4.45
14	Bill Tuttle	4.42
15	Bert Campaneris	4.28
16	Gino Cimoli	4.25
17	Danny Cater	4.08
18	Ken Harrelson	4.05
19	Jose Tartabull	3.97
20	Dick Green	3.52

Batting Average

(minimum 1000 Plate Appearances)

1	Vic Power	.299
2	Harry Simpson	.291
3	Norm Siebern	.289
4	Bob Cerv	.288
5	Hal Smith	.287
6	Danny Cater	.280
7	Jerry Lumpe	.279
8	Hector Lopez	.278
9	Dick Williams	.276
10	Wayne Causey	.270
11	Ed Charles	.268
12	Gino Cimoli	.267
13	Dick Howser	.263
14	Jose Tartabull	.263
15	Bill Tuttle	.261
16	Bert Campaneris	.261
17	Mike Hershberger	.246
18	Gus Zernial	.240
19	Dick Green	.239
20	Ken Harrelson	.239

On-Base Percentage

(minimum 1000 Plate Appearances)

1	Norm Siebern	.381
2	Dick Howser	.359
3	Wayne Causey	.350
4	Harry Simpson	.349
5	Bill Tuttle	.342
6	Bob Cerv	.342
7	Hector Lopez	.337
8	Ed Charles	.337
9	Bobby Del Greco	.336
10	Jerry Lumpe	.334
11	Hal Smith	.332
12	Vic Power	.330
13	Dick Williams	.327
14	Danny Cater	.325
15	Ken Harrelson	.318
16	Gino Cimoli	.315
17	Jose Tartabull	.311
18	Bert Campaneris	.308
19	Mike Hershberger	.306
20	Gus Zernial	.301

Slugging Percentage

(minimum 1000 Plate Appearances)

1	Bob Cerv	.509
2	Gus Zernial	.479
3	Norm Siebern	.463
4	Harry Simpson	.458
5	Vic Power	.452
6	Dick Williams	.442
7	Hector Lopez	.433
8	Hal Smith	.421
9	Ed Charles	.406
10	Ken Harrelson	.399
11	Gino Cimoli	.389
12	Jerry Lumpe	.377
13	Wayne Causey	.371
14	Bill Tuttle	.369
15	Bert Campaneris	.365
16	Danny Cater	.364
17	Bobby Del Greco	.362
18	Dick Green	.359
19	Dick Howser	.351
20	Jose Tartabull	.332

Teams: Athletics

Kansas City Athletics Team Pitching Leaders—Career

Wins

1	Bud Daley	39
2	Ray Herbert	37
3	Diego Segui	33
4	Ned Garver	32
5	Orlando Pena	30
	Catfish Hunter	30
7	John Wyatt	27
8	Tom Gorman	26
9	Dave Wickersham	25
	Lew Krausse	25
	Ed Rakow	25
12	Art Ditmar	24
	Alex Kellner	24
	Jim Nash	24
15	John O'Donoghue	19
16	Ralph Terry	18
17	Jerry Walker	16
18	Jack Urban	15
	Jack Aker	15
20	Six tied at	14

Losses

1	Ray Herbert	48
2	Diego Segui	47
3	Ned Garver	46
4	Orlando Pena	44
5	Art Ditmar	41
6	Bud Daley	39
7	Lew Krausse	37
8	Catfish Hunter	36
9	Ed Rakow	35
10	Ralph Terry	33
	John O'Donoghue	33
12	Moe Drabowsky	32
13	Tom Gorman	29
14	John Wyatt	28
15	Jerry Walker	23
16	Wally Burnette	21
	Johnny Kucks	21
18	Dave Wickersham	20
19	Four tied at	19

Winning Percentage
(minimum 50 decisions)

1	Bud Daley	.500
2	John Wyatt	.491
3	Tom Gorman	.473
4	Catfish Hunter	.455
5	Ray Herbert	.435
6	Ed Rakow	.417
7	Diego Segui	.413
8	Ned Garver	.410
9	Orlando Pena	.405
10	Lew Krausse	.403
11	Art Ditmar	.369
12	John O'Donoghue	.365
13	Ralph Terry	.353

Games

1	John Wyatt	292
2	Tom Gorman	214
3	Diego Segui	191
4	Jack Aker	166
5	Ray Herbert	152
6	Wes Stock	148
7	Ed Rakow	121
8	Bud Daley	118
9	Ned Garver	115
10	Lew Krausse	108
11	Art Ditmar	105
12	Moe Drabowsky	103
13	Orlando Pena	100
14	Catfish Hunter	97
15	Bill Fischer	94
16	Jim Dickson	92
17	Ted Bowsfield	91
18	Dave Wickersham	90
19	Paul Lindblad	88
20	Two tied at	85

Games Started

1	Diego Segui	99
2	Ray Herbert	98
3	Ned Garver	96
4	Orlando Pena	82
5	Catfish Hunter	80
6	Bud Daley	79
7	Ed Rakow	72
8	Ralph Terry	69
9	Alex Kellner	68
10	Art Ditmar	66
11	John O'Donoghue	63
12	Lew Krausse	58
13	Moe Drabowsky	51
	Jim Nash	51
15	Jerry Walker	45
16	Fred Talbot	44
17	Dave Wickersham	43
	Chuck Dobson	43
19	Rollie Sheldon	42
20	Johnny Kucks	40

Complete Games

1	Ray Herbert	32
2	Ned Garver	30
3	Bud Daley	28
4	Art Ditmar	21
5	Orlando Pena	20
	Catfish Hunter	20
7	Ed Rakow	19
8	Diego Segui	16
9	Alex Kellner	14
10	Ralph Terry	13
	Jim Nash	13
12	Moe Drabowsky	10
13	Dick Hall	9
	Jim Archer	9
15	Jack Urban	8
	Bob Grim	8
17	Johnny Kucks	7
	Dave Wickersham	7
	Jerry Walker	7
20	Four tied at	6

Shutouts

1	Ned Garver	8
2	Catfish Hunter	7
3	Ralph Terry	4
	Diego Segui	4
	Orlando Pena	4
6	Art Ditmar	3
	Alex Kellner	3
	Bud Daley	3
	Ed Rakow	3
	Blue Moon Odom	3
11	Ray Herbert	2
	Bob Grim	2
	Lew Krausse	2
	Jim Archer	2
	Norm Bass	2
	Moe Drabowsky	2
	John O'Donoghue	2
	Ted Bowsfield	2
	Rollie Sheldon	2
	Jim Nash	2

Saves

1	John Wyatt	73
2	Jack Aker	47
3	Tom Gorman	33
4	Wes Stock	12
5	Virgil Trucks	10
6	Bobby Shantz	9
	Lew Krausse	9
8	Tom Morgan	7
	Bob Grim	7
	Dick Tomanek	7
	Bill Fischer	7
	Diego Segui	7
	Paul Lindblad	7
	Don Mossi	7
	Tony Pierce	7
16	Dave Wickersham	6
	Gordon Jones	6
18	Four tied at	5

Innings Pitched

1	Ray Herbert	782.2
2	Diego Segui	733.2
3	Ned Garver	670.0
4	Bud Daley	581.2
5	Catfish Hunter	569.1
6	Orlando Pena	561.1
7	Ed Rakow	534.1
8	Tom Gorman	515.0
9	Art Ditmar	505.1
10	John Wyatt	464.2
11	Ralph Terry	457.2
12	Lew Krausse	433.0
13	Alex Kellner	420.2
14	Moe Drabowsky	409.1
15	Dave Wickersham	377.0
16	John O'Donoghue	357.1
17	Jim Nash	349.1
18	Jerry Walker	311.1
19	Chuck Dobson	281.1
20	Jack Aker	268.2

Walks

1	Diego Segui	311
2	Ray Herbert	259
3	John Wyatt	248
4	Art Ditmar	230
5	Ed Rakow	208
6	Bud Daley	199
7	Ned Garver	198
8	Catfish Hunter	194
9	Lew Krausse	193
10	Jerry Walker	174
11	Tom Gorman	171
12	Orlando Pena	166
13	Moe Drabowsky	164
14	Alex Kellner	142
	Ralph Terry	142
	Dan Pfister	142
17	Norm Bass	137
18	Blue Moon Odom	134
	Jim Nash	134
20	John O'Donoghue	133

Strikeouts

1	Diego Segui	513
2	Ray Herbert	393
3	Orlando Pena	392
4	Catfish Hunter	381
5	John Wyatt	362
6	Ed Rakow	344
7	Bud Daley	326
8	Jim Nash	284
9	Ralph Terry	282
10	Moe Drabowsky	272
11	Lew Krausse	246
12	Ned Garver	244
13	Art Ditmar	237
14	Tom Gorman	221
15	Alex Kellner	213
16	Dave Wickersham	192
17	Wes Stock	184
18	Chuck Dobson	171
19	Jack Aker	166
20	Paul Lindblad	164

Strikeouts/9 Innings
(minimum 500 Innings Pitched)

1	Diego Segui	6.29
2	Orlando Pena	6.29
3	Catfish Hunter	6.02
4	Ed Rakow	5.79
5	Bud Daley	5.04
6	Ray Herbert	4.52
7	Art Ditmar	4.22
8	Tom Gorman	3.86
9	Ned Garver	3.28

ERA
(minimum 500 Innings Pitched)

1	Catfish Hunter	3.53
2	Tom Gorman	3.84
3	Ned Garver	3.86
4	Bud Daley	3.93
5	Orlando Pena	4.07
6	Diego Segui	4.15
7	Ray Herbert	4.25
8	Ed Rakow	4.26
9	Art Ditmar	4.86

Component ERA
(minimum 500 Innings Pitched)

1	Catfish Hunter	3.07
2	Ned Garver	3.42
3	Tom Gorman	3.85
4	Orlando Pena	4.00
5	Ray Herbert	4.06
6	Diego Segui	4.07
7	Bud Daley	4.23
8	Ed Rakow	4.30
9	Art Ditmar	4.69

Opponent Average
(minimum 500 Innings Pitched)

1	Catfish Hunter	.232
2	Ned Garver	.247
3	Diego Segui	.253
4	Tom Gorman	.258
5	Orlando Pena	.259
6	Ed Rakow	.262
7	Bud Daley	.266
8	Art Ditmar	.270
9	Ray Herbert	.272

Opponent OBP
(minimum 500 Innings Pitched)

1	Catfish Hunter	.297
2	Ned Garver	.302
3	Orlando Pena	.314
4	Tom Gorman	.319
5	Diego Segui	.327
6	Ray Herbert	.329
7	Bud Daley	.332
8	Ed Rakow	.333
9	Art Ditmar	.351

Oakland Athletics Team Batting Leaders—Career

Games

1	Rickey Henderson	1,552
2	Sal Bando	1,410
3	Mark McGwire	1,329
4	Reggie Jackson	1,311
5	Bert Campaneris	1,295
6	Dwayne Murphy	1,213
7	Carney Lansford	1,203
8	Terry Steinbach	1,199
9	Joe Rudi	1,088
10	Jose Canseco	1,058
11	Wayne Gross	876
12	Tony Phillips	835
13	Mike Bordick	823
14	Gene Tenace	805
15	Mike Davis	788
16	Mike Gallego	772
17	Dick Green	750
18	Mike Heath	725
19	Dave Henderson	702
20	Tony Armas	694

At-Bats

1	Rickey Henderson	5,598
2	Bert Campaneris	5,159
3	Sal Bando	4,991
4	Reggie Jackson	4,568
	Carney Lansford	4,568
6	Mark McGwire	4,448
7	Terry Steinbach	4,162
8	Dwayne Murphy	4,047
9	Jose Canseco	3,970
10	Joe Rudi	3,950
11	Mike Bordick	2,643
12	Tony Phillips	2,588
13	Wayne Gross	2,566
14	Dave Henderson	2,553
15	Mike Davis	2,545
16	Tony Armas	2,484
17	Gene Tenace	2,458
18	Bill North	2,447
19	Mike Heath	2,438
20	Dick Green	2,205

Runs

1	Rickey Henderson	1,169
2	Mark McGwire	773
3	Reggie Jackson	743
4	Sal Bando	725
5	Bert Campaneris	722
6	Jose Canseco	662
7	Carney Lansford	617
8	Dwayne Murphy	614
9	Terry Steinbach	498
10	Joe Rudi	483
11	Bill North	379
12	Gene Tenace	369
	Mike Davis	369
14	Dave Henderson	366
15	Tony Phillips	354
16	Mitchell Page	295
17	Wayne Gross	289
18	Stan Javier	286
19	Geronimo Berroa	283
20	Two tied at	280

Hits

1	Rickey Henderson	1,640
2	Bert Campaneris	1,355
3	Carney Lansford	1,317
4	Sal Bando	1,279
5	Reggie Jackson	1,207
6	Mark McGwire	1,157
7	Terry Steinbach	1,144
8	Joe Rudi	1,079
9	Jose Canseco	1,048
10	Dwayne Murphy	999
11	Mike Bordick	682
12	Mike Davis	680
13	Dave Henderson	672
14	Bill North	664
15	Tony Phillips	649
16	Tony Armas	622
17	Mike Heath	612
18	Gene Tenace	603
19	Wayne Gross	602
20	Mitchell Page	556

Doubles

1	Rickey Henderson	273
2	Reggie Jackson	230
3	Joe Rudi	214
4	Sal Bando	208
5	Terry Steinbach	205
6	Carney Lansford	201
7	Mark McGwire	195
8	Jose Canseco	186
9	Bert Campaneris	175
10	Mike Davis	143
	Dave Henderson	143
12	Dwayne Murphy	129
13	Wayne Gross	109
14	Tony Phillips	107
15	Mike Heath	99
16	Scott Brosius	95
17	Mike Bordick	94
18	Gene Tenace	89
19	Jason Giambi	88
20	Two tied at	84

Triples

1	Rickey Henderson	40
2	Bert Campaneris	39
3	Joe Rudi	32
4	Tony Phillips	25
5	Reggie Jackson	23
	Bill North	23
	Carney Lansford	23
8	Sal Bando	22
9	Rick Monday	21
	Mitchell Page	21
11	Dwayne Murphy	20
12	Tony Armas	19
13	Claudell Washington	18
	Mike Heath	18
	Alfredo Griffin	18
	Luis Polonia	18
17	Phil Garner	17
18	Mike Bordick	15
19	Dave Revering	14
	Terry Steinbach	14

Home Runs

1	Mark McGwire	363
2	Reggie Jackson	268
3	Jose Canseco	254
4	Sal Bando	192
5	Dwayne Murphy	153
	Rickey Henderson	153
7	Terry Steinbach	132
8	Gene Tenace	121
9	Joe Rudi	116
10	Tony Armas	111
11	Dave Henderson	104
12	Dave Kingman	100
13	Carney Lansford	94
14	Wayne Gross	88
15	Geronimo Berroa	87
16	Mike Davis	84
17	Scott Brosius	76
18	Mitchell Page	72
19	Ruben Sierra	60
20	Jeff Newman	59

RBI

1	Mark McGwire	941
2	Jose Canseco	793
3	Sal Bando	789
4	Reggie Jackson	770
5	Terry Steinbach	595
6	Rickey Henderson	591
7	Dwayne Murphy	563
8	Carney Lansford	548
9	Joe Rudi	539
10	Bert Campaneris	391
11	Gene Tenace	389
12	Dave Henderson	377
13	Tony Armas	374
14	Mike Davis	335
15	Wayne Gross	314
16	Dave Kingman	303
17	Geronimo Berroa	301
18	Mike Heath	281
19	Mitchell Page	259
	Tony Phillips	259

Walks

1	Rickey Henderson	1,109
2	Mark McGwire	847
3	Sal Bando	775
4	Dwayne Murphy	694
5	Reggie Jackson	623
6	Gene Tenace	475
7	Jose Canseco	469
8	Bert Campaneris	387
9	Wayne Gross	368
10	Carney Lansford	353
11	Bill North	342
	Tony Phillips	342
13	Terry Steinbach	307
14	Joe Rudi	267
15	Rick Monday	251
16	Mitchell Page	242
17	Mike Bordick	240
18	Dave Henderson	233
19	Dick Green	209
20	Mike Gallego	205

Strikeouts

1	Reggie Jackson	1,180
2	Jose Canseco	1,096
3	Mark McGwire	1,043
4	Dwayne Murphy	883
5	Rickey Henderson	801
6	Terry Steinbach	689
7	Sal Bando	675
8	Bert Campaneris	667
9	Tony Armas	599
10	Dave Henderson	570
11	Joe Rudi	559
12	Gene Tenace	538
13	Tony Phillips	490
14	Mike Davis	450
15	Mitchell Page	445
16	Rick Monday	435
17	Dick Green	409
18	Bill North	388
19	Wayne Gross	379
20	Scott Brosius	372

Stolen Bases

1	Rickey Henderson	801
2	Bert Campaneris	398
3	Bill North	232
4	Carney Lansford	146
5	Reggie Jackson	144
6	Jose Canseco	135
7	Mike Davis	121
8	Mitchell Page	104
9	Stan Javier	103
10	Dwayne Murphy	99
11	Claudell Washington	83
	Alfredo Griffin	83
13	Luis Polonia	66
14	Matt Alexander	63
15	Davey Lopes	62
16	Sal Bando	59
17	Miguel Dilone	56
	Tony Phillips	56
19	Lance Blankenship	54
20	Don Baylor	52

Runs Created

1	Rickey Henderson	1,157
2	Mark McGwire	954
3	Reggie Jackson	840
4	Sal Bando	809
5	Jose Canseco	703
6	Carney Lansford	639
7	Dwayne Murphy	631
8	Bert Campaneris	625
9	Terry Steinbach	572
10	Joe Rudi	546
11	Gene Tenace	437
12	Mike Davis	363
13	Dave Henderson	358
14	Wayne Gross	355
15	Bill North	350
16	Tony Phillips	327
17	Mitchell Page	317
18	Tony Armas	301
19	Geronimo Berroa	300
20	Mike Bordick	292

Runs Created/27 Outs

(minimum 2000 Plate Appearances)

1	Mark McGwire	7.39
2	Rickey Henderson	7.24
3	Reggie Jackson	6.41
4	Jose Canseco	6.05
5	Gene Tenace	6.03
6	Sal Bando	5.56
7	Mitchell Page	5.14
8	Dwayne Murphy	5.12
9	Carney Lansford	4.91
10	Dave Henderson	4.88
11	Mike Davis	4.87
12	Joe Rudi	4.81
13	Bill North	4.81
14	Terry Steinbach	4.77
15	Wayne Gross	4.63
16	Tony Phillips	4.21
17	Scott Brosius	4.19
18	Tony Armas	4.13
19	Bert Campaneris	4.11
20	Stan Javier	4.11

Batting Average

(minimum 2000 Plate Appearances)

1	Rickey Henderson	.293
2	Carney Lansford	.288
3	Terry Steinbach	.275
4	Joe Rudi	.273
5	Bill North	.271
6	Mike Davis	.267
7	Mitchell Page	.266
8	Reggie Jackson	.264
9	Jose Canseco	.264
10	Dave Henderson	.263
11	Bert Campaneris	.263
12	Mark McGwire	.260
13	Mike Bordick	.258
14	Sal Bando	.256
15	Stan Javier	.255
16	Mike Heath	.251
17	Tony Phillips	.251
18	Tony Armas	.250
19	Scott Brosius	.248
20	Dwayne Murphy	.247

On-Base Percentage

(minimum 2000 Plate Appearances)

1	Rickey Henderson	.412
2	Mark McGwire	.380
3	Gene Tenace	.374
4	Bill North	.364
5	Sal Bando	.360
6	Reggie Jackson	.357
7	Dwayne Murphy	.356
8	Mitchell Page	.345
9	Jose Canseco	.344
10	Carney Lansford	.343
11	Tony Phillips	.338
12	Wayne Gross	.332
13	Terry Steinbach	.328
14	Stan Javier	.328
15	Dave Henderson	.325
16	Mike Bordick	.324
17	Joe Rudi	.320
18	Mike Davis	.319
19	Bert Campaneris	.316
20	Scott Brosius	.315

Slugging Percentage

(minimum 2000 Plate Appearances)

1	Mark McGwire	.551
2	Jose Canseco	.507
3	Reggie Jackson	.501
4	Dave Henderson	.445
5	Rickey Henderson	.438
6	Gene Tenace	.435
7	Tony Armas	.434
8	Mike Davis	.433
9	Joe Rudi	.432
10	Mitchell Page	.429
11	Terry Steinbach	.426
12	Sal Bando	.422
13	Scott Brosius	.416
14	Carney Lansford	.404
15	Dwayne Murphy	.402
16	Wayne Gross	.386
17	Mike Heath	.364
18	Jeff Newman	.363
19	Tony Phillips	.350
20	Stan Javier	.346

Teams: Athletics

Oakland Athletics Team Pitching Leaders—Career

Wins

1	Catfish Hunter	131
2	Vida Blue	124
3	Dave Stewart	119
4	Bob Welch	96
5	Ken Holtzman	77
6	Rick Langford	73
7	Blue Moon Odom	71
8	Rollie Fingers	67
9	Mike Moore	66
10	Curt Young	65
11	Steve McCatty	63
12	Chuck Dobson	58
	Mike Norris	58
14	Matt Keough	50
15	Paul Lindblad	42
16	Dennis Eckersley	41
17	Chris Codiroli	38
	Storm Davis	38
19	Ron Darling	37
20	Steve Ontiveros	31

Losses

1	Rick Langford	105
2	Vida Blue	86
3	Dave Stewart	78
4	Catfish Hunter	77
5	Matt Keough	75
6	Steve McCatty	63
7	Rollie Fingers	61
	Blue Moon Odom	61
9	Bob Welch	60
10	Mike Norris	59
11	Ken Holtzman	55
12	Curt Young	51
13	Chuck Dobson	48
14	Mike Moore	46
15	Brian Kingman	45
16	Ron Darling	44
17	Chris Codiroli	42
18	Bill Krueger	31
	Dennis Eckersley	31
20	Todd Van Poppel	29

Winning Percentage
(minimum 75 decisions)

1	Catfish Hunter	.630
2	Bob Welch	.615
3	Dave Stewart	.604
4	Vida Blue	.590
5	Mike Moore	.589
6	Ken Holtzman	.583
7	Curt Young	.560
8	Chuck Dobson	.547
9	Blue Moon Odom	.538
10	Rollie Fingers	.523
11	Steve McCatty	.500
12	Mike Norris	.496
13	Chris Codiroli	.475
14	Ron Darling	.457
15	Rick Langford	.410
16	Matt Keough	.400

Games

1	Dennis Eckersley	525
2	Rollie Fingers	502
3	Paul Lindblad	391
4	Rick Honeycutt	387
5	Gene Nelson	281
6	Vida Blue	273
7	Catfish Hunter	266
8	Dave Stewart	257
9	Rick Langford	248
10	Curt Young	228
11	Bob Lacey	227
12	Steve McCatty	221
13	Blue Moon Odom	220
14	Bob Welch	214
15	Mike Mohler	205
16	Mike Norris	201
17	Darold Knowles	194
18	Steve Ontiveros	179
19	Matt Keough	170
20	Billy Taylor	168

Games Started

1	Vida Blue	262
2	Catfish Hunter	260
3	Dave Stewart	245
4	Rick Langford	195
	Bob Welch	195
6	Blue Moon Odom	178
7	Steve McCatty	161
8	Mike Norris	157
9	Matt Keough	155
	Curt Young	155
11	Ken Holtzman	153
12	Chuck Dobson	140
13	Mike Moore	137
14	Ron Darling	120
15	Chris Codiroli	104
16	Brian Kingman	82
17	Storm Davis	77
18	Steve Ontiveros	67
19	Bill Krueger	66
20	Bobby Witt	63

Complete Games

1	Vida Blue	105
2	Catfish Hunter	96
3	Rick Langford	85
4	Ken Holtzman	54
5	Matt Keough	53
6	Mike Norris	52
7	Dave Stewart	49
8	Steve McCatty	45
9	Chuck Dobson	42
10	Blue Moon Odom	34
11	Brian Kingman	21
12	Jim Nash	15
	Mike Torrez	15
	Curt Young	15
15	Bob Welch	14
	Mike Moore	14
17	Chris Codiroli	13
18	Ron Darling	12
19	Bobby Witt	10
20	Three tied at	8

Shutouts

1	Vida Blue	28
2	Catfish Hunter	24
3	Ken Holtzman	13
4	Blue Moon Odom	11
5	Chuck Dobson	10
	Rick Langford	10
7	Dave Stewart	9
8	Jim Nash	7
	Mike Norris	7
	Matt Keough	7
	Steve McCatty	7
12	Bob Welch	5
13	Mike Torrez	4
	Mike Moore	4
	Bobby Witt	4
16	Brian Kingman	3
	Curt Young	3
	Ron Darling	3
19	Six tied at	2

Saves

1	Dennis Eckersley	320
2	Rollie Fingers	136
3	Jay Howell	61
4	Billy Taylor	41
5	Bill Caudill	37
6	Paul Lindblad	34
7	Rick Honeycutt	32
8	Darold Knowles	30
9	Mudcat Grant	27
10	Dave Beard	25
11	Bob Lacey	22
12	Bob Locker	20
13	Dave Heaverlo	19
	Steve Ontiveros	19
15	Jim Todd	18
16	Elias Sosa	14
	Gene Nelson	14
18	Doug Bair	12
	Tom Underwood	12
	Todd Burns	12

Innings Pitched

1	Vida Blue	1,945.2
2	Catfish Hunter	1,887.0
3	Dave Stewart	1,717.1
4	Rick Langford	1,468.0
5	Bob Welch	1,271.1
6	Blue Moon Odom	1,202.2
7	Steve McCatty	1,188.1
8	Mike Norris	1,124.1
9	Ken Holtzman	1,084.1
10	Matt Keough	1,060.1
11	Curt Young	1,039.1
12	Rollie Fingers	1,016.0
13	Chuck Dobson	919.0
14	Mike Moore	874.0
15	Ron Darling	723.1
16	Chris Codiroli	640.2
17	Dennis Eckersley	637.0
18	Paul Lindblad	629.2
19	Steve Ontiveros	597.2
20	Brian Kingman	547.0

Walks

1	Dave Stewart	655
2	Vida Blue	617
3	Blue Moon Odom	598
4	Steve McCatty	520
5	Mike Norris	499
6	Catfish Hunter	493
7	Bob Welch	469
8	Matt Keough	456
9	Rick Langford	402
10	Mike Moore	375
11	Curt Young	349
12	Chuck Dobson	325
13	Rollie Fingers	293
14	Ron Darling	287
15	Ken Holtzman	277
16	Todd Van Poppel	242
17	Chris Codiroli	234
18	Bill Krueger	228
19	Eric Plunk	215
20	Brian Kingman	204

Strikeouts

1	Vida Blue	1,315
2	Dave Stewart	1,152
3	Catfish Hunter	1,139
4	Rollie Fingers	784
5	Bob Welch	677
6	Blue Moon Odom	675
7	Dennis Eckersley	658
8	Rick Langford	654
9	Mike Norris	636
10	Chuck Dobson	557
11	Steve McCatty	541
12	Ken Holtzman	530
13	Curt Young	516
14	Mike Moore	515
15	Matt Keough	510
16	Ron Darling	431
17	Steve Ontiveros	350
18	Paul Lindblad	326
19	Gene Nelson	315
20	Jose Rijo	308

Strikeouts/9 Innings
(minimum 750 Innings Pitched)

1	Rollie Fingers	6.94
2	Vida Blue	6.08
3	Dave Stewart	6.04
4	Chuck Dobson	5.45
5	Catfish Hunter	5.43
6	Mike Moore	5.30
7	Mike Norris	5.09
8	Blue Moon Odom	5.05
9	Bob Welch	4.79
10	Curt Young	4.47
11	Ken Holtzman	4.40
12	Matt Keough	4.33
13	Steve McCatty	4.10
14	Rick Langford	4.01

ERA
(minimum 750 Innings Pitched)

1	Rollie Fingers	2.91
2	Ken Holtzman	2.92
3	Vida Blue	2.94
4	Catfish Hunter	3.00
5	Blue Moon Odom	3.38
6	Mike Moore	3.54
7	Chuck Dobson	3.61
8	Dave Stewart	3.73
9	Mike Norris	3.89
10	Bob Welch	3.94
11	Rick Langford	3.97
12	Steve McCatty	3.99
13	Matt Keough	4.13
14	Curt Young	4.33

Component ERA
(minimum 750 Innings Pitched)

1	Rollie Fingers	2.76
2	Vida Blue	2.80
3	Catfish Hunter	2.82
4	Ken Holtzman	2.94
5	Chuck Dobson	3.59
6	Mike Norris	3.60
7	Mike Moore	3.61
8	Blue Moon Odom	3.62
9	Dave Stewart	3.66
10	Rick Langford	3.94
11	Bob Welch	4.10
12	Steve McCatty	4.25
13	Curt Young	4.30
14	Matt Keough	4.34

Opponent Average
(minimum 750 Innings Pitched)

1	Catfish Hunter	.227
2	Vida Blue	.230
3	Rollie Fingers	.232
4	Mike Norris	.233
5	Blue Moon Odom	.239
6	Ken Holtzman	.243
7	Mike Moore	.246
8	Dave Stewart	.248
9	Chuck Dobson	.248
10	Steve McCatty	.258
11	Bob Welch	.261
12	Curt Young	.263
13	Matt Keough	.263
14	Rick Langford	.270

Opponent OBP
(minimum 750 Innings Pitched)

1	Catfish Hunter	.279
2	Vida Blue	.291
3	Rollie Fingers	.292
4	Ken Holtzman	.293
5	Chuck Dobson	.313
6	Rick Langford	.318
7	Dave Stewart	.318
8	Mike Norris	.319
9	Mike Moore	.324
10	Curt Young	.325
11	Bob Welch	.330
12	Blue Moon Odom	.331
13	Steve McCatty	.336
14	Matt Keough	.339

Athletics Franchise Batting Leaders—Single Season

Games

1	Norm Siebern	1962	162
	Sal Bando	1968	162
	Sal Bando	1969	162
	Sal Bando	1973	162
	Alfredo Griffin	1985	162
	Alfredo Griffin	1986	162
7	Rocky Colavito	1964	160
	Gene Tenace	1973	160
	Sal Bando	1975	160
	Phil Garner	1975	160
11	Bert Campaneris	1968	159
	Phil Garner	1976	159
	Dwayne Murphy	1980	159
	Jose Canseco	1987	159
	Mike Gallego	1991	159
	Mike Bordick	1993	159
17	Eleven tied at		158

At-Bats

1	Al Simmons	1932	670
2	Doc Cramer	1933	661
3	Al Simmons	1925	658
4	Lou Finney	1936	653
5	Doc Cramer	1934	649
	Wally Moses	1937	649
7	Doc Cramer	1935	644
8	Bert Campaneris	1968	642
9	Jerry Lumpe	1962	641
10	Jose Canseco	1987	630
	Ruben Sierra	1993	630
12	Whitey Witt	1921	629
13	Tony Armas	1980	628
14	Bert Campaneris	1972	625
15	Dave Philley	1953	620
16	Irv Hall	1945	616
17	Eddie Robinson	1953	615
18	Alfredo Griffin	1985	614
19	Jimmy Dykes	1921	613
20	Dick Siebert	1942	612

Runs

1	Al Simmons	1930	152
2	Jimmie Foxx	1932	151
3	Nap Lajoie	1901	145
4	Al Simmons	1932	144
5	Eddie Collins	1912	137
6	Eddie Joost	1949	128
7	Jimmie Foxx	1930	127
8	Eddie Collins	1913	125
	Jimmie Foxx	1933	125
10	Jimmie Foxx	1929	123
	Reggie Jackson	1969	123
12	Eddie Collins	1914	122
	Al Simmons	1925	122
14	Jimmie Foxx	1934	120
	Jose Canseco	1988	120
16	Rickey Henderson	1982	119
	Rickey Henderson	1990	119
18	Mickey Cochrane	1932	118
	Jimmie Foxx	1935	118
20	Max Bishop	1930	117

Hits

1	Al Simmons	1925	253
2	Nap Lajoie	1901	232
3	Al Simmons	1932	216
4	Doc Cramer	1935	214
5	Jimmie Foxx	1932	213
6	Al Simmons	1929	212
7	Al Simmons	1930	211
8	Wally Moses	1937	208
9	Jimmie Foxx	1933	204
10	Bill Lamar	1925	202
	Doc Cramer	1934	202
	Wally Moses	1936	202
13	Home Run Baker	1912	200
	Al Simmons	1931	200
15	Al Simmons	1926	199
16	Eddie Collins	1909	198
	Home Run Baker	1911	198
	Whitey Witt	1921	198
19	Lou Finney	1936	197
20	Doc Cramer	1933	195

Doubles

1	Al Simmons	1926	53
2	Nap Lajoie	1901	48
	Wally Moses	1937	48
4	Harry Davis	1905	47
	Eric McNair	1932	47
6	Socks Seybold	1903	45
7	Bob Johnson	1933	44
8	Harry Davis	1902	43
	Al Simmons	1925	43
	Bing Miller	1931	43
	Ferris Fain	1952	43
12	Home Run Baker	1911	42
	Mickey Cochrane	1930	42
14	Mule Haas	1929	41
	Al Simmons	1929	41
	Al Simmons	1930	41
	Wally Moses	1940	41
	Hank Majeski	1948	41
	Jason Giambi	1997	41
20	Four tied at		40

Triples

1	Home Run Baker	1912	21
2	Home Run Baker	1909	19
3	Danny Murphy	1910	18
4	Danny Murphy	1904	17
5	Amos Strunk	1915	16
	Bing Miller	1929	16
	Al Simmons	1930	16
8	Home Run Baker	1910	15
	Eddie Collins	1910	15
	Whitey Witt	1916	15
	Gino Cimoli	1962	15
12	Socks Seybold	1901	14
	Nap Lajoie	1901	14
	Topsy Hartsel	1903	14
	Danny Murphy	1909	14
	Rube Oldring	1910	14
	Home Run Baker	1911	14
	Rube Oldring	1911	14
	Eddie Collins	1914	14
	Bob Johnson	1936	14

Home Runs

1	Jimmie Foxx	1932	58
2	Mark McGwire	1996	52
3	Mark McGwire	1987	49
4	Jimmie Foxx	1933	48
5	Reggie Jackson	1969	47
6	Jimmie Foxx	1934	44
	Jose Canseco	1991	44
8	Gus Zernial	1953	42
	Jose Canseco	1988	42
	Mark McGwire	1992	42
11	Mark McGwire	1990	39
	Mark McGwire	1995	39
13	Bob Cerv	1958	38
14	Tilly Walker	1922	37
	Jimmie Foxx	1930	37
	Jose Canseco	1990	37
17	Al Simmons	1930	36
	Jimmie Foxx	1935	36
	Reggie Jackson	1975	36
	Geronimo Berroa	1996	36

RBI

1	Jimmie Foxx	1932	169
2	Al Simmons	1930	165
3	Jimmie Foxx	1933	163
4	Al Simmons	1929	157
5	Jimmie Foxx	1930	156
6	Al Simmons	1932	151
7	Home Run Baker	1912	130
	Jimmie Foxx	1934	130
9	Al Simmons	1925	129
10	Al Simmons	1931	128
11	Nap Lajoie	1901	125
	Gus Zernial	1951	125
13	Jose Canseco	1988	124
14	Jose Canseco	1991	122
15	Bob Johnson	1936	121
16	Jimmie Foxx	1931	120
	Hank Majeski	1948	120
18	Reggie Jackson	1969	118
	Dave Kingman	1984	118
	Mark McGwire	1987	118

Walks

1	Eddie Joost	1949	149
2	Ferris Fain	1949	136
3	Ferris Fain	1950	133
4	Max Bishop	1929	128
	Max Bishop	1930	128
6	Eddie Joost	1952	122
7	Topsy Hartsel	1905	121
8	Eddie Joost	1948	119
	Elmer Valo	1949	119
10	Sal Bando	1970	118
11	Rickey Henderson	1980	117
12	Max Bishop	1926	116
	Jimmie Foxx	1932	116
	Rickey Henderson	1982	116
	Mark McGwire	1996	116
16	Jimmie Foxx	1935	114
	Eddie Joost	1947	114
	Reggie Jackson	1969	114
19	Ferris Fain	1948	113
20	Max Bishop	1931	112

Strikeouts

1	Jose Canseco	1986	175
2	Reggie Jackson	1968	171
3	Reggie Jackson	1971	161
4	Jose Canseco	1990	158
5	Jose Canseco	1987	157
6	Jose Canseco	1991	152
7	Nelson Mathews	1964	143
	Rick Monday	1968	143
9	Reggie Jackson	1969	142
10	Reggie Jackson	1970	135
11	Reggie Jackson	1975	133
12	Mark McGwire	1987	131
	Dave Henderson	1989	131
14	Tony Armas	1980	128
	Tony Armas	1982	128
	Jose Canseco	1988	128
17	Gene Tenace	1975	127
18	Dave Kingman	1986	126
19	Reggie Jackson	1972	125
20	Dwayne Murphy	1985	123

Stolen Bases

1	Rickey Henderson	1982	130
2	Rickey Henderson	1983	108
3	Rickey Henderson	1980	100
4	Eddie Collins	1910	81
5	Bill North	1976	75
6	Eddie Collins	1909	67
7	Rickey Henderson	1984	66
8	Rickey Henderson	1990	65
9	Eddie Collins	1912	63
10	Bert Campaneris	1968	62
	Bert Campaneris	1969	62
12	Eddie Collins	1914	58
	Rickey Henderson	1991	58
14	Rickey Henderson	1981	56
15	Eddie Collins	1913	55
	Bert Campaneris	1967	55
17	Bill North	1974	54
	Bert Campaneris	1976	54
19	Bill North	1973	53
20	Four tied at		52

Runs Created

1	Jimmie Foxx	1932	189
2	Nap Lajoie	1901	169
3	Jimmie Foxx	1933	166
4	Al Simmons	1930	156
5	Jimmie Foxx	1930	150
6	Jimmie Foxx	1929	145
7	Jimmie Foxx	1934	144
8	Al Simmons	1929	141
9	Al Simmons	1925	140
10	Jimmie Foxx	1935	139
11	Reggie Jackson	1969	138
12	Jose Canseco	1988	137
13	Al Simmons	1932	135
14	Al Simmons	1931	134
	Mark McGwire	1996	134
16	Home Run Baker	1912	132
17	Eddie Collins	1914	128
18	Eddie Collins	1912	127
	Bob Johnson	1939	127
20	Three tied at		125

Runs Created/27 Outs

(minimum 3.1 Plate Appearances/Tm Gm)

1	Nap Lajoie	1901	13.99
2	Jimmie Foxx	1932	13.19
3	Jimmie Foxx	1933	11.85
4	Mark McGwire	1996	11.79
5	Al Simmons	1930	11.28
6	Al Simmons	1931	11.19
7	Jimmie Foxx	1929	10.64
8	Jimmie Foxx	1934	10.38
9	Jimmie Foxx	1935	10.31
10	Jimmie Foxx	1930	9.84
11	Al Simmons	1929	9.54
12	Eddie Collins	1911	9.42
13	Mickey Cochrane	1933	9.24
14	Rickey Henderson	1990	9.19
15	Mickey Cochrane	1931	9.08
16	Reggie Jackson	1969	9.05
17	Socks Seybold	1901	8.92
18	Mickey Cochrane	1930	8.86
19	Bob Johnson	1939	8.82
20	Home Run Baker	1912	8.66

Batting Average

(minimum 3.1 Plate Appearances/Tm Gm)

1	Nap Lajoie	1901	.426
2	Al Simmons	1931	.390
3	Al Simmons	1925	.384
4	Al Simmons	1930	.381
5	Eddie Collins	1911	.365
6	Al Simmons	1929	.365
7	Jimmie Foxx	1932	.364
8	Mickey Cochrane	1930	.357
9	Ty Cobb	1927	.357
10	Jimmie Foxx	1933	.356
11	Bill Lamar	1925	.356
12	Jimmie Foxx	1929	.354
13	George Burns	1918	.352
14	Al Simmons	1928	.351
15	Mickey Cochrane	1931	.349
16	Eddie Collins	1912	.348
17	Home Run Baker	1912	.347
18	Eddie Collins	1909	.346
19	Jimmie Foxx	1935	.346
20	Wally Moses	1936	.345

On-Base Percentage

(minimum 3.1 Plate Appearances/Tm Gm)

1	Jimmie Foxx	1932	.469
2	Mark McGwire	1996	.467
3	Jimmie Foxx	1929	.463
4	Nap Lajoie	1901	.463
5	Jimmie Foxx	1935	.461
6	Mickey Cochrane	1933	.459
7	Eddie Collins	1914	.452
8	Eddie Collins	1911	.451
9	Ferris Fain	1951	.451
10	Eddie Collins	1912	.450
11	Jimmie Foxx	1933	.449
12	Jimmie Foxx	1934	.449
13	Max Bishop	1933	.446
14	Al Simmons	1931	.444
15	Max Bishop	1927	.442
16	Eddie Collins	1913	.441
17	Bob Johnson	1939	.440
18	Ty Cobb	1927	.440
19	Rickey Henderson	1990	.439
20	Ferris Fain	1952	.438

Slugging Percentage

(minimum 3.1 Plate Appearances/Tm Gm)

1	Jimmie Foxx	1932	.749
2	Mark McGwire	1996	.730
3	Al Simmons	1930	.708
4	Jimmie Foxx	1933	.703
5	Jimmie Foxx	1934	.653
6	Nap Lajoie	1901	.643
7	Al Simmons	1929	.642
8	Al Simmons	1931	.641
9	Jimmie Foxx	1930	.637
10	Jimmie Foxx	1935	.636
11	Jimmie Foxx	1929	.625
12	Mark McGwire	1987	.618
13	Reggie Jackson	1969	.608
14	Al Simmons	1925	.596
15	Bob Cerv	1958	.592
16	Mark McGwire	1992	.585
17	Rickey Henderson	1990	.577
18	Jose Canseco	1988	.569
19	Jimmie Foxx	1931	.567
20	Al Simmons	1926	.566

Teams: Athletics

Athletics Franchise Pitching Leaders—Single Season

Wins

1	Jack Coombs	1910	31
	Lefty Grove	1931	31
3	Jack Coombs	1911	28
	Lefty Grove	1930	28
5	Rube Waddell	1905	27
	Eddie Rommel	1922	27
	Bob Welch	1990	27
8	Eddie Plank	1904	26
	Eddie Plank	1912	26
10	Rube Waddell	1904	25
	Lefty Grove	1932	25
	Catfish Hunter	1974	25
13	Rube Waddell	1902	24
	Eddie Plank	1905	24
	Eddie Plank	1907	24
	Lefty Grove	1928	24
	George Earnshaw	1929	24
	Lefty Grove	1933	24
	Bobby Shantz	1952	24
	Vida Blue	1971	24

Losses

1	Scott Perry	1920	25
2	Joe Bush	1916	24
3	Elmer Myers	1916	23
	Rollie Naylor	1920	23
	Eddie Rommel	1921	23
6	John Wyckoff	1915	22
	Art Ditmar	1956	22
8	Harry Kelley	1937	21
	Lum Harris	1943	21
10	Jack Nabors	1916	20
	Slim Harriss	1922	20
	Gordon Rhodes	1936	20
	George Caster	1938	20
	Bobo Newsom	1945	20
	Alex Kellner	1950	20
	Harry Byrd	1953	20
	Orlando Pena	1963	20
	Brian Kingman	1980	20
19	Nine tied at		19

Winning Percentage
(minimum 15 decisions)

1	Lefty Grove	1931	.886
2	Chief Bender	1914	.850
3	Lefty Grove	1930	.848
4	Chief Bender	1910	.821
5	Bob Welch	1990	.818
6	Eddie Plank	1912	.813
7	Catfish Hunter	1973	.808
8	Roy Mahaffey	1931	.789
9	Jack Coombs	1910	.775
10	Rube Waddell	1902	.774
	Bobby Shantz	1952	.774
12	Chief Bender	1911	.773
13	Lefty Grove	1929	.769
14	Eddie Plank	1906	.760
15	Nine tied at		.750

Games

1	John Wyatt	1964	81
2	Buddy Groom	1997	78
3	Rollie Fingers	1974	76
4	Rollie Fingers	1975	75
5	Bob Lacey	1978	74
6	Mudcat Grant	1970	72
	Buddy Groom	1996	72
	Mike Mohler	1996	72
	Billy Taylor	1997	72
10	Aaron Small	1997	71
11	Rollie Fingers	1976	70
12	Dave Heaverlo	1978	69
	Dennis Eckersley	1992	69
14	Jim Dickson	1965	68
	Paul Lindblad	1975	68
	Elias Sosa	1978	68
	Bill Caudill	1984	68
18	Dennis Eckersley	1991	67
19	Jack Aker	1966	66
	Jeff Parrett	1992	66

Games Started

1	Rube Waddell	1904	46
2	Eddie Plank	1904	43
3	Eddie Plank	1905	41
	Catfish Hunter	1974	41
5	Eddie Plank	1903	40
	Eddie Plank	1907	40
	Jack Coombs	1911	40
	George Caster	1938	40
	Catfish Hunter	1970	40
	Chuck Dobson	1970	40
	Ken Holtzman	1973	40
	Vida Blue	1974	40
13	George Earnshaw	1930	39
	Vida Blue	1971	39
	Mike Torrez	1976	39
16	Six tied at		38

Complete Games

1	Rube Waddell	1904	39
2	Eddie Plank	1904	37
3	Chick Fraser	1901	35
	Eddie Plank	1905	35
	Jack Coombs	1910	35
6	Rube Waddell	1903	34
7	Eddie Plank	1903	33
	Eddie Plank	1907	33
9	Eddie Plank	1902	31
	Weldon Henley	1904	31
	Elmer Myers	1916	31
12	Scott Perry	1918	30
13	Chief Bender	1903	29
14	Eddie Plank	1901	28
	Rick Langford	1980	28
16	Rube Waddell	1905	27
	Lefty Grove	1931	27
	Lefty Grove	1932	27
	Bobby Shantz	1952	27
20	Three tied at		26

Shutouts

1	Jack Coombs	1910	13
2	Rube Waddell	1904	8
	Rube Waddell	1906	8
	Eddie Plank	1907	8
	Joe Bush	1916	8
	Vida Blue	1971	8
7	Eddie Plank	1904	7
	Rube Waddell	1905	7
	Rube Waddell	1907	7
	Harry Krause	1909	7
	Eddie Plank	1913	7
	Chief Bender	1914	7
13	Rube Vickers	1908	6
	Jack Coombs	1909	6
	Eddie Plank	1911	6
	Jim Nash	1968	6
	Catfish Hunter	1974	6
	Vida Blue	1976	6
19	Twelve tied at		5

Saves

1	Dennis Eckersley	1992	51
2	Dennis Eckersley	1990	48
3	Dennis Eckersley	1988	45
4	Dennis Eckersley	1991	43
5	Bill Caudill	1984	36
	Dennis Eckersley	1993	36
7	Dennis Eckersley	1989	33
8	Jack Aker	1966	32
9	Jay Howell	1985	29
	Dennis Eckersley	1995	29
11	Mudcat Grant	1970	24
	Rollie Fingers	1975	24
13	Billy Taylor	1997	23
14	Rollie Fingers	1973	22
15	John Wyatt	1963	21
	Rollie Fingers	1972	21
17	John Wyatt	1964	20
	Rollie Fingers	1976	20
19	Dennis Eckersley	1994	19
20	Three tied at		18

Innings Pitched

1	Rube Waddell	1904	383.0
2	Eddie Plank	1904	357.1
3	Jack Coombs	1910	353.0
4	Eddie Plank	1905	346.2
5	Eddie Plank	1907	343.2
6	Jack Coombs	1911	336.2
7	Eddie Plank	1903	336.0
8	Scott Perry	1918	332.1
9	Chick Fraser	1901	331.0
10	Rube Waddell	1905	328.2
11	Rube Waddell	1903	324.0
12	Catfish Hunter	1974	318.1
13	Rube Vickers	1908	317.0
14	Elmer Myers	1916	315.0
15	Vida Blue	1971	312.0
16	Eddie Plank	1902	300.0
17	Vida Blue	1976	298.1
18	Eddie Rommel	1923	297.2
19	Ken Holtzman	1973	297.1
20	George Earnshaw	1930	296.0

Walks

1	Elmer Myers	1916	168
2	John Wyckoff	1915	165
3	Phil Marchildon	1947	141
4	Phil Marchildon	1942	140
5	George Earnshaw	1930	139
6	Sugar Cain	1933	137
7	Chick Fraser	1901	132
8	Lefty Grove	1925	131
	Phil Marchildon	1948	131
10	Joe Bush	1916	130
11	Alex Kellner	1949	129
12	Sugar Cain	1934	128
13	Joe Coleman	1949	127
14	George Earnshaw	1929	125
15	Byron Houck	1913	122
	Roy Moore	1921	122
17	Jack Coombs	1911	119
18	Four tied at		118

Strikeouts

1	Rube Waddell	1904	349
2	Rube Waddell	1903	302
3	Vida Blue	1971	301
4	Rube Waddell	1905	287
5	Rube Waddell	1907	232
6	Jack Coombs	1910	224
7	Rube Waddell	1902	210
	Eddie Plank	1905	210
9	Lefty Grove	1930	209
10	Dave Stewart	1987	205
	Todd Stottlemyre	1995	205
12	Eddie Plank	1904	201
13	Rube Waddell	1906	196
	Catfish Hunter	1967	196
15	Lefty Grove	1926	194
16	George Earnshaw	1930	193
17	Dave Stewart	1988	192
18	Catfish Hunter	1972	191
19	Vida Blue	1975	189
20	Lefty Grove	1932	188

Strikeouts/9 Innings
(minimum 1 Inning Pitched/Tm Gm)

1	Todd Stottlemyre	1995	8.80
2	Vida Blue	1971	8.68
3	Rube Waddell	1903	8.39
4	Rube Waddell	1904	8.20
5	Jose Rijo	1986	8.18
6	Rube Waddell	1905	7.86
7	Orlando Pena	1964	7.55
8	Jim Nash	1967	7.53
9	Bobby Witt	1994	7.36
10	Rube Waddell	1907	7.33
11	Dave Stewart	1987	7.06
12	Rube Waddell	1902	6.84
13	Catfish Hunter	1967	6.79
14	Lefty Grove	1926	6.77
15	Chuck Dobson	1968	6.71
16	Jim Nash	1968	6.65
17	George Earnshaw	1928	6.65
18	Catfish Hunter	1968	6.62
19	Chief Bender	1904	6.58
20	Diego Segui	1965	6.57

ERA
(minimum 1 Inning Pitched/Tm Gm)

1	Jack Coombs	1910	1.30
2	Harry Krause	1909	1.39
3	Rube Waddell	1905	1.48
4	Cy Morgan	1910	1.55
5	Chief Bender	1910	1.58
6	Rube Waddell	1904	1.62
7	Cy Morgan	1909	1.65
8	Chief Bender	1909	1.66
9	Eddie Plank	1909	1.76
10	Vida Blue	1971	1.82
11	Andy Coakley	1905	1.84
12	Scott Perry	1918	1.98
13	Eddie Plank	1910	2.01
14	Catfish Hunter	1972	2.04
15	Chief Bender	1907	2.05
16	Rube Waddell	1902	2.05
17	Lefty Grove	1931	2.06
18	Eddie Plank	1911	2.10
19	Rube Waddell	1907	2.15
20	Chief Bender	1911	2.16

Component ERA
(minimum 1 Inning Pitched/Tm Gm)

1	Chief Bender	1910	1.56
2	Harry Krause	1909	1.65
3	Rube Waddell	1905	1.66
4	Chief Bender	1909	1.68
5	Catfish Hunter	1972	1.70
6	Jack Coombs	1910	1.72
7	Cy Morgan	1909	1.72
8	Chief Bender	1907	1.76
9	Vida Blue	1971	1.81
10	Eddie Plank	1908	1.91
11	Eddie Plank	1909	1.95
12	Rube Waddell	1904	1.98
13	Rube Vickers	1908	2.01
14	Jack Coombs	1909	2.09
15	Chief Bender	1904	2.11
16	Rube Waddell	1902	2.11
17	Eddie Plank	1906	2.13
18	Eddie Plank	1905	2.14
19	Rube Waddell	1907	2.15
20	Jimmy Dygert	1907	2.15

Opponent Average
(minimum 1 Inning Pitched/Tm Gm)

1	Catfish Hunter	1972	.189
2	Vida Blue	1971	.189
3	Cy Morgan	1909	.191
4	Rube Waddell	1905	.198
5	Jack Coombs	1910	.201
6	Harry Krause	1909	.204
7	Chief Bender	1910	.207
8	Mike Norris	1980	.209
9	Steve McCatty	1981	.211
10	Jack Coombs	1909	.213
11	Jimmy Dygert	1907	.213
12	Chief Bender	1909	.214
13	Byron Houck	1913	.214
14	Moe Drabowsky	1963	.214
15	Blue Moon Odom	1969	.215
16	Blue Moon Odom	1968	.216
17	Cy Morgan	1910	.216
18	Rube Waddell	1904	.217
19	Lew Krausse	1968	.217
20	Steve Ontiveros	1994	.217

Opponent OBP
(minimum 1 Inning Pitched/Tm Gm)

1	Catfish Hunter	1972	.241
2	Vida Blue	1971	.251
3	Chief Bender	1909	.254
4	Chief Bender	1907	.254
5	Chief Bender	1910	.255
6	Catfish Hunter	1974	.258
7	Rube Waddell	1905	.261
8	Harry Krause	1909	.266
9	Jim Nash	1968	.269
10	Eddie Plank	1908	.269
11	Mike Norris	1980	.270
12	Cy Morgan	1909	.271
13	Lefty Grove	1931	.271
14	Steve Ontiveros	1994	.271
15	Rube Waddell	1904	.272
16	Bobby Shantz	1952	.272
17	Jack Coombs	1910	.273
18	Lefty Grove	1928	.274
19	Ken Holtzman	1972	.276
20	Rube Waddell	1902	.276

Philadelphia/Kansas City/Oakland A's Capsule

Best Season: *1929/1958/1989.* The 1929 Philadelphia Athletics won the American League pennant by 18 games. In the World Series, they staged dramatic late-inning comebacks in Games 4 and 5, with the latter one finishing off the Chicago Cubs. During their 13 years in Kansas City, the A's posted their least pitiful won-lost record in 1958 (73-81). Although the Oakland A's put together three straight World Championships from 1972 through 1974, their most impressive championship of all was won in 1989. They won seven more regular-season games than any other club, and brushed aside the Toronto Blue Jays and San Francisco Giants with eight wins in nine postseason contests.

Worst Season: *1916/1961/1979.* Connie Mack's first fire sale led to 117 losses in 1916, setting an AL record that still stands. In 1961, Kansas City lost 100 games as ex-Athletics Roger Maris and Ralph Terry starred for the World Champion New York Yankees. After Oakland lost virtually its entire team through trades and free agency, the 1979 club staggered through a 108-loss season.

Best Player: *Jimmie Foxx/Norm Siebern/Rickey Henderson.*

Best Pitcher: *Lefty Grove/Bud Daley/Catfish Hunter.*

Best Reliever: *Eddie Rommel/John Wyatt/Dennis Eckersley.*

Best Defensive Player: *Ferris Fain/Vic Power/Dwayne Murphy.* Fain was lauded as the best defensive first baseman since Hal Chase, a mantle that Power later inherited. Murphy was a six-time Gold-Glover in center field.

Hall of Famers: *Home Run Baker, Chief Bender, Mickey Cochrane, Eddie Collins, Jimmie Foxx, Lefty Grove, Connie Mack, Eddie Plank, Al Simmons* and *Rube Waddell* from Philadelphia; no one from Kansas City; *Rollie Fingers, Catfish Hunter* and *Reggie Jackson* from Oakland.

Franchise All-Star Team:

C	*Mickey Cochrane/Hal Smith/Terry Steinbach*
1B	*Jimmie Foxx/Norm Siebern/Mark McGwire*
2B	*Eddie Collins/Jerry Lumpe/Dick Green*
3B	*Home Run Baker/Hector Lopez/Sal Bando*
SS	*Eddie Joost/Wayne Causey/Bert Campaneris*
LF	*Al Simmons/Gus Zernial/Rickey Henderson*
CF	*Sam Chapman/Bill Tuttle/Dwayne Murphy*
RF	*Bob Johnson/Bob Cerv/Reggie Jackson*
DH	*—/—/Jose Canseco*
SP	*Lefty Grove/Bud Daley/Catfish Hunter*
RP	*Eddie Rommel/John Wyatt/Dennis Eckersley*

Biggest Flake: *Rube Waddell/Ken Harrelson/Mike Norris.* Waddell was, among other things, an incorrigible fire engine chaser. Harrelson was well-known for his outlandish wardrobe, which included the short-lived Nehru jacket; he achieved every Athletic's dream when he secured his release from owner Charlie Finley after calling Finley "a menace to baseball." Norris was a free spirit whose star burned brightly for one season before flaming out.

Strangest Career: *Scott Perry/Manny Jimenez/Mitchell Page.* Perry came out of nowhere in 1918 to post a 1.98 ERA, the fourth-best in the AL. He accounted for 20 of the last-place Athletics' 52 wins. Connie Mack thought so much of Perry that when the Boston Braves put forth an apparently legitimate claim on Perry, Mack went to court and secured an injunction in order to retain him. Perry hardly justified the aggravation, going 18-48 over the remaining three years of his career. Jimenez batted .301 with 69 RBI as a 23-year-old rookie in 1962; due to the A's mismanagement, he never was given the chance to play regularly again. Page finished second to Eddie Murray in the AL Rookie of the Year balloting in 1977 after batting .307 with 21 home runs and 42 stolen bases. Over the next three years, his average dropped to .285, .247 and .244, ending his days as a regular.

What Might Have Been: *Bill McCahan/Jim Finigan/Mike Warren.* McCahan went 10-5 with a 3.32 ERA and tossed a no-hitter as a rookie in 1947. He hurt his arm moving oil drums over the winter, and pitched ineffectively for two more years. In 1954, third baseman Finigan batted .302 and finished second in the AL Rookie of the Year race. Switched to second base the following year, he slumped to .255. The year after that, he batted .216 and lost his job. Mike Warren was the Bill McCahan of the '80s. He went 5-3 as a rookie in 1983, capping his season with a no-hitter on September 29. Between the majors and two minor league stops, he went 17-8 with 202 strikeouts. He pitched poorly over the next two years and was released in 1985.

Best Trade: *Buddy Rosar/Joe Rudi/Dennis Eckersley.* Connie Mack continually bought and sold players, but rarely traded them, and under his command, the A's acquired very few significant players via the trade route. In May of 1945, catcher Rosar was acquired from the Cleveland Indians for Frankie Hayes. Rosar made the All-Star team in each of the next three seasons. The Kansas City A's dealt outfielder Jim Landis to the Indians for Joe Rudi and catcher Phil Roof in 1965, although they didn't reap the benfits of the trade until after they'd moved to Oakland. Eckersley was acquired from the Cubs in '87 for a handful of minor-leaguers who never amounted to anything.

Worst Trade: *Joe Jackson/Roger Maris/Jose Rijo.* The Athletics traded the young Joe Jackson to the Indians in 1910 for outfielder Bris Lord. They also traded Nellie Fox to the White Sox for Joe Tipton in 1949. Kansas City traded Maris and two players to the Yankees for Norm Siebern and two players on December 11, 1959. Rijo was sent to Cincinnati for Dave Parker in 1987.

Best-Looking Player: *Jimmie Foxx/Whitey Herzog/Rick Monday.*

Ugliest Player: *Eddie Plank/Ralph Terry/Eric Plunk.*

Best Nicknames: Philadelphia had *Boardwalk Brown, Kite Thomas, Skeeter Kell, Jing Johnson, Socks Seybold, Beauty McGowen, "Good Time Bill" Lamar,* and *Bris Lord, "The Human Eyeball."* Kansas City had *Harry "Suitcase" Simpson, "The Immortal Azcue," Joe Azcue; Ken "Hawk" Harrelson;* and *Lou Skizas, "The Nervous Greek."* Oakland had *Blue Moon Odom, Catfish Hunter* and *Shooty Babitt.*

Most Unappreciated Player: *Danny Murphy/Tom Gorman/Dwayne Murphy.* Danny Murphy was a fine second baseman for five years before Eddie Collins bumped him to the outfield. Murphy remained a quality hitter and was a key player on Philadelphia's pennant-winning clubs in 1910 and 1911. Gorman was a useful reliever and swingman in Kansas City for several years. Dwayne Murphy was a terrific defensive center fielder who drew walks and hit for power.

Most Overrated Player: *Mule Haas/Joe DeMaestri/Walt Weiss.* Haas played in a hitters' park in the heart of the lively-ball era. For an outfielder in his time and place, his production was distinctly unimpressive. DeMaestri was a weak-hitting shortstop who made the All-Star team one year purely by default. Weiss was equally inept at the plate, but won accolades with a few well-timed defensive gems before a postseason audience.

Most Admirable Star: *Lou Brissie/Bud Daley/Joe Rudi.* Brissie suffered severe injuries in World War II and underwent 23 operations. Pitching with a heavy brace on his leg, he won 37 games for the Athletics. Daley was a natural righthander who was forced to throw lefthanded after contracting polio as a child. Rudi excelled in all facets of the game and was a consistent, dependable contributor on a club loaded with volatile personalities.

Least Admirable Star: *Bob Dillinger/Ken Harrelson/Dave Kingman.*

Best Season, Player: *Jimmie Foxx, 1932/Bob Cerv, 1958/Rickey Henderson, 1990.* Foxx came up two short in his bid for Babe Ruth's home-run record, and he would have been awarded the Triple Crown under modern rules. Cerv's 1958 season and Norm Siebern's 1962 season are fairly comparable; we give the nod to Cerv for his pre-expansion slugging. Reggie Jackson, Mark McGwire and Jose Canseco enjoyed some fine seasons in Oakland, but none of the three could match Henderson's across-the-board brilliance in 1990.

Best Season, Pitcher: *Lefty Grove, 1931/Jim Nash, 1966/Vida Blue, 1971.* Grove went 31-4 in 1931 and posted an ERA less than one-half of the league average. (One could argue that Rube Waddell had an even greater year in 1902 when he joined the Athletics 50 games into the season and went 24-7.) Rookie righthander Nash went 12-1 in 1966; only one other Kansas City pitcher ever finished more than four games over .500 in a season. Blue won the AL MVP Award for his 24 wins and 301 strikeouts in 1971.

Most Impressive Individual Record: *Jimmie Foxx/None/Rickey Henderson.* Foxx nearly won consecutive Triple Crowns in 1932 and 1933. In '32, he led the league with 58 home runs and 169 RBI, but lost the batting title to Dale Alexander by three points, .367-.364. Alexander had only 392 at-bats, however, and wouldn't have qualified for the batting championship under the modern rules. Foxx came back the next year to win the Triple Crown—uncontested. Henderson set both the single-season and career stolen-base records with Oakland.

Biggest Tragedy: *Doc Powers.* Powers, the Athletics' popular catcher, was seized by abdominal pains while catching the season opener in 1905. Afterward, he collapsed in the clubhouse. Surgery revealed that his intestines had folded inward upon themselves, and a foot of gangrenous intestine was removed. Powers underwent a second operation, but died two weeks later. The A's have been oddly immune to personal tragedy ever since Powers' demise.

Fan Favorite: *Rube Waddell/Jerry Lumpe/Reggie Jackson.*

—Mat Olkin

Seattle Mariners (1977-1997)

Year	Lg	Pos	W-L	Pct	GB	Manager	Att.	R	OR	HR	Avg	OBP	Slg	Opponent				Park Index	
														HR	Avg	OBP	ERA	Runs	HR
1977	AL	6th-W	64-98	.395	38.0	Darrell Johnson	1,338,511	624	855	133	.256	.312	.381	194	.272	.344	4.83	95	119
1978	AL	7th-W	56-104	.350	35.0	Darrell Johnson	877,440	614	834	97	.248	.314	.359	155	.280	.348	4.67	110	146
1979	AL	6th-W	67-95	.414	21.0	Darrell Johnson	844,447	711	820	132	.269	.331	.404	165	.281	.348	4.58	103	158
1980	AL	7th-W	59-103	.364	38.0	Darrell Johnson/Maury Wills	836,204	610	793	104	.248	.308	.356	159	.278	.341	4.38	108	192
1981	AL	6th-W	21-36	.368	14.5	Maury Wills/Rene Lachemann													
	AL	5th-W	23-29	.442	6.5	Rene Lachemann	636,276	426	521	89	.251	.314	.368	76	.271	.334	4.23	101	160
1982	AL	4th-W	76-86	.469	17.0	Rene Lachemann	1,070,404	651	712	130	.254	.311	.381	173	.256	.324	3.88	120	150
1983	AL	7th-W	60-102	.370	39.0	Rene Lachemann/Del Crandall	813,537	558	740	111	.240	.301	.360	145	.268	.337	4.12	100	129
1984	AL	5th-W	74-88	.457	10.0	Del Crandall/Chuck Cottier	870,372	682	774	129	.258	.324	.384	138	.270	.345	4.31	107	128
1985	AL	6th-W	74-88	.457	17.0	Chuck Cottier	1,128,696	719	818	171	.255	.326	.412	154	.265	.343	4.68	90	104
1986	AL	7th-W	67-95	.414	25.0	C. Cottier/M. Martinez/D. Williams	1,029,045	718	835	158	.253	.326	.399	171	.283	.353	4.65	114	144
1987	AL	4th-W	78-84	.481	7.0	Dick Williams	1,134,255	760	801	161	.272	.335	.428	199	.272	.332	4.49	106	154
1988	AL	7th-W	68-93	.422	35.5	Dick Williams/Jimmy Snyder	1,022,398	664	744	148	.257	.317	.398	144	.256	.327	4.15	118	154
1989	AL	6th-W	73-89	.451	26.0	Jim Lefebvre	1,298,443	694	728	134	.257	.320	.384	114	.259	.330	4.00	108	119
1990	AL	5th-W	77-85	.475	26.0	Jim Lefebvre	1,509,727	640	680	107	.259	.333	.373	120	.243	.321	3.69	97	92
1991	AL	5th-W	83-79	.512	12.0	Jim Lefebvre	2,147,905	702	674	126	.255	.328	.383	136	.253	.332	3.79	101	111
1992	AL	7th-W	64-98	.395	32.0	Bill Plummer	1,651,367	679	799	149	.263	.323	.402	129	.266	.348	4.55	104	103
1993	AL	4th-W	82-80	.506	12.0	Lou Piniella	2,052,638	734	731	161	.260	.339	.406	135	.259	.337	4.20	99	90
1994	AL	3rd-W	49-63	.438	2.0	Lou Piniella	1,103,798	569	616	153	.269	.335	.451	109	.274	.357	4.99	110	107
1995	AL	1st-W	79-66	.545	—	Lou Piniella	1,640,992	796	708	182	.276	.350	.448	149	.268	.347	4.50	103	109
1996	AL	2nd-W	85-76	.528	4.5	Lou Piniella	2,722,392	993	895	245	.287	.366	.484	216	.279	.353	5.21	94	104
1997	AL	1st-W	90-72	.556	—	Lou Piniella	3,197,084	925	833	264	.280	.355	.485	192	.267	.342	4.79	102	104

Team Nicknames: Seattle Mariners 1977-1997.

Team Ballparks: Kingdome 1977-1997.

Seattle Mariners Individual Season Batting Leaders

Year	Batting Average		On-Base Percentage		Slugging Percentage		Home Runs		RBI		Stolen Bases	
1977	Lee Stanton	.275	Steve Braun	.351	Lee Stanton	.511	Lee Stanton	27	Dan Meyer	90	Dave Collins	25
1978	Leon Roberts	.301	Leon Roberts	.364	Leon Roberts	.515	Leon Roberts	22	Leon Roberts	92	Julio Cruz	59
1979	Bruce Bochte	.316	Bruce Bochte	.385	Bruce Bochte	.493	Willie Horton	29	Willie Horton	106	Julio Cruz	49
1980	Bruce Bochte	.300	Bruce Bochte	.381	Bruce Bochte	.456	Tom Paciorek	15	Bruce Bochte	78	Julio Cruz	45
1981	Tom Paciorek	.326	Tom Paciorek	.379	Tom Paciorek	.509	Richie Zisk	16	Tom Paciorek	66	Julio Cruz	43
1982	Bruce Bochte	.297	Bruce Bochte	.380	Richie Zisk	.477	Richie Zisk	21	Al Cowens	78	Julio Cruz	46
1983	Pat Putnam	.269	Pat Putnam	.326	Pat Putnam	.448	Pat Putnam	19	Pat Putnam	67	John Moses	11
1984	Jack Perconte	.294	Alvin Davis	.391	Alvin Davis	.497	Alvin Davis	27	Alvin Davis	116	Jack Perconte	29
1985	Phil Bradley	.300	Alvin Davis	.381	Phil Bradley	.498	Gorman Thomas	32	Phil Bradley	88	Jack Perconte	31
1986	Phil Bradley	.310	Phil Bradley	.405	Danny Tartabull	.489	Jim Presley	27	Jim Presley	107	Harold Reynolds	30
1987	Phil Bradley	.297	Phil Bradley	.387	Alvin Davis	.516	Alvin Davis	29	Alvin Davis	100	Harold Reynolds	60
1988	Alvin Davis	.295	Alvin Davis	.412	Alvin Davis	.462	Alvin Davis	18	Alvin Davis	69	Harold Reynolds	35
1989	Alvin Davis	.305	Alvin Davis	.424	Alvin Davis	.496	Jeffrey Leonard	24	Alvin Davis	95	Harold Reynolds	25
1990	Edgar Martinez	.302	Edgar Martinez	.397	Ken Griffey Jr.	.481	Ken Griffey Jr.	22	Ken Griffey Jr.	80	Harold Reynolds	31
1991	Ken Griffey Jr.	.327	Edgar Martinez	.405	Ken Griffey Jr.	.527	Jay Buhner	27	Ken Griffey Jr.	100	Harold Reynolds	28
1992	Edgar Martinez	.343	Edgar Martinez	.404	Edgar Martinez	.544	Ken Griffey Jr.	27	Ken Griffey Jr.	103	Henry Cotto	23
1993	Ken Griffey Jr.	.309	Ken Griffey Jr.	.408	Ken Griffey Jr.	.617	Ken Griffey Jr.	45	Ken Griffey Jr.	109	Rich Amaral	19
1994	Ken Griffey Jr.	.323	Ken Griffey Jr.	.402	Ken Griffey Jr.	.674	Ken Griffey Jr.	40	Ken Griffey Jr.	90	Ken Griffey Jr.	11
1995	Edgar Martinez	.356	Edgar Martinez	.479	Edgar Martinez	.628	Jay Buhner	40	Jay Buhner	121	Rich Amaral	21
1996	Alex Rodriguez	.358	Edgar Martinez	.464	Alex Rodriguez	.631	Ken Griffey Jr.	49	Ken Griffey Jr.	140	Rich Amaral	25
1997	Edgar Martinez	.330	Edgar Martinez	.456	Ken Griffey Jr.	.646	Ken Griffey Jr.	56	Ken Griffey Jr.	147	Alex Rodriguez	29

Seattle Mariners Individual Season Pitching Leaders

Year	ERA		Baserunners/9 IP		Innings Pitched		Strikeouts		Wins		Saves	
1977	John Montague	4.29	Glenn Abbott	12.3	Glenn Abbott	204.1	Enrique Romo	105	Glenn Abbott	12	Enrique Romo	16
1978	Paul Mitchell	4.23	Paul Mitchell	13.6	Paul Mitchell	168.0	Byron McLaughlin	87	Enrique Romo	11	Enrique Romo	10
1979	Mike Parrott	3.77	Mike Parrott	12.7	Mike Parrott	229.1	Mike Parrott	127	Mike Parrott	14	Byron McLaughlin	14
1980	Floyd Bannister	3.47	Floyd Bannister	11.1	Floyd Bannister	217.2	Floyd Bannister	155	Glenn Abbott	12	Shane Rawley	13
1981	Glenn Abbott	3.94	Glenn Abbott	10.7	Glenn Abbott	130.1	Floyd Bannister	85	Floyd Bannister	9	Shane Rawley	8
1982	Jim Beattie	3.34	Floyd Bannister	11.1	Floyd Bannister	247.0	Floyd Bannister	209	Floyd Bannister / Bill Caudill	12	Bill Caudill	26
1983	Matt Young	3.27	Matt Young	11.7	Matt Young	203.2	Jim Beattie	132	Matt Young	11	Bill Caudill	26
1984	Mark Langston	3.40	Jim Beattie	12.2	Mark Langston	225.0	Mark Langston	204	Mark Langston	17	Mike Stanton	8
1985	Mike Moore	3.46	Mike Moore	11.1	Mike Moore	247.0	Mike Moore	155	Mike Moore	17	Edwin Nunez	16
1986	Mike Moore	4.30	Mike Moore	13.0	Mike Moore	266.0	Mark Langston	245	Mark Langston	12	Matt Young	13
1987	Mark Langston	3.84	Mark Langston	11.9	Mark Langston	272.0	Mark Langston	262	Mark Langston	19	Edwin Nunez	12
1988	Mark Langston	3.34	Mike Moore	10.3	Mark Langston	261.1	Mark Langston	235	Mark Langston	15	Mike Schooler	15
1989	Scott Bankhead	3.34	Scott Bankhead	10.8	Scott Bankhead	210.1	Scott Bankhead	140	Scott Bankhead	14	Mike Schooler	33
1990	Erik Hanson	3.24	Erik Hanson	10.5	Erik Hanson	236.0	Erik Hanson	211	Erik Hanson	18	Mike Schooler	30
1991	Bill Krueger	3.60	Erik Hanson	12.4	Randy Johnson	201.1	Randy Johnson	228	Brian Holman / Randy Johnson	13	Bill Swift	17
1992	Dave Fleming	3.39	Dave Fleming	11.4	Dave Fleming	228.1	Randy Johnson	241	Dave Fleming	17	Mike Schooler	13
1993	Randy Johnson	3.24	Randy Johnson	10.6	Randy Johnson	255.1	Randy Johnson	308	Randy Johnson	19	Norm Charlton	18
1994	Randy Johnson	3.19	Randy Johnson	11.0	Randy Johnson	172.0	Randy Johnson	204	Randy Johnson	13	Bobby Ayala	18
1995	Randy Johnson	2.48	Randy Johnson	9.7	Randy Johnson	214.1	Randy Johnson	294	Randy Johnson	18	Bobby Ayala	19
1996	Sterling Hitchcock	5.35	Sterling Hitchcock	14.9	Sterling Hitchcock	196.2	Sterling Hitchcock	132	Sterling Hitchcock	13	Norm Charlton	20
1997	Randy Johnson	2.28	Randy Johnson	9.9	Jeff Fassero	234.1	Randy Johnson	291	Randy Johnson	20	Norm Charlton	14

Mariners Franchise Batting Leaders—Career

Games

1	Ken Griffey Jr.	1,214
2	Alvin Davis	1,166
3	Harold Reynolds	1,155
4	Jay Buhner	1,150
5	Edgar Martinez	1,091
6	Dave Valle	846
7	Jim Presley	799
8	Julio Cruz	742
9	Bruce Bochte	681
10	Omar Vizquel	660
11	Dan Meyer	655
12	Dave Henderson	654
13	Phil Bradley	607
14	Henry Cotto	588
15	Scott Bradley	562
16	Al Cowens	545
17	Tino Martinez	543
18	Rich Amaral	533
19	Ken Phelps	529
20	Dan Wilson	494

At-Bats

1	Ken Griffey Jr.	4,593
2	Alvin Davis	4,136
3	Harold Reynolds	4,090
4	Jay Buhner	4,003
5	Edgar Martinez	3,818
6	Jim Presley	2,946
7	Julio Cruz	2,667
8	Dave Valle	2,502
9	Bruce Bochte	2,404
10	Dan Meyer	2,334
11	Phil Bradley	2,159
12	Dave Henderson	2,123
13	Omar Vizquel	2,111
14	Al Cowens	1,974
15	Tino Martinez	1,896
16	Ruppert Jones	1,691
17	Dan Wilson	1,680
18	Henry Cotto	1,612
19	Spike Owen	1,590
20	Scott Bradley	1,552

Runs

1	Ken Griffey Jr.	820
2	Edgar Martinez	708
3	Jay Buhner	666
4	Alvin Davis	563
5	Harold Reynolds	543
6	Julio Cruz	402
7	Jim Presley	351
8	Phil Bradley	346
9	Bruce Bochte	298
10	Dave Valle	279
11	Dave Henderson	277
12	Dan Meyer	267
13	Alex Rodriguez	260
14	Joey Cora	259
15	Ken Phelps	254
16	Tino Martinez	250
17	Rich Amaral	249
18	Ruppert Jones	242
19	Al Cowens	235
20	Omar Vizquel	223

Hits

1	Ken Griffey Jr.	1,389
2	Edgar Martinez	1,210
3	Alvin Davis	1,163
4	Harold Reynolds	1,063
5	Jay Buhner	1,035
6	Jim Presley	736
7	Bruce Bochte	697
8	Julio Cruz	649
	Phil Bradley	649
10	Dan Meyer	618
11	Dave Valle	588
12	Dave Henderson	545
13	Omar Vizquel	531
14	Al Cowens	504
15	Tino Martinez	502
16	Joey Cora	453
17	Dan Wilson	449
18	Alex Rodriguez	435
19	Ruppert Jones	434
20	Henry Cotto	420

Doubles

1	Edgar Martinez	291
2	Ken Griffey Jr.	261
3	Alvin Davis	212
4	Harold Reynolds	200
5	Jay Buhner	191
6	Jim Presley	147
7	Bruce Bochte	134
8	Al Cowens	128
9	Dave Henderson	114
10	Phil Bradley	112
11	Tino Martinez	106
12	Dave Valle	104
13	Alex Rodriguez	100
14	Dan Meyer	98
15	Joey Cora	96
16	Dan Wilson	91
17	Tom Paciorek	90
18	Julio Cruz	86
19	Ruppert Jones	79
20	Scott Bradley	72

Triples

1	Harold Reynolds	48
2	Phil Bradley	26
3	Ken Griffey Jr.	24
4	Spike Owen	23
5	Ruppert Jones	20
6	Dan Meyer	19
7	Jay Buhner	18
8	Al Cowens	17
9	Julio Cruz	16
	Leon Roberts	16
11	Omar Vizquel	15
12	Larry Milbourne	13
	Bruce Bochte	13
	Jim Presley	13
15	Bill Stein	12
	Dave Henderson	12
	Edgar Martinez	12
	Joey Cora	12
19	Jack Perconte	11
20	Twelve tied at	10

Home Runs

1	Ken Griffey Jr.	294
2	Jay Buhner	250
3	Alvin Davis	160
4	Edgar Martinez	145
5	Jim Presley	115
6	Ken Phelps	105
7	Tino Martinez	88
8	Dave Henderson	79
9	Dave Valle	72
10	Dan Meyer	64
	Alex Rodriguez	64
12	Bruce Bochte	58
13	Al Cowens	56
14	Paul Sorrento	54
15	Mike Blowers	53
16	Phil Bradley	52
17	Ruppert Jones	51
18	Richie Zisk	49
19	Leon Roberts	47
20	Dan Wilson	45

RBI

1	Ken Griffey Jr.	872
2	Jay Buhner	781
3	Alvin Davis	667
4	Edgar Martinez	592
5	Jim Presley	418
6	Bruce Bochte	329
7	Dave Valle	318
8	Dan Meyer	313
9	Tino Martinez	312
10	Harold Reynolds	295
11	Dave Henderson	271
12	Al Cowens	266
13	Ken Phelps	255
14	Dan Wilson	235
15	Phil Bradley	234
16	Alex Rodriguez	228
17	Mike Blowers	224
18	Ruppert Jones	200
19	Tom Paciorek	197
20	Pete O'Brien	194

Walks

1	Edgar Martinez	674
2	Alvin Davis	672
3	Jay Buhner	614
4	Ken Griffey Jr.	580
5	Harold Reynolds	391
6	Julio Cruz	330
7	Ken Phelps	317
8	Bruce Bochte	313
9	Phil Bradley	258
10	Dave Valle	225
11	Tino Martinez	198
12	Ruppert Jones	195
13	Dave Henderson	184
14	Jim Presley	177
15	Omar Vizquel	173
16	Pete O'Brien	154
17	Mike Blowers	149
18	Rich Amaral	141
19	Leon Roberts	140
20	Gorman Thomas	139

Strikeouts

1	Jay Buhner	1,097
2	Ken Griffey Jr.	755
3	Jim Presley	713
4	Edgar Martinez	551
5	Alvin Davis	549
6	Phil Bradley	448
7	Dave Henderson	439
8	Dave Valle	356
9	Harold Reynolds	352
10	Mike Blowers	339
11	Julio Cruz	338
12	Ken Phelps	337
13	Bruce Bochte	316
14	Tino Martinez	309
15	Ruppert Jones	283
16	Dan Wilson	280
17	Al Cowens	276
18	Alex Rodriguez	265
19	Henry Cotto	247
20	Rich Amaral	225

Stolen Bases

1	Julio Cruz	290
2	Harold Reynolds	228
3	Ken Griffey Jr.	123
4	Phil Bradley	107
5	Henry Cotto	102
6	Rich Amaral	86
7	John Moses	70
8	Ruppert Jones	68
9	Jack Perconte	60
10	Greg Briley	59
11	Alex Rodriguez	51
12	Joe Simpson	43
13	Dan Meyer	41
14	Omar Vizquel	39
15	Spike Owen	38
16	Mickey Brantley	34
17	Edgar Martinez	32
18	Al Cowens	31
19	Joey Cora	29
20	Bobby Brown	28

Runs Created

1	Ken Griffey Jr.	928
2	Edgar Martinez	782
3	Alvin Davis	722
4	Jay Buhner	715
5	Harold Reynolds	490
6	Bruce Bochte	371
	Phil Bradley	371
8	Jim Presley	340
9	Julio Cruz	321
10	Ken Phelps	292
11	Dave Henderson	285
12	Tino Martinez	273
13	Dan Meyer	271
14	Dave Valle	266
15	Alex Rodriguez	263
16	Ruppert Jones	232
17	Al Cowens	230
18	Joey Cora	228
19	Dan Wilson	223
20	Four tied at	205

Runs Created/27 Outs

(minimum 2000 Plate Appearances)

1	Edgar Martinez	7.57
2	Ken Griffey Jr.	7.36
3	Alvin Davis	6.19
4	Phil Bradley	6.14
5	Jay Buhner	6.12
6	Bruce Bochte	5.42
7	Tino Martinez	4.94
8	Dave Henderson	4.65
9	Harold Reynolds	4.00
10	Julio Cruz	3.98
11	Dan Meyer	3.97
12	Al Cowens	3.95
13	Jim Presley	3.89
14	Dave Valle	3.47
15	Omar Vizquel	2.93

Batting Average

(minimum 2000 Plate Appearances)

1	Edgar Martinez	.317
2	Ken Griffey Jr.	.302
3	Phil Bradley	.301
4	Bruce Bochte	.290
5	Alvin Davis	.281
6	Dan Meyer	.265
7	Tino Martinez	.265
8	Harold Reynolds	.260
9	Jay Buhner	.259
10	Dave Henderson	.257
11	Al Cowens	.255
12	Omar Vizquel	.252
13	Jim Presley	.250
14	Julio Cruz	.243
15	Dave Valle	.235

On-Base Percentage

(minimum 2000 Plate Appearances)

1	Edgar Martinez	.423
2	Phil Bradley	.382
3	Alvin Davis	.381
4	Ken Griffey Jr.	.381
5	Bruce Bochte	.370
6	Jay Buhner	.360
7	Tino Martinez	.334
8	Julio Cruz	.327
9	Harold Reynolds	.326
10	Dave Henderson	.317
11	Dave Valle	.311
12	Omar Vizquel	.309
13	Dan Meyer	.305
14	Al Cowens	.301
15	Jim Presley	.293

Slugging Percentage

(minimum 2000 Plate Appearances)

1	Ken Griffey Jr.	.562
2	Edgar Martinez	.513
3	Jay Buhner	.503
4	Tino Martinez	.466
5	Alvin Davis	.453
6	Phil Bradley	.449
7	Dave Henderson	.433
8	Bruce Bochte	.429
9	Jim Presley	.426
10	Al Cowens	.422
11	Dan Meyer	.405
12	Dave Valle	.371
13	Harold Reynolds	.345
14	Julio Cruz	.307
15	Omar Vizquel	.303

Teams: Mariners

Mariners Franchise Pitching Leaders—Career

Wins

1	Randy Johnson	121
2	Mark Langston	74
3	Mike Moore	66
4	Erik Hanson	56
5	Matt Young	45
6	Glenn Abbott	44
7	Jim Beattie	43
8	Floyd Bannister	40
9	Dave Fleming	38
10	Scott Bankhead	33
11	Brian Holman	32
12	Bill Swift	30
13	Chris Bosio	27
14	Rick Honeycutt	26
	Bobby Ayala	26
16	Mike Morgan	24
17	Mike Jackson	23
	Jamie Moyer	23
19	Ed Vande Berg	21
20	Shane Rawley	20

Losses

1	Mike Moore	96
2	Jim Beattie	72
3	Mark Langston	67
4	Matt Young	66
5	Randy Johnson	64
6	Glenn Abbott	62
7	Erik Hanson	54
8	Floyd Bannister	50
9	Rick Honeycutt	41
10	Bill Swift	40
11	Mike Parrott	39
12	Mike Morgan	35
	Brian Holman	35
14	Shane Rawley	31
	Scott Bankhead	31
	Dave Fleming	31
	Chris Bosio	31
18	Mike Schooler	29
19	Rich DeLucia	27
20	Mike Jackson	26

Winning Percentage
(minimum 50 decisions)

1	Randy Johnson	.654
2	Dave Fleming	.551
3	Mark Langston	.525
4	Scott Bankhead	.516
5	Erik Hanson	.509
6	Brian Holman	.478
7	Chris Bosio	.466
8	Floyd Bannister	.444
9	Bill Swift	.429
10	Glenn Abbott	.415
11	Mike Moore	.407
12	Mike Morgan	.407
13	Matt Young	.405
14	Shane Rawley	.392
15	Rick Honeycutt	.388
16	Jim Beattie	.374
17	Mike Parrott	.328

Games

1	Mike Jackson	335
2	Ed Vande Berg	272
3	Bill Swift	253
4	Randy Johnson	251
5	Mike Schooler	243
6	Bobby Ayala	230
7	Mike Moore	227
	Jeff Nelson	227
9	Shane Rawley	205
	Edwin Nunez	205
	Norm Charlton	205
12	Matt Young	191
13	Mike Stanton	184
14	Mark Langston	176
15	Jim Beattie	163
16	Glenn Abbott	155
	Dennis Powell	155
18	Jerry Reed	152
	Russ Swan	152
20	Erik Hanson	145

Games Started

1	Randy Johnson	243
2	Mike Moore	217
3	Mark Langston	173
4	Jim Beattie	147
5	Glenn Abbott	146
6	Erik Hanson	143
7	Matt Young	127
8	Floyd Bannister	117
9	Scott Bankhead	92
	Dave Fleming	92
11	Bill Swift	86
12	Rick Honeycutt	85
13	Chris Bosio	83
14	Brian Holman	80
15	Mike Parrott	68
16	Mike Morgan	66
17	Bob Wolcott	52
18	Gaylord Perry	48
	Rich DeLucia	48
20	Paul Mitchell	44

Complete Games

1	Mike Moore	56
2	Randy Johnson	45
3	Mark Langston	41
4	Jim Beattie	30
5	Glenn Abbott	28
6	Floyd Bannister	24
7	Rick Honeycutt	21
	Erik Hanson	21
9	Matt Young	19
10	Mike Morgan	17
11	Mike Parrott	14
	Brian Holman	14
13	Dave Fleming	9
14	Gaylord Perry	8
15	Bill Swift	7
	Scott Bankhead	7
	Chris Bosio	7
18	Ten tied at	5

Shutouts

1	Randy Johnson	17
2	Mike Moore	9
	Mark Langston	9
4	Floyd Bannister	7
5	Jim Beattie	6
6	Matt Young	5
	Brian Holman	5
	Dave Fleming	5
9	Glenn Abbott	3
	Rick Honeycutt	3
	Mike Morgan	3
	Scott Bankhead	3
	Erik Hanson	3
14	Paul Mitchell	2
	Mike Parrott	2
	Bob Stoddard	2
17	Twenty tied at	1

Saves

1	Mike Schooler	98
2	Norm Charlton	66
3	Bill Caudill	52
4	Bobby Ayala	48
5	Shane Rawley	36
6	Edwin Nunez	35
7	Mike Jackson	34
8	Enrique Romo	26
9	Bill Swift	24
10	Mike Stanton	23
11	Ed Vande Berg	20
12	Byron McLaughlin	16
13	Matt Young	14
14	Ted Power	13
15	Bill Wilkinson	12
16	Russ Swan	11
17	Heathcliff Slocumb	10
18	Jeff Nelson	9
19	Jerry Reed	8
20	John Montague	7

Innings Pitched

1	Randy Johnson	1,678.1
2	Mike Moore	1,457.0
3	Mark Langston	1,197.2
4	Erik Hanson	967.1
5	Jim Beattie	944.2
6	Glenn Abbott	904.0
7	Matt Young	864.1
8	Floyd Bannister	768.1
9	Bill Swift	759.0
10	Dave Fleming	578.1
11	Scott Bankhead	568.1
12	Rick Honeycutt	560.2
13	Brian Holman	544.2
14	Chris Bosio	520.0
15	Mike Parrott	490.2
16	Mike Jackson	436.2
17	Mike Morgan	429.1
18	Bryan Clark	381.1
19	Shane Rawley	377.2
20	Bob Stoddard	356.2

Walks

1	Randy Johnson	824
2	Mark Langston	575
3	Mike Moore	535
4	Jim Beattie	369
5	Matt Young	365
6	Erik Hanson	285
7	Bill Swift	253
8	Floyd Bannister	250
9	Glenn Abbott	230
10	Dave Fleming	229
11	Brian Holman	205
12	Mike Jackson	199
13	Bryan Clark	195
14	Shane Rawley	192
	Chris Bosio	192
16	Mike Parrott	188
17	Rick Honeycutt	187
18	Scott Bankhead	166
19	Byron McLaughlin	149
20	John Montague	146

Strikeouts

1	Randy Johnson	1,949
2	Mark Langston	1,078
3	Mike Moore	937
4	Erik Hanson	740
5	Matt Young	597
6	Floyd Bannister	564
7	Jim Beattie	563
8	Mike Jackson	383
9	Scott Bankhead	375
10	Glenn Abbott	343
11	Brian Holman	311
12	Chris Bosio	310
13	Bobby Ayala	306
14	Bill Swift	292
15	Dave Fleming	289
16	Mike Parrott	264
17	Edwin Nunez	247
	Jeff Nelson	247
19	Norm Charlton	234
20	Four tied at	232

Strikeouts/9 Innings
(minimum 500 Innings Pitched)

1	Randy Johnson	10.45
2	Mark Langston	8.10
3	Erik Hanson	6.88
4	Floyd Bannister	6.61
5	Matt Young	6.22
6	Scott Bankhead	5.94
7	Mike Moore	5.79
8	Chris Bosio	5.37
9	Jim Beattie	5.36
10	Brian Holman	5.14
11	Dave Fleming	4.50
12	Rick Honeycutt	3.68
13	Bill Swift	3.46
14	Glenn Abbott	3.41

ERA
(minimum 500 Innings Pitched)

1	Randy Johnson	3.33
2	Erik Hanson	3.69
3	Brian Holman	3.73
4	Floyd Bannister	3.75
5	Mark Langston	4.01
6	Bill Swift	4.04
7	Matt Young	4.13
8	Jim Beattie	4.14
9	Scott Bankhead	4.16
10	Rick Honeycutt	4.22
11	Mike Moore	4.38
12	Chris Bosio	4.43
13	Glenn Abbott	4.54
14	Dave Fleming	4.73

Component ERA
(minimum 500 Innings Pitched)

1	Randy Johnson	3.18
2	Erik Hanson	3.48
3	Floyd Bannister	3.75
4	Scott Bankhead	3.80
5	Mark Langston	3.96
6	Brian Holman	4.03
7	Jim Beattie	4.11
8	Bill Swift	4.11
9	Mike Moore	4.19
10	Matt Young	4.22
11	Rick Honeycutt	4.32
12	Glenn Abbott	4.45
13	Chris Bosio	4.53
14	Dave Fleming	4.83

Opponent Average
(minimum 500 Innings Pitched)

1	Randy Johnson	.210
2	Mark Langston	.240
3	Floyd Bannister	.250
4	Scott Bankhead	.256
5	Erik Hanson	.258
6	Matt Young	.262
7	Brian Holman	.263
8	Jim Beattie	.266
9	Mike Moore	.267
10	Rick Honeycutt	.275
11	Chris Bosio	.277
12	Bill Swift	.281
13	Dave Fleming	.282
14	Glenn Abbott	.283

Opponent OBP
(minimum 500 Innings Pitched)

1	Scott Bankhead	.309
2	Floyd Bannister	.310
3	Randy Johnson	.310
4	Erik Hanson	.313
5	Mark Langston	.328
6	Glenn Abbott	.328
7	Mike Moore	.332
8	Rick Honeycutt	.334
9	Brian Holman	.334
10	Jim Beattie	.336
11	Matt Young	.339
12	Chris Bosio	.341
13	Bill Swift	.343
14	Dave Fleming	.349

Mariners Franchise Batting Leaders—Single Season

Games

1	Willie Horton	1979	162
	Ruppert Jones	1979	162
3	Harold Reynolds	1991	161
4	Ruppert Jones	1977	160
	Harold Reynolds	1987	160
	Harold Reynolds	1990	160
7	Dan Meyer	1977	159
	Phil Bradley	1985	159
9	Phil Bradley	1987	158
	Harold Reynolds	1988	158
	Jay Buhner	1993	158
	Omar Vizquel	1993	158
13	Alvin Davis	1987	157
	Jay Buhner	1997	157
	Ken Griffey Jr.	1997	157
16	Ken Griffey Jr.	1993	156
17	Six tied at		155

At-Bats

1	Willie Horton	1979	646
2	Harold Reynolds	1990	642
3	Phil Bradley	1985	641
4	Harold Reynolds	1991	631
5	Ruppert Jones	1979	622
6	Jim Presley	1986	616
7	Harold Reynolds	1989	613
8	Jack Perconte	1984	612
9	Ken Griffey Jr.	1997	608
10	Phil Bradley	1987	603
11	Alex Rodriguez	1996	601
12	Harold Reynolds	1988	598
13	Ruppert Jones	1977	597
	Ken Griffey Jr.	1990	597
15	Alex Rodriguez	1997	587
16	Dan Meyer	1977	582
	Ken Griffey Jr.	1993	582
18	Alvin Davis	1987	580
19	Alvin Davis	1985	578
20	Mickey Brantley	1988	577

Runs

1	Alex Rodriguez	1996	141
2	Ken Griffey Jr.	1996	125
	Ken Griffey Jr.	1997	125
4	Edgar Martinez	1995	121
	Edgar Martinez	1996	121
6	Ken Griffey Jr.	1993	113
7	Ruppert Jones	1979	109
8	Jay Buhner	1996	107
9	Joey Cora	1997	105
10	Jay Buhner	1997	104
	Edgar Martinez	1997	104
12	Phil Bradley	1987	101
13	Phil Bradley	1985	100
	Harold Reynolds	1990	100
	Edgar Martinez	1992	100
	Alex Rodriguez	1997	100
17	Edgar Martinez	1991	98
18	Harold Reynolds	1991	95
19	Ken Griffey Jr.	1994	94
20	Jack Perconte	1984	93

Hits

1	Alex Rodriguez	1996	215
2	Phil Bradley	1985	192
3	Ken Griffey Jr.	1997	185
4	Harold Reynolds	1989	184
5	Edgar Martinez	1995	182
6	Edgar Martinez	1992	181
7	Willie Horton	1979	180
	Jack Perconte	1984	180
	Ken Griffey Jr.	1993	180
10	Phil Bradley	1987	179
	Ken Griffey Jr.	1990	179
	Ken Griffey Jr.	1991	179
	Edgar Martinez	1997	179
14	Alex Rodriguez	1997	176
15	Bruce Bochte	1979	175
16	Ken Griffey Jr.	1992	174
17	Joey Cora	1997	172
18	Alvin Davis	1987	171
19	Harold Reynolds	1988	169
20	Edgar Martinez	1991	167

Doubles

1	Alex Rodriguez	1996	54
2	Edgar Martinez	1995	52
	Edgar Martinez	1996	52
4	Edgar Martinez	1992	46
5	Ken Griffey Jr.	1991	42
6	Joey Cora	1997	40
	Alex Rodriguez	1997	40
8	Al Cowens	1982	39
	Ken Griffey Jr.	1992	39
10	Bruce Bochte	1979	38
	Phil Bradley	1987	38
	Ken Griffey Jr.	1993	38
13	Alvin Davis	1987	37
	Joey Cora	1996	37
15	Harold Reynolds	1990	36
16	Edgar Martinez	1991	35
	Tino Martinez	1995	35
	Edgar Martinez	1997	35
19	Five tied at		34

Triples

1	Harold Reynolds	1988	11
2	Phil Bradley	1987	10
3	Ruppert Jones	1979	9
	Harold Reynolds	1989	9
5	Ruppert Jones	1977	8
	Al Cowens	1982	8
	Spike Owen	1984	8
	Phil Bradley	1985	8
	Harold Reynolds	1987	8
10	Craig Reynolds	1978	7
	Leon Roberts	1978	7
	Dan Meyer	1979	7
	Jack Perconte	1985	7
	Ken Griffey Jr.	1990	7
15	Ten tied at		6

Home Runs

1	Ken Griffey Jr.	1997	56
2	Ken Griffey Jr.	1996	49
3	Ken Griffey Jr.	1993	45
4	Jay Buhner	1996	44
5	Ken Griffey Jr.	1994	40
	Jay Buhner	1995	40
	Jay Buhner	1997	40
8	Alex Rodriguez	1996	36
9	Gorman Thomas	1985	32
10	Tino Martinez	1995	31
	Paul Sorrento	1997	31
12	Willie Horton	1979	29
	Alvin Davis	1987	29
	Edgar Martinez	1995	29
15	Jim Presley	1985	28
	Edgar Martinez	1997	28
17	Seven tied at		27

RBI

1	Ken Griffey Jr.	1997	147
2	Ken Griffey Jr.	1996	140
3	Jay Buhner	1996	138
4	Alex Rodriguez	1996	123
5	Jay Buhner	1995	121
6	Alvin Davis	1984	116
7	Edgar Martinez	1995	113
8	Tino Martinez	1995	111
9	Ken Griffey Jr.	1993	109
	Jay Buhner	1997	109
11	Edgar Martinez	1997	108
12	Jim Presley	1986	107
13	Willie Horton	1979	106
14	Ken Griffey Jr.	1992	103
	Edgar Martinez	1996	103
16	Bruce Bochte	1979	100
	Alvin Davis	1987	100
	Ken Griffey Jr.	1991	100
19	Jay Buhner	1993	98
20	Two tied at		96

Walks

1	Edgar Martinez	1996	123
2	Jay Buhner	1997	119
	Edgar Martinez	1997	119
4	Edgar Martinez	1995	116
5	Alvin Davis	1989	101
6	Jay Buhner	1993	100
7	Alvin Davis	1984	97
8	Ken Griffey Jr.	1993	96
9	Alvin Davis	1988	95
10	Alvin Davis	1985	90
11	Ken Phelps	1986	88
12	Ruppert Jones	1979	85
	Alvin Davis	1990	85
14	Gorman Thomas	1985	84
	Phil Bradley	1987	84
	Edgar Martinez	1991	84
	Jay Buhner	1996	84
18	Harold Reynolds	1990	81
19	Steve Braun	1977	80
	Ken Phelps	1987	80

Strikeouts

1	Jay Buhner	1997	175
2	Jim Presley	1986	172
3	Jay Buhner	1996	159
4	Danny Tartabull	1986	157
	Jim Presley	1987	157
6	Jay Buhner	1992	146
7	Jay Buhner	1993	144
8	Phil Bradley	1986	134
9	Phil Bradley	1985	129
10	Mike Blowers	1995	128
11	Gorman Thomas	1985	126
12	Jeffrey Leonard	1989	125
13	Ken Griffey Jr.	1997	121
14	Ruppert Jones	1977	120
	Jay Buhner	1995	120
16	Phil Bradley	1987	119
17	Jay Buhner	1991	117
18	Lee Stanton	1977	115
19	Jim Presley	1988	114
20	Two tied at		112

Stolen Bases

1	Harold Reynolds	1987	60
2	Julio Cruz	1978	59
3	Julio Cruz	1979	49
4	Julio Cruz	1982	46
5	Julio Cruz	1980	45
6	Julio Cruz	1981	43
7	Phil Bradley	1987	40
8	Harold Reynolds	1988	35
9	Ruppert Jones	1979	33
	Julio Cruz	1983	33
11	Jack Perconte	1985	31
	Harold Reynolds	1990	31
13	Harold Reynolds	1986	30
14	Jack Perconte	1984	29
	Alex Rodriguez	1997	29
16	Bobby Brown	1982	28
	Harold Reynolds	1991	28
18	Henry Cotto	1988	27
19	Four tied at		25

Runs Created

1	Edgar Martinez	1995	151
2	Ken Griffey Jr.	1997	148
3	Alex Rodriguez	1996	147
4	Ken Griffey Jr.	1996	132
5	Edgar Martinez	1997	127
6	Ken Griffey Jr.	1993	124
	Edgar Martinez	1996	124
8	Jay Buhner	1996	120
9	Alvin Davis	1989	116
10	Phil Bradley	1985	111
	Ken Griffey Jr.	1991	111
12	Alvin Davis	1984	110
13	Phil Bradley	1987	107
14	Ken Griffey Jr.	1992	106
15	Alvin Davis	1987	104
16	Jay Buhner	1993	103
	Tino Martinez	1995	103
18	Edgar Martinez	1992	102
19	Ken Griffey Jr.	1994	100
	Alex Rodriguez	1997	100

Runs Created/27 Outs

(minimum 3.1 Plate Appearances/Tm Gm)

1	Edgar Martinez	1995	11.67
2	Alex Rodriguez	1996	9.47
3	Edgar Martinez	1996	9.33
4	Ken Griffey Jr.	1996	8.98
5	Ken Griffey Jr.	1997	8.82
6	Ken Griffey Jr.	1994	8.76
7	Edgar Martinez	1997	8.67
8	Alvin Davis	1989	8.47
9	Ken Griffey Jr.	1993	7.71
10	Ken Griffey Jr.	1991	7.55
11	Jay Buhner	1996	7.46
12	Edgar Martinez	1992	7.40
13	Jay Buhner	1994	7.19
14	Tino Martinez	1995	7.17
15	Alvin Davis	1984	7.00
16	Edgar Martinez	1994	7.00
17	Ken Griffey Jr.	1992	6.91
18	Phil Bradley	1986	6.88
19	Leon Roberts	1978	6.74
20	Alvin Davis	1988	6.63

Batting Average

(minimum 3.1 Plate Appearances/Tm Gm)

1	Alex Rodriguez	1996	.358
2	Edgar Martinez	1995	.356
3	Edgar Martinez	1992	.343
4	Edgar Martinez	1997	.330
5	Edgar Martinez	1996	.327
6	Ken Griffey Jr.	1991	.327
7	Tom Paciorek	1981	.326
8	Ken Griffey Jr.	1994	.323
9	Felix Fermin	1994	.317
10	Bruce Bochte	1979	.316
11	Richie Zisk	1981	.311
12	Phil Bradley	1986	.310
13	Ken Griffey Jr.	1993	.309
14	Ken Griffey Jr.	1992	.308
15	Edgar Martinez	1991	.307
16	Alvin Davis	1989	.305
17	Ken Griffey Jr.	1997	.304
18	Ken Griffey Jr.	1996	.303
19	Edgar Martinez	1990	.302
20	Leon Roberts	1978	.301

On-Base Percentage

(minimum 3.1 Plate Appearances/Tm Gm)

1	Edgar Martinez	1995	.479
2	Edgar Martinez	1996	.464
3	Edgar Martinez	1997	.456
4	Alvin Davis	1989	.424
5	Alex Rodriguez	1996	.414
6	Alvin Davis	1988	.412
7	Ken Griffey Jr.	1993	.408
8	Edgar Martinez	1991	.405
9	Phil Bradley	1986	.405
10	Edgar Martinez	1992	.404
11	Ken Griffey Jr.	1994	.402
12	Ken Griffey Jr.	1991	.399
13	Edgar Martinez	1990	.397
14	Jay Buhner	1994	.394
15	Ken Griffey Jr.	1996	.392
16	Alvin Davis	1984	.391
17	Phil Bradley	1987	.387
18	Edgar Martinez	1994	.387
19	Alvin Davis	1990	.387
20	Bruce Bochte	1979	.385

Slugging Percentage

(minimum 3.1 Plate Appearances/Tm Gm)

1	Ken Griffey Jr.	1994	.674
2	Ken Griffey Jr.	1997	.646
3	Alex Rodriguez	1996	.631
4	Edgar Martinez	1995	.628
5	Ken Griffey Jr.	1996	.628
6	Ken Griffey Jr.	1993	.617
7	Edgar Martinez	1996	.595
8	Jay Buhner	1995	.566
9	Jay Buhner	1996	.557
10	Edgar Martinez	1997	.554
11	Tino Martinez	1995	.551
12	Edgar Martinez	1992	.544
13	Jay Buhner	1994	.542
14	Ken Griffey Jr.	1992	.535
15	Ken Griffey Jr.	1991	.527
16	Alvin Davis	1987	.516
17	Leon Roberts	1978	.515
18	Paul Sorrento	1997	.514
19	Lee Stanton	1977	.511
20	Tom Paciorek	1981	.509

Teams: Mariners

Mariners Franchise Pitching Leaders—Single Season

Wins

1	Randy Johnson	1997	20
2	Mark Langston	1987	19
	Randy Johnson	1993	19
4	Erik Hanson	1990	18
	Randy Johnson	1995	18
6	Mark Langston	1984	17
	Mike Moore	1985	17
	Dave Fleming	1992	17
	Jamie Moyer	1997	17
10	Jeff Fassero	1997	16
11	Mark Langston	1988	15
12	Mike Parrott	1979	14
	Scott Bankhead	1989	14
	Randy Johnson	1990	14
15	Brian Holman	1991	13
	Randy Johnson	1991	13
	Randy Johnson	1994	13
	Sterling Hitchcock	1996	13
19	Twelve tied at		12

Losses

1	Matt Young	1985	19
	Mike Moore	1987	19
3	Matt Young	1990	18
4	Rick Honeycutt	1980	17
	Bob Stoddard	1983	17
	Mike Moore	1984	17
	Mike Morgan	1986	17
	Mike Morgan	1987	17
	Erik Hanson	1992	17
10	Mike Parrott	1980	16
	Jim Beattie	1984	16
12	Glenn Abbott	1978	15
	Floyd Bannister	1979	15
	Jim Beattie	1980	15
	Jim Beattie	1983	15
	Matt Young	1983	15
	Mike Moore	1988	15
18	Six tied at		14

Winning Percentage
(minimum 15 decisions)

1	Randy Johnson	1995	.900
2	Randy Johnson	1997	.833
3	Jamie Moyer	1997	.773
4	Lee Guetterman	1987	.733
5	Dave Fleming	1993	.706
6	Randy Johnson	1993	.704
7	Scott Bankhead	1989	.700
8	Randy Johnson	1994	.684
9	Erik Hanson	1990	.667
	Bobby Ayala	1997	.667
11	Jeff Fassero	1997	.640
12	Bob Wells	1996	.632
13	Mark Langston	1984	.630
	Mike Moore	1985	.630
	Dave Fleming	1992	.630
16	Enrique Romo	1978	.611
17	Bill Risley	1994	.600
18	Mark Langston	1987	.594
19	Sterling Hitchcock	1996	.591
20	Bill Krueger	1991	.579

Games

1	Ed Vande Berg	1982	78
2	Ed Vande Berg	1985	76
3	Mike Jackson	1996	73
4	Mike Jackson	1991	72
5	Bill Swift	1991	71
	Jeff Nelson	1993	71
	Norm Charlton	1997	71
	Bobby Ayala	1997	71
9	Bill Caudill	1982	70
	Edwin Nunez	1985	70
	Norm Charlton	1996	70
12	Ed Vande Berg	1983	68
13	Mike Schooler	1989	67
14	Jeff Nelson	1992	66
15	Matt Young	1986	65
	Mike Jackson	1989	65
17	Bill Caudill	1983	63
	Mike Jackson	1990	63
	Russ Swan	1991	63
	Bobby Ayala	1995	63

Games Started

1	Mike Moore	1986	37
2	Mark Langston	1986	36
3	Floyd Bannister	1982	35
	Matt Young	1985	35
	Mark Langston	1987	35
	Mark Langston	1988	35
	Sterling Hitchcock	1996	35
	Jeff Fassero	1997	35
9	Glenn Abbott	1977	34
	Mike Moore	1985	34
	Randy Johnson	1993	34
12	Ten tied at		33

Complete Games

1	Mike Moore	1985	14
	Mark Langston	1987	14
3	Mike Parrott	1979	13
4	Jim Beattie	1984	12
	Mike Moore	1987	12
6	Mike Moore	1986	11
7	Randy Johnson	1993	10
8	Rick Honeycutt	1980	9
	Mike Morgan	1986	9
	Mark Langston	1986	9
	Mike Moore	1988	9
	Mark Langston	1988	9
	Randy Johnson	1994	9
14	Glenn Abbott	1978	8
	Rick Honeycutt	1979	8
	Floyd Bannister	1980	8
	Jim Beattie	1983	8
	Mike Morgan	1987	8
19	Five tied at		7

Shutouts

1	Dave Fleming	1992	4
	Randy Johnson	1994	4
3	Floyd Bannister	1982	3
	Mark Langston	1987	3
	Mike Moore	1988	3
	Mark Langston	1988	3
	Brian Holman	1991	3
	Randy Johnson	1993	3
	Randy Johnson	1995	3
10	Eighteen tied at		2

Saves

1	Mike Schooler	1989	33
2	Mike Schooler	1990	30
3	Bill Caudill	1982	26
	Bill Caudill	1983	26
5	Norm Charlton	1996	20
6	Bobby Ayala	1995	19
7	Norm Charlton	1993	18
	Bobby Ayala	1994	18
9	Bill Swift	1991	17
10	Enrique Romo	1977	16
	Edwin Nunez	1985	16
12	Mike Schooler	1988	15
13	Byron McLaughlin	1979	14
	Mike Jackson	1991	14
	Norm Charlton	1995	14
	Norm Charlton	1997	14
17	Shane Rawley	1980	13
	Matt Young	1986	13
	Mike Schooler	1992	13
	Ted Power	1993	13

Innings Pitched

1	Mark Langston	1987	272.0
2	Mike Moore	1986	266.0
3	Mark Langston	1988	261.1
4	Randy Johnson	1993	255.1
5	Floyd Bannister	1982	247.0
	Mike Moore	1985	247.0
7	Mark Langston	1986	239.1
8	Erik Hanson	1990	236.0
9	Jeff Fassero	1997	234.1
10	Mike Moore	1987	231.0
11	Mike Parrott	1979	229.1
12	Mike Moore	1988	228.2
13	Dave Fleming	1992	228.1
14	Matt Young	1990	225.1
15	Mark Langston	1984	225.0
16	Randy Johnson	1990	219.2
17	Matt Young	1985	218.1
18	Floyd Bannister	1980	217.2
19	Gaylord Perry	1982	216.2
20	Mike Morgan	1986	216.1

Walks

1	Randy Johnson	1991	152
2	Randy Johnson	1992	144
3	Mark Langston	1986	123
4	Randy Johnson	1990	120
5	Mark Langston	1984	118
6	Mark Langston	1987	114
7	Mark Langston	1988	110
8	Matt Young	1990	107
9	Randy Johnson	1993	99
10	Jim Beattie	1980	98
11	Mike Moore	1986	94
12	Mark Langston	1985	91
13	Tim Belcher	1995	88
14	Mike Parrott	1979	86
	Mike Morgan	1986	86
16	Mike Moore	1984	85
17	Mike Moore	1987	84
	Jeff Fassero	1997	84
19	Three tied at		79

Strikeouts

1	Randy Johnson	1993	308
2	Randy Johnson	1995	294
3	Randy Johnson	1997	291
4	Mark Langston	1987	262
5	Mark Langston	1986	245
6	Randy Johnson	1992	241
7	Mark Langston	1988	235
8	Randy Johnson	1991	228
9	Erik Hanson	1990	211
10	Floyd Bannister	1982	209
11	Mark Langston	1984	204
	Randy Johnson	1994	204
13	Randy Johnson	1990	194
14	Jeff Fassero	1997	189
15	Mike Moore	1988	182
16	Matt Young	1990	176
17	Erik Hanson	1993	163
18	Mike Moore	1984	158
19	Floyd Bannister	1980	155
	Mike Moore	1985	155

Strikeouts/9 Innings
(minimum 1 Inning Pitched/Tm Gm)

1	Randy Johnson	1995	12.35
2	Randy Johnson	1997	12.30
3	Randy Johnson	1993	10.86
4	Randy Johnson	1994	10.67
5	Randy Johnson	1992	10.31
6	Randy Johnson	1991	10.19
7	Mark Langston	1986	9.21
8	Mark Langston	1987	8.67
9	Mark Langston	1984	8.16
10	Mark Langston	1988	8.09
11	Erik Hanson	1990	8.05
12	Randy Johnson	1990	7.95
13	Floyd Bannister	1982	7.62
14	Erik Hanson	1991	7.37
15	Jim Beattie	1982	7.31
16	Jeff Fassero	1997	7.26
17	Mike Moore	1988	7.16
18	Matt Young	1990	7.03
19	Erik Hanson	1993	6.82
20	Mike Moore	1984	6.71

ERA
(minimum 1 Inning Pitched/Tm Gm)

1	Randy Johnson	1997	2.28
2	Randy Johnson	1995	2.48
3	Randy Johnson	1994	3.19
4	Erik Hanson	1990	3.24
5	Randy Johnson	1993	3.24
6	Matt Young	1983	3.27
7	Scott Bankhead	1989	3.34
8	Mark Langston	1988	3.34
9	Jim Beattie	1982	3.34
10	Dave Fleming	1992	3.39
11	Mark Langston	1984	3.40
12	Jim Beattie	1984	3.41
13	Floyd Bannister	1982	3.43
14	Chris Bosio	1993	3.45
15	Mike Moore	1985	3.46
16	Floyd Bannister	1980	3.47
17	Erik Hanson	1993	3.47
18	Matt Young	1990	3.51
19	Bill Krueger	1991	3.60
20	Jeff Fassero	1997	3.61

Component ERA
(minimum 1 Inning Pitched/Tm Gm)

1	Randy Johnson	1995	2.18
2	Randy Johnson	1997	2.47
3	Erik Hanson	1990	2.72
4	Randy Johnson	1993	2.73
5	Mike Moore	1988	2.94
6	Randy Johnson	1994	2.99
7	Chris Bosio	1993	3.10
8	Scott Bankhead	1989	3.10
9	Jim Beattie	1982	3.13
10	Mike Moore	1985	3.16
11	Dave Fleming	1992	3.26
12	Floyd Bannister	1980	3.26
13	Glenn Abbott	1981	3.30
14	Matt Young	1983	3.38
15	Floyd Bannister	1982	3.51
16	Matt Young	1990	3.53
17	Erik Hanson	1993	3.55
18	Jamie Moyer	1997	3.56
19	Mark Langston	1984	3.56
20	Jim Beattie	1983	3.59

Opponent Average
(minimum 1 Inning Pitched/Tm Gm)

1	Randy Johnson	1997	.194
2	Randy Johnson	1995	.201
3	Randy Johnson	1993	.203
4	Randy Johnson	1992	.206
5	Randy Johnson	1991	.213
6	Randy Johnson	1994	.216
7	Randy Johnson	1990	.216
8	Chris Bosio	1993	.229
9	Mark Langston	1984	.230
10	Mike Moore	1988	.232
11	Erik Hanson	1990	.232
12	Mark Langston	1988	.233
13	Jim Beattie	1982	.233
14	Matt Young	1983	.236
15	Matt Young	1990	.237
16	Mark Langston	1987	.238
17	Scott Bankhead	1989	.239
18	Floyd Bannister	1980	.239
19	Floyd Bannister	1982	.243
20	Mike Moore	1985	.247

Opponent OBP
(minimum 1 Inning Pitched/Tm Gm)

1	Randy Johnson	1995	.266
2	Randy Johnson	1997	.277
3	Mike Moore	1988	.286
4	Erik Hanson	1990	.287
5	Randy Johnson	1993	.290
6	Floyd Bannister	1980	.295
7	Scott Bankhead	1989	.295
8	Glenn Abbott	1981	.296
9	Mike Moore	1985	.300
10	Floyd Bannister	1982	.301
11	Chris Bosio	1993	.303
12	Jim Beattie	1982	.303
13	Jamie Moyer	1997	.303
14	Randy Johnson	1994	.304
15	Dave Fleming	1992	.306
16	Matt Young	1983	.312
17	Jeff Fassero	1997	.312
18	Mark Langston	1988	.313
19	Glenn Abbott	1980	.314
20	Erik Hanson	1993	.315

Mariners Capsule

Best Season: *1995.* Not only was it their first trip to the postseason, but they staged one of the most dramatic comeback victories of all time in the American League Division Series.

Worst Season: *1978.* They lost 98 games in '77 and then their hitters went into a slump.

Best Player: *Ken Griffey Jr.* Few players accomplished more before their 28th birthday.

Best Pitcher: *Randy Johnson.* From August 10, 1992 through the end of the 1997 season, he won 80 of 102 decisions (.784) and fanned 1,299 men in 1,001 innings.

Best Reliever: *Mike Schooler.* The best of a weak lot. Bill Caudill, Bobby Ayala and Norm Charlton had their moments, but none of them lasted very long.

Best Defensive Player: *Omar Vizquel.* On April 22, 1993, Chris Bosio was one out away from completing a no-hitter when Ernie Riles chopped a ball over the mound. Bosio *knew* it was a hit, and he bowed his head and swore in frustration. Vizquel scampered over from shortstop and in one motion, grabbed the ball shoulder-high with his bare hand and fired it to first, nailing the runner by a half-step to save Bosio's gem. Such plays were routine for Vizquel.

Hall of Famers: *Gaylord Perry* spent a season and a half with the Mariners at the end of his career. He is the only Cooperstown inductee who has played for Seattle.

Franchise All-Star Team:

C	Dan Wilson	**LF**	Phil Bradley
1B	Alvin Davis	**CF**	Ken Griffey Jr.
2B	Harold Reynolds	**RF**	Jay Buhner
3B	Jim Presley	**DH**	Edgar Martinez
SS	Alex Rodriguez	**SP**	Randy Johnson
		RP	Mike Schooler

Biggest Flakes: *Bill Caudill, Tom Paciorek, Larry Andersen.*

Strangest Career: *Ruppert Jones.* The Mariners selected Jones with their first pick in the expansion draft; the Royals had made him available when they opted to protect Willie Wilson instead. In the Mariners' inaugural season, Jones, a 22-year-old center fielder, emerged as their biggest star, batting .263 with 25 homers while showing fine range afield. His sophomore season was ruined by a midseason attack of appendicitis, but he came back strong in '79, scoring 109 runs while hitting 21 homers and stealing 33 bases. Then the Mariners cashed him in, sending him to the New York Yankees for pitcher Jim Beattie, catcher Jerry Narron and outfielder Juan Beniquez. The trade was a disaster for Seattle: Beattie had four decent seasons, but the other two players were complete washouts. Jones played between injuries—sometimes well, sometimes poorly—for the remainder of his career.

What Might Have Been: *Roger Salkeld* was only 20 years old when he went 10-9, 3.28 with 180 strikeouts in the high minors in 1991. He was seen as one of the top prospects in baseball at the time, but he missed the entire 1992 season with shoulder problems and was never the same.

Best Trade: The M's got *Jay Buhner* and two minor leaguers from the Yankees for DH Ken Phelps on July 21, 1988.

Worst Trade: The infamous *Kevin Mitchell* trade. Seattle sent pitchers Billy Swift, Mike Jackson and Dave Burba to the San Francisco Giants on December 11, 1992 for the portly slugger. Swift won the NL ERA title the following year and won 21 games the year after that; Jackson remained one of the game's best setup men through 1997; and Burba developed into a useful swingman. In his only year in Seattle, Mitchell played just 99 games and hit only nine home runs.

Best-Looking Player: *Ken Griffey Jr.,* whether he's smiling, swinging the bat, or gliding to the wall.

Ugliest Player: *Randy Johnson,* except when he's on the mound.

Best Nickname: *Randy Johnson, "The Big Unit."*

Most Unappreciated Player: Either *Phil Bradley* or *Ken Phelps.*

Most Overrated Player: *Matt Young.* Young had great stuff, but seemed haunted by an incurable fear of failure. He had a mental block about throwing to the bases. He constantly threw away comebackers, and rarely attempted a pickoff.

In crucial spots, he invariably came unglued, leading to far more losses than a pitcher of his caliber should have accumulated.

Most Admirable Star: *Randy Johnson.* His performance in the '95 postseason—when he very nearly pitched the M's into the World Series, seemingly on sheer will—was a display of pure heart.

Least Admirable Star: *Rey Quinones.* He constantly missed games with dubious injuries, and *The Ballplayers* frankly describes him as an "unstable person."

Best Season, Player: *Alex Rodriguez, 1996.* Possibly the best offensive season by a shortstop in history.

Best Season, Pitcher: *Randy Johnson, 1995.* He was as unbeatable that year as any pitcher in recent memory has been over a whole season. In 30 regular-season starts, he allowed two runs or less a total of 20 times. He three-hit the Angels in a one-game playoff to give Seattle the AL West title, and brought back the Mariners from an 0-2 deficit in the Division Series by beating the Yankees in Game 3 and coming out of the bullpen to beat them again in Game 5.

Most Impressive Individual Record: From 1995 through 1997, *Randy Johnson* posted the best three-year record in history: 43-6 (minimum 45 games started).

Biggest Tragedy: *Rod Scurry.* Cocaine addiction ruined more than just Scurry's career. The southpaw's final major league season came with the Mariners in 1988. Four years later, sheriff's deputies in Reno, Nev., responded to a call and found Scurry on his front lawn, complaining that snakes were in his house, biting and crawling on him. When they tried to calm him, he grew more agitated, and they decided to take him into custody. As they tried to handcuff him, he flew into a violent rage and suddenly stopped breathing. After a week in intensive care, he died.

Fan Favorite: *Ken Griffey Jr., Alex Rodriguez, Joey Cora.*

—Mat Olkin

Washington Senators/Texas Rangers (1961-1997)

Year	Lg	Pos	W-L	Pct	GB	Manager	Att.	R	OR	HR	Avg	OBP	Slg	Opponent HR	Avg	OBP	ERA	Park Index Runs	HR
1961	AL	9th	61-100	.379	47.5	Mickey Vernon	597,287	618	776	119	.244	.315	.367	131	.260	.333	4.23	92	55
1962	AL	10th	60-101	.373	35.5	Mickey Vernon	729,775	599	716	132	.250	.308	.373	151	.256	.328	4.04	101	105
1963	AL	10th	56-106	.346	48.5	Mickey Vernon/Eddie Yost/Gil Hodges	535,604	578	812	138	.227	.293	.351	176	.266	.331	4.42	102	88
1964	AL	9th	62-100	.383	37.0	Gil Hodges	600,106	578	733	125	.231	.299	.348	172	.259	.322	3.98	106	127
1965	AL	8th	70-92	.432	32.0	Gil Hodges	560,083	591	721	136	.228	.304	.350	160	.254	.334	3.93	104	100
1966	AL	8th	71-88	.447	25.5	Gil Hodges	576,260	557	659	126	.234	.295	.355	154	.242	.302	3.70	90	113
1967	AL	6th	76-85	.472	15.5	Gil Hodges	770,868	550	637	115	.223	.288	.326	113	.242	.307	3.38	107	96
1968	AL	10th	65-96	.404	37.5	Jim Lemon	546,661	524	665	124	.224	.287	.336	118	.258	.325	3.64	87	77
1969	AL	4th-E	86-76	.531	23.0	Ted Williams	918,106	694	644	148	.251	.330	.378	135	.244	.328	3.49	93	97
1970	AL	6th-E	70-92	.432	38.0	Ted Williams	824,789	626	689	138	.238	.321	.358	139	.252	.328	3.80	93	92
1971	AL	5th-E	63-96	.396	38.5	Ted Williams	655,156	537	660	86	.230	.307	.326	132	.258	.331	3.70	86	72
1972	AL	6th-W	54-100	.351	38.5	Ted Williams	662,974	461	628	56	.217	.290	.290	92	.246	.329	3.53	92	100
1973	AL	6th-W	57-105	.352	37.0	Whitey Herzog/Del Wilber/Billy Martin	686,085	619	844	110	.255	.318	.361	130	.273	.353	4.64	99	69
1974	AL	2nd-W	84-76	.525	5.0	Billy Martin	1,193,902	690	698	99	.272	.336	.377	126	.260	.318	3.82	91	80
1975	AL	3rd-W	79-83	.488	19.0	Billy Martin/Frank Lucchesi	1,127,924	714	733	134	.256	.330	.371	123	.261	.327	3.86	100	93
1976	AL	4th-W	76-86	.469	14.0	Frank Lucchesi	1,164,982	616	652	80	.250	.321	.341	106	.262	.320	3.45	105	109
1977	AL	2nd-W	94-68	.580	8.0	Lucchesi/Stanky/Ryan/Hunter	1,250,722	767	657	135	.270	.342	.405	134	.255	.315	3.56	107	109
1978	AL	2nd-W	87-75	.537	5.0	Billy Hunter/Pat Corrales	1,447,963	692	632	132	.253	.332	.381	108	.259	.312	3.70	90	84
1979	AL	3rd-W	83-79	.512	5.0	Pat Corrales	1,519,671	750	698	140	.278	.334	.409	135	.253	.321	3.86	98	92
1980	AL	4th-W	76-85	.472	20.5	Pat Corrales	1,198,175	756	752	124	.284	.339	.405	119	.277	.339	4.02	99	91
1981	AL	2nd-W	33-22	.600	1.5	Don Zimmer													
	AL	3rd-W	24-26	.580	4.5	Don Zimmer	850,076	452	389	49	.270	.326	.369	67	.243	.308	3.40	79	55
1982	AL	6th-W	64-98	.395	29.0	Don Zimmer/Darrell Johnson	1,154,432	590	749	115	.249	.308	.359	128	.280	.339	4.28	86	81
1983	AL	3rd-W	77-85	.475	22.0	Doug Rader	1,363,469	639	609	106	.255	.310	.366	97	.252	.313	3.31	99	62
1984	AL	7th-W	69-92	.429	14.5	Doug Rader	1,102,471	656	714	120	.261	.313	.377	148	.260	.325	3.91	101	89
1985	AL	7th-W	62-99	.385	28.5	Doug Rader/Bobby Valentine	1,112,497	617	785	129	.253	.322	.381	173	.269	.331	4.56	121	145
1986	AL	2nd-W	87-75	.537	5.0	Bobby Valentine	1,692,002	771	743	184	.267	.331	.428	145	.249	.340	4.11	90	82
1987	AL	6th-W	75-87	.463	10.0	Bobby Valentine	1,763,053	823	849	194	.266	.333	.430	199	.253	.347	4.63	109	108
1988	AL	6th-W	70-91	.435	33.5	Bobby Valentine	1,581,901	637	735	112	.252	.320	.368	129	.244	.329	4.05	104	106
1989	AL	4th-W	83-79	.512	16.0	Bobby Valentine	2,043,993	695	714	122	.263	.326	.394	119	.239	.324	3.91	105	134
1990	AL	3rd-W	83-79	.512	20.0	Bobby Valentine	2,057,911	676	696	110	.259	.331	.376	113	.248	.327	3.83	102	120
1991	AL	3rd-W	85-77	.525	10.0	Bobby Valentine	2,297,720	829	814	177	.270	.341	.424	151	.262	.341	4.47	96	91
1992	AL	4th-W	77-85	.475	19.0	Bobby Valentine/Toby Harrah	2,198,231	682	753	159	.250	.321	.393	113	.264	.337	4.10	93	97
1993	AL	2nd-W	86-76	.531	8.0	Kevin Kennedy	2,244,616	835	751	181	.267	.329	.431	144	.267	.337	4.28	91	99
1994	AL	1st-W	52-62	.456	—	Kevin Kennedy	2,502,538	613	697	124	.280	.353	.436	157	.288	.351	5.45	89	70
1995	AL	3rd-W	74-70	.514	4.5	Johnny Oates	1,985,910	691	720	138	.265	.338	.410	152	.278	.346	4.66	113	113
1996	AL	1st-W	90-72	.556	—	Johnny Oates	2,888,920	928	799	221	.284	.358	.469	168	.278	.347	4.65	113	104
1997	AL	3rd-W	77-85	.475	13.0	Johnny Oates	2,945,244	807	823	187	.274	.334	.438	169	.283	.347	4.70	105	109

Team Nicknames: Washington Senators 1961-1972, Texas Rangers 1973-1997.

Team Ballparks: Griffith Stadium 1961, RFK Stadium 1962-1971, Arlington Stadium 1972-1993, The Ballpark at Arlington 1994-1997.

Washington Senators/Texas Rangers Individual Season Batting Leaders

Year	Batting Average		On-Base Percentage		Slugging Percentage		Home Runs		RBI		Stolen Bases	
1961	Danny O'Connell	.260	Danny O'Connell	.361	Willie Tasby	.389	Gene Green	18	Willie Tasby	63	Chuck Hinton	22
1962	Chuck Hinton	.310	Chuck Hinton	.361	Chuck Hinton	.472	Harry Bright	17	Chuck Hinton	75	Chuck Hinton	28
							Chuck Hinton					
1963	Chuck Hinton	.269	Chuck Hinton	.340	Don Lock	.446	Don Lock	27	Don Lock	82	Chuck Hinton	25
1964	Chuck Hinton	.274	Don Lock	.346	Don Lock	.461	Don Lock	28	Don Lock	80	Chuck Hinton	17
1965	Frank Howard	.289	Frank Howard	.358	Frank Howard	.477	Frank Howard	21	Frank Howard	84	Ken Hamlin	8
1966	Frank Howard	.278	Fred Valentine	.351	Fred Valentine	.455	Frank Howard	18	Frank Howard	71	Fred Valentine	22
1967	Frank Howard	.256	Frank Howard	.338	Frank Howard	.511	Frank Howard	36	Frank Howard	89	Fred Valentine	17
1968	Frank Howard	.274	Frank Howard	.338	Frank Howard	.552	Frank Howard	44	Frank Howard	106	Del Unser	11
1969	Frank Howard	.296	Frank Howard	.402	Frank Howard	.574	Frank Howard	48	Frank Howard	111	Hank Allen	12
											Ed Stroud	
1970	Frank Howard	.283	Frank Howard	.416	Frank Howard	.546	Frank Howard	44	Frank Howard	126	Ed Stroud	29
1971	Frank Howard	.279	Frank Howard	.367	Frank Howard	.474	Frank Howard	26	Frank Howard	83	Dave Nelson	17
1972	Dick Billings	.254	Frank Howard	.324	Ted Ford	.382	Ted Ford	14	Dick Billings	58	Dave Nelson	51
1973	Alex Johnson	.287	Jeff Burroughs	.355	Jeff Burroughs	.487	Jeff Burroughs	30	Jeff Burroughs	85	Dave Nelson	43
1974	Lenny Randle	.302	Jeff Burroughs	.397	Jeff Burroughs	.504	Jeff Burroughs	25	Jeff Burroughs	118	Lenny Randle	26
1975	Mike Hargrove	.303	Toby Harrah	.403	Toby Harrah	.458	Jeff Burroughs	29	Jeff Burroughs	94	Toby Harrah	23
1976	Mike Hargrove	.287	Mike Hargrove	.397	Tom Grieve	.418	Tom Grieve	20	Jeff Burroughs	86	Lenny Randle	30
1977	Mike Hargrove	.305	Mike Hargrove	.420	Toby Harrah	.479	Toby Harrah	27	Toby Harrah	87	Bump Wills	28
1978	Al Oliver	.324	Mike Hargrove	.388	Bobby Bonds	.497	Bobby Bonds	29	Al Oliver	89	Bump Wills	52
1979	Al Oliver	.323	Al Oliver	.367	Al Oliver	.470	3 tied with	18	Buddy Bell	101	Bump Wills	35
1980	Mickey Rivers	.333	Buddy Bell	.379	Buddy Bell	.498	Al Oliver	19	Al Oliver	117	Bump Wills	34
							Richie Zisk					
1981	Al Oliver	.309	Jim Sundberg	.369	Buddy Bell	.428	Buddy Bell	10	Buddy Bell	64	Bump Wills	12
1982	Buddy Bell	.296	Buddy Bell	.376	Buddy Bell	.426	Dave Hostetler	22	Buddy Bell	67	Lee Mazzilli	11
									Dave Hostetler			
1983	Buddy Bell	.277	Buddy Bell	.332	Larry Parrish	.474	Larry Parrish	26	Larry Parrish	88	Billy Sample	44
1984	Buddy Bell	.315	Buddy Bell	.382	Larry Parrish	.465	Larry Parrish	22	Larry Parrish	101	Wayne Tolleson	22
1985	Gary Ward	.287	Toby Harrah	.432	Pete O'Brien	.452	Pete O'Brien	22	Pete O'Brien	92	Gary Ward	26
1986	Scott Fletcher	.300	Pete O'Brien	.385	Larry Parrish	.509	Pete Incaviglia	30	Larry Parrish	94	Oddibe McDowell	33
1987	Scott Fletcher	.287	Jerry Browne	.358	Pete Incaviglia	.497	Larry Parrish	32	Ruben Sierra	109	Jerry Browne	27
1988	Scott Fletcher	.276	Scott Fletcher	.364	Ruben Sierra	.424	Ruben Sierra	23	Ruben Sierra	91	Cecil Espy	33
											Oddibe McDowell	
1989	Julio Franco	.316	Julio Franco	.386	Ruben Sierra	.543	Ruben Sierra	29	Ruben Sierra	119	Cecil Espy	45
1990	Rafael Palmeiro	.319	Julio Franco	.383	Rafael Palmeiro	.468	Pete Incaviglia	24	Ruben Sierra	96	Gary Pettis	38
1991	Julio Franco	.341	Julio Franco	.408	Rafael Palmeiro	.532	Juan Gonzalez	27	Ruben Sierra	116	Julio Franco	36
1992	Ruben Sierra	.278	Rafael Palmeiro	.352	Juan Gonzalez	.529	Juan Gonzalez	43	Juan Gonzalez	109	Jeff Huson	18
1993	Juan Gonzalez	.310	Rafael Palmeiro	.371	Juan Gonzalez	.632	Juan Gonzalez	46	Juan Gonzalez	118	David Hulse	29
1994	Will Clark	.329	Will Clark	.431	Jose Canseco	.552	Jose Canseco	31	Jose Canseco	90	David Hulse	18
1995	Ivan Rodriguez	.303	Mickey Tettleton	.396	Mickey Tettleton	.510	Mickey Tettleton	32	Will Clark	92	Otis Nixon	50
1996	Rusty Greer	.332	Rusty Greer	.397	Juan Gonzalez	.643	Juan Gonzalez	47	Juan Gonzalez	144	Mark McLemore	27
1997	Rusty Greer	.321	Rusty Greer	.405	Juan Gonzalez	.589	Juan Gonzalez	42	Juan Gonzalez	131	Damon Buford	18

Washington Senators/Texas Rangers Individual Season Pitching Leaders

Year	ERA		Baserunners/9 IP		Innings Pitched		Strikeouts		Wins		Saves	
1961	Dick Donovan	2.40	Dick Donovan	9.4	Bennie Daniels	212.0	Bennie Daniels	110	Bennie Daniels	12	Dave Sisler	11
					Joe McClain							
1962	Tom Cheney	3.17	Don Rudolph	11.8	Dave Stenhouse	197.0	Tom Cheney	147	Dave Stenhouse	11	Jim Hannan	4
1963	Claude Osteen	3.35	Bennie Daniels	11.8	Claude Osteen	212.1	Claude Osteen	109	Claude Osteen	9	Ron Kline	17
1964	Claude Osteen	3.33	Claude Osteen	11.3	Claude Osteen	257.0	Claude Osteen	133	Claude Osteen	15	Ron Kline	14
1965	Pete Richert	2.60	Pete Richert	10.8	Pete Richert	194.0	Pete Richert	161	Pete Richert	15	Ron Kline	29
1966	Pete Richert	3.37	Pete Richert	9.7	Pete Richert	245.2	Pete Richert	195	Pete Richert	14	Ron Kline	23
1967	Phil Ortega	3.03	Phil Ortega	10.3	Phil Ortega	219.2	Phil Ortega	122	Camilo Pascual	12	Darold Knowles	14
1968	Camilo Pascual	2.69	Camilo Pascual	10.9	Joe Coleman	223.0	Joe Coleman	139	Camilo Pascual	13	Dennis Higgins	13
1969	Dick Bosman	2.19	Dick Bosman	9.2	Joe Coleman	247.2	Joe Coleman	182	Dick Bosman	14	Dennis Higgins	16
1970	Dick Bosman	3.00	Dick Bosman	11.1	Dick Bosman	230.2	Joe Coleman	152	Dick Bosman	16	Darold Knowles	27
1971	Dick Bosman	3.73	Dick Bosman	12.2	Dick Bosman	236.2	Dick Bosman	113	Dick Bosman	12	Paul Lindblad	8
1972	Mike Paul	2.17	Mike Paul	11.3	Pete Broberg	176.1	Pete Broberg	133	Rich Hand	10	Horacio Pina	15
1973	Jim Bibby	3.24	Jim Bibby	11.6	Jim Bibby	180.1	Jim Bibby	155	Jim Bibby	9	Steve Foucault	8
1974	Fergie Jenkins	2.82	Fergie Jenkins	9.3	Fergie Jenkins	328.1	Fergie Jenkins	225	Fergie Jenkins	25	Steve Foucault	12
1975	Gaylord Perry	3.03	Gaylord Perry	9.6	Gaylord Perry	270.0	Fergie Jenkins	157	Fergie Jenkins	17	Steve Foucault	10
1976	Bert Blyleven	2.76	Gaylord Perry	10.2	Gaylord Perry	250.1	Bert Blyleven	144	Gaylord Perry	15	Joe Hoerner	8
1977	Bert Blyleven	2.72	Bert Blyleven	9.9	Gaylord Perry	238.0	Bert Blyleven	182	Doyle Alexander	17	Adrian Devine	15
1978	Jon Matlack	2.27	Fergie Jenkins	9.8	Jon Matlack	270.0	Fergie Jenkins	157	Fergie Jenkins	18	Reggie Cleveland	12
									Jon Matlack			
1979	Steve Comer	3.68	Fergie Jenkins	11.7	Fergie Jenkins	259.0	Fergie Jenkins	164	Steve Comer	17	Jim Kern	29
1980	Jon Matlack	3.68	Fergie Jenkins	11.2	Jon Matlack	234.2	Jon Matlack	142	Doc Medich	14	Danny Darwin	8
											Sparky Lyle	
1981	Doc Medich	3.08	Rick Honeycutt	9.7	Danny Darwin	146.0	Danny Darwin	98	Rick Honeycutt	11	Steve Comer	6
											Jim Kern	
1982	Charlie Hough	3.95	Charlie Hough	11.7	Charlie Hough	228.0	Charlie Hough	128	Charlie Hough	16	Danny Darwin	7
1983	Rick Honeycutt	2.42	Rick Honeycutt	10.9	Charlie Hough	252.0	Charlie Hough	152	Charlie Hough	15	Odell Jones	10
1984	Frank Tanana	3.25	Mike Mason	10.4	Charlie Hough	266.0	Charlie Houghs	164	Charlie Houghs	16	Dave Schmidt	12
1985	Charlie Hough	3.31	Charlie Hough	10.4	Charlie Hough	250.1	Charlie Hough	141	Charlie Hough	14	Greg Harris	11
1986	Charlie Hough	3.79	Charlie Hough	11.2	Charlie Hough	230.1	Edwin Correa	189	Charlie Hough	17	Greg Harris	20
1987	Charlie Hough	3.79	Charlie Hough	12.0	Charlie Hough	285.1	Charlie Hough	223	Charlie Hough	18	Dale Mohorcic	16
1988	Charlie Hough	3.32	Jose Guzman	11.6	Charlie Hough	252.0	Charlie Hough	174	Charlie Hough	15	Mitch Williams	18
1989	Nolan Ryan	3.20	Nolan Ryan	10.1	Nolan Ryan	239.1	Nolan Ryan	301	Nolan Ryan	16	Jeff Russell	38
1990	Bobby Witt	3.36	Nolan Ryan	9.6	Bobby Witt	222.0	Nolan Ryan	232	Bobby Witt	17	Kenny Rogers	15
1991	Nolan Ryan	2.91	Nolan Ryan	9.3	Kevin Brown	210.2	Nolan Ryan	203	Jose Guzman	13	Jeff Russell	30
1992	Kevin Brown	3.32	Kevin Brown	11.8	Kevin Brown	265.2	Jose Guzman	179	Kevin Brown	21	Jeff Russell	28
1993	Roger Pavlik	3.41	Kevin Brown	12.2	Kevin Brown	233.0	Kevin Brown	142	Kenny Rogers	16	Tom Henke	40
1994	Kenny Rogers	4.46	Kenny Rogers	12.0	Kevin Brown	170.0	Kevin Brown	123	Kenny Rogers	11	Tom Henke	15
1995	Kenny Rogers	3.38	Kenny Rogers	11.7	Kenny Rogers	208.0	Roger Pavlik	149	Kenny Rogers	17	Jeff Russell	20
1996	Ken Hill	3.63	Ken Hill	12.6	Ken Hill	250.2	Ken Hill	170	Ken Hill	16	Mike Henneman	31
									Bobby Witt			
1997	Darren Oliver	4.20	John Burkett	13.0	Bobby Witt	209.0	John Burkett	139	Darren Oliver	13	John Wetteland	31

Senators/Rangers Franchise Batting Leaders—Career

Games

1	Jim Sundberg	1,512
2	Toby Harrah	1,355
3	Frank Howard	1,172
4	Ed Brinkman	1,143
5	Ruben Sierra	1,033
6	Buddy Bell	958
7	Juan Gonzalez	950
8	Pete O'Brien	946
9	Steve Buechele	889
10	Ivan Rodriguez	880
11	Larry Parrish	872
12	Jim King	796
13	Rafael Palmeiro	788
14	Geno Petralli	784
15	Dean Palmer	774
16	Ken McMullen	767
17	Mike Hargrove	726
18	Bump Wills	703
19	Jeff Burroughs	700
20	Pete Incaviglia	694

At-Bats

1	Jim Sundberg	4,684
2	Toby Harrah	4,572
3	Frank Howard	4,120
4	Ruben Sierra	4,043
5	Ed Brinkman	3,847
6	Juan Gonzalez	3,663
7	Buddy Bell	3,623
8	Pete O'Brien	3,351
9	Ivan Rodriguez	3,264
10	Larry Parrish	3,223
11	Rafael Palmeiro	2,993
12	Ken McMullen	2,820
13	Dean Palmer	2,745
14	Steve Buechele	2,723
15	Bump Wills	2,611
16	Jeff Burroughs	2,527
17	Mike Hargrove	2,494
18	Pete Incaviglia	2,449
19	Julio Franco	2,358
20	Paul Casanova	2,310

Runs

1	Toby Harrah	631
2	Ruben Sierra	571
3	Juan Gonzalez	567
4	Frank Howard	544
5	Jim Sundberg	482
6	Buddy Bell	471
	Rafael Palmeiro	471
8	Ivan Rodriguez	445
9	Dean Palmer	425
10	Larry Parrish	419
	Pete O'Brien	419
12	Bump Wills	408
13	Julio Franco	388
14	Mike Hargrove	380
15	Ed Brinkman	350
	Ken McMullen	350
17	Steve Buechele	337
18	Pete Incaviglia	333
19	Jeff Burroughs	332
20	Billy Sample	330

Hits

1	Jim Sundberg	1,180
2	Toby Harrah	1,174
3	Frank Howard	1,141
4	Ruben Sierra	1,132
5	Buddy Bell	1,060
6	Juan Gonzalez	1,045
7	Ivan Rodriguez	948
8	Pete O'Brien	914
9	Rafael Palmeiro	887
10	Ed Brinkman	868
11	Larry Parrish	852
12	Mike Hargrove	730
13	Julio Franco	725
14	Ken McMullen	709
15	Bump Wills	693
16	Dean Palmer	677
17	Al Oliver	668
18	Steve Buechele	654
19	Jeff Burroughs	645
20	Pete Incaviglia	607

Doubles

1	Ruben Sierra	226
2	Jim Sundberg	200
3	Buddy Bell	197
4	Juan Gonzalez	196
5	Ivan Rodriguez	192
6	Toby Harrah	187
7	Rafael Palmeiro	174
8	Pete O'Brien	161
9	Frank Howard	155
10	Larry Parrish	147
11	Al Oliver	135
12	Dean Palmer	134
13	Ed Brinkman	125
14	Julio Franco	123
15	Mike Hargrove	122
16	Pete Incaviglia	120
	Rusty Greer	120
18	Steve Buechele	115
19	Billy Sample	111
20	Bump Wills	110

Triples

1	Ruben Sierra	43
2	Chuck Hinton	30
3	Ed Brinkman	27
	Jim Sundberg	27
5	Ed Stroud	24
6	Del Unser	22
	Toby Harrah	22
	Oddibe McDowell	22
9	Buddy Bell	21
10	Frank Howard	20
	Bump Wills	20
12	Rafael Palmeiro	19
13	Lenny Randle	18
	Curtis Wilkerson	18
15	Chuck Cottier	16
	Ken McMullen	16
	George Wright	16
	Pete O'Brien	16
	Gary Ward	16
	Juan Gonzalez	16

Home Runs

1	Juan Gonzalez	256
2	Frank Howard	246
3	Dean Palmer	154
4	Ruben Sierra	153
5	Larry Parrish	149
6	Toby Harrah	124
	Pete Incaviglia	124
8	Pete O'Brien	114
9	Jeff Burroughs	108
10	Rafael Palmeiro	107
11	Don Lock	99
12	Steve Buechele	94
13	Jim King	89
14	Ivan Rodriguez	88
15	Buddy Bell	87
16	Ken McMullen	86
17	Mike Epstein	74
18	Rusty Greer	67
19	Tom Grieve	63
20	Jim Sundberg	60

RBI

1	Juan Gonzalez	790
2	Frank Howard	701
3	Ruben Sierra	656
4	Toby Harrah	568
5	Larry Parrish	522
6	Buddy Bell	499
7	Pete O'Brien	487
8	Jim Sundberg	480
9	Dean Palmer	451
10	Rafael Palmeiro	431
11	Ivan Rodriguez	417
12	Jeff Burroughs	412
13	Pete Incaviglia	388
14	Steve Buechele	338
15	Al Oliver	337
16	Julio Franco	331
17	Ken McMullen	327
18	Mike Hargrove	295
	Will Clark	295
20	Rusty Greer	294

Walks

1	Toby Harrah	708
2	Frank Howard	575
3	Jim Sundberg	544
4	Mike Hargrove	435
5	Pete O'Brien	404
6	Jeff Burroughs	335
	Buddy Bell	335
8	Rafael Palmeiro	316
9	Don Lock	293
10	Jim King	290
	Julio Franco	290
12	Ed Brinkman	289
13	Ruben Sierra	284
14	Dean Palmer	279
15	Ken McMullen	275
16	Larry Parrish	272
17	Mike Epstein	270
18	Bump Wills	264
19	Will Clark	252
20	Steve Buechele	248

Strikeouts

1	Frank Howard	909
2	Pete Incaviglia	788
3	Dean Palmer	757
4	Juan Gonzalez	716
5	Larry Parrish	715
6	Jim Sundberg	687
7	Don Lock	592
8	Ruben Sierra	588
9	Toby Harrah	575
10	Ed Brinkman	574
11	Steve Buechele	523
12	Jeff Burroughs	522
13	Ken McMullen	442
14	Mike Epstein	431
15	Oddibe McDowell	424
16	Ivan Rodriguez	419
17	Tom Grieve	400
18	Pete O'Brien	373
19	Bump Wills	365
20	Paul Casanova	349

Stolen Bases

1	Bump Wills	161
2	Toby Harrah	153
3	Dave Nelson	144
4	Oddibe McDowell	129
5	Julio Franco	98
6	Chuck Hinton	92
	Billy Sample	92
8	Cecil Espy	91
9	Ruben Sierra	86
10	Wayne Tolleson	79
11	Lenny Randle	77
12	Gary Pettis	67
13	Ed Stroud	58
14	Mark McLemore	55
15	Juan Beniquez	53
	Curtis Wilkerson	53
17	Bert Campaneris	50
	David Hulse	50
	Otis Nixon	50
20	Mickey Rivers	48

Runs Created

1	Frank Howard	737
2	Toby Harrah	679
3	Juan Gonzalez	663
4	Ruben Sierra	628
5	Jim Sundberg	533
6	Buddy Bell	528
7	Rafael Palmeiro	500
8	Pete O'Brien	495
9	Larry Parrish	454
10	Ivan Rodriguez	441
11	Mike Hargrove	436
12	Julio Franco	419
13	Dean Palmer	401
14	Jeff Burroughs	371
15	Ken McMullen	356
16	Rusty Greer	352
17	Pete Incaviglia	349
18	Bump Wills	331
	Al Oliver	331
20	Four tied at	320

Runs Created/27 Outs

(minimum 2000 Plate Appearances)

1	Rusty Greer	7.14
2	Juan Gonzalez	6.46
3	Julio Franco	6.43
4	Frank Howard	6.33
5	Mike Hargrove	6.26
6	Rafael Palmeiro	6.01
7	Al Oliver	5.84
8	Mike Epstein	5.59
9	Ruben Sierra	5.47
10	Chuck Hinton	5.19
11	Buddy Bell	5.17
12	Pete O'Brien	5.13
13	Jeff Burroughs	5.04
14	Toby Harrah	5.01
15	Dean Palmer	5.00
16	Mickey Rivers	4.92
17	Jim King	4.88
18	Larry Parrish	4.88
19	Don Lock	4.85
20	Pete Incaviglia	4.84

Batting Average

(minimum 2000 Plate Appearances)

1	Al Oliver	.319
2	Rusty Greer	.312
3	Julio Franco	.307
4	Mickey Rivers	.303
5	Rafael Palmeiro	.296
6	Mike Hargrove	.293
7	Buddy Bell	.293
8	Ivan Rodriguez	.290
9	Juan Gonzalez	.285
10	Ruben Sierra	.280
11	Chuck Hinton	.280
12	Scott Fletcher	.280
13	Frank Howard	.277
14	Pete O'Brien	.273
15	Billy Sample	.270
16	Geno Petralli	.266
17	Bump Wills	.265
18	Larry Parrish	.264
19	Toby Harrah	.257
20	Del Unser	.256

On-Base Percentage

(minimum 2000 Plate Appearances)

1	Mike Hargrove	.399
2	Rusty Greer	.392
3	Julio Franco	.382
4	Frank Howard	.367
5	Rafael Palmeiro	.366
6	Mike Epstein	.365
7	Al Oliver	.358
8	Toby Harrah	.357
9	Scott Fletcher	.354
10	Buddy Bell	.351
11	Pete O'Brien	.348
12	Chuck Hinton	.347
13	Geno Petralli	.343
14	Jeff Burroughs	.341
15	Don Lock	.334
16	Juan Gonzalez	.334
17	Jim King	.333
18	Bump Wills	.333
19	Ivan Rodriguez	.330
20	Jim Sundberg	.330

Slugging Percentage

(minimum 2000 Plate Appearances)

1	Juan Gonzalez	.557
2	Frank Howard	.503
3	Rusty Greer	.500
4	Rafael Palmeiro	.474
5	Ruben Sierra	.471
6	Dean Palmer	.470
7	Al Oliver	.466
8	Pete Incaviglia	.459
9	Larry Parrish	.454
10	Julio Franco	.440
11	Ivan Rodriguez	.439
12	Pete O'Brien	.432
13	Buddy Bell	.431
14	Chuck Hinton	.428
15	Jeff Burroughs	.428
16	Don Lock	.427
17	Mike Epstein	.425
18	Jim King	.415
19	Mike Hargrove	.409
20	Oddibe McDowell	.402

Senators/Rangers Franchise Pitching Leaders—Career

Wins

1	Charlie Hough	139
2	Bobby Witt	99
3	Fergie Jenkins	93
4	Kevin Brown	78
5	Kenny Rogers	70
6	Jose Guzman	66
7	Dick Bosman	59
8	Danny Darwin	55
9	Nolan Ryan	51
10	Doc Medich	50
11	Gaylord Perry	48
12	Roger Pavlik	46
13	Joe Coleman	43
	Jon Matlack	43
15	Jeff Russell	42
16	Jim Hannan	39
	Phil Ortega	39
	Casey Cox	39
	Steve Comer	39
20	Bennie Daniels	37

Losses

1	Charlie Hough	123
2	Bobby Witt	100
3	Fergie Jenkins	72
4	Dick Bosman	64
	Kevin Brown	64
6	Jose Guzman	62
7	Bennie Daniels	60
8	Danny Darwin	52
9	Kenny Rogers	51
10	Joe Coleman	50
11	Phil Ortega	49
	Frank Tanana	49
13	Jim Hannan	47
14	Jon Matlack	45
15	Gaylord Perry	43
	Doc Medich	43
17	Claude Osteen	41
	Casey Cox	41
19	Jeff Russell	40
20	Nolan Ryan	39

Winning Percentage

(minimum 75 decisions)

1	Kenny Rogers	.579
2	Nolan Ryan	.567
3	Fergie Jenkins	.564
4	Kevin Brown	.549
5	Roger Pavlik	.548
6	Doc Medich	.538
7	Charlie Hough	.531
8	Gaylord Perry	.527
9	Jose Guzman	.516
10	Danny Darwin	.514
11	Jeff Russell	.512
12	Bobby Witt	.497
13	Jon Matlack	.489
14	Casey Cox	.488
15	Dick Bosman	.480
16	Joe Coleman	.462
17	Jim Hannan	.453
18	Phil Ortega	.443
19	Frank Tanana	.388
20	Bennie Daniels	.381

Games

1	Jeff Russell	445
2	Kenny Rogers	376
3	Charlie Hough	344
4	Casey Cox	302
5	Darold Knowles	271
6	Bobby Witt	262
7	Ron Kline	260
8	Jim Hannan	248
9	Mitch Williams	232
10	Danny Darwin	224
11	Matt Whiteside	223
12	Bob Humphreys	214
13	Steve Foucault	206
14	Dick Bosman	204
15	Fergie Jenkins	197
16	Kevin Brown	187
17	Bennie Daniels	177
	Horacio Pina	177
19	Dale Mohorcic	175
20	Greg Harris	173

Games Started

1	Charlie Hough	313
2	Bobby Witt	256
3	Fergie Jenkins	190
4	Kevin Brown	186
5	Dick Bosman	155
6	Jose Guzman	152
7	Nolan Ryan	129
8	Roger Pavlik	125
9	Joe Coleman	123
10	Jon Matlack	119
11	Bennie Daniels	115
12	Doc Medich	114
13	Gaylord Perry	112
14	Phil Ortega	110
15	Jim Hannan	100
	Frank Tanana	100
	Kenny Rogers	100
18	Danny Darwin	94
19	Claude Osteen	90
20	Mike Mason	86

Complete Games

1	Charlie Hough	98
2	Fergie Jenkins	90
3	Gaylord Perry	55
4	Kevin Brown	40
5	Joe Coleman	36
6	Bobby Witt	33
7	Jon Matlack	32
8	Bert Blyleven	29
9	Claude Osteen	28
10	Jim Bibby	26
11	Bennie Daniels	25
12	Jose Guzman	24
13	Dick Bosman	23
14	Doc Medich	22
15	Danny Darwin	21
16	Doyle Alexander	19
	Frank Tanana	19
18	Steve Hargan	18
19	Rick Honeycutt	17
20	Pete Broberg	16

Shutouts

1	Fergie Jenkins	17
2	Gaylord Perry	12
3	Bert Blyleven	11
	Charlie Hough	11
5	Dick Bosman	9
6	Jim Bibby	8
7	Tom Cheney	7
	Joe Coleman	7
	Doc Medich	7
10	Phil Ortega	6
	Kevin Brown	6
	Nolan Ryan	6
13	Bennie Daniels	5
	Camilo Pascual	5
	Jim Umbarger	5
	Danny Darwin	5
	Rick Honeycutt	5
	Bobby Witt	5
19	Fifteen tied at	4

Saves

1	Jeff Russell	134
2	Ron Kline	83
3	Darold Knowles	64
4	Tom Henke	58
5	Jim Kern	37
6	Steve Foucault	35
7	Mitch Williams	32
8	Greg Harris	31
	Mike Henneman	31
	John Wetteland	31
11	Dennis Higgins	29
12	Dale Mohorcic	28
	Kenny Rogers	28
14	Dave Schmidt	26
15	Horacio Pina	23
	Paul Lindblad	23
17	Dave Baldwin	21
	Sparky Lyle	21
19	Casey Cox	20
20	Six tied at	15

Innings Pitched

1	Charlie Hough	2,308.0
2	Bobby Witt	1,611.1
3	Fergie Jenkins	1,410.1
4	Kevin Brown	1,278.2
5	Dick Bosman	1,103.1
6	Jose Guzman	1,013.2
7	Kenny Rogers	943.1
8	Jon Matlack	915.0
9	Danny Darwin	872.0
10	Joe Coleman	850.1
11	Nolan Ryan	840.0
12	Gaylord Perry	827.1
13	Bennie Daniels	821.1
14	Doc Medich	790.1
15	Jim Hannan	778.2
16	Jeff Russell	752.2
17	Casey Cox	747.1
18	Roger Pavlik	729.0
19	Phil Ortega	712.1
20	Frank Tanana	677.2

Walks

1	Bobby Witt	968
2	Charlie Hough	965
3	Kevin Brown	428
4	Jose Guzman	395
5	Jim Hannan	378
6	Kenny Rogers	370
7	Nolan Ryan	353
8	Roger Pavlik	346
9	Fergie Jenkins	315
10	Bennie Daniels	309
11	Dick Bosman	303
12	Danny Darwin	298
13	Joe Coleman	297
14	Jeff Russell	295
15	Phil Ortega	269
16	Jim Bibby	257
17	Doc Medich	251
18	Casey Cox	230
19	Darren Oliver	226
20	Doyle Alexander	222

Strikeouts

1	Charlie Hough	1,452
2	Bobby Witt	1,375
3	Nolan Ryan	939
4	Fergie Jenkins	895
5	Kevin Brown	742
6	Jose Guzman	715
7	Kenny Rogers	680
8	Gaylord Perry	575
9	Dick Bosman	573
10	Danny Darwin	566
11	Joe Coleman	561
12	Roger Pavlik	518
13	Jon Matlack	493
14	Jeff Russell	474
15	Jim Hannan	415
16	Pete Richert	397
17	Phil Ortega	388
	Frank Tanana	388
19	Bennie Daniels	379
20	Jim Bibby	341

Strikeouts/9 Innings

(minimum 750 Innings Pitched)

1	Nolan Ryan	10.06
2	Bobby Witt	7.68
3	Kenny Rogers	6.49
4	Jose Guzman	6.35
5	Gaylord Perry	6.26
6	Joe Coleman	5.94
7	Danny Darwin	5.84
8	Fergie Jenkins	5.71
9	Jeff Russell	5.67
10	Charlie Hough	5.66
11	Kevin Brown	5.22
12	Jon Matlack	4.85
13	Jim Hannan	4.80
14	Dick Bosman	4.67
15	Bennie Daniels	4.15
16	Doc Medich	3.67

ERA

(minimum 750 Innings Pitched)

1	Gaylord Perry	3.26
2	Dick Bosman	3.35
3	Jon Matlack	3.41
4	Nolan Ryan	3.43
5	Joe Coleman	3.51
6	Fergie Jenkins	3.56
7	Charlie Hough	3.68
8	Danny Darwin	3.72
9	Jeff Russell	3.73
10	Kevin Brown	3.81
11	Jim Hannan	3.84
12	Kenny Rogers	3.88
13	Jose Guzman	3.90
14	Doc Medich	3.95
15	Bennie Daniels	4.14
16	Bobby Witt	4.73

Component ERA

(minimum 750 Innings Pitched)

1	Nolan Ryan	2.56
2	Gaylord Perry	3.05
3	Fergie Jenkins	3.26
4	Dick Bosman	3.37
5	Danny Darwin	3.50
6	Joe Coleman	3.55
7	Charlie Hough	3.58
8	Jon Matlack	3.63
9	Bennie Daniels	3.83
10	Doc Medich	3.84
11	Kevin Brown	3.93
12	Jeff Russell	3.96
13	Jose Guzman	3.97
14	Kenny Rogers	3.98
15	Jim Hannan	4.28
16	Bobby Witt	4.66

Opponent Average

(minimum 750 Innings Pitched)

1	Nolan Ryan	.197
2	Charlie Hough	.233
3	Joe Coleman	.248
4	Fergie Jenkins	.249
5	Gaylord Perry	.251
6	Danny Darwin	.252
7	Jose Guzman	.255
8	Bobby Witt	.255
9	Kenny Rogers	.256
10	Dick Bosman	.257
11	Jeff Russell	.257
12	Bennie Daniels	.258
13	Jim Hannan	.261
14	Kevin Brown	.267
15	Jon Matlack	.272
16	Doc Medich	.273

Opponent OBP

(minimum 750 Innings Pitched)

1	Nolan Ryan	.286
2	Fergie Jenkins	.292
3	Gaylord Perry	.296
4	Dick Bosman	.308
5	Jon Matlack	.314
6	Charlie Hough	.315
7	Joe Coleman	.315
8	Danny Darwin	.316
9	Bennie Daniels	.324
10	Jose Guzman	.326
11	Kenny Rogers	.327
12	Jeff Russell	.328
13	Doc Medich	.329
14	Kevin Brown	.330
15	Jim Hannan	.346
16	Bobby Witt	.356

Teams: Rangers

Washington Senators II Team Batting Leaders—Career

Games

1	Ed Brinkman	1,142
2	Frank Howard	1,077
3	Jim King	796
4	Ken McMullen	767
5	Paul Casanova	686
6	Don Lock	653
7	Del Unser	581
8	Tim Cullen	556
9	Chuck Hinton	545
10	Bernie Allen	530
11	Mike Epstein	514
12	Fred Valentine	448
13	Ed Stroud	444
14	Chuck Cottier	430
15	Don Blasingame	409
16	Hank Allen	324
17	Don Zimmer	299
18	Ken Hamlin	281
19	Willie Kirkland	279
	Dick Nen	279

At-Bats

1	Ed Brinkman	3,845
2	Frank Howard	3,833
3	Ken McMullen	2,820
4	Paul Casanova	2,310
5	Jim King	2,138
6	Del Unser	2,119
7	Don Lock	2,072
8	Chuck Hinton	1,961
9	Mike Epstein	1,587
10	Bernie Allen	1,482
11	Tim Cullen	1,464
12	Don Blasingame	1,363
13	Fred Valentine	1,307
14	Chuck Cottier	1,255
15	Ed Stroud	1,149
16	Don Zimmer	865
17	Ken Hamlin	812
18	Hank Allen	760
19	Danny O'Connell	729
20	Dick Nen	724

Runs

1	Frank Howard	516
2	Ed Brinkman	350
	Ken McMullen	350
4	Jim King	286
5	Don Lock	278
6	Chuck Hinton	275
7	Del Unser	235
8	Mike Epstein	206
9	Paul Casanova	183
10	Ed Stroud	181
11	Fred Valentine	166
12	Don Blasingame	150
13	Chuck Cottier	134
14	Tim Cullen	129
15	Bernie Allen	126
16	Hank Allen	97
17	Don Zimmer	95
18	Ken Hamlin	87
19	Bob Johnson	85
	Danny O'Connell	85

Hits

1	Frank Howard	1,071
2	Ed Brinkman	868
3	Ken McMullen	709
4	Chuck Hinton	549
5	Del Unser	543
6	Paul Casanova	527
7	Jim King	511
8	Don Lock	498
9	Mike Epstein	398
10	Bernie Allen	351
11	Don Blasingame	333
12	Fred Valentine	326
13	Tim Cullen	319
14	Ed Stroud	281
15	Chuck Cottier	278
16	Ken Hamlin	207
17	Don Zimmer	203
18	Bob Johnson	200
19	Hank Allen	191
20	Danny O'Connell	190

Doubles

1	Frank Howard	146
2	Ed Brinkman	125
3	Ken McMullen	97
4	Jim King	84
5	Chuck Hinton	83
6	Paul Casanova	77
7	Don Lock	71
8	Del Unser	56
9	Fred Valentine	52
	Bernie Allen	52
11	Chuck Cottier	50
12	Mike Epstein	49
13	Don Blasingame	44
14	Tim Cullen	42
15	Ken Hamlin	40
16	Danny O'Connell	37
17	Don Zimmer	34
18	Bob Johnson	33
19	Ed Stroud	31
	Aurelio Rodriguez	31

Triples

1	Chuck Hinton	30
2	Ed Brinkman	27
3	Ed Stroud	24
4	Del Unser	22
5	Frank Howard	20
6	Chuck Cottier	16
	Ken McMullen	16
8	Jim King	13
9	Don Blasingame	12
	Paul Casanova	12
11	Mike Epstein	11
	Bernie Allen	11
13	Marty Keough	9
	Don Lock	9
	Hank Allen	9
16	Fred Valentine	8
	Tim Cullen	8
18	Bud Zipfel	6
	John Kennedy	6
20	Aurelio Rodriguez	5

Home Runs

1	Frank Howard	237
2	Don Lock	99
3	Jim King	89
4	Ken McMullen	86
5	Mike Epstein	73
6	Chuck Hinton	49
7	Paul Casanova	41
8	Fred Valentine	34
9	Ed Brinkman	31
10	Bernie Allen	30
11	Don Zimmer	27
12	Willie Kirkland	25
13	Del Unser	22
14	Harry Bright	21
	Dale Long	21
16	Brant Alyea	19
	Aurelio Rodriguez	19
18	Bob Johnson	18
	Gene Green	18
	Dick Nen	18

RBI

1	Frank Howard	670
2	Ken McMullen	327
3	Jim King	290
4	Don Lock	286
5	Ed Brinkman	273
6	Chuck Hinton	217
7	Paul Casanova	216
8	Mike Epstein	212
9	Del Unser	158
10	Bernie Allen	154
11	Fred Valentine	131
12	Tim Cullen	106
13	Chuck Cottier	105
14	Don Zimmer	99
15	Ed Stroud	94
16	Dick Nen	90
17	Harry Bright	88
18	Willie Kirkland	84
19	Aurelio Rodriguez	76
20	Don Blasingame	75

Walks

1	Frank Howard	533
2	Don Lock	293
3	Jim King	290
4	Ed Brinkman	289
5	Ken McMullen	275
6	Mike Epstein	256
7	Chuck Hinton	208
8	Del Unser	193
9	Bernie Allen	172
10	Fred Valentine	138
11	Tim Cullen	127
12	Jim French	121
13	Chuck Cottier	117
	Don Blasingame	117
15	Ed Stroud	115
16	Danny O'Connell	100
17	Paul Casanova	81
18	Gene Woodling	74
19	Don Zimmer	71
20	Joe Cunningham	69

Strikeouts

1	Frank Howard	854
2	Don Lock	592
3	Ed Brinkman	573
4	Ken McMullen	442
5	Mike Epstein	412
6	Paul Casanova	349
7	Chuck Hinton	303
8	Jim King	294
9	Del Unser	217
10	Don Zimmer	210
11	Chuck Cottier	204
12	Fred Valentine	199
13	Ed Stroud	191
14	Tim Cullen	179
15	Bernie Allen	161
16	John Kennedy	148
17	Willie Kirkland	145
18	Dick Nen	132
19	Don Blasingame	128
20	Joe Coleman	119

Stolen Bases

1	Chuck Hinton	92
2	Ed Stroud	58
3	Fred Valentine	47
4	Del Unser	31
5	Ed Brinkman	27
	Chuck Cottier	27
7	Jim King	20
	Danny O'Connell	20
9	Dave Nelson	19
10	Don Lock	18
	Don Blasingame	18
12	Ken Hamlin	16
	Jimmy Piersall	16
14	Ken McMullen	15
	Hank Allen	15
	Aurelio Rodriguez	15
17	Bob Johnson	13
18	Marty Keough	12
	Bob Saverine	12
20	Four tied at	10

Runs Created

1	Frank Howard	700
2	Ken McMullen	356
3	Jim King	306
4	Ed Brinkman	303
5	Don Lock	298
6	Chuck Hinton	292
7	Mike Epstein	264
8	Del Unser	236
9	Fred Valentine	179
10	Paul Casanova	169
	Bernie Allen	169
12	Don Blasingame	136
13	Ed Stroud	129
14	Chuck Cottier	117
15	Tim Cullen	108
16	Danny O'Connell	93
17	Don Zimmer	92
18	Bob Johnson	88
19	Gene Woodling	85
	Ken Hamlin	85

Runs Created/27 Outs

(minimum 1000 Plate Appearances)

1	Frank Howard	6.49
2	Mike Epstein	5.75
3	Chuck Hinton	5.19
4	Jim King	4.88
5	Don Lock	4.85
6	Fred Valentine	4.66
7	Ken McMullen	4.31
8	Bernie Allen	3.89
9	Del Unser	3.88
10	Ed Stroud	3.76
11	Don Blasingame	3.45
12	Chuck Cottier	3.05
13	Ed Brinkman	2.60
14	Paul Casanova	2.43
15	Tim Cullen	2.38

Batting Average

(minimum 1000 Plate Appearances)

1	Chuck Hinton	.280
2	Frank Howard	.279
3	Del Unser	.256
4	Ken McMullen	.251
5	Mike Epstein	.251
6	Fred Valentine	.249
7	Ed Stroud	.245
8	Don Blasingame	.244
9	Don Lock	.240
10	Jim King	.239
11	Bernie Allen	.237
12	Paul Casanova	.228
13	Ed Brinkman	.226
14	Chuck Cottier	.222
15	Tim Cullen	.218

On-Base Percentage

(minimum 1000 Plate Appearances)

1	Frank Howard	.369
2	Mike Epstein	.367
3	Chuck Hinton	.347
4	Don Lock	.334
5	Jim King	.333
6	Fred Valentine	.332
7	Del Unser	.318
8	Bernie Allen	.317
9	Ken McMullen	.317
10	Ed Stroud	.316
11	Don Blasingame	.304
12	Chuck Cottier	.287
13	Ed Brinkman	.283
14	Tim Cullen	.282
15	Paul Casanova	.255

Slugging Percentage

(minimum 1000 Plate Appearances)

1	Frank Howard	.513
2	Mike Epstein	.434
3	Chuck Hinton	.428
4	Don Lock	.427
5	Jim King	.415
6	Ken McMullen	.389
7	Fred Valentine	.379
8	Ed Stroud	.350
9	Bernie Allen	.348
10	Del Unser	.335
11	Paul Casanova	.325
12	Chuck Cottier	.325
13	Don Blasingame	.305
14	Ed Brinkman	.296
15	Tim Cullen	.272

Teams: Rangers

Washington Senators II Team Pitching Leaders—Career

Wins

1	Dick Bosman	49
2	Joe Coleman	43
3	Jim Hannan	39
	Phil Ortega	39
5	Bennie Daniels	37
6	Casey Cox	36
7	Claude Osteen	33
8	Pete Richert	31
9	Camilo Pascual	27
10	Ron Kline	26
11	Barry Moore	23
12	Bob Humphreys	21
13	Darold Knowles	20
14	Mike McCormick	19
15	Tom Cheney	17
16	Dave Stenhouse	16
	Don Rudolph	16
	Steve Ridzik	16
19	Three tied at	14

Losses

1	Bennie Daniels	60
2	Joe Coleman	50
3	Phil Ortega	49
	Dick Bosman	49
5	Jim Hannan	47
6	Claude Osteen	41
7	Casey Cox	36
8	Don Rudolph	32
	Pete Richert	32
10	Dave Stenhouse	28
	Barry Moore	28
12	Buster Narum	27
	Darold Knowles	27
	Camilo Pascual	27
15	Tom Cheney	25
	Ron Kline	25
	Jim Shellenback	25
18	Jim Duckworth	23
19	Three tied at	22

Winning Percentage
(minimum 50 decisions)

1	Ron Kline	.510
2	Dick Bosman	.500
	Casey Cox	.500
	Camilo Pascual	.500
5	Pete Richert	.492
6	Joe Coleman	.462
7	Jim Hannan	.453
8	Barry Moore	.451
9	Claude Osteen	.446
10	Phil Ortega	.443
11	Bennie Daniels	.381

Games

1	Casey Cox	267
2	Ron Kline	260
3	Jim Hannan	248
4	Darold Knowles	229
5	Bob Humphreys	214
6	Bennie Daniels	177
7	Dick Bosman	168
8	Dave Baldwin	145
9	Joe Coleman	143
10	Phil Ortega	133
11	Steve Ridzik	132
12	Horacio Pina	117
13	Dennis Higgins	114
14	Pete Burnside	111
15	Jim Shellenback	109
16	Claude Osteen	108
17	Dick Lines	107
18	Marty Kutyna	104
19	Barry Moore	103
20	Don Rudolph	102

Games Started

1	Joe Coleman	123
2	Dick Bosman	119
3	Bennie Daniels	115
4	Phil Ortega	110
5	Jim Hannan	100
6	Claude Osteen	90
7	Barry Moore	80
8	Pete Richert	73
9	Camilo Pascual	71
10	Tom Cheney	58
	Buster Narum	58
12	Don Rudolph	57
13	Dave Stenhouse	56
14	Casey Cox	54
15	Mike McCormick	53
16	Frank Bertaina	45
17	Jim Shellenback	40
18	Pete Burnside	37
19	Joe McClain	33
20	Denny McLain	32

Complete Games

1	Joe Coleman	36
2	Claude Osteen	28
3	Bennie Daniels	25
4	Dick Bosman	21
5	Phil Ortega	15
6	Pete Richert	14
7	Camilo Pascual	13
8	Tom Cheney	12
	Dave Stenhouse	12
10	Dick Donovan	11
	Mike McCormick	11
12	Pete Burnside	10
	Don Rudolph	10
14	Jim Hannan	9
	Buster Narum	9
	Denny McLain	9
17	Barry Moore	8
18	Joe McClain	7
	Jim Shellenback	7
	Pete Broberg	7

Shutouts

1	Tom Cheney	7
	Joe Coleman	7
	Dick Bosman	7
4	Phil Ortega	6
5	Bennie Daniels	5
	Camilo Pascual	5
7	Claude Osteen	4
	Jim Hannan	4
	Mike McCormick	4
	Frank Bertaina	4
11	Dave Stenhouse	3
	Denny McLain	3
13	Joe McClain	2
	Pete Burnside	2
	Dick Donovan	2
	Don Rudolph	2
	Buster Narum	2
	Jim Shellenback	2
19	Nine tied at	1

Saves

1	Ron Kline	83
2	Darold Knowles	60
3	Dennis Higgins	29
4	Dave Baldwin	21
5	Casey Cox	16
6	Bob Humphreys	14
7	Dave Sisler	11
	Steve Ridzik	11
	Joe Grzenda	11
10	Horacio Pina	8
	Paul Lindblad	8
12	Jim Hannan	7
13	Dick Lines	6
14	John Gabler	4
	Bennie Daniels	4
	Pete Burnside	4
	Ed Roebuck	4
	Bob Priddy	4
19	Three tied at	3

Innings Pitched

1	Dick Bosman	889.2
2	Joe Coleman	850.1
3	Bennie Daniels	821.1
4	Jim Hannan	778.2
5	Phil Ortega	712.1
6	Casey Cox	682.0
7	Claude Osteen	638.0
8	Pete Richert	494.0
9	Barry Moore	458.2
10	Camilo Pascual	421.0
11	Don Rudolph	420.2
12	Bob Humphreys	396.1
13	Tom Cheney	393.1
14	Buster Narum	387.2
15	Mike McCormick	374.0
16	Darold Knowles	373.2
17	Dave Stenhouse	372.0
18	Ron Kline	364.2
19	Pete Burnside	330.1
20	Jim Shellenback	322.0

Walks

1	Jim Hannan	378
2	Bennie Daniels	309
3	Joe Coleman	297
4	Phil Ortega	269
5	Dick Bosman	238
6	Barry Moore	220
7	Casey Cox	204
8	Tom Cheney	182
9	Claude Osteen	180
10	Dave Stenhouse	174
11	Buster Narum	172
12	Pete Richert	168
13	Darold Knowles	159
14	Jim Shellenback	148
15	Bob Humphreys	146
16	Camilo Pascual	140
17	Jim Duckworth	138
18	Frank Bertaina	129
19	Pete Burnside	126
20	Steve Ridzik	109

Strikeouts

1	Joe Coleman	561
2	Dick Bosman	454
3	Jim Hannan	415
4	Pete Richert	397
5	Phil Ortega	388
6	Bennie Daniels	379
7	Claude Osteen	315
8	Tom Cheney	292
9	Darold Knowles	268
10	Casey Cox	266
11	Camilo Pascual	251
12	Bob Humphreys	247
13	Buster Narum	215
14	Dave Stenhouse	214
15	Jim Duckworth	210
16	Barry Moore	209
17	Mike McCormick	189
18	Ron Kline	187
19	Steve Ridzik	179
20	Frank Bertaina	173

Strikeouts/9 Innings
(minimum 500 Innings Pitched)

1	Joe Coleman	5.94
2	Phil Ortega	4.90
3	Jim Hannan	4.80
4	Dick Bosman	4.59
5	Claude Osteen	4.44
6	Bennie Daniels	4.15
7	Casey Cox	3.51

ERA
(minimum 500 Innings Pitched)

1	Dick Bosman	3.26
2	Claude Osteen	3.46
3	Joe Coleman	3.51
4	Casey Cox	3.60
5	Jim Hannan	3.84
6	Phil Ortega	4.12
7	Bennie Daniels	4.14

Component ERA
(minimum 500 Innings Pitched)

1	Dick Bosman	3.24
2	Claude Osteen	3.53
3	Joe Coleman	3.55
4	Casey Cox	3.63
5	Phil Ortega	3.68
6	Bennie Daniels	3.83
7	Jim Hannan	4.28

Opponent Average
(minimum 500 Innings Pitched)

1	Phil Ortega	.241
2	Joe Coleman	.248
3	Dick Bosman	.253
4	Bennie Daniels	.258
5	Claude Osteen	.259
6	Jim Hannan	.261
7	Casey Cox	.265

Opponent OBP
(minimum 500 Innings Pitched)

1	Dick Bosman	.303
2	Claude Osteen	.310
3	Phil Ortega	.313
4	Joe Coleman	.315
5	Casey Cox	.320
6	Bennie Daniels	.324
7	Jim Hannan	.346

Teams: Rangers

Texas Rangers Team Batting Leaders—Career

Games

1	Jim Sundberg	1,512
2	Toby Harrah	1,220
3	Ruben Sierra	1,033
4	Buddy Bell	958
5	Juan Gonzalez	950
6	Pete O'Brien	946
7	Steve Buechele	889
8	Ivan Rodriguez	880
9	Larry Parrish	872
10	Rafael Palmeiro	788
11	Geno Petralli	784
12	Dean Palmer	774
13	Mike Hargrove	726
14	Bump Wills	703
15	Pete Incaviglia	694
16	Billy Sample	675
17	Jeff Burroughs	635
18	Julio Franco	632
19	Curtis Wilkerson	610
20	Oddibe McDowell	572

At-Bats

1	Jim Sundberg	4,684
2	Toby Harrah	4,188
3	Ruben Sierra	4,043
4	Juan Gonzalez	3,663
5	Buddy Bell	3,623
6	Pete O'Brien	3,351
7	Ivan Rodriguez	3,264
8	Larry Parrish	3,223
9	Rafael Palmeiro	2,993
10	Dean Palmer	2,745
11	Steve Buechele	2,723
12	Bump Wills	2,611
13	Mike Hargrove	2,494
14	Pete Incaviglia	2,449
15	Julio Franco	2,358
16	Jeff Burroughs	2,334
17	Billy Sample	2,177
18	Al Oliver	2,094
19	George Wright	2,043
20	Oddibe McDowell	2,005

Runs

1	Toby Harrah	582
2	Ruben Sierra	571
3	Juan Gonzalez	567
4	Jim Sundberg	482
5	Buddy Bell	471
	Rafael Palmeiro	471
7	Ivan Rodriguez	445
8	Dean Palmer	425
9	Larry Parrish	419
	Pete O'Brien	419
11	Bump Wills	408
12	Julio Franco	388
13	Mike Hargrove	380
14	Steve Buechele	337
15	Pete Incaviglia	333
16	Billy Sample	330
17	Oddibe McDowell	322
18	Jeff Burroughs	311
19	Rusty Greer	302
20	Two tied at	283

Hits

1	Jim Sundberg	1,180
2	Ruben Sierra	1,132
3	Toby Harrah	1,086
4	Buddy Bell	1,060
5	Juan Gonzalez	1,045
6	Ivan Rodriguez	948
7	Pete O'Brien	914
8	Rafael Palmeiro	887
9	Larry Parrish	852
10	Mike Hargrove	730
11	Julio Franco	725
12	Bump Wills	693
13	Dean Palmer	677
14	Al Oliver	668
15	Steve Buechele	654
16	Pete Incaviglia	607
17	Jeff Burroughs	601
18	Mickey Rivers	596
19	Billy Sample	587
20	Rusty Greer	573

Doubles

1	Ruben Sierra	226
2	Jim Sundberg	200
3	Buddy Bell	197
4	Juan Gonzalez	196
5	Ivan Rodriguez	192
6	Toby Harrah	176
7	Rafael Palmeiro	174
8	Pete O'Brien	161
9	Larry Parrish	147
10	Al Oliver	135
11	Dean Palmer	134
12	Julio Franco	123
13	Mike Hargrove	122
14	Pete Incaviglia	120
	Rusty Greer	120
16	Steve Buechele	115
17	Billy Sample	111
18	Bump Wills	110
19	Will Clark	105
20	Scott Fletcher	95

Triples

1	Ruben Sierra	43
2	Jim Sundberg	27
3	Oddibe McDowell	22
4	Buddy Bell	21
5	Bump Wills	20
6	Toby Harrah	19
	Rafael Palmeiro	19
8	Lenny Randle	18
	Curtis Wilkerson	18
10	George Wright	16
	Pete O'Brien	16
	Gary Ward	16
	Juan Gonzalez	16
14	Ivan Rodriguez	15
15	Mike Hargrove	14
	Scott Fletcher	14
	David Hulse	14
18	Seven tied at	13

Home Runs

1	Juan Gonzalez	256
2	Dean Palmer	154
3	Ruben Sierra	153
4	Larry Parrish	149
5	Pete Incaviglia	124
6	Toby Harrah	122
7	Pete O'Brien	114
8	Rafael Palmeiro	107
9	Jeff Burroughs	103
10	Steve Buechele	94
11	Ivan Rodriguez	88
12	Buddy Bell	87
13	Rusty Greer	67
14	Tom Grieve	60
	Jim Sundberg	60
16	Richie Zisk	59
	Mickey Tettleton	59
18	Oddibe McDowell	57
19	Julio Franco	55
20	Will Clark	54

RBI

1	Juan Gonzalez	790
2	Ruben Sierra	656
3	Toby Harrah	546
4	Larry Parrish	522
5	Buddy Bell	499
6	Pete O'Brien	487
7	Jim Sundberg	480
8	Dean Palmer	451
9	Rafael Palmeiro	431
10	Ivan Rodriguez	417
11	Pete Incaviglia	388
12	Jeff Burroughs	386
13	Steve Buechele	338
14	Al Oliver	337
15	Julio Franco	331
16	Mike Hargrove	295
	Will Clark	295
18	Rusty Greer	294
19	Bump Wills	264
20	Tom Grieve	236

Walks

1	Toby Harrah	668
2	Jim Sundberg	544
3	Mike Hargrove	435
4	Pete O'Brien	404
5	Buddy Bell	335
6	Rafael Palmeiro	316
7	Jeff Burroughs	311
8	Julio Franco	290
9	Ruben Sierra	284
10	Dean Palmer	279
11	Larry Parrish	272
12	Bump Wills	264
13	Will Clark	252
14	Steve Buechele	248
15	Juan Gonzalez	247
16	Rusty Greer	246
17	Oddibe McDowell	221
18	Pete Incaviglia	219
19	Geno Petralli	211
20	Scott Fletcher	208

Strikeouts

1	Pete Incaviglia	788
2	Dean Palmer	757
3	Juan Gonzalez	716
4	Larry Parrish	715
5	Jim Sundberg	687
6	Ruben Sierra	588
7	Toby Harrah	527
8	Steve Buechele	523
9	Jeff Burroughs	462
10	Oddibe McDowell	424
11	Ivan Rodriguez	419
12	Pete O'Brien	373
13	Bump Wills	365
14	Tom Grieve	362
15	Rafael Palmeiro	347
16	Julio Franco	342
17	Buddy Bell	297
18	George Wright	286
19	Rusty Greer	285
20	Mike Hargrove	278

Stolen Bases

1	Bump Wills	161
2	Toby Harrah	143
3	Oddibe McDowell	129
4	Dave Nelson	125
5	Julio Franco	98
6	Billy Sample	92
7	Cecil Espy	91
8	Ruben Sierra	86
9	Wayne Tolleson	79
10	Lenny Randle	76
11	Gary Pettis	67
12	Mark McLemore	55
13	Juan Beniquez	53
	Curtis Wilkerson	53
15	Bert Campaneris	50
	David Hulse	50
	Otis Nixon	50
18	Mickey Rivers	48
19	Gary Ward	45
20	Jeff Huson	38

Runs Created

1	Juan Gonzalez	663
2	Toby Harrah	647
3	Ruben Sierra	628
4	Jim Sundberg	533
5	Buddy Bell	528
6	Rafael Palmeiro	500
7	Pete O'Brien	495
8	Larry Parrish	454
9	Ivan Rodriguez	441
10	Mike Hargrove	436
11	Julio Franco	419
12	Dean Palmer	401
13	Rusty Greer	352
14	Jeff Burroughs	349
	Pete Incaviglia	349
16	Bump Wills	331
	Al Oliver	331
18	Steve Buechele	320
	Will Clark	320
20	Billy Sample	291

Runs Created/27 Outs

(minimum 2000 Plate Appearances)

1	Rusty Greer	7.14
2	Juan Gonzalez	6.46
3	Julio Franco	6.43
4	Mike Hargrove	6.26
5	Rafael Palmeiro	6.01
6	Al Oliver	5.84
7	Ruben Sierra	5.47
8	Toby Harrah	5.23
9	Buddy Bell	5.17
10	Jeff Burroughs	5.13
11	Pete O'Brien	5.13
12	Dean Palmer	5.00
13	Mickey Rivers	4.92
14	Larry Parrish	4.88
15	Pete Incaviglia	4.84
16	Ivan Rodriguez	4.80
17	Oddibe McDowell	4.71
18	Billy Sample	4.61
19	Scott Fletcher	4.56
20	Bump Wills	4.25

Batting Average

(minimum 2000 Plate Appearances)

1	Al Oliver	.319
2	Rusty Greer	.312
3	Julio Franco	.307
4	Mickey Rivers	.303
5	Rafael Palmeiro	.296
6	Mike Hargrove	.293
7	Buddy Bell	.293
8	Ivan Rodriguez	.290
9	Juan Gonzalez	.285
10	Ruben Sierra	.280
11	Scott Fletcher	.280
12	Pete O'Brien	.273
13	Billy Sample	.270
14	Geno Petralli	.266
15	Bump Wills	.265
16	Larry Parrish	.264
17	Toby Harrah	.259
18	Jeff Burroughs	.257
19	Lenny Randle	.257
20	Jim Sundberg	.252

On-Base Percentage

(minimum 2000 Plate Appearances)

1	Mike Hargrove	.399
2	Rusty Greer	.392
3	Julio Franco	.382
4	Rafael Palmeiro	.366
5	Toby Harrah	.361
6	Al Oliver	.358
7	Scott Fletcher	.354
8	Buddy Bell	.351
9	Pete O'Brien	.348
10	Geno Petralli	.343
11	Jeff Burroughs	.343
12	Juan Gonzalez	.334
13	Bump Wills	.333
14	Ivan Rodriguez	.330
15	Jim Sundberg	.330
16	Mickey Rivers	.327
17	Billy Sample	.327
18	Oddibe McDowell	.325
19	Ruben Sierra	.324
20	Larry Parrish	.323

Slugging Percentage

(minimum 2000 Plate Appearances)

1	Juan Gonzalez	.557
2	Rusty Greer	.500
3	Rafael Palmeiro	.474
4	Ruben Sierra	.471
5	Dean Palmer	.470
6	Al Oliver	.466
7	Pete Incaviglia	.459
8	Larry Parrish	.454
9	Julio Franco	.440
10	Ivan Rodriguez	.439
11	Jeff Burroughs	.434
12	Pete O'Brien	.432
13	Buddy Bell	.431
14	Mike Hargrove	.409
15	Oddibe McDowell	.402
16	Toby Harrah	.398
17	Mickey Rivers	.397
18	Steve Buechele	.396
19	Billy Sample	.383
20	George Wright	.366

Teams: Rangers

Texas Rangers Team Pitching Leaders—Career

Wins

1	Charlie Hough	139
2	Bobby Witt	99
3	Fergie Jenkins	93
4	Kevin Brown	78
5	Kenny Rogers	70
6	Jose Guzman	66
7	Danny Darwin	55
8	Nolan Ryan	51
9	Doc Medich	50
10	Gaylord Perry	48
11	Roger Pavlik	46
12	Jon Matlack	43
13	Jeff Russell	42
14	Steve Comer	39
15	Darren Oliver	35
16	Doyle Alexander	31
	Rick Honeycutt	31
	Frank Tanana	31
19	Jim Bibby	30
	Steve Hargan	30

Losses

1	Charlie Hough	123
2	Bobby Witt	100
3	Fergie Jenkins	72
4	Kevin Brown	64
5	Jose Guzman	62
6	Danny Darwin	52
7	Kenny Rogers	51
8	Frank Tanana	49
9	Jon Matlack	45
10	Gaylord Perry	43
	Doc Medich	43
12	Jeff Russell	40
13	Nolan Ryan	39
14	Roger Pavlik	38
15	Mike Mason	37
16	Jim Bibby	35
17	Rick Honeycutt	33
18	Steve Comer	29
19	Jim Umbarger	28
	Doyle Alexander	28

Winning Percentage
(minimum 50 decisions)

1	Darren Oliver	.636
2	Kenny Rogers	.579
3	Steve Comer	.574
4	Nolan Ryan	.567
5	Fergie Jenkins	.564
6	Kevin Brown	.549
7	Roger Pavlik	.548
8	Doc Medich	.538
9	Charlie Hough	.531
10	Gaylord Perry	.527
11	Steve Hargan	.526
12	Doyle Alexander	.525
13	Jose Guzman	.516
14	Danny Darwin	.514
15	Jeff Russell	.512
16	Steve Foucault	.510
17	Bobby Witt	.497
18	Jon Matlack	.489
19	Rick Honeycutt	.484
20	Two tied at	.461

Games

1	Jeff Russell	445
2	Kenny Rogers	376
3	Charlie Hough	344
4	Bobby Witt	262
5	Mitch Williams	232
6	Danny Darwin	224
7	Matt Whiteside	223
8	Steve Foucault	206
9	Fergie Jenkins	197
10	Kevin Brown	187
11	Dale Mohorcic	175
12	Greg Harris	173
13	Dave Schmidt	172
14	Jose Guzman	159
15	Jon Matlack	158
16	Steve Comer	151
17	Mike Jeffcoat	149
18	Tom Henke	144
19	Ed Vosberg	138
20	Two tied at	132

Games Started

1	Charlie Hough	313
2	Bobby Witt	256
3	Fergie Jenkins	190
4	Kevin Brown	186
5	Jose Guzman	152
6	Nolan Ryan	129
7	Roger Pavlik	125
8	Jon Matlack	119
9	Doc Medich	114
10	Gaylord Perry	112
11	Frank Tanana	100
	Kenny Rogers	100
13	Danny Darwin	94
14	Mike Mason	86
15	Doyle Alexander	80
16	Jim Bibby	76
17	Rick Honeycutt	71
18	Darren Oliver	69
19	Steve Comer	62
20	Steve Hargan	61

Complete Games

1	Charlie Hough	98
2	Fergie Jenkins	90
3	Gaylord Perry	55
4	Kevin Brown	40
5	Bobby Witt	33
6	Jon Matlack	32
7	Bert Blyleven	29
8	Jim Bibby	26
9	Jose Guzman	24
10	Doc Medich	22
11	Danny Darwin	21
12	Doyle Alexander	19
	Frank Tanana	19
14	Steve Hargan	18
15	Rick Honeycutt	17
16	Nolan Ryan	15
17	Jim Umbarger	14
	Kenny Rogers	14
19	Jackie Brown	13
	Mike Smithson	13

Shutouts

1	Fergie Jenkins	17
2	Gaylord Perry	12
3	Bert Blyleven	11
	Charlie Hough	11
5	Jim Bibby	8
6	Doc Medich	7
7	Kevin Brown	6
	Nolan Ryan	6
9	Jim Umbarger	5
	Danny Darwin	5
	Rick Honeycutt	5
	Bobby Witt	5
13	Jackie Brown	4
	Steve Hargan	4
	Jon Matlack	4
16	Six tied at	3

Saves

1	Jeff Russell	134
2	Tom Henke	58
3	Jim Kern	37
4	Steve Foucault	35
5	Mitch Williams	32
6	Greg Harris	31
	Mike Henneman	31
	John Wetteland	31
9	Dale Mohorcic	28
	Kenny Rogers	28
11	Dave Schmidt	26
12	Sparky Lyle	21
13	Horacio Pina	15
	Paul Lindblad	15
	Adrian Devine	15
	Danny Darwin	15
17	Dave Tobik	14
18	Steve Comer	13
19	Three tied at	12

Innings Pitched

1	Charlie Hough	2,308.0
2	Bobby Witt	1,611.1
3	Fergie Jenkins	1,410.1
4	Kevin Brown	1,278.2
5	Jose Guzman	1,013.2
6	Kenny Rogers	943.1
7	Jon Matlack	915.0
8	Danny Darwin	872.0
9	Nolan Ryan	840.0
10	Gaylord Perry	827.1
11	Doc Medich	790.1
12	Jeff Russell	752.2
13	Roger Pavlik	729.0
14	Frank Tanana	677.2
15	Steve Comer	575.2
16	Mike Mason	561.0
17	Doyle Alexander	541.1
18	Jim Bibby	529.0
19	Steve Hargan	512.2
20	Rick Honeycutt	491.1

Walks

1	Bobby Witt	968
2	Charlie Hough	965
3	Kevin Brown	428
4	Jose Guzman	395
5	Kenny Rogers	370
6	Nolan Ryan	353
7	Roger Pavlik	346
8	Fergie Jenkins	315
9	Danny Darwin	298
10	Jeff Russell	295
11	Jim Bibby	257
12	Doc Medich	251
13	Darren Oliver	226
14	Doyle Alexander	222
15	Mitch Williams	220
16	Jon Matlack	219
	Mike Mason	217
18	Steve Comer	210
19	Frank Tanana	208
20	Gaylord Perry	190

Strikeouts

1	Charlie Hough	1,452
2	Bobby Witt	1,375
3	Nolan Ryan	939
4	Fergie Jenkins	895
5	Kevin Brown	742
6	Jose Guzman	715
7	Kenny Rogers	680
8	Gaylord Perry	575
9	Danny Darwin	566
10	Roger Pavlik	518
11	Jon Matlack	493
12	Jeff Russell	474
13	Frank Tanana	388
14	Jim Bibby	341
15	Mike Mason	328
16	Bert Blyleven	326
17	Doc Medich	322
18	Greg Harris	312
19	Darren Oliver	309
20	Mitch Williams	280

Strikeouts/9 Innings
(minimum 500 Innings Pitched)

1	Nolan Ryan	10.06
2	Bobby Witt	7.68
3	Kenny Rogers	6.49
4	Roger Pavlik	6.40
5	Jose Guzman	6.35
6	Gaylord Perry	6.26
7	Danny Darwin	5.84
8	Jim Bibby	5.80
9	Fergie Jenkins	5.71
10	Jeff Russell	5.67
11	Charlie Hough	5.66
12	Mike Mason	5.26
13	Kevin Brown	5.22
14	Frank Tanana	5.15
15	Jon Matlack	4.85
16	Steve Hargan	4.63
17	Doc Medich	3.67
18	Doyle Alexander	3.54
19	Steve Comer	3.20

ERA
(minimum 500 Innings Pitched)

1	Gaylord Perry	3.26
2	Jon Matlack	3.41
3	Nolan Ryan	3.43
4	Fergie Jenkins	3.56
5	Charlie Hough	3.68
6	Danny Darwin	3.72
7	Jeff Russell	3.73
8	Steve Comer	3.80
9	Kevin Brown	3.81
10	Frank Tanana	3.81
11	Kenny Rogers	3.88
12	Doyle Alexander	3.89
13	Jose Guzman	3.90
14	Steve Hargan	3.93
15	Doc Medich	3.95
16	Jim Bibby	4.25
17	Mike Mason	4.38
18	Roger Pavlik	4.59
19	Bobby Witt	4.73

Component ERA
(minimum 500 Innings Pitched)

1	Nolan Ryan	2.56
2	Gaylord Perry	3.05
3	Fergie Jenkins	3.26
4	Danny Darwin	3.50
5	Charlie Hough	3.58
6	Jon Matlack	3.63
7	Frank Tanana	3.73
8	Jim Bibby	3.75
9	Doc Medich	3.84
10	Kevin Brown	3.93
11	Doyle Alexander	3.94
12	Jeff Russell	3.96
13	Jose Guzman	3.97
14	Kenny Rogers	3.98
15	Steve Hargan	4.03
16	Steve Comer	4.15
17	Mike Mason	4.25
18	Roger Pavlik	4.59
19	Bobby Witt	4.66

Opponent Average
(minimum 500 Innings Pitched)

1	Nolan Ryan	.197
2	Charlie Hough	.233
3	Jim Bibby	.239
4	Fergie Jenkins	.249
5	Gaylord Perry	.251
6	Danny Darwin	.252
7	Frank Tanana	.254
8	Jose Guzman	.255
9	Bobby Witt	.255
10	Kenny Rogers	.256
11	Jeff Russell	.257
12	Doyle Alexander	.259
13	Roger Pavlik	.262
14	Mike Mason	.266
15	Kevin Brown	.267
16	Jon Matlack	.272
17	Doc Medich	.273
18	Steve Hargan	.275
19	Steve Comer	.275

Opponent OBP
(minimum 500 Innings Pitched)

1	Nolan Ryan	.286
2	Fergie Jenkins	.292
3	Gaylord Perry	.296
4	Frank Tanana	.312
5	Jon Matlack	.314
6	Charlie Hough	.315
7	Danny Darwin	.316
8	Jose Guzman	.326
9	Kenny Rogers	.327
10	Steve Hargan	.328
11	Jeff Russell	.328
12	Doc Medich	.329
13	Jim Bibby	.330
14	Doyle Alexander	.330
15	Kevin Brown	.330
16	Mike Mason	.333
17	Steve Comer	.340
18	Roger Pavlik	.346
19	Bobby Witt	.356

Senators/Rangers Franchise Batting Leaders—Single Season

Games

	Player	Year	
1	Al Oliver	1980	163
2	Buddy Bell	1979	162
	George Wright	1983	162
	Ruben Sierra	1989	162
5	Frank Howard	1969	161
	Frank Howard	1970	161
	Toby Harrah	1974	161
	Ruben Sierra	1991	161
9	Rafael Palmeiro	1993	160
10	Toby Harrah	1977	159
	Pete O'Brien	1985	159
	Pete O'Brien	1987	159
	Ruben Sierra	1990	159
	Rafael Palmeiro	1991	159
	Rafael Palmeiro	1992	159
16	Seven tied at		158

At-Bats

	Player	Year	
1	Buddy Bell	1979	670
2	Ruben Sierra	1991	661
3	Al Oliver	1980	656
4	Ruben Sierra	1987	643
5	Ivan Rodriguez	1996	639
6	Del Unser	1968	635
7	George Wright	1983	634
	Ruben Sierra	1989	634
9	Rafael Palmeiro	1991	631
10	Mickey Rivers	1980	630
11	Darryl Hamilton	1996	627
12	Ed Brinkman	1970	625
13	Alex Johnson	1973	624
14	Buddy Bell	1983	618
15	Ruben Sierra	1988	615
16	Larry Parrish	1984	613
17	Ruben Sierra	1990	608
	Rafael Palmeiro	1992	608
19	Jeff Burroughs	1976	604
20	Gary Ward	1984	602

Runs

	Player	Year	
1	Rafael Palmeiro	1993	124
2	Ivan Rodriguez	1996	116
3	Rafael Palmeiro	1991	115
4	Rusty Greer	1997	112
5	Frank Howard	1969	111
6	Ruben Sierra	1991	110
7	Julio Franco	1991	108
8	Oddibe McDowell	1986	105
	Juan Gonzalez	1993	105
10	Bump Wills	1980	102
11	Ruben Sierra	1989	101
12	Mike Hargrove	1977	98
	Dean Palmer	1996	98
	Ivan Rodriguez	1997	98
15	Gary Ward	1984	97
	Ruben Sierra	1987	97
17	Mickey Rivers	1980	96
	Al Oliver	1980	96
	Julio Franco	1990	96
	Rusty Greer	1996	96

Hits

	Player	Year	
1	Mickey Rivers	1980	210
2	Al Oliver	1980	209
3	Ruben Sierra	1991	203
	Rafael Palmeiro	1991	203
5	Julio Franco	1991	201
6	Buddy Bell	1979	200
7	Ruben Sierra	1989	194
8	Rusty Greer	1997	193
9	Ivan Rodriguez	1996	192
10	Rafael Palmeiro	1990	191
11	Ivan Rodriguez	1997	187
12	Darryl Hamilton	1996	184
13	Rusty Greer	1996	180
14	Alex Johnson	1973	179
15	Rafael Palmeiro	1993	176
16	Frank Howard	1969	175
	George Wright	1983	175
	Larry Parrish	1984	175
19	Buddy Bell	1984	174
	Otis Nixon	1995	174

Doubles

	Player	Year	
1	Rafael Palmeiro	1991	49
2	Ivan Rodriguez	1996	47
3	Ruben Sierra	1991	44
4	Al Oliver	1980	43
5	Buddy Bell	1979	42
	Larry Parrish	1984	42
	Rusty Greer	1997	42
8	Rusty Greer	1996	41
9	Rafael Palmeiro	1993	40
10	Ruben Sierra	1990	37
11	Buddy Bell	1984	36
12	Al Oliver	1978	35
	Buddy Bell	1983	35
	Ruben Sierra	1987	35
	Ruben Sierra	1989	35
	Rafael Palmeiro	1990	35
17	Pete O'Brien	1985	34
	Scott Fletcher	1986	34
	Juan Gonzalez	1991	34
	Ivan Rodriguez	1997	34

Triples

	Player	Year	
1	Ruben Sierra	1989	14
2	Chuck Hinton	1963	12
3	Ed Stroud	1968	10
	Ruben Sierra	1986	10
	David Hulse	1993	10
6	Marty Keough	1961	9
	Ed Brinkman	1966	9
8	Don Blasingame	1965	8
	Del Unser	1969	8
	Gary Pettis	1990	8
11	Chuck Hinton	1964	7
	Fred Valentine	1966	7
	Del Unser	1968	7
	Vic Harris	1973	7
	Lenny Randle	1975	7
	Bert Campaneris	1977	7
	Gary Ward	1984	7
	Gary Ward	1985	7
	Oddibe McDowell	1986	7
	Cecil Espy	1989	7

Home Runs

	Player	Year	
1	Frank Howard	1969	48
2	Juan Gonzalez	1996	47
3	Juan Gonzalez	1993	46
4	Frank Howard	1968	44
	Frank Howard	1970	44
6	Juan Gonzalez	1992	43
7	Juan Gonzalez	1997	42
8	Dean Palmer	1996	38
9	Rafael Palmeiro	1993	37
10	Frank Howard	1967	36
11	Dean Palmer	1993	33
12	Larry Parrish	1987	32
	Mickey Tettleton	1995	32
14	Jose Canseco	1994	31
15	Mike Epstein	1969	30
	Jeff Burroughs	1973	30
	Pete Incaviglia	1986	30
	Ruben Sierra	1987	30
19	Three tied at		29

RBI

	Player	Year	
1	Juan Gonzalez	1996	144
2	Juan Gonzalez	1997	131
3	Frank Howard	1970	126
4	Ruben Sierra	1989	119
5	Jeff Burroughs	1974	118
	Juan Gonzalez	1993	118
7	Al Oliver	1980	117
8	Ruben Sierra	1991	116
9	Frank Howard	1969	111
10	Ruben Sierra	1987	109
	Juan Gonzalez	1992	109
12	Dean Palmer	1996	107
13	Frank Howard	1968	106
14	Rafael Palmeiro	1993	105
15	Juan Gonzalez	1991	102
16	Buddy Bell	1979	101
	Larry Parrish	1984	101
18	Larry Parrish	1987	100
	Rusty Greer	1996	100
20	Kevin Elster	1996	99

Walks

	Player	Year	
1	Frank Howard	1970	132
2	Toby Harrah	1985	113
3	Toby Harrah	1977	109
4	Mike Hargrove	1978	107
	Mickey Tettleton	1995	107
6	Mike Hargrove	1977	103
7	Frank Howard	1969	102
8	Toby Harrah	1975	98
9	Mike Hargrove	1976	97
10	Mickey Tettleton	1996	95
11	Jeff Burroughs	1974	91
	Toby Harrah	1976	91
13	Pete O'Brien	1986	87
	Mark McLemore	1996	87
15	Mike Epstein	1969	85
16	Toby Harrah	1978	83
	Rusty Greer	1997	83
18	Julio Franco	1990	82
19	Three tied at		79

Strikeouts

	Player	Year	
1	Pete Incaviglia	1986	185
2	Pete Incaviglia	1987	168
3	Frank Howard	1967	155
	Jeff Burroughs	1975	155
5	Larry Parrish	1987	154
	Dean Palmer	1992	154
	Dean Palmer	1993	154
8	Pete Incaviglia	1988	153
9	Don Lock	1963	151
10	Benji Gil	1995	147
11	Pete Incaviglia	1990	146
12	Dean Palmer	1996	145
13	Juan Gonzalez	1992	143
14	Frank Howard	1968	141
15	Kevin Elster	1996	138
16	Don Lock	1964	137
	Mickey Tettleton	1996	137
18	Pete Incaviglia	1989	136
19	Don Lock	1966	126
20	Frank Howard	1970	125

Stolen Bases

	Player	Year	
1	Bump Wills	1978	52
2	Dave Nelson	1972	51
3	Otis Nixon	1995	50
4	Cecil Espy	1989	45
5	Billy Sample	1983	44
6	Dave Nelson	1973	43
7	Gary Pettis	1990	38
8	Bobby Bonds	1978	37
9	Julio Franco	1991	36
10	Bump Wills	1979	35
11	Bump Wills	1980	34
12	Wayne Tolleson	1983	33
	Oddibe McDowell	1986	33
	Cecil Espy	1988	33
	Oddibe McDowell	1988	33
16	Toby Harrah	1978	31
	Julio Franco	1990	31
18	Lenny Randle	1976	30
19	Three tied at		29

Runs Created

	Player	Year	
1	Juan Gonzalez	1993	130
2	Frank Howard	1969	128
3	Rafael Palmeiro	1993	127
4	Ruben Sierra	1989	125
5	Ruben Sierra	1991	121
6	Frank Howard	1970	120
7	Juan Gonzalez	1996	116
	Rusty Greer	1997	116
9	Rusty Greer	1996	114
10	Frank Howard	1968	110
	Jeff Burroughs	1974	110
	Rafael Palmeiro	1991	110
13	Julio Franco	1991	109
14	Toby Harrah	1977	107
	Julio Franco	1989	107
16	Toby Harrah	1975	106
	Mike Hargrove	1977	106
18	Al Oliver	1980	105
19	Juan Gonzalez	1997	104
20	Three tied at		98

Runs Created/27 Outs

(minimum 3.1 Plate Appearances/Tm Gm)

	Player	Year	
1	Juan Gonzalez	1993	9.10
2	Will Clark	1994	8.77
3	Juan Gonzalez	1996	8.14
4	Rusty Greer	1996	8.06
5	Frank Howard	1969	7.72
6	Rafael Palmeiro	1993	7.70
7	Frank Howard	1970	7.43
8	Ruben Sierra	1989	7.32
9	Rusty Greer	1997	7.30
10	Toby Harrah	1975	7.27
11	Will Clark	1995	7.26
12	Mike Hargrove	1977	7.20
13	Mickey Tettleton	1995	7.20
14	Julio Franco	1991	7.16
15	Jeff Burroughs	1974	7.10
16	Juan Gonzalez	1997	7.04
17	Julio Franco	1989	7.00
18	Jose Canseco	1994	6.84
19	Toby Harrah	1977	6.73
20	Ruben Sierra	1991	6.71

Batting Average

(minimum 3.1 Plate Appearances/Tm Gm)

	Player	Year	
1	Julio Franco	1991	.341
2	Mickey Rivers	1980	.333
3	Rusty Greer	1996	.332
4	Will Clark	1994	.329
5	Buddy Bell	1980	.329
6	Al Oliver	1978	.324
7	Al Oliver	1979	.323
8	Rafael Palmeiro	1991	.322
9	Rusty Greer	1997	.321
10	Rafael Palmeiro	1990	.319
11	Al Oliver	1980	.319
12	Julio Franco	1989	.316
13	Buddy Bell	1984	.315
14	Juan Gonzalez	1996	.314
15	Ivan Rodriguez	1997	.313
16	Chuck Hinton	1962	.310
17	Juan Gonzalez	1993	.310
18	Al Oliver	1981	.309
19	Ruben Sierra	1991	.307
20	Ruben Sierra	1989	.306

On-Base Percentage

(minimum 3.1 Plate Appearances/Tm Gm)

	Player	Year	
1	Toby Harrah	1985	.432
2	Will Clark	1994	.431
3	Mike Hargrove	1977	.420
4	Frank Howard	1970	.416
5	Julio Franco	1991	.408
6	Rusty Greer	1997	.405
7	Toby Harrah	1975	.403
8	Frank Howard	1969	.402
9	Jeff Burroughs	1974	.397
10	Rusty Greer	1996	.397
11	Mike Hargrove	1976	.397
12	Mickey Tettleton	1995	.396
13	Mike Hargrove	1975	.395
14	Toby Harrah	1977	.393
15	Will Clark	1995	.389
16	Mark McLemore	1996	.389
17	Rafael Palmeiro	1991	.389
18	Mike Hargrove	1978	.388
19	Julio Franco	1989	.386
20	Jose Canseco	1994	.386

Slugging Percentage

(minimum 3.1 Plate Appearances/Tm Gm)

	Player	Year	
1	Juan Gonzalez	1996	.643
2	Juan Gonzalez	1993	.632
3	Juan Gonzalez	1997	.589
4	Frank Howard	1969	.574
5	Rafael Palmeiro	1993	.554
6	Jose Canseco	1994	.552
7	Frank Howard	1968	.552
8	Frank Howard	1970	.546
9	Ruben Sierra	1989	.543
10	Rafael Palmeiro	1991	.532
11	Rusty Greer	1997	.531
12	Rusty Greer	1996	.530
13	Juan Gonzalez	1992	.529
14	Dean Palmer	1996	.527
15	Frank Howard	1967	.511
16	Mickey Tettleton	1995	.510
17	Larry Parrish	1986	.509
18	Jeff Burroughs	1974	.504
19	Dean Palmer	1993	.503
20	Ruben Sierra	1991	.502

Senators/Rangers Franchise Pitching Leaders—Single Season

Wins

1	Fergie Jenkins	1974	25
2	Kevin Brown	1992	21
3	Jim Bibby	1974	19
4	Fergie Jenkins	1978	18
	Charlie Hough	1987	18
6	Fergie Jenkins	1975	17
	Doyle Alexander	1977	17
	Steve Comer	1979	17
	Charlie Hough	1986	17
	Bobby Witt	1990	17
	Kenny Rogers	1995	17
12	Dick Bosman	1970	16
	Fergie Jenkins	1979	16
	Charlie Hough	1982	16
	Charlie Hough	1984	16
	Nolan Ryan	1989	16
	Jose Guzman	1992	16
	Kenny Rogers	1993	16
	Bobby Witt	1996	16
	Ken Hill	1996	16

Losses

1	Denny McLain	1971	22
2	Don Rudolph	1963	19
	Jim Bibby	1974	19
4	Joe McClain	1961	18
	Fergie Jenkins	1975	18
	Frank Tanana	1982	18
7	Rick Honeycutt	1982	17
8	Bennie Daniels	1962	16
	Joe Coleman	1968	16
	Dick Bosman	1971	16
	Charlie Hough	1985	16
	Charlie Hough	1988	16
13	Buster Narum	1964	15
	Phil Ortega	1965	15
	Frank Tanana	1984	15
	Mike Mason	1985	15
	Jose Guzman	1986	15
	Paul Kilgus	1988	15
	Kevin Gross	1995	15
20	Twelve tied at		14

Winning Percentage
(minimum 15 decisions)

1	Danny Darwin	1980	.765
2	Dick Bosman	1969	.737
3	Jim Kern	1979	.722
4	Kenny Rogers	1995	.708
5	Darren Oliver	1996	.700
6	Fergie Jenkins	1978	.692
7	Steve Comer	1978	.688
8	Fergie Jenkins	1974	.676
9	Nolan Ryan	1991	.667
	Roger Pavlik	1993	.667
11	Kevin Brown	1992	.656
12	Roger Pavlik	1996	.652
13	Jose Guzman	1991	.650
14	Adrian Devine	1977	.647
	Rick Honeycutt	1981	.647
16	Rick Honeycutt	1983	.636
17	Casey Cox	1969	.632
18	Charlie Hough	1986	.630
	Bobby Witt	1990	.630
20	Five tied at		.625

Games

1	Mitch Williams	1987	85
2	Kenny Rogers	1992	81
3	Mitch Williams	1986	80
4	Ron Kline	1965	74
	Dale Mohorcic	1987	74
6	Greg Harris	1986	73
	Kenny Rogers	1989	73
8	Darold Knowles	1970	71
	Jim Kern	1979	71
	Jeff Russell	1989	71
11	Mike Jeffcoat	1991	70
12	Steve Foucault	1974	69
	Kenny Rogers	1990	69
14	Jeff Russell	1991	68
15	Sparky Lyle	1979	67
	Mitch Williams	1988	67
17	Casey Cox	1966	66
	Paul Lindblad	1972	66
	Tom Henke	1993	66
20	Roger McDowell	1995	64

Games Started

1	Jim Bibby	1974	41
	Fergie Jenkins	1974	41
3	Charlie Hough	1987	40
4	Fergie Jenkins	1975	37
	Fergie Jenkins	1979	37
6	Claude Osteen	1964	36
	Joe Coleman	1969	36
	Steve Comer	1979	36
	Charlie Hough	1984	36
10	Dick Bosman	1971	35
	Frank Tanana	1984	35
	Kevin Brown	1992	35
	Ken Hill	1996	35
14	Eleven tied at		34

Complete Games

1	Fergie Jenkins	1974	29
2	Fergie Jenkins	1975	22
3	Gaylord Perry	1976	21
4	Jon Matlack	1978	18
5	Charlie Hough	1984	17
6	Fergie Jenkins	1978	16
7	Gaylord Perry	1975	15
	Bert Blyleven	1977	15
9	Bert Blyleven	1976	14
	Charlie Hough	1985	14
11	Claude Osteen	1964	13
	Gaylord Perry	1977	13
	Charlie Hough	1987	13
	Bobby Witt	1988	13
15	Seven tied at		12

Shutouts

1	Fergie Jenkins	1974	6
	Bert Blyleven	1976	6
3	Jim Bibby	1974	5
	Bert Blyleven	1977	5
5	Tom Cheney	1963	4
	Frank Bertaina	1967	4
	Camilo Pascual	1968	4
	Joe Coleman	1969	4
	Gaylord Perry	1975	4
	Fergie Jenkins	1975	4
	Gaylord Perry	1977	4
	Fergie Jenkins	1978	4
	Doc Medich	1981	4
14	Ten tied at		3

Saves

1	Tom Henke	1993	40
2	Jeff Russell	1989	38
3	Mike Henneman	1996	31
	John Wetteland	1997	31
5	Jeff Russell	1991	30
6	Ron Kline	1965	29
	Jim Kern	1979	29
8	Jeff Russell	1992	28
9	Darold Knowles	1970	27
10	Ron Kline	1966	23
11	Greg Harris	1986	20
	Jeff Russell	1995	20
13	Mitch Williams	1988	18
14	Ron Kline	1963	17
15	Dennis Higgins	1969	16
	Dale Mohorcic	1987	16
17	Horacio Pina	1972	15
	Adrian Devine	1977	15
	Kenny Rogers	1990	15
	Tom Henke	1994	15

Innings Pitched

1	Fergie Jenkins	1974	328.1
2	Charlie Hough	1987	285.1
3	Fergie Jenkins	1975	270.0
	Jon Matlack	1978	270.0
5	Charlie Hough	1984	266.0
6	Kevin Brown	1992	265.2
7	Jim Bibby	1974	264.0
8	Fergie Jenkins	1979	259.0
9	Claude Osteen	1964	257.0
10	Charlie Hough	1983	252.0
	Charlie Hough	1988	252.0
12	Ken Hill	1996	250.2
13	Gaylord Perry	1976	250.1
	Charlie Hough	1985	250.1
15	Fergie Jenkins	1978	249.0
16	Joe Coleman	1969	247.2
17	Frank Tanana	1984	246.1
18	Pete Richert	1966	245.2
19	Steve Comer	1979	242.1
20	Nolan Ryan	1989	239.1

Walks

1	Bobby Witt	1986	143
2	Bobby Witt	1987	140
3	Edwin Correa	1986	126
	Charlie Hough	1988	126
5	Charlie Hough	1987	124
6	Charlie Hough	1990	119
7	Bobby Witt	1989	114
8	Jim Bibby	1974	113
9	Bobby Witt	1990	110
10	Jim Bibby	1973	106
11	Rich Hand	1972	103
12	Bobby Witt	1988	101
13	Joe Coleman	1969	100
14	Nolan Ryan	1989	98
15	Tom Cheney	1962	97
	Phil Ortega	1965	97
17	Bobby Witt	1996	96
18	Four tied at		95

Strikeouts

1	Nolan Ryan	1989	301
2	Nolan Ryan	1990	232
3	Fergie Jenkins	1974	225
4	Charlie Hough	1987	223
5	Bobby Witt	1990	221
6	Nolan Ryan	1991	203
7	Pete Richert	1966	195
8	Edwin Correa	1986	189
9	Joe Coleman	1969	182
	Bert Blyleven	1977	182
11	Jose Guzman	1992	179
12	Gaylord Perry	1977	177
13	Bobby Witt	1986	174
	Charlie Hough	1988	174
15	Kevin Brown	1992	173
16	Ken Hill	1996	170
17	Bobby Witt	1989	166
18	Fergie Jenkins	1979	164
	Charlie Hough	1984	164
20	Pete Richert	1965	161

Strikeouts/9 Innings
(minimum 1 Inning Pitched/Tm Gm)

1	Nolan Ryan	1989	11.32
2	Nolan Ryan	1991	10.56
3	Nolan Ryan	1990	10.24
4	Bobby Witt	1990	8.96
5	Edwin Correa	1986	8.41
6	Jim Bibby	1973	7.74
7	Bobby Witt	1989	7.69
8	Bobby Witt	1988	7.64
9	Tom Cheney	1962	7.63
10	Pete Richert	1965	7.47
11	Gaylord Perry	1975	7.24
12	Jose Guzman	1992	7.19
13	Pete Richert	1966	7.14
14	Roger Pavlik	1993	7.09
15	Bobby Witt	1996	7.08
16	Charlie Hough	1987	7.03
17	Roger Pavlik	1995	7.00
18	Bert Blyleven	1977	6.98
19	Jose Guzman	1988	6.84
20	Pete Broberg	1972	6.79

ERA
(minimum 1 Inning Pitched/Tm Gm)

1	Mike Paul	1972	2.17
2	Dick Bosman	1969	2.19
3	Jon Matlack	1978	2.27
4	Dick Donovan	1961	2.40
5	Rick Honeycutt	1983	2.42
6	Pete Richert	1965	2.60
7	Camilo Pascual	1968	2.69
8	Bert Blyleven	1977	2.72
9	Bert Blyleven	1976	2.76
10	Casey Cox	1969	2.78
11	Fergie Jenkins	1974	2.82
12	Dock Ellis	1977	2.90
13	Nolan Ryan	1991	2.91
14	Dick Bosman	1970	3.00
15	Phil Ortega	1967	3.03
16	Gaylord Perry	1975	3.03
17	Fergie Jenkins	1978	3.04
18	Jose Guzman	1991	3.08
9	Doc Medich	1981	3.08
20	Jim Umbarger	1976	3.15

Component ERA
(minimum 1 Inning Pitched/Tm Gm)

1	Nolan Ryan	1991	1.98
2	Dick Bosman	1969	2.14
3	Dick Donovan	1961	2.21
4	Nolan Ryan	1990	2.28
5	Nolan Ryan	1989	2.31
6	Gaylord Perry	1975	2.37
7	Fergie Jenkins	1974	2.38
8	Bert Blyleven	1977	2.53
9	Jon Matlack	1978	2.65
10	Gaylord Perry	1976	2.70
11	Rick Honeycutt	1981	2.71
12	Fergie Jenkins	1978	2.71
13	Phil Ortega	1967	2.72
14	Charlie Hough	1985	2.77
15	Bert Blyleven	1976	2.77
16	Mike Paul	1972	2.79
17	Pete Richert	1966	2.80
18	Pete Richert	1965	2.85
19	Mike Mason	1984	2.88
20	Phil Ortega	1966	2.88

Opponent Average
(minimum 1 Inning Pitched/Tm Gm)

1	Nolan Ryan	1991	.172
2	Nolan Ryan	1989	.187
3	Nolan Ryan	1990	.188
4	Jim Bibby	1973	.192
5	Pete Richert	1965	.210
6	Tom Cheney	1962	.213
7	Bert Blyleven	1977	.214
8	Charlie Hough	1985	.215
9	Pete Richert	1966	.215
10	Bobby Witt	1988	.216
11	Danny Darwin	1981	.218
12	Phil Ortega	1966	.218
13	Dick Bosman	1969	.220
14	Charlie Hough	1986	.221
15	Charlie Hough	1988	.221
16	Charlie Hough	1987	.223
17	Edwin Correa	1986	.223
18	Dick Donovan	1961	.224
19	Rich Hand	1972	.226
20	Gaylord Perry	1975	.227

Opponent OBP
(minimum 1 Inning Pitched/Tm Gm)

1	Dick Bosman	1969	.260
2	Fergie Jenkins	1974	.262
3	Nolan Ryan	1991	.263
4	Gaylord Perry	1975	.267
5	Dick Donovan	1961	.267
6	Nolan Ryan	1990	.267
7	Pete Richert	1966	.270
8	Rick Honeycutt	1981	.272
9	Phil Ortega	1966	.274
10	Nolan Ryan	1989	.275
11	Fergie Jenkins	1978	.278
12	Bert Blyleven	1977	.278
13	Mike McCormick	1966	.281
14	Jon Matlack	1978	.283
15	Charlie Hough	1985	.283
16	Gaylord Perry	1976	.285
17	Mike Mason	1984	.285
18	Phil Ortega	1967	.286
19	Camilo Pascual	1967	.288
20	Bert Blyleven	1976	.292

Rangers Capsule

Best Season: *1996.* The Rangers won the American League West with a 90-72 record and went to the postseason for the first time in the history of the franchise.

Worst Season: *1973.* Despite the fact that they began the season with Whitey Herzog at the helm and ended it under the direction of Billy Martin, the Rangers lost 105 games, 14 more than any other club in the league.

Best Player: *Juan Gonzalez.*

Best Pitcher: *Charlie Hough.* The ageless knuckleballer was a consistent winner for many years on losing teams.

Best Reliever: *Jeff Russell.*

Best Defensive Player: *Jim Sundberg.* Only two AL catchers have ever won six consecutive Gold Gloves, and both of them have done it with the Rangers: Jim Sundberg and Ivan Rodriguez. Pudge hasn't excelled for quite as long, so the nod goes to Sundberg.

Hall of Famers: *Ferguson Jenkins* and *Gaylord Perry.* Nolan Ryan will join them when he becomes eligible.

Franchise All-Star Team:

C	Ivan Rodriguez		**LF**	Jeff Burroughs
1B	Rafael Palmeiro		**CF**	Oddibe McDowell
2B	Julio Franco		**RF**	Ruben Sierra
3B	Buddy Bell		**DH**	Juan Gonzalez
SS	Toby Harrah		**SP**	Charlie Hough
			RP	Jeff Russell

Biggest Flake: *Jim Kern.*

Strangest Career: *Lee Stevens.* The lefthanded first baseman was billed as a potential star when he first came up with the Angels, but he hit only .225 in 618 at-bats spread over three years. After spending a few seasons in Japan, he came back to the United States and had a huge season in the Rangers' system in '96. The following year, he made the big club and had the kind of year that people had stopped expecting from him long ago.

What Might Have Been: *Bobby Witt.* He came up as a hard-throwing wild man with vast potential, but for his first four-and-a-half seasons in the majors, he fought his control and was more of a curiosity than anything. Then, it suddenly came together for him over the second half of 1990. Over his last 19 starts, he went 14-2, 2.40. But he suffered a partially torn rotator cuff the following spring, and irreversibly reverted to his pre-1990 form.

Best Trade: *Julio Franco.* The Rangers acquired Franco from the Indians after the 1988 season for three players who never amounted to much afterward: Pete O'Brien, Oddibe McDowell and Jerry Browne. Franco had four good years for the Rangers and won the AL batting title in 1991.

Worst Trade: *Harold Baines.* To pry him loose from the White Sox in July 1989, they gave up outfielder Sammy Sosa, shortstop Scott Fletcher and lefthander Wilson Alvarez. Thirteen months later, they traded Baines to the A's for virtually nothing. Alvarez and Sosa became stars.

Best-Looking Player: *Billy Sample.*

Ugliest Player: *Mickey Tettleton.*

Best Nickname: *Ivan "Pudge" Rodriguez.* If it were anyone else, Carlton Fisk would be entitled to take offense at the usurpation of his nickname.

Most Unappreciated Player: *Rafael Palmeiro.* The Rangers let him leave via free agency so they could sign Will Clark instead.

Most Overrated Player: *Dean Palmer.* Power was the only thing he could put on his résumé, but for some reason, the Texas fans took to the stoic third baseman.

Most Admirable Star: *Nolan Ryan.*

Least Admirable Star: *Jose Canseco.*

Best Season, Player: *Juan Gonzalez, 1996.* Forty-seven homers, 144 RBI in 134 games, and one MVP trophy. In Texas' first trip to the postseason, he smashed five home runs in four games.

Best Season, Pitcher: *Fergie Jenkins, 1974,* with a franchise-record 25 victories.

Most Impressive Individual Record: *Dale Mohorcic* set an AL record and tied the major league record by relieving in 13 consecutive games in August 1986.

Biggest Tragedy: *Danny Thompson.* The infielder was acquired by the Rangers during the 1976 season. He died of leukemia that winter.

Fan Favorite: *Nolan Ryan.*

—Mat Olkin

Toronto Blue Jays (1977-1997)

Year	Lg	Pos	W-L	Pct	GB	Manager	Att.	R	OR	HR	Avg	OBP	Slg	Opponent HR	Opponent Avg	Opponent OBP	ERA	Park Index Runs	Park Index HR
1977	AL	7th-E	54-107	.335	45.5	Roy Hartsfield	1,701,052	605	822	100	.252	.316	.365	152	.278	.350	4.57	109	125
1978	AL	7th-E	59-102	.366	40.0	Roy Hartsfield	1,562,585	590	775	98	.250	.308	.359	149	.279	.351	4.54	104	101
1979	AL	7th-E	53-109	.327	50.5	Roy Hartsfield	1,431,651	613	862	95	.251	.311	.363	165	.281	.353	4.82	111	91
1980	AL	7th-E	67-95	.414	36.0	Bobby Mattick	1,400,327	624	762	126	.251	.309	.383	135	.274	.348	4.19	101	101
1981	AL	7th-E	16-42	.276	19.0	Bobby Mattick													
	AL	7th-E	21-27	.438	7.5	Bobby Mattick	755,083	329	466	61	.226	.286	.330	72	.252	.326	3.81	126	129
1982	AL	6th-E	78-84	.481	17.0	Bobby Cox	1,275,978	651	701	106	.262	.314	.383	147	.257	.319	3.95	118	109
1983	AL	4th-E	89-73	.549	9.0	Bobby Cox	1,930,415	795	726	167	.277	.338	.436	145	.259	.325	4.12	118	146
1984	AL	2nd-E	89-73	.549	15.0	Bobby Cox	2,110,009	750	696	143	.273	.331	.421	140	.257	.323	3.86	101	94
1985	AL	1st-E	99-62	.615	—	Bobby Cox	2,468,925	759	588	158	.269	.331	.425	147	.243	.306	3.31	97	102
1986	AL	4th-E	86-76	.531	9.5	Jimy Williams	2,455,477	809	733	181	.269	.329	.427	164	.261	.322	4.08	109	104
1987	AL	2nd-E	96-66	.593	2.0	Jimy Williams	2,778,429	845	655	215	.269	.336	.446	158	.244	.316	3.74	98	97
1988	AL	3rd-E	87-75	.537	2.0	Jimy Williams	2,595,175	763	680	158	.268	.332	.419	143	.256	.326	3.80	98	101
1989	AL	1st-E	89-73	.549	—	Jimy Williams/Cito Gaston	3,375,883	731	651	142	.260	.323	.398	99	.255	.317	3.58	86	90
1990	AL	2nd-E	86-76	.531	2.0	Cito Gaston	3,885,284	767	661	167	.265	.328	.419	143	.260	.317	3.84	103	130
1991	AL	1st-E	91-71	.562	—	Cito Gaston/Gene Tenace/Cito Gaston	4,001,527	684	622	133	.257	.322	.400	121	.238	.307	3.50	117	137
1992	AL	1st-E	96-66	.593	—	Cito Gaston	4,028,318	780	682	163	.263	.333	.414	124	.248	.318	3.92	98	94
1993	AL	1st-E	95-67	.586	—	Cito Gaston	4,057,947	847	742	159	.279	.350	.436	134	.261	.336	4.21	109	140
1994	AL	3rd-E	55-60	.478	16.0	Cito Gaston	2,907,933	566	579	115	.269	.336	.424	127	.266	.348	4.70	93	105
1995	AL	5th-E	56-88	.389	30.0	Cito Gaston	2,826,483	642	777	140	.260	.328	.409	145	.268	.356	4.88	100	114
1996	AL	4th-E	74-88	.457	18.0	Cito Gaston	2,559,563	766	809	177	.259	.331	.420	187	.266	.340	4.57	102	108
1997	AL	5th-E	76-86	.469	22.0	Cito Gaston/Mel Queen	2,589,299	654	694	147	.244	.310	.389	167	.263	.326	3.93	93	80

Team Nicknames: Toronto Blue Jays 1977-1997.

Team Ballparks: Exhibition Stadium 1977-1988, Exhibition Stadium & SkyDome (shared) 1989, SkyDome 1990-1997.

Toronto Blue Jays Individual Season Batting Leaders

Year	Batting Average		On-Base Percentage		Slugging Percentage		Home Runs		RBI		Stolen Bases	
1977	Bob Bailor	.310	Ron Fairly	.362	Ron Fairly	.465	Ron Fairly	19	Doug Ault / Ron Fairly	64	Bob Bailor	15
1978	Roy Howell	.270	John Mayberry	.329	John Mayberry	.416	John Mayberry	22	John Mayberry	70	Rick Bosetti	6
1979	Alfredo Griffin	.287	John Mayberry	.372	John Mayberry	.461	John Mayberry	21	John Mayberry	74	Alfredo Griffin	21
1980	Damaso Garcia	.278	John Mayberry	.349	John Mayberry	.473	John Mayberry	30	John Mayberry	82	Alfredo Griffin	18
1981	John Mayberry	.248	John Mayberry	.360	John Mayberry	.452	John Mayberry	17	John Mayberry / Lloyd Moseby	43	Damaso Garcia	13
1982	Damaso Garcia	.310	Damaso Garcia	.338	Willie Upshaw	.443	Willie Upshaw	21	Willie Upshaw	75	Damaso Garcia	54
1983	Lloyd Moseby	.315	Lloyd Moseby	.376	Willie Upshaw	.515	Jesse Barfield / Willie Upshaw	27	Willie Upshaw	104	Dave Collins / Damaso Garcia	31
1984	George Bell	.292	Lloyd Moseby	.368	George Bell	.498	George Bell	26	Lloyd Moseby	92	Dave Collins	60
1985	Jesse Barfield	.289	Jesse Barfield	.369	Jesse Barfield	.536	George Bell	28	George Bell	95	Lloyd Moseby	37
1986	Tony Fernandez	.310	Jesse Barfield	.368	Jesse Barfield	.559	Jesse Barfield	40	Jesse Barfield / George Bell	108	Lloyd Moseby	32
1987	Tony Fernandez	.322	Tony Fernandez	.379	George Bell	.605	George Bell	47	George Bell	134	Lloyd Moseby	39
1988	Tony Fernandez	.287	Fred McGriff	.376	Fred McGriff	.552	Fred McGriff	34	George Bell	97	Lloyd Moseby	31
1989	George Bell	.297	Fred McGriff	.399	Fred McGriff	.525	Fred McGriff	36	George Bell	104	Lloyd Moseby	24
1990	Fred McGriff	.300	Fred McGriff	.400	Fred McGriff	.530	Fred McGriff	35	Kelly Gruber	118	Tony Fernandez	26
1991	Roberto Alomar	.295	Roberto Alomar	.354	Joe Carter	.503	Joe Carter	33	Joe Carter	108	Roberto Alomar	53
1992	Roberto Alomar	.310	Roberto Alomar	.405	Joe Carter	.498	Joe Carter	34	Joe Carter	119	Roberto Alomar	49
1993	John Olerud	.363	John Olerud	.473	John Olerud	.599	Joe Carter	33	Joe Carter	121	Roberto Alomar	55
1994	Paul Molitor	.341	Paul Molitor	.410	Joe Carter	.524	Joe Carter	27	Joe Carter	103	Paul Molitor	20
1995	Roberto Alomar	.300	John Olerud	.398	Roberto Alomar	.449	Joe Carter	25	Joe Carter	76	Roberto Alomar	30
1996	Otis Nixon	.286	Otis Nixon	.377	Ed Sprague	.496	Ed Sprague	36	Joe Carter	107	Otis Nixon	54
1997	Carlos Delgado	.262	Carlos Delgado	.350	Carlos Delgado	.528	Carlos Delgado	30	Joe Carter	102	Otis Nixon	47

Toronto Blue Jays Individual Season Pitching Leaders

Year	ERA		Baserunners/9 IP		Innings Pitched		Strikeouts		Wins		Saves	
1977	Jerry Garvin	4.19	Jerry Garvin	12.4	Dave Lemanczyk	252.0	Jerry Garvin	127	Dave Lemanczyk	13	Pete Vuckovich	8
1978	Jim Clancy	4.09	Jesse Jefferson	12.9	Jesse Jefferson	211.2	Tom Underwood	139	Jim Clancy	10	Victor Cruz	9
1979	Tom Underwood	3.69	Tom Underwood	12.6	Tom Underwood	227.0	Tom Underwood	127	Tom Underwood	9	Tom Buskey	7
1980	Jim Clancy	3.30	Dave Stieb	11.9	Jim Clancy	250.2	Jim Clancy	152	Jim Clancy	13	Jerry Garvin	8
1981	Dave Stieb	3.19	Dave Stieb	10.8	Dave Stieb	183.2	Dave Stieb	89	Dave Stieb	11	Joey McLaughlin	10
1982	Dave Stieb	3.25	Dave Stieb	11.0	Dave Stieb	288.1	Dave Stieb	141	Dave Stieb	17	Dale Murray	11
1983	Dave Stieb	3.04	Dave Stieb	10.7	Dave Stieb	278.0	Dave Stieb	187	Dave Stieb	17	Randy Moffitt	10
1984	Dave Stieb	2.83	Doyle Alexander	10.3	Dave Stieb	267.0	Dave Stieb	198	Doyle Alexander	17	Roy Lee Jackson / Jimmy Key	10
1985	Dave Stieb	2.48	Jimmy Key	10.2	Dave Stieb	265.0	Dave Stieb	167	Doyle Alexander	17	Bill Caudill	14
1986	Jimmy Key	3.57	Jim Clancy	11.0	Jimmy Key	232.0	Mark Eichhorn	166	3 tied with	14	Tom Henke	27
1987	Jimmy Key	2.76	Jimmy Key	9.6	Jimmy Key	261.0	Jim Clancy	180	Jimmy Key	17	Tom Henke	34
1988	Dave Stieb	3.04	Dave Stieb	10.8	Mike Flanagan	211.0	Dave Stieb	147	Dave Stieb	16	Tom Henke	25
1989	John Cerutti	3.07	Jimmy Key	10.7	Jimmy Key	216.0	Duane Ward	122	Dave Stieb	17	Tom Henke	20
1990	Dave Stieb	2.93	David Wells	10.1	Dave Stieb	208.2	Dave Stieb	125	Dave Stieb	18	Tom Henke	32
1991	Jimmy Key	3.05	David Wells	10.8	Todd Stottlemyre	219.0	Duane Ward	132	Jimmy Key	16	Tom Henke	32
1992	Juan Guzman	2.64	Juan Guzman	10.4	Jack Morris	240.2	Juan Guzman	165	Jack Morris	21	Tom Henke	34
1993	Pat Hentgen	3.87	Pat Hentgen	12.3	Juan Guzman	221.0	Juan Guzman	194	Pat Hentgen	19	Duane Ward	45
1994	Pat Hentgen	3.40	Pat Hentgen	11.3	Pat Hentgen	174.2	Pat Hentgen	147	Pat Hentgen	13	Darren Hall	17
1995	Al Leiter	3.64	Al Leiter	13.6	Pat Hentgen	200.2	Al Leiter	153	Al Leiter	11	Tony Castillo	13
1996	Juan Guzman	2.93	Juan Guzman	10.5	Pat Hentgen	265.2	Pat Hentgen	177	Pat Hentgen	20	Mike Timlin	31
1997	Roger Clemens	2.05	Roger Clemens	9.7	Roger Clemens / Pat Hentgen	264.0	Roger Clemens	292	Roger Clemens	21	Kelvim Escobar	14

Blue Jays Franchise Batting Leaders—Career

	Games			At-Bats			Runs			Hits	
1	Lloyd Moseby	1,392	1	Lloyd Moseby	5,124	1	Lloyd Moseby	768	1	Lloyd Moseby	1,319
2	Ernie Whitt	1,218	2	George Bell	4,528	2	George Bell	641	2	George Bell	1,294
3	George Bell	1,181	3	Tony Fernandez	4,305	3	Joe Carter	578	3	Tony Fernandez	1,250
4	Tony Fernandez	1,122	4	Joe Carter	4,093	4	Tony Fernandez	555	4	Joe Carter	1,051
5	Willie Upshaw	1,115	5	Willie Upshaw	3,710	5	Willie Upshaw	538	5	Damaso Garcia	1,028
	Rance Mulliniks	1,115	6	Damaso Garcia	3,572	6	Jesse Barfield	530	6	Willie Upshaw	982
7	Joe Carter	1,039	7	Ernie Whitt	3,514	7	John Olerud	464	7	Jesse Barfield	919
8	Jesse Barfield	1,032	8	Jesse Barfield	3,463	8	Damaso Garcia	453	8	John Olerud	910
9	Alfredo Griffin	982	9	Alfredo Griffin	3,396	9	Devon White	452	9	Ernie Whitt	888
10	Garth Iorg	931	10	John Olerud	3,103	10	Roberto Alomar	451	10	Alfredo Griffin	844
11	Kelly Gruber	921	11	Kelly Gruber	3,094	11	Ernie Whitt	424	11	Rance Mulliniks	843
12	John Olerud	920	12	Rance Mulliniks	3,013	12	Kelly Gruber	421	12	Roberto Alomar	832
13	Damaso Garcia	902	13	Ed Sprague	2,774	13	Alfredo Griffin	382	13	Kelly Gruber	800
14	Ed Sprague	783	14	Devon White	2,711		Rance Mulliniks	382	14	Devon White	733
15	Manuel Lee	753	15	Roberto Alomar	2,706	15	Fred McGriff	348	15	Ed Sprague	682
16	Pat Borders	741	16	Garth Iorg	2,450	16	Ed Sprague	339	16	Garth Iorg	633
17	Roberto Alomar	703	17	Pat Borders	2,295	17	Paul Molitor	270	17	Pat Borders	587
18	Devon White	656	18	Manuel Lee	2,152	18	Garth Iorg	251	18	Manuel Lee	547
19	Al Woods	595	19	Al Woods	1,958	19	Manuel Lee	231	19	Fred McGriff	540
20	Fred McGriff	578	20	Roy Howell	1,954	20	Bob Bailor	230	20	Roy Howell	532

	Doubles			Triples			Home Runs			RBI	
1	Lloyd Moseby	242	1	Tony Fernandez	70	1	Joe Carter	203	1	George Bell	740
2	George Bell	237	2	Lloyd Moseby	60	2	George Bell	202	2	Joe Carter	736
3	Joe Carter	218	3	Alfredo Griffin	50	3	Jesse Barfield	179	3	Lloyd Moseby	651
4	John Olerud	213	4	Willie Upshaw	42	4	Lloyd Moseby	149	4	Jesse Barfield	527
5	Tony Fernandez	210	5	Roberto Alomar	36	5	Ernie Whitt	131	5	Ernie Whitt	518
6	Rance Mulliniks	204	6	Devon White	34	6	Fred McGriff	125	6	Willie Upshaw	478
7	Willie Upshaw	177	7	George Bell	32	7	Kelly Gruber	114	7	John Olerud	471
8	Damaso Garcia	172	8	Joe Carter	28	8	Willie Upshaw	112	8	Tony Fernandez	454
9	Ernie Whitt	164	9	Jesse Barfield	27	9	John Olerud	109	9	Kelly Gruber	434
10	Jesse Barfield	162	10	Damaso Garcia	26	10	Ed Sprague	96	10	Rance Mulliniks	389
11	Devon White	155	11	Kelly Gruber	24	11	John Mayberry	92	11	Ed Sprague	367
12	Roberto Alomar	152	12	Bob Bailor	19	12	Otto Velez	72	12	Roberto Alomar	342
13	Ed Sprague	150		Dave Collins	19		Devon White	72	13	Fred McGriff	305
14	Kelly Gruber	145	14	Roy Howell	17	14	Rance Mulliniks	68	14	Damaso Garcia	296
15	Alfredo Griffin	127		Manuel Lee	17	15	Carlos Delgado	67	15	Devon White	274
	Pat Borders	127	16	Garth Iorg	16	16	Roberto Alomar	55	16	John Mayberry	272
17	Garth Iorg	125	17	Ernie Whitt	15	17	Cliff Johnson	54	17	Pat Borders	269
18	Roy Howell	101		Junior Felix	15	18	Pat Borders	53	18	Paul Molitor	246
19	Fred McGriff	99	19	Six tied at	14	19	Paul Molitor	51	19	Otto Velez	243
20	Paul Molitor	98				20	Tony Fernandez	44	20	Garth Iorg	238

	Walks			Strikeouts			Stolen Bases			Runs Created	
1	Lloyd Moseby	547	1	Lloyd Moseby	1,015	1	Lloyd Moseby	255	1	Lloyd Moseby	725
2	John Olerud	514	2	Jesse Barfield	855	2	Roberto Alomar	206	2	George Bell	692
3	Rance Mulliniks	416	3	Joe Carter	696	3	Damaso Garcia	194	3	Tony Fernandez	608
4	Ernie Whitt	403	4	Willie Upshaw	576	4	Tony Fernandez	153		Joe Carter	608
5	Willie Upshaw	390	5	Ed Sprague	574	5	Devon White	126	5	John Olerud	544
6	Fred McGriff	352	6	Devon White	572	6	Otis Nixon	101	6	Jesse Barfield	530
7	Jesse Barfield	342	7	George Bell	563	7	Dave Collins	91	7	Willie Upshaw	527
8	Roberto Alomar	322	8	Fred McGriff	495	8	Kelly Gruber	80	8	Ernie Whitt	478
9	Tony Fernandez	316	9	Kelly Gruber	493	9	Alfredo Griffin	79	9	Roberto Alomar	477
10	Joe Carter	286	10	Rance Mulliniks	465	10	Joe Carter	78	10	Rance Mulliniks	455
11	Otto Velez	278	11	Ernie Whitt	450	11	Willie Upshaw	76	11	Kelly Gruber	415
12	John Mayberry	257	12	John Olerud	430	12	George Bell	59	12	Damaso Garcia	404
13	George Bell	255	13	Manuel Lee	426	13	Jesse Barfield	55	13	Devon White	384
14	Ed Sprague	246	14	Tony Fernandez	370	14	Paul Molitor	54	14	Fred McGriff	379
15	Devon White	209	15	Pat Borders	362	15	Bob Bailor	46	15	Ed Sprague	325
16	Kelly Gruber	195	16	Alex Gonzalez	352		Mookie Wilson	46	16	Paul Molitor	317
17	Paul Molitor	193	17	Carlos Delgado	344	17	Nelson Liriano	44	17	Alfredo Griffin	296
18	Roy Howell	178	18	Roy Howell	337	18	Alex Gonzalez	38	18	John Mayberry	293
	Cliff Johnson	178	19	Otto Velez	334	19	Barry Bonnell	31	19	Otto Velez	268
20	Al Woods	164	20	Alfredo Griffin	312		Junior Felix	31	20	Roy Howell	263

	Runs Created/27 Outs			Batting Average			On-Base Percentage			Slugging Percentage	
	(minimum 2000 Plate Appearances)			(minimum 2000 Plate Appearances)			(minimum 2000 Plate Appearances)			(minimum 2000 Plate Appearances)	
1	Fred McGriff	6.94	1	Roberto Alomar	.307	1	John Olerud	.395	1	Fred McGriff	.530
2	Roberto Alomar	6.31	2	John Olerud	.293	2	Fred McGriff	.389	2	George Bell	.486
3	John Olerud	6.30	3	Tony Fernandez	.290	3	Roberto Alomar	.382	3	Jesse Barfield	.483
4	John Mayberry	5.62	4	Damaso Garcia	.288	4	Rance Mulliniks	.365	4	Joe Carter	.473
5	George Bell	5.43	5	George Bell	.286	5	John Mayberry	.352	5	John Olerud	.471
6	Rance Mulliniks	5.30	6	Rance Mulliniks	.280	6	Tony Fernandez	.340	6	Roberto Alomar	.451
7	Jesse Barfield	5.30	7	Fred McGriff	.278	7	Willie Upshaw	.336	7	John Mayberry	.450
8	Joe Carter	5.11	8	Roy Howell	.272	8	Roy Howell	.335	8	Devon White	.432
9	Devon White	5.02	9	Devon White	.270	9	Jesse Barfield	.334	9	Kelly Gruber	.431
10	Tony Fernandez	4.99	10	Al Woods	.270	10	Lloyd Moseby	.333	10	Willie Upshaw	.426
11	Willie Upshaw	4.93	11	Jesse Barfield	.265	11	Devon White	.327	11	Rance Mulliniks	.424
12	Lloyd Moseby	4.81	12	Willie Upshaw	.265	12	Ernie Whitt	.327	12	Ernie Whitt	.420
13	Roy Howell	4.73	13	Bob Bailor	.264	13	Al Woods	.325	13	Lloyd Moseby	.415
14	Ernie Whitt	4.61	14	Kelly Gruber	.259	14	George Bell	.325	14	Ed Sprague	.411
15	Kelly Gruber	4.54	15	Garth Iorg	.258	15	Ed Sprague	.317	15	Roy Howell	.407
16	Al Woods	4.28	16	Lloyd Moseby	.257	16	Bob Bailor	.314	16	Tony Fernandez	.402
17	Ed Sprague	3.98	17	Joe Carter	.257	17	Damaso Garcia	.312	17	Pat Borders	.388
18	Damaso Garcia	3.97	18	Pat Borders	.256	18	Joe Carter	.308	18	Al Woods	.385
19	Bob Bailor	3.72	19	John Mayberry	.256	19	Kelly Gruber	.307	19	Damaso Garcia	.377
20	Pat Borders	3.32	20	Manuel Lee	.254	20	Manuel Lee	.304	20	Garth Iorg	.347

Blue Jays Franchise Pitching Leaders—Career

Wins

1	Dave Stieb	174
2	Jim Clancy	128
3	Jimmy Key	116
4	Pat Hentgen	82
5	Juan Guzman	70
6	Todd Stottlemyre	69
7	Luis Leal	51
8	David Wells	47
9	Doyle Alexander	46
	John Cerutti	46
11	Duane Ward	32
12	Mark Eichhorn	29
	Tom Henke	29
14	Jack Morris	28
15	Dave Lemanczyk	27
16	Jim Acker	26
	Mike Flanagan	26
	Al Leiter	26
19	Roy Lee Jackson	24
20	Mike Timlin	23

Losses

1	Jim Clancy	140
2	Dave Stieb	132
3	Jimmy Key	81
4	Todd Stottlemyre	70
5	Luis Leal	58
6	Jesse Jefferson	56
7	Pat Hentgen	53
8	Juan Guzman	50
9	Dave Lemanczyk	45
10	Jerry Garvin	41
11	John Cerutti	37
	David Wells	37
13	Duane Ward	36
14	Tom Underwood	30
	Jim Gott	30
16	Tom Henke	29
17	Mike Flanagan	27
18	Doyle Alexander	26
19	Woody Williams	25
20	Four tied at	24

Winning Percentage
(minimum 50 decisions)

1	Doyle Alexander	.639
2	Pat Hentgen	.607
3	Jimmy Key	.589
4	Juan Guzman	.583
5	Dave Stieb	.569
6	David Wells	.560
7	John Cerutti	.554
8	Al Leiter	.520
9	Tom Henke	.500
10	Todd Stottlemyre	.496
11	Mike Flanagan	.491
12	Jim Clancy	.478
13	Duane Ward	.471
14	Luis Leal	.468
15	Jim Gott	.412
16	Dave Lemanczyk	.375
17	Jerry Garvin	.328
18	Jesse Jefferson	.282

Games

1	Duane Ward	452
2	Tom Henke	446
3	Dave Stieb	420
4	Jim Clancy	352
5	Jimmy Key	317
6	Mike Timlin	305
7	Jim Acker	281
8	Mark Eichhorn	279
9	David Wells	237
10	Tony Castillo	218
11	Todd Stottlemyre	206
12	Jerry Garvin	196
13	Joey McLaughlin	195
14	John Cerutti	191
15	Roy Lee Jackson	190
16	Pat Hentgen	189
17	Juan Guzman	173
18	Luis Leal	165
19	Dennis Lamp	149
20	Mike Willis	144

Games Started

1	Dave Stieb	405
2	Jim Clancy	345
3	Jimmy Key	250
4	Todd Stottlemyre	175
5	Juan Guzman	173
6	Pat Hentgen	159
7	Luis Leal	151
8	John Cerutti	108
9	Doyle Alexander	103
10	Jesse Jefferson	91
11	Dave Lemanczyk	82
12	Mike Flanagan	76
13	David Wells	69
14	Jerry Garvin	65
	Jim Gott	65
16	Tom Underwood	62
17	Al Leiter	61
	Jack Morris	61
19	Dave Stewart	48
20	Woody Williams	44

Complete Games

1	Dave Stieb	103
2	Jim Clancy	73
3	Pat Hentgen	30
4	Jimmy Key	28
5	Luis Leal	27
6	Dave Lemanczyk	25
	Doyle Alexander	25
8	Jesse Jefferson	21
9	Tom Underwood	19
10	Jerry Garvin	15
	Todd Stottlemyre	15
12	Juan Guzman	13
13	Jack Morris	10
14	Roger Clemens	9
15	Jim Gott	8
16	Balor Moore	7
	Jackson Todd	7
	John Cerutti	7
19	David Cone	5
20	Four tied at	4

Shutouts

1	Dave Stieb	30
2	Jim Clancy	11
3	Jimmy Key	10
4	Pat Hentgen	9
5	Jesse Jefferson	4
	Todd Stottlemyre	4
7	Dave Lemanczyk	3
	Luis Leal	3
	Jim Gott	3
	Doyle Alexander	3
	Roger Clemens	3
12	Tom Underwood	2
	John Cerutti	2
	Mike Flanagan	2
	Al Leiter	2
	Juan Guzman	2
	Jack Morris	2
	David Cone	2
19	Twelve tied at	1

Saves

1	Tom Henke	217
2	Duane Ward	121
3	Mike Timlin	52
4	Joey McLaughlin	31
5	Roy Lee Jackson	30
6	Darren Hall	20
7	Bill Caudill	16
	Tony Castillo	16
9	Mike Willis	15
	Mark Eichhorn	15
11	Jim Acker	14
	Kelvim Escobar	14
13	Dennis Lamp	13
	David Wells	13
15	Dale Murray	11
16	Randy Moffitt	10
	Jimmy Key	10
18	Tom Murphy	9
	Victor Cruz	9
	Gary Lavelle	9

Innings Pitched

1	Dave Stieb	2,822.2
2	Jim Clancy	2,204.2
3	Jimmy Key	1,695.2
4	Pat Hentgen	1,179.0
5	Todd Stottlemyre	1,139.0
6	Juan Guzman	1,070.2
7	Luis Leal	946.0
8	John Cerutti	772.1
9	Doyle Alexander	750.0
10	David Wells	687.1
11	Jesse Jefferson	666.1
12	Duane Ward	650.2
13	Jerry Garvin	606.0
14	Dave Lemanczyk	575.0
15	Tom Henke	563.0
16	Jim Acker	524.1
17	Mark Eichhorn	493.0
18	Mike Flanagan	452.1
19	Tom Underwood	424.2
20	Jim Gott	422.1

Walks

1	Dave Stieb	1,003
2	Jim Clancy	814
3	Juan Guzman	481
4	Pat Hentgen	423
5	Todd Stottlemyre	414
6	Jimmy Key	404
7	Luis Leal	320
8	Duane Ward	278
9	Jesse Jefferson	266
10	John Cerutti	254
11	Al Leiter	240
12	Jerry Garvin	219
13	Dave Lemanczyk	212
14	Jim Acker	206
15	David Wells	201
16	Jim Gott	183
17	Tom Underwood	182
18	Doyle Alexander	172
19	Woody Williams	170
20	Four tied at	167

Strikeouts

1	Dave Stieb	1,631
2	Jim Clancy	1,237
3	Jimmy Key	944
4	Juan Guzman	917
5	Pat Hentgen	783
6	Duane Ward	671
7	Todd Stottlemyre	662
8	Tom Henke	644
9	Luis Leal	491
10	David Wells	449
11	Doyle Alexander	392
12	Mark Eichhorn	372
13	John Cerutti	369
14	Mike Timlin	331
15	Al Leiter	329
16	Jerry Garvin	320
17	Jesse Jefferson	307
18	Roger Clemens	292
19	Woody Williams	288
20	Jim Gott	276

Strikeouts/9 Innings
(minimum 500 Innings Pitched)

1	Tom Henke	10.29
2	Duane Ward	9.28
3	Juan Guzman	7.71
4	Pat Hentgen	5.98
5	David Wells	5.88
6	Todd Stottlemyre	5.23
7	Dave Stieb	5.20
8	Jim Clancy	5.05
9	Jimmy Key	5.01
10	Jerry Garvin	4.75
11	Doyle Alexander	4.70
12	Jim Acker	4.69
13	Luis Leal	4.67
14	John Cerutti	4.30
15	Jesse Jefferson	4.15
16	Dave Lemanczyk	3.76

ERA
(minimum 500 Innings Pitched)

1	Tom Henke	2.48
2	Duane Ward	3.18
3	Dave Stieb	3.39
4	Jimmy Key	3.42
5	Doyle Alexander	3.56
6	David Wells	3.78
7	John Cerutti	3.87
8	Pat Hentgen	3.88
9	Juan Guzman	4.03
10	Jim Acker	4.07
11	Jim Clancy	4.10
12	Luis Leal	4.14
13	Todd Stottlemyre	4.39
14	Jerry Garvin	4.43
15	Dave Lemanczyk	4.68
16	Jesse Jefferson	4.75

Component ERA
(minimum 500 Innings Pitched)

1	Tom Henke	2.18
2	Duane Ward	2.84
3	Jimmy Key	3.25
4	Dave Stieb	3.29
5	David Wells	3.50
6	Doyle Alexander	3.58
7	Juan Guzman	3.73
8	Jim Clancy	3.96
9	Pat Hentgen	3.97
10	Luis Leal	4.07
11	Jim Acker	4.30
12	Todd Stottlemyre	4.31
13	John Cerutti	4.40
14	Jerry Garvin	4.51
15	Dave Lemanczyk	4.67
16	Jesse Jefferson	4.76

Opponent Average
(minimum 500 Innings Pitched)

1	Tom Henke	.203
2	Duane Ward	.224
3	Dave Stieb	.238
4	Juan Guzman	.240
5	Jimmy Key	.252
6	David Wells	.253
7	Pat Hentgen	.256
8	Jim Clancy	.259
9	Doyle Alexander	.261
10	Luis Leal	.265
11	Jim Acker	.269
12	Todd Stottlemyre	.270
13	John Cerutti	.270
14	Jerry Garvin	.277
15	Jesse Jefferson	.281
16	Dave Lemanczyk	.287

Opponent OBP
(minimum 500 Innings Pitched)

1	Tom Henke	.262
2	Jimmy Key	.296
3	Doyle Alexander	.304
4	Duane Ward	.307
5	David Wells	.308
6	Dave Stieb	.310
7	Pat Hentgen	.322
8	Juan Guzman	.323
9	Jim Clancy	.324
10	Luis Leal	.325
11	John Cerutti	.329
12	Todd Stottlemyre	.336
13	Jerry Garvin	.340
14	Jim Acker	.343
15	Jesse Jefferson	.347
16	Dave Lemanczyk	.350

Blue Jays Franchise Batting Leaders—Single Season

Games

1	Tony Fernandez	1986	163
2	Rick Bosetti	1979	162
	Alfredo Griffin	1982	162
	Alfredo Griffin	1983	162
	Joe Carter	1991	162
6	Tony Fernandez	1985	161
	Fred McGriff	1989	161
	Tony Fernandez	1990	161
	Roberto Alomar	1991	161
10	Willie Upshaw	1982	160
	Willie Upshaw	1983	160
	Paul Molitor	1993	160
13	George Bell	1984	159
	George Bell	1986	159
	Jesse Barfield	1987	159
	Ed Sprague	1996	159
17	Five tied at		158

At-Bats

1	Tony Fernandez	1986	687
2	Alfredo Griffin	1980	653
3	Tony Fernandez	1988	648
4	Devon White	1991	642
5	George Bell	1986	641
	Devon White	1992	641
7	Joe Carter	1991	638
8	Roberto Alomar	1991	637
9	Paul Molitor	1993	636
10	Tony Fernandez	1990	635
11	Damaso Garcia	1984	633
12	Joe Carter	1996	625
13	Alfredo Griffin	1979	624
14	Joe Carter	1992	622
15	Bob Bailor	1978	621
16	Rick Bosetti	1979	619
17	George Bell	1988	614
18	George Bell	1989	613
19	Joe Carter	1997	612
20	George Bell	1987	610

Runs

1	Paul Molitor	1993	121
2	Devon White	1993	116
3	George Bell	1987	111
4	Devon White	1991	110
5	Roberto Alomar	1993	109
	John Olerud	1993	109
7	Jesse Barfield	1986	107
8	Lloyd Moseby	1987	106
9	Roberto Alomar	1992	105
10	Lloyd Moseby	1983	104
11	George Bell	1986	101
12	Fred McGriff	1988	100
13	Willie Upshaw	1983	99
14	Fred McGriff	1989	98
	Devon White	1992	98
16	Lloyd Moseby	1984	97
	Joe Carter	1992	97
18	Jesse Barfield	1985	94
19	Four tied at		92

Hits

1	Tony Fernandez	1986	213
2	Paul Molitor	1993	211
3	John Olerud	1993	200
4	George Bell	1986	198
5	Roberto Alomar	1993	192
6	George Bell	1987	188
	Roberto Alomar	1991	188
8	Tony Fernandez	1987	186
	Tony Fernandez	1988	186
10	Damaso Garcia	1982	185
11	George Bell	1989	182
12	Devon White	1991	181
13	Damaso Garcia	1984	180
14	Alfredo Griffin	1979	179
15	Willie Upshaw	1983	177
	George Bell	1984	177
	Roberto Alomar	1992	177
18	Tony Fernandez	1990	175
19	Joe Carter	1991	174
20	Two tied at		170

Doubles

1	John Olerud	1993	54
2	Joe Carter	1991	42
	Devon White	1993	42
	Carlos Delgado	1997	42
5	Tony Fernandez	1988	41
	George Bell	1989	41
	Roberto Alomar	1991	41
8	Devon White	1991	40
9	George Bell	1984	39
10	George Bell	1986	38
11	Paul Molitor	1993	37
12	Mookie Wilson	1990	36
	Kelly Gruber	1990	36
14	Rick Bosetti	1979	35
	Jesse Barfield	1986	35
	Fred McGriff	1988	35
	Roberto Alomar	1993	35
	Joe Carter	1996	35
	Ed Sprague	1996	35
20	Two tied at		34

Triples

1	Tony Fernandez	1990	17
2	Alfredo Griffin	1980	15
	Dave Collins	1984	15
	Lloyd Moseby	1984	15
5	Roberto Alomar	1991	11
6	Alfredo Griffin	1979	10
	Tony Fernandez	1985	10
	Devon White	1991	10
9	Roy Howell	1980	9
	Lloyd Moseby	1982	9
	Alfredo Griffin	1983	9
	Willie Upshaw	1984	9
	Jesse Barfield	1985	9
	Tony Fernandez	1986	9
	Tony Fernandez	1989	9
	Tony Fernandez	1993	9
17	Five tied at		8

Home Runs

1	George Bell	1987	47
2	Jesse Barfield	1986	40
3	Fred McGriff	1989	36
	Ed Sprague	1996	36
5	Fred McGriff	1990	35
6	Fred McGriff	1988	34
	Joe Carter	1992	34
8	Joe Carter	1991	33
	Joe Carter	1993	33
10	George Bell	1986	31
	Kelly Gruber	1990	31
12	John Mayberry	1980	30
	Joe Carter	1996	30
	Carlos Delgado	1997	30
15	George Bell	1985	28
	Jesse Barfield	1987	28
17	Willie Upshaw	1983	27
	Jesse Barfield	1983	27
	Jesse Barfield	1985	27
	Joe Carter	1994	27

RBI

1	George Bell	1987	134
2	Joe Carter	1993	121
3	Joe Carter	1992	119
4	Kelly Gruber	1990	118
5	Paul Molitor	1993	111
6	Jesse Barfield	1986	108
	George Bell	1986	108
	Joe Carter	1991	108
	Dave Winfield	1992	108
10	John Olerud	1993	107
	Joe Carter	1996	107
12	Willie Upshaw	1983	104
	George Bell	1989	104
14	Joe Carter	1994	103
15	Joe Carter	1997	102
16	Ed Sprague	1996	101
17	George Bell	1988	97
18	Lloyd Moseby	1987	96
19	George Bell	1985	95
20	Roberto Alomar	1993	93

Walks

1	Fred McGriff	1989	119
2	John Olerud	1993	114
3	Fred McGriff	1990	94
4	Roberto Alomar	1992	87
5	John Olerud	1995	84
6	Dave Winfield	1992	82
7	Roberto Alomar	1993	80
8	Fred McGriff	1988	79
9	Lloyd Moseby	1984	78
	Willie Upshaw	1986	78
11	John Mayberry	1980	77
	Paul Molitor	1993	77
13	Lloyd Moseby	1985	76
14	Tony Fernandez	1990	71
	Otis Nixon	1996	71
16	Lloyd Moseby	1987	70
	Lloyd Moseby	1988	70
	John Olerud	1992	70
19	John Mayberry	1979	69
	Jesse Barfield	1986	69

Strikeouts

1	Fred McGriff	1988	149
2	Jesse Barfield	1986	146
	Ed Sprague	1996	146
4	Jesse Barfield	1985	143
5	Jesse Barfield	1987	141
6	Carlos Delgado	1996	139
7	Devon White	1991	135
8	Devon White	1992	133
	Carlos Delgado	1997	133
10	Fred McGriff	1989	132
11	Devon White	1993	127
	Alex Gonzalez	1996	127
13	Lloyd Moseby	1987	124
14	Lloyd Moseby	1984	122
	Lloyd Moseby	1986	122
16	Alex Gonzalez	1995	114
17	Joe Carter	1993	113
18	Joe Carter	1991	112
	Candy Maldonado	1992	112
20	Jesse Barfield	1983	110

Stolen Bases

1	Dave Collins	1984	60
2	Roberto Alomar	1993	55
3	Damaso Garcia	1982	54
	Otis Nixon	1996	54
5	Roberto Alomar	1991	53
6	Roberto Alomar	1992	49
7	Otis Nixon	1997	47
8	Damaso Garcia	1984	46
9	Lloyd Moseby	1984	39
	Lloyd Moseby	1987	39
11	Lloyd Moseby	1985	37
	Devon White	1992	37
13	Devon White	1993	34
14	Devon White	1991	33
15	Lloyd Moseby	1986	32
	Tony Fernandez	1987	32
17	Dave Collins	1983	31
	Damaso Garcia	1983	31
	Lloyd Moseby	1988	31
20	Roberto Alomar	1995	30

Runs Created

1	John Olerud	1993	144
2	Paul Molitor	1993	134
3	George Bell	1987	122
4	Jesse Barfield	1986	118
	Roberto Alomar	1993	118
6	Roberto Alomar	1992	117
7	George Bell	1986	113
	Fred McGriff	1989	113
9	Kelly Gruber	1990	110
	Fred McGriff	1990	110
11	Dave Winfield	1992	108
12	Willie Upshaw	1983	106
13	Lloyd Moseby	1987	105
14	Joe Carter	1991	103
15	Jesse Barfield	1985	102
	Roberto Alomar	1991	102
17	Lloyd Moseby	1984	101
	Paul Molitor	1994	101
19	Tony Fernandez	1986	100
20	Two tied at		99

Runs Created/27 Outs

(minimum 3.1 Plate Appearances/Tm Gm)

1	John Olerud	1993	10.40
2	Paul Molitor	1994	8.57
3	Paul Molitor	1993	7.98
4	Roberto Alomar	1992	7.54
5	Roberto Alomar	1993	7.31
6	George Bell	1987	7.30
7	Fred McGriff	1990	7.30
8	Jesse Barfield	1986	7.19
9	Fred McGriff	1989	7.11
10	John Olerud	1994	6.91
11	Dave Winfield	1992	6.77
12	Lloyd Moseby	1983	6.73
13	Jesse Barfield	1985	6.73
14	Willie Upshaw	1983	6.69
15	Carlos Delgado	1997	6.52
16	Fred McGriff	1988	6.51
17	Joe Carter	1994	6.48
18	George Bell	1986	6.44
19	Kelly Gruber	1990	6.43
20	Lloyd Moseby	1987	6.28

Batting Average

(minimum 3.1 Plate Appearances/Tm Gm)

1	John Olerud	1993	.363
2	Paul Molitor	1994	.341
3	Paul Molitor	1993	.332
4	Roberto Alomar	1993	.326
5	Tony Fernandez	1987	.322
6	Lloyd Moseby	1983	.315
7	Bob Bailor	1977	.310
8	Tony Fernandez	1986	.310
9	Roberto Alomar	1992	.310
10	Damaso Garcia	1982	.310
11	George Bell	1986	.309
12	George Bell	1987	.308
13	Damaso Garcia	1983	.307
14	Roberto Alomar	1994	.306
15	Willie Upshaw	1983	.306
16	Fred McGriff	1990	.300
17	Roberto Alomar	1995	.300
18	George Bell	1989	.297
19	John Olerud	1994	.297
20	Roberto Alomar	1991	.295

On-Base Percentage

(minimum 3.1 Plate Appearances/Tm Gm)

1	John Olerud	1993	.473
2	Paul Molitor	1994	.410
3	Roberto Alomar	1993	.408
4	Roberto Alomar	1992	.405
5	Paul Molitor	1993	.402
6	Fred McGriff	1990	.400
7	Fred McGriff	1989	.399
8	John Olerud	1995	.398
9	John Olerud	1994	.393
10	Roberto Alomar	1994	.386
11	Tony Fernandez	1987	.379
12	Otis Nixon	1996	.377
13	Dave Winfield	1992	.377
14	Lloyd Moseby	1983	.376
15	Fred McGriff	1988	.376
16	John Olerud	1992	.375
17	Willie Upshaw	1983	.373
18	John Mayberry	1979	.372
19	Jesse Barfield	1985	.369
20	Jesse Barfield	1986	.368

Slugging Percentage

(minimum 3.1 Plate Appearances/Tm Gm)

1	George Bell	1987	.605
2	John Olerud	1993	.599
3	Jesse Barfield	1986	.559
4	Fred McGriff	1988	.552
5	Jesse Barfield	1985	.536
6	George Bell	1986	.532
7	Fred McGriff	1990	.530
8	Carlos Delgado	1997	.528
9	Fred McGriff	1989	.525
10	Joe Carter	1994	.524
11	Paul Molitor	1994	.518
12	Willie Upshaw	1983	.515
13	Kelly Gruber	1990	.512
14	Paul Molitor	1993	.509
15	Joe Carter	1991	.503
16	Lloyd Moseby	1983	.499
17	Joe Carter	1992	.498
18	George Bell	1984	.498
19	Ed Sprague	1996	.496
20	Roberto Alomar	1993	.492

Teams: Blue Jays

Blue Jays Franchise Pitching Leaders—Single Season

Wins

1	Jack Morris	1992	21
	Roger Clemens	1997	21
3	Pat Hentgen	1996	20
4	Pat Hentgen	1993	19
5	Dave Stieb	1990	18
6	Dave Stieb	1982	17
	Dave Stieb	1983	17
	Doyle Alexander	1984	17
	Doyle Alexander	1985	17
	Jimmy Key	1987	17
	Dave Stieb	1989	17
12	Jim Clancy	1982	16
	Dave Stieb	1984	16
	Dave Stieb	1988	16
	Jimmy Key	1991	16
	Juan Guzman	1992	16
17	Five tied at		15

Losses

1	Jerry Garvin	1977	18
	Phil Huffman	1979	18
3	Jesse Jefferson	1977	17
	Todd Stottlemyre	1990	17
	Erik Hanson	1996	17
6	Dave Lemanczyk	1977	16
	Jesse Jefferson	1978	16
	Tom Underwood	1979	16
	Jim Clancy	1980	16
10	Dave Stieb	1980	15
	Luis Leal	1982	15
	Jim Clancy	1984	15
13	Eleven tied at		14

Winning Percentage
(minimum 15 decisions)

1	Juan Guzman	1993	.824
2	Jack Morris	1992	.778
3	Juan Guzman	1992	.762
4	Dave Stieb	1990	.750
	Roger Clemens	1997	.750
6	Doyle Alexander	1984	.739
7	John Cerutti	1987	.733
8	Jeff Musselman	1987	.706
	Jimmy Key	1988	.706
10	Jimmy Key	1985	.700
	Mark Eichhorn	1986	.700
12	Jimmy Key	1987	.680
	Dave Stieb	1989	.680
14	Pat Hentgen	1993	.679
15	Dave Stieb	1984	.667
	Dave Stieb	1988	.667
	Pat Hentgen	1996	.667
18	Todd Stottlemyre	1991	.652
19	Jimmy Key	1990	.650
20	Two tied at		.647

Games

1	Mark Eichhorn	1987	89
2	Duane Ward	1991	81
3	Duane Ward	1992	79
4	Paul Quantrill	1997	77
5	Duane Ward	1990	73
	Dan Plesac	1997	73
7	Tom Henke	1987	72
8	Duane Ward	1993	71
9	Gary Lavelle	1985	69
	Mark Eichhorn	1986	69
11	Jeff Musselman	1987	68
12	Bill Caudill	1985	67
13	Duane Ward	1989	66
14	Duane Ward	1988	64
	Tom Henke	1989	64
16	Jimmy Key	1984	63
	Tom Henke	1986	63
	Mike Timlin	1991	63
19	Three tied at		61

Games Started

1	Jim Clancy	1982	40
2	Luis Leal	1982	38
	Dave Stieb	1982	38
4	Jim Clancy	1987	37
5	Dave Stieb	1983	36
	Jim Clancy	1984	36
	Doyle Alexander	1985	36
	Dave Stieb	1985	36
	Jimmy Key	1987	36
10	Luis Leal	1983	35
	Doyle Alexander	1984	35
	Luis Leal	1984	35
	Dave Stieb	1984	35
	Jimmy Key	1986	35
	Erik Hanson	1996	35
	Pat Hentgen	1996	35
	Pat Hentgen	1997	35
18	Ten tied at		34

Complete Games

1	Dave Stieb	1982	19
2	Jim Clancy	1980	15
3	Dave Stieb	1980	14
	Dave Stieb	1983	14
5	Jerry Garvin	1977	12
	Tom Underwood	1979	12
7	Dave Lemanczyk	1977	11
	Dave Lemanczyk	1979	11
	Dave Stieb	1981	11
	Jim Clancy	1982	11
	Jim Clancy	1983	11
	Doyle Alexander	1984	11
	Dave Stieb	1984	11
14	Luis Leal	1982	10
	Pat Hentgen	1996	10
16	Jesse Jefferson	1978	9
	Roger Clemens	1997	9
	Pat Hentgen	1997	9
19	Four tied at		8

Shutouts

1	Dave Stieb	1982	5
2	Dave Stieb	1980	4
	Dave Stieb	1983	4
	Dave Stieb	1988	4
5	Dave Lemanczyk	1979	3
	Jim Clancy	1982	3
	Jim Clancy	1986	3
	Pat Hentgen	1994	3
	Pat Hentgen	1996	3
	Roger Clemens	1997	3
	Pat Hentgen	1997	3
12	Sixteen tied at		2

Saves

1	Duane Ward	1993	45
2	Tom Henke	1987	34
	Tom Henke	1992	34
4	Tom Henke	1990	32
	Tom Henke	1991	32
6	Mike Timlin	1996	31
7	Tom Henke	1986	27
8	Tom Henke	1988	25
9	Duane Ward	1991	23
10	Tom Henke	1989	20
11	Darren Hall	1994	17
12	Duane Ward	1988	15
	Duane Ward	1989	15
14	Bill Caudill	1985	14
	Kelvim Escobar	1997	14
16	Tom Henke	1985	13
	Tony Castillo	1995	13
18	Duane Ward	1992	12
19	Dale Murray	1982	11
	Duane Ward	1990	11

Innings Pitched

1	Dave Stieb	1982	288.1
2	Dave Stieb	1983	278.0
3	Dave Stieb	1984	267.0
4	Jim Clancy	1982	266.2
5	Pat Hentgen	1996	265.2
6	Dave Stieb	1985	265.0
7	Roger Clemens	1997	264.0
	Pat Hentgen	1997	264.0
9	Doyle Alexander	1984	261.2
10	Jimmy Key	1987	261.0
11	Doyle Alexander	1985	260.2
12	Dave Lemanczyk	1977	252.0
13	Jim Clancy	1980	250.2
14	Luis Leal	1982	249.2
15	Jerry Garvin	1977	244.2
16	Dave Stieb	1980	242.2
17	Jim Clancy	1987	241.1
18	Jack Morris	1992	240.2
19	Jimmy Key	1986	232.0
20	Tom Underwood	1979	227.0

Walks

1	Jim Clancy	1980	128
2	Juan Guzman	1993	110
3	Al Leiter	1995	108
4	Erik Hanson	1996	102
5	Dave Stieb	1985	96
6	Tom Underwood	1979	95
7	Pat Hentgen	1996	94
8	Dave Stieb	1983	93
9	Jim Clancy	1978	91
10	Pat Hentgen	1995	90
11	Jim Clancy	1984	88
	Dave Stieb	1984	88
13	Dave Lemanczyk	1977	87
	Tom Underwood	1978	87
	Dave Stieb	1986	87
	Dave Stieb	1987	87
17	Jesse Jefferson	1978	86
18	Jerry Garvin	1977	85
19	Jesse Jefferson	1977	83
	Dave Stieb	1980	83

Strikeouts

1	Roger Clemens	1997	292
2	Dave Stieb	1984	198
3	Juan Guzman	1993	194
4	Dave Stieb	1983	187
5	Jim Clancy	1987	180
6	Pat Hentgen	1996	177
7	Dave Stieb	1985	167
8	Mark Eichhorn	1986	166
9	Juan Guzman	1992	165
	Juan Guzman	1996	165
11	Jimmy Key	1987	161
12	Pat Hentgen	1997	160
13	Erik Hanson	1996	156
14	Al Leiter	1995	153
15	Jim Clancy	1980	152
16	Dave Stieb	1988	147
	Pat Hentgen	1994	147
18	Doyle Alexander	1985	142
19	Dave Stieb	1982	141
	Jimmy Key	1986	141

Strikeouts/9 Innings
(minimum 1 Inning Pitched/Tm Gm)

1	Roger Clemens	1997	9.95
2	Juan Guzman	1992	8.22
3	Juan Guzman	1996	7.91
4	Juan Guzman	1993	7.90
5	Juan Guzman	1994	7.57
6	Pat Hentgen	1994	7.57
7	Al Leiter	1995	7.52
8	Dave Stewart	1994	7.49
9	Todd Stottlemyre	1994	6.72
10	Jim Clancy	1987	6.71
11	Dave Stieb	1984	6.67
12	Erik Hanson	1996	6.54
13	Dave Stieb	1988	6.38
14	Tom Underwood	1978	6.33
15	Jim Gott	1983	6.16
16	Pat Hentgen	1995	6.05
17	Dave Stieb	1983	6.05
18	Pat Hentgen	1996	6.00
19	Woody Williams	1997	5.73
20	Dave Stieb	1985	5.67

ERA
(minimum 1 Inning Pitched/Tm Gm)

1	Roger Clemens	1997	2.05
2	Dave Stieb	1985	2.48
3	Juan Guzman	1992	2.64
4	Jimmy Key	1987	2.76
5	Dave Stieb	1984	2.83
6	Juan Guzman	1996	2.93
7	Dave Stieb	1990	2.93
8	Jimmy Key	1985	3.00
9	Dave Stieb	1988	3.04
10	Dave Stieb	1983	3.04
11	Jimmy Key	1991	3.05
12	John Cerutti	1989	3.07
13	Doyle Alexander	1984	3.13
14	David Wells	1990	3.14
15	Dave Stieb	1981	3.19
16	Pat Hentgen	1996	3.22
17	Dave Stieb	1982	3.25
18	Jim Clancy	1980	3.30
19	Dave Stieb	1989	3.35
20	Pat Hentgen	1994	3.40

Component ERA
(minimum 1 Inning Pitched/Tm Gm)

1	Roger Clemens	1997	2.17
2	Juan Guzman	1992	2.34
3	Jimmy Key	1987	2.48
4	David Wells	1990	2.67
5	Dave Stieb	1981	2.74
6	Dave Stieb	1985	2.75
7	Dave Stieb	1984	2.77
8	Dave Stieb	1983	2.78
9	Dave Stieb	1988	2.81
10	Dave Stieb	1989	2.83
11	Dave Stieb	1990	2.84
12	Doyle Alexander	1984	2.86
13	Jimmy Key	1985	2.91
14	Jimmy Key	1991	2.99
15	Juan Guzman	1996	3.00
16	Jimmy Key	1989	3.20
17	Dave Stieb	1982	3.24
18	Pat Hentgen	1996	3.26
19	Jim Clancy	1986	3.33
20	Jim Clancy	1982	3.36

Opponent Average
(minimum 1 Inning Pitched/Tm Gm)

1	Juan Guzman	1992	.207
2	Dave Stieb	1988	.210
3	Roger Clemens	1997	.213
4	Dave Stieb	1985	.213
5	Dave Stieb	1983	.219
6	Dave Stieb	1989	.219
7	Jimmy Key	1987	.221
8	Dave Stieb	1984	.221
9	Dave Stieb	1981	.223
10	Juan Guzman	1996	.228
11	Dave Stieb	1990	.230
12	Jim Clancy	1980	.233
13	Todd Stottlemyre	1991	.235
14	David Wells	1990	.235
15	Jimmy Key	1985	.237
16	Al Leiter	1995	.238
17	Dave Stieb	1987	.239
18	Pat Hentgen	1994	.240
19	Pat Hentgen	1996	.241
20	Dave Stewart	1993	.242

Opponent OBP
(minimum 1 Inning Pitched/Tm Gm)

1	Jimmy Key	1987	.272
2	Roger Clemens	1997	.273
3	Jimmy Key	1985	.282
4	David Wells	1990	.283
5	Doyle Alexander	1984	.284
6	Juan Guzman	1992	.286
7	Juan Guzman	1996	.289
8	Dave Stieb	1985	.290
9	Dave Stieb	1983	.291
10	Dave Stieb	1984	.292
11	Jimmy Key	1989	.292
12	Jimmy Key	1991	.293
13	Dave Stieb	1988	.295
14	Dave Stieb	1990	.296
15	Dave Stieb	1981	.296
16	Jim Clancy	1986	.296
17	David Wells	1991	.297
18	Dave Stieb	1982	.298
19	Jimmy Key	1992	.298
20	Dave Stieb	1989	.301

Blue Jays Capsule

Best Season: *1992.* The Blue Jays won the American League East by four games with a 96-66 record, defeated the Oakland A's in a six-game ALCS, and downed the Atlanta Braves in the World Series, four games to two, for their first World Championship.

Worst Season: *1979.* They finished 50.5 games out of first place and lost a major league-high 109 ballgames, two more losses than they'd suffered during their inaugural season.

Best Player: *Roberto Alomar.*

Best Pitcher: *Dave Stieb.*

Best Reliever: *Tom Henke.*

Best Defensive Players: *Roberto Alomar* and *Devon White.*

Hall of Famers: None yet.

Franchise All-Star Team:

C	Ernie Whitt	LF	Joe Carter
1B	Fred McGriff	CF	Lloyd Moseby
2B	Roberto Alomar	RF	Jesse Barfield
3B	Kelly Gruber	DH	George Bell
SS	Tony Fernandez	SP	Dave Stieb
		RP	Tom Henke

Biggest Flake: *Mike Maksudian.* The man ate bugs. Bill Caudill was the biggest flake who was around for a significant amount of time.

Strangest Career: *Lloyd Moseby.* For his first three years, he was awful, batting between .229 and .236 with nine home runs each season. In 1983, he burst forth as a multi-dimensional talent, batting .315 while doubling his home-run output and stealing 27 bases. For a five-year stretch from 1983 through 1987, he was one of the most complete center fielders in baseball, combining power, speed, walks and defense. But in 1988, he suddenly reverted to his pre-breakthrough form, dropping to .239 with 10 homers. The next year, it was more of the same, and then he moved on to Detroit. All in all, he spent 10 years in Toronto. Five were very good and five were very bad, so you might say he broke even.

What Might Have Been: *Cecil Fielder.* The Jays allowed him to leave for Japan after the 1988 season. It's scary to think what might have happened if they'd found a way to get both Fred McGriff and Fielder into the lineup.

Best Trade: *Roberto Alomar/Joe Carter.* It was one of the biggest trades of the '90s: the Blue Jays sent first baseman Fred McGriff and shortstop Tony Fernandez to the Padres for Alomar and Carter. Alomar developed into the superstar that Fernandez never became, and Carter was able to take advantage of SkyDome well enough to replace McGriff in the lineup. The trade also enabled them to open up first base for John Olerud.

Worst Trade: *Carlos Garcia/Orlando Merced.* It was trumpeted as a coup when the Blue Jays acquired Garcia, Merced and lefty reliever Dan Plesac from the Pirates for a package of five prospects in the winter of '96. But Garcia and Merced turned out to be massive disappointments, helping to ruin the Jays' 1997 season. Meanwhile, the Pirates expect at least two or three of the prospects to develop into major league regulars.

Best-Looking Player: *Danny Ainge.*

Ugliest Player: *Cliff Johnson.*

Best Nickname: *"The Crime Dog," Fred McGriff.*

Most Unappreciated Player: *John Olerud .* After batting .363 in 1993, Olerud remained productive but never was able to fulfill the expectations he'd unwittingly created. The Jays even began platooning him in 1996, before trading him over the offseason and replacing him with an inferior player.

Most Overrated Player: *Joe Carter.* For many years, Carter was a respectable power hitter, and he was durable. This enabled him to drive in over 100 runs year after year. Because people often give undue weight to players' RBI counts, Carter came to be seen as far more valuable than he actually was. As a result, he was allowed to remain in the heart of the Jays' batting order much longer than he deserved to. He was their cleanup hitter in 1995, when Toronto's cleanup men finished last in the league in RBI. He remained in the No. 4 spot the following season, when they moved up to 10th, and hit cleanup again in 1997, when the Blue Jays once again got the fewest RBI in the league from that spot in the order.

Most Admirable Star: *Joe Carter.* Overrated, but admirable.

Least Admirable Star: *George Bell.* Bell openly defied manager Jimy Williams in 1988 when Williams tried to move Bell from left field to DH. The battle divided the team and virtually took them out of the running before the season even started.

Worst Karate Demonstration: *George Bell.* In 1985, Bell charged the mound after getting drilled by Red Sox pitcher Bruce Kison. When he reached the mound, he leapt into the air and attempted to deliver a karate kick to Kison's midsection. Kison coolly took one step to the left and held out his right fist. Bell's kick hit nothing but air, but his face impacted Kison's fist with considerable force.

Best Season, Player: *John Olerud, 1993.* George Bell won the MVP Award in 1987, but Olerud's '93 season was better. Olerud took a .400 average into August before finishing at .363, with 54 doubles and 114 walks. His slugging percentage, .599, was only six points lower than Bell's was in his MVP season, and Olerud's on-base percentage was 121 points higher.

Best Season, Pitcher: *Roger Clemens, 1997.* It was quite possibly the best season of Clemens' career, which should say enough right there. He went 21-7 and won the Cy Young Award with a last-place club.

Most Impressive Individual Record: *Roberto Alomar* set the major league record for second basemen by accepting 484 consecutive chances without an error from June 21, 1994 through July 4, 1995.

Biggest Tragedy: *The sea gull.* In 1983, a warmup throw from Yankees outfielder Dave Winfield hit and killed a sea gull. Indignant Toronto fans booed Winfield for the rest of the game, and afterward Winfield was taken downtown and charged with cruelty to animals. The charges were later dropped. The Blue Jays have been fortunate. There have been no accidents involving a loss of human life.

Fan Favorite: *Joe Carter.* His World Series-clinching home run in 1993 made him the Bobby Thomson of Toronto, forever.

—Mat Olkin

Boston/Milwaukee/Atlanta Braves (1876-1997)

Year	Lg	Pos	W-L	Pct	GB	Manager	Att.	R	OR	HR	Avg	OBP	Slg	Opponent HR	Opponent Avg	Opponent OBP	ERA	Park Index Runs	Park Index HR
1876	NL	4th	39-31	.557	15.0	Harry Wright	—	471	450	9	.266	.281	.328	7	.268	.295	2.51	91	94
1877	NL	1st	42-18	.700	—	Harry Wright	—	419	263	4	.296	.314	.370	5	.249	.261	2.15	104	11
1878	NL	1st	41-19	.683	—	Harry Wright	—	298	241	2	.241	.253	.300	6	.272	.284	2.32	104	100
1879	NL	2nd	54-30	.643	5.0	Harry Wright	—	562	348	20	.274	.294	.368	9	.251	.262	2.19	108	81
1880	NL	6th	40-44	.476	27.0	Harry Wright	—	416	456	20	.253	.278	.343	2	.276	.296	3.08	86	214
1881	NL	6th	38-45	.458	17.5	Harry Wright	—	349	410	5	.251	.279	.317	9	.258	.292	2.71	79	77
1882	NL	3rd	45-39	.536	10.0	John Morrill	—	472	414	15	.264	.294	.347	10	.239	.258	2.80	106	150
1883	NL	1st	63-35	.643	—	Jack Burdock/John Morrill	—	669	456	34	.276	.300	.408	11	.243	.262	2.55	107	114
1884	NL	2nd	73-38	.658	10.5	John Morrill	—	684	468	36	.254	.289	.351	30	.226	.250	2.47	78	37
1885	NL	5th	46-66	.411	41.0	John Morrill	—	528	589	22	.232	.267	.312	26	.261	.294	3.03	90	33
1886	NL	5th	56-61	.479	30.5	John Morrill	—	657	661	24	.260	.301	.341	33	.252	.302	3.24	98	71
1887	NL	5th	61-60	.504	16.5	King Kelly/John Morrill	—	831	792	53	.277	.333	.394	55	.273	.338	4.41	96	75
1888	NL	4th	70-64	.522	15.5	John Morrill	—	669	619	56	.245	.291	.351	36	.232	.280	2.61	115	76
1889	NL	2nd	83-45	.648	1.0	Jim Hart	—	826	626	42	.270	.343	.363	41	.248	.309	3.36	97	82
1890	NL	5th	76-57	.571	12.0	Frank Selee	147,539	763	593	31	.258	.342	.341	27	.245	.298	2.93	115	117
1891	NL	1st	87-51	.630	—	Frank Selee	184,472	847	658	53	.255	.337	.356	51	.248	.300	2.76	124	171
1892	NL	1st	52-22	.703	—	Frank Selee													
	NL	2nd	50-26	.658	3.0	Frank Selee	146,421	862	649	34	.250	.325	.327	41	.225	.289	2.86	123	168
1893	NL	1st	86-43	.667	—	Frank Selee	193,300	1008	795	65	.290	.372	.391	66	.279	.336	4.43	103	215
1894	NL	3rd	83-49	.629	8.0	Frank Selee	152,800	1220	1002	103	.331	.401	.484	89	.312	.365	5.41	126	358
1895	NL	5th	71-60	.542	16.5	Frank Selee	242,000	907	826	54	.290	.365	.391	56	.285	.335	4.27	103	382
1896	NL	4th	74-57	.565	17.0	Frank Selee	240,000	860	761	36	.300	.363	.392	57	.275	.333	3.78	117	197
1897	NL	1st	93-39	.705	—	Frank Selee	334,800	1025	665	45	.319	.378	.426	39	.271	.333	3.65	109	163
1898	NL	1st	102-47	.685	—	Frank Selee	229,275	872	614	53	.290	.344	.377	37	.235	.308	2.98	104	272
1899	NL	2nd	95-57	.625	8.0	Frank Selee	200,384	858	645	39	.287	.345	.377	44	.251	.318	3.26	107	334
1900	NL	4th	66-72	.478	17.0	Frank Selee	202,000	778	739	48	.283	.342	.373	59	.264	.336	3.72	148	326
1901	NL	5th	69-69	.500	20.5	Frank Selee	146,502	531	556	28	.249	.298	.310	29	.247	.302	2.90	117	144
1902	NL	3rd	73-64	.533	29.0	Al Buckenberger	116,960	572	516	14	.249	.313	.305	16	.256	.316	2.61	88	394
1903	NL	6th	58-80	.420	32.0	Al Buckenberger	143,155	578	699	25	.245	.312	.318	30	.278	.343	3.34	96	131
1904	NL	7th	55-98	.359	51.0	Al Buckenberger	140,694	491	749	24	.237	.287	.300	25	.272	.343	3.43	97	83
1905	NL	7th	51-103	.331	54.5	Fred Tenney	150,003	468	733	17	.234	.284	.293	36	.265	.324	3.52	98	118
1906	NL	8th	49-102	.325	66.5	Fred Tenney	143,280	408	649	16	.226	.286	.281	24	.259	.325	3.14	109	210
1907	NL	7th	58-90	.392	47.0	Fred Tenney	203,221	502	652	22	.243	.308	.309	28	.270	.341	3.33	96	218
1908	NL	6th	63-91	.409	36.0	Joe Kelley	253,750	537	622	17	.239	.303	.293	29	.239	.302	2.79	116	254
1909	NL	8th	45-108	.294	65.5	Harry Smith/Frank Bowerman	195,188	435	683	14	.223	.285	.274	23	.263	.339	3.20	102	113
1910	NL	8th	53-100	.346	50.5	Fred Lake	149,027	495	701	31	.246	.301	.317	36	.265	.349	3.22	134	290
1911	NL	8th	44-107	.291	54.0	Fred Tenney	116,000	699	1021	37	.267	.340	.355	76	.296	.381	5.08	125	211
1912	NL	8th	52-101	.340	52.0	Johnny Kling	121,000	693	861	35	.273	.335	.361	43	.291	.359	4.17	125	172
1913	NL	5th	69-82	.457	31.5	George Stallings	208,000	641	690	32	.256	.326	.335	37	.263	.324	3.19	95	63
1914	NL	1st	94-59	.614	—	George Stallings	382,913	657	548	35	.251	.323	.335	38	.249	.319	2.74	107	93
1915	NL	2nd	83-69	.546	7.0	George Stallings	376,283	582	545	17	.240	.321	.319	23	.247	.303	2.57	93	25
1916	NL	3rd	89-63	.586	4.0	George Stallings	313,495	542	453	22	.233	.299	.307	24	.235	.285	2.19	85	31
1917	NL	6th	72-81	.471	25.5	George Stallings	174,253	536	552	22	.246	.309	.320	19	.251	.304	2.78	87	63
1918	NL	7th	53-71	.427	28.5	George Stallings	84,938	424	469	13	.244	.307	.307	14	.266	.316	2.90	88	48
1919	NL	6th	57-82	.410	38.5	George Stallings	167,401	465	563	24	.253	.311	.324	29	.275	.326	3.17	100	65
1920	NL	7th	62-90	.408	30.0	George Stallings	162,483	523	670	23	.260	.315	.339	39	.280	.337	3.54	97	38
1921	NL	4th	79-74	.516	15.0	Fred Mitchell	318,627	721	697	61	.290	.339	.400	54	.280	.337	3.90	84	49
1922	NL	8th	53-100	.346	39.5	Fred Mitchell	167,965	596	822	32	.263	.317	.341	57	.298	.361	4.37	91	32
1923	NL	7th	54-100	.351	41.5	Fred Mitchell	227,802	636	798	32	.273	.331	.353	64	.302	.352	4.21	101	55
1924	NL	8th	53-100	.346	40.0	D. Bancroft/D. Rudolph/D. Bancroft	177,478	520	800	25	.256	.306	.327	49	.270	.353	4.46	90	30
1925	NL	5th	70-83	.458	25.0	Dave Bancroft	313,528	708	802	41	.292	.345	.390	67	.291	.348	4.39	87	37
1926	NL	7th	66-86	.434	22.0	Dave Bancroft	303,598	624	719	16	.277	.335	.350	46	.294	.354	4.01	70	17
1927	NL	7th	60-94	.390	34.0	Dave Bancroft	288,685	651	771	37	.279	.326	.363	43	.296	.356	4.22	90	26
1928	NL	7th	50-103	.327	44.5	Jack Slattery/Rogers Hornsby	227,001	631	878	52	.275	.335	.367	100	.298	.363	4.83	102	132
1929	NL	8th	56-98	.364	43.0	Judge Fuchs	372,351	657	876	33	.280	.335	.375	103	.302	.367	5.12	89	58
1930	NL	6th	70-84	.455	22.0	Bill McKechnie	464,835	693	835	66	.281	.326	.393	117	.302	.360	4.91	91	78
1931	NL	7th	64-90	.416	37.0	Bill McKechnie	515,005	533	680	34	.258	.309	.341	66	.272	.325	3.90	97	67
1932	NL	5th	77-77	.500	13.0	Bill McKechnie	507,606	649	655	63	.265	.311	.366	61	.272	.328	3.53	81	61
1933	NL	4th	83-71	.539	9.0	Bill McKechnie	517,803	552	531	54	.252	.299	.345	54	.261	.309	2.96	86	99
1934	NL	4th	78-73	.517	16.0	Bill McKechnie	303,205	683	714	83	.272	.323	.378	78	.279	.331	4.11	68	65
1935	NL	8th	38-115	.248	61.5	Bill McKechnie	232,754	575	852	75	.263	.311	.362	81	.303	.354	4.93	97	96
1936	NL	6th	71-83	.461	21.0	Bill McKechnie	340,585	631	715	67	.265	.322	.356	69	.281	.337	3.94	86	55
1937	NL	5th	79-73	.520	16.0	Bill McKechnie	385,339	579	556	63	.247	.314	.339	60	.259	.310	3.22	72	50
1938	NL	5th	77-75	.507	12.0	Casey Stengel	341,149	561	618	54	.250	.309	.333	66	.258	.322	3.40	69	36
1939	NL	7th	63-88	.417	32.5	Casey Stengel	285,994	572	659	56	.264	.314	.348	63	.271	.339	3.71	82	32
1940	NL	7th	65-87	.428	34.5	Casey Stengel	241,616	623	745	59	.256	.311	.349	83	.274	.349	4.36	101	65
1941	NL	7th	62-92	.403	38.0	Casey Stengel	263,680	592	720	48	.251	.312	.334	75	.269	.341	3.95	86	59
1942	NL	7th	59-89	.399	44.0	Casey Stengel	285,332	515	645	68	.240	.307	.329	82	.260	.331	3.76	93	100
1943	NL	6th	68-85	.444	36.5	Bob Coleman/Casey Stengel	271,289	465	612	39	.233	.299	.309	66	.255	.314	3.25	113	127
1944	NL	6th	65-89	.422	40.0	Bob Coleman	208,691	593	674	79	.246	.308	.353	80	.267	.335	3.67	88	145
1945	NL	6th	67-85	.441	30.0	Bob Coleman/Del Bissonette	374,178	721	728	101	.267	.334	.374	99	.272	.342	4.04	132	205
1946	NL	4th	81-72	.529	15.5	Billy Southworth	969,673	630	592	44	.264	.337	.353	76	.248	.313	3.35	88	61
1947	NL	3rd	86-68	.558	8.0	Billy Southworth	1,277,361	701	622	85	.275	.346	.390	93	.255	.316	3.62	88	62
1948	NL	1st	91-62	.595	—	Billy Southworth	1,455,439	739	584	95	.275	.359	.399	93	.254	.311	3.38	97	63
1949	NL	4th	75-79	.487	22.0	Billy Southworth/Johnny Cooney	1,081,795	706	719	103	.258	.345	.374	110	.270	.336	3.99	89	60
1950	NL	4th	83-71	.539	8.0	Billy Southworth	944,391	785	736	148	.263	.342	.405	129	.263	.336	4.14	72	60
1951	NL	4th	76-78	.494	20.5	Billy Southworth/Tommy Holmes	487,475	723	662	130	.262	.336	.394	96	.259	.337	3.75	96	74
1952	NL	7th	64-89	.418	32.0	Tommy Holmes/Charlie Grimm	281,278	569	651	110	.233	.301	.343	106	.259	.329	3.78	89	75
1953	NL	2nd	92-62	.597	13.0	Charlie Grimm	1,826,397	738	589	156	.266	.325	.415	107	.245	.318	3.30	83	58
1954	NL	3rd	89-65	.578	8.0	Charlie Grimm	2,131,388	670	556	139	.265	.327	.401	106	.250	.323	3.19	78	42
1955	NL	2nd	85-69	.552	13.5	Charlie Grimm	2,005,836	743	668	182	.261	.326	.427	138	.256	.331	3.85	83	65
1956	NL	2nd	92-62	.597	1.0	Charlie Grimm/Fred Haney	2,046,331	709	569	177	.259	.323	.423	133	.247	.309	3.11	93	74

Year	Lg	Pos	W-L	Pct	GB	Manager	Att.	R	OR	HR	Avg	OBP	Slg	Opponent HR	Opponent Avg	Opponent OBP	ERA	Park Index Runs	Park Index HR
1957	NL	1st	95-59	.617	—	Fred Haney	2,215,404	772	613	199	.269	.327	.442	124	.253	.325	3.47	77	64
1958	NL	1st	92-62	.597	—	Fred Haney	1,971,101	675	541	167	.266	.329	.412	125	.244	.303	3.21	69	70
1959	NL	2nd	86-70	.551	2.0	Fred Haney	1,749,112	724	623	177	.265	.326	.417	128	.260	.315	3.51	86	93
1960	NL	2nd	88-66	.571	7.0	Chuck Dressen	1,497,799	724	658	170	.265	.323	.417	130	.251	.320	3.76	79	95
1961	NL	4th	83-71	.539	10.0	Chuck Dressen/Birdie Tebbetts	1,101,441	712	656	188	.258	.328	.415	153	.258	.322	3.89	79	84
1962	NL	5th	86-76	.531	15.5	Birdie Tebbetts	766,921	730	665	181	.252	.326	.403	151	.263	.315	3.68	95	101
1963	NL	6th	84-78	.519	15.0	Bobby Bragan	773,018	677	603	139	.244	.312	.370	149	.241	.304	3.27	103	107
1964	NL	5th	88-74	.543	5.0	Bobby Bragan	910,911	803	744	159	.272	.333	.418	160	.257	.314	4.12	97	110
1965	NL	5th	86-76	.531	11.0	Bobby Bragan	555,584	708	633	196	.256	.310	.416	123	.246	.316	3.52	108	118
1966	NL	5th	85-77	.525	10.0	Bobby Bragan/Billy Hitchcock	1,539,801	782	683	207	.263	.326	.424	129	.257	.317	3.68	99	149
1967	NL	7th	77-85	.475	24.5	Billy Hitchcock/Ken Silvestri	1,389,222	631	640	158	.240	.307	.372	118	.251	.310	3.47	111	149
1968	NL	5th	81-81	.500	16.0	Lum Harris	1,126,540	514	549	80	.252	.307	.339	87	.241	.290	2.92	83	104
1969	NL	1st-W	93-69	.574	—	Lum Harris	1,458,320	691	631	141	.258	.321	.380	144	.258	.321	3.53	106	130
1970	NL	5th-W	76-86	.469	26.0	Lum Harris	1,078,848	736	772	160	.270	.334	.404	185	.261	.320	4.33	111	157
1971	NL	3rd-W	82-80	.506	8.0	Lum Harris	1,006,320	643	699	153	.257	.312	.385	152	.269	.328	3.75	124	152
1972	NL	4th-W	70-84	.455	25.0	Lum Harris/Eddie Mathews	752,973	628	730	144	.258	.328	.382	155	.266	.331	4.27	117	139
1973	NL	5th-W	76-85	.472	22.5	Eddie Mathews	800,655	799	774	206	.266	.339	.427	144	.263	.332	4.25	134	143
1974	NL	3rd-W	88-74	.543	14.0	Eddie Mathews/Clyde King	981,085	661	563	120	.249	.319	.363	97	.244	.307	3.05	105	101
1975	NL	5th-W	67-94	.416	40.5	Clyde King/Connie Ryan	534,672	583	739	107	.244	.313	.346	101	.278	.341	3.91	92	141
1976	NL	6th-W	70-92	.432	32.0	Dave Bristol	818,179	620	700	82	.245	.320	.334	86	.261	.332	3.86	127	143
1977	NL	6th-W	61-101	.377	37.0	D. Bristol/T. Turner/V. Benson/D. Bristol	872,464	678	895	139	.254	.320	.376	169	.279	.360	4.85	135	208
1978	NL	6th-W	69-93	.426	26.0	Bobby Cox	904,494	600	750	123	.244	.315	.363	132	.257	.335	4.08	130	223
1979	NL	6th-W	66-94	.412	23.5	Bobby Cox	769,465	669	763	126	.256	.318	.377	132	.272	.335	4.18	124	149
1980	NL	4th-W	81-80	.503	11.0	Bobby Cox	1,048,411	630	660	144	.250	.307	.380	131	.258	.316	3.77	103	147
1981	NL	4th-W	25-29	.463	9.5	Bobby Cox													
	NL	5th-W	25-27	.481	7.5	Bobby Cox	535,418	395	416	64	.243	.306	.349	62	.257	.318	3.45	101	189
1982	NL	1st-W	89-73	.549	—	Joe Torre	1,801,985	739	702	146	.256	.325	.383	126	.267	.328	3.82	116	199
1983	NL	2nd-W	88-74	.543	3.0	Joe Torre	2,119,935	746	640	130	.272	.341	.400	132	.260	.327	3.67	111	112
1984	NL	2nd-W	80-82	.494	12.0	Joe Torre	1,724,892	632	655	111	.247	.317	.361	122	.257	.322	3.57	121	116
1985	NL	5th-W	66-96	.407	29.0	Eddie Haas/Bobby Wine	1,350,137	632	781	126	.246	.315	.363	134	.271	.347	4.19	119	126
1986	NL	6th-W	72-89	.447	23.5	Chuck Tanner	1,387,181	615	719	138	.250	.319	.381	117	.266	.338	3.97	106	137
1987	NL	5th-W	69-92	.429	20.5	Chuck Tanner	1,217,402	747	829	152	.258	.339	.403	163	.276	.347	4.63	122	116
1988	NL	6th-W	54-106	.338	39.5	Chuck Tanner/Russ Nixon	848,089	555	741	96	.242	.298	.348	108	.268	.334	4.09	115	125
1989	NL	6th-W	63-97	.394	28.0	Russ Nixon	984,930	584	680	128	.234	.298	.350	114	.250	.309	3.70	106	94
1990	NL	6th-W	65-97	.401	26.0	Russ Nixon/Bobby Cox	980,129	682	821	162	.250	.311	.396	128	.275	.343	4.58	108	115
1991	NL	1st-W	94-68	.580	—	Bobby Cox	2,140,217	749	644	141	.258	.328	.393	118	.240	.303	3.49	129	151
1992	NL	1st-W	98-64	.605	—	Bobby Cox	3,077,400	682	569	138	.254	.316	.388	89	.242	.305	3.14	102	106
1993	NL	1st-W	104-58	.642	—	Bobby Cox	3,884,720	767	559	169	.262	.331	.408	101	.240	.303	3.14	98	93
1994	NL	2nd-E	68-46	.596	6.0	Bobby Cox	2,539,240	542	448	137	.267	.333	.434	76	.242	.311	3.57	93	91
1995	NL	1st-E	90-54	.625	—	Bobby Cox	2,561,831	645	540	168	.250	.326	.409	107	.244	.309	3.44	109	139
1996	NL	1st-E	96-66	.593	—	Bobby Cox	2,901,242	773	648	197	.270	.333	.432	120	.247	.304	3.52	107	119
1997	NL	1st-E	101-61	.623	—	Bobby Cox	3,463,988	791	581	174	.270	.343	.426	111	.242	.301	3.18	98	85

Team Nicknames: Boston Red Stockings 1876-1889, Boston Beaneaters 1890-1913, Boston Braves 1914-1953, Milwaukee Braves 1954-1966, Atlanta Braves 1967-1997.

Team Ballparks: South End Grounds I 1876-1887, South End Grounds II 1888-1893, South End Grounds II & III & Congress Street Grounds (shared) 1894, South End Grounds III 1895-1914, Fenway Park I & Braves Field (shared) 1915, Braves Field 1916-1952, County Stadium 1953-1965, Atlanta-Fulton County Stadium 1966-1996, Ted Turner Field 1997.

Boston/Milwaukee/Atlanta Braves Individual Season Batting Leaders

Year	Batting Average		On-Base Percentage		Slugging Percentage		Home Runs		RBI		Stolen Bases	
1876	Jim O'Rourke	.327	Jim O'Rourke	.358	Jim O'Rourke	.420	4 tied with	2	Jim O'Rourke	43	Statistic unavailable	
1877	Deacon White	.387	Jim O'Rourke	.407	Deacon White	.545	Deacon White	2	Deacon White	49	Statistic unavailable	
1878	Jim O'Rourke	.278	Jim O'Rourke	.292	Jim O'Rourke	.412	Jim O'Rourke	1	Jim O'Rourke	29	Statistic unavailable	
							Ezra Sutton		Ezra Sutton			
1879	John O'Rourke	.341	Charley Jones	.367	John O'Rourke	.521	Charley Jones	9	Charley Jones	62	Statistic unavailable	
									John O'Rourke			
1880	Charley Jones	.300	Charley Jones	.326	Jim O'Rourke	.441	Jim O'Rourke	6	Jim O'Rourke	45	Statistic unavailable	
1881	Ezra Sutton	.291	Ezra Sutton	.318	John Morrill	.379	Joe Hornung	2	John Morrill	39	Statistic unavailable	
1882	Jim Whitney	.323	Jim Whitney	.382	Jim Whitney	.510	Jim Whitney	5	John Morrill	54	Statistic unavailable	
1883	Jack Burdock	.330	Jack Burdock	.353	John Morrill	.525	Joe Hornung	8	Jack Burdock	88	Statistic unavailable	
1884	Ezra Sutton	.346	Ezra Sutton	.384	Ezra Sutton	.455	Joe Hornung	7	3 tied with	61	Statistic unavailable	
1885	Ezra Sutton	.313	Ezra Sutton	.338	Ezra Sutton	.425	3 tied with	4	Ezra Sutton	47	Statistic unavailable	
1886	Sam Wise	.289	Sam Wise	.345	Sam Wise	.432	John Morrill	7	Sam Wise	72	Tom Poorman	31
											Sam Wise	
1887	Sam Wise	.334	King Kelly	.393	Sam Wise	.522	John Morrill	12	Billy Nash	94	King Kelly	84
1888	King Kelly	.318	King Kelly	.368	King Kelly	.480	Dick Johnston	12	Billy Nash	75	King Kelly	56
1889	Dan Brouthers	.373	Dan Brouthers	.462	Dan Brouthers	.507	King Kelly	9	Dan Brouthers	118	King Kelly	68
1890	Steve Brodie	.296	Steve Brodie	.387	Marty Sullivan	.386	Herman Long	8	Steve Brodie	67	Herman Long	49
1891	Herman Long	.282	Herman Long	.377	Harry Stovey	.498	Harry Stovey	16	Billy Nash	95	Herman Long	60
									Harry Stovey			
1892	Hugh Duffy	.301	Tommy Tucker	.365	Hugh Duffy	.410	Herman Long	6	Billy Nash	95	Herman Long	57
1893	Hugh Duffy	.363	Tommy McCarthy	.429	Tommy McCarthy	.465	Bobby Lowe	14	Billy Nash	123	Tommy McCarthy	46
1894	Hugh Duffy	.440	Hugh Duffy	.502	Hugh Duffy	.694	Hugh Duffy	18	Hugh Duffy	145	Hugh Duffy	48
1895	Hugh Duffy	.352	Hugh Duffy	.425	Hugh Duffy	.482	Billy Nash	10	Billy Nash	108	Hugh Duffy	42
1896	Billy Hamilton	.365	Billy Hamilton	.477	Herman Long	.463	Herman Long	6	Hugh Duffy	113	Billy Hamilton	83
1897	Chick Stahl	.354	Billy Hamilton	.461	Chick Stahl	.499	Hugh Duffy	11	Jimmy Collins	132	Billy Hamilton	66
1898	Billy Hamilton	.369	Billy Hamilton	.480	Jimmy Collins	.479	Jimmy Collins	15	Jimmy Collins	111	Billy Hamilton	54
1899	Chick Stahl	.351	Chick Stahl	.426	Chick Stahl	.493	Chick Stahl	7	Hugh Duffy	102	Chick Stahl	33
1900	Billy Hamilton	.333	Billy Hamilton	.449	Buck Freeman	.452	Herman Long	12	Jimmy Collins	95	Billy Hamilton	32
1901	Gene DeMontreville	.300	Fred Tenney	.340	Gene DeMontreville	.364	Gene DeMontreville	5	Gene DeMontreville	72	Gene DeMontreville	25
1902	Fred Tenney	.315	Fred Tenney	.409	Fred Tenney	.376	5 tied with	2	Pat Carney	65	Billy Lush	30
									Ed Gremminger			
1903	Fred Tenney	.313	Fred Tenney	.415	Pat Moran	.406	Pat Moran	7	Duff Cooley	70	Charlie Dexter	32
1904	Jim Delahanty	.285	Fred Tenney	.351	Jim Delahanty	.389	Duff Cooley	5	Duff Cooley	70	Ed Abbaticchio	24
1905	Fred Tenney	.288	Fred Tenney	.368	Ed Abbaticchio	.374	Jim Delahanty	5	Jim Delahanty	55	Ed Abbaticchio	30
									Harry Wolverton			
1906	Fred Tenney	.283	Fred Tenney	.357	Johnny Bates	.349	Johnny Bates	6	Johnny Bates	54	3 tied with	17
									Del Howard			
1907	Ginger Beaumont	.322	Fred Tenney	.371	Ginger Beaumont	.424	Dave Brain	10	Ginger Beaumont	62	Ginger Beaumont	25
1908	Claude Ritchey	.273	Claude Ritchey	.361	Ginger Beaumont	.347	Bill Dahlen	3	Dan McGann	55	Johnny Bates	25
1909	Beals Becker	.246	Beals Becker	.305	Beals Becker	.326	Beals Becker	6	Ginger Beaumont	60	Bill Sweeney	25
1910	Doc Miller	.286	Bill Sweeney	.349	Fred Beck	.415	Fred Beck	10	Fred Beck	64	Bill Collins	36
1911	Doc Miller	.333	Bill Sweeney	.404	Doc Miller	.442	Doc Miller	7	Doc Miller	91	Bill Sweeney	33
1912	Bill Sweeney	.344	Bill Sweeney	.416	Bill Sweeney	.445	Ben Houser	8	Bill Sweeney	100	Bill Sweeney	27
1913	Joe Connolly	.281	Joe Connolly	.379	Joe Connolly	.410	Bris Lord	6	Joe Connolly	57	Hap Myers	57
1914	Butch Schmidt	.285	Johnny Evers	.390	Butch Schmidt	.356	Joe Connolly	9	Rabbit Maranville	78	Rabbit Maranville	28
1915	Sherry Magee	.280	Sherry Magee	.350	Sherry Magee	.392	6 tied with	2	Sherry Magee	87	Rabbit Maranville	18
1916	Ed Konetchy	.260	Red Smith	.333	Ed Konetchy	.373	Rabbit Maranville	4	Ed Konetchy	70	Rabbit Maranville	32
1917	Red Smith	.295	Red Smith	.369	Red Smith	.392	Ray Powell	4	Red Smith	62	Rabbit Maranville	27
1918	Red Smith	.298	Red Smith	.373	Al Wickland	.398	Al Wickland	4	Red Smith	65	Joe Kelly	12
											Al Wickland	
1919	Walter Holke	.292	Walter Holke	.325	Rabbit Maranville	.377	Rabbit Maranville	5	Walter Holke	48	Walter Holke	19
1920	Walter Holke	.294	Les Mann	.341	Walter Holke	.377	Ray Powell	6	Walter Holke	64	Tony Boeckel	18
1921	Tony Boeckel	.313	Tony Boeckel	.370	Ray Powell	.462	Ray Powell	12	Tony Boeckel	84	Billy Southworth	22
1922	Ray Powell	.296	Ray Powell	.369	Ray Powell	.409	Tony Boeckel	6	Hod Ford	60	Tony Boeckel	14
							Ray Powell					
1923	Billy Southworth	.319	Billy Southworth	.383	Billy Southworth	.448	Tony Boeckel	7	Stuffy McInnis	95	Billy Southworth	14
1924	Stuffy McInnis	.291	Casey Stengel	.348	Casey Stengel	.382	Cotton Tierney	6	Stuffy McInnis	59	Casey Stengel	13
1925	Dick Burrus	.340	Dave Bancroft	.400	Dick Burrus	.449	Jimmy Welsh	7	Dick Burrus	87	Doc Gautreau	11
1926	Eddie Brown	.328	Dave Bancroft	.399	Eddie Brown	.415	Dick Burrus	3	Eddie Brown	84	Doc Gautreau	17
							Jimmy Welsh					
1927	Lance Richbourg	.309	Lance Richbourg	.342	Jimmy Welsh	.423	Jack Fournier	10	Eddie Brown	75	Lance Richbourg	24
1928	Rogers Hornsby	.387	Rogers Hornsby	.498	Rogers Hornsby	.632	Rogers Hornsby	21	Rogers Hornsby	94	Lance Richbourg	11
											George Sisler	
1929	George Sisler	.326	George Harper	.389	George Harper	.433	George Harper	10	George Sisler	79	Rabbit Maranville	13
1930	Wally Berger	.310	Wally Berger	.375	Wally Berger	.614	Wally Berger	38	Wally Berger	119	Lance Richbourg	13
1931	Wally Berger	.323	Wally Berger	.380	Wally Berger	.512	Wally Berger	19	Wally Berger	84	Wally Berger	13
1932	Wally Berger	.307	Wally Berger	.346	Wally Berger	.468	Wally Berger	17	Wally Berger	73	Billy Urbanski	8
1933	Wally Berger	.313	Wally Berger	.365	Wally Berger	.566	Wally Berger	27	Wally Berger	106	Buck Jordan	4
											Billy Urbanski	
1934	Buck Jordan	.311	Buck Jordan	.358	Wally Berger	.546	Wally Berger	34	Wally Berger	121	Pinky Whitney	7
1935	Wally Berger	.295	Wally Berger	.355	Wally Berger	.548	Wally Berger	34	Wally Berger	130	4 tied with	3
1936	Buck Jordan	.323	Buck Jordan	.375	Wally Berger	.483	Wally Berger	25	Wally Berger	91	Gene Moore	6
1937	Gene Moore	.283	Gene Moore	.358	Gene Moore	.456	Gene Moore	16	Tony Cuccinello	80	Gene Moore	11
1938	Debs Garms	.315	Debs Garms	.371	Elbie Fletcher	.378	Vince DiMaggio	14	Tony Cuccinello	76	Vince DiMaggio	11
1939	Buddy Hassett	.308	Max West	.364	Max West	.497	Max West	19	Max West	82	Buddy Hassett	13
1940	Bama Rowell	.305	Chet Ross	.352	Chet Ross	.460	Chet Ross	17	Chet Ross	89	Bama Rowell	12
1941	Max West	.277	Max West	.373	Max West	.426	Max West	12	Eddie Miller	68	Bama Rowell	11
									Max West			
1942	Tommy Holmes	.278	Max West	.354	Max West	.409	Max West	16	Max West	56	Nanny Fernandez	15
1943	Tommy Holmes	.270	Tommy Holmes	.334	Tommy Holmes	.378	Chuck Workman	10	Chuck Workman	67	Chuck Workman	12
1944	Tommy Holmes	.309	Tommy Holmes	.372	Tommy Holmes	.456	Butch Nieman	16	Tommy Holmes	73	Connie Ryan	13
1945	Tommy Holmes	.352	Tommy Holmes	.420	Tommy Holmes	.577	Tommy Holmes	28	Tommy Holmes	117	Tommy Holmes	15
1946	Johnny Hopp	.333	Johnny Hopp	.386	Johnny Hopp	.440	Danny Litwhiler	8	Tommy Holmes	79	Johnny Hopp	21
1947	Bob Elliott	.317	Bob Elliott	.410	Bob Elliott	.517	Bob Elliott	22	Bob Elliott	113	Johnny Hopp	13

Teams: Braves

Year	Batting Average		On-Base Percentage		Slugging Percentage		Home Runs		RBI		Stolen Bases	
1948	Tommy Holmes	.325	Bob Elliott	.423	Bob Elliott	.474	Bob Elliott	23	Bob Elliott	100	Earl Torgeson	19
1949	Eddie Stanky	.285	Eddie Stanky	.417	Bob Elliott	.467	Bob Elliott	17	Bob Elliott	76	Al Dark	5
1950	Bob Elliott	.305	Earl Torgeson	.412	Sid Gordon	.557	Sid Gordon	27	Bob Elliott	107	Sam Jethroe	35
1951	Sid Gordon	.287	Sid Gordon	.383	Sid Gordon	.500	Sid Gordon	29	Sid Gordon	109	Sam Jethroe	35
1952	Sid Gordon	.289	Sid Gordon	.384	Sid Gordon	.483	Sid Gordon	25	Sid Gordon	75	Sam Jethroe	28
							Eddie Mathews					
1953	Eddie Mathews	.302	Eddie Mathews	.406	Eddie Mathews	.627	Eddie Mathews	47	Eddie Mathews	135	Bill Bruton	26
1954	Joe Adcock	.308	Eddie Mathews	.423	Eddie Mathews	.603	Eddie Mathews	40	Eddie Mathews	103	Bill Bruton	34
1955	Hank Aaron	.314	Eddie Mathews	.413	Eddie Mathews	.601	Eddie Mathews	41	Hank Aaron	106	Bill Bruton	25
1956	Hank Aaron	.328	Eddie Mathews	.373	Joe Adcock	.597	Joe Adcock	38	Joe Adcock	103	Bill Bruton	8
1957	Hank Aaron	.322	Eddie Mathews	.387	Hank Aaron	.600	Hank Aaron	44	Hank Aaron	132	Bill Bruton	11
1958	Hank Aaron	.326	Hank Aaron	.386	Hank Aaron	.546	Eddie Mathews	31	Hank Aaron	95	Eddie Mathews	5
1959	Hank Aaron	.355	Hank Aaron	.401	Hank Aaron	.636	Eddie Mathews	46	Hank Aaron	123	Bill Bruton	13
1960	Joe Adcock	.298	Eddie Mathews	.397	Hank Aaron	.566	Hank Aaron	40	Hank Aaron	126	Bill Bruton	22
1961	Hank Aaron	.327	Eddie Mathews	.402	Hank Aaron	.594	Joe Adcock	35	Hank Aaron	120	Hank Aaron	21
1962	Hank Aaron	.323	Hank Aaron	.390	Hank Aaron	.618	Hank Aaron	45	Hank Aaron	128	Hank Aaron	15
1963	Hank Aaron	.319	Eddie Mathews	.399	Hank Aaron	.586	Hank Aaron	44	Hank Aaron	130	Hank Aaron	31
1964	Rico Carty	.330	Hank Aaron	.393	Rico Carty	.554	Hank Aaron	24	Joe Torre	109	Hank Aaron	22
1965	Hank Aaron	.318	Hank Aaron	.379	Hank Aaron	.560	Hank Aaron	32	Eddie Mathews	95	Hank Aaron	24
							Eddie Mathews					
1966	Felipe Alou	.327	Rico Carty	.391	Joe Torre	.560	Hank Aaron	44	Hank Aaron	127	Hank Aaron	21
1967	Hank Aaron	.307	Hank Aaron	.369	Hank Aaron	.573	Hank Aaron	39	Hank Aaron	109	Hank Aaron	17
1968	Felipe Alou	.317	Felipe Alou	.365	Hank Aaron	.498	Hank Aaron	29	Hank Aaron	86	Hank Aaron	28
1969	Hank Aaron	.300	Hank Aaron	.396	Hank Aaron	.607	Hank Aaron	44	Hank Aaron	97	Felix Millan	14
1970	Rico Carty	.366	Rico Carty	.454	Rico Carty	.584	Hank Aaron	38	Hank Aaron	118	Felix Millan	16
1971	Ralph Garr	.343	Hank Aaron	.410	Hank Aaron	.669	Hank Aaron	47	Hank Aaron	118	Ralph Garr	30
1972	Ralph Garr	.325	Hank Aaron	.390	Hank Aaron	.514	Hank Aaron	34	Earl Williams	87	Ralph Garr	25
1973	Ralph Garr	.299	Darrell Evans	.403	Darrell Evans	.556	Dave Johnson	43	Darrell Evans	104	Ralph Garr	35
1974	Ralph Garr	.353	Ralph Garr	.383	Ralph Garr	.503	Darrell Evans	25	Darrell Evans	79	Ralph Garr	26
1975	Ralph Garr	.278	Darrell Evans	.361	Darrell Evans	.421	Darrell Evans	22	Darrell Evans	73	Ralph Garr	14
1976	Ken Henderson	.262	Jimmy Wynn	.377	Ken Henderson	.395	Jimmy Wynn	17	Jimmy Wynn	66	Jerry Royster	24
1977	Willie Montanez	.287	Jeff Burroughs	.362	Jeff Burroughs	.520	Jeff Burroughs	41	Jeff Burroughs	114	Jerry Royster	28
1978	Jeff Burroughs	.301	Jeff Burroughs	.432	Jeff Burroughs	.529	3 tied with	23	Dale Murphy	79	Jerry Royster	27
1979	Bob Horner	.314	Gary Matthews	.363	Bob Horner	.552	Bob Horner	33	Bob Horner	98	Jerry Royster	35
1980	Chris Chambliss	.282	Dale Murphy	.349	Dale Murphy	.510	Bob Horner	35	Bob Horner	89	Jerry Royster	22
									Dale Murphy			
1981	Claudell Washington	.291	Bob Horner	.345	Bob Horner	.460	Bob Horner	15	Chris Chambliss	51	Eddie Miller	23
1982	Dale Murphy	.281	Dale Murphy	.378	Dale Murphy	.507	Dale Murphy	36	Dale Murphy	109	Claudell Washington	33
1983	Dale Murphy	.302	Dale Murphy	.393	Dale Murphy	.540	Dale Murphy	36	Dale Murphy	121	Brett Butler	39
1984	Dale Murphy	.290	Dale Murphy	.372	Dale Murphy	.547	Dale Murphy	36	Dale Murphy	100	Claudell Washington	21
1985	Dale Murphy	.300	Dale Murphy	.388	Dale Murphy	.539	Dale Murphy	37	Dale Murphy	111	Claudell Washington	14
1986	Bob Horner	.273	Ken Oberkfell	.373	Dale Murphy	.477	Dale Murphy	29	Bob Horner	87	Rafael Ramirez	19
1987	Dion James	.312	Dale Murphy	.417	Dale Murphy	.580	Dale Murphy	44	Dale Murphy	105	Gerald Perry	42
1988	Gerald Perry	.300	Gerald Perry	.338	Ron Gant	.439	Dale Murphy	24	Dale Murphy	77	Gerald Perry	29
1989	Lonnie Smith	.315	Lonnie Smith	.415	Lonnie Smith	.533	Lonnie Smith	21	Dale Murphy	84	Lonnie Smith	25
1990	Lonnie Smith	.305	Lonnie Smith	.384	Ron Gant	.539	Ron Gant	32	Ron Gant	84	Ron Gant	33
1991	Terry Pendleton	.319	Terry Pendleton	.363	Terry Pendleton	.517	Ron Gant	32	Ron Gant	105	Otis Nixon	72
1992	Terry Pendleton	.311	David Justice	.359	Terry Pendleton	.473	David Justice	21	Terry Pendleton	105	Otis Nixon	41
							Terry Pendleton					
1993	Jeff Blauser	.305	Jeff Blauser	.401	David Justice	.515	David Justice	40	David Justice	120	Otis Nixon	47
1994	Fred McGriff	.318	David Justice	.427	Fred McGriff	.623	Fred McGriff	34	Fred McGriff	94	Deion Sanders	19
1995	Fred McGriff	.280	David Justice	.365	Fred McGriff	.489	Fred McGriff	27	Fred McGriff	93	Marquis Grissom	29
1996	Chipper Jones	.309	Chipper Jones	.393	Ryan Klesko	.530	Ryan Klesko	34	Chipper Jones	110	Marquis Grissom	28
1997	Kenny Lofton	.333	Kenny Lofton	.409	Ryan Klesko	.490	Ryan Klesko	24	Chipper Jones	111	Kenny Lofton	27

Teams: Braves

Boston/Milwaukee/Atlanta Braves Individual Season Pitching Leaders

Year	ERA		Baserunners/9 IP		Innings Pitched		Strikeouts		Wins		Saves	
1876	Jack Manning	2.14	Jack Manning	11.2	Joe Borden	218.1	Joe Borden	34	Jack Manning	18	Jack Manning	5
1877	Tommy Bond	2.11	Tommy Bond	9.8	Tommy Bond	521.0	Tommy Bond	170	Tommy Bond	40	Tommy Bond / Will White	0
1878	Tommy Bond	2.06	Tommy Bond	10.2	Tommy Bond	532.2	Tommy Bond	182	Tommy Bond	40	Tommy Bond / Jack Manning	0
1879	Tommy Bond	1.96	Tommy Bond	9.2	Tommy Bond	555.1	Tommy Bond	155	Tommy Bond	43	4 tied with	0
1880	Tommy Bond	2.67	Tommy Bond	11.0	Tommy Bond	493.0	Tommy Bond	118	Tommy Bond	26	4 tied with	0
1881	Jim Whitney	2.48	Jim Whitney	10.4	Jim Whitney	552.1	Jim Whitney	162	Jim Whitney	31	Bobby Mathews	2
1882	Jim Whitney	2.64	Bobby Mathews	9.5	Jim Whitney	420.0	Jim Whitney	180	Jim Whitney	24	4 tied with	0
1883	Jim Whitney	2.24	Jim Whitney	9.2	Jim Whitney	514.0	Jim Whitney	345	Jim Whitney	37	Jim Whitney	2
1884	Jim Whitney	2.09	Jim Whitney	8.0	Charlie Buffinton	587.0	Charlie Buffinton	417	Charlie Buffinton	48	John Morrill	0
1885	Charlie Buffinton	2.88	Jim Whitney	11.0	Jim Whitney	441.1	Charlie Buffinton	242	Charlie Buffinton	22	4 tied with	0
1886	Old Hoss Radbourn	3.00	Old Hoss Radbourn	11.2	Old Hoss Radbourn	509.1	Bill Stemmeyer	239	Old Hoss Radbourn	27	5 tied with	0
1887	Kid Madden	3.79	Kid Madden	12.9	Old Hoss Radbourn	425.0	Old Hoss Radbourn	87	Old Hoss Radbourn	24	Bill Stemmeyer	1
1888	Bill Sowders	2.07	Kid Madden	9.9	John Clarkson	483.1	John Clarkson	223	John Clarkson	33	5 tied with	0
1889	John Clarkson	2.73	John Clarkson	11.7	John Clarkson	620.0	John Clarkson	284	John Clarkson	49	Bill Sowders	2
1890	Kid Nichols	2.23	Kid Nichols	10.6	Kid Nichols	424.0	Kid Nichols	222	Kid Nichols	27	John Taber	1
1891	Kid Nichols	2.39	Harry Staley	10.9	John Clarkson	460.2	Kid Nichols	240	John Clarkson	33	John Clarkson / Kid Nichols	3
1892	Kid Nichols	2.84	Kid Nichols	10.6	Kid Nichols	453.0	Kid Nichols	187	Kid Nichols / Jack Stivetts	35	Jack Stivetts	1
1893	Kid Nichols	3.52	Kid Nichols	11.9	Kid Nichols	425.0	Kid Nichols	94	Kid Nichols	34	Jack Stivetts	1
1894	Kid Nichols	4.75	Kid Nichols	13.7	Kid Nichols	407.0	Kid Nichols	113	Kid Nichols	32	Tom Smith	1
1895	Kid Nichols	3.41	Kid Nichols	12.0	Kid Nichols	379.2	Kid Nichols	140	Kid Nichols	26	Kid Nichols	3
1896	Kid Nichols	2.83	Kid Nichols	12.0	Kid Nichols	372.1	Kid Nichols	102	Kid Nichols	30	3 tied with	1
1897	Kid Nichols	2.64	Kid Nichols	10.6	Kid Nichols	368.0	Kid Nichols	127	Kid Nichols	31	Kid Nichols	3
1898	Kid Nichols	2.13	Kid Nichols	9.6	Kid Nichols	388.0	Vic Willis	160	Kid Nichols	31	Kid Nichols	4
1899	Vic Willis	2.50	Kid Nichols	10.9	Kid Nichols	343.1	Vic Willis	120	Vic Willis	27	Vic Willis	2
1900	Kid Nichols	3.07	Kid Nichols	11.6	Bill Dinneen	320.2	Bill Dinneen	107	Bill Dinneen	20	Rome Chambers / Nig Cuppy	1
1901	Vic Willis	2.36	Vic Willis	10.3	Kid Nichols	321.0	Kid Nichols	143	Vic Willis	20	5 tied with	0
1902	Vic Willis	2.20	Vic Willis	10.7	Vic Willis	410.0	Vic Willis	225	Togie Pittinger / Vic Willis	27	Vic Willis	3
1903	Vic Willis	2.98	Vic Willis	11.5	Togie Pittinger	351.2	Togie Pittinger	140	Togie Pittinger	18	Togie Pittinger	1
1904	Togie Pittinger	2.66	Togie Pittinger	12.2	Vic Willis	350.0	Vic Willis	196	Vic Willis	18	8 tied with	0
1905	Irv Young	2.90	Irv Young	9.9	Irv Young	378.0	Irv Young	156	Irv Young	20	10 tied with	0
1906	Vive Lindaman	2.43	Irv Young	11.0	Irv Young	358.1	Big Jeff Pfeffer	158	Irv Young	16	9 tied with	0
1907	Patsy Flaherty	2.70	Patsy Flaherty	10.9	Gus Dorner	271.1	Vive Lindaman	90	Gus Dorner / Patsy Flaherty	12	Vive Lindaman / Irv Young	1
1908	Vive Lindaman	2.36	Vive Lindaman	10.8	Vive Lindaman	270.2	George Ferguson	98	Patsy Flaherty / Vive Lindaman	12	Vive Lindaman	1
1909	Al Mattern	2.85	Al Mattern	12.3	Al Mattern	316.1	Al Mattern	98	Al Mattern	15	Al Mattern	3
1910	Buster Brown	2.67	Buster Brown	11.9	Al Mattern	305.0	Sam Frock	170	Al Mattern	16	4 tied with	2
1911	Buster Brown	4.29	Al Mattern	14.1	Buster Brown	241.0	Lefty Tyler	90	Buster Brown	8	Buster Brown / Big Jeff Pfeffer	2
1912	Otto Hess	3.76	Buster Brown	11.4	Lefty Tyler	256.1	Lefty Tyler	144	Hub Perdue	13	Hub Perdue	3
1913	Lefty Tyler	2.79	Hub Perdue	10.3	Lefty Tyler	290.1	Lefty Tyler	143	Hub Perdue / Lefty Tyler	16	Lefty Tyler	2
1914	Bill James	1.90	Dick Rudolph	9.4	Dick Rudolph	336.1	Bill James	156	Bill James / Dick Rudolph	26	Bill James / Lefty Tyler	2
1915	Tom Hughes	2.12	Tom Hughes	8.9	Dick Rudolph	341.1	Tom Hughes	171	Dick Rudolph	22	Tom Hughes	9
1916	Lefty Tyler	2.02	Dick Rudolph	8.9	Dick Rudolph	312.0	Dick Rudolph	133	Dick Rudolph	19	Tom Hughes	5
1917	Art Nehf	2.16	Art Nehf	9.3	Jesse Barnes	295.0	Jesse Barnes	107	Art Nehf	17	3 tied with	1
1918	Bunny Hearn	2.49	Dick Rudolph	10.2	Art Nehf	284.1	Art Nehf	96	Art Nehf	15	14 tied with	0
1919	Dick Rudolph	2.17	Art Nehf	10.5	Dick Rudolph	273.2	Dick Rudolph	76	Dick Rudolph	13	Al Demaree	3
1920	Dana Fillingim	3.11	Hugh McQuillan	12.0	Joe Oeschger	299.0	Jack Scott	94	Joe Oeschger	15	Hugh McQuillan	5
1921	Dana Fillingim	3.45	Dana Fillingim	11.5	Joe Oeschger	299.0	Hugh McQuillan	94	Joe Oeschger	20	Hugh McQuillan	5
1922	Frank Miller	3.51	Frank Miller	12.4	Mule Watson	201.0	Frank Miller	65	Rube Marquard / Frank Miller	11	Dana Fillingim	2
1923	Jesse Barnes	2.76	Jesse Barnes	11.4	Rube Marquard	239.0	Rube Marquard	78	Joe Genewich	13	Jesse Barnes / Joe Oeschger	2
1924	Johnny Cooney	3.18	Johnny Cooney	11.4	Jesse Barnes	267.2	Johnny Cooney	67	Jesse Barnes	15	Johnny Cooney	2
1925	Larry Benton	3.09	Johnny Cooney	11.7	Johnny Cooney	245.2	Johnny Cooney	65	Larry Benton / Johnny Cooney	14	Rosy Ryan	2
1926	Johnny Werts	3.28	Bob Smith	12.2	Larry Benton	231.2	Larry Benton	103	Larry Benton	14	George Mogridge	3
1927	Bob Smith	3.76	Kent Greenfield	12.6	Bob Smith	260.2	Bob Smith	81	Joe Genewich / Kent Greenfield	11	George Mogridge	5
1928	Art Delaney	3.79	Art Delaney	11.9	Bob Smith	244.1	Ed Brandt	84	Bob Smith	13	Art Delaney / Bob Smith	2
1929	Ben Cantwell	4.47	Bob Smith	12.8	Bob Smith	231.0	Percy Jones	69	Socks Seibold	12	Johnny Cooney / Bob Smith	3
1930	Socks Seibold	4.12	Socks Seibold	13.4	Socks Seibold	251.0	Bob Smith	84	Socks Seibold	15	Bob Smith	5
1931	Ed Brandt	2.92	Ed Brandt	11.1	Ed Brandt	250.0	Ed Brandt	112	Ed Brandt	18	3 tied with	2
1932	Huck Betts	2.80	Huck Betts	10.7	Ed Brandt	254.0	Bob Brown	110	Ed Brandt	16	Ben Cantwell	5
1933	Ed Brandt	2.60	Huck Betts	10.4	Ed Brandt	287.2	Ed Brandt	104	Ben Cantwell	20	Huck Betts / Ed Brandt	4
1934	Fred Frankhouse	3.20	Ed Brandt	11.9	Ed Brandt	255.0	Ed Brandt	106	Huck Betts / Fred Frankhouse	17	3 tied with	5
1935	Bob Smith	3.94	Ben Cantwell	12.0	Fred Frankhouse	230.2	Fred Frankhouse	64	Fred Frankhouse	11	Bob Smith	5
1936	Danny MacFayden	2.87	Danny MacFayden	11.4	Danny MacFayden	266.2	Tiny Chaplin / Danny MacFayden	86	Danny MacFayden	17	Bob Smith	8
1937	Jim Turner	2.38	Jim Turner	9.8	Lou Fette	259.0	Lou Fette / Danny MacFayden	70	Lou Fette / Jim Turner	20	Bob Smith	3
1938	Danny MacFayden	2.95	Jim Turner	10.9	Jim Turner	268.0	Lou Fette	83	Danny MacFayden / Jim Turner	14	Dick Errickson	6

Teams: Braves

Year	ERA		Baserunners/9 IP		Innings Pitched		Strikeouts		Wins		Saves	
1939	Danny MacFayden	3.90	Bill Posedel	12.2	Bill Posedel	220.2	Bill Posedel	73	Bill Posedel	15	Fred Frankhouse	4
											Johnny Lanning	
1940	Manny Salvo	3.08	Manny Salvo	11.0	Dick Errickson	236.1	Bill Posedel	86	Dick Errickson	12	Dick Coffman	3
									Bill Posedel		Dick Errickson	
1941	Jim Tobin	3.10	Jim Tobin	10.9	Jim Tobin	238.0	Art Johnson	70	Jim Tobin	12	Tom Earley	3
1942	Al Javery	3.03	Al Javery	11.4	Jim Tobin	287.2	Al Javery	85	Al Javery	12	Johnny Sain	6
									Jim Tobin			
1943	Nate Andrews	2.57	Nate Andrews	10.6	Al Javery	303.0	Al Javery	134	Al Javery	17	Dave Odom	2
1944	Jim Tobin	3.01	Jim Tobin	11.1	Jim Tobin	299.1	Al Javery	137	Jim Tobin	18	Al Javery	3
											Jim Tobin	
1945	Bob Logan	3.18	Johnny Hutchings	12.3	Jim Tobin	196.2	Johnny Hutchings	99	Jim Tobin	9	Don Hendrickson	5
1946	Johnny Sain	2.21	Mort Cooper	9.9	Johnny Sain	265.0	Johnny Sain	129	Johnny Sain	20	Bill Posedel	4
1947	Warren Spahn	2.33	Warren Spahn	10.3	Warren Spahn	289.2	Johnny Sain	132	Johnny Sain	21	Andy Karl	3
									Warren Spahn		Warren Spahn	
1948	Johnny Sain	2.60	Johnny Sain	11.0	Johnny Sain	314.2	Johnny Sain	137	Johnny Sain	24	Clyde Shoun	4
1949	Warren Spahn	3.07	Warren Spahn	11.1	Warren Spahn	302.1	Warren Spahn	151	Warren Spahn	21	Nels Potter	7
1950	Warren Spahn	3.16	Warren Spahn	11.1	Vern Bickford	311.2	Warren Spahn	191	Warren Spahn	21	Bobby Hogue	7
1951	Chet Nichols	2.88	Warren Spahn	11.2	Warren Spahn	310.2	Warren Spahn	164	Warren Spahn	22	Bob Chipman	4
1952	Warren Spahn	2.98	Warren Spahn	10.6	Warren Spahn	290.0	Warren Spahn	183	Warren Spahn	14	Lew Burdette	7
1953	Warren Spahn	2.10	Warren Spahn	9.6	Warren Spahn	265.2	Warren Spahn	148	Warren Spahn	23	Lew Burdette	8
1954	Lew Burdette	2.76	Lew Burdette	11.0	Warren Spahn	283.1	Warren Spahn	136	Warren Spahn	21	Dave Jolly	10
1955	Bob Buhl	3.21	Warren Spahn	11.6	Warren Spahn	245.2	Bob Buhl	117	Warren Spahn	17	Ernie Johnson	4
1956	Lew Burdette	2.70	Warren Spahn	9.7	Warren Spahn	281.1	Warren Spahn	128	Warren Spahn	20	Dave Jolly	7
1957	Warren Spahn	2.69	Warren Spahn	10.7	Warren Spahn	271.0	Bob Buhl	117	Warren Spahn	21	Don McMahon	9
1958	Lew Burdette	2.91	Warren Spahn	10.4	Warren Spahn	290.0	Warren Spahn	150	Warren Spahn	22	Don McMahon	8
1959	Bob Buhl	2.86	Warren Spahn	10.9	Warren Spahn	292.0	Warren Spahn	143	Lew Burdette	21	Don McMahon	15
									Warren Spahn			
1960	Bob Buhl	3.09	Lew Burdette	10.3	Lew Burdette	275.2	Warren Spahn	154	Warren Spahn	21	Don McMahon	10
1961	Warren Spahn	3.02	Warren Spahn	10.4	Lew Burdette	272.1	Warren Spahn	115	Warren Spahn	21	Don McMahon	8
1962	Bob Shaw	2.80	Warren Spahn	10.2	Warren Spahn	269.1	Bob Shaw	124	Warren Spahn	18	Claude Raymond	10
1963	Warren Spahn	2.60	Warren Spahn	10.1	Warren Spahn	259.2	Denny Lemaster	190	Warren Spahn	23	Bob Shaw	13
1964	Tony Cloninger	3.56	Tony Cloninger	10.8	Tony Cloninger	242.2	Denny Lemaster	185	Tony Cloninger	19	Bobby Tiefenauer	13
1965	Ken Johnson	3.21	Ken Johnson	10.3	Tony Cloninger	279.0	Tony Cloninger	211	Tony Cloninger	24	Billy O'Dell	18
1966	Ken Johnson	3.30	Ken Johnson	10.8	Tony Cloninger	257.2	Tony Cloninger	178	Tony Cloninger	14	Clay Carroll	11
									Ken Johnson			
1967	Phil Niekro	1.87	Phil Niekro	9.8	Denny Lemaster	215.1	Denny Lemaster	148	Pat Jarvis	15	Phil Niekro	9
1968	Phil Niekro	2.59	Pat Jarvis	8.9	Phil Niekro	257.0	Phil Niekro	157	Pat Jarvis	16	Cecil Upshaw	13
1969	Phil Niekro	2.56	Phil Niekro	9.4	Phil Niekro	284.1	Phil Niekro	193	Phil Niekro	23	Cecil Upshaw	27
1970	Pat Jarvis	3.61	Pat Jarvis	11.1	Pat Jarvis	254.0	Pat Jarvis	173	Pat Jarvis	16	Hoyt Wilhelm	13
1971	Phil Niekro	2.98	Phil Niekro	10.8	Phil Niekro	268.2	Phil Niekro	173	Phil Niekro	15	Cecil Upshaw	17
1972	Phil Niekro	3.06	Phil Niekro	9.9	Phil Niekro	282.1	Phil Niekro	164	Phil Niekro	16	Cecil Upshaw	13
1973	Phil Niekro	3.31	Phil Niekro	11.3	Carl Morton	256.1	Phil Niekro	131	Carl Morton	15	Danny Frisella	8
1974	Buzz Capra	2.28	Phil Niekro	10.2	Phil Niekro	302.1	Phil Niekro	195	Phil Niekro	20	Tom House	11
1975	Phil Niekro	3.20	Phil Niekro	12.0	Carl Morton	277.2	Phil Niekro	144	Carl Morton	17	Tom House	11
1976	Andy Messersmith	3.04	Andy Messersmith	10.5	Phil Niekro	270.2	Phil Niekro	173	Phil Niekro	17	Adrian Devine	9
1977	Phil Niekro	4.03	Phil Niekro	13.3	Phil Niekro	330.1	Phil Niekro	262	Phil Niekro	16	Dave Campbell	13
1978	Phil Niekro	2.88	Phil Niekro	11.0	Phil Niekro	334.1	Phil Niekro	248	Phil Niekro	19	Gene Garber	22
1979	Phil Niekro	3.39	Phil Niekro	11.4	Phil Niekro	342.0	Phil Niekro	208	Phil Niekro	21	Gene Garber	25
1980	Tommy Boggs	3.42	Tommy Boggs	10.8	Phil Niekro	275.0	Phil Niekro	176	Phil Niekro	15	Rick Camp	22
1981	Rick Mahler	2.80	Phil Niekro	11.4	Gaylord Perry	150.2	Tommy Boggs	81	Rick Camp	9	Rick Camp	17
1982	Phil Niekro	3.61	Phil Niekro	11.6	Phil Niekro	234.1	Phil Niekro	144	Phil Niekro	17	Gene Garber	30
1983	Craig McMurtry	3.08	Pascual Perez	11.2	Craig McMurtry	224.2	Pascual Perez	144	Craig McMurtry	15	Steve Bedrosian	19
									Pascual Perez			
1984	Rick Mahler	3.12	Rick Mahler	11.1	Rick Mahler	222.0	Pascual Perez	145	Pascual Perez	14	Donnie Moore	16
1985	Rick Mahler	3.48	Rick Mahler	11.9	Rick Mahler	266.2	Steve Bedrosian	134	Rick Mahler	17	Bruce Sutter	23
1986	David Palmer	3.65	David Palmer	12.4	Rick Mahler	237.2	David Palmer	170	Rick Mahler	14	Gene Garber	24
1987	Zane Smith	4.09	Zane Smith	12.7	Zane Smith	242.0	Zane Smith	130	Zane Smith	15	Jim Acker	14
1988	Pete Smith	3.69	Rick Mahler	11.9	Rick Mahler	249.0	Rick Mahler	131	Rick Mahler	9	Bruce Sutter	14
1989	John Smoltz	2.94	John Smoltz	10.1	John Smoltz	208.0	John Smoltz	168	Tom Glavine	14	Joe Boever	21
1990	Charlie Leibrandt	3.16	Charlie Leibrandt	11.3	John Smoltz	231.1	John Smoltz	170	John Smoltz	14	Joe Boever	8
1991	Tom Glavine	2.55	Tom Glavine	9.9	Tom Glavine	246.2	Tom Glavine	192	Tom Glavine	20	Juan Berenguer	17
1992	Tom Glavine	2.76	John Smoltz	10.6	John Smoltz	246.2	John Smoltz	215	Tom Glavine	20	Alejandro Pena	15
1993	Greg Maddux	2.36	Greg Maddux	9.6	Greg Maddux	267.0	John Smoltz	208	Tom Glavine	22	Mike Stanton	27
1994	Greg Maddux	1.56	Greg Maddux	8.3	Greg Maddux	202.0	Greg Maddux	156	Greg Maddux	16	Greg McMichael	21
1995	Greg Maddux	1.63	Greg Maddux	7.5	Greg Maddux	209.2	John Smoltz	193	Greg Maddux	19	Mark Wohlers	25
1996	Greg Maddux	2.72	John Smoltz	9.1	John Smoltz	253.2	John Smoltz	276	John Smoltz	24	Mark Wohlers	39
1997	Greg Maddux	2.20	Greg Maddux	8.7	John Smoltz	256.0	John Smoltz	241	Denny Neagle	20	Mark Wohlers	33

Teams: Braves

Braves Franchise Batting Leaders—Career

Games

1	Hank Aaron	3,076
2	Eddie Mathews	2,223
3	Dale Murphy	1,926
4	Rabbit Maranville	1,795
5	Fred Tenney	1,737
6	Herman Long	1,646
7	Bobby Lowe	1,410
8	Del Crandall	1,394
9	Johnny Logan	1,351
10	Tommy Holmes	1,289
11	Mike Lum	1,225
12	John Morrill	1,219
13	Joe Adcock	1,207
14	Glenn Hubbard	1,196
15	Billy Nash	1,186
16	Jeff Blauser	1,184
17	Hugh Duffy	1,152
18	Jerry Royster	1,118
19	Wally Berger	1,057
20	Bill Bruton	1,052

At-Bats

1	Hank Aaron	11,628
2	Eddie Mathews	8,049
3	Dale Murphy	7,098
4	Herman Long	6,775
5	Rabbit Maranville	6,724
6	Fred Tenney	6,637
7	Bobby Lowe	5,617
8	Tommy Holmes	4,956
9	Johnny Logan	4,931
10	John Morrill	4,759
11	Hugh Duffy	4,656
12	Del Crandall	4,583
13	Billy Nash	4,561
14	Joe Adcock	4,232
15	Wally Berger	4,153
16	Bill Bruton	4,079
17	Ezra Sutton	4,045
18	Glenn Hubbard	4,016
19	Jeff Blauser	3,961
20	Joe Torre	3,700

Runs

1	Hank Aaron	2,107
2	Eddie Mathews	1,452
3	Herman Long	1,291
4	Fred Tenney	1,134
5	Dale Murphy	1,103
6	Bobby Lowe	999
7	Hugh Duffy	996
8	Billy Nash	855
9	Rabbit Maranville	801
10	John Morrill	800
11	Tommy Holmes	696
12	Ezra Sutton	694
13	Billy Hamilton	651
	Wally Berger	651
15	Tommy Tucker	648
16	Johnny Logan	624
17	Bill Bruton	622
18	Jeff Blauser	601
19	Joe Adcock	564
20	Joe Hornung	560

Hits

1	Hank Aaron	3,600
2	Eddie Mathews	2,201
3	Fred Tenney	1,994
4	Dale Murphy	1,901
5	Herman Long	1,900
6	Rabbit Maranville	1,696
7	Bobby Lowe	1,606
8	Hugh Duffy	1,544
9	Tommy Holmes	1,503
10	Johnny Logan	1,329
11	Billy Nash	1,283
12	Wally Berger	1,263
13	John Morrill	1,247
14	Joe Adcock	1,206
15	Del Crandall	1,176
16	Ezra Sutton	1,161
17	Bill Bruton	1,126
18	Joe Torre	1,087
19	Jeff Blauser	1,060
20	Tommy Tucker	1,025

Doubles

1	Hank Aaron	600
2	Eddie Mathews	338
3	Dale Murphy	306
4	Herman Long	295
5	Tommy Holmes	291
6	Wally Berger	248
7	Rabbit Maranville	244
8	Fred Tenney	242
9	John Morrill	234
10	Hugh Duffy	220
11	Johnny Logan	207
12	Jeff Blauser	201
13	Billy Nash	199
14	Joe Adcock	197
15	Glenn Hubbard	196
16	Bobby Lowe	186
17	Ezra Sutton	178
18	Del Crandall	167
	Bill Bruton	167
20	Felipe Alou	163

Triples

1	Rabbit Maranville	103
2	Hank Aaron	96
3	Herman Long	91
4	John Morrill	80
5	Bill Bruton	79
6	Fred Tenney	74
7	Hugh Duffy	73
8	Sam Wise	71
	Bobby Lowe	71
10	Eddie Mathews	70
11	Billy Nash	69
12	Ray Powell	67
13	Ezra Sutton	66
14	Joe Hornung	58
15	Chick Stahl	56
16	Dick Johnston	54
17	Wally Berger	52
18	Lance Richbourg	48
19	Tommy Holmes	47
20	Jimmy Collins	43

Home Runs

1	Hank Aaron	733
2	Eddie Mathews	493
3	Dale Murphy	371
4	Joe Adcock	239
5	Bob Horner	215
6	Wally Berger	199
7	Del Crandall	170
8	David Justice	160
9	Ron Gant	147
10	Joe Torre	142
11	Darrell Evans	131
12	Fred McGriff	130
13	Rico Carty	109
	Jeff Blauser	109
15	Bob Elliott	101
16	Sid Gordon	100
	Ryan Klesko	100
18	Felipe Alou	94
19	Johnny Logan	92
20	Seven tied at	88

RBI

1	Hank Aaron	2,202
2	Eddie Mathews	1,388
3	Dale Murphy	1,143
4	Herman Long	963
5	Hugh Duffy	927
6	Bobby Lowe	872
7	Billy Nash	809
8	Joe Adcock	760
9	Wally Berger	746
10	Bob Horner	652
11	Del Crandall	628
12	John Morrill	625
13	Fred Tenney	609
14	Tommy Holmes	580
15	Rabbit Maranville	558
16	Joe Torre	552
17	Tommy Tucker	533
18	David Justice	522
19	Johnny Logan	521
20	Ezra Sutton	487

Walks

1	Eddie Mathews	1,376
2	Hank Aaron	1,297
3	Dale Murphy	912
4	Fred Tenney	750
5	Billy Nash	598
6	Darrell Evans	563
7	Rabbit Maranville	561
8	Billy Hamilton	545
9	Herman Long	536
10	Glenn Hubbard	487
11	Jeff Blauser	483
12	Earl Torgeson	478
13	Tommy Holmes	476
14	Hugh Duffy	457
15	David Justice	452
16	Bob Elliott	441
17	Bobby Lowe	420
18	Johnny Logan	417
19	Joe Adcock	377
20	Del Crandall	374

Strikeouts

1	Dale Murphy	1,581
2	Eddie Mathews	1,387
3	Hank Aaron	1,294
4	Jeff Blauser	792
5	Joe Adcock	732
6	John Morrill	632
7	Ron Gant	600
8	Glenn Hubbard	570
9	Wally Berger	544
10	Bill Bruton	536
11	Joe Torre	518
12	Rabbit Maranville	515
13	Mack Jones	502
	Darrell Evans	502
15	David Justice	492
16	Bob Horner	489
17	Warren Spahn	470
18	Ray Powell	461
19	Sam Wise	455
20	Fred McGriff	454

Stolen Bases

1	Herman Long	431
2	Hugh Duffy	331
3	Billy Hamilton	274
4	Bobby Lowe	260
	Fred Tenney	260
6	Hank Aaron	240
7	King Kelly	238
8	Billy Nash	232
9	Rabbit Maranville	194
10	Jerry Royster	174
11	Tommy McCarthy	160
	Dale Murphy	160
	Otis Nixon	160
14	Ron Gant	157
15	Bill Sweeney	153
16	Bill Bruton	143
17	Tommy Tucker	138
18	Ralph Garr	137
19	Dick Johnston	132
20	Claudell Washington	115

Runs Created

1	Hank Aaron	2,346
2	Eddie Mathews	1,598
3	Dale Murphy	1,202
4	Herman Long	1,195
5	Fred Tenney	1,115
6	Hugh Duffy	1,083
7	Bobby Lowe	966
8	Billy Nash	916
9	John Morrill	803
10	Tommy Holmes	787
11	Wally Berger	776
12	Rabbit Maranville	722
13	Ezra Sutton	714
14	Joe Adcock	695
15	Billy Hamilton	687
16	Tommy Tucker	660
17	Johnny Logan	624
18	Jeff Blauser	609
19	Bob Horner	591
20	Joe Torre	570

Runs Created/27 Outs

(minimum 2000 Plate Appearances)

1	Billy Hamilton	10.00
2	Hugh Duffy	8.70
3	Chick Stahl	7.90
4	Tommy McCarthy	7.85
5	Hank Aaron	7.44
6	Billy Nash	7.24
7	Eddie Mathews	7.08
8	Wally Berger	6.93
9	David Justice	6.91
10	Sid Gordon	6.90
11	Jimmy Collins	6.82
12	Bob Elliott	6.80
13	Rico Carty	6.75
14	Tommy Tucker	6.69
15	Ezra Sutton	6.64
16	Sam Wise	6.57
17	Fred McGriff	6.46
18	Jeff Burroughs	6.38
19	Herman Long	6.15
20	John Morrill	6.15

Batting Average

(minimum 2000 Plate Appearances)

1	Billy Hamilton	.338
2	Hugh Duffy	.332
3	Chick Stahl	.327
4	Ralph Garr	.317
5	Rico Carty	.317
6	Lance Richbourg	.311
7	Hank Aaron	.310
8	Jimmy Collins	.309
9	Wally Berger	.304
10	Tommy Holmes	.303
11	Buck Jordan	.301
12	Fred Tenney	.300
13	Tommy McCarthy	.296
14	Felipe Alou	.295
15	Bob Elliott	.295
16	Joe Torre	.294
17	Fred McGriff	.293
18	Jimmy Welsh	.289
19	Sid Gordon	.289
20	Gary Matthews	.288

On-Base Percentage

(minimum 2000 Plate Appearances)

1	Billy Hamilton	.456
2	Bob Elliott	.398
3	Hugh Duffy	.394
4	Rico Carty	.388
5	Chick Stahl	.387
6	Earl Torgeson	.385
7	Sid Gordon	.385
8	Tommy McCarthy	.382
9	Eddie Mathews	.379
10	Hank Aaron	.377
11	Jeff Burroughs	.377
12	Fred Tenney	.376
13	David Justice	.374
14	Tommy Tucker	.369
15	Fred McGriff	.369
16	Darrell Evans	.368
17	Billy Nash	.368
18	Tommy Holmes	.367
19	Jimmy Collins	.365
20	Wally Berger	.362

Slugging Percentage

(minimum 2000 Plate Appearances)

1	Hank Aaron	.567
2	Wally Berger	.533
3	Eddie Mathews	.517
4	Fred McGriff	.516
5	Joe Adcock	.511
6	Bob Horner	.508
7	Sid Gordon	.500
8	David Justice	.499
9	Rico Carty	.496
10	Bob Elliott	.485
11	Dale Murphy	.478
12	Jeff Burroughs	.472
13	Ron Gant	.466
14	Joe Torre	.462
15	Gary Matthews	.456
16	Chick Stahl	.456
17	Hugh Duffy	.455
18	Terry Pendleton	.445
19	Felipe Alou	.440
20	Mack Jones	.440

Teams: Braves

Braves Franchise Pitching Leaders—Career

Wins

1	Warren Spahn	356
2	Kid Nichols	329
3	Phil Niekro	268
4	Lew Burdette	179
5	Tom Glavine	153
6	Vic Willis	151
7	Tommy Bond	149
	John Clarkson	149
9	Jim Whitney	133
10	Jack Stivetts	131
11	John Smoltz	129
12	Dick Rudolph	121
13	Bob Buhl	109
14	Charlie Buffinton	104
	Johnny Sain	104
16	Ed Brandt	94
17	Lefty Tyler	92
18	Greg Maddux	89
19	Tony Cloninger	86
20	Four tied at	83

Losses

1	Phil Niekro	230
2	Warren Spahn	229
3	Kid Nichols	183
4	Vic Willis	147
5	Jim Whitney	121
6	Bob Smith	120
	Lew Burdette	120
8	Ed Brandt	119
9	Dick Rudolph	107
10	Ben Cantwell	106
11	John Smoltz	102
12	Tom Glavine	99
13	Lefty Tyler	92
14	Johnny Sain	91
15	Rick Mahler	89
16	Ron Reed	88
17	Tommy Bond	87
18	Jesse Barnes	86
19	Togie Pittinger	84
20	Jim Tobin	83

Winning Percentage
(minimum 100 decisions)

1	Greg Maddux	.730
2	Harry Staley	.655
3	John Clarkson	.645
4	Kid Nichols	.643
5	Tommy Bond	.631
6	Jack Stivetts	.627
7	Ted Lewis	.624
8	Warren Spahn	.609
9	Tom Glavine	.607
10	Bob Buhl	.602
11	Lew Burdette	.599
12	Charlie Buffinton	.598
13	Tony Cloninger	.581
14	John Smoltz	.558
15	Vern Bickford	.541
16	Phil Niekro	.538
17	Steve Avery	.537
18	Pat Jarvis	.535
19	Johnny Sain	.533
	Rick Camp	.533

Games

1	Phil Niekro	740
2	Warren Spahn	714
3	Gene Garber	557
4	Kid Nichols	556
5	Lew Burdette	468
6	Rick Camp	414
7	Mark Wohlers	359
8	Steve Bedrosian	350
9	Bob Smith	349
10	Tom Glavine	331
11	Vic Willis	320
12	Rick Mahler	307
13	Mike Stanton	304
14	John Smoltz	301
15	Ben Cantwell	290
16	Ed Brandt	283
17	Bob Buhl	282
18	Dick Rudolph	275
19	Jim Whitney	266
20	Greg McMichael	265

Games Started

1	Warren Spahn	635
2	Phil Niekro	595
3	Kid Nichols	501
4	Tom Glavine	331
5	Lew Burdette	330
6	Vic Willis	302
7	John Smoltz	301
8	Jim Whitney	254
9	Tommy Bond	241
10	Dick Rudolph	240
11	John Clarkson	237
12	Bob Buhl	220
13	Rick Mahler	218
14	Ed Brandt	210
15	Jack Stivetts	207
16	Johnny Sain	206
17	Ron Reed	203
18	Steve Avery	201
19	Lefty Tyler	197
20	Bob Smith	183

Complete Games

1	Kid Nichols	475
2	Warren Spahn	374
3	Vic Willis	268
4	Jim Whitney	242
5	John Clarkson	226
	Phil Niekro	226
7	Tommy Bond	225
8	Jack Stivetts	176
9	Dick Rudolph	171
10	Charlie Buffinton	166
11	Old Hoss Radbourn	157
12	Lew Burdette	146
13	Togie Pittinger	141
14	Lefty Tyler	132
15	Ed Brandt	126
16	Jim Tobin	125
17	Johnny Sain	121
18	Irv Young	107
19	Ted Lewis	105
20	Bob Smith	102

Shutouts

1	Warren Spahn	63
2	Kid Nichols	44
3	Phil Niekro	43
4	Lew Burdette	30
5	Tommy Bond	29
6	Dick Rudolph	27
7	Vic Willis	26
8	Lefty Tyler	22
9	John Clarkson	20
10	Charlie Buffinton	19
11	Jim Whitney	18
12	Togie Pittinger	16
	Bob Buhl	16
14	Irv Young	15
	Al Javery	15
	Johnny Sain	15
	Tom Glavine	15
18	Jesse Barnes	14
	Lou Fette	14
20	Six tied at	13

Saves

1	Gene Garber	141
2	Mark Wohlers	104
3	Cecil Upshaw	78
4	Rick Camp	57
5	Mike Stanton	55
6	Don McMahon	50
7	Greg McMichael	44
8	Steve Bedrosian	41
9	Bruce Sutter	40
10	Bob Smith	36
11	Claude Raymond	33
12	Joe Boever	30
13	Phil Niekro	29
14	Warren Spahn	28
	Tom House	28
16	Alejandro Pena	26
17	Billy O'Dell	24
18	Lew Burdette	23
	Donnie Moore	23
20	Ben Cantwell	20

Innings Pitched

1	Warren Spahn	5,046.0
2	Phil Niekro	4,622.2
3	Kid Nichols	4,538.0
4	Lew Burdette	2,638.1
5	Vic Willis	2,575.0
6	Jim Whitney	2,263.2
7	Tom Glavine	2,196.1
8	Tommy Bond	2,127.1
9	John Clarkson	2,092.2
10	John Smoltz	2,060.1
11	Dick Rudolph	2,035.0
12	Bob Smith	1,813.1
13	Jack Stivetts	1,798.2
14	Ed Brandt	1,761.2
15	Lefty Tyler	1,687.2
16	Johnny Sain	1,624.1
17	Bob Buhl	1,599.2
18	Rick Mahler	1,558.2
19	Charlie Buffinton	1,547.1
20	Togie Pittinger	1,471.2

Walks

1	Phil Niekro	1,458
2	Warren Spahn	1,378
3	Kid Nichols	1,159
4	Vic Willis	854
5	Bob Buhl	782
6	Tom Glavine	743
7	John Smoltz	690
8	Lefty Tyler	678
9	John Clarkson	676
10	Jack Stivetts	651
11	Ed Brandt	611
12	Bob Smith	561
13	Lew Burdette	557
14	Togie Pittinger	545
15	Johnny Sain	502
16	Tony Cloninger	501
	Rick Mahler	501
18	Vern Bickford	466
19	Al Javery	452
20	Ted Lewis	420

Strikeouts

1	Phil Niekro	2,912
2	Warren Spahn	2,493
3	John Smoltz	1,769
4	Kid Nichols	1,667
5	Tom Glavine	1,364
6	Vic Willis	1,161
7	Jim Whitney	1,157
8	Lew Burdette	923
9	Charlie Buffinton	911
10	Greg Maddux	883
11	Denny Lemaster	842
12	John Clarkson	834
	Tony Cloninger	834
14	Lefty Tyler	827
15	Steve Avery	815
16	Bob Buhl	791
17	Ron Reed	778
18	Dick Rudolph	777
19	Rick Mahler	765
20	Pat Jarvis	736

Strikeouts/9 Innings
(minimum 1000 Innings Pitched)

1	John Smoltz	7.73
2	Denny Lemaster	7.03
3	Greg Maddux	6.87
4	Tony Cloninger	6.18
5	Steve Avery	6.00
6	Phil Niekro	5.67
7	Tom Glavine	5.59
8	Pat Jarvis	5.32
9	Charlie Buffinton	5.30
10	Ron Reed	4.93
11	Jim Whitney	4.60
12	Bob Buhl	4.45
13	Warren Spahn	4.45
14	Rick Mahler	4.42
15	Lefty Tyler	4.41
16	Vic Willis	4.06
17	Johnny Sain	3.87
18	Vern Bickford	3.78
19	Togie Pittinger	3.77
20	Al Javery	3.70

ERA
(minimum 1000 Innings Pitched)

1	Greg Maddux	2.13
2	Tommy Bond	2.21
3	Jim Whitney	2.49
4	Dick Rudolph	2.62
5	John Clarkson	2.82
6	Vic Willis	2.82
7	Charlie Buffinton	2.83
8	Kid Nichols	3.00
9	Warren Spahn	3.05
10	Lefty Tyler	3.06
11	Jesse Barnes	3.07
12	Togie Pittinger	3.08
13	Irv Young	3.15
14	Phil Niekro	3.20
15	Bob Buhl	3.27
16	Jim Tobin	3.36
17	John Smoltz	3.40
18	Tom Glavine	3.40
19	Danny MacFayden	3.45
20	Johnny Sain	3.49

Component ERA
(minimum 1000 Innings Pitched)

1	Greg Maddux	1.90
2	Jim Whitney	2.23
3	Tommy Bond	2.48
4	Charlie Buffinton	2.57
5	Dick Rudolph	2.59
6	John Clarkson	2.89
7	Irv Young	2.90
8	Kid Nichols	2.96
9	Vic Willis	2.98
10	Warren Spahn	2.99
11	John Smoltz	3.00
12	Jesse Barnes	3.03
13	Lefty Tyler	3.05
14	Pat Jarvis	3.05
15	Jim Tobin	3.25
16	Phil Niekro	3.25
17	Tom Glavine	3.31
18	Old Hoss Radbourn	3.37
19	Ron Reed	3.41
20	Steve Avery	3.45

Opponent Average
(minimum 1000 Innings Pitched)

1	Greg Maddux	.224
2	John Smoltz	.232
3	John Clarkson	.236
4	Denny Lemaster	.242
5	Bob Buhl	.242
6	Jim Whitney	.243
7	Phil Niekro	.243
8	Warren Spahn	.243
9	Pat Jarvis	.243
10	Charlie Buffinton	.245
11	Lefty Tyler	.245
12	Vic Willis	.247
13	Tony Cloninger	.247
14	Tom Glavine	.250
15	Kid Nichols	.251
16	Vern Bickford	.254
17	Steve Avery	.255
18	Jim Tobin	.256
19	Dick Rudolph	.257
20	Ted Lewis	.258

Opponent OBP
(minimum 1000 Innings Pitched)

1	Greg Maddux	.254
2	Jim Whitney	.261
3	Tommy Bond	.274
4	Charlie Buffinton	.278
5	Warren Spahn	.295
6	John Clarkson	.296
7	John Smoltz	.297
8	Pat Jarvis	.297
9	Dick Rudolph	.297
10	Kid Nichols	.301
11	Lew Burdette	.304
12	Phil Niekro	.304
13	Denny Lemaster	.305
14	Ron Reed	.306
15	Old Hoss Radbourn	.310
16	Jesse Barnes	.310
17	Jim Tobin	.310
18	Steve Avery	.311
19	Tom Glavine	.312
20	Irv Young	.314

Teams: Braves

Boston Braves Team Batting Leaders—Career

Games

1	Rabbit Maranville	1,795
2	Fred Tenney	1,737
3	Herman Long	1,646
4	Bobby Lowe	1,410
5	Tommy Holmes	1,289
6	John Morrill	1,219
7	Billy Nash	1,186
8	Hugh Duffy	1,152
9	Wally Berger	1,057
10	Ezra Sutton	977
11	Sibby Sisti	969
12	Phil Masi	945
13	Tommy Tucker	916
14	Bill Sweeney	902
15	Ray Powell	873
16	Johnny Cooney	858
17	Hank Gowdy	852
18	Billy Urbanski	763
19	Jack Burdock	760
20	Al Spohrer	754

At-Bats

1	Herman Long	6,775
2	Rabbit Maranville	6,724
3	Fred Tenney	6,637
4	Bobby Lowe	5,617
5	Tommy Holmes	4,956
6	John Morrill	4,759
7	Hugh Duffy	4,656
8	Billy Nash	4,561
9	Wally Berger	4,153
10	Ezra Sutton	4,045
11	Tommy Tucker	3,565
12	Ray Powell	3,324
13	Bill Sweeney	3,219
14	Joe Hornung	3,077
15	Billy Urbanski	3,046
16	Jack Burdock	3,029
17	Sibby Sisti	2,976
18	Sam Wise	2,825
19	Phil Masi	2,668
20	Jimmy Collins	2,653

Runs

1	Herman Long	1,291
2	Fred Tenney	1,134
3	Bobby Lowe	999
4	Hugh Duffy	996
5	Billy Nash	855
6	Rabbit Maranville	801
7	John Morrill	800
8	Tommy Holmes	696
9	Ezra Sutton	694
10	Billy Hamilton	651
	Wally Berger	651
12	Tommy Tucker	648
13	Joe Hornung	560
14	Sam Wise	488
15	Jimmy Collins	470
16	Ray Powell	467
17	Jack Burdock	461
18	Tommy McCarthy	450
19	Bob Elliott	436
20	Earl Torgeson	428

Hits

1	Fred Tenney	1,994
2	Herman Long	1,900
3	Rabbit Maranville	1,696
4	Bobby Lowe	1,606
5	Hugh Duffy	1,544
6	Tommy Holmes	1,503
7	Billy Nash	1,283
8	Wally Berger	1,263
9	John Morrill	1,247
10	Ezra Sutton	1,161
11	Tommy Tucker	1,025
12	Bill Sweeney	902
13	Ray Powell	890
14	Billy Hamilton	884
15	Jimmy Collins	821
16	Joe Hornung	810
17	Billy Urbanski	791
18	Bob Elliott	763
19	Jack Burdock	761
20	Lance Richbourg	758

Doubles

1	Herman Long	295
2	Tommy Holmes	291
3	Wally Berger	248
4	Rabbit Maranville	244
5	Fred Tenney	242
6	John Morrill	234
7	Hugh Duffy	220
8	Billy Nash	199
9	Bobby Lowe	186
10	Ezra Sutton	178
11	Bob Elliott	145
12	Bill Sweeney	139
13	Sam Wise	136
14	Tommy Tucker	133
15	Jimmy Collins	129
	Phil Masi	129
17	Red Smith	124
18	Billy Urbanski	123
19	Sibby Sisti	120
20	Max West	119

Triples

1	Rabbit Maranville	103
2	Herman Long	91
3	John Morrill	80
4	Fred Tenney	74
5	Hugh Duffy	73
6	Sam Wise	71
	Bobby Lowe	71
8	Billy Nash	69
9	Ray Powell	67
10	Ezra Sutton	66
11	Joe Hornung	58
12	Chick Stahl	56
13	Dick Johnston	54
14	Wally Berger	52
15	Lance Richbourg	48
16	Tommy Holmes	47
17	Jimmy Collins	43
18	Jimmy Welsh	42
19	Les Mann	41
20	Tommy Tucker	39

Home Runs

1	Wally Berger	199
2	Bob Elliott	101
3	Herman Long	88
	Tommy Holmes	88
5	Earl Torgeson	82
6	Sid Gordon	81
7	Bobby Lowe	70
8	Hugh Duffy	69
9	Max West	64
10	Billy Nash	51
11	Sam Jethroe	49
12	Chuck Workman	48
13	Gene Moore	42
	Walker Cooper	42
15	John Morrill	41
16	Butch Nieman	37
17	Ray Powell	35
18	Jimmy Collins	34
	Chet Ross	34
	Phil Masi	34

RBI

1	Herman Long	963
2	Hugh Duffy	927
3	Bobby Lowe	872
4	Billy Nash	809
5	Wally Berger	746
6	John Morrill	625
7	Fred Tenney	609
8	Tommy Holmes	580
9	Rabbit Maranville	558
10	Tommy Tucker	533
11	Ezra Sutton	487
12	Jimmy Collins	484
13	Bob Elliott	466
14	Tommy McCarthy	384
15	Sam Wise	383
16	Earl Torgeson	377
17	Bill Sweeney	350
18	Jack Burdock	349
19	Joe Hornung	341
	Max West	341

Walks

1	Fred Tenney	750
2	Billy Nash	598
3	Rabbit Maranville	561
4	Billy Hamilton	545
5	Herman Long	536
6	Earl Torgeson	478
7	Tommy Holmes	476
8	Hugh Duffy	457
9	Bob Elliott	441
10	Bobby Lowe	420
11	Bill Sweeney	369
12	Wally Berger	346
13	John Morrill	326
14	Ray Powell	321
15	Tommy Tucker	311
16	Phil Masi	302
17	Max West	294
18	Tommy McCarthy	293
19	Red Smith	286
20	Sibby Sisti	278

Strikeouts

1	John Morrill	632
2	Wally Berger	544
3	Rabbit Maranville	515
4	Ray Powell	461
5	Sam Wise	455
6	Sibby Sisti	438
7	Joe Hornung	333
8	Billy Nash	319
9	Earl Torgeson	294
10	Sam Jethroe	293
11	Chet Ross	281
12	Bob Elliott	278
13	Max West	275
14	Connie Ryan	274
15	Jack Burdock	272
16	Red Smith	258
17	Billy Urbanski	252
18	Vince DiMaggio	245
19	Gene Moore	242
20	Phil Masi	222

Stolen Bases

1	Herman Long	431
2	Hugh Duffy	331
3	Billy Hamilton	274
4	Bobby Lowe	260
	Fred Tenney	260
6	King Kelly	238
7	Billy Nash	232
8	Rabbit Maranville	194
9	Tommy McCarthy	160
10	Bill Sweeney	153
11	Tommy Tucker	138
12	Dick Johnston	132
13	Tom Brown	109
14	Sam Wise	107
15	Sam Jethroe	98
16	Jimmy Bannon	91
17	Joe Hornung	86
18	Chick Stahl	84
19	Earl Torgeson	80
20	Ed Abbaticchio	79

Runs Created

1	Herman Long	1,195
2	Fred Tenney	1,115
3	Hugh Duffy	1,083
4	Bobby Lowe	966
5	Billy Nash	916
6	John Morrill	803
7	Tommy Holmes	787
8	Wally Berger	776
9	Rabbit Maranville	722
10	Ezra Sutton	714
11	Billy Hamilton	687
12	Tommy Tucker	660
13	Sam Wise	515
14	Jimmy Collins	503
15	Bob Elliott	490
16	Tommy McCarthy	477
17	Joe Hornung	468
18	Bill Sweeney	453
19	Chick Stahl	443
20	Earl Torgeson	434

Runs Created/27 Outs

(minimum 2000 Plate Appearances)

1	Billy Hamilton	10.00
2	Hugh Duffy	8.70
3	Chick Stahl	7.90
4	Tommy McCarthy	7.85
5	Billy Nash	7.24
6	Wally Berger	6.93
7	Jimmy Collins	6.82
8	Bob Elliott	6.80
9	Tommy Tucker	6.69
10	Ezra Sutton	6.64
11	Sam Wise	6.57
12	Herman Long	6.15
13	John Morrill	6.15
14	Bobby Lowe	6.07
15	Earl Torgeson	6.03
16	Fred Tenney	5.84
17	Tommy Holmes	5.81
18	Gene Moore	5.58
19	Joe Hornung	5.51
20	Max West	5.37

Batting Average

(minimum 2000 Plate Appearances)

1	Billy Hamilton	.338
2	Hugh Duffy	.332
3	Chick Stahl	.327
4	Lance Richbourg	.311
5	Jimmy Collins	.309
6	Wally Berger	.304
7	Tommy Holmes	.303
8	Buck Jordan	.301
9	Fred Tenney	.300
10	Tommy McCarthy	.296
11	Bob Elliott	.295
12	Jimmy Welsh	.289
13	Tommy Tucker	.288
14	Ezra Sutton	.287
15	Johnny Cooney	.286
16	Randy Moore	.286
17	Bobby Lowe	.286
18	Tony Boeckel	.286
19	Gene Moore	.284
20	Walter Holke	.283

On-Base Percentage

(minimum 2000 Plate Appearances)

1	Billy Hamilton	.456
2	Bob Elliott	.398
3	Hugh Duffy	.394
4	Chick Stahl	.387
5	Earl Torgeson	.385
6	Tommy McCarthy	.382
7	Fred Tenney	.376
8	Tommy Tucker	.369
9	Billy Nash	.368
10	Tommy Holmes	.367
11	Jimmy Collins	.365
12	Wally Berger	.362
13	Red Smith	.359
14	Bill Sweeney	.356
15	Lance Richbourg	.356
16	Elbie Fletcher	.348
17	Max West	.348
18	Gene Moore	.345
19	Tony Cuccinello	.343
20	Tony Boeckel	.343

Slugging Percentage

(minimum 2000 Plate Appearances)

1	Wally Berger	.533
2	Bob Elliott	.485
3	Chick Stahl	.456
4	Hugh Duffy	.455
5	Tommy Holmes	.434
6	Jimmy Collins	.429
7	Gene Moore	.429
8	Earl Torgeson	.427
9	Max West	.414
10	Billy Hamilton	.412
11	Jimmy Welsh	.411
12	Lance Richbourg	.405
13	Sam Wise	.401
14	Buck Jordan	.400
15	Randy Moore	.391
16	Herman Long	.390
17	Billy Nash	.389
18	Tony Boeckel	.388
19	Les Mann	.388
20	Tommy McCarthy	.385

Boston Braves Team Pitching Leaders—Career

Wins

1	Kid Nichols	329
2	Vic Willis	151
3	Tommy Bond	149
	John Clarkson	149
5	Jim Whitney	133
6	Jack Stivetts	131
7	Warren Spahn	122
8	Dick Rudolph	121
9	Charlie Buffinton	104
	Johnny Sain	104
11	Ed Brandt	94
12	Lefty Tyler	92
13	Bob Smith	83
14	Old Hoss Radbourn	78
	Ted Lewis	78
16	Togie Pittinger	75
17	Ben Cantwell	74
18	Harry Staley	72
	Jim Tobin	72
20	Vern Bickford	64

Losses

1	Kid Nichols	183
2	Vic Willis	147
3	Jim Whitney	121
4	Bob Smith	120
5	Ed Brandt	119
6	Dick Rudolph	107
7	Ben Cantwell	106
8	Lefty Tyler	92
9	Johnny Sain	91
	Warren Spahn	91
11	Tommy Bond	87
12	Jesse Barnes	86
13	Togie Pittinger	84
14	Jim Tobin	83
15	John Clarkson	82
16	Old Hoss Radbourn	81
17	Jack Stivetts	78
	Irv Young	78
19	Joe Genewich	76
20	Al Javery	74

Winning Percentage
(minimum 100 decisions)

1	Harry Staley	.655
2	John Clarkson	.645
3	Kid Nichols	.643
4	Tommy Bond	.631
5	Jack Stivetts	.627
6	Ted Lewis	.624
7	Charlie Buffinton	.598
8	Warren Spahn	.573
9	Vern Bickford	.557
10	Johnny Sain	.533
11	Dick Rudolph	.531
12	Jim Whitney	.524
13	Fred Frankhouse	.508
14	Vic Willis	.507
15	Lefty Tyler	.500
16	Old Hoss Radbourn	.491
17	Danny MacFayden	.484
18	Togie Pittinger	.472
19	Jim Tobin	.465
20	Ed Brandt	.441

Games

1	Kid Nichols	556
2	Bob Smith	349
3	Vic Willis	320
4	Ben Cantwell	290
5	Ed Brandt	283
6	Dick Rudolph	275
7	Jim Whitney	266
8	Warren Spahn	262
9	Johnny Sain	257
10	Tommy Bond	247
	Lefty Tyler	247
12	John Clarkson	242
13	Jack Stivetts	237
14	Fred Frankhouse	233
15	Joe Genewich	207
16	Al Javery	205
17	Jesse Barnes	192
18	Jim Tobin	188
19	Dana Fillingim	187
20	Charlie Buffinton	184

Games Started

1	Kid Nichols	501
2	Vic Willis	302
3	Jim Whitney	254
4	Tommy Bond	241
5	Dick Rudolph	240
6	John Clarkson	237
7	Warren Spahn	236
8	Ed Brandt	210
9	Jack Stivetts	207
10	Johnny Sain	206
11	Lefty Tyler	197
12	Bob Smith	183
13	Charlie Buffinton	180
14	Old Hoss Radbourn	163
15	Togie Pittinger	162
16	Jim Tobin	161
17	Ben Cantwell	159
18	Al Javery	147
19	Danny MacFayden	141
20	Vern Bickford	139

Complete Games

1	Kid Nichols	475
2	Vic Willis	268
3	Jim Whitney	242
4	John Clarkson	226
5	Tommy Bond	225
6	Jack Stivetts	176
7	Dick Rudolph	171
8	Charlie Buffinton	166
9	Old Hoss Radbourn	157
10	Warren Spahn	142
11	Togie Pittinger	141
12	Lefty Tyler	132
13	Ed Brandt	126
14	Jim Tobin	125
15	Johnny Sain	121
16	Irv Young	107
17	Ted Lewis	105
18	Bob Smith	102
19	Harry Staley	98
20	Jesse Barnes	88

Shutouts

1	Kid Nichols	44
2	Tommy Bond	29
3	Dick Rudolph	27
	Warren Spahn	27
5	Vic Willis	26
6	Lefty Tyler	22
7	John Clarkson	20
8	Charlie Buffinton	19
9	Jim Whitney	18
10	Togie Pittinger	16
11	Irv Young	15
	Al Javery	15
	Johnny Sain	15
14	Jesse Barnes	14
	Lou Fette	14
16	Art Nehf	13
	Bob Smith	13
	Ed Brandt	13
19	Joe Oeschger	11
20	Three tied at	10

Saves

1	Bob Smith	36
2	Ben Cantwell	20
3	Kid Nichols	16
4	Tom Hughes	14
5	Ed Brandt	13
6	Dick Errickson	12
	Bobby Hogue	12
8	Hugh McQuillan	11
	Johnny Sain	11
10	Warren Spahn	9
	Nels Potter	9
12	George Mogridge	8
	Fred Frankhouse	8
	Huck Betts	8
15	Lew Burdette	7
16	Six tied at	6

Innings Pitched

1	Kid Nichols	4,538.0
2	Vic Willis	2,575.0
3	Jim Whitney	2,263.2
4	Tommy Bond	2,127.1
5	John Clarkson	2,092.2
6	Dick Rudolph	2,035.0
7	Warren Spahn	1,884.0
8	Bob Smith	1,813.1
9	Jack Stivetts	1,798.2
10	Ed Brandt	1,761.2
11	Lefty Tyler	1,687.2
12	Johnny Sain	1,624.1
13	Charlie Buffinton	1,547.1
14	Togie Pittinger	1,471.2
15	Ben Cantwell	1,464.2
16	Old Hoss Radbourn	1,418.1
17	Jim Tobin	1,368.0
18	Jesse Barnes	1,182.2
19	Al Javery	1,142.2
20	Joe Genewich	1,097.1

Walks

1	Kid Nichols	1,159
2	Vic Willis	854
3	Lefty Tyler	678
4	John Clarkson	676
5	Jack Stivetts	651
6	Ed Brandt	611
7	Warren Spahn	587
8	Bob Smith	561
9	Togie Pittinger	545
10	Johnny Sain	502
11	Al Javery	452
12	Vern Bickford	431
13	Ted Lewis	420
14	Jim Tobin	402
15	Dick Rudolph	400
16	Fred Frankhouse	384
17	Ben Cantwell	367
18	Old Hoss Radbourn	361
19	Joe Oeschger	352
20	Buster Brown	335

Strikeouts

1	Kid Nichols	1,667
2	Vic Willis	1,161
3	Jim Whitney	1,157
4	Warren Spahn	1,000
5	Charlie Buffinton	911
6	John Clarkson	834
7	Lefty Tyler	827
8	Dick Rudolph	777
9	Johnny Sain	698
10	Ed Brandt	661
11	Tommy Bond	627
12	Togie Pittinger	616
13	Jack Stivetts	527
14	Bob Smith	502
15	Al Javery	470
16	Old Hoss Radbourn	468
17	Irv Young	425
	Vern Bickford	425
19	Fred Frankhouse	352
20	Jim Tobin	334

Strikeouts/9 Innings
(minimum 1000 Innings Pitched)

1	Charlie Buffinton	5.30
2	Warren Spahn	4.78
3	Jim Whitney	4.60
4	Lefty Tyler	4.41
5	Vic Willis	4.06
6	Johnny Sain	3.87
7	Vern Bickford	3.77
8	Togie Pittinger	3.77
9	Al Javery	3.70
10	John Clarkson	3.59
11	Irv Young	3.59
12	Dick Rudolph	3.44
13	Ed Brandt	3.38
14	Kid Nichols	3.31
15	Old Hoss Radbourn	2.97
16	Fred Frankhouse	2.90
17	Tommy Bond	2.65
18	Harry Staley	2.64
19	Jack Stivetts	2.64
20	Danny MacFayden	2.55

ERA
(minimum 1000 Innings Pitched)

1	Tommy Bond	2.21
2	Jim Whitney	2.49
3	Dick Rudolph	2.62
4	John Clarkson	2.82
5	Vic Willis	2.82
6	Charlie Buffinton	2.83
7	Kid Nichols	3.00
8	Warren Spahn	3.04
9	Lefty Tyler	3.06
10	Jesse Barnes	3.07
11	Togie Pittinger	3.08
12	Irv Young	3.15
13	Jim Tobin	3.36
14	Danny MacFayden	3.45
15	Johnny Sain	3.49
16	Dana Fillingim	3.51
17	Ted Lewis	3.53
18	Old Hoss Radbourn	3.58
19	Vern Bickford	3.60
20	Al Javery	3.80

Component ERA
(minimum 1000 Innings Pitched)

1	Jim Whitney	2.23
2	Tommy Bond	2.48
3	Charlie Buffinton	2.57
4	Dick Rudolph	2.59
5	John Clarkson	2.89
6	Irv Young	2.90
7	Warren Spahn	2.92
8	Kid Nichols	2.96
9	Vic Willis	2.98
10	Jesse Barnes	3.03
11	Lefty Tyler	3.05
12	Jim Tobin	3.25
13	Old Hoss Radbourn	3.37
14	Danny MacFayden	3.50
15	Togie Pittinger	3.50
16	Dana Fillingim	3.52
17	Ben Cantwell	3.54
18	Johnny Sain	3.56
19	Ted Lewis	3.57
20	Al Javery	3.66

Opponent Average
(minimum 1000 Innings Pitched)

1	John Clarkson	.236
2	Warren Spahn	.237
3	Jim Whitney	.243
4	Charlie Buffinton	.245
5	Lefty Tyler	.245
6	Vic Willis	.247
7	Kid Nichols	.251
8	Vern Bickford	.253
9	Jim Tobin	.256
10	Dick Rudolph	.257
11	Ted Lewis	.258
12	Johnny Sain	.260
13	Tommy Bond	.262
14	Old Hoss Radbourn	.262
15	Al Javery	.264
16	Togie Pittinger	.265
17	Jesse Barnes	.268
18	Irv Young	.269
19	Jack Stivetts	.271
20	Ed Brandt	.271

Opponent OBP
(minimum 1000 Innings Pitched)

1	Jim Whitney	.261
2	Tommy Bond	.274
3	Charlie Buffinton	.278
4	John Clarkson	.296
5	Warren Spahn	.297
6	Dick Rudolph	.297
7	Kid Nichols	.301
8	Old Hoss Radbourn	.310
9	Jesse Barnes	.310
10	Jim Tobin	.310
11	Irv Young	.314
12	Vic Willis	.317
13	Johnny Sain	.317
14	Ben Cantwell	.320
15	Danny MacFayden	.324
16	Harry Staley	.326
17	Lefty Tyler	.326
18	Ted Lewis	.330
19	Vern Bickford	.331
20	Jack Stivetts	.332

Teams: Braves

Milwaukee Braves Team Batting Leaders—Career

Games

1	Eddie Mathews	1,944
2	Hank Aaron	1,806
3	Del Crandall	1,248
4	Joe Adcock	1,207
5	Johnny Logan	1,172
6	Bill Bruton	1,052
7	Frank Bolling	680
8	Andy Pafko	658
9	Joe Torre	639
10	Lee Maye	593
11	Frank Torre	514
12	Wes Covington	468
13	Warren Spahn	465
14	Lew Burdette	459
15	Danny O'Connell	457
16	Denis Menke	418
17	Felix Mantilla	402
18	Roy McMillan	399
19	Mack Jones	355
20	Bobby Thomson	327

At-Bats

1	Hank Aaron	7,080
2	Eddie Mathews	7,069
3	Johnny Logan	4,306
4	Joe Adcock	4,232
5	Del Crandall	4,100
6	Bill Bruton	4,079
7	Frank Bolling	2,420
8	Joe Torre	2,253
9	Lee Maye	2,028
10	Andy Pafko	1,897
11	Danny O'Connell	1,675
12	Wes Covington	1,435
13	Denis Menke	1,350
14	Roy McMillan	1,306
15	Frank Torre	1,202
16	Mack Jones	1,169
17	Warren Spahn	1,134
18	Red Schoendienst	1,050
19	Bobby Thomson	1,041
20	Felipe Alou	970

Runs

1	Eddie Mathews	1,300
2	Hank Aaron	1,289
3	Bill Bruton	622
4	Joe Adcock	564
5	Johnny Logan	554
6	Del Crandall	510
7	Lee Maye	310
8	Frank Bolling	294
9	Joe Torre	275
10	Andy Pafko	240
11	Danny O'Connell	208
12	Mack Jones	178
13	Wes Covington	177
14	Denis Menke	165
15	Roy McMillan	144
16	Felipe Alou	140
17	Gene Oliver	135
18	Felix Mantilla	134
19	Frank Torre	129
20	Red Schoendienst	124

Hits

1	Hank Aaron	2,266
2	Eddie Mathews	1,960
3	Joe Adcock	1,206
4	Johnny Logan	1,163
5	Bill Bruton	1,126
6	Del Crandall	1,060
7	Joe Torre	668
8	Frank Bolling	606
9	Lee Maye	568
10	Andy Pafko	521
11	Danny O'Connell	415
12	Wes Covington	407
13	Denis Menke	336
14	Frank Torre	324
15	Roy McMillan	310
16	Red Schoendienst	292
17	Mack Jones	291
18	Felipe Alou	270
19	Gene Oliver	257
20	Bobby Thomson	252

Doubles

1	Hank Aaron	391
2	Eddie Mathews	294
3	Joe Adcock	197
4	Johnny Logan	179
5	Bill Bruton	167
6	Del Crandall	146
7	Joe Torre	105
8	Lee Maye	100
9	Frank Bolling	88
10	Andy Pafko	74
11	Danny O'Connell	69
12	Frank Torre	63
13	Denis Menke	61
14	Red Schoendienst	55
	Felipe Alou	55
16	Wes Covington	54
17	Mack Jones	49
18	Gene Oliver	47
19	Rico Carty	46
20	Warren Spahn	42

Triples

1	Hank Aaron	80
2	Bill Bruton	79
3	Eddie Mathews	61
4	Johnny Logan	36
5	Joe Adcock	22
6	Danny O'Connell	18
	Lee Maye	18
8	Andy Pafko	17
	Mack Jones	17
10	Del Crandall	16
11	Joe Torre	15
12	Frank Bolling	14
13	Wes Covington	13
14	Frank Torre	11
	Denis Menke	11
16	Bobby Thomson	10
17	Red Schoendienst	6
	Ty Cline	6
19	Five tied at	5

Home Runs

1	Eddie Mathews	452
2	Hank Aaron	398
3	Joe Adcock	239
4	Del Crandall	162
5	Johnny Logan	88
6	Joe Torre	76
7	Wes Covington	64
8	Lee Maye	51
9	Andy Pafko	50
10	Bill Bruton	48
11	Gene Oliver	45
12	Mack Jones	44
13	Frank Bolling	41
14	Bobby Thomson	38
15	Denis Menke	37
16	Rico Carty	32
	Felipe Alou	32
18	Warren Spahn	28
19	Frank Thomas	25
20	Roy McMillan	23

RBI

1	Hank Aaron	1,305
2	Eddie Mathews	1,277
3	Joe Adcock	760
4	Del Crandall	557
5	Johnny Logan	463
6	Joe Torre	328
7	Bill Bruton	327
8	Andy Pafko	249
9	Wes Covington	235
10	Frank Bolling	226
11	Lee Maye	215
12	Bobby Thomson	168
13	Gene Oliver	154
14	Frank Torre	149
	Denis Menke	149
16	Mack Jones	145
17	Felipe Alou	129
18	Danny O'Connell	127
19	Rico Carty	123
20	Roy McMillan	120

Walks

1	Eddie Mathews	1,254
2	Hank Aaron	663
3	Joe Adcock	377
4	Johnny Logan	368
5	Del Crandall	352
6	Bill Bruton	275
7	Joe Torre	191
8	Frank Bolling	178
9	Danny O'Connell	161
10	Lee Maye	147
11	Denis Menke	139
12	Roy McMillan	138
13	Andy Pafko	130
14	Frank Torre	120
15	Mack Jones	111
16	Wes Covington	108
17	Bobby Thomson	97
18	Gene Oliver	80
19	Sid Gordon	71
	Red Schoendienst	71

Strikeouts

1	Eddie Mathews	1,190
2	Hank Aaron	736
3	Joe Adcock	732
4	Bill Bruton	536
5	Del Crandall	395
6	Johnny Logan	385
7	Joe Torre	310
8	Mack Jones	309
9	Warren Spahn	291
10	Lee Maye	267
11	Denis Menke	249
12	Frank Bolling	239
13	Bob Buhl	237
14	Lew Burdette	234
15	Bobby Thomson	183
16	Wes Covington	181
17	Roy McMillan	166
18	Gene Oliver	161
19	Andy Pafko	159
20	Danny O'Connell	151

Stolen Bases

1	Hank Aaron	149
2	Bill Bruton	143
3	Eddie Mathews	59
4	Lee Maye	45
5	Mack Jones	25
6	Del Crandall	23
7	Johnny Logan	18
8	Felix Mantilla	14
9	Sandy Alomar	13
	Felipe Alou	13
11	Gene Oliver	12
12	Joe Adcock	11
	Al Spangler	11
	Frank Bolling	11
	Denis Menke	11
16	Jim Pendleton	8
	Danny O'Connell	8
18	Joe Torre	7
19	Six tied at	6

Runs Created

1	Eddie Mathews	1,452
2	Hank Aaron	1,418
3	Joe Adcock	695
4	Johnny Logan	553
5	Bill Bruton	523
6	Del Crandall	517
7	Joe Torre	348
8	Lee Maye	295
9	Frank Bolling	252
10	Andy Pafko	243
11	Wes Covington	214
12	Danny O'Connell	179
13	Denis Menke	177
14	Mack Jones	169
15	Frank Torre	151
16	Felipe Alou	142
17	Gene Oliver	139
18	Rico Carty	138
19	Roy McMillan	132
20	Bobby Thomson	126

Runs Created/27 Outs

(minimum 1500 Plate Appearances)

1	Hank Aaron	7.45
2	Eddie Mathews	7.36
3	Joe Adcock	5.76
4	Joe Torre	5.55
5	Wes Covington	5.30
6	Lee Maye	5.25
7	Bill Bruton	4.51
8	Denis Menke	4.45
9	Andy Pafko	4.43
10	Johnny Logan	4.40
11	Del Crandall	4.22
12	Danny O'Connell	3.59
13	Frank Bolling	3.48

Batting Average

(minimum 1500 Plate Appearances)

1	Hank Aaron	.320
2	Joe Torre	.296
3	Joe Adcock	.285
4	Wes Covington	.284
5	Lee Maye	.280
6	Eddie Mathews	.277
7	Bill Bruton	.276
8	Andy Pafko	.275
9	Johnny Logan	.270
10	Del Crandall	.259
11	Frank Bolling	.250
12	Denis Menke	.249
13	Danny O'Connell	.248

On-Base Percentage

(minimum 1500 Plate Appearances)

1	Eddie Mathews	.385
2	Hank Aaron	.376
3	Joe Torre	.356
4	Joe Adcock	.343
5	Wes Covington	.336
6	Lee Maye	.331
7	Johnny Logan	.331
8	Andy Pafko	.324
9	Bill Bruton	.323
10	Denis Menke	.321
11	Del Crandall	.317
12	Danny O'Connell	.316
13	Frank Bolling	.303

Slugging Percentage

(minimum 1500 Plate Appearances)

1	Hank Aaron	.567
2	Eddie Mathews	.528
3	Joe Adcock	.511
4	Wes Covington	.473
5	Joe Torre	.458
6	Lee Maye	.423
7	Del Crandall	.420
8	Andy Pafko	.411
9	Denis Menke	.393
10	Bill Bruton	.391
11	Johnny Logan	.390
12	Frank Bolling	.349
13	Danny O'Connell	.330

Teams: Braves

Milwaukee Braves Team Pitching Leaders—Career

Wins

1	Warren Spahn	234
2	Lew Burdette	173
3	Bob Buhl	109
4	Tony Cloninger	67
5	Gene Conley	42
6	Denny Lemaster	38
7	Ernie Johnson	28
	Carl Willey	28
9	Ray Crone	25
	Bob Hendley	25
	Hank Fischer	25
	Wade Blasingame	25
13	Joey Jay	24
14	Don McMahon	23
	Juan Pizarro	23
16	Bob Shaw	22
17	Bob Sadowski	19
18	Chet Nichols	18
19	Bob Rush	17
20	Dave Jolly	16

Losses

1	Warren Spahn	138
2	Lew Burdette	109
3	Bob Buhl	72
4	Denny Lemaster	42
5	Tony Cloninger	41
6	Gene Conley	40
	Carl Willey	40
8	Bob Hendley	29
9	Bob Sadowski	26
10	Hank Fischer	25
11	Joey Jay	24
12	Ray Crone	20
	Chet Nichols	20
	Bob Shaw	20
15	Ernie Johnson	19
	Don McMahon	19
	Juan Pizarro	19
18	Wade Blasingame	15
19	Dave Jolly	14
20	Two tied at	12

Winning Percentage
(minimum 50 decisions)

1	Warren Spahn	.629
2	Tony Cloninger	.620
3	Lew Burdette	.613
4	Bob Buhl	.602
5	Gene Conley	.512
6	Hank Fischer	.500
7	Denny Lemaster	.475
8	Bob Hendley	.463
9	Carl Willey	.412

Games

1	Warren Spahn	452
2	Lew Burdette	420
3	Bob Buhl	282
4	Don McMahon	233
5	Ernie Johnson	197
6	Tony Cloninger	162
7	Dave Jolly	159
8	Gene Conley	142
	Carl Willey	142
10	Denny Lemaster	134
11	Hank Fischer	128
12	Joey Jay	115
13	Bob Sadowski	104
14	Ron Piche	100
15	Ray Crone	98
16	Bob Hendley	95
17	Bob Trowbridge	94
18	Juan Pizarro	90
19	Bob Shaw	86
20	Claude Raymond	84

Games Started

1	Warren Spahn	399
2	Lew Burdette	321
3	Bob Buhl	220
4	Tony Cloninger	115
5	Denny Lemaster	101
6	Gene Conley	92
7	Carl Willey	83
8	Bob Hendley	66
9	Hank Fischer	53
10	Juan Pizarro	51
11	Wade Blasingame	49
	Bob Sadowski	49
13	Joey Jay	45
	Bob Shaw	45
15	Ray Crone	43
16	Chet Nichols	41
17	Jim Wilson	37
18	Bob Rush	29
19	Johnny Antonelli	26
	Ken Johnson	26

Complete Games

1	Warren Spahn	232
2	Lew Burdette	141
3	Bob Buhl	83
4	Tony Cloninger	42
5	Gene Conley	33
6	Denny Lemaster	27
7	Carl Willey	20
8	Juan Pizarro	19
9	Bob Hendley	17
10	Ray Crone	15
	Bob Shaw	15
12	Joey Jay	14
13	Wade Blasingame	13
	Bob Sadowski	13
15	Hank Fischer	12
16	Max Surkont	11
	Johnny Antonelli	11
	Jim Wilson	11
	Chet Nichols	11
20	Ken Johnson	8

Shutouts

1	Warren Spahn	36
2	Lew Burdette	30
3	Bob Buhl	16
4	Carl Willey	7
	Tony Cloninger	7
6	Denny Lemaster	6
	Bob Shaw	6
8	Joey Jay	5
	Bob Hendley	5
	Hank Fischer	5
11	Jim Wilson	4
	Gene Conley	4
13	Juan Pizarro	3
	Bob Rush	3
15	Max Surkont	2
	Johnny Antonelli	2
	Wade Blasingame	2
18	Six tied at	1

Saves

1	Don McMahon	50
2	Dave Jolly	19
	Warren Spahn	19
4	Billy O'Dell	18
5	Ernie Johnson	17
	Claude Raymond	17
7	Lew Burdette	16
8	Bob Shaw	15
	Bobby Tiefenauer	15
10	Ron Piche	10
11	Bob Sadowski	8
12	Gene Conley	6
	Don Nottebart	6
	Hank Fischer	6
	Phil Niekro	6
	Dan Osinski	6
17	Bob Buhl	5
	Chi Chi Olivo	5
19	Four tied at	4

Innings Pitched

1	Warren Spahn	3,162.0
2	Lew Burdette	2,497.0
3	Bob Buhl	1,599.2
4	Tony Cloninger	862.0
5	Gene Conley	730.2
6	Denny Lemaster	691.0
7	Carl Willey	634.2
8	Bob Hendley	466.1
9	Juan Pizarro	444.1
10	Joey Jay	414.0
11	Ernie Johnson	411.2
12	Bob Sadowski	406.1
13	Hank Fischer	402.2
14	Ray Crone	401.1
15	Bob Shaw	384.0
16	Don McMahon	344.2
17	Wade Blasingame	344.1
18	Dave Jolly	291.1
19	Chet Nichols	270.1
20	Bob Rush	263.2

Walks

1	Warren Spahn	791
2	Bob Buhl	782
3	Lew Burdette	505
4	Tony Cloninger	343
5	Gene Conley	264
6	Denny Lemaster	250
7	Juan Pizarro	240
8	Carl Willey	234
9	Joey Jay	200
10	Dave Jolly	198
11	Don McMahon	178
12	Wade Blasingame	169
13	Ernie Johnson	168
14	Bob Hendley	162
15	Chet Nichols	135
16	Hank Fischer	126
17	Bob Trowbridge	122
18	Bob Sadowski	121
19	Ray Crone	120
20	Bob Shaw	99

Strikeouts

1	Warren Spahn	1,493
2	Lew Burdette	875
3	Bob Buhl	791
4	Tony Cloninger	594
5	Denny Lemaster	555
6	Gene Conley	402
7	Juan Pizarro	366
8	Carl Willey	365
9	Hank Fischer	279
10	Joey Jay	272
11	Bob Hendley	261
12	Don McMahon	246
	Bob Sadowski	246
14	Ernie Johnson	230
15	Bob Shaw	229
16	Ray Crone	197
17	Wade Blasingame	193
18	Bob Trowbridge	168
19	Bob Rush	156
20	Dave Jolly	155

Strikeouts/9 Innings
(minimum 500 Innings Pitched)

1	Denny Lemaster	7.23
2	Tony Cloninger	6.20
3	Carl Willey	5.18
4	Gene Conley	4.95
5	Bob Buhl	4.45
6	Warren Spahn	4.25
7	Lew Burdette	3.15

ERA
(minimum 500 Innings Pitched)

1	Warren Spahn	3.05
2	Bob Buhl	3.27
3	Gene Conley	3.49
4	Lew Burdette	3.53
5	Denny Lemaster	3.69
6	Tony Cloninger	3.77
7	Carl Willey	3.94

Component ERA
(minimum 500 Innings Pitched)

1	Warren Spahn	3.03
2	Lew Burdette	3.44
3	Tony Cloninger	3.52
4	Denny Lemaster	3.56
5	Bob Buhl	3.68
6	Gene Conley	3.78
7	Carl Willey	3.91

Opponent Average
(minimum 500 Innings Pitched)

1	Tony Cloninger	.241
2	Denny Lemaster	.242
3	Bob Buhl	.242
4	Warren Spahn	.247
5	Carl Willey	.254
6	Gene Conley	.259
7	Lew Burdette	.265

Opponent OBP
(minimum 500 Innings Pitched)

1	Warren Spahn	.293
2	Lew Burdette	.302
3	Denny Lemaster	.310
4	Tony Cloninger	.313
5	Carl Willey	.322
6	Gene Conley	.325
7	Bob Buhl	.330

Atlanta Braves Team Batting Leaders—Career

Games

1	Dale Murphy	1,926
2	Hank Aaron	1,270
3	Mike Lum	1,225
4	Glenn Hubbard	1,196
5	Jeff Blauser	1,184
6	Jerry Royster	1,118
7	Mark Lemke	1,038
8	Bruce Benedict	982
9	Bob Horner	960
10	Rafael Ramirez	927
11	Chris Chambliss	886
12	Darrell Evans	866
13	Ron Gant	858
14	David Justice	817
15	Ralph Garr	800
16	Felix Millan	799
17	Rowland Office	752
18	Marty Perez	690
19	Phil Niekro	689
20	Rafael Belliard	664

At-Bats

1	Dale Murphy	7,098
2	Hank Aaron	4,548
3	Glenn Hubbard	4,016
4	Jeff Blauser	3,961
5	Bob Horner	3,571
6	Rafael Ramirez	3,537
7	Jerry Royster	3,451
8	Ralph Garr	3,222
9	Ron Gant	3,192
10	Mark Lemke	3,139
11	Felix Millan	3,114
12	Mike Lum	3,089
13	Darrell Evans	2,896
14	Bruce Benedict	2,878
15	David Justice	2,858
16	Chris Chambliss	2,668
17	Marty Perez	2,394
18	Fred McGriff	2,388
19	Felipe Alou	2,378
20	Two tied at	2,330

Runs

1	Dale Murphy	1,103
2	Hank Aaron	818
3	Jeff Blauser	601
4	Bob Horner	545
5	Ron Gant	515
6	Glenn Hubbard	498
7	David Justice	475
8	Ralph Garr	470
9	Jerry Royster	459
10	Darrell Evans	453
11	Felix Millan	391
12	Rafael Ramirez	387
13	Fred McGriff	383
14	Mike Lum	355
15	Claudell Washington	347
16	Gary Matthews	340
17	Mark Lemke	339
18	Felipe Alou	324
19	Chris Chambliss	319
	Terry Pendleton	319

Hits

1	Dale Murphy	1,901
2	Hank Aaron	1,334
3	Jeff Blauser	1,060
4	Ralph Garr	1,022
5	Bob Horner	994
6	Glenn Hubbard	983
7	Rafael Ramirez	929
8	Felix Millan	874
9	Jerry Royster	848
10	Ron Gant	836
11	David Justice	786
12	Mark Lemke	778
13	Mike Lum	773
14	Chris Chambliss	727
15	Felipe Alou	719
16	Darrell Evans	712
17	Fred McGriff	700
18	Bruce Benedict	696
19	Terry Pendleton	669
20	Claudell Washington	647

Doubles

1	Dale Murphy	306
2	Hank Aaron	209
3	Jeff Blauser	201
4	Glenn Hubbard	196
5	Bob Horner	160
6	Ron Gant	158
7	Chris Chambliss	140
8	Rafael Ramirez	139
9	Ralph Garr	132
	Fred McGriff	132
11	Terry Pendleton	130
12	David Justice	127
13	Jerry Royster	125
14	Mark Lemke	121
15	Felix Millan	118
16	Claudell Washington	116
17	Mike Lum	114
18	Dusty Baker	111
19	Felipe Alou	108
20	Ken Oberkfell	100

Triples

1	Ralph Garr	40
2	Dale Murphy	37
3	Jerry Royster	30
4	Jeff Blauser	28
5	Ron Gant	27
6	Felix Millan	26
7	Claudell Washington	25
8	Deion Sanders	22
9	Rafael Ramirez	21
10	Sonny Jackson	20
	Glenn Hubbard	20
12	Mike Lum	18
	Gary Matthews	18
14	Hank Aaron	16
	Darrell Evans	16
	Marty Perez	16
	Brett Butler	16
	Lonnie Smith	16
	David Justice	16
20	Four tied at	15

Home Runs

1	Dale Murphy	371
2	Hank Aaron	335
3	Bob Horner	215
4	David Justice	160
5	Ron Gant	147
6	Darrell Evans	131
7	Fred McGriff	130
8	Jeff Blauser	109
9	Ryan Klesko	100
10	Jeff Burroughs	88
11	Earl Williams	81
	Gary Matthews	81
13	Chris Chambliss	80
14	Rico Carty	77
	Dusty Baker	77
16	Mike Lum	74
	Orlando Cepeda	74
	Javy Lopez	74
	Chipper Jones	74
20	Terry Pendleton	71

RBI

1	Dale Murphy	1,143
2	Hank Aaron	897
3	Bob Horner	652
4	David Justice	522
5	Ron Gant	480
6	Jeff Blauser	461
7	Fred McGriff	446
8	Darrell Evans	424
9	Glenn Hubbard	403
10	Chris Chambliss	366
11	Mike Lum	365
12	Rico Carty	328
13	Dusty Baker	324
14	Terry Pendleton	322
15	Chipper Jones	307
16	Rafael Ramirez	301
17	Ryan Klesko	300
18	Gary Matthews	291
19	Jeff Burroughs	289
20	Claudell Washington	279

Walks

1	Dale Murphy	912
2	Hank Aaron	634
3	Darrell Evans	563
4	Glenn Hubbard	487
5	Jeff Blauser	483
6	David Justice	452
7	Mark Lemke	342
8	Bob Horner	337
9	Bruce Benedict	328
10	Jerry Royster	323
11	Jeff Burroughs	311
12	Mike Lum	308
13	Chris Chambliss	304
14	Ron Gant	300
15	Fred McGriff	285
16	Rico Carty	262
17	Dusty Baker	253
18	Chipper Jones	237
19	Gary Matthews	230
20	Ken Oberkfell	229

Strikeouts

1	Dale Murphy	1,581
2	Jeff Blauser	792
3	Ron Gant	600
4	Glenn Hubbard	570
5	Hank Aaron	558
6	Darrell Evans	502
7	David Justice	492
8	Bob Horner	489
9	Fred McGriff	454
10	Mike Lum	426
	Claudell Washington	426
12	Jerry Royster	418
13	Ryan Klesko	388
14	Rafael Ramirez	386
15	Jeff Burroughs	350
	Gary Matthews	350
17	Chris Chambliss	339
18	Terry Pendleton	327
19	Mark Lemke	326
20	Phil Niekro	311

Stolen Bases

1	Jerry Royster	174
2	Dale Murphy	160
	Otis Nixon	160
4	Ron Gant	157
5	Ralph Garr	137
6	Claudell Washington	115
7	Gerald Perry	105
8	Rafael Ramirez	93
9	Hank Aaron	91
10	Deion Sanders	75
11	Brett Butler	69
12	Albert Hall	64
13	Jeff Blauser	61
14	Gary Matthews	59
15	Dusty Baker	58
16	Marquis Grissom	57
17	Felix Millan	56
18	Sonny Jackson	53
19	Lonnie Smith	52
20	Two tied at	42

Runs Created

1	Dale Murphy	1,202
2	Hank Aaron	928
3	Jeff Blauser	609
4	Bob Horner	591
5	David Justice	553
6	Darrell Evans	482
	Glenn Hubbard	482
8	Ron Gant	477
9	Ralph Garr	464
10	Fred McGriff	429
11	Chris Chambliss	390
12	Rico Carty	363
13	Gary Matthews	360
14	Jerry Royster	358
15	Mike Lum	356
16	Rafael Ramirez	352
17	Claudell Washington	347
18	Felipe Alou	341
19	Dusty Baker	339
20	Felix Millan	330

Runs Created/27 Outs

(minimum 2000 Plate Appearances)

1	Hank Aaron	7.43
2	David Justice	6.91
3	Rico Carty	6.64
4	Fred McGriff	6.46
5	Jeff Burroughs	6.38
6	Dale Murphy	5.94
7	Bob Horner	5.85
8	Gary Matthews	5.80
9	Darrell Evans	5.73
10	Dusty Baker	5.40
11	Ralph Garr	5.35
12	Jeff Blauser	5.33
13	Felipe Alou	5.32
14	Claudell Washington	5.21
15	Chris Chambliss	5.18
16	Ron Gant	5.15
17	Terry Pendleton	5.03
18	Gerald Perry	4.35
19	Ken Oberkfell	4.34
20	Glenn Hubbard	4.05

Batting Average

(minimum 2000 Plate Appearances)

1	Ralph Garr	.317
2	Rico Carty	.316
3	Felipe Alou	.302
4	Hank Aaron	.293
5	Fred McGriff	.293
6	Gary Matthews	.288
7	Terry Pendleton	.287
8	Felix Millan	.281
9	Bob Horner	.278
10	Dusty Baker	.278
11	Claudell Washington	.278
12	David Justice	.275
13	Chris Chambliss	.272
14	Ken Oberkfell	.271
15	Gerald Perry	.270
16	Dale Murphy	.268
17	Jeff Blauser	.268
18	Jeff Burroughs	.268
19	Rafael Ramirez	.263
20	Ron Gant	.262

On-Base Percentage

(minimum 2000 Plate Appearances)

1	Rico Carty	.393
2	Hank Aaron	.378
3	Jeff Burroughs	.377
4	David Justice	.374
5	Fred McGriff	.369
6	Darrell Evans	.368
7	Jeff Blauser	.355
8	Gary Matthews	.354
9	Dale Murphy	.351
10	Dusty Baker	.351
11	Ralph Garr	.350
12	Ken Oberkfell	.346
13	Chris Chambliss	.345
14	Felipe Alou	.343
15	Bob Horner	.339
16	Claudell Washington	.339
17	Gerald Perry	.337
18	Glenn Hubbard	.328
19	Terry Pendleton	.327
20	Ron Gant	.326

Slugging Percentage

(minimum 2000 Plate Appearances)

1	Hank Aaron	.567
2	Fred McGriff	.516
3	Bob Horner	.508
4	David Justice	.499
5	Rico Carty	.484
6	Dale Murphy	.478
7	Jeff Burroughs	.472
8	Ron Gant	.466
9	Gary Matthews	.456
10	Terry Pendleton	.445
11	Dusty Baker	.440
12	Felipe Alou	.439
13	Claudell Washington	.435
14	Ralph Garr	.429
15	Darrell Evans	.426
16	Chris Chambliss	.422
17	Jeff Blauser	.415
18	Clete Boyer	.384
19	Gerald Perry	.376
20	Mike Lum	.371

Teams: Braves

Atlanta Braves Team Pitching Leaders—Career

Wins

1	Phil Niekro	266
2	Tom Glavine	153
3	John Smoltz	129
4	Greg Maddux	89
5	Pat Jarvis	83
6	Ron Reed	80
7	Rick Mahler	79
8	Steve Avery	72
9	Rick Camp	56
10	Gene Garber	53
11	Carl Morton	52
12	George Stone	43
13	Steve Bedrosian	40
14	Zane Smith	39
	Charlie Leibrandt	39
16	Pascual Perez	34
17	Ken Johnson	32
18	Kent Mercker	31
	Mark Wohlers	31
20	Four tied at	30

Losses

1	Phil Niekro	227
2	John Smoltz	102
3	Tom Glavine	99
4	Rick Mahler	89
5	Ron Reed	88
6	Gene Garber	73
7	Pat Jarvis	72
8	Steve Avery	62
9	Zane Smith	58
10	Rick Camp	49
11	Pete Smith	48
12	Carl Morton	47
13	Steve Bedrosian	45
14	George Stone	44
15	Dick Ruthven	36
16	Craig McMurtry	35
17	Tommy Boggs	34
18	Pascual Perez	33
	Greg Maddux	33
20	Charlie Leibrandt	31

Winning Percentage
(minimum 75 decisions)

1	Greg Maddux	.730
2	Tom Glavine	.607
3	John Smoltz	.558
4	Phil Niekro	.540
5	Steve Avery	.537
6	Pat Jarvis	.535
7	Rick Camp	.533
8	Carl Morton	.525
9	George Stone	.494
10	Ron Reed	.476
11	Steve Bedrosian	.471
12	Rick Mahler	.470
13	Gene Garber	.421
14	Zane Smith	.402
15	Pete Smith	.385

Games

1	Phil Niekro	689
2	Gene Garber	557
3	Rick Camp	414
4	Mark Wohlers	359
5	Steve Bedrosian	350
6	Tom Glavine	331
7	Rick Mahler	307
8	Mike Stanton	304
9	John Smoltz	301
10	Greg McMichael	265
11	Cecil Upshaw	241
12	Kent Mercker	233
13	Jeff Dedmon	229
14	Paul Assenmacher	226
15	Pat Jarvis	221
16	Ron Reed	218
17	Steve Avery	203
18	Brad Clontz	191
19	Tom House	185
20	Jim Acker	169

Games Started

1	Phil Niekro	594
2	Tom Glavine	331
3	John Smoltz	301
4	Rick Mahler	218
5	Ron Reed	203
6	Steve Avery	201
7	Pat Jarvis	169
8	Greg Maddux	157
9	Carl Morton	138
10	Zane Smith	128
11	Pete Smith	113
12	George Stone	101
13	Pascual Perez	96
14	Charlie Leibrandt	91
15	Ken Johnson	78
16	Craig McMurtry	76
17	Tommy Boggs	75
18	Dick Ruthven	72
19	Doyle Alexander	68
20	Larry McWilliams	67

Complete Games

1	Phil Niekro	226
2	Ron Reed	47
3	John Smoltz	44
4	Pat Jarvis	42
5	Tom Glavine	39
6	Greg Maddux	38
7	Rick Mahler	36
8	Carl Morton	29
9	George Stone	20
10	Denny Lemaster	18
	Ken Johnson	18
12	Zane Smith	17
13	Buzz Capra	16
	Dick Ruthven	16
15	Steve Avery	14
16	Andy Messersmith	13
17	Tony Cloninger	12
	Doyle Alexander	12
19	Twenty tied at	11

Shutouts

1	Phil Niekro	43
2	Tom Glavine	15
3	John Smoltz	11
4	Greg Maddux	10
5	Pat Jarvis	8
	Carl Morton	8
7	Dick Ruthven	7
8	Ron Reed	6
	Rick Mahler	6
	Zane Smith	6
	Steve Avery	6
12	Denny Lemaster	5
	George Stone	5
	Buzz Capra	5
	Charlie Leibrandt	5
16	Dick Kelley	4
	Tommy Boggs	4
	Pete Smith	4
	Denny Neagle	4
20	Forty tied at	3

Saves

1	Gene Garber	141
2	Mark Wohlers	104
3	Cecil Upshaw	78
4	Rick Camp	57
5	Mike Stanton	55
6	Greg McMichael	44
7	Steve Bedrosian	41
8	Bruce Sutter	40
9	Joe Boever	30
10	Tom House	28
11	Alejandro Pena	26
12	Phil Niekro	23
	Donnie Moore	23
14	Terry Forster	19
	Kent Mercker	19
16	Juan Berenguer	18
17	Hoyt Wilhelm	17
18	Claude Raymond	16
	Adrian Devine	16
	Jim Acker	16

Innings Pitched

1	Phil Niekro	4,533.0
2	Tom Glavine	2,196.1
3	John Smoltz	2,060.1
4	Rick Mahler	1,558.2
5	Ron Reed	1,419.2
6	Pat Jarvis	1,244.2
7	Steve Avery	1,222.1
8	Greg Maddux	1,156.1
9	Carl Morton	949.0
10	Rick Camp	942.1
11	Gene Garber	856.0
12	Zane Smith	853.0
13	George Stone	738.2
14	Steve Bedrosian	696.0
15	Pete Smith	663.2
16	Pascual Perez	601.2
17	Ken Johnson	590.0
18	Charlie Leibrandt	585.0
19	Craig McMurtry	532.2
20	Kent Mercker	515.2

Walks

1	Phil Niekro	1,425
2	Tom Glavine	743
3	John Smoltz	690
4	Rick Mahler	501
5	Steve Avery	371
6	Zane Smith	366
	Pat Jarvis	364
8	Ron Reed	353
9	Rick Camp	336
10	Steve Bedrosian	311
11	Carl Morton	286
12	Pete Smith	269
13	Craig McMurtry	260
14	Preston Hanna	246
15	Kent Mercker	242
16	Gene Garber	233
17	Buzz Capra	198
18	George Stone	197
19	Dick Ruthven	180
20	Pascual Perez	176

Strikeouts

1	Phil Niekro	2,855
2	John Smoltz	1,769
3	Tom Glavine	1,364
4	Greg Maddux	883
5	Steve Avery	815
6	Ron Reed	778
7	Rick Mahler	765
8	Pat Jarvis	736
9	Steve Bedrosian	559
10	Gene Garber	540
11	Zane Smith	487
12	George Stone	463
13	Pete Smith	431
14	Kent Mercker	426
15	Mark Wohlers	415
16	Rick Camp	407
17	Pascual Perez	375
18	Carl Morton	345
19	Charlie Leibrandt	308
20	Greg McMichael	288

Strikeouts/9 Innings
(minimum 750 Innings Pitched)

1	John Smoltz	7.73
2	Greg Maddux	6.87
3	Steve Avery	6.00
4	Gene Garber	5.68
5	Phil Niekro	5.67
6	Tom Glavine	5.59
7	Pat Jarvis	5.32
8	Zane Smith	5.14
9	Ron Reed	4.93
10	Rick Mahler	4.42
11	Rick Camp	3.89
12	Carl Morton	3.27

ERA
(minimum 750 Innings Pitched)

1	Greg Maddux	2.13
2	Phil Niekro	3.20
3	Gene Garber	3.34
4	Rick Camp	3.37
5	John Smoltz	3.40
6	Tom Glavine	3.40
7	Carl Morton	3.47
8	Pat Jarvis	3.59
9	Ron Reed	3.74
10	Steve Avery	3.83
11	Rick Mahler	4.00
12	Zane Smith	4.06

Component ERA
(minimum 750 Innings Pitched)

1	Greg Maddux	1.90
2	John Smoltz	3.00
3	Pat Jarvis	3.05
4	Phil Niekro	3.24
5	Tom Glavine	3.31
6	Gene Garber	3.35
7	Ron Reed	3.41
8	Steve Avery	3.45
9	Carl Morton	3.81
10	Rick Camp	3.91
11	Zane Smith	4.02
12	Rick Mahler	4.05

Opponent Average
(minimum 750 Innings Pitched)

1	Greg Maddux	.224
2	John Smoltz	.232
3	Phil Niekro	.243
4	Pat Jarvis	.243
5	Tom Glavine	.250
6	Steve Avery	.255
7	Ron Reed	.260
8	Gene Garber	.261
9	Rick Camp	.269
10	Zane Smith	.270
11	Rick Mahler	.276
12	Carl Morton	.277

Opponent OBP
(minimum 750 Innings Pitched)

1	Greg Maddux	.254
2	John Smoltz	.297
3	Pat Jarvis	.297
4	Phil Niekro	.304
5	Ron Reed	.306
6	Gene Garber	.311
7	Steve Avery	.311
8	Tom Glavine	.312
9	Carl Morton	.329
10	Rick Mahler	.332
11	Rick Camp	.333
12	Zane Smith	.346

Braves Franchise Batting Leaders—Single Season

Games

	Player	Year	
1	Felix Millan	1969	162
	Dale Murphy	1982	162
	Dale Murphy	1983	162
	Dale Murphy	1984	162
	Dale Murphy	1985	162
6	Hank Aaron	1963	161
	Darrell Evans	1973	161
	Terry Pendleton	1993	161
	Jeff Blauser	1993	161
10	Felipe Alou	1968	160
	Hank Aaron	1968	160
	Darrell Evans	1974	160
	Dale Murphy	1986	160
	Terry Pendleton	1992	160
15	Dusty Baker	1973	159
	Dale Murphy	1987	159
	Fred McGriff	1996	159
18	Five tied at		158

At-Bats

	Player	Year	
1	Marquis Grissom	1996	671
2	Ralph Garr	1973	668
3	Felipe Alou	1966	666
4	Felipe Alou	1968	662
5	Felix Millan	1969	652
6	Herman Long	1892	646
7	Terry Pendleton	1992	640
8	Ralph Garr	1971	639
9	Gene Moore	1936	637
10	Tommy Holmes	1945	636
	Bill Bruton	1955	636
12	Terry Pendleton	1993	633
13	Tommy Holmes	1944	631
	Hank Aaron	1963	631
	Gary Matthews	1979	631
16	George Sisler	1929	629
	Tommy Holmes	1943	629
	Hank Aaron	1959	629
	Bill Bruton	1960	629
20	Ralph Garr	1975	625

Runs

	Player	Year	
1	Hugh Duffy	1894	160
2	Bobby Lowe	1894	158
3	Billy Hamilton	1896	152
	Billy Hamilton	1897	152
5	Herman Long	1893	149
6	Hugh Duffy	1893	147
7	Herman Long	1894	136
8	Billy Nash	1894	132
9	Dale Murphy	1983	131
10	Bobby Lowe	1893	130
	Jimmy Bannon	1894	130
	Hugh Duffy	1897	130
13	Herman Long	1891	129
14	Hank Aaron	1962	127
15	Hugh Duffy	1892	125
	Fred Tenney	1897	125
	Tommy Holmes	1945	125
18	Hardy Richardson	1889	122
	Chick Stahl	1899	122
	Felipe Alou	1966	122

Hits

	Player	Year	
1	Hugh Duffy	1894	237
2	Tommy Holmes	1945	224
3	Hank Aaron	1959	223
4	Ralph Garr	1971	219
5	Felipe Alou	1966	218
6	Ralph Garr	1974	214
7	Bobby Lowe	1894	212
8	Felipe Alou	1968	210
9	Fred Tenney	1899	209
10	Marquis Grissom	1996	207
11	Lance Richbourg	1928	206
12	George Sisler	1929	205
13	Bill Sweeney	1912	204
14	Hugh Duffy	1893	203
15	Chick Stahl	1899	202
16	Eddie Brown	1926	201
	Hank Aaron	1963	201
18	Dick Burrus	1925	200
	Hank Aaron	1956	200
	Ralph Garr	1973	200

Doubles

	Player	Year	
1	Hugh Duffy	1894	51
2	Tommy Holmes	1945	47
3	Hank Aaron	1959	46
4	Wally Berger	1931	44
	Lee Maye	1964	44
6	Rogers Hornsby	1928	42
	Tommy Holmes	1944	42
8	King Kelly	1889	41
	Dick Burrus	1925	41
	Chipper Jones	1997	41
11	George Sisler	1929	40
	Hank Aaron	1965	40
13	Wally Berger	1935	39
	Al Dark	1948	39
	Hank Aaron	1961	39
	Terry Pendleton	1992	39
17	Gene Moore	1936	38
18	Eight tied at		37

Triples

	Player	Year	
1	Dick Johnston	1887	20
	Harry Stovey	1891	20
3	Chick Stahl	1899	19
4	Dick Johnston	1888	18
	Ray Powell	1921	18
6	Sam Wise	1887	17
	Fred Tenney	1899	17
	Ralph Garr	1974	17
9	John Morrill	1883	16
	Hugh Duffy	1894	16
	Chick Stahl	1900	16
	Billy Southworth	1923	16
13	Ezra Sutton	1883	15
	Billy Nash	1888	15
	Rabbit Maranville	1920	15
	Billy Southworth	1921	15
	Bill Bruton	1956	15
18	Six tied at		14

Home Runs

	Player	Year	
1	Eddie Mathews	1953	47
	Hank Aaron	1971	47
3	Eddie Mathews	1959	46
4	Hank Aaron	1962	45
5	Hank Aaron	1957	44
	Hank Aaron	1963	44
	Hank Aaron	1966	44
	Hank Aaron	1969	44
	Dale Murphy	1987	44
10	Dave Johnson	1973	43
11	Eddie Mathews	1955	41
	Darrell Evans	1973	41
	Jeff Burroughs	1977	41
14	Eddie Mathews	1954	40
	Hank Aaron	1960	40
	Hank Aaron	1973	40
	David Justice	1993	40
18	Hank Aaron	1959	39
	Eddie Mathews	1960	39
	Hank Aaron	1967	39

RBI

	Player	Year	
1	Hugh Duffy	1894	145
2	Eddie Mathews	1953	135
3	Jimmy Collins	1897	132
	Hank Aaron	1957	132
5	Wally Berger	1935	130
	Hank Aaron	1963	130
7	Hugh Duffy	1897	129
8	Hank Aaron	1962	128
9	Hank Aaron	1966	127
10	Tommy McCarthy	1894	126
	Hank Aaron	1960	126
12	Eddie Mathews	1960	124
13	Billy Nash	1893	123
	Hank Aaron	1959	123
15	Wally Berger	1934	121
	Dale Murphy	1983	121
17	Hank Aaron	1961	120
	David Justice	1993	120
19	Wally Berger	1930	119
20	Four tied at		118

Walks

	Player	Year	
1	Bob Elliott	1948	131
2	Jimmy Wynn	1976	127
3	Darrell Evans	1974	126
4	Eddie Mathews	1963	124
	Darrell Evans	1973	124
6	Earl Torgeson	1950	119
7	Jeff Burroughs	1978	117
8	Dale Murphy	1987	115
9	Eddie Stanky	1949	113
	Eddie Mathews	1954	113
11	Eddie Mathews	1960	111
12	Billy Hamilton	1896	110
13	Eddie Mathews	1955	109
14	Billy Hamilton	1900	107
	Rogers Hornsby	1928	107
16	Billy Hamilton	1897	105
	Darrell Evans	1975	105
18	Earl Torgeson	1951	102
19	Eddie Mathews	1962	101
20	Eddie Mathews	1953	99

Strikeouts

	Player	Year	
1	Dale Murphy	1978	145
2	Dale Murphy	1989	142
3	Dale Murphy	1985	141
	Dale Murphy	1986	141
5	Dale Murphy	1987	136
6	Vince DiMaggio	1938	134
	Dale Murphy	1982	134
	Dale Murphy	1984	134
9	Dale Murphy	1980	133
10	Jim Presley	1990	130
	Ryan Klesko	1997	130
12	Ryan Klesko	1996	129
13	Chet Ross	1940	127
14	Jeff Burroughs	1977	126
15	Dale Murphy	1988	125
16	Mack Jones	1965	122
17	Eddie Mathews	1963	119
18	Earl Williams	1972	118
	Ron Gant	1988	118
20	Ron Gant	1993	117

Stolen Bases

	Player	Year	
1	King Kelly	1887	84
2	Billy Hamilton	1896	83
3	Otis Nixon	1991	72
4	King Kelly	1889	68
5	Billy Hamilton	1897	66
6	Tom Brown	1889	63
7	Herman Long	1891	60
8	Harry Stovey	1891	57
	Herman Long	1892	57
	Hap Myers	1913	57
11	King Kelly	1888	56
12	Billy Hamilton	1898	54
13	Tommy McCarthy	1892	53
14	Dick Johnston	1887	52
15	Hugh Duffy	1892	51
16	Herman Long	1890	49
17	Hugh Duffy	1894	48
18	Hardy Richardson	1889	47
	Jimmy Bannon	1894	47
	Otis Nixon	1993	47

Runs Created

	Player	Year	
1	Hugh Duffy	1894	204
2	Billy Hamilton	1896	155
3	Bobby Lowe	1894	153
4	Tommy Holmes	1945	151
5	Hugh Duffy	1893	147
6	Chick Stahl	1899	146
	Hank Aaron	1963	146
8	Eddie Mathews	1953	145
9	Hank Aaron	1959	143
10	Tommy McCarthy	1894	141
11	Hugh Duffy	1895	139
12	Dan Brouthers	1889	138
	Billy Hamilton	1897	138
14	Hugh Duffy	1897	135
	Rogers Hornsby	1928	135
16	Harry Stovey	1891	134
	Jimmy Bannon	1894	134
	Hank Aaron	1962	134
19	Tommy McCarthy	1893	132
	Dale Murphy	1987	132

Runs Created/27 Outs

(minimum 3.1 Plate Appearances/Tm Gm)

	Player	Year	
1	Hugh Duffy	1894	16.77
2	Deacon White	1877	12.73
3	Billy Hamilton	1898	12.54
4	Dan Brouthers	1889	11.80
5	Billy Hamilton	1896	11.75
6	Tommy McCarthy	1893	11.41
7	John O'Rourke	1879	11.12
8	Rogers Hornsby	1928	10.87
9	Charley Jones	1879	10.84
10	Hugh Duffy	1893	10.75
11	Jim O'Rourke	1877	10.64
12	Jim O'Rourke	1876	10.56
13	Billy Hamilton	1897	10.46
14	Jimmy Bannon	1894	10.29
15	Ezra Sutton	1884	10.23
16	King Kelly	1887	10.14
17	Tommy McCarthy	1894	10.05
18	Jim Whitney	1882	10.00
19	Sam Wise	1887	9.95
20	Hugh Duffy	1895	9.92

Batting Average

(minimum 3.1 Plate Appearances/Tm Gm)

	Player	Year	
1	Hugh Duffy	1894	.440
2	Deacon White	1877	.387
3	Rogers Hornsby	1928	.387
4	Dan Brouthers	1889	.373
5	Billy Hamilton	1898	.369
6	Rico Carty	1970	.366
7	Billy Hamilton	1896	.365
8	Hugh Duffy	1893	.363
9	Jim O'Rourke	1877	.362
10	Hank Aaron	1959	.355
11	Chick Stahl	1897	.354
12	Ralph Garr	1974	.353
13	Tommy Holmes	1945	.352
	Hugh Duffy	1895	.352
15	Chick Stahl	1899	.351
16	Jimmy Bannon	1895	.350
17	Tommy McCarthy	1894	.349
18	Fred Tenney	1899	.347
19	Tommy McCarthy	1893	.346
20	Ezra Sutton	1884	.346

On-Base Percentage

(minimum 3.1 Plate Appearances/Tm Gm)

	Player	Year	
1	Hugh Duffy	1894	.502
2	Rogers Hornsby	1928	.498
3	Billy Hamilton	1898	.480
4	Billy Hamilton	1896	.477
5	Dan Brouthers	1889	.462
6	Billy Hamilton	1897	.461
7	Rico Carty	1970	.454
8	Billy Hamilton	1900	.449
9	Jeff Burroughs	1978	.432
10	Tommy McCarthy	1893	.429
11	David Justice	1994	.427
12	Chick Stahl	1899	.426
13	Hugh Duffy	1895	.425
14	Bob Elliott	1948	.423
15	Eddie Mathews	1954	.423
16	Tommy Holmes	1945	.420
17	Jimmy Bannon	1895	.420
18	Tommy McCarthy	1894	.419
19	Eddie Stanky	1949	.417
20	Dale Murphy	1987	.417

Slugging Percentage

(minimum 3.1 Plate Appearances/Tm Gm)

	Player	Year	
1	Hugh Duffy	1894	.694
2	Hank Aaron	1971	.669
3	Hank Aaron	1959	.636
4	Rogers Hornsby	1928	.632
5	Eddie Mathews	1953	.627
6	Fred McGriff	1994	.623
7	Hank Aaron	1962	.618
8	Wally Berger	1930	.614
9	Hank Aaron	1969	.607
10	Eddie Mathews	1954	.603
11	Eddie Mathews	1955	.601
12	Hank Aaron	1957	.600
13	Joe Adcock	1956	.597
14	Hank Aaron	1961	.594
15	Eddie Mathews	1959	.593
16	Hank Aaron	1963	.586
17	Rico Carty	1970	.584
18	Dale Murphy	1987	.580
19	Tommy Holmes	1945	.577
20	Hank Aaron	1970	.574

Teams: Braves

Braves Franchise Pitching Leaders—Single Season

Wins

1	John Clarkson	1889	49
2	Charlie Buffinton	1884	48
3	Tommy Bond	1879	43
4	Tommy Bond	1877	40
	Tommy Bond	1878	40
6	Jim Whitney	1883	37
7	Kid Nichols	1892	35
	Jack Stivetts	1892	35
9	Kid Nichols	1893	34
10	John Clarkson	1888	33
	John Clarkson	1891	33
12	Kid Nichols	1894	32
13	Jim Whitney	1881	31
	Kid Nichols	1897	31
	Kid Nichols	1898	31
16	Kid Nichols	1891	30
	Kid Nichols	1896	30
18	Five tied at		27

Losses

1	Jim Whitney	1881	33
2	Jim Whitney	1885	32
3	Old Hoss Radbourn	1886	31
4	Tommy Bond	1880	29
	Vic Willis	1905	29
6	Charlie Buffinton	1885	27
7	Vic Willis	1904	25
	Irv Young	1906	25
	Gus Dorner	1906	25
	Ben Cantwell	1935	25
11	Cliff Curtis	1910	24
12	Old Hoss Radbourn	1887	23
	Kaiser Wilhelm	1905	23
	Vive Lindaman	1906	23
	Irv Young	1907	23
	George Ferguson	1909	23
	Buster Brown	1910	23
18	Togie Pittinger	1903	22
	Big Jeff Pfeffer	1906	22
	Lefty Tyler	1912	22

Winning Percentage
(minimum 15 decisions)

1	Greg Maddux	1995	.905
2	Tom Hughes	1916	.842
3	Greg Maddux	1997	.826
4	Phil Niekro	1982	.810
5	Denny Neagle	1997	.800
6	Fred Klobedanz	1897	.788
	Bill James	1914	.788
8	Tom Glavine	1993	.786
9	Jack Manning	1876	.783
10	Vic Willis	1899	.771
11	Warren Spahn	1953	.767
	Warren Spahn	1963	.767
13	Ted Lewis	1898	.765
14	Charlie Buffinton	1884	.750
	Hank Gastright	1893	.750
	Lew Burdette	1953	.750
	Steve Avery	1993	.750
	John Smoltz	1996	.750
19	Kid Nichols	1897	.738
20	Jack Stivetts	1897	.733

Games

1	Brad Clontz	1996	81
2	Rick Camp	1980	77
	Mark Wohlers	1996	77
4	Mike Stanton	1991	74
	Greg McMichael	1993	74
6	John Clarkson	1889	73
	Clay Carroll	1966	73
	Greg McMichael	1996	73
9	Mark Stanton	1997	71
10	Steve Bedrosian	1983	70
11	Gene Garber	1982	69
12	Gene Garber	1979	68
	Gene Garber	1980	68
	Jim Acker	1987	68
15	Charlie Buffinton	1884	67
	Greg McMichael	1995	67
17	Jim Whitney	1881	66
	Rick Camp	1985	66
	Joe Boever	1989	66
	Alan Embree	1997	66

Games Started

1	John Clarkson	1889	72
2	Charlie Buffinton	1884	67
3	Tommy Bond	1879	64
4	Jim Whitney	1881	63
5	Tommy Bond	1878	59
6	Tommy Bond	1877	58
	Old Hoss Radbourn	1886	58
8	Tommy Bond	1880	57
9	Jim Whitney	1883	56
10	John Clarkson	1888	54
11	John Clarkson	1891	51
	Kid Nichols	1892	51
13	Charlie Buffinton	1885	50
	Jim Whitney	1885	50
	Old Hoss Radbourn	1887	50
16	Jim Whitney	1882	48
	Kid Nichols	1891	48
	Jack Stivetts	1892	48
19	Kid Nichols	1890	47
20	Two tied at		46

Complete Games

1	John Clarkson	1889	68
2	Charlie Buffinton	1884	63
3	Tommy Bond	1879	59
4	Tommy Bond	1877	58
5	Tommy Bond	1878	57
	Jim Whitney	1881	57
	Old Hoss Radbourn	1886	57
8	Jim Whitney	1883	54
9	John Clarkson	1888	53
10	Jim Whitney	1885	50
11	Tommy Bond	1880	49
	Charlie Buffinton	1885	49
	Kid Nichols	1892	49
14	Old Hoss Radbourn	1887	48
15	Kid Nichols	1890	47
	John Clarkson	1891	47
17	Jim Whitney	1882	46
18	Kid Nichols	1891	45
	Jack Stivetts	1892	45
	Vic Willis	1902	45

Shutouts

1	Tommy Bond	1879	11
2	Tommy Bond	1878	9
3	Charlie Buffinton	1884	8
	John Clarkson	1889	8
5	Kid Nichols	1890	7
	Togie Pittinger	1902	7
	Irv Young	1905	7
	Warren Spahn	1947	7
	Warren Spahn	1951	7
	Warren Spahn	1963	7
11	Eleven tied at		6

Saves

1	Mark Wohlers	1996	39
2	Mark Wohlers	1997	33
3	Gene Garber	1982	30
4	Cecil Upshaw	1969	27
	Mike Stanton	1993	27
6	Gene Garber	1979	25
	Mark Wohlers	1995	25
8	Gene Garber	1986	24
9	Bruce Sutter	1985	23
10	Gene Garber	1978	22
	Rick Camp	1980	22
12	Joe Boever	1989	21
	Greg McMichael	1994	21
14	Steve Bedrosian	1983	19
	Greg McMichael	1993	19
16	Billy O'Dell	1965	18
17	Cecil Upshaw	1971	17
	Rick Camp	1981	17
	Juan Berenguer	1991	17
20	Donnie Moore	1984	16

Innings Pitched

1	John Clarkson	1889	620.0
2	Charlie Buffinton	1884	587.0
3	Tommy Bond	1879	555.1
4	Jim Whitney	1881	552.1
5	Tommy Bond	1878	532.2
6	Tommy Bond	1877	521.0
7	Jim Whitney	1883	514.0
8	Old Hoss Radbourn	1886	509.1
9	Tommy Bond	1880	493.0
10	John Clarkson	1888	483.1
11	John Clarkson	1891	460.2
12	Kid Nichols	1892	453.0
13	Jim Whitney	1885	441.1
14	Charlie Buffinton	1885	434.1
15	Kid Nichols	1891	425.1
16	Old Hoss Radbourn	1887	425.0
	Kid Nichols	1893	425.0
18	Kid Nichols	1890	424.0
19	Jim Whitney	1882	420.0
20	Jack Stivetts	1892	415.2

Walks

1	John Clarkson	1889	203
2	Jack Stivetts	1892	171
3	Phil Niekro	1977	164
4	John Clarkson	1891	154
5	Chick Fraser	1905	149
6	Vic Willis	1898	148
7	Bill Stemmeyer	1886	144
	Togie Pittinger	1904	144
9	Togie Pittinger	1903	143
10	John Clarkson	1890	140
11	Old Hoss Radbourn	1887	133
12	Togie Pittinger	1902	128
13	Jack Stivetts	1894	127
14	Lefty Tyler	1912	126
15	Fred Klobedanz	1897	125
	Ted Lewis	1897	125
17	Cliff Curtis	1910	124
18	Kid Madden	1887	122
	Vern Bickford	1950	122
20	Four tied at		121

Strikeouts

1	Charlie Buffinton	1884	417
2	Jim Whitney	1883	345
3	John Clarkson	1889	284
4	John Smoltz	1996	276
5	Jim Whitney	1884	270
6	Phil Niekro	1977	262
7	Phil Niekro	1978	248
8	Charlie Buffinton	1885	242
9	John Smoltz	1997	241
10	Kid Nichols	1891	240
11	Bill Stemmeyer	1886	239
12	Vic Willis	1902	225
13	John Clarkson	1888	223
14	Kid Nichols	1890	222
15	Old Hoss Radbourn	1886	218
16	John Smoltz	1992	215
17	Tony Cloninger	1965	211
18	Phil Niekro	1979	208
	John Smoltz	1993	208
20	Jim Whitney	1885	200

Strikeouts/9 Innings
(minimum 1 Inning Pitched/Tm Gm)

1	John Smoltz	1996	9.79
2	John Smoltz	1995	9.02
3	John Smoltz	1997	8.47
4	John Smoltz	1992	7.84
5	Greg Maddux	1995	7.77
6	John Smoltz	1993	7.68
7	Tom Glavine	1994	7.62
8	John Smoltz	1994	7.55
9	Denny Lemaster	1964	7.53
10	Steve Avery	1995	7.32
11	Denny Lemaster	1966	7.32
12	David Palmer	1986	7.30
13	John Smoltz	1989	7.27
14	Steve Avery	1994	7.24
15	Jim Whitney	1884	7.23
16	Denny Lemaster	1963	7.22
17	Phil Niekro	1977	7.14
18	Tom Glavine	1991	7.01
19	Greg Maddux	1994	6.95
20	Tom Glavine	1996	6.92

ERA
(minimum 1 Inning Pitched/Tm Gm)

1	Greg Maddux	1994	1.56
2	Greg Maddux	1995	1.63
3	Phil Niekro	1967	1.87
4	Bill James	1914	1.90
5	Tommy Bond	1879	1.96
6	Lefty Tyler	1916	2.02
7	Tommy Bond	1878	2.06
8	Bill Sowders	1888	2.07
9	Pat Ragan	1916	2.08
10	Jim Whitney	1884	2.09
11	Warren Spahn	1953	2.10
12	Tommy Bond	1877	2.11
13	Tom Hughes	1915	2.12
14	Kid Nichols	1898	2.13
15	Jack Manning	1876	2.14
16	Charlie Buffinton	1884	2.15
17	Art Nehf	1917	2.16
18	Dick Rudolph	1916	2.16
19	Dick Rudolph	1919	2.17
20	Vic Willis	1902	2.20

Component ERA
(minimum 1 Inning Pitched/Tm Gm)

1	Greg Maddux	1995	1.41
2	Jim Whitney	1884	1.55
3	Greg Maddux	1994	1.59
4	Tom Hughes	1915	1.65
5	Charlie Buffinton	1884	1.83
6	Dick Rudolph	1916	1.89
7	Pat Ragan	1916	1.92
8	Greg Maddux	1997	1.95
9	Pat Jarvis	1968	1.97
10	Art Nehf	1917	1.98
11	Kid Nichols	1898	1.99
12	Jim Whitney	1883	2.00
13	Bobby Mathews	1882	2.03
14	Tom Hughes	1916	2.03
15	Lefty Tyler	1916	2.04
16	Jim Whitney	1882	2.06
17	Jesse Barnes	1917	2.10
18	Tommy Bond	1879	2.12
19	Dick Rudolph	1914	2.16
20	John Smoltz	1996	2.17

Opponent Average
(minimum 1 Inning Pitched/Tm Gm)

1	Greg Maddux	1995	.197
2	Greg Maddux	1994	.207
3	Jim Whitney	1884	.207
4	Buzz Capra	1974	.208
5	John Smoltz	1989	.212
6	Tom Hughes	1915	.213
7	Pat Jarvis	1968	.214
8	Tom Hughes	1916	.215
9	John Smoltz	1996	.216
10	Kid Nichols	1898	.217
11	Warren Spahn	1953	.217
12	Jack Stivetts	1892	.217
13	Phil Niekro	1967	.218
14	Pat Ragan	1916	.218
15	Bill Stemmeyer	1886	.218
16	Andy Messersmith	1976	.219
17	Charlie Buffinton	1884	.219
18	Phil Niekro	1969	.221
19	Vic Willis	1899	.222
20	Tom Glavine	1991	.222

Opponent OBP
(minimum 1 Inning Pitched/Tm Gm)

1	Jim Whitney	1884	.223
2	Greg Maddux	1995	.224
3	Greg Maddux	1994	.243
4	Charlie Buffinton	1884	.244
5	Bobby Mathews	1882	.246
6	Jim Whitney	1883	.251
7	Pat Jarvis	1968	.252
8	Jim Whitney	1882	.255
9	Greg Maddux	1997	.256
10	Tommy Bond	1879	.259
11	John Smoltz	1996	.260
12	Dick Rudolph	1916	.261
13	Tommy Bond	1877	.261
14	Greg Maddux	1996	.264
15	Phil Niekro	1969	.264
16	Tom Hughes	1915	.265
17	Kid Nichols	1898	.267
18	Curry Foley	1879	.268
19	Art Nehf	1917	.268
20	Pat Ragan	1916	.270

Boston/Milwaukee/Atlanta Braves Capsule

Best Season: *1914/1957/1995.* The 1914 "Miracle Braves" were dead last in the league on July 4 with a 26-40 record, but won 68 of their final 87 games to win the pennant. In the World Series, they swept Connie Mack's heavily favored Philadelphia Athletics. The Braves won their first pennant in Milwaukee in 1957. Lew Burdette came back on two days' rest to blank the Yankees in the seventh game of the World Series, giving the Braves their first World Championship since 1914. After losing the World Series in both 1991 and 1992, and falling to the Phillies in the 1993 National League Championship Series, the Braves were in danger of being labeled "chokers." They redeemed themselves with a six-game World Series victory over the Cleveland Indians in 1995 after overcoming a three-games-to-one deficit against the St. Louis Cardinals in the NLCS.

Worst Season: *1935/1965/1988.* The 1935 Boston Braves posted the worst won-lost record in NL history, 38-115. Babe Ruth quit on June 2; less than two months later, club president Judge Emil Fuchs was forced to step down after threatening to turn Braves Field into a dog track. In 1965, it was an open secret in Milwaukee that the Braves were planning to move to Atlanta after the season, and the fans reacted with predictable disgust. Attendance dropped to 555,584, less than one-quarter of what it had been during their championship season of 1957. The 1988 club was composed of over-the-hill veterans and green youngsters, and finished with an NL-worst 56-104 record.

Best Player: *King Kelly/Hank Aaron/Hank Aaron.*

Best Pitcher: *Kid Nichols/Warren Spahn/Greg Maddux.*

Best Reliever: *Tom Hughes/Don McMahon/Mark Wohlers.* Hughes, who led the NL in saves and relief wins in 1915, was the best of a weak class. The Braves were a decade or two behind the league in adopting a modern bullpen. Their first modern reliever was Don McMahon, who helped them take the pennant with his superb pitching in the second half of 1957. Their relief work has remained inconsistent even in Atlanta; Mark Wohlers has been one of their few closers who's been able to put together three solid seasons in a row.

Best Defensive Player: *Rabbit Maranville/Del Crandall/Dale Murphy.*

Hall of Famers: *Hank Aaron, John Clarkson, Hugh Duffy, King Kelly, Rabbit Maranville, Eddie Mathews, Tommy McCarthy, Kid Nichols, Phil Niekro, Warren Spahn, Vic Willis, George Wright.*

Franchise All-Star Team:

C	*King Kelly/Del Crandall/Joe Torre*
1B	*Fred Tenney/Joe Adcock/Fred McGriff*
2B	*Bill Sweeney/Frank Bolling/Felix Millan*
3B	*Bob Elliott/Eddie Mathews/Bob Horner*
SS	*Herman Long/Johnny Logan/Jeff Blauser*
LF	*Hugh Duffy/Rico Carty/Ron Gant*
CF	*Wally Berger/Bill Bruton/Dale Murphy*
RF	*Tommy Holmes/Hank Aaron/Hank Aaron*
SP	*Kid Nichols/Warren Spahn/Greg Maddux*
RP	*Tom Hughes/Don McMahon/Mark Wohlers*

Biggest Flake: *Rabbit Maranville/Gene Conley/Pascual Perez.* Maranville was one of the game's most colorful characters, both during and after the game. Conley once jumped the Boston Red Sox and tried to fly to Israel, and he might have succeeded if he'd been sober enough to remember his passport. Perez showed up late for a game and explained that he'd gotten lost driving to the stadium and circled the park three times before running out of gas.

Strangest Career: *Socks Seibold/Danny O'Connell/Earl Williams.* Seibold debuted with the 1916 Philadelphia Athletics as a 19-year-old infielder. He was converted to the mound the following year, and made the club as a pitcher. He went 4-16 in 1917, and went back to the minors after the 1919 season. He kicked around the minors during the 1920s, and even retired for a four-year stretch. But somehow, he made the Braves in 1929 and spent four years in their rotation. The 10-year gap in his major league career is one of the largest ever. The Braves sent six players and $100,000 to the Pirates in 1953 for second baseman Danny O'Connell, who was 26 years old and coming off a .294 season. O'Connell batted .279 in his first year with the club, but his hitting dropped off precipitously after that, and the Braves were forced to deal him midway through the 1957 season. Williams blasted 33 homers as a rookie catcher in 1971, but his career flamed out due to his unwillingness to catch.

What Might Have Been: *Paul Strand/Bob Hazle/Brad Komminsk.* Strand came up as a 19-year-old lefthanded pitcher in 1913. He pitched decently, if sparingly, for three years before returning to the minors, where he switched to the outfield and became a sensational hitter. In 1923, he won the Pacific Coast League's Triple Crown while compiling 325 hits, the highest total in the history of Organized Baseball. In July 1957, outfielder Bob Hazle was batting .279 in the minors when the Braves called him up. He immediately launched one of the most memorable hot streaks in history, rapping out 34 hits in his first 67 at-bats. He finished the season at .403, the Braves won the World Series and "Hurricane" Hazle was suddenly famous. The fairy tale ended in 1958, as several injuries and a serious beaning knocked him out of the lineup. He was sold to Detroit, got buried on the bench and played two more years in the minors before retiring. Komminsk was touted as a can't-miss prospect after batting .334-24-103 at Triple-A in 1983. He was a miserable failure at the major league level, however.

Best Trade: *Lew Burdette/Felipe Alou/John Smoltz.* The Braves got Burdette and $50,000 from the Yankees for Johnny Sain in August 1951. Burdette won 179 games for the Braves; Sain won 33 for the Yankees. (Nine years before, they'd gotten Tommy Holmes from the Yankees for essentially nothing. Bob Elliott and Joe Adcock also came over in one-sided deals.) After the 1963 season, the Braves got Alou and change from the Giants for an empty package. Alou gave them five good years. Smoltz was acquired from Detroit in August of 1987 for Doyle Alexander. Alexander helped the Tigers win the American League East, but Smoltz blossomed into a Cy Young Award winner.

Worst Trade: *Alvin Dark/Johnny Antonelli/Brett Butler.* After the 1949 season, the Braves traded their double-play combination, second baseman Eddie Stanky and shortstop Dark, to the Giants for outfielder Sid Gordon and three players. Gordon gave the Braves four good years, but Dark remained a solid shortstop for a decade. Four years later, they sent the Giants Johnny Antonelli, Billy Klaus, two more players and $50,000 for Bobby Thomson and change. Antonelli won 102 games over the next six seasons. The Braves made a stretch-run deal with the Indians in August 1983 that sent Brett Butler, Brook Jacoby and $150,000 to Cleveland for pitcher Len Barker. Barker went 1-3 in six starts, and the Braves lost the division by three games. Butler remained a top leadoff man for 12 years, and Jacoby had seven solid seasons at third base for the Tribe.

Best-Looking Player: *King Kelly/Eddie Mathews/Dale Murphy.*

Ugliest Player: *Johnny Sain/Bob Buhl/Bob Horner.*

Best Nicknames: *"Glass Arm" Eddie Brown/Bob "Hurricane" Hazle/Steve "Bedrock" Bedrosian.*

Most Unappreciated Player: *Joe Genewich/Denis Menke/Rick Mahler.* Genewich was the mound ace of the hard-luck Braves clubs of the 1920s. Menke was a competent shortstop and a productive hitter who knew how to get on base. Mahler was a workhorse during Atlanta's run of last-place finishes in the late 1980s.

Most Overrated Player: *Walter Holke/Frank Torre/Andres Thomas.* Holke was the Terry Francona of his day: a first baseman who didn't hit for power and never walked. In the late '50s, Torre was allowed to take at-bats away from a far superior hitter, Joe Adcock. Thomas' athleticism often was enough to blind people to his flaws, and the thought that the Pirates would trade Barry Bonds for him—as was rumored in the late 1980s—now seems laughable.

Most Admirable Star: *Kid Nichols/Warren Spahn/Phil Niekro.*

Least Admirable Star: *Max West/None/Deion Sanders.*

Best Season, Player: *Hugh Duffy, 1894/Hank Aaron, 1959/Hank Aaron, 1971.* Duffy's .440 average in 1894 has never been equaled, and he also won the Triple Crown, albeit retroactively. Aaron had his best seasons in 1959, when he won the batting title with a .355 average, and in 1971, when he hit a career-high 47 home runs.

Best Season, Pitcher: *John Clarkson, 1889/Warren Spahn, 1953/Greg Maddux, 1995.* Clarkson was the best pitcher in the league in 1889, but it's the distance between him and the rest of the league that's truly staggering. He won 49 games, 21 more than any other pitcher. He also had the best winning percentage in the league, .721. He threw 620 innings, 200 more than any other NL hurler, and led the loop in strikeouts (284) and ERA (2.73). In 1953, Spahn topped the majors with a 2.10 ERA and tied for the lead with 23 victories. Greg Maddux' 1995 season featured 19 wins against only two defeats, and an ERA (1.63) almost a full run lower than anyone else in baseball.

Most Impressive Individual Record: For Boston, *Hugh Duffy's* .440 batting average in 1894. For Milwaukee and Atlanta, *Hank Aaron's* 755 home runs, of course.

Biggest Tragedy: *Marty Bergen/Red Schoendienst/Nick Esasky.* Bergen brutally murdered his wife and son before taking his own life on January 19, 1900. Schoendienst contracted tuberculosis and missed almost all of the 1959 season, although he ultimately recovered. Esasky signed a big free-agent contract with the Braves in 1990, but came down with vertigo and had to retire after playing only nine games with Atlanta.

Fan Favorite: *King Kelly/Andy Pafko/Dale Murphy.*

—Mat Olkin

Chicago Cubs (1876-1997)

Year	Lg	Pos	W-L	Pct	GB	Manager	Att.	R	OR	HR	Avg	OBP	Slg	HR	Avg	OBP	ERA	Runs	HR
														Opponent				Park Index	
1876	NL	1st	52-14	.788	—	Al Spalding	—	624	257	8	.337	.353	.417	6	.247	.256	1.76	145	45
1877	NL	5th	26-33	.441	15.5	Al Spalding	—	366	375	0	.278	.296	.340	7	.274	.292	3.37	99	138
1878	NL	4th	30-30	.500	11.0	Bob Ferguson	—	371	331	3	.290	.316	.350	4	.253	.265	2.37	117	95
1879	NL	4th	46-33	.582	10.5	Cap Anson/Silver Flint	—	437	411	3	.259	.276	.336	5	.244	.258	2.46	102	29
1880	NL	1st	67-17	.798	—	Cap Anson	—	538	317	4	.279	.303	.360	8	.209	.242	1.93	102	9
1881	NL	1st	56-28	.667	—	Cap Anson	—	550	379	12	.295	.325	.380	14	.243	.273	2.43	114	100
1882	NL	1st	55-29	.655	—	Cap Anson	—	604	353	15	.277	.307	.389	13	.221	.246	2.22	95	134
1883	NL	2nd	59-39	.602	4.0	Cap Anson	—	679	540	13	.273	.298	.393	21	.260	.284	2.78	119	100
1884	NL	4th	62-50	.554	22.0	Cap Anson	—	834	647	142	.281	.324	.446	83	.250	.290	3.03	121	704
1885	NL	1st	87-25	.777	—	Cap Anson	—	834	470	54	.264	.320	.385	37	.221	.259	2.23	122	420
1886	NL	1st	90-34	.726	—	Cap Anson	—	900	555	53	.279	.348	.401	49	.232	.277	2.54	126	343
1887	NL	3rd	71-50	.587	6.5	Cap Anson	—	813	716	80	.271	.336	.412	55	.257	.317	3.46	130	440
1888	NL	2nd	77-58	.570	9.0	Cap Anson	—	734	659	77	.260	.308	.383	63	.246	.301	2.96	116	190
1889	NL	3rd	67-65	.508	19.0	Cap Anson	—	867	814	79	.263	.338	.377	71	.272	.328	3.73	99	234
1890	NL	2nd	84-53	.613	6.0	Cap Anson	102,536	847	692	67	.260	.336	.356	41	.232	.303	3.24	119	316
1891	NL	2nd	82-53	.607	3.5	Cap Anson	201,188	832	730	60	.253	.332	.358	53	.249	.316	3.47	116	169
1892	NL	8th	31-39	.443	19.0	Cap Anson													
	NL	7th	39-37	.513	14.0	Cap Anson	109,067	635	735	26	.235	.299	.316	35	.246	.304	3.16	82	48
1893	NL	9th	56-71	.441	29.0	Cap Anson	223,500	829	874	32	.279	.348	.379	26	.280	.358	4.81	111	116
1894	NL	8th	57-75	.432	34.0	Cap Anson	239,000	1041	1066	65	.314	.380	.441	43	.322	.391	5.68	121	58
1895	NL	4th	72-58	.554	15.0	Cap Anson	382,300	866	854	55	.298	.361	.405	38	.300	.358	4.67	101	128
1896	NL	5th	71-57	.555	18.5	Cap Anson	317,500	815	799	34	.286	.349	.390	30	.282	.348	4.41	118	113
1897	NL	9th	59-73	.447	34.0	Cap Anson	327,160	832	894	38	.282	.347	.386	30	.303	.367	4.53	97	84
1898	NL	4th	85-65	.567	17.5	Tom Burns	424,352	828	679	18	.274	.343	.350	17	.261	.320	2.83	101	46
1899	NL	8th	75-73	.507	26.0	Tom Burns	352,130	812	763	27	.277	.338	.359	20	.275	.329	3.37	90	115
1900	NL	5th	65-75	.464	19.0	Tom Loftus	248,577	635	751	33	.260	.317	.342	21	.276	.331	3.23	80	40
1901	NL	6th	53-86	.381	37.0	Tom Loftus	205,071	578	699	18	.258	.310	.326	27	.274	.330	3.33	105	56
1902	NL	5th	68-69	.496	34.0	Frank Selee	263,700	530	501	6	.250	.307	.298	7	.253	.299	2.21	85	44
1903	NL	3rd	82-56	.594	8.0	Frank Selee	386,205	695	599	9	.275	.340	.347	14	.250	.307	2.77	84	57
1904	NL	2nd	93-60	.608	13.0	Frank Selee	439,100	599	517	22	.248	.295	.315	16	.224	.285	2.30	96	74
1905	NL	3rd	92-61	.601	13.0	Frank Selee/Frank Chance	509,900	667	442	12	.245	.313	.314	14	.225	.287	2.04	102	80
1906	NL	1st	116-36	.763	—	Frank Chance	654,300	705	381	20	.262	.328	.339	12	.207	.280	1.75	103	67
1907	NL	1st	107-45	.704	—	Frank Chance	422,550	574	390	13	.250	.318	.311	11	.216	.281	1.73	108	45
1908	NL	1st	99-55	.643	—	Frank Chance	665,325	624	461	19	.249	.311	.321	20	.221	.287	2.14	106	160
1909	NL	2nd	104-49	.680	6.5	Frank Chance	633,480	635	390	20	.245	.308	.322	6	.215	.273	1.75	89	45
1910	NL	1st	104-50	.675	—	Frank Chance	526,152	712	499	34	.268	.344	.366	18	.235	.307	2.51	93	108
1911	NL	2nd	92-62	.597	7.5	Frank Chance	576,000	757	607	54	.260	.341	.374	26	.245	.320	2.90	91	90
1912	NL	3rd	91-59	.607	11.5	Frank Chance	514,000	756	668	43	.277	.354	.387	33	.261	.332	3.42	108	111
1913	NL	3rd	88-65	.575	13.5	Johnny Evers	419,000	720	630	59	.257	.335	.369	39	.260	.332	3.13	94	135
1914	NL	4th	78-76	.506	16.5	Hank O'Day	202,516	605	638	42	.243	.317	.337	37	.233	.311	2.71	95	117
1915	NL	4th	73-80	.477	17.5	Roger Bresnahan	217,058	570	620	53	.244	.303	.342	28	.247	.316	3.11	107	140
1916	NL	5th	67-86	.438	26.5	Joe Tinker	453,685	520	541	46	.239	.298	.325	32	.244	.299	2.65	138	245
1917	NL	5th	74-80	.481	24.0	Fred Mitchell	360,218	552	567	17	.239	.299	.313	34	.253	.307	2.62	107	96
1918	NL	1st	84-45	.651	—	Fred Mitchell	337,256	538	393	21	.265	.325	.342	13	.239	.291	2.18	94	49
1919	NL	3rd	75-65	.536	21.0	Fred Mitchell	424,430	454	407	21	.256	.308	.332	14	.242	.291	2.21	93	103
1920	NL	5th	75-79	.487	18.0	Fred Mitchell	480,783	619	635	34	.264	.326	.354	37	.276	.328	3.27	99	92
1921	NL	7th	64-89	.418	30.0	Johnny Evers/Bill Killefer	410,107	668	773	37	.292	.339	.378	67	.303	.357	4.39	119	138
1922	NL	5th	80-74	.519	13.0	Bill Killefer	542,283	771	808	42	.293	.359	.390	77	.292	.356	4.34	87	101
1923	NL	4th	83-71	.539	12.5	Bill Killefer	703,705	756	704	90	.288	.348	.406	86	.269	.328	3.82	107	214
1924	NL	5th	81-72	.529	12.0	Bill Killefer	716,922	698	699	66	.276	.340	.378	89	.275	.333	3.83	103	185
1925	NL	8th	68-86	.442	27.5	B. Killefer/R. Maranville/G. Gibson	622,610	723	773	86	.275	.329	.397	102	.292	.353	4.41	94	176
1926	NL	4th	82-72	.532	7.0	Joe McCarthy	885,063	682	602	66	.278	.338	.390	39	.273	.340	3.26	110	98
1927	NL	4th	85-68	.556	8.5	Joe McCarthy	1,159,168	750	661	74	.284	.346	.400	50	.273	.342	3.65	98	79
1928	NL	3rd	91-63	.591	4.0	Joe McCarthy	1,143,740	714	615	92	.278	.345	.402	56	.267	.336	3.40	82	64
1929	NL	1st	98-54	.645	—	Joe McCarthy	1,485,166	982	758	139	.303	.373	.452	77	.285	.352	4.16	96	115
1930	NL	2nd	90-64	.584	2.0	Joe McCarthy/Rogers Hornsby	1,463,624	998	870	171	.309	.378	.481	111	.294	.357	4.80	113	127
1931	NL	3rd	84-70	.545	17.0	Rogers Hornsby	1,086,422	828	710	84	.289	.360	.422	54	.268	.337	3.97	89	82
1932	NL	1st	90-64	.584	—	Rogers Hornsby/Charlie Grimm	974,688	720	633	69	.278	.330	.392	68	.264	.319	3.44	105	88
1933	NL	3rd	86-68	.558	6.0	Charlie Grimm	594,112	646	536	72	.271	.325	.380	51	.254	.312	2.93	89	134
1934	NL	3rd	86-65	.570	8.0	Charlie Grimm	707,525	705	639	101	.279	.330	.402	80	.269	.325	3.76	89	111
1935	NL	1st	100-54	.649	—	Charlie Grimm	692,604	847	597	88	.288	.347	.414	85	.263	.317	3.26	92	92
1936	NL	2nd	87-67	.565	5.0	Charlie Grimm	699,370	755	603	76	.287	.349	.392	77	.265	.324	3.54	105	96
1937	NL	2nd	93-61	.604	3.0	Charlie Grimm	895,020	811	682	96	.287	.355	.416	91	.267	.332	3.97	105	101
1938	NL	1st	89-63	.586	—	Charlie Grimm/Gabby Hartnett	951,640	713	598	65	.269	.338	.377	71	.263	.322	3.37	103	89
1939	NL	4th	84-70	.545	13.0	Gabby Hartnett	726,663	724	678	91	.266	.336	.391	74	.276	.331	3.80	103	90
1940	NL	5th	75-79	.487	25.5	Gabby Hartnett	534,878	681	636	86	.262	.331	.384	74	.262	.318	3.54	97	82
1941	NL	6th	70-84	.455	30.0	Jimmie Wilson	545,159	666	670	99	.253	.327	.365	60	.267	.327	3.72	86	56
1942	NL	6th	68-86	.442	38.0	Jimmie Wilson	590,972	591	665	75	.254	.321	.353	70	.267	.334	3.60	96	77
1943	NL	5th	74-79	.484	30.5	Jimmie Wilson	508,247	632	600	52	.261	.336	.351	53	.258	.311	3.31	99	74
1944	NL	4th	75-79	.487	30.0	J. Wilson/R. Johnson/C. Grimm	640,110	702	669	71	.261	.328	.360	75	.272	.330	3.59	101	97
1945	NL	1st	98-56	.636	—	Charlie Grimm	1,036,386	735	532	57	.277	.349	.372	57	.249	.303	2.98	90	59
1946	NL	3rd	82-71	.536	14.5	Charlie Grimm	1,342,970	626	581	56	.254	.331	.346	58	.256	.325	3.24	83	89
1947	NL	6th	69-85	.448	25.0	Charlie Grimm	1,364,039	567	722	71	.259	.321	.361	106	.274	.353	4.04	101	78
1948	NL	8th	64-90	.416	27.5	Charlie Grimm	1,237,792	597	706	87	.262	.322	.369	104	.261	.341	4.00	87	69
1949	NL	8th	61-93	.396	36.0	Charlie Grimm/Frank Frisch	1,143,139	593	773	97	.256	.312	.373	104	.280	.352	4.50	91	83
1950	NL	7th	64-89	.418	26.5	Frank Frisch	1,165,944	643	772	161	.248	.315	.401	130	.271	.347	4.28	116	94
1951	NL	8th	62-92	.403	34.5	Frank Frisch/Phil Cavarretta	894,415	614	750	103	.250	.315	.364	125	.265	.340	4.34	96	84
1952	NL	5th	77-77	.500	19.5	Phil Cavarretta	1,024,826	628	631	107	.264	.321	.383	101	.240	.314	3.58	105	78
1953	NL	7th	65-89	.422	40.0	Phil Cavarretta	763,658	633	835	137	.260	.328	.399	151	.276	.347	4.79	110	99
1954	NL	7th	64-90	.416	33.0	Stan Hack	748,183	700	766	159	.263	.325	.412	131	.264	.340	4.51	105	100
1955	NL	6th	72-81	.471	26.0	Stan Hack	875,800	626	713	164	.247	.305	.398	153	.251	.330	4.17	101	82
1956	NL	8th	60-94	.390	33.0	Stan Hack	720,118	597	708	142	.244	.302	.382	161	.252	.332	3.96	103	105

Teams: Cubs

Year	Lg	Pos	W-L	Pct	GB	Manager	Att.	R	OR	HR	Avg	OBP	Slg	Opponent				Park Index	
														HR	Avg	OBP	ERA	Runs	HR
1957	NL	7th	62-92	.403	33.0	Bob Scheffing	670,629	628	722	147	.244	.305	.380	144	.261	.336	4.13	94	105
1958	NL	5th	72-82	.468	20.0	Bob Scheffing	979,904	709	725	182	.265	.330	.426	142	.254	.336	4.22	104	115
1959	NL	5th	74-80	.481	13.0	Bob Scheffing	858,255	673	688	163	.249	.317	.398	152	.254	.321	4.01	96	107
1960	NL	7th	60-94	.390	35.0	Charlie Grimm/Lou Boudreau	809,770	634	776	119	.243	.313	.369	152	.260	.333	4.35	105	92
1961	NL	7th	64-90	.416	29.0	Himsl/Craft/Himsl/Tappe/Craft/ Himsl/Tappe/Klein/Tappe	673,057	689	800	176	.255	.325	.418	165	.277	.336	4.48	105	116
1962	NL	9th	59-103	.364	42.5	El Tappe/Lou Klein/Charlie Metro	609,802	632	827	126	.253	.317	.377	159	.272	.346	4.54	118	138
1963	NL	7th	82-80	.506	17.0	Bob Kennedy	979,551	570	578	127	.238	.297	.363	119	.249	.301	3.08	109	118
1964	NL	8th	76-86	.469	17.0	Bob Kennedy	751,647	649	724	145	.251	.314	.390	144	.270	.321	4.08	115	145
1965	NL	8th	72-90	.444	25.0	Bob Kennedy/Lou Klein	641,361	635	723	134	.238	.307	.358	154	.260	.320	3.78	110	150
1966	NL	10th	59-103	.364	36.0	Leo Durocher	635,891	644	809	140	.254	.313	.380	184	.268	.326	4.33	107	125
1967	NL	3rd	87-74	.540	14.0	Leo Durocher	977,226	702	624	128	.251	.316	.378	142	.246	.306	3.48	104	137
1968	NL	3rd	84-78	.519	13.0	Leo Durocher	1,043,409	612	611	130	.242	.298	.366	138	.254	.304	3.41	132	163
1969	NL	2nd-E	92-70	.568	8.0	Leo Durocher	1,674,993	720	611	142	.253	.323	.384	118	.248	.310	3.34	114	132
1970	NL	2nd-E	84-78	.519	5.0	Leo Durocher	1,642,705	806	679	179	.259	.333	.415	143	.256	.316	3.76	143	170
1971	NL	3rd-E	83-79	.512	14.0	Leo Durocher	1,653,007	637	648	128	.258	.325	.378	132	.262	.314	3.61	122	124
1972	NL	2nd-E	85-70	.548	11.0	Leo Durocher/Whitey Lockman	1,299,163	685	567	133	.257	.330	.387	112	.251	.309	3.22	127	149
1973	NL	5th-E	77-84	.478	5.0	Whitey Lockman	1,351,705	614	655	117	.247	.320	.357	128	.267	.322	3.66	118	131
1974	NL	6th-E	66-96	.407	22.0	Whitey Lockman/Jim Marshall	1,015,378	669	826	110	.251	.327	.365	122	.277	.344	4.28	106	149
1975	NL	5th-E	75-87	.463	17.5	Jim Marshall	1,034,819	712	827	95	.259	.338	.368	130	.281	.347	4.49	114	125
1976	NL	4th-E	75-87	.463	26.0	Jim Marshall	1,026,217	611	728	105	.251	.313	.356	123	.268	.327	3.93	124	212
1977	NL	4th-E	81-81	.500	20.0	Herman Franks	1,439,834	692	739	111	.266	.330	.387	128	.266	.325	4.01	132	172
1978	NL	3rd-E	79-83	.488	11.0	Herman Franks	1,525,311	664	724	72	.264	.331	.361	125	.265	.331	4.05	125	143
1979	NL	5th-E	80-82	.494	18.0	Herman Franks/Joey Amalfitano	1,648,587	706	707	135	.269	.329	.403	127	.270	.335	3.88	128	136
1980	NL	6th-E	64-98	.395	27.0	Preston Gomez/Joey Amalfitano	1,206,776	614	728	107	.251	.309	.365	109	.272	.340	3.89	117	116
1981	NL	6th-E	15-37	.288	17.5	Joey Amalfitano													
	NL	5th-E	23-28	.451	6.0	Joey Amalfitano	565,637	370	483	57	.236	.303	.340	59	.270	.340	4.01	111	172
1982	NL	5th-E	73-89	.451	19.0	Lee Elia	1,249,278	676	709	102	.260	.317	.375	125	.272	.327	3.92	109	103
1983	NL	5th-E	71-91	.438	19.0	Lee Elia/Charlie Fox	1,479,717	701	719	140	.261	.319	.401	117	.274	.335	4.08	104	120
1984	NL	1st-E	96-65	.596	—	Jim Frey	2,107,655	762	658	136	.260	.331	.397	99	.267	.321	3.75	121	200
1985	NL	4th-E	77-84	.478	23.5	Jim Frey	2,161,534	686	729	150	.254	.324	.390	156	.271	.333	4.16	140	197
1986	NL	5th-E	70-90	.438	37.0	Jim Frey/John Vukovich/Gene Michael	1,859,102	680	781	155	.256	.318	.398	143	.279	.344	4.49	119	129
1987	NL	6th-E	76-85	.472	18.5	Gene Michael/Frank Lucchesi	2,035,130	720	801	209	.264	.326	.432	159	.275	.349	4.55	104	126
1988	NL	4th-E	77-85	.475	24.0	Don Zimmer	2,089,034	660	694	113	.261	.310	.383	115	.265	.325	3.84	113	130
1989	NL	1st-E	93-69	.574	—	Don Zimmer	2,491,942	702	623	124	.261	.319	.387	106	.250	.317	3.43	117	119
1990	NL	4th-E	77-85	.475	18.0	Don Zimmer	2,243,791	690	774	136	.263	.314	.392	121	.271	.340	4.34	124	136
1991	NL	4th-E	77-83	.481	20.0	Don Zimmer/Joe Altobelli/Jim Essian	2,314,250	695	734	159	.253	.309	.390	117	.257	.324	4.03	112	144
1992	NL	4th-E	78-84	.481	18.0	Jim Lefebvre	2,126,720	593	624	104	.254	.307	.364	107	.246	.320	3.39	101	105
1993	NL	4th-E	84-78	.519	13.0	Jim Lefebvre	2,653,763	738	739	161	.270	.325	.414	153	.273	.332	4.18	107	118
1994	NL	5th-C	49-64	.434	16.5	Tom Trebelhorn	1,845,208	500	549	109	.259	.325	.404	120	.268	.336	4.47	84	97
1995	NL	3rd-C	73-71	.507	12.0	Jim Riggleman	1,918,265	693	671	158	.265	.327	.433	162	.262	.333	4.13	102	108
1996	NL	4th-C	76-86	.469	12.0	Jim Riggleman	2,219,110	772	771	175	.251	.320	.401	184	.260	.330	4.36	104	110
1997	NL	5th-C	68-94	.420	16.0	Jim Riggleman	2,190,368	687	759	127	.263	.321	.396	185	.266	.339	4.44	113	146

Team Nicknames: Chicago White Stockings 1876-1891, Chicago Colts 1892-1898, Chicago Orphans 1899-1902, Chicago Cubs 1903-1997.

Team Ballparks: 23rd Street Grounds 1876-1877, Lake Front Park I 1878-1882, Lake Front Park II 1883-1884, West Side Park 1885-1890, West Side Park & South Side Park II (shared) 1891, South Side Park II 1892-1893, West Side Grounds 1894-1915, Weeghman Park/Wrigley Field (Chi) 1916-1997.

Chicago Cubs Individual Season Batting Leaders

Year	Batting Average		On-Base Percentage		Slugging Percentage		Home Runs		RBI		Stolen Bases	
1876	Ross Barnes	.429	Ross Barnes	.462	Ross Barnes	.590	Cap Anson Paul Hines	2	Deacon White	60	Statistic unavailable	
1877	Cal McVey	.368	Cal McVey	.387	Cal McVey	.455	18 tied with	0	John Peters	41	Statistic unavailable	
1878	Bob Ferguson	.351	Bob Ferguson	.375	Joe Start	.439	3 tied with	1	Cap Anson	40	Statistic unavailable	
1879	Orator Shaffer	.304	Ned Williamson	.343	Ned Williamson	.447	3 tied with	1	Silver Flint	41	Statistic unavailable	
1880	George Gore	.360	George Gore	.399	George Gore	.463	George Gore	2	Cap Anson	74	Statistic unavailable	
1881	Cap Anson	.399	Cap Anson	.442	Cap Anson	.510	Tom Burns	4	Cap Anson	82	Statistic unavailable	
1882	Cap Anson	.362	Cap Anson	.397	Cap Anson	.500	Silver Flint	4	Cap Anson	83	Statistic unavailable	
1883	George Gore	.334	George Gore	.377	George Gore	.472	King Kelly	3	Cap Anson	68	Statistic unavailable	
1884	King Kelly	.354	King Kelly	.414	Ned Williamson	.554	Ned Williamson	27	Cap Anson	102	Statistic unavailable	
1885	George Gore	.313	George Gore	.405	Cap Anson	.461	Abner Dalrymple	11	Cap Anson	108	Statistic unavailable	
1886	King Kelly	.388	King Kelly	.483	Cap Anson	.544	Cap Anson	10	Cap Anson	147	King Kelly	53
1887	Cap Anson	.347	Cap Anson	.422	Cap Anson	.517	Fred Pfeffer	16	Cap Anson	102	Fred Pfeffer	57
1888	Cap Anson	.344	Cap Anson	.400	Jimmy Ryan	.515	Jimmy Ryan	16	Cap Anson	84	Fred Pfeffer	64
1889	Cap Anson	.311	Cap Anson	.414	Jimmy Ryan	.498	Jimmy Ryan	17	Cap Anson	117	Hugh Duffy	52
1890	Cap Anson	.312	Cap Anson	.443	Walt Wilmot	.415	Walt Wilmot	13	Cap Anson	107	Walt Wilmot	76
1891	Cap Anson	.291	Cap Anson	.378	Jimmy Ryan	.434	Walt Wilmot	11	Cap Anson	120	Walt Wilmot	42
1892	Jimmy Ryan	.293	Jimmy Ryan	.375	Jimmy Ryan	.438	Jimmy Ryan	10	Cap Anson	74	Bill Dahlen	60
1893	Cap Anson	.314	Cap Anson	.415	Bill Dahlen	.452	Bill Lange	8	Cap Anson	91	Bill Lange	47
1894	Jimmy Ryan	.361	Bill Dahlen	.444	Bill Dahlen	.566	Bill Dahlen	15	Walt Wilmot	130	Walt Wilmot	74
1895	Bill Lange	.389	Bill Lange	.456	Bill Lange	.575	Bill Lange	10	Bill Lange	98	Bill Lange	67
1896	Bill Dahlen	.352	Bill Dahlen	.438	Bill Dahlen	.553	Bill Dahlen	9	Bill Lange	92	Bill Lange	84
1897	Bill Lange	.340	Bill Lange	.406	Bill Lange	.480	Bill Lange	6	Jimmy Ryan	85	Bill Lange	73
1898	Jimmy Ryan	.323	Jimmy Ryan	.405	Jimmy Ryan	.446	Bill Lange	5	Bill Dahlen Jimmy Ryan	79	Jimmy Ryan	29
1899	Bill Everitt	.310	Jimmy Ryan	.357	Sam Mertes	.467	Sam Mertes	9	Sam Mertes	81	Sam Mertes	45
1900	Sam Mertes	.295	Sam Mertes	.356	Sam Mertes	.407	Sam Mertes	7	Sam Mertes	60	Sam Mertes	38
1901	Topsy Hartsel	.335	Topsy Hartsel	.414	Topsy Hartsel	.475	Topsy Hartsel	7	Charlie Dexter	66	Topsy Hartsel	41
1902	Jimmy Slagle	.315	Jimmy Slagle	.387	Jimmy Slagle	.357	Charlie Dexter Joe Tinker	2	Johnny Kling	57	Jimmy Slagle	40
1903	Frank Chance	.327	Frank Chance	.439	Frank Chance	.440	Johnny Kling	3	Frank Chance	81	Frank Chance	67
1904	Frank Chance	.310	Frank Chance	.382	Frank Chance	.430	Frank Chance	6	Jack McCarthy	51	Frank Chance	42
1905	Frank Chance	.316	Frank Chance	.450	Frank Chance	.434	3 tied with	2	Frank Chance	70	Billy Maloney	59
1906	Harry Steinfeldt	.327	Frank Chance	.419	Harry Steinfeldt	.430	Wildfire Schulte	7	Harry Steinfeldt	83	Frank Chance	57
1907	Solly Hofman	.268	Jimmy Sheckard	.373	Harry Steinfeldt	.336	Johnny Evers Wildfire Schulte	2	Harry Steinfeldt	70	Johnny Evers	46
1908	Johnny Evers	.300	Johnny Evers	.402	Joe Tinker	.392	Joe Tinker	6	Joe Tinker	68	Johnny Evers	36
1909	Solly Hofman	.285	Johnny Evers	.369	Joe Tinker	.372	Wildfire Schulte	4	Wildfire Schulte	60	Frank Chance	29
							Joe Tinker					
1910	Solly Hofman	.325	Johnny Evers	.413	Solly Hofman	.461	Wildfire Schulte	10	Solly Hofman	86	Solly Hofman	29
1911	Heinie Zimmerman	.307	Jimmy Sheckard	.434	Wildfire Schulte	.534	Wildfire Schulte	21	Wildfire Schulte	107	Jimmy Sheckard	32
1912	Heinie Zimmerman	.372	Johnny Evers	.431	Heinie Zimmerman	.571	Heinie Zimmerman	14	Heinie Zimmerman	99	Joe Tinker	25
1913	Heinie Zimmerman	.313	Tommy Leach	.391	Heinie Zimmerman	.490	Vic Saier	14	Heinie Zimmerman	95	Vic Saier	26
1914	Heinie Zimmerman	.296	Vic Saier	.357	Heinie Zimmerman	.424	Vic Saier	18	Heinie Zimmerman	87	Wilbur Good	31
1915	Tom Fisher	.287	Vic Saier	.350	Vic Saier	.445	Cy Williams	13	Vic Saier Cy Williams	64	Vic Saier	29
1916	Cy Williams	.279	Cy Williams	.372	Cy Williams	.459	Cy Williams	12	Cy Williams	66	Max Flack	24
1917	Fred Merkle	.266	Max Flack	.325	Fred Merkle	.370	Larry Doyle	6	Larry Doyle	61	Max Flack Rollie Zeider	17
1918	Charlie Hollocher	.316	Charlie Hollocher	.379	Charlie Hollocher	.397	Max Flack	4	Fred Merkle	65	Charlie Hollocher	26
1919	Max Flack	.294	Charlie Hollocher	.347	Max Flack	.392	Max Flack	6	Fred Merkle	62	Fred Merkle	20
1920	Max Flack	.302	Max Flack	.373	Dave Robertson	.462	Dave Robertson	10	Dave Robertson	75	Charlie Hollocher	20
1921	Ray Grimes	.321	Ray Grimes	.406	Ray Grimes	.449	Max Flack Ray Grimes	6	Ray Grimes	79	Max Flack George Maisel	17
1922	Ray Grimes	.354	Ray Grimes	.442	Ray Grimes	.572	Ray Grimes	14	Ray Grimes	99	Charlie Hollocher	19
1923	Jigger Statz	.319	Bob O'Farrell	.408	Hack Miller	.482	Hack Miller	20	Bernie Friberg Hack Miller	88	George Grantham	43
1924	George Grantham	.316	George Grantham	.390	George Grantham	.458	Gabby Hartnett	16	Bernie Friberg	82	Cliff Heathcote	26
1925	Howard Freigau	.307	Charlie Grimm	.354	Howard Freigau	.445	Gabby Hartnett	24	Charlie Grimm	76	Sparky Adams	26
1926	Hack Wilson	.321	Hack Wilson	.406	Hack Wilson	.539	Hack Wilson	21	Hack Wilson	109	Sparky Adams	27
1927	Riggs Stephenson	.344	Riggs Stephenson	.415	Hack Wilson	.579	Hack Wilson	30	Hack Wilson	129	Sparky Adams	26
1928	Riggs Stephenson	.324	Riggs Stephenson	.407	Hack Wilson	.588	Hack Wilson	31	Hack Wilson	120	Kiki Cuyler	37
1929	Rogers Hornsby	.380	Rogers Hornsby	.459	Rogers Hornsby	.679	Rogers Hornsby	39	Hack Wilson	159	Kiki Cuyler	43
							Hack Wilson					
1930	Hack Wilson	.356	Hack Wilson	.454	Hack Wilson	.723	Hack Wilson	56	Hack Wilson	190	Kiki Cuyler	37
1931	Charlie Grimm	.331	Kiki Cuyler	.404	Kiki Cuyler	.473	Rogers Hornsby	16	Rogers Hornsby	90	Kiki Cuyler	13
1932	Riggs Stephenson	.324	Riggs Stephenson	.383	Riggs Stephenson	.443	Johnny Moore	13	Riggs Stephenson	85	Billy Herman	14
1933	Babe Herman	.289	Babe Herman	.353	Babe Herman	.502	Gabby Hartnett Babe Herman	16	Babe Herman	93	Babe Herman	6
1934	Kiki Cuyler	.338	Kiki Cuyler	.377	Chuck Klein	.510	Gabby Hartnett	22	Gabby Hartnett	90	Kiki Cuyler	15
1935	Billy Herman	.341	Stan Hack	.406	Chuck Klein	.488	Chuck Klein	21	Gabby Hartnett	91	Augie Galan	22
1936	Frank Demaree	.350	Frank Demaree	.400	Frank Demaree	.496	Frank Demaree	16	Frank Demaree	96	Stan Hack	17
1937	Billy Herman	.335	Billy Herman	.396	Frank Demaree	.485	Augie Galan	18	Frank Demaree	115	Augie Galan	23
1938	Stan Hack	.320	Stan Hack	.411	Stan Hack	.432	Ripper Collins	13	Augie Galan	69	Stan Hack	16
1939	Billy Herman	.307	Augie Galan	.392	Billy Herman	.453	Hank Leiber	24	Hank Leiber	88	Stan Hack	17
1940	Stan Hack	.317	Stan Hack	.395	Bill Nicholson	.534	Bill Nicholson	25	Bill Nicholson	98	Stan Hack	21
1941	Stan Hack	.317	Stan Hack	.417	Bill Nicholson	.453	Bill Nicholson	26	Bill Nicholson	98	Stan Hack	10
1942	Lou Novikoff	.300	Stan Hack	.402	Bill Nicholson	.476	Bill Nicholson	21	Bill Nicholson	78	Lennie Merullo	14
1943	Bill Nicholson	.309	Bill Nicholson	.386	Bill Nicholson	.531	Bill Nicholson	29	Bill Nicholson	128	Peanuts Lowrey	13
1944	Phil Cavarretta	.321	Bill Nicholson	.391	Bill Nicholson	.545	Bill Nicholson	33	Bill Nicholson	122	Roy Hughes	16
1945	Phil Cavarretta	.355	Phil Cavarretta	.449	Phil Cavarretta	.500	Bill Nicholson	13	Andy Pafko	110	Stan Hack	12
1946	Phil Cavarretta	.294	Phil Cavarretta	.401	Phil Cavarretta	.435	Phil Cavarretta Bill Nicholson	8	Phil Cavarretta	78	Peanuts Lowrey	10
1947	Phil Cavarretta	.314	Phil Cavarretta	.391	Bill Nicholson	.466	Bill Nicholson	26	Bill Nicholson	75	Lennie Merullo Andy Pafko	4

Year	Batting Average	On-Base Percentage	Slugging Percentage	Home Runs	RBI	Stolen Bases
1948	Andy Pafko .312	Andy Pafko .375	Andy Pafko .516	Andy Pafko 26	Andy Pafko 101	Eddie Waitkus 11
1949	Andy Pafko .281	Andy Pafko .369	Andy Pafko .449	Hank Sauer 27	Hank Sauer 83	Hal Jeffcoat 12
1950	Andy Pafko .304	Andy Pafko .397	Andy Pafko .591	Andy Pafko 36	Hank Sauer 103	Wayne Terwilliger 13
1951	Frankie Baumholtz .284	Frankie Baumholtz .346	Hank Sauer .486	Hank Sauer 30	Hank Sauer 89	Randy Jackson 14
1952	Dee Fondy .300	Hank Sauer .361	Hank Sauer .531	Hank Sauer 37	Hank Sauer 121	Dee Fondy 13
1953	Dee Fondy .309	Ralph Kiner .394	Ralph Kiner .529	Ralph Kiner 28	Ralph Kiner 87	Eddie Miksis 13
1954	Hank Sauer .288	Hank Sauer .375	Hank Sauer .563	Hank Sauer 41	Hank Sauer 103	Dee Fondy 20
1955	Ernie Banks .295	Ernie Banks .345	Ernie Banks .596	Ernie Banks 44	Ernie Banks 117	Gene Baker / Ernie Banks 9
1956	Ernie Banks .297	Ernie Banks .358	Ernie Banks .530	Ernie Banks 28	Ernie Banks 85	Solly Drake / Dee Fondy 9
1957	Walt Moryn .289	Ernie Banks .360	Ernie Banks .579	Ernie Banks 43	Ernie Banks 102	Ernie Banks 8
1958	Ernie Banks .313	Lee Walls .370	Ernie Banks .614	Ernie Banks 47	Ernie Banks 129	Tony Taylor 21
1959	Ernie Banks .304	Ernie Banks .374	Ernie Banks .596	Ernie Banks 45	Ernie Banks 143	Tony Taylor 23
1960	Richie Ashburn .291	Richie Ashburn .415	Ernie Banks .554	Ernie Banks 41	Ernie Banks 117	Richie Ashburn 16
1961	George Altman .303	Ron Santo .362	George Altman .560	Ernie Banks 29	George Altman 96	Richie Ashburn 7
1962	George Altman .318	George Altman .393	George Altman .511	Ernie Banks 37	Ernie Banks 104	George Altman 19
1963	Ron Santo .297	Billy Williams .358	Billy Williams .497	Billy Williams 25 / Billy Williams	Ron Santo 99	Lou Brock 24
1964	Ron Santo .313	Ron Santo .398	Ron Santo .564	Billy Williams 33	Ron Santo 114	Billy Cowan 12
1965	Billy Williams .315	Ron Santo .378	Billy Williams .552	Billy Williams 34	Billy Williams 108	Don Landrum 14
1966	Ron Santo .312	Ron Santo .412	Ron Santo .538	Ron Santo 30	Ron Santo 94	Adolfo Phillips 32
1967	Ron Santo .300	Ron Santo .395	Ron Santo .512	Ron Santo 31	Ron Santo 98	Adolfo Phillips 24
1968	Glenn Beckert .294	Ron Santo .354	Billy Williams .500	Ernie Banks 32	Ron Santo 98 / Billy Williams	Don Kessinger / Adolfo Phillips 9
1969	Billy Williams .293	Ron Santo .384	Ron Santo .485	Ron Santo 29	Ron Santo 123	Don Kessinger 11
1970	Billy Williams .322	Jim Hickman .419	Billy Williams .586	Billy Williams 42	Billy Williams 129	Don Kessinger 12
1971	Glenn Beckert .342	Billy Williams .383	Billy Williams .505	Billy Williams 28	Billy Williams 93	Don Kessinger 15
1972	Billy Williams .333	Billy Williams .398	Billy Williams .606	Billy Williams 37	Billy Williams 122	Jose Cardenal 25
1973	Jose Cardenal .303	Jose Cardenal .375	Rick Monday .469	Rick Monday 26	Billy Williams 86	Jose Cardenal 19
1974	Bill Madlock .313	Rick Monday .375	Rick Monday .467	Rick Monday 20	Jerry Morales 82	Jose Cardenal 23
1975	Bill Madlock .354	Bill Madlock .402	Bill Madlock .479	Andre Thornton 18	Jerry Morales 91	Jose Cardenal 34
1976	Bill Madlock .339	Bill Madlock .412	Rick Monday .507	Rick Monday 32	Bill Madlock 84	Jose Cardenal 23
1977	Steve Ontiveros .299	Steve Ontiveros .390	Bobby Murcer .455	Bobby Murcer 27	Bobby Murcer 89	Ivan DeJesus 24
1978	Bobby Murcer .281	Bobby Murcer .376	Bobby Murcer .403	Dave Kingman 28	Dave Kingman 79	Ivan DeJesus 41
1979	Dave Kingman .288	Steve Ontiveros .362	Dave Kingman .613	Dave Kingman 48	Dave Kingman 115	Ivan DeJesus 24
1980	Bill Buckner .324	Bill Buckner .353	Bill Buckner .457	Jerry Martin 23	Jerry Martin 73	Ivan DeJesus 44
1981	Bill Buckner .311	Steve Henderson .382	Bill Buckner .480	Bill Buckner / Leon Durham 10	Bill Buckner 75	Leon Durham 25
1982	Leon Durham .312	Leon Durham .388	Leon Durham .521	Leon Durham 22	Bill Buckner 105	Bump Wills 35
1983	Keith Moreland .302	Keith Moreland .378	Jody Davis .480	Ron Cey 24 / Jody Davis	Ron Cey 90	Ryne Sandberg 37
1984	Ryne Sandberg .314	Gary Matthews .410	Ryne Sandberg .520	Ron Cey 25	Ron Cey 97	Bob Dernier 45
1985	Keith Moreland .307	Keith Moreland .374	Ryne Sandberg .504	Ryne Sandberg 26	Keith Moreland 106	Ryne Sandberg 54
1986	Ryne Sandberg .284	Leon Durham .350	Leon Durham .452	Jody Davis 21 / Gary Matthews	Keith Moreland 79	Ryne Sandberg 34
1987	Ryne Sandberg .294	Dave Martinez .372	Andre Dawson .568	Andre Dawson 49	Andre Dawson 137	Ryne Sandberg 21
1988	Rafael Palmeiro .307	Mark Grace .371	Andre Dawson .504	Andre Dawson 24	Andre Dawson 79	Shawon Dunston 30
1989	Mark Grace .314	Mark Grace .405	Ryne Sandberg .497	Ryne Sandberg 30	Mark Grace 79	Jerome Walton 24
1990	Andre Dawson .310	Mark Grace .372	Ryne Sandberg .559	Ryne Sandberg 40	Andre Dawson 100 / Ryne Sandberg	Shawon Dunston 25 / Ryne Sandberg
1991	Ryne Sandberg .291	Ryne Sandberg .379	Andre Dawson .488	Andre Dawson 31	Andre Dawson 104	Ced Landrum 27
1992	Mark Grace .307	Mark Grace .380	Ryne Sandberg .510	Ryne Sandberg 26	Andre Dawson 90	Ryne Sandberg 17
1993	Mark Grace .325	Mark Grace .393	Sammy Sosa .485	Sammy Sosa 33	Mark Grace 98	Sammy Sosa 36
1994	Sammy Sosa .300	Mark Grace .370	Sammy Sosa .545	Sammy Sosa 25	Sammy Sosa 70	Sammy Sosa 22
1995	Mark Grace .326	Mark Grace .395	Mark Grace .516	Sammy Sosa 36	Sammy Sosa 119	Sammy Sosa 34
1996	Mark Grace .331	Mark Grace .396	Sammy Sosa .564	Sammy Sosa 40	Sammy Sosa 100	Brian McRae 37
1997	Mark Grace .319	Mark Grace .409	Sammy Sosa .480	Sammy Sosa 36	Sammy Sosa 119	Shawon Dunston 29

Chicago Cubs Individual Season Pitching Leaders

Year	ERA		Baserunners/9 IP		Innings Pitched		Strikeouts		Wins		Saves	
1876	Al Spalding	1.75	Al Spalding	9.7	Al Spalding	528.2	Al Spalding	39	Al Spalding	47	Cal McVey	2
1877	George Bradley	3.31	George Bradley	11.2	George Bradley	394.0	George Bradley	59	George Bradley	18	Cal McVey	2
1878	Terry Larkin	2.24	Terry Larkin	9.6	Terry Larkin	506.0	Terry Larkin	163	Terry Larkin	29	3 tied with	0
1879	Terry Larkin	2.44	Terry Larkin	9.5	Terry Larkin	513.1	Terry Larkin	142	Terry Larkin	31	Frank Hankinson	0
											Terry Larkin	
1880	Fred Goldsmith	1.75	Larry Corcoran	8.4	Larry Corcoran	536.1	Larry Corcoran	268	Larry Corcoran	43	Larry Corcoran	2
1881	Larry Corcoran	2.31	Fred Goldsmith	10.1	Larry Corcoran	396.2	Larry Corcoran	150	Larry Corcoran	31	3 tied with	0
1882	Larry Corcoran	1.95	Larry Corcoran	8.7	Fred Goldsmith	405.0	Larry Corcoran	170	Fred Goldsmith	28	3 tied with	0
1883	Larry Corcoran	2.49	Larry Corcoran	10.7	Larry Corcoran	473.2	Larry Corcoran	216	Larry Corcoran	34	Cap Anson	1
1884	John Clarkson	2.14	John Clarkson	9.1	Larry Corcoran	516.2	Larry Corcoran	272	Larry Corcoran	35	14 tied with	0
1885	John Clarkson	1.85	John Clarkson	8.6	John Clarkson	623.0	John Clarkson	308	John Clarkson	53	Fred Pfeffer	2
											Ned Williamson	
1886	Jocko Flynn	2.24	Jocko Flynn	9.5	John Clarkson	466.2	John Clarkson	313	John Clarkson	36	3 tied with	1
1887	John Clarkson	3.08	John Clarkson	10.5	John Clarkson	523.0	John Clarkson	237	John Clarkson	38	3 tied with	1
1888	Gus Krock	2.44	Gus Krock	9.2	Gus Krock	339.2	Gus Krock	161	Gus Krock	25	George Van Haltren	1
1889	Bill Hutchison	3.54	Bill Hutchison	12.2	Bill Hutchison	318.0	Bill Hutchison	136	3 tied with	16	Bill Bishop	2
1890	Bill Hutchison	2.70	Bill Hutchison	10.5	Bill Hutchison	603.0	Bill Hutchison	289	Bill Hutchison	42	Bill Hutchison	2
1891	Bill Hutchison	2.81	Bill Hutchison	11.0	Bill Hutchison	561.0	Bill Hutchison	261	Bill Hutchison	44	3 tied with	1
1892	Bill Hutchison	2.76	Bill Hutchison	11.0	Bill Hutchison	622.0	Bill Hutchison	312	Bill Hutchison	37	Bill Hutchison	1
1893	Hal Mauck	4.41	Hal Mauck	14.3	Bill Hutchison	348.1	Willie McGill	91	Willie McGill	17	Frank Donnelly	2
1894	Clark Griffith	4.92	Clark Griffith	14.2	Bill Hutchison	277.2	Clark Griffith	71	Clark Griffith	21	8 tied with	0
1895	Clark Griffith	3.93	Clark Griffith	13.4	Clark Griffith	353.0	Adonis Terry	88	Clark Griffith	26	Walter Thornton	1
1896	Clark Griffith	3.54	Clark Griffith	12.5	Clark Griffith	317.2	Danny Friend	86	Clark Griffith	23	Buttons Briggs	1
1897	Clark Griffith	3.72	Clark Griffith	13.4	Clark Griffith	343.2	Clark Griffith	102	Clark Griffith	21	Clark Griffith	1
1898	Clark Griffith	1.88	Clark Griffith	10.8	Clark Griffith	325.2	Clark Griffith	97	Clark Griffith	24	12 tied with	0
1899	Clark Griffith	2.79	Clark Griffith	11.5	Jack Taylor	354.2	Nixey Callahan	77	Clark Griffith	22	Bill Phyle	1
1900	Ned Garvin	2.41	Ned Garvin	11.2	Nixey Callahan	285.1	Ned Garvin	107	Clark Griffith	14	Jack Taylor	1
1901	Rube Waddell	2.81	Rube Waddell	11.6	Long Tom Hughes	308.1	Long Tom Hughes	225	Rube Waddell	14	7 tied with	0
1902	Jack Taylor	1.33	Jack Taylor	9.0	Jack Taylor	324.2	Pop Williams	94	Jack Taylor	23	Bob Rhoads	1
											Jack Taylor	
1903	Jake Weimer	2.30	Jack Taylor	9.8	Jack Taylor	312.1	Jake Weimer	128	Jack Taylor	21	Carl Lundgren	3
1904	Three Finger Brown	1.86	Three Finger Brown	8.9	Jake Weimer	307.0	Jake Weimer	177	Jake Weimer	20	Buttons Briggs	3
1905	Ed Reulbach	1.42	Ed Reulbach	9.2	Ed Reulbach	291.2	Ed Reulbach	152	3 tied with	18	Ed Reulbach	1
											Jake Weimer	
1906	Three Finger Brown	1.04	Three Finger Brown	8.5	Three Finger Brown	277.1	Jack Pfiester	153	Three Finger Brown	26	Three Finger Brown	3
											Ed Reulbach	
1907	Jack Pfiester	1.15	Three Finger Brown	8.7	Orval Overall	268.1	Orval Overall	141	Orval Overall	23	Three Finger Brown	3
											Orval Overall	
1908	Three Finger Brown	1.47	Three Finger Brown	7.7	Three Finger Brown	312.1	Orval Overall	167	Three Finger Brown	29	Three Finger Brown	5
1909	Three Finger Brown	1.31	Three Finger Brown	8.0	Three Finger Brown	342.2	Orval Overall	205	Three Finger Brown	27	Three Finger Brown	7
1910	King Cole	1.80	Three Finger Brown	9.9	Three Finger Brown	295.1	Three Finger Brown	143	Three Finger Brown	25	Three Finger Brown	7
1911	Lew Richie	2.31	Three Finger Brown	10.9	Three Finger Brown	270.0	Three Finger Brown	129	Three Finger Brown	21	Three Finger Brown	13
1912	Larry Cheney	2.85	Larry Cheney	11.3	Larry Cheney	303.1	Larry Cheney	140	Larry Cheney	26	Ed Reulbach	4
1913	George Pearce	2.31	Bert Humphries	9.7	Larry Cheney	305.0	Larry Cheney	136	Larry Cheney	21	Larry Cheney	11
1914	Hippo Vaughn	2.05	Bert Humphries	10.6	Larry Cheney	311.1	Hippo Vaughn	165	Hippo Vaughn	21	Larry Cheney	5
1915	Bert Humphries	2.31	Jimmy Lavender	10.4	Hippo Vaughn	269.2	Hippo Vaughn	148	Hippo Vaughn	20	Jimmy Lavender	4
1916	Hippo Vaughn	2.20	George McConnell	9.3	Hippo Vaughn	294.0	Hippo Vaughn	144	Hippo Vaughn	17	Gene Packard	5
1917	Hippo Vaughn	2.01	Phil Douglas	10.0	Hippo Vaughn	295.2	Hippo Vaughn	195	Hippo Vaughn	23	Vic Aldridge	2
											Paul Carter	
1918	Hippo Vaughn	1.74	Hippo Vaughn	9.3	Hippo Vaughn	290.1	Hippo Vaughn	148	Hippo Vaughn	22	Paul Carter	2
											Phil Douglas	
1919	Pete Alexander	1.72	Pete Alexander	8.3	Hippo Vaughn	306.2	Hippo Vaughn	141	Hippo Vaughn	21	Speed Martin	2
1920	Pete Alexander	1.91	Pete Alexander	10.0	Pete Alexander	363.1	Pete Alexander	173	Pete Alexander	27	Pete Alexander	5
1921	Pete Alexander	3.39	Pete Alexander	11.4	Pete Alexander	252.0	Speed Martin	86	Pete Alexander	15	Buck Freeman	3
1922	Vic Aldridge	3.52	Pete Alexander	11.7	Vic Aldridge	258.1	Tiny Osborne	81	Vic Aldridge	16	Tony Kaufmann	3
									Pete Alexander		Tiny Osborne	
1923	Vic Keen	3.00	Pete Alexander	10.0	Pete Alexander	305.0	Pete Alexander	72	Pete Alexander	22	Fred Fussell	3
							Tony Kaufmann				Tony Kaufmann	
1924	Pete Alexander	3.03	Pete Alexander	11.1	Vic Aldridge	244.1	Tony Kaufmann	79	Tony Kaufmann	16	Vic Keen	3
1925	Pete Alexander	3.39	Pete Alexander	11.5	Pete Alexander	236.0	Sheriff Blake	93	Pete Alexander	15	Guy Bush	4
1926	Charlie Root	2.82	Guy Bush	11.1	Charlie Root	271.1	Charlie Root	127	Charlie Root	18	6 tied with	2
1927	Guy Bush	3.03	Hal Carlson	11.2	Charlie Root	309.0	Charlie Root	145	Charlie Root	26	Guy Bush	2
											Charlie Root	
1928	Sheriff Blake	2.47	Charlie Root	11.2	Pat Malone	250.2	Pat Malone	155	Pat Malone	18	Hal Carlson	4
1929	Charlie Root	3.47	Charlie Root	12.3	Charlie Root	272.0	Pat Malone	166	Pat Malone	22	Guy Bush	8
1930	Pat Malone	3.94	Charlie Root	12.9	Pat Malone	271.2	Pat Malone	142	Pat Malone	20	Pat Malone	4
1931	Bob Smith	3.22	Bob Smith	11.3	Charlie Root	251.0	Charlie Root	131	Charlie Root	17	4 tied with	3
1932	Lon Warneke	2.37	Lon Warneke	10.2	Lon Warneke	277.0	Pat Malone	120	Lon Warneke	22	Charlie Root	3
1933	Lon Warneke	2.00	Lon Warneke	10.6	Lon Warneke	287.1	Lon Warneke	133	Guy Bush	20	Burleigh Grimes	3
1934	Lon Warneke	3.21	Lon Warneke	10.5	Lon Warneke	291.1	Lon Warneke	143	Lon Warneke	22	Bud Tinning	3
											Lon Warneke	
1935	Larry French	2.96	Lon Warneke	10.7	Lon Warneke	261.2	Lon Warneke	120	Bill Lee	20	Lon Warneke	4
									Lon Warneke			
1936	Bill Lee	3.31	Larry French	11.5	Bill Lee	258.2	Lon Warneke	113	Larry French	18	Larry French	3
									Bill Lee			
1937	Tex Carleton	3.15	Charlie Root	10.5	Bill Lee	272.1	Bill Lee	108	Tex Carleton	16	Charlie Root	5
									Larry French			
1938	Bill Lee	2.66	Charlie Root	10.9	Bill Lee	291.0	Clay Bryant	135	Bill Lee	22	Charlie Root	8
1939	Claude Passeau	3.05	Claude Passeau	10.9	Bill Lee	282.1	Claude Passeau	108	Bill Lee	19	Charlie Root	4
1940	Claude Passeau	2.50	Claude Passeau	10.3	Claude Passeau	280.2	Claude Passeau	124	Claude Passeau	20	Claude Passeau	5
1941	Vern Olsen	3.15	Bill Lee	12.0	Claude Passeau	231.0	Paul Erickson	85	Claude Passeau	14	Jake Mooty	4
1942	Claude Passeau	2.68	Claude Passeau	11.7	Claude Passeau	278.1	Claude Passeau	89	Claude Passeau	19	Tot Pressnell	4
1943	Hi Bithorn	2.60	Hi Bithorn	10.6	Claude Passeau	257.0	Claude Passeau	93	Hi Bithorn	18	Hank Wyse	5
1944	Claude Passeau	2.89	Claude Passeau	11.3	Hank Wyse	257.1	Claude Passeau	89	Hank Wyse	16	Paul Derringer	3
											Claude Passeau	

Year	ERA		Baserunners/9 IP		Innings Pitched		Strikeouts		Wins		Saves	
1945	Ray Prim	2.40	Ray Prim	9.0	Hank Wyse	278.1	Claude Passeau	98	Hank Wyse	22	Paul Derringer	4
1946	Johnny Schmitz	2.61	Johnny Schmitz	11.2	Johnny Schmitz	224.1	Johnny Schmitz	135	Hank Wyse	14	3 tied with	2
1947	Johnny Schmitz	3.22	Hank Borowy	12.5	Johnny Schmitz	207.0	Johnny Schmitz	97	Johnny Schmitz	13	Emil Kush	5
1948	Johnny Schmitz	2.64	Johnny Schmitz	10.6	Johnny Schmitz	242.0	Johnny Schmitz	100	Johnny Schmitz	18	Bob Chipman	4
1949	Bob Rush	4.07	Bob Rush	12.4	Johnny Schmitz	207.0	Dutch Leonard	83	Johnny Schmitz	11	Monk Dubiel	4
											Bob Rush	
1950	Bob Rush	3.71	Bob Rush	12.7	Bob Rush	254.2	Paul Minner	99	Bob Rush	13	Dutch Leonard	6
1951	Paul Minner	3.79	Bob Rush	12.1	Bob Rush	211.1	Bob Rush	129	Bob Rush	11	Dutch Leonard	3
1952	Warren Hacker	2.58	Warren Hacker	8.6	Bob Rush	250.1	Bob Rush	157	Bob Rush	17	Dutch Leonard	11
1953	Paul Minner	4.21	Warren Hacker	11.4	Warren Hacker	221.2	Johnny Klippstein	113	Warren Hacker	12	Dutch Leonard	8
									Paul Minner			
1954	Bob Rush	3.77	Warren Hacker	11.2	Bob Rush	236.1	Bob Rush	124	Bob Rush	13	Hal Jeffcoat	7
1955	Paul Minner	3.48	Warren Hacker	10.4	Sam Jones	241.2	Sam Jones	198	Sam Jones	14	Hal Jeffcoat	6
1956	Bob Rush	3.19	Bob Rush	10.2	Bob Rush	239.2	Sam Jones	176	Bob Rush	13	Turk Lown	13
1957	Moe Drabowsky	3.53	Moe Drabowsky	11.9	Moe Drabowsky	239.2	Moe Drabowsky	170	Dick Drott	15	Turk Lown	12
							Dick Drott					
1958	Glen Hobbie	3.74	Taylor Phillips	13.9	Taylor Phillips	170.1	Dick Drott	127	Glen Hobbie	10	Don Elston	10
1959	Dave Hillman	3.53	Dave Hillman	10.5	Bob Anderson	235.1	Glen Hobbie	138	Glen Hobbie	16	Don Elston	13
1960	Dick Ellsworth	3.72	Don Cardwell	12.2	Glen Hobbie	258.2	Glen Hobbie	134	Glen Hobbie	16	Don Elston	11
1961	Don Cardwell	3.82	Don Cardwell	11.8	Don Cardwell	259.1	Don Cardwell	156	Don Cardwell	15	Bob Anderson	8
											Don Elston	
1962	Bob Buhl	3.69	Don Cardwell	12.6	Bob Buhl	212.0	Dick Ellsworth	113	Bob Buhl	12	Don Elston	8
1963	Dick Ellsworth	2.11	Dick Ellsworth	9.3	Dick Ellsworth	290.2	Dick Ellsworth	185	Dick Ellsworth	22	Lindy McDaniel	22
1964	Larry Jackson	3.14	Larry Jackson	9.8	Larry Jackson	297.2	Dick Ellsworth	148	Larry Jackson	24	Lindy McDaniel	15
							Larry Jackson					
1965	Cal Koonce	3.69	Larry Jackson	11.5	Larry Jackson	257.1	Larry Jackson	131	Dick Ellsworth	14	Ted Abernathy	31
									Larry Jackson			
1966	Fergie Jenkins	3.31	Fergie Jenkins	9.9	Dick Ellsworth	269.1	Ken Holtzman	171	Ken Holtzman	11	Bob Hendley	7
1967	Fergie Jenkins	2.80	Fergie Jenkins	9.9	Fergie Jenkins	289.1	Fergie Jenkins	236	Fergie Jenkins	20	Chuck Hartenstein	10
1968	Fergie Jenkins	2.63	Bill Hands	9.2	Fergie Jenkins	308.0	Fergie Jenkins	260	Fergie Jenkins	20	Phil Regan	25
1969	Bill Hands	2.49	Bill Hands	10.4	Fergie Jenkins	311.1	Fergie Jenkins	273	Fergie Jenkins	21	Phil Regan	17
1970	Ken Holtzman	3.38	Fergie Jenkins	9.5	Fergie Jenkins	313.0	Fergie Jenkins	274	Fergie Jenkins	22	Phil Regan	12
1971	Fergie Jenkins	2.77	Fergie Jenkins	9.6	Fergie Jenkins	325.0	Fergie Jenkins	263	Fergie Jenkins	24	Phil Regan	6
1972	Milt Pappas	2.77	Fergie Jenkins	10.0	Fergie Jenkins	289.1	Fergie Jenkins	184	Fergie Jenkins	20	Jack Aker	17
1973	Rick Reuschel	3.00	Fergie Jenkins	10.9	Fergie Jenkins	271.0	Fergie Jenkins	170	3 tied with	14	Bob Locker	18
1974	Bill Bonham	3.86	Rick Reuschel	13.1	Bill Bonham	242.2	Bill Bonham	191	Rick Reuschel	13	Oscar Zamora	10
1975	Rick Reuschel	3.73	Steve Stone	11.9	Ray Burris	238.1	Bill Bonham	165	Ray Burris	15	Darold Knowles	15
1976	Ray Burris	3.11	Steve Renko	11.4	Rick Reuschel	260.0	Rick Reuschel	146	Ray Burris	15	Bruce Sutter	10
1977	Rick Reuschel	2.79	Rick Reuschel	11.1	Rick Reuschel	252.0	Rick Reuschel	166	Rick Reuschel	20	Bruce Sutter	31
1978	Dennis Lamp	3.30	Rick Reuschel	10.9	Rick Reuschel	242.2	Rick Reuschel	115	Rick Reuschel	14	Bruce Sutter	27
1979	Dennis Lamp	3.50	Dennis Lamp	12.3	Rick Reuschel	239.0	Lynn McGlothen	147	Rick Reuschel	18	Bruce Sutter	37
1980	Rick Reuschel	3.40	Rick Reuschel	12.6	Rick Reuschel	257.0	Rick Reuschel	140	Lynn McGlothen	12	Bruce Sutter	28
1981	Randy Martz	3.68	Mike Krukow	12.7	Mike Krukow	144.1	Mike Krukow	101	Mike Krukow	9	Dick Tidrow	9
1982	Fergie Jenkins	3.15	Fergie Jenkins	12.2	Fergie Jenkins	217.1	Fergie Jenkins	134	Fergie Jenkins	14	Lee Smith	17
1983	Fergie Jenkins	4.30	Fergie Jenkins	12.3	Chuck Rainey	191.0	Bill Campbell	97	Chuck Rainey	14	Lee Smith	29
1984	Steve Trout	3.41	Steve Trout	12.6	Steve Trout	190.0	Rick Sutcliffe	155	Rick Sutcliffe	16	Lee Smith	33
1985	Dennis Eckersley	3.08	Dennis Eckersley	8.9	Dennis Eckersley	169.1	Dennis Eckersley	117	Dennis Eckersley	11	Lee Smith	33
1986	Scott Sanderson	4.19	Scott Sanderson	10.8	Dennis Eckersley	201.0	Dennis Eckersley	137	Scott Sanderson	9	Lee Smith	31
									Lee Smith			
1987	Rick Sutcliffe	3.68	Rick Sutcliffe	12.6	Rick Sutcliffe	237.1	Rick Sutcliffe	174	Rick Sutcliffe	18	Lee Smith	36
1988	Greg Maddux	3.18	Greg Maddux	11.6	Greg Maddux	249.0	Rick Sutcliffe	144	Greg Maddux	18	Goose Gossage	13
1989	Greg Maddux	2.95	Rick Sutcliffe	10.7	Greg Maddux	238.1	Rick Sutcliffe	153	Greg Maddux	19	Mitch Williams	36
1990	Mike Harkey	3.26	Mike Harkey	11.3	Greg Maddux	237.0	Greg Maddux	144	Greg Maddux	15	Mitch Williams	16
1991	Greg Maddux	3.35	Greg Maddux	10.4	Greg Maddux	263.0	Greg Maddux	198	Greg Maddux	15	Dave Smith	17
1992	Greg Maddux	2.18	Greg Maddux	9.6	Greg Maddux	268.0	Greg Maddux	199	Greg Maddux	20	Bob Scanlan	14
1993	Greg Hibbard	3.96	Greg Hibbard	12.2	Mike Morgan	207.2	Jose Guzman	163	Greg Hibbard	15	Randy Myers	53
1994	Steve Trachsel	3.21	Anthony Young	11.7	Steve Trachsel	146.0	Steve Trachsel	108	Steve Trachsel	9	Randy Myers	21
1995	Frank Castillo	3.21	Frank Castillo	11.3	Jaime Navarro	200.1	Kevin Foster	146	Jaime Navarro	14	Randy Myers	38
1996	Steve Trachsel	3.03	Steve Trachsel	11.0	Jaime Navarro	236.2	Jaime Navarro	158	Jaime Navarro	15	Turk Wendell	18
1997	Steve Trachsel	4.51	Steve Trachsel	13.4	Steve Trachsel	201.1	Steve Trachsel	160	Jeremi Gonzalez	11	Terry Adams	18

Teams: Cubs

Cubs Franchise Batting Leaders—Career

Games

1	Ernie Banks	2,528
2	Cap Anson	2,276
3	Billy Williams	2,213
4	Ryne Sandberg	2,151
5	Ron Santo	2,126
6	Phil Cavarretta	1,953
7	Stan Hack	1,938
8	Gabby Hartnett	1,926
9	Jimmy Ryan	1,660
10	Don Kessinger	1,648
11	Wildfire Schulte	1,564
12	Joe Tinker	1,536
13	Mark Grace	1,448
14	Johnny Evers	1,409
15	Bill Nicholson	1,349
16	Billy Herman	1,344
17	Charlie Grimm	1,334
18	Frank Chance	1,274
19	Shawon Dunston	1,254
20	Glenn Beckert	1,247

At-Bats

1	Ernie Banks	9,421
2	Cap Anson	9,101
3	Billy Williams	8,479
4	Ryne Sandberg	8,379
5	Ron Santo	7,768
6	Stan Hack	7,278
7	Jimmy Ryan	6,757
8	Phil Cavarretta	6,592
9	Don Kessinger	6,355
10	Gabby Hartnett	6,282
11	Wildfire Schulte	5,837
12	Joe Tinker	5,547
13	Billy Herman	5,532
14	Mark Grace	5,458
15	Glenn Beckert	5,020
16	Charlie Grimm	4,917
17	Tom Burns	4,881
18	Johnny Evers	4,858
19	Bill Nicholson	4,857
20	Shawon Dunston	4,570

Runs

1	Cap Anson	1,719
2	Jimmy Ryan	1,409
3	Ryne Sandberg	1,316
4	Billy Williams	1,306
5	Ernie Banks	1,305
6	Stan Hack	1,239
7	Ron Santo	1,109
8	Phil Cavarretta	968
9	Bill Dahlen	896
10	Billy Herman	875
11	Gabby Hartnett	847
12	Wildfire Schulte	827
13	Frank Chance	794
14	Bill Dahlen	783
15	George Gore	772
16	Don Kessinger	769
17	Woody English	747
18	Ned Williamson	744
19	Fred Pfeffer	742
	Johnny Evers	742

Hits

1	Cap Anson	2,995
2	Ernie Banks	2,583
3	Billy Williams	2,510
4	Ryne Sandberg	2,385
5	Stan Hack	2,193
6	Ron Santo	2,171
7	Jimmy Ryan	2,073
8	Phil Cavarretta	1,927
9	Gabby Hartnett	1,867
10	Billy Herman	1,710
11	Mark Grace	1,691
12	Don Kessinger	1,619
13	Wildfire Schulte	1,590
14	Charlie Grimm	1,454
15	Joe Tinker	1,436
16	Glenn Beckert	1,423
17	Johnny Evers	1,340
18	Bill Nicholson	1,323
19	Tom Burns	1,291
20	Frank Chance	1,268

Doubles

1	Cap Anson	528
2	Ernie Banks	407
3	Ryne Sandberg	403
4	Billy Williams	402
5	Gabby Hartnett	391
6	Stan Hack	363
7	Jimmy Ryan	362
8	Ron Santo	353
9	Billy Herman	346
10	Phil Cavarretta	341
11	Mark Grace	332
12	Charlie Grimm	270
13	Wildfire Schulte	254
14	Bill Nicholson	245
15	Riggs Stephenson	237
16	Tom Burns	236
17	Bill Buckner	235
18	Shawon Dunston	226
19	Joe Tinker	221
20	Kiki Cuyler	220

Triples

1	Jimmy Ryan	142
2	Cap Anson	124
3	Wildfire Schulte	117
4	Bill Dahlen	106
5	Phil Cavarretta	99
6	Joe Tinker	93
7	Ernie Banks	90
8	Billy Williams	87
9	Stan Hack	81
10	Ned Williamson	80
	Bill Lange	80
	Heinie Zimmerman	80
13	Frank Chance	79
14	Ryne Sandberg	76
15	Fred Pfeffer	72
16	Don Kessinger	71
17	Tom Burns	69
	Billy Herman	69
19	Kiki Cuyler	66
	Ron Santo	66

Home Runs

1	Ernie Banks	512
2	Billy Williams	392
3	Ron Santo	337
4	Ryne Sandberg	282
5	Gabby Hartnett	231
6	Bill Nicholson	205
7	Hank Sauer	198
8	Hack Wilson	190
9	Sammy Sosa	178
10	Andre Dawson	174
11	Leon Durham	138
12	Andy Pafko	126
13	Jody Davis	122
14	Shawon Dunston	107
15	Rick Monday	106
16	Mark Grace	104
17	Keith Moreland	100
18	Jimmy Ryan	99
19	Cap Anson	97
	Jim Hickman	97

RBI

1	Cap Anson	1,879
2	Ernie Banks	1,636
3	Billy Williams	1,353
4	Ron Santo	1,290
5	Gabby Hartnett	1,153
6	Ryne Sandberg	1,061
7	Jimmy Ryan	914
8	Phil Cavarretta	896
9	Bill Nicholson	833
10	Hack Wilson	768
11	Mark Grace	742
12	Wildfire Schulte	712
13	Charlie Grimm	697
14	Tom Burns	679
15	Fred Pfeffer	677
16	Joe Tinker	670
17	Stan Hack	642
18	Ned Williamson	622
19	Kiki Cuyler	602
20	Frank Chance	590

Walks

1	Stan Hack	1,092
2	Ron Santo	1,071
3	Cap Anson	952
4	Billy Williams	911
5	Phil Cavarretta	794
6	Ernie Banks	763
7	Ryne Sandberg	761
8	Bill Nicholson	696
9	Gabby Hartnett	691
10	Jimmy Ryan	683
11	Mark Grace	675
12	Jimmy Sheckard	629
13	Johnny Evers	556
14	Don Kessinger	550
15	Frank Chance	546
16	Woody English	498
17	Bill Dahlen	472
18	Billy Herman	470
19	Ned Williamson	465
20	Hack Wilson	463

Strikeouts

1	Ron Santo	1,271
2	Ryne Sandberg	1,259
3	Ernie Banks	1,236
4	Billy Williams	934
5	Shawon Dunston	770
6	Sammy Sosa	732
7	Bill Nicholson	684
8	Gabby Hartnett	683
9	Jody Davis	647
10	Don Kessinger	629
11	Leon Durham	608
12	Phil Cavarretta	585
13	Rick Monday	540
14	Randy Hundley	519
15	Ned Williamson	482
16	Woody English	470
17	Stan Hack	466
18	Hack Wilson	461
19	Hank Sauer	454
20	Andre Dawson	453

Stolen Bases

1	Frank Chance	400
2	Bill Lange	399
3	Jimmy Ryan	369
4	Ryne Sandberg	344
5	Joe Tinker	304
6	Johnny Evers	291
7	Walt Wilmot	290
8	Bill Dahlen	285
9	Fred Pfeffer	263
10	Cap Anson	247
11	Wildfire Schulte	214
12	Jimmy Slagle	198
13	Bill Everitt	179
14	Shawon Dunston	175
15	Stan Hack	165
16	Jimmy Sheckard	163
17	Tom Burns	161
	Kiki Cuyler	161
19	Solly Hofman	158
20	Ivan DeJesus	154

Runs Created

1	Cap Anson	2,108
2	Billy Williams	1,506
3	Ernie Banks	1,481
4	Jimmy Ryan	1,427
5	Ryne Sandberg	1,329
6	Ron Santo	1,313
7	Stan Hack	1,240
8	Gabby Hartnett	1,128
9	Phil Cavarretta	1,051
10	Mark Grace	916
11	Frank Chance	866
12	Wildfire Schulte	864
13	Bill Dahlen	859
14	Bill Nicholson	855
15	Billy Herman	854
16	Tom Burns	807
17	Ned Williamson	799
18	Bill Lange	762
19	Johnny Evers	736
20	Fred Pfeffer	733

Runs Created/27 Outs

(minimum 2000 Plate Appearances)

1	George Gore	9.46
2	King Kelly	9.32
3	Cap Anson	9.08
4	Bill Lange	8.95
5	Hack Wilson	8.38
6	Bill Dahlen	7.91
7	Jimmy Ryan	7.80
8	Abner Dalrymple	7.77
9	Riggs Stephenson	7.17
10	Frank Chance	7.14
11	Ned Williamson	7.13
12	Walt Wilmot	6.99
13	Kiki Cuyler	6.85
14	Bill Everitt	6.76
15	Billy Williams	6.51
16	Gabby Hartnett	6.41
17	Bill Nicholson	6.35
18	Stan Hack	6.30
19	Mark Grace	6.18
20	Leon Durham	6.07

Batting Average

(minimum 2000 Plate Appearances)

1	Riggs Stephenson	.336
2	Bill Lange	.330
3	Cap Anson	.329
4	Kiki Cuyler	.325
5	Bill Everitt	.323
6	Hack Wilson	.322
7	King Kelly	.316
8	George Gore	.315
9	Mark Grace	.310
10	Frank Demaree	.309
11	Billy Herman	.309
12	Jimmy Ryan	.307
13	Charlie Hollocher	.304
14	Heinie Zimmerman	.304
15	Stan Hack	.301
16	Bill Buckner	.300
17	Bill Dahlen	.299
18	Gabby Hartnett	.297
19	Frank Chance	.297
20	Jose Cardenal	.296

On-Base Percentage

(minimum 2000 Plate Appearances)

1	Hack Wilson	.412
2	Riggs Stephenson	.408
3	Bill Lange	.401
4	Cap Anson	.395
5	Stan Hack	.394
6	Frank Chance	.394
7	Kiki Cuyler	.391
8	George Gore	.386
9	Bill Dahlen	.384
10	Mark Grace	.384
11	Jimmy Ryan	.376
12	Jimmy Sheckard	.374
13	Phil Cavarretta	.371
14	Bill Everitt	.371
15	Dom Dallessandro	.370
16	Gabby Hartnett	.370
17	Charlie Hollocher	.370
18	Bill Nicholson	.368
19	Woody English	.368
20	King Kelly	.367

Slugging Percentage

(minimum 2000 Plate Appearances)

1	Hack Wilson	.590
2	Hank Sauer	.512
3	Andre Dawson	.507
4	Billy Williams	.503
5	Sammy Sosa	.500
6	Ernie Banks	.500
7	Gabby Hartnett	.490
8	Kiki Cuyler	.485
9	Leon Durham	.484
10	Ron Santo	.472
11	Bill Nicholson	.471
12	Riggs Stephenson	.469
13	Andy Pafko	.468
14	Jim Hickman	.467
15	Rick Monday	.460
16	Bill Lange	.459
17	George Altman	.458
18	King Kelly	.453
19	Walt Moryn	.452
20	Ryne Sandberg	.452

Cubs Franchise Pitching Leaders—Career

Wins

1	Charlie Root	201
2	Three Finger Brown	188
3	Bill Hutchison	182
4	Larry Corcoran	175
5	Fergie Jenkins	167
6	Clark Griffith	152
	Guy Bush	152
8	Hippo Vaughn	151
9	Bill Lee	139
10	John Clarkson	137
11	Ed Reulbach	136
12	Rick Reuschel	135
13	Pete Alexander	128
14	Claude Passeau	124
15	Pat Malone	115
16	Bob Rush	110
17	Jack Taylor	109
	Lon Warneke	109
19	Fred Goldsmith	107
20	Four tied at	95

Losses

1	Bill Hutchison	158
2	Charlie Root	156
3	Bob Rush	140
4	Fergie Jenkins	132
5	Rick Reuschel	127
6	Bill Lee	123
7	Dick Ellsworth	110
8	Hippo Vaughn	105
9	Guy Bush	101
10	Clark Griffith	96
11	Claude Passeau	94
12	Sheriff Blake	92
13	Jack Taylor	90
14	Bill Hands	86
15	Larry Corcoran	85
	Three Finger Brown	85
17	Larry French	84
18	Pete Alexander	83
19	Ken Holtzman	81
20	Johnny Schmitz	80

Winning Percentage
(minimum 100 decisions)

1	John Clarkson	.706
2	Three Finger Brown	.689
3	Ed Reulbach	.677
4	Larry Corcoran	.673
5	Orval Overall	.662
6	Jack Pfiester	.633
7	Fred Goldsmith	.629
8	Carl Lundgren	.623
9	Clark Griffith	.613
10	Pete Alexander	.607
11	Lon Warneke	.602
12	Guy Bush	.601
13	Larry Cheney	.598
14	Pat Malone	.593
15	Hippo Vaughn	.590
16	Nixey Callahan	.584
17	Claude Passeau	.569
18	Charlie Root	.563
19	Hank Wyse	.561
20	Greg Maddux	.559

Games

1	Charlie Root	605
2	Lee Smith	458
3	Don Elston	449
4	Guy Bush	428
5	Fergie Jenkins	401
6	Bill Hutchison	367
7	Bill Lee	364
8	Rick Reuschel	358
9	Three Finger Brown	346
10	Bob Rush	339
11	Willie Hernandez	323
12	Hippo Vaughn	305
13	Bruce Sutter	300
14	Claude Passeau	292
15	Ed Reulbach	281
16	Paul Assenmacher	279
17	Bill Hands	276
18	Larry French	272
19	Glen Hobbie	271
20	Larry Corcoran	270

Games Started

1	Fergie Jenkins	347
2	Rick Reuschel	343
3	Bill Hutchison	339
	Charlie Root	339
5	Bill Lee	296
6	Bob Rush	292
7	Hippo Vaughn	270
8	Larry Corcoran	262
9	Clark Griffith	252
	Guy Bush	252
11	Three Finger Brown	241
12	Dick Ellsworth	236
13	Claude Passeau	234
14	Pete Alexander	223
15	Ed Reulbach	216
16	Bill Hands	213
17	Ken Holtzman	209
18	Greg Maddux	208
19	Pat Malone	200
20	John Clarkson	197

Complete Games

1	Bill Hutchison	317
2	Larry Corcoran	252
3	Clark Griffith	240
4	Three Finger Brown	206
5	Jack Taylor	188
6	John Clarkson	186
7	Hippo Vaughn	177
	Charlie Root	177
9	Fred Goldsmith	164
10	Pete Alexander	159
11	Fergie Jenkins	154
12	Bill Lee	153
13	Ed Reulbach	149
14	Claude Passeau	143
15	Guy Bush	127
16	Carl Lundgren	125
17	Lon Warneke	122
18	Nixey Callahan	116
19	Terry Larkin	113
20	Bob Rush	112

Shutouts

1	Three Finger Brown	49
2	Hippo Vaughn	35
3	Ed Reulbach	31
4	Fergie Jenkins	29
5	Orval Overall	28
6	Bill Lee	25
7	Pete Alexander	24
8	Larry Corcoran	22
	Claude Passeau	22
10	Bill Hutchison	21
	Charlie Root	21
	Larry French	21
13	Carl Lundgren	19
14	Jack Pfiester	17
	Lon Warneke	17
	Rick Reuschel	17
17	Fred Goldsmith	16
	Pat Malone	16
19	John Clarkson	15
	Ken Holtzman	15

Saves

1	Lee Smith	180
2	Bruce Sutter	133
3	Randy Myers	112
4	Don Elston	63
5	Phil Regan	60
6	Mitch Williams	52
7	Charlie Root	40
8	Three Finger Brown	39
	Lindy McDaniel	39
	Ted Abernathy	39
11	Paul Assenmacher	33
12	Jack Aker	29
13	Dutch Leonard	28
	Turk Lown	28
15	Guy Bush	27
16	Dick Tidrow	25
17	Darold Knowles	24
18	Oscar Zamora	23
	Terry Adams	23
20	Four tied at	22

Innings Pitched

1	Charlie Root	3,137.1
2	Bill Hutchison	3,021.0
3	Fergie Jenkins	2,673.2
4	Larry Corcoran	2,338.1
5	Three Finger Brown	2,329.0
6	Rick Reuschel	2,290.0
7	Bill Lee	2,271.1
8	Hippo Vaughn	2,216.1
9	Guy Bush	2,201.1
10	Clark Griffith	2,188.2
11	Bob Rush	2,132.2
12	Claude Passeau	1,914.2
13	Pete Alexander	1,884.1
14	Ed Reulbach	1,864.2
15	Jack Taylor	1,801.0
16	John Clarkson	1,730.2
17	Pat Malone	1,632.0
18	Lon Warneke	1,624.2
19	Dick Ellsworth	1,613.1
20	Bill Hands	1,564.0

Walks

1	Bill Hutchison	1,109
2	Charlie Root	871
3	Guy Bush	734
4	Bob Rush	725
5	Bill Lee	704
6	Sheriff Blake	688
7	Ed Reulbach	650
8	Rick Reuschel	640
9	Hippo Vaughn	621
10	Fergie Jenkins	600
11	Pat Malone	577
12	Ken Holtzman	530
13	Johnny Schmitz	523
14	Bill Hands	521
15	Clark Griffith	517
16	Rick Sutcliffe	481
17	Glen Hobbie	480
18	Carl Lundgren	476
19	Claude Passeau	474
20	Larry Corcoran	462

Strikeouts

1	Fergie Jenkins	2,038
2	Charlie Root	1,432
3	Rick Reuschel	1,367
4	Bill Hutchison	1,222
5	Hippo Vaughn	1,138
6	Larry Corcoran	1,086
7	Bob Rush	1,076
8	Three Finger Brown	1,043
9	Ken Holtzman	988
10	John Clarkson	960
11	Greg Maddux	937
12	Rick Sutcliffe	909
13	Dick Ellsworth	905
14	Bill Hands	900
15	Pat Malone	878
16	Bill Lee	874
17	Bill Bonham	811
18	Ed Reulbach	799
19	Claude Passeau	754
20	Orval Overall	729

Strikeouts/9 Innings
(minimum 1000 Innings Pitched)

1	Fergie Jenkins	6.86
2	Rick Sutcliffe	6.46
3	Bill Bonham	6.33
4	Ken Holtzman	6.15
5	Greg Maddux	5.85
6	Orval Overall	5.78
7	Rick Reuschel	5.37
8	Bill Hands	5.18
9	Dick Ellsworth	5.05
10	John Clarkson	4.99
11	Glen Hobbie	4.90
12	Pat Malone	4.84
13	Hippo Vaughn	4.62
14	Bob Rush	4.54
15	Ray Burris	4.46
16	Larry Cheney	4.34
17	Jack Pfiester	4.22
18	Larry Corcoran	4.18
19	Jimmy Lavender	4.13
20	Johnny Schmitz	4.13

ERA
(minimum 1000 Innings Pitched)

1	Three Finger Brown	1.80
2	Jack Pfiester	1.85
3	Orval Overall	1.91
4	Ed Reulbach	2.24
5	Larry Corcoran	2.26
6	Hippo Vaughn	2.33
7	Terry Larkin	2.34
8	John Clarkson	2.39
9	Carl Lundgren	2.42
10	Jack Taylor	2.66
11	Larry Cheney	2.74
12	Fred Goldsmith	2.78
13	Lon Warneke	2.84
14	Pete Alexander	2.84
15	Claude Hendrix	2.84
16	Claude Passeau	2.96
17	Jimmy Lavender	3.03
18	Hank Wyse	3.03
19	Bill Hands	3.18
20	Fergie Jenkins	3.20

Component ERA
(minimum 1000 Innings Pitched)

1	Three Finger Brown	1.82
2	Orval Overall	2.00
3	Jack Pfiester	2.02
4	Terry Larkin	2.12
5	John Clarkson	2.16
6	Larry Corcoran	2.16
7	Ed Reulbach	2.28
8	Hippo Vaughn	2.54
9	Carl Lundgren	2.59
10	Fred Goldsmith	2.64
11	Larry Cheney	2.69
12	Jack Taylor	2.72
13	Pete Alexander	2.79
14	Lon Warneke	2.88
15	Fergie Jenkins	2.90
16	Claude Hendrix	2.91
17	Claude Passeau	3.04
18	Jimmy Lavender	3.12
19	Bill Hands	3.14
20	Greg Maddux	3.17

Opponent Average
(minimum 1000 Innings Pitched)

1	Orval Overall	.212
2	Jack Pfiester	.219
3	Ed Reulbach	.220
4	Three Finger Brown	.222
5	Larry Corcoran	.225
6	John Clarkson	.225
7	Larry Cheney	.232
8	Carl Lundgren	.235
9	Fergie Jenkins	.239
10	Hippo Vaughn	.241
11	Terry Larkin	.243
12	Jimmy Lavender	.248
13	Greg Maddux	.249
14	Bill Hands	.249
15	Rick Sutcliffe	.250
16	Bob Rush	.250
17	Lon Warneke	.250
18	Johnny Schmitz	.251
19	Ken Holtzman	.253
20	Jack Taylor	.256

Opponent OBP
(minimum 1000 Innings Pitched)

1	Terry Larkin	.254
2	John Clarkson	.259
3	Larry Corcoran	.261
4	Three Finger Brown	.265
5	Fred Goldsmith	.276
6	Jack Pfiester	.279
7	Orval Overall	.280
8	Fergie Jenkins	.283
9	Pete Alexander	.293
10	Bill Hands	.297
11	Ed Reulbach	.297
12	Lon Warneke	.299
13	Hippo Vaughn	.299
14	Jack Taylor	.299
15	Warren Hacker	.302
16	Claude Passeau	.303
17	Carl Lundgren	.308
18	Larry Cheney	.310
19	Greg Maddux	.311
20	Bob Rush	.312

Cubs Franchise Batting Leaders—Single Season

Games

1	Ron Santo	1965	164
	Billy Williams	1965	164
3	Ernie Banks	1965	163
	Billy Williams	1968	163
	Billy Williams	1969	163
6	Ron Santo	1962	162
	Ron Santo	1963	162
	Billy Williams	1964	162
	Billy Williams	1966	162
	Billy Williams	1967	162
	Ron Santo	1968	162
	Sammy Sosa	1997	162
13	Billy Williams	1963	161
	Ron Santo	1964	161
	Ron Santo	1967	161
	Billy Williams	1970	161
	Bill Buckner	1982	161
	Keith Moreland	1985	161
19	Eight tied at		160

At-Bats

1	Billy Herman	1935	666
2	Don Kessinger	1969	664
3	Ken Hubbs	1962	661
4	Bill Buckner	1982	657
5	Billy Herman	1932	656
	Glenn Beckert	1966	656
7	Jigger Statz	1923	655
	Don Kessinger	1968	655
9	Billy Williams	1966	648
10	Sparky Adams	1927	647
11	Augie Galan	1935	646
12	Billy Williams	1964	645
	Billy Williams	1965	645
14	Glenn Beckert	1968	643
	Kiki Cuyler	1930	642
	Billy Williams	1968	642
	Billy Williams	1969	642
	Sammy Sosa	1997	642
19	Stan Hack	1939	641
20	Woody English	1930	638

Runs

1	Rogers Hornsby	1929	156
2	King Kelly	1886	155
	Kiki Cuyler	1930	155
4	Woody English	1930	152
5	George Gore	1886	150
6	Bill Dahlen	1894	149
7	Hack Wilson	1930	146
8	Hugh Duffy	1889	144
9	Jimmy Ryan	1889	140
10	Bill Dahlen	1896	137
	Billy Williams	1970	137
12	Hack Wilson	1929	135
13	Cliff Carroll	1890	134
	Walt Wilmot	1894	134
15	Augie Galan	1935	133
16	Jimmy Ryan	1894	132
17	Woody English	1929	131
18	Bill Everitt	1896	130
19	Bill Everitt	1895	129
20	Two tied at		126

Hits

1	Rogers Hornsby	1929	229
2	Kiki Cuyler	1930	228
3	Billy Herman	1935	227
4	Woody English	1930	214
5	Frank Demaree	1936	212
6	Billy Herman	1936	211
7	Jigger Statz	1923	209
8	Hack Wilson	1930	208
9	Heinie Zimmerman	1912	207
10	Billy Herman	1932	206
11	Billy Williams	1970	205
12	Augie Galan	1935	203
	Billy Williams	1965	203
14	Woody English	1931	202
	Kiki Cuyler	1931	202
16	Charlie Hollocher	1922	201
	Billy Williams	1964	201
	Bill Buckner	1982	201
19	Ryne Sandberg	1984	200
20	Two tied at		199

Doubles

1	Billy Herman	1935	57
	Billy Herman	1936	57
3	Mark Grace	1995	51
4	Kiki Cuyler	1930	50
5	Ned Williamson	1883	49
	Riggs Stephenson	1932	49
7	Rogers Hornsby	1929	47
8	Riggs Stephenson	1927	46
9	Walt Wilmot	1894	45
	Ray Grimes	1922	45
11	Billy Herman	1932	42
	Charlie Grimm	1932	42
	Kiki Cuyler	1934	42
14	Heinie Zimmerman	1912	41
	Augie Galan	1935	41
	Bill Buckner	1980	41
	Rafael Palmeiro	1988	41
18	Five tied at		39

Triples

1	Wildfire Schulte	1911	21
	Vic Saier	1913	21
3	Bill Dahlen	1892	19
	Bill Dahlen	1896	19
	Ryne Sandberg	1984	19
6	Billy Herman	1939	18
7	Jimmy Ryan	1897	17
	Heinie Zimmerman	1911	17
	Woody English	1930	17
	Kiki Cuyler	1930	17
11	Marty Sullivan	1887	16
	Bill Lange	1895	16
	Bill Lange	1896	16
	Sam Mertes	1899	16
	Topsy Hartsel	1901	16
	Solly Hofman	1910	16
17	Jimmy Ryan	1891	15
	Bill Dahlen	1893	15
	Wildfire Schulte	1910	15
	Phil Cavarretta	1944	15

Home Runs

1	Hack Wilson	1930	56
2	Andre Dawson	1987	49
3	Dave Kingman	1979	48
4	Ernie Banks	1958	47
5	Ernie Banks	1959	45
6	Ernie Banks	1955	44
7	Ernie Banks	1957	43
8	Billy Williams	1970	42
9	Hank Sauer	1954	41
	Ernie Banks	1960	41
11	Ryne Sandberg	1990	40
	Sammy Sosa	1996	40
13	Hack Wilson	1929	39
	Rogers Hornsby	1929	39
15	Gabby Hartnett	1930	37
	Hank Sauer	1952	37
	Ernie Banks	1962	37
	Billy Williams	1972	37
19	Three tied at		36

RBI

1	Hack Wilson	1930	190
2	Hack Wilson	1929	159
3	Rogers Hornsby	1929	149
4	Cap Anson	1886	147
5	Ernie Banks	1959	143
6	Andre Dawson	1987	137
7	Kiki Cuyler	1930	134
8	Walt Wilmot	1894	130
9	Hack Wilson	1927	129
	Ernie Banks	1958	129
	Billy Williams	1970	129
12	Bill Nicholson	1943	128
13	Ron Santo	1969	123
14	Gabby Hartnett	1930	122
	Bill Nicholson	1944	122
	Billy Williams	1972	122
17	Hank Sauer	1952	121
18	Cap Anson	1891	120
	Hack Wilson	1928	120
20	Two tied at		119

Walks

1	Jimmy Sheckard	1911	147
2	Jimmy Sheckard	1912	122
3	Richie Ashburn	1960	116
4	Cap Anson	1890	113
5	Johnny Evers	1910	108
6	Hack Wilson	1930	105
7	Gary Matthews	1984	103
8	George Gore	1886	102
9	Woody English	1930	100
10	Stan Hack	1941	99
	Stan Hack	1945	99
12	Jimmy Slagle	1905	97
13	Ron Santo	1967	96
	Ron Santo	1968	96
	Ron Santo	1969	96
16	Ron Santo	1966	95
17	Vic Saier	1914	94
	Stan Hack	1938	94
	Stan Hack	1942	94
20	Two tied at		93

Strikeouts

1	Sammy Sosa	1997	174
2	Byron Browne	1966	143
3	Adolfo Phillips	1966	135
	Sammy Sosa	1993	135
5	Sammy Sosa	1995	134
	Sammy Sosa	1996	134
7	Dave Kingman	1979	131
8	Ken Hubbs	1962	129
9	Billy Cowan	1964	128
10	Rick Monday	1976	125
11	Rick Monday	1973	124
12	Lou Brock	1963	122
13	Ryne Sandberg	1996	116
14	Roy Smalley	1950	114
	Shawon Dunston	1986	114
16	Randy Hundley	1966	113
17	Dave Kingman	1978	111
18	Jody Davis	1986	110
19	Ron Santo	1965	109
20	Three tied at		108

Stolen Bases

1	Bill Lange	1896	84
2	Walt Wilmot	1890	76
3	Walt Wilmot	1894	74
4	Bill Lange	1897	73
5	Bill Lange	1895	67
	Frank Chance	1903	67
7	Bill Lange	1894	65
8	Fred Pfeffer	1888	64
9	Jimmy Ryan	1888	60
	Bill Dahlen	1892	60
11	Bill Maloney	1905	59
12	Fred Pfeffer	1887	57
	Frank Chance	1906	57
14	Ryne Sandberg	1985	54
15	King Kelly	1886	53
16	Hugh Duffy	1889	52
17	Bill Dahlen	1896	51
18	Jimmy Ryan	1887	50
19	Johnny Evers	1906	49
20	Three tied at		47

Runs Created

1	Rogers Hornsby	1929	178
2	Hack Wilson	1930	171
3	King Kelly	1886	156
4	Cap Anson	1886	152
5	Hack Wilson	1929	148
6	Bill Dahlen	1894	146
7	Jimmy Ryan	1889	145
8	Bill Lange	1895	144
	Billy Williams	1970	144
10	Kiki Cuyler	1930	143
11	Woody English	1930	138
12	Augie Galan	1935	135
13	Bill Dahlen	1896	134
14	Jimmy Ryan	1888	132
	Walt Wilmot	1894	132
	Bill Nicholson	1944	132
17	Jimmy Ryan	1898	131
	Billy Williams	1965	131
19	Billy Williams	1972	130
20	Heinie Zimmerman	1912	129

Runs Created/27 Outs

(minimum 3.1 Plate Appearances/Tm Gm)

1	Ross Barnes	1876	17.46
2	King Kelly	1886	14.63
3	Cap Anson	1886	12.41
4	Bill Lange	1895	12.29
5	Cap Anson	1881	12.25
6	Cap Anson	1882	11.74
7	Rogers Hornsby	1929	11.58
8	King Kelly	1884	11.28
9	Bill Dahlen	1894	11.25
10	Cap Anson	1876	11.14
11	Hack Wilson	1930	11.12
12	George Gore	1885	10.86
13	George Gore	1880	10.74
14	Cal McVey	1877	10.71
15	George Gore	1883	10.48
16	Cap Anson	1884	10.34
17	George Gore	1886	10.30
18	Bill Dahlen	1896	10.28
19	Cap Anson	1887	10.13
20	Deacon White	1876	10.00

Batting Average

(minimum 3.1 Plate Appearances/Tm Gm)

1	Ross Barnes	1876	.429
2	Cap Anson	1881	.399
3	Bill Lange	1895	.389
4	King Kelly	1886	.388
5	Rogers Hornsby	1929	.380
6	Heinie Zimmerman	1912	.372
7	Cap Anson	1886	.371
8	Cal McVey	1877	.368
9	Cap Anson	1882	.362
10	Riggs Stephenson	1929	.362
11	Jimmy Ryan	1894	.361
12	George Gore	1880	.360
13	Kiki Cuyler	1929	.360
14	Bill Everitt	1895	.358
15	Bill Dahlen	1894	.357
16	Cap Anson	1876	.356
17	Hack Wilson	1930	.356
18	Phil Cavarretta	1945	.355
19	Kiki Cuyler	1930	.355
20	Bill Madlock	1975	.354

On-Base Percentage

(minimum 3.1 Plate Appearances/Tm Gm)

1	King Kelly	1886	.483
2	Ross Barnes	1876	.462
3	Rogers Hornsby	1929	.459
4	Bill Lange	1895	.456
5	Hack Wilson	1930	.454
6	Frank Chance	1905	.450
7	Phil Cavarretta	1945	.449
8	Riggs Stephenson	1929	.445
9	Bill Dahlen	1894	.444
10	Cap Anson	1890	.443
11	Ray Grimes	1922	.442
12	Cap Anson	1881	.442
13	Frank Chance	1903	.439
14	Kiki Cuyler	1929	.438
15	Bill Dahlen	1896	.438
16	George Gore	1886	.434
17	Jimmy Sheckard	1911	.434
18	Cap Anson	1886	.433
19	Johnny Evers	1912	.431
20	Woody English	1930	.430

Slugging Percentage

(minimum 3.1 Plate Appearances/Tm Gm)

1	Hack Wilson	1930	.723
2	Rogers Hornsby	1929	.679
3	Gabby Hartnett	1930	.630
4	Hack Wilson	1929	.618
5	Ernie Banks	1958	.614
6	Dave Kingman	1979	.613
7	Billy Williams	1972	.606
8	Ernie Banks	1959	.596
9	Ernie Banks	1955	.596
10	Andy Pafko	1950	.591
11	Ross Barnes	1876	.590
12	Hack Wilson	1928	.588
13	Billy Williams	1970	.586
14	Jim Hickman	1970	.582
15	Ernie Banks	1957	.579
16	Hack Wilson	1927	.579
17	Bill Lange	1895	.575
18	Ray Grimes	1922	.572
19	Heinie Zimmerman	1912	.571
20	Andre Dawson	1987	.568

Teams: Cubs

Cubs Franchise Pitching Leaders—Single Season

Wins

1	John Clarkson	1885	53
2	Al Spalding	1876	47
3	Bill Hutchison	1891	44
4	Larry Corcoran	1880	43
5	Bill Hutchison	1890	42
6	John Clarkson	1887	38
7	Bill Hutchison	1892	37
8	John Clarkson	1886	36
9	Larry Corcoran	1884	35
10	Larry Corcoran	1883	34
11	Terry Larkin	1879	31
	Larry Corcoran	1881	31
	Jim McCormick	1886	31
14	Terry Larkin	1878	29
	Three Finger Brown	1908	29
16	Fred Goldsmith	1882	28
17	Larry Corcoran	1882	27
	Three Finger Brown	1909	27
	Pete Alexander	1920	27
20	Four tied at		26

Losses

1	Bill Hutchison	1892	36
2	Terry Larkin	1878	26
3	Bill Hutchison	1890	25
4	Bill Hutchison	1893	24
5	George Bradley	1877	23
	Terry Larkin	1879	23
	Larry Corcoran	1884	23
	Long Tom Hughes	1901	23
9	Dick Ellsworth	1966	22
	Bill Bonham	1974	22
11	John Clarkson	1887	21
	Bill Hutchison	1895	21
	Jack Taylor	1899	21
	Larry Jackson	1965	21
15	Larry Corcoran	1883	20
	Phil Douglas	1917	20
	Bob Rush	1950	20
	Sam Jones	1955	20
	Glen Hobbie	1960	20
	Dick Ellsworth	1962	20

Winning Percentage

(minimum 15 decisions)

1	Rick Sutcliffe	1984	.941
2	Fred Goldsmith	1880	.875
3	Jim McCormick	1885	.833
	King Cole	1910	.833
5	Ed Reulbach	1906	.826
6	Three Finger Brown	1906	.813
7	Ed Reulbach	1907	.810
8	Orval Overall	1906	.800
	Jack Taylor	1906	.800
	Bert Humphries	1913	.800
11	Al Spalding	1876	.797
12	Jocko Flynn	1886	.793
13	Lon Warneke	1932	.786
14	Ed Reulbach	1908	.774
15	Three Finger Brown	1907	.769
	Bill Lee	1935	.769
17	John Clarkson	1885	.768
18	Three Finger Brown	1908	.763
19	Charlie Root	1929	.760
20	Larry Corcoran	1880	.754

Games

1	Ted Abernathy	1965	84
	Dick Tidrow	1980	84
3	Bill Campbell	1983	82
4	Bob Patterson	1996	79
5	Mitch Williams	1989	76
	Bob Patterson	1997	76
7	Bill Hutchison	1892	75
	Willie Hernandez	1982	75
	Paul Assenmacher	1991	75
10	Paul Assenmacher	1990	74
	Terry Adams	1997	74
12	Randy Myers	1993	73
13	Bill Caudill	1980	72
	Lee Smith	1982	72
	Chuck McElroy	1992	72
16	Bill Hutchison	1890	71
	Lindy McDaniel	1965	71
	Phil Regan	1969	71
	Donnie Moore	1978	71
	Chuck McElroy	1991	71

Games Started

1	John Clarkson	1885	70
	Bill Hutchison	1892	70
3	Bill Hutchison	1890	66
4	Al Spalding	1876	60
	Larry Corcoran	1880	60
6	Larry Corcoran	1884	59
	John Clarkson	1887	59
8	Terry Larkin	1879	58
	Bill Hutchison	1891	58
10	Terry Larkin	1878	56
11	John Clarkson	1886	55
12	Larry Corcoran	1883	53
13	Fred Goldsmith	1882	45
	Fred Goldsmith	1883	45
	Ad Gumbert	1892	45
16	George Bradley	1877	44
	Larry Corcoran	1881	44
18	Jim McCormick	1886	42
	Fergie Jenkins	1969	42
20	Two tied at		41

Complete Games

1	John Clarkson	1885	68
2	Bill Hutchison	1892	67
3	Bill Hutchison	1890	65
4	Terry Larkin	1879	57
	Larry Corcoran	1880	57
	Larry Corcoran	1884	57
7	Terry Larkin	1878	56
	John Clarkson	1887	56
	Bill Hutchison	1891	56
10	Al Spalding	1876	53
11	Larry Corcoran	1883	51
12	John Clarkson	1886	50
13	Fred Goldsmith	1882	45
14	Larry Corcoran	1881	43
15	Fred Goldsmith	1883	40
16	Gus Krock	1888	39
	Ad Gumbert	1892	39
	Clark Griffith	1895	39
	Jack Taylor	1899	39
20	Four tied at		38

Shutouts

1	John Clarkson	1885	10
2	Three Finger Brown	1906	9
	Three Finger Brown	1908	9
	Orval Overall	1909	9
	Pete Alexander	1919	9
	Bill Lee	1938	9
7	Al Spalding	1876	8
	Orval Overall	1907	8
	Three Finger Brown	1909	8
	Lefty Tyler	1918	8
	Hippo Vaughn	1918	8
12	Larry Corcoran	1884	7
	Jack Taylor	1902	7
	Carl Lundgren	1907	7
	Ed Reulbach	1908	7
	Three Finger Brown	1910	7
	Pete Alexander	1920	7
	Hi Bithorn	1943	7
	Fergie Jenkins	1969	7
20	Five tied at		6

Saves

1	Randy Myers	1993	53
2	Randy Myers	1995	38
3	Bruce Sutter	1979	37
4	Lee Smith	1987	36
	Mitch Williams	1989	36
6	Lee Smith	1984	33
	Lee Smith	1985	33
8	Ted Abernathy	1965	31
	Bruce Sutter	1977	31
	Lee Smith	1986	31
11	Lee Smith	1983	29
12	Bruce Sutter	1980	28
13	Bruce Sutter	1978	27
14	Phil Regan	1968	25
15	Lindy McDaniel	1963	22
16	Randy Myers	1994	21
17	Bob Locker	1973	18
	Turk Wendell	1996	18
	Terry Adams	1997	18
20	Four tied at		17

Innings Pitched

1	John Clarkson	1885	623.0
2	Bill Hutchison	1892	622.0
3	Bill Hutchison	1890	603.0
4	Bill Hutchison	1891	561.0
5	Larry Corcoran	1880	536.1
6	Al Spalding	1876	528.2
7	John Clarkson	1887	523.0
8	Larry Corcoran	1884	516.2
9	Terry Larkin	1879	513.1
10	Terry Larkin	1878	506.0
11	Larry Corcoran	1883	473.2
12	John Clarkson	1886	466.2
13	Fred Goldsmith	1882	405.0
14	Larry Corcoran	1881	396.2
15	George Bradley	1877	394.0
16	Fred Goldsmith	1883	383.1
17	Ad Gumbert	1892	382.2
18	Pete Alexander	1920	363.1
19	Larry Corcoran	1882	355.2
20	Jack Taylor	1899	354.2

Walks

1	Bill Hutchison	1890	199
2	Bill Hutchison	1892	190
3	Sam Jones	1955	185
4	Willie McGill	1893	181
5	Bill Hutchison	1891	178
6	Bill Hutchison	1893	156
7	Bill Hutchison	1894	140
	Larry Cheney	1914	140
9	Danny Friend	1896	139
10	Adonis Terry	1895	131
11	King Cole	1910	130
	Sheriff Blake	1929	130
13	Bill Hutchison	1895	129
	Dick Drott	1957	129
15	Clay Bryant	1938	125
16	Adonis Terry	1894	123
17	Mark Baldwin	1887	122
18	Bill Hutchison	1889	117
	Willie McGill	1894	117
	Charlie Root	1927	117

Strikeouts

1	John Clarkson	1886	313
2	Bill Hutchison	1892	312
3	John Clarkson	1885	308
4	Bill Hutchison	1890	289
5	Fergie Jenkins	1970	274
6	Fergie Jenkins	1969	273
7	Larry Corcoran	1884	272
8	Larry Corcoran	1880	268
9	Fergie Jenkins	1971	263
10	Bill Hutchison	1891	261
11	Fergie Jenkins	1968	260
12	John Clarkson	1887	237
13	Fergie Jenkins	1967	236
14	Long Tom Hughes	1901	225
15	Larry Corcoran	1883	216
16	Orval Overall	1909	205
17	Ken Holtzman	1970	202
18	Greg Maddux	1992	199
19	Sam Jones	1955	198
	Greg Maddux	1991	198

Strikeouts/9 Innings

(minimum 1 Inning Pitched/Tm Gm)

1	Dick Selma	1969	8.59
2	Sam Jones	1956	8.40
3	Fergie Jenkins	1969	7.89
4	Fergie Jenkins	1970	7.88
5	Kevin Foster	1995	7.84
6	John Clarkson	1884	7.78
7	Jose Guzman	1993	7.68
8	Fergie Jenkins	1968	7.60
9	Calvin Schiraldi	1988	7.58
10	Sam Jones	1955	7.37
11	Fergie Jenkins	1967	7.34
12	Fergie Jenkins	1966	7.32
13	Fergie Jenkins	1971	7.28
14	Steve Trachsel	1997	7.15
15	Bill Bonham	1974	7.08
16	Ken Holtzman	1966	6.97
17	Frank Castillo	1996	6.86
18	Dick Drott	1958	6.83
19	Greg Maddux	1991	6.78
20	Greg Maddux	1992	6.68

ERA

(minimum 1 Inning Pitched/Tm Gm)

1	Three Finger Brown	1906	1.04
2	Jack Pfiester	1907	1.15
3	Carl Lundgren	1907	1.17
4	Three Finger Brown	1909	1.31
5	Jack Taylor	1902	1.33
6	Three Finger Brown	1907	1.39
7	Ed Reulbach	1905	1.42
8	Orval Overall	1909	1.42
9	Three Finger Brown	1908	1.47
10	Jack Pfiester	1906	1.51
11	Ed Reulbach	1906	1.65
12	Orval Overall	1907	1.68
13	Ed Reulbach	1907	1.69
14	Pete Alexander	1919	1.72
15	Hippo Vaughn	1918	1.74
16	Al Spalding	1876	1.75
17	Fred Goldsmith	1880	1.75
18	Ed Reulbach	1909	1.78
19	Hippo Vaughn	1919	1.79
20	King Cole	1910	1.80

Component ERA

(minimum 1 Inning Pitched/Tm Gm)

1	Three Finger Brown	1908	1.31
2	Three Finger Brown	1909	1.42
3	Larry Corcoran	1880	1.52
4	Three Finger Brown	1906	1.53
5	Pete Alexander	1919	1.56
6	Larry Corcoran	1882	1.58
7	Three Finger Brown	1904	1.60
8	Jack Pfiester	1906	1.63
9	Jack Pfiester	1907	1.67
10	Ed Reulbach	1905	1.68
11	Ed Reulbach	1906	1.68
12	Orval Overall	1909	1.68
13	Carl Lundgren	1907	1.68
14	John Clarkson	1885	1.69
15	Three Finger Brown	1907	1.70
16	Jack Taylor	1902	1.73
17	Hippo Vaughn	1918	1.79
18	Fred Goldsmith	1880	1.82
19	Orval Overall	1907	1.84
20	Phil Douglas	1919	1.87

Opponent Average

(minimum 1 Inning Pitched/Tm Gm)

1	Ed Reulbach	1906	.175
2	Carl Lundgren	1907	.185
3	Three Finger Brown	1908	.195
4	Jack Pfiester	1906	.197
5	Orval Overall	1909	.198
6	Larry Corcoran	1880	.199
7	Three Finger Brown	1904	.199
8	Larry Corcoran	1882	.200
9	Ed Reulbach	1905	.201
10	Three Finger Brown	1909	.202
11	Three Finger Brown	1906	.202
12	Jake Weimer	1904	.204
13	Sam Jones	1955	.206
14	Jack Pfiester	1907	.207
15	John Clarkson	1884	.208
16	Orval Overall	1907	.208
17	Orval Overall	1908	.208
18	Hippo Vaughn	1918	.208
19	John Clarkson	1885	.208
20	Greg Maddux	1992	.210

Opponent OBP

(minimum 1 Inning Pitched/Tm Gm)

1	Three Finger Brown	1908	.232
2	Larry Corcoran	1882	.234
3	Larry Corcoran	1880	.236
4	John Clarkson	1885	.239
5	Three Finger Brown	1909	.239
6	Pete Alexander	1919	.245
7	Warren Hacker	1952	.247
8	Fred Goldsmith	1880	.247
9	John Clarkson	1884	.249
10	Terry Larkin	1879	.250
11	Three Finger Brown	1906	.252
12	Three Finger Brown	1904	.253
13	Fred Goldsmith	1882	.254
14	Jack Taylor	1902	.254
15	Dennis Eckersley	1985	.254
16	Al Spalding	1876	.256
17	Ray Prim	1945	.256
18	Jocko Flynn	1886	.257
19	Terry Larkin	1878	.257
20	Gus Krock	1888	.258

Cubs Capsule

Best Season: *1907.* The Cubs went 107-45, winning the National League pennant by 17 games. In the World Series, they beat the Tigers four games to nothing, with one tie.

Worst Season: *1962.* Piloted by their infamous "college of coaches," the Cubs lost 103 games despite the presence of Ernie Banks, Ron Santo, Billy Williams and Lou Brock.

Best Player: *Cap Anson.*

Best Pitcher: *Three Finger Brown.*

Best Reliever: *Bruce Sutter.*

Best Defensive Player: *Ryne Sandberg.*

Hall of Famers: Players who spent the better parts of their careers with Cubs are: *Cap Anson, Ernie Banks, Three Finger Brown, Frank Chance, Kiki Cuyler, Johnny Evers, Gabby Hartnett, Billy Herman, Ferguson Jenkins, King Kelly, Joe Tinker, Billy Williams* and *Hack Wilson.* If Ron Santo gets in, it will give the Cubs at least one Hall of Famer at every position on the diamond, with an outfielder and two middle infielders to spare.

Franchise All-Star Team:

C	*Gabby Hartnett*	**LF**	*Billy Williams*
1B	*Cap Anson*	**CF**	*Hack Wilson*
2B	*Ryne Sandberg*	**RF**	*King Kelly*
3B	*Ron Santo*	**SP**	*Three Finger Brown*
SS	*Ernie Banks*	**RP**	Bruce Sutter

Biggest Flakes: *Lou Novikoff, Jose Cardenal.*

Strangest Career: *Hal Jeffcoat* broke in as a strong-armed center fielder in 1948, but never developed as a hitter. A broken collarbone in 1950 rendered him a backup, and after batting .235 in 1953, he decided to try to put his arm to better use on the mound. After a season of transition, he emerged as a useful reliever in 1955, sporting a 2.95 ERA out of the bullpen. Traded to the Reds, he put up three decent seasons as a swingman before calling it a career—and a unique one at that.

What Might Have Been: *Charlie Hollocher* was one of the NL's best shortstops from 1918, when he batted .316 as a rookie, through 1922, when he batted .340 and struck out only five times all season. The following year he began to complain of stomach pains. Many were skeptical, because doctors were unable to pinpoint the affliction, but it apparently was very real to Hollocher. He played part-time for two more seasons before retiring at age 28. He committed suicide at age 44.

Best Trades: *Three Finger Brown, Ryne Sandberg, Ferguson Jenkins* and *Kiki Cuyler.* The Cubs stole Brown and a catcher from the Cardinals in 1903 for pitcher Jack Taylor. Sandberg came from the Phillies in a swap of shortstops in 1982. The Phillies also sent Jenkins to the Cubs, along with outfielder Adolfo Phillips, for a couple of pitchers who didn't last long. Cuyler came from Pittsburgh for second baseman Sparky Adams and a spare outfielder.

Worst Trade: *Lou Brock* for Ernie Broglio and garnish, 1964.

Best-Looking Players: *King Kelly, Frank Chance, Kiki Cuyler, Chuck Connors.*

Ugliest Player: *Rick Reuschel.*

Best Nicknames: *Peanuts Lowrey, Kiki Cuyler, Cupid Childs, Egyptian Healy, Davy "Kangaroo" Jones, "The Peerless Leader," Frank Chance, Sheriff Blake, Abraham "Sweetbreads" Bailey, "Handsome Ransom" Jackson, "Jolly Cholly" Grimm, "Sad Sam" Jones, "Shufflin' Phil" Douglas, "Jittery Joe" Berry, "Fidgety Phil" Collins.*

Most Unappreciated Player: *Ed Reulbach,* who was overshadowed by Three Finger Brown but compiled a formidable record in his own right.

Most Overrated Player: *Bill Buckner.*

Most Admirable Star: *Frank Chance.*

Least Admirable Star: *Cap Anson.* Great ballplayer. White supremacist.

Best Season, Player: *Hack Wilson, 1930.* Most recall his NL-record 56 home runs and major league-record 190 RBI, but few remember that he also led the league in walks. Imagine how many runs he could have driven in if he'd gone up there hackin'.

Best Season, Pitcher: *Three Finger Brown, 1906.* He went 26-6, 1.04 and allowed exactly one home run all season.

Most Impressive Individual Record: *Jack Taylor* completed 187 consecutive starts from June 20, 1901 through August 9, 1906. It's safe to say that one may stand for a while longer.

Biggest Tragedy: Young second baseman *Ken Hubbs* was voted the NL Rookie of the Year in 1962. Two years later, he was killed in a plane crash.

Fan Favorite: *Ernie Banks.*

—Mat Olkin

Cincinnati Reds (1882-1997)

Year	Lg	Pos	W-L	Pct	GB	Manager	Att.	R	OR	HR	Avg	OBP	Slg	Opponent HR	Opponent Avg	Opponent OBP	ERA	Park Index Runs	Park Index HR
1882	AA	1st	55-25	.688	—	Pop Snyder	—	489	268	5	.264	.289	.332	7	.218	.252	1.65	101	65
1883	AA	3rd	61-37	.622	5.0	Pop Snyder	—	662	413	34	.262	.289	.363	17	.224	.260	2.26	98	448
1884	AA	5th	68-41	.624	8.0	Will White/Pop Snyder	—	754	512	36	.254	.289	.354	27	.244	.291	3.33	107	402
1885	AA	2nd	63-49	.563	16.0	Ollie Caylor	—	642	575	26	.258	.294	.342	24	.253	.309	3.26	106	213
1886	AA	5th	65-73	.471	27.5	Ollie Caylor	—	883	865	45	.249	.311	.345	25	.255	.327	4.18	90	206
1887	AA	2nd	81-54	.600	14.0	Gus Schmelz	—	892	745	37	.268	.329	.371	28	.257	.322	3.58	111	144
1888	AA	4th	80-54	.597	11.5	Gus Schmelz	—	745	628	32	.242	.301	.323	19	.238	.285	2.73	93	92
1889	AA	4th	76-63	.547	18.0	Gus Schmelz	—	897	769	52	.270	.340	.382	35	.260	.325	3.50	108	163
1890	NL	4th	77-55	.583	10.5	Tom Loftus	131,980	753	633	27	.259	.329	.360	41	.238	.300	2.79	108	148
1891	NL	7th	56-81	.409	30.5	Tom Loftus	97,500	646	790	40	.242	.308	.335	40	.254	.319	3.55	80	85
1892	NL	4th	44-31	.587	8.5	Charlie Comiskey													
	NL	8th	38-37	.507	14.5	Charlie Comiskey	196,473	766	731	44	.241	.311	.322	39	.244	.312	3.17	107	144
1893	NL	6th	65-63	.508	20.5	Charlie Comiskey	194,250	759	814	29	.259	.342	.341	38	.274	.349	4.55	103	148
1894	NL	10th	55-75	.423	35.0	Charlie Comiskey	158,000	910	1085	61	.294	.368	.410	85	.325	.387	5.99	103	147
1895	NL	8th	66-64	.508	21.0	Buck Ewing	281,000	903	854	36	.298	.359	.416	39	.305	.354	4.81	117	26
1896	NL	3rd	77-50	.606	12.0	Buck Ewing	373,000	783	620	20	.294	.357	.388	27	.282	.329	3.67	104	16
1897	NL	4th	76-56	.576	17.0	Buck Ewing	336,800	763	705	22	.290	.353	.383	18	.294	.347	4.09	113	21
1898	NL	3rd	92-60	.605	11.5	Buck Ewing	336,678	831	740	19	.271	.335	.359	16	.273	.336	3.50	116	13
1899	NL	6th	83-67	.553	19.0	Buck Ewing	259,536	856	770	13	.275	.345	.360	26	.277	.333	3.70	107	22
1900	NL	7th	62-77	.446	21.5	Bob Allen	170,000	703	745	33	.266	.318	.354	28	.277	.338	3.83	82	67
1901	NL	8th	52-87	.374	38.0	Bid McPhee	205,728	561	818	38	.251	.303	.338	51	.288	.344	4.17	98	167
1902	NL	4th	70-70	.500	33.5	Bid McPhee/Frank Bancroft/Joe Kelley	217,300	633	566	18	.282	.328	.362	15	.259	.317	2.67	122	136
1903	NL	4th	74-65	.532	16.5	Joe Kelley	351,680	765	656	28	.288	.346	.390	14	.274	.336	3.07	116	68
1904	NL	3rd	88-65	.575	18.0	Joe Kelley	391,915	695	547	21	.255	.313	.338	13	.241	.295	2.34	133	128
1905	NL	5th	79-74	.516	26.0	Joe Kelley	313,927	735	698	27	.269	.332	.354	22	.272	.335	3.01	111	38
1906	NL	6th	64-87	.424	51.5	Ned Hanlon	330,056	530	582	16	.238	.302	.304	14	.250	.320	2.69	137	197
1907	NL	6th	66-87	.431	41.5	Ned Hanlon	317,500	526	519	15	.247	.304	.318	16	.251	.322	2.41	91	33
1908	NL	5th	73-81	.474	26.0	John Ganzel	399,200	489	544	14	.227	.288	.294	19	.243	.307	2.37	106	94
1909	NL	4th	77-76	.503	33.5	Clark Griffith	424,643	606	599	22	.250	.319	.323	5	.240	.314	2.52	92	35
1910	NL	5th	75-79	.487	29.0	Clark Griffith	380,622	620	684	23	.259	.332	.333	27	.261	.338	3.08	106	40
1911	NL	6th	70-83	.458	29.0	Clark Griffith	300,000	682	706	21	.261	.337	.346	36	.265	.332	3.26	80	22
1912	NL	4th	75-78	.490	29.0	Hank O'Day	344,000	656	722	21	.256	.323	.339	28	.279	.343	3.42	81	22
1913	NL	7th	64-89	.418	37.5	Joe Tinker	258,000	607	717	27	.261	.325	.347	40	.273	.338	3.46	109	73
1914	NL	8th	60-94	.390	34.5	Buck Herzog	100,791	530	651	16	.236	.305	.300	30	.248	.320	2.94	113	25
1915	NL	7th	71-83	.461	20.0	Buck Herzog	218,878	516	585	15	.253	.308	.331	28	.250	.321	2.84	106	44
1916	NL	7th	60-93	.392	33.5	B. Herzog/I. Wingo/C. Mathewson	255,846	505	617	14	.254	.307	.331	35	.261	.326	3.10	99	41
1917	NL	4th	78-76	.506	20.0	Christy Mathewson	269,056	601	611	26	.264	.309	.354	20	.259	.315	2.68	90	39
1918	NL	3rd	68-60	.531	15.5	Christy Mathewson/Heine Groh	163,009	530	496	15	.278	.330	.366	19	.268	.332	3.00	97	58
1919	NL	1st	96-44	.686	—	Pat Moran	532,501	577	401	20	.263	.327	.342	21	.239	.288	2.23	103	56
1920	NL	3rd	82-71	.536	10.5	Pat Moran	568,107	639	569	18	.277	.332	.349	26	.258	.314	2.90	76	16
1921	NL	6th	70-83	.458	24.0	Pat Moran	311,227	618	649	20	.278	.333	.370	37	.287	.328	3.46	99	14
1922	NL	2nd	86-68	.558	7.0	Pat Moran	493,754	766	677	45	.296	.353	.401	49	.278	.322	3.53	88	29
1923	NL	2nd	91-63	.591	4.5	Pat Moran	575,063	708	629	45	.285	.344	.392	28	.273	.322	3.21	89	15
1924	NL	4th	83-70	.542	10.0	Jack Hendricks	473,707	649	579	36	.290	.337	.397	30	.267	.309	3.12	95	10
1925	NL	3rd	80-73	.523	15.0	Jack Hendricks	464,920	690	643	44	.285	.339	.387	35	.272	.317	3.38	88	26
1926	NL	2nd	87-67	.565	2.0	Jack Hendricks	672,987	747	651	35	.290	.349	.400	40	.271	.316	3.42	84	28
1927	NL	5th	75-78	.490	18.5	Jack Hendricks	442,164	643	653	29	.278	.332	.367	36	.281	.325	3.54	97	25
1928	NL	5th	78-74	.513	16.0	Jack Hendricks	490,490	648	686	32	.280	.333	.368	58	.289	.342	3.94	90	28
1929	NL	7th	66-88	.429	33.0	Jack Hendricks	295,040	686	760	34	.281	.336	.379	61	.292	.346	4.41	97	36
1930	NL	7th	59-95	.383	33.0	Dan Howley	386,727	665	857	74	.281	.339	.400	75	.310	.361	5.08	78	38
1931	NL	8th	58-96	.377	43.0	Dan Howley	263,316	592	742	21	.269	.323	.352	51	.294	.346	4.22	92	14
1932	NL	8th	60-94	.390	30.0	Dan Howley	356,950	575	715	47	.263	.320	.362	69	.274	.311	3.79	91	23
1933	NL	8th	58-94	.382	33.0	Donie Bush	218,281	496	643	34	.246	.298	.320	47	.279	.314	3.42	98	21
1934	NL	8th	52-99	.344	42.0	B. O'Farrell/B. Shotton/C. Dressen	206,773	590	801	55	.266	.311	.364	61	.299	.348	4.37	108	53
1935	NL	6th	68-85	.444	31.5	Chuck Dressen	448,247	646	772	73	.265	.319	.378	65	.278	.336	4.30	86	36
1936	NL	5th	74-80	.481	18.0	Chuck Dressen	466,345	722	760	82	.274	.329	.388	51	.287	.341	4.22	94	46
1937	NL	8th	56-98	.364	40.0	Chuck Dressen/Bobby Wallace	411,221	612	707	73	.254	.315	.360	38	.270	.339	3.94	83	31
1938	NL	4th	82-68	.547	6.0	Bill McKechnie	706,756	723	634	110	.277	.327	.406	75	.254	.316	3.62	92	74
1939	NL	1st	97-57	.630	—	Bill McKechnie	981,443	767	595	98	.278	.343	.405	81	.255	.322	3.27	101	89
1940	NL	1st	100-53	.654	—	Bill McKechnie	850,180	707	528	89	.266	.327	.379	73	.240	.302	3.05	93	106
1941	NL	3rd	88-66	.571	12.0	Bill McKechnie	643,513	616	564	64	.247	.313	.337	61	.248	.317	3.17	92	72
1942	NL	4th	76-76	.500	29.0	Bill McKechnie	427,031	527	545	66	.231	.299	.321	47	.230	.302	2.82	99	86
1943	NL	2nd	87-67	.565	18.0	Bill McKechnie	379,122	608	543	43	.256	.315	.340	38	.251	.328	3.13	95	65
1944	NL	3rd	89-65	.578	16.0	Bill McKechnie	409,567	573	537	51	.254	.313	.338	60	.245	.299	2.97	81	49
1945	NL	7th	61-93	.396	37.0	Bill McKechnie	290,070	536	694	56	.249	.304	.333	70	.271	.341	4.00	88	62
1946	NL	6th	67-87	.435	30.0	Bill McKechnie/Hank Gowdy	715,751	523	570	65	.239	.307	.327	70	.252	.314	3.08	104	129
1947	NL	5th	73-81	.474	21.0	Johnny Neun	899,975	681	755	95	.259	.330	.375	102	.274	.349	4.41	82	93
1948	NL	7th	64-89	.418	27.0	Johnny Neun/Bucky Walters	823,386	588	752	104	.247	.313	.365	104	.270	.344	4.47	111	135
1949	NL	7th	62-92	.403	35.0	Bucky Walters/Luke Sewell	707,782	627	770	86	.260	.316	.368	124	.266	.348	4.33	93	98
1950	NL	6th	66-87	.431	24.5	Luke Sewell	538,794	654	734	99	.260	.327	.376	145	.259	.338	4.32	112	121
1951	NL	6th	68-86	.442	28.5	Luke Sewell	588,268	559	667	88	.248	.304	.351	119	.255	.323	3.70	99	77
1952	NL	6th	69-85	.448	27.5	L. Sewell/E. Brucker/R. Hornsby	604,197	615	659	104	.249	.314	.366	111	.267	.338	4.01	100	67
1953	NL	6th	68-86	.442	37.0	Rogers Hornsby/Buster Mills	548,086	714	788	166	.261	.325	.403	179	.279	.343	4.64	102	116
1954	NL	5th	74-80	.481	23.0	Birdie Tebbetts	704,167	729	763	147	.262	.333	.406	169	.282	.351	4.50	112	170
1955	NL	5th	75-79	.487	23.5	Birdie Tebbetts	693,662	761	684	181	.270	.341	.425	161	.264	.322	3.95	113	130
1956	NL	3rd	91-63	.591	2.0	Birdie Tebbetts	1,125,928	775	658	221	.266	.336	.441	141	.265	.325	3.85	117	128
1957	NL	4th	80-74	.519	15.0	Birdie Tebbetts	1,070,850	747	781	187	.269	.338	.432	179	.275	.331	4.62	118	149
1958	NL	4th	76-78	.494	16.0	Birdie Tebbetts/Jimmy Dykes	788,582	695	621	123	.258	.331	.389	148	.267	.322	3.73	114	138
1959	NL	5th	74-80	.481	13.0	Mayo Smith/Fred Hutchinson	801,298	764	738	161	.274	.337	.427	162	.275	.335	4.31	111	134
1960	NL	6th	67-87	.435	28.0	Fred Hutchinson	663,486	640	692	140	.250	.318	.388	134	.267	.326	4.00	99	109
1961	NL	1st	93-61	.604	—	Fred Hutchinson	1,117,603	710	653	158	.270	.325	.421	147	.250	.318	3.78	106	91
1962	NL	3rd	98-64	.605	3.5	Fred Hutchinson	982,095	802	685	167	.270	.332	.417	149	.254	.327	3.75	102	107

														Opponent				Park Index	
Year	Lg	Pos	W-L	Pct	GB	Manager	Att.	R	OR	HR	Avg	OBP	Slg	HR	Avg	OBP	ERA	Runs	HR
1963	NL	5th	86-76	.531	13.0	Fred Hutchinson	858,805	648	594	122	.246	.310	.371	117	.242	.300	3.29	108	87
1964	NL	2nd	92-70	.568	1.0	Hutchinson/Sisler/Hutchinson/Sisler	862,466	660	566	130	.249	.308	.372	112	.238	.296	3.07	104	100
1965	NL	4th	89-73	.549	8.0	Dick Sisler	1,047,824	825	704	183	.273	.339	.439	136	.247	.322	3.88	110	125
1966	NL	7th	76-84	.475	18.0	Don Heffner/Dave Bristol	742,958	692	702	149	.260	.309	.395	153	.258	.322	4.08	134	160
1967	NL	4th	87-75	.537	14.5	Dave Bristol	958,300	604	563	109	.248	.297	.372	101	.241	.306	3.05	117	141
1968	NL	4th	83-79	.512	14.0	Dave Bristol	733,354	690	673	106	.273	.320	.389	114	.250	.321	3.56	133	122
1969	NL	3rd-W	89-73	.549	4.0	Dave Bristol	987,991	798	768	171	.277	.335	.422	149	.262	.338	4.11	99	115
1970	NL	1st-W	102-60	.630	—	Sparky Anderson	1,803,568	775	681	191	.270	.336	.436	118	.251	.325	3.69	106	105
1971	NL	4th-W	79-83	.488	11.0	Sparky Anderson	1,501,122	586	581	138	.241	.300	.366	112	.243	.310	3.35	90	92
1972	NL	1st-W	95-59	.617	—	Sparky Anderson	1,611,459	707	557	124	.251	.330	.380	129	.247	.305	3.21	83	88
1973	NL	1st-W	99-63	.611	—	Sparky Anderson	2,017,601	741	621	137	.254	.332	.383	135	.252	.318	3.40	83	72
1974	NL	2nd-W	98-64	.605	4.0	Sparky Anderson	2,164,307	776	631	135	.260	.343	.394	126	.247	.314	3.41	95	109
1975	NL	1st-W	108-54	.667	—	Sparky Anderson	2,315,603	840	586	124	.271	.353	.401	112	.257	.319	3.37	105	107
1976	NL	1st-W	102-60	.630	—	Sparky Anderson	2,629,708	857	633	141	.280	.357	.424	100	.258	.318	3.51	105	98
1977	NL	2nd-W	88-74	.543	10.0	Sparky Anderson	2,519,670	802	725	181	.274	.345	.436	156	.267	.334	4.21	100	97
1978	NL	2nd-W	92-69	.571	2.5	Sparky Anderson	2,532,497	710	688	136	.256	.334	.393	122	.261	.329	3.81	107	111
1979	NL	1st-W	90-71	.559	—	John McNamara	2,356,933	731	644	132	.264	.338	.396	103	.260	.319	3.58	93	113
1980	NL	3rd-W	89-73	.549	3.5	John McNamara	2,022,450	707	670	113	.262	.327	.386	113	.255	.317	3.85	105	151
1981	NL	2nd-W	35-21	.625	0.5	John McNamara													
	NL	2nd-W	31-21	.596	1.5	John McNamara	1,093,730	464	440	64	.267	.335	.385	67	.241	.315	3.73	102	105
1982	NL	6th-W	61-101	.377	28.0	John McNamara/Russ Nixon	1,326,528	545	661	82	.251	.310	.350	105	.258	.328	3.66	106	82
1983	NL	6th-W	74-88	.457	17.0	Russ Nixon	1,190,419	623	710	107	.239	.314	.356	135	.253	.330	3.98	108	92
1984	NL	5th-W	70-92	.432	22.0	Vern Rapp/Pete Rose	1,275,887	627	747	106	.244	.313	.356	128	.259	.328	4.16	116	127
1985	NL	2nd-W	89-72	.553	5.5	Pete Rose	1,834,619	677	666	114	.255	.327	.376	131	.248	.315	3.71	109	86
1986	NL	2nd-W	86-76	.531	10.0	Pete Rose	1,692,432	732	717	144	.254	.325	.387	136	.264	.326	3.91	110	131
1987	NL	2nd-W	84-78	.519	6.0	Pete Rose	2,185,205	783	752	192	.266	.330	.427	170	.267	.326	4.24	108	112
1988	NL	2nd-W	87-74	.540	7.0	Pete Rose/Tommy Helms/Pete Rose	2,072,528	641	596	122	.246	.309	.368	121	.237	.303	3.35	110	152
1989	NL	5th-W	75-87	.463	17.0	Pete Rose/Tommy Helms	1,979,320	632	691	128	.247	.309	.370	125	.253	.323	3.73	109	106
1990	NL	1st-W	91-71	.562	—	Lou Piniella	2,400,892	693	597	125	.265	.325	.399	124	.246	.316	3.39	100	135
1991	NL	5th-W	74-88	.457	20.0	Lou Piniella	2,372,377	689	691	164	.258	.320	.403	127	.253	.323	3.83	119	165
1992	NL	2nd-W	90-72	.556	8.0	Lou Piniella	2,315,946	660	609	99	.260	.328	.382	109	.251	.312	3.46	103	136
1993	NL	5th-W	73-89	.451	31.0	Tony Perez/Davey Johnson	2,453,232	722	785	137	.264	.324	.396	158	.272	.336	4.51	98	103
1994	NL	1st-C	66-48	.579	—	Davey Johnson	1,897,681	609	490	124	.286	.350	.449	117	.262	.322	3.78	100	99
1995	NL	1st-C	85-59	.590	—	Davey Johnson	1,843,649	747	623	161	.270	.342	.440	131	.260	.320	4.03	95	85
1996	NL	3rd-C	81-81	.500	7.0	Ray Knight	1,861,428	778	773	191	.256	.331	.422	167	.263	.336	4.32	100	96
1997	NL	3rd-C	76-86	.469	8.0	Ray Knight/Jack McKeon	1,785,788	651	764	142	.253	.321	.389	173	.256	.330	4.42	107	109

Team Nicknames: Cincinnati Reds 1992-1997.

Team Ballparks: Bank Street Grounds 1882-1883, League Park I (Cin) 1884-1893, League Park II (Cin) 1894-1901, Palace of the Fans 1902-1911, Redland Field/Crosley Field 1912-1969, Riverfront Stadium/Cinergy Field 1970-1997.

Cincinnati Reds Individual Season Batting Leaders

Year	Batting Average		On-Base Percentage		Slugging Percentage		Home Runs		RBI		Stolen Bases	
1882	Hick Carpenter	.342	Hick Carpenter	.360	Hick Carpenter	.422	5 tied with	1	Hick Carpenter	62	Statistic unavailable	
1883	John Reilly	.311	Charley Jones	.328	John Reilly	.485	Charley Jones	10	Statistic unavailable		Statistic unavailable	
1884	John Reilly	.339	Charley Jones	.376	John Reilly	.551	John Reilly	11	Statistic unavailable		Statistic unavailable	
1885	Charley Jones	.322	Charley Jones	.362	Charley Jones	.462	Frank Fennelly	10	Frank Fennelly	89	Statistic unavailable	
1886	Charley Jones	.270	Charley Jones	.356	Bid McPhee	.395	Bid McPhee	8	Pop Corkhill	97	Bid McPhee	40
1887	Pop Corkhill	.311	Frank Fennelly	.369	John Reilly	.477	John Reilly	10	Pop Corkhill / Frank Fennelly	97	Hugh Nicol	138
1888	John Reilly	.321	John Reilly	.363	John Reilly	.501	John Reilly	13	John Reilly	103	Hugh Nicol	103
1889	Bug Holliday	.321	Bug Holliday	.372	Bug Holliday	.497	Bug Holliday	19	Bug Holliday	104	Hugh Nicol	80
1890	Joe Knight	.312	Joe Knight	.367	John Reilly	.472	John Reilly	6	John Reilly	86	Bid McPhee	55
1891	Bug Holliday	.319	Bug Holliday	.376	Bug Holliday	.473	Bug Holliday	9	Bug Holliday	84	Arlie Latham	87
1892	Bug Holliday	.292	Bid McPhee	.373	Bug Holliday	.449	Bug Holliday	13	Bug Holliday	91	Arlie Latham	66
1893	Bug Holliday	.310	Bug Holliday	.401	Bug Holliday	.428	Jim Canavan / Bug Holliday	5	Farmer Vaughn	108	Arlie Latham	57
1894	Bug Holliday	.372	Bid McPhee	.420	Bug Holliday	.523	Jim Canavan / Bug Holliday	13	Bug Holliday	119	Arlie Latham	59
1895	Dusty Miller	.335	Bid McPhee	.409	Dusty Miller	.510	Dusty Miller	10	Dusty Miller	112	Dummy Hoy	50
1896	Eddie Burke	.340	Dummy Hoy	.403	Dusty Miller	.468	Dummy Hoy / Dusty Miller	4	Dusty Miller	93	Dusty Miller	76
1897	Dusty Miller	.316	Dusty Miller	.393	Dusty Miller	.409	Jake Beckley	7	Jake Beckley	76	Dummy Hoy	37
1898	Elmer Smith	.342	Elmer Smith	.425	Elmer Smith	.432	Jake Beckley	4	Dusty Miller	90	Dusty Miller	32
1899	Jake Beckley	.333	Jake Beckley	.393	Jake Beckley	.466	Jake Beckley / Kip Selbach	3	Jake Beckley	99	Kip Selbach	38
1900	Jake Beckley	.341	Jimmy Barrett	.400	Jake Beckley	.434	Sam Crawford	7	Jake Beckley	94	Jimmy Barrett	44
1901	Sam Crawford	.330	Sam Crawford	.378	Sam Crawford	.524	Sam Crawford	16	Sam Crawford	104	Dick Harley	37
1902	Sam Crawford	.333	Sam Crawford	.386	Sam Crawford	.461	Jake Beckley	5	Sam Crawford	78	Tommy Corcoran	20
1903	Mike Donlin	.351	Mike Donlin	.420	Mike Donlin	.516	Mike Donlin / Cy Seymour	7	Harry Steinfeldt	83	Mike Donlin	26
1904	Cy Seymour	.313	Miller Huggins	.377	Cy Seymour	.439	Cozy Dolan	6	Tommy Corcoran	74	Fred Odwell	30
1905	Cy Seymour	.377	Cy Seymour	.429	Cy Seymour	.559	Fred Odwell	9	Cy Seymour	121	Tommy Corcoran	28
1906	Miller Huggins	.292	Miller Huggins	.376	Miller Huggins	.338	Admiral Schlei / Cy Seymour	4	Admiral Schlei	54	Miller Huggins	41
1907	Mike Mitchell	.292	Miller Huggins	.346	Mike Mitchell	.382	John Kane / Mike Mitchell	3	John Ganzel	64	Hans Lobert	30
1908	Hans Lobert	.293	Hans Lobert	.348	Hans Lobert	.407	Hans Lobert	4	Hans Lobert	63	Hans Lobert	47
1909	Mike Mitchell	.310	Mike Mitchell	.378	Mike Mitchell	.430	3 tied with	4	Mike Mitchell	86	Bob Bescher	54
1910	Dode Paskert	.300	Dode Paskert	.389	Mike Mitchell	.401	Mike Mitchell	5	Mike Mitchell	88	Bob Bescher	70
1911	Johnny Bates	.292	Johnny Bates	.415	Mike Mitchell	.427	Doc Hoblitzell	11	Doc Hoblitzell	91	Bob Bescher	80
1912	Doc Hoblitzell	.294	Bob Bescher	.381	Doc Hoblitzell	.405	Bob Bescher / Mike Mitchell	4	Doc Hoblitzell	85	Bob Bescher	67
1913	Doc Hoblitzell	.285	Johnny Bates	.388	Johnny Bates	.388	Johnny Bates	6	Doc Hoblitzell	62	Bob Bescher	38
1914	Heine Groh	.288	Heine Groh	.391	Heine Groh	.358	Bert Niehoff	4	Bert Niehoff	49	Buck Herzog	46
1915	Tommy Griffith	.307	Tommy Griffith	.355	Tommy Griffith	.436	Tommy Griffith	4	Tommy Griffith	85	Buck Herzog	35
1916	Hal Chase	.339	Heine Groh	.370	Hal Chase	.459	Hal Chase	4	Hal Chase	82	Hal Chase	22
1917	Edd Roush	.341	Heine Groh	.385	Edd Roush	.454	3 tied with	4	Hal Chase	86	Greasy Neale	25
1918	Edd Roush	.333	Heine Groh	.395	Edd Roush	.455	Edd Roush	5	Sherry Magee	76	Edd Roush	24
1919	Edd Roush	.321	Heine Groh	.392	Heine Groh	.431	Heine Groh	5	Edd Roush	71	Greasy Neale	28
1920	Edd Roush	.339	Edd Roush	.386	Edd Roush	.453	Jake Daubert / Edd Roush	4	Edd Roush	90	Edd Roush	36
1921	Pat Duncan	.308	Pat Duncan	.367	Pat Duncan	.408	Edd Roush	4	Edd Roush	71	Sammy Bohne	26
1922	Jake Daubert	.336	Jake Daubert	.395	Jake Daubert	.492	Jake Daubert	12	Pat Duncan	94	George Burns	30
1923	Edd Roush	.351	Edd Roush	.406	Edd Roush	.531	Bubbles Hargrave	10	Edd Roush	88	Sammy Bohne	16
1924	Edd Roush	.348	Edd Roush	.376	Edd Roush	.501	4 tied with	4	Edd Roush	72	Babe Pinelli	23
1925	Edd Roush	.339	Curt Walker	.387	Edd Roush	.494	Edd Roush / Elmer Smith	8	Edd Roush	83	Edd Roush	22
1926	Edd Roush	.323	Curt Walker	.372	Edd Roush	.462	Edd Roush	7	Wally Pipp	99	3 tied with	8
1927	Curt Walker	.292	Chuck Dressen	.376	Chuck Dressen	.405	Curt Walker	6	Curt Walker	80	Ethan Allen	12
1928	Ethan Allen	.305	Chuck Dressen	.355	Val Picinich	.412	Val Picinich	7	Curt Walker	73	Curt Walker	19
1929	Curt Walker	.313	Curt Walker	.416	Curt Walker	.474	Curt Walker	7	George Kelly	103	Evar Swanson	33
1930	Harry Heilmann	.333	Harry Heilmann	.416	Harry Heilmann	.577	Harry Heilmann	19	Harry Heilmann	91	Joe Stripp	15
1931	Harvey Hendrick	.315	Harvey Hendrick	.379	Tony Cuccinello	.431	Nick Cullop	8	Tony Cuccinello	93	Joe Stripp	5
1932	Babe Herman	.326	Babe Herman	.389	Babe Herman	.541	Babe Herman	16	Babe Herman	87	Babe Herman	7
1933	Chick Hafey	.303	Chick Hafey	.351	Chick Hafey	.421	Jim Bottomley	13	Jim Bottomley	83	Jo-Jo Morrissey	5
1934	Chick Hafey	.293	Chick Hafey	.359	Chick Hafey	.471	Chick Hafey	18	Jim Bottomley	78	Tony Piet / Gordon Slade	6
1935	Lew Riggs	.278	Lew Riggs	.334	Ival Goodman	.429	Ival Goodman / Ernie Lombardi	12	Ival Goodman	72	Ival Goodman	14
1936	Kiki Cuyler	.326	Kiki Cuyler	.380	Ival Goodman	.476	Ival Goodman	17	Kiki Cuyler	74	Kiki Cuyler	16
1937	Ival Goodman	.273	Ival Goodman	.347	Ival Goodman	.428	Alex Kampouris	17	Alex Kampouris	71	Kiki Cuyler / Ival Goodman	10
1938	Ernie Lombardi	.342	Ernie Lombardi	.391	Ival Goodman	.533	Ival Goodman	30	Frank McCormick	106	Lonny Frey	4
1939	Frank McCormick	.332	Ival Goodman	.401	Ival Goodman	.515	Ernie Lombardi	20	Frank McCormick	128	Bill Werber	15
1940	Frank McCormick	.309	Frank McCormick	.367	Frank McCormick	.482	Frank McCormick	19	Frank McCormick	127	Lonny Frey	22
1941	Frank McCormick	.269	Lonny Frey	.345	Frank McCormick	.421	Frank McCormick	17	Frank McCormick	97	Lonny Frey	16
1942	Frank McCormick	.277	Lonny Frey	.373	Frank McCormick	.388	Frank McCormick	13	Frank McCormick	89	Gee Walker	11
1943	Frank McCormick	.303	Eric Tipton	.395	Eric Tipton	.424	Eric Tipton	9	Eddie Miller	71	Max Marshall / Eddie Miller	8
1944	Frank McCormick	.305	Eric Tipton	.380	Frank McCormick	.482	Frank McCormick	20	Frank McCormick	102	Eddie Miller	9
1945	Al Libke	.283	Frank McCormick	.345	Frank McCormick	.384	Eddie Miller	13	Frank McCormick	81	Dain Clay	19
1946	Grady Hatton	.271	Grady Hatton	.369	Grady Hatton	.422	Grady Hatton	14	Grady Hatton	69	Bert Haas	22
1947	Augie Galan	.314	Augie Galan	.449	Eddie Miller	.457	Eddie Miller	19	Eddie Miller	87	Bobby Adams / Bert Haas	9
1948	Johnny Wyrostek	.273	Johnny Wyrostek	.344	Hank Sauer	.504	Hank Sauer	35	Hank Sauer	97	Frankie Baumholtz	8
1949	Ted Kluszewski	.309	Grady Hatton	.342	Grady Hatton	.413	Walker Cooper	16	Grady Hatton	69	Johnny Wyrostek	7
1950	Ted Kluszewski	.307	Grady Hatton	.366	Ted Kluszewski	.515	Ted Kluszewski	25	Ted Kluszewski	111	Bobby Adams	7

Teams: Reds

Year	Batting Average		On-Base Percentage		Slugging Percentage		Home Runs		RBI		Stolen Bases	
1951	Johnny Wyrostek	.311	Johnny Wyrostek	.376	Connie Ryan	.391	Connie Ryan	16	Ted Kluszewski	77	Connie Ryan	11
1952	Ted Kluszewski	.320	Ted Kluszewski	.383	Ted Kluszewski	.509	Ted Kluszewski	16	Ted Kluszewski	86	Bobby Adams	11
1953	Ted Kluszewski	.316	Ted Kluszewski	.380	Ted Kluszewski	.570	Ted Kluszewski	40	Ted Kluszewski	108	Rocky Bridges Jim Greengrass	6
1954	Ted Kluszewski	.326	Ted Kluszewski	.407	Ted Kluszewski	.642	Ted Kluszewski	49	Ted Kluszewski	141	Johnny Temple	21
1955	Ted Kluszewski	.314	Ted Kluszewski	.382	Ted Kluszewski	.585	Ted Kluszewski	47	Ted Kluszewski	113	Johnny Temple	19
1956	Ted Kluszewski	.302	Frank Robinson	.379	Frank Robinson	.558	Frank Robinson	38	Ted Kluszewski	102	Johnny Temple	14
1957	Frank Robinson	.322	Johnny Temple	.387	Frank Robinson	.529	George Crowe	31	George Crowe	92	Johnny Temple	19
1958	Johnny Temple	.306	Johnny Temple	.405	Frank Robinson	.504	Frank Robinson	31	Frank Robinson	83	Johnny Temple	15
1959	Vada Pinson	.316	Frank Robinson	.391	Frank Robinson	.583	Frank Robinson	36	Frank Robinson	125	Vada Pinson	21
1960	Frank Robinson	.297	Frank Robinson	.407	Frank Robinson	.595	Frank Robinson	31	Frank Robinson	83	Vada Pinson	32
1961	Vada Pinson	.343	Frank Robinson	.404	Frank Robinson	.611	Frank Robinson	37	Frank Robinson	124	Vada Pinson	23
1962	Frank Robinson	.342	Frank Robinson	.421	Frank Robinson	.624	Frank Robinson	39	Frank Robinson	136	Vada Pinson	26
1963	Vada Pinson	.313	Frank Robinson	.379	Vada Pinson	.514	Vada Pinson	22	Vada Pinson	106	Vada Pinson	27
1964	Frank Robinson	.306	Frank Robinson	.396	Frank Robinson	.548	Frank Robinson	29	Frank Robinson	96	Tommy Harper	24
1965	Pete Rose	.312	Frank Robinson	.386	Frank Robinson	.540	Frank Robinson	33	Deron Johnson	130	Tommy Harper	35
1966	Pete Rose	.313	Pete Rose	.351	Deron Johnson	.461	Deron Johnson	24	Leo Cardenas Deron Johnson	81	Tommy Harper	29
1967	Pete Rose	.301	Pete Rose	.364	Tony Perez	.490	Tony Perez	26	Tony Perez	102	Vada Pinson	26
1968	Pete Rose	.335	Pete Rose	.391	Pete Rose	.470	Lee May	22	Tony Perez	92	Vada Pinson	17
1969	Pete Rose	.348	Pete Rose	.428	Lee May	.529	Lee May	38	Tony Perez	122	Bobby Tolan	26
1970	Tony Perez	.317	Tony Perez	.401	Tony Perez	.589	Johnny Bench	45	Johnny Bench	148	Bobby Tolan	57
1971	Pete Rose	.304	Pete Rose	.373	Lee May	.532	Lee May	39	Lee May	98	Pete Rose	13
1972	Pete Rose	.307	Joe Morgan	.417	Johnny Bench	.541	Johnny Bench	40	Johnny Bench	125	Joe Morgan	58
1973	Pete Rose	.338	Joe Morgan	.406	Tony Perez	.527	Tony Perez	27	Johnny Bench	104	Joe Morgan	67
1974	Joe Morgan	.293	Joe Morgan	.427	Johnny Bench	.507	Johnny Bench	33	Johnny Bench	129	Joe Morgan	58
1975	Joe Morgan	.327	Joe Morgan	.466	Johnny Bench	.519	Johnny Bench	28	Johnny Bench	110	Joe Morgan	67
1976	Ken Griffey Sr.	.336	Joe Morgan	.444	Joe Morgan	.576	George Foster	29	George Foster	121	Joe Morgan	60
1977	George Foster	.320	Joe Morgan	.417	George Foster	.631	George Foster	52	George Foster	149	Joe Morgan	49
1978	Pete Rose	.302	Pete Rose	.362	George Foster	.546	George Foster	40	George Foster	120	Dan Driessen	28
1979	Ray Knight	.318	George Foster	.386	George Foster	.561	George Foster	30	George Foster	98	Joe Morgan	28
1980	Dave Collins	.303	Dan Driessen	.377	George Foster	.473	George Foster	25	George Foster	93	Dave Collins	79
1981	Ken Griffey Sr.	.311	George Foster	.373	George Foster	.519	George Foster	22	George Foster	90	Dave Collins	26
1982	Cesar Cedeno	.289	Dan Driessen	.368	Dan Driessen	.421	Dan Driessen	17	Cesar Cedeno Dan Driessen	57	Eddie Milner	18
1983	Ron Oester	.264	Gary Redus	.352	Gary Redus	.444	Gary Redus	17	Ron Oester	58	Eddie Milner	41
1984	Dave Parker	.285	Dave Parker	.328	Dave Parker	.410	Dave Parker	16	Dave Parker	94	Gary Redus	48
1985	Dave Parker	.312	Dave Parker	.365	Dave Parker	.551	Dave Parker	34	Dave Parker	125	Gary Redus	48
1986	Buddy Bell	.278	Buddy Bell	.362	Dave Parker	.477	Dave Parker	31	Dave Parker	116	Eric Davis	80
1987	Eric Davis	.293	Eric Davis	.399	Eric Davis	.593	Eric Davis	37	Eric Davis	100	Eric Davis	50
1988	Barry Larkin	.296	Kal Daniels	.397	Eric Davis	.489	Eric Davis	26	Eric Davis	93	Chris Sabo	46
1989	Eric Davis	.281	Eric Davis	.367	Eric Davis	.541	Eric Davis	34	Eric Davis	101	Eric Davis	21
1990	Barry Larkin	.301	Barry Larkin	.358	Eric Davis	.486	Chris Sabo	25	Eric Davis	86	Billy Hatcher Barry Larkin	30
1991	Hal Morris	.318	Barry Larkin	.378	Barry Larkin	.506	Paul O'Neill	28	Paul O'Neill	91	Barry Larkin	24
1992	Bip Roberts	.323	Bip Roberts	.393	Barry Larkin	.454	Paul O'Neill	14	Barry Larkin	78	Bip Roberts	44
1993	Reggie Sanders	.274	Reggie Sanders	.343	Reggie Sanders	.444	Chris Sabo	21	Reggie Sanders	83	Reggie Sanders	27
1994	Hal Morris	.335	Kevin Mitchell	.429	Kevin Mitchell	.681	Kevin Mitchell	30	Hal Morris	78	Barry Larkin	26
1995	Barry Larkin	.319	Reggie Sanders	.397	Reggie Sanders	.579	Ron Gant	29	Reggie Sanders	99	Barry Larkin	51
1996	Hal Morris	.313	Barry Larkin	.410	Barry Larkin	.567	Barry Larkin	33	Barry Larkin	89	Barry Larkin	36
1997	Deion Sanders	.273	Willie Greene	.354	Willie Greene	.459	Willie Greene	26	Willie Greene	91	Deion Sanders	56

Teams: Reds

Cincinnati Reds Individual Season Pitching Leaders

Year	ERA		Baserunners/9 IP		Innings Pitched		Strikeouts		Wins		Saves	
1882	Harry McCormick	1.52	Harry McCormick	9.0	Will White	480.0	Will White	122	Will White	40	3 tied with	0
1883	Will White	2.09	Will White	9.0	Will White	577.0	Will White	141	Will White	43	5 tied with	0
1884	Billy Mountjoy	2.93	Billy Mountjoy	10.4	Will White	456.0	Will White	118	Will White	34	5 tied with	0
1885	Larry McKeon	2.86	Larry McKeon	10.4	Will White	293.1	Larry McKeon	117	Larry McKeon	20	Pop Corkhill	1
1886	Tony Mullane	3.70	Tony Mullane	11.6	Tony Mullane	529.2	Tony Mullane	250	Tony Mullane	33	14 tied with	0
1887	Elmer Smith	2.94	Elmer Smith	10.8	Elmer Smith	447.1	Elmer Smith	176	Elmer Smith	34	Billy Serad	1
1888	Lee Viau	2.65	Tony Mullane	9.8	Lee Viau	387.2	Tony Mullane	186	Lee Viau	27	Pop Corkhill	1
											Tony Mullane	
1889	Jesse Duryea	2.56	Jesse Duryea	11.2	Jesse Duryea	401.0	Jesse Duryea	183	Jesse Duryea	32	Tony Mullane	5
1890	Billy Rhines	1.95	Billy Rhines	10.1	Billy Rhines	401.1	Billy Rhines	182	Billy Rhines	28	Tony Mullane	1
1891	Billy Rhines	2.87	Billy Rhines	11.8	Tony Mullane	426.1	Billy Rhines	138	Tony Mullane	23	Billy Rhines	1
1892	Frank Dwyer	2.31	Frank Dwyer	10.4	Elton Chamberlin	406.1	Elton Chamberlin	169	Tony Mullane	21	Frank Dwyer	1
											Tony Mullane	
1893	Elton Chamberlin	3.73	Frank Dwyer	13.3	Frank Dwyer	287.1	Elton Chamberlin	59	Frank Dwyer	18	Frank Dwyer	2
1894	Frank Dwyer	5.07	Frank Dwyer	14.9	Frank Dwyer	348.0	Tom Parrott	61	Frank Dwyer	19	3 tied with	1
1895	Frank Foreman	4.11	Billy Rhines	13.4	Frank Dwyer	280.1	Billy Rhines	72	Billy Rhines	19	Tom Parrott	3
1896	Billy Rhines	2.45	Billy Rhines	11.1	Frank Dwyer	288.2	Red Ehret	60	Frank Dwyer	24	Chauncey Fisher	2
1897	Ted Breitenstein	3.62	Ted Breitenstein	12.5	Ted Breitenstein	320.1	Ted Breitenstein	98	Ted Breitenstein	23	Red Ehret	2
1898	Frank Dwyer	3.04	Frank Dwyer	11.8	Pink Hawley	331.0	Bill Hill	75	Pink Hawley	27	Bill Dammann	2
1899	Noodles Hahn	2.68	Noodles Hahn	10.4	Noodles Hahn	309.0	Noodles Hahn	145	Noodles Hahn	23	Jack Taylor	2
1900	Noodles Hahn	3.27	Noodles Hahn	11.6	Ed Scott	315.0	Noodles Hahn	132	Ed Scott	17	Ed Scott	1
1901	Noodles Hahn	2.71	Noodles Hahn	10.7	Noodles Hahn	375.1	Noodles Hahn	239	Noodles Hahn	22	14 tied with	0
1902	Noodles Hahn	1.77	Noodles Hahn	9.7	Noodles Hahn	321.0	Noodles Hahn	142	Noodles Hahn	23	Henry Thielman	1
1903	Noodles Hahn	2.52	Noodles Hahn	10.7	Noodles Hahn	296.0	Noodles Hahn	127	Noodles Hahn	22	Bob Ewing	1
1904	Noodles Hahn	2.06	Noodles Hahn	9.1	Noodles Hahn	297.2	Jack Harper	125	Jack Harper	23	Win Kellum	2
1905	Bob Ewing	2.51	Bob Ewing	10.8	Orval Overall	318.0	Orval Overall	173	Bob Ewing	20	Jack Harper	1
											Ollie Johns	
1906	Jake Weimer	2.22	Bob Ewing	9.7	Jake Weimer	304.2	Bob Ewing	145	Jake Weimer	20	Charlie Chech	3
1907	Bob Ewing	1.73	Bob Ewing	10.0	Bob Ewing	332.2	Bob Ewing	147	Andy Coakley	17	Andy Coakley	1
									Bob Ewing		Fred Smith	
1908	Andy Coakley	1.86	Bob Ewing	9.5	Bob Ewing	293.2	Bob Ewing	95	Bob Ewing	17	Bob Ewing	3
									Bob Spade			
1909	Art Fromme	1.90	Art Fromme	9.6	Art Fromme	279.1	Art Fromme	126	Art Fromme	19	3 tied with	2
									Harry Gaspar			
1910	George Suggs	2.40	George Suggs	10.5	Harry Gaspar	275.0	Jack Rowan	108	George Suggs	20	Harry Gaspar	7
1911	Bobby Keefe	2.69	Bobby Keefe	10.6	George Suggs	260.2	Art Fromme	107	George Suggs	15	Harry Gaspar	4
1912	Art Fromme	2.74	George Suggs	11.5	George Suggs	303.0	Rube Benton	162	George Suggs	19	George Suggs	3
1913	Red Ames	2.88	Three Finger Brown	11.4	Chief Johnson	269.0	Chief Johnson	107	Chief Johnson	14	Three Finger Brown	6
1914	Phil Douglas	2.56	Phil Douglas	10.9	Red Ames	297.0	Red Ames	128	Rube Benton	16	Red Ames	6
1915	Fred Toney	1.58	Fred Toney	9.5	Gene Dale	296.2	Pete Schneider	108	Gene Dale	18	Rube Benton	4
								Fred Toney				
1916	Fred Toney	2.28	Fred Toney	10.0	Fred Toney	300.0	Fred Toney	146	Fred Toney	14	Al Schulz	2
1917	Pete Schneider	1.98	Fred Toney	10.1	Pete Schneider	341.2	Pete Schneider	142	Fred Toney	24	Jimmy Ring	2
1918	Hod Eller	2.36	Hod Eller	11.2	Hod Eller	217.2	Hod Eller	84	Hod Eller	16	Mike Regan	2
											Fred Toney	
1919	Dutch Ruether	1.82	Ray Fisher	9.3	Hod Eller	248.1	Hod Eller	137	Slim Sallee	21	Dolf Luque	3
											Jimmy Ring	
1920	Dutch Ruether	2.47	Dolf Luque	10.1	Jimmy Ring	266.2	Dutch Ruether	99	Jimmy Ring	17	Dutch Ruether	3
1921	Eppa Rixey	2.78	Dolf Luque	11.3	Dolf Luque	304.0	Dolf Luque	102	Eppa Rixey	19	Dolf Luque	3
1922	Pete Donohue	3.12	Eppa Rixey	11.1	Eppa Rixey	313.1	Eppa Rixey	80	Eppa Rixey	25	3 tied with	1
1923	Dolf Luque	1.93	Dolf Luque	10.4	Dolf Luque	322.0	Dolf Luque	151	Dolf Luque	27	Pete Donohue	3
1924	Eppa Rixey	2.76	Eppa Rixey	10.1	Eppa Rixey	238.1	Dolf Luque	86	Carl Mays	20	Jakie May	6
1925	Dolf Luque	2.63	Dolf Luque	10.6	Pete Donohue	301.0	Dolf Luque	140	Pete Donohue	21	4 tied with	2
									Eppa Rixey			
1926	Carl Mays	3.14	Pete Donohue	10.9	Pete Donohue	285.2	Jakie May	103	Pete Donohue	20	Jakie May	3
1927	Dolf Luque	3.20	Red Lucas	10.1	Red Lucas	239.2	Jakie May	121	Red Lucas	18	Art Nehf	4
1928	Ray Kolp	3.19	Red Lucas	11.1	Eppa Rixey	291.1	Dolf Luque	72	Eppa Rixey	19	Ray Kolp	3
1929	Red Lucas	3.60	Red Lucas	10.9	Red Lucas	270.0	Jakie May	92	Red Lucas	19	Jakie May	3
1930	Ray Kolp	4.22	Ray Kolp	11.4	Benny Frey	245.0	Red Lucas	53	Red Lucas	14	Archie Campbell	4
1931	Larry Benton	3.35	Red Lucas	11.3	Si Johnson	262.1	Si Johnson	95	Red Lucas	14	Larry Benton	2
											Benny Frey	
1932	Red Lucas	2.84	Red Lucas	9.9	Red Lucas	269.1	Si Johnson	94	Si Johnson	13	Larry Benton	2
									Red Lucas		Si Johnson	
1933	Paul Derringer	3.23	Red Lucas	11.0	Paul Derringer	231.0	Paul Derringer	86	Larry Benton	10	Ray Kolp	3
									Red Lucas			
1934	Benny Frey	3.52	Benny Frey	12.2	Paul Derringer	261.0	Paul Derringer	122	Paul Derringer	15	Paul Derringer	4
1935	Paul Derringer	3.51	Paul Derringer	11.3	Paul Derringer	276.2	Paul Derringer	120	Paul Derringer	22	Don Brennan	5
1936	Gene Schott	3.80	Paul Derringer	12.0	Paul Derringer	282.1	Paul Derringer	121	Paul Derringer	19	Don Brennan	9
1937	Lee Grissom	3.26	Lee Grissom	11.7	Lee Grissom	223.2	Lee Grissom	149	Lee Grissom	12	Lee Grissom	6
1938	Paul Derringer	2.93	Paul Derringer	10.7	Paul Derringer	307.0	Paul Derringer	132	Paul Derringer	21	Joe Cascarella	4
1939	Bucky Walters	2.29	Bucky Walters	10.3	Bucky Walters	319.0	Bucky Walters	137	Bucky Walters	27	Peaches Davis	2
1940	Bucky Walters	2.48	Paul Derringer	10.0	Bucky Walters	305.0	Paul Derringer	115	Bucky Walters	22	Joe Beggs	7
								Bucky Walters				
1941	Elmer Riddle	2.24	Elmer Riddle	10.1	Bucky Walters	302.0	Johnny Vander Meer	202	Elmer Riddle	19	Joe Beggs	5
										Bucky Walters			
1942	Johnny Vander Meer	2.43	Bucky Walters	10.7	Ray Starr	276.2	Johnny Vander Meer	186	Johnny Vander Meer	18	Joe Beggs	8
1943	Elmer Riddle	2.66	Elmer Riddle	11.9	Johnny Vander Meer	289.0	Johnny Vander Meer	174	Elmer Riddle	21	Clyde Shoun	7
1944	Ed Heusser	2.38	Ed Heusser	9.7	Bucky Walters	285.0	Bucky Walters	77	Bucky Walters	23	Arnold Carter	3
1945	Bucky Walters	2.68	Bucky Walters	11.7	Ed Heusser	223.0	Joe Bowman	71	Joe Bowman	11	6 tied with	1
										Ed Heusser			
1946	Joe Beggs	2.32	Joe Beggs	10.2	Johnny Vander Meer	204.1	Ewell Blackwell	100	Joe Beggs	12	Harry Gumbert	4
1947	Ewell Blackwell	2.47	Ewell Blackwell	10.7	Ewell Blackwell	273.0	Ewell Blackwell	193	Ewell Blackwell	22	Harry Gumbert	10
1948	Johnny Vander Meer	3.41	Ken Raffensberger	11.2	Johnny Vander Meer	232.0	Johnny Vander Meer	120	Johnny Vander Meer	17	Harry Gumbert	17
1949	Ken Raffensberger	3.39	Ken Raffensberger	11.8	Ken Raffensberger	284.0	Ken Raffensberger	103	Ken Raffensberger	18	Harry Gumbert	2

Teams: Reds

Year	ERA		Baserunners/9 IP		Innings Pitched		Strikeouts		Wins		Saves	
1950	Ewell Blackwell	2.97	Ewell Blackwell	11.3	Ewell Blackwell	261.0	Ewell Blackwell	188	Ewell Blackwell	17	Ewell Blackwell Herm Wehmeier	4
1951	Ken Raffensberger	3.44	Ken Raffensberger	10.0	Ken Raffensberger	248.2	Ewell Blackwell	120	Ewell Blackwell Ken Raffensberger	16	Frank Smith	11
1952	Ken Raffensberger	2.81	Ken Raffensberger	10.7	Ken Raffensberger	247.0	Ken Raffensberger	93	Ken Raffensberger	17	Frank Smith	7
1953	Ken Raffensberger	3.93	Ken Raffensberger	12.1	Harry Perkowski	193.0	Bud Podbielan	74	Harry Perkowski	12	Jackie Collum	3
1954	Art Fowler	3.83	Corky Valentine	12.7	Art Fowler	227.2	Art Fowler	93	3 tied with	12	Frank Smith	20
1955	Joe Nuxhall	3.47	Joe Nuxhall	11.3	Joe Nuxhall	257.0	Joe Nuxhall	98	Joe Nuxhall	17	Hersh Freeman	11
1956	Joe Nuxhall	3.72	Art Fowler	11.4	Brooks Lawrence	218.2	Brooks Lawrence	120	Brooks Lawrence	19	Hersh Freeman	18
1957	Brooks Lawrence	3.52	Brooks Lawrence	11.4	Brooks Lawrence	250.1	Brooks Lawrence	121	Brooks Lawrence	16	Hersh Freeman	8
1958	Harvey Haddix	3.52	Bob Purkey	11.2	Bob Purkey	250.0	Joe Nuxhall	111	Bob Purkey	17	Hal Jeffcoat	9
1959	Don Newcombe	3.16	Don Newcombe	10.1	Don Newcombe	222.0	Don Newcombe	100	Don Newcombe Bob Purkey	13	Brooks Lawrence	10
1960	Bob Purkey	3.60	Bob Purkey	11.6	Bob Purkey	252.2	Jim O'Toole	124	Bob Purkey	17	Bill Henry	17
1961	Jim O'Toole	3.10	Bob Purkey	11.0	Jim O'Toole	252.2	Jim O'Toole	178	Joey Jay	21	Jim Brosnan Bill Henry	16
1962	Bob Purkey	2.81	Bob Purkey	10.6	Bob Purkey	288.1	Jim O'Toole	170	Bob Purkey	23	Jim Brosnan	13
1963	Joe Nuxhall	2.61	Joe Nuxhall	9.9	Jim Maloney	250.1	Jim Maloney	265	Jim Maloney	23	Bill Henry	14
1964	Jim O'Toole	2.66	Jim O'Toole	10.0	Jim O'Toole	220.0	Jim Maloney	214	Jim O'Toole	17	Sammy Ellis	14
1965	Jim Maloney	2.54	Jim Maloney	10.7	Sammy Ellis	263.2	Jim Maloney	244	Sammy Ellis	22	Billy McCool	21
1966	Jim Maloney	2.80	Jim Maloney	11.0	Jim Maloney	224.2	Jim Maloney	216	Jim Maloney	16	Billy McCool	18
1967	Gary Nolan	2.58	Mel Queen	9.8	Gary Nolan	226.2	Gary Nolan	206	Milt Pappas	16	Ted Abernathy	28
1968	George Culver	3.22	Gerry Arrigo	11.5	George Culver	226.1	Jim Maloney	181	Jim Maloney	16	Clay Carroll	17
1969	Jim Maloney	2.77	Jim Maloney	11.2	Jim Merritt	251.0	Jim Merritt	144	Jim Merritt	17	Wayne Granger	27
1970	Wayne Simpson	3.02	Wayne Simpson	11.0	Gary Nolan	250.2	Gary Nolan	181	Jim Merritt	20	Wayne Granger	35
1971	Don Gullett	2.65	Gary Nolan	9.9	Gary Nolan	244.2	Gary Nolan	146	Don Gullett	16	Clay Carroll	15
1972	Gary Nolan	1.99	Gary Nolan	9.1	Jack Billingham	217.2	Jack Billingham	137	Gary Nolan	15	Clay Carroll	37
1973	Jack Billingham	3.04	Don Gullett	10.6	Jack Billingham	293.1	Jack Billingham	155	Jack Billingham	19	Pedro Borbon Clay Carroll	14
1974	Don Gullett	3.04	Don Gullett	10.8	Don Gullett	243.0	Don Gullett	183	Jack Billingham	19	Pedro Borbon	14
1975	Gary Nolan	3.16	Gary Nolan	9.9	Gary Nolan	210.2	Fred Norman	119	3 tied with	15	Rawly Eastwick	22
1976	Pat Zachry	2.74	Gary Nolan	9.8	Gary Nolan	239.1	Pat Zachry	143	Gary Nolan	15	Rawly Eastwick	26
1977	Tom Seaver	2.34	Tom Seaver	8.6	Fred Norman	221.1	Fred Norman	160	Fred Norman Tom Seaver	14	Pedro Borbon	18
1978	Tom Seaver	2.88	Tom Seaver	10.6	Tom Seaver	259.2	Tom Seaver	226	Tom Seaver	16	Doug Bair	28
1979	Tom Hume	2.76	Tom Seaver	10.4	Tom Seaver	215.0	Tom Seaver	131	Tom Seaver	16	Tom Hume	17
1980	Mario Soto	3.07	Frank Pastore	9.9	Mario Soto	190.1	Mario Soto	182	Frank Pastore	13	Tom Hume	25
1981	Tom Seaver	2.54	Tom Seaver	10.2	Mario Soto	175.0	Mario Soto	151	Tom Seaver	14	Tom Hume	13
1982	Mario Soto	2.79	Mario Soto	9.7	Mario Soto	257.2	Mario Soto	274	Mario Soto	14	Tom Hume	17
1983	Mario Soto	2.70	Mario Soto	10.1	Mario Soto	273.2	Mario Soto	242	Mario Soto	17	Bill Scherrer	10
1984	Mario Soto	3.53	Mario Soto	10.4	Mario Soto	237.1	Mario Soto	185	Mario Soto	18	Ted Power	11
1985	Tom Browning	3.55	Mario Soto	10.6	Tom Browning	261.1	Mario Soto	214	Tom Browning	20	Ted Power	27
1986	Bill Gullickson	3.38	Tom Browning	10.9	Tom Browning	244.2	Tom Browning	147	Bill Gullickson	15	John Franco	29
1987	Ted Power	4.50	Bill Gullickson	11.6	Ted Power	204.0	Ted Power	133	3 tied with	10	John Franco	32
1988	Jose Rijo	2.39	Danny Jackson	9.6	Danny Jackson	260.2	Danny Jackson	161	Danny Jackson	23	John Franco	39
1989	Tom Browning	3.39	Tom Browning	11.1	Tom Browning	249.2	Rob Dibble	141	Tom Browning	15	John Franco	32
1990	Jose Rijo	2.70	Jose Rijo	10.6	Tom Browning	227.2	Jose Rijo	152	Tom Browning	15	Randy Myers	31
1991	Jose Rijo	2.51	Jose Rijo	9.8	Tom Browning	230.1	Jose Rijo	172	Jose Rijo	15	Rob Dibble	31
1992	Jose Rijo	2.56	Jose Rijo	9.9	Tim Belcher	227.2	Jose Rijo	171	Tim Belcher Jose Rijo	15	Norm Charlton	26
1993	Jose Rijo	2.48	Jose Rijo	9.9	Jose Rijo	257.1	Jose Rijo	227	Jose Rijo	14	Rob Dibble	19
1994	Jose Rijo	3.08	John Smiley	11.9	Jose Rijo	172.1	Jose Rijo	171	John Smiley	11	Jeff Brantley	15
1995	Pete Schourek	3.22	Pete Schourek	10.0	Pete Schourek	190.1	Pete Schourek	160	Pete Schourek	18	Jeff Brantley	28
1996	John Smiley	3.64	John Smiley	11.0	John Smiley	217.1	John Smiley	171	John Smiley	13	Jeff Brantley	44
1997	Mike Morgan	4.78	Mike Morgan	12.3	Mike Morgan	162.0	Mike Remlinger	145	Dave Burba Brett Tomko	11	Jeff Shaw	42

Teams: Reds

Reds Franchise Batting Leaders—Career

Games

1	Pete Rose	2,722
2	Dave Concepcion	2,488
3	Johnny Bench	2,158
4	Bid McPhee	2,135
5	Tony Perez	1,948
6	Vada Pinson	1,565
7	Frank Robinson	1,502
8	Dan Driessen	1,480
9	Barry Larkin	1,401
10	Edd Roush	1,399
11	Roy McMillan	1,348
12	Ted Kluszewski	1,339
13	Ron Oester	1,276
14	George Foster	1,253
15	Gus Bell	1,235
16	Tommy Corcoran	1,228
	Frank McCormick	1,228
18	Ken Griffey Sr.	1,224
19	Heine Groh	1,211
20	Four tied at	1,203

At-Bats

1	Pete Rose	10,934
2	Dave Concepcion	8,723
3	Bid McPhee	8,291
4	Johnny Bench	7,658
5	Tony Perez	6,846
6	Vada Pinson	6,335
7	Frank Robinson	5,527
8	Edd Roush	5,384
9	Barry Larkin	5,170
10	Ted Kluszewski	4,961
11	Tommy Corcoran	4,849
12	Frank McCormick	4,787
13	Dan Driessen	4,717
14	Gus Bell	4,667
15	George Foster	4,454
16	Heine Groh	4,439
17	John Reilly	4,412
18	Roy McMillan	4,319
19	Ron Oester	4,214
20	Ken Griffey Sr.	4,206

Runs

1	Pete Rose	1,741
2	Bid McPhee	1,678
3	Johnny Bench	1,091
4	Frank Robinson	1,043
5	Dave Concepcion	993
6	Vada Pinson	978
7	Tony Perez	936
8	John Reilly	877
9	Barry Larkin	862
10	Joe Morgan	816
11	Edd Roush	815
12	Ted Kluszewski	745
13	Bug Holliday	728
14	Ken Griffey Sr.	709
15	George Foster	680
16	Heine Groh	665
17	Dan Driessen	661
18	Eric Davis	635
19	Gus Bell	634
20	Frank McCormick	631

Hits

1	Pete Rose	3,358
2	Dave Concepcion	2,326
3	Bid McPhee	2,250
4	Johnny Bench	2,048
5	Tony Perez	1,934
6	Vada Pinson	1,881
7	Edd Roush	1,784
8	Frank Robinson	1,673
9	Barry Larkin	1,547
10	Ted Kluszewski	1,499
11	Frank McCormick	1,439
12	Gus Bell	1,343
13	Heine Groh	1,323
14	John Reilly	1,296
15	Dan Driessen	1,277
16	George Foster	1,276
17	Ken Griffey Sr.	1,275
18	Ernie Lombardi	1,238
19	Tommy Corcoran	1,205
20	Joe Morgan	1,155

Doubles

1	Pete Rose	601
2	Dave Concepcion	389
3	Johnny Bench	381
4	Vada Pinson	342
5	Tony Perez	339
6	Frank Robinson	318
7	Bid McPhee	303
8	Frank McCormick	285
9	Barry Larkin	271
10	Edd Roush	260
11	Ted Kluszewski	244
12	Dan Driessen	240
13	Gus Bell	228
14	Heine Groh	224
15	Ernie Lombardi	220
	Joe Morgan	220
17	Ken Griffey Sr.	212
18	John Reilly	207
	George Foster	207
20	Hal Morris	201

Triples

1	Bid McPhee	188
2	Edd Roush	152
3	John Reilly	135
4	Pete Rose	115
5	Vada Pinson	96
6	Curt Walker	94
7	Mike Mitchell	88
8	Ival Goodman	79
9	Jake Daubert	78
10	Jake Beckley	77
11	Heine Groh	75
12	Tommy Corcoran	72
13	Bug Holliday	71
14	Hughie Critz	66
15	Frank Fennelly	65
	Doc Hoblitzell	65
17	Ken Griffey Sr.	63
18	Harry Steinfeldt	62
19	Six tied at	60

Home Runs

1	Johnny Bench	389
2	Frank Robinson	324
3	Tony Perez	287
4	Ted Kluszewski	251
5	George Foster	244
6	Eric Davis	203
7	Vada Pinson	186
8	Wally Post	172
9	Gus Bell	160
10	Pete Rose	152
	Joe Morgan	152
12	Lee May	147
13	Barry Larkin	139
14	Dan Driessen	133
15	Ernie Lombardi	120
16	Reggie Sanders	111
17	Frank McCormick	110
18	Dave Parker	107
19	Chris Sabo	104
20	Dave Concepcion	101

RBI

1	Johnny Bench	1,376
2	Tony Perez	1,192
3	Pete Rose	1,036
4	Frank Robinson	1,009
5	Bid McPhee	961
6	Dave Concepcion	950
7	Ted Kluszewski	886
8	George Foster	861
9	Vada Pinson	814
10	Frank McCormick	803
11	Edd Roush	763
12	Gus Bell	711
13	Ernie Lombardi	682
14	Dan Driessen	670
15	Barry Larkin	646
16	Bug Holliday	617
17	Eric Davis	615
18	Tommy Corcoran	613
19	Joe Morgan	612
20	Jake Beckley	570

Walks

1	Pete Rose	1,210
2	Bid McPhee	981
3	Johnny Bench	891
4	Joe Morgan	881
5	Dave Concepcion	736
6	Frank Robinson	698
7	Dan Driessen	678
8	Tony Perez	671
9	Barry Larkin	592
10	Heine Groh	513
11	Lonny Frey	499
12	Eric Davis	494
13	Grady Hatton	479
14	Johnny Temple	471
15	George Foster	470
16	Roy McMillan	469
17	Ken Griffey Sr.	455
18	Miller Huggins	431
19	Bob Bescher	425
20	Vada Pinson	409

Strikeouts

1	Tony Perez	1,306
2	Johnny Bench	1,278
3	Dave Concepcion	1,186
4	Pete Rose	972
5	George Foster	882
6	Eric Davis	874
7	Vada Pinson	831
8	Frank Robinson	789
9	Leo Cardenas	728
10	Ron Oester	681
11	Cesar Geronimo	662
12	Reggie Sanders	640
13	Dan Driessen	639
14	Lee May	597
15	Wally Post	593
16	Nick Esasky	581
17	Ken Griffey Sr.	549
18	Barry Larkin	507
19	Paul O'Neill	456
20	Gus Bell	452

Stolen Bases

1	Bid McPhee	568
2	Joe Morgan	406
3	Hugh Nicol	345
4	Arlie Latham	337
5	Dave Concepcion	321
6	Bob Bescher	319
7	Barry Larkin	289
8	Eric Davis	270
9	Bug Holliday	248
10	John Reilly	245
11	Vada Pinson	221
12	Edd Roush	199
13	Dusty Miller	198
14	Tommy Corcoran	186
15	Dummy Hoy	175
16	Hans Lobert	168
17	Mike Mitchell	165
18	Frank Robinson	161
19	Hick Carpenter	158
	Heine Groh	158

Runs Created

1	Pete Rose	1,767
2	Bid McPhee	1,600
3	Johnny Bench	1,199
4	Frank Robinson	1,147
5	Tony Perez	1,082
6	Vada Pinson	1,007
7	Dave Concepcion	971
8	John Reilly	923
9	Edd Roush	907
10	Barry Larkin	898
11	Joe Morgan	875
12	Ted Kluszewski	869
13	Bug Holliday	776
14	George Foster	758
15	Frank McCormick	725
16	Dan Driessen	716
17	Gus Bell	696
18	Heine Groh	694
19	Ken Griffey Sr.	671
20	Eric Davis	657

Runs Created/27 Outs

(minimum 2000 Plate Appearances)

1	Charley Jones	9.56
2	Bug Holliday	7.98
3	John Reilly	7.83
4	Joe Morgan	7.80
5	Frank Robinson	7.54
6	Frank Fennelly	7.52
7	Cy Seymour	7.21
8	Dummy Hoy	7.08
9	Eric Davis	7.06
10	Dusty Miller	6.90
11	Jake Beckley	6.88
12	Bid McPhee	6.85
13	Arlie Latham	6.72
14	Ted Kluszewski	6.46
15	Barry Larkin	6.28
16	Bubbles Hargrave	6.20
17	Edd Roush	6.12
18	George Foster	6.09
19	Pete Rose	6.03
20	Ken Griffey Sr.	5.90

Batting Average

(minimum 2000 Plate Appearances)

1	Cy Seymour	.332
2	Edd Roush	.331
3	Jake Beckley	.325
4	Bubbles Hargrave	.314
5	Rube Bressler	.311
6	Ernie Lombardi	.311
7	Bug Holliday	.311
8	Dusty Miller	.308
9	Pete Rose	.307
10	Pat Duncan	.307
11	Hal Morris	.307
12	Ken Griffey Sr.	.303
13	Curt Walker	.303
14	Frank Robinson	.303
15	Ted Kluszewski	.302
16	Charley Jones	.301
17	Jake Daubert	.301
18	Frank McCormick	.301
19	Barry Larkin	.299
20	Heine Groh	.298

On-Base Percentage

(minimum 2000 Plate Appearances)

1	Joe Morgan	.415
2	Dummy Hoy	.390
3	Frank Robinson	.389
4	Pete Rose	.379
5	Rube Bressler	.379
6	Heine Groh	.378
7	Curt Walker	.378
8	Cy Seymour	.378
9	Edd Roush	.377
10	Bubbles Hargrave	.377
11	Bug Holliday	.376
12	Jake Beckley	.375
13	Barry Larkin	.373
14	Johnny Temple	.372
15	Ken Griffey Sr.	.370
16	Eric Davis	.367
17	Bob Bescher	.365
18	Hal Morris	.363
19	Miller Huggins	.362
20	Dan Driessen	.361

Slugging Percentage

(minimum 2000 Plate Appearances)

1	Frank Robinson	.554
2	George Foster	.514
3	Ted Kluszewski	.512
4	Eric Davis	.510
5	Wally Post	.498
6	Lee May	.490
7	Reggie Sanders	.488
8	Johnny Bench	.476
9	Tony Perez	.474
10	Joe Morgan	.470
11	Vada Pinson	.469
12	Dave Parker	.469
13	Ernie Lombardi	.469
14	Deron Johnson	.467
15	Cy Seymour	.463
16	Edd Roush	.462
17	Bubbles Hargrave	.461
18	Gus Bell	.454
19	Barry Larkin	.452
20	John Reilly	.449

Reds Franchise Pitching Leaders—Career

Wins

1	Eppa Rixey	179
2	Tony Mullane	163
3	Paul Derringer	161
4	Bucky Walters	160
5	Dolf Luque	153
6	Will White	136
7	Jim Maloney	134
8	Frank Dwyer	132
9	Joe Nuxhall	130
10	Noodles Hahn	127
	Pete Donohue	127
12	Tom Browning	123
13	Johnny Vander Meer	116
14	Gary Nolan	110
15	Red Lucas	109
16	Bob Ewing	108
17	Bob Purkey	103
18	Mario Soto	100
19	Billy Rhines	97
20	Jim O'Toole	94

Losses

1	Dolf Luque	152
2	Paul Derringer	150
3	Eppa Rixey	148
4	Tony Mullane	124
5	Johnny Vander Meer	116
6	Pete Donohue	110
7	Joe Nuxhall	109
8	Bucky Walters	107
9	Bob Ewing	103
10	Frank Dwyer	101
11	Red Lucas	99
	Ken Raffensberger	99
13	Noodles Hahn	92
	Rube Benton	92
	Mario Soto	92
16	Tom Browning	88
17	Si Johnson	86
18	Pete Schneider	85
19	Jim O'Toole	81
	Jim Maloney	81

Winning Percentage
(minimum 100 decisions)

1	Don Gullett	.674
2	Will White	.663
3	Jim Maloney	.623
4	Clay Carroll	.623
5	Gary Nolan	.621
6	Tom Seaver	.620
7	Jose Rijo	.617
8	Hod Eller	.604
9	Bucky Walters	.599
10	Ted Breitenstein	.595
11	Tom Browning	.583
12	Jack Billingham	.580
13	Noodles Hahn	.580
14	Bob Purkey	.575
15	Elmer Smith	.575
16	Fred Norman	.570
17	Tony Mullane	.568
18	Frank Dwyer	.567
19	Billy Rhines	.551
20	Eppa Rixey	.547

Games

1	Pedro Borbon	531
2	Clay Carroll	486
3	Joe Nuxhall	484
4	Tom Hume	457
5	Eppa Rixey	440
6	Dolf Luque	395
7	Paul Derringer	393
	John Franco	393
9	Rob Dibble	354
10	Ted Power	349
11	Tony Mullane	316
	Pete Donohue	316
13	Johnny Vander Meer	313
14	Bucky Walters	312
15	Tom Browning	300
16	Mario Soto	297
17	Jim Maloney	289
18	Rube Benton	265
19	Frank Dwyer	262
20	Red Lucas	257

Games Started

1	Eppa Rixey	356
2	Paul Derringer	322
3	Dolf Luque	319
4	Tom Browning	298
5	Bucky Walters	296
6	Tony Mullane	285
7	Johnny Vander Meer	278
8	Joe Nuxhall	274
9	Jim Maloney	258
10	Pete Donohue	256
11	Gary Nolan	242
12	Bob Ewing	228
	Jim O'Toole	228
14	Frank Dwyer	227
15	Noodles Hahn	225
16	Mario Soto	224
17	Bob Purkey	217
18	Will White	207
19	Jose Rijo	206
20	Ken Raffensberger	205

Complete Games

1	Tony Mullane	264
2	Noodles Hahn	209
3	Will White	204
4	Bucky Walters	195
5	Paul Derringer	189
6	Frank Dwyer	188
7	Bob Ewing	184
8	Dolf Luque	183
9	Eppa Rixey	180
10	Red Lucas	158
11	Billy Rhines	153
12	Pete Donohue	133
13	Johnny Vander Meer	131
14	Elmer Smith	111
	Bill Phillips	111
16	Ted Breitenstein	103
17	Ken Raffensberger	93
18	Lee Viau	87
19	Rube Benton	85
	Pete Schneider	85

Shutouts

1	Bucky Walters	32
2	Johnny Vander Meer	30
	Jim Maloney	30
4	Ken Raffensberger	25
5	Noodles Hahn	24
	Dolf Luque	24
	Paul Derringer	24
8	Will White	23
	Eppa Rixey	23
10	Joe Nuxhall	20
11	Red Lucas	18
	Jack Billingham	18
13	Fred Toney	17
	Jim O'Toole	17
15	Pete Donohue	16
	Ewell Blackwell	16
17	Tony Mullane	15
	Bob Ewing	15
19	Gary Nolan	14
20	Four tied at	13

Saves

1	John Franco	148
2	Clay Carroll	119
3	Tom Hume	88
	Rob Dibble	88
	Jeff Brantley	88
6	Pedro Borbon	76
7	Wayne Granger	73
8	Bill Henry	64
9	Rawly Eastwick	57
10	Billy McCool	50
	Doug Bair	50
12	Jeff Shaw	46
13	Ted Power	44
14	Frank Smith	43
	Jim Brosnan	43
16	Ted Abernathy	41
17	Hersh Freeman	37
	Randy Myers	37
19	Harry Gumbert	35
20	Norm Charlton	29

Innings Pitched

1	Eppa Rixey	2,890.2
2	Dolf Luque	2,668.2
3	Paul Derringer	2,615.1
4	Tony Mullane	2,599.0
5	Bucky Walters	2,355.2
6	Joe Nuxhall	2,169.1
7	Johnny Vander Meer	2,028.0
8	Bob Ewing	2,020.1
9	Pete Donohue	1,996.1
10	Frank Dwyer	1,992.2
11	Noodles Hahn	1,987.1
12	Tom Browning	1,911.0
13	Will White	1,832.1
14	Jim Maloney	1,818.2
15	Red Lucas	1,768.2
16	Mario Soto	1,730.1
17	Gary Nolan	1,656.1
18	Bob Purkey	1,588.0
19	Jim O'Toole	1,561.0
20	Billy Rhines	1,548.0

Walks

1	Johnny Vander Meer	1,072
2	Tony Mullane	926
3	Bucky Walters	806
4	Jim Maloney	786
5	Dolf Luque	756
6	Joe Nuxhall	706
7	Mario Soto	657
8	Eppa Rixey	603
9	Herm Wehmeier	591
10	Ewell Blackwell	532
11	Fred Norman	531
12	Jim O'Toole	528
13	Bob Ewing	513
14	Tom Browning	506
15	Rube Benton	501
16	Paul Derringer	491
17	Frank Dwyer	489
18	Billy Rhines	483
19	Pete Schneider	478
20	Jose Rijo	424

Strikeouts

1	Jim Maloney	1,592
2	Mario Soto	1,449
3	Joe Nuxhall	1,289
4	Johnny Vander Meer	1,251
5	Jose Rijo	1,201
6	Paul Derringer	1,062
7	Gary Nolan	1,035
8	Jim O'Toole	1,002
9	Tom Browning	997
10	Tony Mullane	993
11	Dolf Luque	970
12	Noodles Hahn	900
13	Bob Ewing	884
14	Bucky Walters	879
15	Fred Norman	864
16	Ewell Blackwell	819
17	Don Gullett	777
18	Tom Seaver	731
19	Joey Jay	708
20	Eppa Rixey	660

Strikeouts/9 Innings
(minimum 1000 Innings Pitched)

1	Jim Maloney	7.88
2	Jose Rijo	7.81
3	Mario Soto	7.54
4	Tom Seaver	6.06
5	Fred Norman	5.91
6	Don Gullett	5.89
7	Joey Jay	5.78
8	Jim O'Toole	5.78
9	Ewell Blackwell	5.75
10	Gary Nolan	5.62
11	Johnny Vander Meer	5.55
12	Joe Nuxhall	5.35
13	Tom Browning	4.70
14	Jakie May	4.65
15	Jack Billingham	4.44
16	Noodles Hahn	4.08
17	Herm Wehmeier	3.96
18	Elmer Smith	3.95
19	Bob Ewing	3.94
20	Rube Benton	3.67

ERA
(minimum 1000 Innings Pitched)

1	Bob Ewing	2.37
2	Will White	2.51
3	Noodles Hahn	2.52
4	Pete Schneider	2.61
5	Jose Rijo	2.71
6	Bucky Walters	2.93
7	Gary Nolan	3.02
8	George Suggs	3.03
9	Don Gullett	3.03
10	Dolf Luque	3.09
11	Tony Mullane	3.15
12	Jim Maloney	3.16
13	Tom Seaver	3.18
14	Billy Rhines	3.28
15	Rube Benton	3.28
16	Elmer Smith	3.31
17	Ewell Blackwell	3.32
18	Eppa Rixey	3.33
19	Paul Derringer	3.36
20	Johnny Vander Meer	3.41

Component ERA
(minimum 1000 Innings Pitched)

1	Will White	2.38
2	Noodles Hahn	2.49
3	Bob Ewing	2.51
4	Jose Rijo	2.80
5	Gary Nolan	2.81
6	Tom Seaver	2.94
7	Elmer Smith	2.97
8	Mario Soto	2.97
9	Tony Mullane	2.97
10	Bucky Walters	3.00
11	Don Gullett	3.00
12	George Suggs	3.04
13	Dolf Luque	3.04
14	Jim Maloney	3.08
15	Red Lucas	3.11
16	Ewell Blackwell	3.13
17	Paul Derringer	3.15
18	Billy Rhines	3.16
19	Pete Schneider	3.19
20	Eppa Rixey	3.27

Opponent Average
(minimum 1000 Innings Pitched)

1	Mario Soto	.220
2	Jim Maloney	.223
3	Tom Seaver	.230
4	Don Gullett	.232
5	Johnny Vander Meer	.232
6	Jose Rijo	.234
7	Will White	.234
8	Ewell Blackwell	.235
9	Gary Nolan	.237
10	Tony Mullane	.240
11	Fred Norman	.241
12	Bucky Walters	.243
13	Elmer Smith	.244
14	Bob Ewing	.246
15	Noodles Hahn	.248
16	Jim O'Toole	.251
17	Joey Jay	.253
18	Billy Rhines	.256
19	Pete Schneider	.258
20	Bob Purkey	.260

Opponent OBP
(minimum 1000 Innings Pitched)

1	Will White	.273
2	Gary Nolan	.284
3	Noodles Hahn	.288
4	Tom Seaver	.292
5	Jose Rijo	.293
6	Mario Soto	.294
7	Don Gullett	.298
8	Bob Ewing	.299
9	Bob Purkey	.303
10	Paul Derringer	.303
11	Red Lucas	.304
12	Ken Raffensberger	.306
13	Jim Maloney	.306
14	Elmer Smith	.307
15	Tony Mullane	.308
16	Bucky Walters	.308
17	Tom Browning	.310
18	Billy Rhines	.313
19	Jim O'Toole	.313
20	Dolf Luque	.314

Teams: Reds

Reds Franchise Batting Leaders—Single Season

Games

	Player	Year	
1	Leo Cardenas	1964	163
	Pete Rose	1974	163
3	Frank Robinson	1962	162
	Vada Pinson	1963	162
	Pete Rose	1965	162
	Pete Rose	1975	162
	Pete Rose	1976	162
	Pete Rose	1977	162
	Ray Knight	1980	162
	Dave Parker	1986	162
11	Todd Benzinger	1989	161
12	Ten tied at		160

At-Bats

	Player	Year	
1	Pete Rose	1973	680
2	Pete Rose	1965	670
3	Vada Pinson	1965	669
4	Pete Rose	1976	665
5	Pete Rose	1975	662
6	Dain Clay	1945	656
7	Pete Rose	1977	655
	Pete Rose	1978	655
9	Pete Rose	1966	654
10	Woody Williams	1944	653
11	Vada Pinson	1960	652
	Vada Pinson	1963	652
	Pete Rose	1974	652
14	Vada Pinson	1967	650
15	Pete Rose	1970	649
16	Vada Pinson	1959	648
17	Tommy Harper	1965	646
18	Pete Rose	1972	645
19	Frankie Baumholtz	1947	643
20	Hughie Critz	1928	641

Runs

	Player	Year	
1	Bid McPhee	1886	139
2	Bid McPhee	1887	137
3	Frank Robinson	1962	134
4	Frank Fennelly	1887	133
5	Vada Pinson	1959	131
6	Pete Rose	1976	130
7	Arlie Latham	1894	129
8	Tommy Harper	1965	126
9	Bid McPhee	1890	125
10	George Foster	1977	124
11	Hugh Nicol	1887	122
	Frank Robinson	1956	122
	Joe Morgan	1972	122
14	Eddie Burke	1896	120
	Dummy Hoy	1896	120
	Bob Bescher	1912	120
	Pete Rose	1969	120
	Pete Rose	1970	120
	Eric Davis	1987	120
20	Two tied at		119

Hits

	Player	Year	
1	Pete Rose	1973	230
2	Cy Seymour	1905	219
3	Pete Rose	1969	218
4	Pete Rose	1976	215
5	Pete Rose	1968	210
	Pete Rose	1975	210
7	Frank McCormick	1938	209
	Frank McCormick	1939	209
	Pete Rose	1965	209
10	Vada Pinson	1961	208
	Frank Robinson	1962	208
12	Jake Daubert	1922	205
	Vada Pinson	1959	205
	Pete Rose	1966	205
	Pete Rose	1970	205
16	Vada Pinson	1963	204
	Vada Pinson	1965	204
	Pete Rose	1977	204
19	Pat Duncan	1922	199
20	Three tied at		198

Doubles

	Player	Year	
1	Frank Robinson	1962	51
	Pete Rose	1978	51
3	Vada Pinson	1959	47
	Pete Rose	1975	47
5	George Kelly	1929	45
	Pete Rose	1974	45
7	Pat Duncan	1922	44
	Frank McCormick	1940	44
9	Harry Heilmann	1930	43
10	Pete Rose	1968	42
	Pete Rose	1976	42
	Dave Parker	1985	42
13	Edd Roush	1923	41
	Frank McCormick	1939	41
15	Cy Seymour	1905	40
	Frank McCormick	1938	40
	Johnny Bench	1968	40
	Chris Sabo	1988	40
19	Five tied at		39

Triples

	Player	Year	
1	John Reilly	1890	26
2	Bid McPhee	1890	22
	Sam Crawford	1902	22
	Mike Mitchell	1911	22
	Jake Daubert	1922	22
6	Cy Seymour	1905	21
	Edd Roush	1924	21
8	Curt Walker	1926	20
9	John Reilly	1884	19
	Bid McPhee	1887	19
	Babe Herman	1932	19
12	Mike Donlin	1903	18
	Hans Lobert	1908	18
	Mike Mitchell	1910	18
	Edd Roush	1923	18
	Ival Goodman	1935	18
17	Five tied at		17

Home Runs

	Player	Year	
1	George Foster	1977	52
2	Ted Kluszewski	1954	49
3	Ted Kluszewski	1955	47
4	Johnny Bench	1970	45
5	Ted Kluszewski	1953	40
	Wally Post	1955	40
	Tony Perez	1970	40
	Johnny Bench	1972	40
	George Foster	1978	40
10	Frank Robinson	1962	39
	Lee May	1971	39
12	Frank Robinson	1956	38
	Lee May	1969	38
14	Frank Robinson	1961	37
	Tony Perez	1969	37
	Eric Davis	1987	37
17	Wally Post	1956	36
	Frank Robinson	1959	36
19	Hank Sauer	1948	35
	Ted Kluszewski	1956	35

RBI

	Player	Year	
1	George Foster	1977	149
2	Johnny Bench	1970	148
3	Ted Kluszewski	1954	141
4	Frank Robinson	1962	136
5	Deron Johnson	1965	130
6	Tony Perez	1970	129
	Johnny Bench	1974	129
8	Frank McCormick	1939	128
9	Frank McCormick	1940	127
10	Frank Robinson	1959	125
	Johnny Bench	1972	125
	Dave Parker	1985	125
13	Frank Robinson	1961	124
14	Tony Perez	1969	122
15	Cy Seymour	1905	121
	George Foster	1976	121
17	George Foster	1978	120
18	Bug Holliday	1894	119
19	Dave Parker	1986	116
20	Gus Bell	1959	115

Walks

	Player	Year	
1	Joe Morgan	1975	132
2	Joe Morgan	1974	120
3	Joe Morgan	1977	117
4	Joe Morgan	1972	115
5	Joe Morgan	1976	114
6	Joe Morgan	1973	111
7	Pete Rose	1974	106
8	Miller Huggins	1905	103
	Johnny Bates	1911	103
10	Bob Bescher	1911	102
11	George Burns	1923	101
12	Johnny Bench	1972	100
13	Barry Larkin	1996	96
14	Bid McPhee	1893	94
	Bob Bescher	1913	94
	Augie Galan	1947	94
	Johnny Temple	1957	94
	Bernie Carbo	1970	94
19	Joe Morgan	1979	93
	Dan Driessen	1980	93

Strikeouts

	Player	Year	
1	Lee May	1969	142
2	George Foster	1978	138
3	Lee May	1971	135
4	Tony Perez	1970	134
	Eric Davis	1987	134
6	Tony Perez	1969	131
7	Tommy Harper	1965	127
8	Dave Parker	1986	126
9	Lee May	1970	125
10	Wally Post	1956	124
	Eric Davis	1988	124
12	Reggie Sanders	1995	122
13	Tony Perez	1972	121
	Eric Davis	1996	121
15	Tony Perez	1971	120
	Todd Benzinger	1989	120
17	Reggie Sanders	1993	118
18	Tony Perez	1973	117
19	Eric Davis	1989	116
20	Reggie Sanders	1994	114

Stolen Bases

	Player	Year	
1	Hugh Nicol	1887	138
2	Hugh Nicol	1888	103
3	Bid McPhee	1887	95
4	Arlie Latham	1891	87
5	John Reilly	1888	82
6	Hugh Nicol	1889	80
	Bob Bescher	1911	80
	Eric Davis	1986	80
9	Dave Collins	1980	79
10	Dusty Miller	1896	76
11	Frank Fennelly	1887	74
12	Bob Bescher	1910	70
13	Bob Bescher	1912	67
	Joe Morgan	1973	67
	Joe Morgan	1975	67
16	Arlie Latham	1892	66
17	Bid McPhee	1889	63
18	W. Wings Tebeau	1889	61
19	Joe Morgan	1976	60
20	Two tied at		59

Runs Created

	Player	Year	
1	Frank Robinson	1962	152
2	Cy Seymour	1905	147
3	Charley Jones	1884	142
4	Ted Kluszewski	1954	141
5	John Reilly	1884	137
	Joe Morgan	1975	137
7	Pete Rose	1969	133
8	Bug Holliday	1889	130
9	Bug Holliday	1894	129
	George Foster	1977	129
11	Ted Kluszewski	1955	127
	Frank Robinson	1961	127
	Joe Morgan	1973	127
14	John Reilly	1887	125
	Bug Holliday	1892	125
	Joe Morgan	1976	125
17	John Reilly	1888	124
	Frank Robinson	1964	124
	Tony Perez	1970	124
20	Dusty Miller	1895	122

Runs Created/27 Outs

(minimum 3.1 Plate Appearances/Tm Gm)

	Player	Year	
1	John Reilly	1884	12.30
2	Charley Jones	1884	11.64
3	Joe Morgan	1975	10.52
4	Cy Seymour	1905	10.18
5	Bug Holliday	1894	10.18
6	Joe Morgan	1976	9.85
7	John Reilly	1883	9.59
8	Frank Robinson	1962	9.56
9	Charley Jones	1885	9.49
10	Ted Kluszewski	1954	9.39
11	Hick Carpenter	1882	9.37
12	Charley Jones	1883	9.36
13	Mike Donlin	1903	9.34
14	John Reilly	1888	9.14
15	Elmer Smith	1898	8.94
16	Eric Davis	1987	8.88
17	Kevin Mitchell	1994	8.83
18	Bug Holliday	1889	8.78
19	Dusty Miller	1895	8.73
20	Bug Holliday	1893	8.63

Batting Average

(minimum 3.1 Plate Appearances/Tm Gm)

	Player	Year	
1	Cy Seymour	1905	.377
2	Bug Holliday	1894	.372
3	Edd Roush	1923	.351
4	Mike Donlin	1903	.351
5	Edd Roush	1924	.348
6	Pete Rose	1969	.348
7	Vada Pinson	1961	.343
8	Cy Seymour	1903	.342
9	Hick Carpenter	1882	.342
10	Elmer Smith	1898	.342
11	Frank Robinson	1962	.342
12	Ernie Lombardi	1938	.342
13	Edd Roush	1917	.341
14	Jake Beckley	1900	.341
15	Eddie Burke	1896	.340
16	Hal Chase	1916	.339
17	John Reilly	1884	.339
18	Edd Roush	1925	.339
19	Edd Roush	1920	.339
20	Pete Rose	1973	.338

On-Base Percentage

(minimum 3.1 Plate Appearances/Tm Gm)

	Player	Year	
1	Joe Morgan	1975	.466
2	Augie Galan	1947	.449
3	Joe Morgan	1976	.444
4	Cy Seymour	1905	.429
5	Kevin Mitchell	1994	.429
6	Pete Rose	1969	.428
7	Joe Morgan	1974	.427
8	Elmer Smith	1898	.425
9	Frank Robinson	1962	.421
10	Bid McPhee	1894	.420
11	Mike Donlin	1903	.420
12	Bug Holliday	1894	.420
13	Joe Morgan	1977	.417
14	Joe Morgan	1972	.417
15	Curt Walker	1929	.416
16	Harry Heilmann	1930	.416
17	Dummy Hoy	1894	.416
18	Johnny Bates	1911	.415
19	Barry Larkin	1996	.410
20	Bid McPhee	1895	.409

Slugging Percentage

(minimum 3.1 Plate Appearances/Tm Gm)

	Player	Year	
1	Kevin Mitchell	1994	.681
2	Ted Kluszewski	1954	.642
3	George Foster	1977	.631
4	Frank Robinson	1962	.624
5	Frank Robinson	1961	.611
6	Frank Robinson	1960	.595
7	Eric Davis	1987	.593
8	Tony Perez	1970	.589
9	Johnny Bench	1970	.587
10	Ted Kluszewski	1955	.585
11	Frank Robinson	1959	.583
12	Reggie Sanders	1995	.579
13	Harry Heilmann	1930	.577
14	Joe Morgan	1976	.576
15	Wally Post	1955	.574
16	Ted Kluszewski	1953	.570
17	Barry Larkin	1996	.567
18	George Foster	1979	.561
19	Cy Seymour	1905	.559
20	Frank Robinson	1956	.558

Teams: Reds

Reds Franchise Pitching Leaders—Single Season

Wins

1	Will White	1883	43
2	Will White	1882	40
3	Will White	1884	34
	Elmer Smith	1887	34
5	Tony Mullane	1886	33
6	Jesse Duryea	1889	32
7	Tony Mullane	1887	31
8	Billy Rhines	1890	28
9	Lee Viau	1888	27
	Pink Hawley	1898	27
	Dolf Luque	1923	27
	Bucky Walters	1939	27
13	Tony Mullane	1888	26
14	Eppa Rixey	1922	25
	Paul Derringer	1939	25
16	Frank Dwyer	1896	24
	Fred Toney	1917	24
18	Nine tied at		23

Losses

1	Tony Mullane	1886	27
2	Tony Mullane	1891	26
3	Paul Derringer	1933	25
4	Billy Rhines	1891	24
5	Elton Chamberlin	1892	23
	Orval Overall	1905	23
	Red Ames	1914	23
	Dolf Luque	1922	23
9	Will White	1883	22
	Frank Dwyer	1894	22
	Si Johnson	1934	22
12	George Pechiney	1886	21
	Rube Benton	1912	21
	Paul Derringer	1934	21
15	Lee Viau	1889	20
	Ed Scott	1900	20
	Noodles Hahn	1900	20
	Chick Fraser	1906	20
19	Fifteen tied at		19

Winning Percentage
(minimum 15 decisions)

1	Tom Seaver	1981	.875
2	Elmer Riddle	1941	.826
3	Wayne Simpson	1970	.824
	Tom Seaver	1977	.824
5	Bob Purkey	1962	.821
6	Joe Beggs	1940	.800
	John Franco	1985	.800
8	Don Gullett	1975	.789
9	Tom Browning	1988	.783
10	Paul Derringer	1939	.781
11	Dolf Luque	1923	.771
12	Will White	1882	.769
13	Jim Maloney	1963	.767
14	Dutch Ruether	1919	.760
15	Mike Sullivan	1892	.750
	Ed Poole	1902	.750
	Slim Sallee	1919	.750
	Gary Nolan	1972	.750
	Fred Norman	1975	.750
20	Three tied at		.742

Games

1	Wayne Granger	1969	90
2	Rob Murphy	1987	87
3	Frank Williams	1987	85
4	Stan Belinda	1997	84
5	Pedro Borbon	1973	80
6	Ted Abernathy	1968	78
	Tom Hume	1980	78
	Ted Power	1984	78
	Jeff Shaw	1996	78
	Jeff Shaw	1997	78
11	Rob Murphy	1988	76
12	John Franco	1986	74
	Rob Dibble	1989	74
14	Pedro Borbon	1974	73
	Pedro Borbon	1977	73
	Bill Scherrer	1983	73
17	Clay Carroll	1969	71
	Rawly Eastwick	1976	71
19	Six tied at		70

Games Started

1	Will White	1883	64
2	Tony Mullane	1886	56
3	Will White	1882	54
4	Will White	1884	52
	Elmer Smith	1887	52
6	Elton Chamberlin	1892	49
7	Tony Mullane	1887	48
	Jesse Duryea	1889	48
9	Tony Mullane	1891	47
10	Billy Rhines	1890	45
11	Billy Rhines	1891	43
12	Lee Viau	1888	42
	Tony Mullane	1888	42
	Lee Viau	1889	42
	Noodles Hahn	1901	42
	Pete Schneider	1917	42
	Fred Toney	1917	42
18	Four tied at		40

Complete Games

1	Will White	1883	64
2	Tony Mullane	1886	55
3	Will White	1882	52
	Will White	1884	52
5	Elmer Smith	1887	49
6	Tony Mullane	1887	47
7	Billy Rhines	1890	45
8	Elton Chamberlin	1892	43
9	Lee Viau	1888	42
	Tony Mullane	1891	42
11	Tony Mullane	1888	41
	Noodles Hahn	1901	41
13	Billy Rhines	1891	40
14	Jesse Duryea	1889	38
	Lee Viau	1889	38
16	Elmer Smith	1888	37
17	George Pechiney	1886	35
	Noodles Hahn	1902	35
19	Frank Dwyer	1894	34
	Noodles Hahn	1903	34

Shutouts

1	Will White	1882	8
2	Will White	1884	7
	Fred Toney	1917	7
	Hod Eller	1919	7
	Jack Billingham	1973	7
6	Will White	1883	6
	Tony Mullane	1887	6
	Billy Rhines	1890	6
	Noodles Hahn	1902	6
	Jack Harper	1904	6
	Jake Weimer	1906	6
	Fred Toney	1915	6
	Dolf Luque	1923	6
	J. Vander Meer	1941	6
	Bucky Walters	1944	6
	Ewell Blackwell	1946	6
	Ewell Blackwell	1947	6
	Ken Raffensberger	1952	6
	Jim Maloney	1963	6
	Danny Jackson	1988	6

Saves

1	Jeff Brantley	1996	44
2	Jeff Shaw	1997	42
3	John Franco	1988	39
4	Clay Carroll	1972	37
5	Wayne Granger	1970	35
6	John Franco	1987	32
	John Franco	1989	32
8	Randy Myers	1990	31
	Rob Dibble	1991	31
10	John Franco	1986	29
11	Ted Abernathy	1967	28
	Doug Bair	1978	28
	Jeff Brantley	1995	28
14	Wayne Granger	1969	27
	Ted Power	1985	27
16	Rawly Eastwick	1976	26
	Norm Charlton	1992	26
18	Tom Hume	1980	25
	Rob Dibble	1992	25
20	Rawly Eastwick	1975	22

Innings Pitched

1	Will White	1883	577.0
2	Tony Mullane	1886	529.2
3	Will White	1882	480.0
4	Will White	1884	456.0
5	Elmer Smith	1887	447.1
6	Tony Mullane	1891	426.1
7	Tony Mullane	1887	416.1
8	Elton Chamberlin	1892	406.1
9	Billy Rhines	1890	401.1
10	Jesse Duryea	1889	401.0
11	Lee Viau	1888	387.2
12	Tony Mullane	1888	380.1
13	Noodles Hahn	1901	375.1
14	Lee Viau	1889	373.0
15	Billy Rhines	1891	372.2
16	Elmer Smith	1888	348.1
17	Frank Dwyer	1894	348.0
18	Pete Schneider	1917	341.2
19	Fred Toney	1917	339.2
20	Bob Ewing	1907	332.2

Walks

1	Tony Mullane	1891	187
2	Elton Chamberlin	1892	170
3	Tony Mullane	1886	166
4	J. Vander Meer	1943	162
5	Orval Overall	1905	147
6	Lee Viau	1889	136
7	Herm Wehmeier	1950	135
8	George Pechiney	1886	133
9	Jesse Duryea	1889	127
	Tony Mullane	1892	127
11	Elmer Smith	1887	126
	Tom Parrott	1894	126
	J. Vander Meer	1941	126
14	Billy Rhines	1891	124
	J. Vander Meer	1948	124
16	Ted Breitenstein	1898	123
17	Tony Mullane	1887	121
18	Bill Hill	1898	119
	Pete Schneider	1917	119
20	Rube Benton	1912	118

Strikeouts

1	Mario Soto	1982	274
2	Jim Maloney	1963	265
3	Tony Mullane	1886	250
4	Jim Maloney	1965	244
5	Mario Soto	1983	242
6	Noodles Hahn	1901	239
7	Jose Rijo	1993	227
8	Tom Seaver	1978	226
9	Jim Maloney	1966	216
10	Jim Maloney	1964	214
	Mario Soto	1985	214
12	Gary Nolan	1967	206
13	J. Vander Meer	1941	202
14	Ewell Blackwell	1947	193
15	Ewell Blackwell	1950	188
16	Tony Mullane	1888	186
	J. Vander Meer	1942	186
18	Mario Soto	1984	185
19	Three tied at		183

Strikeouts/9 Innings
(minimum 1 Inning Pitched/Tm Gm)

1	Mario Soto	1982	9.57
2	Jim Maloney	1963	9.53
3	Jose Rijo	1994	8.93
4	Jim Maloney	1964	8.92
5	Jose Rijo	1988	8.89
6	Jim Maloney	1966	8.65
7	Mario Soto	1980	8.61
8	Jim Maloney	1965	8.60
9	Gary Nolan	1967	8.18
10	J. Vander Meer	1941	8.03
11	Mario Soto	1983	7.96
12	Jose Rijo	1993	7.94
13	Jim Maloney	1968	7.87
14	Tom Seaver	1978	7.83
15	Mario Soto	1981	7.77
16	Jose Rijo	1991	7.58
17	Bruce Berenyi	1981	7.57
18	Pete Schourek	1995	7.57
19	Mario Soto	1985	7.50
20	John Tsitouris	1964	7.49

ERA
(minimum 1 Inning Pitched/Tm Gm)

1	Harry McCormick	1882	1.52
2	Will White	1882	1.54
3	Fred Toney	1915	1.58
4	Bob Ewing	1907	1.73
5	Noodles Hahn	1902	1.77
6	Dutch Ruether	1919	1.82
7	Andy Coakley	1908	1.86
8	Art Fromme	1909	1.90
9	Dolf Luque	1923	1.93
10	Billy Rhines	1890	1.95
11	Pete Schneider	1917	1.98
12	Gary Nolan	1972	1.99
13	Harry Gaspar	1909	2.01
14	Slim Sallee	1919	2.06
15	Noodles Hahn	1904	2.06
16	Will White	1883	2.09
17	Ray Fisher	1919	2.17
18	Fred Toney	1917	2.20
19	Bob Ewing	1908	2.21
20	Jake Weimer	1906	2.22

Component ERA
(minimum 1 Inning Pitched/Tm Gm)

1	Fred Toney	1915	1.80
2	Art Fromme	1909	1.81
3	Will White	1882	1.82
4	Harry McCormick	1882	1.83
5	Will White	1883	1.83
6	Tom Seaver	1977	1.89
7	Noodles Hahn	1904	1.90
8	Ray Fisher	1919	2.00
9	Bob Ewing	1908	2.03
10	Noodles Hahn	1902	2.07
11	Bob Ewing	1906	2.13
12	Bob Ewing	1907	2.15
13	Mario Soto	1980	2.15
14	Ren Deagle	1883	2.17
15	Jimmy Ring	1919	2.19
16	Harry Gaspar	1909	2.22
17	Gary Nolan	1972	2.22
18	Billy Rhines	1890	2.22
19	Jose Rijo	1991	2.23
20	Danny Jackson	1988	2.23

Opponent Average
(minimum 1 Inning Pitched/Tm Gm)

1	Mario Soto	1980	.187
2	Wayne Simpson	1970	.198
3	Art Fromme	1909	.201
4	Tony Mullane	1892	.201
5	Tom Seaver	1977	.201
6	Jim Maloney	1963	.202
7	Tom Seaver	1981	.205
8	Harry McCormick	1882	.206
9	Jim Maloney	1965	.206
10	Fred Toney	1915	.207
11	Mario Soto	1983	.208
12	Jim Maloney	1969	.208
13	J. Vander Meer	1942	.208
14	Jose Rijo	1988	.209
15	Mario Soto	1984	.209
16	Ewell Blackwell	1950	.210
17	Bruce Berenyi	1981	.211
18	Mario Soto	1985	.211
19	Jose Rijo	1990	.212
20	Gus Shallix	1884	.212

Opponent OBP
(minimum 1 Inning Pitched/Tm Gm)

1	Harry McCormick	1882	.243
2	Tom Seaver	1977	.248
3	Will White	1883	.249
4	Will White	1882	.250
5	Gary Nolan	1972	.259
6	Noodles Hahn	1904	.262
7	Ren Deagle	1883	.267
8	Noodles Hahn	1902	.270
9	Mel Queen	1967	.271
10	Ray Fisher	1919	.271
11	Mario Soto	1982	.271
12	Jose Rijo	1991	.272
13	Danny Jackson	1988	.273
14	Red Lucas	1932	.275
15	Gary Nolan	1971	.275
16	Jim Maloney	1963	.275
17	Gary Nolan	1976	.275
18	Frank Pastore	1980	.275
19	Ed Heusser	1944	.275
20	Gary Nolan	1975	.275

Teams: Reds

Reds Capsule

Best Season: *1976.* The Reds won 102 games and went undefeated in the postseason to become the first National League team in 54 years to win back-to-back World Championships.

Worst Season: *1982.* After posting the best overall record in the majors in 1981, the Reds collapsed, dropping into the cellar with a 61-101 record, the worst mark in the history of the franchise.

Best Player: *Joe Morgan.* Sparky Anderson called him, "The single greatest player I ever saw in my lifetime," and even with all of Sparky's Mantle comparisons, he never said the same of anyone else. Johnny Bench, George Foster, Pete Rose and Edd Roush really don't come that close to Morgan. In fact, Bid McPhee may be second-best.

Best Pitcher: *Eppa Rixey.* Dolf Luque is Rixey's main competition. The two pitchers spent their prime years as teammates from 1921 through 1929, and Luque demonstrably outperformed Rixey in only one of those nine seasons.

Best Reliever: *John Franco.*

Best Defensive Player: *Johnny Bench.* Dave Concepcion and Roy McMillan were superb as well.

Hall of Famers: *Johnny Bench, Ernie Lombardi, Joe Morgan, Frank Robinson, Eppa Rixey, Edd Roush.* Manager *Bill McKechnie* spent more time in Cincinnati than anywhere else.

Franchise All-Star Team:

C	*Johnny Bench*		**LF**	*George Foster*
1B	*Tony Perez*		**CF**	*Edd Roush*
2B	*Joe Morgan*		**RF**	*Frank Robinson*
3B	*Heinie Groh*		**SP**	*Eppa Rixey*
SS	*Barry Larkin*		**RP**	*John Franco*

Biggest Flake: *Brad Lesley,* who often unleashed a primal scream after a satisfying strikeout.

Strangest Career: *Gary Nolan.* Only three teenage pitchers in history have struck out 200 hitters in a season: Bob Feller, Dwight Gooden and Gary Nolan. As a 19-year-old rookie in 1967, Nolan finished fourth in the NL in both strikeouts (206) and ERA (2.58). The following spring, he began to have arm problems, and his strikeout rate dropped dramatically. He managed to stay healthy during 1970 and 1971, and enjoyed his best season in 1972 when given a lighter workload. But he missed almost all of '73 with shoulder problems, and he eventually succumbed to surgery in May 1974. He returned in '75 after missing almost two full seasons and went 15-9, although he was a vastly different pitcher. Relying on a changeup, he had become the consummate control pitcher, leading the majors in fewest walks per nine innings by a wide margin. He posted a nearly identical record the following year before another shoulder injury ended his career in 1977.

What Might Have Been: *Wayne Simpson.* On July 5, 1970, the 21-year-old rookie righthander owned a 13-1 record and had already thrown a one-hitter, a two-hitter and a three-hitter. Then he hurt his shoulder and pitched sparingly for the rest of the season. He compiled a 23-30 record over parts of six seasons after his arm went bad.

Best Trades: There have been quite a few of them. They got Hall of Famer *Edd Roush* from the Giants in 1916 for an over-the-hill Buck Herzog. Roush starred for the Reds for the next 11 years. Catcher *Ernie Lombardi* came over from the Dodgers as a throw-in in a 1932 trade. Lombardi spent 10 years behind the plate for Cincinnati, winning the batting title and the MVP Award in 1938. The Reds sent catcher Spud Davis, pitcher Al Hollingsworth and $50,000 to the Phillies for pitcher *Bucky Walters* in 1938; Walter won the MVP the following year. They got *Paul Derringer* from the Cardinals in 1933 in a deal that boiled down to Derringer for Leo Durocher. Durocher became a key component of the "Gas House Gang," but Derringer ultimately won 194 games for the Reds. They dealt Jimmy Ring and change to the Phillies in 1921 for *Eppa Rixey,* who was a big winner for the next 10 years. The Reds' best trade of all time came in the 1971 offseason, at the expense of the Houston Astros, and helped to build the "Big Red Machine." The principals were *Joe Morgan,* Jack Billingham and Cesar Geronimo, who came to Cincinnati, and Lee May and Tommy Helms, who went to Houston. A few months later, they sent shortstop Frank Duffy to the Giants for *George Foster.* The Reds' best trade of recent years was the 1987 deal that sent Dave Parker to Oakland for *Jose Rijo.*

Worst Trades: *Christy Mathewson* and *Frank Robinson.* On December 15, 1900, they dealt the 22-year-old Mathewson to the Giants for washed-up superstar Amos Rusie. Over the winter of 1965, they traded Robinson to the Orioles for pitcher Milt Pappas and a couple of spare parts. Another loser was the 1959 deal that sent pitcher Harvey Haddix, catcher Smoky Burgess and third baseman Don Hoak to the Pirates for Frank Thomas and three players who proved useless.

Best-Looking Player: *Johnny Bench.*

Ugliest Players: *Ernie Lombardi, Hans Lobert* and *George Foster.*

Best Nickname: *Ernie "The Schnozz" Lombardi.*

Best Genes: *The Reds of the early 1970s.* Seven Reds from the early '70s fathered major league ballplayers—Pedro Borbon Sr., Ken Griffey Sr., Julian Javier, Hal McRae, Tony Perez, Pete Rose and Ed Sprague Sr.

Most Unappreciated Player: *Bob Bescher.* It was Bescher's NL single-season stolen-base record that Maury Wills broke in 1962. Bescher spent five years as the Reds' leadoff man and center fielder from 1909 to 1913. He led the NL in stolen bases during four of those years, and led the league in runs once and walks once. He finished fifth in the NL Chalmers Award balloting in 1912, but is virtually forgotten today. Even the Reds' 1998 media guide misspells his name.

Most Overrated Player: *Dan Driessen.* He batted .301 as a rookie and finished third in the NL Rookie of the Year balloting in 1973. After the 1976 season, the Reds traded first baseman Tony Perez and gave his job to Driessen. Driessen responded to the challenge by batting .300 with 17 homers and 91 RBI. That performance enabled him to keep the first-base job for another six years, though he never matched those totals again.

Most Admirable Star: *Tony Perez.* On a team loaded with stars, Perez never sought the spotlight or showed an ounce of jealousy. His quiet leadership had a lot to do with keeping the club's strong personalities working as a team.

Least Admirable Stars: *Pete Rose, Rob Dibble.* Rose's transgressions have been well-chronicled. Dibble's notable achievements included a clubhouse wrestling match with manager Lou Piniella that was captured on camera. On one occasion he fielded a bunt from Doug Dascenzo and, realizing that Dascenzo was going to beat it out, fired the ball into the back of Dascenzo's thigh, apparently intentionally. He was suspended twice in one season in two different years, and totaled six suspensions during his major league career.

Best Season, Player: *Joe Morgan, 1976.* Others have put up more impressive Triple Crown stats, but Morgan led the league in both on-base percentage and slugging percentage while stealing 60 bases, playing Gold Glove defense and finishing in the top five in all three Triple Crown categories. Honorable mention goes to George Foster, 1977 (.320-52-149); Johnny Bench, 1970 (.293-45-148); Cy Seymour, 1905 (.377-8-121); Frank Robinson, 1962 (.342-39-126); and Ted Kluszewski, 1954 (.326-49-141).

Best Season, Pitcher: *Dolf Luque, 1923.* Luque led the Senior Circuit in wins (27), winning percentage (.771) and ERA (1.93). His ERA was less than half of the league average. Honorable mention goes to Bucky Walters, 1939 (27-11, 2.29) and Ewell Blackwell, 1947 (22-8, 2.47).

Most Impressive Individual Record: *Johnny Vander Meer.* His consecutive no-hitters are a feat that may never be matched, much less exceeded.

Biggest Tragedies: *Willard Hershberger, Jake Daubert, Fred Hutchinson* Hershberger committed suicide during the 1940 pennant race, for reasons that may never be fully known. Daubert died of complications following an appendectomy in 1924. Hutchinson battled cancer before stepping down as Reds' manager in August 1964. He died three months later.

Fan Favorite: *Pete Rose,* but to a lesser extent after 1989.

—Mat Olkin

Colorado Rockies (1993-1997)

Year	Lg	Pos	W-L	Pct	GB	Manager	Att.	R	OR	HR	Avg	OBP	Slg	Opponent HR	Opponent Avg	Opponent OBP	ERA	Park Index Runs	Park Index HR
1993	NL	6th-W	67-95	.414	37.0	Don Baylor	4,483,350	758	967	142	.273	.323	.422	181	.294	.362	5.41	152	132
1994	NL	3rd-W	53-64	.453	6.5	Don Baylor	3,281,511	573	638	125	.274	.337	.439	120	.292	.366	5.15	132	101
1995	NL	2nd-W	77-67	.535	1.0	Don Baylor	3,390,037	785	783	200	.282	.350	.471	160	.286	.355	4.97	164	203
1996	NL	3rd-W	83-79	.512	8.0	Don Baylor	3,891,014	961	964	221	.287	.355	.472	198	.285	.362	5.59	172	183
1997	NL	3rd-W	83-79	.512	7.0	Don Baylor	3,696,184	923	908	239	.288	.357	.478	196	.300	.367	5.25	133	129

Team Nicknames: Colorado Rockies 1993-1997.

Team Ballparks: Mile High Stadium 1993-1994, Coors Field 1995-1997.

Colorado Rockies Individual Season Batting Leaders

Year	Batting Average		On-Base Percentage		Slugging Percentage		Home Runs		RBI		Stolen Bases	
1993	Andres Galarraga	.370	Andres Galarraga	.403	Andres Galarraga	.602	Charlie Hayes	25	Andres Galarraga	98	Eric Young	42
									Charlie Hayes			
1994	Andres Galarraga	.319	Andres Galarraga	.356	Andres Galarraga	.592	Andres Galarraga	31	Dante Bichette	95	Dante Bichette	21
1995	Dante Bichette	.340	Walt Weiss	.403	Dante Bichette	.620	Dante Bichette	40	Dante Bichette	128	Eric Young	35
1996	Ellis Burks	.344	Ellis Burks	.408	Ellis Burks	.639	Andres Galarraga	47	Andres Galarraga	150	Eric Young	53
1997	Larry Walker	.366	Larry Walker	.452	Larry Walker	.720	Larry Walker	49	Andres Galarraga	140	Larry Walker	33

Colorado Rockies Individual Season Pitching Leaders

Year	ERA		Baserunners/9 IP		Innings Pitched		Strikeouts		Wins		Saves	
1993	Armando Reynoso	4.00	Armando Reynoso	13.2	Armando Reynoso	189.0	Bruce Ruffin	126	Armando Reynoso	12	Darren Holmes	25
1994	Dave Nied	4.80	Dave Nied	13.9	Greg Harris	130.0	Greg Harris	82	Marvin Freeman	10	Bruce Ruffin	16
1995	Kevin Ritz	4.21	Kevin Ritz	12.6	Kevin Ritz	173.1	Kevin Ritz	120	Kevin Ritz	11	Darren Holmes	14
1996	Armando Reynoso	4.96	Armando Reynoso	13.5	Kevin Ritz	213.0	Kevin Ritz	105	Kevin Ritz	17	Bruce Ruffin	24
1997	Roger Bailey	4.29	John Thomson	13.5	Roger Bailey	191.0	John Thomson	106	Roger Bailey	9	Jerry Dipoto	16
									Darren Holmes			

Rockies Franchise Batting Leaders—Career

Games

1	Dante Bichette	706
2	Andres Galarraga	679
3	Vinny Castilla	615
4	Eric Young	613
5	Walt Weiss	523
6	Ellis Burks	420
7	John VanderWal	376
8	Larry Walker	367
9	Steve Reed	329
10	Joe Girardi	304
11	Quinton McCracken	274
12	Charlie Hayes	270
13	Jason Bates	266
14	Darren Holmes	263
15	Mike Munoz	260
16	Bruce Ruffin	246
17	Curt Leskanic	227
18	Mike Kingery	224
19	Jeff Reed	206
20	Jerald Clark	140

At-Bats

1	Dante Bichette	2,795
2	Andres Galarraga	2,667
3	Vinny Castilla	2,235
4	Eric Young	2,120
5	Walt Weiss	1,760
6	Ellis Burks	1,464
7	Larry Walker	1,334
8	Joe Girardi	1,102
9	Charlie Hayes	996
10	Mike Kingery	651
11	Quinton McCracken	609
12	Jason Bates	603
13	Jeff Reed	597
14	Jerald Clark	478
15	John VanderWal	454
16	Nelson Liriano	406
17	Roberto Mejia	397
18	Neifi Perez	358
19	Alex Cole	348
20	Kirt Manwaring	337

Runs

1	Andres Galarraga	476
2	Dante Bichette	464
3	Eric Young	378
4	Vinny Castilla	325
5	Ellis Burks	307
6	Larry Walker	297
7	Walt Weiss	264
8	Joe Girardi	145
9	Charlie Hayes	135
10	Mike Kingery	122
11	Quinton McCracken	119
12	Jason Bates	78
13	Jeff Reed	77
14	Nelson Liriano	67
15	Jerald Clark	65
16	Jayhawk Owens	54
	John VanderWal	54
18	Alex Cole	50
	Neifi Perez	50
20	Roberto Mejia	47

Hits

1	Dante Bichette	882
2	Andres Galarraga	843
3	Vinny Castilla	669
4	Eric Young	626
5	Walt Weiss	469
6	Ellis Burks	456
7	Larry Walker	434
8	Joe Girardi	302
9	Charlie Hayes	297
10	Mike Kingery	199
11	Quinton McCracken	177
12	Jeff Reed	173
13	Jason Bates	148
14	Jerald Clark	135
15	John VanderWal	116
16	Nelson Liriano	111
17	Neifi Perez	98
18	Alex Cole	89
	Roberto Mejia	89
20	Danny Sheaffer	84

Doubles

1	Dante Bichette	184
2	Andres Galarraga	155
3	Vinny Castilla	113
4	Eric Young	102
5	Larry Walker	95
6	Ellis Burks	82
7	Walt Weiss	71
8	Charlie Hayes	68
9	Mike Kingery	45
10	Joe Girardi	40
11	Jason Bates	35
12	Jeff Reed	30
13	Jerald Clark	26
14	Quinton McCracken	24
15	Nelson Liriano	23
	Roberto Mejia	23
17	John VanderWal	19
18	Jayhawk Owens	16
19	Daryl Boston	15
	Neifi Perez	15

Triples

1	Eric Young	28
2	Ellis Burks	19
3	Dante Bichette	14
	Walt Weiss	14
5	Andres Galarraga	13
	Larry Walker	13
7	Vinny Castilla	12
	Mike Kingery	12
9	Joe Girardi	11
10	Neifi Perez	10
11	Nelson Liriano	8
12	Quinton McCracken	7
13	Charlie Hayes	6
	Jerald Clark	6
	Roberto Mejia	6
16	Chris Jones	5
	Jason Bates	5
18	Alex Cole	4
	John VanderWal	4
	Kirt Manwaring	4

Home Runs

1	Andres Galarraga	172
2	Dante Bichette	145
3	Vinny Castilla	124
4	Larry Walker	103
5	Ellis Burks	99
6	Charlie Hayes	35
7	Eric Young	30
8	Jeff Reed	25
9	John VanderWal	16
10	Joe Girardi	15
11	Daryl Boston	14
	Walt Weiss	14
13	Jerald Clark	13
14	Mike Kingery	12
	Jason Bates	12
16	Jayhawk Owens	11
17	Roberto Mejia	10
	Howard Johnson	10
19	Chris Jones	6
	Quinton McCracken	6

RBI

1	Andres Galarraga	579
2	Dante Bichette	571
3	Vinny Castilla	364
4	Larry Walker	289
5	Ellis Burks	283
6	Eric Young	227
7	Charlie Hayes	148
8	Walt Weiss	143
9	Joe Girardi	120
10	Jeff Reed	84
11	Mike Kingery	78
	John VanderWal	78
13	Quinton McCracken	76
14	Jerald Clark	67
15	Jason Bates	66
16	Nelson Liriano	46
17	Danny Sheaffer	44
18	Daryl Boston	40
	Howard Johnson	40
20	Roberto Mejia	38

Walks

1	Walt Weiss	300
2	Eric Young	254
3	Andres Galarraga	169
4	Ellis Burks	163
5	Larry Walker	147
6	Dante Bichette	144
7	Vinny Castilla	129
8	Jason Bates	80
9	Charlie Hayes	79
10	Jeff Reed	78
11	Mike Kingery	75
12	Joe Girardi	74
	Quinton McCracken	74
14	John VanderWal	61
15	Nelson Liriano	60
16	Alex Cole	43
17	Howard Johnson	39
18	Jayhawk Owens	38
19	Kirt Manwaring	30
20	Roberto Mejia	28

Strikeouts

1	Andres Galarraga	610
2	Dante Bichette	460
3	Vinny Castilla	351
4	Ellis Burks	300
5	Walt Weiss	249
6	Larry Walker	220
7	Joe Girardi	165
8	Eric Young	155
9	Charlie Hayes	153
10	Jason Bates	131
11	John VanderWal	125
	Quinton McCracken	125
13	Jeff Reed	120
14	Roberto Mejia	113
15	Jayhawk Owens	104
16	Kirt Manwaring	78
17	Kevin Ritz	76
18	Howard Johnson	73
19	Nelson Liriano	66
	Mike Kingery	66

Stolen Bases

1	Eric Young	180
2	Dante Bichette	85
3	Larry Walker	67
4	Andres Galarraga	55
5	Ellis Burks	49
6	Quinton McCracken	45
7	Walt Weiss	42
8	Alex Cole	30
9	Mike Kingery	18
10	Vinny Castilla	15
11	Charlie Hayes	14
12	Joe Girardi	12
13	Howard Johnson	11
14	Jerald Clark	9
	Chris Jones	9
16	Roberto Mejia	7
17	Nelson Liriano	6
	John VanderWal	6
	Neifi Perez	6
20	Four tied at	5

Runs Created

1	Andres Galarraga	548
2	Dante Bichette	516
3	Vinny Castilla	360
4	Eric Young	339
5	Larry Walker	308
6	Ellis Burks	301
7	Walt Weiss	233
8	Charlie Hayes	162
9	Joe Girardi	134
10	Mike Kingery	103
11	Jeff Reed	100
12	Quinton McCracken	96
13	Jason Bates	83
14	John VanderWal	76
15	Jerald Clark	71
16	Nelson Liriano	59
17	Alex Cole	43
	Neifi Perez	43
19	Jayhawk Owens	42
20	Howard Johnson	39

Runs Created/27 Outs

(minimum 500 Plate Appearances)

1	Larry Walker	8.66
2	Andres Galarraga	7.66
3	Ellis Burks	7.56
4	Dante Bichette	6.77
5	Jeff Reed	5.90
6	Vinny Castilla	5.79
7	Charlie Hayes	5.78
8	John VanderWal	5.77
9	Mike Kingery	5.58
10	Eric Young	5.57
11	Quinton McCracken	5.40
12	Jerald Clark	5.25
13	Jason Bates	4.66
14	Walt Weiss	4.57
15	Joe Girardi	4.11

Batting Average

(minimum 500 Plate Appearances)

1	Larry Walker	.325
2	Andres Galarraga	.316
3	Dante Bichette	.316
4	Ellis Burks	.311
5	Mike Kingery	.306
6	Vinny Castilla	.299
7	Charlie Hayes	.298
8	Eric Young	.295
9	Quinton McCracken	.291
10	Jeff Reed	.290
11	Jerald Clark	.282
12	Joe Girardi	.274
13	Walt Weiss	.266
14	John VanderWal	.256
15	Jason Bates	.245

On-Base Percentage

(minimum 500 Plate Appearances)

1	Larry Walker	.404
2	Ellis Burks	.383
3	Eric Young	.378
4	Walt Weiss	.375
5	Mike Kingery	.374
6	Jeff Reed	.374
7	Quinton McCracken	.368
8	Andres Galarraga	.367
9	Charlie Hayes	.352
10	Dante Bichette	.350
11	John VanderWal	.342
12	Jason Bates	.340
13	Vinny Castilla	.340
14	Jerald Clark	.324
15	Joe Girardi	.323

Slugging Percentage

(minimum 500 Plate Appearances)

1	Larry Walker	.648
2	Ellis Burks	.596
3	Andres Galarraga	.577
4	Dante Bichette	.547
5	Vinny Castilla	.527
6	Charlie Hayes	.484
7	Jeff Reed	.469
8	Mike Kingery	.467
9	Jerald Clark	.444
10	John VanderWal	.421
11	Eric Young	.412
12	Quinton McCracken	.383
13	Jason Bates	.380
14	Joe Girardi	.371
15	Walt Weiss	.347

Rockies Franchise Pitching Leaders—Career

Wins

1	Kevin Ritz	39
2	Armando Reynoso	30
3	Steve Reed	25
4	Darren Holmes	23
5	Marvin Freeman	20
6	Curt Leskanic	19
7	Roger Bailey	18
8	Bruce Ruffin	17
9	Mark Thompson	15
10	Dave Nied	14
	Bill Swift	14
12	Mike Munoz	13
	Lance Painter	13
14	Jamey Wright	12
15	Bryan Rekar	7
	John Thomson	7
17	Willie Blair	6
	Kent Bottenfield	6
	Frank Castillo	6
20	Eight tied at	5

Losses

1	Kevin Ritz	36
2	Armando Reynoso	31
3	Greg Harris	20
4	Roger Bailey	19
5	Bruce Ruffin	18
	Steve Reed	18
	Dave Nied	18
	Marvin Freeman	18
	Mark Thompson	18
10	Jamey Wright	16
11	Willie Blair	15
12	Curt Leskanic	14
13	Darren Holmes	13
14	Mike Munoz	12
15	Lance Painter	10
	Bill Swift	10
	Bryan Rekar	10
18	John Thomson	9
19	Butch Henry	8
20	Eight tied at	6

Winning Percentage
(minimum 30 decisions)

1	Darren Holmes	.639
2	Steve Reed	.581
3	Curt Leskanic	.576
4	Marvin Freeman	.526
5	Kevin Ritz	.520
6	Armando Reynoso	.492
7	Roger Bailey	.486
8	Bruce Ruffin	.486
9	Mark Thompson	.455
10	Dave Nied	.438

Games

1	Steve Reed	329
2	Darren Holmes	263
3	Mike Munoz	260
4	Bruce Ruffin	246
5	Curt Leskanic	227
6	Kevin Ritz	99
7	Willie Blair	93
8	Lance Painter	92
	Roger Bailey	92
10	Armando Reynoso	89
11	Jerry Dipoto	74
12	Marvin Freeman	67
13	Gary Wayne	65
14	Mark Thompson	63
15	Marcus Moore	56
16	Mike DeJean	55
17	Dave Nied	46
18	Greg Harris	42
	Jamey Wright	42
20	Four tied at	40

Games Started

1	Kevin Ritz	96
2	Armando Reynoso	87
3	Marvin Freeman	59
4	Roger Bailey	46
5	Mark Thompson	41
	Jamey Wright	41
7	Dave Nied	39
8	Bill Swift	35
9	Greg Harris	32
10	Bryan Rekar	27
	John Thomson	27
12	Lance Painter	22
13	Willie Blair	19
14	Butch Henry	15
	Kent Bottenfield	15
16	Frank Castillo	14
17	Mike Harkey	13
18	Bruce Ruffin	12
19	Curt Leskanic	11
	Juan Acevedo	11

Complete Games

1	Armando Reynoso	5
	Roger Bailey	5
3	Dave Nied	3
	Kevin Ritz	3
	Mark Thompson	3
6	John Thomson	2
7	Greg Harris	1
	Willie Blair	1
	Butch Henry	1
	Kent Bottenfield	1
	Lance Painter	1
	Bryan Rekar	1
	Jamey Wright	1

Shutouts

1	Roger Bailey	2
2	Dave Nied	1
	Mark Thompson	1
	John Thomson	1

Saves

1	Bruce Ruffin	60
2	Darren Holmes	46
3	Curt Leskanic	18
4	Jerry Dipoto	16
5	Steve Reed	15
6	Mike Munoz	5
7	Willie Blair	3
8	Kevin Ritz	2
	Bill Swift	2
	Mike DeJean	2
11	Mark Grant	1
	Jeff Parrett	1
	Greg Harris	1
	Gary Wayne	1
	Andy Ashby	1
	Kent Bottenfield	1
	Keith Shepherd	1
	Lance Painter	1
	Roger Bailey	1

Innings Pitched

1	Kevin Ritz	567.1
2	Armando Reynoso	503.0
3	Steve Reed	369.2
4	Roger Bailey	356.0
5	Marvin Freeman	337.0
6	Darren Holmes	328.0
7	Bruce Ruffin	321.0
8	Curt Leskanic	309.1
9	Mark Thompson	259.1
10	Jamey Wright	241.0
11	Willie Blair	223.2
12	Dave Nied	218.2
13	Lance Painter	208.2
14	Greg Harris	203.1
15	Mike Munoz	197.2
16	Bill Swift	189.1
17	John Thomson	166.1
18	Bryan Rekar	152.2
19	Kent Bottenfield	101.1
20	Jerry Dipoto	95.2

Walks

1	Kevin Ritz	251
2	Armando Reynoso	170
3	Bruce Ruffin	165
4	Roger Bailey	161
5	Darren Holmes	136
6	Curt Leskanic	132
7	Steve Reed	123
8	Marvin Freeman	121
9	Mark Thompson	117
10	Jamey Wright	112
11	Dave Nied	100
12	Mike Munoz	96
13	Greg Harris	82
14	Willie Blair	81
15	Bill Swift	74
16	Lance Painter	70
17	Bryan Rekar	56
18	John Thomson	51
19	Kent Bottenfield	48
20	Jeff Parrett	45

Strikeouts

1	Kevin Ritz	334
2	Bruce Ruffin	319
3	Darren Holmes	297
4	Curt Leskanic	283
5	Steve Reed	275
6	Armando Reynoso	270
7	Marvin Freeman	199
8	Roger Bailey	162
9	Mike Munoz	156
10	Willie Blair	152
11	Mark Thompson	143
12	Lance Painter	141
13	Dave Nied	127
14	Greg Harris	122
15	John Thomson	106
16	Jamey Wright	104
17	Bill Swift	102
18	Bryan Rekar	89
19	Jerry Dipoto	74
20	Jeff Parrett	66

Strikeouts/9 Innings
(minimum 300 Innings Pitched)

1	Bruce Ruffin	8.94
2	Curt Leskanic	8.23
3	Darren Holmes	8.15
4	Steve Reed	6.70
5	Marvin Freeman	5.31
6	Kevin Ritz	5.30
7	Armando Reynoso	4.83
8	Roger Bailey	4.10

ERA
(minimum 300 Innings Pitched)

1	Steve Reed	3.68
2	Bruce Ruffin	3.84
3	Darren Holmes	4.42
4	Armando Reynoso	4.65
5	Roger Bailey	4.90
6	Marvin Freeman	4.91
7	Curt Leskanic	5.00
8	Kevin Ritz	5.11

Component ERA
(minimum 300 Innings Pitched)

1	Steve Reed	3.78
2	Bruce Ruffin	3.91
3	Curt Leskanic	4.34
4	Darren Holmes	4.36
5	Armando Reynoso	5.09
6	Marvin Freeman	5.18
7	Kevin Ritz	5.19
8	Roger Bailey	5.24

Opponent Average
(minimum 300 Innings Pitched)

1	Steve Reed	.245
2	Bruce Ruffin	.246
3	Curt Leskanic	.262
4	Darren Holmes	.268
5	Roger Bailey	.284
6	Kevin Ritz	.287
7	Armando Reynoso	.289
8	Marvin Freeman	.290

Opponent OBP
(minimum 300 Innings Pitched)

1	Steve Reed	.313
2	Bruce Ruffin	.335
3	Curt Leskanic	.335
4	Darren Holmes	.339
5	Armando Reynoso	.352
6	Marvin Freeman	.354
7	Roger Bailey	.363
8	Kevin Ritz	.364

Teams: Rockies

Rockies Franchise Batting Leaders—Single Season

Games

1	Vinny Castilla	1996	160
2	Andres Galarraga	1996	159
	Dante Bichette	1996	159
	Vinny Castilla	1997	159
5	Charlie Hayes	1993	157
6	Ellis Burks	1996	156
7	Walt Weiss	1996	155
8	Andres Galarraga	1997	154
9	Larry Walker	1997	153
10	Dante Bichette	1997	151
11	Quinton McCracken	1997	147
12	Eric Young	1993	144
13	Andres Galarraga	1995	143
14	Dante Bichette	1993	141
	Eric Young	1996	141
16	Jerald Clark	1993	140
17	Dante Bichette	1995	139
	Vinny Castilla	1995	139
19	Walt Weiss	1995	137
20	Larry Walker	1995	131

At-Bats

1	Dante Bichette	1996	633
2	Vinny Castilla	1996	629
3	Andres Galarraga	1996	626
4	Ellis Burks	1996	613
5	Vinny Castilla	1997	612
6	Andres Galarraga	1997	600
7	Dante Bichette	1995	579
8	Charlie Hayes	1993	573
9	Eric Young	1996	568
	Larry Walker	1997	568
11	Dante Bichette	1997	561
12	Andres Galarraga	1995	554
13	Dante Bichette	1993	538
14	Vinny Castilla	1995	527
15	Walt Weiss	1996	517
16	Larry Walker	1995	494
17	Eric Young	1993	490
18	Dante Bichette	1994	484
19	Jerald Clark	1993	478
20	Andres Galarraga	1993	470

Runs

1	Larry Walker	1997	143
2	Ellis Burks	1996	142
3	Andres Galarraga	1997	120
4	Andres Galarraga	1996	119
5	Dante Bichette	1996	114
6	Eric Young	1996	113
7	Dante Bichette	1995	102
8	Vinny Castilla	1996	97
9	Larry Walker	1995	96
10	Vinny Castilla	1997	94
11	Dante Bichette	1993	93
12	Ellis Burks	1997	91
13	Charlie Hayes	1993	89
	Andres Galarraga	1995	89
	Walt Weiss	1996	89
16	Eric Young	1993	82
	Vinny Castilla	1995	82
18	Dante Bichette	1997	81
19	Eric Young	1997	78
20	Andres Galarraga	1994	77

Hits

1	Ellis Burks	1996	211
2	Larry Walker	1997	208
3	Dante Bichette	1996	198
4	Dante Bichette	1995	197
5	Vinny Castilla	1996	191
	Andres Galarraga	1997	191
7	Andres Galarraga	1996	190
8	Vinny Castilla	1997	186
9	Eric Young	1996	184
10	Charlie Hayes	1993	175
11	Andres Galarraga	1993	174
12	Dante Bichette	1997	173
13	Dante Bichette	1993	167
14	Vinny Castilla	1995	163
15	Andres Galarraga	1995	155
16	Larry Walker	1995	151
17	Dante Bichette	1994	147
18	Walt Weiss	1996	146
19	Jerald Clark	1993	135
20	Andres Galarraga	1994	133

Doubles

1	Larry Walker	1997	46
2	Charlie Hayes	1993	45
	Ellis Burks	1996	45
4	Dante Bichette	1993	43
5	Andres Galarraga	1996	39
	Dante Bichette	1996	39
7	Dante Bichette	1995	38
8	Andres Galarraga	1993	35
9	Vinny Castilla	1995	34
	Vinny Castilla	1996	34
11	Dante Bichette	1994	33
12	Larry Walker	1995	31
	Andres Galarraga	1997	31
	Dante Bichette	1997	31
15	Andres Galarraga	1995	29
	Eric Young	1997	29
17	Mike Kingery	1994	27
18	Jerald Clark	1993	26
19	Vinny Castilla	1997	25
20	Three tied at		23

Triples

1	Neifi Perez	1997	10
2	Eric Young	1995	9
3	Eric Young	1993	8
	Mike Kingery	1994	8
	Ellis Burks	1996	8
6	Vinny Castilla	1993	7
7	Jerald Clark	1993	6
	Ellis Burks	1995	6
	Quinton McCracken	1996	6
	Eric Young	1997	6
11	Dante Bichette	1993	5
	Joe Girardi	1993	5
	Roberto Mejia	1993	5
	Nelson Liriano	1994	5
	Larry Walker	1995	5
	Walt Weiss	1997	5
17	Twelve tied at		4

Home Runs

1	Larry Walker	1997	49
2	Andres Galarraga	1996	47
3	Andres Galarraga	1997	41
4	Dante Bichette	1995	40
	Ellis Burks	1996	40
	Vinny Castilla	1996	40
	Vinny Castilla	1997	40
8	Larry Walker	1995	36
9	Vinny Castilla	1995	32
	Ellis Burks	1997	32
11	Andres Galarraga	1994	31
	Andres Galarraga	1995	31
	Dante Bichette	1996	31
14	Dante Bichette	1994	27
15	Dante Bichette	1997	26
16	Charlie Hayes	1993	25
17	Andres Galarraga	1993	22
18	Dante Bichette	1993	21
19	Larry Walker	1996	18
20	Jeff Reed	1997	17

RBI

1	Andres Galarraga	1996	150
2	Dante Bichette	1996	141
3	Andres Galarraga	1997	140
4	Larry Walker	1997	130
5	Dante Bichette	1995	128
	Ellis Burks	1996	128
7	Dante Bichette	1997	118
8	Vinny Castilla	1996	113
	Vinny Castilla	1997	113
10	Andres Galarraga	1995	106
11	Larry Walker	1995	101
12	Andres Galarraga	1993	98
	Charlie Hayes	1993	98
14	Dante Bichette	1994	95
15	Vinny Castilla	1995	90
16	Dante Bichette	1993	89
17	Andres Galarraga	1994	85
18	Ellis Burks	1997	82
19	Eric Young	1996	74
20	Jerald Clark	1993	67

Walks

1	Walt Weiss	1995	98
2	Walt Weiss	1996	80
3	Larry Walker	1997	78
4	Walt Weiss	1997	66
5	Eric Young	1993	63
6	Ellis Burks	1996	61
7	Eric Young	1997	57
8	Walt Weiss	1994	56
9	Andres Galarraga	1997	54
10	Larry Walker	1995	49
	Eric Young	1995	49
12	Eric Young	1996	47
	Ellis Burks	1997	47
14	Mike Kingery	1995	45
	Dante Bichette	1996	45
16	Vinny Castilla	1997	44
17	Charlie Hayes	1993	43
	Alex Cole	1993	43
	Jeff Reed	1996	43
20	Three tied at		42

Strikeouts

1	Andres Galarraga	1996	157
2	Andres Galarraga	1995	146
3	Andres Galarraga	1997	141
4	Ellis Burks	1996	114
5	Vinny Castilla	1997	108
6	Dante Bichette	1996	105
7	Dante Bichette	1993	99
8	Dante Bichette	1995	96
9	Andres Galarraga	1994	93
10	Dante Bichette	1997	90
	Larry Walker	1997	90
12	Vinny Castilla	1996	88
13	Vinny Castilla	1995	87
14	Charlie Hayes	1993	82
15	Walt Weiss	1996	78
	Kirt Manwaring	1997	78
17	Joe Girardi	1995	76
18	Ellis Burks	1997	75
19	Andres Galarraga	1993	73
	Howard Johnson	1994	73

Stolen Bases

1	Eric Young	1996	53
2	Eric Young	1993	42
3	Eric Young	1995	35
4	Larry Walker	1997	33
5	Ellis Burks	1996	32
	Eric Young	1997	32
7	Dante Bichette	1996	31
8	Alex Cole	1993	30
9	Quinton McCracken	1997	28
10	Dante Bichette	1994	21
11	Eric Young	1994	18
	Andres Galarraga	1996	18
	Larry Walker	1996	18
14	Quinton McCracken	1996	17
15	Larry Walker	1995	16
16	Walt Weiss	1995	15
	Andres Galarraga	1997	15
18	Dante Bichette	1993	14
19	Mike Kingery	1995	13
	Dante Bichette	1995	13

Runs Created

1	Larry Walker	1997	158
2	Andres Galarraga	1996	150
3	Ellis Burks	1996	146
4	Dante Bichette	1996	124
5	Dante Bichette	1995	123
6	Andres Galarraga	1997	118
7	Vinny Castilla	1996	113
	Vinny Castilla	1997	113
9	Andres Galarraga	1993	110
10	Charlie Hayes	1993	103
11	Larry Walker	1995	99
12	Dante Bichette	1993	97
13	Eric Young	1996	95
14	Dante Bichette	1997	94
15	Andres Galarraga	1995	93
16	Vinny Castilla	1995	83
	Ellis Burks	1997	83
18	Dante Bichette	1994	78
19	Andres Galarraga	1994	77
20	Walt Weiss	1996	72

Runs Created/27 Outs

(minimum 3.1 Plate Appearances/Tm Gm)

1	Larry Walker	1997	10.99
2	Andres Galarraga	1993	9.43
3	Ellis Burks	1996	9.14
4	Andres Galarraga	1996	8.86
5	Dante Bichette	1995	8.04
6	Larry Walker	1995	7.36
7	Andres Galarraga	1997	7.29
8	Dante Bichette	1996	7.06
9	Andres Galarraga	1994	6.88
10	Vinny Castilla	1997	6.75
11	Dante Bichette	1993	6.65
12	Vinny Castilla	1996	6.59
13	Charlie Hayes	1993	6.35
14	Eric Young	1996	6.13
15	Dante Bichette	1997	6.13
16	Andres Galarraga	1995	5.99
17	Dante Bichette	1994	5.78
18	Vinny Castilla	1995	5.66
19	Jerald Clark	1993	5.25
20	Charlie Hayes	1994	4.99

Batting Average

(minimum 3.1 Plate Appearances/Tm Gm)

1	Andres Galarraga	1993	.370
2	Larry Walker	1997	.366
3	Ellis Burks	1996	.344
4	Dante Bichette	1995	.340
5	Eric Young	1996	.324
6	Andres Galarraga	1994	.319
7	Andres Galarraga	1997	.318
8	Dante Bichette	1996	.313
9	Dante Bichette	1993	.310
10	Vinny Castilla	1995	.309
11	Dante Bichette	1997	.308
12	Larry Walker	1995	.306
13	Charlie Hayes	1993	.305
14	Vinny Castilla	1997	.304
15	Dante Bichette	1994	.304
16	Vinny Castilla	1996	.304
17	Andres Galarraga	1996	.304
18	Charlie Hayes	1994	.288
19	Jerald Clark	1993	.282
20	Walt Weiss	1996	.282

On-Base Percentage

(minimum 3.1 Plate Appearances/Tm Gm)

1	Larry Walker	1997	.452
2	Ellis Burks	1996	.408
3	Andres Galarraga	1993	.403
4	Walt Weiss	1995	.403
5	Eric Young	1996	.393
6	Andres Galarraga	1997	.389
7	Walt Weiss	1996	.381
8	Larry Walker	1995	.381
9	Dante Bichette	1995	.364
10	Eric Young	1997	.363
11	Dante Bichette	1996	.359
12	Andres Galarraga	1996	.357
13	Andres Galarraga	1994	.356
14	Vinny Castilla	1997	.356
15	Eric Young	1993	.355
16	Charlie Hayes	1993	.355
17	Charlie Hayes	1994	.348
18	Dante Bichette	1993	.348
19	Vinny Castilla	1995	.347
20	Vinny Castilla	1996	.343

Slugging Percentage

(minimum 3.1 Plate Appearances/Tm Gm)

1	Larry Walker	1997	.720
2	Ellis Burks	1996	.639
3	Dante Bichette	1995	.620
4	Larry Walker	1995	.607
5	Andres Galarraga	1993	.602
6	Andres Galarraga	1996	.601
7	Andres Galarraga	1994	.592
8	Andres Galarraga	1997	.585
9	Vinny Castilla	1995	.564
10	Vinny Castilla	1996	.548
11	Dante Bichette	1994	.548
12	Vinny Castilla	1997	.547
13	Dante Bichette	1996	.531
14	Dante Bichette	1993	.526
15	Charlie Hayes	1993	.522
16	Andres Galarraga	1995	.511
17	Dante Bichette	1997	.510
18	Jerald Clark	1993	.444
19	Charlie Hayes	1994	.433
20	Eric Young	1996	.421

Rockies Franchise Pitching Leaders—Single Season

Wins

1	Kevin Ritz	1996	17
2	Armando Reynoso	1993	12
3	Kevin Ritz	1995	11
4	Marvin Freeman	1994	10
5	Steve Reed	1993	9
	Dave Nied	1994	9
	Bill Swift	1995	9
	Mark Thompson	1996	9
	Darren Holmes	1997	9
	Roger Bailey	1997	9
11	Armando Reynoso	1996	8
	Jamey Wright	1997	8
13	Armando Reynoso	1995	7
	Roger Bailey	1995	7
	Bruce Ruffin	1996	7
	Marvin Freeman	1996	7
	Curt Leskanic	1996	7
	John Thomson	1997	7
19	Six tied at		6

Losses

1	Greg Harris	1994	12
	Jamey Wright	1997	12
3	Armando Reynoso	1993	11
	Kevin Ritz	1995	11
	Kevin Ritz	1996	11
	Mark Thompson	1996	11
7	Willie Blair	1993	10
	Roger Bailey	1997	10
9	Dave Nied	1993	9
	Marvin Freeman	1996	9
	Armando Reynoso	1996	9
	John Thomson	1997	9
13	Greg Harris	1993	8
	Butch Henry	1993	8
	Kevin Ritz	1997	8
16	Dave Nied	1994	7
	Marvin Freeman	1995	7
	Armando Reynoso	1995	7
19	Eight tied at		6

Winning Percentage
(minimum 15 decisions)

1	Kevin Ritz	1996	.607
2	Dave Nied	1994	.563
3	Armando Reynoso	1993	.522
4	Kevin Ritz	1995	.500
5	Roger Bailey	1997	.474
6	Armando Reynoso	1996	.471
7	Mark Thompson	1996	.450
8	Marvin Freeman	1996	.438
	John Thomson	1997	.438
10	Jamey Wright	1997	.400
11	Willie Blair	1993	.375
12	Greg Harris	1994	.200

Games

1	Curt Leskanic	1995	76
2	Jerry Dipoto	1997	74
3	Steve Reed	1995	71
	Bruce Ruffin	1996	71
5	Steve Reed	1996	70
	Curt Leskanic	1996	70
7	Darren Holmes	1995	68
8	Gary Wayne	1993	65
9	Steve Reed	1993	64
	Mike Munoz	1995	64
	Mike Munoz	1997	64
12	Steve Reed	1997	63
13	Darren Holmes	1993	62
	Darren Holmes	1996	62
15	Steve Reed	1994	61
16	Bruce Ruffin	1993	59
17	Mike Munoz	1994	57
18	Bruce Ruffin	1994	56
19	Curt Leskanic	1997	55
	Mike DeJean	1997	55

Games Started

1	Kevin Ritz	1996	35
2	Armando Reynoso	1993	30
	Armando Reynoso	1996	30
4	Roger Bailey	1997	29
5	Kevin Ritz	1995	28
	Mark Thompson	1996	28
7	John Thomson	1997	27
8	Jamey Wright	1997	26
9	Marvin Freeman	1996	23
10	Dave Nied	1994	22
11	Greg Harris	1994	19
	Bill Swift	1995	19
13	Willie Blair	1993	18
	Marvin Freeman	1994	18
	Marvin Freeman	1995	18
	Armando Reynoso	1995	18
	Kevin Ritz	1997	18
18	Dave Nied	1993	16
19	Three tied at		15

Complete Games

1	Roger Bailey	1997	5
2	Armando Reynoso	1993	4
3	Mark Thompson	1996	3
4	Dave Nied	1994	2
	Kevin Ritz	1996	2
	John Thomson	1997	2
7	Willie Blair	1993	1
	Butch Henry	1993	1
	Kent Bottenfield	1993	1
	Dave Nied	1993	1
	Lance Painter	1993	1
	Greg Harris	1994	1
	Armando Reynoso	1994	1
	Bryan Rekar	1995	1
	Kevin Ritz	1997	1
	Jamey Wright	1997	1

Shutouts

1	Roger Bailey	1997	2
2	Dave Nied	1994	1
	Mark Thompson	1996	1
	John Thomson	1997	1

Saves

1	Darren Holmes	1993	25
2	Bruce Ruffin	1996	24
3	Bruce Ruffin	1994	16
	Jerry Dipoto	1997	16
5	Darren Holmes	1995	14
6	Bruce Ruffin	1995	11
7	Curt Leskanic	1995	10
8	Bruce Ruffin	1997	7
9	Curt Leskanic	1996	6
	Steve Reed	1997	6
11	Steve Reed	1993	3
	Willie Blair	1994	3
	Darren Holmes	1994	3
	Steve Reed	1994	3
	Steve Reed	1995	3
	Darren Holmes	1997	3
17	Seven tied at		2

Innings Pitched

1	Kevin Ritz	1996	213.0
2	Roger Bailey	1997	191.0
3	Armando Reynoso	1993	189.0
4	Kevin Ritz	1995	173.1
5	Mark Thompson	1996	169.2
6	Armando Reynoso	1996	168.2
7	John Thomson	1997	166.1
8	Jamey Wright	1997	149.2
9	Willie Blair	1993	146.0
10	Bruce Ruffin	1993	139.2
11	Greg Harris	1994	130.0
12	Marvin Freeman	1996	129.2
13	Dave Nied	1994	122.0
14	Marvin Freeman	1994	112.2
15	Kevin Ritz	1997	107.1
16	Bill Swift	1995	105.2
17	Curt Leskanic	1995	98.0
18	Jerry Dipoto	1997	95.2
19	Marvin Freeman	1995	94.2
20	Armando Reynoso	1995	93.0

Walks

1	Kevin Ritz	1996	105
2	Mark Thompson	1996	74
3	Jamey Wright	1997	71
4	Roger Bailey	1997	70
5	Bruce Ruffin	1993	69
6	Kevin Ritz	1995	65
7	Armando Reynoso	1993	63
8	Marvin Freeman	1996	57
9	Greg Harris	1994	52
	Roger Bailey	1996	52
11	John Thomson	1997	51
12	Armando Reynoso	1996	49
13	Dave Nied	1994	47
14	Kevin Ritz	1997	46
15	Jeff Parrett	1993	45
16	Bill Swift	1995	43
17	Willie Blair	1993	42
	Dave Nied	1993	42
19	Marvin Freeman	1995	41
	Jamey Wright	1996	41

Strikeouts

1	Bruce Ruffin	1993	126
2	Kevin Ritz	1995	120
3	Armando Reynoso	1993	117
4	Curt Leskanic	1995	107
5	John Thomson	1997	106
6	Kevin Ritz	1996	105
7	Mark Thompson	1996	99
8	Armando Reynoso	1996	88
9	Willie Blair	1993	84
	Roger Bailey	1997	84
11	Greg Harris	1994	82
12	Steve Reed	1995	79
13	Curt Leskanic	1996	76
14	Dave Nied	1994	74
	Bruce Ruffin	1996	74
	Jerry Dipoto	1997	74
17	Darren Holmes	1996	73
18	Marvin Freeman	1996	71
19	Darren Holmes	1997	70
20	Two tied at		68

Strikeouts/9 Innings
(minimum 1 Inning Pitched/Tm Gm)

1	Kevin Ritz	1995	6.23
2	John Thomson	1997	5.74
3	Greg Harris	1994	5.68
4	Armando Reynoso	1993	5.57
5	Dave Nied	1994	5.46
6	Mark Thompson	1996	5.25
7	Armando Reynoso	1996	4.70
8	Kevin Ritz	1996	4.44
9	Roger Bailey	1997	3.96

ERA
(minimum 1 Inning Pitched/Tm Gm)

1	Armando Reynoso	1993	4.00
2	Kevin Ritz	1995	4.21
3	Roger Bailey	1997	4.29
4	John Thomson	1997	4.71
5	Dave Nied	1994	4.80
6	Armando Reynoso	1996	4.96
7	Kevin Ritz	1996	5.28
8	Mark Thompson	1996	5.30
9	Greg Harris	1994	6.65

Component ERA
(minimum 1 Inning Pitched/Tm Gm)

1	Kevin Ritz	1995	3.98
2	Armando Reynoso	1993	4.55
3	John Thomson	1997	4.74
4	Dave Nied	1994	4.99
5	Roger Bailey	1997	5.16
6	Armando Reynoso	1996	5.26
7	Kevin Ritz	1996	5.40
8	Mark Thompson	1996	5.59
9	Greg Harris	1994	5.79

Opponent Average
(minimum 1 Inning Pitched/Tm Gm)

1	Kevin Ritz	1995	.259
2	Armando Reynoso	1993	.277
3	Kevin Ritz	1996	.282
4	Roger Bailey	1997	.283
5	Mark Thompson	1996	.285
6	Dave Nied	1994	.287
7	Armando Reynoso	1996	.291
8	John Thomson	1997	.296
9	Greg Harris	1994	.300

Opponent OBP
(minimum 1 Inning Pitched/Tm Gm)

1	Kevin Ritz	1995	.329
2	Armando Reynoso	1993	.337
3	Armando Reynoso	1996	.347
4	John Thomson	1997	.351
5	Roger Bailey	1997	.354
6	Dave Nied	1994	.354
7	Greg Harris	1994	.366
8	Mark Thompson	1996	.367
9	Kevin Ritz	1996	.368

Teams: Rockies

1409

Rockies Capsule

Best Season: *1995.* The Rockies reached the postseason in their third year of existence by winning the National League wild card with a 77-67 record. No expansion franchise ever made it into the playoffs more quickly.

Worst Season: *1993.* Their inaugural season was the only one where they were truly out of contention, but it was hardly considered a failure. They won three more games than their expansion mates, the Florida Marlins, and led the majors in attendance by a wide margin.

Best Player: *Larry Walker.* Unlike Dante Bichette, Ellis Burks, Vinny Castilla or Andres Galarraga, Walker joined the Rockies as a bona fide star. His 1997 performance with the Rockies only confirmed that he still was the best hitter of the bunch.

Best Pitcher: *Kevin Ritz.* He had a fine year in 1995, and followed it with a franchise-record 17 victories in '96.

Best Reliever: *Bruce Ruffin.* Honorable mention to Steve Reed, who was more consistent but was used only in middle relief.

Best Defensive Player: *Larry Walker.* Walt Weiss was good, but Colorado's only Gold Glove winner is Walker.

Hall of Famers: Dale Murphy, who has a chance of reaching Cooperstown, played 26 games for the Rockies in 1993.

Franchise All-Star Team:

C	*Jeff Reed*		**LF**	*Dante Bichette*
1B	*Andres Galarraga*		**CF**	*Ellis Burks*
2B	*Eric Young*		**RF**	*Larry Walker*
3B	*Vinny Castilla*		**SP**	*Kevin Ritz*
SS	*Walt Weiss*		**RP**	*Bruce Ruffin*

Biggest Flake: *Curt Leskanic.* He once claimed that he added velocity to his fastball by shaving his arm every few weeks to improve its aerodynamics.

Strangest Career: *Bryan Rekar.* The young righthander pitched in 31 games for the Rockies from 1995 through 1997, and might have been one of the best young pitchers in the league. His record on the road over those three years was 5-5 with a 3.26 ERA in 80 innings. National League pitchers with comparable road ERAs over the same period include Tom Glavine (3.25), Curt Schilling (3.26) and Denny Neagle (3.37). Pitchers with higher road ERAs over the same span include Ramon Martinez (3.71), Ismael Valdes (3.75), Andy Ashby (3.97), Shawn Estes (4.03), Andy Benes (4.06), Hideo Nomo (4.09) and Chan Ho Park (4.43). But while most of those other pitchers enjoyed some sort of home-field advantage, Rekar was victimized by his home park to a staggering extent. In 17 games at Coors Field, he went 2-5 with a 10.16 ERA, allowing 120 hits and 85 runs in only 72.2 innings. Each of the Rockies' young starters has struggled to adjust to pitching at Coors, but none of them have been hurt by the park nearly as badly as Rekar was. His overall record with the Rockies was 7-10, 6.54, and he was selected by the Devil Rays in the 1997 expansion draft when the Rockies left him unprotected.

What Might Have Been: *David Nied.* The Rockies took him with the first overall pick in the expansion draft, and big things were expected of him. The season before, he'd gone 14-9 at Triple-A before posting a 3-0, 1.17 mark in a late-season call-up with the Braves. And the season before that, he posted a combined 15-6 mark at two levels of the minors. He started the first game in Rockies history in 1993, and won three of his first four starts before suffering through a five-game losing streak. Three weeks after a 139-pitch outing, he suffered a slightly torn elbow ligament in an exhibition start and didn't return until September. He rebounded in '94 to post a 9-4 record over his first 17 starts, but got pounded over his final five appearances, going 0-3, 7.06. It turned out to be a sign of things to come, as he suffered an elbow injury the following spring that virtually ended his career.

Best Trade: *Dante Bichette.* Even if he wasn't as good as his numbers, he was a heck of a lot better than Kevin Reimer, whom the Rockies traded to the Brewers for Bichette in 1992.

Worst Trade: *Andy Ashby.* The Rockies sent him to the Padres in July 1993, with catcher Brad Ausmus and middle reliever Doug Bochtler, for a pair of pitchers, Bruce Hurst and Greg Harris. Hurst went 0-1 for the Rockies, and Harris went 4-20.

Best-Looking Player: *Daryl Boston.*

Ugliest Player: *Dante Bichette.*

Best Nickname: *"The Big Cat," Andres Galarraga.*

Most Unappreciated Player: *Vinny Castilla.* He was consistent, durable and productive, but always seemed to be overshadowed by the other big bats in the lineup. He combined good power and defense, and his productivity wasn't entirely a Coors Field illusion. In another park, his all-around performance would have been very comparable to that of Travis Fryman.

Most Overrated Player: *Dante Bichette.* He's gotten more help from his home park than any star in history except Chuck Klein.

Most Admirable Star: *Darryl Kile.* Any pitcher who willingly risks his reputation at Coors Field is worthy of admiration.

Least Admirable Star: *Dante Bichette.* Major league body, Worldwide Wrestling Federation head.

Best Season, Player: *Larry Walker, 1997.* His MVP season was *not* one of the 100 best seasons in history; in fact it wasn't even close. But it was the best one ever put together by a Rockies hitter.

Best Season, Pitcher: *Marvin Freeman, 1994.* How he posted a 2.80 ERA while pitching his home games at Mile High Stadium is an enduring mystery. He would have placed third in the NL in ERA if he'd been able to throw just 4.1 more innings. He didn't allow more than four runs in any of his 18 starts, and he pitched so well in his only two defeats that they easily could have turned out as wins.

Most Impressive Individual Record: *Larry Walker's* 29 road homers in 1997—only two less than George Foster's NL mark.

Biggest Tragedy: *Doug Million.* The Rockies' first-round pick in the 1994 draft never made it to the majors. He died of an asthma attack on September 24, 1997 at age 21.

Fan Favorite: *Dante Bichette.*

—Mat Olkin

Florida Marlins (1993-1997)

Year	Lg	Pos	W-L	Pct	GB	Manager	Att.	R	OR	HR	Avg	OBP	Slg	Opponent HR	Opponent Avg	Opponent OBP	ERA	Park Index Runs	Park Index HR
1993	NL	6th-E	64-98	.395	33.0	Rene Lachemann	3,064,847	581	724	94	.248	.314	.346	135	.261	.334	4.13	105	103
1994	NL	5th-E	51-64	.443	23.5	Rene Lachemann	1,937,467	468	576	94	.266	.330	.396	120	.274	.349	4.50	121	112
1995	NL	4th-E	67-76	.469	22.5	Rene Lachemann	1,700,466	673	673	144	.262	.335	.406	139	.264	.343	4.27	95	84
1996	NL	3rd-E	80-82	.494	16.0	R. Lachemann/C. Rojas/J. Boles	1,746,767	688	703	150	.257	.329	.393	113	.256	.334	3.95	87	80
1997	NL	2nd-E	92-70	.568	9.0	Jim Leyland	2,321,542	740	669	136	.259	.346	.395	131	.250	.334	3.83	94	92

Team Nicknames: Florida Marlins 1993-1997.

Team Ballparks: Joe Robbie Stadium/Pro Player Stadium 1993-1997.

Florida Marlins Individual Season Batting Leaders

Year	Batting Average		On-Base Percentage		Slugging Percentage		Home Runs		RBI		Stolen Bases	
1993	Jeff Conine	.292	Walt Weiss	.367	Orestes Destrade	.406	Orestes Destrade	20	Orestes Destrade	87	Chuck Carr	58
1994	Jeff Conine	.319	Jerry Browne	.392	Gary Sheffield	.584	Gary Sheffield	27	Jeff Conine	82	Chuck Carr	32
1995	Jeff Conine	.302	Quilvio Veras	.384	Jeff Conine	.520	Jeff Conine	25	Jeff Conine	105	Quilvio Veras	56
1996	Gary Sheffield	.314	Gary Sheffield	.465	Gary Sheffield	.624	Gary Sheffield	42	Gary Sheffield	120	Devon White	22
1997	Bobby Bonilla	.297	Gary Sheffield	.424	Moises Alou	.493	Moises Alou	23	Moises Alou	115	Edgar Renteria	32

Florida Marlins Individual Season Pitching Leaders

Year	ERA		Baserunners/9 IP		Innings Pitched		Strikeouts		Wins		Saves	
1993	Charlie Hough	4.27	Charlie Hough	12.4	Charlie Hough	204.1	Charlie Hough	126	Chris Hammond	11	Bryan Harvey	45
1994	Pat Rapp	3.85	Pat Rapp	14.0	Dave Weathers	135.0	Pat Rapp	75	Dave Weathers	8	Robb Nen	15
1995	Pat Rapp	3.44	Chris Hammond	11.9	John Burkett	188.1	John Burkett	126	John Burkett	14	Robb Nen	23
							Chris Hammond		Pat Rapp			
1996	Kevin Brown	1.89	Kevin Brown	9.1	Kevin Brown	233.0	Al Leiter	200	Kevin Brown	17	Robb Nen	35
1997	Kevin Brown	2.69	Alex Fernandez	10.8	Kevin Brown	237.1	Kevin Brown	205	Alex Fernandez	17	Robb Nen	35

Teams: Marlins

Marlins Franchise Batting Leaders—Career

Games

1	Jeff Conine	718
2	Gary Sheffield	518
3	Kurt Abbott	424
4	Alex Arias	423
5	Chuck Carr	353
6	Charles Johnson	345
7	Greg Colbrunn	326
8	Robb Nen	269
9	Edgar Renteria	260
10	Terry Pendleton	244
11	Benito Santiago	240
12	Devon White	220
13	Bret Barberie	206
14	Quilvio Veras	197
15	Orestes Destrade	192
16	Jerry Browne	178
	Jesus Tavarez	178
18	Yorkis Perez	177
19	Walt Weiss	158
20	Bobby Bonilla	153

At-Bats

1	Jeff Conine	2,531
2	Gary Sheffield	1,734
3	Kurt Abbott	1,337
4	Chuck Carr	1,292
5	Greg Colbrunn	1,194
6	Charles Johnson	1,128
7	Edgar Renteria	1,048
8	Terry Pendleton	919
9	Alex Arias	895
10	Devon White	817
11	Benito Santiago	806
12	Bret Barberie	747
13	Orestes Destrade	699
14	Quilvio Veras	693
15	Bobby Bonilla	562
16	Moises Alou	538
17	Jerry Browne	513
18	Walt Weiss	500
19	Dave Magadan	438
20	Luis Castillo	427

Runs

1	Gary Sheffield	344
2	Jeff Conine	337
3	Chuck Carr	190
4	Kurt Abbott	173
5	Edgar Renteria	158
6	Greg Colbrunn	147
7	Quilvio Veras	126
8	Charles Johnson	122
9	Devon White	114
10	Terry Pendleton	100
11	Alex Arias	93
12	Moises Alou	88
13	Bret Barberie	85
14	Benito Santiago	84
15	Bobby Bonilla	77
16	Orestes Destrade	73
17	Jerry Browne	63
18	Luis Castillo	53
19	Dave Magadan	52
20	Walt Weiss	50

Hits

1	Jeff Conine	737
2	Gary Sheffield	501
3	Kurt Abbott	343
4	Greg Colbrunn	339
5	Chuck Carr	331
6	Edgar Renteria	304
7	Charles Johnson	272
8	Terry Pendleton	251
9	Alex Arias	237
10	Bret Barberie	216
	Devon White	216
12	Benito Santiago	200
13	Quilvio Veras	179
14	Orestes Destrade	172
15	Bobby Bonilla	167
16	Moises Alou	157
17	Jerry Browne	144
18	Walt Weiss	133
19	Dave Magadan	123
20	Luis Castillo	106

Doubles

1	Jeff Conine	122
2	Gary Sheffield	87
3	Kurt Abbott	71
4	Chuck Carr	58
	Greg Colbrunn	58
6	Charles Johnson	55
7	Terry Pendleton	52
8	Devon White	50
9	Edgar Renteria	39
	Bobby Bonilla	39
11	Bret Barberie	36
12	Benito Santiago	33
13	Alex Arias	32
14	Moises Alou	29
15	Quilvio Veras	28
16	Orestes Destrade	24
17	Jerry Browne	21
18	Dave Magadan	19
	Jim Eisenreich	19
20	Walt Weiss	14

Triples

1	Kurt Abbott	19
2	Jeff Conine	14
3	Benito Santiago	8
	Quilvio Veras	8
5	Devon White	7
6	Gary Sheffield	6
	Edgar Renteria	6
8	Alex Arias	5
	Moises Alou	5
10	Chuck Carr	4
	Bret Barberie	4
	Jerry Browne	4
13	Orestes Destrade	3
	Bob Natal	3
	Greg Colbrunn	3
	Charles Johnson	3
	Andre Dawson	3
	Bobby Bonilla	3
19	Twenty-two tied at	2

Home Runs

1	Gary Sheffield	116
2	Jeff Conine	98
3	Greg Colbrunn	45
4	Charles Johnson	44
5	Kurt Abbott	40
6	Orestes Destrade	25
7	Benito Santiago	24
8	Devon White	23
	Moises Alou	23
10	Terry Pendleton	21
11	Bobby Bonilla	17
12	Bret Barberie	10
	Andre Dawson	10
14	Alex Arias	9
	Quilvio Veras	9
	Edgar Renteria	9
17	Chuck Carr	8
18	Junior Felix	7
19	Tommy Gregg	6
	Cliff Floyd	6

RBI

1	Jeff Conine	422
2	Gary Sheffield	352
3	Greg Colbrunn	189
4	Kurt Abbott	156
5	Charles Johnson	143
6	Terry Pendleton	136
7	Devon White	118
8	Moises Alou	115
9	Orestes Destrade	102
10	Alex Arias	98
11	Bobby Bonilla	96
12	Benito Santiago	91
	Chuck Carr	91
14	Edgar Renteria	83
15	Bret Barberie	64
16	Andre Dawson	51
17	Jerry Browne	47
18	Dave Magadan	46
	Quilvio Veras	46
20	Walt Weiss	39

Walks

1	Gary Sheffield	398
2	Jeff Conine	277
3	Charles Johnson	147
4	Quilvio Veras	131
5	Chuck Carr	117
6	Kurt Abbott	88
7	Alex Arias	87
8	Dave Magadan	83
9	Walt Weiss	79
10	Edgar Renteria	78
11	Orestes Destrade	77
	Jerry Browne	77
13	Bobby Bonilla	73
14	Devon White	70
	Moises Alou	70
16	Terry Pendleton	64
17	Benito Santiago	62
18	Bret Barberie	56
	Greg Colbrunn	56
20	Luis Castillo	41

Strikeouts

1	Jeff Conine	531
2	Kurt Abbott	375
3	Charles Johnson	275
4	Gary Sheffield	274
5	Chuck Carr	194
6	Edgar Renteria	176
7	Greg Colbrunn	172
8	Devon White	164
9	Orestes Destrade	162
10	Terry Pendleton	159
11	Benito Santiago	145
12	Bret Barberie	123
13	Quilvio Veras	110
14	Luis Castillo	99
15	Alex Arias	97
16	Bobby Bonilla	94
17	Darrell Whitmore	92
18	Moises Alou	85
19	Pat Rapp	82
20	Walt Weiss	73

Stolen Bases

1	Chuck Carr	115
2	Gary Sheffield	70
3	Quilvio Veras	64
4	Edgar Renteria	48
5	Devon White	35
6	Luis Castillo	33
7	Greg Colbrunn	16
8	Kurt Abbott	13
	Jesus Tavarez	13
10	Henry Cotto	11
	Benito Santiago	11
12	Moises Alou	9
13	Jeff Conine	8
14	Walt Weiss	7
15	Greg Briley	6
	Bobby Bonilla	6
	Cliff Floyd	6
18	Carl Everett	5
	John Cangelosi	5
20	Eight tied at	4

Runs Created

1	Gary Sheffield	401
2	Jeff Conine	393
3	Greg Colbrunn	164
	Kurt Abbott	164
5	Chuck Carr	139
6	Charles Johnson	132
7	Terry Pendleton	127
8	Devon White	126
	Edgar Renteria	126
10	Quilvio Veras	101
11	Moises Alou	100
12	Alex Arias	95
13	Bobby Bonilla	93
14	Benito Santiago	90
	Bret Barberie	90
16	Orestes Destrade	87
17	Walt Weiss	66
18	Jerry Browne	65
19	Dave Magadan	59
20	Jesus Tavarez	43

Runs Created/27 Outs

(minimum 500 Plate Appearances)

1	Gary Sheffield	8.20
2	Moises Alou	6.63
3	Bobby Bonilla	5.86
4	Jeff Conine	5.60
5	Devon White	5.32
6	Terry Pendleton	4.92
7	Greg Colbrunn	4.85
8	Quilvio Veras	4.84
9	Dave Magadan	4.78
10	Walt Weiss	4.64
11	Jerry Browne	4.42
12	Bret Barberie	4.37
13	Kurt Abbott	4.23
14	Orestes Destrade	4.22
15	Edgar Renteria	4.15
16	Charles Johnson	3.86
17	Benito Santiago	3.77
18	Alex Arias	3.64
19	Chuck Carr	3.60

Batting Average

(minimum 500 Plate Appearances)

1	Bobby Bonilla	.297
2	Moises Alou	.292
3	Jeff Conine	.291
4	Edgar Renteria	.290
5	Bret Barberie	.289
6	Gary Sheffield	.289
7	Greg Colbrunn	.284
8	Dave Magadan	.281
9	Jerry Browne	.281
10	Terry Pendleton	.273
11	Walt Weiss	.266
12	Alex Arias	.265
13	Devon White	.264
14	Quilvio Veras	.258
15	Kurt Abbott	.257
16	Chuck Carr	.256
17	Benito Santiago	.248
18	Orestes Destrade	.246
19	Charles Johnson	.241

On-Base Percentage

(minimum 500 Plate Appearances)

1	Gary Sheffield	.429
2	Dave Magadan	.393
3	Quilvio Veras	.383
4	Bobby Bonilla	.378
5	Jerry Browne	.376
6	Moises Alou	.373
7	Walt Weiss	.367
8	Jeff Conine	.360
9	Bret Barberie	.350
10	Edgar Renteria	.340
11	Alex Arias	.335
12	Charles Johnson	.331
13	Devon White	.329
14	Greg Colbrunn	.325
15	Orestes Destrade	.322
16	Terry Pendleton	.321
17	Chuck Carr	.320
18	Kurt Abbott	.308
19	Benito Santiago	.304

Slugging Percentage

(minimum 500 Plate Appearances)

1	Gary Sheffield	.547
2	Moises Alou	.493
3	Bobby Bonilla	.468
4	Jeff Conine	.467
5	Greg Colbrunn	.451
6	Kurt Abbott	.428
7	Devon White	.427
8	Charles Johnson	.412
9	Terry Pendleton	.403
10	Benito Santiago	.398
11	Orestes Destrade	.396
12	Bret Barberie	.388
13	Edgar Renteria	.365
14	Quilvio Veras	.361
15	Jerry Browne	.361
16	Dave Magadan	.358
17	Alex Arias	.342
18	Chuck Carr	.326
19	Walt Weiss	.308

Teams: Marlins

Marlins Franchise Pitching Leaders—Career

Wins

1	Pat Rapp	37
2	Kevin Brown	33
3	Chris Hammond	29
4	Al Leiter	27
5	Robb Nen	20
	John Burkett	20
7	Alex Fernandez	17
8	Dave Weathers	16
9	Charlie Hough	14
10	Ryan Bowen	11
	Jay Powell	11
12	Jack Armstrong	9
	Mark Gardner	9
	Livan Hernandez	9
15	Luis Aquino	8
	Terry Mathews	8
	Yorkis Perez	8
	Mark Hutton	8
19	Richie Lewis	7
20	Felix Heredia	6

Losses

1	Pat Rapp	43
2	Chris Hammond	30
3	Charlie Hough	25
4	John Burkett	24
5	Dave Weathers	22
6	Al Leiter	21
7	Kevin Brown	19
8	Jack Armstrong	17
	Ryan Bowen	17
10	Robb Nen	16
11	Alex Fernandez	12
12	Yorkis Perez	10
13	Luis Aquino	9
	Mark Gardner	9
	Terry Mathews	9
16	Richie Lewis	8
17	Kurt Miller	7
	Bobby Witt	7
	Rick Helling	7
20	Tony Saunders	6

Winning Percentage
(minimum 30 decisions)

1	Kevin Brown	.635
2	Al Leiter	.563
3	Robb Nen	.556
4	Chris Hammond	.492
5	Pat Rapp	.463
6	John Burkett	.455
7	Dave Weathers	.421
8	Charlie Hough	.359

Games

1	Robb Nen	269
2	Yorkis Perez	177
3	Jay Powell	150
4	Terry Mathews	138
5	Richie Lewis	123
6	Pat Rapp	117
7	Chris Hammond	108
8	Dave Weathers	97
9	Felix Heredia	77
10	Bryan Harvey	72
11	Luis Aquino	67
12	Kevin Brown	65
13	Al Leiter	60
14	Joe Klink	59
	Mark Gardner	59
	Dennis Cook	59
17	Charlie Hough	55
	Matt Turner	55
19	John Burkett	54
20	Randy Veres	47

Games Started

1	Pat Rapp	115
2	Chris Hammond	78
3	Kevin Brown	65
4	Al Leiter	60
5	Charlie Hough	55
6	John Burkett	54
7	Dave Weathers	53
8	Ryan Bowen	38
9	Jack Armstrong	33
10	Alex Fernandez	32
11	Mark Gardner	25
12	Tony Saunders	21
13	Bobby Witt	19
14	Livan Hernandez	17
15	Luis Aquino	14
16	Rick Helling	12
17	Marc Valdes	11
18	Kurt Miller	9
	Willie Banks	9
	Mark Hutton	9

Complete Games

1	Kevin Brown	11
2	Pat Rapp	7
3	Chris Hammond	5
	John Burkett	5
	Alex Fernandez	5
6	Ryan Bowen	3
7	Al Leiter	2
8	Charlie Hough	1
	Mark Gardner	1
	Bobby Witt	1

Shutouts

1	Kevin Brown	5
2	Pat Rapp	4
3	Chris Hammond	3
4	Charlie Hough	1
	Ryan Bowen	1
	Mark Gardner	1
	Al Leiter	1
	Alex Fernandez	1

Saves

1	Robb Nen	108
2	Bryan Harvey	51
3	Jeremy Hernandez	9
4	Terry Mathews	7
5	Jay Powell	4
6	Trevor Hoffman	2
7	Rich Rodriguez	1
	Mark Gardner	1
	Yorkis Perez	1
	Randy Veres	1
	Ed Vosberg	1
	Robby Stanifer	1

Innings Pitched

1	Pat Rapp	665.2
2	Chris Hammond	506.1
3	Kevin Brown	470.1
4	Al Leiter	366.2
5	Dave Weathers	342.1
	John Burkett	342.1
7	Charlie Hough	318.0
8	Robb Nen	314.0
9	Ryan Bowen	220.2
	Alex Fernandez	220.2
11	Jack Armstrong	196.1
12	Mark Gardner	194.2
13	Terry Mathews	180.2
14	Richie Lewis	167.1
15	Luis Aquino	161.1
16	Jay Powell	159.1
17	Yorkis Perez	135.0
18	Tony Saunders	111.1
19	Bobby Witt	110.2
20	Mark Hutton	104.0

Walks

1	Pat Rapp	326
2	Al Leiter	210
3	Chris Hammond	163
4	Dave Weathers	152
5	Charlie Hough	123
6	Robb Nen	121
7	Ryan Bowen	118
8	John Burkett	99
	Kevin Brown	99
10	Richie Lewis	96
11	Jack Armstrong	78
12	Mark Gardner	73
	Yorkis Perez	73
14	Jay Powell	72
15	Alex Fernandez	69
16	Tony Saunders	64
17	Terry Mathews	63
18	Luis Aquino	62
19	Rick Helling	55
20	Four tied at	47

Strikeouts

1	Pat Rapp	384
2	Kevin Brown	364
3	Al Leiter	332
4	Robb Nen	328
5	Chris Hammond	324
6	John Burkett	234
7	Dave Weathers	206
8	Charlie Hough	191
9	Alex Fernandez	183
10	Ryan Bowen	145
11	Mark Gardner	144
12	Richie Lewis	142
	Terry Mathews	142
14	Yorkis Perez	135
15	Jay Powell	121
16	Jack Armstrong	118
17	Tony Saunders	102
18	Bobby Witt	95
19	Luis Aquino	89
20	Bryan Harvey	83

Strikeouts/9 Innings
(minimum 300 Innings Pitched)

1	Robb Nen	9.40
2	Al Leiter	8.15
3	Kevin Brown	6.97
4	John Burkett	6.15
5	Chris Hammond	5.76
6	Dave Weathers	5.42
7	Charlie Hough	5.41
8	Pat Rapp	5.19

ERA
(minimum 300 Innings Pitched)

1	Kevin Brown	2.30
2	Robb Nen	3.41
3	Al Leiter	3.51
4	Pat Rapp	4.18
5	John Burkett	4.31
6	Chris Hammond	4.46
7	Charlie Hough	4.58
8	Dave Weathers	5.28

Component ERA
(minimum 300 Innings Pitched)

1	Kevin Brown	2.45
2	Robb Nen	3.27
3	Al Leiter	3.61
4	John Burkett	4.12
5	Charlie Hough	4.37
6	Chris Hammond	4.37
7	Pat Rapp	4.72
8	Dave Weathers	5.47

Opponent Average
(minimum 300 Innings Pitched)

1	Al Leiter	.219
2	Kevin Brown	.231
3	Robb Nen	.238
4	Charlie Hough	.265
5	John Burkett	.274
6	Pat Rapp	.277
7	Chris Hammond	.278
8	Dave Weathers	.303

Opponent OBP
(minimum 300 Innings Pitched)

1	Kevin Brown	.283
2	Robb Nen	.308
3	John Burkett	.328
4	Chris Hammond	.335
5	Al Leiter	.335
6	Charlie Hough	.337
7	Pat Rapp	.363
8	Dave Weathers	.377

Marlins Franchise Batting Leaders—Single Season

Games

1	Jeff Conine	1993	162
2	Gary Sheffield	1996	161
3	Walt Weiss	1993	158
4	Jeff Conine	1996	157
5	Edgar Renteria	1997	154
6	Orestes Destrade	1993	153
	Bobby Bonilla	1997	153
8	Jeff Conine	1997	151
9	Moises Alou	1997	150
10	Devon White	1996	146
11	Chuck Carr	1993	142
12	Greg Colbrunn	1996	141
13	Benito Santiago	1993	139
14	Greg Colbrunn	1995	138
15	Gary Sheffield	1997	135
16	Terry Pendleton	1995	133
	Jeff Conine	1995	133
18	Quilvio Veras	1995	124
	Charles Johnson	1997	124
20	Five tied at		120

At-Bats

1	Edgar Renteria	1997	617
2	Jeff Conine	1996	597
3	Jeff Conine	1993	595
4	Orestes Destrade	1993	569
5	Bobby Bonilla	1997	562
6	Devon White	1996	552
7	Chuck Carr	1993	551
8	Moises Alou	1997	538
9	Greg Colbrunn	1995	528
10	Gary Sheffield	1996	519
11	Terry Pendleton	1995	513
12	Greg Colbrunn	1996	511
13	Walt Weiss	1993	500
14	Jeff Conine	1995	483
15	Benito Santiago	1993	469
16	Jeff Conine	1994	451
17	Gary Sheffield	1997	444
18	Quilvio Veras	1995	440
19	Chuck Carr	1994	433
20	Edgar Renteria	1996	431

Runs

1	Gary Sheffield	1996	118
2	Edgar Renteria	1997	90
3	Moises Alou	1997	88
4	Quilvio Veras	1995	86
	Gary Sheffield	1997	86
6	Jeff Conine	1996	84
7	Devon White	1996	77
	Bobby Bonilla	1997	77
9	Chuck Carr	1993	75
	Jeff Conine	1993	75
11	Jeff Conine	1995	72
12	Terry Pendleton	1995	70
	Greg Colbrunn	1995	70
14	Edgar Renteria	1996	68
15	Orestes Destrade	1993	61
	Gary Sheffield	1994	61
	Chuck Carr	1994	61
18	Jeff Conine	1994	60
	Kurt Abbott	1995	60
	Greg Colbrunn	1996	60

Hits

1	Jeff Conine	1996	175
2	Jeff Conine	1993	174
3	Edgar Renteria	1997	171
4	Bobby Bonilla	1997	167
5	Gary Sheffield	1996	163
6	Moises Alou	1997	157
7	Devon White	1996	151
8	Terry Pendleton	1995	149
9	Chuck Carr	1993	147
10	Jeff Conine	1995	146
	Greg Colbrunn	1995	146
	Greg Colbrunn	1996	146
13	Orestes Destrade	1993	145
14	Jeff Conine	1994	144
15	Walt Weiss	1993	133
	Edgar Renteria	1996	133
17	Quilvio Veras	1995	115
18	Chuck Carr	1994	114
19	Bret Barberie	1994	112
20	Gary Sheffield	1997	111

Doubles

1	Bobby Bonilla	1997	39
2	Devon White	1996	37
3	Gary Sheffield	1996	33
4	Terry Pendleton	1995	32
	Jeff Conine	1996	32
6	Moises Alou	1997	29
7	Jeff Conine	1994	27
8	Jeff Conine	1995	26
	Greg Colbrunn	1996	26
	Charles Johnson	1997	26
11	Jeff Conine	1993	24
12	Greg Colbrunn	1995	22
	Gary Sheffield	1997	22
14	Edgar Renteria	1997	21
15	Orestes Destrade	1993	20
	Bret Barberie	1994	20
	Chuck Carr	1995	20
	Quilvio Veras	1995	20
	Terry Pendleton	1996	20
20	Four tied at		19

Triples

1	Kurt Abbott	1995	7
	Quilvio Veras	1995	7
	Kurt Abbott	1996	7
4	Benito Santiago	1993	6
	Jeff Conine	1994	6
	Devon White	1996	6
7	Moises Alou	1997	5
8	Jerry Browne	1994	4
9	Orestes Destrade	1993	3
	Gary Sheffield	1993	3
	Jeff Conine	1993	3
	Kurt Abbott	1994	3
	Andre Dawson	1995	3
	Edgar Renteria	1996	3
	Bobby Bonilla	1997	3
	Edgar Renteria	1997	3
17	Twenty tied at		2

Home Runs

1	Gary Sheffield	1996	42
2	Gary Sheffield	1994	27
3	Jeff Conine	1996	26
4	Jeff Conine	1995	25
5	Greg Colbrunn	1995	23
	Moises Alou	1997	23
7	Gary Sheffield	1997	21
8	Orestes Destrade	1993	20
9	Charles Johnson	1997	19
10	Jeff Conine	1994	18
11	Kurt Abbott	1995	17
	Devon White	1996	17
	Bobby Bonilla	1997	17
	Jeff Conine	1997	17
15	Gary Sheffield	1995	16
	Greg Colbrunn	1996	16
17	Terry Pendleton	1995	14
18	Benito Santiago	1993	13
	Charles Johnson	1996	13
20	Jeff Conine	1993	12

RBI

1	Gary Sheffield	1996	120
2	Moises Alou	1997	115
3	Jeff Conine	1995	105
4	Bobby Bonilla	1997	96
5	Jeff Conine	1996	95
6	Greg Colbrunn	1995	89
7	Orestes Destrade	1993	87
8	Devon White	1996	84
9	Jeff Conine	1994	82
10	Jeff Conine	1993	79
11	Gary Sheffield	1994	78
	Terry Pendleton	1995	78
13	Gary Sheffield	1997	71
14	Greg Colbrunn	1996	69
15	Charles Johnson	1997	63
16	Jeff Conine	1997	61
17	Kurt Abbott	1995	60
18	Terry Pendleton	1996	58
19	Edgar Renteria	1997	52
20	Benito Santiago	1993	50

Walks

1	Gary Sheffield	1996	142
2	Gary Sheffield	1997	121
3	Quilvio Veras	1995	80
4	Walt Weiss	1993	79
5	Bobby Bonilla	1997	73
6	Moises Alou	1997	70
7	Jeff Conine	1995	66
8	Jeff Conine	1996	62
9	Charles Johnson	1997	60
10	Orestes Destrade	1993	58
11	Jeff Conine	1997	57
12	Gary Sheffield	1995	55
13	Jeff Conine	1993	52
	Jerry Browne	1994	52
15	Gary Sheffield	1994	51
	Quilvio Veras	1996	51
17	Chuck Carr	1993	49
18	Chuck Carr	1995	46
	Charles Johnson	1995	46
20	Edgar Renteria	1997	45

Strikeouts

1	Jeff Conine	1993	135
2	Orestes Destrade	1993	130
3	Jeff Conine	1996	121
4	Kurt Abbott	1995	110
5	Charles Johnson	1997	109
6	Edgar Renteria	1997	108
7	Devon White	1996	99
	Kurt Abbott	1996	99
9	Kurt Abbott	1994	98
10	Jeff Conine	1995	94
	Bobby Bonilla	1997	94
12	Jeff Conine	1994	92
13	Charles Johnson	1996	91
14	Jeff Conine	1997	89
15	Benito Santiago	1993	88
16	Moises Alou	1997	85
17	Terry Pendleton	1995	84
18	Gary Sheffield	1997	79
19	Greg Colbrunn	1996	76
20	Terry Pendleton	1996	75

Stolen Bases

1	Chuck Carr	1993	58
2	Quilvio Veras	1995	56
3	Chuck Carr	1994	32
	Edgar Renteria	1997	32
5	Chuck Carr	1995	25
6	Devon White	1996	22
7	Gary Sheffield	1995	19
8	Luis Castillo	1996	17
9	Gary Sheffield	1996	16
	Edgar Renteria	1996	16
	Luis Castillo	1997	16
12	Devon White	1997	13
13	Gary Sheffield	1993	12
	Gary Sheffield	1994	12
15	Henry Cotto	1993	11
	Greg Colbrunn	1995	11
	Gary Sheffield	1997	11
18	Benito Santiago	1993	10
19	Moises Alou	1997	9
20	Quilvio Veras	1996	8

Runs Created

1	Gary Sheffield	1996	145
2	Moises Alou	1997	100
3	Jeff Conine	1995	93
	Bobby Bonilla	1997	93
5	Jeff Conine	1996	90
6	Devon White	1996	88
	Gary Sheffield	1997	88
8	Jeff Conine	1993	87
9	Terry Pendleton	1995	79
10	Greg Colbrunn	1995	77
11	Orestes Destrade	1993	76
12	Jeff Conine	1994	72
13	Gary Sheffield	1994	70
14	Quilvio Veras	1995	69
15	Walt Weiss	1993	66
	Edgar Renteria	1997	66
17	Chuck Carr	1993	61
	Greg Colbrunn	1996	61
19	Edgar Renteria	1996	60
20	Charles Johnson	1997	59

Runs Created/27 Outs

(minimum 3.1 Plate Appearances/Tm Gm)

1	Gary Sheffield	1996	10.13
2	Gary Sheffield	1994	7.43
3	Jeff Conine	1995	6.95
4	Gary Sheffield	1997	6.79
5	Moises Alou	1997	6.63
6	Jeff Conine	1994	6.05
7	Bobby Bonilla	1997	5.86
8	Terry Pendleton	1995	5.67
9	Devon White	1996	5.56
10	Jeff Conine	1996	5.41
11	Jerry Browne	1994	5.35
12	Jeff Conine	1993	5.30
13	Quilvio Veras	1995	5.16
14	Greg Colbrunn	1995	5.16
15	Walt Weiss	1993	4.64
16	Kurt Abbott	1995	4.61
17	Bret Barberie	1994	4.56
18	Orestes Destrade	1993	4.56
19	Benito Santiago	1994	4.39
20	Greg Colbrunn	1996	4.16

Batting Average

(minimum 3.1 Plate Appearances/Tm Gm)

1	Jeff Conine	1994	.319
2	Gary Sheffield	1996	.314
3	Jeff Conine	1995	.302
4	Bret Barberie	1994	.301
5	Bobby Bonilla	1997	.297
6	Jerry Browne	1994	.295
7	Jeff Conine	1996	.293
8	Jeff Conine	1993	.292
9	Moises Alou	1997	.292
10	Terry Pendleton	1995	.290
11	Greg Colbrunn	1996	.286
12	Edgar Renteria	1997	.277
13	Greg Colbrunn	1995	.277
14	Gary Sheffield	1994	.276
15	Devon White	1996	.274
16	Benito Santiago	1994	.273
17	Chuck Carr	1993	.267
18	Walt Weiss	1993	.266
19	Chuck Carr	1994	.263
20	Quilvio Veras	1995	.261

On-Base Percentage

(minimum 3.1 Plate Appearances/Tm Gm)

1	Gary Sheffield	1996	.465
2	Gary Sheffield	1997	.424
3	Jerry Browne	1994	.392
4	Quilvio Veras	1995	.384
5	Gary Sheffield	1994	.380
6	Jeff Conine	1995	.379
7	Bobby Bonilla	1997	.378
8	Moises Alou	1997	.373
9	Jeff Conine	1994	.373
10	Walt Weiss	1993	.367
11	Jeff Conine	1996	.360
12	Bret Barberie	1994	.356
13	Jeff Conine	1993	.351
14	Terry Pendleton	1995	.339
15	Greg Colbrunn	1996	.333
16	Edgar Renteria	1997	.327
17	Chuck Carr	1993	.327
18	Devon White	1996	.325
19	Orestes Destrade	1993	.324
20	Benito Santiago	1994	.322

Slugging Percentage

(minimum 3.1 Plate Appearances/Tm Gm)

1	Gary Sheffield	1996	.624
2	Gary Sheffield	1994	.584
3	Jeff Conine	1994	.525
4	Jeff Conine	1995	.520
5	Moises Alou	1997	.493
6	Jeff Conine	1996	.484
7	Bobby Bonilla	1997	.468
8	Devon White	1996	.455
9	Greg Colbrunn	1995	.453
10	Kurt Abbott	1995	.452
11	Gary Sheffield	1997	.446
12	Terry Pendleton	1995	.439
13	Greg Colbrunn	1996	.438
14	Benito Santiago	1994	.424
15	Orestes Destrade	1993	.406
16	Bret Barberie	1994	.406
17	Jeff Conine	1993	.403
18	Jerry Browne	1994	.398
19	Kurt Abbott	1994	.394
20	Benito Santiago	1993	.380

Marlins Franchise Pitching Leaders—Single Season

Wins

1	Kevin Brown	1996	17
	Alex Fernandez	1997	17
3	Al Leiter	1996	16
	Kevin Brown	1997	16
5	John Burkett	1995	14
	Pat Rapp	1995	14
7	Chris Hammond	1993	11
	Al Leiter	1997	11
9	Charlie Hough	1993	9
	Jack Armstrong	1993	9
	Chris Hammond	1995	9
	Robb Nen	1997	9
	Livan Hernandez	1997	9
14	Ryan Bowen	1993	8
	Dave Weathers	1994	8
	Pat Rapp	1996	8
17	Pat Rapp	1994	7
	Jay Powell	1997	7
19	Three tied at		6

Losses

1	Jack Armstrong	1993	17
2	Charlie Hough	1993	16
	Pat Rapp	1996	16
4	John Burkett	1995	14
5	Chris Hammond	1993	12
	Ryan Bowen	1993	12
	Dave Weathers	1994	12
	Al Leiter	1996	12
	Alex Fernandez	1997	12
10	Kevin Brown	1996	11
11	John Burkett	1996	10
12	Charlie Hough	1994	9
	Al Leiter	1997	9
14	Luis Aquino	1993	8
	Pat Rapp	1994	8
	Chris Hammond	1996	8
	Kevin Brown	1997	8
18	Bobby Witt	1995	7
	Pat Rapp	1995	7
	Robb Nen	1995	7

Winning Percentage
(minimum 15 decisions)

1	Pat Rapp	1995	.667
	Kevin Brown	1997	.667
3	Kevin Brown	1996	.607
4	Chris Hammond	1995	.600
5	Alex Fernandez	1997	.586
6	Al Leiter	1996	.571
7	Al Leiter	1997	.550
8	John Burkett	1995	.500
9	Chris Hammond	1993	.478
10	Pat Rapp	1994	.467
11	Ryan Bowen	1993	.400
	Dave Weathers	1994	.400
13	John Burkett	1996	.375
14	Charlie Hough	1993	.360
15	Jack Armstrong	1993	.346
16	Pat Rapp	1996	.333

Games

1	Robb Nen	1996	75
2	Jay Powell	1997	74
3	Robb Nen	1997	73
4	Yorkis Perez	1995	69
5	Jay Powell	1996	67
6	Yorkis Perez	1996	64
7	Robb Nen	1995	62
8	Joe Klink	1993	59
	Bryan Harvey	1993	59
	Dennis Cook	1997	59
11	Richie Lewis	1993	57
	Terry Mathews	1995	57
	Terry Mathews	1996	57
14	Felix Heredia	1997	56
15	Matt Turner	1993	55
16	Randy Veres	1995	47
17	Richie Lewis	1994	45
18	Yorkis Perez	1994	44
	Robb Nen	1994	44
20	Mark Gardner	1995	39

Games Started

1	Charlie Hough	1993	34
2	Jack Armstrong	1993	33
	Al Leiter	1996	33
	Kevin Brown	1997	33
5	Chris Hammond	1993	32
	Kevin Brown	1996	32
	Alex Fernandez	1997	32
8	John Burkett	1995	30
9	Pat Rapp	1996	29
10	Pat Rapp	1995	28
11	Ryan Bowen	1993	27
	Al Leiter	1997	27
13	Dave Weathers	1994	24
	Chris Hammond	1995	24
	John Burkett	1996	24
16	Pat Rapp	1994	23
17	Charlie Hough	1994	21
	Tony Saunders	1997	21
19	Bobby Witt	1995	19
	Pat Rapp	1997	19

Complete Games

1	Kevin Brown	1997	6
2	Kevin Brown	1996	5
	Alex Fernandez	1997	5
4	John Burkett	1995	4
5	Chris Hammond	1995	3
	Pat Rapp	1995	3
7	Ryan Bowen	1993	2
	Pat Rapp	1994	2
	Al Leiter	1996	2
10	Chris Hammond	1993	1
	Pat Rapp	1993	1
	Charlie Hough	1994	1
	Chris Hammond	1994	1
	Ryan Bowen	1994	1
	Bobby Witt	1995	1
	Mark Gardner	1995	1
	John Burkett	1996	1
	Pat Rapp	1997	1

Shutouts

1	Kevin Brown	1996	3
2	Chris Hammond	1995	2
	Pat Rapp	1995	2
	Kevin Brown	1997	2
5	Ryan Bowen	1993	1
	Charlie Hough	1994	1
	Chris Hammond	1994	1
	Pat Rapp	1994	1
	Mark Gardner	1995	1
	Al Leiter	1996	1
	Alex Fernandez	1997	1
	Pat Rapp	1997	1

Saves

1	Bryan Harvey	1993	45
2	Robb Nen	1996	35
	Robb Nen	1997	35
4	Robb Nen	1995	23
5	Robb Nen	1994	15
6	Jeremy Hernandez	1994	9
7	Bryan Harvey	1994	6
8	Terry Mathews	1996	4
9	Terry Mathews	1995	3
10	Trevor Hoffman	1993	2
	Jay Powell	1996	2
	Jay Powell	1997	2
13	Rich Rodriguez	1993	1
	Mark Gardner	1995	1
	Randy Veres	1995	1
	Yorkis Perez	1995	1
	Ed Vosberg	1997	1
	Robby Stanifer	1997	1

Innings Pitched

1	Kevin Brown	1997	237.1
2	Kevin Brown	1996	233.0
3	Alex Fernandez	1997	220.2
4	Al Leiter	1996	215.1
5	Charlie Hough	1993	204.1
6	Jack Armstrong	1993	196.1
7	Chris Hammond	1993	191.0
8	John Burkett	1995	188.1
9	Pat Rapp	1995	167.1
10	Pat Rapp	1996	162.1
11	Chris Hammond	1995	161.0
12	Ryan Bowen	1993	156.2
13	John Burkett	1996	154.0
14	Al Leiter	1997	151.1
15	Dave Weathers	1994	135.0
16	Pat Rapp	1994	133.1
17	Charlie Hough	1994	113.2
18	Tony Saunders	1997	111.1
19	Luis Aquino	1993	110.2
	Bobby Witt	1995	110.2

Walks

1	Al Leiter	1996	119
2	Pat Rapp	1996	91
	Al Leiter	1997	91
4	Ryan Bowen	1993	87
5	Jack Armstrong	1993	78
6	Pat Rapp	1995	76
7	Charlie Hough	1993	71
8	Pat Rapp	1994	69
	Alex Fernandez	1997	69
10	Chris Hammond	1993	66
	Kevin Brown	1997	66
12	Tony Saunders	1997	64
13	Dave Weathers	1994	59
14	John Burkett	1995	57
15	Charlie Hough	1994	52
	Dave Weathers	1995	52
17	Pat Rapp	1997	51
18	Rick Helling	1997	48
19	Bobby Witt	1995	47
	Chris Hammond	1995	47

Strikeouts

1	Kevin Brown	1997	205
2	Al Leiter	1996	200
3	Alex Fernandez	1997	183
4	Kevin Brown	1996	159
5	Al Leiter	1997	132
6	Charlie Hough	1993	126
	John Burkett	1995	126
	Chris Hammond	1995	126
9	Jack Armstrong	1993	118
10	Chris Hammond	1993	108
	John Burkett	1996	108
12	Pat Rapp	1995	102
	Tony Saunders	1997	102
14	Ryan Bowen	1993	98
15	Bobby Witt	1995	95
16	Robb Nen	1996	92
17	Mark Gardner	1995	87
18	Pat Rapp	1996	86
19	Robb Nen	1997	81
20	Pat Rapp	1994	75

Strikeouts/9 Innings
(minimum 1 Inning Pitched/Tm Gm)

1	Al Leiter	1996	8.36
2	Kevin Brown	1997	7.77
3	Alex Fernandez	1997	7.46
4	Chris Hammond	1995	7.04
5	Kevin Brown	1996	6.14
6	John Burkett	1995	6.02
7	Charlie Hough	1993	5.55
8	Pat Rapp	1995	5.49
9	Jack Armstrong	1993	5.41
10	Chris Hammond	1993	5.09
11	Pat Rapp	1994	5.06
12	Dave Weathers	1994	4.80
13	Pat Rapp	1996	4.77

ERA
(minimum 1 Inning Pitched/Tm Gm)

1	Kevin Brown	1996	1.89
2	Kevin Brown	1997	2.69
3	Al Leiter	1996	2.93
4	Pat Rapp	1995	3.44
5	Alex Fernandez	1997	3.59
6	Chris Hammond	1995	3.80
7	Pat Rapp	1994	3.85
8	Charlie Hough	1993	4.27
9	John Burkett	1995	4.30
10	Jack Armstrong	1993	4.49
11	Chris Hammond	1993	4.66
12	Pat Rapp	1996	5.10
13	Dave Weathers	1994	5.27

Component ERA
(minimum 1 Inning Pitched/Tm Gm)

1	Kevin Brown	1996	2.00
2	Kevin Brown	1997	2.92
3	Al Leiter	1996	3.09
4	Alex Fernandez	1997	3.24
5	Chris Hammond	1995	3.75
6	Pat Rapp	1995	3.90
7	Charlie Hough	1993	3.93
8	Chris Hammond	1993	4.31
9	John Burkett	1995	4.53
10	Pat Rapp	1994	4.73
11	Jack Armstrong	1993	4.82
12	Pat Rapp	1996	5.46
13	Dave Weathers	1994	5.52

Opponent Average
(minimum 1 Inning Pitched/Tm Gm)

1	Al Leiter	1996	.202
2	Kevin Brown	1996	.220
3	Alex Fernandez	1997	.238
4	Kevin Brown	1997	.240
5	Pat Rapp	1995	.253
6	Chris Hammond	1995	.256
7	Charlie Hough	1993	.259
8	Pat Rapp	1994	.266
9	Jack Armstrong	1993	.271
10	Chris Hammond	1993	.277
11	John Burkett	1995	.282
12	Pat Rapp	1996	.301
13	Dave Weathers	1994	.306

Opponent OBP
(minimum 1 Inning Pitched/Tm Gm)

1	Kevin Brown	1996	.262
2	Alex Fernandez	1997	.299
3	Kevin Brown	1997	.303
4	Chris Hammond	1995	.315
5	Al Leiter	1996	.318
6	Charlie Hough	1993	.325
7	Chris Hammond	1993	.336
8	Jack Armstrong	1993	.339
9	John Burkett	1995	.339
10	Pat Rapp	1995	.340
11	Pat Rapp	1994	.361
12	Dave Weathers	1994	.376
13	Pat Rapp	1996	.390

Marlins Capsule

Best Season: *1997.* After gaining entrance to the postseason via the wild-card route, they downed the San Francisco Giants in three straight games before upsetting the Braves in the National League Championship Series. They went on to defeat Cleveland in the World Series with a dramatic extra-inning victory in Game 7.

Worst Season: *1996.* Despite having signed free agents Kevin Brown and Al Leiter, the Marlins dug themselves a deep hole by losing 21 of their first 31 games. Rene Lachemann, the club's first and only manager to that time, was fired on July 7 with the club at 40-47 and 14 games out of first. The Marlins failed to finish above .500 despite getting career years from Brown, Leiter, Gary Sheffield and Robb Nen.

Best Player: *Gary Sheffield,* whenever he was healthy. He batted .292 with 10 homers in 72 games in 1993 after coming over in a midseason trade. The following season, he slugged 27 homers in only 87 games, and the year after that, he hit .324 with 16 homers despite missing more than half of the season with a thumb injury. In 1996, his only healthy, full season with the club, he hit .314 with 42 homers and 120 RBI to finish sixth in the NL MVP balloting. He played through injuries in '97 but still finished fifth in the league in on-base percentage.

Best Pitcher: *Kevin Brown.* He was robbed of the Cy Young Award in '96, and remained highly effective in '97. Poor run support cost him several wins each season, but he still won a total of 33 games in his two years in Florida.

Best Reliever: *Robb Nen.*

Best Defensive Player: *Charles Johnson.* He won the Gold Glove during each of his first three seasons in the majors, and nearly went through the entire 1997 season without committing a passed ball or an error.

Hall of Famers: Andre Dawson is the only man who played for the Marlins in their first five seasons who seems destined for Cooperstown.

Franchise All-Star Team:

C	*Charles Johnson*	LF	*Moises Alou*
1B	*Jeff Conine*	CF	*Devon White*
2B	*Quilvio Veras*	RF	*Gary Sheffield*
3B	*Bobby Bonilla*	SP	*Kevin Brown*
SS	*Edgar Renteria*	RP	*Robb Nen*

Biggest Flakes: *Gregg Zaun.* He is believed to be the first major league player in history to post movie reviews on the Internet.

Strangest Career: *Chris Hammond.* Few pitchers ran hot and cold quite the way Hammond did. In 1993, his first year with the club, he was on a 20-win pace in early July with a 10-4 record and a 3.71 ERA, but went 1-8, 5.87 the rest of the way. The next season, he went 4-3, 1.79 in his first nine starts before straining his lower back. He went 0-1, 7.00 the remainder of the year. In late July 1995, his record stood at 7-3, 2.50, but he went 2-3, 6.19 over the last two months. And in '96, he spent the year pitching his way in and out of the rotation, posting a 3.38 ERA out of the pen and a 10.60 ERA as a starter.

What Might Have Been: *Josh Booty.* He was considered the top high school quarterback in the country in 1994, but the Marlins signed him by offering a record $1.6 million bonus. Booty initially flopped as a baseball player and later asked for his release, but the Marlins insisted that their bonus be returned first. Booty was unable to come up with the cash, so he had no choice but to continue playing the wrong sport.

Best Trade: *Robb Nen.* In mid-1993, they got Nen from the Rangers for a pitcher who never panned out.

Worst Trade: *Danny Jackson.* After selecting Jackson in the expansion draft, the Marlins sent him to Philadelphia for two pitchers who never developed. Jackson pitched well for the next two seasons.

Best-Looking Player: *Darren Daulton,* if only for a few months.

Ugliest Player: *David Weathers.* He won ugly, he lost ugly and he even no-decisioned ugly.

Best Nickname: *"Devo,"* Devon White.

Most Unappreciated Player: *Quilvio Veras.* As a rookie in 1995, he stole 56 bases, led the team in runs scored, and posted the second-best on-base percentage on the team. The following year, hamstring injuries prevented him from stealing bases, and the Marlins shunned him in favor of Luis Castillo. They even shipped Veras to the minors, despite the fact that he still had the second-best on-base percentage on the club. He was traded over the winter, and the second-base job and leadoff spot were given to Castillo, who barely made it past the All-Star break before being shipped back to Triple-A.

Most Overrated Player: *Greg Colbrunn.* His overall numbers looked decent enough, but he was slow, he didn't draw walks and his power was subpar by first basemen's standards.

Most Admirable Star: *Jeff Conine.* He did whatever was asked of him, whether it was learning to play the outfield or accepting a part-time role after succeeding as a regular. Through it all, he remained both positive and productive.

Least Admirable Star: *Gary Sheffield.* Perhaps Sheffield's biggest sin was that he was simply too open with the media, but his Florida career seemed to be littered with an endless stream of complaints, accusations and ultimatums.

Best Season, Player: *Gary Sheffield, 1996.* Hands down.

Best Season, Pitcher: *Kevin Brown, 1996.* Brown lost the Cy Young Award to John Smoltz, but Brown can't be faulted for that. If his teammates hadn't stuck him with the league's worst run support, he easily would have posted a better won-lost record than Smoltz did.

Most Impressive Individual Record: As a 22-year-old rookie in 1997, *Livan Hernandez* set an NLCS record with 15 strikeouts in Game 5.

Biggest Tragedy: The Marlins' first president, *Carl Barger,* collapsed and died at the 1992 Winter Meetings from a ruptured aortic aneurysm. Barger helped to get the franchise up and running, but didn't live to see the Marlins take the field for the first time.

Fan Favorite: *Jeff Conine.*

—Mat Olkin

Houston Astros (1962-1997)

Year	Lg	Pos	W-L	Pct	GB	Manager	Att.	R	OR	HR	Avg	OBP	Slg	Opp HR	Opp Avg	Opp OBP	ERA	Park Runs	Park HR
1962	NL	8th	64-96	.400	36.5	Harry Craft	924,456	592	717	105	.246	.310	.351	113	.259	.319	3.83	87	64
1963	NL	9th	66-96	.407	33.0	Harry Craft	719,502	464	640	62	.220	.283	.301	95	.245	.295	3.44	84	60
1964	NL	9th	66-96	.407	27.0	Harry Craft/Lum Harris	725,773	495	628	70	.229	.285	.315	105	.260	.306	3.41	91	72
1965	NL	9th	65-97	.401	32.0	Lum Harris	2,151,470	569	711	97	.237	.305	.340	123	.260	.310	3.84	79	35
1966	NL	8th	72-90	.444	23.0	Grady Hatton	1,872,108	612	695	112	.255	.318	.365	130	.262	.313	3.76	94	66
1967	NL	9th	69-93	.426	32.5	Grady Hatton	1,348,303	626	742	93	.249	.317	.364	120	.260	.322	4.03	91	42
1968	NL	10th	72-90	.444	25.0	Grady Hatton/Harry Walker	1,312,887	510	588	66	.231	.298	.317	68	.249	.311	3.26	100	63
1969	NL	5th-W	81-81	.500	12.0	Harry Walker	1,442,995	676	668	104	.240	.330	.352	111	.247	.318	3.60	104	72
1970	NL	4th-W	79-83	.488	23.0	Harry Walker	1,253,444	744	763	129	.259	.332	.391	131	.265	.336	4.23	87	79
1971	NL	4th-W	79-83	.488	11.0	Harry Walker	1,261,589	585	567	71	.240	.302	.340	75	.241	.307	3.13	82	45
1972	NL	2nd-W	84-69	.549	10.5	Harry Walker/Salty Parker/Leo Durocher	1,469,247	708	636	134	.258	.326	.393	114	.256	.323	3.77	115	84
1973	NL	4th-W	82-80	.506	17.0	Leo Durocher	1,394,004	681	672	134	.251	.312	.376	111	.252	.323	3.75	89	83
1974	NL	4th-W	81-81	.500	21.0	Preston Gomez	1,090,728	653	632	110	.263	.322	.378	84	.255	.331	3.46	94	92
1975	NL	6th-W	64-97	.398	43.5	Preston Gomez/Bill Virdon	858,002	664	711	84	.254	.320	.359	106	.262	.343	4.04	89	77
1976	NL	3rd-W	80-82	.494	22.0	Bill Virdon	886,146	625	657	66	.256	.322	.347	82	.250	.332	3.56	71	61
1977	NL	3rd-W	81-81	.500	17.0	Bill Virdon	1,109,560	680	650	114	.254	.320	.385	110	.251	.319	3.54	82	48
1978	NL	5th-W	74-88	.457	21.0	Bill Virdon	1,126,145	605	634	70	.258	.313	.355	86	.247	.320	3.63	88	61
1979	NL	2nd-W	89-73	.549	1.5	Bill Virdon	1,900,312	583	582	49	.256	.315	.344	90	.237	.304	3.20	76	49
1980	NL	1st-W	93-70	.571	—	Bill Virdon	2,278,217	637	589	75	.261	.326	.367	69	.246	.305	3.10	92	51
1981	NL	3rd-W	28-29	.491	8.0	Bill Virdon													
	NL	1st-W	33-20	.623	—	Bill Virdon	1,321,282	394	331	45	.257	.318	.356	40	.231	.289	2.66	69	48
1982	NL	5th-W	77-85	.475	12.0	Bill Virdon/Bob Lillis	1,558,555	569	620	74	.247	.302	.349	87	.247	.310	3.42	97	55
1983	NL	3rd-W	85-77	.525	6.0	Bob Lillis	1,351,962	643	646	97	.257	.320	.375	94	.236	.309	3.45	78	38
1984	NL	2nd-W	80-82	.494	12.0	Bob Lillis	1,229,862	693	630	79	.264	.323	.371	91	.248	.311	3.32	83	38
1985	NL	3rd-W	83-79	.512	12.0	Bob Lillis	1,184,314	706	691	121	.261	.319	.388	119	.254	.321	3.67	92	66
1986	NL	1st-W	96-66	.593	—	Hal Lanier	1,734,276	654	569	125	.255	.322	.381	116	.225	.295	3.15	101	77
1987	NL	3rd-W	76-86	.469	14.0	Hal Lanier	1,909,902	648	678	122	.253	.318	.373	141	.250	.317	3.84	83	58
1988	NL	5th-W	82-80	.506	12.5	Hal Lanier	1,933,505	617	631	96	.244	.306	.351	123	.243	.304	3.41	85	61
1989	NL	3rd-W	86-76	.531	6.0	Art Howe	1,834,908	647	669	97	.239	.306	.345	105	.247	.315	3.64	106	82
1990	NL	4th-W	75-87	.463	16.0	Art Howe	1,310,927	573	656	94	.242	.313	.345	130	.255	.318	3.61	86	58
1991	NL	6th-W	65-97	.401	29.0	Art Howe	1,196,152	605	717	79	.244	.309	.347	129	.247	.328	4.00	92	52
1992	NL	4th-W	81-81	.500	17.0	Art Howe	1,211,412	608	668	96	.246	.313	.359	114	.252	.320	3.74	87	75
1993	NL	3rd-W	85-77	.525	19.0	Art Howe	2,084,618	716	630	138	.267	.330	.409	117	.251	.313	3.49	93	86
1994	NL	2nd-C	66-49	.574	0.5	Terry Collins	1,561,136	602	503	120	.278	.347	.445	102	.265	.331	3.97	93	98
1995	NL	2nd-C	76-68	.528	9.0	Terry Collins	1,363,801	747	674	109	.275	.353	.399	118	.266	.331	4.06	77	64
1996	NL	2nd-C	82-80	.506	6.0	Terry Collins	1,975,888	753	792	129	.262	.336	.397	154	.274	.342	4.37	85	77
1997	NL	1st-C	84-78	.519	—	Larry Dierker	2,046,815	777	660	133	.259	.344	.403	134	.252	.319	3.67	87	76

Team Nicknames: Houston Colt .45s 1962-1966, Houston Astros 1967-1997.

Team Ballparks: Colt Stadium 1962-1964, Astrodome 1965-1997.

Houston Astros Individual Season Batting Leaders

Year	Batting Average		On-Base Percentage		Slugging Percentage		Home Runs		RBI		Stolen Bases	
1962	Roman Mejias	.286	Norm Larker	.358	Roman Mejias	.445	Roman Mejias	24	Roman Mejias	76	Roman Mejias	12
1963	Carl Warwick	.254	Carl Warwick	.319	Carl Warwick	.348	John Bateman	10	John Bateman	59	Johnny Temple	7
1964	Bob Aspromonte	.280	Bob Aspromonte	.329	Walt Bond	.420	Walt Bond	20	Walt Bond	85	Joe Gaines	8
1965	Jimmy Wynn	.275	Joe Morgan	.373	Jimmy Wynn	.470	Jimmy Wynn	22	Jimmy Wynn	73	Jimmy Wynn	43
1966	Sonny Jackson	.292	Joe Morgan	.410	Rusty Staub	.412	Rusty Staub	18	Rusty Staub	81	Sonny Jackson	49
1967	Rusty Staub	.333	Rusty Staub	.398	Jimmy Wynn	.495	Jimmy Wynn	37	Jimmy Wynn	107	Joe Morgan	29
1968	Rusty Staub	.291	Jimmy Wynn	.376	Jimmy Wynn	.474	Jimmy Wynn	26	Rusty Staub	72	Jimmy Wynn	11
1969	Denis Menke	.269	Jimmy Wynn	.436	Jimmy Wynn	.507	Jimmy Wynn	33	Denis Menke	90	Joe Morgan	49
1970	Denis Menke	.304	Jimmy Wynn	.394	Jimmy Wynn	.493	Jimmy Wynn	27	Denis Menke	92	Joe Morgan	42
1971	Bob Watson	.288	Joe Morgan	.351	Joe Morgan	.407	Joe Morgan	13	Cesar Cedeno	81	Joe Morgan	40
1972	Cesar Cedeno	.320	Jimmy Wynn	.389	Cesar Cedeno	.537	Lee May	29	Lee May	98	Cesar Cedeno	55
1973	Cesar Cedeno	.320	Bob Watson	.403	Cesar Cedeno	.537	Lee May	28	Lee May	105	Cesar Cedeno	56
1974	Greg Gross	.314	Greg Gross	.393	Cesar Cedeno	.461	Cesar Cedeno	26	Cesar Cedeno	102	Cesar Cedeno	57
1975	Bob Watson	.324	Bob Watson	.375	Bob Watson	.495	Cliff Johnson	20	Bob Watson	85	Cesar Cedeno	50
1976	Bob Watson	.313	Bob Watson	.377	Bob Watson	.458	Cesar Cedeno	18	Bob Watson	102	Cesar Cedeno	58
1977	Jose Cruz	.299	Joe Ferguson	.379	Bob Watson	.498	Bob Watson	22	Bob Watson	110	Cesar Cedeno	61
1978	Jose Cruz	.315	Jose Cruz	.376	Jose Cruz	.460	Bob Watson	14	Jose Cruz	83	Jose Cruz	37
1979	Jose Cruz	.289	Jose Cruz	.367	Jose Cruz	.421	Jose Cruz	9	Jose Cruz	72	Enos Cabell	37
1980	Cesar Cedeno	.309	Cesar Cedeno	.389	Cesar Cedeno	.465	Terry Puhl	13	Jose Cruz	91	Cesar Cedeno	48
1981	Art Howe	.296	Art Howe	.365	Jose Cruz	.425	Jose Cruz	13	Jose Cruz	55	Terry Puhl	22
1982	Ray Knight	.294	Ray Knight	.344	Phil Garner	.423	Phil Garner	13	Phil Garner	83	Dickie Thon	37
1983	Jose Cruz	.318	Jose Cruz	.385	Jose Cruz	.463	Dickie Thon	20	Jose Cruz	92	Dickie Thon	34
1984	Jose Cruz	.312	Jose Cruz	.381	Jose Cruz	.462	Jose Cruz	12	Jose Cruz	95	Jose Cruz	22
1985	Jose Cruz	.300	Bill Doran	.362	Bill Doran	.434	Glenn Davis	20	Jose Cruz	79	Bill Doran	23
1986	Kevin Bass	.311	Bill Doran	.368	Glenn Davis	.493	Glenn Davis	31	Glenn Davis	101	Bill Doran	42
1987	Billy Hatcher	.296	Bill Doran	.365	Glenn Davis	.458	Glenn Davis	27	Glenn Davis	93	Billy Hatcher	53
1988	Rafael Ramirez	.276	Glenn Davis	.341	Glenn Davis	.478	Glenn Davis	30	Glenn Davis	99	Gerald Young	65
1989	Glenn Davis	.269	Glenn Davis	.350	Glenn Davis	.492	Glenn Davis	34	Glenn Davis	89	Gerald Young	34
1990	Craig Biggio	.276	Craig Biggio	.342	Craig Biggio	.348	Franklin Stubbs	23	Franklin Stubbs	71	Eric Yelding	64
1991	Craig Biggio	.295	Jeff Bagwell	.387	Jeff Bagwell	.437	Jeff Bagwell	15	Jeff Bagwell	82	Steve Finley	34
1992	Ken Caminiti	.294	Craig Biggio	.378	Jeff Bagwell	.444	Eric Anthony	19	Jeff Bagwell	96	Steve Finley	44
1993	Jeff Bagwell	.320	Jeff Bagwell	.388	Craig Biggio	.516	Jeff Bagwell	21	Jeff Bagwell	88	Luis Gonzalez	20
1994	Jeff Bagwell	.368	Jeff Bagwell	.451	Jeff Bagwell	.750	Jeff Bagwell	39	Jeff Bagwell	116	Craig Biggio	39
1995	Derek Bell	.334	Craig Biggio	.406	Jeff Bagwell	.496	Craig Biggio	22	Craig Biggio	87	Craig Biggio	33
1996	Jeff Bagwell	.315	Jeff Bagwell	.451	Jeff Bagwell	.570	Jeff Bagwell	31	Jeff Bagwell	120	Brian Hunter	35
1997	Craig Biggio	.309	Jeff Bagwell	.425	Jeff Bagwell	.592	Jeff Bagwell	43	Jeff Bagwell	135	Craig Biggio	47

Houston Astros Individual Season Pitching Leaders

Year	ERA		Baserunners/9 IP		Innings Pitched		Strikeouts		Wins		Saves	
1962	Turk Farrell	3.02	Turk Farrell	10.1	Turk Farrell	241.2	Turk Farrell	203	Bob Bruce / Turk Farrell	10	Don McMahon	8
1963	Ken Johnson	2.65	Turk Farrell	8.8	Ken Johnson	224.0	Ken Johnson	148	Turk Farrell	14	Hal Woodeshick	10
1964	Bob Bruce	2.76	Bob Bruce	10.1	Ken Johnson	218.0	Bob Bruce	135	Bob Bruce	15	Hal Woodeshick	23
1965	Turk Farrell	3.50	Turk Farrell	10.4	Bob Bruce	229.2	Bob Bruce	145	Turk Farrell	11	Jim Owens	8
1966	Mike Cuellar	2.22	Mike Cuellar	9.7	Mike Cuellar	227.1	Mike Cuellar	175	Dave Giusti	15	Claude Raymond	16
1967	Don Wilson	2.79	Don Wilson	10.6	Mike Cuellar	246.1	Mike Cuellar	203	Mike Cuellar	16	Larry Sherry	6
1968	Mike Cuellar	2.74	Mike Cuellar	10.4	Dave Giusti	251.0	Dave Giusti	186	Don Wilson	13	Steve Shea	6
1969	Larry Dierker	2.33	Larry Dierker	9.2	Larry Dierker	305.1	Don Wilson	235	Larry Dierker	20	Fred Gladding	29
1970	Larry Dierker	3.87	Larry Dierker	11.7	Larry Dierker	269.2	Larry Dierker	191	Larry Dierker	16	Fred Gladding	18
1971	Don Wilson	2.45	Don Wilson	9.4	Don Wilson	268.0	Don Wilson	180	Don Wilson	16	Fred Gladding	12
1972	Don Wilson	2.68	Don Wilson	10.4	Don Wilson	228.1	Jerry Reuss	174	Larry Dierker / Don Wilson	15	Fred Gladding	14
1973	Dave Roberts	2.85	Don Wilson	10.8	Jerry Reuss	279.1	Jerry Reuss	177	Dave Roberts	17	3 tied with	6
1974	Larry Dierker	2.90	Larry Dierker	11.1	Larry Dierker	223.2	Larry Dierker	150	Tom Griffin	14	Ken Forsch	10
1975	Larry Dierker	4.00	Dave Roberts	11.7	Larry Dierker	232.0	J.R. Richard	176	Larry Dierker	14	Mike Cosgrove / Wayne Granger	5
1976	J.R. Richard	2.75	J.R. Richard	11.6	J.R. Richard	291.0	J.R. Richard	214	J.R. Richard	20	Ken Forsch	19
1977	J.R. Richard	2.97	J.R. Richard	10.7	J.R. Richard	267.0	J.R. Richard	214	J.R. Richard	18	Ken Forsch	8
1978	J.R. Richard	3.11	J.R. Richard	11.0	J.R. Richard	275.1	J.R. Richard	303	J.R. Richard	18	Joe Sambito	11
1979	J.R. Richard	2.71	Ken Forsch	9.6	J.R. Richard	292.1	J.R. Richard	313	Joe Niekro	21	Joe Sambito	22
1980	Ken Forsch	3.20	Ken Forsch	11.3	Joe Niekro	256.0	Nolan Ryan	200	Joe Niekro	20	Joe Sambito	17
1981	Nolan Ryan	1.69	Don Sutton	9.2	Joe Niekro	166.0	Nolan Ryan	140	Nolan Ryan / Don Sutton	11	Joe Sambito	10
1982	Joe Niekro	2.47	Joe Niekro	9.8	Joe Niekro	270.0	Nolan Ryan	245	Joe Niekro	17	Dave Smith	11
1983	Nolan Ryan	2.98	Nolan Ryan	11.0	Joe Niekro	263.2	Nolan Ryan	183	Joe Niekro	15	Frank DiPino	20
1984	Nolan Ryan	3.04	Nolan Ryan	10.6	Joe Niekro	248.1	Nolan Ryan	197	Joe Niekro	16	Frank DiPino	14
1985	Mike Scott	3.29	Mike Scott	11.2	Bob Knepper	241.0	Nolan Ryan	209	Mike Scott	18	Dave Smith	27
1986	Mike Scott	2.22	Mike Scott	8.4	Mike Scott	275.1	Mike Scott	306	Mike Scott	18	Dave Smith	33
1987	Nolan Ryan	2.76	Mike Scott	10.2	Mike Scott	247.2	Nolan Ryan	270	Mike Scott	16	Dave Smith	24
1988	Mike Scott	2.92	Mike Scott	9.2	Nolan Ryan	220.0	Nolan Ryan	228	Bob Knepper / Mike Scott	14	Dave Smith	27
1989	Jim Deshaies	2.91	Mike Scott	9.6	Mike Scott	229.0	Mike Scott	172	Mike Scott	20	Dave Smith	25
1990	Danny Darwin	2.21	Danny Darwin	9.5	Jim Deshaies	209.1	Mark Portugal	136	Danny Darwin / Mark Portugal	11	Dave Smith	23
1991	Pete Harnisch	2.70	Pete Harnisch	10.7	Pete Harnisch	216.2	Pete Harnisch	172	Pete Harnisch	12	Al Osuna	12
1992	Pete Harnisch	3.70	Pete Harnisch	10.9	Pete Harnisch	206.2	Pete Harnisch	164	Doug Jones	11	Doug Jones	36
1993	Mark Portugal	2.77	Pete Harnisch	10.6	Doug Drabek	237.2	Pete Harnisch	185	Mark Portugal	18	Doug Jones	26
1994	Doug Drabek	2.84	Doug Drabek	9.8	Doug Drabek	164.2	Doug Drabek	121	Doug Drabek	12	John Hudek	16
1995	Mike Hampton	3.35	Shane Reynolds	11.2	Shane Reynolds	189.1	Shane Reynolds	175	3 tied with	10	Todd Jones	15
1996	Shane Reynolds	3.65	Shane Reynolds	10.5	Shane Reynolds	239.0	Darryl Kile	219	Shane Reynolds	16	Todd Jones	17
1997	Darryl Kile	2.57	Darryl Kile	11.0	Darryl Kile	255.2	Darryl Kile	205	Darryl Kile	19	Billy Wagner	23

Astros Franchise Batting Leaders—Career

	Games			At-Bats			Runs			Hits	
1	Jose Cruz	1,870	1	Jose Cruz	6,629	1	Cesar Cedeno	890	1	Jose Cruz	1,937
2	Terry Puhl	1,516	2	Cesar Cedeno	5,732	2	Craig Biggio	874	2	Cesar Cedeno	1,659
3	Cesar Cedeno	1,512	3	Craig Biggio	5,104	3	Jose Cruz	871	3	Craig Biggio	1,470
4	Jimmy Wynn	1,426	4	Jimmy Wynn	5,063	4	Jimmy Wynn	829	4	Bob Watson	1,448
5	Bob Watson	1,381	5	Bob Watson	4,883	5	Terry Puhl	676	5	Terry Puhl	1,357
6	Craig Biggio	1,379	6	Terry Puhl	4,837	6	Jeff Bagwell	654	6	Jimmy Wynn	1,291
7	Doug Rader	1,178	7	Bill Doran	4,264	7	Bob Watson	640	7	Bill Doran	1,139
8	Craig Reynolds	1,170	8	Doug Rader	4,232	8	Bill Doran	611	8	Enos Cabell	1,124
9	Bill Doran	1,165	9	Enos Cabell	4,005	9	Joe Morgan	597	9	Jeff Bagwell	1,112
10	Kevin Bass	1,122	10	Joe Morgan	3,729	10	Enos Cabell	522	10	Doug Rader	1,060
11	Denny Walling	1,072	11	Roger Metzger	3,678	11	Doug Rader	520	11	Kevin Bass	990
12	Enos Cabell	1,067	12	Jeff Bagwell	3,657	12	Kevin Bass	465	12	Joe Morgan	972
13	Joe Morgan	1,032	13	Bob Aspromonte	3,588	13	Glenn Davis	427	13	Bob Aspromonte	925
14	Roger Metzger	1,021	14	Kevin Bass	3,558	14	Ken Caminiti	409	14	Ken Caminiti	896
15	Jeff Bagwell	1,008	15	Ken Caminiti	3,441	15	Roger Metzger	407	15	Craig Reynolds	860
16	Bob Aspromonte	1,007	16	Craig Reynolds	3,418	16	Craig Reynolds	373	16	Roger Metzger	844
17	Alan Ashby	965	17	Glenn Davis	3,032	17	Denny Walling	351	17	Glenn Davis	795
18	Ken Caminiti	948	18	Alan Ashby	2,926	18	Luis Gonzalez	344	18	Rusty Staub	792
19	Rusty Staub	833	19	Rusty Staub	2,906	19	Phil Garner	337	19	Alan Ashby	736
20	Glenn Davis	830	20	Denny Walling	2,618	20	Bob Aspromonte	336	20	Denny Walling	726

	Doubles			Triples			Home Runs			RBI	
1	Cesar Cedeno	343	1	Jose Cruz	80	1	Jimmy Wynn	223	1	Jose Cruz	942
2	Jose Cruz	335	2	Joe Morgan	63	2	Jeff Bagwell	187	2	Bob Watson	782
3	Craig Biggio	282	3	Roger Metzger	62	3	Glenn Davis	166	3	Cesar Cedeno	778
4	Jeff Bagwell	246	4	Terry Puhl	56	4	Cesar Cedeno	163	4	Jeff Bagwell	724
5	Bob Watson	241	5	Cesar Cedeno	55	5	Bob Watson	139	5	Jimmy Wynn	719
6	Jimmy Wynn	228		Craig Reynolds	55	6	Jose Cruz	138	6	Doug Rader	600
7	Terry Puhl	226	7	Enos Cabell	45	7	Doug Rader	128	7	Craig Biggio	545
8	Doug Rader	197	8	Steve Finley	41	8	Craig Biggio	116	8	Glenn Davis	518
9	Kevin Bass	194	9	Craig Biggio	36	9	Kevin Bass	87	9	Kevin Bass	468
10	Bill Doran	180	10	Bill Doran	35	10	Lee May	81	10	Ken Caminiti	445
	Ken Caminiti	180	11	Jimmy Wynn	32	11	Ken Caminiti	75	11	Terry Puhl	432
12	Enos Cabell	175	12	Bob Watson	30	12	Joe Morgan	72	12	Enos Cabell	405
13	Rusty Staub	156		Doug Rader	30	13	Alan Ashby	69	13	Bill Doran	404
14	Joe Morgan	153		Denny Walling	30		Bill Doran	69	14	Alan Ashby	388
	Luis Gonzalez	153		Phil Garner	30	15	Terry Puhl	62	15	Bob Aspromonte	385
16	Glenn Davis	150		Kevin Bass	30		Luis Gonzalez	62	16	Rusty Staub	370
17	Alan Ashby	136	17	Luis Gonzalez	25	17	Rusty Staub	57	17	Luis Gonzalez	366
18	Denny Walling	125	18	Bob Aspromonte	24	18	Cliff Johnson	52	18	Denny Walling	345
19	Art Howe	121	19	Six tied at	22	19	Bob Aspromonte	51	19	Joe Morgan	327
20	Phil Garner	119				20	Four tied at	49	20	Phil Garner	320

	Walks			Strikeouts			Stolen Bases			Runs Created	
1	Jimmy Wynn	847	1	Jimmy Wynn	1,088	1	Cesar Cedeno	487	1	Jose Cruz	1,019
2	Jose Cruz	730	2	Doug Rader	848	2	Jose Cruz	288	2	Cesar Cedeno	930
3	Joe Morgan	678	3	Jose Cruz	841	3	Craig Biggio	268	3	Craig Biggio	876
4	Craig Biggio	634	4	Craig Biggio	753	4	Joe Morgan	219	4	Jimmy Wynn	861
5	Jeff Bagwell	627	5	Cesar Cedeno	735	5	Terry Puhl	217	5	Bob Watson	780
6	Bill Doran	585	6	Jeff Bagwell	689	6	Enos Cabell	191	6	Jeff Bagwell	778
7	Cesar Cedeno	534	7	Bob Watson	635		Bill Doran	191	7	Terry Puhl	669
8	Bob Watson	508	8	Ken Caminiti	564	8	Jimmy Wynn	180	8	Joe Morgan	620
9	Terry Puhl	502	9	Bill Doran	513	9	Gerald Young	153	9	Bill Doran	609
10	Doug Rader	402	10	Terry Puhl	505	10	Billy Hatcher	145	10	Doug Rader	537
11	Rusty Staub	323	11	Glenn Davis	490	11	Kevin Bass	120	11	Kevin Bass	508
	Alan Ashby	323	12	Enos Cabell	481	12	Steve Finley	110	12	Glenn Davis	476
13	Roger Metzger	317	13	Kevin Bass	468	13	Jeff Bagwell	109	13	Enos Cabell	448
14	Glenn Davis	310	14	Alan Ashby	435	14	Dickie Thon	94	14	Ken Caminiti	417
15	Ken Caminiti	298	15	Joe Morgan	415	15	Eric Yelding	86	15	Rusty Staub	396
16	Denis Menke	296	16	Roger Metzger	399	16	James Mouton	79	16	Bob Aspromonte	369
17	Denny Walling	281	17	Luis Gonzalez	395	17	Sonny Jackson	73	17	Denny Walling	362
18	Bob Aspromonte	274	18	Phil Garner	387	18	Derek Bell	71	18	Luis Gonzalez	346
19	Kevin Bass	259	19	Bob Aspromonte	383	19	Phil Garner	68	19	Alan Ashby	337
20	Luis Gonzalez	251	20	Lee May	364	20	Roger Metzger	64	20	Craig Reynolds	333

	Runs Created/27 Outs			Batting Average			On-Base Percentage			Slugging Percentage	
	(minimum 2000 Plate Appearances)			(minimum 2000 Plate Appearances)			(minimum 2000 Plate Appearances)			(minimum 2000 Plate Appearances)	
1	Jeff Bagwell	7.67	1	Jeff Bagwell	.304	1	Jeff Bagwell	.409	1	Jeff Bagwell	.536
2	Craig Biggio	6.13	2	Bob Watson	.297	2	Craig Biggio	.377	2	Glenn Davis	.483
3	Jimmy Wynn	5.82	3	Jose Cruz	.292	3	Joe Morgan	.374	3	Cesar Cedeno	.454
4	Bob Watson	5.82	4	Cesar Cedeno	.289	4	Bob Watson	.364	4	Jimmy Wynn	.445
5	Joe Morgan	5.77	5	Craig Biggio	.288	5	Jimmy Wynn	.362	5	Bob Watson	.444
6	Cesar Cedeno	5.70	6	Enos Cabell	.281	6	Jose Cruz	.359	6	Jose Cruz	.429
7	Jose Cruz	5.53	7	Terry Puhl	.281	7	Denis Menke	.355	7	Craig Biggio	.426
8	Glenn Davis	5.51	8	Steve Finley	.281	8	Bill Doran	.355	8	Kevin Bass	.423
9	Kevin Bass	5.05	9	Kevin Bass	.278	9	Cesar Cedeno	.352	9	Luis Gonzalez	.417
10	Bill Doran	4.96	10	Denny Walling	.277	10	Terry Puhl	.349	10	Steve Finley	.406
11	Denny Walling	4.95	11	Rusty Staub	.273	11	Rusty Staub	.346	11	Doug Rader	.402
12	Terry Puhl	4.86	12	Dickie Thon	.270	12	Denny Walling	.345	12	Denny Walling	.402
13	Denis Menke	4.83	13	Art Howe	.269	13	Art Howe	.337	13	Dickie Thon	.395
14	Rusty Staub	4.79	14	Bill Doran	.267	14	Glenn Davis	.337	14	Art Howe	.394
15	Steve Finley	4.62	15	Denis Menke	.266	15	Luis Gonzalez	.335	15	Joe Morgan	.393
16	Luis Gonzalez	4.62	16	Billy Hatcher	.266	16	Steve Finley	.331	16	Rusty Staub	.393
17	Dickie Thon	4.48	17	Luis Gonzalez	.266	17	Kevin Bass	.330	17	Phil Garner	.389
18	Art Howe	4.39	18	Glenn Davis	.262	18	Gerald Young	.330	18	Terry Puhl	.389
19	Doug Rader	4.33	19	Joe Morgan	.261	19	Dickie Thon	.329	19	Ken Caminiti	.386
20	Billy Hatcher	4.29	20	Phil Garner	.260	20	Alan Ashby	.324	20	Enos Cabell	.381

Teams: Astros

Astros Franchise Pitching Leaders—Career

Wins

1	Joe Niekro	144
2	Larry Dierker	137
3	Mike Scott	110
4	J.R. Richard	107
5	Nolan Ryan	106
6	Don Wilson	104
7	Bob Knepper	93
8	Ken Forsch	78
9	Darryl Kile	71
10	Jim Deshaies	61
11	Turk Farrell	53
	Dave Smith	53
13	Mark Portugal	52
14	Dave Giusti	47
	Dave Roberts	47
	Danny Darwin	47
17	Tom Griffin	45
	Pete Harnisch	45
19	Joaquin Andujar	44
	Shane Reynolds	44

Losses

1	Larry Dierker	117
2	Joe Niekro	116
3	Bob Knepper	100
4	Nolan Ryan	94
5	Don Wilson	92
6	Ken Forsch	81
	Mike Scott	81
8	J.R. Richard	71
9	Darryl Kile	65
10	Turk Farrell	64
11	Tom Griffin	60
12	Jim Deshaies	59
13	Bob Bruce	58
14	Dave Giusti	53
	Joaquin Andujar	53
16	Ken Johnson	51
17	Dave Smith	47
18	Denny Lemaster	46
	Vern Ruhle	46
20	Dave Roberts	44

Winning Percentage
(minimum 75 decisions)

1	Mark Portugal	.634
2	J.R. Richard	.601
3	Pete Harnisch	.577
4	Mike Scott	.576
5	Danny Darwin	.573
6	Joe Niekro	.554
7	Larry Dierker	.539
8	Don Wilson	.531
9	Shane Reynolds	.530
10	Nolan Ryan	.530
	Dave Smith	.530
12	Darryl Kile	.522
13	Dave Roberts	.516
14	Jim Deshaies	.508
15	Ken Forsch	.491
16	Bob Knepper	.482
17	Doug Drabek	.475
18	Dave Giusti	.470
19	Vern Ruhle	.459
20	Joaquin Andujar	.454

Games

1	Dave Smith	563
2	Ken Forsch	421
3	Joe Niekro	397
4	Joe Sambito	353
5	Larry Dierker	345
6	Bob Knepper	284
7	Nolan Ryan	282
8	Jim Ray	280
9	Xavier Hernandez	273
10	Larry Andersen	268
11	Don Wilson	266
12	Mike Scott	263
13	Juan Agosto	261
14	J.R. Richard	238
15	Fred Gladding	233
16	Danny Darwin	220
17	Darryl Kile	209
18	Joaquin Andujar	202
19	Frank DiPino	201
20	Tom Griffin	199

Games Started

1	Larry Dierker	320
2	Joe Niekro	301
3	Nolan Ryan	282
4	Bob Knepper	267
5	Mike Scott	259
6	Don Wilson	245
7	J.R. Richard	221
8	Darryl Kile	182
9	Jim Deshaies	178
10	Ken Forsch	153
11	Bob Bruce	138
12	Turk Farrell	132
13	Tom Griffin	123
	Mark Portugal	123
15	Dave Roberts	121
16	Dave Giusti	118
	Doug Drabek	118
18	Pete Harnisch	117
19	Shane Reynolds	115
20	Joaquin Andujar	113

Complete Games

1	Larry Dierker	106
2	Joe Niekro	82
3	Don Wilson	78
4	J.R. Richard	76
5	Mike Scott	42
6	Turk Farrell	41
	Bob Knepper	41
8	Mike Cuellar	38
	Nolan Ryan	38
10	Ken Forsch	36
11	Dave Roberts	34
12	Dave Giusti	33
13	Bob Bruce	24
	Tom Griffin	24
15	Joaquin Andujar	23
16	Denny Lemaster	21
17	Ken Johnson	19
18	Jack Billingham	17
19	Six tied at	16

Shutouts

1	Larry Dierker	25
2	Joe Niekro	21
	Mike Scott	21
4	Don Wilson	20
5	J.R. Richard	19
6	Bob Knepper	18
7	Nolan Ryan	13
8	Dave Roberts	11
9	Tom Griffin	9
	Ken Forsch	9
11	Dave Giusti	8
	Vern Ruhle	8
13	Bob Bruce	6
	Mike Cuellar	6
	Jim Deshaies	6
	Pete Harnisch	6
	Darryl Kile	6
18	Eight tied at	5

Saves

1	Dave Smith	199
2	Fred Gladding	76
3	Joe Sambito	72
4	Doug Jones	62
5	Ken Forsch	50
6	Frank DiPino	43
7	Todd Jones	39
8	Hal Woodeshick	36
9	Billy Wagner	32
10	John Hudek	29
11	Claude Raymond	26
	Frank LaCorte	26
13	Xavier Hernandez	25
14	Jim Ray	23
15	Bill Dawley	21
16	Larry Andersen	20
17	Jim Owens	16
18	Al Osuna	14
19	Don McMahon	13
20	Four tied at	12

Innings Pitched

1	Larry Dierker	2,294.1
2	Joe Niekro	2,270.0
3	Nolan Ryan	1,854.2
4	Don Wilson	1,748.1
5	Bob Knepper	1,738.0
6	Mike Scott	1,704.0
7	J.R. Richard	1,606.0
8	Ken Forsch	1,493.2
9	Darryl Kile	1,200.0
10	Jim Deshaies	1,102.0
11	Turk Farrell	1,015.0
12	Dave Giusti	913.1
13	Bob Bruce	907.0
14	Tom Griffin	863.1
15	Joaquin Andujar	860.0
16	Dave Roberts	843.2
17	Mark Portugal	782.1
18	Shane Reynolds	769.2
19	Danny Darwin	769.0
20	Doug Drabek	762.2

Walks

1	Joe Niekro	818
2	Nolan Ryan	796
3	J.R. Richard	770
4	Larry Dierker	695
5	Don Wilson	640
6	Darryl Kile	562
7	Bob Knepper	521
8	Mike Scott	505
9	Tom Griffin	441
10	Ken Forsch	428
11	Jim Deshaies	423
12	Joaquin Andujar	361
13	Mark Portugal	281
14	Pete Harnisch	265
15	Dave Giusti	263
16	Dave Smith	260
17	Dave Roberts	257
18	Bob Bruce	242
	Jim Ray	242
20	Denny Lemaster	231

Strikeouts

1	Nolan Ryan	1,866
2	J.R. Richard	1,493
3	Larry Dierker	1,487
4	Mike Scott	1,318
5	Don Wilson	1,283
6	Joe Niekro	1,178
7	Darryl Kile	973
8	Bob Knepper	946
9	Ken Forsch	815
10	Jim Deshaies	731
11	Turk Farrell	694
12	Shane Reynolds	661
13	Tom Griffin	652
14	Dave Giusti	625
15	Bob Bruce	609
16	Pete Harnisch	583
17	Doug Drabek	558
18	Mike Cuellar	557
19	Danny Darwin	543
20	Mark Portugal	535

Strikeouts/9 Innings
(minimum 750 Innings Pitched)

1	Nolan Ryan	9.05
2	J.R. Richard	8.37
3	Shane Reynolds	7.73
4	Darryl Kile	7.30
5	Mike Scott	6.96
6	Tom Griffin	6.80
7	Don Wilson	6.60
8	Doug Drabek	6.58
9	Danny Darwin	6.36
10	Dave Smith	6.25
11	Dave Giusti	6.16
12	Mark Portugal	6.15
13	Turk Farrell	6.15
14	Bob Bruce	6.04
15	Jim Deshaies	5.97
16	Larry Dierker	5.83
17	Ken Forsch	4.91
18	Bob Knepper	4.90
19	Joe Niekro	4.67
20	Dave Roberts	4.30

ERA
(minimum 750 Innings Pitched)

1	Dave Smith	2.53
2	Nolan Ryan	3.13
3	Don Wilson	3.15
4	J.R. Richard	3.15
5	Ken Forsch	3.18
6	Danny Darwin	3.21
7	Joe Niekro	3.22
8	Larry Dierker	3.28
9	Mike Scott	3.30
10	Mark Portugal	3.34
11	Turk Farrell	3.42
12	Bob Knepper	3.66
13	Jim Deshaies	3.67
14	Joaquin Andujar	3.67
15	Dave Roberts	3.69
16	Shane Reynolds	3.72
17	Bob Bruce	3.78
18	Darryl Kile	3.79
19	Doug Drabek	4.00
20	Dave Giusti	4.02

Component ERA
(minimum 750 Innings Pitched)

1	Dave Smith	2.58
2	Nolan Ryan	2.79
3	Mike Scott	2.79
4	J.R. Richard	2.79
5	Turk Farrell	2.96
6	Don Wilson	2.97
7	Danny Darwin	2.97
8	Larry Dierker	3.14
9	Joe Niekro	3.20
10	Ken Forsch	3.23
11	Jim Deshaies	3.35
12	Mark Portugal	3.36
13	Shane Reynolds	3.44
14	Dave Giusti	3.51
15	Bob Bruce	3.59
16	Joaquin Andujar	3.63
17	Bob Knepper	3.66
18	Dave Roberts	3.77
19	Doug Drabek	3.84
20	Darryl Kile	4.02

Opponent Average
(minimum 750 Innings Pitched)

1	J.R. Richard	.212
2	Nolan Ryan	.213
3	Mike Scott	.228
4	Don Wilson	.228
5	Dave Smith	.230
6	Jim Deshaies	.236
7	Danny Darwin	.240
8	Joe Niekro	.242
9	Larry Dierker	.242
10	Ken Forsch	.244
11	Turk Farrell	.247
12	Darryl Kile	.251
13	Tom Griffin	.252
14	Joaquin Andujar	.254
15	Ken Forsch	.255
16	Dave Giusti	.257
17	Bob Bruce	.262
18	Bob Knepper	.264
19	Shane Reynolds	.264
20	Doug Drabek	.268

Opponent OBP
(minimum 750 Innings Pitched)

1	Mike Scott	.286
2	Turk Farrell	.287
3	Danny Darwin	.293
4	Dave Smith	.297
5	Nolan Ryan	.298
6	Don Wilson	.299
7	Larry Dierker	.301
8	Shane Reynolds	.304
9	J.R. Richard	.305
10	Jim Deshaies	.308
11	Ken Forsch	.308
12	Dave Giusti	.309
13	Joe Niekro	.310
14	Mark Portugal	.312
15	Bob Bruce	.314
16	Bob Knepper	.318
17	Doug Drabek	.321
18	Dave Roberts	.325
19	Joaquin Andujar	.329
20	Darryl Kile	.341

Teams: Astros

Astros Franchise Batting Leaders—Single Season

Games

1	Enos Cabell	1978	162
	Bill Doran	1987	162
	Craig Biggio	1992	162
	Steve Finley	1992	162
	Jeff Bagwell	1992	162
	Craig Biggio	1996	162
	Jeff Bagwell	1996	162
	Craig Biggio	1997	162
	Jeff Bagwell	1997	162
10	Rusty Staub	1968	161
	Cesar Cedeno	1971	161
	Ken Caminiti	1989	161
13	Joe Morgan	1971	160
	Cesar Cedeno	1974	160
	Jose Cruz	1980	160
	Jose Cruz	1983	160
	Jose Cruz	1984	160
18	Steve Finley	1991	159
19	Six tied at		158

At-Bats

1	Enos Cabell	1978	660
2	Roger Metzger	1972	641
3	Derek Bell	1996	627
4	Enos Cabell	1977	625
	Bill Doran	1987	625
6	Dickie Thon	1983	619
	Craig Biggio	1997	619
8	Craig Biggio	1992	613
9	Jose Cruz	1980	612
10	Cesar Cedeno	1971	611
11	Cesar Cedeno	1974	610
	Craig Biggio	1993	610
13	Ray Knight	1982	609
14	Steve Finley	1992	607
15	Craig Biggio	1996	605
16	Enos Cabell	1980	604
17	Enos Cabell	1979	603
18	Joe Morgan	1965	601
19	Terry Puhl	1979	600
	Jose Cruz	1984	600

Runs

1	Craig Biggio	1997	146
2	Craig Biggio	1995	123
3	Jimmy Wynn	1972	117
4	Jimmy Wynn	1969	113
	Craig Biggio	1996	113
6	Jeff Bagwell	1996	111
7	Jeff Bagwell	1997	109
8	Jeff Bagwell	1994	104
9	Cesar Cedeno	1972	103
10	Jimmy Wynn	1967	102
	Joe Morgan	1970	102
12	Enos Cabell	1977	101
13	Joe Morgan	1965	100
14	Craig Biggio	1993	98
15	Bob Watson	1973	97
16	Jose Cruz	1984	96
	Billy Hatcher	1987	96
	Craig Biggio	1992	96
19	Cesar Cedeno	1974	95
20	Joe Morgan	1969	94

Hits

1	Enos Cabell	1978	195
2	Craig Biggio	1997	191
3	Jose Cruz	1983	189
4	Jose Cruz	1984	187
5	Greg Gross	1974	185
	Jose Cruz	1980	185
7	Kevin Bass	1986	184
8	Bob Watson	1976	183
9	Rusty Staub	1967	182
10	Cesar Cedeno	1972	179
	Bob Watson	1973	179
	Ray Knight	1982	179
	Jeff Bagwell	1996	179
14	Jose Cruz	1978	178
15	Dickie Thon	1983	177
	Bill Doran	1987	177
	Steve Finley	1992	177
18	Enos Cabell	1977	176
19	Craig Biggio	1993	175
20	Two tied at		174

Doubles

1	Jeff Bagwell	1996	48
2	Rusty Staub	1967	44
	Craig Biggio	1994	44
4	Craig Biggio	1993	41
5	Cesar Cedeno	1971	40
	Derek Bell	1996	40
	Jeff Bagwell	1997	40
8	Cesar Cedeno	1972	39
9	Bob Watson	1977	38
	Sean Berry	1996	38
11	Rusty Staub	1968	37
	Jeff Bagwell	1993	37
	Craig Biggio	1997	37
14	Enos Cabell	1977	36
	Cesar Cedeno	1977	36
	Ray Knight	1982	36
	Ray Knight	1983	36
18	Cesar Cedeno	1973	35
	Glenn Davis	1987	35
20	Four tied at		34

Triples

1	Roger Metzger	1973	14
2	Jose Cruz	1984	13
	Steve Finley	1992	13
	Steve Finley	1993	13
5	Joe Morgan	1965	12
	Craig Reynolds	1981	12
7	Joe Morgan	1967	11
	Roger Metzger	1971	11
	Joe Morgan	1971	11
	Omar Moreno	1983	11
	Craig Reynolds	1984	11
	Bill Doran	1984	11
13	Roger Metzger	1974	10
	Greg Gross	1975	10
	Jose Cruz	1977	10
	Dickie Thon	1982	10
	Phil Garner	1985	10
	Steve Finley	1991	10
19	Nine tied at		9

Home Runs

1	Jeff Bagwell	1997	43
2	Jeff Bagwell	1994	39
3	Jimmy Wynn	1967	37
4	Glenn Davis	1989	34
5	Jimmy Wynn	1969	33
6	Glenn Davis	1986	31
	Jeff Bagwell	1996	31
8	Glenn Davis	1988	30
9	Lee May	1972	29
10	Lee May	1973	28
11	Jimmy Wynn	1970	27
	Glenn Davis	1987	27
13	Jimmy Wynn	1968	26
	Cesar Cedeno	1974	26
15	Doug Rader	1970	25
	Cesar Cedeno	1973	25
17	Roman Mejias	1962	24
	Jimmy Wynn	1972	24
	Lee May	1974	24
20	Franklin Stubbs	1990	23

RBI

1	Jeff Bagwell	1997	135
2	Jeff Bagwell	1996	120
3	Jeff Bagwell	1994	116
4	Derek Bell	1996	113
5	Bob Watson	1977	110
6	Jimmy Wynn	1967	107
7	Lee May	1973	105
8	Cesar Cedeno	1974	102
	Bob Watson	1976	102
10	Glenn Davis	1986	101
11	Glenn Davis	1988	99
12	Lee May	1972	98
13	Jeff Bagwell	1992	96
14	Jose Cruz	1984	95
	Sean Berry	1996	95
16	Bob Watson	1973	94
17	Glenn Davis	1987	93
18	Denis Menke	1970	92
	Jose Cruz	1983	92
20	Jose Cruz	1980	91

Walks

1	Jimmy Wynn	1969	148
2	Jeff Bagwell	1996	135
3	Jeff Bagwell	1997	127
4	Joe Morgan	1969	110
5	Jimmy Wynn	1970	106
6	Jimmy Wynn	1972	103
7	Joe Morgan	1970	102
8	Joe Morgan	1965	97
9	Craig Biggio	1992	94
10	Joe Morgan	1980	93
11	Jimmy Wynn	1973	91
12	Jimmy Wynn	1968	90
13	Joe Morgan	1966	89
14	Joe Morgan	1971	88
15	Denis Menke	1969	87
16	Bill Doran	1983	86
17	Bob Watson	1973	85
	Joe Ferguson	1977	85
19	Three tied at		84

Strikeouts

1	Lee May	1972	145
2	Jimmy Wynn	1969	142
3	Jimmy Wynn	1967	137
4	Jimmy Wynn	1968	131
	Doug Rader	1974	131
6	Howie Goss	1963	128
7	Jimmy Wynn	1965	126
8	Glenn Davis	1989	123
	Derek Bell	1996	123
10	Lee May	1973	122
	Jeff Bagwell	1997	122
12	Doug Rader	1972	120
13	Jeff Bagwell	1991	116
	Orlando Miller	1996	116
15	Franklin Stubbs	1990	114
	Jeff Bagwell	1996	114
17	Doug Rader	1971	112
18	Craig Biggio	1997	107
19	Three tied at		103

Stolen Bases

1	Gerald Young	1988	65
2	Eric Yelding	1990	64
3	Cesar Cedeno	1977	61
4	Cesar Cedeno	1976	58
5	Cesar Cedeno	1974	57
6	Cesar Cedeno	1973	56
7	Cesar Cedeno	1972	55
8	Billy Hatcher	1987	53
9	Cesar Cedeno	1975	50
10	Sonny Jackson	1966	49
	Joe Morgan	1969	49
12	Cesar Cedeno	1980	48
13	Craig Biggio	1997	47
14	Jose Cruz	1977	44
	Steve Finley	1992	44
16	Jimmy Wynn	1965	43
17	Joe Morgan	1970	42
	Enos Cabell	1977	42
	Bill Doran	1986	42
20	Joe Morgan	1971	40

Runs Created

1	Jeff Bagwell	1996	149
2	Craig Biggio	1997	147
3	Jeff Bagwell	1997	142
4	Jimmy Wynn	1969	124
5	Cesar Cedeno	1972	116
6	Jeff Bagwell	1994	114
	Craig Biggio	1996	114
8	Jimmy Wynn	1970	113
9	Craig Biggio	1995	112
10	Jose Cruz	1984	110
11	Jimmy Wynn	1972	107
	Cesar Cedeno	1973	107
	Bob Watson	1973	107
14	Jimmy Wynn	1965	104
15	Denis Menke	1970	102
	Glenn Davis	1989	102
	Craig Biggio	1993	102
18	Joe Morgan	1965	100
	Bob Watson	1976	100
	Jose Cruz	1983	100

Runs Created/27 Outs

(minimum 3.1 Plate Appearances/Tm Gm)

1	Jeff Bagwell	1994	11.02
2	Jeff Bagwell	1996	9.66
3	Craig Biggio	1997	8.89
4	Jeff Bagwell	1997	8.85
5	Jimmy Wynn	1969	8.79
6	Craig Biggio	1994	8.07
7	Cesar Cedeno	1972	7.58
8	Cesar Cedeno	1973	7.38
9	Craig Biggio	1995	7.25
10	Jimmy Wynn	1970	7.19
11	Jimmy Wynn	1972	7.05
12	Bob Watson	1973	6.93
13	Bob Watson	1972	6.90
14	Jeff Bagwell	1995	6.88
15	Bob Watson	1975	6.78
16	Jose Cruz	1984	6.76
17	Craig Biggio	1996	6.65
18	Denis Menke	1970	6.59
19	Rusty Staub	1967	6.55
20	Jeff Bagwell	1993	6.53

Batting Average

(minimum 3.1 Plate Appearances/Tm Gm)

1	Jeff Bagwell	1994	.368
2	Derek Bell	1995	.334
3	Rusty Staub	1967	.333
4	Bob Watson	1975	.324
5	Cesar Cedeno	1972	.320
6	Cesar Cedeno	1973	.320
7	Jeff Bagwell	1993	.320
8	Jose Cruz	1983	.318
9	Craig Biggio	1994	.318
10	Jeff Bagwell	1996	.315
11	Jose Cruz	1978	.315
12	Greg Gross	1974	.314
13	Bob Watson	1976	.313
14	Bob Watson	1973	.312
15	Bob Watson	1972	.312
16	Jose Cruz	1984	.312
17	Kevin Bass	1986	.311
18	Cesar Cedeno	1980	.309
19	Craig Biggio	1997	.309
20	Denis Menke	1970	.304

On-Base Percentage

(minimum 3.1 Plate Appearances/Tm Gm)

1	Jeff Bagwell	1994	.451
2	Jeff Bagwell	1996	.451
3	Jimmy Wynn	1969	.436
4	Jeff Bagwell	1997	.425
5	Craig Biggio	1997	.415
6	Craig Biggio	1994	.411
7	Joe Morgan	1966	.410
8	Craig Biggio	1995	.406
9	Bob Watson	1973	.403
10	Jeff Bagwell	1995	.399
11	Rusty Staub	1967	.398
12	Jimmy Wynn	1970	.394
13	Greg Gross	1974	.393
14	Denis Menke	1970	.392
15	Jimmy Wynn	1972	.389
16	Cesar Cedeno	1980	.389
17	Jeff Bagwell	1993	.388
18	Jeff Bagwell	1991	.387
19	Craig Biggio	1996	.386
20	Derek Bell	1995	.385

Slugging Percentage

(minimum 3.1 Plate Appearances/Tm Gm)

1	Jeff Bagwell	1994	.750
2	Jeff Bagwell	1997	.592
3	Jeff Bagwell	1996	.570
4	Cesar Cedeno	1973	.537
5	Cesar Cedeno	1972	.537
6	Jeff Bagwell	1993	.516
7	Jimmy Wynn	1969	.507
8	Craig Biggio	1997	.501
9	Bob Watson	1977	.498
10	Jeff Bagwell	1995	.496
11	Ken Caminiti	1994	.495
12	Jimmy Wynn	1967	.495
13	Bob Watson	1975	.495
14	Glenn Davis	1986	.493
15	Jimmy Wynn	1970	.493
16	Glenn Davis	1989	.492
17	Lee May	1972	.490
18	Kevin Bass	1986	.486
19	Craig Biggio	1994	.483
20	Craig Biggio	1995	.483

Teams: Astros

Astros Franchise Pitching Leaders—Single Season

Wins

1	Joe Niekro	1979	21
2	Larry Dierker	1969	20
	J.R. Richard	1976	20
	Joe Niekro	1980	20
	Mike Scott	1989	20
6	Darryl Kile	1997	19
7	J.R. Richard	1977	18
	J.R. Richard	1978	18
	J.R. Richard	1979	18
	Mike Scott	1985	18
	Mike Scott	1986	18
	Mark Portugal	1993	18
13	Dave Roberts	1973	17
	Joe Niekro	1982	17
	Bob Knepper	1986	17
16	Ten tied at		16

Losses

1	Turk Farrell	1962	20
2	Bob Bruce	1965	18
	Doug Drabek	1993	18
4	Ken Johnson	1963	17
	Denny Lemaster	1969	17
	Bob Knepper	1987	17
7	Ken Johnson	1962	16
	Hal Woodeshick	1962	16
	Ken Johnson	1964	16
	Don Wilson	1968	16
	Jack Billingham	1971	16
	Don Wilson	1973	16
	Larry Dierker	1975	16
	Nolan Ryan	1987	16
15	Seven tied at		15

Winning Percentage
(minimum 15 decisions)

1	Mark Portugal	1993	.818
2	Vern Ruhle	1980	.750
3	Bob Knepper	1988	.737
4	Bill Dawley	1984	.733
	Danny Darwin	1989	.733
	Danny Darwin	1990	.733
7	Darryl Kile	1997	.731
8	Jim Deshaies	1986	.706
9	Mike Scott	1985	.692
10	Nolan Ryan	1981	.688
11	Larry Dierker	1971	.667
	Mike Scott	1989	.667
	Doug Drabek	1994	.667
14	Joe Niekro	1979	.656
15	Larry Dierker	1972	.652
	Darryl Kile	1993	.652
17	Don Wilson	1970	.647
	Ken Forsch	1979	.647
	Jim Deshaies	1987	.647
20	Mike Scott	1986	.643

Games

1	Juan Agosto	1990	82
2	Joe Boever	1992	81
3	Doug Jones	1992	80
4	Xavier Hernandez	1992	77
5	Juan Agosto	1988	75
6	Xavier Hernandez	1993	72
	Dave Veres	1995	72
8	Juan Agosto	1989	71
	Al Osuna	1991	71
	Doug Jones	1993	71
11	Ken Forsch	1974	70
12	Danny Darwin	1989	68
	Todd Jones	1995	68
14	Larry Andersen	1987	67
15	Al Osuna	1992	66
16	Joe Sambito	1980	64
	Dave Smith	1985	64
18	Fred Gladding	1970	63
	Joe Sambito	1979	63
20	Three tied at		62

Games Started

1	Jerry Reuss	1973	40
2	J.R. Richard	1976	39
3	Joe Niekro	1979	38
	J.R. Richard	1979	38
	Joe Niekro	1983	38
	Joe Niekro	1984	38
	Bob Knepper	1986	38
8	Larry Dierker	1969	37
	Denny Lemaster	1969	37
	Bob Knepper	1985	37
	Mike Scott	1986	37
12	Larry Dierker	1970	36
	Dave Roberts	1973	36
	J.R. Richard	1977	36
	J.R. Richard	1978	36
	Joe Niekro	1980	36
	Mike Scott	1987	36
18	Seven tied at		35

Complete Games

1	Larry Dierker	1969	20
2	J.R. Richard	1979	19
3	Don Wilson	1971	18
4	Larry Dierker	1970	17
5	Mike Cuellar	1967	16
	J.R. Richard	1978	16
	Joe Niekro	1982	16
8	Larry Dierker	1975	14
	J.R. Richard	1976	14
10	Don Wilson	1969	13
	Don Wilson	1972	13
	J.R. Richard	1977	13
13	Turk Farrell	1963	12
	Dave Giusti	1968	12
	Larry Dierker	1972	12
	Jerry Reuss	1973	12
	Dave Roberts	1973	12
18	Seven tied at		11

Shutouts

1	Dave Roberts	1973	6
2	Larry Dierker	1972	5
	Joe Niekro	1979	5
	Bob Knepper	1981	5
	Joe Niekro	1982	5
	Bob Knepper	1986	5
	Mike Scott	1986	5
	Mike Scott	1988	5
9	Bob Bruce	1964	4
	Dave Giusti	1966	4
	Larry Dierker	1969	4
	Don Wilson	1974	4
	Joaquin Andujar	1976	4
	Larry Dierker	1976	4
	J.R. Richard	1979	4
	J.R. Richard	1980	4
	Pete Harnisch	1993	4
	Darryl Kile	1997	4
19	Twenty-five tied at		3

Saves

1	Doug Jones	1992	36
2	Dave Smith	1986	33
3	Fred Gladding	1969	29
4	Dave Smith	1985	27
	Dave Smith	1988	27
6	Doug Jones	1993	26
7	Dave Smith	1989	25
8	Dave Smith	1987	24
9	Hal Woodeshick	1964	23
	Dave Smith	1990	23
	Billy Wagner	1997	23
12	Joe Sambito	1979	22
13	Frank DiPino	1983	20
14	Ken Forsch	1976	19
15	Fred Gladding	1970	18
16	Joe Sambito	1980	17
	Todd Jones	1996	17
18	Claude Raymond	1966	16
	John Hudek	1994	16
20	Todd Jones	1995	15

Innings Pitched

1	Larry Dierker	1969	305.1
2	J.R. Richard	1979	292.1
3	J.R. Richard	1976	291.0
4	Jerry Reuss	1973	279.1
5	J.R. Richard	1978	275.1
	Mike Scott	1986	275.1
7	Joe Niekro	1982	270.0
8	Larry Dierker	1970	269.2
9	Don Wilson	1971	268.0
10	J.R. Richard	1977	267.0
11	Joe Niekro	1979	263.2
	Joe Niekro	1983	263.2
13	Bob Knepper	1986	258.0
14	Joe Niekro	1980	256.0
15	Darryl Kile	1997	255.2
16	Dave Giusti	1968	251.0
17	Nolan Ryan	1982	250.1
18	Dave Roberts	1973	249.1
19	Joe Niekro	1984	248.1
20	Mike Scott	1987	247.2

Walks

1	J.R. Richard	1976	151
2	J.R. Richard	1978	141
3	J.R. Richard	1975	138
4	Jerry Reuss	1973	117
5	Nolan Ryan	1982	109
6	Joe Niekro	1979	107
7	J.R. Richard	1977	104
8	Joe Niekro	1983	101
	Nolan Ryan	1983	101
10	Don Wilson	1974	100
11	Joe Niekro	1985	99
12	J.R. Richard	1979	98
	Nolan Ryan	1980	98
14	Don Wilson	1969	97
	Darryl Kile	1996	97
16	Nolan Ryan	1985	95
17	Darryl Kile	1997	94
18	Tom Griffin	1969	93
19	Don Wilson	1973	92
20	Larry Dierker	1975	91

Strikeouts

1	J.R. Richard	1979	313
2	Mike Scott	1986	306
3	J.R. Richard	1978	303
4	Nolan Ryan	1987	270
5	Nolan Ryan	1982	245
6	Don Wilson	1969	235
7	Mike Scott	1987	233
8	Larry Dierker	1969	232
9	Nolan Ryan	1988	228
10	Darryl Kile	1996	219
11	J.R. Richard	1976	214
	J.R. Richard	1977	214
13	Nolan Ryan	1985	209
14	Darryl Kile	1997	205
15	Shane Reynolds	1996	204
16	Turk Farrell	1962	203
	Mike Cuellar	1967	203
18	Tom Griffin	1969	200
	Nolan Ryan	1980	200
20	Nolan Ryan	1984	197

Strikeouts/9 Innings
(minimum 1 Inning Pitched/Tm Gm)

1	Nolan Ryan	1987	11.48
2	Mike Scott	1986	10.00
3	J.R. Richard	1978	9.90
4	Nolan Ryan	1986	9.81
5	Nolan Ryan	1984	9.65
6	J.R. Richard	1979	9.64
7	Tom Griffin	1969	9.56
8	Don Wilson	1969	9.40
9	Nolan Ryan	1988	9.33
10	Darryl Kile	1996	9.00
11	Nolan Ryan	1982	8.81
12	Mike Scott	1987	8.47
13	Nolan Ryan	1981	8.46
14	Nolan Ryan	1983	8.39
15	Shane Reynolds	1995	8.32
16	Jerry Reuss	1972	8.16
17	Ken Johnson	1962	8.13
18	Nolan Ryan	1985	8.11
19	Shane Reynolds	1994	7.98
20	Mike Scott	1988	7.82

ERA
(minimum 1 Inning Pitched/Tm Gm)

1	Nolan Ryan	1981	1.69
2	Bob Knepper	1981	2.18
3	Danny Darwin	1990	2.21
4	Mike Cuellar	1966	2.22
5	Mike Scott	1986	2.22
6	Larry Dierker	1969	2.33
7	Don Wilson	1971	2.45
8	Joe Niekro	1982	2.47
9	Ken Forsch	1971	2.53
10	Darryl Kile	1997	2.57
11	Don Sutton	1981	2.61
12	Ken Johnson	1963	2.65
13	Don Wilson	1972	2.68
14	Pete Harnisch	1991	2.70
15	J.R. Richard	1979	2.71
16	Mike Cuellar	1968	2.74
17	J.R. Richard	1976	2.75
18	Bob Bruce	1964	2.76
19	Nolan Ryan	1987	2.76
20	Mark Portugal	1993	2.77

Component ERA
(minimum 1 Inning Pitched/Tm Gm)

1	Mike Scott	1986	1.67
2	Turk Farrell	1963	1.98
3	Nolan Ryan	1981	2.02
4	Don Sutton	1981	2.05
5	Don Wilson	1971	2.10
6	Larry Dierker	1969	2.11
7	Mike Scott	1988	2.15
8	J.R. Richard	1979	2.23
9	Mike Cuellar	1966	2.25
10	Bob Knepper	1981	2.26
11	Danny Darwin	1990	2.31
12	Joe Niekro	1982	2.35
13	Don Nottebart	1963	2.39
14	Mike Scott	1989	2.43
15	Nolan Ryan	1986	2.46
16	Don Sutton	1982	2.47
17	Bob Bruce	1964	2.49
18	Nolan Ryan	1987	2.50
19	Doug Drabek	1994	2.52
20	J.R. Richard	1978	2.53

Opponent Average
(minimum 1 Inning Pitched/Tm Gm)

1	Mike Scott	1986	.186
2	Nolan Ryan	1981	.188
3	Nolan Ryan	1986	.188
4	Nolan Ryan	1983	.195
5	J.R. Richard	1978	.196
6	Nolan Ryan	1987	.200
7	Don Wilson	1971	.202
8	Mike Scott	1988	.204
9	J.R. Richard	1979	.209
10	Don Wilson	1967	.209
11	Nolan Ryan	1984	.211
12	J.R. Richard	1976	.212
13	Mike Scott	1989	.212
14	Pete Harnisch	1991	.212
15	Nolan Ryan	1982	.213
16	Don Wilson	1973	.213
17	Larry Dierker	1969	.214
18	Pete Harnisch	1993	.214
19	Jim Deshaies	1989	.217
20	Mike Scott	1987	.217

Opponent OBP
(minimum 1 Inning Pitched/Tm Gm)

1	Mike Scott	1986	.242
2	Turk Farrell	1963	.255
3	Mike Scott	1988	.260
4	Larry Dierker	1969	.261
5	Don Sutton	1981	.265
6	Don Wilson	1971	.266
7	Danny Darwin	1990	.266
8	Mike Scott	1989	.267
9	Don Nottebart	1963	.272
10	Mike Cuellar	1966	.273
11	Ken Forsch	1979	.273
12	Doug Drabek	1994	.275
13	J.R. Richard	1979	.276
14	Bob Bruce	1964	.277
15	Don Sutton	1982	.277
16	Joe Niekro	1982	.277
17	Bob Knepper	1981	.278
18	Turk Farrell	1962	.279
19	Nolan Ryan	1981	.280
20	Mike Scott	1987	.281

Astros Capsule

Best Season: *1986.* The Astros won 96 to take the National League West title and nearly defeated the heavily favored New York Mets in the NLCS in one of the most exciting postseason series in history.

Worst Season: *1975.* Don Wilson died over the winter, and the Astros went on to finish last with a 64-97 record as ex-Astro Joe Morgan won the MVP Award and led the Cincinnati Reds to the World Championship.

Best Player: *Jeff Bagwell.*

Best Pitcher: *J.R. Richard.* You could make an argument for Nolan Ryan, Joe Niekro or Larry Dierker.

Best Reliever: *Dave Smith.*

Best Defensive Player: *Doug Rader* won five straight Gold Gloves at the hot corner.

Hall of Famers: *Nellie Fox, Eddie Mathews, Joe Morgan, Robin Roberts, Nolan Ryan* and *Don Sutton.* None spent his prime years in Houston, and Morgan was the only one developed by Houston's farm system.

Franchise All-Star Team:

C	*Alan Ashby*	**LF**	*Jose Cruz*
1B	*Jeff Bagwell*	**CF**	*Cesar Cedeno*
2B	*Craig Biggio*	**RF**	*Jimmy Wynn*
3B	*Doug Rader*	**SP**	*J.R. Richard*
SS	*Craig Reynolds*	**RP**	*Dave Smith*

Biggest Flakes: *Doug Rader, Charley Kerfeld.*

Strangest Career: *Gerald Young* batted .321 in 71 games in 1987, finishing fifth in the NL Rookie of the Year race. Then he slumped to .257 and .233 before losing his job.

What Might Have Been: *Cesar Cedeno.* In 1973, at age 22, the budding superstar batted .320 with 20+ homers and 50+ steals for the second straight season. Over the winter, his mistress was shot and killed in a hotel room. The only person who witnessed the shooting was Cedeno, and his gun was the murder weapon. At the trial, he claimed that she had shot herself. He was convicted of involuntary manslaughter and fined 100 pesos. Although he avoided a jail sentence, he never performed as well on the field again.

Best Trade: First baseman *Jeff Bagwell* has a terrific shot at becoming one of the few Hall of Famers to be traded before playing a single major league game. He was acquired from Boston for relief pitcher Larry Andersen on August 31, 1990.

Worst Trader: *Spec Richardson.* If it hadn't been for Houston GM Spec Richardson, the dominant NL team of the mid-'70s might have been the Astros, rather than the Cincinnati Reds. From the end of the 1968 season to the beginning of the 1974 season, Richardson committed five major trading blunders that cost the Astros a total of seven star players: first baseman John Mayberry; second baseman Joe Morgan; center fielder Cesar Geronimo; starters Mike Cuellar, Jerry Reuss and Jack Billingham; and reliever Mike Marshall. All Houston got in return was one season from Curt Blefary, two from Milt May, and three apiece from Lee May and Tommy Helms. A team comprised of all that lost talent, plus Cesar Cedeno, Larry Dierker, Ken Forsch, Doug Rader, J.R. Richard, Bob Watson and Jimmy Wynn, would have been a monster.

Best-Looking Player: *Ken Caminiti.*

Ugliest Player: *Vern Ruhle.*

Best Nickname: *Jimmy Wynn, "The Toy Cannon."*

Most Unappreciated Player: *Jose Cruz* was a consistent .300 hitter and run producer for a full decade. His ability was masked by the Astrodome, which deflated his offensive numbers considerably. Had he played in a ballpark more conducive to hitting, he might have been recognized as one of the best hitters of his time.

Most Overrated Player: *Enos Cabell.* The Rick Cerone of third basemen.

Most Admirable Star: *Jeff Bagwell.*

Least Admirable Star: *Cesar Cedeno.*

Best Season, Player: *Jeff Bagwell, 1994.* Yes, he really did slug .750. His Triple Crown stats projected to a full season: .368-55-163.

Best Season, Pitcher: *Mike Scott, 1986.* He held batters to a .186 average, clinched the Astros' division title with a no-hitter, beat the Mets twice in the NLCS, and won the Cy Young Award. His 18-10 record was due to a lack of run-support; half of his losses came in games in which he allowed three runs or less.

Most Impressive Individual Record: *Jeff Bagwell's* unanimous selection as the NL MVP in 1994, only the third unanimous pick in league history.

Biggest Tragedies: *Don Wilson, J.R. Richard, Walt Bond* and *Dickie Thon.* Wilson died when he passed out and left his car running in his garage. Richard's career was ended by a stroke. Bond died of leukemia. Thon was developing into one of the game's best shortstops before he was hit in the face by a Mike Torrez fastball in early 1984.

Fan Favorite: *Nolan Ryan.*

—Mat Olkin

Brooklyn/Los Angeles Dodgers (1884-1997)

														Opponent				Park Index	
Year	Lg	Pos	W-L	Pct	GB	Manager	Att.	R	OR	HR	Avg	OBP	Slg	HR	Avg	OBP	ERA	Runs	HR
1884	AA	9th	40-64	.385	33.5	George Taylor	—	476	644	16	.225	.263	.292	20	.254	.288	3.79	100	100
1885	AA	5th	53-59	.473	26.0	Charlie Hackett/Charlie Byrne	—	624	650	14	.245	.295	.319	27	.240	.283	3.46	111	119
1886	AA	3rd	76-61	.555	16.0	Charlie Byrne	—	832	832	16	.250	.311	.330	17	.243	.312	3.42	99	96
1887	AA	6th	60-74	.448	34.5	Charlie Byrne	—	904	918	25	.261	.330	.350	27	.281	.348	4.47	94	130
1888	AA	2nd	88-52	.629	6.5	Bill McGunnigle	—	758	584	25	.242	.300	.321	15	.215	.258	2.33	106	214
1889	AA	1st	93-44	.679	—	Bill McGunnigle	—	995	706	47	.263	.344	.364	33	.256	.314	3.61	86	145
1890	NL	1st	86-43	.667	—	Bill McGunnigle	121,412	884	620	43	.264	.346	.369	27	.246	.308	3.06	96	79
1891	NL	6th	61-76	.445	25.5	Monte Ward	181,477	765	820	23	.260	.330	.345	40	.262	.325	3.86	97	82
1892	NL	2nd	51-26	.662	2.5	Monte Ward													
	NL	3rd	44-33	.571	9.5	Monte Ward	183,727	935	733	30	.262	.344	.350	26	.234	.309	3.25	103	68
1893	NL	6th	65-63	.508	20.5	Dave Foutz	235,000	775	845	45	.266	.341	.371	41	.270	.347	4.55	77	83
1894	NL	5th	70-61	.534	20.5	Dave Foutz	214,000	1021	1007	42	.313	.378	.440	41	.303	.375	5.51	89	79
1895	NL	5th	71-60	.542	16.5	Dave Foutz	230,000	867	834	39	.282	.346	.379	41	.290	.346	4.94	86	112
1896	NL	9th	58-73	.443	33.0	Dave Foutz	201,000	692	764	28	.284	.340	.379	39	.293	.349	4.25	75	99
1897	NL	6th	61-71	.462	32.0	Billy Barnie	220,831	802	845	24	.279	.336	.366	34	.292	.353	4.60	108	104
1898	NL	10th	54-91	.372	46.0	Billy Barnie/Mike Griffin/Charlie Ebbets	122,514	638	811	17	.256	.309	.322	34	.281	.348	4.01	94	100
1899	NL	1st	101-47	.682	—	Ned Hanlon	269,641	892	658	27	.291	.368	.383	32	.269	.338	3.25	105	102
1900	NL	1st	82-54	.603	—	Ned Hanlon	183,000	816	722	26	.293	.359	.383	30	.283	.347	3.89	119	112
1901	NL	3rd	79-57	.581	9.5	Ned Hanlon	198,200	744	600	32	.287	.335	.387	18	.263	.332	3.14	110	61
1902	NL	2nd	75-63	.543	27.5	Ned Hanlon	199,868	564	519	19	.256	.310	.319	10	.238	.298	2.69	84	63
1903	NL	5th	70-66	.515	19.0	Ned Hanlon	224,670	667	682	15	.265	.348	.339	18	.276	.339	3.44	99	92
1904	NL	6th	56-97	.366	50.0	Ned Hanlon	214,600	497	614	15	.232	.297	.295	27	.256	.320	2.70	92	52
1905	NL	8th	48-104	.316	56.5	Ned Hanlon	227,924	506	807	29	.246	.297	.317	24	.274	.343	3.76	99	152
1906	NL	5th	66-86	.434	50.0	Patsy Donovan	277,400	496	625	25	.236	.297	.308	15	.249	.316	3.13	76	68
1907	NL	5th	65-83	.439	40.0	Patsy Donovan	312,500	446	522	18	.232	.287	.298	16	.249	.319	2.38	86	123
1908	NL	7th	53-101	.344	46.0	Patsy Donovan	275,600	377	516	28	.213	.266	.277	17	.238	.309	2.47	90	73
1909	NL	6th	55-98	.359	55.5	Harry Lumley	321,300	444	627	16	.229	.279	.296	31	.257	.334	3.10	99	76
1910	NL	6th	64-90	.416	40.0	Bill Dahlen	279,321	497	623	25	.229	.294	.305	17	.259	.335	3.07	91	49
1911	NL	7th	64-86	.427	33.5	Bill Dahlen	269,000	539	659	28	.237	.301	.311	27	.263	.344	3.39	90	65
1912	NL	7th	58-95	.379	46.0	Bill Dahlen	243,000	651	754	32	.268	.336	.358	45	.273	.343	3.64	93	94
1913	NL	6th	65-84	.436	34.5	Bill Dahlen	347,000	595	613	39	.270	.321	.363	33	.255	.321	3.13	108	86
1914	NL	5th	75-79	.487	19.5	Wilbert Robinson	122,671	622	618	31	.269	.323	.355	36	.253	.320	2.82	104	98
1915	NL	3rd	80-72	.526	10.0	Wilbert Robinson	297,766	536	560	14	.248	.295	.317	29	.245	.318	2.66	103	112
1916	NL	1st	94-60	.610	—	Wilbert Robinson	447,747	585	471	28	.261	.313	.345	24	.233	.289	2.12	102	117
1917	NL	7th	70-81	.464	26.5	Wilbert Robinson	221,619	511	559	25	.247	.296	.322	32	.247	.307	2.78	113	100
1918	NL	5th	57-69	.452	25.5	Wilbert Robinson	83,831	360	463	10	.250	.291	.315	22	.248	.307	2.81	103	133
1919	NL	5th	69-71	.493	27.0	Wilbert Robinson	360,721	525	513	25	.263	.304	.340	21	.262	.308	2.73	85	94
1920	NL	1st	93-61	.604	—	Wilbert Robinson	808,722	660	528	28	.277	.324	.367	25	.259	.304	2.62	118	137
1921	NL	5th	77-75	.507	16.5	Wilbert Robinson	613,245	667	681	59	.280	.325	.386	46	.293	.342	3.70	109	104
1922	NL	6th	76-78	.494	17.0	Wilbert Robinson	498,865	743	754	56	.290	.335	.392	74	.294	.357	4.05	87	84
1923	NL	6th	76-78	.494	19.5	Wilbert Robinson	564,666	753	741	62	.285	.340	.387	55	.274	.336	3.74	96	83
1924	NL	2nd	92-62	.597	1.5	Wilbert Robinson	818,883	717	675	72	.287	.345	.391	58	.270	.326	3.64	96	76
1925	NL	6th	68-85	.444	27.0	Wilbert Robinson	659,435	786	866	64	.296	.351	.406	75	.301	.362	4.77	90	89
1926	NL	6th	71-82	.464	17.5	Wilbert Robinson	650,819	623	705	40	.263	.328	.358	50	.276	.339	3.82	96	121
1927	NL	6th	65-88	.425	28.5	Wilbert Robinson	637,230	541	619	39	.253	.306	.342	63	.265	.323	3.36	103	128
1928	NL	6th	77-76	.503	17.5	Wilbert Robinson	664,863	665	640	66	.266	.340	.374	59	.261	.324	3.25	93	80
1929	NL	6th	70-83	.458	28.5	Wilbert Robinson	731,886	755	888	99	.291	.355	.427	92	.290	.360	4.92	90	111
1930	NL	4th	86-68	.558	6.0	Wilbert Robinson	1,097,329	871	738	122	.304	.364	.454	115	.278	.330	4.03	95	146
1931	NL	4th	79-73	.520	21.0	Wilbert Robinson	753,133	681	673	71	.276	.331	.390	56	.283	.329	3.84	104	111
1932	NL	3rd	81-73	.526	9.0	Max Carey	681,827	752	747	110	.283	.334	.420	72	.282	.334	4.27	93	95
1933	NL	6th	65-88	.425	26.5	Max Carey	526,815	617	695	62	.263	.316	.359	51	.275	.326	3.68	99	120
1934	NL	6th	71-81	.467	23.5	Casey Stengel	434,188	748	795	79	.281	.350	.396	81	.285	.346	4.48	93	100
1935	NL	5th	70-83	.458	29.5	Casey Stengel	470,517	711	767	59	.277	.333	.376	88	.281	.337	4.22	90	106
1936	NL	7th	67-87	.435	25.0	Casey Stengel	489,618	662	752	33	.272	.323	.353	84	.266	.333	3.98	115	109
1937	NL	6th	62-91	.405	33.5	Burleigh Grimes	482,481	616	772	37	.265	.327	.354	68	.274	.336	4.13	114	95
1938	NL	7th	69-80	.463	18.5	Burleigh Grimes	663,087	704	710	61	.257	.338	.367	88	.278	.338	4.07	96	131
1939	NL	3rd	84-69	.549	12.5	Leo Durocher	955,668	708	645	78	.265	.338	.380	93	.263	.317	3.64	107	107
1940	NL	2nd	88-65	.575	12.0	Leo Durocher	975,978	697	621	93	.260	.327	.383	101	.248	.302	3.50	118	92
1941	NL	1st	100-54	.649	—	Leo Durocher	1,214,910	800	581	101	.272	.347	.405	81	.233	.300	3.14	104	109
1942	NL	2nd	104-50	.675	2.0	Leo Durocher	1,037,765	742	510	62	.265	.338	.362	73	.232	.302	2.84	96	88
1943	NL	3rd	81-72	.529	23.5	Leo Durocher	661,739	716	674	39	.272	.346	.357	59	.254	.338	3.88	104	107
1944	NL	7th	63-91	.409	42.0	Leo Durocher	605,905	690	832	56	.269	.331	.366	75	.275	.358	4.68	109	89
1945	NL	3rd	87-67	.565	11.0	Leo Durocher	1,059,220	795	724	57	.271	.349	.376	74	.253	.330	3.70	91	90
1946	NL	2nd	96-60	.615	2.0	Leo Durocher	1,796,824	701	570	55	.260	.348	.361	58	.243	.331	3.05	104	57
1947	NL	1st	94-60	.610	—	Clyde Sukeforth/Burt Shotton	1,807,526	774	668	83	.272	.364	.384	104	.251	.336	3.82	109	101
1948	NL	3rd	84-70	.545	7.5	Leo Durocher/Ray Blades/Burt Shotton	1,398,967	744	667	91	.261	.338	.381	119	.253	.337	3.75	110	112
1949	NL	1st	97-57	.630	—	Burt Shotton	1,633,747	879	651	152	.274	.354	.419	132	.248	.326	3.80	100	127
1950	NL	2nd	89-65	.578	2.0	Burt Shotton	1,185,896	847	724	194	.272	.349	.444	163	.263	.339	4.28	113	133
1951	NL	2nd	97-60	.618	1.0	Chuck Dressen	1,282,628	855	672	184	.275	.352	.434	150	.253	.326	3.88	92	120
1952	NL	1st	96-57	.627	—	Chuck Dressen	1,088,704	775	603	153	.262	.348	.399	121	.247	.321	3.53	103	123
1953	NL	1st	105-49	.682	—	Chuck Dressen	1,163,419	955	689	208	.285	.366	.474	169	.253	.320	4.10	107	104
1954	NL	2nd	92-62	.597	5.0	Walter Alston	1,020,531	778	740	186	.270	.349	.444	164	.261	.328	4.31	104	123
1955	NL	1st	98-55	.641	—	Walter Alston	1,033,589	857	650	201	.271	.356	.448	168	.248	.313	3.68	106	122
1956	NL	1st	93-61	.604	—	Walter Alston	1,213,562	720	601	179	.258	.342	.419	171	.244	.305	3.57	103	120
1957	NL	3rd	84-70	.545	11.0	Walter Alston	1,028,258	690	591	147	.253	.325	.387	144	.244	.305	3.35	133	145
1958	NL	7th	71-83	.461	21.0	Walter Alston	1,845,556	668	761	172	.251	.317	.402	173	.267	.344	4.47	115	127
1959	NL	1st	88-68	.564	—	Walter Alston	2,071,045	705	670	148	.257	.334	.396	157	.247	.329	3.79	103	129
1960	NL	4th	82-72	.532	13.0	Walter Alston	2,253,887	662	593	126	.255	.324	.383	154	.234	.311	3.40	132	198
1961	NL	2nd	89-65	.578	4.0	Walter Alston	1,804,250	735	697	157	.262	.338	.405	167	.256	.329	4.04	104	145
1962	NL	2nd	102-63	.618	1.0	Walter Alston	2,755,184	842	697	140	.268	.337	.400	115	.245	.317	3.62	82	50
1963	NL	1st	99-63	.611	—	Walter Alston	2,538,602	640	550	110	.251	.309	.357	111	.239	.293	2.85	84	63
1964	NL	6th	80-82	.494	13.0	Walter Alston	2,228,751	614	572	79	.250	.305	.340	88	.232	.292	2.95	78	62

Year	Lg	Pos	W-L	Pct	GB	Manager	Att.	R	OR	HR	Avg	OBP	Slg	Opponent HR	Opponent Avg	Opponent OBP	ERA	Park Index Runs	Park Index HR
1965	NL	1st	97-65	.599	—	Walter Alston	2,553,577	608	521	78	.245	.312	.335	127	.224	.283	2.81	76	49
1966	NL	1st	95-67	.586	—	Walter Alston	2,617,029	606	490	108	.256	.314	.362	84	.237	.286	2.62	86	70
1967	NL	8th	73-89	.451	28.5	Walter Alston	1,664,362	519	595	82	.236	.301	.332	93	.254	.306	3.21	73	68
1968	NL	7th	76-86	.469	21.0	Walter Alston	1,581,093	470	509	67	.230	.289	.319	65	.241	.297	2.69	77	59
1969	NL	4th-W	85-77	.525	8.0	Walter Alston	1,784,527	645	561	97	.254	.315	.359	122	.242	.299	3.08	94	78
1970	NL	2nd-W	87-74	.540	14.5	Walter Alston	1,697,142	749	684	87	.270	.334	.382	164	.250	.314	3.82	77	86
1971	NL	2nd-W	89-73	.549	1.0	Walter Alston	2,064,594	663	587	95	.266	.325	.370	110	.250	.301	3.23	95	93
1972	NL	3rd-W	85-70	.548	10.5	Walter Alston	1,860,858	584	527	98	.256	.319	.360	83	.230	.291	2.78	84	90
1973	NL	2nd-W	95-66	.590	3.5	Walter Alston	2,136,192	675	565	110	.263	.323	.371	129	.231	.292	3.00	95	108
1974	NL	1st-W	102-60	.630	—	Walter Alston	2,632,474	798	561	139	.272	.342	.401	112	.233	.294	2.97	80	90
1975	NL	2nd-W	88-74	.543	20.0	Walter Alston	2,539,349	648	534	118	.248	.325	.365	104	.225	.285	2.92	84	109
1976	NL	2nd-W	92-70	.568	10.0	Walter Alston/Tom Lasorda	2,386,301	608	543	91	.251	.313	.349	97	.243	.305	3.02	95	92
1977	NL	1st-W	98-64	.605	—	Tom Lasorda	2,955,087	769	582	191	.266	.336	.418	119	.251	.308	3.22	95	108
1978	NL	1st-W	95-67	.586	—	Tom Lasorda	3,347,845	727	573	149	.264	.338	.402	107	.250	.307	3.12	95	115
1979	NL	3rd-W	79-83	.488	11.5	Tom Lasorda	2,860,954	739	717	183	.263	.331	.412	101	.260	.329	3.83	101	131
1980	NL	2nd-W	92-71	.564	1.0	Tom Lasorda	3,249,287	663	591	148	.263	.323	.388	105	.247	.306	3.25	90	122
1981	NL	1st-W	36-21	.632	—	Tom Lasorda													
	NL	4th-W	27-26	.509	6.0	Tom Lasorda	2,381,292	450	356	82	.262	.323	.374	54	.245	.302	3.01	91	105
1982	NL	2nd-W	88-74	.543	1.0	Tom Lasorda	3,608,881	691	612	138	.264	.327	.388	81	.244	.303	3.26	86	72
1983	NL	1st-W	91-71	.562	—	Tom Lasorda	3,510,313	654	609	146	.250	.318	.379	97	.244	.307	3.10	96	105
1984	NL	4th-W	79-83	.488	13.0	Tom Lasorda	3,134,266	580	600	102	.244	.306	.348	76	.250	.313	3.17	106	100
1985	NL	1st-W	95-67	.586	—	Tom Lasorda	3,264,593	682	579	129	.261	.328	.382	102	.234	.295	2.96	82	78
1986	NL	5th-W	73-89	.451	23.0	Tom Lasorda	3,023,208	638	679	130	.251	.313	.370	115	.256	.319	3.76	88	73
1987	NL	4th-W	73-89	.451	17.0	Tom Lasorda	2,797,409	635	675	125	.252	.309	.371	130	.255	.325	3.72	81	73
1988	NL	1st-W	94-67	.584	—	Tom Lasorda	2,980,262	628	544	99	.248	.305	.352	84	.237	.299	2.96	108	90
1989	NL	4th-W	77-83	.481	14.0	Tom Lasorda	2,944,653	554	536	89	.240	.306	.339	95	.237	.304	2.95	82	80
1990	NL	2nd-W	86-76	.531	5.0	Tom Lasorda	3,002,396	728	685	129	.262	.328	.382	137	.249	.310	3.72	91	91
1991	NL	2nd-W	93-69	.574	1.0	Tom Lasorda	3,348,170	665	565	108	.253	.326	.359	96	.241	.306	3.06	102	102
1992	NL	6th-W	63-99	.389	35.0	Tom Lasorda	2,473,266	548	636	72	.248	.313	.339	82	.257	.326	3.41	89	62
1993	NL	4th-W	81-81	.500	23.0	Tom Lasorda	3,170,393	675	662	130	.261	.321	.383	103	.254	.324	3.50	94	96
1994	NL	1st-W	58-56	.509	—	Tom Lasorda	2,279,355	532	509	115	.270	.333	.414	90	.267	.331	4.17	78	94
1995	NL	1st-W	78-66	.542	—	Tom Lasorda	2,766,251	634	609	140	.264	.329	.400	125	.243	.311	3.66	81	71
1996	NL	2nd-W	90-72	.556	1.0	Tom Lasorda/Bill Russell	3,188,454	703	652	150	.252	.316	.384	125	.249	.317	3.46	79	68
1997	NL	2nd-W	88-74	.543	2.0	Bill Russell	3,318,822	742	645	174	.268	.330	.418	163	.241	.313	3.63	82	91

Team Nicknames: Brooklyn Bridegrooms 1884-1899, Brooklyn Superbas 1900-1905, Brooklyn Dodgers 1906-1958, Los Angeles Dodgers 1959-1997.

Team Ballparks: Washington Park I 1884-1888, Washington Park II 1889-1890, Eastern Park 1891-1897, Washington Park III 1898-1912, Ebbets Field 1913-1957, Los Angeles Memorial Coliseum 1958-1961, Dodger Stadium 1962-1997.

Brooklyn/Los Angeles Dodgers Individual Season Batting Leaders

Year	Batting Average		On-Base Percentage		Slugging Percentage		Home Runs		RBI		Stolen Bases	
1884	Oscar Walker	.270	Oscar Walker	.292	Oscar Walker	.359	3 tied with	3	Statistic unavailable		Statistic unavailable	
1885	Bill Phillips	.302	Bill Phillips	.364	Bill Phillips	.422	Germany Smith	4	Bill Phillips	63	Statistic unavailable	
1886	Ed Swartwood	.280	Ed Swartwood	.377	Jim McTamany	.371	Jimmy Peoples	3	Ernie Burch	72	Bill McClellan	43
									Ed Swartwood			
									Bill Phillips			
1887	Germany Smith	.294	Jim McTamany	.365	Germany Smith	.439	Germany Smith	4	Bill Phillips	101	Bill McClellan	70
1888	Darby O'Brien	.280	George Pinckney	.358	Dave Foutz	.375	Bob Caruthers	5	Dave Foutz	99	Darby O'Brien	55
1889	Oyster Burns	.304	Oyster Burns	.391	Oyster Burns	.423	Pop Corkhill	8	Dave Foutz	113	Darby O'Brien	91
							Joe Visner					
1890	George Pinckney	.309	George Pinckney	.411	Oyster Burns	.464	Oyster Burns	13	Oyster Burns	128	Hub Collins	85
1891	Oyster Burns	.285	George Pinckney	.366	Oyster Burns	.417	Darby O'Brien	5	Oyster Burns	83	Mike Griffin	65
1892	Dan Brouthers	.335	Dan Brouthers	.432	Dan Brouthers	.480	Bill Joyce	6	Dan Brouthers	124	Monte Ward	88
1893	Tom Daly	.289	Mike Griffin	.396	Tom Daly	.445	Tom Daly	8	Tom Daly	70	Dave Foutz	39
1894	Mike Griffin	.358	Mike Griffin	.467	George Treadway	.518	Tom Daly	8	Oyster Burns	107	Tom Daly	51
1895	Mike Griffin	.333	Mike Griffin	.444	Mike Griffin	.457	John Anderson	9	Candy LaChance	108	Candy LaChance	37
1896	Fielder Jones	.354	Fielder Jones	.427	John Anderson	.453	Candy LaChance	7	Tommy Corcoran	73	John Anderson	37
1897	John Anderson	.325	Mike Griffin	.416	John Anderson	.455	3 tied with	4	Billy Shindle	105	Fielder Jones	48
1898	Fielder Jones	.304	Mike Griffin	.379	Mike Griffin	.367	Candy LaChance	5	Fielder Jones	69	Fielder Jones	36
1899	Willie Keeler	.379	Willie Keeler	.425	Willie Keeler	.451	Joe Kelley	6	Joe Kelley	93	Willie Keeler	45
1900	Willie Keeler	.362	Willie Keeler	.402	Joe Kelley	.485	Joe Kelley	6	Joe Kelley	91	Willie Keeler	41
1901	Jimmy Sheckard	.354	Jimmy Sheckard	.407	Jimmy Sheckard	.534	Jimmy Sheckard	11	Jimmy Sheckard	104	Jimmy Sheckard	35
1902	Willie Keeler	.333	Willie Keeler	.365	Willie Keeler	.386	Tom McCreery	4	Bill Dahlen	74	Cozy Dolan	24
							Jimmy Sheckard					
1903	Jimmy Sheckard	.332	Jimmy Sheckard	.423	Jimmy Sheckard	.476	Jimmy Sheckard	9	Jack Doyle	91	Jimmy Sheckard	67
1904	Harry Lumley	.279	Charlie Babb	.345	Harry Lumley	.428	Harry Lumley	9	Harry Lumley	78	Charlie Babb	34
1905	Harry Lumley	.293	Jimmy Sheckard	.380	Harry Lumley	.412	Harry Lumley	7	Emil Batch	49	Doc Gessler	26
1906	Harry Lumley	.324	Harry Lumley	.386	Harry Lumley	.477	Tim Jordan	12	Tim Jordan	78	Billy Maloney	38
1907	Tim Jordan	.274	Tim Jordan	.371	Harry Lumley	.425	Harry Lumley	9	Harry Lumley	66	Billy Maloney	25
1908	Tim Jordan	.247	Tim Jordan	.328	Tim Jordan	.371	Tim Jordan	12	Tim Jordan	60	Harry Pattee	24
1909	John Hummel	.280	Ed Lennox	.337	John Hummel	.363	John Hummel	4	John Hummel	52	Al Burch	38
1910	Zack Wheat	.284	Zack Wheat	.341	Zack Wheat	.403	Jake Daubert	6	John Hummel	74	Bill Davidson	27
1911	Jake Daubert	.307	Jake Daubert	.366	Zack Wheat	.412	Tex Erwin	7	Zack Wheat	76	Bob Coulson	32
											Jake Daubert	
1912	Jake Daubert	.308	Jake Daubert	.369	Zack Wheat	.450	Zack Wheat	8	Jake Daubert	66	Jake Daubert	29
1913	Jake Daubert	.350	Jake Daubert	.405	Red Smith	.441	3 tied with	7	George Cutshaw	80	George Cutshaw	39
1914	Jake Daubert	.329	Casey Stengel	.404	Zack Wheat	.452	Zack Wheat	9	Zack Wheat	89	George Cutshaw	34
1915	Jake Daubert	.301	Jake Daubert	.368	Jake Daubert	.381	Zack Wheat	5	Zack Wheat	66	George Cutshaw	28
1916	Jake Daubert	.316	Jake Daubert	.371	Zack Wheat	.461	Zack Wheat	9	Zack Wheat	73	George Cutshaw	27
1917	Ivy Olson	.269	Jake Daubert	.341	Casey Stengel	.375	Jim Hickman	6	Casey Stengel	73	George Cutshaw	22
							Casey Stengel					
1918	Zack Wheat	.335	Zack Wheat	.369	Jake Daubert	.429	Hi Myers	4	Zack Wheat	51	Jimmy Johnston	22
1919	Hi Myers	.307	Zack Wheat	.344	Hi Myers	.436	Tommy Griffith	6	Hi Myers	73	Ivy Olson	26
1920	Zack Wheat	.328	Zack Wheat	.385	Zack Wheat	.463	Zack Wheat	9	Hi Myers	80	Jimmy Johnston	19
1921	Jimmy Johnston	.325	Zack Wheat	.372	Zack Wheat	.484	Zack Wheat	14	Zack Wheat	85	Jimmy Johnston	28
1922	Zack Wheat	.335	Zack Wheat	.388	Zack Wheat	.503	Zack Wheat	16	Zack Wheat	112	Jimmy Johnston	18
1923	Jack Fournier	.351	Jack Fournier	.411	Jack Fournier	.588	Jack Fournier	22	Jack Fournier	102	Jimmy Johnston	16
1924	Zack Wheat	.375	Jack Fournier	.428	Zack Wheat	.549	Jack Fournier	27	Jack Fournier	116	Jack Fournier	7
1925	Zack Wheat	.359	Jack Fournier	.446	Jack Fournier	.569	Jack Fournier	22	Jack Fournier	130	Milt Stock	8
1926	Babe Herman	.319	Babe Herman	.375	Babe Herman	.500	Jack Fournier	11	Babe Herman	81	William Marriott	12
							Babe Herman					
1927	Harvey Hendrick	.310	Harvey Hendrick	.350	Harvey Hendrick	.424	Babe Herman	14	Babe Herman	73	Max Carey	32
1928	Babe Herman	.340	Rube Bressler	.398	Del Bissonette	.543	Del Bissonette	25	Del Bissonette	106	Max Carey	18
1929	Babe Herman	.381	Babe Herman	.436	Babe Herman	.612	Johnny Frederick	24	Babe Herman	113	Babe Herman	21
1930	Babe Herman	.393	Babe Herman	.455	Babe Herman	.678	Babe Herman	35	Babe Herman	130	Babe Herman	18
1931	Lefty O'Doul	.336	Lefty O'Doul	.396	Babe Herman	.525	Babe Herman	18	Babe Herman	97	Babe Herman	17
1932	Lefty O'Doul	.368	Lefty O'Doul	.423	Lefty O'Doul	.555	Hack Wilson	23	Hack Wilson	123	Joe Stripp	14
1933	Johnny Frederick	.308	Johnny Frederick	.355	Johnny Frederick	.410	3 tied with	9	Tony Cuccinello	65	Jake Flowers	13
1934	Sam Leslie	.332	Len Koenecke	.411	Len Koenecke	.509	Tony Cuccinello	14	Sam Leslie	102	Danny Taylor	12
							Len Koenecke					
1935	Sam Leslie	.308	Sam Leslie	.379	Lonny Frey	.437	Lonny Frey	11	Sam Leslie	93	Frenchy Bordagaray	18
1936	Buddy Hassett	.310	Lonny Frey	.369	Buddy Hassett	.405	Babe Phelps	5	Buddy Hassett	82	Frenchy Bordagaray	12
1937	Heinie Manush	.333	Heinie Manush	.389	Heinie Manush	.442	Cookie Lavagetto	8	Heinie Manush	73	Buddy Hassett	13
											Cookie Lavagetto	
1938	Ernie Koy	.299	Dolph Camilli	.393	Dolph Camilli	.485	Dolph Camilli	24	Dolph Camilli	100	Ernie Koy	15
											Cookie Lavagetto	
1939	Cookie Lavagetto	.300	Dolph Camilli	.409	Dolph Camilli	.524	Dolph Camilli	26	Dolph Camilli	104	Cookie Lavagetto	14
1940	Dixie Walker	.308	Dolph Camilli	.397	Dolph Camilli	.529	Dolph Camilli	23	Dolph Camilli	96	Pee Wee Reese	15
1941	Pete Reiser	.343	Dolph Camilli	.407	Pete Reiser	.558	Dolph Camilli	34	Dolph Camilli	120	Pee Wee Reese	10
1942	Pete Reiser	.310	Pete Reiser	.375	Dolph Camilli	.471	Dolph Camilli	26	Dolph Camilli	109	Pete Reiser	20
1943	Billy Herman	.330	Augie Galan	.412	Billy Herman	.417	Augie Galan	9	Billy Herman	100	Arky Vaughan	20
1944	Dixie Walker	.357	Dixie Walker	.434	Dixie Walker	.529	Dixie Walker	13	Augie Galan	93	Luis Olmo	10
1945	Goody Rosen	.325	Augie Galan	.423	Luis Olmo	.462	Goody Rosen	12	Dixie Walker	124	Luis Olmo	15
1946	Dixie Walker	.319	Eddie Stanky	.436	Dixie Walker	.448	Pete Reiser	11	Dixie Walker	116	Pete Reiser	34
1947	Dixie Walker	.306	Dixie Walker	.415	Dixie Walker	.427	Pee Wee Reese	12	Dixie Walker	94	Jackie Robinson	29
							Jackie Robinson					
1948	Jackie Robinson	.296	Jackie Robinson	.367	Jackie Robinson	.453	Gene Hermanski	15	Jackie Robinson	85	Pee Wee Reese	25
1949	Jackie Robinson	.342	Jackie Robinson	.432	Jackie Robinson	.528	Gil Hodges	23	Jackie Robinson	124	Jackie Robinson	37
							Duke Snider					
1950	Jackie Robinson	.328	Jackie Robinson	.423	Duke Snider	.553	Gil Hodges	32	Gil Hodges	113	Pee Wee Reese	17
1951	Jackie Robinson	.338	Jackie Robinson	.429	Roy Campanella	.590	Gil Hodges	40	Roy Campanella	108	Jackie Robinson	25
1952	Jackie Robinson	.308	Jackie Robinson	.440	Gil Hodges	.500	Gil Hodges	32	Gil Hodges	102	Pee Wee Reese	30
1953	Carl Furillo	.344	Jackie Robinson	.425	Duke Snider	.627	Duke Snider	42	Roy Campanella	142	Pee Wee Reese	22
1954	Duke Snider	.341	Duke Snider	.423	Duke Snider	.647	Gil Hodges	42	Gil Hodges	130	3 tied with	8
									Duke Snider			
1955	Roy Campanella	.318	Duke Snider	.418	Duke Snider	.628	Duke Snider	42	Duke Snider	136	Jim Gilliam	15
1956	Jim Gilliam	.300	Duke Snider	.399	Duke Snider	.598	Duke Snider	43	Duke Snider	101	Jim Gilliam	21

Teams: Dodgers

Year	Batting Average		On-Base Percentage		Slugging Percentage		Home Runs		RBI		Stolen Bases	
1957	Gil Hodges	.299	Duke Snider	.368	Duke Snider	.587	Duke Snider	40	Gil Hodges	98	Jim Gilliam	26
1958	Don Zimmer	.262	Jim Gilliam	.352	Charlie Neal	.438	Gil Hodges Charlie Neal	22	Carl Furillo	83	Jim Gilliam	18
1959	Wally Moon	.302	Wally Moon	.394	Wally Moon	.495	Gil Hodges	25	Duke Snider	88	Jim Gilliam	23
1960	Norm Larker	.323	Wally Moon	.383	Frank Howard	.464	Frank Howard	23	Norm Larker	78	Maury Wills	50
1961	Wally Moon	.328	Wally Moon	.434	Wally Moon	.505	John Roseboro	18	Wally Moon	88	Maury Wills	35
1962	Tommy Davis	.346	Ron Fairly	.379	Frank Howard	.560	Frank Howard	31	Tommy Davis	153	Maury Wills	104
1963	Tommy Davis	.326	Tommy Davis	.359	Tommy Davis	.457	Frank Howard	28	Tommy Davis	88	Maury Wills	40
1964	Willie Davis	.294	Ron Fairly	.349	Willie Davis	.413	Frank Howard	24	Tommy Davis	86	Maury Wills	53
1965	Maury Wills	.286	Ron Fairly	.361	Lou Johnson	.391	Lou Johnson Jim Lefebvre	12	Ron Fairly	70	Maury Wills	94
1966	Willie Davis	.284	Wes Parker	.351	Jim Lefebvre	.460	Jim Lefebvre	24	Jim Lefebvre	74	Maury Wills	38
1967	Jim Lefebvre	.261	Jim Lefebvre	.322	Willie Davis	.367	Al Ferrara	16	Ron Fairly	55	Willie Davis	20
1968	Tom Haller	.285	Tom Haller	.345	Tom Haller	.388	Len Gabrielson	10	Tom Haller	53	Willie Davis	36
1969	Willie Davis	.311	Willie Davis	.356	Willie Davis	.456	Andy Kosco	19	Andy Kosco	74	Maury Wills	25
1970	Wes Parker	.319	Billy Grabarkewitz	.399	Wes Parker	.458	Billy Grabarkewitz	17	Wes Parker	111	Willie Davis	38
1971	Willie Davis	.309	Dick Allen	.395	Dick Allen	.468	Dick Allen	23	Dick Allen	90	Willie Davis	20
1972	Willie Davis	.289	Wes Parker	.367	Willie Davis	.441	Willie Davis Frank Robinson	19	Willie Davis	79	Willie Davis	20
1973	Willie Crawford	.295	Willie Crawford	.396	Joe Ferguson	.470	Joe Ferguson	25	Joe Ferguson	88	Davey Lopes	36
1974	Bill Buckner	.314	Jimmy Wynn	.387	Jimmy Wynn	.497	Jimmy Wynn	32	Steve Garvey	111	Davey Lopes	59
1975	Steve Garvey	.319	Jimmy Wynn	.403	Steve Garvey	.476	Ron Cey	25	Ron Cey	101	Davey Lopes	77
1976	Steve Garvey	.317	Ron Cey	.386	Ron Cey	.462	Ron Cey	23	Ron Cey Steve Garvey	80	Davey Lopes	63
1977	Reggie Smith	.307	Reggie Smith	.427	Reggie Smith	.576	Steve Garvey	33	Steve Garvey	115	Davey Lopes	47
1978	Steve Garvey	.316	Reggie Smith	.382	Reggie Smith	.559	Reggie Smith	29	Steve Garvey	113	Davey Lopes	45
1979	Steve Garvey	.315	Ron Cey	.389	Ron Cey	.499	3 tied with	28	Steve Garvey	110	Davey Lopes	44
1980	Steve Garvey	.304	Ron Cey	.342	Dusty Baker	.503	Dusty Baker	29	Steve Garvey	106	Rudy Law	40
1981	Dusty Baker	.320	Ron Cey	.372	Ron Cey	.474	Ron Cey	13	Steve Garvey	64	Davey Lopes	20
1982	Pedro Guerrero	.304	Pedro Guerrero	.378	Pedro Guerrero	.536	Pedro Guerrero	32	Pedro Guerrero	100	Steve Sax	49
1983	Pedro Guerrero	.298	Pedro Guerrero	.373	Pedro Guerrero	.531	Pedro Guerrero	32	Pedro Guerrero	103	Steve Sax	56
1984	Pedro Guerrero	.303	Pedro Guerrero	.358	Pedro Guerrero	.462	Mike Marshall	21	Pedro Guerrero	72	Steve Sax	34
1985	Pedro Guerrero	.320	Pedro Guerrero	.422	Pedro Guerrero	.577	Pedro Guerrero	33	Mike Marshall	95	Mariano Duncan	38
1986	Steve Sax	.332	Steve Sax	.390	Steve Sax	.441	Franklin Stubbs	23	Bill Madlock	60	Mariano Duncan	48
1987	Pedro Guerrero	.338	Pedro Guerrero	.416	Pedro Guerrero	.539	Pedro Guerrero	27	Pedro Guerrero	89	Steve Sax	37
1988	Kirk Gibson	.290	Kirk Gibson	.377	Kirk Gibson	.483	Kirk Gibson	25	Mike Marshall	82	Steve Sax	42
1989	Willie Randolph	.282	Willie Randolph	.366	Eddie Murray	.401	Eddie Murray	20	Eddie Murray	88	Kirk Gibson	12
1990	Eddie Murray	.330	Eddie Murray	.414	Kal Daniels	.531	Kal Daniels	27	Eddie Murray	95	Juan Samuel	38
1991	Brett Butler	.296	Brett Butler	.401	Darryl Strawberry	.491	Darryl Strawberry	28	Darryl Strawberry	99	Brett Butler	38
1992	Brett Butler	.309	Brett Butler	.413	Eric Karros	.426	Eric Karros	20	Eric Karros	88	Brett Butler	41
1993	Mike Piazza	.318	Brett Butler	.387	Mike Piazza	.561	Mike Piazza	35	Mike Piazza	112	Brett Butler	39
1994	Mike Piazza	.319	Brett Butler	.411	Mike Piazza	.541	Mike Piazza	24	Mike Piazza	92	Brett Butler Delino DeShields	27
1995	Mike Piazza	.346	Mike Piazza	.400	Mike Piazza	.606	Eric Karros Mike Piazza	32	Eric Karros	105	Delino DeShields	39
1996	Mike Piazza	.336	Mike Piazza	.422	Mike Piazza	.563	Mike Piazza	36	Eric Karros	111	Delino DeShields	48
1997	Mike Piazza	.362	Mike Piazza	.431	Mike Piazza	.638	Mike Piazza	40	Mike Piazza	124	Raul Mondesi	32

Brooklyn/Los Angeles Dodgers Individual Season Pitching Leaders

Year	ERA		Baserunners/9 IP		Innings Pitched		Strikeouts		Wins		Saves	
1884	Adonis Terry	3.49	Adonis Terry	10.6	Adonis Terry	485.0	Adonis Terry	233	Adonis Terry	20	5 tied with	0
1885	Henry Porter	2.78	Henry Porter	10.3	Henry Porter	481.2	Henry Porter	197	Henry Porter	33	Adonis Terry	1
1886	Adonis Terry	3.09	Henry Porter	12.0	Henry Porter	424.0	Henry Porter	163	Henry Porter	27	6 tied with	0
1887	Adonis Terry	4.02	Adonis Terry	12.4	Henry Porter	339.2	Adonis Terry	138	Adonis Terry	16	Adonis Terry	3
1888	Adonis Terry	2.03	Bob Caruthers	9.0	Bob Caruthers	391.2	Mickey Hughes	159	Bob Caruthers	29	5 tied with	0
1889	Bob Caruthers	3.13	Bob Caruthers	11.1	Bob Caruthers	445.0	Adonis Terry	186	Bob Caruthers	40	Bob Caruthers	1
1890	Tom Lovett	2.78	Tom Lovett	11.3	Tom Lovett	372.0	Adonis Terry	185	Tom Lovett	30	Dave Foutz	2
1891	Bob Caruthers	3.12	Tom Lovett	12.1	Tom Lovett	365.2	Tom Lovett	129	Tom Lovett	23	3 tied with	1
1892	Ed Stein	2.84	Ed Stein	11.0	George Haddock	381.1	Ed Stein	190	George Haddock	29	5 tied with	1
1893	Brickyard Kennedy	3.72	Ed Stein	12.5	Brickyard Kennedy	382.2	Brickyard Kennedy	107	Brickyard Kennedy	25	3 tied with	1
1894	Ed Stein	4.54	Ed Stein	14.2	Brickyard Kennedy	360.2	Brickyard Kennedy	107	Ed Stein	27	Hank Gastright Brickyard Kennedy	2
1895	Dan Daub	4.29	Dan Daub	12.8	Brickyard Kennedy	279.2	Ed Stein	55	Brickyard Kennedy	19	Jack Cronin	2
1896	Harley Payne	3.39	Dan Daub	12.7	Brickyard Kennedy	305.2	Brickyard Kennedy	76	Brickyard Kennedy	17	Brickyard Kennedy	1
1897	Brickyard Kennedy	3.91	Jack Dunn	13.5	Brickyard Kennedy	343.1	Harley Payne	86	Brickyard Kennedy	18	Chauncey Fisher Brickyard Kennedy	1
1898	Brickyard Kennedy	3.37	Jack Dunn	12.5	Brickyard Kennedy	339.1	Brickyard Kennedy	73	Jack Dunn	16	12 tied with	0
1899	Jim Hughes	2.68	Jim Hughes	11.8	Jack Dunn	299.1	Doc McJames	105	Jim Hughes	28	Jack Dunn Brickyard Kennedy	2
1900	Joe McGinnity	2.94	Frank Kitson	12.4	Joe McGinnity	343.0	Joe McGinnity	93	Joe McGinnity	28	Frank Kitson	4
1901	Wild Bill Donovan	2.77	Wild Bill Donovan	12.4	Wild Bill Donovan	351.0	Wild Bill Donovan	226	Wild Bill Donovan	25	Frank Kitson	2
1902	Doc Newton	2.42	Doc Newton	10.4	Wild Bill Donovan	297.2	Wild Bill Donovan	170	Frank Kitson	19	Wild Bill Donovan	1
1903	Oscar Jones	2.94	Ned Garvin	11.3	Oscar Jones	324.1	Ned Garvin	154	Henry Schmidt	22	Ned Garvin Henry Schmidt	2
1904	Ned Garvin	1.68	Jack Cronin	10.9	Oscar Jones	376.2	Jack Cronin	110	Oscar Jones	17	Ed Poole Bill Reidy	1
1905	Doc Scanlan	2.92	Doc Scanlan	12.0	Harry McIntire	308.2	Harry McIntire Doc Scanlan	135	Doc Scanlan	14	3 tied with	1
1906	Elmer Stricklett	2.72	Elmer Stricklett	11.0	Elmer Stricklett	291.2	Harry McIntire	121	Doc Scanlan	18	Elmer Stricklett	5
1907	Nap Rucker	2.06	George Bell	10.4	Nap Rucker	275.1	Nap Rucker	131	Jim Pastorius	16	George Bell	1
1908	Kaiser Wilhelm	1.87	Kaiser Wilhelm	9.6	Nap Rucker	333.1	Nap Rucker	199	Nap Rucker	17	Harry McIntire	2
1909	Nap Rucker	2.24	Nap Rucker	10.5	Nap Rucker	309.1	Nap Rucker	201	George Bell	16	3 tied with	1
1910	Nap Rucker	2.58	George Bell	10.2	Nap Rucker	320.1	Nap Rucker	147	Nap Rucker	17	Doc Scanlan	2
1911	Nap Rucker	2.74	Nap Rucker	10.6	Nap Rucker	315.2	Nap Rucker	190	Nap Rucker	22	Nap Rucker Bill Schardt	4
1912	Nap Rucker	2.21	Nap Rucker	10.5	Nap Rucker	297.2	Nap Rucker	151	Nap Rucker	18	Nap Rucker	4
1913	Frank Allen	2.83	Nap Rucker	10.7	Pat Ragan	264.2	Nap Rucker	111	Pat Ragan	15	Nap Rucker	3
1914	Jeff Pfeffer	1.97	Jeff Pfeffer	10.3	Jeff Pfeffer	315.0	Jeff Pfeffer	135	Jeff Pfeffer	23	Jeff Pfeffer	4
1915	Jeff Pfeffer	2.10	Jeff Pfeffer	10.4	Jeff Pfeffer	291.2	Wheezer Dell	94	Jeff Pfeffer	19	Jeff Pfeffer	3
1916	Rube Marquard	1.58	Rube Marquard	9.1	Jeff Pfeffer	328.2	Larry Cheney	166	Jeff Pfeffer	25	Rube Marquard	5
1917	Jeff Pfeffer	2.23	Rube Marquard	10.1	Jeff Pfeffer	266.0	Rube Marquard	117	Rube Marquard	19	Leon Cadore Sherry Smith	3
1918	Burleigh Grimes	2.14	Burleigh Grimes	9.7	Burleigh Grimes	269.2	Burleigh Grimes	113	Burleigh Grimes	19	Larry Cheney Burleigh Grimes	1
1919	Sherry Smith	2.24	Leon Cadore	9.8	Jeff Pfeffer	267.0	Leon Cadore	94	Jeff Pfeffer	17	Sherry Smith	1
1920	Burleigh Grimes	2.22	Burleigh Grimes	10.1	Burleigh Grimes	303.2	Burleigh Grimes	131	Burleigh Grimes	23	Al Mamaux	4
1921	Burleigh Grimes	2.83	Burleigh Grimes	11.7	Burleigh Grimes	302.1	Burleigh Grimes	136	Burleigh Grimes	22	Sherry Smith	4
1922	Dutch Ruether	3.53	Dutch Ruether	13.1	Dutch Ruether	267.1	Dazzy Vance	134	Dutch Ruether	21	Al Mamaux	3
1923	Dazzy Vance	3.50	Dazzy Vance	12.0	Burleigh Grimes	327.0	Dazzy Vance	197	Burleigh Grimes	21	Art Decatur	3
1924	Dazzy Vance	2.16	Dazzy Vance	9.5	Burleigh Grimes	310.2	Dazzy Vance	262	Dazzy Vance	28	Dutch Ruether	3
1925	Dazzy Vance	3.53	Dazzy Vance	11.0	Dazzy Vance	265.1	Dazzy Vance	221	Dazzy Vance	22	4 tied with	1
1926	Jesse Petty	2.84	Jesse Petty	10.7	Jesse Petty	275.2	Dazzy Vance	140	Jesse Petty	17	Rube Ehrhardt	4
1927	Dazzy Vance	2.70	Dazzy Vance	10.4	Dazzy Vance	273.1	Dazzy Vance	184	Dazzy Vance	16	Jumbo Elliott	3
1928	Dazzy Vance	2.09	Dazzy Vance	9.8	Dazzy Vance	280.1	Dazzy Vance	200	Dazzy Vance	22	Watty Clark Bill Doak	3
1929	Watty Clark	3.74	Dazzy Vance	11.7	Watty Clark	279.0	Watty Clark	140	Watty Clark	16	Johnny Morrison	8
1930	Dazzy Vance	2.61	Dazzy Vance	10.5	Dazzy Vance	258.2	Dazzy Vance	173	Dazzy Vance	17	Watty Clark	6
1931	Watty Clark	3.20	Dazzy Vance	11.3	Watty Clark	233.1	Dazzy Vance	150	Watty Clark	14	Jack Quinn	15
1932	Watty Clark	3.49	Watty Clark	11.0	Watty Clark	273.0	Van Lingle Mungo	107	Watty Clark	20	Jack Quinn	8
1933	Van Lingle Mungo	2.72	Van Lingle Mungo	11.1	Boom-Boom Beck	257.0	Van Lingle Mungo	110	Van Lingle Mungo	16	Sloppy Thurston	3
1934	Dutch Leonard	3.28	Van Lingle Mungo	11.6	Van Lingle Mungo	315.1	Van Lingle Mungo	184	Van Lingle Mungo	18	Dutch Leonard	5
1935	Watty Clark	3.30	Watty Clark	10.6	Van Lingle Mungo	214.1	Van Lingle Mungo	143	Van Lingle Mungo	16	Dutch Leonard	8
1936	Van Lingle Mungo	3.35	Van Lingle Mungo	11.4	Van Lingle Mungo	311.2	Van Lingle Mungo	238	Van Lingle Mungo	18	George Jeffcoat Van Lingle Mungo	3
1937	Van Lingle Mungo	2.91	Van Lingle Mungo	10.9	Max Butcher	191.2	Van Lingle Mungo	122	Max Butcher Luke Hamlin	11	Van Lingle Mungo	3
1938	Freddie Fitzsimmons	3.02	Freddie Fitzsimmons	11.1	Luke Hamlin	237.1	Luke Hamlin	97	Luke Hamlin Vito Tamulis	12	Luke Hamlin	6
1939	Hugh Casey	2.93	Luke Hamlin	10.3	Luke Hamlin	269.2	Luke Hamlin	88	Luke Hamlin	20	Vito Tamulis	4
1940	Luke Hamlin	3.06	Luke Hamlin	10.8	Whit Wyatt	239.1	Whit Wyatt	124	Freddie Fitzsimmons	16	5 tied with	2
1941	Whit Wyatt	2.34	Whit Wyatt	9.6	Kirby Higbe	298.0	Whit Wyatt	176	Kirby Higbe Whit Wyatt	22	Hugh Casey	7
1942	Curt Davis	2.36	Curt Davis	10.4	Kirby Higbe	221.2	Kirby Higbe	115	Whit Wyatt	19	Hugh Casey	13
1943	Whit Wyatt	2.49	Whit Wyatt	9.1	Kirby Higbe	185.0	Kirby Higbe	108	Whit Wyatt	14	Les Webber	10
1944	Curt Davis	3.34	Curt Davis	11.6	Hal Gregg	197.2	Hal Gregg	92	Curt Davis	10	Curt Davis	4
1945	Vic Lombardi	3.31	Hal Gregg	12.3	Hal Gregg	254.1	Hal Gregg	139	Hal Gregg	18	Cy Buker	5
1946	Joe Hatten	2.84	Vic Lombardi	11.9	Joe Hatten	222.0	Kirby Higbe	134	Kirby Higbe	17	Hugh Casey Art Herring	5
1947	Ralph Branca	2.67	Ralph Branca	11.4	Ralph Branca	280.0	Ralph Branca	148	Ralph Branca	21	Hugh Casey	18
1948	Preacher Roe	2.63	Preacher Roe	9.7	Rex Barney	246.2	Rex Barney	138	Rex Barney	15	Hank Behrman	7
1949	Preacher Roe	2.79	Preacher Roe	10.5	Don Newcombe	244.1	Don Newcombe	149	Don Newcombe	17	Erv Palica	6
1950	Preacher Roe	3.30	Don Newcombe	11.3	Don Newcombe	267.1	Erv Palica	131	Don Newcombe Preacher Roe	19	Ralph Branca	7
1951	Preacher Roe	3.04	Preacher Roe	10.9	Don Newcombe	272.0	Don Newcombe	164	Preacher Roe	22	Clyde King	6

Teams: Dodgers

Year	ERA		Baserunners/9 IP		Innings Pitched		Strikeouts		Wins		Saves	
1952	Billy Loes	2.69	Carl Erskine	10.5	Carl Erskine	206.2	Carl Erskine	131	Joe Black	15	Joe Black	15
1953	Carl Erskine	3.54	Carl Erskine	11.3	Carl Erskine	246.2	Carl Erskine	187	Carl Erskine	20	Jim Hughes	9
1954	Russ Meyer	3.99	Carl Erskine	11.6	Carl Erskine	260.1	Carl Erskine	166	Carl Erskine	18	Jim Hughes	24
1955	Don Newcombe	3.20	Don Newcombe	10.1	Don Newcombe	233.2	Don Newcombe	143	Don Newcombe	20	Ed Roebuck	12
1956	Sal Maglie	2.87	Don Newcombe	9.0	Don Newcombe	268.0	Don Newcombe	139	Don Newcombe	27	Clem Labine	19
1957	Johnny Podres	2.66	Johnny Podres	9.8	Don Drysdale	221.0	Don Drysdale	148	Don Drysdale	17	Clem Labine	17
1958	Johnny Podres	3.72	Johnny Podres	12.3	Don Drysdale	211.2	Johnny Podres	143	Johnny Podres	13	Clem Labine	14
1959	Don Drysdale	3.46	Don Drysdale	11.6	Don Drysdale	270.2	Don Drysdale	242	Don Drysdale	17	Clem Labine	9
1960	Don Drysdale	2.84	Don Drysdale	9.9	Don Drysdale	269.0	Don Drysdale	246	Don Drysdale	15	Ed Roebuck	8
1961	Sandy Koufax	3.52	Sandy Koufax	10.9	Sandy Koufax	255.2	Sandy Koufax	269	Sandy Koufax Johnny Podres	18	Larry Sherry	15
1962	Sandy Koufax	2.54	Sandy Koufax	9.4	Don Drysdale	314.1	Don Drysdale	232	Don Drysdale	25	Ron Perranoski	20
1963	Sandy Koufax	1.88	Sandy Koufax	8.0	Don Drysdale	315.1	Sandy Koufax	306	Sandy Koufax	25	Ron Perranoski	21
1964	Sandy Koufax	1.74	Sandy Koufax	8.4	Don Drysdale	321.1	Sandy Koufax	237	Sandy Koufax	19	Ron Perranoski	14
1965	Sandy Koufax	2.04	Sandy Koufax	7.8	Sandy Koufax	335.2	Sandy Koufax	382	Sandy Koufax	26	Ron Perranoski	17
1966	Sandy Koufax	1.73	Sandy Koufax	8.9	Sandy Koufax	323.0	Sandy Koufax	317	Sandy Koufax	27	Phil Regan	21
1967	Bill Singer	2.64	Don Drysdale	10.8	Claude Osteen	288.1	Don Drysdale	196	Claude Osteen	17	Ron Perranoski	16
1968	Don Drysdale	2.15	Don Drysdale	10.1	Bill Singer	256.1	Bill Singer	227	Don Drysdale	14	Jim Brewer	14
1969	Bill Singer	2.34	Bill Singer	9.4	Claude Osteen	321.0	Bill Singer	247	Claude Osteen Bill Singer	20	Jim Brewer	20
1970	Claude Osteen	3.83	Claude Osteen	11.7	Don Sutton	260.1	Don Sutton	201	Claude Osteen	16	Jim Brewer	24
1971	Don Sutton	2.54	Don Sutton	9.9	Don Sutton	265.1	Don Sutton	194	Al Downing	20	Jim Brewer	22
1972	Don Sutton	2.08	Don Sutton	8.4	Don Sutton	272.2	Don Sutton	207	Claude Osteen	20	Jim Brewer	17
1973	Don Sutton	2.42	Don Sutton	9.0	Don Sutton	256.1	Don Sutton	200	Don Sutton	18	Jim Brewer	20
1974	Mike Marshall	2.42	Andy Messersmith	10.0	Andy Messersmith	292.1	Andy Messersmith	221	Andy Messersmith	20	Mike Marshall	21
1975	Andy Messersmith	2.29	Don Sutton	9.4	Andy Messersmith	321.2	Andy Messersmith	213	Andy Messersmith	19	Mike Marshall	13
1976	Doug Rau	2.57	Burt Hooton	10.5	Don Sutton	267.2	Don Sutton	161	Don Sutton	21	Charlie Hough	18
1977	Burt Hooton	2.62	Burt Hooton	10.0	Don Sutton	240.1	Burt Hooton	153	Tommy John	20	Charlie Hough	22
1978	Burt Hooton	2.71	Burt Hooton	9.8	Don Sutton	238.1	Don Sutton	154	Burt Hooton	19	Terry Forster	22
1979	Burt Hooton	2.97	Don Sutton	10.5	Rick Sutcliffe	242.0	Don Sutton	146	Rick Sutcliffe	17	Bobby Castillo	7
1980	Don Sutton	2.20	Don Sutton	9.0	Jerry Reuss	229.1	Bob Welch	141	Jerry Reuss	18	Steve Howe	17
1981	Burt Hooton	2.28	Fernando Valenzuela	9.5	Fernando Valenzuela	192.1	Fernando Valenzuela	180	Fernando Valenzuela	13	Steve Howe	8
1982	Fernando Valenzuela	2.87	Jerry Reuss	10.0	Fernando Valenzuela	285.0	Fernando Valenzuela	199	Fernando Valenzuela	19	Steve Howe	13
1983	Bob Welch	2.65	Alejandro Pena	10.4	Fernando Valenzuela	257.0	Fernando Valenzuela	189	Fernando Valenzuela Bob Welch	15	Steve Howe	18
1984	Alejandro Pena	2.48	Orel Hershiser	10.2	Fernando Valenzuela	261.0	Fernando Valenzuela	240	Bob Welch	13	Tom Niedenfuer	11
1985	Orel Hershiser	2.03	Orel Hershiser	9.5	Fernando Valenzuela	272.1	Fernando Valenzuela	208	Orel Hershiser	19	Tom Niedenfuer	19
1986	Fernando Valenzuela	3.14	Fernando Valenzuela	10.4	Fernando Valenzuela	269.1	Fernando Valenzuela	242	Fernando Valenzuela	21	Ken Howell	12
1987	Orel Hershiser	3.06	Bob Welch	10.5	Orel Hershiser	264.2	Bob Welch	196	Orel Hershiser	16	Alejandro Pena Matt Young	11
1988	Orel Hershiser	2.26	Orel Hershiser	9.6	Orel Hershiser	267.0	Tim Leary	180	Orel Hershiser	23	Jay Howell	21
1989	Orel Hershiser	2.31	Tim Belcher	10.5	Orel Hershiser	256.2	Tim Belcher	200	Tim Belcher Orel Hershiser	15	Jay Howell	28
1990	Ramon Martinez	2.92	Ramon Martinez	10.1	Ramon Martinez	234.1	Ramon Martinez	223	Ramon Martinez	20	Jay Howell	16
1991	Tim Belcher	2.62	Mike Morgan	9.9	Mike Morgan	236.1	Tim Belcher	156	Ramon Martinez	17	Jay Howell	16
1992	Tom Candiotti	3.00	Tom Candiotti	10.7	Orel Hershiser	210.2	Kevin Gross	158	Tom Candiotti	11	Roger McDowell	14
1993	Tom Candiotti	3.12	Tom Candiotti	11.3	Orel Hershiser	215.2	Tom Candiotti	155	Pedro Astacio	14	Jim Gott	25
1994	Kevin Gross	3.60	Pedro Astacio	11.7	Ramon Martinez	170.0	Kevin Gross	124	Ramon Martinez	12	Todd Worrell	11
1995	Hideo Nomo	2.54	Hideo Nomo	9.7	Ramon Martinez	206.1	Hideo Nomo	236	Ramon Martinez	17	Todd Worrell	32
1996	Hideo Nomo	3.19	Hideo Nomo	10.5	Hideo Nomo	228.1	Hideo Nomo	234	Hideo Nomo	16	Todd Worrell	44
1997	Ismael Valdes	2.65	Ismael Valdes	10.1	Hideo Nomo	207.1	Hideo Nomo	233	Hideo Nomo Chan Ho Park	14	Todd Worrell	35

Dodgers Franchise Batting Leaders—Career

Games

1	Zack Wheat	2,322
2	Bill Russell	2,181
3	Pee Wee Reese	2,166
4	Gil Hodges	2,006
5	Jim Gilliam	1,956
6	Willie Davis	1,952
7	Duke Snider	1,923
8	Carl Furillo	1,806
9	Steve Garvey	1,727
10	Maury Wills	1,593
11	Ron Cey	1,481
12	Mike Scioscia	1,441
13	Jackie Robinson	1,382
14	Ron Fairly	1,306
15	John Roseboro	1,289
16	Wes Parker	1,288
17	Jimmy Johnston	1,266
18	Steve Yeager	1,219
19	Roy Campanella	1,215
20	Jake Daubert	1,213

At-Bats

1	Zack Wheat	8,859
2	Pee Wee Reese	8,058
3	Willie Davis	7,495
4	Bill Russell	7,318
5	Jim Gilliam	7,119
6	Gil Hodges	6,881
7	Duke Snider	6,640
8	Steve Garvey	6,543
9	Carl Furillo	6,378
10	Maury Wills	6,156
11	Ron Cey	5,216
12	Jackie Robinson	4,877
13	Jimmy Johnston	4,841
14	Davey Lopes	4,590
15	Jake Daubert	4,552
16	Dixie Walker	4,492
17	Hi Myers	4,448
18	Mike Scioscia	4,373
19	Steve Sax	4,312
20	Ivy Olson	4,212

Runs

1	Pee Wee Reese	1,338
2	Zack Wheat	1,255
3	Duke Snider	1,199
4	Jim Gilliam	1,163
5	Gil Hodges	1,088
6	Willie Davis	1,004
7	Jackie Robinson	947
8	Carl Furillo	895
9	Mike Griffin	881
10	Maury Wills	876
11	Steve Garvey	852
12	Bill Russell	796
13	Tom Daly	787
14	George Pinckney	761
15	Davey Lopes	759
16	Jimmy Johnston	727
17	Ron Cey	715
18	Dixie Walker	666
19	Jake Daubert	648
20	Roy Campanella	627

Hits

1	Zack Wheat	2,804
2	Pee Wee Reese	2,170
3	Willie Davis	2,091
4	Duke Snider	1,995
5	Steve Garvey	1,968
6	Bill Russell	1,926
7	Carl Furillo	1,910
8	Jim Gilliam	1,889
9	Gil Hodges	1,884
10	Maury Wills	1,732
11	Jackie Robinson	1,518
12	Jimmy Johnston	1,440
13	Dixie Walker	1,395
14	Jake Daubert	1,387
15	Ron Cey	1,378
16	Hi Myers	1,253
17	Steve Sax	1,218
18	Davey Lopes	1,204
19	Tom Daly	1,181
20	Mike Griffin	1,166

Doubles

1	Zack Wheat	464
2	Duke Snider	343
3	Steve Garvey	333
4	Pee Wee Reese	330
5	Carl Furillo	324
6	Willie Davis	321
7	Jim Gilliam	304
8	Gil Hodges	294
9	Bill Russell	293
10	Dixie Walker	274
11	Jackie Robinson	273
12	Babe Herman	232
13	Ron Cey	223
14	Mike Griffin	210
15	Johnny Frederick	200
16	Mike Scioscia	198
17	Wes Parker	194
18	Tom Daly	190
19	Jimmy Johnston	181
20	Dusty Baker	179

Triples

1	Zack Wheat	171
2	Willie Davis	110
3	Hi Myers	97
4	Jake Daubert	87
5	Oyster Burns	85
6	John Hummel	82
	Duke Snider	82
8	Pee Wee Reese	80
9	Tom Daly	76
	Jimmy Sheckard	76
11	Jimmy Johnston	73
12	Jim Gilliam	71
13	Harry Lumley	66
	Babe Herman	66
15	Dave Foutz	65
16	Mike Griffin	64
17	John Anderson	57
	Bill Russell	57
19	Five tied at	56

Home Runs

1	Duke Snider	389
2	Gil Hodges	361
3	Roy Campanella	242
4	Ron Cey	228
5	Steve Garvey	211
6	Carl Furillo	192
7	Pedro Guerrero	171
8	Mike Piazza	168
9	Willie Davis	154
	Eric Karros	154
11	Dusty Baker	144
12	Dolph Camilli	139
13	Jackie Robinson	137
	Mike Marshall	137
15	Zack Wheat	131
16	Pee Wee Reese	126
17	Frank Howard	123
18	Babe Herman	112
19	Steve Yeager	100
	Raul Mondesi	100

RBI

1	Duke Snider	1,271
2	Gil Hodges	1,254
3	Zack Wheat	1,210
4	Carl Furillo	1,058
5	Steve Garvey	992
6	Pee Wee Reese	885
7	Roy Campanella	856
8	Willie Davis	849
9	Ron Cey	842
10	Jackie Robinson	734
11	Dixie Walker	725
12	Bill Russell	627
13	Tom Daly	614
14	Oyster Burns	606
15	Babe Herman	594
16	Dusty Baker	586
17	Pedro Guerrero	585
18	Dolph Camilli	572
19	Jim Gilliam	558
20	Dave Foutz	548

Walks

1	Pee Wee Reese	1,210
2	Jim Gilliam	1,036
3	Gil Hodges	925
4	Duke Snider	893
5	Ron Cey	765
6	Jackie Robinson	740
7	Zack Wheat	632
8	Davey Lopes	603
9	Dolph Camilli	584
10	Mike Scioscia	567
11	Mike Griffin	544
12	Dixie Walker	539
13	Roy Campanella	533
14	Wes Parker	532
15	Tom Daly	526
16	Ron Fairly	522
17	Carl Furillo	514
18	Bill Russell	483
19	Maury Wills	456
20	John Roseboro	444

Strikeouts

1	Duke Snider	1,123
2	Gil Hodges	1,108
3	Pee Wee Reese	890
4	Ron Cey	838
5	Willie Davis	815
6	Steve Garvey	751
7	Mike Marshall	724
8	Steve Yeager	703
9	Bill Russell	667
10	Davey Lopes	629
11	Wes Parker	615
12	Pedro Guerrero	611
13	Eric Karros	596
14	Willie Crawford	581
15	John Roseboro	566
16	Maury Wills	562
17	Zack Wheat	554
18	Dolph Camilli	539
19	Frank Howard	515
20	Dusty Baker	509

Stolen Bases

1	Maury Wills	490
2	Davey Lopes	418
3	Willie Davis	335
4	Tom Daly	298
5	Steve Sax	290
6	George Pinckney	280
7	Darby O'Brien	272
8	Mike Griffin	264
9	Dave Foutz	241
10	Pee Wee Reese	232
11	Jimmy Sheckard	212
12	Zack Wheat	203
	Jim Gilliam	203
14	Jackie Robinson	197
15	Hub Collins	195
16	Jake Daubert	187
17	Brett Butler	179
18	Oyster Burns	172
19	Bill Russell	167
20	George Cutshaw	166

Runs Created

1	Zack Wheat	1,462
2	Duke Snider	1,362
3	Gil Hodges	1,216
4	Pee Wee Reese	1,204
5	Jim Gilliam	1,011
6	Carl Furillo	1,000
7	Willie Davis	987
8	Jackie Robinson	985
9	Steve Garvey	931
10	Mike Griffin	849
11	Tom Daly	838
12	Ron Cey	817
13	Dixie Walker	798
14	Maury Wills	755
15	Roy Campanella	748
16	Bill Russell	738
17	George Pinckney	735
18	Oyster Burns	693
19	Jake Daubert	687
20	Davey Lopes	678

Runs Created/27 Outs

(minimum 2000 Plate Appearances)

1	Jack Fournier	8.40
2	Mike Griffin	8.15
3	Oyster Burns	8.05
4	Mike Piazza	8.01
5	Babe Herman	7.61
6	Augie Galan	7.57
7	Tom Daly	7.54
8	Dolph Camilli	7.45
9	Duke Snider	7.41
10	Jackie Robinson	7.28
11	Darby O'Brien	7.20
12	Reggie Smith	7.12
13	George Pinckney	7.09
14	Willie Keeler	6.95
15	Pete Reiser	6.95
16	Fielder Jones	6.89
17	Pedro Guerrero	6.83
18	Jimmy Sheckard	6.75
19	Dixie Walker	6.66
20	John Anderson	6.56

Batting Average

(minimum 2000 Plate Appearances)

1	Willie Keeler	.352
2	Babe Herman	.339
3	Jack Fournier	.337
4	Mike Piazza	.334
5	Zack Wheat	.317
6	Manny Mota	.315
7	Fielder Jones	.313
8	Jackie Robinson	.311
9	Dixie Walker	.311
10	Pedro Guerrero	.309
11	Johnny Frederick	.308
12	Pete Reiser	.306
13	Mike Griffin	.305
14	Del Bissonette	.305
15	Jake Daubert	.305
16	Tommy Davis	.304
17	Steve Garvey	.301
18	Augie Galan	.301
19	Duke Snider	.300
20	Oyster Burns	.300

On-Base Percentage

(minimum 2000 Plate Appearances)

1	Jack Fournier	.421
2	Augie Galan	.416
3	Jackie Robinson	.409
4	Eddie Stanky	.405
5	Mike Griffin	.399
6	Mike Piazza	.398
7	Babe Herman	.396
8	Dolph Camilli	.392
9	Brett Butler	.392
10	Willie Keeler	.389
11	Fielder Jones	.388
12	Reggie Smith	.387
13	Dixie Walker	.386
14	Pete Reiser	.384
15	Duke Snider	.384
16	Tom Daly	.382
17	Pedro Guerrero	.381
18	Wally Moon	.377
19	Jimmy Sheckard	.376
20	Manny Mota	.374

Slugging Percentage

(minimum 2000 Plate Appearances)

1	Mike Piazza	.576
2	Babe Herman	.557
3	Duke Snider	.553
4	Jack Fournier	.552
5	Reggie Smith	.528
6	Pedro Guerrero	.512
7	Raul Mondesi	.511
8	Roy Campanella	.500
9	Dolph Camilli	.497
10	Frank Howard	.495
11	Gil Hodges	.488
12	Del Bissonette	.486
13	Johnny Frederick	.477
14	Jackie Robinson	.474
15	Pete Reiser	.460
16	Steve Garvey	.459
17	Carl Furillo	.458
18	Eric Karros	.455
19	Zack Wheat	.452
20	Mike Marshall	.449

Dodgers Franchise Pitching Leaders—Career

Wins

1	Don Sutton	233
2	Don Drysdale	209
3	Dazzy Vance	190
4	Brickyard Kennedy	177
5	Sandy Koufax	165
6	Burleigh Grimes	158
7	Claude Osteen	147
8	Fernando Valenzuela	141
9	Johnny Podres	136
10	Nap Rucker	134
	Orel Hershiser	134
12	Adonis Terry	127
13	Don Newcombe	123
14	Carl Erskine	122
15	Ramon Martinez	116
16	Bob Welch	115
17	Jeff Pfeffer	113
18	Burt Hooton	112
19	Bob Caruthers	110
20	Watty Clark	106

Losses

1	Don Sutton	181
2	Don Drysdale	166
3	Brickyard Kennedy	149
4	Adonis Terry	139
5	Nap Rucker	134
6	Dazzy Vance	131
7	Claude Osteen	126
8	Burleigh Grimes	121
9	Fernando Valenzuela	116
10	Johnny Podres	104
11	Orel Hershiser	102
12	Van Lingle Mungo	99
13	Harry McIntire	98
14	Watty Clark	88
15	Sandy Koufax	87
16	Bob Welch	86
17	Burt Hooton	84
18	Jeff Pfeffer	80
19	George Bell	79
20	Carl Erskine	78

Winning Percentage
(minimum 100 decisions)

1	Preacher Roe	.715
2	Bob Caruthers	.683
3	Tommy John	.674
4	Sandy Koufax	.655
5	Don Newcombe	.651
6	Kirby Higbe	.648
7	Whit Wyatt	.640
8	Hugh Casey	.631
9	Tom Lovett	.619
10	Ramon Martinez	.611
11	Carl Erskine	.610
12	Dazzy Vance	.592
13	Jeff Pfeffer	.585
14	Ralph Branca	.580
	Doug Rau	.580
16	Ed Stein	.580
17	Clem Labine	.574
18	Bob Welch	.572
19	Burt Hooton	.571
20	Orel Hershiser	.568

Games

1	Don Sutton	550
2	Don Drysdale	518
3	Jim Brewer	474
4	Ron Perranoski	457
5	Clem Labine	425
6	Charlie Hough	401
7	Sandy Koufax	397
8	Brickyard Kennedy	381
9	Dazzy Vance	378
10	Johnny Podres	366
11	Orel Hershiser	343
12	Claude Osteen	339
13	Nap Rucker	336
14	Carl Erskine	335
15	Fernando Valenzuela	331
16	Watty Clark	322
	Ed Roebuck	322
	Burt Hooton	322
19	Burleigh Grimes	318
20	Tom Niedenfuer	310

Games Started

1	Don Sutton	533
2	Don Drysdale	465
3	Claude Osteen	335
4	Brickyard Kennedy	332
5	Dazzy Vance	326
6	Fernando Valenzuela	320
7	Sandy Koufax	314
8	Johnny Podres	310
9	Orel Hershiser	303
10	Burleigh Grimes	285
11	Adonis Terry	276
12	Nap Rucker	272
13	Bob Welch	267
14	Burt Hooton	265
15	Ramon Martinez	247
16	Don Newcombe	230
17	Carl Erskine	216
18	Van Lingle Mungo	215
19	Jerry Reuss	201
20	Jeff Pfeffer	200

Complete Games

1	Brickyard Kennedy	279
2	Adonis Terry	256
3	Dazzy Vance	212
4	Burleigh Grimes	205
5	Nap Rucker	186
6	Don Drysdale	167
7	Jeff Pfeffer	157
8	Don Sutton	156
9	Bob Caruthers	147
10	Henry Porter	139
11	Sandy Koufax	137
12	Ed Stein	136
13	Harry McIntire	119
14	Van Lingle Mungo	114
15	Don Newcombe	111
16	Tom Lovett	107
	Fernando Valenzuela	107
18	Doc Scanlan	100
	Claude Osteen	100
20	George Bell	92

Shutouts

1	Don Sutton	52
2	Don Drysdale	49
3	Sandy Koufax	40
4	Nap Rucker	38
5	Claude Osteen	34
6	Dazzy Vance	30
7	Fernando Valenzuela	29
8	Jeff Pfeffer	25
9	Orel Hershiser	24
10	Johnny Podres	23
	Bob Welch	23
12	Don Newcombe	22
	Burt Hooton	22
14	Burleigh Grimes	20
	Ramon Martinez	20
16	Bill Singer	18
17	George Bell	17
	Whit Wyatt	17
19	Van Lingle Mungo	16
	Jerry Reuss	16

Saves

1	Todd Worrell	127
2	Jim Brewer	125
3	Ron Perranoski	101
4	Jay Howell	85
5	Clem Labine	83
6	Tom Niedenfuer	64
7	Charlie Hough	60
8	Steve Howe	59
9	Hugh Casey	50
10	Ed Roebuck	43
11	Mike Marshall	42
12	Jim Hughes	39
	Larry Sherry	39
14	Jim Gott	38
15	Alejandro Pena	32
16	Ken Howell	31
17	Phil Regan	27
	Terry Forster	27
19	Bob Miller	24
20	Four tied at	23

Innings Pitched

1	Don Sutton	3,816.1
2	Don Drysdale	3,432.0
3	Brickyard Kennedy	2,857.0
4	Dazzy Vance	2,757.2
5	Burleigh Grimes	2,425.2
6	Claude Osteen	2,396.2
7	Adonis Terry	2,385.1
8	Nap Rucker	2,375.1
9	Fernando Valenzuela	2,348.2
10	Sandy Koufax	2,324.1
11	Orel Hershiser	2,156.0
12	Johnny Podres	2,029.1
13	Burt Hooton	1,861.1
14	Bob Welch	1,820.2
15	Jeff Pfeffer	1,748.1
16	Van Lingle Mungo	1,739.1
17	Carl Erskine	1,718.2
18	Don Newcombe	1,662.2
19	Watty Clark	1,659.0
20	Ramon Martinez	1,630.0

Walks

1	Brickyard Kennedy	1,128
2	Don Sutton	996
3	Fernando Valenzuela	915
4	Don Drysdale	855
5	Sandy Koufax	817
6	Dazzy Vance	764
7	Burleigh Grimes	744
8	Adonis Terry	737
9	Nap Rucker	701
10	Van Lingle Mungo	697
11	Johnny Podres	670
12	Ramon Martinez	663
13	Orel Hershiser	653
14	Carl Erskine	646
15	Ed Stein	593
16	Ralph Branca	589
17	Doc Scanlan	582
18	Claude Osteen	568
19	Bob Welch	565
20	Burt Hooton	540

Strikeouts

1	Don Sutton	2,696
2	Don Drysdale	2,486
3	Sandy Koufax	2,396
4	Dazzy Vance	1,918
5	Fernando Valenzuela	1,759
6	Orel Hershiser	1,443
7	Johnny Podres	1,331
8	Bob Welch	1,292
9	Ramon Martinez	1,223
10	Nap Rucker	1,217
11	Adonis Terry	1,203
12	Claude Osteen	1,162
13	Burt Hooton	1,042
14	Van Lingle Mungo	1,031
15	Bill Singer	989
16	Carl Erskine	981
17	Burleigh Grimes	952
18	Don Newcombe	913
19	Ralph Branca	757
20	Brickyard Kennedy	749

Strikeouts/9 Innings
(minimum 1000 Innings Pitched)

1	Sandy Koufax	9.28
2	Bill Singer	6.98
3	Ramon Martinez	6.75
4	Fernando Valenzuela	6.74
5	Don Drysdale	6.52
6	Bob Welch	6.39
7	Don Sutton	6.36
8	Dazzy Vance	6.26
9	Tom Candiotti	6.17
10	Orel Hershiser	6.02
11	Johnny Podres	5.90
12	Van Lingle Mungo	5.33
13	Ralph Branca	5.15
14	Carl Erskine	5.14
15	Burt Hooton	5.04
16	Doug Rau	4.99
17	Don Newcombe	4.94
18	Tommy John	4.88
19	Nap Rucker	4.61
20	Adonis Terry	4.54

ERA
(minimum 1000 Innings Pitched)

1	Jeff Pfeffer	2.31
2	Nap Rucker	2.42
3	Sandy Koufax	2.76
4	George Bell	2.85
5	Whit Wyatt	2.86
6	Sherry Smith	2.91
7	Bob Caruthers	2.92
8	Don Drysdale	2.95
9	Doc Scanlan	2.95
10	Tommy John	2.97
11	Orel Hershiser	3.00
12	Bill Singer	3.03
13	Claude Osteen	3.09
14	Don Sutton	3.09
15	Harry McIntire	3.11
16	Leon Cadore	3.11
17	Jerry Reuss	3.11
18	Burt Hooton	3.14
19	Bob Welch	3.14
20	Dazzy Vance	3.17

Component ERA
(minimum 1000 Innings Pitched)

1	Sandy Koufax	2.50
2	Whit Wyatt	2.51
3	Jeff Pfeffer	2.54
4	Nap Rucker	2.60
5	George Bell	2.70
6	Don Sutton	2.72
7	Bill Singer	2.77
8	Bob Caruthers	2.81
9	Burt Hooton	2.89
10	Orel Hershiser	2.91
11	Dazzy Vance	2.92
12	Adonis Terry	2.92
13	Doc Scanlan	2.92
14	Don Drysdale	2.96
15	Jerry Reuss	3.03
16	Bob Welch	3.05
17	Henry Porter	3.07
18	Leon Cadore	3.09
19	Tommy John	3.09
20	Curt Davis	3.11

Opponent Average
(minimum 1000 Innings Pitched)

1	Sandy Koufax	.205
2	Whit Wyatt	.229
3	Bill Singer	.230
4	Don Sutton	.231
5	Doc Scanlan	.235
6	Ramon Martinez	.237
7	Don Drysdale	.239
8	Orel Hershiser	.239
9	Burt Hooton	.239
10	Bob Welch	.240
11	Fernando Valenzuela	.240
12	Ralph Branca	.242
13	Adonis Terry	.243
14	Nap Rucker	.243
15	Jeff Pfeffer	.244
16	Van Lingle Mungo	.245
17	Don Newcombe	.247
18	Bob Caruthers	.248
19	Dazzy Vance	.249
20	Carl Erskine	.252

Opponent OBP
(minimum 1000 Innings Pitched)

1	Sandy Koufax	.275
2	Don Sutton	.282
3	Whit Wyatt	.286
4	Bill Singer	.292
5	Bob Caruthers	.292
6	Don Drysdale	.293
7	Burt Hooton	.293
8	Don Newcombe	.295
9	Jeff Pfeffer	.298
10	Orel Hershiser	.299
11	Luke Hamlin	.299
12	Bob Welch	.300
13	Curt Davis	.300
14	Adonis Terry	.300
15	Jerry Reuss	.301
16	Tommy John	.302
17	Henry Porter	.302
18	Claude Osteen	.303
19	Preacher Roe	.304
20	Dazzy Vance	.305

Teams: Dodgers

Brooklyn Dodgers Team Batting Leaders—Career

	Games			At-Bats			Runs			Hits	
1	Zack Wheat	2,322	1	Zack Wheat	8,859	1	Pee Wee Reese	1,317	1	Zack Wheat	2,804
2	Pee Wee Reese	2,107	2	Pee Wee Reese	7,911	2	Zack Wheat	1,255	2	Pee Wee Reese	2,137
3	Carl Furillo	1,626	3	Carl Furillo	5,864	3	Duke Snider	994	3	Carl Furillo	1,762
4	Gil Hodges	1,531	4	Gil Hodges	5,581	4	Jackie Robinson	947	4	Duke Snider	1,609
5	Duke Snider	1,425	5	Duke Snider	5,317	5	Gil Hodges	916	5	Gil Hodges	1,556
6	Jackie Robinson	1,382	6	Jackie Robinson	4,877	6	Mike Griffin	881	6	Jackie Robinson	1,518
7	Jimmy Johnston	1,266	7	Jimmy Johnston	4,841	7	Carl Furillo	832	7	Jimmy Johnston	1,440
8	Roy Campanella	1,215	8	Jake Daubert	4,552	8	Tom Daly	787	8	Dixie Walker	1,395
9	Jake Daubert	1,213	9	Dixie Walker	4,492	9	George Pinckney	761	9	Jake Daubert	1,387
10	Dixie Walker	1,207	10	Hi Myers	4,448	10	Jimmy Johnston	727	10	Hi Myers	1,253
11	Hi Myers	1,166	11	Ivy Olson	4,212	11	Dixie Walker	666	11	Tom Daly	1,181
12	John Hummel	1,139	12	Roy Campanella	4,205	12	Jake Daubert	648	12	Mike Griffin	1,166
13	Tom Daly	1,094	13	Tom Daly	4,013	13	Roy Campanella	627	13	Roy Campanella	1,161
14	Ivy Olson	1,053	14	John Hummel	3,845	14	Oyster Burns	591	14	Ivy Olson	1,100
15	Mike Griffin	986	15	Mike Griffin	3,820	15	Dave Foutz	580	15	Babe Herman	1,093
16	George Pinckney	931	16	George Pinckney	3,730	16	Jimmy Sheckard	566	16	George Pinckney	1,012
17	Otto Miller	927	17	Dave Foutz	3,339	17	Babe Herman	540	17	John Hummel	973
18	Babe Herman	888	18	Jimmy Sheckard	3,272		Dolph Camilli	540	18	Jimmy Sheckard	966
19	Jimmy Sheckard	871	19	Babe Herman	3,221	19	Jim Gilliam	533	19	Oyster Burns	955
20	George Cutshaw	845	20	Oyster Burns	3,188	20	Hi Myers	512	20	Johnny Frederick	954

	Doubles			Triples			Home Runs			RBI	
1	Zack Wheat	464	1	Zack Wheat	171	1	Duke Snider	316	1	Zack Wheat	1,210
2	Pee Wee Reese	323	2	Hi Myers	97	2	Gil Hodges	298	2	Gil Hodges	1,049
3	Carl Furillo	301	3	Jake Daubert	87	3	Roy Campanella	242	3	Duke Snider	1,003
4	Duke Snider	288	4	Oyster Burns	85	4	Carl Furillo	174	4	Carl Furillo	961
5	Dixie Walker	274	5	John Hummel	82	5	Dolph Camilli	139	5	Pee Wee Reese	868
6	Jackie Robinson	273	6	Pee Wee Reese	78	6	Jackie Robinson	137	6	Roy Campanella	856
7	Gil Hodges	248	7	Tom Daly	76	7	Zack Wheat	131	7	Jackie Robinson	734
8	Babe Herman	232		Jimmy Sheckard	76	8	Pee Wee Reese	122	8	Dixie Walker	725
9	Mike Griffin	210	9	Jimmy Johnston	73	9	Babe Herman	112	9	Tom Daly	614
10	Johnny Frederick	200	10	Harry Lumley	66	10	Johnny Frederick	85	10	Oyster Burns	606
11	Tom Daly	190		Babe Herman	66	11	Jack Fournier	82	11	Babe Herman	594
12	Jimmy Johnston	181		Duke Snider	66	12	Dixie Walker	67	12	Dolph Camilli	572
13	Roy Campanella	178	13	Dave Foutz	65	13	Del Bissonette	66	13	Dave Foutz	548
14	Jimmy Sheckard	160	14	Mike Griffin	64	14	Billy Cox	46	14	Hi Myers	496
15	Oyster Burns	155	15	John Anderson	57	15	Tom Daly	44	15	Mike Griffin	477
	Hi Myers	155	16	Dixie Walker	56		Glenn Wright	44	16	George Pinckney	436
17	Dolph Camilli	151	17	Dolph Camilli	55		Pete Reiser	44	17	Jimmy Sheckard	420
18	George Pinckney	146	18	Jackie Robinson	54	18	Tony Cuccinello	43	18	Jake Daubert	415
	Augie Galan	146	19	Tommy Corcoran	53		Babe Phelps	43	19	Jack Fournier	396
20	Cookie Lavagetto	143	20	Two tied at	52	20	Sandy Amoros	42	20	Cookie Lavagetto	395

	Walks			Strikeouts			Stolen Bases			Runs Created	
1	Pee Wee Reese	1,184	1	Pee Wee Reese	875	1	Tom Daly	298	1	Zack Wheat	1,462
2	Gil Hodges	765	2	Duke Snider	874	2	George Pinckney	280	2	Pee Wee Reese	1,184
3	Jackie Robinson	740	3	Gil Hodges	849	3	Darby O'Brien	272	3	Duke Snider	1,103
4	Duke Snider	692	4	Zack Wheat	554	4	Mike Griffin	264	4	Gil Hodges	1,027
5	Zack Wheat	632	5	Dolph Camilli	539	5	Dave Foutz	241	5	Jackie Robinson	985
6	Dolph Camilli	584	6	Roy Campanella	501	6	Pee Wee Reese	231	6	Carl Furillo	926
7	Mike Griffin	544	7	Carl Furillo	395	7	Jimmy Sheckard	212	7	Mike Griffin	849
8	Dixie Walker	539	8	Jake Daubert	363	8	Zack Wheat	203	8	Tom Daly	838
9	Roy Campanella	533	9	Hi Myers	329	9	Jackie Robinson	197	9	Dixie Walker	798
10	Tom Daly	526	10	Tom Daly	322	10	Hub Collins	195	10	Roy Campanella	748
11	Carl Furillo	472	11	Babe Herman	303	11	Jimmy Johnston	187	11	George Pinckney	735
12	Eddie Stanky	432	12	Otto Miller	301	12	Oyster Burns	172	12	Oyster Burns	693
13	George Pinckney	429	13	Jackie Robinson	291	13	George Cutshaw	166	13	Jake Daubert	687
14	Cookie Lavagetto	420	14	Casey Stengel	281	14	Jimmy Johnston	164	14	Jimmy Johnston	651
15	Augie Galan	413	15	Dazzy Vance	271	15	Fielder Jones	153	15	Babe Herman	650
16	Jim Gilliam	405	16	Del Bissonette	269	16	Monte Ward	145	16	Jimmy Sheckard	622
17	Jake Daubert	393		Pete Reiser	269	17	Bill Dahlen	137	17	Dolph Camilli	621
18	Jimmy Sheckard	381	18	John Hummel	261	18	Germany Smith	135	18	Dave Foutz	586
19	Jimmy Johnston	371	19	Jimmy Johnston	229	19	Willie Keeler	130	19	Hi Myers	531
20	Oyster Burns	339	20	Darby O'Brien	224	20	Bill McClellan	126	20	Johnny Frederick	504

	Runs Created/27 Outs			Batting Average			On-Base Percentage			Slugging Percentage	
	(minimum 2000 Plate Appearances)			(minimum 2000 Plate Appearances)			(minimum 2000 Plate Appearances)			(minimum 2000 Plate Appearances)	
1	Jack Fournier	8.40	1	Willie Keeler	.352	1	Jack Fournier	.421	1	Duke Snider	.560
2	Mike Griffin	8.15	2	Babe Herman	.339	2	Augie Galan	.416	2	Babe Herman	.557
3	Oyster Burns	8.05	3	Jack Fournier	.337	3	Jackie Robinson	.409	3	Jack Fournier	.552
4	Babe Herman	7.61	4	Zack Wheat	.317	4	Eddie Stanky	.405	4	Roy Campanella	.500
5	Augie Galan	7.57	5	Fielder Jones	.313	5	Mike Griffin	.399	5	Gil Hodges	.499
6	Tom Daly	7.54	6	Jackie Robinson	.311	6	Babe Herman	.396	6	Dolph Camilli	.497
7	Duke Snider	7.52	7	Dixie Walker	.311	7	Dolph Camilli	.392	7	Del Bissonette	.486
8	Dolph Camilli	7.45	8	Johnny Frederick	.308	8	Willie Keeler	.389	8	Johnny Frederick	.477
9	Jackie Robinson	7.28	9	Pete Reiser	.306	9	Fielder Jones	.388	9	Jackie Robinson	.474
10	Darby O'Brien	7.20	10	Mike Griffin	.305	10	Dixie Walker	.386	10	Pete Reiser	.460
11	George Pinckney	7.09	11	Del Bissonette	.305	11	Pete Reiser	.384	11	Carl Furillo	.459
12	Willie Keeler	6.95	12	Jake Daubert	.305	12	Duke Snider	.383	12	Zack Wheat	.452
13	Pete Reiser	6.95	13	Duke Snider	.303	13	Tom Daly	.382	13	Dixie Walker	.441
14	Fielder Jones	6.89	14	Augie Galan	.301	14	Jimmy Sheckard	.376	14	Oyster Burns	.439
15	Jimmy Sheckard	6.75	15	Carl Furillo	.300	15	Cookie Lavagetto	.372	15	Augie Galan	.438
16	Dixie Walker	6.66	16	Oyster Burns	.300	16	Oyster Burns	.371	16	John Anderson	.430
17	John Anderson	6.56	17	Jimmy Johnston	.297	17	Del Bissonette	.371	17	Willie Keeler	.425
18	Gil Hodges	6.48	18	John Anderson	.297	18	Billy Herman	.367	18	Jimmy Sheckard	.424
19	Candy LaChance	6.37	19	Joe Stripp	.295	19	Zack Wheat	.367	19	Candy LaChance	.420
20	Bill McClellan	6.30	20	Jimmy Sheckard	.295	20	Pee Wee Reese	.366	20	Mike Griffin	.416

Teams: Dodgers

Brooklyn Dodgers Team Pitching Leaders—Career

Wins

1	Dazzy Vance	190
2	Brickyard Kennedy	177
3	Burleigh Grimes	158
4	Nap Rucker	134
5	Adonis Terry	127
6	Don Newcombe	123
7	Carl Erskine	118
8	Jeff Pfeffer	113
9	Bob Caruthers	110
10	Watty Clark	106
11	Van Lingle Mungo	102
12	Preacher Roe	93
13	Ed Stein	91
14	Whit Wyatt	80
	Ralph Branca	80
16	Henry Porter	75
17	Tom Lovett	73
18	Hugh Casey	70
	Kirby Higbe	70
20	Sherry Smith	69

Losses

1	Brickyard Kennedy	149
2	Adonis Terry	139
3	Nap Rucker	134
4	Dazzy Vance	131
5	Burleigh Grimes	121
6	Van Lingle Mungo	99
7	Harry McIntire	98
8	Watty Clark	88
9	Jeff Pfeffer	80
10	George Bell	79
11	Leon Cadore	71
	Carl Erskine	71
13	Sherry Smith	70
14	Doc Scanlan	67
15	Ed Stein	66
16	Henry Porter	64
17	Don Newcombe	60
18	Jesse Petty	59
19	Ralph Branca	58
20	Luke Hamlin	57

Winning Percentage
(minimum 100 decisions)

1	Preacher Roe	.715
2	Bob Caruthers	.683
3	Don Newcombe	.672
4	Kirby Higbe	.648
5	Whit Wyatt	.640
6	Hugh Casey	.631
7	Carl Erskine	.624
8	Tom Lovett	.619
9	Dazzy Vance	.592
10	Jeff Pfeffer	.585
11	Ralph Branca	.580
12	Ed Stein	.580
13	Burleigh Grimes	.566
14	Curt Davis	.550
15	Watty Clark	.546
16	Jack Dunn	.544
17	Brickyard Kennedy	.543
18	Henry Porter	.540
19	Rube Marquard	.538
20	Luke Hamlin	.513

Games

1	Brickyard Kennedy	381
2	Dazzy Vance	378
3	Nap Rucker	336
4	Watty Clark	322
5	Burleigh Grimes	318
6	Clem Labine	304
7	Carl Erskine	294
8	Hugh Casey	293
9	Adonis Terry	291
10	Van Lingle Mungo	284
11	Ralph Branca	283
12	Don Newcombe	247
13	Sherry Smith	229
14	Jeff Pfeffer	226
15	Preacher Roe	201
16	Joe Hatten	197
17	Leon Cadore	189
18	Luke Hamlin	186
19	Erv Palica	184
20	Ed Stein	182

Games Started

1	Brickyard Kennedy	332
2	Dazzy Vance	326
3	Burleigh Grimes	285
4	Adonis Terry	276
5	Nap Rucker	272
6	Don Newcombe	222
7	Van Lingle Mungo	215
8	Carl Erskine	204
9	Jeff Pfeffer	200
10	Watty Clark	196
11	Preacher Roe	173
12	Ralph Branca	166
13	Bob Caruthers	158
14	Ed Stein	156
15	Harry McIntire	149
16	Whit Wyatt	148
17	Leon Cadore	146
18	Doc Scanlan	145
19	Henry Porter	142
20	Luke Hamlin	136

Complete Games

1	Brickyard Kennedy	279
2	Adonis Terry	256
3	Dazzy Vance	212
4	Burleigh Grimes	205
5	Nap Rucker	186
6	Jeff Pfeffer	157
7	Bob Caruthers	147
8	Henry Porter	139
9	Ed Stein	136
10	Harry McIntire	119
11	Van Lingle Mungo	114
12	Don Newcombe	110
13	Tom Lovett	107
14	Doc Scanlan	100
15	George Bell	92
16	Watty Clark	90
17	John Harkins	88
18	Jack Dunn	86
19	Oscar Jones	83
	Leon Cadore	83

Shutouts

1	Nap Rucker	38
2	Dazzy Vance	30
3	Jeff Pfeffer	25
4	Don Newcombe	22
5	Burleigh Grimes	20
6	George Bell	17
	Whit Wyatt	17
8	Van Lingle Mungo	16
9	Adonis Terry	15
	Doc Scanlan	15
11	Bob Caruthers	14
	Harry McIntire	14
	Watty Clark	14
14	Curt Davis	13
	Ralph Branca	13
	Carl Erskine	13
17	Preacher Roe	12
18	Brickyard Kennedy	11
	Sherry Smith	11
	Johnny Podres	11

Saves

1	Clem Labine	59
2	Hugh Casey	50
3	Jim Hughes	39
4	Jack Quinn	23
5	Ed Roebuck	21
6	Joe Black	20
7	Hank Behrman	19
8	Ralph Branca	18
9	Sherry Smith	16
	Watty Clark	16
11	Nap Rucker	14
	Van Lingle Mungo	14
	Dutch Leonard	14
	Les Webber	14
15	Curt Davis	13
16	Carl Erskine	12
	Don Bessent	12
18	Ed Head	11
19	Vic Lombardi	10
	Erv Palica	10

Innings Pitched

1	Brickyard Kennedy	2,857.0
2	Dazzy Vance	2,757.2
3	Burleigh Grimes	2,425.2
4	Adonis Terry	2,385.1
5	Nap Rucker	2,375.1
6	Jeff Pfeffer	1,748.1
7	Van Lingle Mungo	1,739.1
8	Watty Clark	1,659.0
9	Don Newcombe	1,628.1
10	Carl Erskine	1,597.0
11	Bob Caruthers	1,433.2
12	Ed Stein	1,403.1
13	Ralph Branca	1,324.0
14	Harry McIntire	1,300.1
15	Preacher Roe	1,277.1
16	Leon Cadore	1,251.0
17	Henry Porter	1,245.1
18	Doc Scanlan	1,221.1
19	Sherry Smith	1,197.2
20	George Bell	1,086.0

Walks

1	Brickyard Kennedy	1,128
2	Dazzy Vance	764
3	Burleigh Grimes	744
4	Adonis Terry	737
5	Nap Rucker	701
6	Van Lingle Mungo	697
7	Carl Erskine	598
8	Ed Stein	593
9	Ralph Branca	589
10	Doc Scanlan	582
11	Kirby Higbe	452
12	Harry McIntire	450
13	Joe Hatten	430
14	Jeff Pfeffer	415
15	Rex Barney	410
16	Don Newcombe	405
17	Hal Gregg	377
18	Tom Lovett	370
19	Doug McWeeny	361
20	Watty Clark	353

Strikeouts

1	Dazzy Vance	1,918
2	Nap Rucker	1,217
3	Adonis Terry	1,203
4	Van Lingle Mungo	1,031
5	Burleigh Grimes	952
6	Carl Erskine	912
7	Don Newcombe	897
8	Ralph Branca	757
9	Brickyard Kennedy	749
10	Jeff Pfeffer	656
11	Preacher Roe	632
12	Watty Clark	620
13	Doc Scanlan	574
14	Whit Wyatt	540
15	Harry McIntire	497
16	Kirby Higbe	488
17	Rube Marquard	444
18	Leon Cadore	440
19	Henry Porter	434
20	Ed Stein	432

Strikeouts/9 Innings
(minimum 1000 Innings Pitched)

1	Dazzy Vance	6.26
2	Van Lingle Mungo	5.33
3	Ralph Branca	5.15
4	Carl Erskine	5.14
5	Don Newcombe	4.96
6	Nap Rucker	4.61
7	Adonis Terry	4.54
8	Whit Wyatt	4.53
9	Preacher Roe	4.45
10	Doc Scanlan	4.23
11	Luke Hamlin	3.80
12	Burleigh Grimes	3.53
13	Harry McIntire	3.44
14	Jeff Pfeffer	3.38
15	Watty Clark	3.36
16	Leon Cadore	3.17
17	Henry Porter	3.14
18	George Bell	3.12
19	Tom Lovett	3.05
20	Ed Stein	2.77

ERA
(minimum 1000 Innings Pitched)

1	Jeff Pfeffer	2.31
2	Nap Rucker	2.42
3	George Bell	2.85
4	Whit Wyatt	2.86
5	Sherry Smith	2.91
6	Bob Caruthers	2.92
7	Doc Scanlan	2.95
8	Harry McIntire	3.11
9	Leon Cadore	3.11
10	Dazzy Vance	3.17
11	Curt Davis	3.23
12	Preacher Roe	3.26
13	Henry Porter	3.39
14	Adonis Terry	3.41
15	Van Lingle Mungo	3.41
16	Don Newcombe	3.42
17	Burleigh Grimes	3.46
18	Watty Clark	3.55
19	Luke Hamlin	3.61
20	Ralph Branca	3.70

Component ERA
(minimum 1000 Innings Pitched)

1	Whit Wyatt	2.51
2	Jeff Pfeffer	2.54
3	Nap Rucker	2.60
4	George Bell	2.70
5	Bob Caruthers	2.81
6	Dazzy Vance	2.92
7	Adonis Terry	2.92
8	Doc Scanlan	2.92
9	Henry Porter	3.07
10	Leon Cadore	3.09
11	Curt Davis	3.11
12	Sherry Smith	3.13
13	Harry McIntire	3.16
14	Don Newcombe	3.18
15	Luke Hamlin	3.19
16	Van Lingle Mungo	3.24
17	Tom Lovett	3.29
18	Watty Clark	3.33
19	Burleigh Grimes	3.50
20	Preacher Roe	3.56

Opponent Average
(minimum 1000 Innings Pitched)

1	Whit Wyatt	.229
2	Doc Scanlan	.235
3	Ralph Branca	.242
4	Adonis Terry	.243
5	Nap Rucker	.243
6	Jeff Pfeffer	.244
7	Don Newcombe	.245
8	Van Lingle Mungo	.245
9	Bob Caruthers	.248
10	Carl Erskine	.248
11	Dazzy Vance	.249
12	Tom Lovett	.253
13	Henry Porter	.254
14	George Bell	.254
15	Luke Hamlin	.255
16	Harry McIntire	.258
17	Preacher Roe	.258
18	Curt Davis	.261
19	Ed Stein	.261
20	Leon Cadore	.268

Opponent OBP
(minimum 1000 Innings Pitched)

1	Whit Wyatt	.286
2	Bob Caruthers	.292
3	Don Newcombe	.293
4	Jeff Pfeffer	.298
5	Luke Hamlin	.299
6	Curt Davis	.300
7	Adonis Terry	.300
8	Henry Porter	.302
9	Preacher Roe	.304
10	Dazzy Vance	.305
11	Nap Rucker	.306
12	George Bell	.310
13	Watty Clark	.311
14	Tom Lovett	.313
15	Leon Cadore	.313
16	Carl Erskine	.317
17	Sherry Smith	.318
18	Van Lingle Mungo	.319
19	Ralph Branca	.325
20	Doc Scanlan	.329

Teams: Dodgers

Los Angeles Dodgers Team Batting Leaders—Career

## Games		## At-Bats		## Runs		## Hits	
1 Bill Russell	2,181	1 Willie Davis	7,495	1 Willie Davis	1,004	1 Willie Davis	2,091
2 Willie Davis	1,952	2 Bill Russell	7,318	2 Maury Wills	876	2 Steve Garvey	1,968
3 Steve Garvey	1,727	3 Steve Garvey	6,543	3 Steve Garvey	852	3 Bill Russell	1,926
4 Maury Wills	1,593	4 Maury Wills	6,156	4 Bill Russell	796	4 Maury Wills	1,732
5 Ron Cey	1,481	5 Ron Cey	5,216	5 Davey Lopes	759	5 Ron Cey	1,378
6 Mike Scioscia	1,441	6 Davey Lopes	4,590	6 Ron Cey	715	6 Steve Sax	1,218
7 Ron Fairly	1,306	7 Mike Scioscia	4,373	7 Jim Gilliam	630	7 Davey Lopes	1,204
8 Wes Parker	1,288	8 Steve Sax	4,312	8 Steve Sax	574	8 Dusty Baker	1,144
9 John Roseboro	1,254	9 Jim Gilliam	4,158	9 Pedro Guerrero	561	9 Mike Scioscia	1,131
10 Steve Yeager	1,219	10 Wes Parker	4,157	10 Dusty Baker	549	10 Pedro Guerrero	1,113
11 Jim Gilliam	1,210	11 Dusty Baker	4,073	11 Wes Parker	548	11 Wes Parker	1,110
12 Davey Lopes	1,207	12 John Roseboro	3,951	12 Ron Fairly	491	12 Jim Gilliam	1,084
13 Dusty Baker	1,117	13 Ron Fairly	3,880	13 Brett Butler	455	13 Ron Fairly	1,010
14 Steve Sax	1,091	14 Pedro Guerrero	3,602	14 Eric Karros	441	14 John Roseboro	999
15 Pedro Guerrero	1,036	15 Steve Yeager	3,454	15 Willie Crawford	437	15 Tommy Davis	912
16 Willie Crawford	989	16 Eric Karros	3,371	16 John Roseboro	435	16 Eric Karros	891
17 Mike Marshall	928	17 Mike Marshall	3,249	17 Mike Piazza	423	17 Mike Marshall	882
18 Jim Lefebvre	922	18 Jim Lefebvre	3,014	18 Mike Scioscia	398	18 Mike Piazza	854
19 Eric Karros	891	19 Tommy Davis	2,999	19 Mike Marshall	395	19 Bill Buckner	837
20 Ken Landreaux	868	20 Bill Buckner	2,895	20 Tommy Davis	392	Brett Butler	837

## Doubles		## Triples		## Home Runs		## RBI	
1 Steve Garvey	333	1 Willie Davis	110	1 Ron Cey	228	1 Steve Garvey	992
2 Willie Davis	321	2 Bill Russell	57	2 Steve Garvey	211	2 Willie Davis	849
3 Bill Russell	293	3 Maury Wills	56	3 Pedro Guerrero	171	3 Ron Cey	842
4 Ron Cey	223	4 John Roseboro	44	4 Mike Piazza	168	4 Bill Russell	627
5 Mike Scioscia	198	5 Brett Butler	41	5 Willie Davis	154	5 Dusty Baker	586
6 Wes Parker	194	6 Davey Lopes	39	Eric Karros	154	6 Pedro Guerrero	585
7 Dusty Baker	179	7 Steve Garvey	35	7 Dusty Baker	144	7 Ron Fairly	541
8 Jim Gilliam	176	Steve Sax	35	8 Mike Marshall	137	8 Eric Karros	535
9 Pedro Guerrero	169	9 Wes Parker	32	9 Frank Howard	123	9 Mike Piazza	533
10 Ron Fairly	168	10 Willie Crawford	29	10 Steve Yeager	100	10 Mike Marshall	484
11 Davey Lopes	165	11 Raul Mondesi	27	Raul Mondesi	100	11 Wes Parker	470
Eric Karros	165	12 Jim Gilliam	26	12 Davey Lopes	99	12 John Roseboro	465
13 John Roseboro	160	13 Wally Moon	24	13 Reggie Smith	97	Tommy Davis	465
14 Steve Sax	159	Pedro Guerrero	24	14 Joe Ferguson	91	14 Mike Scioscia	446
15 Mike Marshall	155	Jose Offerman	24	15 Ron Fairly	90	15 Jim Lefebvre	404
16 Maury Wills	150	16 Ken Landreaux	23	John Roseboro	90	16 Steve Yeager	398
17 Raul Mondesi	135	17 Ron Fairly	22	17 Tommy Davis	86	17 Davey Lopes	384
18 Jim Lefebvre	126	Tommy Davis	22	18 Willie Crawford	74	18 Frank Howard	382
19 Willie Crawford	125	Manny Mota	22	Jim Lefebvre	74	19 Maury Wills	374
20 Bill Buckner	121	20 Charlie Neal	20	20 Two tied at	73	20 Willie Crawford	335

## Walks		## Strikeouts		## Stolen Bases		## Runs Created	
1 Ron Cey	765	1 Ron Cey	838	1 Maury Wills	490	1 Willie Davis	987
2 Jim Gilliam	631	2 Willie Davis	815	2 Davey Lopes	418	2 Steve Garvey	931
3 Davey Lopes	603	3 Steve Garvey	751	3 Willie Davis	335	3 Ron Cey	817
4 Mike Scioscia	567	4 Mike Marshall	724	4 Steve Sax	290	4 Maury Wills	755
5 Wes Parker	532	5 Steve Yeager	703	5 Brett Butler	179	5 Bill Russell	738
6 Ron Fairly	522	6 Bill Russell	667	6 Bill Russell	167	6 Davey Lopes	678
7 Bill Russell	483	7 Davey Lopes	629	7 Ken Landreaux	119	7 Pedro Guerrero	667
8 Maury Wills	456	8 Wes Parker	615	8 Delino DeShields	114	8 Dusty Baker	586
9 John Roseboro	434	9 Pedro Guerrero	611	9 Jim Gilliam	112	9 Jim Gilliam	577
10 Brett Butler	432	10 Eric Karros	596	10 Mariano Duncan	100	10 Wes Parker	571
11 Pedro Guerrero	417	11 Willie Crawford	581	11 Bill Buckner	93	11 Ron Fairly	555
12 Dusty Baker	392	12 Maury Wills	562	12 Raul Mondesi	88	12 Mike Scioscia	546
13 Joe Ferguson	382	13 John Roseboro	546	13 Pedro Guerrero	86	13 Steve Sax	539
14 Steve Garvey	367	14 Frank Howard	515	14 Steve Garvey	77	14 Mike Piazza	535
15 Steve Sax	363	15 Dusty Baker	509	15 Dusty Baker	73	15 John Roseboro	519
16 Willie Crawford	360	16 Ron Fairly	485	16 Kirk Gibson	69	16 Mike Marshall	454
17 Willie Davis	350	17 Jim Lefebvre	447	17 Tommy Davis	65	17 Eric Karros	450
18 Wally Moon	337	18 Joe Ferguson	423	18 Juan Samuel	63	18 Tommy Davis	442
19 Steve Yeager	330	19 Raul Mondesi	417	19 Jose Offerman	61	19 Brett Butler	425
20 Jim Lefebvre	322	20 Rick Monday	415	20 Wes Parker	60	20 Willie Crawford	413

## Runs Created/27 Outs		## Batting Average		## On-Base Percentage		## Slugging Percentage	
(minimum 2000 Plate Appearances)		(minimum 2000 Plate Appearances)		(minimum 2000 Plate Appearances)		(minimum 2000 Plate Appearances)	
1 Mike Piazza	8.01	1 Mike Piazza	.334	1 Mike Piazza	.398	1 Mike Piazza	.576
2 Reggie Smith	7.12	2 Manny Mota	.315	2 Brett Butler	.392	2 Reggie Smith	.528
3 Pedro Guerrero	6.83	3 Pedro Guerrero	.309	3 Reggie Smith	.387	3 Pedro Guerrero	.512
4 Raul Mondesi	5.95	4 Tommy Davis	.304	4 Pedro Guerrero	.381	4 Raul Mondesi	.511
5 Wally Moon	5.82	5 Steve Garvey	.301	5 Wally Moon	.377	5 Frank Howard	.495
6 Frank Howard	5.59	6 Raul Mondesi	.299	6 Manny Mota	.374	6 Steve Garvey	.459
7 Ron Cey	5.43	7 Brett Butler	.298	7 Ron Cey	.359	7 Eric Karros	.455
8 Brett Butler	5.30	8 Reggie Smith	.297	8 Joe Ferguson	.359	8 Mike Marshall	.449
9 Tommy Davis	5.30	9 Bill Buckner	.289	9 Jim Gilliam	.358	9 Ron Cey	.445
10 Joe Ferguson	5.20	10 Wally Moon	.286	10 Willie Crawford	.351	10 Tommy Davis	.441
11 Willie Crawford	5.20	11 Steve Sax	.282	11 Wes Parker	.351	11 Dusty Baker	.437
12 Steve Garvey	5.16	12 Maury Wills	.281	12 Davey Lopes	.349	12 Wally Moon	.435
13 Manny Mota	5.12	13 Dusty Baker	.281	13 Ron Fairly	.347	13 Joe Ferguson	.419
14 Dusty Baker	5.08	14 Willie Davis	.279	14 Mike Scioscia	.344	14 Willie Crawford	.413
15 Davey Lopes	5.06	15 Mike Marshall	.271	15 Jose Offerman	.344	15 Willie Davis	.413
16 Mike Marshall	4.93	16 Frank Howard	.269	16 Dusty Baker	.343	16 Charlie Neal	.411
17 Ron Fairly	4.90	17 Willie Crawford	.268	17 Steve Sax	.339	17 Ken Landreaux	.394
18 Jim Gilliam	4.76	18 Wes Parker	.267	18 Raul Mondesi	.339	18 Manny Mota	.391
19 Wes Parker	4.72	19 Eric Karros	.264	19 Tommy Davis	.338	19 Ron Fairly	.385
20 Willie Davis	4.64	20 Ron Cey	.264	20 Steve Garvey	.337	20 John Roseboro	.384

Teams: Dodgers

Los Angeles Dodgers Team Pitching Leaders—Career

Wins

1	Don Sutton	233
2	Don Drysdale	187
3	Sandy Koufax	156
4	Claude Osteen	147
5	Fernando Valenzuela	141
6	Orel Hershiser	134
7	Ramon Martinez	116
8	Bob Welch	115
9	Burt Hooton	112
10	Johnny Podres	95
11	Tommy John	87
12	Jerry Reuss	86
13	Doug Rau	80
14	Bill Singer	69
15	Jim Brewer	61
16	Stan Williams	57
17	Andy Messersmith	55
18	Ron Perranoski	54
19	Tom Candiotti	52
20	Tim Belcher	50

Losses

1	Don Sutton	181
2	Don Drysdale	152
3	Claude Osteen	126
4	Fernando Valenzuela	116
5	Orel Hershiser	102
6	Bob Welch	86
7	Burt Hooton	84
8	Sandy Koufax	77
9	Bill Singer	76
10	Johnny Podres	74
	Ramon Martinez	74
12	Jerry Reuss	69
13	Tom Candiotti	64
14	Doug Rau	58
15	Jim Brewer	51
16	Pedro Astacio	47
17	Stan Williams	46
	Charlie Hough	46
19	Rick Honeycutt	45
20	Kevin Gross	44

Winning Percentage
(minimum 75 decisions)

1	Tommy John	.674
2	Sandy Koufax	.670
3	Andy Messersmith	.618
4	Ramon Martinez	.611
5	Doug Rau	.580
6	Bob Welch	.572
7	Burt Hooton	.571
8	Ron Perranoski	.568
9	Tim Belcher	.568
10	Orel Hershiser	.568
11	Don Sutton	.563
12	Johnny Podres	.562
13	Jerry Reuss	.555
14	Al Downing	.554
15	Stan Williams	.553
16	Don Drysdale	.552
17	Fernando Valenzuela	.549
18	Jim Brewer	.545
19	Claude Osteen	.538
20	Charlie Hough	.505

Games

1	Don Sutton	550
2	Jim Brewer	474
3	Don Drysdale	459
4	Ron Perranoski	457
5	Charlie Hough	401
6	Orel Hershiser	343
7	Claude Osteen	339
8	Sandy Koufax	335
9	Fernando Valenzuela	331
10	Burt Hooton	322
11	Tom Niedenfuer	310
12	Bob Welch	292
13	Alejandro Pena	281
	Tim Crews	281
15	Bob Miller	275
16	Jim Gott	272
17	Todd Worrell	269
18	Jerry Reuss	253
19	Ramon Martinez	251
20	Johnny Podres	246

Games Started

1	Don Sutton	533
2	Don Drysdale	424
3	Claude Osteen	335
4	Fernando Valenzuela	320
5	Orel Hershiser	303
6	Sandy Koufax	286
7	Bob Welch	267
8	Burt Hooton	265
9	Ramon Martinez	247
10	Johnny Podres	220
11	Jerry Reuss	201
12	Doug Rau	184
13	Bill Singer	179
14	Tommy John	174
15	Tom Candiotti	159
16	Pedro Astacio	132
17	Stan Williams	129
18	Andy Messersmith	123
19	Al Downing	120
20	Tim Belcher	119

Complete Games

1	Don Drysdale	156
	Don Sutton	156
3	Sandy Koufax	133
4	Fernando Valenzuela	107
5	Claude Osteen	100
6	Orel Hershiser	65
7	Burt Hooton	61
8	Bill Singer	52
9	Johnny Podres	50
10	Bob Welch	47
11	Jerry Reuss	44
12	Andy Messersmith	43
13	Tommy John	37
14	Ramon Martinez	36
15	Doug Rau	33
16	Al Downing	25
17	Stan Williams	24
18	Rick Rhoden	21
	Tim Belcher	21
20	Roger Craig	16

Shutouts

1	Don Sutton	52
2	Don Drysdale	45
3	Sandy Koufax	38
4	Claude Osteen	34
5	Fernando Valenzuela	29
6	Orel Hershiser	24
7	Bob Welch	23
8	Burt Hooton	22
9	Ramon Martinez	20
10	Bill Singer	18
11	Jerry Reuss	16
12	Andy Messersmith	13
13	Johnny Podres	12
	Al Downing	12
	Tim Belcher	12
16	Doug Rau	11
	Tommy John	11
18	Pedro Astacio	9
19	Three tied at	7

Saves

1	Todd Worrell	127
2	Jim Brewer	125
3	Ron Perranoski	101
4	Jay Howell	85
5	Tom Niedenfuer	64
6	Charlie Hough	60
7	Steve Howe	59
8	Mike Marshall	42
9	Larry Sherry	39
10	Jim Gott	38
11	Alejandro Pena	32
12	Ken Howell	31
13	Phil Regan	27
	Terry Forster	27
15	Clem Labine	24
	Bob Miller	24
17	Roger McDowell	23
18	Ed Roebuck	22
19	Pete Mikkelsen	20
20	Bobby Castillo	18

Innings Pitched

1	Don Sutton	3,816.1
2	Don Drysdale	3,112.0
3	Claude Osteen	2,396.2
4	Fernando Valenzuela	2,348.2
5	Orel Hershiser	2,156.0
6	Sandy Koufax	2,119.2
7	Burt Hooton	1,861.1
8	Bob Welch	1,820.2
9	Ramon Martinez	1,630.0
10	Jerry Reuss	1,407.2
11	Johnny Podres	1,407.1
12	Bill Singer	1,274.1
13	Doug Rau	1,250.2
14	Tommy John	1,198.0
15	Tom Candiotti	1,048.0
16	Andy Messersmith	926.0
17	Al Downing	897.2
18	Pedro Astacio	886.2
19	Stan Williams	872.0
20	Jim Brewer	822.1

Walks

1	Don Sutton	996
2	Fernando Valenzuela	915
3	Don Drysdale	763
4	Sandy Koufax	709
5	Ramon Martinez	663
6	Orel Hershiser	653
7	Claude Osteen	568
8	Bob Welch	565
9	Burt Hooton	540
10	Johnny Podres	452
11	Stan Williams	429
12	Charlie Hough	417
13	Bill Singer	392
14	Doug Rau	378
15	Jerry Reuss	333
16	Tom Candiotti	329
17	Al Downing	326
18	Andy Messersmith	301
19	Jim Brewer	298
20	Tommy John	296

Strikeouts

1	Don Sutton	2,696
2	Don Drysdale	2,283
3	Sandy Koufax	2,214
4	Fernando Valenzuela	1,759
5	Orel Hershiser	1,443
6	Bob Welch	1,292
7	Ramon Martinez	1,223
8	Claude Osteen	1,162
9	Burt Hooton	1,042
10	Bill Singer	989
11	Johnny Podres	947
12	Tom Candiotti	718
13	Hideo Nomo	703
14	Doug Rau	694
15	Jerry Reuss	685
16	Jim Brewer	672
17	Stan Williams	657
18	Tommy John	649
19	Andy Messersmith	637
20	Tim Belcher	633

Strikeouts/9 Innings
(minimum 750 Innings Pitched)

1	Sandy Koufax	9.40
2	Jim Brewer	7.35
3	Tim Belcher	7.07
4	Bill Singer	6.98
5	Stan Williams	6.78
6	Ramon Martinez	6.75
7	Fernando Valenzuela	6.74
8	Alejandro Pena	6.68
9	Don Drysdale	6.60
10	Bob Welch	6.39
11	Don Sutton	6.36
12	Andy Messersmith	6.19
13	Tom Candiotti	6.17
14	Pedro Astacio	6.07
15	Johnny Podres	6.06
16	Charlie Hough	6.03
17	Orel Hershiser	6.02
18	Ron Perranoski	5.41
19	Al Downing	5.33
20	Burt Hooton	5.04

ERA
(minimum 750 Innings Pitched)

1	Ron Perranoski	2.56
2	Jim Brewer	2.62
3	Sandy Koufax	2.64
4	Andy Messersmith	2.67
5	Alejandro Pena	2.92
6	Tommy John	2.97
7	Don Drysdale	2.98
8	Tim Belcher	2.99
9	Orel Hershiser	3.00
10	Bill Singer	3.03
11	Claude Osteen	3.09
12	Don Sutton	3.09
13	Jerry Reuss	3.11
14	Burt Hooton	3.14
15	Bob Welch	3.14
16	Al Downing	3.16
17	Doug Rau	3.30
18	Fernando Valenzuela	3.31
19	Ramon Martinez	3.48
20	Charlie Hough	3.50

Component ERA
(minimum 750 Innings Pitched)

1	Sandy Koufax	2.35
2	Jim Brewer	2.45
3	Andy Messersmith	2.60
4	Don Sutton	2.72
5	Bill Singer	2.77
6	Tim Belcher	2.81
7	Burt Hooton	2.89
8	Alejandro Pena	2.91
9	Orel Hershiser	2.91
10	Don Drysdale	2.94
11	Jerry Reuss	3.03
12	Ron Perranoski	3.05
13	Bob Welch	3.05
14	Tommy John	3.09
15	Claude Osteen	3.17
16	Fernando Valenzuela	3.21
17	Al Downing	3.30
18	Ramon Martinez	3.46
19	Pedro Astacio	3.52
20	Tom Candiotti	3.53

Opponent Average
(minimum 750 Innings Pitched)

1	Sandy Koufax	.202
2	Andy Messersmith	.215
3	Jim Brewer	.216
4	Charlie Hough	.221
5	Tim Belcher	.228
6	Bill Singer	.230
7	Don Sutton	.231
8	Stan Williams	.233
9	Ramon Martinez	.237
10	Don Drysdale	.239
11	Orel Hershiser	.239
12	Alejandro Pena	.239
13	Burt Hooton	.239
14	Bob Welch	.240
15	Fernando Valenzuela	.240
16	Al Downing	.242
17	Ron Perranoski	.247
18	Tom Candiotti	.253
19	Pedro Astacio	.254
20	Tommy John	.255

Opponent OBP
(minimum 750 Innings Pitched)

1	Sandy Koufax	.269
2	Andy Messersmith	.281
3	Don Sutton	.282
4	Jim Brewer	.287
5	Bill Singer	.292
6	Tim Belcher	.292
7	Don Drysdale	.292
8	Burt Hooton	.293
9	Orel Hershiser	.299
10	Alejandro Pena	.299
11	Bob Welch	.300
12	Jerry Reuss	.301
13	Tommy John	.302
14	Claude Osteen	.303
15	Al Downing	.310
16	Fernando Valenzuela	.312
17	Pedro Astacio	.314
18	Tom Candiotti	.314
19	Ramon Martinez	.315
20	Doug Rau	.318

Dodgers Franchise Batting Leaders—Single Season

Games

	Player	Year	G
1	Maury Wills	1962	165
2	Tommy Davis	1962	163
	Steve Garvey	1980	163
4	Bill Russell	1973	162
	Steve Garvey	1976	162
	Steve Garvey	1977	162
	Steve Garvey	1978	162
	Steve Garvey	1979	162
	Steve Garvey	1982	162
	Eric Karros	1997	162
11	Wes Parker	1970	161
	Brett Butler	1991	161
13	Jim Gilliam	1962	160
	Willie Davis	1968	160
	Bill Russell	1974	160
	Steve Garvey	1975	160
	Pedro Guerrero	1983	160
	Steve Sax	1988	160
	Eddie Murray	1989	160
	Todd Zeile	1997	160

At-Bats

	Player	Year	AB
1	Maury Wills	1962	695
2	Carl Furillo	1951	667
3	Tommy Davis	1962	665
4	Steve Garvey	1975	659
5	Steve Garvey	1980	658
6	Ivy Olson	1921	652
7	Maury Wills	1965	650
8	Steve Garvey	1979	648
9	Steve Garvey	1977	646
10	Willie Davis	1968	643
11	Steve Garvey	1974	642
	Bill Buckner	1976	642
13	Willie Davis	1971	641
14	Steve Garvey	1978	639
15	Steve Sax	1982	638
16	Ivy Olson	1920	637
17	Jimmy Johnston	1920	635
	Buddy Hassett	1936	635
19	Bill Russell	1977	634
	Raul Mondesi	1996	634

Runs

	Player	Year	R
1	Hub Collins	1890	148
2	Darby O'Brien	1889	146
3	Babe Herman	1930	143
4	Mike Griffin	1895	140
	Willie Keeler	1899	140
6	Hub Collins	1889	139
7	Mike Griffin	1897	136
8	Tom Daly	1894	135
9	George Pinckney	1888	134
	Fielder Jones	1897	134
11	George Pinckney	1887	133
12	Pee Wee Reese	1949	132
	Duke Snider	1953	132
14	Bill McClellan	1886	131
15	Maury Wills	1962	130
16	Eddie Stanky	1945	128
17	Johnny Frederick	1929	127
18	Goody Rosen	1945	126
	Duke Snider	1955	126
20	Three tied at		125

Hits

	Player	Year	H
1	Babe Herman	1930	241
2	Tommy Davis	1962	230
3	Zack Wheat	1925	221
4	Lefty O'Doul	1932	219
5	Babe Herman	1929	217
6	Willie Keeler	1899	216
7	Zack Wheat	1924	212
8	Steve Garvey	1975	210
	Steve Sax	1986	210
10	Maury Wills	1962	208
11	Johnny Frederick	1929	206
	Johnny Frederick	1930	206
13	Willie Keeler	1900	204
	Steve Garvey	1979	204
15	Jimmy Johnston	1921	203
	Jimmy Johnston	1923	203
	Jackie Robinson	1949	203
18	Willie Keeler	1901	202
	Milt Stock	1925	202
	Steve Garvey	1978	202

Doubles

	Player	Year	2B
1	Johnny Frederick	1929	52
2	Babe Herman	1930	48
3	Wes Parker	1970	47
4	Johnny Frederick	1930	44
5	Babe Herman	1931	43
	Augie Galan	1944	43
	Steve Sax	1986	43
8	Zack Wheat	1925	42
	Babe Herman	1929	42
	Dixie Walker	1945	42
	Raul Mondesi	1997	42
12	Jimmy Johnston	1921	41
	Zack Wheat	1924	41
	Billy Herman	1943	41
15	Red Smith	1913	40
	Raul Mondesi	1996	40
17	Five tied at		39

Triples

	Player	Year	3B
1	George Treadway	1894	26
2	Hi Myers	1920	22
3	Dan Brouthers	1892	20
	Tommy Corcoran	1894	20
5	Jimmy Sheckard	1901	19
6	Oyster Burns	1892	18
	Harry Lumley	1904	18
8	John Anderson	1896	17
	Joe Kelley	1900	17
	Pete Reiser	1941	17
	Jim Gilliam	1953	17
12	Germany Smith	1887	16
	Candy LaChance	1897	16
	Whitey Alperman	1907	16
	Jake Daubert	1912	16
	Jack Fournier	1925	16
	Babe Herman	1931	16
	Willie Davis	1970	16
19	Four tied at		15

Home Runs

	Player	Year	HR
1	Duke Snider	1956	43
2	Duke Snider	1953	42
	Gil Hodges	1954	42
	Duke Snider	1955	42
5	Roy Campanella	1953	41
6	Gil Hodges	1951	40
	Duke Snider	1954	40
	Duke Snider	1957	40
	Mike Piazza	1997	40
10	Mike Piazza	1996	36
11	Babe Herman	1930	35
	Mike Piazza	1993	35
13	Dolph Camilli	1941	34
	Eric Karros	1996	34
15	Roy Campanella	1951	33
	Steve Garvey	1977	33
	Pedro Guerrero	1985	33
18	Ten tied at		32

RBI

	Player	Year	RBI
1	Tommy Davis	1962	153
2	Roy Campanella	1953	142
3	Duke Snider	1955	136
4	Jack Fournier	1925	130
	Babe Herman	1930	130
	Duke Snider	1954	130
	Gil Hodges	1954	130
8	Oyster Burns	1890	128
9	Glenn Wright	1930	126
	Duke Snider	1953	126
11	Dan Brouthers	1892	124
	Dixie Walker	1945	124
	Jackie Robinson	1949	124
	Mike Piazza	1997	124
15	Hack Wilson	1932	123
16	Gil Hodges	1953	122
17	Dolph Camilli	1941	120
18	Frank Howard	1962	119
19	Jack Fournier	1924	116
	Dixie Walker	1946	116

Walks

	Player	Year	BB
1	Eddie Stanky	1945	148
2	Eddie Stanky	1946	137
3	Dolph Camilli	1938	119
4	Pee Wee Reese	1949	116
5	Augie Galan	1945	114
6	Dolph Camilli	1939	110
	Jimmy Wynn	1975	110
8	Jimmy Wynn	1974	108
	Brett Butler	1991	108
10	Gil Hodges	1952	107
11	Jackie Robinson	1952	106
12	Dolph Camilli	1941	104
	Pee Wee Reese	1947	104
	Duke Snider	1955	104
	Reggie Smith	1977	104
16	Augie Galan	1943	103
	Eddie Stanky	1947	103
18	Augie Galan	1944	101
19	Jim Gilliam	1953	100
20	Duke Snider	1956	99

Strikeouts

	Player	Year	SO
1	Billy Grabarkewitz	1970	149
2	Cory Snyder	1993	147
3	Mike Marshall	1985	137
4	Juan Samuel	1991	133
5	John Shelby	1988	128
6	Mike Marshall	1983	127
7	Juan Samuel	1990	126
8	Darryl Strawberry	1991	125
9	Delino DeShields	1996	124
10	Raul Mondesi	1996	122
11	Eric Karros	1996	121
12	Kirk Gibson	1988	120
	Greg Gagne	1997	120
14	Frank Howard	1963	116
	Kal Daniels	1991	116
	Eric Karros	1997	116
17	Dolph Camilli	1941	115
	Eric Karros	1995	115
19	Three tied at		113

Stolen Bases

	Player	Year	SB
1	Maury Wills	1962	104
2	Maury Wills	1965	94
3	Darby O'Brien	1889	91
4	Monte Ward	1892	88
5	Hub Collins	1890	85
6	Davey Lopes	1975	77
7	Bill McClellan	1887	70
8	Jimmy Sheckard	1903	67
9	Jim McTamany	1887	66
10	Hub Collins	1889	65
	Mike Griffin	1891	65
12	Davey Lopes	1976	63
13	George Pinckney	1887	59
	Davey Lopes	1974	59
15	Monte Ward	1891	57
	Darby O'Brien	1892	57
17	Steve Sax	1983	56
18	Darby O'Brien	1888	55
19	Maury Wills	1964	53
20	Two tied at		51

Runs Created

	Player	Year	RC
1	Babe Herman	1930	163
2	Darby O'Brien	1889	151
3	Dan Brouthers	1892	149
4	Duke Snider	1953	148
5	Mike Griffin	1895	144
6	Duke Snider	1954	140
7	Jackie Robinson	1949	139
8	Duke Snider	1955	137
	Mike Piazza	1997	137
10	Jimmy Sheckard	1901	135
11	Tommy Davis	1962	132
12	Tom Daly	1894	131
13	Jack Fournier	1925	130
14	George Pinckney	1890	129
	Lefty O'Doul	1932	129
16	Hub Collins	1890	128
	Babe Herman	1929	128
18	Four tied at		127

Runs Created/27 Outs

(minimum 3.1 Plate Appearances/Tm Gm)

	Player	Year	
1	Mike Griffin	1894	11.41
2	Babe Herman	1930	10.79
3	Mike Griffin	1895	10.42
4	Tom Daly	1894	10.24
5	George Pinckney	1890	10.02
6	Dan Brouthers	1892	10.01
7	Darby O'Brien	1889	9.82
8	Jimmy Sheckard	1901	9.80
9	Mike Piazza	1997	9.71
10	George Treadway	1894	9.60
11	Duke Snider	1953	9.50
12	Oyster Burns	1894	9.49
13	Dixie Walker	1944	9.44
14	Oyster Burns	1889	9.34
15	Duke Snider	1955	9.25
16	Duke Snider	1954	9.21
17	Bill Phillips	1885	9.21
18	Jack Fournier	1925	9.17
19	Hub Collins	1890	9.05
20	Jack Fournier	1923	9.02

Batting Average

(minimum 3.1 Plate Appearances/Tm Gm)

	Player	Year	
1	Babe Herman	1930	.393
2	Babe Herman	1929	.381
3	Willie Keeler	1899	.379
4	Zack Wheat	1924	.375
5	Lefty O'Doul	1932	.368
6	Willie Keeler	1900	.362
7	Mike Piazza	1997	.362
8	Zack Wheat	1925	.359
9	Mike Griffin	1894	.358
10	Dixie Walker	1944	.357
11	Oyster Burns	1894	.354
12	Fielder Jones	1896	.354
13	Jimmy Sheckard	1901	.354
14	Jack Fournier	1923	.351
15	Jack Fournier	1925	.350
16	Jake Daubert	1913	.350
17	Tommy Davis	1962	.346
18	Mike Piazza	1995	.346
19	Carl Furillo	1953	.344
20	Pete Reiser	1941	.343

On-Base Percentage

(minimum 3.1 Plate Appearances/Tm Gm)

	Player	Year	
1	Mike Griffin	1894	.467
2	Babe Herman	1930	.455
3	Jack Fournier	1925	.446
4	Mike Griffin	1895	.444
5	Jackie Robinson	1952	.440
6	Babe Herman	1929	.436
7	Eddie Stanky	1946	.436
8	Tom Daly	1894	.436
9	Wally Moon	1961	.434
10	Dixie Walker	1944	.434
11	Jackie Robinson	1949	.432
12	Dan Brouthers	1892	.432
13	Mike Piazza	1997	.431
14	Jackie Robinson	1951	.429
15	Jack Fournier	1924	.428
16	Zack Wheat	1924	.428
17	Fielder Jones	1896	.427
18	Reggie Smith	1977	.427
19	Augie Galan	1944	.426
20	Willie Keeler	1899	.425

Slugging Percentage

(minimum 3.1 Plate Appearances/Tm Gm)

	Player	Year	
1	Babe Herman	1930	.678
2	Duke Snider	1954	.647
3	Mike Piazza	1997	.638
4	Duke Snider	1955	.628
5	Duke Snider	1953	.627
6	Babe Herman	1929	.612
7	Roy Campanella	1953	.611
8	Mike Piazza	1995	.606
9	Duke Snider	1956	.598
10	Roy Campanella	1951	.590
11	Jack Fournier	1923	.588
12	Duke Snider	1957	.587
13	Roy Campanella	1955	.583
14	Carl Furillo	1953	.580
15	Gil Hodges	1954	.579
16	Pedro Guerrero	1985	.577
17	Reggie Smith	1977	.576
18	Jack Fournier	1925	.569
19	Mike Piazza	1996	.563
20	Mike Piazza	1993	.561

Teams: Dodgers

Dodgers Franchise Pitching Leaders—Single Season

Wins

1	Bob Caruthers	1889	40
2	Henry Porter	1885	33
3	Tom Lovett	1890	30
4	Bob Caruthers	1888	29
	George Haddock	1892	29
6	Jim Hughes	1899	28
	Joe McGinnity	1900	28
	Dazzy Vance	1924	28
9	Henry Porter	1886	27
	Ed Stein	1892	27
	Ed Stein	1894	27
	Don Newcombe	1956	27
	Sandy Koufax	1966	27
14	Adonis Terry	1890	26
	Sandy Koufax	1965	26
16	Six tied at		25

Losses

1	Adonis Terry	1884	35
2	George Bell	1910	27
3	Oscar Jones	1904	25
	Harry McIntire	1905	25
5	Henry Porter	1887	24
6	Jack Cronin	1904	23
7	Joe Yeager	1898	22
	Brickyard Kennedy	1898	22
	Kaiser Wilhelm	1908	22
10	Henry Porter	1885	21
	Jack Dunn	1898	21
	Mal Eason	1905	21
	Harry McIntire	1906	21
	Nap Rucker	1912	21
15	Nine tied at		20

Winning Percentage
(minimum 15 decisions)

1	Phil Regan	1966	.933
2	F. Fitzsimmons	1940	.889
3	Preacher Roe	1951	.880
4	Orel Hershiser	1985	.864
5	Ron Perranoski	1963	.842
6	Sandy Koufax	1963	.833
7	Jim Hughes	1899	.824
	Dazzy Vance	1924	.824
9	Tommy John	1974	.813
10	Don Newcombe	1955	.800
	Rick Rhoden	1976	.800
12	Don Newcombe	1956	.794
13	Sandy Koufax	1964	.792
14	Larry French	1942	.789
	Joe Black	1952	.789
16	Bob Caruthers	1889	.784
17	Johnny Podres	1961	.783
18	Joe McGinnity	1900	.778
	Bob Welch	1985	.778
20	Three tied at		.769

Games

1	Mike Marshall	1974	106
2	Charlie Hough	1976	77
3	Scott Radinsky	1997	75
4	Bob Miller	1964	74
5	Antonio Osuna	1996	73
6	Ron Perranoski	1964	72
	Todd Worrell	1996	72
8	Ron Perranoski	1962	70
	Ron Perranoski	1967	70
	Charlie Hough	1977	70
11	Ron Perranoski	1963	69
12	Jim Gott	1992	68
13	Steve Howe	1982	66
	Tom Niedenfuer	1983	66
	Tim Crews	1990	66
	Mark Guthrie	1996	66
17	Phil Regan	1966	65
	Roger McDowell	1992	65
	Pedro Martinez	1993	65
	Todd Worrell	1997	65

Games Started

1	Adonis Terry	1884	56
2	Henry Porter	1885	54
3	Bob Caruthers	1889	50
4	Henry Porter	1886	48
5	Adonis Terry	1890	44
	George Haddock	1892	44
	Brickyard Kennedy	1893	44
8	Bob Caruthers	1888	43
	Tom Lovett	1891	43
10	Ed Stein	1892	42
	Don Drysdale	1963	42
	Don Drysdale	1965	42
13	Nine tied at		41

Complete Games

1	Adonis Terry	1884	55
2	Henry Porter	1885	53
3	Henry Porter	1886	48
4	Bob Caruthers	1889	46
5	Bob Caruthers	1888	42
6	Sam Kimber	1884	40
	Mickey Hughes	1888	40
	Brickyard Kennedy	1893	40
9	Tom Lovett	1890	39
	Tom Lovett	1891	39
	George Haddock	1892	39
12	Henry Porter	1887	38
	Adonis Terry	1890	38
	Ed Stein	1892	38
	Ed Stein	1894	38
	Brickyard Kennedy	1898	38
	Oscar Jones	1904	38
18	Brickyard Kennedy	1897	36
	Wild Bill Donovan	1901	36
20	Two tied at		35

Shutouts

1	Sandy Koufax	1963	11
2	Don Sutton	1972	9
3	Sandy Koufax	1965	8
	Don Drysdale	1968	8
	F. Valenzuela	1981	8
	Orel Hershiser	1988	8
	Tim Belcher	1989	8
8	Bob Caruthers	1889	7
	Burleigh Grimes	1918	7
	Whit Wyatt	1941	7
	Sandy Koufax	1964	7
	Don Drysdale	1965	7
	Claude Osteen	1969	7
	Andy Messersmith	1975	7
15	Fourteen tied at		6

Saves

1	Todd Worrell	1996	44
2	Todd Worrell	1997	35
3	Todd Worrell	1995	32
4	Jay Howell	1989	28
5	Jim Gott	1993	25
6	Jim Hughes	1954	24
	Jim Brewer	1970	24
8	Jim Brewer	1971	22
	Charlie Hough	1977	22
	Terry Forster	1978	22
11	Ron Perranoski	1963	21
	Phil Regan	1966	21
	Mike Marshall	1974	21
	Jay Howell	1988	21
15	Ron Perranoski	1962	20
	Jim Brewer	1969	20
	Jim Brewer	1973	20
18	Clem Labine	1956	19
	Tom Niedenfuer	1985	19
20	Three tied at		18

Innings Pitched

1	Adonis Terry	1884	485.0
2	Henry Porter	1885	481.2
3	Bob Caruthers	1889	445.0
4	Henry Porter	1886	424.0
5	Bob Caruthers	1888	391.2
6	Brickyard Kennedy	1893	382.2
7	George Haddock	1892	381.1
8	Ed Stein	1892	377.1
9	Oscar Jones	1904	376.2
10	Tom Lovett	1890	372.0
11	Adonis Terry	1890	370.0
12	Tom Lovett	1891	365.2
13	Mickey Hughes	1888	363.0
14	Brickyard Kennedy	1894	360.2
15	Ed Stein	1894	359.0
16	Sam Kimber	1884	352.1
17	Wild Bill Donovan	1901	351.0
18	Brickyard Kennedy	1897	343.1
19	Joe McGinnity	1900	343.0
20	Henry Porter	1887	339.2

Walks

1	Ed Stein	1894	171
2	Brickyard Kennedy	1893	168
3	George Haddock	1892	163
4	Wild Bill Donovan	1901	152
5	Ed Stein	1892	150
6	Brickyard Kennedy	1894	149
	Brickyard Kennedy	1897	149
8	Tom Lovett	1890	141
9	Hal Gregg	1944	137
10	Adonis Terry	1890	133
11	Kirby Higbe	1941	132
12	Brickyard Kennedy	1896	130
13	Tom Lovett	1891	129
14	Doc Scanlan	1906	127
15	Adonis Terry	1889	126
16	Nap Rucker	1908	125
17	F. Valenzuela	1987	124
18	Brickyard Kennedy	1898	123
19	Doc McJames	1899	122
	Rex Barney	1948	122

Strikeouts

1	Sandy Koufax	1965	382
2	Sandy Koufax	1966	317
3	Sandy Koufax	1963	306
4	Sandy Koufax	1961	269
5	Dazzy Vance	1924	262
6	Don Drysdale	1963	251
7	Bill Singer	1969	247
8	Don Drysdale	1960	246
9	Don Drysdale	1959	242
	F. Valenzuela	1986	242
11	F. Valenzuela	1984	240
12	Van Lingle Mungo	1936	238
13	Don Drysdale	1964	237
14	Hideo Nomo	1995	236
15	Hideo Nomo	1996	234
16	Adonis Terry	1884	233
	Hideo Nomo	1997	233
18	Don Drysdale	1962	232
19	Bill Singer	1968	227
20	Wild Bill Donovan	1901	226

Strikeouts/9 Innings
(minimum 1 Inning Pitched/Tm Gm)

1	Hideo Nomo	1995	11.10
2	Sandy Koufax	1962	10.55
3	Sandy Koufax	1965	10.24
4	Sandy Koufax	1960	10.13
5	Hideo Nomo	1997	10.11
6	Sandy Koufax	1961	9.47
7	Hideo Nomo	1996	9.22
8	Sandy Koufax	1964	9.00
9	Sandy Koufax	1963	8.86
10	Sandy Koufax	1966	8.83
11	Ramon Martinez	1990	8.56
12	F. Valenzuela	1981	8.42
13	Don Sutton	1966	8.34
14	F. Valenzuela	1984	8.28
15	Don Drysdale	1960	8.23
16	F. Valenzuela	1986	8.09
17	Don Drysdale	1959	8.05
18	Bill Singer	1968	7.97
19	Stan Williams	1961	7.84
20	Tim Belcher	1989	7.83

ERA
(minimum 1 Inning Pitched/Tm Gm)

1	Rube Marquard	1916	1.58
2	Ned Garvin	1904	1.68
3	Sandy Koufax	1966	1.73
4	Sandy Koufax	1964	1.74
5	Kaiser Wilhelm	1908	1.87
6	Sandy Koufax	1963	1.88
7	Jeff Pfeffer	1916	1.92
8	Larry Cheney	1916	1.92
9	Jeff Pfeffer	1914	1.97
10	Orel Hershiser	1985	2.03
11	Adonis Terry	1888	2.03
12	Sandy Koufax	1965	2.04
13	Nap Rucker	1907	2.06
14	Nap Rucker	1908	2.08
15	Don Sutton	1972	2.08
16	Dazzy Vance	1928	2.09
17	Jeff Pfeffer	1915	2.10
18	Mickey Hughes	1888	2.13
19	Burleigh Grimes	1918	2.14
20	Don Drysdale	1968	2.15

Component ERA
(minimum 1 Inning Pitched/Tm Gm)

1	Sandy Koufax	1963	1.55
2	Sandy Koufax	1965	1.56
3	Don Sutton	1972	1.63
4	Sandy Koufax	1964	1.66
5	Whit Wyatt	1943	1.81
6	Bob Caruthers	1888	1.86
7	Rube Marquard	1916	1.87
8	Mickey Hughes	1888	1.89
9	Don Drysdale	1964	1.89
10	Kaiser Wilhelm	1908	1.89
11	Sandy Koufax	1966	1.92
12	Adonis Terry	1888	1.94
13	Dave Foutz	1888	1.95
14	Burleigh Grimes	1918	1.95
15	Orel Hershiser	1985	2.01
16	Dazzy Vance	1924	2.02
17	Whit Wyatt	1941	2.06
18	Jerry Reuss	1980	2.08
19	Don Sutton	1973	2.08
20	Larry Cheney	1916	2.09

Opponent Average
(minimum 1 Inning Pitched/Tm Gm)

1	Sandy Koufax	1965	.179
2	Hideo Nomo	1995	.182
3	Sandy Koufax	1963	.189
4	Don Sutton	1972	.189
5	Sandy Koufax	1964	.191
6	Adonis Terry	1888	.191
7	Sandy Koufax	1962	.197
8	Larry Cheney	1916	.198
9	Sandy Koufax	1966	.205
10	F. Valenzuela	1981	.205
11	Mickey Hughes	1888	.206
12	Orel Hershiser	1985	.206
13	Don Drysdale	1964	.207
14	Whit Wyatt	1943	.207
15	Sandy Koufax	1960	.207
16	Don Sutton	1973	.209
17	Burt Hooton	1975	.210
18	Bill Singer	1969	.210
19	Stan Williams	1960	.210
20	Don Sutton	1980	.211

Opponent OBP
(minimum 1 Inning Pitched/Tm Gm)

1	Sandy Koufax	1965	.227
2	Sandy Koufax	1963	.230
3	Don Sutton	1972	.240
4	Sandy Koufax	1964	.240
5	Bob Caruthers	1888	.248
6	Sandy Koufax	1966	.252
7	Whit Wyatt	1943	.255
8	Don Drysdale	1964	.255
9	Don Newcombe	1956	.257
10	Don Sutton	1973	.257
11	Adonis Terry	1888	.257
	Don Sutton	1980	.257
13	Mickey Hughes	1888	.259
14	Jerry Reuss	1980	.260
15	Sandy Koufax	1962	.261
16	Bill Singer	1969	.261
17	Don Sutton	1975	.263
18	Burt Hooton	1975	.265
19	Al Mays	1888	.265
20	Orel Hershiser	1985	.267

Brooklyn/Los Angeles Dodgers Capsule

Best Season: *1955/1988.* From 1947 through 1954, the Dodgers won four pennants—and lost the World Series to the hated New York Yankees every single time, leaving Brooklyn fans muttering, "Wait 'til next year." In 1955, "next year" finally came, as Johnny Podres shut out the Yankees in Game 7 of the World Series to bring Brooklyn its first World Series championship. The 1988 club shocked the baseball world, first by winning the National League West, and then by upsetting two heavily favored opponents in the postseason. They defeated the New York Mets in a seven-game NLCS on the strength of Orel Hershiser's pitching, and beat the Oakland Athletics in a five-game World Series after Kirk Gibson's dramatic ninth-inning, two-run homer off Dennis Eckersley won Game 1.

Worst Season: *1905/1967.* The Brooklyn Superbas, as they were then known, finished last in the NL with a 48-104 record in 1905, the franchise's worst season in the modern era. Los Angeles won three pennants in four years from 1963 through 1966, but then Sandy Koufax retired, and the club fell to a 73-89, eighth-place finish in 1967.

Best Player: *Duke Snider/Mike Piazza.* Snider was the center fielder and leading hitter for the Dodgers' great teams of the mid-1950s, just as Mickey Mantle and Willie Mays were for the intracity rival New York Yankees and New York Giants, respectively. From 1993 through 1997, Mike Piazza put together the most productive five-year stretch by a catcher in history and placed in the top 10 in the NL MVP voting in all five seasons.

Best Pitcher: *Dazzy Vance/Sandy Koufax.* Vance was the most dominant NL pitcher of the 1920s, leading the league in strikeouts for seven straight seasons while winning three ERA titles. Koufax' five-year run from 1962 through 1966 is perhaps the strongest in history: he went 111-34 while leading the NL in ERA all five seasons.

Best Reliever: *Clem Labine/Jim Brewer.* Labine led the NL in relief wins in two seasons and in saves in two other years. Several Los Angeles relievers have performed brilliantly for a few years at a time, including Ron Perranoski, Phil Regan and Mike Marshall, but Brewer's 11 straight solid campaigns are unmatched.

Best Defensive Player: *Billy Cox/Wes Parker.* Cox, a converted shortstop, was the premier defensive third baseman of his generation. Parker won six straight Gold Gloves at first base and retired with the highest lifetime fielding percentage in history for a first sacker with 1,000 or more games. (His record has since been eclipsed, by mere percentage points, by Steve Garvey and Don Mattingly.)

Hall of Famers: Nine Hall of Fame players spent the bulk of their careers with the team—*Roy Campanella, Burleigh Grimes, Pee Wee Reese, Jackie Robinson, Duke Snider* and *Zack Wheat* in Brooklyn, and *Don Drysdale, Sandy Koufax* and *Don Sutton* in Los Angeles. The franchise also is responsible for more non-playing Cooperstown honorees than any other—executives *Larry MacPhail* and *Branch Rickey,* and managers *Walter Alston, Leo Durocher, Tom Lasorda* and *Wilbert Robinson.*

Franchise All-Star Team:

C	Roy Campanella/Mike Piazza	LF	Zack Wheat/Pedro Guerrero
1B	Gil Hodges/Steve Garvey	CF	Duke Snider/Willie Davis
2B	Jackie Robinson/Davey Lopes	RF	Carl Furillo/Raul Mondesi
3B	Billy Cox/Ron Cey	SP	Dazzy Vance/Sandy Koufax
SS	Pee Wee Reese/Maury Wills	RP	Clem Labine/Jim Brewer

Biggest Flake: *Casey Stengel/Jay Johnstone.* In his first major league game, Stengel, a lefthanded hitter, hit safely in his first four at-bats. When he came up to hit for the fifth time, he discovered that a lefthanded pitcher was now on the mound. Unfazed, he switched over to bat from the right side and earned a walk. Unlike the old Brooklyn clubs that were continually populated with colorful characters, the Los Angeles players' personalities have been unfailingly bland. This may be in part a result of the modern Dodgers' antiseptic, corporate image. The managers probably have played a large role as well. Walter Alston and Tom Lasorda have skippered the club for most of the time it's been on the West Coast. Alston was akin to Jack Webb with a lineup card, and didn't suffer fools lightly; Lasorda was the King of Schmooze and always had to be the biggest character in the room. Jay Johnstone was one of the few who refused to behave and got away with it.

Strangest Career: *Bill Bergen/Joe Ferguson.* No matter what Bergen did, he just couldn't play his way out of the lineup. He caught at least 51 games for eight straight years from 1904 to 1911 without batting over .190 in any one season. He batted .162 and hit exactly one home run during those eight years. His strong throwing arm was well-respected, but it's hard to see how it could have made up for his bat. Ferguson was signed as an outfielder but was converted to catcher in the minors. In his first full season in the majors, 1973, he hit 25 homers, drove in 88 runs, and set a major league record for fielding percentage by a catcher. Despite that, he slowly lost his job to light-hitting Steve Yeager before being traded away in 1976. Reacquired in midseason in 1978, he hit 20 homers as a part-time catcher in 1979 before losing his job to Yeager again in 1980.

What Might Have Been: *Pete Reiser, Karl Spooner/Joe Moeller, Bobby Valentine.* Reiser was one of the game's brightest young stars when he crashed into the center-field wall at Sportsman's Park in July of 1942. He suffered a separated shoulder and a severe concussion, and developed headaches and dizziness that plagued him for the rest of his career. This, combined with a stint in the military and various other injuries, wrecked his career. Spooner went 21-9 with 262 strikeouts in the minors in 1954. Called up to the big club in late September, the 23-year-old southpaw fanned the first six batters he faced and ended up with a 15-strikeout, complete-game victory in his debut. He pitched once more before the close of the season, notching his second straight shutout while striking out 12. He hurt his arm the following spring and won only eight more games. Moeller had a huge year in the minors in 1961 at age 18, going 20-9 with 295 strikeouts at three stops. He made the majors the following year, but fought injuries and never became a big winner. Valentine won the Pacific Coast League batting title in 1970 at age 20. He played for the Dodgers for two years before being dealt to the California Angels, where his career was wrecked by a broken leg.

Best Trade: *Burleigh Grimes/Pedro Guerrero.* On January 9, 1918, the Dodgers acquired Hall of Famer Burleigh Grimes from the Pirates, along with infielder Chuck Ward and pitcher Al Mamaux, for outfielder Casey Stengel and second baseman George Cutshaw. Stengel and Cutshaw remained useful for a few more years, but Grimes won 158 games for the Dodgers, third on Brooklyn's all-time list. The Dodgers stole Pedro Guerrero from the Cleveland Indians for pitcher Bruce Ellingsen on April 3, 1974. Ellingsen pitched in 16 major league games, while Guerrero became one of the NL's most productive hitters of the 1980s.

Worst Trade: *Ernie Lombardi/John Wetteland.* The Dodgers traded 23-year-old future Hall of Fame catcher Ernie Lombardi to the Reds on Marsh 14, 1932. Outfielder Babe Herman and third baseman Wally Gilbert were included in the deal that brought catcher Clyde Sukeforth, second baseman Tony Cuccinello and third baseman Joe Stripp. The latter two remained quality players for several more years, but so did Herman, and Lombardi went on to win two batting titles and an MVP Award. Wetteland was a throw-in in the November 27, 1991 deal that sent pitcher Tim Belcher to the Reds for outfielder Eric Davis and pitcher Kip Gross. Davis produced virtually nothing for the Dodgers while Wetteland (who was subsequently traded to Montreal) immediately became one of the game's top closers.

Best-Looking Player: *Duke Snider/Don Drysdale.*

Ugliest Player: *Jack Banta/Ron Roenicke.*

Best Nicknames: *Dixie Walker, "The People's Cherce,"* and *Walter "Boom-Boom" Beck/Phil Regan, "The Vulture,"* and *Bill Singer, "The Singer Throwing Machine."*

Most Unappreciated Player: *Don Newcombe/Willie Davis.* Newcombe was an outstanding pitcher and hitter, but was derided for failing to win the "big games." Davis was a fine hitter, fielder and baserunner for many years, in a time and place that depressed his numbers.

Most Overrated Player: *Buddy Hassett/Steve Garvey.*

Most Admirable Star: *Jackie Robinson/Brett Butler.*

Least Admirable Star: *Joe Medwick/Steve Garvey.*

Best Season, Player: *Roy Campanella, 1953/Mike Piazza, 1997.* Campanella set the single-season home-run record for catchers (later tied) and drove in 142 runs. In 1997, Piazza had the greatest offensive season by a catcher in history.

Best Season, Pitcher: *Dazzy Vance, 1924/Sandy Koufax, 1965.* Vance's 28-6 record earned him the MVP Award over St. Louis' Rogers Hornsby, who batted .424 that year. Koufax went 26-8 with a league-leading 2.04 ERA in 1965, and set the season record for strikeouts (since broken by Nolan Ryan) with 382. He threw two shutouts in the World Series, including one in Game 7 on two days' rest to give Los Angeles the championship.

Most Impressive Individual Record: *Joe Oeschger/Orel Hershiser.* Pitcher Joe Oeschger went the distance in the longest game of the modern era, holding the Braves to one run over 26 innings on May 1, 1920. He didn't allow a single hit over the last nine innings before the game was called with the score tied 1-1. Hershiser threw 59 consecutive scoreless innings during the 1988 stretch run, breaking fellow Dodger Don Drysdale's record.

Biggest Tragedy: *Roy Campanella/Sandy Koufax.* Campanella was paralyzed in an auto accident in the winter of 1958. Koufax retired in 1966 at the height of his stardom due to an arthritic elbow.

Fan Favorite: *Dixie Walker/Fernando Valenzuela.* "Fernandomania" swept Los Angeles in 1981 when Valenzuela won the Rookie of the Year and Cy Young Awards and helped the Dodgers win the World Series.

—Mat Olkin

Montreal Expos (1969-1997)

Year	Lg	Pos	W-L	Pct	GB	Manager	Att.	R	OR	HR	Avg	OBP	Slg	Opponent HR	Opponent Avg	Opponent OBP	ERA	Park Index Runs	Park Index HR
1969	NL	6th-E	52-110	.321	48.0	Gene Mauch	1,212,608	582	791	125	.240	.310	.359	145	.263	.350	4.33	107	145
1970	NL	6th-E	73-89	.451	16.0	Gene Mauch	1,424,683	687	807	136	.237	.323	.365	162	.261	.349	4.50	103	132
1971	NL	5th-E	71-90	.441	25.5	Gene Mauch	1,290,963	622	729	88	.246	.322	.343	133	.260	.341	4.12	100	116
1972	NL	5th-E	70-86	.449	26.5	Gene Mauch	1,142,145	513	609	91	.234	.303	.325	103	.245	.321	3.59	105	120
1973	NL	4th-E	79-83	.488	3.5	Gene Mauch	1,246,863	668	702	125	.251	.340	.364	128	.250	.334	3.71	110	111
1974	NL	4th-E	79-82	.491	8.5	Gene Mauch	1,019,134	662	657	86	.254	.335	.350	99	.249	.319	3.60	109	117
1975	NL	5th-E	75-87	.463	17.5	Gene Mauch	908,292	601	690	98	.244	.317	.348	102	.259	.339	3.72	119	122
1976	NL	6th-E	55-107	.340	46.0	Karl Kuehl/Charlie Fox	646,704	531	734	94	.235	.291	.340	89	.266	.347	3.99	105	91
1977	NL	5th-E	75-87	.463	26.0	Dick Williams	1,433,757	665	736	138	.260	.318	.402	135	.255	.325	4.01	97	92
1978	NL	4th-E	76-86	.469	14.0	Dick Williams	1,427,007	633	611	121	.254	.306	.379	117	.249	.323	3.42	90	68
1979	NL	2nd-E	95-65	.594	2.0	Dick Williams	2,102,173	701	581	143	.264	.319	.408	116	.253	.310	3.14	101	83
1980	NL	2nd-E	90-72	.556	1.0	Dick Williams	2,208,175	694	629	114	.257	.324	.388	100	.261	.317	3.48	97	76
1981	NL	3rd-E	30-25	.545	4.0	Dick Williams													
	NL	1st-E	30-23	.566	—	Dick Williams/Jim Fanning	1,534,564	443	394	81	.246	.316	.370	58	.247	.300	3.30	96	75
1982	NL	3rd-E	86-76	.531	6.0	Jim Fanning	2,318,292	697	616	133	.262	.325	.396	110	.250	.306	3.31	110	104
1983	NL	3rd-E	82-80	.506	8.0	Bill Virdon	2,320,651	677	646	102	.264	.326	.386	120	.254	.315	3.58	101	76
1984	NL	5th-E	78-83	.484	18.0	Bill Virdon/Jim Fanning	1,606,531	593	585	96	.251	.312	.362	114	.249	.310	3.31	80	92
1985	NL	3rd-E	84-77	.522	16.5	Buck Rodgers	1,502,494	633	636	118	.247	.310	.375	99	.247	.312	3.55	86	70
1986	NL	4th-E	78-83	.484	29.5	Buck Rodgers	1,128,981	637	688	110	.254	.322	.379	119	.246	.318	3.78	95	76
1987	NL	3rd-E	91-71	.562	4.0	Buck Rodgers	1,850,324	741	720	120	.265	.328	.401	145	.257	.313	3.92	112	105
1988	NL	3rd-E	81-81	.500	20.0	Buck Rodgers	1,478,659	628	592	107	.251	.309	.373	122	.238	.301	3.08	109	91
1989	NL	4th-E	81-81	.500	12.0	Buck Rodgers	1,783,533	632	630	100	.247	.319	.361	120	.245	.312	3.48	105	110
1990	NL	3rd-E	85-77	.525	10.0	Buck Rodgers	1,373,087	662	598	114	.250	.322	.370	127	.245	.311	3.37	90	84
1991	NL	6th-E	71-90	.441	26.5	Buck Rodgers/Tom Runnells	934,742	579	655	95	.246	.308	.357	111	.244	.320	3.64	78	67
1992	NL	2nd-E	87-75	.537	9.0	Tom Runnells/Felipe Alou	1,669,127	648	581	102	.252	.313	.370	92	.238	.309	3.25	118	102
1993	NL	2nd-E	94-68	.580	3.0	Felipe Alou	1,641,437	732	682	122	.257	.326	.386	119	.249	.302	3.55	93	87
1994	NL	1st-E	74-40	.649	—	Felipe Alou	1,276,250	585	454	108	.278	.343	.435	100	.247	.302	3.56	108	89
1995	NL	5th-E	66-78	.458	24.0	Felipe Alou	1,309,618	621	638	118	.259	.320	.394	128	.262	.325	4.11	97	66
1996	NL	2nd-E	88-74	.543	8.0	Felipe Alou	1,618,573	741	668	148	.262	.327	.406	152	.247	.313	3.78	111	110
1997	NL	4th-E	78-84	.481	23.0	Felipe Alou	1,497,603	691	740	172	.258	.316	.425	149	.251	.325	4.14	105	88

Team Nicknames: Montreal Expos 1969-1997.

Team Ballparks: Parc Jarry 1969-1976, Stade Olympique 1977-1997.

Montreal Expos Individual Season Batting Leaders

Year	Batting Average		On-Base Percentage		Slugging Percentage		Home Runs		RBI		Stolen Bases	
1969	Rusty Staub	.302	Rusty Staub	.426	Rusty Staub	.526	Rusty Staub	29	Coco Laboy	83	Maury Wills	15
1970	Rusty Staub	.274	Rusty Staub	.394	Rusty Staub	.497	Rusty Staub	30	Rusty Staub	94	Rusty Staub	12
1971	Rusty Staub	.311	Ron Hunt	.402	Rusty Staub	.482	Rusty Staub	19	Rusty Staub	97	Bob Bailey	13
1972	Ron Fairly	.278	Ron Hunt	.363	Ron Fairly	.430	Ron Fairly	17	Ron Fairly	68	Mike Jorgensen	12
1973	Ken Singleton	.302	Ken Singleton	.425	Bob Bailey	.489	Bob Bailey	26	Ken Singleton	103	Mike Jorgensen	16
1974	Willie Davis	.295	Bob Bailey	.396	Bob Bailey	.446	Bob Bailey	20	Willie Davis	89	Larry Lintz	50
1975	Larry Parrish	.274	Mike Jorgensen	.378	Mike Jorgensen	.422	Mike Jorgensen	18	Gary Carter	68	Pepe Mangual	33
1976	Tim Foli	.264	Larry Parrish	.285	Tim Foli	.366	Larry Parrish	11	Larry Parrish	61	Pepe Mangual	17
1977	Ellis Valentine	.293	Gary Carter	.356	Gary Carter	.525	Gary Carter	31	Tony Perez	91	Dave Cash / Andre Dawson	21
1978	Warren Cromartie	.297	Warren Cromartie	.337	Ellis Valentine	.489	Andre Dawson / Ellis Valentine	25	Tony Perez	78	Andre Dawson	28
1979	Larry Parrish	.307	Larry Parrish	.357	Larry Parrish	.551	Larry Parrish	30	Andre Dawson	92	Rodney Scott	39
1980	Andre Dawson	.308	Andre Dawson	.358	Andre Dawson	.492	Gary Carter	29	Gary Carter	101	Ron LeFlore	97
1981	Warren Cromartie	.304	Tim Raines	.391	Andre Dawson	.553	Andre Dawson	24	Gary Carter	68	Tim Raines	71
1982	Al Oliver	.331	Al Oliver	.392	Al Oliver	.514	Gary Carter	29	Al Oliver	109	Tim Raines	78
1983	Al Oliver	.300	Tim Raines	.393	Andre Dawson	.539	Andre Dawson	32	Andre Dawson	113	Tim Raines	90
1984	Tim Raines	.309	Tim Raines	.393	Gary Carter	.487	Gary Carter	27	Gary Carter	106	Tim Raines	75
1985	Tim Raines	.320	Tim Raines	.405	Tim Raines	.475	Andre Dawson	23	Hubie Brooks	100	Tim Raines	70
1986	Tim Raines	.334	Tim Raines	.413	Andre Dawson	.478	Andre Dawson	20	Andre Dawson	78	Tim Raines	70
1987	Tim Raines	.330	Tim Raines	.429	Tim Raines	.526	Tim Wallach	26	Tim Wallach	123	Tim Raines	50
1988	Andres Galarraga	.302	Andres Galarraga	.352	Andres Galarraga	.540	Andres Galarraga	29	Andres Galarraga	92	Otis Nixon	46
1989	Tim Raines	.286	Tim Raines	.395	Andres Galarraga	.434	Andres Galarraga	23	Andres Galarraga	85	Tim Raines	41
1990	Tim Wallach	.296	Tim Raines	.379	Tim Wallach	.471	Tim Wallach	21	Tim Wallach	98	Otis Nixon	50
1991	Ivan Calderon	.300	Ivan Calderon	.368	Ivan Calderon	.481	Ivan Calderon	19	Ivan Calderon	75	Marquis Grissom	76
1992	Larry Walker	.301	Delino DeShields	.359	Larry Walker	.506	Larry Walker	23	Larry Walker	93	Marquis Grissom	78
1993	Marquis Grissom	.298	Delino DeShields	.389	Moises Alou	.483	Larry Walker	22	Marquis Grissom	95	Marquis Grissom	53
1994	Moises Alou	.339	Moises Alou	.397	Moises Alou	.592	Moises Alou	22	Larry Walker	86	Marquis Grissom	36
1995	Rondell White	.295	Rondell White	.356	Rondell White	.464	3 tied with	14	Mike Lansing	62	Mike Lansing	27
1996	Mark Grudzielanek	.306	Mike Lansing	.341	Henry Rodriguez	.562	Henry Rodriguez	36	Henry Rodriguez	103	Mark Grudzielanek	33
1997	David Segui	.307	David Segui	.380	David Segui	.505	Rondell White	28	Henry Rodriguez	83	Mark Grudzielanek	25

Montreal Expos Individual Season Pitching Leaders

Year	ERA		Baserunners/9 IP		Innings Pitched		Strikeouts		Wins		Saves	
1969	Jerry Robertson	3.96	Jerry Robertson	13.6	Bill Stoneman	235.2	Bill Stoneman	185	Bill Stoneman	11	Dan McGinn	6
1970	Carl Morton	3.60	Steve Renko	12.7	Carl Morton	284.2	Bill Stoneman	176	Carl Morton	18	Claude Raymond	23
1971	Bill Stoneman	3.15	Bill Stoneman	12.0	Bill Stoneman	294.2	Bill Stoneman	251	Bill Stoneman	17	Mike Marshall	23
1972	Bill Stoneman	2.98	Bill Stoneman	11.4	Bill Stoneman	250.2	Bill Stoneman	171	Mike Torrez	16	Mike Marshall	18
1973	Mike Marshall	2.66	Steve Renko	11.2	Steve Renko	249.2	Steve Renko	164	Steve Renko	15	Mike Marshall	31
1974	Mike Torrez	3.57	Steve Renko	12.0	Steve Rogers	253.2	Steve Rogers	154	Steve Rogers / Mike Torrez	15	Chuck Taylor	11
1975	Dan Warthen	3.11	Dan Warthen	11.7	Steve Rogers	251.2	Steve Rogers	137	Dale Murray	15	Dale Murray	9
1976	Steve Rogers	3.21	Steve Rogers	11.2	Steve Rogers	230.0	Steve Rogers	150	Woodie Fryman	13	Dale Murray	13
1977	Steve Rogers	3.10	Steve Rogers	10.7	Steve Rogers	301.2	Steve Rogers	206	Steve Rogers	17	Joe Kerrigan	11
1978	Steve Rogers	2.47	Steve Rogers	10.4	Ross Grimsley	263.0	Steve Rogers	126	Ross Grimsley	20	Mike Garman	13
1979	Dan Schatzeder	2.83	Dan Schatzeder	10.9	Steve Rogers	248.2	Steve Rogers	143	Bill Lee	16	Elias Sosa	18
1980	Steve Rogers	2.98	Steve Rogers	10.7	Steve Rogers	281.0	Steve Rogers	147	Steve Rogers / Scott Sanderson	16	Woodie Fryman	17
1981	Bill Gullickson	2.80	Scott Sanderson	10.1	Steve Rogers	160.2	Bill Gullickson	115	Steve Rogers	12	Woodie Fryman	7
1982	Steve Rogers	2.40	Charlie Lea	10.2	Steve Rogers	277.0	Steve Rogers	179	Steve Rogers	19	Jeff Reardon	26
1983	Charlie Lea	3.12	Bill Gullickson	10.9	Steve Rogers	273.0	Steve Rogers	146	Bill Gullickson / Steve Rogers	17	Jeff Reardon	21
1984	Charlie Lea	2.89	Bill Gullickson	10.6	Bill Gullickson	226.2	Charlie Lea	123	Charlie Lea	15	Jeff Reardon	23
1985	Bryn Smith	2.91	Bryn Smith	9.5	Bryn Smith	222.1	Bryn Smith	127	Bryn Smith	18	Jeff Reardon	41
1986	Floyd Youmans	3.53	Floyd Youmans	11.0	Floyd Youmans	219.0	Floyd Youmans	202	Floyd Youmans	13	Jeff Reardon	35
1987	Bob Sebra	4.42	Neal Heaton	11.5	Neal Heaton	193.1	Bob Sebra	156	Neal Heaton	13	Tim Burke	18
1988	Pascual Perez	2.44	Pascual Perez	8.8	Dennis Martinez	235.1	Pascual Perez	131	Dennis Martinez	15	Tim Burke	18
1989	Mark Langston	2.39	Bryn Smith	9.8	Dennis Martinez	232.0	Mark Langston	175	Dennis Martinez	16	Tim Burke	28
1990	Oil Can Boyd	2.93	Dennis Martinez	9.8	Dennis Martinez	226.0	Dennis Martinez	156	Bill Sampen	12	Tim Burke	20
1991	Dennis Martinez	2.39	Dennis Martinez	10.3	Dennis Martinez	222.0	Dennis Martinez	123	Dennis Martinez	14	Barry Jones	13
1992	Dennis Martinez	2.47	Dennis Martinez	9.6	Dennis Martinez	226.1	Ken Hill	150	Ken Hill / Dennis Martinez	16	John Wetteland	37
1993	Ken Hill	3.23	Dennis Martinez	11.5	Dennis Martinez	224.2	Jeff Fassero	140	Dennis Martinez	15	John Wetteland	43
1994	Jeff Fassero	2.99	Jeff Fassero	10.4	Ken Hill	154.2	Pedro Martinez	142	Ken Hill	16	John Wetteland	25
1995	Pedro Martinez	3.51	Pedro Martinez	10.9	Pedro Martinez	194.2	Pedro Martinez	174	Pedro Martinez	14	Mel Rojas	30
1996	Jeff Fassero	3.30	Jeff Fassero	10.7	Jeff Fassero	231.2	Jeff Fassero / Pedro Martinez	222	Jeff Fassero	15	Mel Rojas	36
1997	Pedro Martinez	1.90	Pedro Martinez	8.7	Pedro Martinez	241.1	Pedro Martinez	305	Pedro Martinez	17	Ugueth Urbina	27

Expos Franchise Batting Leaders—Career

Games

1	Tim Wallach	1,767
2	Gary Carter	1,503
3	Andre Dawson	1,443
4	Tim Raines	1,405
5	Warren Cromartie	1,038
6	Larry Parrish	967
7	Bob Bailey	951
8	Chris Speier	895
9	Andres Galarraga	847
10	Ron Fairly	718
11	Tim Foli	710
12	Marquis Grissom	698
13	Mike Lansing	677
14	Larry Walker	674
15	Mike Jorgensen	670
16	Tom Foley	661
17	Hubie Brooks	647
18	Darrin Fletcher	643
19	Ellis Valentine	638
20	Mike Fitzgerald	633

At-Bats

1	Tim Wallach	6,529
2	Andre Dawson	5,628
3	Tim Raines	5,305
4	Gary Carter	5,303
5	Warren Cromartie	3,796
6	Larry Parrish	3,411
7	Andres Galarraga	3,082
8	Bob Bailey	2,991
9	Chris Speier	2,902
10	Marquis Grissom	2,678
11	Tim Foli	2,614
12	Mike Lansing	2,565
13	Hubie Brooks	2,471
14	Larry Walker	2,366
15	Ellis Valentine	2,351
16	Ron Fairly	2,226
17	Moises Alou	2,144
18	Delino DeShields	2,073
19	Darrin Fletcher	1,957
20	Mike Jorgensen	1,880

Runs

1	Tim Raines	934
2	Andre Dawson	828
3	Tim Wallach	737
4	Gary Carter	707
5	Warren Cromartie	446
6	Marquis Grissom	430
7	Larry Parrish	421
8	Bob Bailey	412
9	Andres Galarraga	394
10	Larry Walker	368
11	Moises Alou	343
12	Mike Lansing	340
13	Delino DeShields	309
14	Ron Fairly	303
15	Ellis Valentine	297
16	Hubie Brooks	291
17	Rusty Staub	290
18	Chris Speier	277
19	Ron Hunt	272
20	Mitch Webster	255

Hits

1	Tim Wallach	1,694
2	Tim Raines	1,598
3	Andre Dawson	1,575
4	Gary Carter	1,427
5	Warren Cromartie	1,063
6	Larry Parrish	896
7	Andres Galarraga	830
8	Bob Bailey	791
9	Marquis Grissom	747
10	Chris Speier	710
11	Mike Lansing	709
12	Hubie Brooks	689
13	Ellis Valentine	676
14	Larry Walker	666
15	Tim Foli	642
16	Moises Alou	626
17	Ron Fairly	615
18	Delino DeShields	575
19	Rusty Staub	531
20	Darrin Fletcher	520

Doubles

1	Tim Wallach	360
2	Andre Dawson	295
3	Gary Carter	274
4	Tim Raines	273
5	Warren Cromartie	222
6	Larry Parrish	208
7	Andres Galarraga	168
8	Mike Lansing	165
9	Larry Walker	147
10	Hubie Brooks	139
11	Moises Alou	138
12	Ellis Valentine	136
13	Marquis Grissom	130
14	Chris Speier	123
15	Bob Bailey	116
16	Darrin Fletcher	111
17	Wil Cordero	101
18	Mark Grudzielanek	100
19	Tim Foli	99
	Tony Perez	99

Triples

1	Tim Raines	81
2	Andre Dawson	67
3	Tim Wallach	31
4	Warren Cromartie	30
5	Mitch Webster	25
	Delino DeShields	25
7	Gary Carter	24
	Larry Parrish	24
9	Bob Bailey	23
	Marquis Grissom	23
11	Chris Speier	22
	Dave Martinez	22
13	Rodney Scott	21
14	Spike Owen	20
15	Rusty Staub	18
	Hubie Brooks	18
17	Larry Walker	16
	Moises Alou	16
19	Rondell White	15
20	Andres Galarraga	14

Home Runs

1	Andre Dawson	225
2	Gary Carter	220
3	Tim Wallach	204
4	Bob Bailey	118
5	Andres Galarraga	106
6	Larry Parrish	100
7	Larry Walker	99
8	Tim Raines	96
9	Ellis Valentine	95
10	Ron Fairly	86
11	Moises Alou	84
12	Rusty Staub	81
13	Hubie Brooks	75
14	Henry Rodriguez	63
15	Darrin Fletcher	61
16	Warren Cromartie	60
17	Mike Jorgensen	57
18	Marquis Grissom	54
19	Rondell White	51
20	Mike Lansing	49

RBI

1	Tim Wallach	905
2	Andre Dawson	838
3	Gary Carter	823
4	Tim Raines	552
5	Bob Bailey	466
6	Larry Parrish	444
7	Andres Galarraga	433
8	Hubie Brooks	390
9	Larry Walker	384
10	Moises Alou	373
11	Warren Cromartie	371
12	Ellis Valentine	358
13	Ron Fairly	331
14	Darrin Fletcher	300
15	Rusty Staub	284
16	Marquis Grissom	276
17	Mike Lansing	265
18	Chris Speier	255
19	Mike Jorgensen	243
20	Tony Perez	242

Walks

1	Tim Raines	775
2	Gary Carter	582
3	Tim Wallach	514
4	Bob Bailey	502
5	Ron Fairly	370
6	Andre Dawson	354
7	Chris Speier	337
8	Mike Jorgensen	321
9	Rusty Staub	310
	Warren Cromartie	310
11	Delino DeShields	287
12	Ken Singleton	286
13	Larry Walker	264
14	Larry Parrish	249
15	Mike Fitzgerald	243
16	Spike Owen	238
17	Andres Galarraga	224
18	Ron Hunt	216
19	Marquis Grissom	208
20	Mike Lansing	193

Strikeouts

1	Tim Wallach	1,009
2	Andre Dawson	896
3	Andres Galarraga	790
4	Gary Carter	691
5	Larry Parrish	612
6	Bob Bailey	607
7	Tim Raines	563
8	Larry Walker	474
9	Hubie Brooks	427
10	Delino DeShields	419
11	Warren Cromartie	385
12	Chris Speier	377
13	Marquis Grissom	373
14	Mike Lansing	335
15	Ellis Valentine	330
16	Mike Fitzgerald	321
17	Henry Rodriguez	320
18	Moises Alou	304
19	Tony Perez	297
20	Mike Jorgensen	290

Stolen Bases

1	Tim Raines	634
2	Marquis Grissom	266
3	Andre Dawson	253
4	Delino DeShields	187
5	Rodney Scott	139
6	Otis Nixon	133
7	Larry Walker	98
8	Ron LeFlore	97
9	Mitch Webster	96
	Mike Lansing	96
11	Larry Lintz	79
12	Dave Martinez	68
13	Mark Grudzielanek	66
14	Herm Winningham	65
15	Pepe Mangual	57
	Rondell White	57
17	Ellis Valentine	56
18	Andres Galarraga	54
19	Jerry White	53
	Moises Alou	53

Runs Created

1	Tim Raines	994
2	Andre Dawson	842
3	Tim Wallach	815
4	Gary Carter	793
5	Warren Cromartie	479
6	Bob Bailey	477
7	Larry Parrish	424
8	Andres Galarraga	408
9	Larry Walker	397
10	Ron Fairly	390
11	Marquis Grissom	377
12	Moises Alou	372
13	Rusty Staub	361
14	Mike Lansing	351
15	Ellis Valentine	344
16	Hubie Brooks	326
17	Delino DeShields	302
18	Chris Speier	297
19	Mike Jorgensen	282
20	Ron Hunt	264

Runs Created/27 Outs

(minimum 2000 Plate Appearances)

1	Rusty Staub	7.16
2	Tim Raines	6.83
3	Ron Fairly	6.23
4	Moises Alou	6.20
5	Larry Walker	5.94
6	Bob Bailey	5.41
7	Andre Dawson	5.28
8	Ron Hunt	5.27
9	Gary Carter	5.24
10	Ellis Valentine	5.20
11	Mike Jorgensen	5.13
12	Delino DeShields	5.00
13	Marquis Grissom	4.97
14	Mike Lansing	4.75
15	Andres Galarraga	4.68
16	Hubie Brooks	4.63
17	Warren Cromartie	4.46
18	Tim Wallach	4.32
19	Darrin Fletcher	4.30
20	Larry Parrish	4.28

Batting Average

(minimum 2000 Plate Appearances)

1	Tim Raines	.301
2	Rusty Staub	.295
3	Moises Alou	.292
4	Ellis Valentine	.288
5	Larry Walker	.281
6	Warren Cromartie	.280
7	Andre Dawson	.280
8	Marquis Grissom	.279
9	Hubie Brooks	.279
10	Delino DeShields	.277
11	Ron Hunt	.277
12	Mike Lansing	.276
13	Ron Fairly	.276
14	Andres Galarraga	.269
15	Gary Carter	.269
16	Darrin Fletcher	.266
17	Bob Bailey	.264
18	Larry Parrish	.263
19	Tim Wallach	.259
20	Mike Jorgensen	.254

On-Base Percentage

(minimum 2000 Plate Appearances)

1	Rusty Staub	.402
2	Tim Raines	.390
3	Ron Hunt	.390
4	Ron Fairly	.381
5	Bob Bailey	.368
6	Delino DeShields	.367
7	Mike Jorgensen	.365
8	Larry Walker	.357
9	Moises Alou	.349
10	Gary Carter	.342
11	Warren Cromartie	.335
12	Mike Lansing	.333
13	Marquis Grissom	.331
14	Mike Fitzgerald	.331
15	Ellis Valentine	.329
16	Andres Galarraga	.326
17	Andre Dawson	.326
18	Chris Speier	.323
19	Darrin Fletcher	.322
20	Hubie Brooks	.322

Slugging Percentage

(minimum 2000 Plate Appearances)

1	Rusty Staub	.497
2	Moises Alou	.489
3	Larry Walker	.483
4	Andre Dawson	.476
5	Ellis Valentine	.476
6	Gary Carter	.454
7	Hubie Brooks	.441
8	Ron Fairly	.440
9	Tim Raines	.438
10	Bob Bailey	.437
11	Andres Galarraga	.436
12	Larry Parrish	.426
13	Darrin Fletcher	.422
14	Tim Wallach	.418
15	Marquis Grissom	.405
16	Mike Lansing	.405
17	Warren Cromartie	.402
18	Mike Jorgensen	.391
19	Delino DeShields	.373
20	Mike Fitzgerald	.359

Expos Franchise Pitching Leaders—Career

Wins

1	Steve Rogers	158
2	Dennis Martinez	100
3	Bryn Smith	81
4	Bill Gullickson	72
5	Steve Renko	68
6	Jeff Fassero	58
7	Scott Sanderson	56
8	Charlie Lea	55
	Pedro Martinez	55
10	Bill Stoneman	51
	Woodie Fryman	51
12	Tim Burke	43
13	Ken Hill	41
14	Mike Torrez	40
15	David Palmer	38
16	Dan Schatzeder	37
17	Mike Marshall	36
18	Carl Morton	35
19	Chris Nabholz	34
20	Four tied at	32

Losses

1	Steve Rogers	152
2	Steve Renko	82
3	Bill Stoneman	72
	Dennis Martinez	72
5	Bryn Smith	71
6	Bill Gullickson	61
7	Woodie Fryman	52
8	Ernie McAnally	49
9	Jeff Fassero	48
10	Scott Sanderson	47
11	Carl Morton	45
12	Charlie Lea	41
13	Jeff Reardon	37
14	Mike Marshall	34
15	Mark Gardner	33
	Pedro Martinez	33
17	Mike Torrez	32
18	Dan Schatzeder	31
19	Six tied at	29

Winning Percentage
(minimum 75 decisions)

1	Pedro Martinez	.625
2	Dennis Martinez	.581
3	Charlie Lea	.573
4	Jeff Fassero	.547
5	Scott Sanderson	.544
6	Bill Gullickson	.541
7	Bryn Smith	.533
8	Steve Rogers	.510
9	Woodie Fryman	.495
10	Steve Renko	.453
11	Carl Morton	.438
12	Bill Stoneman	.415
13	Ernie McAnally	.380

Games

1	Tim Burke	425
2	Steve Rogers	399
3	Mel Rojas	385
4	Jeff Reardon	359
5	Woodie Fryman	297
6	Bryn Smith	284
7	Jeff Fassero	262
8	Andy McGaffigan	258
9	Mike Marshall	247
10	Dan Schatzeder	241
11	Dennis Martinez	239
12	Steve Renko	238
13	Stan Bahnsen	204
14	Dale Murray	201
15	John Wetteland	189
16	Bill Stoneman	186
17	Tim Scott	179
18	Bill Gullickson	176
19	Joe Hesketh	174
20	Elias Sosa	161

Games Started

1	Steve Rogers	393
2	Dennis Martinez	233
3	Bryn Smith	193
4	Steve Renko	192
5	Bill Gullickson	170
6	Bill Stoneman	157
7	Scott Sanderson	136
8	Charlie Lea	121
9	Pedro Martinez	117
10	Carl Morton	104
11	Jeff Fassero	100
12	Mike Torrez	97
	Ernie McAnally	97
14	Chris Nabholz	88
15	Mark Gardner	87
16	David Palmer	86
17	Ken Hill	84
18	Floyd Youmans	80
19	Dan Schatzeder	75
20	Ross Grimsley	70

Complete Games

1	Steve Rogers	129
2	Bill Stoneman	46
3	Dennis Martinez	41
4	Steve Renko	40
5	Bill Gullickson	31
6	Scott Sanderson	24
7	Carl Morton	22
	Mike Torrez	22
	Charlie Lea	22
10	Ernie McAnally	21
	Ross Grimsley	21
12	Bryn Smith	20
	Pedro Martinez	20
14	Woodie Fryman	15
15	Floyd Youmans	10
	Carlos Perez	10
17	Balor Moore	9
	Don Stanhouse	9
19	Ten tied at	8

Shutouts

1	Steve Rogers	37
2	Bill Stoneman	15
3	Dennis Martinez	13
4	Woodie Fryman	8
	Scott Sanderson	8
	Charlie Lea	8
	Bryn Smith	8
	Pedro Martinez	8
9	Steve Renko	6
	Ernie McAnally	6
	Bill Gullickson	6
	Floyd Youmans	6
	Carlos Perez	6
14	Carl Morton	5
15	Balor Moore	4
	Kevin Gross	4
	Mark Langston	4
	Oil Can Boyd	4
	Ken Hill	4
20	Eight tied at	3

Saves

1	Jeff Reardon	152
2	Mel Rojas	109
3	John Wetteland	105
4	Tim Burke	101
5	Mike Marshall	75
6	Woodie Fryman	52
7	Dale Murray	33
8	Elias Sosa	30
9	Ugueth Urbina	27
10	Claude Raymond	24
11	Andy McGaffigan	21
12	Chuck Taylor	17
	Stan Bahnsen	17
	Bob James	17
15	Joe Hesketh	14
16	Mike Garman	13
	Bob McClure	13
	Dave Schmidt	13
	Barry Jones	13
20	Four tied at	12

Innings Pitched

1	Steve Rogers	2,837.2
2	Dennis Martinez	1,609.0
3	Bryn Smith	1,400.1
4	Steve Renko	1,359.1
5	Bill Gullickson	1,186.1
6	Bill Stoneman	1,085.1
7	Scott Sanderson	883.0
8	Jeff Fassero	850.0
9	Pedro Martinez	797.1
10	Charlie Lea	793.1
11	Dan Schatzeder	749.2
12	Woodie Fryman	721.2
13	Carl Morton	699.2
14	Mike Torrez	640.2
15	Ernie McAnally	623.1
16	Tim Burke	600.1
17	David Palmer	576.2
18	Ken Hill	556.1
19	Chris Nabholz	535.1
20	Mark Gardner	527.0

Walks

1	Steve Rogers	876
2	Steve Renko	624
3	Bill Stoneman	535
4	Dennis Martinez	407
5	Bryn Smith	341
6	Mike Torrez	303
7	Charlie Lea	291
8	Bill Gullickson	288
9	Carl Morton	279
10	Woodie Fryman	274
	Jeff Fassero	274
12	Ernie McAnally	268
13	Dan Schatzeder	263
14	Floyd Youmans	255
15	Pedro Martinez	248
16	Scott Sanderson	240
17	Chris Nabholz	226
18	David Palmer	209
19	Mark Gardner	207
20	Mike Marshall	201

Strikeouts

1	Steve Rogers	1,621
2	Dennis Martinez	973
3	Pedro Martinez	843
4	Bryn Smith	838
5	Bill Stoneman	831
6	Steve Renko	810
7	Jeff Fassero	750
8	Bill Gullickson	678
9	Scott Sanderson	603
10	Woodie Fryman	469
11	Charlie Lea	463
12	Dan Schatzeder	438
13	Mel Rojas	418
14	Floyd Youmans	404
15	Jeff Reardon	398
16	Tim Burke	395
	Mark Gardner	395
18	David Palmer	370
19	Chris Nabholz	356
20	Four tied at	354

Strikeouts/9 Innings
(minimum 750 Innings Pitched)

1	Pedro Martinez	9.52
2	Jeff Fassero	7.94
3	Bill Stoneman	6.89
4	Scott Sanderson	6.15
5	Dennis Martinez	5.44
6	Bryn Smith	5.39
7	Steve Renko	5.36
8	Charlie Lea	5.25
9	Bill Gullickson	5.14
10	Steve Rogers	5.14

ERA
(minimum 750 Innings Pitched)

1	Pedro Martinez	3.06
2	Dennis Martinez	3.06
3	Steve Rogers	3.17
4	Jeff Fassero	3.20
5	Bryn Smith	3.28
6	Charlie Lea	3.32
7	Scott Sanderson	3.33
8	Bill Gullickson	3.44
9	Steve Renko	3.90
10	Bill Stoneman	3.98

Component ERA
(minimum 750 Innings Pitched)

1	Pedro Martinez	2.63
2	Dennis Martinez	2.91
3	Bryn Smith	3.03
4	Steve Rogers	3.05
5	Jeff Fassero	3.10
6	Bill Gullickson	3.16
7	Charlie Lea	3.24
8	Scott Sanderson	3.31
9	Steve Renko	3.90
10	Bill Stoneman	4.13

Opponent Average
(minimum 750 Innings Pitched)

1	Pedro Martinez	.214
2	Dennis Martinez	.238
3	Charlie Lea	.241
4	Jeff Fassero	.243
5	Steve Renko	.246
6	Bryn Smith	.247
7	Steve Rogers	.248
8	Bill Stoneman	.249
9	Scott Sanderson	.251
10	Bill Gullickson	.254

Opponent OBP
(minimum 750 Innings Pitched)

1	Pedro Martinez	.283
2	Dennis Martinez	.291
3	Bryn Smith	.295
4	Bill Gullickson	.299
5	Scott Sanderson	.301
6	Jeff Fassero	.303
7	Steve Rogers	.306
8	Charlie Lea	.309
9	Steve Renko	.327
10	Bill Stoneman	.340

Teams: Expos

Expos Franchise Batting Leaders—Single Season

Games

1	Rusty Staub	1971	162
	Ken Singleton	1973	162
	Warren Cromartie	1980	162
4	Tim Wallach	1990	161
5	Rusty Staub	1970	160
	Al Oliver	1982	160
	Tim Raines	1984	160
	Tim Wallach	1984	160
9	Bobby Wine	1970	159
	Dave Cash	1978	159
	Warren Cromartie	1978	159
	Andre Dawson	1983	159
	Gary Carter	1984	159
	Tim Wallach	1988	159
	Marquis Grissom	1992	159
	Mike Lansing	1996	159
17	Rusty Staub	1969	158
	Warren Cromartie	1979	158
	Tim Wallach	1982	158
20	Seven tied at		157

At-Bats

1	Warren Cromartie	1979	659
2	Dave Cash	1978	658
3	Mark Grudzielanek	1996	657
4	Marquis Grissom	1992	653
5	Dave Cash	1977	650
6	Mark Grudzielanek	1997	649
7	Tim Raines	1982	647
8	Mike Lansing	1996	641
9	Andre Dawson	1979	639
10	Andre Dawson	1983	633
11	Marquis Grissom	1993	630
12	Tim Wallach	1990	626
13	Tim Raines	1984	622
14	Warren Cromartie	1977	620
15	Al Oliver	1982	617
16	Tim Raines	1983	615
17	Al Oliver	1983	614
18	Willie Davis	1974	611
19	Andre Dawson	1978	609
	Andres Galarraga	1988	609

Runs

1	Tim Raines	1983	133
2	Tim Raines	1987	123
3	Tim Raines	1985	115
4	Andre Dawson	1982	107
5	Tim Raines	1984	106
6	Andre Dawson	1983	104
	Marquis Grissom	1993	104
8	Mitch Webster	1987	101
9	Ken Singleton	1973	100
10	Andres Galarraga	1988	99
	Marquis Grissom	1992	99
	Mike Lansing	1996	99
	Mark Grudzielanek	1996	99
14	Rusty Staub	1970	98
15	Andre Dawson	1980	96
	Marquis Grissom	1994	96
17	Ron LeFlore	1980	95
18	Rusty Staub	1971	94
19	Three tied at		91

Hits

1	Al Oliver	1982	204
2	Mark Grudzielanek	1996	201
3	Tim Raines	1986	194
4	Tim Raines	1984	192
5	Andre Dawson	1983	189
6	Dave Cash	1977	188
	Marquis Grissom	1993	188
8	Rusty Staub	1971	186
9	Tim Wallach	1990	185
10	Al Oliver	1983	184
	Tim Raines	1985	184
	Andres Galarraga	1988	184
13	Andre Dawson	1982	183
	Tim Raines	1983	183
	Mike Lansing	1996	183
16	Warren Cromartie	1979	181
17	Willie Davis	1974	180
	Warren Cromartie	1978	180
	Marquis Grissom	1992	180
20	Tim Raines	1982	179

Doubles

1	Mark Grudzielanek	1997	54
2	Warren Cromartie	1979	46
3	Mike Lansing	1997	45
4	Larry Walker	1994	44
5	Al Oliver	1982	43
6	Dave Cash	1977	42
	Tim Wallach	1987	42
	Andres Galarraga	1988	42
	Tim Wallach	1989	42
	Henry Rodriguez	1996	42
11	Warren Cromartie	1977	41
	Andre Dawson	1980	41
13	Andres Galarraga	1987	40
	Mike Lansing	1996	40
15	Larry Parrish	1978	39
	Larry Parrish	1979	39
	Marquis Grissom	1992	39
18	Tony Perez	1978	38
	Al Oliver	1983	38
	Tim Raines	1984	38

Triples

1	Rodney Scott	1980	13
	Tim Raines	1985	13
	Mitch Webster	1986	13
4	Andre Dawson	1979	12
5	Ron LeFlore	1980	11
6	Andre Dawson	1983	10
	Tim Raines	1986	10
8	Willie Davis	1974	9
	Andre Dawson	1977	9
	Tim Raines	1984	9
	Marquis Grissom	1991	9
12	Andre Dawson	1978	8
	Tim Raines	1982	8
	Tim Raines	1983	8
	Tim Raines	1987	8
	Mitch Webster	1987	8
	Andres Galarraga	1988	8
	Spike Owen	1991	8
	Delino DeShields	1992	8
20	Ten tied at		7

Home Runs

1	Henry Rodriguez	1996	36
2	Andre Dawson	1983	32
3	Gary Carter	1977	31
4	Rusty Staub	1970	30
	Larry Parrish	1979	30
6	Rusty Staub	1969	29
	Gary Carter	1980	29
	Gary Carter	1982	29
	Andres Galarraga	1988	29
10	Bob Bailey	1970	28
	Tim Wallach	1982	28
	Rondell White	1997	28
13	Gary Carter	1984	27
14	Bob Bailey	1973	26
	Tim Wallach	1987	26
	Henry Rodriguez	1997	26
17	Ellis Valentine	1977	25
	Andre Dawson	1978	25
	Ellis Valentine	1978	25
	Andre Dawson	1979	25

RBI

1	Tim Wallach	1987	123
2	Andre Dawson	1983	113
3	Al Oliver	1982	109
4	Gary Carter	1984	106
5	Ken Singleton	1973	103
	Henry Rodriguez	1996	103
7	Gary Carter	1980	101
8	Hubie Brooks	1985	100
9	Tim Wallach	1990	98
10	Rusty Staub	1971	97
	Gary Carter	1982	97
	Tim Wallach	1982	97
13	Moises Alou	1996	96
14	Marquis Grissom	1993	95
15	Rusty Staub	1970	94
16	Larry Walker	1992	93
17	Andre Dawson	1979	92
	Andres Galarraga	1988	92
19	Tony Perez	1977	91
	Andre Dawson	1985	91

Walks

1	Ken Singleton	1973	123
2	Rusty Staub	1970	112
3	Rusty Staub	1969	110
4	Bob Bailey	1974	100
5	Bob Bailey	1971	97
	Tim Raines	1983	97
7	Delino DeShields	1991	95
8	Ken Singleton	1974	93
	Tim Raines	1989	93
10	Tim Raines	1987	90
11	Bob Bailey	1973	88
12	Tim Raines	1984	87
13	Ron Fairly	1973	86
	Vance Law	1985	86
15	Ron Fairly	1971	81
	Tim Raines	1985	81
17	Larry Walker	1993	80
18	Mike Jorgensen	1975	79
19	Gary Carter	1982	78
	Tim Raines	1986	78

Strikeouts

1	Andres Galarraga	1990	169
2	Henry Rodriguez	1996	160
3	Andres Galarraga	1989	158
4	Andres Galarraga	1988	153
5	Delino DeShields	1991	151
6	Henry Rodriguez	1997	149
7	Andre Dawson	1978	128
8	Andres Galarraga	1987	127
9	Shane Andrews	1996	119
10	Pepe Mangual	1975	115
	Andre Dawson	1979	115
12	Bob Bailey	1972	112
	Larry Walker	1990	112
14	Tony Perez	1977	111
	Rondell White	1997	111
16	Mack Jones	1969	110
17	Hubie Brooks	1988	108
	Hubie Brooks	1989	108
	Delino DeShields	1992	108
20	Bob Bailey	1974	107

Stolen Bases

1	Ron LeFlore	1980	97
2	Tim Raines	1983	90
3	Tim Raines	1982	78
	Marquis Grissom	1992	78
5	Marquis Grissom	1991	76
6	Tim Raines	1984	75
7	Tim Raines	1981	71
8	Tim Raines	1985	70
	Tim Raines	1986	70
10	Rodney Scott	1980	63
11	Delino DeShields	1991	56
12	Marquis Grissom	1993	53
13	Larry Lintz	1974	50
	Tim Raines	1987	50
	Otis Nixon	1990	50
16	Tim Raines	1990	49
17	Otis Nixon	1988	46
	Delino DeShields	1992	46
19	Delino DeShields	1993	43
20	Delino DeShields	1990	42

Runs Created

1	Tim Raines	1987	124
2	Tim Raines	1985	120
3	Rusty Staub	1969	118
4	Rusty Staub	1970	117
	Tim Raines	1986	117
6	Al Oliver	1982	114
7	Rusty Staub	1971	113
	Tim Raines	1984	113
9	Tim Raines	1983	112
10	Ken Singleton	1973	108
11	Andres Galarraga	1988	107
12	Andre Dawson	1983	106
13	Larry Parrish	1979	102
	Tim Wallach	1987	102
15	Andre Dawson	1982	101
16	Andre Dawson	1980	100
	Gary Carter	1982	100
18	Marquis Grissom	1993	99
19	Gary Carter	1984	98
	Mitch Webster	1987	98

Runs Created/27 Outs

(minimum 3.1 Plate Appearances/Tm Gm)

1	Tim Raines	1987	9.01
2	Larry Walker	1994	8.08
3	Moises Alou	1994	7.90
4	Rusty Staub	1969	7.87
5	Tim Raines	1985	7.86
6	Tim Raines	1986	7.85
7	Andre Dawson	1981	7.61
8	Tim Raines	1981	7.41
9	Ron Fairly	1973	7.36
10	Al Oliver	1982	7.20
11	Rusty Staub	1970	7.11
12	Larry Parrish	1979	7.00
13	Rusty Staub	1971	6.86
14	Ken Singleton	1973	6.78
15	Tim Raines	1984	6.75
16	Andres Galarraga	1988	6.57
17	Tim Raines	1989	6.55
18	Tim Raines	1983	6.53
19	Henry Rodriguez	1996	6.51
20	Larry Walker	1992	6.44

Batting Average

(minimum 3.1 Plate Appearances/Tm Gm)

1	Moises Alou	1994	.339
2	Tim Raines	1986	.334
3	Al Oliver	1982	.331
4	Tim Raines	1987	.330
5	Larry Walker	1994	.322
6	Tim Raines	1985	.320
7	Rusty Staub	1971	.311
8	Tim Raines	1984	.309
9	Andre Dawson	1980	.308
10	David Segui	1997	.307
11	Larry Parrish	1979	.307
12	Mark Grudzielanek	1996	.306
13	Andres Galarraga	1987	.305
14	Warren Cromartie	1981	.304
15	Tim Raines	1981	.304
16	Rusty Staub	1969	.302
17	Andres Galarraga	1988	.302
18	Andre Dawson	1981	.302
19	Ken Singleton	1973	.302
20	Larry Walker	1992	.301

On-Base Percentage

(minimum 3.1 Plate Appearances/Tm Gm)

1	Tim Raines	1987	.429
2	Rusty Staub	1969	.426
3	Ken Singleton	1973	.425
4	Ron Fairly	1973	.422
5	Tim Raines	1986	.413
6	Tim Raines	1985	.405
7	Ron Hunt	1971	.402
8	Moises Alou	1994	.397
9	Bob Bailey	1974	.396
10	Tim Raines	1989	.395
11	Rusty Staub	1970	.394
12	Larry Walker	1994	.394
13	Tim Raines	1984	.393
14	Tim Raines	1983	.393
15	Al Oliver	1982	.392
16	Rusty Staub	1971	.392
17	Tim Raines	1981	.391
18	Delino DeShields	1993	.389
19	Ken Singleton	1974	.385
20	Gary Carter	1982	.381

Slugging Percentage

(minimum 3.1 Plate Appearances/Tm Gm)

1	Moises Alou	1994	.592
2	Larry Walker	1994	.587
3	Henry Rodriguez	1996	.562
4	Andre Dawson	1981	.553
5	Larry Parrish	1979	.551
6	Andres Galarraga	1988	.540
7	Andre Dawson	1983	.539
8	Tim Raines	1987	.526
9	Rusty Staub	1969	.526
10	Gary Carter	1977	.525
11	Tim Wallach	1987	.514
12	Al Oliver	1982	.514
13	Gary Carter	1982	.510
14	Larry Walker	1992	.506
15	David Segui	1997	.505
16	Ellis Valentine	1977	.504
17	Andre Dawson	1982	.498
18	Rusty Staub	1970	.497
19	Andre Dawson	1980	.492
20	Ellis Valentine	1978	.489

Teams: Expos

Expos Franchise Pitching Leaders—Single Season

Wins

1	Ross Grimsley	1978	20
2	Steve Rogers	1982	19
3	Carl Morton	1970	18
	Bryn Smith	1985	18
5	Bill Stoneman	1971	17
	Steve Rogers	1977	17
	Bill Gullickson	1983	17
	Steve Rogers	1983	17
	Pedro Martinez	1997	17
10	Mike Torrez	1972	16
	Bill Lee	1979	16
	Steve Rogers	1980	16
	Scott Sanderson	1980	16
	Charlie Lea	1983	16
	Dennis Martinez	1989	16
	Dennis Martinez	1992	16
	Ken Hill	1992	16
	Ken Hill	1994	16
19	Nine tied at		15

Losses

1	Steve Rogers	1974	22
2	Bill Stoneman	1969	19
3	Carl Morton	1971	18
4	Steve Rogers	1976	17
5	Jerry Robertson	1969	16
	Bill Stoneman	1971	16
	Balor Moore	1973	16
	Steve Renko	1974	16
	Steve Rogers	1977	16
10	Bill Stoneman	1970	15
	Ernie McAnally	1972	15
	Dennis Blair	1975	15
	Steve Rogers	1984	15
	Bob Sebra	1987	15
15	Mike Wegener	1969	14
	Steve Renko	1971	14
	Bill Stoneman	1972	14
	Bill Gullickson	1982	14
	Ray Burris	1982	14
	Jeff Fassero	1995	14

Winning Percentage
(minimum 15 decisions)

1	Bryn Smith	1985	.783
2	Ken Hill	1994	.762
3	Jeff Parrett	1988	.750
4	Dennis Martinez	1987	.733
5	Jeff Fassero	1993	.706
6	Steve Rogers	1982	.704
7	Dennis Martinez	1989	.696
8	Pedro Martinez	1994	.688
	Jeff Juden	1997	.688
10	Pedro Martinez	1997	.680
11	Steve Rogers	1973	.667
	Dan Schatzeder	1979	.667
	Bill Gullickson	1980	.667
	Joe Hesketh	1985	.667
	Andy McGaffigan	1986	.667
	Ugueth Urbina	1996	.667
17	Mike Torrez	1974	.652
	Dale Murray	1975	.652
19	Ross Grimsley	1978	.645
20	Ken Hill	1992	.640

Games

1	Mike Marshall	1973	92
2	Dale Murray	1976	81
3	Tim Burke	1985	78
4	Barry Jones	1991	77
5	Jeff Reardon	1982	75
6	Dan McGinn	1969	74
	Mel Rojas	1996	74
8	Jeff Fassero	1992	70
	John Wetteland	1993	70
	Mike Dyer	1996	70
11	Will McEnaney	1977	69
	Andy McGaffigan	1987	69
13	Jeff Reardon	1984	68
	Tim Burke	1986	68
	Tim Burke	1989	68
	Mel Rojas	1992	68
	Dave Veres	1996	68
18	Elias Sosa	1980	67
	John Wetteland	1992	67
20	Four tied at		66

Games Started

1	Steve Rogers	1977	40
2	Bill Stoneman	1971	39
3	Steve Rogers	1974	38
4	Carl Morton	1970	37
	Steve Renko	1971	37
	Steve Rogers	1979	37
	Steve Rogers	1980	37
8	Bill Stoneman	1969	36
	Ross Grimsley	1978	36
	Steve Rogers	1983	36
11	Carl Morton	1971	35
	Bill Stoneman	1972	35
	Steve Renko	1974	35
	Steve Rogers	1975	35
	Steve Rogers	1982	35
16	Seven tied at		34

Complete Games

1	Bill Stoneman	1971	20
2	Ross Grimsley	1978	19
3	Steve Rogers	1977	17
4	Steve Rogers	1980	14
	Steve Rogers	1982	14
6	Mike Torrez	1972	13
	Bill Stoneman	1972	13
	Steve Rogers	1979	13
	Steve Rogers	1983	13
	Pedro Martinez	1997	13
11	Steve Rogers	1975	12
12	Steve Rogers	1974	11
	Steve Rogers	1978	11
14	Carl Morton	1970	10
	Bill Gullickson	1983	10
16	Steve Renko	1971	9
	Carl Morton	1971	9
	Steve Renko	1973	9
	Dennis Martinez	1988	9
	Dennis Martinez	1991	9

Shutouts

1	Bill Stoneman	1969	5
	Steve Rogers	1979	5
	Steve Rogers	1983	5
	Dennis Martinez	1991	5
	Carlos Perez	1997	5
6	Carl Morton	1970	4
	Bill Stoneman	1972	4
	Steve Rogers	1976	4
	Steve Rogers	1977	4
	Steve Rogers	1980	4
	Steve Rogers	1982	4
	Charlie Lea	1983	4
	Mark Langston	1989	4
	Pedro Martinez	1997	4
15	Ninteen tied at		3

Saves

1	John Wetteland	1993	43
2	Jeff Reardon	1985	41
3	John Wetteland	1992	37
4	Mel Rojas	1996	36
5	Jeff Reardon	1986	35
6	Mike Marshall	1973	31
7	Mel Rojas	1995	30
8	Tim Burke	1989	28
9	Ugueth Urbina	1997	27
10	Jeff Reardon	1982	26
11	John Wetteland	1994	25
12	Claude Raymond	1970	23
	Mike Marshall	1971	23
	Jeff Reardon	1984	23
15	Jeff Reardon	1983	21
16	Tim Burke	1990	20
17	Mike Marshall	1972	18
	Elias Sosa	1979	18
	Tim Burke	1987	18
	Tim Burke	1988	18

Innings Pitched

1	Steve Rogers	1977	301.2
2	Bill Stoneman	1971	294.2
3	Carl Morton	1970	284.2
4	Steve Rogers	1980	281.0
5	Steve Rogers	1982	277.0
6	Steve Renko	1971	275.2
7	Steve Rogers	1983	273.0
8	Ross Grimsley	1978	263.0
9	Steve Rogers	1974	253.2
10	Steve Rogers	1975	251.2
11	Bill Stoneman	1972	250.2
12	Steve Renko	1973	249.2
13	Steve Rogers	1979	248.2
14	Mike Torrez	1972	243.1
15	Bill Gullickson	1983	242.1
16	Pedro Martinez	1997	241.1
17	Bill Gullickson	1982	236.2
18	Bill Stoneman	1969	235.2
19	Dennis Martinez	1988	235.1
20	Dennis Martinez	1989	232.0

Walks

1	Bill Stoneman	1971	146
2	Steve Renko	1971	135
3	Carl Morton	1970	125
4	Bill Stoneman	1969	123
5	Floyd Youmans	1986	118
6	Mike Torrez	1973	115
7	Bill Stoneman	1970	109
	Balor Moore	1973	109
9	Steve Renko	1973	108
10	Dennis Blair	1975	106
11	Steve Renko	1970	104
12	Mike Torrez	1972	103
13	Bill Stoneman	1972	102
14	Mike Wegener	1969	96
15	Mark Langston	1989	93
16	Don Stanhouse	1976	92
17	Steve Rogers	1975	88
	Kevin Gross	1989	88
19	Ernie McAnally	1971	87
	Dan Warthen	1975	87

Strikeouts

1	Pedro Martinez	1997	305
2	Bill Stoneman	1971	251
3	Jeff Fassero	1996	222
	Pedro Martinez	1996	222
5	Steve Rogers	1977	206
6	Floyd Youmans	1986	202
7	Bill Stoneman	1969	185
8	Steve Rogers	1982	179
9	Bill Stoneman	1970	176
10	Mark Langston	1989	175
11	Pedro Martinez	1995	174
12	Bill Stoneman	1972	171
13	Steve Renko	1973	164
	Jeff Fassero	1995	164
15	Balor Moore	1972	161
16	Scott Sanderson	1982	158
	Kevin Gross	1989	158
18	Bob Sebra	1987	156
	Dennis Martinez	1990	156
20	Bill Gullickson	1982	155

Strikeouts/9 Innings
(minimum 1 Inning Pitched/Tm Gm)

1	Pedro Martinez	1997	11.37
2	Pedro Martinez	1996	9.22
3	Mark Langston	1989	8.92
4	Pedro Martinez	1994	8.83
5	Jeff Fassero	1996	8.62
6	Floyd Youmans	1986	8.30
7	Pedro Martinez	1995	8.04
8	Bob Sebra	1987	7.92
9	Jeff Fassero	1995	7.81
10	Jeff Fassero	1994	7.72
11	Balor Moore	1973	7.71
12	Bill Stoneman	1971	7.67
13	Bill Stoneman	1970	7.63
14	Scott Sanderson	1979	7.39
15	Bill Stoneman	1969	7.07
16	Kevin Gross	1989	7.06
17	Pascual Perez	1989	6.90
18	Dan Warthen	1975	6.87
19	Mike Wegener	1969	6.74
20	Jerry Robertson	1969	6.66

ERA
(minimum 1 Inning Pitched/Tm Gm)

1	Pedro Martinez	1997	1.90
2	Dennis Martinez	1991	2.39
3	Mark Langston	1989	2.39
4	Steve Rogers	1982	2.40
5	Pascual Perez	1988	2.44
6	Dennis Martinez	1992	2.47
7	Steve Rogers	1978	2.47
8	Mike Marshall	1973	2.66
9	Ken Hill	1992	2.68
10	Dennis Martinez	1988	2.72
11	Bill Gullickson	1981	2.80
12	Steve Renko	1973	2.81
13	Dan Schatzeder	1979	2.83
14	Bryn Smith	1989	2.84
15	Charlie Lea	1984	2.89
16	Bryn Smith	1985	2.91
17	Oil Can Boyd	1990	2.93
18	Dennis Martinez	1990	2.95
19	Scott Sanderson	1981	2.95
20	Steve Rogers	1980	2.98

Component ERA
(minimum 1 Inning Pitched/Tm Gm)

1	Pedro Martinez	1997	1.79
2	Pascual Perez	1988	1.94
3	Dennis Martinez	1992	2.19
4	Bryn Smith	1985	2.29
5	Bill Gullickson	1981	2.42
6	Dennis Martinez	1990	2.44
7	Dennis Martinez	1991	2.46
8	Bryn Smith	1989	2.47
9	Steve Rogers	1982	2.54
10	Floyd Youmans	1986	2.62
11	Scott Sanderson	1981	2.64
12	Charlie Lea	1982	2.67
13	Steve Rogers	1978	2.68
14	Pascual Perez	1989	2.69
15	Bryn Smith	1988	2.73
16	Ross Grimsley	1978	2.79
17	Steve Rogers	1980	2.80
18	Steve Rogers	1977	2.81
19	Pedro Martinez	1994	2.81
20	Jeff Fassero	1994	2.82

Opponent Average
(minimum 1 Inning Pitched/Tm Gm)

1	Pedro Martinez	1997	.184
2	Floyd Youmans	1986	.188
3	Pascual Perez	1988	.196
4	Dennis Martinez	1992	.211
5	Dan Warthen	1975	.217
6	Mark Langston	1989	.218
7	Steve Renko	1973	.218
8	Pedro Martinez	1994	.220
9	Charlie Lea	1982	.222
10	Bryn Smith	1989	.223
11	Dan Schatzeder	1979	.225
12	Bill Stoneman	1971	.225
13	Dennis Martinez	1991	.226
14	Pedro Martinez	1995	.227
15	Dennis Martinez	1990	.228
16	Ernie McAnally	1971	.228
17	Bill Stoneman	1972	.229
18	Jeff Fassero	1994	.229
19	Mark Gardner	1991	.230
20	Ken Hill	1992	.230

Opponent OBP
(minimum 1 Inning Pitched/Tm Gm)

1	Pedro Martinez	1997	.250
2	Pascual Perez	1988	.252
3	Bryn Smith	1985	.268
4	Dennis Martinez	1992	.271
5	Bryn Smith	1989	.274
6	Dennis Martinez	1990	.274
7	Scott Sanderson	1981	.278
8	Dennis Martinez	1991	.282
9	Bryn Smith	1988	.282
10	Pascual Perez	1989	.282
11	Charlie Lea	1982	.283
12	Bill Gullickson	1981	.283
13	Jeff Fassero	1994	.285
14	Steve Rogers	1982	.285
15	Dennis Martinez	1988	.286
16	Oil Can Boyd	1990	.288
17	Jeff Fassero	1996	.289
18	Ross Grimsley	1978	.291
19	Steve Rogers	1978	.293
20	Pedro Martinez	1996	.294

Expos Capsule

Best Season: *1981.* After barely missing the National League East title in both 1979 and 1980, the Expos finished with the best record in the division in the second half of the 1981 split season (despite firing manager Dick Williams on September 8). They defeated the Philadelphia Phillies in a five-game Division Series to advance to the NLCS, where they battled the Los Angeles Dodgers for the full five games. Game 5 was tied with two out in the top of the ninth when Los Angeles' Rick Monday homered off Steve Rogers to dash the Expos' World Series hopes.

Worst Season: *1976.* Gene Mauch, the only manager the club had ever had, was fired after the 1975 season. Karl Kuehl took over and the results were disastrous. Shortstop Tim Foli soon took to openly challenging him. After Foli upbraided him in full view of the team and suffered no disciplinary action, Kuehl lost all remaining support. He was fired in late August, and the team finished with a major league-worst 55-107 record.

Best Player: *Andre Dawson.* Before his knees really started to trouble him, he was a .300 hitter with power and speed and a perennial Gold Glover. He finished second in the MVP balloting twice in the span of three seasons. Tim Raines or Gary Carter would be excellent selections as well. Raines was the premier NL leadoff man of the 1980s while Carter was one of the most durable and productive catchers of all time. Both placed high in the MVP balloting several different times.

Best Pitcher: *Steve Rogers.* Montreal's all-time victory leader pitched for the Expos for five seasons before they climbed above .500, and once they did, he posted a winning record for seven years in a row. Rogers finished in the top five in the NL Cy Young voting three times.

Best Reliever: *Jeff Reardon* saved 152 games for the Expos in six seasons and led the NL with 41 saves in 1985. Honorable mention goes to John Wetteland, who was brilliant during his three short seasons in an Expos' uniform.

Best Defensive Player: *Andre Dawson.* He won six Gold Gloves in center and right field, not only for his speed and athleticism but also for his throwing arm, which was among the best in the game for his entire career.

Hall of Famers: Andre Dawson has an excellent chance to be enshrined, as do Gary Carter and Tim Raines.

Franchise All-Star Team:

C	*Gary Carter*		**LF**	*Tim Raines*
1B	*Andres Galarraga*		**CF**	*Andre Dawson*
2B	*Delino DeShields*		**RF**	*Larry Walker*
3B	*Tim Wallach*		**SP**	*Steve Rogers*
SS	*Tim Foli*		**RP**	*Jeff Reardon*

Biggest Flake: Tough call. The Expos seem to attract free spirits. Lefthander *Ross Grimsley* refused to bathe on the days he pitched and liked to moon passing motorists from the team bus. As a member of the Atlanta Braves, *Pascual Perez* became instantly famous when he showed up late to a game and explained that he'd gotten lost on his way to the ballpark and had been driving around for hours (he never had any such problems with the Expos, despite the French traffic signs). Years later, his younger brother *Carlos* joined the team and became known for his odd strikeout dance, which resembled a full-body muscle spasm. *Bill "Spaceman" Lee* and *Don "Stan The Man Unusual" Stanhouse* both ruminated on the meaning of life from Olympic Stadium's mound.

Strangest Career: *Bill Lee.* The inscrutable southpaw was acquired from the Red Sox after the 1978 season for little-used utilityman Stan Papi, and won 16 games the next season as the Expos zoomed into contention for the first time in their history. But he won only four games in 1980 due to injuries—one of which was allegedly suffered when he fell after climbing out the window of a woman's apartment. (The door wasn't an option because the woman's husband was entering through it at the time.) He lost his spot in the rotation in '81, but posted a fine 2.93 ERA out of the bullpen. Still, he was released in '82 after pitching just 12 more games. No one picked him up. Lee claimed he'd been blacklisted.

What Might Have Been: *David Palmer.* Persistent injuries prevented him from pitching a full season for the Expos. During two of his eight years in Montreal, he wasn't able to pitch at all. When he was able to take the mound, he was terrific. His career numbers with Montreal included a 3.26 ERA and a .594 winning percentage.

Best Trade: The Expos acquired *Dennis Martinez* from the Baltimore Orioles for infielder Rene Gonzalez on June 16, 1986. Martinez, recovered from alcoholism and physical problems, became Montreal's ace for the next seven years. Honorable mention goes to the May 29, 1981 trade that sent Ellis Valentine to the New York Mets for closer Jeff Reardon.

Worst Trade: On December 4, 1974, the Expos sent outfielder *Ken Singleton* and pitcher *Mike Torrez* to the Orioles for pitcher Dave McNally and outfielder Rich Coggins. Torrez won 20 games the following year and remained a winner for many years, while Singleton had a long and productive career. The Expos got essentially nothing out of the deal. McNally hurt his arm and soon retired, while Coggins was sold to the Yankees after only 13 games.

Best-Looking Player: *Tim Wallach.*

Ugliest Player: *Zane Smith.*

The All-Nickname Team:

C	*Gary "The Kid" Carter*	**LF**	*"Oh! Henry" Rodriguez*
1B	*Andres Galarraga, "The Big Cat"*	**CF**	Andre "The Hawk" Dawson
2B	*Rex "The Wonder Dog" Hudler*	**RF**	*Rusty Staub, "Le Grand Orange"*
3B	*Tim "Eli" Wallach*	**SP**	Bill "Spaceman" Lee
SS	*Rodney Scott, "Cool Breeze"*	**RP**	Don *"Stan The Man Unusual" Stanhouse*

Most Unappreciated Player: Middle reliever *Andy McGaffigan,* who posted sub-3.00 ERAs in four of his five years with the club.

Most Overrated Player: *Warren Cromartie.* Despite his .280 average, his lack of power or plate discipline made him a below-average performer as a left fielder or first baseman.

Most Admirable Star: *Andre Dawson.*

Least Admirable Star: *Ellis Valentine.*

Best Season, Player: *Andre Dawson, 1981.* In the strike-shortened season, Dawson batted .301 and finished second in the NL with 24 homers. He also stole 26 bases in 30 attempts while playing Gold Glove defense in center field.

Best Season, Pitcher: *Pedro Martinez, 1997.* Martinez went 19-8 and won the NL Cy Young while leading the majors with 305 strikeouts and a 1.90 ERA.

Most Impressive Individual Record: *Ron Hunt's* incredible total of 50 hit-by-pitches in 1971, a modern record. Hunt was a prolific HBP artist, but he nearly doubled his next-best season total that year.

Biggest Tragedy: *The labor strife that brought a premature end to the 1994 season.* At the time, the Expos owned the best record in baseball and held a six-game lead over the Atlanta Braves in the NL East Division race. It all went for naught as the playoffs and World Series were cancelled. During the offseason, the Expos lost four of their best players (outfielders Larry Walker and Marquis Grissom and pitchers John Wetteland and Ken Hill) to money-related trades or free agency, and they fell into last place the following year.

Fan Favorite: *Rusty Staub.*

—Mat Olkin

New York Mets (1962-1997)

Year	Lg	Pos	W-L	Pct	GB	Manager	Att.	R	OR	HR	Avg	OBP	Slg	HR	Avg	OBP	ERA	Runs	HR
1962	NL	10th	40-120	.250	60.5	Casey Stengel	922,530	617	948	139	.240	.318	.361	192	.281	.349	5.04	117	181
1963	NL	10th	51-111	.315	48.0	Casey Stengel	1,080,108	501	774	96	.219	.285	.315	162	.263	.330	4.12	106	148
1964	NL	10th	53-109	.327	40.0	Casey Stengel	1,732,597	569	776	103	.246	.296	.348	130	.272	.332	4.25	97	104
1965	NL	10th	50-112	.309	47.0	Casey Stengel/Wes Westrum	1,768,389	495	752	107	.221	.277	.327	147	.262	.326	4.06	105	107
1966	NL	9th	66-95	.410	28.5	Wes Westrum	1,932,693	587	761	98	.239	.301	.342	166	.272	.337	4.17	91	120
1967	NL	10th	61-101	.377	40.5	Wes Westrum/Salty Parker	1,565,492	498	672	83	.238	.288	.325	124	.253	.321	3.73	101	111
1968	NL	9th	73-89	.451	24.0	Gil Hodges	1,781,657	473	499	81	.228	.281	.315	87	.230	.290	2.72	103	143
1969	NL	1st-E	100-62	.617	—	Gil Hodges	2,175,373	632	541	109	.242	.311	.351	119	.227	.296	2.99	96	99
1970	NL	3rd-E	83-79	.512	6.0	Gil Hodges	2,697,479	695	630	120	.249	.333	.370	135	.233	.307	3.45	105	115
1971	NL	3rd-E	83-79	.512	14.0	Gil Hodges	2,266,680	588	550	98	.249	.319	.351	100	.227	.299	3.00	89	98
1972	NL	3rd-E	83-73	.532	13.5	Yogi Berra	2,134,185	528	578	105	.225	.307	.332	118	.240	.306	3.26	88	83
1973	NL	1st-E	82-79	.509	—	Yogi Berra	1,912,390	608	588	85	.246	.315	.338	127	.245	.307	3.26	98	88
1974	NL	5th-E	71-91	.438	17.0	Yogi Berra	1,722,209	572	646	96	.235	.311	.329	99	.257	.320	3.42	98	89
1975	NL	3rd-E	82-80	.506	10.5	Yogi Berra/Roy McMillan	1,730,566	646	625	101	.256	.319	.361	99	.246	.319	3.39	88	100
1976	NL	3rd-E	86-76	.531	15.0	Joe Frazier	1,468,754	615	538	102	.246	.319	.352	97	.233	.290	2.94	78	74
1977	NL	6th-E	64-98	.395	37.0	Joe Frazier/Joe Torre	1,066,825	587	663	88	.244	.313	.346	118	.254	.317	3.77	91	103
1978	NL	6th-E	66-96	.407	24.0	Joe Torre	1,007,328	607	690	86	.245	.314	.352	114	.265	.330	3.87	98	97
1979	NL	6th-E	63-99	.389	35.0	Joe Torre	788,905	593	706	74	.250	.313	.350	120	.266	.338	3.84	92	83
1980	NL	5th-E	67-95	.414	24.0	Joe Torre	1,192,073	611	702	61	.257	.319	.345	140	.267	.328	3.85	93	130
1981	NL	5th-E	17-34	.333	15.0	Joe Torre													
	NL	4th-E	24-28	.462	5.5	Joe Torre	704,244	348	432	57	.248	.308	.356	74	.259	.323	3.55	104	110
1982	NL	6th-E	65-97	.401	27.0	George Bamberger	1,323,036	609	723	97	.247	.305	.350	119	.273	.341	3.88	99	100
1983	NL	6th-E	68-94	.420	22.0	George Bamberger/Frank Howard	1,112,774	575	680	112	.241	.300	.344	97	.256	.331	3.68	98	122
1984	NL	2nd-E	90-72	.556	6.5	Davey Johnson	1,842,695	652	676	107	.257	.320	.369	104	.252	.324	3.60	100	95
1985	NL	2nd-E	98-64	.605	3.0	Davey Johnson	2,761,601	695	568	134	.257	.323	.385	111	.237	.302	3.11	90	90
1986	NL	1st-E	108-54	.667	—	Davey Johnson	2,767,601	783	578	148	.263	.339	.401	103	.236	.302	3.11	86	98
1987	NL	2nd-E	92-70	.568	3.0	Davey Johnson	3,034,129	823	698	192	.268	.339	.434	135	.254	.319	3.84	95	91
1988	NL	1st-E	100-60	.625	—	Davey Johnson	3,055,445	703	532	152	.256	.325	.396	78	.235	.291	2.91	75	78
1989	NL	2nd-E	87-75	.537	6.0	Davey Johnson	2,918,710	683	595	147	.246	.311	.385	115	.231	.301	3.29	91	105
1990	NL	2nd-E	91-71	.562	4.0	Davey Johnson/Bud Harrelson	2,732,745	775	613	172	.256	.323	.408	119	.246	.304	3.43	95	90
1991	NL	5th-E	77-84	.478	20.5	Bud Harrelson/Mike Cubbage	2,284,484	640	646	117	.244	.317	.365	108	.257	.309	3.56	108	95
1992	NL	5th-E	72-90	.444	24.0	Jeff Torborg	1,779,534	599	653	93	.235	.310	.342	98	.256	.318	3.68	90	91
1993	NL	7th-E	59-103	.364	38.0	Jeff Torborg/Dallas Green	1,873,183	672	744	158	.248	.305	.390	139	.269	.324	4.05	96	98
1994	NL	3rd-E	55-58	.487	18.5	Dallas Green	1,151,471	506	526	117	.250	.316	.394	117	.271	.328	4.13	109	106
1995	NL	2nd-E	69-75	.479	21.0	Dallas Green	1,273,183	657	618	125	.267	.330	.400	133	.262	.320	3.88	89	103
1996	NL	4th-E	71-91	.438	25.0	Dallas Green/Bobby Valentine	1,588,323	746	779	147	.270	.324	.412	159	.272	.337	4.22	82	80
1997	NL	3rd-E	88-74	.543	13.0	Bobby Valentine	1,766,154	777	709	153	.262	.332	.405	160	.262	.326	3.95	98	86

Team Nicknames: New York Mets 1962-1997.

Team Ballparks: Polo Grounds V 1962-1963, Shea Stadium 1964-1997.

New York Mets Individual Season Batting Leaders

Year	Batting Average		On-Base Percentage		Slugging Percentage		Home Runs		RBI		Stolen Bases	
1962	Felix Mantilla	.275	Felix Mantilla	.330	Frank Thomas	.496	Frank Thomas	34	Frank Thomas	94	Richie Ashburn	12
											Elio Chacon	
1963	Ron Hunt	.272	Ron Hunt	.334	Jim Hickman	.399	Jim Hickman	17	Frank Thomas	60	Rod Kanehl	6
1964	Ron Hunt	.303	Joe Christopher	.360	Joe Christopher	.466	Charley Smith	20	Joe Christopher	76	3 tied with	6
1965	Ed Kranepool	.253	Johnny Lewis	.331	Charley Smith	.393	Ron Swoboda	19	Charley Smith	62	Joe Christopher	4
											Johnny Lewis	
1966	Ron Hunt	.288	Ron Hunt	.356	Ken Boyer	.415	Ed Kranepool	16	Ken Boyer	61	Cleon Jones	16
1967	Tommy Davis	.302	Tommy Davis	.342	Tommy Davis	.440	Tommy Davis	16	Tommy Davis	73	Bud Harrelson	12
											Cleon Jones	
1968	Cleon Jones	.297	Cleon Jones	.341	Cleon Jones	.452	Ed Charles	15	Ron Swoboda	59	Cleon Jones	23
1969	Cleon Jones	.340	Cleon Jones	.422	Cleon Jones	.482	Tommie Agee	26	Tommie Agee	76	Cleon Jones	16
1970	Tommie Agee	.286	Cleon Jones	.352	Tommie Agee	.469	Tommie Agee	24	Donn Clendenon	97	Tommie Agee	31
1971	Cleon Jones	.319	Cleon Jones	.382	Cleon Jones	.473	3 tied with	14	Cleon Jones	69	Tommie Agee	28
											Bud Harrelson	
1972	Tommie Agee	.227	Tommie Agee	.317	Tommie Agee	.374	John Milner	17	Cleon Jones	52	Bud Harrelson	12
1973	Felix Millan	.290	Rusty Staub	.361	John Milner	.432	John Milner	23	Rusty Staub	76	Wayne Garrett	6
1974	Cleon Jones	.282	Rusty Staub	.347	Cleon Jones	.421	John Milner	20	Rusty Staub	78	John Milner	10
1975	Del Unser	.294	Rusty Staub	.371	Dave Kingman	.494	Dave Kingman	36	Rusty Staub	105	Dave Kingman	7
1976	Felix Millan	.282	John Milner	.362	Dave Kingman	.506	Dave Kingman	37	Dave Kingman	86	Bruce Boisclair	9
											Bud Harrelson	
1977	Lenny Randle	.304	Lenny Randle	.383	Lenny Randle	.404	3 tied with	12	Steve Henderson	65	Lenny Randle	33
1978	Lee Mazzilli	.273	John Stearns	.364	Lee Mazzilli	.432	Willie Montanez	17	Willie Montanez	96	John Stearns	25
1979	Lee Mazzilli	.303	Lee Mazzilli	.395	Lee Mazzilli	.449	Joel Youngblood	16	Richie Hebner	79	Frank Taveras	42
									Lee Mazzilli			
1980	Steve Henderson	.290	Lee Mazzilli	.370	Lee Mazzilli	.431	Lee Mazzilli	16	Lee Mazzilli	76	Lee Mazzilli	41
1981	Hubie Brooks	.307	Hubie Brooks	.345	Dave Kingman	.456	Dave Kingman	22	Dave Kingman	59	Mookie Wilson	24
1982	Mookie Wilson	.279	Mookie Wilson	.314	Dave Kingman	.432	Dave Kingman	37	Dave Kingman	99	Mookie Wilson	58
1983	Mookie Wilson	.276	Mookie Wilson	.300	George Foster	.419	George Foster	28	George Foster	90	Mookie Wilson	54
1984	Keith Hernandez	.311	Keith Hernandez	.409	Darryl Strawberry	.467	Darryl Strawberry	26	Darryl Strawberry	97	Mookie Wilson	46
1985	Keith Hernandez	.309	Keith Hernandez	.384	Gary Carter	.488	Gary Carter	32	Gary Carter	100	Wally Backman	30
1986	Keith Hernandez	.310	Keith Hernandez	.413	Darryl Strawberry	.507	Darryl Strawberry	27	Gary Carter	105	Lenny Dykstra	31
1987	Keith Hernandez	.290	Darryl Strawberry	.398	Darryl Strawberry	.583	Darryl Strawberry	39	Darryl Strawberry	104	Darryl Strawberry	36
1988	Kevin McReynolds	.288	Darryl Strawberry	.366	Darryl Strawberry	.545	Darryl Strawberry	39	Darryl Strawberry	101	Lenny Dykstra	30
1989	Howard Johnson	.287	Howard Johnson	.369	Howard Johnson	.559	Howard Johnson	36	Howard Johnson	101	Howard Johnson	41
1990	Dave Magadan	.328	Dave Magadan	.417	Darryl Strawberry	.518	Darryl Strawberry	37	Darryl Strawberry	108	Howard Johnson	34
1991	Gregg Jefferies	.272	Dave Magadan	.378	Howard Johnson	.535	Howard Johnson	38	Howard Johnson	117	Vince Coleman	37
1992	Eddie Murray	.261	Bobby Bonilla	.348	Bobby Bonilla	.432	Bobby Bonilla	19	Eddie Murray	93	Vince Coleman	24
1993	Eddie Murray	.285	Bobby Bonilla	.352	Bobby Bonilla	.522	Bobby Bonilla	34	Eddie Murray	100	Vince Coleman	38
1994	Jeff Kent	.292	Bobby Bonilla	.374	Bobby Bonilla	.504	Bobby Bonilla	20	Jeff Kent	68	John Cangelosi	5
1995	Rico Brogna	.289	Rico Brogna	.342	Rico Brogna	.485	Rico Brogna	22	Rico Brogna	76	Brett Butler	21
1996	Lance Johnson	.333	Bernard Gilkey	.393	Bernard Gilkey	.562	Todd Hundley	41	Bernard Gilkey	117	Lance Johnson	50
1997	Edgardo Alfonzo	.315	John Olerud	.400	Todd Hundley	.549	Todd Hundley	30	John Olerud	102	Carl Everett	17

New York Mets Individual Season Pitching Leaders

Year	ERA		Baserunners/9 IP		Innings Pitched		Strikeouts		Wins		Saves	
1962	Al Jackson	4.40	Al Jackson	12.7	Roger Craig	233.1	Roger Craig	118	Roger Craig	10	Craig Anderson	4
							Al Jackson					
1963	Carl Willey	3.10	Carl Willey	10.9	Roger Craig	236.0	Al Jackson	142	Al Jackson	13	Larry Bearnarth	4
1964	Galen Cisco	3.62	Galen Cisco	11.4	Jack Fisher	227.2	Tracy Stallard	118	Al Jackson	11	Willard Hunter	5
1965	Jack Fisher	3.94	Jack Fisher	11.5	Jack Fisher	253.2	Al Jackson	120	Jack Fisher	8	Dennis Ribant	3
									Al Jackson			
1966	Dennis Ribant	3.20	Dennis Ribant	10.8	Jack Fisher	230.0	Jack Fisher	127	3 tied with	11	Jack Hamilton	13
1967	Tom Seaver	2.76	Tom Seaver	11.0	Tom Seaver	251.0	Tom Seaver	170	Tom Seaver	16	Ron Taylor	8
1968	Jerry Koosman	2.08	Tom Seaver	9.1	Tom Seaver	277.2	Tom Seaver	205	Jerry Koosman	19	Ron Taylor	13
1969	Tom Seaver	2.21	Tom Seaver	9.6	Tom Seaver	273.1	Tom Seaver	208	Tom Seaver	25	Ron Taylor	13
1970	Tom Seaver	2.82	Tom Seaver	9.8	Tom Seaver	290.2	Tom Seaver	283	Tom Seaver	18	Ron Taylor	13
1971	Tom Seaver	1.76	Tom Seaver	8.6	Tom Seaver	286.1	Tom Seaver	289	Tom Seaver	20	Danny Frisella	12
1972	Jon Matlack	2.32	Jim McAndrew	9.9	Tom Seaver	262.0	Tom Seaver	249	Tom Seaver	21	Tug McGraw	27
1973	Tom Seaver	2.08	Tom Seaver	8.9	Tom Seaver	290.0	Tom Seaver	251	Tom Seaver	19	Tug McGraw	25
1974	Jon Matlack	2.41	Jon Matlack	10.2	Jon Matlack	265.1	Tom Seaver	201	Jerry Koosman	15	Harry Parker	4
1975	Tom Seaver	2.38	Tom Seaver	9.9	Tom Seaver	280.1	Tom Seaver	243	Tom Seaver	22	Bob Apodaca	13
1976	Tom Seaver	2.59	Tom Seaver	9.7	Tom Seaver	271.0	Tom Seaver	235	Jerry Koosman	21	Skip Lockwood	19
1977	Nino Espinosa	3.42	Jerry Koosman	11.1	Jerry Koosman	226.2	Jerry Koosman	192	Nino Espinosa	10	Skip Lockwood	20
1978	Craig Swan	2.43	Craig Swan	9.7	Jerry Koosman	235.1	Jerry Koosman	160	Nino Espinosa	11	Skip Lockwood	15
1979	Craig Swan	3.29	Craig Swan	10.7	Craig Swan	251.1	Craig Swan	145	Craig Swan	14	Skip Lockwood	9
1980	Pat Zachry	3.01	Pat Zachry	11.4	Ray Burris	170.1	Pete Falcone	109	Mark Bomback	10	Neil Allen	22
1981	Mike Scott	3.90	Mike Scott	10.9	Pat Zachry	139.0	Pat Zachry	76	Neil Allen	7	Neil Allen	18
									Pat Zachry			
1982	Craig Swan	3.35	Craig Swan	10.9	Pete Falcone	171.0	Pete Falcone	101	Craig Swan	11	Neil Allen	19
					Charlie Puleo							
1983	Tom Seaver	3.55	Tom Seaver	11.3	Tom Seaver	231.0	Tom Seaver	135	Jesse Orosco	13	Jesse Orosco	17
1984	Dwight Gooden	2.60	Dwight Gooden	9.7	Dwight Gooden	218.0	Dwight Gooden	276	Dwight Gooden	17	Jesse Orosco	31
1985	Dwight Gooden	1.53	Dwight Gooden	8.8	Dwight Gooden	276.2	Dwight Gooden	268	Dwight Gooden	24	Roger McDowell	17
											Jesse Orosco	
1986	Bobby Ojeda	2.57	Bobby Ojeda	9.9	Dwight Gooden	250.0	Sid Fernandez	200	Bobby Ojeda	18	Roger McDowell	22
							Dwight Gooden					
1987	Dwight Gooden	3.21	Dwight Gooden	10.9	Ron Darling	207.2	Ron Darling	167	Dwight Gooden	15	Roger McDowell	25
1988	David Cone	2.22	Bobby Ojeda	9.2	Dwight Gooden	248.1	David Cone	213	David Cone	20	Randy Myers	26
1989	Sid Fernandez	2.83	Sid Fernandez	9.8	David Cone	219.2	Sid Fernandez	198	3 tied with	14	Randy Myers	24
1990	Frank Viola	2.67	Sid Fernandez	10.1	Frank Viola	249.2	David Cone	233	Frank Viola	20	John Franco	33
1991	David Cone	3.29	David Cone	10.9	David Cone	232.2	David Cone	241	David Cone	14	John Franco	30
1992	Sid Fernandez	2.73	Sid Fernandez	9.8	Sid Fernandez	214.2	David Cone	214	Sid Fernandez	14	John Franco	15
											Anthony Young	
1993	Dwight Gooden	3.45	Dwight Gooden	11.1	Dwight Gooden	208.2	Dwight Gooden	149	Dwight Gooden	12	John Franco	10
1994	Bret Saberhagen	2.74	Bret Saberhagen	9.4	Bret Saberhagen	177.1	Bret Saberhagen	143	Bret Saberhagen	14	John Franco	30
1995	Bobby Jones	4.19	Dave Mlicki	12.2	Bobby Jones	195.2	Bobby Jones	127	Bobby Jones	10	John Franco	29
1996	Mark Clark	3.43	Mark Clark	11.4	Mark Clark	212.1	Mark Clark	142	Mark Clark	14	John Franco	28
1997	Rick Reed	2.89	Rick Reed	9.6	Rick Reed	208.1	Dave Mlicki	157	Bobby Jones	15	John Franco	36

Teams: Mets

Mets Franchise Batting Leaders—Career

Games

1	Ed Kranepool	1,853
2	Bud Harrelson	1,322
3	Jerry Grote	1,235
4	Cleon Jones	1,201
5	Howard Johnson	1,154
6	Mookie Wilson	1,116
7	Darryl Strawberry	1,109
8	Lee Mazzilli	979
9	Rusty Staub	942
10	Wayne Garrett	883
11	Keith Hernandez	880
12	John Stearns	809
13	Kevin McReynolds	787
14	Todd Hundley	776
15	Wally Backman	765
16	John Milner	741
17	Ron Swoboda	737
18	Dave Magadan	701
19	Ken Boswell	681
	Felix Millan	681

At-Bats

1	Ed Kranepool	5,436
2	Bud Harrelson	4,390
3	Cleon Jones	4,223
4	Mookie Wilson	4,027
5	Howard Johnson	3,968
6	Darryl Strawberry	3,903
7	Jerry Grote	3,881
8	Keith Hernandez	3,164
9	Lee Mazzilli	3,013
10	Kevin McReynolds	2,910
11	Wayne Garrett	2,817
12	John Stearns	2,679
13	Felix Millan	2,677
14	Rusty Staub	2,571
15	Todd Hundley	2,425
16	Tommie Agee	2,416
17	Hubie Brooks	2,400
18	John Milner	2,389
	George Foster	2,389
20	Wally Backman	2,369

Runs

1	Darryl Strawberry	662
2	Howard Johnson	627
3	Mookie Wilson	592
4	Cleon Jones	563
5	Ed Kranepool	536
6	Bud Harrelson	490
7	Keith Hernandez	455
8	Kevin McReynolds	405
9	Lee Mazzilli	404
10	Wayne Garrett	389
11	Wally Backman	359
12	Tommie Agee	344
13	John Stearns	334
14	Todd Hundley	332
15	John Milner	315
16	Jerry Grote	314
17	Felix Millan	308
18	Dave Kingman	302
19	Rusty Staub	296
20	George Foster	290

Hits

1	Ed Kranepool	1,418
2	Cleon Jones	1,188
3	Mookie Wilson	1,112
4	Bud Harrelson	1,029
5	Darryl Strawberry	1,025
6	Howard Johnson	997
7	Jerry Grote	994
8	Keith Hernandez	939
9	Lee Mazzilli	796
10	Kevin McReynolds	791
11	Felix Millan	743
12	Rusty Staub	709
13	John Stearns	695
14	Wally Backman	670
15	Wayne Garrett	667
16	Hubie Brooks	640
17	Tommie Agee	632
18	Dave Magadan	610
19	George Foster	602
20	Todd Hundley	592

Doubles

1	Ed Kranepool	225
2	Howard Johnson	214
3	Darryl Strawberry	187
4	Cleon Jones	182
5	Mookie Wilson	170
6	Keith Hernandez	159
7	Kevin McReynolds	153
8	John Stearns	152
9	Lee Mazzilli	148
10	Jerry Grote	143
11	Rusty Staub	130
12	Bud Harrelson	123
13	Todd Hundley	114
14	Felix Millan	111
15	Dave Magadan	110
16	Joel Youngblood	108
17	Tommie Agee	107
18	Lenny Dykstra	104
19	John Milner	100
20	Jeff Kent	98

Triples

1	Mookie Wilson	62
2	Bud Harrelson	45
3	Cleon Jones	33
4	Steve Henderson	31
5	Darryl Strawberry	30
6	Lance Johnson	27
7	Doug Flynn	26
8	Ed Kranepool	25
9	Lee Mazzilli	22
10	Ron Swoboda	20
	Wayne Garrett	20
12	Jerry Grote	18
	Joel Youngblood	18
	Howard Johnson	18
15	Lenny Dykstra	17
16	Ken Boswell	15
	Lenny Randle	15
18	Sixteen tied at	14

Home Runs

1	Darryl Strawberry	252
2	Howard Johnson	192
3	Dave Kingman	154
4	Kevin McReynolds	122
5	Todd Hundley	121
6	Ed Kranepool	118
7	George Foster	99
8	John Milner	94
9	Cleon Jones	93
10	Bobby Bonilla	91
11	Gary Carter	89
12	Tommie Agee	82
13	Keith Hernandez	80
14	Rusty Staub	75
15	Ron Swoboda	69
16	Lee Mazzilli	68
17	Jeff Kent	67
18	Jim Hickman	60
	Mookie Wilson	60
20	Wayne Garrett	55

RBI

1	Darryl Strawberry	733
2	Howard Johnson	629
3	Ed Kranepool	614
4	Cleon Jones	521
5	Keith Hernandez	468
6	Kevin McReynolds	456
7	Rusty Staub	399
8	Dave Kingman	389
9	Todd Hundley	385
10	George Foster	361
11	Jerry Grote	357
12	Lee Mazzilli	353
13	Gary Carter	349
14	Mookie Wilson	342
15	John Milner	338
16	John Stearns	312
17	Ron Swoboda	304
18	Wayne Garrett	295
19	Bobby Bonilla	277
20	Hubie Brooks	269

Walks

1	Darryl Strawberry	580
2	Bud Harrelson	573
3	Howard Johnson	556
4	Wayne Garrett	482
5	Keith Hernandez	471
6	Ed Kranepool	454
7	Lee Mazzilli	438
8	Jerry Grote	363
9	Cleon Jones	355
10	Dave Magadan	347
11	John Milner	338
12	Rusty Staub	333
13	John Stearns	323
14	Todd Hundley	283
15	Kevin McReynolds	263
16	Wally Backman	260
17	Ron Swoboda	240
	Mookie Wilson	240
19	Tommie Agee	232
20	Four tied at	224

Strikeouts

1	Darryl Strawberry	960
2	Howard Johnson	827
3	Cleon Jones	697
4	Mookie Wilson	692
5	Dave Kingman	672
6	Bud Harrelson	595
7	Ed Kranepool	581
8	Tommie Agee	572
9	Todd Hundley	569
10	Ron Swoboda	549
11	Jerry Grote	509
12	George Foster	496
13	Wayne Garrett	465
14	Keith Hernandez	459
15	Lee Mazzilli	443
16	Jim Hickman	416
17	Hubie Brooks	387
18	Jerry Koosman	386
19	John Milner	368
20	Tom Seaver	355

Stolen Bases

1	Mookie Wilson	281
2	Howard Johnson	202
3	Darryl Strawberry	191
4	Lee Mazzilli	152
5	Lenny Dykstra	116
6	Bud Harrelson	115
7	Wally Backman	106
8	Vince Coleman	99
9	Tommie Agee	92
10	Cleon Jones	91
	John Stearns	91
12	Frank Taveras	90
13	Kevin McReynolds	67
14	Lance Johnson	65
15	Gregg Jefferies	63
16	Steve Henderson	55
17	Lenny Randle	47
18	Daryl Boston	45
19	Keith Miller	44
20	Bob Bailor	40

Runs Created

1	Darryl Strawberry	735
2	Howard Johnson	661
3	Ed Kranepool	641
4	Cleon Jones	583
5	Keith Hernandez	534
6	Mookie Wilson	520
7	Kevin McReynolds	463
8	Bud Harrelson	462
9	Lee Mazzilli	452
10	Jerry Grote	399
11	Rusty Staub	391
12	Wayne Garrett	376
13	Dave Magadan	356
	Todd Hundley	356
15	John Stearns	345
16	John Milner	342
17	Tommie Agee	331
18	Wally Backman	300
	George Foster	300
20	Four tied at	298

Runs Created/27 Outs

(minimum 2000 Plate Appearances)

1	Darryl Strawberry	6.56
2	Dave Magadan	6.18
3	Keith Hernandez	6.17
4	Howard Johnson	5.72
5	Kevin McReynolds	5.66
6	Rusty Staub	5.35
7	Lee Mazzilli	5.19
8	Steve Henderson	5.19
9	Todd Hundley	5.00
10	John Milner	4.88
11	Cleon Jones	4.86
12	Tommie Agee	4.70
13	Mookie Wilson	4.59
14	Joel Youngblood	4.53
15	Wayne Garrett	4.50
16	Wally Backman	4.39
17	Gary Carter	4.37
18	George Foster	4.34
19	John Stearns	4.31
20	Ron Swoboda	4.27

Batting Average

(minimum 2000 Plate Appearances)

1	Keith Hernandez	.297
2	Dave Magadan	.292
3	Steve Henderson	.287
4	Wally Backman	.283
5	Cleon Jones	.281
6	Felix Millan	.278
7	Mookie Wilson	.276
8	Rusty Staub	.276
9	Joel Youngblood	.274
10	Kevin McReynolds	.272
11	Hubie Brooks	.267
12	Lee Mazzilli	.264
13	Darryl Strawberry	.263
14	Tommie Agee	.262
15	Ed Kranepool	.261
16	John Stearns	.259
17	Jerry Grote	.256
18	George Foster	.252
19	Howard Johnson	.251
20	Ken Boswell	.250

On-Base Percentage

(minimum 2000 Plate Appearances)

1	Dave Magadan	.391
2	Keith Hernandez	.387
3	Steve Henderson	.360
4	Darryl Strawberry	.359
5	Rusty Staub	.358
6	Lee Mazzilli	.357
7	Wally Backman	.353
8	Wayne Garrett	.348
9	Howard Johnson	.341
10	John Stearns	.341
11	Cleon Jones	.340
12	John Milner	.339
13	Joel Youngblood	.333
14	Kevin McReynolds	.331
15	Tommie Agee	.329
16	Todd Hundley	.326
17	Felix Millan	.326
18	Bud Harrelson	.324
19	Jerry Grote	.321
20	Ron Swoboda	.319

Slugging Percentage

(minimum 2000 Plate Appearances)

1	Darryl Strawberry	.520
2	Kevin McReynolds	.460
3	Howard Johnson	.459
4	Dave Kingman	.453
5	Todd Hundley	.447
6	Keith Hernandez	.429
7	Steve Henderson	.423
8	George Foster	.422
9	Rusty Staub	.419
10	Tommie Agee	.419
11	John Milner	.415
12	Gary Carter	.412
13	Joel Youngblood	.410
14	Cleon Jones	.406
15	Lee Mazzilli	.396
16	Mookie Wilson	.394
17	Jim Hickman	.392
18	Ron Swoboda	.387
19	Dave Magadan	.386
20	Ed Kranepool	.377

Teams: Mets

Mets Franchise Pitching Leaders—Career

Wins

#	Player	Wins
1	Tom Seaver	198
2	Dwight Gooden	157
3	Jerry Koosman	140
4	Ron Darling	99
5	Sid Fernandez	98
6	Jon Matlack	82
7	David Cone	80
8	Craig Swan	59
9	Bobby Ojeda	51
	Bobby Jones	51
11	Tug McGraw	47
	Jesse Orosco	47
13	Al Jackson	43
14	Gary Gentry	41
	Pat Zachry	41
16	Jack Fisher	38
	Ed Lynch	38
	Frank Viola	38
19	Rick Aguilera	37
20	Jim McAndrew	36

Losses

#	Player	Losses
1	Jerry Koosman	137
2	Tom Seaver	124
3	Dwight Gooden	85
4	Jon Matlack	81
5	Al Jackson	80
6	Sid Fernandez	78
7	Jack Fisher	73
8	Craig Swan	71
9	Ron Darling	70
10	Tug McGraw	55
11	Jim McAndrew	49
12	David Cone	48
13	Jesse Orosco	47
14	Roger Craig	46
	Pat Zachry	46
16	Galen Cisco	43
17	Gary Gentry	42
18	Neil Allen	40
	Ed Lynch	40
	Bobby Ojeda	40

Winning Percentage
(minimum 75 decisions)

#	Player	Pct.
1	Dwight Gooden	.649
2	David Cone	.625
3	Tom Seaver	.615
4	Ron Darling	.586
5	Bobby Jones	.573
6	Bobby Ojeda	.560
7	Sid Fernandez	.557
8	Jerry Koosman	.505
9	Jon Matlack	.503
10	Jesse Orosco	.500
11	Gary Gentry	.494
12	Ed Lynch	.487
13	Pat Zachry	.471
14	Tug McGraw	.461
15	Craig Swan	.454
16	Jim McAndrew	.424
17	Al Jackson	.350
18	Jack Fisher	.342

Games

#	Player	Games
1	Tom Seaver	401
2	John Franco	378
3	Jerry Koosman	376
4	Jesse Orosco	372
5	Tug McGraw	361
6	Dwight Gooden	305
7	Jeff Innis	288
8	Roger McDowell	280
9	Ron Taylor	269
10	Doug Sisk	263
11	Ron Darling	257
12	Sid Fernandez	255
13	Craig Swan	229
14	Skip Lockwood	227
15	Neil Allen	223
16	Jon Matlack	203
17	Randy Myers	185
18	Al Jackson	184
	Bob Apodaca	184
20	David Cone	182

Games Started

#	Player	GS
1	Tom Seaver	395
2	Jerry Koosman	346
3	Dwight Gooden	303
4	Sid Fernandez	250
5	Ron Darling	241
6	Jon Matlack	199
7	Craig Swan	184
8	David Cone	165
9	Al Jackson	138
10	Jack Fisher	133
11	Bobby Jones	124
12	Gary Gentry	121
13	Pat Zachry	113
14	Bobby Ojeda	109
15	Jim McAndrew	105
16	Ed Lynch	98
17	Pete Falcone	86
18	Frank Viola	82
19	Nolan Ryan	74
	Bret Saberhagen	74

Complete Games

#	Player	CG
1	Tom Seaver	171
2	Jerry Koosman	108
3	Dwight Gooden	67
4	Jon Matlack	65
5	Al Jackson	41
6	Jack Fisher	35
7	David Cone	34
8	Roger Craig	27
9	Craig Swan	25
	Ron Darling	25
11	Sid Fernandez	23
12	Gary Gentry	22
13	Pat Zachry	20
14	Jim McAndrew	19
15	Bobby Ojeda	17
16	Jay Hook	16
	Tracy Stallard	16
18	Nolan Ryan	13
	Ray Sadecki	13
	Nino Espinosa	13

Shutouts

#	Player	SHO
1	Tom Seaver	44
2	Jerry Koosman	26
	Jon Matlack	26
4	Dwight Gooden	23
5	David Cone	15
6	Al Jackson	10
	Ron Darling	10
8	Sid Fernandez	9
	Bobby Ojeda	9
10	Gary Gentry	8
11	Craig Swan	7
12	Jim McAndrew	6
	Pat Zachry	6
14	Carl Willey	4
	Jack Fisher	4
	Dick Selma	4
	Don Cardwell	4
	Frank Viola	4
	Bobby Jones	4
20	Ten tied at	3

Saves

#	Player	Saves
1	John Franco	211
2	Jesse Orosco	107
3	Tug McGraw	86
4	Roger McDowell	84
5	Neil Allen	69
6	Skip Lockwood	65
7	Randy Myers	56
8	Ron Taylor	49
9	Doug Sisk	33
10	Bob Apodaca	26
11	Danny Frisella	24
12	Cal Koonce	18
	Anthony Young	18
14	Jack Hamilton	14
15	Doug Henry	13
16	Harry Parker	11
17	Jeff Reardon	10
18	Dale Murray	9
	Alejandro Pena	9
20	Four tied at	8

Innings Pitched

#	Player	IP
1	Tom Seaver	3,045.1
2	Jerry Koosman	2,544.2
3	Dwight Gooden	2,169.2
4	Ron Darling	1,620.0
5	Sid Fernandez	1,584.2
6	Jon Matlack	1,448.0
7	Craig Swan	1,230.2
8	David Cone	1,191.1
9	Al Jackson	980.2
10	Jack Fisher	931.2
11	Bobby Jones	806.1
12	Tug McGraw	792.2
13	Gary Gentry	789.2
14	Bobby Ojeda	764.0
15	Pat Zachry	741.2
16	Ed Lynch	730.1
17	Jim McAndrew	729.2
18	Pete Falcone	607.2
19	Ray Sadecki	600.1
20	Jesse Orosco	595.2

Walks

#	Player	BB
1	Tom Seaver	847
2	Jerry Koosman	820
3	Dwight Gooden	651
4	Ron Darling	614
5	Sid Fernandez	596
6	Jon Matlack	419
7	David Cone	418
8	Craig Swan	368
9	Tug McGraw	350
10	Nolan Ryan	344
11	Gary Gentry	324
12	Al Jackson	304
13	Pat Zachry	300
14	Jack Fisher	242
15	Pete Falcone	241
16	Jesse Orosco	240
	Bobby Jones	240
18	Bobby Ojeda	213
19	Doug Sisk	210
20	Ray Sadecki	206

Strikeouts

#	Player	SO
1	Tom Seaver	2,541
2	Dwight Gooden	1,875
3	Jerry Koosman	1,799
4	Sid Fernandez	1,449
5	David Cone	1,159
6	Ron Darling	1,148
7	Jon Matlack	1,023
8	Craig Swan	671
9	Tug McGraw	618
10	Gary Gentry	563
11	Al Jackson	561
12	Jesse Orosco	506
13	Nolan Ryan	493
14	Bobby Jones	483
15	Jack Fisher	475
16	Bobby Ojeda	459
17	Jim McAndrew	408
18	Pat Zachry	391
19	Bret Saberhagen	388
20	Frank Viola	387

Strikeouts/9 Innings
(minimum 750 Innings Pitched)

#	Player	K/9
1	David Cone	8.76
2	Sid Fernandez	8.23
3	Dwight Gooden	7.78
4	Tom Seaver	7.51
5	Tug McGraw	7.02
6	Gary Gentry	6.42
7	Ron Darling	6.38
8	Jerry Koosman	6.36
9	Jon Matlack	6.36
10	Bobby Ojeda	5.41
11	Bobby Jones	5.39
12	Al Jackson	5.15
13	Craig Swan	4.91
14	Jack Fisher	4.59

ERA
(minimum 750 Innings Pitched)

#	Player	ERA
1	Tom Seaver	2.57
2	Jon Matlack	3.03
3	David Cone	3.08
4	Jerry Koosman	3.09
5	Dwight Gooden	3.10
6	Bobby Ojeda	3.12
7	Sid Fernandez	3.14
8	Tug McGraw	3.17
9	Ron Darling	3.50
10	Gary Gentry	3.56
11	Craig Swan	3.72
12	Bobby Jones	3.86
13	Jack Fisher	4.12
14	Al Jackson	4.26

Component ERA
(minimum 750 Innings Pitched)

#	Player	CERA
1	Tom Seaver	2.42
2	Sid Fernandez	2.57
3	Dwight Gooden	2.81
4	David Cone	2.87
5	Jon Matlack	2.91
6	Bobby Ojeda	2.92
7	Jerry Koosman	3.08
8	Tug McGraw	3.31
9	Gary Gentry	3.35
10	Craig Swan	3.45
11	Ron Darling	3.56
12	Bobby Jones	3.88
13	Jack Fisher	3.94
14	Al Jackson	3.99

Opponent Average
(minimum 750 Innings Pitched)

#	Player	Avg.
1	Sid Fernandez	.204
2	Tom Seaver	.219
3	David Cone	.225
4	Gary Gentry	.229
5	Dwight Gooden	.235
6	Tug McGraw	.237
7	Bobby Ojeda	.241
8	Jerry Koosman	.242
9	Jon Matlack	.242
10	Ron Darling	.244
11	Craig Swan	.255
12	Bobby Jones	.266
13	Al Jackson	.270
14	Jack Fisher	.272

Opponent OBP
(minimum 750 Innings Pitched)

#	Player	OBP
1	Tom Seaver	.276
2	Sid Fernandez	.281
3	Bobby Ojeda	.293
4	Dwight Gooden	.294
5	David Cone	.295
6	Jon Matlack	.296
7	Jerry Koosman	.303
8	Craig Swan	.309
9	Gary Gentry	.309
10	Ron Darling	.315
11	Tug McGraw	.320
12	Bobby Jones	.320
13	Jack Fisher	.321
14	Al Jackson	.327

Teams: Mets

Mets Franchise Batting Leaders—Single Season

Games

1	Felix Millan	1975	162
2	Lance Johnson	1996	160
3	Lee Mazzilli	1977	159
	Willie Montanez	1978	159
	Mookie Wilson	1982	159
6	Lee Mazzilli	1979	158
	Joel Youngblood	1979	158
	Keith Hernandez	1985	158
9	Roy McMillan	1965	157
	Bud Harrelson	1970	157
	Steve Henderson	1978	157
	Doug Flynn	1979	157
	George Foster	1983	157
	Howard Johnson	1987	157
15	Frank Thomas	1962	156
	Doug Flynn	1978	156
	Howard Johnson	1991	156
	Eddie Murray	1992	156
19	Rusty Staub	1975	155
	John Stearns	1979	155

At-Bats

1	Lance Johnson	1996	682
2	Felix Millan	1975	676
3	Mookie Wilson	1982	639
4	Felix Millan	1973	638
	Mookie Wilson	1983	638
6	Tommie Agee	1970	636
7	Frank Taveras	1979	635
8	Eddie Murray	1993	610
9	Willie Montanez	1978	609
10	Gregg Jefferies	1990	604
11	George Foster	1983	601
12	Lee Mazzilli	1979	597
13	Keith Hernandez	1985	593
14	Joel Youngblood	1979	590
	Kevin McReynolds	1987	590
	Howard Johnson	1990	590
17	Steve Henderson	1978	587
	Mookie Wilson	1984	587
	Keith Hernandez	1987	587
20	Hubie Brooks	1983	586

Runs

1	Lance Johnson	1996	117
2	Darryl Strawberry	1987	108
	Howard Johnson	1991	108
	Bernard Gilkey	1996	108
5	Tommie Agee	1970	107
6	Howard Johnson	1989	104
7	Darryl Strawberry	1988	101
8	Tommie Agee	1969	97
9	Gregg Jefferies	1990	96
10	Keith Hernandez	1986	94
11	Rusty Staub	1975	93
	Howard Johnson	1987	93
13	Cleon Jones	1969	92
	Darryl Strawberry	1990	92
15	Mookie Wilson	1983	91
16	Joel Youngblood	1979	90
	Mookie Wilson	1982	90
	John Olerud	1997	90
19	Frank Taveras	1979	89
	Howard Johnson	1990	89

Hits

1	Lance Johnson	1996	227
2	Felix Millan	1975	191
3	Felix Millan	1973	185
4	Keith Hernandez	1985	183
5	Tommie Agee	1970	182
6	Lee Mazzilli	1979	181
	Bernard Gilkey	1996	181
8	Mookie Wilson	1982	178
9	Mookie Wilson	1983	176
10	Tommy Davis	1967	174
	Eddie Murray	1993	174
12	Keith Hernandez	1984	171
	Keith Hernandez	1986	171
	Gregg Jefferies	1990	171
15	Keith Hernandez	1987	170
16	Frank Taveras	1979	167
17	Cleon Jones	1969	164
	Howard Johnson	1989	164
19	Four tied at		163

Doubles

1	Bernard Gilkey	1996	44
2	Howard Johnson	1989	41
3	Gregg Jefferies	1990	40
4	Felix Millan	1975	37
	Joel Youngblood	1979	37
	Lenny Dykstra	1987	37
	Howard Johnson	1990	37
	Eddie Murray	1992	37
9	Rusty Staub	1973	36
10	Lee Mazzilli	1979	34
	Keith Hernandez	1985	34
	Keith Hernandez	1986	34
	Howard Johnson	1991	34
	John Olerud	1997	34
15	Tommy Davis	1967	32
	Willie Montanez	1978	32
	Darryl Strawberry	1987	32
	Kevin McReynolds	1987	32
	Kevin McReynolds	1991	32
	Todd Hundley	1996	32

Triples

1	Lance Johnson	1996	21
2	Mookie Wilson	1984	10
3	Charlie Neal	1962	9
	Steve Henderson	1978	9
	Frank Taveras	1979	9
	Mookie Wilson	1982	9
7	Joe Christopher	1964	8
	Bud Harrelson	1970	8
	Cleon Jones	1970	8
	Doug Flynn	1978	8
	Lenny Randle	1978	8
	Joel Youngblood	1978	8
	Steve Henderson	1979	8
	Doug Flynn	1980	8
	Steve Henderson	1980	8
	Mookie Wilson	1981	8
	Mookie Wilson	1985	8
	Vince Coleman	1993	8
19	Nine tied at		7

Home Runs

1	Todd Hundley	1996	41
2	Darryl Strawberry	1987	39
	Darryl Strawberry	1988	39
4	Howard Johnson	1991	38
5	Dave Kingman	1976	37
	Dave Kingman	1982	37
	Darryl Strawberry	1990	37
8	Dave Kingman	1975	36
	Howard Johnson	1987	36
	Howard Johnson	1989	36
11	Frank Thomas	1962	34
	Bobby Bonilla	1993	34
13	Gary Carter	1985	32
14	Bernard Gilkey	1996	30
	Todd Hundley	1997	30
16	Darryl Strawberry	1985	29
	Kevin McReynolds	1987	29
	Darryl Strawberry	1989	29
19	George Foster	1983	28
20	Three tied at		27

RBI

1	Howard Johnson	1991	117
	Bernard Gilkey	1996	117
3	Todd Hundley	1996	112
4	Darryl Strawberry	1990	108
5	Rusty Staub	1975	105
	Gary Carter	1986	105
7	Darryl Strawberry	1987	104
8	John Olerud	1997	102
9	Darryl Strawberry	1988	101
	Howard Johnson	1989	101
11	Gary Carter	1985	100
	Eddie Murray	1993	100
13	Dave Kingman	1982	99
	Howard Johnson	1987	99
	Kevin McReynolds	1988	99
16	Donn Clendenon	1970	97
	Darryl Strawberry	1984	97
18	Willie Montanez	1978	96
19	Kevin McReynolds	1987	95
20	Two tied at		94

Walks

1	Keith Hernandez	1984	97
	Darryl Strawberry	1987	97
3	Bud Harrelson	1970	95
4	Keith Hernandez	1986	94
5	Lee Mazzilli	1979	93
6	Wayne Garrett	1974	89
7	Howard Johnson	1988	86
8	Darryl Strawberry	1988	85
	John Olerud	1997	85
10	Howard Johnson	1987	83
	Dave Magadan	1991	83
	Todd Hundley	1997	83
13	Lee Mazzilli	1980	82
14	Richie Ashburn	1962	81
	Wayne Garrett	1970	81
	Keith Hernandez	1987	81
17	Todd Hundley	1996	79
18	Howard Johnson	1991	78
19	Five tied at		77

Strikeouts

1	Tommie Agee	1970	156
	Dave Kingman	1982	156
3	Dave Kingman	1975	153
4	Todd Hundley	1996	146
5	Darryl Strawberry	1986	141
6	Tommie Agee	1969	137
7	Dave Kingman	1976	135
8	Darryl Strawberry	1984	131
9	Darryl Strawberry	1983	128
10	Darryl Strawberry	1988	127
11	Howard Johnson	1989	126
12	Bernard Gilkey	1996	125
13	Charley Smith	1965	123
	George Foster	1982	123
15	George Foster	1984	122
	Darryl Strawberry	1987	122
17	Jim Hickman	1963	120
	Howard Johnson	1991	120
19	Johnny Lewis	1965	117
20	Todd Hundley	1997	116

Stolen Bases

1	Mookie Wilson	1982	58
2	Mookie Wilson	1983	54
3	Lance Johnson	1996	50
4	Mookie Wilson	1984	46
5	Frank Taveras	1979	42
6	Lee Mazzilli	1980	41
	Howard Johnson	1989	41
8	Vince Coleman	1993	38
9	Vince Coleman	1991	37
10	Darryl Strawberry	1987	36
11	Lee Mazzilli	1979	34
	Howard Johnson	1990	34
13	Lenny Randle	1977	33
14	Frank Taveras	1980	32
	Wally Backman	1984	32
	Howard Johnson	1987	32
17	Tommie Agee	1970	31
	Lenny Dykstra	1986	31
	Juan Samuel	1989	31
20	Three tied at		30

Runs Created

1	Bernard Gilkey	1996	132
2	Howard Johnson	1989	129
3	Lance Johnson	1996	122
4	Darryl Strawberry	1987	121
5	John Olerud	1997	114
6	Lee Mazzilli	1979	107
	Darryl Strawberry	1990	107
8	Keith Hernandez	1984	105
9	Keith Hernandez	1986	104
	Howard Johnson	1991	104
	Edgardo Alfonzo	1997	104
12	Todd Hundley	1996	103
13	Darryl Strawberry	1988	102
14	Cleon Jones	1969	101
	Tommie Agee	1970	101
	Howard Johnson	1987	101
17	Kevin McReynolds	1988	100
18	Lee Mazzilli	1980	98
	Keith Hernandez	1985	98
20	Two tied at		97

Runs Created/27 Outs

(minimum 3.1 Plate Appearances/Tm Gm)

1	Bernard Gilkey	1996	8.40
2	Howard Johnson	1989	8.26
3	Darryl Strawberry	1987	8.15
4	Cleon Jones	1969	7.98
5	Dave Magadan	1990	7.87
6	John Olerud	1997	7.73
7	Edgardo Alfonzo	1997	7.41
8	Todd Hundley	1997	7.21
9	Keith Hernandez	1984	7.12
10	Keith Hernandez	1986	7.10
11	Darryl Strawberry	1990	7.04
12	Bobby Bonilla	1994	6.90
13	Lance Johnson	1996	6.83
14	Kevin McReynolds	1988	6.73
15	Todd Hundley	1996	6.73
16	Lee Mazzilli	1979	6.62
17	Jeff Kent	1994	6.55
18	Darryl Strawberry	1988	6.53
19	Darryl Strawberry	1986	6.49
20	Cleon Jones	1971	6.38

Batting Average

(minimum 3.1 Plate Appearances/Tm Gm)

1	Cleon Jones	1969	.340
2	Lance Johnson	1996	.333
3	Dave Magadan	1990	.328
4	Cleon Jones	1971	.319
5	Bernard Gilkey	1996	.317
6	Edgardo Alfonzo	1997	.315
7	Keith Hernandez	1984	.311
8	Keith Hernandez	1986	.310
9	Keith Hernandez	1985	.309
10	Hubie Brooks	1981	.307
11	Lenny Randle	1977	.304
12	Lee Mazzilli	1979	.303
13	Ron Hunt	1964	.303
14	Tommy Davis	1967	.302
15	Joe Christopher	1964	.300
16	Ray Knight	1986	.298
17	Cleon Jones	1968	.297
18	John Olerud	1997	.294
19	Del Unser	1975	.294
20	Jeff Kent	1994	.292

On-Base Percentage

(minimum 3.1 Plate Appearances/Tm Gm)

1	Cleon Jones	1969	.422
2	Dave Magadan	1990	.417
3	Keith Hernandez	1986	.413
4	Keith Hernandez	1984	.409
5	John Olerud	1997	.400
6	Darryl Strawberry	1987	.398
7	Lee Mazzilli	1979	.395
8	Todd Hundley	1997	.394
9	Bernard Gilkey	1996	.393
10	Edgardo Alfonzo	1997	.391
11	Keith Hernandez	1985	.384
12	Lenny Randle	1977	.383
13	Cleon Jones	1971	.382
14	Dave Magadan	1991	.378
15	Keith Hernandez	1987	.377
16	Bobby Bonilla	1994	.374
17	Rusty Staub	1975	.371
18	John Stearns	1977	.370
19	Lee Mazzilli	1980	.370
20	Howard Johnson	1989	.369

Slugging Percentage

(minimum 3.1 Plate Appearances/Tm Gm)

1	Darryl Strawberry	1987	.583
2	Bernard Gilkey	1996	.562
3	Howard Johnson	1989	.559
4	Todd Hundley	1996	.550
5	Todd Hundley	1997	.549
6	Darryl Strawberry	1988	.545
7	Howard Johnson	1991	.535
8	Bobby Bonilla	1993	.522
9	Darryl Strawberry	1990	.518
10	Darryl Strawberry	1986	.507
11	Dave Kingman	1976	.506
12	Bobby Bonilla	1994	.504
13	Howard Johnson	1987	.504
14	Butch Huskey	1997	.503
15	Kevin McReynolds	1988	.496
16	Frank Thomas	1962	.496
17	Kevin McReynolds	1987	.495
18	Dave Kingman	1975	.494
19	John Olerud	1997	.489
20	Gary Carter	1985	.488

Mets Franchise Pitching Leaders—Single Season

Wins

1	Tom Seaver	1969	25
2	Dwight Gooden	1985	24
3	Tom Seaver	1975	22
4	Tom Seaver	1972	21
	Jerry Koosman	1976	21
6	Tom Seaver	1971	20
	David Cone	1988	20
	Frank Viola	1990	20
9	Jerry Koosman	1968	19
	Tom Seaver	1973	19
	Dwight Gooden	1990	19
12	Tom Seaver	1970	18
	Bobby Ojeda	1986	18
	Dwight Gooden	1988	18
15	Jerry Koosman	1969	17
	Jon Matlack	1976	17
	Dwight Gooden	1984	17
	Dwight Gooden	1986	17
	Ron Darling	1988	17
20	Five tied at		16

Losses

1	Roger Craig	1962	24
	Jack Fisher	1965	24
3	Roger Craig	1963	22
4	Al Jackson	1962	20
	Tracy Stallard	1964	20
	Al Jackson	1965	20
	Jerry Koosman	1977	20
8	Jay Hook	1962	19
	Galen Cisco	1964	19
10	Jack Fisher	1967	18
11	Craig Anderson	1962	17
	Tracy Stallard	1963	17
	Al Jackson	1963	17
	Jack Fisher	1964	17
	Mike Torrez	1983	17
16	Al Jackson	1964	16
	Jon Matlack	1973	16
	Anthony Young	1993	16
19	Nine tied at		15

Winning Percentage
(minimum 15 decisions)

1	David Cone	1988	.870
2	Dwight Gooden	1985	.857
3	George Stone	1973	.800
4	Bobby Ojeda	1986	.783
5	Tom Seaver	1969	.781
6	Bret Saberhagen	1994	.778
7	Dwight Gooden	1986	.739
8	Sid Fernandez	1989	.737
9	Tug McGraw	1971	.733
10	Dwight Gooden	1990	.731
11	Ron Darling	1985	.727
	Sid Fernandez	1986	.727
13	Ron Darling	1986	.714
14	Tom Seaver	1975	.710
15	Dwight Gooden	1987	.682
16	Jerry Koosman	1976	.677
17	Tom Seaver	1971	.667
	Dwight Gooden	1988	.667
19	Tom Seaver	1973	.655
20	Three tied at		.654

Games

1	Jeff Innis	1992	76
2	Roger McDowell	1986	75
3	Greg McMichael	1997	73
4	Jeff Innis	1991	69
5	Doug Sisk	1983	67
	Jeff Innis	1993	67
7	Randy Myers	1989	65
8	Skip Lockwood	1977	63
9	Bill Wakefield	1964	62
	Jesse Orosco	1983	62
	Roger McDowell	1985	62
	Roger McDowell	1988	62
13	Jeff Reardon	1980	61
14	Tug McGraw	1973	60
	Jesse Orosco	1984	60
16	Ron Taylor	1969	59
	Bob Apodaca	1977	59
	Neil Allen	1980	59
	John Franco	1997	59
20	Nine tied at		58

Games Started

1	Jack Fisher	1965	36
	Tom Seaver	1970	36
	Tom Seaver	1973	36
	Tom Seaver	1975	36
5	Tom Seaver	1968	35
	Tom Seaver	1969	35
	Gary Gentry	1969	35
	Tom Seaver	1971	35
	Tom Seaver	1972	35
	Jerry Koosman	1973	35
	Jerry Koosman	1974	35
	Jon Matlack	1976	35
	Craig Swan	1979	35
	Ron Darling	1985	35
	Dwight Gooden	1985	35
	Frank Viola	1990	35
	Frank Viola	1991	35
18	Seventeen tied at		34

Complete Games

1	Tom Seaver	1971	21
2	Tom Seaver	1970	19
3	Tom Seaver	1967	18
	Tom Seaver	1969	18
	Tom Seaver	1973	18
6	Jerry Koosman	1968	17
	Jerry Koosman	1976	17
8	Jerry Koosman	1969	16
	Jon Matlack	1976	16
	Dwight Gooden	1985	16
11	Tom Seaver	1975	15
12	Roger Craig	1963	14
	Tom Seaver	1968	14
	Jon Matlack	1973	14
	Jon Matlack	1974	14
16	Jay Hook	1962	13
	Roger Craig	1962	13
	Tom Seaver	1972	13
	Jerry Koosman	1974	13
	Tom Seaver	1976	13

Shutouts

1	Dwight Gooden	1985	8
2	Jerry Koosman	1968	7
	Jon Matlack	1974	7
4	Jerry Koosman	1969	6
	Jon Matlack	1976	6
6	Tom Seaver	1968	5
	Tom Seaver	1969	5
	Tom Seaver	1974	5
	Tom Seaver	1975	5
	Tom Seaver	1976	5
	Bobby Ojeda	1988	5
	David Cone	1992	5
13	Al Jackson	1962	4
	Carl Willey	1963	4
	Tom Seaver	1971	4
	Jon Matlack	1972	4
	Jerry Koosman	1975	4
	Ron Darling	1988	4
	David Cone	1988	4
20	Twenty-one tied at		3

Saves

1	John Franco	1997	36
2	John Franco	1990	33
3	Jesse Orosco	1984	31
4	John Franco	1991	30
	John Franco	1994	30
6	John Franco	1995	29
7	John Franco	1996	28
8	Tug McGraw	1972	27
9	Randy Myers	1988	26
10	Tug McGraw	1973	25
	Roger McDowell	1987	25
12	Randy Myers	1989	24
13	Neil Allen	1980	22
	Roger McDowell	1986	22
15	Jesse Orosco	1986	21
16	Skip Lockwood	1977	20
17	Skip Lockwood	1976	19
	Neil Allen	1982	19
19	Neil Allen	1981	18
20	Three tied at		17

Innings Pitched

1	Tom Seaver	1970	290.2
2	Tom Seaver	1973	290.0
3	Tom Seaver	1971	286.1
4	Tom Seaver	1975	280.1
5	Tom Seaver	1968	277.2
6	Dwight Gooden	1985	276.2
7	Tom Seaver	1969	273.1
8	Tom Seaver	1976	271.0
9	Jon Matlack	1974	265.1
10	Jerry Koosman	1974	265.0
11	Jerry Koosman	1968	263.2
12	Jerry Koosman	1973	263.0
13	Tom Seaver	1972	262.0
	Jon Matlack	1976	262.0
15	Jack Fisher	1965	253.2
16	Craig Swan	1979	251.1
17	Tom Seaver	1967	251.0
18	Dwight Gooden	1986	250.0
19	Frank Viola	1990	249.2
20	Dwight Gooden	1988	248.1

Walks

1	Nolan Ryan	1971	116
2	Ron Darling	1985	114
3	Mike Torrez	1983	113
4	Ron Darling	1984	104
5	Jon Matlack	1973	99
6	Jerry Koosman	1975	98
7	Nolan Ryan	1970	97
8	Ron Darling	1987	96
9	Sid Fernandez	1986	91
10	Charlie Puleo	1982	90
11	Jack Hamilton	1966	88
	Tom Seaver	1975	88
13	Gary Gentry	1970	86
	Randy Tate	1975	86
	Tom Seaver	1983	86
16	Jerry Koosman	1974	85
17	Al Jackson	1963	84
	Jerry Koosman	1978	84
19	Tom Seaver	1970	83
20	Three tied at		82

Strikeouts

1	Tom Seaver	1971	289
2	Tom Seaver	1970	283
3	Dwight Gooden	1984	276
4	Dwight Gooden	1985	268
5	Tom Seaver	1973	251
6	Tom Seaver	1972	249
7	Tom Seaver	1975	243
8	David Cone	1991	241
9	Tom Seaver	1976	235
10	David Cone	1990	233
11	Dwight Gooden	1990	223
12	David Cone	1992	214
13	David Cone	1988	213
14	Tom Seaver	1969	208
15	Tom Seaver	1968	205
	Jon Matlack	1973	205
17	Tom Seaver	1974	201
18	Jerry Koosman	1976	200
	Sid Fernandez	1986	200
	Dwight Gooden	1986	200

Strikeouts/9 Innings
(minimum 1 Inning Pitched/Tm Gm)

1	Dwight Gooden	1984	11.39
2	David Cone	1990	9.91
3	David Cone	1992	9.79
4	Sid Fernandez	1985	9.51
5	David Cone	1991	9.32
6	Sid Fernandez	1988	9.10
7	Tom Seaver	1971	9.08
8	Sid Fernandez	1990	9.08
9	Sid Fernandez	1986	8.81
10	Tom Seaver	1970	8.76
11	Dwight Gooden	1985	8.72
12	Dwight Gooden	1990	8.63
13	Tom Seaver	1972	8.55
14	David Cone	1988	8.29
15	Sid Fernandez	1989	8.12
16	Jerry Koosman	1972	8.12
17	Sid Fernandez	1992	8.09
18	Tom Seaver	1976	7.80
19	Tom Seaver	1975	7.80
20	Tom Seaver	1973	7.79

ERA
(minimum 1 Inning Pitched/Tm Gm)

1	Dwight Gooden	1985	1.53
2	Tom Seaver	1971	1.76
3	Tom Seaver	1973	2.08
4	Jerry Koosman	1968	2.08
5	Tom Seaver	1968	2.20
6	Tom Seaver	1969	2.21
7	David Cone	1988	2.22
8	Jerry Koosman	1969	2.28
9	Jon Matlack	1972	2.32
10	Tom Seaver	1975	2.38
11	Jon Matlack	1974	2.41
12	Craig Swan	1978	2.43
13	Bobby Ojeda	1986	2.57
14	Tom Seaver	1976	2.59
15	Dwight Gooden	1984	2.60
16	Frank Viola	1990	2.67
17	Jerry Koosman	1976	2.69
18	Sid Fernandez	1992	2.73
19	Bret Saberhagen	1994	2.74
20	Dick Selma	1968	2.76

Component ERA
(minimum 1 Inning Pitched/Tm Gm)

1	Dwight Gooden	1985	1.83
2	Tom Seaver	1971	1.90
3	Bobby Ojeda	1988	2.02
4	Tom Seaver	1973	2.05
5	Tom Seaver	1968	2.07
6	Dwight Gooden	1984	2.08
7	Tom Seaver	1976	2.23
8	Sid Fernandez	1992	2.24
9	Jerry Koosman	1969	2.24
10	Tom Seaver	1975	2.26
11	Sid Fernandez	1988	2.31
12	Craig Swan	1978	2.31
13	Tom Seaver	1969	2.34
14	David Cone	1988	2.34
15	Jon Matlack	1974	2.35
16	Sid Fernandez	1985	2.36
17	Tom Seaver	1970	2.39
18	Sid Fernandez	1989	2.43
19	Dwight Gooden	1986	2.48
20	Jim McAndrew	1972	2.49

Opponent Average
(minimum 1 Inning Pitched/Tm Gm)

1	Sid Fernandez	1985	.181
2	Sid Fernandez	1988	.191
3	Sid Fernandez	1989	.198
4	Sid Fernandez	1990	.200
5	Dwight Gooden	1985	.201
6	Dwight Gooden	1984	.202
7	Tom Seaver	1971	.206
8	Tom Seaver	1973	.206
9	Tom Seaver	1969	.207
10	Sid Fernandez	1992	.210
11	David Cone	1988	.213
12	Tom Seaver	1976	.213
13	Tom Seaver	1970	.214
14	Tom Seaver	1975	.214
15	Dwight Gooden	1986	.215
16	Sid Fernandez	1986	.216
17	Jerry Koosman	1969	.216
18	Craig Swan	1978	.219
19	Carl Willey	1963	.220
20	Tom Seaver	1968	.222

Opponent OBP
(minimum 1 Inning Pitched/Tm Gm)

1	Tom Seaver	1971	.252
2	Tom Seaver	1973	.252
3	Dwight Gooden	1985	.254
4	Tom Seaver	1968	.261
5	Bobby Ojeda	1988	.261
6	Dwight Gooden	1984	.269
7	Bret Saberhagen	1994	.271
8	Sid Fernandez	1989	.271
9	Sid Fernandez	1988	.271
10	Rick Reed	1997	.272
11	Tom Seaver	1969	.272
12	Tom Seaver	1970	.272
13	Tom Seaver	1976	.272
14	Sid Fernandez	1992	.273
15	Craig Swan	1978	.275
16	Jerry Koosman	1969	.275
17	Jim McAndrew	1972	.276
18	Sid Fernandez	1990	.277
19	Bobby Ojeda	1986	.278
20	Jerry Koosman	1976	.278

Mets Capsule

Best Season: *1969.* In the magical summer of '69, the Mets ended seven seasons of losing baseball by winning 38 of their last 49 games to overtake the Cubs for the National League East title. After sweeping the Braves in the first-ever NLCS, they toppled the heavily favored Baltimore Orioles for their first-ever World Series victory. The 1986 season was thrilling as well, as New York won 108 regular-season games and staged dramatic comebacks to win both the NLCS and the World Series.

Worst Season: *1992.* After finishing either first or second in each of the previous seven seasons, the Mets tumbled all the way to fifth place—this despite having signed several expensive free agents in the offseason. The newcomers proved to be losers both on and off the field, and their exploits were detailed in the book *The Worst Team Money Could Buy,* an insider's account of the Mets' season that deeply embarrassed the organization.

Best Player: *Darryl Strawberry.*

Best Pitcher: *Tom Seaver.*

Best Reliever: *John Franco.*

Best Defensive Player: *Keith Hernandez* won six straight Gold Gloves and was regarded as the premier defensive first baseman of his generation. Second baseman Doug Flynn carried Grade-A leather, and shortstop Rey Ordonez is one of the most exciting and creative defenders in the game today.

Hall of Famer: *Tom Seaver.*

Franchise All-Star Team:

C	Todd Hundley	LF	Rusty Staub
1B	Keith Hernandez	CF	Lee Mazzilli
2B	Felix Millan	RF	Darryl Strawberry
3B	Howard Johnson	SP	Tom Seaver
SS	Bud Harrelson	RP	John Franco

Biggest Flake: Glove-slapping reliever *Tug McGraw* was a constant source of inspiration and colorful quotes.

Strangest Career: Outfielder *Joe Christopher* carried a .244 lifetime batting average in 141 games when the Mets claimed him off the Pirates' roster in the expansion draft. He exactly matched that average while playing 119 games in his first season in New York. He got only 149 at-bats as he slumped to .221 in 1963, but he suddenly put it all together in '64, batting .300 with 16 homers and 76 RBI. He lost it just as quickly as he'd found it, however, falling off to .249 with five home runs in 1965 before disappearing from the majors the following year.

What Might Have Been: The Mets selected pitcher *Tim Leary* with the second overall pick in the 1979 draft. The following year, he led the Texas League with 15 victories and was named the league's MVP. He enjoyed such a terrific spring training in 1981 that the Mets took him north, but he injured his elbow in his very first major league start. He missed most of '81 and all of '82, and was traded away in 1985 after failing to establish himself in the majors. He went on to log a 13-year major league career, but posted a winning record only twice.

Best Trade: *David Cone* was stolen from the Royals for sore-armed-catcher-turned-motivational-speaker Ed Hearn in 1987. The Keith Hernandez trade turned out very well, too. His drug problem prompted the Cardinals to trade him to the Mets midway through the 1983 season for pitchers Neil Allen and Rick Ownbey. Depending on how you look at it, the Ron Darling trade might have been the best of all. He came over from the Rangers in exchange for the washed-up Lee Mazzilli in 1982. The Mets also acquired pitcher Walt Terrell in the deal; three years later they dealt Terrell for third baseman Howard Johnson. Darling and Johnson both became mainstays of the strong Mets teams of the late '80s.

Worst Trade: The Mets came out on the short end of one of the most lopsided trades of all time when they sent *Nolan Ryan* to the Angels for Jim Fregosi and three other players in 1972. They also got burned when they shipped Amos Otis to the Royals in 1969 and Jeff Reardon to the Expos in 1981. The 1989 deal that sent center fielder Lenny Dykstra and reliever Roger McDowell to the Phillies for Juan Samuel turned into an unmitigated disaster. Samuel proved to be a completely inept center fielder, while Dykstra became a star and McDowell remained effective for many years thereafter.

Best-Looking Player: *Tom Seaver.*

Ugliest Player: *Jesse Orosco.*

Best Nickname: *"Marvelous Marv"* *Throneberry.*

Most Unappreciated Player: *Jerry Koosman* was a quality southpaw and a consistent winner, but toiled in Tom Seaver's shadow for most of his career with the Mets.

Most Overrated Player: *Ed Kranepool* must have been the most mediocre player who ever lasted 18 years in the majors. For a first baseman, 16 homers and 58 RBI are unremarkable single-season totals; Kranepool never exceeded either figure.

Most Admirable Star: *Tom Seaver.*

Least Admirable Star: *Vince Coleman.* He openly disrespected manager Jeff Torborg and coach Mike Cubbage in separate incidents, and later tossed a firecracker that injured a child.

Best Season, Player: *Todd Hundley, 1996.* He set the major league single-season record for catchers with 41 homers. Outfielder Bernard Gilkey batted .317 with 44 doubles, 30 homers and 117 RBI the same year. Darryl Strawberry's best year was 1988, when he topped the NL with 39 homers.

Best Season, Pitcher: *Dwight Gooden, 1985.* He led the majors—by a comfortable margin—in wins (24), strikeouts (268) and ERA (1.53).

Most Impressive Individual Record: As a 19-year-old rookie, *Dwight Gooden* set a rookie record with 276 strikeouts in 1984.

Biggest Tragedy: Manager *Gil Hodges* died of a heart attack on April 2, 1972.

Fan Favorite: *Tom Seaver.*

—Mat Olkin

Philadelphia Phillies (1883-1997)

														Opponent				Park Index	
Year	Lg	Pos	W-L	Pct	GB	Manager	Att.	R	OR	HR	Avg	OBP	Slg	HR	Avg	OBP	ERA	Runs	HR
1883	NL	8th	17-81	.173	46.0	Bob Ferguson/Blondie Purcell	—	437	887	3	.240	.269	.320	20	.318	.338	5.34	99	5
1884	NL	6th	39-73	.348	45.0	Harry Wright	—	549	824	14	.234	.272	.301	38	.261	.304	3.93	95	4
1885	NL	3rd	56-54	.509	30.0	Harry Wright	—	513	511	20	.229	.270	.302	18	.224	.266	2.39	104	58
1886	NL	4th	71-43	.623	14.0	Harry Wright	—	621	498	26	.240	.289	.327	29	.224	.271	2.45	90	78
1887	NL	2nd	75-48	.610	3.5	Harry Wright	—	901	702	47	.274	.337	.389	48	.259	.311	3.47	96	103
1888	NL	3rd	69-61	.531	14.5	Harry Wright	—	535	509	16	.225	.276	.290	26	.236	.271	2.38	122	73
1889	NL	4th	63-64	.496	20.5	Harry Wright	—	742	748	44	.266	.327	.362	33	.272	.333	4.00	108	92
1890	NL	3rd	78-54	.591	9.5	Wright/Clements/Reach/Allen/Wright	148,366	823	707	23	.269	.350	.364	22	.255	.325	3.32	115	84
1891	NL	4th	68-69	.496	18.5	Harry Wright	217,282	756	773	21	.252	.326	.322	29	.259	.328	3.73	88	51
1892	NL	3rd	46-30	.605	7.0	Harry Wright													
	NL	5th	41-36	.569	12.5	Harry Wright	193,731	860	690	50	.262	.334	.367	24	.239	.303	2.93	104	117
1893	NL	4th	72-57	.558	14.0	Harry Wright	293,019	1011	841	80	.301	.368	.431	30	.281	.351	4.68	95	110
1894	NL	4th	71-57	.555	18.0	Arthur Irwin	352,773	1143	966	40	.349	.414	.476	62	.315	.377	5.63	91	112
1895	NL	3rd	78-53	.595	9.5	Arthur Irwin	474,971	1068	957	61	.330	.394	.450	36	.305	.368	5.47	99	122
1896	NL	8th	62-68	.477	28.5	Billy Nash	357,025	890	891	49	.295	.363	.413	39	.316	.369	5.20	108	140
1897	NL	10th	55-77	.417	38.0	George Stallings	290,027	752	792	40	.293	.353	.398	28	.300	.357	4.60	92	51
1898	NL	6th	78-71	.523	24.0	George Stallings/Bill Shettsline	265,414	823	784	33	.280	.348	.377	23	.281	.343	3.72	91	56
1899	NL	3rd	94-58	.618	9.0	Bill Shettsline	388,933	916	743	31	.301	.363	.395	17	.270	.329	3.47	89	34
1900	NL	3rd	75-63	.543	8.0	Bill Shettsline	301,913	810	792	29	.290	.356	.378	29	.298	.358	4.12	99	54
1901	NL	2nd	83-57	.593	7.5	Bill Shettsline	234,937	668	543	24	.266	.334	.346	19	.257	.302	2.87	100	67
1902	NL	7th	56-81	.409	46.0	Bill Shettsline	112,066	484	649	5	.247	.305	.293	12	.280	.335	3.50	120	71
1903	NL	7th	49-86	.363	39.5	Chief Zimmer	151,729	617	738	12	.268	.322	.341	21	.285	.352	3.96	90	111
1904	NL	8th	52-100	.342	53.5	Hugh Duffy	140,771	571	784	23	.248	.305	.316	22	.267	.330	3.39	95	52
1905	NL	4th	83-69	.546	21.5	Hugh Duffy	317,932	708	602	16	.260	.318	.336	21	.253	.316	2.81	106	87
1906	NL	4th	71-82	.464	45.5	Hugh Duffy	294,680	528	564	12	.241	.307	.307	18	.234	.302	2.58	82	30
1907	NL	3rd	83-64	.565	21.5	Billy Murray	341,216	512	476	12	.236	.304	.305	13	.253	.327	2.43	103	30
1908	NL	4th	83-71	.539	16.0	Billy Murray	420,660	504	445	11	.244	.298	.316	8	.234	.294	2.10	96	19
1909	NL	5th	74-79	.484	36.5	Billy Murray	303,177	516	518	12	.244	.303	.309	23	.234	.304	2.44	110	83
1910	NL	4th	78-75	.510	25.5	Red Dooin	296,597	674	639	22	.255	.327	.338	36	.253	.330	3.05	91	109
1911	NL	4th	79-73	.520	19.5	Red Dooin	416,000	658	669	60	.259	.328	.359	43	.255	.340	3.30	115	255
1912	NL	5th	73-79	.480	30.5	Red Dooin	250,000	670	688	43	.267	.332	.367	43	.272	.344	3.25	100	150
1913	NL	2nd	88-63	.583	12.5	Red Dooin	470,000	693	636	73	.265	.318	.382	40	.261	.330	3.15	119	187
1914	NL	6th	74-80	.481	20.5	Red Dooin	138,474	651	687	62	.263	.329	.361	26	.270	.335	3.06	106	292
1915	NL	1st	90-62	.592	—	Pat Moran	449,898	589	463	58	.247	.316	.340	26	.234	.288	2.17	109	320
1916	NL	2nd	91-62	.595	2.5	Pat Moran	515,365	581	489	42	.250	.310	.341	28	.244	.292	2.36	87	180
1917	NL	2nd	87-65	.572	10.0	Pat Moran	354,428	578	500	38	.248	.310	.339	25	.246	.295	2.46	114	278
1918	NL	6th	55-68	.447	26.0	Pat Moran	122,266	430	507	25	.244	.305	.313	22	.258	.323	3.15	126	255
1919	NL	8th	47-90	.343	47.5	Jack Coombs/Gavvy Cravath	240,424	510	699	42	.251	.303	.342	40	.294	.356	4.14	125	175
1920	NL	8th	62-91	.405	30.5	Gavvy Cravath	330,998	565	714	64	.263	.305	.364	35	.284	.345	3.63	127	416
1921	NL	8th	51-103	.331	43.5	Wild Bill Donovan/Kaiser Wilhelm	273,961	617	919	88	.284	.324	.397	79	.308	.356	4.48	115	233
1922	NL	7th	57-96	.373	35.5	Kaiser Wilhelm	232,471	738	920	116	.282	.341	.415	89	.307	.365	4.64	141	314
1923	NL	8th	50-104	.325	45.5	Art Fletcher	228,138	748	1008	112	.278	.333	.401	100	.321	.385	5.34	144	273
1924	NL	7th	55-96	.364	37.0	Art Fletcher	299,818	676	849	94	.275	.328	.397	84	.313	.372	4.87	128	221
1925	NL	6th	68-85	.444	27.0	Art Fletcher	304,905	812	930	100	.295	.354	.425	117	.315	.368	5.02	144	207
1926	NL	8th	58-93	.384	29.5	Art Fletcher	240,600	687	900	75	.281	.337	.390	68	.315	.371	4.99	120	162
1927	NL	8th	51-103	.331	43.0	Stuffy McInnis	305,420	678	903	57	.280	.337	.370	84	.317	.374	5.36	103	124
1928	NL	8th	43-109	.283	51.0	Burt Shotton	182,168	660	957	85	.267	.333	.382	108	.315	.397	5.56	123	173
1929	NL	5th	71-82	.464	27.5	Burt Shotton	281,200	897	1032	153	.309	.377	.467	122	.324	.398	6.13	130	141
1930	NL	8th	52-102	.338	40.0	Burt Shotton	299,007	944	1199	126	.315	.367	.458	142	.346	.405	6.71	124	116
1931	NL	6th	66-88	.429	35.0	Burt Shotton	284,849	684	828	81	.279	.336	.400	75	.293	.358	4.58	120	120
1932	NL	4th	78-76	.506	12.0	Burt Shotton	268,914	844	796	122	.292	.348	.442	107	.287	.344	4.47	133	218
1933	NL	7th	60-92	.395	31.0	Burt Shotton	156,421	607	760	60	.274	.326	.369	87	.293	.348	4.34	153	181
1934	NL	7th	56-93	.376	37.0	Jimmie Wilson	169,885	675	794	56	.284	.338	.384	126	.288	.347	4.76	126	134
1935	NL	7th	64-89	.418	35.5	Jimmie Wilson	205,470	685	871	92	.269	.322	.378	106	.295	.358	4.76	137	148
1936	NL	8th	54-100	.351	38.0	Jimmie Wilson	249,219	726	874	103	.281	.339	.401	87	.292	.356	4.64	128	187
1937	NL	7th	61-92	.399	34.5	Jimmie Wilson	212,790	724	869	103	.273	.334	.391	116	.297	.359	5.05	125	168
1938	NL	8th	45-105	.300	43.0	Jimmie Wilson/Hans Lobert	166,111	550	840	40	.254	.312	.333	76	.285	.358	4.93	112	122
1939	NL	8th	45-106	.298	50.5	Doc Prothro	277,973	553	856	49	.261	.318	.351	106	.289	.365	5.17	97	81
1940	NL	8th	50-103	.327	50.0	Doc Prothro	207,177	494	750	75	.238	.300	.331	92	.270	.333	4.40	98	93
1941	NL	8th	43-111	.279	57.0	Doc Prothro	231,401	501	793	64	.244	.307	.331	79	.279	.355	4.50	103	104
1942	NL	8th	42-109	.278	62.5	Hans Lobert	230,183	394	706	44	.232	.289	.306	61	.260	.342	4.12	94	91
1943	NL	7th	64-90	.416	41.0	Bucky Harris/Freddie Fitzsimmons	466,975	571	676	66	.249	.316	.335	59	.267	.326	3.79	90	62
1944	NL	8th	61-92	.399	43.5	Freddie Fitzsimmons	369,586	539	658	55	.251	.316	.336	49	.260	.320	3.64	102	63
1945	NL	8th	46-108	.299	52.0	Freddie Fitzsimmons/Ben Chapman	285,057	548	865	56	.246	.307	.326	61	.285	.361	4.64	101	77
1946	NL	5th	69-85	.448	28.0	Ben Chapman	1,045,247	560	705	80	.258	.315	.359	73	.273	.344	3.99	95	89
1947	NL	7th	62-92	.403	32.0	Ben Chapman	907,332	589	687	60	.258	.321	.352	98	.276	.345	3.96	101	76
1948	NL	6th	66-88	.429	25.5	B. Chapman/D. Cooke/E. Sawyer	767,429	591	729	91	.259	.318	.368	95	.269	.342	4.08	88	71
1949	NL	3rd	81-73	.526	16.0	Eddie Sawyer	819,698	662	668	122	.254	.325	.388	104	.270	.337	3.89	99	74
1950	NL	1st	91-63	.591	—	Eddie Sawyer	1,217,035	722	624	125	.265	.334	.396	122	.250	.320	3.50	87	82
1951	NL	5th	73-81	.474	23.5	Eddie Sawyer	937,658	648	644	108	.260	.326	.375	110	.258	.324	3.81	91	74
1952	NL	4th	87-67	.565	9.5	Eddie Sawyer/Steve O'Neill	755,417	657	552	93	.260	.332	.376	95	.249	.301	3.07	97	85
1953	NL	3rd	83-71	.539	22.0	Steve O'Neill	853,644	716	666	115	.265	.335	.396	138	.265	.320	3.80	93	102
1954	NL	4th	75-79	.487	22.0	Steve O'Neill/Terry Moore	738,991	659	614	102	.267	.341	.395	133	.256	.315	3.59	93	81
1955	NL	4th	77-77	.500	21.5	Mayo Smith	922,886	675	666	132	.255	.340	.395	161	.251	.315	3.93	103	111
1956	NL	5th	71-83	.461	22.0	Mayo Smith	934,798	668	738	121	.252	.329	.381	172	.266	.323	4.20	92	85
1957	NL	5th	77-77	.500	18.0	Mayo Smith	1,146,230	623	656	117	.250	.322	.375	139	.254	.307	3.79	94	88
1958	NL	8th	69-85	.448	23.0	Mayo Smith/Eddie Sawyer	931,110	664	762	124	.266	.339	.400	148	.272	.326	4.32	101	100
1959	NL	8th	64-90	.416	23.0	Eddie Sawyer	802,815	599	725	113	.242	.312	.362	150	.261	.324	4.27	102	85
1960	NL	8th	59-95	.383	36.0	E. Sawyer/A. Cohen/G. Mauch	862,205	546	691	99	.239	.302	.351	133	.270	.325	4.01	119	123
1961	NL	8th	47-107	.305	46.0	Gene Mauch	590,039	584	796	103	.243	.310	.357	155	.273	.340	4.61	93	87
1962	NL	7th	81-80	.503	20.0	Gene Mauch	762,034	705	759	142	.260	.330	.390	155	.268	.341	4.28	90	86
1963	NL	4th	87-75	.537	12.0	Gene Mauch	907,141	642	578	126	.252	.306	.381	113	.235	.309	3.09	104	103

Year	Lg	Pos	W-L	Pct	GB	Manager	Att.	R	OR	HR	Avg	OBP	Slg	Opponent HR	Avg	OBP	ERA	Park Index Runs	HR
1964	NL	2nd	92-70	.568	1.0	Gene Mauch	1,425,891	693	632	130	.258	.315	.391	129	.252	.312	3.36	96	86
1965	NL	6th	85-76	.528	11.5	Gene Mauch	1,166,376	654	667	144	.250	.313	.384	116	.256	.318	3.53	87	104
1966	NL	4th	87-75	.537	8.0	Gene Mauch	1,108,201	696	640	117	.258	.322	.378	137	.258	.315	3.57	102	85
1967	NL	5th	82-80	.506	19.5	Gene Mauch	828,888	612	581	103	.242	.313	.357	86	.250	.304	3.10	108	97
1968	NL	7th	76-86	.469	21.0	Gene Mauch/George Myatt/Bob Skinner	664,546	543	615	100	.233	.294	.333	91	.257	.313	3.36	97	105
1969	NL	5th-E	63-99	.389	37.0	Bob Skinner/George Myatt	519,414	645	745	137	.241	.312	.372	134	.270	.340	4.14	100	105
1970	NL	5th-E	73-88	.453	15.5	Frank Lucchesi	708,247	594	730	101	.238	.305	.356	132	.265	.330	4.17	92	92
1971	NL	6th-E	67-95	.414	30.0	Frank Lucchesi	1,511,223	558	688	123	.233	.298	.350	132	.254	.320	3.71	109	150
1972	NL	6th-E	59-97	.378	37.5	Frank Lucchesi/Paul Owens	1,343,329	503	635	98	.236	.302	.344	117	.251	.321	3.66	95	95
1973	NL	6th-E	71-91	.438	11.5	Danny Ozark	1,475,934	642	717	134	.249	.310	.371	131	.263	.341	3.99	119	148
1974	NL	3rd-E	80-82	.494	8.0	Danny Ozark	1,808,648	676	701	95	.261	.320	.373	111	.257	.341	3.91	108	117
1975	NL	2nd-E	86-76	.531	6.5	Danny Ozark	1,909,233	735	694	125	.269	.342	.402	111	.249	.317	3.82	104	102
1976	NL	1st-E	101-61	.623	—	Danny Ozark	2,480,150	770	557	110	.272	.338	.395	98	.250	.301	3.08	112	117
1977	NL	1st-E	101-61	.623	—	Danny Ozark	2,700,070	847	668	186	.279	.346	.448	134	.263	.323	3.71	99	105
1978	NL	1st-E	90-72	.556	—	Danny Ozark	2,583,389	708	586	133	.258	.328	.388	118	.251	.303	3.33	109	145
1979	NL	4th-E	84-78	.519	14.0	Danny Ozark/Dallas Green	2,775,011	683	718	119	.266	.340	.396	135	.266	.325	4.16	93	95
1980	NL	1st-E	91-71	.562	—	Dallas Green	2,651,650	728	639	117	.270	.327	.400	87	.255	.319	3.43	115	113
1981	NL	1st-E	34-21	.618	—	Dallas Green													
	NL	3rd-E	25-27	.481	4.5	Dallas Green	1,638,752	491	472	69	.273	.341	.389	72	.267	.329	4.05	129	124
1982	NL	2nd-E	89-73	.549	3.0	Pat Corrales	2,376,394	664	654	112	.260	.323	.376	86	.255	.314	3.61	86	108
1983	NL	1st-E	90-72	.556	—	Pat Corrales/Paul Owens	2,128,339	696	635	125	.249	.329	.373	111	.256	.314	3.34	102	107
1984	NL	4th-E	81-81	.500	15.5	Paul Owens	2,062,693	720	690	147	.266	.333	.407	101	.253	.308	3.62	105	100
1985	NL	5th-E	75-87	.463	26.0	John Felske	1,830,350	667	673	141	.245	.312	.383	115	.259	.331	3.68	106	102
1986	NL	2nd-E	86-75	.534	21.5	John Felske	1,933,335	739	713	154	.253	.327	.400	130	.265	.331	3.85	110	92
1987	NL	4th-E	80-82	.494	15.0	John Felske/Lee Elia	2,100,110	702	749	169	.254	.327	.410	167	.263	.335	4.18	109	89
1988	NL	6th-E	65-96	.404	35.5	Lee Elia/John Vukovich	1,990,041	597	734	106	.239	.306	.355	118	.265	.341	4.14	108	130
1989	NL	6th-E	67-95	.414	26.0	Nick Leyva	1,861,985	629	735	123	.243	.314	.364	127	.259	.335	4.04	107	108
1990	NL	4th-E	77-85	.475	18.0	Nick Leyva	1,992,484	646	729	103	.255	.327	.363	124	.253	.334	4.07	97	101
1991	NL	3rd-E	78-84	.481	20.0	Nick Leyva/Jim Fregosi	2,050,012	629	680	111	.241	.303	.358	111	.246	.329	3.86	101	100
1992	NL	6th-E	70-92	.432	26.0	Jim Fregosi	1,927,448	686	717	118	.253	.320	.377	113	.257	.326	4.13	100	101
1993	NL	1st-E	97-65	.599	—	Jim Fregosi	3,137,674	877	740	156	.274	.351	.426	129	.252	.322	3.95	101	93
1994	NL	4th-E	54-61	.470	20.5	Jim Fregosi	2,290,971	521	497	80	.262	.332	.390	98	.261	.328	3.85	92	84
1995	NL	2nd-E	69-75	.479	21.0	Jim Fregosi	2,043,588	615	658	94	.262	.332	.384	134	.254	.333	4.21	120	130
1996	NL	5th-E	67-95	.414	29.0	Jim Fregosi	1,801,677	650	790	132	.256	.325	.387	160	.267	.331	4.48	93	88
1997	NL	5th-E	68-94	.420	33.0	Terry Francona	1,490,638	668	840	116	.255	.322	.385	171	.265	.342	4.87	98	98

Team Nicknames: Philadelphia Phillies 1883-1997.

Team Ballparks: Recreation Park (Phi) 1883-1886, Philadelphia Baseball Grounds 1887-1894, Baker Bowl 1895-1937, Baker Bowl & Shibe Park/Connie Mack Stadium (shared) 1938, Shibe Park/Connie Mack Stadium 1939-1970, Veterans Stadium 1971-1997.

Teams: Phillies

Philadelphia Phillies Individual Season Batting Leaders

Year	Batting Average		On-Base Percentage		Slugging Percentage		Home Runs		RBI		Stolen Bases	
1883	Blondie Purcell	.268	Jack Manning	.300	Jack Manning	.364	3 tied with	1	Jack Manning	37	Statistic unavailable	
1884	Jack Manning	.271	Jack Manning	.334	Jack Manning	.394	Jack Manning	5	Jack Manning	52	Statistic unavailable	
1885	Joe Mulvey	.269	Ed Andrews	.318	Joe Mulvey	.393	Joe Mulvey	6	Joe Mulvey	64	Statistic unavailable	
1886	George Wood	.273	George Wood	.309	George Wood	.407	Sid Farrar	5	Joe Mulvey	53	Ed Andrews	56
1887	Ed Andrews	.325	Jim Fogarty	.376	George Wood	.497	George Wood	14	Charlie Ferguson	85	Jim Fogarty	102
1888	Sid Farrar	.244	Jim Fogarty	.325	George Wood	.342	George Wood	6	Sid Farrar	53	Jim Fogarty	58
1889	Sam Thompson	.296	Jim Fogarty	.352	Sam Thompson	.492	Sam Thompson	20	Sam Thompson	111	Jim Fogarty	99
1890	Billy Hamilton	.325	Billy Hamilton	.430	Jack Clements	.472	Jack Clements	7	Sam Thompson	102	Billy Hamilton	102
1891	Billy Hamilton	.340	Billy Hamilton	.453	Jack Clements	.426	Sam Thompson	7	Sam Thompson	90	Billy Hamilton	111
1892	Billy Hamilton	.330	Billy Hamilton	.423	Ed Delahanty	.495	Roger Connor	12	Sam Thompson	104	Billy Hamilton	57
1893	Billy Hamilton	.380	Billy Hamilton	.490	Ed Delahanty	.583	Ed Delahanty	19	Ed Delahanty	146	Billy Hamilton	43
1894	Sam Thompson	.407	Billy Hamilton	.523	Sam Thompson	.686	Sam Thompson	13	Sam Thompson	141	Billy Hamilton	98
1895	Ed Delahanty	.404	Ed Delahanty	.500	Sam Thompson	.654	Sam Thompson	18	Sam Thompson	165	Billy Hamilton	97
1896	Ed Delahanty	.397	Ed Delahanty	.472	Ed Delahanty	.631	Ed Delahanty	13	Ed Delahanty	126	Ed Delahanty	37
1897	Ed Delahanty	.377	Ed Delahanty	.444	Nap Lajoie	.569	Nap Lajoie	9	Nap Lajoie	127	Duff Cooley	31
1898	Ed Delahanty	.334	Elmer Flick	.430	Nap Lajoie	.461	Elmer Flick	8	Nap Lajoie	127	Ed Delahanty	58
1899	Ed Delahanty	.410	Ed Delahanty	.464	Ed Delahanty	.582	Ed Delahanty	9	Ed Delahanty	137	Roy Thomas	42
1900	Elmer Flick	.367	Roy Thomas	.451	Elmer Flick	.545	Elmer Flick	11	Elmer Flick	110	Roy Thomas	37
1901	Ed Delahanty	.354	Roy Thomas	.437	Ed Delahanty	.528	Ed Delahanty Elmer Flick	8	Ed Delahanty	108	Elmer Flick	30
1902	Shad Barry	.287	Roy Thomas	.414	Shad Barry	.363	Shad Barry	3	Shad Barry	58	Roy Thomas	17
1903	Roy Thomas	.327	Roy Thomas	.453	Harry Wolverton	.383	Bill Keister	3	Bill Keister	63	Shad Barry	26
1904	John Titus	.294	Roy Thomas	.416	John Titus	.387	Red Dooin	6	Sherry Magee	57	Roy Thomas	28
1905	Roy Thomas	.317	Roy Thomas	.417	John Titus	.436	Sherry Magee	5	Sherry Magee	98	Sherry Magee	48
1906	Sherry Magee	.282	Roy Thomas	.393	Sherry Magee	.407	Sherry Magee	6	Sherry Magee	67	Sherry Magee	55
1907	Sherry Magee	.328	Sherry Magee	.396	Sherry Magee	.455	Sherry Magee	4	Sherry Magee	85	Sherry Magee	46
1908	Kitty Bransfield	.304	John Titus	.365	Sherry Magee	.417	Kitty Bransfield	3	Kitty Bransfield	71	Sherry Magee	40
1909	Kitty Bransfield	.292	John Titus	.367	Sherry Magee	.398	John Titus	3	Sherry Magee	66	Sherry Magee	38
1910	Sherry Magee	.331	Sherry Magee	.445	Sherry Magee	.507	Sherry Magee	6	Sherry Magee	123	Sherry Magee	49
1911	Fred Luderus	.301	Hans Lobert	.368	Sherry Magee	.483	Fred Luderus	16	Fred Luderus	99	Hans Lobert	40
1912	Dode Paskert	.315	Dode Paskert	.420	Gavy Cravath	.470	Gavy Cravath	11	Gavy Cravath	70	Dode Paskert	36
1913	Gavy Cravath	.341	Gavy Cravath	.407	Gavy Cravath	.568	Gavy Cravath	19	Gavy Cravath	128	Hans Lobert	41
1914	Beals Becker	.325	Gavy Cravath	.402	Sherry Magee	.509	Gavy Cravath	19	Sherry Magee	103	Hans Lobert	31
1915	Fred Luderus	.315	Gavy Cravath	.393	Gavy Cravath	.510	Gavy Cravath	24	Gavy Cravath	115	Possum Whitted	24
1916	Gavy Cravath	.283	Gavy Cravath	.379	Gavy Cravath	.440	Gavy Cravath	11	Gavy Cravath	70	Possum Whitted	29
1917	Gavy Cravath	.280	Gavy Cravath	.369	Gavy Cravath	.473	Gavy Cravath	12	Gavy Cravath	83	Milt Stock	25
1918	Fred Luderus	.288	Fred Luderus	.351	Irish Meusel	.383	Gavy Cravath	8	Fred Luderus	67	Milt Stock	20
1919	Irish Meusel	.305	Fred Luderus	.365	Irish Meusel	.411	Gavy Cravath	12	Irish Meusel	59	Irish Meusel	24
1920	Cy Williams	.325	Cy Williams	.364	Cy Williams	.497	Cy Williams	15	Cy Williams	72	Cy Williams	18
1921	Cy Williams	.320	Cy Williams	.357	Cy Williams	.488	Cy Williams	18	Cy Williams	75	Irish Meusel	8
1922	Curt Walker	.337	Curt Walker	.399	Cy Williams	.514	Cy Williams	26	Cy Williams	92	Curt Walker Cy Williams	11
1923	Cotton Tierney	.317	Cy Williams	.371	Cy Williams	.576	Cy Williams	41	Cy Williams	114	Curt Walker	12
1924	Cy Williams	.328	Cy Williams	.403	Cy Williams	.552	Cy Williams	24	Cy Williams	93	George Harper	10
1925	George Harper	.349	George Harper	.391	George Harper	.558	George Harper	18	George Harper	97	George Harper	10
1926	Freddy Leach	.329	Johnny Mokan	.365	Freddy Leach	.484	Cy Williams	18	Freddy Leach	71	Clarence Huber	9
1927	Freddy Leach	.306	Heinie Sand	.369	Cy Williams	.502	Cy Williams	30	Cy Williams	98	Fresco Thompson	19
1928	Freddy Leach	.304	Don Hurst	.391	Don Hurst	.508	Don Hurst	19	Pinky Whitney	103	Fresco Thompson	19
1929	Lefty O'Doul	.398	Lefty O'Doul	.465	Chuck Klein	.657	Chuck Klein	43	Chuck Klein	145	Fresco Thompson	16
1930	Chuck Klein	.386	Lefty O'Doul	.453	Chuck Klein	.687	Chuck Klein	40	Chuck Klein	170	Fresco Thompson	7
1931	Chuck Klein	.337	Chuck Klein	.398	Chuck Klein	.584	Chuck Klein	31	Chuck Klein	121	Don Hurst	8
1932	Chuck Klein	.348	Don Hurst	.412	Chuck Klein	.646	Chuck Klein	38	Don Hurst	143	Chuck Klein	20
1933	Chuck Klein	.368	Chuck Klein	.422	Chuck Klein	.602	Chuck Klein	28	Chuck Klein	120	Chick Fullis	18
1934	Johnny Moore	.343	Johnny Moore	.397	Johnny Moore	.515	Dolph Camilli	12	Johnny Moore	93	Dick Bartell	13
1935	Johnny Moore	.323	Johnny Moore	.375	Johnny Moore	.483	Dolph Camilli	25	Johnny Moore	93	Dolph Camilli	9
1936	Johnny Moore	.328	Dolph Camilli	.441	Dolph Camilli	.577	Dolph Camilli	28	Dolph Camilli	102	Lou Chiozza	17
1937	Pinky Whitney	.341	Dolph Camilli	.446	Dolph Camilli	.587	Dolph Camilli	27	Dolph Camilli	80	George Scharein	13
1938	Hersh Martin	.298	Hersh Martin	.347	Hersh Martin	.421	Chuck Klein	8	Morrie Arnovich	72	George Scharein	11
1939	Morrie Arnovich	.324	Morrie Arnovich	.397	Morrie Arnovich	.413	Joe Marty Heinie Mueller	9	Morrie Arnovich	67	Morrie Arnovich	7
1940	Pinky May	.293	Pinky May	.371	Joe Marty	.437	Johnny Rizzo	20	Johnny Rizzo	53	Art Mahan	4
1941	Nick Etten	.311	Nick Etten	.405	Danny Litwhiler	.466	Danny Litwhiler	18	Nick Etten	79	Danny Murtaugh	18
1942	Danny Litwhiler	.271	Nick Etten	.357	Danny Litwhiler	.389	Danny Litwhiler	9	Danny Litwhiler	56	Danny Murtaugh	13
1943	Babe Dahlgren	.287	Danny Murtaugh	.357	Ron Northey	.430	Ron Northey	16	Ron Northey	68	Jimmy Wasdell	6
1944	Ron Northey	.288	Buster Adams	.370	Ron Northey	.496	Ron Northey	22	Ron Northey	104	Tony Lupien	18
1945	Jimmy Wasdell	.300	Jimmy Wasdell	.346	Vince DiMaggio	.451	Vince DiMaggio	19	Vince DiMaggio	84	Vince DiMaggio	12
1946	Del Ennis	.313	Johnny Wyrostek	.366	Del Ennis	.485	Del Ennis	17	Del Ennis	73	Roy Hughes Johnny Wyrostek	7
1947	Harry Walker	.371	Harry Walker	.443	Harry Walker	.500	Andy Seminick	13	Del Ennis	81	Harry Walker	13
1948	Richie Ashburn	.333	Richie Ashburn	.410	Del Ennis	.525	Del Ennis	30	Del Ennis	95	Richie Ashburn	32
1949	Del Ennis	.302	Del Ennis	.367	Del Ennis	.525	Del Ennis	25	Del Ennis	110	Richie Ashburn	9
1950	Del Ennis	.311	Dick Sisler	.373	Del Ennis	.551	Del Ennis	31	Del Ennis	126	Richie Ashburn	14
1951	Richie Ashburn	.344	Richie Ashburn	.393	Puddin' Head Jones	.470	Puddin' Head Jones	22	Puddin' Head Jones	81	Richie Ashburn	29
1952	Del Ennis	.289	Eddie Waitkus	.371	Del Ennis	.475	Del Ennis	20	Del Ennis	107	Richie Ashburn	16
1953	Richie Ashburn	.330	Richie Ashburn	.394	Del Ennis	.484	Del Ennis	29	Del Ennis	125	Richie Ashburn	14
1954	Richie Ashburn	.313	Richie Ashburn	.441	Granny Hamner	.466	Del Ennis	25	Del Ennis	119	Richie Ashburn	11
1955	Richie Ashburn	.338	Richie Ashburn	.449	Del Ennis	.518	Del Ennis	29	Del Ennis	120	Richie Ashburn	12
1956	Richie Ashburn	.303	Richie Ashburn	.384	Stan Lopata	.535	Stan Lopata	32	Del Ennis	95	Richie Ashburn	10
1957	Richie Ashburn	.297	Ed Bouchee	.394	Ed Bouchee	.470	Rip Repulski	20	Ed Bouchee	76	Chico Fernandez	18
1958	Richie Ashburn	.350	Richie Ashburn	.440	Harry Anderson	.524	Harry Anderson	23	Harry Anderson	97	Richie Ashburn	30
1959	Ed Bouchee	.285	Ed Bouchee	.375	Wally Post	.457	Gene Freese	23	Wally Post	94	Richie Ashburn	9
1960	Tony Taylor	.287	Pancho Herrera	.348	Pancho Herrera	.455	Pancho Herrera	17	Pancho Herrera	71	Tony Taylor	24
1961	Tony Gonzalez	.277	Johnny Callison	.363	Tony Gonzalez	.437	Don Demeter	20	Don Demeter	68	Tony Gonzalez	15

Year	Batting Average		On-Base Percentage		Slugging Percentage		Home Runs		RBI		Stolen Bases	
1962	Don Demeter	.307	Johnny Callison	.363	Don Demeter	.520	Don Demeter	29	Don Demeter	107	Tony Taylor	20
1963	Tony Gonzalez	.306	Tony Gonzalez	.372	Johnny Callison	.502	Johnny Callison	26	Don Demeter	83	Tony Taylor	23
1964	Dick Allen	.318	Dick Allen	.382	Dick Allen	.557	Johnny Callison	31	Johnny Callison	104	Tony Taylor	13
1965	Cookie Rojas	.303	Dick Allen	.375	Johnny Callison	.509	Johnny Callison	32	Johnny Callison	101	Dick Allen	15
1966	Dick Allen	.317	Dick Allen	.396	Dick Allen	.632	Dick Allen	40	Dick Allen	110	Bill White	16
1967	Tony Gonzalez	.339	Dick Allen	.404	Dick Allen	.566	Dick Allen	23	Dick Allen	77	Dick Allen	20
1968	Dick Allen	.263	Dick Allen	.352	Dick Allen	.520	Dick Allen	33	Dick Allen	90	Tony Taylor	22
1969	Dick Allen	.288	Dick Allen	.375	Dick Allen	.573	Dick Allen	32	Dick Allen	89	Tony Taylor	19
1970	Don Money	.295	Don Money	.361	Don Money	.463	Deron Johnson	27	Deron Johnson	93	Larry Bowa	24
1971	Tim McCarver	.278	Deron Johnson	.347	Deron Johnson	.490	Deron Johnson	34	Willie Montanez	99	Larry Bowa	28
1972	Greg Luzinski	.281	Greg Luzinski	.332	Greg Luzinski	.453	Greg Luzinski	18	Greg Luzinski	68	Larry Bowa	17
1973	Greg Luzinski	.285	Greg Luzinski	.346	Greg Luzinski	.484	Greg Luzinski	29	Greg Luzinski	97	Larry Bowa	10
1974	Willie Montanez	.304	Mike Schmidt	.395	Mike Schmidt	.546	Mike Schmidt	36	Mike Schmidt	116	Larry Bowa	39
1975	Larry Bowa	.305	Greg Luzinski	.394	Greg Luzinski	.540	Mike Schmidt	38	Greg Luzinski	120	Mike Schmidt	29
1976	Garry Maddox	.330	Garry Maddox	.377	Mike Schmidt	.524	Mike Schmidt	38	Mike Schmidt	107	Larry Bowa	30
1977	Greg Luzinski	.309	Greg Luzinski	.394	Greg Luzinski	.594	Greg Luzinski	39	Greg Luzinski	130	Larry Bowa	32
1978	Larry Bowa	.294	Greg Luzinski	.388	Greg Luzinski	.526	Greg Luzinski	35	Greg Luzinski	101	Garry Maddox	33
1979	Pete Rose	.331	Pete Rose	.418	Mike Schmidt	.564	Mike Schmidt	45	Mike Schmidt	114	Garry Maddox	26
1980	Bake McBride	.309	Mike Schmidt	.380	Mike Schmidt	.624	Mike Schmidt	48	Mike Schmidt	121	Lonnie Smith	33
1981	Pete Rose	.325	Mike Schmidt	.435	Mike Schmidt	.644	Mike Schmidt	31	Mike Schmidt	91	Lonnie Smith	21
1982	Bo Diaz	.288	Mike Schmidt	.403	Mike Schmidt	.547	Mike Schmidt	35	Mike Schmidt	87	Bob Dernier	42
1983	Gary Matthews	.258	Mike Schmidt	.399	Mike Schmidt	.524	Mike Schmidt	40	Mike Schmidt	109	Bob Dernier	35
1984	Von Hayes	.292	Mike Schmidt	.383	Mike Schmidt	.536	Mike Schmidt	36	Mike Schmidt	106	Juan Samuel	72
1985	Mike Schmidt	.277	Mike Schmidt	.375	Mike Schmidt	.532	Mike Schmidt	33	Glenn Wilson	102	Juan Samuel	53
1986	Von Hayes	.305	Mike Schmidt	.390	Mike Schmidt	.547	Mike Schmidt	37	Mike Schmidt	119	Juan Samuel	42
1987	Milt Thompson	.302	Von Hayes	.404	Mike Schmidt	.548	Mike Schmidt	35	Mike Schmidt	113	Milt Thompson	46
1988	Phil Bradley	.264	Phil Bradley	.341	Phil Bradley	.392	Chris James	19	Juan Samuel	67	Juan Samuel	33
1989	Tom Herr	.287	Von Hayes	.376	Von Hayes	.461	Von Hayes	26	Von Hayes	78	Von Hayes	28
1990	Lenny Dykstra	.325	Lenny Dykstra	.418	Lenny Dykstra	.441	Von Hayes	17	Von Hayes	73	Lenny Dykstra	33
1991	John Kruk	.294	John Kruk	.367	John Kruk	.483	John Kruk	21	John Kruk	92	Lenny Dykstra	24
1992	John Kruk	.323	John Kruk	.423	Darren Daulton	.524	Darren Daulton Dave Hollins	27	Darren Daulton	109	Lenny Dykstra	30
1993	John Kruk	.316	John Kruk	.430	Darren Daulton	.482	Darren Daulton Pete Incaviglia	24	Darren Daulton	105	Lenny Dykstra	37
1994	Lenny Dykstra	.273	Lenny Dykstra	.404	Lenny Dykstra	.435	Darren Daulton	15	Darren Daulton	56	Lenny Dykstra	15
1995	Gregg Jefferies	.306	Mickey Morandini	.350	Gregg Jefferies	.448	3 tied with	11	Charlie Hayes	85	Lenny Dykstra Jim Eisenreich	10
1996	Todd Zeile	.268	Todd Zeile	.353	Benito Santiago	.503	Benito Santiago	30	Benito Santiago	85	Mickey Morandini	26
1997	Mickey Morandini	.295	Scott Rolen	.377	Scott Rolen	.469	Scott Rolen	21	Scott Rolen	92	Mickey Morandini Scott Rolen	16

Philadelphia Phillies Individual Season Pitching Leaders

Year	ERA		Baserunners/9 IP		Innings Pitched		Strikeouts		Wins		Saves	
1883	John Coleman	4.87	John Coleman	13.7	John Coleman	538.1	John Coleman	159	John Coleman	12	9 tied with	0
1884	Bill Vinton	2.23	Bill Vinton	9.9	Charlie Ferguson	416.2	Charlie Ferguson	194	Charlie Ferguson	21	Charlie Ferguson	1
1885	Ed Daily	2.21	Ed Daily	9.4	Ed Daily	440.0	Charlie Ferguson	197	Ed Daily Charlie Ferguson	26	4 tied with	0
1886	Charlie Ferguson	1.98	Charlie Ferguson	8.8	Charlie Ferguson	395.2	Charlie Ferguson	212	Charlie Ferguson	30	Charlie Ferguson	2
1887	Dan Casey	2.86	Charlie Ferguson	10.7	Dan Casey	390.1	Charlie Buffinton	160	Dan Casey	28	Charlie Ferguson	1
1888	Ben Sanders	1.90	Charlie Buffinton	8.7	Charlie Buffinton	400.1	Charlie Buffinton	199	Charlie Buffinton	28	George Wood	2
1889	Charlie Buffinton	3.24	Charlie Buffinton	12.2	Charlie Buffinton	380.0	Charlie Buffinton	153	Charlie Buffinton	28	Kid Gleason Ben Sanders	1
1890	Kid Gleason	2.63	Kid Gleason	11.5	Kid Gleason	506.0	Kid Gleason	222	Kid Gleason	38	Kid Gleason	2
1891	Kid Gleason	3.51	John Thornton	12.8	Kid Gleason	418.0	Duke Esper	108	Kid Gleason	24	John Thornton	2
1892	Tim Keefe	2.36	Tim Keefe	10.8	Gus Weyhing	469.2	Gus Weyhing	202	Gus Weyhing	32	Gus Weyhing	3
1893	Jack Taylor	4.24	Jack Taylor	14.1	Gus Weyhing	345.1	Gus Weyhing	101	Gus Weyhing	23	Frank O'Connor Jack Taylor	1
1894	Jack Taylor	4.08	Jack Taylor	13.4	Jack Taylor	298.0	Gus Weyhing	81	Jack Taylor	23	Nixey Callahan	
1895	Jack Taylor	4.49	Jack Taylor	13.1	Kid Carsey	342.1	Kid Carsey	93	Jack Taylor	26	Ernie Beam	3
1896	Al Orth	4.41	Al Orth	13.3	Jack Taylor	359.0	Jack Taylor	97	Jack Taylor	20	Kid Carsey Jack Taylor	1
1897	George Wheeler	3.96	Jack Taylor	13.6	Jack Taylor	317.1	Jack Taylor	88	Jack Taylor	16	Jack Taylor	2
1898	Al Orth	3.02	Wiley Piatt	11.8	Wiley Piatt	306.0	Wiley Piatt	121	Wiley Piatt	24	10 tied with	0
1899	Chick Fraser	3.36	Red Donahue	11.9	Wiley Piatt	305.0	Wiley Piatt	89	Wiley Piatt	23	Jack Fifield Al Orth	1
1900	Chick Fraser	3.14	Al Orth	12.9	Al Orth	262.0	Al Orth	68	3 tied with	15	Bill Bernhard	2
1901	Al Orth	2.27	Al Orth	9.3	Red Donahue	295.1	Doc White	132	Red Donahue Al Orth	20	6 tied with	0
1902	Doc White	2.53	Doc White	10.6	Doc White	306.0	Doc White	185	Doc White	14	Henry Fox Doc White	1
1903	Tully Sparks	2.72	Tully Sparks	11.3	Bill Duggleby	264.1	Chick Fraser	104	Bill Duggleby	13	Bill Duggleby	2
1904	Tully Sparks	2.65	Tully Sparks	11.5	Chick Fraser	302.0	Chick Fraser	127	Chick Fraser	14	Bill Duggleby Chick Fraser	1
1905	Tully Sparks	2.18	Tully Sparks	10.4	Togie Pittinger	337.1	Togie Pittinger	136	Togie Pittinger	23	Togie Pittinger	2
1906	Tully Sparks	2.16	Tully Sparks	9.0	Tully Sparks	316.2	Johnny Lush	151	Tully Sparks	19	Tully Sparks	3
1907	Tully Sparks	2.00	Tully Sparks	9.5	Frank Corridon	274.0	Frank Corridon	131	Tully Sparks	22	Frank Corridon	2
1908	George McQuillan	1.53	George McQuillan	9.0	George McQuillan	359.2	George McQuillan	114	George McQuillan	23	George McQuillan Tully Sparks	2
1909	Earl Moore	2.10	George McQuillan	9.3	Earl Moore	299.2	Earl Moore	173	Earl Moore	18	George McQuillan	2
1910	Earl Moore	2.58	Earl Moore	11.4	Earl Moore	283.0	Earl Moore	185	Earl Moore	22	Bert Humphries	2
1911	Pete Alexander	2.57	Pete Alexander	10.3	Pete Alexander	367.0	Pete Alexander	227	Pete Alexander	28	George Chalmers	4
1912	Eppa Rixey	2.50	Eppa Rixey	11.3	Pete Alexander	310.1	Pete Alexander	195	Pete Alexander	19	Pete Alexander	3
1913	Ad Brennan	2.39	Pete Alexander	10.8	Tom Seaton	322.1	Tom Seaton	168	Tom Seaton	27	Pete Alexander Eppa Rixey	2
1914	Pete Alexander	2.38	Pete Alexander	10.5	Pete Alexander	355.0	Pete Alexander	214	Pete Alexander	27	Erskine Mayer Ben Tincup	2
1915	Pete Alexander	1.22	Pete Alexander	7.8	Pete Alexander	376.1	Pete Alexander	241	Pete Alexander	31	Pete Alexander	3
1916	Pete Alexander	1.55	Pete Alexander	8.9	Pete Alexander	389.0	Pete Alexander	167	Pete Alexander	33	Chief Bender	3
1917	Pete Alexander	1.83	Pete Alexander	9.2	Pete Alexander	388.0	Pete Alexander	200	Pete Alexander	30	Chief Bender	2
1918	Brad Hogg	2.53	Brad Hogg	10.6	Mike Prendergast	252.1	Brad Hogg	81	Brad Hogg Mike Prendergast	13	Joe Oeschger	3
1919	Lee Meadows	2.47	Lee Meadows	11.1	George Smith	184.2	Lee Meadows	88	Lee Meadows	8	Red Ames Gene Packard	1
1920	Lee Meadows	2.84	Eppa Rixey	11.4	Eppa Rixey	284.1	Eppa Rixey	109	Lee Meadows	16	Red Causey	3
1921	Jimmy Ring	4.24	Bill Hubbell	12.7	Jimmy Ring	246.0	Jimmy Ring	88	Lee Meadows	11	Huck Betts	4
1922	Lefty Weinert	3.40	Lee Meadows	13.1	Jimmy Ring	249.1	Jimmy Ring	116	Lee Meadows Jimmy Ring	12	Jesse Winters	2
1923	Jimmy Ring	3.87	Jimmy Ring	13.4	Jimmy Ring	304.1	Jimmy Ring	112	Jimmy Ring	18	Petie Behan	2
1924	Jimmy Ring	3.97	Bill Hubbell	14.1	Jimmy Ring	215.1	Jimmy Ring	72	Bill Hubbell Jimmy Ring	10	Johnny Couch	3
1925	Hal Carlson	4.23	Hal Carlson	13.0	Jimmy Ring	270.0	Jimmy Ring	93	Jimmy Ring	14	Jack Knight	3
1926	Hal Carlson	3.23	Hal Carlson	11.5	Hal Carlson	267.1	Hal Carlson	55	Hal Carlson	17	Jack Knight	2
1927	Dutch Ulrich	3.17	Dutch Ulrich	11.2	Jack Scott	233.1	Hub Pruett	90	Jack Scott	9	Claude Willoughby	2
1928	Ray Benge	4.55	Ray Benge	13.9	Ray Benge	201.2	Jimmy Ring	72	Ray Benge	8	3 tied with	2
1929	Claude Willoughby	4.99	Claude Willoughby	14.8	Claude Willoughby	243.1	Ray Benge	78	Claude Willoughby	15	Phil Collins	5
1930	Phil Collins	4.78	Phil Collins	14.4	Phil Collins	239.0	Phil Collins	87	Phil Collins	16	Phil Collins	3
1931	Ray Benge	3.17	Ray Benge	11.6	Jumbo Elliott	249.0	Ray Benge	117	Jumbo Elliott	19	Jumbo Elliott	5
1932	Snipe Hansen	3.72	Flint Rhem	12.1	Ed Holley	228.0	Ed Holley	89	Phil Collins	14	Ray Benge	6
1933	Ed Holley	3.53	Cy Moore	12.4	Ed Holley	206.2	Ed Holley	56	Ed Holley	13	Phil Collins	6
1934	Curt Davis	2.95	Curt Davis	11.5	Curt Davis	274.1	Curt Davis	99	Curt Davis	19	Curt Davis	5
1935	Syl Johnson	3.56	Syl Johnson	11.1	Curt Davis	231.0	Syl Johnson	89	Curt Davis	16	Syl Johnson	6
1936	Claude Passeau	3.48	Claude Passeau	12.7	Bucky Walters	258.0	Claude Passeau	85	Claude Passeau Bucky Walters	11	Syl Johnson	7
1937	Claude Passeau	4.34	Claude Passeau	13.3	Claude Passeau	292.1	Wayne LaMaster Claude Passeau	135	Wayne LaMaster	15	Wayne LaMaster	4
1938	Al Hollingsworth	3.82	Al Hollingsworth	13.1	Hugh Mulcahy	267.1	Claude Passeau	100	Claude Passeau	11	Pete Sivess	3
1939	Boom-Boom Beck	4.73	Boom-Boom Beck	13.3	Hugh Mulcahy	225.2	Kirby Higbe	79	Kirby Higbe	10	Hugh Mulcahy	4
1940	Hugh Mulcahy	3.60	Kirby Higbe	11.6	Kirby Higbe	283.0	Kirby Higbe	137	Kirby Higbe	14	Lloyd Brown	3
1941	Tommy Hughes	4.45	Johnny Podgajny	13.2	Johnny Podgajny	181.1	Si Johnson	80	Tommy Hughes Johnny Podgajny	9	Ike Pearson	6
1942	Tommy Hughes	3.06	Tommy Hughes	11.5	Tommy Hughes	253.0	Rube Melton	107	Tommy Hughes	12	Rube Melton	4
1943	Dick Barrett	2.39	Dick Barrett	10.1	Al Gerheauser	215.0	Al Gerheauser	92	Schoolboy Rowe	14	Bill Lee	3
1944	Ken Raffensberger	3.06	Ken Raffensberger	10.6	Ken Raffensberger	258.2	Ken Raffensberger	136	Ken Raffensberger Charley Schanz	13	Charley Schanz	3
1945	Andy Karl	2.99	Andy Karl	11.4	Dick Barrett	190.2	Dick Barrett	72	Dick Barrett Andy Karl	8	Andy Karl	15
1946	Oscar Judd	3.53	Ken Raffensberger	11.2	Ken Raffensberger	196.0	Ken Raffensberger	73	Oscar Judd Schoolboy Rowe	11	Ken Raffensberger	6

Teams: Phillies

Year	ERA		Baserunners/9 IP		Innings Pitched		Strikeouts		Wins		Saves	
1947	Dutch Leonard	2.68	Dutch Leonard	10.8	Dutch Leonard	235.0	Dutch Leonard	103	Dutch Leonard	17	Blix Donnelly	5
1948	Dutch Leonard	2.51	Dutch Leonard	11.3	Dutch Leonard	225.2	Dutch Leonard	92	Dutch Leonard	12	Monk Dubiel	4
1949	Ken Heintzelman	3.02	Russ Meyer	11.4	Ken Heintzelman	250.0	Robin Roberts	95	Ken Heintzelman	17	Jim Konstanty	7
									Russ Meyer			
1950	Robin Roberts	3.02	Robin Roberts	10.7	Robin Roberts	304.1	Robin Roberts	146	Robin Roberts	20	Jim Konstanty	22
							Curt Simmons					
1951	Robin Roberts	3.03	Robin Roberts	10.0	Robin Roberts	315.0	Robin Roberts	127	Robin Roberts	21	Jim Konstanty	9
1952	Robin Roberts	2.59	Robin Roberts	9.3	Robin Roberts	330.0	Robin Roberts	148	Robin Roberts	28	Jim Konstanty	6
1953	Robin Roberts	2.75	Robin Roberts	10.0	Robin Roberts	346.2	Robin Roberts	198	Robin Roberts	23	Jim Konstanty	5
1954	Curt Simmons	2.81	Robin Roberts	9.4	Robin Roberts	336.2	Robin Roberts	185	Robin Roberts	23	Robin Roberts	4
1955	Robin Roberts	3.28	Robin Roberts	10.2	Robin Roberts	305.0	Robin Roberts	160	Robin Roberts	23	Jack Meyer	16
1956	Curt Simmons	3.36	Harvey Haddix	11.2	Robin Roberts	297.1	Robin Roberts	157	Robin Roberts	19	Bob Miller	5
1957	Jack Sanford	3.08	Robin Roberts	10.5	Robin Roberts	249.2	Jack Sanford	188	Jack Sanford	19	Turk Farrell	10
1958	Robin Roberts	3.24	Robin Roberts	10.8	Robin Roberts	269.2	Robin Roberts	130	Robin Roberts	17	Turk Farrell	11
1959	Gene Conley	3.00	Gene Conley	10.2	Robin Roberts	257.1	Robin Roberts	137	Robin Roberts	15	Turk Farrell	6
1960	Gene Conley	3.68	Robin Roberts	11.1	Robin Roberts	237.1	Robin Roberts	122	Robin Roberts	12	Turk Farrell	11
1961	Art Mahaffey	4.10	Art Mahaffey	11.6	Art Mahaffey	219.1	Art Mahaffey	158	Art Mahaffey	11	Frank Sullivan	6
1962	Dennis Bennett	3.81	Dennis Bennett	11.2	Art Mahaffey	274.0	Art Mahaffey	177	Art Mahaffey	19	Jack Baldschun	13
1963	Chris Short	2.95	Cal McLish	10.5	Cal McLish	209.2	Ray Culp	176	Ray Culp	14	Jack Baldschun	16
1964	Chris Short	2.20	Chris Short	9.3	Jim Bunning	284.1	Jim Bunning	219	Jim Bunning	19	Jack Baldschun	21
1965	Jim Bunning	2.60	Jim Bunning	10.1	Chris Short	297.1	Jim Bunning	268	Jim Bunning	19	Gary Wagner	7
1966	Jim Bunning	2.41	Jim Bunning	9.6	Jim Bunning	314.0	Jim Bunning	252	Chris Short	20	Darold Knowles	13
1967	Jim Bunning	2.29	Jim Bunning	9.7	Jim Bunning	302.1	Jim Bunning	253	Chris Short	17	Turk Farrell	12
1968	Larry Jackson	2.77	Larry Jackson	10.8	Chris Short	269.2	Chris Short	202	Chris Short	19	Turk Farrell	12
1969	Rick Wise	3.23	Rick Wise	11.4	Grant Jackson	253.0	Grant Jackson	180	Rick Wise	15	John Boozer	6
											Billy Wilson	
1970	Jim Bunning	4.11	Jim Bunning	12.2	Rick Wise	220.1	Dick Selma	153	Rick Wise	13	Dick Selma	22
1971	Rick Wise	2.88	Barry Lersch	10.7	Rick Wise	272.1	Rick Wise	155	Rick Wise	17	Joe Hoerner	9
1972	Steve Carlton	1.97	Steve Carlton	9.0	Steve Carlton	346.1	Steve Carlton	310	Steve Carlton	27	Mac Scarce	4
1973	Wayne Twitchell	2.50	Wayne Twitchell	11.3	Steve Carlton	293.1	Steve Carlton	223	4 tied with	13	Mac Scarce	12
1974	Jim Lonborg	3.21	Jim Lonborg	11.3	Steve Carlton	291.0	Steve Carlton	240	Jim Lonborg	17	Eddie Watt	6
1975	Steve Carlton	3.56	Larry Christenson	10.2	Steve Carlton	255.1	Steve Carlton	192	Steve Carlton	15	Gene Garber	14
											Tug McGraw	
1976	Jim Lonborg	3.08	Steve Carlton	10.6	Steve Carlton	252.2	Steve Carlton	195	Steve Carlton	20	Ron Reed	14
1977	Steve Carlton	2.64	Steve Carlton	10.2	Steve Carlton	283.0	Steve Carlton	198	Steve Carlton	23	Gene Garber	19
1978	Steve Carlton	2.84	Larry Christenson	10.1	Steve Carlton	247.1	Steve Carlton	161	Steve Carlton	16	Ron Reed	17
1979	Steve Carlton	3.62	Steve Carlton	10.6	Steve Carlton	251.0	Steve Carlton	213	Steve Carlton	18	Tug McGraw	16
1980	Steve Carlton	2.34	Steve Carlton	9.9	Steve Carlton	304.0	Steve Carlton	286	Steve Carlton	24	Tug McGraw	20
1981	Steve Carlton	2.42	Steve Carlton	10.2	Steve Carlton	190.0	Steve Carlton	179	Steve Carlton	13	Tug McGraw	10
1982	Steve Carlton	3.10	Steve Carlton	10.3	Steve Carlton	295.2	Steve Carlton	286	Steve Carlton	23	Ron Reed	14
1983	John Denny	2.37	John Denny	10.6	Steve Carlton	283.2	Steve Carlton	275	John Denny	19	Al Holland	25
1984	Jerry Koosman	3.25	Steve Carlton	11.5	Steve Carlton	229.0	Steve Carlton	163	Jerry Koosman	14	Al Holland	29
1985	Shane Rawley	3.31	Charles Hudson	12.3	John Denny	230.0	Kevin Gross	151	Kevin Gross	15	Kent Tekulve	14
1986	Kevin Gross	4.02	Kevin Gross	12.7	Kevin Gross	241.2	Kevin Gross	154	Kevin Gross	12	Steve Bedrosian	29
1987	Don Carman	4.22	Don Carman	11.4	Shane Rawley	229.2	Don Carman	125	Shane Rawley	17	Steve Bedrosian	40
1988	Kevin Gross	3.69	Kevin Gross	12.0	Kevin Gross	231.2	Kevin Gross	162	Kevin Gross	12	Steve Bedrosian	28
1989	Ken Howell	3.44	Ken Howell	10.7	Ken Howell	204.0	Ken Howell	164	Ken Howell	12	Roger McDowell	19
									Jeff Parrett			
1990	Terry Mulholland	3.34	Terry Mulholland	10.8	Pat Combs	183.1	Pat Combs	108	Pat Combs	10	Roger McDowell	22
1991	Tommy Greene	3.38	Tommy Greene	10.7	Terry Mulholland	232.0	Tommy Greene	154	Terry Mulholland	16	Mitch Williams	30
1992	Curt Schilling	2.35	Curt Schilling	8.9	Terry Mulholland	229.0	Curt Schilling	147	Curt Schilling	14	Mitch Williams	29
1993	Terry Mulholland	3.25	Terry Mulholland	10.4	Curt Schilling	235.1	Curt Schilling	186	Tommy Greene	16	Mitch Williams	43
									Curt Schilling			
1994	Danny Jackson	3.26	Danny Jackson	11.6	Danny Jackson	179.1	Danny Jackson	129	Danny Jackson	14	Doug Jones	27
1995	Paul Quantrill	4.67	Paul Quantrill	13.1	Paul Quantrill	179.1	Curt Schilling	114	Paul Quantrill	11	Heathcliff Slocumb	32
1996	Curt Schilling	3.19	Curt Schilling	9.9	Curt Schilling	183.1	Curt Schilling	182	Curt Schilling	9	Ricky Bottalico	34
1997	Curt Schilling	2.97	Curt Schilling	9.6	Curt Schilling	254.1	Curt Schilling	319	Curt Schilling	17	Ricky Bottalico	34

Teams: Phillies

Phillies Franchise Batting Leaders—Career

Games

1	Mike Schmidt	2,404
2	Richie Ashburn	1,794
3	Larry Bowa	1,739
4	Tony Taylor	1,669
5	Del Ennis	1,630
6	Ed Delahanty	1,555
7	Sherry Magee	1,521
8	Puddin' Head Jones	1,520
9	Granny Hamner	1,501
10	Cy Williams	1,463
11	Johnny Callison	1,432
12	Chuck Klein	1,405
13	Garry Maddox	1,328
14	Fred Luderus	1,311
15	Mickey Doolan	1,302
16	Greg Luzinski	1,289
17	Roy Thomas	1,286
18	John Titus	1,219
19	Red Dooin	1,215
20	Von Hayes	1,208

At-Bats

1	Mike Schmidt	8,352
2	Richie Ashburn	7,122
3	Larry Bowa	6,815
4	Ed Delahanty	6,359
5	Del Ennis	6,327
6	Tony Taylor	5,799
7	Granny Hamner	5,772
8	Sherry Magee	5,505
9	Puddin' Head Jones	5,419
10	Johnny Callison	5,306
11	Chuck Klein	5,238
12	Cy Williams	5,077
13	Fred Luderus	4,760
14	Garry Maddox	4,696
15	Greg Luzinski	4,630
16	Roy Thomas	4,629
17	Mickey Doolan	4,572
18	Sam Thompson	4,413
19	John Titus	4,346
20	Pinky Whitney	4,322

Runs

1	Mike Schmidt	1,506
2	Ed Delahanty	1,367
3	Richie Ashburn	1,114
4	Chuck Klein	963
5	Sam Thompson	924
6	Roy Thomas	923
7	Sherry Magee	898
8	Del Ennis	891
9	Billy Hamilton	874
10	Cy Williams	825
11	Larry Bowa	816
12	Johnny Callison	774
13	Tony Taylor	737
14	Puddin' Head Jones	735
15	Granny Hamner	707
16	Dick Allen	697
17	Bill Hallman	676
18	John Titus	649
19	Von Hayes	646
20	Greg Luzinski	618

Hits

1	Mike Schmidt	2,234
2	Richie Ashburn	2,217
3	Ed Delahanty	2,213
4	Del Ennis	1,812
5	Larry Bowa	1,798
6	Chuck Klein	1,705
7	Sherry Magee	1,647
8	Cy Williams	1,553
9	Granny Hamner	1,518
10	Tony Taylor	1,511
11	Sam Thompson	1,469
12	Johnny Callison	1,438
13	Puddin' Head Jones	1,400
14	Roy Thomas	1,364
15	Garry Maddox	1,333
16	Pinky Whitney	1,329
17	Fred Luderus	1,322
18	Greg Luzinski	1,299
19	John Titus	1,209
20	Bill Hallman	1,179

Doubles

1	Ed Delahanty	442
2	Mike Schmidt	408
3	Sherry Magee	337
4	Chuck Klein	336
5	Del Ennis	310
6	Richie Ashburn	287
7	Sam Thompson	272
8	Granny Hamner	271
9	Johnny Callison	265
10	Greg Luzinski	253
11	Fred Luderus	249
	Garry Maddox	249
13	Cy Williams	237
	Pinky Whitney	237
15	Puddin' Head Jones	232
	Von Hayes	232
17	Gavy Cravath	222
18	Tony Taylor	219
19	John Titus	216
20	Larry Bowa	206

Triples

1	Ed Delahanty	157
2	Sherry Magee	127
3	Sam Thompson	106
4	Richie Ashburn	97
5	Johnny Callison	84
6	Larry Bowa	81
7	Gavy Cravath	72
8	Juan Samuel	71
9	Del Ennis	65
10	John Titus	64
	Chuck Klein	64
	Dick Allen	64
13	Mickey Doolan	63
	Tony Taylor	63
15	Nap Lajoie	62
16	Granny Hamner	61
17	Mike Schmidt	59
18	Elmer Flick	57
19	Jack Clements	53
20	Four tied at	52

Home Runs

1	Mike Schmidt	548
2	Del Ennis	259
3	Chuck Klein	243
4	Greg Luzinski	223
5	Cy Williams	217
6	Dick Allen	204
7	Johnny Callison	185
8	Puddin' Head Jones	180
9	Darren Daulton	134
10	Von Hayes	124
11	Andy Seminick	123
12	Gavy Cravath	117
13	Stan Lopata	116
14	Don Hurst	112
15	Granny Hamner	103
16	Juan Samuel	100
17	Sam Thompson	95
18	Dolph Camilli	92
19	Deron Johnson	88
20	Ed Delahanty	87

RBI

1	Mike Schmidt	1,595
2	Ed Delahanty	1,286
3	Del Ennis	1,124
4	Chuck Klein	983
5	Sam Thompson	957
6	Sherry Magee	886
7	Greg Luzinski	811
8	Cy Williams	795
9	Puddin' Head Jones	753
10	Pinky Whitney	734
11	Granny Hamner	705
12	Gavy Cravath	676
13	Johnny Callison	666
14	Dick Allen	655
15	Jack Clements	636
16	Fred Luderus	630
17	Don Hurst	598
18	Bill Hallman	571
19	Von Hayes	568
20	Darren Daulton	567

Walks

1	Mike Schmidt	1,507
2	Roy Thomas	946
	Richie Ashburn	946
4	Puddin' Head Jones	693
5	Ed Delahanty	643
6	Von Hayes	619
7	Darren Daulton	607
8	Greg Luzinski	572
9	Billy Hamilton	551
	Cy Williams	551
11	Sherry Magee	547
12	Del Ennis	539
13	John Titus	536
14	Dick Allen	517
15	Johnny Callison	513
16	Gavy Cravath	503
17	Tony Taylor	477
18	Chuck Klein	471
19	Lenny Dykstra	459
20	Andy Seminick	450

Strikeouts

1	Mike Schmidt	1,883
2	Greg Luzinski	1,098
3	Dick Allen	1,023
4	Johnny Callison	854
5	Juan Samuel	825
6	Tony Taylor	818
7	Darren Daulton	709
8	Von Hayes	677
9	Del Ennis	622
10	Andy Seminick	591
11	Tony Gonzalez	549
12	Garry Maddox	544
13	Gavy Cravath	514
14	Puddin' Head Jones	493
15	Mickey Morandini	492
16	Stan Lopata	481
17	Cy Williams	477
18	Deron Johnson	468
19	Richie Ashburn	455
	Larry Bowa	455

Stolen Bases

1	Billy Hamilton	508
2	Ed Delahanty	411
3	Sherry Magee	387
4	Jim Fogarty	289
5	Larry Bowa	288
6	Juan Samuel	249
7	Roy Thomas	228
8	Von Hayes	202
9	Richie Ashburn	199
10	Sam Thompson	189
	Garry Maddox	189
12	Mike Schmidt	174
13	Tony Taylor	169
	Lenny Dykstra	169
15	Ed Andrews	155
	Bill Hallman	155
17	Dode Paskert	149
18	Red Dooin	132
19	John Titus	131
20	Hans Lobert	125

Runs Created

1	Mike Schmidt	1,662
2	Ed Delahanty	1,546
3	Richie Ashburn	1,137
4	Chuck Klein	1,030
5	Sherry Magee	1,010
6	Sam Thompson	1,001
7	Del Ennis	978
8	Cy Williams	909
9	Roy Thomas	892
10	Billy Hamilton	869
11	Johnny Callison	829
12	Greg Luzinski	789
13	Puddin' Head Jones	761
14	Dick Allen	760
15	Gavy Cravath	703
16	John Titus	695
17	Fred Luderus	691
18	Jack Clements	685
19	Von Hayes	670
20	Larry Bowa	667

Runs Created/27 Outs

(minimum 2000 Plate Appearances)

1	Billy Hamilton	11.71
2	Ed Delahanty	9.49
3	Elmer Flick	8.89
4	Sam Thompson	8.79
5	Nap Lajoie	8.05
6	Dolph Camilli	7.48
7	Chuck Klein	7.47
8	Dick Allen	6.97
9	Mike Schmidt	6.95
10	Gavy Cravath	6.82
11	Roy Thomas	6.70
12	Jack Clements	6.70
13	Jim Fogarty	6.55
14	John Kruk	6.53
15	Cy Williams	6.44
16	Sherry Magee	6.40
17	Don Hurst	6.39
18	Lenny Dykstra	6.35
19	Greg Luzinski	6.10
20	Duff Cooley	6.04

Batting Average

(minimum 2000 Plate Appearances)

1	Billy Hamilton	.361
2	Ed Delahanty	.348
3	Nap Lajoie	.345
4	Elmer Flick	.338
5	Sam Thompson	.333
6	Chuck Klein	.326
7	Spud Davis	.321
8	Freddy Leach	.312
9	Richie Ashburn	.311
10	John Kruk	.309
11	Duff Cooley	.308
12	Pinky Whitney	.307
13	Cy Williams	.306
14	Don Hurst	.303
15	Fresco Thompson	.300
16	Sherry Magee	.299
17	Russ Wrightstone	.298
18	Dave Cash	.296
19	Tony Gonzalez	.295
20	Dolph Camilli	.295

On-Base Percentage

(minimum 2000 Plate Appearances)

1	Billy Hamilton	.468
2	Roy Thomas	.421
3	Elmer Flick	.419
4	Ed Delahanty	.415
5	John Kruk	.400
6	Dolph Camilli	.395
7	Richie Ashburn	.394
8	Lenny Dykstra	.388
9	Sam Thompson	.388
10	Chuck Klein	.382
11	Don Hurst	.382
12	Gavy Cravath	.381
13	Mike Schmidt	.380
14	Cy Williams	.380
15	Spud Davis	.374
16	Nap Lajoie	.374
17	Dick Allen	.371
18	Sherry Magee	.371
19	John Titus	.368
20	Johnny Mokan	.367

Slugging Percentage

(minimum 2000 Plate Appearances)

1	Chuck Klein	.553
2	Dick Allen	.530
3	Mike Schmidt	.527
4	Nap Lajoie	.520
5	Dolph Camilli	.510
6	Ed Delahanty	.508
7	Sam Thompson	.507
8	Cy Williams	.500
9	Gavy Cravath	.489
10	Greg Luzinski	.489
11	Don Hurst	.488
12	Elmer Flick	.487
13	Del Ennis	.479
14	John Kruk	.461
15	Freddy Leach	.460
16	Billy Hamilton	.460
17	Stan Lopata	.459
18	Johnny Callison	.457
19	Spud Davis	.449
20	Sherry Magee	.447

Phillies Franchise Pitching Leaders—Career

Wins

1	Steve Carlton	241
2	Robin Roberts	234
3	Pete Alexander	190
4	Chris Short	132
5	Curt Simmons	115
6	Al Orth	100
7	Charlie Ferguson	99
8	Jack Taylor	96
9	Tully Sparks	95
10	Kid Carsey	94
11	Bill Duggleby	90
12	Jim Bunning	89
13	Eppa Rixey	87
14	Larry Christenson	83
15	Kid Gleason	78
	Dick Ruthven	78
17	Charlie Buffinton	77
18	Erskine Mayer	76
19	Six tied at	75

Losses

1	Robin Roberts	199
2	Steve Carlton	161
3	Chris Short	127
4	Curt Simmons	110
5	Eppa Rixey	103
6	Bill Duggleby	98
	Jimmy Ring	98
8	Tully Sparks	95
9	Pete Alexander	91
10	Hugh Mulcahy	89
11	Ray Benge	82
12	Phil Collins	79
13	Jack Taylor	77
14	Chick Fraser	76
	Rick Wise	76
16	Jim Bunning	73
17	Al Orth	72
18	Kid Carsey	71
	Larry Christenson	71
20	Kid Gleason	70

Winning Percentage
(minimum 100 decisions)

1	Pete Alexander	.676
2	Charlie Ferguson	.607
3	Charlie Buffinton	.606
4	Red Donahue	.600
5	Steve Carlton	.600
6	Al Orth	.581
7	Gus Weyhing	.573
8	Kid Carsey	.570
9	Jim Lonborg	.556
	Curt Schilling	.556
11	Jack Taylor	.555
12	Erskine Mayer	.555
13	Shane Rawley	.551
14	Dan Casey	.550
15	Jim Bunning	.549
16	Frank Corridon	.546
17	Dick Ruthven	.545
18	Robin Roberts	.540
19	Larry Christenson	.539
20	Kid Gleason	.527

Games

1	Robin Roberts	529
2	Steve Carlton	499
3	Tug McGraw	463
4	Chris Short	459
5	Ron Reed	458
6	Turk Farrell	359
7	Pete Alexander	338
8	Jack Baldschun	333
9	Curt Simmons	325
10	Jim Konstanty	314
11	Don Carman	312
12	Kent Tekulve	291
13	Phil Collins	265
14	Bob Miller	261
15	Eppa Rixey	252
16	Gene Garber	250
17	Larry Christenson	243
18	Larry Andersen	241
19	Bill Duggleby	230
20	Jim Bunning	226

Games Started

1	Steve Carlton	499
2	Robin Roberts	472
3	Chris Short	301
4	Pete Alexander	280
5	Curt Simmons	262
6	Larry Christenson	220
7	Jim Bunning	208
8	Tully Sparks	198
	Dick Ruthven	198
10	Eppa Rixey	196
11	Jimmy Ring	192
12	Bill Duggleby	186
13	Rick Wise	178
14	Jim Lonborg	175
15	Al Orth	173
16	Charlie Ferguson	170
17	Jack Taylor	168
18	Kid Carsey	167
19	Kevin Gross	164
20	Terry Mulholland	158

Complete Games

1	Robin Roberts	272
2	Pete Alexander	220
3	Steve Carlton	185
4	Charlie Ferguson	165
5	Bill Duggleby	156
6	Jack Taylor	150
	Tully Sparks	150
8	Al Orth	149
9	Kid Carsey	141
10	Chick Fraser	133
11	Kid Gleason	132
12	Dan Casey	128
13	Charlie Buffinton	115
14	Red Donahue	114
15	Eppa Rixey	110
16	Curt Simmons	109
17	Gus Weyhing	104
18	Jimmy Ring	102
19	Chris Short	88
20	Frank Corridon	81

Shutouts

1	Pete Alexander	61
2	Steve Carlton	39
3	Robin Roberts	35
4	Chris Short	24
5	Jim Bunning	23
6	Tully Sparks	18
	Curt Schilling	18
8	George McQuillan	17
	Earl Moore	17
10	Bill Duggleby	16
	Eppa Rixey	16
12	Al Orth	14
13	Charlie Ferguson	13
	Rick Wise	13
	Woodie Fryman	13
16	Dan Casey	11
	Chick Fraser	11
	Erskine Mayer	11
	Larry Jackson	11
20	Twelve tied at	10

Saves

1	Steve Bedrosian	103
2	Mitch Williams	102
3	Tug McGraw	94
4	Ron Reed	90
5	Ricky Bottalico	69
6	Turk Farrell	65
7	Jack Baldschun	59
8	Al Holland	55
9	Jim Konstanty	54
10	Gene Garber	51
11	Roger McDowell	44
12	Heathcliff Slocumb	32
13	Doug Jones	27
14	Dick Selma	26
15	Kent Tekulve	25
16	Robin Roberts	24
17	Syl Johnson	23
18	Phil Collins	22
	Andy Karl	22
20	Six tied at	21

Innings Pitched

1	Robin Roberts	3,739.1
2	Steve Carlton	3,697.1
3	Pete Alexander	2,513.2
4	Chris Short	2,253.0
5	Curt Simmons	1,939.2
6	Tully Sparks	1,698.0
7	Bill Duggleby	1,684.0
8	Eppa Rixey	1,604.0
9	Jim Bunning	1,520.2
10	Charlie Ferguson	1,514.2
11	Jack Taylor	1,505.1
12	Al Orth	1,504.2
13	Kid Carsey	1,470.2
14	Jimmy Ring	1,458.0
15	Larry Christenson	1,402.2
16	Kid Gleason	1,328.2
17	Chick Fraser	1,270.0
18	Dick Ruthven	1,262.2
19	Rick Wise	1,244.1
20	Phil Collins	1,236.2

Walks

1	Steve Carlton	1,252
2	Chris Short	762
3	Curt Simmons	718
	Robin Roberts	718
5	Jimmy Ring	636
6	Pete Alexander	561
7	Kid Carsey	536
8	Earl Moore	518
9	Kid Gleason	482
10	Hugh Mulcahy	480
11	Eppa Rixey	479
12	Dick Ruthven	475
13	Phil Collins	470
14	Jack Taylor	454
15	Chick Fraser	449
16	Gus Weyhing	442
17	Kevin Gross	430
18	Bill Duggleby	408
19	Larry Christenson	395
20	Claude Willoughby	394

Strikeouts

1	Steve Carlton	3,031
2	Robin Roberts	1,871
3	Chris Short	1,585
4	Pete Alexander	1,409
5	Jim Bunning	1,197
6	Curt Simmons	1,052
7	Curt Schilling	1,006
8	Larry Christenson	781
9	Charlie Ferguson	728
10	Kevin Gross	727
11	Rick Wise	717
	Dick Ruthven	717
13	Eppa Rixey	690
14	Earl Moore	651
15	Art Mahaffey	620
16	Tully Sparks	586
17	Don Carman	581
18	Wayne Twitchell	573
19	Woodie Fryman	571
20	Terry Mulholland	570

Strikeouts/9 Innings
(minimum 1000 Innings Pitched)

1	Curt Schilling	8.25
2	Steve Carlton	7.38
3	Jim Bunning	7.08
4	Chris Short	6.33
5	Kevin Gross	5.92
6	Rick Wise	5.19
7	Dick Ruthven	5.11
8	Earl Moore	5.09
9	Pete Alexander	5.04
10	Larry Christenson	5.01
11	Curt Simmons	4.88
12	Terry Mulholland	4.79
13	Robin Roberts	4.50
14	Charlie Ferguson	4.33
15	Jim Lonborg	4.32
16	Charlie Buffinton	4.14
17	Eppa Rixey	3.87
18	Dan Casey	3.64
19	Ray Benge	3.43
20	Jimmy Ring	3.41

ERA
(minimum 1000 Innings Pitched)

1	Pete Alexander	2.18
2	Tully Sparks	2.48
3	Earl Moore	2.63
4	Charlie Ferguson	2.67
5	Erskine Mayer	2.81
6	Eppa Rixey	2.83
7	Charlie Buffinton	2.89
8	Dan Casey	2.91
9	Jim Bunning	2.93
10	Steve Carlton	3.09
11	Bill Duggleby	3.20
12	Red Donahue	3.26
13	Curt Schilling	3.28
14	Chris Short	3.38
15	Kid Gleason	3.39
16	Robin Roberts	3.46
17	Al Orth	3.49
18	Chick Fraser	3.53
19	Rick Wise	3.60
20	Curt Simmons	3.66

Component ERA
(minimum 1000 Innings Pitched)

1	Pete Alexander	2.20
2	Charlie Ferguson	2.35
3	Tully Sparks	2.45
4	Curt Schilling	2.72
5	Charlie Buffinton	2.72
6	Jim Bunning	2.80
7	Eppa Rixey	2.85
8	Dan Casey	2.90
9	Steve Carlton	3.01
10	Earl Moore	3.01
11	Erskine Mayer	3.06
12	Robin Roberts	3.22
13	Terry Mulholland	3.36
14	Bill Duggleby	3.41
15	Larry Christenson	3.46
16	Chris Short	3.47
17	Al Orth	3.49
18	Kid Gleason	3.51
19	Curt Simmons	3.51
20	Red Donahue	3.54

Opponent Average
(minimum 1000 Innings Pitched)

1	Curt Schilling	.230
2	Pete Alexander	.233
3	Charlie Ferguson	.233
4	Earl Moore	.235
5	Steve Carlton	.235
6	Jim Bunning	.238
7	Dan Casey	.242
8	Charlie Buffinton	.243
9	Tully Sparks	.243
10	Chris Short	.250
11	Curt Simmons	.254
12	Robin Roberts	.256
13	Eppa Rixey	.257
14	Kevin Gross	.258
15	Kid Gleason	.258
16	Dick Ruthven	.259
17	Larry Christenson	.262
18	Erskine Mayer	.263
19	Terry Mulholland	.263
20	Chick Fraser	.265

Opponent OBP
(minimum 1000 Innings Pitched)

1	Charlie Ferguson	.270
2	Curt Schilling	.280
3	Pete Alexander	.281
4	Jim Bunning	.287
5	Charlie Buffinton	.289
6	Tully Sparks	.291
7	Robin Roberts	.292
8	Dan Casey	.295
9	Steve Carlton	.299
10	Terry Mulholland	.302
11	Larry Christenson	.313
12	Chris Short	.315
13	Erskine Mayer	.316
14	Eppa Rixey	.316
15	Rick Wise	.317
16	Curt Simmons	.321
17	Al Orth	.321
18	Jim Lonborg	.322
19	Kid Gleason	.323
20	Bill Duggleby	.324

Phillies Franchise Batting Leaders—Single Season

Games

	Player	Year	
1	Pete Rose	1979	163
2	Dick Allen	1964	162
	Johnny Callison	1964	162
	Larry Bowa	1974	162
	Dave Cash	1974	162
	Mike Schmidt	1974	162
	Dave Cash	1975	162
	Pete Rose	1980	162
	Gary Matthews	1982	162
	Pete Rose	1982	162
11	Dick Allen	1965	161
	Greg Luzinski	1973	161
	Greg Luzinski	1975	161
	Ivan DeJesus	1982	161
	Glenn Wilson	1985	161
	Juan Samuel	1985	161
	Lenny Dykstra	1993	161
18	Seven tied at		160

At-Bats

	Player	Year	
1	Juan Samuel	1984	701
2	Dave Cash	1975	699
3	Dave Cash	1974	687
4	Larry Bowa	1974	669
5	Dave Cash	1976	666
6	Juan Samuel	1985	663
7	Richie Ashburn	1949	662
	Granny Hamner	1949	662
9	Pete Rose	1980	655
	Juan Samuel	1987	655
11	Johnny Callison	1964	654
	Larry Bowa	1978	654
13	Chuck Klein	1932	650
	Larry Bowa	1971	650
15	Chuck Klein	1930	648
16	Chick Fullis	1933	647
17	Ethan Allen	1935	645
18	Richie Ashburn	1951	643
19	Eddie Waitkus	1950	641
20	Tony Taylor	1963	640

Runs

	Player	Year	
1	Billy Hamilton	1894	192
2	Billy Hamilton	1895	166
3	Chuck Klein	1930	158
4	Lefty O'Doul	1929	152
	Chuck Klein	1932	152
6	Ed Delahanty	1895	149
7	Ed Delahanty	1894	147
8	Ed Delahanty	1893	145
9	Lenny Dykstra	1993	143
10	Billy Hamilton	1891	141
11	Roy Thomas	1899	137
12	Ed Delahanty	1899	135
13	Billy Hamilton	1890	133
14	Billy Hamilton	1892	132
	Roy Thomas	1900	132
16	Sam Thompson	1895	131
	Ed Delahanty	1896	131
18	Sam Thompson	1893	130
19	Chuck Klein	1929	126
20	Dick Allen	1964	125

Hits

	Player	Year	
1	Lefty O'Doul	1929	254
2	Chuck Klein	1930	250
3	Ed Delahanty	1899	238
4	Chuck Klein	1932	226
5	Chuck Klein	1933	223
6	Sam Thompson	1893	222
7	Richie Ashburn	1951	221
8	Billy Hamilton	1894	220
9	Ed Delahanty	1893	219
	Chuck Klein	1929	219
11	Richie Ashburn	1958	215
12	Dave Cash	1975	213
13	Sam Thompson	1895	211
14	Pete Rose	1979	208
15	Pinky Whitney	1930	207
16	Dave Cash	1974	206
17	Richie Ashburn	1953	205
18	Lave Cross	1894	204
19	Fresco Thompson	1929	202
	Lefty O'Doul	1930	202

Doubles

	Player	Year	
1	Chuck Klein	1930	59
2	Ed Delahanty	1899	55
3	Chuck Klein	1932	50
4	Ed Delahanty	1895	49
5	Dick Bartell	1932	48
6	Ethan Allen	1935	46
	Von Hayes	1986	46
8	Sam Thompson	1895	45
	Chuck Klein	1929	45
10	Ed Delahanty	1896	44
	Chuck Klein	1933	44
	Lenny Dykstra	1993	44
13	Nap Lajoie	1898	43
	Pinky Whitney	1929	43
	Dick Bartell	1931	43
16	Bert Niehoff	1916	42
	Hal Lee	1932	42
	Ethan Allen	1934	42
	Pete Rose	1980	42
20	Four tied at		41

Triples

	Player	Year	
1	Sam Thompson	1894	27
2	Nap Lajoie	1897	23
3	Ed Delahanty	1892	21
	Sam Thompson	1895	21
5	George Wood	1887	19
	Juan Samuel	1984	19
7	Ed Delahanty	1893	18
	Ed Delahanty	1894	18
9	Jim Fogarty	1889	17
	Ed Delahanty	1896	17
	Elmer Flick	1901	17
	Sherry Magee	1905	17
	Sherry Magee	1910	17
14	Elmer Flick	1900	16
	Ed Delahanty	1901	16
	Sherry Magee	1908	16
	Gavy Cravath	1917	16
	Harry Walker	1947	16
	Johnny Callison	1965	16
20	Five tied at		15

Home Runs

	Player	Year	
1	Mike Schmidt	1980	48
2	Mike Schmidt	1979	45
3	Chuck Klein	1929	43
4	Cy Williams	1923	41
5	Chuck Klein	1930	40
	Dick Allen	1966	40
	Mike Schmidt	1983	40
8	Greg Luzinski	1977	39
9	Chuck Klein	1932	38
	Mike Schmidt	1975	38
	Mike Schmidt	1976	38
	Mike Schmidt	1977	38
13	Mike Schmidt	1986	37
14	Mike Schmidt	1974	36
	Mike Schmidt	1984	36
16	Greg Luzinski	1978	35
	Mike Schmidt	1982	35
	Mike Schmidt	1987	35
19	Deron Johnson	1971	34
	Greg Luzinski	1975	34

RBI

	Player	Year	
1	Chuck Klein	1930	170
2	Sam Thompson	1895	165
3	Ed Delahanty	1893	146
4	Chuck Klein	1929	145
5	Don Hurst	1932	143
6	Sam Thompson	1894	141
7	Ed Delahanty	1899	137
	Chuck Klein	1932	137
9	Ed Delahanty	1894	131
10	Greg Luzinski	1977	130
11	Gavy Cravath	1913	128
12	Nap Lajoie	1897	127
	Nap Lajoie	1898	127
14	Sam Thompson	1893	126
	Ed Delahanty	1896	126
	Del Ennis	1950	126
17	Lave Cross	1894	125
	Don Hurst	1929	125
	Del Ennis	1953	125
20	Pinky Whitney	1932	124

Walks

	Player	Year	
1	Lenny Dykstra	1993	129
2	Mike Schmidt	1983	128
3	Billy Hamilton	1894	126
4	Richie Ashburn	1954	125
5	Von Hayes	1987	121
6	Mike Schmidt	1979	120
7	Darren Daulton	1993	117
8	Roger Connor	1892	116
	Dolph Camilli	1936	116
10	Roy Thomas	1899	115
	Roy Thomas	1900	115
12	John Kruk	1993	111
13	Roy Thomas	1902	107
	Roy Thomas	1903	107
	Roy Thomas	1906	107
	Mike Schmidt	1982	107
17	Mike Schmidt	1974	106
18	Richie Ashburn	1955	105
19	Mike Schmidt	1977	104
20	Two tied at		102

Strikeouts

	Player	Year	
1	Mike Schmidt	1975	180
2	Juan Samuel	1984	168
3	Juan Samuel	1987	162
4	Dick Allen	1968	161
5	Larry Hisle	1969	152
6	Greg Luzinski	1975	151
	Juan Samuel	1988	151
8	Dick Allen	1965	150
9	Mike Schmidt	1976	149
10	Mike Schmidt	1983	148
11	Deron Johnson	1971	146
12	Dick Allen	1969	144
13	Juan Samuel	1986	142
14	Juan Samuel	1985	141
15	Greg Luzinski	1977	140
16	Larry Hisle	1970	139
17	Dick Allen	1964	138
	Mike Schmidt	1974	138
	Scott Rolen	1997	138
20	Four tied at		136

Stolen Bases

	Player	Year	
1	Billy Hamilton	1891	111
2	Jim Fogarty	1887	102
	Billy Hamilton	1890	102
4	Jim Fogarty	1889	99
5	Billy Hamilton	1894	98
6	Billy Hamilton	1895	97
7	Juan Samuel	1984	72
8	Jim Fogarty	1888	58
	Ed Delahanty	1898	58
10	Ed Andrews	1887	57
	Billy Hamilton	1892	57
12	Ed Andrews	1886	56
13	Sherry Magee	1906	55
14	Juan Samuel	1985	53
15	Sherry Magee	1910	49
16	Sherry Magee	1905	48
	Von Hayes	1984	48
18	Ed Delahanty	1895	46
	Sherry Magee	1907	46
	Milt Thompson	1987	46

Runs Created

	Player	Year	
1	Billy Hamilton	1894	187
2	Chuck Klein	1930	171
3	Ed Delahanty	1899	165
4	Ed Delahanty	1893	163
5	Ed Delahanty	1896	162
6	Billy Hamilton	1895	160
7	Ed Delahanty	1895	159
8	Lefty O'Doul	1929	157
9	Billy Hamilton	1891	156
10	Sam Thompson	1895	154
11	Chuck Klein	1932	153
12	Sam Thompson	1893	149
13	Elmer Flick	1900	145
14	Ed Delahanty	1894	144
15	Chuck Klein	1929	140
16	Chuck Klein	1933	138
17	Sam Thompson	1894	137
	Ed Delahanty	1898	137
19	Roger Connor	1892	135
20	Lefty O'Doul	1930	133

Runs Created/27 Outs

(minimum 3.1 Plate Appearances/Tm Gm)

	Player	Year	
1	Billy Hamilton	1894	14.49
2	Ed Delahanty	1895	13.99
3	Ed Delahanty	1896	13.61
4	Billy Hamilton	1893	13.17
5	Sam Thompson	1894	13.16
6	Billy Hamilton	1895	12.65
7	Ed Delahanty	1894	12.52
8	Sam Thompson	1895	12.03
9	Ed Delahanty	1899	11.95
10	Billy Hamilton	1891	11.84
11	Ed Delahanty	1893	11.32
12	Chuck Klein	1930	10.69
13	Elmer Flick	1900	10.55
14	Sam Thompson	1893	10.29
15	Lefty O'Doul	1930	10.17
16	Lefty O'Doul	1929	10.17
17	Dolph Camilli	1937	10.14
18	Billy Hamilton	1890	9.94
19	Ed Delahanty	1897	9.83
20	Mike Schmidt	1981	9.61

Batting Average

(minimum 3.1 Plate Appearances/Tm Gm)

	Player	Year	
1	Ed Delahanty	1899	.410
2	Sam Thompson	1894	.407
3	Ed Delahanty	1894	.407
4	Billy Hamilton	1894	.404
5	Ed Delahanty	1895	.404
6	Lefty O'Doul	1929	.398
7	Ed Delahanty	1896	.397
8	Sam Thompson	1895	.392
9	Billy Hamilton	1895	.389
10	Chuck Klein	1930	.386
11	Lave Cross	1894	.386
12	Lefty O'Doul	1930	.383
13	Billy Hamilton	1893	.380
14	Ed Delahanty	1897	.377
15	Harry Walker	1947	.371
16	Sam Thompson	1893	.370
17	Ed Delahanty	1893	.368
18	Chuck Klein	1933	.368
19	Elmer Flick	1900	.367
20	Nap Lajoie	1897	.361

On-Base Percentage

(minimum 3.1 Plate Appearances/Tm Gm)

	Player	Year	
1	Billy Hamilton	1894	.523
2	Ed Delahanty	1895	.500
3	Ed Delahanty	1899	.490
4	Billy Hamilton	1893	.490
5	Ed Delahanty	1894	.478
6	Ed Delahanty	1896	.472
7	Lefty O'Doul	1929	.465
8	Ed Delahanty	1899	.464
9	Sam Thompson	1894	.458
10	Roy Thomas	1899	.457
11	Roy Thomas	1903	.453
12	Lefty O'Doul	1930	.453
13	Billy Hamilton	1891	.453
14	Roy Thomas	1900	.451
15	Richie Ashburn	1955	.449
16	Dolph Camilli	1937	.446
17	Sherry Magee	1910	.445
18	Ed Delahanty	1897	.444
19	Harry Walker	1947	.443
20	Richie Ashburn	1954	.441

Slugging Percentage

(minimum 3.1 Plate Appearances/Tm Gm)

	Player	Year	
1	Chuck Klein	1930	.687
2	Sam Thompson	1894	.686
3	Chuck Klein	1929	.657
4	Sam Thompson	1895	.654
5	Chuck Klein	1932	.646
6	Mike Schmidt	1981	.644
7	Dick Allen	1966	.632
8	Ed Delahanty	1896	.631
9	Mike Schmidt	1980	.624
10	Lefty O'Doul	1929	.622
11	Ed Delahanty	1895	.617
12	Lefty O'Doul	1930	.604
13	Chuck Klein	1933	.602
14	Greg Luzinski	1977	.594
15	Dolph Camilli	1937	.587
16	Ed Delahanty	1894	.585
17	Chuck Klein	1931	.584
18	Ed Delahanty	1893	.583
19	Ed Delahanty	1899	.582
20	Dolph Camilli	1936	.577

Teams: Phillies

Phillies Franchise Pitching Leaders—Single Season

Wins

1	Kid Gleason	1890	38
2	Pete Alexander	1916	33
3	Gus Weyhing	1892	32
4	Pete Alexander	1915	31
5	Charlie Ferguson	1886	30
	Pete Alexander	1917	30
7	Dan Casey	1887	28
	Charlie Buffinton	1888	28
	Charlie Buffinton	1889	28
	Pete Alexander	1911	28
	Robin Roberts	1952	28
12	Tom Seaton	1913	27
	Pete Alexander	1914	27
	Steve Carlton	1972	27
15	Ed Daily	1885	26
	Charlie Ferguson	1885	26
	Jack Taylor	1895	26
18	Six tied at		24

Losses

1	John Coleman	1883	48
2	Charlie Ferguson	1884	25
3	Chick Fraser	1904	24
4	Ed Daily	1885	23
5	Tom Vickery	1890	22
	Kid Gleason	1891	22
	Eppa Rixey	1920	22
	Hugh Mulcahy	1940	22
	Robin Roberts	1957	22
10	Gus Weyhing	1892	21
	Jack Taylor	1896	21
	Eppa Rixey	1917	21
	Jack Scott	1927	21
	Bucky Walters	1936	21
15	Eleven tied at		20

Winning Percentage
(minimum 15 decisions)

1	Al Orth	1899	.824
2	Robin Roberts	1952	.800
	Tommy Greene	1993	.800
4	Charlie Ferguson	1886	.769
5	Steve Carlton	1981	.765
6	Larry Christenson	1977	.760
	John Denny	1983	.760
8	Pete Alexander	1915	.756
9	Steve Carlton	1976	.741
10	Tully Sparks	1907	.733
	Pete Alexander	1913	.733
	Pete Alexander	1916	.733
	Schoolboy Rowe	1946	.733
	Jim Lonborg	1977	.733
15	Steve Carlton	1972	.730
16	Steve Carlton	1980	.727
17	Red Donahue	1899	.724
18	Dick Ruthven	1978	.722
19	Mitch Williams	1991	.706
20	Two tied at		.704

Games

1	Kent Tekulve	1987	90
2	David West	1993	76
	Jerry Spradlin	1997	76
4	Jim Konstanty	1950	74
5	Dick Selma	1970	73
	Kent Tekulve	1986	73
7	Jeff Parrett	1989	72
	Roger McDowell	1990	72
9	Jack Baldschun	1964	71
	Gene Garber	1975	71
	Don Carman	1985	71
	Darrel Akerfelds	1990	71
13	Kent Tekulve	1988	70
14	Darold Knowles	1966	69
	Mitch Williams	1991	69
	Toby Borland	1996	69
	Ricky Bottalico	1997	69
18	Four tied at		68

Games Started

1	John Coleman	1883	61
2	Kid Gleason	1890	55
3	Ed Daily	1885	50
4	Gus Weyhing	1892	49
5	Charlie Ferguson	1884	47
6	Charlie Buffinton	1888	46
	Tom Vickery	1890	46
8	Charlie Ferguson	1885	45
	Charlie Ferguson	1886	45
	Dan Casey	1887	45
	Pete Alexander	1916	45
12	Dan Casey	1886	44
	Kid Gleason	1891	44
	Pete Alexander	1917	44
15	Charlie Buffinton	1889	43
16	George McQuillan	1908	42
	Pete Alexander	1915	42
18	Four tied at		41

Complete Games

1	John Coleman	1883	59
2	Kid Gleason	1890	54
3	Ed Daily	1885	49
4	Charlie Ferguson	1884	46
	Gus Weyhing	1892	46
6	Charlie Ferguson	1885	45
7	Charlie Ferguson	1886	43
	Dan Casey	1887	43
	Charlie Buffinton	1888	43
10	Tom Vickery	1890	41
11	Kid Gleason	1891	40
12	Dan Casey	1886	39
13	Pete Alexander	1916	38
14	Charlie Buffinton	1889	37
15	Pete Alexander	1915	36
16	Charlie Buffinton	1887	35
	Kid Carsey	1895	35
	Jack Taylor	1896	35
	Jack Taylor	1897	35
	Pete Alexander	1917	35

Shutouts

1	Pete Alexander	1916	16
2	Pete Alexander	1915	12
3	Pete Alexander	1913	9
4	Ben Sanders	1888	8
	Pete Alexander	1917	8
	Steve Carlton	1972	8
7	George McQuillan	1908	7
	Pete Alexander	1911	7
	Jim Bunning	1965	7
10	Thirteen tied at		6

Saves

1	Mitch Williams	1993	43
2	Steve Bedrosian	1987	40
3	Ricky Bottalico	1996	34
	Ricky Bottalico	1997	34
5	Heathcliff Slocumb	1995	32
6	Mitch Williams	1991	30
7	Al Holland	1984	29
	Steve Bedrosian	1986	29
	Mitch Williams	1992	29
10	Steve Bedrosian	1988	28
11	Doug Jones	1994	27
12	Al Holland	1983	25
13	Jim Konstanty	1950	22
	Dick Selma	1970	22
	Roger McDowell	1990	22
16	Jack Baldschun	1964	21
17	Tug McGraw	1980	20
18	Gene Garber	1977	19
	Roger McDowell	1989	19
20	Ron Reed	1978	17

Innings Pitched

1	John Coleman	1883	538.1
2	Kid Gleason	1890	506.0
3	Gus Weyhing	1892	469.2
4	Ed Daily	1885	440.0
5	Kid Gleason	1891	418.0
6	Charlie Ferguson	1884	416.2
7	Charlie Ferguson	1885	405.0
8	Charlie Buffinton	1888	400.1
9	Charlie Ferguson	1886	395.2
10	Dan Casey	1887	390.1
11	Pete Alexander	1916	389.0
12	Pete Alexander	1917	388.0
13	Tom Vickery	1890	382.0
14	Charlie Buffinton	1889	380.0
15	Pete Alexander	1915	376.1
16	Dan Casey	1886	369.0
17	Pete Alexander	1911	367.0
18	George McQuillan	1908	359.2
19	Jack Taylor	1896	359.0
20	Pete Alexander	1914	355.0

Walks

1	Tom Vickery	1890	184
2	Gus Weyhing	1892	168
3	Kid Gleason	1890	167
4	Kid Gleason	1891	165
5	Earl Moore	1911	164
6	Gus Weyhing	1893	145
7	Tom Seaton	1913	136
	Steve Carlton	1974	136
9	Pete Alexander	1911	129
10	Jose DeJesus	1991	128
11	Kid Carsey	1893	124
12	Charlie Buffinton	1889	121
	Duke Esper	1891	121
	Earl Moore	1910	121
	Kirby Higbe	1940	121
16	Hugh Mulcahy	1938	120
17	Johnny Lush	1906	119
	Jimmy Ring	1925	119
19	Kid Carsey	1895	118
20	Two tied at		116

Strikeouts

1	Curt Schilling	1997	319
2	Steve Carlton	1972	310
3	Steve Carlton	1980	286
	Steve Carlton	1982	286
5	Steve Carlton	1983	275
6	Jim Bunning	1965	268
7	Jim Bunning	1967	253
8	Jim Bunning	1966	252
9	Pete Alexander	1915	241
10	Steve Carlton	1974	240
11	Chris Short	1965	237
12	Pete Alexander	1911	227
13	Steve Carlton	1973	223
14	Kid Gleason	1890	222
15	Jim Bunning	1964	219
16	Pete Alexander	1914	214
17	Steve Carlton	1979	213
18	Charlie Ferguson	1886	212
19	Gus Weyhing	1892	202
	Chris Short	1968	202

Strikeouts/9 Innings
(minimum 1 Inning Pitched/Tm Gm)

1	Curt Schilling	1997	11.29
2	Curt Schilling	1996	8.93
3	Steve Carlton	1983	8.73
4	Steve Carlton	1982	8.71
5	Steve Carlton	1981	8.48
6	Steve Carlton	1980	8.47
7	Jim Bunning	1965	8.29
8	Steve Carlton	1972	8.06
9	Ray Culp	1963	7.79
10	Dennis Bennett	1962	7.68
11	Steve Carlton	1979	7.64
12	Jim Bunning	1967	7.53
13	Tommy Greene	1993	7.52
14	Steve Carlton	1974	7.42
15	Chris Short	1964	7.38
16	Mark Leiter	1997	7.29
17	Chris Short	1963	7.27
18	Ken Howell	1989	7.24
19	Jim Bunning	1966	7.22
20	Chris Short	1965	7.17

ERA
(minimum 1 Inning Pitched/Tm Gm)

1	Pete Alexander	1915	1.22
2	George McQuillan	1908	1.53
3	Pete Alexander	1916	1.55
4	Lew Richie	1908	1.83
5	Pete Alexander	1917	1.83
6	Eppa Rixey	1916	1.85
7	Ben Sanders	1888	1.90
8	Charlie Buffinton	1888	1.91
9	Steve Carlton	1972	1.97
10	Charlie Ferguson	1886	1.98
11	Tully Sparks	1907	2.00
12	Earl Moore	1909	2.10
13	Frank Corridon	1909	2.11
14	George McQuillan	1909	2.14
15	Tully Sparks	1906	2.16
16	Tully Sparks	1905	2.18
17	Chris Short	1964	2.20
18	Ed Daily	1885	2.21
19	Charlie Ferguson	1885	2.22
20	Bill Vinton	1884	2.23

Component ERA
(minimum 1 Inning Pitched/Tm Gm)

1	Pete Alexander	1915	1.33
2	George McQuillan	1908	1.64
3	Charlie Buffinton	1888	1.67
4	Charlie Ferguson	1886	1.74
5	Tully Sparks	1906	1.75
6	Pete Alexander	1916	1.83
7	Ben Sanders	1888	1.86
8	Curt Schilling	1992	1.86
9	Steve Carlton	1972	1.92
10	Charlie Ferguson	1885	1.93
11	Pete Alexander	1917	1.94
12	Tully Sparks	1907	1.97
13	George McQuillan	1909	1.97
14	Ed Daily	1885	1.98
15	Al Orth	1901	2.00
16	Chris Short	1964	2.10
17	Frank Corridon	1908	2.13
18	Eppa Rixey	1916	2.14
19	Lew Richie	1908	2.16
20	Bill Vinton	1884	2.17

Opponent Average
(minimum 1 Inning Pitched/Tm Gm)

1	Pete Alexander	1915	.191
2	Curt Schilling	1992	.201
3	Ray Culp	1963	.206
4	Steve Carlton	1972	.206
5	George McQuillan	1908	.207
6	Earl Moore	1909	.210
7	Charlie Ferguson	1886	.210
8	Tully Sparks	1906	.211
9	Charlie Buffinton	1888	.213
10	Ken Howell	1989	.215
11	Jim Bunning	1967	.217
12	Ed Daily	1885	.217
13	Chris Short	1964	.217
14	Steve Carlton	1980	.218
15	Wayne Twitchell	1973	.219
16	Pete Alexander	1911	.219
17	Charlie Ferguson	1885	.219
18	Steve Carlton	1979	.219
19	Tim Keefe	1892	.220
20	Bill Vinton	1884	.220

Opponent OBP
(minimum 1 Inning Pitched/Tm Gm)

1	Pete Alexander	1915	.234
2	Charlie Ferguson	1886	.244
3	Charlie Buffinton	1888	.244
4	Ben Sanders	1888	.253
5	Curt Schilling	1992	.254
6	Bill Vinton	1884	.255
7	Ed Daily	1885	.256
8	Tully Sparks	1906	.257
9	Steve Carlton	1972	.257
10	Charlie Ferguson	1885	.257
11	Pete Alexander	1916	.262
12	Robin Roberts	1952	.263
13	George McQuillan	1908	.263
14	Al Orth	1901	.265
15	Pete Alexander	1917	.266
16	Robin Roberts	1954	.266
17	Chris Short	1964	.266
18	Jim Bunning	1966	.268
19	Curt Schilling	1997	.271
20	Jim Bunning	1967	.271

Phillies Capsule

Best Season: *1980.* They edged the Expos by a single game for the National League East title before beating the Astros in the NLCS with a come-from-behind, extra-inning win in the fifth and final game. To top it all off, they defeated the Royals in a six-game World Series for the first championship in the 98-year history of the Philadelphia franchise.

Worst Season: *1883.* The Phils have had their share of lean years, but none have been worse than their inaugural season, when they lost 81 of 98 games.

Best Player: *Mike Schmidt,* who is arguably the best third baseman of all time.

Best Pitcher: *Steve Carlton.* Pete Alexander was just as good, but Carlton did more in a Phillies uniform.

Best Reliever: *Tug McGraw* and Ron Reed were Philadelphia's lefty-righty bullpen combo from 1976 to 1983, and their overall numbers as Phillies were virtually identical. During those eight seasons, the Phillies won five division titles and two pennants. McGraw gets the nod due his prominent role during the championship season of 1980.

Best Defensive Player: *Mike Schmidt* won 10 Gold Gloves, five more than any other NL third baseman. Center fielders Garry Maddox and Richie Ashburn and catcher Bob Boone were first-rate as well.

Hall of Famers: *Pete Alexander, Richie Ashburn, Ed Delahanty, Billy Hamilton, Chuck Klein, Robin Roberts, Mike Schmidt, Sam Thompson.*

Franchise All-Star Team:

C	Jack Clements	LF	Ed Delahanty
1B	Dick Allen	CF	Richie Ashburn
2B	Granny Hamner	RF	Chuck Klein
3B	Mike Schmidt	SP	Steve Carlton
SS	Larry Bowa	RP	Tug McGraw

Biggest Flakes: *Tug McGraw*

Strangest Career: *Willie Montanez* constantly changed positions, batting styles and teams. He began as a power-hitting center fielder for the Phils in 1971, batting .255 with 30 homers while finishing second in NL Rookie of the Year balloting. The next year, he slumped to .248 with only 13 homers. The season after that, he was shifted to first base, and apparently decided he wanted to swing for singles instead of homers. His average rose to .263, and then to .304, as his power output continued to slide. In early 1975, he was traded to the Giants for Garry Maddox in one of the Phillies' best deals. Montanez batted .302 that year and set a career high with 101 RBI, despite hitting only 10 dingers. He posted the best batting average of his career the following year, .317. Then he went back to swinging for the fences; his average dropped to .287 but he pushed his homer total back up to 20. From then on, both his average and his power tailed off, as he played for six different teams in five years. The last was the Phils, for whom he went 1-for-16 in 18 games in 1982.

What Might Have Been: *Ed Bouchee.* The 24-year-old first baseman had a fine rookie season in 1957, batting .293 with 17 homers and finishing second to teammate Jack Sanford in the NL Rookie of the Year voting. The following year, he was arrested for exposing himself in front of a young girl, and missed two months of the season while receiving psychiatric treatment. He had a decent year in 1959 before being traded to the Cubs in 1960, and he never managed to surpass his rookie numbers.

Best Trade: *Steve Carlton* got on the wrong side of St. Louis Cardinals owner Gussie Busch, so the Cards dealt the future Hall of Famer to the Phillies for Rick Wise in 1972. Other good trades include the one that brought Lenny Dykstra and Roger McDowell over from the Mets in exchange for Juan Samuel in 1989, the trade that netted Garry Maddox from the Giants for Willie Montanez in 1975, and the swap of outfielder Mike Anderson for Cardinals reliever Ron Reed later the same year. Curt Schilling was stolen from the Astros for Jason Grimsley in 1992.

Worst Trades: The Phillies probably have committed more trading blunders than any team this side of the Giants. Each of their two worst deals sent a future Hall of Famer to the Cubs. The first sent *Fergie Jenkins* and two other players to Chicago for an aging Larry Jackson and change. The second deal included *Ryne Sandberg* as a throw-in when the Cubs and Phils swapped shortstops in 1982. There have been many more stinkers. Shortstop Dave Bancroft was traded to the Giants for two players and cash in 1920; Bancroft played for another decade and was ultimately enshrined in Cooperstown. Dolph Camilli was half-traded, half-sold to Brooklyn in 1938. Smoky Burgess was traded to the Reds in a six-player deal in 1955 that netted the Phils virtually nothing. Burgess played solidly for another decade. Eppa Rixey was sent to the Reds for Jimmy Ring and a player in 1920. Ring pitched well for Philadelphia for five years, but Rixey pitched even more effectively for Cincinnati—for twice as long. The great Pete Alexander was sent to the Cubs for a couple of not-so-great players and a great amount of money in 1920.

Best-Looking Player: *Chuck Klein.*

Ugliest Player: *Greg Luzinski.*

Best Nicknames: *Sheriff Blake, Blix Donnelly, Willie "Puddin' Head" Jones, Bill "Swish" Nicholson, Putsy Caballero, Hugh "Losing Pitcher" Mulcahy.*

Most Unappreciated Player: *Dick Allen.* He may not have been an angel, but he certainly deserved better treatment than he received from the Phillies' fans, who virtually booed him out of town.

Most Overrated Player: Shortstop *Larry Bowa* was celebrated for his surehandedness, while his unremarkable range and tepid hitting were overlooked.

Most Admirable Star: *Richie Ashburn.*

Least Admirable Star: *John Denny.* To phrase it in a way that won't invite a lawsuit, Denny just didn't like people.

Left Out: *Jack Clements* and *Bill Hulen.* The Phillies had the major leagues' last regular lefthanded-throwing catcher (Jack Clements, 1895) and the last regular lefthanded shortstop (Bill Hulen, 1896).

Best Season, Player: *Mike Schmidt, 1981.* Chuck Klein won the NL Triple Crown in 1933, but Schmidt nearly did the same in 1981—and his year was better. He led the league with 31 home runs and 91 RBI in only 107 games, and finished third in the batting race with a .316 average, nine points behind NL batting champ Pete Rose. He led the loop in on-base and slugging percentage by wide margins, and topped the charts in runs and walks as well. On defense, he won his sixth straight Gold Glove.

Best Season, Pitcher: *Steve Carlton, 1972.* He went 27-10 for a club that finished 59-97. A tip of the cap goes to Robin Roberts for his 28-win 1952 season, Kid Gleason for his 38 wins in 1890, Pete Alexander for his impeccable work in 1915 and 1916 (31-10 and 33-12), and Curt Schilling for his strong pitching for a weak club in 1997 (17-11, 2.97).

Most Impressive Individual Record: *Steve Carlton.* In 1972, he singlehandedly accounted for nearly half of the Phillies' victories, receiving credit for 27 of their 59 wins. No 20th-century pitcher has won a higher percentage of his team's games in a single season.

Biggest Tragedies: *Walt Lerian* and *Mickey Finn.* Lerian, the Phils' regular catcher in 1928 and 1929, was struck and killed by a car in October 1929. Finn died of complications from a duodenal ulcer in 1933.

Fan Favorite: *Tug McGraw.*

—Mat Olkin

Pittsburgh Pirates (1882-1997)

Year	Lg	Pos	W-L	Pct	GB	Manager	Att.	R	OR	HR	Avg	OBP	Slg	Opponent HR	Avg	OBP	ERA	Park Index Runs	HR
1882	AA	4th	39-39	.500	15.0	Al Pratt	—	428	418	18	.251	.274	.348	4	.245	.267	2.79	92	263
1883	AA	7th	31-67	.316	35.0	Al Pratt/Ormond Butler/Joe Battin	—	525	728	13	.247	.280	.324	21	.293	.319	4.62	96	62
1884	AA	11th	30-78	.278	45.5	McKnight/Ferguson/Battin/ Creamer/Phillips	—	406	725	2	.211	.248	.268	25	.265	.312	4.35	99	22
1885	AA	3rd	56-55	.505	22.5	Horace Phillips	—	547	539	5	.240	.282	.315	14	.232	.275	2.92	110	44
1886	AA	2nd	80-57	.584	12.0	Horace Phillips	—	810	647	16	.241	.314	.329	10	.235	.285	2.83	76	20
1887	NL	6th	55-69	.444	24.0	Horace Phillips	—	621	750	20	.258	.314	.349	39	.281	.322	4.12	86	19
1888	NL	6th	66-68	.493	19.5	Horace Phillips	—	534	580	14	.227	.264	.289	23	.249	.287	2.67	86	3
1889	NL	5th	61-71	.462	25.0	H. Phillips/F. Dunlap/N. Hanlon	—	726	801	42	.253	.320	.351	42	.282	.336	4.51	79	10
1890	NL	8th	23-113	.169	66.5	Guy Hecker	16,064	597	1235	20	.230	.299	.294	52	.297	.376	5.97	90	31
1891	NL	8th	55-80	.407	30.5	Ned Hanlon/Bill McGunnigle	128,000	679	744	29	.239	.308	.318	31	.244	.311	2.89	100	65
1892	NL	6th	37-39	.487	16.0	Al Buckenberger/Tom Burns													
	NL	4th	43-34	.558	10.5	Tom Burns/Al Buckenberger	177,205	802	796	38	.236	.297	.322	28	.245	.314	3.10	86	179
1893	NL	2nd	81-48	.628	5.0	Al Buckenberger	184,000	970	766	37	.299	.377	.411	29	.264	.335	4.08	107	77
1894	NL	7th	65-65	.500	25.0	Al Buckenberger/Connie Mack	159,000	955	972	48	.312	.379	.443	39	.318	.376	5.60	88	56
1895	NL	7th	71-61	.538	17.0	Connie Mack	188,000	811	787	26	.290	.352	.386	17	.272	.343	4.05	93	40
1896	NL	6th	66-63	.512	24.0	Connie Mack	197,000	787	741	27	.292	.353	.385	18	.280	.342	4.03	82	18
1897	NL	8th	60-71	.458	32.5	Patsy Donovan	165,950	676	835	25	.276	.337	.370	22	.297	.350	4.67	92	48
1898	NL	8th	72-76	.486	29.5	Bill Watkins	150,900	634	694	14	.258	.314	.328	14	.270	.324	3.41	91	49
1899	NL	7th	76-73	.510	25.5	Bill Watkins/Patsy Donovan	251,834	834	765	27	.289	.343	.384	27	.275	.338	3.60	92	47
1900	NL	2nd	79-60	.568	4.5	Fred Clarke	264,000	733	612	26	.272	.327	.368	24	.260	.312	3.06	99	71
1901	NL	1st	90-49	.647	—	Fred Clarke	251,955	776	534	29	.286	.345	.379	20	.250	.295	2.58	93	90
1902	NL	1st	103-36	.741	—	Fred Clarke	243,826	775	440	18	.286	.344	.374	4	.240	.286	2.30	99	96
1903	NL	1st	91-49	.650	—	Fred Clarke	326,855	793	613	34	.286	.341	.393	9	.255	.316	2.91	105	115
1904	NL	4th	87-66	.569	19.0	Fred Clarke	340,615	675	592	15	.258	.314	.338	13	.248	.306	2.89	93	32
1905	NL	2nd	96-57	.627	9.0	Fred Clarke	369,124	692	570	22	.266	.320	.350	12	.248	.308	2.86	104	17
1906	NL	3rd	93-60	.608	23.5	Fred Clarke	394,877	623	470	12	.261	.324	.327	13	.245	.294	2.21	105	94
1907	NL	2nd	91-63	.591	17.0	Fred Clarke	319,506	634	510	19	.254	.325	.324	12	.241	.299	2.30	109	49
1908	NL	2nd	98-56	.636	1.0	Fred Clarke	382,444	585	469	25	.247	.309	.332	16	.223	.287	2.12	84	64
1909	NL	1st	110-42	.724	—	Fred Clarke	534,950	699	447	25	.260	.327	.353	12	.232	.284	2.07	104	74
1910	NL	3rd	86-67	.562	17.5	Fred Clarke	436,586	655	576	33	.266	.328	.360	20	.249	.310	2.83	122	90
1911	NL	3rd	85-69	.552	14.5	Fred Clarke	432,000	744	557	49	.262	.336	.372	36	.248	.306	2.84	97	70
1912	NL	2nd	93-58	.616	10.0	Fred Clarke	384,000	751	565	39	.264	.340	.398	28	.251	.323	2.85	88	55
1913	NL	4th	78-71	.523	21.5	Fred Clarke	296,000	673	585	35	.263	.319	.356	26	.260	.320	2.90	88	43
1914	NL	7th	69-85	.448	25.5	Fred Clarke	139,620	503	540	18	.233	.295	.303	27	.249	.308	2.70	79	26
1915	NL	5th	73-81	.474	18.0	Fred Clarke	225,743	557	520	24	.246	.309	.334	21	.246	.304	2.60	97	45
1916	NL	6th	65-89	.422	29.0	Nixey Callahan	289,132	484	586	20	.240	.298	.316	24	.247	.311	2.76	112	47
1917	NL	8th	51-103	.331	47.0	N. Callahan/H. Wagner/H. Bezdek	192,807	464	595	9	.238	.298	.298	14	.253	.314	3.01	101	34
1918	NL	4th	65-60	.520	17.0	Hugo Bezdek	213,610	466	412	15	.248	.315	.321	13	.243	.300	2.48	112	73
1919	NL	4th	71-68	.511	24.5	Hugo Bezdek	276,810	472	466	17	.249	.306	.325	23	.244	.290	2.88	108	59
1920	NL	4th	79-75	.513	14.0	George Gibson	429,037	530	552	16	.257	.310	.332	25	.261	.301	2.89	99	32
1921	NL	2nd	90-63	.588	4.0	George Gibson	701,567	692	595	37	.285	.330	.387	37	.271	.316	3.17	100	46
1922	NL	3rd	85-69	.552	8.0	George Gibson/Bill McKechnie	523,675	865	736	52	.308	.360	.419	52	.296	.343	3.98	105	56
1923	NL	3rd	87-67	.565	8.5	Bill McKechnie	611,082	786	696	49	.295	.347	.404	53	.284	.337	3.87	90	32
1924	NL	3rd	90-63	.588	3.0	Bill McKechnie	736,883	724	588	44	.287	.336	.400	42	.267	.333	3.27	108	75
1925	NL	1st	95-58	.621	—	Bill McKechnie	804,354	912	715	78	.307	.369	.449	81	.287	.339	3.87	101	57
1926	NL	3rd	84-69	.549	4.5	Bill McKechnie	798,542	769	689	44	.285	.343	.396	50	.272	.334	3.67	127	56
1927	NL	1st	94-60	.610	—	Donie Bush	869,720	817	659	54	.305	.361	.412	58	.267	.323	3.66	98	71
1928	NL	4th	85-67	.559	9.0	Donie Bush	495,070	837	704	52	.309	.364	.421	66	.274	.335	3.95	115	33
1929	NL	2nd	88-65	.575	10.5	Donie Bush/Jewel Ens	491,377	904	780	60	.303	.364	.430	96	.284	.340	4.36	104	70
1930	NL	5th	80-74	.519	12.0	Jewel Ens	357,795	891	928	86	.303	.365	.449	128	.313	.367	5.24	95	57
1931	NL	5th	75-79	.487	26.0	Jewel Ens	260,392	636	691	41	.266	.330	.360	55	.274	.331	3.66	102	75
1932	NL	2nd	86-68	.558	4.0	George Gibson	287,262	701	711	48	.285	.333	.395	86	.270	.314	3.75	98	55
1933	NL	2nd	87-67	.565	5.0	George Gibson	288,747	667	619	39	.285	.333	.383	54	.264	.308	3.27	89	37
1934	NL	5th	74-76	.493	19.5	George Gibson/Pie Traynor	322,622	735	713	52	.287	.344	.398	78	.284	.332	4.20	114	81
1935	NL	4th	86-67	.562	13.5	Pie Traynor	352,885	743	647	66	.285	.343	.402	63	.265	.307	3.42	112	78
1936	NL	4th	84-70	.545	8.0	Pie Traynor	372,524	804	718	60	.286	.349	.397	74	.269	.318	3.89	91	57
1937	NL	3rd	86-68	.558	10.0	Pie Traynor	459,679	704	646	47	.285	.343	.384	71	.264	.321	3.56	102	52
1938	NL	2nd	86-64	.573	2.0	Pie Traynor	641,033	707	630	65	.279	.340	.388	71	.266	.324	3.46	98	45
1939	NL	6th	68-85	.444	28.5	Pie Traynor	376,734	666	721	63	.276	.338	.384	70	.287	.342	4.15	102	65
1940	NL	4th	78-76	.506	22.5	Frank Frisch	507,934	809	783	76	.276	.346	.394	72	.283	.345	4.36	95	52
1941	NL	4th	81-73	.526	19.0	Frank Frisch	482,241	690	643	56	.268	.338	.368	66	.260	.323	3.48	105	65
1942	NL	5th	66-81	.449	36.5	Frank Frisch	448,897	585	631	54	.245	.320	.330	62	.262	.320	3.58	105	43
1943	NL	4th	80-74	.519	25.0	Frank Frisch	498,740	669	605	42	.262	.335	.357	44	.263	.341	3.08	107	65
1944	NL	2nd	90-63	.588	14.5	Frank Frisch	604,278	744	662	70	.265	.338	.379	65	.265	.321	3.44	115	66
1945	NL	4th	82-72	.532	16.0	Frank Frisch	604,694	753	686	72	.267	.342	.377	61	.272	.330	3.76	106	69
1946	NL	7th	63-91	.409	34.0	Frank Frisch/Spud Davis	749,962	552	668	60	.250	.328	.344	50	.268	.341	3.72	112	75
1947	NL	7th	62-92	.403	32.0	Billy Herman/Bill Burwell	1,283,531	744	817	156	.263	.340	.406	155	.275	.341	4.68	111	141
1948	NL	4th	83-71	.539	8.5	Billy Meyer	1,517,021	706	699	108	.263	.338	.380	120	.260	.334	4.15	113	136
1949	NL	6th	71-83	.461	26.0	Billy Meyer	1,449,435	681	760	126	.259	.332	.384	142	.276	.346	4.57	105	131
1950	NL	8th	57-96	.373	33.5	Billy Meyer	1,166,267	681	857	138	.264	.338	.406	152	.275	.353	4.96	112	121
1951	NL	7th	64-90	.416	32.5	Billy Meyer	980,590	689	845	137	.258	.331	.397	157	.274	.354	4.79	125	113
1952	NL	8th	42-112	.273	54.5	Billy Meyer	686,673	515	793	92	.231	.300	.331	133	.266	.346	4.65	107	108
1953	NL	8th	50-104	.325	55.0	Fred Haney	572,757	622	887	99	.247	.319	.356	168	.285	.356	5.22	112	112
1954	NL	8th	53-101	.344	44.0	Fred Haney	475,494	557	845	76	.248	.323	.350	128	.287	.354	4.92	99	46
1955	NL	8th	60-94	.390	38.5	Fred Haney	469,397	560	767	91	.244	.308	.361	142	.281	.354	4.39	97	57
1956	NL	7th	66-88	.429	27.0	Bobby Bragan	949,878	588	653	110	.257	.307	.380	142	.267	.327	3.74	100	58
1957	NL	7th	62-92	.403	33.0	Bobby Bragan/Danny Murtaugh	850,732	586	696	92	.268	.315	.384	158	.270	.323	3.88	86	41
1958	NL	2nd	84-70	.545	8.0	Danny Murtaugh	1,311,988	662	607	134	.264	.317	.410	123	.261	.323	3.56	85	46
1959	NL	4th	78-76	.506	9.0	Danny Murtaugh	1,359,917	651	680	112	.265	.320	.384	134	.267	.320	3.90	105	68
1960	NL	1st	95-59	.617	—	Danny Murtaugh	1,705,828	734	593	120	.276	.335	.407	105	.257	.307	3.49	96	63
1961	NL	6th	75-79	.487	18.0	Danny Murtaugh	1,199,128	694	675	128	.273	.328	.410	121	.274	.326	3.92	98	71

Year	Lg	Pos	W-L	Pct	GB	Manager	Att.	R	OR	HR	Avg	OBP	Slg	Opponent HR	Opponent Avg	Opponent OBP	ERA	Park Index Runs	Park Index HR
1962	NL	4th	93-68	.578	8.0	Danny Murtaugh	1,090,648	706	626	108	.268	.321	.394	118	.262	.320	3.37	101	84
1963	NL	8th	74-88	.457	25.0	Danny Murtaugh	783,648	567	595	108	.250	.309	.359	99	.249	.311	3.10	96	75
1964	NL	6th	80-82	.494	13.0	Danny Murtaugh	759,496	663	636	121	.264	.315	.389	92	.260	.320	3.52	102	68
1965	NL	3rd	90-72	.556	7.0	Harry Walker	909,279	675	580	111	.265	.317	.382	89	.241	.304	3.01	97	60
1966	NL	3rd	92-70	.568	3.0	Harry Walker	1,196,618	759	641	158	.279	.329	.428	125	.261	.321	3.52	100	51
1967	NL	6th	81-81	.500	20.5	Harry Walker/Danny Murtaugh	907,012	679	693	91	.277	.324	.380	108	.261	.330	3.74	101	86
1968	NL	6th	80-82	.494	17.0	Larry Shepard	693,485	583	532	80	.252	.306	.343	73	.240	.304	2.74	100	70
1969	NL	3rd-E	88-74	.543	12.0	Larry Shepard/Alex Grammas	769,369	725	652	119	.277	.334	.398	96	.248	.320	3.61	88	52
1970	NL	1st-E	89-73	.549	—	Danny Murtaugh	1,341,947	729	664	130	.270	.325	.406	106	.255	.334	3.70	91	54
1971	NL	1st-E	97-65	.599	—	Danny Murtaugh	1,501,132	788	599	154	.274	.330	.416	108	.257	.316	3.31	96	80
1972	NL	1st-E	96-59	.619	—	Bill Virdon	1,427,460	691	512	110	.274	.324	.397	90	.243	.302	2.81	102	76
1973	NL	3rd-E	80-82	.494	2.5	Bill Virdon/Danny Murtaugh	1,319,913	704	693	154	.261	.315	.405	110	.258	.329	3.73	83	76
1974	NL	1st-E	88-74	.543	—	Danny Murtaugh	1,110,552	751	657	114	.274	.335	.391	93	.256	.323	3.49	94	62
1975	NL	1st-E	92-69	.571	—	Danny Murtaugh	1,270,018	712	565	138	.263	.323	.402	79	.243	.313	3.01	95	100
1976	NL	2nd-E	92-70	.568	9.0	Danny Murtaugh	1,025,945	708	630	110	.267	.321	.391	95	.253	.310	3.36	100	92
1977	NL	2nd-E	96-66	.593	5.0	Chuck Tanner	1,237,349	734	665	133	.274	.331	.413	149	.252	.311	3.61	103	99
1978	NL	2nd-E	88-73	.547	1.5	Chuck Tanner	964,106	684	637	115	.257	.320	.385	103	.249	.313	3.41	111	117
1979	NL	1st-E	98-64	.605	—	Chuck Tanner	1,435,454	775	643	148	.272	.330	.416	125	.254	.311	3.41	109	124
1980	NL	3rd-E	83-79	.512	8.0	Chuck Tanner	1,646,757	666	646	116	.266	.322	.388	110	.259	.316	3.58	107	105
1981	NL	4th-E	25-23	.521	5.5	Chuck Tanner													
	NL	6th-E	21-33	.389	9.5	Chuck Tanner	541,789	407	425	55	.257	.311	.369	60	.266	.331	3.56	94	106
1982	NL	4th-E	84-78	.519	8.0	Chuck Tanner	1,024,106	724	696	134	.273	.327	.408	118	.257	.321	3.81	124	129
1983	NL	2nd-E	84-78	.519	6.0	Chuck Tanner	1,225,916	659	648	121	.264	.325	.383	109	.252	.321	3.55	106	115
1984	NL	6th-E	75-87	.463	21.5	Chuck Tanner	773,500	615	567	98	.255	.310	.363	102	.246	.308	3.11	86	85
1985	NL	6th-E	57-104	.354	43.5	Chuck Tanner	735,900	568	708	80	.247	.311	.347	107	.255	.329	3.97	109	98
1986	NL	6th-E	64-98	.395	44.0	Jim Leyland	1,000,917	663	700	111	.250	.325	.374	138	.255	.327	3.90	102	99
1987	NL	4th-E	80-82	.494	15.0	Jim Leyland	1,161,193	723	744	131	.264	.330	.403	164	.253	.324	4.20	110	111
1988	NL	2nd-E	85-75	.531	15.0	Jim Leyland	1,866,713	651	616	110	.247	.317	.369	108	.250	.311	3.47	95	92
1989	NL	5th-E	74-88	.457	19.0	Jim Leyland	1,374,141	637	680	95	.241	.311	.359	121	.248	.314	3.64	86	98
1990	NL	1st-E	95-67	.586	—	Jim Leyland	2,049,908	733	619	138	.259	.330	.405	135	.251	.305	3.40	93	81
1991	NL	1st-E	98-64	.605	—	Jim Leyland	2,065,302	768	632	126	.263	.338	.398	117	.256	.308	3.44	92	85
1992	NL	1st-E	96-66	.593	—	Jim Leyland	1,829,395	693	595	106	.255	.324	.381	101	.254	.312	3.35	99	74
1993	NL	5th-E	75-87	.463	22.0	Jim Leyland	1,650,593	707	806	110	.267	.335	.393	153	.280	.339	4.77	101	99
1994	NL	3rd-C	53-61	.465	13.0	Jim Leyland	1,222,520	466	580	80	.259	.322	.384	117	.281	.347	4.64	101	101
1995	NL	5th-C	58-86	.403	27.0	Jim Leyland	905,517	629	736	125	.259	.323	.396	130	.283	.350	4.70	113	114
1996	NL	5th-C	73-89	.451	15.0	Jim Leyland	1,326,640	776	833	138	.266	.329	.407	183	.281	.339	4.61	105	96
1997	NL	2nd-C	79-83	.488	5.0	Gene Lamont	1,657,022	725	760	129	.262	.329	.404	143	.271	.343	4.28	105	114

Team Nicknames: Pittsburgh Alleghenys 1882-1890, Pittsburgh Innocents 1891, Pittsburgh Pirates 1892-1997.

Team Ballparks: Exposition Park I (Pit) 1882, Exposition Park I & II (Pit) (shared) 1883, Recreation Park (Pit) 1884-1890, Exposition Park III (Pit) 1891-1908, Exposition Park III (Pit) & Forbes Field (shared) 1909, Forbes Field 1910-1969, Forbes Field & Three Rivers Stadium (shared) 1970, Three Rivers Stadium 1971-1997.

Teams: Pirates

Pittsburgh Pirates Individual Season Batting Leaders

Year	Batting Average		On-Base Percentage		Slugging Percentage		Home Runs		RBI		Stolen Bases	
1882	Ed Swartwood	.329	Ed Swartwood	.370	Ed Swartwood	.489	Ed Swartwood	4	Statistic unavailable		Statistic unavailable	
1883	Ed Swartwood	.356	Ed Swartwood	.391	Ed Swartwood	.475	3 tied with	3	Statistic unavailable		Statistic unavailable	
1884	Ed Swartwood	.288	Ed Swartwood	.365	Ed Swartwood	.366	Charlie Eden Mike Mansell	1	Statistic unavailable		Statistic unavailable	
1885	Tom Brown	.307	Tom Brown	.366	Tom Brown	.426	Tom Brown	4	Tom Brown	68	Statistic unavailable	
1886	Fred Carroll	.288	Tom Brown	.365	Fred Carroll	.422	Fred Carroll	5	Sam Barkley	69	Pop Smith	38
1887	Fred Carroll	.328	Fred Carroll	.383	Fred Carroll	.499	Fred Carroll	6	3 tied with	54	Doggie Miller	33
1888	Billy Sunday	.236	John Coleman	.285	Bill Kuehne	.336	Pop Smith	4	Bill Kuehne	62	Billy Sunday	71
1889	Jake Beckley	.301	Jake Beckley	.345	Jake Beckley	.437	Jake Beckley	9	Jake Beckley	97	Ned Hanlon	53
1890	Doggie Miller	.273	Doggie Miller	.357	Doggie Miller	.350	Harry Decker	5	Doggie Miller	66	Billy Sunday	56
1891	Jake Beckley	.292	Doggie Miller	.357	Jake Beckley	.419	4 tied with	4	Jake Beckley	73	Ned Hanlon	54
1892	Elmer Smith	.274	Elmer Smith	.375	Elmer Smith	.384	Jake Beckley	10	Jake Beckley	96	Patsy Donovan	40
1893	Elmer Smith	.346	Elmer Smith	.435	Elmer Smith	.525	Elmer Smith	7	Jake Beckley	106	Patsy Donovan	46
1894	Elmer Smith	.356	Jake Stenzel	.441	Jake Stenzel	.580	Jake Stenzel	13	Jake Stenzel	121	Jake Stenzel	61
1895	Jake Stenzel	.374	Jake Stenzel	.447	Jake Stenzel	.539	Jake Stenzel	7	Jake Beckley	110	Jake Stenzel	53
1896	Elmer Smith	.362	Elmer Smith	.454	Elmer Smith	.500	Elmer Smith	6	Elmer Smith	94	Jake Stenzel	57
1897	Patsy Donovan	.322	Elmer Smith	.408	Harry Davis	.473	Elmer Smith	6	Bones Ely	74	Patsy Donovan	34
1898	Patsy Donovan	.302	Patsy Donovan	.346	Jack McCarthy	.380	Jack McCarthy	4	Jack McCarthy	78	Patsy Donovan	41
1899	Jimmy Williams	.355	Jimmy Williams	.417	Jimmy Williams	.532	Jimmy Williams	9	Jimmy Williams	116	Ginger Beaumont	31
1900	Honus Wagner	.381	Honus Wagner	.434	Honus Wagner	.573	Ginger Beaumont Jimmy Williams	5	Honus Wagner	100	Honus Wagner	38
1901	Honus Wagner	.353	Honus Wagner	.416	Honus Wagner	.494	Ginger Beaumont	8	Honus Wagner	126	Honus Wagner	49
1902	Ginger Beaumont	.357	Ginger Beaumont	.404	Honus Wagner	.463	Tommy Leach	6	Honus Wagner	91	Honus Wagner	43
1903	Honus Wagner	.355	Fred Clarke	.414	Fred Clarke	.532	Ginger Beaumont Tommy Leach	7	Honus Wagner	101	Honus Wagner	46
1904	Honus Wagner	.349	Honus Wagner	.423	Honus Wagner	.520	Honus Wagner	4	Honus Wagner	75	Honus Wagner	53
1905	Honus Wagner	.363	Honus Wagner	.427	Honus Wagner	.505	Honus Wagner	6	Honus Wagner	101	Honus Wagner	57
1906	Honus Wagner	.339	Honus Wagner	.416	Honus Wagner	.459	Jim Nealon	3	Jim Nealon	83	Honus Wagner	53
1907	Honus Wagner	.350	Honus Wagner	.408	Honus Wagner	.513	Honus Wagner	6	Ed Abbaticchio Honus Wagner	82	Honus Wagner	61
1908	Honus Wagner	.354	Honus Wagner	.415	Honus Wagner	.542	Honus Wagner	10	Honus Wagner	109	Honus Wagner	53
1909	Honus Wagner	.339	Honus Wagner	.420	Honus Wagner	.489	Tommy Leach	6	Honus Wagner	100	Honus Wagner	35
1910	Honus Wagner	.320	Honus Wagner	.390	Honus Wagner	.432	John Flynn	6	Honus Wagner	81	Bobby Byrne	36
1911	Honus Wagner	.334	Honus Wagner	.423	Honus Wagner	.507	Chief Wilson	12	Chief Wilson	107	Max Carey	27
1912	Honus Wagner	.324	Honus Wagner	.395	Chief Wilson	.513	Chief Wilson	11	Honus Wagner	102	Max Carey	45
1913	Jim Viox	.317	Jim Viox	.399	Jim Viox	.427	Chief Wilson	10	Dots Miller	90	Max Carey	61
1914	Jim Viox	.265	Jim Viox	.351	Max Carey	.347	Ed Konetchy	4	Jim Viox	57	Max Carey	38
1915	Bill Hinchman	.307	Bill Hinchman	.368	Bill Hinchman	.438	Honus Wagner	6	Honus Wagner	78	Max Carey	36
1916	Bill Hinchman	.315	Bill Hinchman	.378	Bill Hinchman	.427	Max Carey	7	Bill Hinchman	76	Max Carey	63
1917	Max Carey	.296	Max Carey	.369	Max Carey	.378	William Fischer	3	Max Carey	51	Max Carey	46
1918	George Cutshaw	.285	Max Carey	.363	George Cutshaw	.395	George Cutshaw	5	George Cutshaw	68	Max Carey	58
1919	Billy Southworth	.280	Carson Bigbee	.332	Billy Southworth	.400	Billy Southworth Casey Stengel	4	Billy Southworth	61	George Cutshaw	36
1920	Max Carey	.289	Max Carey	.369	Carson Bigbee	.391	Carson Bigbee Fred Nicholson	4	Possum Whitted	74	Max Carey	52
1921	Carson Bigbee	.323	Max Carey	.395	Max Carey	.430	3 tied with	7	Charlie Grimm	71	Max Carey	37
1922	Carson Bigbee	.350	Max Carey	.408	Cotton Tierney	.515	Reb Russell	12	Carson Bigbee	99	Max Carey	51
1923	Charlie Grimm	.345	Charlie Grimm	.389	Pie Traynor	.489	Pie Traynor	12	Pie Traynor	101	Max Carey	51
1924	Kiki Cuyler	.354	Kiki Cuyler	.402	Kiki Cuyler	.539	Kiki Cuyler	9	Glenn Wright	111	Max Carey	49
1925	Kiki Cuyler	.357	Kiki Cuyler	.423	Kiki Cuyler	.598	Kiki Cuyler Glenn Wright	18	Glenn Wright	121	Max Carey	46
1926	Paul Waner	.336	Paul Waner	.413	Paul Waner	.528	4 tied with	8	Kiki Cuyler Pie Traynor	92	Kiki Cuyler	35
1927	Paul Waner	.380	Paul Waner	.437	Paul Waner	.543	Paul Waner Glenn Wright	9	Paul Waner	131	Kiki Cuyler	20
1928	Paul Waner	.370	Paul Waner	.446	Paul Waner	.547	George Grantham	10	Pie Traynor	124	Pie Traynor	12
1929	Pie Traynor	.356	Paul Waner	.424	Paul Waner	.534	Paul Waner	15	Pie Traynor	108	Adam Comorosky	19
1930	Paul Waner	.368	Paul Waner	.428	George Grantham	.534	George Grantham	18	Adam Comorosky	119	Paul Waner	18
1931	Paul Waner	.322	Paul Waner	.404	Paul Waner	.453	George Grantham	10	Pie Traynor	103	Adam Comorosky	11
1932	Paul Waner	.341	Paul Waner	.397	Paul Waner	.510	Paul Waner	8	Tony Piet	85	Tony Piet	19
1933	Arky Vaughan	.314	Arky Vaughan	.388	Arky Vaughan	.478	Gus Suhr	10	Arky Vaughan	97	Tony Piet	12
1934	Paul Waner	.362	Arky Vaughan	.431	Paul Waner	.539	Gus Suhr	14	Gus Suhr	103	Arky Vaughan	10
1935	Arky Vaughan	.385	Arky Vaughan	.491	Arky Vaughan	.607	Arky Vaughan	19	Arky Vaughan	99	Woody Jensen	9
1936	Paul Waner	.373	Arky Vaughan	.453	Paul Waner	.520	Gus Suhr	11	Gus Suhr	118	Gus Suhr	8
1937	Paul Waner	.354	Paul Waner	.413	Arky Vaughan	.463	Pep Young	9	Gus Suhr	97	Arky Vaughan	7
1938	Arky Vaughan	.322	Arky Vaughan	.433	Johnny Rizzo	.514	Johnny Rizzo	23	Johnny Rizzo	111	Arky Vaughan	14
1939	Paul Waner	.328	Arky Vaughan	.385	Paul Waner	.438	Elbie Fletcher	12	Elbie Fletcher	71	Lee Handley	17
1940	Arky Vaughan	.300	Elbie Fletcher	.418	Arky Vaughan	.453	Vince DiMaggio	19	Maurice Van Robays	116	Bob Elliott	13
1941	Elbie Fletcher	.288	Elbie Fletcher	.421	Elbie Fletcher	.457	Vince DiMaggio	21	Vince DiMaggio	100	Lee Handley	16
1942	Bob Elliott	.296	Elbie Fletcher	.417	Bob Elliott	.416	Vince DiMaggio	15	Bob Elliott	89	Johnny Barrett Vince DiMaggio	10
1943	Bob Elliott	.315	Elbie Fletcher	.395	Bob Elliott	.444	Vince DiMaggio	15	Bob Elliott	101	Frankie Gustine Jim Russell	12
1944	Jim Russell	.312	Jim Russell	.399	Bob Elliott	.465	Babe Dahlgren	12	Bob Elliott	108	Johnny Barrett	28
1945	Bob Elliott	.290	Jim Russell	.377	Jim Russell	.433	Johnny Barrett Bill Salkeld	15	Bob Elliott	108	Johnny Barrett	25
1946	Jim Russell	.277	Elbie Fletcher	.384	Ralph Kiner	.430	Ralph Kiner	23	Ralph Kiner	81	Jim Russell	11
1947	Ralph Kiner	.313	Ralph Kiner	.417	Ralph Kiner	.639	Ralph Kiner	51	Ralph Kiner	127	Jim Russell	7
1948	Stan Rojek	.290	Ralph Kiner	.391	Ralph Kiner	.533	Ralph Kiner	40	Ralph Kiner	123	Stan Rojek	24
1949	Ralph Kiner	.310	Ralph Kiner	.432	Ralph Kiner	.658	Ralph Kiner	54	Ralph Kiner	127	Johnny Hopp	9
1950	Wally Westlake	.285	Ralph Kiner	.408	Ralph Kiner	.590	Ralph Kiner	47	Ralph Kiner	118	Johnny Hopp Danny O'Connell	7
1951	Ralph Kiner	.309	Ralph Kiner	.452	Ralph Kiner	.627	Ralph Kiner	42	Ralph Kiner	109	3 tied with	4
1952	Gus Bell	.250	Ralph Kiner	.384	Ralph Kiner	.500	Ralph Kiner	37	Ralph Kiner	87	Brandy Davis	9

1474

Year	Batting Average		On-Base Percentage		Slugging Percentage		Home Runs		RBI		Stolen Bases	
1953	Danny O'Connell	.294	Cal Abrams	.368	Frank Thomas	.505	Frank Thomas	30	Frank Thomas	102	Carlos Bernier	15
1954	Frank Thomas	.298	Frank Thomas	.359	Frank Thomas	.497	Frank Thomas	23	Frank Thomas	94	Curt Roberts	6
1955	Dale Long	.291	Dale Long	.362	Dale Long	.513	Frank Thomas	25	Dale Long	79	Gene Freese	5
1956	Bill Virdon	.334	Bill Virdon	.374	Dale Long	.485	Dale Long	27	Dale Long	91	Roberto Clemente Bill Virdon	6
1957	Dick Groat	.315	Dick Groat	.350	Frank Thomas	.460	Frank Thomas	23	Frank Thomas	89	Dee Fondy	11
1958	Bob Skinner	.321	Bob Skinner	.387	Frank Thomas	.528	Frank Thomas	35	Frank Thomas	109	Bob Skinner	12
1959	Don Hoak	.294	Don Hoak	.374	Don Hoak	.399	Dick Stuart	27	Dick Stuart	78	Bob Skinner	10
1960	Dick Groat	.325	Dick Groat	.371	Dick Stuart	.479	Dick Stuart	23	Roberto Clemente	94	Bob Skinner	11
1961	Roberto Clemente	.351	Roberto Clemente	.390	Dick Stuart	.581	Dick Stuart	35	Dick Stuart	117	Joe Christopher	6
1962	Roberto Clemente	.312	Bob Skinner	.395	Bob Skinner	.504	Bob Skinner	20	Bill Mazeroski	81	Donn Clendenon	16
1963	Roberto Clemente	.320	Roberto Clemente	.356	Roberto Clemente	.470	Roberto Clemente	17	Roberto Clemente	76	Donn Clendenon	22
1964	Roberto Clemente	.339	Roberto Clemente	.388	Roberto Clemente	.484	Willie Stargell	21	Roberto Clemente	87	Donn Clendenon	12
1965	Roberto Clemente	.329	Roberto Clemente	.378	Willie Stargell	.501	Willie Stargell	27	Willie Stargell	107	Bob Bailey	10
1966	Matty Alou	.342	Willie Stargell	.381	Willie Stargell	.581	Willie Stargell	33	Roberto Clemente	119	Matty Alou	23
1967	Roberto Clemente	.357	Roberto Clemente	.400	Roberto Clemente	.554	Roberto Clemente	23	Roberto Clemente	110	Maury Wills	29
1968	Matty Alou	.332	Matty Alou	.362	Roberto Clemente	.482	Willie Stargell	24	Donn Clendenon	87	Maury Wills	52
1969	Roberto Clemente	.345	Roberto Clemente	.411	Willie Stargell	.556	Willie Stargell	29	Willie Stargell	92	Matty Alou	22
1970	Manny Sanguillen	.325	Manny Sanguillen	.344	Willie Stargell	.511	Willie Stargell	31	Willie Stargell	85	Matty Alou	19
1971	Roberto Clemente	.341	Willie Stargell	.398	Willie Stargell	.628	Willie Stargell	48	Willie Stargell	125	Gene Clines	15
1972	Al Oliver	.312	Richie Hebner	.378	Willie Stargell	.558	Willie Stargell	33	Willie Stargell	112	Vic Davalillo	14
1973	Willie Stargell	.299	Willie Stargell	.392	Willie Stargell	.646	Willie Stargell	44	Willie Stargell	119	Gene Clines	8
1974	Al Oliver	.321	Willie Stargell	.407	Willie Stargell	.537	Willie Stargell	25	Richie Zisk	100	Gene Clines	14
1975	Manny Sanguillen	.328	Manny Sanguillen	.391	Dave Parker	.541	Dave Parker	25	Dave Parker	101	Frank Taveras	17
1976	Dave Parker	.313	Dave Parker	.349	Dave Parker	.475	Bill Robinson Richie Zisk	21	Dave Parker	90	Frank Taveras	58
1977	Dave Parker	.338	Dave Parker	.397	Dave Parker	.531	Bill Robinson	26	Bill Robinson	104	Frank Taveras	70
1978	Dave Parker	.334	Dave Parker	.394	Dave Parker	.585	Dave Parker	30	Dave Parker	117	Omar Moreno	71
1979	Dave Parker	.310	Dave Parker	.380	Dave Parker	.526	Willie Stargell	32	Dave Parker	94	Omar Moreno	77
1980	Dave Parker	.295	Bill Madlock	.341	Dave Parker	.458	Mike Easler	21	Dave Parker	79	Omar Moreno	96
1981	Bill Madlock	.341	Bill Madlock	.413	Bill Madlock	.495	Jason Thompson	15	Dave Parker	48	Omar Moreno	39
1982	Bill Madlock	.319	Jason Thompson	.391	Jason Thompson	.511	Jason Thompson	31	Jason Thompson	101	Omar Moreno	60
1983	Bill Madlock	.323	Bill Madlock	.386	Bill Madlock	.444	Jason Thompson	18	Jason Thompson	76	Lee Lacy	31
1984	Lee Lacy	.321	Lee Lacy	.362	Lee Lacy	.464	Jason Thompson	17	Tony Pena	78	Marvell Wynne	24
1985	Johnny Ray	.274	Johnny Ray	.325	Johnny Ray	.375	Jason Thompson	12	Johnny Ray	70	Joe Orsulak	24
1986	Johnny Ray	.301	Johnny Ray	.363	Jim Morrison	.482	Jim Morrison	23	Jim Morrison	88	Barry Bonds	36
1987	Bobby Bonilla	.300	Andy Van Slyke	.359	Andy Van Slyke	.507	Barry Bonds	25	Andy Van Slyke	82	Andy Van Slyke	34
1988	Andy Van Slyke	.288	Barry Bonds	.368	Andy Van Slyke	.506	Andy Van Slyke	25	Bobby Bonilla Andy Van Slyke	100	Andy Van Slyke	30
1989	Bobby Bonilla	.281	Bobby Bonilla	.358	Bobby Bonilla	.490	Bobby Bonilla	24	Bobby Bonilla	86	Barry Bonds	32
1990	Barry Bonds	.301	Barry Bonds	.406	Barry Bonds	.565	Barry Bonds	33	Bobby Bonilla	120	Barry Bonds	52
1991	Bobby Bonilla	.302	Barry Bonds	.410	Barry Bonds	.514	Barry Bonds	25	Barry Bonds	116	Barry Bonds	43
1992	Andy Van Slyke	.324	Barry Bonds	.456	Barry Bonds	.624	Barry Bonds	34	Barry Bonds	103	Barry Bonds	39
1993	Orlando Merced	.313	Orlando Merced	.414	Al Martin	.481	Al Martin	18	Jeff King	98	Carlos Garcia	18
1994	Carlos Garcia	.277	Jay Bell	.353	Jay Bell	.441	Brian Hunter	11	Orlando Merced	51	Carlos Garcia	18
1995	Orlando Merced	.300	Orlando Merced	.365	Orlando Merced	.468	Jeff King	18	Jeff King	87	Jacob Brumfield	22
1996	Al Martin	.300	Orlando Merced	.357	Jeff King	.497	Jeff King	30	Jeff King	111	Al Martin	38
1997	Jason Kendall	.294	Jason Kendall	.391	Jason Kendall	.434	Kevin Young	18	Kevin Young	74	Tony Womack	60

Teams: Pirates

Pittsburgh Pirates Individual Season Pitching Leaders

Year	ERA		Baserunners/9 IP		Innings Pitched		Strikeouts		Wins		Saves	
1882	Denny Driscoll	1.21	Denny Driscoll	7.8	Harry Salisbury	335.0	Harry Salisbury	135	Harry Salisbury	20	7 tied with	0
1883	Denny Driscoll	3.99	Denny Driscoll	12.5	Denny Driscoll	336.1	Bob Barr	81	Denny Driscoll	18	Bob Barr	1
1884	Jack Neagle	3.73	Jack Neagle	12.2	Fleury Sullivan	441.0	Fleury Sullivan	189	Fleury Sullivan	16	10 tied with	0
1885	Ed Morris	2.35	Ed Morris	8.9	Ed Morris	581.0	Ed Morris	298	Ed Morris	39	8 tied with	0
1886	Ed Morris	2.45	Ed Morris	9.4	Ed Morris	555.1	Ed Morris	326	Ed Morris	41	Ed Morris	1
1887	Pud Galvin	3.29	Pud Galvin	11.6	Pud Galvin	440.2	Ed Morris	91	Pud Galvin	28	5 tied with	0
1888	Ed Morris	2.31	Ed Morris	10.4	Ed Morris	480.0	Ed Morris	135	Ed Morris	29	6 tied with	0
1889	Harry Staley	3.51	Harry Staley	11.9	Harry Staley	420.0	Harry Staley	159	Pud Galvin	23	Harry Staley	1
1890	Kirtley Baker	5.60	Kirtley Baker	15.7	Kirtley Baker	178.1	Kirtley Baker	76	Billy Gumbert	4	22 tied with	0
1891	Mark Baldwin	2.76	Pud Galvin	12.0	Mark Baldwin	437.2	Mark Baldwin	197	Mark Baldwin	22	Silver King Al Maul	1
1892	Adonis Terry	2.51	Red Ehret	10.6	Mark Baldwin	440.1	Mark Baldwin	157	Mark Baldwin	26	Adonis Terry	1
1893	Red Ehret	3.44	Frank Killen	11.7	Frank Killen	415.0	Frank Killen	99	Frank Killen	36	Tom Colcolough	1
1894	Frank Killen	4.50	Red Ehret	14.8	Red Ehret	346.2	Red Ehret	102	Red Ehret	19	11 tied with	0
1895	Pink Hawley	3.18	Pink Hawley	11.6	Pink Hawley	444.1	Pink Hawley	142	Pink Hawley	31	Brownie Foreman Jake Hewitt	2
1896	Frank Killen	3.41	Frank Killen	12.4	Frank Killen	432.1	Pink Hawley	137	Frank Killen	30	Charlie Hastings	1
1897	Jesse Tannehill	4.25	Jesse Tannehill	12.9	Frank Killen	337.1	Frank Killen	99	Pink Hawley	18	Jim Hughey Jesse Tannehill	1
1898	Jesse Tannehill	2.95	Jesse Tannehill	11.4	Jesse Tannehill	326.2	Jesse Tannehill	93	Jesse Tannehill	25	Jesse Tannehill	2
1899	Jesse Tannehill	2.73	Sam Leever	11.5	Sam Leever	379.0	Sam Leever	121	Jesse Tannehill	24	Sam Leever	3
1900	Rube Waddell	2.37	Deacon Phillippe	10.5	Deacon Phillippe	279.0	Rube Waddell	130	Deacon Phillippe Jesse Tannehill	20	Jack Chesbro	1
1901	Jesse Tannehill	2.18	Deacon Phillippe	9.8	Deacon Phillippe	296.0	Jack Chesbro	129	Deacon Phillippe	22	Deacon Phillippe	2
1902	Jesse Tannehill	1.95	Jesse Tannehill	9.3	Jack Chesbro	286.1	Jack Chesbro	136	Jack Chesbro	28	Sam Leever	2
1903	Sam Leever	2.06	Deacon Phillippe	9.4	Deacon Phillippe	289.1	Deacon Phillippe	123	Sam Leever Deacon Phillippe	25	Ed Doheny Deacon Phillippe	2
1904	Patsy Flaherty	2.05	Sam Leever	10.1	Sam Leever	253.1	Mike Lynch	95	Patsy Flaherty	19	Deacon Phillippe	1
1905	Deacon Phillippe	2.19	Deacon Phillippe	9.5	Deacon Phillippe	279.0	Deacon Phillippe	133	Sam Leever Deacon Phillippe	20	Mike Lynch	2
1906	Vic Willis	1.73	Sam Leever	9.9	Vic Willis	322.0	Vic Willis	124	Vic Willis	23	Lefty Leifield Vic Willis	1
1907	Sam Leever	1.66	Vic Willis	9.5	Vic Willis	292.2	Lefty Leifield	112	Vic Willis	21	Deacon Phillippe	2
1908	Howie Camnitz	1.56	Vic Willis	9.3	Vic Willis	304.2	Howie Camnitz	118	Nick Maddox Vic Willis	23	3 tied with	2
1909	Howie Camnitz	1.62	Howie Camnitz	9.0	Vic Willis	289.2	Howie Camnitz	133	Howie Camnitz	25	Howie Camnitz	3
1910	Babe Adams	2.24	Babe Adams	10.4	Howie Camnitz	260.0	Howie Camnitz	120	Babe Adams	18	Deacon Phillippe	4
1911	Babe Adams	2.33	Babe Adams	9.3	Lefty Leifield	318.0	Howie Camnitz	139	Babe Adams	22	Jack Ferry	3
1912	Hank Robinson	2.26	Hank Robinson	9.6	Claude Hendrix	288.2	Claude Hendrix	176	Claude Hendrix	24	Howie Camnitz Hank Robinson	2
1913	Babe Adams	2.15	Babe Adams	9.2	Babe Adams	313.2	Babe Adams	144	Babe Adams	21	Claude Hendrix	3
1914	Wilbur Cooper	2.13	Babe Adams	9.5	Babe Adams	283.0	Wilbur Cooper	102	Wilbur Cooper	16	George McQuillan	4
1915	Al Mamaux	2.04	Babe Adams	9.7	Bob Harmon	269.2	Al Mamaux	152	Al Mamaux	21	Wilbur Cooper	4
1916	Wilbur Cooper	1.87	Wilbur Cooper	9.8	Al Mamaux	310.0	Al Mamaux	163	Al Mamaux	21	3 tied with	2
1917	Wilbur Cooper	2.36	Wilbur Cooper	10.1	Wilbur Cooper	297.2	Wilbur Cooper	99	Wilbur Cooper	17	Elmer Jacobs	2
1918	Wilbur Cooper	2.11	Wilbur Cooper	9.7	Wilbur Cooper	273.1	Wilbur Cooper	117	Wilbur Cooper	19	Wilbur Cooper	3
1919	Babe Adams	1.98	Babe Adams	8.2	Wilbur Cooper	286.2	Wilbur Cooper	106	Wilbur Cooper	19	4 tied with	1
1920	Babe Adams	2.16	Babe Adams	8.9	Wilbur Cooper	327.0	Wilbur Cooper	114	Wilbur Cooper	24	Hal Carlson Earl Hamilton	3
1921	Babe Adams	2.64	Babe Adams	9.7	Wilbur Cooper	327.0	Wilbur Cooper	134	Wilbur Cooper	22	Hal Carlson Jimmy Zinn	4
1922	Wilbur Cooper	3.18	Babe Adams	11.0	Wilbur Cooper	294.2	Wilbur Cooper	129	Wilbur Cooper	23	Hal Carlson Earl Hamilton	2
1923	Lee Meadows	3.01	Lee Meadows	11.7	Johnny Morrison	301.2	Johnny Morrison	114	Johnny Morrison	25	Jim Bagby	3
1924	Emil Yde	2.83	Johnny Morrison	11.0	Wilbur Cooper	268.2	Johnny Morrison	85	Wilbur Cooper	20	Johnny Morrison	2
1925	Vic Aldridge	3.63	Ray Kremer	12.1	Lee Meadows	255.1	Vic Aldridge	88	Lee Meadows	19	Emil Yde	4
1926	Ray Kremer	2.61	Ray Kremer	10.7	Ray Kremer	231.1	Ray Kremer	74	Ray Kremer Lee Meadows	20	Ray Kremer	5
1927	Ray Kremer	2.47	Ray Kremer	10.3	Lee Meadows	299.1	Carmen Hill	95	Carmen Hill	22	Johnny Morrison	3
1928	Burleigh Grimes	2.99	Burleigh Grimes	10.8	Burleigh Grimes	330.2	Burleigh Grimes	97	Burleigh Grimes	25	Joe Dawson Burleigh Grimes	3
1929	Burleigh Grimes	3.13	Ray Kremer	11.7	Burleigh Grimes	232.2	Erv Brame	68	Ray Kremer	18	Steve Swetonic	5
1930	Larry French	4.36	Erv Brame	13.4	Ray Kremer	276.0	Larry French	90	Ray Kremer	20	Steve Swetonic	5
1931	Heinie Meine	2.98	Heinie Meine	11.8	Heinie Meine	284.0	Larry French	73	Heinie Meine	19	Glenn Spencer	3
1932	Steve Swetonic	2.82	Bill Swift	9.8	Larry French	274.1	Larry French	72	Larry French	18	Larry French Bill Swift	4
1933	Larry French	2.72	Bill Swift	10.5	Larry French	291.1	Larry French	88	Larry French	18	Bill Harris	5
1934	Waite Hoyt	2.93	Waite Hoyt	10.8	Larry French	263.2	Waite Hoyt	105	Waite Hoyt	15	Waite Hoyt	5
1935	Cy Blanton	2.58	Cy Blanton	9.8	Cy Blanton	254.1	Cy Blanton	142	Cy Blanton	18	Waite Hoyt	6
1936	Red Lucas	3.18	Red Lucas	10.6	Bill Swift	262.1	Cy Blanton	127	Bill Swift	16	Cy Blanton Mace Brown	3
1937	Russ Bauers	2.88	Bill Swift	10.8	Cy Blanton	242.2	Cy Blanton	143	Cy Blanton	14	Mace Brown	7
1938	Bob Klinger	2.99	Bob Klinger	11.3	Russ Bauers	243.0	Russ Bauers	117	Mace Brown	15	Mace Brown	5
1939	Mace Brown	3.37	Rip Sewell	12.8	Bob Klinger	225.0	Mace Brown	71	Bob Klinger	14	Mace Brown	7
1940	Rip Sewell	2.80	Rip Sewell	11.3	Rip Sewell	189.2	Mace Brown	73	Rip Sewell	16	Mace Brown	7
1941	Max Butcher	3.05	Rip Sewell	11.3	Rip Sewell	249.0	Ken Heintzelman	81	Max Butcher	17	Bob Klinger	4
1942	Bob Klinger	3.24	Bob Klinger	11.7	Rip Sewell	248.0	Rip Sewell	69	Rip Sewell	17	Dutch Dietz	3
1943	Rip Sewell	2.54	Bob Klinger	11.2	Rip Sewell	265.1	Bob Klinger Rip Sewell	65	Rip Sewell	21	Hank Gornicki	4
1944	Fritz Ostermueller	2.73	Nick Strincevich	10.9	Rip Sewell	286.0	Preacher Roe	88	Rip Sewell	21	Xavier Rescigno	5
1945	Preacher Roe	2.87	Preacher Roe	10.5	Preacher Roe	235.0	Preacher Roe	148	Nick Strincevich	16	Xavier Rescigno	9
1946	Fritz Ostermueller	2.84	Fritz Ostermueller	11.7	Fritz Ostermueller	193.1	Jack Hallett	64	Fritz Ostermueller	13	Preacher Roe	2
1947	Kirby Higbe	3.72	Fritz Ostermueller	12.3	Kirby Higbe	225.0	Kirby Higbe	99	Fritz Ostermueller	12	Kirby Higbe	5
1948	Kirby Higbe	3.36	Vic Lombardi	12.4	Bob Chesnes	194.1	Kirby Higbe	86	Bob Chesnes	14	Kirby Higbe	10

1476

Teams: Pirates

Year	ERA		Baserunners/9 IP		Innings Pitched		Strikeouts		Wins		Saves	
1949	Murry Dickson	3.29	Murry Dickson	12.1	Murry Dickson	224.1	Bill Werle	106	Cliff Chambers	13	Hugh Casey	5
1950	Murry Dickson	3.80	Murry Dickson	12.5	Cliff Chambers	249.1	Cliff Chambers	93	Cliff Chambers	12	Bill Werle	8
1951	Murry Dickson	4.02	Murry Dickson	12.5	Murry Dickson	288.2	Mel Queen	123	Murry Dickson	20	Ted Wilks	12
1952	Murry Dickson	3.57	Murry Dickson	11.5	Murry Dickson	277.2	Murry Dickson	112	Murry Dickson	14	Ted Wilks	4
1953	Murry Dickson	4.53	Paul LaPalme	13.0	Murry Dickson	200.2	Johnny Lindell	102	Murry Dickson	10	Murry Dickson	4
1954	Dick Littlefield	3.60	Max Surkont	12.9	Max Surkont	208.1	Dick Littlefield	92	Dick Littlefield	10	Johnny Hetki	9
1955	Bob Friend	2.83	Bob Friend	10.4	Vern Law	200.2	Bob Friend	98	Bob Friend	14	Roy Face	5
1956	Ron Kline	3.38	Bob Friend	11.4	Bob Friend	314.1	Bob Friend	166	Bob Friend	17	Roy Face	6
1957	Vern Law	2.87	Vern Law	10.7	Bob Friend	277.0	Bob Friend	143	Bob Friend	14	Roy Face	10
1958	Ron Kline	3.53	Ron Kline	11.8	Bob Friend	274.0	Bob Friend	135	Bob Friend	22	Roy Face	20
1959	Vern Law	2.98	Harvey Haddix	9.6	Vern Law	266.0	Harvey Haddix	149	Roy Face Vern Law	18	Roy Face	10
1960	Bob Friend	3.00	Bob Friend	10.2	Bob Friend	275.2	Bob Friend	183	Vern Law	20	Roy Face	24
1961	Joe Gibbon	3.32	Joe Gibbon	11.3	Bob Friend	236.0	Joe Gibbon	145	Bob Friend	14	Roy Face	17
1962	Bob Friend	3.06	Bob Friend	11.5	Bob Friend	261.2	Bob Friend	144	Bob Friend	18	Roy Face	28
1963	Bob Friend	2.34	Bob Friend	9.5	Bob Friend	268.2	Bob Friend	144	Bob Friend	17	Roy Face	16
1964	Bob Veale	2.74	Vern Law	11.1	Bob Veale	279.2	Bob Veale	250	Bob Veale	18	Al McBean	22
1965	Vern Law	2.15	Vern Law	9.1	Bob Veale	266.0	Bob Veale	276	Vern Law Bob Veale	17	Al McBean	18
1966	Bob Veale	3.02	Bob Veale	11.2	Bob Veale	268.1	Bob Veale	229	Bob Veale	16	Roy Face	18
1967	Tommie Sisk	3.34	Dennis Ribant	12.0	Tommie Sisk	207.2	Bob Veale	179	Bob Veale	16	Roy Face	17
1968	Bob Veale	2.05	Bob Moose	9.5	Bob Veale	245.1	Bob Veale	171	Steve Blass	18	Roy Face	13
1969	Bob Moose	2.91	Bob Moose	11.4	Bob Veale	225.2	Bob Veale	213	Steve Blass	16	Chuck Hartenstein	10
1970	Luke Walker	3.04	Bob Moose	12.0	Bob Veale	202.0	Bob Veale	178	Luke Walker	15	Dave Giusti	26
1971	Steve Blass	2.85	Dock Ellis	10.8	Steve Blass	240.0	Dock Ellis	137	Dock Ellis	19	Dave Giusti	30
1972	Steve Blass	2.49	Bob Moose	10.5	Steve Blass	249.2	Bob Moose	144	Steve Blass	19	Dave Giusti	22
1973	Nelson Briles	2.84	Jim Rooker	10.4	Nelson Briles	218.2	Dock Ellis Jim Rooker	122	Nelson Briles	14	Dave Giusti	20
1974	Jim Rooker	2.78	Dock Ellis	10.7	Jim Rooker	262.2	Jim Rooker	139	Jerry Reuss	16	Dave Giusti	12
1975	Jerry Reuss	2.54	Jerry Reuss	11.5	Jerry Reuss	237.1	Jerry Reuss	131	Jerry Reuss	18	Dave Giusti	17
1976	Bruce Kison	3.08	John Candelaria	9.6	John Candelaria	220.0	John Candelaria	138	John Candelaria	16	Bob Moose	10
1977	John Candelaria	2.34	John Candelaria	9.7	John Candelaria	230.2	Goose Gossage	151	John Candelaria	20	Goose Gossage	26
1978	Bert Blyleven	3.03	Don Robinson	10.4	Bert Blyleven	243.2	Bert Blyleven	182	Bert Blyleven Don Robinson	14	Kent Tekulve	31
1979	Bruce Kison	3.19	John Candelaria	10.7	Bert Blyleven	237.1	Bert Blyleven	172	John Candelaria	14	Kent Tekulve	31
1980	Jim Bibby	3.32	Jim Bibby	11.5	Jim Bibby	238.1	Bert Blyleven	168	Jim Bibby	19	Kent Tekulve	21
1981	Eddie Solomon	3.12	Eddie Solomon	11.6	Rick Rhoden	136.1	Rick Rhoden	76	Rick Rhoden	9	Enrique Romo	9
1982	John Candelaria	2.94	John Candelaria	10.7	Rick Rhoden	230.1	Don Robinson	165	Don Robinson	15	Kent Tekulve	20
1983	Rick Rhoden	3.09	John Candelaria	10.8	Rick Rhoden	244.1	Larry McWilliams	199	John Candelaria Larry McWilliams	15	Kent Tekulve	18
1984	Rick Rhoden	2.72	John Candelaria	10.4	Rick Rhoden	238.1	Jose DeLeon	153	Rick Rhoden	14	Kent Tekulve	13
1985	Rick Reuschel	2.27	Rick Reuschel	9.6	Rick Rhoden	213.1	Jose DeLeon	149	Rick Reuschel	14	John Candelaria	9
1986	Rick Rhoden	2.84	Rick Rhoden	10.3	Rick Rhoden	253.2	Rick Rhoden	159	Rick Rhoden	15	Don Robinson	14
1987	Rick Reuschel	2.75	Rick Reuschel	10.4	Brian Fisher	185.1	Doug Drabek	120	Mike Dunne	13	Jim Gott	13
1988	Bob Walk	2.71	Doug Drabek	10.3	Doug Drabek	219.1	John Smiley	129	Doug Drabek	15	Jim Gott	34
1989	Doug Drabek	2.80	John Smiley	9.9	Doug Drabek	244.1	Doug Drabek	123	Doug Drabek	14	Bill Landrum	26
1990	Doug Drabek	2.76	Doug Drabek	9.7	Doug Drabek	231.1	Doug Drabek	131	Doug Drabek	22	Bill Landrum	13
1991	Randy Tomlin	2.98	John Smiley	10.4	Doug Drabek	234.2	Doug Drabek	142	John Smiley	20	Bill Landrum	17
1992	Doug Drabek	2.77	Doug Drabek	9.7	Doug Drabek	256.2	Doug Drabek	177	Doug Drabek	15	Stan Belinda	18
1993	Steve Cooke	3.89	Steve Cooke	11.5	Steve Cooke	210.2	Steve Cooke	132	Bob Walk	13	Stan Belinda	19
1994	Zane Smith	3.27	Zane Smith	11.2	Zane Smith	157.0	Denny Neagle	122	Zane Smith	10	Alejandro Pena	7
1995	Denny Neagle	3.43	Denny Neagle	11.5	Denny Neagle	209.2	Denny Neagle	150	Denny Neagle	13	Danny Miceli	21
1996	Denny Neagle	3.05	Denny Neagle	11.0	Denny Neagle	182.2	Denny Neagle	131	Denny Neagle	14	Francisco Cordova	12
1997	Francisco Cordova	3.63	Jon Lieber	11.7	Esteban Loaiza	196.1	Jon Lieber	160	3 tied with	11	Rich Loiselle	29

Teams: Pirates   1477

Pirates Franchise Batting Leaders—Career

Games

1	Honus Wagner	2,433
	Roberto Clemente	2,433
3	Willie Stargell	2,360
4	Max Carey	2,178
5	Bill Mazeroski	2,163
6	Paul Waner	2,154
7	Pie Traynor	1,941
8	Lloyd Waner	1,803
9	Tommy Leach	1,574
10	Fred Clarke	1,479
11	Bill Virdon	1,415
12	Arky Vaughan	1,411
13	Gus Suhr	1,365
14	Al Oliver	1,302
15	Dave Parker	1,301
16	Manny Sanguillen	1,296
17	Dick Groat	1,258
18	Gene Alley	1,195
19	Frankie Gustine	1,176
20	George Gibson	1,174

At-Bats

1	Roberto Clemente	9,454
2	Honus Wagner	9,034
3	Paul Waner	8,429
4	Max Carey	8,406
5	Willie Stargell	7,927
6	Bill Mazeroski	7,755
7	Pie Traynor	7,559
8	Lloyd Waner	7,256
9	Tommy Leach	5,910
10	Fred Clarke	5,472
11	Bill Virdon	5,375
12	Arky Vaughan	5,268
13	Al Oliver	5,026
14	Gus Suhr	4,953
15	Dick Groat	4,950
16	Dave Parker	4,848
17	Manny Sanguillen	4,491
18	Frankie Gustine	4,302
19	Carson Bigbee	4,192
20	Jay Bell	4,179

Runs

1	Honus Wagner	1,521
2	Paul Waner	1,492
3	Roberto Clemente	1,416
4	Max Carey	1,414
5	Willie Stargell	1,195
6	Pie Traynor	1,183
7	Lloyd Waner	1,151
8	Fred Clarke	1,015
9	Tommy Leach	1,009
10	Arky Vaughan	936
11	Patsy Donovan	839
12	Bill Mazeroski	769
13	Ginger Beaumont	757
14	Ralph Kiner	754
15	Dave Parker	728
16	Jake Beckley	699
17	Gus Suhr	689
	Al Oliver	689
19	Barry Bonds	672
20	Bill Virdon	667

Hits

1	Roberto Clemente	3,000
2	Honus Wagner	2,967
3	Paul Waner	2,868
4	Max Carey	2,416
	Pie Traynor	2,416
6	Lloyd Waner	2,317
7	Willie Stargell	2,232
8	Bill Mazeroski	2,016
9	Arky Vaughan	1,709
10	Fred Clarke	1,638
11	Tommy Leach	1,603
12	Al Oliver	1,490
13	Dave Parker	1,479
14	Dick Groat	1,435
15	Bill Virdon	1,431
16	Gus Suhr	1,379
17	Manny Sanguillen	1,343
18	Ginger Beaumont	1,292
19	Patsy Donovan	1,283
20	Carson Bigbee	1,205

Doubles

1	Paul Waner	556
2	Honus Wagner	551
3	Roberto Clemente	440
4	Willie Stargell	423
5	Max Carey	375
6	Pie Traynor	371
7	Dave Parker	296
8	Bill Mazeroski	294
9	Arky Vaughan	291
10	Gus Suhr	276
	Al Oliver	276
12	Lloyd Waner	269
13	Fred Clarke	238
14	Jay Bell	233
15	Dick Groat	226
16	Barry Bonds	220
17	Bill Virdon	217
18	Bob Elliott	213
19	Frankie Gustine	208
20	Andy Van Slyke	203

Triples

1	Honus Wagner	232
2	Paul Waner	186
3	Roberto Clemente	166
4	Pie Traynor	164
5	Fred Clarke	156
6	Max Carey	148
7	Tommy Leach	139
8	Arky Vaughan	116
9	Lloyd Waner	114
10	Jake Beckley	112
	Gus Suhr	112
12	Elmer Smith	99
13	Chief Wilson	94
14	Carson Bigbee	75
	Bill Virdon	75
16	George Grantham	69
17	Bob Elliott	68
18	Bill Kuehne	67
	Andy Van Slyke	67
20	Four tied at	65

Home Runs

1	Willie Stargell	475
2	Ralph Kiner	301
3	Roberto Clemente	240
4	Barry Bonds	176
5	Dave Parker	166
6	Frank Thomas	163
7	Bill Mazeroski	138
8	Al Oliver	135
9	Richie Hebner	128
10	Dick Stuart	117
	Andy Van Slyke	117
12	Bobby Bonilla	114
13	Paul Waner	109
	Bill Robinson	109
15	Donn Clendenon	106
	Bob Robertson	106
17	Jeff King	99
18	Wally Westlake	97
19	Jason Thompson	93
20	Bob Skinner	90

RBI

1	Willie Stargell	1,540
2	Honus Wagner	1,475
3	Roberto Clemente	1,305
4	Pie Traynor	1,273
5	Paul Waner	1,177
6	Bill Mazeroski	853
7	Ralph Kiner	801
8	Gus Suhr	789
9	Arky Vaughan	764
10	Dave Parker	758
11	Max Carey	719
12	Al Oliver	717
13	Jake Beckley	661
14	Bob Elliott	633
15	Tommy Leach	626
16	Fred Clarke	622
17	Lloyd Waner	577
18	Andy Van Slyke	564
19	Frank Thomas	562
20	Barry Bonds	556

Walks

1	Willie Stargell	937
2	Max Carey	918
3	Paul Waner	909
4	Honus Wagner	877
5	Ralph Kiner	795
6	Arky Vaughan	778
7	Gus Suhr	679
8	Fred Clarke	630
9	Elbie Fletcher	625
10	Roberto Clemente	621
11	Barry Bonds	611
12	Tommy Leach	516
13	George Grantham	488
14	Pie Traynor	472
15	Bill Mazeroski	447
16	Bob Skinner	435
17	Andy Van Slyke	431
18	Jason Thompson	430
19	Bob Elliott	429
20	Jay Bell	426

Strikeouts

1	Willie Stargell	1,936
2	Roberto Clemente	1,230
3	Donn Clendenon	840
4	Jay Bell	780
5	Dave Parker	777
6	Andy Van Slyke	733
7	Bill Mazeroski	706
8	Max Carey	646
9	Omar Moreno	633
10	Gene Alley	622
11	Barry Bonds	590
12	Bill Virdon	575
13	Ralph Kiner	546
14	Bob Skinner	525
15	Bob Robertson	498
16	Dick Stuart	483
17	Vince DiMaggio	479
18	Al Martin	474
19	Bill Robinson	469
20	Frank Thomas	465

Stolen Bases

1	Max Carey	688
2	Honus Wagner	640
3	Omar Moreno	412
4	Patsy Donovan	312
5	Tommy Leach	271
6	Fred Clarke	261
7	Barry Bonds	251
8	Doggie Miller	209
9	Frank Taveras	206
10	Ginger Beaumont	200
11	Jake Stenzel	188
12	Carson Bigbee	182
13	Billy Sunday	174
14	Elmer Smith	173
15	Pie Traynor	158
16	Lee Lacy	140
17	Jake Beckley	138
18	Andy Van Slyke	134
19	Kiki Cuyler	130
20	Dave Parker	123

Runs Created

1	Honus Wagner	1,876
2	Paul Waner	1,642
3	Roberto Clemente	1,487
4	Willie Stargell	1,451
5	Max Carey	1,297
6	Pie Traynor	1,173
7	Arky Vaughan	1,058
8	Lloyd Waner	1,033
9	Fred Clarke	1,016
10	Ralph Kiner	865
11	Tommy Leach	853
12	Bill Mazeroski	799
13	Gus Suhr	793
	Dave Parker	793
15	Jake Beckley	752
16	Al Oliver	724
17	Barry Bonds	719
18	Patsy Donovan	711
19	Elmer Smith	702
20	Ginger Beaumont	699

Runs Created/27 Outs

(minimum 2000 Plate Appearances)

1	Elmer Smith	8.98
2	Ralph Kiner	7.92
3	Honus Wagner	7.69
4	Arky Vaughan	7.65
5	Kiki Cuyler	7.53
6	Paul Waner	7.42
7	George Grantham	7.33
8	Fred Carroll	7.32
9	Jake Beckley	7.23
10	Barry Bonds	7.07
11	Willie Stargell	6.63
12	Elbie Fletcher	6.52
13	Fred Clarke	6.49
14	Ginger Beaumont	6.30
15	Richie Zisk	6.24
16	Patsy Donovan	6.18
17	Dave Parker	6.02
18	Bobby Bonilla	5.95
19	Orlando Merced	5.92
20	Roberto Clemente	5.86

Batting Average

(minimum 2000 Plate Appearances)

1	Paul Waner	.340
2	Kiki Cuyler	.336
3	Honus Wagner	.328
4	Matty Alou	.327
5	Elmer Smith	.324
6	Arky Vaughan	.324
7	Ginger Beaumont	.321
8	Pie Traynor	.320
9	Lloyd Waner	.319
10	Roberto Clemente	.317
11	George Grantham	.315
12	Patsy Donovan	.307
13	Dave Parker	.305
14	Jake Beckley	.300
15	Fred Clarke	.299
16	Richie Zisk	.299
17	Manny Sanguillen	.299
18	Glenn Wright	.298
19	Bill Madlock	.297
20	Al Oliver	.296

On-Base Percentage

(minimum 2000 Plate Appearances)

1	Arky Vaughan	.415
2	Elmer Smith	.415
3	George Grantham	.410
4	Paul Waner	.407
5	Ralph Kiner	.405
6	Elbie Fletcher	.403
7	Kiki Cuyler	.399
8	Honus Wagner	.394
9	Barry Bonds	.380
10	Fred Clarke	.379
11	Jason Thompson	.376
12	Ginger Beaumont	.369
13	Jim Russell	.367
14	Gus Suhr	.366
15	Richie Zisk	.366
16	Fred Carroll	.365
17	Orlando Merced	.364
18	Don Hoak	.364
19	Mike LaValliere	.363
20	Bob Elliott	.363

Slugging Percentage

(minimum 2000 Plate Appearances)

1	Ralph Kiner	.567
2	Willie Stargell	.529
3	Kiki Cuyler	.513
4	Dick Stuart	.512
5	Barry Bonds	.503
6	Dave Parker	.494
7	George Grantham	.491
8	Paul Waner	.489
9	Wally Westlake	.484
10	Bobby Bonilla	.481
11	Bill Robinson	.477
12	Richie Zisk	.477
13	Roberto Clemente	.475
14	Frank Thomas	.474
15	Arky Vaughan	.472
16	Honus Wagner	.468
17	Elmer Smith	.466
18	Al Martin	.460
19	Andy Van Slyke	.458
20	Al Oliver	.454

Teams: Pirates

Pirates Franchise Pitching Leaders—Career

Wins

1	Wilbur Cooper	202
2	Sam Leever	195
3	Babe Adams	194
4	Bob Friend	191
5	Deacon Phillippe	168
6	Vern Law	162
7	Ray Kremer	143
	Rip Sewell	143
9	Ed Morris	129
10	Pud Galvin	125
11	John Candelaria	124
12	Jesse Tannehill	116
	Howie Camnitz	116
	Bob Veale	116
15	Frank Killen	112
16	Lefty Leifield	109
17	Steve Blass	103
18	Roy Face	100
19	Dock Ellis	96
20	Doug Drabek	92

Losses

1	Bob Friend	218
2	Wilbur Cooper	159
3	Vern Law	147
4	Babe Adams	139
5	Pud Galvin	110
6	Ed Morris	102
7	Sam Leever	100
8	Rip Sewell	97
9	Roy Face	93
10	Deacon Phillippe	92
11	Ron Kline	91
	Bob Veale	91
13	John Candelaria	87
14	Ray Kremer	85
	Murry Dickson	85
16	Howie Camnitz	84
	Lefty Leifield	84
18	Larry French	83
19	Frank Killen	82
20	Dock Ellis	80

Winning Percentage
(minimum 100 decisions)

1	Jesse Tannehill	.667
2	Sam Leever	.661
3	Vic Willis	.659
4	Jack Chesbro	.648
5	Deacon Phillippe	.646
6	Lee Meadows	.629
7	Ray Kremer	.627
8	Al McBean	.602
9	Doug Drabek	.597
10	Rip Sewell	.596
11	John Smiley	.588
12	John Candelaria	.588
13	Babe Adams	.583
14	Howie Camnitz	.580
15	Frank Killen	.577
16	Steve Blass	.575
17	Bob Walk	.573
18	Jerry Reuss	.570
19	Heinie Meine	.569
20	Lefty Leifield	.565

Games

1	Roy Face	802
2	Kent Tekulve	722
3	Bob Friend	568
4	Vern Law	483
5	Babe Adams	481
6	Wilbur Cooper	469
7	Dave Giusti	410
8	Sam Leever	388
9	Rip Sewell	385
10	Al McBean	376
11	John Candelaria	345
12	Don Robinson	343
13	Bob Veale	341
14	Deacon Phillippe	330
15	Ray Kremer	308
16	Bill Swift	305
17	Bob Moose	289
18	Ron Kline	288
19	Steve Blass	282
20	Four tied at	278

Games Started

1	Bob Friend	477
2	Wilbur Cooper	369
3	Vern Law	364
4	Babe Adams	354
5	Sam Leever	299
6	John Candelaria	271
7	Bob Veale	255
8	Deacon Phillippe	250
9	Ray Kremer	247
10	Rip Sewell	243
11	Pud Galvin	242
12	Ed Morris	240
13	Steve Blass	231
14	Rick Rhoden	213
15	Dock Ellis	208
16	Frank Killen	201
17	Bob Walk	196
	Doug Drabek	196
19	Howie Camnitz	195
20	Lefty Leifield	192

Complete Games

1	Wilbur Cooper	263
2	Sam Leever	241
3	Ed Morris	235
4	Pud Galvin	225
5	Deacon Phillippe	209
6	Babe Adams	206
7	Frank Killen	163
8	Bob Friend	161
9	Jesse Tannehill	148
10	Rip Sewell	137
11	Ray Kremer	134
12	Lefty Leifield	125
13	Vern Law	119
14	Howie Camnitz	116
15	Pink Hawley	114
16	Vic Willis	108
17	Larry French	103
18	Red Ehret	95
19	Mark Baldwin	93
	Lee Meadows	93

Shutouts

1	Babe Adams	44
2	Sam Leever	39
3	Bob Friend	35
4	Wilbur Cooper	34
5	Lefty Leifield	29
6	Vern Law	28
7	Ed Morris	25
	Deacon Phillippe	25
9	Vic Willis	23
10	Rip Sewell	20
	Bob Veale	20
12	Howie Camnitz	18
13	Jesse Tannehill	17
	Jack Chesbro	17
15	Pud Galvin	16
	Steve Blass	16
	Doug Drabek	16
18	Larry French	15
19	Ray Kremer	14
20	Ten tied at	13

Saves

1	Roy Face	188
2	Kent Tekulve	158
3	Dave Giusti	133
4	Stan Belinda	61
5	Al McBean	59
6	Bill Landrum	56
7	Jim Gott	50
8	Don Robinson	43
9	Ramon Hernandez	39
10	Grant Jackson	36
11	Rod Scurry	34
12	Mace Brown	29
	Rich Loiselle	29
14	Goose Gossage	26
	Enrique Romo	26
16	Danny Miceli	24
17	Cecilio Guante	20
18	Bob Moose	19
19	Bill Swift	18
	Waite Hoyt	18

Innings Pitched

1	Bob Friend	3,480.1
2	Wilbur Cooper	3,199.0
3	Babe Adams	2,991.1
4	Vern Law	2,672.0
5	Sam Leever	2,660.2
6	Deacon Phillippe	2,286.0
7	Rip Sewell	2,108.2
8	Ed Morris	2,104.0
9	Pud Galvin	2,084.2
10	Ray Kremer	1,954.2
11	John Candelaria	1,873.0
12	Bob Veale	1,868.2
13	Howie Camnitz	1,754.1
14	Frank Killen	1,661.1
15	Steve Blass	1,597.1
16	Lefty Leifield	1,578.0
17	Bill Swift	1,555.0
18	Larry French	1,502.2
19	Jesse Tannehill	1,499.0
20	Rick Rhoden	1,448.0

Walks

1	Bob Friend	869
2	Bob Veale	839
3	Wilbur Cooper	762
4	Rip Sewell	740
5	Vern Law	597
	Steve Blass	597
7	Sam Leever	587
8	Howie Camnitz	532
9	Frank Killen	519
10	Ray Kremer	483
11	Lefty Leifield	481
12	Jim Rooker	479
13	Bruce Kison	469
14	Ron Kline	459
15	Bob Walk	451
16	Don Robinson	441
17	Rick Rhoden	440
18	Dock Ellis	438
19	John Candelaria	436
20	Johnny Morrison	429

Strikeouts

1	Bob Friend	1,682
2	Bob Veale	1,652
3	Wilbur Cooper	1,191
4	John Candelaria	1,159
5	Vern Law	1,092
6	Babe Adams	1,036
7	Steve Blass	896
8	Ed Morris	890
9	Dock Ellis	869
10	Deacon Phillippe	861
11	Rick Rhoden	852
12	Sam Leever	847
13	Roy Face	842
14	Bob Moose	827
15	Don Robinson	825
16	Doug Drabek	820
17	Howie Camnitz	806
18	Bruce Kison	735
19	Jim Rooker	672
20	Bob Walk	650

Strikeouts/9 Innings
(minimum 1000 Innings Pitched)

1	Bob Veale	7.96
2	Don Robinson	6.17
3	Roy Face	5.76
4	Bob Moose	5.71
5	John Candelaria	5.57
6	Dock Ellis	5.47
7	Doug Drabek	5.42
8	Rick Rhoden	5.30
9	Bruce Kison	5.22
10	Steve Blass	5.05
11	Kent Tekulve	4.88
12	Al McBean	4.85
13	Jim Rooker	4.59
14	Jerry Reuss	4.50
15	Bob Walk	4.49
16	Bob Friend	4.35
17	Howie Camnitz	4.13
18	Ron Kline	3.96
19	Ed Morris	3.81
20	Vern Law	3.68

ERA
(minimum 1000 Innings Pitched)

1	Vic Willis	2.08
2	Lefty Leifield	2.38
3	Sam Leever	2.47
4	Deacon Phillippe	2.50
5	Howie Camnitz	2.64
6	Kent Tekulve	2.68
7	Jesse Tannehill	2.73
8	Babe Adams	2.73
9	Wilbur Cooper	2.74
10	Ed Morris	2.81
11	Doug Drabek	3.02
12	Bob Veale	3.06
13	Al McBean	3.08
14	Pud Galvin	3.10
15	Dock Ellis	3.16
16	John Candelaria	3.17
17	Jim Rooker	3.29
18	Max Butcher	3.34
19	Rip Sewell	3.43
20	Roy Face	3.46

Component ERA
(minimum 1000 Innings Pitched)

1	Vic Willis	2.11
2	Ed Morris	2.35
3	Deacon Phillippe	2.36
4	Babe Adams	2.39
5	Sam Leever	2.49
6	Howie Camnitz	2.56
7	Lefty Leifield	2.67
8	Kent Tekulve	2.77
9	Wilbur Cooper	2.84
10	Jesse Tannehill	2.89
11	Doug Drabek	2.92
12	John Candelaria	3.11
13	Pud Galvin	3.11
14	Dock Ellis	3.17
15	Bill Swift	3.18
16	Bob Veale	3.21
17	Johnny Morrison	3.34
18	Jim Rooker	3.39
19	Bruce Kison	3.42
20	Roy Face	3.42

Opponent Average
(minimum 1000 Innings Pitched)

1	Vic Willis	.228
2	Ed Morris	.234
3	Bob Veale	.235
4	Howie Camnitz	.239
5	Kent Tekulve	.240
6	Doug Drabek	.242
7	Lefty Leifield	.243
8	Bruce Kison	.245
9	Sam Leever	.245
10	Jim Rooker	.248
11	Dock Ellis	.249
12	John Candelaria	.250
13	Deacon Phillippe	.250
14	Babe Adams	.253
15	Don Robinson	.254
16	Rip Sewell	.256
17	Steve Blass	.258
18	Wilbur Cooper	.258
19	Bob Walk	.259
20	Roy Face	.259

Opponent OBP
(minimum 1000 Innings Pitched)

1	Ed Morris	.274
2	Deacon Phillippe	.279
3	Vic Willis	.280
4	Babe Adams	.283
5	Doug Drabek	.290
6	Sam Leever	.293
7	John Candelaria	.294
8	Pud Galvin	.299
9	Bill Swift	.302
10	Howie Camnitz	.303
11	Jesse Tannehill	.304
12	Kent Tekulve	.307
13	Roy Face	.307
14	Dock Ellis	.308
15	Wilbur Cooper	.308
16	Lefty Leifield	.310
17	Vern Law	.312
18	Bob Friend	.313
19	Jim Rooker	.314
20	Bruce Kison	.317

Pirates Franchise Batting Leaders—Single Season

Games

1	Bill Mazeroski	1967	163
	Bobby Bonilla	1989	163
3	Bill Mazeroski	1964	162
	Donn Clendenon	1965	162
	Bill Mazeroski	1966	162
	Matty Alou	1969	162
	Omar Moreno	1979	162
	Omar Moreno	1980	162
	Johnny Ray	1982	162
10	Dick Groat	1962	161
	Dale Berra	1983	161
12	Bobby Bonilla	1990	160
13	Bill Mazeroski	1962	159
	Bob Bailey	1965	159
	Dave Parker	1977	159
	Bobby Bonilla	1988	159
	Barry Bonds	1989	159
	Jay Bell	1990	159
	Jay Bell	1992	159
20	Six tied at		158

At-Bats

1	Matty Alou	1969	698
2	Woody Jensen	1936	696
3	Omar Moreno	1979	695
4	Lloyd Waner	1931	681
5	Dick Groat	1962	678
6	Matty Alou	1970	677
7	Omar Moreno	1980	676
8	Rennie Stennett	1974	673
9	Rabbit Maranville	1922	672
10	Bill Virdon	1962	663
11	Lloyd Waner	1929	662
12	Lloyd Waner	1928	659
13	Al Oliver	1973	654
	Rennie Stennett	1976	654
	Frank Taveras	1978	654
16	Marvell Wynne	1984	653
17	Lou Bierbauer	1892	649
18	Johnny Ray	1982	647
19	Omar Moreno	1982	645
20	Two tied at		641

Runs

1	Jake Stenzel	1894	148
2	Patsy Donovan	1894	145
3	Kiki Cuyler	1925	144
4	Paul Waner	1928	142
5	Max Carey	1922	140
6	Ginger Beaumont	1903	137
7	Lloyd Waner	1929	134
8	Lloyd Waner	1927	133
9	Paul Waner	1929	131
10	George Van Haltren	1893	129
11	Elmer Smith	1894	128
12	Jimmy Williams	1899	126
	Tommy Leach	1909	126
14	Ralph Kiner	1951	124
15	Paul Waner	1934	122
	Arky Vaughan	1936	122
17	Elmer Smith	1893	121
	Jake Beckley	1894	121
	Elmer Smith	1896	121
	Lloyd Waner	1928	121

Hits

1	Paul Waner	1927	237
2	Lloyd Waner	1929	234
3	Matty Alou	1969	231
4	Lloyd Waner	1927	223
	Paul Waner	1928	223
6	Lloyd Waner	1928	221
7	Kiki Cuyler	1925	220
8	Jimmy Williams	1899	219
	Paul Waner	1937	219
10	Paul Waner	1936	218
11	Paul Waner	1930	217
	Paul Waner	1934	217
13	Carson Bigbee	1922	215
	Paul Waner	1932	215
	Dave Parker	1977	215
16	Lloyd Waner	1931	214
17	Roberto Clemente	1964	211
18	Ginger Beaumont	1903	209
	Roberto Clemente	1967	209
20	Pie Traynor	1923	208

Doubles

1	Paul Waner	1932	62
2	Paul Waner	1936	53
3	Paul Waner	1928	50
4	Adam Comorosky	1930	47
5	Honus Wagner	1900	45
	Dave Parker	1979	45
	Andy Van Slyke	1992	45
8	Honus Wagner	1904	44
	Dave Parker	1977	44
	Bobby Bonilla	1991	44
11	Bobby Byrne	1910	43
	Kiki Cuyler	1925	43
	Paul Waner	1929	43
	Willie Stargell	1973	43
15	Arky Vaughan	1934	41
	Vince DiMaggio	1943	41
	Matty Alou	1969	41
18	Five tied at		40

Triples

1	Chief Wilson	1912	36
2	Harry Davis	1897	28
3	Jimmy Williams	1899	27
4	Kiki Cuyler	1925	26
5	Elmer Smith	1893	23
	Adam Comorosky	1930	23
7	Honus Wagner	1900	22
	Tommy Leach	1902	22
	Paul Waner	1926	22
10	Jake Stenzel	1894	20
	Honus Wagner	1912	20
	Dots Miller	1913	20
	Rabbit Maranville	1924	20
	Lloyd Waner	1929	20
15	Thirteen tied at		19

Home Runs

1	Ralph Kiner	1949	54
2	Ralph Kiner	1947	51
3	Willie Stargell	1971	48
4	Ralph Kiner	1950	47
5	Willie Stargell	1973	44
6	Ralph Kiner	1951	42
7	Ralph Kiner	1948	40
8	Ralph Kiner	1952	37
9	Frank Thomas	1958	35
	Dick Stuart	1961	35
11	Barry Bonds	1992	34
12	Willie Stargell	1966	33
	Willie Stargell	1972	33
	Barry Bonds	1990	33
15	Willie Stargell	1979	32
	Bobby Bonilla	1990	32
17	Willie Stargell	1970	31
	Jason Thompson	1982	31
19	Three tied at		30

RBI

1	Paul Waner	1927	131
2	Ralph Kiner	1947	127
	Ralph Kiner	1949	127
4	Honus Wagner	1901	126
5	Willie Stargell	1971	125
6	Pie Traynor	1928	124
7	Ralph Kiner	1948	123
8	Jake Stenzel	1894	121
	Glenn Wright	1925	121
10	Jake Beckley	1894	120
	Bobby Bonilla	1990	120
12	Adam Comorosky	1930	119
	Pie Traynor	1930	119
	Roberto Clemente	1966	119
	Willie Stargell	1973	119
16	Gus Suhr	1936	118
	Ralph Kiner	1950	118
18	Dick Stuart	1961	117
	Dave Parker	1978	117
20	Three tied at		116

Walks

1	Ralph Kiner	1951	137
2	Barry Bonds	1992	127
3	Ralph Kiner	1950	122
4	Elbie Fletcher	1940	119
5	Arky Vaughan	1936	118
	Elbie Fletcher	1941	118
7	Ralph Kiner	1949	117
8	Ralph Kiner	1948	112
9	Elbie Fletcher	1946	111
10	Ralph Kiner	1952	110
11	Barry Bonds	1991	107
12	Elbie Fletcher	1942	105
13	Arky Vaughan	1938	104
	Hank Greenberg	1947	104
15	Jason Thompson	1982	101
16	Jason Thompson	1983	99
17	Ralph Kiner	1947	98
18	Denny Lyons	1893	97
	Arky Vaughan	1935	97
20	Two tied at		95

Strikeouts

1	Donn Clendenon	1968	163
2	Willie Stargell	1971	154
3	Donn Clendenon	1966	142
4	Donn Clendenon	1963	136
5	Willie Stargell	1972	129
	Willie Stargell	1973	129
7	Donn Clendenon	1965	128
	Jason Thompson	1983	128
9	Willie Stargell	1965	127
10	Vince DiMaggio	1943	126
	Andy Van Slyke	1988	126
12	Andy Van Slyke	1987	122
	Jay Bell	1993	122
	Al Martin	1993	122
15	Dick Stuart	1961	121
	Omar Moreno	1982	121
17	Willie Stargell	1969	120
18	Willie Stargell	1970	119
19	Al Martin	1996	116
20	Jay Bell	1995	110

Stolen Bases

1	Omar Moreno	1980	96
2	Omar Moreno	1979	77
3	Billy Sunday	1888	71
	Omar Moreno	1978	71
5	Frank Taveras	1977	70
6	Max Carey	1916	63
7	Jake Stenzel	1894	61
	Honus Wagner	1907	61
	Max Carey	1913	61
10	Omar Moreno	1982	60
	Tony Womack	1997	60
12	Max Carey	1918	58
	Frank Taveras	1976	58
14	Jake Stenzel	1896	57
	Honus Wagner	1905	57
16	Billy Sunday	1890	56
17	Ned Hanlon	1891	54
18	Six tied at		53

Runs Created

1	Jake Stenzel	1894	153
2	Honus Wagner	1900	150
3	Kiki Cuyler	1925	149
4	Jimmy Williams	1899	148
5	Ralph Kiner	1949	147
6	Jake Stenzel	1895	144
	Ralph Kiner	1951	144
8	Paul Waner	1928	143
9	Arky Vaughan	1935	142
	Ralph Kiner	1947	142
11	Paul Waner	1927	141
12	Elmer Smith	1893	140
13	Honus Wagner	1905	136
	Paul Waner	1929	136
15	Honus Wagner	1901	133
	Paul Waner	1936	133
17	Arky Vaughan	1936	132
18	Elmer Smith	1894	131
	Honus Wagner	1908	131
	Paul Waner	1934	131

Runs Created/27 Outs

(minimum 3.1 Plate Appearances/Tm Gm)

1	Arky Vaughan	1935	11.93
2	Honus Wagner	1900	11.61
3	Jake Stenzel	1894	11.48
4	Jake Stenzel	1895	11.28
5	Elmer Smith	1893	10.78
6	Elmer Smith	1894	10.34
7	Ed Swartwood	1883	10.34
8	Ralph Kiner	1951	10.28
9	Elmer Smith	1896	10.25
10	Honus Wagner	1904	10.11
11	Barry Bonds	1992	10.08
12	Ralph Kiner	1949	10.07
13	Honus Wagner	1905	9.82
14	Honus Wagner	1903	9.58
15	Ed Swartwood	1882	9.55
16	Honus Wagner	1901	9.55
17	Paul Waner	1928	9.48
18	Ralph Kiner	1947	9.36
19	Paul Waner	1936	9.29
20	Jake Stenzel	1896	9.28

Batting Average

(minimum 3.1 Plate Appearances/Tm Gm)

1	Arky Vaughan	1935	.385
2	Honus Wagner	1900	.381
3	Paul Waner	1927	.380
4	Jake Stenzel	1895	.374
5	Paul Waner	1936	.373
6	Paul Waner	1928	.370
7	Paul Waner	1930	.368
8	Pie Traynor	1930	.366
9	Honus Wagner	1905	.363
10	Paul Waner	1934	.362
11	Elmer Smith	1896	.362
12	Jake Stenzel	1896	.361
13	Roberto Clemente	1967	.357
14	Ginger Beaumont	1902	.357
15	Kiki Cuyler	1925	.357
16	Ed Swartwood	1883	.356
17	Elmer Smith	1894	.356
18	Pie Traynor	1929	.356
19	Honus Wagner	1903	.355
20	Jimmy Williams	1899	.355

On-Base Percentage

(minimum 3.1 Plate Appearances/Tm Gm)

1	Arky Vaughan	1935	.491
2	Barry Bonds	1992	.456
3	Elmer Smith	1896	.454
4	Arky Vaughan	1936	.453
5	Ralph Kiner	1951	.452
6	Jake Stenzel	1895	.447
7	Paul Waner	1928	.446
8	Paul Waner	1936	.446
9	Jake Stenzel	1894	.441
10	Paul Waner	1927	.437
11	Elmer Smith	1894	.436
12	Elmer Smith	1893	.435
13	Honus Wagner	1900	.434
14	Arky Vaughan	1938	.433
15	Ralph Kiner	1949	.432
16	Arky Vaughan	1934	.431
17	Denny Lyons	1893	.430
18	Paul Waner	1934	.429
19	Paul Waner	1930	.428
20	Honus Wagner	1905	.427

Slugging Percentage

(minimum 3.1 Plate Appearances/Tm Gm)

1	Ralph Kiner	1949	.658
2	Willie Stargell	1973	.646
3	Ralph Kiner	1947	.639
4	Willie Stargell	1971	.628
5	Ralph Kiner	1951	.627
6	Barry Bonds	1992	.624
7	Arky Vaughan	1935	.607
8	Kiki Cuyler	1925	.598
9	Ralph Kiner	1950	.590
10	Dave Parker	1978	.585
11	Willie Stargell	1966	.581
12	Dick Stuart	1961	.581
13	Jake Stenzel	1894	.580
14	Honus Wagner	1900	.573
15	Barry Bonds	1990	.565
16	Roberto Clemente	1961	.559
17	Willie Stargell	1972	.558
18	Willie Stargell	1969	.556
19	Roberto Clemente	1967	.554
20	Paul Waner	1928	.547

Pirates Franchise Pitching Leaders—Single Season

Wins

1	Ed Morris	1886	41
2	Ed Morris	1885	39
3	Frank Killen	1893	36
4	Pink Hawley	1895	31
5	Frank Killen	1896	30
6	Pud Galvin	1886	29
	Ed Morris	1888	29
8	Pud Galvin	1887	28
	Jack Chesbro	1902	28
10	Mark Baldwin	1892	26
11	Jesse Tannehill	1898	25
	Deacon Phillippe	1903	25
	Sam Leever	1903	25
	Howie Camnitz	1909	25
	Johnny Morrison	1923	25
	Burleigh Grimes	1928	25
17	Jesse Tannehill	1899	24
	Claude Hendrix	1912	24
	Wilbur Cooper	1920	24
20	Six tied at		23

Losses

1	Fleury Sullivan	1884	35
2	Silver King	1891	29
3	Mark Baldwin	1891	28
4	Mark Baldwin	1892	27
5	Jack Neagle	1884	26
	Harry Staley	1889	26
7	Pud Galvin	1888	25
8	Ed Morris	1885	24
9	Jim McCormick	1887	23
	Ed Morris	1888	23
	Frank Killen	1897	23
	Sam Leever	1899	23
13	Ed Morris	1887	22
	Pink Hawley	1895	22
15	Denny Driscoll	1883	21
	Pud Galvin	1886	21
	Pud Galvin	1887	21
	Red Ehret	1894	21
	Pink Hawley	1896	21
	Murry Dickson	1952	21

Winning Percentage
(minimum 15 decisions)

1	Roy Face	1959	.947
2	Deacon Phillippe	1910	.875
3	Emil Yde	1924	.842
4	Jack Chesbro	1902	.824
	Bob Moose	1969	.824
6	Rip Sewell	1948	.813
	Al McBean	1963	.813
8	Howie Camnitz	1909	.806
9	Ed Doheny	1902	.800
	Sam Leever	1905	.800
	Babe Adams	1909	.800
	John Candelaria	1977	.800
13	Red Lucas	1936	.789
14	Doug Drabek	1990	.786
15	Sam Leever	1903	.781
16	Jesse Tannehill	1900	.769
	Jesse Tannehill	1902	.769
	Ray Kremer	1926	.769
19	Rip Sewell	1940	.762
20	Jim Bibby	1980	.760

Games

1	Kent Tekulve	1979	94
2	Kent Tekulve	1978	91
3	Kent Tekulve	1982	85
4	Enrique Romo	1979	84
5	Kent Tekulve	1980	78
6	Rod Scurry	1982	76
	Kent Tekulve	1983	76
8	Jeff Robinson	1988	75
9	Enrique Romo	1980	74
10	Dan Plesac	1996	73
11	Kent Tekulve	1977	72
	Goose Gossage	1977	72
	Grant Jackson	1979	72
	Kent Tekulve	1984	72
	Rich Loiselle	1997	72
16	Pete Mikkelsen	1966	71
17	Marc Wilkins	1997	70
18	Roy Face	1956	68
	Roy Face	1960	68
20	Two tied at		67

Games Started

1	Ed Morris	1885	63
	Ed Morris	1886	63
3	Ed Morris	1888	55
4	Mark Baldwin	1892	53
5	Fleury Sullivan	1884	51
6	Pud Galvin	1886	50
	Pud Galvin	1888	50
	Mark Baldwin	1891	50
	Pink Hawley	1895	50
	Frank Killen	1896	50
11	Pud Galvin	1887	48
	Frank Killen	1893	48
13	Harry Staley	1889	47
14	Silver King	1891	44
15	Pink Hawley	1896	43
16	Bob Friend	1956	42
17	Frank Killen	1897	41
18	Denny Driscoll	1883	40
	Pud Galvin	1889	40
20	Three tied at		39

Complete Games

1	Ed Morris	1885	63
	Ed Morris	1886	63
3	Ed Morris	1888	54
4	Fleury Sullivan	1884	51
5	Pud Galvin	1886	49
	Pud Galvin	1888	49
7	Mark Baldwin	1891	48
8	Pud Galvin	1887	47
9	Harry Staley	1889	46
10	Mark Baldwin	1892	45
11	Pink Hawley	1895	44
	Frank Killen	1896	44
13	Silver King	1891	40
14	Harry Salisbury	1882	38
	Pud Galvin	1889	38
	Frank Killen	1893	38
	Frank Killen	1897	38
18	Jack Neagle	1884	37
	Ed Morris	1887	37
	Pink Hawley	1896	37

Shutouts

1	Ed Morris	1886	12
2	Jack Chesbro	1902	8
	Lefty Leifield	1906	8
	Al Mamaux	1915	8
	Babe Adams	1920	8
6	Ed Morris	1885	7
	Sam Leever	1903	7
	Vic Willis	1908	7
	Wilbur Cooper	1917	7
	Bob Veale	1965	7
	Steve Blass	1968	7
12	Pud Galvin	1888	6
	Jack Chesbro	1901	6
	Sam Leever	1906	6
	Vic Willis	1906	6
	Lefty Leifield	1907	6
	Vic Willis	1907	6
	Babe Adams	1911	6
	Babe Adams	1919	6
	Jerry Reuss	1975	6

Saves

1	Jim Gott	1988	34
2	Kent Tekulve	1978	31
	Kent Tekulve	1979	31
4	Dave Giusti	1971	30
5	Rich Loiselle	1997	29
6	Roy Face	1962	28
7	Dave Giusti	1970	26
	Goose Gossage	1977	26
	Bill Landrum	1989	26
10	Roy Face	1960	24
11	Al McBean	1964	22
	Dave Giusti	1972	22
13	Kent Tekulve	1980	21
	Danny Miceli	1995	21
15	Roy Face	1958	20
	Dave Giusti	1973	20
	Kent Tekulve	1982	20
18	Stan Belinda	1993	19
19	Four tied at		18

Innings Pitched

1	Ed Morris	1885	581.0
2	Ed Morris	1886	555.1
3	Ed Morris	1888	480.0
4	Pink Hawley	1895	444.1
5	Fleury Sullivan	1884	441.0
6	Pud Galvin	1887	440.2
7	Mark Baldwin	1892	440.1
8	Mark Baldwin	1891	437.2
9	Pud Galvin	1888	437.1
10	Pud Galvin	1886	434.2
11	Frank Killen	1896	432.1
12	Harry Staley	1889	420.0
13	Frank Killen	1893	415.0
14	Silver King	1891	384.1
15	Sam Leever	1899	379.0
16	Pink Hawley	1896	378.0
17	Red Ehret	1894	346.2
18	Pud Galvin	1889	341.0
19	Frank Killen	1897	337.1
20	Denny Driscoll	1883	336.1

Walks

1	Mark Baldwin	1891	227
2	Mark Baldwin	1892	194
3	Marty O'Toole	1912	159
4	Pink Hawley	1896	157
5	Silver King	1891	144
6	Frank Killen	1893	140
7	Al Mamaux	1916	136
8	Bill Hart	1895	135
9	Red Ehret	1894	128
10	Bob Veale	1964	124
11	Pink Hawley	1895	122
	Sam Leever	1899	122
13	Frank Killen	1896	119
	Bob Veale	1965	119
	Bob Veale	1967	119
16	Ed Morris	1886	118
17	Harry Staley	1889	116
	Johnny Lindell	1953	116
19	Red Ehret	1893	115
20	Two tied at		110

Strikeouts

1	Ed Morris	1886	326
2	Ed Morris	1885	298
3	Bob Veale	1965	276
4	Bob Veale	1964	250
5	Bob Veale	1966	229
6	Bob Veale	1969	213
7	Larry McWilliams	1983	199
8	Mark Baldwin	1891	197
9	Fleury Sullivan	1884	189
10	Bob Friend	1960	183
11	Bert Blyleven	1978	182
12	Bob Veale	1967	179
13	Bob Veale	1970	178
14	Doug Drabek	1992	177
15	Claude Hendrix	1912	176
16	Dock Ellis	1969	173
17	Bert Blyleven	1979	172
18	Bob Veale	1968	171
19	Bert Blyleven	1980	168
20	Bob Friend	1956	166

Strikeouts/9 Innings
(minimum 1 Inning Pitched/Tm Gm)

1	Bob Veale	1965	9.34
2	Bob Moose	1969	8.74
3	Bob Veale	1969	8.49
4	Jose DeLeon	1985	8.24
5	Bob Veale	1964	8.05
6	Denny Neagle	1994	8.01
7	Bob Veale	1967	7.94
8	Bob Veale	1970	7.93
9	Bob Veale	1966	7.68
10	Jon Lieber	1997	7.65
11	Larry McWilliams	1983	7.53
12	Jose DeLeon	1984	7.16
13	John Candelaria	1983	7.15
14	Dock Ellis	1969	7.12
15	Bert Blyleven	1980	6.98
16	John Candelaria	1982	6.85
17	Luke Walker	1970	6.85
18	Bert Blyleven	1978	6.72
19	Joe Gibbon	1961	6.68
20	Bob Moose	1968	6.62

ERA
(minimum 1 Inning Pitched/Tm Gm)

1	Denny Driscoll	1882	1.21
2	Howie Camnitz	1908	1.56
3	Howie Camnitz	1909	1.62
4	Sam Leever	1907	1.66
5	Vic Willis	1906	1.73
6	Lefty Leifield	1906	1.87
7	Wilbur Cooper	1916	1.87
8	Jesse Tannehill	1902	1.95
9	Babe Adams	1919	1.98
10	Al Mamaux	1915	2.04
11	Patsy Flaherty	1904	2.05
12	Deacon Phillippe	1902	2.05
13	Bob Veale	1968	2.05
14	Sam Leever	1903	2.06
15	Vic Willis	1908	2.07
16	Lefty Leifield	1908	2.10
17	Sam Leever	1908	2.10
18	Wilbur Cooper	1918	2.11
19	Steve Blass	1968	2.12
20	Wilbur Cooper	1914	2.13

Component ERA
(minimum 1 Inning Pitched/Tm Gm)

1	Denny Driscoll	1882	1.44
2	Babe Adams	1919	1.52
3	Howie Camnitz	1909	1.64
4	Ed Morris	1885	1.67
5	Vic Willis	1908	1.82
6	Ed Morris	1886	1.86
7	Howie Camnitz	1907	1.91
8	Jesse Tannehill	1902	1.93
9	Deacon Phillippe	1905	1.93
10	Babe Adams	1920	1.94
11	Vic Willis	1907	1.97
12	Bob Moose	1968	1.99
13	Wilbur Cooper	1918	2.00
14	Wilbur Cooper	1916	2.00
15	Babe Adams	1911	2.01
16	Babe Adams	1913	2.03
17	Frank Miller	1919	2.06
18	Howie Camnitz	1908	2.06
19	Cy Blanton	1935	2.08
20	Harry Salisbury	1882	2.10

Opponent Average
(minimum 1 Inning Pitched/Tm Gm)

1	Adonis Terry	1892	.205
2	Denny Driscoll	1882	.206
3	Al Mamaux	1915	.208
4	Ed Morris	1885	.208
5	Howie Camnitz	1908	.210
6	Howie Camnitz	1909	.211
7	Bob Veale	1968	.211
8	Howie Camnitz	1907	.211
9	Lefty Leifield	1908	.212
10	Vic Willis	1908	.213
11	Ed Morris	1886	.214
12	Jose DeLeon	1984	.214
13	Wilbur Cooper	1916	.215
14	Rick Reuschel	1985	.215
15	John Candelaria	1976	.216
16	Bob Veale	1964	.217
17	Bob Moose	1968	.218
18	Vic Willis	1907	.219
19	Luke Walker	1970	.219
20	Babe Adams	1919	.220

Opponent OBP
(minimum 1 Inning Pitched/Tm Gm)

1	Denny Driscoll	1882	.218
2	Babe Adams	1919	.241
3	Ed Morris	1885	.247
4	Harry Salisbury	1882	.253
5	Ed Morris	1886	.258
6	Babe Adams	1920	.259
7	Vern Law	1965	.261
8	Vic Willis	1908	.262
9	Deacon Phillippe	1903	.263
10	Jesse Tannehill	1902	.267
11	Babe Adams	1913	.267
12	Howie Camnitz	1909	.267
13	Bob Friend	1963	.267
14	Bob Moose	1968	.268
15	Harvey Haddix	1959	.271
16	John Candelaria	1976	.271
17	Rick Reuschel	1985	.271
18	Vic Willis	1907	.271
19	Babe Adams	1911	.271
20	Deacon Phillippe	1901	.271

Pirates Capsule

Best Season: *1909.* Honus Wagner's Pirates won a franchise-record 110 games and bested Ty Cobb's Detroit Tigers in a seven-game World Series.

Worst Season: *1985.* While the Pirates staggered to a last-place finish with a 57-104 record, the Pittsburgh Drug Trial became one of the biggest stories of the season. Seven players testified in court under grants of immunity. Several Pirates and ex-Pirates either admitted or were implicated in drug use.

Best Player: *Honus Wagner.*

Best Pitcher: *Babe Adams.* One could make a case for Wilbur Cooper, Sam Leever, Ray Kremer or Deacon Phillippe. Cooper is the strongest challenger, but Adams' won-lost record is slightly superior. Adams might have had a good chance of winning 300 games, but two things prevented that. He wasn't brought to the majors until he was 27, and when he came up with a sore arm in 1916, the Pirates farmed him out to the minors, where he dominated the competition for two years before Pittsburgh was persuaded to bring him back.

Best Reliever: *Roy Face.*

Best Defensive Player: *Bill Mazeroski.*

Hall of Famers: *Max Carey, Fred Clarke, Roberto Clemente, Ralph Kiner, Willie Stargell, Pie Traynor, Arky Vaughn, Honus Wagner, Lloyd Waner, Paul Waner.* About two dozen more Hall of Famers played for the Pirates at one time or another.

Franchise All-Star Team:

C	*Manny Sanguillen*	LF	*Barry Bonds*
1B	*Willie Stargell*	CF	*Max Carey*
2B	*Bill Mazeroski*	RF	*Roberto Clemente*
3B	*Pie Traynor*	SP	*Babe Adams*
SS	*Honus Wagner*	RP	*Roy Face*

Biggest Flakes: *Dick Stuart, Manny Sanguillen.*

Strangest Career: *Nick Maddox.* In 1907, 20-year-old righthander Maddox made six starts for the Pirates, completing all six of them. One of them was a no-hitter, the first in the history of the franchise. (It was Maddox' third no-hitter of the season; he'd already thrown two for Wheeling of the Central League.) He went 5-1 for Pittsburgh, allowing only five earned runs for an 0.83 ERA. The following season, he posted a 23-8 record, tying for fourth place in the NL in wins. On the way to his 23-win season, he set a major league record by recording the 20th victory of his major league career in only his 30th appearance. In Pittsburgh's championship season of 1909, he missed most of the first half with an unspecified illness, but rebounded to finish with a 13-8 record. He notched the Pirates' first win in the history of Forbes Field on July 2, and won his only World Series start that fall. The following spring, the *Pittsburgh Sun* reported that Maddox had recovered from "an injured ligament in his flinging arm. . . and if the cure is permanent, Nick should be a power on the mound." It all ended for him that year, though, as he took ill during spring training once again. He was used sparingly during the first two months of the season, and pitched so poorly in June and July that he was reduced to a mop-up role by August, where he remained even as the Pirates' starters struggled. His record stood at 2-3 when he was released in late September. Curiously, his meteoric rise and swift decline were not well-chronicled, and little survives to explain his odd career. He left behind a major league record of 43-20 with a 2.29 ERA, and later he went back to the minors, where his effectiveness returned. (Research contributed by Pittsburgh-area SABR member Mike Emeigh.)

What Might Have Been: *Ron Necciai.* As a 19-year-old pitcher in the Class-D Appalachian League in 1952, Necciai tossed a no-hitter and struck out 27 batters, which is still the record for a nine-inning professional game. He fanned 24 men in his next start. After six starts, his record stood at 4-0 with an 0.42 ERA and 109 strikeouts in 43 innings. Promoted to the Class-B Carolina League, he went 7-9 for a team that won only 45 games all year, posting a 1.57 ERA while fanning 172 in 126 innings. That got him a call to Pittsburgh, but the teenager was no help to the hapless Bucs, going 1-6 with a fat 7.04 ERA. Arm trouble ended his big-league career the following summer.

Best Trades: *Andy Van Slyke, Doug Drabek* and *Bobby Bonilla.* Pittsburgh GM Syd Thrift pulled off three steals in 10 months from July 1986 through April 1987. First, he sent pitcher Jose DeLeon to the White Sox for Bonilla. Then he packaged starter Rick Rhoden and a couple of relievers to the Yankees for pitchers Drabek, Brian Fisher and a minor leaguer. Finally, he sent catcher Tony Pena to St. Louis for Van Slyke, catcher Mike LaValliere and pitcher

Mike Dunne. Bonilla, Drabek and Van Slyke teamed with Barry Bonds to form the core of the Pittsburgh club that won three straight division titles from 1990 through 1992.

Worst Trade: *Joe Kelley* was traded to Baltimore for George Van Haltren in September 1892. Van Haltren spent only one season with the Pirates, while Kelley played for another 15 years and was eventually voted into the Hall of Fame. The Pirates also traded Larry French to the Cubs in 1934, when French still had 110 victories left in his arm.

Best Rookie Crop: *1924.* If the Rookie of the Year Award had existed back then, the voters would have had to choose between these four Pirates: outfielder Kiki Cuyler (.354-9-85, 32 stolen bases), shortstop Glenn Wright (.287-7-111), and pitchers Emil Yde (16-3, 2.83) and Ray Kremer (18-10, 3.19).

Best-Looking Player: *Babe Adams.*

Ugliest Player: *Ravelo Manzanillo.*

Best Nicknames: *Paul and Lloyd Waner, "Big Poison" and "Little Poison"; Benny Distefano, "Mr. Excitement."*

Most Unappreciated Player: *Wally Westlake.*

Most Overrated Player: *Lloyd Waner.* He put together his three best seasons at the start of his career, creating the impression that he was a comparable ballplayer to his brother Paul. He wasn't—and over the next 15 years, he proved it—but the impression stuck.

Most Admirable Stars: *Honus Wagner, Roberto Clemente.*

Least Admirable Star: *Dave Parker.*

Best Season, Player: *Barry Bonds, 1992.* Honus Wagner had more *great* seasons, but none of them were as impressive as Bonds' '92 campaign.

Best Season, Pitcher: *Roy Face, 1959.* He didn't go 18-1 by vulturing wins; 13 of his victories came after he entered a tie game and two came after he entered with Pittsburgh trailing. Only three of the wins came when he failed to hold a lead he inherited. He also recorded 10 saves, although they weren't officially credited at the time. But the point is this: he was doing the job of both a modern closer and a modern setup man. He was coming into the game in the seventh or eighth inning, and holding the opposition scoreless until the Pirates could break through, time after time.

Most Impressive Individual Record: *Owen "Chief" Wilson* legged out 36 triples in 1912, the highest single-season total in history by a margin of 10. Honorable mention goes to *Harvey Haddix,* who pitched 12 perfect innings against the Milwaukee Braves on May 29, 1959. Some have called it the best single-game pitching performance of all time.

Biggest Tragedy: *Roberto Clemente.* On New Year's Eve 1972, Clemente flew out of Puerto Rico on a plane loaded with relief supplies for earthquake victims in Nicaragua. He knew that the plane was overloaded with cargo and that it had a history of mechanical problems. The plane crashed into the ocean a few miles offshore.

Fan Favorites: *Fred Clarke, Honus Wagner, Kiki Cuyler, Willie Stargell.*

—Mat Olkin

St. Louis Cardinals (1882-1997)

Year	Lg	Pos	W-L	Pct	GB	Manager	Att.	R	OR	HR	Avg	OBP	Slg	Opponent HR	Avg	OBP	ERA	Park Index Runs	HR
1882	AA	5th	37-43	.463	18.0	Ned Cuthbert	—	399	496	11	.231	.260	.302	7	.256	.282	2.92	109	82
1883	AA	2nd	65-33	.663	1.0	Ted Sullivan/Charlie Comiskey	—	549	409	7	.255	.280	.321	7	.214	.247	2.23	107	133
1884	AA	4th	67-40	.626	8.0	Jimmy Williams/Charlie Comiskey	—	658	539	11	.250	.288	.327	16	.226	.266	2.67	117	148
1885	AA	1st	79-33	.705	—	Charlie Comiskey	—	677	461	17	.246	.297	.321	12	.228	.268	2.44	75	63
1886	AA	1st	93-46	.669	—	Charlie Comiskey	—	944	592	20	.273	.333	.360	13	.227	.281	2.49	116	152
1887	AA	1st	95-40	.704	—	Charlie Comiskey	—	1131	761	39	.307	.371	.413	19	.258	.311	3.77	109	223
1888	AA	1st	92-43	.681	—	Charlie Comiskey	—	789	501	36	.250	.316	.324	19	.205	.242	2.09	113	117
1889	AA	2nd	90-45	.667	2.0	Charlie Comiskey	—	957	680	58	.266	.339	.370	39	.240	.299	3.00	116	291
1890	AA	3rd	77-58	.570	12.5	McCarthy/Kerins/Roseman/ Campau/McCarthy/Gerhardt	—	870	736	48	.273	.350	.370	38	.223	.286	3.67	139	537
1891	AA	2nd	85-51	.625	8.5	Charlie Comiskey	—	976	753	58	.266	.357	.355	50	.245	.330	3.27	125	173
1892	NL	9th	31-42	.425	20.5	J. Glasscock/C. Stricker/J. Crooks													
	NL	11th	25-52	.325	28.5	J. Crooks/G. Gore/B. Caruthers	192,442	703	922	45	.226	.312	.298	47	.267	.333	4.20	92	241
1893	NL	10th	57-75	.432	30.5	Bill Watkins	195,000	745	829	10	.264	.343	.341	38	.266	.340	4.06	99	69
1894	NL	9th	56-76	.424	35.0	Doggie Miller	155,000	771	953	54	.286	.354	.408	48	.299	.366	5.29	101	82
1895	NL	11th	39-92	.298	48.5	Buckenberger/Von Der Ahe/ Quinn/Phelan	170,000	747	1032	38	.281	.338	.374	64	.320	.376	5.76	101	147
1896	NL	11th	40-90	.308	50.5	Diddlebock/Latham/Von Der Ahe/ Connor/Dowd	184,000	593	929	37	.257	.313	.346	40	.309	.371	5.33	95	143
1897	NL	12th	29-102	.221	63.5	Dowd/Nicol/Hallman/Von Der Ahe	136,400	588	1083	31	.275	.336	.356	54	.330	.396	6.21	97	310
1898	NL	12th	39-111	.260	63.5	Tim Hurst	151,700	571	929	13	.247	.309	.305	32	.295	.351	4.53	120	140
1899	NL	5th	84-67	.556	18.5	Patsy Tebeau	373,909	819	739	47	.285	.347	.378	41	.277	.325	3.36	120	342
1900	NL	5th	65-75	.464	19.0	Patsy Tebeau/Louie Heilbroner	270,000	744	748	36	.291	.356	.375	37	.284	.331	3.75	85	95
1901	NL	4th	76-64	.543	14.5	Patsy Donovan	379,988	792	689	39	.284	.337	.381	39	.266	.318	3.68	94	102
1902	NL	6th	56-78	.418	44.5	Patsy Donovan	226,417	517	695	10	.258	.306	.304	16	.288	.339	3.47	100	55
1903	NL	8th	43-94	.314	46.5	Patsy Donovan	226,538	505	795	8	.251	.297	.313	25	.284	.349	3.67	102	142
1904	NL	5th	75-79	.487	31.5	Kid Nichols	386,750	602	595	24	.253	.306	.327	23	.238	.286	2.64	98	170
1905	NL	6th	58-96	.377	47.5	Kid Nichols/Jimmy Burke/Matt Robison	292,800	535	734	20	.248	.307	.321	28	.279	.333	3.59	86	92
1906	NL	7th	52-98	.347	63.0	John McCloskey	283,770	475	607	10	.235	.291	.296	17	.246	.317	3.04	103	142
1907	NL	8th	52-101	.340	55.5	John McCloskey	185,377	419	608	19	.232	.283	.288	20	.242	.317	2.69	96	82
1908	NL	8th	49-105	.318	50.0	John McCloskey	205,129	371	626	17	.223	.271	.283	16	.232	.296	2.64	93	154
1909	NL	7th	54-98	.355	56.0	Roger Bresnahan	299,982	583	731	15	.243	.326	.303	22	.263	.331	3.41	106	138
1910	NL	7th	63-90	.412	40.5	Roger Bresnahan	355,668	639	718	15	.248	.345	.319	30	.275	.350	3.78	87	62
1911	NL	5th	75-74	.503	22.0	Roger Bresnahan	447,768	671	745	26	.252	.337	.340	39	.254	.350	3.68	106	56
1912	NL	6th	63-90	.412	41.0	Roger Bresnahan	241,759	659	830	27	.268	.340	.352	31	.287	.361	3.85	105	65
1913	NL	8th	51-99	.340	49.0	Miller Huggins	203,531	528	755	15	.247	.316	.316	57	.280	.347	4.23	88	67
1914	NL	3rd	81-72	.529	13.0	Miller Huggins	256,099	558	540	33	.248	.314	.333	26	.249	.313	2.38	107	138
1915	NL	6th	72-81	.471	18.5	Miller Huggins	252,666	590	601	20	.254	.320	.333	30	.256	.314	2.89	105	70
1916	NL	7th	60-93	.392	33.5	Miller Huggins	224,308	476	629	25	.243	.295	.318	31	.265	.330	3.14	99	94
1917	NL	3rd	82-70	.539	15.0	Miller Huggins	288,491	531	567	26	.250	.303	.333	29	.248	.311	3.03	107	120
1918	NL	8th	51-78	.395	33.0	Jack Hendricks	110,599	454	527	27	.244	.301	.325	16	.261	.321	2.96	90	76
1919	NL	7th	54-83	.394	40.5	Branch Rickey	167,059	463	552	18	.256	.305	.326	25	.256	.326	3.23	90	78
1920	NL	5th	75-79	.487	18.0	Branch Rickey	326,836	675	682	32	.289	.337	.385	30	.277	.343	3.43	98	49
1921	NL	3rd	87-66	.569	7.0	Branch Rickey	384,773	809	681	83	.308	.358	.437	61	.282	.337	3.62	88	88
1922	NL	3rd	85-69	.552	8.0	Branch Rickey	536,998	863	819	107	.301	.357	.444	61	.300	.358	4.44	105	115
1923	NL	5th	79-74	.516	16.0	Branch Rickey	338,551	746	732	63	.286	.343	.398	70	.284	.344	3.87	79	58
1924	NL	6th	65-89	.422	28.5	Branch Rickey	272,885	740	750	67	.290	.341	.411	70	.290	.354	4.15	109	101
1925	NL	4th	77-76	.503	18.0	Branch Rickey/Rogers Hornsby	404,959	828	764	109	.299	.356	.445	86	.283	.347	4.36	104	123
1926	NL	1st	89-65	.578	—	Rogers Hornsby	668,428	817	678	90	.286	.348	.415	76	.269	.322	3.67	106	137
1927	NL	2nd	92-61	.601	1.5	Bob O'Farrell	749,340	754	665	84	.278	.343	.408	72	.271	.320	3.57	114	193
1928	NL	1st	95-59	.617	—	Bill McKechnie	761,574	807	636	113	.281	.353	.425	86	.270	.323	3.38	95	131
1929	NL	4th	78-74	.513	20.0	B. Southworth/G. Street/B. McKechnie	399,887	831	806	100	.293	.354	.438	101	.297	.357	4.66	98	98
1930	NL	1st	92-62	.597	—	Gabby Street	508,501	1004	784	104	.314	.372	.471	87	.294	.354	4.36	107	115
1931	NL	1st	101-53	.656	—	Gabby Street	608,535	815	614	60	.286	.342	.411	65	.273	.332	3.45	110	87
1932	NL	6th	72-82	.468	18.0	Gabby Street	279,219	684	717	76	.269	.324	.385	76	.282	.340	3.97	103	97
1933	NL	5th	82-71	.536	9.5	Gabby Street/Frank Frisch	256,171	687	609	57	.276	.329	.378	55	.261	.321	3.37	103	62
1934	NL	1st	95-58	.621	—	Frank Frisch	325,056	799	656	104	.288	.337	.425	77	.268	.323	3.69	125	119
1935	NL	2nd	96-58	.623	4.0	Frank Frisch	506,084	829	625	86	.284	.335	.405	68	.267	.318	3.52	103	75
1936	NL	2nd	87-67	.565	5.0	Frank Frisch	448,078	795	794	88	.281	.336	.410	89	.289	.344	4.50	92	87
1937	NL	4th	81-73	.526	15.0	Frank Frisch	430,811	789	733	94	.282	.331	.406	95	.281	.337	3.98	104	117
1938	NL	6th	71-80	.470	17.5	Frank Frisch/Mike Gonzalez	291,418	725	721	91	.279	.331	.407	77	.272	.333	3.84	133	152
1939	NL	2nd	92-61	.601	4.5	Ray Blades	400,245	779	633	98	.294	.354	.432	76	.260	.326	3.59	108	146
1940	NL	3rd	84-69	.549	16.0	R. Blades/M. Gonzalez/B. Southworth	324,078	747	699	119	.275	.336	.411	83	.267	.330	3.83	101	133
1941	NL	2nd	97-56	.634	2.5	Billy Southworth	633,645	734	589	70	.272	.340	.377	85	.242	.310	3.19	121	137
1942	NL	1st	106-48	.688	—	Billy Southworth	553,552	755	482	60	.268	.338	.379	49	.228	.294	2.55	110	102
1943	NL	1st	105-49	.682	—	Billy Southworth	517,135	679	475	70	.279	.333	.391	33	.237	.303	2.57	102	90
1944	NL	1st	105-49	.682	—	Billy Southworth	461,968	772	490	100	.275	.344	.402	55	.233	.298	2.67	90	53
1945	NL	2nd	95-59	.617	3.0	Billy Southworth	594,630	756	583	64	.273	.338	.371	70	.253	.319	3.24	95	76
1946	NL	1st	98-58	.628	—	Eddie Dyer	1,061,807	712	545	81	.265	.334	.381	63	.253	.320	3.01	110	115
1947	NL	2nd	89-65	.578	5.0	Eddie Dyer	1,247,913	780	634	115	.270	.347	.401	106	.266	.330	3.53	107	74
1948	NL	2nd	85-69	.552	6.5	Eddie Dyer	1,111,440	742	616	105	.263	.340	.389	103	.264	.326	3.91	98	76
1949	NL	2nd	96-58	.623	1.0	Eddie Dyer	1,430,676	766	616	102	.277	.348	.404	87	.254	.322	3.44	119	75
1950	NL	5th	78-75	.510	12.5	Eddie Dyer	1,093,411	693	670	102	.259	.339	.386	119	.268	.339	3.97	104	74
1951	NL	3rd	81-73	.526	15.5	Marty Marion	1,013,429	683	671	95	.264	.339	.382	119	.263	.337	3.95	102	85
1952	NL	3rd	88-66	.571	8.5	Eddie Stanky	913,113	677	630	97	.267	.340	.391	119	.247	.317	3.66	94	95
1953	NL	3rd	83-71	.539	22.0	Eddie Stanky	880,242	768	713	140	.273	.347	.424	139	.262	.333	4.23	98	77
1954	NL	6th	72-82	.468	25.0	Eddie Stanky	1,039,698	799	790	119	.281	.350	.421	170	.275	.343	4.50	106	104
1955	NL	7th	68-86	.442	30.5	Eddie Stanky/Harry Walker	849,130	654	757	143	.261	.321	.400	185	.262	.334	4.56	104	116
1956	NL	4th	76-78	.494	17.0	Fred Hutchinson	1,029,773	678	698	124	.268	.333	.399	155	.257	.327	3.97	99	89
1957	NL	2nd	87-67	.565	8.0	Fred Hutchinson	1,183,575	737	666	132	.274	.333	.405	140	.257	.322	3.78	101	97
1958	NL	5th	72-82	.468	20.0	Fred Hutchinson/Stan Hack	1,063,730	619	704	111	.261	.329	.380	158	.264	.338	4.12	116	126
1959	NL	7th	71-83	.461	16.0	Solly Hemus	929,953	641	725	118	.269	.331	.400	137	.271	.341	4.34	113	101
1960	NL	3rd	86-68	.558	9.0	Solly Hemus	1,096,632	639	616	138	.254	.321	.393	127	.253	.319	3.64	114	115

Year	Lg	Pos	W-L	Pct	GB	Manager	Att.	R	OR	HR	Avg	OBP	Slg	Opponent HR	Avg	OBP	ERA	Park Index Runs	HR
1961	NL	5th	80-74	.519	13.0	Solly Hemus/Johnny Keane	855,305	703	668	103	.271	.334	.393	136	.256	.330	3.74	130	106
1962	NL	6th	84-78	.519	17.5	Johnny Keane	953,895	774	664	137	.271	.335	.394	149	.252	.318	3.55	115	106
1963	NL	2nd	93-69	.574	6.0	Johnny Keane	1,170,546	747	628	128	.271	.326	.403	124	.241	.303	3.32	117	145
1964	NL	1st	93-69	.574	—	Johnny Keane	1,143,294	715	652	109	.272	.324	.392	133	.255	.308	3.43	127	137
1965	NL	7th	80-81	.497	16.5	Red Schoendienst	1,241,201	707	674	109	.254	.314	.371	166	.255	.315	3.77	114	162
1966	NL	6th	83-79	.512	12.0	Red Schoendienst	1,712,980	571	577	108	.251	.298	.368	130	.246	.306	3.11	96	89
1967	NL	1st	101-60	.627	—	Red Schoendienst	2,090,145	695	557	115	.263	.320	.379	97	.239	.297	3.05	99	101
1968	NL	1st	97-65	.599	—	Red Schoendienst	2,011,167	583	472	73	.249	.298	.346	82	.234	.285	2.49	85	74
1969	NL	4th-E	87-75	.537	13.0	Red Schoendienst	1,682,783	595	540	90	.253	.316	.359	99	.237	.305	2.94	95	82
1970	NL	4th-E	76-86	.469	13.0	Red Schoendienst	1,629,736	744	747	113	.263	.331	.379	102	.263	.337	4.06	114	79
1971	NL	2nd-E	90-72	.556	7.0	Red Schoendienst	1,604,671	739	699	95	.275	.338	.385	104	.263	.333	3.85	104	78
1972	NL	4th-E	75-81	.481	21.5	Red Schoendienst	1,196,894	568	600	70	.260	.317	.355	87	.247	.317	3.42	111	80
1973	NL	2nd-E	81-81	.500	1.5	Red Schoendienst	1,574,046	643	603	75	.259	.325	.357	105	.248	.310	3.25	78	46
1974	NL	2nd-E	86-75	.534	1.5	Red Schoendienst	1,838,413	677	643	83	.265	.331	.365	97	.254	.329	3.48	107	101
1975	NL	3rd-E	82-80	.506	10.5	Red Schoendienst	1,695,270	662	689	81	.273	.327	.375	98	.260	.328	3.57	108	90
1976	NL	5th-E	72-90	.444	29.0	Red Schoendienst	1,207,079	629	671	63	.260	.323	.359	91	.258	.329	3.60	110	77
1977	NL	3rd-E	83-79	.512	18.0	Vern Rapp	1,659,287	737	688	96	.270	.330	.388	139	.260	.326	3.81	90	63
1978	NL	5th-E	69-93	.426	21.0	Vern Rapp/Jack Krol/Ken Boyer	1,278,215	600	657	79	.249	.303	.358	94	.245	.323	3.58	90	54
1979	NL	3rd-E	86-76	.531	12.0	Ken Boyer	1,627,256	731	693	100	.278	.331	.401	127	.258	.318	3.72	112	99
1980	NL	4th-E	74-88	.457	17.0	Boyer/Krol/Herzog/Schoendienst	1,385,147	738	710	101	.275	.328	.400	90	.265	.326	3.93	108	77
1981	NL	2nd-E	30-20	.600	1.5	Whitey Herzog													
	NL	2nd-E	29-23	.558	0.5	Whitey Herzog	1,010,247	464	417	50	.265	.336	.377	52	.255	.312	3.63	102	82
1982	NL	1st-E	92-70	.568	—	Whitey Herzog	2,111,906	685	609	67	.264	.334	.364	94	.258	.320	3.37	105	87
1983	NL	4th-E	79-83	.488	11.0	Whitey Herzog	2,317,914	679	710	83	.270	.335	.384	115	.266	.330	3.79	97	94
1984	NL	3rd-E	84-78	.519	12.5	Whitey Herzog	2,037,448	652	645	75	.252	.317	.351	94	.262	.324	3.58	97	72
1985	NL	1st-E	101-61	.623	—	Whitey Herzog	2,637,563	747	572	87	.264	.335	.379	98	.246	.305	3.10	87	68
1986	NL	3rd-E	79-82	.491	28.5	Whitey Herzog	2,471,974	601	611	58	.236	.309	.327	135	.250	.311	3.37	105	86
1987	NL	1st-E	95-67	.586	—	Whitey Herzog	3,072,122	798	693	94	.263	.340	.378	129	.266	.331	3.91	95	84
1988	NL	5th-E	76-86	.469	25.0	Whitey Herzog	2,892,799	578	633	71	.249	.309	.337	91	.252	.312	3.47	109	72
1989	NL	3rd-E	86-76	.531	7.0	Whitey Herzog	3,080,980	632	608	73	.258	.321	.363	84	.243	.306	3.36	102	67
1990	NL	6th-E	70-92	.432	25.0	W. Herzog/R. Schoendienst/J. Torre	2,573,225	599	698	73	.256	.320	.358	98	.261	.320	3.87	112	111
1991	NL	2nd-E	84-78	.519	14.0	Joe Torre	2,448,699	651	648	68	.255	.322	.357	114	.255	.315	3.69	90	62
1992	NL	3rd-E	83-79	.512	13.0	Joe Torre	2,418,699	631	604	94	.262	.323	.375	118	.252	.303	3.38	102	102
1993	NL	3rd-E	87-75	.537	10.0	Joe Torre	2,844,977	758	744	118	.272	.341	.395	152	.276	.324	4.09	87	78
1994	NL	3rd-C	53-61	.465	13.0	Joe Torre	1,866,544	535	621	108	.263	.339	.414	134	.289	.351	5.14	98	95
1995	NL	4th-C	62-81	.434	22.5	Joe Torre/Mike Jorgensen	1,748,709	563	658	107	.247	.314	.374	135	.268	.333	4.09	104	88
1996	NL	1st-C	88-74	.543	—	Tony La Russa	2,659,239	759	706	142	.267	.330	.407	173	.251	.319	3.97	96	92
1997	NL	4th-C	73-89	.451	11.0	Tony La Russa	2,089,335	689	708	144	.255	.324	.396	124	.259	.329	3.88	92	90

Team Nicknames: St. Louis Browns 1882-1899, St. Louis Perfectos 1900-1901, St. Louis Cardinals 1902-1997.

Team Ballparks: Sportsman's Park I 1882-1892, Robison Field 1893-1919, Robison Field & Sportsman's Park III/Busch Stadium I (shared) 1920, Sportsman's Park III/Busch Stadium I 1921-1966, Busch Stadium II 1967-1997.

Teams: Cardinals

St. Louis Cardinals Individual Season Batting Leaders

Year	Batting Average		On-Base Percentage		Slugging Percentage		Home Runs		RBI		Stolen Bases	
1882	Bill Gleason	.288	Jack Gleason	.310	Oscar Walker	.396	Oscar Walker	7	Statistic unavailable		Statistic unavailable	
1883	Charlie Comiskey	.294	Hugh Nicol	.321	Charlie Comiskey	.397	Charlie Comiskey	2	Statistic unavailable		Statistic unavailable	
							Bill Gleason					
1884	Arlie Latham	.274	Bill Gleason	.326	Arlie Latham	.367	Tip O'Neill	3	Statistic unavailable		Statistic unavailable	
1885	Curt Welch	.271	Curt Welch	.318	Sam Barkley	.380	4 tied with	3	Curt Welch	69	Statistic unavailable	
1886	Tip O'Neill	.328	Tip O'Neill	.385	Tip O'Neill	.440	Bob Caruthers	4	Tip O'Neill	107	Arlie Latham	60
1887	Tip O'Neill	.435	Tip O'Neill	.490	Tip O'Neill	.691	Tip O'Neill	14	Tip O'Neill	123	Arlie Latham	129
1888	Tip O'Neill	.335	Yank Robinson	.400	Tip O'Neill	.446	Charlie Comiskey	6	Tip O'Neill	98	Arlie Latham	109
1889	Tip O'Neill	.335	Tip O'Neill	.419	Tip O'Neill	.478	Charlie Duffee	16	Tip O'Neill	110	Arlie Latham	69
1890	Tommy McCarthy	.350	Tommy McCarthy	.430	Tommy McCarthy	.467	Count Campau	9	Count Campau	75	Tommy McCarthy	83
1891	Tip O'Neill	.321	Denny Lyons	.445	Denny Lyons	.455	Denny Lyons	11	Tommy McCarthy	95	Dummy Hoy	59
									Tip O'Neill			
1892	Bob Caruthers	.277	Jack Crooks	.400	Bob Caruthers	.357	Perry Werden	8	Perry Werden	84	Cliff Carroll	30
1893	Steve Brodie	.318	Jack Crooks	.408	Perry Werden	.442	Perry Werden	2	Perry Werden	94	Tommy Dowd	59
1894	Doggie Miller	.339	Doggie Miller	.414	Roger Connor	.582	Bones Ely	12	Bones Ely	89	Tommy Dowd	31
1895	Duff Cooley	.339	Roger Connor	.423	Roger Connor	.508	Roger Connor	8	Roger Connor	77	Tom Brown	34
1896	Tom Parrott	.291	Roger Connor	.356	Roger Connor	.433	Roger Connor	11	Roger Connor	72	Monte Cross	40
											Tommy Dowd	
1897	Klondike Douglass	.329	Klondike Douglass	.403	Klondike Douglass	.405	Mike Grady	7	Fred Hartman	67	Monte Cross	38
1898	Lave Cross	.317	Lave Cross	.348	Lave Cross	.405	Jack Clements	3	Lave Cross	79	Jake Stenzel	21
							Lave Cross					
1899	Jesse Burkett	.396	Jesse Burkett	.463	Jesse Burkett	.500	Bobby Wallace	12	Bobby Wallace	108	Emmett Heidrick	55
1900	Jesse Burkett	.363	John McGraw	.505	Jesse Burkett	.474	Mike Donlin	10	Bill Keister	72	Patsy Donovan	45
1901	Jesse Burkett	.376	Jesse Burkett	.440	Jesse Burkett	.509	Jesse Burkett	10	Bobby Wallace	91	Emmett Heidrick	32
1902	Patsy Donovan	.315	Patsy Donovan	.363	Homer Smoot	.380	George Barclay	3	George Barclay	53	Patsy Donovan	34
							Homer Smoot					
1903	Patsy Donovan	.327	Patsy Donovan	.370	Homer Smoot	.396	Homer Smoot	4	Dave Brain	60	Jimmy Burke	28
1904	Jake Beckley	.325	Jake Beckley	.375	Dave Brain	.408	Dave Brain	7	Dave Brain	72	Danny Shay	36
1905	Homer Smoot	.311	Homer Smoot	.359	Homer Smoot	.433	Mike Grady	4	Homer Smoot	58	Spike Shannon	27
							Homer Smoot					
1906	Pug Bennett	.262	Pug Bennett	.334	Pug Bennett	.318	Mike Grady	3	Jake Beckley	44	Pug Bennett	20
1907	Red Murray	.262	Bobby Byrne	.307	Red Murray	.367	Red Murray	7	Red Murray	46	Red Murray	23
1908	Red Murray	.282	Red Murray	.332	Red Murray	.400	Red Murray	7	Red Murray	62	Red Murray	48
1909	Ed Konetchy	.286	Ed Konetchy	.366	Ed Konetchy	.396	Ed Konetchy	4	Ed Konetchy	80	Ed Konetchy	25
1910	Ed Konetchy	.302	Miller Huggins	.399	Ed Konetchy	.425	Rube Ellis	4	Ed Konetchy	78	Miller Huggins	34
1911	Steve Evans	.294	Miller Huggins	.385	Ed Konetchy	.433	Ed Konetchy	6	Ed Konetchy	88	Miller Huggins	37
1912	Ed Konetchy	.314	Miller Huggins	.422	Ed Konetchy	.455	Ed Konetchy	8	Ed Konetchy	82	Miller Huggins	35
1913	Rebel Oakes	.293	Miller Huggins	.432	Ed Konetchy	.427	Ed Konetchy	8	Ed Konetchy	68	Ed Konetchy	27
1914	Dots Miller	.290	Miller Huggins	.396	Chief Wilson	.393	Chief Wilson	9	Dots Miller	88	Cozy Dolan	42
1915	Frank Snyder	.298	Frank Snyder	.353	Tom Long	.446	Bob Bescher	4	Dots Miller	72	Bob Bescher	27
											Dots Miller	
1916	Rogers Hornsby	.313	Rogers Hornsby	.369	Rogers Hornsby	.444	3 tied with	6	Rogers Hornsby	65	Bob Bescher	39
1917	Rogers Hornsby	.327	Rogers Hornsby	.385	Rogers Hornsby	.484	Rogers Hornsby	8	Rogers Hornsby	66	Jack Smith	25
1918	Rogers Hornsby	.281	Rogers Hornsby	.349	Rogers Hornsby	.416	Walton Cruise	6	Rogers Hornsby	60	Doug Baird	25
1919	Rogers Hornsby	.318	Rogers Hornsby	.384	Rogers Hornsby	.430	Rogers Hornsby	8	Rogers Hornsby	71	Jack Smith	30
1920	Rogers Hornsby	.370	Rogers Hornsby	.431	Rogers Hornsby	.559	Austin McHenry	10	Rogers Hornsby	94	Jack Fournier	26
1921	Rogers Hornsby	.397	Rogers Hornsby	.458	Rogers Hornsby	.639	Rogers Hornsby	21	Rogers Hornsby	126	Jack Fournier	20
1922	Rogers Hornsby	.401	Rogers Hornsby	.459	Rogers Hornsby	.722	Rogers Hornsby	42	Rogers Hornsby	152	Jack Smith	18
1923	Rogers Hornsby	.384	Rogers Hornsby	.459	Rogers Hornsby	.627	Rogers Hornsby	17	Milt Stock	96	Jack Smith	32
1924	Rogers Hornsby	.424	Rogers Hornsby	.507	Rogers Hornsby	.696	Rogers Hornsby	25	Jim Bottomley	111	Jack Smith	24
1925	Rogers Hornsby	.403	Rogers Hornsby	.489	Rogers Hornsby	.756	Rogers Hornsby	39	Rogers Hornsby	143	Jack Smith	20
1926	Les Bell	.325	Ray Blades	.409	Les Bell	.518	Jim Bottomley	19	Jim Bottomley	120	Taylor Douthit	23
1927	Frankie Frisch	.337	Jim Bottomley	.387	Jim Bottomley	.509	Jim Bottomley	19	Jim Bottomley	124	Frankie Frisch	48
1928	Chick Hafey	.337	Jim Bottomley	.402	Jim Bottomley	.628	Jim Bottomley	31	Jim Bottomley	136	Frankie Frisch	29
1929	Chick Hafey	.338	Taylor Douthit	.416	Chick Hafey	.632	Jim Bottomley	29	Jim Bottomley	137	Frankie Frisch	24
							Chick Hafey					
1930	Frankie Frisch	.346	Chick Hafey	.407	Chick Hafey	.652	Chick Hafey	26	Frankie Frisch	114	Frankie Frisch	15
1931	Chick Hafey	.349	Chick Hafey	.404	Chick Hafey	.569	Chick Hafey	16	Chick Hafey	95	Frankie Frisch	28
1932	George Watkins	.312	George Watkins	.384	Ripper Collins	.474	Ripper Collins	21	Ripper Collins	91	Frankie Frisch	18
											George Watkins	
1933	Pepper Martin	.316	Pepper Martin	.387	Joe Medwick	.497	Joe Medwick	18	Joe Medwick	98	Pepper Martin	26
1934	Ripper Collins	.333	Ripper Collins	.393	Ripper Collins	.615	Ripper Collins	35	Ripper Collins	128	Pepper Martin	23
1935	Joe Medwick	.353	Joe Medwick	.386	Joe Medwick	.576	Ripper Collins	23	Joe Medwick	126	Pepper Martin	20
							Joe Medwick					
1936	Joe Medwick	.351	Joe Medwick	.387	Joe Medwick	.577	Johnny Mize	19	Joe Medwick	138	Pepper Martin	23
1937	Joe Medwick	.374	Johnny Mize	.427	Joe Medwick	.641	Joe Medwick	31	Joe Medwick	154	Terry Moore	13
1938	Johnny Mize	.337	Johnny Mize	.422	Johnny Mize	.614	Johnny Mize	27	Joe Medwick	122	Don Gutteridge	14
1939	Johnny Mize	.349	Johnny Mize	.444	Johnny Mize	.626	Johnny Mize	28	Joe Medwick	117	4 tied with	6
1940	Johnny Mize	.314	Johnny Mize	.404	Johnny Mize	.636	Johnny Mize	43	Johnny Mize	137	Terry Moore	18
1941	Johnny Mize	.317	Johnny Mize	.406	Johnny Mize	.535	Johnny Mize	16	Johnny Mize	100	Johnny Hopp	15
1942	Enos Slaughter	.318	Enos Slaughter	.412	Enos Slaughter	.494	Enos Slaughter	13	Enos Slaughter	98	Johnny Hopp	14
1943	Stan Musial	.357	Stan Musial	.425	Stan Musial	.562	Whitey Kurowski	13	Walker Cooper	81	Lou Klein	9
							Stan Musial		Stan Musial		Stan Musial	
1944	Stan Musial	.347	Stan Musial	.440	Stan Musial	.549	Whitey Kurowski	20	Ray Sanders	102	Johnny Hopp	15
1945	Whitey Kurowski	.323	Whitey Kurowski	.383	Whitey Kurowski	.511	Whitey Kurowski	21	Whitey Kurowski	102	Red Schoendienst	26
1946	Stan Musial	.365	Stan Musial	.434	Stan Musial	.587	Enos Slaughter	18	Enos Slaughter	130	Red Schoendienst	12
											Harry Walker	
1947	Stan Musial	.312	Whitey Kurowski	.420	Whitey Kurowski	.544	Whitey Kurowski	27	Whitey Kurowski	104	Red Schoendienst	6
1948	Stan Musial	.376	Stan Musial	.450	Stan Musial	.702	Stan Musial	39	Stan Musial	131	Stan Musial	7
1949	Stan Musial	.338	Stan Musial	.438	Stan Musial	.624	Stan Musial	36	Stan Musial	123	Red Schoendienst	8
1950	Stan Musial	.346	Stan Musial	.437	Stan Musial	.596	Stan Musial	28	Stan Musial	109	Tommy Glaviano	6
1951	Stan Musial	.355	Stan Musial	.449	Stan Musial	.614	Stan Musial	32	Stan Musial	108	Solly Hemus	7
											Enos Slaughter	
1952	Stan Musial	.336	Stan Musial	.432	Stan Musial	.538	Stan Musial	21	Enos Slaughter	101	Red Schoendienst	9
1953	Red Schoendienst	.342	Stan Musial	.437	Stan Musial	.609	Stan Musial	30	Stan Musial	113	Enos Slaughter	4

1486

Year	Batting Average		On-Base Percentage		Slugging Percentage		Home Runs		RBI		Stolen Bases	
1954	Stan Musial	.330	Stan Musial	.428	Stan Musial	.607	Stan Musial	35	Stan Musial	126	Wally Moon	18
1955	Stan Musial	.319	Stan Musial	.408	Stan Musial	.566	Stan Musial	33	Stan Musial	108	Ken Boyer	22
1956	Stan Musial	.310	Wally Moon	.390	Stan Musial	.522	Stan Musial	27	Stan Musial	109	Wally Moon	12
1957	Stan Musial	.351	Stan Musial	.422	Stan Musial	.612	Stan Musial	29	Del Ennis	105	Don Blasingame	21
1958	Stan Musial	.337	Stan Musial	.423	Stan Musial	.528	Ken Boyer	23	Ken Boyer	90	Don Blasingame	20
1959	Joe Cunningham	.345	Joe Cunningham	.453	Ken Boyer	.508	Ken Boyer	28	Ken Boyer	94	Don Blasingame Bill White	15
1960	Ken Boyer	.304	Ken Boyer	.370	Ken Boyer	.562	Ken Boyer	32	Ken Boyer	97	Julian Javier	19
1961	Ken Boyer	.329	Ken Boyer	.397	Ken Boyer	.533	Ken Boyer	24	Ken Boyer	95	Julian Javier	11
1962	Stan Musial	.330	Ken Boyer	.416	Stan Musial	.508	Ken Boyer	24	Bill White	102	Julian Javier	26
1963	Dick Groat	.319	Dick Groat	.377	Bill White	.491	Bill White	27	Ken Boyer	111	Julian Javier	18
1964	Curt Flood	.311	Ken Boyer	.365	Ken Boyer	.489	Ken Boyer	24	Ken Boyer	119	Lou Brock	33
1965	Curt Flood	.310	Curt Flood	.366	Bill White	.481	Bill White	24	Curt Flood	83	Lou Brock	63
1966	Orlando Cepeda	.303	Orlando Cepeda	.362	Orlando Cepeda	.469	Orlando Cepeda	17	Curt Flood	78	Lou Brock	74
1967	Curt Flood	.335	Orlando Cepeda	.399	Orlando Cepeda	.524	Orlando Cepeda	25	Orlando Cepeda	111	Lou Brock	52
1968	Curt Flood	.301	Curt Flood	.339	Lou Brock	.418	Orlando Cepeda	16	Mike Shannon	79	Lou Brock	62
1969	Lou Brock	.298	Joe Torre	.361	Joe Torre	.447	Joe Torre	18	Joe Torre	101	Lou Brock	53
1970	Joe Torre	.325	Joe Torre	.398	Dick Allen	.560	Dick Allen	34	Dick Allen	101	Lou Brock	51
1971	Joe Torre	.363	Joe Torre	.421	Joe Torre	.555	Joe Torre	24	Joe Torre	137	Lou Brock	64
1972	Lou Brock	.311	Lou Brock	.359	Ted Simmons	.465	Ted Simmons	16	Ted Simmons	96	Lou Brock	63
1973	Ted Simmons	.310	Joe Torre	.376	Ted Simmons	.438	Ted Simmons Joe Torre	13	Ted Simmons	91	Lou Brock	70
1974	Bake McBride	.309	Reggie Smith	.389	Reggie Smith	.528	Reggie Smith	23	Ted Simmons	103	Lou Brock	118
1975	Ted Simmons	.332	Ted Simmons	.396	Ted Simmons	.491	Reggie Smith	19	Ted Simmons	100	Lou Brock	56
1976	Lou Brock	.301	Ted Simmons	.371	Ted Simmons	.394	Heity Cruz	13	Ted Simmons	75	Lou Brock	56
1977	Garry Templeton	.322	Ted Simmons	.408	Ted Simmons	.500	Ted Simmons	21	Ted Simmons	95	Lou Brock	35
1978	Ted Simmons	.287	Ted Simmons	.377	Ted Simmons	.512	Ted Simmons	22	Ted Simmons	80	Garry Templeton	34
1979	Keith Hernandez	.344	Keith Hernandez	.417	Keith Hernandez	.513	Ted Simmons	26	Keith Hernandez	105	Tony Scott	37
1980	Keith Hernandez	.321	Keith Hernandez	.408	Ted Simmons	.505	George Hendrick	25	George Hendrick	109	Garry Templeton	31
1981	Keith Hernandez	.306	Keith Hernandez	.401	George Hendrick	.485	George Hendrick	18	George Hendrick	61	Tom Herr	23
1982	Lonnie Smith	.307	Keith Hernandez	.397	George Hendrick	.450	George Hendrick	19	George Hendrick	104	Lonnie Smith	68
1983	Lonnie Smith	.321	Lonnie Smith	.381	George Hendrick	.493	George Hendrick	18	George Hendrick	97	Lonnie Smith	43
1984	Willie McGee	.291	Lonnie Smith	.349	Willie McGee	.394	David Green	15	George Hendrick	69	Lonnie Smith	50
1985	Willie McGee	.353	Jack Clark	.393	Willie McGee	.503	Jack Clark	22	Tom Herr	110	Vince Coleman	110
1986	Ozzie Smith	.280	Ozzie Smith	.376	Willie McGee	.370	Andy Van Slyke	13	Tom Herr Andy Van Slyke	61	Vince Coleman	107
1987	Ozzie Smith	.303	Jack Clark	.459	Jack Clark	.597	Jack Clark	35	Jack Clark	106	Vince Coleman	109
1988	Willie McGee	.292	Ozzie Smith	.350	Tom Brunansky	.428	Tom Brunansky	22	Tom Brunansky	79	Vince Coleman	81
1989	Pedro Guerrero	.311	Pedro Guerrero	.391	Pedro Guerrero	.477	Tom Brunansky	20	Pedro Guerrero	117	Vince Coleman	65
1990	Willie McGee	.335	Willie McGee	.382	Willie McGee	.437	Todd Zeile	15	Pedro Guerrero	80	Vince Coleman	77
1991	Felix Jose	.305	Ozzie Smith	.380	Felix Jose	.438	Todd Zeile	11	Todd Zeile	81	Ray Lankford	44
1992	Ozzie Smith	.295	Ray Lankford	.371	Ray Lankford	.480	Ray Lankford	20	Ray Lankford	86	Ozzie Smith	43
1993	Gregg Jefferies	.342	Gregg Jefferies	.408	Gregg Jefferies	.485	Mark Whiten	25	Todd Zeile	103	Gregg Jefferies	46
1994	Gregg Jefferies	.325	Gregg Jefferies	.391	Gregg Jefferies	.489	Ray Lankford Todd Zeile	19	Todd Zeile	75	Bernard Gilkey	15
1995	Bernard Gilkey	.298	Ray Lankford	.360	Ray Lankford	.513	Ray Lankford	25	Ray Lankford	82	Brian Jordan Ray Lankford	24
1996	Brian Jordan	.310	Ray Lankford	.366	Ray Lankford	.486	Ron Gant	30	Brian Jordan	104	Ray Lankford	35
1997	Delino DeShields	.295	Ray Lankford	.411	Ray Lankford	.585	Ray Lankford	31	Ray Lankford	98	Delino DeShields	55

Teams: Cardinals

St. Louis Cardinals Individual Season Pitching Leaders

Year	ERA		Baserunners/9 IP		Innings Pitched		Strikeouts		Wins		Saves	
1882	Jumbo McGinnis	2.60	Jumbo McGinnis	10.3	Jumbo McGinnis	388.1	Jumbo McGinnis	134	Jumbo McGinnis	25	Eddie Fusselback	1
1883	Tony Mullane	2.19	Tony Mullane	8.7	Tony Mullane	460.2	Tony Mullane	191	Tony Mullane	35	Tony Mullane	1
1884	Dave Foutz	2.18	Dave Foutz	9.2	Jumbo McGinnis	354.1	Daisy Davis	143	Jumbo McGinnis	24	6 tied with	0
1885	Bob Caruthers	2.07	Bob Caruthers	9.4	Bob Caruthers	482.1	Bob Caruthers	190	Bob Caruthers	40	3 tied with	0
1886	Dave Foutz	2.11	Bob Caruthers	9.7	Dave Foutz	504.0	Dave Foutz	283	Dave Foutz	41	Dave Foutz Nat Hudson	1
1887	Bob Caruthers	3.30	Bob Caruthers	10.9	Silver King	390.0	Silver King	128	Silver King	32	Silver King Yank Robinson	1
1888	Silver King	1.64	Silver King	7.9	Silver King	585.2	Silver King	258	Silver King	45	7 tied with	0
1889	Jack Stivetts	2.25	Jack Stivetts	10.4	Silver King	458.0	Elton Chamberlin	202	Silver King	34	3 tied with	1
1890	Jack Stivetts	3.52	Toad Ramsey	11.3	Jack Stivetts	419.1	Jack Stivetts	289	Jack Stivetts	27	Bill Whitrock	1
1891	Jack Stivetts	2.86	Jack Stivetts	12.0	Jack Stivetts	440.0	Jack Stivetts	259	Jack Stivetts	33	5 tied with	1
1892	Pink Hawley	3.19	Pink Hawley	12.1	Kid Gleason	400.0	Kid Gleason	133	Kid Gleason	20	Bob Caruthers	1
1893	Ted Breitenstein	3.18	Ted Breitenstein	12.1	Ted Breitenstein	382.2	Ted Breitenstein	102	Kid Gleason	21	4 tied with	1
1894	Ted Breitenstein	4.79	Ted Breitenstein	13.8	Ted Breitenstein	447.1	Ted Breitenstein	140	Ted Breitenstein	27	8 tied with	0
1895	Ted Breitenstein	4.44	Ted Breitenstein	13.3	Ted Breitenstein	429.2	Ted Breitenstein	127	Ted Breitenstein	19	Ted Breitenstein	1
1896	Ted Breitenstein	4.48	Ted Breitenstein	13.6	Ted Breitenstein	339.2	Ted Breitenstein	114	Ted Breitenstein	18	Bill Kissinger	1
1897	Red Donahue	6.13	Red Donahue	15.8	Red Donahue	348.0	Bill Hart	67	Red Donahue	10	Red Donahue	1
1898	Jack Taylor	3.90	Jim Hughey	12.9	Jack Taylor	397.1	Jack Taylor	89	Jack Taylor	15	Willie Sudhoff Jack Taylor	1
1899	Cy Young	2.58	Cy Young	10.2	Jack Powell	373.0	Cy Young	111	Cy Young	26	Cy Young	1
1900	Cy Young	3.00	Cy Young	10.6	Cy Young	321.1	Cy Young	115	Cy Young	19	8 tied with	0
1901	Willie Sudhoff	3.52	Jack Powell	11.0	Jack Powell	338.1	Jack Powell	133	Jack Harper	23	Jack Powell	3
1902	Mike O'Neill	2.90	Mike O'Neill	11.7	Mike O'Neill	288.1	Mike O'Neill	105	Mike O'Neill	16	Wiley Dunham Ed Murphy	1
1903	Three Finger Brown	2.60	Chappie McFarland	12.1	Chappie McFarland	229.0	Three Finger Brown	83	Three Finger Brown Chappie McFarland	9	Clarence Currie Jim Hackett	1
1904	Kid Nichols	2.02	Kid Nichols	9.2	Jack Taylor	352.0	Kid Nichols	134	Kid Nichols	21	Kid Nichols Jack Taylor	1
1905	Buster Brown	2.97	Jack Taylor	11.6	Jack Taylor	309.0	Jack Taylor	102	Jack Taylor Jake Thielman	15	Chappie McFarland Jack Taylor	1
1906	Jack Taylor	2.15	Fred Beebe	10.8	Buster Brown	238.1	Fred Beebe	116	Fred Beebe	9	Ed Karger Chappie McFarland	1
1907	Ed Karger	2.03	Ed Karger	9.4	Stoney McGlynn	352.1	Fred Beebe	141	Ed Karger	15	Ed Karger Stoney McGlynn	1
1908	Bugs Raymond	2.03	Bugs Raymond	9.6	Bugs Raymond	324.1	Bugs Raymond	145	Bugs Raymond	15	Bugs Raymond	2
1909	Slim Sallee	2.42	Fred Beebe	11.5	Fred Beebe	287.2	Fred Beebe	105	Fred Beebe	15	Steve Melter	3
1910	Johnny Lush	3.20	Vic Willis	12.1	Bob Harmon	236.0	Bob Harmon	87	Johnny Lush	14	Frank Corridon Vic Willis	3
1911	Slim Sallee	2.76	Slim Sallee	11.1	Bob Harmon	348.0	Bob Harmon	144	Bob Harmon	23	Bob Harmon	4
1912	Slim Sallee	2.60	Slim Sallee	11.2	Slim Sallee	294.0	Slim Sallee	108	Bob Harmon	18	Slim Sallee	6
1913	Slim Sallee	2.71	Slim Sallee	10.3	Slim Sallee	276.0	Slim Sallee	106	Slim Sallee	19	Slim Sallee	5
1914	Bill Doak	1.72	Bill Doak	10.1	Pol Perritt	286.0	Bill Doak	118	Bill Doak	19	Slim Sallee	6
1915	Bill Doak	2.64	Slim Sallee	10.0	Bill Doak	276.0	Bill Doak	124	Bill Doak	16	Dan Griner Slim Sallee	3
1916	Lee Meadows	2.58	Bill Doak	11.0	Lee Meadows	289.0	Lee Meadows	120	Bill Doak Lee Meadows	12	Red Ames	8
1917	Red Ames	2.71	Red Ames	10.7	Bill Doak	281.1	Bill Doak	111	Bill Doak	16	Red Ames	3
1918	Red Ames	2.31	Red Ames	10.8	Bill Doak	211.0	Bill Doak	74	Gene Packard	12	Gene Packard	2
1919	Marv Goodwin	2.51	Marv Goodwin	10.3	Bill Doak	202.2	Bill Doak	69	Bill Doak	13	Oscar Tuero	4
1920	Bill Doak	2.53	Bill Doak	11.4	Jesse Haines	301.2	Jesse Haines	120	Bill Doak	20	Bill Sherdel	6
1921	Bill Doak	2.59	Bill Doak	11.4	Jesse Haines	244.1	Jesse Haines	84	Jesse Haines	18	Lou North	7
1922	Jeff Pfeffer	3.58	Jeff Pfeffer	12.2	Jeff Pfeffer	261.1	Lou North	84	Jeff Pfeffer	19	Lou North	4
1923	Jesse Haines	3.11	Jesse Haines	12.3	Jesse Haines	266.0	Bill Sherdel	78	Jesse Haines	20	Johnny Stuart	3
1924	Bill Sherdel	3.42	Bill Sherdel	12.3	Jesse Haines	222.2	Jesse Haines	69	Allen Sothoron	10	Bill Doak	3
1925	Bill Sherdel	3.11	Bill Sherdel	11.7	Jesse Haines	207.0	Allen Sothoron	67	Bill Sherdel	15	Eddie Dyer	3
1926	Flint Rhem	3.21	Flint Rhem	11.1	Flint Rhem	258.0	Flint Rhem	72	Flint Rhem	20	Pete Alexander Hi Bell	2
1927	Pete Alexander	2.52	Pete Alexander	10.1	Jesse Haines	300.2	Jesse Haines	89	Jesse Haines	24	Bill Sherdel	6
1928	Bill Sherdel	2.86	Pete Alexander	11.1	Bill Sherdel	248.2	Jesse Haines	77	Bill Sherdel	21	Hal Haid Bill Sherdel	5
1929	Syl Johnson	3.60	Syl Johnson	12.3	Bill Sherdel	195.2	Syl Johnson	80	Jesse Haines Syl Johnson	13	Hal Haid	4
1930	Jesse Haines	4.30	Syl Johnson	12.3	Wild Bill Hallahan	237.1	Wild Bill Hallahan	177	Wild Bill Hallahan	15	Hi Bell	8
1931	Syl Johnson	3.00	Syl Johnson	10.5	Wild Bill Hallahan	248.2	Wild Bill Hallahan	159	Wild Bill Hallahan	19	Jim Lindsey	7
1932	Wild Bill Hallahan	3.11	Wild Bill Hallahan	12.1	Dizzy Dean	286.0	Dizzy Dean	191	Dizzy Dean	18	Jim Lindsey	3
1933	Dizzy Dean	3.04	Dizzy Dean	10.7	Dizzy Dean	293.0	Dizzy Dean	199	Dizzy Dean	20	Dizzy Dean	4
1934	Dizzy Dean	2.66	Dizzy Dean	10.7	Dizzy Dean	311.2	Dizzy Dean	195	Dizzy Dean	30	Dizzy Dean	7
1935	Dizzy Dean	3.04	Paul Dean	10.8	Dizzy Dean	325.1	Dizzy Dean	190	Dizzy Dean	28	Paul Dean Dizzy Dean	5
1936	Dizzy Dean	3.17	Dizzy Dean	10.5	Dizzy Dean	315.0	Dizzy Dean	195	Dizzy Dean	24	Dizzy Dean	11
1937	Dizzy Dean	2.69	Dizzy Dean	10.7	Bob Weiland	264.1	Dizzy Dean	120	Lon Warneke	18	4 tied with	1
1938	Bill McGee	3.21	Curt Davis	11.2	Bob Weiland	228.1	Bob Weiland	117	Bob Weiland	16	Bill McGee	5
1939	Bob Bowman	2.60	Bob Bowman	10.7	Curt Davis	248.0	Mort Cooper	130	Curt Davis	22	Bob Bowman Clyde Shoun	9
1940	Lon Warneke	3.14	Clyde Shoun	11.0	Lon Warneke	232.0	Mort Cooper	95	Bill McGee Lon Warneke	16	Clyde Shoun	5
1941	Ernie White	2.40	Ernie White	10.5	Lon Warneke	246.0	Mort Cooper	118	Lon Warneke Ernie White	17	Bill Crouch	6
1942	Mort Cooper	1.78	Mort Cooper	9.0	Mort Cooper	278.2	Mort Cooper	152	Mort Cooper	22	Harry Gumbert	5
1943	Max Lanier	1.90	Mort Cooper	10.2	Mort Cooper	274.0	Mort Cooper	141	Mort Cooper	21	Harry Brecheen	4
1944	Mort Cooper	2.46	Ted Wilks	9.7	Mort Cooper	252.1	Max Lanier	141	Mort Cooper	22	Freddy Schmidt	5
1945	Harry Brecheen	2.52	Red Barrett	10.3	Red Barrett	246.2	Blix Donnelly	76	Red Barrett	21	4 tied with	2
1946	Howie Pollet	2.10	Murry Dickson	10.7	Howie Pollet	266.0	Harry Brecheen	117	Howie Pollet	21	Howie Pollet	5

Teams: Cardinals

Year	ERA		Baserunners/9 IP		Innings Pitched		Strikeouts		Wins		Saves	
1947	Al Brazle	2.84	Harry Brecheen	11.6	Murry Dickson	231.2	George Munger	123	Harry Brecheen George Munger	16	Ted Wilks	5
1948	Harry Brecheen	2.24	Harry Brecheen	9.4	Murry Dickson	252.1	Harry Brecheen	149	Harry Brecheen	20	Ted Wilks	13
1949	Gerry Staley	2.73	Gerry Staley	10.4	Howie Pollet	230.2	Howie Pollet	108	Howie Pollet	20	Ted Wilks	9
1950	Max Lanier	3.13	Harry Brecheen	11.0	Howie Pollet	232.1	Howie Pollet	117	Howie Pollet	14	Al Brazle	6
1951	Max Lanier	3.26	Max Lanier	11.3	Gerry Staley	227.0	Tom Poholsky	70	Gerry Staley	19	Al Brazle	7
1952	Gerry Staley	3.27	Gerry Staley	11.2	Gerry Staley	239.2	Vinegar Bend Mizell	146	Gerry Staley	17	Al Brazle	16
1953	Harvey Haddix	3.06	Harvey Haddix	10.4	Harvey Haddix	253.0	Vinegar Bend Mizell	173	Harvey Haddix	20	Al Brazle	18
1954	Harvey Haddix	3.57	Harvey Haddix	11.3	Harvey Haddix	259.2	Harvey Haddix	184	Harvey Haddix	18	Al Brazle	8
1955	Luis Arroyo	4.19	Harvey Haddix	12.2	Harvey Haddix	208.0	Harvey Haddix	150	Harvey Haddix	12	Barney Schultz	4
1956	Murry Dickson	3.07	Murry Dickson	10.7	Vinegar Bend Mizell	208.2	Vinegar Bend Mizell	153	Vinegar Bend Mizell	14	Larry Jackson	9
1957	Larry Jackson	3.47	Larry Jackson	11.0	Larry Jackson	210.1	Sam Jones	154	Larry Jackson Lindy McDaniel	15	Hoyt Wilhelm	11
1958	Sam Jones	2.88	Sam Jones	11.4	Sam Jones	250.0	Sam Jones	225	Sam Jones	14	Larry Jackson	8
1959	Larry Jackson	3.30	Larry Jackson	11.9	Larry Jackson	256.0	Larry Jackson	145	Larry Jackson Lindy McDaniel	14	Lindy McDaniel	15
1960	Ernie Broglio	2.74	Ernie Broglio	10.9	Larry Jackson	282.0	Ernie Broglio	188	Ernie Broglio	21	Lindy McDaniel	26
1961	Curt Simmons	3.13	Larry Jackson	11.2	Ray Sadecki	222.2	Bob Gibson	166	Larry Jackson Ray Sadecki	14	Lindy McDaniel	9
1962	Bob Gibson	2.85	Bob Gibson	10.7	Larry Jackson	252.1	Bob Gibson	208	Larry Jackson	16	Lindy McDaniel	14
1963	Curt Simmons	2.48	Curt Simmons	10.2	Bob Gibson	254.2	Bob Gibson	204	Ernie Broglio Bob Gibson	18	Bobby Shantz Ron Taylor	11
1964	Bob Gibson	3.01	Curt Simmons	10.6	Bob Gibson	287.1	Bob Gibson	245	Ray Sadecki	20	Barney Schultz	14
1965	Bob Gibson	3.07	Bob Gibson	10.7	Bob Gibson	299.0	Bob Gibson	270	Bob Gibson	20	Hal Woodeshick	15
1966	Bob Gibson	2.44	Bob Gibson	9.4	Bob Gibson	280.1	Bob Gibson	225	Bob Gibson	21	Joe Hoerner	13
1967	Dick Hughes	2.67	Dick Hughes	8.8	Dick Hughes	222.1	Steve Carlton	168	Dick Hughes	16	Joe Hoerner	15
1968	Bob Gibson	1.12	Bob Gibson	7.9	Bob Gibson	304.2	Bob Gibson	268	Bob Gibson	22	Joe Hoerner	17
1969	Steve Carlton	2.17	Bob Gibson	10.2	Bob Gibson	314.0	Bob Gibson	269	Bob Gibson	20	Joe Hoerner	15
1970	Bob Gibson	3.12	Bob Gibson	10.8	Bob Gibson	294.0	Bob Gibson	274	Bob Gibson	23	Chuck Taylor	8
1971	Bob Gibson	3.04	Bob Gibson	10.9	Steve Carlton	273.1	Bob Gibson	185	Steve Carlton	20	Moe Drabowsky	8
1972	Bob Gibson	2.46	Bob Gibson	10.3	Bob Gibson	278.0	Bob Gibson	208	Bob Gibson	19	Diego Segui	9
1973	Bob Gibson	2.77	Bob Gibson	10.1	Rick Wise	259.0	Rick Wise	144	Rick Wise	16	Diego Segui	17
1974	Lynn McGlothen	2.69	Lynn McGlothen	11.5	Bob Gibson	240.0	Lynn McGlothen	142	Lynn McGlothen	16	Al Hrabosky	9
1975	Bob Forsch	2.86	Bob Forsch	11.2	Lynn McGlothen	239.0	Lynn McGlothen	146	Bob Forsch Lynn McGlothen	15	Al Hrabosky	22
1976	John Denny	2.52	Pete Falcone	11.4	Pete Falcone	212.0	Pete Falcone	138	Lynn McGlothen	13	Al Hrabosky	13
1977	Eric Rasmussen	3.48	Eric Rasmussen	11.2	Eric Rasmussen	233.0	Eric Rasmussen	120	Bob Forsch	20	Al Hrabosky	10
1978	Pete Vuckovich	2.54	John Denny	10.8	John Denny	234.0	Pete Vuckovich	149	John Denny	14	Mark Littell	11
1979	Silvio Martinez	3.27	Bob Forsch	11.1	Pete Vuckovich	233.0	Pete Vuckovich	145	Silvio Martinez Pete Vuckovich	15	Mark Littell	13
1980	Pete Vuckovich	3.40	Bob Forsch	11.0	Pete Vuckovich	222.1	Pete Vuckovich	132	Pete Vuckovich	12	John Littlefield	9
1981	Bob Forsch	3.18	Bob Forsch	10.1	Lary Sorensen	140.1	Bruce Sutter	57	Bob Forsch	10	Bruce Sutter	25
1982	Joaquin Andujar	2.47	Joaquin Andujar	10.0	Joaquin Andujar	265.2	Joaquin Andujar	137	Joaquin Andujar Bob Forsch	15	Bruce Sutter	36
1983	John Stuper	3.68	Joaquin Andujar	11.7	Joaquin Andujar	225.0	Joaquin Andujar	125	Dave LaPoint John Stuper	12	Bruce Sutter	21
1984	Joaquin Andujar	3.34	Joaquin Andujar	10.2	Joaquin Andujar	261.1	Joaquin Andujar	147	Joaquin Andujar	20	Bruce Sutter	45
1985	John Tudor	1.93	John Tudor	8.6	John Tudor	275.0	John Tudor	169	Joaquin Andujar John Tudor	21	Jeff Lahti	19
1986	Danny Cox	2.90	Danny Cox	10.3	Bob Forsch	230.0	Danny Cox	108	Bob Forsch	14	Todd Worrell	36
1987	Joe Magrane	3.54	Greg Mathews	11.6	Danny Cox	199.1	Greg Mathews	108	3 tied with	11	Todd Worrell	33
1988	Joe Magrane	2.18	Joe Magrane	10.1	Jose DeLeon	225.1	Jose DeLeon	208	Jose DeLeon	13	Todd Worrell	32
1989	Joe Magrane	2.91	Jose DeLeon	9.5	Jose DeLeon	244.2	Jose DeLeon	201	Joe Magrane	18	Todd Worrell	20
1990	Joe Magrane	3.59	Joe Magrane	12.0	Joe Magrane	203.1	Jose DeLeon	164	John Tudor	12	Lee Smith	27
1991	Jose DeLeon	2.71	Bryn Smith	10.9	Bryn Smith	198.2	Ken Hill	121	Bryn Smith	12	Lee Smith	47
1992	Bob Tewksbury	2.16	Bob Tewksbury	9.3	Bob Tewksbury	233.0	Omar Olivares	124	Bob Tewksbury	16	Lee Smith	43
1993	Rene Arocha	3.78	Rene Arocha	11.1	Bob Tewksbury	213.2	Bob Tewksbury	97	Bob Tewksbury	17	Lee Smith	43
1994	Vicente Palacios	4.44	Vicente Palacios	11.5	Bob Tewksbury	155.2	Vicente Palacios	95	Bob Tewksbury	12	Mike Perez	12
1995	No qualifier		No qualifier		Mark Petkovsek	137.1	Donovan Osborne	82	Rich DeLucia	8	Tom Henke	36
1996	Donovan Osborne	3.53	Donovan Osborne	11.3	Andy Benes	230.1	Todd Stottlemyre	194	Andy Benes	18	Dennis Eckersley	30
1997	Andy Benes	3.10	Andy Benes	10.9	Matt Morris	217.0	Andy Benes	175	Matt Morris Todd Stottlemyre	12	Dennis Eckersley	36

Cardinals Franchise Batting Leaders—Career

Games

1	Stan Musial	3,026
2	Lou Brock	2,289
3	Ozzie Smith	1,990
4	Enos Slaughter	1,820
5	Red Schoendienst	1,795
6	Curt Flood	1,738
7	Ken Boyer	1,667
8	Rogers Hornsby	1,580
9	Julian Javier	1,578
10	Ted Simmons	1,564
11	Marty Marion	1,502
12	Willie McGee	1,409
13	Jim Bottomley	1,392
14	Frankie Frisch	1,311
15	Terry Moore	1,298
16	Joe Medwick	1,216
17	Dal Maxvill	1,205
18	Pepper Martin	1,189
19	Tim McCarver	1,181
20	Keith Hernandez	1,165

At-Bats

1	Stan Musial	10,972
2	Lou Brock	9,125
3	Ozzie Smith	7,160
4	Red Schoendienst	6,841
5	Enos Slaughter	6,775
6	Ken Boyer	6,334
7	Curt Flood	6,318
8	Rogers Hornsby	5,881
9	Ted Simmons	5,725
10	Julian Javier	5,631
11	Jim Bottomley	5,314
12	Marty Marion	5,313
13	Willie McGee	5,194
14	Frankie Frisch	5,059
15	Joe Medwick	4,747
16	Terry Moore	4,700
17	Charlie Comiskey	4,389
18	Bill White	4,165
19	Pepper Martin	4,117
20	Keith Hernandez	4,076

Runs

1	Stan Musial	1,949
2	Lou Brock	1,427
3	Rogers Hornsby	1,089
4	Enos Slaughter	1,071
5	Red Schoendienst	1,025
6	Ozzie Smith	991
7	Ken Boyer	988
8	Jim Bottomley	921
9	Curt Flood	845
10	Arlie Latham	832
11	Frankie Frisch	831
12	Charlie Comiskey	816
13	Joe Medwick	811
14	Pepper Martin	756
15	Ted Simmons	736
16	Terry Moore	719
	Julian Javier	719
18	Willie McGee	708
19	Tip O'Neill	697
20	Jack Smith	678

Hits

1	Stan Musial	3,630
2	Lou Brock	2,713
3	Rogers Hornsby	2,110
4	Enos Slaughter	2,064
5	Red Schoendienst	1,980
6	Ozzie Smith	1,944
7	Ken Boyer	1,855
8	Curt Flood	1,853
9	Jim Bottomley	1,727
10	Ted Simmons	1,704
11	Joe Medwick	1,590
12	Frankie Frisch	1,577
13	Willie McGee	1,547
14	Julian Javier	1,450
15	Marty Marion	1,402
16	Terry Moore	1,318
17	Bill White	1,241
18	Pepper Martin	1,227
19	Keith Hernandez	1,217
20	Charlie Comiskey	1,199

Doubles

1	Stan Musial	725
2	Lou Brock	434
3	Joe Medwick	377
4	Rogers Hornsby	367
5	Enos Slaughter	366
6	Red Schoendienst	352
7	Jim Bottomley	344
8	Ozzie Smith	338
9	Ted Simmons	332
10	Frankie Frisch	286
11	Curt Flood	271
12	Pepper Martin	270
13	Ken Boyer	269
14	Keith Hernandez	265
15	Terry Moore	263
16	Marty Marion	261
17	Chick Hafey	242
18	Willie McGee	238
19	Ray Lankford	222
20	Johnny Mize	218

Triples

1	Stan Musial	177
2	Rogers Hornsby	143
3	Enos Slaughter	135
4	Lou Brock	121
5	Jim Bottomley	119
6	Ed Konetchy	93
7	Willie McGee	82
8	Joe Medwick	81
9	Pepper Martin	75
10	Tip O'Neill	70
11	Garry Templeton	69
12	Johnny Mize	66
13	Red Schoendienst	65
14	Jack Smith	63
15	Frankie Frisch	61
	Ken Boyer	61
17	Charlie Comiskey	58
18	Vince Coleman	56
19	Julian Javier	55
20	Four tied at	51

Home Runs

1	Stan Musial	475
2	Ken Boyer	255
3	Rogers Hornsby	193
4	Jim Bottomley	181
5	Ted Simmons	172
6	Johnny Mize	158
7	Joe Medwick	152
8	Enos Slaughter	146
9	Bill White	140
10	Ray Lankford	135
11	Lou Brock	129
12	Chick Hafey	127
13	George Hendrick	122
14	Ripper Collins	106
	Whitey Kurowski	106
16	Joe Torre	98
17	Curt Flood	84
18	Keith Hernandez	81
19	Terry Moore	80
20	Wally Moon	78

RBI

1	Stan Musial	1,951
2	Enos Slaughter	1,148
3	Jim Bottomley	1,105
4	Rogers Hornsby	1,072
5	Ken Boyer	1,001
6	Ted Simmons	929
7	Joe Medwick	923
8	Lou Brock	814
9	Frankie Frisch	720
10	Ozzie Smith	664
11	Johnny Mize	653
12	Red Schoendienst	651
13	Curt Flood	633
14	Bill White	631
15	Willie McGee	624
16	Chick Hafey	618
17	Marty Marion	605
18	Keith Hernandez	595
19	George Hendrick	582
20	Tip O'Neill	571

Walks

1	Stan Musial	1,599
2	Ozzie Smith	876
3	Enos Slaughter	838
4	Lou Brock	681
5	Rogers Hornsby	660
6	Ken Boyer	631
7	Ted Simmons	624
8	Keith Hernandez	585
9	Miller Huggins	572
10	Jim Bottomley	509
11	Ray Lankford	502
12	Red Schoendienst	497
13	Marty Marion	451
14	Frankie Frisch	448
15	Curt Flood	439
16	Tom Herr	438
17	Johnny Mize	424
18	Yank Robinson	419
19	Jose Oquendo	414
20	Terry Moore	406

Strikeouts

1	Lou Brock	1,469
2	Ray Lankford	880
3	Ken Boyer	859
4	Willie McGee	817
5	Julian Javier	801
6	Stan Musial	696
7	Vince Coleman	628
8	Curt Flood	606
9	Bill White	601
10	Keith Hernandez	536
11	Mike Shannon	525
12	Marty Marion	520
13	Rogers Hornsby	480
14	Joe Torre	476
15	Dal Maxvill	470
16	Ted Simmons	453
17	George Hendrick	448
18	Pepper Martin	438
19	Terry Pendleton	430
20	Four tied at	429

Stolen Bases

1	Lou Brock	888
2	Vince Coleman	549
3	Ozzie Smith	433
4	Arlie Latham	369
5	Charlie Comiskey	336
6	Willie McGee	287
7	Tommy McCarthy	270
8	Yank Robinson	221
9	Jack Smith	203
10	Ray Lankford	199
11	Frankie Frisch	195
12	Tommy Dowd	187
13	Miller Huggins	174
14	Lonnie Smith	173
15	Tom Herr	152
16	Ed Konetchy	151
17	Curt Welch	148
18	Pepper Martin	146
19	Shorty Fuller	140
20	Garry Templeton	138

Runs Created

1	Stan Musial	2,418
2	Lou Brock	1,368
3	Rogers Hornsby	1,318
4	Enos Slaughter	1,206
5	Jim Bottomley	1,060
6	Ken Boyer	1,018
7	Ozzie Smith	953
8	Joe Medwick	920
9	Ted Simmons	910
10	Red Schoendienst	886
11	Tip O'Neill	855
12	Curt Flood	835
13	Frankie Frisch	810
14	Johnny Mize	743
15	Charlie Comiskey	739
16	Keith Hernandez	707
17	Willie McGee	701
18	Bill White	688
19	Pepper Martin	676
20	Terry Moore	662

Runs Created/27 Outs

(minimum 2000 Plate Appearances)

1	Tip O'Neill	10.69
2	Johnny Mize	9.31
3	Rogers Hornsby	8.69
4	Stan Musial	8.42
5	Yank Robinson	8.11
6	Tommy McCarthy	7.85
7	Chick Hafey	7.58
8	Joe Medwick	7.46
9	Jim Bottomley	7.33
10	Ripper Collins	7.26
11	Bill Gleason	6.85
12	Joe Cunningham	6.81
13	Enos Slaughter	6.58
14	Ray Blades	6.58
15	George Watkins	6.53
16	Arlie Latham	6.36
17	Keith Hernandez	6.31
18	Joe Torre	6.19
19	Charlie Comiskey	6.11
20	Pepper Martin	6.10

Batting Average

(minimum 2000 Plate Appearances)

1	Rogers Hornsby	.359
2	Tip O'Neill	.343
3	Johnny Mize	.336
4	Joe Medwick	.335
5	Stan Musial	.331
6	Chick Hafey	.326
7	Jim Bottomley	.325
8	Patsy Donovan	.314
9	Frankie Frisch	.312
10	George Watkins	.309
11	Joe Torre	.308
12	Ripper Collins	.307
13	Tommy McCarthy	.307
14	Ernie Orsatti	.306
15	Milt Stock	.305
16	Garry Templeton	.305
17	Enos Slaughter	.305
18	Joe Cunningham	.304
19	Austin McHenry	.302
20	Ray Blades	.301

On-Base Percentage

(minimum 2000 Plate Appearances)

1	Rogers Hornsby	.427
2	Johnny Mize	.419
3	Stan Musial	.417
4	Joe Cunningham	.413
5	Tip O'Neill	.406
6	Miller Huggins	.402
7	Ray Blades	.395
8	Solly Hemus	.392
9	Yank Robinson	.392
10	Jim Bottomley	.387
11	Keith Hernandez	.385
12	Enos Slaughter	.384
13	Joe Torre	.382
14	Chick Hafey	.379
15	Taylor Douthit	.373
16	Joe Medwick	.372
17	Ray Sanders	.372
18	Tommy McCarthy	.371
19	Ripper Collins	.370
20	Frankie Frisch	.370

Slugging Percentage

(minimum 2000 Plate Appearances)

1	Johnny Mize	.600
2	Rogers Hornsby	.568
3	Chick Hafey	.568
4	Stan Musial	.559
5	Joe Medwick	.545
6	Jim Bottomley	.537
7	Ripper Collins	.517
8	Tip O'Neill	.489
9	Ken Boyer	.475
10	George Watkins	.474
11	Bill White	.472
12	Ray Lankford	.470
13	George Hendrick	.470
14	Enos Slaughter	.463
15	Ray Blades	.460
16	Ted Simmons	.459
17	Joe Torre	.458
18	Whitey Kurowski	.455
19	Wally Moon	.454
20	Keith Hernandez	.448

Teams: Cardinals

Cardinals Franchise Pitching Leaders—Career

Wins

1	Bob Gibson	251
2	Jesse Haines	210
3	Bob Forsch	163
4	Bill Sherdel	153
5	Bill Doak	144
6	Dizzy Dean	134
7	Harry Brecheen	128
8	Dave Foutz	114
9	Silver King	111
10	Bob Caruthers	108
11	Slim Sallee	106
12	Mort Cooper	105
13	Max Lanier	101
	Larry Jackson	101
15	Howie Pollet	97
	Al Brazle	97
17	Ted Breitenstein	94
18	Wild Bill Hallahan	93
19	Gerry Staley	89
20	Jumbo McGinnis	88

Losses

1	Bob Gibson	174
2	Jesse Haines	158
3	Bill Doak	136
4	Bill Sherdel	131
5	Bob Forsch	127
6	Ted Breitenstein	125
7	Slim Sallee	107
8	Larry Jackson	86
9	Bob Harmon	81
10	Harry Brecheen	79
11	Gerry Staley	76
12	Dizzy Dean	75
13	Vinegar Bend Mizell	70
14	Max Lanier	69
15	Wild Bill Hallahan	68
16	Lee Meadows	67
17	Howie Pollet	65
18	Al Brazle	64
	Ray Sadecki	64
20	Flint Rhem	63

Winning Percentage
(minimum 100 decisions)

1	Dave Foutz	.704
2	Silver King	.694
3	Bob Caruthers	.692
4	Mort Cooper	.677
5	Dizzy Dean	.641
6	Lon Warneke	.629
7	Harry Brecheen	.618
8	Al Brazle	.602
9	George Munger	.602
10	Howie Pollet	.599
11	Max Lanier	.594
12	Jack Stivetts	.593
13	Bob Tewksbury	.593
14	Jumbo McGinnis	.591
15	Bob Gibson	.591
16	Wild Bill Hallahan	.578
17	Murry Dickson	.571
18	Jesse Haines	.571
19	Flint Rhem	.563
20	Bob Forsch	.562

Games

1	Jesse Haines	554
2	Bob Gibson	528
3	Bill Sherdel	465
4	Bob Forsch	455
5	Al Brazle	441
6	Bill Doak	376
7	Todd Worrell	348
8	Lindy McDaniel	336
9	Larry Jackson	330
10	Al Hrabosky	329
11	Ken Dayley	327
12	Slim Sallee	317
13	Gerry Staley	301
14	Harry Brecheen	292
15	Ted Wilks	282
16	Max Lanier	277
17	Dizzy Dean	273
18	Wild Bill Hallahan	259
19	Ted Breitenstein	250
20	Bruce Sutter	249

Games Started

1	Bob Gibson	482
2	Bob Forsch	401
3	Jesse Haines	388
4	Bill Doak	319
5	Bill Sherdel	244
6	Harry Brecheen	224
7	Ted Breitenstein	221
8	Slim Sallee	214
9	Larry Jackson	209
10	Dizzy Dean	196
11	Max Lanier	187
12	Wild Bill Hallahan	186
	Mort Cooper	186
14	Vinegar Bend Mizell	185
15	Howie Pollet	177
16	Steve Carlton	172
17	Curt Simmons	171
18	Dave Foutz	166
19	Ray Sadecki	165
20	Flint Rhem	164

Complete Games

1	Bob Gibson	255
2	Jesse Haines	209
3	Ted Breitenstein	197
4	Dave Foutz	156
5	Silver King	154
6	Bob Caruthers	151
7	Jumbo McGinnis	145
8	Bill Doak	144
	Bill Sherdel	144
10	Dizzy Dean	141
11	Slim Sallee	123
12	Harry Brecheen	122
13	Mort Cooper	105
14	Jack Powell	101
15	Willie Sudhoff	100
16	Jack Stivetts	99
17	Howie Pollet	96
18	Jack Taylor	90
19	Kid Gleason	86
20	Max Lanier	85

Shutouts

1	Bob Gibson	56
2	Bill Doak	32
3	Mort Cooper	28
4	Harry Brecheen	25
5	Jesse Haines	24
6	Dizzy Dean	23
7	Max Lanier	20
	Howie Pollet	20
9	Bob Forsch	19
10	Jumbo McGinnis	18
	Ernie Broglio	18
12	Slim Sallee	17
13	Dave Foutz	16
	Curt Simmons	16
	Steve Carlton	16
16	Larry Jackson	15
17	Lon Warneke	14
18	Wild Bill Hallahan	13
	George Munger	13
	Joaquin Andujar	13

Saves

1	Lee Smith	160
2	Todd Worrell	129
3	Bruce Sutter	127
4	Dennis Eckersley	66
5	Lindy McDaniel	64
6	Al Brazle	60
	Joe Hoerner	60
8	Al Hrabosky	59
9	Ken Dayley	39
10	Tom Henke	36
11	Dizzy Dean	30
12	Ted Wilks	29
13	Mark Littell	28
14	Slim Sallee	26
	Diego Segui	26
16	Bill Sherdel	25
17	Barney Schultz	21
	Hal Woodeshick	21
19	Six tied at	20

Innings Pitched

1	Bob Gibson	3,884.1
2	Jesse Haines	3,203.2
3	Bob Forsch	2,658.2
4	Bill Sherdel	2,450.2
5	Bill Doak	2,387.0
6	Ted Breitenstein	1,925.1
7	Slim Sallee	1,905.1
8	Harry Brecheen	1,790.1
9	Dizzy Dean	1,737.1
10	Larry Jackson	1,672.1
11	Mort Cooper	1,480.1
12	Dave Foutz	1,457.2
13	Max Lanier	1,454.2
14	Wild Bill Hallahan	1,453.1
15	Silver King	1,433.2
16	Howie Pollet	1,401.2
17	Bob Caruthers	1,395.0
18	Al Brazle	1,376.2
19	Jumbo McGinnis	1,325.0
20	Bob Harmon	1,284.1

Walks

1	Bob Gibson	1,336
2	Jesse Haines	870
3	Ted Breitenstein	839
4	Bob Forsch	780
5	Bill Doak	740
6	Wild Bill Hallahan	648
7	Bill Sherdel	595
8	Bob Harmon	594
9	Vinegar Bend Mizell	568
10	Max Lanier	524
11	Harry Brecheen	505
12	Al Brazle	492
13	Jack Stivetts	479
	Larry Jackson	479
15	Mort Cooper	478
16	Howie Pollet	473
	Ernie Broglio	473
18	Slim Sallee	467
19	Six tied at	449

Strikeouts

1	Bob Gibson	3,117
2	Dizzy Dean	1,095
3	Bob Forsch	1,079
4	Jesse Haines	979
5	Steve Carlton	951
6	Bill Doak	938
7	Larry Jackson	899
8	Harry Brecheen	857
9	Vinegar Bend Mizell	789
10	Wild Bill Hallahan	784
11	Bill Sherdel	779
12	Max Lanier	764
13	Jose DeLeon	763
14	Mort Cooper	758
15	Ernie Broglio	747
16	Jack Stivetts	691
17	Ray Sadecki	665
18	Ray Washburn	663
19	Slim Sallee	652
20	Howie Pollet	635

Strikeouts/9 Innings
(minimum 1000 Innings Pitched)

1	Bob Gibson	7.22
2	Steve Carlton	6.77
3	Ernie Broglio	5.98
4	Jack Stivetts	5.92
5	Vinegar Bend Mizell	5.83
6	Dizzy Dean	5.67
7	Ray Sadecki	5.42
8	Ray Washburn	5.22
9	Wild Bill Hallahan	4.86
10	Larry Jackson	4.84
11	Max Lanier	4.73
12	Mort Cooper	4.61
13	Joaquin Andujar	4.51
14	Harry Brecheen	4.31
15	Curt Simmons	4.28
16	Murry Dickson	4.24
17	George Munger	4.20
18	Howie Pollet	4.08
19	Dave Foutz	3.82
20	Bob Forsch	3.65

ERA
(minimum 1000 Innings Pitched)

1	Slim Sallee	2.67
2	Dave Foutz	2.67
3	Silver King	2.71
4	Jumbo McGinnis	2.73
5	Bob Caruthers	2.75
6	Mort Cooper	2.77
7	Max Lanier	2.84
8	Harry Brecheen	2.91
9	Bob Gibson	2.91
10	Bill Doak	2.93
11	Dizzy Dean	2.99
12	Lee Meadows	3.00
13	Jack Stivetts	3.01
14	Howie Pollet	3.06
15	Steve Carlton	3.10
16	Curt Simmons	3.25
17	Al Brazle	3.31
18	Joaquin Andujar	3.33
19	Ray Washburn	3.34
20	Murry Dickson	3.38

Component ERA
(minimum 1000 Innings Pitched)

1	Jumbo McGinnis	2.27
2	Bob Caruthers	2.30
3	Silver King	2.38
4	Dave Foutz	2.41
5	Mort Cooper	2.72
6	Slim Sallee	2.79
7	Bob Gibson	2.86
8	Harry Brecheen	2.86
9	Dizzy Dean	2.93
10	Max Lanier	3.01
11	Joaquin Andujar	3.01
12	Bill Doak	3.03
13	Jack Stivetts	3.05
14	Howie Pollet	3.26
15	Lee Meadows	3.27
16	Steve Carlton	3.30
17	Ray Washburn	3.39
18	Ernie Broglio	3.39
19	Murry Dickson	3.41
20	Curt Simmons	3.41

Opponent Average
(minimum 1000 Innings Pitched)

1	Bob Gibson	.228
2	Dave Foutz	.229
3	Ernie Broglio	.232
4	Bob Caruthers	.234
5	Silver King	.234
6	Jumbo McGinnis	.235
7	Mort Cooper	.235
8	Jack Stivetts	.239
9	Harry Brecheen	.240
10	Vinegar Bend Mizell	.240
11	Max Lanier	.245
12	Steve Carlton	.246
13	Joaquin Andujar	.246
14	Murry Dickson	.249
15	Dizzy Dean	.252
16	Howie Pollet	.252
17	Slim Sallee	.256
18	Ray Washburn	.257
19	Bob Forsch	.258
20	Bill Doak	.258

Opponent OBP
(minimum 1000 Innings Pitched)

1	Jumbo McGinnis	.267
2	Bob Caruthers	.272
3	Silver King	.277
4	Dave Foutz	.280
5	Bob Gibson	.297
6	Harry Brecheen	.297
7	Dizzy Dean	.297
8	Mort Cooper	.299
9	Joaquin Andujar	.300
10	Slim Sallee	.305
11	Curt Simmons	.306
12	Ray Washburn	.307
13	Ernie Broglio	.310
14	Steve Carlton	.311
15	Bob Forsch	.312
16	Lon Warneke	.312
17	Max Lanier	.313
18	Murry Dickson	.315
19	Howie Pollet	.316
20	Larry Jackson	.316

Cardinals Franchise Batting Leaders—Single Season

Games

1	Jose Oquendo	1989	163
2	Bill White	1963	162
	Curt Flood	1964	162
	Ken Boyer	1964	162
	Pedro Guerrero	1989	162
	Terry Pendleton	1989	162
7	Julian Javier	1963	161
	Dick Groat	1964	161
	Joe Torre	1970	161
	Joe Torre	1971	161
	Ted Simmons	1973	161
	Ken Reitz	1975	161
	Keith Hernandez	1977	161
	Keith Hernandez	1979	161
15	Ken Boyer	1962	160
	Bill White	1964	160
	Curt Flood	1966	160
	Lou Brock	1973	160
	Keith Hernandez	1982	160
20	Twelve tied at		159

At-Bats

1	Lou Brock	1967	689
2	Curt Flood	1964	679
3	Garry Templeton	1979	672
4	Taylor Douthit	1930	664
	Lou Brock	1970	664
6	Curt Flood	1963	662
7	Lou Brock	1968	660
8	Red Schoendienst	1947	659
9	Bill White	1963	658
10	Lou Brock	1969	655
11	Don Blasingame	1957	650
	Lou Brock	1973	650
13	Taylor Douthit	1928	648
14	Jack Rothrock	1934	647
	Garry Templeton	1978	647
16	Jimmy Brown	1939	645
17	Lou Brock	1966	643
18	Red Schoendienst	1950	642
19	Red Schoendienst	1949	640
	Lou Brock	1971	640

Runs

1	Tip O'Neill	1887	167
2	Arlie Latham	1887	163
3	Arlie Latham	1886	152
4	Jesse Burkett	1901	142
5	Rogers Hornsby	1922	141
6	Charlie Comiskey	1887	139
7	Tommy McCarthy	1890	137
8	Tommy McCarthy	1889	136
	Dummy Hoy	1891	136
10	Bill Gleason	1887	135
	Stan Musial	1948	135
12	Rogers Hornsby	1925	133
13	Joe Medwick	1935	132
14	Rogers Hornsby	1921	131
15	Taylor Douthit	1929	128
	Stan Musial	1949	128
17	Tommy McCarthy	1891	127
	Stan Musial	1953	127
19	Lou Brock	1971	126
20	Three tied at		124

Hits

1	Rogers Hornsby	1922	250
2	Joe Medwick	1937	237
3	Rogers Hornsby	1921	235
4	Stan Musial	1948	230
	Joe Torre	1971	230
6	Stan Musial	1946	228
7	Rogers Hornsby	1924	227
	Jim Bottomley	1925	227
9	Jesse Burkett	1901	226
10	Tip O'Neill	1887	225
11	Joe Medwick	1935	224
12	Joe Medwick	1936	223
13	Jesse Burkett	1899	221
14	Stan Musial	1943	220
15	Rogers Hornsby	1920	218
16	Willie McGee	1985	216
17	Curt Flood	1964	211
	Garry Templeton	1979	211
19	Keith Hernandez	1979	210
20	Frankie Frisch	1927	208

Doubles

1	Joe Medwick	1936	64
2	Joe Medwick	1937	56
3	Stan Musial	1953	53
4	Tip O'Neill	1887	52
	Enos Slaughter	1939	52
6	Stan Musial	1944	51
7	Stan Musial	1946	50
8	Joe Medwick	1939	48
	Stan Musial	1943	48
	Keith Hernandez	1979	48
11	Chick Hafey	1929	47
	Joe Medwick	1938	47
13	Rogers Hornsby	1922	46
	Chick Hafey	1928	46
	Frankie Frisch	1930	46
	Sparky Adams	1931	46
	Joe Medwick	1935	46
	Stan Musial	1948	46
	Lou Brock	1968	46
20	Four tied at		44

Triples

1	Perry Werden	1893	29
2	Roger Connor	1894	25
	Tom Long	1915	25
4	Duff Cooley	1895	20
	Rogers Hornsby	1920	20
	Jim Bottomley	1928	20
	Stan Musial	1943	20
	Stan Musial	1946	20
9	Tip O'Neill	1887	19
	Garry Templeton	1979	19
11	Frank Shugart	1894	18
	Rogers Hornsby	1921	18
	Joe Medwick	1934	18
	Stan Musial	1948	18
	Garry Templeton	1977	18
	Willie McGee	1985	18
17	Tommy Dowd	1895	17
	Ed Konetchy	1913	17
	Rogers Hornsby	1917	17
	Enos Slaughter	1942	17

Home Runs

1	Johnny Mize	1940	43
2	Rogers Hornsby	1922	42
3	Rogers Hornsby	1925	39
	Stan Musial	1948	39
5	Stan Musial	1949	36
6	Ripper Collins	1934	35
	Stan Musial	1954	35
	Jack Clark	1987	35
9	Dick Allen	1970	34
10	Stan Musial	1955	33
11	Stan Musial	1951	32
	Ken Boyer	1960	32
13	Jim Bottomley	1928	31
	Joe Medwick	1937	31
	Ray Lankford	1997	31
16	Stan Musial	1953	30
	Ron Gant	1996	30
18	Chick Hafey	1929	29
	Jim Bottomley	1929	29
	Stan Musial	1957	29

RBI

1	Joe Medwick	1937	154
2	Rogers Hornsby	1922	152
3	Rogers Hornsby	1925	143
4	Joe Medwick	1936	138
5	Jim Bottomley	1929	137
	Johnny Mize	1940	137
	Joe Torre	1971	137
8	Jim Bottomley	1928	136
9	Stan Musial	1948	131
10	Enos Slaughter	1946	130
11	Jim Bottomley	1925	128
	Ripper Collins	1934	128
13	Rogers Hornsby	1921	126
	Joe Medwick	1935	126
	Stan Musial	1954	126
16	Chick Hafey	1929	125
17	Jim Bottomley	1927	124
18	Tip O'Neill	1887	123
	Stan Musial	1949	123
20	Two tied at		122

Walks

1	Jack Crooks	1892	136
	Jack Clark	1987	136
3	Jack Crooks	1893	121
4	Dummy Hoy	1891	119
5	Yank Robinson	1889	118
6	Yank Robinson	1888	116
	Miller Huggins	1910	116
8	Stan Musial	1949	107
9	Miller Huggins	1914	105
	Stan Musial	1953	105
11	Stan Musial	1954	103
12	Keith Hernandez	1982	100
13	Stan Musial	1951	98
14	Miller Huggins	1911	96
	Solly Hemus	1952	96
	Stan Musial	1952	96
17	Ray Lankford	1997	95
18	Yank Robinson	1887	92
	Miller Huggins	1913	92
	Johnny Mize	1939	92

Strikeouts

1	Ron Gant	1997	162
2	Ray Lankford	1992	147
3	Jack Clark	1987	139
4	Lou Brock	1966	134
5	Ray Lankford	1996	133
6	Vince Coleman	1987	126
7	Steve Bilko	1953	125
	Ray Lankford	1997	125
9	Lou Brock	1968	124
10	Heity Cruz	1976	119
11	Dick Allen	1970	118
12	Lou Brock	1965	116
13	Lou Brock	1969	115
	Vince Coleman	1985	115
15	Mike Shannon	1968	114
	Ray Lankford	1991	114
17	Felix Jose	1991	113
	Ray Lankford	1994	113
19	Lou Brock	1973	112
20	Two tied at		111

Stolen Bases

1	Arlie Latham	1887	129
2	Lou Brock	1974	118
3	Charlie Comiskey	1887	117
4	Vince Coleman	1985	110
5	Arlie Latham	1888	109
	Vince Coleman	1987	109
7	Vince Coleman	1986	107
8	Tommy McCarthy	1888	93
9	Curt Welch	1887	89
10	Tommy McCarthy	1890	83
11	Vince Coleman	1988	81
12	Vince Coleman	1990	77
13	Yank Robinson	1887	75
14	Lou Brock	1966	74
15	Charlie Comiskey	1888	72
16	Lou Brock	1973	70
17	Arlie Latham	1889	69
18	Lonnie Smith	1982	68
19	Charlie Comiskey	1889	65
	Vince Coleman	1989	65

Runs Created

1	Tip O'Neill	1887	192
2	Rogers Hornsby	1922	179
3	Stan Musial	1948	177
4	Joe Medwick	1937	163
5	Rogers Hornsby	1924	162
6	Rogers Hornsby	1925	158
7	Stan Musial	1949	155
8	Jesse Burkett	1901	153
9	Rogers Hornsby	1921	152
	Stan Musial	1946	152
11	Tip O'Neill	1889	147
	Stan Musial	1951	147
13	Stan Musial	1953	145
14	Dummy Hoy	1891	144
15	Joe Medwick	1935	143
	Johnny Mize	1937	143
17	Stan Musial	1954	141
18	Five tied at		138

Runs Created/27 Outs

(minimum 3.1 Plate Appearances/Tm Gm)

1	Tip O'Neill	1887	16.99
2	Bob Caruthers	1887	13.03
3	Rogers Hornsby	1925	12.88
4	Rogers Hornsby	1924	12.73
5	Stan Musial	1948	11.72
6	Rogers Hornsby	1922	11.70
7	Jack Clark	1987	10.84
8	Tip O'Neill	1889	10.69
9	Denny Lyons	1891	10.64
10	Joe Medwick	1937	10.62
11	Jesse Burkett	1901	10.60
12	Johnny Mize	1937	10.53
13	Dave Foutz	1887	10.45
14	Rogers Hornsby	1921	10.41
15	Stan Musial	1951	10.30
16	Yank Robinson	1887	10.28
17	Rogers Hornsby	1923	10.27
18	John McGraw	1900	10.26
19	Jesse Burkett	1899	10.01
20	Stan Musial	1946	10.01

Batting Average

(minimum 3.1 Plate Appearances/Tm Gm)

1	Tip O'Neill	1887	.435
2	Rogers Hornsby	1924	.424
3	Rogers Hornsby	1925	.403
4	Rogers Hornsby	1922	.401
5	Rogers Hornsby	1921	.397
6	Jesse Burkett	1899	.396
7	Rogers Hornsby	1923	.384
8	Stan Musial	1948	.376
9	Jesse Burkett	1901	.376
10	Joe Medwick	1937	.374
11	Jim Bottomley	1923	.371
12	Rogers Hornsby	1920	.370
13	Jim Bottomley	1925	.367
14	Stan Musial	1946	.365
15	Johnny Mize	1937	.364
16	Jesse Burkett	1900	.363
17	Joe Torre	1971	.363
18	Bob Caruthers	1887	.357
19	Dave Foutz	1887	.357
20	Stan Musial	1943	.357

On-Base Percentage

(minimum 3.1 Plate Appearances/Tm Gm)

1	Rogers Hornsby	1924	.507
2	John McGraw	1900	.505
3	Tip O'Neill	1887	.490
4	Rogers Hornsby	1925	.489
5	Bob Caruthers	1887	.463
6	Jesse Burkett	1899	.463
7	Jack Clark	1987	.459
8	Rogers Hornsby	1922	.459
9	Rogers Hornsby	1923	.459
10	Rogers Hornsby	1921	.458
11	Joe Cunningham	1959	.453
12	Stan Musial	1948	.450
13	Stan Musial	1951	.449
14	Yank Robinson	1887	.445
15	Denny Lyons	1891	.445
16	Johnny Mize	1939	.444
17	Stan Musial	1944	.440
18	Jesse Burkett	1901	.440
19	Stan Musial	1949	.438
20	Stan Musial	1950	.437

Slugging Percentage

(minimum 3.1 Plate Appearances/Tm Gm)

1	Rogers Hornsby	1925	.756
2	Rogers Hornsby	1922	.722
3	Stan Musial	1948	.702
4	Rogers Hornsby	1924	.696
5	Tip O'Neill	1887	.691
6	Chick Hafey	1930	.652
7	Joe Medwick	1937	.641
8	Rogers Hornsby	1921	.639
9	Johnny Mize	1940	.636
10	Chick Hafey	1929	.632
11	Jim Bottomley	1928	.628
12	Rogers Hornsby	1923	.627
13	Johnny Mize	1939	.626
14	Stan Musial	1949	.624
15	Ripper Collins	1934	.615
16	Stan Musial	1951	.614
17	Johnny Mize	1938	.614
18	Stan Musial	1957	.612
19	Stan Musial	1953	.609
20	Stan Musial	1954	.607

Cardinals Franchise Pitching Leaders—Single Season

Wins

1	Silver King	1888	45
2	Dave Foutz	1886	41
3	Bob Caruthers	1885	40
4	Tony Mullane	1883	35
5	Silver King	1889	34
6	Dave Foutz	1885	33
	Jack Stivetts	1891	33
8	Silver King	1887	32
	Elton Chamberlin	1889	32
10	Bob Caruthers	1886	30
	Dizzy Dean	1934	30
12	Bob Caruthers	1887	29
13	Jumbo McGinnis	1883	28
	Dizzy Dean	1935	28
15	Jack Stivetts	1890	27
	Ted Breitenstein	1894	27
17	Cy Young	1899	26
18	Jumbo McGinnis	1882	25
	Dave Foutz	1887	25
	Nat Hudson	1888	25

Losses

1	Red Donahue	1897	35
2	Ted Breitenstein	1895	30
3	Bill Hart	1896	29
	Jack Taylor	1898	29
5	Pink Hawley	1894	27
	Bill Hart	1897	27
	Willie Sudhoff	1898	27
8	Ted Breitenstein	1896	26
9	Stoney McGlynn	1907	25
	Bugs Raymond	1908	25
11	Kid Gleason	1892	24
	Ted Breitenstein	1893	24
	Red Donahue	1896	24
	Jim Hughey	1898	24
15	Ted Breitenstein	1894	23
	Lee Meadows	1916	23
17	Jack Stivetts	1891	22
	Kid Gleason	1893	22
	Dan Griner	1913	22
20	Seven tied at		21

Winning Percentage
(minimum 15 decisions)

1	Howie Krist	1942	.813
	Al Hrabosky	1975	.813
3	Dizzy Dean	1934	.811
4	Ted Wilks	1944	.810
5	Jesse Haines	1931	.800
6	Harry Brecheen	1945	.789
7	Johnny Beazley	1942	.778
8	Bob Gibson	1970	.767
9	Jesse Haines	1926	.765
10	Bob Caruthers	1887	.763
11	Harry Brecheen	1944	.762
	George Munger	1947	.762
	Bob Tewksbury	1992	.762
14	Bill Doak	1914	.760
15	Mort Cooper	1942	.759
	Mort Cooper	1944	.759
17	Bob Caruthers	1885	.755
18	Bill Walker	1934	.750
	Lindy McDaniel	1960	.750
	John Tudor	1990	.750

Games

1	Mike Perez	1992	77
2	Todd Worrell	1987	75
3	Todd Worrell	1986	74
4	Cris Carpenter	1992	73
	Rob Murphy	1993	73
6	Mark Littell	1978	72
	Juan Agosto	1991	72
8	Bruce Sutter	1984	71
	Ken Dayley	1989	71
	Bob McClure	1992	71
	Tony Fossas	1997	71
12	Bruce Sutter	1982	70
	Lee Smith	1992	70
14	Al Hrabosky	1976	68
	Todd Worrell	1988	68
16	Ricky Horton	1987	67
	Frank DiPino	1989	67
	Lee Smith	1991	67
	Todd Worrell	1992	67
	T.J. Mathews	1996	67

Games Started

1	Silver King	1888	65
2	Dave Foutz	1886	57
3	Jack Stivetts	1891	56
4	Bob Caruthers	1885	53
	Silver King	1889	53
6	Elton Chamberlin	1889	51
7	Ted Breitenstein	1894	50
	Ted Breitenstein	1895	50
9	Tony Mullane	1883	49
10	Jack Taylor	1898	47
11	Dave Foutz	1885	46
	Jack Stivetts	1890	46
13	Jumbo McGinnis	1882	45
	Jumbo McGinnis	1883	45
	Kid Gleason	1892	45
	Kid Gleason	1893	45
17	Silver King	1887	44
18	Bob Caruthers	1886	43
	Ted Breitenstein	1896	43
	Jack Powell	1899	43

Complete Games

1	Silver King	1888	64
2	Dave Foutz	1886	55
3	Bob Caruthers	1885	53
4	Tony Mullane	1883	49
5	Silver King	1889	47
6	Dave Foutz	1885	46
	Ted Breitenstein	1894	46
	Ted Breitenstein	1895	46
9	Elton Chamberlin	1889	44
10	Jumbo McGinnis	1882	43
	Silver King	1887	43
	Kid Gleason	1892	43
13	Bob Caruthers	1886	42
	Jack Taylor	1898	42
15	Jumbo McGinnis	1883	41
	Jack Stivetts	1890	41
17	Jack Stivetts	1891	40
	Jack Powell	1899	40
	Cy Young	1899	40
20	Three tied at		39

Shutouts

1	Bob Gibson	1968	13
2	Dave Foutz	1886	11
3	Mort Cooper	1942	10
	John Tudor	1985	10
5	Bill Doak	1914	7
	Dizzy Dean	1934	7
	Mort Cooper	1944	7
	Harry Brecheen	1948	7
9	Jumbo McGinnis	1883	6
	Bob Caruthers	1885	6
	Silver King	1888	6
	Ed Karger	1907	6
	Jesse Haines	1927	6
	Mort Cooper	1943	6
	George Munger	1947	6
	Harvey Haddix	1953	6
	Curt Simmons	1963	6
	Bob Gibson	1965	6
19	Seventeen tied at		5

Saves

1	Lee Smith	1991	47
2	Bruce Sutter	1984	45
3	Lee Smith	1992	43
	Lee Smith	1993	43
5	Bruce Sutter	1982	36
	Todd Worrell	1986	36
	Tom Henke	1995	36
	Dennis Eckersley	1997	36
9	Todd Worrell	1987	33
10	Todd Worrell	1988	32
11	Dennis Eckersley	1996	30
12	Lee Smith	1990	27
13	Lindy McDaniel	1960	26
14	Bruce Sutter	1981	25
15	Al Hrabosky	1975	22
16	Bruce Sutter	1983	21
17	Todd Worrell	1989	20
18	Jeff Lahti	1985	19
19	Al Brazle	1953	18
20	Two tied at		17

Innings Pitched

1	Silver King	1888	585.2
2	Dave Foutz	1886	504.0
3	Bob Caruthers	1885	482.1
4	Tony Mullane	1883	460.2
5	Silver King	1889	458.0
6	Ted Breitenstein	1894	447.1
7	Jack Stivetts	1891	440.0
8	Ted Breitenstein	1895	429.2
9	Elton Chamberlin	1889	421.2
10	Jack Stivetts	1890	419.1
11	Dave Foutz	1885	407.2
12	Kid Gleason	1892	400.0
13	Jack Taylor	1898	397.1
14	Pink Hawley	1894	392.2
15	Silver King	1887	390.0
16	Jumbo McGinnis	1882	388.1
17	Bob Caruthers	1886	387.1
18	Jumbo McGinnis	1883	382.2
	Ted Breitenstein	1893	382.2
20	Kid Gleason	1893	380.1

Walks

1	Jack Stivetts	1891	232
2	Ted Breitenstein	1894	191
3	Kid Gleason	1893	187
4	Bob Harmon	1911	181
5	Jack Stivetts	1890	179
6	Ted Breitenstein	1895	178
7	Elton Chamberlin	1889	165
8	Ted Breitenstein	1893	156
9	Kid Gleason	1892	151
10	Pink Hawley	1894	149
11	Ted Breitenstein	1892	148
	Bill Hart	1897	148
13	Dave Foutz	1886	144
14	Bill Hart	1896	141
15	Ted Breitenstein	1896	138
16	Bob Harmon	1910	133
17	Willie McGill	1891	131
18	Roy Golden	1911	129
19	Ferdie Schupp	1920	127
20	Wild Bill Hallahan	1930	126

Strikeouts

1	Jack Stivetts	1890	289
2	Dave Foutz	1886	283
3	Bob Gibson	1970	274
4	Bob Gibson	1965	270
5	Bob Gibson	1969	269
6	Bob Gibson	1968	268
7	Jack Stivetts	1891	259
8	Silver King	1888	258
9	Toad Ramsey	1890	257
10	Bob Gibson	1964	245
11	Sam Jones	1958	225
	Bob Gibson	1966	225
13	Steve Carlton	1969	210
14	Bob Gibson	1962	208
	Bob Gibson	1972	208
	Jose DeLeon	1988	208
17	Bob Gibson	1963	204
18	Elton Chamberlin	1889	202
19	Jose DeLeon	1989	201
20	Dizzy Dean	1933	199

Strikeouts/9 Innings
(minimum 1 Inning Pitched/Tm Gm)

1	Andy Benes	1997	8.90
2	Bob Gibson	1970	8.39
3	Jose DeLeon	1988	8.31
4	Bob Gibson	1965	8.13
5	Sam Jones	1958	8.10
6	Jose DeLeon	1990	8.08
7	Bob Gibson	1962	8.01
8	Steve Carlton	1969	8.00
9	Todd Stottlemyre	1997	7.96
10	Bob Gibson	1968	7.92
11	Steve Carlton	1967	7.83
12	Todd Stottlemyre	1996	7.82
13	Bob Gibson	1969	7.71
14	Bob Gibson	1964	7.67
15	Sam Jones	1957	7.59
16	Bob Gibson	1967	7.55
17	Ernie Broglio	1960	7.48
18	Jose DeLeon	1989	7.39
19	Vicente Palacios	1994	7.27
20	Bob Gibson	1966	7.22

ERA
(minimum 1 Inning Pitched/Tm Gm)

1	Bob Gibson	1968	1.12
2	Silver King	1888	1.64
3	Bill Doak	1914	1.72
4	Mort Cooper	1942	1.78
5	Max Lanier	1943	1.90
6	John Tudor	1985	1.93
7	Kid Nichols	1904	2.02
8	Bugs Raymond	1908	2.03
9	Ed Karger	1907	2.03
10	Bob Caruthers	1885	2.07
11	Mike O'Neill	1904	2.09
12	Howie Pollet	1946	2.10
13	Slim Sallee	1914	2.10
14	Dave Foutz	1886	2.11
15	Johnny Lush	1908	2.12
16	Johnny Beazley	1942	2.13
17	Jack Taylor	1906	2.15
18	Bob Tewksbury	1992	2.16
19	Steve Carlton	1969	2.17
20	Two tied at		2.18

Component ERA
(minimum 1 Inning Pitched/Tm Gm)

1	Silver King	1888	1.44
2	Bob Gibson	1968	1.44
3	Tony Mullane	1883	1.63
4	Mort Cooper	1942	1.81
5	Bugs Raymond	1908	1.83
6	Jumbo McGinnis	1883	1.83
7	Kid Nichols	1904	1.83
8	John Tudor	1985	1.84
9	Ed Karger	1907	1.91
10	Dave Foutz	1884	1.93
11	Bob Caruthers	1886	1.96
12	Bob Caruthers	1885	1.98
13	Nat Hudson	1888	2.01
14	Harry Brecheen	1948	2.01
15	Jumbo McGinnis	1884	2.07
16	Bill Doak	1914	2.07
17	Jumbo McGinnis	1885	2.09
18	Dick Hughes	1967	2.09
19	Dave Foutz	1886	2.14
20	Jose DeLeon	1989	2.16

Opponent Average
(minimum 1 Inning Pitched/Tm Gm)

1	Bob Gibson	1968	.184
2	Fred Beebe	1908	.193
3	Silver King	1888	.197
4	Jose DeLeon	1989	.197
5	Dick Hughes	1967	.203
6	Bob Gibson	1962	.204
7	Mort Cooper	1942	.204
8	Jack Stivetts	1889	.205
9	Bob Gibson	1966	.207
10	Bugs Raymond	1908	.207
11	Fred Beebe	1906	.208
12	John Tudor	1985	.209
13	Tony Mullane	1883	.211
14	Dave Foutz	1884	.212
15	Ernie Broglio	1960	.213
16	Ernie Broglio	1963	.216
17	Steve Carlton	1969	.216
18	Dave Foutz	1886	.216
19	Bill Doak	1914	.216
20	Bob Caruthers	1886	.217

Opponent OBP
(minimum 1 Inning Pitched/Tm Gm)

1	Silver King	1888	.224
2	Bob Gibson	1968	.233
3	Tony Mullane	1883	.242
4	John Tudor	1985	.249
5	Dick Hughes	1967	.251
6	Jumbo McGinnis	1883	.252
7	Dave Foutz	1884	.255
8	Nat Hudson	1888	.256
9	Mort Cooper	1942	.258
10	Jumbo McGinnis	1884	.258
11	Bob Caruthers	1885	.260
12	Kid Nichols	1904	.260
13	Bob Caruthers	1886	.263
14	Ed Karger	1907	.265
15	Bob Tewksbury	1992	.265
16	Harry Brecheen	1948	.265
17	Bob Gibson	1966	.265
18	Fred Beebe	1908	.267
19	Jumbo McGinnis	1885	.267
20	Jose DeLeon	1989	.268

Cardinals Capsule

Best Season: *1946.* The Cardinals and Dodgers finished in a dead heat. In a three-game playoff, the Cardinals won the first two games to advance to the World Series. The Fall Classic went down to the late innings of Game 7 before Enos Slaughter's mad dash home secured the championship for St. Louis.

Worst Season: *1897.* The club went 29-102, finished 23.5 games behind the next-worst club in the National League, and didn't win a single series all year. The team went through four managers before owner Chris von der Ahe took the reins. Contemporary publications rated their performance "the worst in history."

Best Player: *Stan Musial.* Rogers Hornsby might have been better at his peak, but Musial was productive for a much longer period and he didn't get himself traded out of town.

Best Pitcher: *Bob Gibson.*

Best Reliever: *Bruce Sutter.*

Best Defensive Player: *Ozzie Smith* set the standard with his artistry at shortstop. Other St. Louis defensive greats include Terry Moore, Ken Boyer, Bill White, Bob Gibson, Curt Flood, Keith Hernandez and Terry Pendleton.

Hall of Famers: *Jim Bottomley, Lou Brock, Dizzy Dean, Frankie Frisch, Bob Gibson, Chick Hafey, Jesse Haines, Rogers Hornsby, Joe Medwick, Johnny Mize, Stan Musial, Red Schoendienst, Enos Slaughter.*

Franchise All-Star Team:

C	Ted Simmons	LF	Stan Musial
1B	Johnny Mize	CF	Ray Lankford
2B	Rogers Hornsby	RF	Enos Slaughter
3B	Ken Boyer	SP	Bob Gibson
SS	Ozzie Smith	RP	Bruce Sutter

Biggest Flakes: *Flint Rhem, Dizzy Dean* and *Pepper Martin.* Rhem is remembered for his creative explanation of his absence after a two-day bender: he said he'd been kidnapped and forced to drink whiskey. Dean's unique personality made him one of baseball's biggest drawing cards. Martin, who preferred not to play third base, was said to aim his throws at batters who bunted on him.

Strangest Career: *George Watkins* batted .373 in 391 at-bats during his rookie year in 1930. Some sources credit him with the highest rookie batting average of all time. He batted over .300 just once more during the remaining six years of his career. The fact that he was 30 years old when he broke in provides only a partial explanation.

What Might Have Been: In 1942, rookie righthander *Johnny Beazley* went 21-6 with a 2.13 ERA, finishing second in the league to teammate Mort Cooper in both victories and ERA. He spent the next three years in the service, where he hurt his arm while pitching an exhibition game. He won only nine more major league games after returning from the war.

Best Trades: *Curt Flood, Lou Brock, Willie McGee, Joaquin Andujar, John Tudor* and *George Hendrick.* Flood was acquired from the Reds in the winter of '57 in a five-player deal that cost the Cardinals little more than reliever Willard Schmidt. Seven years later, Brock was added to the outfield via a six-player deal that sent over-the-hill hurler Ernie Broglio to the Cubs. In 1981, the Cardinals stole minor league outfielder McGee from the Yankees for washed-up southpaw Bob Sykes, and nabbed Andujar in a midsummer deal that sent outfielder Tony Scott to Houston. In 1985, the Cardinals captured the NL pennant on the strength of the arms of Andujar and Tudor. The latter came over from Pittsburgh in a 1984 trade for outfielder Hendrick. Hendrick had given the Cardinals seven good years after the Padres traded him to St. Louis for pitcher Eric Rasmussen in 1978.

Worst Trades: *Three Finger Brown, Paul Derringer* and *Steve Carlton;* few teams have given away three finer arms. After going 9-13 as a rookie in 1903, Brown was dealt to the Cubs in a disastrous four-player swap. Derringer was lost to the Reds in a 1933 deal that netted shortstop Leo Durocher and little more. Finally, Carlton was traded straight-up for Rick Wise in 1972. In their post-Cardinals career, Brown, Derringer and Carlton won 230, 194 and 252 games, respectively. By comparison, the only two pitchers who've won more than 163 games for the Cardinals are Bob Gibson (251) and Jesse Haines (210).

Best-Looking Players: *Allen Sothoron, Joe Magrane, Bob Gibson, Bill White.*

Ugliest Players: *Branch Rickey, Slim Sallee, Fred Beebe, Willie McGee.*

I Don't Know: *Third Base.* For nearly three-quarters of a century, the Cardinals have been taking players from all over the diamond and converting them into third basemen. It all began in 1924, when they put shortstop Howard Freigau at the hot corner, where he remained for three years. They tried outfielder Wattie Holm at third in '28, and used second baseman Sparky Adams there in '30 and '31. Outfielder Pepper Martin served a three-year stint at third from 1933 through 1935 before returning to the outfield. Middle infielder Jimmy Brown was pressed into service at third in 1941 and 1942. Whitey Kurowski, Ray Jablonski and Ken Boyer gave the Cards three legitimate third basemen from World War II through the mid-'60s, but when they needed a third baseman in 1967, outfielder Mike Shannon got the call. When his career was ended in mid-1970 by a kidney ailment, catcher Joe Torre shed his shinguards and moved to third. He remained there until '73. Ken Reitz held down the position for most of the 1970s, but when he was traded after the 1980 season, second baseman Ken Oberkfell was next in line. He was succeeded in 1984 by minor league second baseman Terry Pendleton, who hadn't ever played third base prior to that season. When Pendleton left as a free agent after the 1990 season, catcher Todd Zeile was shifted to third by someone who'd made the same move himself, manager Joe Torre.

Best Nicknames: *"Harry the Cat" Brecheen; Harvey "Kitten" Haddix; "The Big Cat;" Johnny Mize; Jim "Kitty" Kaat; Bad News Galloway; Pink Hawley; John "Soldier Boy" Murphy; Dots Miller; Dizzy Dean; Peanuts Lowrey; Vinegar Bend Mizell; Rebel Oakes; Cotton Pippen; Creepy Crespi; Joe "Ducky" Medwick.*

Most Unappreciated Player: First baseman *Ed Konetchy* was one of the Senior Circuit's premier run producers for five years before being dealt to Pittsburgh following the 1913 season. Center fielder Terry Moore was well-respected in his day, but has been largely forgotten.

Most Overrated Player: *Vince Coleman.* Great basestealer. Awful ballplayer.

Most Admirable Stars: *Stan Musial* and *Ozzie Smith.*

Least Admirable Stars: *Rogers Hornsby* and *Garry Templeton.*

Best Season; Player: *Rogers Hornsby; 1922.* Hornsby won the Triple Crown by the widest margin in history. He batted .401; 47 points higher than anyone in the NL. He hit 42 homers (no one else in the NL hit more than 26) and drove in 154 runs (20 more than the next-closest batter).

Best Season; Pitcher: *Bob Gibson; 1968.* Even in "The Year of the Pitcher," Gibson's 1.12 ERA was 63 percent lower than the league ERA. Since the advent of the lively ball, no other pitcher has bested his league's ERA by more than 57 percent. Although his won-lost record was "only" 22-9, three of those losses were by the score of 1-0. By the same token, he won four 1-0 games that year. When the Cardinals scored three runs or more for him, he went 13-1. When they gave him one or two runs, he went 8-5. From June 6 through July 30 he made 11 starts and went 11-0, 0.27.

Most Impressive Individual Record: *Bob Gibson's* NL-record seven World Series victories. In nine World Series starts, he went 7-1 with a 1.89 ERA and won Game 7 in both the 1964 and 1967 World Series. He might have won Game 7 in 1968 if Curt Flood hadn't misjudged a flyball.

Biggest Tragedy: Center fielder *Austin McHenry* finished second in the NL batting race with a .350 average in 1921. He also finished fourth in the circuit with 17 home runs, third with 102 RBI and second with a .531 slugging percentage. The following year; a brain tumor killed him.

Fan Favorites: *Dizzy Dean, Stan Musial, Ozzie Smith.*

—Mat Olkin

San Diego Padres (1969-1997)

Year	Lg	Pos	W-L	Pct	GB	Manager	Att.	R	OR	HR	Avg	OBP	Slg	HR	Avg	OBP	ERA	Runs	HR
														Opponent				Park Index	
1969	NL	6th-W	52-110	.321	41.0	Preston Gomez	512,970	468	746	99	.225	.285	.329	113	.267	.341	4.24	97	80
1970	NL	6th-W	63-99	.389	39.0	Preston Gomez	643,679	681	788	172	.246	.312	.391	149	.267	.341	4.37	92	63
1971	NL	6th-W	61-100	.379	28.5	Preston Gomez	557,513	486	610	96	.233	.293	.332	93	.249	.321	3.22	92	81
1972	NL	6th-W	58-95	.379	36.5	Preston Gomez/Don Zimmer	644,273	488	665	102	.227	.283	.332	121	.255	.334	3.78	78	81
1973	NL	6th-W	60-102	.370	39.0	Don Zimmer	611,826	548	770	112	.244	.296	.351	157	.267	.334	4.16	91	95
1974	NL	6th-W	60-102	.370	42.0	John McNamara	1,075,399	541	830	99	.229	.302	.330	124	.275	.359	4.58	91	83
1975	NL	4th-W	71-91	.438	37.0	John McNamara	1,281,747	552	683	78	.244	.310	.335	99	.266	.329	3.48	100	67
1976	NL	5th-W	73-89	.451	29.0	John McNamara	1,458,478	570	662	64	.247	.310	.337	87	.253	.321	3.65	76	84
1977	NL	5th-W	69-93	.426	29.0	John McNamara/Bob Skinner/Alvin Dark	1,376,269	692	834	120	.249	.324	.375	160	.276	.353	4.43	78	78
1978	NL	4th-W	84-78	.519	11.0	Roger Craig	1,670,107	591	598	75	.252	.321	.348	74	.257	.317	3.28	82	57
1979	NL	5th-W	68-93	.422	22.0	Roger Craig	1,456,967	603	681	93	.242	.311	.348	108	.263	.326	3.69	93	69
1980	NL	6th-W	73-89	.451	19.5	Jerry Coleman	1,139,026	591	654	67	.255	.324	.342	97	.267	.331	3.65	84	61
1981	NL	6th-W	23-33	.411	12.5	Frank Howard													
	NL	6th-W	18-36	.333	15.5	Frank Howard	519,161	382	455	32	.256	.313	.346	64	.268	.341	3.72	88	60
1982	NL	4th-W	81-81	.500	8.0	Dick Williams	1,607,516	675	673	81	.257	.311	.359	139	.244	.307	3.52	82	98
1983	NL	4th-W	81-81	.500	10.0	Dick Williams	1,539,815	653	653	93	.250	.311	.351	144	.253	.320	3.62	99	132
1984	NL	1st-W	92-70	.568	—	Dick Williams	1,983,904	686	634	109	.259	.317	.371	122	.244	.315	3.48	95	110
1985	NL	3rd-W	83-79	.512	12.0	Dick Williams	2,210,352	650	622	109	.255	.320	.368	127	.257	.313	3.40	103	146
1986	NL	4th-W	74-88	.457	22.0	Steve Boros	1,805,716	656	723	136	.261	.321	.388	150	.258	.333	3.99	91	123
1987	NL	6th-W	65-97	.401	25.0	Larry Bowa	1,454,061	668	763	113	.260	.332	.378	175	.256	.332	4.27	94	120
1988	NL	3rd-W	83-78	.516	11.0	Larry Bowa/Jack McKeon	1,506,896	594	583	94	.247	.310	.351	112	.247	.304	3.28	93	118
1989	NL	2nd-W	89-73	.549	3.0	Jack McKeon	2,009,031	642	626	120	.251	.319	.369	133	.249	.310	3.38	101	141
1990	NL	4th-W	75-87	.463	16.0	Jack McKeon/Greg Riddoch	1,856,396	673	673	123	.257	.320	.380	147	.258	.320	3.68	105	109
1991	NL	3rd-W	84-78	.519	10.0	Greg Riddoch	1,804,289	636	646	121	.244	.310	.362	139	.252	.308	3.58	98	111
1992	NL	3rd-W	82-80	.506	16.0	Greg Riddoch/Jim Riggleman	1,721,406	617	636	135	.255	.313	.386	111	.261	.315	3.58	116	159
1993	NL	7th-W	61-101	.377	43.0	Jim Riggleman	1,375,432	679	772	153	.252	.312	.389	148	.266	.334	4.23	99	123
1994	NL	4th-W	47-70	.402	12.5	Jim Riggleman	953,857	479	531	92	.275	.330	.401	99	.252	.321	4.08	100	137
1995	NL	3rd-W	70-74	.486	8.0	Bruce Bochy	1,041,805	668	672	116	.272	.334	.397	142	.255	.331	4.13	85	97
1996	NL	1st-W	91-71	.562	—	Bruce Bochy	2,187,886	771	682	147	.265	.338	.402	138	.248	.313	3.72	91	107
1997	NL	4th-W	76-86	.469	14.0	Bruce Bochy	1,690,831	795	891	152	.271	.342	.407	172	.280	.352	4.99	87	112

Team Nicknames: San Diego Padres 1969-1997.

Team Ballparks: San Diego Stadium/Jack Murphy Stadium/Qualcomm Stadium 1969-1997.

Teams: Padres

San Diego Padres Individual Season Batting Leaders

Year	Batting Average		On-Base Percentage		Slugging Percentage		Home Runs		RBI		Stolen Bases	
1969	Ollie Brown	.264	Nate Colbert	.322	Nate Colbert	.482	Nate Colbert	24	Nate Colbert	66	Jose Arcia	14
1970	Cito Gaston	.318	Cito Gaston	.364	Cito Gaston	.543	Nate Colbert	38	Cito Gaston	93	Dave Campbell	18
1971	Ollie Brown	.273	Ollie Brown	.346	Nate Colbert	.462	Nate Colbert	27	Nate Colbert	84	Enzo Hernandez	21
1972	Nate Colbert	.250	Nate Colbert	.333	Nate Colbert	.508	Nate Colbert	38	Nate Colbert	111	Enzo Hernandez	24
1973	Dave Roberts	.286	Nate Colbert	.343	Dave Roberts	.472	Nate Colbert	22	Nate Colbert	80	Enzo Hernandez Derrel Thomas	15
1974	John Grubb	.286	John Grubb	.355	Dave Winfield	.438	Willie McCovey	22	Dave Winfield	75	Enzo Hernandez	37
1975	Tito Fuentes	.280	Dave Winfield	.354	Dave Winfield	.403	Willie McCovey	23	Dave Winfield	76	Dave Winfield	23
1976	Dave Winfield	.283	Dave Winfield	.366	Dave Winfield	.431	Dave Winfield	13	Mike Ivie	70	Dave Winfield	26
1977	George Hendrick	.311	Gene Tenace	.415	George Hendrick	.492	Dave Winfield	25	Dave Winfield	92	Gene Richards	56
1978	Dave Winfield	.308	Gene Tenace	.392	Dave Winfield	.499	Dave Winfield	24	Dave Winfield	97	Ozzie Smith	40
1979	Dave Winfield	.308	Gene Tenace	.403	Dave Winfield	.558	Dave Winfield	34	Dave Winfield	118	Ozzie Smith	28
1980	Gene Richards	.301	Dave Winfield	.365	Dave Winfield	.450	Dave Winfield	20	Dave Winfield	87	Gene Richards	61
1981	Luis Salazar	.303	Gene Richards	.373	Gene Richards	.407	Joe Lefebvre	8	Gene Richards	42	Ozzie Smith	22
1982	Terry Kennedy	.295	Sixto Lezcano	.388	Terry Kennedy	.486	Terry Kennedy	21	Terry Kennedy	97	Alan Wiggins	33
1983	Terry Kennedy	.284	Alan Wiggins	.360	Terry Kennedy	.434	Terry Kennedy	17	Terry Kennedy	98	Alan Wiggins	66
1984	Tony Gwynn	.351	Tony Gwynn	.410	Kevin McReynolds	.465	Kevin McReynolds Graig Nettles	20	Steve Garvey	86	Alan Wiggins	70
1985	Tony Gwynn	.317	Tony Gwynn	.364	Carmelo Martinez	.434	Carmelo Martinez	21	Steve Garvey	81	Garry Templeton	16
1986	Tony Gwynn	.329	Tony Gwynn	.381	Kevin McReynolds	.504	Kevin McReynolds	26	Kevin McReynolds	96	Tony Gwynn	37
1987	Tony Gwynn	.370	Tony Gwynn	.447	Tony Gwynn	.511	John Kruk	20	John Kruk	91	Tony Gwynn	56
1988	Tony Gwynn	.313	Tony Gwynn	.373	Tony Gwynn	.415	Carmelo Martinez	18	Tony Gwynn	70	Tony Gwynn	26
1989	Tony Gwynn	.336	Jack Clark	.410	Jack Clark	.459	Jack Clark	26	Jack Clark	94	Roberto Alomar	42
1990	Bip Roberts	.309	Bip Roberts	.375	Bip Roberts	.433	Jack Clark	25	Joe Carter	115	Bip Roberts	46
1991	Tony Gwynn	.317	Fred McGriff	.396	Fred McGriff	.494	Fred McGriff	31	Fred McGriff	106	Bip Roberts	26
1992	Gary Sheffield	.330	Fred McGriff	.394	Gary Sheffield	.580	Fred McGriff	35	Fred McGriff	104	Tony Fernandez	20
1993	Tony Gwynn	.358	Tony Gwynn	.398	Phil Plantier	.509	Phil Plantier	34	Phil Plantier	100	Derek Bell	26
1994	Tony Gwynn	.394	Tony Gwynn	.454	Tony Gwynn	.568	Phil Plantier	18	Tony Gwynn	64	Derek Bell	24
1995	Tony Gwynn	.368	Tony Gwynn	.404	Ken Caminiti	.513	Ken Caminiti	26	Ken Caminiti	94	Steve Finley	36
1996	Ken Caminiti	.326	Rickey Henderson	.410	Ken Caminiti	.621	Ken Caminiti	40	Ken Caminiti	130	Rickey Henderson	37
1997	Tony Gwynn	.372	Tony Gwynn	.409	Tony Gwynn	.547	Steve Finley	28	Tony Gwynn	119	Quilvio Veras	33

San Diego Padres Individual Season Pitching Leaders

Year	ERA		Baserunners/9 IP		Innings Pitched		Strikeouts		Wins		Saves	
1969	Joe Niekro	3.70	Joe Niekro	11.5	Clay Kirby	215.2	Clay Kirby	113	Joe Niekro Al Santorini	8	Billy McCool	7
1970	Danny Coombs	3.30	Dave Roberts	11.2	Pat Dobson	251.0	Pat Dobson	185	Pat Dobson	14	Tom Dukes	10
1971	Dave Roberts	2.10	Dave Roberts	10.1	Dave Roberts	269.2	Clay Kirby	231	Clay Kirby	15	Al Severinsen	8
1972	Clay Kirby	3.13	Clay Kirby	11.9	Steve Arlin	250.0	Clay Kirby	175	Clay Kirby	12	Mike Corkins	6
1973	Bill Greif	3.21	Bill Greif	11.2	Bill Greif	199.1	Clay Kirby	129	Steve Arlin	11	Mike Caldwell	10
1974	Dave Freisleben	3.66	Randy Jones	13.0	Bill Greif	226.0	Bill Greif	137	4 tied with	9	Vicente Romo	9
1975	Randy Jones	2.24	Randy Jones	9.4	Randy Jones	285.0	Dan Spillner	104	Randy Jones	20	Danny Frisella Bill Greif	9
1976	Randy Jones	2.74	Randy Jones	9.4	Randy Jones	315.1	Brent Strom	103	Randy Jones	22	Butch Metzger	16
1977	Bob Shirley	3.70	Bob Shirley	13.4	Bob Shirley	214.0	Bob Shirley	146	Bob Shirley	12	Rollie Fingers	35
1978	Gaylord Perry	2.73	Gaylord Perry	10.7	Gaylord Perry	260.2	Gaylord Perry	154	Gaylord Perry	21	Rollie Fingers	37
1979	Gaylord Perry	3.06	Randy Jones	11.1	Randy Jones	263.0	Gaylord Perry	140	Gaylord Perry	12	Rollie Fingers	13
1980	John Curtis	3.51	John Curtis	12.2	John Curtis	187.0	Steve Mura	109	Rollie Fingers Bob Shirley	11	Rollie Fingers	23
1981	Juan Eichelberger	3.50	Chris Welsh	11.9	Juan Eichelberger	141.1	Juan Eichelberger	81	Juan Eichelberger	8	Gary Lucas	13
1982	Tim Lollar	3.13	John Montefusco	10.8	Tim Lollar	232.2	Tim Lollar	150	Tim Lollar	16	Gary Lucas	16
1983	Dave Dravecky	3.58	Dave Dravecky	11.2	Eric Show	200.2	Tim Lollar	135	Eric Show	15	Gary Lucas	17
1984	Mark Thurmond	2.97	Ed Whitson	10.8	Eric Show	206.2	Tim Lollar	131	Eric Show	15	Goose Gossage	25
1985	Dave Dravecky	2.93	LaMarr Hoyt	9.9	Eric Show	233.0	Eric Show	141	Andy Hawkins	18	Goose Gossage	26
1986	Andy Hawkins	4.30	Andy Hawkins	12.8	Andy Hawkins	209.1	Andy Hawkins	117	Andy Hawkins Lance McCullers	10	Goose Gossage	21
1987	Eric Show	3.84	Ed Whitson	11.6	Eric Show	206.1	Ed Whitson	135	Ed Whitson	10	Lance McCullers	16
1988	Eric Show	3.26	Eric Show	10.0	Eric Show	234.2	Eric Show	144	Eric Show	16	Mark Davis	28
1989	Ed Whitson	2.66	Ed Whitson	10.0	Bruce Hurst	244.2	Bruce Hurst	179	Ed Whitson	16	Mark Davis	44
1990	Ed Whitson	2.60	Bruce Hurst	10.1	Ed Whitson	228.2	Bruce Hurst	162	Ed Whitson	14	Craig Lefferts	23
1991	Andy Benes	3.03	Andy Benes	10.4	Andy Benes	223.0	Andy Benes	167	Andy Benes Bruce Hurst	15	Craig Lefferts	23
1992	Andy Benes	3.35	Bruce Hurst	11.3	Andy Benes	231.1	Andy Benes	169	Bruce Hurst	14	Randy Myers	38
1993	Andy Benes	3.78	Andy Benes	11.3	Andy Benes	230.2	Andy Benes	179	Andy Benes	15	Gene Harris	23
1994	Andy Ashby	3.40	Andy Ashby	10.5	Andy Benes	172.1	Andy Benes	189	Joey Hamilton	9	Trevor Hoffman	20
1995	Andy Ashby	2.94	Joey Hamilton	11.3	Joey Hamilton	204.1	Andy Ashby	150	Andy Ashby	12	Trevor Hoffman	31
1996	Fernando Valenzuela	3.62	Bob Tewksbury	11.8	Joey Hamilton	211.2	Joey Hamilton	184	Joey Hamilton	15	Trevor Hoffman	42
1997	Andy Ashby	4.13	Andy Ashby	11.7	Andy Ashby	200.2	Andy Ashby	144	Joey Hamilton	12	Trevor Hoffman	37

Teams: Padres

Padres Franchise Batting Leaders—Career

Games

1	Tony Gwynn	2,095
2	Garry Templeton	1,286
3	Dave Winfield	1,117
4	Tim Flannery	972
5	Gene Richards	939
6	Nate Colbert	866
7	Terry Kennedy	835
8	Benito Santiago	789
9	Carmelo Martinez	783
10	Cito Gaston	766
11	Fred Kendall	754
12	Enzo Hernandez	710
13	Luis Salazar	704
14	Bip Roberts	667
15	Jerry Turner	638
16	Steve Garvey	605
17	Ozzie Smith	583
18	Gene Tenace	573
19	John Grubb	513
20	Derrel Thomas	512

At-Bats

1	Tony Gwynn	8,187
2	Garry Templeton	4,512
3	Dave Winfield	3,997
4	Gene Richards	3,414
5	Nate Colbert	3,080
6	Terry Kennedy	2,987
7	Benito Santiago	2,872
8	Cito Gaston	2,615
9	Tim Flannery	2,473
10	Carmelo Martinez	2,325
11	Enzo Hernandez	2,324
12	Steve Garvey	2,292
13	Bip Roberts	2,258
14	Luis Salazar	2,237
15	Ozzie Smith	2,236
16	Fred Kendall	2,218
17	John Grubb	1,791
18	Kevin McReynolds	1,789
19	Derrel Thomas	1,779
20	Steve Finley	1,777

Runs

1	Tony Gwynn	1,237
2	Dave Winfield	599
3	Gene Richards	484
4	Nate Colbert	442
5	Garry Templeton	430
6	Bip Roberts	378
7	Steve Finley	331
8	Benito Santiago	312
9	Terry Kennedy	308
10	Steve Garvey	291
11	Carmelo Martinez	286
12	Ken Caminiti	275
13	Cito Gaston	269
14	Ozzie Smith	266
15	Tim Flannery	255
16	Roberto Alomar	246
17	Enzo Hernandez	241
18	Alan Wiggins	236
19	John Grubb	235
20	Four tied at	233

Hits

1	Tony Gwynn	2,780
2	Garry Templeton	1,135
3	Dave Winfield	1,134
4	Gene Richards	994
5	Terry Kennedy	817
6	Nate Colbert	780
7	Benito Santiago	758
8	Bip Roberts	673
9	Cito Gaston	672
10	Tim Flannery	631
	Steve Garvey	631
12	Luis Salazar	598
13	Carmelo Martinez	577
14	Enzo Hernandez	522
15	Fred Kendall	516
	Ozzie Smith	516
17	John Grubb	513
18	Steve Finley	508
19	Roberto Alomar	497
20	Ken Caminiti	478

Doubles

1	Tony Gwynn	460
2	Garry Templeton	195
3	Dave Winfield	179
4	Terry Kennedy	158
5	Nate Colbert	130
6	Benito Santiago	124
7	Gene Richards	123
8	Carmelo Martinez	111
9	Steve Garvey	107
10	John Grubb	101
11	Bip Roberts	98
	Ken Caminiti	98
13	Steve Finley	94
14	Cito Gaston	93
15	Kevin McReynolds	84
16	Roberto Alomar	78
17	Tim Flannery	77
18	Luis Salazar	73
19	Fred Kendall	72
20	Four tied at	70

Triples

1	Tony Gwynn	84
2	Gene Richards	63
3	Dave Winfield	39
4	Garry Templeton	36
5	Cito Gaston	29
6	Tim Flannery	25
7	Luis Salazar	24
8	Nate Colbert	22
	Steve Finley	22
10	Bip Roberts	21
11	Ozzie Smith	19
12	Kevin McReynolds	17
13	Benito Santiago	15
14	Derrel Thomas	14
15	Ivan Murrell	13
	Enzo Hernandez	13
	Bill Almon	13
	Gene Tenace	13
19	Alan Wiggins	12
	Roberto Alomar	12

Home Runs

1	Nate Colbert	163
2	Dave Winfield	154
3	Tony Gwynn	107
4	Ken Caminiti	92
5	Benito Santiago	85
6	Fred McGriff	84
7	Carmelo Martinez	82
8	Cito Gaston	77
9	Terry Kennedy	76
10	Gene Tenace	68
	Steve Finley	68
12	Kevin McReynolds	65
13	Steve Garvey	61
14	Phil Plantier	57
15	Ollie Brown	52
	Willie McCovey	52
17	Graig Nettles	51
	Jack Clark	51
19	Darrin Jackson	44
20	Four tied at	43

RBI

1	Tony Gwynn	973
2	Dave Winfield	626
3	Nate Colbert	481
4	Garry Templeton	427
5	Terry Kennedy	424
6	Benito Santiago	375
7	Carmelo Martinez	337
8	Cito Gaston	316
	Steve Garvey	316
10	Ken Caminiti	314
11	Kevin McReynolds	260
12	Fred McGriff	256
13	Gene Richards	251
14	Gene Tenace	239
15	Steve Finley	231
16	Luis Salazar	226
17	Jerry Turner	209
	Tim Flannery	209
19	Ollie Brown	208
20	Fred Kendall	201

Walks

1	Tony Gwynn	707
2	Dave Winfield	463
3	Gene Tenace	423
4	Nate Colbert	350
5	Gene Richards	338
6	Carmelo Martinez	327
7	Tim Flannery	277
8	Garry Templeton	272
9	Fred McGriff	243
10	Jack Clark	236
11	Ken Caminiti	227
12	John Kruk	215
13	Bip Roberts	212
14	John Grubb	208
15	Terry Kennedy	200
16	Ozzie Smith	196
	Rickey Henderson	196
18	Enzo Hernandez	189
19	Willie McCovey	174
20	Fred Kendall	172

Strikeouts

1	Nate Colbert	773
2	Garry Templeton	684
3	Cito Gaston	595
4	Dave Winfield	585
5	Benito Santiago	516
6	Terry Kennedy	508
7	Gene Richards	408
8	Carmelo Martinez	403
9	Tony Gwynn	389
10	Gene Tenace	386
11	Luis Salazar	369
12	Ken Caminiti	311
13	Bip Roberts	305
14	Fred McGriff	298
15	Tim Flannery	293
16	Dave Roberts	292
17	Ivan Murrell	273
18	Archi Cianfrocco	267
19	Kevin McReynolds	262
20	Ollie Brown	258

Stolen Bases

1	Tony Gwynn	308
2	Gene Richards	242
3	Alan Wiggins	171
4	Bip Roberts	148
5	Ozzie Smith	147
6	Dave Winfield	133
7	Enzo Hernandez	129
8	Garry Templeton	101
9	Luis Salazar	93
10	Roberto Alomar	90
11	Steve Finley	73
12	Rickey Henderson	66
13	Benito Santiago	62
14	Jerry Mumphrey	52
15	Derek Bell	50
16	Bobby Brown	49
17	Nate Colbert	48
18	Bill Almon	47
19	Jerry Turner	44
20	Tony Fernandez	43

Runs Created

1	Tony Gwynn	1,418
2	Dave Winfield	633
3	Gene Richards	485
4	Nate Colbert	463
5	Garry Templeton	429
6	Terry Kennedy	382
7	Bip Roberts	341
8	Ken Caminiti	326
9	Carmelo Martinez	324
10	Benito Santiago	306
11	Cito Gaston	295
12	Gene Tenace	293
13	Steve Finley	285
14	Tim Flannery	278
15	Steve Garvey	270
16	John Grubb	261
17	Fred McGriff	250
18	Kevin McReynolds	247
19	Luis Salazar	245
20	Roberto Alomar	234

Runs Created/27 Outs

(minimum 2000 Plate Appearances)

1	Tony Gwynn	6.54
2	Gene Tenace	6.11
3	Dave Winfield	5.64
4	Bip Roberts	5.41
5	John Grubb	5.28
6	Nate Colbert	5.16
7	Gene Richards	5.07
8	Carmelo Martinez	4.75
9	Terry Kennedy	4.53
10	Steve Garvey	4.12
11	Cito Gaston	3.94
12	Tim Flannery	3.85
13	Luis Salazar	3.78
14	Benito Santiago	3.64
15	Garry Templeton	3.22
16	Fred Kendall	2.71
17	Ozzie Smith	2.70
18	Enzo Hernandez	2.58

Batting Average

(minimum 2000 Plate Appearances)

1	Tony Gwynn	.340
2	Bip Roberts	.298
3	Gene Richards	.291
4	John Grubb	.286
5	Dave Winfield	.284
6	Steve Garvey	.275
7	Terry Kennedy	.274
8	Luis Salazar	.267
9	Benito Santiago	.264
10	Cito Gaston	.257
11	Tim Flannery	.255
12	Nate Colbert	.253
13	Garry Templeton	.252
14	Carmelo Martinez	.248
15	Gene Tenace	.237
16	Fred Kendall	.233
17	Ozzie Smith	.231
18	Enzo Hernandez	.225

On-Base Percentage

(minimum 2000 Plate Appearances)

1	Gene Tenace	.403
2	Tony Gwynn	.390
3	John Grubb	.363
4	Bip Roberts	.361
5	Dave Winfield	.357
6	Gene Richards	.357
7	Carmelo Martinez	.341
8	Tim Flannery	.335
9	Nate Colbert	.331
10	Terry Kennedy	.319
11	Steve Garvey	.309
12	Benito Santiago	.298
13	Luis Salazar	.298
14	Cito Gaston	.298
15	Ozzie Smith	.295
16	Garry Templeton	.293
17	Fred Kendall	.287
18	Enzo Hernandez	.283

Slugging Percentage

(minimum 2000 Plate Appearances)

1	Nate Colbert	.469
2	Dave Winfield	.464
3	Tony Gwynn	.455
4	Gene Tenace	.422
5	Steve Garvey	.409
6	Carmelo Martinez	.408
7	Terry Kennedy	.407
8	Benito Santiago	.406
9	Cito Gaston	.403
10	John Grubb	.397
11	Gene Richards	.387
12	Bip Roberts	.387
13	Luis Salazar	.375
14	Garry Templeton	.339
15	Tim Flannery	.317
16	Fred Kendall	.312
17	Ozzie Smith	.278
18	Enzo Hernandez	.267

Padres Franchise Pitching Leaders—Career

Wins

1	Eric Show	100
2	Randy Jones	92
3	Ed Whitson	77
4	Andy Benes	69
5	Andy Hawkins	60
6	Bruce Hurst	55
7	Dave Dravecky	53
8	Clay Kirby	52
9	Craig Lefferts	42
	Joey Hamilton	42
11	Dennis Rasmussen	41
	Greg Harris	41
13	Bob Shirley	39
	Andy Ashby	39
15	Tim Lollar	36
16	Rollie Fingers	34
17	Gaylord Perry	33
18	Steve Arlin	32
19	Dave Freisleben	31
	Mark Thurmond	31

Losses

1	Randy Jones	105
2	Eric Show	87
3	Clay Kirby	81
4	Andy Benes	75
5	Ed Whitson	72
6	Steve Arlin	62
7	Bill Greif	61
8	Andy Hawkins	58
9	Bob Shirley	57
10	Dave Freisleben	53
11	Dave Dravecky	50
12	Andy Ashby	43
13	Tim Lollar	42
	Dennis Rasmussen	42
15	Dan Spillner	41
16	Rollie Fingers	40
	Craig Lefferts	40
18	Bob Owchinko	39
	Greg Harris	39
20	Bruce Hurst	38

Winning Percentage
(minimum 75 decisions)

1	Bruce Hurst	.591
2	Eric Show	.535
3	Ed Whitson	.517
4	Dave Dravecky	.515
5	Greg Harris	.513
6	Craig Lefferts	.512
7	Andy Hawkins	.508
8	Dennis Rasmussen	.494
9	Andy Benes	.479
10	Andy Ashby	.476
11	Randy Jones	.467
12	Tim Lollar	.462
13	Bob Shirley	.406
14	Clay Kirby	.391
15	Dave Freisleben	.369
16	Steve Arlin	.340
17	Bill Greif	.322

Games

1	Craig Lefferts	375
2	Eric Show	309
3	Trevor Hoffman	281
4	Rollie Fingers	265
5	Randy Jones	264
6	Dave Tomlin	239
7	Gary Lucas	230
	Mark Davis	230
9	Lance McCullers	229
10	Ed Whitson	227
11	Gary Ross	219
12	Dave Dravecky	199
	Andy Hawkins	199
14	Bob Shirley	197
	Goose Gossage	197
16	Greg Harris	194
17	Dan Spillner	192
18	Rich Rodriguez	191
19	Andy Benes	187
20	Luis DeLeon	185

Games Started

1	Randy Jones	253
2	Eric Show	230
3	Ed Whitson	208
4	Andy Benes	186
5	Andy Hawkins	172
6	Clay Kirby	170
7	Bruce Hurst	131
8	Andy Ashby	121
9	Dave Dravecky	119
10	Steve Arlin	113
11	Dennis Rasmussen	110
12	Dave Freisleben	109
13	Joey Hamilton	108
14	Tim Lollar	106
15	Bill Greif	94
16	Bob Shirley	92
17	Mark Thurmond	85
18	Bob Owchinko	83
19	Greg Harris	71
20	Gaylord Perry	69

Complete Games

1	Randy Jones	71
2	Eric Show	35
3	Clay Kirby	34
4	Steve Arlin	31
5	Bruce Hurst	29
6	Dave Dravecky	23
7	Ed Whitson	22
8	Andy Hawkins	19
9	Bill Greif	18
10	Dave Roberts	17
	Dave Freisleben	17
12	Fred Norman	16
13	Gaylord Perry	15
	Andy Benes	15
15	Brent Strom	14
16	Juan Eichelberger	12
17	Dennis Rasmussen	11
18	Bob Shirley	10
19	Eight tied at	9

Shutouts

1	Randy Jones	18
2	Steve Arlin	11
	Eric Show	11
4	Bruce Hurst	10
5	Andy Benes	8
6	Clay Kirby	7
	Andy Hawkins	7
8	Fred Norman	6
	Dave Freisleben	6
	Dave Dravecky	6
	Ed Whitson	6
12	Bill Greif	5
	Eric Rasmussen	5
14	Dave Roberts	4
	Tim Lollar	4
	Joey Hamilton	4
17	Fourteen tied at	3

Saves

1	Trevor Hoffman	133
2	Rollie Fingers	108
3	Goose Gossage	83
4	Mark Davis	78
5	Craig Lefferts	64
6	Gary Lucas	49
7	Randy Myers	38
8	Lance McCullers	36
9	Luis DeLeon	31
10	Gene Harris	23
11	Vicente Romo	16
	Butch Metzger	16
13	Greg Harris	15
	Larry Andersen	15
15	Bill Greif	13
	John D'Acquisto	13
17	Mike Caldwell	12
	Bob Shirley	12
19	Tom Dukes	11
20	Four tied at	10

Innings Pitched

1	Randy Jones	1,766.0
2	Eric Show	1,603.1
3	Ed Whitson	1,354.1
4	Andy Benes	1,235.0
5	Clay Kirby	1,128.0
6	Andy Hawkins	1,102.2
7	Bruce Hurst	911.2
8	Dave Dravecky	900.1
9	Andy Ashby	777.1
10	Steve Arlin	745.0
11	Dave Freisleben	730.0
12	Bob Shirley	722.0
13	Joey Hamilton	717.1
14	Tim Lollar	680.2
15	Dennis Rasmussen	680.0
16	Greg Harris	673.1
17	Craig Lefferts	659.0
18	Bill Greif	645.0
19	Dan Spillner	570.0
20	Bob Owchinko	526.0

Walks

1	Eric Show	593
2	Clay Kirby	505
3	Randy Jones	414
4	Andy Hawkins	412
5	Andy Benes	402
6	Steve Arlin	351
7	Ed Whitson	350
8	Dave Freisleben	346
9	Tim Lollar	328
10	Bob Shirley	274
11	Dave Dravecky	270
12	Dan Spillner	255
13	Bill Greif	253
14	Mike Corkins	248
15	Bruce Hurst	242
16	Joey Hamilton	237
17	Dennis Rasmussen	227
18	John D'Acquisto	225
19	Juan Eichelberger	214
20	Andy Ashby	212

Strikeouts

1	Andy Benes	1,036
2	Eric Show	951
3	Clay Kirby	802
4	Ed Whitson	767
5	Randy Jones	677
6	Bruce Hurst	616
7	Andy Ashby	544
8	Joey Hamilton	492
9	Andy Hawkins	489
10	Greg Harris	462
11	Dave Dravecky	456
12	Tim Lollar	454
13	Steve Arlin	443
14	Bob Shirley	432
15	Craig Lefferts	404
16	Bill Greif	396
17	Trevor Hoffman	395
18	Scott Sanders	391
19	Dave Freisleben	376
20	Four tied at	346

Strikeouts/9 Innings
(minimum 750 Innings Pitched)

1	Andy Benes	7.55
2	Clay Kirby	6.40
3	Andy Ashby	6.30
4	Bruce Hurst	6.08
5	Eric Show	5.34
6	Ed Whitson	5.10
7	Dave Dravecky	4.56
8	Andy Hawkins	3.99
9	Randy Jones	3.45

ERA
(minimum 750 Innings Pitched)

1	Dave Dravecky	3.12
2	Bruce Hurst	3.27
3	Randy Jones	3.30
4	Andy Benes	3.57
5	Eric Show	3.59
6	Andy Ashby	3.62
7	Ed Whitson	3.69
8	Clay Kirby	3.73
9	Andy Hawkins	3.84

Component ERA
(minimum 750 Innings Pitched)

1	Bruce Hurst	3.00
2	Randy Jones	3.01
3	Dave Dravecky	3.15
4	Andy Benes	3.29
5	Ed Whitson	3.46
6	Andy Ashby	3.57
7	Eric Show	3.60
8	Clay Kirby	3.80
9	Andy Hawkins	3.90

Opponent Average
(minimum 750 Innings Pitched)

1	Andy Benes	.242
2	Clay Kirby	.243
3	Dave Dravecky	.243
4	Bruce Hurst	.244
5	Eric Show	.245
6	Ed Whitson	.256
7	Randy Jones	.256
8	Andy Ashby	.257
9	Andy Hawkins	.261

Opponent OBP
(minimum 750 Innings Pitched)

1	Bruce Hurst	.294
2	Randy Jones	.299
3	Dave Dravecky	.301
4	Ed Whitson	.303
5	Andy Benes	.304
6	Andy Ashby	.310
7	Eric Show	.316
8	Clay Kirby	.325
9	Andy Hawkins	.329

Padres Franchise Batting Leaders—Single Season

	Games				At-Bats				Runs				Hits		
1	Dave Winfield	1980	162	1	Steve Finley	1996	655	1	Steve Finley	1996	126	1	Tony Gwynn	1997	220
	Steve Garvey	1985	162	2	Steve Garvey	1985	654	2	Tony Gwynn	1987	119	2	Tony Gwynn	1987	218
	Joe Carter	1990	162	3	Gene Richards	1980	642	3	Rickey Henderson	1996	110	3	Tony Gwynn	1984	213
4	Steve Garvey	1984	161		Tony Gwynn	1986	642	4	Ken Caminiti	1996	109	4	Tony Gwynn	1986	211
	Steve Finley	1996	161	5	Joe Carter	1990	634	5	Tony Gwynn	1986	107	5	Tony Gwynn	1989	203
6	Jerry Mumphrey	1980	160	6	Roberto Alomar	1989	623	6	Alan Wiggins	1984	106	6	Tony Gwynn	1985	197
	Tony Gwynn	1986	160	7	Tony Gwynn	1985	622	7	Dave Winfield	1977	104		Tony Gwynn	1995	197
8	Ozzie Smith	1978	159		Tony Fernandez	1992	622		Bip Roberts	1990	104	8	Steve Finley	1996	195
	Dave Winfield	1979	159	9	Steve Garvey	1984	617		Steve Finley	1995	104	9	Gene Richards	1980	193
10	Dave Winfield	1978	158	10	Dave Winfield	1977	615	10	Steve Finley	1997	101	10	Cito Gaston	1970	186
	Gene Richards	1980	158	11	Bill Almon	1977	613	11	Dave Winfield	1979	97	11	Dave Winfield	1979	184
	Ozzie Smith	1980	158	12	Ozzie Smith	1980	609		Tony Gwynn	1997	97		Steve Garvey	1985	184
	Alan Wiggins	1984	158	13	Tony Gwynn	1984	606	13	Cito Gaston	1970	92		Roberto Alomar	1989	184
	Tony Gwynn	1984	158	14	Tony Gwynn	1989	604		Ken Caminiti	1997	92		Gary Sheffield	1992	184
	Kevin McReynolds	1986	158	15	Dave Winfield	1979	597	15	Gene Richards	1980	91	15	Dave Winfield	1978	181
	Tony Gwynn	1989	158	16	Alan Wiggins	1984	596	16	Gene Richards	1978	90	16	Ken Caminiti	1996	178
	Roberto Alomar	1989	158	17	Tony Gwynn	1997	592		Tony Gwynn	1985	90	17	Tony Gwynn	1990	177
18	Dave Winfield	1977	157	18	Ozzie Smith	1978	590	18	Dave Winfield	1980	89	18	Steve Garvey	1984	175
	Tony Gwynn	1987	157	19	Tony Gwynn	1987	589		Kevin McReynolds	1986	89		Tony Gwynn	1993	175
20	Three tied at		156	20	Three tied at		587	20	Two tied at		88	20	Bip Roberts	1990	172

	Doubles				Triples				Home Runs				RBI		
1	Tony Gwynn	1997	49	1	Tony Gwynn	1987	13	1	Ken Caminiti	1996	40	1	Ken Caminiti	1996	130
2	Steve Finley	1996	45	2	Gene Richards	1978	12	2	Nate Colbert	1970	38	2	Tony Gwynn	1997	119
3	Terry Kennedy	1982	42		Gene Richards	1981	12		Nate Colbert	1972	38	3	Dave Winfield	1979	118
4	Tony Gwynn	1993	41	4	Bill Almon	1977	11	4	Fred McGriff	1992	35	4	Joe Carter	1990	115
5	Ken Caminiti	1996	37		Gene Richards	1977	11	5	Dave Winfield	1979	34	5	Nate Colbert	1972	111
6	John Grubb	1975	36		Tony Gwynn	1991	11		Phil Plantier	1993	34	6	Fred McGriff	1991	106
	Tony Gwynn	1987	36	7	Willie Davis	1976	10	7	Gary Sheffield	1992	33	7	Fred McGriff	1992	104
	Bip Roberts	1990	36		Dave Winfield	1979	10	8	Fred McGriff	1991	31	8	Gary Sheffield	1992	100
9	Tony Gwynn	1994	35		Tony Gwynn	1984	10	9	Steve Finley	1996	30		Phil Plantier	1993	100
10	Ollie Brown	1970	34		Tony Gwynn	1990	10	10	Cito Gaston	1970	29	10	Terry Kennedy	1983	98
	Ruppert Jones	1981	34	11	Nate Colbert	1969	9	11	Steve Finley	1997	28	11	Dave Winfield	1978	97
	Steve Garvey	1985	34		Cito Gaston	1970	9	12	Nate Colbert	1971	27		Terry Kennedy	1982	97
	Gary Sheffield	1992	34		Cito Gaston	1971	9	13	Kevin McReynolds	1986	26	13	Kevin McReynolds	1986	96
14	Tony Gwynn	1986	33		Gene Richards	1979	9		Jack Clark	1989	26	14	Steve Finley	1996	95
	Benito Santiago	1987	33		Steve Finley	1996	9		Ken Caminiti	1995	26	15	Jack Clark	1989	94
	Tony Gwynn	1995	33	16	Gene Richards	1980	8		Ken Caminiti	1997	26		Ken Caminiti	1995	94
	Ken Caminiti	1995	33		Gene Richards	1982	8	17	Dave Winfield	1977	25	17	Cito Gaston	1970	93
18	Tony Fernandez	1992	32		Garry Templeton	1982	8		Jack Clark	1990	25	18	Dave Winfield	1977	92
19	Kevin McReynolds	1986	31		Bip Roberts	1989	8	19	Three tied at		24		Steve Finley	1997	92
20	Three tied at		30		Steve Finley	1995	8					20	John Kruk	1987	91

	Walks				Strikeouts				Stolen Bases				Runs Created		
1	Jack Clark	1989	132	1	Nate Colbert	1970	150	1	Alan Wiggins	1984	70	1	Tony Gwynn	1997	138
2	Gene Tenace	1977	125	2	Nate Colbert	1973	146	2	Alan Wiggins	1983	66	2	Ken Caminiti	1996	136
	Rickey Henderson	1996	125	3	Jack Clark	1989	145	3	Gene Richards	1980	61	3	Tony Gwynn	1987	128
4	Gene Tenace	1979	105	4	Cito Gaston	1970	142	4	Ozzie Smith	1980	57	4	Dave Winfield	1979	125
	Fred McGriff	1991	105	5	Fred McGriff	1991	135	5	Gene Richards	1977	56	5	Steve Finley	1996	115
6	Jack Clark	1990	104	6	Nate Colbert	1972	127		Tony Gwynn	1987	56	6	Tony Gwynn	1984	113
7	Gene Tenace	1978	101	7	Phil Plantier	1993	124	7	Jerry Mumphrey	1980	52	7	Cito Gaston	1970	109
8	Willie McCovey	1974	96	8	Nate Colbert	1969	123	8	Bip Roberts	1990	46	8	Tony Gwynn	1986	108
	Fred McGriff	1992	96	9	Derek Bell	1993	122	9	Roberto Alomar	1989	42		Gary Sheffield	1992	108
10	Gene Tenace	1980	92	10	Cito Gaston	1971	121	10	Ozzie Smith	1978	40	10	Fred McGriff	1992	106
11	Carmelo Martinez	1985	87	11	Nate Colbert	1971	119		Tony Gwynn	1989	40	11	Jack Clark	1989	103
12	Dave Winfield	1979	85		Gene Tenace	1977	119	12	Enzo Hernandez	1974	37	12	Tony Gwynn	1995	101
13	Tony Gwynn	1987	82	13	Ken Caminiti	1997	118		Gene Richards	1978	37	13	Fred McGriff	1991	100
14	John Kruk	1988	80	14	Cito Gaston	1969	117		Tony Gwynn	1986	37	14	Tony Gwynn	1989	99
	Ken Caminiti	1997	80	15	Dave Campbell	1970	115		Rickey Henderson	1996	37	15	George Hendrick	1977	98
16	Dave Winfield	1980	79	16	Bill Almon	1977	114	16	Steve Finley	1995	36	16	Kevin McReynolds	1986	97
17	Sixto Lezcano	1982	78		Benito Santiago	1991	114	17	Stan Jefferson	1987	34		Ken Caminiti	1995	97
	Ken Caminiti	1996	78		Chris Gomez	1997	114	18	Alan Wiggins	1982	33	18	Dave Winfield	1978	96
19	Alan Wiggins	1984	75	19	Benito Santiago	1987	112		Tony Gwynn	1984	33	19	Nate Colbert	1972	95
20	John Kruk	1987	73	20	Greg Vaughn	1997	110		Quilvio Veras	1997	33		Bip Roberts	1990	95

Runs Created/27 Outs				Batting Average				On-Base Percentage				Slugging Percentage			
(minimum 3.1 Plate Appearances/Tm Gm)				(minimum 3.1 Plate Appearances/Tm Gm)				(minimum 3.1 Plate Appearances/Tm Gm)				(minimum 3.1 Plate Appearances/Tm Gm)			
1	Tony Gwynn	1997	9.24	1	Tony Gwynn	1994	.394	1	Tony Gwynn	1994	.454	1	Ken Caminiti	1996	.621
2	Ken Caminiti	1996	9.24	2	Tony Gwynn	1997	.372	2	Tony Gwynn	1987	.447	2	Gary Sheffield	1992	.580
3	Tony Gwynn	1987	8.60	3	Tony Gwynn	1987	.370	3	Gene Tenace	1977	.415	3	Tony Gwynn	1994	.568
4	Tony Gwynn	1994	8.00	4	Tony Gwynn	1995	.368	4	Rickey Henderson	1996	.410	4	Dave Winfield	1979	.558
5	Dave Winfield	1979	7.81	5	Tony Gwynn	1993	.358	5	Jack Clark	1989	.410	5	Fred McGriff	1992	.556
6	Jack Clark	1989	7.75	6	Tony Gwynn	1984	.351	6	Tony Gwynn	1984	.410	6	Tony Gwynn	1997	.547
7	Tony Gwynn	1995	7.41	7	Tony Gwynn	1989	.336	7	Tony Gwynn	1997	.409	7	Cito Gaston	1970	.543
8	Gary Sheffield	1992	7.24	8	Gary Sheffield	1992	.330	8	Ken Caminiti	1996	.408	8	Steve Finley	1996	.531
9	Tony Gwynn	1993	7.21	9	Tony Gwynn	1986	.329	9	John Kruk	1987	.406	9	Ken Caminiti	1995	.513
10	Fred McGriff	1992	7.14	10	Wally Joyner	1997	.327	10	Tony Gwynn	1995	.404	10	Tony Gwynn	1987	.511
11	Sixto Lezcano	1982	7.13	11	Ken Caminiti	1996	.326	11	Gene Tenace	1979	.403	11	Nate Colbert	1970	.509
12	Cito Gaston	1970	7.09	12	Bip Roberts	1994	.320	12	Tony Gwynn	1993	.398	12	Phil Plantier	1993	.509
13	Tony Gwynn	1984	7.06	13	Cito Gaston	1970	.318	13	Fred McGriff	1991	.396	13	Ken Caminiti	1997	.508
14	John Kruk	1987	6.88	14	Tony Gwynn	1992	.317	14	Dave Winfield	1979	.395	14	Nate Colbert	1972	.508
15	Ken Caminiti	1997	6.84	15	Tony Gwynn	1991	.317	15	Fred McGriff	1992	.394	15	Kevin McReynolds	1986	.504
16	George Hendrick	1977	6.81	16	Tony Gwynn	1985	.317	16	Gene Tenace	1978	.392	16	Dave Winfield	1978	.499
17	Ken Caminiti	1995	6.75	17	John Kruk	1987	.313	17	Wally Joyner	1997	.390	17	Tony Gwynn	1993	.497
18	Fred McGriff	1991	6.71	18	Tony Gwynn	1988	.313	18	Tony Gwynn	1989	.389	18	Fred McGriff	1991	.494
19	Wally Joyner	1997	6.67	19	Derek Bell	1994	.311	19	Ken Caminiti	1997	.389	19	George Hendrick	1977	.492
20	Gene Tenace	1977	6.62	20	George Hendrick	1977	.311	20	Sixto Lezcano	1982	.388	20	Ollie Brown	1970	.489

Padres Franchise Pitching Leaders—Single Season

Wins

1	Randy Jones	1976	22
2	Gaylord Perry	1978	21
3	Randy Jones	1975	20
4	Andy Hawkins	1985	18
5	Tim Lollar	1982	16
	LaMarr Hoyt	1985	16
	Eric Show	1988	16
	Ed Whitson	1989	16
9	Clay Kirby	1971	15
	Eric Show	1983	15
	Eric Show	1984	15
	Bruce Hurst	1989	15
	Bruce Hurst	1991	15
	Andy Benes	1991	15
	Andy Benes	1993	15
	Joey Hamilton	1996	15
17	Nine tied at		14

Losses

1	Randy Jones	1974	22
2	Steve Arlin	1972	21
3	Clay Kirby	1969	20
4	Steve Arlin	1971	19
	Bill Greif	1974	19
6	Clay Kirby	1973	18
	Bob Shirley	1977	18
8	Joe Niekro	1969	17
	Dave Roberts	1971	17
	Bill Greif	1973	17
11	Clay Kirby	1970	16
	Bill Greif	1972	16
	Brent Strom	1976	16
	Bob Shirley	1979	16
	Eric Show	1987	16
16	Pat Dobson	1970	15
	Joe McIntosh	1975	15
	Dennis Rasmussen	1990	15
	Andy Benes	1993	15
20	Fifteen tied at		14

Winning Percentage
(minimum 15 decisions)

1	Gaylord Perry	1978	.778
	Dennis Rasmussen	1988	.778
3	Butch Metzger	1976	.733
4	Andy Hawkins	1985	.692
5	LaMarr Hoyt	1985	.667
6	Bruce Hurst	1991	.652
7	Tim Lollar	1982	.640
8	Ed Whitson	1984	.636
	Mark Thurmond	1984	.636
10	Joey Hamilton	1997	.632
11	Randy Jones	1975	.625
	Eric Show	1982	.625
	Eric Show	1984	.625
	Goose Gossage	1984	.625
	Joey Hamilton	1996	.625
16	F. Valenzuela	1996	.619
17	Randy Jones	1976	.611
18	Ed Whitson	1990	.609
	Bruce Hurst	1992	.609
20	Joey Hamilton	1994	.600

Games

1	Craig Lefferts	1986	83
2	Rollie Fingers	1977	78
	Lance McCullers	1987	78
4	Butch Metzger	1976	77
5	Larry Hardy	1974	76
	Dave Tomlin	1977	76
	Dan Spillner	1977	76
8	Greg Harris	1990	73
9	Lance McCullers	1986	70
	Mark Davis	1989	70
	Trevor Hoffman	1996	70
	Trevor Hoffman	1997	70
13	Frank Reberger	1969	67
	Dave Tomlin	1975	67
	Rollie Fingers	1978	67
16	Rollie Fingers	1980	66
	Randy Myers	1992	66
18	Danny Frisella	1975	65
	Gary Lucas	1982	65
20	Three tied at		64

Games Started

1	Randy Jones	1976	40
2	Randy Jones	1979	39
3	Steve Arlin	1972	37
	Gaylord Perry	1978	37
5	Clay Kirby	1971	36
	Randy Jones	1975	36
	Randy Jones	1978	36
8	Clay Kirby	1969	35
	Bill Greif	1974	35
	Bob Shirley	1977	35
	Eric Show	1985	35
	Andy Hawkins	1986	35
13	Eleven tied at		34

Complete Games

1	Randy Jones	1976	25
2	Randy Jones	1975	18
3	Dave Roberts	1971	14
4	Clay Kirby	1971	13
	Eric Show	1988	13
6	Steve Arlin	1972	12
7	Steve Arlin	1971	10
	Fred Norman	1972	10
	Gaylord Perry	1979	10
	Bruce Hurst	1989	10
11	Clay Kirby	1972	9
	Bill Greif	1973	9
	Dave Dravecky	1983	9
	Bruce Hurst	1990	9
15	Joe Niekro	1969	8
	Pat Dobson	1970	8
	Brent Strom	1976	8
	Juan Eichelberger	1982	8
	LaMarr Hoyt	1985	8
20	Four tied at		7

Shutouts

1	Fred Norman	1972	6
	Randy Jones	1975	6
3	Randy Jones	1976	5
4	Steve Arlin	1971	4
	Bruce Hurst	1990	4
	Bruce Hurst	1992	4
7	Joe Niekro	1969	3
	Steve Arlin	1972	3
	Bill Greif	1973	3
	Steve Arlin	1973	3
	Dave Freisleben	1976	3
	Eric Rasmussen	1979	3
	Randy Jones	1980	3
	LaMarr Hoyt	1985	3
	Eric Show	1987	3
	Ed Whitson	1990	3
17	Thirty-one tied at		2

Saves

1	Mark Davis	1989	44
2	Trevor Hoffman	1996	42
3	Randy Myers	1992	38
4	Rollie Fingers	1978	37
	Trevor Hoffman	1997	37
6	Rollie Fingers	1977	35
7	Trevor Hoffman	1995	31
8	Mark Davis	1988	28
9	Goose Gossage	1985	26
10	Goose Gossage	1984	25
11	Rollie Fingers	1980	23
	Craig Lefferts	1990	23
	Craig Lefferts	1991	23
	Gene Harris	1993	23
15	Goose Gossage	1986	21
16	Trevor Hoffman	1994	20
17	Gary Lucas	1983	17
18	Butch Metzger	1976	16
	Gary Lucas	1982	16
	Lance McCullers	1987	16

Innings Pitched

1	Randy Jones	1976	315.1
2	Randy Jones	1975	285.0
3	Dave Roberts	1971	269.2
4	Clay Kirby	1971	267.1
5	Randy Jones	1979	263.0
6	Gaylord Perry	1978	260.2
7	Randy Jones	1978	253.0
8	Pat Dobson	1970	251.0
9	Steve Arlin	1972	250.0
10	Bruce Hurst	1989	244.2
11	Clay Kirby	1972	238.2
12	Eric Show	1988	234.2
13	Eric Show	1985	233.0
14	Gaylord Perry	1979	232.2
	Tim Lollar	1982	232.2
16	Andy Benes	1992	231.1
17	Andy Benes	1993	230.2
18	Andy Hawkins	1985	228.2
	Ed Whitson	1990	228.2
20	Steve Arlin	1971	227.2

Walks

1	Steve Arlin	1972	122
2	Clay Kirby	1970	120
3	Clay Kirby	1972	116
4	Dave Freisleben	1974	112
5	Tim Lollar	1984	105
6	Steve Arlin	1971	103
	Clay Kirby	1971	103
8	Clay Kirby	1969	100
	Bob Shirley	1977	100
10	Bill Greif	1974	95
11	Fred Norman	1972	88
	Tom Griffin	1977	88
	Eric Show	1984	88
14	Tim Lollar	1982	87
	Eric Show	1985	87
16	John D'Acquisto	1979	86
	Steve Mura	1980	86
	Andy Benes	1993	86
19	Tim Lollar	1983	85
	Eric Show	1987	85

Strikeouts

1	Clay Kirby	1971	231
2	Andy Benes	1994	189
3	Pat Dobson	1970	185
4	Joey Hamilton	1996	184
5	Bruce Hurst	1989	179
	Andy Benes	1993	179
7	Clay Kirby	1972	175
8	Andy Benes	1992	169
9	Fred Norman	1972	167
	Andy Benes	1991	167
11	Bruce Hurst	1990	162
12	Steve Arlin	1972	159
13	Scott Sanders	1996	157
14	Steve Arlin	1971	156
15	Clay Kirby	1970	154
	Gaylord Perry	1978	154
17	Tim Lollar	1982	150
	Andy Ashby	1995	150
19	Bob Shirley	1977	146
20	Two tied at		144

Strikeouts/9 Innings
(minimum 1 Inning Pitched/Tm Gm)

1	Andy Benes	1994	9.87
2	Joey Hamilton	1996	7.82
3	Clay Kirby	1971	7.78
4	Fred Norman	1972	7.10
5	Andy Ashby	1995	7.01
6	Andy Benes	1993	6.98
7	Tim Lollar	1983	6.92
8	Andy Benes	1991	6.74
9	Pat Dobson	1970	6.63
10	Andy Ashby	1994	6.63
11	Clay Kirby	1972	6.60
12	Bruce Hurst	1989	6.58
13	Andy Benes	1992	6.57
14	Andy Benes	1990	6.55
15	Bruce Hurst	1990	6.52
16	Andy Ashby	1997	6.46
17	Clay Kirby	1970	6.46
18	Steve Arlin	1971	6.17
19	Bob Shirley	1977	6.14
20	Clay Kirby	1973	6.06

ERA
(minimum 1 Inning Pitched/Tm Gm)

1	Dave Roberts	1971	2.10
2	Randy Jones	1975	2.24
3	Ed Whitson	1990	2.60
4	Ed Whitson	1989	2.66
5	Bruce Hurst	1989	2.69
6	Gaylord Perry	1978	2.73
7	Randy Jones	1976	2.74
8	Clay Kirby	1971	2.83
9	Randy Jones	1978	2.88
10	Dave Dravecky	1985	2.93
11	Andy Ashby	1995	2.94
12	Mark Thurmond	1984	2.97
13	Andy Benes	1991	3.03
14	Gaylord Perry	1979	3.06
15	Joey Hamilton	1995	3.08
16	Eric Show	1985	3.09
17	Clay Kirby	1972	3.13
18	Tim Lollar	1982	3.13
19	Bruce Hurst	1990	3.14
20	Andy Hawkins	1985	3.15

Component ERA
(minimum 1 Inning Pitched/Tm Gm)

1	Randy Jones	1976	2.19
2	Randy Jones	1975	2.27
3	Dave Roberts	1971	2.43
4	Bruce Hurst	1989	2.68
5	Ed Whitson	1989	2.72
6	Clay Kirby	1971	2.72
7	Gaylord Perry	1978	2.72
8	Eric Show	1988	2.73
9	Bruce Hurst	1990	2.75
10	Ed Whitson	1990	2.76
11	Andy Ashby	1994	2.82
12	Andy Benes	1991	2.92
13	LaMarr Hoyt	1985	2.93
14	Bruce Hurst	1991	2.95
15	Tim Lollar	1982	2.99
16	Brent Strom	1976	3.08
17	Randy Jones	1978	3.10
18	Dave Dravecky	1985	3.11
19	Randy Jones	1979	3.11
20	John Montefusco	1982	3.12

Opponent Average
(minimum 1 Inning Pitched/Tm Gm)

1	Clay Kirby	1971	.216
2	Tim Lollar	1982	.224
3	Clay Kirby	1972	.226
4	Bruce Hurst	1990	.228
5	Eric Show	1988	.231
6	Randy Jones	1975	.232
7	Andy Benes	1993	.232
8	Andy Benes	1991	.232
9	Andy Ashby	1994	.233
10	Randy Jones	1976	.234
11	Eric Show	1984	.234
12	Tim Lollar	1984	.234
13	Ed Whitson	1989	.235
14	Steve Arlin	1972	.237
15	Bruce Hurst	1989	.237
16	Andy Benes	1994	.237
17	Brent Strom	1976	.239
18	Dave Roberts	1971	.240
19	Bruce Hurst	1991	.241
20	Dave Freisleben	1974	.241

Opponent OBP
(minimum 1 Inning Pitched/Tm Gm)

1	Randy Jones	1976	.265
2	Randy Jones	1975	.269
3	Ed Whitson	1989	.278
4	Eric Show	1988	.279
5	LaMarr Hoyt	1985	.280
6	Bruce Hurst	1990	.284
7	Andy Benes	1991	.285
8	Dave Roberts	1971	.285
9	Andy Ashby	1994	.285
10	Bruce Hurst	1989	.288
11	Ed Whitson	1990	.289
12	John Montefusco	1982	.290
13	Clay Kirby	1971	.291
14	Bruce Hurst	1991	.292
15	Andy Benes	1994	.293
16	Gaylord Perry	1978	.295
17	Ed Whitson	1984	.296
18	Tim Lollar	1982	.297
19	Ed Whitson	1988	.298
20	Dave Dravecky	1985	.299

Padres Capsule

Best Season: *1984.* Manager Dick Williams took a team with three aging infielders, an outfielder at second base, and an outfield full of first-time regulars, and won the National League pennant with them. They overcame a two-games-to-nothing deficit in the five-game NLCS, but the Detroit Tigers pounded their starting pitchers in a five-game World Series loss.

Worst Season: *1993.* Owner Tom Werner ordered the club to cut payroll, instigating trades of several of the club's central players, including Gary Sheffield and Fred McGriff. Shorn of talent and motivation, the club plunged into last place with a 61-101 record.

Best Player: *Tony Gwynn.*

Best Pitcher: *Randy Jones.*

Best Reliever: *Trevor Hoffman.*

Best Defensive Player: *Ozzie Smith.*

Hall of Famers: *Rollie Fingers, Willie McCovey* and *Gaylord Perry.* Tony Gwynn, Ozzie Smith and Dave Winfield are expected to be enshrined when they become eligible.

Franchise All-Star Team:

C	Terry Kennedy	LF	Gene Richards
1B	Nate Colbert	CF	Dave Winfield
2B	Roberto Alomar	RF	Tony Gwynn
3B	Ken Caminiti	SP	Randy Jones
SS	Ozzie Smith	RP	Trevor Hoffman

Biggest Flake: *Kurt Bevacqua.*

Strangest Career: *Cito Gaston.* Gaston enjoyed one of the greatest fluke years of all time in 1970, batting .318 with 29 homers and 93 RBI. The season before, he'd hit .230 with two home runs and 28 RBI, and he hit .228-17-61 the following year.

What Might Have Been: *Mike Ivie.* He's still regarded as the best high school catcher of the past 30 years. The Padres had the first pick of the 1970 draft, and they took Ivie without a second thought. He soon developed a phobia about throwing the ball to the pitcher, though, and refused to catch. He made the Padres and spent a few years as their first baseman before being traded away, but his career was a massive disappointment.

What Might Have Been II: *Randy Bass.* The Padres passed on the lefthanded-hitting first baseman after giving him a short trial in 1980, '81 and '82. Bass later went on to star in Japan, clubbing 202 home runs in six seasons for the Hanshin Tigers. In 1985 he came within a single homer of tying Sadaharu Oh's single-season home-run record, and he finished his pro career with 449 homers. Only nine of them came in the American major leagues.

Best Trade: The Padres got *Gaylord Perry* from the Rangers on January 25, 1978 for Dave Tomlin and cash. Perry went on to win the NL Cy Young Award that season.

Worst Trade: Over the winter of 1981, when the Padres traded *Ozzie Smith* and change to the Cardinals for Garry Templeton and change, there was plenty of debate about whether Templeton's bat was more valuable than Smith's glove. Over the remainder of their careers, Smith out-hit Templeton by 22 points while establishing a reputation as the greatest defensive shortstop of his era.

Best-Looking Player: *Wally Joyner.*

Ugliest Player: *Benito Santiago.*

Best Nickname: *Bip Roberts.* He was born to be a Bip, and the last thing baseball needed was another Leon Roberts.

Most Unappreciated Player: Southpaw *Bob Shirley.* He had one of the three best ERAs on the staff during all four of his seasons in San Diego, but the Padres constantly shuttled him back and forth between the rotation and the bullpen, and ultimately included him as a throw-in in the trade that sent Rollie Fingers to St. Louis.

Most Overrated Player: *Benito Santiago.*

Most Admirable Star: *Tony Gwynn.*

Least Admirable Star: *LaMarr Hoyt.*

Best Season, Player: *Ken Caminiti, 1996.* Caminiti won the MVP Award and was an unstoppable force down the stretch as the Padres battled for a postseason berth. In 53 games in August and September, he batted .359 with 23 home runs and 61 RBI.

Best Season, Pitcher: *Randy Jones, 1976.* Jones went 22-14 for the fifth-place Padres, notching almost one-third of his team's wins. He also earned the Cy Young Award.

Most Impressive Individual Record: *Tony Gwynn's* total of eight batting titles, which ties him for second on the all-time list with Honus Wagner. Only Ty Cobb won more batting crowns, 12.

Biggest Tragedies: *Alan Wiggins* and *Eric Show.* Wiggins was traded to Baltimore in June 1985 after repeated drug-related suspensions and relapses. He played for two more years, then contracted AIDS and ultimately died in 1991. Show battled drug problems for several years before turning up dead at a California drug rehabilitation center in 1994.

Fan Favorite: *Tony Gwynn.*

—Mat Olkin

New York/San Francisco Giants (1883-1997)

Year	Lg	Pos	W-L	Pct	GB	Manager	Att.	R	OR	HR	Avg	OBP	Slg	Opponent HR	Avg	OBP	ERA	Park Index Runs	HR
1883	NL	6th	46-50	.479	16.0	John Clapp	—	530	577	24	.255	.281	.354	19	.253	.287	2.94	104	456
1884	NL	4th	62-50	.554	22.0	Jim Price/Monte Ward	—	693	623	23	.255	.298	.341	28	.245	.300	3.12	94	31
1885	NL	2nd	85-27	.759	2.0	Jim Mutrie	—	691	370	16	.269	.307	.359	11	.205	.258	1.72	107	96
1886	NL	3rd	75-44	.630	12.5	Jim Mutrie	—	692	558	21	.269	.307	.356	23	.246	.294	2.86	73	47
1887	NL	4th	68-55	.553	10.5	Jim Mutrie	—	816	723	48	.279	.339	.389	27	.250	.314	3.57	98	60
1888	NL	1st	84-47	.641	—	Jim Mutrie	—	659	479	55	.242	.287	.336	27	.199	.256	1.96	74	55
1889	NL	1st	83-43	.659	—	Jim Mutrie	—	935	708	52	.282	.360	.393	38	.243	.324	3.47	104	60
1890	NL	6th	63-68	.481	24.0	Jim Mutrie	60,667	713	698	25	.259	.315	.354	14	.229	.320	3.06	86	36
1891	NL	3rd	71-61	.538	13.0	Jim Mutrie	210,568	754	711	46	.263	.329	.360	26	.234	.320	2.99	84	136
1892	NL	10th	31-43	.419	21.0	Pat Powers													
	NL	6th	40-37	.519	13.5	Pat Powers	130,566	811	826	39	.251	.320	.338	32	.227	.313	3.29	97	108
1893	NL	5th	68-64	.515	19.5	Monte Ward	290,000	941	845	61	.293	.366	.410	36	.263	.342	4.29	106	204
1894	NL	2nd	88-44	.667	3.0	Monte Ward	387,000	940	789	43	.301	.368	.409	37	.271	.345	3.83	94	167
1895	NL	9th	66-65	.504	21.5	G. Davis/J. Doyle/H. Watkins	240,000	852	834	32	.288	.355	.389	34	.291	.349	4.51	86	48
1896	NL	7th	64-67	.489	27.0	Arthur Irwin/Bill Joyce	274,000	829	821	40	.297	.364	.394	33	.287	.345	4.54	98	94
1897	NL	3rd	83-48	.634	9.5	Bill Joyce	390,340	895	695	31	.299	.361	.392	26	.264	.342	3.47	98	84
1898	NL	7th	77-73	.513	25.5	Bill Joyce/Cap Anson/Bill Joyce	206,700	837	800	34	.266	.328	.353	21	.260	.345	3.44	88	109
1899	NL	10th	60-90	.400	42.0	John Day/Fred Hoey	121,384	734	863	23	.281	.337	.352	19	.287	.376	4.29	100	47
1900	NL	8th	60-78	.435	23.0	Buck Ewing/George Davis	190,000	713	823	23	.279	.338	.357	26	.294	.364	3.96	100	75
1901	NL	7th	52-85	.380	37.0	George Davis	297,650	544	755	19	.253	.303	.318	24	.285	.344	3.87	88	80
1902	NL	8th	48-88	.353	53.5	H. Fogel/H. Smith/J. McGraw	302,875	401	590	6	.238	.283	.289	16	.254	.311	2.82	106	100
1903	NL	2nd	84-55	.604	6.5	John McGraw	579,530	729	567	20	.272	.338	.344	20	.259	.317	2.94	110	94
1904	NL	1st	106-47	.693	—	John McGraw	609,826	744	476	31	.262	.328	.344	36	.223	.277	2.17	100	328
1905	NL	1st	105-48	.686	—	John McGraw	552,700	780	505	39	.273	.351	.368	25	.229	.284	2.39	94	451
1906	NL	2nd	96-56	.632	20.0	John McGraw	402,850	625	510	15	.255	.343	.321	13	.240	.299	2.49	96	159
1907	NL	4th	82-71	.536	25.5	John McGraw	538,350	574	510	23	.251	.331	.317	25	.239	.295	2.45	114	395
1908	NL	2nd	98-56	.636	1.0	John McGraw	910,000	652	456	20	.267	.342	.333	26	.233	.277	2.14	109	84
1909	NL	3rd	92-61	.601	18.5	John McGraw	783,700	623	546	26	.254	.329	.328	28	.238	.295	2.27	101	345
1910	NL	2nd	91-63	.591	13.0	John McGraw	511,785	715	567	31	.275	.354	.366	30	.250	.308	2.68	88	150
1911	NL	1st	99-54	.647	—	John McGraw	675,000	756	542	41	.279	.358	.390	33	.246	.300	2.69	99	126
1912	NL	1st	103-48	.682	—	John McGraw	638,000	823	571	47	.286	.360	.395	36	.259	.307	2.58	102	175
1913	NL	1st	101-51	.664	—	John McGraw	630,000	684	515	30	.273	.338	.361	38	.243	.289	2.42	103	179
1914	NL	2nd	84-70	.545	10.5	John McGraw	364,313	672	576	30	.265	.338	.348	47	.253	.306	2.94	89	97
1915	NL	8th	69-83	.454	21.0	John McGraw	391,850	582	628	24	.251	.300	.329	40	.260	.308	3.11	84	124
1916	NL	4th	86-66	.566	7.0	John McGraw	552,056	597	504	42	.253	.307	.343	41	.245	.293	2.60	87	110
1917	NL	1st	98-56	.636	—	John McGraw	500,264	635	457	39	.261	.317	.343	29	.234	.283	2.27	87	123
1918	NL	2nd	71-53	.573	10.5	John McGraw	256,618	480	415	13	.260	.310	.330	20	.243	.287	2.64	92	243
1919	NL	2nd	87-53	.621	9.0	John McGraw	708,857	605	470	40	.269	.322	.366	34	.247	.296	2.70	96	160
1920	NL	2nd	86-68	.558	7.0	John McGraw	929,609	682	543	46	.269	.327	.363	44	.261	.303	2.80	94	228
1921	NL	1st	94-59	.614	—	John McGraw	973,477	840	637	75	.298	.359	.421	79	.286	.326	3.55	91	151
1922	NL	1st	93-61	.604	—	John McGraw	945,809	852	658	80	.305	.363	.428	71	.272	.324	3.45	102	125
1923	NL	1st	95-58	.621	—	John McGraw	820,780	854	679	85	.295	.356	.415	82	.271	.328	3.90	100	137
1924	NL	1st	93-60	.608	—	J. McGraw/H. Jennings/J. McGraw	844,068	857	641	95	.300	.358	.432	77	.274	.326	3.62	77	111
1925	NL	2nd	86-66	.566	8.5	J. McGraw/H. Jennings/J. McGraw	778,993	736	702	114	.283	.337	.415	73	.289	.342	3.94	94	101
1926	NL	5th	74-77	.490	13.5	John McGraw	700,362	663	668	73	.278	.325	.384	70	.269	.328	3.77	94	158
1927	NL	3rd	92-62	.597	2.0	John McGraw/Rogers Hornsby	858,190	817	720	109	.297	.356	.427	77	.283	.341	3.97	98	160
1928	NL	2nd	93-61	.604	2.0	John McGraw	916,191	807	653	118	.293	.349	.430	77	.273	.327	3.67	99	183
1929	NL	3rd	84-67	.556	13.5	John McGraw	868,806	897	709	136	.296	.358	.436	102	.287	.337	3.97	96	136
1930	NL	3rd	87-67	.565	5.0	John McGraw	868,714	959	814	143	.319	.369	.473	117	.288	.345	4.61	92	142
1931	NL	2nd	87-65	.572	13.0	John McGraw	812,163	768	599	101	.289	.340	.416	71	.255	.313	3.30	89	275
1932	NL	6th	72-82	.468	18.0	John McGraw/Bill Terry	484,868	755	706	116	.276	.322	.406	112	.280	.330	3.83	97	189
1933	NL	1st	91-61	.599	—	Bill Terry	604,471	636	515	82	.263	.312	.361	61	.250	.307	2.71	90	231
1934	NL	2nd	93-60	.608	2.0	Bill Terry	730,851	760	583	126	.275	.329	.405	75	.260	.308	3.19	88	148
1935	NL	3rd	91-62	.595	8.5	Bill Terry	748,748	770	675	123	.286	.336	.416	106	.263	.318	3.78	90	187
1936	NL	1st	92-62	.597	—	Bill Terry	837,952	742	621	97	.281	.337	.395	75	.273	.327	3.46	95	238
1937	NL	1st	95-57	.625	—	Bill Terry	926,887	732	602	111	.278	.334	.403	85	.258	.314	3.43	95	217
1938	NL	3rd	83-67	.553	5.0	Bill Terry	799,633	705	637	125	.271	.334	.396	87	.261	.314	3.62	103	239
1939	NL	5th	77-74	.510	18.5	Bill Terry	702,457	703	685	116	.272	.340	.396	86	.275	.340	4.07	99	246
1940	NL	6th	72-80	.474	27.5	Bill Terry	747,852	663	659	91	.267	.329	.374	110	.262	.325	3.79	100	209
1941	NL	5th	74-79	.484	25.5	Bill Terry	763,098	667	706	95	.260	.326	.371	90	.269	.337	3.94	108	282
1942	NL	3rd	85-67	.559	20.0	Mel Ott	779,621	675	600	109	.254	.330	.361	94	.250	.316	3.31	106	249
1943	NL	8th	55-98	.359	49.5	Mel Ott	466,095	558	713	81	.247	.313	.335	80	.272	.350	4.08	93	247
1944	NL	5th	67-87	.435	38.0	Mel Ott	674,483	682	773	93	.263	.331	.370	116	.265	.341	4.29	113	353
1945	NL	5th	78-74	.513	19.0	Mel Ott	1,016,468	668	700	114	.269	.336	.379	85	.263	.332	4.06	99	184
1946	NL	8th	61-93	.396	36.0	Mel Ott	1,219,873	612	685	121	.255	.328	.374	114	.256	.343	3.92	109	180
1947	NL	4th	81-73	.526	13.0	Mel Ott	1,600,793	830	761	221	.271	.335	.454	122	.272	.347	4.44	103	154
1948	NL	5th	78-76	.506	13.5	Mel Ott/Leo Durocher	1,459,269	780	704	164	.256	.334	.408	122	.269	.341	3.93	99	149
1949	NL	5th	73-81	.474	24.0	Leo Durocher	1,218,446	736	693	147	.261	.340	.401	132	.251	.323	3.82	106	161
1950	NL	3rd	86-68	.558	5.0	Leo Durocher	1,008,876	735	643	133	.258	.342	.392	140	.244	.320	3.71	92	127
1951	NL	1st	98-59	.624	—	Leo Durocher	1,059,539	781	641	179	.260	.347	.418	148	.248	.312	3.48	100	168
1952	NL	2nd	92-62	.597	4.5	Leo Durocher	984,940	722	639	151	.256	.329	.399	121	.248	.323	3.59	105	186
1953	NL	5th	70-84	.455	35.0	Leo Durocher	811,518	768	747	176	.271	.336	.422	146	.264	.343	4.25	95	144
1954	NL	1st	97-57	.630	—	Leo Durocher	1,155,067	732	550	186	.264	.332	.424	113	.243	.326	3.09	103	171
1955	NL	3rd	80-74	.519	18.5	Leo Durocher	824,112	702	673	169	.260	.325	.402	155	.257	.332	3.77	95	128
1956	NL	6th	67-87	.435	26.0	Bill Rigney	629,179	540	650	145	.244	.299	.382	144	.250	.324	3.78	93	165
1957	NL	6th	69-85	.448	26.0	Bill Rigney	653,923	643	701	157	.252	.311	.393	150	.267	.327	4.01	107	152
1958	NL	3rd	80-74	.519	12.0	Bill Rigney	1,272,625	727	698	170	.263	.331	.422	166	.263	.330	3.98	101	106
1959	NL	3rd	83-71	.539	4.0	Bill Rigney	1,422,130	705	613	167	.261	.322	.414	139	.246	.314	3.47	86	88
1960	NL	5th	79-75	.513	16.0	Bill Rigney/Tom Sheehan	1,795,356	671	631	130	.255	.317	.393	107	.245	.313	3.44	74	51
1961	NL	3rd	85-69	.552	8.0	Alvin Dark	1,390,679	773	655	183	.264	.329	.423	152	.249	.316	3.77	93	108
1962	NL	1st	103-62	.624	—	Alvin Dark	1,592,594	878	690	204	.278	.341	.441	148	.251	.314	3.79	100	110
1963	NL	3rd	88-74	.543	11.0	Alvin Dark	1,571,306	725	641	197	.258	.316	.414	126	.246	.306	3.35	91	104

Year	Lg	Pos	W-L	Pct	GB	Manager	Att.	R	OR	HR	Avg	OBP	Slg	Opponent HR	Avg	OBP	ERA	Park Index Runs	HR
1964	NL	4th	90-72	.556	3.0	Alvin Dark	1,504,364	656	587	165	.246	.310	.382	118	.241	.304	3.19	97	111
1965	NL	2nd	95-67	.586	2.0	Herman Franks	1,546,075	682	593	159	.252	.313	.385	137	.238	.293	3.20	119	121
1966	NL	2nd	93-68	.578	1.5	Herman Franks	1,657,192	675	626	181	.248	.303	.392	140	.244	.292	3.24	92	108
1967	NL	2nd	91-71	.562	10.5	Herman Franks	1,242,480	652	551	140	.245	.313	.372	113	.234	.294	2.92	98	94
1968	NL	2nd	88-74	.543	9.0	Herman Franks	837,220	599	529	108	.239	.307	.341	86	.236	.282	2.71	92	90
1969	NL	2nd-W	90-72	.556	3.0	Clyde King	873,603	713	636	136	.242	.334	.361	120	.248	.307	3.26	101	117
1970	NL	3rd-W	86-76	.531	16.0	Clyde King/Charlie Fox	740,720	831	826	165	.262	.351	.409	156	.267	.339	4.50	93	101
1971	NL	1st-W	90-72	.556	—	Charlie Fox	1,106,043	706	644	140	.247	.329	.378	128	.242	.303	3.32	99	93
1972	NL	5th-W	69-86	.445	26.5	Charlie Fox	647,744	662	649	150	.244	.309	.384	130	.250	.318	3.69	102	119
1973	NL	3rd-W	88-74	.543	11.0	Charlie Fox	834,193	739	702	161	.262	.335	.407	145	.257	.318	3.79	111	115
1974	NL	5th-W	72-90	.444	30.0	Charlie Fox/Wes Westrum	519,987	634	723	93	.252	.322	.358	116	.257	.325	3.78	119	113
1975	NL	3rd-W	80-81	.497	27.5	Wes Westrum	522,919	659	671	84	.259	.333	.365	92	.259	.336	3.74	104	70
1976	NL	4th-W	74-88	.457	28.0	Bill Rigney	626,868	595	686	85	.246	.312	.345	68	.263	.325	3.53	108	99
1977	NL	4th-W	75-87	.463	23.0	Joe Altobelli	700,056	673	711	134	.253	.323	.383	114	.267	.331	3.75	110	91
1978	NL	3rd-W	89-73	.549	6.0	Joe Altobelli	1,740,477	613	594	117	.248	.318	.374	84	.252	.309	3.30	80	62
1979	NL	4th-W	71-91	.438	19.5	Joe Altobelli/Dave Bristol	1,456,402	672	751	125	.246	.319	.365	143	.269	.338	4.16	86	74
1980	NL	5th-W	75-86	.466	17.0	Dave Bristol	1,096,115	573	634	80	.244	.308	.342	92	.261	.323	3.46	90	60
1981	NL	5th-W	27-32	.458	10.0	Frank Robinson													
	NL	3rd-W	29-23	.558	3.5	Frank Robinson	632,274	427	414	63	.250	.320	.357	57	.256	.327	3.28	110	70
1982	NL	3rd-W	87-75	.537	2.0	Frank Robinson	1,200,948	673	687	133	.253	.327	.376	109	.270	.326	3.64	87	82
1983	NL	5th-W	79-83	.488	12.0	Frank Robinson	1,251,530	687	697	142	.247	.325	.375	127	.259	.323	3.70	103	109
1984	NL	6th-W	66-96	.407	26.0	Frank Robinson/Danny Ozark	1,001,545	682	807	112	.265	.328	.375	125	.278	.342	4.39	97	99
1985	NL	6th-W	62-100	.383	33.0	Jim Davenport/Roger Craig	818,697	556	674	115	.233	.299	.348	125	.247	.319	3.61	87	109
1986	NL	3rd-W	83-79	.512	13.0	Roger Craig	1,528,748	698	618	114	.253	.322	.375	121	.236	.313	3.33	89	90
1987	NL	1st-W	90-72	.556	—	Roger Craig	1,917,168	783	669	205	.260	.324	.430	146	.255	.324	3.68	89	118
1988	NL	4th-W	83-79	.512	11.5	Roger Craig	1,785,297	670	626	113	.248	.318	.368	99	.242	.298	3.39	87	89
1989	NL	1st-W	92-70	.568	—	Roger Craig	2,059,701	699	600	141	.250	.316	.390	120	.243	.304	3.30	92	91
1990	NL	3rd-W	85-77	.525	6.0	Roger Craig	1,975,528	719	710	152	.262	.323	.396	131	.267	.333	4.08	102	114
1991	NL	4th-W	75-87	.463	19.0	Roger Craig	1,737,478	649	697	141	.246	.309	.381	143	.257	.326	4.03	83	86
1992	NL	5th-W	72-90	.444	26.0	Roger Craig	1,560,998	574	647	105	.244	.302	.355	128	.253	.318	3.61	97	101
1993	NL	2nd-W	103-59	.636	1.0	Dusty Baker	2,606,354	808	636	168	.276	.340	.427	168	.253	.313	3.61	83	94
1994	NL	2nd-W	55-60	.478	3.5	Dusty Baker	1,704,608	504	500	123	.249	.318	.402	122	.262	.330	3.99	97	104
1995	NL	4th-W	67-77	.465	11.0	Dusty Baker	1,241,497	652	776	152	.253	.323	.404	173	.275	.345	4.86	88	90
1996	NL	4th-W	68-94	.420	23.0	Dusty Baker	1,413,687	752	862	153	.253	.331	.388	194	.273	.345	4.71	100	105
1997	NL	1st-W	90-72	.556	—	Dusty Baker	2,614,857	784	793	172	.258	.337	.414	160	.270	.340	4.43	94	92

Team Nicknames: New York Gothams 1883-1885, New York Giants 1886-1958, San Francisco Giants 1959-1997.

Team Ballparks: Polo Grounds I 1883-1888, Polo Grounds III 1889-1890, Polo Grounds IV 1891-1910, Hilltop Park & Polo Grounds V (shared) 1911, Polo Grounds V 1912-1957, Seals Stadium 1958-1959, Candlestick Park/3Com Park 1960-1997.

New York/San Francisco Giants Individual Season Batting Leaders

Year	Batting Average		On-Base Percentage		Slugging Percentage		Home Runs		RBI		Stolen Bases	
1883	Roger Connor	.357	Roger Connor	.394	Roger Connor	.506	Buck Ewing	10	Pete Gillespie	62	Statistic unavailable	
1884	Roger Connor	.317	Roger Connor	.367	Buck Ewing	.445	Roger Connor	4	Roger Connor	82	Statistic unavailable	
							Alex McKinnon					
1885	Roger Connor	.371	Roger Connor	.435	Roger Connor	.495	Buck Ewing	6	Roger Connor	65	Statistic unavailable	
1886	Roger Connor	.355	Roger Connor	.405	Roger Connor	.540	Roger Connor	7	Monte Ward	81	Monte Ward	36
1887	Monte Ward	.338	Roger Connor	.392	Roger Connor	.541	Roger Connor	17	Roger Connor	104	Monte Ward	111
1888	Buck Ewing	.306	Roger Connor	.389	Roger Connor	.480	Roger Connor	14	Roger Connor	71	Buck Ewing	53
1889	Mike Tiernan	.335	Mike Tiernan	.447	Roger Connor	.528	Roger Connor	13	Roger Connor	130	Monte Ward	62
1890	Jack Glasscock	.336	Jack Glasscock	.395	Mike Tiernan	.495	Mike Tiernan	13	Jack Glasscock	66	Mike Tiernan	56
1891	Mike Tiernan	.306	Roger Connor	.399	Mike Tiernan	.494	Mike Tiernan	16	Jim O'Rourke	95	Mike Tiernan	53
1892	Jim O'Rourke	.304	Mike Tiernan	.369	Mike Tiernan	.400	Buck Ewing	8	Buck Ewing	76	3 tied with	42
							Denny Lyons					
1893	George Davis	.355	Roger Connor	.413	George Davis	.554	Mike Tiernan	15	George Davis	119	Eddie Burke	54
1894	Jack Doyle	.367	George Davis	.435	George Davis	.537	George Davis	8	George Van Haltren	104	George Van Haltren	43
1895	Mike Tiernan	.347	Mike Tiernan	.427	Mike Tiernan	.527	George Van Haltren	8	George Van Haltren	103	George Davis	48
1896	Mike Tiernan	.369	Mike Tiernan	.452	Mike Tiernan	.516	Mike Tiernan	7	George Davis	99	George Davis	48
1897	George Davis	.353	Bill Joyce	.441	George Davis	.509	George Davis	10	George Davis	136	George Davis	65
1898	George Van Haltren	.312	Bill Joyce	.386	George Van Haltren	.413	Bill Joyce	10	Bill Joyce	91	George Van Haltren	36
1899	George Van Haltren	.301	George Van Haltren	.378	Tom O'Brien	.400	Tom O'Brien	6	Tom O'Brien	77	Jack Doyle	35
1900	Kip Selbach	.337	Kip Selbach	.425	Charlie Hickman	.482	Charlie Hickman	9	Charlie Hickman	91	George Van Haltren	45
1901	George Van Haltren	.335	George Van Haltren	.396	George Davis	.426	George Davis	7	John Ganzel	66	Sammy Strang	40
1902	Steve Brodie	.281	Steve Brodie	.327	Steve Brodie	.332	Steve Brodie	3	Billy Lauder	44	Heinie Smith	32
1903	Roger Bresnahan	.350	Roger Bresnahan	.443	Roger Bresnahan	.493	Sam Mertes	7	Sam Mertes	104	Sam Mertes	45
1904	Dan McGann	.286	Art Devlin	.371	Sam Mertes	.393	Dan McGann	6	Bill Dahlen	80	Bill Dahlen	47
											Sam Mertes	
1905	Mike Donlin	.356	Mike Donlin	.413	Mike Donlin	.495	Bill Dahlen	7	Sam Mertes	108	Art Devlin	59
							Mike Donlin					
1906	Art Devlin	.299	Roger Bresnahan	.418	Art Devlin	.390	Cy Seymour	4	Art Devlin	65	Art Devlin	54
							Sammy Strang					
1907	Cy Seymour	.294	Art Devlin	.376	Cy Seymour	.400	George Browne	5	Cy Seymour	75	Art Devlin	38
1908	Mike Donlin	.334	Roger Bresnahan	.401	Mike Donlin	.452	Mike Donlin	6	Mike Donlin	106	Mike Donlin	30
1909	Larry Doyle	.302	Al Bridwell	.386	Larry Doyle	.419	Red Murray	7	Red Murray	91	Red Murray	48
1910	Fred Snodgrass	.321	Fred Snodgrass	.440	Fred Merkle	.441	Larry Doyle	8	Red Murray	87	Red Murray	57
1911	Larry Doyle	.310	Larry Doyle	.397	Larry Doyle	.527	Larry Doyle	13	Fred Merkle	84	Josh Devore	61
1912	Larry Doyle	.330	Larry Doyle	.393	Larry Doyle	.471	Fred Merkle	11	Red Murray	92	Fred Snodgrass	43
1913	Art Fletcher	.297	Fred Snodgrass	.373	Tillie Shafer	.398	Larry Doyle	5	Larry Doyle	73	George Burns	40
							Tillie Shafer					
1914	George Burns	.303	George Burns	.403	George Burns	.417	Fred Merkle	7	Art Fletcher	79	George Burns	62
1915	Larry Doyle	.320	Larry Doyle	.358	Larry Doyle	.442	Larry Doyle	4	Art Fletcher	74	George Burns	27
							Fred Merkle					
1916	Dave Robertson	.307	Benny Kauff	.348	Dave Robertson	.426	Dave Robertson	12	Benny Kauff	74	Benny Kauff	40
1917	Benny Kauff	.308	George Burns	.380	George Burns	.412	Dave Robertson	12	Heinie Zimmerman	102	George Burns	40
1918	Ross Youngs	.302	Ross Youngs	.368	George Burns	.389	George Burns	4	Heinie Zimmerman	56	George Burns	40
1919	Ross Youngs	.311	George Burns	.396	Benny Kauff	.422	Benny Kauff	10	Benny Kauff	67	George Burns	40
1920	Ross Youngs	.351	Ross Youngs	.427	Ross Youngs	.477	George Kelly	11	George Kelly	94	Frankie Frisch	34
1921	Frankie Frisch	.341	Ross Youngs	.411	George Kelly	.528	George Kelly	23	George Kelly	122	Frankie Frisch	49
1922	Ross Youngs	.331	Ross Youngs	.398	Irish Meusel	.509	George Kelly	17	Irish Meusel	132	Frankie Frisch	31
1923	Frankie Frisch	.348	Ross Youngs	.412	Frankie Frisch	.485	Irish Meusel	19	Irish Meusel	125	Frankie Frisch	29
1924	Ross Youngs	.356	Ross Youngs	.441	George Kelly	.531	George Kelly	21	George Kelly	136	Frankie Frisch	22
1925	Frankie Frisch	.331	Frankie Frisch	.374	Irish Meusel	.548	Irish Meusel	21	Irish Meusel	111	Frankie Frisch	21
1926	Frankie Frisch	.314	Frankie Frisch	.353	George Kelly	.445	George Kelly	13	George Kelly	80	Frankie Frisch	23
1927	Rogers Hornsby	.361	Rogers Hornsby	.448	Rogers Hornsby	.586	Rogers Hornsby	26	Rogers Hornsby	125	Edd Roush	18
1928	Freddy Lindstrom	.358	Mel Ott	.397	Mel Ott	.524	Mel Ott	18	Freddy Lindstrom	107	Freddy Lindstrom	15
1929	Bill Terry	.372	Mel Ott	.449	Mel Ott	.635	Mel Ott	42	Mel Ott	151	4 tied with	10
1930	Bill Terry	.401	Mel Ott	.458	Bill Terry	.619	Mel Ott	25	Bill Terry	129	Freddy Lindstrom	15
1931	Bill Terry	.349	Bill Terry	.397	Mel Ott	.545	Mel Ott	29	Mel Ott	115	Chick Fullis	13
											Travis Jackson	
1932	Bill Terry	.350	Mel Ott	.424	Mel Ott	.601	Mel Ott	38	Mel Ott	123	Freddy Lindstrom	6
											Mel Ott	
1933	Bill Terry	.322	Bill Terry	.375	Mel Ott	.467	Mel Ott	23	Mel Ott	103	Kiddo Davis	10
1934	Bill Terry	.354	Mel Ott	.415	Mel Ott	.591	Mel Ott	35	Mel Ott	135	Jo-Jo Moore	5
1935	Bill Terry	.341	Mel Ott	.407	Mel Ott	.555	Mel Ott	31	Mel Ott	114	Mel Ott	7
											Bill Terry	
1936	Mel Ott	.328	Mel Ott	.448	Mel Ott	.588	Mel Ott	33	Mel Ott	135	Burgess Whitehead	14
1937	Jo-Jo Moore	.310	Mel Ott	.408	Mel Ott	.523	Mel Ott	31	Mel Ott	95	3 tied with	7
1938	Mel Ott	.311	Mel Ott	.442	Mel Ott	.583	Mel Ott	36	Mel Ott	116	George Myatt	10
1939	Zeke Bonura	.321	Mel Ott	.449	Mel Ott	.581	Mel Ott	27	Zeke Bonura	85	Jo-Jo Moore	5
1940	Frank Demaree	.302	Mel Ott	.407	Mel Ott	.457	Mel Ott	19	Babe Young	101	Burgess Whitehead	9
1941	Billy Jurges	.293	Mel Ott	.403	Mel Ott	.495	Mel Ott	27	Babe Young	104	Johnny Rucker	8
1942	Johnny Mize	.305	Mel Ott	.415	Mel Ott	.521	Mel Ott	30	Johnny Mize	110	Bill Werber	9
1943	Mickey Witek	.314	Mickey Witek	.356	Sid Gordon	.373	Mel Ott	18	Sid Gordon	63	Mel Ott	7
1944	Joe Medwick	.337	Mel Ott	.423	Mel Ott	.544	Mel Ott	26	Joe Medwick	85	Buddy Kerr	14
1945	Mel Ott	.308	Mel Ott	.411	Mel Ott	.499	Mel Ott	21	Mel Ott	79	George Hausmann	7
											Johnny Rucker	
1946	Sid Gordon	.293	Sid Gordon	.380	Willard Marshall	.406	Johnny Mize	22	Johnny Mize	70	Buddy Blattner	12
1947	Walker Cooper	.305	Johnny Mize	.384	Johnny Mize	.614	Johnny Mize	51	Johnny Mize	138	Bill Rigney	7
1948	Sid Gordon	.299	Johnny Mize	.395	Johnny Mize	.564	Johnny Mize	40	Johnny Mize	125	Buddy Kerr	9
1949	Bobby Thomson	.309	Sid Gordon	.404	Bobby Thomson	.518	Bobby Thomson	27	Bobby Thomson	109	Whitey Lockman	12
1950	Eddie Stanky	.300	Eddie Stanky	.460	Hank Thompson	.463	Bobby Thomson	25	Hank Thompson	91	Al Dark	9
											Eddie Stanky	
1951	Monte Irvin	.312	Monte Irvin	.415	Bobby Thomson	.562	Bobby Thomson	32	Monte Irvin	121	Al Dark	12
											Monte Irvin	
1952	Al Dark	.301	Whitey Lockman	.363	Bobby Thomson	.482	Bobby Thomson	24	Bobby Thomson	108	Al Dark	6
1953	Don Mueller	.333	Monte Irvin	.406	Monte Irvin	.541	Bobby Thomson	26	Bobby Thomson	106	Al Dark	7
1954	Willie Mays	.345	Willie Mays	.411	Willie Mays	.667	Willie Mays	41	Willie Mays	110	Willie Mays	8

Teams: Giants

Year	Batting Average		On-Base Percentage		Slugging Percentage		Home Runs		RBI		Stolen Bases	
1955	Willie Mays	.319	Willie Mays	.400	Willie Mays	.659	Willie Mays	51	Willie Mays	127	Willie Mays	24
1956	Willie Mays	.296	Willie Mays	.369	Willie Mays	.557	Willie Mays	36	Willie Mays	84	Willie Mays	40
1957	Willie Mays	.333	Willie Mays	.407	Willie Mays	.626	Willie Mays	35	Willie Mays	97	Willie Mays	38
1958	Willie Mays	.347	Willie Mays	.419	Willie Mays	.583	Willie Mays	29	Orlando Cepeda / Willie Mays	96	Willie Mays	31
1959	Orlando Cepeda	.317	Willie Mays	.381	Willie Mays	.583	Willie Mays	34	Orlando Cepeda	105	Willie Mays	27
1960	Willie Mays	.319	Willie Mays	.381	Willie Mays	.555	Willie Mays	29	Willie Mays	103	Willie Mays	25
1961	Orlando Cepeda	.311	Willie Mays	.393	Orlando Cepeda	.609	Orlando Cepeda	46	Orlando Cepeda	142	Willie Mays	18
1962	Felipe Alou	.316	Willie Mays	.384	Willie Mays	.615	Willie Mays	49	Willie Mays	141	Willie Mays	18
1963	Orlando Cepeda	.316	Willie Mays	.380	Willie Mays	.582	Willie McCovey	44	Willie Mays	103	Felipe Alou	11
1964	Orlando Cepeda	.304	Willie Mays	.383	Willie Mays	.607	Willie Mays	47	Willie Mays	111	Willie Mays	19
1965	Willie Mays	.317	Willie Mays	.398	Willie Mays	.645	Willie Mays	52	Willie Mays	112	Matty Alou	10
1966	Willie McCovey	.295	Willie McCovey	.391	Willie McCovey	.586	Willie Mays	37	Willie Mays	103	Tito Fuentes	6
1967	Jesus Alou	.292	Willie McCovey	.378	Willie McCovey	.535	Willie McCovey	31	Jim Ray Hart	99	Willie Mays	6
1968	Willie McCovey	.293	Willie McCovey	.378	Willie McCovey	.545	Willie McCovey	36	Willie McCovey	105	Bobby Bonds	16
1969	Willie McCovey	.320	Willie McCovey	.453	Willie McCovey	.656	Willie McCovey	45	Willie McCovey	126	Bobby Bonds	45
1970	Bobby Bonds	.302	Willie McCovey	.444	Willie McCovey	.612	Willie McCovey	39	Willie McCovey	126	Bobby Bonds	48
1971	Bobby Bonds	.288	Willie Mays	.425	Bobby Bonds	.512	Bobby Bonds	33	Bobby Bonds	102	Bobby Bonds	26
1972	Chris Speier	.269	Chris Speier	.361	Dave Kingman	.462	Dave Kingman	29	Dave Kingman	83	Bobby Bonds	44
1973	Garry Maddox	.319	Bobby Bonds	.370	Bobby Bonds	.530	Bobby Bonds	39	Bobby Bonds	96	Bobby Bonds	43
1974	Gary Matthews	.287	Gary Matthews	.368	Gary Matthews	.442	Bobby Bonds	21	Gary Matthews	82	Bobby Bonds	41
1975	Von Joshua	.318	Bobby Murcer	.396	Von Joshua	.448	Gary Matthews	12	Bobby Murcer	91	Derrel Thomas	28
1976	Gary Matthews	.279	Bobby Murcer	.362	Gary Matthews	.443	Bobby Murcer	23	Bobby Murcer	90	3 tied with	16
1977	Bill Madlock	.302	Willie McCovey	.367	Willie McCovey	.500	Willie McCovey	28	Willie McCovey	86	Gary Thomasson	16
1978	Bill Madlock	.309	Bill Madlock	.378	Jack Clark	.537	Jack Clark	25	Jack Clark	98	Bill Madlock	16
1979	Jack Clark	.273	Bill North	.386	Jack Clark	.476	Mike Ivie	27	Mike Ivie	89	Bill North	58
1980	Jack Clark	.284	Jack Clark	.382	Jack Clark	.517	Jack Clark	22	Jack Clark	82	Bill North	45
1981	Milt May	.310	Milt May	.376	Jack Clark	.460	Jack Clark	17	Jack Clark	53	Bill North	26
1982	Joe Morgan	.289	Joe Morgan	.400	Jack Clark	.481	Jack Clark	27	Jack Clark	103	Chili Davis / Joe Morgan	24
1983	Jeffrey Leonard	.279	Darrell Evans	.378	Darrell Evans	.516	Darrell Evans	30	Jeffrey Leonard	87	Johnnie LeMaster	39
1984	Chili Davis	.315	Chili Davis	.368	Chili Davis	.507	Chili Davis / Jeffrey Leonard	21	Jeffrey Leonard	86	Dan Gladden	31
1985	Chili Davis	.270	Chili Davis	.349	Chili Davis	.412	Bob Brenly	19	Jeffrey Leonard	62	Dan Gladden	32
1986	Chili Davis	.278	Chili Davis	.375	Chili Davis	.416	Candy Maldonado	18	Candy Maldonado	85	Dan Gladden	27
1987	Will Clark	.308	Will Clark	.371	Will Clark	.580	Will Clark	35	Will Clark	91	3 tied with	16
1988	Brett Butler	.287	Brett Butler	.393	Will Clark	.508	Will Clark	29	Will Clark	109	Brett Butler	43
1989	Will Clark	.333	Will Clark	.407	Kevin Mitchell	.635	Kevin Mitchell	47	Kevin Mitchell	125	Brett Butler	31
1990	Brett Butler	.309	Brett Butler	.397	Kevin Mitchell	.544	Kevin Mitchell	35	Matt Williams	122	Brett Butler	51
1991	Willie McGee	.312	Will Clark	.359	Will Clark	.536	Matt Williams	34	Will Clark	116	Mike Felder	21
1992	Will Clark	.300	Will Clark	.384	Will Clark	.476	Matt Williams	20	Will Clark	73	Darren Lewis	28
1993	Barry Bonds	.336	Barry Bonds	.458	Barry Bonds	.677	Barry Bonds	46	Barry Bonds	123	Darren Lewis	46
1994	Barry Bonds	.312	Barry Bonds	.426	Barry Bonds	.647	Matt Williams	43	Matt Williams	96	Darren Lewis	30
1995	Barry Bonds	.294	Barry Bonds	.431	Barry Bonds	.577	Barry Bonds	33	Barry Bonds	104	Barry Bonds	31
1996	Barry Bonds	.308	Barry Bonds	.461	Barry Bonds	.615	Barry Bonds	42	Barry Bonds	129	Barry Bonds	40
1997	Barry Bonds	.291	Barry Bonds	.446	Barry Bonds	.585	Barry Bonds	40	Jeff Kent	121	Barry Bonds	37

Teams: Giants

New York/San Francisco Giants Individual Season Pitching Leaders

Year	ERA		Baserunners/9 IP		Innings Pitched		Strikeouts		Wins		Saves	
1883	Monte Ward	2.70	Monte Ward	10.0	Mickey Welch	426.0	Mickey Welch	144	Mickey Welch	25	5 tied with	0
1884	Mickey Welch	2.50	Mickey Welch	10.9	Mickey Welch	557.1	Mickey Welch	345	Mickey Welch	39	6 tied with	0
1885	Tim Keefe	1.58	Tim Keefe	9.0	Mickey Welch	492.0	Mickey Welch	258	Mickey Welch	44	Jim Devlin	1
1886	Tim Keefe	2.53	Tim Keefe	9.6	Tim Keefe	540.0	Tim Keefe	291	Tim Keefe	42	Jim Devlin	1
1887	Tim Keefe	3.10	Tim Keefe	10.6	Tim Keefe	478.2	Tim Keefe	186	Tim Keefe	35	Mike Tiernan	1
1888	Tim Keefe	1.74	Tim Keefe	8.7	Tim Keefe	434.1	Tim Keefe	333	Tim Keefe	35	Ed Crane	1
1889	Mickey Welch	3.02	Tim Keefe	11.8	Mickey Welch	375.0	Tim Keefe	209	Tim Keefe	28	Mickey Welch	2
1890	Amos Rusie	2.56	Amos Rusie	11.9	Amos Rusie	548.2	Amos Rusie	341	Amos Rusie	29	Amos Rusie	1
1891	John Ewing	2.27	John Ewing	11.4	Amos Rusie	500.1	Amos Rusie	337	Amos Rusie	33	3 tied with	1
1892	Amos Rusie	2.88	Amos Rusie	11.4	Amos Rusie	532.0	Amos Rusie	288	Amos Rusie	31	Ed Crane	1
1893	Amos Rusie	3.23	Amos Rusie	12.5	Amos Rusie	482.0	Amos Rusie	208	Amos Rusie	33	Mark Baldwin	2
1894	Amos Rusie	2.78	Jouett Meekin	12.7	Amos Rusie	444.0	Amos Rusie	195	Amos Rusie	36	Jouett Meekin	2
1895	Dad Clarke	3.39	Amos Rusie	12.4	Amos Rusie	393.1	Amos Rusie	201	Amos Rusie	23	Dad Clarke	1
1896	Jouett Meekin	3.82	Mike Sullivan	12.6	Dad Clarke	351.0	Jouett Meekin	110	Jouett Meekin	26	Dad Clarke Charlie Gettig	1
1897	Amos Rusie	2.54	Amos Rusie	11.5	Amos Rusie	322.1	Cy Seymour	149	Amos Rusie	28	Mike Sullivan	2
1898	Amos Rusie	3.03	Amos Rusie	12.0	Cy Seymour	356.2	Cy Seymour	239	Cy Seymour	25	Amos Rusie	1
1899	Cy Seymour	3.56	Cy Seymour	14.7	Bill Carrick	361.2	Cy Seymour	142	Bill Carrick	16	11 tied with	0
1900	Pink Hawley	3.53	Pink Hawley	13.3	Bill Carrick	341.2	Pink Hawley	80	Bill Carrick	19	9 tied with	0
1901	Christy Mathewson	2.41	Christy Mathewson	10.7	Luther Taylor	353.1	Christy Mathewson	221	Christy Mathewson	20	Bill Phyle	1
1902	Joe McGinnity	2.06	Joe McGinnity	9.6	Christy Mathewson	276.2	Christy Mathewson	159	Christy Mathewson	14	Tully Sparks	1
1903	Christy Mathewson	2.26	Christy Mathewson	10.6	Joe McGinnity	434.0	Christy Mathewson	267	Joe McGinnity	31	Roscoe Miller	3
1904	Joe McGinnity	1.61	Joe McGinnity	9.0	Joe McGinnity	408.0	Christy Mathewson	212	Joe McGinnity	35	Joe McGinnity	5
1905	Christy Mathewson	1.28	Christy Mathewson	8.4	Christy Mathewson	338.2	Christy Mathewson	206	Christy Mathewson	31	Claude Elliott	6
1906	Luther Taylor	2.20	Hooks Wiltse	10.4	Joe McGinnity	339.2	Red Ames	156	Joe McGinnity	27	George Ferguson	7
1907	Christy Mathewson	2.00	Christy Mathewson	8.7	Christy Mathewson	315.0	Christy Mathewson	178	Christy Mathewson	24	Joe McGinnity	4
1908	Christy Mathewson	1.43	Christy Mathewson	7.6	Christy Mathewson	390.2	Christy Mathewson	259	Christy Mathewson	37	Christy Mathewson Joe McGinnity	5
1909	Christy Mathewson	1.14	Christy Mathewson	7.5	Christy Mathewson	275.1	Red Ames	156	Christy Mathewson	25	Doc Crandall	6
1910	Christy Mathewson	1.89	Christy Mathewson	10.0	Christy Mathewson	318.1	Christy Mathewson	184	Christy Mathewson	27	Doc Crandall	5
1911	Christy Mathewson	1.99	Red Ames	10.0	Christy Mathewson	307.0	Rube Marquard	237	Christy Mathewson	26	Doc Crandall	5
1912	Jeff Tesreau	1.96	Christy Mathewson	10.1	Christy Mathewson	310.0	Rube Marquard	175	Rube Marquard	26	Christy Mathewson	4
1913	Christy Mathewson	2.06	Christy Mathewson	9.2	Christy Mathewson	306.0	Jeff Tesreau	167	Christy Mathewson	25	Doc Crandall	6
1914	Jeff Tesreau	2.37	Christy Mathewson	9.8	Jeff Tesreau	322.1	Jeff Tesreau	189	Jeff Tesreau	26	3 tied with	2
1915	Jeff Tesreau	2.29	Jeff Tesreau	9.3	Jeff Tesreau	306.0	Jeff Tesreau	176	Jeff Tesreau	19	Jeff Tesreau	3
1916	Pol Perritt	2.62	Rube Benton	10.5	Jeff Tesreau	268.1	Rube Benton Pol Perritt	115	Pol Perritt	18	5 tied with	2
1917	Fred Anderson	1.44	Fred Anderson	8.8	Ferdie Schupp	272.0	Ferdie Schupp	147	Ferdie Schupp	21	Slim Sallee	4
1918	Slim Sallee	2.25	Slim Sallee	9.1	Pol Perritt	233.0	Pol Perritt	60	Pol Perritt	18	Fred Anderson	3
1919	Fred Toney	1.84	Jesse Barnes	9.1	Jesse Barnes	295.2	Jesse Barnes	92	Jesse Barnes	25	Jean Dubuc Jesse Winters	3
1920	Jesse Barnes	2.64	Jesse Barnes	10.1	Jesse Barnes	292.2	Fred Toney	81	Art Nehf Fred Toney	21	4 tied with	2
1921	Jesse Barnes	3.10	Art Nehf	11.2	Art Nehf	260.2	Art Nehf	67	Art Nehf	20	Jesse Barnes	6
1922	Phil Douglas	2.63	Phil Douglas	11.0	Art Nehf	268.1	Rosy Ryan	75	Art Nehf	19	Claude Jonnard	5
1923	Hugh McQuillan	3.40	Rosy Ryan	11.3	Hugh McQuillan	230.1	Jack Bentley	80	Rosy Ryan	16	Claude Jonnard	5
1924	Hugh McQuillan	2.69	Hugh McQuillan	11.0	Virgil Barnes	229.1	Art Nehf	72	Virgil Barnes Jack Bentley	16	Claude Jonnard Rosy Ryan	5
1925	Jack Scott	3.15	Jack Scott	11.6	Jack Scott	239.2	Jack Scott	87	Virgil Barnes	15	Jack Scott	3
1926	Virgil Barnes	2.87	Hugh McQuillan	11.5	Jack Scott	226.0	Jack Scott	82	Freddie Fitzsimmons	14	Chick Davies	6
1927	Burleigh Grimes	3.54	Dutch Henry	11.8	Burleigh Grimes	259.2	Burleigh Grimes	102	Burleigh Grimes	19	Dutch Henry	4
1928	Larry Benton	2.73	Larry Benton	10.7	Larry Benton	310.1	Larry Benton	90	Larry Benton	25	Larry Benton	4
1929	Bill Walker	3.09	Carl Hubbell	11.6	Carl Hubbell	268.0	Carl Hubbell	106	Carl Hubbell	18	Carl Mays	4
1930	Carl Hubbell	3.87	Freddie Fitzsimmons	11.6	Bill Walker	245.1	Carl Hubbell	117	Freddie Fitzsimmons	19	Joe Heving	6
1931	Bill Walker	2.26	Carl Hubbell	10.2	Freddie Fitzsimmons	253.2	Carl Hubbell	155	Freddie Fitzsimmons	18	3 tied with	3
1932	Carl Hubbell	2.50	Carl Hubbell	9.6	Carl Hubbell	284.0	Carl Hubbell	137	Carl Hubbell	18	Dolf Luque	5
1933	Carl Hubbell	1.66	Carl Hubbell	8.9	Carl Hubbell	308.2	Carl Hubbell	156	Carl Hubbell	23	Hi Bell Carl Hubbell	5
1934	Carl Hubbell	2.30	Carl Hubbell	9.3	Carl Hubbell	313.0	Carl Hubbell	118	Hal Schumacher	23	Carl Hubbell	8
1935	Hal Schumacher	2.89	Hal Schumacher	10.7	Carl Hubbell	302.2	Carl Hubbell	150	Carl Hubbell	23	Al Smith Allyn Stout	5
1936	Carl Hubbell	2.31	Carl Hubbell	9.7	Carl Hubbell	304.0	Carl Hubbell	123	Carl Hubbell	26	Dick Coffman	7
1937	Cliff Melton	2.61	Cliff Melton	10.1	Carl Hubbell	261.2	Cliff Melton	159	Carl Hubbell	22	Cliff Melton	7
1938	Carl Hubbell	3.07	Carl Hubbell	10.4	Cliff Melton	243.0	Cliff Melton	104	Harry Gumbert	15	Dick Coffman	12
1939	Carl Hubbell	2.75	Carl Hubbell	10.3	Harry Gumbert	243.2	Cliff Melton	95	Harry Gumbert	18	Jumbo Brown	7
1940	Hal Schumacher	3.25	Bill Lohrman	11.4	Harry Gumbert	237.0	Hal Schumacher	123	Hal Schumacher	13	Jumbo Brown	7
1941	Cliff Melton	3.01	Cliff Melton	11.3	Hal Schumacher	206.0	Cliff Melton	100	Hal Schumacher	12	Jumbo Brown	8
1942	Bill Lohrman	2.56	Bill Lohrman	10.1	Hal Schumacher	216.0	Carl Hubbell Cliff Melton	61	Bill Lohrman	13	Ace Adams	11
1943	Cliff Melton	3.19	Cliff Melton	12.4	Cliff Melton	186.1	Ken Chase	86	Ace Adams	11	Ace Adams	9
1944	Bill Voiselle	3.02	Bill Voiselle	11.5	Bill Voiselle	312.2	Bill Voiselle	161	Bill Voiselle	21	Ace Adams	13
1945	Van Lingle Mungo	3.20	Van Lingle Mungo	11.6	Bill Voiselle	232.1	Bill Voiselle	115	Van Lingle Mungo Bill Voiselle	14	Ace Adams	15
1946	Monte Kennedy	3.42	Dave Koslo	12.1	Dave Koslo	265.1	Dave Koslo	121	Dave Koslo	14	Junior Thompson	4
1947	Larry Jansen	3.16	Larry Jansen	10.9	Larry Jansen	248.0	Larry Jansen	104	Larry Jansen	21	Ken Trinkle	10
1948	Sheldon Jones	3.35	Larry Jansen	11.0	Larry Jansen	277.0	Larry Jansen	126	Larry Jansen	18	Ken Trinkle	7
1949	Dave Koslo	2.50	Dave Koslo	10.0	Larry Jansen	259.2	Larry Jansen	113	Larry Jansen Sheldon Jones	15	Dave Koslo	4
1950	Sal Maglie	2.71	Larry Jansen	9.6	Larry Jansen	275.0	Larry Jansen	161	Larry Jansen	19	3 tied with	3
1951	Sal Maglie	2.93	Larry Jansen	10.1	Sal Maglie	298.0	Sal Maglie	146	Larry Jansen Sal Maglie	23	George Spencer	6
1952	Hoyt Wilhelm	2.43	Hoyt Wilhelm	10.7	Jim Hearn	223.2	Sal Maglie	112	Sal Maglie	18	Hoyt Wilhelm	11
1953	Ruben Gomez	3.40	Larry Jansen	11.8	Ruben Gomez	204.0	Ruben Gomez	113	Ruben Gomez	13	Hoyt Wilhelm	15
1954	Johnny Antonelli	2.30	Johnny Antonelli	10.7	Johnny Antonelli	258.2	Johnny Antonelli	152	Johnny Antonelli	21	Marv Grissom	19

Teams: Giants

Year	ERA		Baserunners/9 IP		Innings Pitched		Strikeouts		Wins		Saves	
1955	Johnny Antonelli	3.33	Johnny Antonelli	11.4	Johnny Antonelli	235.1	Johnny Antonelli	143	Johnny Antonelli Jim Hearn	14	Marv Grissom	8
1956	Johnny Antonelli	2.86	Johnny Antonelli	10.6	Johnny Antonelli	258.1	Johnny Antonelli	145	Johnny Antonelli	20	Hoyt Wilhelm	8
1957	Curt Barclay	3.44	Al Worthington	11.5	Ruben Gomez	238.1	Johnny Antonelli	114	Ruben Gomez	15	Marv Grissom	14
1958	Stu Miller	2.47	Stu Miller	10.4	Johnny Antonelli	241.2	Johnny Antonelli	143	Johnny Antonelli	16	Marv Grissom	10
1959	Sam Jones	2.83	Johnny Antonelli	10.4	Johnny Antonelli	282.0	Sam Jones	209	Sam Jones	21	Stu Miller	8
1960	Mike McCormick	2.70	Mike McCormick	10.5	Mike McCormick	253.0	Sam Jones	190	Sam Jones	18	Johnny Antonelli	11
1961	Mike McCormick	3.20	Mike McCormick	11.2	Mike McCormick	250.0	Mike McCormick	163	Stu Miller	14	Stu Miller	17
1962	Juan Marichal	3.36	Jack Sanford	11.1	Billy O'Dell	280.2	Billy O'Dell	195	Jack Sanford	24	Stu Miller	19
1963	Juan Marichal	2.41	Juan Marichal	9.0	Juan Marichal	321.1	Juan Marichal	248	Juan Marichal	25	Billy Pierce	8
1964	Juan Marichal	2.48	Juan Marichal	9.8	Juan Marichal	269.0	Juan Marichal	206	Juan Marichal	21	Bob Shaw	11
1965	Juan Marichal	2.13	Juan Marichal	8.3	Juan Marichal	295.1	Juan Marichal	240	Juan Marichal	22	Frank Linzy	21
1966	Juan Marichal	2.23	Juan Marichal	7.9	Juan Marichal	307.1	Juan Marichal	222	Juan Marichal	25	Frank Linzy	16
1967	Gaylord Perry	2.61	Gaylord Perry	9.8	Gaylord Perry	293.0	Gaylord Perry	230	Mike McCormick	22	Frank Linzy	17
1968	Bobby Bolin	1.99	Bobby Bolin	9.1	Juan Marichal	326.0	Juan Marichal	218	Juan Marichal	26	Frank Linzy	12
1969	Juan Marichal	2.10	Juan Marichal	9.1	Gaylord Perry	325.1	Gaylord Perry	233	Juan Marichal	21	Frank Linzy	11
1970	Gaylord Perry	3.20	Gaylord Perry	10.5	Gaylord Perry	328.2	Gaylord Perry	214	Gaylord Perry	23	Don McMahon	19
1971	Gaylord Perry	2.76	Juan Marichal	9.8	Gaylord Perry	280.0	Juan Marichal	159	Gaylord Perry	18	Jerry Johnson	18
1972	Jim Barr	2.87	Jim Barr	10.6	Ron Bryant	214.0	Sam McDowell	122	Ron Bryant	14	Jerry Johnson	8
1973	Ron Bryant	3.53	Tom Bradley	11.4	Ron Bryant	270.0	Ron Bryant	143	Ron Bryant	24	Elias Sosa	18
1974	Jim Barr	2.74	Jim Barr	10.2	Jim Barr	239.2	John D'Acquisto	167	Mike Caldwell	14	Randy Moffitt	15
1975	John Montefusco	2.88	John Montefusco	11.2	Jim Barr John Montefusco	244.0	John Montefusco	215	John Montefusco	15	Randy Moffitt	11
1976	John Montefusco	2.85	John Montefusco	10.7	John Montefusco	253.0	John Montefusco	172	John Montefusco	16	Randy Moffitt	14
1977	Ed Halicki	3.32	Ed Halicki	11.1	Ed Halicki	257.2	Ed Halicki	168	Ed Halicki	16	Gary Lavelle	20
1978	Bob Knepper	2.63	Ed Halicki	9.9	Bob Knepper	260.0	John Montefusco	177	Bob Knepper	18	Gary Lavelle	14
1979	Bob Knepper	4.64	Vida Blue	13.6	Vida Blue	237.0	Vida Blue	138	Vida Blue	14	Gary Lavelle	20
1980	Vida Blue	2.97	Vida Blue	10.6	Vida Blue	224.0	Vida Blue	129	Vida Blue	14	Greg Minton	19
1981	Vida Blue	2.45	Vida Blue	11.0	Doyle Alexander	152.1	Tom Griffin	83	Doyle Alexander	11	Greg Minton	21
1982	Bill Laskey	3.14	Bill Laskey	11.0	Bill Laskey	189.1	Bill Laskey Atlee Hammaker	102	Bill Laskey	13	Greg Minton	30
1983	Atlee Hammaker	2.25	Atlee Hammaker	9.5	Fred Breining	202.2	Mike Krukow	136	Bill Laskey	13	Greg Minton	22
1984	Bill Laskey	4.33	Bill Laskey	12.0	Bill Laskey	207.2	Mike Krukow	141	Mike Krukow	11	Greg Minton	19
1985	Mike Krukow	3.38	Mike Krukow	10.5	Dave LaPoint	206.2	Mike Krukow	150	Scott Garrelts	9	Scott Garrelts	13
1986	Mike Krukow	3.05	Mike Krukow	9.7	Mike Krukow	245.0	Mike Krukow	178	Mike Krukow	20	Scott Garrelts	10
1987	Atlee Hammaker	3.58	Atlee Hammaker	11.7	Kelly Downs	186.0	Kelly Downs	137	Mike LaCoss	13	Scott Garrelts	12
1988	Don Robinson	2.45	Kelly Downs	10.2	Rick Reuschel	245.0	Don Robinson	122	Rick Reuschel	19	Scott Garrelts	13
1989	Scott Garrelts	2.28	Scott Garrelts	9.1	Rick Reuschel	208.1	Scott Garrelts	119	Rick Reuschel	17	Craig Lefferts	20
1990	John Burkett	3.79	John Burkett	11.7	John Burkett	204.0	John Burkett	118	John Burkett	14	Jeff Brantley	19
1991	Trevor Wilson	3.56	Trevor Wilson	11.4	Bud Black	214.1	Trevor Wilson	139	Trevor Wilson	13	Dave Righetti	24
1992	Bill Swift	2.08	Bill Swift	10.4	John Burkett	189.2	John Burkett	107	John Burkett	13	Rod Beck	17
1993	Bill Swift	2.82	Bill Swift	9.9	John Burkett	232.2	Bill Swift	157	John Burkett	22	Rod Beck	48
1994	John Burkett	3.62	Mark Portugal	12.2	John Burkett	159.1	Mark Portugal	87	Mark Portugal	10	Rod Beck	28
1995	Mark Leiter	3.82	Mark Leiter	11.8	Mark Leiter	195.2	Mark Leiter	129	Mark Leiter	10	Rod Beck	33
1996	Mark Gardner	4.42	Allen Watson	12.7	Allen Watson	185.2	Mark Gardner	145	Mark Gardner	12	Rod Beck	35
1997	Shawn Estes	3.18	Kirk Rueter	11.6	Shawn Estes	201.0	Shawn Estes	181	Shawn Estes	19	Rod Beck	37

Giants Franchise Batting Leaders—Career

## Games			## At-Bats			## Runs			## Hits		
1	Willie Mays	2,857	1	Willie Mays	10,477	1	Willie Mays	2,011	1	Willie Mays	3,187
2	Mel Ott	2,730	2	Mel Ott	9,456	2	Mel Ott	1,859	2	Mel Ott	2,876
3	Willie McCovey	2,256	3	Willie McCovey	7,214	3	Mike Tiernan	1,313	3	Bill Terry	2,193
4	Bill Terry	1,721	4	Bill Terry	6,428	4	Bill Terry	1,120	4	Willie McCovey	1,974
5	Travis Jackson	1,656	5	Travis Jackson	6,086	5	Willie McCovey	1,113	5	Mike Tiernan	1,834
6	Larry Doyle	1,622	6	Larry Doyle	5,995	6	George Van Haltren	973	6	Travis Jackson	1,768
7	Jim Davenport	1,501	7	Mike Tiernan	5,906	7	Roger Connor	946	7	Larry Doyle	1,751
8	Whitey Lockman	1,485	8	Whitey Lockman	5,584	8	Larry Doyle	906	8	Jo-Jo Moore	1,615
9	Mike Tiernan	1,476	9	Jo-Jo Moore	5,427	9	George Burns	877	9	George Van Haltren	1,575
10	George Burns	1,362	10	George Burns	5,311	10	George Davis	838	10	Whitey Lockman	1,571
11	Jo-Jo Moore	1,335	11	George Van Haltren	4,906	11	Travis Jackson	833	11	George Burns	1,541
12	Art Fletcher	1,321	12	Art Fletcher	4,766	12	Monte Ward	828	12	Ross Youngs	1,491
13	Robby Thompson	1,304	13	Ross Youngs	4,627	13	Ross Youngs	812	13	George Davis	1,427
14	George Van Haltren	1,221	14	Robby Thompson	4,612	14	Jo-Jo Moore	809	14	Roger Connor	1,388
15	Ross Youngs	1,211	15	Monte Ward	4,461	15	Whitey Lockman	799	15	Freddy Lindstrom	1,347
16	Don Mueller	1,171	16	Jim Davenport	4,427	16	Bobby Bonds	765	16	Art Fletcher	1,311
17	Will Clark	1,160	17	Roger Connor	4,346	17	Freddy Lindstrom	705	17	Frankie Frisch	1,303
18	George Kelly	1,136	18	George Davis	4,303	18	Frankie Frisch	701	18	Orlando Cepeda	1,286
19	Bobby Thomson	1,135	19	Will Clark	4,269	19	Will Clark	687	19	Will Clark	1,278
20	Four tied at	1,120	20	Freddy Lindstrom	4,242	20	Robby Thompson	671	20	George Kelly	1,270

## Doubles			## Triples			## Home Runs			## RBI		
1	Willie Mays	504	1	Mike Tiernan	162	1	Willie Mays	646	1	Mel Ott	1,860
2	Mel Ott	488	2	Willie Mays	139	2	Mel Ott	511	2	Willie Mays	1,859
3	Bill Terry	373	3	Roger Connor	131	3	Willie McCovey	469	3	Willie McCovey	1,388
4	Willie McCovey	308	4	Larry Doyle	117	4	Matt Williams	247	4	Bill Terry	1,078
5	Travis Jackson	291	5	Bill Terry	112	5	Orlando Cepeda	226	5	Travis Jackson	929
6	Larry Doyle	275	6	Buck Ewing	109	6	Barry Bonds	198	6	Mike Tiernan	851
7	George Burns	267	7	George Davis	98	7	Bobby Thomson	189	7	George Davis	816
8	Jo-Jo Moore	258	8	Ross Youngs	93	8	Bobby Bonds	186	8	Roger Connor	786
9	Mike Tiernan	256	9	George Van Haltren	88	9	Will Clark	176	9	Orlando Cepeda	767
10	Will Clark	249	10	Travis Jackson	86	10	Jack Clark	163	10	George Kelly	762
11	Roger Connor	242	11	George Burns	82	11	Johnny Mize	157	11	Matt Williams	732
12	Robby Thompson	238	12	Frankie Frisch	77		Jim Ray Hart	157	12	Larry Doyle	725
13	Ross Youngs	236	13	Mel Ott	72	13	Bill Terry	154	13	Will Clark	709
14	George Davis	227	14	Art Fletcher	65	14	Kevin Mitchell	143	14	Bobby Thomson	704
15	Orlando Cepeda	226	15	Irish Meusel	64	15	Darrell Evans	142	15	George Van Haltren	604
16	George Kelly	218	16	Red Murray	63	16	Travis Jackson	135	16	Freddy Lindstrom	603
17	Whitey Lockman	216		Freddy Lindstrom	63	17	Hank Thompson	129	17	Jack Clark	595
18	Freddy Lindstrom	212	18	Jim O'Rourke	60	18	George Kelly	123	18	Ross Youngs	592
19	Al Dark	205	19	Fred Merkle	58	19	Robby Thompson	119	19	Art Fletcher	584
20	Jack Clark	197	20	Monte Ward	57	20	Whitey Lockman	113	20	Irish Meusel	571

## Walks			## Strikeouts			## Stolen Bases			## Runs Created		
1	Mel Ott	1,708	1	Willie Mays	1,436	1	Mike Tiernan	428	1	Willie Mays	2,220
2	Willie Mays	1,393	2	Willie McCovey	1,351	2	George Davis	354	2	Mel Ott	2,127
3	Willie McCovey	1,168	3	Bobby Bonds	1,016	3	Willie Mays	336	3	Willie McCovey	1,426
4	Mike Tiernan	747	4	Robby Thompson	987	4	George Burns	334	4	Mike Tiernan	1,353
5	George Burns	631	5	Mel Ott	896	5	Monte Ward	332	5	Bill Terry	1,242
6	Barry Bonds	616	6	Matt Williams	872	6	George Van Haltren	320	6	Roger Connor	1,101
7	Darrell Evans	605	7	Will Clark	744	7	Larry Doyle	291	7	George Van Haltren	972
8	Roger Connor	578	8	Jim Davenport	673	8	Art Devlin	266	8	George Davis	961
9	Larry Doyle	576	9	Orlando Cepeda	636	9	Bobby Bonds	263	9	Larry Doyle	957
10	Ross Youngs	550	10	Jeffrey Leonard	586	10	Jack Doyle	254	10	Travis Jackson	887
11	Bill Terry	537	11	Chili Davis	578	11	Red Murray	239	11	George Burns	845
12	Whitey Lockman	520	12	Travis Jackson	565	12	Frankie Frisch	224	12	Ross Youngs	843
13	Will Clark	506	13	Jack Clark	556	13	Fred Merkle	212	13	Will Clark	823
14	Bobby Bonds	500	14	Johnnie LeMaster	542	14	Fred Snodgrass	201	14	Jo-Jo Moore	786
15	Jack Clark	497	15	Jim Ray Hart	521	15	Buck Ewing	178	15	Whitey Lockman	785
16	Art Devlin	496	16	Chris Speier	519	16	Barry Bonds	166	16	Orlando Cepeda	749
17	Wes Westrum	489	17	Wes Westrum	514	17	Sam Mertes	165	17	Monte Ward	726
18	George Van Haltren	486	18	George Kelly	503	18	Kid Gleason	162		Bobby Bonds	726
19	Hank Thompson	483	19	Bobby Thomson	477	19	Roger Connor	161	19	Freddy Lindstrom	691
20	Chris Speier	466	20	Darrell Evans	475	20	Four tied at	153	20	Barry Bonds	685

## Runs Created/27 Outs			## Batting Average			## On-Base Percentage			## Slugging Percentage		
(minimum 2000 Plate Appearances)			(minimum 2000 Plate Appearances)			(minimum 2000 Plate Appearances)			(minimum 2000 Plate Appearances)		
1	Barry Bonds	10.05	1	Bill Terry	.341	1	Barry Bonds	.446	1	Barry Bonds	.619
2	Roger Connor	9.78	2	George Davis	.332	2	Mel Ott	.414	2	Willie Mays	.564
3	Buck Ewing	8.57	3	Ross Youngs	.322	3	Roger Bresnahan	.403	3	Johnny Mize	.549
4	Mike Tiernan	8.55	4	Frankie Frisch	.321	4	Roger Connor	.402	4	Kevin Mitchell	.536
5	George Davis	8.43	5	George Van Haltren	.321	5	Ross Youngs	.399	5	Orlando Cepeda	.535
6	Mel Ott	8.34	6	Roger Connor	.319	6	Bill Terry	.393	6	Mel Ott	.533
7	Johnny Mize	8.08	7	Freddy Lindstrom	.318	7	George Davis	.393	7	Willie McCovey	.524
8	Willie Mays	7.77	8	Irish Meusel	.314	8	Mike Tiernan	.392	8	Bill Terry	.506
9	Bill Terry	7.35	9	Shanty Hogan	.311	9	Johnny Mize	.389	9	Will Clark	.499
10	George Van Haltren	7.34	10	Mike Tiernan	.311	10	Monte Irvin	.389	10	Matt Williams	.498
11	Jim O'Rourke	7.17	11	Dave Bancroft	.310	11	Willie Mays	.385	11	Roger Connor	.488
12	Will Clark	7.09	12	Barry Bonds	.308	12	George Van Haltren	.385	12	Bobby Thomson	.484
13	Willie McCovey	7.05	13	Orlando Cepeda	.308	13	Dave Bancroft	.382	13	Bobby Bonds	.478
14	George Gore	7.01	14	Buck Ewing	.306	14	Brett Butler	.381	14	Monte Irvin	.477
15	Roger Bresnahan	6.75	15	Jack Doyle	.306	15	George Gore	.378	15	Irish Meusel	.477
16	Jack Doyle	6.71	16	Willie Mays	.304	16	Willie McCovey	.377	16	Jack Clark	.477
17	Ross Youngs	6.63	17	Mel Ott	.304	17	Chief Meyers	.376	17	Jim Ray Hart	.474
18	Monte Irvin	6.59	18	Chief Meyers	.301	18	Fred Snodgrass	.374	18	Buck Ewing	.469
19	Orlando Cepeda	6.55	19	George Kelly	.301	19	Hank Thompson	.373	19	George Davis	.467
20	Bobby Bonds	6.39	20	Will Clark	.299	20	Will Clark	.373	20	Felipe Alou	.466

Teams: Giants

Giants Franchise Pitching Leaders—Career

Wins

1	Christy Mathewson	372
2	Carl Hubbell	253
3	Mickey Welch	240
4	Juan Marichal	238
5	Amos Rusie	233
6	Tim Keefe	173
7	Freddie Fitzsimmons	170
8	Hal Schumacher	158
9	Joe McGinnity	151
10	Hooks Wiltse	136
11	Gaylord Perry	134
12	Larry Jansen	120
13	Jouett Meekin	116
14	Luther Taylor	115
	Jeff Tesreau	115
16	Red Ames	108
	Johnny Antonelli	108
18	Art Nehf	107
	Mike McCormick	107
20	Rube Marquard	103

Losses

1	Christy Mathewson	188
2	Amos Rusie	163
3	Carl Hubbell	154
4	Mickey Welch	147
5	Juan Marichal	140
6	Hal Schumacher	121
7	Freddie Fitzsimmons	114
8	Gaylord Perry	109
9	Dave Koslo	104
10	Luther Taylor	103
11	Mike McCormick	96
	Jim Barr	96
13	Joe McGinnity	88
14	Larry Jansen	86
15	Hooks Wiltse	85
16	Johnny Antonelli	84
17	Tim Keefe	82
18	Cliff Melton	80
19	Red Ames	77
20	Rube Marquard	76

Winning Percentage
(minimum 100 decisions)

1	Sal Maglie	.693
2	Tim Keefe	.678
3	Christy Mathewson	.664
4	Jesse Barnes	.656
5	Doc Crandall	.650
6	Art Nehf	.641
7	Joe McGinnity	.632
8	Juan Marichal	.630
9	Carl Hubbell	.622
10	Mickey Welch	.620
11	Hooks Wiltse	.615
12	Jeff Tesreau	.615
13	John Burkett	.615
14	Jouett Meekin	.611
15	Freddie Fitzsimmons	.599
16	Amos Rusie	.588
17	Red Ames	.584
18	Larry Jansen	.583
19	Pol Perritt	.576
20	Rube Marquard	.575

Games

1	Gary Lavelle	647
2	Christy Mathewson	634
3	Greg Minton	552
4	Carl Hubbell	535
5	Randy Moffitt	459
6	Juan Marichal	458
7	Mickey Welch	426
	Amos Rusie	426
9	Rod Beck	416
10	Freddie Fitzsimmons	403
11	Jim Barr	394
12	Hal Schumacher	391
13	Gaylord Perry	367
14	Mike McCormick	357
15	Scott Garrelts	352
16	Bobby Bolin	345
17	Hooks Wiltse	339
18	Dave Koslo	332
19	Hoyt Wilhelm	319
20	Frank Linzy	308

Games Started

1	Christy Mathewson	550
2	Juan Marichal	446
3	Carl Hubbell	431
4	Mickey Welch	412
5	Amos Rusie	403
6	Freddie Fitzsimmons	329
	Hal Schumacher	329
8	Gaylord Perry	283
9	Tim Keefe	269
10	Mike McCormick	252
11	Joe McGinnity	237
12	Luther Taylor	233
13	Larry Jansen	230
14	Hooks Wiltse	223
15	Jim Barr	220
16	Johnny Antonelli	219
17	Red Ames	211
	Jack Sanford	211
19	Jouett Meekin	207
	Jeff Tesreau	207

Complete Games

1	Christy Mathewson	433
2	Mickey Welch	391
3	Amos Rusie	371
4	Carl Hubbell	260
5	Tim Keefe	251
6	Juan Marichal	244
7	Joe McGinnity	186
8	Jouett Meekin	178
9	Luther Taylor	155
10	Hooks Wiltse	153
11	Freddie Fitzsimmons	150
12	Hal Schumacher	138
13	Red Ames	128
14	Gaylord Perry	125
15	Jeff Tesreau	123
16	Larry Jansen	105
17	Cy Seymour	104
18	Rube Marquard	99
19	Art Nehf	95
20	Ed Doheny	93

Shutouts

1	Christy Mathewson	79
2	Juan Marichal	52
3	Carl Hubbell	36
4	Amos Rusie	29
	Hal Schumacher	29
6	Mickey Welch	28
7	Hooks Wiltse	27
	Jeff Tesreau	27
9	Joe McGinnity	26
10	Tim Keefe	22
11	Freddie Fitzsimmons	21
	Johnny Antonelli	21
	Gaylord Perry	21
14	Luther Taylor	20
	Pol Perritt	20
	Sal Maglie	20
	Jim Barr	20
18	Mike McCormick	19
19	Larry Jansen	17
20	Five tied at	16

Saves

1	Rod Beck	199
2	Gary Lavelle	127
3	Greg Minton	125
4	Randy Moffitt	83
5	Frank Linzy	78
6	Marv Grissom	58
7	Ace Adams	49
8	Scott Garrelts	48
9	Stu Miller	47
10	Jeff Brantley	42
11	Hoyt Wilhelm	41
12	Don McMahon	36
13	Craig Lefferts	35
14	Steve Bedrosian	34
15	Carl Hubbell	33
16	Hooks Wiltse	29
	Jerry Johnson	29
18	Christy Mathewson	28
	Dave Righetti	28
20	Four tied at	27

Innings Pitched

1	Christy Mathewson	4,771.2
2	Carl Hubbell	3,590.1
3	Mickey Welch	3,579.0
4	Amos Rusie	3,522.2
5	Juan Marichal	3,444.0
6	Freddie Fitzsimmons	2,514.1
7	Hal Schumacher	2,482.1
8	Gaylord Perry	2,294.2
9	Tim Keefe	2,270.0
10	Joe McGinnity	2,151.1
11	Hooks Wiltse	2,053.0
12	Luther Taylor	1,882.1
13	Mike McCormick	1,822.2
14	Red Ames	1,802.2
15	Jim Barr	1,800.1
16	Jouett Meekin	1,741.0
17	Larry Jansen	1,731.0
18	Jeff Tesreau	1,679.0
19	Johnny Antonelli	1,600.2
20	Dave Koslo	1,559.2

Walks

1	Amos Rusie	1,585
2	Mickey Welch	1,077
3	Hal Schumacher	902
4	Christy Mathewson	843
5	Carl Hubbell	725
6	Juan Marichal	690
7	Freddie Fitzsimmons	670
8	Cy Seymour	652
9	Jouett Meekin	648
10	Red Ames	620
11	Mike McCormick	616
12	Gaylord Perry	581
13	Tim Keefe	580
14	Jeff Tesreau	572
15	Luther Taylor	543
16	Johnny Antonelli	528
17	Dave Koslo	526
18	Ruben Gomez	498
19	Monte Kennedy	495
20	Ed Doheny	493

Strikeouts

1	Christy Mathewson	2,499
2	Juan Marichal	2,281
3	Amos Rusie	1,819
4	Carl Hubbell	1,677
5	Gaylord Perry	1,606
6	Mickey Welch	1,570
7	Tim Keefe	1,278
8	Red Ames	1,169
9	Mike McCormick	1,030
10	Bobby Bolin	977
11	Hooks Wiltse	948
12	Johnny Antonelli	919
13	Hal Schumacher	906
14	Rube Marquard	897
15	Jeff Tesreau	880
16	John Montefusco	869
17	Larry Jansen	826
18	Mike Krukow	802
19	Joe McGinnity	787
20	Jack Sanford	781

Strikeouts/9 Innings
(minimum 1000 Innings Pitched)

1	Bobby Bolin	6.86
2	John Montefusco	6.62
3	Gaylord Perry	6.30
4	Mike Krukow	6.25
5	Ed Halicki	6.05
6	Juan Marichal	5.96
7	Red Ames	5.84
8	Vida Blue	5.60
9	Rube Marquard	5.22
10	Atlee Hammaker	5.21
11	Johnny Antonelli	5.17
12	Cy Seymour	5.11
13	Mike McCormick	5.09
14	Tim Keefe	5.07
15	Jack Sanford	5.00
16	Jeff Tesreau	4.72
17	Christy Mathewson	4.71
18	Amos Rusie	4.65
19	Sal Maglie	4.54
20	Larry Jansen	4.29

ERA
(minimum 1000 Innings Pitched)

1	Christy Mathewson	2.12
2	Joe McGinnity	2.38
3	Jeff Tesreau	2.43
4	Red Ames	2.45
5	Hooks Wiltse	2.48
6	Tim Keefe	2.53
7	Mickey Welch	2.69
8	Luther Taylor	2.76
9	Rube Benton	2.79
10	Juan Marichal	2.84
11	Rube Marquard	2.85
12	Doc Crandall	2.89
13	Amos Rusie	2.89
14	Jesse Barnes	2.92
15	Gaylord Perry	2.96
16	Carl Hubbell	2.98
17	Johnny Antonelli	3.13
18	Sal Maglie	3.13
19	Bobby Bolin	3.26
20	Hal Schumacher	3.36

Component ERA
(minimum 1000 Innings Pitched)

1	Christy Mathewson	2.13
2	Tim Keefe	2.15
3	Jeff Tesreau	2.35
4	Joe McGinnity	2.38
5	Hooks Wiltse	2.49
6	Red Ames	2.52
7	Rube Benton	2.60
8	Juan Marichal	2.70
9	Mickey Welch	2.71
10	Rube Marquard	2.76
11	Gaylord Perry	2.81
12	Jesse Barnes	2.87
13	Carl Hubbell	2.88
14	Amos Rusie	2.96
15	Luther Taylor	3.04
16	Doc Crandall	3.05
17	Johnny Antonelli	3.21
18	Atlee Hammaker	3.21
19	Bobby Bolin	3.22
20	Ed Halicki	3.24

Opponent Average
(minimum 1000 Innings Pitched)

1	Tim Keefe	.220
2	Jeff Tesreau	.223
3	Bobby Bolin	.227
4	Amos Rusie	.230
5	Red Ames	.234
6	Christy Mathewson	.236
7	Juan Marichal	.236
8	Mickey Welch	.237
9	Joe McGinnity	.238
10	Gaylord Perry	.238
11	Johnny Antonelli	.239
12	Hooks Wiltse	.241
13	Jack Sanford	.242
14	Cy Seymour	.244
15	Ed Halicki	.246
16	Vida Blue	.246
17	Sal Maglie	.248
18	Rube Marquard	.248
19	Jim Hearn	.249
20	Mike McCormick	.251

Opponent OBP
(minimum 1000 Innings Pitched)

1	Tim Keefe	.272
2	Christy Mathewson	.273
3	Juan Marichal	.275
4	Joe McGinnity	.286
5	Gaylord Perry	.289
6	Hooks Wiltse	.291
7	Carl Hubbell	.291
8	Mickey Welch	.293
9	Jeff Tesreau	.295
10	Rube Benton	.296
11	Jesse Barnes	.299
12	Atlee Hammaker	.300
13	Larry Jansen	.302
14	Johnny Antonelli	.302
15	Bobby Bolin	.303
16	Red Ames	.303
17	Rube Marquard	.304
18	Ed Halicki	.305
19	Doc Crandall	.307
20	Jim Barr	.309

New York Giants Team Batting Leaders—Career

Games

1	Mel Ott	2,730
2	Bill Terry	1,721
3	Travis Jackson	1,656
4	Larry Doyle	1,622
5	Mike Tiernan	1,476
6	Whitey Lockman	1,393
7	George Burns	1,362
8	Jo-Jo Moore	1,335
9	Art Fletcher	1,321
10	George Van Haltren	1,221
11	Ross Youngs	1,211
12	Don Mueller	1,171
13	George Kelly	1,136
14	Bobby Thomson	1,135
15	Roger Connor	1,120
16	Art Devlin	1,116
17	Fred Merkle	1,105
18	George Davis	1,096
19	Freddy Lindstrom	1,087
20	Monte Ward	1,070

At-Bats

1	Mel Ott	9,456
2	Bill Terry	6,428
3	Travis Jackson	6,086
4	Larry Doyle	5,995
5	Mike Tiernan	5,906
6	Whitey Lockman	5,462
7	Jo-Jo Moore	5,427
8	George Burns	5,311
9	George Van Haltren	4,906
10	Art Fletcher	4,766
11	Ross Youngs	4,627
12	Monte Ward	4,461
13	Roger Connor	4,346
14	George Davis	4,303
15	Freddy Lindstrom	4,242
16	Bobby Thomson	4,223
17	George Kelly	4,213
18	Don Mueller	4,194
19	Frankie Frisch	4,053
20	Fred Merkle	3,831

Runs

1	Mel Ott	1,859
2	Mike Tiernan	1,313
3	Bill Terry	1,120
4	George Van Haltren	973
5	Roger Connor	946
6	Larry Doyle	906
7	George Burns	877
8	George Davis	838
9	Travis Jackson	833
10	Monte Ward	828
11	Ross Youngs	812
12	Jo-Jo Moore	809
13	Whitey Lockman	784
14	Freddy Lindstrom	705
15	Frankie Frisch	701
16	Bobby Thomson	648
17	Buck Ewing	643
18	George Kelly	608
19	Al Dark	605
20	Art Fletcher	602

Hits

1	Mel Ott	2,876
2	Bill Terry	2,193
3	Mike Tiernan	1,834
4	Travis Jackson	1,768
5	Larry Doyle	1,751
6	Jo-Jo Moore	1,615
7	George Van Haltren	1,575
8	Whitey Lockman	1,542
9	George Burns	1,541
10	Ross Youngs	1,491
11	George Davis	1,427
12	Roger Connor	1,388
13	Freddy Lindstrom	1,347
14	Art Fletcher	1,311
15	Frankie Frisch	1,303
16	George Kelly	1,270
17	Don Mueller	1,248
18	Monte Ward	1,245
19	Bobby Thomson	1,171
20	Al Dark	1,106

Doubles

1	Mel Ott	488
2	Bill Terry	373
3	Travis Jackson	291
4	Larry Doyle	275
5	George Burns	267
6	Jo-Jo Moore	258
7	Mike Tiernan	256
8	Roger Connor	242
9	Ross Youngs	236
10	George Davis	227
11	George Kelly	218
12	Freddy Lindstrom	212
13	Whitey Lockman	211
14	Al Dark	205
15	George Van Haltren	194
16	Art Fletcher	193
17	Fred Merkle	192
	Bobby Thomson	192
19	Frankie Frisch	180
20	Jim O'Rourke	170

Triples

1	Mike Tiernan	162
2	Roger Connor	131
3	Larry Doyle	117
4	Bill Terry	112
5	Buck Ewing	109
6	George Davis	98
7	Ross Youngs	93
8	George Van Haltren	88
9	Travis Jackson	86
10	George Burns	82
11	Frankie Frisch	77
12	Mel Ott	72
13	Art Fletcher	65
14	Irish Meusel	64
15	Red Murray	63
	Freddy Lindstrom	63
	Willie Mays	63
18	Jim O'Rourke	60
19	Fred Merkle	58
20	Monte Ward	57

Home Runs

1	Mel Ott	511
2	Bobby Thomson	189
3	Willie Mays	187
4	Johnny Mize	157
5	Bill Terry	154
6	Travis Jackson	135
7	Hank Thompson	129
8	George Kelly	123
9	Whitey Lockman	111
10	Mike Tiernan	107
11	Al Dark	98
12	Wes Westrum	96
13	Freddy Lindstrom	91
14	Sid Gordon	90
15	Willard Marshall	86
16	Monte Irvin	84
17	Jo-Jo Moore	79
18	Roger Connor	76
19	Irish Meusel	70
20	Larry Doyle	67

RBI

1	Mel Ott	1,860
2	Bill Terry	1,078
3	Travis Jackson	929
4	Mike Tiernan	851
5	George Davis	816
6	Roger Connor	786
7	George Kelly	762
8	Larry Doyle	725
9	Bobby Thomson	704
10	George Van Haltren	604
11	Freddy Lindstrom	603
12	Ross Youngs	592
13	Art Fletcher	584
14	Irish Meusel	571
15	Monte Ward	546
16	Whitey Lockman	536
17	Frankie Frisch	524
18	Jo-Jo Moore	513
19	Willie Mays	509
20	Fred Merkle	508

Walks

1	Mel Ott	1,708
2	Mike Tiernan	747
3	George Burns	631
4	Roger Connor	578
5	Larry Doyle	576
6	Ross Youngs	550
7	Bill Terry	537
8	Whitey Lockman	507
9	Art Devlin	496
10	Wes Westrum	489
11	George Van Haltren	486
12	Hank Thompson	483
13	Travis Jackson	412
14	Roger Bresnahan	410
15	George Davis	399
16	Willie Mays	361
17	Bobby Thomson	360
18	Sid Gordon	356
19	Jo-Jo Moore	348
20	Fred Snodgrass	345

Strikeouts

1	Mel Ott	896
2	Travis Jackson	565
3	Wes Westrum	514
4	George Kelly	503
5	Bobby Thomson	477
6	Bill Terry	449
7	George Burns	440
8	Fred Merkle	414
9	Ross Youngs	390
10	Whitey Lockman	354
11	Hank Thompson	330
12	Willie Mays	321
13	Mike Tiernan	318
14	Art Fletcher	306
15	Fred Snodgrass	296
16	Roger Connor	276
	Dick Bartell	276
18	Mickey Welch	273
19	Al Dark	257
20	Johnny Rucker	248

Stolen Bases

1	Mike Tiernan	428
2	George Davis	354
3	George Burns	334
4	Monte Ward	332
5	George Van Haltren	320
6	Larry Doyle	291
7	Art Devlin	266
8	Jack Doyle	254
9	Red Murray	239
10	Frankie Frisch	224
11	Fred Merkle	212
12	Fred Snodgrass	201
13	Buck Ewing	178
14	Sam Mertes	165
15	Kid Gleason	162
16	Roger Connor	161
17	Jim O'Rourke	153
	Ross Youngs	153
19	Art Fletcher	152
20	Dan McGann	151

Runs Created

1	Mel Ott	2,127
2	Mike Tiernan	1,353
3	Bill Terry	1,242
4	Roger Connor	1,101
5	George Van Haltren	972
6	George Davis	961
7	Larry Doyle	957
8	Travis Jackson	887
9	George Burns	845
10	Ross Youngs	843
11	Jo-Jo Moore	786
12	Whitey Lockman	772
13	Monte Ward	726
14	Freddy Lindstrom	691
15	George Kelly	683
16	Bobby Thomson	675
17	Frankie Frisch	672
18	Buck Ewing	667
19	Jim O'Rourke	621
20	Willie Mays	619

Runs Created/27 Outs

(minimum 2000 Plate Appearances)

1	Roger Connor	9.78
2	Buck Ewing	8.57
3	Mike Tiernan	8.55
4	George Davis	8.43
5	Mel Ott	8.34
6	Johnny Mize	8.08
7	Willie Mays	7.84
8	Bill Terry	7.35
9	George Van Haltren	7.34
10	Jim O'Rourke	7.17
11	George Gore	7.01
12	Roger Bresnahan	6.75
13	Jack Doyle	6.71
14	Ross Youngs	6.63
15	Monte Irvin	6.59
16	Pete Gillespie	6.21
17	Hank Thompson	6.20
18	Sam Mertes	6.13
19	Dave Bancroft	6.07
20	Frankie Frisch	6.03

Batting Average

(minimum 2000 Plate Appearances)

1	Bill Terry	.341
2	George Davis	.332
3	Ross Youngs	.322
4	Frankie Frisch	.321
5	George Van Haltren	.321
6	Roger Connor	.319
7	Freddy Lindstrom	.318
8	Irish Meusel	.314
9	Willie Mays	.311
10	Shanty Hogan	.311
11	Mike Tiernan	.311
12	Dave Bancroft	.310
13	Buck Ewing	.306
14	Jack Doyle	.306
15	Mel Ott	.304
16	Chief Meyers	.301
17	George Kelly	.301
18	Johnny Mize	.299
19	Jim O'Rourke	.299
20	Jo-Jo Moore	.298

On-Base Percentage

(minimum 2000 Plate Appearances)

1	Mel Ott	.414
2	Roger Bresnahan	.403
3	Roger Connor	.402
4	Ross Youngs	.399
5	Bill Terry	.393
6	George Davis	.393
7	Mike Tiernan	.392
8	Johnny Mize	.389
9	Monte Irvin	.389
10	Willie Mays	.387
11	George Van Haltren	.385
12	Dave Bancroft	.382
13	George Gore	.378
14	Chief Meyers	.376
15	Fred Snodgrass	.374
16	Hank Thompson	.373
17	Al Bridwell	.372
18	Sid Gordon	.368
19	George Burns	.368
20	Frankie Frisch	.367

Slugging Percentage

(minimum 2000 Plate Appearances)

1	Willie Mays	.593
2	Johnny Mize	.549
3	Mel Ott	.533
4	Bill Terry	.506
5	Roger Connor	.488
6	Bobby Thomson	.484
7	Monte Irvin	.477
8	Irish Meusel	.477
9	Buck Ewing	.469
10	George Davis	.467
11	George Kelly	.465
12	Mike Tiernan	.463
13	Freddy Lindstrom	.462
14	Hank Thompson	.457
15	Sid Gordon	.448
16	Hank Leiber	.446
17	Frankie Frisch	.444
18	Babe Young	.441
19	Ross Youngs	.441
20	Al Dark	.439

1512

New York Giants Team Pitching Leaders—Career

Wins

1	Christy Mathewson	372
2	Carl Hubbell	253
3	Mickey Welch	240
4	Amos Rusie	233
5	Tim Keefe	173
6	Freddie Fitzsimmons	170
7	Hal Schumacher	158
8	Joe McGinnity	151
9	Hooks Wiltse	136
10	Larry Jansen	120
11	Jouett Meekin	116
12	Luther Taylor	115
	Jeff Tesreau	115
14	Red Ames	108
15	Art Nehf	107
16	Rube Marquard	103
17	Sal Maglie	95
18	Dave Koslo	91
19	Cliff Melton	86
20	Jesse Barnes	82

Losses

1	Christy Mathewson	188
2	Amos Rusie	163
3	Carl Hubbell	154
4	Mickey Welch	147
5	Hal Schumacher	121
6	Freddie Fitzsimmons	114
7	Dave Koslo	104
8	Luther Taylor	103
9	Joe McGinnity	88
10	Larry Jansen	86
11	Hooks Wiltse	85
12	Tim Keefe	82
13	Cliff Melton	80
14	Red Ames	77
15	Rube Marquard	76
16	Jouett Meekin	74
17	Jeff Tesreau	72
18	Ed Doheny	69
19	Jim Hearn	66
20	Two tied at	60

Winning Percentage
(minimum 100 decisions)

1	Sal Maglie	.693
2	Tim Keefe	.678
3	Christy Mathewson	.664
4	Jesse Barnes	.656
5	Doc Crandall	.650
6	Art Nehf	.641
7	Joe McGinnity	.632
8	Carl Hubbell	.622
9	Mickey Welch	.620
10	Hooks Wiltse	.615
11	Jeff Tesreau	.615
12	Jouett Meekin	.611
13	Freddie Fitzsimmons	.599
14	Amos Rusie	.588
15	Red Ames	.584
16	Larry Jansen	.583
17	Pol Perritt	.576
18	Rube Marquard	.575
19	Jack Scott	.574
20	Hal Schumacher	.566

Games

1	Christy Mathewson	634
2	Carl Hubbell	535
3	Mickey Welch	426
	Amos Rusie	426
5	Freddie Fitzsimmons	403
6	Hal Schumacher	391
7	Hooks Wiltse	339
8	Dave Koslo	332
9	Hoyt Wilhelm	319
10	Ace Adams	302
11	Joe McGinnity	300
12	Larry Jansen	283
13	Red Ames	282
14	Tim Keefe	272
	Cliff Melton	272
16	Luther Taylor	270
17	Monte Kennedy	249
18	Jeff Tesreau	247
19	Rube Marquard	239
20	Marv Grissom	234

Games Started

1	Christy Mathewson	550
2	Carl Hubbell	431
3	Mickey Welch	412
4	Amos Rusie	403
5	Freddie Fitzsimmons	329
	Hal Schumacher	329
7	Tim Keefe	269
8	Joe McGinnity	237
9	Luther Taylor	233
10	Larry Jansen	230
11	Hooks Wiltse	223
12	Red Ames	211
13	Jouett Meekin	207
	Jeff Tesreau	207
15	Rube Marquard	188
	Dave Koslo	188
17	Jim Hearn	186
18	Art Nehf	181
19	Cliff Melton	179
20	Sal Maglie	171

Complete Games

1	Christy Mathewson	433
2	Mickey Welch	391
3	Amos Rusie	371
4	Carl Hubbell	260
5	Tim Keefe	251
6	Joe McGinnity	186
7	Jouett Meekin	178
8	Luther Taylor	155
9	Hooks Wiltse	153
10	Freddie Fitzsimmons	150
11	Hal Schumacher	138
12	Red Ames	128
13	Jeff Tesreau	123
14	Larry Jansen	105
15	Cy Seymour	104
16	Rube Marquard	99
17	Art Nehf	95
18	Ed Doheny	93
19	Jesse Barnes	80
20	Sal Maglie	77

Shutouts

1	Christy Mathewson	79
2	Carl Hubbell	36
3	Amos Rusie	29
	Hal Schumacher	29
5	Mickey Welch	28
6	Hooks Wiltse	27
	Jeff Tesreau	27
8	Joe McGinnity	26
9	Tim Keefe	22
10	Freddie Fitzsimmons	21
11	Luther Taylor	20
	Pol Perritt	20
	Sal Maglie	20
14	Larry Jansen	17
15	Rube Marquard	16
	Dave Koslo	16
	Johnny Antonelli	16
18	Red Ames	15
19	Art Nehf	14
20	Two tied at	13

Saves

1	Ace Adams	49
2	Marv Grissom	48
3	Hoyt Wilhelm	41
4	Carl Hubbell	33
5	Hooks Wiltse	29
6	Christy Mathewson	28
7	Jumbo Brown	27
8	Dick Coffman	25
9	Doc Crandall	24
10	Joe McGinnity	21
	Dave Koslo	21
12	Ken Trinkle	19
13	Claude Jonnard	16
	Dolf Luque	16
	Cliff Melton	16
16	Rosy Ryan	15
17	Jack Scott	13
	Hi Bell	13
19	Four tied at	12

Innings Pitched

1	Christy Mathewson	4,771.2
2	Carl Hubbell	3,590.1
3	Mickey Welch	3,579.0
4	Amos Rusie	3,522.2
5	Freddie Fitzsimmons	2,514.1
6	Hal Schumacher	2,482.1
7	Tim Keefe	2,270.0
8	Joe McGinnity	2,151.1
9	Hooks Wiltse	2,053.0
10	Luther Taylor	1,882.1
11	Red Ames	1,802.2
12	Jouett Meekin	1,741.0
13	Larry Jansen	1,731.0
14	Jeff Tesreau	1,679.0
15	Dave Koslo	1,559.2
16	Rube Marquard	1,546.0
17	Cliff Melton	1,453.2
18	Art Nehf	1,436.0
19	Sal Maglie	1,297.2
20	Jim Hearn	1,242.2

Walks

1	Amos Rusie	1,585
2	Mickey Welch	1,077
3	Hal Schumacher	902
4	Christy Mathewson	843
5	Carl Hubbell	725
6	Freddie Fitzsimmons	670
7	Cy Seymour	652
8	Jouett Meekin	648
9	Red Ames	620
10	Tim Keefe	580
11	Jeff Tesreau	572
12	Luther Taylor	543
13	Dave Koslo	526
14	Monte Kennedy	495
15	Ed Doheny	493
16	Hooks Wiltse	491
17	Jim Hearn	477
18	Joe McGinnity	464
19	Sal Maglie	434
20	Cliff Melton	431

Strikeouts

1	Christy Mathewson	2,499
2	Amos Rusie	1,819
3	Carl Hubbell	1,677
4	Mickey Welch	1,570
5	Tim Keefe	1,278
6	Red Ames	1,169
7	Hooks Wiltse	948
8	Hal Schumacher	906
9	Rube Marquard	897
10	Jeff Tesreau	880
11	Larry Jansen	826
12	Joe McGinnity	787
13	Luther Taylor	759
14	Freddie Fitzsimmons	693
15	Cliff Melton	660
16	Sal Maglie	654
17	Dave Koslo	596
18	Cy Seymour	582
19	Johnny Antonelli	554
20	Jouett Meekin	514

Strikeouts/9 Innings
(minimum 1000 Innings Pitched)

1	Red Ames	5.84
2	Rube Marquard	5.22
3	Cy Seymour	5.11
4	Tim Keefe	5.07
5	Jeff Tesreau	4.72
6	Christy Mathewson	4.71
7	Amos Rusie	4.65
8	Sal Maglie	4.54
9	Larry Jansen	4.29
10	Carl Hubbell	4.20
11	Hooks Wiltse	4.16
12	Cliff Melton	4.09
13	Ruben Gomez	4.01
14	Mickey Welch	3.95
15	Luther Taylor	3.63
16	Doc Crandall	3.60
17	Jim Hearn	3.50
18	Dave Koslo	3.44
19	Joe McGinnity	3.29
20	Hal Schumacher	3.28

ERA
(minimum 1000 Innings Pitched)

1	Christy Mathewson	2.12
2	Joe McGinnity	2.38
3	Jeff Tesreau	2.43
4	Red Ames	2.45
5	Hooks Wiltse	2.48
6	Tim Keefe	2.53
7	Mickey Welch	2.69
8	Luther Taylor	2.76
9	Rube Benton	2.79
10	Rube Marquard	2.85
11	Doc Crandall	2.89
12	Amos Rusie	2.89
13	Jesse Barnes	2.92
14	Carl Hubbell	2.98
15	Sal Maglie	3.13
16	Hal Schumacher	3.36
17	Cliff Melton	3.42
18	Art Nehf	3.45
19	Virgil Barnes	3.53
20	Freddie Fitzsimmons	3.54

Component ERA
(minimum 1000 Innings Pitched)

1	Christy Mathewson	2.13
2	Tim Keefe	2.15
3	Jeff Tesreau	2.35
4	Joe McGinnity	2.38
5	Hooks Wiltse	2.49
6	Red Ames	2.52
7	Rube Benton	2.60
8	Mickey Welch	2.71
9	Rube Marquard	2.76
10	Jesse Barnes	2.87
11	Carl Hubbell	2.88
12	Amos Rusie	2.96
13	Luther Taylor	3.04
14	Doc Crandall	3.05
15	Art Nehf	3.27
16	Cliff Melton	3.30
17	Larry Jansen	3.42
18	Sal Maglie	3.44
19	Hal Schumacher	3.45
20	Virgil Barnes	3.50

Opponent Average
(minimum 1000 Innings Pitched)

1	Tim Keefe	.220
2	Jeff Tesreau	.223
3	Amos Rusie	.230
4	Red Ames	.234
5	Christy Mathewson	.236
6	Mickey Welch	.237
7	Joe McGinnity	.238
8	Hooks Wiltse	.241
9	Cy Seymour	.244
10	Sal Maglie	.248
11	Rube Marquard	.248
12	Jim Hearn	.249
13	Rube Benton	.251
14	Carl Hubbell	.251
15	Ruben Gomez	.252
16	Hal Schumacher	.255
17	Luther Taylor	.255
18	Larry Jansen	.258
19	Doc Crandall	.258
20	Cliff Melton	.259

Opponent OBP
(minimum 1000 Innings Pitched)

1	Tim Keefe	.272
2	Christy Mathewson	.273
3	Joe McGinnity	.286
4	Hooks Wiltse	.291
5	Carl Hubbell	.291
6	Mickey Welch	.293
7	Jeff Tesreau	.295
8	Rube Benton	.296
9	Jesse Barnes	.299
10	Larry Jansen	.302
11	Red Ames	.303
12	Rube Marquard	.304
13	Doc Crandall	.307
14	Art Nehf	.311
15	Sal Maglie	.312
16	Amos Rusie	.313
17	Luther Taylor	.313
18	Cliff Melton	.314
19	Jim Hearn	.320
20	Dave Koslo	.320

San Francisco Giants Team Batting Leaders—Career

Games

1	Willie McCovey	2,256
2	Willie Mays	2,095
3	Jim Davenport	1,501
4	Robby Thompson	1,304
5	Will Clark	1,160
6	Matt Williams	1,120
7	Orlando Cepeda	1,114
	Chris Speier	1,114
9	Hal Lanier	1,101
10	Darrell Evans	1,094
11	Tito Fuentes	1,054
12	Jack Clark	1,044
13	Bobby Bonds	1,014
14	Jim Ray Hart	1,001
15	Johnnie LeMaster	986
16	Jose Uribe	985
17	Chili Davis	874
18	Bob Brenly	823
19	Jeffrey Leonard	789
20	Tom Haller	761

At-Bats

1	Willie Mays	7,578
2	Willie McCovey	7,214
3	Robby Thompson	4,612
4	Jim Davenport	4,427
5	Will Clark	4,269
6	Orlando Cepeda	4,178
7	Matt Williams	4,139
8	Bobby Bonds	4,047
9	Tito Fuentes	3,823
10	Jack Clark	3,731
11	Chris Speier	3,730
12	Darrell Evans	3,728
13	Hal Lanier	3,514
14	Jim Ray Hart	3,425
15	Chili Davis	3,148
16	Johnnie LeMaster	3,089
17	Jose Uribe	2,992
18	Jeffrey Leonard	2,946
19	Bob Brenly	2,527
20	Barry Bonds	2,485

Runs

1	Willie Mays	1,480
2	Willie McCovey	1,113
3	Bobby Bonds	765
4	Will Clark	687
5	Robby Thompson	671
6	Orlando Cepeda	652
7	Jack Clark	597
8	Matt Williams	594
9	Barry Bonds	572
10	Jim Davenport	552
11	Darrell Evans	534
12	Jim Ray Hart	488
13	Chris Speier	445
14	Chili Davis	432
15	Tito Fuentes	417
16	Jeffrey Leonard	381
17	Kevin Mitchell	351
18	Felipe Alou	337
19	Gary Matthews	318
20	Brett Butler	317

Hits

1	Willie Mays	2,284
2	Willie McCovey	1,974
3	Orlando Cepeda	1,286
4	Will Clark	1,278
5	Robby Thompson	1,187
6	Jim Davenport	1,142
7	Bobby Bonds	1,106
8	Matt Williams	1,092
9	Jack Clark	1,034
10	Tito Fuentes	1,000
11	Jim Ray Hart	965
12	Darrell Evans	952
13	Chris Speier	924
14	Chili Davis	840
15	Jeffrey Leonard	809
16	Hal Lanier	803
17	Barry Bonds	766
18	Jose Uribe	721
19	Johnnie LeMaster	695
20	Felipe Alou	655

Doubles

1	Willie Mays	376
2	Willie McCovey	308
3	Will Clark	249
4	Robby Thompson	238
5	Orlando Cepeda	226
6	Jack Clark	197
7	Bobby Bonds	188
8	Matt Williams	179
9	Jim Davenport	177
10	Darrell Evans	159
11	Chris Speier	153
12	Tito Fuentes	152
13	Chili Davis	144
14	Jeffrey Leonard	139
	Barry Bonds	139
16	Jim Ray Hart	135
17	Felipe Alou	119
18	Bob Brenly	116
19	Johnnie LeMaster	109
	Kevin Mitchell	109

Triples

1	Willie Mays	76
2	Willie McCovey	45
3	Bobby Bonds	42
4	Larry Herndon	39
	Robby Thompson	39
6	Jim Davenport	37
	Will Clark	37
8	Jose Uribe	34
9	Tito Fuentes	33
10	Jack Clark	30
11	Jim Ray Hart	27
	Chris Speier	27
13	Matt Williams	25
14	Gary Matthews	24
	Jeffrey Leonard	24
16	Derrel Thomas	23
	Darren Lewis	23
18	Orlando Cepeda	22
	Gary Thomasson	22
	Brett Butler	22

Home Runs

1	Willie McCovey	469
2	Willie Mays	459
3	Matt Williams	247
4	Orlando Cepeda	226
5	Barry Bonds	198
6	Bobby Bonds	186
7	Will Clark	176
8	Jack Clark	163
9	Jim Ray Hart	157
10	Kevin Mitchell	143
11	Darrell Evans	142
12	Robby Thompson	119
13	Tom Haller	107
14	Chili Davis	101
15	Jeffrey Leonard	99
16	Bob Brenly	90
17	Felipe Alou	85
18	Jim Davenport	77
	Dave Kingman	77
20	Chris Speier	70

RBI

1	Willie McCovey	1,388
2	Willie Mays	1,350
3	Orlando Cepeda	767
4	Matt Williams	732
5	Will Clark	709
6	Jack Clark	595
7	Bobby Bonds	552
8	Barry Bonds	538
9	Jim Ray Hart	526
10	Darrell Evans	525
11	Robby Thompson	458
12	Jim Davenport	456
13	Jeffrey Leonard	435
14	Chili Davis	418
15	Kevin Mitchell	411
16	Chris Speier	409
17	Bob Brenly	327
18	Felipe Alou	325
19	Tom Haller	320
20	Tito Fuentes	306

Walks

1	Willie McCovey	1,168
2	Willie Mays	1,032
3	Barry Bonds	616
4	Darrell Evans	605
5	Will Clark	506
6	Bobby Bonds	500
7	Jack Clark	497
8	Chris Speier	466
9	Robby Thompson	439
10	Jim Davenport	382
11	Chili Davis	361
12	Jim Ray Hart	341
13	Dick Dietz	318
14	Tom Haller	311
15	Bob Brenly	308
16	Ken Henderson	283
17	Gary Matthews	275
18	Matt Williams	272
19	Kevin Mitchell	264
20	Orlando Cepeda	259

Strikeouts

1	Willie McCovey	1,351
2	Willie Mays	1,115
3	Bobby Bonds	1,016
4	Robby Thompson	987
5	Matt Williams	872
6	Will Clark	744
7	Jim Davenport	673
8	Orlando Cepeda	636
9	Jeffrey Leonard	586
10	Chili Davis	578
11	Jack Clark	556
12	Johnnie LeMaster	542
13	Jim Ray Hart	521
14	Chris Speier	519
15	Darrell Evans	475
16	Dave Kingman	422
17	Bob Brenly	421
18	Jose Uribe	418
19	Hal Lanier	413
20	Tito Fuentes	405

Stolen Bases

1	Bobby Bonds	263
2	Willie Mays	215
3	Barry Bonds	166
4	Darren Lewis	138
5	Bill North	129
6	Brett Butler	125
7	Jeffrey Leonard	115
8	Robby Thompson	103
9	Chili Davis	95
10	Dan Gladden	94
11	Johnnie LeMaster	93
12	Orlando Cepeda	92
13	Jose Uribe	72
14	Royce Clayton	66
15	Tito Fuentes	63
16	Jack Clark	60
	Larry Herndon	60
18	Ken Henderson	59
	Garry Maddox	59
20	Darrell Evans	55

Runs Created

1	Willie Mays	1,601
2	Willie McCovey	1,426
3	Will Clark	823
4	Orlando Cepeda	749
5	Bobby Bonds	726
6	Barry Bonds	685
7	Matt Williams	623
8	Jack Clark	622
9	Robby Thompson	605
10	Darrell Evans	592
11	Jim Ray Hart	555
12	Jim Davenport	523
13	Chris Speier	451
14	Chili Davis	447
15	Tito Fuentes	402
16	Jeffrey Leonard	400
17	Kevin Mitchell	394
18	Tom Haller	360
19	Felipe Alou	354
20	Two tied at	350

Runs Created/27 Outs

(minimum 2000 Plate Appearances)

1	Barry Bonds	10.05
2	Willie Mays	7.75
3	Will Clark	7.09
4	Willie McCovey	7.05
5	Orlando Cepeda	6.55
6	Bobby Bonds	6.39
7	Kevin Mitchell	6.36
8	Jack Clark	5.81
9	Gary Matthews	5.78
10	Jim Ray Hart	5.75
11	Brett Butler	5.53
12	Felipe Alou	5.51
13	Darrell Evans	5.48
14	Matt Williams	5.23
15	Tom Haller	5.20
16	Ken Henderson	5.06
17	Chili Davis	4.87
18	Harvey Kuenn	4.81
19	Jeffrey Leonard	4.73
20	Bob Brenly	4.69

Batting Average

(minimum 2000 Plate Appearances)

1	Barry Bonds	.308
2	Orlando Cepeda	.308
3	Willie Mays	.301
4	Will Clark	.299
5	Brett Butler	.293
6	Gary Matthews	.287
7	Felipe Alou	.286
8	Jim Ray Hart	.282
9	Harvey Kuenn	.280
10	Jesus Alou	.279
11	Kevin Mitchell	.278
12	Jack Clark	.277
13	Jeffrey Leonard	.275
14	Willie McCovey	.274
15	Bobby Bonds	.273
16	Larry Herndon	.267
17	Chili Davis	.267
18	Matt Williams	.264
19	Dave Rader	.262
20	Tito Fuentes	.262

On-Base Percentage

(minimum 2000 Plate Appearances)

1	Barry Bonds	.446
2	Willie Mays	.384
3	Brett Butler	.381
4	Willie McCovey	.377
5	Will Clark	.373
6	Gary Matthews	.367
7	Jack Clark	.359
8	Darrell Evans	.358
9	Kevin Mitchell	.356
10	Bobby Bonds	.356
11	Orlando Cepeda	.352
12	Jim Ray Hart	.348
13	Harvey Kuenn	.346
14	Ken Henderson	.345
15	Chili Davis	.340
16	Tom Haller	.340
17	Chris Speier	.333
18	Bob Brenly	.333
19	Dave Rader	.332
20	Robby Thompson	.329

Slugging Percentage

(minimum 2000 Plate Appearances)

1	Barry Bonds	.619
2	Willie Mays	.553
3	Kevin Mitchell	.536
4	Orlando Cepeda	.535
5	Willie McCovey	.524
6	Will Clark	.499
7	Matt Williams	.498
8	Bobby Bonds	.478
9	Jack Clark	.477
10	Jim Ray Hart	.474
11	Felipe Alou	.466
12	Gary Matthews	.443
13	Jeffrey Leonard	.439
14	Tom Haller	.431
15	Darrell Evans	.422
16	Chili Davis	.422
17	Bob Brenly	.408
18	Robby Thompson	.403
19	Ken Henderson	.403
20	Brett Butler	.378

San Francisco Giants Team Pitching Leaders—Career

Wins

1	Juan Marichal	238
2	Gaylord Perry	134
3	Mike McCormick	104
4	Jim Barr	90
5	Jack Sanford	89
6	Bobby Bolin	73
	Gary Lavelle	73
8	Vida Blue	72
9	Scott Garrelts	69
10	John Burkett	67
11	Mike Krukow	66
12	John Montefusco	59
13	Atlee Hammaker	58
14	Ron Bryant	57
15	Billy O'Dell	56
16	Bob Knepper	53
17	Ed Halicki	52
18	Frank Linzy	48
19	Three tied at	47

Losses

1	Juan Marichal	140
2	Gaylord Perry	109
3	Jim Barr	96
4	Mike McCormick	94
5	Jack Sanford	67
	Gary Lavelle	67
7	Ed Halicki	65
8	John Montefusco	62
9	Atlee Hammaker	59
10	Vida Blue	58
11	Bobby Bolin	56
	Mike Krukow	56
13	Ron Bryant	55
	Bob Knepper	55
15	Scott Garrelts	53
16	Greg Minton	52
17	Billy O'Dell	49
	Mike LaCoss	49
19	Bill Laskey	48
20	Two tied at	46

Winning Percentage
(minimum 75 decisions)

1	Juan Marichal	.630
2	John Burkett	.615
3	Jack Sanford	.571
4	Bobby Bolin	.566
5	Scott Garrelts	.566
6	Don Robinson	.560
7	Sam Jones	.560
8	Vida Blue	.554
9	Kelly Downs	.553
10	Frank Linzy	.552
11	Gaylord Perry	.551
12	Mike Krukow	.541
13	Stu Miller	.533
	Billy O'Dell	.533
15	Mike McCormick	.525
16	Gary Lavelle	.521
17	Ron Bryant	.509
18	Atlee Hammaker	.496
19	Bob Knepper	.491
20	Mike LaCoss	.490

Games

1	Gary Lavelle	647
2	Greg Minton	552
3	Randy Moffitt	459
4	Juan Marichal	458
5	Rod Beck	416
6	Jim Barr	394
7	Gaylord Perry	367
8	Scott Garrelts	352
9	Bobby Bolin	345
10	Mike McCormick	330
11	Frank Linzy	308
12	Jeff Brantley	299
13	Stu Miller	269
14	Charlie Williams	237
15	Jack Sanford	233
16	Ron Herbel	230
	Mark Davis	230
18	Atlee Hammaker	214
19	Don McMahon	210
20	Billy O'Dell	204

Games Started

1	Juan Marichal	446
2	Gaylord Perry	283
3	Mike McCormick	245
4	Jim Barr	220
5	Jack Sanford	211
6	Mike Krukow	182
7	John Montefusco	175
8	Vida Blue	166
9	John Burkett	157
10	Ed Halicki	151
11	Bob Knepper	146
12	Bobby Bolin	144
	Atlee Hammaker	144
14	Ron Bryant	131
15	Billy O'Dell	118
16	Trevor Wilson	115
17	Mike LaCoss	111
18	Kelly Downs	110
19	Bill Laskey	109
20	Ray Sadecki	96

Complete Games

1	Juan Marichal	244
2	Gaylord Perry	125
3	Mike McCormick	77
4	Jim Barr	59
5	Jack Sanford	54
6	Billy O'Dell	41
7	Bob Knepper	37
8	Ed Halicki	36
9	Johnny Antonelli	31
	Sam Jones	31
	Vida Blue	31
12	Ray Sadecki	30
	John Montefusco	30
14	Bobby Bolin	29
15	Mike Krukow	25
16	Ron Bryant	23
17	Atlee Hammaker	18
18	Rick Reuschel	12
	Don Robinson	12
20	Two tied at	11

Shutouts

1	Juan Marichal	52
2	Gaylord Perry	21
3	Jim Barr	20
4	Mike McCormick	19
5	Ed Halicki	13
6	Ray Sadecki	12
	Bob Knepper	12
8	John Montefusco	11
9	Bobby Bolin	10
10	Jack Sanford	9
11	Sam Jones	7
	Billy O'Dell	7
	Vida Blue	7
14	Ron Bryant	6
	Atlee Hammaker	6
	Kelly Downs	6
17	Johnny Antonelli	5
	Mike Krukow	5
19	Three tied at	4

Saves

1	Rod Beck	199
2	Gary Lavelle	127
3	Greg Minton	125
4	Randy Moffitt	83
5	Frank Linzy	78
6	Scott Garrelts	48
7	Stu Miller	46
8	Jeff Brantley	42
9	Don McMahon	36
10	Craig Lefferts	35
11	Steve Bedrosian	34
12	Jerry Johnson	29
13	Dave Righetti	28
14	Elias Sosa	27
15	Bobby Bolin	21
16	Al Holland	19
17	Jeff Robinson	18
18	Johnny Antonelli	15
19	Don Larsen	14
	Don Robinson	14

Innings Pitched

1	Juan Marichal	3,444.0
2	Gaylord Perry	2,294.2
3	Jim Barr	1,800.1
4	Mike McCormick	1,741.1
5	Jack Sanford	1,405.2
6	Bobby Bolin	1,282.1
7	John Montefusco	1,182.0
8	Mike Krukow	1,154.0
9	Vida Blue	1,131.1
10	Ed Halicki	1,027.2
11	Atlee Hammaker	1,008.0
12	John Burkett	997.1
13	Gary Lavelle	980.1
14	Bob Knepper	970.0
15	Scott Garrelts	959.1
16	Billy O'Dell	921.0
17	Ron Bryant	908.1
18	Greg Minton	870.1
19	Mike LaCoss	765.0
20	Kelly Downs	762.0

Walks

1	Juan Marichal	690
2	Gaylord Perry	581
3	Mike McCormick	574
4	Jack Sanford	491
5	Bobby Bolin	477
6	Vida Blue	453
7	Scott Garrelts	413
8	Jim Barr	391
9	John Montefusco	383
10	Gary Lavelle	382
11	Greg Minton	376
12	Ron Bryant	372
13	Mike Krukow	353
14	Bob Knepper	336
15	Ed Halicki	323
16	Mike LaCoss	308
17	Trevor Wilson	300
18	John D'Acquisto	279
19	Billy O'Dell	276
20	Kelly Downs	267

Strikeouts

1	Juan Marichal	2,281
2	Gaylord Perry	1,606
3	Bobby Bolin	977
4	Mike McCormick	976
5	John Montefusco	869
6	Mike Krukow	802
7	Jack Sanford	781
8	Vida Blue	704
9	Scott Garrelts	703
10	Gary Lavelle	696
11	Ed Halicki	691
12	Jim Barr	650
13	Billy O'Dell	620
14	John Burkett	591
15	Atlee Hammaker	583
16	Bob Knepper	527
17	Ray Sadecki	517
18	Sam Jones	504
19	Ron Bryant	502
20	Kelly Downs	494

Strikeouts/9 Innings
(minimum 750 Innings Pitched)

1	Bobby Bolin	6.86
2	John Montefusco	6.62
3	Scott Garrelts	6.60
4	Gary Lavelle	6.39
5	Gaylord Perry	6.30
6	Mike Krukow	6.25
7	Billy O'Dell	6.06
8	Ed Halicki	6.05
9	Juan Marichal	5.96
10	Kelly Downs	5.83
11	Vida Blue	5.60
12	John Burkett	5.33
13	Atlee Hammaker	5.21
14	Mike McCormick	5.04
15	Jack Sanford	5.00
16	Ron Bryant	4.97
17	Bob Knepper	4.89
18	Mike LaCoss	4.49
19	Greg Minton	3.64
20	Jim Barr	3.25

ERA
(minimum 750 Innings Pitched)

1	Gary Lavelle	2.82
2	Juan Marichal	2.84
3	Gaylord Perry	2.96
4	Greg Minton	3.23
5	Bobby Bolin	3.26
6	Scott Garrelts	3.29
7	Jim Barr	3.41
8	John Montefusco	3.47
9	Atlee Hammaker	3.51
10	Vida Blue	3.52
11	Billy O'Dell	3.55
12	Ed Halicki	3.58
13	Jack Sanford	3.61
14	Kelly Downs	3.64
15	Mike McCormick	3.64
16	Bob Knepper	3.71
17	Mike LaCoss	3.79
18	John Burkett	3.83
19	Mike Krukow	3.84
20	Ron Bryant	3.90

Component ERA
(minimum 750 Innings Pitched)

1	Juan Marichal	2.70
2	Gaylord Perry	2.81
3	Gary Lavelle	3.13
4	Scott Garrelts	3.20
5	Atlee Hammaker	3.21
6	Bobby Bolin	3.22
7	Ed Halicki	3.24
8	Kelly Downs	3.29
9	Jack Sanford	3.35
10	Jim Barr	3.38
11	Billy O'Dell	3.43
12	John Montefusco	3.43
13	Vida Blue	3.46
14	Mike McCormick	3.52
15	Greg Minton	3.54
16	John Burkett	3.64
17	Mike Krukow	3.66
18	Mike LaCoss	3.71
19	Ron Bryant	3.80
20	Bob Knepper	3.86

Opponent Average
(minimum 750 Innings Pitched)

1	Bobby Bolin	.227
2	Scott Garrelts	.232
3	Juan Marichal	.236
4	Gaylord Perry	.238
5	Jack Sanford	.242
6	Kelly Downs	.245
7	Ed Halicki	.246
8	Vida Blue	.246
9	Gary Lavelle	.249
10	Mike McCormick	.249
11	Ron Bryant	.252
12	John Montefusco	.253
13	Atlee Hammaker	.253
14	Mike Krukow	.255
15	Billy O'Dell	.255
16	Mike LaCoss	.259
17	Greg Minton	.263
18	Bob Knepper	.264
19	John Burkett	.267
20	Jim Barr	.270

Opponent OBP
(minimum 750 Innings Pitched)

1	Juan Marichal	.275
2	Gaylord Perry	.289
3	Atlee Hammaker	.300
4	Bobby Bolin	.303
5	Ed Halicki	.305
6	Jim Barr	.309
7	Jack Sanford	.309
8	Mike McCormick	.309
9	Billy O'Dell	.311
10	Kelly Downs	.311
11	Mike Krukow	.311
12	John Montefusco	.312
13	Scott Garrelts	.313
14	John Burkett	.315
15	Vida Blue	.318
16	Gary Lavelle	.320
17	Bob Knepper	.326
18	Ron Bryant	.326
19	Mike LaCoss	.332
20	Greg Minton	.339

Giants Franchise Batting Leaders—Single Season

Games

1	Jose Pagan	1962	164
2	Orlando Cepeda	1962	162
	Willie Mays	1962	162
	Will Clark	1988	162
5	Chuck Hiller	1962	161
6	Willie McCovey	1965	160
	Jim Ray Hart	1965	160
	Bobby Bonds	1973	160
	Tito Fuentes	1973	160
	Darrell Evans	1979	160
	Brett Butler	1990	160
12	Hal Lanier	1965	159
	Darrell Evans	1978	159
	Will Clark	1989	159
	Matt Williams	1990	159
	Barry Bonds	1993	159
	Barry Bonds	1997	159
18	Jim Ray Hart	1967	158
	Bobby Bonds	1969	158
	Barry Bonds	1996	158

At-Bats

1	Jo-Jo Moore	1935	681
2	Bobby Bonds	1970	663
3	Hughie Critz	1932	659
4	Tito Fuentes	1973	656
5	George Van Haltren	1898	654
6	Dave Bancroft	1922	651
7	Jo-Jo Moore	1936	649
8	Al Dark	1953	647
9	Freddy Lindstrom	1928	646
	Al Dark	1951	646
11	Al Dark	1954	644
12	Bill Terry	1932	643
	Bobby Bonds	1973	643
14	Frankie Frisch	1923	641
	Bobby Thomson	1949	641
	Chili Davis	1982	641
17	Bill Terry	1930	633
18	Burgess Whitehead	1936	632
19	George Burns	1920	631
20	Tito Fuentes	1971	630

Runs

1	Mike Tiernan	1889	147
2	Bill Terry	1930	139
3	Mel Ott	1929	138
4	Johnny Mize	1947	137
5	George Van Haltren	1896	136
6	Bobby Bonds	1970	134
7	Rogers Hornsby	1927	133
8	George Gore	1889	132
	Mike Tiernan	1890	132
	Mike Tiernan	1896	132
11	Bobby Bonds	1973	131
12	Willie Mays	1962	130
13	Monte Ward	1893	129
	George Van Haltren	1898	129
	Willie Mays	1961	129
	Barry Bonds	1993	129
17	Mike Tiernan	1895	127
	Freddy Lindstrom	1930	127
19	Al Dark	1953	126
20	Willie Mays	1959	125

Hits

1	Bill Terry	1930	254
2	Freddy Lindstrom	1928	231
	Freddy Lindstrom	1930	231
4	Bill Terry	1929	226
5	Bill Terry	1932	225
6	Frankie Frisch	1923	223
7	Mike Donlin	1905	216
8	Bill Terry	1931	213
	Bill Terry	1934	213
10	Don Mueller	1954	212
11	Frankie Frisch	1921	211
12	Dave Bancroft	1922	209
13	Willie Mays	1958	208
14	Rogers Hornsby	1927	205
	Jo-Jo Moore	1936	205
16	George Van Haltren	1898	204
	Ross Youngs	1920	204
	Irish Meusel	1922	204
19	Hank Leiber	1935	203
	Bill Terry	1935	203

Doubles

1	Jack Clark	1978	46
2	Bill Terry	1931	43
	Willie Mays	1959	43
4	George Kelly	1921	42
	Bill Terry	1932	42
6	Dave Bancroft	1922	41
	Al Dark	1951	41
	Al Dark	1953	41
9	Larry Doyle	1915	40
	Will Clark	1992	40
11	Freddy Lindstrom	1928	39
	Bill Terry	1929	39
	Freddy Lindstrom	1930	39
	Bill Terry	1930	39
	Willie McCovey	1970	39
16	Six tied at		38

Triples

1	George Davis	1893	27
2	Larry Doyle	1911	25
3	Roger Connor	1887	22
4	Mike Tiernan	1890	21
	Mike Tiernan	1895	21
	George Van Haltren	1896	21
7	Buck Ewing	1884	20
	Roger Connor	1886	20
	Red Murray	1912	20
	Bill Terry	1931	20
	Willie Mays	1957	20
12	George Davis	1894	19
	George Van Haltren	1895	19
14	Roger Connor	1888	17
	Roger Connor	1889	17
	Charlie Hickman	1900	17
	Sam Mertes	1905	17
	Frankie Frisch	1921	17
	Irish Meusel	1922	17
20	Five tied at		16

Home Runs

1	Willie Mays	1965	52
2	Johnny Mize	1947	51
	Willie Mays	1955	51
4	Willie Mays	1962	49
5	Willie Mays	1964	47
	Kevin Mitchell	1989	47
7	Orlando Cepeda	1961	46
	Barry Bonds	1993	46
9	Willie McCovey	1969	45
10	Willie McCovey	1963	44
11	Matt Williams	1994	43
12	Mel Ott	1929	42
	Barry Bonds	1996	42
14	Willie Mays	1954	41
15	Johnny Mize	1948	40
	Willie Mays	1961	40
	Barry Bonds	1997	40
18	Willie McCovey	1965	39
	Willie McCovey	1970	39
	Bobby Bonds	1973	39

RBI

1	Mel Ott	1929	151
2	Orlando Cepeda	1961	142
3	Willie Mays	1962	141
4	Johnny Mize	1947	138
5	George Davis	1897	136
	George Kelly	1924	136
7	Mel Ott	1934	135
	Mel Ott	1936	135
9	Irish Meusel	1922	132
10	Roger Connor	1889	130
11	Bill Terry	1930	129
	Barry Bonds	1996	129
13	Willie Mays	1955	127
14	Willie McCovey	1969	126
	Willie McCovey	1970	126
16	Irish Meusel	1923	125
	Rogers Hornsby	1927	125
	Johnny Mize	1948	125
	Kevin Mitchell	1989	125
20	Three tied at		123

Walks

1	Barry Bonds	1996	151
2	Barry Bonds	1997	145
3	Eddie Stanky	1950	144
4	Willie McCovey	1970	137
5	Eddie Stanky	1951	127
6	Barry Bonds	1993	126
7	Willie McCovey	1969	121
8	Barry Bonds	1995	120
9	Mel Ott	1938	118
10	Mel Ott	1929	113
11	Willie Mays	1971	112
12	Mel Ott	1936	111
13	Mel Ott	1942	109
	Dick Dietz	1970	109
15	Willie McCovey	1973	105
	Darrell Evans	1978	105
17	Wes Westrum	1951	104
18	Mel Ott	1930	103
19	Mel Ott	1937	102
20	Five tied at		100

Strikeouts

1	Bobby Bonds	1970	189
2	Bobby Bonds	1969	187
3	Bobby Bonds	1973	148
4	Dave Kingman	1972	140
5	Matt Williams	1990	138
6	Bobby Bonds	1971	137
	Bobby Bonds	1972	137
8	Bobby Bonds	1974	134
9	Robby Thompson	1989	133
	Jeff Kent	1997	133
11	Will Clark	1988	129
12	Matt Williams	1991	128
13	Dave Kingman	1974	125
14	J.T. Snow	1997	124
15	Willie Mays	1971	123
	Jeffrey Leonard	1984	123
17	Dave Kingman	1973	122
18	Willie McCovey	1963	119
19	Willie McCovey	1965	118
20	Jeffrey Leonard	1983	116

Stolen Bases

1	Monte Ward	1887	111
2	George Davis	1897	65
3	Monte Ward	1889	62
	George Burns	1914	62
5	Josh Devore	1911	61
6	Art Devlin	1905	59
7	Bill North	1979	58
8	Red Murray	1910	57
9	Mike Tiernan	1890	56
10	Jack Glasscock	1890	54
	Eddie Burke	1893	54
	Art Devlin	1906	54
13	Buck Ewing	1888	53
	Mike Tiernan	1891	53
15	Mike Tiernan	1888	52
	Sam Mertes	1905	52
17	Fred Snodgrass	1911	51
	Brett Butler	1990	51
19	George Van Haltren	1897	50
20	Two tied at		49

Runs Created

1	Barry Bonds	1993	162
2	Bill Terry	1930	160
	Barry Bonds	1996	160
4	Mel Ott	1929	155
5	Willie Mays	1955	146
	Willie Mays	1962	146
7	Mike Tiernan	1889	145
8	Mel Ott	1932	143
	Mel Ott	1934	143
10	George Davis	1893	142
11	Roger Connor	1889	141
	Will Clark	1989	141
13	Mel Ott	1936	140
	Willie McCovey	1969	140
15	Rogers Hornsby	1927	139
	Willie Mays	1954	139
	Willie Mays	1965	139
18	Freddy Lindstrom	1930	138
	Johnny Mize	1947	138
	Willie Mays	1958	138

Runs Created/27 Outs

(minimum 3.1 Plate Appearances/Tm Gm)

1	Roger Connor	1885	11.96
2	Mike Tiernan	1889	11.36
3	Barry Bonds	1996	11.33
4	Barry Bonds	1993	11.27
5	Roger Connor	1886	11.08
6	Roger Connor	1889	10.82
7	Willie McCovey	1969	10.75
8	George Davis	1894	10.65
9	Roger Connor	1883	10.61
10	Mel Ott	1929	10.60
11	Mel Bresnahan	1903	10.52
12	Mike Tiernan	1895	10.49
13	George Davis	1893	10.47
14	Mike Tiernan	1896	10.44
15	Bill Terry	1930	10.33
16	George Davis	1895	10.21
17	Jack Doyle	1894	10.13
18	Mel Ott	1936	10.02
19	George Davis	1897	9.96
20	Barry Bonds	1994	9.88

Batting Average

(minimum 3.1 Plate Appearances/Tm Gm)

1	Bill Terry	1930	.401
2	Freddy Lindstrom	1930	.379
3	Bill Terry	1929	.372
4	Roger Connor	1885	.371
5	Mike Tiernan	1896	.369
6	Jack Doyle	1894	.367
7	Rogers Hornsby	1927	.361
8	Freddy Lindstrom	1928	.358
9	Roger Connor	1883	.357
10	Mike Donlin	1905	.356
11	Ross Youngs	1924	.356
12	George Davis	1893	.355
13	Roger Connor	1886	.355
14	Bill Terry	1934	.354
15	George Davis	1897	.353
16	George Davis	1894	.352
17	Ross Youngs	1920	.351
18	George Van Haltren	1896	.351
19	Bill Terry	1932	.350
20	Roger Bresnahan	1903	.350

On-Base Percentage

(minimum 3.1 Plate Appearances/Tm Gm)

1	Barry Bonds	1996	.461
2	Eddie Stanky	1950	.460
3	Mel Ott	1930	.458
4	Barry Bonds	1993	.458
5	Willie McCovey	1969	.453
6	Mike Tiernan	1896	.452
7	Bill Terry	1930	.452
8	Mel Ott	1929	.449
9	Mel Ott	1939	.449
10	Rogers Hornsby	1927	.448
11	Mel Ott	1936	.448
12	Mike Tiernan	1889	.447
13	Barry Bonds	1997	.446
14	Willie McCovey	1970	.444
15	Roger Bresnahan	1903	.443
16	Mel Ott	1938	.442
17	Bill Joyce	1897	.441
18	Ross Youngs	1924	.441
19	Fred Snodgrass	1910	.440
20	George Harper	1927	.435

Slugging Percentage

(minimum 3.1 Plate Appearances/Tm Gm)

1	Barry Bonds	1993	.677
2	Willie Mays	1954	.667
3	Willie Mays	1955	.659
4	Willie McCovey	1969	.656
5	Barry Bonds	1994	.647
6	Willie Mays	1965	.645
7	Kevin Mitchell	1989	.635
8	Mel Ott	1929	.635
9	Willie Mays	1957	.626
10	Bill Terry	1930	.619
11	Willie Mays	1962	.615
12	Barry Bonds	1996	.615
13	Johnny Mize	1947	.614
14	Willie McCovey	1970	.612
15	Orlando Cepeda	1961	.609
16	Willie Mays	1964	.607
17	Matt Williams	1994	.607
18	Mel Ott	1932	.601
19	Mel Ott	1934	.591
20	Mel Ott	1936	.588

Giants Franchise Pitching Leaders—Single Season

Wins

	Player	Year	
1	Mickey Welch	1885	44
2	Tim Keefe	1886	42
3	Mickey Welch	1884	39
4	Christy Mathewson	1908	37
5	Amos Rusie	1894	36
6	Tim Keefe	1887	35
	Tim Keefe	1888	35
	Joe McGinnity	1904	35
9	Mickey Welch	1886	33
	Amos Rusie	1891	33
	Amos Rusie	1893	33
	Jouett Meekin	1894	33
	Christy Mathewson	1904	33
14	Tim Keefe	1885	32
15	Amos Rusie	1892	31
	Joe McGinnity	1903	31
	Christy Mathewson	1905	31
18	Christy Mathewson	1903	30
19	Amos Rusie	1890	29
20	Two tied at		28

Losses

	Player	Year	
1	Amos Rusie	1890	34
2	Amos Rusie	1892	31
3	Bill Carrick	1899	27
	Luther Taylor	1901	27
5	Silver King	1892	24
	Ed Crane	1892	24
	Dad Clarke	1896	24
8	Mickey Welch	1883	23
	Amos Rusie	1895	23
10	Mickey Welch	1886	22
	Bill Carrick	1900	22
	Rube Marquard	1914	22
13	Mickey Welch	1884	21
	Amos Rusie	1893	21
15	Tim Keefe	1886	20
	Amos Rusie	1891	20
	Mark Baldwin	1893	20
	Joe McGinnity	1903	20
19	Five tied at		19

Winning Percentage
(minimum 15 decisions)

	Player	Year	
1	Hoyt Wilhelm	1952	.833
2	Sal Maglie	1950	.818
3	Joe McGinnity	1904	.814
4	Hooks Wiltse	1904	.813
	Carl Hubbell	1936	.813
6	Doc Crandall	1910	.810
7	Larry Jansen	1947	.808
8	Christy Mathewson	1909	.806
	Juan Marichal	1966	.806
10	Mickey Welch	1885	.800
11	Sal Maglie	1951	.793
12	Shawn Estes	1997	.792
13	Jouett Meekin	1894	.786
14	Art Nehf	1924	.778
15	Christy Mathewson	1905	.775
16	Rube Marquard	1911	.774
	Jack Sanford	1962	.774
18	Christy Mathewson	1908	.771
19	Al Demaree	1913	.765
	Bill Lohrman	1942	.765

Games

	Player	Year	
1	Julian Tavarez	1997	89
2	Mike Jackson	1993	81
3	Greg Minton	1982	78
	Mark Dewey	1996	78
5	Gary Lavelle	1984	77
	Mark Davis	1985	77
7	Rod Beck	1993	76
8	Doug Henry	1997	75
9	Greg Minton	1984	74
	Scott Garrelts	1985	74
11	Gary Lavelle	1977	73
	Greg Minton	1983	73
	Rod Beck	1997	73
14	Hoyt Wilhelm	1952	71
	Elias Sosa	1973	71
	Rich Rodriguez	1997	71
17	Ace Adams	1943	70
	Randy Moffitt	1978	70
	Gary Lavelle	1979	70
	Craig Lefferts	1989	70

Games Started

	Player	Year	
1	Mickey Welch	1884	65
2	Tim Keefe	1886	64
3	Amos Rusie	1890	63
4	Amos Rusie	1892	61
5	Mickey Welch	1886	59
6	Amos Rusie	1891	57
7	Tim Keefe	1887	56
8	Mickey Welch	1885	55
9	Mickey Welch	1883	52
	Amos Rusie	1893	52
11	Tim Keefe	1888	51
12	Amos Rusie	1894	50
13	Jouett Meekin	1894	48
	Joe McGinnity	1903	48
15	Mickey Welch	1888	47
	Silver King	1892	47
	Amos Rusie	1895	47
18	Tim Keefe	1885	46
	Christy Mathewson	1904	46
20	Tim Keefe	1889	45

Complete Games

	Player	Year	
1	Mickey Welch	1884	62
	Tim Keefe	1886	62
3	Amos Rusie	1892	58
4	Mickey Welch	1886	56
	Amos Rusie	1890	56
6	Mickey Welch	1885	55
7	Tim Keefe	1887	54
8	Amos Rusie	1891	52
9	Amos Rusie	1893	50
10	Tim Keefe	1888	48
11	Mickey Welch	1888	47
12	Mickey Welch	1883	46
	Silver King	1892	46
14	Tim Keefe	1885	45
	Amos Rusie	1894	45
16	Joe McGinnity	1903	44
17	Amos Rusie	1895	42
18	Jouett Meekin	1894	40
	Bill Carrick	1899	40
20	Three tied at		39

Shutouts

	Player	Year	
1	Christy Mathewson	1908	11
2	Carl Hubbell	1933	10
	Juan Marichal	1965	10
4	Joe McGinnity	1904	9
5	Tim Keefe	1888	8
	Christy Mathewson	1902	8
	Christy Mathewson	1905	8
	Christy Mathewson	1907	8
	Christy Mathewson	1909	8
	Jeff Tesreau	1914	8
	Jeff Tesreau	1915	8
	Juan Marichal	1969	8
13	Tim Keefe	1885	7
	Mickey Welch	1885	7
	Hooks Wiltse	1908	7
	Hal Schumacher	1933	7
17	Ten tied at		6

Saves

	Player	Year	
1	Rod Beck	1993	48
2	Rod Beck	1997	37
3	Rod Beck	1996	35
4	Rod Beck	1995	33
5	Greg Minton	1982	30
6	Rod Beck	1994	28
7	Dave Righetti	1991	24
8	Greg Minton	1983	22
9	Frank Linzy	1965	21
	Greg Minton	1981	21
11	Gary Lavelle	1977	20
	Gary Lavelle	1979	20
	Gary Lavelle	1983	20
	Craig Lefferts	1989	20
15	Marv Grissom	1954	19
	Stu Miller	1962	19
	Don McMahon	1970	19
	Greg Minton	1980	19
	Greg Minton	1984	19
	Jeff Brantley	1990	19

Innings Pitched

	Player	Year	
1	Mickey Welch	1884	557.1
2	Amos Rusie	1890	548.2
3	Tim Keefe	1886	540.0
4	Amos Rusie	1892	532.0
5	Amos Rusie	1891	500.1
6	Mickey Welch	1886	500.0
7	Mickey Welch	1885	492.0
8	Amos Rusie	1893	482.0
9	Tim Keefe	1887	478.2
10	Amos Rusie	1894	444.0
11	Tim Keefe	1888	434.1
12	Joe McGinnity	1903	434.0
13	Mickey Welch	1883	426.0
14	Mickey Welch	1888	425.1
15	Silver King	1892	419.1
16	Jouett Meekin	1894	409.0
17	Joe McGinnity	1904	408.0
18	Tim Keefe	1885	398.0
19	Amos Rusie	1895	393.1
20	Christy Mathewson	1908	390.2

Walks

	Player	Year	
1	Amos Rusie	1890	289
2	Amos Rusie	1892	267
3	Amos Rusie	1891	262
4	Amos Rusie	1893	218
5	Cy Seymour	1898	213
6	Amos Rusie	1894	200
7	Ed Crane	1892	189
8	Silver King	1892	174
9	Jouett Meekin	1894	171
10	Cy Seymour	1899	170
11	Cy Seymour	1897	164
12	Mickey Welch	1886	163
13	Amos Rusie	1895	159
14	Ed Doheny	1899	156
15	Tim Keefe	1889	151
16	Mickey Welch	1889	149
17	Mickey Welch	1884	146
18	Mark Baldwin	1893	141
19	Ed Crane	1889	136
20	Mickey Welch	1885	131

Strikeouts

	Player	Year	
1	Mickey Welch	1884	345
2	Amos Rusie	1890	341
3	Amos Rusie	1891	337
4	Tim Keefe	1888	333
5	Tim Keefe	1886	291
6	Amos Rusie	1892	288
7	Mickey Welch	1886	272
8	Christy Mathewson	1903	267
9	Christy Mathewson	1908	259
10	Mickey Welch	1885	258
11	Juan Marichal	1963	248
12	Juan Marichal	1965	240
13	Cy Seymour	1898	239
14	Rube Marquard	1911	237
15	Gaylord Perry	1969	233
16	Tim Keefe	1885	230
	Gaylord Perry	1967	230
18	Juan Marichal	1966	222
19	Christy Mathewson	1901	221
20	Juan Marichal	1968	218

Strikeouts/9 Innings
(minimum 1 Inning Pitched/Tm Gm)

	Player	Year	
1	Shawn Estes	1997	8.10
2	John Montefusco	1975	7.93
3	Gaylord Perry	1965	7.82
4	Rube Marquard	1911	7.68
5	Bobby Bolin	1964	7.52
6	Bobby Bolin	1965	7.45
7	Juan Marichal	1967	7.38
8	Juan Marichal	1965	7.31
9	Sam Jones	1960	7.31
10	Ray Sadecki	1968	7.30
11	Mark Gardner	1996	7.28
12	Gaylord Perry	1966	7.08
13	Gaylord Perry	1967	7.06
14	John D'Acquisto	1974	6.99
15	Sam Jones	1959	6.95
16	Juan Marichal	1963	6.95
17	Ray Sadecki	1967	6.94
18	Mike Krukow	1985	6.93
19	Red Ames	1906	6.90
20	Tim Keefe	1888	6.90

ERA
(minimum 1 Inning Pitched/Tm Gm)

	Player	Year	
1	Christy Mathewson	1909	1.14
2	Christy Mathewson	1905	1.28
3	Christy Mathewson	1908	1.43
4	Fred Anderson	1917	1.44
5	Tim Keefe	1885	1.58
6	Joe McGinnity	1904	1.61
7	Carl Hubbell	1933	1.66
8	Mickey Welch	1885	1.66
9	Tim Keefe	1888	1.74
10	Fred Toney	1919	1.84
11	Pol Perritt	1917	1.88
12	Christy Mathewson	1910	1.89
13	Mickey Welch	1888	1.93
14	Ferdie Schupp	1917	1.95
15	Jeff Tesreau	1912	1.96
16	Bobby Bolin	1968	1.99
17	Christy Mathewson	1911	1.99
18	Christy Mathewson	1907	2.00
19	Hooks Wiltse	1909	2.00
20	Christy Mathewson	1904	2.03

Component ERA
(minimum 1 Inning Pitched/Tm Gm)

	Player	Year	
1	Christy Mathewson	1909	1.29
2	Christy Mathewson	1908	1.34
3	Christy Mathewson	1905	1.54
4	Tim Keefe	1888	1.56
5	Fred Anderson	1917	1.62
6	Christy Mathewson	1907	1.67
7	Tim Keefe	1885	1.71
8	Joe McGinnity	1904	1.71
9	Mickey Welch	1885	1.73
10	Cannonball Titcomb	1888	1.75
11	Juan Marichal	1966	1.80
12	Ferdie Schupp	1917	1.82
13	Jeff Tesreau	1915	1.84
14	Carl Hubbell	1933	1.84
15	Joe McGinnity	1902	1.87
16	Bobby Bolin	1968	1.89
17	Juan Marichal	1965	1.92
18	Hooks Wiltse	1908	1.96
19	Mickey Welch	1888	1.97
20	Luther Taylor	1904	1.99

Opponent Average
(minimum 1 Inning Pitched/Tm Gm)

	Player	Year	
1	Tim Keefe	1888	.195
2	Christy Mathewson	1909	.200
3	Bobby Bolin	1968	.200
4	Christy Mathewson	1908	.200
5	Cannonball Titcomb	1888	.201
6	Tim Keefe	1885	.201
7	Juan Marichal	1966	.202
8	Amos Rusie	1892	.203
9	Mickey Welch	1885	.203
10	Jeff Tesreau	1912	.204
11	Juan Marichal	1965	.205
12	Christy Mathewson	1905	.205
13	Mickey Welch	1888	.207
14	Amos Rusie	1891	.207
15	Joe McGinnity	1904	.208
16	Ferdie Schupp	1917	.209
17	Fred Anderson	1917	.209
18	Jeff Tesreau	1914	.209
19	Bobby Bolin	1966	.211
20	Scott Garrelts	1989	.212

Opponent OBP
(minimum 1 Inning Pitched/Tm Gm)

	Player	Year	
1	Christy Mathewson	1908	.225
2	Christy Mathewson	1909	.228
3	Juan Marichal	1966	.230
4	Juan Marichal	1965	.239
5	Tim Keefe	1888	.243
6	Christy Mathewson	1905	.245
7	Christy Mathewson	1907	.251
8	Cannonball Titcomb	1888	.253
9	Tim Keefe	1885	.254
10	Fred Anderson	1917	.255
11	Juan Marichal	1963	.255
12	Mickey Welch	1885	.256
13	Scott Garrelts	1989	.258
14	Bobby Bolin	1968	.258
15	Joe McGinnity	1904	.258
16	Slim Sallee	1918	.259
17	Jesse Barnes	1919	.260
18	Carl Hubbell	1933	.260
19	Juan Marichal	1969	.261
20	Carl Hubbell	1934	.263

New York/San Francisco Giants Capsule

Best Season: *1905/1962.* The Giants won the 1904 pennant but refused to play the American League champion Boston Pilgrims, due to lingering animosity between John McGraw and Ban Johnson, among other things. The following season, the Giants won 105 games and defeated the Philadelphia Athletics in a five-game World Series, giving McGraw his first uncontested championship. The 1962 Giants tied the Los Angeles Dodgers on the last day of the season to force a three-game playoff for the National League pennant. After the two teams split the first two games, the Dodgers took a 4-2 lead into the ninth inning of Game 3, but the Giants plated four runs to take the flag. The World Series went right down to the wire as well, with the Yankees and Giants splitting the first six games. In Game 7, the Giants trailed by a run as Willie McCovey came up with two out and the winning runs on base in the bottom of the ninth. McCovey ripped a shot—right to Yankees second baseman Bobby Richardson. The Giants missed winning the Series by inches, and no San Francisco club has ever come closer.

Worst Season: *1902/1985.* The 1902 Giants had the worst record in baseball with a 48-88 mark. On the bright side, John McGraw took over the club for the second half of the season, and went on to lead them to a first- or second-place finish 10 times in the next 12 years. In 1985, rookie manager Jim Davenport was overmatched and didn't survive the season as the Giants lost 100 games for the first time in franchise history.

Best Player: *Buck Ewing/Willie Mays.*

Best Pitcher: *Christy Mathewson/Juan Marichal.*

Best Reliever: *Doc Crandall/Rod Beck.*

Best Defensive Player: *Bill Terry/Willie Mays.* Terry was one of the best-fielding first basemen of his era. Mays patrolled the Polo Grounds' vast center field with legendary grace.

Hall of Famers: Many. The Manhattanites had *Roger Bresnahan, Roger Connor, George Davis, Buck Ewing, Travis Jackson, Frankie Frisch, Carl Hubbell, Monte Irvin, Tim Keefe, George Kelly, Fred Lindstrom, Rube Marquard, Christy Mathewson, Joe McGinnity, Johnny Mize, Jim O'Rourke, Mel Ott, Bill Terry, Monte Ward, Mickey Welch, Hoyt Wilhelm, Ross Youngs* and *manager John McGraw.* The San Franciscans had *Juan Marichal, Willie Mays, Willie McCovey* and *Gaylord Perry.*

Franchise All-Star Team:

C	*Buck Ewing/Tom Haller*	**LF**	*Monte Irvin/Barry Bonds*
1B	*Bill Terry/Willie McCovey*	**CF**	*Willie Mays/Willie Mays*
2B	*Frankie Frisch/Robby Thompson*	**RF**	*Mel Ott/Jack Clark*
3B	*Fred Lindstrom/Matt Williams*	**SP**	*Christy Mathewson/Juan Marichal*
SS	*George Davis/Chris Speier*	**RP**	*Doc Crandall/Rod Beck*

Biggest Flake: *Charles "Victory" Faust /John Montefusco.*

Strangest Career: *Mike Donlin/Mike McCormick.* Donlin was traded to the Giants in 1904. In 1905, his first full year with the team, he batted .356 and led the league in runs scored. A broken leg kept him out for most of 1906, and he held out for the entire season in 1907. He came back the next year to hit .334 with 106 RBI, and then retired for two years to pursue a career in Vaudeville. He returned in 1911 and played 12 games with the Giants before being sold to the Braves. Bonus baby Mike McCormick won 11 games in 1958 at age 19, then posted a 15-12 won-lost record and won the National League ERA crown two years later. He suffered from a sore arm in 1962 and was traded to Baltimore after the season. He spent the next four years pitching for the Orioles and Senators with little success, but the Giants reacquired him in 1967. He had his best season that year, going 22-10 and winning the Cy Young Award. His effectiveness declined in subsequent seasons, and he was traded to the Yankees in 1970.

What Might Have Been: *Hank Leiber/Atlee Hammaker.* Outfielder Hank Leiber had a terrific season in 1935. In his first year as a regular, he finished fifth in the NL in batting average (.331) and RBI (107). He lost playing time to Jimmy Ripple in 1936 but remained productive. While batting against Bob Feller in an exhibition game on April 4, 1937, he was beaned so severely that he missed most of the season. He played part-time for the Giants in 1938 and was traded after the season, never to play regularly again. Hammaker emerged as one of the best young lefthanders in baseball during the first half of the 1983 season. He was torched for seven runs in the All-Star Game, however, and began complaining of a sore arm soon thereafter. He underwent two major arm surgeries in 1984 and never again threw the way he had in '83.

Best Trade: *Christy Mathewson/Kevin Mitchell.* The Giants stole Mathewson from the Reds for washed-up Amos Rusie on December 15, 1900. Mitchell was acquired from the Padres along with pitchers Craig Lefferts and Dave Dravecky in July of 1987 for a package that included Mark Davis. Davis had two outstanding seasons in San Diego, but his career disintegrated after that. Mitchell developed into one of the NL's premier power hitters, and he won the MVP Award in 1989. During the winter of 1991, the Giants traded him to Seattle for pitchers Billy Swift, Mike Jackson and Dave Burba. Swift won the ERA title in his first year with San Francisco and won 21 games the following season, while Jackson enjoyed three strong seasons out of the bullpen. Mitchell played for four more teams and never played regularly again.

Worst Trade: *Edd Roush/George Foster.* On July 20, 1916, John McGraw and the Giants engineered a trade that sent Mathewson and Roush to Cincinnati. McGraw, Mathewson's close friend, was glad to help Matty get the chance to manage the Cincinnati club, and gave him a going-away present by including Roush in the deal and advising Matty to play him. Matty followed McGraw's advice, and Roush ended up in the Hall of Fame—wearing a Reds cap. The Giants gave away plenty of talent after the move to San Francisco, but the single worst deal may have been the one that sent Foster to Cincinnati for infielder Frank Duffy and pitcher Vern Geishert in 1971. Foster became one of the NL's premier power hitters. Once again, the Reds were the beneficiaries.

Best-Looking Player: *Christy Mathewson/Barry Bonds.*

Ugliest Player: *Cliff Melton/Ron Herbel.*

Best Nickname: *Don Mueller, "Mandrake the Magician"/John "The Count" Montefusco.*

Most Unappreciated Player: *George Burns/Darrell Evans.* Burns was the Giants' left fielder and leadoff man for nine seasons, and he led the NL in runs scored five times over that period. Evans spent seven-plus seasons with the Giants, playing primarily third base. He was a lefthanded hitter with decent power and an ability to reach base, and he played good defense. Unfortunately, his skills were often overlooked as people focused instead on his unimpressive batting average.

Most Overrated Player: *Fred Lindstrom/Johnnie LeMaster.* Lindstrom had two good seasons, and each of them came in a hitters' park at the peak of a hitters' era. His name found its way into some important men's reminiscences, and he was voted into the Hall of Fame by a bunch of guys who were willing to take his two good years at face value while overlooking the absence of any accompanying credentials. LeMaster was the Giants' starting shortstop for seven years, and the Giants seemed to get a perverse thrill out of his tolerable fielding and pathetic hitting. In 1982, he batted .216 and scored 34 runs in 130 games; the following season, they made him their leadoff hitter.

Most Admirable Star: *Christy Mathewson/Willie Mays.*

Least Admirable Star: *Alvin Dark/Jack Clark.*

Best Season, Player: *Willie Mays, 1955/Barry Bonds, 1993.*

Best Season, Pitcher: *Christy Mathewson, 1908/Juan Marichal, 1968.*

Most Impressive Individual Record: *Christy Mathewson/Rod Beck.* It's safe to say that Mathewson's three shutouts in the 1905 World Series is a record that never will be broken. Beck converted all 28 of his save opportunities in 1994, which is a record that may stand for a while, too.

Biggest Tragedy: *Ross Youngs/Dave Dravecky.* Youngs, one of the Giants' best outfielders of the John McGraw era, died of a kidney ailment in 1927 at age 30. Dravecky had a cancerous tumor removed from his pitching arm in 1988, and the doctors told him that they were forced to remove so much of his deltoid muscle that he would never be able to pitch again. He made a miraculous comeback in August 1989, defeating the Reds in his first start. He was doing well in his next start when he broke his arm while throwing a pitch. The Giants won their division that season, and Dravecky re-broke the same arm during the celebration. Ultimately, doctors were forced to amputate the entire arm.

From Surplus to Deficit: From 1956 through 1963, the Giants' farm system was spectacularly productive, churning out eight hitters who went on to have long, successful careers. The only problem was that all eight of them were either outfielders or first basemen, and the Giants just couldn't find room for them all. (In fact, in 1958 and 1959, the Giants produced back-to-back Rookie of the Year-winning first basemen, *Orlando Cepeda* and *Willie McCovey.* No other NL team has ever produced consecutive Rookie winners who played the same position.) The Giants addressed the problem by keeping McCovey and trading away the other seven. All seven deals were losers. Taken together, they gave up eight good years of *Bill White,* seven of Cepeda, 10 of *Felipe Alou,* eight of *Matty Alou,* seven of *Leon Wagner,* at least 10 of *Manny Mota,* and 12 of *Jose Cardenal,* all for a half-dozen pitchers who had a few decent years and moved on, and a couple of forgettable infielders.

Fan Favorite: *Mel Ott/Will Clark.*

—Mat Olkin

Team Batting Leaders—Single Season

Runs

1	Boston Beaneaters	1894	1220
2	Baltimore Orioles	1894	1171
3	Philadelphia Phillies	1894	1143
4	St. Louis Browns	1887	1131
5	Philadelphia Phillies	1895	1068
6	New York Yankees	1931	1067
7	New York Yankees	1936	1065
8	New York Yankees	1930	1062
9	Chicago Colts	1894	1041
10	Boston Red Stockings	1891	1028
11	Boston Red Sox	1950	1027
12	Boston Beaneaters	1897	1025
13	Brooklyn Bridegrooms	1894	1021
14	New York Giants	1890	1018
15	Philadelphia Phillies	1893	1011
16	Baltimore Orioles	1895	1009
17	Boston Beaneaters	1893	1008
18	St. Louis Cardinals	1930	1004
19	New York Yankees	1932	1002
20	Chicago Cubs	1930	998

Hits

1	Philadelphia Phillies	1930	1783
2	New York Giants	1930	1769
3	Philadelphia Phillies	1894	1732
	St. Louis Cardinals	1930	1732
5	Detroit Tigers	1921	1724
6	Chicago Cubs	1930	1722
7	Cleveland Indians	1936	1715
8	Pittsburgh Pirates	1922	1698
9	St. Louis Browns	1922	1693
	Philadelphia Phillies	1929	1693
11	Boston Red Sox	1997	1684
12	New York Yankees	1930	1683
13	New York Yankees	1936	1676
14	Detroit Tigers	1929	1671
15	New York Yankees	1931	1667
16	Boston Red Sox	1950	1665
	Cleveland Indians	1996	1665
18	Philadelphia Phillies	1895	1664
19	Pittsburgh Pirates	1929	1663
20	New York Giants	1922	1661

Doubles

1	St. Louis Cardinals	1930	373
	Boston Red Sox	1997	373
3	Cleveland Indians	1930	358
4	Cleveland Indians	1936	357
5	Cleveland Indians	1921	355
6	St. Louis Cardinals	1931	353
7	Detroit Tigers	1934	349
8	Philadelphia Phillies	1930	345
9	Seattle Mariners	1996	343
10	Chicago Cubs	1931	340
	Cleveland Indians	1934	340
12	Detroit Tigers	1929	339
	Montreal Expos	1997	339
14	Cleveland Indians	1996	335
15	Cleveland Indians	1926	333
16	St. Louis Cardinals	1936	332
	St. Louis Cardinals	1939	332
	Minnesota Twins	1996	332
19	Philadelphia Phillies	1932	330
20	St. Louis Browns	1937	327

Triples

1	Baltimore Orioles	1894	150
2	Philadelphia Phillies	1894	131
3	Brooklyn Bridegrooms	1894	130
4	Pittsburgh Pirates	1912	129
5	Pittsburgh Pirates	1893	127
6	Detroit Wolverines	1887	126
7	Pittsburgh Pirates	1894	124
8	Philadelphia Athletic	1891	123
9	Pittsburgh Pirates	1924	122
10	Pittsburgh Pirates	1899	121
11	Cincinnati Reds	1890	120
	Cincinnati Reds	1926	120
13	Pittsburgh Pirates	1930	119
14	Washington Senators	1894	118
15	Pittsburgh Pirates	1929	116
16	Philadelphia Quakers	1890	113
	Pittsburgh Burghers	1890	113
	St. Louis Browns	1894	113
	Boston Pilgrims	1903	113
20	Four tied with		111

Home Runs

1	Seattle Mariners	1997	264
2	Baltimore Orioles	1996	257
3	Seattle Mariners	1996	245
4	Oakland Athletics	1996	243
5	New York Yankees	1961	240
6	Colorado Rockies	1997	239
7	Detroit Tigers	1987	225
	Minnesota Twins	1963	225
9	Minnesota Twins	1964	221
	New York Giants	1947	221
	Cincinnati Reds	1956	221
	Texas Rangers	1996	221
	Colorado Rockies	1996	221
14	Cleveland Indians	1997	220
15	Cleveland Indians	1996	218
16	Milwaukee Brewers	1982	216
17	Toronto Blue Jays	1987	215
18	Baltimore Orioles	1985	214
19	Boston Red Sox	1977	213
20	Baltimore Orioles	1987	211

Walks

1	Boston Red Sox	1949	835
2	Boston Red Sox	1948	823
3	Philadelphia Athletics	1949	783
4	St. Louis Browns	1941	775
5	New York Yankees	1932	766
6	Detroit Tigers	1993	765
7	Detroit Tigers	1947	762
8	Boston Red Sox	1951	756
9	Detroit Tigers	1949	751
10	New York Yankees	1938	749
11	New York Yankees	1931	748
12	Brooklyn Dodgers	1947	732
13	New York Yankees	1949	731
14	San Francisco Giants	1970	729
15	Boston Red Sox	1956	727
16	Philadelphia Athletics	1948	726
17	Cleveland Indians	1955	723
18	Detroit Tigers	1950	722
19	Boston Red Sox	1950	719
20	Baltimore Orioles	1970	717

Strikeouts

1	Detroit Tigers	1996	1268
2	New York Mets	1968	1203
3	St. Louis Cardinals	1997	1191
4	Los Angeles Dodgers	1996	1190
5	San Francisco Giants	1996	1189
6	Detroit Tigers	1991	1185
7	Oakland Athletics	1997	1181
8	San Diego Padres	1970	1164
	Detroit Tigers	1997	1164
10	Pittsburgh Pirates	1997	1161
11	Atlanta Braves	1997	1160
12	Philadelphia Phillies	1986	1154
13	Seattle Mariners	1986	1148
14	San Diego Padres	1969	1143
15	Toronto Blue Jays	1997	1138
16	Cincinnati Reds	1996	1134
17	Philadelphia Phillies	1969	1130
18	New York Mets	1965	1129
	San Diego Padres	1997	1129
20	Washington Senators	1965	1125

Stolen Bases

1	St. Louis Browns	1887	581
2	Baltimore Orioles	1887	545
3	Cincinnati Reds	1887	527
4	Philadelphia Athletics	1887	476
5	Kansas City Blues	1889	472
6	Cincinnati Reds	1888	469
7	St. Louis Browns	1888	468
8	Louisville Colonels	1887	466
9	Cincinnati Reds	1889	462
10	Boston Red Stockings	1891	447
11	Baltimore Orioles	1896	441
12	Philadelphia Athletics	1888	434
13	Toledo Maumees	1890	421
14	New York Giants	1887	415
15	Boston Red Stockings	1890	412
16	Brooklyn Bridegrooms	1887	409
	Brooklyn Bridegrooms	1892	409
18	Baltimore Orioles	1897	401
19	Brooklyn Bridegrooms	1889	389
20	Chicago White Stockings	1887	382

Caught Stealing

1	New York Yankees	1914	191
2	St. Louis Browns	1914	189
3	Philadelphia Athletics	1914	188
4	Chicago White Sox	1915	183
5	Boston Red Sox	1914	176
6	Washington Senators	1914	163
7	St. Louis Browns	1915	160
8	Cleveland Bronchos	1914	157
9	Detroit Tigers	1914	154
10	Chicago White Sox	1914	152
11	Chicago Cubs	1924	149
12	Detroit Tigers	1915	146
13	St. Louis Cardinals	1915	144
14	Chicago Cubs	1923	143
15	Cincinnati Reds	1915	142
16	New York Giants	1915	137
17	Cincinnati Reds	1922	136
18	New York Yankees	1915	133
19	Chicago Cubs	1920	129
20	Cincinnati Reds	1920	128

Hit By Pitch

1	Baltimore Orioles	1898	159
2	Brooklyn Superbas	1899	125
3	Baltimore Orioles	1899	122
4	Baltimore Orioles	1896	120
5	Baltimore Orioles	1897	115
6	Baltimore Orioles	1891	111
7	Baltimore Orioles	1895	106
8	Houston Astros	1997	100
9	Baltimore Orioles	1894	98
10	Buffalo Bisons	1890	96
11	St. Louis Browns	1890	95
12	Toronto Blue Jays	1996	92
	Pittsburgh Pirates	1997	92
14	New York Giants	1903	91
15	St. Louis Cardinals	1901	90
	New York Giants	1905	90
17	Philadelphia Athletics	1890	87
	St. Louis Browns	1891	87
	Washington Senators	1899	87
20	New York Giants	1911	85

Sacrifice Hits

1	Boston Red Sox	1917	310
2	Philadelphia Phillies	1909	283
3	Chicago Cubs	1908	270
	Chicago White Sox	1915	270
5	Boston Red Sox	1915	265
6	Detroit Tigers	1923	257
7	Cleveland Indians	1917	255
8	Cleveland Indians	1920	254
9	New York Giants	1908	250
10	Philadelphia Athletics	1909	248
	Chicago White Sox	1923	248
12	Chicago Cubs	1909	246
13	Detroit Tigers	1922	244
14	Chicago White Sox	1905	241
15	Cincinnati Reds	1926	239
16	Philadelphia Athletics	1926	238
17	Detroit Tigers	1926	237
18	Three tied with		236

Sacrifice Flies

1	Oakland Athletics	1984	77
2	Kansas City Royals	1979	76
3	Philadelphia Phillies	1977	74
	Cleveland Indians	1980	74
5	Kansas City Royals	1978	72
	Milwaukee Brewers	1992	72
	Cleveland Indians	1993	72
	New York Yankees	1974	72
	New York Yankees	1996	72
10	Milwaukee Brewers	1990	71
	Kansas City Royals	1976	71
12	New York Yankees	1997	70
13	Chicago White Sox	1992	69
	Texas Rangers	1996	69
15	New York Yankees	1995	68
16	Pittsburgh Pirates	1982	67
	Cleveland Indians	1984	67
	Philadelphia Phillies	1976	67
	Baltimore Orioles	1996	67
20	Six tied with		66

GDP

1	Boston Red Sox	1990	174
2	Minnesota Twins	1996	172
3	Boston Red Sox	1982	171
	Boston Red Sox	1983	171
5	Philadelphia Athletics	1950	170
6	Boston Red Sox	1989	169
	Boston Red Sox	1949	169
	Boston Red Sox	1951	169
9	St. Louis Cardinals	1958	166
10	Cleveland Indians	1980	165
11	Boston Red Sox	1985	164
	Detroit Tigers	1949	164
	Cleveland Indians	1996	164
14	Oakland Athletics	1989	163
15	Detroit Tigers	1950	162
16	Chicago Cubs	1933	161
	Cincinnati Reds	1933	161
18	Philadelphia Athletics	1949	160
19	Four tied with		159

Batting Average

1	Philadelphia Phillies	1894	.349
2	Baltimore Orioles	1894	.343
3	Chicago White Stockings	1876	.337
4	Boston Beaneaters	1894	.331
5	Philadelphia Phillies	1895	.330
6	Baltimore Orioles	1896	.328
7	Baltimore Orioles	1897	.325
8	Baltimore Orioles	1895	.324
9	Boston Beaneaters	1897	.319
10	New York Giants	1930	.319
11	Detroit Tigers	1921	.316
12	Philadelphia Phillies	1930	.315
13	St. Louis Cardinals	1930	.314
14	Chicago Colts	1894	.314
15	Brooklyn Bridegrooms	1894	.313
16	St. Louis Browns	1922	.313
17	Pittsburgh Pirates	1894	.312
18	New York Yankees	1930	.309
19	Pittsburgh Pirates	1928	.309
20	Philadelphia Phillies	1929	.309

On-Base Percentage

1	Baltimore Orioles	1894	.418
2	Philadelphia Phillies	1894	.414
3	Boston Beaneaters	1894	.401
4	Philadelphia Phillies	1895	.394
5	Baltimore Orioles	1897	.394
6	Baltimore Orioles	1896	.393
7	Boston Red Sox	1950	.385
8	Detroit Tigers	1921	.385
9	Baltimore Orioles	1895	.384
10	New York Yankees	1930	.384
11	Cleveland Indians	1921	.383
12	New York Yankees	1927	.383
13	New York Yankees	1931	.383
14	Baltimore Orioles	1898	.382
15	Cleveland Indians	1923	.381
16	Boston Red Sox	1949	.381
17	New York Yankees	1936	.381
18	Washington Senators	1894	.381
19	Chicago Colts	1894	.380
20	Detroit Tigers	1925	.379

Slugging Percentage

1	New York Yankees	1927	.489
2	New York Yankees	1930	.488
3	Seattle Mariners	1997	.485
4	Boston Beaneaters	1894	.484
5	Cleveland Indians	1994	.484
6	Seattle Mariners	1996	.484
7	New York Yankees	1936	.483
8	Baltimore Orioles	1894	.483
9	Chicago Cubs	1930	.481
10	Cleveland Indians	1995	.479
11	Colorado Rockies	1997	.478
12	Philadelphia Phillies	1894	.476
13	Cleveland Indians	1996	.475
14	Brooklyn Dodgers	1953	.474
15	New York Giants	1930	.473
16	Colorado Rockies	1996	.472
17	Baltimore Orioles	1996	.472
18	St. Louis Cardinals	1930	.471
19	Colorado Rockies	1995	.471
20	Texas Rangers	1996	.469

Team Pitching Leaders—Single Season

Wins

1 Chicago Cubs	1906	116
2 Cleveland Indians	1954	111
3 Pittsburgh Pirates	1909	110
New York Yankees	1927	110
5 Baltimore Orioles	1969	109
New York Yankees	1961	109
7 New York Mets	1986	108
Baltimore Orioles	1970	108
Cincinnati Reds	1975	108
10 Chicago Cubs	1907	107
Philadelphia Athletics	1931	107
New York Yankees	1932	107
13 New York Giants	1904	106
New York Yankees	1939	106
St. Louis Cardinals	1942	106
16 Five tied with		105

Losses

1 Cleveland Spiders	1899	134
2 New York Mets	1962	120
3 Philadelphia Athletics	1916	117
4 Boston Braves	1935	115
5 Pittsburgh Innocents	1890	113
Washington Senators	1904	113
7 New York Mets	1965	112
Pittsburgh Pirates	1952	112
9 New York Mets	1963	111
Louisville Colonels	1889	111
St. Louis Browns	1898	111
Boston Red Sox	1932	111
St. Louis Browns	1939	111
Philadelphia Phillies	1941	111
15 Montreal Expos	1969	110
San Diego Padres	1969	110
Washington Senators	1909	110
18 Six tied with		109

Winning Percentage

1 St. Louis Maroons	1884	.832
2 Chicago White Stockings	1880	.798
3 Chicago White Stockings	1876	.788
4 Chicago White Stockings	1885	.777
5 Chicago Cubs	1906	.763
6 New York Giants	1885	.759
7 Providence Grays	1884	.750
8 Pittsburgh Pirates	1902	.741
9 Chicago White Stockings	1886	.726
10 Pittsburgh Pirates	1909	.724
11 Cleveland Indians	1954	.721
12 New York Yankees	1927	.714
13 Detroit Wolverines	1886	.707
14 St. Louis Browns	1885	.705
15 Boston Beaneaters	1897	.705
16 Chicago Cubs	1907	.704
Philadelphia Athletics	1931	.704
18 St. Louis Browns	1887	.704
19 StL Brown Stockings	1876	.703
20 Providence Grays	1879	.702

Complete Games

1 Boston Pilgrims	1904	148
2 Louisville Colonels	1892	147
Chicago Orphans	1899	147
4 St. Louis Cardinals	1904	146
5 Detroit Tigers	1904	143
6 Boston Beaneaters	1892	142
Cleveland Spiders	1898	142
Cincinnati Reds	1904	142
9 New York Giants	1898	141
Cleveland Bronchos	1904	141
11 Cleveland Spiders	1892	140
Cleveland Bronchos	1905	140
13 St. Louis Browns	1892	139
New York Giants	1892	139
Chicago Cubs	1904	139
Boston Beaneaters	1905	139
17 Six tied with		138

Shutouts

1 Chicago White Sox	1906	32
Chicago Cubs	1907	32
Chicago Cubs	1909	32
4 St. Louis Cardinals	1968	30
Chicago Cubs	1906	30
6 Chicago Cubs	1908	29
7 Los Angeles Angels	1964	28
New York Mets	1969	28
9 Cleveland Bronchos	1906	27
Pittsburgh Pirates	1906	27
Philadelphia Athletics	1907	27
Philadelphia Athletics	1909	27
13 Chicago White Sox	1904	26
Philadelphia Athletics	1904	26
Chicago White Sox	1909	26
Boston Red Sox	1918	26
St. Louis Cardinals	1944	26
Cleveland Indians	1948	26
19 Six tied with		25

Saves

1 Chicago White Sox	1990	68
2 Oakland Athletics	1988	64
Oakland Athletics	1990	64
4 Montreal Expos	1993	61
5 Toronto Blue Jays	1991	60
Cincinnati Reds	1970	60
Cincinnati Reds	1972	60
8 Baltimore Orioles	1997	59
9 New York Yankees	1986	58
Oakland Athletics	1992	58
Minnesota Twins	1970	58
12 Oakland Athletics	1989	57
13 Chicago Cubs	1993	56
14 San Diego Padres	1978	55
Chicago Cubs	1989	55
Cincinnati Reds	1992	55
17 St. Louis Cardinals	1993	54
18 Three tied with		53

Hits Allowed

1 Philadelphia Phillies	1930	1993
2 Cleveland Spiders	1899	1844
3 Philadelphia Phillies	1923	1801
4 St. Louis Browns	1936	1776
5 St. Louis Browns	1937	1768
6 Philadelphia Phillies	1925	1753
7 Philadelphia Phillies	1929	1743
8 Oakland Athletics	1997	1734
9 Pittsburgh Pirates	1930	1730
10 St. Louis Browns	1939	1724
11 Philadelphia Phillies	1927	1710
12 Philadelphia Phillies	1926	1699
Detroit Tigers	1996	1699
14 Colorado Rockies	1997	1697
15 Philadelphia Phillies	1922	1692
16 Philadelphia Phillies	1924	1689
17 Philadelphia Athletics	1939	1687
18 Washington Senators	1935	1672
19 St. Louis Browns	1935	1667
20 Philadelphia Phillies	1921	1665

Runs Allowed

1 Cleveland Spiders	1899	1252
2 Pittsburgh Innocents	1890	1235
3 Buffalo Bisons	1890	1199
Philadelphia Phillies	1930	1199
5 Washington Senators	1894	1122
6 Cleveland Spiders	1887	1112
7 Detroit Tigers	1996	1103
8 New York Metropolitans	1887	1093
9 Louisville Colonels	1889	1091
10 Louisville Colonels	1895	1090
11 Cincinnati Reds	1894	1085
12 St. Louis Browns	1897	1083
13 Washington Senators	1891	1067
14 Chicago Colts	1894	1066
15 St. Louis Browns	1936	1064
16 Washington Senators	1895	1048
17 Philadelphia Athletics	1936	1045
18 St. Louis Browns	1939	1035
19 Three tied with		1032

Walks

1 Philadelphia Athletics	1915	827
2 New York Yankees	1949	812
3 St. Louis Browns	1951	801
4 Detroit Tigers	1996	784
5 Washington Senators	1949	779
6 Cleveland Indians	1971	770
7 Texas Rangers	1987	760
8 Philadelphia Athletics	1949	758
9 Boston Red Sox	1950	748
10 St. Louis Browns	1939	739
11 St. Louis Browns	1938	737
St. Louis Browns	1948	737
13 Texas Rangers	1986	736
14 Washington Senators	1948	734
Chicago White Sox	1950	734
16 Washington Senators	1956	730
17 Philadelphia Athletics	1950	729
18 Boston Red Sox	1996	722
19 Montreal Expos	1970	716
20 Two tied with		715

Strikeouts

1 Atlanta Braves	1996	1245
2 Los Angeles Dodgers	1997	1232
3 Houston Astros	1969	1221
4 New York Mets	1990	1217
5 Los Angeles Dodgers	1996	1212
6 Philadelphia Phillies	1997	1209
7 Seattle Mariners	1997	1207
8 Montreal Expos	1996	1206
9 Atlanta Braves	1997	1196
10 San Diego Padres	1996	1194
11 Cleveland Indians	1967	1189
12 Florida Marlins	1997	1188
13 Boston Red Sox	1996	1165
New York Yankees	1997	1165
15 Houston Astros	1996	1163
16 Cleveland Indians	1964	1162
17 Houston Astros	1986	1160
18 Cincinnati Reds	1997	1159
19 Two tied with		1157

Strikeouts/9 Innings

1 Chicago Browns	1884	7.79
2 Philadelphia Phillies	1997	7.66
3 Houston Astros	1969	7.65
4 Atlanta Braves	1996	7.63
5 New York Mets	1990	7.61
6 Los Angeles Dodgers	1997	7.60
7 Atlanta Braves	1994	7.59
8 Atlanta Braves	1995	7.57
9 Montreal Expos	1996	7.53
10 Seattle Mariners	1997	7.50
11 Seattle Mariners	1995	7.46
12 Los Angeles Dodgers	1996	7.44
13 San Diego Padres	1994	7.42
14 Florida Marlins	1997	7.39
15 Los Angeles Dodgers	1995	7.37
16 Atlanta Braves	1997	7.34
17 San Diego Padres	1995	7.33
18 Toronto Blue Jays	1994	7.31
19 Cleveland Indians	1967	7.24
20 Houston Astros	1996	7.23

Home Runs Allowed

1 Detroit Tigers	1996	241
2 Minnesota Twins	1996	233
3 Baltimore Orioles	1987	226
4 Kansas City Athletics	1964	220
5 Cleveland Indians	1987	219
California Angels	1996	219
7 Seattle Mariners	1996	216
8 Milwaukee Brewers	1996	213
9 California Angels	1987	212
10 Minnesota Twins	1987	210
Minnesota Twins	1995	210
12 Baltimore Orioles	1996	209
13 Minnesota Twins	1982	208
14 Oakland Athletics	1996	205
15 Anaheim Angels	1997	202
16 Minnesota Twins	1986	200
17 Seattle Mariners	1987	199
Texas Rangers	1987	199
Kansas City Athletics	1962	199
20 Colorado Rockies	1996	198

ERA

1 StL Brown Stockings	1876	1.22
2 Providence Grays	1884	1.61
3 Providence Grays	1880	1.64
4 Cincinnati Reds	1882	1.65
5 Hartford Dark Blues	1876	1.67
6 Louisville Grays	1876	1.69
7 New York Giants	1885	1.72
8 Chicago Cubs	1907	1.73
9 Chicago Cubs	1909	1.75
10 Chicago Cubs	1906	1.75
11 Chicago White Stockings	1876	1.76
12 Philadelphia Athletics	1910	1.79
13 Cincinnati Red Stockings	1878	1.84
14 Cleveland Blues	1880	1.90
15 Chicago White Stockings	1880	1.93
16 Philadelphia Athletics	1909	1.93
17 St. Louis Maroons	1884	1.96
18 New York Giants	1888	1.96
19 Chicago White Sox	1905	1.99
20 Cleveland Bronchos	1908	2.02

Component ERA

1 StL Brown Stockings	1876	1.45
2 Providence Grays	1880	1.50
3 New York Metropolitans	1884	1.62
4 Chicago White Stockings	1880	1.64
5 St. Louis Browns	1888	1.66
6 Hartford Dark Blues	1876	1.67
7 Louisville Colonels	1884	1.67
8 Providence Grays	1884	1.68
9 St. Louis Maroons	1884	1.71
10 New York Giants	1885	1.78
11 Louisville Grays	1876	1.79
12 New York Giants	1888	1.80
13 St. Louis Browns	1883	1.81
14 Chicago White Stockings	1882	1.83
15 New York Metropolitans	1883	1.85
16 Cincinnati Reds	1882	1.89
17 Cleveland Blues	1880	1.90
18 Chicago Cubs	1909	1.93
19 Chicago White Sox	1908	1.93
20 Chicago Cubs	1906	1.93

Opponent Average

1 New York Giants	1888	.199
2 New York Giants	1885	.205
3 Cleveland Indians	1968	.206
4 St. Louis Browns	1888	.206
5 Chicago Cubs	1906	.207
6 Providence Grays	1884	.209
7 Chicago White Stockings	1880	.209
8 New York Metropolitans	1884	.209
9 StL Brown Stockings	1876	.210
10 St. Louis Browns	1883	.211
11 Baltimore Orioles	1968	.212
12 St. Louis Maroons	1884	.214
13 Columbus Colts	1890	.214
14 Cincinnati Reds	1882	.214
15 Providence Grays	1880	.215
16 Chicago Cubs	1909	.215
17 Brooklyn Bridegrooms	1888	.215
18 Philadelphia Athletics	1888	.215
19 Louisville Colonels	1884	.216
20 Chicago Cubs	1907	.216

Opponent OBP

1 StL Brown Stockings	1876	.224
2 Providence Grays	1880	.228
3 St. Louis Maroons	1884	.235
4 Hartford Dark Blues	1876	.235
5 New York Metropolitans	1884	.237
6 Louisville Grays	1876	.240
7 Louisville Colonels	1884	.241
8 Providence Grays	1884	.242
9 Chicago White Stockings	1880	.242
10 St. Louis Browns	1888	.244
11 St. Louis Browns	1883	.244
12 Cincinnati Outlaw Reds	1884	.245
13 Chicago White Stockings	1882	.246
14 Cincinnati Reds	1882	.247
15 Providence Grays	1882	.250
16 Boston Red Stockings	1884	.250
17 Boston Unions	1884	.251
18 Cleveland Blues	1880	.253
19 New York Metropolitans	1883	.253
20 Buffalo Bisons	1879	.254

Postseason

World Series

League Championship Series

Division Series

For each of the modern World Series (1903, 1905-1993 and 1995-1997), League Championship Series (1969-1993 and 1995-1997) and Division Series (1981 and 1995-1997), we provide a summary, detailed box scores for every game and composite statistics.

Register

In the format of our player register in the companion volume, *STATS All-Time Major League Handbook*, we provide yearly and career totals, broken down by the type of series, for all players who have seen postseason action since 1903. We provide biographical information and, where pertinent, 23 batting, 27 pitching and six fielding statistics.

Player Profiles

For select players, we offer detailed breakdowns of their entire postseason careers. For hitters and pitchers, we list home/road and left/right splits as well as how they did in five other situations: with runners in scoring position, close & late (seventh inning or later, and the batting team is ahead by one run, tied or has the potential tying run on base, at the plate or on deck), with the bases empty and none out, with the bases empty and with runners on.

We also show which opponents the players performed the best and worst against, with a minimum on 10 plate appearances in each matchup.

Leaders

We list the top 20 career leaders in 16 hitting and 16 pitching categories, for World Series play, League Championship Series play and 20th century postseason play as a whole. Minimums for the World Series and League Championship Series percentage categories are 50 plate appearances for hitters and five decisions (winning percentage only) or 25 innings for pitchers. For the overall postseason, the minimums are 75 plate appearances for batters and eight decisions (winning percentage only) or 40 innings for pitchers.

19th Century Championships

There were 13 World Series or similar postseason series played before the American League became a major league in 1901. For each of these 19th century championships, we provide a summary, line scores for every game and composite statistics.

Abbreviations & Formulas

A complete list of team and statistical abbreviations are listed in the back of the book, along with an appendix explaining formulas and the availability of certain statistics.

1903 Boston Pilgrims (AL) 5, Pittsburgh Pirates (NL) 3

The National League champions met the top American League club for the first time as the Pittsburgh Pirates defended the Senior Circuit's honor against the Boston Pilgrims in a best-of-nine series. With the Pittsburgh pitching staff weakened by Sam Leever's sore wing and Ed Doheny's absence, Deacon Phillippe was sent to the hill to take on Cy Young in the opener. Phillippe proved worthy of the assignment, besting Young, 7-3, but Bill Dinneen put Boston even with a 3-0 shutout the next day. Phillippe was back on the mound for Game 3, and came away with a 4-2 victory. Three days later, he won Game 4, 5-4, despite allowing three runs in the ninth. Young got his first win of the Series in Game 5 by the score of 11-2, and Dinneen squared the Series once more with a 6-3 win in Game 6. Game 7 was a rematch of the opening-game starters, but Phillippe was worse for the wear and fell to Young, 7-3. When the eighth game was played three days later, the Pirates still didn't have anyone to turn to but Phillippe, who fell to Dinneen, 3-0, as the Pilgrims captured the flag in the first modern World Series.

Game 1

Thursday, October 1

Pirates	AB	R	H	RBI	BB	K	Avg
Ginger Beaumont, cf	5	1	0	0	0	1	.000
Fred Clarke, lf	5	0	2	0	0	1	.400
Tommy Leach, 3b	5	1	4	1	0	0	.800
Honus Wagner, ss	3	1	1	1	2	0	.333
Kitty Bransfield, 1b	5	2	1	0	0	0	.200
Claude Ritchey, 2b	4	1	0	0	1	1	.000
Jimmy Sebring, rf	5	1	3	4	0	0	.600
Ed Phelps, c	4	0	1	0	0	1	.250
Deacon Phillippe, p	4	0	0	0	0	1	.000
TOTALS	40	7	12	6	3	5	.300

Pilgrims	AB	R	H	RBI	BB	K	Avg
Patsy Dougherty, lf	4	0	0	0	0	1	.000
Jimmy Collins, 3b	4	0	0	0	0	1	.000
Chick Stahl, cf	4	0	1	0	0	1	.250
Buck Freeman, rf	4	2	2	0	0	0	.500
Freddy Parent, ss	4	1	2	1	0	1	.500
Candy LaChance, 1b	4	0	0	2	0	1	.000
Hobe Ferris, 2b	3	0	1	0	0	2	.333
Lou Criger, c	3	0	0	0	0	1	.000
Jack O'Brien, ph	1	0	0	0	0	1	.000
Cy Young, p	3	0	0	0	0	1	.000
Duke Farrell, ph	1	0	0	0	0	0	.000
TOTALS	35	3	6	3	0	10	.171

	1	2	3	4	5	6	7	8	9	R	H	E
Pirates	4	0	1	1	0	0	1	0	0	7	12	2
Pilgrims	0	0	0	0	0	0	2	0	1	3	6	4

E—Ferris 2, Leach, Wagner, Criger 2. LOB—Pirates 9, Pilgrims 6. Scoring Position—Pirates 4-for-10, Pilgrims 1-for-6. 3B—Leach 2 (2), Bransfield (1), Freeman (1), Parent (1). HR—Sebring (1). SB—Wagner (1), Bransfield (1), Ritchey (1). CS—Leach (1).

Pirates	IP	H	R	ER	BB	K	ERA
Deacon Phillippe (W, 1-0)	9.0	6	3	2	0	10	2.00

Pilgrims	IP	H	R	ER	BB	K	ERA
Cy Young (L, 0-1)	9.0	12	7	3	3	5	3.00

HBP—Ferris by Phillippe. Time—1:55. Attendance—16,242. Umpires—HP, O'Day. Bases, Connolly.

Game 2

Friday, October 2

Pirates	AB	R	H	RBI	BB	K	Avg
Ginger Beaumont, cf	3	0	0	0	1	1	.000
Fred Clarke, lf	3	0	1	0	1	1	.375
Tommy Leach, 3b	3	0	0	0	0	1	.500
Honus Wagner, ss	3	0	0	0	0	0	.167
Kitty Bransfield, 1b	3	0	0	0	0	1	.125
Claude Ritchey, 2b	3	0	1	0	0	2	.143
Jimmy Sebring, rf	3	0	1	0	0	2	.500
Harry Smith, c	3	0	0	0	0	0	.000
Sam Leever, p	0	0	0	0	0	0	—
Bucky Veil, p	2	0	0	0	0	2	.000
Ed Phelps, ph	1	0	0	0	0	1	.200
TOTALS	27	0	3	0	2	11	.238

Pilgrims	AB	R	H	RBI	BB	K	Avg
Patsy Dougherty, lf	4	2	3	2	0	0	.375
Jimmy Collins, 3b	4	0	1	0	1	0	.125
Chick Stahl, cf	4	1	1	0	0	1	.250
Buck Freeman, rf	4	0	2	1	0	0	.500
Freddy Parent, ss	3	0	1	0	1	0	.429
Candy LaChance, 1b	2	0	0	0	1	0	.000
Hobe Ferris, 2b	4	0	0	0	0	0	.143
Lou Criger, c	3	0	0	0	1	0	.000
Bill Dinneen, p	1	0	0	0	2	0	.000
TOTALS	29	3	8	3	6	1	.237

	1	2	3	4	5	6	7	8	9	R	H	E
Pirates	0	0	0	0	0	0	0	0	0	0	3	2
Pilgrims	2	0	0	0	0	1	0	0	x	3	8	0

E—Veil, Smith. DP—Pirates 2 (Ritchey to Wagner to Bransfield; Wagner to Ritchey to Bransfield), Pilgrims 1 (Ferris). LOB—Pirates 2, Pilgrims 11. Scoring Position—Pirates 0-for-2, Pilgrims 2-for-11. 2B—Stahl (1). HR—Dougherty 2 (2). S—LaChance, Dinneen. GDP—Collins, Criger. SB—Collins 2 (2).

Pirates	IP	H	R	ER	BB	K	ERA
Sam Leever (L, 0-1)	1.0	3	2	2	1	0	18.00
Bucky Veil	7.0	5	1	1	5	1	1.29

Pilgrims	IP	H	R	ER	BB	K	ERA
Bill Dinneen (W, 1-0)	9.0	3	0	0	2	11	0.00

HBP—Dougherty by Veil. Time—1:47. Attendance—9,415. Umpires—HP, O'Day. Bases, Connolly.

Game 3

Saturday, October 3

Pirates	AB	R	H	RBI	BB	K	Avg
Ginger Beaumont, cf	4	1	0	0	1	0	.000
Fred Clarke, lf	4	0	1	0	0	0	.333
Tommy Leach, 3b	4	1	1	1	0	0	.417
Honus Wagner, ss	3	1	1	0	0	0	.222
Kitty Bransfield, 1b	3	0	0	0	0	0	.091
Claude Ritchey, 2b	4	1	2	1	0	1	.273
Jimmy Sebring, rf	3	0	0	0	1	1	.364
Ed Phelps, c	4	0	2	1	0	0	.333
Deacon Phillippe, p	4	0	0	0	0	0	.000
TOTALS	33	4	7	3	2	2	.232

Pilgrims	AB	R	H	RBI	BB	K	Avg
Patsy Dougherty, lf	4	0	0	0	0	2	.250
Jimmy Collins, 3b	4	2	2	0	0	0	.250
Chick Stahl, cf	3	0	1	1	1	0	.273
Buck Freeman, rf	3	0	0	0	1	0	.364
Freddy Parent, ss	4	0	0	1	0	0	.273
Candy LaChance, 1b	3	0	1	0	1	0	.111
Hobe Ferris, 2b	4	0	0	0	0	2	.091
Lou Criger, c	3	0	0	0	0	0	.000
Long Tom Hughes, p	0	0	0	0	0	0	—
Cy Young, p	3	0	0	0	0	2	.000
TOTALS	31	2	4	2	3	6	.196

	1	2	3	4	5	6	7	8	9	R	H	E
Pirates	0	1	2	0	0	0	0	1	0	4	7	1
Pilgrims	0	0	0	1	0	0	0	1	0	2	4	2

E—Parent, Bransfield, Young. DP—Pilgrims 1 (Dougherty to Collins). LOB—Pirates 6, Pilgrims 5. Scoring Position—Pirates 3-for-9, Pilgrims 1-for-5. 2B—Clarke (1), Wagner (1), Ritchey (1), Phelps 2 (2), Collins (1), LaChance (1). S—Bransfield.

Pirates	IP	H	R	ER	BB	K	ERA
Deacon Phillippe (W, 2-0)	9.0	4	2	2	3	6	2.00

Pilgrims	IP	H	R	ER	BB	K	ERA
Long Tom Hughes (L, 0-1)	2.0	4	2	2	2	0	9.00
Cy Young	7.0	3	2	1	0	2	2.25

Hughes pitched to three batters in the 3rd.

HBP—Wagner by Young. Time—1:50. Attendance—18,801. Umpires—HP, O'Day. Bases, Connolly.

Game 4

Tuesday, October 6

Pilgrims	AB	R	H	RBI	BB	K	Avg
Patsy Dougherty, lf	4	0	0	0	0	1	.188
Jimmy Collins, 3b	4	1	1	0	0	0	.250
Chick Stahl, cf	4	1	2	0	0	0	.333
Buck Freeman, rf	4	0	1	1	0	0	.333
Freddy Parent, ss	4	1	1	1	0	0	.267
Candy LaChance, 1b	4	1	2	0	0	0	.231
Hobe Ferris, 2b	4	0	1	0	0	0	.133
Lou Criger, c	3	0	1	1	0	1	.083
Duke Farrell, ph	1	0	0	1	0	0	.000
Bill Dinneen, p	3	0	0	0	0	0	.000
Jack O'Brien, ph	1	0	0	0	0	0	.000
TOTALS	36	4	9	4	0	2	.216

Pirates	AB	R	H	RBI	BB	K	Avg
Ginger Beaumont, cf	4	2	3	0	0	0	.188
Fred Clarke, lf	4	1	1	0	0	0	.313
Tommy Leach, 3b	4	1	2	3	0	0	.438
Honus Wagner, ss	4	0	3	1	0	1	.385
Kitty Bransfield, 1b	4	0	1	1	0	3	.133
Claude Ritchey, 2b	3	0	0	0	1	0	.214
Jimmy Sebring, rf	4	0	0	0	0	1	.267
Ed Phelps, c	4	0	1	0	0	1	.308
Deacon Phillippe, p	3	1	1	0	0	1	.091
TOTALS	34	5	12	5	1	7	.264

	1	2	3	4	5	6	7	8	9	R	H	E
Pilgrims	0	0	0	0	1	0	0	0	3	4	9	1
Pirates	1	0	0	0	1	0	3	0	x	5	12	1

E—Dougherty, Bransfield. DP—Pirates 1 (Ritchey to Bransfield). LOB—Pilgrims 5, Pirates 6. Scoring Position—Pilgrims 3-for-7, Pirates 5-for-8. 3B—Beaumont (1), Leach (3). SB—Wagner (2). CS—Wagner (1).

Pilgrims	IP	H	R	ER	BB	K	ERA
Bill Dinneen (L, 1-1)	8.0	12	5	5	1	7	2.65

Pirates	IP	H	R	ER	BB	K	ERA
Deacon Phillippe (W, 3-0)	9.0	9	4	4	0	2	2.67

Time—1:30. Attendance—7,600. Umpires—HP, O'Day. Bases, Connolly.

Game 5

Wednesday, October 7

Pilgrims	AB	R	H	RBI	BB	K	Avg
Patsy Dougherty, lf	6	0	3	3	0	0	.273
Jimmy Collins, 3b	6	0	2	0	0	0	.273
Chick Stahl, cf	5	2	1	0	0	0	.300
Buck Freeman, rf	4	2	2	1	1	1	.368
Freddy Parent, ss	5	1	2	0	0	0	.300
Candy LaChance, 1b	4	2	1	1	1	0	.235
Hobe Ferris, 2b	5	2	1	2	0	2	.150
Lou Criger, c	3	1	0	0	1	1	.067
Cy Young, p	5	1	2	3	0	0	.182
TOTALS	43	11	14	10	3	4	.247

Pirates	AB	R	H	RBI	BB	K	Avg
Ginger Beaumont, cf	4	1	1	0	0	0	.200
Fred Clarke, lf	4	1	0	0	0	0	.250
Tommy Leach, 3b	4	0	2	2	0	0	.450
Honus Wagner, ss	4	0	0	0	0	1	.294
Kitty Bransfield, 1b	4	0	0	0	0	1	.105
Claude Ritchey, 2b	4	0	1	0	0	1	.222
Jimmy Sebring, rf	4	0	1	0	0	0	.263
Ed Phelps, c	3	0	0	0	0	1	.250
Brickyard Kennedy, p	2	0	1	0	0	0	.500
Gus Thompson, p	1	0	0	0	0	0	.000
TOTALS	34	2	6	2	0	4	.257

	1	2	3	4	5	6	7	8	9	R	H	E
Pilgrims	0	0	0	0	0	6	4	1	0	11	14	2
Pirates	0	0	0	0	0	0	0	2	0	2	6	4

E—Parent, Leach, Wagner 2, Clarke, LaChance. LOB—Pilgrims 9, Pirates 6. Scoring Position—Pilgrims 5-for-18, Pirates 1-for-8. 2B—Kennedy (1). 3B—Dougherty 2 (2), Collins (1), Stahl (1), Young (1), Leach (4). S—Criger, Phelps. SB—Collins (3), Stahl (1).

Pilgrims	IP	H	R	ER	BB	K	ERA
Cy Young (W, 1-1)	9.0	6	2	0	0	4	1.44

Pirates	IP	H	R	ER	BB	K	ERA
Brickyard Kennedy (L, 0-1)	7.0	11	10	4	3	3	5.14
Gus Thompson	2.0	3	1	1	0	1	4.50

Time—2:00. Attendance—12,322. Umpires—HP, Connolly. Bases, O'Brien.

Game 6

Thursday, October 8

Pilgrims	AB	R	H	RBI	BB	K	Avg
Patsy Dougherty, lf	3	1	1	0	2	0	.280
Jimmy Collins, 3b	5	1	1	1	0	0	.259
Chick Stahl, cf	5	1	2	1	0	0	.320
Buck Freeman, rf	5	0	0	1	0	1	.292
Freddy Parent, ss	4	2	1	0	0	0	.292
Candy LaChance, 1b	4	0	1	1	0	0	.238
Hobe Ferris, 2b	4	0	2	0	0	0	.208
Lou Criger, c	4	0	1	0	0	0	.105
Bill Dinneen, p	4	1	1	0	0	1	.125
TOTALS	38	6	10	4	2	2	.249

Pirates	AB	R	H	RBI	BB	K	Avg
Ginger Beaumont, cf	5	1	4	1	0	0	.320
Fred Clarke, lf	5	0	2	2	0	2	.280
Tommy Leach, 3b	5	0	0	0	0	0	.360
Honus Wagner, ss	3	0	0	0	1	0	.250
Kitty Bransfield, 1b	3	0	1	0	1	0	.136
Claude Ritchey, 2b	3	0	0	0	1	0	.190
Jimmy Sebring, rf	4	1	2	0	0	0	.304
Ed Phelps, c	4	1	1	0	0	1	.250
Sam Leever, p	4	0	0	0	0	0	.000
TOTALS	36	3	10	3	3	3	.259

	1	2	3	4	5	6	7	8	9	R	H	E
Pilgrims	0	0	3	0	2	0	1	0	0	6	10	1
Pirates	0	0	0	0	0	0	3	0	0	3	10	3

E—Leach 2, Wagner, Criger. DP—Pilgrims 1 (Parent to LaChance), Pirates 1 (Ritchey to Wagner to Bransfield). LOB—Pilgrims 8, Pirates 9. Scoring Position—Pilgrims 4-for-12, Pirates 2-for-11. 2B—LaChance (2), Clarke (2). 3B—Stahl (2), Parent (2). GDP—LaChance. SB—Stahl (2), Beaumont 2 (2), Clarke (1), Leach (1).

Pilgrims	IP	H	R	ER	BB	K	ERA
Bill Dinneen (W, 2-1)	9.0	10	3	3	3	3	2.77

Pirates	IP	H	R	ER	BB	K	ERA
Sam Leever (L, 0-2)	9.0	10	6	4	2	2	5.40

HBP—Parent by Leever. Time—2:02. Attendance—11,556. Umpires—HP, O'Day. Bases, Connolly.

Game 7

Saturday, October 10

Pilgrims	AB	R	H	RBI	BB	K	Avg
Patsy Dougherty, lf	5	0	1	0	0	1	.267
Jimmy Collins, 3b	5	1	1	0	0	0	.250
Chick Stahl, cf	4	1	2	1	0	0	.345
Buck Freeman, rf	4	1	1	0	0	0	.286
Freddy Parent, ss	4	2	2	1	0	0	.321
Candy LaChance, 1b	3	1	0	0	0	1	.208
Hobe Ferris, 2b	3	1	2	0	0	0	.259
Lou Criger, c	4	0	2	3	0	0	.174
Cy Young, p	4	0	0	0	0	0	.133
TOTALS	36	7	11	5	0	2	.258

Pirates	AB	R	H	RBI	BB	K	Avg
Ginger Beaumont, cf	5	0	1	0	0	0	.300
Fred Clarke, lf	5	1	1	0	0	0	.267
Tommy Leach, 3b	5	0	0	0	0	0	.300
Honus Wagner, ss	3	0	0	1	0	1	.217
Kitty Bransfield, 1b	4	1	3	0	0	0	.231
Claude Ritchey, 2b	4	0	0	1	0	1	.160
Jimmy Sebring, rf	4	1	2	0	0	0	.333
Ed Phelps, c	3	0	1	0	1	0	.261
Deacon Phillippe, p	4	0	2	1	0	1	.200
TOTALS	37	3	10	3	1	6	.258

	1	2	3	4	5	6	7	8	9	R	H	E
Pilgrims	2	0	0	2	0	2	0	1	0	7	11	4
Pirates	0	0	0	1	0	1	0	0	1	3	10	3

E—Phelps, Parent, Phillippe, Wagner, Collins, LaChance 2. DP—Pilgrims 1 (Ferris to LaChance), Pirates 1 (Wagner to Ritchey to Bransfield). LOB—Pilgrims 4, Pirates 9. Scoring Position—Pilgrims 3-for-7, Pirates 1-for-11. 3B—Collins (2), Stahl (3), Freeman (2), Parent (3), Ferris (1), Clarke (1), Bransfield (2). S—LaChance, Ferris, Wagner. GDP—Young, Leach. CS—Stahl (1), Freeman (1), Sebring (1).

Pilgrims	IP	H	R	ER	BB	K	ERA
Cy Young (W, 2-1)	9.0	10	3	3	1	6	1.85

Pirates	IP	H	R	ER	BB	K	ERA
Deacon Phillippe (L, 3-1)	9.0	11	7	4	0	2	3.00

WP—Phillippe. Time—1:45. Attendance—17,038. Umpires—HP, Connolly. Bases, O'Brien.

Game 8

Tuesday, October 13

Pirates	AB	R	H	RBI	BB	K	Avg
Ginger Beaumont, cf	4	0	0	0	0	2	.265
Fred Clarke, lf	4	0	1	0	0	1	.265
Tommy Leach, 3b	3	0	0	0	1	0	.273
Honus Wagner, ss	4	0	1	0	0	1	.222
Kitty Bransfield, 1b	3	0	0	0	0	1	.207
Claude Ritchey, 2b	2	0	0	0	1	1	.148
Jimmy Sebring, rf	3	0	1	0	0	0	.333
Ed Phelps, c	3	0	0	0	0	1	.231
Deacon Phillippe, p	3	0	1	0	0	0	.222
TOTALS	29	0	4	0	2	7	.244

Pilgrims	AB	R	H	RBI	BB	K	Avg
Patsy Dougherty, rf	4	0	0	0	0	1	.235
Jimmy Collins, 3b	4	0	1	0	0	0	.250
Chick Stahl, cf	4	0	0	0	0	0	.303
Buck Freeman, lf	4	1	1	0	0	0	.281
Freddy Parent, ss	4	1	0	0	0	0	.281
Candy LaChance, 1b	3	1	1	0	0	0	.222
Hobe Ferris, 2b	4	0	2	3	0	0	.290
Lou Criger, c	3	0	2	0	0	0	.231
Bill Dinneen, p	3	0	1	0	0	1	.182
TOTALS	33	3	8	3	0	2	.260

	1	2	3	4	5	6	7	8	9	R	H	E
Pirates	0	0	0	0	0	0	0	0	0	0	4	3
Pilgrims	0	0	0	2	0	1	0	0	x	3	8	0

E—Phelps, Bransfield, Wagner. LOB—Pirates 4, Pilgrims 7. Scoring Position—Pirates 0-for-1, Pilgrims 3-for-6. 3B—Sebring (1), Freeman (3), LaChance (1). S—LaChance. SB—Wagner (3). CS—Leach (2).

Pirates	IP	H	R	ER	BB	K	ERA
Deacon Phillippe (L, 3-2)	8.0	8	3	2	0	2	2.86

Pilgrims	IP	H	R	ER	BB	K	ERA
Bill Dinneen (W, 3-1)	9.0	4	0	0	2	7	2.06

Time—1:35. Attendance—7,455. Umpires—HP, O'Day. Bases, Connolly.

1903 World Series—Composite Statistics

Batting

Pilgrims	G	AB	R	H	RBI	2B	3B	HR	BB	SO	SB	CS	Avg	OBP	Slg
Jimmy Collins	8	36	5	9	1	1	2	0	1	1	3	0	.250	.270	.389
Lou Criger	8	26	1	6	4	0	0	0	2	3	0	0	.231	.286	.231
Bill Dinneen	4	11	1	2	0	0	0	0	2	2	0	0	.182	.308	.182
Patsy Dougherty	8	34	3	8	5	0	2	2	2	6	0	0	.235	.297	.529
Duke Farrell	2	2	0	0	1	0	0	0	0	0	0	0	.000	.000	.000
Hobe Ferris	8	31	3	9	5	0	1	0	0	6	0	0	.290	.313	.355
Buck Freeman	8	32	6	9	4	0	3	0	2	2	0	1	.281	.324	.469
Candy LaChance	8	27	5	6	4	2	1	0	3	2	0	0	.222	.300	.370
Jack O'Brien	2	2	0	0	0	0	0	0	0	1	0	0	.000	.000	.000
Freddy Parent	8	32	8	9	4	0	3	0	1	1	0	0	.281	.324	.469
Chick Stahl	8	33	6	10	3	1	3	0	1	2	2	1	.303	.324	.515
Cy Young	4	15	1	2	3	0	1	0	0	3	0	0	.133	.133	.267
Totals	8	281	39	70	34	4	16	2	14	29	5	2	.249	.292	.399

Batting

Pirates	G	AB	R	H	RBI	2B	3B	HR	BB	SO	SB	CS	Avg	OBP	Slg
Ginger Beaumont	8	34	6	9	1	0	1	0	2	4	2	0	.265	.306	.324
Kitty Bransfield	8	29	3	6	1	0	2	0	1	6	1	0	.207	.233	.345
Fred Clarke	8	34	3	9	2	2	1	0	1	5	1	0	.265	.286	.382
Brickyard Kennedy	1	2	0	1	0	1	0	0	0	0	0	0	.500	.500	1.000
Tommy Leach	8	33	3	9	7	0	4	0	1	4	1	2	.273	.294	.515
Sam Leever	2	4	0	0	0	0	0	0	0	0	0	0	.000	.000	.000
Ed Phelps	8	26	1	6	1	2	0	0	1	6	0	0	.231	.259	.308
Deacon Phillippe	5	18	1	4	1	0	0	0	0	3	0	0	.222	.222	.222
Claude Ritchey	8	27	2	4	2	1	0	0	4	7	1	0	.148	.258	.185
Jimmy Sebring	8	30	3	10	4	0	1	1	1	4	0	1	.333	.355	.500
Harry Smith	1	3	0	0	0	0	0	0	0	0	0	0	.000	.000	.000
Gus Thompson	1	1	0	0	0	0	0	0	0	0	0	0	.000	.000	.000
Bucky Veil	1	2	0	0	0	0	0	0	0	2	0	0	.000	.000	.000
Honus Wagner	8	27	2	6	3	1	0	0	3	4	3	1	.222	.323	.259
Totals	8	270	24	64	22	7	9	1	14	45	9	4	.237	.277	.341

Pitching

Pilgrims	G	GS	CG	IP	H	R	ER	BB	SO	W-L	Sv-Op	Hld	ERA
Bill Dinneen	4	4	4	35.0	29	8	8	8	28	3-1	0-0	0	2.06
Long Tom Hughes	1	1	0	2.0	4	2	2	2	0	0-1	0-0	0	9.00
Cy Young	4	3	3	34.0	31	14	7	4	17	2-1	0-0	0	1.85
Totals	8	8	7	71.0	64	24	17	14	45	5-3	0-0	0	2.15

Pitching

Pirates	G	GS	CG	IP	H	R	ER	BB	SO	W-L	Sv-Op	Hld	ERA
Brickyard Kennedy	1	1	0	7.0	11	10	4	3	3	0-1	0-0	0	5.14
Sam Leever	2	2	1	10.0	13	8	6	3	2	0-2	0-0	0	5.40
Deacon Phillippe	5	5	5	44.0	38	19	14	3	22	3-2	0-0	0	2.86
Gus Thompson	1	0	0	2.0	3	1	1	0	1	0-0	0-0	0	4.50
Bucky Veil	1	0	0	7.0	5	1	1	5	1	0-0	0-0	0	1.29
Totals	8	8	6	70.0	70	39	26	14	29	3-5	0-0	0	3.34

Fielding

Pilgrims	Pos	G	PO	Ast	E	DP	PB	FPct
Jimmy Collins	3b	8	9	18	1	1	—	.964
Lou Criger	c	8	54	5	3	0	0	.952
Bill Dinneen	p	4	2	9	0	0	—	1.000
Patsy Dougherty	lf	7	10	3	1	1	—	.929
	rf	1	2	0	0	0	—	1.000
Hobe Ferris	2b	8	18	23	2	2	—	.953
Buck Freeman	rf	7	8	0	0	0	—	1.000
	lf	1	3	0	0	0	—	1.000
Long Tom Hughes	p	1	0	0	0	0	—	—
Candy LaChance	1b	8	77	3	3	2	—	.964
Freddy Parent	ss	8	16	28	3	1	—	.936
Chick Stahl	cf	8	14	1	0	0	—	1.000
Cy Young	p	4	0	8	1	0	—	.889
Totals		8	213	98	14	7	0	.957

Fielding

Pirates	Pos	G	PO	Ast	E	DP	PB	FPct
Ginger Beaumont	cf	8	21	0	0	0	—	1.000
Kitty Bransfield	1b	8	81	6	3	5	—	.967
Fred Clarke	lf	8	18	0	1	0	—	.947
Brickyard Kennedy	p	1	0	1	0	0	—	1.000
Tommy Leach	3b	8	5	16	4	0	—	.840
Sam Leever	p	2	0	2	0	0	—	1.000
Ed Phelps	c	7	36	5	2	0	0	.953
Deacon Phillippe	p	5	2	9	1	0	—	.917
Claude Ritchey	2b	8	20	29	0	5	—	1.000
Jimmy Sebring	rf	8	13	1	0	0	—	1.000
Harry Smith	c	1	2	1	1	0	0	.750
Gus Thompson	p	1	0	1	0	0	—	1.000
Bucky Veil	p	1	0	0	1	0	—	.000
Honus Wagner	ss	8	12	30	6	4	—	.875
Totals		8	210	101	19	14	0	.942

1905 New York Giants (NL) 4, Philadelphia Athletics (AL) 1

Never has one pitcher so dominated a World Series as the New York Giants' Christy Mathewson did in 1905. In the opener, he shut out the Philadelphia Athletics 3-0 on four hits. Chief Bender was equally effective for the Athletics in Game 2, blanking the Giants on four safeties. Mathewson duplicated his Game 1 gem in the third contest, tossing another four-hit shutout, as the Giants won 9-0 on four Athletics errors. Joe McGinnity beat Eddie Plank 1-0 in Game 4, with the only run of the game resulting from errors by Lave Cross and Monte Cross. Mathewson won it for New York with his third shutout of the Series, a 2-0 Game 5 victory in which he allowed six hits and scored the final run of the game himself. In 27 innings, Mathewson allowed 14 hits, no runs and one walk while striking out 18.

Game 1

Monday, October 9

Giants	AB	R	H	RBI	BB	K	Avg
Roger Bresnahan, c	3	1	1	1	1	0	.333
George Browne, rf	5	0	0	0	0	0	.000
Mike Donlin, cf	5	1	2	1	0	0	.400
Dan McGann, 1b	3	0	1	0	1	0	.333
Sam Mertes, lf	4	0	1	1	0	1	.250
Bill Dahlen, ss	4	0	0	0	0	1	.000
Art Devlin, 3b	4	0	1	0	0	2	.250
Billy Gilbert, 2b	4	1	3	0	0	0	.750
Christy Mathewson, p	3	0	1	0	1	0	.333
TOTALS	35	3	10	3	2	5	.286

Athletics	AB	R	H	RBI	BB	K	Avg
Topsy Hartsel, lf	4	0	1	0	0	1	.250
Bris Lord, cf	4	0	0	0	0	1	.000
Harry Davis, 1b	4	0	1	0	0	1	.250
Lave Cross, 3b	4	0	0	0	0	0	.000
Socks Seybold, rf	3	0	0	0	0	0	.000
Danny Murphy, 2b	3	0	1	0	0	1	.333
Monte Cross, ss	3	0	0	0	0	1	.000
Ossee Schreckengost, c	3	0	1	0	0	0	.333
Eddie Plank, p	3	0	0	0	0	2	.000
TOTALS	31	0	4	0	0	6	.129

	1	2	3	4	5	6	7	8	9		R	H	E
Giants	0	0	0	0	2	0	0	0	1		3	10	1
Athletics	0	0	0	0	0	0	0	0	0		0	4	0

E—Donlin. DP—Giants 1 (Dahlen to McGann). LOB—Giants 9, Athletics 4. Scoring Position—Giants 3-for-11, Athletics 0-for-6. 2B—McGann (1), Mertes (1), Davis (1), Murphy (1), Schreckengost (1). S—Mathewson (1). GDP—Plank. SB—Bresnahan (1), Donlin (1), Devlin (1), Gilbert (1). CS—Gilbert (1).

Giants	IP	H	R	ER	BB	K	ERA
Christy Mathewson (W, 1-0)	9.0	4	0	0	0	6	0.00

Athletics	IP	H	R	ER	BB	K	ERA
Eddie Plank (L, 0-1)	9.0	10	3	3	2	5	3.00

WP—Mathewson. HBP—Bresnahan by Plank. Time—1:46. Attendance—17,955. Umpires—HP, Sheridan. Bases, O'Day.

Game 2

Tuesday, October 10

Athletics	AB	R	H	RBI	BB	K	Avg
Topsy Hartsel, lf	4	1	2	0	0	0	.375
Bris Lord, cf	4	0	2	2	0	0	.250
Harry Davis, 1b	4	0	0	0	0	0	.125
Lave Cross, 3b	3	0	0	0	1	0	.000
Socks Seybold, rf	4	0	0	0	0	0	.000
Danny Murphy, 2b	4	0	1	0	0	1	.286
Monte Cross, ss	4	0	0	0	0	2	.000
Ossee Schreckengost, c	4	2	1	0	0	0	.286
Chief Bender, p	2	0	0	0	0	0	.000
TOTALS	33	3	6	2	1	3	.164

Giants	AB	R	H	RBI	BB	K	Avg
Roger Bresnahan, c	4	0	1	0	0	0	.286
George Browne, rf	4	0	0	0	0	0	.000
Mike Donlin, cf	4	0	2	0	0	0	.444
Dan McGann, 1b	3	0	0	0	1	3	.167
Sam Mertes, lf	4	0	0	0	0	2	.125
Bill Dahlen, ss	3	0	0	0	1	0	.000
Art Devlin, 3b	3	0	1	0	1	0	.286
Billy Gilbert, 2b	3	0	0	0	0	1	.429
Joe McGinnity, p	2	0	0	0	0	2	.000
Sammy Strang, ph	1	0	0	0	0	1	.000
Red Ames, p	0	0	0	0	0	0	—
TOTALS	31	0	4	0	3	9	.206

	1	2	3	4	5	6	7	8	9		R	H	E
Athletics	0	0	1	0	0	0	0	2	0		3	6	2
Giants	0	0	0	0	0	0	0	0	0		0	4	2

E—Murphy, Bresnahan, McGann, MCross. LOB—Athletics 5, Giants 7. Scoring Position—Athletics 2-for-5, Giants 0-for-11. 2B—Hartsel (1), Bresnahan (1), Donlin (1). S—Bender. SB—Dahlen (1), Devlin (2). CS—Donlin (1), Dahlen (1).

Athletics	IP	H	R	ER	BB	K	ERA
Chief Bender (W, 1-0)	9.0	4	0	0	3	9	0.00

Giants	IP	H	R	ER	BB	K	ERA
Joe McGinnity (L, 0-1)	8.0	5	3	0	0	2	0.00
Red Ames	1.0	1	0	0	1	1	0.00

Time—1:55. Attendance—24,992. Umpires—HP, O'Day. Bases, Sheridan.

Game 3

Thursday, October 12

Giants	AB	R	H	RBI	BB	K	Avg
Roger Bresnahan, c	3	2	0	0	1	0	.200
George Browne, rf	5	2	1	0	0	1	.071
Mike Donlin, cf	3	3	1	0	2	0	.417
Dan McGann, 1b	5	1	3	4	0	0	.364
Sam Mertes, lf	3	0	1	1	1	0	.182
Bill Dahlen, ss	3	1	0	1	1	0	.000
Art Devlin, 3b	4	0	1	1	0	0	.273
Billy Gilbert, 2b	4	0	0	0	1	0	.273
Christy Mathewson, p	4	0	1	0	0	0	.286
TOTALS	34	9	8	7	5	2	.227

Athletics	AB	R	H	RBI	BB	K	Avg
Topsy Hartsel, lf	4	0	0	0	0	1	.250
Bris Lord, cf	4	0	0	0	3	0	.167
Harry Davis, 1b	4	0	1	0	0	0	.167
Lave Cross, 3b	4	0	1	0	0	0	.091
Socks Seybold, rf	3	0	1	0	1	1	.100
Danny Murphy, 2b	3	0	0	0	0	0	.200
Monte Cross, ss	3	0	1	0	0	2	.100
Ossee Schreckengost, c	2	0	0	0	0	0	.222
Mike Powers, c	1	0	0	0	0	0	.000
Andy Coakley, p	2	0	0	0	0	1	.000
TOTALS	30	0	4	0	1	8	.157

	1	2	3	4	5	6	7	8	9		R	H	E
Giants	2	0	0	0	5	0	0	0	2		9	8	1
Athletics	0	0	0	0	0	0	0	0	0		0	4	4

E—Devlin, Murphy 3, Hartsel. DP—Giants 1 (Bresnahan to Dahlen), Athletics 2 (Coakley to Schreckengost to Davis; Seybold to Davis). LOB—Giants 4, Athletics 5. Scoring Position—Giants 4-for-9, Athletics 0-for-2. 2B—McGann (2). GDP—Devlin. SB—Browne 2 (2), Donlin (2), Dahlen (2), Devlin (3), Hartsel (1). CS—McGann (1), Mertes (1), Murphy (1).

Giants	IP	H	R	ER	BB	K	ERA
Christy Mathewson (W, 2-0)	9.0	4	0	0	1	8	0.00

Athletics	IP	H	R	ER	BB	K	ERA
Andy Coakley (L, 0-1)	9.0	8	9	2	5	2	2.00

HBP—Bresnahan by Coakley, Coakley by Mathewson. Time—1:55. Attendance—10,991. Umpires—HP, Sheridan. Bases, O'Day.

Game 4

Friday, October 13

Athletics	AB	R	H	RBI	BB	K	Avg
Topsy Hartsel, lf	1	0	0	0	2	0	.231
Bris Lord, cf	4	0	0	0	0	0	.125
Harry Davis, 1b	4	0	1	0	0	0	.188
Lave Cross, 3b	4	0	1	0	0	0	.133
Socks Seybold, rf	3	0	0	0	1	1	.077
Danny Murphy, 2b	3	0	1	0	0	0	.231
Monte Cross, ss	4	0	1	0	0	2	.143
Mike Powers, c	3	0	0	0	0	0	.000
Danny Hoffman, ph	1	0	0	0	0	1	.000
Eddie Plank, p	3	0	1	0	0	0	.167
TOTALS	30	0	5	0	3	4	.153

Giants	AB	R	H	RBI	BB	K	Avg
Roger Bresnahan, c	2	0	1	0	2	0	.250
George Browne, rf	4	0	2	0	0	1	.167
Mike Donlin, cf	3	0	0	0	0	0	.333
Dan McGann, 1b	3	0	0	0	0	2	.286
Sam Mertes, lf	4	1	0	0	0	2	.133
Bill Dahlen, ss	3	0	0	0	0	0	.000
Art Devlin, 3b	3	0	1	0	0	1	.286
Billy Gilbert, 2b	3	0	0	1	0	0	.214
Joe McGinnity, p	3	0	0	0	0	0	.000
TOTALS	28	1	4	1	2	6	.200

	1	2	3	4	5	6	7	8	9		R	H	E
Athletics	0	0	0	0	0	0	0	0	0		0	5	2
Giants	0	0	0	1	0	0	0	0	x		1	4	0

E—MCross, LCross. LOB—Athletics 8, Giants 7. Scoring Position—Athletics 0-for-7, Giants 0-for-8. 2B—Devlin (1). S—Hartsel, Murphy, Donlin, McGann. SB—Hartsel (2).

Athletics	IP	H	R	ER	BB	K	ERA
Eddie Plank (L, 0-2)	8.0	4	1	0	2	6	1.59

Giants	IP	H	R	ER	BB	K	ERA
Joe McGinnity (W, 1-1)	9.0	5	0	0	3	4	0.00

WP—Plank. Time—1:55. Attendance—13,598. Umpires—HP, O'Day. Bases, Sheridan.

Game 5

Saturday, October 14

Athletics	AB	R	H	RBI	BB	K	Avg
Topsy Hartsel, lf	4	0	2	0	0	1	.294
Bris Lord, cf	4	0	0	0	0	1	.100
Harry Davis, 1b	4	0	1	0	0	0	.200
Lave Cross, 3b	4	0	0	0	0	1	.105
Socks Seybold, rf	3	0	1	0	0	1	.125
Danny Murphy, 2b	3	0	0	0	0	0	.188
Monte Cross, ss	3	0	1	0	0	0	.176
Mike Powers, c	3	0	0	0	0	0	.143
Chief Bender, p	3	0	0	0	0	0	.000
TOTALS	31	0	6	0	0	4	.161

Giants	AB	R	H	RBI	BB	K	Avg
Roger Bresnahan, c	4	0	2	0	0	0	.313
George Browne, rf	4	0	1	1	0	0	.182
Mike Donlin, cf	4	0	0	0	0	1	.263
Dan McGann, 1b	3	0	0	0	0	2	.235
Sam Mertes, lf	2	1	1	0	1	0	.176
Bill Dahlen, ss	2	0	0	0	1	1	.000
Art Devlin, 3b	2	0	0	0	0	0	.250
Billy Gilbert, 2b	3	0	1	1	0	0	.235
Christy Mathewson, p	1	1	0	0	1	0	.250
TOTALS	25	2	5	2	3	4	.211

	1	2	3	4	5	6	7	8	9		R	H	E
Athletics	0	0	0	0	0	0	0	0	0		0	6	0
Giants	0	0	0	1	0	0	0	1	x		2	5	1

E—Mathewson. DP—Giants 1 (Dahlen to McGann). LOB—Athletics 4, Giants 4. Scoring Position—Athletics 0-for-1, Giants 0-for-6. 2B—Powers (1), Bresnahan (2). S—Devlin, Mathewson. GDP—Murphy. CS—MCross (1), Mertes (2).

Athletics	IP	H	R	ER	BB	K	ERA
Chief Bender (L, 1-1)	8.0	5	2	2	3	4	1.06

Giants	IP	H	R	ER	BB	K	ERA
Christy Mathewson (W, 3-0)	9.0	6	0	0	0	4	0.00

Time—1:35. Attendance—24,187. Umpires—HP, Sheridan. Bases, O'Day.

1905 World Series—Composite Statistics

Batting

Giants	G	AB	R	H	RBI	2B	3B	HR	BB	SO	SB	CS	Avg	OBP	Slg
Roger Bresnahan	5	16	3	5	1	2	0	0	4	0	1	0	.313	.500	.438
George Browne	5	22	2	4	1	0	0	0	0	2	2	0	.182	.182	.182
Bill Dahlen	5	15	1	0	1	0	0	0	3	2	2	1	.000	.167	.000
Art Devlin	5	16	0	4	1	1	0	0	1	3	3	0	.250	.294	.313
Mike Donlin	5	19	4	5	1	1	0	0	2	1	2	0	.263	.333	.316
Billy Gilbert	5	17	1	4	2	0	0	0	0	2	1	1	.235	.235	.235
Christy Mathewson	3	8	1	2	0	0	0	0	1	1	0	0	.250	.333	.250
Dan McGann	5	17	1	4	4	2	0	0	2	7	0	1	.235	.316	.353
Joe McGinnity	2	5	0	0	0	0	0	0	0	2	0	0	.000	.000	.000
Sam Mertes	5	17	2	3	2	1	0	0	2	5	0	2	.176	.263	.235
Sammy Strang	1	1	0	0	0	0	0	0	0	1	0	0	.000	.000	.000
Totals	5	153	15	31	13	7	0	0	15	26	11	6	.203	.282	.248

Batting

Athletics	G	AB	R	H	RBI	2B	3B	HR	BB	SO	SB	CS	Avg	OBP	Slg
Chief Bender	2	5	0	0	0	0	0	0	0	1	0	0	.000	.000	.000
Andy Coakley	1	2	0	0	0	0	0	0	0	1	0	0	.000	.333	.000
Lave Cross	5	19	0	2	0	0	0	0	1	1	0	0	.105	.150	.105
Monte Cross	5	17	0	3	0	0	0	0	0	7	0	1	.176	.176	.176
Harry Davis	5	20	0	4	0	1	0	0	0	1	0	0	.200	.200	.250
Topsy Hartsel	5	17	1	5	0	1	0	0	2	1	2	0	.294	.368	.353
Danny Hoffman	1	1	0	0	0	0	0	0	0	0	0	0	.000	.000	.000
Bris Lord	5	20	0	2	2	0	0	0	0	5	0	0	.100	.100	.100
Danny Murphy	5	16	0	3	0	1	0	0	0	2	0	1	.188	.188	.250
Eddie Plank	2	6	0	1	0	0	0	0	0	2	0	0	.167	.167	.167
Mike Powers	3	7	0	1	0	1	0	0	0	0	0	0	.143	.143	.286
Ossee Schreckengost	3	9	2	2	0	1	0	0	0	0	0	0	.222	.222	.333
Socks Seybold	5	16	0	2	0	0	0	0	2	3	0	0	.125	.222	.125
Totals	5	155	3	25	2	5	0	0	5	25	2	2	.161	.193	.194

Pitching

Giants	G	GS	CG	IP	H	R	ER	BB	SO	W-L	Sv-Op	Hld	ERA
Red Ames	1	0	0	1.0	1	0	0	1	1	0-0	0-0	0	0.00
Christy Mathewson	3	3	3	27.0	14	0	0	1	18	3-0	0-0	0	0.00
Joe McGinnity	2	2	1	17.0	10	3	0	3	6	1-1	0-0	0	0.00
Totals	5	5	4	45.0	25	3	0	5	25	4-1	0-0	0	0.00

Pitching

Athletics	G	GS	CG	IP	H	R	ER	BB	SO	W-L	Sv-Op	Hld	ERA
Chief Bender	2	2	2	17.0	9	2	2	6	13	1-1	0-0	0	1.06
Andy Coakley	1	1	1	9.0	8	9	2	5	2	0-1	0-0	0	2.00
Eddie Plank	2	2	2	17.0	14	4	3	4	11	0-2	0-0	0	1.59
Totals	5	5	5	43.0	31	15	7	15	26	1-4	0-0	0	1.47

Fielding

Giants	Pos	G	PO	Ast	E	DP	PB	FPct
Red Ames	p	1	0	1	0	0	—	1.000
Roger Bresnahan	c	5	27	8	1	1	0	.972
George Browne	rf	5	3	0	0	0	—	1.000
Bill Dahlen	ss	5	10	19	0	3	—	1.000
Art Devlin	3b	5	7	15	1	0	—	.957
Mike Donlin	cf	5	16	0	1	0	—	.941
Billy Gilbert	2b	5	9	15	0	0	—	1.000
Christy Mathewson	p	3	1	9	1	0	—	.909
Dan McGann	1b	5	59	1	1	2	—	.984
Joe McGinnity	p	2	0	6	0	0	—	1.000
Sam Mertes	lf	5	3	1	0	0	—	1.000
Totals		5	135	75	5	6	0	.977

Fielding

Athletics	Pos	G	PO	Ast	E	DP	PB	FPct
Chief Bender	p	2	0	4	0	0	—	1.000
Andy Coakley	p	1	0	2	0	1	—	1.000
Lave Cross	3b	5	5	6	1	0	—	.917
Monte Cross	ss	5	13	12	2	0	—	.926
Harry Davis	1b	5	52	1	0	2	—	1.000
Topsy Hartsel	lf	5	9	1	1	0	—	.909
Bris Lord	cf	5	12	0	0	0	—	1.000
Danny Murphy	2b	5	3	12	4	0	—	.789
Eddie Plank	p	2	1	6	0	0	—	1.000
Mike Powers	c	3	13	5	0	0	0	1.000
Ossee Schreckengost	c	3	17	4	0	1	0	1.000
Socks Seybold	rf	5	4	1	0	1	—	1.000
Totals		5	129	54	8	5	0	.958

1906 Chicago White Sox (AL) 4, Chicago Cubs (NL) 2

The Chicago White Sox upset the Cubs in a clash of crosstown rivals. Three Finger Brown and Nick Altrock were equally effective in Game 1, with Frank Isbell's seventh-inning single plating the decisive run for the White Sox. The Cubs' Ed Reulbach evened the Series with a one-hit, 7-1 win in Game 2. The White Sox' Ed Walsh tossed a two-hit shutout in Game 3 before the Cubs' ace, Brown, turned the same trick in Game 4. The "Hitless Wonders" shook off their nickname with some heavy hitting in the final two games. Frank Isbell smacked four doubles in the White Sox' 8-6 victory in Game 5, and Eddie Hahn enjoyed a four-hit game in Game 6 as the White Sox sent the Cubs to an 8-3 defeat.

Game 1

Tuesday, October 9

White Sox	AB	R	H	RBI	BB	K	Avg
Ed Hahn, rf	3	0	0	0	0	1	.000
Fielder Jones, cf	4	1	1	0	0	0	.250
Frank Isbell, 2b	4	0	1	1	0	1	.250
George Rohe, 3b	4	1	1	0	0	0	.250
Jiggs Donahue, 1b	4	0	0	0	0	3	.000
Patsy Dougherty, lf	3	0	0	0	0	0	.000
Billy Sullivan, c	3	0	0	0	0	0	.000
Lee Tannehill, ss	3	0	0	0	0	1	.000
Nick Altrock, p	2	0	1	0	1	1	.500
TOTALS	30	2	4	1	1	7	.133

Cubs	AB	R	H	RBI	BB	K	Avg
Solly Hofman, cf	3	0	0	0	0	1	.000
Jimmy Sheckard, lf	3	0	0	0	0	0	.000
Pat Moran, ph	1	0	0	0	0	0	.000
Wildfire Schulte, rf	4	0	1	0	0	0	.250
Frank Chance, 1b	4	0	1	0	0	0	.250
Harry Steinfeldt, 3b	4	0	0	0	0	0	.000
Joe Tinker, ss	3	0	0	0	0	0	.000
Johnny Evers, 2b	3	0	0	0	0	1	.000
Johnny Kling, c	2	1	1	0	1	0	.500
Three Finger Brown, p	2	0	1	0	0	1	.500
TOTALS	29	1	4	0	1	3	.138

	1	2	3	4	5	6	7	8	9		R	H	E
White Sox	0	0	0	0	1	1	0	0	0		2	4	1
Cubs	0	0	0	0	0	1	0	0	0		1	4	2

E—Brown, Kling, Isbell. LOB—White Sox 3, Cubs 4. Scoring Position—White Sox 2-for-10, Cubs 0-for-4. 3B—Rohe (1). S—Hahn, Hofman, Brown. SB—Isbell (1), Dougherty (1). CS—Hahn (1), Schulte (1).

White Sox	IP	H	R	ER	BB	K	ERA
Nick Altrock (W, 1-0)	9.0	4	1	1	1	3	1.00

Cubs	IP	H	R	ER	BB	K	ERA
Three Finger Brown (L, 0-1)	9.0	4	2	1	1	7	1.00

WP—Brown, Altrock. PB—Kling 2. Time—1:45. Attendance—12,693. Umpires—HP, Johnstone. Bases, O'Loughlin.

Game 2

Wednesday, October 10

Cubs	AB	R	H	RBI	BB	K	Avg
Solly Hofman, cf	4	0	1	1	1	0	.143
Jimmy Sheckard, lf	4	0	0	0	0	0	.000
Wildfire Schulte, rf	4	0	1	0	1	0	.250
Frank Chance, 1b	5	2	1	0	0	1	.222
Harry Steinfeldt, 3b	3	1	3	1	0	0	.429
Joe Tinker, ss	3	3	2	1	1	0	.333
Johnny Evers, 2b	4	1	1	0	0	0	.143
Johnny Kling, c	2	0	1	0	2	1	.500
Ed Reulbach, p	3	0	0	1	0	1	.000
TOTALS	32	7	10	4	5	3	.224

White Sox	AB	R	H	RBI	BB	K	Avg
Ed Hahn, rf	3	0	0	0	1	0	.000
Fielder Jones, cf	3	0	0	0	1	1	.143
Frank Isbell, 2b	4	0	0	0	0	0	.125
George Rohe, 3b	2	0	0	0	1	0	.167
Jiggs Donahue, 1b	3	0	1	0	1	0	.143
Patsy Dougherty, lf	2	1	0	0	2	0	.000
Billy Sullivan, c	4	0	0	0	0	1	.000
Lee Tannehill, ss	3	0	0	0	0	0	.000
Doc White, p	0	0	0	0	0	0	—
Babe Towne, ph	1	0	0	0	0	0	.000
Frank Owen, p	2	0	0	0	0	1	.000
TOTALS	27	1	1	0	6	3	.073

	1	2	3	4	5	6	7	8	9		R	H	E
Cubs	0	3	1	0	0	1	0	2	0		7	10	2
White Sox	0	0	0	0	1	0	0	0	0		1	1	3

E—Evers, Tinker, Sullivan 2, Isbell. DP—Cubs 2 (Sheckard to Kling; Evers to Chance). LOB—Cubs 6, White Sox 6. Scoring Position—Cubs 3-for-12, White Sox 0-for-7. 2B—Kling (1). S—Sheckard, Steinfeldt, Reulbach. GDP—Donahue. SB—Hofman (1), Chance 2 (2), Tinker 2 (2), Evers (1). CS—Schulte (2), Steinfeldt (1), Hahn (2).

Cubs	IP	H	R	ER	BB	K	ERA
Ed Reulbach (W, 1-0)	9.0	1	1	0	6	3	0.00

White Sox	IP	H	R	ER	BB	K	ERA
Doc White (L, 0-1)	3.0	4	4	0	2	1	0.00
Frank Owen	6.0	6	3	2	3	2	3.00

WP—Reulbach, Owen. HBP—Rohe by Reulbach. Time—1:58. Attendance—12,595. Umpires—HP, O'Loughlin. Bases, Johnstone.

Game 3

Thursday, October 11

White Sox	AB	R	H	RBI	BB	K	Avg
Ed Hahn, rf	2	0	0	0	0	0	.000
Bill O'Neill, pr-rf	1	1	0	0	0	0	.000
Fielder Jones, cf	4	0	1	0	0	1	.182
Frank Isbell, 2b	4	0	0	0	0	3	.083
George Rohe, 3b	3	0	1	3	1	0	.222
Jiggs Donahue, 1b	3	0	1	0	0	0	.200
Patsy Dougherty, lf	4	0	0	0	0	1	.000
Billy Sullivan, c	3	0	0	0	0	2	.000
Lee Tannehill, ss	3	1	1	0	0	1	.111
Ed Walsh, p	2	1	0	0	1	0	.000
TOTALS	29	3	4	3	2	9	.099

Cubs	AB	R	H	RBI	BB	K	Avg
Solly Hofman, cf	4	0	1	0	0	1	.182
Jimmy Sheckard, lf	4	0	0	0	0	2	.000
Wildfire Schulte, rf	4	0	1	0	0	3	.250
Frank Chance, 1b	2	0	0	0	1	0	.182
Harry Steinfeldt, 3b	3	0	0	0	0	0	.300
Joe Tinker, ss	3	0	0	0	0	2	.222
Johnny Evers, 2b	3	0	0	0	0	2	.100
Johnny Kling, c	3	0	0	0	0	1	.286
Jack Pfiester, p	2	0	0	0	0	1	.000
Doc Gessler, ph	1	0	0	0	0	0	.000
TOTALS	29	0	2	0	1	12	.179

	1	2	3	4	5	6	7	8	9		R	H	E
White Sox	0	0	0	0	3	0	0	0	0		3	4	1
Cubs	0	0	0	0	0	0	0	0	0		0	2	2

E—Pfiester, Tinker, Isbell. LOB—White Sox 4, Cubs 3. Scoring Position—White Sox 1-for-9, Cubs 0-for-3. 2B—Schulte (1). 3B—Rohe (2), Donahue (1). S—Donahue, Sullivan. SB—Rohe (1). CS—Jones (1), Donahue (1), Hofman (1).

White Sox	IP	H	R	ER	BB	K	ERA
Ed Walsh (W, 1-0)	9.0	2	0	0	1	12	0.00

Cubs	IP	H	R	ER	BB	K	ERA
Jack Pfiester (L, 0-1)	9.0	4	3	3	2	9	3.00

PB—Sullivan. HBP—Hahn by Pfiester. Time—2:10. Attendance—13,667. Umpires—HP, Johnstone. Bases, O'Loughlin.

Game 4

Friday, October 12

Cubs	AB	R	H	RBI	BB	K	Avg
Solly Hofman, cf	4	0	2	0	0	0	.267
Jimmy Sheckard, lf	3	0	0	0	1	0	.000
Wildfire Schulte, rf	4	0	0	0	0	0	.188
Frank Chance, 1b	4	1	2	0	0	0	.267
Harry Steinfeldt, 3b	2	0	1	0	0	0	.333
Joe Tinker, ss	1	0	0	0	0	0	.200
Johnny Evers, 2b	3	0	1	1	0	0	.154
Johnny Kling, c	3	0	0	0	0	0	.200
Three Finger Brown, p	3	0	1	0	0	2	.200
TOTALS	27	1	7	1	1	2	.209

White Sox	AB	R	H	RBI	BB	K	Avg
Ed Hahn, rf	4	0	1	0	0	0	.083
Fielder Jones, cf	3	0	0	0	1	0	.143
Frank Isbell, 2b	4	0	0	0	0	1	.063
George Rohe, 3b	3	0	0	0	0	0	.167
Jiggs Donahue, 1b	1	0	0	0	1	0	.182
Patsy Dougherty, lf	3	0	1	0	0	1	.083
George Davis, ss	3	0	0	0	0	1	.000
Billy Sullivan, c	3	0	0	0	0	2	.000
Nick Altrock, p	2	0	0	0	0	0	.250
Ed McFarland, ph	1	0	0	0	0	0	.000
TOTALS	27	0	2	0	2	5	.102

	1	2	3	4	5	6	7	8	9		R	H	E
Cubs	0	0	0	0	0	0	1	0	0		1	7	1
White Sox	0	0	0	0	0	0	0	0	0		0	2	1

E—Steinfeldt, Davis. DP—Cubs 1 (Kling to Evers), White Sox 1 (Altrock to Donahue to Sullivan). LOB—Cubs 5, White Sox 3. Scoring Position—Cubs 1-for-6, White Sox 0-for-3. 2B—Hofman (1). S—Steinfeldt 2, Tinker 3, Donahue. SB—Sheckard (1). CS—Schulte (3), Evers (1), Donahue (2), Davis (1).

Cubs	IP	H	R	ER	BB	K	ERA
Three Finger Brown (W, 1-1)	9.0	2	0	0	2	5	0.50

White Sox	IP	H	R	ER	BB	K	ERA
Nick Altrock (L, 1-1)	9.0	7	1	1	1	2	1.00

PB—Kling. Time—1:36. Attendance—18,385. Umpires—HP, O'Loughlin. Bases, Johnstone.

Game 5

Saturday, October 13

White Sox	AB	R	H	RBI	BB	K	Avg
Ed Hahn, rf	5	2	1	0	0	0	.118
Fielder Jones, cf	4	1	1	0	0	1	.167
Frank Isbell, 2b	5	3	4	2	0	1	.238
George Davis, ss	5	2	2	3	0	0	.250
George Rohe, 3b	4	0	3	1	1	1	.313
Jiggs Donahue, 1b	3	0	1	1	1	0	.214
Patsy Dougherty, lf	5	0	0	0	0	1	.059
Billy Sullivan, c	4	0	0	0	0	2	.000
Ed Walsh, p	2	0	0	0	2	2	.000
Doc White, p	0	0	0	0	0	0	—
TOTALS	37	8	12	7	4	8	.159

Cubs	AB	R	H	RBI	BB	K	Avg
Solly Hofman, cf	3	2	1	0	2	2	.278
Jimmy Sheckard, lf	4	0	0	0	0	2	.000
Wildfire Schulte, rf	5	1	3	2	0	0	.286
Frank Chance, 1b	4	0	1	0	0	0	.263
Harry Steinfeldt, 3b	5	1	1	1	0	0	.294
Joe Tinker, ss	4	1	0	0	1	0	.143
Johnny Evers, 2b	3	0	0	0	1	0	.125
Pat Moran, ph	1	0	0	0	0	0	.000
Johnny Kling, c	3	0	0	0	1	1	.154
Ed Reulbach, p	0	0	0	0	0	0	.000
Jack Pfiester, p	0	0	0	0	0	0	.000
Orval Overall, p	2	1	0	0	1	1	.000
TOTALS	34	6	6	3	6	6	.186

	1	2	3	4	5	6	7	8	9		R	H	E
White Sox	1	0	2	4	0	1	0	0	0		8	12	6
Cubs	3	0	0	1	0	2	0	0	0		6	6	0

E—Walsh, Rohe 2, Isbell 2, Davis. DP—Cubs 1 (Schulte to Evers to Kling). LOB—White Sox 8, Cubs 10. Scoring Position—White Sox 6-for-15, Cubs 2-for-17. 2B—Isbell 4 (4), Davis 2 (2), Rohe (1), Donahue (1), Schulte (2), Chance (1), Steinfeldt (1). S—Jones, Sheckard, Reulbach. SB—Davis (1), Dougherty (2), Tinker (3), Evers (2).

White Sox	IP	H	R	ER	BB	K	ERA
Ed Walsh (W, 2-0)	6.0	5	6	2	5	5	1.20
Doc White (S, 1)	3.0	1	0	0	1	1	0.00

Cubs	IP	H	R	ER	BB	K	ERA
Ed Reulbach	2.0	5	3	3	2	1	2.45
Jack Pfiester (L, 0-2)	1.1	3	4	4	1	2	6.10
Orval Overall	5.2	4	1	1	1	5	1.59

Reulbach pitched to two batters in the 3rd. Walsh pitched to one batter in the 7th.

WP—Walsh, Overall. HBP—Donahue by Pfiester, Chance by Walsh. Time—2:40. Attendance—23,257. Umpires—HP, Johnstone. Bases, O'Loughlin.

Game 6

Sunday, October 14

Cubs	AB	R	H	RBI	BB	K	Avg
Solly Hofman, cf	5	1	2	1	0	1	.304
Jimmy Sheckard, lf	3	0	0	1	1	0	.000
Wildfire Schulte, rf	5	0	1	1	0	0	.269
Frank Chance, 1b	2	0	0	0	1	0	.238
Harry Steinfeldt, 3b	3	0	0	0	1	0	.250
Joe Tinker, ss	4	0	1	0	0	0	.167
Johnny Evers, 2b	4	1	1	0	0	0	.150
Johnny Kling, c	4	1	1	0	0	0	.176
Three Finger Brown, p	1	0	0	0	0	1	.333
Orval Overall, p	2	0	1	0	0	0	.250
Doc Gessler, ph	0	0	0	0	1	0	.000
TOTALS	33	3	7	3	4	2	.203

White Sox	AB	R	H	RBI	BB	K	Avg
Ed Hahn, rf	5	2	4	0	0	0	.273
Fielder Jones, cf	3	2	0	0	1	0	.143
Frank Isbell, 2b	5	1	3	1	0	0	.308
George Davis, ss	5	2	2	3	0	0	.308
George Rohe, 3b	5	1	2	0	0	0	.333
Jiggs Donahue, 1b	4	0	2	3	0	1	.278
Patsy Dougherty, lf	3	0	1	1	1	0	.100
Billy Sullivan, c	4	0	0	0	0	2	.000
Doc White, p	3	0	0	0	1	0	.000
TOTALS	37	8	14	8	3	3	.212

	1	2	3	4	5	6	7	8	9		R	H	E
Cubs	1	0	0	0	1	0	0	0	1		3	7	0
White Sox	3	4	0	0	0	0	0	1	x		8	14	3

E—Dougherty, Rohe, Donahue. DP—White Sox 1 (Davis to Donahue). LOB—Cubs 9, White Sox 9. Scoring Position—Cubs 2-for-13, White Sox 7-for-13. 2B—Schulte (3), Evers (1), Davis (3), Donahue (2), Overall (1). S—Sheckard, Jones. GDP—Kling. SB—Rohe (2). CS—Chance (1).

Cubs	IP	H	R	ER	BB	K	ERA
Three Finger Brown (L, 1-2)	1.2	8	7	7	1	0	3.66
Orval Overall	6.1	6	1	1	2	3	1.50

White Sox	IP	H	R	ER	BB	K	ERA
Doc White (W, 1-1)	9.0	7	3	3	4	2	1.80

HBP—Chance by White. Time—1:55. Attendance—19,249. Umpires—HP, O'Loughlin. Bases, Johnstone.

1906 World Series—Composite Statistics

Batting

White Sox	G	AB	R	H	RBI	2B	3B	HR	BB	SO	SB	CS	Avg	OBP	Slg
Nick Altrock	2	4	0	1	0	0	0	0	1	1	0	0	.250	.400	.250
George Davis	3	13	4	4	6	3	0	0	0	1	1	1	.308	.308	.538
Jiggs Donahue	6	18	0	5	4	2	1	0	3	4	0	2	.278	.409	.500
Patsy Dougherty	6	20	1	2	1	0	0	0	3	3	2	0	.100	.217	.100
Ed Hahn	6	22	4	6	0	0	0	0	1	1	0	2	.273	.333	.273
Frank Isbell	6	26	4	8	4	4	0	0	0	6	1	0	.308	.308	.462
Fielder Jones	6	21	4	3	0	0	0	0	3	3	0	1	.143	.250	.143
Ed McFarland	1	1	0	0	0	0	0	0	0	0	0	0	.000	.000	.000
Bill O'Neill	1	1	1	0	0	0	0	0	0	0	0	0	.000	.000	.000
Frank Owen	1	2	0	0	0	0	0	0	0	1	0	0	.000	.000	.000
George Rohe	6	21	2	7	4	1	2	0	3	1	2	0	.333	.440	.571
Billy Sullivan	6	21	0	0	0	0	0	0	0	9	0	0	.000	.000	.000
Lee Tannehill	3	9	1	1	0	0	0	0	2	2	0	0	.111	.111	.111
Babe Towne	1	1	0	0	0	0	0	0	0	0	0	0	.000	.000	.000
Ed Walsh	2	4	1	0	0	0	0	0	3	3	0	0	.000	.429	.000
Doc White	3	3	0	0	0	0	0	0	1	0	0	0	.000	.250	.000
Totals	6	187	22	37	19	10	3	0	18	35	6	6	.198	.279	.283

Cubs	G	AB	R	H	RBI	2B	3B	HR	BB	SO	SB	CS	Avg	OBP	Slg
Three Finger Brown	3	6	0	2	0	0	0	0	0	4	0	0	.333	.333	.333
Frank Chance	6	21	3	5	0	1	0	0	2	1	2	1	.238	.360	.286
Johnny Evers	6	20	2	3	1	1	0	0	1	3	2	1	.150	.190	.200
Doc Gessler	2	1	0	0	0	0	0	0	1	0	0	0	.000	.500	.000
Solly Hofman	6	23	3	7	2	1	0	0	3	5	1	1	.304	.385	.348
Johnny Kling	6	17	2	3	0	1	0	0	4	3	0	0	.176	.333	.235
Pat Moran	2	2	0	0	0	0	0	0	0	0	0	0	.000	.000	.000
Orval Overall	2	4	1	1	0	1	0	0	1	1	0	0	.250	.400	.500
Jack Pfiester	2	2	0	0	0	0	0	0	0	1	0	0	.000	.000	.000
Ed Reulbach	2	3	0	0	1	0	0	0	0	1	0	0	.000	.000	.000
Wildfire Schulte	6	26	1	7	3	3	0	0	1	3	0	3	.269	.296	.385
Jimmy Sheckard	6	21	0	0	0	0	0	0	2	4	1	0	.000	.087	.000
Harry Steinfeldt	6	20	2	5	2	1	0	0	1	0	0	1	.250	.286	.300
Joe Tinker	6	18	4	3	1	0	0	0	2	2	3	0	.167	.250	.167
Totals	6	184	18	36	11	9	0	0	18	28	9	7	.196	.275	.245

Pitching

White Sox	G	GS	CG	IP	H	R	ER	BB	SO	W-L	Sv-Op	Hld	ERA
Nick Altrock	2	2	2	18.0	11	2	2	2	5	1-1	0-0	0	1.00
Frank Owen	1	0	0	6.0	6	3	2	3	2	0-0	0-0	0	3.00
Ed Walsh	2	2	1	15.0	7	6	2	6	17	2-0	0-0	0	1.20
Doc White	3	2	1	15.0	12	7	3	7	4	1-1	1-1	0	1.80
Totals	6	6	4	54.0	36	18	9	18	28	4-2	1-1	0	1.50

Cubs	G	GS	CG	IP	H	R	ER	BB	SO	W-L	Sv-Op	Hld	ERA
Three Finger Brown	3	3	2	19.2	14	9	8	4	12	1-2	0-0	0	3.66
Orval Overall	2	0	0	12.0	10	2	2	3	8	0-0	0-0	0	1.50
Jack Pfiester	2	1	1	10.1	7	7	7	3	11	0-2	0-0	0	6.10
Ed Reulbach	2	2	1	11.0	6	4	3	8	4	1-0	0-0	0	2.45
Totals	6	6	4	53.0	37	22	20	18	35	2-4	0-0	0	3.40

Fielding

White Sox	Pos	G	PO	Ast	E	DP	PB	FPct
Nick Altrock	p	2	6	11	0	1	—	1.000
George Davis	ss	3	7	15	2	1	—	.917
Jiggs Donahue	1b	6	80	8	1	2	—	.989
Patsy Dougherty	lf	6	4	0	1	0	—	.800
Ed Hahn	rf	6	3	0	0	0	—	1.000
Frank Isbell	2b	6	11	16	5	0	—	.844
Fielder Jones	cf	6	9	0	0	0	—	1.000
Bill O'Neill	rf	1	1	0	0	0	—	1.000
Frank Owen	p	1	0	4	0	0	—	1.000
George Rohe	3b	6	4	17	3	0	—	.875
Billy Sullivan	c	6	35	10	2	1	1	.957
Lee Tannehill	ss	3	1	8	0	0	—	1.000
Ed Walsh	p	2	0	4	1	0	—	.800
Doc White	p	3	1	3	0	0	—	1.000
Totals		6	162	96	15	5	1	.945

Cubs	Pos	G	PO	Ast	E	DP	PB	FPct
Three Finger Brown	p	3	1	11	1	0	—	.923
Frank Chance	1b	6	60	2	0	1	—	1.000
Johnny Evers	2b	6	14	19	1	3	—	.971
Solly Hofman	cf	6	10	1	0	0	—	1.000
Johnny Kling	c	6	45	9	1	3	3	.982
Orval Overall	p	2	0	2	0	0	—	1.000
Jack Pfiester	p	2	0	2	1	0	—	.667
Ed Reulbach	p	2	0	4	0	0	—	1.000
Wildfire Schulte	rf	6	5	1	0	1	—	1.000
Jimmy Sheckard	lf	6	10	1	0	1	—	1.000
Harry Steinfeldt	3b	6	4	8	1	0	—	.923
Joe Tinker	ss	6	10	20	2	0	—	.938
Totals		6	159	80	7	9	3	.972

1907 Chicago Cubs (NL) 4, Detroit Tigers (AL) 0, 1 Tie

After an opening-game tie, the Chicago Cubs completely shut down the Detroit Tigers' attack, beating them four times without a defeat. Detroit nearly got its only win in the opener, taking a 3-1 lead into the bottom of the ninth before the Cubs tied it on an RBI groundout and a run-scoring passed ball. After 12 innings, the game was called on account of darkness, tied 3-3. In Game 2, the Tigers pulled the hidden ball trick on Jimmy Slagle in the first inning, but he got his revenge by singling in the go-ahead run and coming around to score another in the fourth, as Jack Pfiester bested George Mullin, 3-1. The next day, Ed Reulbach beat Detroit, 5-1. Detroit held a 1-0 lead in the fifth inning of Game 4 when rain halted play for 15 minutes, and when the game resumed, Detroit pitcher Bill Donovan's arm stiffened, and the Cubs prevailed, 6-1. Three Finger Brown blanked Detroit in the finale to clinch it for the Cubs.

Game 1

Tuesday, October 8

Tigers	AB	R	H	RBI	BB	K	Avg
Davy Jones, lf	5	1	3	0	1	0	.600
Germany Schaefer, 2b	6	1	1	0	0	0	.167
Sam Crawford, cf	5	1	3	2	0	1	.600
Ty Cobb, rf	5	0	0	0	0	0	.000
Claude Rossman, 1b	4	0	0	1	1	0	.000
Bill Coughlin, 3b	5	0	0	0	0	2	.000
Boss Schmidt, c	5	0	2	0	0	0	.400
Charley O'Leary, ss	4	0	0	0	0	1	.000
Wild Bill Donovan, p	5	0	0	0	0	3	.000
TOTALS	44	3	9	3	2	7	.205

Cubs	AB	R	H	RBI	BB	K	Avg
Jimmy Slagle, cf	6	0	2	0	0	0	.333
Jimmy Sheckard, lf	5	0	1	0	0	2	.200
Frank Chance, 1b	4	2	1	0	2	2	.250
Harry Steinfeldt, 3b	3	1	1	0	0	0	.333
Johnny Kling, c	4	0	2	1	1	1	.500
Johnny Evers, 2b-ss	4	0	2	0	0	0	.500
Wildfire Schulte, rf	5	0	1	1	0	1	.200
Joe Tinker, ss	3	0	0	0	0	3	.000
Del Howard, ph	1	0	0	0	0	1	.000
Heinie Zimmerman, 2b	1	0	0	0	0	1	.000
Orval Overall, p	3	0	0	0	0	1	.000
Pat Moran, ph	0	0	0	0	0	0	.000
Ed Reulbach, p	2	0	0	0	0	0	.000
TOTALS	41	3	10	2	3	12	.244

	1	2	3	4	5	6	7	8	9	10	11	12	R	H	E
Tigers	0	0	0	0	0	0	0	3	0	0	0	0	3	9	3
Cubs	0	0	0	1	0	0	0	0	2	0	0	0	3	10	5

E—Schmidt 2, Evers 2, Tinker, Kling, Coughlin, Steinfeldt. DP—Tigers 1 (Schaefer to Rossman), Cubs 1 (Evers to Tinker). LOB—Tigers 8, Cubs 9. Scoring Position—Tigers 3-for-15, Cubs 2-for-13. S—O'Leary, Steinfeldt, Evers. SB—Jones 2 (2), Slagle 2 (2), Sheckard (1), Chance (1), Steinfeldt (1), Evers (1), Howard (1). CS—Schaefer (1), Slagle (1), Evers (1).

Tigers	IP	H	R	ER	BB	K	ERA
Wild Bill Donovan	12.0	10	3	1	3	12	0.75

Cubs	IP	H	R	ER	BB	K	ERA
Orval Overall	9.0	9	3	1	2	5	1.00
Ed Reulbach	3.0	0	0	0	0	2	0.00

PB—Schmidt. HBP—Steinfeldt by Donovan, Sheckard by Donovan. Time—2:40. Attendance—24,377. Umpires—HP, O'Day. Bases, Sheridan.

Game 2

Wednesday, October 9

Tigers	AB	R	H	RBI	BB	K	Avg
Davy Jones, lf	4	0	2	0	0	0	.556
Germany Schaefer, 2b	4	0	1	0	0	0	.200
Sam Crawford, cf	4	0	0	0	0	1	.333
Ty Cobb, rf	3	0	0	0	0	0	.125
Claude Rossman, 1b	4	1	3	0	0	0	.375
Bill Coughlin, 3b	4	0	0	0	0	1	.000
Fred Payne, c	4	0	1	1	0	0	.250
Charley O'Leary, ss	2	0	1	0	1	0	.167
George Mullin, p	3	0	0	0	0	1	.000
TOTALS	32	1	9	1	1	3	.242

Cubs	AB	R	H	RBI	BB	K	Avg
Jimmy Slagle, cf	3	1	2	1	1	1	.444
Jimmy Sheckard, lf	3	0	1	1	0	1	.250
Frank Chance, 1b	3	0	1	0	1	0	.286
Harry Steinfeldt, 3b	3	0	0	0	0	1	.167
Johnny Kling, c	4	1	1	0	0	1	.375
Johnny Evers, 2b	4	0	2	0	0	1	.500
Wildfire Schulte, rf	4	0	1	0	0	1	.222
Joe Tinker, ss	2	1	1	1	1	0	.111
Jack Pfiester, p	2	0	0	0	0	1	.000
TOTALS	28	3	9	3	3	6	.306

	1	2	3	4	5	6	7	8	9	R	H	E
Tigers	0	1	0	0	0	0	0	0	0	1	9	1
Cubs	0	1	0	2	0	0	0	0	x	3	9	1

E—Payne, Tinker. DP—Tigers 1 (Crawford to Schaefer), Cubs 2 (Tinker to Chance; Tinker to Chance). LOB—Tigers 6, Cubs 7. Scoring Position—Tigers 1-for-6, Cubs 3-for-12. 2B—Sheckard (1). 3B—Rossman (1). S—Sheckard, Pfiester. GDP—Cobb. SB—Payne (1), Slagle 2 (4), Chance (2), Evers (2). CS—Jones (1), Schaefer (2), O'Leary (1), Sheckard (1).

Tigers	IP	H	R	ER	BB	K	ERA
George Mullin (L, 0-1)	8.0	9	3	3	3	6	3.38

Cubs	IP	H	R	ER	BB	K	ERA
Jack Pfiester (W, 1-0)	9.0	9	1	1	1	3	1.00

HBP—Cobb by Pfiester, Steinfeldt by Mullin. Time—2:13. Attendance—21,901. Umpires—HP, Sheridan. Bases, O'Day.

Game 3

Thursday, October 10

Tigers	AB	R	H	RBI	BB	K	Avg
Davy Jones, lf	3	0	0	0	1	0	.417
Germany Schaefer, 2b	4	0	1	0	0	0	.214
Sam Crawford, cf	4	0	1	1	0	0	.308
Ty Cobb, rf	4	0	1	0	0	1	.167
Claude Rossman, 1b	4	0	2	0	0	0	.417
Bill Coughlin, 3b	3	0	0	0	1	0	.000
Boss Schmidt, c	3	0	0	0	1	0	.250
Charley O'Leary, ss	4	0	0	0	0	1	.100
Ed Siever, p	1	0	0	0	0	0	.000
Ed Killian, p	2	1	1	0	0	0	.500
TOTALS	32	1	6	1	3	2	.240

Cubs	AB	R	H	RBI	BB	K	Avg
Jimmy Slagle, cf	4	0	0	0	1	0	.308
Jimmy Sheckard, lf	4	0	1	0	0	1	.250
Frank Chance, 1b	4	1	1	0	0	0	.273
Harry Steinfeldt, 3b	3	1	2	1	1	0	.333
Johnny Kling, c	3	1	1	0	0	0	.364
Johnny Evers, 2b	4	0	3	1	0	0	.583
Wildfire Schulte, rf	4	1	1	1	0	0	.231
Joe Tinker, ss	4	1	0	0	0	0	.111
Ed Reulbach, p	3	0	1	1	0	0	.200
TOTALS	33	5	10	4	1	2	.305

	1	2	3	4	5	6	7	8	9	R	H	E
Tigers	0	0	0	0	0	1	0	0	0	1	6	1
Cubs	0	1	0	3	1	0	0	0	x	5	10	1

E—Evers, Jones. DP—Cubs 2 (Tinker to Evers to Chance; Steinfeldt to Evers to Chance). LOB—Tigers 7, Cubs 6. Scoring Position—Tigers 1-for-7, Cubs 4-for-8. 2B—Sheckard (2), Chance (1), Steinfeldt (1), Evers 2 (2). S—Kling. GDP—Schaefer.

Tigers	IP	H	R	ER	BB	K	ERA
Ed Siever (L, 0-1)	4.0	7	4	2	0	1	4.50
Ed Killian	4.0	3	1	1	1	1	2.25

Cubs	IP	H	R	ER	BB	K	ERA
Ed Reulbach (W, 1-0)	9.0	6	1	1	3	2	0.75

Time—1:35. Attendance—13,114. Umpires—HP, O'Day. Bases, Sheridan.

Game 4

Friday, October 11

Cubs	AB	R	H	RBI	BB	K	Avg
Jimmy Slagle, cf	5	1	1	2	0	0	.278
Jimmy Sheckard, lf	5	0	2	1	0	0	.294
Frank Chance, 1b	3	0	0	0	0	0	.214
Harry Steinfeldt, 3b	4	0	2	0	0	1	.385
Johnny Kling, c	4	0	0	0	0	2	.267
Johnny Evers, 2b	4	1	0	0	0	1	.438
Wildfire Schulte, rf	3	2	1	0	1	0	.250
Joe Tinker, ss	1	2	0	0	1	0	.100
Orval Overall, p	2	0	1	2	0	0	.200
TOTALS	31	6	7	5	2	4	.282

Tigers	AB	R	H	RBI	BB	K	Avg
Davy Jones, lf	2	0	0	0	1	0	.357
Germany Schaefer, 2b	3	0	0	0	0	2	.176
Sam Crawford, cf	4	0	0	0	0	1	.235
Ty Cobb, rf	4	1	1	0	0	0	.188
Claude Rossman, 1b	4	0	1	1	0	0	.375
Bill Coughlin, 3b	4	3	0	0	0	1	.188
Boss Schmidt, c	3	0	0	0	1	1	.182
Charley O'Leary, ss	4	0	0	0	0	1	.071
Wild Bill Donovan, p	3	0	0	0	0	0	.000
TOTALS	31	1	5	1	2	6	.209

	1	2	3	4	5	6	7	8	9	R	H	E
Cubs	0	0	0	0	2	0	3	0	1	6	7	2
Tigers	0	0	0	1	0	0	0	0	0	1	5	2

E—O'Leary 2, Tinker, Slagle. DP—Cubs 1 (Tinker). LOB—Cubs 5, Tigers 7. Scoring Position—Cubs 3-for-7, Tigers 1-for-8. 3B—Cobb (1). S—Tinker 2, Overall 2, Jones, Schaefer. SB—Slagle (5), Chance (3). CS—Sheckard (2), Chance (1).

Cubs	IP	H	R	ER	BB	K	ERA
Orval Overall (W, 1-0)	9.0	5	1	1	2	6	1.00

Tigers	IP	H	R	ER	BB	K	ERA
Wild Bill Donovan (L, 0-1)	9.0	7	6	3	2	4	1.71

HBP—Chance by Donovan. Time—1:45. Attendance—11,306. Umpires—HP, Sheridan. Bases, O'Day.

Game 5

Saturday, October 12

Cubs	AB	R	H	RBI	BB	K	Avg
Jimmy Slagle, cf	4	1	1	1	1	1	.273
Jimmy Sheckard, lf	4	0	0	0	0	0	.238
Del Howard, 1b	4	0	1	0	0	1	.200
Harry Steinfeldt, 3b	4	0	3	1	0	0	.471
Johnny Kling, c	4	0	0	0	0	0	.211
Johnny Evers, 2b	4	1	0	0	0	0	.350
Wildfire Schulte, rf	4	0	1	0	0	0	.250
Joe Tinker, ss	3	0	1	0	1	0	.154
Three Finger Brown, p	3	0	0	0	1	0	.000
TOTALS	34	2	7	2	3	2	.271

Tigers	AB	R	H	RBI	BB	K	Avg
Davy Jones, lf	3	0	1	0	1	0	.353
Germany Schaefer, 2b	4	0	0	0	0	1	.143
Sam Crawford, cf	4	0	1	0	0	0	.238
Ty Cobb, rf	4	0	1	0	0	2	.200
Claude Rossman, 1b	4	0	2	0	0	0	.400
Fred Payne, pr	0	0	0	0	0	0	.250
Bill Coughlin, 3b	4	0	2	0	0	0	.250
Jimmy Archer, c	3	0	0	0	0	1	.000
Boss Schmidt, ph	1	0	0	0	0	0	.167
Charley O'Leary, ss	3	0	0	0	0	0	.059
George Mullin, p	3	0	0	0	0	0	.000
TOTALS	33	0	7	0	1	4	.217

	1	2	3	4	5	6	7	8	9	R	H	E
Cubs	1	1	0	0	0	0	0	0	0	2	7	1
Tigers	0	0	0	0	0	0	0	0	0	0	7	2

E—Schulte, Rossman, Coughlin. LOB—Cubs 8, Tigers 7. Scoring Position—Cubs 1-for-6, Tigers 1-for-9. 2B—Crawford (1). 3B—Steinfeldt (1). SB—Slagle (6), Evers (3), Tinker (1), Jones (3), Rossman (1), Coughlin (1). CS—Slagle (2), Cobb (1).

Cubs	IP	H	R	ER	BB	K	ERA
Three Finger Brown (W, 1-0)	9.0	7	0	0	1	4	0.00

Tigers	IP	H	R	ER	BB	K	ERA
George Mullin (L, 0-2)	9.0	7	2	1	3	2	2.12

Time—1:42. Attendance—7,370. Umpires—HP, O'Day. Bases, Sheridan.

1907 World Series—Composite Statistics

Batting

Cubs	G	AB	R	H	RBI	2B	3B	HR	BB	SO	SB	CS	Avg	OBP	Slg
Three Finger Brown	1	3	0	0	0	0	0	0	0	1	0	0	.000	.250	.000
Frank Chance	4	14	3	3	0	1	0	0	3	2	3	1	.214	.389	.286
Johnny Evers	5	20	2	7	1	2	0	0	0	1	3	1	.350	.350	.450
Del Howard	2	5	0	1	0	0	0	0	0	2	1	0	.200	.200	.200
Johnny Kling	5	19	2	4	1	0	0	0	1	4	0	0	.211	.250	.211
Pat Moran	1	0	0	0	0	0	0	0	0	0	0	0	—	—	—
Orval Overall	2	5	0	1	2	0	0	0	0	1	0	0	.200	.200	.200
Jack Pfiester	1	2	0	0	0	0	0	0	0	1	0	0	.000	.000	.000
Ed Reulbach	2	5	0	1	1	0	0	0	0	0	0	0	.200	.200	.200
Wildfire Schulte	5	20	3	5	2	0	0	0	1	2	0	0	.250	.286	.250
Jimmy Sheckard	5	21	0	5	2	2	0	0	0	4	1	2	.238	.273	.333
Jimmy Slagle	5	22	3	6	4	0	0	0	2	3	6	2	.273	.333	.273
Harry Steinfeldt	5	17	2	8	2	1	1	0	1	2	1	0	.471	.550	.647
Joe Tinker	5	13	4	2	1	0	0	0	3	3	1	0	.154	.313	.154
Heinie Zimmerman	1	1	0	0	0	0	0	0	0	1	0	0	.000	.000	.000
Totals	**5**	**167**	**19**	**43**	**16**	**6**	**1**	**0**	**12**	**26**	**16**	**6**	**.257**	**.322**	**.305**

Batting

Tigers	G	AB	R	H	RBI	2B	3B	HR	BB	SO	SB	CS	Avg	OBP	Slg
Jimmy Archer	1	3	0	0	0	0	0	0	0	1	0	0	.000	.000	.000
Ty Cobb	5	20	1	4	0	0	1	0	0	3	0	1	.200	.238	.300
Bill Coughlin	5	20	0	5	0	0	0	0	1	4	1	0	.250	.286	.250
Sam Crawford	5	21	1	5	3	1	0	0	0	3	0	0	.238	.238	.286
Wild Bill Donovan	2	8	0	0	0	0	0	0	0	3	0	0	.000	.000	.000
Davy Jones	5	17	1	6	0	0	0	0	4	0	3	1	.353	.476	.353
Ed Killian	1	2	1	1	0	0	0	0	0	0	0	0	.500	.500	.500
George Mullin	2	6	0	0	0	0	0	0	0	1	0	0	.000	.000	.000
Charley O'Leary	5	17	0	1	0	0	0	0	1	3	0	1	.059	.111	.059
Fred Payne	2	4	0	1	0	0	0	0	0	0	1	0	.250	.250	.250
Claude Rossman	5	20	1	8	2	0	1	0	1	0	1	0	.400	.429	.500
Germany Schaefer	5	21	1	3	0	0	0	0	0	3	0	2	.143	.143	.143
Boss Schmidt	4	12	0	2	0	0	0	0	2	1	0	0	.167	.286	.167
Ed Siever	1	1	0	0	0	0	0	0	0	0	0	0	.000	.000	.000
Totals	**5**	**172**	**6**	**36**	**6**	**1**	**2**	**0**	**9**	**22**	**6**	**5**	**.209**	**.253**	**.238**

Pitching

Cubs	G	GS	CG	IP	H	R	ER	BB	SO	W-L	Sv-Op	Hld	ERA
Three Finger Brown	1	1	1	9.0	7	0	0	1	4	1-0	0-0	0	0.00
Orval Overall	2	2	1	18.0	14	4	2	4	11	1-0	0-0	0	1.00
Jack Pfiester	1	1	1	9.0	9	1	1	1	3	1-0	0-0	0	1.00
Ed Reulbach	2	1	1	12.0	6	1	1	3	4	1-0	0-0	0	0.75
Totals	**5**	**5**	**4**	**48.0**	**36**	**6**	**4**	**9**	**22**	**4-0**	**0-0**	**0**	**0.75**

Pitching

Tigers	G	GS	CG	IP	H	R	ER	BB	SO	W-L	Sv-Op	Hld	ERA
Wild Bill Donovan	2	2	2	21.0	17	9	4	5	16	0-1	0-0	0	1.71
Ed Killian	1	0	0	4.0	3	1	1	1	1	0-0	0-0	0	2.25
George Mullin	2	2	2	17.0	16	5	4	6	8	0-2	0-0	0	2.12
Ed Siever	1	1	0	4.0	7	4	2	0	1	0-1	0-0	0	4.50
Totals	**5**	**5**	**4**	**46.0**	**43**	**19**	**11**	**12**	**26**	**0-4**	**0-0**	**0**	**2.15**

Fielding

Cubs	Pos	G	PO	Ast	E	DP	PB	FPct
Three Finger Brown	p	1	1	1	0	0	—	1.000
Frank Chance	1b	4	44	1	0	3	—	1.000
Johnny Evers	2b	5	11	12	2	2	—	.920
	ss	1	0	0	1	0	—	.000
Del Howard	1b	1	10	1	0	0	—	1.000
Johnny Kling	c	5	25	10	1	0	0	.972
Orval Overall	p	2	0	7	0	0	—	1.000
Jack Pfiester	p	1	0	0	0	0	—	—
Ed Reulbach	p	2	1	3	0	0	—	1.000
Wildfire Schulte	rf	5	4	2	1	0	—	.857
Jimmy Sheckard	lf	5	10	0	0	0	—	1.000
Jimmy Slagle	cf	5	13	0	1	0	—	.929
Harry Steinfeldt	3b	5	9	6	1	1	—	.938
Joe Tinker	ss	5	16	23	3	5	—	.929
Heinie Zimmerman	2b	1	0	2	0	0	—	1.000
Totals		**5**	**144**	**68**	**10**	**11**	**0**	**.955**

Fielding

Tigers	Pos	G	PO	Ast	E	DP	PB	FPct
Jimmy Archer	c	1	4	1	0	0	0	1.000
Ty Cobb	rf	5	10	0	0	0	—	1.000
Bill Coughlin	3b	5	9	7	2	0	—	.889
Sam Crawford	cf	5	6	2	0	1	—	1.000
Wild Bill Donovan	p	2	2	3	0	0	—	1.000
Davy Jones	lf	5	10	2	1	0	—	.923
Ed Killian	p	1	0	0	0	0	—	—
George Mullin	p	2	1	5	0	0	—	1.000
Charley O'Leary	ss	5	12	15	2	0	—	.931
Fred Payne	c	1	6	1	1	0	0	.875
Claude Rossman	1b	5	47	4	1	1	—	.981
Germany Schaefer	2b	5	11	18	0	2	—	1.000
Boss Schmidt	c	3	20	6	2	0	1	.929
Ed Siever	p	1	0	0	0	0	—	—
Totals		**5**	**138**	**64**	**9**	**4**	**1**	**.957**

1908 Chicago Cubs (NL) 4, Detroit Tigers (AL) 1

The Chicago Cubs, who had fought so hard to hold off the New York Giants for the National League pennant, defeated the American League champion Detroit Tigers with relative ease. The Cubs won Game 1, 10-6, with a five-run ninth-inning outburst. The contest was played under intermittent showers and was marred by sloppy fielding on both sides. Orval Overall and Wild Bill Donovan matched goose eggs for seven innings before Joe Tinker's two-run homer sent the Cubs on their way to a 6-1 victory in Game 2. The Tigers got their only win in Game 3, an 8-3 decision, behind George Mullin's sharp pitching and Ty Cobb's four-hit game. Three Finger Brown put the Cubs up three games to one with a four-hit shutout in Game 4, and Overall iced it with a three-hit whitewash in Game 5.

Game 1

Saturday, October 10

Cubs	AB	R	H	RBI	BB	K	Avg
Jimmy Sheckard, lf	6	1	3	0	0	0	.500
Johnny Evers, 2b	4	1	2	0	0	1	.500
Wildfire Schulte, rf	4	2	2	1	0	0	.500
Frank Chance, 1b	4	2	1	0	1	0	.250
Harry Steinfeldt, 3b	3	2	2	2	1	0	.667
Solly Hofman, cf	4	1	1	2	1	0	.250
Joe Tinker, ss	5	1	2	2	0	0	.400
Johnny Kling, c	3	0	1	2	1	0	.333
Ed Reulbach, p	3	0	0	0	0	1	.000
Orval Overall, p	1	0	0	0	0	1	.000
Three Finger Brown, p	0	0	0	0	0	0	—
TOTALS	37	10	14	9	4	3	.378

Tigers	AB	R	H	RBI	BB	K	Avg
Matty McIntyre, lf	3	1	2	0	1	0	.667
Charley O'Leary, ss	4	0	1	0	0	1	.250
Ira Thomas, ph	1	0	1	0	0	0	1.000
George Winter, pr	0	0	0	0	0	0	—
Sam Crawford, cf	4	1	0	0	1	1	.000
Ty Cobb, rf	4	2	2	1	0	0	.500
Claude Rossman, 1b	4	1	2	1	0	1	.500
Germany Schaefer, 3b	3	0	0	0	0	1	.000
Boss Schmidt, c	4	0	0	1	0	0	.000
Red Downs, 2b	4	1	1	1	0	0	.250
Ed Killian, p	0	0	0	0	0	0	—
Ed Summers, p	3	0	1	1	0	1	.333
Davy Jones, ph	1	0	0	0	0	1	.000
TOTALS	35	6	10	5	2	6	.286

	1	2	3	4	5	6	7	8	9	R	H	E
Cubs	0	0	4	0	0	0	1	0	5	10	14	2
Tigers	1	0	0	0	0	0	3	2	0	6	10	3

E—Downs, Evers, Schaefer, McIntyre, Chance. LOB—Cubs 9, Tigers 7. Scoring Position—Cubs 7-for-19, Tigers 4-for-12. 2B—Sheckard 2 (2), Downs (1). S—Evers, Schulte, Kling, Cobb, Schaefer, Brown. SF—Steinfeldt. SB—Chance 2 (2), Hofman (1), Tinker 2 (2), McIntyre (1). CS—Kling (1).

Cubs	IP	H	R	ER	BB	K	ERA
Ed Reulbach	6.2	8	4	4	0	5	5.40
Orval Overall (H, 1)	0.1	0	1	1	1	0	27.00
T. F. Brown (BS, 1; W, 1-0)	2.0	2	1	0	1	1	0.00

Tigers	IP	H	R	ER	BB	K	ERA
Ed Killian	2.1	5	4	3	3	1	11.57
Ed Summers (L, 0-1)	6.2	9	6	5	1	2	6.75

Overall pitched to one batter in the 8th.

WP—Brown. HBP—McIntyre by Overall. Time—2:10. Attendance—10,812. Umpires—HP, Sheridan. Bases, O'Day.

Game 2

Sunday, October 11

Tigers	AB	R	H	RBI	BB	K	Avg
Matty McIntyre, lf	4	0	0	0	0	2	.286
Charley O'Leary, ss	3	0	0	0	0	1	.143
Davy Jones, ph	0	1	0	0	1	0	.000
Sam Crawford, cf	4	0	0	0	0	0	.000
Ty Cobb, rf	4	0	1	1	0	0	.375
Claude Rossman, 1b	4	0	0	0	0	0	.250
Germany Schaefer, 3b	3	0	2	0	0	0	.333
Boss Schmidt, c	3	0	1	0	0	0	.143
Red Downs, 2b	2	0	0	0	1	2	.167
Wild Bill Donovan, p	2	0	0	0	0	0	.000
TOTALS	29	1	4	1	2	5	.200

Cubs	AB	R	H	RBI	BB	K	Avg
Jimmy Sheckard, lf	4	1	1	1	0	0	.400
Johnny Evers, 2b	4	1	1	1	0	0	.375
Wildfire Schulte, rf	4	1	1	1	0	1	.375
Frank Chance, 1b	3	0	0	0	1	1	.143
Harry Steinfeldt, 3b	4	0	0	0	0	2	.286
Solly Hofman, cf	3	1	1	0	0	1	.286
Joe Tinker, ss	3	1	1	2	0	0	.375
Johnny Kling, c	3	1	1	0	0	2	.333
Orval Overall, p	3	0	1	0	0	0	.250
TOTALS	31	6	7	5	1	7	.323

	1	2	3	4	5	6	7	8	9	R	H	E
Tigers	0	0	0	0	0	0	0	0	1	1	4	1
Cubs	0	0	0	0	0	0	6	x		6	7	0

E—Donovan. DP—Tigers 1 (Downs to O'Leary to Rossman). LOB—Tigers 4, Cubs 2. Scoring Position—Tigers 1-for-5, Cubs 3-for-5. 2B—Kling (1). 3B—Schulte (1). HR—Tinker (1). S—Donovan. GDP—Rossman, Sheckard. SB—Schaefer (1), Sheckard (1), Evers (1), Chance (3).

Tigers	IP	H	R	ER	BB	K	ERA
Wild Bill Donovan (L, 0-1)	8.0	7	6	6	1	7	6.75

Cubs	IP	H	R	ER	BB	K	ERA
Orval Overall (W, 1-0)	9.0	4	1	1	2	5	1.93

WP—Donovan. Time—1:30. Attendance—17,760. Umpires—HP, Klem. Bases, Connolly.

Game 3

Monday, October 12

Tigers	AB	R	H	RBI	BB	K	Avg
Matty McIntyre, lf	4	1	1	0	1	0	.273
Charley O'Leary, ss	5	2	1	0	0	0	.167
Sam Crawford, cf	4	1	1	1	0	0	.083
Ty Cobb, rf	5	1	4	2	0	0	.538
Claude Rossman, 1b	4	2	2	2	1	0	.333
Germany Schaefer, 2b	4	0	0	0	0	0	.200
Ira Thomas, c	3	0	1	1	1	0	.500
Bill Coughlin, 3b	3	0	0	1	0	1	.000
George Mullin, p	3	1	1	1	1	0	.333
TOTALS	35	8	11	8	4	1	.275

Cubs	AB	R	H	RBI	BB	K	Avg
Jimmy Sheckard, lf	4	0	0	0	0	2	.286
Johnny Evers, 2b	3	1	0	0	1	0	.273
Wildfire Schulte, rf	4	0	1	0	0	0	.333
Frank Chance, 1b	4	1	2	1	0	0	.273
Harry Steinfeldt, 3b	4	1	1	0	0	2	.273
Solly Hofman, cf	4	0	2	1	0	1	.364
Joe Tinker, ss	3	0	1	0	0	1	.364
Johnny Kling, c	3	0	0	0	0	0	.222
Jack Pfiester, p	2	0	0	0	0	2	.000
Del Howard, ph	1	0	0	0	0	0	.000
Ed Reulbach, p	0	0	0	0	0	0	.000
TOTALS	32	3	7	2	1	8	.281

	1	2	3	4	5	6	7	8	9	R	H	E
Tigers	1	0	0	0	0	5	0	2	0	8	11	4
Cubs	0	0	0	3	0	0	0	0	0	3	7	1

E—Rossman 2, O'Leary, Coughlin, Steinfeldt. DP—Tigers 2 (Schaefer to Rossman; O'Leary to Schaefer to Rossman), Cubs 2 (Evers to Chance; Hofman to Kling). LOB—Tigers 6, Cubs 3. Scoring Position—Tigers 6-for-11, Cubs 2-for-7. 2B—Cobb (1), Thomas (1). 3B—Hofman (1). S—Crawford. SF—Coughlin. GDP—Sheckard, Kling. SB—Cobb 2 (2), Rossman (1), Chance 2 (5), Steinfeldt (1). CS—Cobb (1), Evers (1), Schulte (1), Tinker (1).

Tigers	IP	H	R	ER	BB	K	ERA
George Mullin (W, 1-0)	9.0	7	3	0	1	8	0.00

Cubs	IP	H	R	ER	BB	K	ERA
Jack Pfiester (L, 0-1)	8.0	10	8	7	3	1	7.88
Ed Reulbach	1.0	1	0	0	1	0	4.70

Time—2:10. Attendance—14,543. Umpires—HP, O'Day. Bases, Sheridan.

Game 4

Tuesday, October 13

Cubs	AB	R	H	RBI	BB	K	Avg
Jimmy Sheckard, lf	4	0	0	0	1	1	.222
Johnny Evers, 2b	5	1	1	0	0	1	.250
Wildfire Schulte, rf	3	1	2	0	2	0	.400
Frank Chance, 1b	4	1	2	0	1	0	.333
Harry Steinfeldt, 3b	3	0	1	1	0	0	.286
Solly Hofman, cf	4	0	2	1	0	0	.400
Joe Tinker, ss	4	0	0	0	0	1	.267
Johnny Kling, c	4	0	2	0	0	0	.308
Three Finger Brown, p	4	0	0	0	0	2	.000
TOTALS	35	3	10	2	4	5	.296

Tigers	AB	R	H	RBI	BB	K	Avg
Matty McIntyre, lf	4	0	0	0	0	0	.200
Charley O'Leary, ss	4	0	2	0	0	0	.250
Sam Crawford, cf	4	0	2	0	0	0	.188
Ty Cobb, rf	3	0	0	0	0	1	.438
Claude Rossman, 1b	3	0	0	0	0	1	.267
Germany Schaefer, 2b	3	0	0	0	0	1	.154
Boss Schmidt, c	3	0	0	0	0	0	.100
Bill Coughlin, 3b	2	0	0	0	0	0	.000
Ed Summers, p	2	0	0	0	0	1	.200
Davy Jones, ph	1	0	0	0	0	0	.000
George Winter, p	0	0	0	0	0	0	—
TOTALS	29	0	4	0	0	4	.221

	1	2	3	4	5	6	7	8	9	R	H	E
Cubs	0	0	2	0	0	0	0	0	1	3	10	0
Tigers	0	0	0	0	0	0	0	0	0	0	4	1

E—Cobb. DP—Cubs 1 (Brown to Tinker to Chance). LOB—Cubs 10, Tigers 3. Scoring Position—Cubs 3-for-10, Tigers 0-for-2. 2B—Crawford (1). S—Steinfeldt. GDP—Crawford. SB—Evers (2), Schulte 2 (2), Hofman (2). CS—Schulte (2), Kling (2).

Cubs	IP	H	R	ER	BB	K	ERA
Three Finger Brown (W, 2-0)	9.0	4	0	0	0	4	0.00

Tigers	IP	H	R	ER	BB	K	ERA
Ed Summers (L, 0-2)	8.0	9	2	2	3	5	4.30
George Winter	1.0	1	1	0	1	0	0.00

PB—Schmidt, Kling. HBP—Coughlin by Brown. Time—1:35. Attendance—12,907. Umpires—HP, Connolly. Bases, Klem.

Game 5

Wednesday, October 14

Cubs	AB	R	H	RBI	BB	K	Avg
Jimmy Sheckard, lf	3	0	1	0	1	0	.238
Johnny Evers, 2b	4	1	3	1	0	0	.350
Wildfire Schulte, rf	3	0	1	0	0	0	.389
Frank Chance, 1b	4	0	3	1	0	0	.421
Harry Steinfeldt, 3b	2	0	0	0	1	1	.250
Solly Hofman, cf	4	0	0	0	0	2	.316
Joe Tinker, ss	4	0	1	0	0	0	.263
Johnny Kling, c	3	1	0	0	1	0	.250
Orval Overall, p	2	0	1	0	0	0	.333
TOTALS	29	2	10	2	3	3	.312

Tigers	AB	R	H	RBI	BB	K	Avg
Matty McIntyre, lf	3	0	1	0	1	0	.222
Charley O'Leary, ss	4	0	0	0	0	1	.200
Sam Crawford, cf	4	0	1	0	0	1	.200
Ty Cobb, rf	3	0	0	0	1	1	.368
Claude Rossman, 1b	4	0	0	0	0	2	.211
Germany Schaefer, 2b	3	0	0	0	1	2	.125
Boss Schmidt, c	4	0	0	0	0	2	.071
Bill Coughlin, 3b	3	0	1	0	0	0	.125
Wild Bill Donovan, p	2	0	0	0	1	1	.000
TOTALS	30	0	3	0	4	10	.196

	1	2	3	4	5	6	7	8	9	R	H	E
Cubs	1	0	0	0	1	0	0	0	0	2	10	0
Tigers	0	0	0	0	0	0	0	0	0	0	3	0

DP—Tigers 2 (Schmidt to Schaefer; O'Leary to Rossman to Coughlin). LOB—Cubs 6, Tigers 7. Scoring Position—Cubs 3-for-9, Tigers 0-for-6. 2B—Evers (1), McIntyre (1). S—Schulte, Steinfeldt, Overall. SB—Donovan (1). CS—Sheckard (1), Evers (2), Steinfeldt (1), Schaefer (1).

Cubs	IP	H	R	ER	BB	K	ERA
Orval Overall (W, 2-0)	9.0	3	0	0	4	10	0.98

Tigers	IP	H	R	ER	BB	K	ERA
Wild Bill Donovan (L, 0-2)	9.0	10	2	2	3	3	4.24

WP—Overall. Time—1:25. Attendance—6,210. Umpires—HP, Sheridan. Bases, O'Day.

1908 World Series—Composite Statistics

Batting

Cubs	G	AB	R	H	RBI	2B	3B	HR	BB	SO	SB	CS	Avg	OBP	Slg
Three Finger Brown	2	4	0	0	0	0	0	0	0	0	2	0	.000	.000	.000
Frank Chance	5	19	4	8	2	0	0	0	3	1	5	0	.421	.500	.421
Johnny Evers	5	20	5	7	2	1	0	0	1	2	2	2	.350	.381	.400
Solly Hofman	5	19	2	6	4	0	1	0	1	4	2	0	.316	.350	.421
Del Howard	1	1	0	0	0	0	0	0	0	0	0	0	.000	.000	.000
Johnny Kling	5	16	2	4	2	1	0	0	2	2	0	2	.250	.333	.313
Orval Overall	3	6	0	2	0	0	0	0	0	1	0	0	.333	.333	.333
Jack Pfiester	1	2	0	0	0	0	0	0	0	2	0	0	.000	.000	.000
Ed Reulbach	2	3	0	0	0	0	0	0	0	1	0	0	.000	.000	.000
Wildfire Schulte	5	18	4	7	2	0	1	0	2	1	0	2	.389	.450	.500
Jimmy Sheckard	5	21	2	5	1	2	0	0	2	3	1	1	.238	.304	.333
Harry Steinfeldt	5	16	3	4	3	0	0	0	2	5	1	1	.250	.316	.250
Joe Tinker	5	19	2	5	4	0	0	1	0	2	2	1	.263	.263	.421
Totals	**5**	**164**	**24**	**48**	**20**	**4**	**2**	**1**	**13**	**26**	**15**	**9**	**.293**	**.343**	**.360**

Pitching

Cubs	G	GS	CG	IP	H	R	ER	BB	SO	W-L	Sv-Op	Hld	ERA
Three Finger Brown	2	1	1	11.0	6	1	0	1	5	2-0	0-1	0	0.00
Orval Overall	3	2	2	18.1	7	2	2	7	15	2-0	0-0	1	0.98
Jack Pfiester	1	1	0	8.0	10	8	7	3	1	0-1	0-0	0	7.88
Ed Reulbach	2	1	0	7.2	9	4	4	1	5	0-0	0-0	0	4.70
Totals	**5**	**5**	**3**	**45.0**	**32**	**15**	**13**	**12**	**26**	**4-1**	**0-1**	**1**	**2.60**

Fielding

Cubs	Pos	G	PO	Ast	E	DP	PB	FPct
Three Finger Brown	p	2	0	6	0	1	—	1.000
Frank Chance	1b	5	66	0	1	3	—	.985
Johnny Evers	2b	5	5	20	1	1	—	.962
Solly Hofman	cf	5	10	1	0	1	—	1.000
Johnny Kling	c	5	32	6	0	1	1	1.000
Orval Overall	p	3	0	2	0	0	—	1.000
Jack Pfiester	p	1	0	0	0	0	—	—
Ed Reulbach	p	2	0	5	0	0	—	1.000
Wildfire Schulte	rf	5	3	1	0	0	—	1.000
Jimmy Sheckard	lf	5	7	0	0	0	—	1.000
Harry Steinfeldt	3b	5	4	11	1	0	—	.938
Joe Tinker	ss	5	8	20	0	2	—	1.000
Totals		**5**	**135**	**72**	**3**	**9**	**1**	**.986**

Batting

Tigers	G	AB	R	H	RBI	2B	3B	HR	BB	SO	SB	CS	Avg	OBP	Slg
Ty Cobb	5	19	3	7	4	1	0	0	1	2	2	1	.368	.400	.421
Bill Coughlin	3	8	0	1	1	0	0	0	0	1	0	0	.125	.200	.125
Sam Crawford	5	20	2	4	1	1	0	0	1	2	0	0	.200	.238	.250
Wild Bill Donovan	2	4	0	0	0	0	0	0	1	1	1	0	.000	.200	.000
Red Downs	2	6	1	1	1	0	0	1	2	0	0	.167	.286	.333
Davy Jones	3	2	1	0	0	0	0	0	1	1	0	0	.000	.333	.000
Matty McIntyre	5	18	2	4	0	1	0	0	3	2	1	0	.222	.364	.278
George Mullin	1	3	1	1	1	0	0	0	1	0	0	0	.333	.500	.333
Charley O'Leary	5	20	2	4	0	0	0	0	0	3	0	0	.200	.200	.200
Claude Rossman	5	19	3	4	3	0	0	0	1	4	1	0	.211	.250	.211
Germany Schaefer	5	16	0	2	0	0	0	0	1	4	1	1	.125	.176	.125
Boss Schmidt	4	14	0	1	1	0	0	0	0	2	0	0	.071	.071	.071
Ed Summers	2	5	0	1	1	0	0	0	0	2	0	0	.200	.200	.200
Ira Thomas	2	4	0	2	1	1	0	0	1	0	0	0	.500	.600	.750
Totals	**5**	**158**	**15**	**32**	**14**	**5**	**0**	**0**	**12**	**26**	**6**	**2**	**.203**	**.266**	**.234**

Pitching

Tigers	G	GS	CG	IP	H	R	ER	BB	SO	W-L	Sv-Op	Hld	ERA
Wild Bill Donovan	2	2	2	17.0	17	8	8	4	10	0-2	0-0	0	4.24
Ed Killian	1	1	0	2.1	5	4	3	3	1	0-0	0-0	0	11.57
George Mullin	1	1	1	9.0	7	3	0	1	8	1-0	0-0	0	0.00
Ed Summers	2	1	0	14.2	18	8	7	4	7	0-2	0-0	0	4.30
George Winter	1	0	0	1.0	1	1	0	1	0	0-0	0-0	0	0.00
Totals	**5**	**5**	**3**	**44.0**	**48**	**24**	**18**	**13**	**26**	**1-4**	**0-0**	**0**	**3.68**

Fielding

Tigers	Pos	G	PO	Ast	E	DP	PB	FPct
Ty Cobb	rf	5	3	0	1	0	—	.750
Bill Coughlin	3b	3	3	6	1	1	—	.900
Sam Crawford	cf	5	16	0	0	0	—	1.000
Wild Bill Donovan	p	2	1	2	1	0	—	.750
Red Downs	2b	2	2	8	1	1	—	.909
Ed Killian	p	1	0	1	0	0	—	1.000
Matty McIntyre	lf	5	10	0	1	0	—	.909
George Mullin	p	1	0	1	0	0	—	1.000
Charley O'Leary	ss	5	7	12	1	3	—	.950
Claude Rossman	1b	5	49	5	2	4	—	.964
Germany Schaefer	2b	3	9	8	0	3	—	1.000
	3b	2	1	3	1	0	—	.800
Boss Schmidt	c	4	22	5	0	1	1	1.000
Ed Summers	p	2	0	7	0	0	—	1.000
Ira Thomas	c	1	9	2	0	0	0	1.000
George Winter	p	1	0	0	0	0	—	—
Totals		**5**	**132**	**60**	**9**	**13**	**1**	**.955**

1909 Pittsburgh Pirates (NL) 4, Detroit Tigers (AL) 3

Babe Adams was the surprise hero for the Pittsburgh Pirates, leading them to a seven-game World Series victory over the Detroit Tigers. Adams got the nod in the opener and beat George Mullin, 4-1, as Tommy Leach made two fine grabs in center field. Detroit took the second meeting, 7-2, as Jim Delahanty's bases-loaded two-run single in the third put the Tigers ahead to stay. Honus Wagner had three hits and stole three bases as the Pirates won Game 3, 8-6. Mullin tossed a five-hit shutout in near-freezing conditions for a 5-0 Detroit victory in Game 4. Adams won the fifth game, 8-4, as Fred Clarke hit a tie-breaking, three-run homer in the seventh. Mullin surrendered three runs in the first inning of Game 6, but recovered to win the game, 5-4. Adams earned his third win of the Series in Game 7, an 8-0 shutout, as the Pirates clinched the title.

Game 1

Friday, October 8

Tigers	AB	R	H	RBI	BB	K	Avg
Davy Jones, lf	3	0	2	0	1	0	.667
Donie Bush, ss	2	0	0	0	1	0	.000
Ty Cobb, rf	3	1	0	0	1	0	.000
Sam Crawford, cf	4	0	1	0	0	0	.250
Jim Delahanty, 2b	4	0	1	1	0	1	.250
George Moriarty, 3b	4	0	1	0	0	0	.250
Tom Jones, 1b	3	0	0	0	0	0	.000
Matty McIntyre, ph	1	0	0	0	0	0	.000
Boss Schmidt, c	3	0	0	0	1	0	.000
George Mullin, p	4	0	1	0	0	1	.250
TOTALS	31	1	6	1	4	2	.194

Pirates	AB	R	H	RBI	BB	K	Avg
Bobby Byrne, 3b	3	0	0	0	0	1	.000
Tommy Leach, cf	3	0	1	0	0	1	.000
Fred Clarke, lf	4	1	1	1	0	0	.250
Honus Wagner, ss	3	1	1	0	0	0	.333
Dots Miller, 2b	4	0	1	0	0	0	.250
Bill Abstein, 1b	3	1	0	1	1	1	.000
Chief Wilson, rf	3	0	1	0	0	0	.333
George Gibson, c	3	1	1	1	0	0	.333
Babe Adams, p	3	0	0	0	0	0	.000
TOTALS	29	4	5	4	1	4	.172

	1	2	3	4	5	6	7	8	9		R	H	E
Tigers	1	0	0	0	0	0	0	0	0		1	6	4
Pirates	0	0	0	1	2	1	0	0	x		4	5	0

E—Bush, Schmidt, Cobb, Delahanty. LOB—Tigers 8, Pirates 5. Scoring Position—Tigers 2-for-5, Pirates 1-for-8. 2B—Wagner (1), Gibson (1). HR—Clarke (1). S—Bush. SF—Leach. SB—Cobb (1), Miller (1), Wilson (1).

Tigers	IP	H	R	ER	BB	K	ERA
George Mullin (L, 0-1)	8.0	5	4	1	1	4	1.13

Pirates	IP	H	R	ER	BB	K	ERA
Babe Adams (W, 1-0)	9.0	6	1	1	4	2	1.00

HBP—Byrne by Mullin, Wagner by Mullin. Time—1:55. Attendance—29,264. Umpires—HP, Johnstone. Bases, O'Loughlin.

Game 2

Saturday, October 9

Tigers	AB	R	H	RBI	BB	K	Avg
Davy Jones, lf	5	1	1	0	0	0	.375
Donie Bush, ss	3	1	1	0	1	1	.200
Ty Cobb, rf	3	1	1	0	1	0	.167
Sam Crawford, cf	4	1	1	0	0	1	.250
Jim Delahanty, 2b	3	1	1	2	1	1	.286
George Moriarty, 3b	3	1	1	0	1	0	.286
Tom Jones, 1b	3	1	1	0	1	0	.167
Boss Schmidt, c	4	0	2	4	0	0	.286
Wild Bill Donovan, p	4	0	0	0	0	1	.000
TOTALS	32	7	9	6	5	4	.241

Pirates	AB	R	H	RBI	BB	K	Avg
Bobby Byrne, 3b	3	1	0	0	1	1	.000
Tommy Leach, cf	4	1	2	1	0	0	.286
Fred Clarke, lf	3	0	0	0	0	0	.143
Honus Wagner, ss	4	0	1	0	0	1	.286
Dots Miller, 2b	4	0	1	1	0	1	.250
Bill Abstein, 1b	4	0	1	0	0	3	.143
Chief Wilson, rf	5	0	0	0	0	0	.125
George Gibson, c	2	0	0	0	1	0	.200
Howie Camnitz, p	1	0	0	0	0	0	.000
Vic Willis, p	2	0	0	0	0	1	.000
TOTALS	32	2	5	2	2	7	.172

	1	2	3	4	5	6	7	8	9		R	H	E
Tigers	0	2	3	0	2	0	0	0	0		7	9	3
Pirates	2	0	0	0	0	0	0	0	0		2	5	1

E—Abstein, Schmidt, Delahanty, Donovan. DP—Tigers 1 (Bush to TJones to Moriarty), Pirates 1 (Miller to Abstein to Byrne). LOB—Tigers 4, Pirates 6. Scoring Position—Tigers

---

3-for-8, Pirates 1-for-12. 2B—Crawford (1), Schmidt (1), Leach 2 (2), Miller (1). S—Bush, Clarke. GDP—Crawford, Gibson. SB—Cobb (2), Wagner (1), Gibson (1). CS—DJones (1), Bush (1), Wagner (1).

Tigers	IP	H	R	ER	BB	K	ERA
Wild Bill Donovan (W, 1-0)	9.0	5	2	2	2	7	2.00

Pirates	IP	H	R	ER	BB	K	ERA
Howie Camnitz (L, 0-1)	2.1	6	5	4	1	2	15.43
Vic Willis	6.2	3	2	2	4	2	2.70

Time—1:45. Attendance—30,915. Umpires—HP, Evans. Bases, Klem.

Game 3

Monday, October 11

Pirates	AB	R	H	RBI	BB	K	Avg
Bobby Byrne, 3b	5	1	2	0	0	0	.182
Tommy Leach, cf	4	3	2	0	0	0	.364
Fred Clarke, lf	3	1	0	1	0	0	.100
Honus Wagner, ss	5	1	3	2	0	0	.417
Dots Miller, 2b	4	1	0	0	1	1	.167
Bill Abstein, 1b	4	1	2	0	0	0	.273
Chief Wilson, rf	4	0	1	1	0	0	.167
George Gibson, c	4	0	0	0	0	0	.111
Nick Maddox, p	4	0	0	0	1	1	.000
TOTALS	37	8	10	4	1	2	.217

Tigers	AB	R	H	RBI	BB	K	Avg
Davy Jones, lf	5	2	1	0	0	0	.308
Donie Bush, ss	5	1	3	2	0	0	.400
Ty Cobb, rf	5	0	2	2	0	1	.273
Sam Crawford, cf	5	0	0	1	0	0	.154
Jim Delahanty, 2b	5	1	3	0	0	0	.417
George Moriarty, 3b	3	1	0	0	1	1	.200
Tom Jones, 1b	3	1	1	1	1	0	.222
Boss Schmidt, c	4	0	0	0	0	0	.182
Ed Summers, p	0	0	0	0	0	0	—
Ed Willett, p	2	0	0	0	0	0	.000
Matty McIntyre, ph	1	0	0	0	0	1	.000
Ralph Works, p	0	0	0	0	0	0	—
George Mullin, ph	1	0	0	0	0	1	.200
TOTALS	39	6	10	6	2	4	.255

	1	2	3	4	5	6	7	8	9		R	H	E
Pirates	5	1	0	0	0	0	0	0	2		8	10	2
Tigers	0	0	0	0	0	0	4	0	2		6	10	5

E—Bush 2, Abstein 2, Willett, Schmidt, Crawford. LOB—Pirates 6, Tigers 8. Scoring Position—Pirates 2-for-13, Tigers 5-for-14. 2B—Leach (3), Abstein (1), Cobb (1), Delahanty 2 (2). SF—Clarke. SB—Wagner 3 (4). CS—Leach (1), Wagner (2), Moriarty (1).

Pirates	IP	H	R	ER	BB	K	ERA
Nick Maddox (W, 1-0)	9.0	10	6	1	2	4	1.00

Tigers	IP	H	R	ER	BB	K	ERA
Ed Summers (L, 0-1)	0.1	3	5	0	1	0	0.00
Ed Willett	6.2	3	1	0	0	0	0.00
Ralph Works	2.0	4	2	2	0	2	9.00

WP—Summers. HBP—Leach by Willett, Clarke by Willett. Time—1:56. Attendance—18,277. Umpires—HP, O'Loughlin. 1B, Johnstone. 2B, Evans. 3B, Klem.

Game 4

Tuesday, October 12

Pirates	AB	R	H	RBI	BB	K	Avg
Bobby Byrne, 3b	4	0	1	0	0	1	.200
Tommy Leach, cf	3	0	0	0	1	0	.286
Fred Clarke, lf	4	0	0	0	0	2	.071
Honus Wagner, ss	3	0	0	0	1	1	.333
Dots Miller, 2b	4	0	1	0	0	2	.188
Bill Abstein, 1b	4	0	1	0	0	1	.267
Chief Wilson, rf	4	0	1	0	0	0	.188
George Gibson, c	3	0	1	0	0	0	.167
Lefty Leifield, p	1	0	0	0	0	1	.000
Paddy O'Connor, ph	1	0	0	0	0	1	.000
Deacon Phillippe, p	1	0	0	0	0	1	.000
TOTALS	32	0	5	0	2	10	.208

Tigers	AB	R	H	RBI	BB	K	Avg
Davy Jones, lf	4	1	1	0	0	0	.294
Donie Bush, ss	5	1	1	1	0	0	.333
Ty Cobb, rf	3	0	1	2	0	0	.286
Sam Crawford, cf	4	0	1	0	0	0	.176
Jim Delahanty, 2b	3	0	0	0	0	0	.333
George Moriarty, 3b	4	1	2	0	0	0	.286
Tom Jones, 1b	3	1	1	0	0	0	.250
Oscar Stanage, c	3	0	1	2	0	0	.333
George Mullin, p	3	1	0	0	1	1	.125
TOTALS	32	5	8	5	2	1	.270

	1	2	3	4	5	6	7	8	9		R	H	E
Pirates	0	0	0	0	0	0	0	0	0		0	5	6
Tigers	0	2	0	3	0	0	0	0	x		5	8	0

E—Miller, Abstein 2, Phillippe 2, Wagner. DP—Pirates 1 (Wagner to Abstein). LOB—Pirates 7, Tigers 9. Scoring Position—Pirates 0-for-5, Tigers 3-for-10. 2B—Byrne (1), Bush (1), Cobb (2). S—TJones, Stanage. GDP—Stanage. SB—Byrne (1), Leach (1). CS—DJones (2), Cobb (1).

Pirates	IP	H	R	ER	BB	K	ERA
Lefty Leifield (L, 0-1)	4.0	7	5	5	1	0	11.25
Deacon Phillippe	4.0	1	0	0	1	1	0.00

Tigers	IP	H	R	ER	BB	K	ERA
George Mullin (W, 1-1)	9.0	5	0	0	2	10	0.53

HBP—Cobb by Leifield, Delahanty by Leifield. Time—1:57. Attendance—17,036. Umpires—HP, Klem. 1B, Evans. 2B, Johnstone. 3B, O'Loughlin.

Game 5
Wednesday, October 13

Tigers	AB	R	H	RBI	BB	K	Avg
Davy Jones, lf	4	1	1	1	0	0	.286
Donie Bush, ss	3	0	0	0	1	2	.278
Ty Cobb, rf	4	1	1	0	0	0	.278
Sam Crawford, cf	4	2	3	2	0	0	.286
Jim Delahanty, 2b	4	0	0	0	0	2	.263
George Moriarty, 3b	4	0	0	0	0	0	.222
Tom Jones, 1b	4	0	1	0	0	0	.250
Oscar Stanage, c	2	0	0	0	0	2	.200
Matty McIntyre, ph	1	0	0	0	0	0	.000
Boss Schmidt, c	1	0	0	0	0	0	.167
Ed Summers, p	3	0	0	0	0	2	.000
Ed Willett, p	0	0	0	0	0	0	.000
George Mullin, ph	1	0	0	0	0	0	.111
TOTALS	35	4	6	3	1	8	.236

Pirates	AB	R	H	RBI	BB	K	Avg
Bobby Byrne, 3b	5	2	2	0	0	1	.250
Tommy Leach, cf	4	1	2	0	0	0	.333
Fred Clarke, lf	2	2	2	3	1	0	.188
Honus Wagner, ss	2	1	1	0	1	0	.353
Dots Miller, 2b	4	0	0	1	0	1	.150
Bill Abstein, 1b	3	0	0	1	1	1	.222
Chief Wilson, rf	4	1	1	0	0	1	.200
George Gibson, c	4	1	2	1	0	0	.250
Babe Adams, p	3	0	0	0	0	1	.000
TOTALS	31	8	10	6	3	5	.232

	1	2	3	4	5	6	7	8	9		R	H	E
Tigers	1	0	0	0	0	2	0	1	0		4	6	1
Pirates	1	1	1	0	0	0	4	1	x		8	10	2

E—Schmidt, Wagner 2. LOB—Tigers 5, Pirates 5. Scoring Position—Tigers 0-for-10, Pirates 2-for-11. 2B—Crawford (2), TJones (1), Wilson (1). HR—DJones (1), Crawford (1), Clarke (2). S—Clarke, Adams. SB—Crawford (2), TJones (1), Wagner 2 (6), Gibson (2). CS—Gibson (1).

Tigers	IP	H	R	ER	BB	K	ERA
Ed Summers (L, 0-2)	7.0	10	8	7	3	4	8.59
Ed Willett	1.0	0	0	0	0	1	0.00

Pirates	IP	H	R	ER	BB	K	ERA
Babe Adams (W, 2-0)	9.0	6	4	3	1	8	2.00

Summers pitched to two batters in the 8th.

WP—Summers. HBP—Wagner by Summers. Time—1:46. Attendance—21,706. Umpires—HP, Johnstone. 1B, O'Loughlin. 2B, Klem. 3B, Evans.

Game 6
Thursday, October 14

Pirates	AB	R	H	RBI	BB	K	Avg
Bobby Byrne, 3b	4	1	1	0	0	0	.250
Tommy Leach, cf	4	1	1	0	0	1	.318
Fred Clarke, lf	3	1	1	1	0	1	.211
Honus Wagner, ss	4	0	1	2	0	0	.333
Dots Miller, 2b	3	1	2	0	1	0	.217
Bill Abstein, 1b	4	0	1	0	0	2	.227
Chief Wilson, rf	3	0	0	0	0	0	.174
George Gibson, c	4	0	1	0	0	1	.250
Vic Willis, p	2	0	0	0	0	0	.000
Howie Camnitz, p	0	0	0	0	0	0	.000
Ham Hyatt, ph	1	0	0	0	0	0	.000
Deacon Phillippe, p	0	0	0	0	0	0	.000
Ed Abbaticchio, ph	1	0	0	0	0	1	.000
TOTALS	33	4	8	3	1	5	.236

Tigers	AB	R	H	RBI	BB	K	Avg
Davy Jones, lf-cf	5	1	0	0	0	0	.231
Donie Bush, ss	2	2	1	0	2	0	.300
Ty Cobb, rf	4	0	1	1	0	1	.273
Sam Crawford, cf-1b	3	1	1	1	1	0	.292
Jim Delahanty, 2b	4	0	2	1	0	1	.304
George Moriarty, 3b	3	1	1	1	1	0	.238
Tom Jones, 1b	4	0	1	1	0	0	.250
Matty McIntyre, lf	0	0	0	0	0	0	.000
Boss Schmidt, c	3	0	1	0	1	0	.200
George Mullin, p	4	0	2	0	0	0	.231
TOTALS	32	5	10	5	5	2	.257

	1	2	3	4	5	6	7	8	9		R	H	E
Pirates	3	0	0	0	0	0	0	0	1		4	8	3
Tigers	1	0	0	2	1	1	0	0	x		5	10	2

E—Miller, Bush, Wilson, TJones, Clarke. DP—Pirates 1 (Byrne to Abstein), Tigers 1 (Schmidt to Bush). LOB—Pirates 5, Tigers 9. Scoring Position—Pirates 2-for-10, Tigers 4-for-14. 2B—Wagner (2), Cobb (3), Crawford (3), Delahanty (3), Mullin (1). S—Clarke, Wilson. SB—Miller (2), DJones (1), Bush (1). CS—Wilson (1).

Pirates	IP	H	R	ER	BB	K	ERA
Vic Willis (L, 0-1)	5.0	7	4	2	4	1	3.09
Howie Camnitz	1.0	2	1	1	1	0	13.50
Deacon Phillippe	2.0	1	0	0	0	1	0.00

Tigers	IP	H	R	ER	BB	K	ERA
George Mullin (W, 2-1)	9.0	8	4	3	1	5	1.38

HBP—Bush by Willis. Time—2:00. Attendance—10,535. Umpires—HP, Evans. 1B, Klem. 2B, O'Loughlin. 3B, Johnstone.

Game 7
Saturday, October 16

Pirates	AB	R	H	RBI	BB	K	Avg
Bobby Byrne, 3b	0	0	0	0	0	0	.250
Ham Hyatt, cf	3	1	0	1	1	0	.000
Tommy Leach, cf-3b	3	2	2	0	1	0	.360
Fred Clarke, lf	0	2	0	1	4	0	.211
Honus Wagner, ss	3	1	1	2	2	0	.333
Dots Miller, 2b	5	0	2	2	0	0	.250
Bill Abstein, 1b	4	1	1	0	1	1	.231
Chief Wilson, rf	4	1	0	0	0	0	.148
George Gibson, c	5	0	1	0	0	0	.240
Babe Adams, p	3	0	0	0	1	0	.000
TOTALS	30	8	7	6	10	1	.237

Tigers	AB	R	H	RBI	BB	K	Avg
Davy Jones, lf	4	0	1	0	0	1	.233
Donie Bush, ss	3	0	0	0	0	0	.261
Ty Cobb, rf	4	0	0	0	0	0	.231
Sam Crawford, cf	4	0	0	0	0	0	.250
Jim Delahanty, 2b	3	0	2	0	1	0	.346
George Moriarty, 3b	1	0	1	0	0	0	.273
Charley O'Leary, pr-3b	3	0	0	0	0	0	.000
Tom Jones, 1b	4	0	1	0	0	0	.250
Boss Schmidt, c	3	0	1	0	0	0	.222
Wild Bill Donovan, p	0	0	0	0	0	0	.000
George Mullin, ph-p	3	0	0	0	0	0	.188
TOTALS	32	0	6	0	1	1	.245

	1	2	3	4	5	6	7	8	9		R	H	E
Pirates	0	2	0	2	0	3	0	1	0		8	7	0
Tigers	0	0	0	0	0	0	0	0	0		0	6	3

E—Bush, DJones, Crawford. DP—Tigers 1 (Bush to Schmidt to Delahanty). LOB—Pirates 11, Tigers 7. Scoring Position—Pirates 2-for-13, Tigers 0-for-7. 2B—Leach (4), Abstein (2), Gibson (2), Delahanty (4), Moriarty (1), Schmidt (2). 3B—Wagner (1). S—Leach, Clarke, Wilson, Adams. SF—Hyatt. SB—Clarke 2 (3), Miller (3), Abstein (1). CS—Byrne (1), Bush (2).

Pirates	IP	H	R	ER	BB	K	ERA
Babe Adams (W, 3-0)	9.0	6	0	0	1	1	1.33

Tigers	IP	H	R	ER	BB	K	ERA
Wild Bill Donovan (L, 1-1)	3.0	2	2	2	6	0	3.00
George Mullin	6.0	5	6	4	4	1	2.25

HBP—Byrne by Donovan, Bush by Adams. Time—2:10. Attendance—17,562. Umpires—HP, O'Loughlin. 1B, Johnstone. 2B, Evans. 3B, Klem.

1909 World Series—Composite Statistics

Batting

Pirates	G	AB	R	H	RBI	2B	3B	HR	BB	SO	SB	CS	Avg	OBP	Slg
Ed Abbaticchio	1	1	0	0	0	0	0	0	0	1	0	0	.000	.000	.000
Bill Abstein	7	26	3	6	2	2	0	0	3	9	1	0	.231	.310	.308
Babe Adams	3	9	0	0	0	0	0	0	1	1	0	0	.000	.100	.000
Bobby Byrne	7	24	5	6	0	1	0	0	1	4	1	1	.250	.333	.292
Howie Camnitz	2	1	0	0	0	0	0	0	0	0	0	0	.000	.000	.000
Fred Clarke	7	19	7	4	7	0	0	2	5	3	3	0	.211	.385	.526
George Gibson	7	25	2	6	2	2	0	0	1	1	2	1	.240	.269	.320
Ham Hyatt	2	4	1	0	1	0	0	0	1	0	0	0	.000	.167	.000
Tommy Leach	7	25	8	9	2	4	0	0	2	1	1	1	.360	.414	.520
Lefty Leifield	1	1	0	0	0	0	0	0	0	1	0	0	.000	.000	.000
Nick Maddox	1	4	0	0	0	0	0	0	0	1	0	0	.000	.000	.000
Dots Miller	7	28	2	7	4	1	0	0	2	5	3	0	.250	.300	.286
Paddy O'Connor	1	1	0	0	0	0	0	0	0	1	0	0	.000	.000	.000
Deacon Phillippe	2	1	0	0	0	0	0	0	0	1	0	0	.000	.000	.000
Honus Wagner	7	24	4	8	6	2	1	0	4	2	6	2	.333	.467	.500
Vic Willis	2	4	0	0	0	0	0	0	0	1	0	0	.000	.000	.000
Chief Wilson	7	27	2	4	1	1	0	0	0	2	1	1	.148	.148	.185
Totals	**7**	**224**	**34**	**50**	**25**	**13**	**1**	**2**	**20**	**34**	**18**	**6**	**.223**	**.300**	**.317**

Batting

Tigers	G	AB	R	H	RBI	2B	3B	HR	BB	SO	SB	CS	Avg	OBP	Slg
Donie Bush	7	23	5	6	3	1	0	0	5	3	1	2	.261	.433	.304
Ty Cobb	7	26	3	6	5	3	0	0	2	2	2	1	.231	.310	.346
Sam Crawford	7	28	4	7	4	3	0	1	1	1	1	0	.250	.276	.464
Jim Delahanty	7	26	2	9	4	4	0	0	2	5	0	0	.346	.414	.500
Wild Bill Donovan	2	4	0	0	0	0	0	0	0	1	0	0	.000	.000	.000
Davy Jones	7	30	6	7	1	0	0	1	2	1	1	2	.233	.281	.333
Tom Jones	7	24	3	6	2	1	0	0	2	0	1	0	.250	.308	.292
Matty McIntyre	4	3	0	0	0	0	0	0	0	1	0	0	.000	.000	.000
George Moriarty	7	22	4	6	1	1	0	0	3	1	0	1	.273	.360	.318
George Mullin	6	16	1	3	0	1	0	0	1	3	0	0	.188	.235	.250
Charley O'Leary	1	3	0	0	0	0	0	0	0	0	0	0	.000	.000	.000
Boss Schmidt	6	18	0	4	4	2	0	0	2	0	0	0	.222	.300	.333
Oscar Stanage	2	5	0	1	2	0	0	0	0	2	0	0	.200	.200	.200
Ed Summers	2	3	0	0	0	0	0	0	0	2	0	0	.000	.000	.000
Ed Willett	2	2	0	0	0	0	0	0	0	0	0	0	.000	.000	.000
Totals	**7**	**233**	**28**	**55**	**26**	**16**	**0**	**2**	**20**	**22**	**6**	**6**	**.236**	**.307**	**.330**

Pitching

Pirates	G	GS	CG	IP	H	R	ER	BB	SO	W-L	Sv-Op	Hld	ERA
Babe Adams	3	3	3	27.0	18	5	4	6	11	3-0	0-0	0	1.33
Howie Camnitz	2	1	0	3.1	8	6	5	2	2	0-1	0-0	0	13.50
Lefty Leifield	1	1	0	4.0	7	5	5	1	0	0-1	0-0	0	11.25
Nick Maddox	1	1	1	9.0	10	6	1	2	4	1-0	0-0	0	1.00
Deacon Phillippe	2	0	0	6.0	2	0	0	1	2	0-0	0-0	0	0.00
Vic Willis	2	1	0	11.2	10	6	4	8	3	0-1	0-0	0	3.09
Totals	**7**	**7**	**4**	**61.0**	**55**	**28**	**19**	**20**	**22**	**4-3**	**0-0**	**0**	**2.80**

Pitching

Tigers	G	GS	CG	IP	H	R	ER	BB	SO	W-L	Sv-Op	Hld	ERA
Wild Bill Donovan	2	2	1	12.0	7	4	4	8	7	1-1	0-0	0	3.00
George Mullin	4	3	3	32.0	23	14	8	8	20	2-1	0-0	0	2.25
Ed Summers	2	2	0	7.1	13	13	7	4	4	0-2	0-0	0	8.59
Ed Willett	2	0	0	7.2	3	1	0	0	1	0-0	0-0	0	0.00
Ralph Works	1	0	0	2.0	4	2	2	0	2	0-0	0-0	0	9.00
Totals	**7**	**7**	**4**	**61.0**	**50**	**34**	**21**	**20**	**34**	**3-4**	**0-0**	**0**	**3.10**

Fielding

Pirates	Pos	G	PO	Ast	E	DP	PB	FPct
Bill Abstein	1b	7	71	4	5	3	—	.938
Babe Adams	p	3	0	5	0	0	—	1.000
Bobby Byrne	3b	6	11	16	0	3	—	1.000
Howie Camnitz	p	2	0	2	0	0	—	1.000
Fred Clarke	lf	7	19	0	1	0	—	.950
George Gibson	c	7	28	9	0	1	0	1.000
Ham Hyatt	cf	1	0	0	0	0	—	—
Tommy Leach	cf	6	16	1	0	0	—	1.000
	3b	1	4	2	0	0	—	1.000
Lefty Leifield	p	1	0	5	0	0	—	1.000
Nick Maddox	p	1	0	1	0	0	—	1.000
Dots Miller	2b	7	16	14	2	1	—	.938
Deacon Phillippe	p	2	1	2	2	0	—	.600
Honus Wagner	ss	7	13	23	3	1	—	.923
Vic Willis	p	2	1	2	0	0	—	1.000
Chief Wilson	rf	7	3	1	1	0	—	.800
Totals		**7**	**183**	**87**	**14**	**9**	**0**	**.951**

Fielding

Tigers	Pos	G	PO	Ast	E	DP	PB	FPct
Donie Bush	ss	7	9	18	5	3	—	.844
Ty Cobb	rf	7	8	0	1	0	—	.889
Sam Crawford	cf	7	17	0	2	0	—	.895
	1b	1	0	1	0	0	—	1.000
Jim Delahanty	2b	7	10	17	2	1	—	.931
Wild Bill Donovan	p	2	0	5	1	0	—	.833
Davy Jones	lf	7	14	0	1	0	—	.933
	cf	1	0	0	0	0	—	—
Tom Jones	1b	7	73	1	1	1	—	.987
Matty McIntyre	lf	1	0	0	0	0	—	—
George Moriarty	3b	7	7	15	0	1	—	1.000
George Mullin	p	4	0	12	0	0	—	1.000
Charley O'Leary	3b	1	1	1	0	0	—	1.000
Boss Schmidt	c	6	31	10	4	2	0	.911
Oscar Stanage	c	2	12	2	0	0	0	1.000
Ed Summers	p	2	0	2	0	0	—	1.000
Ed Willett	p	2	1	3	1	0	—	.800
Ralph Works	p	1	0	1	0	0	—	1.000
Totals		**7**	**183**	**88**	**18**	**8**	**0**	**.938**

1910 Philadelphia Athletics (AL) 4, Chicago Cubs (NL) 1

Using only two pitchers, Jack Coombs and Chief Bender, the Philadelphia Athletics downed the Chicago Cubs in a five-game World Series. Home Run Baker rapped two doubles and a single as Chief Bender won the opener, 4-1. Eddie Collins starred in Game 2, stealing two bases and scoring two runs with a single and a pair of doubles. Coombs started Game 3 on only one day's rest, but won 12-5 while driving in three runs himself. The Athletics held a 3-2 lead in the ninth inning of Game 4, and were three outs away from completing a sweep of the Series, when Frank Chance tied the score with an RBI triple. Jimmy Sheckard's 10th-inning RBI single won it for the Cubs. Coombs won his third game of the Series in Game 5, wrapping up Philadelphia's title with a 7-2 victory.

Game 1

Monday, October 17

Cubs	AB	R	H	RBI	BB	K	Avg
Jimmy Sheckard, lf	4	0	0	0	0	2	.000
Wildfire Schulte, rf	2	0	1	0	2	1	.500
Solly Hofman, cf	4	0	0	0	0	1	.000
Frank Chance, 1b	3	0	0	0	0	0	.000
Heinie Zimmerman, 2b	3	0	0	0	0	2	.000
Harry Steinfeldt, 3b	3	0	0	0	0	1	.000
Joe Tinker, ss	3	1	1	0	0	0	.333
Johnny Kling, c	3	0	1	1	0	0	.333
John Kane, pr	0	0	0	0	0	0	—
Orval Overall, p	1	0	0	0	0	0	.000
Harry McIntire, p	1	0	0	0	0	1	.000
Ginger Beaumont, ph	1	0	0	0	0	0	.000
TOTALS	28	1	3	1	2	8	.107

Athletics	AB	R	H	RBI	BB	K	Avg
Amos Strunk, cf	3	0	0	0	1	0	.000
Bris Lord, lf	4	1	1	0	0	1	.250
Eddie Collins, 2b	2	1	1	0	1	0	.500
Home Run Baker, 3b	4	1	3	2	0	0	.750
Harry Davis, 1b	3	0	0	0	0	1	.000
Danny Murphy, rf	3	1	1	1	0	0	.333
Jack Barry, ss	3	0	0	0	0	0	.000
Ira Thomas, c	1	0	0	0	2	1	.000
Chief Bender, p	3	0	1	1	0	1	.333
TOTALS	26	4	7	4	4	4	.269

	1 2 3	4 5 6	7 8 9	R	H	E
Cubs	0 0 0	0 0 0	0 0 1	1	3	1
Athletics	0 2 1	0 0 0	0 1 x	4	7	2

E—Strunk, Thomas, McIntire. LOB—Cubs 2, Athletics 4. Scoring Position—Cubs 1-for-3, Athletics 4-for-7. 2B—Lord (1), Baker 2 (2). S—Collins, Davis. SB—Murphy (1). CS—Schulte 2 (2), Strunk (1), Collins (1), Baker (1).

Cubs	IP	H	R	ER	BB	K	ERA
Orval Overall (L, 0-1)	3.0	6	3	3	1	1	9.00
Harry McIntire	5.0	1	1	0	3	3	0.00

Athletics	IP	H	R	ER	BB	K	ERA
Chief Bender (W, 1-0)	9.0	3	1	0	2	8	0.00

Time—1:54. Attendance—26,891. Umpires—HP, Connolly. 1B, O'Day. 2B, Rigler. 3B, Sheridan.

Game 2

Tuesday, October 18

Cubs	AB	R	H	RBI	BB	K	Avg
Jimmy Sheckard, lf	1	1	1	0	3	0	.200
Wildfire Schulte, rf	3	1	0	0	0	0	.200
Solly Hofman, cf	2	1	1	0	3	0	.167
Frank Chance, 1b	5	0	2	1	0	1	.250
Heinie Zimmerman, 2b	3	0	1	2	1	0	.167
Harry Steinfeldt, 3b	5	0	1	0	0	1	.125
Joe Tinker, ss	4	0	2	0	1	0	.429
Johnny Kling, c	4	0	0	0	1	1	.143
Three Finger Brown, p	3	0	0	0	0	1	.000
Ginger Beaumont, ph	1	0	0	0	0	1	.000
Lew Richie, p	0	0	0	0	0	0	—
TOTALS	31	3	8	3	9	5	.193

Athletics	AB	R	H	RBI	BB	K	Avg
Amos Strunk, cf	5	1	2	1	0	3	.250
Bris Lord, lf	5	1	1	0	0	0	.222
Eddie Collins, 2b	4	2	3	1	1	0	.667
Home Run Baker, 3b	4	1	1	0	1	0	.500
Harry Davis, 1b	5	1	2	2	0	0	.250
Danny Murphy, rf	4	1	1	2	1	0	.286
Jack Barry, ss	3	0	1	0	0	1	.167
Ira Thomas, c	3	2	2	1	1	0	.500
Jack Coombs, p	4	0	1	0	0	2	.250
TOTALS	37	9	14	7	4	6	.333

	1 2 3	4 5 6	7 8 9	R	H	E
Cubs	1 0 0	0 0 0	1 0 1	3	8	3
Athletics	0 0 2	0 1 0	6 0 x	9	14	4

E—Coombs 2, Steinfeldt 2, Sheckard, Davis 2. DP—Cubs 1 (Tinker to Chance), Athletics 3 (Collins to Davis; Murphy to Thomas; Collins to Davis). LOB—Cubs 14, Athletics 9. Scoring Position—Cubs 3-for-16, Athletics 6-for-17. 2B—Sheckard (1), Zimmerman (1), Steinfeldt (1), Tinker (1), Strunk (1), Collins 2 (2), Davis (1), Murphy (1). S—Sheckard, Schulte 2, Barry. SF—Zimmerman. GDP—Barry. SB—Collins 2 (2). CS—Tinker (1), Lord (1).

Cubs	IP	H	R	ER	BB	K	ERA
Three Finger Brown (L, 0-1)	7.0	13	9	6	4	6	7.71
Lew Richie	1.0	1	0	0	0	0	0.00

Athletics	IP	H	R	ER	BB	K	ERA
Jack Coombs (W, 1-0)	9.0	8	3	3	9	5	3.00

Time—2:25. Attendance—24,597. Umpires—HP, Rigler. 1B, Sheridan. 2B, O'Day. 3B, Connolly.

Game 3

Thursday, October 20

Athletics	AB	R	H	RBI	BB	K	Avg
Amos Strunk, cf	5	1	1	0	1	1	.231
Bris Lord, lf	4	0	1	0	0	0	.231
Eddie Collins, 2b	5	1	1	0	0	0	.455
Home Run Baker, 3b	5	2	2	2	0	0	.462
Harry Davis, 1b	3	3	3	0	1	0	.455
Danny Murphy, rf	5	2	1	3	0	0	.250
Jack Barry, ss	5	3	3	3	0	0	.364
Ira Thomas, c	4	0	0	0	1	0	.250
Jack Coombs, p	5	0	3	3	0	0	.444
TOTALS	41	12	15	11	3	1	.347

Cubs	AB	R	H	RBI	BB	K	Avg
Jimmy Sheckard, lf	1	2	0	0	3	0	.167
Wildfire Schulte, rf	4	0	2	2	0	1	.333
Solly Hofman, cf	3	1	1	1	0	1	.222
Frank Chance, 1b	1	0	0	0	0	1	.222
Jimmy Archer, 1b	3	0	0	0	0	1	.000
Heinie Zimmerman, 2b	4	0	0	0	0	1	.100
Harry Steinfeldt, 3b	4	0	0	0	0	1	.083
Joe Tinker, ss	4	1	3	0	0	0	.545
Johnny Kling, c	4	0	0	0	0	1	.091
Ed Reulbach, p	0	0	0	0	0	0	—
Ginger Beaumont, ph	0	1	0	0	1	0	.000
Harry McIntire, p	0	0	0	0	0	0	.000
Jack Pfiester, p	2	0	0	0	0	1	.000
Tom Needham, ph	1	0	0	0	0	0	.000
TOTALS	31	5	6	3	4	8	.198

	1 2 3	4 5 6	7 8 9	R	H	E
Athletics	1 2 5	0 0 0	4 0 0	12	15	1
Cubs	1 2 0	0 0 0	0 2 0	5	6	5

E—Baker, Schulte, Hofman, Tinker 2, Steinfeldt. DP—Athletics 2 (Barry to Collins to Davis; Murphy to Davis), Cubs 1 (Zimmerman to Tinker to Archer). LOB—Athletics 7, Cubs 4. Scoring Position—Athletics 7-for-14, Cubs 1-for-7. 2B—Davis (2), Barry 2 (2), Coombs (1), Schulte 2 (2), Tinker (2). HR—Murphy (1). S—Lord. SF—Hofman. GDP—Coombs, Kling. SB—Tinker (1). CS—Collins (2), Baker (2).

Athletics	IP	H	R	ER	BB	K	ERA
Jack Coombs (W, 2-0)	9.0	6	5	5	4	8	4.00

Cubs	IP	H	R	ER	BB	K	ERA
Ed Reulbach	2.0	3	3	3	2	0	13.50
Harry McIntire (L, 0-1)	0.1	3	4	4	0	0	6.75
Jack Pfiester	6.2	9	5	0	1	1	0.00

WP—Coombs. HBP—Davis by McIntire. Time—2:07. Attendance—26,210. Umpires—HP, O'Day. 1B, Sheridan. 2B, Rigler. 3B, Connolly.

Game 4

Saturday, October 22

Athletics	AB	R	H	RBI	BB	K	Avg
Amos Strunk, cf	5	0	2	1	0	1	.278
Bris Lord, lf	5	0	0	0	0	1	.167
Eddie Collins, 2b	5	1	1	0	0	0	.375
Home Run Baker, 3b	4	1	3	0	1	0	.529
Harry Davis, 1b	3	0	1	0	1	2	.429
Danny Murphy, rf	4	0	2	2	0	0	.313
Jack Barry, ss	4	0	0	0	0	2	.267
Ira Thomas, c	4	0	1	0	0	0	.250
Chief Bender, p	3	1	1	0	1	0	.333
TOTALS	37	3	11	3	3	6	.326

Cubs	AB	R	H	RBI	BB	K	Avg
Jimmy Sheckard, lf	4	1	1	1	1	0	.200
Wildfire Schulte, rf	4	2	2	0	0	1	.385
Solly Hofman, cf	3	0	2	1	0	0	.333
Frank Chance, 1b	4	0	2	2	0	0	.308
Heinie Zimmerman, 2b	4	0	1	0	0	0	.143
Harry Steinfeldt, 3b	4	0	0	0	0	1	.063
Joe Tinker, ss	3	0	0	0	1	1	.429
Jimmy Archer, c	4	1	1	0	0	1	.143
King Cole, p	2	0	0	0	0	2	.000
Johnny Kling, ph	1	0	0	0	0	0	.083
John Kane, pr	0	0	0	0	0	0	—
Three Finger Brown, p	1	0	0	0	0	0	.000
TOTALS	34	4	9	4	2	6	.222

	1 2 3	4 5 6	7 8 9 10	R	H	E
Athletics	0 0 1	2 0 0	0 0 0 0	3	11	3
Cubs	1 0 0	1 0 0	0 0 1 1	4	9	1

E—Baker, Collins, Brown, Davis. DP—Athletics 2 (Baker to Collins to Davis; Bender to Baker to Davis), Cubs 1 (Cole to Archer to Chance). LOB—Athletics 10, Cubs 4. Scoring Position—Athletics 3-for-11, Cubs 4-for-9. 2B—Baker (3), Davis (3), Murphy (2), Schulte (3), Archer (1). 3B—Strunk (1), Chance (1). S—Davis, Murphy, Hofman. GDP—Thomas, Zimmerman. SB—Sheckard (1). CS—Baker (3), Schulte (3), Zimmerman (1), Tinker (2).

Athletics	IP	H	R	ER	BB	K	ERA
Chief Bender (L, 1-1)	9.2	9	4	4	2	6	1.93

Cubs	IP	H	R	ER	BB	K	ERA
King Cole	8.0	10	3	3	3	5	3.38
Three Finger Brown (W, 1-1)	2.0	1	0	0	0	1	6.00

HBP—Barry by Cole. Time—2:14. Attendance—19,150. Umpires—HP, Connolly. 1B, Rigler. 2B, Sheridan. 3B, O'Day.

Game 5

Sunday, October 23

Athletics	AB	R	H	RBI	BB	K	Avg
Topsy Hartsel, lf	5	2	1	0	0	1	.200
Bris Lord, cf	4	1	1	1	1	1	.182
Eddie Collins, 2b	5	0	3	2	0	0	.429
Home Run Baker, 3b	5	1	0	0	0	1	.409
Harry Davis, 1b	3	1	0	0	1	1	.353
Danny Murphy, rf	4	2	2	1	0	0	.350
Jack Barry, ss	2	0	0	0	1	0	.235
Jack Lapp, c	4	0	1	1	0	2	.250
Jack Coombs, p	4	0	1	0	0	1	.385
TOTALS	36	7	9	5	3	7	.326

Cubs	AB	R	H	RBI	BB	K	Avg
Jimmy Sheckard, lf	4	1	2	0	0	0	.286
Wildfire Schulte, rf	4	0	1	0	0	0	.353
Solly Hofman, cf	3	0	0	0	1	1	.267
Frank Chance, 1b	4	1	2	1	0	0	.353
Heinie Zimmerman, 2b	3	0	2	0	0	0	.235
Harry Steinfeldt, 3b	4	0	1	1	0	0	.100
Joe Tinker, ss	4	0	0	0	0	1	.333
Jimmy Archer, c	4	0	1	0	0	2	.182
Three Finger Brown, p	3	0	0	0	0	0	.000
Johnny Kling, ph	1	0	0	0	0	0	.077
TOTALS	34	2	9	2	1	4	.235

	1 2 3	4 5 6	7 8 9	R	H	E
Athletics	1 0 0	0 1 0	0 5 0	7	9	1
Cubs	0 1 0	0 0 0	0 1 0	2	9	2

E—Baker, Zimmerman, Steinfeldt. LOB—Athletics 6, Cubs 7. Scoring Position—Athletics 5-for-11, Cubs 2-for-8. 2B—Lord (2), Collins 2 (4), Murphy (3), Sheckard (2), Chance (1). S—Barry, Zimmerman. SB—Hartsel 2 (2), Collins 2 (4), Zimmerman (1). CS—Schulte 2 (5).

Athletics	IP	H	R	ER	BB	K	ERA
Jack Coombs (W, 3-0)	9.0	9	2	2	1	4	3.33

Cubs	IP	H	R	ER	BB	K	ERA
Three Finger Brown (L, 1-2)	9.0	9	7	4	3	7	5.00

WP—Brown. Time—2:06. Attendance—27,374. Umpires—HP, O'Day. 1B, Sheridan. 2B, Rigler. 3B, Connolly.

1910 World Series—Composite Statistics

Batting

Athletics

Athletics	G	AB	R	H	RBI	2B	3B	HR	BB	SO	SB	CS	Avg	OBP	Slg
Home Run Baker	5	22	6	9	4	3	0	0	2	1	0	3	.409	.458	.545
Jack Barry	5	17	3	4	3	2	0	0	1	3	0	0	.235	.316	.353
Chief Bender	2	6	1	2	1	0	0	0	1	1	0	0	.333	.429	.333
Eddie Collins	5	21	5	9	3	4	0	0	2	0	4	2	.429	.478	.619
Jack Coombs	3	13	0	5	3	1	0	0	0	3	0	0	.385	.385	.462
Harry Davis	5	17	5	6	2	3	0	0	3	4	0	0	.353	.476	.529
Topsy Hartsel	1	5	2	1	0	0	0	0	0	1	2	0	.200	.200	.200
Jack Lapp	1	4	0	1	1	0	0	0	0	2	0	0	.250	.250	.250
Bris Lord	5	22	3	4	1	2	0	0	1	3	0	1	.182	.217	.273
Danny Murphy	5	20	6	7	9	3	0	1	1	0	1	0	.350	.350	.650
Amos Strunk	4	18	2	5	2	1	1	0	2	5	0	1	.278	.350	.444
Ira Thomas	4	12	2	3	1	0	0	0	4	1	0	0	.250	.438	.250
Totals	5	177	35	56	30	19	1	1	17	24	7	7	.316	.383	.452

Cubs

Cubs	G	AB	R	H	RBI	2B	3B	HR	BB	SO	SB	CS	Avg	OBP	Slg
Jimmy Archer	3	11	1	2	0	1	0	0	0	4	0	0	.182	.182	.273
Ginger Beaumont	3	2	1	0	0	0	0	0	1	1	0	0	.000	.333	.000
Three Finger Brown	3	7	0	0	0	0	0	0	0	1	0	0	.000	.000	.000
Frank Chance	5	17	1	6	4	1	1	0	0	2	0	0	.353	.353	.529
King Cole	1	2	0	0	0	0	0	0	0	0	0	0	.000	.000	.000
Solly Hofman	5	15	2	4	2	0	0	0	4	3	0	0	.267	.400	.267
John Kane	2	0	0	0	0	0	0	0	0	0	0	0	—	—	—
Johnny Kling	5	13	0	1	1	0	0	0	1	2	0	0	.077	.143	.077
Harry McIntire	2	1	0	0	0	0	0	0	0	1	0	0	.000	.000	.000
Tom Needham	1	1	0	0	0	0	0	0	0	0	0	0	.000	.000	.000
Orval Overall	1	1	0	0	0	0	0	0	0	0	0	0	.000	.000	.000
Jack Pfiester	1	2	0	0	0	0	0	0	0	1	0	0	.000	.000	.000
Wildfire Schulte	5	17	3	6	2	3	0	0	2	3	0	5	.353	.421	.529
Jimmy Sheckard	5	14	5	4	1	2	0	0	7	2	1	0	.286	.524	.429
Harry Steinfeldt	5	20	0	2	1	1	0	0	0	4	0	0	.100	.100	.150
Joe Tinker	5	18	2	6	0	2	0	0	2	2	1	2	.333	.400	.444
Heinie Zimmerman	5	17	0	4	2	1	0	0	1	3	1	1	.235	.263	.294
Totals	5	158	15	35	13	11	1	0	18	31	3	8	.222	.298	.304

Pitching

Athletics

Athletics	G	GS	CG	IP	H	R	ER	BB	SO	W-L	Sv-Op	Hld	ERA
Chief Bender	2	2	2	18.2	12	5	4	4	14	1-1	0-0	0	1.93
Jack Coombs	3	3	3	27.0	23	10	10	14	17	3-0	0-0	0	3.33
Totals	5	5	5	45.2	35	15	14	18	31	4-1	0-0	0	2.76

Cubs

Cubs	G	GS	CG	IP	H	R	ER	BB	SO	W-L	Sv-Op	Hld	ERA
Three Finger Brown	3	2	1	18.0	23	16	10	7	14	1-2	0-0	0	5.00
King Cole	1	1	0	8.0	10	3	3	5	5	0-0	0-0	0	3.38
Harry McIntire	2	0	0	5.1	4	5	4	3	3	0-1	0-0	0	6.75
Orval Overall	1	1	0	3.0	6	3	3	1	1	0-1	0-0	0	9.00
Jack Pfiester	1	0	0	6.2	9	5	0	1	1	0-0	0-0	0	0.00
Ed Reulbach	1	1	0	2.0	3	3	3	2	0	0-0	0-0	0	13.50
Lew Richie	1	0	0	1.0	1	0	0	0	0	0-0	0-0	0	0.00
Totals	5	5	1	44.0	56	35	23	17	24	1-4	0-0	0	4.70

Fielding

Athletics

Athletics	Pos	G	PO	Ast	E	DP	PB	FPct
Home Run Baker	3b	5	8	11	3	2	—	.864
Jack Barry	ss	5	9	12	0	1	—	1.000
Chief Bender	p	2	1	2	0	1	—	1.000
Eddie Collins	2b	5	17	18	1	4	—	.972
Jack Coombs	p	3	1	3	2	0	—	.667
Harry Davis	1b	5	44	2	3	6	—	.939
Topsy Hartsel	lf	1	2	0	0	0	—	1.000
Jack Lapp	c	1	4	2	0	0	0	1.000
Bris Lord	lf	4	6	0	0	0	—	1.000
	cf	1	5	0	0	0	—	1.000
Danny Murphy	rf	5	6	2	0	2	—	1.000
Amos Strunk	cf	4	7	0	1	0	—	.875
Ira Thomas	c	4	27	8	1	1	0	.972
Totals		5	137	60	11	17	0	.947

Cubs

Cubs	Pos	G	PO	Ast	E	DP	PB	FPct
Jimmy Archer	c	2	18	4	0	1	0	1.000
	1b	1	9	0	0	1	—	1.000
Three Finger Brown	p	3	0	10	1	0	—	.909
Frank Chance	1b	5	52	3	0	2	—	1.000
King Cole	p	1	1	3	0	1	—	1.000
Solly Hofman	cf	5	7	0	1	0	—	.875
Johnny Kling	c	3	11	7	0	0	0	1.000
Harry McIntire	p	2	0	1	1	0	—	.500
Orval Overall	p	1	0	0	0	0	—	—
Jack Pfiester	p	1	0	1	0	0	—	1.000
Ed Reulbach	p	1	0	1	0	0	—	1.000
Lew Richie	p	1	0	0	0	0	—	—
Wildfire Schulte	rf	5	4	0	1	0	—	.800
Jimmy Sheckard	lf	5	7	2	1	0	—	.900
Harry Steinfeldt	3b	5	2	12	4	0	—	.778
Joe Tinker	ss	5	10	14	2	2	—	.923
Heinie Zimmerman	2b	5	11	18	1	1	—	.967
Totals		5	132	76	12	8	0	.945

1911 Philadelphia Athletics (AL) 4, New York Giants (NL) 2

Frank "Home Run" Baker earned his nickname, swatting two clutch home runs to help the Philadelphia Athletics defeat the New York Giants in six games. Christy Mathewson and the Giants took Game 1, 2-1, on Josh Devore's seventh-inning RBI double. Eddie Plank was sharp in the second game and Baker made the difference with a tie-breaking, two-run blast in the sixth. Jack Coombs beat Mathewson 3-2 in 11 innings in Game 3. Baker hit a game-tying homer off Matty in the ninth, and the Athletics tallied two in the 11th and held on to win, 3-2. After a week of rain, Chief Bender defeated Mathewson, 4-2. The Giants staved off elimination with a last-gasp, 4-3 victory in the fifth game. Run-scoring safeties by Doc Crandall and Devore tied it in the bottom of the ninth, and won it in the 10th on Fred Merkle's sacrifice fly. The Athletics took Game 6 in a rout, 13-2.

Game 1

Saturday, October 14

Athletics	AB	R	H	RBI	BB	K	Avg
Bris Lord, lf	4	0	0	0	0	2	.000
Rube Oldring, cf	4	0	2	0	0	1	.500
Eddie Collins, 2b	3	0	0	0	1	0	.000
Home Run Baker, 3b	4	1	2	0	0	1	.500
Danny Murphy, rf	3	0	0	0	0	0	.000
Harry Davis, 1b	4	0	1	1	0	0	.250
Jack Barry, ss	3	0	0	0	0	1	.000
Ira Thomas, c	3	0	0	0	0	0	.000
Chief Bender, p	3	0	1	0	0	0	.333
TOTALS	31	1	6	1	1	5	.194

Giants	AB	R	H	RBI	BB	K	Avg
Josh Devore, lf	3	0	1	1	1	1	.333
Larry Doyle, 2b	3	0	1	0	1	0	.333
Fred Snodgrass, cf	2	1	0	0	1	2	.000
Red Murray, rf	3	0	0	0	0	1	.000
Fred Merkle, 1b	4	0	1	0	0	2	.250
Buck Herzog, 3b	3	0	0	0	1	1	.000
Art Fletcher, ss	4	0	0	0	0	2	.000
Chief Meyers, c	3	1	1	0	0	0	.333
Christy Mathewson, p	3	0	1	0	0	2	.333
TOTALS	28	2	5	1	4	11	.179

	1	2	3	4	5	6	7	8	9	R	H	E
Athletics	0	1	0	0	0	0	0	0	0	1	6	2
Giants	0	0	0	1	0	0	1	0	x	2	5	0

E—Baker, Collins. LOB—Athletics 5, Giants 8. Scoring Position—Athletics 1-for-4, Giants 1-for-8. 2B—Oldring 2 (2), Devore (1), Meyers (1). S—Murphy, Murray. SB—Doyle (1). CS—Baker (1), Snodgrass 2 (2).

Athletics	IP	H	R	ER	BB	K	ERA
Chief Bender (L, 0-1)	8.0	5	2	1	4	11	1.13

Giants	IP	H	R	ER	BB	K	ERA
Christy Mathewson (W, 1-0)	9.0	6	1	1	1	5	1.00

PB—Meyers. HBP—Snodgrass by Bender. Time—2:12. Attendance—38,281. Umpires—HP, Klem. 1B, Dinneen. 2B, Brennan. 3B, Connolly.

Game 2

Monday, October 16

Giants	AB	R	H	RBI	BB	K	Avg
Josh Devore, lf	4	0	0	0	0	4	.143
Larry Doyle, 2b	4	0	0	0	0	0	.143
Fred Snodgrass, cf	3	0	2	0	0	1	.400
Red Murray, rf	4	0	0	0	0	1	.000
Fred Merkle, 1b	3	0	1	0	0	0	.286
Buck Herzog, 3b	3	1	1	0	0	0	.167
Art Fletcher, ss	3	0	0	0	0	0	.000
Chief Meyers, c	3	0	1	1	0	0	.333
Rube Marquard, p	2	0	0	0	0	2	.000
Doc Crandall, ph-p	1	0	0	0	0	0	.000
TOTALS	30	1	5	1	0	8	.164

Athletics	AB	R	H	RBI	BB	K	Avg
Bris Lord, lf	4	1	1	0	0	2	.125
Rube Oldring, cf	3	0	0	0	0	0	.286
Eddie Collins, 2b	3	1	2	0	0	0	.333
Home Run Baker, 3b	3	1	1	2	0	1	.429
Danny Murphy, rf	3	0	0	0	0	1	.000
Harry Davis, 1b	3	0	0	0	0	0	.143
Jack Barry, ss	3	0	0	0	0	0	.000
Ira Thomas, c	3	0	0	0	0	0	.000
Eddie Plank, p	3	0	0	0	0	2	.000
TOTALS	28	3	4	2	0	6	.161

	1	2	3	4	5	6	7	8	9	R	H	E
Giants	0	1	0	0	0	0	0	0	0	1	5	3
Athletics	1	0	0	0	0	2	0	0	x	3	4	0

E—Devore, Merkle, Murray. LOB—Giants 3, Athletics 2. Scoring Position—Giants 1-for-2, Athletics 1-for-3. 2B—Herzog (1), Collins (1). HR—Baker (1). S—Oldring.

Giants	IP	H	R	ER	BB	K	ERA
Rube Marquard (L, 0-1)	7.0	4	3	2	0	4	2.57
Doc Crandall	1.0	0	0	0	0	2	0.00

Athletics	IP	H	R	ER	BB	K	ERA
Eddie Plank (W, 1-0)	9.0	5	1	1	0	8	1.00

WP—Marquard. HBP—Snodgrass by Plank. Time—1:52. Attendance—26,286. Umpires—HP, Connolly. 1B, Brennan. 2B, Klem. 3B, Dinneen.

Game 3

Tuesday, October 17

Athletics	AB	R	H	RBI	BB	K	Avg
Bris Lord, lf	5	0	0	0	0	0	.077
Rube Oldring, cf	5	0	0	0	0	1	.167
Eddie Collins, 2b	5	1	2	0	0	1	.364
Home Run Baker, 3b	5	2	2	1	0	0	.417
Danny Murphy, rf	5	0	0	1	0	0	.000
Harry Davis, 1b	5	0	2	1	0	1	.250
Jack Barry, ss	3	0	2	0	0	0	.222
Jack Lapp, c	4	0	1	0	0	0	.250
Jack Coombs, p	4	0	0	0	0	0	.000
TOTALS	41	3	9	3	0	3	.205

Giants	AB	R	H	RBI	BB	K	Avg
Josh Devore, lf	4	0	0	1	0	1	.091
Larry Doyle, 2b	4	0	0	0	0	1	.091
Fred Snodgrass, cf	3	0	0	0	1	2	.250
Red Murray, rf	2	0	0	0	1	0	.000
Fred Merkle, 1b	3	0	0	0	1	0	.200
Buck Herzog, 3b	3	1	1	0	1	1	.222
Art Fletcher, ss	4	0	0	0	0	0	.000
Chief Meyers, c	4	1	1	0	0	1	.300
Christy Mathewson, p	3	0	1	0	0	1	.333
Beals Becker, ph	1	0	0	0	0	0	.000
TOTALS	31	2	3	1	4	7	.151

	1	2	3	4	5	6	7	8	9	10	11	R	H	E
Athletics	0	0	0	0	0	0	0	1	0	2		3	9	2
Giants	0	0	1	0	0	0	0	0	0	0	1	2	3	5

E—Fletcher 2, Herzog 3, Collins 2. DP—Giants 1 (Doyle to Fletcher). LOB—Athletics 6, Giants 1. Scoring Position—Athletics 2-for-12, Giants 0-for-5. 2B—Barry (1), Herzog (2). HR—Baker (2). S—Barry, Murray. SB—Collins (1), Barry (1). CS—Davis (1), Devore (1), Murray (1), Merkle (1), Herzog (1), Becker (1).

Athletics	IP	H	R	ER	BB	K	ERA
Jack Coombs (W, 1-0)	11.0	3	2	1	4	7	0.82

Giants	IP	H	R	ER	BB	K	ERA
Christy Mathewson (L, 1-1)	11.0	9	3	1	0	3	0.90

Time—2:25. Attendance—37,216. Umpires—HP, Brennan. 1B, Connolly. 2B, Klem. 3B, Dinneen.

Game 4
Tuesday, October 24

Giants	AB	R	H	RBI	BB	K	Avg
Josh Devore, lf	4	1	2	0	0	0	.200
Larry Doyle, 2b	3	1	1	1	1	0	.143
Fred Snodgrass, cf	3	0	0	1	0	1	.182
Red Murray, rf	4	0	0	0	0	0	.000
Fred Merkle, 1b	4	0	1	0	0	3	.214
Buck Herzog, 3b	4	0	0	0	0	0	.154
Art Fletcher, ss	4	0	2	0	0	0	.133
Chief Meyers, c	4	0	1	0	0	0	.286
Christy Mathewson, p	1	0	0	0	1	0	.286
Beals Becker, ph	1	0	0	0	0	0	.000
Hooks Wiltse, p	0	0	0	0	0	0	—
TOTALS	32	2	7	2	2	4	.169

Athletics	AB	R	H	RBI	BB	K	Avg
Bris Lord, lf	4	0	1	0	0	1	.118
Rube Oldring, cf	3	0	0	0	0	1	.133
Eddie Collins, 2b	3	1	2	0	0	1	.429
Home Run Baker, 3b	3	1	2	1	1	1	.467
Danny Murphy, rf	4	1	2	1	0	1	.133
Harry Davis, 1b	4	1	1	1	0	1	.250
Jack Barry, ss	4	0	3	0	0	0	.385
Ira Thomas, c	3	0	0	1	0	0	.000
Chief Bender, p	4	0	0	0	0	0	.143
TOTALS	32	4	11	4	1	6	.240

	1 2 3 4 5 6 7 8 9	R H E
Giants	2 0 0 0 0 0 0 0 0	2 7 3
Athletics	0 0 0 3 1 0 0 0 x	4 11 1

E—Fletcher, Baker, Murray, Mathewson. DP—Athletics 1 (Baker to Davis). LOB—Giants 6, Athletics 8. Scoring Position—Giants 0-for-4, Athletics 2-for-10. 2B—Merkle (1), Meyers (2), Baker 2 (2), Murphy 2 (2), Davis (1), Barry 2 (3). 3B—Doyle (1). S—Oldring, Collins. SF—Snodgrass, Thomas. CS—Murphy (1).

Giants	IP	H	R	ER	BB	K	ERA
Christy Mathewson (L, 1-2)	7.0	10	4	4	1	5	2.00
Hooks Wiltse	1.0	1	0	0	0	1	0.00

Athletics	IP	H	R	ER	BB	K	ERA
Chief Bender (W, 1-1)	9.0	7	2	2	2	4	1.59

Time—1:49. Attendance—24,355. Umpires—HP, Dinneen. 1B, Klem. 2B, Connolly. 3B, Brennan.

Game 5
Wednesday, October 25

Athletics	AB	R	H	RBI	BB	K	Avg
Bris Lord, lf	5	0	0	0	0	0	.091
Rube Oldring, cf	5	1	2	3	0	0	.200
Eddie Collins, 2b	3	0	0	0	1	0	.353
Home Run Baker, 3b	4	0	0	0	0	1	.368
Danny Murphy, rf	4	0	1	0	0	1	.158
Harry Davis, 1b	4	0	0	0	0	1	.200
Jack Barry, ss	4	0	1	0	0	0	.353
Jack Lapp, c	4	1	1	0	0	1	.250
Jack Coombs, p	4	1	2	0	0	0	.250
Amos Strunk, pr	0	0	0	0	0	0	—
Eddie Plank, p	0	0	0	0	0	0	.000
TOTALS	37	3	7	3	1	4	.235

Giants	AB	R	H	RBI	BB	K	Avg
Josh Devore, lf	5	0	1	1	0	1	.200
Larry Doyle, 2b	5	1	4	0	0	0	.316
Fred Snodgrass, cf	4	0	0	0	0	1	.133
Red Murray, rf	5	0	0	0	0	3	.000
Fred Merkle, 1b	2	1	0	1	1	1	.188
Buck Herzog, 3b	4	0	1	0	0	0	.176
Art Fletcher, ss	4	1	1	0	0	1	.158
Chief Meyers, c	3	0	1	1	0	1	.294
Rube Marquard, p	0	0	0	0	0	0	.000
Beals Becker, ph	1	0	0	0	0	0	.000
Red Ames, p	1	0	0	0	0	0	.000
Doc Crandall, ph-p	1	1	1	1	1	0	.500
TOTALS	35	4	9	4	2	9	.181

	1 2 3 4 5 6 7 8 9 10	R H E
Athletics	0 0 3 0 0 0 0 0 0 0	3 7 1
Giants	0 0 0 0 0 1 0 2 1	4 9 2

E—Fletcher, Doyle, Collins. DP—Athletics 1 (Lapp to Collins), Giants 1 (Meyers to Doyle). LOB—Athletics 5, Giants 8. Scoring Position—Athletics 1-for-7, Giants 2-for-15. 2B—Doyle 2 (2), Fletcher (1), Crandall (1). HR—Oldring (1). S—Snodgrass. SF—Merkle, Meyers. SB—Collins (2), Barry (2), Doyle (2), Herzog (1). CS—Murphy (2), Barry (1), Devore (2), Meyers (1).

Athletics	IP	H	R	ER	BB	K	ERA
Jack Coombs	9.0	8	3	2	2	9	1.35
Eddie Plank (L, 1-1)	0.2	1	1	1	0	0	1.86

Giants	IP	H	R	ER	BB	K	ERA
Rube Marquard	3.0	3	3	0	1	2	1.80
Red Ames	4.0	2	0	0	0	0	0.00
Doc Crandall (W, 1-0)	3.0	2	0	0	0	0	0.00

WP—Crandall. HBP—Merkle by Coombs. Time—2:33. Attendance—33,228. Umpires—HP, Klem. 1B, Dinneen. 2B, Connolly. 3B, Brennan.

Game 6
Thursday, October 26

Giants	AB	R	H	RBI	BB	K	Avg
Josh Devore, lf	4	0	0	0	0	1	.167
Larry Doyle, 2b	4	1	1	0	0	0	.304
Fred Snodgrass, cf	4	0	0	0	0	0	.105
Red Murray, rf	3	0	0	0	0	1	.000
Fred Merkle, 1b	4	0	0	0	0	0	.150
Buck Herzog, 3b	4	1	1	0	0	1	.190
Art Fletcher, ss	4	0	0	1	0	1	.130
Chief Meyers, c	3	0	1	0	0	0	.300
Art Wilson, c	1	0	0	0	0	0	.000
Red Ames, p	1	0	1	0	0	0	.500
Doc Crandall, ph	0	0	0	0	1	0	.500
Hooks Wiltse, p	1	0	0	0	0	1	.000
Rube Marquard, p	0	0	0	0	0	0	.000
TOTALS	33	2	4	1	2	5	.173

Athletics	AB	R	H	RBI	BB	K	Avg
Bris Lord, lf	5	1	3	1	0	0	.185
Rube Oldring, cf	5	1	1	0	0	1	.200
Eddie Collins, 2b	4	1	0	1	0	1	.286
Home Run Baker, 3b	5	2	2	1	0	1	.375
Danny Murphy, rf	4	3	4	1	0	0	.304
Harry Davis, 1b	4	2	1	2	0	0	.208
Stuffy McInnis, 1b	0	0	0	0	0	0	—
Jack Barry, ss	2	2	1	2	0	1	.368
Ira Thomas, c	3	1	1	0	1	2	.083
Chief Bender, p	4	0	0	0	0	1	.091
TOTALS	36	13	13	8	1	7	.247

	1 2 3 4 5 6 7 8 9	R H E
Giants	1 0 0 0 0 0 0 0 1	2 4 3
Athletics	0 0 1 4 0 1 7 0 x	13 13 5

E—Barry 3, Merkle, Murray, Oldring, Ames, Murphy. LOB—Giants 6, Athletics 3. Scoring Position—Giants 0-for-6, Athletics 5-for-13. 2B—Doyle (3), Lord 2 (2), Murphy (3), Barry (4). S—Collins, Barry. SF—Barry. SB—Herzog (2). CS—Devore (3), Thomas (1).

Giants	IP	H	R	ER	BB	K	ERA
Red Ames (L, 0-1)	4.0	4	5	2	1	4	2.25
Hooks Wiltse	2.1	7	8	7	0	1	18.90
Rube Marquard	1.2	2	0	0	0	2	1.54

Athletics	IP	H	R	ER	BB	K	ERA
Chief Bender (W, 2-1)	9.0	4	2	0	2	5	1.04

WP—Bender, Marquard. Time—2:12. Attendance—20,485. Umpires—HP, Connolly. 1B, Brennan. 2B, Klem. 3B, Dinneen.

Postseason: World Series

1911 World Series—Composite Statistics

Batting

Athletics	G	AB	R	H	RBI	2B	3B	HR	BB	SO	SB	CS	Avg	OBP	Slg
Home Run Baker	6	24	7	9	5	2	0	2	1	5	0	1	.375	.400	.708
Jack Barry	6	19	2	7	2	4	0	0	0	2	2	1	.368	.350	.579
Chief Bender	3	11	0	1	0	0	0	0	0	1	0	0	.091	.091	.091
Eddie Collins	6	21	4	6	1	1	0	0	2	3	2	0	.286	.348	.333
Jack Coombs	2	8	1	2	0	0	0	0	0	0	0	0	.250	.250	.250
Harry Davis	6	24	3	5	5	1	0	0	0	3	0	1	.208	.208	.250
Jack Lapp	2	8	1	2	0	0	0	0	0	1	0	0	.250	.250	.250
Bris Lord	6	27	2	5	1	2	0	0	0	5	0	0	.185	.185	.259
Danny Murphy	6	23	4	7	3	3	0	0	0	3	0	2	.304	.304	.435
Rube Oldring	6	25	2	5	3	2	0	1	0	4	0	0	.200	.200	.400
Eddie Plank	2	3	0	0	0	0	0	0	0	2	0	0	.000	.000	.000
Amos Strunk	1	0	0	0	0	0	0	0	0	0	0	0	—	—	—
Ira Thomas	4	12	1	1	1	0	0	0	1	2	0	1	.083	.143	.083
Totals	**6**	**205**	**27**	**50**	**21**	**15**	**0**	**3**	**4**	**31**	**4**	**6**	**.244**	**.256**	**.361**

Giants	G	AB	R	H	RBI	2B	3B	HR	BB	SO	SB	CS	Avg	OBP	Slg
Red Ames	2	2	0	1	0	0	0	0	0	1	0	0	.500	.500	.500
Beals Becker	3	3	0	0	0	0	0	0	0	0	0	1	.000	.000	.000
Doc Crandall	3	2	1	1	1	1	0	0	2	0	0	0	.500	.750	1.000
Josh Devore	6	24	1	4	3	1	0	0	1	8	0	3	.167	.200	.208
Larry Doyle	6	23	3	7	1	3	1	0	2	1	2	0	.304	.360	.522
Art Fletcher	6	23	1	3	1	1	0	0	0	4	0	0	.130	.130	.174
Buck Herzog	6	21	3	4	0	2	0	0	2	3	2	1	.190	.261	.286
Rube Marquard	3	2	0	0	0	0	0	0	0	2	0	0	.000	.000	.000
Christy Mathewson	3	7	0	2	0	0	0	0	1	3	0	0	.286	.375	.286
Fred Merkle	6	20	1	3	1	1	0	0	2	6	0	1	.150	.250	.200
Chief Meyers	6	20	2	6	2	2	0	0	0	3	0	1	.300	.286	.400
Red Murray	6	21	0	0	0	0	0	0	2	5	0	1	.000	.087	.000
Fred Snodgrass	6	19	1	2	1	0	0	0	2	7	0	2	.105	.250	.105
Art Wilson	1	1	0	0	0	0	0	0	0	0	0	0	.000	.000	.000
Hooks Wiltse	2	1	0	0	0	0	0	0	0	1	0	0	.000	.000	.000
Totals	**6**	**189**	**13**	**33**	**10**	**11**	**1**	**0**	**14**	**44**	**4**	**10**	**.175**	**.239**	**.243**

Pitching

Athletics	G	GS	CG	IP	H	R	ER	BB	SO	W-L	Sv-Op	Hld	ERA
Chief Bender	3	3	3	26.0	16	6	3	8	20	2-1	0-0	0	1.04
Jack Coombs	2	2	1	20.0	11	5	3	6	16	1-0	0-0	0	1.35
Eddie Plank	2	1	1	9.2	6	2	2	0	8	1-1	0-0	0	1.86
Totals	**6**	**6**	**5**	**55.2**	**33**	**13**	**8**	**14**	**44**	**4-2**	**0-0**	**0**	**1.29**

Giants	G	GS	CG	IP	H	R	ER	BB	SO	W-L	Sv-Op	Hld	ERA
Red Ames	2	1	0	8.0	6	5	2	1	6	0-1	0-0	0	2.25
Doc Crandall	2	0	0	4.0	2	0	0	0	2	1-0	0-0	0	0.00
Rube Marquard	3	2	0	11.2	9	6	2	1	8	0-1	0-0	0	1.54
Christy Mathewson	3	3	2	27.0	25	8	6	2	13	1-2	0-0	0	2.00
Hooks Wiltse	2	0	0	3.1	8	8	7	0	2	0-0	0-0	0	18.90
Totals	**6**	**6**	**2**	**54.0**	**50**	**27**	**17**	**4**	**31**	**2-4**	**0-0**	**0**	**2.83**

Fielding

Athletics	Pos	G	PO	Ast	E	DP	PB	FPct
Home Run Baker	3b	6	10	11	2	1	—	.913
Jack Barry	ss	6	8	12	3	0	—	.870
Chief Bender	p	3	1	6	0	0	—	1.000
Eddie Collins	2b	6	13	22	4	1	—	.897
Jack Coombs	p	2	1	2	0	0	—	1.000
Harry Davis	1b	6	54	3	0	1	—	1.000
Jack Lapp	c	2	18	8	0	1	0	1.000
Bris Lord	lf	6	14	1	0	0	—	1.000
Stuffy McInnis	1b	1	1	0	0	0	—	1.000
Danny Murphy	rf	6	8	0	1	0	—	.889
Rube Oldring	cf	6	8	0	1	0	—	.889
Eddie Plank	p	2	0	2	0	0	—	1.000
Ira Thomas	c	4	31	4	0	0	0	1.000
Totals		**6**	**167**	**71**	**11**	**4**	**0**	**.956**

Giants	Pos	G	PO	Ast	E	DP	PB	FPct
Red Ames	p	2	0	1	1	0	—	.500
Doc Crandall	p	2	0	2	0	0	—	1.000
Josh Devore	lf	6	15	0	1	0	—	.938
Larry Doyle	2b	6	13	15	1	2	—	.966
Art Fletcher	ss	6	11	18	4	1	—	.879
Buck Herzog	3b	6	7	13	3	0	—	.870
Rube Marquard	p	3	0	2	0	0	—	1.000
Christy Mathewson	p	3	2	9	1	0	—	.917
Fred Merkle	1b	6	62	4	2	0	—	.971
Chief Meyers	c	6	37	12	0	1	1	1.000
Red Murray	rf	6	4	1	3	0	—	.625
Fred Snodgrass	cf	6	10	0	0	0	—	1.000
Art Wilson	c	1	1	0	0	0	0	1.000
Hooks Wiltse	p	2	0	2	0	0	—	1.000
Totals		**6**	**162**	**79**	**16**	**4**	**1**	**.938**

1912 Boston Red Sox (AL) 4, New York Giants (NL) 3, 1 Tie

The Boston Red Sox defeated the New York Giants, four games to three (with one tie) in one of the greatest World Series ever played. Steve Yerkes' key two-run single helped Joe Wood give the Red Sox a 4-3 victory in the opener. The second game was called on account of darkness after 11 innings, tied 6-6. Rube Marquard won the third game, 2-1, before Wood came back to take Game 4, 3-1. Yerkes tripled in a run and scored on Larry Doyle's miscue as Hugh Bedient beat Christy Mathewson in Game 5, 2-1. Marquard defeated the Red Sox for the second time with a 5-2 win in Game 6, and the Giants jumped all over Wood in Game 7, running away with an 11-4 victory. Mathewson was masterful in Game 8, taking a 1-0 lead into the seventh until Olaf Henriksen's pinch-hit RBI double tied the game. Fred Merkle gave the Giants a one-run lead in the top of the 10th on an RBI single, but disaster struck the Giants in the bottom of the frame. Center fielder Fred Snodgrass muffed Clyde Engle's fly to open the inning, although he made a fantastic grab of Harry Hooper's fly on the next play. After Merkle and Chief Meyers let Tris Speaker's foul fly drop untouched, Speaker tied the game with a single, and Larry Gardner won it for Boston with a sacrifice fly.

Game 1

Tuesday, October 8

Red Sox	AB	R	H	RBI	BB	K	Avg
Harry Hooper, rf	3	1	1	1	1	1	.333
Steve Yerkes, 2b	4	0	1	2	0	0	.250
Tris Speaker, cf	3	1	1	0	1	1	.333
Duffy Lewis, lf	4	0	0	0	0	0	.000
Larry Gardner, 3b	4	0	0	0	0	2	.000
Jake Stahl, 1b	4	0	0	0	0	2	.000
Heinie Wagner, ss	3	1	2	0	1	0	.667
Hick Cady, c	3	0	1	0	0	0	.333
Joe Wood, p	3	1	0	0	1	0	.000
TOTALS	31	4	6	4	4	6	.194

Giants	AB	R	H	RBI	BB	K	Avg
Josh Devore, lf	3	1	0	0	1	1	.000
Larry Doyle, 2b	4	1	2	0	0	0	.500
Fred Snodgrass, cf	4	0	1	0	0	1	.250
Red Murray, rf	3	0	1	2	1	0	.333
Fred Merkle, 1b	4	1	1	0	0	1	.250
Buck Herzog, 3b	4	0	2	0	0	1	.500
Chief Meyers, c	3	0	1	0	1	1	.333
Beals Becker, pr	0	0	0	0	0	0	—
Art Fletcher, ss	4	0	0	0	0	3	.000
Jeff Tesreau, p	2	0	0	0	0	2	.000
Moose McCormick, ph	1	0	0	0	0	0	.000
Doc Crandall, p	1	0	0	0	0	1	.000
TOTALS	33	3	8	3	2	11	.242

	1	2	3	4	5	6	7	8	9	R	H	E
Red Sox	0	0	0	0	0	1	3	0	0	4	6	1
Giants	0	0	2	0	0	0	0	0	1	3	8	1

E—Fletcher, Wagner. DP—Red Sox 1 (Stahl to Wood). LOB—Red Sox 6, Giants 6. Scoring Position—Red Sox 2-for-10, Giants 2-for-7. 2B—Hooper (1), Wagner (1), Doyle (1). 3B—Speaker (1). S—Hooper, Cady. CS—Stahl (1).

Red Sox	IP	H	R	ER	BB	K	ERA
Joe Wood (W, 1-0)	9.0	8	3	3	2	11	3.00

Giants	IP	H	R	ER	BB	K	ERA
Jeff Tesreau (L, 0-1)	7.0	5	4	4	4	4	5.14
Doc Crandall	2.0	1	0	0	0	2	0.00

HBP—Meyers by Wood. Time—2:10. Attendance—35,730. Umpires—HP, Klem. 1B, Evans. 2B, Rigler. 3B, O'Loughlin.

Game 2

Wednesday, October 9

Giants	AB	R	H	RBI	BB	K	Avg
Fred Snodgrass, lf-rf	4	1	1	0	1	1	.250
Larry Doyle, 2b	5	0	1	0	1	2	.333
Beals Becker, cf	4	1	0	0	2	0	.000
Red Murray, rf-lf	5	2	3	1	0	0	.500
Fred Merkle, 1b	5	1	1	0	0	1	.222
Buck Herzog, 3b	4	1	3	3	0	0	.625
Chief Meyers, c	4	0	2	1	1	0	.429
Tillie Shafer, pr-ss	0	0	0	0	0	0	—
Art Fletcher, ss	4	0	0	0	0	0	.000
Moose McCormick, ph	0	0	0	1	0	0	.000
Art Wilson, c	0	0	0	0	0	0	—
Christy Mathewson, p	5	0	0	0	0	2	.000
TOTALS	40	6	11	6	5	6	.284

Red Sox	AB	R	H	RBI	BB	K	Avg
Harry Hooper, rf	5	1	3	0	0	0	.500
Steve Yerkes, 2b	5	1	1	1	0	0	.222
Tris Speaker, cf	5	2	2	0	0	0	.375
Duffy Lewis, lf	5	2	3	0	0	0	.333
Larry Gardner, 3b	4	0	1	2	0	0	.000
Jake Stahl, 1b	5	0	1	2	0	1	.111
Heinie Wagner, ss	5	0	0	0	1	0	.250
Bill Carrigan, c	5	0	0	0	0	0	.000
Ray Collins, p	3	0	0	0	0	2	.000
Sea Lion Hall, p	1	0	0	0	0	0	.000
Hugh Bedient, p	1	0	0	0	0	0	.000
TOTALS	44	6	10	4	0	4	.217

	1	2	3	4	5	6	7	8	9	10	11	R	H	E
Giants	0	1	0	1	0	0	0	3	0	1	0	6	11	5
Red Sox	3	0	0	0	1	0	0	0	1	0	1	6	10	1

E—Lewis, Fletcher 3, Wilson, Doyle. DP—Giants 1 (Fletcher to Herzog). LOB—Giants 9, Red Sox 6. Scoring Position—Giants 3-for-14, Red Sox 3-for-14. 2B—Snodgrass (1), Murray (1), Herzog (1), Hooper (2), Lewis 2 (2). 3B—Murray (1), Merkle (1), Herzog (1), Yerkes (1), Speaker (2). S—Gardner. SF—Herzog, McCormick. SB—Snodgrass (1), Herzog (1), Hooper 2 (2), Stahl (1). CS—Becker (1), Murray (1).

Giants	IP	H	R	ER	BB	K	ERA
Christy Mathewson	11.0	10	6	1	0	4	0.82

Red Sox	IP	H	R	ER	BB	K	ERA
Ray Collins	7.1	9	5	3	0	5	3.68
Sea Lion Hall (BS, 1)	2.2	2	1	1	4	0	3.38
Hugh Bedient	1.0	0	0	0	1	1	0.00

HBP—Snodgrass by Bedient. Time—2:38. Attendance—30,148. Umpires—HP, O'Loughlin. 1B, Rigler. 2B, Klem. 3B, Evans.

Game 3

Thursday, October 10

Giants	AB	R	H	RBI	BB	K	Avg
Josh Devore, rf	4	0	2	0	0	1	.286
Larry Doyle, 2b	3	0	0	0	1	0	.250
Fred Snodgrass, cf	4	0	1	0	0	0	.250
Red Murray, lf	4	1	1	0	0	0	.417
Fred Merkle, 1b	3	0	0	0	0	1	.167
Buck Herzog, 3b	2	1	1	1	0	0	.600
Chief Meyers, c	4	0	1	0	0	1	.364
Art Fletcher, ss	3	0	1	1	1	0	.091
Rube Marquard, p	1	0	0	0	1	0	.000
TOTALS	28	2	7	2	3	3	.295

Red Sox	AB	R	H	RBI	BB	K	Avg
Harry Hooper, rf	3	0	0	0	1	1	.364
Steve Yerkes, 2b	4	0	1	0	0	1	.231
Tris Speaker, cf	4	0	1	0	0	0	.333
Duffy Lewis, lf	4	1	2	0	0	0	.385
Larry Gardner, 3b	3	0	1	1	0	0	.091
Jake Stahl, 1b	4	0	2	0	0	0	.231
Olaf Henriksen, pr	0	0	0	0	0	0	—
Heinie Wagner, ss	4	0	0	0	0	1	.167
Bill Carrigan, c	2	0	0	0	0	0	.000
Clyde Engle, ph	1	0	0	0	0	0	.000
Hick Cady, c	1	0	0	0	0	0	.250
Buck O'Brien, p	2	0	0	0	0	2	.000
Neal Ball, ph	1	0	0	0	0	1	.000
Hugh Bedient, p	0	0	0	0	0	0	.000
TOTALS	33	1	7	1	1	6	.228

	1	2	3	4	5	6	7	8	9	R	H	E
Giants	0	1	0	0	1	0	0	0	0	2	7	1
Red Sox	0	0	0	0	0	0	0	0	1	1	7	0

E—Merkle. DP—Red Sox 1 (Speaker to Stahl). LOB—Giants 6, Red Sox 7. Scoring Position—Giants 1-for-8, Red Sox 0-for-5. 2B—Murray (2), Herzog (2), Gardner (1), Stahl (1). S—Merkle, Marquard, Gardner. SF—Herzog. SB—Devore (1), Fletcher (1), Wagner (1). CS—Devore (1), Herzog (1), Stahl (2).

Giants	IP	H	R	ER	BB	K	ERA
Rube Marquard (W, 1-0)	9.0	7	1	1	1	6	1.00

Red Sox	IP	H	R	ER	BB	K	ERA
Buck O'Brien (L, 0-1)	8.0	6	2	2	3	3	2.25
Hugh Bedient	1.0	1	0	0	0	0	0.00

HBP—Herzog by Bedient. Time—2:15. Attendance—34,624. Umpires—HP, Evans. 1B, Klem. 2B, O'Loughlin. 3B, Rigler.

Game 4

Friday, October 11

Red Sox	AB	R	H	RBI	BB	K	Avg
Harry Hooper, rf	4	0	1	0	1	0	.333
Steve Yerkes, 2b	3	0	1	0	0	0	.250
Tris Speaker, cf	4	0	1	0	0	0	.313
Duffy Lewis, lf	4	0	0	0	0	1	.294
Larry Gardner, 3b	3	2	2	0	1	0	.214
Jake Stahl, 1b	3	1	0	0	0	1	.188
Heinie Wagner, ss	3	0	0	0	1	1	.133
Hick Cady, c	4	0	1	1	0	2	.250
Joe Wood, p	4	0	2	1	0	0	.286
TOTALS	32	3	8	2	3	5	.250

Giants	AB	R	H	RBI	BB	K	Avg
Josh Devore, lf	4	0	1	0	0	1	.273
Larry Doyle, 2b	4	0	1	0	0	0	.250
Fred Snodgrass, cf	4	0	0	0	0	1	.188
Red Murray, rf	4	0	1	0	0	2	.375
Fred Merkle, 1b	4	0	1	0	0	2	.188
Buck Herzog, 3b	4	1	2	0	0	0	.571
Chief Meyers, c	4	0	0	0	0	1	.267
Art Fletcher, ss	4	0	1	1	0	0	.133
Jeff Tesreau, p	2	0	1	0	0	1	.250
Moose McCormick, ph	1	0	1	0	0	0	.500
Red Ames, p	0	0	0	0	0	0	—
TOTALS	35	1	9	1	0	8	.280

	1	2	3	4	5	6	7	8	9	R	H	E
Red Sox	0	1	0	1	0	0	0	0	1	3	8	1
Giants	0	0	0	0	0	0	1	0	0	1	9	1

E—Meyers, Wagner. DP—Giants 1 (Fletcher to Merkle). LOB—Red Sox 7, Giants 7. Scoring Position—Red Sox 2-for-11, Giants 1-for-7. 2B—Speaker (1), Fletcher (1). 3B—Gardner (1). S—Yerkes, Stahl. GDP—Speaker. SB—Stahl (2), Merkle (1). CS—Speaker (1).

Red Sox	IP	H	R	ER	BB	K	ERA
Joe Wood (W, 2-0)	9.0	9	1	1	0	8	2.00

Giants	IP	H	R	ER	BB	K	ERA
Jeff Tesreau (L, 0-2)	7.0	5	2	2	2	5	3.86
Red Ames	2.0	3	1	1	1	0	4.50

WP—Tesreau. Time—2:06. Attendance—36,502. Umpires—HP, Rigler. 1B, O'Loughlin. 2B, Evans. 3B, Klem.

Game 5

Saturday, October 12

Giants	AB	R	H	RBI	BB	K	Avg
Josh Devore, lf	2	0	0	0	2	1	.231
Larry Doyle, 2b	4	0	0	0	0	0	.200
Fred Snodgrass, cf	4	0	0	0	0	1	.150
Red Murray, rf	3	0	0	0	1	0	.316
Fred Merkle, 1b	4	1	1	0	0	1	.200
Buck Herzog, 3b	4	0	0	0	0	0	.444
Chief Meyers, c	3	0	1	0	0	0	.278
Art Fletcher, ss	2	0	0	0	0	0	.118
Moose McCormick, ph	1	0	0	0	0	0	.333
Tillie Shafer, pr-ss	0	0	0	0	0	0	—
Christy Mathewson, p	3	0	1	0	0	1	.125
TOTALS	30	1	3	0	3	4	.237

Red Sox	AB	R	H	RBI	BB	K	Avg
Harry Hooper, rf	4	1	2	0	0	0	.368
Steve Yerkes, 2b	4	1	1	1	0	0	.250
Tris Speaker, cf	3	0	1	1	0	0	.316
Duffy Lewis, lf	3	0	0	0	0	0	.250
Larry Gardner, 3b	3	0	0	0	0	1	.176
Jake Stahl, 1b	3	0	0	0	0	0	.158
Heinie Wagner, ss	3	0	1	0	0	1	.167
Hick Cady, c	3	0	0	0	0	0	.182
Hugh Bedient, p	3	0	0	0	0	0	.000
TOTALS	29	2	5	2	0	2	.231

	1	2	3	4	5	6	7	8	9		R	H	E
Giants	0	0	0	0	0	0	1	0	0		1	3	1
Red Sox	0	0	2	0	0	0	0	0	x		2	5	1

E—Gardner, Doyle. DP—Red Sox 1 (Wagner to Yerkes to Stahl). LOB—Giants 5, Red Sox 3. Scoring Position—Giants 0-for-7, Red Sox 1-for-5. 2B—Merkle (1). 3B—Hooper (1), Yerkes (2). GDP—Snodgrass.

Giants	IP	H	R	ER	BB	K	ERA
Christy Mathewson (L, 0-1)	8.0	5	2	2	0	2	1.42

Red Sox	IP	H	R	ER	BB	K	ERA
Hugh Bedient (W, 1-0)	9.0	3	1	1	3	4	0.82

Time—1:43. Attendance—34,683. Umpires—HP, O'Loughlin. 1B, Rigler. 2B, Klem. 3B, Evans.

Game 6

Monday, October 14

Red Sox	AB	R	H	RBI	BB	K	Avg
Harry Hooper, rf	4	0	1	0	0	0	.348
Steve Yerkes, 2b	4	0	2	0	0	0	.292
Tris Speaker, cf	3	0	0	0	1	0	.273
Duffy Lewis, lf	4	0	0	0	0	0	.208
Larry Gardner, 3b	4	1	0	0	0	1	.143
Jake Stahl, 1b	4	1	2	0	0	1	.217
Heinie Wagner, ss	4	0	0	0	0	1	.136
Hick Cady, c	3	0	1	0	0	0	.214
Buck O'Brien, p	0	0	0	0	0	0	.000
Clyde Engle, ph	1	0	1	2	0	0	.500
Ray Collins, p	2	0	0	0	0	0	.000
TOTALS	33	2	7	2	1	3	.225

Giants	AB	R	H	RBI	BB	K	Avg
Josh Devore, lf	4	0	1	0	0	1	.235
Larry Doyle, 2b	4	1	1	0	0	0	.208
Fred Snodgrass, cf	4	0	1	0	0	1	.167
Red Murray, rf	3	1	2	0	0	0	.364
Fred Merkle, 1b	3	1	2	1	0	0	.261
Buck Herzog, 3b	3	1	1	1	0	0	.429
Chief Meyers, c	3	1	2	0	0	0	.333
Art Fletcher, ss	3	0	1	1	0	0	.150
Rube Marquard, p	3	0	0	0	0	0	.000
TOTALS	30	5	11	3	0	2	.261

	1	2	3	4	5	6	7	8	9		R	H	E
Red Sox	0	2	0	0	0	0	0	0	0		2	7	2
Giants	5	0	0	0	0	0	0	0	x		5	11	1

E—Cady, Yerkes, Marquard. DP—Red Sox 1 (Hooper to Stahl), Giants 1 (Fletcher to Doyle to Merkle). LOB—Red Sox 5, Giants 1. Scoring Position—Red Sox 1-for-6, Giants 5-for-8. 2B—Merkle (2), Herzog (3), Engle (1). 3B—Meyers (1). GDP—Collins. SB—Speaker (1), Doyle (1), Herzog (2), Meyers (1). CS—Hooper (1), Snodgrass (1), Merkle (1).

Red Sox	IP	H	R	ER	BB	K	ERA
Buck O'Brien (L, 0-2)	1.0	6	5	3	0	1	5.00
Ray Collins	7.0	5	0	0	0	1	1.88

Giants	IP	H	R	ER	BB	K	ERA
Rube Marquard (W, 2-0)	9.0	7	2	0	1	3	0.50

Balk—O'Brien. Time—1:58. Attendance—30,622. Umpires—HP, Klem. 1B, Evans. 2B, O'Loughlin. 3B, Rigler.

Game 7

Tuesday, October 15

Giants	AB	R	H	RBI	BB	K	Avg
Josh Devore, rf	4	2	1	0	2	0	.238
Larry Doyle, 2b	4	3	3	2	1	0	.286
Fred Snodgrass, cf	5	1	2	2	0	0	.207
Red Murray, lf	4	0	0	0	0	0	.308
Fred Merkle, 1b	5	1	2	1	0	0	.286
Buck Herzog, 3b	4	2	1	0	1	1	.400
Chief Meyers, c	4	1	3	1	0	0	.400
Art Wilson, c	1	0	1	0	0	0	1.000
Art Fletcher, ss	5	1	1	0	0	0	.160
Jeff Tesreau, p	4	0	2	2	1	0	.375
TOTALS	40	11	16	8	5	1	.292

Red Sox	AB	R	H	RBI	BB	K	Avg
Harry Hooper, rf	3	0	1	1	1	2	.346
Steve Yerkes, 2b	4	0	0	0	1	1	.250
Tris Speaker, cf	4	1	1	0	1	0	.269
Duffy Lewis, lf	4	1	1	0	1	0	.214
Larry Gardner, 3b	4	1	1	2	0	1	.160
Jake Stahl, 1b	5	0	1	0	0	0	.214
Heinie Wagner, ss	5	0	1	0	0	1	.148
Hick Cady, c	4	1	0	0	0	1	.167
Joe Wood, p	0	0	0	0	0	0	.286
Sea Lion Hall, p	3	0	3	0	1	0	.750
TOTALS	36	4	9	3	5	6	.235

	1	2	3	4	5	6	7	8	9		R	H	E
Giants	6	1	0	0	0	2	1	0	1		11	16	4
Red Sox	0	1	0	0	0	0	2	1	0		4	9	3

E—Devore, Gardner, Merkle, Speaker, Doyle 2, Hall. DP—Giants 1 (Devore to Meyers), Red Sox 1 (Speaker). LOB—Giants 8, Red Sox 12. Scoring Position—Giants 5-for-16, Red Sox 1-for-13. 2B—Snodgrass (2), Lewis (3), Hall (1). HR—Doyle (1), Gardner (1). S—Murray. SF—Hooper. SB—Devore 2 (3), Doyle (2). CS—Tesreau (1).

Giants	IP	H	R	ER	BB	K	ERA
Jeff Tesreau (W, 1-2)	9.0	9	4	2	5	6	3.13

Red Sox	IP	H	R	ER	BB	K	ERA
Joe Wood (L, 2-1)	1.0	7	6	4	0	0	3.79
Sea Lion Hall	8.0	9	5	3	5	1	3.38

WP—Tesreau 2. HBP—Gardner by Tesreau. Time—2:21. Attendance—32,694. Umpires—HP, Evans. 1B, Klem. 2B, O'Loughlin. 3B, Rigler.

Game 8

Wednesday, October 16

Giants	AB	R	H	RBI	BB	K	Avg
Josh Devore, rf	3	1	1	0	2	0	.250
Larry Doyle, 2b	5	0	0	0	0	0	.242
Fred Snodgrass, cf	4	0	1	0	1	0	.212
Red Murray, lf	5	1	2	1	0	0	.323
Fred Merkle, 1b	5	0	1	1	0	1	.273
Buck Herzog, 3b	5	0	2	0	0	1	.400
Chief Meyers, c	3	0	0	0	1	0	.357
Art Fletcher, ss	3	0	1	0	0	1	.179
Moose McCormick, ph	1	0	0	0	0	1	.250
Tillie Shafer, ss	0	0	0	0	0	0	—
Christy Mathewson, p	4	0	1	0	0	0	.167
TOTALS	38	2	9	2	4	4	.273

Red Sox	AB	R	H	RBI	BB	K	Avg
Harry Hooper, rf	5	0	0	0	0	0	.290
Steve Yerkes, 2b	4	1	1	0	1	1	.250
Tris Speaker, cf	4	0	2	1	1	1	.300
Duffy Lewis, lf	4	0	0	1	0	1	.188
Larry Gardner, 3b	3	0	1	1	1	0	.179
Jake Stahl, 1b	4	1	2	0	0	0	.250
Heinie Wagner, ss	3	0	1	0	1	0	.167
Hick Cady, c	4	0	0	0	0	0	.136
Hugh Bedient, p	2	0	0	0	0	0	.000
Olaf Henriksen, ph	1	0	1	1	0	0	1.000
Joe Wood, p	0	0	0	0	0	0	.286
Clyde Engle, ph	1	1	0	0	0	0	.333
TOTALS	35	3	8	3	5	4	.224

	1	2	3	4	5	6	7	8	9	10		R	H	E
Giants	0	0	1	0	0	0	0	0	1			2	9	2
Red Sox	0	0	0	0	0	0	1	0	0	2		3	8	5

E—Gardner 2, Snodgrass, Speaker, Doyle, Stahl, Wagner. LOB—Giants 11, Red Sox 9. Scoring Position—Giants 2-for-11, Red Sox 2-for-11. 2B—Murray 2 (4), Herzog (4), Gardner (2), Stahl (2), Henriksen (1). S—Meyers. SF—Gardner. SB—Devore (4). CS—Devore (2), Snodgrass (2), Meyers (1).

Giants	IP	H	R	ER	BB	K	ERA
Christy Mathewson (L, 0-2)	9.2	8	3	1	5	4	1.26

Red Sox	IP	H	R	ER	BB	K	ERA
Hugh Bedient	7.0	6	1	1	3	2	1.00
Joe Wood (W, 3-1)	3.0	3	1	1	1	2	3.68

Time—2:37. Attendance—17,034. Umpires—HP, O'Loughlin. 1B, Rigler. 2B, Klem. 3B, Evans.

1912 World Series—Composite Statistics

Batting

Red Sox	G	AB	R	H	RBI	2B	3B	HR	BB	SO	SB	CS	Avg	OBP	Slg
Neal Ball	1	1	0	0	0	0	0	0	0	0	1	0	.000	.000	.000
Hugh Bedient	4	6	0	0	0	0	0	0	0	0	0	0	.000	.000	.000
Hick Cady	7	22	1	3	1	0	0	0	0	3	0	0	.136	.136	.136
Bill Carrigan	2	7	0	0	0	0	0	0	0	0	0	0	.000	.000	.000
Ray Collins	2	5	0	0	0	0	0	0	2	0	0	0	.000	.000	.000
Clyde Engle	3	3	1	1	2	1	0	0	0	0	0	0	.333	.333	.667
Larry Gardner	8	28	4	5	5	2	1	1	2	5	0	0	.179	.250	.429
Sea Lion Hall	2	4	0	3	0	1	0	0	1	0	0	0	.750	.800	1.000
Olaf Henriksen	2	1	0	1	1	1	0	0	0	0	0	0	1.000	1.000	2.000
Harry Hooper	8	31	3	9	2	2	1	0	4	4	2	1	.290	.361	.419
Duffy Lewis	8	32	4	6	1	3	0	0	2	2	0	0	.188	.235	.281
Buck O'Brien	2	2	0	0	0	0	0	0	0	2	0	0	.000	.000	.000
Tris Speaker	8	30	4	9	2	1	2	0	4	2	1	1	.300	.382	.467
Jake Stahl	8	32	3	8	2	2	0	0	0	6	2	2	.250	.250	.313
Heinie Wagner	8	30	1	5	0	1	0	0	3	6	1	0	.167	.242	.200
Joe Wood	4	7	1	2	1	0	0	0	1	0	0	0	.286	.375	.286
Steve Yerkes	8	32	3	8	4	0	2	0	2	3	0	0	.250	.294	.375
Totals	8	273	25	60	21	14	6	1	19	36	6	4	.220	.271	.326

Giants	G	AB	R	H	RBI	2B	3B	HR	BB	SO	SB	CS	Avg	OBP	Slg
Beals Becker	2	4	1	0	0	0	0	0	0	2	0	1	.000	.333	.000
Doc Crandall	1	1	0	0	0	0	0	0	0	1	0	0	.000	.000	.000
Josh Devore	7	24	4	6	0	0	0	0	7	5	4	2	.250	.419	.250
Larry Doyle	8	33	5	8	2	1	0	1	3	2	2	0	.242	.306	.364
Art Fletcher	8	28	1	5	3	1	0	0	1	4	1	0	.179	.207	.214
Buck Herzog	8	30	6	12	5	4	1	0	1	3	2	1	.400	.412	.600
Rube Marquard	2	4	0	0	0	0	0	0	1	0	0	0	.000	.200	.000
Christy Mathewson	3	12	0	2	0	0	0	0	0	4	0	0	.167	.167	.167
Moose McCormick	5	4	0	1	1	0	0	0	0	0	0	0	.250	.200	.250
Fred Merkle	8	33	5	9	3	2	1	0	0	7	1	1	.273	.273	.394
Chief Meyers	8	28	2	10	0	1	0	1	0	2	3	1	.357	.419	.429
Red Murray	8	31	5	10	4	4	1	0	2	2	0	1	.323	.364	.516
Fred Snodgrass	8	33	2	7	2	2	0	0	2	5	1	2	.212	.278	.273
Jeff Tesreau	3	8	0	3	2	0	0	0	1	3	0	1	.375	.444	.375
Art Wilson	2	1	0	1	0	0	0	0	0	0	0	1	1.000	1.000	1.000
Totals	8	274	31	74	25	14	4	1	22	39	12	10	.270	.328	.361

Pitching

Red Sox	G	GS	CG	IP	H	R	ER	BB	SO	W-L	Sv-Op	Hld	ERA
Hugh Bedient	4	2	1	18.0	10	2	2	7	7	1-0	0-0	0	1.00
Ray Collins	2	1	0	14.1	14	5	3	0	6	0-0	0-0	0	1.88
Sea Lion Hall	2	0	0	10.2	11	6	4	9	1	0-0	0-1	0	3.38
Buck O'Brien	2	2	0	9.0	12	7	5	3	4	0-2	0-0	0	5.00
Joe Wood	4	3	2	22.0	27	11	9	3	21	3-1	0-0	0	3.68
Totals	8	8	3	74.0	74	31	23	22	39	4-3	0-1	0	2.80

Giants	G	GS	CG	IP	H	R	ER	BB	SO	W-L	Sv-Op	Hld	ERA
Red Ames	1	0	0	2.0	3	1	1	1	0	0-0	0-0	0	4.50
Doc Crandall	1	0	0	2.0	1	0	0	2	0	0-0	0-0	0	0.00
Rube Marquard	2	2	2	18.0	14	3	1	2	9	2-0	0-0	0	0.50
Christy Mathewson	3	3	3	28.2	23	11	4	5	10	0-2	0-0	0	1.26
Jeff Tesreau	3	3	1	23.0	19	10	8	11	15	1-2	0-0	0	3.13
Totals	8	8	6	73.2	60	25	14	19	36	3-4	0-0	0	1.71

Fielding

Red Sox	Pos	G	PO	Ast	E	DP	PB	FPct
Hugh Bedient	p	4	0	1	0	0	—	1.000
Hick Cady	c	7	35	8	1	0	0	.977
Bill Carrigan	c	2	10	4	0	0	0	1.000
Ray Collins	p	2	0	3	0	0	—	1.000
Larry Gardner	3b	8	9	13	4	0	—	.846
Sea Lion Hall	p	2	0	5	1	0	—	.833
Harry Hooper	rf	8	16	2	0	1	—	1.000
Duffy Lewis	lf	8	14	0	1	0	—	.933
Buck O'Brien	p	2	1	6	0	0	—	1.000
Tris Speaker	cf	8	21	2	2	2	—	.920
Jake Stahl	1b	8	76	3	1	4	—	.988
Heinie Wagner	ss	8	25	24	3	1	—	.942
Joe Wood	p	4	1	6	0	1	—	1.000
Steve Yerkes	2b	8	14	22	1	1	—	.973
Totals		8	222	99	14	10	0	.958

Giants	Pos	G	PO	Ast	E	DP	PB	FPct
Red Ames	p	1	0	1	0	0	—	1.000
Beals Becker	cf	1	0	0	0	0	—	—
Doc Crandall	p	1	0	1	0	0	—	1.000
Josh Devore	lf	4	3	0	0	0	—	1.000
	rf	3	9	2	1	1	—	.917
Larry Doyle	2b	8	15	26	5	1	—	.891
Art Fletcher	ss	8	16	24	4	3	—	.909
Buck Herzog	3b	8	11	15	0	1	—	1.000
Rube Marquard	p	2	0	4	1	0	—	.800
Christy Mathewson	p	3	1	12	0	0	—	1.000
Fred Merkle	1b	8	83	0	2	2	—	.976
Chief Meyers	c	8	42	4	1	1	0	.979
Red Murray	rf	5	12	1	0	0	—	1.000
	lf	4	9	0	0	0	—	1.000
Tillie Shafer	ss	3	1	4	0	0	—	1.000
Fred Snodgrass	cf	7	17	1	1	0	—	.947
	lf	1	0	0	0	0	—	—
	rf	1	0	0	0	0	—	—
Jeff Tesreau	p	3	0	10	0	0	—	1.000
Art Wilson	c	2	2	1	1	0	0	.750
Totals		8	221	106	16	9	0	.953

1913 Philadelphia Athletics (AL) 4, New York Giants (NL) 1

The Philadelphia Athletics' Eddie Plank defeated the New York Giants' Christy Mathewson in Game 5 as the Athletics defeated the Giants. Home Run Baker laced two singles and a two-run homer in Game 1 as Chief Bender defeated New York's Rube Marquard, 6-4. Mathewson starred in the second game, tossing 10 innings of shutout ball and driving in the go-ahead run to beat Eddie Plank, 3-0. Wally Schang homered in the Athletics' 8-2 victory in Game 3, and Bender survived a late rally to win Game 4, 6-5. Plank and Mathewson were again brilliant in Game 5, but this time Plank came out on top with a 3-1 win. Baker batted .450 during the Series and drove in seven of the Athletics' 23 runs.

Game 1

Tuesday, October 7

Athletics	AB	R	H	RBI	BB	K	Avg
Eddie Murphy, rf	4	0	1	0	1	0	.250
Rube Oldring, lf	4	0	1	0	0	0	.250
Eddie Collins, 2b	3	3	3	0	1	0	1.000
Home Run Baker, 3b	4	1	3	3	0	0	.750
Stuffy McInnis, 1b	3	0	1	1	0	0	.333
Amos Strunk, cf	4	1	0	0	0	2	.000
Jack Barry, ss	4	1	1	0	0	0	.250
Wally Schang, c	4	0	1	2	0	0	.250
Chief Bender, p	4	0	0	0	0	1	.000
TOTALS	34	6	11	6	2	3	.324

Giants	AB	R	H	RBI	BB	K	Avg
Tillie Shafer, cf	5	0	1	0	0	1	.200
Larry Doyle, 2b	4	1	2	2	0	0	.500
Art Fletcher, ss	4	0	2	1	0	0	.500
George Burns, lf	4	0	1	1	0	1	.250
Buck Herzog, 3b	4	0	0	0	0	0	.000
Red Murray, rf	4	0	2	0	0	1	.500
Chief Meyers, c	4	0	0	0	0	0	.000
Fred Merkle, 1b	4	2	2	0	0	1	.500
Rube Marquard, p	0	0	0	0	0	0	—
Moose McCormick, ph	1	1	1	0	0	0	1.000
Doc Crandall, p	1	0	0	0	0	0	.000
Jeff Tesreau, p	0	0	0	0	0	0	—
Larry McLean, ph	1	0	0	0	0	0	.000
TOTALS	36	4	11	4	0	4	.306

	1 2 3	4 5 6	7 8 9	R	H	E
Athletics	0 0 0	3 2 0	0 1 0	6	11	1
Giants	0 0 1	0 3 0	0 0 0	4	11	0

E—Barry. DP—Athletics 1 (Barry to Collins to McInnis). LOB—Athletics 4, Giants 6. Scoring Position—Athletics 4-for-8, Giants 2-for-8. 2B—McInnis (1), Barry (1), Burns (1). 3B—Collins (1), Schang (1). HR—Baker (1). S—McInnis, Marquard. GDP—Fletcher. SB—Collins (1). CS—Murphy (1), Baker (1), Fletcher (1).

Athletics	IP	H	R	ER	BB	K	ERA
Chief Bender (W, 1-0)	9.0	11	4	3	0	4	3.00

Giants	IP	H	R	ER	BB	K	ERA
Rube Marquard (L, 0-1)	5.0	8	5	5	1	1	9.00
Doc Crandall	2.0	3	1	1	0	1	4.50
Jeff Tesreau	2.0	0	0	0	1	1	0.00

Crandall pitched to three batters in the 8th.

Time—2:06. Attendance—36,291. Umpires—HP, Klem. 1B, Egan. 2B, Rigler. 3B, Connolly.

Game 2

Wednesday, October 8

Giants	AB	R	H	RBI	BB	K	Avg
Buck Herzog, 3b	5	1	0	0	0	0	.000
Larry Doyle, 2b	4	0	0	0	0	0	.250
Art Fletcher, ss	5	0	2	2	0	1	.444
George Burns, lf	4	0	0	0	1	3	.125
Tillie Shafer, cf	5	0	0	0	0	0	.100
Red Murray, rf	4	0	0	0	0	1	.250
Larry McLean, c	4	0	2	0	0	0	.400
Eddie Grant, pr	0	1	0	0	0	0	—
Art Wilson, c	0	0	0	0	0	0	—
Fred Snodgrass, 1b	1	0	1	0	0	0	1.000
Hooks Wiltse, pr-1b	2	0	0	0	0	1	.000
Christy Mathewson, p	3	1	2	1	1	0	.667
TOTALS	37	3	7	3	2	6	.238

Athletics	AB	R	H	RBI	BB	K	Avg
Eddie Murphy, rf	5	0	0	0	0	0	.111
Rube Oldring, lf	5	0	1	0	0	0	.222
Eddie Collins, 2b	4	0	1	0	0	2	.571
Home Run Baker, 3b	5	0	2	0	0	1	.556
Stuffy McInnis, 1b	4	0	0	0	0	1	.143
Amos Strunk, cf	3	0	1	0	1	0	.143
Jack Barry, ss	4	0	1	0	0	0	.250
Jack Lapp, c	4	0	1	0	0	1	.250
Eddie Plank, p	4	0	1	0	0	0	.250
TOTALS	38	0	8	0	1	5	.281

	1 2 3	4 5 6	7 8 9 10	R	H	E
Giants	0 0 0	0 0 0	0 0 0 3	3	7	2
Athletics	0 0 0	0 0 0	0 0 0 0	0	8	2

E—Baker, Doyle 2, Collins. LOB—Giants 8, Athletics 10. Scoring Position—Giants 2-for-9, Athletics 0-for-7. S—Collins, Wiltse. CS—Shafer (1).

Giants	IP	H	R	ER	BB	K	ERA
Christy Mathewson (W, 1-0)	10.0	8	0	0	1	5	0.00

Athletics	IP	H	R	ER	BB	K	ERA
Eddie Plank (L, 0-1)	10.0	7	3	2	2	6	1.80

HBP—Doyle by Plank. Time—2:22. Attendance—20,563. Umpires—HP, Connolly. 1B, Rigler. 2B, Klem. 3B, Egan.

Game 3

Thursday, October 9

Athletics	AB	R	H	RBI	BB	K	Avg
Eddie Murphy, rf	5	1	2	0	0	0	.214
Rube Oldring, lf	5	3	2	0	0	0	.286
Eddie Collins, 2b	5	2	3	3	0	0	.583
Home Run Baker, 3b	4	1	2	2	0	0	.538
Stuffy McInnis, 1b	4	0	0	0	0	1	.091
Amos Strunk, cf	4	0	0	0	0	0	.091
Jack Barry, ss	4	0	1	0	0	0	.250
Wally Schang, c	4	1	1	1	0	2	.250
Joe Bush, p	4	0	1	0	0	1	.250
TOTALS	39	8	12	6	0	4	.293

Giants	AB	R	H	RBI	BB	K	Avg
Buck Herzog, 3b	4	0	0	0	0	0	.000
Larry Doyle, 2b	4	0	1	0	0	0	.250
Art Fletcher, ss	2	0	1	0	1	0	.455
George Burns, lf	4	0	0	0	0	1	.083
Tillie Shafer, cf	3	1	1	0	1	0	.154
Red Murray, rf	3	1	1	1	1	0	.273
Larry McLean, c	2	0	1	1	0	0	.429
Claude Cooper, pr	0	0	0	0	0	0	—
Art Wilson, c	2	0	0	0	0	1	.000
Fred Merkle, 1b	2	0	0	0	1	0	.333
Hooks Wiltse, pr-1b	0	0	0	0	0	0	.000
Jeff Tesreau, p	2	0	0	0	0	1	.000
Doc Crandall, p	1	0	0	0	0	0	.000
TOTALS	29	2	5	2	4	3	.204

	1 2 3	4 5 6	7 8 9	R	H	E
Athletics	3 2 0	0 0 0	2 1 0	8	12	1
Giants	0 0 0	0 1 0	1 0 0	2	5	1

E—Schang, Fletcher. DP—Athletics 3 (Collins to Barry; Bush to Barry to McInnis; Schang to Collins), Giants 1 (Doyle). LOB—Athletics 4, Giants 5. Scoring Position—Athletics 3-for-6, Giants 2-for-6. 2B—Shafer (1). 3B—Collins (2). HR—Schang (1). GDP—Burns. SB—Oldring (1), Collins (2), Baker (1), Fletcher (1), Murray (1), Cooper (1). CS—Murray (1).

Athletics	IP	H	R	ER	BB	K	ERA
Joe Bush (W, 1-0)	9.0	5	2	1	4	3	1.00

Giants	IP	H	R	ER	BB	K	ERA
Jeff Tesreau (L, 0-1)	6.1	11	7	6	0	3	6.48
Doc Crandall	2.2	1	1	1	0	1	3.86

HBP—Fletcher by Bush. Time—2:11. Attendance—36,896. Umpires—HP, Rigler. 1B, Connolly. 2B, Klem. 3B, Egan.

Game 4

Friday, October 10

Giants	AB	R	H	RBI	BB	K	Avg
Fred Snodgrass, cf	2	0	0	0	0	0	.333
Buck Herzog, 3b	2	0	1	0	0	0	.067
Larry Doyle, 2b	4	0	0	0	0	1	.188
Art Fletcher, ss	4	1	0	0	0	0	.333
George Burns, lf	4	2	2	1	0	0	.188
Tillie Shafer, 3b-cf	4	0	1	1	0	2	.176
Red Murray, rf	2	1	1	0	1	0	.308
Larry McLean, c	2	0	2	0	0	0	.556
Claude Cooper, pr	0	0	0	0	0	0	—
Art Wilson, c	1	0	0	0	0	1	.000
Doc Crandall, ph	1	0	0	0	0	0	.000
Fred Merkle, 1b	4	1	1	3	0	1	.300
Al Demaree, p	1	0	0	0	0	0	.000
Moose McCormick, ph	1	0	0	0	0	0	.500
Rube Marquard, p	1	0	0	0	0	0	.000
Eddie Grant, ph	1	0	0	0	0	0	.000
TOTALS	34	5	8	5	1	5	.232

Athletics	AB	R	H	RBI	BB	K	Avg
Eddie Murphy, rf	5	0	0	0	0	0	.158
Rube Oldring, lf	4	0	2	0	0	1	.333
Eddie Collins, 2b	4	0	0	0	0	0	.438
Home Run Baker, 3b	4	0	0	0	0	1	.412
Stuffy McInnis, 1b	4	1	1	0	0	0	.133
Amos Strunk, cf	2	2	1	0	1	0	.154
Jack Barry, ss	4	2	3	1	0	0	.375
Wally Schang, c	2	1	2	4	2	0	.400
Chief Bender, p	4	0	0	1	0	0	.000
TOTALS	33	6	9	6	3	2	.280

	1 2 3	4 5 6	7 8 9	R	H	E
Giants	0 0 0	0 0 0	3 2 0	5	8	2
Athletics	0 1 0	3 2 0	0 0 x	6	9	0

E—Merkle 2. LOB—Giants 4, Athletics 7. Scoring Position—Giants 2-for-7, Athletics 3-for-9. 2B—Burns (2), Barry 2 (3). 3B—Shafer (1), Oldring (1). HR—Merkle (1). S—Strunk. SB—Burns (1), Murray (2), Collins (3). CS—Cooper (1).

Giants	IP	H	R	ER	BB	K	ERA
Al Demaree (L, 0-1)	4.0	7	4	2	1	0	4.50
Rube Marquard	4.0	2	2	2	2	2	7.00

Athletics	IP	H	R	ER	BB	K	ERA
Chief Bender (W, 2-0)	9.0	8	5	5	1	5	4.00

PB—McLean. HBP—Murray by Bender. Time—2:09. Attendance—20,568. Umpires—HP, Egan. 1B, Klem. 2B, Connolly. 3B, Rigler.

Game 5

Saturday, October 11

Athletics	AB	R	H	RBI	BB	K	Avg
Eddie Murphy, rf	3	1	2	0	1	0	.227
Rube Oldring, lf	4	2	0	0	0	0	.273
Eddie Collins, 2b	3	0	1	0	0	0	.421
Home Run Baker, 3b	3	0	2	2	0	0	.450
Stuffy McInnis, 1b	2	0	0	1	0	0	.118
Amos Strunk, cf	4	0	0	0	0	0	.118
Jack Barry, ss	4	0	0	0	0	0	.300
Wally Schang, c	4	0	1	0	0	2	.357
Eddie Plank, p	3	0	0	0	0	0	.143
TOTALS	30	3	6	3	1	2	.278

Giants	AB	R	H	RBI	BB	K	Avg
Buck Herzog, 3b	4	0	0	0	0	1	.053
Larry Doyle, 2b	4	0	0	0	0	0	.150
Art Fletcher, ss	3	0	0	0	0	0	.278
George Burns, lf	3	0	0	0	0	0	.158
Tillie Shafer, cf	2	1	0	0	1	0	.158
Red Murray, rf	3	0	0	0	0	0	.250
Larry McLean, c	3	0	1	1	0	0	.500
Fred Merkle, 1b	3	0	0	0	0	0	.231
Christy Mathewson, p	2	0	1	0	0	0	.600
Doc Crandall, ph	1	0	0	0	0	0	.000
TOTALS	28	1	2	1	1	1	.214

	1 2 3	4 5 6	7 8 9	R	H	E
Athletics	1 0 2	0 0 0	0 0 0	3	6	1
Giants	0 0 0	0 1 0	0 0 0	1	2	2

E—Burns, Doyle, Plank. DP—Athletics 2 (Collins to Barry to McInnis; Barry to Collins to McInnis). LOB—Athletics 5, Giants 1. Scoring Position—Athletics 1-for-4, Giants 1-for-2. S—Collins, McInnis. SF—Baker, McInnis. GDP—Herzog, Merkle.

Athletics	IP	H	R	ER	BB	K	ERA
Eddie Plank (W, 1-1)	9.0	2	1	0	1	1	0.95

Giants	IP	H	R	ER	BB	K	ERA
Christy Mathewson (L, 1-1)	9.0	6	3	2	1	2	0.95

Time—1:39. Attendance—36,632. Umpires—HP, Klem. 1B, Egan. 2B, Rigler. 3B, Connolly.

1913 World Series—Composite Statistics

Batting

Athletics	G	AB	R	H	RBI	2B	3B	HR	BB	SO	SB	CS	Avg	OBP	Slg
Home Run Baker	5	20	2	9	7	0	0	1	0	2	1	1	.450	.429	.600
Jack Barry	5	20	3	6	1	3	0	0	0	0	0	0	.300	.300	.450
Chief Bender	2	8	0	0	1	0	0	0	0	1	0	0	.000	.000	.000
Joe Bush	1	4	0	1	0	0	0	0	0	1	0	0	.250	.250	.250
Eddie Collins	5	19	5	8	3	0	2	0	1	2	3	0	.421	.450	.632
Jack Lapp	1	4	0	1	0	0	0	0	0	0	0	0	.250	.250	.250
Stuffy McInnis	5	17	1	2	2	1	0	0	0	2	0	0	.118	.111	.176
Eddie Murphy	5	22	2	5	0	0	0	0	2	0	0	1	.227	.292	.227
Rube Oldring	5	22	5	6	0	0	1	0	0	1	1	0	.273	.273	.364
Eddie Plank	2	7	0	1	0	0	0	0	0	0	0	0	.143	.143	.143
Wally Schang	4	14	2	5	7	0	1	1	2	4	0	0	.357	.438	.714
Amos Strunk	5	17	3	2	0	0	0	0	2	2	0	0	.118	.211	.118
Totals	5	174	23	46	21	4	4	2	7	16	5	2	.264	.290	.368

Batting

Giants	G	AB	R	H	RBI	2B	3B	HR	BB	SO	SB	CS	Avg	OBP	Slg
George Burns	5	19	2	3	2	2	0	0	1	5	1	0	.158	.200	.263
Claude Cooper	2	0	0	0	0	0	0	0	0	0	1	1	—	—	—
Doc Crandall	4	4	0	0	0	0	0	0	0	0	0	0	.000	.000	.000
Al Demaree	1	1	0	0	0	0	0	0	0	0	0	0	.000	.000	.000
Larry Doyle	5	20	2	3	0	0	0	0	1	0	0	0	.150	.150	.150
Art Fletcher	5	18	1	5	3	0	0	0	1	1	1	1	.278	.350	.278
Eddie Grant	2	1	1	0	0	0	0	0	0	0	0	0	.000	.000	.000
Buck Herzog	5	19	1	1	0	0	0	0	0	1	0	0	.053	.053	.053
Rube Marquard	2	1	0	0	0	0	0	0	0	0	0	0	.000	.000	.000
Christy Mathewson	2	5	1	3	1	0	0	0	1	0	0	0	.600	.667	.600
Moose McCormick	2	2	1	1	0	0	0	0	0	0	0	0	.500	.500	.500
Larry McLean	5	12	0	6	2	0	0	0	0	0	0	0	.500	.500	.500
Fred Merkle	4	13	3	3	3	0	0	1	1	2	0	0	.231	.286	.462
Chief Meyers	1	4	0	0	0	0	0	0	0	0	0	0	.000	.000	.000
Red Murray	5	16	2	4	1	0	0	0	2	2	2	1	.250	.368	.250
Tillie Shafer	5	19	2	3	1	1	1	0	2	3	0	1	.158	.238	.316
Fred Snodgrass	2	3	0	1	0	0	0	0	0	0	0	0	.333	.333	.333
Jeff Tesreau	2	2	0	0	0	0	0	0	0	1	0	0	.000	.000	.000
Art Wilson	3	3	0	0	0	0	0	0	0	2	0	0	.000	.000	.000
Hooks Wiltse	2	2	0	0	0	0	0	0	0	1	0	0	.000	.000	.000
Totals	5	164	15	33	15	3	1	1	8	19	5	4	.201	.251	.250

Pitching

Athletics	G	GS	CG	IP	H	R	ER	BB	SO	W-L	Sv-Op	Hld	ERA
Chief Bender	2	2	2	18.0	19	9	8	1	9	2-0	0-0	0	4.00
Joe Bush	1	1	1	9.0	5	2	1	4	3	1-0	0-0	0	1.00
Eddie Plank	2	2	2	19.0	9	4	2	3	7	1-1	0-0	0	0.95
Totals	5	5	5	46.0	33	15	11	8	19	4-1	0-0	0	2.15

Pitching

Giants	G	GS	CG	IP	H	R	ER	BB	SO	W-L	Sv-Op	Hld	ERA
Doc Crandall	2	0	0	4.2	4	2	2	0	2	0-0	0-0	0	3.86
Al Demaree	1	1	0	4.0	7	4	2	1	0	0-1	0-0	0	4.50
Rube Marquard	2	1	0	9.0	10	7	7	3	3	0-1	0-0	0	7.00
Christy Mathewson	2	2	2	19.0	14	3	2	2	7	1-1	0-0	0	0.95
Jeff Tesreau	2	1	0	8.1	11	7	6	1	4	0-1	0-0	0	6.48
Totals	5	5	2	45.0	46	23	19	7	16	1-4	0-0	0	3.80

Fielding

Athletics	Pos	G	PO	Ast	E	DP	PB	FPct
Home Run Baker	3b	5	6	5	1	0	—	.917
Jack Barry	ss	5	8	15	1	5	—	.958
Chief Bender	p	2	0	5	0	0	—	1.000
Joe Bush	p	1	0	1	0	1	—	1.000
Eddie Collins	2b	5	17	18	1	5	—	.972
Jack Lapp	c	1	7	1	0	0	0	1.000
Stuffy McInnis	1b	5	45	0	0	4	—	1.000
Eddie Murphy	rf	5	14	0	0	0	—	1.000
Rube Oldring	lf	5	10	0	0	0	—	1.000
Eddie Plank	p	2	1	3	1	0	—	.800
Wally Schang	c	4	16	4	1	1	0	.952
Amos Strunk	cf	5	14	0	0	0	—	1.000
Totals		5	138	52	5	16	0	.974

Fielding

Giants	Pos	G	PO	Ast	E	DP	PB	FPct
George Burns	lf	5	14	0	1	0	—	.933
Doc Crandall	p	2	0	2	0	0	—	1.000
Al Demaree	p	1	0	2	0	0	—	1.000
Larry Doyle	2b	5	13	19	3	1	—	.914
Art Fletcher	ss	5	8	10	1	0	—	.947
Buck Herzog	3b	5	6	7	0	0	—	1.000
Rube Marquard	p	2	0	8	0	0	—	1.000
Christy Mathewson	p	2	0	5	0	0	—	1.000
Larry McLean	c	4	14	2	0	0	1	1.000
Fred Merkle	1b	4	37	1	2	0	—	.950
Chief Meyers	c	1	4	1	0	0	0	1.000
Red Murray	rf	5	9	0	0	0	—	1.000
Tillie Shafer	cf	5	7	0	0	0	—	1.000
	3b	1	1	0	0	0	—	1.000
Fred Snodgrass	cf	1	2	0	0	0	—	1.000
	1b	1	1	1	0	0	—	1.000
Jeff Tesreau	p	2	0	1	0	0	—	1.000
Art Wilson	c	3	4	1	0	0	—	1.000
Hooks Wiltse	1b	2	15	2	0	0	—	1.000
Totals		5	135	62	7	1	1	.966

1914 Boston Braves (NL) 4, Philadelphia Athletics (AL) 0

Boston's "Miracle Braves" stunned the Philadelphia Athletics, sweeping them in four straight games. Boston catcher Hank Gowdy singled, doubled and tripled as Dick Rudolph won Game 1, 7-1. Les Mann's ninth-inning RBI single helped Boston's Bill James beat Eddie Plank 1-0 in Game 2. The Athletics took a 4-2 lead in the top of the 10th inning of Game 3, but the Braves tied it on a home run from Gowdy and a sacrifice fly from Joe Connolly. After Gowdy doubled leading off the 12th, the Braves won it on Joe Bush's throwing error. Johnny Evers' two-run single was the difference in Game 4, as Dick Rudolph won 3-1 to complete the Braves' improbable transformation from cellar dwellers to World Champions.

Game 1

Friday, October 9

Braves	AB	R	H	RBI	BB	K	Avg
Herbie Moran, rf	5	0	0	0	0	1	.000
Johnny Evers, 2b	4	1	1	0	0	1	.250
Joe Connolly, lf	3	1	1	0	1	1	.333
Possum Whitted, cf	3	2	1	2	1	0	.333
Butch Schmidt, 1b	4	1	2	1	0	0	.500
Hank Gowdy, c	3	2	3	1	1	0	1.000
Rabbit Maranville, ss	4	0	2	2	0	1	.500
Charlie Deal, 3b	4	0	0	0	0	0	.000
Dick Rudolph, p	4	0	1	0	0	1	.250
TOTALS	34	7	11	6	3	5	.324

Athletics	AB	R	H	RBI	BB	K	Avg
Eddie Murphy, rf	4	0	1	0	0	1	.250
Rube Oldring, lf	3	0	0	0	0	2	.000
Eddie Collins, 2b	3	0	0	0	1	0	.000
Home Run Baker, 3b	4	0	1	0	0	1	.250
Stuffy McInnis, 1b	2	1	0	0	2	1	.000
Amos Strunk, cf	4	0	2	0	0	0	.500
Jack Barry, ss	4	0	0	0	0	2	.000
Wally Schang, c	2	0	0	0	0	1	.000
Jack Lapp, c	1	0	0	0	0	0	.000
Chief Bender, p	2	0	0	0	0	0	.000
John Wyckoff, p	1	0	1	0	0	0	1.000
TOTALS	30	1	5	0	3	8	.167

	1	2	3	4	5	6	7	8	9		R	H	E
Braves	0	2	0	0	1	3	0	1	0		7	11	2
Athletics	0	1	0	0	0	0	0	0	0		1	5	0

E—Moran, Evers. DP—Braves 1 (Schmidt to Deal), Athletics 5 (Barry to Collins to McInnis; Bender to Barry to McInnis; Bender to McInnis; Baker to McInnis; Lapp to Baker). LOB—Braves 3, Athletics 6. Scoring Position—Braves 4-for-8, Athletics 0-for-12. 2B—Gowdy (1), Baker (1), Wyckoff (1). 3B—Whitted (1), Gowdy (1). S—Oldring. GDP—Whitted, Deal 2. SB—Moran (1), Schmidt (1).

Braves	IP	H	R	ER	BB	K	ERA
Dick Rudolph (W, 1-0)	9.0	5	1	0	3	8	0.00

Athletics	IP	H	R	ER	BB	K	ERA
Chief Bender (L, 0-1)	5.1	8	6	6	2	3	10.13
John Wyckoff	3.2	3	1	1	1	2	2.45

Time—1:58. Attendance—20,562. Umpires—HP, Dinneen. 1B, Klem. 2B, Byron. 3B, Hildebrand.

Game 2

Saturday, October 10

Braves	AB	R	H	RBI	BB	K	Avg
Les Mann, rf	5	0	2	1	0	1	.400
Johnny Evers, 2b	4	0	2	0	1	0	.375
Ted Cather, lf	5	0	0	0	0	1	.000
Possum Whitted, cf	3	0	0	0	1	0	.167
Butch Schmidt, 1b	4	0	1	0	0	0	.375
Hank Gowdy, c	2	0	0	0	2	0	.600
Rabbit Maranville, ss	2	0	1	0	0	0	.500
Charlie Deal, 3b	4	1	1	0	0	0	.125
Bill James, p	4	0	0	0	0	4	.000
TOTALS	33	1	7	1	4	6	.291

Athletics	AB	R	H	RBI	BB	K	Avg
Eddie Murphy, rf	3	0	0	0	1	1	.143
Rube Oldring, lf	3	0	0	0	0	1	.000
Eddie Collins, 2b	3	0	1	0	0	0	.167
Home Run Baker, 3b	3	0	0	0	0	0	.143
Stuffy McInnis, 1b	3	0	0	0	0	2	.000
Amos Strunk, cf	3	0	0	0	0	2	.286
Jack Barry, ss	2	0	0	0	1	0	.000
Wally Schang, c	3	0	1	0	0	1	.200
Eddie Plank, p	2	0	0	0	0	0	.000
Jimmy Walsh, ph	0	0	0	0	1	0	—
TOTALS	25	0	2	0	3	8	.118

	1	2	3	4	5	6	7	8	9		R	H	E
Braves	0	0	0	0	0	0	0	0	1		1	7	1
Athletics	0	0	0	0	0	0	0	0	0		0	2	1

E—Maranville, Barry. LOB—Braves 11, Athletics 1. Scoring Position—Braves 1-for-8, Athletics 0-for-1. 2B—Deal (1), Schang (1). S—Maranville. GDP—Murphy. SB—Deal 2 (2), Barry (1). CS—Evers (1), Murphy (1), Schang (1).

Braves	IP	H	R	ER	BB	K	ERA
Bill James (W, 1-0)	9.0	2	0	0	3	8	0.00

Athletics	IP	H	R	ER	BB	K	ERA
Eddie Plank (L, 0-1)	9.0	7	1	1	4	6	1.00

PB—Schang. HBP—Maranville by Plank. Time—1:56. Attendance—20,562. Umpires—HP, Hildebrand. 1B, Byron. 2B, Klem. 3B, Dinneen.

Game 3

Monday, October 12

Athletics	AB	R	H	RBI	BB	K	Avg
Eddie Murphy, rf	5	2	2	0	1	0	.250
Rube Oldring, lf	5	0	0	0	0	1	.000
Eddie Collins, 2b	4	0	1	1	1	0	.200
Home Run Baker, 3b	5	0	2	2	1	2	.250
Stuffy McInnis, 1b	5	1	1	0	1	0	.100
Jimmy Walsh, cf	4	0	1	1	1	0	.250
Jack Barry, ss	5	0	0	0	0	0	.000
Wally Schang, c	4	1	1	0	1	0	.222
Joe Bush, p	5	0	0	0	0	2	.000
TOTALS	42	4	8	4	6	5	.143

Braves	AB	R	H	RBI	BB	K	Avg
Herbie Moran, rf	4	1	0	0	1	0	.000
Johnny Evers, 2b	5	0	3	0	0	0	.462
Joe Connolly, lf	4	0	0	1	0	0	.143
Possum Whitted, cf	5	0	0	0	0	1	.091
Butch Schmidt, 1b	5	1	1	0	0	1	.308
Charlie Deal, 3b	5	0	1	0	0	0	.154
Rabbit Maranville, ss	4	1	1	1	1	0	.400
Hank Gowdy, c	4	1	3	2	1	0	.667
Les Mann, pr	0	1	0	0	0	0	.400
Lefty Tyler, p	3	0	0	0	0	1	.000
Josh Devore, ph	1	0	0	0	0	1	.000
Bill James, p	0	0	0	0	0	0	.000
Larry Gilbert, ph	0	0	0	0	1	0	—
TOTALS	40	5	9	4	4	4	.265

	1	2	3	4	5	6	7	8	9	10	11	12	R	H	E
Athletics	1	0	0	1	0	0	0	0	0	2	0	0	4	8	2
Braves	0	1	0	1	0	0	0	0	2	0	1	5	9	1	

E—Schang, Connolly, Bush. DP—Braves 1 (Evers to Maranville to Schmidt). LOB—Athletics 10, Braves 8. Scoring Position—Athletics 2-for-9, Braves 2-for-5. 2B—Murphy 2 (2), Baker (2), McInnis (1), Deal (2), Gowdy 2 (3). HR—Gowdy (1). S—Oldring, Moran. SF—Collins, Connolly. SB—Collins (1), Evers (1), Maranville 2 (2). CS—Maranville (1).

Athletics	IP	H	R	ER	BB	K	ERA
Joe Bush (L, 0-1)	11.0	9	5	4	4	4	3.27

Braves	IP	H	R	ER	BB	K	ERA
Lefty Tyler	10.0	8	4	4	3	4	3.60
Bill James (W, 2-0)	2.0	0	0	0	3	1	0.00

Bush pitched to three batters in the 12th.

Time—3:06. Attendance—35,520. Umpires—HP, Klem. 1B, Dinneen. 2B, Byron. 3B, Hildebrand.

Game 4

Tuesday, October 13

Athletics	AB	R	H	RBI	BB	K	Avg
Eddie Murphy, rf	4	0	0	0	0	0	.188
Rube Oldring, lf	4	0	1	0	0	1	.067
Eddie Collins, 2b	4	0	1	0	0	1	.214
Home Run Baker, 3b	4	0	1	0	0	0	.250
Stuffy McInnis, 1b	4	0	1	0	0	0	.143
Jimmy Walsh, cf	2	0	1	0	1	1	.333
Jack Barry, ss	3	1	1	0	0	1	.071
Wally Schang, c	3	0	0	0	0	2	.167
Bob Shawkey, p	2	0	1	1	0	1	.500
Herb Pennock, p	1	0	0	0	0	0	.000
TOTALS	31	1	7	1	1	7	.173

Braves	AB	R	H	RBI	BB	K	Avg
Herbie Moran, rf	4	1	1	0	0	0	.077
Johnny Evers, 2b	3	1	1	2	1	1	.438
Joe Connolly, lf	2	0	0	0	0	0	.111
Les Mann, ph-lf	2	0	0	0	0	0	.286
Possum Whitted, cf	3	0	2	0	1	0	.214
Butch Schmidt, 1b	4	0	1	1	0	1	.294
Hank Gowdy, c	2	0	0	0	1	1	.545
Rabbit Maranville, ss	3	0	0	0	0	0	.308
Charlie Deal, 3b	3	0	0	0	0	0	.125
Dick Rudolph, p	2	1	1	0	1	0	.333
TOTALS	28	3	6	3	4	3	.270

	1	2	3	4	5	6	7	8	9		R	H	E
Athletics	0	0	0	0	1	0	0	0	0		1	7	0
Braves	0	0	0	1	2	0	0	0	x		3	6	0

DP—Braves 1 (Gowdy to Evers). LOB—Athletics 4, Braves 5. Scoring Position—Athletics 1-for-7, Braves 2-for-6. 2B—Walsh (1), Shawkey (1), Moran (1). SB—Whitted (1). CS—Oldring (1), Schmidt (1).

Athletics	IP	H	R	ER	BB	K	ERA
Bob Shawkey (L, 0-1)	5.0	4	3	2	2	0	3.60
Herb Pennock	3.0	2	0	0	2	3	0.00

Braves	IP	H	R	ER	BB	K	ERA
Dick Rudolph (W, 2-0)	9.0	7	1	1	1	7	0.50

WP—Rudolph. PB—Schang. Time—1:49. Attendance—34,365. Umpires—HP, Byron. 1B, Hildebrand. 2B, Klem. 3B, Dinneen.

1914 World Series—Composite Statistics

Batting

Braves	G	AB	R	H	RBI	2B	3B	HR	BB	SO	SB	CS	Avg	OBP	Slg
Ted Cather	1	5	0	0	0	0	0	0	0	1	0	0	.000	.000	.000
Joe Connolly	3	9	1	1	1	0	0	0	1	1	0	0	.111	.182	.111
Charlie Deal	4	16	1	2	0	2	0	0	0	2	0	0	.125	.125	.250
Josh Devore	1	1	0	0	0	0	0	0	0	1	0	0	.000	.000	.000
Johnny Evers	4	16	2	7	2	0	0	0	2	2	1	1	.438	.500	.438
Larry Gilbert	1	0	0	0	0	0	0	0	1	0	0	0	—	1.000	—
Hank Gowdy	4	11	3	6	3	3	1	1	5	1	1	0	.545	.688	1.273
Bill James	2	4	0	0	0	0	0	0	0	4	0	0	.000	.000	.000
Les Mann	3	7	1	2	1	0	0	0	0	1	0	0	.286	.286	.286
Rabbit Maranville	4	13	1	4	3	0	0	0	1	1	2	1	.308	.400	.308
Herbie Moran	3	13	2	1	0	1	0	0	1	1	0	0	.077	.143	.154
Dick Rudolph	2	6	1	2	0	0	0	0	1	1	0	0	.333	.429	.333
Butch Schmidt	4	17	2	5	2	0	0	0	0	2	1	1	.294	.294	.294
Lefty Tyler	1	3	0	0	0	0	0	0	0	1	0	0	.000	.000	.000
Possum Whitted	4	14	2	3	2	0	1	0	3	1	1	0	.214	.353	.357
Totals	4	135	16	33	14	6	2	1	15	18	9	3	.244	.322	.341

Athletics	G	AB	R	H	RBI	2B	3B	HR	BB	SO	SB	CS	Avg	OBP	Slg
Home Run Baker	4	16	0	4	2	2	0	0	1	3	0	0	.250	.294	.375
Jack Barry	4	14	1	1	0	0	0	0	1	3	1	0	.071	.133	.071
Chief Bender	1	2	0	0	0	0	0	0	0	0	0	0	.000	.000	.000
Joe Bush	1	5	0	0	0	0	0	0	0	2	0	0	.000	.000	.000
Eddie Collins	4	14	0	3	1	0	0	0	2	1	1	0	.214	.294	.214
Jack Lapp	1	1	0	0	0	0	0	0	0	1	0	0	.000	.000	.000
Stuffy McInnis	4	14	2	2	0	1	0	0	3	3	0	0	.143	.294	.214
Eddie Murphy	4	16	2	3	0	2	0	0	2	2	0	1	.188	.278	.313
Rube Oldring	4	15	0	1	0	0	0	0	0	5	0	1	.067	.067	.067
Herb Pennock	1	1	0	0	0	0	0	0	0	0	0	0	.000	.000	.000
Eddie Plank	1	2	0	0	0	0	0	0	0	1	0	0	.000	.000	.000
Wally Schang	4	12	1	2	0	1	0	0	1	4	0	1	.167	.231	.250
Bob Shawkey	1	2	0	1	1	1	0	0	0	1	0	0	.500	.500	1.000
Amos Strunk	2	7	0	2	0	0	0	0	0	2	0	0	.286	.286	.286
Jimmy Walsh	3	6	0	2	1	1	0	0	3	1	0	0	.333	.556	.500
John Wyckoff	1	1	0	1	0	1	0	0	0	0	0	1	1.000	1.000	2.000
Totals	4	128	6	22	5	9	0	0	13	28	2	3	.172	.246	.242

Pitching

Braves	G	GS	CG	IP	H	R	ER	BB	SO	W-L	Sv-Op	Hld	ERA
Bill James	2	1	1	11.0	2	0	0	6	9	2-0	0-0	0	0.00
Dick Rudolph	2	2	2	18.0	12	2	1	4	15	2-0	0-0	0	0.50
Lefty Tyler	1	1	0	10.0	8	4	4	3	4	0-0	0-0	0	3.60
Totals	4	4	3	39.0	22	6	5	13	28	4-0	0-0	0	1.15

Athletics	G	GS	CG	IP	H	R	ER	BB	SO	W-L	Sv-Op	Hld	ERA
Chief Bender	1	1	0	5.1	8	6	6	2	3	0-1	0-0	0	10.13
Joe Bush	1	1	1	11.0	9	5	4	4	4	0-1	0-0	0	3.27
Herb Pennock	1	0	0	3.0	2	0	0	2	3	0-0	0-0	0	0.00
Eddie Plank	1	1	1	9.0	7	1	1	4	6	0-1	0-0	0	1.00
Bob Shawkey	1	1	0	5.0	4	3	2	2	0	0-1	0-0	0	3.60
John Wyckoff	1	0	0	3.2	3	1	1	1	2	0-0	0-0	0	2.45
Totals	4	4	2	37.0	33	16	14	15	18	0-4	0-0	0	3.41

Fielding

Braves	Pos	G	PO	Ast	E	DP	PB	FPct
Ted Cather	lf	1	2	0	0	0	—	1.000
Joe Connolly	lf	3	1	2	1	0	—	.750
Charlie Deal	3b	4	6	11	0	1	—	1.000
Johnny Evers	2b	4	8	16	1	2	—	.960
Hank Gowdy	c	4	31	4	0	1	0	1.000
Bill James	p	2	0	4	0	0	—	1.000
Les Mann	lf	1	1	0	0	0	—	1.000
	rf	1	0	0	0	0	—	—
Rabbit Maranville	ss	4	7	13	1	2	—	.952
Herbie Moran	rf	3	2	0	1	0	—	.667
Dick Rudolph	p	2	0	3	0	0	—	1.000
Butch Schmidt	1b	4	52	3	0	3	—	1.000
Lefty Tyler	p	1	1	5	0	0	—	1.000
Possum Whitted	cf	4	6	0	0	0	—	1.000
Totals		4	117	61	4	9	0	.978

Athletics	Pos	G	PO	Ast	E	DP	PB	FPct
Home Run Baker	3b	4	10	15	0	2	—	1.000
Jack Barry	ss	4	5	20	1	2	—	.962
Chief Bender	p	1	1	3	0	2	—	1.000
Joe Bush	p	1	0	5	1	0	—	.833
Eddie Collins	2b	4	9	12	0	1	—	1.000
Jack Lapp	c	1	2	1	0	1	0	1.000
Stuffy McInnis	1b	4	50	1	0	4	—	1.000
Eddie Murphy	rf	4	4	0	0	0	—	1.000
Rube Oldring	lf	4	6	0	0	0	—	1.000
Herb Pennock	p	1	0	0	0	0	—	—
Eddie Plank	p	1	0	1	0	0	—	1.000
Wally Schang	c	4	17	4	1	0	2	.955
Bob Shawkey	p	1	0	3	0	0	—	1.000
Amos Strunk	cf	2	4	0	0	0	—	1.000
Jimmy Walsh	cf	2	2	0	0	0	—	1.000
John Wyckoff	p	1	1	0	0	0	—	1.000
Totals		4	111	65	3	12	2	.983

1915 Boston Red Sox (AL) 4, Philadelphia Phillies (NL) 1

The Boston Red Sox beat the Philadelphia Phillies in a tense, low-scoring World Series that went five games. Boston's Ernie Shore and Philly's Pete Alexander were both sharp in Game 1. Gavy Cravath's RBI groundout in the bottom of the eighth proved to be the difference as Philadelphia prevailed, 3-1. Boston's Rube Foster pitched a gem in Game 2, and won 2-1 when he singled in the winning run in the top of the ninth. The Red Sox won the third game by the same score as well as in the same fashion, as Duffy Lewis knocked in the winning run in the last of the ninth. Shore bested George Chalmers in Game 4 as the Red Sox won by the score of 2-1 for the third straight game. In the fifth and final contest, Harry Hooper slugged his second homer of the day in the ninth inning to give the Red Sox a 5-4 victory and the World Championship.

Game 1

Friday, October 8

Red Sox	AB	R	H	RBI	BB	K	Avg
Harry Hooper, rf	5	0	1	0	0	1	.200
Everett Scott, ss	3	0	1	0	0	0	.333
Tris Speaker, cf	2	1	0	0	2	0	.000
Doc Hoblitzell, 1b	4	0	1	0	0	0	.250
Duffy Lewis, lf	4	0	2	1	0	2	.500
Larry Gardner, 3b	3	0	1	0	0	0	.333
Jack Barry, 2b	4	0	1	0	0	1	.250
Hick Cady, c	2	0	0	0	0	1	.000
Olaf Henriksen, ph	1	0	0	0	0	0	.000
Ernie Shore, p	3	0	1	0	0	1	.333
Babe Ruth, ph	1	0	0	0	0	0	.000
TOTALS	32	1	8	1	2	6	.250

Phillies	AB	R	H	RBI	BB	K	Avg
Milt Stock, 3b	3	1	0	0	1	0	.000
Dave Bancroft, ss	4	1	1	0	0	0	.250
Dode Paskert, cf	3	1	1	0	1	0	.333
Gavy Cravath, rf	2	0	0	1	1	0	.000
Fred Luderus, 1b	4	0	1	1	0	0	.250
Possum Whitted, lf	2	0	1	1	1	0	.500
Bert Niehoff, 2b	3	0	0	0	0	1	.000
Ed Burns, c	3	0	0	0	0	1	.000
Pete Alexander, p	3	0	1	0	0	0	.333
TOTALS	27	3	5	3	4	2	.185

	1 2 3	4 5 6	7 8 9	R	H	E
Red Sox	0 0 0	0 0 0	0 1 0	1	8	1
Phillies	0 0 0	1 0 0	0 2 x	3	5	1

E—Shore, Luderus. LOB—Red Sox 9, Phillies 5. Scoring Position—Red Sox 1-for-9, Phillies 2-for-5. S—Scott, Gardner, Cady, Cravath. SB—Hoblitzell (1), Whitted (1). CS—Luderus 2 (2).

Red Sox	IP	H	R	ER	BB	K	ERA
Ernie Shore (L, 0-1)	8.0	5	3	3	4	2	3.38

Phillies	IP	H	R	ER	BB	K	ERA
Pete Alexander (W, 1-0)	9.0	8	1	1	2	6	1.00

Time—1:58. Attendance—19,343. Umpires—HP, Klem. 1B, O'Loughlin. 2B, Evans. 3B, Rigler.

Game 2

Saturday, October 9

Red Sox	AB	R	H	RBI	BB	K	Avg
Harry Hooper, rf	3	1	1	0	2	2	.250
Everett Scott, ss	3	0	0	0	0	1	.167
Olaf Henriksen, ph	1	0	0	0	0	0	.000
Hick Cady, c	0	0	0	0	0	0	.000
Tris Speaker, cf	4	0	1	0	0	0	.167
Doc Hoblitzell, 1b	4	0	1	0	0	0	.250
Duffy Lewis, lf	4	0	1	0	0	2	.375
Larry Gardner, 3b	4	1	2	0	0	0	.429
Jack Barry, 2b	4	0	1	0	0	1	.250
Pinch Thomas, c	3	0	0	0	0	0	.000
Hal Janvrin, ss	1	0	0	0	0	0	.000
Rube Foster, p	4	0	3	1	0	1	.750
TOTALS	35	2	10	1	2	7	.270

Phillies	AB	R	H	RBI	BB	K	Avg
Milt Stock, 3b	4	0	0	0	0	0	.000
Dave Bancroft, ss	4	0	1	0	0	2	.250
Dode Paskert, cf	4	0	0	0	0	0	.143
Gavy Cravath, rf	3	1	1	0	0	2	.200
Fred Luderus, 1b	3	0	1	1	0	1	.286
Possum Whitted, lf	3	0	0	0	0	0	.200
Bert Niehoff, 2b	3	0	0	0	0	1	.000
Ed Burns, c	3	0	0	0	0	1	.000
Erskine Mayer, p	3	0	0	0	0	1	.000
TOTALS	30	1	3	1	0	8	.130

	1 2 3	4 5 6	7 8 9	R	H	E
Red Sox	1 0 0	0 0 0	0 0 1	2	10	0
Phillies	0 0 0	0 1 0	0 0 0	1	3	1

E—Burns. LOB—Red Sox 8, Phillies 2. Scoring Position—Red Sox 2-for-5, Phillies 1-for-4. 2B—Foster (1), Cravath (1), Luderus (1). CS—Speaker (1), Hoblitzell (1).

Red Sox	IP	H	R	ER	BB	K	ERA
Rube Foster (W, 1-0)	9.0	3	1	1	0	8	1.00

Phillies	IP	H	R	ER	BB	K	ERA
Erskine Mayer (L, 0-1)	9.0	10	2	1	2	7	1.00

Time—2:05. Attendance—20,306. Umpires—HP, Rigler. 1B, Evans. 2B, O'Loughlin. 3B, Klem.

Game 3

Monday, October 11

Phillies	AB	R	H	RBI	BB	K	Avg
Milt Stock, 3b	3	0	1	0	0	0	.100
Dave Bancroft, ss	3	0	1	1	0	0	.273
Dode Paskert, cf	4	0	0	0	0	0	.091
Gavy Cravath, rf	4	0	0	0	0	1	.111
Fred Luderus, 1b	3	0	0	0	0	3	.200
Possum Whitted, lf	3	0	0	0	0	0	.125
Bert Niehoff, 2b	3	0	0	0	0	1	.000
Ed Burns, c	3	1	1	0	0	0	.111
Pete Alexander, p	2	0	0	0	0	1	.200
TOTALS	28	1	3	1	0	6	.134

Red Sox	AB	R	H	RBI	BB	K	Avg
Harry Hooper, rf	4	1	1	0	0	0	.250
Everett Scott, ss	3	0	0	0	0	1	.111
Tris Speaker, cf	3	1	2	0	1	0	.333
Doc Hoblitzell, 1b	3	0	0	1	0	0	.182
Duffy Lewis, lf	4	0	3	1	0	0	.500
Larry Gardner, 3b	3	0	0	0	0	0	.300
Jack Barry, 2b	3	0	0	0	0	0	.182
Bill Carrigan, c	2	0	0	0	1	1	.000
Dutch Leonard, p	3	0	0	0	0	2	.000
TOTALS	28	2	6	2	2	4	.253

	1 2 3	4 5 6	7 8 9	R	H	E
Phillies	0 0 1	0 0 0	0 0 0	1	3	0
Red Sox	0 0 0	1 0 0	0 0 1	2	6	1

E—Hoblitzell. DP—Phillies 1 (Burns to Bancroft to Luderus). LOB—Phillies 3, Red Sox 4. Scoring Position—Phillies 1-for-5, Red Sox 1-for-2. 2B—Stock (1). 3B—Speaker (1). S—Stock, Bancroft, Alexander, Scott. SF—Hoblitzell. GDP—Hoblitzell. CS—Lewis (1).

Phillies	IP	H	R	ER	BB	K	ERA
Pete Alexander (L, 1-1)	8.2	6	2	2	2	4	1.53

Red Sox	IP	H	R	ER	BB	K	ERA
Dutch Leonard (W, 1-0)	9.0	3	1	1	0	6	1.00

Time—1:48. Attendance—42,300. Umpires—HP, O'Loughlin. 1B, Klem. 2B, Rigler. 3B, Evans.

Game 4

Tuesday, October 12

Phillies	AB	R	H	RBI	BB	K	Avg
Milt Stock, 3b	4	0	1	0	0	0	.143
Dave Bancroft, ss	2	0	0	0	2	0	.231
Dode Paskert, cf	4	0	0	0	0	2	.067
Gavy Cravath, rf	4	1	1	0	0	1	.154
Fred Luderus, 1b	4	0	3	1	0	0	.357
Oscar Dugey, pr	0	0	0	0	0	0	—
Beals Becker, lf	0	0	0	0	0	0	—
Possum Whitted, lf-1b	3	0	0	0	0	0	.091
Bert Niehoff, 2b	3	0	0	0	1	0	.000
Ed Burns, c	3	0	1	0	1	0	.167
George Chalmers, p	3	0	1	0	0	1	.333
Bobby Byrne, ph	1	0	0	0	0	0	.000
TOTALS	31	1	7	1	4	4	.157

Red Sox	AB	R	H	RBI	BB	K	Avg
Harry Hooper, rf	4	0	1	1	0	1	.250
Everett Scott, ss	4	0	0	0	0	1	.077
Tris Speaker, cf	3	0	1	0	1	0	.333
Doc Hoblitzell, 1b	4	1	3	0	0	1	.333
Duffy Lewis, lf	2	0	1	1	1	0	.500
Larry Gardner, 3b	4	0	0	0	0	0	.214
Jack Barry, 2b	2	1	0	0	1	0	.154
Hick Cady, c	3	0	2	0	0	1	.400
Ernie Shore, p	2	0	0	0	0	2	.200
TOTALS	28	2	8	2	3	6	.271

	1 2 3	4 5 6	7 8 9	R	H	E
Phillies	0 0 0	0 0 0	0 1 0	1	7	0
Red Sox	0 0 1	0 0 1	0 0 x	2	8	1

E—Barry. DP—Phillies 1 (Chalmers to Burns to Whitted), Red Sox 1 (Scott to Barry to Hoblitzell). LOB—Phillies 8, Red Sox 7. Scoring Position—Phillies 1-for-7, Red Sox 1-for-8. 2B—Lewis (1). 3B—Cravath (1). S—Whitted, Lewis, Shore. GDP—Gardner. SB—Dugey (1). CS—Bancroft (1), Speaker (2).

Phillies	IP	H	R	ER	BB	K	ERA
George Chalmers (L, 0-1)	8.0	8	2	2	3	6	2.25

Red Sox	IP	H	R	ER	BB	K	ERA
Ernie Shore (W, 1-1)	9.0	7	1	1	4	4	2.12

Time—2:05. Attendance—41,096. Umpires—HP, Evans. 1B, Rigler. 2B, O'Loughlin. 3B, Klem.

Game 5

Wednesday, October 13

Red Sox	AB	R	H	RBI	BB	K	Avg
Harry Hooper, rf	4	2	3	2	0	0	.350
Everett Scott, ss	5	0	0	0	0	0	.056
Tris Speaker, cf	5	0	1	0	0	1	.294
Doc Hoblitzell, 1b	1	0	0	0	0	0	.313
Del Gainer, ph-1b	3	1	1	0	0	0	.333
Duffy Lewis, lf	4	1	1	2	0	0	.444
Larry Gardner, 3b	3	1	1	0	1	0	.235
Jack Barry, 2b	4	0	1	1	0	0	.176
Pinch Thomas, c	2	0	1	0	0	0	.200
Hick Cady, ph-c	1	0	0	0	1	0	.333
Rube Foster, p	4	0	1	0	0	1	.500
TOTALS	36	5	10	5	2	2	.283

Phillies	AB	R	H	RBI	BB	K	Avg
Milt Stock, 3b	3	0	0	0	0	0	.118
Dave Bancroft, ss	4	1	2	0	0	0	.294
Dode Paskert, cf	4	1	2	0	0	0	.158
Gavy Cravath, rf	3	0	0	0	1	2	.125
Oscar Dugey, pr	0	0	0	0	0	0	—
Beals Becker, rf	0	0	0	0	0	0	—
Fred Luderus, 1b	2	1	2	3	1	0	.438
Possum Whitted, lf	4	0	0	0	0	0	.067
Bert Niehoff, 2b	4	1	1	0	0	2	.063
Ed Burns, c	4	0	1	0	0	0	.188
Erskine Mayer, p	1	0	0	0	0	1	.000
Eppa Rixey, p	2	0	1	0	0	0	.500
Bill Killefer, ph	1	0	0	0	0	0	.000
TOTALS	32	4	9	3	2	5	.180

	1 2 3	4 5 6	7 8 9	R	H	E
Red Sox	0 1 1	0 0 0	0 2 1	5	10	1
Phillies	2 0 0	2 0 0	0 0 0	4	9	1

E—Bancroft, Hooper. DP—Red Sox 1 (Foster to Thomas to Hoblitzell), Phillies 1 (Bancroft to Luderus). LOB—Red Sox 7, Phillies 5. Scoring Position—Red Sox 1-for-6, Phillies 2-for-5. 2B—Luderus (2). 3B—Gardner (1). HR—Hooper 2 (2), Lewis (1), Luderus (1). GDP—Cravath, Gainer. CS—Speaker (3), Bancroft (2), Paskert (1), Luderus (3).

Red Sox	IP	H	R	ER	BB	K	ERA
Rube Foster (W, 2-0)	9.0	9	4	3	2	5	2.00

Phillies	IP	H	R	ER	BB	K	ERA
Erskine Mayer	2.1	6	2	2	0	0	2.38
Eppa Rixey (L, 0-1)	6.2	4	3	3	2	2	4.05

HBP—Hooper by Rixey, Stock by Foster, Luderus by Foster. Time—2:15. Attendance—20,306. Umpires—HP, Klem. 1B, O'Loughlin. 2B, Evans. 3B, Rigler.

1915 World Series—Composite Statistics

Batting

Red Sox	G	AB	R	H	RBI	2B	3B	HR	BB	SO	SB	CS	Avg	OBP	Slg
Jack Barry	5	17	1	3	1	0	0	0	1	2	0	0	.176	.222	.176
Hick Cady	4	6	0	2	0	0	0	0	1	2	0	0	.333	.429	.333
Bill Carrigan	1	2	0	0	0	0	0	0	1	1	0	0	.000	.333	.000
Rube Foster	2	8	0	4	1	1	0	0	0	2	0	0	.500	.500	.625
Del Gainer	1	3	1	1	0	0	0	0	0	0	0	0	.333	.333	.333
Larry Gardner	5	17	2	4	0	0	1	0	1	0	0	0	.235	.278	.353
Olaf Henriksen	2	2	0	0	0	0	0	0	0	0	0	0	.000	.000	.000
Doc Hoblitzell	5	16	1	5	1	0	0	0	0	1	1	1	.313	.294	.313
Harry Hooper	5	20	4	7	3	0	0	2	2	4	0	0	.350	.435	.650
Hal Janvrin	1	1	0	0	0	0	0	0	0	0	0	0	.000	.000	.000
Dutch Leonard	1	3	0	0	0	0	0	0	0	2	0	0	.000	.000	.000
Duffy Lewis	5	18	1	8	5	1	0	1	1	4	0	1	.444	.474	.667
Babe Ruth	1	1	0	0	0	0	0	0	0	0	0	0	.000	.000	.000
Everett Scott	5	18	0	1	0	0	0	0	0	3	0	0	.056	.056	.056
Ernie Shore	2	5	0	1	0	0	0	0	0	3	0	0	.200	.200	.200
Tris Speaker	5	17	2	5	0	0	1	0	4	1	0	3	.294	.429	.412
Pinch Thomas	2	5	0	1	0	0	0	0	0	0	0	0	.200	.200	.200
Totals	5	159	12	42	11	2	2	3	11	25	1	5	.264	.314	.358

Batting

Phillies	G	AB	R	H	RBI	2B	3B	HR	BB	SO	SB	CS	Avg	OBP	Slg
Pete Alexander	2	5	0	1	0	0	0	0	0	1	0	0	.200	.200	.200
Dave Bancroft	5	17	2	5	1	0	0	0	2	2	0	2	.294	.368	.294
Ed Burns	5	16	1	3	0	0	0	0	1	2	0	0	.188	.235	.188
Bobby Byrne	1	1	0	0	0	0	0	0	0	0	0	0	.000	.000	.000
George Chalmers	1	3	0	1	0	0	0	0	0	1	0	0	.333	.333	.333
Gavy Cravath	5	16	2	2	1	1	1	0	2	6	0	0	.125	.222	.313
Oscar Dugey	2	0	0	0	0	0	0	0	0	0	1	0	—	—	—
Bill Killefer	1	1	0	0	0	0	0	0	0	0	0	0	.000	.000	.000
Fred Luderus	5	16	1	7	6	2	0	1	1	4	0	3	.438	.500	.750
Erskine Mayer	2	4	0	0	0	0	0	0	0	2	0	0	.000	.000	.000
Bert Niehoff	5	16	1	1	0	0	0	0	1	5	0	0	.063	.118	.063
Dode Paskert	5	19	2	3	0	0	0	0	1	2	0	1	.158	.200	.158
Eppa Rixey	1	2	0	1	0	0	0	0	0	0	0	0	.500	.500	.500
Milt Stock	5	17	1	2	0	0	0	0	1	0	0	0	.118	.211	.176
Possum Whitted	5	15	0	1	1	0	0	0	1	0	1	0	.067	.125	.067
Totals	5	148	10	27	9	4	1	1	10	25	2	6	.182	.244	.243

Pitching

Red Sox	G	GS	CG	IP	H	R	ER	BB	SO	W-L	Sv-Op	Hld	ERA
Rube Foster	2	2	2	18.0	12	5	4	2	13	2-0	0-0	0	2.00
Dutch Leonard	1	1	1	9.0	3	1	1	0	6	1-0	0-0	0	1.00
Ernie Shore	2	2	2	17.0	12	4	4	8	6	1-1	0-0	0	2.12
Totals	5	5	5	44.0	27	10	9	10	25	4-1	0-0	0	1.84

Pitching

Phillies	G	GS	CG	IP	H	R	ER	BB	SO	W-L	Sv-Op	Hld	ERA
Pete Alexander	2	2	2	17.2	14	3	3	4	10	1-1	0-0	0	1.53
George Chalmers	1	1	1	8.0	8	2	2	3	6	0-1	0-0	0	2.25
Erskine Mayer	2	2	1	11.1	16	4	3	2	7	0-1	0-0	0	2.38
Eppa Rixey	1	0	0	6.2	4	3	3	2	2	0-1	0-0	0	4.05
Totals	5	5	4	43.2	42	12	11	11	25	1-4	0-0	0	2.27

Fielding

Red Sox	Pos	G	PO	Ast	E	DP	PB	FPct
Jack Barry	2b	5	10	8	1	1	—	.947
Hick Cady	c	4	14	4	0	0	0	1.000
Bill Carrigan	c	1	8	0	0	0	0	1.000
Rube Foster	p	2	4	3	0	1	—	1.000
Del Gainer	1b	1	9	0	0	0	—	1.000
Larry Gardner	3b	5	5	14	0	0	—	1.000
Doc Hoblitzell	1b	5	35	5	1	2	—	.976
Harry Hooper	rf	5	8	0	1	0	—	.889
Hal Janvrin	ss	1	1	0	0	0	—	1.000
Dutch Leonard	p	1	0	2	0	0	—	1.000
Duffy Lewis	lf	5	10	1	0	0	—	1.000
Everett Scott	ss	5	8	12	0	1	—	1.000
Ernie Shore	p	2	0	5	1	0	—	.833
Tris Speaker	cf	5	10	0	0	0	—	1.000
Pinch Thomas	c	2	10	3	0	1	0	1.000
Totals		5	132	57	4	6	0	.979

Fielding

Phillies	Pos	G	PO	Ast	E	DP	PB	FPct
Pete Alexander	p	2	2	5	0	0	—	1.000
Dave Bancroft	ss	5	13	10	1	2	—	.958
Beals Becker	lf	1	0	0	0	0	—	—
	rf	1	0	0	0	0	—	—
Ed Burns	c	5	28	8	1	2	0	.973
George Chalmers	p	1	0	4	0	1	—	1.000
Gavy Cravath	rf	5	5	0	0	0	—	1.000
Fred Luderus	1b	5	39	4	1	2	—	.977
Erskine Mayer	p	2	2	3	0	0	—	1.000
Bert Niehoff	2b	5	10	10	0	0	—	1.000
Dode Paskert	cf	5	17	0	0	0	—	1.000
Eppa Rixey	p	1	0	1	0	0	—	1.000
Milt Stock	3b	5	1	8	0	0	—	1.000
Possum Whitted	lf	5	12	0	0	0	—	1.000
	1b	1	2	0	0	1	—	1.000
Totals		5	131	53	3	8	0	.984

1916 Boston Red Sox (AL) 4, Brooklyn Dodgers (NL) 1

The Boston Red Sox beat the Brooklyn Dodgers in five games with solid pitching and defense. The Red Sox almost blew a 6-1 lead in the ninth inning of Game 1, but Carl Mays induced Jake Daubert to ground out with the bases loaded to preserve Boston's 6-5 victory. Babe Ruth won Game 2 when Del Gainer drove in the winning run in the 14th inning with a pinch-hit RBI single. Jack Coombs beat Mays 4-3 in Game 3, but Boston came back to take Game 4 behind Dutch Leonard, 6-2. Ernie Shore tossed a three-hitter in Game 5 to defeat Brooklyn, 4-1, clinching the title for Boston. Boston third baseman Larry Gardner drove in six runs with a pair of homers and sparkled afield.

Game 1
Saturday, October 7

Dodgers	AB	R	H	RBI	BB	K	Avg
Hi Myers, cf	5	0	2	1	0	0	.400
Jake Daubert, 1b	4	0	0	0	1	2	.000
Casey Stengel, rf	4	2	2	0	0	1	.500
Zack Wheat, lf	4	1	2	1	0	0	.500
George Cutshaw, 2b	3	1	0	0	0	0	.000
Mike Mowrey, 3b	3	1	1	1	1	0	.333
Ivy Olson, ss	4	0	1	0	0	1	.250
Chief Meyers, c	4	0	1	0	0	0	.250
Rube Marquard, p	2	0	0	0	0	1	.000
Jimmy Johnston, ph	1	0	1	0	0	0	1.000
Jeff Pfeffer, p	0	0	0	0	0	0	—
Fred Merkle, ph	0	0	0	1	1	0	—
TOTALS	34	5	10	4	3	5	.294

Red Sox	AB	R	H	RBI	BB	K	Avg
Harry Hooper, rf	4	2	1	0	1	1	.250
Hal Janvrin, 2b	4	1	2	0	0	2	.500
Tilly Walker, cf	4	1	2	1	1	1	.500
Doc Hoblitzell, 1b	5	2	1	0	0	0	.200
Duffy Lewis, lf	3	0	1	1	1	0	.333
Larry Gardner, 3b	4	0	1	1	0	1	.250
Everett Scott, ss	2	0	0	1	0	0	.000
Hick Cady, c	1	0	0	0	3	0	.000
Pinch Thomas, c	0	0	0	0	0	0	—
Ernie Shore, p	4	0	0	0	0	1	.000
Carl Mays, p	0	0	0	0	0	0	—
TOTALS	31	6	8	5	6	6	.258

	1	2	3	4	5	6	7	8	9	R	H	E
Dodgers	0	0	0	1	0	0	0	0	4	5	10	4
Red Sox	0	0	1	0	1	0	3	1	x	6	8	1

E—Stengel, Cutshaw, Janvrin, Olson 2. DP—Red Sox 4 (Janvrin to Scott to Hoblitzell; Hooper to Cady; Gardner to Janvrin to Hoblitzell; Shore to Scott to Janvrin to Hoblitzell). LOB—Dodgers 6, Red Sox 11. Scoring Position—Dodgers 2-for-9, Red Sox 2-for-13. 2B—Hooper (1), Janvrin (1), Lewis (1). 3B—Wheat (1), Meyers (1), Walker (1), Hoblitzell (1). S—Janvrin, Lewis, Scott. SF—Scott. GDP—Myers, Cutshaw, Olson.

Dodgers	IP	H	R	ER	BB	K	ERA
Rube Marquard (L, 0-1)	7.0	7	5	4	4	6	5.14
Jeff Pfeffer	1.0	1	1	0	2	0	0.00

Red Sox	IP	H	R	ER	BB	K	ERA
Ernie Shore (W, 1-0)	8.2	9	5	3	3	5	3.12
Carl Mays (S, 1)	0.1	1	0	0	0	0	0.00

PB—Meyers. HBP—Cutshaw by Shore. Time—2:16. Attendance—36,117. Umpires—HP, Connolly. 1B, O'Day. 2B, Quigley. 3B, Dinneen.

Game 2
Monday, October 9

Dodgers	AB	R	H	RBI	BB	K	Avg
Jimmy Johnston, rf	5	0	1	0	1	0	.333
Jake Daubert, 1b	5	0	0	0	1	1	.000
Hi Myers, cf	6	1	1	1	0	1	.273
Zack Wheat, lf	5	0	0	0	0	0	.222
George Cutshaw, 2b	5	0	0	0	0	1	.000
Mike Mowrey, 3b	5	0	1	0	0	0	.250
Ivy Olson, ss	2	0	1	0	1	1	.333
Otto Miller, c	5	0	1	0	0	0	.200
Sherry Smith, p	5	0	1	0	0	0	.200
TOTALS	43	1	6	1	3	4	.194

Red Sox	AB	R	H	RBI	BB	K	Avg
Harry Hooper, rf	6	0	1	0	0	0	.200
Hal Janvrin, 2b	6	0	1	0	0	0	.300
Tilly Walker, cf	3	0	0	0	0	0	.286
Jimmy Walsh, ph-cf	3	0	0	0	0	0	.000
Doc Hoblitzell, 1b	2	0	0	0	4	0	.143
Mike McNally, pr	0	1	0	0	0	0	—
Duffy Lewis, lf	3	0	1	0	1	0	.333
Larry Gardner, 3b	5	0	0	0	0	0	.111
Del Gainer, ph	1	0	1	1	0	0	1.000
Everett Scott, ss	4	1	2	0	1	0	.333
Pinch Thomas, c	4	0	1	0	0	0	.250
Babe Ruth, p	5	0	0	1	0	2	.000
TOTALS	42	2	7	2	6	2	.221

	1	2	3	4	5	6	7	8	9	10	11	12	13	14	R	H	E
Dodgers	1	0	0	0	0	0	0	0	0	0	0	0	0	0	1	6	2
Red Sox	0	0	1	0	0	0	0	0	0	0	0	0	0	1	2	7	1

E—Cutshaw, Gardner, Mowrey. DP—Dodgers 2 (Mowrey to Cutshaw to Daubert; Myers to Miller), Red Sox 1 (Scott to Janvrin to Hoblitzell). LOB—Dodgers 5, Red Sox 9. Scoring Position—Dodgers 1-for-5, Red Sox 2-for-11. 2B—Smith (1), Janvrin (2). 3B—Scott (1), Thomas (1). HR—Myers (1). S—Olson 2, Lewis 2, Thomas. GDP—Myers, Lewis. CS—Johnston 2 (2).

Dodgers	IP	H	R	ER	BB	K	ERA
Sherry Smith (L, 0-1)	13.1	7	2	2	6	2	1.35

Red Sox	IP	H	R	ER	BB	K	ERA
Babe Ruth (W, 1-0)	14.0	6	1	1	3	4	0.64

Time—2:32. Attendance—47,373. Umpires—HP, Dinneen. 1B, Quigley. 2B, Connolly. 3B, O'Day.

Game 3
Tuesday, October 10

Red Sox	AB	R	H	RBI	BB	K	Avg
Harry Hooper, rf	4	1	2	1	0	0	.286
Hal Janvrin, 2b	4	0	0	0	0	1	.214
Chick Shorten, cf	4	0	3	1	0	0	.750
Doc Hoblitzell, 1b	4	0	1	0	0	0	.182
Duffy Lewis, lf	4	0	0	0	0	0	.200
Larry Gardner, 3b	3	1	1	1	0	0	.167
Everett Scott, ss	3	0	0	0	0	0	.222
Pinch Thomas, c	3	0	0	0	0	1	.143
Carl Mays, p	1	0	0	0	0	1	.000
Olaf Henriksen, ph	0	1	0	0	1	0	—
Rube Foster, p	1	0	0	0	0	1	.000
TOTALS	31	3	7	3	1	4	.229

Dodgers	AB	R	H	RBI	BB	K	Avg
Hi Myers, cf	3	0	0	0	0	1	.214
Jake Daubert, 1b	4	1	3	0	0	0	.231
Casey Stengel, rf	3	0	1	0	0	0	.429
Zack Wheat, lf	2	1	1	0	2	0	.273
George Cutshaw, 2b	4	0	1	1	0	0	.083
Mike Mowrey, 3b	3	1	0	0	1	1	.182
Ivy Olson, ss	4	1	2	2	0	0	.400
Otto Miller, c	3	0	0	0	0	1	.125
Jack Coombs, p	3	0	1	0	0	0	.333
Jeff Pfeffer, p	1	0	1	0	0	0	1.000
TOTALS	30	4	10	4	3	3	.244

	1	2	3	4	5	6	7	8	9	R	H	E
Red Sox	0	0	0	0	0	2	1	0	0	3	7	1
Dodgers	0	0	1	1	2	0	0	0	x	4	10	0

E—Gardner. LOB—Red Sox 2, Dodgers 9. Scoring Position—Red Sox 1-for-2, Dodgers 3-for-11. 3B—Hooper (1), Daubert (1), Olson (1). HR—Gardner (1). S—Myers, Stengel, Miller. SB—Wheat (1). CS—Hooper (1), Shorten (1).

Red Sox	IP	H	R	ER	BB	K	ERA
Carl Mays (L, 0-1)	5.0	7	4	3	3	2	5.06
Rube Foster	3.0	3	0	0	0	1	0.00

Dodgers	IP	H	R	ER	BB	K	ERA
Jack Coombs (W, 1-0)	6.1	7	3	3	1	1	4.26
Jeff Pfeffer (S, 1)	2.2	0	0	0	0	3	0.00

HBP—Myers by Mays. Time—2:01. Attendance—21,087. Umpires—HP, O'Day. 1B, Connolly. 2B, Quigley. 3B, Dinneen.

Game 4
Wednesday, October 11

Red Sox	AB	R	H	RBI	BB	K	Avg
Harry Hooper, rf	4	1	2	0	1	0	.333
Hal Janvrin, 2b	5	1	0	0	0	3	.158
Tilly Walker, cf	4	0	1	0	0	1	.273
Doc Hoblitzell, 1b	3	1	2	1	1	0	.286
Duffy Lewis, lf	4	2	2	0	0	1	.286
Larry Gardner, 3b	3	1	1	3	0	1	.200
Everett Scott, ss	4	0	0	0	0	1	.154
Bill Carrigan, c	3	0	2	1	0	1	.667
Dutch Leonard, p	3	0	0	0	1	3	.000
TOTALS	33	6	10	5	3	11	.245

Dodgers	AB	R	H	RBI	BB	K	Avg
Jimmy Johnston, rf	4	1	1	0	0	0	.300
Hi Myers, cf	4	1	1	1	0	0	.222
Fred Merkle, 1b	3	0	1	0	1	0	.333
Zack Wheat, lf	4	0	1	0	0	0	.267
George Cutshaw, 2b	4	0	1	1	0	0	.125
Mike Mowrey, 3b	3	0	0	0	1	1	.143
Ivy Olson, ss	3	0	0	0	1	0	.308
Chief Meyers, c	3	0	0	0	1	0	.143
Casey Stengel, pr	0	0	0	0	0	0	.429
Rube Marquard, p	1	0	0	0	0	0	.000
Jeff Pfeffer, ph	1	0	0	0	0	1	.500
Larry Cheney, p	0	0	0	0	0	0	—
Ollie O'Mara, ph	1	0	0	0	0	1	.000
Nap Rucker, p	0	0	0	0	0	0	—
Gus Getz, ph	1	0	0	0	0	0	.000
TOTALS	32	2	5	2	4	3	.227

	1	2	3	4	5	6	7	8	9		R	H	E
Red Sox	0	3	0	1	1	0	1	0	0		6	10	1
Dodgers	2	0	0	0	0	0	0	0	0		2	5	4

E—Cheney, Janvrin, Johnston, Wheat, Merkle. LOB—Red Sox 5, Dodgers 7. Scoring Position—Red Sox 4-for-9, Dodgers 1-for-9. 2B—Hoblitzell (1), Lewis (2), Cutshaw (1). 3B—Johnston (1). HR—Gardner (2). S—Gardner, Carrigan. SB—Hooper (1). CS—Hooper (2), Walker (1), Carrigan (1), Wheat (1).

Red Sox	IP	H	R	ER	BB	K	ERA
Dutch Leonard (W, 1-0)	9.0	5	2	1	4	3	1.00

Dodgers	IP	H	R	ER	BB	K	ERA
Rube Marquard (L, 0-2)	4.0	5	4	4	2	3	6.55
Larry Cheney	3.0	4	2	1	1	5	3.00
Nap Rucker	2.0	1	0	0	0	3	0.00

WP—Leonard. Time—2:30. Attendance—21,662. Umpires—HP, Quigley. 1B, Dinneen. 2B, O'Day. 3B, Connolly.

Game 5
Thursday, October 12

Dodgers	AB	R	H	RBI	BB	K	Avg
Hi Myers, cf	4	0	0	0	0	1	.182
Jake Daubert, 1b	4	0	0	0	0	0	.176
Casey Stengel, rf	4	0	1	0	0	0	.364
Zack Wheat, lf	4	0	0	0	0	2	.211
George Cutshaw, 2b	3	1	0	0	1	0	.105
Mike Mowrey, 3b	3	0	1	0	0	0	.176
Ivy Olson, ss	3	0	0	0	0	0	.250
Chief Meyers, c	3	0	1	0	0	0	.200
Jeff Pfeffer, p	2	0	0	0	0	1	.250
Fred Merkle, ph	1	0	0	0	0	0	.250
Wheezer Dell, p	0	0	0	0	0	0	—
TOTALS	31	1	3	0	1	4	.201

Red Sox	AB	R	H	RBI	BB	K	Avg
Harry Hooper, rf	3	2	1	0	1	0	.333
Hal Janvrin, 2b	4	0	2	1	0	0	.217
Chick Shorten, cf	3	0	1	1	0	1	.571
Doc Hoblitzell, 1b	3	0	0	0	1	0	.235
Duffy Lewis, lf	3	1	2	0	0	0	.353
Larry Gardner, 3b	2	0	0	1	0	0	.176
Everett Scott, ss	3	0	0	0	0	0	.125
Hick Cady, c	3	1	1	0	0	0	.250
Ernie Shore, p	3	0	0	0	0	1	.000
TOTALS	27	4	7	3	2	2	.248

	1	2	3	4	5	6	7	8	9		R	H	E
Dodgers	0	1	0	0	0	0	0	0	0		1	3	3
Red Sox	0	1	2	0	1	0	0	0	x		4	7	2

E—Scott 2, Olson 2, Mowrey. LOB—Dodgers 5, Red Sox 4. Scoring Position—Dodgers 0-for-3, Red Sox 1-for-8. 2B—Janvrin (3). 3B—Lewis (1). S—Mowrey, Shorten, Lewis. SF—Gardner. CS—Janvrin (1), Shorten (2).

Dodgers	IP	H	R	ER	BB	K	ERA
Jeff Pfeffer (L, 0-1)	7.0	6	4	2	2	2	1.69
Wheezer Dell	1.0	1	0	0	0	0	0.00

Red Sox	IP	H	R	ER	BB	K	ERA
Ernie Shore (W, 2-0)	9.0	3	1	0	1	4	1.53

WP—Pfeffer 2. PB—Cady. Time—1:43. Attendance—43,620. Umpires—HP, Connolly. 1B, O'Day. 2B, Dinneen. 3B, Quigley.

1916 World Series—Composite Statistics

Batting

Red Sox	G	AB	R	H	RBI	2B	3B	HR	BB	SO	SB	CS	Avg	OBP	Slg
Hick Cady	2	4	1	1	0	0	0	0	0	3	0	0	.250	.571	.250
Bill Carrigan	1	3	0	2	1	0	0	0	0	1	0	1	.667	.667	.667
Rube Foster	1	1	0	0	0	0	0	0	0	1	0	0	.000	.000	.000
Del Gainer	1	1	0	1	1	0	0	0	0	0	0	0	1.000	1.000	1.000
Larry Gardner	5	17	2	3	6	0	0	2	0	2	0	0	.176	.167	.529
Olaf Henriksen	1	0	1	0	0	0	0	0	1	0	0	0	—	1.000	—
Doc Hoblitzell	5	17	3	4	2	1	1	0	6	0	0	0	.235	.435	.412
Harry Hooper	5	21	6	7	1	1	1	0	3	1	1	2	.333	.417	.476
Hal Janvrin	5	23	2	5	1	3	0	0	0	6	0	1	.217	.217	.348
Dutch Leonard	1	3	0	0	0	0	0	0	1	3	0	0	.000	.250	.000
Duffy Lewis	5	17	3	6	1	2	1	0	2	1	0	0	.353	.421	.588
Carl Mays	2	1	0	0	0	0	0	0	0	1	0	0	.000	.000	.000
Mike McNally	1	0	1	0	0	0	0	0	0	0	0	0	—	—	—
Babe Ruth	1	5	0	0	1	0	0	0	0	2	0	0	.000	.000	.000
Everett Scott	5	16	1	2	1	0	1	0	1	1	0	0	.125	.167	.250
Ernie Shore	2	7	0	0	0	0	0	0	0	2	0	0	.000	.000	.000
Chick Shorten	2	7	0	4	2	0	0	0	0	1	0	2	.571	.571	.571
Pinch Thomas	3	7	0	1	0	0	1	0	0	1	0	0	.143	.143	.429
Tilly Walker	3	11	1	3	1	0	1	0	1	2	0	1	.273	.333	.455
Jimmy Walsh	1	3	0	0	0	0	0	0	0	0	0	0	.000	.000	.000
Totals	5	164	21	39	18	7	6	2	18	25	1	7	.238	.310	.390

Batting

Dodgers	G	AB	R	H	RBI	2B	3B	HR	BB	SO	SB	CS	Avg	OBP	Slg
Jack Coombs	1	3	0	1	1	0	0	0	0	0	0	0	.333	.333	.333
George Cutshaw	5	19	2	2	2	1	0	0	1	1	0	0	.105	.190	.158
Jake Daubert	4	17	1	3	0	0	1	0	2	3	0	0	.176	.263	.294
Gus Getz	1	1	0	0	0	0	0	0	0	0	0	0	.000	.000	.000
Jimmy Johnston	3	10	1	3	0	0	1	0	1	0	0	2	.300	.364	.500
Rube Marquard	2	3	0	0	0	0	0	0	0	0	1	0	.000	.000	.000
Fred Merkle	3	4	0	1	1	0	0	0	2	0	0	0	.250	.500	.250
Chief Meyers	3	10	0	2	0	0	1	0	1	0	0	0	.200	.273	.400
Otto Miller	2	8	0	1	0	0	0	0	0	1	0	0	.125	.125	.125
Mike Mowrey	5	17	2	3	1	0	0	0	3	2	0	0	.176	.300	.176
Hi Myers	5	22	2	4	3	0	0	1	0	3	0	0	.182	.217	.318
Ollie O'Mara	1	1	0	0	0	0	0	0	0	1	0	0	.000	.000	.000
Ivy Olson	5	16	1	4	2	0	1	0	2	2	0	0	.250	.333	.375
Jeff Pfeffer	4	4	0	1	0	0	0	0	0	2	0	0	.250	.250	.250
Sherry Smith	1	5	0	1	0	1	0	0	0	0	0	0	.200	.200	.400
Casey Stengel	4	11	2	4	0	0	0	0	0	1	0	0	.364	.364	.364
Zack Wheat	5	19	2	4	1	0	1	0	2	2	1	1	.211	.286	.316
Totals	5	170	13	34	11	2	5	1	14	19	1	3	.200	.269	.288

Pitching

Red Sox	G	GS	CG	IP	H	R	ER	BB	SO	W-L	Sv-Op	Hld	ERA
Rube Foster	1	0	0	3.0	3	0	0	0	1	0-0	0-0	0	0.00
Dutch Leonard	1	1	1	9.0	5	2	1	4	3	1-0	0-0	0	1.00
Carl Mays	2	1	0	5.1	8	4	3	3	2	0-1	1-1	0	5.06
Babe Ruth	1	1	1	14.0	6	1	1	3	4	1-0	0-0	0	0.64
Ernie Shore	2	2	1	17.2	12	6	3	4	9	2-0	0-0	0	1.53
Totals	5	5	3	49.0	34	13	8	14	19	4-1	1-1	0	1.47

Pitching

Dodgers	G	GS	CG	IP	H	R	ER	BB	SO	W-L	Sv-Op	Hld	ERA
Larry Cheney	1	0	0	3.0	4	2	1	1	5	0-0	0-0	0	3.00
Jack Coombs	1	1	0	6.1	7	3	3	1	1	1-0	0-0	0	4.26
Wheezer Dell	1	0	0	1.0	0	0	0	0	0	0-0	0-0	0	0.00
Rube Marquard	2	2	0	11.0	12	9	8	6	9	0-2	0-0	0	6.55
Jeff Pfeffer	3	1	0	10.2	7	5	2	4	5	0-1	1-1	0	1.69
Nap Rucker	1	0	0	2.0	1	0	0	0	3	0-0	0-0	0	0.00
Sherry Smith	1	1	1	13.1	7	2	2	6	2	0-1	0-0	0	1.35
Totals	5	5	1	47.1	39	21	16	18	25	1-4	1-1	0	3.04

Fielding

Red Sox	Pos	G	PO	Ast	E	DP	PB	FPct
Hick Cady	c	2	11	1	0	1	1	1.000
Bill Carrigan	c	1	3	1	0	0	0	1.000
Rube Foster	p	1	1	2	0	0	—	1.000
Larry Gardner	3b	5	7	19	2	1	—	.929
Doc Hoblitzell	1b	5	69	4	0	4	—	1.000
Harry Hooper	rf	5	8	2	0	1	—	1.000
Hal Janvrin	2b	5	8	15	2	4	—	.920
Dutch Leonard	p	1	0	1	0	0	—	1.000
Duffy Lewis	lf	5	9	1	0	0	—	1.000
Carl Mays	p	2	0	4	0	0	—	1.000
Babe Ruth	p	1	2	4	0	0	—	1.000
Everett Scott	ss	5	9	24	2	3	—	.943
Ernie Shore	p	2	2	7	0	1	—	1.000
Chick Shorten	cf	2	3	0	0	0	—	1.000
Pinch Thomas	c	3	10	4	0	0	0	1.000
Tilly Walker	cf	3	4	1	0	0	—	1.000
Jimmy Walsh	cf	1	1	0	0	0	—	1.000
Totals		5	147	90	6	15	1	.975

Fielding

Dodgers	Pos	G	PO	Ast	E	DP	PB	FPct
Larry Cheney	p	1	0	0	1	0	—	.000
Jack Coombs	p	1	0	2	0	0	—	1.000
George Cutshaw	2b	5	18	12	2	1	—	.938
Jake Daubert	1b	4	41	2	0	1	—	1.000
Wheezer Dell	p	1	0	0	0	0	—	—
Jimmy Johnston	rf	2	1	0	1	0	—	.500
Rube Marquard	p	2	0	2	0	0	—	1.000
Fred Merkle	1b	1	9	1	1	0	—	.909
Chief Meyers	c	3	21	8	0	1	1	1.000
Otto Miller	c	2	8	3	0	1	0	1.000
Mike Mowrey	3b	5	8	15	2	1	—	.920
Hi Myers	cf	5	9	1	0	1	—	1.000
Ivy Olson	ss	5	9	12	4	0	—	.840
Jeff Pfeffer	p	3	0	2	0	0	—	1.000
Nap Rucker	p	1	0	0	0	0	—	—
Sherry Smith	p	1	1	7	0	0	—	1.000
Casey Stengel	rf	3	3	1	1	0	—	.800
Zack Wheat	lf	5	14	0	1	0	—	.933
Totals		5	142	68	13	5	1	.942

1917 Chicago White Sox (AL) 4, New York Giants (NL) 2

Red Faber won the final two games as the Chicago White Sox beat the New York Giants in six games. Eddie Cicotte beat Slim Sallee 2-1 in the opener with a solo homer from Happy Felsch. Faber won Game 2, 7-2, as Joe Jackson got three hits. Rube Benton and Ferdie Schupp blanked the Sox in Games 3 and 4, respectively, and the Giants had the Sox on the ropes when Slim Sallee took a 5-2 lead into the bottom of the seventh in Game 5. Chick Gandil's two-run double cut it to 5-4, and moments later, an error enabled Gandil to score the tying run. Giants manager John McGraw left Sallee in to start the eighth, and Eddie Collins soon reached him for an RBI single to send the Sox on the way to an 8-5 victory. Faber got the win in relief, and notched his third victory of the Series two days later as the Sox beat New York 4-2 to capture the World Championship.

Game 1

Saturday, October 6

Giants	AB	R	H	RBI	BB	K	Avg
George Burns, lf	3	0	1	0	1	0	.333
Buck Herzog, 2b	4	0	1	0	0	1	.250
Benny Kauff, cf	4	0	0	0	0	1	.000
Heinie Zimmerman, 3b	4	0	0	0	0	0	.000
Art Fletcher, ss	4	0	0	0	0	0	.000
Dave Robertson, rf	4	0	1	0	0	0	.250
Walter Holke, 1b	3	0	2	0	0	0	.667
Lew McCarty, c	3	1	1	0	0	0	.333
Slim Sallee, p	3	0	1	1	0	0	.333
TOTALS	32	1	7	1	1	2	.219

White Sox	AB	R	H	RBI	BB	K	Avg
Shano Collins, rf	4	1	3	0	0	0	.750
Fred McMullin, 3b	3	0	1	1	0	0	.333
Eddie Collins, 2b	3	0	0	0	0	1	.000
Joe Jackson, lf	3	0	0	0	0	0	.000
Happy Felsch, cf	3	1	1	1	0	0	.333
Chick Gandil, 1b	3	0	1	0	0	0	.333
Buck Weaver, ss	3	0	0	0	0	1	.000
Ray Schalk, c	3	0	0	0	0	0	.000
Eddie Cicotte, p	3	0	1	0	0	0	.333
TOTALS	28	2	7	2	0	2	.250

	1	2	3	4	5	6	7	8	9		R	H	E
Giants	0	0	0	0	1	0	0	0	0		1	7	1
White Sox	0	0	1	1	0	0	0	0	x		2	7	1

E—McCarty, Weaver. DP—White Sox 1 (Weaver to ECollins to Gandil). LOB—Giants 5, White Sox 3. Scoring Position—Giants 1-for-4, White Sox 1-for-6. 2B—Robertson (1), SCollins (1), McMullin (1). 3B—McCarty (1). HR—Felsch (1). S—McMullin. GDP—Burns. SB—Burns (1), Gandil (1). CS—Kauff (1), McMullin (1).

Giants	IP	H	R	ER	BB	K	ERA
Slim Sallee (L, 0-1)	8.0	7	2	2	0	2	2.25

White Sox	IP	H	R	ER	BB	K	ERA
Eddie Cicotte (W, 1-0)	9.0	7	1	1	1	2	1.00

Time—1:48. Attendance—32,000. Umpires—HP, O'Loughlin. 1B, Klem. 2B, Rigler. 3B, Evans.

Game 2

Sunday, October 7

Giants	AB	R	H	RBI	BB	K	Avg
George Burns, lf	3	0	1	0	1	0	.333
Buck Herzog, 2b	4	0	0	0	0	1	.125
Benny Kauff, cf	4	0	0	0	0	0	.000
Heinie Zimmerman, 3b	4	0	0	0	0	0	.000
Art Fletcher, ss	4	0	1	0	0	0	.125
Dave Robertson, rf	3	1	2	0	0	0	.429
Walter Holke, 1b	3	1	1	0	0	0	.500
Lew McCarty, c	1	0	1	1	0	0	.500
Bill Rariden, c	2	0	1	0	0	0	.500
Ferdie Schupp, p	1	0	0	0	0	0	.000
Fred Anderson, p	0	0	0	0	0	0	
Pol Perritt, p	1	0	1	0	0	0	1.000
Joe Wilhoit, ph	1	0	0	0	0	0	.000
Jeff Tesreau, p	0	0	0	0	0	0	—
TOTALS	31	2	8	1	1	1	.233

White Sox	AB	R	H	RBI	BB	K	Avg
Shano Collins, rf	1	0	0	0	0	0	.600
Nemo Leibold, ph-rf	3	1	1	1	1	1	.333
Fred McMullin, 3b	5	1	1	1	0	1	.250
Eddie Collins, 2b	4	1	2	1	0	1	.286
Joe Jackson, lf	3	1	3	2	1	0	.500
Happy Felsch, cf	4	1	1	0	0	1	.286
Chick Gandil, 1b	4	0	1	1	0	1	.286
Buck Weaver, ss	4	1	3	1	0	0	.429
Ray Schalk, c	4	1	1	0	0	0	.143
Red Faber, p	3	0	1	0	1	1	.333
TOTALS	35	7	14	7	3	6	.333

	1	2	3	4	5	6	7	8	9		R	H	E
Giants	0	2	0	0	0	0	0	0	0		2	8	1
White Sox	0	2	0	5	0	0	0	0	x		7	14	1

E—Schalk, Fletcher. DP—Giants 1 (Herzog), White Sox 3 (Faber to Weaver to Gandil; Felsch to ECollins to Weaver; Weaver to Gandil). LOB—Giants 3, White Sox 7. Scoring Position—Giants 1-for-4, White Sox 7-for-14. GDP—Burns. SB—ECollins 2 (2), Jackson (1). CS—Holke (1), Weaver (1), Leibold (1).

Giants	IP	H	R	ER	BB	K	ERA
Ferdie Schupp	1.1	4	2	2	1	2	13.50
Fred Anderson (L, 0-1)	2.0	5	4	4	0	3	18.00
Pol Perritt	3.2	5	1	1	1	0	2.45
Jeff Tesreau	1.0	0	0	0	1	1	0.00

White Sox	IP	H	R	ER	BB	K	ERA
Red Faber (W, 1-0)	9.0	8	2	2	1	1	2.00

PB—McCarty. Time—2:13. Attendance—32,000. Umpires—HP, Evans. 1B, Rigler. 2B, Klem. 3B, O'Loughlin.

Game 3

Wednesday, October 10

White Sox	AB	R	H	RBI	BB	K	Avg
Shano Collins, rf	4	0	0	0	0	0	.333
Fred McMullin, 3b	4	0	0	0	0	1	.167
Eddie Collins, 2b	4	0	2	0	0	0	.364
Joe Jackson, lf	4	0	0	0	0	0	.300
Happy Felsch, cf	3	0	1	0	0	1	.300
Chick Gandil, 1b	3	0	0	0	0	0	.200
Buck Weaver, ss	3	0	2	0	0	0	.500
Ray Schalk, c	3	0	0	0	0	1	.100
Eddie Cicotte, p	3	0	0	0	0	2	.167
TOTALS	31	0	5	0	0	5	.273

Giants	AB	R	H	RBI	BB	K	Avg
George Burns, lf	4	0	1	1	0	2	.300
Buck Herzog, 2b	4	0	1	0	0	1	.167
Benny Kauff, cf	4	0	0	0	0	0	.000
Heinie Zimmerman, 3b	4	0	1	0	0	0	.083
Art Fletcher, ss	4	0	0	0	0	1	.083
Dave Robertson, rf	4	1	3	0	0	0	.545
Walter Holke, 1b	4	1	1	1	0	2	.400
Bill Rariden, c	2	0	1	0	0	0	.500
Rube Benton, p	3	0	0	0	0	2	.000
TOTALS	33	2	8	2	0	8	.221

	1	2	3	4	5	6	7	8	9		R	H	E
White Sox	0	0	0	0	0	0	0	0	0		0	5	3
Giants	0	0	0	2	0	0	0	0	x		2	8	2

E—Holke, SCollins 2, Fletcher, Cicotte. DP—Giants 1 (Rariden to Herzog). LOB—White Sox 4, Giants 8. Scoring Position—White Sox 0-for-2, Giants 3-for-11. 2B—Weaver (1), Holke (1). 3B—Robertson (1). S—Rariden. SB—Robertson (1). CS—Weaver (2), Schalk (1).

White Sox	IP	H	R	ER	BB	K	ERA
Eddie Cicotte (L, 1-1)	8.0	8	2	2	0	8	1.59

Giants	IP	H	R	ER	BB	K	ERA
Rube Benton (W, 1-0)	9.0	5	0	0	0	5	0.00

Time—1:55. Attendance—33,616. Umpires—HP, Klem. 1B, O'Loughlin. 2B, Evans. 3B, Rigler.

Game 4
Thursday, October 11

White Sox	AB	R	H	RBI	BB	K	Avg
Shano Collins, rf	4	0	2	0	0	1	.385
Fred McMullin, 3b	4	0	1	0	0	2	.188
Eddie Collins, 2b	3	0	1	0	1	1	.357
Joe Jackson, lf	4	0	0	0	0	0	.214
Happy Felsch, cf	4	0	0	0	0	2	.214
Chick Gandil, 1b	4	0	1	0	0	0	.214
Buck Weaver, ss	3	0	0	0	0	1	.385
Ray Schalk, c	3	0	2	0	0	0	.231
Red Faber, p	2	0	0	0	0	0	.200
Swede Risberg, ph	1	0	0	0	0	0	.000
Dave Danforth, p	0	0	0	0	0	0	—
TOTALS	32	0	7	0	1	7	.265

Giants	AB	R	H	RBI	BB	K	Avg
George Burns, lf	4	0	1	0	0	2	.286
Buck Herzog, 2b	3	1	1	0	0	0	.200
Benny Kauff, cf	4	2	2	3	0	0	.125
Heinie Zimmerman, 3b	4	0	1	0	0	0	.125
Art Fletcher, ss	4	1	2	0	0	1	.188
Dave Robertson, rf	3	1	1	0	0	0	.500
Walter Holke, 1b	2	0	1	0	0	1	.417
Bill Rariden, c	3	0	0	1	0	0	.286
Ferdie Schupp, p	3	0	1	1	0	1	.250
TOTALS	30	5	10	5	0	5	.254

	1 2 3	4 5 6	7 8 9	R H E
White Sox	0 0 0	0 0 0	0 0 0	0 7 0
Giants	0 0 0	1 1 0	1 2 x	5 10 1

E—Herzog. DP—White Sox 1 (Faber to Schalk to Gandil), Giants 1 (Herzog to Fletcher to Holke). LOB—White Sox 6, Giants 3. Scoring Position—White Sox 0-for-5, Giants 2-for-9. 2B—ECollins (1). 3B—Zimmerman (1). HR—Kauff 2 (2). S—Herzog. GDP—Weaver, Rariden. SB—ECollins (3). CS—SCollins (1), ECollins (1), Zimmerman (1).

White Sox	IP	H	R	ER	BB	K	ERA
Red Faber (L, 1-1)	7.0	7	3	3	0	3	2.81
Dave Danforth	1.0	3	2	2	0	2	18.00

Giants	IP	H	R	ER	BB	K	ERA
Ferdie Schupp (W, 1-0)	9.0	7	0	0	1	7	1.74

WP—Faber. HBP—Holke by Faber. Time—2:09. Attendance—27,746. Umpires—HP, Rigler. 1B, Evans. 2B, O'Loughlin. 3B, Klem.

Game 5
Saturday, October 13

Giants	AB	R	H	RBI	BB	K	Avg
George Burns, lf	4	2	1	1	1	2	.278
Buck Herzog, 2b	5	0	1	0	0	1	.200
Benny Kauff, cf	5	0	2	2	0	0	.190
Heinie Zimmerman, 3b	5	1	1	0	0	0	.143
Art Fletcher, ss	5	1	1	0	0	0	.190
Jim Thorpe, rf	0	0	0	0	0	0	—
Dave Robertson, ph-rf	5	0	3	1	0	0	.526
Walter Holke, 1b	5	0	0	0	0	2	.294
Bill Rariden, c	3	1	3	1	1	0	.500
Slim Sallee, p	3	0	0	0	0	2	.167
Pol Perritt, p	0	0	0	0	0	0	1.000
TOTALS	40	5	12	5	2	7	.273

White Sox	AB	R	H	RBI	BB	K	Avg
Shano Collins, rf	5	1	1	0	0	1	.333
Fred McMullin, 3b	3	0	0	0	1	0	.158
Eddie Collins, 2b	4	2	3	1	1	0	.444
Joe Jackson, lf	5	2	3	0	0	0	.316
Happy Felsch, cf	5	1	3	2	0	0	.316
Chick Gandil, 1b	5	1	1	2	0	0	.211
Buck Weaver, ss	4	1	1	0	0	0	.353
Ray Schalk, c	3	0	1	0	1	0	.250
Reb Russell, p	0	0	0	0	0	0	—
Eddie Cicotte, p	1	0	0	0	1	0	.143
Swede Risberg, ph	1	0	1	1	0	0	.500
Lefty Williams, p	0	0	0	0	0	0	—
Byrd Lynn, ph	1	0	0	0	0	1	.000
Red Faber, p	0	0	0	0	0	0	.200
TOTALS	37	8	14	6	4	2	.288

	1 2 3	4 5 6	7 8 9	R H E
Giants	2 0 0	2 0 0	1 0 0	5 12 3
White Sox	0 0 1	0 0 1	3 3 x	8 14 6

E—Williams, Weaver 3, SCollins, Gandil, Fletcher, Herzog, Zimmerman. DP—White Sox 2 (McMullin to Gandil; McMullin to ECollins to Gandil). LOB—Giants 11, White Sox 10. Scoring Position—Giants 4-for-17, White Sox 4-for-13. 2B—Kauff (1), Fletcher (1), Felsch (1), Gandil (1). S—Sallee, McMullin. GDP—Zimmerman. SB—Kauff (1), Schalk (1). CS—Felsch (1).

Giants	IP	H	R	ER	BB	K	ERA
Slim Sallee (L, 0-2)	7.1	13	8	7	4	2	5.28
Pol Perritt	0.2	1	0	0	0	0	2.08

White Sox	IP	H	R	ER	BB	K	ERA
Reb Russell	0.0	2	2	2	1	0	—
Eddie Cicotte	6.0	8	2	1	1	3	1.57
Lefty Williams	1.0	2	1	1	0	3	9.00
Red Faber (W, 2-1)	2.0	0	0	0	0	1	2.50

Russell pitched to three batters in the 1st.

Time—2:37. Attendance—27,323. Umpires—HP, O'Loughlin. 1B, Klem. 2B, Rigler. 3B, Evans.

Game 6
Monday, October 15

White Sox	AB	R	H	RBI	BB	K	Avg
Shano Collins, rf	3	0	0	0	0	0	.286
Nemo Leibold, ph-rf	2	0	1	1	0	0	.400
Fred McMullin, 3b	5	0	0	0	0	2	.125
Eddie Collins, 2b	4	1	1	0	0	0	.409
Joe Jackson, lf	4	1	1	0	0	0	.304
Happy Felsch, cf	3	1	0	1	1	0	.273
Chick Gandil, 1b	4	0	2	2	0	1	.261
Buck Weaver, ss	4	1	1	0	0	0	.333
Ray Schalk, c	3	0	1	0	1	0	.263
Red Faber, p	2	0	0	0	1	2	.143
TOTALS	34	4	7	3	3	6	.278

Giants	AB	R	H	RBI	BB	K	Avg
George Burns, lf	4	1	0	0	0	0	.227
Buck Herzog, 2b	4	0	2	2	0	0	.250
Benny Kauff, cf	4	0	0	0	0	1	.160
Heinie Zimmerman, 3b	4	0	0	0	0	0	.120
Art Fletcher, ss	4	0	1	0	0	0	.200
Dave Robertson, rf	3	0	1	0	0	0	.500
Walter Holke, 1b	4	0	1	0	0	1	.286
Bill Rariden, c	3	1	0	0	1	1	.385
Rube Benton, p	1	0	0	0	0	1	.000
Joe Wilhoit, ph	0	0	0	0	1	0	.000
Pol Perritt, p	1	0	1	0	0	0	1.000
Lew McCarty, ph	1	0	0	0	0	0	.400
TOTALS	33	2	6	2	2	4	.259

	1 2 3	4 5 6	7 8 9	R H E
White Sox	0 0 0	3 0 0	0 0 1	4 7 1
Giants	0 0 0	0 2 0	0 0 0	2 6 3

E—Schalk, Robertson, Zimmerman 2. LOB—White Sox 7, Giants 7. Scoring Position—White Sox 2-for-6, Giants 1-for-7. 2B—Holke (2). 3B—Herzog (1). S—Faber. CS—Felsch (2).

White Sox	IP	H	R	ER	BB	K	ERA
Red Faber (W, 3-1)	9.0	6	2	2	4		2.33

Giants	IP	H	R	ER	BB	K	ERA
Rube Benton (L, 1-1)	5.0	4	3	0	1	3	0.00
Pol Perritt	4.0	3	1	1	2	3	2.16

PB—Schalk. HBP—Robertson by Faber. Time—2:18. Attendance—33,969. Umpires—HP, Klem. 1B, O'Loughlin. 2B, Evans. 3B, Rigler.

1917 World Series—Composite Statistics

Batting

White Sox	G	AB	R	H	RBI	2B	3B	HR	BB	SO	SB	CS	Avg	OBP	Slg
Eddie Cicotte	3	7	0	1	0	0	0	0	1	2	0	0	.143	.250	.143
Eddie Collins	6	22	4	9	2	1	0	0	2	3	3	1	.409	.458	.455
Shano Collins	6	21	2	6	0	1	0	0	0	2	0	1	.286	.286	.333
Red Faber	4	7	0	1	0	0	0	0	2	3	0	0	.143	.333	.143
Happy Felsch	6	22	4	6	3	1	0	1	1	5	0	2	.273	.304	.455
Chick Gandil	6	23	1	6	5	1	0	0	0	2	1	0	.261	.261	.304
Joe Jackson	6	23	4	7	2	0	0	0	1	0	1	0	.304	.333	.304
Nemo Leibold	2	5	1	2	2	0	0	0	1	1	0	1	.400	.500	.400
Byrd Lynn	1	1	0	0	0	0	0	0	0	1	0	0	.000	.000	.000
Fred McMullin	6	24	1	3	2	1	0	0	1	6	0	1	.125	.160	.167
Swede Risberg	2	2	0	1	1	0	0	0	0	0	0	0	.500	.500	.500
Ray Schalk	6	19	1	5	0	0	0	0	2	1	1	1	.263	.333	.263
Buck Weaver	6	21	3	7	1	1	0	0	0	2	0	2	.333	.333	.381
Totals	6	197	21	54	18	6	0	1	11	28	6	9	.274	.313	.320

Batting

Giants	G	AB	R	H	RBI	2B	3B	HR	BB	SO	SB	CS	Avg	OBP	Slg
Rube Benton	2	4	0	0	0	0	0	0	0	3	0	0	.000	.000	.000
George Burns	6	22	3	5	2	0	0	0	3	6	1	0	.227	.320	.227
Art Fletcher	6	25	2	5	0	1	0	0	0	2	0	0	.200	.200	.240
Buck Herzog	6	24	1	6	2	0	1	0	0	4	0	0	.250	.250	.333
Walter Holke	6	21	2	6	1	2	0	0	0	6	0	1	.286	.318	.381
Benny Kauff	6	25	2	4	5	1	0	2	0	2	1	1	.160	.160	.440
Lew McCarty	3	5	1	2	1	0	1	0	0	0	0	0	.400	.400	.800
Pol Perritt	3	2	0	2	0	0	0	0	0	0	0	0	1.000	1.000	1.000
Bill Rariden	5	13	2	5	2	0	0	0	2	1	0	0	.385	.467	.385
Dave Robertson	6	22	3	11	1	1	1	0	0	0	1	0	.500	.522	.636
Slim Sallee	2	6	0	1	1	0	0	0	0	2	0	0	.167	.167	.167
Ferdie Schupp	2	4	0	1	1	0	0	0	0	1	0	0	.250	.250	.250
Jim Thorpe	1	0	0	0	0	0	0	0	0	0	0	0	—	—	—
Joe Wilhoit	2	1	0	0	0	0	0	0	1	0	0	0	.000	.500	.000
Heinie Zimmerman	6	25	1	3	0	1	0	0	0	0	0	1	.120	.120	.200
Totals	6	199	17	51	16	5	4	2	6	27	3	3	.256	.285	.352

Pitching

White Sox	G	GS	CG	IP	H	R	ER	BB	SO	W-L	Sv-Op	Hld	ERA
Eddie Cicotte	3	2	2	23.0	23	5	4	2	13	1-1	0-0	0	1.57
Dave Danforth	1	0	0	1.0	3	2	2	0	2	0-0	0-0	0	18.00
Red Faber	4	3	2	27.0	21	7	7	3	9	3-1	0-0	0	2.33
Reb Russell	1	1	0	0.0	2	2	2	1	0	0-0	0-0	0	—
Lefty Williams	1	0	0	1.0	2	1	1	0	3	0-0	0-0	0	9.00
Totals	6	6	4	52.0	51	17	16	6	27	4-2	0-0	0	2.77

Pitching

Giants	G	GS	CG	IP	H	R	ER	BB	SO	W-L	Sv-Op	Hld	ERA
Fred Anderson	1	0	0	2.0	5	4	4	0	3	0-1	0-0	0	18.00
Rube Benton	2	2	1	14.0	9	3	0	1	8	1-1	0-0	0	0.00
Pol Perritt	3	0	0	8.1	9	2	2	3	3	0-0	0-0	0	2.16
Slim Sallee	2	2	1	15.1	20	10	9	4	4	0-2	0-0	0	5.28
Ferdie Schupp	2	2	1	10.1	11	2	2	2	9	1-0	0-0	0	1.74
Jeff Tesreau	1	0	0	1.0	0	0	0	1	1	0-0	0-0	0	0.00
Totals	6	6	3	51.0	54	21	17	11	28	2-4	0-0	0	3.00

Fielding

White Sox	Pos	G	PO	Ast	E	DP	PB	FPct
Eddie Cicotte	p	3	0	7	1	0	—	.875
Eddie Collins	2b	6	11	23	0	3	—	1.000
Shano Collins	rf	6	4	1	3	0	—	.625
Dave Danforth	p	1	0	1	0	0	—	1.000
Red Faber	p	4	1	9	0	2	—	1.000
Happy Felsch	cf	6	16	2	0	1	—	1.000
Chick Gandil	1b	6	67	4	1	6	—	.986
Joe Jackson	lf	6	9	1	0	0	—	1.000
Nemo Leibold	rf	2	1	0	0	0	—	1.000
Fred McMullin	3b	6	2	14	0	2	—	1.000
Reb Russell	p	1	0	0	0	0	—	—
Ray Schalk	c	6	32	6	2	1	1	.950
Buck Weaver	ss	6	13	14	4	4	—	.871
Lefty Williams	p	1	0	0	1	0	—	.000
Totals		6	156	82	12	19	1	.952

Fielding

Giants	Pos	G	PO	Ast	E	DP	PB	FPct
Fred Anderson	p	1	0	1	0	0	—	1.000
Rube Benton	p	2	1	3	0	0	—	1.000
George Burns	lf	6	11	0	0	0	—	1.000
Art Fletcher	ss	6	9	17	3	1	—	.897
Buck Herzog	2b	6	11	11	2	3	—	.917
Walter Holke	1b	6	67	0	1	1	—	.985
Benny Kauff	cf	6	6	0	0	0	—	1.000
Lew McCarty	c	2	7	1	1	0	1	.889
Pol Perritt	p	3	0	1	0	0	—	1.000
Bill Rariden	c	5	25	11	0	1	0	1.000
Dave Robertson	rf	6	6	3	1	0	—	.900
Slim Sallee	p	2	0	8	0	0	—	1.000
Ferdie Schupp	p	2	1	4	0	0	—	1.000
Jeff Tesreau	p	1	0	0	0	0	—	—
Heinie Zimmerman	3b	6	9	15	3	0	—	.889
Totals		6	153	75	11	6	1	.954

1918 Boston Red Sox (AL) 4, Chicago Cubs (NL) 2

Babe Ruth and the Boston Red Sox beat the Chicago Cubs in six games in one of the lowest-scoring Series of all time. Ruth beat Hippo Vaughn in the opener, 1-0, when Stuffy McInnis' hit-and-run single plated a run in the fourth. Chicago's Lefty Tyler knocked in the eventual winning runs as he pitched the Cubs to a 3-1 victory in Game 2. Carl Mays beat Vaughn 2-1 in the third game, as Chicago's Charlie Pick was thrown out at the plate to end the game. In Game 4, Babe Ruth gave himself a 2-0 lead with a two-run triple in the fourth. After the Cubs tied it in the top of the eighth, the Red Sox tallied the eventual game-winner in the bottom of the frame when Wally Schang scored on Phil Douglas' wild throw. Hippo Vaughn blanked the Sox on five hits in Game 5 after the players staged a brief rebellion over their World Series shares. With two out and two on base in the third inning of the sixth game, Max Flack dropped a line drive to allow two runs to score for Boston. That was all Mays needed, as he beat Tyler 2-1 to sew up Boston's last World Championship.

Game 1

Thursday, September 5

Red Sox	AB	R	H	RBI	BB	K	Avg
Harry Hooper, rf	4	0	1	0	0	0	.250
Dave Shean, 2b	2	1	1	0	2	1	.500
Amos Strunk, cf	3	0	0	0	0	0	.000
George Whiteman, lf	4	0	2	0	0	1	.500
Stuffy McInnis, 1b	2	0	1	1	1	0	.500
Everett Scott, ss	4	0	0	0	0	0	.000
Fred Thomas, 3b	3	0	0	0	0	2	.000
Sam Agnew, c	3	0	0	0	0	0	.000
Babe Ruth, p	3	0	0	0	0	2	.000
TOTALS	28	1	5	1	3	6	.179

Cubs	AB	R	H	RBI	BB	K	Avg
Max Flack, rf	3	0	1	0	0	1	.333
Charlie Hollocher, ss	3	0	0	0	0	0	.000
Les Mann, lf	4	0	1	0	0	0	.250
Dode Paskert, cf	4	0	2	0	0	1	.500
Fred Merkle, 1b	3	0	1	0	1	0	.333
Charlie Pick, 2b	3	0	0	0	0	1	.000
Bob O'Farrell, ph	1	0	0	0	0	0	.000
Charlie Deal, 3b	4	0	1	0	0	0	.250
Bill McCabe, pr	0	0	0	0	0	0	—
Bill Killefer, c	4	0	0	0	0	0	.000
Hippo Vaughn, p	3	0	0	0	0	1	.000
TOTALS	32	0	6	0	1	4	.188

	1	2	3	4	5	6	7	8	9	R	H	E
Red Sox	0 0 0	1 0 0	0 0 0							1	5	0
Cubs	0 0 0	0 0 0	0 0 0							0	6	0

LOB—Red Sox 5, Cubs 8. Scoring Position—Red Sox 1-for-7, Cubs 0-for-5. S—Strunk, McInnis, Hollocher. CS—Hooper (1), Strunk (1).

Red Sox	IP	H	R	ER	BB	K	ERA
Babe Ruth (W, 1-0)	9.0	6	0	0	1	4	0.00

Cubs	IP	H	R	ER	BB	K	ERA
Hippo Vaughn (L, 0-1)	9.0	5	1	1	3	6	1.00

HBP—Flack by Ruth. Time—1:50. Attendance—19,274. Umpires—HP, O'Day. 1B, Hildebrand. 2B, Klem. 3B, Owens.

Game 2

Friday, September 6

Red Sox	AB	R	H	RBI	BB	K	Avg
Harry Hooper, rf	3	0	1	0	1	0	.286
Dave Shean, 2b	4	0	1	0	0	1	.333
Amos Strunk, cf	4	1	1	0	0	0	.143
George Whiteman, lf	3	0	1	1	1	0	.429
Stuffy McInnis, 1b	4	0	1	0	0	0	.333
Everett Scott, ss	2	0	0	0	1	0	.000
Fred Thomas, 3b	3	0	0	0	0	0	.000
Jean Dubuc, ph	1	0	0	0	0	1	.000
Sam Agnew, c	2	0	0	0	0	0	.000
Wally Schang, ph-c	2	0	1	0	0	0	.500
Joe Bush, p	2	0	0	0	1	0	.000
TOTALS	30	1	6	1	4	2	.200

Cubs	AB	R	H	RBI	BB	K	Avg
Max Flack, rf	4	0	2	0	0	0	.429
Charlie Hollocher, ss	4	0	1	0	0	0	.143
Les Mann, lf	4	0	0	0	0	0	.125
Dode Paskert, cf	4	0	0	0	0	0	.250
Fred Merkle, 1b	2	1	1	0	1	0	.400
Charlie Pick, 2b	2	1	1	0	1	0	.200
Charlie Deal, 3b	2	0	0	0	0	0	.167
Bill Killefer, c	2	1	1	1	1	0	.167
Lefty Tyler, p	3	0	1	2	0	0	.333
TOTALS	27	3	7	3	3	0	.236

	1	2	3	4	5	6	7	8	9	R	H	E
Red Sox	0 0 0	0 0 0	0 0 1							1	6	1
Cubs	0 3 0	0 0 0	0 0 x							3	7	1

E—Deal, Whiteman. DP—Cubs 2 (Killefer to Hollocher; Hollocher to Pick to Merkle). LOB—Red Sox 7, Cubs 4. Scoring Position—Red Sox 1-for-6, Cubs 2-for-8. 2B—Killefer (1). 3B—Strunk (1), Whiteman (1), Hollocher (1). GDP—Whiteman. CS—Hooper (2), Flack (1), Merkle (1), Pick (1).

Red Sox	IP	H	R	ER	BB	K	ERA
Joe Bush (L, 0-1)	8.0	7	3	3	3	0	3.38

Cubs	IP	H	R	ER	BB	K	ERA
Lefty Tyler (W, 1-0)	9.0	6	1	1	4	2	1.00

Time—1:58. Attendance—20,040. Umpires—HP, Hildebrand. 1B, Klem. 2B, Owens. 3B, O'Day.

Game 3

Saturday, September 7

Red Sox	AB	R	H	RBI	BB	K	Avg
Harry Hooper, rf	3	0	1	0	1	1	.300
Dave Shean, 2b	4	0	0	0	0	0	.200
Amos Strunk, cf	4	0	0	0	0	2	.091
George Whiteman, lf	3	1	1	0	0	0	.400
Stuffy McInnis, 1b	4	1	1	0	0	1	.300
Wally Schang, c	4	0	2	1	0	2	.500
Everett Scott, ss	4	0	1	1	0	1	.100
Fred Thomas, 3b	3	0	1	0	0	0	.111
Carl Mays, p	3	0	0	0	0	0	.000
TOTALS	32	2	7	2	1	7	.228

Cubs	AB	R	H	RBI	BB	K	Avg
Max Flack, rf	3	0	0	0	1	0	.300
Charlie Hollocher, ss	3	0	0	0	0	1	.100
Les Mann, lf	4	0	2	0	0	0	.250
Dode Paskert, cf	4	0	1	0	0	1	.250
Fred Merkle, 1b	4	0	0	0	0	1	.222
Charlie Pick, 2b	4	1	2	0	0	0	.333
Charlie Deal, 3b	3	0	1	0	0	0	.222
Turner Barber, ph	0	0	0	0	0	0	—
Bill Killefer, c	3	0	1	1	0	0	.222
Hippo Vaughn, p	3	0	0	0	0	1	.000
TOTALS	31	1	7	1	1	4	.221

	1	2	3	4	5	6	7	8	9	R	H	E
Red Sox	0 0 0	2 0 0	0 0 0							2	7	0
Cubs	0 0 0	0 1 0	0 0 0							1	7	1

E—Hollocher. DP—Cubs 2 (Hollocher to Merkle; Vaughn to Merkle). LOB—Red Sox 5, Cubs 5. Scoring Position—Red Sox 3-for-7, Cubs 1-for-8. 2B—Mann (1), Pick (1). S—Hollocher. SB—Whiteman (1), Schang (1), Pick (1). CS—Killefer (1).

Red Sox	IP	H	R	ER	BB	K	ERA
Carl Mays (W, 1-0)	9.0	7	1	1	1	4	1.00

Cubs	IP	H	R	ER	BB	K	ERA
Hippo Vaughn (L, 0-2)	9.0	7	2	2	1	7	1.50

PB—Schang. HBP—Whiteman by Vaughn. Time—1:57. Attendance—27,054. Umpires—HP, Klem. 1B, Owens. 2B, O'Day. 3B, Hildebrand.

Game 4
Monday, September 9

Cubs	AB	R	H	RBI	BB	K	Avg
Max Flack, rf	4	0	1	0	0	0	.286
Charlie Hollocher, ss	4	0	0	1	0	0	.071
Les Mann, lf	4	0	1	1	0	0	.250
Dode Paskert, cf	4	0	0	0	0	0	.188
Fred Merkle, 1b	3	0	1	0	1	0	.250
Charlie Pick, 2b	2	0	2	0	0	0	.455
Rollie Zeider, ph-3b	0	0	0	0	2	0	—
Charlie Deal, 3b	2	0	1	0	0	0	.273
Bob O'Farrell, ph	1	0	0	0	0	0	.000
Chuck Wortman, 2b	1	0	0	0	0	0	.000
Bill Killefer, c	2	1	0	0	1	0	.182
Turner Barber, ph	1	0	0	0	0	0	.000
Lefty Tyler, p	0	0	0	0	2	0	.333
Claude Hendrix, ph	1	0	1	0	0	0	1.000
Bill McCabe, pr	0	1	0	0	0	0	—
Phil Douglas, p	0	0	0	0	0	0	—
TOTALS	29	2	7	2	6	0	.239

Red Sox	AB	R	H	RBI	BB	K	Avg
Harry Hooper, rf	3	0	0	0	0	0	.231
Dave Shean, 2b	3	0	1	0	1	0	.231
Amos Strunk, cf	4	0	0	0	0	1	.067
George Whiteman, lf	3	1	0	0	1	0	.308
Joe Bush, p	0	0	0	0	0	0	.000
Stuffy McInnis, 1b	3	1	1	0	0	0	.308
Babe Ruth, p-lf	2	0	1	2	0	0	.200
Everett Scott, ss	3	0	0	0	0	0	.077
Fred Thomas, 3b	3	0	0	0	0	0	.083
Sam Agnew, c	2	0	0	0	0	0	.000
Wally Schang, ph-c	1	1	1	0	0	0	.571
TOTALS	27	3	4	2	2	1	.195

	1	2	3	4	5	6	7	8	9		R	H	E
Cubs	0	0	0	0	0	0	0	2	0		2	7	1
Red Sox	0	0	0	2	0	0	0	1	x		3	4	0

E—Douglas. DP—Red Sox 2 (Ruth to Scott to McInnis; Scott to Shean to McInnis). LOB—Cubs 6, Red Sox 4. Scoring Position—Cubs 1-for-8, Red Sox 1-for-9. 2B—Shean (1). 3B—Ruth (1). S—Hooper, Ruth. GDP—Killefer, O'Farrell, Barber. SB—Shean (1).

Cubs	IP	H	R	ER	BB	K	ERA
Lefty Tyler	7.0	3	2	2	2	1	1.69
Phil Douglas (L, 0-1)	1.0	1	1	0	0	0	0.00

Red Sox	IP	H	R	ER	BB	K	ERA
Babe Ruth (W, 2-0)	8.0	7	2	2	6	0	1.06
Joe Bush (S, 1)	1.0	0	0	0	0	0	3.00

Ruth pitched to two batters in the 9th.

WP—Ruth. PB—Killefer. Time—1:50. Attendance—22,183. Umpires—HP, Owens. 1B, O'Day. 2B, Hildebrand. 3B, Klem.

Game 5
Tuesday, September 10

Cubs	AB	R	H	RBI	BB	K	Avg
Max Flack, rf	2	1	0	0	2	0	.250
Charlie Hollocher, ss	3	2	3	0	1	0	.235
Les Mann, lf	3	0	1	1	0	0	.263
Dode Paskert, cf	3	0	0	2	1	0	.211
Fred Merkle, 1b	3	0	1	0	1	1	.267
Charlie Pick, 2b	4	0	1	0	0	0	.400
Charlie Deal, 3b	4	0	0	0	0	1	.200
Bill Killefer, c	4	0	0	0	0	0	.133
Hippo Vaughn, p	4	0	0	0	0	3	.000
TOTALS	30	3	7	3	5	5	.227

Red Sox	AB	R	H	RBI	BB	K	Avg
Harry Hooper, rf	4	0	1	0	0	1	.235
Dave Shean, 2b	3	0	1	0	0	0	.250
Amos Strunk, cf	4	0	1	0	0	2	.105
George Whiteman, lf	3	0	1	0	0	0	.313
Stuffy McInnis, 1b	3	0	0	0	0	0	.250
Everett Scott, ss	3	0	0	0	0	0	.063
Fred Thomas, 3b	3	0	1	0	0	0	.133
Sam Agnew, c	2	0	0	0	0	0	.000
Wally Schang, ph-c	1	0	0	0	0	1	.500
Sad Sam Jones, p	1	0	0	0	1	0	.000
Hack Miller, ph	1	0	0	0	0	0	.000
TOTALS	28	0	5	0	1	4	.194

	1	2	3	4	5	6	7	8	9		R	H	E
Cubs	0	0	1	0	0	0	0	2	0		3	7	0
Red Sox	0	0	0	0	0	0	0	0	0		0	5	0

DP—Cubs 3 (Merkle to Hollocher; Hollocher to Pick to Merkle; Hollocher to Pick to Merkle), Red Sox 1 (Whiteman to Shean). LOB—Cubs 6, Red Sox 3. Scoring Position—Cubs 4-for-11, Red Sox 0-for-4. 2B—Mann (2), Paskert (1), Strunk (1). S—Mann, Shean. GDP—McInnis, Agnew. SB—Hollocher (1).

Cubs	IP	H	R	ER	BB	K	ERA
Hippo Vaughn (W, 1-2)	9.0	5	0	0	1	4	1.00

Red Sox	IP	H	R	ER	BB	K	ERA
Sad Sam Jones (L, 0-1)	9.0	7	3	3	5	5	3.00

Time—1:42. Attendance—24,694. Umpires—HP, O'Day. 1B, Hildebrand. 2B, Klem. 3B, Owens.

Game 6
Wednesday, September 11

Cubs	AB	R	H	RBI	BB	K	Avg
Max Flack, rf	3	1	1	0	1	0	.263
Charlie Hollocher, ss	4	0	0	0	0	0	.190
Les Mann, lf	3	0	0	0	0	0	.227
Dode Paskert, cf	2	0	0	0	1	0	.190
Fred Merkle, 1b	3	0	1	1	0	1	.278
Charlie Pick, 2b	3	0	1	0	0	0	.389
Charlie Deal, 3b	2	0	0	0	0	0	.176
Turner Barber, ph	1	0	0	0	0	0	.000
Rollie Zeider, 3b	0	0	0	0	0	0	—
Bill Killefer, c	2	0	0	0	0	0	.118
Bob O'Farrell, ph-c	1	0	0	0	0	0	.000
Lefty Tyler, p	2	0	0	0	0	0	.200
Bill McCabe, ph	1	0	0	0	0	0	.000
Claude Hendrix, p	0	0	0	0	0	0	1.000
TOTALS	27	1	3	1	2	1	.224

Red Sox	AB	R	H	RBI	BB	K	Avg
Harry Hooper, rf	3	0	0	0	0	0	.200
Dave Shean, 2b	3	1	0	0	1	1	.211
Amos Strunk, cf	4	0	2	0	0	0	.174
George Whiteman, lf	4	0	0	0	0	0	.250
Babe Ruth, lf	0	0	0	0	0	0	.200
Stuffy McInnis, 1b	4	0	1	0	0	0	.250
Everett Scott, ss	4	0	1	0	0	0	.100
Fred Thomas, 3b	2	0	0	0	1	0	.118
Wally Schang, c	1	0	0	0	2	0	.444
Carl Mays, p	2	1	1	0	1	0	.200
TOTALS	27	2	5	0	5	1	.203

	1	2	3	4	5	6	7	8	9		R	H	E
Cubs	0	0	0	1	0	0	0	0	0		1	3	2
Red Sox	0	0	2	0	0	0	0	0	x		2	5	0

E—Flack, Tyler. LOB—Cubs 2, Red Sox 8. Scoring Position—Cubs 1-for-2, Red Sox 1-for-5. S—Hooper, Thomas. SB—Flack (1). CS—Mann (1), Schang (1).

Cubs	IP	H	R	ER	BB	K	ERA
Lefty Tyler (L, 1-1)	7.0	5	2	0	5	1	1.17
Claude Hendrix	1.0	0	0	0	0	0	0.00

Red Sox	IP	H	R	ER	BB	K	ERA
Carl Mays (W, 2-0)	9.0	3	1	1	2	1	1.00

HBP—Mann by Mays. Time—1:46. Attendance—15,238. Umpires—HP, Hildebrand. 1B, Klem. 2B, Owens. 3B, O'Day.

1918 World Series—Composite Statistics

Batting

Red Sox	G	AB	R	H	RBI	2B	3B	HR	BB	SO	SB	CS	Avg	OBP	Slg
Sam Agnew	4	9	0	0	0	0	0	0	0	0	0	0	.000	.000	.000
Joe Bush	2	2	0	0	0	0	0	0	1	0	0	0	.000	.333	.000
Jean Dubuc	1	1	0	0	0	0	0	0	0	1	0	0	.000	.000	.000
Harry Hooper	6	20	0	4	0	0	0	0	2	2	0	2	.200	.273	.200
Sad Sam Jones	1	1	0	0	0	0	0	0	0	1	0	0	.000	.500	.000
Carl Mays	2	5	1	1	0	0	0	0	1	0	0	0	.200	.333	.200
Stuffy McInnis	6	20	2	5	1	0	0	0	1	1	0	0	.250	.286	.250
Hack Miller	1	1	0	0	0	0	0	0	0	0	0	0	.000	.000	.000
Babe Ruth	3	5	0	1	2	0	1	0	0	2	0	0	.200	.200	.600
Wally Schang	5	9	1	4	1	0	0	0	2	3	1	1	.444	.545	.444
Everett Scott	6	20	0	2	1	0	0	0	1	1	0	0	.100	.143	.100
Dave Shean	6	19	2	4	0	1	0	0	4	3	1	0	.211	.348	.263
Amos Strunk	6	23	1	4	0	1	1	0	0	5	0	1	.174	.174	.304
Fred Thomas	6	17	0	2	0	0	0	0	1	2	0	0	.118	.167	.118
George Whiteman	6	20	2	5	1	0	1	0	2	1	1	0	.250	.348	.350
Totals	**6**	**172**	**9**	**32**	**6**	**2**	**3**	**0**	**16**	**21**	**3**	**4**	**.186**	**.259**	**.233**

Batting

Cubs	G	AB	R	H	RBI	2B	3B	HR	BB	SO	SB	CS	Avg	OBP	Slg
Turner Barber	3	2	0	0	0	0	0	0	0	0	0	0	.000	.000	.000
Charlie Deal	6	17	0	3	0	0	0	0	0	1	0	0	.176	.176	.176
Max Flack	6	19	2	5	0	0	0	0	4	1	1	1	.263	.417	.263
Claude Hendrix	2	1	0	1	0	0	0	0	0	0	0	0	1.000	1.000	1.000
Charlie Hollocher	6	21	2	4	1	0	1	0	1	1	1	0	.190	.227	.286
Bill Killefer	6	17	2	2	2	1	0	0	2	0	0	1	.118	.211	.176
Les Mann	6	22	0	5	2	2	0	0	0	0	0	1	.227	.261	.318
Bill McCabe	3	1	1	0	0	0	0	0	0	0	0	0	.000	.000	.000
Fred Merkle	6	18	1	5	1	0	0	0	4	3	0	1	.278	.409	.278
Bob O'Farrell	3	3	0	0	0	0	0	0	0	0	0	0	.000	.000	.000
Dode Paskert	6	21	0	4	2	1	0	0	2	2	0	0	.190	.261	.238
Charlie Pick	6	18	2	7	0	1	0	0	1	1	1	1	.389	.421	.444
Lefty Tyler	3	5	0	1	2	0	0	0	2	0	0	0	.200	.429	.200
Hippo Vaughn	3	10	0	0	0	0	0	0	0	5	0	0	.000	.000	.000
Chuck Wortman	1	1	0	0	0	0	0	0	0	0	0	0	.000	.000	.000
Rollie Zeider	2	0	0	0	0	0	0	0	2	0	0	0	—	1.000	—
Totals	**6**	**176**	**10**	**37**	**10**	**5**	**1**	**0**	**18**	**14**	**3**	**5**	**.210**	**.291**	**.250**

Pitching

Red Sox	G	GS	CG	IP	H	R	ER	BB	SO	W-L	Sv-Op	Hld	ERA
Joe Bush	2	1	1	9.0	7	3	3	3	0	0-1	1-1	0	3.00
Sad Sam Jones	1	1	1	9.0	7	3	3	5	5	0-1	0-0	0	3.00
Carl Mays	2	2	2	18.0	10	2	2	3	5	2-0	0-0	0	1.00
Babe Ruth	2	2	1	17.0	13	2	2	7	4	2-0	0-0	0	1.06
Totals	**6**	**6**	**5**	**53.0**	**37**	**10**	**10**	**18**	**14**	**4-2**	**1-1**	**0**	**1.70**

Pitching

Cubs	G	GS	CG	IP	H	R	ER	BB	SO	W-L	Sv-Op	Hld	ERA
Phil Douglas	1	0	0	1.0	1	1	0	0	0	0-1	0-0	0	0.00
Claude Hendrix	1	0	0	1.0	0	0	0	0	0	0-0	0-0	0	0.00
Lefty Tyler	3	3	1	23.0	14	5	3	11	4	1-1	0-0	0	1.17
Hippo Vaughn	3	3	3	27.0	17	3	3	5	17	1-2	0-0	0	1.00
Totals	**6**	**6**	**4**	**52.0**	**32**	**9**	**6**	**16**	**21**	**2-4**	**0-0**	**0**	**1.04**

Fielding

Red Sox	Pos	G	PO	Ast	E	DP	PB	FPct
Sam Agnew	c	4	12	6	0	0	0	1.000
Joe Bush	p	2	0	3	0	0	—	1.000
Harry Hooper	rf	6	11	0	0	0	—	1.000
Sad Sam Jones	p	1	1	3	0	0	—	1.000
Carl Mays	p	2	0	8	0	0	—	1.000
Stuffy McInnis	1b	6	70	2	0	3	—	1.000
Babe Ruth	lf	2	1	0	0	0	—	1.000
	p	2	0	5	0	1	—	1.000
Wally Schang	c	5	9	4	0	0	1	1.000
Everett Scott	ss	6	11	26	0	3	—	1.000
Dave Shean	2b	6	15	16	0	3	—	1.000
Amos Strunk	cf	6	8	2	0	0	—	1.000
Fred Thomas	3b	6	6	10	0	0	—	1.000
George Whiteman	lf	6	15	2	1	1	—	.944
Totals		**6**	**159**	**87**	**1**	**11**	**1**	**.996**

Fielding

Cubs	Pos	G	PO	Ast	E	DP	PB	FPct
Charlie Deal	3b	6	7	9	1	0	—	.941
Phil Douglas	p	1	0	0	1	0	—	.000
Max Flack	rf	6	14	2	1	0	—	.941
Claude Hendrix	p	1	0	0	0	0	—	—
Charlie Hollocher	ss	6	11	17	1	6	—	.966
Bill Killefer	c	6	26	6	0	1	1	1.000
Les Mann	lf	6	7	0	0	0	—	1.000
Fred Merkle	1b	6	52	9	0	6	—	1.000
Bob O'Farrell	c	1	0	0	0	0	0	—
Dode Paskert	cf	6	17	0	0	0	—	1.000
Charlie Pick	2b	6	12	11	0	3	—	1.000
Lefty Tyler	p	3	2	9	1	0	—	.917
Hippo Vaughn	p	3	6	11	0	1	—	1.000
Chuck Wortman	2b	1	1	0	0	0	—	1.000
Rollie Zeider	3b	2	1	2	0	0	—	1.000
Totals		**6**	**156**	**76**	**5**	**17**	**1**	**.979**

1919 Cincinnati Reds (NL) 5, Chicago White Sox (AL) 3

The Chicago White Sox fell to the Cincinnati Reds, five games to three, in a Series that marked one of baseball's darkest hours. Dutch Ruether drove in three runs with two triples and a single, and pitched the Reds to a 9-1 victory in Game 1. Larry Kopf's two-run triple sent the Reds to a 4-2 victory in Game 2. Chicago's Kerr gave an honest effort in Game 3 and tossed a three-hit shutout. Eddie Cicotte lost to Jimmy Ring 2-0 in the fourth game. The only two runs came in the fifth when Cicotte committed two straight misplays. Hod Eller blanked the Sox 5-0 in Game 5. Kerr won the sixth game 5-4 when Chick Gandil singled in the winning run in the 10th. Cicotte reverted to form in Game 7, winning 4-1, but Lefty Williams was knocked out in the first inning of Game 8 as the Sox went out with a 10-5 defeat. After the Series, it was revealed that eight members of the White Sox had conspired with gamblers to throw the Series. Cicotte, Happy Felsch, Gandil, Joe Jackson, Fred McMullin, Swede Risberg, Buck Weaver(who wasn't in on the fix but did not share his knowledge of it) and Williams were all banned from basaeball for life. This was the first time since 1903 that a nine-game format was used.

Game 1

Wednesday, October 1

White Sox	AB	R	H	RBI	BB	K	Avg
Shano Collins, rf	4	0	1	0	0	0	.250
Eddie Collins, 2b	4	0	1	0	0	0	.250
Buck Weaver, 3b	4	0	1	0	0	0	.250
Joe Jackson, lf	4	1	0	0	0	0	.000
Happy Felsch, cf	3	0	0	0	0	0	.000
Chick Gandil, 1b	4	0	2	1	0	0	.500
Swede Risberg, ss	2	0	0	0	1	0	.000
Ray Schalk, c	3	0	0	0	0	0	.000
Eddie Cicotte, p	1	0	0	0	0	1	.000
Roy Wilkinson, p	1	0	0	0	0	0	.000
Fred McMullin, ph	1	0	1	0	0	0	1.000
Grover Lowdermilk, p	0	0	0	0	0	0	—
TOTALS	31	1	6	1	1	1	.194

Reds	AB	R	H	RBI	BB	K	Avg
Morrie Rath, 2b	3	2	1	1	0	0	.333
Jake Daubert, 1b	4	1	3	1	0	0	.750
Heine Groh, 3b	3	1	1	2	1	0	.333
Edd Roush, cf	3	0	0	0	1	0	.000
Pat Duncan, lf	4	0	2	1	0	0	.500
Larry Kopf, ss	4	1	0	0	0	1	.000
Greasy Neale, rf	4	2	3	0	0	0	.750
Ivy Wingo, c	3	1	1	1	0	1	.333
Dutch Ruether, p	3	1	3	3	1	0	1.000
TOTALS	31	9	14	9	3	2	.452

	1	2	3	4	5	6	7	8	9	R	H	E
White Sox	0	1	0	0	0	0	0	0	0	1	6	1
Reds	1	0	0	5	0	0	2	1	x	9	14	1

E—Kopf, Gandil. DP—White Sox 2 (Risberg to ECollins; Risberg to ECollins to Gandil). LOB—White Sox 5, Reds 7. Scoring Position—White Sox 1-for-3, Reds 6-for-14. 2B—Rath (1). 3B—Daubert (1), Ruether 2 (2). S—Felsch, Rath, Roush, Wingo. SF—Groh. GDP—Kopf. SB—Roush (1). CS—ECollins (1), Gandil (1), Daubert (1), Duncan (1).

White Sox	IP	H	R	ER	BB	K	ERA
Eddie Cicotte (L, 0-1)	3.2	7	6	6	2	1	14.73
Roy Wilkinson	3.1	5	2	1	0	1	2.70
Grover Lowdermilk	1.0	2	1	1	1	0	9.00

Reds	IP	H	R	ER	BB	K	ERA
Dutch Ruether (W, 1-0)	9.0	6	1	0	1	1	0.00

HBP—Daubert by Lowdermilk, Rath by Cicotte. Time—1:42. Attendance—30,511. Umpires—HP, Rigler. 1B, Evans. 2B, Nallin. 3B, Quigley.

Game 2

Thursday, October 2

White Sox	AB	R	H	RBI	BB	K	Avg
Shano Collins, rf	4	0	0	0	0	0	.125
Eddie Collins, 2b	3	0	0	0	1	0	.143
Buck Weaver, 3b	4	0	2	0	0	0	.375
Joe Jackson, lf	4	0	3	0	0	1	.375
Happy Felsch, cf	2	0	0	0	0	0	.000
Chick Gandil, 1b	4	0	1	0	0	0	.375
Swede Risberg, ss	4	1	1	0	0	0	.167
Ray Schalk, c	4	1	2	0	0	0	.286
Lefty Williams, p	3	0	1	0	0	1	.333
Fred McMullin, ph	1	0	0	0	0	0	.500
TOTALS	33	2	10	0	1	2	.258

Reds	AB	R	H	RBI	BB	K	Avg
Morrie Rath, 2b	3	1	0	0	1	0	.167
Jake Daubert, 1b	3	0	0	0	0	0	.429
Heine Groh, 3b	2	1	0	0	2	0	.200
Edd Roush, cf	2	1	1	2	0	0	.200
Pat Duncan, lf	1	1	0	0	1	0	.400
Larry Kopf, ss	3	0	1	2	0	0	.143
Greasy Neale, rf	3	0	1	0	0	1	.571
Bill Rariden, c	3	0	1	0	0	0	.333
Slim Sallee, p	3	0	0	0	0	0	.000
TOTALS	23	4	4	4	6	1	.292

	1	2	3	4	5	6	7	8	9	R	H	E
White Sox	0	0	0	0	0	0	2	0	0	2	10	1
Reds	0	0	0	3	0	1	0	0	x	4	4	2

E—Risberg, Neale, Daubert. DP—White Sox 2 (ECollins to Gandil; Felsch to Gandil), Reds 2 (Kopf to Daubert; Rath to Kopf to Daubert). LOB—White Sox 7, Reds 3. Scoring Position—White Sox 0-for-7, Reds 3-for-7. 2B—Weaver (1), Jackson (1). 3B—Kopf (1). S—Felsch 2, Daubert, Duncan. GDP—Risberg. SB—Gandil (1). CS—Roush (1), Neale (1).

White Sox	IP	H	R	ER	BB	K	ERA
Lefty Williams (L, 0-1)	8.0	4	4	4	6	1	4.50

Reds	IP	H	R	ER	BB	K	ERA
Slim Sallee (W, 1-0)	9.0	10	2	0	1	2	0.00

Balk—Sallee. Time—1:42. Attendance—29,698. Umpires—HP, Evans. 1B, Quigley. 2B, Nallin. 3B, Rigler.

Game 3

Friday, October 3

Reds	AB	R	H	RBI	BB	K	Avg
Morrie Rath, 2b	4	0	0	0	0	0	.100
Jake Daubert, 1b	4	0	0	0	0	1	.273
Heine Groh, 3b	3	0	0	0	1	1	.125
Edd Roush, cf	3	0	0	0	0	0	.125
Pat Duncan, lf	3	0	1	0	0	1	.375
Larry Kopf, ss	3	0	1	0	0	0	.200
Greasy Neale, rf	3	0	0	0	0	1	.400
Bill Rariden, c	3	0	0	0	0	0	.167
Ray Fisher, p	2	0	1	0	0	0	.500
Sherry Magee, ph	1	0	0	0	0	0	.000
Dolf Luque, p	0	0	0	0	0	0	—
TOTALS	29	0	3	0	1	4	.230

White Sox	AB	R	H	RBI	BB	K	Avg
Nemo Leibold, rf	4	0	0	0	0	1	.000
Eddie Collins, 2b	4	0	1	0	0	0	.182
Buck Weaver, 3b	4	0	1	0	0	0	.333
Joe Jackson, lf	3	1	2	0	0	0	.455
Happy Felsch, cf	2	1	0	1	0	0	.000
Chick Gandil, 1b	3	0	1	2	0	1	.364
Swede Risberg, ss	2	1	1	0	1	0	.250
Ray Schalk, c	3	0	1	1	0	0	.300
Dickie Kerr, p	3	0	0	0	0	0	.000
TOTALS	28	3	7	3	2	2	.260

	1	2	3	4	5	6	7	8	9	R	H	E
Reds	0	0	0	0	0	0	0	0	0	0	3	1
White Sox	0	2	0	1	0	0	0	0	x	3	7	0

E—Fisher. DP—Reds 1 (Groh to Rath to Daubert), White Sox 1 (Risberg to Collins). LOB—Reds 3, White Sox 3. Scoring Position—Reds 0-for-3, White Sox 2-for-7. 3B—Risberg (1). GDP—Felsch. CS—Jackson (1), Felsch (1), Schalk (1).

Reds	IP	H	R	ER	BB	K	ERA
Ray Fisher (L, 0-1)	7.0	7	3	2	2	1	2.57
Dolf Luque	1.0	0	0	0	0	1	0.00

White Sox	IP	H	R	ER	BB	K	ERA
Dickie Kerr (W, 1-0)	9.0	3	0	0	1	4	0.00

Time—1:30. Attendance—29,126. Umpires—HP, Quigley. 1B, Nallin. 2B, Rigler. 3B, Evans.

Game 4

Saturday, October 4

Reds	AB	R	H	RBI	BB	K	Avg
Morrie Rath, 2b	4	0	1	0	0	0	.143
Jake Daubert, 1b	4	0	0	0	0	0	.200
Heine Groh, 3b	4	0	0	0	0	0	.083
Edd Roush, cf	3	0	0	0	0	0	.091
Pat Duncan, lf	3	1	0	0	0	0	.273
Larry Kopf, ss	3	1	1	1	0	1	.231
Greasy Neale, rf	3	0	1	1	0	0	.385
Ivy Wingo, c	3	0	2	0	0	0	.500
Jimmy Ring, p	3	0	0	0	0	1	.000
TOTALS	30	2	5	2	0	2	.214

White Sox	AB	R	H	RBI	BB	K	Avg
Nemo Leibold, rf	5	0	0	0	0	0	.000
Eddie Collins, 2b	3	0	0	0	0	0	.143
Buck Weaver, 3b	4	0	0	0	0	0	.250
Joe Jackson, lf	4	0	1	0	0	1	.400
Happy Felsch, cf	3	0	1	0	0	1	.100
Chick Gandil, 1b	4	0	1	0	0	1	.333
Swede Risberg, ss	3	0	0	0	1	0	.182
Ray Schalk, c	1	0	0	0	2	0	.273
Eddie Cicotte, p	3	0	0	0	0	0	.000
Eddie Murphy, ph	1	0	0	0	0	0	.000
TOTALS	31	0	3	0	3	2	.217

	1	2	3	4	5	6	7	8	9	R	H	E
Reds	0	0	0	0	2	0	0	0	0	2	5	2
White Sox	0	0	0	0	0	0	0	0	0	0	3	2

E—Groh, Rath, Cicotte 2. DP—White Sox 2 (Collins to Risberg to Gandil; Cicotte to Risberg to Gandil). LOB—Reds 1, White Sox 10. Scoring Position—Reds 2-for-4, White Sox 0-for-5. 2B—Neale (1), Jackson (2). S—Felsch. GDP—Daubert, Ring. SB—Risberg (1). CS—Wingo (1).

Reds	IP	H	R	ER	BB	K	ERA
Jimmy Ring (W, 1-0)	9.0	3	0	0	3	2	0.00

White Sox	IP	H	R	ER	BB	K	ERA
Eddie Cicotte (L, 0-2)	9.0	5	2	0	0	2	4.26

HBP—Schalk by Ring, Collins by Ring. Time—1:37. Attendance—34,363. Umpires—HP, Nallin. 1B, Rigler. 2B, Evans. 3B, Quigley.

Postseason: World Series

Game 5

Monday, October 6

Reds	AB	R	H	RBI	BB	K	Avg
Morrie Rath, 2b	3	1	1	1	1	0	.176
Jake Daubert, 1b	2	0	0	0	0	0	.176
Heine Groh, 3b	3	1	0	0	1	0	.067
Edd Roush, cf	4	2	1	2	0	0	.133
Pat Duncan, lf	2	0	0	1	1	1	.231
Larry Kopf, ss	3	0	1	0	0	0	.250
Greasy Neale, rf	4	0	0	1	0	1	.294
Bill Rariden, c	4	0	0	0	0	1	.100
Hod Eller, p	3	1	1	0	0	1	.333
TOTALS	28	5	4	5	3	3	.187

White Sox	AB	R	H	RBI	BB	K	Avg
Nemo Leibold, rf	3	0	0	0	1	1	.000
Eddie Collins, 2b	4	0	0	0	0	1	.111
Buck Weaver, 3b	4	0	2	0	0	0	.300
Joe Jackson, lf	4	0	0	0	0	0	.316
Happy Felsch, cf	3	0	0	0	0	1	.077
Chick Gandil, 1b	3	0	0	0	0	1	.278
Swede Risberg, ss	3	0	0	0	0	1	.143
Ray Schalk, c	2	0	1	0	0	1	.308
Byrd Lynn, c	1	0	0	0	0	0	.000
Lefty Williams, p	2	0	0	0	0	2	.200
Eddie Murphy, ph	1	0	0	0	0	1	.000
Erskine Mayer, p	0	0	0	0	0	0	—
TOTALS	30	0	3	0	1	9	.200

	1	2	3	4	5	6	7	8	9		R	H	E
Reds	0	0	0	0	0	4	0	0	1		5	4	0
White Sox	0	0	0	0	0	0	0	0	0		0	3	3

E—Risberg, Felsch, Collins. LOB—Reds 3, White Sox 4. Scoring Position—Reds 2-for-7, White Sox 1-for-4. 2B—Eller (1). 3B—Roush (1), Weaver (1). S—Daubert 2, Kopf. SF—Duncan. SB—Roush (2). CS—Neale (2).

Reds	IP	H	R	ER	BB	K	ERA
Hod Eller (W, 1-0)	9.0	3	0	0	1	9	0.00

White Sox	IP	H	R	ER	BB	K	ERA
Lefty Williams (L, 0-2)	8.0	4	4	4	2	3	4.50
Erskine Mayer	1.0	0	1	0	1	0	0.00

Time—1:45. Attendance—34,379. Umpires—HP, Rigler. 1B, Evans. 2B, Quigley. 3B, Nallin.

Game 6

Tuesday, October 7

White Sox	AB	R	H	RBI	BB	K	Avg
Shano Collins, rf	3	0	0	0	0	0	.091
Nemo Leibold, ph-rf	1	0	0	0	1	0	.000
Eddie Collins, 2b	4	0	0	1	0	0	.091
Buck Weaver, 3b	5	2	3	0	0	0	.360
Joe Jackson, lf	4	1	2	1	1	0	.348
Happy Felsch, cf	5	1	2	1	0	1	.167
Chick Gandil, 1b	4	0	1	1	1	0	.273
Swede Risberg, ss	4	1	0	0	1	0	.111
Ray Schalk, c	2	0	1	1	2	1	.333
Dickie Kerr, p	3	0	1	0	0	0	.167
TOTALS	35	5	10	5	6	2	.214

Reds	AB	R	H	RBI	BB	K	Avg
Morrie Rath, 2b	5	0	1	0	0	0	.182
Jake Daubert, 1b	4	1	2	0	0	0	.238
Heine Groh, 3b	4	0	1	0	1	1	.105
Edd Roush, cf	4	1	1	0	0	0	.158
Pat Duncan, lf	5	0	1	2	0	0	.222
Larry Kopf, ss	4	0	0	0	1	0	.200
Greasy Neale, rf	4	1	3	0	0	0	.381
Bill Rariden, c	4	0	1	0	0	0	.143
Dutch Ruether, p	2	1	1	1	0	0	.800
Jimmy Ring, p	2	0	0	0	0	1	.000
TOTALS	38	4	11	3	2	2	.220

	1	2	3	4	5	6	7	8	9	10	R	H	E
White Sox	0	0	0	0	0	1	3	0	0	1	5	10	3
Reds	0	0	2	0	0	0	0	0	0	0	4	11	0

E—Risberg 2, Felsch. DP—White Sox 2 (Jackson to Schalk; Risberg to ECollins to Gandil), Reds 3 (Roush to Groh; Roush to Rath; Kopf to Rath). LOB—White Sox 8, Reds 8. Scoring Position—White Sox 5-for-15, Reds 3-for-13. 2B—Weaver 2 (3), Felsch (1), Groh (1), Duncan (1), Ruether (1). 3B—Neale (1). S—Kerr, Daubert. SF—ECollins. GDP—Roush. SB—Schalk (1), Rath (1), Daubert (1), Leibold (1). CS—Groh (1), Neale (3).

White Sox	IP	H	R	ER	BB	K	ERA
Dickie Kerr (W, 2-0)	10.0	11	4	3	2	2	1.42

Reds	IP	H	R	ER	BB	K	ERA
Dutch Ruether	5.0	6	4	4	3	0	2.57
Jimmy Ring (BS, 1; L, 1-1)	5.0	4	1	1	3	2	0.64

Ruether pitched to three batters in the 6th.

HBP—Roush by Kerr. Time—2:06. Attendance—32,006. Umpires—HP, Evans. 1B, Quigley. 2B, Nallin. 3B, Rigler.

Game 7

Wednesday, October 8

White Sox	AB	R	H	RBI	BB	K	Avg
Shano Collins, rf	5	2	3	0	0	0	.250
Eddie Collins, 2b	4	1	2	0	0	1	.154
Buck Weaver, 3b	4	1	0	0	0	1	.310
Joe Jackson, lf	4	0	2	2	0	0	.370
Happy Felsch, cf	4	0	2	2	0	1	.227
Chick Gandil, 1b	4	0	0	0	0	0	.231
Swede Risberg, ss	4	0	0	0	0	1	.091
Ray Schalk, c	4	0	1	0	0	0	.316
Eddie Cicotte, p	4	0	0	0	0	2	.000
TOTALS	37	4	10	4	0	6	.236

Reds	AB	R	H	RBI	BB	K	Avg
Morrie Rath, 2b	5	0	1	0	0	0	.185
Jake Daubert, 1b	4	0	0	0	0	1	.200
Heine Groh, 3b	4	1	1	0	0	1	.130
Edd Roush, cf	4	0	0	0	0	0	.130
Pat Duncan, lf	4	0	1	1	0	0	.227
Larry Kopf, ss	4	0	1	0	0	0	.208
Greasy Neale, rf	4	0	1	0	0	1	.360
Ivy Wingo, c	1	0	1	0	3	0	.571
Slim Sallee, p	1	0	0	0	0	0	.000
Ray Fisher, p	0	0	0	0	0	0	.500
Dutch Ruether, ph	1	0	0	0	0	0	.667
Dolf Luque, p	1	0	0	0	0	1	.000
Sherry Magee, ph	1	0	1	0	0	0	.500
Jimmy Smith, pr	0	0	0	0	0	0	—
TOTALS	34	1	7	1	3	4	.236

	1	2	3	4	5	6	7	8	9		R	H	E
White Sox	1	0	1	0	2	0	0	0	0		4	10	1
Reds	0	0	0	0	0	1	0	0	0		1	7	4

E—Roush, Groh, Daubert, Rath, ECollins. DP—Reds 1 (Kopf to Daubert). LOB—White Sox 7, Reds 9. Scoring Position—White Sox 3-for-10, Reds 1-for-6. 2B—SCollins (1), Groh (2). S—ECollins. CS—Kopf (1).

White Sox	IP	H	R	ER	BB	K	ERA
Eddie Cicotte (W, 1-2)	9.0	7	1	1	3	4	2.91

Reds	IP	H	R	ER	BB	K	ERA
Slim Sallee (L, 1-1)	4.1	9	4	2	0	0	1.35
Ray Fisher	0.2	0	0	0	0	1	2.35
Dolf Luque	4.0	1	0	0	0	5	0.00

Time—1:47. Attendance—13,923. Umpires—HP, Quigley. 1B, Nallin. 2B, Rigler. 3B, Evans.

Game 8

Thursday, October 9

Reds	AB	R	H	RBI	BB	K	Avg
Morrie Rath, 2b	4	1	2	0	2	1	.226
Jake Daubert, 1b	4	2	2	0	1	0	.241
Heine Groh, 3b	6	2	2	0	0	1	.172
Edd Roush, cf	5	2	3	4	0	0	.214
Pat Duncan, lf	4	1	2	3	0	0	.269
Larry Kopf, ss	3	1	1	0	2	0	.222
Greasy Neale, rf	3	0	1	1	2	1	.357
Bill Rariden, c	5	0	2	2	0	0	.211
Hod Eller, p	4	1	1	0	0	1	.286
TOTALS	38	10	16	10	7	4	.241

White Sox	AB	R	H	RBI	BB	K	Avg
Nemo Leibold, cf	5	0	1	0	0	1	.056
Eddie Collins, 2b	5	1	3	0	0	1	.226
Buck Weaver, 3b	5	1	2	0	0	1	.324
Joe Jackson, lf	5	2	2	3	0	0	.375
Happy Felsch, cf	4	0	0	0	0	1	.192
Chick Gandil, 1b	4	1	1	1	0	0	.233
Swede Risberg, ss	3	0	0	0	1	1	.080
Ray Schalk, c	4	0	1	0	0	0	.304
Lefty Williams, p	0	0	0	0	0	0	.200
Bill James, p	2	0	0	0	0	1	.000
Roy Wilkinson, p	1	0	0	0	0	1	.000
Eddie Murphy, ph	0	0	0	0	0	0	.000
TOTALS	38	5	10	4	1	6	.230

	1	2	3	4	5	6	7	8	9		R	H	E
Reds	4	1	0	0	1	3	0	1	0		10	16	2
White Sox	0	0	1	0	0	0	0	4	0		5	10	1

E—Roush, Schalk, Rariden. LOB—Reds 12, White Sox 8. Scoring Position—Reds 8-for-20, White Sox 2-for-11. 2B—Roush 2 (2), Duncan (2), Collins (3). 3B—Kopf (2), Gandil (1). HR—Jackson (1). S—Daubert, Duncan. SB—Rath (2), Neale (1), Rariden (1), Collins (1). CS—Neale (4).

Reds	IP	H	R	ER	BB	K	ERA
Hod Eller (W, 2-0)	9.0	10	5	4	1	6	2.00

White Sox	IP	H	R	ER	BB	K	ERA
Lefty Williams (L, 0-3)	0.1	4	4	4	0	0	6.61
Bill James	4.2	8	4	3	3	2	5.79
Roy Wilkinson	4.0	4	2	1	4	2	2.45

James pitched to two batters in the 6th.

HBP—Eller by James, Roush by Wilkinson, Murphy by Eller. Time—2:27. Attendance—32,930. Umpires—HP, Nallin. 1B, Rigler. 2B, Evans. 3B, Quigley.

1919 World Series—Composite Statistics

Batting

Reds	G	AB	R	H	RBI	2B	3B	HR	BB	SO	SB	CS	Avg	OBP	Slg
Jake Daubert	8	29	4	7	1	0	1	0	1	2	1	1	.241	.290	.310
Pat Duncan	8	26	3	7	8	2	0	0	2	2	0	1	.269	.310	.346
Hod Eller	2	7	2	2	0	1	0	0	0	2	0	0	.286	.375	.429
Ray Fisher	2	2	0	1	0	0	0	0	0	0	0	0	.500	.500	.500
Heine Groh	8	29	6	5	2	2	0	0	6	4	0	1	.172	.306	.241
Larry Kopf	8	27	3	6	3	0	2	0	3	2	0	1	.222	.300	.370
Dolf Luque	2	1	0	0	0	0	0	0	0	1	0	0	.000	.000	.000
Sherry Magee	2	2	0	1	0	0	0	0	0	0	0	0	.500	.500	.500
Greasy Neale	8	28	3	10	4	1	1	0	2	5	1	4	.357	.400	.464
Bill Rariden	5	19	0	4	2	0	0	0	0	1	0	0	.211	.211	.211
Morrie Rath	8	31	5	7	2	1	0	0	4	1	2	0	.226	.333	.258
Jimmy Ring	2	5	0	0	0	0	0	0	0	2	0	0	.000	.000	.000
Edd Roush	8	28	6	6	7	2	1	0	3	0	2	1	.214	.333	.357
Dutch Ruether	3	6	2	4	4	1	2	0	1	0	0	0	.667	.714	1.500
Slim Sallee	2	4	0	0	0	0	0	0	0	0	0	0	.000	.000	.000
Jimmy Smith	1	0	0	0	0	0	0	0	0	0	0	0	—	—	—
Ivy Wingo	3	7	1	4	1	0	0	0	3	1	0	1	.571	.700	.571
Totals	8	251	35	64	34	10	7	0	25	22	7	10	.255	.332	.351

White Sox	G	AB	R	H	RBI	2B	3B	HR	BB	SO	SB	CS	Avg	OBP	Slg
Eddie Cicotte	3	8	0	0	0	0	0	0	0	3	0	0	.000	.000	.000
Eddie Collins	8	31	2	7	1	1	0	0	1	2	1	1	.226	.265	.258
Shano Collins	4	16	2	4	0	1	0	0	0	0	0	0	.250	.250	.313
Happy Felsch	8	26	2	5	3	1	0	0	1	4	0	1	.192	.222	.231
Chick Gandil	8	30	1	7	5	0	1	0	1	3	1	1	.233	.258	.300
Joe Jackson	8	32	5	12	6	3	0	1	1	2	0	1	.375	.394	.563
Bill James	1	2	0	0	0	0	0	0	0	1	0	0	.000	.000	.000
Dickie Kerr	2	6	0	1	0	0	0	0	0	0	0	0	.167	.167	.167
Nemo Leibold	5	18	0	1	0	0	0	0	2	3	1	0	.056	.150	.056
Byrd Lynn	1	1	0	0	0	0	0	0	0	0	0	0	.000	.000	.000
Fred McMullin	2	2	0	1	0	0	0	0	0	0	0	0	.500	.500	.500
Eddie Murphy	3	2	0	0	0	0	0	0	0	1	0	0	.000	.333	.000
Swede Risberg	8	25	3	2	0	1	0	0	5	3	1	0	.080	.233	.160
Ray Schalk	8	23	1	7	2	0	0	0	4	2	1	1	.304	.429	.304
Buck Weaver	8	34	4	11	0	4	1	0	0	2	0	0	.324	.324	.500
Roy Wilkinson	2	2	0	0	0	0	0	0	0	1	0	0	.000	.000	.000
Lefty Williams	3	5	0	1	0	0	0	0	0	3	0	0	.200	.200	.200
Totals	8	263	20	59	17	10	3	1	15	30	5	5	.224	.273	.297

Pitching

Reds	G	GS	CG	IP	H	R	ER	BB	SO	W-L	Sv-Op	Hld	ERA
Hod Eller	2	2	2	18.0	13	5	4	2	15	2-0	0-0	0	2.00
Ray Fisher	2	1	0	7.2	7	3	2	2	2	0-1	0-0	0	2.35
Dolf Luque	2	0	0	5.0	1	0	0	0	6	0-0	0-0	0	0.00
Jimmy Ring	2	1	1	14.0	7	1	1	6	4	1-1	0-1	0	0.64
Dutch Ruether	2	2	1	14.0	12	5	4	4	1	1-0	0-0	0	2.57
Slim Sallee	2	2	1	13.1	19	6	2	1	2	1-1	0-0	0	1.35
Totals	8	8	5	72.0	59	20	13	15	30	5-3	0-1	0	1.63

White Sox	G	GS	CG	IP	H	R	ER	BB	SO	W-L	Sv-Op	Hld	ERA
Eddie Cicotte	3	3	2	21.2	19	9	7	5	7	1-2	0-0	0	2.91
Bill James	1	0	0	4.2	8	4	3	3	2	0-0	0-0	0	5.79
Dickie Kerr	2	2	2	19.0	14	4	3	3	6	2-0	0-0	0	1.42
Grover Lowdermilk	1	0	0	1.0	2	1	1	1	0	0-0	0-0	0	9.00
Erskine Mayer	1	0	0	1.0	0	1	0	1	0	0-0	0-0	0	0.00
Roy Wilkinson	2	0	0	7.1	9	4	2	4	3	0-0	0-0	0	2.45
Lefty Williams	3	3	1	16.1	12	12	12	8	4	0-3	0-0	0	6.61
Totals	8	8	5	71.0	64	35	28	25	22	3-5	0-0	0	3.55

Fielding

Reds	Pos	G	PO	Ast	E	DP	PB	FPct
Jake Daubert	1b	8	81	4	2	4	—	.977
Pat Duncan	lf	8	9	0	0	0	—	1.000
Hod Eller	p	2	0	2	0	0	—	1.000
Ray Fisher	p	2	0	6	1	0	—	.857
Heine Groh	3b	8	8	18	2	2	—	.929
Larry Kopf	ss	8	11	28	1	4	—	.975
Dolf Luque	p	2	1	0	0	0	—	1.000
Greasy Neale	rf	8	19	0	1	0	—	.950
Bill Rariden	c	5	25	3	1	0	0	.966
Morrie Rath	2b	8	21	16	2	4	—	.949
Jimmy Ring	p	2	1	3	0	0	—	1.000
Edd Roush	cf	8	31	3	2	2	—	.944
Dutch Ruether	p	2	0	2	0	0	—	1.000
Slim Sallee	p	2	1	4	0	0	—	1.000
Ivy Wingo	c	3	8	3	0	0	0	1.000
Totals		8	216	92	12	16	0	.963

White Sox	Pos	G	PO	Ast	E	DP	PB	FPct
Eddie Cicotte	p	3	0	6	2	1	—	.750
Eddie Collins	2b	8	21	30	2	6	—	.962
Shano Collins	rf	4	5	0	0	0	—	1.000
Happy Felsch	cf	7	21	1	2	1	—	.917
	rf	1	2	0	0	0	—	1.000
Chick Gandil	1b	8	79	2	1	6	—	.988
Joe Jackson	lf	8	16	1	0	1	—	1.000
Bill James	p	1	0	0	0	0	—	—
Dickie Kerr	p	2	1	4	0	0	—	1.000
Nemo Leibold	rf	4	3	0	0	0	—	1.000
	cf	1	2	2	0	0	—	1.000
Grover Lowdermilk	p	1	0	1	0	0	—	1.000
Byrd Lynn	c	1	1	0	0	0	0	1.000
Erskine Mayer	p	1	0	0	0	0	—	—
Swede Risberg	ss	8	23	30	4	6	—	.930
Ray Schalk	c	8	29	15	1	1	0	.978
Buck Weaver	3b	8	9	18	0	0	—	1.000
Roy Wilkinson	p	2	0	2	0	0	—	1.000
Lefty Williams	p	3	1	2	0	0	—	1.000
Totals		8	213	114	12	22	0	.965

1920 Cleveland Indians (AL) 5, Brooklyn Dodgers (NL) 2

Stan Coveleski pitched the Cleveland Indians to a five-games-to-two World Series victory over the Brooklyn Dodgers. Coveleski got his first victory in the opener, beating the Dodgers, 3-1. Burleigh Grimes blanked the Tribe in Game 2 to even the Series. Brooklyn knocked Ray Caldwell out of the box in the first inning of Game 3 and held on for a 2-1 win. Coveleski won again in Game 4 by the score of 5-1. Cleveland right fielder Elmer Smith tripled, homered and drove in four runs, and second baseman Bill Wambsganss turned an unassisted triple play as Cleveland took Game 5, 8-1. Duster Mails blanked Brooklyn 1-0 in Game 6. Coveleski put Brooklyn to rest with a five-hit shutout in the seventh and final game. He finished the Series with a 3-0 record and an 0.67 ERA in 27 innings.

Game 1

Tuesday, October 5

Indians	AB	R	H	RBI	BB	K	Avg
Joe Evans, lf	2	0	0	0	1	0	.000
Charlie Jamieson, ph-lf	1	0	0	0	0	0	.000
Bill Wambsganss, 2b	3	0	0	0	0	1	.000
Tris Speaker, cf	4	0	0	0	0	1	.000
George Burns, 1b	3	1	1	0	0	1	.333
Elmer Smith, ph-rf	1	0	0	0	0	0	.000
Larry Gardner, 3b	4	0	0	0	0	0	.000
Joe Wood, rf	2	2	1	0	1	1	.500
Doc Johnston, ph-1b	1	0	0	0	0	0	.000
Joe Sewell, ss	3	0	1	0	0	1	.333
Steve O'Neill, c	3	0	2	2	0	1	.667
Stan Coveleski, p	3	0	0	0	0	1	.000
TOTALS	30	3	5	2	2	7	.167

Dodgers	AB	R	H	RBI	BB	K	Avg
Ivy Olson, ss	3	0	2	0	1	0	.667
Jimmy Johnston, 3b	3	0	0	0	0	0	.000
Tommy Griffith, rf	4	0	1	0	0	0	.250
Zack Wheat, lf	4	1	1	0	0	0	.250
Hi Myers, cf	4	0	0	0	0	0	.000
Ed Konetchy, 1b	4	0	0	1	0	1	.000
Pete Kilduff, 2b	3	0	0	0	0	1	.000
Ernie Krueger, c	3	0	0	0	0	0	.000
Rube Marquard, p	1	0	0	0	0	0	.000
Bill Lamar, ph	1	0	0	0	0	0	.000
Al Mamaux, p	0	0	0	0	0	0	—
Clarence Mitchell, ph	1	0	1	0	0	0	1.000
Bernie Neis, pr	0	0	0	0	0	0	—
Leon Cadore, p	0	0	0	0	0	0	—
TOTALS	31	1	5	1	1	3	.161

	1	2	3	4	5	6	7	8	9		R	H	E
Indians	0	2	0	1	0	0	0	0	0		3	5	0
Dodgers	0	0	0	0	0	1	0	0			1	5	1

E—Konetchy. DP—Dodgers 1 (Konetchy to Krueger to JJohnston). LOB—Indians 3, Dodgers 5. Scoring Position—Indians 2-for-7, Dodgers 0-for-7. 2B—Wood (1), O'Neill 2 (2), Wheat (1). S—Wambsganss, JJohnston.

Indians	IP	H	R	ER	BB	K	ERA
Stan Coveleski (W, 1-0)	9.0	5	1	1	1	3	1.00

Dodgers	IP	H	R	ER	BB	K	ERA
Rube Marquard (L, 0-1)	6.0	5	3	2	2	4	3.00
Al Mamaux	2.0	0	0	0	0	3	0.00
Leon Cadore	1.0	0	0	0	0	0	0.00

Time—1:41. Attendance—23,573. Umpires—HP, Klem. 1B, Connolly. 2B, O'Day. 3B, Dinneen.

Game 2

Wednesday, October 6

Indians	AB	R	H	RBI	BB	K	Avg
Charlie Jamieson, lf	4	0	1	0	1	0	.200
Bill Wambsganss, 2b	3	0	0	0	1	0	.000
George Burns, ph	0	0	0	0	1	0	.333
Harry Lunte, 2b	0	0	0	0	0	0	—
Tris Speaker, cf	3	0	2	0	1	0	.286
Elmer Smith, rf	4	0	0	0	0	1	.000
Larry Gardner, 3b	3	0	2	0	1	0	.286
Doc Johnston, 1b	4	0	0	0	0	0	.000
Joe Sewell, ss	4	0	0	0	0	0	.143
Steve O'Neill, c	4	0	1	0	0	0	.429
Jim Bagby, p	2	0	0	0	0	0	.000
Jack Graney, ph	1	0	0	0	0	1	.000
George Uhle, p	0	0	0	0	0	0	—
Les Nunamaker, ph	1	0	1	0	0	0	1.000
TOTALS	33	0	7	0	4	2	.196

Dodgers	AB	R	H	RBI	BB	K	Avg
Ivy Olson, ss	4	1	1	0	0	1	.429
Jimmy Johnston, 3b	4	1	1	0	0	0	.143
Tommy Griffith, rf	4	0	2	2	0	1	.375
Zack Wheat, lf	3	0	1	1	1	0	.286
Hi Myers, cf	3	0	1	0	0	0	.143
Ed Konetchy, 1b	3	0	0	0	0	0	.000
Pete Kilduff, 2b	3	0	0	0	0	0	.000
Otto Miller, c	3	0	0	0	0	1	.000
Burleigh Grimes, p	3	1	1	0	0	0	.333
TOTALS	30	3	7	3	1	3	.200

	1	2	3	4	5	6	7	8	9		R	H	E
Indians	0	0	0	0	0	0	0	0	0		0	7	1
Dodgers	1	0	1	0	1	0	0	0	x		3	7	0

E—Bagby. DP—Indians 1 (Gardner to O'Neill to DJohnston). LOB—Indians 10, Dodgers 4. Scoring Position—Indians 0-for-8, Dodgers 3-for-7. 2B—Speaker (1), Gardner (1), Griffith (1), Wheat (2). SB—JJohnston (1). CS—DJohnston (1), Griffith (1).

Indians	IP	H	R	ER	BB	K	ERA
Jim Bagby (L, 0-1)	6.0	7	3	2	1	0	3.00
George Uhle	2.0	0	0	0	0	3	0.00

Dodgers	IP	H	R	ER	BB	K	ERA
Burleigh Grimes (W, 1-0)	9.0	7	0	0	4	2	0.00

Time—1:55. Attendance—22,559. Umpires—HP, Connolly. 1B, O'Day. 2B, Dinneen. 3B, Klem.

Game 3

Thursday, October 7

Indians	AB	R	H	RBI	BB	K	Avg
Joe Evans, lf	4	0	0	0	0	0	.000
Bill Wambsganss, 2b	3	0	0	0	1	0	.000
Tris Speaker, cf	4	1	1	0	0	0	.273
George Burns, 1b	3	0	0	0	0	1	.167
Larry Gardner, 3b	3	0	0	0	0	0	.200
Joe Wood, rf	3	0	0	0	0	1	.200
Joe Sewell, ss	2	0	0	0	1	0	.111
Steve O'Neill, c	3	0	2	0	0	0	.500
Charlie Jamieson, pr	0	0	0	0	0	0	.200
George Uhle, p	0	0	0	0	0	0	—
Ray Caldwell, p	0	0	0	0	0	0	—
Duster Mails, p	2	0	0	0	0	0	.000
Les Nunamaker, ph-c	1	0	0	0	0	0	.500
TOTALS	28	1	3	0	2	2	.200

Dodgers	AB	R	H	RBI	BB	K	Avg
Ivy Olson, ss	2	1	1	0	2	0	.444
Jimmy Johnston, 3b	3	0	0	0	0	1	.100
Tommy Griffith, rf	1	1	0	0	0	0	.333
Bernie Neis, ph-rf	3	0	0	0	0	0	.000
Zack Wheat, lf	4	0	3	1	0	0	.455
Hi Myers, cf	4	0	2	1	0	0	.273
Ed Konetchy, 1b	3	0	0	0	1	0	.000
Pete Kilduff, 2b	1	0	0	0	1	0	.000
Otto Miller, c	1	0	0	0	1	0	.000
Sherry Smith, p	3	0	0	0	0	1	.000
TOTALS	25	2	6	2	5	2	.208

	1	2	3	4	5	6	7	8	9		R	H	E
Indians	0	0	0	1	0	0	0	0	0		1	3	1
Dodgers	2	0	0	0	0	0	0	0	x		2	6	1

E—Sewell, Wheat. DP—Indians 2 (Mails to Burns; Wambsganss to Sewell to Burns), Dodgers 2 (Olson to Kilduff to Konetchy; Johnston to Kilduff to Konetchy). LOB—Indians 2, Dodgers 7. Scoring Position—Indians 0-for-2, Dodgers 2-for-10. 2B—Speaker (2). S—Johnston, Kilduff, Miller. GDP—Konetchy, Mails, Nunamaker. CS—Olson (1).

Indians	IP	H	R	ER	BB	K	ERA
Ray Caldwell (L, 0-1)	0.1	2	2	1	1	0	27.00
Duster Mails	6.2	3	0	0	4	2	0.00
George Uhle	1.0	1	0	0	0	0	0.00

Dodgers	IP	H	R	ER	BB	K	ERA
Sherry Smith (W, 1-0)	9.0	3	1	0	2	2	0.00

Time—1:47. Attendance—25,088. Umpires—HP, O'Day. 1B, Dinneen. 2B, Klem. 3B, Connolly.

Game 4

Saturday, October 9

Dodgers	AB	R	H	RBI	BB	K	Avg
Ivy Olson, ss	4	0	1	0	0	0	.385
Jimmy Johnston, 3b	4	1	2	0	0	0	.214
Bernie Neis, pr	0	0	0	0	0	0	.000
Tommy Griffith, rf	4	0	1	1	0	0	.308
Zack Wheat, lf	4	0	0	0	0	0	.333
Hi Myers, cf	3	0	0	0	0	1	.214
Ed Konetchy, 1b	2	0	0	0	1	0	.000
Pete Kilduff, 2b	3	0	1	0	0	2	.100
Otto Miller, c	3	0	0	0	0	0	.000
Leon Cadore, p	0	0	0	0	0	0	—
Al Mamaux, p	1	0	0	0	0	1	.000
Rube Marquard, p	0	0	0	0	0	0	.000
Bill Lamar, ph	1	0	0	0	0	0	.000
Jeff Pfeffer, p	1	0	0	0	0	0	.000
TOTALS	30	1	5	1	1	4	.198

Indians	AB	R	H	RBI	BB	K	Avg
Charlie Jamieson, lf	2	0	0	0	0	0	.143
Joe Evans, ph-lf	3	0	1	0	0	0	.111
Bill Wambsganss, 2b	4	2	1	1	1	0	.154
Tris Speaker, cf	5	2	2	0	0	0	.313
Elmer Smith, rf	1	0	1	1	0	0	.167
George Burns, ph-1b	2	0	1	1	1	1	.250
Larry Gardner, 3b	3	0	1	1	0	1	.231
Doc Johnston, 1b	1	0	0	0	0	1	.000
Joe Wood, ph-rf	2	0	0	0	0	0	.143
Jack Graney, ph-rf	1	0	0	0	0	0	.000
Joe Sewell, ss	4	0	2	0	0	0	.231
Steve O'Neill, c	2	0	1	0	2	1	.500
Stan Coveleski, p	4	1	1	0	0	1	.143
TOTALS	34	5	12	4	4	5	.218

	1	2	3	4	5	6	7	8	9		R	H	E
Dodgers	0	0	0	1	0	0	0	0	0		1	5	1
Indians	2	0	2	0	0	1	0	0	x		5	12	1

E—Burns, Wheat. DP—Dodgers 1 (Myers to Olson to Kilduff), Indians 2 (Sewell to Wambsganss to Burns; Gardner to Wambsganss to Burns). LOB—Dodgers 3, Indians 10. Scoring Position—Dodgers 0-for-3, Indians 5-for-15. 2B—Griffith (2). SF—Gardner. GDP—Miller 2.

Dodgers	IP	H	R	ER	BB	K	ERA
Leon Cadore (L, 0-1)	1.0	4	2	2	1	1	9.00
Al Mamaux	1.0	2	2	2	0	1	6.00
Rube Marquard	3.0	2	0	0	1	2	2.00
Jeff Pfeffer	3.0	4	1	1	2	1	3.00

Indians	IP	H	R	ER	BB	K	ERA
Stan Coveleski (W, 2-0)	9.0	5	1	1	1	4	1.00

Cadore pitched to two batters in the 2nd. Mamaux pitched to three batters in the 3rd.

WP—Pfeffer. PB—Miller. Time—1:54. Attendance—25,734. Umpires—HP, Dinneen. 1B, Klem. 2B, Connolly. 3B, O'Day.

Game 5
Sunday, October 10

Dodgers	AB	R	H	RBI	BB	K	Avg
Ivy Olson, ss	4	0	2	0	0	0	.412
Jack Sheehan, 3b	3	0	1	0	0	0	.333
Tommy Griffith, rf	4	0	0	0	0	1	.235
Zack Wheat, lf	4	1	2	0	0	1	.368
Hi Myers, cf	4	0	2	0	0	0	.278
Ed Konetchy, 1b	4	0	2	1	0	1	.125
Pete Kilduff, 2b	4	0	1	0	0	0	.143
Otto Miller, c	2	0	2	0	0	0	.222
Ernie Krueger, c	2	0	1	0	0	0	.200
Burleigh Grimes, p	1	0	0	0	0	0	.250
Clarence Mitchell, p	2	0	0	0	0	0	.333
TOTALS	34	1	13	1	0	3	.264

Indians	AB	R	H	RBI	BB	K	Avg
Charlie Jamieson, lf	4	1	2	0	0	0	.273
Jack Graney, ph-lf	1	0	0	0	0	1	.000
Bill Wambsganss, 2b	5	1	1	0	0	0	.167
Tris Speaker, cf	3	2	1	0	1	0	.316
Elmer Smith, rf	4	1	3	4	0	0	.400
Larry Gardner, 3b	4	0	1	1	0	0	.235
Doc Johnston, 1b	3	1	2	0	0	0	.222
Joe Sewell, ss	3	0	0	0	1	0	.188
Steve O'Neill, c	2	1	0	0	2	0	.429
Pinch Thomas, c	0	0	0	0	0	0	—
Jim Bagby, p	4	1	2	3	0	0	.333
TOTALS	33	8	12	8	4	1	.268

	1	2	3	4	5	6	7	8	9	R	H	E
Dodgers	0	0	0	0	0	0	0	0	1	1	13	1
Indians	4	0	0	3	1	0	0	0	x	8	12	2

E—Sheehan, O'Neill, Gardner. DP—Dodgers 1 (Olson to Kilduff to Konetchy), Indians 3 (Jamieson to O'Neill; Gardner to Wambsganss to Johnston; Johnston to Sewell). TP—Indians 1 (Wambsganss). LOB—Dodgers 7, Indians 6. Scoring Position—Dodgers 1-for-9, Indians 4-for-8. 3B—Konetchy (1), Smith (1). HR—Smith (1), Bagby (1). S—Sheehan, Johnston. GDP—Grimes, Sewell, Mitchell. CS—Myers 2 (2), Jamieson (1), Sewell (1).

Dodgers	IP	H	R	ER	BB	K	ERA
Burleigh Grimes (L, 1-1)	3.1	9	7	7	1	0	5.11
Clarence Mitchell	4.2	3	1	0	3	1	0.00

Indians	IP	H	R	ER	BB	K	ERA
Jim Bagby (W, 1-1)	9.0	13	1	1	0	3	1.80

WP—Bagby. PB—Miller. Time—1:49. Attendance—26,884. Umpires—HP, Klem. 1B, Connolly. 2B, O'Day. 3B, Dinneen.

Game 6
Monday, October 11

Dodgers	AB	R	H	RBI	BB	K	Avg
Ivy Olson, ss	4	0	1	0	0	0	.381
Jack Sheehan, 3b	4	0	0	0	0	1	.143
Bernie Neis, rf	2	0	0	0	1	0	.000
Ernie Krueger, ph	1	0	0	0	0	0	.167
Tommy Griffith, rf	0	0	0	0	0	0	.235
Zack Wheat, lf	4	0	0	0	0	1	304
Hi Myers, cf	4	0	1	0	0	0	.273
Ed Konetchy, 1b	3	0	1	0	1	0	.158
Bill McCabe, pr	0	0	0	0	0	0	—
Pete Kilduff, 2b	4	0	0	0	0	1	.111
Otto Miller, c	3	0	0	0	0	0	.167
Sherry Smith, p	3	0	0	0	0	1	.000
TOTALS	32	0	3	0	2	4	.218

Indians	AB	R	H	RBI	BB	K	Avg
Joe Evans, lf	4	0	3	0	0	0	.308
Bill Wambsganss, 2b	4	0	0	0	0	0	.136
Tris Speaker, cf	3	1	1	0	0	0	.318
Larry Gardner, 3b	2	0	1	1	1	0	.300
Joe Wood, rf	3	0	0	0	0	0	.200
George Burns, 1b	3	0	1	0	0	0	.200
Joe Sewell, ss	3	0	1	0	0	0	.211
Steve O'Neill, c	3	0	0	0	0	0	.353
Duster Mails, p	3	0	0	0	0	1	.000
TOTALS	28	1	7	1	1	1	.239

	1	2	3	4	5	6	7	8	9	R	H	E
Dodgers	0	0	0	0	0	0	0	0	0	0	3	0
Indians	0	0	0	0	0	1	0	0	x	1	7	3

E—Sewell 2, Gardner. LOB—Dodgers 7, Indians 4. Scoring Position—Dodgers 0-for-6, Indians 0-for-3. 2B—Olson (1), Burns (1). CS—Evans (1), Sewell (2).

Dodgers	IP	H	R	ER	BB	K	ERA
Sherry Smith (L, 1-1)	8.0	7	1	1	1	1	0.53

Indians	IP	H	R	ER	BB	K	ERA
Duster Mails (W, 1-0)	9.0	3	0	0	2	4	0.00

Time—1:34. Attendance—27,194. Umpires—HP, Connolly. 1B, O'Day. 2B, Dinneen. 3B, Klem.

Game 7
Tuesday, October 12

Dodgers	AB	R	H	RBI	BB	K	Avg
Ivy Olson, ss	4	0	0	0	0	0	.320
Jack Sheehan, 3b	4	0	1	0	0	0	.182
Tommy Griffith, rf	4	0	0	0	0	0	.190
Zack Wheat, lf	4	0	2	0	0	0	.333
Hi Myers, cf	4	0	0	0	0	0	.231
Ed Konetchy, 1b	4	0	1	0	0	0	.174
Pete Kilduff, 2b	3	0	0	0	0	0	.095
Otto Miller, c	2	0	0	0	0	1	.143
Bill Lamar, ph	1	0	0	0	0	0	.000
Ernie Krueger, c	0	0	0	0	0	0	.167
Burleigh Grimes, p	2	0	1	0	0	0	.333
Ray Schmandt, ph	1	0	0	0	0	0	.000
Al Mamaux, p	0	0	0	0	0	0	.000
TOTALS	33	0	5	0	0	1	.216

Indians	AB	R	H	RBI	BB	K	Avg
Charlie Jamieson, lf	4	1	2	1	0	0	.333
Bill Wambsganss, 2b	4	0	1	0	0	0	.154
Tris Speaker, cf	3	0	1	1	1	0	.320
Elmer Smith, rf	3	0	0	0	1	0	.308
Larry Gardner, 3b	4	1	1	0	0	0	.208
Doc Johnston, 1b	2	0	1	0	2	0	.273
Joe Sewell, ss	4	0	0	0	0	0	.174
Steve O'Neill, c	4	0	1	0	0	1	.333
Stan Coveleski, p	3	1	0	0	0	2	.100
TOTALS	31	3	7	2	4	3	.244

	1	2	3	4	5	6	7	8	9	R	H	E
Dodgers	0	0	0	0	0	0	0	0	0	0	5	2
Indians	0	0	0	1	1	0	1	0	x	3	7	3

E—Sheehan, Sewell 2, Grimes, Coveleski. LOB—Dodgers 6, Indians 8. Scoring Position—Dodgers 1-for-3, Indians 2-for-10. 2B—Jamieson (1), O'Neill (3). 3B—Speaker (1). SB—Jamieson (1), Johnston (1). CS—Johnston (2).

Dodgers	IP	H	R	ER	BB	K	ERA
Burleigh Grimes (L, 1-2)	7.0	7	3	2	4	2	4.19
Al Mamaux	1.0	0	0	0	0	1	4.50

Indians	IP	H	R	ER	BB	K	ERA
Stan Coveleski (W, 3-0)	9.0	5	0	0	0	1	0.67

Time—1:55. Attendance—27,525. Umpires—HP, O'Day. 1B, Dinneen. 2B, Klem. 3B, Connolly.

1920 World Series—Composite Statistics

Batting

Indians	G	AB	R	H	RBI	2B	3B	HR	BB	SO	SB	CS	Avg	OBP	Slg
Jim Bagby	2	6	1	2	3	0	0	1	0	0	0	0	.333	.333	.833
George Burns	5	10	1	3	2	1	0	0	3	3	0	0	.300	.462	.400
Stan Coveleski	3	10	2	1	0	0	0	0	0	4	0	0	.100	.100	.100
Joe Evans	4	13	0	4	0	0	0	0	1	0	0	1	.308	.357	.308
Larry Gardner	7	24	1	5	2	1	0	0	1	1	0	0	.208	.231	.250
Jack Graney	3	3	0	0	0	0	0	0	0	2	0	0	.000	.000	.000
Charlie Jamieson	6	15	2	5	1	1	0	0	1	0	1	1	.333	.375	.400
Doc Johnston	5	11	1	3	0	0	0	0	2	1	1	2	.273	.385	.273
Duster Mails	2	5	0	0	0	0	0	0	0	1	0	0	.000	.000	.000
Les Nunamaker	2	2	0	1	0	0	0	0	0	0	0	0	.500	.500	.500
Steve O'Neill	7	21	1	7	2	3	0	0	4	3	0	0	.333	.440	.476
Joe Sewell	7	23	0	4	0	0	0	0	2	1	0	2	.174	.240	.174
Elmer Smith	5	13	1	4	5	0	1	1	1	1	0	0	.308	.357	.692
Tris Speaker	7	25	6	8	1	2	1	0	3	1	0	0	.320	.393	.480
Bill Wambsganss	7	26	3	4	1	0	0	0	2	1	0	0	.154	.214	.154
Joe Wood	4	10	2	2	0	1	0	0	1	2	0	0	.200	.273	.300
Totals	7	217	21	53	17	9	2	2	21	21	2	6	.244	.310	.332

Batting

Dodgers	G	AB	R	H	RBI	2B	3B	HR	BB	SO	SB	CS	Avg	OBP	Slg
Tommy Griffith	7	21	1	4	3	2	0	0	0	2	0	1	.190	.190	.286
Burleigh Grimes	3	6	1	2	0	0	0	0	0	0	0	0	.333	.333	.333
Jimmy Johnston	4	14	2	3	0	0	0	0	0	2	1	0	.214	.214	.214
Pete Kilduff	7	21	0	2	0	0	0	0	1	4	0	0	.095	.136	.095
Ed Konetchy	7	23	0	4	2	0	1	0	3	2	0	0	.174	.269	.261
Ernie Krueger	4	6	0	1	0	0	0	0	0	0	0	0	.167	.167	.167
Bill Lamar	3	3	0	0	0	0	0	0	0	0	0	0	.000	.000	.000
Al Mamaux	3	1	0	0	0	0	0	0	0	1	0	0	.000	.000	.000
Rube Marquard	2	1	0	0	0	0	0	0	0	0	0	0	.000	.000	.000
Bill McCabe	1	0	0	0	0	0	0	0	0	0	0	0	—	—	—
Otto Miller	6	14	0	2	0	0	0	0	1	2	0	0	.143	.200	.143
Clarence Mitchell	2	3	0	1	0	0	0	0	0	0	0	0	.333	.333	.333
Hi Myers	7	26	0	6	1	0	0	0	0	1	0	2	.231	.231	.231
Bernie Neis	4	5	0	0	0	0	0	0	0	1	0	0	.000	.167	.000
Ivy Olson	7	25	2	8	0	1	0	0	3	1	0	1	.320	.393	.360
Jeff Pfeffer	1	1	0	0	0	0	0	0	0	0	0	0	.000	.000	.000
Ray Schmandt	1	1	0	0	0	0	0	0	0	0	0	0	.000	.000	.000
Jack Sheehan	3	11	0	2	0	0	0	0	0	1	0	0	.182	.182	.182
Sherry Smith	2	6	0	0	0	0	0	0	0	2	0	0	.000	.000	.000
Zack Wheat	7	27	2	9	2	2	0	0	1	2	0	0	.333	.357	.407
Totals	7	215	8	44	8	5	1	0	10	20	1	4	.205	.240	.237

Pitching

Indians	G	GS	CG	IP	H	R	ER	BB	SO	W-L	Sv-Op	Hld	ERA
Jim Bagby	2	2	1	15.0	20	4	3	1	3	1-1	0-0	0	1.80
Ray Caldwell	1	1	0	0.1	2	2	1	1	0	0-1	0-0	0	27.00
Stan Coveleski	3	3	3	27.0	15	2	2	2	8	3-0	0-0	0	0.67
Duster Mails	2	1	1	15.2	6	0	0	6	6	1-0	0-0	0	0.00
George Uhle	2	0	0	3.0	1	0	0	0	3	0-0	0-0	0	0.00
Totals	7	7	5	61.0	44	8	6	10	20	5-2	0-0	0	0.89

Pitching

Dodgers	G	GS	CG	IP	H	R	ER	BB	SO	W-L	Sv-Op	Hld	ERA
Leon Cadore	2	1	0	2.0	4	2	2	1	1	0-1	0-0	0	9.00
Burleigh Grimes	3	3	1	19.1	23	10	9	9	4	1-2	0-0	0	4.19
Al Mamaux	3	0	0	4.0	2	2	2	0	5	0-0	0-0	0	4.50
Rube Marquard	2	1	0	9.0	7	3	2	3	6	0-1	0-0	0	2.00
Clarence Mitchell	1	0	0	4.2	3	1	0	3	1	0-0	0-0	0	0.00
Jeff Pfeffer	1	0	0	3.0	4	1	1	2	1	0-0	0-0	0	3.00
Sherry Smith	2	2	2	17.0	10	2	1	3	3	1-1	0-0	0	0.53
Totals	7	7	3	59.0	53	21	17	21	21	2-5	0-0	0	2.59

Fielding

Indians	Pos	G	PO	Ast	E	DP	PB	FPct
Jim Bagby	p	2	2	3	1	0	—	.833
George Burns	1b	4	38	1	1	4	—	.975
Ray Caldwell	p	1	0	0	0	0	—	—
Stan Coveleski	p	3	2	5	1	0	—	.875
Joe Evans	lf	4	7	0	0	0	—	1.000
Larry Gardner	3b	7	8	14	2	3	—	.917
Jack Graney	lf	1	0	0	0	0	—	—
	rf	1	0	0	0	0	—	—
Charlie Jamieson	lf	5	8	1	0	1	—	1.000
Doc Johnston	1b	5	29	6	0	3	—	1.000
Harry Lunte	2b	1	0	0	0	0	—	—
Duster Mails	p	2	1	4	0	1	—	1.000
Les Nunamaker	c	1	0	0	0	0	0	—
Steve O'Neill	c	7	23	6	1	2	0	.967
Joe Sewell	ss	7	12	28	5	3	—	.889
Elmer Smith	rf	5	7	1	0	0	—	1.000
Tris Speaker	cf	7	18	0	0	0	—	1.000
Pinch Thomas	c	1	1	0	0	0	0	1.000
George Uhle	p	2	0	1	0	0	—	1.000
Bill Wambsganss	2b	7	20	17	0	4	—	1.000
Joe Wood	rf	4	7	0	0	0	—	1.000
Totals		7	183	87	11	21	0	.961

Fielding

Dodgers	Pos	G	PO	Ast	E	DP	PB	FPct
Leon Cadore	p	2	1	1	0	0	—	1.000
Tommy Griffith	rf	7	10	0	0	0	—	1.000
Burleigh Grimes	p	3	1	7	1	0	—	.889
Jimmy Johnston	3b	4	2	8	0	2	—	1.000
Pete Kilduff	2b	7	15	28	0	4	—	1.000
Ed Konetchy	1b	7	70	7	1	4	—	.987
Ernie Krueger	c	3	10	2	0	1	0	1.000
Al Mamaux	p	3	0	1	0	0	—	1.000
Rube Marquard	p	2	0	1	0	0	—	1.000
Otto Miller	c	6	17	6	0	0	2	1.000
Clarence Mitchell	p	1	1	0	0	0	—	1.000
Hi Myers	cf	7	15	1	0	1	—	1.000
Bernie Neis	rf	2	3	0	0	0	—	1.000
Ivy Olson	ss	7	12	20	0	3	—	1.000
Jeff Pfeffer	p	1	0	0	0	0	—	—
Jack Sheehan	3b	3	3	5	2	0	—	.800
Sherry Smith	p	2	2	4	0	0	—	1.000
Zack Wheat	lf	7	15	0	2	0	—	.882
Totals		7	177	91	6	15	2	.978

1921 New York Giants (NL) 5, New York Yankees (AL) 3

In the first World Series clash between New York clubs, the Giants topped the Yankees, five games to three. Carl Mays blanked the Giants on five hits in the opener, and Waite Hoyt tossed a two-hitter in Game 2 for the Yankees' second straight shutout. George Burns rapped two singles, a double and a triple as the Giants romped, 13-5, in Game 3. Burns drove in the go-ahead run the next day as the Giants' Phil Douglas bested Mays, 4-2. Hoyt won again in Game 5, posting a 3-1 victory. Irish Meusel and Frank Snyder homered as the Giants took Game 6, 8-5. Douglas beat Mays again in Game 7 when Snyder doubled in tho go-ahead run in the seventh. The Giants scored in the first inning of Game 8 on shortstop Roger Peckinpaugh's error, and Art Nehf made it stand up for a 1-0 victory over Hoyt, who didn't allow a single earned run in 27 innings.

Game 1

Wednesday, October 5

Yankees	AB	R	H	RBI	BB	K	Avg
Elmer Miller, cf	4	1	1	0	0	0	.250
Roger Peckinpaugh, ss	3	1	1	0	0	1	.333
Babe Ruth, lf	3	0	1	1	1	2	.333
Bob Meusel, rf	4	0	0	1	0	0	.000
Wally Pipp, 1b	2	0	0	0	1	0	.000
Aaron Ward, 2b	3	0	1	0	1	1	.333
Mike McNally, 3b	4	1	2	0	0	0	.500
Wally Schang, c	2	0	0	0	1	2	.000
Carl Mays, p	3	0	1	0	0	1	.333
TOTALS	28	3	7	2	4	7	.250

Giants	AB	R	H	RBI	BB	K	Avg
George Burns, cf	4	0	0	0	0	0	.000
Dave Bancroft, ss	4	0	0	0	0	0	.000
Frankie Frisch, 3b	4	0	4	0	0	0	1.000
Ross Youngs, rf	3	0	0	0	0	0	.000
George Kelly, 1b	4	0	0	0	0	1	.000
Irish Meusel, lf	3	0	0	0	0	0	.000
Johnny Rawlings, 2b	2	0	1	0	0	0	.500
Frank Snyder, c	3	0	0	0	0	0	.000
Phil Douglas, p	2	0	0	0	0	0	.000
Earl Smith, ph	1	0	0	0	0	0	.000
Jesse Barnes, p	0	0	0	0	0	0	—
TOTALS	30	0	5	0	0	1	.167

	1 2 3	4 5 6	7 8 9	R	H	E
Yankees	1 0 0	0 1 1	0 0 0	3	7	0
Giants	0 0 0	0 0 0	0 0 0	0	5	0

DP—Giants 1 (Frisch to Rawlings to Kelly). LOB—Yankees 5, Giants 5. Scoring Position—Yankees 1-for-7, Giants 0-for-3. 2B—McNally (1). 3B—Frisch (1). S—Peckinpaugh, Pipp, Schang, Youngs. GDP—BMeusel, Kelly. SB—McNally 2 (2), Frisch (1). CS—Pipp (1).

Yankees	IP	H	R	ER	BB	K	ERA
Carl Mays (W, 1-0)	9.0	5	0	0	0	1	0.00

Giants	IP	H	R	ER	BB	K	ERA
Phil Douglas (L, 0-1)	8.0	5	3	3	4	6	3.38
Jesse Barnes	1.0	2	0	0	0	1	0.00

PB—Snyder. HBP—Rawlings by Mays. Time—1:38. Attendance—30,203. Umpires—HP, Rigler. 1B, Moriarty. 2B, Quigley. 3B, Chill.

Game 2

Thursday, October 6

Giants	AB	R	H	RBI	BB	K	Avg
George Burns, cf	3	0	0	0	1	1	.000
Dave Bancroft, ss	4	0	1	0	0	0	.000
Frankie Frisch, 3b	4	0	1	0	0	0	.625
Ross Youngs, rf	2	0	0	0	2	0	.000
George Kelly, 1b	4	0	0	0	0	2	.000
Irish Meusel, lf	2	0	0	0	0	0	.000
Johnny Rawlings, 2b	3	0	1	0	0	0	.400
Earl Smith, c	3	0	0	0	0	0	.000
Art Nehf, p	2	0	0	0	1	1	.000
TOTALS	27	0	2	0	5	5	.135

Yankees	AB	R	H	RBI	BB	K	Avg
Elmer Miller, cf	3	0	0	0	1	0	.143
Roger Peckinpaugh, ss	3	0	0	0	1	0	.167
Babe Ruth, lf	1	1	0	0	3	0	.250
Bob Meusel, rf	4	1	1	0	0	0	.125
Wally Pipp, 1b	3	0	0	1	1	0	.000
Aaron Ward, 2b	4	1	1	0	0	0	.286
Mike McNally, 3b	3	0	0	0	0	0	.286
Wally Schang, c	2	0	0	1	1	0	.000
Waite Hoyt, p	3	0	1	1	0	0	.333
TOTALS	26	3	3	2	7	0	.176

	1 2 3	4 5 6	7 8 9	R	H	E
Giants	0 0 0	0 0 0	0 0 0	0	2	3
Yankees	0 0 0	1 0 0	0 2 x	3	3	0

E—Frisch, Smith, Nehf. DP—Giants 2 (Frisch to Rawlings; Rawlings to Kelly to Smith), Yankees 1 (McNally to Ward to Pipp). LOB—Giants 5, Yankees 6. Scoring Position—Giants 0-for-2, Yankees 0-for-6. GDP—Kelly. SB—Ruth 2 (2), BMeusel (1). CS—Burns (1), McNally (1).

Giants	IP	H	R	ER	BB	K	ERA
Art Nehf (L, 0-1)	8.0	3	3	1	7	0	1.13

Yankees	IP	H	R	ER	BB	K	ERA
Waite Hoyt (W, 1-0)	9.0	2	0	0	5	5	0.00

Time—1:55. Attendance—34,939. Umpires—HP, Moriarty. 1B, Quigley. 2B, Chill. 3B, Rigler.

Game 3

Friday, October 7

Yankees	AB	R	H	RBI	BB	K	Avg
Elmer Miller, cf	5	1	1	1	0	2	.167
Roger Peckinpaugh, ss	3	1	0	0	1	0	.111
Babe Ruth, lf	3	0	1	2	1	2	.286
Chick Fewster, pr-lf	0	1	0	0	0	0	—
Bob Meusel, rf	3	0	2	0	1	1	.273
Wally Pipp, 1b	3	0	0	1	0	0	.000
Aaron Ward, 2b	4	0	2	1	0	1	.364
Mike McNally, 3b	3	0	0	0	0	1	.200
Wally Schang, c	2	1	1	0	1	0	.167
Al DeVormer, c	1	0	0	0	0	0	.000
Bob Shawkey, p	1	1	1	0	0	0	1.000
Jack Quinn, p	2	0	0	0	0	1	.000
Rip Collins, p	0	0	0	0	0	0	—
Tom Rogers, p	0	0	0	0	0	0	—
Home Run Baker, ph	1	0	0	0	0	0	.000
TOTALS	31	5	8	5	4	8	.203

Giants	AB	R	H	RBI	BB	K	Avg
George Burns, cf	6	1	4	0	0	0	.308
Dave Bancroft, ss	5	1	1	1	0	1	.077
Frankie Frisch, 3b	2	3	2	0	3	0	.700
Ross Youngs, rf	3	2	2	4	2	0	.250
George Kelly, 1b	3	1	0	1	2	1	.000
Irish Meusel, lf	5	2	3	0	0	0	.300
Johnny Rawlings, 2b	5	0	2	3	0	1	.400
Frank Snyder, c	5	1	4	1	0	0	.500
Fred Toney, p	0	0	0	0	0	0	—
Jesse Barnes, p	5	2	2	0	0	0	.400
TOTALS	39	13	20	13	7	3	.307

	1 2 3	4 5 6	7 8 9	R	H	E
Yankees	0 0 4	0 0 0	0 1 0	5	8	0
Giants	0 0 4	0 0 0	8 1 x	13	20	0

DP—Yankees 2 (Ward to Pipp; Quinn to Peckinpaugh to Pipp). LOB—Yankees 5, Giants 10. Scoring Position—Yankees 3-for-10, Giants 6-for-15. 2B—BMeusel (1), Burns (1), Youngs (1), IMeusel (1). 3B—Burns (1), Youngs (1). S—Pipp. SF—Bancroft. GDP—Barnes. SB—Burns (1), Frisch (2), IMeusel (1). CS—Ruth (1), BMeusel (1), Rawlings (1), Snyder (1).

Yankees	IP	H	R	ER	BB	K	ERA
Bob Shawkey	2.1	4	4	4	2	2	15.43
Jack Quinn (L, 0-1)	3.2	7	4	4	2	2	9.82
Rip Collins	0.2	5	4	4	1	0	54.00
Tom Rogers	1.1	3	1	1	0	1	6.75

Giants	IP	H	R	ER	BB	K	ERA
Fred Toney	2.0	4	4	4	2	1	18.00
Jesse Barnes (W, 1-0)	7.0	4	1	1	2	7	1.13

Toney pitched to five batters in the 3rd. Quinn pitched to four batters in the 7th.

WP—Barnes. HBP—McNally by Barnes. Time—2:40. Attendance—36,509. Umpires—HP, Quigley. 1B, Chill. 2B, Rigler. 3B, Moriarty.

Game 4

Sunday, October 9

Giants	AB	R	H	RBI	BB	K	Avg
George Burns, cf	4	0	2	2	0	1	.353
Dave Bancroft, ss	4	0	0	0	0	0	.059
Frankie Frisch, 3b	4	0	0	0	0	0	.500
Ross Youngs, rf	4	0	1	0	0	0	.250

Giants	AB	R	H	RBI	BB	K	Avg
George Kelly, 1b	4	1	1	0	0	0	.067
Irish Meusel, lf	4	1	2	1	0	0	.357
Johnny Rawlings, 2b	4	1	2	1	0	0	.429
Frank Snyder, c	4	1	1	0	0	0	.417
Phil Douglas, p	2	0	0	0	0	0	.000
TOTALS	34	4	9	4	0	1	.286

Yankees	AB	R	H	RBI	BB	K	Avg
Elmer Miller, cf	4	0	0	0	0	2	.125
Roger Peckinpaugh, ss	4	0	1	0	0	0	.154
Babe Ruth, lf	4	1	2	1	0	1	.364
Bob Meusel, rf	4	0	0	0	0	1	.200
Wally Pipp, 1b	4	0	1	0	0	0	.083
Aaron Ward, 2b	2	0	0	0	2	0	.308
Mike McNally, 3b	3	1	1	0	0	1	.231
Wally Schang, c	3	0	2	1	0	1	.333
Carl Mays, p	3	0	0	0	0	0	.167
TOTALS	31	2	7	2	0	8	.213

	1 2 3	4 5 6	7 8 9	R	H	E
Giants	0 0 0	0 0 0	0 3 1	4	9	1
Yankees	0 0 0	0 1 0	0 0 1	2	7	1

E—McNally, Bancroft. DP—Yankees 1 (Ward to Peckinpaugh to Pipp). LOB—Giants 4, Yankees 3. Scoring Position—Giants 3-for-6, Yankees 0-for-3. 2B—Burns (2), Kelly (1). 3B—IMeusel (1), Schang (1). HR—Ruth (1). S—Douglas, Ward. GDP—Kelly. CS—IMeusel (1), Peckinpaugh (1), McNally (2).

Giants	IP	H	R	ER	BB	K	ERA
Phil Douglas (W, 1-1)	9.0	7	2	2	0	8	2.65

Yankees	IP	H	R	ER	BB	K	ERA
Carl Mays (L, 1-1)	9.0	9	4	4	0	1	2.00

Time—1:38. Attendance—36,372. Umpires—HP, Chill. 1B, Rigler. 2B, Moriarty. 3B, Quigley.

Game 5

Monday, October 10

Yankees	AB	R	H	RBI	BB	K	Avg
Elmer Miller, cf	3	0	1	1	0	0	.158
Roger Peckinpaugh, ss	4	0	1	0	0	0	.176
Babe Ruth, lf	4	1	1	0	0	3	.333
Bob Meusel, rf	4	1	2	1	0	0	.263
Wally Pipp, 1b	3	0	0	0	0	0	.067
Aaron Ward, 2b	3	0	0	1	0	1	.250
Mike McNally, 3b	2	1	0	0	1	0	.200
Wally Schang, c	3	0	1	0	0	0	.333
Waite Hoyt, p	3	0	0	0	0	1	.167
TOTALS	29	3	6	3	1	5	.216

Giants	AB	R	H	RBI	BB	K	Avg
George Burns, cf	5	0	1	0	0	2	.318
Dave Bancroft, ss	4	1	1	0	0	0	.095
Frankie Frisch, 3b	4	0	2	0	0	0	.500
Ross Youngs, rf	3	0	1	0	1	0	.267
George Kelly, 1b	4	0	3	1	0	1	.211
Irish Meusel, lf	4	0	1	0	0	1	.333
Johnny Rawlings, 2b	4	0	1	0	0	0	.389
Earl Smith, c	3	0	0	0	1	0	.000
Art Nehf, p	3	0	0	0	0	1	.000
Frank Snyder, ph	1	0	0	0	0	1	.385
TOTALS	35	1	10	1	2	6	.282

	1 2 3	4 5 6	7 8 9	R	H	E
Yankees	0 0 1	2 0 0	0 0 0	3	6	1
Giants	1 0 0	0 0 0	0 0 0	1	10	1

E—Frisch, McNally. LOB—Yankees 3, Giants 9. Scoring Position—Yankees 0-for-4, Giants 1-for-8. 2B—Miller (1), BMeusel (2), Schang (1), IMeusel (2), Rawlings (1). S—Pipp. SF—Miller, Ward. CS—BMeusel (2), Smith (1).

Yankees	IP	H	R	ER	BB	K	ERA
Waite Hoyt (W, 2-0)	9.0	10	1	0	2	6	0.00

Giants	IP	H	R	ER	BB	K	ERA
Art Nehf (L, 0-2)	9.0	6	3	3	1	5	2.12

Time—1:52. Attendance—35,758. Umpires—HP, Rigler. 1B, Moriarty. 2B, Quigley. 3B, Chill.

Game 6

Tuesday, October 11

Giants	AB	R	H	RBI	BB	K	Avg
George Burns, cf	3	1	1	0	1	0	.320
Dave Bancroft, ss	5	0	2	2	0	1	.154
Frankie Frisch, 3b	4	2	0	0	1	2	.409
Ross Youngs, rf	5	0	1	0	0	2	.250
George Kelly, 1b	4	1	3	3	1	1	.304
Irish Meusel, lf	4	1	2	2	1	0	.364
Johnny Rawlings, 2b	5	0	0	0	0	2	.304
Frank Snyder, c	4	2	2	1	0	0	.412
Fred Toney, p	0	0	0	0	0	0	—
Jesse Barnes, p	4	1	2	0	0	0	.444
TOTALS	38	8	13	8	4	8	.316

Yankees	AB	R	H	RBI	BB	K	Avg
Chick Fewster, lf	3	2	1	2	2	1	.333
Roger Peckinpaugh, ss	5	0	0	0	0	1	.136
Elmer Miller, cf	5	1	1	0	0	1	.167
Bob Meusel, rf	3	1	1	1	1	1	.273
Wally Pipp, 1b	4	0	1	0	0	1	.105
Aaron Ward, 2b	4	0	1	2	0	2	.250
Mike McNally, 3b	4	0	0	0	0	1	.158
Wally Schang, c	2	0	1	0	2	1	.357
Harry Harper, p	0	0	0	0	0	0	—
Bob Shawkey, p	3	1	1	0	0	1	.500
Home Run Baker, ph	1	0	0	0	0	0	.000
Bill Piercy, p	0	0	0	0	0	0	—
TOTALS	34	5	7	5	5	10	.208

	1 2 3	4 5 6	7 8 9	R	H	E
Giants	0 3 0	4 0 1	0 0 0	8	13	0
Yankees	3 2 0	0 0 0	0 0 0	5	7	2

E—Ward, McNally. DP—Yankees 2 (Schang to McNally; Schang to Peckinpaugh). LOB—Giants 8, Yankees 7. Scoring Position—Giants 3-for-11, Yankees 2-for-7. HR—IMeusel (1), Snyder (1), Fewster (1). S—Burns. SB—Frisch (3), Pipp (1). CS—Bancroft (1), Youngs (1), Kelly (1).

Giants	IP	H	R	ER	BB	K	ERA
Fred Toney	0.2	3	3	3	1	0	23.63
Jesse Barnes (W, 2-0)	8.1	4	2	2	4	10	1.65

Yankees	IP	H	R	ER	BB	K	ERA
Harry Harper	1.1	3	3	3	2	1	20.25
Bob Shawkey (L, 0-1)	6.2	8	5	3	2	5	7.00
Bill Piercy	1.0	2	0	0	0	2	0.00

Time—2:31. Attendance—34,283. Umpires—HP, Moriarty. 1B, Quigley. 2B, Chill. 3B, Rigler.

Game 7

Wednesday, October 12

Yankees	AB	R	H	RBI	BB	K	Avg
Chick Fewster, lf	4	0	1	0	0	1	.286
Roger Peckinpaugh, ss	4	0	2	0	0	1	.192
Elmer Miller, cf	3	0	0	0	1	0	.148
Bob Meusel, rf	4	0	0	0	0	1	.231
Wally Pipp, 1b	4	1	1	0	0	0	.130
Aaron Ward, 2b	3	0	0	0	0	0	.217
Mike McNally, 3b	1	0	1	1	0	0	.200
Home Run Baker, 3b	3	0	2	0	0	0	.400
Al DeVormer, pr	0	0	0	0	0	0	.000
Wally Schang, c	4	0	1	0	0	0	.333
Carl Mays, p	3	0	0	0	0	0	.111
TOTALS	33	1	8	1	1	3	.205

Giants	AB	R	H	RBI	BB	K	Avg
George Burns, cf	4	0	2	0	0	0	.345
Dave Bancroft, ss	4	0	1	0	0	1	.167
Frankie Frisch, 3b	4	0	0	0	0	1	.346
Ross Youngs, rf	3	1	1	0	0	0	.261
George Kelly, 1b	3	0	0	0	0	2	.269
Irish Meusel, lf	3	0	1	1	0	1	.360
Johnny Rawlings, 2b	3	1	0	0	0	0	.269
Frank Snyder, c	3	0	1	1	0	0	.400
Phil Douglas, p	3	0	0	0	0	2	.000
TOTALS	30	2	6	2	0	7	.288

	1 2 3	4 5 6	7 8 9	R	H	E
Yankees	0 1 0	0 0 0	0 0 0	1	8	1
Giants	0 0 0	1 0 0	1 0 x	2	6	0

E—Ward. LOB—Yankees 7, Giants 4. Scoring Position—Yankees 1-for-4, Giants 1-for-6. 2B—Peckinpaugh (1), Pipp (1), Burns 2 (4), Bancroft (1), Snyder (1). S—Ward. SB—Youngs (1).

Yankees	IP	H	R	ER	BB	K	ERA
Carl Mays (L, 1-2)	8.0	6	2	1	0	7	1.73

Giants	IP	H	R	ER	BB	K	ERA
Phil Douglas (W, 2-1)	9.0	8	1	1	1	3	2.08

WP—Douglas. Time—1:40. Attendance—36,503. Umpires—HP, Quigley. 1B, Chill. 2B, Rigler. 3B, Moriarty.

Game 8

Thursday, October 13

Giants	AB	R	H	RBI	BB	K	Avg
George Burns, cf	4	0	1	0	1	1	.333
Dave Bancroft, ss	3	1	0	0	1	1	.152
Frankie Frisch, 3b	4	0	0	0	0	0	.300
Ross Youngs, rf	2	0	1	0	2	0	.280
George Kelly, 1b	4	0	0	0	0	2	.233
Irish Meusel, lf	4	0	1	0	0	1	.345
Johnny Rawlings, 2b	4	0	3	0	0	0	.333
Frank Snyder, c	2	0	0	0	0	1	.364
Art Nehf, p	4	0	0	0	0	1	.000
TOTALS	31	1	6	0	4	7	.278

Yankees	AB	R	H	RBI	BB	K	Avg
Chick Fewster, lf	3	0	0	0	1	1	.200
Roger Peckinpaugh, ss	2	0	0	0	2	0	.179
Elmer Miller, cf	4	0	1	0	0	0	.161
Bob Meusel, rf	4	0	0	0	0	1	.200
Wally Pipp, 1b	3	0	1	0	0	1	.154
Babe Ruth, ph	1	0	0	0	0	0	.313
Aaron Ward, 2b	3	0	1	0	1	0	.231
Home Run Baker, 3b	3	0	0	0	1	0	.250
Wally Schang, c	3	0	0	0	0	0	.286
Waite Hoyt, p	3	0	1	0	0	0	.222
TOTALS	29	0	4	0	5	3	.210

	1 2 3	4 5 6	7 8 9	R	H	E
Giants	1 0 0	0 0 0	0 0 0	1	6	0
Yankees	0 0 0	0 0 0	0 0 0	0	4	1

E—Peckinpaugh. DP—Giants 1 (Bancroft to Rawlings to Kelly). LOB—Giants 9, Yankees 7. Scoring Position—Giants 0-for-8, Yankees 0-for-3. 2B—Rawlings 2 (3). S—Snyder 2. GDP—Peckinpaugh. SB—Youngs (2). CS—IMeusel (2).

Giants	IP	H	R	ER	BB	K	ERA
Art Nehf (W, 1-2)	9.0	4	0	0	5	3	1.38

Yankees	IP	H	R	ER	BB	K	ERA
Waite Hoyt (L, 2-1)	9.0	6	1	0	4	7	0.00

WP—Nehf. Time—1:57. Attendance—25,410. Umpires—HP, Chill. 1B, Rigler. 2B, Moriarty. 3B, Quigley.

1921 World Series—Composite Statistics

Batting

Giants	G	AB	R	H	RBI	2B	3B	HR	BB	SO	SB	CS	Avg	OBP	Slg
Dave Bancroft	8	33	3	5	3	1	0	0	1	5	0	1	.152	.171	.182
Jesse Barnes	3	9	3	4	0	0	0	0	0	0	0	0	.444	.444	.444
George Burns	8	33	2	11	2	4	1	0	3	5	1	1	.333	.389	.515
Phil Douglas	3	7	0	0	0	0	0	0	0	2	0	0	.000	.000	.000
Frankie Frisch	8	30	5	9	0	0	1	0	4	3	3	0	.300	.382	.367
George Kelly	8	30	3	7	5	1	0	0	3	10	0	1	.233	.303	.267
Irish Meusel	8	29	4	10	7	2	1	1	2	3	1	2	.345	.387	.586
Art Nehf	3	9	0	0	0	0	0	0	1	3	0	0	.000	.100	.000
Johnny Rawlings	8	30	2	10	4	3	0	0	0	3	0	1	.333	.355	.433
Earl Smith	3	7	0	0	0	0	0	0	1	0	0	1	.000	.125	.000
Frank Snyder	7	22	4	8	3	1	0	1	0	2	0	1	.364	.364	.545
Ross Youngs	8	25	3	7	4	1	1	0	7	2	2	1	.280	.438	.400
Totals	8	264	29	71	28	13	4	2	22	38	7	9	.269	.326	.371

Yankees	G	AB	R	H	RBI	2B	3B	HR	BB	SO	SB	CS	Avg	OBP	Slg
Home Run Baker	4	8	0	2	0	0	0	0	1	0	0	0	.250	.333	.250
Al DeVormer	2	1	0	0	0	0	0	0	0	0	0	0	.000	.000	.000
Chick Fewster	4	10	3	2	2	0	0	1	3	3	0	0	.200	.385	.500
Waite Hoyt	3	9	0	2	1	0	0	0	0	1	0	0	.222	.222	.222
Carl Mays	3	9	0	1	0	0	0	0	0	1	0	0	.111	.111	.111
Mike McNally	7	20	3	4	1	1	0	0	1	3	2	2	.200	.273	.250
Bob Meusel	8	30	3	6	3	2	0	0	2	5	1	2	.200	.250	.267
Elmer Miller	8	31	3	5	2	1	0	0	2	5	0	0	.161	.206	.194
Roger Peckinpaugh	8	28	2	5	0	1	0	0	4	3	0	1	.179	.281	.214
Wally Pipp	8	26	1	4	2	1	0	0	2	3	1	1	.154	.214	.192
Jack Quinn	1	2	0	0	0	0	0	0	0	0	0	0	.000	.000	.000
Babe Ruth	6	16	3	5	4	0	0	1	5	8	2	1	.313	.476	.500
Wally Schang	8	21	1	6	1	1	1	0	5	4	0	0	.286	.423	.429
Bob Shawkey	2	4	2	2	0	0	0	0	0	1	0	0	.500	.500	.500
Aaron Ward	8	26	1	6	4	0	0	0	2	6	0	0	.231	.276	.231
Totals	8	241	22	50	20	7	1	2	27	44	6	7	.207	.288	.270

Pitching

Giants	G	GS	CG	IP	H	R	ER	BB	SO	W-L	Sv-Op	Hld	ERA
Jesse Barnes	3	0	0	16.1	10	3	3	6	18	2-0	0-0	0	1.65
Phil Douglas	3	3	2	26.0	20	6	6	5	17	2-1	0-0	0	2.08
Art Nehf	3	3	3	26.0	13	6	4	13	8	1-2	0-0	0	1.38
Fred Toney	2	2	0	2.2	7	7	7	3	1	0-0	0-0	0	23.63
Totals	8	8	5	71.0	50	22	20	27	44	5-3	0-0	0	2.54

Yankees	G	GS	CG	IP	H	R	ER	BB	SO	W-L	Sv-Op	Hld	ERA
Rip Collins	1	0	0	0.2	5	4	4	1	0	0-0	0-0	0	54.00
Harry Harper	1	1	0	1.1	3	3	3	2	1	0-0	0-0	0	20.25
Waite Hoyt	3	3	3	27.0	18	2	0	11	18	2-1	0-0	0	0.00
Carl Mays	3	3	2	26.0	20	6	5	0	9	1-2	0-0	0	1.73
Bill Piercy	1	0	0	1.0	2	0	0	0	2	0-0	0-0	0	0.00
Jack Quinn	1	0	0	3.2	7	4	4	2	2	0-1	0-0	0	9.82
Tom Rogers	1	0	0	1.1	3	1	1	0	1	0-0	0-0	0	6.75
Bob Shawkey	2	1	0	9.0	13	9	7	6	5	0-1	0-0	0	7.00
Totals	8	8	6	70.0	71	29	24	22	38	3-5	0-0	0	3.09

Fielding

Giants	Pos	G	PO	Ast	E	DP	PB	FPct
Dave Bancroft	ss	8	16	17	1	1	—	.971
Jesse Barnes	p	3	1	1	0	0	—	1.000
George Burns	cf	8	9	0	0	0	—	1.000
Phil Douglas	p	3	3	8	0	0	—	1.000
Frankie Frisch	3b	8	12	23	2	3	—	.946
George Kelly	1b	8	86	6	0	4	—	1.000
Irish Meusel	lf	8	8	2	0	0	—	1.000
Art Nehf	p	3	1	4	1	0	—	.833
Johnny Rawlings	2b	8	20	27	0	5	—	1.000
Earl Smith	c	2	7	2	1	1	0	.900
Frank Snyder	c	6	43	5	0	0	1	1.000
Fred Toney	p	2	0	1	0	0	—	1.000
Ross Youngs	rf	8	7	1	0	0	—	1.000
Totals		8	213	97	5	14	1	.984

Yankees	Pos	G	PO	Ast	E	DP	PB	FPct
Home Run Baker	3b	2	2	3	0	0	—	1.000
Rip Collins	p	1	0	0	0	0	—	—
Al DeVormer	c	1	1	0	0	0	0	1.000
Chick Fewster	lf	4	7	0	0	0	—	1.000
Harry Harper	p	1	0	0	0	0	—	—
Waite Hoyt	p	3	0	6	0	0	—	1.000
Carl Mays	p	3	0	9	0	0	—	1.000
Mike McNally	3b	7	5	11	3	2	—	.842
Bob Meusel	rf	8	10	2	0	0	—	1.000
Elmer Miller	cf	8	10	1	0	0	—	1.000
Roger Peckinpaugh	ss	8	17	29	1	4	—	.979
Bill Piercy	p	1	0	0	0	0	—	—
Wally Pipp	1b	8	91	1	0	5	—	1.000
Jack Quinn	p	1	0	1	0	1	—	1.000
Tom Rogers	p	1	0	1	0	0	—	1.000
Babe Ruth	lf	5	9	0	0	0	—	1.000
Wally Schang	c	8	39	10	0	2	0	1.000
Bob Shawkey	p	2	0	0	0	0	—	—
Aaron Ward	2b	8	19	32	2	4	—	.962
Totals		8	210	106	6	18	0	.981

1922 New York Giants (NL) 4, New York Yankees (AL) 0, 1 Tie

In a battle between two teams that called the Polo Grounds home, the New York Giants beat the New York Yankees four games to none, with one tie, as the World Series returned to a seven-game format. The Yanks' Joe Bush took a 2-0 lead into the eighth inning of Game 1, but the Giants loaded the bases, and Irish Meusel lashed a game-tying single to knock out Bush. Ross Youngs followed with a sacrifice fly off Waite Hoyt, and the Giants won, 3-2. Game 2 was called after 10 innings on account of darkness with the score knotted at three apiece. Jack Scott blanked the Yanks on four hits in Game 3. The Giants' Hugh McQuillan bested the Yankees' Carl Mays in Game 4 by the score of 4-3. George Kelly's two-run single in the bottom of the eighth gave the Giants a 5-3 victory in Game 5 to wrap it up. The Giants held Babe Ruth to a pair of singles in 17 at-bats in the Series.

Game 1
Wednesday, October 4

Yankees	AB	R	H	RBI	BB	K	Avg
Whitey Witt, cf	4	0	1	0	0	1	.250
Joe Dugan, 3b	4	1	1	0	0	0	.250
Babe Ruth, rf	4	0	1	1	0	2	.250
Wally Pipp, 1b	4	0	1	0	0	1	.250
Bob Meusel, lf	4	1	2	0	0	1	.500
Wally Schang, c	2	0	1	0	0	0	.500
Aaron Ward, 2b	1	0	0	1	1	0	.000
Everett Scott, ss	3	0	0	0	0	0	.000
Joe Bush, p	3	0	0	0	0	0	.000
Waite Hoyt, p	0	0	0	0	0	0	—
TOTALS	29	2	7	2	1	5	.241

Giants	AB	R	H	RBI	BB	K	Avg
Dave Bancroft, ss	4	1	1	0	0	0	.250
Heine Groh, 3b	3	1	3	0	1	0	1.000
Frankie Frisch, 2b	4	1	2	0	0	0	.500
Irish Meusel, lf	4	0	1	2	0	0	.250
Ross Youngs, rf	3	0	0	1	0	1	.000
George Kelly, 1b	4	0	2	0	0	2	.500
Casey Stengel, cf	4	0	1	0	0	1	.250
Frank Snyder, c	3	0	1	0	0	0	.333
Art Nehf, p	2	0	0	0	0	0	.000
Earl Smith, ph	1	0	0	0	0	0	.000
Rosy Ryan, p	0	0	0	0	0	0	—
TOTALS	32	3	11	3	1	5	.344

	1	2	3	4	5	6	7	8	9		R	H	E
Yankees	0	0	0	0	0	1	1	0	0		2	7	0
Giants	0	0	0	0	0	0	0	3	x		3	11	2

E—Youngs, Nehf. DP—Yankees 1 (Scott to Ward to Pipp), Giants 3 (Snyder to Bancroft; Youngs to Frisch; Frisch to Kelly). LOB—Yankees 4, Giants 7. Scoring Position—Yankees 1-for-6, Giants 3-for-7. 3B—Witt (1), Groh (1). S—Schang 2. SF—Ward, Youngs. GDP—Smith. CS—Ruth (1), Groh (1).

Yankees	IP	H	R	ER	BB	K	ERA
Joe Bush (L, 0-1)	7.0	11	3	3	1	3	3.86
Waite Hoyt	1.0	0	0	0	0	2	0.00

Giants	IP	H	R	ER	BB	K	ERA
Art Nehf	7.0	6	2	1	1	3	1.29
Rosy Ryan (W, 1-0)	2.0	1	0	0	0	2	0.00

Bush pitched to four batters in the 8th.

PB—Schang. Time—2:08. Attendance—36,514. Umpires—HP, Klem. 1B, Hildebrand. 2B, McCormick. 3B, Owens.

Game 2
Thursday, October 5

Giants	AB	R	H	RBI	BB	K	Avg
Dave Bancroft, ss	5	0	1	0	0	0	.222
Heine Groh, 3b	4	1	1	0	1	0	.571
Frankie Frisch, 2b	4	1	2	0	0	0	.500
Irish Meusel, lf	4	1	1	3	0	0	.250
Ross Youngs, rf	3	0	1	0	1	0	.167
George Kelly, 1b	4	0	0	0	0	1	.250
Casey Stengel, cf	1	0	1	0	0	0	.400
Bill Cunningham, pr-cf	2	0	0	0	0	1	.000
Earl Smith, ph	1	0	0	0	0	1	.000
Lee King, cf	0	0	0	0	0	0	—
Frank Snyder, c	4	0	1	0	0	0	.286
Jesse Barnes, p	4	0	0	0	0	1	.000
TOTALS	36	3	8	3	2	4	.288

Yankees	AB	R	H	RBI	BB	K	Avg
Whitey Witt, cf	5	0	1	0	0	1	.222
Joe Dugan, 3b	5	1	2	0	0	1	.333
Babe Ruth, rf	4	1	1	0	1	0	.250
Wally Pipp, 1b	5	0	1	1	0	0	.222
Bob Meusel, lf	4	0	1	1	1	0	.375
Wally Schang, c	4	0	0	0	0	1	.167
Aaron Ward, 2b	4	1	1	1	0	2	.200
Everett Scott, ss	4	0	1	0	0	0	.143
Bob Shawkey, p	4	0	0	0	0	1	.000
TOTALS	39	3	8	3	2	6	.231

	1	2	3	4	5	6	7	8	9	10		R	H	E
Giants	3	0	0	0	0	0	0	0	0	0		3	8	1
Yankees	1	0	0	1	0	0	0	1	0	0		3	8	0

E—Bancroft. DP—Yankees 1 (Scott to Ward to Pipp). LOB—Giants 5, Yankees 8. Scoring Position—Giants 1-for-5, Yankees 2-for-8. 2B—Dugan (1), Ruth (1), BMeusel (1). HR—IMeusel (1), Ward (1). GDP—Barnes. SB—Frisch (1).

Giants	IP	H	R	ER	BB	K	ERA
Jesse Barnes	10.0	8	3	2	2	6	1.80

Yankees	IP	H	R	ER	BB	K	ERA
Bob Shawkey	10.0	8	3	3	2	4	2.70

WP—Shawkey. Time—2:40. Attendance—37,020. Umpires—HP, Hildebrand. 1B, McCormick. 2B, Owens. 3B, Klem.

Game 3
Friday, October 6

Yankees	AB	R	H	RBI	BB	K	Avg
Whitey Witt, cf	3	0	0	0	1	0	.167
Joe Dugan, 3b	4	0	0	0	0	0	.231
Babe Ruth, rf	3	0	0	0	0	0	.182
Wally Pipp, 1b	4	0	1	0	0	1	.231
Bob Meusel, lf	4	0	1	0	0	0	.333
Wally Schang, c	3	0	1	0	0	0	.222
Aaron Ward, 2b	2	0	0	0	0	0	.143
Elmer Smith, ph	1	0	0	0	0	1	.000
Mike McNally, 2b	0	0	0	0	0	0	
Everett Scott, ss	3	0	0	0	0	0	.100
Waite Hoyt, p	2	0	1	0	0	0	.500
Home Run Baker, ph	1	0	0	0	0	0	.000
Sad Sam Jones, p	0	0	0	0	0	0	—
TOTALS	30	0	4	0	1	2	.209

Giants	AB	R	H	RBI	BB	K	Avg
Dave Bancroft, ss	3	2	0	0	1	1	.167
Heine Groh, 3b	4	1	2	0	0	0	.545
Frankie Frisch, 2b	2	0	2	2	1	0	.600
Irish Meusel, lf	4	0	1	1	0	0	.250
Ross Youngs, rf	4	0	3	0	0	0	.400
George Kelly, 1b	3	0	1	0	0	0	.273
Bill Cunningham, cf	3	0	1	0	1	0	.200
Earl Smith, c	4	0	1	0	0	0	.167
Jack Scott, p	4	0	1	0	0	1	.250
TOTALS	31	3	12	3	3	2	.333

	1	2	3	4	5	6	7	8	9		R	H	E
Yankees	0	0	0	0	0	0	0	0	0		0	4	1
Giants	0	0	2	0	0	0	1	0	x		3	12	1

E—Frisch, Ward. DP—Yankees 1 (Ward to Pipp). LOB—Yankees 5, Giants 9. Scoring Position—Yankees 0-for-3, Giants 2-for-7. 2B—Schang (1). S—Kelly. SF—Frisch. SB—Pipp (1). CS—Frisch (1), Kelly (1).

Yankees	IP	H	R	ER	BB	K	ERA
Waite Hoyt (L, 0-1)	7.0	11	3	1	2	2	1.13
Sad Sam Jones	1.0	1	0	0	1	0	0.00

Giants	IP	H	R	ER	BB	K	ERA
Jack Scott (W, 1-0)	9.0	4	0	0	1	2	0.00

HBP—Ruth by JScott. Time—1:48. Attendance—37,630. Umpires—HP, McCormick. 1B, Owens. 2B, Klem. 3B, Hildebrand.

Game 4

Saturday, October 7

Giants	AB	R	H	RBI	BB	K	Avg
Dave Bancroft, ss	3	1	2	2	1	0	.267
Heine Groh, 3b	4	1	1	0	0	0	.467
Frankie Frisch, 2b	3	0	0	0	0	0	.462
Irish Meusel, lf	4	0	1	1	0	0	.250
Ross Youngs, rf	4	0	2	1	0	0	.429
George Kelly, 1b	4	0	0	0	0	0	.200
Bill Cunningham, cf	3	0	0	0	1	0	.125
Frank Snyder, c	4	1	2	0	0	0	.364
Hugh McQuillan, p	4	1	1	0	0	1	.250
TOTALS	33	4	9	4	2	1	.324

Yankees	AB	R	H	RBI	BB	K	Avg
Whitey Witt, cf	4	1	2	0	0	0	.250
Joe Dugan, 3b	4	1	1	0	0	0	.235
Babe Ruth, rf	3	0	0	0	1	0	.143
Wally Pipp, 1b	4	0	2	1	0	0	.294
Bob Meusel, lf	4	0	1	1	0	1	.313
Wally Schang, c	4	0	1	0	0	1	.231
Aaron Ward, 2b	4	1	1	1	0	1	.182
Everett Scott, ss	2	0	0	0	1	0	.083
Carl Mays, p	2	0	0	0	0	0	.000
Elmer Smith, ph	1	0	0	0	0	1	.000
Sad Sam Jones, p	0	0	0	0	0	0	—
TOTALS	32	3	8	3	2	4	.217

	1	2	3	4	5	6	7	8	9		R	H	E
Giants	0	0	0	0	4	0	0	0	0		4	9	1
Yankees	2	0	0	0	0	0	1	0	0		3	8	0

E—Snyder. DP—Giants 1 (Frisch to Bancroft to Kelly), Yankees 1 (Pipp to Scott). LOB—Giants 5, Yankees 4. Scoring Position—Giants 2-for-5, Yankees 2-for-8. 2B—McQuillan (1), Witt (1), Pipp (1). HR—Ward (2). S—Frisch. GDP—Kelly, Witt. SB—BMeusel (1). CS—Youngs (1).

Giants	IP	H	R	ER	BB	K	ERA
Hugh McQuillan (W, 1-0)	9.0	8	3	3	2	4	3.00

Yankees	IP	H	R	ER	BB	K	ERA
Carl Mays (L, 0-1)	8.0	9	4	4	2	1	4.50
Sad Sam Jones	1.0	0	0	0	0	0	0.00

Time—1:41. Attendance—36,242. Umpires—HP, Owens. 1B, Klem. 2B, Hildebrand. 3B, McCormick.

Game 5

Sunday, October 8

Yankees	AB	R	H	RBI	BB	K	Avg
Whitey Witt, cf	2	0	0	0	0	0	.222
Norm McMillan, ph-cf	2	0	0	0	0	0	.000
Joe Dugan, 3b	3	1	1	0	0	0	.250
Babe Ruth, rf	3	0	0	0	0	1	.118
Wally Pipp, 1b	4	0	1	1	0	0	.286
Bob Meusel, lf	4	1	1	0	0	1	.300
Wally Schang, c	3	0	0	0	0	1	.188
Aaron Ward, 2b	2	1	0	0	2	0	.154
Everett Scott, ss	2	0	1	1	0	0	.143
Joe Bush, p	3	0	1	1	0	0	.167
TOTALS	28	3	5	3	2	3	.211

Giants	AB	R	H	RBI	BB	K	Avg
Dave Bancroft, ss	4	0	0	0	0	0	.211
Heine Groh, 3b	4	0	2	0	0	1	.474
Frankie Frisch, 2b	4	1	2	0	0	1	.471
Irish Meusel, lf	4	2	1	0	0	0	.250
Ross Youngs, rf	2	2	0	0	2	0	.375
George Kelly, 1b	3	0	2	2	0	0	.278
Bill Cunningham, cf	2	0	1	2	0	0	.200
Earl Smith, ph	1	0	0	0	0	1	.143
Lee King, cf	1	0	1	1	0	0	1.000
Frank Snyder, c	4	0	1	0	0	1	.333
Art Nehf, p	1	0	0	0	2	0	.000
TOTALS	30	5	10	5	4	3	.317

	1	2	3	4	5	6	7	8	9		R	H	E
Yankees	1	0	0	0	1	0	1	0	0		3	5	0
Giants	0	2	0	0	0	0	0	3	x		5	10	0

DP—Yankees 3 (Bush to Scott to Pipp; Bush to Scott to Pipp; Ward to Scott to Pipp). LOB—Yankees 4, Giants 6. Scoring Position—Yankees 2-for-5, Giants 3-for-7. 2B—Frisch (1). S—Ruth, Schang, Kelly. SF—Scott. GDP—Bancroft, Frisch, Cunningham.

Yankees	IP	H	R	ER	BB	K	ERA
Joe Bush (L, 0-2)	8.0	10	5	5	4	3	4.80

Giants	IP	H	R	ER	BB	K	ERA
Art Nehf (W, 1-0)	9.0	5	3	3	2	3	2.25

WP—Nehf. HBP—Dugan by Nehf. Time—2:00. Attendance—38,551. Umpires—HP, Klem. 1B, Hildebrand. 2B, McCormick. 3B, Owens.

1922 World Series—Composite Statistics

Batting

Batting (left)

Giants	G	AB	R	H	RBI	2B	3B	HR	BB	SO	SB	CS	Avg	OBP	Slg
Dave Bancroft	5	19	4	4	2	0	0	0	2	1	0	0	.211	.286	.211
Jesse Barnes	1	4	0	0	0	0	0	0	0	1	0	0	.000	.000	.000
Bill Cunningham	4	10	0	2	2	0	0	0	2	1	0	0	.200	.333	.200
Frankie Frisch	5	17	3	8	2	1	0	0	1	0	1	1	.471	.474	.529
Heine Groh	5	19	4	9	0	0	1	0	2	1	0	1	.474	.524	.579
George Kelly	5	18	0	5	2	0	0	0	0	3	0	1	.278	.278	.278
Lee King	2	1	0	1	1	0	0	0	0	0	0	0	1.000	1.000	1.000
Hugh McQuillan	1	4	1	1	0	1	0	0	0	1	0	0	.250	.250	.500
Irish Meusel	5	20	3	5	7	0	0	1	0	1	0	0	.250	.250	.400
Art Nehf	2	3	0	0	0	0	0	0	2	0	0	0	.000	.400	.000
Jack Scott	1	4	0	1	0	0	0	0	0	1	0	0	.250	.250	.250
Earl Smith	4	7	0	1	0	0	0	0	0	2	0	0	.143	.143	.143
Frank Snyder	4	15	1	5	0	0	0	0	0	1	0	0	.333	.333	.333
Casey Stengel	2	5	0	2	0	0	0	0	0	1	0	0	.400	.400	.400
Ross Youngs	5	16	2	6	2	0	0	0	3	1	0	1	.375	.450	.375
Totals	**5**	**162**	**18**	**50**	**18**	**2**	**1**	**1**	**12**	**15**	**1**	**4**	**.309**	**.352**	**.352**

Batting (right)

Yankees	G	AB	R	H	RBI	2B	3B	HR	BB	SO	SB	CS	Avg	OBP	Slg
Home Run Baker	1	1	0	0	0	0	0	0	0	0	0	0	.000	.000	.000
Joe Bush	2	6	0	1	1	0	0	0	0	0	0	0	.167	.167	.167
Joe Dugan	5	20	4	5	0	1	0	0	1	0	0	0	.250	.286	.300
Waite Hoyt	2	2	0	1	0	0	0	0	0	0	0	0	.500	.500	.500
Carl Mays	1	2	0	0	0	0	0	0	0	0	0	0	.000	.000	.000
Norm McMillan	1	2	0	0	0	0	0	0	0	0	0	0	.000	.000	.000
Bob Meusel	5	20	2	6	2	1	0	0	1	3	1	0	.300	.333	.350
Wally Pipp	5	21	0	6	3	1	0	0	0	2	1	0	.286	.286	.333
Babe Ruth	5	17	1	2	1	1	0	0	2	3	0	1	.118	.250	.176
Wally Schang	5	16	0	3	0	1	0	0	0	3	0	0	.188	.188	.250
Everett Scott	5	14	0	2	1	0	0	0	1	0	0	0	.143	.188	.143
Bob Shawkey	1	4	0	0	0	0	0	0	0	1	0	0	.000	.000	.000
Elmer Smith	2	2	0	0	0	0	0	0	0	2	0	0	.000	.000	.000
Aaron Ward	5	13	3	2	3	0	0	2	3	3	0	0	.154	.294	.615
Whitey Witt	5	18	1	4	0	1	1	0	1	2	0	0	.222	.263	.389
Totals	**5**	**158**	**11**	**32**	**11**	**6**	**1**	**2**	**8**	**20**	**2**	**1**	**.203**	**.247**	**.291**

Pitching

Pitching (left)

Giants	G	GS	CG	IP	H	R	ER	BB	SO	W-L	Sv-Op	Hld	ERA
Jesse Barnes	1	1	1	10.0	8	3	2	2	6	0-0	0-0	0	1.80
Hugh McQuillan	1	1	1	9.0	8	3	3	2	4	1-0	0-0	0	3.00
Art Nehf	2	2	1	16.0	11	5	4	3	6	1-0	0-0	0	2.25
Rosy Ryan	1	0	0	2.0	1	0	0	0	2	1-0	0-0	0	0.00
Jack Scott	1	1	1	9.0	4	0	0	1	2	1-0	0-0	0	0.00
Totals	**5**	**5**	**4**	**46.0**	**32**	**11**	**9**	**8**	**20**	**4-0**	**0-0**	**0**	**1.76**

Pitching (right)

Yankees	G	GS	CG	IP	H	R	ER	BB	SO	W-L	Sv-Op	Hld	ERA
Joe Bush	2	2	1	15.0	21	8	8	5	6	0-2	0-0	0	4.80
Waite Hoyt	2	1	0	8.0	11	3	1	2	4	0-1	0-0	0	1.13
Sad Sam Jones	2	0	0	2.0	1	0	0	1	0	0-0	0-0	0	0.00
Carl Mays	1	1	0	8.0	9	4	4	2	1	0-1	0-0	0	4.50
Bob Shawkey	1	1	1	10.0	8	3	3	2	4	0-0	0-0	0	2.70
Totals	**5**	**5**	**2**	**43.0**	**50**	**18**	**16**	**12**	**15**	**0-4**	**0-0**	**0**	**3.35**

Fielding

Fielding (left)

Giants	Pos	G	PO	Ast	E	DP	PB	FPct
Dave Bancroft	ss	5	9	16	1	2	—	.962
Jesse Barnes	p	1	0	4	0	0	—	1.000
Bill Cunningham	cf	4	10	2	0	0	—	1.000
Frankie Frisch	2b	5	10	19	1	3	—	.967
Heine Groh	3b	5	6	16	0	0	—	1.000
George Kelly	1b	5	61	1	0	2	—	1.000
Lee King	cf	2	0	0	0	0	—	—
Hugh McQuillan	p	1	0	0	0	0	—	—
Irish Meusel	lf	5	3	0	0	0	—	1.000
Art Nehf	p	2	0	3	1	0	—	.750
Rosy Ryan	p	1	0	0	0	0	—	—
Jack Scott	p	1	1	1	0	0	—	1.000
Earl Smith	c	1	2	1	0	0	0	1.000
Frank Snyder	c	4	23	3	1	1	0	.963
Casey Stengel	cf	2	4	0	0	0	—	1.000
Ross Youngs	rf	5	9	2	1	1	—	.917
Totals		**5**	**138**	**68**	**5**	**9**	**0**	**.976**

Fielding (right)

Yankees	Pos	G	PO	Ast	E	DP	PB	FPct
Joe Bush	p	2	1	3	0	2	—	1.000
Joe Dugan	3b	5	5	8	0	0	—	1.000
Waite Hoyt	p	2	1	2	0	0	—	1.000
Sad Sam Jones	p	2	0	1	0	0	—	1.000
Carl Mays	p	1	0	4	0	0	—	1.000
Norm McMillan	cf	1	1	0	0	0	—	1.000
Mike McNally	2b	1	1	1	0	0	—	1.000
Bob Meusel	lf	5	7	1	0	0	—	1.000
Wally Pipp	1b	5	51	3	0	7	—	1.000
Babe Ruth	rf	5	9	0	0	0	—	1.000
Wally Schang	c	5	19	4	0	0	1	1.000
Everett Scott	ss	5	14	15	0	6	—	1.000
Bob Shawkey	p	1	0	2	0	0	—	1.000
Aaron Ward	2b	5	13	16	1	4	—	.967
Whitey Witt	cf	5	7	1	0	0	—	1.000
Totals		**5**	**129**	**61**	**1**	**19**	**1**	**.995**

1923 New York Yankees (AL) 4, New York Giants (NL) 2

The New York Yankees capped off Yankee Stadium's inaugural season with a six-game World Series victory over their ex-landlords, the New York Giants. Casey Stengel's inside-the-park homer in the top of the ninth gave the Giants a 5-4 victory in the opener. Babe Ruth hit a pair of homers—including one over the Polo Grounds' right field roof—as the Yanks took Game 2, 4-2. Stengel's seventh-inning homer was the only run of Game 3 as the Giants prevailed, 1-0. A six-run second inning sent the Yanks to an 8-4 victory in the fourth game. Yankee third baseman Joe Dugan had three singles, a homer and three RBI in New York's 8-1 win in Game 5. The Yanks trailed 4-1 before loading the bases in the eighth inning of Game 6. Two walks brought home two runs, and Bob Meusel put the Yanks on the road to victory with a two-run single. The Yankees won 6-4 to capture their first Championship.

Game 1

Wednesday, October 10

Giants	AB	R	H	RBI	BB	K	Avg
Dave Bancroft, ss	4	1	1	1	0	0	.250
Heine Groh, 3b	4	1	2	2	0	0	.500
Frankie Frisch, 2b	4	0	1	1	0	0	.250
Ross Youngs, rf	3	0	0	0	1	0	.000
Irish Meusel, lf	4	0	0	0	0	0	.000
Casey Stengel, cf	3	1	2	1	1	0	.667
Bill Cunningham, cf	0	0	0	0	0	0	—
George Kelly, 1b	4	1	1	0	0	0	.250
Hank Gowdy, c	0	0	0	0	1	0	—
Freddie Maguire, pr	0	1	0	0	0	0	—
Frank Snyder, c	2	0	0	0	0	1	.000
Mule Watson, p	0	0	0	0	0	0	—
Jack Bentley, ph	1	0	1	0	0	0	1.000
Dinty Gearin, pr	0	0	0	0	0	0	—
Rosy Ryan, p	2	0	0	0	0	1	.000
TOTALS	31	5	8	5	3	2	.258

Yankees	AB	R	H	RBI	BB	K	Avg
Whitey Witt, cf	5	0	1	2	0	0	.200
Joe Dugan, 3b	4	1	1	1	1	0	.250
Babe Ruth, rf	4	1	1	0	0	0	.250
Bob Meusel, lf	4	0	1	1	0	0	.250
Wally Pipp, 1b	4	0	2	0	0	0	.500
Aaron Ward, 2b	4	1	2	0	0	0	.500
Wally Schang, c	3	1	2	0	1	0	.667
Everett Scott, ss	2	0	0	0	0	1	.000
Harvey Hendrick, ph	1	0	0	0	0	0	.000
Ernie Johnson, ss	0	0	0	0	0	0	—
Waite Hoyt, p	1	0	0	0	0	1	.000
Joe Bush, p	3	1	2	0	0	0	.667
TOTALS	35	4	12	4	2	3	.343

	1	2	3	4	5	6	7	8	9	R	H	E
Giants	0	0	4	0	0	0	0	0	1	5	8	0
Yankees	1	2	0	0	0	0	1	0	0	4	12	1

E—Schang. DP—Giants 2 (Ryan to Groh to Frisch; Frisch to Snyder), Yankees 2 (Scott to Ward to Pipp; Scott to Ward to Pipp). LOB—Giants 2, Yankees 7. Scoring Position—Giants 3-for-6, Yankees 1-for-8. 2B—BMeusel (1), Schang (1), Bush (1). 3B—Groh (1), Dugan (1), Ruth (1). HR—Stengel (1). S—Scott. GDP—Kelly 2. SB—Bancroft (1). CS—Frisch (1), Youngs (1).

Giants	IP	H	R	ER	BB	K	ERA
Mule Watson	2.0	4	3	3	1	1	13.50
Rosy Ryan (W, 1-0)	7.0	8	1	1	1	2	1.29

Yankees	IP	H	R	ER	BB	K	ERA
Waite Hoyt	2.1	4	4	4	1	0	15.43
Joe Bush (L, 0-1)	6.2	4	1	1	2	2	1.35

WP—Ryan. Time—2:05. Attendance—55,307. Umpires—HP, Evans. 1B, O'Day. 2B, Nallin. 3B, Hart.

Game 2

Thursday, October 11

Yankees	AB	R	H	RBI	BB	K	Avg
Whitey Witt, cf	5	0	0	0	0	0	.100
Joe Dugan, 3b	4	0	1	0	1	0	.250
Babe Ruth, rf	3	2	2	2	2	0	.429
Bob Meusel, lf	4	0	1	0	0	1	.250
Wally Pipp, 1b	3	1	1	0	1	0	.429
Aaron Ward, 2b	4	1	2	1	0	0	.500
Wally Schang, c	4	0	1	0	0	0	.429
Everett Scott, ss	4	0	2	1	0	0	.333
Herb Pennock, p	3	0	0	0	0	0	.000
TOTALS	34	4	10	4	4	1	.313

Giants	AB	R	H	RBI	BB	K	Avg
Dave Bancroft, ss	4	0	0	0	0	0	.125
Heine Groh, 3b	3	1	1	0	1	0	.429
Frankie Frisch, 2b	4	0	2	0	0	0	.375
Ross Youngs, rf	4	0	2	1	0	0	.286
Irish Meusel, lf	4	1	2	1	0	0	.250
Bill Cunningham, cf	3	0	0	0	0	0	.000
Hank Gowdy, ph	1	0	0	0	0	0	.000
Casey Stengel, cf	0	0	0	0	0	0	.667
George Kelly, 1b	4	0	1	0	0	1	.250
Frank Snyder, c	4	0	0	0	0	0	.000
Hugh McQuillan, p	1	0	0	0	0	0	.000
Jack Bentley, p	2	0	1	0	0	0	.667
Travis Jackson, ph	1	0	0	0	0	0	.000
TOTALS	35	2	9	2	1	1	.266

	1	2	3	4	5	6	7	8	9	R	H	E
Yankees	0	1	0	2	1	0	0	0	0	4	10	0
Giants	0	1	0	0	0	1	0	0	0	2	9	2

E—Youngs 2. DP—Yankees 1 (Scott to Ward to Pipp), Giants 2 (Bancroft to Frisch to Kelly; Bancroft to Frisch to Kelly). LOB—Yankees 8, Giants 7. Scoring Position—Yankees 1-for-8, Giants 1-for-6. 2B—Dugan (1), Bentley (1). HR—Ruth 2 (2), Ward (1), IMeusel (1). GDP—BMeusel, Pennock, Cunningham. CS—Ruth (1).

Yankees	IP	H	R	ER	BB	K	ERA
Herb Pennock (W, 1-0)	9.0	9	2	2	1	1	2.00

Giants	IP	H	R	ER	BB	K	ERA
Hugh McQuillan (L, 0-1)	3.2	5	3	3	2	1	7.36
Jack Bentley	5.1	5	1	1	2	0	1.69

HBP—Pennock by Bentley. Time—2:08. Attendance—40,402. Umpires—HP, O'Day. 1B, Nallin. 2B, Hart. 3B, Evans.

Game 3

Friday, October 12

Giants	AB	R	H	RBI	BB	K	Avg
Dave Bancroft, ss	3	0	0	0	1	1	.091
Heine Groh, 3b	4	0	0	0	0	1	.273
Frankie Frisch, 2b	4	0	2	0	0	0	.417
Ross Youngs, rf	4	0	0	0	0	0	.182
Irish Meusel, lf	4	0	0	0	0	0	.167
Casey Stengel, cf	3	1	1	1	1	0	.500
George Kelly, 1b	3	0	0	0	0	0	.182
Frank Snyder, c	3	0	0	0	0	0	.000
Art Nehf, p	3	0	1	0	0	1	.333
TOTALS	31	1	4	1	2	3	.221

Yankees	AB	R	H	RBI	BB	K	Avg
Whitey Witt, cf	4	0	1	0	0	1	.143
Joe Dugan, 3b	4	0	1	0	0	0	.250
Babe Ruth, rf-1b	2	0	1	0	2	1	.444
Bob Meusel, lf	4	0	0	0	0	0	.167
Wally Pipp, 1b	2	0	0	0	1	0	.333
Hinkey Haines, rf	1	0	0	0	0	0	.000
Aaron Ward, 2b	4	0	1	0	0	1	.417
Wally Schang, c	4	0	1	0	0	0	.364
Everett Scott, ss	3	0	1	0	0	0	.333
Sad Sam Jones, p	2	0	0	0	0	1	.000
Fred Hofmann, ph	1	0	0	0	0	0	.000
Joe Bush, p	0	0	0	0	0	0	.667
TOTALS	31	0	6	0	3	4	.295

	1	2	3	4	5	6	7	8	9	R	H	E
Giants	0	0	0	0	0	0	1	0	0	1	4	0
Yankees	0	0	0	0	0	0	0	0	0	0	6	1

E—Scott. DP—Giants 2 (Bancroft to Frisch to Kelly; Frisch to Bancroft to Kelly), Yankees 1 (Jones to Scott to Pipp). LOB—Giants 5, Yankees 7. Scoring Position—Giants 0-for-1, Yankees 0-for-5. 2B—Dugan (2). HR—Stengel (2). GDP—Kelly, BMeusel, Jones.

Giants	IP	H	R	ER	BB	K	ERA
Art Nehf (W, 1-0)	9.0	6	0	0	3	4	0.00

Yankees	IP	H	R	ER	BB	K	ERA
Sad Sam Jones (L, 0-1)	8.0	4	1	1	2	3	1.13
Joe Bush	1.0	0	0	0	0	0	1.17

Time—2:05. Attendance—62,430. Umpires—HP, Nallin. 1B, Hart. 2B, Evans. 3B, O'Day.

Game 4

Saturday, October 13

Yankees	AB	R	H	RBI	BB	K	Avg
Whitey Witt, cf	4	0	3	2	0	0	.278
Joe Dugan, 3b	5	1	0	0	0	0	.176
Babe Ruth, rf	3	2	1	0	2	2	.417
Bob Meusel, lf	5	0	1	2	0	1	.176
Wally Pipp, 1b	4	1	2	0	1	0	.385
Aaron Ward, 2b	4	2	2	1	1	0	.438
Wally Schang, c	3	1	1	0	0	1	.357
Everett Scott, ss	5	1	2	2	0	0	.357
Bob Shawkey, p	3	0	1	1	0	0	.333
Herb Pennock, p	1	0	0	0	0	1	.000
TOTALS	37	8	13	8	4	5	.305

Giants	AB	R	H	RBI	BB	K	Avg
Dave Bancroft, ss	5	0	1	0	0	0	.125
Heine Groh, 3b	3	0	0	0	2	0	.214
Frankie Frisch, 2b	5	0	2	0	0	0	.412
Ross Youngs, rf	5	2	4	1	0	0	.375
Irish Meusel, lf	5	1	1	0	0	1	.176
Casey Stengel, cf	2	1	2	1	2	0	.625
Bill Cunningham, ph	1	0	0	0	0	1	.000
George Kelly, 1b	5	0	2	1	0	0	.250
Frank Snyder, c	4	0	0	1	0	0	.000
Jack Scott, p	0	0	0	0	0	0	—
Rosy Ryan, p	0	0	0	0	0	0	.000
Hugh McQuillan, p	2	0	0	0	0	1	.000
Jack Bentley, ph	1	0	1	0	0	0	.750
Freddie Maguire, pr	0	0	0	0	0	0	—
Claude Jonnard, p	0	0	0	0	0	0	—
Jimmy O'Connell, ph	0	0	0	0	0	0	—
Jesse Barnes, p	0	0	0	0	0	0	—
TOTALS	38	4	13	4	4	3	.254

	1	2	3	4	5	6	7	8	9		R	H	E
Yankees	0	6	1	1	0	0	0	0	0		8	13	1
Giants	0	0	0	0	0	0	0	3	1		4	13	1

E—JScott, Ruth. DP—Yankees 2 (Shawkey to Dugan to Pipp; Dugan to Pipp). LOB—Yankees 10, Giants 12. Scoring Position—Yankees 5-for-17, Giants 2-for-13. 2B—Witt 2 (2), Ruth (1). 3B—BMeusel (1). HR—Youngs (1). S—Witt, Schang 2. SF—Shawkey. GDP—Snyder.

Yankees	IP	H	R	ER	BB	K	ERA
Bob Shawkey (W, 1-0)	7.2	12	3	3	4	2	3.52
Herb Pennock (S, 1)	1.1	1	1	1	0	1	2.61

Giants	IP	H	R	ER	BB	K	ERA
Jack Scott (L, 0-1)	1.0	4	4	3	0	1	27.00
Rosy Ryan	0.2	2	2	0	1	0	1.17
Hugh McQuillan	5.1	6	2	2	2	2	5.00
Claude Jonnard	1.0	1	0	0	0	0	0.00
Jesse Barnes	1.0	0	0	0	0	2	0.00

JScott pitched to four batters in the 2nd.

HBP—O'Connell by Shawkey. Time—2:32. Attendance—46,302. Umpires—HP, Hart. 1B, Evans. 2B, O'Day. 3B, Nallin.

Game 5

Sunday, October 14

Giants	AB	R	H	RBI	BB	K	Avg
Dave Bancroft, ss	4	0	0	0	0	1	.100
Heine Groh, 3b	4	0	0	0	0	0	.167
Frankie Frisch, 2b	4	0	0	0	0	0	.333
Ross Youngs, rf	3	0	0	0	1	0	.316
Irish Meusel, lf	4	1	3	0	0	0	.286
Casey Stengel, cf	3	0	0	1	0	0	.455
George Kelly, 1b	2	0	0	0	1	0	.222
Hank Gowdy, c	3	0	0	0	0	0	.000
Jack Bentley, p	0	0	0	0	0	0	.750
Jack Scott, p	1	0	0	0	0	0	.000
Jesse Barnes, p	1	0	0	0	0	1	.000
Jimmy O'Connell, ph	1	0	0	0	0	1	.000
Claude Jonnard, p	0	0	0	0	0	0	—
TOTALS	30	1	3	1	2	3	.259

Yankees	AB	R	H	RBI	BB	K	Avg
Whitey Witt, cf	4	1	1	0	1	0	.273
Joe Dugan, 3b	5	3	4	3	0	0	.318
Babe Ruth, rf	4	2	1	0	1	1	.375
Bob Meusel, lf	5	1	3	3	0	0	.273
Wally Pipp, 1b	3	0	0	2	1	1	.313
Aaron Ward, 2b	4	0	2	0	0	1	.450
Wally Schang, c	4	0	1	0	0	1	.333
Everett Scott, ss	4	0	1	0	0	0	.333
Joe Bush, p	4	1	1	0	0	1	.429
TOTALS	37	8	14	8	3	5	.335

	1	2	3	4	5	6	7	8	9		R	H	E
Giants	0	1	0	0	0	0	0	0	0		1	3	2
Yankees	3	4	0	1	0	0	0	0	x		8	14	0

E—Frisch, Kelly. DP—Giants 1 (Bancroft to Frisch). LOB—Giants 4, Yankees 9. Scoring Position—Giants 0-for-3, Yankees 3-for-10. 2B—IMeusel (1). 3B—IMeusel (1), BMeusel (2). HR—Dugan (1). SF—Pipp. SB—Ward (1).

Giants	IP	H	R	ER	BB	K	ERA
Jack Bentley (L, 0-1)	1.1	5	7	6	2	1	9.45
Jack Scott	2.0	5	1	1	1	1	12.00
Jesse Barnes	3.2	4	0	0	0	2	0.00
Claude Jonnard	1.0	0	0	0	0	1	0.00

Yankees	IP	H	R	ER	BB	K	ERA
Joe Bush (W, 1-1)	9.0	3	1	1	2	3	1.08

Time—1:55. Attendance—62,817. Umpires—HP, Evans. 1B, O'Day. 2B, Nallin. 3B, Hart.

Game 6

Monday, October 15

Yankees	AB	R	H	RBI	BB	K	Avg
Whitey Witt, cf	3	0	0	0	0	0	.240
Joe Bush, ph	0	0	0	1	1	0	.429
Ernie Johnson, pr	0	1	0	0	0	0	—
Sad Sam Jones, p	0	0	0	0	0	0	.000
Joe Dugan, 3b	3	1	0	1	1	0	.280
Babe Ruth, rf	3	1	1	1	1	2	.368
Bob Meusel, lf	4	0	1	2	0	1	.269
Wally Pipp, 1b	4	0	0	0	0	0	.250
Aaron Ward, 2b	4	0	1	0	0	0	.417
Wally Schang, c	4	1	1	0	0	0	.318
Everett Scott, ss	4	1	1	0	0	0	.318
Herb Pennock, p	2	0	0	0	0	1	.000
Fred Hofmann, ph	0	0	0	0	1	0	.000
Hinkey Haines, pr-cf	0	1	0	0	0	0	.000
TOTALS	31	6	5	5	4	4	.295

Giants	AB	R	H	RBI	BB	K	Avg
Dave Bancroft, ss	4	0	0	0	0	0	.083
Heine Groh, 3b	4	1	1	0	0	0	.182
Frankie Frisch, 2b	4	2	3	0	0	0	.400
Ross Youngs, rf	4	0	2	1	0	0	.348
Irish Meusel, lf	4	0	1	1	0	1	.280
Bill Cunningham, cf	3	0	1	1	0	0	.143
Casey Stengel, ph-cf	1	0	0	0	0	0	.417
George Kelly, 1b	4	0	0	0	0	1	.182
Frank Snyder, c	4	1	2	1	0	1	.118
Art Nehf, p	3	0	0	0	0	3	.167
Rosy Ryan, p	0	0	0	0	0	0	.000
Jack Bentley, ph	1	0	0	0	0	0	.600
TOTALS	36	4	10	4	0	6	.247

	1	2	3	4	5	6	7	8	9		R	H	E
Yankees	1	0	0	0	0	0	0	5	0		6	5	0
Giants	1	0	0	1	1	1	0	0	0		4	10	1

E—Cunningham. DP—Giants 1 (Nehf to Bancroft to Kelly). LOB—Yankees 2, Giants 5. Scoring Position—Yankees 1-for-4, Giants 3-for-7. 3B—Frisch (1). HR—Ruth (3), Snyder (1). GDP—Schang.

Yankees	IP	H	R	ER	BB	K	ERA
Herb Pennock (W, 2-0)	7.0	9	4	4	0	6	3.63
Sad Sam Jones (S, 1)	2.0	1	0	0	0	0	0.90

Giants	IP	H	R	ER	BB	K	ERA
Art Nehf (L, 1-1)	7.1	4	5	5	3	3	2.76
Rosy Ryan (BS, 1)	1.2	1	1	0	1	1	0.96

Time—2:05. Attendance—34,172. Umpires—HP, O'Day. 1B, Nallin. 2B, Hart. 3B, Evans.

1923 World Series—Composite Statistics

Batting

Yankees	G	AB	R	H	RBI	2B	3B	HR	BB	SO	SB	CS	Avg	OBP	Slg
Joe Bush	4	7	2	3	1	1	0	0	1	1	0	0	.429	.500	.571
Joe Dugan	6	25	5	7	5	2	1	1	3	0	0	0	.280	.357	.560
Hinkey Haines	2	1	1	0	0	0	0	0	0	0	0	0	.000	.000	.000
Harvey Hendrick	1	1	0	0	0	0	0	0	0	0	0	0	.000	.000	.000
Fred Hofmann	2	1	0	0	0	0	0	0	1	0	0	0	.000	.500	.000
Waite Hoyt	1	1	0	0	0	0	0	0	0	1	0	0	.000	.000	.000
Ernie Johnson	2	0	1	0	0	0	0	0	0	0	0	0	—	—	—
Sad Sam Jones	2	2	0	0	0	0	0	0	0	1	0	0	.000	.000	.000
Bob Meusel	6	26	1	7	8	1	2	0	0	3	0	0	.269	.269	.462
Herb Pennock	3	6	0	0	0	0	0	0	0	2	0	0	.000	.143	.000
Wally Pipp	6	20	2	5	2	0	0	0	4	1	0	0	.250	.360	.250
Babe Ruth	6	19	8	7	3	1	1	3	8	6	0	1	.368	.556	1.000
Wally Schang	6	22	3	7	0	1	0	0	1	2	0	0	.318	.348	.364
Everett Scott	6	22	2	7	3	0	0	0	1	0	0	0	.318	.318	.318
Bob Shawkey	1	3	0	1	1	0	0	0	0	0	0	0	.333	.250	.333
Aaron Ward	6	24	4	10	2	0	0	1	1	3	1	0	.417	.440	.542
Whitey Witt	6	25	1	6	4	2	0	0	1	1	0	0	.240	.269	.320
Totals	6	205	30	60	29	8	4	5	20	22	1	1	.293	.355	.444

Batting

Giants	G	AB	R	H	RBI	2B	3B	HR	BB	SO	SB	CS	Avg	OBP	Slg
Dave Bancroft	6	24	1	2	1	0	0	0	1	2	1	0	.083	.120	.083
Jesse Barnes	2	1	0	0	0	0	0	0	0	1	0	0	.000	.000	.000
Jack Bentley	5	5	0	3	0	1	0	0	0	0	0	0	.600	.600	.800
Bill Cunningham	4	7	0	1	1	0	0	0	0	1	0	0	.143	.143	.143
Frankie Frisch	6	25	2	10	1	0	1	0	0	0	0	1	.400	.400	.480
Dinty Gearin	1	0	0	0	0	0	0	0	0	0	0	0	—	—	—
Hank Gowdy	3	4	0	0	0	0	0	0	1	0	0	0	.000	.200	.000
Heine Groh	6	22	3	4	2	0	1	0	3	1	0	0	.182	.280	.273
Travis Jackson	1	1	0	0	0	0	0	0	0	0	0	0	.000	.000	.000
George Kelly	6	22	1	4	1	0	0	0	1	2	0	0	.182	.217	.182
Freddie Maguire	2	0	1	0	0	0	0	0	0	0	0	0	—	—	—
Hugh McQuillan	2	3	0	0	0	0	0	0	0	1	0	0	.000	.000	.000
Irish Meusel	6	25	3	7	2	1	1	1	0	2	0	0	.280	.280	.520
Art Nehf	2	6	0	1	0	0	0	0	0	4	0	0	.167	.167	.167
Jimmy O'Connell	2	1	0	0	0	0	0	0	1	0	0	0	.000	.500	.000
Rosy Ryan	3	2	0	0	0	0	0	0	0	1	0	0	.000	.000	.000
Jack Scott	2	1	0	0	0	0	0	0	0	0	0	0	.000	.000	.000
Frank Snyder	5	17	1	2	2	0	0	1	0	2	0	0	.118	.118	.294
Casey Stengel	6	12	3	5	4	0	0	2	4	0	0	0	.417	.563	.917
Ross Youngs	6	23	2	8	3	0	0	1	2	0	0	1	.348	.400	.478
Totals	6	201	17	47	17	2	3	5	12	18	1	2	.234	.280	.348

Pitching

Yankees	G	GS	CG	IP	H	R	ER	BB	SO	W-L	Sv-Op	Hld	ERA
Joe Bush	3	1	1	16.2	7	2	2	4	5	1-1	0-0	0	1.08
Waite Hoyt	1	1	0	2.1	4	4	4	1	0	0-0	0-0	0	15.43
Sad Sam Jones	2	1	0	10.0	5	1	1	2	3	0-1	1-1	0	0.90
Herb Pennock	3	2	1	17.1	19	7	7	1	8	2-0	1-1	0	3.63
Bob Shawkey	1	1	0	7.2	12	3	3	4	2	1-0	0-0	0	3.52
Totals	6	6	2	54.0	47	17	17	12	18	4-2	2-2	0	2.83

Pitching

Giants	G	GS	CG	IP	H	R	ER	BB	SO	W-L	Sv-Op	Hld	ERA
Jesse Barnes	2	0	0	4.2	4	0	0	0	4	0-0	0-0	0	0.00
Jack Bentley	2	1	0	6.2	10	8	7	4	1	0-1	0-0	0	9.45
Claude Jonnard	2	0	0	2.0	1	0	0	1	1	0-0	0-0	0	0.00
Hugh McQuillan	2	1	0	9.0	11	5	5	4	3	0-1	0-0	0	5.00
Art Nehf	2	2	1	16.1	10	5	5	6	7	1-1	0-0	0	2.76
Rosy Ryan	3	0	0	9.1	11	4	1	3	3	1-0	0-1	0	0.96
Jack Scott	2	1	0	3.0	9	5	4	1	2	0-1	0-0	0	12.00
Mule Watson	1	1	0	2.0	4	3	3	1	1	0-0	0-0	0	13.50
Totals	6	6	1	53.0	60	30	25	20	22	2-4	0-1	0	4.25

Fielding

Yankees	Pos	G	PO	Ast	E	DP	PB	FPct
Joe Bush	p	3	2	3	0	0	—	1.000
Joe Dugan	3b	6	7	13	0	2	—	1.000
Hinkey Haines	cf	1	0	0	0	0	—	—
	rf	1	0	0	0	0	—	—
Waite Hoyt	p	1	0	0	0	0	—	—
Ernie Johnson	ss	1	0	1	0	0	—	1.000
Sad Sam Jones	p	2	0	3	0	1	—	1.000
Bob Meusel	lf	6	14	0	0	0	—	1.000
Herb Pennock	p	3	0	2	0	0	—	1.000
Wally Pipp	1b	6	63	3	0	6	—	.938
Babe Ruth	rf	6	15	0	1	0	—	.938
	1b	1	2	0	0	0	—	1.000
Wally Schang	c	6	21	2	1	0	0	.958
Everett Scott	ss	6	8	20	1	4	—	.966
Bob Shawkey	p	1	1	2	0	1	—	1.000
Aaron Ward	2b	6	11	26	0	3	—	1.000
Whitey Witt	cf	6	18	1	0	0	—	1.000
Totals		6	162	76	3	17	0	.988

Fielding

Giants	Pos	G	PO	Ast	E	DP	PB	FPct
Dave Bancroft	ss	6	11	23	0	6	—	1.000
Jesse Barnes	p	2	1	2	0	0	—	1.000
Jack Bentley	p	2	0	2	0	0	—	1.000
Bill Cunningham	cf	3	2	0	1	0	—	.667
Frankie Frisch	2b	6	17	17	1	7	—	.971
Hank Gowdy	c	3	7	0	0	0	0	1.000
Heine Groh	3b	6	4	17	0	1	—	1.000
Claude Jonnard	p	2	0	1	0	0	—	1.000
George Kelly	1b	6	63	3	1	5	—	.985
Hugh McQuillan	p	2	0	1	0	0	—	1.000
Irish Meusel	lf	6	13	0	0	0	—	1.000
Art Nehf	p	2	0	6	0	1	—	1.000
Rosy Ryan	p	3	1	2	0	1	—	1.000
Jack Scott	p	2	0	0	1	0	—	.000
Frank Snyder	c	5	24	3	0	1	0	1.000
Casey Stengel	cf	6	11	0	0	0	—	1.000
Mule Watson	p	1	0	1	0	0	—	1.000
Ross Youngs	rf	6	5	1	2	0	—	.750
Totals		6	159	79	6	22	0	.975

1924 Washington Senators (AL) 4, New York Giants (NL) 3

The Washington Senators caught three lucky breaks in the 12th inning of the seventh game to send the New York Giants to defeat. Walter Johnson went 11 solid innings in the opener before faltering and allowing a pair of runs in the 12th. Bucky Harris drove in a run in the bottom of the frame, but with the tying run on third base, Goose Goslin grounded out to end the game. The Giants tied up Game 2 with a two-run rally in the ninth, but Roger Peckinpaugh won it with an RBI double in the bottom of the inning. After the Giants took the third game, 6-4, to take a 2-to-1 lead in the Series, Goslin homered and drove in four runs to give the Senators a 7-4 win in Game 4. The Giants beat Johnson for a second time in Game 5, a 6-2 decision, but the Senators knotted the Series when Tom Zachary won Game 6, 2-1, on Harris' two-run single. Harris came through in Game 7 as well, singling in two runs to tie the score in the bottom of the eighth. Johnson came on to pitch in the ninth and the game went into extra innings. In the bottom of the 12th, catcher Hank Gowdy tripped over his mask and missed Muddy Ruel's foul pop. Ruel doubled, and Johnson reached base when Travis Jackson muffed his grounder. Earl McNeely lined the ball toward third baseman Fred Lindstrom, but the ball skipped oddly over his head as Ruel scored the winning run.

Game 1

Saturday, October 4

Giants	AB	R	H	RBI	BB	K	Avg
Freddy Lindstrom, 3b	5	0	0	0	0	2	.000
Jack Bentley, ph	0	0	0	0	1	0	—
Billy Southworth, pr-cf	0	1	0	0	0	0	—
Frankie Frisch, 2b-3b	5	0	2	0	1	0	.400
Ross Youngs, rf	6	0	2	1	0	3	.333
George Kelly, cf-2b	5	1	1	2	0	2	.200
Bill Terry, 1b	5	1	3	1	1	0	.600
Hack Wilson, lf	6	0	2	0	0	3	.333
Travis Jackson, ss	3	0	0	0	1	1	.000
Hank Gowdy, c	3	0	1	0	2	1	.333
Art Nehf, p	5	1	3	0	0	0	.600
TOTALS	43	4	14	4	6	12	.326

Senators	AB	R	H	RBI	BB	K	Avg
Earl McNeely, cf	5	1	1	0	1	0	.200
Bucky Harris, 2b	6	0	2	1	0	0	.333
Sam Rice, rf	5	0	2	1	1	0	.400
Goose Goslin, lf	6	0	1	0	0	1	.167
Joe Judge, 1b	4	0	1	0	1	0	.250
Ossie Bluege, 3b	5	1	1	0	0	1	.200
Roger Peckinpaugh, ss	5	0	2	1	0	0	.400
Muddy Ruel, c	3	0	0	0	2	0	.000
Walter Johnson, p	4	0	0	0	0	0	.000
Mule Shirley, ph	1	1	0	0	0	0	.000
TOTALS	44	3	10	3	5	3	.227

	1	2	3	4	5	6	7	8	9	10	11	12	R	H	E
Giants	0	1	0	1	0	0	0	0	0	0	0	2	4	14	1
Senators	0	0	0	0	1	0	0	1	0	0	0	1	3	10	1

E—McNeely, Jackson. DP—Giants 1 (Jackson to Frisch to Terry), Senators 2 (Peckinpaugh to Harris; Bluege to Harris to Judge). LOB—Giants 11, Senators 10. Scoring Position—Giants 3-for-10, Senators 1-for-11. 2B—Frisch (1), Youngs (1), McNeely (1), Peckinpaugh (1). HR—Kelly (1), Terry (1). S—Jackson. SF—Kelly. GDP—Jackson, Johnson. SB—Frisch (1), Rice (1), Peckinpaugh (1). CS—Youngs (1), Goslin (1).

Giants	IP	H	R	ER	BB	K	ERA
Art Nehf (W, 1-0)	12.0	10	3	2	5	3	1.50

Senators	IP	H	R	ER	BB	K	ERA
Walter Johnson (L, 0-1)	12.0	14	4	3	6	12	2.25

WP—Johnson. Time—3:07. Attendance—35,760. Umpires—HP, Connolly. 1B, Klem. 2B, Dinneen. 3B, Quigley.

Game 2

Sunday, October 5

Giants	AB	R	H	RBI	BB	K	Avg
Freddy Lindstrom, 3b	3	0	1	0	1	0	.125
Frankie Frisch, 2b	3	1	1	0	1	0	.375
Ross Youngs, rf	4	0	1	0	0	0	.300
George Kelly, 1b	3	2	1	1	1	0	.250
Irish Meusel, lf	4	0	1	0	0	0	.250
Hack Wilson, cf	4	0	1	1	0	0	.300
Travis Jackson, ss	4	0	0	0	0	1	.000
Hank Gowdy, c	3	0	0	0	0	0	.167
Jack Bentley, p	3	0	0	0	0	0	.000
TOTALS	31	3	6	2	3	1	.219

Senators	AB	R	H	RBI	BB	K	Avg
Earl McNeely, cf	4	0	0	0	0	0	.111
Bucky Harris, 2b	3	1	1	1	1	0	.333
Sam Rice, rf	3	1	2	0	0	0	.500
Goose Goslin, lf	4	1	1	2	0	2	.200
Joe Judge, 1b	2	1	1	0	2	0	.333
Ossie Bluege, 3b	3	0	0	0	0	1	.125
Roger Peckinpaugh, ss	4	0	1	1	0	0	.333
Muddy Ruel, c	3	0	0	0	0	1	.000

Tom Zachary, p	2	0	0	0	1	2	.000
Firpo Marberry, p	0	0	0	0	0	0	—
TOTALS	28	4	6	4	4	6	.239

	1	2	3	4	5	6	7	8	9	R	H	E
Giants	0	0	0	0	0	0	1	0	2	3	6	0
Senators	2	0	0	0	1	0	0	0	1	4	6	1

E—Harris. DP—Senators 3 (Bluege to Harris to Judge; Harris to Peckinpaugh to Judge; Bluege to Harris to Judge). LOB—Giants 4, Senators 5. Scoring Position—Giants 1-for-6, Senators 2-for-3. 2B—Peckinpaugh (2). HR—Harris (1), Goslin (1). S—Rice, Bluege. GDP—Kelly, Meusel, Wilson. SB—Rice (2). CS—Judge (1).

Giants	IP	H	R	ER	BB	K	ERA
Jack Bentley (L, 0-1)	8.1	6	4	4	4	6	4.32

Senators	IP	H	R	ER	BB	K	ERA
Tom Zachary	8.2	6	3	3	3	0	3.12
Firpo Marberry (W, 1-0)	0.1	0	0	0	0	1	0.00

Time—1:58. Attendance—35,922. Umpires—HP, Klem. 1B, Dinneen. 2B, Quigley. 3B, Connolly.

Game 3

Monday, October 6

Senators	AB	R	H	RBI	BB	K	Avg
Nemo Leibold, cf	4	0	0	0	1	0	.000
Bucky Harris, 2b	5	1	1	0	0	1	.286
Sam Rice, rf	3	1	1	0	2	0	.455
Goose Goslin, lf	5	0	1	0	0	0	.200
Joe Judge, 1b	5	1	3	0	0	0	.455
Ossie Bluege, 3b-ss	3	1	1	0	2	1	.182
Roger Peckinpaugh, ss	1	0	0	0	0	0	.300
Ralph Miller, 3b	2	0	1	1	1	0	.500
Muddy Ruel, c	3	0	0	0	2	0	.000
Firpo Marberry, p	1	0	0	0	0	0	.000
Bennie Tate, ph	0	0	0	1	1	0	—
Allan Russell, p	0	0	0	0	0	0	—
Earl McNeely, ph	1	0	0	0	0	0	.100
Joe Martina, p	0	0	0	0	0	0	—
Mule Shirley, ph	1	0	1	1	0	0	.500
Byron Speece, p	0	0	0	0	0	0	—
TOTALS	34	4	9	3	9	2	.250

Giants	AB	R	H	RBI	BB	K	Avg
Freddy Lindstrom, 3b	4	0	1	1	1	0	.167
Frankie Frisch, 2b	4	0	2	0	0	0	.417
Ross Youngs, rf	4	0	1	0	0	1	.286
George Kelly, cf	4	1	2	0	0	1	.333
Billy Southworth, cf	0	0	0	0	0	0	—
Bill Terry, 1b	4	1	2	0	0	0	.556
Hack Wilson, lf	4	0	0	0	0	1	.214
Travis Jackson, ss	4	2	1	0	0	1	.091
Hank Gowdy, c	4	1	2	2	0	0	.300
Hugh McQuillan, p	0	0	0	0	1	0	—
Rosy Ryan, p	2	1	1	1	0	0	.500
Claude Jonnard, p	0	0	0	0	0	0	—
Mule Watson, p	0	0	0	0	0	0	—
TOTALS	34	6	12	4	2	5	.292

	1	2	3	4	5	6	7	8	9	R	H	E
Senators	0	0	0	2	0	0	0	1	1	4	9	2
Giants	0	2	1	1	0	1	0	1	x	6	12	0

E—Miller, Harris. DP—Senators 1 (Marberry to Bluege to Harris to Judge), Giants 1 (McQuillan to Frisch to Terry). LOB—Senators 13, Giants 8. Scoring Position—Senators 2-for-8, Giants 4-for-9. 2B—Judge (1), Lindstrom (1). HR—Ryan (1). S—Ryan. SF—Miller. GDP—Bluege, Wilson. SB—Jackson (1).

Game 4

Tuesday, October 7

Senators	AB	R	H	RBI	BB	K	Avg
Earl McNeely, cf	5	2	3	0	0	1	.267
Bucky Harris, 2b	5	2	2	0	0	1	.316
Sam Rice, rf	5	0	0	0	0	0	.313
Goose Goslin, lf	4	2	4	4	0	0	.368
Joe Judge, 1b	4	1	1	0	0	0	.400
Ossie Bluege, ss	4	0	3	2	0	0	.333
Muddy Ruel, c	3	0	0	0	0	0	.000
Ralph Miller, 3b	4	0	0	0	0	0	.167
George Mogridge, p	4	0	0	0	0	4	.000
Firpo Marberry, p	0	0	0	0	0	0	.000
TOTALS	38	7	13	6	0	6	.279

Giants	AB	R	H	RBI	BB	K	Avg
Freddy Lindstrom, 3b	4	1	3	1	1	0	.313
Frankie Frisch, 2b	4	0	0	0	1	0	.313
Ross Youngs, rf	4	1	0	0	1	1	.222
George Kelly, 1b	5	1	1	0	0	2	.294
Irish Meusel, lf	2	0	0	0	2	0	.167
Hack Wilson, cf	4	0	1	2	0	0	.222
Travis Jackson, ss	4	0	0	0	0	0	.067
Hank Gowdy, c	4	1	1	0	0	0	.286
Virgil Barnes, p	0	0	0	0	0	1	—
Bill Terry, ph	1	0	0	0	0	0	.500
Harry Baldwin, p	0	0	0	0	0	0	—
Billy Southworth, ph	1	0	0	0	0	0	.000
Wayland Dean, p	0	0	0	0	0	0	—
Jack Bentley, ph	1	0	0	0	0	1	.000
TOTALS	34	4	6	3	6	4	.252

	1	2	3	4	5	6	7	8	9	R	H	E
Senators	0	0	3	0	2	0	2	0	0	7	13	3
Giants	1	0	0	0	0	1	0	1	1	4	6	1

E—Bluege, Miller, Rice, Meusel. LOB—Senators 5, Giants 9. Scoring Position—Senators 3-for-14, Giants 2-for-11. 2B—McNeely (2), Kelly (1), Wilson (1). HR—Goslin (2). S—Ruel. CS—Goslin (2).

Senators	IP	H	R	ER	BB	K	ERA
George Mogridge (W, 1-0)	7.1	3	3	2	5	2	2.45
Firpo Marberry (S, 1)	1.2	3	1	0	1	2	1.80

Giants	IP	H	R	ER	BB	K	ERA
Virgil Barnes (L, 0-1)	5.0	9	5	5	0	3	9.00
Harry Baldwin	2.0	1	0	0	0	1	0.00
Wayland Dean	2.0	3	2	1	0	2	4.50

WP—Barnes. Time—2:10. Attendance—49,243. Umpires—HP, Quigley. 1B, Connolly. 2B, Klem. 3B, Dinneen.

Senators	IP	H	R	ER	BB	K	ERA
Firpo Marberry (L, 1-1)	3.0	5	3	1	2	4	2.70
Allan Russell	3.0	4	2	1	0	0	3.00
Joe Martina	1.0	0	0	0	0	1	0.00
Byron Speece	1.0	3	1	1	0	0	9.00

Giants	IP	H	R	ER	BB	K	ERA
Hugh McQuillan (W, 1-0)	3.2	2	2	2	5	0	4.91
Rosy Ryan	4.2	7	2	2	3	2	3.86
Claude Jonnard	0.0	0	0	0	1	0	—
Mule Watson (S, 1)	0.2	0	0	0	0	0	0.00

Jonnard pitched to one batter in the 9th.

WP—Marberry. HBP—Frisch by Marberry. Time—2:25. Attendance—47,608. Umpires—HP, Dinneen. 1B, Quigley. 2B, Connolly. 3B, Klem.

Game 5

Wednesday, October 8

Senators	AB	R	H	RBI	BB	K	Avg
Earl McNeely, cf	4	0	1	0	1	1	.263
Bucky Harris, 2b	5	0	1	0	0	1	.292
Sam Rice, rf	4	0	0	0	0	1	.250
Goose Goslin, lf	4	1	2	1	0	1	.391
Joe Judge, 1b	4	1	3	0	0	0	.474
Ossie Bluege, ss	3	0	0	0	0	1	.278
Muddy Ruel, c	2	0	0	0	2	0	.000
Ralph Miller, 3b	3	0	1	1	0	0	.222
Nemo Leibold, ph	1	0	0	0	0	0	.000
Walter Johnson, p	3	0	1	0	0	0	.143
Bennie Tate, ph	0	0	0	0	1	0	—
Tommy Taylor, pr	0	0	0	0	0	0	—
TOTALS	33	2	9	2	4	5	.272

Giants	AB	R	H	RBI	BB	K	Avg
Freddy Lindstrom, 3b	5	0	4	2	0	0	.429
Frankie Frisch, 2b	5	0	1	0	0	0	.286
Ross Youngs, rf	3	0	1	0	0	0	.238
George Kelly, cf	4	1	1	0	0	1	.286
Bill Terry, 1b	2	1	1	0	2	0	.500
Hack Wilson, lf	3	0	0	0	0	1	.190
Travis Jackson, ss	3	1	1	1	0	0	.111
Hank Gowdy, c	4	2	1	0	0	1	.278
Jack Bentley, p	3	1	2	2	0	0	.286
Hugh McQuillan, p	1	0	1	1	0	0	1.000
TOTALS	33	6	13	6	2	3	.286

	1	2	3	4	5	6	7	8	9	R	H	E
Senators	0	0	0	1	0	0	0	1	0	2	9	1
Giants	0	0	1	0	2	0	0	3	x	6	13	0

E—Johnson. DP—Senators 2 (Rice to Johnson to Ruel; Bluege to Harris to Judge). LOB—Senators 9, Giants 8. Scoring Position—Senators 1-for-10, Giants 3-for-10. 2B—Frisch (2). 3B—Terry (1). HR—Goslin (3), Bentley (1). S—Bluege, Wilson. SF—Jackson. GDP—Kelly. CS—Lindstrom 2 (2).

Senators	IP	H	R	ER	BB	K	ERA
Walter Johnson (L, 0-2)	8.0	13	6	3	2	3	2.70

Giants	IP	H	R	ER	BB	K	ERA
Jack Bentley (W, 1-1)	7.1	9	2	2	3	4	3.45
Hugh McQuillan (S, 1)	1.2	0	0	0	1	1	3.38

HBP—Youngs by Johnson. Time—2:30. Attendance—49,271. Umpires—HP, Connolly. 1B, Klem. 2B, Dinneen. 3B, Quigley.

Game 6

Thursday, October 9

Giants	AB	R	H	RBI	BB	K	Avg
Freddy Lindstrom, 3b	4	0	0	0	0	1	.360
Frankie Frisch, 2b	4	0	2	0	0	0	.320
Ross Youngs, rf	4	1	0	0	0	0	.200
George Kelly, 1b	4	0	2	1	0	0	.320
Billy Southworth, pr	0	0	0	0	0	0	.000
Irish Meusel, lf	4	0	0	0	0	0	.100
Hack Wilson, cf	4	0	2	0	0	2	.240
Travis Jackson, ss	3	0	0	0	0	0	.095
Hank Gowdy, c	3	0	1	0	0	0	.286
Art Nehf, p	2	0	0	0	0	0	.429
Frank Snyder, ph	1	0	0	0	0	0	.000
Rosy Ryan, p	0	0	0	0	0	0	.500
TOTALS	33	1	7	1	0	3	.261

Senators	AB	R	H	RBI	BB	K	Avg
Earl McNeely, cf	2	1	0	0	2	0	.238
Bucky Harris, 2b	4	0	1	2	0	0	.286
Sam Rice, rf	4	0	1	0	0	1	.250
Goose Goslin, lf	4	0	0	0	0	2	.333
Joe Judge, 1b	3	0	0	0	1	1	.409
Ossie Bluege, 3b-ss	3	0	0	0	1	0	.238
Roger Peckinpaugh, ss	2	1	2	0	1	0	.417
Tommy Taylor, 3b	0	0	0	0	0	0	—
Muddy Ruel, c	2	0	0	0	0	0	.000
Tom Zachary, p	3	0	0	0	0	1	.000
TOTALS	27	2	4	2	5	5	.267

	1	2	3	4	5	6	7	8	9	R	H	E
Giants	1	0	0	0	0	0	0	0	0	1	7	1
Senators	0	0	0	0	2	0	0	0	x	2	4	0

E—Kelly. DP—Senators 1 (Harris to Peckinpaugh to Judge). LOB—Giants 5, Senators 7. Scoring Position—Giants 1-for-4, Senators 1-for-5. 2B—Frisch 2 (4). S—Ruel. GDP—Jackson. SB—McNeely (1), Bluege (1). CS—Harris (1).

Giants	IP	H	R	ER	BB	K	ERA
Art Nehf (L, 1-1)	7.0	4	2	2	4	4	1.89
Rosy Ryan	1.0	0	0	0	1	1	3.18

Senators	IP	H	R	ER	BB	K	ERA
Tom Zachary (W, 1-0)	9.0	7	1	1	0	3	2.04

Time—1:57. Attendance—34,254. Umpires—HP, Klem. 1B, Dinneen. 2B, Quigley. 3B, Connolly.

Game 7

Friday, October 10

Giants	AB	R	H	RBI	BB	K	Avg
Freddy Lindstrom, 3b	5	0	1	0	0	2	.333
Frankie Frisch, 2b	5	0	2	0	1	1	.333
Ross Youngs, rf-lf-rf	2	1	0	0	4	1	.185
George Kelly, cf-1b	6	1	1	0	0	2	.290
Bill Terry, 1b	2	0	0	0	0	1	.429
Irish Meusel, ph-lf-rf-lf	3	0	1	1	0	0	.154
Hack Wilson, lf-cf	5	1	1	0	1	2	.233
Travis Jackson, ss	6	0	0	0	0	1	.074
Hank Gowdy, c	6	0	1	0	0	0	.259
Virgil Barnes, p	4	0	0	0	0	2	.000
Art Nehf, p	0	0	0	0	0	0	.429
Hugh McQuillan, p	0	0	0	0	0	0	1.000
Heine Groh, ph	1	0	1	0	0	0	1.000
Billy Southworth, pr	0	0	0	0	0	0	.000
Jack Bentley, p	0	0	0	0	0	0	.286
TOTALS	45	3	8	1	6	12	.260

Senators	AB	R	H	RBI	BB	K	Avg
Earl McNeely, cf	6	0	1	1	0	2	.222
Bucky Harris, 2b	5	1	3	3	0	1	.333
Sam Rice, rf	5	0	0	0	0	0	.207
Goose Goslin, lf	5	0	2	0	0	1	.344
Joe Judge, 1b	4	0	1	0	1	0	.385
Ossie Bluege, ss	5	0	0	0	0	0	.192
Tommy Taylor, 3b	2	0	0	0	0	2	.000
Nemo Leibold, ph	1	1	1	0	0	0	.167
Ralph Miller, 3b	2	0	0	0	0	0	.182
Muddy Ruel, c	5	2	2	0	0	0	.095
Curly Ogden, p	0	0	0	0	0	0	—
George Mogridge, p	1	0	0	0	0	1	.000
Firpo Marberry, p	1	0	0	0	0	0	.000
Bennie Tate, ph	0	0	0	0	1	0	—
Mule Shirley, pr	0	0	0	0	0	0	.500
Walter Johnson, p	2	0	0	0	0	0	.111
TOTALS	44	4	10	4	2	7	.242

	1	2	3	4	5	6	7	8	9	10	11	12	R	H	E
Giants	0	0	0	0	0	3	0	0	0	0	0	0	3	8	3
Senators	0	0	0	1	0	0	0	2	0	0	0	1	4	10	4

E—Taylor, Jackson 2, Bluege 2, Judge, Gowdy. DP—Giants 2 (Kelly to Jackson; Jackson to Frisch to Kelly), Senators 1 (Johnson to Bluege to Judge). LOB—Giants 14, Senators 8. Scoring Position—Giants 0-for-11, Senators 3-for-8. 2B—Lindstrom (2), McNeely (3), Harris 2 (2), Goslin 2 (2), Judge (2), Ruel 2 (2), Leibold (1). 3B—Frisch (1). HR—Harris (2). S—Lindstrom. SF—Meusel. GDP—Gowdy, Rice, Miller. SB—Youngs (1).

Giants	IP	H	R	ER	BB	K	ERA
Virgil Barnes	7.2	6	3	3	1	6	5.68
Art Nehf	0.2	1	0	0	0	0	1.83
Hugh McQuillan	1.2	0	0	0	0	1	2.57
Jack Bentley (L, 1-2)	1.1	3	1	1	1	0	3.71

Senators	IP	H	R	ER	BB	K	ERA
Curly Ogden	0.1	0	0	0	1	1	0.00
George Mogridge	4.2	4	2	1	1	3	2.25
Firpo Marberry (BS, 1)	3.0	1	1	0	1	3	1.13
Walter Johnson (W, 1-2)	4.0	3	0	0	3	5	2.25

Mogridge pitched to two batters in the 6th.

Time—3:00. Attendance—31,667. Umpires—HP, Dinneen. 1B, Quigley. 2B, Connolly. 3B, Klem.

1924 World Series—Composite Statistics

Batting

Senators	G	AB	R	H	RBI	2B	3B	HR	BB	SO	SB	CS	Avg	OBP	Slg
Ossie Bluege	7	26	2	5	2	0	0	0	3	4	1	0	.192	.276	.192
Goose Goslin	7	32	4	11	7	2	0	3	0	7	0	2	.344	.344	.688
Bucky Harris	7	33	5	11	7	2	0	2	1	4	0	1	.333	.353	.576
Walter Johnson	3	9	0	1	0	0	0	0	0	0	0	0	.111	.111	.111
Joe Judge	7	26	4	10	0	2	0	0	5	2	0	1	.385	.484	.462
Nemo Leibold	3	6	1	1	0	1	0	0	1	0	0	0	.167	.286	.333
Firpo Marberry	4	2	0	0	0	0	0	0	0	0	0	0	.000	.000	.000
Earl McNeely	7	27	4	6	1	3	0	0	4	4	1	0	.222	.323	.333
Ralph Miller	4	11	0	2	2	0	0	0	1	0	0	0	.182	.231	.182
George Mogridge	2	5	0	0	0	0	0	0	0	5	0	0	.000	.000	.000
Roger Peckinpaugh	4	12	1	5	2	2	0	0	1	0	1	0	.417	.462	.583
Sam Rice	7	29	2	6	1	0	0	0	3	2	2	0	.207	.281	.207
Muddy Ruel	7	21	2	2	0	2	0	0	6	1	0	0	.095	.296	.190
Mule Shirley	3	2	1	1	0	0	0	0	0	0	0	0	.500	.500	.500
Bennie Tate	3	0	0	0	1	0	0	0	3	0	0	0	—	1.000	—
Tommy Taylor	3	2	0	0	0	0	0	0	0	2	0	0	.000	.000	.000
Tom Zachary	2	5	0	0	0	0	0	0	1	3	0	0	.000	.167	.000
Totals	7	248	26	61	24	14	0	5	29	34	5	4	.246	.324	.363

Giants	G	AB	R	H	RBI	2B	3B	HR	BB	SO	SB	CS	Avg	OBP	Slg
Virgil Barnes	2	4	0	0	0	0	0	0	1	2	0	0	.000	.200	.000
Jack Bentley	5	7	1	2	2	0	0	1	1	1	0	0	.286	.375	.714
Frankie Frisch	7	30	1	10	0	4	1	0	4	1	1	0	.333	.429	.533
Hank Gowdy	7	27	4	7	2	0	0	0	2	2	0	0	.259	.310	.259
Heine Groh	1	1	0	1	0	0	0	0	0	0	0	0	1.000	1.000	1.000
Travis Jackson	7	27	3	2	1	0	0	0	1	4	1	0	.074	.103	.074
George Kelly	7	31	7	9	4	1	0	1	1	8	0	0	.290	.303	.419
Freddy Lindstrom	7	30	1	10	4	2	0	0	3	6	0	2	.333	.394	.400
Hugh McQuillan	3	1	0	1	0	0	0	0	1	0	0	0	1.000	1.000	1.000
Irish Meusel	4	13	0	2	1	0	0	0	2	0	0	0	.154	.250	.154
Art Nehf	3	7	1	3	0	0	0	0	0	0	0	0	.429	.429	.429
Rosy Ryan	2	2	1	1	1	0	0	1	0	0	0	0	.500	.500	2.000
Frank Snyder	1	1	0	0	0	0	0	0	0	0	0	0	.000	.000	.000
Billy Southworth	5	1	1	0	0	0	0	0	0	0	0	0	.000	.000	.000
Bill Terry	5	14	3	6	1	0	1	1	3	1	0	0	.429	.529	.786
Hack Wilson	7	30	1	7	3	1	0	0	1	9	0	0	.233	.258	.267
Ross Youngs	7	27	3	5	1	1	0	0	5	6	1	1	.185	.333	.222
Totals	7	253	27	66	21	9	2	4	25	40	3	3	.261	.329	.360

Pitching

Senators	G	GS	CG	IP	H	R	ER	BB	SO	W-L	Sv-Op	Hld	ERA
Walter Johnson	3	2	2	24.0	30	10	6	11	20	1-2	0-0	0	2.25
Firpo Marberry	4	1	0	8.0	9	5	1	4	10	1-1	1-2	0	1.13
Joe Martina	1	0	0	1.0	0	0	0	0	1	0-0	0-0	0	0.00
George Mogridge	2	1	0	12.0	7	5	3	6	5	1-0	0-0	0	2.25
Curly Ogden	1	1	0	0.1	0	0	0	1	1	0-0	0-0	0	0.00
Allan Russell	1	0	0	3.0	4	2	1	0	0	0-0	0-0	0	3.00
Byron Speece	1	0	0	1.0	3	1	1	0	0	0-0	0-0	0	9.00
Tom Zachary	2	2	1	17.2	13	4	4	3	3	1-0	0-0	0	2.04
Totals	7	7	3	67.0	66	27	16	25	40	4-3	1-2	0	2.15

Giants	G	GS	CG	IP	H	R	ER	BB	SO	W-L	Sv-Op	Hld	ERA
Harry Baldwin	1	0	0	2.0	1	0	0	0	1	0-0	0-0	0	0.00
Virgil Barnes	2	2	0	12.2	15	8	8	1	9	0-1	0-0	0	5.68
Jack Bentley	3	2	1	17.0	18	7	7	8	10	1-2	0-0	0	3.71
Wayland Dean	1	0	0	2.0	3	2	1	0	2	0-0	0-0	0	4.50
Claude Jonnard	1	0	0	0.0	0	0	0	0	0	0-0	0-0	0	—
Hugh McQuillan	3	1	0	7.0	2	2	2	6	2	1-0	1-1	0	2.57
Art Nehf	3	2	1	19.2	15	5	4	9	7	1-1	0-0	0	1.83
Rosy Ryan	2	0	0	5.2	7	2	2	4	3	0-0	0-0	0	3.18
Mule Watson	1	0	0	0.2	0	0	0	0	0	0-0	1-1	0	0.00
Totals	7	7	2	66.2	61	26	24	29	34	3-4	2-2	0	3.24

Fielding

Senators	Pos	G	PO	Ast	E	DP	PB	FPct
Ossie Bluege	ss	5	3	13	3	3	—	.842
	3b	4	4	11	0	3	—	1.000
Goose Goslin	lf	7	15	1	0	0	—	1.000
Bucky Harris	2b	7	27	27	2	8	—	.964
Walter Johnson	p	3	1	4	1	2	—	.833
Joe Judge	1b	7	62	4	1	8	—	.985
Nemo Leibold	cf	1	2	0	0	0	—	1.000
Firpo Marberry	p	4	1	1	0	1	—	1.000
Joe Martina	p	1	0	0	0	0	—	—
Earl McNeely	cf	6	8	0	1	0	—	.889
Ralph Miller	3b	4	6	4	2	0	—	.833
George Mogridge	p	2	0	0	0	0	—	—
Curly Ogden	p	1	0	0	0	0	—	—
Roger Peckinpaugh	ss	4	7	14	0	3	—	1.000
Sam Rice	rf	7	13	4	1	1	—	.944
Muddy Ruel	c	7	51	4	0	1	0	1.000
Allan Russell	p	1	0	1	0	0	—	1.000
Byron Speece	p	1	0	2	0	0	—	1.000
Tommy Taylor	3b	2	0	3	1	0	—	.750
Tom Zachary	p	2	1	4	0	0	—	1.000
Totals		7	201	97	12	30	0	.961

Giants	Pos	G	PO	Ast	E	DP	PB	FPct
Harry Baldwin	p	1	0	0	0	0	—	—
Virgil Barnes	p	2	2	3	0	0	—	1.000
Jack Bentley	p	3	1	3	0	0	—	1.000
Wayland Dean	p	1	0	0	0	0	—	—
Frankie Frisch	2b	7	17	26	0	3	—	1.000
	3b	1	0	0	0	0	—	—
Hank Gowdy	c	7	37	5	1	0	0	.977
Travis Jackson	ss	7	8	20	3	3	—	.903
Claude Jonnard	p	1	0	0	0	0	—	—
George Kelly	1b	4	44	5	1	2	—	.980
	cf	4	7	0	0	0	—	1.000
	2b	1	1	1	0	0	—	1.000
Freddy Lindstrom	3b	7	7	18	0	0	—	1.000
Hugh McQuillan	p	3	0	2	0	1	—	1.000
Irish Meusel	lf	4	5	0	1	0	—	.833
	rf	1	0	0	0	0	—	—
Art Nehf	p	3	0	6	0	0	—	1.000
Rosy Ryan	p	2	0	1	0	0	—	1.000
Billy Southworth	cf	2	1	1	0	0	—	1.000
Bill Terry	1b	4	43	2	0	2	—	1.000
Mule Watson	p	1	0	0	0	0	—	—
Hack Wilson	lf	4	12	1	0	0	—	1.000
	cf	4	7	0	0	0	—	1.000
Ross Youngs	rf	7	8	1	0	0	—	1.000
	lf	1	0	0	0	0	—	—
Totals		7	200	95	6	11	0	.980

1925 Pittsburgh Pirates (NL) 4, Washington Senators (AL) 3

Roger Peckinpaugh's unsteady fielding fueled a late comeback by the Pittsburgh Pirates in Game 7 and the Washington Senators came up just short at the end. Walter Johnson nailed down a 4-1 victory for Washington in the opener. With Game 2 knotted 1-1 in the eighth, Peckinpaugh's error put a runner on base before Kiki Cuyler's two-run homer, and Washington was able to get only one back in the top of the ninth after loading the bases with no one out. Pittsburgh hung on to win, 3-2. Joe Harris' RBI single in the bottom of the seventh gave the Senators a 4-3 win in Game 3. Johnson was even sharper in Game 4, and Goose Goslin socked a three-run homer as Washington came away with a 4-0 win. Cuyler's seventh-inning single off third baseman Ossie Bluege's glove plated the go-ahead run in the Pirates' 6-3 win in Game 5. Ray Kremer won the sixth game, 3-2. Walter Johnson held a 6-4 lead in the seventh inning of Game 7, until a Peckinpaugh error helped the Pirates to tie the score. Peckinpaugh atoned with a solo homer in the top of the eighth, but with two outs in the bottom of the inning, Carson Bigbee tied it up again with an RBI double. Cuyler doubled in two more, and the Pirates took the flag with a 9-7 win.

Game 1

Wednesday, October 7

Senators	AB	R	H	RBI	BB	K	Avg
Sam Rice, cf-rf	4	0	2	2	0	0	.500
Bucky Harris, 2b	3	0	0	0	1	0	.000
Goose Goslin, lf	4	1	1	0	0	0	.250
Joe Judge, 1b	3	0	0	0	0	0	.000
Joe Harris, rf	4	2	2	1	0	1	.500
Earl McNeely, cf	0	0	0	0	0	0	—
Ossie Bluege, 3b	4	1	2	1	0	2	.500
Roger Peckinpaugh, ss	4	0	1	0	0	0	.250
Muddy Ruel, c	3	0	0	0	0	0	.000
Walter Johnson, p	3	0	0	0	0	1	.000
TOTALS	32	4	8	4	0	5	.250

Pirates	AB	R	H	RBI	BB	K	Avg
Eddie Moore, 2b	4	0	0	0	0	0	.000
Max Carey, cf	2	0	0	0	0	1	.000
Kiki Cuyler, rf	4	0	1	0	0	0	.250
Clyde Barnhart, lf	4	0	1	0	0	2	.250
Pie Traynor, 3b	4	1	2	1	0	0	.500
Glenn Wright, ss	4	0	0	0	0	2	.000
George Grantham, 1b	3	0	0	0	0	1	.000
Earl Smith, c	3	0	1	0	0	0	.333
Carson Bigbee, pr	0	0	0	0	0	0	—
Johnny Gooch, c	0	0	0	0	0	0	—
Lee Meadows, p	1	0	0	0	1	1	.000
Stuffy McInnis, ph	1	0	0	0	0	1	.000
Johnny Morrison, p	0	0	0	0	0	0	—
TOTALS	30	1	5	1	1	10	.167

	1	2	3	4	5	6	7	8	9		R	H	E
Senators	0	1	0	0	2	0	0	0	1		4	8	1
Pirates	0	0	0	0	1	0	0	0	0		1	5	0

E—Peckinpaugh. DP—Senators 1 (Peckinpaugh to Judge), Pirates 1 (Grantham). LOB—Senators 3, Pirates 5. Scoring Position—Senators 3-for-7, Pirates 0-for-5. HR—JHarris (1), Traynor (1). S—Judge. GDP—Moore. SB—Grantham (1), Bigbee (1). CS—Carey (1), Cuyler (1).

Senators	IP	H	R	ER	BB	K	ERA
Walter Johnson (W, 1-0)	9.0	5	1	1	1	10	1.00

Pirates	IP	H	R	ER	BB	K	ERA
Lee Meadows (L, 0-1)	8.0	6	3	3	0	4	3.38
Johnny Morrison	1.0	2	1	1	0	1	9.00

HBP—BHarris by Meadows, Carey by Johnson, Carey by Johnson. Time—1:57. Attendance—41,723. Umpires—HP, Rigler. 1B, Owens. 2B, McCormick. 3B, Moriarty.

Game 2

Thursday, October 8

Senators	AB	R	H	RBI	BB	K	Avg
Sam Rice, cf	5	0	2	0	0	0	.444
Bucky Harris, 2b	3	0	0	0	0	1	.000
Goose Goslin, lf	4	0	0	0	0	0	.125
Joe Judge, 1b	4	1	1	1	0	0	.143
Joe Harris, rf	3	0	2	0	1	0	.571
Earl McNeely, pr	0	1	0	0	0	0	—
Ossie Bluege, 3b	2	0	0	0	0	0	.333
Buddy Myer, pr-3b	1	0	1	0	0	0	1.000
Roger Peckinpaugh, ss	3	0	1	0	1	0	.286
Muddy Ruel, c	3	0	1	0	0	1	.167
Bobby Veach, ph	0	0	0	1	0	0	—
Stan Coveleski, p	2	0	0	0	0	1	.000
Dutch Ruether, ph	1	0	0	0	0	1	.000
TOTALS	31	2	8	2	2	4	.267

Pirates	AB	R	H	RBI	BB	K	Avg
Eddie Moore, 2b	4	1	0	0	0	0	.000
Max Carey, cf	4	0	2	0	0	1	.333
Kiki Cuyler, rf	3	1	1	2	0	0	.286

(continued top of next column)

Clyde Barnhart, lf	4	0	1	0	0	0	.250
Pie Traynor, 3b	3	0	0	0	1	0	.286
Glenn Wright, ss	4	1	2	1	0	0	.250
George Grantham, 1b	4	0	0	0	0	0	.000
Earl Smith, c	3	0	1	0	0	1	.333
Vic Aldridge, p	3	0	0	0	0	0	.000
TOTALS	32	3	7	3	1	3	.200

	1	2	3	4	5	6	7	8	9		R	H	E
Senators	0	1	0	0	0	0	0	0	1		2	8	2
Pirates	0	0	0	1	0	0	0	2	x		3	7	0

E—Peckinpaugh 2. LOB—Senators 8, Pirates 7. Scoring Position—Senators 0-for-8, Pirates 1-for-7. HR—Judge (1), Cuyler (1), Wright (1). S—BHarris, Coveleski, Cuyler. SF—Veach. CS—JHarris (1), Myer (1).

Senators	IP	H	R	ER	BB	K	ERA
Stan Coveleski (L, 0-1)	8.0	7	3	2	1	3	2.25

Pirates	IP	H	R	ER	BB	K	ERA
Vic Aldridge (W, 1-0)	9.0	8	2	2	4	2.00

Balk—Aldridge. PB—Ruel. HBP—Bluege by Aldridge. Time—2:04. Attendance—43,364. Umpires—HP, Owens. 1B, McCormick. 2B, Moriarty. 3B, Rigler.

Game 3

Saturday, October 10

Pirates	AB	R	H	RBI	BB	K	Avg
Eddie Moore, 2b	3	0	1	0	2	1	.091
Max Carey, cf	4	0	2	0	0	1	.400
Kiki Cuyler, rf	4	1	1	0	0	0	.273
Clyde Barnhart, lf	5	0	1	1	0	0	.231
Pie Traynor, 3b	4	1	1	0	1	0	.273
Glenn Wright, ss	3	1	0	1	0	1	.182
George Grantham, 1b	4	0	0	0	0	2	.000
Earl Smith, c	3	0	1	0	1	0	.333
Ray Kremer, p	3	0	1	1	0	2	.333
Carson Bigbee, ph	1	0	0	0	0	0	.000
TOTALS	34	3	8	3	4	7	.220

Senators	AB	R	H	RBI	BB	K	Avg
Sam Rice, cf-rf	5	1	2	0	0	0	.429
Bucky Harris, 2b	3	1	1	0	0	0	.111
Goose Goslin, lf	4	1	2	1	0	1	.250
Joe Judge, 1b	3	0	1	2	0	0	.200
Joe Harris, rf	4	0	2	1	0	1	.545
Firpo Marberry, p	0	0	0	0	0	0	—
Buddy Myer, 3b	3	0	0	0	1	1	.250
Roger Peckinpaugh, ss	4	0	1	0	0	0	.273
Muddy Ruel, c	3	0	1	0	1	0	.222
Alex Ferguson, p	2	0	0	0	0	2	.000
Nemo Leibold, ph	0	0	0	0	1	0	—
Earl McNeely, pr-cf	0	1	0	0	0	0	—
TOTALS	31	4	10	4	3	5	.293

	1	2	3	4	5	6	7	8	9		R	H	E
Pirates	0	1	0	1	0	1	0	0	0		3	8	2
Senators	0	0	1	0	0	1	2	0	x		4	10	1

E—Wright, Carey, Peckinpaugh. DP—Pirates 1 (Moore to Grantham), Senators 1 (Peckinpaugh to BHarris to Judge). LOB—Pirates 11, Senators 9. Scoring Position—Pirates 2-for-12, Senators 3-for-9. 2B—Carey (1), Cuyler (1), Judge (1). 3B—Traynor (1). HR—Goslin (1). S—BHarris, Marberry. SF—Wright, Judge. GDP—Barnhart, BHarris. CS—Peckinpaugh (1).

Pirates	IP	H	R	ER	BB	K	ERA
Ray Kremer (L, 0-1)	8.0	10	4	4	3	5	4.50

Senators	IP	H	R	ER	BB	K	ERA
Alex Ferguson (W, 1-0)	7.0	6	3	2	4	5	2.57
Firpo Marberry (S, 1)	2.0	2	0	0	0	2	0.00

PB—Smith. HBP—Cuyler by Marberry, Carey by Ferguson.

Time—2:10. Attendance—36,495. Umpires—HP, McCormick. 1B, Moriarty. 2B, Rigler. 3B, Owens.

Game 4

Sunday, October 11

Pirates	AB	R	H	RBI	BB	K	Avg
Eddie Moore, 2b	4	0	1	0	0	0	.133
Max Carey, cf	3	0	1	0	1	0	.385
Kiki Cuyler, rf	4	0	0	0	0	1	.200
Clyde Barnhart, lf	3	0	0	0	1	1	.188
Pie Traynor, 3b	4	0	2	0	0	0	.333
Glenn Wright, ss	4	0	0	0	0	0	.133
George Grantham, 1b	3	0	2	0	0	0	.143
Johnny Gooch, c	3	0	0	0	0	0	.000
Emil Yde, p	1	0	0	0	0	0	.000
Johnny Morrison, p	1	0	0	0	0	0	.000
Carson Bigbee, ph	1	0	0	0	0	0	.000
Babe Adams, p	0	0	0	0	0	0	—
TOTALS	31	0	6	0	2	2	.200

Senators	AB	R	H	RBI	BB	K	Avg
Sam Rice, cf	5	1	2	0	0	0	.421
Bucky Harris, 2b	3	1	1	0	1	0	.167
Goose Goslin, lf	3	1	2	3	1	1	.333
Joe Harris, rf	4	1	1	0	1	0	.467
Joe Judge, 1b	3	0	0	0	1	0	.154
Roger Peckinpaugh, ss	4	0	1	0	0	1	.267
Muddy Ruel, c	3	0	3	0	0	0	.417
Buddy Myer, 3b	4	0	1	0	0	1	.250
Walter Johnson, p	4	0	1	0	0	1	.143
TOTALS	33	4	12	4	4	5	.310

	1	2	3	4	5	6	7	8	9		R	H	E
Pirates	0	0	0	0	0	0	0	0	0		0	6	1
Senators	0	0	4	0	0	0	0	0	x		4	12	0

E—Wright. DP—Pirates 1 (Traynor to Moore to Grantham), Senators 2 (BHarris to Judge; BHarris to Judge). LOB—Pirates 6, Senators 9. Scoring Position—Pirates 0-for-4, Senators 2-for-9. 2B—Ruel (1). HR—Goslin (2), JHarris (2). GDP—Traynor, JHarris. SB—Carey (1), Peckinpaugh (1). CS—BHarris (1), Judge (1).

Pirates	IP	H	R	ER	BB	K	ERA
Emil Yde (L, 0-1)	2.1	5	4	3	3	1	11.57
Johnny Morrison	4.2	5	0	0	1	4	1.59
Babe Adams	1.0	2	0	0	0	0	0.00

Senators	IP	H	R	ER	BB	K	ERA
Walter Johnson (W, 2-0)	9.0	6	0	0	2	2	0.50

Time—2:00. Attendance—38,701. Umpires—HP, Moriarty. 1B, Rigler. 2B, Owens. 3B, McCormick.

Game 5
Monday, October 12

Pirates	AB	R	H	RBI	BB	K	Avg
Eddie Moore, 2b	4	1	1	0	1	0	.158
Max Carey, cf	4	2	2	0	1	0	.412
Kiki Cuyler, rf	4	1	2	1	1	0	.263
Clyde Barnhart, lf	4	1	2	2	1	0	.250
Pie Traynor, 3b	3	0	1	1	1	1	.333
Glenn Wright, ss	5	1	2	1	0	0	.200
Stuffy McInnis, 1b	5	0	1	1	0	0	.167
Earl Smith, c	3	0	2	0	0	0	.417
Vic Aldridge, p	4	0	0	0	0	0	.000
TOTALS	36	6	13	6	5	1	.261

Senators	AB	R	H	RBI	BB	K	Avg
Sam Rice, cf	5	1	2	1	0	0	.417
Bucky Harris, 2b	3	0	0	0	0	0	.133
Goose Goslin, lf	4	0	1	1	0	0	.316
Joe Judge, 1b	3	0	0	0	1	1	.125
Joe Harris, rf	3	1	2	1	1	0	.500
Roger Peckinpaugh, ss	3	0	0	0	0	1	.222
Muddy Ruel, c	3	0	1	0	0	1	.400
Ossie Bluege, 3b	4	0	1	0	0	2	.300
Stan Coveleski, p	1	0	0	0	1	1	.000
Win Ballou, p	0	0	0	0	0	0	—
Nemo Leibold, ph	1	1	1	0	0	0	1.000
Tom Zachary, p	0	0	0	0	0	0	—
Firpo Marberry, p	0	0	0	0	0	0	—
Spencer Adams, ph	1	0	0	0	0	0	.000
TOTALS	31	3	8	3	4	5	.307

	1	2	3	4	5	6	7	8	9		R	H	E
Pirates	0	0	2	0	0	0	2	1	1		6	13	0
Senators	1	0	0	1	0	0	1	0	0		3	8	1

E—Peckinpaugh. DP—Pirates 1 (Smith to Traynor), Senators 2 (Bluege to BHarris to Judge; Coveleski to Peckinpaugh to Judge). LOB—Pirates 10, Senators 8. Scoring Position—Pirates 5-for-12, Senators 2-for-9. 2B—Wright (1), Goslin (1), Bluege (1), Leibold (1). HR—JHarris (3). S—Smith, BHarris 2, Peckinpaugh. SF—Traynor. GDP—Smith, Aldridge. SB—Carey (2), Barnhart (1). CS—Cuyler (2), JHarris (2).

Pirates	IP	H	R	ER	BB	K	ERA
Vic Aldridge (W, 2-0)	9.0	8	3	3	4	5	2.50

Senators	IP	H	R	ER	BB	K	ERA
Stan Coveleski (L, 0-2)	6.1	9	4	4	4	0	3.77
Win Ballou	0.2	0	0	0	0	1	0.00
Tom Zachary	1.2	3	2	2	1	0	10.80
Firpo Marberry	0.1	1	0	0	0	0	0.00

Time—2:26. Attendance—35,899. Umpires—HP, Rigler. 1B, Owens. 2B, McCormick. 3B, Moriarty.

Game 6
Tuesday, October 13

Senators	AB	R	H	RBI	BB	K	Avg
Sam Rice, cf	4	0	0	0	0	0	.357
Bucky Harris, 2b	3	0	0	0	0	0	.111
Bobby Veach, ph	1	0	0	0	0	0	.000
Win Ballou, p	0	0	0	0	0	0	—
Goose Goslin, lf-lf	3	1	1	1	1	0	.318
Joe Harris, rf	4	0	1	0	0	1	.455
Joe Judge, 1b	4	0	1	0	0	1	.150
Ossie Bluege, 3b	4	1	1	0	0	0	.286
Roger Peckinpaugh, ss	3	0	1	1	0	0	.238
Hank Severeid, c	3	0	1	0	0	0	.333
Earl McNeely, pr	0	0	0	0	0	0	—
Spencer Adams, 2b	0	0	0	0	0	0	.000
Alex Ferguson, p	2	0	0	0	0	1	.000
Nemo Leibold, ph	1	0	0	0	0	0	.500
Muddy Ruel, c	0	0	0	0	0	0	.400
TOTALS	32	2	6	2	1	3	.287

Pirates	AB	R	H	RBI	BB	K	Avg
Eddie Moore, 2b	3	2	2	1	1	0	.227
Max Carey, cf	2	1	0	0	0	0	.368
Kiki Cuyler, rf	3	0	0	0	0	0	.227
Clyde Barnhart, lf	3	0	1	1	1	0	.261
Pie Traynor, 3b	4	0	2	1	0	0	.364
Glenn Wright, ss	3	0	0	0	1	1	.174
Stuffy McInnis, 1b	4	0	1	0	0	1	.200
Earl Smith, c	4	0	1	0	0	1	.375
Ray Kremer, p	3	0	0	0	0	3	.167
TOTALS	29	3	7	3	3	6	.270

	1	2	3	4	5	6	7	8	9		R	H	E
Senators	1	1	0	0	0	0	0	0	0		2	6	2
Pirates	0	0	2	0	1	0	0	0	x		3	7	1

E—Kremer, Severeid, Peckinpaugh. DP—Senators 1 (Judge). LOB—Senators 4, Pirates 8. Scoring Position—Senators 0-for-7, Pirates 1-for-9. 2B—JHarris (1), Peckinpaugh (1), Barnhart (1). HR—Goslin (3), Moore (1). S—Carey 2, Cuyler. SB—Traynor (1), McNeely (1). CS—Bluege (1).

Senators	IP	H	R	ER	BB	K	ERA
Alex Ferguson (L, 1-1)	7.0	7	3	3	2	6	3.21
Win Ballou	1.0	0	0	0	1	0	0.00

Pirates	IP	H	R	ER	BB	K	ERA
Ray Kremer (W, 1-1)	9.0	6	2	2	1	3	3.18

Time—1:57. Attendance—43,810. Umpires—HP, Owens. 1B, McCormick. 2B, Moriarty. 3B, Rigler.

Game 7
Thursday, October 15

Senators	AB	R	H	RBI	BB	K	Avg
Sam Rice, cf	5	2	2	0	0	1	.364
Bucky Harris, 2b	5	0	0	0	0	2	.087
Goose Goslin, lf	4	2	1	0	1	1	.308
Joe Harris, rf	3	1	1	2	1	0	.440
Joe Judge, 1b	3	1	1	0	1	0	.174
Ossie Bluege, 3b	4	0	1	1	0	0	.278
Roger Peckinpaugh, ss	3	1	1	2	0	0	.250
Muddy Ruel, c	4	0	0	1	0	0	.316
Walter Johnson, p	4	0	0	0	0	1	.091
TOTALS	35	7	7	6	3	5	.272

Pirates	AB	R	H	RBI	BB	K	Avg
Eddie Moore, 2b	4	3	1	1	1	0	.231
Max Carey, cf	5	3	4	2	0	0	.458
Kiki Cuyler, rf	4	0	2	3	0	1	.269
Clyde Barnhart, lf	5	0	1	0	0	2	.250
Red Oldham, p	0	0	0	0	0	0	—
Pie Traynor, 3b	4	0	1	1	0	0	.346
Glenn Wright, ss	4	0	1	0	0	0	.185
Stuffy McInnis, 1b	4	0	2	0	0	0	.286
Earl Smith, c	4	0	1	0	0	0	.350
Emil Yde, pr	0	1	0	0	0	0	.000
Johnny Gooch, c	0	0	0	0	0	0	—
Vic Aldridge, p	0	0	0	0	0	0	.000
Johnny Morrison, p	1	1	1	0	0	0	.500
George Grantham, ph	1	0	0	0	0	0	.133
Ray Kremer, p	1	0	0	0	0	0	.143
Carson Bigbee, ph-lf	1	1	1	1	0	0	.333
TOTALS	38	9	15	9	1	3	.266

	1	2	3	4	5	6	7	8	9		R	H	E
Senators	4	0	0	2	0	0	0	1	0		7	7	2
Pirates	0	0	3	0	1	0	2	3	x		9	15	3

E—Moore, Cuyler, Smith, Peckinpaugh 2. DP—Senators 1 (BHarris to Judge). LOB—Senators 5, Pirates 7. Scoring Position—Senators 2-for-7, Pirates 7-for-16. 2B—JHarris (2), Moore (1), Carey 3 (4), Cuyler 2 (3), Smith (1), Bigbee (1). 3B—Traynor (2). HR—Peckinpaugh (1). S—Cuyler. GDP—Smith. SB—Carey (3).

Senators	IP	H	R	ER	BB	K	ERA
Walter Johnson (L, 2-1)	8.0	15	9	5	1	3	2.08

Pirates	IP	H	R	ER	BB	K	ERA
Vic Aldridge	0.1	2	4	4	3	0	4.42
Johnny Morrison	3.2	4	2	2	0	2	2.89
Ray Kremer (W, 2-1)	4.0	1	1	1	0	1	3.00
Red Oldham (S, 1)	1.0	0	0	0	0	2	0.00

Reached, Catcher's Interference—Senators 1, Peckinpaugh by Smith. Pirates 0. WP—Aldridge 2. Time—2:31. Attendance—42,856. Umpires—HP, McCormick. 1B, Moriarty. 2B, Rigler. 3B, Owens.

1925 World Series—Composite Statistics

Batting

Pirates

Pirates	G	AB	R	H	RBI	2B	3B	HR	BB	SO	SB	CS	Avg	OBP	Slg
Vic Aldridge	3	7	0	0	0	0	0	0	0	0	0	0	.000	.000	.000
Clyde Barnhart	7	28	1	7	5	1	0	0	3	5	1	0	.250	.323	.206
Carson Bigbee	4	3	1	1	1	1	0	0	0	0	1	0	.333	.333	.667
Max Carey	7	24	6	11	2	4	0	0	2	3	3	1	.458	.552	.625
Kiki Cuyler	7	26	3	7	6	3	0	1	1	4	0	2	.269	.321	.500
Johnny Gooch	3	3	0	0	0	0	0	0	0	0	0	0	.000	.000	.000
George Grantham	5	15	0	2	0	0	0	0	0	3	1	0	.133	.133	.133
Ray Kremer	3	7	0	1	1	0	0	0	0	5	0	0	.143	.143	.143
Stuffy McInnis	4	14	0	4	1	0	0	0	0	2	0	0	.286	.286	.286
Lee Meadows	1	1	0	0	0	0	0	0	0	1	1	0	.000	.500	.000
Eddie Moore	7	26	7	6	2	1	0	1	5	2	0	0	.231	.355	.385
Johnny Morrison	3	2	1	1	0	0	0	0	0	0	0	0	.500	.500	.500
Earl Smith	6	20	0	7	0	1	0	0	1	2	0	0	.350	.381	.400
Pie Traynor	7	26	2	9	4	0	2	1	3	1	1	0	.346	.400	.615
Glenn Wright	7	27	3	5	3	1	0	1	1	4	0	0	.185	.207	.333
Emil Yde	2	1	1	0	0	0	0	0	0	0	0	0	.000	.000	.000
Totals	7	230	25	61	25	12	2	4	17	32	7	3	.265	.324	.387

Senators

Senators	G	AB	R	H	RBI	2B	3B	HR	BB	SO	SB	CS	Avg	OBP	Slg
Spencer Adams	2	1	0	0	0	0	0	0	0	0	0	0	.000	.000	.000
Ossie Bluege	5	18	2	5	2	1	0	0	0	4	0	1	.278	.316	.333
Stan Coveleski	2	3	0	0	0	0	0	0	1	2	0	0	.000	.250	.000
Alex Ferguson	2	4	0	0	0	0	0	0	0	3	0	0	.000	.000	.000
Goose Goslin	7	26	6	8	6	1	0	3	3	3	0	0	.308	.379	.692
Bucky Harris	7	23	2	2	0	0	0	0	1	3	0	1	.087	.160	.087
Joe Harris	7	25	5	11	6	2	0	3	3	4	0	2	.440	.500	.880
Walter Johnson	3	11	0	1	0	0	0	0	0	3	0	0	.091	.091	.091
Joe Judge	7	23	2	4	3	1	0	1	3	2	0	1	.174	.259	.348
Nemo Leibold	3	2	1	1	0	1	0	0	1	0	0	0	.500	.667	1.000
Firpo Marberry	2	0	0	0	0	0	0	0	0	0	0	0	—	—	—
Earl McNeely	4	0	2	0	0	0	0	0	0	0	1	0	—	—	—
Buddy Myer	3	8	0	2	0	0	0	0	1	2	0	1	.250	.333	.250
Roger Peckinpaugh	7	24	1	6	3	1	0	1	1	2	1	1	.250	.280	.417
Sam Rice	7	33	5	12	3	0	0	0	1	0	0	0	.364	.364	.364
Muddy Ruel	7	19	0	6	1	1	0	0	3	2	0	0	.316	.409	.368
Dutch Ruether	1	1	0	0	0	0	0	0	0	1	0	0	.000	.000	.000
Hank Severeid	1	3	0	1	0	0	0	0	0	0	0	0	.333	.333	.333
Bobby Veach	2	1	0	0	1	0	0	0	0	0	0	0	.000	.000	.000
Totals	7	225	26	59	25	8	0	8	17	32	2	7	.262	.317	.404

Pitching

Pirates

Pirates	G	GS	CG	IP	H	R	ER	BB	SO	W-L	Sv-Op	Hld	ERA
Babe Adams	1	0	0	1.0	2	0	0	0	0	0-0	0-0	0	0.00
Vic Aldridge	3	3	2	18.1	18	9	9	9	9	2-0	0-0	0	4.42
Ray Kremer	3	2	2	21.0	17	7	7	4	9	2-1	0-0	0	3.00
Lee Meadows	1	1	0	8.0	6	3	3	0	4	0-1	0-0	0	3.38
Johnny Morrison	3	0	0	9.1	11	3	3	1	7	0-0	0-0	0	2.89
Red Oldham	1	0	0	1.0	0	0	0	0	2	0-0	1-1	0	0.00
Emil Yde	1	1	0	2.1	5	4	3	3	1	0-1	0-0	0	11.57
Totals	7	7	4	61.0	59	26	25	17	32	4-3	1-1	0	3.69

Senators

Senators	G	GS	CG	IP	H	R	ER	BB	SO	W-L	Sv-Op	Hld	ERA
Win Ballou	2	0	0	1.2	0	0	0	0	1	0-0	0-0	0	0.00
Stan Coveleski	2	2	1	14.1	16	7	6	5	3	0-2	0-0	0	3.77
Alex Ferguson	2	2	0	14.0	13	6	5	6	11	1-1	0-0	0	3.21
Walter Johnson	3	3	3	26.0	26	10	6	4	15	2-1	0-0	0	2.08
Firpo Marberry	2	0	0	2.1	3	0	0	0	2	0-0	1-1	0	0.00
Tom Zachary	1	0	0	1.2	3	2	2	1	0	0-0	0-0	0	10.80
Totals	7	7	4	60.0	61	25	19	17	32	3-4	1-1	0	2.85

Fielding

Pirates

Pirates	Pos	G	PO	Ast	E	DP	PB	FPct
Babe Adams	p	1	0	0	0	0	—	—
Vic Aldridge	p	3	0	4	0	0	—	1.000
Clyde Barnhart	lf	7	12	1	0	0	—	1.000
Carson Bigbee	lf	1	0	0	0	0	—	—
Max Carey	cf	7	14	0	1	0	—	.933
Kiki Cuyler	rf	7	12	0	1	0	—	.923
Johnny Gooch	c	3	9	3	0	0	0	1.000
George Grantham	1b	4	41	6	0	3	—	1.000
Ray Kremer	p	3	2	3	1	0	—	.833
Stuffy McInnis	1b	3	30	3	0	0	—	1.000
Lee Meadows	p	1	0	2	0	0	—	1.000
Eddie Moore	2b	7	16	14	1	2	—	.968
Johnny Morrison	p	3	0	3	0	0	—	1.000
Red Oldham	p	1	0	0	0	0	—	—
Earl Smith	c	6	29	7	1	1	1	.973
Pie Traynor	3b	7	6	18	0	2	—	1.000
Glenn Wright	ss	7	12	23	2	0	—	.946
Emil Yde	p	1	0	0	0	0	—	—
Totals		7	183	87	7	8	1	.975

Senators

Senators	Pos	G	PO	Ast	E	DP	PB	FPct
Spencer Adams	2b	1	0	0	0	0	—	—
Win Ballou	p	2	0	0	0	0	—	—
Ossie Bluege	3b	5	1	13	0	1	—	1.000
Stan Coveleski	p	2	0	4	0	1	—	1.000
Alex Ferguson	p	2	0	1	0	0	—	1.000
Goose Goslin	lf	7	15	0	0	0	—	1.000
Bucky Harris	2b	7	23	18	0	5	—	1.000
Joe Harris	rf	7	11	1	0	0	—	1.000
Walter Johnson	p	3	0	4	0	0	—	1.000
Joe Judge	1b	7	60	2	0	8	—	1.000
Firpo Marberry	p	2	0	0	0	0	—	—
Earl McNeely	cf	2	3	0	0	0	—	1.000
Buddy Myer	3b	1	1	1	0	0	—	1.000
Roger Peckinpaugh	ss	7	10	22	8	3	—	.800
Sam Rice	cf	7	14	0	0	0	—	1.000
	rf	2	1	0	0	0	—	1.000
Muddy Ruel	c	7	35	5	0	0	1	1.000
Hank Severeid	c	1	6	0	1	0	0	.857
Tom Zachary	p	1	0	3	0	0	—	1.000
Totals		7	180	74	9	18	1	.966

1926 St. Louis Cardinals (NL) 4, New York Yankees (AL) 3

In a big upset, the St. Louis Cardinals defeated the New York Yankees in seven games to win their first World Series. New York's Herb Pennock won the opener with a three-hitter, 2-1. Billy Southworth's three-run homer in the top of the seventh sent the Cards to a 6-2 win in Game 2. St. Louis' Jesse Haines stole the show in Game 3, blanking the Yanks on five hits while belting a two-run homer. Babe Ruth swatted three home runs in Game 4 as the Yanks romped, 10-5. Tony Lazzeri's sacrifice fly in the top of the 10th won Game 5 for New York, 3-2. Les Bell had a homer and a pair of singles in St. Louis' 10-2 win in Game 6. The Cards took Game 7, 3-2, as Pete Alexander came in to strike out Lazzeri to end a Yankees threat in the seventh. Ruth was thrown out stealing on a hit-and-run to end the Series.

Game 1

Saturday, October 2

Cardinals	AB	R	H	RBI	BB	K	Avg
Taylor Douthit, cf	3	1	1	0	1	0	.333
Billy Southworth, rf	3	0	0	0	0	0	.000
Wattie Holm, ph-rf	1	0	0	0	0	0	.000
Rogers Hornsby, 2b	4	0	0	0	0	0	.000
Jim Bottomley, 1b	4	0	2	1	0	1	.500
Les Bell, 3b	3	0	0	0	1	1	.000
Chick Hafey, lf	4	0	0	0	0	0	.000
Bob O'Farrell, c	2	0	0	0	1	0	.000
Tommy Thevenow, ss	2	0	0	0	0	0	.000
Bill Sherdel, p	2	0	0	0	0	1	.000
Jake Flowers, ph	1	0	0	0	0	0	.000
Jesse Haines, p	0	0	0	0	0	0	—
TOTALS	29	1	3	1	3	4	.103

Yankees	AB	R	H	RBI	BB	K	Avg
Earle Combs, cf	3	1	1	0	1	0	.333
Mark Koenig, ss	4	0	1	0	0	0	.250
Babe Ruth, rf	3	1	1	0	1	0	.333
Bob Meusel, lf	1	0	0	0	2	0	.000
Lou Gehrig, 1b	4	0	1	2	0	0	.250
Tony Lazzeri, 2b	4	0	1	0	0	1	.250
Joe Dugan, 3b	3	0	1	0	0	0	.333
Hank Severeid, c	3	0	0	0	0	0	.000
Herb Pennock, p	2	0	0	0	0	0	.000
TOTALS	27	2	6	2	4	1	.222

	1	2	3	4	5	6	7	8	9	R	H	E
Cardinals	1	0	0	0	0	0	0	0	0	1	3	1
Yankees	1	0	0	0	0	1	0	0	x	2	6	0

E—Bell. DP—Cardinals 1 (Thevenow to Hornsby to Bottomley). LOB—Cardinals 5, Yankees 7. Scoring Position—Cardinals 1-for-5, Yankees 1-for-7. 2B—Douthit (1). S—Thevenow, Meusel, Pennock. GDP—Koenig.

Cardinals	IP	H	R	ER	BB	K	ERA
Bill Sherdel (L, 0-1)	7.0	6	2	2	3	1	2.57
Jesse Haines	1.0	0	0	0	1	0	0.00

Yankees	IP	H	R	ER	BB	K	ERA
Herb Pennock (W, 1-0)	9.0	3	1	1	3	4	1.00

Time—1:48. Attendance—61,658. Umpires—HP, Dinneen. 1B, O'Day. 2B, Hildebrand. 3B, Klem.

Game 2

Sunday, October 3

Cardinals	AB	R	H	RBI	BB	K	Avg
Taylor Douthit, cf	4	1	1	0	1	1	.286
Billy Southworth, rf	5	2	3	3	0	0	.375
Rogers Hornsby, 2b	3	0	1	0	1	0	.143
Jim Bottomley, 1b	5	0	2	2	0	0	.444
Les Bell, 3b	4	0	0	0	0	1	.000
Chick Hafey, lf	4	0	0	0	0	1	.000
Bob O'Farrell, c	4	1	2	0	0	0	.333
Tommy Thevenow, ss	4	2	3	1	0	0	.500
Pete Alexander, p	4	0	0	0	0	2	.000
TOTALS	37	6	12	6	2	5	.242

Yankees	AB	R	H	RBI	BB	K	Avg
Earle Combs, cf	3	0	1	0	1	0	.333
Mark Koenig, ss	4	0	0	0	0	1	.125
Babe Ruth, rf	4	0	0	0	0	1	.143
Bob Meusel, lf	4	1	1	0	0	1	.200
Lou Gehrig, 1b	3	0	0	0	1	0	.143
Tony Lazzeri, 2b	3	1	1	1	0	1	.286
Joe Dugan, 3b	3	0	1	0	0	1	.333
Hank Severeid, c	2	0	0	0	0	1	.000
Ben Paschal, ph	1	0	0	0	0	1	.000
Pat Collins, c	0	0	0	0	0	0	—
Urban Shocker, p	2	0	0	0	0	2	.000
Bob Shawkey, p	0	0	0	0	0	0	—
Dutch Ruether, ph	1	0	0	0	0	0	.000
Sad Sam Jones, p	0	0	0	0	0	0	—
TOTALS	30	2	4	1	1	10	.182

	1	2	3	4	5	6	7	8	9	R	H	E
Cardinals	0	0	2	0	0	0	3	0	1	6	12	1
Yankees	0	2	0	0	0	0	0	0	0	2	4	0

E—Alexander. DP—Cardinals 1 (Alexander to Thevenow to Hornsby to Bottomley). LOB—Cardinals 7, Yankees 2. Scoring Position—Cardinals 3-for-8, Yankees 1-for-3. 2B—Hornsby (1), O'Farrell (1). HR—Southworth (1), Thevenow (1). S—Hornsby. GDP—Koenig. CS—Bottomley (1), Lazzeri (1).

Cardinals	IP	H	R	ER	BB	K	ERA
Pete Alexander (W, 1-0)	9.0	4	2	1	1	10	1.00

Yankees	IP	H	R	ER	BB	K	ERA
Urban Shocker (L, 0-1)	7.0	10	5	5	0	2	6.43
Bob Shawkey	1.0	0	0	0	0	0	0.00
Sad Sam Jones	1.0	2	1	1	2	1	9.00

Shocker pitched to one batter in the 8th.

Time—1:57. Attendance—63,600. Umpires—HP, O'Day. 1B, Hildebrand. 2B, Klem. 3B, Dinneen.

Game 3

Tuesday, October 5

Yankees	AB	R	H	RBI	BB	K	Avg
Earle Combs, cf	3	0	1	0	1	1	.333
Mark Koenig, ss	4	0	0	0	0	1	.083
Babe Ruth, rf	3	0	1	0	1	0	.200
Bob Meusel, lf	4	0	0	0	0	0	.111
Lou Gehrig, 1b	4	0	2	0	0	0	.273
Tony Lazzeri, 2b	4	0	0	0	0	1	.182
Joe Dugan, 3b	3	0	1	0	0	0	.333
Hank Severeid, c	2	0	0	0	0	0	.000
Dutch Ruether, p	2	0	0	0	0	0	.000
Bob Shawkey, p	0	0	0	0	0	0	—
Ben Paschal, ph	0	0	0	0	1	0	.000
Myles Thomas, p	0	0	0	0	0	0	—
TOTALS	29	0	5	0	3	3	.183

Cardinals	AB	R	H	RBI	BB	K	Avg
Taylor Douthit, cf	3	0	0	0	1	1	.200
Billy Southworth, rf	3	1	2	0	0	0	.455
Rogers Hornsby, 2b	4	0	1	0	0	0	.182
Jim Bottomley, 1b	4	0	1	1	0	0	.385
Les Bell, 3b	4	1	1	0	0	1	.091
Chick Hafey, lf	3	0	1	0	0	0	.091
Bob O'Farrell, c	2	0	0	0	1	0	.250
Tommy Thevenow, ss	3	1	0	0	0	0	.333
Jesse Haines, p	3	1	2	2	0	0	.667
TOTALS	29	4	8	3	2	2	.264

	1	2	3	4	5	6	7	8	9	R	H	E
Yankees	0	0	0	0	0	0	0	0	0	0	5	1
Cardinals	0	0	0	3	1	0	0	0	x	4	8	0

E—Koenig. DP—Yankees 1 (Koenig to Lazzeri to Gehrig), Cardinals 1 (Hornsby to Thevenow to Bottomley). LOB—Yankees 6, Cardinals 5. Scoring Position—Yankees 0-for-7, Cardinals 0-for-8. 2B—Hafey (1). HR—Haines (1). S—Severeid, Southworth, Hafey. GDP—Koenig, Lazzeri, Bell.

Yankees	IP	H	R	ER	BB	K	ERA
Dutch Ruether (L, 0-1)	4.1	7	4	2	2	1	4.15
Bob Shawkey	2.2	0	0	0	0	1	0.00
Myles Thomas	1.0	1	0	0	0	0	0.00

Cardinals	IP	H	R	ER	BB	K	ERA
Jesse Haines (W, 1-0)	9.0	5	0	0	3	3	0.00

Time—1:41. Attendance—37,708. Umpires—HP, Hildebrand. 1B, Klem. 2B, Dinneen. 3B, O'Day.

Game 4

Wednesday, October 6

Yankees	AB	R	H	RBI	BB	K	Avg
Earle Combs, cf	5	2	2	1	1	1	.357
Mark Koenig, ss	6	1	1	1	0	3	.111
Babe Ruth, lf	3	4	3	4	2	0	.385
Bob Meusel, rf	2	1	1	0	3	0	.182
Lou Gehrig, 1b	3	0	2	1	1	1	.357
Tony Lazzeri, 2b	3	1	1	1	1	0	.214
Joe Dugan, 3b	4	0	1	2	1	0	.308
Hank Severeid, c	4	1	3	0	1	0	.273
Waite Hoyt, p	4	0	0	0	1	0	.000
TOTALS	34	10	14	10	10	6	.259

Cardinals	AB	R	H	RBI	BB	K	Avg
Taylor Douthit, cf	5	1	2	1	0	0	.267
Billy Southworth, rf	5	0	3	0	0	0	.500
Rogers Hornsby, 2b	5	1	2	1	0	2	.250
Jim Bottomley, 1b	4	0	1	0	0	0	.353
Les Bell, 3b	4	0	1	1	0	0	.133
Chick Hafey, lf	5	1	1	0	0	2	.125
Bob O'Farrell, c	4	1	2	0	0	0	.333
Tommy Thevenow, ss	4	1	2	1	0	1	.385
Flint Rhem, p	1	0	0	0	0	1	.000
Specs Toporcer, ph	0	0	0	1	0	0	—
Art Reinhart, p	0	0	0	0	0	0	—
Hi Bell, p	0	0	0	0	0	0	—
Jake Flowers, ph	1	0	0	0	0	1	.000
Wild Bill Hallahan, p	0	0	0	0	0	0	—
Wattie Holm, ph	1	0	0	0	0	1	.000
Vic Keen, p	0	0	0	0	0	0	—
TOTALS	39	5	14	5	1	8	.280

	1	2	3	4	5	6	7	8	9	R	H	E
Yankees	1	0	1	1	4	2	1	0	0	10	14	1
Cardinals	1	0	0	3	0	0	0	0	1	5	14	0

E—Koenig. LOB—Yankees 10, Cardinals 10. Scoring Position—Yankees 2-for-8, Cardinals 5-for-11. 2B—Combs (1), Koenig (1), Gehrig (1), Lazzeri (1), Dugan (1), Douthit (2), Thevenow (1). HR—Ruth 3 (3). S—Gehrig, Hoyt. SF—Lazzeri, LBell, Toporcer. SB—Hornsby (1).

Yankees	IP	H	R	ER	BB	K	ERA
Waite Hoyt (W, 1-0)	9.0	14	5	2	1	8	2.00

Cardinals	IP	H	R	ER	BB	K	ERA
Flint Rhem	4.0	7	3	3	2	4	6.75
Art Reinhart (L, 0-1)	0.0	1	4	4	4	0	—
Hi Bell	2.0	4	2	2	1	1	9.00
Wild Bill Hallahan	2.0	2	1	1	3	1	4.50
Vic Keen	1.0	0	0	0	0	0	0.00

Reinhart pitched to five batters in the 5th.

Balk—HBell. Time—2:38. Attendance—38,825. Umpires—HP, Klem. 1B, Dinneen. 2B, O'Day. 3B, Hildebrand.

Game 5
Thursday, October 7

Yankees	AB	R	H	RBI	BB	K	Avg
Earle Combs, cf	4	0	1	0	1	0	.333
Mark Koenig, ss	5	1	2	1	0	0	.174
Babe Ruth, lf	3	0	0	0	2	1	.313
Bob Meusel, rf	3	0	0	0	0	0	.143
Lou Gehrig, 1b	3	1	2	0	2	1	.412
Tony Lazzeri, 2b	4	0	2	1	0	0	.278
Joe Dugan, 3b	3	0	0	0	0	0	.250
Ben Paschal, ph	1	0	1	1	0	0	.500
Mike Gazella, 3b	0	0	0	0	0	0	—
Hank Severeid, c	5	0	0	0	0	0	.188
Herb Pennock, p	4	1	1	0	0	0	.167
TOTALS	35	3	9	3	5	2	.260

Cardinals	AB	R	H	RBI	BB	K	Avg
Wattie Holm, cf	4	0	0	0	1	1	.000
Billy Southworth, rf	4	0	0	0	0	0	.400
Rogers Hornsby, 2b	4	0	0	0	0	0	.200
Jim Bottomley, 1b	4	1	1	0	0	1	.333
Les Bell, 3b	4	1	2	1	0	1	.211
Chick Hafey, lf	4	0	0	0	0	0	.100
Bob O'Farrell, c	4	0	3	1	0	0	.438
Tommy Thevenow, ss	4	0	1	0	0	0	.353
Bill Sherdel, p	3	0	0	0	0	1	.000
Jake Flowers, ph	1	0	0	0	0	0	.259
TOTALS	36	2	7	2	1	4	.259

	1 2 3	4 5 6	7 8 9 10	R	H	E
Yankees	0 0 0	0 0 1	0 0 1 1	3	9	1
Cardinals	0 0 0	1 0 0	1 0 0 0	2	7	1

E—Koenig, Thevenow. DP—Yankees 1 (Lazzeri to Koenig to Gehrig), Cardinals 1 (Hornsby to Bottomley). LOB—Yankees 11, Cardinals 5. Scoring Position—Yankees 3-for-10, Cardinals 2-for-7. 2B—Gehrig (2), Pennock (1), Bottomley (1), Bell (1). S—Meusel. SF—Meusel, Lazzeri. GDP—Dugan, Hornsby. CS—Bell (1).

Yankees	IP	H	R	ER	BB	K	ERA
Herb Pennock (W, 2-0)	10.0	7	2	2	1	4	1.42

Cardinals	IP	H	R	ER	BB	K	ERA
Bill Sherdel (L, 0-2)	10.0	9	3	2	5	2	2.12

WP—Sherdel. PB—Severeid. HBP—Gazella by Sherdel. Time—2:28. Attendance—39,552. Umpires—HP, Dinneen. 1B, O'Day. 2B, Hildebrand. 3B, Klem.

Game 6
Saturday, October 9

Cardinals	AB	R	H	RBI	BB	K	Avg
Wattie Holm, cf	5	1	2	1	0	0	.182
Billy Southworth, rf	5	3	2	1	0	0	.400
Rogers Hornsby, 2b	4	1	1	3	1	0	.208
Jim Bottomley, 1b	5	2	2	1	0	0	.346
Les Bell, 3b	4	1	3	4	1	1	.304
Chick Hafey, lf	3	0	1	0	0	2	.130
Bob O'Farrell, c	4	0	0	0	0	2	.350
Tommy Thevenow, ss	3	1	2	0	0	0	.400
Pete Alexander, p	2	1	0	0	0	0	.000
TOTALS	35	10	13	10	2	5	.287

Yankees	AB	R	H	RBI	BB	K	Avg
Earle Combs, cf	5	0	2	1	0	0	.348
Mark Koenig, ss	5	0	0	0	0	1	.143
Babe Ruth, rf	3	0	0	1	1	0	.263
Bob Meusel, lf	3	1	2	0	1	0	.235
Lou Gehrig, 1b	4	0	1	1	0	1	.381
Tony Lazzeri, 2b	4	0	0	0	0	0	.227
Joe Dugan, 3b	4	1	2	0	0	0	.300
Hank Severeid, c	3	0	1	0	0	1	.211
Spencer Adams, pr	0	0	0	0	0	0	—
Pat Collins, c	1	0	0	0	0	1	.000
Bob Shawkey, p	2	0	0	0	0	1	.000
Urban Shocker, p	0	0	0	0	0	0	.000
Ben Paschal, ph	1	0	0	0	0	1	.333
Myles Thomas, p	0	0	0	0	0	0	—
Dutch Ruether, ph	1	0	0	0	0	0	.000
TOTALS	36	2	8	2	2	6	.249

	1 2 3	4 5 6	7 8 9	R	H	E
Cardinals	3 0 0	0 1 0	5 0 1	10	13	2
Yankees	0 0 0	1 0 0	1 0 0	2	8	1

E—Lazzeri, Thevenow, Bell. DP—Cardinals 1 (Southworth to Thevenow), Yankees 1 (Gehrig to Koenig). LOB—Cardinals 4, Yankees 9. Scoring Position—Cardinals 5-for-12, Yankees 1-for-15. 2B—Southworth (1), Bottomley 2 (3), Hafey (2), Combs (2), Meusel (1). 3B—Southworth (1), Meusel (1). HR—Bell (1). S—Hafey, Alexander 2. GDP—Holm. SB—Ruth (1). CS—Bell (2).

Cardinals	IP	H	R	ER	BB	K	ERA
Pete Alexander (W, 2-0)	9.0	8	2	2	6		1.50

Yankees	IP	H	R	ER	BB	K	ERA
Bob Shawkey (L, 0-1)	6.1	8	7	6	2	4	5.40
Urban Shocker	0.2	3	2	2	0	1	8.22
Myles Thomas	2.0	2	1	1	0	0	3.00

HBP—Thevenow by Thomas. Time—2:05. Attendance—48,615. Umpires—HP, O'Day. 1B, Hildebrand. 2B, Klem. 3B, Dinneen.

Game 7
Sunday, October 10

Cardinals	AB	R	H	RBI	BB	K	Avg
Wattie Holm, cf	5	0	0	0	0	0	.125
Billy Southworth, rf	4	0	0	0	0	0	.345
Rogers Hornsby, 2b	4	0	2	0	0	0	.250
Jim Bottomley, 1b	3	1	1	0	0	0	.345
Les Bell, 3b	4	1	0	0	0	0	.259
Chick Hafey, lf	4	1	2	0	0	1	.185
Bob O'Farrell, c	3	0	0	1	0	0	.304
Tommy Thevenow, ss	4	0	2	2	0	0	.417
Jesse Haines, p	2	0	1	0	0	1	.600
Pete Alexander, p	1	0	0	0	0	0	.000
TOTALS	34	3	8	3	0	2	.284

Yankees	AB	R	H	RBI	BB	K	Avg
Earle Combs, cf	5	0	2	0	0	0	.357
Mark Koenig, ss	4	0	0	0	0	0	.125
Babe Ruth, rf	1	1	1	1	4	0	.300
Bob Meusel, lf	4	0	1	0	0	0	.238
Lou Gehrig, 1b	2	0	0	0	2	0	.348
Tony Lazzeri, 2b	4	0	0	0	0	3	.192
Joe Dugan, 3b	4	1	2	0	0	0	.333
Hank Severeid, c	3	0	2	1	0	0	.273
Spencer Adams, pr	0	0	0	0	0	0	—
Pat Collins, c	1	0	0	0	0	0	.000
Waite Hoyt, p	2	0	0	0	0	0	.000
Ben Paschal, ph	1	0	0	0	0	0	.250
Herb Pennock, p	1	0	0	0	0	0	.143
TOTALS	32	2	8	2	6	3	.251

	1 2 3	4 5 6	7 8 9	R	H	E
Cardinals	0 0 0	3 0 0	0 0 0	3	8	0
Yankees	0 0 1	0 0 1	0 0 0	2	8	3

E—Koenig, Meusel, Dugan. LOB—Cardinals 7, Yankees 10. Scoring Position—Cardinals 3-for-9, Yankees 0-for-6. 2B—Severeid (1). HR—Ruth (4). S—Bottomley, Haines, Koenig. SF—O'Farrell. CS—Hafey (1), Ruth (1), Dugan (1).

Cardinals	IP	H	R	ER	BB	K	ERA
Jesse Haines (W, 2-0)	6.2	8	2	2	5	2	1.08
Pete Alexander (S, 1)	2.1	0	0	0	1	1	1.33

Yankees	IP	H	R	ER	BB	K	ERA
Waite Hoyt (L, 1-1)	6.0	5	3	0	0	2	1.20
Herb Pennock	3.0	3	0	0	0	0	1.23

Time—2:15. Attendance—38,093. Umpires—HP, Hildebrand. 1B, Klem. 2B, Dinneen. 3B, O'Day.

1926 World Series—Composite Statistics

Batting

Cardinals	G	AB	R	H	RBI	2B	3B	HR	BB	SO	SB	CS	Avg	OBP	Slg
Pete Alexander	3	7	1	0	0	0	0	0	0	2	0	0	.000	.000	.000
Les Bell	7	27	4	7	6	1	0	1	2	5	0	2	.259	.300	.407
Jim Bottomley	7	29	4	10	5	3	0	0	1	2	0	1	.345	.367	.448
Taylor Douthit	4	15	3	4	1	2	0	0	3	2	0	0	.267	.389	.400
Jake Flowers	3	3	0	0	0	0	0	0	0	1	0	0	.000	.000	.000
Chick Hafey	7	27	2	5	0	2	0	0	0	7	0	1	.185	.185	.259
Jesse Haines	3	5	1	3	2	0	0	1	0	1	0	0	.600	.600	1.200
Wattie Holm	5	16	1	2	1	0	0	0	1	2	0	0	.125	.176	.125
Rogers Hornsby	7	28	2	7	4	1	0	0	2	2	1	0	.250	.300	.286
Bob O'Farrell	7	23	2	7	2	1	0	0	2	2	0	0	.304	.346	.348
Flint Rhem	1	1	0	0	0	0	0	0	0	1	0	0	.000	.000	.000
Bill Sherdel	2	5	0	0	0	0	0	0	0	2	0	0	.000	.000	.000
Billy Southworth	7	29	6	10	4	1	1	1	0	0	0	0	.345	.345	.552
Tommy Thevenow	7	24	5	10	4	1	0	1	0	1	0	0	.417	.440	.583
Specs Toporcer	1	0	0	0	1	0	0	0	0	0	0	0	—	.000	—
Totals	7	239	31	65	30	12	1	4	11	30	1	4	.272	.303	.381

Yankees	G	AB	R	H	RBI	2B	3B	HR	BB	SO	SB	CS	Avg	OBP	Slg
Spencer Adams	2	0	0	0	0	0	0	0	0	0	0	0	—	—	—
Pat Collins	3	2	0	0	0	0	0	0	1	0	0	0	.000	.000	.000
Earle Combs	7	28	3	10	2	2	0	0	5	2	0	0	.357	.455	.429
Joe Dugan	7	24	2	8	2	1	0	0	1	1	0	1	.333	.360	.375
Mike Gazella	1	0	0	0	0	0	0	0	0	0	0	0	—	1.000	—
Lou Gehrig	7	23	1	8	4	2	0	0	5	4	0	0	.348	.464	.435
Waite Hoyt	2	6	0	0	0	0	0	0	0	1	0	0	.000	.000	.000
Mark Koenig	7	32	2	4	2	1	0	0	0	6	0	0	.125	.125	.156
Tony Lazzeri	7	26	2	5	3	1	0	1	6	0	1	.192	.207	.231
Bob Meusel	7	21	3	5	0	1	1	0	6	1	0	0	.238	.393	.381
Ben Paschal	5	4	0	1	1	0	0	0	1	2	0	0	.250	.400	.250
Herb Pennock	3	7	1	1	0	1	0	0	0	0	0	0	.143	.143	.286
Dutch Ruether	3	4	0	0	0	0	0	0	0	0	0	0	.000	.000	.000
Babe Ruth	7	20	6	6	5	0	0	4	11	2	1	1	.300	.548	.900
Hank Severeid	7	22	1	6	1	1	0	0	1	2	0	0	.273	.304	.318
Bob Shawkey	3	2	0	0	0	0	0	0	0	1	0	0	.000	.000	.000
Urban Shocker	2	2	0	0	0	0	0	0	0	2	0	0	.000	.000	.000
Totals	7	223	21	54	20	10	1	4	31	31	1	3	.242	.333	.350

Pitching

Cardinals	G	GS	CG	IP	H	R	ER	BB	SO	W-L	Sv-Op	Hld	ERA
Pete Alexander	3	2	2	20.1	12	4	3	4	17	2-0	1-1	0	1.33
Hi Bell	1	0	0	2.0	4	2	2	1	1	0-0	0-0	0	9.00
Jesse Haines	3	2	1	16.2	13	2	2	9	5	2-0	0-0	0	1.08
Wild Bill Hallahan	1	0	0	2.0	2	1	1	3	1	0-0	0-0	0	4.50
Vic Keen	1	0	0	1.0	0	0	0	0	0	0-0	0-0	0	0.00
Art Reinhart	1	0	0	0.0	1	4	4	4	0	0-1	0-0	0	—
Flint Rhem	1	1	0	4.0	7	3	3	2	4	0-0	0-0	0	6.75
Bill Sherdel	2	2	1	17.0	15	5	4	8	3	0-2	0-0	0	2.12
Totals	7	7	4	63.0	54	21	19	31	31	4-3	1-1	0	2.71

Yankees	G	GS	CG	IP	H	R	ER	BB	SO	W-L	Sv-Op	Hld	ERA
Waite Hoyt	2	2	1	15.0	19	8	2	1	10	1-1	0-0	0	1.20
Sad Sam Jones	1	0	0	1.0	2	1	1	2	1	0-0	0-0	0	9.00
Herb Pennock	3	2	2	22.0	13	3	3	4	8	2-0	0-0	0	1.23
Dutch Ruether	1	1	0	4.1	7	4	2	2	1	0-1	0-0	0	4.15
Bob Shawkey	3	1	0	10.0	8	7	6	2	7	0-1	0-0	0	5.40
Urban Shocker	2	1	0	7.2	13	7	7	0	3	0-1	0-0	0	8.22
Myles Thomas	2	0	0	3.0	3	1	1	0	0	0-0	0-0	0	3.00
Totals	7	7	3	63.0	65	31	22	11	30	3-4	0-0	0	3.14

Fielding

Cardinals	Pos	G	PO	Ast	E	DP	PB	FPct
Pete Alexander	p	3	0	6	1	1	—	.857
Hi Bell	p	1	0	0	0	0	—	—
Les Bell	3b	7	7	16	2	0	—	.920
Jim Bottomley	1b	7	79	1	0	5	—	1.000
Taylor Douthit	cf	4	5	2	0	0	—	1.000
Chick Hafey	lf	7	20	1	0	0	—	1.000
Jesse Haines	p	3	0	6	0	0	—	1.000
Wild Bill Hallahan	p	1	1	0	0	0	—	1.000
Wattie Holm	cf	3	7	0	0	0	—	1.000
	rf	1	0	0	0	0	—	—
Rogers Hornsby	2b	7	16	21	0	5	—	1.000
Vic Keen	p	1	0	1	0	0	—	1.000
Bob O'Farrell	c	7	35	8	0	0	0	1.000
Art Reinhart	p	1	0	0	0	0	—	—
Flint Rhem	p	1	0	1	0	0	—	1.000
Bill Sherdel	p	2	2	5	0	0	—	1.000
Billy Southworth	rf	7	8	3	0	1	—	1.000
Tommy Thevenow	ss	7	9	26	2	5	—	.946
Totals		7	189	97	5	17	0	.983

Yankees	Pos	G	PO	Ast	E	DP	PB	FPct
Pat Collins	c	3	1	0	0	0	0	1.000
Earle Combs	cf	7	17	0	0	0	—	1.000
Joe Dugan	3b	7	7	14	1	0	—	.955
Mike Gazella	3b	1	1	2	0	0	—	1.000
Lou Gehrig	1b	7	77	1	0	3	—	1.000
Waite Hoyt	p	2	0	1	0	0	—	1.000
Sad Sam Jones	p	1	0	0	0	0	—	—
Mark Koenig	ss	7	12	24	4	3	—	.900
Tony Lazzeri	2b	7	15	19	1	2	—	.971
Bob Meusel	lf	5	12	0	1	0	—	.923
	rf	2	1	0	0	0	—	1.000
Herb Pennock	p	3	0	6	0	0	—	1.000
Dutch Ruether	p	1	0	2	0	0	—	1.000
Babe Ruth	rf	5	4	1	0	0	—	1.000
	lf	2	4	1	0	0	—	1.000
Hank Severeid	c	7	38	7	0	0	1	1.000
Bob Shawkey	p	3	0	1	0	0	—	1.000
Urban Shocker	p	2	0	2	0	0	—	1.000
Myles Thomas	p	2	0	2	0	0	—	1.000
Totals		7	189	83	7	8	1	.975

1927 New York Yankees (AL) 4, Pittsburgh Pirates (NL) 0

The New York Yankees' superlative slugging, combined with the Pittsburgh Pirates' sloppy play, led to a four-game New York sweep. The Pirates self destructed in Game 1, fueling a critical three-run Yankees rally with two errors and a bases-loaded walk, as Waite Hoyt and Wilcy Moore combined for a 5-4 victory. Lou Gehrig's double, an error and two sacrifice flies keyed a three-run third-inning rally as the Yanks took Game 2, 6-2. Herb Pennock took a perfect game into the eighth inning and Babe Ruth hit a three-run homer in the Yankees' 8-1 Game 3 victory. The fourth game was tied 3-3 with the bases loaded in the bottom of the ninth when Pittsburgh pitcher Johnny Miljus threw a wild pitch that enabled Earle Combs to scoot home with the winning run. Ruth drove in seven runs and hit the only two homers of the Series.

Game 1

Wednesday, October 5

Yankees	AB	R	H	RBI	BB	K	Avg
Earle Combs, cf	4	0	0	0	0	1	.000
Mark Koenig, ss	4	2	1	0	0	1	.250
Babe Ruth, rf	4	2	3	0	0	1	.750
Lou Gehrig, 1b	2	1	1	2	1	0	.500
Bob Meusel, lf	3	0	0	1	1	1	.000
Tony Lazzeri, 2b	4	0	1	1	0	0	.250
Joe Dugan, 3b	3	0	0	0	0	0	.000
Pat Collins, c	2	0	0	2	0	0	.000
Waite Hoyt, p	3	0	0	0	0	0	.000
Wilcy Moore, p	1	0	0	0	0	1	.000
TOTALS	30	5	6	4	4	4	.200

Pirates	AB	R	H	RBI	BB	K	Avg
Lloyd Waner, cf	4	2	1	0	0	0	.250
Clyde Barnhart, lf	5	0	1	1	0	0	.200
Paul Waner, rf	4	0	3	1	0	0	.750
Glenn Wright, ss	2	1	1	1	0	0	.500
Pie Traynor, 3b	4	0	1	0	0	0	.250
George Grantham, 2b	3	0	0	0	1	0	.000
Joe Harris, 1b	4	0	1	1	0	0	.250
Earl Smith, c	4	0	0	0	0	0	.000
Ray Kremer, p	2	1	1	0	0	1	.500
Johnny Miljus, p	1	0	0	0	0	1	.000
George Brickell, ph	1	0	0	0	0	0	.000
TOTALS	34	4	9	4	1	2	.265

	1	2	3	4	5	6	7	8	9		R	H	E
Yankees	1	0	3	0	1	0	0	0	0		5	6	1
Pirates	1	0	1	0	1	0	0	1	0		4	9	2

E—Grantham, Meusel, Smith. DP—Yankees 1 (Lazzeri to Gehrig), Pirates 1 (Wright to Grantham to Harris). LOB—Yankees 4, Pirates 7. Scoring Position—Yankees 0-for-5, Pirates 3-for-11. 2B—Koenig (1), Lazzeri (1), LWaner (1), PWaner (1), Kremer (1). 3B—Gehrig (1). S—Dugan. SF—Gehrig, Wright 2. GDP—Hoyt, Harris. CS—Ruth (1).

Yankees	IP	H	R	ER	BB	K	ERA
Waite Hoyt (W, 1-0)	7.1	8	4	4	1	2	4.91
Wilcy Moore (S, 1)	1.2	1	0	0	0	0	0.00

Pirates	IP	H	R	ER	BB	K	ERA
Ray Kremer (L, 0-1)	5.0	5	5	2	3	1	3.60
Johnny Miljus	4.0	1	0	0	1	3	0.00

Kremer pitched to one batter in the 6th.

HBP—LWaner by Hoyt. Time—2:04. Attendance—41,467. Umpires—HP, Quigley. 1B, Nallin. 2B, Moran. 3B, Ormsby.

Game 2

Thursday, October 6

Yankees	AB	R	H	RBI	BB	K	Avg
Earle Combs, cf	4	1	1	1	0	1	.125
Mark Koenig, ss	5	1	3	1	0	0	.444
Babe Ruth, rf	3	0	0	1	1	1	.429
Lou Gehrig, 1b	3	1	1	0	1	0	.400
Bob Meusel, lf	5	1	2	0	0	1	.250
Tony Lazzeri, 2b	4	0	2	1	0	0	.375
Joe Dugan, 3b	5	1	1	0	0	0	.125
Benny Bengough, c	3	1	0	0	1	0	.000
George Pipgras, p	3	0	1	0	1	1	.333
TOTALS	35	6	11	4	4	4	.288

Pirates	AB	R	H	RBI	BB	K	Avg
Lloyd Waner, cf	3	2	1	0	1	0	.286
Clyde Barnhart, lf	3	0	2	1	0	0	.375
Paul Waner, rf	3	0	1	1	0	1	.571
Glenn Wright, ss	4	0	0	0	0	0	.167
Pie Traynor, 3b	4	0	1	0	0	0	.250
George Grantham, 2b	4	0	2	0	0	1	.286
Joe Harris, 1b	4	0	0	0	0	0	.125
Johnny Gooch, c	3	0	0	0	0	0	.000
Vic Aldridge, p	2	0	0	0	0	0	.000
Mike Cvengros, p	0	0	0	0	0	0	—
Earl Smith, ph	1	0	0	0	0	0	.000
Joe Dawson, p	0	0	0	0	0	0	—
TOTALS	31	2	7	2	1	2	.246

	1	2	3	4	5	6	7	8	9		R	H	E
Yankees	0	0	3	0	0	0	0	3	0		6	11	0
Pirates	1	0	0	0	0	0	0	1	0		2	7	2

E—LWaner, Wright. DP—Yankees 1 (Lazzeri to Koenig). LOB—Yankees 10, Pirates 5. Scoring Position—Yankees 2-for-9, Pirates 0-for-5. 2B—Gehrig (1), Grantham (1). 3B—LWaner (1). SF—Ruth, Gehrig, Lazzeri, Barnhart, PWaner. SB—Meusel (1).

Yankees	IP	H	R	ER	BB	K	ERA
George Pipgras (W, 1-0)	9.0	7	2	2	1	2	2.00

Pirates	IP	H	R	ER	BB	K	ERA
Vic Aldridge (L, 0-1)	7.1	10	6	6	4	4	7.36
Mike Cvengros	0.2	1	0	0	0	0	0.00
Joe Dawson	1.0	0	0	0	0	0	0.00

WP—Aldridge. HBP—Combs by Cvengros. Time—2:20. Attendance—41,634. Umpires—HP, Nallin. 1B, Moran. 2B, Ormsby. 3B, Quigley.

Game 3

Friday, October 7

Pirates	AB	R	H	RBI	BB	K	Avg
Lloyd Waner, cf	4	0	1	0	0	0	.273
Hal Rhyne, 2b	4	0	0	0	0	0	.000
Paul Waner, rf	4	0	0	0	0	0	.364
Glenn Wright, ss	3	0	0	0	0	0	.111
Pie Traynor, 3b	3	1	1	0	0	0	.273
Clyde Barnhart, lf	3	0	1	1	0	0	.364
Joe Harris, 1b	3	0	0	0	0	0	.091
Johnny Gooch, c	2	0	0	0	0	1	.000
Roy Spencer, ph-c	1	0	0	0	0	0	.000
Lee Meadows, p	2	0	0	0	0	0	.000
Mike Cvengros, p	0	0	0	0	0	0	—
Heine Groh, ph	1	0	0	0	0	0	.000
TOTALS	30	1	3	1	0	1	.208

Yankees	AB	R	H	RBI	BB	K	Avg
Earle Combs, cf	4	2	2	1	0	0	.250
Mark Koenig, ss	4	2	2	1	0	0	.462
Babe Ruth, rf	4	1	1	3	0	1	.364
Lou Gehrig, 1b	3	0	2	2	1	1	.500
Bob Meusel, lf	4	0	0	0	0	3	.167
Tony Lazzeri, 2b	4	1	1	0	0	0	.333
Joe Dugan, 3b	3	1	1	0	0	0	.182
Johnny Grabowski, c	2	0	0	0	0	0	.000
Cedric Durst, ph	1	0	0	0	0	0	.000
Benny Bengough, c	1	0	0	0	0	0	.000
Herb Pennock, p	4	1	0	1	0	0	.000
TOTALS	34	8	9	8	1	8	.278

	1	2	3	4	5	6	7	8	9		R	H	E
Yankees	0	0	3	0	0	0	0	3	0		6	11	0
Pirates	1	0	0	0	0	0	0	1	0		2	7	2

E—LWaner, Wright. DP—Yankees 1 (Lazzeri to Koenig). LOB—Yankees 10, Pirates 5. Scoring Position—Yankees 2-for-9, Pirates 0-for-5. 2B—Gehrig (1), Grantham (1). 3B—LWaner (1). SF—Ruth, Gehrig, Lazzeri, Barnhart, PWaner. SB—Meusel (1).

Pirates	IP	H	R	ER	BB	K	ERA
Lee Meadows (L, 0-1)	6.1	7	7	7	1	6	9.95
Mike Cvengros	1.2	2	1	1	0	2	3.86

Yankees	IP	H	R	ER	BB	K	ERA
Herb Pennock (W, 1-0)	9.0	3	1	1	0	1	1.00

Time—2:04. Attendance—60,695. Umpires—HP, Moran. 1B, Ormsby. 2B, Quigley. 3B, Nallin.

Game 4

Saturday, October 8

Pirates	AB	R	H	RBI	BB	K	Avg
Lloyd Waner, cf	4	1	3	0	0	0	.400
Clyde Barnhart, lf	5	0	1	1	0	0	.313
Paul Waner, rf	4	0	1	1	0	0	.333
Glenn Wright, ss	4	0	1	0	0	0	.154
Pie Traynor, 3b	4	0	0	0	0	1	.200
George Grantham, 2b	4	0	2	0	0	1	.364
Joe Harris, 1b	4	0	0	0	0	0	.200
Earl Smith, c	3	0	0	0	0	0	.000
Emil Yde, pr	0	1	0	0	0	0	—
Johnny Gooch, c	0	0	0	0	0	1	.000
Carmen Hill, p	1	0	0	0	0	1	.000
George Brickell, ph	1	1	0	0	0	0	.000
Johnny Miljus, p	1	0	0	0	0	1	.000
TOTALS	35	3	10	3	2	2	.237

Yankees	AB	R	H	RBI	BB	K	Avg
Earle Combs, cf	4	3	2	0	1	0	.313
Mark Koenig, ss	5	0	3	0	0	1	.500
Babe Ruth, rf	4	1	2	3	1	0	.400
Lou Gehrig, 1b	5	0	0	0	0	0	.308
Bob Meusel, lf	5	0	0	0	0	2	.118
Tony Lazzeri, 2b	3	0	0	0	1	2	.267
Joe Dugan, 3b	4	0	1	0	0	0	.200
Pat Collins, c	3	0	3	0	0	0	.600
Wilcy Moore, p	4	0	1	0	0	2	.200
TOTALS	37	4	12	3	4	9	.311

	1	2	3	4	5	6	7	8	9		R	H	E
Pirates	1	0	0	0	0	0	2	0	0		3	10	1
Yankees	1	0	0	0	2	0	0	0	1		4	12	2

E—Moore, LWaner, Lazzeri. DP—Pirates 1 (Traynor to Wright to Harris), Yankees 2 (Lazzeri to Gehrig; Dugan to Lazzeri to Gehrig). LOB—Pirates 9, Yankees 11. Scoring Position—Pirates 3-for-7, Yankees 1-for-11. 2B—Collins (1). HR—Ruth (2). S—LWaner. SF—PWaner. GDP—Barnhart, Wright, Ruth. SB—Ruth (1).

Pirates	IP	H	R	ER	BB	K	ERA
Carmen Hill	6.0	9	3	3	1	6	4.50
Johnny Miljus (L, 0-1)	2.2	3	1	1	3	3	1.35

Yankees	IP	H	R	ER	BB	K	ERA
Wilcy Moore (W, 1-0)	9.0	10	3	1	2	2	0.84

WP—Miljus 2. Time—2:15. Attendance—57,909. Umpires—HP, Ormsby. 1B, Quigley. 2B, Nallin. 3B, Moran.

1927 World Series—Composite Statistics

Batting

Yankees	G	AB	R	H	RBI	2B	3B	HR	BB	SO	SB	CS	Avg	OBP	Slg
Benny Bengough	2	4	1	0	0	0	0	0	1	0	0	0	.000	.200	.000
Pat Collins	2	5	0	3	0	1	0	0	3	0	0	0	.600	.750	.800
Earle Combs	4	16	6	5	2	0	0	0	1	2	0	0	.313	.389	.313
Joe Dugan	4	15	2	3	0	0	0	0	0	0	0	0	.200	.200	.200
Cedric Durst	1	1	0	0	0	0	0	0	0	0	0	0	.000	.000	.000
Lou Gehrig	4	13	2	4	4	2	2	0	3	3	0	0	.308	.389	.769
Johnny Grabowski	1	2	0	0	0	0	0	0	0	0	0	0	.000	.000	.000
Waite Hoyt	1	3	0	0	0	0	0	0	0	0	0	0	.000	.000	.000
Mark Koenig	4	18	5	9	2	2	0	0	0	2	0	0	.500	.500	.611
Tony Lazzeri	4	15	1	4	2	1	0	0	1	4	0	0	.267	.294	.333
Bob Meusel	4	17	1	2	1	0	0	0	1	7	1	0	.118	.167	.118
Wilcy Moore	2	5	0	1	0	0	0	0	0	3	0	0	.200	.200	.200
Herb Pennock	1	4	1	0	1	0	0	0	0	1	0	0	.000	.000	.000
George Pipgras	1	3	0	1	0	0	0	0	1	1	0	0	.333	.500	.333
Babe Ruth	4	15	4	6	7	0	0	2	2	2	1	1	.400	.444	.800
Totals	4	136	23	38	19	6	2	2	13	25	2	1	.279	.338	.397

Pirates	G	AB	R	H	RBI	2B	3B	HR	BB	SO	SB	CS	Avg	OBP	Slg
Vic Aldridge	1	2	0	0	0	0	0	0	0	0	0	0	.000	.000	.000
Clyde Barnhart	4	16	0	5	4	1	0	0	0	0	0	0	.313	.294	.375
George Brickell	2	2	1	0	0	0	0	0	0	0	0	0	.000	.000	.000
Johnny Gooch	3	5	0	0	0	0	0	0	1	1	0	0	.000	.167	.000
George Grantham	3	11	0	4	0	1	0	0	1	1	0	0	.364	.417	.455
Heine Groh	1	1	0	0	0	0	0	0	0	0	0	0	.000	.000	.000
Joe Harris	4	15	0	3	1	0	0	0	0	0	0	0	.200	.200	.200
Carmen Hill	1	1	0	0	0	0	0	0	1	0	0	0	.000	.500	.000
Ray Kremer	1	2	1	1	0	1	0	0	0	1	0	0	.500	.500	1.000
Lee Meadows	1	2	0	0	0	0	0	0	0	0	0	0	.000	.000	.000
Johnny Miljus	2	2	0	0	0	0	0	0	0	2	0	0	.000	.000	.000
Hal Rhyne	1	4	0	0	0	0	0	0	0	0	0	0	.000	.000	.000
Earl Smith	3	8	0	0	0	0	0	0	0	0	0	0	.000	.000	.000
Roy Spencer	1	1	0	0	0	0	0	0	0	0	0	0	.000	.000	.000
Pie Traynor	4	15	1	3	0	1	0	0	0	1	0	0	.200	.200	.267
Lloyd Waner	4	15	5	6	0	1	1	0	1	0	0	0	.400	.471	.600
Paul Waner	4	15	0	5	3	1	0	0	0	1	0	0	.333	.294	.400
Glenn Wright	4	13	1	2	2	0	0	0	0	0	0	0	.154	.133	.154
Emil Yde	1	0	1	0	0	0	0	0	0	0	0	0	—	—	—
Totals	4	130	10	29	10	6	1	0	4	7	0	0	.223	.243	.285

Pitching

Yankees	G	GS	CG	IP	H	R	ER	BB	SO	W-L	Sv-Op	Hld	ERA
Waite Hoyt	1	1	0	7.1	8	4	4	1	2	1-0	0-0	0	4.91
Wilcy Moore	2	1	1	10.2	11	3	1	2	2	1-0	1-1	0	0.84
Herb Pennock	1	1	1	9.0	3	1	1	0	1	1-0	0-0	0	1.00
George Pipgras	1	1	1	9.0	7	2	2	1	2	1-0	0-0	0	2.00
Totals	4	4	3	36.0	29	10	8	4	7	4-0	1-1	0	2.00

Pirates	G	GS	CG	IP	H	R	ER	BB	SO	W-L	Sv-Op	Hld	ERA
Vic Aldridge	1	1	0	7.1	10	6	6	4	4	0-1	0-0	0	7.36
Mike Cvengros	2	0	0	2.1	3	1	1	0	2	0-0	0-0	0	3.86
Joe Dawson	1	0	0	1.0	0	0	0	0	0	0-0	0-0	0	0.00
Carmen Hill	1	1	0	6.0	9	3	3	1	6	0-0	0-0	0	4.50
Ray Kremer	1	1	0	5.0	5	5	2	3	1	0-1	0-0	0	3.60
Lee Meadows	1	1	0	6.1	7	7	7	1	6	0-1	0-0	0	9.95
Johnny Miljus	2	0	0	6.2	4	1	1	4	6	0-1	0-0	0	1.35
Totals	4	4	0	34.2	38	23	20	13	25	0-4	0-0	0	5.19

Fielding

Yankees	Pos	G	PO	Ast	E	DP	PB	FPct
Benny Bengough	c	2	4	0	0	0	0	1.000
Pat Collins	c	2	5	1	0	0	0	1.000
Earle Combs	cf	4	16	0	0	0	—	1.000
Joe Dugan	3b	4	3	6	0	1	—	1.000
Lou Gehrig	1b	4	41	3	0	3	—	1.000
Johnny Grabowski	c	1	3	0	0	0	0	1.000
Waite Hoyt	p	1	0	0	0	0	—	—
Mark Koenig	ss	4	6	8	0	1	—	1.000
Tony Lazzeri	2b	4	10	18	1	4	—	.966
Bob Meusel	lf	4	8	0	1	0	—	.889
Wilcy Moore	p	2	0	5	1	0	—	.833
Herb Pennock	p	1	1	1	0	0	—	1.000
George Pipgras	p	1	1	2	0	0	—	1.000
Babe Ruth	rf	4	10	0	0	0	—	1.000
Totals		4	108	44	3	9	0	.981

Pirates	Pos	G	PO	Ast	E	DP	PB	FPct
Vic Aldridge	p	1	0	2	0	0	—	1.000
Clyde Barnhart	lf	4	6	0	0	0	—	1.000
Mike Cvengros	p	2	0	0	0	0	—	—
Joe Dawson	p	1	0	0	0	0	—	—
Johnny Gooch	c	3	19	1	0	0	0	1.000
George Grantham	2b	3	7	7	1	1	—	.933
Joe Harris	1b	4	35	1	0	2	—	1.000
Carmen Hill	p	1	0	0	0	0	—	—
Ray Kremer	p	1	0	0	0	0	—	—
Lee Meadows	p	1	0	1	0	0	—	1.000
Johnny Miljus	p	2	1	2	0	0	—	1.000
Hal Rhyne	2b	1	0	6	0	0	—	1.000
Earl Smith	c	2	10	1	1	0	0	.917
Roy Spencer	c	1	0	0	0	0	0	—
Pie Traynor	3b	4	5	9	1	1	—	.933
Lloyd Waner	cf	4	8	1	2	0	—	.818
Paul Waner	rf	4	8	0	0	0	—	1.000
Glenn Wright	ss	4	5	13	1	2	—	.947
Totals		4	104	44	6	6	0	.961

1928 New York Yankees (AL) 4, St. Louis Cardinals (NL) 0

Babe Ruth and Lou Gehrig teamed up to destroy the St. Louis Cardinals, as the Yankees took the Series in four games. Game 1 saw Waite Hoyt beat St. Louis' Bill Sherdel, 4-1. Gehrig's three-run homer helped the Yanks to beat Pete Alexander in Game 2, 9-3. The score was tied 3-3 in the sixth inning of Game 3 when Babe Ruth tried to score on an overthrow. The throw beat him, but he knocked the ball out of catcher Jimmie Wilson's glove to score the go-ahead run. Bob Meusel then stole home on the front end of a double steal, and the Yanks rode to victory, 7-3, as Gehrig drove in three runs with a pair of homers. Ruth hit a game-tying homer off Bill Sherdel in the fourth inning of Game 4, and batted again in the seventh with the Yankees down a run. Sherdel got two strikes on Ruth and threw a "quick pitch" by Ruth for strike three, but umpire Charles Pfirman disallowed it. Ruth homered to tie the score, and Gehrig followed with another dinger to put the Yanks ahead for good. Ruth later added his third homer of the game as New York finished the sweep with a 7-3 victory.

Game 1

Thursday, October 4

Cardinals	AB	R	H	RBI	BB	K	Avg
Taylor Douthit, cf	3	0	0	1	1	.000
Andy High, 3b	4	0	0	0	0	2	.000
Frankie Frisch, 2b	4	0	0	0	0	0	.000
Jim Bottomley, 1b	3	1	2	1	1	0	.667
Chick Hafey, lf	4	0	0	0	0	2	.000
George Harper, rf	3	0	1	0	0	0	.333
Jimmie Wilson, c	3	0	0	0	0	0	.000
Rabbit Maranville, ss	2	0	0	0	0	0	.000
Ernie Orsatti, ph	0	0	0	0	1	0	—
Tommy Thevenow, ss	0	0	0	0	0	0	—
Bill Sherdel, p	2	0	0	0	0	1	.000
Wattie Holm, ph	1	0	0	0	0	0	.000
Syl Johnson, p	0	0	0	0	0	0	—
TOTALS	29	1	3	1	3	6	.103

Yankees	AB	R	H	RBI	BB	K	Avg
Ben Paschal, cf	4	0	0	0	0	0	.000
Cedric Durst, cf	0	0	0	0	0	0	—
Mark Koenig, ss	4	1	1	0	0	0	.250
Babe Ruth, rf	4	2	3	0	0	1	.750
Lou Gehrig, 1b	4	0	2	2	0	0	.500
Bob Meusel, lf	4	1	1	2	0	0	.250
Tony Lazzeri, 2b	2	0	0	0	0	0	.000
Leo Durocher, 2b	1	0	0	0	0	1	.000
Joe Dugan, 3b	3	0	0	0	0	0	.000
Benny Bengough, c	3	0	0	0	0	0	.000
Waite Hoyt, p	3	0	0	0	0	0	.000
TOTALS	32	4	7	4	0	2	.219

	1	2	3	4	5	6	7	8	9	R	H	E
Cardinals	0	0	0	0	0	0	1	0	0	1	3	1
Yankees	1	0	0	2	0	0	0	1	x	4	7	0

E—Maranville. LOB—Cardinals 4, Yankees 4. Scoring Position—Cardinals 0-for-0, Yankees 3-for-6. 2B—Ruth 2 (2), Gehrig (1). HR—Bottomley (1), Meusel (1). CS—Wilson (1).

Cardinals	IP	H	R	ER	BB	K	ERA
Bill Sherdel (L, 0-1)	7.0	4	3	3	0	2	3.86
Syl Johnson	1.0	3	1	1	0	0	9.00

Yankees	IP	H	R	ER	BB	K	ERA
Waite Hoyt (W, 1-0)	9.0	3	1	1	3	6	1.00

Time—1:49. Attendance—61,425. Umpires—HP, Owens. 1B, Rigler. 2B, McGowan. 3B, Pfirman.

Game 2

Friday, October 5

Cardinals	AB	R	H	RBI	BB	K	Avg
Taylor Douthit, cf	4	0	0	1	0	0	.000
Andy High, 3b	3	0	0	0	1	0	.000
Frankie Frisch, 2b	3	0	2	0	1	1	.286
Jim Bottomley, 1b	4	0	0	0	0	3	.286
Chick Hafey, lf	4	0	0	0	0	1	.000
George Harper, rf	3	1	0	0	1	1	.167
Jimmie Wilson, c	4	1	1	1	0	1	.143
Rabbit Maranville, ss	3	1	1	0	1	1	.200
Pete Alexander, p	1	0	0	1	0	0	.000
Clarence Mitchell, p	2	0	0	0	0	0	.000
Ernie Orsatti, ph	1	0	0	0	0	0	.000
TOTALS	32	3	4	3	4	8	.121

Yankees	AB	R	H	RBI	BB	K	Avg
Cedric Durst, cf	2	1	2	1	0	0	1.000
Ben Paschal, ph-cf	2	0	1	1	1	0	.167
Mark Koenig, ss	5	0	0	0	0	1	.111
Babe Ruth, rf	3	2	2	0	1	1	.714
Lou Gehrig, 1b	3	2	1	3	1	0	.429
Bob Meusel, lf	3	2	1	1	1	1	.286
Tony Lazzeri, 2b	3	0	0	0	0	0	.000
Leo Durocher, 2b	0	0	0	0	0	0	.000
Gene Robertson, 3b	2	1	0	0	1	0	.000
Joe Dugan, ph-3b	0	0	0	1	0	0	.000
Benny Bengough, c	3	1	1	1	1	0	.167
George Pipgras, p	2	0	0	1	0	1	.000
TOTALS	28	9	8	9	6	4	.263

	1	2	3	4	5	6	7	8	9	R	H	E
Cardinals	0	3	0	0	0	0	0	0	0	3	4	1
Yankees	3	1	4	0	0	0	1	0	x	9	8	2

E—Lazzeri, Koenig, Mitchell. DP—Cardinals 1 (Frisch to Maranville to Bottomley), Yankees 1 (Koenig to Lazzeri to Gehrig). LOB—Cardinals 6, Yankees 5. Scoring Position—Cardinals 1-for-9, Yankees 5-for-10. 2B—Wilson (1), Ruth (3), Meusel (1). HR—Gehrig (1). S—Lazzeri, Pipgras. SF—Dugan. GDP—Douthit, Bengough. SB—Frisch 2 (2), Meusel (1).

Cardinals	IP	H	R	ER	BB	K	ERA
Pete Alexander (L, 0-1)	2.1	6	8	8	4	1	30.86
Clarence Mitchell	5.2	2	1	1	2	3	1.59

Yankees	IP	H	R	ER	BB	K	ERA
George Pipgras (W, 1-0)	9.0	4	3	2	4	8	2.00

HBP—Pipgras by Mitchell. Time—2:04. Attendance—60,714. Umpires—HP, Rigler. 1B, McGowan. 2B, Pfirman. 3B, Owens.

Game 3

Sunday, October 7

Yankees	AB	R	H	RBI	BB	K	Avg
Cedric Durst, cf	5	1	0	0	0	1	.286
Mark Koenig, ss	5	0	1	0	0	0	.143
Babe Ruth, rf	4	2	1	0	0	0	.636
Lou Gehrig, 1b	2	2	2	3	2	0	.556
Bob Meusel, rf	3	1	0	0	1	2	.200
Tony Lazzeri, 2b	3	1	0	0	1	0	.000
Leo Durocher, 2b	0	0	0	0	0	0	.000
Gene Robertson, 3b	4	0	1	1	0	0	.167
Benny Bengough, c	4	0	1	0	0	1	.200
Tom Zachary, p	4	0	0	0	0	1	.000
TOTALS	34	7	7	5	4	5	.263

Cardinals	AB	R	H	RBI	BB	K	Avg
Taylor Douthit, cf	4	1	1	0	0	0	.091
Andy High, 3b	5	1	2	1	0	1	.167
Frankie Frisch, 2b	2	1	1	0	1	0	.333
Jim Bottomley, 1b	4	0	1	2	0	1	.273
Chick Hafey, lf	4	0	2	0	0	0	.167
Wattie Holm, rf	4	0	1	0	0	1	.200
Jimmie Wilson, c	4	0	0	0	0	2	.091
Rabbit Maranville, ss	4	0	1	0	0	0	.222
Jesse Haines, p	2	0	0	0	0	0	.000
Syl Johnson, p	0	0	0	0	0	0	—
Ray Blades, ph	1	0	0	0	0	1	.000
Flint Rhem, p	0	0	0	0	0	0	—
Ernie Orsatti, ph	1	0	0	0	0	1	.000
TOTALS	35	3	9	3	1	7	.176

	1	2	3	4	5	6	7	8	9	R	H	E
Yankees	0	1	0	2	0	3	1	0	0	7	7	2
Cardinals	2	0	0	0	1	0	0	0	0	3	9	3

E—Lazzeri, Hafey, Wilson 2, Robertson. DP—Yankees 1 (Koenig to Durocher to Gehrig), Cardinals 1 (High to Frisch to Bottomley). LOB—Yankees 4, Cardinals 8. Scoring Position—Yankees 2-for-5, Cardinals 1-for-9. 2B—High (1). 3B—Bottomley (1). HR—Gehrig 2 (3). S—Frisch. GDP—Lazzeri, Wilson. SB—Meusel (2), Lazzeri (1).

Yankees	IP	H	R	ER	BB	K	ERA
Tom Zachary (W, 1-0)	9.0	9	3	3	1	7	3.00

Cardinals	IP	H	R	ER	BB	K	ERA
Jesse Haines (L, 0-1)	6.0	6	6	3	3	4	4.50
Syl Johnson	1.0	1	1	0	1	1	4.50
Flint Rhem	2.0	0	0	0	0	1	0.00

HBP—Douthit by Zachary. Time—2:09. Attendance—39,602. Umpires—HP, McGowan. 1B, Pfirman. 2B, Owens. 3B, Rigler.

Game 4

Tuesday, October 9

Yankees	AB	R	H	RBI	BB	K	Avg
Ben Paschal, cf	4	0	1	0	0	0	.200
Cedric Durst, cf	1	1	1	1	0	0	.375
Mark Koenig, ss	5	0	1	0	0	0	.158
Babe Ruth, lf	5	3	3	3	0	0	.625
Lou Gehrig, 1b	2	1	1	1	3	0	.545
Bob Meusel, rf	5	1	1	0	0	2	.200
Tony Lazzeri, 2b	4	1	3	0	0	0	.250
Leo Durocher, 2b	1	0	0	0	0	0	.000
Joe Dugan, 3b	4	0	1	1	0	0	.143
Gene Robertson, 3b	1	0	0	0	0	0	.143
Benny Bengough, c	3	0	1	0	0	0	.231
Earle Combs, ph	0	0	0	1	0	0	—
Pat Collins, c	1	0	1	0	0	0	1.000
Waite Hoyt, p	4	0	1	0	0	0	.143
TOTALS	40	7	15	7	3	2	.289

Cardinals	AB	R	H	RBI	BB	K	Avg
Ernie Orsatti, cf	5	1	2	0	0	2	.286
Andy High, 3b	5	0	3	0	0	0	.294
Frankie Frisch, 2b	4	0	1	0	1	0	.231
Jim Bottomley, 1b	3	0	0	0	1	2	.214
Chick Hafey, lf	3	0	1	0	1	1	.200
George Harper, rf	3	0	0	1	1	1	.111
Earl Smith, c	4	0	3	0	0	0	.750
Pepper Martin, pr	0	1	0	0	0	0	—
Rabbit Maranville, ss	4	1	2	0	0	0	.308
Bill Sherdel, p	3	0	0	0	0	1	.000
Pete Alexander, p	0	0	0	0	0	0	.000
Wattie Holm, ph	1	0	0	1	0	0	.167
TOTALS	35	3	11	2	3	8	.240

	1	2	3	4	5	6	7	8	9	R	H	E
Yankees	0	0	0	1	0	0	4	2	0	7	15	2
Cardinals	0	0	1	0	0	1	0	0	1	3	11	0

E—Koenig, Hoyt. DP—Yankees 1 (Koenig to Gehrig), Cardinals 1 (Bottomley to Maranville). LOB—Yankees 11, Cardinals 9. Scoring Position—Yankees 0-for-12, Cardinals 1-for-10. 2B—Lazzeri (1), Orsatti (1), High (2), Maranville (1), Collins (1). HR—Ruth 3 (3), Gehrig (4), Durst (1). S—Hoyt. SF—Frisch, Combs. GDP—Ruth, Harper. SB—Lazzeri (2), Maranville (1). CS—Smith (1).

Yankees	IP	H	R	ER	BB	K	ERA
Waite Hoyt (W, 2-0)	9.0	11	3	2	3	8	1.50

Cardinals	IP	H	R	ER	BB	K	ERA
Bill Sherdel (L, 0-2)	6.1	11	4	4	3	2	4.73
Pete Alexander	2.2	4	3	3	0	1	19.80

Time—2:25. Attendance—37,331. Umpires—HP, Pfirman. 1B, Owens. 2B, Rigler. 3B, McGowan.

1928 World Series—Composite Statistics

Batting

Yankees	G	AB	R	H	RBI	2B	3B	HR	BB	SO	SB	CS	Avg	OBP	Slg
Benny Bengough	4	13	1	3	1	0	0	0	1	1	0	0	.231	.286	.231
Pat Collins	1	1	0	1	0	1	0	0	0	0	0	0	1.000	1.000	2.000
Earle Combs	1	0	0	0	1	0	0	0	0	0	0	0	—	.000	—
Joe Dugan	3	7	0	1	2	0	0	0	0	0	0	0	.143	.125	.143
Leo Durocher	4	2	0	0	0	0	0	0	0	1	0	0	.000	.000	.000
Cedric Durst	4	8	3	3	2	0	0	1	0	1	0	0	.375	.375	.750
Lou Gehrig	4	11	5	6	9	1	0	4	6	0	0	0	.545	.706	1.727
Waite Hoyt	2	7	0	1	0	0	0	0	0	0	0	0	.143	.143	.143
Mark Koenig	4	19	1	3	0	0	0	0	0	1	0	0	.158	.158	.158
Tony Lazzeri	4	12	2	3	0	1	0	0	1	0	2	0	.250	.308	.333
Bob Meusel	4	15	5	3	3	1	0	1	2	5	2	0	.200	.294	.467
Ben Paschal	3	10	0	2	1	0	0	0	1	0	0	0	.200	.273	.200
George Pipgras	1	2	0	0	1	0	0	0	0	1	0	0	.000	.333	.000
Gene Robertson	3	7	1	1	1	0	0	0	1	0	0	0	.143	.250	.143
Babe Ruth	4	16	9	10	4	3	0	3	1	2	0	0	.625	.647	1.375
Tom Zachary	1	4	0	0	0	0	0	0	0	1	0	0	.000	.000	.000
Totals	**4**	**134**	**27**	**37**	**25**	**7**	**0**	**9**	**13**	**13**	**4**	**0**	**.276**	**.340**	**.530**

Cardinals	G	AB	R	H	RBI	2B	3B	HR	BB	SO	SB	CS	Avg	OBP	Slg
Pete Alexander	2	1	0	0	1	0	0	0	0	0	0	0	.000	.000	.000
Ray Blades	1	1	0	0	0	0	0	0	0	1	0	0	.000	.000	.000
Jim Bottomley	4	14	1	3	3	0	1	1	2	6	0	0	.214	.313	.571
Taylor Douthit	3	11	1	1	1	0	0	0	1	1	0	0	.091	.231	.091
Frankie Frisch	4	13	1	3	1	0	0	0	2	2	1	0	.231	.313	.231
Chick Hafey	4	15	0	3	0	0	0	0	1	4	0	0	.200	.250	.200
Jesse Haines	1	2	0	0	0	0	0	0	0	0	0	0	.000	.000	.000
George Harper	3	9	1	1	0	0	0	0	2	2	0	0	.111	.273	.111
Andy High	4	17	1	5	1	2	0	0	1	3	0	0	.294	.333	.412
Wattie Holm	3	6	0	1	1	0	0	0	0	1	0	0	.167	.167	.167
Rabbit Maranville	4	13	2	4	0	1	0	0	1	1	1	0	.308	.357	.385
Pepper Martin	1	0	1	0	0	0	0	0	0	0	0	0	—	—	—
Clarence Mitchell	1	2	0	0	0	0	0	0	0	0	0	0	.000	.000	.000
Ernie Orsatti	4	7	1	2	0	1	0	0	1	3	0	0	.286	.375	.429
Bill Sherdel	2	5	0	0	0	0	0	0	0	2	0	0	.000	.000	.000
Earl Smith	1	4	0	3	0	0	0	0	0	0	0	1	.750	.750	.750
Jimmie Wilson	3	11	1	1	1	1	0	0	0	3	0	1	.091	.091	.182
Totals	**4**	**131**	**10**	**27**	**9**	**5**	**1**	**1**	**11**	**29**	**3**	**2**	**.206**	**.271**	**.282**

Pitching

Yankees	G	GS	CG	IP	H	R	ER	BB	SO	W-L	Sv-Op	Hld	ERA
Waite Hoyt	2	2	2	18.0	14	4	3	6	14	2-0	0-0	0	1.50
George Pipgras	1	1	1	9.0	4	3	2	4	8	1-0	0-0	0	2.00
Tom Zachary	1	1	1	9.0	9	3	3	1	7	1-0	0-0	0	3.00
Totals	**4**	**4**	**4**	**36.0**	**27**	**10**	**8**	**11**	**29**	**4-0**	**0-0**	**0**	**2.00**

Cardinals	G	GS	CG	IP	H	R	ER	BB	SO	W-L	Sv-Op	Hld	ERA
Pete Alexander	2	1	0	5.0	10	11	11	4	2	0-1	0-0	0	19.80
Jesse Haines	1	1	0	6.0	6	6	3	3	3	0-1	0-0	0	4.50
Syl Johnson	2	0	0	2.0	4	2	1	1	1	0-0	0-0	0	4.50
Clarence Mitchell	1	0	0	5.2	2	1	1	2	4	0-0	0-0	0	1.59
Flint Rhem	1	0	0	2.0	0	0	0	0	1	0-0	0-0	0	0.00
Bill Sherdel	2	2	0	13.1	15	7	7	3	3	0-2	0-0	0	4.73
Totals	**4**	**4**	**0**	**34.0**	**37**	**27**	**23**	**13**	**13**	**0-4**	**0-0**	**0**	**6.09**

Fielding

Yankees	Pos	G	PO	Ast	E	DP	PB	FPct
Benny Bengough	c	4	33	2	0	0	0	1.000
Pat Collins	c	1	2	0	0	0	0	1.000
Joe Dugan	3b	3	3	0	0	0	—	1.000
Leo Durocher	2b	4	1	1	0	1	—	1.000
Cedric Durst	cf	4	3	0	0	0	—	1.000
Lou Gehrig	1b	4	33	0	0	3	—	1.000
Waite Hoyt	p	2	0	3	1	0	—	.750
Mark Koenig	ss	4	8	11	2	3	—	.905
Tony Lazzeri	2b	4	2	7	2	1	—	.818
Bob Meusel	lf	2	4	0	0	0	—	1.000
	rf	2	3	0	0	0	—	1.000
Ben Paschal	cf	3	8	0	0	0	—	1.000
George Pipgras	p	1	0	1	0	0	—	1.000
Gene Robertson	3b	3	2	1	1	0	—	.750
Babe Ruth	rf	2	4	0	0	0	—	1.000
	lf	2	2	1	0	0	—	1.000
Tom Zachary	p	1	0	1	0	0	—	1.000
Totals		**4**	**108**	**28**	**6**	**8**	**0**	**.958**

Cardinals	Pos	G	PO	Ast	E	DP	PB	FPct
Pete Alexander	p	2	0	4	0	0	—	1.000
Jim Bottomley	1b	4	36	2	0	3	—	1.000
Taylor Douthit	cf	3	6	1	0	0	—	1.000
Frankie Frisch	2b	4	8	13	0	2	—	1.000
Chick Hafey	lf	4	8	0	1	0	—	.889
Jesse Haines	p	1	0	1	0	0	—	1.000
George Harper	rf	3	5	0	0	0	—	1.000
Andy High	3b	4	2	5	0	1	—	1.000
Wattie Holm	rf	1	4	0	0	0	—	1.000
Syl Johnson	p	2	0	0	0	0	—	—
Rabbit Maranville	ss	4	11	3	1	2	—	.933
Clarence Mitchell	p	1	0	1	1	0	—	.500
Ernie Orsatti	cf	1	4	0	0	0	—	1.000
Flint Rhem	p	1	0	0	0	0	—	—
Bill Sherdel	p	2	0	4	0	0	—	1.000
Earl Smith	c	1	3	1	0	0	0	1.000
Tommy Thevenow	ss	1	1	0	0	0	—	1.000
Jimmie Wilson	c	3	14	2	2	0	0	.889
Totals		**4**	**102**	**37**	**5**	**8**	**0**	**.965**

1929 Philadelphia Athletics (AL) 4, Chicago Cubs (NL) 1

The Philadelphia Athletics downed the Chicago Cubs in a wild and unpredictable five-game World Series. Philadelphia manager Connie Mack named Howard Ehmke as his surprise opening-game pitcher, and the sidearmer set a World Series record with 13 strikeouts en route to a 3-1 victory. Jimmie Foxx' three-run homer led the Athletics to a 9-3 win in the second game. Guy Bush got the Cubs their first win with a 3-1 victory in Game 3. Game 4 featured the greatest comeback in World Series history. Trailing 8-0 in the bottom of the seventh, the Athletics routed four Chicago pitchers for 10 runs, emerging with a 10-8 victory. The Cubs led 2-0 in the ninth inning of Game 5 before Mule Haas rapped a game-tying homer. Bing Miller followed with an RBI double to win the Series for Philadelphia.

Game 1

Monday, October 7

Athletics	AB	R	H	RBI	BB	K	Avg
Max Bishop, 2b	4	0	0	0	0	0	.000
Mule Haas, cf	3	0	0	0	1	1	.000
Mickey Cochrane, c	3	1	1	0	1	0	.333
Al Simmons, lf	4	1	0	0	0	1	.000
Jimmie Foxx, 1b	4	1	2	1	0	0	.500
Bing Miller, rf	4	0	1	2	0	1	.250
Jimmy Dykes, 3b	4	0	1	0	0	1	.250
Joe Boley, ss	4	0	0	0	0	0	.000
Howard Ehmke, p	4	0	1	0	0	0	.250
TOTALS	34	3	6	3	2	5	.176

Cubs	AB	R	H	RBI	BB	K	Avg
Norm McMillan, 3b	4	0	1	0	0	1	.250
Woody English, ss	4	0	2	0	0	1	.500
Rogers Hornsby, 2b	4	0	0	0	0	2	.000
Hack Wilson, cf	4	0	0	0	0	2	.000
Kiki Cuyler, rf	4	1	1	0	0	2	.250
Riggs Stephenson, lf	4	0	2	1	0	1	.500
Charlie Grimm, 1b	2	0	2	0	1	0	1.000
Zack Taylor, c	2	0	0	0	0	0	.000
Cliff Heathcote, ph	1	0	0	0	0	0	.000
Mike Gonzalez, c	0	0	0	0	0	0	—
Footsie Blair, ph	1	0	0	0	0	0	.000
Charlie Root, p	2	0	0	0	0	2	.000
Gabby Hartnett, ph	1	0	0	0	0	1	.000
Guy Bush, p	0	0	0	0	0	0	—
Chick Tolson, ph	1	0	0	0	0	1	.000
TOTALS	34	1	8	1	1	13	.235

	1 2 3	4 5 6	7 8 9	R H E
Athletics	0 0 0	0 0 0	1 0 2	3 6 1
Cubs	0 0 0	0 0 0	0 0 1	1 8 2

E—English 2, Dykes. DP—Cubs 1 (English to Hornsby to Grimm). LOB—Athletics 6, Cubs 8. Scoring Position—Athletics 1-for-6, Cubs 1-for-7. 2B—English (1). HR—Foxx (1). S—Grimm. GDP—Boley. CS—Grimm (1).

Athletics	IP	H	R	ER	BB	K	ERA
Howard Ehmke (W, 1-0)	9.0	8	1	0	1	13	0.00

Cubs	IP	H	R	ER	BB	K	ERA
Charlie Root (L, 0-1)	7.0	3	1	1	2	5	1.29
Guy Bush	2.0	3	2	0	0	0	0.00

Time—2:03. Attendance—50,740. Umpires—HP, Klem. 1B, Dinneen. 2B, Moran. 3B, Van Graflan.

Game 2

Wednesday, October 9

Athletics	AB	R	H	RBI	BB	K	Avg
Max Bishop, 2b	4	0	0	0	1	2	.000
Mule Haas, cf	5	1	1	1	0	1	.125
Mickey Cochrane, c	2	2	1	0	3	0	.400
Al Simmons, lf	4	2	2	4	1	1	.250
Jimmie Foxx, 1b	5	2	3	3	0	0	.556
Bing Miller, rf	4	0	1	0	0	1	.250
Jimmy Dykes, 3b	4	1	3	1	1	0	.500
Joe Boley, ss	3	0	1	0	0	0	.143
George Earnshaw, p	3	1	0	0	0	2	.000
Lefty Grove, p	2	0	0	0	0	1	.000
TOTALS	36	9	12	9	6	8	.258

Cubs	AB	R	H	RBI	BB	K	Avg
Norm McMillan, 3b	4	0	0	0	1	2	.125
Woody English, ss	5	0	1	0	0	2	.333
Rogers Hornsby, 2b	4	1	1	0	1	2	.125
Hack Wilson, cf	3	1	3	0	2	0	.429
Kiki Cuyler, rf	4	0	0	0	1	3	.125
Riggs Stephenson, lf	5	1	1	1	0	0	.333
Charlie Grimm, 1b	4	0	2	0	0	0	.667
Zack Taylor, c	4	0	2	1	0	1	.333
Pat Malone, p	1	0	0	0	0	1	.000
Sheriff Blake, p	1	0	1	0	0	0	1.000
Cliff Heathcote, ph	0	0	0	0	0	0	.000
Gabby Hartnett, ph	1	0	0	0	0	1	.000
Hal Carlson, p	0	0	0	0	0	0	—
Mike Gonzalez, c	1	0	0	0	0	1	.000
Art Nehf, p	0	0	0	0	0	0	—
TOTALS	37	3	11	3	5	13	.284

	1 2 3	4 5 6	7 8 9	R H E
Athletics	0 0 3	3 0 0	1 2 0	9 12 0
Cubs	0 0 0	3 0 0	0 0 0	3 11 1

E—English. DP—Athletics 1 (Bishop to Boley to Foxx), Cubs 1 (English to Hornsby to Grimm). LOB—Athletics 9, Cubs 12. Scoring Position—Athletics 3-for-10, Cubs 3-for-10. 2B—Foxx (1), English (2). HR—Simmons (1), Foxx (2). S—Miller, Boley 2. GDP—Cochrane, Stephenson.

Athletics	IP	H	R	ER	BB	K	ERA
George Earnshaw	4.2	8	3	3	4	7	5.79
Lefty Grove (W, 1-0)	4.1	3	0	0	1	6	0.00

Cubs	IP	H	R	ER	BB	K	ERA
Pat Malone (L, 0-1)	3.2	5	6	3	5	5	7.36
Sheriff Blake	1.1	2	0	0	1	0	0.00
Hal Carlson	3.0	5	3	3	1	2	9.00
Art Nehf	1.0	0	0	0	0	0	0.00

Time—2:29. Attendance—49,987. Umpires—HP, Dinneen. 1B, Moran. 2B, Van Graflan. 3B, Klem.

Game 3

Friday, October 11

Cubs	AB	R	H	RBI	BB	K	Avg
Norm McMillan, 3b	4	0	0	0	0	1	.083
Woody English, ss	4	1	0	0	0	1	.231
Rogers Hornsby, 2b	4	1	2	1	0	2	.250
Hack Wilson, cf	3	0	2	0	1	0	.500
Kiki Cuyler, rf	4	0	1	2	0	1	.167
Riggs Stephenson, lf	4	0	1	0	0	0	.308
Charlie Grimm, 1b	4	0	0	0	0	1	.400
Zack Taylor, c	4	0	0	0	0	1	.200
Guy Bush, p	3	1	0	0	1	3	.000
TOTALS	34	3	6	3	2	10	.253

Athletics	AB	R	H	RBI	BB	K	Avg
Max Bishop, 2b	4	0	1	0	1	0	.083
Mule Haas, cf	5	0	2	0	0	0	.231
Mickey Cochrane, c	3	1	2	0	1	0	.500
Al Simmons, lf	3	0	0	0	0	0	.182
Jimmie Foxx, 1b	4	0	0	0	0	1	.385
Bing Miller, rf	4	0	1	1	0	0	.250
Jimmy Dykes, 3b	4	0	1	0	0	0	.417
Joe Boley, ss	4	0	2	0	0	0	.273
George Earnshaw, p	2	0	0	0	0	2	.000
Homer Summa, ph	1	0	0	0	0	1	.000
TOTALS	34	1	9	1	2	4	.265

	1 2 3	4 5 6	7 8 9	R H E
Cubs	0 0 0	0 0 3	0 0 0	3 6 1
Athletics	0 0 0	0 1 0	0 0 0	1 9 1

E—English, Dykes. LOB—Cubs 6, Athletics 10. Scoring Position—Cubs 2-for-9, Athletics 1-for-8. 2B—Hornsby (1), Stephenson (1). 3B—Wilson (1). S—Earnshaw. SF—Simmons. CS—Miller (1).

Cubs	IP	H	R	ER	BB	K	ERA
Guy Bush (W, 1-0)	9.0	9	1	1	2	4	0.82

Athletics	IP	H	R	ER	BB	K	ERA
George Earnshaw (L, 0-1)	9.0	6	3	1	2	10	2.63

WP—Bush. Time—2:09. Attendance—29,921. Umpires—HP, Moran. 1B, Van Graflan. 2B, Klem. 3B, Dinneen.

Game 4

Saturday, October 12

Cubs	AB	R	H	RBI	BB	K	Avg
Norm McMillan, 3b	4	0	0	0	1	2	.063
Woody English, ss	4	0	0	0	1	1	.176
Rogers Hornsby, 2b	5	2	2	0	0	1	.294
Hack Wilson, cf	3	1	2	0	1	0	.538
Kiki Cuyler, rf	4	2	3	2	0	1	.313
Riggs Stephenson, lf	4	1	1	1	0	0	.294
Charlie Grimm, 1b	4	2	2	2	0	0	.429
Zack Taylor, c	3	0	0	1	0	1	.154
Charlie Root, p	3	0	0	0	0	1	.000
Art Nehf, p	0	0	0	0	0	0	—
Sheriff Blake, p	0	0	0	0	0	0	1.000
Pat Malone, p	0	0	0	0	0	0	.000
Gabby Hartnett, ph	1	0	0	0	0	0	.000
Hal Carlson, p	0	0	0	0	0	0	—
TOTALS	35	8	10	6	3	8	.263

Athletics	AB	R	H	RBI	BB	K	Avg
Max Bishop, 2b	5	1	2	1	0	0	.176
Mule Haas, cf	4	1	1	3	0	0	.235
Mickey Cochrane, c	4	1	2	0	1	0	.500
Al Simmons, lf	5	2	2	1	0	2	.250
Jimmie Foxx, 1b	4	2	2	1	0	0	.412
Bing Miller, rf	3	1	2	0	0	0	.333
Jimmy Dykes, 3b	4	1	3	3	0	0	.500
Joe Boley, ss	3	1	1	1	0	1	.286
Jack Quinn, p	2	0	0	0	0	2	.000
Rube Walberg, p	0	0	0	0	0	0	—
Eddie Rommel, p	0	0	0	0	0	0	—
George Burns, ph	2	0	0	0	0	1	.000
Lefty Grove, p	0	0	0	0	0	0	.000
TOTALS	36	10	15	10	1	6	.315

	1	2	3	4	5	6	7	8	9		R	H	E
Cubs	0	0	0	2	0	5	1	0	0		8	10	2
Athletics	0	0	0	0	0	0	10	0	x		10	15	2

E—Wilson, Walberg, Cuyler, Miller. DP—Athletics 1 (Dykes to Bishop to Foxx). LOB—Cubs 4, Athletics 6. Scoring Position—Cubs 5-for-8, Athletics 7-for-14. 2B—Cochrane (1), Dykes (1). 3B—Hornsby (1). HR—Grimm (1), Haas (1), Simmons (2). S—Haas, Boley. SF—Taylor. GDP—Stephenson. CS—Miller (2).

Cubs	IP	H	R	ER	BB	K	ERA
Charlie Root	6.1	9	6	6	0	3	4.73
Art Nehf	0.0	1	2	2	1	0	18.00
Sheriff Blake (BS, 1; L, 0-1)	0.0	2	2	2	0	0	13.50
Pat Malone	0.2	1	0	0	0	2	6.23
Hal Carlson	1.0	2	0	0	0	1	6.75

Athletics	IP	H	R	ER	BB	K	ERA
Jack Quinn	5.0	7	6	5	2	2	9.00
Rube Walberg	1.0	1	1	0	0	2	0.00
Eddie Rommel (W, 1-0)	1.0	2	1	1	1	0	9.00
Lefty Grove (S, 1)	2.0	0	0	0	0	4	0.00

Quinn pitched to four batters in the 6th. Nehf pitched to two batters in the 7th. Blake pitched to two batters in the 7th.

HBP—Miller by Malone. Time—2:12. Attendance—29,921. Umpires—HP, Van Graflan. 1B, Klem. 2B, Dinneen. 3B, Moran.

Game 5

Monday, October 14

Cubs	AB	R	H	RBI	BB	K	Avg
Norm McMillan, 3b	4	0	1	0	0	0	.100
Woody English, ss	4	0	1	0	0	1	.190
Rogers Hornsby, 2b	4	0	0	0	0	1	.238
Hack Wilson, cf	4	0	1	0	0	1	.471
Kiki Cuyler, rf	4	1	1	0	0	0	.300
Riggs Stephenson, lf	2	1	1	0	2	1	.316
Charlie Grimm, 1b	4	0	1	1	0	1	.389
Zack Taylor, c	4	0	1	1	0	0	.176
Pat Malone, p	3	0	1	0	0	1	.250
TOTALS	33	2	8	2	2	6	.268

Athletics	AB	R	H	RBI	BB	K	Avg
Max Bishop, 2b	4	1	1	0	0	1	.190
Mule Haas, cf	4	1	1	2	0	1	.238
Mickey Cochrane, c	3	0	0	0	1	0	.400
Al Simmons, lf	4	1	2	0	0	0	.300
Jimmie Foxx, 1b	3	0	0	0	1	0	.350
Bing Miller, rf	4	0	2	1	0	0	.368
Jimmy Dykes, 3b	3	0	0	0	0	0	.421
Joe Boley, ss	3	0	0	0	0	1	.235
Howard Ehmke, p	1	0	0	0	0	0	.200
Rube Walberg, p	1	0	0	0	0	0	.000
Walt French, ph	1	0	0	0	0	1	.000
TOTALS	31	3	6	3	2	4	.302

	1	2	3	4	5	6	7	8	9		R	H	E
Cubs	0	0	0	2	0	0	0	0	0		2	8	1
Athletics	0	0	0	0	0	0	0	0	3		3	6	0

E—Hornsby. DP—Cubs 2 (Hornsby to Grimm; English to Hornsby to Grimm). LOB—Cubs 6, Athletics 4. Scoring Position—Cubs 2-for-6, Athletics 1-for-3. 2B—Cuyler (1), Malone (1), Simmons (1), Miller (1). HR—Haas (2). GDP—Foxx 2. SB—McMillan (1). CS—English (1), Cuyler (1).

Cubs	IP	H	R	ER	BB	K	ERA
Pat Malone (L, 0-2)	8.2	6	3	3	2	4	4.15

Athletics	IP	H	R	ER	BB	K	ERA
Howard Ehmke	3.2	6	2	2	2	0	1.42
Rube Walberg (W, 1-0)	5.1	2	0	0	0	6	0.00

Time—1:42. Attendance—29,921. Umpires—HP, Klem. 1B, Dinneen. 2B, Moran. 3B, Van Graflan.

1929 World Series—Composite Statistics

Batting

Athletics	G	AB	R	H	RBI	2B	3B	HR	BB	SO	SB	CS	Avg	OBP	Slg
Max Bishop	5	21	2	4	1	0	0	0	2	3	0	0	.190	.261	.190
Joe Boley	5	17	1	4	1	0	0	0	0	3	0	0	.235	.235	.235
George Burns	1	2	0	0	0	0	0	0	0	1	0	0	.000	.000	.000
Mickey Cochrane	5	15	5	6	0	1	0	0	7	0	0	0	.400	.591	.467
Jimmy Dykes	5	19	2	8	4	1	0	0	1	1	0	0	.421	.450	.474
George Earnshaw	2	5	1	0	0	0	0	0	0	4	0	0	.000	.000	.000
Howard Ehmke	2	5	0	1	0	0	0	0	0	3	0	0	.200	.200	.200
Jimmie Foxx	5	20	5	7	5	1	0	2	1	1	0	0	.350	.381	.700
Walt French	1	1	0	0	0	0	0	0	0	1	0	0	.000	.000	.000
Lefty Grove	2	2	0	0	0	0	0	0	0	1	0	0	.000	.000	.000
Mule Haas	5	21	3	5	6	0	0	2	1	3	0	0	.238	.273	.524
Bing Miller	5	19	1	7	4	1	0	0	0	2	0	2	.368	.400	.421
Jack Quinn	1	2	0	0	0	0	0	0	0	0	0	0	.000	.000	.000
Al Simmons	5	20	6	6	5	1	0	2	1	4	0	0	.300	.318	.650
Homer Summa	1	1	0	0	0	0	0	0	0	1	0	0	.000	.000	.000
Rube Walberg	2	1	0	0	0	0	0	0	0	0	0	0	.000	.000	.000
Totals	5	171	26	48	26	5	0	6	13	27	0	2	.281	.333	.415

Batting

Cubs	G	AB	R	H	RBI	2B	3B	HR	BB	SO	SB	CS	Avg	OBP	Slg
Footsie Blair	1	1	0	0	0	0	0	0	0	0	0	0	.000	.000	.000
Sheriff Blake	2	1	0	1	0	0	0	0	0	0	0	0	1.000	1.000	1.000
Guy Bush	2	3	1	0	0	0	0	0	1	3	0	0	.000	.250	.000
Kiki Cuyler	5	20	4	6	4	1	0	0	1	7	0	1	.300	.333	.350
Woody English	5	21	1	4	0	2	0	0	1	6	0	1	.190	.227	.286
Mike Gonzalez	2	1	0	0	0	0	0	0	0	1	0	0	.000	.000	.000
Charlie Grimm	5	18	2	7	4	0	0	1	1	2	0	1	.389	.421	.556
Gabby Hartnett	3	3	0	0	0	0	0	0	0	3	0	0	.000	.000	.000
Cliff Heathcote	2	1	0	0	0	0	0	0	0	0	0	0	.000	.000	.000
Rogers Hornsby	5	21	4	5	1	1	1	0	1	8	0	0	.238	.273	.381
Pat Malone	3	4	0	1	0	1	0	0	0	2	0	0	.250	.250	.500
Norm McMillan	5	20	0	2	0	0	0	0	2	6	1	0	.100	.182	.100
Charlie Root	2	5	0	0	0	0	0	0	0	3	0	0	.000	.000	.000
Riggs Stephenson	5	19	3	6	3	1	0	0	2	2	0	0	.316	.381	.368
Zack Taylor	5	17	0	3	3	0	0	0	0	3	0	0	.176	.167	.176
Chick Tolson	1	1	0	0	0	0	0	0	0	1	0	0	.000	.000	.000
Hack Wilson	5	17	2	8	0	0	1	0	4	3	0	0	.471	.571	.588
Totals	5	173	17	43	15	6	2	1	13	50	1	3	.249	.299	.324

Pitching

Athletics	G	GS	CG	IP	H	R	ER	BB	SO	W-L	Sv-Op	Hld	ERA
George Earnshaw	2	2	1	13.2	14	6	4	6	17	0-1	0-0	0	2.63
Howard Ehmke	2	2	1	12.2	14	3	2	3	13	1-0	0-0	0	1.42
Lefty Grove	2	0	0	6.1	3	0	0	1	10	1-0	1-1	0	0.00
Jack Quinn	1	1	0	5.0	7	6	5	2	2	0-0	0-0	0	9.00
Eddie Rommel	1	0	0	1.0	2	1	1	1	0	1-0	0-0	0	9.00
Rube Walberg	2	0	0	6.1	3	1	0	0	8	1-0	0-0	0	0.00
Totals	5	5	2	45.0	43	17	12	13	50	4-1	1-1	0	2.40

Pitching

Cubs	G	GS	CG	IP	H	R	ER	BB	SO	W-L	Sv-Op	Hld	ERA
Sheriff Blake	2	0	0	1.1	4	2	2	0	1	0-1	0-1	0	13.50
Guy Bush	2	1	1	11.0	12	3	1	2	4	1-0	0-0	0	0.82
Hal Carlson	2	0	0	4.0	7	3	3	1	3	0-0	0-0	0	6.75
Pat Malone	3	2	1	13.0	12	9	6	7	11	0-2	0-0	0	4.15
Art Nehf	2	0	0	1.0	1	2	2	1	0	0-0	0-0	0	18.00
Charlie Root	2	2	0	13.1	12	7	7	2	8	0-1	0-0	0	4.73
Totals	5	5	2	43.2	48	26	21	13	27	1-4	0-1	0	4.33

Fielding

Athletics	Pos	G	PO	Ast	E	DP	PB	FPct
Max Bishop	2b	5	9	13	0	2	—	1.000
Joe Boley	ss	5	4	12	0	1	—	1.000
Mickey Cochrane	c	5	59	2	0	0	0	1.000
Jimmy Dykes	3b	5	3	4	2	1	—	.778
George Earnshaw	p	2	0	2	0	0	—	1.000
Howard Ehmke	p	2	0	4	0	0	—	1.000
Jimmie Foxx	1b	5	38	1	0	2	—	1.000
Lefty Grove	p	2	0	1	0	0	—	1.000
Mule Haas	cf	5	5	0	0	0	—	1.000
Bing Miller	rf	5	13	0	1	0	—	.929
Jack Quinn	p	1	0	0	0	0	—	—
Eddie Rommel	p	1	0	0	0	0	—	—
Al Simmons	lf	5	4	0	0	0	—	1.000
Rube Walberg	p	2	0	1	1	0	—	.500
Totals		5	135	40	4	6	0	.978

Fielding

Cubs	Pos	G	PO	Ast	E	DP	PB	FPct
Sheriff Blake	p	2	0	0	0	0	—	
Guy Bush	p	2	0	3	0	0	—	1.000
Hal Carlson	p	2	0	2	0	0	—	1.000
Kiki Cuyler	rf	5	8	0	1	0	—	.889
Woody English	ss	5	9	11	4	3	—	.833
Mike Gonzalez	c	1	2	0	0	0	0	1.000
Charlie Grimm	1b	5	40	1	0	4	—	1.000
Rogers Hornsby	2b	5	8	11	1	4	—	.950
Pat Malone	p	3	0	1	0	0	—	1.000
Norm McMillan	3b	5	6	9	0	0	—	1.000
Art Nehf	p	2	0	0	0	0	—	—
Charlie Root	p	2	0	0	0	0	—	
Riggs Stephenson	lf	5	13	1	0	0	—	1.000
Zack Taylor	c	5	31	4	0	0	0	1.000
Hack Wilson	cf	5	14	0	1	0	—	.933
Totals		5	131	43	7	11	0	.961

1930 Philadelphia Athletics (AL) 4, St. Louis Cardinals (NL) 2

At the very height of their power, Connie Mack's powerhouse Philadelphia Athletics club dispatched the St. Louis Cardinals in six games. Homers from Mickey Cochrane and Al Simmons helped the A's take the opener, 5-2, behind Lefty Grove. Cochrane went deep again the next day as George Earnshaw six-hit the Cards for a 6-1 victory. The Cards came right back to even the Series 2-2 when Bill Hallahan blanked the A's in Game 3 and Jesse Haines bested Lefty Grove in Game 4 by the score of 3-1. Game 5 was scoreless in the top of the ninth when the A's reasserted their superiority in the power department, as Jimmie Foxx blasted a monstrous two-run homer in the ninth for a 2-0 win. Jimmy Dykes and Simmons swatted homers in Game 6 as Earnshaw came back on one day's rest to beat the Cardinals, 7-1.

Game 1

Wednesday, October 1

Cardinals	AB	R	H	RBI	BB	K	Avg
Taylor Douthit, cf	4	0	0	1	0	0	.000
Sparky Adams, 3b	3	0	1	1	0	1	.333
Frankie Frisch, 2b	4	0	2	0	0	0	.500
Jim Bottomley, 1b	4	0	0	0	0	1	.000
Chick Hafey, lf	4	0	1	0	0	0	.250
Ray Blades, rf	3	0	0	0	1	1	.000
Gus Mancuso, c	4	1	1	0	0	0	.250
Charlie Gelbert, ss	4	1	2	0	0	1	.500
Burleigh Grimes, p	3	0	2	0	0	1	.667
George Puccinelli, ph	1	0	0	0	0	0	.000
TOTALS	34	2	9	2	1	5	.265

Athletics	AB	R	H	RBI	BB	K	Avg
Max Bishop, 2b	3	1	0	0	1	1	.000
Jimmy Dykes, 3b	4	0	1	1	0	0	.250
Mickey Cochrane, c	3	1	1	1	1	1	.333
Al Simmons, lf	3	1	1	1	0	0	.333
Jimmie Foxx, 1b	3	1	1	0	0	2	.333
Bing Miller, rf	2	0	0	1	0	0	.000
Mule Haas, cf	3	1	1	0	0	0	.333
Joe Boley, ss	2	0	0	1	0	0	.000
Lefty Grove, p	3	0	0	0	0	2	.000
TOTALS	26	5	5	5	3	6	.192

	1	2	3	4	5	6	7	8	9		R	H	E
Cardinals	0	0	2	0	0	0	0	0	0		2	9	0
Athletics	0	1	0	1	0	1	1	1	x		5	5	0

LOB—Cardinals 8, Athletics 2. Scoring Position—Cardinals 1-for-7, Athletics 0-for-2. 2B—Frisch (1), Hafey (1), Dykes (1). 3B—Foxx (1), Haas (1). HR—Cochrane (1), Simmons (1). S—Boley. SF—Douthit, Adams, Miller. CS—Cochrane (1).

Cardinals	IP	H	R	ER	BB	K	ERA
Burleigh Grimes (L, 0-1)	8.0	5	5	5	3	6	5.63

Athletics	IP	H	R	ER	BB	K	ERA
Lefty Grove (W, 1-0)	9.0	9	2	2	1	5	2.00

Time—1:48. Attendance—32,295. Umpires—HP, Moriarty. 1B, Rigler. 2B, Geisel. 3B, Reardon.

Game 2

Thursday, October 2

Cardinals	AB	R	H	RBI	BB	K	Avg
Taylor Douthit, cf	4	0	0	0	0	0	.000
Sparky Adams, 3b	4	0	1	0	0	0	.286
Frankie Frisch, 2b	4	0	1	0	0	0	.375
Jim Bottomley, 1b	4	0	0	0	0	1	.000
Chick Hafey, lf	4	0	0	0	0	1	.125
George Watkins, rf	4	1	1	1	0	1	.250
Gus Mancuso, c	3	0	1	0	1	2	.286
Charlie Gelbert, ss	3	0	1	0	0	1	.429
Flint Rhem, p	1	0	0	0	0	1	.000
Jim Lindsey, p	1	0	1	0	0	0	1.000
Showboat Fisher, ph	1	0	0	0	0	1	.000
Syl Johnson, p	0	0	0	0	0	0	—
TOTALS	33	1	6	1	1	8	.217

Athletics	AB	R	H	RBI	BB	K	Avg
Max Bishop, 2b	2	1	0	0	2	0	.000
Jimmy Dykes, 3b	3	0	1	2	0	1	.286
Mickey Cochrane, c	3	2	1	1	1	0	.333
Al Simmons, lf	4	2	2	1	0	0	.429
Jimmie Foxx, 1b	3	0	1	1	1	1	.333
Bing Miller, rf	4	0	1	1	0	1	.167
Mule Haas, cf	4	0	0	0	0	2	.143
Joe Boley, ss	4	1	1	0	0	1	.167
George Earnshaw, p	3	0	0	0	0	2	.000
TOTALS	30	6	7	6	4	7	.226

	1	2	3	4	5	6	7	8	9		R	H	E
Cardinals	0	1	0	0	0	0	0	0	0		1	6	2
Athletics	2	0	2	2	0	0	0	x			6	7	2

E—Boley, Cochrane, Rhem, Frisch. DP—Cardinals 1 (Gelbert), Athletics 1 (Dykes to Foxx). LOB—Cardinals 6, Athletics 5. Scoring Position—Cardinals 0-for-4, Athletics 2-for-7. 2B—Frisch (2), Dykes (2), Simmons (1), Foxx (1). HR—Watkins (1), Cochrane (2). S—Dykes. SB—Frisch (1).

Cardinals	IP	H	R	ER	BB	K	ERA
Flint Rhem (L, 0-1)	3.1	7	6	4	2	3	10.80
Jim Lindsey	2.2	0	0	0	0	2	0.00
Syl Johnson	2.0	0	0	0	2	2	0.00

Athletics	IP	H	R	ER	BB	K	ERA
George Earnshaw (W, 1-0)	9.0	6	1	1	1	8	1.00

Time—1:47. Attendance—32,295. Umpires—HP, Rigler. 1B, Geisel. 2B, Reardon. 3B, Moriarty.

Game 3

Saturday, October 4

Athletics	AB	R	H	RBI	BB	K	Avg
Max Bishop, 2b	4	0	3	0	1	0	.333
Jimmy Dykes, 3b	4	0	0	0	1	2	.182
Mickey Cochrane, c	2	0	0	0	2	0	.250
Al Simmons, lf	4	0	2	0	0	1	.455
Jimmie Foxx, 1b	4	0	1	0	0	0	.300
Bing Miller, rf	4	0	0	0	0	1	.100
Mule Haas, cf	3	0	0	0	0	1	.100
Jimmy Moore, ph	1	0	1	0	0	0	1.000
Joe Boley, ss	4	0	0	0	0	0	.100
Rube Walberg, p	2	0	0	0	0	1	.000
Bill Shores, p	0	0	0	0	1	0	—
Jack Quinn, p	0	0	0	0	0	0	—
Eric McNair, ph	1	0	0	0	0	0	.000
TOTALS	33	0	7	0	5	6	.229

Cardinals	AB	R	H	RBI	BB	K	Avg
Taylor Douthit, cf	4	1	2	1	0	0	.167
Sparky Adams, 3b	4	0	0	0	0	0	.182
Frankie Frisch, 2b	4	0	0	0	0	0	.250
Jim Bottomley, 1b	4	1	1	0	0	2	.083
Chick Hafey, lf	4	1	2	1	0	1	.250
Ray Blades, rf	2	1	1	0	0	0	.200
George Watkins, rf	2	1	1	0	0	0	.333
Jimmie Wilson, c	4	0	2	2	0	0	.500
Charlie Gelbert, ss	3	0	1	0	0	0	.400
Wild Bill Hallahan, p	2	0	0	1	1	1	.000
TOTALS	33	5	10	5	1	4	.233

	1	2	3	4	5	6	7	8	9		R	H	E
Athletics	0	0	0	0	0	0	0	0	0		0	7	0
Cardinals	0	0	0	1	1	0	2	1	x		5	10	0

DP—Cardinals 1 (Gelbert to Frisch to Bottomley). LOB—Athletics 11, Cardinals 5. Scoring Position—Athletics 1-for-9, Cardinals 3-for-7. 2B—Simmons (2), Bottomley (1), Hafey (2). HR—Douthit (1). GDP—Simmons.

Athletics	IP	H	R	ER	BB	K	ERA
Rube Walberg (L, 0-1)	4.2	4	2	2	1	3	3.86
Bill Shores	1.1	3	2	2	0	0	13.50
Jack Quinn	2.0	3	1	1	0	1	4.50

Cardinals	IP	H	R	ER	BB	K	ERA
Wild Bill Hallahan (W, 1-0)	9.0	7	0	0	5	6	0.00

Shores pitched to four batters in the 7th.

Time—1:55. Attendance—36,944. Umpires—HP, Geisel. 1B, Reardon. 2B, Moriarty. 3B, Rigler.

Game 4
Sunday, October 5

Athletics	AB	R	H	RBI	BB	K	Avg
Max Bishop, 2b	3	1	1	0	1	0	.333
Jimmy Dykes, 3b	2	0	0	0	1	0	.154
Mickey Cochrane, c	4	0	0	0	0	0	.167
Al Simmons, lf	3	0	2	1	1	0	.500
Jimmie Foxx, 1b	4	0	1	0	0	0	.286
Bing Miller, rf	4	0	0	0	0	1	.071
Mule Haas, cf	3	0	0	0	1	0	.077
Joe Boley, ss	4	0	0	0	0	0	.071
Lefty Grove, p	3	0	0	0	0	1	.000
TOTALS	30	1	4	1	4	2	.196

Cardinals	AB	R	H	RBI	BB	K	Avg
Taylor Douthit, cf	4	0	0	0	0	1	.125
Sparky Adams, 3b	4	0	0	0	0	1	.133
Frankie Frisch, 2b	4	0	0	0	0	0	.188
Jim Bottomley, 1b	4	0	0	0	0	1	.063
Chick Hafey, lf	3	1	1	0	0	0	.267
Ray Blades, rf	3	1	0	0	0	0	.125
Jimmie Wilson, c	3	0	1	0	0	0	.429
Charlie Gelbert, ss	2	1	2	1	1	0	.500
Jesse Haines, p	2	0	1	1	0	0	.500
TOTALS	29	3	5	2	1	3	.215

	1	2	3	4	5	6	7	8	9		R	H	E
Athletics	1	0	0	0	0	0	0	0	0		1	4	1
Cardinals	0	0	1	2	0	0	0	0	x		3	5	1

E—Frisch, Dykes. DP—Cardinals 1 (Gelbert to Frisch to Bottomley). LOB—Athletics 7, Cardinals 4. Scoring Position—Athletics 1-for-6, Cardinals 2-for-5. 2B—Hafey (3). 3B—Gelbert (1). S—Dykes, Haines. GDP—Foxx.

Athletics	IP	H	R	ER	BB	K	ERA
Lefty Grove (L, 1-1)	8.0	5	3	1	1	3	1.59

Cardinals	IP	H	R	ER	BB	K	ERA
Jesse Haines (W, 1-0)	9.0	4	1	1	4	2	1.00

WP—Haines. Time—1:41. Attendance—39,946. Umpires—HP, Reardon. 1B, Moriarty. 2B, Rigler. 3B, Geisel.

Game 5
Monday, October 6

Athletics	AB	R	H	RBI	BB	K	Avg
Max Bishop, 2b	4	0	0	0	0	2	.250
Jimmy Dykes, 3b	3	0	0	0	1	0	.125
Mickey Cochrane, c	3	1	1	0	1	1	.200
Al Simmons, lf	4	0	0	0	0	0	.389
Jimmie Foxx, 1b	4	1	2	2	0	1	.333
Bing Miller, rf	4	0	0	0	0	1	.056
Mule Haas, cf	4	0	1	0	0	0	.118
Joe Boley, ss	3	0	1	0	1	0	.118
George Earnshaw, p	2	0	0	0	0	1	.000
Jimmy Moore, ph	0	0	0	0	1	0	1.000
Lefty Grove, p	0	0	0	0	0	0	.000
TOTALS	31	2	5	2	3	7	.190

Cardinals	AB	R	H	RBI	BB	K	Avg
Taylor Douthit, cf	4	0	0	0	0	0	.100
Sparky Adams, 3b	4	0	1	0	0	1	.158
Frankie Frisch, 2b	4	0	1	0	0	0	.200
Jim Bottomley, 1b	4	0	0	0	0	3	.050
Chick Hafey, lf	3	0	0	0	1	1	.222
George Watkins, rf	3	0	0	0	0	1	.222
Ray Blades, ph	0	0	0	0	1	0	.125
Jimmie Wilson, c	4	0	1	0	0	0	.364
Charlie Gelbert, ss	2	0	0	0	2	1	.429
Burleigh Grimes, p	2	0	0	0	0	0	.400
TOTALS	30	0	3	0	4	7	.201

	1	2	3	4	5	6	7	8	9		R	H	E
Athletics	0	0	0	0	0	0	0	0	2		2	5	0
Cardinals	0	0	0	0	0	0	0	0	0		0	3	1

E—Frisch. DP—Cardinals 1 (Adams to Frisch to Bottomley). LOB—Athletics 5, Cardinals 8. Scoring Position—Athletics 1-for-3, Cardinals 0-for-5. 2B—Wilson (1). HR—Foxx (1). S—Grimes. GDP—Haas. CS—Haas (1).

Athletics	IP	H	R	ER	BB	K	ERA
George Earnshaw	7.0	2	0	0	3	5	0.56
Lefty Grove (W, 2-1)	2.0	1	0	0	1	2	1.42

Cardinals	IP	H	R	ER	BB	K	ERA
Burleigh Grimes (L, 0-2)	9.0	5	2	2	3	7	3.71

Time—1:58. Attendance—38,844. Umpires—HP, Moriarty. 1B, Rigler. 2B, Geisel. 3B, Reardon.

Game 6
Wednesday, October 8

Cardinals	AB	R	H	RBI	BB	K	Avg
Taylor Douthit, cf	4	0	0	0	0	1	.083
Sparky Adams, 3b	2	0	0	0	0	1	.143
Andy High, ph-3b	2	1	1	0	0	0	.500
George Watkins, rf	3	0	0	0	1	1	.167
Frankie Frisch, 2b	4	0	1	0	0	0	.208
Chick Hafey, lf	4	0	2	1	0	0	.273
Jim Bottomley, 1b	2	0	0	0	2	1	.045
Jimmie Wilson, c	4	0	0	0	0	1	.267
Charlie Gelbert, ss	3	0	0	0	0	0	.353
Wild Bill Hallahan, p	0	0	0	0	0	0	.000
Showboat Fisher, ph	1	0	1	0	0	0	.500
Syl Johnson, p	0	0	0	0	0	0	—
Ray Blades, ph	1	0	0	0	0	1	.111
Jim Lindsey, p	0	0	0	0	0	0	1.000
Ernie Orsatti, ph	1	0	0	0	0	0	.000
Hi Bell, p	0	0	0	0	0	0	—
TOTALS	31	1	5	1	3	6	.190

Athletics	AB	R	H	RBI	BB	K	Avg
Max Bishop, 2b	2	2	0	0	2	0	.222
Jimmy Dykes, 3b	2	2	2	2	2	0	.222
Mickey Cochrane, c	3	1	1	2	0	0	.222
Al Simmons, cf-lf	4	1	1	0	1	0	.364
Jimmie Foxx, 1b	3	1	1	0	1	0	.333
Bing Miller, rf	3	0	2	1	0	0	.143
Jimmy Moore, lf	2	0	0	0	0	1	.333
Mule Haas, cf	1	0	0	1	0	0	.111
Joe Boley, ss	4	0	0	0	0	0	.095
George Earnshaw, p	4	0	0	0	0	2	.000
TOTALS	28	7	7	7	5	4	.207

	1	2	3	4	5	6	7	8	9		R	H	E
Cardinals	0	0	0	0	0	0	0	0	1		1	5	1
Athletics	2	0	1	2	1	1	0	0	x		7	7	0

E—Watkins. DP—Athletics 1 (Foxx). LOB—Cardinals 6, Athletics 6. Scoring Position—Cardinals 1-for-5, Athletics 1-for-7. 2B—Hafey 2 (5), Dykes (3), Cochrane (1), Foxx (2), Miller 2 (2), Fisher (2). HR—Dykes (1), Simmons (2). S—Miller. SF—Cochrane, Haas.

Cardinals	IP	H	R	ER	BB	K	ERA
Wild Bill Hallahan (L, 1-1)	2.0	2	2	2	3	2	1.64
Syl Johnson	3.0	4	4	4	1	2	7.20
Jim Lindsey	2.0	1	1	1	1	0	1.93
Hi Bell	1.0	0	0	0	0	0	0.00

Athletics	IP	H	R	ER	BB	K	ERA
George Earnshaw (W, 2-0)	9.0	5	1	1	3	6	0.72

PB—Wilson. HBP—Bishop by Hallahan. Time—1:46. Attendance—32,295. Umpires—HP, Rigler. 1B, Geisel. 2B, Reardon. 3B, Moriarty.

1930 World Series—Composite Statistics

Batting

Athletics	G	AB	R	H	RBI	2B	3B	HR	BB	SO	SB	CS	Avg	OBP	Slg
Max Bishop	6	18	5	4	0	0	0	0	7	3	0	0	.222	.462	.222
Joe Boley	6	21	1	2	1	0	0	0	1	0	0	0	.095	.095	.095
Mickey Cochrane	6	18	5	4	4	1	0	2	5	2	0	1	.222	.375	.611
Jimmy Dykes	6	18	2	4	5	3	0	1	5	3	0	0	.222	.391	.556
George Earnshaw	3	9	0	0	0	0	0	0	0	5	0	0	.000	.000	.000
Jimmie Foxx	6	21	3	7	3	2	1	1	2	4	0	0	.333	.391	.667
Lefty Grove	3	6	0	0	0	0	0	0	0	3	0	0	.000	.000	.000
Mule Haas	6	18	1	2	1	0	1	0	1	3	0	1	.111	.150	.222
Eric McNair	1	1	0	0	0	0	0	0	0	0	0	0	.000	.000	.000
Bing Miller	6	21	0	3	3	2	0	0	4	0	0	0	.143	.136	.238
Jimmy Moore	3	3	0	1	0	0	0	0	1	1	0	0	.333	.500	.333
Bill Shores	1	0	0	0	0	0	0	0	1	0	0	0	—	1.000	—
Al Simmons	6	22	4	8	4	2	0	2	2	2	0	0	.364	.417	.727
Rube Walberg	1	2	0	0	0	0	0	0	0	1	0	0	.000	.000	.000
Totals	6	178	21	35	21	10	2	6	24	32	0	2	.197	.291	.376

Batting

Cardinals	G	AB	R	H	RBI	2B	3B	HR	BB	SO	SB	CS	Avg	OBP	Slg
Sparky Adams	6	21	0	3	1	0	0	0	0	4	0	0	.143	.136	.143
Ray Blades	5	9	2	1	0	0	0	0	2	2	0	0	.111	.273	.111
Jim Bottomley	6	22	1	1	0	1	0	0	2	9	0	0	.045	.125	.091
Taylor Douthit	6	24	1	2	2	0	0	1	0	2	0	0	.083	.080	.208
Showboat Fisher	2	2	0	1	0	1	0	0	0	1	0	0	.500	.500	1.000
Frankie Frisch	6	24	0	5	0	2	0	0	0	1	0	0	.208	.208	.292
Charlie Gelbert	6	17	2	6	2	0	1	0	3	3	0	0	.353	.450	.471
Burleigh Grimes	2	5	0	2	0	0	0	0	0	1	0	0	.400	.400	.400
Chick Hafey	6	22	2	6	2	5	0	0	1	3	0	0	.273	.304	.500
Jesse Haines	1	2	0	1	1	0	0	0	0	0	0	0	.500	.500	.500
Wild Bill Hallahan	2	2	0	0	0	0	0	0	1	1	0	0	.000	.333	.000
Andy High	1	2	1	1	0	0	0	0	0	0	0	0	.500	.500	.500
Jim Lindsey	2	1	0	1	0	0	0	0	0	0	0	0	1.000	1.000	1.000
Gus Mancuso	2	7	1	2	0	0	0	0	1	2	0	0	.286	.375	.286
Ernie Orsatti	1	1	0	0	0	0	0	0	0	0	0	0	.000	.000	.000
George Puccinelli	1	1	0	0	0	0	0	0	0	0	0	0	.000	.000	.000
Flint Rhem	1	1	0	0	0	0	0	0	0	0	0	0	.000	.000	.000
George Watkins	4	12	2	2	1	0	0	1	1	3	0	0	.167	.231	.417
Jimmie Wilson	4	15	0	4	2	1	0	0	0	1	0	0	.267	.267	.333
Totals	6	190	12	38	11	10	1	2	11	33	1	0	.200	.241	.295

Pitching

Athletics	G	GS	CG	IP	H	R	ER	BB	SO	W-L	Sv-Op	Hld	ERA
George Earnshaw	3	3	2	25.0	13	2	2	7	19	2-0	0-0	0	0.72
Lefty Grove	3	2	2	19.0	15	5	3	3	10	2-1	0-0	0	1.42
Jack Quinn	1	0	0	2.0	3	1	1	0	1	0-0	0-0	0	4.50
Bill Shores	1	0	0	1.1	3	2	2	0	0	0-0	0-0	0	13.50
Rube Walberg	1	1	0	4.2	4	2	2	1	3	0-1	0-0	0	3.86
Totals	6	6	4	52.0	38	12	10	11	33	4-2	0-0	0	1.73

Pitching

Cardinals	G	GS	CG	IP	H	R	ER	BB	SO	W-L	Sv-Op	Hld	ERA
Hi Bell	1	0	0	1.0	0	0	0	0	0	0-0	0-0	0	0.00
Burleigh Grimes	2	2	2	17.0	10	7	7	6	13	0-2	0-0	0	3.71
Jesse Haines	1	1	1	9.0	4	1	1	4	2	1-0	0-0	0	1.00
Wild Bill Hallahan	2	2	1	11.0	9	2	2	8	8	1-1	0-0	0	1.64
Syl Johnson	2	0	0	5.0	4	4	4	3	4	0-0	0-0	0	7.20
Jim Lindsey	2	0	0	4.2	1	1	1	1	2	0-0	0-0	0	1.93
Flint Rhem	1	1	0	3.1	7	6	4	2	3	0-1	0-0	0	10.80
Totals	6	6	4	51.0	35	21	19	24	32	2-4	0-0	0	3.35

Fielding

Athletics	Pos	G	PO	Ast	E	DP	PB	FPct
Max Bishop	2b	6	8	9	0	0	—	1.000
Joe Boley	ss	6	9	13	1	0	—	.957
Mickey Cochrane	c	6	40	1	1	0	—	.976
Jimmy Dykes	3b	6	8	6	1	1	—	.933
George Earnshaw	p	3	1	6	0	0	—	1.000
Jimmie Foxx	1b	6	52	3	0	2	—	1.000
Lefty Grove	p	3	0	1	0	0	—	1.000
Mule Haas	cf	6	13	0	0	0	—	1.000
Bing Miller	rf	6	13	0	0	0	—	1.000
Jimmy Moore	lf	1	0	0	0	0	—	—
Jack Quinn	p	1	0	1	0	0	—	1.000
Bill Shores	p	1	0	0	0	0	—	—
Al Simmons	lf	6	9	1	0	0	—	1.000
	cf	1	3	0	0	0	—	1.000
Rube Walberg	p	1	0	0	0	0	—	—
Totals		6	156	41	3	3	0	.985

Fielding

Cardinals	Pos	G	PO	Ast	E	DP	PB	FPct
Sparky Adams	3b	6	4	7	0	1	—	1.000
Hi Bell	p	1	0	1	0	0	—	1.000
Ray Blades	rf	3	10	0	0	0	—	1.000
Jim Bottomley	1b	6	57	2	0	3	—	1.000
Taylor Douthit	cf	6	14	0	0	0	—	1.000
Frankie Frisch	2b	6	13	14	3	3	—	.900
Charlie Gelbert	ss	6	5	23	0	3	—	1.000
Burleigh Grimes	p	2	0	3	0	0	—	1.000
Chick Hafey	lf	6	9	0	0	0	—	1.000
Jesse Haines	p	1	0	1	0	0	—	1.000
Wild Bill Hallahan	p	2	0	1	0	0	—	1.000
Andy High	3b	1	0	0	0	0	—	—
Syl Johnson	p	2	0	0	0	0	—	—
Jim Lindsey	p	2	0	1	0	0	—	1.000
Gus Mancuso	c	2	13	1	0	0	0	1.000
Flint Rhem	p	1	0	0	1	0	—	.000
George Watkins	rf	4	5	0	1	0	—	.833
Jimmie Wilson	c	4	23	1	0	0	1	1.000
Totals		6	153	55	5	10	1	.977

1931 St. Louis Cardinals (NL) 4, Philadelphia Athletics (AL) 3

The St. Louis Cardinals topped the Philadelphia Athletics in an entertaining seven-game set. Al Simmons socked a two-run homer as Lefty Grove won the opener for Philadelphia, 6-2. Wild Bill Hallahan tossed a three-hitter to give the Cardinals a 2-0 win in Game 2. Burleigh Grimes avenged his two World Series losses from the year before with a two-hit, 5-2 victory over the Athletics in Game 3. George Earnshaw returned the favor with a two-hit, 3-0 win over St. Louis in the fourth game. Pepper Martin drove in four runs with a pair of singles and a homer as Hallahan won the fifth game, 5-1. Grove was overpowering in Game 6, winning 8-1, but Grimes extracted further revenge by winning the deciding game for St. Louis, 4-2.

Game 1

Thursday, October 1

Athletics	AB	R	H	RBI	BB	K	Avg
Max Bishop, 2b	5	1	1	0	0	1	.200
Mule Haas, cf	5	1	1	1	0	1	.200
Mickey Cochrane, c	4	2	2	0	1	0	.500
Al Simmons, lf	4	1	1	3	1	2	.250
Jimmie Foxx, 1b	4	0	2	2	0	1	.500
Bing Miller, rf	4	0	0	0	0	1	.000
Jimmy Dykes, 3b	3	0	2	0	1	0	.667
Dib Williams, ss	4	1	2	0	0	2	.500
Lefty Grove, p	4	0	0	0	0	3	.000
TOTALS	37	6	11	6	3	11	.297

Cardinals	AB	R	H	RBI	BB	K	Avg
Andy High, 3b	4	0	1	0	0	1	.250
Gus Mancuso, ph	1	0	0	0	0	0	.000
Wally Roettger, rf	5	1	2	0	0	1	.400
Frankie Frisch, 2b	4	1	2	0	0	0	.500
Jim Bottomley, 1b	4	0	1	1	0	0	.250
Chick Hafey, lf	4	0	1	0	0	2	.250
Pepper Martin, cf	4	0	3	1	0	1	.750
Jimmie Wilson, c	4	0	0	0	0	0	.000
Charlie Gelbert, ss	4	0	2	0	0	0	.500
Paul Derringer, p	2	0	0	0	0	1	.000
Jake Flowers, ph	1	0	0	0	0	0	.000
Syl Johnson, p	0	0	0	0	0	0	—
Ray Blades, ph	1	0	0	0	0	1	.000
TOTALS	38	2	12	2	0	7	.316

	1	2	3	4	5	6	7	8	9	R	H	E
Athletics	0	0	4	0	0	0	2	0	0	6	11	0
Cardinals	2	0	0	0	0	0	0	0	0	2	12	0

DP—Athletics 1 (Bishop to Williams to Foxx), Cardinals 1 (Bottomley). LOB—Athletics 7, Cardinals 9. Scoring Position—Athletics 2-for-8, Cardinals 2-for-10. 2B—Haas (1), Martin (1), Gelbert (1). HR—Simmons (1). GDP—Wilson. SB—Hafey (1), Martin (1).

Athletics	IP	H	R	ER	BB	K	ERA
Lefty Grove (W, 1-0)	9.0	12	2	2	0	7	2.00

Cardinals	IP	H	R	ER	BB	K	ERA
Paul Derringer (L, 0-1)	7.0	11	6	6	3	9	7.71
Syl Johnson	2.0	0	0	0	0	2	0.00

Time—1:55. Attendance—38,529. Umpires—HP, Klem. 1B, Nallin. 2B, Stark. 3B, McGowan.

Game 2

Friday, October 2

Athletics	AB	R	H	RBI	BB	K	Avg
Max Bishop, 2b	5	0	0	0	0	1	.100
Mule Haas, cf	4	0	1	0	0	1	.222
Mickey Cochrane, c	2	0	0	0	2	1	.333
Al Simmons, lf	4	0	0	0	0	0	.125
Jimmie Foxx, 1b	2	0	1	0	2	0	.500
Bing Miller, rf	4	0	1	0	0	1	.125
Jimmy Dykes, 3b	2	0	0	0	1	0	.400
Dib Williams, ss	2	0	0	0	2	2	.333
George Earnshaw, p	3	0	0	0	0	1	.000
Jimmy Moore, ph	1	0	0	0	0	1	.000
TOTALS	29	0	3	0	7	8	.226

Cardinals	AB	R	H	RBI	BB	K	Avg
Jake Flowers, 3b	4	0	0	0	0	0	.000
George Watkins, rf	4	0	2	0	0	1	.500
Frankie Frisch, 2b	4	0	1	0	0	0	.375
Jim Bottomley, 1b	3	0	0	0	1	1	.143
Chick Hafey, lf	4	0	0	0	0	1	.125
Pepper Martin, cf	3	2	2	0	0	0	.714
Jimmie Wilson, c	3	0	0	1	0	0	.000
Charlie Gelbert, ss	2	0	1	1	0	0	.500
Wild Bill Hallahan, p	2	0	0	0	0	2	.000
TOTALS	29	2	6	2	1	5	.278

	1	2	3	4	5	6	7	8	9	R	H	E
Athletics	0	0	0	0	0	0	0	0	0	0	3	0
Cardinals	0	1	0	0	0	0	1	0	x	2	6	1

E—Wilson. DP—Cardinals 1 (Frisch to Gelbert to Bottomley). LOB—Athletics 10, Cardinals 6. Scoring Position—Athletics 0-for-5, Cardinals 0-for-7. 2B—Watkins (1), Frisch (1), Martin (2). S—Dykes, Gelbert, Hallahan. GDP—Earnshaw. SB—Martin 2 (3).

Athletics	IP	H	R	ER	BB	K	ERA
George Earnshaw (L, 0-1)	8.0	6	2	2	1	5	2.25

Cardinals	IP	H	R	ER	BB	K	ERA
Wild Bill Hallahan (W, 1-0)	9.0	3	0	0	7	8	0.00

WP—Hallahan. Time—1:49. Attendance—35,947. Umpires—HP, Nallin. 1B, Stark. 2B, McGowan. 3B, Klem.

Game 3

Monday, October 5

Cardinals	AB	R	H	RBI	BB	K	Avg
Sparky Adams, 3b	3	0	0	0	0	1	.000
Jake Flowers, 3b	1	0	0	0	1	0	.000
Wally Roettger, rf	5	0	1	0	0	0	.300
George Watkins, pr-rf	0	1	0	0	0	0	.500
Frankie Frisch, 2b	5	0	1	0	0	0	.308
Jim Bottomley, 1b	4	1	1	1	1	0	.182
Chick Hafey, lf	5	1	1	0	0	0	.154
Pepper Martin, cf	4	2	2	0	0	0	.636
Jimmie Wilson, c	4	0	3	1	0	0	.273
Charlie Gelbert, ss	4	0	1	1	0	1	.400
Burleigh Grimes, p	4	0	2	2	0	0	.500
TOTALS	39	5	12	5	2	2	.302

Athletics	AB	R	H	RBI	BB	K	Avg
Max Bishop, 2b	3	0	0	0	1	1	.077
Mule Haas, cf	4	0	0	0	0	1	.154
Mickey Cochrane, c	3	0	0	0	1	1	.222
Eric McNair, pr	0	1	0	0	0	0	—
Al Simmons, lf	4	1	1	2	0	0	.167
Jimmie Foxx, 1b	2	0	0	0	2	1	.375
Bing Miller, rf	3	0	1	0	0	0	.182
Jimmy Dykes, 3b	3	0	0	0	0	0	.250
Dib Williams, ss	3	0	0	0	0	1	.222
Lefty Grove, p	2	0	0	0	0	1	.000
Doc Cramer, ph	1	0	0	0	0	0	.000
Roy Mahaffey, p	0	0	0	0	0	0	—
TOTALS	28	2	2	2	4	5	.178

	1	2	3	4	5	6	7	8	9	R	H	E
Cardinals	0	2	0	2	0	0	0	0	1	5	12	0
Athletics	0	0	0	0	0	0	0	0	2	2	2	0

DP—Cardinals 1 (Gelbert to Frisch to Bottomley). LOB—Cardinals 9, Athletics 3. Scoring Position—Cardinals 4-for-11, Athletics 0-for-3. 2B—Roettger (1), Bottomley (1), Martin (3). HR—Simmons (2). GDP—Dykes.

Cardinals	IP	H	R	ER	BB	K	ERA
Burleigh Grimes (W, 1-0)	9.0	2	2	2	4	5	2.00

Athletics	IP	H	R	ER	BB	K	ERA
Lefty Grove (L, 1-1)	8.0	11	4	4	1	2	3.18
Roy Mahaffey	1.0	1	1	1	1	0	9.00

Time—2:10. Attendance—32,295. Umpires—HP, Stark. 1B, McGowan. 2B, Klem. 3B, Nallin.

Game 4

Tuesday, October 6

Cardinals	AB	R	H	RBI	BB	K	Avg
Jake Flowers, 3b	1	0	0	0	0	0	.000
Andy High, 3b	3	0	0	0	0	0	.143
George Watkins, rf	4	0	0	0	0	0	.250
Frankie Frisch, 2b	3	0	0	0	1	0	.250
Jim Bottomley, 1b	3	0	0	0	0	2	.143
Chick Hafey, lf	3	0	0	0	0	0	.125
Pepper Martin, cf	3	0	2	0	0	1	.643
Jimmie Wilson, c	3	0	0	0	0	1	.214
Charlie Gelbert, ss	3	0	0	0	0	1	.308
Syl Johnson, p	2	0	0	0	0	2	.000
Jim Lindsey, p	0	0	0	0	0	0	—
Ripper Collins, ph	1	0	0	0	0	1	.000
Paul Derringer, p	0	0	0	0	0	0	.000
TOTALS	29	0	2	0	1	8	.237

Athletics	AB	R	H	RBI	BB	K	Avg
Max Bishop, 2b	4	1	2	0	0	0	.176
Mule Haas, cf	3	0	1	0	0	1	.188
Mickey Cochrane, c	3	0	0	0	1	0	.167
Al Simmons, lf	4	0	2	1	0	0	.250
Jimmie Foxx, 1b	3	1	1	1	1	0	.364
Bing Miller, rf	4	1	1	0	0	1	.200
Jimmy Dykes, 3b	4	0	2	1	0	0	.333
Dib Williams, ss	4	0	1	0	0	2	.231
George Earnshaw, p	3	0	0	0	0	1	.000
TOTALS	32	3	10	3	2	5	.220

	1	2	3	4	5	6	7	8	9	R	H	E
Cardinals	0	0	0	0	0	0	0	0	0	0	2	1
Athletics	1	0	0	0	0	2	0	0	x	3	10	0

E—Bottomley. DP—Cardinals 1 (Frisch to Gelbert to Bottomley). LOB—Cardinals 3, Athletics 8. Scoring Position—Cardinals 0-for-5, Athletics 2-for-7. 2B—Martin (4), Simmons (1), Miller (1). HR—Foxx (1). S—Haas. GDP—Simmons. SB—Frisch (1), Martin (4).

Cardinals	IP	H	R	ER	BB	K	ERA
Syl Johnson (L, 0-1)	5.2	9	3	3	1	2	3.52
Jim Lindsey	1.1	1	0	0	1	2	0.00
Paul Derringer	1.0	0	0	0	0	1	6.75

Athletics	IP	H	R	ER	BB	K	ERA
George Earnshaw (W, 1-1)	9.0	2	0	0	1	8	1.06

Time—1:58. Attendance—32,295. Umpires—HP, McGowan. 1B, Klem. 2B, Nallin. 3B, Stark.

Game 5

Wednesday, October 7

Cardinals	AB	R	H	RBI	BB	K	Avg
Sparky Adams, 3b	1	0	1	0	0	0	1.000
Andy High, pr-3b	4	1	0	0	0	1	.000
George Watkins, rf	3	1	0	0	1	0	.000
Frankie Frisch, 2b	4	1	2	0	0	0	.500
Pepper Martin, cf	4	1	3	4	0	0	.750
Chick Hafey, lf	4	0	1	0	0	1	.250
Jim Bottomley, 1b	4	1	2	0	0	0	.500
Jimmie Wilson, c	4	0	2	0	0	0	.500
Charlie Gelbert, ss	4	0	1	1	0	0	.250
Wild Bill Hallahan, p	4	0	0	0	0	1	.000
TOTALS	36	5	12	5	1	3	.333

Athletics	AB	R	H	RBI	BB	K	Avg
Max Bishop, 2b	2	0	0	0	0	0	.000
Eric McNair, ph-2b	2	0	0	0	0	1	.000
Mule Haas, cf	2	0	0	0	0	0	.000
Jimmy Moore, ph-lf	2	0	1	0	0	0	.500
Mickey Cochrane, c	4	0	1	0	0	0	.250
Al Simmons, lf-cf	4	1	3	0	0	0	.750
Jimmie Foxx, 1b	3	0	2	0	1	0	.667
Bing Miller, rf	4	0	0	1	0	0	.000
Jimmy Dykes, 3b	4	0	1	0	0	0	.250
Dib Williams, ss	4	0	1	0	0	1	.250
Waite Hoyt, p	2	0	0	0	0	0	.000
Rube Walberg, p	0	0	0	0	0	0	—
Johnny Heving, ph	1	0	0	0	0	0	.000
Eddie Rommel, p	0	0	0	0	0	0	—
Joe Boley, ph	1	0	0	0	0	1	.000
TOTALS	35	1	9	1	1	4	.257

	1	2	3	4	5	6	7	8	9		R	H	E
Cardinals	1	0	0	0	0	2	0	1	1		5	12	0
Athletics	0	0	0	0	0	0	0	1	0		1	9	0

DP—Cardinals 1 (Gelbert to Bottomley to Wilson), Athletics 1 (Bishop to Foxx). LOB—Cardinals 5, Athletics 8. Scoring Position—Cardinals 3-for-9, Athletics 0-for-9. 2B—Frisch (1), Simmons (1). HR—Martin (1). SB—Watkins (1). CS—Martin (1), Wilson (1).

Cardinals	IP	H	R	ER	BB	K	ERA
Wild Bill Hallahan (W, 1-0)	9.0	9	1	1	1	4	1.00

Athletics	IP	H	R	ER	BB	K	ERA
Waite Hoyt (L, 0-1)	6.0	7	3	3	0	1	4.50
Rube Walberg	2.0	2	1	1	1	2	4.50
Eddie Rommel	1.0	3	1	1	0	0	9.00

Time—1:56. Attendance—32,295. Umpires—HP, Klem. 1B, Nallin. 2B, Stark. 3B, McGowan.

Game 6

Friday, October 9

Athletics	AB	R	H	RBI	BB	K	Avg
Max Bishop, 2b	4	2	1	0	1	1	.190
Mule Haas, cf	2	0	0	1	2	1	.167
Mickey Cochrane, c	5	0	1	1	0	0	.176
Al Simmons, lf	4	1	1	2	1	0	.250
Jimmie Foxx, 1b	5	2	2	0	0	1	.375
Bing Miller, rf	3	1	1	0	0	1	.222
Jimmy Dykes, 3b	3	1	0	1	2	0	.267
Dib Williams, ss	4	1	2	1	0	0	.294
Lefty Grove, p	4	0	0	0	0	3	.000
TOTALS	34	8	8	6	6	7	.224

Cardinals	AB	R	H	RBI	BB	K	Avg
Jake Flowers, 3b	4	1	1	0	0	0	.091
Wally Roettger, rf	4	0	1	0	0	2	.286
Frankie Frisch, 2b	4	0	1	1	0	2	.250
Pepper Martin, cf	3	0	0	0	1	0	.529
Chick Hafey, lf	4	0	1	0	0	1	.150
Jim Bottomley, 1b	4	0	0	0	0	0	.111
Jimmie Wilson, c	3	0	0	0	0	0	.176
Gus Mancuso, c	0	0	0	0	0	0	.000
Charlie Gelbert, ss	3	0	1	0	0	1	.313
Paul Derringer, p	0	0	0	0	0	0	.000
Syl Johnson, p	0	0	0	0	0	0	.000
Ray Blades, ph	1	0	0	0	0	1	.000
Jim Lindsey, p	0	0	0	0	0	0	—
Ripper Collins, ph	1	0	0	0	0	0	.000
Flint Rhem, p	0	0	0	0	0	0	—
TOTALS	31	1	5	1	1	7	.225

	1	2	3	4	5	6	7	8	9		R	H	E
Athletics	0	0	0	4	0	4	0	0			8	8	1
Cardinals	0	0	0	0	0	1	0	0	0		1	5	2

E—Cochrane, Hafey, Flowers. DP—Athletics 1 (Bishop to Williams to Foxx), Cardinals 1 (Frisch to Gelbert to Bottomley). LOB—Athletics 8, Cardinals 5. Scoring Position—Athletics 3-for-10, Cardinals 1-for-5. 2B—Williams (1), Flowers (1). S—Haas, Miller, Derringer. GDP—Cochrane, Frisch.

Athletics	IP	H	R	ER	BB	K	ERA
Lefty Grove (W, 2-1)	9.0	5	1	1	1	7	2.42

Cardinals	IP	H	R	ER	BB	K	ERA
Paul Derringer (L, 0-2)	4.2	3	4	0	4	4	4.26
Syl Johnson	1.1	1	0	0	0	2	3.00
Jim Lindsey	2.0	3	4	2	2	0	5.40
Flint Rhem	1.0	1	0	0	0	1	0.00

WP—Derringer. HBP—Miller by Lindsey. Time—1:57. Attendance—39,401. Umpires—HP, Nallin. 1B, Stark. 2B, McGowan. 3B, Klem.

Game 7

Saturday, October 10

Athletics	AB	R	H	RBI	BB	K	Avg
Max Bishop, 2b	4	0	0	0	1	1	.160
Mule Haas, cf	3	0	0	0	1	0	.143
Mickey Cochrane, c	4	0	0	0	0	0	.143
Al Simmons, lf	3	0	1	0	1	1	.261
Jimmie Foxx, 1b	4	0	0	0	0	2	.300
Bing Miller, rf	4	1	3	0	0	0	.318
Jimmy Dykes, 3b	3	1	0	0	1	1	.222
Dib Williams, ss	4	0	2	0	0	1	.333
George Earnshaw, p	2	0	0	0	0	0	.000
Phil Todt, ph	0	0	0	0	1	0	—
Rube Walberg, p	0	0	0	0	0	0	—
Doc Cramer, ph	1	0	1	2	0	0	.500
TOTALS	32	2	7	2	5	6	.227

Cardinals	AB	R	H	RBI	BB	K	Avg
Andy High, 3b	4	2	3	0	0	0	.364
George Watkins, rf	3	2	2	2	1	0	.364
Frankie Frisch, 2b	3	0	0	0	0	0	.217
Pepper Martin, cf	3	0	0	0	1	1	.450
Ernie Orsatti, lf	3	0	0	0	0	3	.000
Jim Bottomley, 1b	3	0	0	0	0	2	.095
Jimmie Wilson, c	2	0	0	0	1	0	.158
Charlie Gelbert, ss	3	0	0	0	0	1	.263
Burleigh Grimes, p	3	0	0	0	0	2	.286
Wild Bill Hallahan, p	0	0	0	0	0	0	.000
TOTALS	27	4	5	2	3	9	.250

	1	2	3	4	5	6	7	8	9		R	H	E
Athletics	0	0	0	0	0	0	0	2			2	7	1
Cardinals	2	0	2	0	0	0	0	x			4	5	0

E—Foxx. DP—Athletics 1 (Dykes to Bishop to Foxx), Cardinals 1 (Frisch to Gelbert to Bottomley). LOB—Athletics 8, Cardinals 3. Scoring Position—Athletics 3-for-8, Cardinals 0-for-4. HR—Watkins (1). S—Frisch. GDP—Earnshaw, Gelbert. SB—Martin (5).

Athletics	IP	H	R	ER	BB	K	ERA
George Earnshaw (L, 1-2)	7.0	4	4	3	2	7	1.88
Rube Walberg	1.0	1	0	0	1	2	0.00

Cardinals	IP	H	R	ER	BB	K	ERA
Burleigh Grimes (W, 2-0)	8.2	7	2	2	5	6	2.04
Wild Bill Hallahan (S, 1)	0.1	0	0	0	0	0	0.00

WP—Earnshaw. Time—1:57. Attendance—20,805. Umpires—HP, Stark. 1B, McGowan. 2B, Klem. 3B, Nallin.

1931 World Series—Composite Statistics

Batting

Cardinals	G	AB	R	H	RBI	2B	3B	HR	BB	SO	SB	CS	Avg	OBP	Slg
Sparky Adams	2	4	0	1	0	0	0	0	0	1	0	0	.250	.250	.250
Ray Blades	2	2	0	0	0	0	0	0	0	2	0	0	.000	.000	.000
Jim Bottomley	7	25	2	4	2	1	0	0	2	5	0	0	.160	.222	.200
Ripper Collins	2	2	0	0	0	0	0	0	0	1	0	0	.000	.000	.000
Paul Derringer	3	2	0	0	0	0	0	0	0	1	0	0	.000	.000	.000
Jake Flowers	5	11	1	1	0	1	0	0	1	0	0	0	.091	.167	.182
Frankie Frisch	7	27	2	7	1	2	0	1	2	1	2	0	.259	.286	.333
Charlie Gelbert	7	23	0	6	3	1	0	0	0	4	0	0	.261	.261	.304
Burleigh Grimes	2	7	0	2	2	0	0	0	0	2	0	0	.286	.286	.286
Chick Hafey	6	24	1	4	0	0	0	0	0	5	1	0	.167	.167	.167
Wild Bill Hallahan	3	6	0	0	0	0	0	0	0	3	0	0	.000	.000	.000
Andy High	4	15	3	4	0	0	0	0	0	2	0	0	.267	.267	.267
Syl Johnson	3	2	0	0	0	0	0	0	0	2	0	0	.000	.000	.000
Gus Mancuso	2	1	0	0	0	0	0	0	0	0	0	0	.000	.000	.000
Pepper Martin	7	24	5	12	5	4	0	1	2	3	5	1	.500	.538	.792
Ernie Orsatti	1	3	0	0	0	0	0	0	0	3	0	0	.000	.000	.000
Wally Roettger	3	14	1	4	0	1	0	0	0	3	0	0	.286	.286	.357
George Watkins	5	14	4	4	2	1	0	1	2	1	1	0	.286	.375	.571
Jimmie Wilson	7	23	0	5	2	0	0	0	1	1	0	1	.217	.250	.217
Totals	**7**	**229**	**19**	**54**	**17**	**11**	**0**	**2**	**9**	**41**	**8**	**2**	**.236**	**.265**	**.310**

Athletics	G	AB	R	H	RBI	2B	3B	HR	BB	SO	SB	CS	Avg	OBP	Slg
Max Bishop	7	27	4	4	0	0	0	0	3	5	0	0	.148	.200	.148
Joe Boley	1	1	0	0	0	0	0	0	0	1	0	0	.000	.000	.000
Mickey Cochrane	7	25	2	4	1	0	0	0	5	2	0	0	.160	.300	.160
Doc Cramer	2	2	0	1	2	0	0	0	0	0	0	0	.500	.500	.500
Jimmy Dykes	7	22	2	5	2	0	0	0	5	1	0	0	.227	.370	.227
George Earnshaw	3	8	0	0	0	0	0	0	0	2	0	0	.000	.000	.000
Jimmie Foxx	7	23	3	8	3	0	0	1	6	5	0	0	.348	.483	.478
Lefty Grove	3	10	0	0	0	0	0	0	0	7	0	0	.000	.000	.000
Mule Haas	7	23	1	3	2	1	0	0	3	5	0	0	.130	.231	.174
Johnny Heving	1	1	0	0	0	0	0	0	0	0	0	0	.000	.000	.000
Waite Hoyt	1	2	0	0	0	0	0	0	0	0	0	0	.000	.000	.000
Eric McNair	2	1	0	0	0	0	0	0	0	1	0	0	.000	.000	.000
Bing Miller	7	26	3	7	1	1	0	0	0	4	0	0	.269	.296	.308
Jimmy Moore	2	3	0	1	0	0	0	0	0	1	0	0	.333	.333	.333
Al Simmons	7	27	4	9	8	2	0	2	3	3	0	0	.333	.400	.630
Phil Todt	1	0	0	0	0	0	0	0	1	0	0	0	—	1.000	—
Dib Williams	7	25	2	8	1	1	0	0	2	9	0	0	.320	.370	.360
Totals	**7**	**227**	**22**	**50**	**20**	**5**	**0**	**3**	**28**	**46**	**0**	**0**	**.220**	**.309**	**.282**

Pitching

Cardinals	G	GS	CG	IP	H	R	ER	BB	SO	W-L	Sv-Op	Hld	ERA
Paul Derringer	3	2	0	12.2	14	10	6	7	14	0-2	0-0	0	4.26
Burleigh Grimes	2	2	1	17.2	9	4	4	9	11	2-0	0-0	0	2.04
Wild Bill Hallahan	3	2	2	18.1	12	1	1	8	12	2-0	1-1	0	0.49
Syl Johnson	3	1	0	9.0	10	3	3	1	6	0-1	0-0	0	3.00
Jim Lindsey	2	0	0	3.1	4	4	2	3	2	0-0	0-0	0	5.40
Flint Rhem	1	0	0	1.0	1	0	0	0	1	0-0	0-0	0	0.00
Totals	**7**	**7**	**3**	**62.0**	**50**	**22**	**16**	**28**	**46**	**4-3**	**1-1**	**0**	**2.32**

Athletics	G	GS	CG	IP	H	R	ER	BB	SO	W-L	Sv-Op	Hld	ERA
George Earnshaw	3	3	2	24.0	12	6	5	4	20	1-2	0-0	0	1.88
Lefty Grove	3	3	2	26.0	28	7	7	2	16	2-1	0-0	0	2.42
Waite Hoyt	1	1	0	6.0	7	3	3	0	1	0-1	0-0	0	4.50
Roy Mahaffey	1	0	0	1.0	1	1	1	1	0	0-0	0-0	0	9.00
Eddie Rommel	1	0	0	1.0	3	1	1	0	0	0-0	0-0	0	9.00
Rube Walberg	2	0	0	3.0	3	1	1	2	4	0-0	0-0	0	3.00
Totals	**7**	**7**	**4**	**61.0**	**54**	**19**	**18**	**9**	**41**	**3-4**	**0-0**	**0**	**2.66**

Fielding

Cardinals	Pos	G	PO	Ast	E	DP	PB	FPct
Sparky Adams	3b	1	0	1	0	0	—	1.000
Jim Bottomley	1b	7	61	2	1	7	—	.984
Paul Derringer	p	3	0	2	0	0	—	1.000
Jake Flowers	3b	4	3	4	1	0	—	.875
Frankie Frisch	2b	7	23	19	0	5	—	1.000
Charlie Gelbert	ss	7	13	29	0	6	—	1.000
Burleigh Grimes	p	2	0	3	0	0	—	1.000
Chick Hafey	lf	6	8	0	1	0	—	.889
Wild Bill Hallahan	p	3	0	0	0	0	—	—
Andy High	3b	4	3	9	0	0	—	1.000
Syl Johnson	p	3	0	1	0	0	—	1.000
Jim Lindsey	p	2	0	0	0	0	—	—
Gus Mancuso	c	1	2	0	0	0	0	1.000
Pepper Martin	cf	7	11	0	0	0	—	1.000
Ernie Orsatti	lf	1	0	0	0	0	—	—
Flint Rhem	p	1	0	0	0	0	—	—
Wally Roettger	rf	3	4	0	0	0	—	1.000
George Watkins	rf	5	8	0	0	0	—	1.000
Jimmie Wilson	c	7	50	2	1	1	0	.981
Totals		**7**	**186**	**72**	**4**	**19**	**0**	**.985**

Athletics	Pos	G	PO	Ast	E	DP	PB	FPct
Max Bishop	2b	7	12	18	0	4	—	1.000
Mickey Cochrane	c	7	40	4	1	0	0	.978
Jimmy Dykes	3b	7	4	12	0	1	—	1.000
George Earnshaw	p	3	1	7	0	0	—	1.000
Jimmie Foxx	1b	7	69	2	1	4	—	.986
Lefty Grove	p	3	0	0	0	0	—	—
Mule Haas	cf	7	15	0	0	0	—	1.000
Waite Hoyt	p	1	0	0	0	0	—	—
Roy Mahaffey	p	1	0	1	0	0	—	1.000
Eric McNair	2b	1	1	1	0	0	—	1.000
Bing Miller	rf	7	13	0	0	0	—	1.000
Jimmy Moore	lf	1	1	0	0	0	—	1.000
Eddie Rommel	p	1	0	0	0	0	—	—
Al Simmons	lf	7	19	0	0	0	—	1.000
	cf	1	1	0	0	0	—	1.000
Rube Walberg	p	2	0	0	0	0	—	—
Dib Williams	ss	7	7	24	0	2	—	1.000
Totals		**7**	**183**	**69**	**2**	**11**	**0**	**.992**

1932 New York Yankees (AL) 4, Chicago Cubs (NL) 0

Lou Gehrig's heavy hitting led the Yankees to a four-game sweep of the Chicago Cubs. Ben Chapman made a spectacular running catch in the top of the fourth in Game 1, and Gehrig's two-run homer in the bottom of the frame gave New York the lead, as they went on to win, 12-6. Lefty Gomez won Game 2, 5-2. In the fifth inning of Game 3, Babe Ruth hit his second homer of the game off Charlie Root to put the Yanks ahead 5-4, and Gehrig with followed his second circuit shot of the afternoon to knock Root out of the box. (If Ruth had indeed "called his shot," the editors of the *Spalding Guide* deemed it unworthy of mention.) The Yankees took the game, 7-5, before concluding the sweep with a 13-6 victory the next day. Gehrig batted .529 and drove in eight runs with three homers and a double.

Game 1

Wednesday, September 28

Cubs	AB	R	H	RBI	BB	K	Avg
Billy Herman, 2b	5	2	2	1	0	0	.400
Woody English, 3b	4	1	1	0	1	1	.250
Kiki Cuyler, rf	5	1	1	0	0	2	.200
Riggs Stephenson, lf	5	0	3	3	0	0	.600
Johnny Moore, cf	4	0	0	0	1	1	.000
Charlie Grimm, 1b	3	0	0	0	2	2	.000
Gabby Hartnett, c	5	1	2	0	0	2	.400
Mark Koenig, ss	4	1	1	1	1	0	.250
Guy Bush, p	1	0	0	0	1	0	.000
Burleigh Grimes, p	1	0	0	0	0	1	.000
Marv Gudat, ph	1	0	0	0	0	1	.000
Bob Smith, p	0	0	0	0	0	0	—
TOTALS	38	6	10	5	6	10	.263

Yankees	AB	R	H	RBI	BB	K	Avg
Earle Combs, cf	4	2	2	1	1	1	.500
Joe Sewell, 3b	4	1	1	1	1	0	.250
Babe Ruth, rf	3	3	1	1	2	0	.333
Lou Gehrig, 1b	4	3	2	2	1	0	.500
Tony Lazzeri, 2b	4	1	1	1	0	0	.250
Bill Dickey, c	3	0	1	2	0	0	.333
Ben Chapman, lf	4	1	0	2	0	0	.000
Frankie Crosetti, ss	2	1	0	1	1	1	.000
Red Ruffing, p	4	0	0	0	0	1	.000
TOTALS	32	12	8	11	6	3	.250

	1	2	3	4	5	6	7	8	9		R	H	E
Cubs	2	0	0	0	0	0	2	2	0		6	10	1
Yankees	0	0	0	3	0	5	3	1	x		12	8	2

E—Crosetti, English, Ruth. DP—Cubs 1 (Herman to Koenig to Grimm). LOB—Cubs 11, Yankees 4. Scoring Position—Cubs 3-for-11, Yankees 5-for-13. 2B—Hartnett 2 (2), Combs (1). 3B—Koenig (1). HR—Gehrig (1). S—Crosetti. GDP—Combs. SB—Cuyler (1).

Cubs	IP	H	R	ER	BB	K	ERA
Guy Bush (L, 0-1)	5.1	3	8	8	5	2	13.50
Burleigh Grimes	1.2	3	3	3	1	0	16.20
Bob Smith	1.0	2	1	1	0	1	9.00

Yankees	IP	H	R	ER	BB	K	ERA
Red Ruffing (W, 1-0)	9.0	10	6	3	6	10	3.00

WP—Grimes. HBP—Dickey by Grimes. Time—2:31. Attendance—41,459. Umpires—HP, Dinneen. 1B, Klem. 2B, Van Graflan. 3B, Magerkurth.

Game 2

Thursday, September 29

Cubs	AB	R	H	RBI	BB	K	Avg
Billy Herman, 2b	4	1	1	0	0	2	.333
Woody English, 3b	4	0	1	0	0	1	.250
Kiki Cuyler, rf	4	0	1	0	0	0	.222
Riggs Stephenson, lf	4	1	2	1	0	0	.556
Frank Demaree, cf	4	0	1	1	0	0	.250
Charlie Grimm, 1b	4	0	2	0	0	0	.286
Gabby Hartnett, c	3	0	1	0	1	1	.375
Billy Jurges, ss	3	0	0	0	0	0	.000
Lon Warneke, p	3	0	0	0	0	3	.000
Rollie Hemsley, ph	1	0	0	0	0	1	.000
TOTALS	34	2	9	2	1	8	.295

Yankees	AB	R	H	RBI	BB	K	Avg
Earle Combs, cf	3	1	1	0	1	0	.429
Joe Sewell, 3b	3	1	1	0	1	0	.286
Babe Ruth, rf	3	1	1	0	1	1	.333
Lou Gehrig, 1b	4	2	3	1	0	0	.625
Tony Lazzeri, 2b	4	0	1	0	0	0	.250
Bill Dickey, c	3	0	2	2	1	0	.500
Ben Chapman, lf	4	0	1	2	0	3	.125
Frankie Crosetti, ss	3	0	0	0	0	1	.000
Lefty Gomez, p	3	0	0	0	0	2	.000
TOTALS	30	5	10	5	4	7	.310

	1	2	3	4	5	6	7	8	9		R	H	E
Cubs	1	0	1	0	0	0	0	0	0		2	9	0
Yankees	2	0	2	0	1	0	0	0	x		5	10	1

E—Crosetti. DP—Cubs 4 (Warneke to Hartnett to Jurges; Hartnett to Herman; Herman to Jurges to Grimm; Herman to Jurges to Grimm). LOB—Cubs 7, Yankees 5. Scoring Position—Cubs 1-for-9, Yankees 4-for-10. 2B—Herman (1), Stephenson (1). 3B—Cuyler (1). S—Jurges. GDP—Gehrig, Dickey. CS—Dickey (1).

Cubs	IP	H	R	ER	BB	K	ERA
Lon Warneke (L, 0-1)	8.0	10	5	5	4	7	5.63

Yankees	IP	H	R	ER	BB	K	ERA
Lefty Gomez (W, 1-0)	9.0	9	2	1	1	8	1.00

Time—1:46. Attendance—50,709. Umpires—HP, Klem. 1B, Van Graflan. 2B, Magerkurth. 3B, Dinneen.

Game 3

Saturday, October 1

Yankees	AB	R	H	RBI	BB	K	Avg
Earle Combs, cf	5	1	0	0	0	2	.250
Joe Sewell, 3b	2	1	0	0	2	0	.222
Babe Ruth, rf	4	2	2	4	1	0	.400
Lou Gehrig, 1b	5	2	2	2	0	1	.538
Tony Lazzeri, 2b	4	1	0	0	1	1	.167
Bill Dickey, c	4	0	1	0	1	0	.400
Ben Chapman, lf	4	0	2	1	1	1	.250
Frankie Crosetti, ss	4	0	1	0	1	0	.111
George Pipgras, p	5	0	0	0	0	5	.000
Herb Pennock, p	0	0	0	0	0	0	—
TOTALS	37	7	8	7	7	10	.283

Cubs	AB	R	H	RBI	BB	K	Avg
Billy Herman, 2b	4	1	0	0	1	0	.231
Woody English, 3b	4	0	0	0	1	0	.167
Kiki Cuyler, rf	4	1	3	2	0	0	.385
Riggs Stephenson, lf	4	0	1	0	0	0	.462
Johnny Moore, cf	3	1	0	0	1	0	.000
Charlie Grimm, 1b	4	0	1	1	0	0	.273
Gabby Hartnett, c	4	1	1	1	0	0	.333
Billy Jurges, ss	4	1	3	0	0	0	.429
Charlie Root, p	2	0	0	0	0	1	.000
Pat Malone, p	0	0	0	0	0	0	—
Marv Gudat, ph	1	0	0	0	0	0	.000
Jakie May, p	0	0	0	0	0	0	—
Bud Tinning, p	0	0	0	0	0	0	—
Mark Koenig, ph	0	0	0	0	0	0	.250
Rollie Hemsley, ph	1	0	0	0	0	1	.000
TOTALS	35	5	9	4	3	2	.276

	1	2	3	4	5	6	7	8	9		R	H	E
Yankees	3	0	1	0	2	0	0	0	1		7	8	1
Cubs	1	0	2	1	0	0	0	0	1		5	9	4

E—Herman, Jurges 2, Lazzeri, Hartnett. DP—Yankees 1 (Sewell to Lazzeri to Gehrig), Cubs 1 (Herman to Jurges to Grimm). LOB—Yankees 11, Cubs 6. Scoring Position—Yankees 2-for-8, Cubs 0-for-8. 2B—Chapman (1), Cuyler (1), Grimm (1), Jurges (1). HR—Ruth 2 (2), Gehrig 2 (3), Cuyler (1), Hartnett (1). GDP—Ruth, Stephenson. SB—Jurges 2 (2). CS—Chapman (1), English (1).

Yankees	IP	H	R	ER	BB	K	ERA
George Pipgras (W, 1-0)	8.0	9	5	4	3	1	4.50
Herb Pennock (S, 1)	1.0	0	0	0	0	1	0.00

Cubs	IP	H	R	ER	BB	K	ERA
Charlie Root (L, 0-1)	4.1	6	6	5	3	4	10.38
Pat Malone	2.2	1	0	0	4	4	0.00
Jakie May	1.1	1	1	0	0	1	0.00
Bud Tinning	0.2	0	0	0	0	1	0.00

Pipgras pitched to two batters in the 9th.

HBP—Sewell by May. Time—2:11. Attendance—49,986. Umpires—HP, Van Graflan. 1B, Magerkurth. 2B, Dinneen. 3B, Klem.

Game 4

Sunday, October 2

Yankees	AB	R	H	RBI	BB	K	Avg
Earle Combs, cf	4	4	3	2	2	0	.375
Joe Sewell, 3b	6	1	3	2	0	0	.333
Babe Ruth, lf	5	0	1	1	0	2	.333
Sammy Byrd, lf	0	0	0	0	0	0	—
Lou Gehrig, 1b	4	2	3	1	0	.529
Tony Lazzeri, 2b	5	2	3	4	1	0	.294
Bill Dickey, c	6	2	3	0	0	1	.438
Ben Chapman, rf	5	0	2	1	1	0	.294
Frankie Crosetti, ss	6	1	1	0	0	1	.133
Johnny Allen, p	0	0	0	0	0	0	—
Wilcy Moore, p	3	0	1	0	0	2	.333
Red Ruffing, ph	0	0	0	0	1	0	.000
Myril Hoag, pr	0	1	0	0	0	0	—
Herb Pennock, p	1	0	0	0	0	0	.000
TOTALS	45	13	19	13	6	6	.331

Cubs	AB	R	H	RBI	BB	K	Avg
Billy Herman, 2b	5	1	1	0	0	1	.222
Woody English, 3b	5	1	1	1	0	0	.176
Kiki Cuyler, rf	5	0	0	0	0	1	.278
Riggs Stephenson, lf	5	1	2	0	0	0	.444
Frank Demaree, cf	3	1	1	3	1	0	.286
Charlie Grimm, 1b	4	2	2	0	0	0	.333
Gabby Hartnett, c	4	0	1	0	0	0	.313
Stan Hack, pr	0	0	0	0	0	0	—
Burleigh Grimes, p	0	0	0	0	0	0	.000
Billy Jurges, ss	4	0	1	1	0	1	.364
Guy Bush, p	0	0	0	0	0	0	.000
Lon Warneke, p	1	0	0	0	0	0	.000
Jakie May, p	2	0	0	0	0	0	.000
Bud Tinning, p	0	0	0	0	0	0	.000
Rollie Hemsley, ph-c	1	0	0	0	0	1	.000
TOTALS	39	6	9	5	1	4	.275

	1	2	3	4	5	6	7	8	9		R	H	E
Yankees	1	0	2	0	0	2	4	0	4		13	19	4
Cubs	4	0	0	0	0	1	0	0	1		6	9	1

E—Demaree, Crosetti 2, Gehrig, Sewell. DP—Cubs 1 (Herman to Jurges to Grimm). LOB—Yankees 13, Cubs 7. Scoring Position—Yankees 6-for-18, Cubs 2-for-12. 2B—Sewell (1), Gehrig (1), Chapman (2), Crosetti (1), Grimm (2). HR—Combs (1), Lazzeri 2 (2), Demaree (1). GDP—Crosetti.

Yankees	IP	H	R	ER	BB	K	ERA
Johnny Allen	0.2	5	4	3	0	0	40.50
Wilcy Moore (W, 1-0)	5.1	2	1	0	0	1	0.00
Herb Pennock (S, 2)	3.0	2	1	1	1	3	2.25

Cubs	IP	H	R	ER	BB	K	ERA
Guy Bush	0.1	2	1	1	1	0	14.29
Lon Warneke	2.2	5	2	2	1	1	5.91
Jakie May (L, 0-1)	3.1	8	6	6	3	3	11.57
Bud Tinning	1.2	0	0	0	0	2	0.00
Burleigh Grimes	1.0	4	4	1	0	0	23.63

Warneke pitched to two batters in the 4th.

HBP—Gehrig by May, Ruth by Bush. Time—2:27. Attendance—49,844. Umpires—HP, Magerkurth. 1B, Dinneen. 2B, Klem. 3B, Van Graflan.

1932 World Series—Composite Statistics

Batting

Yankees	G	AB	R	H	RBI	2B	3B	HR	BB	SO	SB	CS	Avg	OBP	Slg
Ben Chapman	4	17	1	5	6	2	0	0	2	4	0	1	.294	.368	.412
Earle Combs	4	16	8	6	4	1	0	1	4	3	0	0	.375	.500	.625
Frankie Crosetti	4	15	2	2	0	1	0	0	2	3	0	0	.133	.235	.200
Bill Dickey	4	16	2	7	4	0	0	0	2	1	0	1	.438	.526	.438
Lou Gehrig	4	17	9	9	8	1	0	3	2	1	0	0	.529	.600	1.118
Lefty Gomez	1	3	0	0	0	0	0	0	0	2	0	0	.000	.000	.000
Myril Hoag	1	0	1	0	0	0	0	0	0	0	0	0	—	—	—
Tony Lazzeri	4	17	4	5	5	0	0	2	2	1	0	0	.294	.368	.647
Wilcy Moore	1	3	0	1	0	0	0	0	0	2	0	0	.333	.333	.333
Herb Pennock	2	1	0	0	0	0	0	0	0	0	0	0	.000	.000	.000
George Pipgras	1	5	0	0	0	0	0	0	0	5	0	0	.000	.000	.000
Red Ruffing	2	4	0	0	0	0	0	0	1	1	0	0	.000	.200	.000
Babe Ruth	4	15	6	5	6	0	0	2	4	3	0	0	.333	.500	.733
Joe Sewell	4	15	4	5	3	1	0	0	4	0	0	0	.333	.500	.400
Totals	4	144	37	45	36	6	0	8	23	26	0	2	.313	.421	.521

Cubs	G	AB	R	H	RBI	2B	3B	HR	BB	SO	SB	CS	Avg	OBP	Slg
Guy Bush	2	1	0	0	0	0	0	0	1	0	0	0	.000	.500	.000
Kiki Cuyler	4	18	2	5	2	1	1	1	0	3	1	0	.278	.278	.611
Frank Demaree	2	7	1	2	4	0	0	1	1	0	0	0	.286	.375	.714
Woody English	4	17	2	3	1	0	0	0	2	2	0	1	.176	.263	.176
Burleigh Grimes	2	1	0	0	0	0	0	0	0	1	0	0	.000	.000	.000
Charlie Grimm	4	15	2	5	1	2	0	0	2	2	0	0	.333	.412	.467
Marv Gudat	2	2	0	0	0	0	0	0	0	1	0	0	.000	.000	.000
Stan Hack	1	0	0	0	0	0	0	0	0	0	0	0	—	—	—
Gabby Hartnett	4	16	2	5	1	2	0	1	1	3	0	0	.313	.353	.625
Rollie Hemsley	3	3	0	0	0	0	0	0	0	3	0	0	.000	.000	.000
Billy Herman	4	18	5	4	1	1	0	0	1	3	0	0	.222	.263	.278
Billy Jurges	3	11	1	4	1	1	0	0	0	2	0	0	.364	.364	.455
Mark Koenig	2	4	1	1	1	0	1	0	1	0	0	0	.250	.400	.750
Jakie May	2	2	0	0	0	0	0	0	0	0	0	0	.000	.000	.000
Johnny Moore	2	7	1	0	0	0	0	0	2	1	0	0	.000	.222	.000
Charlie Root	1	2	0	0	0	0	0	0	0	1	0	0	.000	.000	.000
Riggs Stephenson	4	18	2	8	4	1	0	0	0	3	0	0	.444	.444	.500
Lon Warneke	2	4	0	0	0	0	0	0	0	3	0	0	.000	.000	.000
Totals	4	146	19	37	16	8	2	3	11	24	3	1	.253	.306	.397

Pitching

Yankees	G	GS	CG	IP	H	R	ER	BB	SO	W-L	Sv-Op	Hld	ERA
Johnny Allen	1	1	0	0.2	5	4	3	0	0	0-0	0-0	0	40.50
Lefty Gomez	1	1	1	9.0	9	2	1	1	8	1-0	0-0	0	1.00
Wilcy Moore	1	0	0	5.1	2	1	0	0	1	1-0	0-0	0	0.00
Herb Pennock	2	0	0	4.0	2	1	1	1	4	0-0	2-2	0	2.25
George Pipgras	1	1	0	8.0	9	5	4	3	1	1-0	0-0	0	4.50
Red Ruffing	1	1	1	9.0	10	6	3	6	10	1-0	0-0	0	3.00
Totals	4	4	2	36.0	37	19	12	11	24	4-0	2-2	0	3.00

Cubs	G	GS	CG	IP	H	R	ER	BB	SO	W-L	Sv-Op	Hld	ERA
Guy Bush	2	2	0	5.2	5	9	9	6	2	0-1	0-0	0	14.29
Burleigh Grimes	2	0	0	2.2	7	7	7	2	0	0-0	0-0	0	23.63
Pat Malone	1	0	0	2.2	1	0	0	4	4	0-0	0-0	0	0.00
Jakie May	2	0	0	4.2	9	7	6	3	4	0-1	0-0	0	11.57
Charlie Root	1	1	0	4.1	6	6	5	3	4	0-1	0-0	0	10.38
Bob Smith	1	0	0	1.0	2	1	1	0	1	0-0	0-0	0	9.00
Bud Tinning	2	0	0	2.1	0	0	0	3	0	0-0	0-0	0	0.00
Lon Warneke	2	1	1	10.2	15	7	7	5	8	0-1	0-0	0	5.91
Totals	4	4	1	34.0	45	37	35	23	26	0-4	0-0	0	9.26

Fielding

Yankees	Pos	G	PO	Ast	E	DP	PB	FPct
Johnny Allen	p	1	0	0	0	0	—	—
Sammy Byrd	lf	1	0	0	0	0	—	—
Ben Chapman	lf	3	4	1	0	0	—	1.000
	rf	1	4	0	0	0	—	1.000
Earle Combs	cf	4	10	0	0	0	—	1.000
Frankie Crosetti	ss	4	9	13	4	0	—	.846
Bill Dickey	c	4	25	1	0	0	0	1.000
Lou Gehrig	1b	4	37	2	1	1	—	.975
Lefty Gomez	p	1	0	3	0	0	—	1.000
Tony Lazzeri	2b	4	8	11	1	1	—	.950
Wilcy Moore	p	1	0	1	0	0	—	1.000
Herb Pennock	p	2	0	1	0	0	—	1.000
George Pipgras	p	1	0	0	0	0	—	—
Red Ruffing	p	1	1	3	0	0	—	1.000
Babe Ruth	rf	3	4	0	1	0	—	.800
	lf	1	2	0	0	0	—	1.000
Joe Sewell	3b	4	4	6	1	1	—	.909
Totals		4	108	42	8	3	0	.949

Cubs	Pos	G	PO	Ast	E	DP	PB	FPct
Guy Bush	p	2	0	2	0	0	—	1.000
Kiki Cuyler	rf	4	5	0	0	0	—	1.000
Frank Demaree	cf	2	4	0	1	0	—	.800
Woody English	3b	4	3	4	1	0	—	.875
Burleigh Grimes	p	2	0	0	0	0	—	—
Charlie Grimm	1b	4	28	3	0	5	—	1.000
Gabby Hartnett	c	4	32	5	1	2	0	.974
Rollie Hemsley	c	1	0	0	0	0	0	—
Billy Herman	2b	4	5	12	1	6	—	.944
Billy Jurges	ss	3	11	8	2	5	—	.905
Mark Koenig	ss	1	4	3	0	1	—	1.000
Pat Malone	p	1	0	0	0	0	—	—
Jakie May	p	2	1	0	0	0	—	1.000
Johnny Moore	cf	2	4	0	0	0	—	1.000
Charlie Root	p	1	0	0	0	0	—	—
Bob Smith	p	1	0	0	0	0	—	—
Riggs Stephenson	lf	4	4	0	0	0	—	1.000
Bud Tinning	p	2	0	1	0	0	—	1.000
Lon Warneke	p	2	1	2	0	1	—	1.000
Totals		4	102	40	6	20	0	.959

1933 New York Giants (NL) 4, Washington Senators (AL) 1

Bill Terry, in his first full year following John McGraw's 31-year reign as the manager of the New York Giants, piloted the Giants to a five-game World Series victory over the Washington Senators. Mel Ott drove in three runs in the opener with a homer and three singles as Carl Hubbell beat Lefty Stewart, 4-2. Consecutive RBI singles by Lefty O'Doul, Travis Jackson and Gus Mancuso helped the Giants to a 6-1 win in Game 2, before Washington's Earl Whitehill blanked the Giants 4-0 in Game 3. Game 4 went 11 innings before New York's Blondy Ryan knocked in the go-ahead run, and Hubbell escaped a one-out, bases-loaded jam in the bottom of the frame by inducing pinch-hitter Cliff Bolton to tap into a game-ending double play. The fifth game also went into extra innings before Mel Ott homered in the 10th to give the Giants the go-ahead run in their 4-3 victory.

Game 1

Tuesday, October 3

Senators	AB	R	H	RBI	BB	K	Avg
Buddy Myer, 2b	4	1	1	0	0	1	.250
Goose Goslin, rf	4	0	0	0	0	1	.000
Heinie Manush, lf	4	1	0	0	0	1	.000
Joe Cronin, ss	4	0	2	1	0	0	.500
Fred Schulte, cf	4	0	2	0	0	1	.500
Joe Kuhel, 1b	4	0	0	1	0	1	.000
Ossie Bluege, 3b	4	0	0	0	0	3	.000
Luke Sewell, c	3	0	0	0	1	0	.000
Lefty Stewart, p	1	0	0	0	0	1	.000
Jack Russell, p	1	0	0	0	0	1	.000
Dave Harris, ph	0	0	0	0	1	0	—
Bud Thomas, p	0	0	0	0	0	0	—
TOTALS	33	2	5	2	2	10	.152

Giants	AB	R	H	RBI	BB	K	Avg
Jo-Jo Moore, lf	4	1	0	0	0	0	.000
Hughie Critz, 2b	4	1	1	0	0	0	.250
Bill Terry, 1b	4	1	1	0	0	0	.250
Mel Ott, rf	4	1	4	3	0	0	1.000
Kiddo Davis, cf	4	0	2	0	0	2	.500
Travis Jackson, 3b	4	0	0	1	0	1	.000
Gus Mancuso, c	4	0	0	0	0	0	.000
Blondy Ryan, ss	4	0	1	0	0	2	.250
Carl Hubbell, p	3	0	1	0	0	0	.333
TOTALS	35	4	10	4	0	5	.286

	1	2	3	4	5	6	7	8	9		R	H	E
Senators	0	0	0	1	0	0	0	0	1		2	5	3
Giants	2	0	2	0	0	0	0	0	x		4	10	2

E—Ryan, Myer 3, Critz. DP—Giants 1 (Mancuso to Ryan). LOB—Senators 6, Giants 7. Scoring Position—Senators 1-for-9, Giants 1-for-8. HR—Ott (1). CS—Schulte (1), Ott (1).

Senators	IP	H	R	ER	BB	K	ERA
Lefty Stewart (L, 0-1)	2.0	6	4	2	0	0	9.00
Jack Russell	5.0	4	0	0	0	3	0.00
Bud Thomas	1.0	0	0	0	0	2	0.00

Giants	IP	H	R	ER	BB	K	ERA
Carl Hubbell (W, 1-0)	9.0	5	2	0	2	10	0.00

Stewart pitched to three batters in the 3rd.

Time—2:07. Attendance—46,672. Umpires—HP, Moran. 1B, Moriarty. 2B, Pfirman. 3B, Ormsby.

Game 2

Wednesday, October 4

Senators	AB	R	H	RBI	BB	K	Avg
Buddy Myer, 2b	3	0	0	0	1	0	.143
Goose Goslin, rf	4	1	2	1	0	0	.250
Heinie Manush, lf	3	0	1	0	1	0	.143
Joe Cronin, ss	4	0	0	0	0	1	.250
Fred Schulte, cf	4	0	0	0	0	0	.250
Joe Kuhel, 1b	3	0	0	0	1	0	.000
Ossie Bluege, 3b	2	0	0	0	1	1	.000
Dave Harris, ph	1	0	0	0	0	0	.000
Luke Sewell, c	3	0	0	0	0	0	.000
Cliff Bolton, ph	1	0	0	0	0	0	.000
General Crowder, p	2	0	1	0	0	0	.500
Bud Thomas, p	0	0	0	0	0	0	—
Sam Rice, ph	1	0	1	0	0	0	1.000
Alex McColl, p	0	0	0	0	0	0	—
TOTALS	31	1	5	1	4	2	.161

Giants	AB	R	H	RBI	BB	K	Avg
Jo-Jo Moore, lf	4	0	2	1	0	1	.250
Hughie Critz, 2b	3	1	1	0	1	0	.286
Bill Terry, 1b	4	1	1	0	0	0	.250
Mel Ott, rf	2	1	0	0	2	0	.667
Kiddo Davis, cf	2	0	1	0	0	0	.500
Lefty O'Doul, ph	1	1	1	2	0	0	1.000
Homer Peel, cf	1	0	0	0	0	0	.000
Travis Jackson, 3b	3	1	1	1	0	0	.143
Gus Mancuso, c	4	1	1	1	0	0	.125
Blondy Ryan, ss	4	0	1	0	0	0	.250
Hal Schumacher, p	4	0	1	1	0	1	.250
TOTALS	32	6	10	6	3	3	.297

	1	2	3	4	5	6	7	8	9		R	H	E
Senators	0	0	1	0	0	0	0	0	0		1	5	0
Giants	0	0	0	0	6	0	0	x			6	10	0

DP—Senators 1 (Cronin to Myer to Kuhel), Giants 1 (Jackson to Critz to Terry). LOB—Senators 7, Giants 6. Scoring Position—Senators 0-for-5, Giants 6-for-10. 2B—Terry (1). HR—Goslin (1). S—Jackson. GDP—Cronin, Schumacher.

Senators	IP	H	R	ER	BB	K	ERA
General Crowder (L, 0-1)	5.2	9	6	6	3	3	9.53
Bud Thomas	0.1	1	0	0	0	0	0.00
Alex McColl	2.0	0	0	0	0	0	0.00

Giants	IP	H	R	ER	BB	K	ERA
Hal Schumacher (W, 1-0)	9.0	5	1	1	4	2	1.00

WP—Schumacher. Time—2:09. Attendance—35,461. Umpires—HP, Moriarty. 1B, Pfirman. 2B, Ormsby. 3B, Moran.

Game 3

Thursday, October 5

Giants	AB	R	H	RBI	BB	K	Avg
Jo-Jo Moore, lf	4	0	0	0	0	0	.167
Hughie Critz, 2b	4	0	1	0	0	0	.273
Bill Terry, 1b	4	0	0	0	0	0	.167
Mel Ott, rf	3	0	0	0	1	2	.444
Kiddo Davis, cf	4	0	1	0	0	0	.400
Travis Jackson, 3b	3	0	1	0	1	0	.200
Gus Mancuso, c	4	0	0	0	0	0	.083
Blondy Ryan, ss	3	0	0	0	0	0	.182
Freddie Fitzsimmons, p	2	0	1	0	0	0	.500
Homer Peel, ph	1	0	1	0	0	0	.500
Hi Bell, p	0	0	0	0	0	0	—
TOTALS	32	0	5	0	2	2	.242

Senators	AB	R	H	RBI	BB	K	Avg
Buddy Myer, 2b	4	1	3	2	0	1	.364
Goose Goslin, rf	4	1	1	0	0	1	.250
Heinie Manush, lf	4	0	0	0	0	0	.091
Joe Cronin, ss	4	0	1	1	0	0	.250
Fred Schulte, cf	4	0	2	1	0	0	.333
Joe Kuhel, 1b	3	0	0	0	0	0	.000
Ossie Bluege, 3b	3	1	1	0	0	0	.111
Luke Sewell, c	3	1	1	0	0	0	.111
Earl Whitehill, p	3	0	0	0	0	0	—
TOTALS	32	4	9	4	0	2	.191

	1	2	3	4	5	6	7	8	9		R	H	E
Giants	0	0	0	0	0	0	0	0	0		0	5	0
Senators	2	1	0	0	0	0	1	0	x		4	9	1

E—Cronin. DP—Giants 1 (Moore to Mancuso), Senators 1 (Cronin to Myer to Kuhel). LOB—Giants 7, Senators 4. Scoring Position—Giants 0-for-7, Senators 3-for-10. 2B—Jackson (1), Myer (1), Goslin (1), Schulte (1), Bluege (1). GDP—Mancuso. SB—Sewell (1). CS—Kuhel (1).

Giants	IP	H	R	ER	BB	K	ERA
Freddie Fitzsimmons (L, 0-1)	7.0	9	4	4	0	2	5.14
Hi Bell	1.0	0	0	0	0	0	0.00

Senators	IP	H	R	ER	BB	K	ERA
Earl Whitehill (W, 0-1)	9.0	5	0	0	2	2	0.00

WP—Whitehill. Time—1:55. Attendance—25,727. Umpires—HP, Pfirman. 1B, Ormsby. 2B, Moran. 3B, Moriarty.

Game 4
Friday, October 6

Giants	AB	R	H	RBI	BB	K	Avg
Jo-Jo Moore, lf	5	0	2	0	1	1	.235
Hughie Critz, 2b	6	0	0	0	0	0	.176
Bill Terry, 1b	5	1	2	1	0	0	.235
Mel Ott, rf	4	0	2	0	1	0	.462
Kiddo Davis, cf	4	0	1	0	0	1	.357
Travis Jackson, 3b	5	1	1	0	0	1	.200
Gus Mancuso, c	2	0	0	0	2	0	.071
Blondy Ryan, ss	5	0	2	1	0	1	.250
Carl Hubbell, p	4	0	1	0	0	0	.286
TOTALS	40	2	11	2	4	4	.246

Senators	AB	R	H	RBI	BB	K	Avg
Buddy Myer, 2b	4	0	2	0	1	0	.400
Goose Goslin, rf-lf	4	0	1	0	0	0	.250
Heinie Manush, lf	2	0	0	0	1	0	.077
Dave Harris, rf	1	0	0	0	1	0	.000
Joe Cronin, ss	5	0	1	0	0	1	.235
Fred Schulte, cf	5	0	1	0	0	0	.294
Joe Kuhel, 1b	5	1	1	0	0	2	.067
Ossie Bluege, 3b	3	0	0	0	0	0	.083
Luke Sewell, c	4	0	2	1	1	0	.231
Montie Weaver, p	4	0	0	0	0	2	.000
Jack Russell, p	0	0	0	0	0	0	.000
Cliff Bolton, ph	1	0	0	0	0	0	.000
TOTALS	38	1	8	1	4	5	.197

	1	2	3	4	5	6	7	8	9	10	11		R	H	E
Giants	0	0	0	1	0	0	0	0	0	0	1		2	11	1
Senators	0	0	0	0	0	0	1	0	0	0	0		1	8	0

E—Hubbell. DP—Senators 1 (Myer to Kuhel). LOB—Giants 12, Senators 11. Scoring Position—Giants 1-for-12, Senators 1-for-8. 2B—Moore (1). HR—Terry (1). S—Davis, Mancuso, Hubbell, Goslin, Bluege 2. GDP—Bolton.

Giants	IP	H	R	ER	BB	K	ERA
Carl Hubbell (W, 2-0)	11.0	8	1	0	4	5	0.00

Senators	IP	H	R	ER	BB	K	ERA
Montie Weaver (L, 0-1)	10.1	11	2	2	4	3	1.74
Jack Russell	0.2	0	0	0	0	1	0.00

Time—2:59. Attendance—26,762. Umpires—HP, Ormsby. 1B, Moran. 2B, Moriarty. 3B, Pfirman.

Game 5
Saturday, October 7

Giants	AB	R	H	RBI	BB	K	Avg
Jo-Jo Moore, lf	5	0	1	0	0	1	.227
Hughie Critz, 2b	5	0	0	0	0	0	.136
Bill Terry, 1b	5	0	2	0	0	0	.273
Mel Ott, rf	5	1	1	1	0	2	.389
Kiddo Davis, cf	5	1	2	0	0	0	.368
Travis Jackson, 3b	3	1	1	0	0	1	.222
Gus Mancuso, c	3	1	1	1	1	0	.118
Blondy Ryan, ss	2	0	1	0	1	1	.278
Hal Schumacher, p	3	0	1	2	0	2	.286
Dolf Luque, p	1	0	1	0	0	0	1.000
TOTALS	37	4	11	4	2	7	.256

Senators	AB	R	H	RBI	BB	K	Avg
Buddy Myer, 2b	5	0	0	0	0	1	.300
Goose Goslin, rf	4	0	1	0	1	1	.250
Heinie Manush, lf	5	1	1	0	0	0	.111
Joe Cronin, ss	5	1	3	0	0	0	.318
Fred Schulte, cf	4	1	2	3	1	0	.333
John Kerr, pr	0	0	0	0	0	0	—
Joe Kuhel, 1b	5	0	2	0	0	1	.150
Ossie Bluege, 3b	4	0	1	0	0	2	.125
Luke Sewell, c	4	0	0	0	0	0	.176
General Crowder, p	2	0	0	0	0	0	.250
Jack Russell, p	1	0	0	0	1	1	.000
TOTALS	39	3	10	3	3	6	.225

	1	2	3	4	5	6	7	8	9	10		R	H	E
Giants	0	2	0	0	1	0	0	0	1			4	11	1
Senators	0	0	0	0	3	0	0	0	0			3	10	0

E—Jackson. DP—Giants 1 (Jackson to Terry), Senators 1 (Cronin to Kuhel). LOB—Giants 7, Senators 9. Scoring Position—Giants 2-for-8, Senators 1-for-6. 2B—Davis (1), Mancuso (1). HR—Ott (2), Schulte (1). S—Jackson, Ryan. GDP—Jackson.

Giants	IP	H	R	ER	BB	K	ERA
Hal Schumacher	5.2	8	3	3	1	1	2.45
Dolf Luque (W, 1-0)	4.1	2	0	0	2	5	0.00

Senators	IP	H	R	ER	BB	K	ERA
General Crowder	5.1	7	3	3	2	4	7.36
Jack Russell (L, 0-1)	4.2	4	1	1	0	3	0.87

WP—Crowder, Schumacher. Time—2:38. Attendance—28,454. Umpires—HP, Moran. 1B, Moriarty. 2B, Pfirman. 3B, Ormsby.

1933 World Series—Composite Statistics

Batting

Giants	G	AB	R	H	RBI	2B	3B	HR	BB	SO	SB	CS	Avg	OBP	Slg
Hughie Critz	5	22	2	3	0	0	0	0	1	0	0	0	.136	.174	.136
Kiddo Davis	5	19	1	7	0	1	0	0	0	3	0	0	.368	.368	.421
Freddie Fitzsimmons	1	2	0	1	0	0	0	0	0	0	0	0	.500	.500	.500
Carl Hubbell	2	7	0	2	0	0	0	0	0	0	0	0	.286	.286	.286
Travis Jackson	5	18	3	4	2	1	0	0	1	3	0	0	.222	.263	.278
Dolf Luque	1	1	0	1	0	0	0	0	0	0	0	0	1.000	1.000	1.000
Gus Mancuso	5	17	2	2	2	1	0	0	3	0	0	0	.118	.250	.176
Jo-Jo Moore	5	22	1	5	1	1	0	0	1	3	0	0	.227	.261	.273
Lefty O'Doul	1	1	1	1	2	0	0	0	0	0	0	0	1.000	1.000	1.000
Mel Ott	5	18	3	7	4	0	0	2	4	4	0	1	.389	.500	.722
Homer Peel	2	2	0	1	0	0	0	0	0	0	0	0	.500	.500	.500
Blondy Ryan	5	18	0	5	1	0	0	0	1	5	0	0	.278	.316	.278
Hal Schumacher	2	7	0	2	3	0	0	0	0	3	0	0	.286	.286	.286
Bill Terry	5	22	3	6	1	1	0	1	0	0	0	0	.273	.273	.455
Totals	5	176	16	47	16	5	0	3	11	21	0	1	.267	.310	.347

Batting

Senators	G	AB	R	H	RBI	2B	3B	HR	BB	SO	SB	CS	Avg	OBP	Slg
Ossie Bluege	5	16	1	2	0	1	0	0	1	6	0	0	.125	.176	.188
Cliff Bolton	2	2	0	0	0	0	0	0	0	0	0	0	.000	.000	.000
Joe Cronin	5	22	1	7	2	0	0	0	2	0	0	0	.318	.318	.318
General Crowder	2	4	0	1	0	0	0	0	0	0	0	0	.250	.250	.250
Goose Goslin	5	20	2	5	1	1	0	1	1	3	0	0	.250	.286	.450
Dave Harris	3	2	0	0	0	0	0	0	2	0	0	0	.000	.000	.000
John Kerr	1	0	0	0	0	0	0	0	0	0	0	0	—	—	—
Joe Kuhel	5	20	1	3	1	0	0	0	1	4	0	1	.150	.190	.150
Heinie Manush	5	18	2	2	0	0	0	0	2	1	0	0	.111	.200	.111
Buddy Myer	5	20	2	6	2	1	0	0	2	3	0	0	.300	.364	.350
Sam Rice	1	1	0	1	0	0	0	0	0	0	0	0	1.000	1.000	1.000
Jack Russell	3	2	0	0	0	0	0	0	1	2	0	0	.000	.333	.000
Fred Schulte	5	21	1	7	4	1	0	1	1	1	0	1	.333	.364	.524
Luke Sewell	5	17	1	3	1	0	0	0	2	0	1	0	.176	.263	.176
Lefty Stewart	1	1	0	0	0	0	0	0	0	1	0	0	.000	.000	.000
Montie Weaver	1	4	0	0	0	0	0	0	0	2	0	0	.000	.000	.000
Earl Whitehill	1	3	0	0	0	0	0	0	0	0	0	0	.000	.000	.000
Totals	5	173	11	37	11	4	0	2	13	25	1	2	.214	.269	.272

Pitching

Giants	G	GS	CG	IP	H	R	ER	BB	SO	W-L	Sv-Op	Hld	ERA
Hi Bell	1	0	0	1.0	0	0	0	0	0	0-0	0-0	0	0.00
Freddie Fitzsimmons	1	1	0	7.0	9	4	4	0	2	0-1	0-0	0	5.14
Carl Hubbell	2	2	2	20.0	13	3	0	6	15	2-0	0-0	0	0.00
Dolf Luque	1	0	0	4.1	2	0	0	2	5	1-0	0-0	0	0.00
Hal Schumacher	2	2	1	14.2	13	4	4	5	3	1-0	0-0	0	2.45
Totals	5	5	3	47.0	37	11	8	13	25	4-1	0-0	0	1.53

Pitching

Senators	G	GS	CG	IP	H	R	ER	BB	SO	W-L	Sv-Op	Hld	ERA
General Crowder	2	2	0	11.0	16	9	9	5	7	0-1	0-0	0	7.36
Alex McColl	1	0	0	2.0	0	0	0	0	0	0-0	0-0	0	0.00
Jack Russell	3	0	0	10.1	8	1	1	0	7	0-1	0-0	0	0.87
Lefty Stewart	1	1	0	2.0	6	4	2	0	0	0-1	0-0	0	9.00
Bud Thomas	2	0	0	1.1	1	0	0	0	2	0-0	0-0	0	0.00
Montie Weaver	1	1	0	10.1	11	2	2	4	3	0-1	0-0	0	1.74
Earl Whitehill	1	1	1	9.0	5	0	0	2	2	1-0	0-0	0	0.00
Totals	5	5	1	46.0	47	16	14	11	21	1-4	0-0	0	2.74

Fielding

Giants	Pos	G	PO	Ast	E	DP	PB	FPct
Hi Bell	p	1	0	0	0	0	—	—
Hughie Critz	2b	5	16	18	1	2	—	.971
Kiddo Davis	cf	5	6	0	0	0	—	1.000
Freddie Fitzsimmons	p	1	0	1	0	0	—	1.000
Carl Hubbell	p	2	1	4	1	0	—	.833
Travis Jackson	3b	5	3	16	1	2	—	.950
Dolf Luque	p	1	1	0	0	0	—	1.000
Gus Mancuso	c	5	32	4	0	2	0	1.000
Jo-Jo Moore	lf	5	13	1	0	1	—	1.000
Mel Ott	rf	5	10	0	0	0	—	1.000
Homer Peel	cf	1	0	0	0	0	—	—
Blondy Ryan	ss	5	9	19	1	2	—	.966
Hal Schumacher	p	2	0	2	0	0	—	1.000
Bill Terry	1b	5	50	1	0	3	—	1.000
Totals		5	141	66	4	12	0	.981

Fielding

Senators	Pos	G	PO	Ast	E	DP	PB	FPct
Ossie Bluege	3b	5	3	14	0	0	—	1.000
Joe Cronin	ss	5	7	15	1	3	—	.957
General Crowder	p	2	0	3	0	0	—	1.000
Goose Goslin	rf	5	8	1	0	0	—	1.000
	lf	1	2	0	0	0	—	1.000
Dave Harris	rf	1	0	0	0	0	—	—
Joe Kuhel	1b	5	59	3	0	4	—	1.000
Heinie Manush	lf	5	10	0	0	0	—	1.000
Alex McColl	p	1	0	1	0	0	—	1.000
Buddy Myer	2b	5	15	12	3	3	—	.900
Jack Russell	p	3	1	5	0	0	—	1.000
Fred Schulte	cf	5	9	0	0	0	—	1.000
Luke Sewell	c	5	23	2	0	0	0	1.000
Lefty Stewart	p	1	0	0	0	0	—	—
Bud Thomas	p	2	0	0	0	0	—	—
Montie Weaver	p	1	1	5	0	0	—	1.000
Earl Whitehill	p	1	0	4	0	0	—	1.000
Totals		5	138	65	4	10	0	.981

1934 St. Louis Cardinals (NL) 4, Detroit Tigers (AL) 3

The Dean brothers won two games apiece as the St. Louis Cardinals defeated the Detroit Tigers in seven games. The Tigers fumbled away Game 1 while Dizzy Dean pitched the Cards to an 8-3 victory. Bill Hallahan held a 2-1 lead in the ninth inning of Game 2, until Gee Walker's pinch-hit single tied the game. In the bottom of the 12th, Goose Goslin drove in Charlie Gehringer with the game-winning run. Paul Dean won Game 3, 4-1, but Hank Greenberg drove in three runs with two singles and two doubles as the Tigers took the fourth game, 10-4. Tommy Bridges put the Tigers a game away from a championship when he beat Dizzy Dean 3-1 in Game 5, but Paul Dean saved the Cards when he drove in the go-ahead run and pitched the Cards to a 4-3 victory in Game 6. Dizzy came back on one day's rest to finish the job, pitching an 11-0 shuout in a seventh game interrupted by angry Tigers fans, who pelted Joe Medwick with garbage.

Game 1

Wednesday, October 3

Cardinals	AB	R	H	RBI	BB	K	Avg
Pepper Martin, 3b	5	1	1	1	0	1	.200
Jack Rothrock, rf	4	0	2	2	0	0	.500
Frankie Frisch, 2b	4	0	0	0	0	0	.000
Joe Medwick, lf	5	2	4	2	0	0	.800
Ripper Collins, 1b	4	2	1	0	1	0	.250
Bill Delancey, c	5	0	1	2	0	0	.200
Ernie Orsatti, cf	4	1	2	0	0	0	.500
Chick Fullis, cf	1	0	1	0	0	0	1.000
Leo Durocher, ss	5	0	0	0	0	0	.000
Dizzy Dean, p	5	2	1	0	0	1	.200
TOTALS	42	8	13	7	1	2	.310

Tigers	AB	R	H	RBI	BB	K	Avg
Jo-Jo White, cf	2	1	0	0	2	1	.000
Mickey Cochrane, c	4	0	1	0	0	0	.250
Charlie Gehringer, 2b	4	0	2	1	0	0	.500
Hank Greenberg, 1b	4	2	2	1	0	1	.500
Goose Goslin, lf	4	0	2	1	0	0	.500
Billy Rogell, ss	4	0	1	0	0	1	.250
Marv Owen, 3b	4	0	0	0	0	2	.000
Pete Fox, rf	4	0	0	0	0	0	.000
General Crowder, p	1	0	0	0	0	0	.000
Frank Doljack, ph	1	0	0	0	0	0	.000
Firpo Marberry, p	0	0	0	0	0	0	—
Chief Hogsett, p	1	0	0	0	0	0	.000
Gee Walker, ph	1	0	0	0	1	0	.000
TOTALS	34	3	8	3	2	6	.235

	1	2	3	4	5	6	7	8	9		R	H	E
Cardinals	0	2	1	0	1	4	0	0	0		8	13	2
Tigers	0	0	1	0	0	1	0	1	0		3	8	5

E—Owen 2, Greenberg, Orsatti 2, Rogell, Gehringer. DP—Cardinals 1 (Delancey to Frisch). LOB—Cardinals 10, Tigers 6. Scoring Position—Cardinals 4-for-13, Tigers 2-for-5. 2B—Delancey (1), Dean (1). HR—Medwick (1), Greenberg (1). S—Rothrock, Frisch. CS—Goslin (1).

Cardinals	IP	H	R	ER	BB	K	ERA
Dizzy Dean (W, 1-0)	9.0	8	3	3	2	6	3.00

Tigers	IP	H	R	ER	BB	K	ERA
General Crowder (L, 0-1)	5.0	6	4	1	1	1	1.80
Firpo Marberry	0.2	4	4	4	0	0	54.00
Chief Hogsett	3.1	3	0	0	0	1	0.00

Time—2:13. Attendance—42,505. Umpires—HP, Owens. 1B, Klem. 2B, Geisel. 3B, Reardon.

Game 2

Thursday, October 4

Cardinals	AB	R	H	RBI	BB	K	Avg
Pepper Martin, 3b	5	1	2	0	0	0	.300
Jack Rothrock, rf	4	0	0	0	0	1	.250
Frankie Frisch, 2b	5	0	1	0	0	0	.111
Joe Medwick, lf	5	0	1	1	0	2	.500
Ripper Collins, 1b	5	0	1	0	0	1	.222
Bill Delancey, c	5	1	1	0	0	1	.200
Ernie Orsatti, cf	4	0	1	1	0	0	.375
Leo Durocher, ss	4	0	0	0	0	0	.000
Wild Bill Hallahan, p	3	0	0	0	0	1	.000
Bill Walker, p	1	0	0	0	0	1	.000
TOTALS	41	2	7	2	0	7	.234

Tigers	AB	R	H	RBI	BB	K	Avg
Jo-Jo White, cf	4	0	0	0	0	0	.000
Gee Walker, ph	1	0	1	1	0	0	.500
Frank Doljack, cf	1	0	0	0	0	0	.000
Mickey Cochrane, c	4	0	0	0	2	1	.125
Charlie Gehringer, 2b	4	1	1	0	2	0	.375
Hank Greenberg, 1b	4	0	0	0	2	2	.250
Goose Goslin, lf	6	0	2	1	0	0	.400
Billy Rogell, ss	4	1	1	0	1	0	.250
Marv Owen, 3b	5	0	0	0	0	1	.000
Pete Fox, rf	5	1	2	1	0	0	.222
Schoolboy Rowe, p	4	0	0	0	0	4	.000
TOTALS	42	3	7	3	7	8	.203

	1	2	3	4	5	6	7	8	9	10	11	12	R	H	E
Cardinals	0	1	1	0	0	0	0	0	0	0	0	0	2	7	3
Tigers	0	0	0	1	0	0	0	0	1	0	0	1	3	7	0

E—Martin, Hallahan, Frisch. LOB—Cardinals 4, Tigers 13. Scoring Position—Cardinals 2-for-7, Tigers 3-for-9. 2B—Martin (1), Rogell (1), Fox (1). 3B—Orsatti (1). S—Rothrock, Rowe. SB—Gehringer (1). CS—GWalker (1).

Cardinals	IP	H	R	ER	BB	K	ERA
Wild Bill Hallahan	8.1	6	2	2	4	6	2.16
Bill Walker (L, 0-1)	3.0	1	1	1	3	2	3.00

Tigers	IP	H	R	ER	BB	K	ERA
Schoolboy Rowe (W, 1-0)	12.0	7	2	2	0	7	1.50

Time—2:49. Attendance—43,451. Umpires—HP, Klem. 1B, Geisel. 2B, Reardon. 3B, Owens.

Game 3

Friday, October 5

Tigers	AB	R	H	RBI	BB	K	Avg
Jo-Jo White, cf	5	1	2	0	0	0	.182
Mickey Cochrane, c	3	0	0	0	2	1	.091
Charlie Gehringer, 2b	5	0	2	0	0	0	.385
Hank Greenberg, 1b	4	0	1	1	1	0	.250
Goose Goslin, lf	4	0	1	0	1	1	.357
Billy Rogell, ss	4	0	1	0	0	0	.250
Marv Owen, 3b	3	0	0	0	0	1	.000
Pete Fox, rf	4	0	1	0	0	1	.231
Tommy Bridges, p	1	0	0	0	1	1	.000
Chief Hogsett, p	2	0	0	0	0	1	.000
TOTALS	35	1	8	1	5	7	.216

Cardinals	AB	R	H	RBI	BB	K	Avg
Pepper Martin, 3b	3	2	2	0	1	0	.385
Jack Rothrock, rf	4	1	1	2	0	0	.250
Frankie Frisch, 2b	4	0	2	0	0	0	.231
Joe Medwick, lf	4	0	1	0	0	2	.429
Ripper Collins, 1b	4	1	2	0	0	0	.308
Bill Delancey, c	4	0	1	0	0	1	.214
Ernie Orsatti, cf	2	0	0	0	1	1	.300
Leo Durocher, ss	3	0	0	0	0	0	.000
Paul Dean, p	3	0	1	0	1	0	.000
TOTALS	31	4	9	4	2	5	.260

	1	2	3	4	5	6	7	8	9		R	H	E
Tigers	0	0	0	0	0	0	0	0	1		1	8	2
Cardinals	1	1	0	0	2	0	0	0	x		4	9	1

E—Rothrock, Rogell 2. DP—Tigers 2 (Cochrane to Gehringer; Rogell to Gehringer to Greenberg). LOB—Tigers 13, Cardinals 6. Scoring Position—Tigers 0-for-10, Cardinals 2-for-8. 2B—Gehringer (1), Martin (2), Delancey (2). 3B—Greenberg (1), Martin (1), Rothrock (1). GDP—Medwick. CS—Martin (1), Frisch (1), Collins (1).

Tigers	IP	H	R	ER	BB	K	ERA
Tommy Bridges (L, 0-1)	4.0	8	4	4	1	3	9.00
Chief Hogsett	4.0	1	0	0	1	2	0.00

Cardinals	IP	H	R	ER	BB	K	ERA
Paul Dean (W, 1-0)	9.0	8	1	1	5	7	1.00

Bridges pitched to three batters in the 5th.

HBP—Owen by Dean, Orsatti by Bridges. Time—2:07. Attendance—34,073. Umpires—HP, Geisel. 1B, Reardon. 2B, Owens. 3B, Klem.

Game 4

Saturday, October 6

Tigers	AB	R	H	RBI	BB	K	Avg
Jo-Jo White, cf	4	2	1	0	2	1	.200
Mickey Cochrane, c	5	2	1	0	0	1	.125
Charlie Gehringer, 2b	4	2	2	0	1	0	.412
Goose Goslin, lf	3	2	0	2	0	0	.294
Billy Rogell, ss	5	1	2	4	0	1	.294
Hank Greenberg, 1b	5	1	4	3	0	0	.412
Marv Owen, 3b	5	0	2	1	0	0	.118
Pete Fox, rf	4	0	1	0	1	2	.235
Eldon Auker, p	4	0	0	0	0	2	.000
TOTALS	39	10	13	8	6	7	.255

Cardinals	AB	R	H	RBI	BB	K	Avg
Pepper Martin, 3b	4	0	1	1	1	0	.353
Jack Rothrock, rf	5	0	0	0	0	0	.176
Frankie Frisch, 2b	5	1	1	0	0	0	.222
Joe Medwick, lf	3	1	2	0	1	0	.471
Ripper Collins, 1b	4	0	2	1	0	0	.353
Bill Delancey, c	2	0	0	0	2	0	.188
Ernie Orsatti, cf	4	1	2	1	0	0	.357
Leo Durocher, ss	4	1	1	1	0	0	.063
Tex Carleton, p	1	0	0	0	0	0	.000
Dazzy Vance, p	0	0	0	0	0	0	—
Spud Davis, ph	1	0	1	1	0	0	1.000
Dizzy Dean, pr	0	0	0	0	0	0	.200
Bill Walker, p	1	0	0	0	0	1	.000
Jesse Haines, p	0	0	0	0	0	0	—
Pat Crawford, ph	1	0	0	0	0	0	.000
Jim Mooney, p	0	0	0	0	0	0	—
TOTALS	35	4	10	4	4	1	.268

	1	2	3	4	5	6	7	8	9		R	H	E
Tigers	0	0	3	1	0	0	1	5	0		10	13	1
Cardinals	0	1	1	2	0	0	0	0	0		4	10	6

E—Delancey 2, Martin 3, Walker, Gehringer. DP—Tigers 3 (Auker to Rogell to Greenberg; Greenberg to Rogell; Rogell to Greenberg). LOB—Tigers 12, Cardinals 8. Scoring Position—Tigers 7-for-17, Cardinals 2-for-8. 2B—Cochrane (1), Greenberg 2 (2), Fox (2), Collins (1). S—Cochrane, Gehringer, Goslin, Auker. GDP—Rothrock, Frisch. SB—White (1), Greenberg (1), Owen (1).

Tigers	IP	H	R	ER	BB	K	ERA
Eldon Auker (W, 1-0)	9.0	10	4	3	4	1	3.00

Cardinals	IP	H	R	ER	BB	K	ERA
Tex Carleton	2.2	4	3	3	2	2	10.13
Dazzy Vance	1.1	2	1	0	1	3	0.00
Bill Walker (L, 0-2)	3.1	5	6	3	3	0	5.68
Jesse Haines	0.2	1	0	0	0	2	0.00
Jim Mooney	1.0	1	0	0	0	0	0.00

WP—Vance. Time—2:43. Attendance—37,492. Umpires—HP, Reardon. 1B, Owens. 2B, Klem. 3B, Geisel.

Game 5

Sunday, October 7

Tigers	AB	R	H	RBI	BB	K	Avg
Jo-Jo White, cf	2	0	0	0	2	0	.176
Mickey Cochrane, c	4	0	1	0	0	0	.150
Charlie Gehringer, 2b	4	1	1	1	0	0	.381
Goose Goslin, lf	4	0	1	0	0	0	.286
Billy Rogell, ss	4	1	2	0	0	1	.333
Hank Greenberg, 1b	3	1	0	1	1	1	.350
Marv Owen, 3b	4	0	0	0	0	1	.095
Pete Fox, rf	4	0	1	1	0	1	.238
Tommy Bridges, p	4	0	1	0	0	2	.200
TOTALS	33	3	7	3	3	6	.251

Cardinals	AB	R	H	RBI	BB	K	Avg
Pepper Martin, 3b	4	0	2	0	0	0	.381
Jack Rothrock, rf	4	0	0	0	0	0	.143
Frankie Frisch, 2b	4	0	1	0	0	1	.227
Joe Medwick, lf	4	0	0	0	0	2	.381
Ripper Collins, 1b	4	0	1	0	0	0	.333
Bill Delancey, c	4	1	1	1	0	3	.200
Chick Fullis, cf	3	0	0	0	0	0	.250
Ernie Orsatti, ph	1	0	0	0	0	0	.333
Leo Durocher, ss	2	0	1	0	0	0	.111
Spud Davis, ph	1	0	1	0	0	0	1.000
Burgess Whitehead, pr-ss	0	0	0	0	0	0	—
Dizzy Dean, p	2	0	0	0	0	1	.143
Pat Crawford, ph	1	0	0	0	0	0	.000
Tex Carleton, p	0	0	0	0	0	0	.000
TOTALS	34	1	7	1	0	7	.263

	1	2	3	4	5	6	7	8	9		R	H	E
Tigers	0	1	0	0	0	2	0	0	0		3	7	0
Cardinals	0	0	0	0	0	0	1	0	0		1	7	1

E—Fullis. DP—Cardinals 1 (Collins to Durocher). LOB—Tigers 7, Cardinals 6. Scoring Position—Tigers 1-for-7, Cardinals 0-for-5. 2B—Goslin (1), Fox (3), Martin (3). HR—Gehringer (1), Delancey (1). GDP—Cochrane. SB—Rogell (1).

Tigers	IP	H	R	ER	BB	K	ERA
Tommy Bridges (W, 1-1)	9.0	7	1	1	0	7	3.46

Cardinals	IP	H	R	ER	BB	K	ERA
Dizzy Dean (L, 1-1)	8.0	6	3	2	3	6	2.65
Tex Carleton	1.0	1	0	0	0	0	7.36

WP—Bridges. HBP—White by Dean. Time—1:58. Attendance—38,536. Umpires—HP, Owens. 1B, Klem. 2B, Geisel. 3B, Reardon.

Game 6

Monday, October 8

Cardinals	AB	R	H	RBI	BB	K	Avg
Pepper Martin, 3b	5	1	1	1	0	1	.346
Jack Rothrock, rf	4	1	2	1	0	0	.200
Frankie Frisch, 2b	4	0	0	0	0	0	.192
Joe Medwick, lf	4	0	2	1	0	1	.400
Ripper Collins, 1b	4	0	0	0	0	0	.280
Bill Delancey, c	4	0	0	0	0	2	.167
Ernie Orsatti, cf	4	0	1	0	0	0	.316
Leo Durocher, ss	4	2	3	0	0	0	.227
Paul Dean, p	3	0	1	1	0	0	.167
TOTALS	36	4	10	4	0	5	.263

Tigers	AB	R	H	RBI	BB	K	Avg
Jo-Jo White, cf	2	2	0	0	2	1	.158
Mickey Cochrane, c	4	0	3	1	0	0	.250
Charlie Gehringer, 2b	4	1	1	0	0	0	.360
Goose Goslin, lf	4	0	1	0	0	0	.280
Billy Rogell, ss	4	0	0	0	0	1	.280
Hank Greenberg, 1b	4	0	1	1	0	1	.333
Marv Owen, 3b	4	0	0	0	0	0	.080
Pete Fox, rf	4	0	1	0	0	0	.240
Schoolboy Rowe, p	3	0	0	0	0	1	.000
TOTALS	33	3	7	2	2	4	.241

	1	2	3	4	5	6	7	8	9		R	H	E
Cardinals	1	0	0	0	2	0	1	0	0		4	10	2
Tigers	0	0	1	0	0	2	0	0	0		3	7	1

E—Dean, Goslin, Frisch. LOB—Cardinals 6, Tigers 6. Scoring Position—Cardinals 3-for-8, Tigers 2-for-10. 2B—Rothrock (1), Durocher (1), Fox (4). S—Dean, Rowe. CS—White 2 (2).

Cardinals	IP	H	R	ER	BB	K	ERA
Paul Dean (W, 2-0)	9.0	7	3	1	2	4	1.00

Tigers	IP	H	R	ER	BB	K	ERA
Schoolboy Rowe (L, 1-1)	9.0	10	4	3	0	5	2.14

Time—1:58. Attendance—44,551. Umpires—HP, Klem. 1B, Geisel. 2B, Reardon. 3B, Owens.

Game 7

Tuesday, October 9

Cardinals	AB	R	H	RBI	BB	K	Avg
Pepper Martin, 3b	5	3	2	1	1	1	.355
Jack Rothrock, rf	5	1	2	1	1	1	.233
Frankie Frisch, 2b	5	1	1	3	0	0	.194
Joe Medwick, lf	4	1	1	1	0	0	.379
Chick Fullis, lf	1	0	1	0	0	0	.400
Ripper Collins, 1b	5	1	4	2	0	0	.367
Bill Delancey, c	5	1	1	1	0	1	.172
Ernie Orsatti, cf	3	1	1	0	2	0	.318
Leo Durocher, ss	5	1	2	0	0	0	.259
Dizzy Dean, p	5	1	2	1	0	1	.250
TOTALS	43	11	17	10	4	4	.285

Tigers	AB	R	H	RBI	BB	K	Avg
Jo-Jo White, cf	4	0	0	0	0	1	.130
Mickey Cochrane, c	4	0	0	0	0	0	.214
Ray Hayworth, c	0	0	0	0	0	0	—
Charlie Gehringer, 2b	4	0	2	0	0	0	.379
Goose Goslin, lf	4	0	0	0	0	0	.241
Billy Rogell, ss	4	0	1	0	0	0	.276
Hank Greenberg, 1b	4	0	1	0	0	3	.321
Marv Owen, 3b	4	0	0	0	0	0	.069
Pete Fox, rf	3	0	2	0	0	0	.286
Eldon Auker, p	0	0	0	0	0	0	.000
Schoolboy Rowe, p	0	0	0	0	0	0	.000
Chief Hogsett, p	0	0	0	0	0	0	.000
Tommy Bridges, p	2	0	0	0	0	1	.143
Firpo Marberry, p	0	0	0	0	0	0	—
Gee Walker, ph	1	0	0	0	0	0	.333
General Crowder, p	0	0	0	0	0	0	.000
TOTALS	34	0	6	0	0	5	.226

	1	2	3	4	5	6	7	8	9		R	H	E
Cardinals	0	0	7	0	0	2	2	0	0		11	17	1
Tigers	0	0	0	0	0	0	0	0	0		0	6	3

E—White, Collins, Gehringer, Goslin. DP—Tigers 1 (Owen to Gehringer to Greenberg). LOB—Cardinals 9, Tigers 7. Scoring Position—Cardinals 8-for-19, Tigers 0-for-7. 2B—Rothrock (3), Frisch (1), Delancey (3), Dean (2), Fox 2 (6). 3B—Medwick (1), Durocher (1). GDP—Delancey. SB—Martin 2 (2). CS—Orsatti (1).

Cardinals	IP	H	R	ER	BB	K	ERA
Dizzy Dean (W, 2-1)	9.0	6	0	0	0	5	1.73

Tigers	IP	H	R	ER	BB	K	ERA
Eldon Auker (L, 1-1)	2.1	6	4	4	1	1	5.56
Schoolboy Rowe	0.1	2	2	2	0	0	2.95
Chief Hogsett	0.0	2	1	1	2	0	1.23
Tommy Bridges	4.1	6	4	2	0	2	3.63
Firpo Marberry	1.0	1	0	0	1	0	21.60
General Crowder	1.0	0	0	0	0	1	1.50

Hogsett pitched to four batters in the 3rd.

Time—2:19. Attendance—40,902. Umpires—HP, Geisel. 1B, Reardon. 2B, Owens. 3B, Klem.

1934 World Series—Composite Statistics

Batting

Cardinals	G	AB	R	H	RBI	2B	3B	HR	BB	SO	SB	CS	Avg	OBP	Slg
Tex Carleton	2	1	0	0	0	0	0	0	0	0	0	0	.000	.000	.000
Ripper Collins	7	30	4	11	3	1	0	0	1	2	0	1	.367	.387	.400
Pat Crawford	2	2	0	0	0	0	0	0	0	0	0	0	.000	.000	.000
Spud Davis	2	2	0	2	1	0	0	0	0	0	0	0	1.000	1.000	1.000
Dizzy Dean	4	12	3	3	1	2	0	0	0	3	0	0	.250	.250	.417
Paul Dean	2	6	0	1	2	0	0	0	0	1	0	0	.167	.167	.167
Bill Delancey	7	29	3	5	4	3	0	1	2	8	0	0	.172	.226	.379
Leo Durocher	7	27	4	7	0	1	1	0	0	0	0	0	.259	.259	.370
Frankie Frisch	7	31	2	6	4	1	0	0	0	1	0	1	.194	.194	.226
Chick Fullis	3	5	0	2	0	0	0	0	0	0	0	0	.400	.400	.400
Wild Bill Hallahan	1	3	0	0	0	0	0	0	0	2	0	0	.000	.000	.000
Pepper Martin	7	31	8	11	4	3	1	0	3	3	2	1	.355	.412	.516
Joe Medwick	7	29	4	11	5	0	1	1	1	7	0	0	.379	.400	.552
Ernie Orsatti	7	22	3	7	2	0	1	0	3	1	0	1	.318	.423	.409
Jack Rothrock	7	30	3	7	6	3	1	0	1	2	0	0	.233	.258	.400
Bill Walker	2	2	0	0	0	0	0	0	0	2	0	0	.000	.000	.000
Totals	7	262	34	73	32	14	5	2	11	31	2	4	.279	.310	.393

Batting

Tigers	G	AB	R	H	RBI	2B	3B	HR	BB	SO	SB	CS	Avg	OBP	Slg
Eldon Auker	2	4	0	0	0	0	0	0	0	2	0	0	.000	.000	.000
Tommy Bridges	3	7	0	1	0	0	0	0	1	4	0	0	.143	.250	.143
Mickey Cochrane	7	28	2	6	1	1	0	0	4	3	0	0	.214	.313	.250
General Crowder	2	1	0	0	0	0	0	0	0	0	0	0	.000	.000	.000
Frank Doljack	2	2	0	0	0	0	0	0	0	0	0	0	.000	.000	.000
Pete Fox	7	28	1	8	2	6	0	0	1	4	0	0	.286	.310	.500
Charlie Gehringer	7	29	5	11	2	1	0	1	3	0	1	0	.379	.438	.517
Goose Goslin	7	29	2	7	2	1	0	0	3	1	0	1	.241	.313	.276
Hank Greenberg	7	28	4	9	7	2	1	1	4	9	1	0	.321	.406	.571
Chief Hogsett	3	3	0	0	0	0	0	0	0	1	0	0	.000	.000	.000
Marv Owen	7	29	0	2	1	0	0	0	0	5	1	0	.069	.100	.069
Billy Rogell	7	29	3	8	4	1	0	0	1	4	1	0	.276	.300	.310
Schoolboy Rowe	3	7	0	0	0	0	0	0	0	5	0	0	.000	.000	.000
Gee Walker	3	3	0	1	1	0	0	0	0	1	0	1	.333	.333	.333
Jo-Jo White	7	23	6	3	0	0	0	0	8	4	1	2	.130	.375	.130
Totals	7	250	23	56	20	12	1	2	25	43	5	4	.224	.300	.304

Pitching

Cardinals	G	GS	CG	IP	H	R	ER	BB	SO	W-L	Sv-Op	Hld	ERA
Tex Carleton	2	1	0	3.2	5	3	3	2	2	0-0	0-0	0	7.36
Dizzy Dean	3	3	2	26.0	20	6	5	5	17	2-1	0-0	0	1.73
Paul Dean	2	2	2	18.0	15	4	2	7	11	2-0	0-0	0	1.00
Jesse Haines	1	0	0	0.2	1	0	0	0	2	0-0	0-0	0	0.00
Wild Bill Hallahan	1	1	0	8.1	6	2	2	4	6	0-0	0-0	0	2.16
Jim Mooney	1	0	0	1.0	1	0	0	0	0	0-0	0-0	0	0.00
Dazzy Vance	1	0	0	1.1	2	1	0	1	3	0-0	0-0	0	0.00
Bill Walker	2	0	0	6.1	6	7	4	6	2	0-2	0-0	0	5.68
Totals	7	7	4	65.1	56	23	16	25	43	4-3	0-0	0	2.20

Pitching

Tigers	G	GS	CG	IP	H	R	ER	BB	SO	W-L	Sv-Op	Hld	ERA
Eldon Auker	2	2	1	11.1	16	8	7	5	2	1-1	0-0	0	5.56
Tommy Bridges	3	2	1	17.1	21	9	7	1	12	1-1	0-0	0	3.63
General Crowder	2	1	0	6.0	6	4	1	1	2	0-1	0-0	0	1.50
Chief Hogsett	3	0	0	7.1	6	1	1	3	3	0-0	0-0	0	1.23
Firpo Marberry	2	0	0	1.2	5	4	4	1	0	0-0	0-0	0	21.60
Schoolboy Rowe	3	2	2	21.1	19	8	7	0	12	1-1	0-0	0	2.95
Totals	7	7	4	65.0	73	34	27	11	31	3-4	0-0	0	3.74

Fielding

Cardinals	Pos	G	PO	Ast	E	DP	PB	FPct
Tex Carleton	p	2	0	0	0	0	—	—
Ripper Collins	1b	7	56	7	1	1	—	.984
Dizzy Dean	p	3	2	2	0	0	—	1.000
Paul Dean	p	2	0	0	1	0	—	.000
Bill Delancey	c	7	50	6	2	1	0	.966
Leo Durocher	ss	7	13	17	0	1	—	1.000
Frankie Frisch	2b	7	17	26	2	1	—	.956
Chick Fullis	cf	2	5	0	1	0	—	.833
	lf	1	1	0	0	0	—	1.000
Jesse Haines	p	1	0	0	0	0	—	—
Wild Bill Hallahan	p	1	1	3	1	0	—	.800
Pepper Martin	3b	7	6	9	4	0	—	.789
Joe Medwick	lf	7	9	0	0	0	—	1.000
Jim Mooney	p	1	0	1	0	0	—	1.000
Ernie Orsatti	cf	6	16	1	2	0	—	.895
Jack Rothrock	rf	7	19	0	1	0	—	.950
Dazzy Vance	p	1	0	0	0	0	—	—
Bill Walker	p	2	0	1	1	0	—	.500
Burgess Whitehead	ss	1	1	0	0	0	—	1.000
Totals		7	196	73	16	4	0	.944

Fielding

Tigers	Pos	G	PO	Ast	E	DP	PB	FPct
Eldon Auker	p	2	0	2	0	1	—	1.000
Tommy Bridges	p	3	0	2	0	0	—	1.000
Mickey Cochrane	c	7	36	5	0	1	0	1.000
General Crowder	p	2	0	0	0	0	—	—
Frank Doljack	cf	1	1	0	0	0	—	1.000
Pete Fox	rf	7	16	0	0	0	—	1.000
Charlie Gehringer	2b	7	18	26	3	3	—	.936
Goose Goslin	lf	7	20	1	2	0	—	.913
Hank Greenberg	1b	7	60	4	1	5	—	.985
Ray Hayworth	c	1	1	0	0	0	0	1.000
Chief Hogsett	p	3	0	2	0	0	—	1.000
Firpo Marberry	p	2	0	1	0	0	—	1.000
Marv Owen	3b	7	9	9	2	1	—	.900
Billy Rogell	ss	7	12	16	3	4	—	.903
Schoolboy Rowe	p	3	1	1	0	0	—	1.000
Jo-Jo White	cf	7	21	0	1	0	—	.955
Totals		7	195	69	12	15	0	.957

1935 Detroit Tigers (AL) 4, Chicago Cubs (NL) 2

Even without Hank Greenberg, the Detroit Tigers downed the Chicago Cubs in a six-game Series. Lon Warneke pitched the Cubs to a 3-0 victory in Game 1. Greenberg broke his wrist and was lost for the Series after homering in the second game, but his two-run shot sent the Tigers on their way to an 8-3 win. The Cubs tied Game 3 with two runs in the bottom of the ninth before Jo-Jo White drove in the eventual game-winner for Detroit in the top of the 11th. Errors by Augie Galan and Billy Jurges gave the Tigers a 2-1 victory in Game 4 behind General Crowder. Warneke beat Schoolboy Rowe 3-1 in Game 5, but Goose Goslin drove in the winning run with two outs in the bottom of the ninth in Game 6 to give the Tigers their first World Championship.

Game 1

Wednesday, October 2

Cubs	AB	R	H	RBI	BB	K	Avg
Augie Galan, lf	4	1	1	0	0	1	.250
Billy Herman, 2b	3	1	0	0	0	0	.000
Freddy Lindstrom, cf	3	0	1	0	0	0	.333
Gabby Hartnett, c	4	0	2	1	0	1	.500
Frank Demaree, rf	4	1	2	1	0	1	.500
Phil Cavarretta, 1b	3	0	0	0	0	2	.000
Stan Hack, 3b	4	0	0	0	0	1	.000
Billy Jurges, ss	4	0	1	0	0	2	.250
Lon Warneke, p	3	0	0	0	0	0	.000
TOTALS	32	3	7	2	0	8	.219

Tigers	AB	R	H	RBI	BB	K	Avg
Jo-Jo White, cf	4	0	1	0	0	1	.250
Mickey Cochrane, c	4	0	0	0	0	0	.000
Charlie Gehringer, 2b	3	0	0	0	1	0	.000
Hank Greenberg, 1b	3	0	0	0	1	0	.000
Goose Goslin, lf	3	0	0	0	1	0	.000
Pete Fox, rf	4	0	2	0	0	0	.500
Billy Rogell, ss	4	0	0	0	0	0	.000
Marv Owen, 3b	3	0	0	0	1	0	.000
Schoolboy Rowe, p	3	0	1	0	0	0	.333
TOTALS	31	0	4	0	4	1	.129

	1	2	3	4	5	6	7	8	9		R	H	E
Cubs	2	0	0	0	0	0	0	0	1		3	7	0
Tigers	0	0	0	0	0	0	0	0	0		0	4	3

E—Rowe, Greenberg, Goslin. DP—Tigers 1 (Cochrane to Gehringer). LOB—Cubs 5, Tigers 8. Scoring Position—Cubs 1-for-8, Tigers 0-for-6. 2B—Galan (1), Fox (1), Rowe (1). HR—Demaree (1). S—Herman, Lindstrom, Cavarretta. CS—Lindstrom (1).

Cubs	IP	H	R	ER	BB	K	ERA
Lon Warneke (W, 1-0)	9.0	4	0	0	4	1	0.00

Tigers	IP	H	R	ER	BB	K	ERA
Schoolboy Rowe (L, 0-1)	9.0	7	3	2	0	8	2.00

PB—Cochrane. Time—1:51. Attendance—47,391. Umpires—HP, Moriarty. 1B, Quigley. 2B, McGowan. 3B, Stark.

Game 2

Thursday, October 3

Cubs	AB	R	H	RBI	BB	K	Avg
Augie Galan, lf	4	0	0	0	1	0	.125
Billy Herman, 2b	4	0	1	2	0	1	.143
Freddy Lindstrom, cf	3	0	0	0	1	1	.167
Gabby Hartnett, c	4	0	1	0	0	0	.375
Frank Demaree, rf	4	0	1	0	0	0	.375
Phil Cavarretta, 1b	4	1	0	0	0	0	.000
Stan Hack, 3b	3	0	1	0	1	0	.143
Billy Jurges, ss	3	1	1	1	1	0	.286
Charlie Root, p	0	0	0	0	0	0	—
Roy Henshaw, p	1	0	0	0	0	0	.000
Fabian Kowalik, p	2	1	1	0	0	0	.500
Chuck Klein, ph	1	0	0	0	0	0	.000
TOTALS	33	3	6	3	4	2	.210

Tigers	AB	R	H	RBI	BB	K	Avg
Jo-Jo White, cf	3	2	1	0	2	0	.286
Mickey Cochrane, c	2	1	1	1	2	0	.167
Charlie Gehringer, 2b	3	2	2	3	1	0	.333
Hank Greenberg, 1b	3	1	1	2	0	0	.167
Goose Goslin, lf	3	0	0	0	1	0	.000
Pete Fox, rf	4	0	1	1	0	0	.375
Billy Rogell, ss	4	0	2	0	0	1	.250
Marv Owen, 3b	2	1	0	0	0	1	.000
Tommy Bridges, p	4	1	1	0	0	1	.250
TOTALS	28	8	9	7	6	3	.214

	1	2	3	4	5	6	7	8	9		R	H	E
Cubs	0	0	0	0	1	0	2	0	0		3	6	1
Tigers	4	0	0	3	0	0	1	0	x		8	9	2

E—Kowalik, Greenberg 2. DP—Cubs 2 (Herman to Cavarretta; Jurges to Herman to Cavarretta), Tigers 2 (Bridges to Rogell to Greenberg; Rogell to Gehringer to Greenberg). LOB—Cubs 7, Tigers 5. Scoring Position—Cubs 2-for-6, Tigers 3-for-7. 2B—Demaree (1), Cochrane (1), Rogell (1). HR—Greenberg (1). S—Owen. GDP—Herman, Hartnett, Greenberg.

Cubs	IP	H	R	ER	BB	K	ERA
Charlie Root (L, 0-1)	0.0	4	4	4	0	0	—
Roy Henshaw	3.2	2	3	3	5	2	7.36
Fabian Kowalik	4.1	3	1	1	1	1	2.08

Tigers	IP	H	R	ER	BB	K	ERA
Tommy Bridges (W, 1-0)	9.0	6	3	2	4	2	2.00

Root pitched to four batters in the 1st.

WP—Henshaw. HBP—Owen by Henshaw, Greenberg by Kowalik. Time—1:59. Attendance—46,742. Umpires—HP, Quigley. 1B, McGowan. 2B, Stark. 3B, Moriarty.

Game 3

Friday, October 4

Tigers	AB	R	H	RBI	BB	K	Avg
Jo-Jo White, cf	5	1	2	1	1	2	.333
Mickey Cochrane, c	5	0	0	0	1	0	.091
Charlie Gehringer, 2b	5	1	2	0	0	0	.364
Goose Goslin, lf	5	2	3	2	0	0	.273
Pete Fox, rf	5	1	2	1	0	0	.385
Billy Rogell, ss	5	0	3	1	0	1	.385
Marv Owen, 1b	5	1	0	0	0	0	.000
Flea Clifton, 3b	4	0	0	0	1	1	.000
Eldon Auker, p	2	0	0	0	0	1	.000
Gee Walker, ph	1	0	0	0	0	0	.000
Chief Hogsett, p	0	0	0	0	0	0	—
Schoolboy Rowe, p	2	0	0	0	0	1	.200
TOTALS	44	6	12	5	3	6	.247

Cubs	AB	R	H	RBI	BB	K	Avg
Augie Galan, lf	4	0	2	2	1	0	.250
Billy Herman, 2b	5	0	1	0	0	1	.167
Freddy Lindstrom, cf-3b	5	0	2	0	0	0	.273
Gabby Hartnett, c	4	0	0	0	0	0	.250
Frank Demaree, rf-cf	4	1	1	1	1	1	.333
Phil Cavarretta, 1b	5	0	0	0	0	0	.000
Stan Hack, 3b-ss	5	2	2	0	0	0	.250
Billy Jurges, ss	1	1	0	0	1	0	.250
Chuck Klein, ph-rf	2	1	1	0	0	1	.333
Bill Lee, p	1	0	0	1	0	0	.000
Lon Warneke, p	0	0	0	0	0	0	.000
Ken O'Dea, ph	1	0	1	1	0	0	1.000
Larry French, p	0	0	0	0	0	0	.000
Walter Stephenson, ph	1	0	0	0	0	1	.000
TOTALS	38	5	10	5	3	4	.220

	1	2	3	4	5	6	7	8	9	10	11		R	H	E
Tigers	0	0	0	0	0	1	0	4	0	0	1		6	12	2
Cubs	0	2	0	0	1	0	0	0	2	0	0		5	10	3

E—Cavarretta, Clifton, Herman, Cochrane, Lindstrom. DP—Tigers 2 (Rogell to Gehringer to Owen; Gehringer to Rogell to Owen), Cubs 1 (Jurges to Herman to Cavarretta). LOB—Tigers 8, Cubs 7. Scoring Position—Tigers 3-for-10, Cubs 3-for-12. 2B—Gehringer (1), Goslin (1), Lindstrom (1). 3B—Fox (1). HR—Demaree (2). S—Hartnett, Lee 2. GDP—Lindstrom, Hartnett, Walker. SB—Hack (1). CS—Rogell (1), Cavarretta (1).

Tigers	IP	H	R	ER	BB	K	ERA
Eldon Auker	6.0	6	3	2	2	1	3.00
Chief Hogsett	1.0	0	0	0	1	0	0.00
Schoolboy Rowe (BS, 1; W, 1-1)	4.0	4	2	2	0	3	2.77

Cubs	IP	H	R	ER	BB	K	ERA
Bill Lee	7.1	7	4	4	3	3	4.91
Lon Warneke	1.2	2	1	1	0	2	0.84
Larry French (L, 0-1)	2.0	3	1	0	0	1	0.00

HBP—Jurges by Hogsett. Time—2:27. Attendance—45,532. Umpires—HP, McGowan. 1B, Stark. 2B, Moriarty. 3B, Quigley.

Game 4
Saturday, October 5

Tigers	AB	R	H	RBI	BB	K	Avg
Jo-Jo White, cf	3	0	1	0	2	2	.333
Mickey Cochrane, c	4	0	1	0	1	0	.133
Charlie Gehringer, 2b	4	0	2	1	0	1	.400
Goose Goslin, lf	3	0	1	0	2	0	.286
Pete Fox, rf	5	0	1	0	0	1	.333
Billy Rogell, ss	3	0	0	0	2	2	.313
Marv Owen, 1b	4	0	0	0	0	0	.000
Flea Clifton, 3b	4	1	0	0	0	0	.000
General Crowder, p	3	1	1	0	1	0	.333
TOTALS	33	2	7	1	8	6	.246

Cubs	AB	R	H	RBI	BB	K	Avg
Augie Galan, lf	4	0	0	0	0	0	.188
Billy Herman, 2b	4	0	1	0	0	0	.188
Freddy Lindstrom, cf	4	0	0	0	0	0	.200
Gabby Hartnett, c	4	1	1	1	0	1	.250
Frank Demaree, rf	4	0	1	0	0	1	.313
Phil Cavarretta, 1b	4	0	2	0	0	1	.125
Stan Hack, 3b	4	0	0	0	0	1	.188
Billy Jurges, ss	1	0	0	0	2	0	.222
Tex Carleton, p	1	0	0	0	1	1	.000
Chuck Klein, ph	1	0	0	0	0	0	.250
Charlie Root, p	0	0	0	0	0	0	—
TOTALS	31	1	5	1	3	5	.208

	1 2 3	4 5 6	7 8 9	R	H	E
Tigers	0 0 1	0 0 1	0 0 0	2	7	0
Cubs	0 1 0	0 0 0	0 0 0	1	5	2

E—Galan, Jurges. DP—Cubs 1 (Jurges to Herman). LOB—Tigers 13, Cubs 6. Scoring Position—Tigers 1-for-12, Cubs 0-for-6. 2B—Gehringer (2), Fox (2), Herman (1). HR—Hartnett (1). S—Gehringer. GDP—Hack. SB—Gehringer (1).

Tigers	IP	H	R	ER	BB	K	ERA
General Crowder (W, 1-0)	9.0	5	1	1	3	5	1.00

Cubs	IP	H	R	ER	BB	K	ERA
Tex Carleton (L, 0-1)	7.0	6	2	1	4	1	1.29
Charlie Root	2.0	1	0	0	1	2	18.00

Balk—Carleton. Time—2:28. Attendance—49,350. Umpires—HP, Stark. 1B, Moriarty. 2B, Quigley. 3B, McGowan.

Game 5
Sunday, October 6

Tigers	AB	R	H	RBI	BB	K	Avg
Jo-Jo White, cf	4	0	0	0	0	2	.263
Mickey Cochrane, c	4	0	2	0	0	0	.211
Charlie Gehringer, 2b	4	1	1	0	0	0	.368
Goose Goslin, lf	3	0	1	0	1	0	.294
Pete Fox, rf	4	0	2	1	0	0	.364
Billy Rogell, ss	4	0	0	0	0	0	.250
Marv Owen, 1b	3	0	0	0	0	1	.000
Gee Walker, ph	1	0	0	0	0	0	.000
Flea Clifton, 3b	3	0	0	0	1	1	.000
Schoolboy Rowe, p	3	0	1	0	0	0	.250
TOTALS	33	1	7	1	2	4	.234

Cubs	AB	R	H	RBI	BB	K	Avg
Augie Galan, lf	4	1	0	0	0	0	.150
Billy Herman, 2b	4	1	2	1	0	0	.250
Chuck Klein, cf	4	1	2	2	0	1	.375
Gabby Hartnett, c	4	0	1	0	0	0	.250
Frank Demaree, rf	4	0	1	0	0	0	.300
Phil Cavarretta, 1b	4	0	0	0	1	0	.100
Stan Hack, 3b	2	0	0	0	1	0	.167
Billy Jurges, ss	3	0	1	0	0	1	.250
Lon Warneke, p	2	0	1	0	0	0	.200
Bill Lee, p	0	0	0	0	0	0	.000
TOTALS	31	3	8	3	1	3	.215

	1 2 3	4 5 6	7 8 9	R	H	E
Tigers	0 0 0	0 0 0	0 0 1	1	7	1
Cubs	0 0 2	0 0 0	1 0 x	3	8	0

E—Owen. DP—Cubs 1 (Jurges to Cavarretta). LOB—Tigers 7, Cubs 6. Scoring Position—Tigers 1-for-8, Cubs 2-for-6. 2B—Herman (2). 3B—Herman (1). HR—Klein (1). S—Lee. GDP—Rogell.

Tigers	IP	H	R	ER	BB	K	ERA
Schoolboy Rowe (L, 1-2)	8.0	8	3	2	1	3	2.57

Cubs	IP	H	R	ER	BB	K	ERA
Lon Warneke (W, 2-0)	6.0	3	0	0	0	2	0.54
Bill Lee (S, 1)	3.0	4	1	1	2	2	4.35

Time—1:49. Attendance—49,237. Umpires—HP, Moriarty. 1B, Quigley. 2B, McGowan. 3B, Stark.

Game 6
Monday, October 7

Cubs	AB	R	H	RBI	BB	K	Avg
Augie Galan, lf	5	0	1	0	0	1	.160
Billy Herman, 2b	4	1	3	3	0	0	.333
Chuck Klein, rf	4	0	1	0	0	0	.333
Gabby Hartnett, c	4	0	2	0	0	1	.292
Frank Demaree, cf	4	0	0	0	0	1	.250
Phil Cavarretta, 1b	4	0	1	0	0	1	.125
Stan Hack, 3b	4	0	2	0	0	0	.227
Billy Jurges, ss	4	1	1	0	0	1	.250
Larry French, p	4	1	1	0	0	2	.250
TOTALS	37	3	12	3	0	7	.240

Tigers	AB	R	H	RBI	BB	K	Avg
Flea Clifton, 3b	5	0	0	0	0	2	.000
Mickey Cochrane, c	5	2	3	0	0	1	.292
Charlie Gehringer, 2b	5	0	2	0	0	0	.375
Goose Goslin, lf	5	0	1	1	0	0	.273
Pete Fox, rf	4	0	2	1	0	0	.385
Gee Walker, cf	2	1	1	0	1	0	.250
Billy Rogell, ss	4	1	2	0	0	1	.292
Marv Owen, 1b	3	0	1	1	1	1	.050
Tommy Bridges, p	4	0	0	1	0	2	.125
TOTALS	37	4	12	4	2	7	.250

	1 2 3	4 5 6	7 8 9	R	H	E
Cubs	0 0 1	0 2 0	0 0 0	3	12	0
Tigers	1 0 0	1 0 1	0 0 1	4	12	1

E—Fox. DP—Tigers 1 (Gehringer to Rogell to Owen). LOB—Cubs 7, Tigers 10. Scoring Position—Cubs 1-for-6, Tigers 3-for-11. 2B—Hack (1), Gehringer (3), Fox (3), Rogell (2). 3B—Hack (1). HR—Herman (1). S—Walker. GDP—Demaree.

Cubs	IP	H	R	ER	BB	K	ERA
Larry French (L, 0-2)	8.2	12	4	4	2	7	3.38

Tigers	IP	H	R	ER	BB	K	ERA
Tommy Bridges (W, 2-0)	9.0	12	3	3	0	7	2.50

Time—1:57. Attendance—48,420. Umpires—HP, Quigley. 1B, McGowan. 2B, Stark. 3B, Moriarty.

1935 World Series—Composite Statistics

Batting

Tigers	G	AB	R	H	RBI	2B	3B	HR	BB	SO	SB	CS	Avg	OBP	Slg
Eldon Auker	1	2	0	0	0	0	0	0	0	1	0	0	.000	.000	.000
Tommy Bridges	2	8	1	1	1	0	0	0	0	3	0	0	.125	.125	.125
Flea Clifton	4	16	1	0	0	0	0	0	2	4	0	0	.000	.111	.000
Mickey Cochrane	6	24	3	7	1	1	0	0	4	1	0	0	.292	.393	.333
General Crowder	1	3	1	1	0	0	0	0	1	0	0	0	.333	.500	.333
Pete Fox	6	26	1	10	4	3	1	0	0	1	0	0	.385	.385	.577
Charlie Gehringer	6	24	4	9	4	3	0	0	2	1	1	0	.375	.423	.500
Goose Goslin	6	22	2	6	3	1	0	0	5	0	0	0	.273	.407	.318
Hank Greenberg	2	6	1	1	2	0	0	1	1	0	0	0	.167	.375	.667
Marv Owen	6	20	2	1	1	0	0	0	2	3	0	0	.050	.174	.050
Billy Rogell	6	24	1	7	1	2	0	0	2	5	0	1	.292	.346	.375
Schoolboy Rowe	3	8	0	2	0	1	0	0	0	1	0	0	.250	.250	.375
Gee Walker	3	4	1	1	0	0	0	0	1	0	0	0	.250	.400	.250
Jo-Jo White	5	19	3	5	1	0	0	0	5	7	0	0	.263	.417	.263
Totals	**6**	**206**	**21**	**51**	**18**	**11**	**1**	**1**	**25**	**27**	**1**	**1**	**.248**	**.335**	**.325**

Cubs	G	AB	R	H	RBI	2B	3B	HR	BB	SO	SB	CS	Avg	OBP	Slg
Tex Carleton	1	1	0	0	0	0	0	0	1	1	0	0	.000	.500	.000
Phil Cavarretta	6	24	1	3	0	0	0	0	0	5	0	1	.125	.125	.125
Frank Demaree	6	24	2	6	2	1	0	2	1	4	0	0	.250	.280	.542
Larry French	2	4	1	1	0	0	0	0	0	2	0	0	.250	.250	.250
Augie Galan	6	25	2	4	2	1	0	0	2	2	0	0	.160	.222	.200
Stan Hack	6	22	2	5	0	1	1	0	2	2	1	0	.227	.292	.364
Gabby Hartnett	6	24	1	7	2	0	0	1	0	3	0	0	.292	.292	.417
Roy Henshaw	1	1	0	0	0	0	0	0	0	0	0	0	.000	.000	.000
Billy Herman	6	24	3	8	6	2	1	1	0	2	0	0	.333	.333	.625
Billy Jurges	6	16	3	4	1	0	0	0	4	4	0	0	.250	.429	.250
Chuck Klein	5	12	2	4	2	0	0	1	0	2	0	0	.333	.333	.583
Fabian Kowalik	1	2	1	1	0	0	0	0	0	0	0	0	.500	.500	.500
Bill Lee	2	1	0	0	1	0	0	0	0	0	0	0	.000	.000	.000
Freddy Lindstrom	4	15	0	3	0	1	0	0	1	1	0	1	.200	.250	.267
Ken O'Dea	1	1	0	1	1	0	0	0	0	0	0	0	1.000	1.000	1.000
Walter Stephenson	1	1	0	0	0	0	0	0	0	1	0	0	.000	.000	.000
Lon Warneke	3	5	0	1	0	0	0	0	0	0	0	0	.200	.200	.200
Totals	**6**	**202**	**18**	**48**	**17**	**6**	**2**	**5**	**11**	**29**	**1**	**2**	**.238**	**.280**	**.361**

Pitching

Tigers	G	GS	CG	IP	H	R	ER	BB	SO	W-L	Sv-Op	Hld	ERA
Eldon Auker	1	1	0	6.0	6	3	2	2	1	0-0	0-0	0	3.00
Tommy Bridges	2	2	2	18.0	18	6	5	4	9	2-0	0-0	0	2.50
General Crowder	1	1	1	9.0	5	1	1	3	5	1-0	0-0	0	1.00
Chief Hogsett	1	0	0	1.0	0	0	0	1	0	0-0	0-0	0	0.00
Schoolboy Rowe	3	2	2	21.0	19	8	6	1	14	1-2	0-1	0	2.57
Totals	**6**	**6**	**5**	**55.0**	**48**	**18**	**14**	**11**	**29**	**4-2**	**0-1**	**0**	**2.29**

Cubs	G	GS	CG	IP	H	R	ER	BB	SO	W-L	Sv-Op	Hld	ERA
Tex Carleton	1	1	0	7.0	6	2	1	7	4	0-1	0-0	0	1.29
Larry French	2	1	1	10.2	15	5	4	2	8	0-2	0-0	0	3.38
Roy Henshaw	1	0	0	3.2	2	3	3	5	2	0-0	0-0	0	7.36
Fabian Kowalik	1	0	0	4.1	3	1	1	1	1	0-0	0-0	0	2.08
Bill Lee	2	1	0	10.1	11	5	5	5	5	0-0	1-1	0	4.35
Charlie Root	2	1	0	2.0	5	4	4	1	2	0-1	0-0	0	18.00
Lon Warneke	3	2	1	16.2	9	1	1	4	5	2-0	0-0	0	0.54
Totals	**6**	**6**	**2**	**54.2**	**51**	**21**	**19**	**25**	**27**	**2-4**	**1-1**	**0**	**3.13**

Fielding

Tigers	Pos	G	PO	Ast	E	DP	PB	FPct
Eldon Auker	p	1	0	2	0	0	—	1.000
Tommy Bridges	p	2	1	5	0	1	—	1.000
Flea Clifton	3b	4	2	9	1	0	—	.917
Mickey Cochrane	c	6	32	4	1	1	1	.973
General Crowder	p	1	2	1	0	0	—	1.000
Pete Fox	rf	6	10	2	1	0	—	.923
Charlie Gehringer	2b	6	14	25	0	6	—	1.000
Goose Goslin	lf	6	12	0	1	0	—	.923
Hank Greenberg	1b	2	17	2	3	2	—	.864
Chief Hogsett	p	1	1	0	0	0	—	1.000
Marv Owen	1b	4	44	5	1	4	—	.980
	3b	2	2	0	0	0	—	1.000
Billy Rogell	ss	6	13	12	0	6	—	1.000
Schoolboy Rowe	p	3	3	5	1	0	—	.889
Gee Walker	cf	1	0	0	0	0	—	—
Jo-Jo White	cf	5	12	0	0	0	—	1.000
Totals		**6**	**165**	**72**	**9**	**20**	**1**	**.963**

Cubs	Pos	G	PO	Ast	E	DP	PB	FPct
Tex Carleton	p	1	0	1	0	0	—	1.000
Phil Cavarretta	1b	6	59	4	1	4	—	.984
Frank Demaree	rf	5	7	2	0	0	—	1.000
	cf	2	0	0	0	0	—	—
Larry French	p	2	1	2	0	0	—	1.000
Augie Galan	lf	6	13	1	1	0	—	.933
Stan Hack	3b	6	4	10	0	0	—	1.000
	ss	1	1	0	0	0	—	1.000
Gabby Hartnett	c	6	33	6	0	0	0	1.000
Roy Henshaw	p	1	0	1	0	0	—	1.000
Billy Herman	2b	6	15	19	1	4	—	.971
Billy Jurges	ss	6	16	15	1	4	—	.969
Chuck Klein	rf	2	1	0	0	0	—	1.000
	cf	1	3	0	0	0	—	1.000
Fabian Kowalik	p	1	0	2	1	0	—	.667
Bill Lee	p	2	1	1	0	0	—	1.000
Freddy Lindstrom	cf	4	7	0	0	0	—	1.000
	3b	1	1	1	1	0	—	.667
Charlie Root	p	2	0	1	0	0	—	1.000
Lon Warneke	p	3	2	9	0	0	—	1.000
Totals		**6**	**164**	**75**	**6**	**12**	**0**	**.976**

1936 New York Yankees (AL) 4, New York Giants (NL) 2

The New York Yankees no longer had Babe Ruth, but they did have an impressive rookie named Joe DiMaggio, and the rest of the talent on hand was more than good enough to hand the New York Giants a six-game defeat in the World Series. The Giants drew first blood with a 6-1 victory in Game 1 behind Carl Hubbell, but the Yanks came back to hand the Giants an 18-4 thrashing in Game 2, as Bill Dickey and Tony Lazzeri each drove in five runs. The Yanks won again in Game 3, as Frankie Crosetti singled in the go-ahead run in the bottom of the eighth for the 2-1 win. Red Rolfe gave the Yanks a 2-1 lead against Carl Hubbell by singling home Crosetti in the third inning of Game 4, and Gehrig followed with a two-run homer as the Yanks triumphed, 5-2. The Giants stayed alive with a 10-inning, 5-4 win in Game 5, but the Yanks took Game 6, blowing the game wide open with a seven-run explosion in the ninth.

Game 1
Wednesday, September 30

Yankees	AB	R	H	RBI	BB	K	Avg
Frankie Crosetti, ss	4	0	1	0	0	0	.250
Red Rolfe, 3b	3	0	1	0	0	0	.333
Joe DiMaggio, cf	4	0	1	0	0	1	.250
Lou Gehrig, 1b	3	0	0	0	0	1	.000
Bill Dickey, c	4	0	0	0	0	0	.000
Jake Powell, lf	4	0	3	0	0	0	.750
Tony Lazzeri, 2b	3	0	0	0	1	2	.000
George Selkirk, rf	4	1	1	1	0	1	.250
Red Ruffing, p	3	0	0	0	0	2	.000
TOTALS	32	1	7	1	1	8	.219

Giants	AB	R	H	RBI	BB	K	Avg
Jo-Jo Moore, lf	5	0	0	0	0	1	.000
Dick Bartell, ss	4	1	2	1	0	0	.500
Bill Terry, 1b	4	1	2	0	0	0	.500
Mel Ott, rf	2	2	2	0	2	0	1.000
Jimmy Ripple, cf	2	0	0	0	0	1	.000
Gus Mancuso, c	3	1	1	1	1	1	.333
Burgess Whitehead, 2b	3	1	0	1	1	0	.000
Travis Jackson, 3b	4	0	0	1	0	1	.000
Carl Hubbell, p	4	0	2	1	0	0	.500
TOTALS	31	6	9	5	4	5	.290

	1	2	3	4	5	6	7	8	9		R	H	E
Yankees	0	0	1	0	0	0	0	0	0		1	7	2
Giants	0	0	0	0	1	1	0	4	x		6	9	1

E—Crosetti, Dickey, Hubbell. DP—Giants 1 (Whitehead to Terry). LOB—Yankees 7, Giants 7. Scoring Position—Yankees 0-for-4, Giants 2-for-7. 2B—Crosetti (1), Powell (1), Ott (1). HR—Selkirk (1), Bartell (1). S—Rolfe, Ripple 2. CS—Powell (1).

Yankees	IP	H	R	ER	BB	K	ERA
Red Ruffing (L, 0-1)	8.0	9	6	4	4	5	4.50

Giants	IP	H	R	ER	BB	K	ERA
Carl Hubbell (W, 1-0)	9.0	7	1	1	1	8	1.00

HBP—Gehrig by Hubbell. Time—2:40. Attendance—39,415. Umpires—HP, Pfirman. 1B, Geisel. 2B, Magerkurth. 3B, Summers.

Game 2
Friday, October 2

Yankees	AB	R	H	RBI	BB	K	Avg
Frankie Crosetti, ss	5	4	3	0	1	0	.444
Red Rolfe, 3b	4	3	2	1	2	0	.429
Joe DiMaggio, cf	5	2	3	2	0	0	.444
Lou Gehrig, 1b	5	1	2	3	1	0	.250
Bill Dickey, c	5	3	2	5	1	0	.222
George Selkirk, rf	5	1	1	0	1	1	.222
Jake Powell, lf	3	2	2	0	2	0	.714
Tony Lazzeri, 2b	4	1	1	5	1	0	.143
Lefty Gomez, p	5	1	1	2	0	2	.200
TOTALS	41	18	17	18	9	3	.343

Giants	AB	R	H	RBI	BB	K	Avg
Jo-Jo Moore, lf	5	0	0	0	0	2	.000
Dick Bartell, ss	3	0	1	1	2	1	.429
Bill Terry, 1b	5	0	2	0	1	0	.444
Hank Leiber, cf	4	0	0	0	1	1	.000
Mel Ott, rf	4	0	0	0	0	0	.333
Gus Mancuso, c	2	2	1	0	2	1	.400
Burgess Whitehead, 2b	4	0	0	0	0	1	.000
Travis Jackson, 3b	4	1	1	0	0	0	.125
Hal Schumacher, p	0	0	0	0	1	0	—
Al Smith, p	0	0	0	0	0	0	—
Dick Coffman, p	0	0	0	0	0	0	—
Kiddo Davis, ph	1	1	1	0	0	0	1.000
Frank Gabler, p	0	0	0	0	1	0	—
Harry Danning, ph	1	0	0	0	0	1	.000
Harry Gumbert, p	0	0	0	0	0	0	—
TOTALS	33	4	6	3	7	8	.224

	1	2	3	4	5	6	7	8	9		R	H	E
Yankees	2	0	7	0	0	1	2	0	6		18	17	0
Giants	0	1	0	3	0	0	0	0	0		4	6	1

E—Jackson. DP—Giants 1 (Leiber to Jackson to Bartell). LOB—Yankees 6, Giants 9. Scoring Position—Yankees 9-for-20, Giants 2-for-11. 2B—DiMaggio (1), Bartell (1), Mancuso (1). HR—Dickey (1), Lazzeri (1). SF—DiMaggio. SB—Powell (1). CS—Gehrig (1), Selkirk (1).

Yankees	IP	H	R	ER	BB	K	ERA
Lefty Gomez (W, 1-0)	9.0	6	4	4	7	8	4.00

Giants	IP	H	R	ER	BB	K	ERA
Hal Schumacher (L, 0-1)	2.0	3	5	4	4	1	18.00
Al Smith	0.1	2	3	3	1	0	81.00
Dick Coffman	1.2	2	1	1	0	1	5.40
Frank Gabler	4.0	5	3	3	3	0	6.75
Harry Gumbert	1.0	5	6	6	1	1	54.00

Schumacher pitched to three batters in the 3rd.

WP—Schumacher, Gomez. Time—2:40. Attendance—43,543. Umpires—HP, Geisel. 1B, Magerkurth. 2B, Summers. 3B, Pfirman.

Game 3
Saturday, October 3

Giants	AB	R	H	RBI	BB	K	Avg
Jo-Jo Moore, lf	5	0	1	0	0	0	.067
Dick Bartell, ss	3	0	1	0	0	0	.400
Bill Terry, 1b	4	0	1	0	0	0	.385
Mel Ott, rf	4	0	2	0	0	0	.400
Jimmy Ripple, cf	4	1	1	1	0	1	.167
Gus Mancuso, c	4	0	1	0	0	0	.333
Burgess Whitehead, 2b	4	0	0	0	0	1	.000
Travis Jackson, 3b	2	0	1	0	1	0	.200
Mark Koenig, ph	1	0	0	0	0	0	.000
Freddie Fitzsimmons, p	3	0	2	0	0	1	.667
Sam Leslie, ph	1	0	1	0	0	0	1.000
Kiddo Davis, pr	0	0	0	0	0	0	1.000
TOTALS	35	1	11	1	1	3	.267

Yankees	AB	R	H	RBI	BB	K	Avg
Frankie Crosetti, ss	4	0	1	1	0	1	.385
Red Rolfe, 3b	4	0	0	0	0	0	.273
Joe DiMaggio, cf	3	0	1	0	0	0	.417
Lou Gehrig, 1b	3	1	1	1	0	0	.273
Bill Dickey, c	2	0	0	0	1	0	.182
George Selkirk, rf	3	0	1	0	0	1	.250
Jake Powell, lf	2	1	0	0	1	1	.556
Tony Lazzeri, 2b	2	0	0	0	0	1	.111
Bump Hadley, p	2	0	0	0	0	1	.000
Red Ruffing, ph	1	0	0	0	0	1	.000
Roy Johnson, pr	0	0	0	0	0	0	—
Pat Malone, p	0	0	0	0	0	0	—
TOTALS	26	2	4	2	2	5	.287

	1	2	3	4	5	6	7	8	9		R	H	E
Giants	0	0	0	0	1	0	0	0	0		1	11	0
Yankees	0	1	0	0	0	0	0	1	x		2	4	0

DP—Giants 1 (Bartell to Whitehead to Terry), Yankees 1 (Crosetti to Gehrig). LOB—Giants 9, Yankees 3. Scoring Position—Giants 1-for-6, Yankees 1-for-5. 2B—DiMaggio (2). HR—Ripple (1), Gehrig (1). S—Bartell, Lazzeri. GDP—Ott, Powell. CS—Whitehead (1).

Giants	IP	H	R	ER	BB	K	ERA
Freddie Fitzsimmons (L, 0-1)	8.0	4	2	2	2	5	2.25

Yankees	IP	H	R	ER	BB	K	ERA
Bump Hadley (W, 1-0)	8.0	10	1	1	1	2	1.13
Pat Malone (S, 1)	1.0	1	0	0	0	1	0.00

Time—2:01. Attendance—64,842. Umpires—HP, Magerkurth. 1B, Summers. 2B, Pfirman. 3B, Geisel.

Game 4

Sunday, October 4

Giants	AB	R	H	RBI	BB	K	Avg
Jo-Jo Moore, lf	3	0	1	0	1	1	.111
Dick Bartell, ss	4	1	1	0	0	1	.357
Bill Terry, 1b	3	0	0	1	1	2	.313
Mel Ott, rf	4	0	0	0	0	1	.286
Jimmy Ripple, cf	4	0	2	1	0	0	.300
Gus Mancuso, c	4	0	0	0	0	1	.231
Burgess Whitehead, 2b	3	0	0	0	0	0	.000
Mark Koenig, ph	1	0	1	0	0	0	.500
Travis Jackson, 3b	4	0	1	0	0	1	.214
Carl Hubbell, p	2	0	0	0	0	0	.333
Sam Leslie, ph	1	0	1	0	0	0	1.000
Kiddo Davis, pr	0	1	0	0	0	0	1.000
Frank Gabler, p	0	0	0	0	0	0	—
TOTALS	33	2	7	2	2	7	.250

Yankees	AB	R	H	RBI	BB	K	Avg
Frankie Crosetti, ss	4	1	2	0	0	0	.412
Red Rolfe, 3b	3	1	2	1	1	0	.357
Joe DiMaggio, cf	4	0	0	0	0	0	.313
Lou Gehrig, 1b	4	2	2	2	0	0	.333
Bill Dickey, c	4	0	0	0	0	1	.133
Jake Powell, lf	4	1	1	1	0	0	.462
Tony Lazzeri, 2b	4	0	0	0	0	0	.077
George Selkirk, rf	3	0	1	1	1	1	.267
Monte Pearson, p	4	0	2	0	0	0	.500
TOTALS	34	5	10	5	2	2	.303

	1	2	3	4	5	6	7	8	9	R	H	E
Giants	0	0	0	1	0	0	0	1	0	2	7	1
Yankees	0	1	3	0	0	0	0	1	x	5	10	1

E—Selkirk, Jackson. DP—Giants 1 (Bartell to Whitehead to Terry). LOB—Giants 6, Yankees 7. Scoring Position—Giants 1-for-8, Yankees 5-for-9. 2B—Crosetti (2), Gehrig (1), Pearson (1). HR—Gehrig (2). GDP—DiMaggio. CS—Moore (1), Ripple (1).

Giants	IP	H	R	ER	BB	K	ERA
Carl Hubbell (L, 1-1)	7.0	8	4	3	1	2	2.25
Frank Gabler	1.0	2	1	1	1	0	7.20

Yankees	IP	H	R	ER	BB	K	ERA
Monte Pearson (W, 1-0)	9.0	7	2	2	2	7	2.00

WP—Hubbell. Time—2:12. Attendance—66,569. Umpires—HP, Summers. 1B, Pfirman. 2B, Geisel. 3B, Magerkurth.

Game 5

Monday, October 5

Giants	AB	R	H	RBI	BB	K	Avg
Jo-Jo Moore, lf	5	2	2	0	0	0	.174
Dick Bartell, ss	4	1	1	1	0	2	.333
Bill Terry, 1b	5	0	0	1	0	1	.238
Mel Ott, rf	5	1	1	0	0	0	.263
Jimmy Ripple, cf	2	1	1	1	2	1	.333
Gus Mancuso, c	3	0	2	0	0	0	.313
Burgess Whitehead, 2b	4	0	1	2	0	0	.056
Travis Jackson, 3b	4	0	0	0	0	1	.167
Hal Schumacher, p	4	0	0	0	0	3	.000
TOTALS	36	5	8	5	2	8	.221

Yankees	AB	R	H	RBI	BB	K	Avg
Frankie Crosetti, ss	5	0	0	1	0	3	.318
Red Rolfe, 3b	5	0	2	0	0	1	.368
Joe DiMaggio, cf	4	0	1	0	1	2	.300
Lou Gehrig, 1b	4	0	1	0	1	1	.316
Bill Dickey, c	5	0	1	0	0	1	.150
Bob Seeds, pr	0	0	0	0	0	0	—
George Selkirk, rf	4	2	2	1	1	0	.316
Jake Powell, lf	4	1	1	0	1	1	.412
Tony Lazzeri, 2b	3	1	1	1	1	0	.125
Red Ruffing, p	1	0	0	0	1	0	.000
Roy Johnson, ph	1	0	0	0	0	1	.000
Pat Malone, p	1	0	1	0	0	0	1.000
TOTALS	37	4	10	3	6	10	.283

	1	2	3	4	5	6	7	8	9	10	R	H	E
Giants	3	0	0	0	0	1	0	0	0	1	5	8	3
Yankees	0	1	1	0	0	2	0	0	0	0	4	10	1

E—Crosetti, Bartell, Ott, Jackson. DP—Giants 3 (Schumacher to Terry to Mancuso; Bartell to Whitehead to Terry; Mancuso to Whitehead), Yankees 1 (Crosetti to Lazzeri to Gehrig). LOB—Giants 5, Yankees 9. Scoring Position—Giants 3-for-11, Yankees 2-for-11. 2B—Moore 2 (2), Bartell (2), Mancuso (2), DiMaggio (3). HR—Selkirk (2). S—Bartell, Mancuso. GDP—Mancuso, Ruffing. CS—Rolfe (1), Seeds (1).

Giants	IP	H	R	ER	BB	K	ERA
Hal Schumacher (W, 1-1)	10.0	10	4	3	6	10	5.25

Yankees	IP	H	R	ER	BB	K	ERA
Red Ruffing	6.0	7	4	3	1	7	4.50
Pat Malone (L, 0-1)	4.0	1	1	1	1	1	1.80

WP—Schumacher. Time—2:45. Attendance—50,024. Umpires—HP, Pfirman. 1B, Geisel. 2B, Magerkurth. 3B, Summers.

Game 6

Tuesday, October 6

Yankees	AB	R	H	RBI	BB	K	Avg
Frankie Crosetti, ss	4	0	0	1	2	1	.269
Red Rolfe, 3b	6	1	3	2	0	0	.400
Joe DiMaggio, cf	6	1	3	1	0	0	.346
Lou Gehrig, 1b	5	1	1	1	1	0	.292
Bill Dickey, c	5	2	0	0	1	1	.120
George Selkirk, rf	5	2	2	0	1	0	.333
Jake Powell, lf	5	3	3	4	0	2	.455
Tony Lazzeri, 2b	4	2	3	1	1	1	.250
Lefty Gomez, p	3	0	1	1	0	1	.250
Johnny Murphy, p	2	1	1	1	0	1	.500
TOTALS	45	13	17	12	6	7	.307

Giants	AB	R	H	RBI	BB	K	Avg
Jo-Jo Moore, lf	5	2	2	1	0	0	.214
Dick Bartell, ss	3	2	2	0	2	0	.381
Bill Terry, 1b	4	0	1	0	0	0	.240
Hank Leiber, cf	2	0	0	0	1	1	.000
Eddie Mayo, 3b	1	0	0	0	0	0	.000
Mel Ott, rf	4	1	2	3	1	0	.304
Gus Mancuso, c	3	0	0	0	0	0	.263
Sam Leslie, ph	1	0	0	0	0	0	.667
Harry Danning, c	1	0	0	0	0	0	.000
Burgess Whitehead, 2b	3	0	0	0	0	0	.048
Jimmy Ripple, ph-cf	0	0	0	0	1	0	.333
Travis Jackson, 3b	3	0	1	0	0	0	.190
Mark Koenig, ph-2b	1	0	0	0	0	1	.333
Freddie Fitzsimmons, p	1	0	0	0	0	0	.500
Slick Castleman, p	2	0	1	0	0	0	.500
Kiddo Davis, ph	1	0	0	0	0	0	.500
Dick Coffman, p	0	0	0	0	0	0	—
Harry Gumbert, p	0	0	0	0	0	0	—
TOTALS	35	5	9	4	5	2	.249

	1	2	3	4	5	6	7	8	9	R	H	E
Yankees	0	2	1	2	0	0	0	1	7	13	17	2
Giants	2	0	0	0	1	0	1	1	0	5	9	1

E—DiMaggio, Danning, Rolfe. LOB—Yankees 11, Giants 10. Scoring Position—Yankees 7-for-17, Giants 2-for-8. 2B—Bartell (3), Ott (2). 3B—Selkirk (1). HR—Powell (1), Moore (1), Ott (1). S—Terry, Leiber.

Yankees	IP	H	R	ER	BB	K	ERA
Lefty Gomez (W, 2-0)	6.1	8	4	3	4	1	4.11
Johnny Murphy (S, 1)	2.2	1	1	1	1	1	3.38

Giants	IP	H	R	ER	BB	K	ERA
Freddie Fitzsimmons (L, 0-2)	3.2	9	5	5	0	1	5.40
Slick Castleman	4.1	3	1	1	2	5	2.08
Dick Coffman	0.0	3	5	5	1	0	32.40
Harry Gumbert	1.0	2	2	2	3	1	36.00

Coffman pitched to six batters in the 9th.

Time—2:50. Attendance—38,427. Umpires—HP, Geisel. 1B, Magerkurth. 2B, Summers. 3B, Pfirman.

1936 World Series—Composite Statistics

Batting

Yankees	G	AB	R	H	RBI	2B	3B	HR	BB	SO	SB	CS	Avg	OBP	Slg
Frankie Crosetti	6	26	5	7	3	2	0	0	3	5	0	0	.269	.345	.346
Bill Dickey	6	25	5	3	5	0	0	1	3	4	0	0	.120	.214	.240
Joe DiMaggio	6	26	3	9	3	3	0	0	1	3	0	0	.346	.357	.462
Lou Gehrig	6	24	5	7	7	1	0	2	3	2	0	1	.292	.393	.583
Lefty Gomez	2	8	1	2	3	0	0	0	0	3	0	0	.250	.250	.250
Bump Hadley	1	2	0	0	0	0	0	0	0	1	0	0	.000	.000	.000
Roy Johnson	2	1	0	0	0	0	0	0	0	1	0	0	.000	.000	.000
Tony Lazzeri	6	20	4	5	7	0	0	1	4	4	0	0	.250	.375	.400
Pat Malone	2	1	0	1	0	0	0	0	0	0	0	0	1.000	1.000	1.000
Johnny Murphy	1	2	1	1	1	0	0	0	0	1	0	0	.500	.500	.500
Monte Pearson	1	4	0	2	0	1	0	0	0	0	0	0	.500	.500	.750
Jake Powell	6	22	8	10	5	1	0	1	4	4	1	1	.455	.538	.636
Red Rolfe	6	25	5	10	4	0	0	0	3	1	0	1	.400	.464	.400
Red Ruffing	3	5	0	0	0	0	0	0	1	2	0	0	.000	.167	.000
Bob Seeds	1	0	0	0	0	0	0	0	0	0	0	1	—	—	—
George Selkirk	6	24	6	8	3	0	1	2	4	4	0	1	.333	.429	.667
Totals	6	215	43	65	41	8	1	7	26	35	1	5	.302	.379	.447

Giants	G	AB	R	H	RBI	2B	3B	HR	BB	SO	SB	CS	Avg	OBP	Slg
Dick Bartell	6	21	5	8	3	3	0	1	4	4	0	0	.381	.480	.667
Slick Castleman	1	2	0	1	0	0	0	0	0	0	0	0	.500	.500	.500
Harry Danning	2	2	0	0	0	0	0	0	0	1	0	0	.000	.000	.000
Kiddo Davis	4	2	2	1	0	0	0	0	0	0	0	0	.500	.500	.500
Freddie Fitzsimmons	2	4	0	2	0	0	0	0	0	1	0	0	.500	.500	.500
Frank Gabler	2	0	0	0	0	0	0	0	1	0	0	0	—	1.000	—
Carl Hubbell	2	6	0	2	1	0	0	0	0	0	0	0	.333	.333	.333
Travis Jackson	6	21	1	4	0	0	0	0	1	3	0	0	.190	.227	.190
Mark Koenig	3	3	0	1	0	0	0	0	0	1	0	0	.333	.333	.333
Hank Leiber	2	6	0	0	0	0	0	0	2	2	0	0	.000	.250	.000
Sam Leslie	3	3	0	2	0	0	0	0	0	0	0	0	.667	.667	.667
Gus Mancuso	6	19	3	5	1	2	0	0	3	3	0	0	.263	.364	.368
Eddie Mayo	1	1	0	0	0	0	0	0	0	0	0	0	.000	.000	.000
Jo-Jo Moore	6	28	4	6	1	2	0	1	1	4	0	1	.214	.241	.393
Mel Ott	6	23	4	7	3	2	0	1	3	1	0	0	.304	.385	.522
Jimmy Ripple	5	12	2	4	3	0	0	1	3	3	0	1	.333	.467	.583
Hal Schumacher	2	4	0	0	0	0	0	0	1	3	0	0	.000	.200	.000
Bill Terry	6	25	1	6	4	0	0	1	4	0	0	0	.240	.269	.240
Burgess Whitehead	6	21	1	1	3	0	0	1	3	0	1	0	.048	.091	.048
Totals	6	203	23	50	20	9	0	4	21	33	0	3	.246	.317	.350

Pitching

Yankees	G	GS	CG	IP	H	R	ER	BB	SO	W-L	Sv-Op	Hld	ERA
Lefty Gomez	2	2	1	15.1	14	8	7	11	9	2-0	0-0	0	4.11
Bump Hadley	1	1	0	8.0	10	1	1	1	2	1-0	0-0	0	1.13
Pat Malone	2	0	0	5.0	2	1	1	1	2	0-1	1-1	0	1.80
Johnny Murphy	1	0	0	2.2	1	1	1	1	1	0-0	1-1	0	3.38
Monte Pearson	1	1	1	9.0	7	2	2	2	7	1-0	0-0	0	2.00
Red Ruffing	2	2	1	14.0	16	10	7	5	12	0-1	0-0	0	4.50
Totals	6	6	3	54.0	50	23	19	21	33	4-2	2-2	0	3.17

Giants	G	GS	CG	IP	H	R	ER	BB	SO	W-L	Sv-Op	Hld	ERA
Slick Castleman	1	0	0	4.1	3	1	1	2	5	0-0	0-0	0	2.08
Dick Coffman	2	0	0	1.2	5	6	6	1	1	0-0	0-0	0	32.40
Freddie Fitzsimmons	2	2	1	11.2	13	7	7	2	6	0-2	0-0	0	5.40
Frank Gabler	2	0	0	5.0	7	4	4	4	0	0-0	0-0	0	7.20
Harry Gumbert	2	0	0	2.0	7	8	8	4	2	0-0	0-0	0	36.00
Carl Hubbell	2	2	1	16.0	15	5	4	2	10	1-1	0-0	0	2.25
Hal Schumacher	2	2	1	12.0	13	9	7	10	11	1-1	0-0	0	5.25
Al Smith	1	0	0	0.1	2	3	3	1	0	0-0	0-0	0	81.00
Totals	6	6	3	53.0	65	43	40	26	35	2-4	0-0	0	6.79

Fielding

Yankees	Pos	G	PO	Ast	E	DP	PB	FPct
Frankie Crosetti	ss	6	13	14	2	2	—	.931
Bill Dickey	c	6	38	4	1	0	0	.977
Joe DiMaggio	cf	6	17	0	1	0	—	.944
Lou Gehrig	1b	6	45	2	0	2	—	1.000
Lefty Gomez	p	2	0	3	0	0	—	1.000
Bump Hadley	p	1	0	3	0	0	—	1.000
Tony Lazzeri	2b	6	12	17	0	1	—	1.000
Pat Malone	p	2	0	2	0	0	—	1.000
Johnny Murphy	p	1	0	0	0	0	—	—
Monte Pearson	p	1	1	2	0	0	—	1.000
Jake Powell	lf	6	12	0	0	0	—	1.000
Red Rolfe	3b	6	14	7	1	0	—	.955
Red Ruffing	p	2	1	3	0	0	—	1.000
George Selkirk	rf	6	9	0	1	0	—	.900
Totals		6	162	57	6	5	0	.973

Giants	Pos	G	PO	Ast	E	DP	PB	FPct
Dick Bartell	ss	6	8	13	1	4	—	.955
Slick Castleman	p	1	0	0	0	0	—	—
Dick Coffman	p	2	0	1	0	0	—	1.000
Harry Danning	c	1	3	0	1	0	0	.750
Freddie Fitzsimmons	p	2	1	2	0	0	—	1.000
Frank Gabler	p	2	1	0	0	0	—	1.000
Harry Gumbert	p	2	0	0	0	0	—	—
Carl Hubbell	p	2	2	2	1	0	—	.800
Travis Jackson	3b	6	2	8	3	1	—	.769
Mark Koenig	2b	1	1	0	0	0	—	1.000
Hank Leiber	cf	2	11	1	0	1	—	1.000
Gus Mancuso	c	6	40	5	0	2	0	1.000
Eddie Mayo	3b	1	0	1	0	0	—	1.000
Jo-Jo Moore	lf	6	11	0	0	0	—	1.000
Mel Ott	rf	6	12	0	1	0	—	.923
Jimmy Ripple	cf	5	8	0	0	0	—	1.000
Hal Schumacher	p	2	0	2	0	1	—	1.000
Al Smith	p	1	0	0	0	0	—	—
Bill Terry	1b	6	45	8	0	5	—	1.000
Burgess Whitehead	2b	6	14	20	0	5	—	1.000
Totals		6	159	63	7	19	0	.969

1937 New York Yankees (AL) 4, New York Giants (NL) 1

The New York Yankees overpowered the New York Giants en route to a five-game World Series triumph. The Yankees trotted out Lefty Gomez against the Giants' Carl Hubbell in Game 1, and after five innings, the Giants led 1-0. In the sixth, the Yanks suddenly exploded for seven runs, turning the game into an 8-1 rout. A similar fate befell the Giants' Cliff Melton the next day, as he took a 1-0 lead into the fifth only to be knocked out of the box by opposing pitcher Red Ruffing, who singled in the go-ahead run as the Yanks went on to win by the same score, 8-1. Monte Pearson five-hit the Giants in Game 3, 5-1. Hubbell was brought back on short rest for Game 4, and he won, 7-3, to avert a sweep. Gomez won Game 5, 4-2, and drove in the go-ahead run himself for his second victory of the Series.

Game 1

Wednesday, October 6

Giants	AB	R	H	RBI	BB	K	Avg
Jo-Jo Moore, lf	4	0	2	0	0	0	.500
Dick Bartell, ss	4	0	1	0	0	0	.250
Mel Ott, 3b	4	0	0	0	0	1	.000
Hank Leiber, cf	4	0	0	0	0	1	.000
Jimmy Ripple, rf	3	1	1	0	1	0	.333
Johnny McCarthy, 1b	4	0	1	0	0	0	.250
Gus Mancuso, c	3	0	0	0	0	0	.000
Burgess Whitehead, 2b	3	0	1	0	0	0	.333
Carl Hubbell, p	2	0	0	0	0	0	.000
Harry Gumbert, p	0	0	0	0	0	0	—
Dick Coffman, p	0	0	0	0	0	0	—
Wally Berger, ph	1	0	0	0	0	0	.000
Al Smith, p	0	0	0	0	0	0	—
TOTALS	32	1	6	0	1	2	.188

Yankees	AB	R	H	RBI	BB	K	Avg
Frankie Crosetti, ss	4	1	1	0	1	0	.250
Red Rolfe, 3b	4	1	1	1	1	1	.250
Joe DiMaggio, cf	4	0	2	2	0	0	.500
Lou Gehrig, 1b	2	1	0	0	2	1	.000
Bill Dickey, c	3	1	1	1	1	0	.333
Myril Hoag, lf	4	1	0	0	0	0	.000
George Selkirk, rf	4	1	1	2	0	0	.250
Tony Lazzeri, 2b	4	1	1	1	0	1	.250
Lefty Gomez, p	2	1	0	0	2	0	.000
TOTALS	31	8	7	7	7	3	.226

	1	2	3	4	5	6	7	8	9		R	H	E
Giants	0	0	0	0	1	0	0	0	0		1	6	2
Yankees	0	0	0	0	0	7	0	1	x		8	7	0

E—Whitehead, Bartell. DP—Giants 1 (Ott to Whitehead to McCarthy), Yankees 1 (Crosetti to Lazzeri to Gehrig). LOB—Giants 5, Yankees 6. Scoring Position—Giants 0-for-2, Yankees 4-for-12. 2B—Whitehead (1). HR—Lazzeri (1). GDP—Mancuso, Hoag.

Giants	IP	H	R	ER	BB	K	ERA
Carl Hubbell (L, 0-1)	5.1	6	7	4	3	3	6.75
Harry Gumbert	0.0	0	0	0	0	0	—
Dick Coffman	1.2	0	0	0	4	0	0.00
Al Smith	1.0	1	1	1	0	0	9.00

Yankees	IP	H	R	ER	BB	K	ERA
Lefty Gomez (W, 1-0)	9.0	6	1	1	1	2	1.00

Gumbert pitched to one batter in the 6th.

Time—2:20. Attendance—60,573. Umpires—HP, Ormsby. 1B, Barr. 2B, Basil. 3B, Stewart.

Game 2

Thursday, October 7

Giants	AB	R	H	RBI	BB	K	Avg
Jo-Jo Moore, lf	5	0	2	0	0	1	.444
Dick Bartell, ss	4	1	2	0	0	2	.375
Mel Ott, 3b	4	0	1	1	0	0	.125
Jimmy Ripple, rf	4	0	0	0	0	1	.143
Johnny McCarthy, 1b	4	0	0	0	0	1	.125
Lou Chiozza, cf	4	0	1	0	0	1	.250
Gus Mancuso, c	4	0	0	0	0	1	.000
Burgess Whitehead, 2b	3	0	1	0	1	0	.333
Cliff Melton, p	1	0	0	0	1	0	.000
Harry Gumbert, p	0	0	0	0	0	0	—
Dick Coffman, p	1	0	0	0	0	1	.000
Sam Leslie, ph	0	0	0	0	1	0	—
TOTALS	34	1	7	1	3	8	.220

Yankees	AB	R	H	RBI	BB	K	Avg
Frankie Crosetti, ss	5	0	0	0	0	2	.111
Red Rolfe, 3b	5	0	0	0	0	0	.111
Joe DiMaggio, cf	4	1	2	0	0	0	.500
Lou Gehrig, 1b	2	1	1	0	2	0	.250
Bill Dickey, c	4	1	2	1	0	1	.429
Myril Hoag, lf	4	2	1	1	0	0	.125
George Selkirk, rf	4	2	2	3	0	0	.375
Tony Lazzeri, 2b	3	1	2	0	1	0	.429
Red Ruffing, p	4	0	2	3	0	0	.500
TOTALS	35	8	12	8	3	4	.297

	1	2	3	4	5	6	7	8	9		R	H	E
Giants	1	0	0	0	0	0	0	0	0		1	7	0
Yankees	0	0	0	2	4	2	0	x			8	12	0

DP—Giants 1 (Bartell to Whitehead to McCarthy). LOB—Giants 9, Yankees 6. Scoring Position—Giants 1-for-8, Yankees 5-for-13. 2B—Moore (1), Bartell (1), Hoag (1), Selkirk (1), Ruffing (1). GDP—Ruffing.

Giants	IP	H	R	ER	BB	K	ERA
Cliff Melton (L, 0-1)	4.0	6	2	2	1	2	4.50
Harry Gumbert	1.1	4	4	4	1	1	27.00
Dick Coffman	2.2	2	2	2	1	1	4.15

Yankees	IP	H	R	ER	BB	K	ERA
Red Ruffing (W, 1-0)	9.0	7	1	1	3	8	1.00

Melton pitched to four batters in the 5th.

Time—2:11. Attendance—57,675. Umpires—HP, Barr. 1B, Basil. 2B, Stewart. 3B, Ormsby.

Game 3

Friday, October 8

Yankees	AB	R	H	RBI	BB	K	Avg
Frankie Crosetti, ss	4	0	0	0	1	0	.077
Red Rolfe, 3b	4	1	2	0	1	0	.231
Joe DiMaggio, cf	5	0	1	0	0	1	.385
Lou Gehrig, 1b	5	1	1	1	0	0	.222
Bill Dickey, c	5	1	1	1	0	0	.333
George Selkirk, rf	4	2	1	1	1	0	.333
Myril Hoag, lf	4	0	2	0	0	0	.250
Tony Lazzeri, 2b	2	0	1	1	2	1	.444
Monte Pearson, p	3	0	0	0	1	1	.000
Johnny Murphy, p	0	0	0	0	0	0	—
TOTALS	36	5	9	4	6	3	.271

Giants	AB	R	H	RBI	BB	K	Avg
Jo-Jo Moore, lf	4	0	1	0	0	0	.385
Dick Bartell, ss	4	0	0	0	0	1	.250
Mel Ott, 3b	4	0	1	0	0	1	.167
Jimmy Ripple, rf	4	1	1	0	0	0	.182
Johnny McCarthy, 1b	3	0	1	1	1	0	.182
Lou Chiozza, cf	3	0	1	0	1	0	.286
Harry Danning, c	4	0	0	0	0	0	.000
Burgess Whitehead, 2b	3	0	0	0	0	0	.222
Hal Schumacher, p	1	0	0	0	0	1	.000
Wally Berger, ph	1	0	0	0	0	1	.000
Cliff Melton, p	0	0	0	0	0	0	.000
Sam Leslie, ph	1	0	0	0	0	0	.000
Don Brennan, p	0	0	0	0	0	0	—
TOTALS	32	1	5	1	2	4	.214

	1	2	3	4	5	6	7	8	9		R	H	E
Yankees	0	1	2	1	1	0	0	0	0		5	9	0
Giants	0	0	0	0	0	0	1	0	0		1	5	4

E—Melton, McCarthy 2, Chiozza. DP—Giants 1 (Whitehead to Bartell to McCarthy). LOB—Yankees 11, Giants 6. Scoring Position—Yankees 5-for-16, Giants 0-for-3. 2B—Rolfe 2 (2), McCarthy (1). 3B—Dickey (1). S—Hoag. GDP—Pearson.

Yankees	IP	H	R	ER	BB	K	ERA
Monte Pearson (W, 1-0)	8.2	5	1	1	2	4	1.04
Johnny Murphy (S, 1)	0.1	0	0	0	0	0	0.00

Giants	IP	H	R	ER	BB	K	ERA
Hal Schumacher (L, 0-1)	6.0	9	5	4	4	3	6.00
Cliff Melton	2.0	0	0	0	2	0	3.00
Don Brennan	1.0	0	0	0	0	0	0.00

WP—Schumacher. Time—2:07. Attendance—37,385. Umpires—HP, Basil. 1B, Stewart. 2B, Ormsby. 3B, Barr.

Game 4
Saturday, October 9

Yankees	AB	R	H	RBI	BB	K	Avg
Frankie Crosetti, ss	4	1	0	0	0	0	.059
Red Rolfe, 3b	4	1	2	0	0	0	.294
Joe DiMaggio, cf	4	0	0	1	0	0	.294
Lou Gehrig, 1b	4	1	1	1	0	1	.231
Bill Dickey, c	4	0	0	0	0	0	.250
Myril Hoag, lf	4	0	2	0	0	1	.313
George Selkirk, rf	3	0	0	0	1	0	.267
Tony Lazzeri, 2b	3	0	1	0	0	0	.417
Bump Hadley, p	0	0	0	0	0	0	—
Ivy Andrews, p	2	0	0	0	0	1	.000
Jake Powell, ph	1	0	0	0	0	1	.000
Kemp Wicker, p	0	0	0	0	0	0	—
TOTALS	33	3	6	2	1	4	.254

Giants	AB	R	H	RBI	BB	K	Avg
Jo-Jo Moore, lf	5	1	1	1	0	0	.333
Dick Bartell, ss	5	1	1	1	0	0	.235
Mel Ott, 3b	5	0	1	0	0	1	.176
Jimmy Ripple, rf	2	0	1	0	2	0	.231
Hank Leiber, cf	3	2	2	2	1	0	.286
Johnny McCarthy, 1b	4	1	2	0	0	0	.267
Harry Danning, c	4	0	3	2	0	0	.375
Burgess Whitehead, 2b	3	1	1	0	1	0	.250
Carl Hubbell, p	4	1	0	0	0	0	.000
TOTALS	35	7	12	7	4	1	.248

	1	2	3	4	5	6	7	8	9		R	H	E
Yankees	1	0	1	0	0	0	0	0	1		3	6	0
Giants	0	6	0	0	0	0	1	0	x		7	12	3

E—Bartell 2, Ott. DP—Giants 2 (Whitehead to Bartell; Hubbell to Whitehead to McCarthy). LOB—Yankees 4, Giants 8. Scoring Position—Yankees 0-for-5, Giants 6-for-12. 2B—Danning (1). 3B—Rolfe (1). HR—Gehrig (1). GDP—Crosetti. SB—Whitehead (1). CS—Ripple (1).

Yankees	IP	H	R	ER	BB	K	ERA
Bump Hadley (L, 0-1)	1.1	6	5	5	0	0	33.75
Ivy Andrews	5.2	6	2	2	4	1	3.18
Kemp Wicker	1.0	0	0	0	0	0	0.00

Giants	IP	H	R	ER	BB	K	ERA
Carl Hubbell (W, 1-1)	9.0	6	3	2	1	4	3.77

Time—1:57. Attendance—44,293. Umpires—HP, Stewart. 1B, Ormsby. 2B, Barr. 3B, Basil.

Game 5
Sunday, October 10

Yankees	AB	R	H	RBI	BB	K	Avg
Frankie Crosetti, ss	4	0	0	0	1	0	.048
Red Rolfe, 3b	3	0	1	0	1	1	.300
Joe DiMaggio, cf	5	1	1	1	0	1	.273
Lou Gehrig, 1b	4	0	2	1	1	2	.294
Bill Dickey, c	3	0	0	0	1	1	.211
Myril Hoag, lf	4	1	1	1	0	0	.300
George Selkirk, rf	4	0	1	0	0	0	.263
Tony Lazzeri, 2b	3	1	1	0	0	1	.400
Lefty Gomez, p	4	1	1	1	0	1	.167
TOTALS	34	4	8	4	4	7	.252

Giants	AB	R	H	RBI	BB	K	Avg
Jo-Jo Moore, lf	5	0	3	0	0	0	.391
Dick Bartell, ss	4	1	1	0	0	0	.238
Mel Ott, 3b	3	1	1	2	1	1	.200
Jimmy Ripple, rf	4	0	2	0	0	0	.294
Hank Leiber, cf	4	0	2	0	0	0	.364
Johnny McCarthy, 1b	4	0	0	0	0	1	.211
Harry Danning, c	4	0	0	0	0	2	.250
Burgess Whitehead, 2b	4	0	1	0	0	0	.250
Cliff Melton, p	1	0	0	0	0	1	.000
Blondy Ryan, ph	1	0	0	0	0	1	.000
Al Smith, p	0	0	0	0	0	0	—
Gus Mancuso, ph	1	0	0	0	0	0	.000
Don Brennan, p	0	0	0	0	0	0	—
Wally Berger, ph	1	0	0	0	0	0	.000
TOTALS	36	2	10	2	1	6	.248

	1	2	3	4	5	6	7	8	9		R	H	E
Yankees	0	1	1	0	2	0	0	0	0		4	8	0
Giants	0	0	2	0	0	0	0	0	0		2	10	0

DP—Yankees 1 (Gehrig). LOB—Yankees 9, Giants 8. Scoring Position—Yankees 2-for-8, Giants 0-for-6. 2B—Gehrig (1), Whitehead (2). 3B—Gehrig (1), Lazzeri (1). HR—DiMaggio (1), Hoag (1), Ott (1). S—Rolfe.

Yankees	IP	H	R	ER	BB	K	ERA
Lefty Gomez (W, 2-0)	9.0	10	2	2	1	6	1.50

Giants	IP	H	R	ER	BB	K	ERA
Cliff Melton (L, 0-2)	5.0	6	4	4	3	5	4.91
Al Smith	2.0	1	0	0	0	1	3.00
Don Brennan	2.0	1	0	0	1	1	0.00

WP—Melton. HBP—Lazzeri by Smith. Time—2:06. Attendance—38,216. Umpires—HP, Ormsby. 1B, Barr. 2B, Basil. 3B, Stewart.

1937 World Series—Composite Statistics

Batting

Yankees	G	AB	R	H	RBI	2B	3B	HR	BB	SO	SB	CS	Avg	OBP	Slg
Ivy Andrews	1	2	0	0	0	0	0	0	0	1	0	0	.000	.000	.000
Frankie Crosetti	5	21	2	1	0	0	0	0	3	2	0	0	.048	.167	.048
Bill Dickey	5	19	3	4	3	0	1	0	2	2	0	0	.211	.286	.316
Joe DiMaggio	5	22	2	6	4	0	0	1	0	3	0	0	.273	.273	.409
Lou Gehrig	5	17	4	5	3	1	1	1	5	4	0	0	.294	.455	.647
Lefty Gomez	2	6	2	1	1	0	0	0	2	1	0	0	.167	.375	.167
Myril Hoag	5	20	4	6	2	1	0	1	0	1	0	0	.300	.300	.500
Tony Lazzeri	5	15	3	6	2	0	1	1	3	3	0	0	.400	.526	.733
Monte Pearson	1	3	0	0	0	0	0	0	1	1	0	0	.000	.250	.000
Jake Powell	1	1	0	0	0	0	0	0	0	1	0	0	.000	.000	.000
Red Rolfe	5	20	3	6	1	2	1	0	3	2	0	0	.300	.391	.500
Red Ruffing	1	4	0	2	3	1	0	0	0	0	0	0	.500	.500	.750
George Selkirk	5	19	5	5	6	1	0	0	2	0	0	0	.263	.333	.316
Totals	5	169	28	42	25	6	4	4	21	21	0	0	.249	.335	.402

Giants	G	AB	R	H	RBI	2B	3B	HR	BB	SO	SB	CS	Avg	OBP	Slg
Dick Bartell	5	21	3	5	1	1	0	0	0	3	0	0	.238	.238	.286
Wally Berger	3	3	0	0	0	0	0	0	0	1	0	0	.000	.000	.000
Lou Chiozza	2	7	0	2	0	0	0	0	1	1	0	0	.286	.375	.286
Dick Coffman	2	1	0	0	0	0	0	0	0	1	0	0	.000	.000	.000
Harry Danning	3	12	0	3	2	1	0	0	0	2	0	0	.250	.250	.333
Carl Hubbell	2	6	1	0	1	0	0	0	0	0	0	0	.000	.000	.000
Hank Leiber	3	11	2	4	2	0	0	0	1	1	0	0	.364	.417	.364
Sam Leslie	2	1	0	0	0	0	0	0	1	0	0	0	.000	.500	.000
Gus Mancuso	3	8	0	0	0	0	0	0	0	1	0	0	.000	.000	.000
Johnny McCarthy	5	19	1	4	1	1	0	0	1	2	0	0	.211	.250	.263
Cliff Melton	3	2	0	0	0	0	0	0	0	1	0	0	.000	.333	.000
Jo-Jo Moore	5	23	1	9	1	1	0	0	0	1	0	0	.391	.391	.435
Mel Ott	5	20	1	4	3	0	0	1	1	4	0	0	.200	.238	.350
Jimmy Ripple	5	17	2	5	0	0	0	0	3	1	0	1	.294	.400	.294
Blondy Ryan	1	1	0	0	0	0	0	0	0	1	0	0	.000	.000	.000
Hal Schumacher	1	1	0	0	0	0	0	0	0	1	0	0	.000	.000	.000
Burgess Whitehead	5	16	1	4	0	2	0	0	2	0	1	0	.250	.333	.375
Totals	5	169	12	40	11	6	0	1	11	21	1	1	.237	.283	.290

Pitching

Yankees	G	GS	CG	IP	H	R	ER	BB	SO	W-L	Sv-Op	Hld	ERA
Ivy Andrews	1	0	0	5.2	6	2	2	4	1	0-0	0-0	0	3.18
Lefty Gomez	2	2	2	18.0	16	3	3	2	8	2-0	0-0	0	1.50
Bump Hadley	1	1	0	1.1	6	5	5	0	0	0-1	0-0	0	33.75
Johnny Murphy	1	0	0	0.1	0	0	0	0	0	0-0	1-1	0	0.00
Monte Pearson	1	1	0	8.2	5	1	1	2	4	1-0	0-0	0	1.04
Red Ruffing	1	1	1	9.0	7	1	1	3	8	1-0	0-0	0	1.00
Kemp Wicker	1	0	0	1.0	0	0	0	0	0	0-0	0-0	0	0.00
Totals	5	5	3	44.0	40	12	12	11	21	4-1	1-1	0	2.45

Giants	G	GS	CG	IP	H	R	ER	BB	SO	W-L	Sv-Op	Hld	ERA
Don Brennan	2	0	0	3.0	1	0	0	1	1	0-0	0-0	0	0.00
Dick Coffman	2	0	0	4.1	2	2	2	5	1	0-0	0-0	0	4.15
Harry Gumbert	2	0	0	1.1	4	4	4	1	1	0-0	0-0	0	27.00
Carl Hubbell	2	2	1	14.1	12	10	6	4	7	1-1	0-0	0	3.77
Cliff Melton	3	2	0	11.0	12	6	6	6	7	0-2	0-0	0	4.91
Hal Schumacher	1	1	0	6.0	9	5	4	4	3	0-1	0-0	0	6.00
Al Smith	2	0	0	3.0	2	1	1	0	1	0-0	0-0	0	3.00
Totals	5	5	1	43.0	42	28	23	21	21	1-4	0-0	0	4.81

Fielding

Yankees	Pos	G	PO	Ast	E	DP	PB	FPct
Ivy Andrews	p	1	0	1	0	0	—	1.000
Frankie Crosetti	ss	5	6	18	0	1	—	1.000
Bill Dickey	c	5	26	1	0	0	0	1.000
Joe DiMaggio	cf	5	18	0	0	0	—	1.000
Lou Gehrig	1b	5	51	1	0	2	—	1.000
Lefty Gomez	p	2	1	3	0	0	—	1.000
Bump Hadley	p	1	0	0	0	0	—	—
Myril Hoag	lf	5	11	0	0	0	—	1.000
Tony Lazzeri	2b	5	10	15	0	1	—	1.000
Johnny Murphy	p	1	0	0	0	0	—	—
Monte Pearson	p	1	0	0	0	0	—	—
Red Rolfe	3b	5	2	6	0	0	—	1.000
Red Ruffing	p	1	0	2	0	0	—	1.000
George Selkirk	rf	5	7	0	0	0	—	1.000
Kemp Wicker	p	1	0	0	0	0	—	—
Totals		5	132	47	0	4	0	1.000

Giants	Pos	G	PO	Ast	E	DP	PB	FPct
Dick Bartell	ss	5	13	11	3	3	—	.889
Don Brennan	p	2	0	0	0	0	—	—
Lou Chiozza	cf	2	6	0	1	0	—	.857
Dick Coffman	p	2	0	1	0	0	—	1.000
Harry Danning	c	3	20	1	0	0	0	1.000
Harry Gumbert	p	2	0	0	0	0	—	—
Carl Hubbell	p	2	0	3	0	1	—	1.000
Hank Leiber	cf	3	7	0	0	0	—	1.000
Gus Mancuso	c	2	8	1	0	0	0	1.000
Johnny McCarthy	1b	5	38	1	2	4	—	.951
Cliff Melton	p	3	0	0	1	0	—	.000
Jo-Jo Moore	lf	5	13	0	0	0	—	1.000
Mel Ott	3b	5	5	9	1	1	—	.933
Jimmy Ripple	rf	5	11	0	0	0	—	1.000
Hal Schumacher	p	1	0	1	0	0	—	1.000
Al Smith	p	2	0	1	0	0	—	1.000
Burgess Whitehead	2b	5	8	17	1	5	—	.962
Totals		5	129	46	9	14	0	.951

1938 New York Yankees (AL) 4, Chicago Cubs (NL) 0

The New York Yankees became the first team in history to win three straight World Series after defeating the Chicago Cubs, four games to none. Bill Dickey went 4-for-4 in the opener as Red Ruffing beat Chicago's Bill Lee, 3-1. Joe DiMaggio and Frankie Crosetti clubbed two-run homers in Game 2 and the Yanks beat Dizzy Dean, 6-3. Joe Gordon singled, homered and drove in three runs as Monte Pearson won the third game, 5-2. Crosetti starred again in Game 4 with a double, a triple, and four RBI, and the Yankees made it a clean sweep with an 8-3 win. Red Ruffing notched his second complete-game victory of the Series.

Game 1

Wednesday, October 5

Yankees	AB	R	H	RBI	BB	K	Avg
Frankie Crosetti, ss	4	0	1	0	0	2	.250
Red Rolfe, 3b	5	0	1	0	0	0	.200
Tommy Henrich, rf	4	1	2	0	0	1	.500
Joe DiMaggio, cf	4	0	0	0	0	0	.000
Lou Gehrig, 1b	3	1	1	0	1	2	.333
Bill Dickey, c	4	1	4	1	0	0	1.000
George Selkirk, lf	4	0	1	1	0	0	.250
Joe Gordon, 2b	4	0	2	1	0	1	.500
Red Ruffing, p	3	0	0	0	0	0	.000
TOTALS	35	3	12	3	1	6	.343

Cubs	AB	R	H	RBI	BB	K	Avg
Stan Hack, 3b	4	0	3	1	0	0	.750
Billy Herman, 2b	4	0	1	0	0	0	.250
Frank Demaree, lf	4	0	0	0	0	1	.000
Phil Cavarretta, rf	4	0	2	0	0	1	.500
Carl Reynolds, cf	4	0	0	0	0	0	.000
Gabby Hartnett, c	3	0	1	0	0	1	.333
Ripper Collins, 1b	3	1	1	0	0	0	.333
Billy Jurges, ss	3	0	1	0	0	2	.333
Bill Lee, p	2	0	0	0	0	0	.000
Ken O'Dea, ph	1	0	0	0	0	0	.000
Jack Russell, p	0	0	0	0	0	0	—
TOTALS	32	1	9	1	0	5	.281

	1 2 3	4 5 6	7 8 9	R H E
Yankees	0 2 0	0 0 1	0 0 0	3 12 1
Cubs	0 0 1	0 0 0	0 0 0	1 9 1

E—Henrich, Herman. DP—Yankees 2 (Crosetti to Gehrig; Gordon to Crosetti to Gehrig), Cubs 2 (Jurges to Herman to Collins). LOB—Yankees 8, Cubs 4. Scoring Position—Yankees 2-for-12, Cubs 2-for-4. 2B—Crosetti (1), Henrich (1), Gordon (1). 3B—Hartnett (1). S—Ruffing. GDP—Ruffing, Hack, Reynolds. SB—Dickey (1). CS—Henrich (1), Hack (1).

Yankees	IP	H	R	ER	BB	K	ERA
Red Ruffing (W, 1-0)	9.0	9	1	1	0	5	1.00

Cubs	IP	H	R	ER	BB	K	ERA
Bill Lee (L, 0-1)	8.0	11	3	3	1	6	3.38
Jack Russell	1.0	1	0	0	0	0	0.00

HBP—Crosetti by Lee. Time—1:53. Attendance—43,642. Umpires—HP, Moran. 1B, Kolls. 2B, Sears. 3B, Hubbard.

Game 2

Thursday, October 6

Yankees	AB	R	H	RBI	BB	K	Avg
Frankie Crosetti, ss	4	1	1	2	0	0	.250
Red Rolfe, 3b	4	0	0	0	0	2	.111
Tommy Henrich, rf	4	1	1	0	0	0	.375
Joe DiMaggio, cf	4	2	2	2	0	0	.250
Lou Gehrig, 1b	3	1	1	0	1	1	.333
Bill Dickey, c	4	0	0	0	0	0	.500
George Selkirk, lf	3	0	1	0	1	0	.286
Jake Powell, lf	0	0	0	0	0	0	—
Joe Gordon, 2b	4	0	1	2	0	1	.375
Lefty Gomez, p	2	0	0	0	0	0	.000
Myril Hoag, ph	1	1	0	0	0	0	.000
Johnny Murphy, p	0	0	0	0	0	0	—
TOTALS	33	6	7	6	2	4	.292

Cubs	AB	R	H	RBI	BB	K	Avg
Stan Hack, 3b	5	2	2	0	0	1	.556
Billy Herman, 2b	4	1	1	0	0	2	.250
Frank Demaree, rf	3	0	1	0	0	1	.143
Joe Marty, cf	4	0	3	3	0	0	.750
Carl Reynolds, lf	3	0	0	0	1	1	.000
Gabby Hartnett, c	4	0	0	0	0	0	.143
Ripper Collins, 1b	4	0	1	0	0	1	.286
Billy Jurges, ss	3	0	0	0	1	0	.167
Dizzy Dean, p	3	0	2	0	0	0	.667
Larry French, p	0	0	0	0	0	0	—
Phil Cavarretta, ph	1	0	1	0	0	0	.600
TOTALS	34	3	11	3	2	6	.317

	1 2 3	4 5 6	7 8 9	R H E
Yankees	0 2 0	0 0 0	0 2 2	6 7 2
Cubs	1 0 2	0 0 0	0 0 0	3 11 0

E—Rolfe 2. DP—Yankees 2 (Crosetti to Gordon to Gehrig; Gordon to Crosetti to Gehrig), Cubs 1 (Herman to Jurges to Collins). LOB—Yankees 2, Cubs 7. Scoring Position—Yankees 1-for-4, Cubs 1-for-6. 2B—Gordon (2), Marty (1). HR—Crosetti (1), DiMaggio (1). S—Demaree. GDP—Dickey, Hack, Reynolds. CS—Marty (1), Dean (1).

Yankees	IP	H	R	ER	BB	K	ERA
Lefty Gomez (W, 1-0)	7.0	9	3	3	1	5	3.86
Johnny Murphy (S, 1)	2.0	2	0	0	1	1	0.00

Cubs	IP	H	R	ER	BB	K	ERA
Dizzy Dean (L, 0-1)	8.0	7	6	6	1	2	6.75
Larry French	1.0	0	0	0	1	2	0.00

Dean pitched to two batters in the 9th.

Time—1:53. Attendance—42,108. Umpires—HP, Kolls. 1B, Sears. 2B, Hubbard. 3B, Moran.

Game 3

Saturday, October 8

Cubs	AB	R	H	RBI	BB	K	Avg
Stan Hack, 3b	3	1	1	0	1	1	.500
Billy Herman, 2b	3	0	0	1	2	.182	
Phil Cavarretta, rf	4	0	1	0	0	0	.444
Joe Marty, cf	4	1	3	2	0	0	.750
Carl Reynolds, lf	4	0	0	0	0	2	.000
Gabby Hartnett, c	4	0	0	0	0	1	.091
Ripper Collins, 1b	4	0	0	0	0	1	.182
Billy Jurges, ss	3	0	0	0	0	1	.111
Tony Lazzeri, ph	1	0	0	0	0	0	.000
Clay Bryant, p	2	0	0	0	0	1	.000
Jack Russell, p	0	0	0	0	0	0	—
Augie Galan, ph	1	0	0	0	0	0	.000
Larry French, p	0	0	0	0	0	0	—
Ken O'Dea, ph	1	0	0	0	0	0	.000
TOTALS	34	2	5	2	2	9	.250

Yankees	AB	R	H	RBI	BB	K	Avg
Frankie Crosetti, ss	3	0	0	0	2	1	.182
Red Rolfe, 3b	4	0	1	1	0	0	.154
Tommy Henrich, rf	4	0	0	0	0	0	.250
Joe DiMaggio, cf	3	1	1	0	1	0	.273
Lou Gehrig, 1b	4	1	1	0	0	0	.300
Bill Dickey, c	3	1	1	1	1	0	.455
George Selkirk, lf	3	0	0	1	1	1	.200
Joe Gordon, 2b	4	1	2	3	0	1	.417
Monte Pearson, p	3	1	1	0	1	0	.333
TOTALS	31	5	7	5	6	3	.280

	1 2 3	4 5 6	7 8 9	R H E
Cubs	0 0 0	0 1 0	0 1 0	2 5 1
Yankees	0 0 0	0 2 2	0 1 x	5 7 2

E—Gordon, Crosetti, Herman. LOB—Cubs 7, Yankees 8. Scoring Position—Cubs 1-for-10, Yankees 2-for-8. 2B—Hack (1). HR—Marty (1), Dickey (1), Gordon (1). CS—Crosetti (1).

Cubs	IP	H	R	ER	BB	K	ERA
Clay Bryant (L, 0-1)	5.1	6	4	4	5	3	6.75
Jack Russell	0.2	0	0	0	1	0	0.00
Larry French	2.0	1	1	1	0	0	3.00

Yankees	IP	H	R	ER	BB	K	ERA
Monte Pearson (W, 1-0)	9.0	5	2	1	2	9	1.00

Time—1:57. Attendance—55,236. Umpires—HP, Sears. 1B, Hubbard. 2B, Moran. 3B, Kolls.

Game 4

Sunday, October 9

Cubs	AB	R	H	RBI	BB	K	Avg
Stan Hack, 3b	5	0	2	0	0	0	.471
Billy Herman, 2b	5	0	1	0	0	0	.188
Phil Cavarretta, rf	4	1	2	0	0	0	.462
Joe Marty, cf	4	0	0	0	0	2	.500
Frank Demaree, lf	3	1	0	0	1	0	.100
Ken O'Dea, c	3	1	1	2	1	0	.200
Ripper Collins, 1b	4	0	0	0	0	1	.133
Billy Jurges, ss	4	0	2	0	0	0	.231
Bill Lee, p	1	0	0	0	0	1	.000
Augie Galan, ph	1	0	0	0	0	1	.000
Charlie Root, p	0	0	0	0	0	0	—
Tony Lazzeri, ph	1	0	0	0	0	1	.000
Vance Page, p	0	0	0	0	0	0	—
Larry French, p	0	0	0	0	0	0	—
Tex Carleton, p	0	0	0	0	0	0	—
Dizzy Dean, p	0	0	0	0	0	0	.667
Carl Reynolds, ph	1	0	0	0	0	0	.000
TOTALS	36	3	8	2	2	6	.260

Yankees	AB	R	H	RBI	BB	K	Avg
Frankie Crosetti, ss	5	0	2	4	0	1	.250
Red Rolfe, 3b	5	1	1	0	0	1	.167
Tommy Henrich, rf	4	1	1	1	0	0	.250
Joe DiMaggio, cf	4	1	1	0	0	1	.267
Lou Gehrig, 1b	4	1	1	0	0	1	.286
Bill Dickey, c	4	0	1	0	0	0	.400
Myril Hoag, lf	4	2	2	1	0	0	.400
Joe Gordon, 2b	3	2	1	0	0	0	.400
Red Ruffing, p	3	1	1	1	1	0	.167
TOTALS	36	8	11	7	2	3	.283

	1 2 3	4 5 6	7 8 9	R H E
Cubs	0 0 0	1 0 0	0 2 0	3 8 1
Yankees	0 3 0	0 0 1	0 4 x	8 11 1

E—Gordon, Jurges. LOB—Cubs 8, Yankees 6. Scoring Position—Cubs 1-for-10, Yankees 4-for-10. 2B—Cavarretta (1), Jurges (1), Crosetti (2), Hoag (1). 3B—Crosetti (1). HR—O'Dea (1), Henrich (1). SB—Rolfe (1), Gordon (1).

Cubs	IP	H	R	ER	BB	K	ERA
Bill Lee (L, 0-2)	3.0	4	3	0	0	2	2.45
Charlie Root	3.0	3	1	1	0	1	3.00
Vance Page	1.1	2	2	2	0	0	13.50
Larry French	0.1	0	0	0	0	0	2.70
Tex Carleton	0.0	1	2	2	2	0	—
Dizzy Dean	0.1	1	0	0	0	0	6.48

Yankees	IP	H	R	ER	BB	K	ERA
Red Ruffing (W, 2-0)	9.0	8	3	2	2	6	1.50

Carleton pitched to three batters in the 8th.

WP—Carleton 2. Time—2:11. Attendance—59,847. Umpires—HP, Hubbard. 1B, Moran. 2B, Kolls. 3B, Sears.

1938 World Series—Composite Statistics

Batting

Yankees	G	AB	R	H	RBI	2B	3B	HR	BB	SO	SB	CS	Avg	OBP	Slg
Frankie Crosetti	4	16	1	4	6	2	1	1	2	4	0	1	.250	.368	.688
Bill Dickey	4	15	2	6	2	0	0	1	1	0	1	0	.400	.438	.600
Joe DiMaggio	4	15	4	4	2	0	0	1	1	1	0	0	.267	.313	.467
Lou Gehrig	4	14	4	4	0	0	0	0	2	3	0	0	.286	.375	.286
Lefty Gomez	1	2	0	0	0	0	0	0	0	0	0	0	.000	.000	.000
Joe Gordon	4	15	3	6	6	2	0	1	1	3	1	0	.400	.438	.733
Tommy Henrich	4	16	3	4	1	1	0	1	0	1	0	1	.250	.250	.500
Myril Hoag	2	5	3	2	1	1	0	0	0	0	0	0	.400	.400	.600
Monte Pearson	1	3	1	1	0	0	0	0	1	0	0	0	.333	.500	.333
Red Rolfe	4	18	0	3	1	0	0	0	0	3	1	0	.167	.167	.167
Red Ruffing	2	6	1	1	1	0	0	0	1	0	0	0	.167	.286	.167
George Selkirk	3	10	0	2	1	0	0	0	2	1	0	0	.200	.333	.200
Totals	4	135	22	37	21	6	1	5	11	16	3	2	.274	.333	.444

Batting

Cubs	G	AB	R	H	RBI	2B	3B	HR	BB	SO	SB	CS	Avg	OBP	Slg
Clay Bryant	1	2	0	0	0	0	0	0	0	1	0	0	.000	.000	.000
Phil Cavarretta	4	13	1	6	0	1	0	0	0	1	0	0	.462	.462	.538
Ripper Collins	4	15	1	2	0	0	0	0	0	3	0	0	.133	.133	.133
Dizzy Dean	2	3	0	2	0	0	0	0	0	0	0	1	.667	.667	.667
Frank Demaree	3	10	1	1	0	0	0	0	1	2	0	0	.100	.182	.100
Augie Galan	2	2	0	0	0	0	0	0	0	1	0	0	.000	.000	.000
Stan Hack	4	17	3	8	1	1	0	0	1	2	0	1	.471	.500	.529
Gabby Hartnett	3	11	0	1	0	0	0	1	0	2	0	0	.091	.091	.273
Billy Herman	4	16	1	3	0	0	0	0	1	4	0	0	.188	.235	.188
Billy Jurges	4	13	0	3	0	1	0	0	1	3	0	0	.231	.286	.308
Tony Lazzeri	2	2	0	0	0	0	0	0	0	1	0	0	.000	.000	.000
Bill Lee	2	3	0	0	0	0	0	0	0	1	0	0	.000	.000	.000
Joe Marty	3	12	1	6	5	1	0	1	0	2	0	1	.500	.500	.833
Ken O'Dea	3	5	1	1	2	0	0	1	1	0	0	0	.200	.333	.800
Carl Reynolds	4	12	0	0	0	0	0	0	1	3	0	0	.000	.077	.000
Totals	4	136	9	33	8	4	1	2	6	26	0	3	.243	.275	.331

Pitching

Yankees	G	GS	CG	IP	H	R	ER	BB	SO	W-L	Sv-Op	Hld	ERA
Lefty Gomez	1	1	0	7.0	9	3	3	1	5	1-0	0-0	0	3.86
Johnny Murphy	1	0	0	2.0	2	0	0	1	1	0-0	1-1	0	0.00
Monte Pearson	1	1	1	9.0	5	2	1	2	9	1-0	0-0	0	1.00
Red Ruffing	2	2	2	18.0	17	4	3	2	11	2-0	0-0	0	1.50
Totals	4	4	3	36.0	33	9	7	6	26	4-0	1-1	0	1.75

Pitching

Cubs	G	GS	CG	IP	H	R	ER	BB	SO	W-L	Sv-Op	Hld	ERA
Clay Bryant	1	1	0	5.1	6	4	4	5	3	0-1	0-0	0	6.75
Tex Carleton	1	0	0	0.0	1	2	2	2	0	0-0	0-0	0	—
Dizzy Dean	2	1	0	8.1	8	6	6	1	2	0-1	0-0	0	6.48
Larry French	3	0	0	3.1	1	1	1	1	2	0-0	0-0	0	2.70
Bill Lee	2	2	0	11.0	15	6	3	1	8	0-2	0-0	0	2.45
Vance Page	1	0	0	1.1	2	2	2	0	0	0-0	0-0	0	13.50
Charlie Root	1	0	0	3.0	3	1	1	0	1	0-0	0-0	0	3.00
Jack Russell	2	0	0	1.2	1	0	0	1	0	0-0	0-0	0	0.00
Totals	4	4	0	34.0	37	22	19	11	16	0-4	0-0	0	5.03

Fielding

Yankees	Pos	G	PO	Ast	E	DP	PB	FPct
Frankie Crosetti	ss	4	16	11	1	4	—	.964
Bill Dickey	c	4	30	5	0	0	0	1.000
Joe DiMaggio	cf	4	10	0	0	0	—	1.000
Lou Gehrig	1b	4	26	3	0	4	—	1.000
Lefty Gomez	p	1	0	1	0	0	—	1.000
Joe Gordon	2b	4	12	11	2	3	—	.920
Tommy Henrich	rf	4	6	0	1	0	—	.857
Myril Hoag	lf	1	1	0	0	0	—	1.000
Johnny Murphy	p	1	0	0	0	0	—	—
Monte Pearson	p	1	2	0	0	0	—	1.000
Jake Powell	lf	1	0	0	0	0	—	—
Red Rolfe	3b	4	0	4	2	0	—	.667
Red Ruffing	p	2	2	4	0	0	—	1.000
George Selkirk	lf	3	3	0	0	0	—	1.000
Totals		4	108	39	6	11	0	.961

Fielding

Cubs	Pos	G	PO	Ast	E	DP	PB	FPct
Clay Bryant	p	1	0	0	0	0	—	—
Tex Carleton	p	1	0	0	0	0	—	—
Phil Cavarretta	rf	3	4	1	0	0	—	1.000
Ripper Collins	1b	4	38	1	0	3	—	1.000
Dizzy Dean	p	2	0	2	0	0	—	1.000
Frank Demaree	lf	2	5	0	0	0	—	1.000
	rf	1	1	0	0	0	—	1.000
Larry French	p	3	0	2	0	0	—	1.000
Stan Hack	3b	4	4	4	0	0	—	1.000
Gabby Hartnett	c	3	14	3	0	0	0	1.000
Billy Herman	2b	4	5	15	2	2	—	.909
Billy Jurges	ss	4	11	7	1	2	—	.947
Bill Lee	p	2	1	0	0	0	—	1.000
Joe Marty	cf	3	7	0	0	0	—	1.000
Ken O'Dea	c	1	5	0	0	0	0	1.000
Vance Page	p	1	0	1	0	0	—	1.000
Carl Reynolds	lf	2	4	0	0	0	—	1.000
	cf	1	3	0	0	0	—	1.000
Charlie Root	p	1	0	0	0	0	—	—
Jack Russell	p	2	0	0	0	0	—	—
Totals		4	102	36	3	7	0	.979

1939 New York Yankees (AL) 4, Cincinnati Reds (NL) 0

The New York Yankees brought home their fourth straight World Championship with a four-game sweep of the Cincinnati Reds. Red Ruffing and Paul Derringer were superb in the opener, with the game going into the ninth tied at 1-1. The Yanks pulled it out in the bottom of the ninth when Charlie Keller tripled and Bill Dickey singled him in. Monte Pearson authored a two-hit shutout and Babe Dahlgren homered as the Yankees took Game 2, 4-0. Keller homered twice and drove in four runs in the Yanks' 7-3 win in Game 3. The Reds held a 4-2 lead in the ninth inning of Game 4, but shortstop Billy Myers muffed a double-play ball, leading to a game-tying two-run New York rally. The Yanks won the game with three runs in the 10th on errors by Myers and Goodman, with Joe DiMaggio scoring the final run after Keller's slide knocked catcher Ernie Lombardi for a loop.

Game 1
Wednesday, October 4

Reds	AB	R	H	RBI	BB	K	Avg
Bill Werber, 3b	4	0	0	0	0	0	.000
Lonny Frey, 2b	4	0	0	0	0	0	.000
Ival Goodman, rf	2	1	0	0	1	1	.000
Frank McCormick, 1b	3	0	2	1	0	0	.667
Ernie Lombardi, c	3	0	0	0	0	0	.000
Harry Craft, cf	3	0	1	0	0	1	.333
Wally Berger, lf	3	0	0	0	0	2	.000
Billy Myers, ss	3	0	1	0	0	0	.333
Paul Derringer, p	3	0	0	0	0	0	.000
TOTALS	28	1	4	1	1	4	.143

Yankees	AB	R	H	RBI	BB	K	Avg
Frankie Crosetti, ss	4	0	0	0	0	1	.000
Red Rolfe, 3b	4	0	0	0	0	0	.000
Charlie Keller, rf	4	1	1	0	0	1	.250
Joe DiMaggio, cf	3	0	1	0	1	0	.333
Bill Dickey, c	4	0	1	1	0	1	.250
George Selkirk, lf	3	0	0	0	0	1	.000
Joe Gordon, 2b	3	1	1	0	0	1	.333
Babe Dahlgren, 1b	3	0	1	0	1	0	.333
Red Ruffing, p	3	0	1	0	0	1	.333
TOTALS	31	2	6	2	1	7	.194

	1	2	3	4	5	6	7	8	9	R	H	E
Reds	0	0	0	1	0	0	0	0	0	1	4	0
Yankees	0	0	0	0	1	0	0	0	1	2	6	0

DP—Yankees 3 (Rolfe to Gordon to Dahlgren; Ruffing to Crosetti to Gordon to Dahlgren; Gordon to Crosetti to Dahlgren). LOB—Reds 1, Yankees 5. Scoring Position—Reds 1-for-1, Yankees 1-for-3. 2B—Dahlgren (1). 3B—Keller (1). GDP—Lombardi, Myers, Derringer. SB—Goodman (1).

Reds	IP	H	R	ER	BB	K	ERA
Paul Derringer (L, 0-1)	8.1	6	2	2	1	7	2.16

Yankees	IP	H	R	ER	BB	K	ERA
Red Ruffing (W, 1-0)	9.0	4	1	1	1	4	1.00

Time—1:33. Attendance—58,541. Umpires—HP, McGowan. 1B, Reardon. 2B, Summers. 3B, Pinelli.

Game 2
Thursday, October 5

Reds	AB	R	H	RBI	BB	K	Avg
Bill Werber, 3b	3	0	1	0	1	0	.143
Lonny Frey, 2b	4	0	0	0	0	1	.000
Ival Goodman, rf	3	0	0	0	0	1	.000
Frank McCormick, 1b	3	0	0	0	0	1	.333
Ernie Lombardi, c	3	0	1	0	0	0	.167
Frenchy Bordagaray, pr	0	0	0	0	0	0	—
Willard Hershberger, c	0	0	0	0	0	0	—
Harry Craft, cf	3	0	0	0	0	3	.167
Wally Berger, lf	3	0	0	0	0	0	.000
Billy Myers, ss	3	0	0	0	0	1	.167
Bucky Walters, p	2	0	0	0	0	0	.000
Lee Gamble, ph	1	0	0	0	0	1	.000
TOTALS	28	0	2	0	1	8	.113

Yankees	AB	R	H	RBI	BB	K	Avg
Frankie Crosetti, ss	4	0	1	1	0	0	.125
Red Rolfe, 3b	4	1	1	0	0	0	.125
Charlie Keller, rf	4	1	2	1	0	0	.375
Joe DiMaggio, cf	4	0	1	0	0	0	.286
Bill Dickey, c	3	0	1	1	0	1	.286
George Selkirk, lf	3	0	1	0	0	1	.167
Joe Gordon, 2b	3	0	0	0	0	1	.167
Babe Dahlgren, 1b	3	2	2	1	0	1	.500
Monte Pearson, p	2	0	0	0	0	1	.000
TOTALS	30	4	9	4	0	5	.241

	1	2	3	4	5	6	7	8	9	R	H	E
Reds	0	0	0	0	0	0	0	0	0	0	2	0
Yankees	0	0	3	1	0	0	0	0	x	4	9	0

DP—Reds 1 (Walters to Myers to McCormick), Yankees 1 (Dickey to Crosetti). LOB—Reds 2, Yankees 3. Scoring Position—Reds 0-for-0, Yankees 2-for-4. 2B—Keller (1), Dahlgren (2). HR—Dahlgren (1). S—Pearson. GDP—DiMaggio. CS—Werber (1).

Reds	IP	H	R	ER	BB	K	ERA
Bucky Walters (L, 0-1)	8.0	9	4	4	0	5	4.50

Yankees	IP	H	R	ER	BB	K	ERA
Monte Pearson (W, 1-0)	9.0	2	0	0	1	8	0.00

Time—1:27. Attendance—59,791. Umpires—HP, Reardon. 1B, Summers. 2B, Pinelli. 3B, McGowan.

Game 3
Saturday, October 7

Yankees	AB	R	H	RBI	BB	K	Avg
Frankie Crosetti, ss	4	1	0	0	1	1	.083
Red Rolfe, 3b	4	1	1	0	0	0	.167
Charlie Keller, rf	3	3	2	4	1	1	.455
Joe DiMaggio, cf	4	1	1	2	0	1	.273
Bill Dickey, c	3	1	1	1	1	0	.300
George Selkirk, lf	2	0	0	0	2	0	.125
Joe Gordon, 2b	4	0	0	0	0	0	.100
Babe Dahlgren, 1b	4	0	0	0	0	1	.300
Lefty Gomez, p	1	0	0	0	0	1	.000
Bump Hadley, p	3	0	0	0	0	0	.000
TOTALS	32	7	5	7	5	5	.216

Reds	AB	R	H	RBI	BB	K	Avg
Bill Werber, 3b	4	1	1	1	1	0	.182
Lonny Frey, 2b	4	0	0	0	1	0	.000
Ival Goodman, rf	5	1	3	1	0	0	.300
Frank McCormick, 1b	5	0	2	0	0	0	.364
Ernie Lombardi, c	3	0	1	1	0	0	.222
Frenchy Bordagaray, pr	0	0	0	0	0	0	—
Willard Hershberger, c	1	0	0	0	0	0	.000
Harry Craft, cf	4	0	0	0	0	1	.100
Wally Berger, lf	4	0	0	0	0	2	.000
Billy Myers, ss	3	1	2	0	1	0	.333
Junior Thompson, p	1	0	1	0	0	0	1.000
Lee Grissom, p	0	0	0	0	0	0	—
Nino Bongiovanni, ph	1	0	0	0	0	0	.000
Whitey Moore, p	1	0	0	0	0	0	.000
TOTALS	36	3	10	3	3	3	.186

	1	2	3	4	5	6	7	8	9	R	H	E
Yankees	2	0	2	0	3	0	0	0	0	7	5	1
Reds	1	2	0	0	0	0	0	0	0	3	10	0

E—Hadley. DP—Yankees 1 (Rolfe to Gordon to Dahlgren). LOB—Yankees 3, Reds 11. Scoring Position—Yankees 1-for-2, Reds 3-for-12. HR—Keller 2 (2), DiMaggio (1), Dickey (1). S—Thompson. GDP—Craft.

Yankees	IP	H	R	ER	BB	K	ERA
Lefty Gomez	1.0	3	1	1	0	1	9.00
Bump Hadley (W, 1-0)	8.0	7	2	2	3	2	2.25

Reds	IP	H	R	ER	BB	K	ERA
Junior Thompson (L, 0-1)	4.2	5	7	7	4	3	13.50
Lee Grissom	1.1	0	0	0	1	0	0.00
Whitey Moore	3.0	0	0	0	0	2	0.00

WP—Thompson. HBP—Lombardi by Hadley. Time—2:01. Attendance—32,723. Umpires—HP, Summers. 1B, Pinelli. 2B, McGowan. 3B, Reardon.

Game 4
Sunday, October 8

Yankees	AB	R	H	RBI	BB	K	Avg
Frankie Crosetti, ss	4	1	0	0	1	0	.063
Red Rolfe, 3b	4	0	0	0	0	0	.125
Charlie Keller, rf	5	3	2	1	0	0	.438
Joe DiMaggio, cf	5	2	2	1	0	0	.313
Bill Dickey, c	5	1	1	2	0	0	.267
George Selkirk, lf	4	0	1	0	1	0	.167
Joe Gordon, 2b	4	0	1	1	0	0	.143
Babe Dahlgren, 1b	4	0	0	0	0	1	.214
Oral Hildebrand, p	1	0	0	0	0	0	.000
Steve Sundra, p	0	0	0	0	1	0	—
Johnny Murphy, p	2	0	0	0	0	1	.000
TOTALS	38	7	7	5	3	3	.213

Reds	AB	R	H	RBI	BB	K	Avg
Bill Werber, 3b	5	0	2	1	0	0	.250
Lonny Frey, 2b	5	0	0	0	0	3	.000
Ival Goodman, rf	5	1	2	0	0	0	.333
Frank McCormick, 1b	4	1	2	0	0	0	.400
Ernie Lombardi, c	5	0	1	0	1	1	.214
Harry Craft, cf	1	0	0	0	0	1	.091
Al Simmons, lf	4	1	1	0	0	1	.250
Wally Berger, lf-cf	5	0	0	1	0	0	.000
Billy Myers, ss	3	1	1	0	1	2	.333
Paul Derringer, p	2	0	1	0	0	0	.200
Willard Hershberger, ph	1	0	1	1	0	0	.500
Bucky Walters, p	1	0	0	0	0	0	.000
TOTALS	41	4	11	4	1	7	.202

	1	2	3	4	5	6	7	8	9	10	R	H	E
Yankees	0	0	0	0	0	0	2	0	2	3	7	7	1
Reds	0	0	0	0	0	0	3	1	0	0	4	11	4

E—Myers 2, Goodman, Rolfe, Lombardi. LOB—Yankees 5, Reds 9. Scoring Position—Yankees 2-for-8, Reds 3-for-12. 2B—Selkirk (1), Goodman (1), McCormick (1), Simmons (1). 3B—Myers (1). HR—Keller (3), Dickey (2). S—Rolfe, McCormick.

Yankees	IP	H	R	ER	BB	K	ERA
Oral Hildebrand	4.0	2	0	0	0	3	0.00
Steve Sundra	2.2	4	3	0	1	2	0.00
Johnny Murphy (W, 1-0)	3.1	5	1	1	0	2	2.70

Reds	IP	H	R	ER	BB	K	ERA
Paul Derringer	7.0	3	2	2	2	2	2.35
Bucky Walters (BS, 1; L, 0-2)	3.0	4	5	2	1	1	4.91

Time—2:04. Attendance—32,794. Umpires—HP, Pinelli. 1B, McGowan. 2B, Reardon. 3B, Summers.

1939 World Series—Composite Statistics

Batting

Yankees	G	AB	R	H	RBI	2B	3B	HR	BB	SO	SB	CS	Avg	OBP	Slg
Frankie Crosetti	4	16	2	1	1	0	0	0	2	2	0	0	.063	.167	.063
Babe Dahlgren	4	14	2	3	2	2	0	1	0	4	0	0	.214	.214	.571
Bill Dickey	4	15	2	4	5	0	0	2	1	2	0	0	.267	.313	.667
Joe DiMaggio	4	16	3	5	3	0	0	1	1	1	0	0	.313	.353	.500
Lefty Gomez	1	1	0	0	0	0	0	0	0	1	0	0	.000	.000	.000
Joe Gordon	4	14	1	2	1	0	0	0	0	2	0	0	.143	.143	.143
Bump Hadley	1	3	0	0	0	0	0	0	0	0	0	0	.000	.000	.000
Oral Hildebrand	1	1	0	0	0	0	0	0	0	1	0	0	.000	.000	.000
Charlie Keller	4	16	8	7	6	1	1	3	1	2	0	0	.438	.471	1.188
Johnny Murphy	1	2	0	0	0	0	0	0	0	1	0	0	.000	.000	.000
Monte Pearson	1	2	0	0	0	0	0	0	0	1	0	0	.000	.000	.000
Red Rolfe	4	16	2	2	0	0	0	0	0	0	0	0	.125	.125	.125
Red Ruffing	1	3	0	1	0	0	0	0	0	1	0	0	.333	.333	.333
George Selkirk	4	12	0	2	0	1	0	0	3	2	0	0	.167	.333	.250
Steve Sundra	1	0	0	0	0	0	0	0	1	0	0	0	—	1.000	—
Totals	4	131	20	27	18	4	1	7	9	20	0	0	.206	.257	.412

Reds	G	AB	R	H	RBI	2B	3B	HR	BB	SO	SB	CS	Avg	OBP	Slg
Wally Berger	4	15	0	0	1	0	0	0	0	4	0	0	.000	.000	.000
Nino Bongiovanni	1	1	0	0	0	0	0	0	0	0	0	0	.000	.000	.000
Frenchy Bordagaray	2	0	0	0	0	0	0	0	0	0	0	0	—	—	—
Harry Craft	4	11	0	1	0	0	0	0	0	6	0	0	.091	.091	.091
Paul Derringer	2	5	0	1	0	0	0	0	0	0	0	0	.200	.200	.200
Lonny Frey	4	17	0	0	0	0	0	0	1	4	0	0	.000	.056	.000
Lee Gamble	1	1	0	0	0	0	0	0	0	1	0	0	.000	.000	.000
Ival Goodman	4	15	3	5	1	1	0	0	1	2	1	0	.333	.375	.400
Willard Hershberger	3	2	0	1	0	0	0	0	0	0	0	0	.500	.500	.500
Ernie Lombardi	4	14	0	3	2	0	0	0	1	0	0	0	.214	.267	.214
Frank McCormick	4	15	1	6	1	1	0	0	1	0	0	0	.400	.400	.467
Whitey Moore	1	1	0	0	0	0	0	0	0	0	0	0	.000	.000	.000
Billy Myers	4	12	2	4	0	0	1	0	2	3	0	0	.333	.429	.500
Al Simmons	1	4	1	1	0	1	0	0	0	0	0	0	.250	.250	.500
Junior Thompson	1	1	0	1	0	0	0	0	0	0	0	0	1.000	1.000	1.000
Bucky Walters	2	3	0	0	0	0	0	0	0	0	0	0	.000	.000	.000
Bill Werber	4	16	1	4	2	0	0	0	2	0	0	1	.250	.333	.250
Totals	4	133	8	27	8	3	1	0	6	22	1	1	.203	.243	.241

Pitching

Yankees	G	GS	CG	IP	H	R	ER	BB	SO	W-L	Sv-Op	Hld	ERA
Lefty Gomez	1	1	0	1.0	3	1	1	0	1	0-0	0-0	0	9.00
Bump Hadley	1	0	0	8.0	7	2	2	3	2	1-0	0-0	0	2.25
Oral Hildebrand	1	1	0	4.0	2	0	0	0	3	0-0	0-0	0	0.00
Johnny Murphy	1	0	0	3.1	5	1	1	0	2	1-0	0-0	0	2.70
Monte Pearson	1	1	1	9.0	2	0	0	1	8	1-0	0-0	0	0.00
Red Ruffing	1	1	1	9.0	4	1	1	1	4	1-0	0-0	0	1.00
Steve Sundra	1	0	0	2.2	4	3	0	1	2	0-0	0-0	0	0.00
Totals	4	4	2	37.0	27	8	5	6	22	4-0	0-0	0	1.22

Reds	G	GS	CG	IP	H	R	ER	BB	SO	W-L	Sv-Op	Hld	ERA
Paul Derringer	2	2	1	15.1	9	4	4	3	9	0-1	0-0	0	2.35
Lee Grissom	1	0	0	1.1	0	0	0	1	0	0-0	0-0	0	0.00
Whitey Moore	1	0	0	3.0	0	0	0	0	2	0-0	0-0	0	0.00
Junior Thompson	1	1	0	4.2	5	7	7	4	3	0-1	0-0	0	13.50
Bucky Walters	2	1	1	11.0	13	9	6	1	6	0-2	0-1	0	4.91
Totals	4	4	2	35.1	27	20	17	9	20	0-4	0-1	0	4.33

Fielding

Yankees	Pos	G	PO	Ast	E	DP	PB	FPct
Frankie Crosetti	ss	4	6	13	0	3	—	1.000
Babe Dahlgren	1b	4	41	2	0	4	—	1.000
Bill Dickey	c	4	27	2	0	1	0	1.000
Joe DiMaggio	cf	4	11	0	0	0	—	1.000
Lefty Gomez	p	1	0	0	0	0	—	—
Joe Gordon	2b	4	6	13	0	4	—	1.000
Bump Hadley	p	1	1	1	1	0	—	.667
Oral Hildebrand	p	1	0	0	0	0	—	—
Charlie Keller	rf	4	5	0	0	0	—	1.000
Johnny Murphy	p	1	0	3	0	0	—	1.000
Monte Pearson	p	1	0	5	0	0	—	1.000
Red Rolfe	3b	4	4	8	1	2	—	.923
Red Ruffing	p	1	0	3	0	1	—	1.000
George Selkirk	lf	4	10	0	0	0	—	1.000
Steve Sundra	p	1	0	0	0	0	—	—
Totals		4	111	50	2	15	0	.988

Reds	Pos	G	PO	Ast	E	DP	PB	FPct
Wally Berger	lf	4	5	0	0	0	—	1.000
	cf	1	3	0	0	0	—	1.000
Harry Craft	cf	4	7	1	0	0	—	1.000
Paul Derringer	p	2	2	0	0	0	—	1.000
Lonny Frey	2b	4	9	9	0	0	—	1.000
Ival Goodman	rf	4	11	2	1	0	—	.929
Lee Grissom	p	1	0	0	0	0	—	—
Willard Hershberger	c	2	1	0	0	0	0	1.000
Ernie Lombardi	c	4	22	1	1	0	0	.958
Frank McCormick	1b	4	32	2	0	1	—	1.000
Whitey Moore	p	1	0	2	0	0	—	1.000
Billy Myers	ss	4	8	9	2	1	—	.895
Al Simmons	lf	1	3	0	0	0	—	1.000
Junior Thompson	p	1	0	0	0	0	—	—
Bucky Walters	p	2	0	3	0	1	—	1.000
Bill Werber	3b	4	3	6	0	0	—	1.000
Totals		4	106	35	4	3	0	.972

1940 Cincinnati Reds (NL) 4, Detroit Tigers (AL) 3

Paul Derringer bested Bobo Newsom in a seventh-game showdown of weary hurlers, as the Cincinnati Reds downed the Detroit Tigers in seven games. Newsom prevailed by the score of 7-2 in an identical pitching matchup in Game 1. Bucky Walters beat Detroit 5-3 in Game 2, as Jimmy Ripple's two-run homer in the third put the Reds ahead to stay. Mike Higgins doubled, homered and drove in three runs in Detroit's 7-4 victory in Game 3. Derringer won Game 4, 5-2, to even the Series. Newsom put the Tigers on the brink of the championship with a three-hit shutout in Game 5, but Bucky Walters answered with a five-hit shutout the next day, smacking a solo homer in the Reds' 4-0 victory. Newsom came back on one day's rest for the seventh game, while Derringer came back on two days' rest. Both pitched brilliantly. Cincinnati scored two in the bottom of the seventh, with the final tally coming on Billy Myers' sacrifice fly, as Detroit fell, 2-1.

Game 1
Wednesday, October 2

Tigers	AB	R	H	RBI	BB	K	Avg
Dick Bartell, ss	4	0	2	2	1	2	.500
Barney McCosky, cf	5	0	2	1	0	0	.400
Charlie Gehringer, 2b	4	0	0	0	1	0	.000
Hank Greenberg, lf	5	1	1	0	0	2	.200
Rudy York, 1b	4	2	2	0	1	2	.500
Bruce Campbell, rf	3	1	2	4	1	1	.667
Mike Higgins, 3b	4	1	1	2	0	1	.250
Billy Sullivan, c	3	1	0	0	1	1	.000
Bobo Newsom, p	4	1	0	0	0	1	.000
TOTALS	36	7	10	7	5	10	.278

Reds	AB	R	H	RBI	BB	K	Avg
Bill Werber, 3b	4	1	1	0	0	0	.250
Mike McCormick, cf	4	0	1	0	0	1	.250
Ival Goodman, rf	4	1	2	1	0	0	.500
Frank McCormick, 1b	3	0	0	0	1	0	.000
Jimmy Ripple, lf	4	0	1	1	0	0	.250
Jimmie Wilson, c	2	0	0	0	0	0	.000
Lew Riggs, ph	1	0	0	0	0	1	.000
Bill Baker, c	1	0	1	0	0	0	1.000
Eddie Joost, 2b	4	0	2	0	0	0	.500
Billy Myers, ss	4	0	0	0	0	1	.000
Paul Derringer, p	0	0	0	0	0	0	—
Whitey Moore, p	2	0	0	0	0	1	.000
Harry Craft, ph	1	0	0	0	0	0	.000
Elmer Riddle, p	0	0	0	0	0	0	—
TOTALS	34	2	8	2	1	4	.235

	1	2	3	4	5	6	7	8	9	R	H	E
Tigers	0	5	0	0	2	0	0	0	0	7	10	1
Reds	0	0	0	1	0	0	0	1	0	2	8	3

E—Baker, Myers, Werber, Bartell. DP—Tigers 1 (Higgins to Gehringer to York), Reds 1 (Wilson to Joost). LOB—Tigers 8, Reds 6. Scoring Position—Tigers 4-for-11, Reds 2-for-7. 2B—Werber (1), MMcCormick (1), Goodman (1). 3B—York (1). HR—Campbell (1). S—Campbell. GDP—Wilson. SB—Bartell (1). CS—Campbell (1), Joost (1).

Tigers	IP	H	R	ER	BB	K	ERA
Bobo Newsom (W, 1-0)	9.0	8	2	2	1	4	2.00

Reds	IP	H	R	ER	BB	K	ERA
Paul Derringer (L, 0-1)	1.1	5	5	4	1	1	27.00
Whitey Moore	6.2	5	2	2	4	7	2.70
Elmer Riddle	1.0	0	0	0	0	2	0.00

Time—2:09. Attendance—31,793. Umpires—HP, Klem. 1B, Ormsby. 2B, Ballanfant. 3B, Basil.

Game 2
Thursday, October 3

Tigers	AB	R	H	RBI	BB	K	Avg
Dick Bartell, ss	3	1	0	0	1	0	.286
Barney McCosky, cf	2	1	0	0	2	0	.286
Charlie Gehringer, 2b	4	1	1	1	0	0	.125
Hank Greenberg, lf	3	0	1	1	1	0	.250
Rudy York, 1b	4	0	0	0	0	2	.250
Bruce Campbell, rf	4	0	0	0	0	0	.286
Mike Higgins, 3b	3	0	1	0	0	0	.286
Birdie Tebbetts, c	3	0	0	0	0	0	.000
Schoolboy Rowe, p	1	0	0	0	0	1	.000
Johnny Gorsica, p	2	0	0	0	0	1	.000
TOTALS	29	3	3	2	4	4	.224

Reds	AB	R	H	RBI	BB	K	Avg
Bill Werber, 3b	3	0	1	1	1	0	.286
Mike McCormick, cf	4	0	0	0	0	1	.125
Ival Goodman, rf	4	1	1	0	0	0	.375
Frank McCormick, 1b	4	1	1	0	0	0	.143
Jimmy Ripple, lf	4	1	1	2	0	0	.250
Jimmie Wilson, c	4	1	2	0	0	0	.333
Eddie Joost, 2b	4	0	1	1	0	0	.375
Billy Myers, ss	3	0	1	1	0	1	.143
Bucky Walters, p	3	1	1	0	0	0	.333
TOTALS	33	5	9	5	1	2	.258

	1	2	3	4	5	6	7	8	9	R	H	E
Tigers	2	0	0	0	0	1	0	0	0	3	3	1
Reds	0	2	2	1	0	0	0	0	x	5	9	0

E—Tebbetts. DP—Reds 1 (Werber to Joost to FMcCormick). LOB—Tigers 5, Reds 5. Scoring Position—Tigers 1-for-7, Reds 3-for-6. 2B—Greenberg (1), Higgins (1), Werber (2), Walters (1). HR—Ripple (1). GDP—Greenberg.

Tigers	IP	H	R	ER	BB	K	ERA
Schoolboy Rowe (L, 0-1)	3.1	8	5	5	1	1	13.50
Johnny Gorsica	4.2	1	0	0	0	1	0.00

Reds	IP	H	R	ER	BB	K	ERA
Bucky Walters (W, 1-0)	9.0	3	3	3	4	4	3.00

Time—1:54. Attendance—30,640. Umpires—HP, Ormsby. 1B, Ballanfant. 2B, Basil. 3B, Klem.

Game 3
Friday, October 4

Reds	AB	R	H	RBI	BB	K	Avg
Bill Werber, 3b	4	1	3	1	1	0	.455
Mike McCormick, cf	5	0	2	1	0	2	.231
Ival Goodman, rf	4	0	1	1	0	0	.333
Frank McCormick, 1b	4	0	0	0	0	0	.091
Jimmy Ripple, lf	4	1	1	0	0	1	.250
Ernie Lombardi, c	3	0	1	0	0	0	.333
Bill Baker, c	1	1	0	0	0	0	.500
Eddie Joost, 2b	4	0	1	0	1	0	.333
Billy Myers, ss	4	0	1	0	0	1	.182
Jim Turner, p	2	0	0	0	0	0	.000
Whitey Moore, p	0	0	0	0	0	0	.000
Lew Riggs, ph	1	1	0	0	0	0	.000
Joe Beggs, p	0	0	0	0	0	0	—
Lonny Frey, ph	1	0	0	0	0	0	.000
TOTALS	37	4	10	4	1	5	.255

Tigers	AB	R	H	RBI	BB	K	Avg
Dick Bartell, ss	4	0	1	0	0	0	.273
Barney McCosky, cf	4	1	2	0	0	0	.364
Charlie Gehringer, 2b	4	0	1	0	0	0	.167
Hank Greenberg, lf	4	2	2	0	0	1	.333
Rudy York, 1b	4	1	2	2	0	2	.333
Bruce Campbell, rf	4	2	3	1	0	0	.455
Mike Higgins, 3b	4	1	2	3	0	1	.364
Birdie Tebbetts, c	4	0	0	0	0	0	.000
Tommy Bridges, p	3	0	0	1	0	1	.000
TOTALS	35	7	13	6	0	5	.289

	1	2	3	4	5	6	7	8	9	R	H	E
Reds	1	0	0	0	0	0	0	1	2	4	10	1
Tigers	0	0	0	1	0	0	4	2	x	7	13	1

E—MMcCormick, Higgins. DP—Reds 2 (Werber to Joost to FMcCormick; Myers to FMcCormick to Baker). LOB—Reds 7, Tigers 4. Scoring Position—Reds 4-for-13, Tigers 2-for-7. 2B—Werber (3), Lombardi (1), McCosky (1), Campbell (1), Higgins (2). 3B—Greenberg (1). HR—York (1), Higgins (1). GDP—Greenberg. CS—Werber (1).

Reds	IP	H	R	ER	BB	K	ERA
Jim Turner (L, 0-1)	6.0	8	5	5	0	4	7.50
Whitey Moore	1.0	2	0	0	0	0	2.35
Joe Beggs	1.0	3	2	2	0	1	18.00

Tigers	IP	H	R	ER	BB	K	ERA
Tommy Bridges (W, 1-0)	9.0	10	4	3	1	5	3.00

Turner pitched to four batters in the 7th.

Time—2:08. Attendance—52,877. Umpires—HP, Ballanfant. 1B, Basil. 2B, Klem. 3B, Ormsby.

Game 4
Saturday, October 5

Reds	AB	R	H	RBI	BB	K	Avg
Bill Werber, 3b	3	2	2	0	2	0	.500
Mike McCosky, cf	5	1	2	1	0	0	.278
Ival Goodman, rf	5	2	2	0	0	0	.353
Frank McCormick, 1b	5	0	2	0	0	0	.188
Jimmy Ripple, lf	2	0	1	1	1	0	.286
Morrie Arnovich, ph-lf	1	0	0	0	0	0	.000
Jimmie Wilson, c	5	0	1	0	0	1	.273
Eddie Joost, 2b	5	0	1	0	0	0	.294
Billy Myers, ss	3	0	0	0	1	0	.143
Paul Derringer, p	4	0	0	0	0	1	.000
TOTALS	38	5	11	4	4	2	.278

Tigers	AB	R	H	RBI	BB	K	Avg
Dick Bartell, ss	4	0	0	0	0	1	.200
Pete Fox, ph	1	0	0	0	0	0	.000
Barney McCosky, cf	2	1	1	0	2	0	.385
Charlie Gehringer, 2b	4	0	0	0	0	0	.125
Hank Greenberg, lf	4	0	1	1	0	0	.313
Rudy York, 1b	2	0	0	0	2	0	.286
Bruce Campbell, rf	4	1	1	0	0	2	.400
Mike Higgins, 3b	4	0	2	1	0	0	.400
Billy Sullivan, c	2	0	0	0	2	0	.000
Dizzy Trout, p	1	0	0	0	0	0	.000
Clay Smith, p	1	0	0	0	0	1	.000
Earl Averill, ph	1	0	0	0	0	0	.000
Archie McKain, p	0	0	0	0	0	0	—
Birdie Tebbetts, ph	1	0	0	0	0	0	.000
TOTALS	31	2	5	2	6	4	.256

	1	2	3	4	5	6	7	8	9	R	H	E
Reds	2	0	1	1	0	0	1	0	0	5	11	1
Tigers	0	0	1	0	0	1	0	0	0	2	5	1

E—Myers, Higgins. DP—Reds 2 (Joost to Myers to FMcCormick; Derringer to Myers to FMcCormick). LOB—Reds 11, Tigers 8. Scoring Position—Reds 2-for-13, Tigers 1-for-4. 2B—MMcCormick (2), Goodman (2), Ripple (1), Greenberg (2). 3B—Higgins (1). S—Arnovich. GDP—Gehringer 2.

Reds	IP	H	R	ER	BB	K	ERA
Paul Derringer (W, 1-1)	9.0	5	2	2	6	4	5.23

Tigers	IP	H	R	ER	BB	K	ERA
Dizzy Trout (L, 0-1)	2.0	6	3	2	1	1	9.00
Clay Smith	4.0	1	1	1	3	1	2.25
Archie McKain	3.0	4	1	1	0	0	3.00

Trout pitched to three batters in the 3rd.

WP—McKain. Time—2:06. Attendance—54,093. Umpires—HP, Basil. 1B, Klem. 2B, Ormsby. 3B, Ballanfant.

Game 5
Sunday, October 6

Reds	AB	R	H	RBI	BB	K	Avg
Bill Werber, 3b	4	0	1	0	0	1	.444
Mike McCormick, cf	4	0	1	0	0	0	.273
Ival Goodman, rf	4	0	0	0	0	1	.286
Frank McCormick, 1b	4	0	1	0	0	1	.200
Jimmy Ripple, lf	2	0	0	0	1	0	.250
Jimmie Wilson, c	1	0	0	0	0	0	.250
Bill Baker, ph-c	2	0	0	0	0	1	.250
Eddie Joost, 2b	3	0	0	0	0	1	.250
Billy Myers, ss	2	0	0	0	1	0	.125
Junior Thompson, p	1	0	0	0	0	1	.000
Whitey Moore, p	0	0	0	0	0	0	.000
Lonny Frey, ph	1	0	0	0	0	0	.000
Johnny Vander Meer, p	0	0	0	0	0	0	—
Lew Riggs, ph	1	0	0	0	0	1	.000
Johnny Hutchings, p	0	0	0	0	0	0	—
TOTALS	29	0	3	0	2	7	.248

Tigers	AB	R	H	RBI	BB	K	Avg
Dick Bartell, ss	4	1	2	1	1	0	.263
Barney McCosky, cf	3	2	2	0	2	0	.438
Charlie Gehringer, 2b	4	2	2	0	1	0	.200
Hank Greenberg, lf	5	2	3	4	0	0	.381
Rudy York, 1b	4	0	0	0	1	1	.222
Bruce Campbell, rf	4	3	3	2	1	1	.474
Mike Higgins, 3b	2	0	0	0	3	1	.353
Billy Sullivan, c	4	1	1	0	1	1	.111
Bobo Newsom, p	4	0	0	0	0	0	.000
TOTALS	34	8	13	7	10	4	.299

	1	2	3	4	5	6	7	8	9		R	H	E
Reds	0	0	0	0	0	0	0	0	0		0	3	0
Tigers	0	0	3	4	0	0	0	1	x		8	13	0

DP—Tigers 1 (Bartell to Gehringer to York). LOB—Reds 4, Tigers 13. Scoring Position—Reds 0-for-2, Tigers 4-for-13. 2B—Bartell (1). HR—Greenberg (1). S—Newsom. GDP—MMcCormick. CS—Campbell (2).

Reds	IP	H	R	ER	BB	K	ERA
Junior Thompson (L, 0-1)	3.1	8	6	6	4	2	16.20
Whitey Moore	0.2	1	1	1	2	0	3.24
Johnny Vander Meer	3.0	2	0	0	3	2	0.00
Johnny Hutchings	1.0	2	1	1	1	0	9.00

Tigers	IP	H	R	ER	BB	K	ERA
Bobo Newsom (W, 2-0)	9.0	3	0	0	2	7	1.00

WP—Hutchings. PB—Wilson. Time—2:26. Attendance—55,189. Umpires—HP, Klem. 1B, Ormsby. 2B, Ballanfant. 3B, Basil.

Game 6
Monday, October 7

Tigers	AB	R	H	RBI	BB	K	Avg
Dick Bartell, ss	3	0	2	0	0	0	.318
Billy Sullivan, ph	1	0	0	0	0	0	.100
Frank Croucher, ss	0	0	0	0	0	0	—
Barney McCosky, cf	4	0	0	0	0	0	.350
Charlie Gehringer, 2b	4	0	0	0	0	0	.167
Hank Greenberg, lf	3	0	0	0	1	1	.333
Rudy York, 1b	4	0	2	0	0	0	.273
Bruce Campbell, rf	3	0	0	0	1	0	.409
Mike Higgins, 3b	3	0	1	0	0	0	.350
Birdie Tebbetts, c	3	0	0	0	0	0	.000
Schoolboy Rowe, p	0	0	0	0	0	0	.000
Johnny Gorsica, p	2	0	0	0	0	1	.000
Earl Averill, ph	1	0	0	0	0	0	.000
Fred Hutchinson, p	0	0	0	0	0	0	—
TOTALS	31	0	5	0	2	2	.269

Reds	AB	R	H	RBI	BB	K	Avg
Bill Werber, 3b	5	1	2	0	0	0	.435
Mike McCormick, cf	3	0	1	0	0	0	.280
Ival Goodman, rf	4	1	2	1	0	0	.320
Frank McCormick, 1b	4	0	1	0	0	0	.208
Jimmy Ripple, lf	2	0	2	1	2	0	.333
Jimmie Wilson, c	3	1	1	0	1	1	.267
Eddie Joost, 2b	3	0	0	0	1	0	.217
Billy Myers, ss	4	0	0	0	0	2	.100
Bucky Walters, p	4	1	1	2	0	1	.286
TOTALS	32	4	10	4	5	4	.272

	1	2	3	4	5	6	7	8	9		R	H	E
Tigers	0	0	0	0	0	0	0	0	0		0	5	0
Reds	2	0	0	0	0	1	0	1	x		4	10	2

E—Myers, FMcCormick. DP—Tigers 1 (Gorsica to Tebbetts to York), Reds 3 (Joost to Myers to FMcCormick; FMcCormick to Myers; Werber to Joost to FMcCormick). LOB—Tigers 6, Reds 11. Scoring Position—Tigers 0-for-6, Reds 2-for-9. 2B—Bartell (2), Werber (4). HR—Walters (1). S—MMcCormick, Goodman. GDP—Gehringer, York, Campbell, Werber.

Tigers	IP	H	R	ER	BB	K	ERA
Schoolboy Rowe (L, 0-2)	0.1	4	2	2	0	0	17.18
Johnny Gorsica	6.2	5	1	1	4	3	0.79
Fred Hutchinson	1.0	1	1	1	1	1	9.00

Reds	IP	H	R	ER	BB	K	ERA
Bucky Walters (W, 2-0)	9.0	5	0	0	2	2	1.50

Time—2:01. Attendance—30,481. Umpires—HP, Ormsby. 1B, Ballanfant. 2B, Basil. 3B, Klem.

Game 7
Tuesday, October 8

Tigers	AB	R	H	RBI	BB	K	Avg
Dick Bartell, ss	4	0	0	0	0	0	.269
Barney McCosky, cf	3	0	0	0	1	0	.304
Charlie Gehringer, 2b	4	0	2	0	0	0	.214
Hank Greenberg, lf	4	0	2	0	0	1	.357
Rudy York, 1b	4	0	0	0	0	0	.231
Bruce Campbell, rf	3	0	0	0	1	0	.360
Mike Higgins, 3b	4	0	1	0	0	0	.333
Billy Sullivan, c	3	1	1	0	1	0	.154
Bobo Newsom, p	2	0	1	0	0	0	.100
Earl Averill, ph	1	0	0	0	0	0	.000
TOTALS	32	1	7	0	3	1	.272

Reds	AB	R	H	RBI	BB	K	Avg
Bill Werber, 3b	4	0	0	0	0	1	.370
Mike McCormick, cf	4	0	2	0	0	2	.310
Ival Goodman, rf	4	0	0	0	0	2	.276
Frank McCormick, 1b	4	1	1	0	0	0	.214
Jimmy Ripple, lf	3	1	1	1	0	1	.333
Jimmie Wilson, c	2	0	2	0	0	0	.353
Eddie Joost, 2b	2	0	0	0	0	0	.200
Ernie Lombardi, ph	0	0	0	0	1	0	.333
Lonny Frey, pr-2b	0	0	0	0	0	0	.000
Billy Myers, ss	3	0	1	1	0	0	.130
Paul Derringer, p	3	0	0	0	0	0	.000
TOTALS	29	2	7	2	1	6	.261

	1	2	3	4	5	6	7	8	9		R	H	E
Tigers	0	0	1	0	0	0	0	0	0		1	7	0
Reds	0	0	0	0	0	0	2	0	x		2	7	1

E—Werber. DP—Tigers 1 (Gehringer to Bartell to York). LOB—Tigers 8, Reds 5. Scoring Position—Tigers 2-for-8, Reds 1-for-4. 2B—Higgins (3), MMcCormick (3), FMcCormick (1), Ripple (2). S—Newsom, Wilson. GDP—Joost. SB—Wilson (1).

Tigers	IP	H	R	ER	BB	K	ERA
Bobo Newsom (L, 2-1)	8.0	7	2	2	1	6	1.38

Reds	IP	H	R	ER	BB	K	ERA
Paul Derringer (W, 2-1)	9.0	7	1	0	3	1	2.79

Time—1:47. Attendance—26,854. Umpires—HP, Ballanfant. 1B, Basil. 2B, Klem. 3B, Ormsby.

1940 World Series—Composite Statistics

Batting

Reds

Reds	G	AD	R	H	RBI	2B	3B	HR	BB	SO	SB	CS	Avg	OBP	Slg
Morrie Arnovich	1	1	0	0	0	0	0	0	0	0	0	0	.000	.000	.000
Bill Baker	3	4	1	1	0	0	0	0	0	1	0	0	.250	.250	.250
Harry Craft	1	1	0	0	0	0	0	0	0	0	0	0	.000	.000	.000
Paul Derringer	3	7	0	0	0	0	0	0	0	1	0	0	.000	.000	.000
Lonny Frey	3	2	0	0	0	0	0	0	0	0	0	0	.000	.000	.000
Ival Goodman	7	29	5	8	5	2	0	0	0	3	0	0	.276	.276	.345
Eddie Joost	7	25	0	5	2	0	0	0	1	2	0	1	.200	.231	.200
Ernie Lombardi	2	3	0	1	0	1	0	0	0	0	0	0	.333	.500	.667
Frank McCormick	7	28	2	6	0	1	0	0	1	1	0	0	.214	.241	.250
Mike McCormick	7	29	1	9	2	3	0	0	1	6	0	0	.310	.333	.414
Whitey Moore	3	2	0	0	0	0	0	0	0	1	0	0	.000	.000	.000
Billy Myers	7	23	0	3	2	0	0	0	2	5	0	0	.130	.200	.130
Lew Riggs	3	3	1	0	0	0	0	0	0	2	0	0	.000	.000	.000
Jimmy Ripple	7	21	3	7	6	2	0	1	4	2	0	0	.333	.440	.571
Junior Thompson	1	1	0	0	0	0	0	0	0	1	0	0	.000	.000	.000
Jim Turner	1	2	0	0	0	0	0	0	0	0	0	0	.000	.000	.000
Bucky Walters	2	7	2	2	2	1	0	1	0	1	0	0	.286	.286	.857
Bill Werber	7	27	5	10	2	4	0	0	4	2	0	1	.370	.452	.519
Jimmie Wilson	6	17	2	6	0	0	0	0	1	2	1	0	.353	.389	.353
Totals	7	232	22	58	21	14	0	2	15	30	1	2	.250	.296	.336

Tigers

Tigers	G	AB	R	H	RBI	2B	3B	HR	BB	SO	SB	CS	Avg	OBP	Slg
Earl Averill	3	3	0	0	0	0	0	0	0	0	0	0	.000	.000	.000
Dick Bartell	7	26	2	7	3	2	0	0	3	3	1	0	.269	.345	.346
Tommy Bridges	1	3	0	0	0	0	0	0	0	1	0	0	.000	.000	.000
Bruce Campbell	7	25	4	9	5	1	0	1	4	4	0	2	.360	.448	.520
Pete Fox	1	1	0	0	0	0	0	0	0	0	0	0	.000	.000	.000
Charlie Gehringer	7	28	3	6	1	0	0	0	2	0	0	0	.214	.267	.214
Johnny Gorsica	2	4	0	0	0	0	0	0	0	0	0	0	.000	.000	.000
Hank Greenberg	7	28	5	10	6	2	1	1	2	5	0	0	.357	.400	.607
Mike Higgins	7	24	2	8	6	3	1	1	3	3	0	0	.333	.407	.667
Barney McCosky	7	23	5	7	1	1	0	0	7	0	0	0	.304	.467	.348
Bobo Newsom	3	10	1	1	0	0	0	0	0	1	0	0	.100	.100	.100
Schoolboy Rowe	2	1	0	0	0	0	0	0	0	0	0	0	.000	.000	.000
Clay Smith	1	1	0	0	0	0	0	0	0	1	0	0	.000	.000	.000
Billy Sullivan	5	13	3	2	0	0	0	0	5	2	0	0	.154	.389	.154
Birdie Tebbetts	4	11	0	0	0	0	0	0	0	0	0	0	.000	.000	.000
Dizzy Trout	1	1	0	0	0	0	0	0	0	0	0	0	.000	.000	.000
Rudy York	7	26	3	6	2	0	1	1	4	7	0	0	.231	.333	.423
Totals	7	228	28	56	24	9	3	4	30	30	1	2	.246	.333	.364

Pitching

Reds

Reds	G	GS	CG	IP	H	R	ER	BB	SO	W-L	Sv-Op	Hld	ERA
Joe Beggs	1	0	0	1.0	3	2	2	0	1	0-0	0-0	0	18.00
Paul Derringer	3	3	2	19.1	17	8	6	10	6	2-1	0-0	0	2.79
Johnny Hutchings	1	0	0	1.0	2	1	1	1	0	0-0	0-0	0	9.00
Whitey Moore	3	0	0	8.1	8	3	3	6	7	0-0	0-0	0	3.24
Elmer Riddle	1	0	0	1.0	0	0	0	0	2	0-0	0-0	0	0.00
Junior Thompson	1	1	0	3.1	8	6	6	4	2	0-1	0-0	0	16.20
Jim Turner	1	1	0	6.0	8	5	5	0	4	0-1	0-0	0	7.50
Johnny Vander Meer	1	0	0	3.0	2	0	0	3	2	0-0	0-0	0	0.00
Bucky Walters	2	2	2	18.0	8	3	3	6	6	2-0	0-0	0	1.50
Totals	7	7	4	61.0	56	28	26	30	30	4-3	0-0	0	3.84

Tigers

Tigers	G	GS	CG	IP	H	R	ER	BB	SO	W-L	Sv-Op	Hld	ERA
Tommy Bridges	1	1	1	9.0	10	4	3	1	5	1-0	0-0	0	3.00
Johnny Gorsica	2	0	0	11.1	6	1	1	4	4	0-0	0-0	0	0.79
Fred Hutchinson	1	0	0	1.0	1	1	1	1	1	0-0	0-0	0	9.00
Archie McKain	1	0	0	3.0	4	1	1	0	0	0-0	0-0	0	3.00
Bobo Newsom	3	3	3	26.0	18	4	4	4	17	2-1	0-0	0	1.38
Schoolboy Rowe	2	2	0	3.2	12	7	7	1	1	0-2	0-0	0	17.18
Clay Smith	1	0	0	4.0	1	1	1	3	1	0-0	0-0	0	2.25
Dizzy Trout	1	1	0	2.0	6	3	2	1	1	0-1	0-0	0	9.00
Totals	7	7	4	60.0	58	22	20	15	30	3-4	0-0	0	3.00

Fielding

Reds

Reds	Pos	G	PO	Ast	E	DP	PB	FPct
Morrie Arnovich	lf	1	2	0	0	0	—	1.000
Bill Baker	c	3	7	0	1	1	0	.875
Joe Beggs	p	1	0	0	0	0	—	—
Paul Derringer	p	3	0	5	0	1	—	1.000
Lonny Frey	2b	1	0	1	0	0	—	1.000
Ival Goodman	rf	7	11	0	0	0	—	1.000
Johnny Hutchings	p	1	0	1	0	0	—	1.000
Eddie Joost	2b	7	14	12	0	6	—	1.000
Ernie Lombardi	c	1	4	0	0	0	0	1.000
Frank McCormick	1b	7	59	4	1	8	—	.984
Mike McCormick	cf	7	23	1	1	0	—	.960
Whitey Moore	p	3	0	1	0	0	—	1.000
Billy Myers	ss	7	14	17	3	5	—	.912
Elmer Riddle	p	1	0	0	0	0	—	—
Jimmy Ripple	lf	7	14	0	0	0	—	1.000
Junior Thompson	p	1	0	1	0	0	—	1.000
Jim Turner	p	1	0	1	0	0	—	1.000
Johnny Vander Meer	p	1	0	0	0	0	—	—
Bucky Walters	p	2	0	4	0	0	—	1.000
Bill Werber	3b	7	9	16	2	3	—	.926
Jimmie Wilson	c	6	26	2	0	1	1	1.000
Totals		7	183	66	8	25	1	.969

Tigers

Tigers	Pos	G	PO	Ast	E	DP	PB	FPct
Dick Bartell	ss	7	12	11	1	2	—	.958
Tommy Bridges	p	1	0	1	0	0	—	1.000
Bruce Campbell	rf	7	17	0	0	0	—	1.000
Frank Croucher	ss	1	0	0	0	0	—	—
Charlie Gehringer	2b	7	18	18	0	3	—	1.000
Johnny Gorsica	p	2	0	6	0	1	—	1.000
Hank Greenberg	lf	7	12	0	0	0	—	1.000
Mike Higgins	3b	7	4	30	2	1	—	.944
Fred Hutchinson	p	1	0	0	0	0	—	—
Barney McCosky	cf	7	19	0	0	0	—	1.000
Archie McKain	p	1	0	1	0	0	—	1.000
Bobo Newsom	p	3	2	0	0	0	—	1.000
Schoolboy Rowe	p	2	0	1	0	0	—	1.000
Clay Smith	p	1	0	1	0	0	—	1.000
Billy Sullivan	c	4	23	2	0	0	0	1.000
Birdie Tebbetts	c	3	13	3	1	1	0	.941
Dizzy Trout	p	1	0	1	0	0	—	1.000
Rudy York	1b	7	60	2	0	4	—	1.000
Totals		7	180	77	4	12	0	.985

1941 New York Yankees (AL) 4, Brooklyn Dodgers (NL) 1

Brooklyn catcher Mickey Owen took the goat horns as the Dodgers fell to the New York Yankees in five games. In the opener, the Yankees' Red Ruffing bested Curt Davis, 3-2. Whit Wyatt evened it up with a complete-game, 3-2 victory in Game 2. Marius Russo and Freddie Fitzsimmons battled for seven scoreless frames in Game 3 before Russo scorched a liner off Fitzsimmons' knee, knocking him out of the game. In the very next inning, the Yankees got a pair of runs off Dodger reliever Hugh Casey, and Russo went the route for a 2-1 win. Owen's moment of infamy came in the ninth inning of the fourth game. Brooklyn led 4-3 with two outs and nobody on base when Hugh Casey fanned Tommy Henrich for what should have been the final out. Owen dropped the ball, Henrich reached first, and a four-run Yankee rally ensued. Tiny Bonham tossed a four-hitter in Game 5, wrapping it up with a 3-1 victory.

Game 1
Wednesday, October 1

Dodgers	AB	R	H	RBI	BB	K	Avg
Dixie Walker, rf	3	0	0	0	1	0	.000
Billy Herman, 2b	3	0	0	0	1	0	.000
Pete Reiser, cf	3	0	0	0	1	1	.000
Dolph Camilli, 1b	4	0	0	0	0	3	.000
Joe Medwick, lf	4	0	1	0	0	1	.250
Cookie Lavagetto, 3b	4	1	0	0	0	0	.000
Pee Wee Reese, ss	4	1	3	0	0	0	.750
Mickey Owen, c	2	0	1	1	0	0	.500
Lew Riggs, ph	1	0	1	1	0	0	1.000
Herman Franks, c	1	0	0	0	0	0	.000
Curt Davis, p	2	0	0	0	0	0	.000
Hugh Casey, p	0	0	0	0	0	0	—
Jimmy Wasdell, ph	1	0	0	0	0	0	.000
Johnny Allen, p	0	0	0	0	0	0	—
TOTALS	32	2	6	2	3	5	.188

Yankees	AB	R	H	RBI	BB	K	Avg
Johnny Sturm, 1b	3	0	1	0	0	0	.333
Red Rolfe, 3b	3	0	1	0	1	1	.333
Tommy Henrich, rf	4	0	0	0	0	0	.000
Joe DiMaggio, cf	4	0	0	0	0	0	.000
Charlie Keller, lf	2	2	0	0	2	0	.000
Bill Dickey, c	4	0	2	1	0	0	.500
Joe Gordon, 2b	2	1	2	2	2	0	1.000
Phil Rizzuto, ss	4	0	0	0	0	0	.000
Red Ruffing, p	3	0	0	0	0	0	.000
TOTALS	29	3	6	3	5	1	.207

	1	2	3	4	5	6	7	8	9		R	H	E
Dodgers	0	0	0	1	0	1	0	0			2	6	0
Yankees	0	1	0	1	0	1	0	0	x		3	6	1

E—Rizzuto. DP—Yankees 1 (Rolfe to Rizzuto). LOB—Dodgers 6, Yankees 8. Scoring Position—Dodgers 1-for-8, Yankees 1-for-4. 2B—Dickey (1). 3B—Owen (1). HR—Gordon (1). GDP—Franks. CS—Sturm (1).

Dodgers	IP	H	R	ER	BB	K	ERA
Curt Davis (L, 0-1)	5.1	6	3	3	3	1	5.06
Hugh Casey	0.2	0	0	0	0	0	0.00
Johnny Allen	2.0	0	0	0	2	0	0.00

Yankees	IP	H	R	ER	BB	K	ERA
Red Ruffing (W, 1-0)	9.0	6	2	1	3	5	1.00

HBP—Sturm by Allen. Time—2:08. Attendance—68,540. Umpires—HP, McGowan. 1B, Pinelli. 2B, Grieve. 3B, Goetz.

Game 2
Thursday, October 2

Dodgers	AB	R	H	RBI	BB	K	Avg
Dixie Walker, rf	4	1	0	0	0	1	.000
Billy Herman, 2b	4	0	1	0	0	0	.143
Pete Reiser, cf	4	0	0	0	0	2	.000
Dolph Camilli, 1b	3	1	1	1	1	0	.143
Joe Medwick, lf	4	1	2	0	0	0	.375
Cookie Lavagetto, 3b	3	0	1	0	1	0	.143
Pee Wee Reese, ss	4	0	0	1	0	0	.375
Mickey Owen, c	2	0	1	1	1	0	.500
Whit Wyatt, p	3	0	0	0	1	0	.000
TOTALS	31	3	6	3	3	4	.190

Yankees	AB	R	H	RBI	BB	K	Avg
Johnny Sturm, 1b	5	0	1	0	0	2	.250
Red Rolfe, 3b	5	0	1	0	0	0	.250
Tommy Henrich, rf	4	1	1	0	1	1	.125
Joe DiMaggio, cf	3	0	0	0	1	0	.000
Charlie Keller, lf	4	1	2	1	0	0	.333
Bill Dickey, c	4	0	0	0	0	1	.250
Frenchy Bordagaray, pr	0	0	0	0	0	0	—
Buddy Rosar, c	0	0	0	0	0	0	—
Joe Gordon, 2b	1	0	1	0	3	0	1.000
Phil Rizzuto, ss	4	0	1	0	0	0	.125
Spud Chandler, p	2	0	1	1	0	0	.500
Johnny Murphy, p	1	0	0	0	0	1	.000
George Selkirk, ph	1	0	1	0	0	0	1.000
TOTALS	34	2	9	2	5	5	.250

	1	2	3	4	5	6	7	8	9		R	H	E
Dodgers	0	0	0	0	2	1	0	0	0		3	6	2
Yankees	0	1	1	0	0	0	0	0	0		2	9	1

E—Reese 2, Gordon. DP—Dodgers 1 (Reese to Herman to Camilli), Yankees 3 (Gordon to Rizzuto to Sturm; Gordon to Rizzuto to Sturm; Dickey to Gordon). LOB—Dodgers 4, Yankees 10. Scoring Position—Dodgers 2-for-7, Yankees 2-for-7. 2B—Medwick (1), Henrich (1). GDP—Lavagetto, Wyatt, DiMaggio. CS—Owen (1).

Dodgers	IP	H	R	ER	BB	K	ERA
Whit Wyatt (W, 1-0)	9.0	9	2	2	5	5	2.00

Yankees	IP	H	R	ER	BB	K	ERA
Spud Chandler (L, 0-1)	5.0	4	3	2	2	2	3.60
Johnny Murphy	4.0	2	0	0	1	2	0.00

Chandler pitched to two batters in the 6th.

Time—2:31. Attendance—66,248. Umpires—HP, Pinelli. 1B, Grieve. 2B, Goetz. 3B, McGowan.

Game 3
Friday, October 3

Yankees	AB	R	H	RBI	BB	K	Avg
Johnny Sturm, 1b	4	0	1	0	0	0	.250
Red Rolfe, 3b	4	1	2	0	0	0	.333
Tommy Henrich, rf	3	1	1	0	1	0	.182
Joe DiMaggio, cf	4	0	2	1	0	0	.182
Charlie Keller, lf	4	0	1	1	0	0	.300
Bill Dickey, c	4	0	0	0	0	0	.167
Joe Gordon, 2b	3	0	1	0	1	0	.667
Phil Rizzuto, ss	3	0	0	0	1	0	.091
Marius Russo, p	4	0	0	0	0	1	.000
TOTALS	33	2	8	2	3	1	.236

Dodgers	AB	R	H	RBI	BB	K	Avg
Pee Wee Reese, ss	4	0	1	1	0	0	.333
Billy Herman, 2b	1	0	0	0	1	0	.125
Pete Coscarart, 2b	2	0	0	0	0	0	.000
Pete Reiser, cf	4	0	1	0	0	1	.091
Joe Medwick, lf	4	0	1	0	0	1	.333
Cookie Lavagetto, 3b	3	0	0	0	1	0	.100
Dolph Camilli, 1b	3	0	0	0	0	2	.100
Dixie Walker, rf	3	1	1	0	0	0	.100
Mickey Owen, c	3	0	0	0	0	0	.286
Freddie Fitzsimmons, p	2	0	0	0	0	0	.000
Hugh Casey, p	0	0	0	0	0	0	—
Larry French, p	0	0	0	0	0	0	—
Augie Galan, ph	1	0	0	0	0	1	.000
Johnny Allen, p	0	0	0	0	0	0	—
TOTALS	30	1	4	1	2	5	.176

	1	2	3	4	5	6	7	8	9		R	H	E
Yankees	0	0	0	0	0	0	0	2	0		2	8	0
Dodgers	0	0	0	0	0	0	0	1	0		1	4	0

DP—Yankees 1 (Rizzuto to Sturm), Dodgers 1 (Reese to Camilli). LOB—Yankees 7, Dodgers 4. Scoring Position—Yankees 2-for-10, Dodgers 1-for-6. 2B—Reiser (1), Walker (1). 3B—Gordon (1). GDP—Dickey, Camilli. SB—Sturm (1), Rizzuto (1).

Yankees	IP	H	R	ER	BB	K	ERA
Marius Russo (W, 1-0)	9.0	4	1	1	2	5	1.00

Dodgers	IP	H	R	ER	BB	K	ERA
Freddie Fitzsimmons	7.0	4	0	0	3	1	0.00
Hugh Casey (L, 0-1)	0.1	4	2	2	0	0	18.00
Larry French	0.2	0	0	0	0	0	0.00
Johnny Allen	1.0	0	0	0	0	0	0.00

Time—2:22. Attendance—33,100. Umpires—HP, Grieve. 1B, Goetz. 2B, McGowan. 3B, Pinelli.

Game 4
Sunday, October 5

Yankees	AB	R	H	RBI	BB	K	Avg
Johnny Sturm, 1b	5	0	2	2	0	0	.294
Red Rolfe, 3b	5	1	2	0	0	0	.353
Tommy Henrich, rf	4	1	0	0	0	1	.133
Joe DiMaggio, cf	4	1	2	0	1	0	.267
Charlie Keller, lf	5	1	4	3	0	0	.467
Bill Dickey, c	2	2	0	0	3	0	.143
Joe Gordon, 2b	5	1	2	2	0	0	.545
Phil Rizzuto, ss	4	0	0	0	1	0	.067
Atley Donald, p	2	0	0	0	0	1	.000
Marv Breuer, p	1	0	0	0	0	0	.000
George Selkirk, ph	1	0	0	0	0	0	.500
Johnny Murphy, p	1	0	0	0	0	0	.000
TOTALS	39	7	12	7	5	2	.270

Dodgers	AB	R	H	RBI	BB	K	Avg
Pee Wee Reese, ss	5	0	0	0	0	0	.235
Dixie Walker, rf	5	1	2	0	0	0	.200
Pete Reiser, cf	5	1	2	2	0	1	.188
Dolph Camilli, 1b	4	0	2	0	0	0	.214
Lew Riggs, 3b	3	0	0	0	1	1	.250
Joe Medwick, lf	2	0	0	0	0	0	.286
Johnny Allen, p	0	0	0	0	0	0	—
Hugh Casey, p	2	0	1	0	0	1	.500
Mickey Owen, c	2	1	0	0	2	0	.222
Pete Coscarart, 2b	3	1	0	0	1	2	.000
Kirby Higbe, p	1	0	1	0	0	0	1.000
Larry French, p	0	0	0	0	0	0	—
Jimmy Wasdell, ph-lf	3	0	1	2	0	0	.250
TOTALS	35	4	9	4	4	5	.228

	1	2	3	4	5	6	7	8	9		R	H	E
Yankees	1	0	0	2	0	0	0	0	4		7	12	0
Dodgers	0	0	0	2	2	0	0	0	0		4	9	1

E—Owen. DP—Yankees 1 (Gordon to Rizzuto to Sturm). LOB—Yankees 11, Dodgers 8. Scoring Position—Yankees 5-for-10, Dodgers 2-for-8. 2B—Keller 2 (2), Gordon (1), Walker (2), Camilli (1), Wasdell (1). HR—Reiser (1). GDP—Reiser.

Yankees	IP	H	R	ER	BB	K	ERA
Atley Donald	4.0	6	4	4	3	2	9.00
Marv Breuer	3.0	3	0	0	1	2	0.00
Johnny Murphy (W, 1-0)	2.0	0	0	0	0	1	0.00

Dodgers	IP	H	R	ER	BB	K	ERA
Kirby Higbe	3.2	6	3	3	2	1	7.36
Larry French	0.1	0	0	0	0	0	0.00
Johnny Allen	0.2	1	0	0	1	0	0.00
Hugh Casey (L, 0-2)	4.1	5	4	0	2	1	3.38

Donald pitched to two batters in the 5th.

HBP—Henrich by Allen. Time—2:54. Attendance—33,813. Umpires—HP, Goetz. 1B, McGowan. 2B, Pinelli. 3B, Grieve.

Game 5
Monday, October 6

Yankees	AB	R	H	RBI	BB	K	Avg
Johnny Sturm, 1b	4	0	1	0	0	0	.286
Red Rolfe, 3b	3	0	0	0	1	0	.300
Tommy Henrich, rf	3	1	1	1	1	1	.167
Joe DiMaggio, cf	4	0	1	0	0	0	.263
Charlie Keller, lf	3	1	0	0	1	1	.389
Bill Dickey, c	4	1	1	0	0	0	.167
Joe Gordon, 2b	3	0	1	1	1	0	.500
Phil Rizzuto, ss	3	0	1	0	1	1	.111
Tiny Bonham, p	4	0	0	0	0	4	.000
TOTALS	31	3	6	2	5	9	.260

Dodgers	AB	R	H	RBI	BB	K	Avg
Dixie Walker, rf	3	0	1	0	1	0	.222
Lew Riggs, 3b	4	0	1	0	0	0	.250
Pete Reiser, cf	4	0	1	1	0	1	.200
Dolph Camilli, 1b	4	0	0	0	0	1	.167
Joe Medwick, lf	3	0	0	0	1	0	.235
Pee Wee Reese, ss	3	0	0	0	0	0	.200
Jimmy Wasdell, ph	1	0	0	0	0	0	.200
Mickey Owen, c	3	0	0	0	0	0	.167
Pete Coscarart, 2b	2	0	0	0	0	0	.000
Augie Galan, ph	1	0	0	0	0	0	.000
Billy Herman, 2b	0	0	0	0	0	0	.125
Whit Wyatt, p	3	1	1	0	0	0	.167
TOTALS	31	1	4	1	2	2	.184

	1	2	3	4	5	6	7	8	9		R	H	E
Yankees	0	2	0	0	1	0	0	0	0		3	6	0
Dodgers	0	0	1	0	0	0	0	0	0		1	4	1

E—Reese. DP—Dodgers 3 (Owen to Riggs; Reese to Coscarart to Camilli; Herman to Reese to Camilli). LOB—Yankees 6, Dodgers 5. Scoring Position—Yankees 1-for-6, Dodgers 1-for-4. 2B—Wyatt (1). 3B—Reiser (1). HR—Henrich (1). GDP—Keller, Gordon. CS—Rolfe (1).

Yankees	IP	H	R	ER	BB	K	ERA
Tiny Bonham (W, 1-0)	9.0	4	1	1	2	2	1.00

Dodgers	IP	H	R	ER	BB	K	ERA
Whit Wyatt (L, 1-1)	9.0	6	3	3	5	9	2.50

WP—Wyatt. Time—2:13. Attendance—34,072. Umpires—HP, McGowan. 1B, Pinelli. 2B, Grieve. 3B, Goetz.

1941 World Series—Composite Statistics

Batting

Yankees	G	AB	R	H	RBI	2B	3B	HR	BB	SO	SB	CS	Avg	OBP	Slg
Tiny Bonham	1	4	0	0	0	0	0	0	0	4	0	0	.000	.000	.000
Frenchy Bordagaray	1	0	0	0	0	0	0	0	0	0	0	0	—	—	—
Marv Breuer	1	1	0	0	0	0	0	0	0	0	0	0	.000	.000	.000
Spud Chandler	1	2	0	1	1	0	0	0	0	0	0	0	.500	.500	.500
Bill Dickey	5	18	3	3	1	1	0	0	3	1	0	0	.167	.286	.222
Joe DiMaggio	5	19	1	5	1	0	0	0	2	2	0	0	.263	.333	.263
Atley Donald	1	2	0	0	0	0	0	0	0	1	0	0	.000	.000	.000
Joe Gordon	5	14	2	7	5	1	1	1	7	0	0	0	.500	.667	.929
Tommy Henrich	5	18	4	3	1	1	0	1	3	3	0	0	.167	.318	.389
Charlie Keller	5	18	5	7	5	2	0	0	3	1	0	0	.389	.476	.500
Johnny Murphy	2	2	0	0	0	0	0	0	0	1	0	0	.000	.000	.000
Phil Rizzuto	5	18	0	2	0	0	0	0	3	1	1	0	.111	.238	.111
Red Rolfe	5	20	2	6	0	0	0	0	2	1	0	1	.300	.364	.300
Red Ruffing	1	3	0	0	0	0	0	0	0	0	0	0	.000	.000	.000
Marius Russo	1	4	0	0	0	0	0	0	0	1	0	0	.000	.000	.000
George Selkirk	2	2	0	1	0	0	0	0	0	0	0	0	.500	.500	.500
Johnny Sturm	5	21	0	6	2	0	0	0	0	2	1	1	.286	.318	.286
Totals	5	166	17	41	16	5	1	2	23	18	2	2	.247	.346	.325

Dodgers	G	AB	R	H	RBI	2B	3B	HR	BB	SO	SB	CS	Avg	OBP	Slg
Dolph Camilli	5	18	1	3	1	1	0	0	1	6	0	0	.167	.211	.222
Hugh Casey	3	2	0	1	0	0	0	0	0	1	0	0	.500	.500	.500
Pete Coscarart	3	7	1	0	0	0	0	0	1	2	0	0	.000	.125	.000
Curt Davis	1	2	0	0	0	0	0	0	0	0	0	0	.000	.000	.000
Freddie Fitzsimmons	1	2	0	0	0	0	0	0	0	0	0	0	.000	.000	.000
Herman Franks	1	1	0	0	0	0	0	0	0	0	0	0	.000	.000	.000
Augie Galan	2	2	0	0	0	0	0	0	0	1	0	0	.000	.000	.000
Billy Herman	4	8	0	1	0	0	0	0	2	0	0	0	.125	.300	.125
Kirby Higbe	1	1	0	0	0	0	0	0	0	0	0	0	1.000	1.000	1.000
Cookie Lavagetto	3	10	1	1	0	0	0	0	2	0	0	0	.100	.250	.100
Joe Medwick	5	17	1	4	0	1	0	0	1	2	0	0	.235	.278	.294
Mickey Owen	5	12	1	2	2	0	1	0	3	0	0	1	.167	.333	.333
Pee Wee Reese	5	20	1	4	2	0	0	0	0	0	0	0	.200	.200	.200
Pete Reiser	5	20	1	4	3	1	1	1	1	6	0	0	.200	.238	.500
Lew Riggs	3	8	0	2	1	0	0	0	1	0	0	0	.250	.333	.250
Dixie Walker	5	18	3	4	0	2	0	0	2	1	0	0	.222	.300	.333
Jimmy Wasdell	3	5	0	1	2	1	0	0	0	0	0	0	.200	.200	.400
Whit Wyatt	2	6	1	1	0	1	0	0	0	1	0	0	.167	.167	.333
Totals	5	159	11	29	11	7	2	1	14	21	0	1	.182	.249	.270

Pitching

Yankees	G	GS	CG	IP	H	R	ER	BB	SO	W-L	Sv-Op	Hld	ERA
Tiny Bonham	1	1	1	9.0	4	1	1	2	2	1-0	0-0	0	1.00
Marv Breuer	1	0	0	3.0	3	0	0	1	2	0-0	0-0	0	0.00
Spud Chandler	1	1	0	5.0	4	3	2	2	2	0-1	0-0	0	3.60
Atley Donald	1	1	0	4.0	6	4	4	3	2	0-0	0-0	0	9.00
Johnny Murphy	2	0	0	6.0	2	0	0	1	3	1-0	0-0	0	0.00
Red Ruffing	1	1	1	9.0	6	2	1	3	5	1-0	0-0	0	1.00
Marius Russo	1	1	1	9.0	4	1	1	2	5	1-0	0-0	0	1.00
Totals	5	5	3	45.0	29	11	9	14	21	4-1	0-0	0	1.80

Dodgers	G	GS	CG	IP	H	R	ER	BB	SO	W-L	Sv-Op	Hld	ERA
Johnny Allen	3	0	0	3.2	1	0	0	3	3	0-0	0-0	0	0.00
Hugh Casey	3	0	0	5.1	9	6	2	2	1	0-2	0-0	0	3.38
Curt Davis	1	1	0	5.1	6	3	3	3	1	0-1	0-0	0	5.06
Freddie Fitzsimmons	1	1	0	7.0	4	0	0	3	1	0-0	0-0	0	0.00
Larry French	2	0	0	1.0	0	0	0	0	0	0-0	0-0	0	0.00
Kirby Higbe	1	1	0	3.2	6	3	3	2	1	0-0	0-0	0	7.36
Whit Wyatt	2	2	2	18.0	15	5	5	10	14	1-1	0-0	0	2.50
Totals	5	5	2	44.0	41	17	13	23	18	1-4	0-0	0	2.66

Fielding

Yankees	Pos	G	PO	Ast	E	DP	PB	FPct
Tiny Bonham	p	1	0	1	0	0	—	1.000
Marv Breuer	p	1	0	1	0	0	—	1.000
Spud Chandler	p	1	0	0	0	0	—	—
Bill Dickey	c	5	24	2	0	1	0	1.000
Joe DiMaggio	cf	5	18	0	0	0	—	1.000
Atley Donald	p	1	0	1	0	0	—	1.000
Joe Gordon	2b	5	7	19	1	5	—	.963
Tommy Henrich	rf	5	6	0	0	0	—	1.000
Charlie Keller	lf	5	12	0	0	0	—	1.000
Johnny Murphy	p	2	1	0	0	0	—	1.000
Phil Rizzuto	ss	5	12	18	1	6	—	.968
Red Rolfe	3b	5	7	8	0	1	—	1.000
Buddy Rosar	c	1	0	0	0	0	0	—
Red Ruffing	p	1	0	0	0	0	—	—
Marius Russo	p	1	0	4	0	0	—	1.000
Johnny Sturm	1b	5	48	1	0	5	—	1.000
Totals		5	135	55	2	18	0	.990

Dodgers	Pos	G	PO	Ast	E	DP	PB	FPct
Johnny Allen	p	3	0	0	0	0	—	—
Dolph Camilli	1b	5	45	4	0	4	—	1.000
Hugh Casey	p	3	0	3	0	0	—	1.000
Pete Coscarart	2b	3	7	8	0	1	—	1.000
Curt Davis	p	1	1	0	0	0	—	1.000
Freddie Fitzsimmons	p	1	0	2	0	0	—	1.000
Herman Franks	c	1	0	1	0	0	0	1.000
Larry French	p	2	0	0	0	0	—	—
Billy Herman	2b	4	4	13	0	2	—	1.000
Kirby Higbe	p	1	0	1	0	0	—	1.000
Cookie Lavagetto	3b	3	2	0	0	0	—	1.000
Joe Medwick	lf	5	8	0	0	0	—	1.000
Mickey Owen	c	5	20	4	1	1	0	.960
Pee Wee Reese	ss	5	13	14	3	4	—	.900
Pete Reiser	cf	5	14	1	0	0	—	1.000
Lew Riggs	3b	2	1	4	0	1	—	1.000
Dixie Walker	rf	5	14	0	0	0	—	1.000
Jimmy Wasdell	lf	1	2	0	0	0	—	1.000
Whit Wyatt	p	2	1	2	0	0	—	1.000
Totals		5	132	57	4	13	0	.979

1942 St. Louis Cardinals (NL) 4, New York Yankees (AL) 1

Whitey Kurowski's two-run homer in the top of the ninth inning of Game 5 gave the St. Louis Cardinals a five-game victory over the New York Yankees. The Yanks took a 7-0 lead into the bottom of the ninth in Game 1 before the Cardinals launched a rally that plated four runs and brought Stan Musial to the plate with the bases loaded and two out. Spud Chandler got him to ground to first to end the contest. In Game 2, Enos Slaughter doubled and scored the go-ahead run in the bottom of the eighth, and then threw out Tuck Stainback at third base in the top of the ninth to help preserve the Cards' 4-3 win. Ernie White spun a six-hit shutout for a 2-0 St. Louis win in Game 3. Mort Cooper was shelled in Game 5, but his brother Walker singled in the decisive run in the seventh as St. Louis prevailed, 9-6. Game 5 was tied 2-2 in the ninth when Kurowski hit his dramatic blow off Red Ruffing.

Game 1

Wednesday, September 30

Yankees	AB	R	H	RBI	BB	K	Avg
Phil Rizzuto, ss	4	0	0	0	1	0	.000
Red Rolfe, 3b	5	2	2	0	0	2	.400
Roy Cullenbine, rf	3	1	1	0	1	0	.333
Joe DiMaggio, cf	5	2	3	1	0	0	.600
Charlie Keller, lf	4	0	0	0	1	2	.000
Joe Gordon, 2b	5	0	0	0	0	3	.000
Bill Dickey, c	4	1	2	0	1	0	.500
Buddy Hassett, 1b	4	1	2	2	0	1	.500
Red Ruffing, p	4	0	1	0	0	0	.250
Spud Chandler, p	0	0	0	0	0	0	—
TOTALS	38	7	11	3	4	8	.289

Cardinals	AB	R	H	RBI	BB	K	Avg
Jimmy Brown, 2b	4	0	1	0	1	0	.250
Terry Moore, cf	4	0	2	1	1	0	.500
Enos Slaughter, rf	3	0	1	0	2	1	.333
Stan Musial, lf	4	0	0	0	1	0	.000
Walker Cooper, c	4	1	1	0	0	1	.250
Johnny Hopp, 1b	4	0	0	0	0	1	.000
Whitey Kurowski, 3b	3	0	0	0	0	3	.000
Ray Sanders, ph	0	1	0	0	1	0	—
Marty Marion, ss	4	1	1	2	0	1	.250
Mort Cooper, p	2	0	0	0	0	0	.000
Harry Gumbert, p	0	0	0	0	0	0	—
Harry Walker, ph	1	0	0	0	0	1	.000
Max Lanier, p	0	0	0	0	0	0	—
Ken O'Dea, ph	1	0	1	1	0	0	1.000
Creepy Crespi, pr	0	1	0	0	0	0	—
TOTALS	34	4	7	4	6	8	.206

	1	2	3	4	5	6	7	8	9		R	H	E
Yankees	0	0	0	1	1	0	0	3	2		7	11	0
Cardinals	0	0	0	0	0	0	0	0	4		4	7	4

E—Lanier 2, Slaughter, Brown. LOB—Yankees 9, Cardinals 9. Scoring Position—Yankees 2-for-9, Cardinals 4-for-8. 2B—Cullenbine (1), Hassett (1). 3B—Marion (1). S—Cullenbine.

Yankees	IP	H	R	ER	BB	K	ERA
Red Ruffing (W, 1-0)	8.2	5	4	4	6	8	4.15
Spud Chandler (S, 1)	0.1	2	0	0	0	0	0.00

Cardinals	IP	H	R	ER	BB	K	ERA
Mort Cooper (L, 0-1)	7.2	10	5	3	3	7	3.52
Harry Gumbert	0.1	0	0	0	0	0	0.00
Max Lanier	1.0	1	2	0	1	1	0.00

Time—2:35. Attendance—34,769. Umpires—HP, Magerkurth. 1B, Summers. 2B, Barr. 3B, Hubbard.

Game 2

Thursday, October 1

Yankees	AB	R	H	RBI	BB	K	Avg
Phil Rizzuto, ss	4	0	1	0	1	1	.125
Red Rolfe, 3b	4	0	1	0	0	0	.333
Roy Cullenbine, rf	4	1	1	0	0	0	.286
Joe DiMaggio, cf	4	1	1	1	0	0	.444
Charlie Keller, lf	4	1	2	2	0	0	.250
Joe Gordon, 2b	4	0	1	0	0	2	.111
Bill Dickey, c	4	0	2	0	0	0	.500
Tuck Stainback, pr	0	0	0	0	0	0	—
Buddy Hassett, 1b	4	0	1	0	0	0	.375
Tiny Bonham, p	2	0	0	0	0	1	.000
Red Ruffing, ph	1	0	0	0	0	0	.200
TOTALS	35	3	10	3	2	4	.288

Cardinals	AB	R	H	RBI	BB	K	Avg
Jimmy Brown, 2b	3	1	0	0	1	0	.143
Terry Moore, cf	3	1	0	0	0	0	.286
Enos Slaughter, rf	4	1	1	0	0	0	.286
Stan Musial, lf	4	0	1	1	0	0	.125
Walker Cooper, c	4	0	1	2	0	0	.250
Johnny Hopp, 1b	3	1	2	0	0	0	.286
Whitey Kurowski, 3b	3	0	1	1	0	0	.167
Marty Marion, ss	3	0	0	0	0	0	.143
Johnny Beazley, p	3	0	0	0	0	3	.000
TOTALS	30	4	6	4	1	3	.200

	1	2	3	4	5	6	7	8	9		R	H	E
Yankees	0	0	0	0	0	0	0	3	0		3	10	2
Cardinals	2	0	0	0	0	0	1	1	x		4	6	0

E—Rizzuto, Hassett. DP—Cardinals 1 (Brown to Marion to Hopp). LOB—Yankees 7, Cardinals 4. Scoring Position—Yankees 1-for-9, Cardinals 2-for-8. 2B—Rolfe (1), Gordon (1), Slaughter (1), Cooper (1). 3B—Kurowski (1). HR—Keller (1). S—Moore. GDP—Rolfe. SB—Rizzuto (1), Cullenbine (1).

Yankees	IP	H	R	ER	BB	K	ERA
Tiny Bonham (L, 0-1)	8.0	6	4	4	1	3	4.50

Cardinals	IP	H	R	ER	BB	K	ERA
Johnny Beazley (W, 1-0)	9.0	10	3	3	2	4	3.00

Time—1:57. Attendance—34,255. Umpires—HP, Summers. 1B, Barr. 2B, Hubbard. 3B, Magerkurth.

Game 3

Saturday, October 3

Cardinals	AB	R	H	RBI	BB	K	Avg
Jimmy Brown, 2b	4	1	1	1	0	0	.182
Terry Moore, cf	4	0	0	0	0	2	.182
Enos Slaughter, rf	4	0	1	0	1	1	.273
Stan Musial, lf	3	0	1	0	1	0	.182
Walker Cooper, c	4	0	0	0	0	0	.167
Johnny Hopp, 1b	4	0	0	0	0	0	.182
Whitey Kurowski, 3b	2	1	1	0	1	0	.250
Marty Marion, ss	3	0	1	0	0	0	.200
Ernie White, p	2	0	0	0	0	0	.000
TOTALS	30	2	5	2	3	3	.195

Yankees	AB	R	H	RBI	BB	K	Avg
Phil Rizzuto, ss	4	0	2	0	0	0	.250
Buddy Hassett, 1b	1	0	0	0	0	0	.333
Frankie Crosetti, 3b	3	0	0	0	0	1	.000
Roy Cullenbine, rf	4	0	1	0	0	1	.273
Joe DiMaggio, cf	4	0	2	0	0	1	.462
Joe Gordon, 2b	4	0	0	0	0	1	.077
Charlie Keller, lf	4	0	0	0	0	0	.167
Bill Dickey, c	3	0	1	0	0	0	.455
Jerry Priddy, 3b-1b	3	0	0	0	0	0	.000
Spud Chandler, p	2	0	0	0	0	1	.000
Red Ruffing, ph	1	0	0	0	0	1	.167
Marv Breuer, p	0	0	0	0	0	0	—
Jim Turner, p	0	0	0	0	0	0	—
TOTALS	33	0	6	0	0	6	.253

	1	2	3	4	5	6	7	8	9		R	H	E
Cardinals	0	0	1	0	0	0	0	0	1		2	5	1
Yankees	0	0	0	0	0	0	0	0	0		0	6	1

E—Cooper, Breuer. DP—Yankees 1 (Keller to Dickey). LOB—Cardinals 4, Yankees 6. Scoring Position—Cardinals 1-for-5, Yankees 0-for-1. S—White. SB—Rizzuto (2). CS—Musial (1).

Cardinals	IP	H	R	ER	BB	K	ERA
Ernie White (W, 1-0)	9.0	6	0	0	0	6	0.00

Yankees	IP	H	R	ER	BB	K	ERA
Spud Chandler (L, 0-1)	8.0	3	1	1	1	3	1.08
Marv Breuer	0.0	2	1	0	0	0	—
Jim Turner	1.0	0	0	0	0	1	0.00

Breuer pitched to four batters in the 9th.

Time—2:30. Attendance—69,123. Umpires—HP, Barr. 1B, Hubbard. 2B, Magerkurth. 3B, Summers.

Game 4

Sunday, October 4

Cardinals	AB	R	H	RBI	BB	K	Avg
Jimmy Brown, 2b	6	0	2	0	0	0	.235
Terry Moore, cf	3	0	2	1	1	0	.286
Enos Slaughter, rf	4	1	0	0	1	0	.200
Stan Musial, lf	3	2	2	1	2	0	.286
Walker Cooper, c	5	1	2	1	0	0	.235
Johnny Hopp, 1b	3	2	1	0	1	0	.214
Whitey Kurowski, 3b	3	1	1	2	1	0	.273
Marty Marion, ss	4	1	0	1	1	1	.143
Mort Cooper, p	3	1	1	2	0	1	.200
Harry Gumbert, p	0	0	0	0	0	0	—
Howie Pollet, p	0	0	0	0	0	0	—
Ray Sanders, ph	1	0	0	0	0	0	.000
Max Lanier, p	1	0	1	1	0	0	1.000
TOTALS	36	9	12	9	7	2	.236

Yankees	AB	R	H	RBI	BB	K	Avg
Phil Rizzuto, ss	5	1	3	0	0	0	.353
Red Rolfe, 3b	4	2	2	0	1	0	.385
Roy Cullenbine, rf	4	1	2	2	0	0	.333
Joe DiMaggio, cf	4	0	0	0	0	0	.353
Charlie Keller, lf	4	1	1	3	0	1	.188
Joe Gordon, 2b	4	1	0	0	0	0	.059
Bill Dickey, c	4	0	0	0	0	0	.333
Jerry Priddy, 1b	4	0	1	1	0	0	.143
Hank Borowy, p	1	0	0	0	0	1	.000
Atley Donald, p	2	0	0	0	0	0	.000
Tiny Bonham, p	0	0	0	0	0	0	.000
Buddy Rosar, ph	1	0	1	0	0	0	1.000
TOTALS	37	6	10	6	1	2	.268

	1	2	3	4	5	6	7	8	9		R	H	E
Cardinals	0	0	0	6	0	0	2	0	1		9	12	1
Yankees	1	0	0	0	0	5	0	0	0		6	10	1

E—Kurowski, Dickey. DP—Cardinals 1 (Marion to Brown). LOB—Cardinals 10, Yankees 5. Scoring Position—Cardinals 6-for-17, Yankees 4-for-7. 2B—Moore (1), Musial (1), Rolfe (2), Priddy (1). HR—Keller (2). S—Moore, Hopp, Kurowski.

Cardinals	IP	H	R	ER	BB	K	ERA
Mort Cooper	5.1	7	5	5	1	2	5.54
Harry Gumbert (BS, 1)	0.1	1	1	0	0	0	0.00
Howie Pollet (W, 1-0)	0.1	0	0	0	0	0	0.00
Max Lanier (S, 1)	3.0	2	0	0	0	0	0.00

Yankees	IP	H	R	ER	BB	K	ERA
Hank Borowy	3.0	6	6	6	3	1	18.00
Atley Donald (L, 0-1)	3.0	3	2	2	1	1	6.00
Tiny Bonham	3.0	3	1	1	2	0	4.09

Borowy pitched to seven batters in the 4th. Donald pitched to four batters in the 7th.

Time—2:28. Attendance—69,902. Umpires—HP, Hubbard. 1B, Magerkurth. 2B, Summers. 3B, Barr.

Game 5

Monday, October 5

Cardinals	AB	R	H	RBI	BB	K	Avg
Jimmy Brown, 2b	3	0	2	0	1	0	.300
Terry Moore, cf	3	1	1	0	0	1	.294
Enos Slaughter, rf	4	1	2	1	0	0	.263
Stan Musial, lf	4	0	0	0	0	0	.222
Walker Cooper, c	4	1	2	1	0	0	.286
Johnny Hopp, 1b	3	0	0	0	0	0	.176
Whitey Kurowski, 3b	4	1	1	2	0	0	.267
Marty Marion, ss	4	0	0	0	0	0	.111
Johnny Beazley, p	4	0	1	0	0	2	.143
TOTALS	33	4	9	4	1	3	.237

Yankees	AB	R	H	RBI	BB	K	Avg
Phil Rizzuto, ss	4	1	2	1	0	0	.381
Red Rolfe, 3b	4	1	1	0	0	0	.353
Roy Cullenbine, rf	4	0	0	0	0	0	.263
Joe DiMaggio, cf	4	0	1	1	0	0	.333
Charlie Keller, lf	4	0	1	0	0	0	.200
Joe Gordon, 2b	4	0	1	0	0	1	.095
Bill Dickey, c	4	0	0	0	0	0	.263
Tuck Stainback, pr	0	0	0	0	0	0	—
Jerry Priddy, 1b	3	0	0	0	1	0	.100
Red Ruffing, p	3	0	1	0	0	1	.222
George Selkirk, ph	1	0	0	0	0	0	.000
TOTALS	35	2	7	2	1	2	.253

	1	2	3	4	5	6	7	8	9		R	H	E
Cardinals	0	0	0	1	0	1	0	0	2		4	9	4
Yankees	1	0	0	1	0	0	0	0	0		2	7	1

E—Beazley, Priddy, Hopp, Brown 2. DP—Cardinals 1 (Hopp to Marion to Brown), Yankees 1 (Gordon to Rizzuto to Priddy). LOB—Cardinals 5, Yankees 7. Scoring Position—Cardinals 1-for-6, Yankees 1-for-7. HR—Slaughter (1), Kurowski (1), Rizzuto (1). S—Moore, Hopp. GDP—Slaughter, Ruffing.

Cardinals	IP	H	R	ER	BB	K	ERA
Johnny Beazley (W, 2-0)	9.0	7	2	2	1	2	2.50

Yankees	IP	H	R	ER	BB	K	ERA
Red Ruffing (L, 1-1)	9.0	9	4	4	1	3	4.08

Time—1:58. Attendance—69,052. Umpires—HP, Magerkurth. 1B, Summers. 2B, Barr. 3B, Hubbard.

1942 World Series—Composite Statistics

Batting

Cardinals	G	AB	R	H	RBI	2B	3B	HR	BB	SO	SB	CS	Avg	OBP	Slg
Johnny Beazley	2	7	0	1	0	0	0	0	0	5	0	0	.143	.143	.143
Jimmy Brown	5	20	2	6	1	0	0	0	3	0	0	0	.300	.391	.300
Mort Cooper	2	5	1	1	2	0	0	0	0	1	0	0	.200	.200	.200
Walker Cooper	5	21	3	6	4	1	0	0	0	1	0	0	.286	.286	.333
Creepy Crespi	1	0	1	0	0	0	0	0	0	0	0	0	—	—	—
Johnny Hopp	5	17	3	3	0	0	0	0	1	1	0	0	.176	.222	.176
Whitey Kurowski	5	15	3	4	5	0	1	1	2	3	0	0	.267	.353	.600
Max Lanier	2	1	0	1	1	0	0	0	0	0	0	0	1.000	1.000	1.000
Marty Marion	5	18	2	2	3	0	1	0	1	2	0	0	.111	.158	.222
Terry Moore	5	17	2	5	2	1	0	0	2	3	0	0	.294	.368	.353
Stan Musial	5	18	2	4	2	1	0	0	4	0	0	0	.222	.364	.278
Ken O'Dea	1	1	0	1	1	0	0	0	0	0	0	0	1.000	1.000	1.000
Ray Sanders	2	1	1	0	0	0	0	0	1	0	0	0	.000	.500	.000
Enos Slaughter	5	19	3	5	2	1	0	1	3	2	0	0	.263	.364	.474
Harry Walker	1	1	0	0	0	0	0	0	0	1	0	0	.000	.000	.000
Ernie White	1	2	0	0	0	0	0	0	0	0	0	0	.000	.000	.000
Totals	5	163	23	39	23	4	2	2	17	19	0	1	.239	.311	.325

Batting

Yankees	G	AB	R	H	RBI	2B	3B	HR	BB	SO	SB	CS	Avg	OBP	Slg
Tiny Bonham	2	2	0	0	0	0	0	0	1	0	0	0	.000	.333	.000
Hank Borowy	1	1	0	0	0	0	0	0	0	1	0	0	.000	.000	.000
Spud Chandler	2	2	0	0	0	0	0	0	0	1	0	0	.000	.000	.000
Frankie Crosetti	1	3	0	0	0	0	0	0	0	1	0	0	.000	.000	.000
Roy Cullenbine	5	19	3	5	2	1	0	0	1	2	1	0	.263	.300	.316
Bill Dickey	5	19	1	5	0	0	0	0	1	0	0	0	.263	.300	.263
Joe DiMaggio	5	21	3	7	3	0	0	0	1	0	0	0	.333	.333	.333
Atley Donald	1	2	0	0	0	0	0	0	0	0	0	0	.000	.000	.000
Joe Gordon	5	21	1	2	0	1	0	0	7	0	0	0	.095	.095	.143
Buddy Hassett	3	9	1	3	2	1	0	0	1	0	0	0	.333	.333	.444
Charlie Keller	5	20	2	4	5	0	0	2	1	3	0	0	.200	.238	.500
Jerry Priddy	3	10	0	1	1	1	0	0	1	0	0	0	.100	.182	.200
Phil Rizzuto	5	21	2	8	1	0	0	1	2	1	2	0	.381	.435	.524
Red Rolfe	4	17	5	6	0	2	0	0	1	2	0	0	.353	.389	.471
Buddy Rosar	1	1	0	1	0	0	0	0	0	0	0	1	1.000	1.000	1.000
Red Ruffing	4	9	0	2	0	0	0	0	0	2	0	0	.222	.222	.222
George Selkirk	1	1	0	0	0	0	0	0	0	0	0	0	.000	.000	.000
Tuck Stainback	2	0	0	0	0	0	0	0	0	0	0	0	—	—	—
Totals	5	178	18	44	14	6	0	3	8	22	3	0	.247	.280	.331

Pitching

Cardinals	G	GS	CG	IP	H	R	ER	BB	SO	W-L	Sv-Op	Hld	ERA
Johnny Beazley	2	2	2	18.0	17	5	5	3	6	2-0	0-0	0	2.50
Mort Cooper	2	2	0	13.0	17	10	8	4	9	0-1	0-0	0	5.54
Harry Gumbert	2	0	0	0.2	1	1	0	0	0	0-1	0-0	0	0.00
Max Lanier	2	0	0	4.0	3	2	0	1	1	0-0	1-1	0	0.00
Howie Pollet	1	0	0	0.1	0	0	0	0	0	1-0	0-0	0	0.00
Ernie White	1	1	1	9.0	6	0	0	0	6	1-0	0-0	0	0.00
Totals	5	5	3	45.0	44	18	13	8	22	4-1	1-2	0	2.60

Pitching

Yankees	G	GS	CG	IP	H	R	ER	BB	SO	W-L	Sv-Op	Hld	ERA
Tiny Bonham	2	1	1	11.0	9	5	5	3	3	0-1	0-0	0	4.09
Hank Borowy	1	1	0	3.0	6	6	6	3	1	0-0	0-0	0	18.00
Marv Breuer	1	0	0	0.0	2	1	0	0	1	0-0	0-0	0	—
Spud Chandler	2	1	0	8.1	5	1	1	1	3	0-1	1-1	0	1.08
Atley Donald	1	0	0	3.0	3	2	2	2	1	0-1	0-0	0	6.00
Red Ruffing	2	2	1	17.2	14	8	8	7	11	1-1	0-0	0	4.08
Jim Turner	1	0	0	1.0	0	0	0	1	0	0-0	0-0	0	0.00
Totals	5	5	2	44.0	39	23	22	17	19	1-4	1-1	0	4.50

Fielding

Cardinals	Pos	G	PO	Ast	E	DP	PB	FPct
Johnny Beazley	p	2	2	0	1	0	—	.667
Jimmy Brown	2b	5	6	16	3	3	—	.880
Mort Cooper	p	2	0	1	0	0	—	1.000
Walker Cooper	c	5	24	2	1	0	0	.963
Harry Gumbert	p	2	0	1	0	0	—	1.000
Johnny Hopp	1b	5	46	3	1	2	—	.980
Whitey Kurowski	3b	5	7	4	1	0	—	.917
Max Lanier	p	2	0	1	2	0	—	.333
Marty Marion	ss	5	13	16	0	3	—	1.000
Terry Moore	cf	5	15	0	0	0	—	1.000
Stan Musial	lf	5	13	0	0	0	—	1.000
Howie Pollet	p	1	0	0	0	0	—	—
Enos Slaughter	rf	5	9	1	1	0	—	.909
Ernie White	p	1	0	0	0	0	—	—
Totals		5	135	45	10	8	0	.947

Fielding

Yankees	Pos	G	PO	Ast	E	DP	PB	FPct
Tiny Bonham	p	2	0	1	0	0	—	1.000
Hank Borowy	p	1	0	1	0	0	—	1.000
Marv Breuer	p	1	0	0	1	0	—	.000
Spud Chandler	p	2	2	2	0	0	—	1.000
Frankie Crosetti	3b	1	1	1	0	0	—	1.000
Roy Cullenbine	rf	5	6	0	0	0	—	1.000
Bill Dickey	c	5	25	1	1	1	0	.963
Joe DiMaggio	cf	5	20	0	0	0	—	1.000
Atley Donald	p	1	0	0	0	0	—	—
Joe Gordon	2b	5	11	12	0	1	—	1.000
Buddy Hassett	1b	3	15	1	1	0	—	.941
Charlie Keller	lf	5	12	1	0	1	—	1.000
Jerry Priddy	1b	3	22	4	1	1	—	.963
	3b	1	0	0	0	0	—	—
Phil Rizzuto	ss	5	15	15	1	1	—	.968
Red Rolfe	3b	4	3	5	0	0	—	1.000
Red Ruffing	p	2	0	1	0	0	—	1.000
Jim Turner	p	1	0	0	0	0	—	—
Totals		5	132	45	5	5	0	.973

1943 New York Yankees (AL) 4, St. Louis Cardinals (NL) 1

After losing to the St. Louis Cardinals in a five-game World Series the year before, the New York Yankees turned the tables, downing the Cardinals in five games. Spud Chandler won the opener, 4-2, as Frankie Crosetti scored the decisive run in the sixth inning, scoring all the way from second base on Max Lanier's wild pitch. Mort Cooper gave the Cards a 4-3 win in Game 2, thanks to home runs from Marty Marion and Ray Sanders. Bill Johnson cleared the bases with a triple in the bottom of the eighth, sending the Yanks to a 6-2 victory in Game 3. New York's Marius Russo did it all in Game 4, going the distance for a 2-1 victory, and scoring the go-ahead run after rapping his second double of the game in the eighth inning. Chandler put the wraps on it with a 2-0 shutout in Game 5, as Bill Dickey's two-run shot provided all the offense the Yanks needed.

Game 1
Tuesday, October 5

Cardinals	AB	R	H	RBI	BB	K	Avg
Lou Klein, 2b	4	0	1	0	0	0	.250
Harry Walker, cf	4	0	0	0	0	1	.000
Stan Musial, rf	4	0	1	0	0	0	.250
Walker Cooper, c	4	1	1	0	0	0	.250
Whitey Kurowski, 3b	3	0	0	0	0	0	.000
Ray Sanders, 1b	4	1	2	0	0	1	.500
Danny Litwhiler, lf	3	0	0	0	1	0	.000
Marty Marion, ss	3	0	1	1	0	0	.333
Max Lanier, p	2	0	1	1	0	0	.500
Debs Garms, ph	1	0	0	0	0	1	.000
Harry Brecheen, p	0	0	0	0	0	0	—
TOTALS	32	2	7	2	1	3	.219

Yankees	AB	R	H	RBI	BB	K	Avg
Tuck Stainback, rf	4	0	1	0	0	1	.250
Frankie Crosetti, ss	4	2	1	0	0	0	.250
Bill Johnson, 3b	4	1	2	0	0	0	.500
Charlie Keller, lf	4	0	1	0	0	1	.250
Joe Gordon, 2b	3	1	1	1	1	1	.333
Bill Dickey, c	4	0	1	1	0	1	.250
Nick Etten, 1b	4	0	0	0	0	0	.000
Johnny Lindell, cf	3	0	0	0	0	2	.000
Spud Chandler, p	3	0	1	0	0	1	.333
TOTALS	33	4	8	2	1	8	.242

	1 2 3	4 5 6	7 8 9	R	H	E
Cardinals	0 1 0	0 1 0	0 0 0	2	7	2
Yankees	0 0 0	2 0 2	0 0 x	4	8	2

E—Klein, Etten, Lanier, Crosetti. DP—Cardinals 1 (Klein to Marion to Sanders), Yankees 1 (Gordon to Crosetti to Etten). LOB—Cardinals 5, Yankees 6. Scoring Position—Cardinals 2-for-6, Yankees 2-for-7. 2B—Marion (1). HR—Gordon (1). S—Kurowski. GDP—Marion, Keller. SB—Crosetti (1).

Cardinals	IP	H	R	ER	BB	K	ERA
Max Lanier (L, 0-1)	7.0	7	4	2	0	7	2.57
Harry Brecheen	1.0	1	0	0	1	1	0.00

Yankees	IP	H	R	ER	BB	K	ERA
Spud Chandler (W, 1-0)	9.0	7	2	1	1	3	1.00

WP—Lanier. Time—2:07. Attendance—68,676. Umpires—HP, Rommel. 1B, Reardon. 2B, Rue. 3B, Stewart.

Game 2
Wednesday, October 6

Cardinals	AB	R	H	RBI	BB	K	Avg
Lou Klein, 2b	4	0	1	0	1	0	.250
Harry Walker, cf	5	0	1	0	0	1	.111
Stan Musial, rf	4	1	1	0	0	0	.250
Walker Cooper, c	3	0	1	0	0	0	.286
Whitey Kurowski, 3b	4	1	1	1	0	3	.143
Ray Sanders, 1b	3	1	1	2	1	1	.429
Danny Litwhiler, lf	3	0	0	0	1	2	.000
Marty Marion, ss	3	1	1	1	1	0	.333
Mort Cooper, p	3	0	0	0	0	2	.000
TOTALS	32	4	7	4	4	9	.213

Yankees	AB	R	H	RBI	BB	K	Avg
Frankie Crosetti, ss	4	1	2	0	0	1	.375
Bud Metheny, rf	3	0	0	0	0	0	.000
Bill Johnson, 3b	4	1	2	0	0	0	.500
Charlie Keller, lf	4	1	1	1	0	0	.250
Bill Dickey, c	3	0	0	0	1	0	.143
Nick Etten, 1b	4	0	0	1	0	1	.000
Joe Gordon, 2b	4	0	1	0	0	1	.286
Tuck Stainback, cf	3	0	0	0	0	1	.143
Tiny Bonham, p	2	0	0	0	0	0	.000
Roy Weatherly, ph	1	0	0	0	0	0	.000
Johnny Murphy, p	0	0	0	0	0	0	—
TOTALS	32	3	6	3	1	4	.220

	1 2 3	4 5 6	7 8 9	R	H	E
Cardinals	0 0 1	3 0 0	0 0 0	4	7	2
Yankees	0 0 0	1 0 0	0 0 2	3	6	0

E—Walker, WCooper. DP—Cardinals 1 (Marion to Klein to Sanders). LOB—Cardinals 7, Yankees 4. Scoring Position—Cardinals 2-for-7, Yankees 1-for-8. 2B—Johnson (1). 3B—Keller (1). HR—Sanders (1), Marion (1). S—WCooper, MCooper. GDP—Johnson. SB—Marion (1).

Cardinals	IP	H	R	ER	BB	K	ERA
Mort Cooper (W, 1-0)	9.0	6	3	3	1	4	3.00

Yankees	IP	H	R	ER	BB	K	ERA
Tiny Bonham (L, 0-1)	8.0	6	4	4	3	9	4.50
Johnny Murphy	1.0	1	0	0	1	0	0.00

Reached, Catcher's Interference—Cardinals 0, Yankees 1, Metheny by WCooper. Time—2:08. Attendance—68,578. Umpires—HP, Reardon. 1B, Rue. 2B, Stewart. 3B, Rommel.

Game 3
Thursday, October 7

Cardinals	AB	R	H	RBI	BB	K	Avg
Lou Klein, 2b	4	0	0	0	0	0	.167
Harry Walker, cf	4	0	1	0	0	0	.154
Stan Musial, rf	3	1	1	0	1	0	.273
Walker Cooper, c	4	0	1	0	0	0	.273
Whitey Kurowski, 3b	3	1	1	0	0	0	.200
Ken O'Dea, ph	1	0	0	0	0	0	.000
Ray Sanders, 1b	3	0	0	0	1	1	.300
Danny Litwhiler, lf	4	0	2	2	0	2	.200
Marty Marion, ss	2	0	0	0	1	1	.250
Al Brazle, p	3	0	0	0	0	1	.000
Howie Krist, p	0	0	0	0	0	0	—
Harry Brecheen, p	0	0	0	0	0	0	—
TOTALS	31	2	6	2	3	5	.213

Yankees	AB	R	H	RBI	BB	K	Avg
Tuck Stainback, cf	4	0	1	0	0	0	.182
Frankie Crosetti, ss	2	1	0	0	1	0	.300
Bill Johnson, 3b	4	1	1	3	0	0	.417
Charlie Keller, lf	3	1	0	0	1	1	.182
Joe Gordon, 2b	4	0	1	1	0	0	.273
Bill Dickey, c	4	0	2	0	0	0	.273
Nick Etten, 1b	4	0	1	0	0	1	.083
Johnny Lindell, rf	3	1	1	0	0	1	.167
Hank Borowy, p	2	1	1	0	0	1	.500
Snuffy Stirnweiss, ph	1	1	0	0	0	0	.000
Johnny Murphy, p	0	0	0	0	0	0	—
TOTALS	31	6	8	5	2	4	.241

	1 2 3	4 5 6	7 8 9	R	H	E
Cardinals	0 0 0	2 0 0	0 0 0	2	6	4
Yankees	0 0 0	0 0 1	0 5 x	6	8	0

E—Kurowski 2, Walker, Marion. DP—Cardinals 1 (Marion to Klein to Sanders), Yankees 1 (Crosetti to Gordon to Etten). LOB—Cardinals 5, Yankees 4. Scoring Position—Cardinals 1-for-4, Yankees 4-for-10. 2B—Walker (1), Kurowski (1), Borowy (1). 3B—Johnson (1). S—Crosetti. GDP—Cooper, Johnson. CS—Cooper (1).

Cardinals	IP	H	R	ER	BB	K	ERA
Al Brazle (L, 0-1)	7.1	5	6	3	2	4	3.68
Howie Krist	0.0	1	0	0	0	0	—
Harry Brecheen	0.2	2	0	0	0	0	0.00

Yankees	IP	H	R	ER	BB	K	ERA
Hank Borowy (W, 1-0)	8.0	6	2	2	3	4	2.25
Johnny Murphy (S, 1)	1.0	0	0	0	0	1	0.00

Krist pitched to one batter in the 8th.

Time—2:10. Attendance—69,990. Umpires—HP, Rue. 1B, Stewart. 2B, Rommel. 3B, Reardon.

Game 4
Sunday, October 10

Yankees	AB	R	H	RBI	BB	K	Avg
Tuck Stainback, cf	3	0	0	0	0	0	.143
Frankie Crosetti, ss	4	0	1	1	0	1	.286
Bill Johnson, 3b	4	0	0	0	0	1	.313
Charlie Keller, lf	4	0	1	0	0	2	.200
Joe Gordon, 2b	4	1	1	0	0	1	.267
Bill Dickey, c	3	0	1	1	1	0	.286
Nick Etten, 1b	4	0	0	0	0	0	.063
Johnny Lindell, rf	3	0	0	0	1	1	.111
Marius Russo, p	3	1	2	0	1	1	.667
TOTALS	32	2	6	2	3	7	.224

Cardinals	AB	R	H	RBI	BB	K	Avg
Lou Klein, 2b	5	0	0	0	0	0	.118
Harry Walker, cf	4	0	0	0	0	0	.118
Stan Musial, rf	4	0	2	0	0	0	.333
Walker Cooper, c	4	0	1	0	0	1	.267
Whitey Kurowski, 3b	4	0	0	0	0	0	.143
Ray Sanders, 1b	4	1	1	0	0	1	.286
Danny Litwhiler, lf	4	0	1	0	0	0	.214
Marty Marion, ss	3	0	2	0	1	0	.364
Max Lanier, p	2	0	0	0	0	0	.250
Frank Demaree, ph	1	0	0	0	0	0	.000
Ernie White, pr	0	0	0	0	0	0	—
Harry Brecheen, p	0	0	0	0	0	0	—
Sam Narron, ph	1	0	0	0	0	0	.000
TOTALS	36	1	7	0	1	2	.220

	1	2	3	4	5	6	7	8	9	R	H	E
Yankees	0	0	0	1	0	0	0	1	0	2	6	2
Cardinals	0	0	0	0	0	0	1	0	0	1	7	1

E—Johnson, Klein, Crosetti. LOB—Yankees 7, Cardinals 9.
Scoring Position—Yankees 2-for-7, Cardinals 0-for-6. 2B—
Gordon (1), Russo 2 (2), Litwhiler (1), Marion (2). S—Stainback.
SB—Keller (1).

Yankees	IP	H	R	ER	BB	K	ERA
Marius Russo (W, 1-0)	9.0	7	1	0	1	2	0.00

Cardinals	IP	H	R	ER	BB	K	ERA
Max Lanier	7.0	4	1	1	1	5	1.93
Harry Brecheen (L, 0-1)	2.0	2	1	1	2	2	2.45

Time—2:06. Attendance—36,196. Umpires—HP, Stewart. 1B,
Rommel. 2B, Reardon. 3B, Rue.

Game 5
Monday, October 11

Yankees	AB	R	H	RBI	BB	K	Avg
Frankie Crosetti, ss	4	0	1	0	1	1	.278
Bud Metheny, rf	5	0	1	0	0	2	.125
Johnny Lindell, rf	0	0	0	0	0	0	.111
Bill Johnson, 3b	4	0	1	0	0	1	.300
Charlie Keller, lf	3	1	1	0	1	1	.222
Bill Dickey, c	4	1	1	2	0	1	.278
Nick Etten, 1b	3	0	1	0	1	0	.105
Joe Gordon, 2b	2	0	0	0	2	0	.235
Tuck Stainback, cf	3	0	1	0	0	0	.176
Spud Chandler, p	3	0	0	0	0	1	.167
TOTALS	31	2	7	2	5	7	.213

Cardinals	AB	R	H	RBI	BB	K	Avg
Lou Klein, 2b	5	0	1	0	0	2	.136
Debs Garms, lf	4	0	0	0	0	1	.000
Stan Musial, rf	3	0	0	0	1	2	.278
Walker Cooper, c	2	0	1	0	0	0	.294
Ken O'Dea, c	2	0	2	0	0	0	.667
Whitey Kurowski, 3b	4	0	2	0	0	0	.222
Ray Sanders, 1b	3	0	1	0	1	0	.294
Johnny Hopp, cf	4	0	0	0	0	1	.000
Marty Marion, ss	3	0	1	0	0	0	.357
Mort Cooper, p	2	0	0	0	0	1	.000
Harry Walker, ph	1	0	1	0	0	0	.167
Max Lanier, p	0	0	0	0	0	0	.250
Murry Dickson, p	0	0	0	0	0	0	—
Danny Litwhiler, ph	1	0	1	0	0	0	.267
TOTALS	34	0	10	0	2	7	.231

	1	2	3	4	5	6	7	8	9	R	H	E
Yankees	0	0	0	0	0	2	0	0	0	2	7	1
Cardinals	0	0	0	0	0	0	0	0	0	0	10	1

E—WCooper, Crosetti. DP—Yankees 1 (Crosetti to Gordon to
Etten), Cardinals 1 (Klein to Marion to Sanders). LOB—Yankees 9, Cardinals 11. Scoring Position—Yankees 0-for-9, Cardinals 0-for-10. HR—Dickey (1). S—Stainback, Chandler,
Garms, Marion. GDP—Dickey, Kurowski.

Yankees	IP	H	R	ER	BB	K	ERA
Spud Chandler (W, 2-0)	9.0	10	0	0	2	7	0.50

Cardinals	IP	H	R	ER	BB	K	ERA
Mort Cooper (L, 1-1)	7.0	5	2	2	2	6	2.81
Max Lanier	1.1	2	0	0	2	1	1.76
Murry Dickson	0.2	0	0	0	1	0	0.00

WP—MCooper. Time—2:24. Attendance—33,872. Umpires—
HP, Reardon. 1B, Rommel. 2B, Rue. 3B, Stewart.

1943 World Series—Composite Statistics

Batting

Yankees	G	AB	R	H	RBI	2B	3B	HR	BB	SO	SB	CS	Avg	OBP	Slg
Tiny Bonham	1	2	0	0	0	0	0	0	0	0	0	0	.000	.000	.000
Hank Borowy	1	2	1	1	0	1	0	0	0	1	0	0	.500	.500	1.000
Spud Chandler	2	6	0	1	0	0	0	0	0	2	0	0	.167	.167	.167
Frankie Crosetti	5	18	4	5	1	0	0	0	2	3	1	0	.278	.350	.278
Bill Dickey	5	18	1	5	4	0	0	1	2	2	0	0	.278	.350	.444
Nick Etten	5	19	0	2	2	0	0	0	1	2	0	0	.105	.150	.105
Joe Gordon	5	17	2	4	2	1	0	1	3	3	0	0	.235	.350	.471
Bill Johnson	5	20	3	6	3	1	1	0	0	3	0	0	.300	.300	.450
Charlie Keller	5	18	3	4	2	0	1	0	2	5	1	0	.222	.300	.333
Johnny Lindell	4	9	1	1	0	0	0	0	1	4	0	0	.111	.200	.111
Bud Metheny	2	8	0	1	0	0	0	0	0	2	0	0	.125	.125	.125
Marius Russo	1	3	1	2	0	2	0	0	1	1	0	0	.667	.750	1.333
Tuck Stainback	5	17	0	3	0	0	0	0	0	2	0	0	.176	.176	.176
Snuffy Stirnweiss	1	1	1	0	0	0	0	0	0	0	0	0	.000	.000	.000
Roy Weatherly	1	1	0	0	0	0	0	0	0	0	0	0	.000	.000	.000
Totals	5	159	17	35	14	5	2	2	12	30	2	0	.220	.275	.314

Cardinals	G	AB	R	H	RBI	2B	3B	HR	BB	SO	SB	CS	Avg	OBP	Slg
Al Brazle	1	3	0	0	0	0	0	0	0	1	0	0	.000	.000	.000
Mort Cooper	2	5	0	0	0	0	0	0	0	3	0	0	.000	.000	.000
Walker Cooper	5	17	1	5	0	0	0	0	0	1	0	1	.294	.294	.294
Frank Demaree	1	1	0	0	0	0	0	0	0	0	0	0	.000	.000	.000
Debs Garms	2	5	0	0	0	0	0	0	0	2	0	0	.000	.000	.000
Johnny Hopp	1	4	0	0	0	0	0	0	0	1	0	0	.000	.000	.000
Lou Klein	5	22	0	3	0	0	0	0	1	2	0	0	.136	.174	.136
Whitey Kurowski	5	18	2	4	1	1	0	0	0	3	0	0	.222	.222	.278
Max Lanier	3	4	0	1	1	0	0	0	0	0	0	0	.250	.250	.250
Danny Litwhiler	5	15	0	4	2	1	0	0	2	4	0	0	.267	.353	.333
Marty Marion	5	14	1	5	2	2	0	1	3	1	1	0	.357	.471	.714
Stan Musial	5	18	2	5	0	0	0	0	2	2	0	0	.278	.350	.278
Sam Narron	1	1	0	0	0	0	0	0	0	0	0	0	.000	.000	.000
Ken O'Dea	2	3	0	2	0	0	0	0	0	0	0	0	.667	.667	.667
Ray Sanders	5	17	3	5	2	0	0	1	3	4	0	0	.294	.400	.471
Harry Walker	5	18	0	3	0	1	0	0	0	2	0	0	.167	.167	.222
Ernie White	1	0	0	0	0	0	0	0	0	0	0	0	—	—	—
Totals	5	165	9	37	8	5	0	2	11	26	1	1	.224	.273	.291

Pitching

Yankees	G	GS	CG	IP	H	R	ER	BB	SO	W-L	Sv-Op	Hld	ERA
Tiny Bonham	1	1	0	8.0	6	4	4	3	9	0-1	0-0	0	4.50
Hank Borowy	1	1	0	8.0	6	2	2	3	4	1-0	0-0	0	2.25
Spud Chandler	2	2	2	18.0	17	2	1	3	10	2-0	0-0	0	0.50
Johnny Murphy	2	0	0	2.0	1	0	0	1	1	0-0	1-1	0	0.00
Marius Russo	1	1	1	9.0	7	1	0	1	2	1-0	0-0	0	0.00
Totals	5	5	3	45.0	37	9	7	11	26	4-1	1-1	0	1.40

Cardinals	G	GS	CG	IP	H	R	ER	BB	SO	W-L	Sv-Op	Hld	ERA
Al Brazle	1	1	0	7.1	5	6	3	2	4	0-1	0-0	0	3.68
Harry Brecheen	3	0	0	3.2	5	1	1	3	3	0-1	0-0	0	2.45
Mort Cooper	2	2	1	16.0	11	5	5	3	10	1-1	0-0	0	2.81
Murry Dickson	1	0	0	0.2	0	0	0	1	0	0-0	0-0	0	0.00
Howie Krist	1	0	0	0.0	1	0	0	0	0	0-0	0-0	0	—
Max Lanier	3	2	0	15.1	13	5	3	3	13	0-1	0-0	0	1.76
Totals	5	5	1	43.0	35	17	12	12	30	1-4	0-0	0	2.51

Fielding

Yankees	Pos	G	PO	Ast	E	DP	PB	FPct
Tiny Bonham	p	1	0	0	0	0	—	—
Hank Borowy	p	1	2	0	0	0	—	1.000
Spud Chandler	p	2	0	4	0	0	—	1.000
Frankie Crosetti	ss	5	9	16	3	3	—	.893
Bill Dickey	c	5	28	3	0	0	0	1.000
Nick Etten	1b	5	46	2	1	3	—	.980
Joe Gordon	2b	5	20	23	0	3	—	1.000
Bill Johnson	3b	5	2	9	1	0	—	.917
Charlie Keller	lf	5	10	1	0	0	—	1.000
Johnny Lindell	rf	3	5	0	0	0	—	1.000
	cf	1	3	0	0	0	—	1.000
Bud Metheny	rf	2	3	0	0	0	—	1.000
Johnny Murphy	p	2	0	1	0	0	—	1.000
Marius Russo	p	1	0	2	0	0	—	1.000
Tuck Stainback	cf	4	5	0	0	0	—	1.000
	rf	1	2	1	0	0	—	1.000
Totals		5	135	62	5	9	0	.975

Cardinals	Pos	G	PO	Ast	E	DP	PB	FPct
Al Brazle	p	1	1	2	0	0	—	1.000
Harry Brecheen	p	3	0	2	0	0	—	1.000
Mort Cooper	p	2	0	1	0	0	—	1.000
Walker Cooper	c	5	28	3	2	0	0	.939
Murry Dickson	p	1	1	0	0	0	—	1.000
Debs Garms	lf	1	1	0	0	0	—	1.000
Johnny Hopp	cf	1	1	0	0	0	—	1.000
Lou Klein	2b	5	10	13	2	4	—	.920
Howie Krist	p	1	0	0	0	0	—	—
Whitey Kurowski	3b	5	8	8	2	0	—	.889
Max Lanier	p	3	0	3	1	0	—	.750
Danny Litwhiler	lf	4	11	0	0	0	—	1.000
Marty Marion	ss	5	8	14	1	4	—	.957
Stan Musial	rf	5	7	2	0	0	—	1.000
Ken O'Dea	c	1	2	0	0	0	0	1.000
Ray Sanders	1b	5	41	5	0	4	—	1.000
Harry Walker	cf	4	10	0	2	0	—	.833
Totals		5	129	53	10	12	0	.948

1944 St. Louis Cardinals (NL) 4, St. Louis Browns (AL) 2

The St. Louis Cardinals became champions of their home town—and thus, the world—by defeating the Browns in a six-game Series. The Browns' Denny Galehouse won the opener, 2-1, on a two-run homer by George McQuinn. Game 2 went 11 innings before Ken O'Dea's pinch-hit RBI single gave the Cards a 3-2 win. The Browns won Game 3 behind Jack Kramer, 6-2, as McQuinn went 3-for-3 with a pair of RBI. The Cardinals, however, came back to take the next three games, holding the Browns to just two runs over the remainder of the Series. Harry Brecheen and Mort Cooper tossed complete-game victories before Max Lanier combined with Ted Wilks to win Game 6.

Game 1
Wednesday, October 4

Browns	AB	R	H	RBI	BB	K	Avg
Don Gutteridge, 2b	4	0	0	0	0	0	.000
Mike Kreevich, cf	4	0	0	0	0	2	.000
Chet Laabs, lf	4	0	0	0	0	2	.000
Vern Stephens, ss	3	0	0	0	1	0	.000
Gene Moore, rf	3	1	1	0	1	1	.333
George McQuinn, 1b	3	1	1	2	0	0	.333
Mark Christman, 3b	3	0	0	0	0	1	.000
Red Hayworth, c	3	0	0	0	0	0	.000
Denny Galehouse, p	2	0	0	0	1	0	.000
TOTALS	29	2	2	2	3	6	.069

Cardinals	AB	R	H	RBI	BB	K	Avg
Johnny Hopp, cf	5	0	1	0	0	0	.200
Ray Sanders, 1b	3	0	1	0	1	1	.333
Stan Musial, rf	3	0	1	0	0	0	.333
Walker Cooper, c	3	0	0	0	1	0	.000
Whitey Kurowski, 3b	4	0	1	0	0	1	.250
Danny Litwhiler, lf	2	0	0	0	1	1	.000
George Fallon, 2b	1	0	0	0	0	0	.000
Marty Marion, ss	4	1	2	0	0	0	.500
Emil Verban, 2b	2	0	1	0	0	0	.500
Augie Bergamo, ph-lf	1	0	0	0	1	0	.000
Mort Cooper, p	2	0	0	0	0	2	.000
Debs Garms, ph	1	0	0	0	0	0	.000
Blix Donnelly, p	0	0	0	0	0	0	—
Ken O'Dea, ph	1	0	0	1	0	0	.000
TOTALS	32	1	7	1	4	5	.219

	1	2	3	4	5	6	7	8	9		R	H	E
Browns	0	0	0	2	0	0	0	0	0		2	2	0
Cardinals	0	0	0	0	0	0	0	0	1		1	7	0

DP—Browns 1 (Gutteridge to Stephens to McQuinn). LOB—Browns 3, Cardinals 9. Scoring Position—Browns 0-for-0, Cardinals 1-for-8. 2B—Marion 2 (2). HR—McQuinn (1). S—Musial. GDP—Musial.

Browns	IP	H	R	ER	BB	K	ERA
Denny Galehouse (W, 1-0)	9.0	7	1	1	4	5	1.00

Cardinals	IP	H	R	ER	BB	K	ERA
Mort Cooper (L, 0-1)	7.0	2	2	2	3	4	2.57
Blix Donnelly	2.0	0	0	0	0	2	0.00

Time—2:05. Attendance—33,242. Umpires—HP, Sears. 1B, McGowan. 2B, Dunn. 3B, Pipgras.

Game 2
Thursday, October 5

Browns	AB	R	H	RBI	BB	K	Avg
Don Gutteridge, 2b	4	0	0	0	1	2	.000
Mike Kreevich, cf	5	0	2	0	0	0	.222
Chet Laabs, lf	4	0	0	0	0	3	.000
Al Zarilla, ph-lf	1	0	0	0	0	0	.000
Vern Stephens, ss	5	0	0	0	0	2	.000
George McQuinn, 1b	2	0	1	0	3	1	.400
Mark Christman, 3b	5	0	0	0	0	2	.000
Gene Moore, rf	5	1	2	0	0	1	.375
Red Hayworth, c	5	1	1	1	0	1	.125
Nels Potter, p	2	0	0	0	0	0	.000
Frank Mancuso, ph	1	0	1	1	0	0	1.000
Tex Shirley, pr	0	0	0	0	0	0	—
Bob Muncrief, p	1	0	0	0	0	1	.000
TOTALS	40	2	7	2	4	13	.134

Cardinals	AB	R	H	RBI	BB	K	Avg
Augie Bergamo, lf	5	0	0	1	0	3	.000
Johnny Hopp, cf	5	0	0	0	0	2	.100
Stan Musial, rf	5	0	1	0	0	0	.250
Walker Cooper, c	4	0	1	0	0	0	.143
Ray Sanders, 1b	3	2	1	0	2	1	.333
Whitey Kurowski, 3b	4	0	2	0	0	0	.375
Marty Marion, ss	3	0	0	0	2	0	.286
Emil Verban, 2b	3	1	1	1	1	0	.400
Ken O'Dea, ph	1	0	1	1	0	0	.500
Max Lanier, p	2	0	0	0	0	0	.000
Blix Donnelly, p	1	0	0	0	0	1	.000
TOTALS	36	3	7	3	5	7	.226

	1	2	3	4	5	6	7	8	9	10	11		R	H
Browns	0	0	0	0	0	0	2	0	0	0	0		2	7
Cardinals	0	0	1	1	0	0	0	0	0	0	1		3	7

E—Christman, Gutteridge, Potter 2. DP—Browns 2 (Stephens to Gutteridge; Stephens to Gutteridge to McQuinn). LOB—Browns 9, Cardinals 10. Scoring Position—Browns 1-for-6, Cardinals 1-for-12. 2B—Kreevich (1), McQuinn (1), Hayworth (1), Cooper (1), Kurowski (1). S—Cooper, Kurowski, Lanier. GDP—Cooper.

Browns	IP	H	R	ER	BB	K	ERA
Nels Potter	6.0	4	2	0	2	3	0.00
Bob Muncrief (L, 0-1)	4.1	3	1	1	3	4	2.08

Cardinals	IP	H	R	ER	BB	K	ERA
Max Lanier	7.0	5	2	2	3	6	2.57
Blix Donnelly (W, 1-0)	4.0	2	0	0	1	7	0.00

Lanier pitched to one batter in the 8th.

Time—2:32. Attendance—35,076. Umpires—HP, McGowan. 1B, Dunn. 2B, Pipgras. 3B, Sears.

Game 3
Friday, October 6

Cardinals	AB	R	H	RBI	BB	K	Avg
Danny Litwhiler, lf	5	0	0	0	0	2	.000
Johnny Hopp, cf	4	1	1	0	0	1	.143
Stan Musial, rf	4	0	1	0	0	0	.250
Walker Cooper, c	4	0	2	1	0	0	.273
Ray Sanders, 1b	3	0	1	0	1	2	.333
Whitey Kurowski, 3b	4	1	0	0	0	1	.250
Marty Marion, ss	4	0	2	1	0	1	.364
Emil Verban, 2b	2	0	0	0	0	0	.286
Debs Garms, ph	1	0	0	0	0	0	.000
George Fallon, 2b	1	0	0	0	0	1	.000
Ted Wilks, p	1	0	0	0	0	1	.000
Freddy Schmidt, p	1	0	0	0	0	1	.000
Augie Bergamo, ph	0	0	0	0	1	0	.000
Al Jurisich, p	0	0	0	0	0	0	—
Bud Byerly, p	0	0	0	0	0	0	—
Ken O'Dea, ph	1	0	0	0	0	0	.333
TOTALS	35	2	7	2	2	10	.214

Browns	AB	R	H	RBI	BB	K	Avg
Don Gutteridge, 2b	4	1	1	0	0	2	.083
Mike Kreevich, cf	4	0	0	0	0	0	.154
Gene Moore, rf	4	1	1	0	0	0	.333
Vern Stephens, ss	2	1	1	0	2	0	.100
George McQuinn, 1b	3	1	3	2	1	0	.625
Al Zarilla, rf	4	1	1	0	1	1	.200
Mark Christman, 3b	4	0	1	1	0	0	.083
Red Hayworth, c	2	0	0	2	0	0	.100
Jack Kramer, p	4	0	0	0	2	2	.000
TOTALS	31	6	8	4	5	5	.186

	1	2	3	4	5	6	7	8	9		R	H	E
Cardinals	1	0	0	0	0	0	1	0	0		2	7	0
Browns	0	0	4	0	0	0	2	0	x		6	8	2

E—Stephens, Gutteridge. DP—Cardinals 1 (Marion to Sanders). LOB—Cardinals 8, Browns 6. Scoring Position—Cardinals 2-for-8, Browns 3-for-10. 2B—Cooper (2), Gutteridge (1), McQuinn (2). GDP—Zarilla.

Cardinals	IP	H	R	ER	BB	K	ERA
Ted Wilks (L, 0-1)	2.2	5	4	4	3	3	13.50
Freddy Schmidt	3.1	1	0	0	1	1	0.00
Al Jurisich	0.2	2	2	2	1	0	27.00
Bud Byerly	1.1	0	0	0	0	1	0.00

Browns	IP	H	R	ER	BB	K	ERA
Jack Kramer (W, 1-0)	9.0	7	2	0	2	10	0.00

WP—Schmidt. PB—Cooper. Time—2:19. Attendance—34,737. Umpires—HP, Dunn. 1B, Pipgras. 2B, Sears. 3B, McGowan.

Game 4
Saturday, October 7

Cardinals	AB	R	H	RBI	BB	K	Avg
Danny Litwhiler, lf	4	1	2	0	1	1	.182
Johnny Hopp, cf	5	1	2	0	0	1	.211
Stan Musial, rf	4	2	3	2	1	0	.375
Walker Cooper, c	4	0	2	1	1	0	.333
Ray Sanders, 1b	5	1	1	0	0	1	.286
Whitey Kurowski, 3b	4	0	0	0	0	1	.188
Marty Marion, ss	4	0	1	1	0	1	.333
Emil Verban, 2b	4	0	1	0	0	0	.273
Harry Brecheen, p	4	0	0	0	0	1	.000
TOTALS	38	5	12	4	3	6	.264

Browns	AB	R	H	RBI	BB	K	Avg
Don Gutteridge, 2b	4	0	2	0	1	1	.188
Mike Kreevich, cf	5	0	1	0	0	0	.167
Gene Moore, rf	3	1	0	0	1	1	.267
Vern Stephens, ss	4	0	1	0	0	0	.143
Chet Laabs, lf	4	0	2	0	0	0	.167
George McQuinn, 1b	3	0	1	0	1	0	.545
Mark Christman, 3b	4	0	1	0	0	2	.125
Red Hayworth, c	2	0	0	0	0	0	.083
Frank Mancuso, c	2	0	1	0	0	0	.667
Sig Jakucki, p	0	0	0	0	0	0	—
Ellis Clary, ph	1	0	0	0	0	0	.000
Al Hollingsworth, p	1	0	0	0	0	0	.000
Milt Byrnes, ph	0	0	0	0	1	0	—
Tex Shirley, p	0	0	0	0	0	0	—
Tom Turner, ph	1	0	0	0	0	0	.000
TOTALS	34	1	9	0	4	4	.208

	1	2	3	4	5	6	7	8	9		R	H	E
Cardinals	2	0	2	0	0	1	0	0	0		5	12	0
Browns	0	0	0	0	0	0	0	1	0		1	9	1

E—Gutteridge. DP—Cardinals 2 (Kurowski to Verban to Sanders; Marion to Verban to Sanders). LOB—Cardinals 9, Browns 10. Scoring Position—Cardinals 1-for-8, Browns 0-for-5. 2B—Musial (1), Marion (3), Laabs (1). 3B—Cooper (1). HR—Musial (1). GDP—Laabs, Hayworth.

Cardinals	IP	H	R	ER	BB	K	ERA
Harry Brecheen (W, 1-0)	9.0	9	1	1	4	4	1.00

Browns	IP	H	R	ER	BB	K	ERA
Sig Jakucki (L, 0-1)	3.0	5	4	3	0	4	9.00
Al Hollingsworth	4.0	5	1	1	2	1	2.25
Tex Shirley	2.0	2	0	0	1	1	0.00

Time—2:22. Attendance—35,455. Umpires—HP, Pipgras. 1B, Sears. 2B, McGowan. 3B, Dunn.

Game 5
Sunday, October 8

Cardinals	AB	R	H	RBI	BB	K	Avg
Danny Litwhiler, lf	4	1	2	1	0	1	.267
Johnny Hopp, cf	4	0	0	0	0	3	.174
Stan Musial, rf	3	0	1	0	1	0	.368
Walker Cooper, c	4	0	0	0	0	2	.263
Ray Sanders, 1b	4	1	1	1	0	2	.278
Whitey Kurowski, 3b	4	0	1	0	0	1	.200
Marty Marion, ss	4	0	0	0	0	1	.263
Emil Verban, 2b	3	0	1	0	0	0	.286
Mort Cooper, p	2	0	0	0	0	0	.000
TOTALS	32	2	6	2	1	10	.252

Browns	AB	R	H	RBI	BB	K	Avg
Don Gutteridge, 2b	2	0	0	0	1	0	.167
Floyd Baker, ph-2b	1	0	0	0	0	1	.000
Mike Kreevich, cf	4	0	2	0	0	1	.227
Gene Moore, rf	4	0	0	0	0	2	.211
Vern Stephens, ss	4	0	3	0	0	0	.278
George McQuinn, 1b	3	0	0	0	1	1	.429
Al Zarilla, lf	4	0	0	0	0	2	.111
Mark Christman, 3b	3	0	0	0	0	1	.105
Milt Byrnes, ph	1	0	0	0	0	1	.000
Red Hayworth, c	3	0	1	0	0	0	.133
Chet Laabs, ph	1	0	0	0	0	1	.154
Denny Galehouse, p	3	0	1	0	0	1	.200
Mike Chartak, ph	1	0	0	0	0	1	.000
TOTALS	34	0	7	0	2	12	.200

	1	2	3	4	5	6	7	8	9		R	H	E
Cardinals	0	0	0	0	0	1	0	1	0		2	6	1
Browns	0	0	0	0	0	0	0	0	0		0	7	1

E—Musial, Stephens. DP—Browns 1 (Stephens to McQuinn). LOB—Cardinals 5, Browns 9. Scoring Position—Cardinals 0-for-7, Browns 0-for-8. 2B—Litwhiler (1), Musial (2), Kreevich (2), Stephens (1). HR—Litwhiler (1), Sanders (1). S—MCooper. GDP—MCooper.

Cardinals	IP	H	R	ER	BB	K	ERA
Mort Cooper (W, 1-1)	9.0	7	0	0	2	12	1.13

Browns	IP	H	R	ER	BB	K	ERA
Denny Galehouse (L, 1-1)	9.0	6	2	2	1	10	1.50

Time—2:04. Attendance—36,568. Umpires—HP, Sears. 1B, Pipgras. 2B, Dunn. 3B, McGowan.

Game 6
Monday, October 9

Browns	AB	R	H	RBI	BB	K	Avg
Don Gutteridge, 2b	3	0	0	0	0	0	.143
Floyd Baker, ph-2b	1	0	0	0	0	1	.000
Mike Kreevich, cf	4	0	1	0	0	2	.231
Gene Moore, rf	3	0	0	0	1	1	.182
Vern Stephens, ss	4	0	0	0	0	1	.227
Chet Laabs, lf	2	1	1	0	2	0	.200
George McQuinn, 1b	2	0	1	1	1	0	.438
Mark Christman, 3b	3	0	0	0	0	0	.091
Milt Byrnes, ph	1	0	0	0	0	1	.000
Red Hayworth, c	2	0	0	0	1	0	.118
Mike Chartak, ph	1	0	0	0	0	1	.000
Nels Potter, p	2	0	0	0	0	1	.000
Bob Muncrief, p	0	0	0	0	0	0	.000
Al Zarilla, ph	1	0	0	0	0	1	.100
Jack Kramer, p	0	0	0	0	0	0	.000
TOTALS	29	1	3	1	5	9	.177

Cardinals	AB	R	H	RBI	BB	K	Avg
Danny Litwhiler, lf	5	0	0	0	0	2	.200
Johnny Hopp, cf	4	0	1	0	0	1	.185
Stan Musial, rf	4	0	0	0	0	0	.304
Walker Cooper, c	3	1	2	0	1	0	.318
Ray Sanders, 1b	3	1	1	0	1	1	.286
Whitey Kurowski, 3b	3	1	1	1	1	0	.217
Marty Marion, ss	3	0	0	0	0	0	.227
Emil Verban, 2b	3	0	3	1	0	0	.412
Max Lanier, p	2	0	2	1	0	0	.500
Ted Wilks, p	1	0	0	0	0	1	.000
TOTALS	31	3	10	3	4	5	.265

	1	2	3	4	5	6	7	8	9		R	H	E
Browns	0	1	0	0	0	0	0	0	0		1	3	2
Cardinals	0	0	0	3	0	0	0	0	x		3	10	0

E—Hayworth, Stephens. LOB—Browns 7, Cardinals 10. Scoring Position—Browns 1-for-6, Cardinals 2-for-11. 2B—Kreevich (3). 3B—Laabs (1). S—McQuinn, Marion, Wilks. CS—Kurowski (1).

Browns	IP	H	R	ER	BB	K	ERA
Nels Potter (L, 0-1)	3.2	6	3	1	1	3	0.93
Bob Muncrief	2.1	2	0	0	1	0	1.35
Jack Kramer	2.0	2	0	0	2	2	0.00

Cardinals	IP	H	R	ER	BB	K	ERA
Max Lanier (W, 1-0)	5.1	3	1	1	5	5	2.19
Ted Wilks (S, 1)	3.2	0	0	0	0	4	5.68

WP—Lanier. Time—2:06. Attendance—31,630. Umpires—HP, McGowan. 1B, Dunn. 2B, Pipgras. 3B, Sears.

1944 World Series—Composite Statistics

Batting

Cardinals	G	AB	R	H	RBI	2B	3B	HR	BB	SO	SB	CS	Avg	OBP	Slg
Augie Bergamo	3	6	0	0	1	0	0	0	2	3	0	0	.000	.250	.000
Harry Brecheen	1	4	0	0	0	0	0	0	1	0	0	0	.000	.000	.000
Mort Cooper	2	4	0	0	0	0	0	0	2	0	0	0	.000	.000	.000
Walker Cooper	6	22	1	7	2	2	1	0	3	2	0	0	.318	.400	.500
Blix Donnelly	2	1	0	0	0	0	0	0	1	0	0	0	.000	.000	.000
George Fallon	2	2	0	0	0	0	0	0	1	0	0	0	.000	.000	.000
Debs Garms	2	2	0	0	0	0	0	0	0	0	0	0	.000	.000	.000
Johnny Hopp	6	27	2	5	0	0	0	0	8	0	0	0	.185	.185	.185
Whitey Kurowski	6	23	2	5	1	1	0	0	1	4	0	1	.217	.250	.261
Max Lanier	2	4	0	1	0	0	0	0	0	0	0	0	.500	.500	.500
Danny Litwhiler	5	20	2	4	1	1	0	1	2	7	0	0	.200	.273	.400
Marty Marion	6	22	1	5	2	3	0	0	2	3	0	0	.227	.292	.364
Stan Musial	6	23	2	7	2	2	0	1	2	0	0	0	.304	.360	.522
Ken O'Dea	3	3	0	1	2	0	0	0	0	0	0	0	.333	.333	.333
Ray Sanders	6	21	5	6	1	0	0	1	5	8	0	0	.286	.423	.429
Freddy Schmidt	1	1	0	0	0	0	0	0	0	1	0	0	.000	.000	.000
Emil Verban	6	17	1	7	2	0	0	0	2	0	0	0	.412	.474	.412
Ted Wilks	2	2	0	0	0	0	0	0	0	2	0	0	.000	.000	.000
Totals	6	204	16	49	15	9	1	3	19	43	0	1	.240	.305	.338

Batting

Browns	G	AB	R	H	RBI	2B	3B	HR	BB	SO	SB	CS	Avg	OBP	Slg
Floyd Baker	2	2	0	0	0	0	0	0	0	2	0	0	.000	.000	.000
Milt Byrnes	3	2	0	0	0	0	0	0	1	2	0	0	.000	.333	.000
Mike Chartak	2	2	0	0	0	0	0	0	0	2	0	0	.000	.000	.000
Mark Christman	6	22	0	2	1	0	0	0	0	6	0	0	.091	.091	.091
Ellis Clary	1	1	0	0	0	0	0	0	0	0	0	0	.000	.000	.000
Denny Galehouse	2	5	0	1	0	0	0	0	1	1	0	0	.200	.333	.200
Don Gutteridge	6	21	1	3	0	1	0	0	3	5	0	0	.143	.250	.190
Red Hayworth	6	17	1	2	1	1	0	0	3	1	0	0	.118	.250	.176
Al Hollingsworth	1	1	0	0	0	0	0	0	0	0	0	0	.000	.000	.000
Jack Kramer	2	4	0	0	0	0	0	0	0	2	0	0	.000	.000	.000
Mike Kreevich	6	26	0	6	0	3	0	0	0	5	0	0	.231	.231	.346
Chet Laabs	5	15	1	3	0	1	1	0	2	6	0	0	.200	.294	.400
Frank Mancuso	2	3	0	2	1	0	0	0	0	0	0	0	.667	.667	.667
George McQuinn	6	16	2	7	5	2	0	1	7	2	0	0	.438	.609	.750
Gene Moore	6	22	4	4	0	0	0	0	3	6	0	0	.182	.280	.182
Bob Muncrief	2	1	0	0	0	0	0	0	0	1	0	0	.000	.000	.000
Nels Potter	2	4	0	0	0	0	0	0	0	1	0	0	.000	.000	.000
Vern Stephens	6	22	2	5	0	1	0	0	3	3	0	0	.227	.320	.273
Tom Turner	1	1	0	0	0	0	0	0	0	0	0	0	.000	.000	.000
Al Zarilla	4	10	1	1	0	1	0	0	0	4	0	0	.100	.100	.100
Totals	6	197	12	36	9	9	1	1	23	49	0	0	.183	.268	.254

Pitching

Cardinals	G	GS	CG	IP	H	R	ER	BB	SO	W-L	Sv-Op	Hld	ERA
Harry Brecheen	1	1	1	9.0	9	1	1	4	4	1-0	0-0	0	1.00
Bud Byerly	1	0	0	1.1	0	0	0	0	1	0-0	0-0	0	0.00
Mort Cooper	2	2	1	16.0	9	2	2	5	16	1-1	0-0	0	1.13
Blix Donnelly	2	0	0	6.0	2	0	0	1	9	1-0	0-0	0	0.00
Al Jurisich	1	0	0	0.2	2	2	2	1	0	0-0	0-0	0	27.00
Max Lanier	2	2	0	12.1	8	3	3	8	11	1-0	0-0	0	2.19
Freddy Schmidt	1	0	0	3.1	1	0	0	1	1	0-0	0-0	0	0.00
Ted Wilks	2	1	0	6.1	5	4	4	3	7	0-1	1-1	0	5.68
Totals	6	6	2	55.0	36	12	12	23	49	4-2	1-1	0	1.96

Pitching

Browns	G	GS	CG	IP	H	R	ER	BB	SO	W-L	Sv-Op	Hld	ERA
Denny Galehouse	2	2	2	18.0	13	3	3	5	15	1-1	0-0	0	1.50
Al Hollingsworth	1	0	0	4.0	5	1	1	2	1	0-0	0-0	0	2.25
Sig Jakucki	1	1	0	3.0	5	4	3	0	4	0-1	0-0	0	9.00
Jack Kramer	2	1	1	11.0	9	2	0	4	12	1-0	0-0	0	0.00
Bob Muncrief	2	0	0	6.2	5	1	1	4	4	0-1	0-0	0	1.35
Nels Potter	2	2	0	9.2	10	5	1	3	6	0-1	0-0	0	0.93
Tex Shirley	1	0	0	2.0	2	0	0	1	1	0-0	0-0	0	0.00
Totals	6	6	3	54.1	49	16	9	19	43	2-4	0-0	0	1.49

Fielding

Cardinals	Pos	G	PO	Ast	E	DP	PB	FPct
Augie Bergamo	lf	2	1	0	0	0	—	1.000
Harry Brecheen	p	1	1	3	0	0	—	1.000
Bud Byerly	p	1	0	0	0	0	—	—
Mort Cooper	p	2	0	6	0	0	—	1.000
Walker Cooper	c	6	55	0	0	0	1	1.000
Blix Donnelly	p	2	0	2	0	0	—	1.000
George Fallon	2b	2	0	0	0	0	—	—
Johnny Hopp	cf	6	14	0	0	0	—	1.000
Al Jurisich	p	1	0	0	0	0	—	—
Whitey Kurowski	3b	6	4	15	0	1	—	1.000
Max Lanier	p	2	1	1	0	0	—	1.000
Danny Litwhiler	lf	5	5	0	0	0	—	1.000
Marty Marion	ss	6	7	22	0	2	—	1.000
Stan Musial	rf	6	11	0	1	0	—	.917
Ray Sanders	1b	6	51	2	0	3	—	1.000
Freddy Schmidt	p	1	0	0	0	0	—	—
Emil Verban	2b	6	15	7	0	2	—	1.000
Ted Wilks	p	2	0	1	0	0	—	1.000
Totals		6	165	59	1	8	1	.996

Fielding

Browns	Pos	G	PO	Ast	E	DP	PB	FPct
Floyd Baker	2b	2	1	0	0	0	—	1.000
Mark Christman	3b	6	3	9	1	0	—	.923
Denny Galehouse	p	2	0	5	0	0	—	1.000
Don Gutteridge	2b	6	15	11	3	3	—	.897
Red Hayworth	c	6	45	2	1	0	0	.979
Al Hollingsworth	p	1	1	0	0	0	—	1.000
Sig Jakucki	p	1	0	1	0	0	—	1.000
Jack Kramer	p	2	0	3	0	0	—	1.000
Mike Kreevich	cf	6	20	2	0	0	—	1.000
Chet Laabs	lf	4	5	1	0	0	—	1.000
Frank Mancuso	c	1	3	0	0	0	—	1.000
George McQuinn	1b	6	50	2	0	3	—	1.000
Gene Moore	rf	6	8	0	0	0	—	1.000
Bob Muncrief	p	2	0	1	0	0	—	1.000
Nels Potter	p	2	2	0	2	0	—	.500
Tex Shirley	p	1	0	1	0	0	—	1.000
Vern Stephens	ss	6	9	19	3	4	—	.903
Al Zarilla	lf	3	2	0	0	0	—	1.000
Totals		6	163	58	10	10	0	.957

1945 Detroit Tigers (AL) 4, Chicago Cubs (NL) 3

After starting and losing Game 5 and winning Game 6 in relief, Hank Borowy proved unable to win Game 7, as the Detroit Tigers defeated the Chicago Cubs in seven games. Borowy beat the Tigers' Hal Newhouser in the opener, 9-0. Detroit's Virgil Trucks won Game 2, 4-1, on Hank Greenberg's three-run homer. Claude Passeau tossed the first one-hit shutout in World Series history for a 3-0 Chicago win in Game 3. Dizzy Trout put the Tigers even again with a 4-1 win in Game 4. Newhouser and Borowy faced off again in Game 5, but this time Newhouser got the win, 8-4. In Game 6, the Cubs pulled out a 12-inning 8-7 victory on Stan Hack's 12th-inning RBI double. Borowy tossed four innings of shutout relief for the victory. Borowy got the nod in Game 7, but was lifted after each of the first three batters he faced hit safely, and the Tigers triumphed, 9-3.

Game 1
Wednesday, October 3

Cubs	AB	R	H	RBI	BB	K	Avg
Stan Hack, 3b	5	0	1	0	0	1	.200
Don Johnson, 2b	5	2	2	0	0	0	.400
Peanuts Lowrey, lf	4	0	0	0	0	0	.000
Phil Cavarretta, 1b	4	3	3	2	1	0	.750
Andy Pafko, cf	4	3	3	1	1	0	.750
Bill Nicholson, rf	4	1	2	3	0	0	.500
Mickey Livingston, c	4	0	2	2	0	0	.500
Roy Hughes, ss	3	0	0	0	1	2	.000
Hank Borowy, p	3	0	0	0	0	2	.000
TOTALS	36	9	13	8	3	5	.361

Tigers	AB	R	H	RBI	BB	K	Avg
Skeeter Webb, ss	4	0	1	0	0	0	.250
John McHale, ph	1	0	0	0	0	0	.000
Eddie Mayo, 2b	4	0	2	0	0	1	.500
Doc Cramer, cf	3	0	0	0	1	0	.000
Hank Greenberg, lf	2	0	1	0	1	1	.500
Roy Cullenbine, rf	3	0	0	0	1	0	.000
Rudy York, 1b	3	0	1	0	1	0	.333
Jimmy Outlaw, 3b	4	0	1	0	0	0	.250
Paul Richards, c	2	0	0	0	1	1	.000
Chuck Hostetler, ph	1	0	0	0	0	0	.000
Hal Newhouser, p	1	0	0	0	0	0	.000
Al Benton, p	0	0	0	0	0	0	—
Zeb Eaton, ph	1	0	0	0	0	1	.000
Jim Tobin, p	1	0	0	0	0	0	.000
Les Mueller, p	0	0	0	0	0	0	—
Red Borom, ph	1	0	0	0	0	0	.000
TOTALS	31	0	6	0	5	4	.194

	1	2	3	4	5	6	7	8	9	R	H	E
Cubs	4	0	3	0	0	0	2	0	0	9	13	0
Tigers	0	0	0	0	0	0	0	0	0	0	6	0

DP—Cubs 2 (Hughes to Johnson to Cavarretta; Johnson to Hughes to Cavarretta). LOB—Cubs 5, Tigers 10. Scoring Position—Cubs 6-for-9, Tigers 0-for-9. 2B—Johnson (1), Pafko (1). 3B—Nicholson (1). HR—Cavarretta (1). S—Lowrey, Borowy. GDP—Cramer, Newhouser. SB—Johnson (1), Pafko (1). CS—Livingston 2 (2).

Cubs	IP	H	R	ER	BB	K	ERA
Hank Borowy (W, 1-0)	9.0	6	0	0	5	4	0.00

Tigers	IP	H	R	ER	BB	K	ERA
Hal Newhouser (L, 0-1)	2.2	8	7	7	1	3	23.63
Al Benton	1.1	4	0	0	1	0	0.00
Jim Tobin	3.0	4	2	2	1	0	6.00
Les Mueller	2.0	0	0	0	1	1	0.00

PB—Richards 2. HBP—Greenberg by Borowy. Time—2:10. Attendance—54,637. Umpires—HP, Summers. 1B, Jorda. 2B, Passarella. 3B, Conlan.

Game 2
Thursday, October 4

Cubs	AB	R	H	RBI	BB	K	Avg
Stan Hack, 3b	3	0	3	0	1	0	.500
Don Johnson, 2b	3	0	0	0	0	2	.250
Peanuts Lowrey, lf	4	0	2	0	0	0	.250
Phil Cavarretta, 1b	4	1	1	0	0	0	.500
Andy Pafko, cf	4	0	0	0	0	0	.375
Bill Nicholson, rf	3	0	1	1	1	0	.429
Paul Gillespie, c	4	0	0	0	0	0	.000
Roy Hughes, ss	3	0	0	0	1	0	.000
Hank Wyse, p	2	0	0	0	0	1	.000
Frank Secory, ph	1	0	0	0	0	0	.000
Paul Erickson, p	0	0	0	0	0	0	—
Heinz Becker, ph	1	0	0	0	0	1	.000
TOTALS	32	1	7	1	3	4	.295

Tigers	AB	R	H	RBI	BB	K	Avg
Skeeter Webb, ss	4	1	2	0	0	0	.375
Eddie Mayo, 2b	3	1	0	0	1	0	.286
Doc Cramer, cf	4	1	3	1	0	0	.429
Hank Greenberg, lf	3	1	1	3	1	0	.400
Roy Cullenbine, rf	2	0	0	0	2	0	.000
Rudy York, 1b	4	0	0	0	0	1	.143
Jimmy Outlaw, 3b	4	0	1	0	0	0	.250
Paul Richards, c	4	0	0	0	0	0	.000
Virgil Trucks, p	3	0	0	0	0	1	.000
TOTALS	31	4	7	4	4	2	.232

	1	2	3	4	5	6	7	8	9	R	H	E
Cubs	0	0	0	1	0	0	0	0	0	1	7	0
Tigers	0	0	0	0	4	0	0	0	x	4	7	0

LOB—Cubs 8, Tigers 7. Scoring Position—Cubs 2-for-9, Tigers 2-for-6. 2B—Hack (1), Cavarretta (1). HR—Greenberg (1). S—Johnson.

Cubs	IP	H	R	ER	BB	K	ERA
Hank Wyse (L, 0-1)	6.0	5	4	4	3	1	6.00
Paul Erickson	2.0	2	0	0	1	1	0.00

Tigers	IP	H	R	ER	BB	K	ERA
Virgil Trucks (W, 1-0)	9.0	7	1	1	3	4	1.00

Time—1:47. Attendance—53,636. Umpires—HP, Jorda. 1B, Passarella. 2B, Conlan. 3B, Summers.

Game 3
Friday, October 5

Cubs	AB	R	H	RBI	BB	K	Avg
Stan Hack, 3b	5	0	2	0	0	0	.462
Don Johnson, 2b	5	0	0	0	0	1	.154
Peanuts Lowrey, lf	4	1	2	0	0	0	.333
Phil Cavarretta, 1b	2	0	1	0	1	0	.500
Andy Pafko, cf	2	1	0	0	1	0	.300
Bill Nicholson, rf	4	0	1	1	0	1	.364
Mickey Livingston, c	4	1	1	0	0	0	.375
Roy Hughes, ss	3	0	1	1	0	0	.111
Claude Passeau, p	4	0	0	1	0	3	.000
TOTALS	33	3	8	3	2	5	.311

Tigers	AB	R	H	RBI	BB	K	Avg
Skeeter Webb, ss	3	0	0	0	0	0	.273
John McHale, ph	1	0	0	0	0	0	.000
Eddie Mayo, 2b	3	0	0	0	0	0	.200
Doc Cramer, cf	3	0	0	0	0	0	.300
Hank Greenberg, lf	3	0	0	0	0	1	.250
Roy Cullenbine, rf	3	0	0	0	0	0	.000
Rudy York, 1b	3	0	1	0	0	0	.200
Jimmy Outlaw, 3b	3	0	0	0	0	0	.182
Bob Swift, c	1	0	0	0	1	0	.000
Red Borom, pr	0	0	0	0	0	0	.000
Paul Richards, c	1	0	0	0	0	0	.000
Stubby Overmire, p	1	0	0	0	0	0	.000
Hub Walker, ph	1	0	0	0	0	0	.000
Al Benton, p	0	0	0	0	0	0	—
Chuck Hostetler, ph	1	0	0	0	0	0	.000
TOTALS	27	0	1	0	1	1	.169

	1	2	3	4	5	6	7	8	9	R	H	E
Cubs	0	0	0	2	0	0	1	0	0	3	8	0
Tigers	0	0	0	0	0	0	0	0	0	0	1	2

E—Mayo 2. DP—Cubs 1 (Johnson to Cavarretta). LOB—Cubs 8, Tigers 1. Scoring Position—Cubs 2-for-11, Tigers 0-for-0. 2B—Hack (2), Lowrey (1), Livingston (1). S—Cavarretta, Pafko, Hughes. GDP—Walker. CS—Hack (1).

Cubs	IP	H	R	ER	BB	K	ERA
Claude Passeau (W, 1-0)	9.0	1	0	0	1	1	0.00

Tigers	IP	H	R	ER	BB	K	ERA
Stubby Overmire (L, 0-1)	6.0	4	2	2	2	2	3.00
Al Benton	3.0	4	1	1	0	3	2.08

Time—1:55. Attendance—55,500. Umpires—HP, Passarella. 1B, Conlan. 2B, Summers. 3B, Jorda.

Game 4
Saturday, October 6

Tigers	AB	R	H	RBI	BB	K	Avg
Skeeter Webb, ss	5	0	0	0	0	1	.188
Eddie Mayo, 2b	3	1	0	0	1	0	.154
Doc Cramer, cf	4	1	2	0	0	0	.357
Hank Greenberg, lf	3	1	1	1	1	2	.273
Roy Cullenbine, rf	3	1	1	1	1	0	.091
Rudy York, 1b	3	0	0	0	1	0	.154
Jimmy Outlaw, 3b	4	0	1	1	0	0	.200
Paul Richards, c	4	0	1	0	1	1	.091
Dizzy Trout, p	4	0	1	0	0	0	.250
TOTALS	33	4	7	4	4	4	.194

Cubs	AB	R	H	RBI	BB	K	Avg
Stan Hack, 3b	4	0	0	0	0	0	.353
Don Johnson, 2b	4	1	2	0	0	0	.235
Peanuts Lowrey, lf	4	0	1	0	0	1	.313
Phil Cavarretta, 1b	4	0	0	0	0	2	.357
Andy Pafko, cf	4	0	0	0	0	0	.214
Bill Nicholson, rf	4	0	0	0	0	2	.267
Mickey Livingston, c	3	0	1	0	0	0	.364
Roy Hughes, ss	1	0	0	0	1	0	.100
Heinz Becker, ph	1	0	1	0	0	0	.500
Lennie Merullo, pr-ss	0	0	0	0	0	0	—
Ray Prim, p	0	0	0	0	0	0	—
Paul Derringer, p	0	0	0	0	0	0	—
Frank Secory, ph	1	0	0	0	0	1	.000
Hy Vandenberg, p	0	0	0	0	0	0	—
Paul Gillespie, ph	1	0	0	0	0	0	.000
Paul Erickson, p	0	0	0	0	0	0	—
TOTALS	31	1	5	0	1	6	.268

	1	2	3	4	5	6	7	8	9	R	H	E
Tigers	0	0	0	4	0	0	0	0	0	4	7	1
Cubs	0	0	0	0	0	1	0	0	0	1	5	1

E—Nicholson, York. LOB—Tigers 6, Cubs 5. Scoring Position—Tigers 3-for-6, Cubs 0-for-5. 2B—Cullenbine (1). 3B—Johnson (1). S—Prim.

Tigers	IP	H	R	ER	BB	K	ERA
Dizzy Trout (W, 1-0)	9.0	5	1	0	1	6	0.00

Cubs	IP	H	R	ER	BB	K	ERA
Ray Prim (L, 0-1)	3.1	3	4	4	1	1	10.80
Paul Derringer	1.2	2	0	0	2	1	0.00
Hy Vandenberg	2.0	0	0	0	0	0	0.00
Paul Erickson	2.0	2	0	0	1	2	0.00

PB—Livingston. Time—2:00. Attendance—42,923. Umpires—HP, Conlan. 1B, Summers. 2B, Jorda. 3B, Passarella.

Game 5
Sunday, October 7

Tigers	AB	R	H	RBI	BB	K	Avg
Skeeter Webb, ss	4	1	1	1	1	0	.200
Eddie Mayo, 2b	4	0	2	0	1	0	.235
Doc Cramer, cf	4	2	1	1	0	0	.333
Hank Greenberg, lf	5	3	3	1	0	0	.375
Roy Cullenbine, rf	4	1	2	2	0	1	.200
Rudy York, 1b	5	1	1	1	0	1	.167
Jimmy Outlaw, 3b	4	0	0	1	0	1	.158
Paul Richards, c	4	0	1	0	1	0	.133
Hal Newhouser, p	3	0	0	1	1	1	.000
TOTALS	37	8	11	8	4	4	.218

Cubs	AB	R	H	RBI	BB	K	Avg
Stan Hack, 3b	3	0	1	1	1	0	.350
Don Johnson, 2b	3	0	0	0	0	2	.200
Peanuts Lowrey, lf	4	1	1	0	0	0	.300
Phil Cavarretta, 1b	3	1	1	0	1	1	.353
Andy Pafko, cf	4	1	0	0	0	3	.167
Bill Nicholson, rf	4	0	1	2	0	0	.263
Mickey Livingston, c	4	0	1	1	0	0	.333
Lennie Merullo, ss	2	0	0	0	0	1	.000
Dewey Williams, ph	1	0	0	0	0	1	.000
Bill Schuster, ss	1	0	0	0	0	0	.000
Hank Borowy, p	1	1	1	0	0	0	.250
Hy Vandenberg, p	0	0	0	0	0	0	—
Bob Chipman, p	0	0	0	0	0	0	—
Eddie Sauer, ph	1	0	0	0	0	1	.000
Paul Derringer, p	0	0	0	0	0	0	—
Frank Secory, ph	1	0	1	0	0	0	.333
Paul Erickson, p	0	0	0	0	0	0	—
TOTALS	32	4	7	4	2	9	.270

	1	2	3	4	5	6	7	8	9	R	H	E
Tigers	0	0	1	0	0	4	1	0	2	8	11	0
Cubs	0	0	1	0	0	0	2	0	1	4	7	2

E—Pafko, Hack. DP—Tigers 1 (Mayo to York to Webb), Cubs 1 (Johnson to Merullo to Cavarretta). LOB—Tigers 9, Cubs 4. Scoring Position—Tigers 4-for-14, Cubs 3-for-8. 2B—Greenberg 3 (3), Cullenbine (2), Cavarretta (2), Livingston (2), Borowy (1). S—Cullenbine, Outlaw, Johnson. GDP—Newhouser. CS—Hack (2).

Tigers	IP	H	R	ER	BB	K	ERA
Hal Newhouser (W, 1-1)	9.0	7	4	4	2	9	8.49

Cubs	IP	H	R	ER	BB	K	ERA
Hank Borowy (L, 1-1)	5.0	8	5	5	1	4	3.21
Hy Vandenberg	0.2	0	0	0	2	0	0.00
Bob Chipman	0.1	0	0	0	1	0	0.00
Paul Derringer	2.0	1	1	1	0	0	2.45
Paul Erickson	1.0	2	2	2	0	0	3.60

Borowy pitched to five batters in the 6th.

HBP—Cramer by Erickson. Time—2:18. Attendance—43,463. Umpires—HP, Summers. 1B, Jorda. 2B, Passarella. 3B, Conlan.

Game 6
Monday, October 8

Tigers	AB	R	H	RBI	BB	K	Avg
Skeeter Webb, ss	3	0	0	0	0	0	.174
Chuck Hostetler, ph	1	0	0	0	0	0	.000
Joe Hoover, ss	3	1	1	1	0	0	.333
Eddie Mayo, 2b	6	0	1	1	0	0	.217
Doc Cramer, cf	6	1	2	1	0	0	.333
Hank Greenberg, lf	5	2	1	1	1	0	.333
Roy Cullenbine, rf	5	1	2	1	1	0	.250
Rudy York, 1b	6	0	2	1	0	1	.208
Jimmy Outlaw, 3b	5	0	1	0	1	0	.167
Paul Richards, c	0	0	0	1	2	0	.133
Bob Maier, ph	1	0	1	0	0	0	1.000
Bob Swift, c	2	1	1	0	1	0	.333
Virgil Trucks, p	1	0	0	0	0	0	.000
George Caster, p	0	0	0	0	0	0	—
John McHale, ph	1	0	0	0	0	1	.000
Tommy Bridges, p	0	0	0	0	0	0	—
Al Benton, p	0	0	0	0	0	0	—
Hub Walker, ph	1	1	1	0	0	0	.500
Dizzy Trout, p	2	0	0	0	0	0	.167
TOTALS	48	7	13	7	7	2	.226

Cubs	AB	R	H	RBI	BB	K	Avg
Stan Hack, 3b	5	1	4	3	2	0	.440
Don Johnson, 2b	4	0	0	0	0	2	.167
Peanuts Lowrey, lf	5	1	1	0	1	1	.280
Phil Cavarretta, 1b	5	1	2	2	1	0	.364
Andy Pafko, cf	6	0	2	0	0	0	.208
Bill Nicholson, rf	5	0	0	1	0	2	.208
Mickey Livingston, c	3	2	2	1	1	0	.389
Paul Gillespie, ph	1	0	0	0	0	0	.000
Dewey Williams, c	1	0	0	0	0	0	.000
Roy Hughes, ss	4	1	3	2	0	1	.286
Heinz Becker, ph	0	0	0	0	1	0	.500
Cy Block, pr	0	0	0	0	0	0	—
Lennie Merullo, ss	0	0	0	0	0	0	.000
Frank Secory, ph	1	0	1	0	0	0	.500
Bill Schuster, pr	0	1	0	0	0	0	.000
Claude Passeau, p	3	1	0	0	0	1	.000
Hank Wyse, p	1	0	0	0	0	1	.000
Ray Prim, p	0	0	0	0	0	0	—
Hank Borowy, p	2	0	0	0	0	1	.167
TOTALS	46	8	15	8	7	9	.263

	1	2	3	4	5	6	7	8	9	10	11	12	R	H	E
Tigers	0	1	0	0	0	0	2	4	0	0	0	0	7	13	1
Cubs	0	0	0	0	4	1	2	0	0	0	0	1	8	15	3

E—Johnson, Richards, Hack 2. DP—Tigers 2 (Mayo to Webb to Richards; Mayo to Hoover to York), Cubs 1 (Merullo to Johnson to Cavarretta). LOB—Tigers 12, Cubs 12. Scoring Position—Tigers 5-for-15, Cubs 4-for-17. 2B—York (1), Hack (3), Pafko (2), Livingston (3), Hughes (1), Walker (1). HR—Greenberg (2). S—Johnson 2. GDP—Greenberg, Lowrey. SB—Cullenbine (1). CS—Hughes (1), Hoover (1).

Tigers	IP	H	R	ER	BB	K	ERA
Virgil Trucks	4.1	7	4	4	2	3	3.38
George Caster	0.2	0	0	0	0	1	0.00
Tommy Bridges	1.2	3	3	3	3	1	16.20
Al Benton	0.1	1	0	0	0	1	1.93
Dizzy Trout (L, 1-1)	4.2	4	1	1	2	3	0.66

Cubs	IP	H	R	ER	BB	K	ERA
Claude Passeau	6.2	5	3	3	6	2	1.72
Hank Wyse (H, 1)	0.2	3	3	2	1	0	8.10
Ray Prim (BS, 1)	0.2	1	1	1	0	0	11.25
Hank Borowy (W, 2-1)	4.0	4	0	0	0	0	2.50

Time—3:28. Attendance—41,708. Umpires—HP, Jorda. 1B, Passarella. 2B, Conlan. 3B, Summers.

Game 7
Wednesday, October 10

Tigers	AB	R	H	RBI	BB	K	Avg
Skeeter Webb, ss	4	2	1	0	1	0	.185
Eddie Mayo, 2b	5	2	2	1	0	1	.250
Doc Cramer, cf	5	2	3	1	0	0	.379
Hank Greenberg, lf	2	0	0	1	2	1	.304
Ed Mierkowicz, lf	0	0	0	0	0	0	—
Roy Cullenbine, rf	2	2	0	0	3	1	.227
Rudy York, 1b	4	0	0	1	1	1	.179
Jimmy Outlaw, 3b	4	1	1	1	1	0	.179
Paul Richards, c	4	0	2	4	0	1	.211
Bob Swift, c	1	0	0	0	0	0	.250
Hal Newhouser, p	4	0	0	0	0	0	.000
TOTALS	35	9	9	9	8	5	.231

Cubs	AB	R	H	RBI	BB	K	Avg
Stan Hack, 3b	5	0	0	0	0	1	.367
Don Johnson, 2b	5	1	1	0	0	1	.172
Peanuts Lowrey, lf	4	1	2	0	0	0	.310
Phil Cavarretta, 1b	4	1	3	1	0	0	.423
Andy Pafko, cf	4	0	1	0	0	2	.214
Bill Nicholson, rf	4	0	1	0	0	0	.214
Mickey Livingston, c	4	0	1	0	0	1	.364
Roy Hughes, ss	3	0	1	0	1	2	.294
Hank Borowy, p	0	0	0	0	0	0	.167
Paul Derringer, p	0	0	0	0	0	0	—
Hy Vandenberg, p	1	0	0	0	0	0	.000
Eddie Sauer, ph	1	0	0	0	0	1	.000
Paul Erickson, p	0	0	0	0	0	0	—
Frank Secory, ph	1	0	0	0	0	1	.400
Claude Passeau, p	0	0	0	0	0	0	.000
Hank Wyse, p	0	0	0	0	0	0	.000
Clyde McCullough, ph	1	0	0	0	0	1	.000
TOTALS	37	3	10	3	1	10	.274

	1	2	3	4	5	6	7	8	9	R	H	E
Tigers	5	1	0	0	0	0	1	2	0	9	9	1
Cubs	1	0	0	1	0	0	0	1	0	3	10	0

E—Newhouser. DP—Tigers 1 (Webb to Mayo to York). LOB—Tigers 8, Cubs 8. Scoring Position—Tigers 2-for-11, Cubs 2-for-10. 2B—Mayo (1), Richards 2 (2), Johnson (2), Nicholson (1). 3B—Pafko (1). S—Greenberg. GDP—Pafko. SB—Cramer (1), Outlaw (1).

Tigers	IP	H	R	ER	BB	K	ERA
Hal Newhouser (W, 2-1)	9.0	10	3	3	1	10	6.10

Cubs	IP	H	R	ER	BB	K	ERA
Hank Borowy (L, 2-2)	0.0	3	3	3	0	0	4.00
Paul Derringer	1.2	2	3	3	5	0	6.75
Hy Vandenberg	3.1	1	0	0	1	3	0.00
Paul Erickson	2.0	2	1	1	2	1	3.86
Claude Passeau	1.0	1	2	2	1	0	2.70
Hank Wyse	1.0	0	0	0	0	1	7.04

Borowy pitched to three batters in the 1st.

WP—Newhouser. Time—2:31. Attendance—41,590. Umpires—HP, Passarella. 1B, Conlan. 2B, Summers. 3B, Jorda.

1945 World Series—Composite Statistics

Batting

Tigers

Tigers	G	AB	R	H	RBI	2B	3B	HR	BB	SO	SB	CS	Avg	OBP	Slg
Red Borom	2	1	0	0	0	0	0	0	0	0	0	0	.000	.000	.000
Doc Cramer	7	29	7	11	4	0	0	0	1	0	1	0	.379	.419	.379
Roy Cullenbine	7	22	5	5	4	2	0	0	8	2	1	0	.227	.433	.318
Zeb Eaton	1	1	0	0	0	0	0	0	0	1	0	0	.000	.000	.000
Hank Greenberg	7	23	7	7	7	3	0	2	6	5	0	0	.304	.467	.696
Joe Hoover	1	3	1	1	1	0	0	0	0	0	0	1	.333	.333	.333
Chuck Hostetler	3	3	0	0	0	0	0	0	0	0	0	0	.000	.000	.000
Bob Maier	1	1	0	1	0	0	0	0	0	0	0	0	1.000	1.000	1.000
Eddie Mayo	7	28	4	7	2	1	0	0	3	2	0	0	.250	.323	.286
John McHale	3	3	0	0	0	0	0	0	0	1	0	0	.000	.000	.000
Hal Newhouser	3	8	0	0	1	0	0	0	1	1	0	0	.000	.111	.000
Jimmy Outlaw	7	28	1	5	3	0	0	0	2	1	1	0	.179	.233	.179
Stubby Overmire	1	1	0	0	0	0	0	0	0	0	0	0	.000	.000	.000
Paul Richards	7	19	0	4	6	2	0	0	4	3	0	0	.211	.348	.316
Bob Swift	3	4	1	1	0	0	0	0	2	0	0	0	.250	.500	.250
Jim Tobin	1	1	0	0	0	0	0	0	0	0	0	0	.000	.000	.000
Dizzy Trout	2	6	0	1	0	0	0	0	0	0	0	0	.167	.167	.167
Virgil Trucks	2	4	0	0	0	0	0	0	1	1	0	0	.000	.200	.000
Hub Walker	2	2	1	1	0	1	0	0	0	0	0	0	.500	.500	1.000
Skeeter Webb	7	27	4	5	1	0	0	0	2	1	0	0	.185	.241	.185
Rudy York	7	28	1	5	3	1	0	0	3	4	0	0	.179	.258	.214
Totals	7	242	32	54	32	10	0	2	33	22	3	1	.223	.321	.289

Cubs

Cubs	G	AB	R	H	RBI	2B	3B	HR	BB	SO	SB	CS	Avg	OBP	Slg
Heinz Becker	3	2	0	1	0	0	0	0	1	1	0	0	.500	.667	.500
Cy Block	1	0	0	0	0	0	0	0	0	0	0	0	—	—	—
Hank Borowy	4	6	1	1	0	1	0	0	0	3	0	0	.167	.167	.333
Phil Cavarretta	7	26	7	11	5	2	0	1	4	3	0	0	.423	.500	.615
Paul Gillespie	3	6	0	0	0	0	0	0	0	0	0	0	.000	.000	.000
Stan Hack	7	30	1	11	4	3	0	0	4	2	0	2	.367	.441	.467
Roy Hughes	6	17	1	5	3	1	0	0	4	5	0	1	.294	.429	.353
Don Johnson	7	29	4	5	0	2	1	0	8	1	0	0	.172	.172	.310
Mickey Livingston	6	22	3	8	4	3	0	0	1	1	0	2	.364	.391	.500
Peanuts Lowrey	7	29	4	9	0	1	0	0	1	2	0	0	.310	.333	.345
Clyde McCullough	1	1	0	0	0	0	0	0	0	1	0	0	.000	.000	.000
Lennie Merullo	3	2	0	0	0	0	0	0	0	1	0	0	.000	.000	.000
Bill Nicholson	7	28	1	6	8	1	1	0	2	5	0	0	.214	.267	.321
Andy Pafko	7	28	5	6	2	2	1	0	2	5	1	0	.214	.267	.357
Claude Passeau	3	7	1	0	1	0	0	0	0	4	0	0	.000	.000	.000
Ray Prim	2	0	0	0	0	0	0	0	0	0	0	0	—	—	—
Eddie Sauer	2	2	0	0	0	0	0	0	0	2	0	0	.000	.000	.000
Bill Schuster	2	1	1	0	0	0	0	0	0	0	0	0	.000	.000	.000
Frank Secory	5	5	0	2	0	0	0	0	0	2	0	0	.400	.400	.400
Hy Vandenberg	3	1	0	0	0	0	0	0	0	0	0	0	.000	.000	.000
Dewey Williams	2	2	0	0	0	0	0	0	0	1	0	0	.000	.000	.000
Hank Wyse	3	3	0	0	0	0	0	0	0	2	0	0	.000	.000	.000
Totals	7	247	29	65	27	16	3	1	19	48	2	5	.263	.316	.364

Pitching

Tigers

Tigers	G	GS	CG	IP	H	R	ER	BB	SO	W-L	Sv-Op	Hld	ERA
Al Benton	3	0	0	4.2	6	1	1	0	5	0-0	0-0	0	1.93
Tommy Bridges	1	0	0	1.2	3	3	3	3	1	0-0	0-0	0	16.20
George Caster	1	0	0	0.2	0	0	0	0	1	0-0	0-0	0	0.00
Les Mueller	1	0	0	2.0	0	0	0	1	0	0-0	0-0	0	0.00
Hal Newhouser	3	3	2	20.2	25	14	14	4	22	2-1	0-0	0	6.10
Stubby Overmire	1	1	0	6.0	4	2	2	2	2	0-1	0-0	0	3.00
Jim Tobin	1	0	0	3.0	4	2	2	1	0	0-0	0-0	0	6.00
Dizzy Trout	2	1	1	13.2	9	2	1	3	9	1-1	0-0	0	0.66
Virgil Trucks	2	2	1	13.1	14	5	5	5	7	1-0	0-0	0	3.38
Totals	7	7	4	65.2	65	29	28	19	48	4-3	0-0	0	3.84

Cubs

Cubs	G	GS	CG	IP	H	R	ER	BB	SO	W-L	Sv-Op	Hld	ERA
Hank Borowy	4	3	1	18.0	21	8	8	6	8	2-2	0-0	0	4.00
Bob Chipman	1	0	0	0.1	0	0	0	1	0	0-0	0-0	0	0.00
Paul Derringer	3	0	0	5.1	5	4	4	7	1	0-0	0-0	0	6.75
Paul Erickson	4	0	0	7.0	8	3	3	3	5	0-0	0-0	0	3.86
Claude Passeau	3	2	1	16.2	7	5	5	8	3	1-0	0-0	0	2.70
Ray Prim	2	1	0	4.0	4	5	5	1	1	0-1	0-1	0	11.25
Hy Vandenberg	3	0	0	6.0	1	0	0	3	3	0-0	0-0	0	0.00
Hank Wyse	3	1	0	7.2	8	7	6	4	1	0-1	0-0	1	7.04
Totals	7	7	2	65.0	54	32	31	33	22	3-4	0-1	1	4.29

Fielding

Tigers

Tigers	Pos	G	PO	Ast	E	DP	PB	FPct
Al Benton	p	3	0	3	0	0	—	1.000
Tommy Bridges	p	1	0	0	0	0	—	—
George Caster	p	1	0	0	0	0	—	—
Doc Cramer	cf	7	21	0	0	0	—	1.000
Roy Cullenbine	rf	7	8	0	0	0	—	1.000
Hank Greenberg	lf	7	8	1	0	0	—	1.000
Joe Hoover	ss	1	1	1	0	1	—	1.000
Eddie Mayo	2b	7	18	13	2	4	—	.939
Ed Mierkowicz	lf	1	0	0	0	0	—	—
Les Mueller	p	1	0	0	0	0	—	—
Hal Newhouser	p	3	2	6	1	0	—	.889
Jimmy Outlaw	3b	7	5	15	0	0	—	1.000
Stubby Overmire	p	1	0	1	0	0	—	1.000
Paul Richards	c	7	46	5	1	1	2	.981
Bob Swift	c	3	9	1	0	0	0	1.000
Jim Tobin	p	1	0	1	0	0	—	1.000
Dizzy Trout	p	2	2	5	0	0	—	1.000
Virgil Trucks	p	2	1	1	0	0	—	1.000
Skeeter Webb	ss	7	9	24	0	3	—	1.000
Rudy York	1b	7	67	8	1	3	—	.987
Totals		7	197	85	5	12	2	.983

Cubs

Cubs	Pos	G	PO	Ast	E	DP	PB	FPct
Hank Borowy	p	4	1	2	0	0	—	1.000
Phil Cavarretta	1b	7	71	3	0	5	—	1.000
Bob Chipman	p	1	0	0	0	0	—	—
Paul Derringer	p	3	0	0	0	0	—	—
Paul Erickson	p	4	0	1	0	0	—	1.000
Paul Gillespie	c	1	3	0	0	0	0	1.000
Stan Hack	3b	7	12	13	3	0	—	.893
Roy Hughes	ss	6	13	18	0	2	—	1.000
Don Johnson	2b	7	11	23	1	5	—	.971
Mickey Livingston	c	6	22	4	0	0	1	1.000
Peanuts Lowrey	lf	7	23	1	0	0	—	1.000
Lennie Merullo	ss	3	4	2	0	2	—	1.000
Bill Nicholson	rf	7	9	0	1	0	—	.900
Andy Pafko	cf	7	22	2	1	0	—	.960
Claude Passeau	p	3	1	3	0	0	—	1.000
Ray Prim	p	2	0	1	0	0	—	1.000
Bill Schuster	ss	1	1	2	0	0	—	1.000
Hy Vandenberg	p	3	1	2	0	0	—	1.000
Dewey Williams	c	1	1	1	0	0	0	1.000
Hank Wyse	p	3	0	0	0	0	—	—
Totals		7	195	78	6	14	1	.978

1946 St. Louis Cardinals (NL) 4, Boston Red Sox (AL) 3

Enos Slaughter raced around from first base to score the go-ahead run in the eighth inning of Game 7, sending the St. Louis Cardinals to a 4-3 win and a seven-game World Series victory over the Boston Red Sox. The Cardinals held a 2-1 lead in Game 1 until Tom McBride tied it with an RBI single in the ninth. Rudy York's homer off Howie Pollet won it for Boston in the following frame. Harry Brecheen evened the score with a four-hit shutout in Game 2. Boo Ferriss returned the favor with a six-hit whitewash of the Cardinals in Game 3. Slaughter, Whitey Kurowski and Joe Garagiola notched four hits apiece as the Cards ran away with a 12-3 win in the fourth game, but Joe Dobson got Boston a 6-3 win in Game 5. Brecheen came through with a 4-1 victory in Game 6 to force a seventh game. With the score tied in the bottom of the eighth, Harry Walker doubled and Boston shortstop Johnny Pesky hesitated, enabling Slaughter to beat his relay to the plate. Brecheen, pitching in relief, notched his third victory.

Game 1

Sunday, October 6

Red Sox	AB	R	H	RBI	BB	K	Avg
Tom McBride, rf	5	0	1	1	0	1	.200
Wally Moses, rf	0	0	0	0	0	0	—
Johnny Pesky, ss	5	0	0	0	0	0	.000
Dom DiMaggio, cf	5	0	2	0	0	0	.400
Ted Williams, lf	3	0	1	0	2	0	.333
Rudy York, 1b	4	2	1	1	0	0	.250
Bobby Doerr, 2b	4	0	1	0	1	1	.250
Mike Higgins, 3b	4	0	2	1	0	0	.500
Don Gutteridge, pr	0	1	0	0	0	0	
Earl Johnson, p	1	0	0	0	0	0	.000
Hal Wagner, c	3	0	0	0	0	0	.000
Rip Russell, ph-3b	1	0	1	0	0	0	1.000
Tex Hughson, p	2	0	0	0	1	0	.000
Roy Partee, ph-c	1	0	0	0	0	1	.000
TOTALS	38	3	9	3	4	3	.237

Cardinals	AB	R	H	RBI	BB	K	Avg
Red Schoendienst, 2b	5	1	2	0	0	0	.400
Terry Moore, cf	4	0	0	0	0	0	.000
Stan Musial, 1b	5	0	1	1	0	0	.200
Enos Slaughter, rf	4	0	1	0	1	0	.250
Whitey Kurowski, 3b	3	1	1	0	0	1	.333
Joe Garagiola, c	4	0	1	1	0	1	.250
Harry Walker, lf	2	0	1	0	1	1	.500
Erv Dusak, ph-lf	1	0	0	0	0	0	.000
Marty Marion, ss	3	0	0	0	0	1	.000
Howie Pollet, p	4	0	0	0	0	1	.000
TOTALS	35	2	7	2	2	6	.200

	1	2	3	4	5	6	7	8	9	10	R	H	E
Red Sox	0	1	0	0	0	0	0	0	1	1	3	9	2
Cardinals	0	0	0	0	1	0	1	0	0	0	2	7	0

E—McBride, Pesky. LOB—Red Sox 10, Cardinals 8. Scoring Position—Red Sox 2-for-7, Cardinals 2-for-10. 2B—Musial (1), Garagiola (1). 3B—Slaughter (1). HR—York (1). S—Moore, Marion. SB—Schoendienst (1).

Red Sox	IP	H	R	ER	BB	K	ERA
Tex Hughson	8.0	7	2	2	2	5	2.25
Earl Johnson (W, 1-0)	2.0	0	0	0	0	1	0.00

Cardinals	IP	H	R	ER	BB	K	ERA
Howie Pollet (L, 0-1)	10.0	9	3	3	4	3	2.70

HBP—York by Pollet, Kurowski by Hughson. Time—2:39. Attendance—36,218. Umpires—HP, Ballanfant. 1B, Hubbard. 2B, Barlick. 3B, Berry.

Game 2

Monday, October 7

Red Sox	AB	R	H	RBI	BB	K	Avg
Tom McBride, rf	4	0	1	0	0	0	.222
Johnny Pesky, ss	4	0	0	0	0	1	.000
Dom DiMaggio, cf	4	0	1	0	0	0	.333
Ted Williams, lf	4	0	0	0	0	1	.143
Rudy York, 1b	2	0	0	0	2	0	.167
Bobby Doerr, 2b	4	0	1	0	0	0	.250
Mike Higgins, 3b	2	0	0	0	1	0	.333
Roy Partee, c	2	0	0	0	0	0	.000
Hal Wagner, c	1	0	0	0	0	1	.000
Mickey Harris, p	2	0	1	0	0	0	.500
Leon Culberson, ph	1	0	0	0	0	1	.000
Joe Dobson, p	0	0	0	0	0	0	—
TOTALS	30	0	4	0	3	4	.188

Cardinals	AB	R	H	RBI	BB	K	Avg
Red Schoendienst, 2b	3	0	0	0	0	0	.250
Terry Moore, cf	3	0	1	1	1	0	.143
Stan Musial, 1b	4	0	0	1	0	1	.111
Whitey Kurowski, 3b	4	0	1	0	0	0	.286
Enos Slaughter, rf	4	0	0	0	0	0	.125
Erv Dusak, lf	2	0	1	0	1	1	.333
Dick Sisler, ph	1	0	0	0	0	0	.000
Harry Walker, lf	0	0	0	0	0	0	.500
Marty Marion, ss	4	0	1	0	0	0	.000
Del Rice, c	2	2	2	0	1	0	1.000
Harry Brecheen, p	3	1	1	1	0	1	.333
TOTALS	30	3	6	3	3	3	.211

	1	2	3	4	5	6	7	8	9	R	H	E
Red Sox	0	0	0	0	0	0	0	0	0	0	4	1
Cardinals	0	0	1	0	2	0	0	0	x	3	6	0

E—Higgins. DP—Cardinals 1 (Marion to Musial). LOB—Red Sox 6, Cardinals 7. Scoring Position—Red Sox 0-for-2, Cardinals 2-for-8. 2B—Dusak (1), Rice (1). S—Schoendienst. GDP—DiMaggio.

Red Sox	IP	H	R	ER	BB	K	ERA
Mickey Harris (L, 0-1)	7.0	6	3	2	3	3	2.57
Joe Dobson	1.0	0	0	0	0	0	0.00

Cardinals	IP	H	R	ER	BB	K	ERA
Harry Brecheen (W, 1-0)	9.0	4	0	0	3	4	0.00

Time—1:56. Attendance—35,815. Umpires—HP, Hubbard. 1B, Barlick. 2B, Berry. 3B, Ballanfant.

Game 3

Wednesday, October 9

Cardinals	AB	R	H	RBI	BB	K	Avg
Red Schoendienst, 2b	4	0	0	0	0	0	.167
Terry Moore, cf	4	0	0	0	0	1	.091
Stan Musial, 1b	3	0	1	0	1	0	.167
Enos Slaughter, rf	4	0	1	0	0	1	.167
Whitey Kurowski, 3b	3	0	0	0	0	0	.200
Joe Garagiola, c	3	0	1	0	0	0	.286
Harry Walker, lf	3	0	1	0	0	0	.400
Marty Marion, ss	3	0	1	0	0	0	.100
Murry Dickson, p	2	0	1	0	0	0	.500
Dick Sisler, ph	1	0	0	0	0	0	.000
Ted Wilks, p	0	0	0	0	0	0	—
TOTALS	30	0	6	0	1	2	.181

Red Sox	AB	R	H	RBI	BB	K	Avg
Wally Moses, rf	3	0	0	0	1	1	.000
Johnny Pesky, ss	4	1	2	0	0	0	.154
Dom DiMaggio, cf	4	0	1	0	0	0	.308
Ted Williams, lf	3	1	1	0	1	1	.200
Rudy York, 1b	4	2	2	3	0	0	.300
Bobby Doerr, 2b	4	0	2	0	0	1	.333
Mike Higgins, 3b	3	0	0	0	1	0	.222
Hal Wagner, c	3	0	0	0	0	0	.000
Boo Ferriss, p	4	0	0	0	0	1	.000
TOTALS	32	4	8	3	4	4	.210

	1	2	3	4	5	6	7	8	9	R	H	E
Cardinals	0	0	0	0	0	0	0	0	0	0	6	1
Red Sox	3	0	0	0	0	0	0	1	x	4	8	0

E—Schoendienst. DP—Red Sox 2 (DiMaggio to Pesky; Pesky to Doerr to York). LOB—Cardinals 4, Red Sox 8. Scoring Position—Cardinals 0-for-2, Red Sox 1-for-10. 2B—Dickson (1), DiMaggio (1), Doerr (1). 3B—Musial (1). HR—York (2). S—Wagner. GDP—Kurowski. SB—Musial (1). CS—Musial (1).

Cardinals	IP	H	R	ER	BB	K	ERA
Murry Dickson (L, 0-1)	7.0	6	3	3	3	4	3.86
Ted Wilks	1.0	2	1	0	0	0	0.00

Red Sox	IP	H	R	ER	BB	K	ERA
Boo Ferriss (W, 1-0)	9.0	6	0	0	1	2	0.00

PB—Garagiola. Time—1:54. Attendance—34,500. Umpires—HP, Barlick. 1B, Barry. 2B, Ballanfant. 3B, Hubbard.

Game 4

Thursday, October 10

Cardinals	AB	R	H	RBI	BB	K	Avg
Red Schoendienst, 2b	6	1	1	0	0	0	.167
Terry Moore, cf	4	1	1	0	1	0	.133
Stan Musial, 1b	5	1	1	2	1	0	.176
Enos Slaughter, rf	6	4	4	1	0	0	.333
Whitey Kurowski, 3b	5	2	4	1	0	0	.400
Joe Garagiola, c	5	1	4	3	0	0	.500
Harry Walker, lf	2	1	1	1	2	1	.429
Marty Marion, ss	4	1	3	3	0	0	.286
George Munger, p	4	0	1	0	0	2	.250
TOTALS	41	12	20	11	4	3	.283

Red Sox	AB	R	H	RBI	BB	K	Avg
Wally Moses, rf	5	0	4	0	0	0	.500
Johnny Pesky, ss	5	0	0	0	0	1	.111
Dom DiMaggio, cf	4	1	0	0	0	0	.235
Ted Williams, lf	3	1	1	0	1	0	.231
Rudy York, 1b	3	0	1	1	1	1	.308
Bobby Doerr, 2b	3	1	2	1	0	0	.400
Don Gutteridge, 2b	0	0	0	0	0	0	—
Mike Higgins, 3b	4	0	1	0	0	0	.231
Hal Wagner, c	4	0	0	0	0	0	.000
Tex Hughson, p	0	0	0	0	0	0	.000
Jim Bagby Jr., p	0	0	0	0	0	0	.000
Catfish Metkovich, ph	1	0	0	0	0	0	.000
Bill Zuber, p	0	0	0	0	0	0	—
Tom McBride, ph	1	0	0	0	0	0	.200
Mace Brown, p	0	0	0	0	0	0	—
Mike Ryba, p	0	0	0	0	0	0	—
Clem Dreisewerd, p	0	0	0	0	0	0	—
Leon Culberson, ph	1	0	0	0	0	0	.000
TOTALS	35	3	9	3	3	2	.226

	1	2	3	4	5	6	7	8	9	R	H	E
Cardinals	0	3	3	0	1	0	1	0	4	12	20	1
Red Sox	0	0	0	1	0	0	0	2	0	3	9	4

E—Pesky, Hughson, Marion, Ryba, Higgins. DP—Cardinals 2 (Slaughter to Garagiola; Schoendienst to Musial), Red Sox 2 (Doerr to Pesky to York; Pesky to Doerr). LOB—Cardinals 10, Red Sox 8. Scoring Position—Cardinals 9-for-19, Red Sox 2-for-6. 2B—Musial (2), Slaughter (1), Kurowski 2 (2), Garagiola (2), Marion (2). 3B—Marion (1), York (1), Doerr (1). S—Moore, Walker, Marion, Munger. GDP—Marion. CS—Walker (1).

Cardinals	IP	H	R	ER	BB	K	ERA
George Munger (W, 1-0)	9.0	9	3	1	3	2	1.00

Red Sox	IP	H	R	ER	BB	K	ERA
Tex Hughson (L, 0-1)	2.0	5	6	3	0	1	4.50
Jim Bagby Jr.	3.0	6	1	1	1	1	3.00
Bill Zuber	2.0	3	1	1	1	1	4.50
Mace Brown	1.0	4	3	3	1	0	27.00
Mike Ryba	0.2	2	1	0	1	0	0.00
Clem Dreisewerd	0.1	0	0	0	0	0	0.00

Hughson pitched to three batters in the 3rd. Brown pitched to four batters in the 9th.

Time—2:31. Attendance—35,645. Umpires—HP, Barry. 1B, Ballanfant. 2B, Hubbard. 3B, Barlick.

Postseason: World Series

Game 5
Friday, October 11

Cardinals	AB	R	H	RBI	BB	K	Avg
Red Schoendienst, 2b	4	0	1	0	0	1	.182
Terry Moore, cf	4	0	0	0	0	2	.105
Stan Musial, 1b	3	1	1	0	1	0	.200
Enos Slaughter, rf	2	0	0	0	0	0	.300
Erv Dusak, lf	1	0	0	0	0	1	.250
Whitey Kurowski, 3b	4	1	0	0	0	2	.316
Joe Garagiola, c	4	1	0	0	0	1	.375
Harry Walker, lf-rf	4	0	2	3	0	0	.455
Marty Marion, ss	4	0	0	0	0	0	.222
Howie Pollet, p	0	0	0	0	0	0	.000
Al Brazle, p	2	0	0	0	0	0	.000
Nippy Jones, ph	1	0	0	0	0	1	.000
Johnny Beazley, p	0	0	0	0	0	0	—
TOTALS	33	3	4	3	1	8	.244

Red Sox	AB	R	H	RBI	BB	K	Avg
Don Gutteridge, 2b	5	0	2	1	0	0	.400
Johnny Pesky, ss	5	1	3	0	0	0	.217
Dom DiMaggio, cf	3	1	1	0	1	0	.250
Ted Williams, lf	5	0	1	1	0	2	.222
Rudy York, 1b	2	1	0	0	3	1	.267
Mike Higgins, 3b	4	1	1	1	0	0	.235
Leon Culberson, rf	3	1	2	1	1	0	.400
Roy Partee, c	3	1	1	1	1	0	.167
Joe Dobson, p	3	0	0	0	0	2	.000
TOTALS	33	6	11	5	6	5	.241

	1	2	3	4	5	6	7	8	9		R	H	E
Cardinals	0	1	0	0	0	0	0	0	2		3	4	1
Red Sox	1	1	0	0	0	1	3	0	x		6	11	3

E—Pesky 2, Marion, York. DP—Cardinals 1 (Marion to Schoendienst to Musial), Red Sox 1 (Partee to Pesky). LOB—Cardinals 5, Red Sox 11. Scoring Position—Cardinals 2-for-6, Red Sox 3-for-19. 2B—Musial (3), Walker (1), DiMaggio (2), Higgins (1). HR—Culberson (1). S—DiMaggio, Dobson. GDP—DiMaggio. SB—Slaughter (1), Pesky (1), Culberson (1). CS—Schoendienst (1), Pesky (1).

Cardinals	IP	H	R	ER	BB	K	ERA
Howie Pollet	0.1	3	2	1	0	0	3.48
Al Brazle (L, 0-1)	6.2	7	4	4	6	4	5.40
Johnny Beazley	1.0	1	0	0	0	1	0.00

Red Sox	IP	H	R	ER	BB	K	ERA
Joe Dobson (W, 1-0)	9.0	4	3	0	1	8	0.00

WP—Beazley. HBP—Slaughter by Dobson. Time—2:23. Attendance—35,982. Umpires—HP, Ballanfant. 1B, Hubbard. 2B, Barlick. 3B, Berry.

Game 6
Sunday, October 13

Red Sox	AB	R	H	RBI	BB	K	Avg
Leon Culberson, rf	4	0	0	0	0	2	.222
Johnny Pesky, ss	3	0	1	0	1	1	.231
Dom DiMaggio, cf	4	0	1	0	0	1	.250
Ted Williams, lf	3	0	1	0	1	1	.238
Rudy York, 1b	4	1	1	0	0	0	.263
Bobby Doerr, 2b	3	0	1	1	0	0	.389
Mike Higgins, 3b	3	0	1	0	0	0	.250
Roy Partee, c	3	0	0	0	0	1	.111
Mickey Harris, p	1	0	0	0	0	0	.333
Tex Hughson, p	1	0	1	0	0	0	.333
Tom McBride, ph	1	0	0	0	0	0	.182
Earl Johnson, p	0	0	0	0	0	0	.000
TOTALS	30	1	7	1	2	6	.250

Cardinals	AB	R	H	RBI	BB	K	Avg
Red Schoendienst, 2b	4	1	1	0	0	0	.192
Terry Moore, cf	4	0	1	1	0	2	.130
Stan Musial, 1b	4	1	1	0	0	1	.208
Whitey Kurowski, 3b	4	0	1	1	0	0	.304
Enos Slaughter, rf	2	0	1	1	2	1	.318
Erv Dusak, lf	0	0	0	0	1	0	.250
Harry Walker, ph-lf	3	1	0	0	0	0	.357
Marty Marion, ss	4	0	2	1	0	0	.273
Del Rice, c	3	0	1	0	1	0	.600
Harry Brecheen, p	4	1	0	0	0	0	.143
TOTALS	32	4	8	4	4	4	.253

	1	2	3	4	5	6	7	8	9		R	H	E
Red Sox	0	0	0	0	0	0	1	0	0		1	7	0
Cardinals	0	0	3	0	0	0	0	1	x		4	8	0

DP—Cardinals 2 (Kurowski to Schoendienst to Musial; Kurowski to Schoendienst to Musial). LOB—Red Sox 4, Cardinals 8. Scoring Position—Red Sox 0-for-2, Cardinals 3-for-7. 2B—Schoendienst (1), Marion (2). 3B—York (1). GDP—DiMaggio, York 2.

Red Sox	IP	H	R	ER	BB	K	ERA
Mickey Harris (L, 0-2)	2.2	5	3	3	1	2	4.66
Tex Hughson	4.1	2	0	0	1	2	3.14
Earl Johnson	1.0	1	1	1	2	0	3.00

Cardinals	IP	H	R	ER	BB	K	ERA
Harry Brecheen (W, 2-0)	9.0	7	1	1	2	6	0.50

Time—1:56. Attendance—35,768. Umpires—HP, Hubbard. 1B, Barlick. 2B, Berry. 3B, Ballanfant.

Game 7
Tuesday, October 15

Red Sox	AB	R	H	RBI	BB	K	Avg
Wally Moses, rf	4	1	1	0	0	1	.417
Johnny Pesky, ss	4	0	1	0	0	0	.233
Dom DiMaggio, cf	3	0	1	3	1	1	.259
Leon Culberson, pr-cf	0	0	0	0	0	0	.222
Ted Williams, lf	4	0	0	0	0	0	.200
Rudy York, 1b	4	0	1	0	0	2	.261
Paul Campbell, pr	0	0	0	0	0	0	—
Bobby Doerr, 2b	4	0	2	0	0	0	.409
Mike Higgins, 3b	4	0	0	0	0	0	.208
Hal Wagner, c	2	0	0	0	0	0	.000
Rip Russell, ph	1	1	1	0	0	0	1.000
Roy Partee, c	1	0	0	0	0	0	.100
Boo Ferriss, p	2	0	0	0	0	0	.000
Joe Dobson, p	0	0	0	0	0	0	.000
Catfish Metkovich, ph	1	1	1	0	0	0	.500
Bob Klinger, p	0	0	0	0	0	0	—
Earl Johnson, p	0	0	0	0	0	0	.000
Tom McBride, ph	1	0	0	0	0	0	.167
TOTALS	35	3	8	3	1	4	.235

Cardinals	AB	R	H	RBI	BB	K	Avg
Red Schoendienst, 2b	4	0	2	1	0	1	.233
Terry Moore, cf	4	0	1	0	0	0	.148
Stan Musial, 1b	3	0	1	0	1	0	.222
Enos Slaughter, rf	3	1	1	0	1	1	.320
Whitey Kurowski, 3b	4	1	1	0	0	0	.296
Joe Garagiola, c	3	0	0	0	0	1	.316
Del Rice, c	1	0	0	0	0	0	.500
Harry Walker, lf	3	1	2	2	1	0	.412
Marty Marion, ss	2	0	0	0	1	0	.250
Murry Dickson, p	3	1	1	1	0	1	.400
Harry Brecheen, p	1	0	0	0	0	0	.125
TOTALS	31	4	9	4	4	4	.270

	1	2	3	4	5	6	7	8	9		R	H	E
Red Sox	1	0	0	0	0	0	0	2	0		3	8	0
Cardinals	0	1	0	0	2	0	0	1	x		4	9	1

E—Kurowski. LOB—Red Sox 6, Cardinals 8. Scoring Position—Red Sox 1-for-11, Cardinals 2-for-9. 2B—DiMaggio (3), Musial (4), Kurowski (3), Walker (2), Dickson (2), Metkovich (1). S—Marion.

Red Sox	IP	H	R	ER	BB	K	ERA
Boo Ferriss	4.1	7	3	3	1	2	2.03
Joe Dobson	2.2	0	0	0	2	2	0.00
Bob Klinger (L, 0-1)	0.2	2	1	1	1	0	13.50
Earl Johnson	0.1	0	0	0	0	0	2.70

Cardinals	IP	H	R	ER	BB	K	ERA
Murry Dickson	7.0	5	3	3	1	3	3.86
Harry Brecheen (BS, 1; W, 3-0)	2.0	3	0	0	0	1	0.45

Dickson pitched to two batters in the 8th.

Time—2:17. Attendance—36,143. Umpires—HP, Barlick. 1B, Berry. 2B, Ballanfant. 3B, Hubbard.

1946 World Series—Composite Statistics

Batting

Cardinals	G	AB	R	H	RBI	2B	3B	HR	BB	SO	SB	CS	Avg	OBP	Slg
Al Brazle	1	2	0	0	0	0	0	0	0	0	0	0	.000	.000	.000
Harry Brecheen	3	8	2	1	1	0	0	0	0	1	0	0	.125	.125	.125
Murry Dickson	2	5	1	2	1	2	0	0	0	1	0	0	.400	.400	.800
Erv Dusak	4	4	0	1	0	1	0	0	2	2	0	0	.250	.500	.500
Joe Garagiola	5	19	2	6	4	2	0	0	0	3	0	0	.316	.316	.421
Nippy Jones	1	1	0	0	0	0	0	0	0	1	0	0	.000	.000	.000
Whitey Kurowski	7	27	5	8	2	3	0	0	0	3	0	0	.296	.321	.407
Marty Marion	7	24	1	6	4	2	0	0	1	1	0	0	.250	.280	.333
Terry Moore	7	27	1	4	2	0	0	0	2	6	0	0	.148	.207	.148
George Munger	1	4	0	1	0	0	0	0	0	2	0	0	.250	.250	.250
Stan Musial	7	27	3	6	4	4	1	0	4	2	1	1	.222	.323	.444
Howie Pollet	2	4	0	0	0	0	0	0	0	1	0	0	.000	.000	.000
Del Rice	3	6	2	3	0	1	0	0	2	0	0	0	.500	.625	.667
Red Schoendienst	7	30	3	7	1	1	0	0	0	2	1	1	.233	.233	.267
Dick Sisler	2	2	0	0	0	0	0	0	0	0	0	0	.000	.000	.000
Enos Slaughter	7	25	5	8	2	1	1	1	4	3	1	0	.320	.433	.560
Harry Walker	7	17	3	7	6	2	0	0	4	2	0	1	.412	.524	.529
Totals	7	232	28	60	27	19	2	1	19	30	3	3	.259	.320	.371

Batting

Red Sox	G	AB	R	H	RBI	2B	3B	HR	BB	SO	SB	CS	Avg	OBP	Slg
Jim Bagby Jr.	1	1	0	0	0	0	0	0	0	0	0	0	.000	.000	.000
Paul Campbell	1	0	0	0	0	0	0	0	0	0	0	0	—	—	—
Leon Culberson	5	9	1	2	1	0	0	1	1	2	1	0	.222	.300	.556
Dom DiMaggio	7	27	2	7	3	3	0	0	2	2	0	0	.259	.310	.370
Joe Dobson	3	3	0	0	0	0	0	0	0	2	0	0	.000	.000	.000
Bobby Doerr	6	22	1	9	3	1	0	1	2	2	0	0	.409	.458	.591
Boo Ferriss	2	6	0	0	0	0	0	0	0	1	0	0	.000	.000	.000
Don Gutteridge	3	5	1	2	1	0	0	0	0	0	0	0	.400	.400	.400
Mickey Harris	2	3	0	1	0	0	0	0	0	1	0	0	.333	.333	.333
Mike Higgins	7	24	1	5	2	1	0	0	2	0	0	0	.208	.269	.250
Tex Hughson	3	3	0	1	0	0	0	0	0	1	0	0	.333	.500	.333
Earl Johnson	3	1	0	0	0	0	0	0	0	0	0	0	.000	.000	.000
Tom McBride	5	12	0	2	1	0	0	0	0	1	0	0	.167	.167	.167
Catfish Metkovich	2	2	1	1	0	0	0	0	0	0	0	0	.500	.500	1.000
Wally Moses	4	12	1	5	0	0	0	0	1	2	0	0	.417	.462	.417
Roy Partee	5	10	1	1	1	0	0	0	1	2	0	0	.100	.182	.100
Johnny Pesky	7	30	2	7	0	0	0	0	1	3	1	1	.233	.258	.233
Rip Russell	2	2	1	2	0	0	0	0	0	0	0	0	1.000	1.000	1.000
Hal Wagner	5	13	0	0	0	0	0	0	0	0	0	0	.000	.000	.000
Ted Williams	7	25	2	5	1	0	0	0	5	5	0	0	.200	.333	.200
Rudy York	7	23	6	6	5	1	1	2	6	4	0	0	.261	.433	.652
Totals	7	233	20	56	18	7	1	4	22	28	2	1	.240	.309	.330

Pitching

Cardinals	G	GS	CG	IP	H	R	ER	BB	SO	W-L	Sv-Op	Hld	ERA
Johnny Beazley	1	0	0	1.0	1	0	0	0	1	0-0	0-0	0	0.00
Al Brazle	1	0	0	6.2	7	4	4	6	4	0-1	0-0	0	5.40
Harry Brecheen	3	2	2	20.0	14	1	1	5	11	3-0	0-1	0	0.45
Murry Dickson	2	2	0	14.0	11	6	6	4	7	0-1	0-0	0	3.86
George Munger	1	1	1	9.0	9	3	1	3	2	1-0	0-0	0	1.00
Howie Pollet	2	2	1	10.1	12	5	4	4	3	0-1	0-0	0	3.48
Ted Wilks	1	0	0	1.0	2	1	0	0	0	0-0	0-0	0	0.00
Totals	7	7	4	62.0	56	20	16	22	28	4-3	0-1	0	2.32

Pitching

Red Sox	G	GS	CG	IP	H	R	ER	BB	SO	W-L	Sv-Op	Hld	ERA
Jim Bagby Jr.	1	0	0	3.0	6	1	1	1	1	0-0	0-0	0	3.00
Mace Brown	1	0	0	1.0	4	3	3	1	0	0-0	0-0	0	27.00
Joe Dobson	3	1	1	12.2	4	3	0	3	10	1-0	0-0	0	0.00
Clem Dreisewerd	1	0	0	0.1	0	0	0	0	0	0-0	0-0	0	0.00
Boo Ferriss	2	2	1	13.1	13	3	3	2	4	1-0	0-0	0	2.03
Mickey Harris	2	2	0	9.2	11	6	5	4	5	0-2	0-0	0	4.66
Tex Hughson	3	2	0	14.1	14	8	5	3	8	0-1	0-0	0	3.14
Earl Johnson	3	0	0	3.1	1	1	1	2	1	1-0	0-0	0	2.70
Bob Klinger	1	0	0	0.2	2	1	1	1	0	0-1	0-0	0	13.50
Mike Ryba	1	0	0	0.2	2	1	0	1	0	0-0	0-0	0	0.00
Bill Zuber	1	0	0	2.0	3	1	1	1	1	0-0	0-0	0	4.50
Totals	7	7	2	61.0	60	28	20	19	30	3-4	0-0	0	2.95

Fielding

Cardinals	Pos	G	PO	Ast	E	DP	PB	FPct
Johnny Beazley	p	1	0	1	0	0	—	1.000
Al Brazle	p	1	0	1	0	0	—	1.000
Harry Brecheen	p	3	0	2	0	1	—	1.000
Murry Dickson	p	2	0	3	0	0	—	1.000
Erv Dusak	lf	4	1	1	0	0	—	1.000
Joe Garagiola	c	5	22	2	0	1	1	1.000
Whitey Kurowski	3b	7	12	10	1	2	—	.957
Marty Marion	ss	7	12	22	2	3	—	.944
Terry Moore	cf	7	18	1	0	0	—	1.000
George Munger	p	1	1	0	0	0	—	1.000
Stan Musial	1b	7	61	2	0	6	—	1.000
Howie Pollet	p	2	0	0	0	0	—	—
Del Rice	c	3	9	1	0	0	0	1.000
Red Schoendienst	2b	7	17	21	1	5	—	.974
Enos Slaughter	rf	7	20	1	0	1	—	1.000
Harry Walker	lf	7	13	0	0	0	—	1.000
	rf	1	0	0	0	0	—	—
Ted Wilks	p	1	0	1	0	0	—	1.000
Totals		7	186	69	4	19	1	.985

Fielding

Red Sox	Pos	G	PO	Ast	E	DP	PB	FPct
Jim Bagby Jr.	p	1	0	1	0	0	—	1.000
Mace Brown	p	1	0	0	0	0	—	—
Leon Culberson	rf	2	7	0	0	0	—	1.000
	cf	1	0	0	0	0	—	—
Dom DiMaggio	cf	7	20	3	0	1	—	1.000
Joe Dobson	p	3	0	2	0	0	—	1.000
Bobby Doerr	2b	6	17	32	0	3	—	1.000
Clem Dreisewerd	p	1	0	0	0	0	—	—
Boo Ferriss	p	2	0	3	0	0	—	1.000
Don Gutteridge	2b	2	0	2	0	0	—	1.000
Mickey Harris	p	2	1	0	0	0	—	1.000
Mike Higgins	3b	7	6	6	2	0	—	.857
Tex Hughson	p	3	0	1	1	0	—	.500
Earl Johnson	p	3	0	2	0	0	—	1.000
Bob Klinger	p	1	1	0	0	0	—	1.000
Tom McBride	rf	2	4	0	1	0	—	.800
Wally Moses	rf	4	5	0	0	0	—	1.000
Roy Partee	c	5	14	1	0	1	0	1.000
Johnny Pesky	ss	7	13	17	4	5	—	.882
Rip Russell	3b	1	0	0	0	0	—	—
Mike Ryba	p	1	0	0	1	0	—	.000
Hal Wagner	c	5	20	2	0	0	0	1.000
Ted Williams	lf	7	15	2	0	0	—	1.000
Rudy York	1b	7	60	3	1	2	—	.984
Bill Zuber	p	1	0	0	0	0	—	—
Totals		7	183	77	10	12	0	.963

1947 New York Yankees (AL) 4, Brooklyn Dodgers (NL) 3

In the first of seven "Subway Series" that New York City enjoyed in the post-WWII era, the Yankees defeated the Brooklyn Dodgers, four games to three. A two-run double from Johnny Lindell and a two-run single from Tommy Henrich helped the Yankees take the opener, 5-3. Allie Reynolds coasted to a 10-3 win in Game 2. In the third game, the Dodgers broke out on top 6-0, before holding on for a 9-8 victory. New York's Bill Bevens took a no-hitter and a 2-1 lead into the bottom of the ninth in Game 4. With two outs and two on, Cookie Lavagetto doubled off the right field wall, ruining the no-no and giving Brooklyn a 3-2 victory. Brooklyn won Game 6, 8-6, before a record 74,065 fans. Al Gionfriddo made a fantastic catch on Joe DiMaggio's drive in the sixth, preventing a game-tying three-run homer. The Yanks took Game 7, 5-2, as Joe Page tossed five shutout innings of relief.

Game 1

Tuesday, September 30

Dodgers	AB	R	H	RBI	BB	K	Avg
Eddie Stanky, 2b	4	0	1	0	0	0	.250
Jackie Robinson, 1b	2	1	0	0	2	0	.000
Pete Reiser, cf-lf	4	1	1	0	0	0	.250
Dixie Walker, rf	4	0	2	1	0	0	.500
Gene Hermanski, lf	2	0	0	0	0	1	.000
Carl Furillo, ph-cf	1	0	1	1	1	0	1.000
Bruce Edwards, c	4	0	0	0	0	0	.000
Spider Jorgensen, 3b	2	0	0	0	0	1	.000
Cookie Lavagetto, ph-3b	2	0	0	0	0	1	.000
Pee Wee Reese, ss	4	1	1	0	0	0	.250
Ralph Branca, p	2	0	0	0	0	1	.000
Hank Behrman, p	0	0	0	0	0	0	—
Eddie Miksis, ph	1	0	0	0	0	0	.000
Hugh Casey, p	0	0	0	0	0	0	—
TOTALS	32	3	6	2	3	5	.188

Yankees	AB	R	H	RBI	BB	K	Avg
Snuffy Stirnweiss, 2b	4	0	0	0	0	1	.000
Tommy Henrich, rf	4	0	1	2	0	1	.250
Yogi Berra, c	4	0	0	0	0	0	.000
Joe DiMaggio, cf	4	1	1	0	0	0	.250
George McQuinn, 1b	3	1	0	0	1	1	.000
Bill Johnson, 3b	2	1	0	0	0	0	.000
Johnny Lindell, lf	3	0	1	2	0	1	.333
Phil Rizzuto, ss	2	1	1	0	1	0	.500
Spec Shea, p	1	0	0	0	0	1	.000
Bobby Brown, ph	0	1	0	1	1	0	—
Joe Page, p	1	0	0	0	0	0	.000
TOTALS	28	5	4	5	3	6	.143

```
          1 2 3  4 5 6  7 8 9        R H E
Dodgers   1 0 0  0 0 1  1 0 0        3 6 0
Yankees   0 0 0  0 5 0  0 0 x        5 4 0
```

DP—Yankees 1 (Johnson to McQuinn). LOB—Dodgers 5, Yankees 3. Scoring Position—Dodgers 2-for-6, Yankees 2-for-7. 2B—Lindell (1). SB—Robinson (1), Reese (1).

Dodgers	IP	H	R	ER	BB	K	ERA
Ralph Branca (L, 0-1)	4.0	2	5	5	3	5	11.25
Hank Behrman	2.0	1	0	0	0	0	0.00
Hugh Casey	2.0	1	0	0	0	1	0.00

Yankees	IP	H	R	ER	BB	K	ERA
Spec Shea (W, 1-0)	5.0	2	1	1	2	3	1.80
Joe Page (S, 1)	4.0	4	2	2	1	2	4.50

Branca pitched to six batters in the 5th.

Balk—Shea. WP—Page. HBP—Johnson by Branca. Time—2:20. Attendance—73,365. Umpires—HP, McGowan. 1B, Pinelli. 2B, Rommel. 3B, Goetz.

Game 2

Wednesday, October 1

Dodgers	AB	R	H	RBI	BB	K	Avg
Eddie Stanky, 2b	4	0	1	0	0	1	.250
Jackie Robinson, 1b	4	0	2	1	0	1	.333
Pete Reiser, cf	4	0	1	0	0	1	.250
Dixie Walker, rf	4	1	1	1	0	0	.375
Gene Hermanski, lf	3	1	0	0	1	1	.000
Bruce Edwards, c	4	0	1	0	0	1	.125
Pee Wee Reese, ss	3	1	2	0	1	0	.429
Spider Jorgensen, 3b	4	0	1	1	0	1	.167
Vic Lombardi, p	2	0	0	0	0	0	.000
Hal Gregg, p	0	0	0	0	0	0	—
Arky Vaughan, ph	1	0	0	0	0	0	.000
Hank Behrman, p	0	0	0	0	0	0	—
Rex Barney, p	0	0	0	0	0	0	—
Al Gionfriddo, ph	1	0	0	0	0	0	.000
TOTALS	34	3	9	3	2	6	.233

Yankees	AB	R	H	RBI	BB	K	Avg
Snuffy Stirnweiss, 2b	4	2	3	1	1	1	.375
Tommy Henrich, rf	4	1	2	1	0	0	.375
Johnny Lindell, lf	4	1	2	2	1	0	.429
Joe DiMaggio, cf	4	0	1	0	1	1	.250
George McQuinn, 1b	5	1	2	0	0	2	.250
Bill Johnson, 3b	5	2	2	1	0	0	.286
Phil Rizzuto, ss	5	0	1	1	0	0	.286
Yogi Berra, c	3	1	0	1	1	0	.000
Allie Reynolds, p	4	2	2	1	0	0	.500
TOTALS	38	10	15	8	4	5	.297

```
          1 2 3  4 5 6  7 8 9        R H E
Dodgers   0 0 1  1 0 0  0 0 1        3 9 2
Yankees   1 0 1  1 2 1  4 0 x       10 15 1
```

E—Berra, Stanky, Reiser. DP—Dodgers 1 (Jorgensen to Stanky to Robinson), Yankees 1 (Stirnweiss to Rizzuto to McQuinn). LOB—Dodgers 6, Yankees 9. Scoring Position—Dodgers 2-for-7, Yankees 6-for-20. 2B—Robinson (1), Lindell (2), Rizzuto (1). 3B—Stirnweiss (1), Lindell (1), Johnson (1). HR—Walker (1), Henrich (1). S—Henrich. GDP—Walker, Lindell. SB—Reese (2). CS—Reese (1).

Dodgers	IP	H	R	ER	BB	K	ERA
Vic Lombardi (L, 0-1)	4.0	9	5	5	1	3	11.25
Hal Gregg	2.0	2	1	1	2		4.50
Hank Behrman	0.1	3	4	4	1	0	15.43
Rex Barney	1.2	1	0	0	1	0	0.00

Yankees	IP	H	R	ER	BB	K	ERA
Allie Reynolds (W, 1-0)	9.0	9	3	3	2	6	3.00

Lombardi pitched to two batters in the 5th.

WP—Behrman, Barney. Time—2:36. Attendance—69,865. Umpires—HP, Pinelli. 1B, Rommel. 2B, Goetz. 3B, McGowan.

Game 3

Thursday, October 2

Yankees	AB	R	H	RBI	BB	K	Avg
Snuffy Stirnweiss, 2b	5	0	2	1	0	2	.385
Tommy Henrich, rf	4	0	1	1	1	0	.333
Johnny Lindell, lf	4	1	2	1	1	0	.455
Joe DiMaggio, cf	4	1	2	3	1	0	.333
George McQuinn, 1b	4	0	0	0	1	2	.167
Bill Johnson, 3b	4	1	1	0	1	1	.273
Phil Rizzuto, ss	5	0	1	0	0	0	.250
Sherm Lollar, c	3	2	2	1	0	0	.667
Yogi Berra, ph-c	2	1	1	1	0	0	.111
Bobo Newsom, p	0	0	0	0	0	0	—
Vic Raschi, p	0	0	0	0	0	0	—
Allie Clark, ph	1	0	0	1	0	0	—
Karl Drews, p	0	0	0	0	0	0	—
Jack Phillips, ph	1	0	0	0	0	0	.000
Spud Chandler, p	0	0	0	0	0	0	—
Bobby Brown, ph	1	1	1	0	0	0	1.000
Joe Page, p	1	0	0	0	0	0	.000
TOTALS	38	8	13	8	6	5	.303

Dodgers	AB	R	H	RBI	BB	K	Avg
Eddie Stanky, 2b	4	2	1	2	1	0	.250
Jackie Robinson, 1b	4	1	2	0	0	0	.400
Pete Reiser, cf	0	0	0	0	1	0	.250
Carl Furillo, ph-cf	3	1	2	2	1	0	.750
Dixie Walker, rf	5	0	2	1	0	0	.385
Gene Hermanski, lf	3	2	1	1	1	0	.125
Bruce Edwards, c	4	1	1	1	1	1	.167
Pee Wee Reese, ss	3	1	1	1	1	1	.400
Spider Jorgensen, 3b	4	0	2	1	0	0	.300
Joe Hatten, p	2	1	1	0	0	0	.500
Ralph Branca, p	1	0	0	0	0	0	.000
Hugh Casey, p	1	0	0	0	0	1	.000
TOTALS	34	9	13	9	6	4	.301

```
          1 2 3  4 5 6  7 8 9        R H E
Yankees   0 0 2  2 2 1  1 0 0        8 13 0
Dodgers   0 6 1  2 0 0  0 0 x        9 13 1
```

E—Furillo. DP—Dodgers 2 (Reese to Stanky to Robinson; Stanky to Robinson). LOB—Yankees 9, Dodgers 9. Scoring Position—Yankees 4-for-14, Dodgers 7-for-18. 2B—Henrich (1), Lollar (1), Stanky (1), Edwards (1), Jorgensen (1), Furillo (1), Brown (1). HR—DiMaggio (1), Berra (1). S—Robinson. GDP—Henrich, DiMaggio. SB—Robinson (2), Walker (1). CS—Reiser (1).

Yankees	IP	H	R	ER	BB	K	ERA
Bobo Newsom (L, 0-1)	1.2	5	5	5	2	0	27.00
Vic Raschi	0.1	2	1	1	0	0	27.00
Karl Drews	1.0	1	1	1	0	0	9.00
Spud Chandler	2.0	2	2	2	3	1	9.00
Joe Page	3.0	3	0	0	1	3	2.57

Dodgers	IP	H	R	ER	BB	K	ERA
Joe Hatten	4.1	8	6	6	3	3	12.46
Ralph Branca	2.0	4	2	2	2	1	10.50
Hugh Casey (BS, 1; W, 1-0)	2.2	1	0	0	1	1	0.00

WP—Drews, Page. PB—Lollar. HBP—Hermanski by Drews. Time—3:05. Attendance—33,098. Umpires—HP, Rommel. 1B, Goetz. 2B, McGowan. 3B, Pinelli.

Game 4

Friday, October 3

Yankees	AB	R	H	RBI	BB	K	Avg
Snuffy Stirnweiss, 2b	4	1	2	0	1	2	.412
Tommy Henrich, rf	5	0	1	0	0	1	.294
Yogi Berra, c	4	0	0	0	0	0	.077
Joe DiMaggio, cf	2	0	0	1	2	0	.286
George McQuinn, 1b	4	0	1	0	0	1	.188
Bill Johnson, 3b	4	1	1	0	0	0	.267
Johnny Lindell, lf	3	0	2	1	1	0	.500
Phil Rizzuto, ss	4	0	1	0	0	0	.250
Bill Bevens, p	3	0	0	0	0	1	.000
TOTALS	33	2	8	2	4	5	.280

Dodgers	AB	R	H	RBI	BB	K	Avg
Eddie Stanky, 2b	1	0	0	0	2	0	.231
Cookie Lavagetto, ph	1	0	1	2	0	0	.333
Pee Wee Reese, ss	4	0	0	1	0	0	.286
Jackie Robinson, 1b	4	0	0	0	0	1	.286
Dixie Walker, rf	2	0	0	0	2	0	.333
Gene Hermanski, lf	4	0	0	0	0	3	.083
Bruce Edwards, c	4	0	0	0	0	3	.125
Carl Furillo, cf	3	0	0	0	1	0	.429
Al Gionfriddo, pr	0	1	0	0	1	0	.000
Spider Jorgensen, 3b	2	1	0	0	2	0	.250
Harry Taylor, p	0	0	0	0	0	0	—
Hal Gregg, p	1	0	0	0	0	1	.000
Arky Vaughan, ph	0	0	0	0	1	0	.000
Hank Behrman, p	0	0	0	0	0	0	—
Hugh Casey, p	0	0	0	0	0	0	—
Pete Reiser, ph	0	0	0	0	1	0	.250
Eddie Miksis, pr	0	1	0	0	0	0	.000
TOTALS	26	3	1	3	10	5	.235

```
          1 2 3  4 5 6  7 8 9        R H E
Yankees   1 0 0  1 0 0  0 0 0        2 8 1
Dodgers   0 0 0  0 1 0  0 0 2        3 1 3
```

E—Jorgensen, Berra, Edwards, Reese. DP—Dodgers 3 (Reese to Stanky to Robinson; Gregg to Reese to Robinson; Casey to Edwards to Robinson). LOB—Yankees 9, Dodgers 8. Scoring Position—Yankees 2-for-11, Dodgers 1-for-7. 2B—Lindell (3), Lavagetto (1). 3B—Johnson (2). S—Bevens, Stanky. GDP—Henrich 2, Johnson. SB—Rizzuto (1), Reese (3), Gionfriddo (1).

Yankees	IP	H	R	ER	BB	K	ERA
Bill Bevens (L, 0-1)	8.2	1	3	3	10	5	3.12

Dodgers	IP	H	R	ER	BB	K	ERA
Harry Taylor	0.0	2	1	0	1	0	—
Hal Gregg	7.0	4	1	1	3	5	2.00
Hank Behrman	1.1	2	0	0	0	0	9.82
Hugh Casey (W, 2-0)	0.2	0	0	0	0	0	0.00

Taylor pitched to four batters in the 1st.

WP—Bevens. Time—2:20. Attendance—33,443. Umpires—HP, Goetz. 1B, McGowan. 2B, Pinelli. 3B, Rommel.

Game 5
Saturday, October 4

Yankees	AB	R	H	RBI	BB	K	Avg
Snuffy Stirnweiss, 2b	3	0	0	0	2	1	.350
Tommy Henrich, rf	4	0	2	0	1	0	.333
Johnny Lindell, lf	2	0	0	0	2	1	.438
Joe DiMaggio, cf	4	1	1	1	1	0	.278
George McQuinn, 1b	4	0	0	0	0	1	.150
Bill Johnson, 3b	3	0	0	0	1	2	.222
Aaron Robinson, c	3	1	0	0	1	0	.000
Phil Rizzuto, ss	2	0	0	0	2	0	.222
Spec Shea, p	4	0	2	1	0	1	.400
TOTALS	29	2	5	2	10	7	.281

Dodgers	AB	R	H	RBI	BB	K	Avg
Eddie Stanky, 2b	3	0	0	0	0	1	.188
Pete Reiser, ph	0	0	0	0	1	0	.250
Eddie Miksis, pr-2b	0	0	0	0	0	0	.000
Pee Wee Reese, ss	2	0	0	0	2	1	.250
Jackie Robinson, 1b	4	0	1	1	0	1	.278
Dixie Walker, rf	4	0	0	0	0	0	.263
Gene Hermanski, lf	4	0	1	0	0	0	.125
Bruce Edwards, c	3	0	1	0	1	1	.158
Vic Lombardi, pr	0	0	0	0	0	0	.000
Carl Furillo, cf	3	0	0	0	0	0	.300
Spider Jorgensen, 3b	4	0	0	0	0	2	.188
Rex Barney, p	1	0	0	0	0	0	.000
Joe Hatten, p	0	0	0	0	0	0	.500
Al Gionfriddo, ph	0	1	0	0	1	0	.000
Hank Behrman, p	0	0	0	0	0	0	—
Arky Vaughan, ph	1	0	1	0	0	0	.500
Hugh Casey, p	0	0	0	0	0	0	.000
Cookie Lavagetto, ph	1	0	0	0	1	0	.250
TOTALS	30	1	4	1	5	7	.217

	1	2	3	4	5	6	7	8	9		R	H	E
Yankees	0	0	0	1	1	0	0	0	0		2	5	0
Dodgers	0	0	0	0	0	1	0	0	0		1	4	1

E—Miksis. DP—Dodgers 2 (Reese to Stanky to JRobinson; Reese to Miksis to JRobinson). LOB—Yankees 11, Dodgers 8. Scoring Position—Yankees 1-for-10, Dodgers 1-for-6. 2B—Henrich (2), Shea (1), Vaughan (1). HR—DiMaggio (2). S—Furillo. GDP—DiMaggio 2. CS—Rizzuto (1).

Yankees	IP	H	R	ER	BB	K	ERA
Spec Shea (W, 2-0)	9.0	4	1	1	5	7	1.29

Dodgers	IP	H	R	ER	BB	K	ERA
Rex Barney (L, 0-1)	4.2	3	2	2	9	3	2.84
Joe Hatten	1.1	0	0	0	0	1	9.53
Hank Behrman	1.0	1	0	0	1	2	7.71
Hugh Casey	2.0	1	0	0	0	1	0.00

WP—Barney. PB—Edwards 2. HBP—Lindell by Casey. Time—2:46. Attendance—34,379. Umpires—HP, McGowan. 1B, Pinelli. 2B, Rommel. 3B, Goetz.

Game 6
Sunday, October 5

Dodgers	AB	R	H	RBI	BB	K	Avg
Eddie Stanky, 2b	5	2	2	0	0	0	.238
Pee Wee Reese, ss	4	2	3	2	1	0	.350
Jackie Robinson, 1b	5	1	2	1	0	0	.304
Dixie Walker, rf	5	0	1	1	0	1	.250
Gene Hermanski, lf	1	0	0	0	1	0	.118
Eddie Miksis, ph-lf	1	0	0	0	0	0	.000
Al Gionfriddo, lf	2	0	0	0	0	0	.000
Bruce Edwards, c	4	1	1	0	0	1	.174
Carl Furillo, cf	4	1	2	0	0	0	.357
Spider Jorgensen, 3b	2	0	0	0	0	0	.167
Cookie Lavagetto, ph-3b	2	0	0	1	0	0	.167
Vic Lombardi, p	1	0	0	0	0	0	.000
Ralph Branca, p	1	0	0	0	0	0	.000
Bobby Bragan, ph	1	0	1	1	0	0	1.000
Dan Bankhead, pr	0	1	0	0	0	0	—
Joe Hatten, p	1	0	0	0	0	0	.333
Hugh Casey, p	0	0	0	0	0	0	.000
TOTALS	39	8	12	6	2	2	.230

Yankees	AB	R	H	RBI	BB	K	Avg
Snuffy Stirnweiss, 2b	5	0	0	1	1	1	.280
Tommy Henrich, rf-lf	5	1	2	0	0	0	.346
Johnny Lindell, lf	2	1	2	1	0	0	.500
Yogi Berra, rf	3	0	2	1	0	0	.188
Joe DiMaggio, cf	5	1	1	0	0	0	.261
Bill Johnson, 3b	5	1	2	1	0	1	.261
Jack Phillips, 1b	1	0	0	0	0	0	.000
Bobby Brown, ph	1	0	1	1	0	0	1.000
George McQuinn, 1b	1	0	0	0	2	0	.143
Phil Rizzuto, ss	4	0	1	0	1	0	.227
Sherm Lollar, c	1	1	1	0	0	0	.750
Aaron Robinson, c	4	1	2	0	0	0	.286
Allie Reynolds, p	0	0	0	0	0	0	.500
Karl Drews, p	2	0	0	0	0	2	.000
Joe Page, p	0	0	0	0	0	0	.000
Bobo Newsom, p	0	0	0	0	0	0	—
Allie Clark, ph	1	0	0	0	0	0	.000
Vic Raschi, p	0	0	0	0	0	0	—
Ralph Houk, p	1	0	1	0	0	0	1.000
Butch Wensloff, p	0	0	0	0	0	0	.000
Lonny Frey, ph	1	0	0	1	0	0	.000
TOTALS	42	6	15	6	4	4	.290

	1	2	3	4	5	6	7	8	9		R	H	E
Dodgers	2	0	2	0	0	4	0	0	0		8	12	1
Yankees	0	0	4	1	0	0	0	0	1		6	15	2

E—Jorgensen, ARobinson, McQuinn. DP—Yankees 1 (Rizzuto to Phillips). LOB—Dodgers 6, Yankees 13. Scoring Position—Dodgers 6-for-10, Yankees 6-for-16. 2B—Reese (1), JRobinson (2), Walker (1), Furillo (2), Lollar (2), Bragan (1). GDP—Walker.

Dodgers	IP	H	R	ER	BB	K	ERA
Vic Lombardi	2.2	5	4	4	0	2	12.15
Ralph Branca (W, 1-1)	2.1	6	1	1	0	2	8.64
Joe Hatten (H, 1)	3.0	3	1	1	4	0	7.27
Hugh Casey (S, 1)	1.0	1	0	0	0	0	0.00

Yankees	IP	H	R	ER	BB	K	ERA
Allie Reynolds	2.1	6	4	3	1	0	4.76
Karl Drews	2.0	1	0	0	1	0	3.00
Joe Page (L, 0-1)	1.0	4	4	4	0	1	6.75
Bobo Newsom	0.2	1	0	0	0	0	19.29
Vic Raschi	1.0	0	0	0	0	1	6.75
Butch Wensloff	2.0	0	0	0	0	0	0.00

Hatten pitched to two batters in the 9th.

WP—Lombardi. PB—Lollar. Time—3:19. Attendance—74,065. Umpires—HP, Pinelli. 1B, Rommel. 2B, Goetz. 3B, McGowan.

Game 7
Monday, October 6

Dodgers	AB	R	H	RBI	BB	K	Avg
Eddie Stanky, 2b	4	0	1	0	0	0	.240
Pee Wee Reese, ss	3	0	0	0	1	1	.304
Jackie Robinson, 1b	4	0	0	0	0	1	.259
Dixie Walker, rf	3	0	0	0	1	0	.222
Gene Hermanski, lf	2	1	1	0	0	0	.158
Eddie Miksis, ph-lf	2	0	1	0	0	0	.250
Bruce Edwards, c	4	1	2	1	0	0	.222
Carl Furillo, cf	3	0	1	0	0	0	.353
Spider Jorgensen, 3b	2	0	1	0	0	0	.200
Cookie Lavagetto, ph-3b	1	0	0	0	0	0	.143
Hal Gregg, p	2	0	0	0	0	0	.000
Hank Behrman, p	0	0	0	0	0	0	—
Joe Hatten, p	0	0	0	0	0	0	.333
Rex Barney, p	0	0	0	0	0	0	.000
Gil Hodges, ph	1	0	0	0	0	1	.000
Hugh Casey, p	0	0	0	0	0	0	.000
TOTALS	31	2	7	2	2	3	.234

Yankees	AB	R	H	RBI	BB	K	Avg
Snuffy Stirnweiss, 2b	2	0	0	0	3	0	.259
Tommy Henrich, lf	5	0	1	0	1	0	.323
Yogi Berra, rf	3	0	0	0	0	0	.158
Allie Clark, ph-rf	1	0	1	1	0	0	.500
Joe DiMaggio, cf	3	0	0	0	1	0	.231
George McQuinn, 1b	2	1	0	0	1	1	.130
Bill Johnson, 3b	3	2	1	0	1	0	.269
Aaron Robinson, c	3	0	0	1	1	1	.200
Phil Rizzuto, ss	4	2	3	1	0	0	.308
Spec Shea, p	0	0	0	0	0	0	.400
Bill Bevens, p	1	0	0	0	0	1	.000
Bobby Brown, ph	1	0	1	1	0	0	1.000
Joe Page, p	2	0	0	0	0	1	.000
TOTALS	30	5	7	5	7	5	.252

	1	2	3	4	5	6	7	8	9		R	H	E
Dodgers	0	2	0	0	0	0	0	0	0		2	7	0
Yankees	0	1	0	2	0	1	1	0	x		5	7	0

LOB—Dodgers 4, Yankees 9. Scoring Position—Dodgers 2-for-4, Yankees 4-for-12. 2B—Jorgensen (2), Brown (2). 3B—Hermanski (1), Johnson (3). S—McQuinn. GDP—Edwards. SB—Rizzuto (2). CS—Stanky (1), Reese (2).

Dodgers	IP	H	R	ER	BB	K	ERA
Hal Gregg (L, 0-1)	3.2	3	3	3	4	3	3.55
Hank Behrman	1.2	2	1	1	3	1	7.11
Joe Hatten	0.1	1	0	0	0	1	7.00
Rex Barney	0.1	0	0	0	0	0	2.70
Hugh Casey	2.0	1	1	1	0	0	0.87

Yankees	IP	H	R	ER	BB	K	ERA
Spec Shea	1.1	4	2	2	1	0	2.35
Bill Bevens	2.2	2	0	0	1	2	2.38
Joe Page (W, 1-1)	5.0	1	0	0	0	1	4.15

Time—2:19. Attendance—71,548. Umpires—HP, Rommel. 1B, Goetz. 2B, McGowan. 3B, Pinelli.

1947 World Series—Composite Statistics

Batting

Yankees	G	AB	R	H	RBI	2B	3B	HR	BB	SO	SB	CS	Avg	OBP	Slg
Yogi Berra	6	19	2	3	2	0	0	1	1	2	0	0	.158	.200	.316
Bill Bevens	2	4	0	0	0	0	0	0	0	2	0	0	.000	.000	.000
Bobby Brown	4	3	2	3	3	2	0	0	1	0	0	0	1.000	1.000	1.667
Allie Clark	3	2	1	1	1	0	0	0	1	0	0	0	.500	.667	.500
Joe DiMaggio	7	26	4	6	5	0	0	2	6	2	0	0	.231	.375	.462
Karl Drews	2	2	0	0	0	0	0	0	0	2	0	0	.000	.000	.000
Lonny Frey	1	1	0	0	0	0	0	0	0	0	0	0	.000	.000	.000
Tommy Henrich	7	31	2	10	5	2	0	1	2	3	0	0	.323	.364	.484
Ralph Houk	1	1	0	1	0	0	0	0	0	0	0	0	1.000	1.000	1.000
Bill Johnson	7	26	8	7	2	0	3	0	3	4	0	0	.269	.367	.500
Johnny Lindell	6	18	3	9	7	3	1	0	5	2	0	0	.500	.625	.778
Sherm Lollar	2	4	3	3	1	2	0	0	0	0	0	0	.750	.750	1.250
George McQuinn	7	23	3	3	1	0	0	0	5	8	0	0	.130	.286	.130
Joe Page	4	4	0	0	0	0	0	0	0	0	1	0	.000	.000	.000
Jack Phillips	2	2	0	0	0	0	0	0	0	0	0	0	.000	.000	.000
Allie Reynolds	2	4	2	2	1	0	0	0	0	0	0	0	.500	.500	.500
Phil Rizzuto	7	26	3	8	2	1	0	0	4	0	2	1	.308	.400	.346
Aaron Robinson	3	10	2	2	1	0	0	0	2	1	0	0	.200	.333	.200
Spec Shea	3	5	0	2	1	1	0	0	0	2	0	0	.400	.400	.600
Snuffy Stirnweiss	7	27	3	7	3	0	1	0	8	8	0	0	.259	.429	.333
Totals	7	238	38	67	36	11	5	4	38	37	2	1	.282	.385	.420

Batting

Dodgers	G	AB	R	H	RBI	2B	3B	HR	BB	SO	SB	CS	Avg	OBP	Slg
Dan Bankhead	1	0	1	0	0	0	0	0	0	0	0	0	—	—	—
Rex Barney	3	1	0	0	0	0	0	0	0	0	0	0	.000	.000	.000
Bobby Bragan	1	1	0	1	1	1	0	0	0	0	0	0	1.000	1.000	2.000
Ralph Branca	3	4	0	0	0	0	0	0	0	1	0	0	.000	.000	.000
Hugh Casey	6	1	0	0	0	0	0	0	0	1	0	0	.000	.000	.000
Bruce Edwards	7	27	3	6	2	1	0	0	2	7	0	0	.222	.276	.259
Carl Furillo	6	17	2	6	3	2	0	0	3	0	0	0	.353	.450	.471
Al Gionfriddo	4	3	2	0	0	0	0	0	1	0	1	0	.000	.250	.000
Hal Gregg	3	3	0	0	0	0	0	0	1	1	0	0	.000	.250	.000
Joe Hatten	4	3	1	1	0	0	0	0	0	0	0	0	.333	.333	.333
Gene Hermanski	7	19	4	3	1	0	1	0	3	3	0	0	.158	.304	.263
Gil Hodges	1	1	0	0	0	0	0	0	0	1	0	0	.000	.000	.000
Spider Jorgensen	7	20	1	4	3	2	0	0	2	4	0	0	.200	.273	.300
Cookie Lavagetto	5	7	0	1	3	1	0	0	0	2	0	0	.143	.143	.286
Vic Lombardi	3	3	0	0	0	0	0	0	0	0	0	0	.000	.000	.000
Eddie Miksis	5	4	1	1	0	0	0	0	0	1	0	0	.250	.250	.250
Pee Wee Reese	7	23	5	7	4	1	0	0	6	3	3	2	.304	.448	.348
Pete Reiser	5	8	1	2	0	0	0	0	3	1	0	1	.250	.455	.250
Jackie Robinson	7	27	3	7	3	2	0	0	2	4	2	0	.259	.310	.333
Eddie Stanky	7	25	4	6	2	1	0	0	3	2	0	1	.240	.321	.280
Arky Vaughan	3	2	0	1	0	1	0	0	1	0	0	0	.500	.667	1.000
Dixie Walker	7	27	1	6	4	1	0	1	3	1	1	0	.222	.300	.370
Totals	7	226	29	52	26	13	1	1	30	32	7	4	.230	.323	.310

Pitching

Yankees	G	GS	CG	IP	H	R	ER	BB	SO	W-L	Sv-Op	Hld	ERA
Bill Bevens	2	1	1	11.1	3	3	3	11	7	0-1	0-0	0	2.38
Spud Chandler	1	0	0	2.0	2	2	2	3	1	0-0	0-0	0	9.00
Karl Drews	2	0	0	3.0	2	1	1	1	0	0-0	0-0	0	3.00
Bobo Newsom	2	1	0	2.1	6	5	5	2	0	0-1	0-0	0	19.29
Joe Page	4	0	0	13.0	12	6	6	2	7	1-1	1-1	0	4.15
Vic Raschi	2	0	0	1.1	2	1	1	0	1	0-0	0-0	0	6.75
Allie Reynolds	2	2	1	11.1	15	7	6	3	6	1-0	0-0	0	4.76
Spec Shea	3	3	1	15.1	10	4	4	8	10	2-0	0-0	0	2.35
Butch Wensloff	1	0	0	2.0	0	0	0	0	0	0-0	0-0	0	0.00
Totals	7	7	3	61.2	52	29	28	30	32	4-3	1-1	0	4.09

Pitching

Dodgers	G	GS	CG	IP	H	R	ER	BB	SO	W-L	Sv-Op	Hld	ERA
Rex Barney	3	1	0	6.2	4	2	2	10	3	0-1	0-0	0	2.70
Hank Behrman	5	0	0	6.1	9	5	5	5	3	0-0	0-0	0	7.11
Ralph Branca	3	1	0	8.1	12	8	8	5	8	1-1	0-0	0	8.64
Hugh Casey	6	0	0	10.1	5	1	1	1	3	2-0	1-2	0	0.87
Hal Gregg	3	1	0	12.2	9	5	5	8	10	0-1	0-0	0	3.55
Joe Hatten	4	1	0	9.0	12	7	7	7	5	0-0	0-0	1	7.00
Vic Lombardi	2	2	0	6.2	14	9	9	1	5	0-1	0-0	0	12.15
Harry Taylor	1	1	0	0.0	2	1	0	1	0	0-0	0-0	0	—
Totals	7	7	0	60.0	67	38	37	38	37	3-4	1-2	1	5.55

Fielding

Yankees	Pos	G	PO	Ast	E	DP	PB	FPct
Yogi Berra	c	4	19	2	2	0	0	.913
	rf	2	3	0	0	0	—	1.000
Bill Bevens	p	2	0	1	0	0	—	1.000
Spud Chandler	p	1	0	0	0	0	—	—
Allie Clark	rf	1	2	0	0	0	—	1.000
Joe DiMaggio	cf	7	23	0	0	0	—	1.000
Karl Drews	p	2	0	3	0	0	—	1.000
Tommy Henrich	rf	6	9	0	0	0	—	1.000
	lf	2	2	0	0	0	—	1.000
Bill Johnson	3b	7	11	14	0	1	—	1.000
Johnny Lindell	lf	6	10	0	0	0	—	1.000
Sherm Lollar	c	2	2	1	0	0	2	1.000
George McQuinn	1b	7	48	4	1	3	—	.981
Bobo Newsom	p	2	0	1	0	0	—	1.000
Joe Page	p	4	1	2	0	0	—	1.000
Jack Phillips	1b	1	4	0	0	1	—	1.000
Vic Raschi	p	2	0	0	0	0	—	—
Allie Reynolds	p	2	1	0	0	0	—	1.000
Phil Rizzuto	ss	7	19	18	0	3	—	1.000
Aaron Robinson	c	3	13	2	1	0	0	.938
Spec Shea	p	3	1	3	0	0	—	1.000
Snuffy Stirnweiss	2b	7	17	18	0	2	—	1.000
Butch Wensloff	p	1	0	1	0	0	—	1.000
Totals		7	185	70	4	10	2	.985

Fielding

Dodgers	Pos	G	PO	Ast	E	DP	PB	FPct
Rex Barney	p	3	0	1	0	0	—	1.000
Hank Behrman	p	5	1	3	0	0	—	1.000
Ralph Branca	p	3	0	1	0	0	—	1.000
Hugh Casey	p	6	2	3	0	1	—	1.000
Bruce Edwards	c	7	44	4	1	1	2	.980
Carl Furillo	cf	6	14	1	1	0	—	.938
Al Gionfriddo	lf	1	1	0	0	0	—	1.000
Hal Gregg	p	3	1	3	0	1	—	1.000
Joe Hatten	p	4	0	0	0	0	—	—
Gene Hermanski	lf	7	15	0	0	0	—	1.000
Spider Jorgensen	3b	7	8	11	2	1	—	.905
Cookie Lavagetto	3b	3	0	1	0	0	—	1.000
Vic Lombardi	p	2	0	0	0	0	—	—
Eddie Miksis	lf	2	2	0	0	0	—	1.000
	2b	1	1	1	1	1	—	.667
Pee Wee Reese	ss	7	8	16	1	5	—	.960
Pete Reiser	cf	3	6	0	1	0	—	.857
	lf	1	1	0	0	0	—	1.000
Jackie Robinson	1b	7	49	6	0	8	—	1.000
Eddie Stanky	2b	7	18	18	1	5	—	.973
Harry Taylor	p	1	0	0	0	0	—	—
Dixie Walker	rf	7	9	1	0	0	—	1.000
Totals		7	180	70	8	23	2	.969

1948 Cleveland Indians (AL) 4, Boston Braves (NL) 2

After defeating the Boston Red Sox in a one-game playoff for the American League pennant, the Cleveland Indians upended the *other* Boston team—the Braves—in a six-game World Series. In Game 1, Boston's Johnny Sain bested Bob Feller, 1-0. In the eighth inning, Feller picked Phil Masi off second base (and photos would later prove Masi was out) but umpire Bill Stewart called him safe. Moments later, Tommy Holmes singled in Masi with the game's only run. Bob Lemon beat Warren Spahn 4-1 in Game 2 to even the Series. Gene Bearden was masterful in Game 3, authoring a five-hit shutout for Cleveland. Cleveland's Steve Gromek outdueled Johnny Sain, 2-1, in the fourth game, but the Braves took Game 5, 11-5, with a six-run seventh inning. Bearden came on in relief in Game 6 to quell a Boston rally and preserve the Indians' 4-3 victory.

Game 1
Wednesday, October 6

Indians	AB	R	H	RBI	BB	K	Avg
Dale Mitchell, lf	4	0	0	0	0	0	.000
Larry Doby, cf	4	0	1	0	0	0	.250
Lou Boudreau, ss	4	0	0	0	0	1	.000
Joe Gordon, 2b	4	0	1	0	0	1	.250
Ken Keltner, 3b	4	0	1	0	0	1	.250
Wally Judnich, rf	4	0	0	0	0	1	.000
Eddie Robinson, 1b	3	0	0	0	0	0	.000
Jim Hegan, c	3	0	1	0	0	0	.333
Bob Feller, p	2	0	0	0	0	2	.000
TOTALS	32	0	4	0	0	6	.125

Braves	AB	R	H	RBI	BB	K	Avg
Tommy Holmes, rf	4	0	1	1	0	0	.250
Al Dark, ss	4	0	0	0	0	0	.000
Earl Torgeson, 1b	2	0	0	0	1	1	.000
Glenn Elliott, 3b	3	0	0	0	0	0	.000
Marv Rickert, lf	3	0	1	0	0	0	.333
Bill Salkeld, c	1	0	0	0	1	1	.000
Phil Masi, pr-c	0	1	0	0	0	0	—
Mike McCormick, cf	2	0	0	0	0	0	.000
Eddie Stanky, 2b	2	0	0	1	0	0	.000
Sibby Sisti, pr-2b	0	0	0	0	0	0	—
Johnny Sain, p	3	0	0	0	0	0	.000
TOTALS	24	1	2	1	3	2	.083

	1	2	3	4	5	6	7	8	9	R	H	E
Indians	0	0	0	0	0	0	0	0	0	0	4	0
Braves	0	0	0	0	0	0	0	1	x	1	2	2

E—Elliott 2. LOB—Indians 6, Braves 4. Scoring Position—Indians 0-for-6, Braves 1-for-6. S—Feller, Salkeld, McCormick. SB—Gordon (1), Hegan (1), Torgeson (1).

Indians	IP	H	R	ER	BB	K	ERA
Bob Feller (L, 0-1)	8.0	2	1	1	3	2	1.13

Braves	IP	H	R	ER	BB	K	ERA
Johnny Sain (W, 1-0)	9.0	4	0	0	0	6	0.00

Time—1:42. Attendance—40,135. Umpires—HP, Barr. 1B, Summers. 2B, Stewart. 3B, Grieve.

Game 2
Thursday, October 7

Indians	AB	R	H	RBI	BB	K	Avg
Dale Mitchell, lf	5	1	1	0	0	0	.111
Allie Clark, rf	3	0	0	0	0	1	.000
Bob Kennedy, rf	1	0	1	1	0	0	1.000
Lou Boudreau, ss	5	1	2	1	0	0	.222
Joe Gordon, 2b	4	1	1	1	0	0	.250
Ken Keltner, 3b	4	0	0	0	0	0	.125
Larry Doby, cf	4	0	2	1	0	2	.375
Eddie Robinson, 1b	3	0	1	0	1	0	.167
Jim Hegan, c	3	1	0	1	0	0	.167
Bob Lemon, p	4	0	0	0	0	0	.000
TOTALS	36	4	8	4	2	3	.194

Braves	AB	R	H	RBI	BB	K	Avg
Tommy Holmes, rf	4	0	0	0	0	0	.125
Al Dark, ss	4	1	1	0	0	1	.125
Earl Torgeson, 1b	4	0	2	0	0	0	.333
Glenn Elliott, 3b	4	0	1	1	0	0	.143
Marv Rickert, lf	4	0	0	0	0	1	.143
Bill Salkeld, c	1	0	1	0	2	0	.500
Phil Masi, pr-c	1	0	0	0	0	0	.000
Mike McCormick, cf	4	0	2	0	0	1	.333
Eddie Stanky, 2b	2	0	1	0	1	0	.250
Warren Spahn, p	2	0	0	0	0	0	.000
Red Barrett, p	0	0	0	0	0	0	—
Frank McCormick, ph	1	0	0	0	0	1	.000
Nels Potter, p	0	0	0	0	0	0	—
Ray Sanders, ph	1	0	0	0	0	0	.000
TOTALS	32	1	8	1	3	5	.189

	1	2	3	4	5	6	7	8	9	R	H	E
Indians	0	0	0	2	1	0	0	0	1	4	8	1
Braves	1	0	0	0	0	0	0	0	0	1	8	3

E—Elliott, Dark 2, Gordon. DP—Indians 2 (Boudreau to Gordon to Robinson; Gordon to Boudreau to Robinson), Braves 1 (Holmes to Torgeson). LOB—Indians 8, Braves 8. Scoring Position—Indians 4-for-11, Braves 1-for-7. 2B—Boudreau (1), Doby (1), Stanky (1). S—Clark, Stanky. GDP—Elliott, Stanky.

Indians	IP	H	R	ER	BB	K	ERA
Bob Lemon (W, 1-0)	9.0	8	1	0	3	5	0.00

Braves	IP	H	R	ER	BB	K	ERA
Warren Spahn (L, 0-1)	4.1	6	3	3	2	1	6.23
Red Barrett	2.2	1	0	0	0	0	0.00
Nels Potter	2.0	1	1	0	0	1	0.00

Time—2:14. Attendance—39,633. Umpires—HP, Summers. 1B, Stewart. 2B, Grieve. 3B, Barr.

Game 3
Friday, October 8

Braves	AB	R	H	RBI	BB	K	Avg
Tommy Holmes, rf	4	0	0	0	0	0	.083
Al Dark, ss	4	0	1	0	0	1	.167
Mike McCormick, lf	4	0	1	0	0	1	.300
Glenn Elliott, 3b	3	0	1	0	0	0	.200
Frank McCormick, 1b	3	0	1	0	0	1	.250
Clint Conatser, cf	3	0	0	0	0	0	.000
Phil Masi, c	3	0	0	0	0	0	.000
Eddie Stanky, 2b	3	0	1	0	0	0	.286
Vern Bickford, p	0	0	0	0	0	0	—
Bill Voiselle, p	1	0	0	0	0	0	.000
Connie Ryan, ph	1	0	0	0	0	1	.000
Red Barrett, p	0	0	0	0	0	0	—
TOTALS	29	0	5	0	0	4	.172

Indians	AB	R	H	RBI	BB	K	Avg
Dale Mitchell, lf	3	0	0	0	1	0	.083
Larry Doby, cf	3	0	1	0	1	0	.364
Lou Boudreau, ss	3	0	0	0	1	0	.167
Joe Gordon, 2b	4	0	0	0	0	0	.167
Ken Keltner, 3b	3	1	0	0	1	0	.091
Wally Judnich, rf	3	0	0	0	1	1	.000
Eddie Robinson, 1b	3	0	1	0	0	0	.222
Jim Hegan, c	3	0	1	1	0	0	.222
Gene Bearden, p	3	1	2	0	0	0	.667
TOTALS	28	2	5	1	5	1	.186

	1	2	3	4	5	6	7	8	9	R	H	E
Braves	0	0	0	0	0	0	0	0	0	0	5	1
Indians	0	0	1	1	0	0	0	0	x	2	5	0

E—Dark. DP—Braves 1 (Dark to Stanky to FMcCormick), Indians 2 (Bearden to Gordon to Robinson; Keltner to Gordon to Robinson). LOB—Braves 3, Indians 7. Scoring Position—Braves 0-for-4, Indians 2-for-6. 2B—Dark (1), Bearden (1). S—Bickford. GDP—FMcCormick, Conatser, Boudreau.

Braves	IP	H	R	ER	BB	K	ERA
Vern Bickford (L, 0-1)	3.1	4	2	1	5	1	2.70
Bill Voiselle	3.2	1	0	0	0	0	0.00
Red Barrett	1.0	0	0	0	0	0	0.00

Indians	IP	H	R	ER	BB	K	ERA
Gene Bearden (W, 1-0)	9.0	5	0	0	0	4	0.00

Time—1:36. Attendance—70,306. Umpires—HP, Stewart. 1B, Grieve. 2B, Barr. 3B, Summers.

Game 4
Saturday, October 9

Braves	AB	R	H	RBI	BB	K	Avg
Tommy Holmes, rf	4	0	0	0	0	0	.063
Al Dark, ss	4	0	0	0	0	0	.125
Earl Torgeson, 1b	3	0	2	0	1	0	.444
Glenn Elliott, 3b	4	0	0	0	0	0	.143
Marv Rickert, lf	4	1	2	1	0	1	.273
Mike McCormick, cf	4	0	1	0	0	1	.286
Phil Masi, c	3	0	0	0	0	0	.000
Bill Salkeld, ph	1	0	0	0	0	0	.333
Eddie Stanky, 2b	3	0	1	0	0	0	.300
Johnny Sain, p	2	0	1	0	0	0	.200
TOTALS	32	1	7	1	1	2	.200

Indians	AB	R	H	RBI	BB	K	Avg
Dale Mitchell, lf	4	1	1	0	0	0	.125
Larry Doby, cf	3	1	1	1	0	0	.357
Lou Boudreau, ss	3	0	1	1	0	0	.200
Joe Gordon, 2b	3	0	0	0	0	0	.133
Ken Keltner, 3b	3	0	0	0	0	0	.071
Wally Judnich, rf	3	0	0	0	0	2	.000
Bob Kennedy, rf	0	0	0	0	0	0	1.000
Eddie Robinson, 1b	3	0	2	0	0	0	.333
Jim Hegan, c	2	0	0	0	0	0	.182
Steve Gromek, p	3	0	0	0	0	1	.000
TOTALS	27	2	5	2	0	3	.180

	1	2	3	4	5	6	7	8	9	R	H	E
Braves	0	0	0	0	0	0	1	0	0	1	7	0
Indians	1	0	1	0	0	0	0	0	x	2	5	0

DP—Indians 1 (Boudreau to Gordon to Robinson). LOB—Braves 6, Indians 2. Scoring Position—Braves 0-for-4, Indians 1-for-3. 2B—Torgeson 2 (2), Boudreau (2). HR—Rickert (1), Doby (1). S—Sain, Hegan. GDP—Elliott.

Braves	IP	H	R	ER	BB	K	ERA
Johnny Sain (L, 1-1)	8.0	5	2	2	0	3	1.06

Indians	IP	H	R	ER	BB	K	ERA
Steve Gromek (W, 1-0)	9.0	7	1	1	1	2	1.00

Time—1:31. Attendance—81,897. Umpires—HP, Grieve. 1B, Barr. 2B, Summers. 3B, Stewart.

Game 5
Sunday, October 10

Braves	AB	R	H	RBI	BB	K	Avg
Tommy Holmes, rf	5	2	2	0	0	0	.143
Al Dark, ss	4	1	1	0	0	0	.150
Earl Torgeson, 1b	5	1	2	1	0	0	.429
Glenn Elliott, 3b	4	3	2	4	1	1	.222
Marv Rickert, lf	5	1	1	1	0	2	.250
Bill Salkeld, c	4	2	1	1	1	0	.286
Mike McCormick, cf	5	1	1	1	0	0	.263
Eddie Stanky, 2b	3	0	1	1	2	0	.308
Nels Potter, p	2	0	1	0	0	1	.500
Warren Spahn, p	2	0	0	1	0	1	.000
TOTALS	39	11	12	10	4	5	.239

Indians	AB	R	H	RBI	BB	K	Avg
Dale Mitchell, lf	3	1	1	1	1	0	.158
Larry Doby, cf	4	0	0	0	0	1	.278
Lou Boudreau, ss	4	0	2	0	0	0	.263
Joe Gordon, 2b	3	1	1	0	1	1	.167
Ken Keltner, 3b	3	1	0	0	1	1	.059
Wally Judnich, rf	3	1	1	1	0	0	.077
Ray Boone, ph	1	0	0	0	0	1	.000
Hal Peck, rf	0	0	0	0	0	0	—
Eddie Robinson, 1b	4	0	0	0	0	0	.250
Jim Hegan, c	4	1	1	3	0	2	.200
Bob Feller, p	2	0	0	0	0	0	.000
Ed Klieman, p	0	0	0	0	0	0	—
Russ Christopher, p	0	0	0	0	0	0	—
Satchel Paige, p	0	0	0	0	0	0	—
Al Rosen, ph	1	0	0	0	0	0	.000
Bob Muncrief, p	0	0	0	0	0	0	—
Joe Tipton, ph	1	0	0	0	0	1	.000
TOTALS	33	5	6	5	3	7	.176

	1	2	3	4	5	6	7	8	9	R	H	E
Braves	3	0	1	0	0	1	6	0	0	11	12	0
Indians	1	0	0	4	0	0	0	0	0	5	6	2

E—Doby, Keltner. LOB—Braves 6, Indians 4. Scoring Position—Braves 5-for-9, Indians 2-for-8. 2B—Boudreau (3). HR—Elliott 2 (2), Salkeld (1), Mitchell (1), Hegan (1). S—Dark.

Braves	IP	H	R	ER	BB	K	ERA
Nels Potter	3.1	5	5	5	2	0	8.44
Warren Spahn (W, 1-1)	5.2	1	0	0	1	7	2.70

Indians	IP	H	R	ER	BB	K	ERA
Bob Feller (L, 0-2)	6.1	8	7	7	2	5	5.02
Ed Klieman	0.0	1	3	3	2	0	—
Russ Christopher	0.0	2	1	1	0	0	—
Satchel Paige	0.2	0	0	0	0	0	0.00
Bob Muncrief	2.0	1	0	0	0	0	0.00

Klieman pitched to four batters in the 7th. Christopher pitched to two batters in the 7th.

Balk—Paige. Time—2:39. Attendance—86,288. Umpires—HP, Barr. 1B, Summers. 2B, Stewart. 3B, Grieve.

Game 6
Monday, October 11

Indians	AB	R	H	RBI	BB	K	Avg
Dale Mitchell, lf	4	1	1	0	0	0	.174
Bob Kennedy, lf	1	0	0	0	0	1	.500
Larry Doby, rf	4	0	2	0	1	1	.318
Lou Boudreau, ss	3	0	1	1	0	0	.273
Joe Gordon, 2b	4	1	1	1	0	0	.182
Ken Keltner, 3b	4	1	0	0	0	1	.095
Thurman Tucker, cf	3	1	1	0	1	0	.333
Eddie Robinson, 1b	4	0	2	1	0	0	.300
Jim Hegan, c	4	0	1	1	0	2	.211
Bob Lemon, p	3	0	0	0	0	0	.000
Gene Bearden, p	1	0	0	0	0	1	.500
TOTALS	35	4	10	4	2	6	.224

Braves	AB	R	H	RBI	BB	K	Avg
Tommy Holmes, rf	5	1	2	0	0	0	.192
Al Dark, ss	4	0	1	0	0	0	.167
Earl Torgeson, 1b	4	1	1	0	0	0	.389
Glenn Elliott, 3b	3	1	3	0	1	0	.333
Marv Rickert, lf	3	0	0	0	0	0	.211
Clint Conatser, ph-cf	1	0	0	1	0	0	.000
Bill Salkeld, c	2	0	0	0	1	0	.222
Phil Masi, ph-c	1	0	1	1	0	0	.125
Mike McCormick, cf-lf	4	0	1	0	1	0	.261
Eddie Stanky, 2b	1	0	0	0	3	0	.286
Connie Ryan, pr	0	0	0	0	0	0	.000
Bill Voiselle, p	1	0	0	0	0	0	.000
Frank McCormick, ph	1	0	0	0	0	0	.200
Warren Spahn, p	0	0	0	0	0	0	.000
Sibby Sisti, ph	1	0	0	0	0	0	.000
TOTALS	31	3	9	3	5	1	.229

	1	2	3	4	5	6	7	8	9	R	H	E
Indians	0	0	1	0	0	2	0	1	0	4	10	0
Braves	0	0	0	1	0	0	0	2	0	3	9	0

DP—Indians 4 (Tucker to Robinson; Lemon to Boudreau to Robinson; Gordon to Boudreau to Robinson; Hegan to Gordon), Braves 1 (Elliott to Stanky to Torgeson). LOB—Indians 7, Braves 7. Scoring Position—Indians 2-for-9, Braves 3-for-10. 2B—Mitchell (1), Boudreau (4), Torgeson (3), Masi (1). HR—Gordon (1). S—Voiselle. GDP—Boudreau, Dark, Rickert. CS—Tucker (1).

Indians	IP	H	R	ER	BB	K	ERA
Bob Lemon (W, 2-0)	7.1	8	3	3	4	1	1.65
Gene Bearden (S, 1)	1.2	1	0	0	1	0	0.00

Braves	IP	H	R	ER	BB	K	ERA
Bill Voiselle (L, 0-1)	7.0	7	3	3	2	2	2.53
Warren Spahn	2.0	3	1	1	0	4	3.00

Balk—Lemon. HBP—Boudreau by Voiselle. Time—2:16. Attendance—40,103. Umpires—HP, Summers. 1B, Stewart. 2B, Grieve. 3B, Barr.

1948 World Series—Composite Statistics

Batting

Indians	G	AB	R	H	HBI	2B	3B	HR	BB	SO	SB	CS	Avg	OBP	Slg
Gene Bearden	2	4	1	2	0	1	0	0	0	1	0	0	.500	.500	.750
Ray Boone	1	1	0	0	0	0	0	0	0	1	0	0	.000	.000	.000
Lou Boudreau	6	22	1	6	3	4	0	0	1	1	0	0	.273	.333	.455
Allie Clark	1	3	0	0	0	0	0	0	0	1	0	0	.000	.000	.000
Larry Doby	6	22	1	7	2	1	0	1	2	4	0	0	.318	.375	.500
Bob Feller	2	4	0	0	0	0	0	0	0	2	0	0	.000	.000	.000
Joe Gordon	6	22	3	4	2	0	0	1	1	2	1	0	.182	.217	.318
Steve Gromek	1	3	0	0	0	0	0	0	0	1	0	0	.000	.000	.000
Jim Hegan	6	19	2	4	5	0	0	1	1	4	1	0	.211	.250	.368
Wally Judnich	4	13	1	1	1	0	0	0	1	4	0	0	.077	.143	.077
Ken Keltner	6	21	3	2	0	0	0	0	2	3	0	0	.095	.174	.095
Bob Kennedy	3	2	0	1	1	0	0	0	0	1	0	0	.500	.500	.500
Bob Lemon	2	7	0	0	0	0	0	0	0	0	0	0	.000	.000	.000
Dale Mitchell	6	23	4	4	1	1	0	1	2	0	0	0	.174	.240	.348
Eddie Robinson	6	20	0	6	1	0	0	0	1	0	0	0	.300	.333	.300
Al Rosen	1	1	0	0	0	0	0	0	0	0	0	0	.000	.000	.000
Joe Tipton	1	1	0	0	0	0	0	0	0	1	0	0	.000	.000	.000
Thurman Tucker	1	3	1	1	0	0	0	0	1	0	0	1	.333	.500	.333
Totals	6	191	17	38	16	7	0	4	12	26	2	1	.199	.250	.298

Batting

Braves	G	AB	R	H	RBI	2B	3B	HR	BB	SO	SB	CS	Avg	OBP	Slg
Vern Bickford	1	0	0	0	0	0	0	0	0	0	0	0	—	—	—
Clint Conatser	2	4	0	0	1	0	0	0	0	0	0	0	.000	.000	.000
Al Dark	6	24	2	4	0	1	0	0	0	2	0	0	.167	.167	.208
Glenn Elliott	6	21	4	7	5	0	0	2	2	2	0	0	.333	.391	.619
Tommy Holmes	6	26	3	5	1	0	0	0	0	0	0	0	.192	.192	.192
Phil Masi	5	8	1	1	1	1	0	0	0	0	0	0	.125	.125	.250
Frank McCormick	3	5	0	1	0	0	0	0	0	2	0	0	.200	.200	.200
Mike McCormick	6	23	1	6	2	0	0	0	4	0	0	0	.261	.261	.261
Nels Potter	2	2	0	1	0	0	0	0	0	1	0	0	.500	.500	.500
Marv Rickert	5	19	2	4	2	0	0	1	0	4	0	0	.211	.211	.368
Connie Ryan	2	1	0	0	0	0	0	0	0	1	0	0	.000	.000	.000
Johnny Sain	2	5	0	1	0	0	0	0	0	0	0	0	.200	.200	.200
Bill Salkeld	5	9	2	2	1	0	0	1	5	1	0	0	.222	.500	.556
Ray Sanders	1	1	0	0	0	0	0	0	0	0	0	0	.000	.000	.000
Sibby Sisti	2	1	0	0	0	0	0	0	0	0	0	0	.000	.000	.000
Warren Spahn	3	4	0	0	1	0	0	0	0	1	0	0	.000	.000	.000
Eddie Stanky	6	14	0	4	1	1	0	0	7	0	0	0	.286	.524	.357
Earl Torgeson	5	18	2	7	1	3	0	0	2	1	1	0	.389	.450	.556
Bill Voiselle	2	2	0	0	0	0	0	0	0	0	0	0	.000	.000	.000
Totals	6	187	17	43	16	6	0	4	16	19	1	0	.230	.291	.326

Pitching

Indians	G	GS	CG	IP	H	R	ER	BB	SO	W-L	Sv-Op	Hld	ERA
Gene Bearden	2	1	1	10.2	6	0	0	1	4	1-0	1-1	0	0.00
Russ Christopher	1	0	0	0.0	2	1	1	0	0	0-0	0-0	0	—
Bob Feller	2	2	1	14.1	10	8	8	5	7	0-2	0-0	0	5.02
Steve Gromek	1	1	1	9.0	7	1	1	1	2	1-0	0-0	0	1.00
Ed Klieman	1	0	0	0.0	1	3	3	2	0	0-0	0-0	0	—
Bob Lemon	2	2	1	16.1	16	4	3	7	6	2-0	0-0	0	1.65
Bob Muncrief	1	0	0	2.0	1	0	0	0	0	0-0	0-0	0	0.00
Satchel Paige	1	0	0	0.2	0	0	0	0	0	0-0	0-0	0	0.00
Totals	6	6	4	53.0	43	17	16	16	19	4-2	1-1	0	2.72

Pitching

Braves	G	GS	CG	IP	H	R	ER	BB	SO	W-L	Sv-Op	Hld	ERA
Red Barrett	2	0	0	3.2	1	0	0	0	1	0-0	0-0	0	0.00
Vern Bickford	1	1	0	3.1	4	2	1	5	1	0-1	0-0	0	2.70
Nels Potter	2	1	0	5.1	6	6	5	2	1	0-0	0-0	0	8.44
Johnny Sain	2	2	2	17.0	9	2	2	0	9	1-1	0-0	0	1.06
Warren Spahn	3	1	0	12.0	10	4	4	3	12	1-1	0-0	0	3.00
Bill Voiselle	2	1	0	10.2	8	3	3	2	2	0-1	0-0	0	2.53
Totals	6	6	2	52.0	38	17	15	12	26	2-4	0-0	0	2.60

Fielding

Indians	Pos	G	PO	Ast	E	DP	PB	FPct
Gene Bearden	p	2	0	7	0	1	—	1.000
Lou Boudreau	ss	6	11	14	0	5	—	1.000
Russ Christopher	p	1	0	0	0	0	—	—
Allie Clark	rf	1	2	0	0	0	—	1.000
Larry Doby	cf	5	10	0	1	0	—	.909
	rf	1	1	0	0	0	—	1.000
Bob Feller	p	2	2	4	0	0	—	1.000
Joe Gordon	2b	6	15	13	1	7	—	.966
Steve Gromek	p	1	1	1	0	0	—	1.000
Jim Hegan	c	6	25	5	0	1	0	1.000
Wally Judnich	rf	4	7	0	0	0	—	1.000
Ken Keltner	3b	6	3	11	1	1	—	.933
Bob Kennedy	rf	2	1	0	0	0	—	1.000
	lf	1	1	0	0	0	—	1.000
Ed Klieman	p	1	0	0	0	0	—	—
Bob Lemon	p	2	3	9	0	1	—	1.000
Dale Mitchell	lf	6	13	0	0	0	—	1.000
Bob Muncrief	p	1	1	0	0	0	—	1.000
Satchel Paige	p	1	0	0	0	0	—	—
Hal Peck	rf	1	0	0	0	0	—	—
Eddie Robinson	1b	6	60	7	0	8	—	1.000
Thurman Tucker	cf	1	3	1	0	1	—	1.000
Totals		6	159	72	3	25	0	.987

Fielding

Braves	Pos	G	PO	Ast	E	DP	PB	FPct
Red Barrett	p	2	0	0	0	0	—	—
Vern Bickford	p	1	0	0	0	0	—	—
Clint Conatser	cf	2	1	0	0	0	—	1.000
Al Dark	ss	6	7	12	3	1	—	.864
Glenn Elliott	3b	6	11	13	3	1	—	.889
Tommy Holmes	rf	6	10	2	0	1	—	1.000
Phil Masi	c	5	10	1	0	0	0	1.000
Frank McCormick	1b	1	5	1	0	1	—	1.000
Mike McCormick	cf	5	11	0	0	0	—	1.000
	lf	2	6	0	0	0	—	1.000
Nels Potter	p	2	1	0	0	0	—	1.000
Marv Rickert	lf	5	20	0	0	0	—	1.000
Johnny Sain	p	2	2	2	0	0	—	1.000
Bill Salkeld	c	4	19	1	0	0	0	1.000
Sibby Sisti	2b	1	0	0	0	0	—	—
Warren Spahn	p	3	0	2	0	0	—	1.000
Eddie Stanky	2b	6	8	13	0	2	—	1.000
Earl Torgeson	1b	5	44	5	0	2	—	1.000
Bill Voiselle	p	2	1	0	0	0	—	1.000
Totals		6	156	52	6	8	0	.972

1949 New York Yankees (AL) 4, Brooklyn Dodgers (NL) 1

The New York Yankees brushed aside the Brooklyn Dodgers in a quiet five-game World Series. Allie Reynolds and Don Newcombe matched zeroes in the opener until New York's Tommy Henrich won it with a solo homer in the bottom of the ninth. Preacher Roe evened the Series with a six-hit shutout in the second game. Jackie Robinson scored the only run of the game on Gil Hodges' RBI single in the second inning. Johnny Mize broke open a tie game with a pinch-hit, two-run single in the top of the ninth inning of Game 3, and a Brooklyn rally in the bottom of the ninth fell just short as the Yanks prevailed, 4-3. Bobby Brown drove in three runs in New York's 6-4 win in Game 4, before the Yanks clinched it with a 10-6 victory in Game 5. A World Series contest was played under the lights for the first time when Ebbets Field's lights were turned on in the ninth inning of Game 5.

Game 1

Wednesday, October 5

Dodgers	AB	R	H	RBI	BB	K	Avg
Pee Wee Reese, ss	4	0	1	0	0	0	.250
Spider Jorgensen, 3b	3	0	1	0	1	1	.333
Duke Snider, cf	4	0	0	0	0	3	.000
Jackie Robinson, 2b	4	0	0	0	0	0	.000
Gene Hermanski, lf	3	0	0	0	1	1	.000
Carl Furillo, rf	3	0	0	0	1	0	.000
Gil Hodges, 1b	2	0	0	0	0	1	.000
Roy Campanella, c	2	0	0	0	1	1	.000
Don Newcombe, p	3	0	0	0	0	2	.000
TOTALS	28	0	2	0	4	9	.071

Yankees	AB	R	H	RBI	BB	K	Avg
Phil Rizzuto, ss	4	0	0	0	0	0	.000
Tommy Henrich, 1b	4	1	1	1	0	0	.250
Yogi Berra, c	3	0	0	0	0	1	.000
Joe DiMaggio, cf	3	0	0	0	0	1	.000
Johnny Lindell, lf	3	0	1	0	0	1	.333
Bill Johnson, 3b	3	0	0	0	0	2	.000
Cliff Mapes, rf	3	0	0	0	0	3	.000
Jerry Coleman, 2b	3	0	1	0	0	2	.333
Allie Reynolds, p	3	0	2	0	0	1	.667
TOTALS	29	1	5	1	0	11	.172

	1	2	3	4	5	6	7	8	9		R	H	E
Dodgers	0	0	0	0	0	0	0	0	0		0	2	0
Yankees	0	0	0	0	0	0	0	0	1		1	5	1

E—Coleman. DP—Yankees 1 (Reynolds to Coleman to Henrich). LOB—Dodgers 6, Yankees 4. Scoring Position—Dodgers 0-for-8, Yankees 0-for-4. 2B—Jorgensen (1), Coleman (1), Reynolds (1). HR—Henrich (1). S—Hodges. GDP—Hodges. SB—Reese (1).

Dodgers	IP	H	R	ER	BB	K	ERA
Don Newcombe (L, 0-1)	8.0	5	1	1	0	11	1.13

Yankees	IP	H	R	ER	BB	K	ERA
Allie Reynolds (W, 1-0)	9.0	2	0	0	4	9	0.00

Newcombe pitched to one batter in the 9th.

Time—2:24. Attendance—66,224. Umpires—HP, Hubbard. 1B, Reardon. 2B, Passarella. 3B, Jorda.

Game 2

Thursday, October 6

Dodgers	AB	R	H	RBI	BB	K	Avg
Pee Wee Reese, ss	4	0	0	0	0	0	.125
Spider Jorgensen, 3b	4	0	1	0	0	0	.286
Duke Snider, cf	4	0	1	0	0	0	.125
Jackie Robinson, 2b	3	1	1	0	0	1	.143
Gene Hermanski, rf	3	0	1	0	0	0	.167
Carl Furillo, ph	1	0	0	0	0	0	.000
Mike McCormick, rf	0	0	0	0	0	0	—
Marv Rackley, lf	2	0	0	0	0	0	.000
Luis Olmo, lf	2	0	1	0	0	0	.500
Gil Hodges, 1b	3	0	1	1	0	0	.200
Roy Campanella, c	2	0	1	0	1	0	.250
Preacher Roe, p	3	0	0	0	0	3	.000
TOTALS	31	1	7	1	1	4	.161

Yankees	AB	R	H	RBI	BB	K	Avg
Phil Rizzuto, ss	3	0	1	0	0	0	.143
Tommy Henrich, 1b	4	0	0	0	0	0	.125
Hank Bauer, rf	4	0	1	0	0	0	.250
Joe DiMaggio, cf	4	0	1	0	0	1	.143
Johnny Lindell, lf	4	0	0	0	0	1	.143
Bill Johnson, 3b	4	0	1	0	0	0	.143
Jerry Coleman, 2b	4	0	1	0	0	0	.286
Charlie Silvera, c	2	0	0	0	0	0	.000
Johnny Mize, ph	1	0	1	0	0	0	1.000
Snuffy Stirnweiss, pr	0	0	0	0	0	0	—
Gus Niarhos, c	0	0	0	0	0	0	—
Vic Raschi, p	2	0	0	0	0	0	.000
Bobby Brown, ph	1	0	0	0	0	1	.000
Joe Page, p	0	0	0	0	0	0	—
TOTALS	33	0	6	0	0	3	.170

	1	2	3	4	5	6	7	8	9		R	H	E
Dodgers	0	1	0	0	0	0	0	0	0		1	7	2
Yankees	0	0	0	0	0	0	0	0	0		0	6	1

E—Lindell, Reese, Roe. DP—Yankees 1 (Rizzuto to Coleman to Henrich). LOB—Dodgers 5, Yankees 7. Scoring Position—Dodgers 1-for-10, Yankees 0-for-6. 2B—Jorgensen (2), Robinson (1), Coleman (2). 3B—Hermanski (1). S—Robinson, Rizzuto. GDP—Hodges. SB—Rizzuto (1), Johnson (1).

Dodgers	IP	H	R	ER	BB	K	ERA
Preacher Roe (W, 1-0)	9.0	6	0	0	0	3	0.00

Yankees	IP	H	R	ER	BB	K	ERA
Vic Raschi (L, 0-1)	8.0	6	1	1	1	4	1.13
Joe Page	1.0	1	0	0	0	0	0.00

Time—2:30. Attendance—70,053. Umpires—HP, Reardon. 1B, Passarella. 2B, Jorda. 3B, Hubbard.

Game 3

Friday, October 7

Yankees	AB	R	H	RBI	BB	K	Avg
Phil Rizzuto, ss	4	0	0	1	0	0	.091
Tommy Henrich, 1b	3	0	0	0	1	0	.091
Yogi Berra, c	3	1	0	0	1	1	.000
Joe DiMaggio, cf	4	0	0	0	0	2	.091
Bobby Brown, 3b	4	1	1	0	0	0	.200
Gene Woodling, lf	3	1	1	0	1	0	.333
Cliff Mapes, rf	2	1	0	0	1	0	.000
Johnny Mize, ph	1	0	1	2	0	0	1.000
Hank Bauer, pr-rf	0	0	0	0	0	0	.250
Jerry Coleman, 2b	4	0	1	1	0	2	.273
Tommy Byrne, p	1	0	1	0	0	0	1.000
Joe Page, p	3	0	0	0	0	2	.000
TOTALS	32	4	5	4	4	7	.164

Dodgers	AB	R	H	RBI	BB	K	Avg
Pee Wee Reese, ss	2	1	1	1	1	0	.200
Eddie Miksis, 3b	4	0	1	0	0	0	.250
Carl Furillo, rf	4	0	1	0	0	0	.125
Jackie Robinson, 2b	2	0	0	0	2	0	.111
Gil Hodges, 1b	3	0	0	0	1	0	.125
Luis Olmo, lf	4	1	1	1	0	0	.333
Duke Snider, cf	4	0	0	0	0	1	.083
Roy Campanella, c	4	1	1	1	0	0	.250
Ralph Branca, p	3	0	0	0	0	3	.000
Jack Banta, p	0	0	0	0	0	0	—
Bruce Edwards, ph	1	0	0	0	0	1	.000
TOTALS	31	3	5	3	4	5	.159

	1	2	3	4	5	6	7	8	9		R	H	E
Yankees	0	0	1	0	0	0	0	0	3		4	5	0
Dodgers	0	0	0	1	0	0	0	0	2		3	5	0

DP—Yankees 1 (Berra to Coleman). LOB—Yankees 5, Dodgers 6. Scoring Position—Yankees 2-for-6, Dodgers 0-for-4. 2B—Woodling (1). HR—Reese (1), Olmo (1), Campanella (1).

Yankees	IP	H	R	ER	BB	K	ERA
Tommy Byrne	3.1	2	1	1	2	1	2.70
Joe Page (W, 1-0)	5.2	3	2	2	4	4	2.70

Dodgers	IP	H	R	ER	BB	K	ERA
Ralph Branca (L, 0-1)	8.2	4	4	4	6	6	4.15
Jack Banta	0.1	1	0	0	0	1	0.00

HBP—Reese by Byrne. Time—2:30. Attendance—32,788. Umpires—HP, Passarella. 1B, Jorda. 2B, Hubbard. 3B, Reardon.

Game 4

Saturday, October 8

Yankees	AB	R	H	RBI	BB	K	Avg
Phil Rizzuto, ss	4	0	2	0	1	0	.200
Tommy Henrich, 1b	4	1	3	0	1	0	.267
Yogi Berra, c	5	1	1	0	0	0	.091
Joe DiMaggio, cf	3	1	0	0	2	1	.071
Bobby Brown, 3b	3	1	2	3	1	0	.375
Gene Woodling, lf	3	1	0	0	1	0	.167
Cliff Mapes, rf	2	1	1	2	0	0	.143
Hank Bauer, ph-rf	2	0	0	0	0	0	.167
Jerry Coleman, 2b	4	0	0	0	0	0	.200
Ed Lopat, p	3	0	1	1	0	0	.333
Allie Reynolds, p	1	0	0	0	0	0	.500
TOTALS	34	6	10	6	6	1	.202

Dodgers	AB	R	H	RBI	BB	K	Avg
Pee Wee Reese, ss	4	1	2	0	0	0	.286
Eddie Miksis, 3b	2	0	0	0	0	1	.167
Billy Cox, ph-3b	2	0	1	0	0	0	.500
Duke Snider, cf	4	0	0	0	0	1	.063
Jackie Robinson, 2b	3	1	1	1	1	0	.167
Gil Hodges, 1b	4	1	0	0	0	1	.167
Luis Olmo, lf	4	1	1	1	0	1	.300
Roy Campanella, c	4	0	1	0	0	0	.250
Gene Hermanski, rf	4	0	2	1	0	2	.300
Don Newcombe, p	1	0	0	0	0	1	.000
Joe Hatten, p	0	0	0	0	0	0	—
Tommy Brown, ph	1	0	0	0	0	0	.000
Carl Erskine, p	0	0	0	0	0	0	—
Spider Jorgensen, ph	1	0	0	0	0	1	.250
Jack Banta, p	0	0	0	0	0	0	—
Dick Whitman, ph	1	0	0	0	0	1	.000
TOTALS	35	4	9	4	1	9	.204

	1 2 3	4 5 6	7 8 9	R	H	E
Yankees	0 0 0	3 3 0	0 0 0	6	10	0
Dodgers	0 0 0	0 0 4	0 0 0	4	9	1

E—Miksis. DP—Yankees 1 (Rizzuto to Henrich), Dodgers 1 (Miksis to Campanella to Robinson). LOB—Yankees 7, Dodgers 5. Scoring Position—Yankees 4-for-10, Dodgers 4-for-9. 2B—BBrown (1), Mapes (1), Lopat (1), Reese (1). 3B—BBrown (1). GDP—Snider.

Yankees	IP	H	R	ER	BB	K	ERA
Ed Lopat (W, 1-0)	5.2	9	4	4	1	4	6.35
Allie Reynolds (S, 1)	3.1	0	0	0	0	5	0.00

Dodgers	IP	H	R	ER	BB	K	ERA
Don Newcombe (L, 0-2)	3.2	5	3	3	3	0	3.09
Joe Hatten	1.1	3	3	3	2	0	20.25
Carl Erskine	1.0	1	0	0	0	0	0.00
Jack Banta	3.0	1	0	0	1	1	0.00

Time—2:42. Attendance—33,934. Umpires—HP, Jorda. 1B, Hubbard. 2B, Reardon. 3B, Passarella.

Game 5

Sunday, October 9

Yankees	AB	R	H	RBI	BB	K	Avg
Phil Rizzuto, ss	3	2	0	0	2	1	.167
Tommy Henrich, 1b	4	2	1	0	1	0	.263
Yogi Berra, c	5	0	0	1	0	1	.063
Joe DiMaggio, cf	4	1	2	2	1	0	.111
Bobby Brown, 3b	4	2	3	2	1	1	.500
Gene Woodling, lf	4	2	3	0	1	0	.400
Cliff Mapes, rf	3	1	0	0	1	1	.100
Jerry Coleman, 2b	5	0	2	3	0	0	.250
Vic Raschi, p	3	0	1	1	1	1	.200
Joe Page, p	1	0	0	0	0	0	.000
TOTALS	36	10	11	9	8	5	.212

Dodgers	AB	R	H	RBI	BB	K	Avg
Pee Wee Reese, ss	5	0	2	1	0	0	.316
Spider Jorgensen, 3b	3	1	0	0	1	0	.182
Eddie Miksis, ph	1	0	1	0	0	0	.286
Duke Snider, cf	5	2	2	0	0	3	.143
Jackie Robinson, 2b	4	0	1	1	1	1	.188
Gene Hermanski, rf	3	1	1	2	0	0	.308
Gil Hodges, 1b	5	1	2	3	0	2	.235
Marv Rackley, lf	3	0	0	0	0	2	.000
Luis Olmo, ph-lf	1	0	0	0	0	1	.273
Roy Campanella, c	3	1	1	0	1	0	.267
Rex Barney, p	0	0	0	0	0	0	—
Jack Banta, p	1	0	0	0	0	0	.000
Tommy Brown, ph	1	0	0	0	0	1	.000
Carl Erskine, p	0	0	0	0	0	0	—
Joe Hatten, p	0	0	0	0	0	0	—
Billy Cox, ph	1	0	0	0	0	1	.333
Erv Palica, p	0	0	0	0	0	0	—
Bruce Edwards, ph	1	0	1	0	0	0	.500
Paul Minner, p	0	0	0	0	0	0	—
TOTALS	37	6	11	6	5	11	.231

	1 2 3	4 5 6	7 8 9	R	H	E
Yankees	2 0 3	1 1 3	0 0 0	10	11	1
Dodgers	0 0 1	0 0 1	4 0 0	6	11	2

E—Mapes, Robinson, Barney. DP—Yankees 1 (Page to Rizzuto to Henrich). LOB—Yankees 9, Dodgers 9. Scoring Position—Yankees 3-for-14, Dodgers 3-for-12. 2B—Woodling 2 (3), Coleman (3), Snider (1), Campanella (1), Miksis (1). 3B—BBrown (2). HR—DiMaggio (1), Hodges (1). S—Rizzuto, Mapes. GDP—Reese.

Yankees	IP	H	R	ER	BB	K	ERA
Vic Raschi (W, 1-1)	6.2	9	6	6	4	7	4.30
Joe Page (S, 1)	2.1	2	0	0	1	4	2.00

Dodgers	IP	H	R	ER	BB	K	ERA
Rex Barney (L, 0-1)	2.2	3	5	5	6	2	16.88
Jack Banta	2.1	3	2	2	0	2	3.18
Carl Erskine	0.2	2	3	3	1	0	16.20
Joe Hatten	0.1	1	0	0	0	0	16.20
Erv Palica	2.0	1	0	0	1	1	0.00
Paul Minner	1.0	1	0	0	0	0	0.00

Time—3:04. Attendance—33,711. Umpires—HP, Hubbard. 1B, Reardon. 2B, Passarella. 3B, Jorda.

1949 World Series—Composite Statistics

Batting

Yankees	G	AB	R	H	RBI	2B	3B	HR	BB	SO	SB	CS	Avg	OBP	Slg
Hank Bauer	3	6	0	1	0	0	0	0	0	0	0	0	.167	.167	.167
Yogi Berra	4	16	2	1	1	0	0	0	1	3	0	0	.063	.118	.063
Bobby Brown	4	12	4	6	5	1	2	0	2	2	0	0	.500	.571	.917
Tommy Byrne	1	1	0	1	0	0	0	0	0	0	0	1	1.000	1.000	1.000
Jerry Coleman	5	20	0	5	4	3	0	0	0	4	0	0	.250	.250	.400
Joe DiMaggio	5	18	2	2	2	0	0	1	3	5	0	0	.111	.238	.278
Tommy Henrich	5	19	4	5	1	0	0	1	3	0	0	0	.263	.364	.421
Bill Johnson	2	7	0	1	0	0	0	0	0	2	1	0	.143	.143	.143
Johnny Lindell	2	7	0	1	0	0	0	0	0	2	0	0	.143	.143	.143
Ed Lopat	1	3	0	1	1	1	0	0	0	0	0	0	.333	.333	.667
Cliff Mapes	4	10	3	1	2	1	0	0	2	4	0	0	.100	.250	.200
Johnny Mize	2	2	0	2	2	0	0	0	0	0	0	0	1.000	1.000	1.000
Joe Page	3	4	0	0	0	0	0	0	0	2	0	0	.000	.000	.000
Vic Raschi	2	5	0	1	1	0	0	0	1	1	0	0	.200	.333	.200
Allie Reynolds	2	4	0	2	0	1	0	0	0	1	0	0	.500	.500	.750
Phil Rizzuto	5	18	2	3	1	0	0	0	3	1	1	0	.167	.286	.167
Charlie Silvera	1	2	0	0	0	0	0	0	0	0	0	0	.000	.000	.000
Snuffy Stirnweiss	1	0	0	0	0	0	0	0	0	0	0	0	—	—	—
Gene Woodling	3	10	4	4	0	3	0	0	3	0	0	0	.400	.538	.700
Totals	**5**	**164**	**21**	**37**	**20**	**10**	**2**	**2**	**18**	**27**	**2**	**0**	**.226**	**.302**	**.348**

Dodgers	G	AB	R	H	RBI	2B	3B	HR	BB	SO	SB	CS	Avg	OBP	Slg
Jack Banta	3	1	0	0	0	0	0	0	0	0	0	0	.000	.000	.000
Ralph Branca	1	3	0	0	0	0	0	0	0	3	0	0	.000	.000	.000
Tommy Brown	2	2	0	0	0	0	0	0	0	1	0	0	.000	.000	.000
Roy Campanella	5	15	2	4	2	1	0	1	3	1	0	0	.267	.389	.533
Billy Cox	2	3	0	1	0	0	0	0	0	1	0	0	.333	.333	.333
Bruce Edwards	2	2	0	1	0	0	0	0	0	1	0	0	.500	.500	.500
Carl Furillo	3	8	0	1	0	0	0	0	1	0	0	0	.125	.222	.125
Gene Hermanski	4	13	1	4	2	0	1	0	3	3	0	0	.308	.438	.462
Gil Hodges	5	17	2	4	4	0	0	1	1	4	0	0	.235	.278	.412
Spider Jorgensen	4	11	1	2	0	2	0	0	2	2	0	0	.182	.308	.364
Eddie Miksis	3	7	0	2	0	1	0	0	0	1	0	0	.286	.286	.429
Don Newcombe	2	4	0	0	0	0	0	0	0	3	0	0	.000	.000	.000
Luis Olmo	4	11	2	3	2	0	0	1	0	2	0	0	.273	.273	.545
Marv Rackley	2	5	0	0	0	0	0	0	0	2	0	0	.000	.000	.000
Pee Wee Reese	5	19	2	6	2	1	0	1	1	0	1	0	.316	.381	.526
Jackie Robinson	5	16	2	3	2	1	0	0	4	2	0	0	.188	.350	.250
Preacher Roe	1	3	0	0	0	0	0	0	0	3	0	0	.000	.000	.000
Duke Snider	5	21	2	3	0	1	0	0	0	8	0	0	.143	.143	.190
Dick Whitman	1	1	0	0	0	0	0	0	0	1	0	0	.000	.000	.000
Totals	**5**	**162**	**14**	**34**	**14**	**7**	**1**	**4**	**15**	**38**	**1**	**0**	**.210**	**.281**	**.340**

Pitching

Yankees	G	GS	CG	IP	H	R	ER	BB	SO	W-L	Sv-Op	Hld	ERA
Tommy Byrne	1	1	0	3.1	2	1	1	2	1	0-0	0-0	0	2.70
Ed Lopat	1	1	0	5.2	9	4	4	1	4	1-0	0-0	0	6.35
Joe Page	3	0	0	9.0	6	2	2	3	8	1-0	1-1	0	2.00
Vic Raschi	2	2	0	14.2	15	7	7	5	11	1-1	0-0	0	4.30
Allie Reynolds	2	1	1	12.1	2	0	0	4	14	1-0	1-1	0	0.00
Totals	**5**	**5**	**1**	**45.0**	**34**	**14**	**14**	**15**	**38**	**4-1**	**2-2**	**0**	**2.80**

Dodgers	G	GS	CG	IP	H	R	ER	BB	SO	W-L	Sv-Op	Hld	ERA
Jack Banta	3	0	0	5.2	5	2	2	1	4	0-0	0-0	0	3.18
Rex Barney	1	1	0	2.2	3	5	5	6	2	0-1	0-0	0	16.88
Ralph Branca	1	1	0	8.2	4	4	4	4	6	0-1	0-0	0	4.15
Carl Erskine	2	0	0	1.2	3	3	3	1	0	0-0	0-0	0	16.20
Joe Hatten	2	0	0	1.2	4	3	3	2	0	0-0	0-0	0	16.20
Paul Minner	1	0	0	1.0	1	0	0	0	0	0-0	0-0	0	0.00
Don Newcombe	2	2	1	11.2	10	4	4	3	11	0-2	0-0	0	3.09
Erv Palica	1	0	0	2.0	1	0	0	1	1	0-0	0-0	0	0.00
Preacher Roe	1	1	1	9.0	6	0	0	0	3	1-0	0-0	0	0.00
Totals	**5**	**5**	**2**	**44.0**	**37**	**21**	**21**	**18**	**27**	**1-4**	**0-0**	**0**	**4.30**

Fielding

Yankees	Pos	G	PO	Ast	E	DP	PB	FPct
Hank Bauer	rf	3	3	0	0	0	—	1.000
Yogi Berra	c	4	37	3	0	1	0	1.000
Bobby Brown	3b	3	0	6	0	0	—	1.000
Tommy Byrne	p	1	0	0	0	0	—	—
Jerry Coleman	2b	5	10	9	1	3	—	.950
Joe DiMaggio	cf	5	7	0	0	0	—	1.000
Tommy Henrich	1b	5	48	1	0	4	—	1.000
Bill Johnson	3b	2	2	5	0	0	—	1.000
Johnny Lindell	lf	2	2	1	1	0	—	.750
Ed Lopat	p	1	0	1	0	0	—	1.000
Cliff Mapes	rf	4	8	0	1	0	—	.889
Gus Niarhos	c	1	0	0	0	0	0	—
Joe Page	p	3	0	2	0	1	—	1.000
Vic Raschi	p	2	0	0	0	0	—	—
Allie Reynolds	p	2	0	1	0	1	—	1.000
Phil Rizzuto	ss	5	5	15	0	3	—	1.000
Charlie Silvera	c	1	6	0	0	0	0	1.000
Gene Woodling	lf	3	7	0	0	0	—	1.000
Totals		**5**	**135**	**44**	**3**	**13**	**0**	**.984**

Dodgers	Pos	G	PO	Ast	E	DP	PB	FPct
Jack Banta	p	3	0	1	0	0	—	1.000
Rex Barney	p	1	1	1	1	0	—	.667
Ralph Branca	p	1	1	0	0	0	—	1.000
Roy Campanella	c	5	32	2	0	1	0	1.000
Billy Cox	3b	1	1	0	0	0	—	1.000
Carl Erskine	p	2	0	0	0	0	—	—
Carl Furillo	rf	2	2	0	0	0	—	1.000
Joe Hatten	p	2	0	0	0	0	—	—
Gene Hermanski	rf	3	6	0	0	0	—	1.000
	lf	1	0	0	0	0	—	—
Gil Hodges	1b	5	38	3	0	0	—	1.000
Spider Jorgensen	3b	3	1	6	0	0	—	1.000
Mike McCormick	rf	1	1	0	0	0	—	1.000
Eddie Miksis	3b	2	3	3	1	1	—	.857
Paul Minner	p	1	0	1	0	0	—	1.000
Don Newcombe	p	2	1	1	0	0	—	1.000
Luis Olmo	lf	4	6	1	0	0	—	1.000
Erv Palica	p	1	0	1	0	0	—	1.000
Marv Rackley	lf	2	3	0	0	0	—	1.000
Pee Wee Reese	ss	5	5	9	1	0	—	.933
Jackie Robinson	2b	5	12	9	1	1	—	.955
Preacher Roe	p	1	1	1	1	0	—	.667
Duke Snider	cf	5	18	1	0	0	—	1.000
Totals		**5**	**132**	**40**	**5**	**3**	**0**	**.972**

1950 New York Yankees (AL) 4, Philadelphia Phillies (NL) 0

Casey Stengel's New York Yankees swept the "Whiz Kids," Eddie Sawyer's Philadelphia Phillies, in one of the lowest-scoring World Series ever. With his starting rotation in shambles due to injuries and an exhausting stretch run, Sawyer selected ace reliever Jim Konstanty as his Game 1 starter. Konstanty had set a major league record during the regular season with 74 relief appearances, and hadn't started a game in four years. He acquitted himself well, pitching eight strong innings, but ultimately lost to Vic Raschi, 1-0. The Yankees took Game 2 on Joe DiMaggio's 10th-inning home run, and tallied single runs in the last two frames of the third game for their third straight one-run victory. In the fourth and final game, 21-year-old rookie southpaw Whitey Ford came within one out of a shutout when left fielder Gene Woodling dropped a fly ball, allowing two runs to score. Allie Reynolds came on to fan Stan Lopata for the final out, and the Yankees wrapped up their second straight World Championship.

Game 1

Wednesday, October 4

Yankees	AB	R	H	RBI	BB	K	Avg
Gene Woodling, lf	3	0	1	0	2	0	.333
Phil Rizzuto, ss	3	0	1	0	0	0	.333
Yogi Berra, c	4	0	0	0	0	0	.000
Joe DiMaggio, cf	2	0	0	0	2	0	.000
Johnny Mize, 1b	4	0	0	0	0	0	.000
Johnny Hopp, 1b	0	0	0	0	0	0	—
Bobby Brown, 3b	4	1	1	0	0	0	.250
Bill Johnson, 3b	0	0	0	0	0	0	—
Hank Bauer, rf	4	0	1	0	0	0	.250
Jerry Coleman, 2b	4	0	0	1	0	0	.000
Vic Raschi, p	3	0	1	0	0	0	.333
TOTALS	31	1	5	1	4	0	.161

Phillies	AB	R	H	RBI	BB	K	Avg
Eddie Waitkus, 1b	3	0	0	0	1	0	.000
Richie Ashburn, cf	4	0	0	0	0	0	.000
Dick Sisler, lf	4	0	0	0	0	2	.000
Del Ennis, rf	3	0	0	0	0	0	.000
Puddin' Head Jones, 3b	3	0	1	0	0	0	.333
Granny Hamner, ss	3	0	0	0	0	0	.000
Andy Seminick, c	3	0	1	0	0	1	.333
Mike Goliat, 2b	3	0	0	0	0	1	.000
Jim Konstanty, p	2	0	0	0	0	1	.000
Dick Whitman, ph	1	0	0	0	0	0	.000
Russ Meyer, p	0	0	0	0	0	0	—
TOTALS	29	0	2	0	1	5	.069

	1	2	3	4	5	6	7	8	9		R	H	E
Yankees	0	0	0	1	0	0	0	0	0		1	5	0
Phillies	0	0	0	0	0	0	0	0	0		0	2	1

E—Jones. LOB—Yankees 9, Phillies 3. Scoring Position—Yankees 0-for-10, Phillies 0-for-1. 2B—Brown (1). S—Rizzuto, Raschi.

Yankees	IP	H	R	ER	BB	K	ERA
Vic Raschi (W, 1-0)	9.0	2	0	0	1	5	0.00

Phillies	IP	H	R	ER	BB	K	ERA
Jim Konstanty (L, 0-1)	8.0	4	1	1	4	0	1.13
Russ Meyer	1.0	1	0	0	0	0	0.00

Time—2:17. Attendance—30,746. Umpires—HP, Conlan. 1B, McGowan. 2B, Boggess. 3B, Berry.

Game 2

Thursday, October 5

Yankees	AB	R	H	RBI	BB	K	Avg
Gene Woodling, lf	5	0	2	1	0	0	.375
Phil Rizzuto, ss	4	0	0	0	1	0	.143
Yogi Berra, c	5	0	1	0	0	1	.111
Joe DiMaggio, cf	5	1	1	1	0	0	.143
Johnny Mize, 1b	4	0	1	0	0	1	.125
Bill Johnson, 3b	1	0	0	0	0	1	.000
Bobby Brown, 3b	3	0	1	0	0	0	.375
Johnny Hopp, pr-1b	1	0	0	0	0	0	.000
Hank Bauer, rf	5	0	1	0	0	0	.222
Jerry Coleman, 2b	3	1	1	0	1	0	.143
Allie Reynolds, p	3	0	1	0	0	2	.333
TOTALS	40	2	10	2	3	5	.206

Phillies	AB	R	H	RBI	BB	K	Avg
Eddie Waitkus, 1b	4	0	2	0	0	0	.286
Richie Ashburn, cf	5	0	2	1	0	0	.222
Dick Sisler, lf	5	0	0	0	0	2	.000
Del Ennis, rf	4	0	0	0	0	0	.000
Puddin' Head Jones, 3b	4	0	0	0	0	1	.143
Granny Hamner, ss	3	0	2	0	1	0	.333
Andy Seminick, c	2	0	0	0	1	1	.200
Putsy Caballero, pr	0	0	0	0	0	0	—
Ken Silvestri, c	0	0	0	0	0	0	—
Dick Whitman, ph	1	0	0	0	1	0	.000
Stan Lopata, c	0	0	0	0	0	0	—
Mike Goliat, 2b	4	1	1	0	0	0	.143
Robin Roberts, p	2	0	0	0	0	1	.000
Jackie Mayo, ph	0	0	0	0	1	0	—
TOTALS	33	1	7	1	4	6	.150

	1	2	3	4	5	6	7	8	9	10		R	H	E
Yankees	0	1	0	0	0	0	0	0	0	1		2	10	0
Phillies	0	0	0	0	1	0	0	0	0	0		1	7	0

DP—Yankees 2 (Johnson to Coleman to Hopp; Rizzuto to Coleman to Hopp). LOB—Yankees 11, Phillies 8. Scoring Position—Yankees 1-for-8, Phillies 0-for-12. 2B—Coleman (1), Waitkus (1), Ashburn (1), Hamner (1). 3B—Hamner (1). HR—DiMaggio (1). S—Waitkus, Roberts. GDP—Ennis, Goliat. SB—Hamner (1).

Yankees	IP	H	R	ER	BB	K	ERA
Allie Reynolds (W, 1-0)	10.0	7	1	1	4	6	0.90

Phillies	IP	H	R	ER	BB	K	ERA
Robin Roberts (L, 0-1)	10.0	10	2	2	3	5	1.80

Time—3:06. Attendance—32,660. Umpires—HP, McGowan. 1B, Boggess. 2B, Berry. 3B, Conlan.

Game 3

Friday, October 6

Phillies	AB	R	H	RBI	BB	K	Avg
Eddie Waitkus, 1b	5	0	1	0	0	0	.250
Richie Ashburn, cf	4	0	1	0	0	3	.231
Puddin' Head Jones, 3b	3	0	1	0	0	1	.200
Del Ennis, rf	4	1	1	0	0	0	.091
Dick Sisler, lf	4	0	1	1	0	0	.077
Jackie Mayo, lf	0	0	0	0	0	0	—
Granny Hamner, ss	4	1	3	0	0	0	.500
Andy Seminick, c	2	0	1	0	0	1	.286
Mike Goliat, 2b	3	0	1	1	1	0	.200
Putsy Caballero, pr	0	0	0	0	0	0	—
Jimmy Bloodworth, 2b	0	0	0	0	0	0	—
Ken Heintzelman, p	2	0	0	0	0	0	.000
Jim Konstanty, p	0	0	0	0	0	0	.000
Dick Whitman, ph	1	0	0	0	0	0	.000
Russ Meyer, p	0	0	0	0	0	0	—
TOTALS	32	2	10	2	1	5	.207

Yankees	AB	R	H	RBI	BB	K	Avg
Phil Rizzuto, ss	3	1	1	0	2	0	.200
Jerry Coleman, 2b	4	1	3	2	1	0	.364
Yogi Berra, c	2	0	0	0	2	0	.091
Joe DiMaggio, cf	3	0	1	0	1	0	.200
Hank Bauer, lf	3	0	0	0	0	0	.167
Bobby Brown, ph	1	0	0	0	0	0	.333
Jackie Jensen, pr	0	0	0	0	0	0	—
Tom Ferrick, p	0	0	0	0	0	0	—
Johnny Mize, 1b	4	0	0	0	0	0	.083
Joe Collins, 1b	0	0	0	0	0	0	—
Bill Johnson, 3b	4	0	0	0	0	2	.000
Cliff Mapes, rf	4	0	0	0	0	1	.000
Ed Lopat, p	2	0	1	0	0	1	.500
Gene Woodling, ph-lf	2	1	1	0	0	0	.400
TOTALS	32	3	7	2	6	4	.208

	1	2	3	4	5	6	7	8	9		R	H	E
Phillies	0	0	0	0	0	1	1	0	0		2	10	2
Yankees	0	0	1	0	0	0	0	1	1		3	7	0

E—Hamner, Seminick. DP—Phillies 1 (Hamner to Waitkus). LOB—Phillies 8, Yankees 9. Scoring Position—Phillies 2-for-10, Yankees 2-for-4. 2B—Ennis (1), Hamner (2). S—Jones, Seminick 2, Heintzelman. SB—Rizzuto (1).

Phillies	IP	H	R	ER	BB	K	ERA
Ken Heintzelman	7.2	4	2	1	6	3	1.17
Jim Konstanty (BS, 1)	0.1	0	0	0	0	0	1.08
Russ Meyer (L, 0-1)	0.2	3	1	1	0	1	5.40

Yankees	IP	H	R	ER	BB	K	ERA
Ed Lopat	8.0	9	2	2	0	5	2.25
Tom Ferrick (W, 1-0)	1.0	1	0	0	1	0	0.00

Time—2:35. Attendance—64,505. Umpires—HP, Boggess. 1B, Berry. 2B, Conlan. 3B, McGowan.

Game 4

Saturday, October 7

Phillies	AB	R	H	RBI	BB	K	Avg
Eddie Waitkus, 1b	3	0	1	0	1	0	.267
Richie Ashburn, cf	4	0	0	0	0	1	.176
Puddin' Head Jones, 3b	4	1	2	0	0	1	.286
Del Ennis, rf	3	0	1	0	0	0	.143
Dick Sisler, lf	4	0	0	0	0	1	.059
Ken Johnson, pr	0	1	0	0	0	0	—
Granny Hamner, ss	4	0	1	0	0	2	.429
Andy Seminick, c	4	0	0	0	0	1	.182
Jackie Mayo, pr	0	0	0	0	0	0	—
Mike Goliat, 2b	4	0	1	0	0	1	.214
Bob Miller, p	0	0	0	0	0	0	—
Jim Konstanty, p	2	0	1	0	0	0	.250
Putsy Caballero, ph	1	0	0	0	0	1	.000
Robin Roberts, p	0	0	0	0	0	0	.000
Stan Lopata, ph	1	0	0	0	0	1	.000
TOTALS	34	2	7	0	1	8	.210

Yankees	AB	R	H	RBI	BB	K	Avg
Gene Woodling, lf	4	1	2	0	0	0	.429
Phil Rizzuto, ss	4	0	0	0	0	0	.143
Yogi Berra, c	4	2	2	2	0	0	.200
Joe DiMaggio, cf	3	1	2	1	0	1	.308
Johnny Mize, 1b	3	0	1	0	0	0	.133
Johnny Hopp, 1b	1	0	0	0	0	0	.000
Bobby Brown, 3b	3	1	1	1	0	0	.333
Bill Johnson, 3b	1	0	0	0	0	0	.000
Hank Bauer, rf	3	0	0	1	0	0	.133
Jerry Coleman, 2b	3	0	0	0	0	0	.286
Whitey Ford, p	3	0	0	0	0	2	.000
Allie Reynolds, p	0	0	0	0	0	0	.333
TOTALS	32	5	8	5	0	3	.222

	1	2	3	4	5	6	7	8	9		R	H	E
Phillies	0	0	0	0	0	0	0	2	0		2	7	1
Yankees	2	0	0	0	3	0	0	0	x		5	8	2

E—Goliat, Brown, Woodling. DP—Yankees 2 (Mize to Berra; Coleman to Rizzuto to Mize). LOB—Phillies 7, Yankees 4. Scoring Position—Phillies 0-for-7, Yankees 3-for-6. 2B—Jones (1), DiMaggio (1). 3B—Brown (1). HR—Berra (1). GDP—Sisler. CS—Woodling (1).

Phillies	IP	H	R	ER	BB	K	ERA
Bob Miller (L, 0-1)	0.1	2	2	1	0	0	27.00
Jim Konstanty	6.2	5	3	3	0	3	2.40
Robin Roberts	1.0	1	0	0	0	0	1.64

Yankees	IP	H	R	ER	BB	K	ERA
Whitey Ford (W, 1-0)	8.2	7	2	0	1	7	0.00
Allie Reynolds (S, 1)	0.1	0	0	0	0	1	0.87

WP—Miller. HBP—Ennis by Ford, DiMaggio by Konstanty. Time—2:05. Attendance—68,098. Umpires—HP, Berry. 1B, Coleman. 2B, McGowan. 3B, Boggess.

1950 World Series—Composite Statistics

Batting

Yankees	G	AB	R	H	RBI	2B	3B	HR	BB	SO	SB	CS	Avg	OBP	Slg
Hank Bauer	4	15	0	2	1	0	0	0	0	0	0	0	.133	.133	.133
Yogi Berra	4	15	2	3	2	0	0	1	2	1	0	0	.200	.294	.400
Bobby Brown	4	12	2	4	1	1	1	0	0	0	0	0	.333	.333	.583
Jerry Coleman	4	14	2	4	3	1	0	0	2	0	0	0	.286	.375	.357
Joe DiMaggio	4	13	2	4	2	1	0	1	3	1	0	0	.308	.471	.615
Whitey Ford	1	3	0	0	0	0	0	0	0	2	0	0	.000	.000	.000
Johnny Hopp	3	2	0	0	0	0	0	0	0	0	0	0	.000	.000	.000
Jackie Jensen	1	0	0	0	0	0	0	0	0	0	0	0	—	—	—
Bill Johnson	4	6	0	0	0	0	0	0	0	3	0	0	.000	.000	.000
Ed Lopat	1	2	0	1	0	0	0	0	0	1	0	0	.500	.500	.500
Cliff Mapes	1	4	0	0	0	0	0	0	0	1	0	0	.000	.000	.000
Johnny Mize	4	15	0	2	0	0	0	0	0	1	0	0	.133	.133	.133
Vic Raschi	1	3	0	1	0	0	0	0	0	0	0	0	.333	.333	.333
Allie Reynolds	2	3	0	1	0	0	0	0	1	2	0	0	.333	.500	.333
Phil Rizzuto	4	14	1	2	0	0	0	0	3	0	1	0	.143	.294	.143
Gene Woodling	4	14	2	6	1	0	0	0	2	0	0	1	.429	.500	.429
Totals	**4**	**135**	**11**	**30**	**10**	**3**	**1**	**2**	**13**	**12**	**1**	**1**	**.222**	**.295**	**.304**

Batting

Phillies	G	AB	R	H	RBI	2B	3B	HR	BB	SO	SB	CS	Avg	OBP	Slg
Richie Ashburn	4	17	0	3	1	1	0	0	0	4	0	0	.176	.176	.235
Putsy Caballero	3	1	0	0	0	0	0	0	0	1	0	0	.000	.000	.000
Del Ennis	4	14	1	2	0	1	0	0	0	1	0	0	.143	.200	.214
Mike Goliat	4	14	1	3	1	0	0	0	1	2	0	0	.214	.267	.214
Granny Hamner	4	14	1	6	0	2	1	0	1	2	1	0	.429	.467	.714
Ken Heintzelman	1	2	0	0	0	0	0	0	0	0	0	0	.000	.000	.000
Ken Johnson	1	0	1	0	0	0	0	0	0	0	0	0	—	—	—
Puddin' Head Jones	4	14	1	4	0	1	0	0	0	3	0	0	.286	.286	.357
Jim Konstanty	3	4	0	1	0	0	0	0	0	1	0	0	.250	.250	.250
Stan Lopata	2	1	0	0	0	0	0	0	0	1	0	0	.000	.000	.000
Jackie Mayo	3	0	0	0	0	0	0	0	1	0	0	0	—	1.000	—
Robin Roberts	2	2	0	0	0	0	0	0	0	1	0	0	.000	.000	.000
Andy Seminick	4	11	0	2	0	0	0	0	1	3	0	0	.182	.250	.182
Dick Sisler	4	17	0	1	1	0	0	0	0	5	0	0	.059	.059	.059
Eddie Waitkus	4	15	0	4	0	1	0	0	2	0	0	0	.267	.353	.333
Dick Whitman	3	2	0	0	0	0	0	0	1	0	0	0	.000	.333	.000
Totals	**4**	**128**	**5**	**26**	**3**	**6**	**1**	**0**	**7**	**24**	**1**	**0**	**.203**	**.250**	**.266**

Pitching

Yankees	G	GS	CG	IP	H	R	ER	BB	SO	W-L	Sv-Op	Hld	ERA
Tom Ferrick	1	0	0	1.0	1	0	0	1	0	1-0	0-0	0	0.00
Whitey Ford	1	1	0	8.2	7	2	0	1	7	1-0	0-0	0	0.00
Ed Lopat	1	1	0	8.0	9	2	2	0	5	0-0	0-0	0	2.25
Vic Raschi	1	1	1	9.0	2	0	0	1	5	1-0	0-0	0	0.00
Allie Reynolds	2	1	1	10.1	7	1	1	4	7	1-0	1-1	0	0.87
Totals	**4**	**4**	**2**	**37.0**	**26**	**5**	**3**	**7**	**24**	**4-0**	**1-1**	**0**	**0.73**

Pitching

Phillies	G	GS	CG	IP	H	R	ER	BB	SO	W-L	Sv-Op	Hld	ERA
Ken Heintzelman	1	1	0	7.2	4	2	1	6	3	0-0	0-0	0	1.17
Jim Konstanty	3	1	0	15.0	9	4	4	4	3	0-1	0-1	0	2.40
Russ Meyer	2	0	0	1.2	4	1	1	0	1	0-1	0-0	0	5.40
Bob Miller	1	1	0	0.1	2	2	1	0	0	0-1	0-0	0	27.00
Robin Roberts	2	1	1	11.0	11	2	2	3	5	0-1	0-0	0	1.64
Totals	**4**	**4**	**1**	**35.2**	**30**	**11**	**9**	**13**	**12**	**0-4**	**0-1**	**0**	**2.27**

Fielding

Yankees	Pos	G	PO	Ast	E	DP	PB	FPct
Hank Bauer	rf	3	7	0	0	0	—	1.000
	lf	1	1	0	0	0	—	1.000
Yogi Berra	c	4	30	1	0	1	0	1.000
Bobby Brown	3b	3	0	1	1	0	—	.500
Jerry Coleman	2b	4	11	12	0	3	—	1.000
Joe Collins	1b	1	1	1	0	0	—	1.000
Joe DiMaggio	cf	4	8	0	0	0	—	1.000
Tom Ferrick	p	1	0	0	0	0	—	—
Whitey Ford	p	1	1	0	0	0	—	1.000
Johnny Hopp	1b	3	7	1	0	2	—	1.000
Bill Johnson	3b	4	1	5	0	1	—	1.000
Ed Lopat	p	1	1	4	0	0	—	1.000
Cliff Mapes	rf	1	3	0	0	0	—	1.000
Johnny Mize	1b	4	27	3	0	2	—	1.000
Vic Raschi	p	1	0	3	0	0	—	1.000
Allie Reynolds	p	2	1	2	0	0	—	1.000
Phil Rizzuto	ss	4	5	8	0	2	—	1.000
Gene Woodling	lf	4	7	0	1	0	—	.875
Totals		**4**	**111**	**41**	**2**	**11**	**0**	**.987**

Fielding

Phillies	Pos	G	PO	Ast	E	DP	PB	FPct
Richie Ashburn	cf	4	9	0	0	0	—	1.000
Jimmy Bloodworth	2b	1	0	0	0	0	—	—
Del Ennis	rf	4	9	0	0	0	—	1.000
Mike Goliat	2b	4	13	9	1	0	—	.957
Granny Hamner	ss	4	6	7	1	1	—	.929
Ken Heintzelman	p	1	0	2	0	0	—	1.000
Puddin' Head Jones	3b	4	8	9	1	0	—	.944
Jim Konstanty	p	3	1	1	0	0	—	1.000
Stan Lopata	c	1	1	0	0	0	0	1.000
Jackie Mayo	lf	1	1	0	0	0	—	1.000
Russ Meyer	p	2	0	1	0	0	—	1.000
Bob Miller	p	1	0	0	0	0	—	—
Robin Roberts	p	2	0	0	0	0	—	—
Andy Seminick	c	4	14	2	1	0	0	.941
Ken Silvestri	c	1	1	0	0	0	0	1.000
Dick Sisler	lf	4	10	1	0	0	—	1.000
Eddie Waitkus	1b	4	34	2	0	1	—	1.000
Totals		**4**	**107**	**34**	**4**	**2**	**0**	**.972**

1951 New York Yankees (AL) 4, New York Giants (NL) 2

After wresting the NL pennant from the Dodgers with the most famous game-winning home run in baseball history, the Giants took two of the first three World Series contests from the New York Yankees, but dropped three straight to lose the Series in six games. Giants skipper Leo Durocher had used his top three starters in the three-game playoff with Brooklyn, and was forced to open with lefty Dave Koslo. Koslo surprised with a 5-1 victory, while Monte Irvin pulled off the first steal of home in 23 years. Eddie Lopat evened the Series with a 3-1 win in the second game, although rookie right fielder Mickey Mantle was lost for the remainder of the Series after tearing ligaments in his right knee while chasing a fly ball. In the fifth inning of the third game, the Yankees called a pitchout and Yogi Berra's peg beat Eddie Stanky to the second base bag, but Stanky kicked the ball out of Phil Rizzuto's glove and scampered to third as the ball rolled away. A five-run rally followed, and the Giants took Game 3 to go ahead, two games to one. A day of rain followed, and it proved to be the turning point. No off-days had been scheduled for the "Subway Series," but the postponement enabled Yankee manager Casey Stengel to get his own rotation back in order. That proved to be all the Yanks needed, as Allie Reynolds, Lopat and Vic Raschi shut down the Giants in the next three games to give the Yankees the championship.

Game 1
Thursday, October 4

Giants	AB	R	H	RBI	BB	K	Avg
Eddie Stanky, 2b	4	1	0	0	1	0	.000
Al Dark, ss	5	1	2	3	0	1	.400
Hank Thompson, rf	3	1	0	0	2	0	.000
Monte Irvin, lf	5	1	4	0	0	0	.800
Whitey Lockman, 1b	4	0	1	1	1	0	.250
Bobby Thomson, 3b	3	0	1	0	2	0	.333
Willie Mays, cf	5	0	0	0	0	1	.000
Wes Westrum, c	3	1	2	0	2	0	.667
Dave Koslo, p	3	0	0	0	0	2	.000
TOTALS	35	5	10	4	8	4	.286

Yankees	AB	R	H	RBI	BB	K	Avg
Mickey Mantle, rf	3	0	0	0	2	0	.000
Phil Rizzuto, ss	4	0	2	0	0	1	.500
Hank Bauer, lf	4	0	0	0	0	0	.000
Joe DiMaggio, cf	4	0	0	0	0	0	.000
Yogi Berra, c	4	0	1	0	0	0	.250
Gil McDougald, 3b	4	1	1	0	0	0	.250
Jerry Coleman, 2b	3	0	1	0	1	0	.333
Joe Collins, 1b	3	0	1	0	0	0	.333
Johnny Mize, ph	1	0	0	0	0	0	.000
Allie Reynolds, p	2	0	1	0	0	0	.500
Bobby Hogue, p	0	0	0	0	0	0	—
Bobby Brown, ph	1	0	0	0	0	1	.000
Tom Morgan, p	0	0	0	0	0	0	—
Gene Woodling, ph	1	0	0	0	0	1	.000
TOTALS	34	1	7	0	3	3	.206

	1	2	3	4	5	6	7	8	9		R	H	E
Giants	2	0	0	0	0	3	0	0	0		5	10	1
Yankees	0	1	0	0	0	0	0	0	0		1	7	1

E—McDougald, Thompson. DP—Yankees 1 (McDougald to Coleman to Collins). LOB—Giants 13, Yankees 9. Scoring Position—Giants 3-for-13, Yankees 1-for-3. 2B—Lockman (1), McDougald (1). 3B—Irvin (1). HR—Dark (1). S—Koslo 2. GDP—Stanky. SB—Irvin (1).

Giants	IP	H	R	ER	BB	K	ERA
Dave Koslo (W, 1-0)	9.0	7	1	1	3	3	1.00

Yankees	IP	H	R	ER	BB	K	ERA
Allie Reynolds (L, 0-1)	6.0	8	5	5	7	1	7.50
Bobby Hogue	1.0	0	0	0	0	0	0.00
Tom Morgan	2.0	2	0	0	1	3	0.00

Time—2:58. Attendance—65,673. Umpires—HP, Summers. 1B, Ballanfant. 2B, Paparella. 3B, Barlick.

Game 2
Friday, October 5

Giants	AB	R	H	RBI	BB	K	Avg
Eddie Stanky, 2b	3	0	0	0	1	0	.000
Al Dark, ss	4	0	1	0	0	0	.333
Bobby Thomson, 3b	4	0	0	0	0	0	.143
Monte Irvin, lf	4	1	3	0	0	0	.778
Whitey Lockman, 1b	4	0	1	0	0	0	.250
Willie Mays, cf	4	0	0	0	0	0	.000
Wes Westrum, c	2	0	0	0	1	0	.400
Hank Schenz, pr	0	0	0	0	0	0	—
Clint Hartung, rf	1	0	0	0	0	0	.000
Hank Thompson, rf	2	0	0	0	0	1	.000
Bill Rigney, ph	1	0	0	1	0	0	.000
George Spencer, p	0	0	0	0	0	0	—
Larry Jansen, p	2	0	0	0	0	0	.000
Ray Noble, ph-c	1	0	0	0	0	0	.000
TOTALS	32	1	5	1	2	1	.234

Yankees	AB	R	H	RBI	BB	K	Avg
Mickey Mantle, rf	2	1	1	0	0	1	.200
Hank Bauer, rf	2	0	0	0	0	0	.000
Phil Rizzuto, ss	4	0	1	0	0	0	.375
Gil McDougald, 2b-3b	3	0	1	1	0	1	.286
Joe DiMaggio, cf	3	0	0	0	0	1	.000
Yogi Berra, c	3	0	0	0	0	1	.143
Gene Woodling, lf	3	0	0	0	0	0	.000
Bobby Brown, 3b	3	0	1	0	0	0	.250
Billy Martin, pr	0	1	0	0	0	0	.000
Jerry Coleman, 2b	0	0	0	0	0	0	.333
Joe Collins, 1b	3	1	1	1	0	0	.333
Ed Lopat, p	3	0	1	1	0	1	.333
TOTALS	29	3	6	3	0	5	.200

	1	2	3	4	5	6	7	8	9		R	H	E
Giants	0	0	0	0	0	0	1	0	0		1	5	1
Yankees	1	1	0	0	0	0	0	1	x		3	6	0

E—Lockman. DP—Giants 1 (Dark to Stanky to Lockman). LOB—Giants 6, Yankees 2. Scoring Position—Giants 0-for-6, Yankees 2-for-4. HR—Collins (1). GDP—DiMaggio. SB—Irvin (2).

Giants	IP	H	R	ER	BB	K	ERA
Larry Jansen (L, 0-1)	6.0	4	2	2	0	5	3.00
George Spencer	2.0	2	1	1	0	0	4.50

Yankees	IP	H	R	ER	BB	K	ERA
Ed Lopat (W, 1-0)	9.0	5	1	1	2	1	1.00

Time—2:05. Attendance—66,018. Umpires—HP, Ballanfant. 1B, Paparella. 2B, Barlick. 3B, Summers.

Game 3
Saturday, October 6

Yankees	AB	R	H	RBI	BB	K	Avg
Gene Woodling, lf	4	1	1	1	1	0	.125
Phil Rizzuto, ss	4	1	1	0	0	0	.333
Gil McDougald, 2b	3	0	2	0	2	0	.400
Joe DiMaggio, cf	4	0	0	0	0	1	.000
Yogi Berra, c	3	0	1	0	1	0	.200
Bobby Brown, 3b	3	0	0	0	1	0	.143
Joe Collins, 1b	3	0	1	1	1	0	.222
Hank Bauer, rf	4	0	0	0	0	0	.000
Vic Raschi, p	1	0	0	0	1	0	.000
Bobby Hogue, p	0	0	0	0	0	0	—
Johnny Hopp, ph	0	0	0	0	1	0	—
Joe Ostrowski, p	0	0	0	0	0	0	—
Johnny Mize, ph	1	0	0	0	0	0	.000
TOTALS	30	2	5	2	8	1	.175

Giants	AB	R	H	RBI	BB	K	Avg
Eddie Stanky, 2b	2	1	1	0	1	1	.111
Al Dark, ss	4	1	1	1	0	0	.308
Hank Thompson, rf	3	1	1	0	1	1	.125
Monte Irvin, lf	3	1	0	0	1	0	.583
Whitey Lockman, 1b	4	1	1	3	0	1	.250
Bobby Thomson, 3b	4	1	1	0	0	0	.182
Willie Mays, cf	4	0	2	1	0	0	.154
Wes Westrum, c	4	0	0	0	0	0	.222
Jim Hearn, p	3	0	0	0	0	1	.000
Sheldon Jones, p	0	0	0	0	0	0	—
TOTALS	31	6	7	5	3	4	.244

	1	2	3	4	5	6	7	8	9		R	H	E
Yankees	0	0	0	0	0	0	0	1	1		2	5	2
Giants	0	1	0	0	5	0	0	0	x		6	7	2

E—Westrum, Berra, Lockman, Rizzuto. DP—Yankees 1 (Rizzuto to McDougald to Collins), Giants 2 (Stanky to Dark to Lockman; Hearn to Dark to Lockman). LOB—Yankees 10, Giants 5. Scoring Position—Yankees 0-for-4, Giants 3-for-5. 2B—Thomson (1). HR—Woodling (1), Lockman (1). GDP—Collins, Westrum. CS—Rizzuto (1), Stanky (1).

Yankees	IP	H	R	ER	BB	K	ERA
Vic Raschi (L, 0-1)	4.1	5	6	1	3	3	2.08
Bobby Hogue	1.2	1	0	0	0	0	0.00
Joe Ostrowski	2.0	1	0	0	0	1	0.00

Giants	IP	H	R	ER	BB	K	ERA
Jim Hearn (W, 1-0)	7.2	4	1	1	8	1	1.17
Sheldon Jones (S, 1)	1.1	1	1	1	0	0	6.75

HBP—Rizzuto by Hearn, Stanky by Raschi. Time—2:42. Attendance—52,035. Umpires—HP, Paparella. 1B, Barlick. 2B, Summers. 3B, Ballanfant.

Game 4

Monday, October 8

Yankees	AB	R	H	RBI	BB	K	Avg
Hank Bauer, rf	4	0	2	0	1	0	.143
Phil Rizzuto, ss	5	1	1	0	0	2	.294
Yogi Berra, c	5	1	1	0	0	0	.200
Joe DiMaggio, cf	5	1	2	2	0	2	.125
Gene Woodling, lf	4	2	1	0	1	1	.167
Gil McDougald, 2b-3b	4	0	1	1	0	1	.357
Bobby Brown, 3b	4	1	2	0	0	0	.273
Jerry Coleman, 2b	0	0	0	0	0	0	.333
Joe Collins, 1b	3	0	1	1	1	0	.250
Allie Reynolds, p	4	0	1	1	0	1	.333
TOTALS	38	6	12	5	3	7	.233

Giants	AB	R	H	RBI	BB	K	Avg
Eddie Stanky, 2b	4	0	1	0	0	1	.154
Al Dark, ss	4	1	3	0	0	0	.412
Hank Thompson, rf	3	1	0	0	1	0	.091
Monte Irvin, lf	4	0	2	1	0	1	.563
Whitey Lockman, 1b	4	0	0	0	0	1	.188
Bobby Thomson, 3b	2	0	2	1	2	0	.308
Willie Mays, cf	4	0	0	0	0	0	.118
Wes Westrum, c	2	0	0	0	1	2	.182
Sal Maglie, p	1	0	0	0	0	1	.000
Jack Lohrke, ph	1	0	0	0	0	0	.000
Sheldon Jones, p	0	0	0	0	0	0	—
Bill Rigney, ph	1	0	0	0	0	1	.000
Monte Kennedy, p	0	0	0	0	0	0	—
TOTALS	30	2	8	2	4	7	.254

	1	2	3	4	5	6	7	8	9	R	H	E
Yankees	0	1	0	1	2	0	2	0	0	6	12	0
Giants	1	0	0	0	0	0	0	0	1	2	8	2

E—Thomson, Stanky. DP—Yankees 3 (Rizzuto to McDougald to Collins; Reynolds to Rizzuto to Collins; Reynolds to Rizzuto to Collins). LOB—Yankees 8, Giants 5. Scoring Position—Yankees 4-for-12, Giants 2-for-10. 2B—Woodling (1), Brown (1), Dark 3 (3). HR—DiMaggio (1). GDP—Dark, Mays 3. CS—Irvin (1).

Yankees	IP	H	R	ER	BB	K	ERA
Allie Reynolds (W, 1-1)	9.0	8	2	2	4	7	4.20

Giants	IP	H	R	ER	BB	K	ERA
Sal Maglie (L, 0-1)	5.0	8	4	4	2	3	7.20
Sheldon Jones	3.0	4	2	0	1	2	2.08
Monte Kennedy	1.0	0	0	0	0	2	0.00

Time—2:57. Attendance—49,010. Umpires—HP, Barlick. 1B, Summers. 2B, Ballanfant. 3B, Paparella.

Game 5

Tuesday, October 9

Yankees	AB	R	H	RBI	BB	K	Avg
Gene Woodling, lf	3	3	1	0	3	1	.200
Phil Rizzuto, ss	4	3	2	3	2	0	.333
Yogi Berra, c	4	2	1	0	1	0	.211
Joe DiMaggio, cf	5	1	3	3	0	0	.238
Johnny Mize, 1b	3	1	1	1	1	0	.200
Hank Bauer, rf	1	0	0	0	0	0	.133
Gil McDougald, 2b-3b	5	1	1	4	0	0	.316
Bobby Brown, 3b	3	0	2	0	1	0	.357
Jerry Coleman, pr-2b	1	1	0	0	0	0	.250
Joe Collins, rf-1b	5	1	1	0	0	1	.235
Ed Lopat, p	5	0	0	0	0	1	.125
TOTALS	39	13	12	11	8	4	.247

Giants	AB	R	H	RBI	BB	K	Avg
Eddie Stanky, 2b	4	0	0	0	0	0	.118
Al Dark, ss	4	1	2	0	0	0	.429
Bobby Thomson, 3b	4	0	0	0	0	0	.235
Monte Irvin, lf	4	0	2	0	0	0	.550
Whitey Lockman, 1b	4	0	0	0	0	0	.150
Willie Mays, cf	2	0	0	0	1	1	.105
Clint Hartung, rf	3	0	0	0	0	0	.000
Wes Westrum, c	3	0	1	0	0	1	.214
Larry Jansen, p	0	0	0	0	0	0	.000
Jack Lohrke, ph	1	0	0	0	0	1	.000
Monte Kennedy, p	0	0	0	0	0	0	—
Bill Rigney, ph	1	0	0	0	0	0	.000
George Spencer, p	0	0	0	0	0	0	—
Al Corwin, p	0	0	0	0	0	0	—
Davey Williams, ph	1	0	0	0	0	0	.000
Alex Konikowski, p	0	0	0	0	0	0	—
TOTALS	31	1	5	0	1	3	.243

	1	2	3	4	5	6	7	8	9	R	H	E
Yankees	0	0	5	2	0	2	4	0	0	13	12	1
Giants	1	0	0	0	0	0	0	0	0	1	5	3

E—Irvin, Hartung, Thomson, Woodling. DP—Yankees 1 (Lopat to McDougald to Mize). LOB—Yankees 7, Giants 4. Scoring Position—Yankees 4-for-12, Giants 0-for-3. 2B—DiMaggio (1), Mize (1), Westrum (1). 3B—Woodling (1). HR—Rizzuto (1), McDougald (1). GDP—Hartung.

Yankees	IP	H	R	ER	BB	K	ERA
Ed Lopat (W, 2-0)	9.0	5	1	0	1	3	0.50

Giants	IP	H	R	ER	BB	K	ERA
Larry Jansen (L, 0-2)	3.0	3	5	5	4	1	7.00
Monte Kennedy	2.0	3	2	2	1	2	6.00
George Spencer	1.1	4	6	6	3	0	18.90
Al Corwin	1.2	1	0	0	0	1	0.00
Alex Konikowski	1.0	1	0	0	0	0	0.00

WP—Corwin. Time—2:31. Attendance—47,530. Umpires—HP, Summers. 1B, Ballanfant. 2B, Paparella. 3B, Barlick.

Game 6

Wednesday, October 10

Giants	AB	R	H	RBI	BB	K	Avg
Eddie Stanky, 2b	5	1	1	1	0	0	.136
Al Dark, ss	3	1	1	0	2	2	.417
Whitey Lockman, 1b	5	0	3	0	0	0	.240
Monte Irvin, lf	4	0	0	1	1	0	.458
Bobby Thomson, 3b	4	0	1	1	1	0	.238
Hank Thompson, rf	3	0	1	0	1	0	.143
Sal Yvars, ph	1	0	0	0	0	0	.000
Wes Westrum, c	3	0	1	0	1	0	.235
Davey Williams, pr	0	0	0	0	0	0	.000
Larry Jansen, p	0	0	0	0	0	0	.000
Willie Mays, cf	3	1	2	0	1	0	.182
Dave Koslo, p	2	0	0	0	0	0	.000
Bill Rigney, ph	1	0	1	0	0	0	.250
Jim Hearn, p	0	0	0	0	0	0	.000
Ray Noble, ph-c	1	0	0	0	0	1	.000
TOTALS	35	3	11	3	7	3	.246

Yankees	AB	R	H	RBI	BB	K	Avg
Phil Rizzuto, ss	4	0	1	0	0	0	.320
Jerry Coleman, 2b	4	1	1	0	0	1	.250
Yogi Berra, c	4	1	2	0	0	0	.261
Joe DiMaggio, cf	2	1	1	0	2	0	.261
Gil McDougald, 3b	4	0	0	1	0	0	.261
Johnny Mize, 1b	2	1	1	0	1	0	.286
Joe Collins, 1b	1	0	0	0	0	0	.222
Hank Bauer, rf	3	0	1	3	0	1	.167
Gene Woodling, lf	3	0	0	0	0	0	.167
Vic Raschi, p	1	0	0	0	1	1	.000
Johnny Sain, p	1	0	0	0	0	0	.000
Bob Kuzava, p	0	0	0	0	0	0	—
TOTALS	29	4	7	4	4	3	.241

	1	2	3	4	5	6	7	8	9	R	H	E
Giants	0	0	0	0	1	0	0	0	2	3	11	1
Yankees	1	0	0	0	0	3	0	0	x	4	7	0

E—Thompson. DP—Giants 1 (Dark to Stanky to Lockman), Yankees 3 (Rizzuto to Mize; Rizzuto to Coleman to Mize; Rizzuto to Mize). LOB—Giants 12, Yankees 5. Scoring Position—Giants 1-for-15, Yankees 1-for-6. 2B—Lockman (2), Berra (1), DiMaggio (2). 3B—Bauer (1). GDP—Lockman, Thompson, Westrum, Rizzuto. CS—McDougald (1).

Giants	IP	H	R	ER	BB	K	ERA
Dave Koslo (L, 1-1)	6.0	5	4	4	4	3	3.00
Jim Hearn	1.0	1	0	0	0	0	1.04
Larry Jansen	1.0	1	0	0	0	0	6.30

Yankees	IP	H	R	ER	BB	K	ERA
Vic Raschi (W, 1-1)	6.0	7	1	0	5	1	0.87
Johnny Sain (H, 1)	2.0	4	2	2	2	2	9.00
Bob Kuzava (S, 1)	1.0	0	0	0	0	0	0.00

Raschi pitched to two batters in the 7th. Sain pitched to three batters in the 9th.

WP—Koslo. PB—Berra. Time—2:59. Attendance—61,711. Umpires—HP, Ballanfant. 1B, Paparella. 2B, Barlick. 3B, Summers.

1951 World Series—Composite Statistics

Batting

Yankees	G	AB	R	H	RBI	2B	3B	HR	BB	SO	SB	CS	Avg	OBP	Slg
Hank Bauer	6	18	0	3	3	0	1	0	1	1	0	0	.167	.211	.278
Yogi Berra	6	23	4	6	0	1	0	0	2	1	0	0	.261	.320	.304
Bobby Brown	5	14	1	5	0	1	0	0	2	1	0	0	.357	.438	.429
Jerry Coleman	5	8	2	2	0	0	0	0	1	2	0	0	.250	.333	.250
Joe Collins	6	18	2	4	3	0	0	1	2	1	0	0	.222	.300	.389
Joe DiMaggio	6	23	3	6	5	2	0	1	2	4	0	0	.261	.320	.478
Johnny Hopp	1	0	0	0	0	0	0	0	1	0	0	0	—	1.000	—
Ed Lopat	2	8	0	1	1	0	0	0	0	2	0	0	.125	.125	.125
Mickey Mantle	2	5	1	1	0	0	0	0	2	1	0	0	.200	.429	.200
Billy Martin	1	0	1	0	0	0	0	0	0	0	0	0	—	—	—
Gil McDougald	6	23	2	6	7	1	0	1	2	2	0	1	.261	.320	.435
Johnny Mize	4	7	2	2	1	1	0	0	2	0	0	0	.286	.444	.429
Vic Raschi	2	2	0	0	0	0	0	0	0	2	1	0	.000	.500	.000
Allie Reynolds	2	6	0	2	1	0	0	0	0	1	0	0	.333	.333	.333
Phil Rizzuto	6	25	5	8	3	0	0	1	2	3	0	1	.320	.393	.440
Johnny Sain	1	1	0	0	0	0	0	0	0	0	0	0	.000	.000	.000
Gene Woodling	6	18	6	3	1	1	1	1	5	3	0	0	.167	.348	.500
Totals	6	199	29	49	25	7	2	5	26	23	0	2	.246	.336	.377

Giants	G	AB	R	H	RBI	2B	3B	HR	BB	SO	SB	CS	Avg	OBP	Slg
Al Dark	6	24	5	10	4	3	0	1	2	3	0	0	.417	.462	.667
Clint Hartung	2	4	0	0	0	0	0	0	0	0	0	0	.000	.000	.000
Jim Hearn	2	3	0	0	0	0	0	0	0	1	0	0	.000	.000	.000
Monte Irvin	6	24	3	11	2	0	1	0	2	1	2	1	.458	.500	.542
Larry Jansen	3	2	0	0	0	0	0	0	0	0	0	0	.000	.000	.000
Dave Koslo	2	5	0	0	0	0	0	0	0	2	0	0	.000	.000	.000
Whitey Lockman	6	25	1	6	4	2	0	1	1	2	0	0	.240	.269	.440
Jack Lohrke	2	2	0	0	0	0	0	0	0	1	0	0	.000	.000	.000
Sal Maglie	1	1	0	0	0	0	0	0	0	1	0	0	.000	.000	.000
Willie Mays	6	22	1	4	1	0	0	0	2	2	0	0	.182	.250	.182
Ray Noble	2	2	0	0	0	0	0	0	0	1	0	0	.000	.000	.000
Bill Rigney	4	4	0	1	1	0	0	0	0	1	0	0	.250	.250	.250
Hank Schenz	1	0	0	0	0	0	0	0	0	0	0	0	.000	.000	.000
Eddie Stanky	6	22	3	3	1	0	0	0	3	2	0	1	.136	.269	.136
Hank Thompson	5	14	3	2	0	0	0	0	5	2	0	0	.143	.368	.143
Bobby Thomson	6	21	1	5	2	1	0	0	5	0	0	0	.238	.385	.286
Wes Westrum	6	17	1	4	0	1	0	0	5	3	0	0	.235	.409	.294
Davey Williams	2	1	0	0	0	0	0	0	0	0	0	0	.000	.000	.000
Sal Yvars	1	1	0	0	0	0	0	0	0	0	0	0	.000	.000	.000
Totals	6	194	18	46	15	7	1	2	25	22	2	2	.237	.327	.314

Pitching

Yankees	G	GS	CG	IP	H	R	ER	BB	SO	W-L	Sv-Op	Hld	ERA
Bobby Hogue	2	0	0	2.2	1	0	0	0	0	0-0	0-0	0	0.00
Bob Kuzava	1	0	0	1.0	0	0	0	0	0	0-0	1-1	0	0.00
Ed Lopat	2	2	2	18.0	10	2	1	3	4	2-0	0-0	0	0.50
Tom Morgan	1	0	0	2.0	2	0	0	1	3	0-0	0-0	0	0.00
Joe Ostrowski	1	0	0	2.0	1	0	0	0	1	0-0	0-0	0	0.00
Vic Raschi	2	2	0	10.1	12	7	1	8	4	1-1	0-0	0	0.87
Allie Reynolds	2	2	1	15.0	16	7	7	11	8	1-1	0-0	0	4.20
Johnny Sain	1	0	0	2.0	4	2	2	2	2	0-0	0-0	1	9.00
Totals	6	6	3	53.0	46	18	11	25	22	4-2	1-1	1	1.87

Giants	G	GS	CG	IP	H	R	ER	BB	SO	W-L	Sv-Op	Hld	ERA
Al Corwin	1	0	0	1.2	1	0	0	0	1	0-0	0-0	0	0.00
Jim Hearn	2	1	0	8.2	5	1	1	8	1	1-0	0-0	0	1.04
Larry Jansen	3	2	0	10.0	8	7	7	4	6	0-2	0-0	0	6.30
Sheldon Jones	2	0	0	4.1	5	3	1	1	2	0-0	1-1	0	2.08
Monte Kennedy	2	0	0	3.0	3	2	2	1	4	0-0	0-0	0	6.00
Alex Konikowski	1	0	0	1.0	1	0	0	0	0	0-0	0-0	0	0.00
Dave Koslo	2	2	1	15.0	12	5	5	7	6	1-1	0-0	0	3.00
Sal Maglie	1	1	0	5.0	8	4	4	2	3	0-1	0-0	0	7.20
George Spencer	2	0	0	3.1	6	7	7	3	0	0-0	0-0	0	18.90
Totals	6	6	1	52.0	49	29	27	26	23	2-4	1-1	0	4.67

Fielding

Yankees	Pos	G	PO	Ast	E	DP	PB	FPct
Hank Bauer	rf	5	7	0	0	0	—	1.000
	lf	1	0	0	0	0	—	—
Yogi Berra	c	6	27	3	1	0	1	.968
Bobby Brown	3b	4	1	8	0	0	—	1.000
Jerry Coleman	2b	5	7	6	0	3	—	1.000
Joe Collins	1b	6	40	2	0	6	—	1.000
	rf	1	0	0	0	0	—	—
Joe DiMaggio	cf	6	17	0	0	0	—	1.000
Bobby Hogue	p	2	0	1	0	0	—	1.000
Bob Kuzava	p	1	0	0	0	0	—	—
Ed Lopat	p	2	2	4	0	1	—	1.000
Mickey Mantle	rf	2	4	0	0	0	—	1.000
Gil McDougald	3b	5	2	8	1	1	—	.909
	2b	4	8	6	0	3	—	1.000
Johnny Mize	1b	2	12	0	0	4	—	1.000
Tom Morgan	p	1	0	1	0	0	—	1.000
Joe Ostrowski	p	1	0	0	0	0	—	—
Vic Raschi	p	2	0	0	0	0	—	—
Allie Reynolds	p	2	0	5	0	2	—	1.000
Phil Rizzuto	ss	6	14	23	1	8	—	.974
Johnny Sain	p	1	0	0	0	0	—	—
Gene Woodling	lf	5	18	0	1	0	—	.947
Totals		6	159	67	4	28	1	.983

Giants	Pos	G	PO	Ast	E	DP	PB	FPct
Al Corwin	p	1	1	0	0	0	—	1.000
Al Dark	ss	6	10	16	0	4	—	1.000
Clint Hartung	rf	2	1	1	1	0	—	.667
Jim Hearn	p	2	0	2	0	1	—	1.000
Monte Irvin	lf	6	17	0	1	0	—	.944
Larry Jansen	p	3	1	2	0	0	—	1.000
Sheldon Jones	p	2	0	1	0	0	—	1.000
Monte Kennedy	p	2	0	1	0	0	—	1.000
Alex Konikowski	p	1	0	0	0	0	—	—
Dave Koslo	p	2	2	1	0	0	—	1.000
Whitey Lockman	1b	6	48	5	2	4	—	.964
Sal Maglie	p	1	0	0	0	0	—	—
Willie Mays	cf	6	16	1	0	0	—	1.000
Ray Noble	c	2	0	1	0	0	0	1.000
George Spencer	p	2	0	1	0	0	—	1.000
Eddie Stanky	2b	6	14	15	1	3	—	.967
Hank Thompson	rf	5	4	0	2	0	—	.667
Bobby Thomson	3b	6	13	15	2	0	—	.933
Wes Westrum	c	6	29	2	1	0	0	.969
Totals		6	156	64	10	12	0	.957

1952 New York Yankees (AL) 4, Brooklyn Dodgers (NL) 3

The New York Yankees spotted the Brooklyn Dodgers a three-games-to-two lead, and then pulled out close decisions in Games 6 and 7 to clinch their fourth straight championship. With the two New York teams scheduled to meet on seven consecutive days, both managers were forced to juggle their rotations. Brooklyn's Charlie Dressen opened with rookie reliever Joe Black, who'd started only twice all year. He won 4-2, thanks to three Brooklyn home runs, but Vic Raschi and Allie Reynolds won two of the next three games for the Yankees, evening the Series at two games apiece. In Game 5, Carl Erskine survived a five-run outburst in the fifth, and ultimately tossed 11 innings before Duke Snider's RBI double brought home the game-winning run. That put Brooklyn only a game away from the crown, but home runs off the bat of young Mickey Mantle provided the margin of victory for the Yankees in both Game 6 and Game 7. Trailing 4-2 in the seventh inning of the finale, the Dodgers loaded the bases for Jackie Robinson. Robinson lifted a high popup that first baseman Joe Collins appeared to lose in the sun, but second baseman Billy Martin raced in to pick the ball off his shoetops and kill the rally.

Game 1

Wednesday, October 1

Yankees	AB	R	H	RBI	BB	K	Avg
Hank Bauer, rf	4	0	0	1	0	1	.000
Phil Rizzuto, ss	4	0	1	0	0	1	.250
Mickey Mantle, cf	4	0	2	0	0	1	.500
Yogi Berra, c	4	0	0	0	0	0	.000
Joe Collins, 1b	4	0	0	0	0	0	.000
Irv Noren, lf	3	0	0	0	1	1	.000
Gil McDougald, 3b	2	1	1	1	1	0	.500
Billy Martin, 2b	3	0	1	0	0	1	.333
Allie Reynolds, p	2	0	0	0	0	1	.000
Gene Woodling, ph	1	1	1	0	0	0	1.000
Ray Scarborough, p	0	0	0	0	0	0	—
TOTALS	31	2	6	2	2	6	.194

Dodgers	AB	R	H	RBI	BB	K	Avg
Billy Cox, 3b	3	0	0	0	1	0	.000
Pee Wee Reese, ss	4	2	2	1	0	1	.500
Duke Snider, cf	4	1	2	0	0	1	.500
Jackie Robinson, 2b	2	1	1	1	1	0	.500
Roy Campanella, c	3	0	1	0	0	0	.333
Andy Pafko, lf	3	0	0	0	0	0	.000
Gil Hodges, 1b	3	0	0	0	0	1	.000
Carl Furillo, rf	3	0	0	0	0	0	.000
Joe Black, p	3	0	0	0	0	3	.000
TOTALS	28	4	6	4	2	5	.214

	1	2	3	4	5	6	7	8	9	R	H	E
Yankees	0	0	1	0	0	0	0	1	0	2	6	2
Dodgers	0	1	0	0	0	2	0	1	x	4	6	0

E—McDougald, Reynolds. DP—Yankees 1 (Martin to Collins), Dodgers 1 (Cox to Robinson to Hodges). LOB—Yankees 4, Dodgers 2. Scoring Position—Yankees 0-for-6, Dodgers 1-for-3. 2B—Snider (1). 3B—Woodling (1). HR—McDougald (1), Reese (1), Snider (1), Robinson (1). GDP—McDougald, Campanella. CS—Cox (1), Campanella (1).

Yankees	IP	H	R	ER	BB	K	ERA
Allie Reynolds (L, 0-1)	7.0	5	3	3	2	4	3.86
Ray Scarborough	1.0	1	1	1	0	1	9.00

Dodgers	IP	H	R	ER	BB	K	ERA
Joe Black (W, 1-0)	9.0	6	2	2	2	6	2.00

WP—Reynolds. Time—2:21. Attendance—34,861. Umpires—HP, Pinelli. 1B, Passarella. 2B, Goetz. 3B, McKinley.

Game 2

Thursday, October 2

Yankees	AB	R	H	RBI	BB	K	Avg
Hank Bauer, rf	4	0	1	0	1	1	.125
Phil Rizzuto, ss	4	0	0	0	0	1	.125
Mickey Mantle, cf	5	2	3	0	0	1	.556
Gene Woodling, lf	4	1	1	0	1	0	.400
Yogi Berra, c	3	0	2	1	1	0	.286
Joe Collins, 1b	3	1	0	0	1	0	.000
Gil McDougald, 3b	3	2	1	1	1	1	.400
Billy Martin, 2b	4	1	2	4	0	0	.429
Vic Raschi, p	3	0	0	0	1	2	.000
TOTALS	33	7	10	6	7	6	.271

Dodgers	AB	R	H	RBI	BB	K	Avg
Billy Cox, 3b	4	0	0	0	0	1	.000
Pee Wee Reese, ss	3	1	1	0	1	1	.429
Duke Snider, cf	4	0	1	0	0	3	.375
Jackie Robinson, 2b	3	0	0	0	1	0	.200
Roy Campanella, c	4	0	1	1	0	0	.286
Andy Pafko, lf	4	0	0	0	0	1	.000
Gil Hodges, 1b	3	0	0	0	1	1	.000
Carl Furillo, rf	3	0	0	0	1	2	.000
Carl Erskine, p	2	0	0	0	0	0	.000
Billy Loes, p	0	0	0	0	0	0	—

(continued in next column)

	AB	R	H	RBI	BB	K	Avg
Rocky Nelson, ph	0	0	0	0	1	0	—
Ken Lehman, p	0	0	0	0	0	0	—
TOTALS	30	1	3	1	5	9	.164

	1	2	3	4	5	6	7	8	9	R	H	E
Yankees	0	0	0	1	1	5	0	0	0	7	10	0
Dodgers	0	0	1	0	0	0	0	0	0	1	3	1

E—Hodges. DP—Dodgers 1 (Reese to Robinson to Hodges). LOB—Yankees 6, Dodgers 7. Scoring Position—Yankees 3-for-14, Dodgers 1-for-5. 2B—Mantle (1). HR—Martin (1). GDP—Bauer. SB—McDougald (1). CS—Bauer (1), Rizzuto (1).

Yankees	IP	H	R	ER	BB	K	ERA
Vic Raschi (W, 1-0)	9.0	3	1	1	5	9	1.00

Dodgers	IP	H	R	ER	BB	K	ERA
Carl Erskine (L, 0-1)	5.0	6	5	4	6	4	7.20
Billy Loes	2.0	2	2	2	0	2	9.00
Ken Lehman	2.0	2	0	0	1	0	0.00

Erskine pitched to four batters in the 6th.

WP—Erskine. Time—2:47. Attendance—33,792. Umpires—HP, Passarella. 1B, Goetz. 2B, McKinley. 3B, Pinelli.

Game 3

Friday, October 3

Dodgers	AB	R	H	RBI	BB	K	Avg
Carl Furillo, rf	5	1	1	0	0	0	.091
Pee Wee Reese, ss	5	1	3	1	0	0	.500
Jackie Robinson, 2b	4	2	2	1	1	0	.333
Roy Campanella, c	5	0	1	0	0	0	.250
Andy Pafko, lf	5	0	2	1	0	0	.167
Duke Snider, cf	5	0	1	0	0	0	.308
Gil Hodges, 1b	3	0	0	1	0	0	.000
Billy Cox, 3b	2	1	1	0	2	0	.111
Preacher Roe, p	2	0	0	0	0	0	.000
TOTALS	36	5	11	3	4	0	.225

Yankees	AB	R	H	RBI	BB	K	Avg
Phil Rizzuto, ss	4	0	0	0	1	0	.083
Joe Collins, 1b	4	0	0	0	0	1	.000
Johnny Sain, ph	1	0	0	0	0	0	.000
Mickey Mantle, cf	4	0	0	0	0	0	.385
Gene Woodling, lf	4	0	1	0	0	2	.333
Yogi Berra, c	4	1	3	1	0	0	.455
Hank Bauer, rf	2	1	0	0	1	0	.100
Gil McDougald, 3b	4	0	0	0	0	1	.222
Billy Martin, 2b	1	0	0	0	2	0	.375
Ed Lopat, p	2	0	1	1	1	1	.500
Tom Gorman, p	0	0	0	0	0	0	—
Johnny Mize, ph	1	1	1	1	0	0	1.000
TOTALS	31	3	6	3	5	5	.253

	1	2	3	4	5	6	7	8	9	R	H	E
Dodgers	0	0	1	0	1	0	0	1	2	5	11	0
Yankees	0	1	0	0	0	0	0	1	1	3	6	2

E—McDougald, Berra. DP—Yankees 2 (Rizzuto to Martin; McDougald to Collins). LOB—Dodgers 10, Yankees 8. Scoring Position—Dodgers 2-for-12, Yankees 1-for-5. 2B—Furillo (1), Berra (1). HR—Berra (1), Mize (1). S—Roe 2, Bauer. SB—Reese (1), Robinson (1), Snider (1). CS—Martin (1).

Dodgers	IP	H	R	ER	BB	K	ERA
Preacher Roe (W, 1-0)	9.0	6	3	3	5	5	3.00

Yankees	IP	H	R	ER	BB	K	ERA
Ed Lopat (L, 0-1)	8.1	10	5	4	0	5	5.40
Tom Gorman	0.2	1	0	0	0	0	0.00

PB—Berra. HBP—Martin by Roe. Time—2:56. Attendance—66,698. Umpires—HP, Goetz. 1B, McKinley. 2B, Pinelli. 3B, Passarella.

Game 4

Saturday, October 4

Dodgers	AB	R	H	RBI	BB	K	Avg
Billy Cox, 3b	3	0	0	0	0	1	.083
Rocky Nelson, ph	1	0	0	0	0	1	.000
Bobby Morgan, 3b	0	0	0	0	0	0	—
Pee Wee Reese, ss	4	0	2	0	0	0	.500
Duke Snider, cf	4	0	0	0	0	0	.235
Jackie Robinson, 2b	4	0	0	0	0	3	.231
Roy Campanella, c	3	0	0	0	1	2	.200
Andy Pafko, lf	3	0	1	0	0	2	.200
Gil Hodges, 1b	2	0	0	0	1	0	.000
Carl Furillo, rf	2	0	1	0	0	0	.154
Joe Black, p	1	0	0	0	0	1	.000
George Shuba, ph	1	0	0	0	0	0	.000
Johnny Rutherford, p	0	0	0	0	0	0	—
TOTALS	28	0	4	0	3	10	.203

Yankees	AB	R	H	RBI	BB	K	Avg
Gil McDougald, 3b	3	0	0	0	1	0	.167
Phil Rizzuto, ss	2	0	0	0	2	0	.071
Mickey Mantle, cf	3	1	1	0	1	0	.375
Johnny Mize, 1b	3	1	2	1	1	0	.750
Joe Collins, pr-1b	0	0	0	0	0	0	.000
Yogi Berra, c	4	0	0	0	0	1	.333
Gene Woodling, lf	3	0	1	0	1	0	.333
Hank Bauer, rf	4	0	0	0	0	1	.071
Billy Martin, 2b	3	0	0	0	0	1	.273
Allie Reynolds, p	3	0	0	0	0	1	.000
TOTALS	28	2	4	1	6	3	.219

	1	2	3	4	5	6	7	8	9	R	H	E
Dodgers	0	0	0	0	0	0	0	0	0	0	4	1
Yankees	0	0	0	1	0	0	0	1	x	2	4	1

E—Martin, Reese. DP—Yankees 1 (Rizzuto to Martin to Mize). LOB—Dodgers 5, Yankees 8. Scoring Position—Dodgers 0-for-3, Yankees 0-for-7. 2B—Mize (1), Woodling (1). 3B—Mantle (1). HR—Mize (2). S—Furillo. GDP—Hodges. CS—Reese (1), Pafko (1).

Dodgers	IP	H	R	ER	BB	K	ERA
Joe Black (L, 1-1)	7.0	3	1	1	5	2	1.69
Johnny Rutherford	1.0	1	1	1	1	1	9.00

Yankees	IP	H	R	ER	BB	K	ERA
Allie Reynolds (W, 1-1)	9.0	4	0	0	3	10	1.69

Time—2:33. Attendance—71,787. Umpires—HP, McKinley. 1B, Pinelli. 2B, Passarella. 3B, Goetz.

Game 5
Sunday, October 5

Dodgers	AB	R	H	RBI	BB	K	Avg
Billy Cox, 3b	5	2	3	0	0	0	.235
Pee Wee Reese, ss	5	0	1	1	0	0	.429
Duke Snider, cf	5	1	3	4	0	1	.318
Jackie Robinson, 2b	2	1	0	0	4	1	.200
George Shuba, lf	2	0	1	0	0	1	.333
Carl Furillo, rf	4	0	1	0	0	1	.176
Roy Campanella, c	5	0	0	0	0	2	.150
Andy Pafko, rf-lf	4	0	1	1	0	0	.211
Tommy Holmes, lf	1	0	0	0	0	0	.000
Gil Hodges, 1b	3	1	0	0	2	1	.176
Carl Erskine, p	4	1	0	0	0	1	.000
TOTALS	40	6	10	6	6	7	.219

Yankees	AB	R	H	RBI	BB	K	Avg
Gil McDougald, 3b	4	1	0	1	1	0	.125
Phil Rizzuto, ss	5	1	1	0	0	1	.105
Mickey Mantle, cf	5	0	1	0	0	1	.333
Johnny Mize, 1b	5	1	1	3	0	1	.444
Yogi Berra, c	4	0	0	0	1	2	.263
Gene Woodling, lf	4	0	0	0	1	0	.250
Hank Bauer, rf	3	1	0	0	1	0	.059
Billy Martin, 2b	4	1	1	0	0	0	.267
Ewell Blackwell, p	1	0	0	0	0	0	.000
Irv Noren, ph	1	0	1	1	0	0	.250
Johnny Sain, p	2	0	0	0	0	0	.000
TOTALS	38	5	5	5	3	6	.214

	1	2	3	4	5	6	7	8	9	10	11	R	H	E
Dodgers	0	1	0	0	3	0	1	0	0	0	1	6	10	0
Yankees	0	0	0	0	5	0	0	0	0	0	0	5	5	1

E—Rizzuto. DP—Yankees 2 (Martin to Rizzuto to Mize; McDougald to Berra to Mize). LOB—Dodgers 11, Yankees 3. Scoring Position—Dodgers 4-for-14, Yankees 2-for-4. 2B—Snider (2), Furillo (2). HR—Snider (2), Mize (3). S—Cox, Reese, Erskine. GDP—Snider, Furillo. SB—Robinson (2).

Dodgers	IP	H	R	ER	BB	K	ERA
Carl Erskine (W, 1-1)	11.0	5	5	5	3	6	5.06

Yankees	IP	H	R	ER	BB	K	ERA
Ewell Blackwell	5.0	4	4	4	3	4	7.20
Johnny Sain (BS, 1; L, 0-1)	6.0	6	2	2	3	3	3.00

HBP—Snider by Sain. Time—3:00. Attendance—70,536. Umpires—HP, Pinelli. 1B, Passarella. 2B, Goetz. 3B, McKinley.

Game 6
Monday, October 6

Yankees	AB	R	H	RBI	BB	K	Avg
Gil McDougald, 3b	4	0	1	0	1	0	.150
Phil Rizzuto, ss	4	0	1	0	1	0	.130
Mickey Mantle, cf	3	1	1	1	2	0	.333
Johnny Mize, 1b	3	0	0	0	1	0	.333
Joe Collins, 1b	1	0	0	0	0	1	.000
Yogi Berra, c	5	1	1	1	0	0	.250
Gene Woodling, lf	3	1	2	0	1	0	.316
Irv Noren, rf	4	0	2	0	0	2	.375
Hank Bauer, rf	0	0	0	0	0	0	.059
Billy Martin, 2b	4	0	0	0	0	1	.211
Vic Raschi, p	3	0	1	1	0	0	.167
Allie Reynolds, p	1	0	0	0	0	0	.000
TOTALS	35	3	9	3	6	4	.205

Dodgers	AB	R	H	RBI	BB	K	Avg
Billy Cox, 3b	5	0	2	0	0	1	.273
Pee Wee Reese, ss	4	0	0	0	0	0	.360
Duke Snider, cf	3	2	2	2	1	0	.360
Jackie Robinson, 2b	4	0	0	0	0	1	.158
George Shuba, lf	4	0	1	0	0	2	.286
Sandy Amoros, pr	0	0	0	0	0	0	—
Tommy Holmes, lf	0	0	0	0	0	0	.000
Roy Campanella, c	4	0	1	0	0	1	.167
Gil Hodges, 1b	3	0	0	0	0	3	.000
Rocky Nelson, ph	1	0	0	0	0	0	.000
Carl Furillo, rf	3	0	1	0	1	0	.200
Billy Loes, p	3	0	1	0	0	1	.333
Preacher Roe, p	0	0	0	0	0	0	.000
Andy Pafko, ph	1	0	0	0	0	0	.200
TOTALS	35	2	8	2	2	11	.225

	1	2	3	4	5	6	7	8	9	R	H	E
Yankees	0	0	0	0	0	0	2	1	0	3	9	0
Dodgers	0	0	0	0	0	1	0	1	0	2	8	1

E—Reese. DP—Dodgers 1 (Hodges to Reese to Robinson). LOB—Yankees 11, Dodgers 8. Scoring Position—Yankees 1-for-8, Dodgers 0-for-5. 2B—Cox (1), Shuba (1). HR—Mantle (1), Berra (2), Snider 2 (4). GDP—Raschi. SB—Loes (1).

Yankees	IP	H	R	ER	BB	K	ERA
Vic Raschi (W, 2-0)	7.2	8	2	2	1	9	1.62
Allie Reynolds (S, 1)	1.1	0	0	0	1	2	1.56

Dodgers	IP	H	R	ER	BB	K	ERA
Billy Loes (L, 0-1)	8.1	9	3	3	5	3	4.35
Preacher Roe	0.2	0	0	0	1	1	2.79

Balk—Loes. Time—2:56. Attendance—30,037. Umpires—HP, Passarella. 1B, Goetz. 2B, McKinley. 3B, Pinelli.

Game 7
Tuesday, October 7

Yankees	AB	R	H	RBI	BB	K	Avg
Gil McDougald, 3b	5	1	2	0	0	0	.200
Phil Rizzuto, ss	4	1	1	0	0	0	.148
Mickey Mantle, cf	5	1	2	2	0	1	.345
Johnny Mize, 1b	3	0	2	1	1	0	.400
Joe Collins, 1b	0	0	0	0	0	0	.000
Yogi Berra, c	4	0	0	0	0	1	.214
Gene Woodling, lf	4	1	2	1	0	0	.348
Irv Noren, rf	2	0	0	0	0	0	.300
Hank Bauer, ph-rf	1	0	0	0	1	0	.056
Billy Martin, 2b	4	0	1	0	0	0	.217
Ed Lopat, p	1	0	0	0	0	0	.333
Allie Reynolds, p	1	0	0	0	0	0	.000
Ralph Houk, ph	1	0	0	0	0	0	.000
Vic Raschi, p	0	0	0	0	0	0	.167
Bob Kuzava, p	1	0	0	0	0	0	.000
TOTALS	36	4	10	4	2	2	.219

Dodgers	AB	R	H	RBI	BB	K	Avg
Billy Cox, 3b	5	1	2	0	0	1	.296
Pee Wee Reese, ss	4	0	1	1	1	0	.345
Duke Snider, cf	4	1	1	0	0	1	.345
Jackie Robinson, 2b	4	0	1	0	0	0	.174
Roy Campanella, c	4	0	2	0	0	1	.214
Gil Hodges, 1b	4	0	0	1	0	0	.000
George Shuba, lf	3	0	1	0	0	1	.300
Andy Pafko, ph	1	0	0	0	0	1	.190
Tommy Holmes, lf	0	0	0	0	0	0	.000
Carl Furillo, rf	3	0	0	0	1	0	.174
Joe Black, p	2	0	0	0	0	2	.000
Preacher Roe, p	0	0	0	0	0	0	.000
Rocky Nelson, ph	1	0	0	0	0	0	.000
Carl Erskine, p	0	0	0	0	0	0	.000
Bobby Morgan, ph	1	0	0	0	0	0	.000
TOTALS	36	2	8	2	2	7	.213

	1	2	3	4	5	6	7	8	9	R	H	E
Yankees	0	0	0	1	1	1	1	0	0	4	10	4
Dodgers	0	0	0	1	1	0	0	0	0	2	8	1

E—McDougald 2, Woodling, Reynolds, Cox. DP—Yankees 1 (Rizzuto to Martin to Mize), Dodgers 1 (Robinson to Reese to Hodges). LOB—Yankees 8, Dodgers 9. Scoring Position—Yankees 2-for-6, Dodgers 2-for-9. 2B—Rizzuto (1), Cox (2). HR—Mantle (2), Woodling (1). S—Rizzuto. GDP—Berra, Hodges.

Yankees	IP	H	R	ER	BB	K	ERA
Ed Lopat	3.0	4	1	1	0	3	4.76
Allie Reynolds (W, 2-1)	3.0	3	1	1	0	2	1.77
Vic Raschi (H, 1)	0.1	1	0	0	2	0	1.59
Bob Kuzava (S, 1)	2.2	0	0	0	0	2	0.00

Dodgers	IP	H	R	ER	BB	K	ERA
Joe Black (L, 1-2)	5.1	6	3	3	1	1	2.53
Preacher Roe	1.2	3	1	1	0	1	3.18
Carl Erskine	2.0	1	0	0	1	0	4.50

Lopat pitched to three batters in the 4th.

Time—2:54. Attendance—33,195. Umpires—HP, Goetz. 1B, McKinley. 2B, Pinelli. 3B, Passarella.

1952 World Series—Composite Statistics

Batting

Yankees	G	AB	R	H	RBI	2B	3B	HR	BB	SO	SB	CS	Avg	OBP	Slg
Hank Bauer	7	18	2	1	1	0	0	0	4	3	0	1	.056	.227	.056
Yogi Berra	7	28	2	6	3	1	0	2	2	4	0	0	.214	.267	.464
Ewell Blackwell	1	1	0	0	0	0	0	0	0	0	0	0	.000	.000	.000
Joe Collins	6	12	1	0	0	0	0	0	1	3	0	0	.000	.077	.000
Ralph Houk	1	1	0	0	0	0	0	0	0	0	0	0	.000	.000	.000
Bob Kuzava	1	1	0	0	0	0	0	0	0	0	0	0	.000	.000	.000
Ed Lopat	2	3	0	1	1	0	0	0	1	1	0	0	.333	.500	.333
Mickey Mantle	7	29	5	10	3	1	1	2	3	4	0	0	.345	.406	.655
Billy Martin	7	23	2	5	4	0	0	1	2	2	0	1	.217	.308	.348
Gil McDougald	7	25	5	5	3	0	0	1	5	2	1	0	.200	.333	.320
Johnny Mize	5	15	3	6	6	1	0	3	3	1	0	0	.400	.500	1.067
Irv Noren	4	10	0	3	1	0	0	0	1	3	0	0	.300	.364	.300
Vic Raschi	3	6	0	1	1	0	0	0	1	2	0	0	.167	.286	.167
Allie Reynolds	4	7	0	0	0	0	0	0	0	2	0	0	.000	.000	.000
Phil Rizzuto	7	27	2	4	0	1	0	0	5	2	0	1	.148	.281	.185
Johnny Sain	2	3	0	0	0	0	0	0	0	0	0	0	.000	.000	.000
Gene Woodling	7	23	4	8	1	1	1	1	3	3	0	0	.348	.423	.609
Totals	**7**	**232**	**26**	**50**	**24**	**5**	**2**	**10**	**31**	**32**	**1**	**3**	**.216**	**.311**	**.384**

Dodgers	G	AB	R	H	RBI	2B	3B	HR	BB	SO	SB	CS	Avg	OBP	Slg
Sandy Amoros	1	0	0	0	0	0	0	0	0	0	0	0	—	—	—
Joe Black	3	6	0	0	0	0	0	0	1	6	0	0	.000	.143	.000
Roy Campanella	7	28	0	6	1	0	0	0	1	6	0	1	.214	.241	.214
Billy Cox	7	27	4	8	0	2	0	0	3	4	0	1	.296	.367	.370
Carl Erskine	3	6	1	0	0	0	0	0	0	1	0	0	.000	.000	.000
Carl Furillo	7	23	1	4	0	2	0	0	3	3	0	0	.174	.269	.261
Gil Hodges	7	21	1	0	1	0	0	0	5	6	0	0	.000	.192	.000
Tommy Holmes	3	1	0	0	0	0	0	0	0	0	0	0	.000	.000	.000
Billy Loes	2	3	0	1	0	0	0	0	0	1	1	0	.333	.333	.333
Bobby Morgan	2	1	0	0	0	0	0	0	0	0	0	0	.000	.000	.000
Rocky Nelson	4	3	0	0	0	0	0	0	1	2	0	0	.000	.250	.000
Andy Pafko	7	21	0	4	2	0	0	0	0	4	1	0	.190	.190	.190
Pee Wee Reese	7	29	4	10	4	0	0	1	2	2	1	1	.345	.387	.448
Jackie Robinson	7	23	4	4	2	0	0	1	7	5	2	0	.174	.367	.304
Preacher Roe	3	2	0	0	0	0	0	0	0	0	0	0	.000	.000	.000
George Shuba	4	10	0	3	0	1	0	0	0	4	0	0	.300	.300	.400
Duke Snider	7	29	5	10	8	2	0	4	1	5	1	0	.345	.387	.828
Totals	**7**	**233**	**20**	**50**	**18**	**7**	**0**	**6**	**24**	**49**	**5**	**4**	**.215**	**.291**	**.322**

Pitching

Yankees	G	GS	CG	IP	H	R	ER	BB	SO	W-L	Sv-Op	Hld	ERA
Ewell Blackwell	1	1	0	5.0	4	4	4	3	4	0-0	0-0	0	7.20
Tom Gorman	1	0	0	0.2	1	0	0	0	0	0-0	0-0	0	0.00
Bob Kuzava	1	0	0	2.2	0	0	0	2	0	1-1	0-0	0	0.00
Ed Lopat	2	2	0	11.1	14	6	6	4	3	0-1	0-0	0	4.76
Vic Raschi	3	2	1	17.0	12	3	3	8	18	2-0	0-0	1	1.59
Allie Reynolds	4	2	1	20.1	12	4	4	6	18	2-1	1-1	0	1.77
Johnny Sain	1	0	0	6.0	6	2	2	3	3	0-1	0-1	0	3.00
Ray Scarborough	1	0	0	1.0	1	1	1	0	1	0-0	0-0	0	9.00
Totals	**7**	**7**	**2**	**64.0**	**50**	**20**	**20**	**24**	**49**	**4-3**	**2-3**	**1**	**2.81**

Dodgers	G	GS	CG	IP	H	R	ER	BB	SO	W-L	Sv-Op	Hld	ERA
Joe Black	3	3	1	21.1	15	6	6	8	9	1-2	0-0	0	2.53
Carl Erskine	3	2	1	18.0	12	10	9	10	10	1-1	0-0	0	4.50
Ken Lehman	1	0	0	2.0	2	0	0	1	0	0-0	0-0	0	0.00
Billy Loes	2	1	0	10.1	11	5	5	5	5	0-1	0-0	0	4.35
Preacher Roe	3	1	1	11.1	9	4	4	6	7	1-0	0-0	0	3.18
Johnny Rutherford	1	0	0	1.0	1	1	1	1	1	0-0	0-0	0	9.00
Totals	**7**	**7**	**3**	**64.0**	**50**	**26**	**25**	**31**	**32**	**3-4**	**0-0**	**0**	**3.52**

Fielding

Yankees	Pos	G	PO	Ast	E	DP	PB	FPct
Hank Bauer	rf	7	10	0	0	0	—	1.000
Yogi Berra	c	7	59	7	1	1	1	.985
Ewell Blackwell	p	1	0	1	0	0	—	1.000
Joe Collins	1b	6	27	1	0	2	—	1.000
Tom Gorman	p	1	0	0	0	0	—	—
Bob Kuzava	p	1	0	0	0	0	—	—
Ed Lopat	p	2	0	1	0	0	—	1.000
Mickey Mantle	cf	7	16	0	0	0	—	1.000
Billy Martin	2b	7	15	16	1	5	—	.969
Gil McDougald	3b	7	4	15	4	2	—	.826
Johnny Mize	1b	4	26	3	0	4	—	1.000
Irv Noren	rf	2	1	0	0	0	—	1.000
	lf	1	1	0	0	0	—	1.000
Vic Raschi	p	3	0	1	0	0	—	1.000
Allie Reynolds	p	4	2	1	2	0	—	.600
Phil Rizzuto	ss	7	13	17	1	4	—	.968
Johnny Sain	p	1	0	2	0	0	—	1.000
Ray Scarborough	p	1	0	1	0	0	—	1.000
Gene Woodling	lf	6	18	0	1	0	—	.947
Totals		**7**	**192**	**66**	**10**	**18**	**1**	**.963**

Dodgers	Pos	G	PO	Ast	E	DP	PB	FPct
Joe Black	p	3	1	2	0	0	—	1.000
Roy Campanella	c	7	39	5	0	0	0	1.000
Billy Cox	3b	7	9	14	1	1	—	.958
Carl Erskine	p	3	0	2	0	0	—	1.000
Carl Furillo	rf	7	13	0	0	0	—	1.000
Gil Hodges	1b	7	60	6	1	4	—	.985
Tommy Holmes	lf	3	2	0	0	0	—	1.000
Ken Lehman	p	1	0	1	0	0	—	1.000
Billy Loes	p	2	0	2	0	0	—	1.000
Bobby Morgan	3b	1	0	1	0	0	—	1.000
Andy Pafko	lf	5	9	1	0	0	—	1.000
	rf	1	3	0	0	0	—	1.000
Pee Wee Reese	ss	7	15	18	2	3	—	.943
Jackie Robinson	2b	7	10	19	0	4	—	1.000
Preacher Roe	p	3	1	0	0	0	—	1.000
Johnny Rutherford	p	1	0	0	0	0	—	—
George Shuba	lf	3	7	0	0	0	—	1.000
Duke Snider	cf	7	23	0	0	0	—	1.000
Totals		**7**	**192**	**71**	**4**	**12**	**0**	**.985**

1953 New York Yankees (AL) 4, Brooklyn Dodgers (NL) 2

The New York Yankees defeated the Brooklyn Dodgers in six games to take their fifth straight World Championship. The Yanks took an early lead in Game 1 before Brooklyn battled back, but New York went ahead for good on Joe Collins' solo homer in the bottom of the seventh and went on to win, 9-5. New York's Eddie Lopat beat Preacher Roe 4-2 in Game 2 on an eighth-inning, two-run homer by Mickey Mantle. Carl Erskine won the third game, 3-2, and set a new World Series record by fanning 14 Yankees. Duke Snider notched two doubles and a homer and drove in four runs in the Dodgers' 7-3 win in Game 4. Mantle's grand slam sent the Yanks to an 11-7 win in Game 5. Brooklyn refused to go down without a fight, as Carl Furillo's ninth-inning, two-run homer tied the sixth game, 3-3. In the bottom of the inning, Billy Martin singled in Hank Bauer with the winning run as the Yanks clinched the title. Martin batted .500 and drove in eight runs in the Series.

Game 1
Wednesday, September 30

Dodgers	AB	R	H	RBI	BB	K	Avg
Jim Gilliam, 2b	5	1	2	1	0	1	.400
Pee Wee Reese, ss	3	0	0	0	2	0	.000
Duke Snider, cf	5	0	2	0	0	1	.400
Jackie Robinson, lf	4	0	0	0	1	0	.000
Roy Campanella, c	4	1	1	0	0	0	.250
Gil Hodges, 1b	5	1	3	1	0	0	.600
Carl Furillo, rf	4	0	1	1	1	1	.250
Billy Cox, 3b	5	1	2	0	0	0	.400
Carl Erskine, p	0	0	0	0	0	0	—
Wayne Belardi, ph	1	0	0	0	0	0	.000
Jim Hughes, p	1	0	0	0	0	1	.000
George Shuba, ph	1	1	1	2	0	0	1.000
Clem Labine, p	1	0	0	0	0	0	.000
Ben Wade, p	0	0	0	0	0	0	—
TOTALS	39	5	12	5	4	6	.308

Yankees	AB	R	H	RBI	BB	K	Avg
Gil McDougald, 3b	5	0	0	0	0	0	.000
Joe Collins, 1b	4	2	2	2	1	0	.500
Hank Bauer, rf	5	1	2	1	0	2	.400
Yogi Berra, c	4	1	2	1	0	2	.500
Mickey Mantle, cf	3	1	1	0	1	1	.333
Gene Woodling, lf	3	1	1	0	1	0	.333
Billy Martin, 2b	4	1	3	3	0	0	.750
Phil Rizzuto, ss	3	1	0	0	1	0	.000
Allie Reynolds, p	1	0	0	0	1	1	.000
Johnny Sain, p	2	1	1	2	0	1	.500
TOTALS	34	9	12	9	5	7	.353

	1	2	3	4	5	6	7	8	9		R	H	E
Dodgers	0	0	0	0	1	3	1	0	0		5	12	2
Yankees	4	0	0	0	1	0	1	3	x		9	12	0

E—Hughes, Furillo. LOB—Dodgers 12, Yankees 6. Scoring Position—Dodgers 1-for-8, Yankees 3-for-9. 2B—Snider (1), Cox (1), Sain (1). 3B—Bauer (1), Martin (1). HR—Gilliam (1), Hodges (1), Collins (1), Berra (1), Shuba (1). SB—Martin (1). CS—Mantle (1), Martin (1).

Dodgers	IP	H	R	ER	BB	K	ERA
Carl Erskine	1.0	2	4	4	3	1	36.00
Jim Hughes	4.0	3	1	1	1	3	2.25
Clem Labine (L, 0-1)	1.2	4	1	1	0	1	5.40
Ben Wade	1.1	3	3	3	1	2	20.25

Yankees	IP	H	R	ER	BB	K	ERA
Allie Reynolds	5.1	7	4	4	3	6	6.75
Johnny Sain (BS, 1; W, 1-0)	3.2	5	1	1	1	0	2.45

HBP—Campanella by Reynolds. Time—3:10. Attendance—69,374. Umpires—HP, Grieve. 1B, Stewart. 2B, Hurley. 3B, Gore.

Game 2
Thursday, October 1

Dodgers	AB	R	H	RBI	BB	K	Avg
Jim Gilliam, 2b	5	0	0	0	0	0	.200
Pee Wee Reese, ss	3	0	2	0	2	0	.333
Duke Snider, cf	5	0	0	0	0	1	.200
Jackie Robinson, lf	4	0	1	0	0	0	.125
Roy Campanella, c	4	0	0	0	0	0	.125
Gil Hodges, 1b	3	1	2	0	1	0	.625
Carl Furillo, rf	4	1	2	0	0	0	.375
Billy Cox, 3b	3	0	1	2	1	0	.375
Preacher Roe, p	3	0	0	0	0	2	.000
Dick Williams, ph	1	0	1	0	0	0	1.000
TOTALS	35	2	9	2	4	3	.286

Yankees	AB	R	H	RBI	BB	K	Avg
Gene Woodling, lf	3	1	0	0	1	1	.167
Joe Collins, 1b	3	0	0	0	1	0	.286
Hank Bauer, rf	4	1	1	0	0	1	.333
Yogi Berra, c	3	0	0	1	1	0	.286
Mickey Mantle, cf	3	1	1	2	1	0	.333
Gil McDougald, 3b	3	0	0	0	0	0	.000
Billy Martin, 2b	3	1	2	1	0	0	.714
Phil Rizzuto, ss	2	0	1	0	0	0	.200
Ed Lopat, p	3	0	0	0	0	2	.000
TOTALS	27	4	5	4	4	4	.276

	1	2	3	4	5	6	7	8	9		R	H	E
Dodgers	0	0	0	2	0	0	0	0	0		2	9	1
Yankees	1	0	0	0	0	0	1	2	x		4	5	0

E—Furillo. DP—Yankees 1 (Martin to Rizzuto to Collins). LOB—Dodgers 10, Yankees 5. Scoring Position—Dodgers 1-for-10, Yankees 0-for-6. 2B—Furillo (1), Cox (2), Rizzuto (1). 3B—Reese (1). HR—Mantle (1), Martin (1). S—Rizzuto. GDP—Furillo. SB—Hodges (1). CS—Berra (1).

Dodgers	IP	H	R	ER	BB	K	ERA
Preacher Roe (L, 0-1)	8.0	5	4	4	4	4	4.50

Yankees	IP	H	R	ER	BB	K	ERA
Ed Lopat (W, 1-0)	9.0	9	2	2	4	3	2.00

HBP—McDougald by Roe. Time—2:42. Attendance—66,786. Umpires—HP, Stewart. 1B, Hurley. 2B, Gore. 3B, Grieve.

Game 3
Friday, October 2

Yankees	AB	R	H	RBI	BB	K	Avg
Gil McDougald, 3b	4	0	1	1	0	1	.083
Irv Noren, ph	0	0	0	0	1	0	—
Joe Collins, 1b	5	0	0	0	0	4	.167
Hank Bauer, rf	4	1	1	0	0	0	.308
Yogi Berra, c	1	0	1	0	1	0	.375
Mickey Mantle, cf	4	0	0	0	0	4	.200
Gene Woodling, lf	4	0	1	1	0	1	.200
Billy Martin, 2b	3	1	1	0	1	0	.600
Phil Rizzuto, ss	3	0	1	0	0	1	.250
Don Bollweg, ph	1	0	0	0	0	1	.000
Vic Raschi, p	2	0	0	0	0	1	.000
Johnny Mize, ph	1	0	0	0	0	1	.000
TOTALS	32	2	6	2	3	14	.253

Dodgers	AB	R	H	RBI	BB	K	Avg
Jim Gilliam, 2b	4	0	1	0	0	0	.214
Pee Wee Reese, ss	4	0	1	0	0	1	.300
Duke Snider, cf	3	1	1	0	1	0	.231
Gil Hodges, 1b	2	0	1	0	2	0	.600
Roy Campanella, c	4	1	1	1	0	1	.167
Carl Furillo, rf	4	0	0	0	0	1	.250
Jackie Robinson, lf	4	1	3	1	0	0	.333
Don Thompson, lf	0	0	0	0	0	0	—
Billy Cox, 3b	3	0	0	1	0	1	.273
Carl Erskine, p	3	0	1	0	0	0	.333
TOTALS	31	3	9	3	3	4	.289

	1	2	3	4	5	6	7	8	9		R	H	E
Yankees	0	0	0	0	1	0	0	1	0		2	6	0
Dodgers	0	0	0	0	1	1	0	1	x		3	9	0

DP—Yankees 1 (Rizzuto to Martin to Collins). LOB—Yankees 9, Dodgers 8. Scoring Position—Yankees 2-for-9, Dodgers 1-for-7. 2B—Robinson (1). HR—Campanella (1). S—Raschi, Cox. GDP—Furillo. CS—Gilliam (1).

Yankees	IP	H	R	ER	BB	K	ERA
Vic Raschi (L, 0-1)	8.0	9	3	3	3	4	3.38

Dodgers	IP	H	R	ER	BB	K	ERA
Carl Erskine (W, 1-0)	9.0	6	2	2	3	14	5.40

Balk—Raschi. WP—Erskine. HBP—Berra by Erskine, Berra by Erskine. Time—3:00. Attendance—35,270. Umpires—HP, Hurley. 1B, Gore. 2B, Grieve. 3B, Stewart.

Game 4

Saturday, October 3

Yankees	AB	R	H	RBI	BB	K	Avg
Mickey Mantle, cf	5	0	1	1	0	2	.200
Joe Collins, 1b	4	0	0	0	0	2	.125
Hank Bauer, rf	4	0	1	0	0	0	.294
Yogi Berra, c	4	0	2	0	0	1	.417
Gene Woodling, lf	3	1	1	0	1	0	.231
Billy Martin, 2b	4	1	2	0	0	0	.571
Gil McDougald, 3b	3	1	1	2	1	0	.133
Phil Rizzuto, ss	4	0	1	0	0	1	.250
Whitey Ford, p	0	0	0	0	0	0	—
Tom Gorman, p	1	0	0	0	0	1	.000
Don Bollweg, ph	1	0	0	0	0	1	.000
Johnny Sain, p	0	0	0	0	0	0	.500
Irv Noren, ph	1	0	0	0	0	0	.000
Art Schallock, p	0	0	0	0	0	0	—
Johnny Mize, ph	1	0	0	0	0	0	.000
TOTALS	35	3	9	3	2	9	.262

Dodgers	AB	R	H	RBI	BB	K	Avg
Jim Gilliam, 2b	5	1	3	2	0	0	.316
Pee Wee Reese, ss	5	0	0	0	0	0	.200
Jackie Robinson, lf	4	0	1	1	0	0	.313
Don Thompson, lf	0	0	0	0	0	0	—
Gil Hodges, 1b	4	1	0	0	0	1	.429
Roy Campanella, c	2	2	0	0	2	0	.143
Duke Snider, cf	4	1	3	4	0	0	.353
Carl Furillo, rf	4	1	1	0	0	1	.250
Billy Cox, 3b	4	1	2	0	0	1	.333
Billy Loes, p	3	0	2	0	0	0	.667
Clem Labine, p	0	0	0	0	0	0	.000
TOTALS	35	7	12	7	2	3	.300

	1 2 3	4 5 6	7 8 9	R	H	E
Yankees	0 0 0	0 2 0	0 0 1	3	9	0
Dodgers	3 0 0	1 0 2	1 0 x	7	12	0

LOB—Yankees 7, Dodgers 7. Scoring Position—Yankees 2-for-4, Dodgers 4-for-13. 2B—Gilliam 3 (3), Snider 2 (3), Cox (3). 3B—Martin (2). HR—McDougald (1), Snider (1). S—Loes.

Yankees	IP	H	R	ER	BB	K	ERA
Whitey Ford (L, 0-1)	1.0	3	3	3	1	0	27.00
Tom Gorman	3.0	4	1	1	0	1	3.00
Johnny Sain	2.0	3	2	2	0	1	4.76
Art Schallock	2.0	2	1	1	1	1	4.50

Dodgers	IP	H	R	ER	BB	K	ERA
Billy Loes (W, 1-0)	8.0	8	3	3	2	8	3.38
Clem Labine (S, 1)	1.0	1	0	0	0	1	3.38

Loes pitched to three batters in the 9th.

WP—Ford. Time—2:46. Attendance—36,775. Umpires—HP, Gore. 1B, Grieve. 2B, Stewart. 3B, Hurley.

Game 5

Sunday, October 4

Yankees	AB	R	H	RBI	BB	K	Avg
Gene Woodling, lf	3	1	1	1	2	0	.250
Joe Collins, 1b	5	2	1	0	0	1	.143
Hank Bauer, rf	3	1	0	0	0	1	.250
Yogi Berra, c	4	2	2	1	1	0	.438
Mickey Mantle, cf	5	1	1	4	0	1	.200
Billy Martin, 2b	5	1	2	2	0	1	.526
Gil McDougald, 3b	5	1	2	1	0	1	.200
Phil Rizzuto, ss	3	2	1	0	2	0	.267
Jim McDonald, p	2	0	1	1	1	1	.500
Bob Kuzava, p	1	0	0	0	0	1	.000
Allie Reynolds, p	0	0	0	0	0	0	.000
TOTALS	36	11	11	10	6	7	.278

Dodgers	AB	R	H	RBI	BB	K	Avg
Jim Gilliam, 2b	4	2	2	1	0	0	.348
Pee Wee Reese, ss	5	0	1	0	0	0	.200
Duke Snider, cf	5	0	2	1	0	1	.364
Jackie Robinson, lf	5	1	1	0	0	0	.286
Roy Campanella, c	4	2	3	0	0	0	.278
Gil Hodges, 1b	4	0	2	0	0	1	.444
Carl Furillo, rf	4	1	1	1	0	0	.250
Billy Cox, 3b	4	1	1	3	0	0	.316
Johnny Podres, p	1	0	1	0	0	0	1.000
Russ Meyer, p	1	0	0	0	0	0	.000
Wayne Belardi, ph	1	0	0	0	0	0	.000
Ben Wade, p	0	0	0	0	0	0	—
George Shuba, ph	0	0	0	0	0	0	1.000
Dick Williams, ph	1	0	0	0	0	1	.500
Joe Black, p	0	0	0	0	0	0	—
TOTALS	39	7	14	6	0	4	.315

	1 2 3	4 5 6	7 8 9	R	H	E
Yankees	1 0 5	0 0 0	3 1 1	11	11	1
Dodgers	0 1 0	0 1 0	0 4 1	7	14	1

E—Hodges, Rizzuto. DP—Yankees 1 (Rizzuto to Collins). LOB—Yankees 7, Dodgers 6. Scoring Position—Yankees 2-for-10, Dodgers 3-for-11. 2B—Collins (1), McDonald (1). 3B—McDougald (1). HR—Woodling (1), Mantle (2), Martin (2), McDougald (2), Gilliam (2), Cox (1). S—Bauer, McDonald. GDP—Robinson, Furillo. SB—Rizzuto (1). CS—Martin (2).

Yankees	IP	H	R	ER	BB	K	ERA
Jim McDonald (W, 1-0)	7.2	12	6	5	0	3	5.87
Bob Kuzava	0.2	2	1	1	0	1	13.50
Allie Reynolds (S, 1)	0.2	0	0	0	0	0	6.00

Dodgers	IP	H	R	ER	BB	K	ERA
Johnny Podres (L, 0-1)	2.2	1	5	1	2	0	3.38
Russ Meyer	4.1	8	4	3	4	5	6.23
Ben Wade	1.0	1	1	1	0	0	15.43
Joe Black	1.0	1	1	1	0	2	9.00

HBP—Bauer by Podres, Gilliam by McDonald. Time—3:02. Attendance—36,775. Umpires—HP, Grieve. 1B, Stewart. 2B, Hurley. 3B, Gore.

Game 6

Monday, October 5

Dodgers	AB	R	H	RBI	BB	K	Avg
Jim Gilliam, 2b	4	0	0	0	0	1	.296
Pee Wee Reese, ss	4	0	1	0	0	0	.208
Jackie Robinson, lf	4	1	2	0	0	0	.320
Roy Campanella, c	4	0	1	1	0	2	.273
Gil Hodges, 1b	4	0	0	0	0	0	.364
Duke Snider, cf	3	1	0	0	1	3	.320
Carl Furillo, rf	4	1	3	2	0	0	.333
Billy Cox, 3b	4	0	1	0	0	0	.304
Carl Erskine, p	1	0	0	0	0	1	.250
Dick Williams, ph	0	0	0	0	1	0	.500
Bob Milliken, p	0	0	0	0	0	0	—
Bobby Morgan, ph	1	0	0	0	0	0	.000
Clem Labine, p	1	0	0	0	0	1	.000
TOTALS	34	3	8	3	2	10	.299

Yankees	AB	R	H	RBI	BB	K	Avg
Gene Woodling, lf	4	1	2	1	1	0	.300
Joe Collins, 1b	3	0	1	0	1	1	.167
Johnny Mize, ph	1	0	0	0	0	0	.000
Don Bollweg, 1b	0	0	0	0	0	0	.000
Hank Bauer, rf	3	2	1	0	2	0	.261
Yogi Berra, c	5	0	2	1	0	0	.429
Mickey Mantle, cf	4	0	1	0	1	0	.208
Billy Martin, 2b	5	0	2	2	0	0	.500
Gil McDougald, 3b	4	0	0	0	0	1	.167
Phil Rizzuto, ss	4	1	2	0	0	0	.316
Whitey Ford, p	3	0	1	0	0	0	.333
Allie Reynolds, p	1	0	1	0	0	0	.500
TOTALS	37	4	13	4	5	2	.286

	1 2 3	4 5 6	7 8 9	R	H	E
Dodgers	0 0 0	0 0 1	0 0 2	3	8	3
Yankees	2 1 0	0 0 0	0 0 1	4	13	0

E—Gilliam, Erskine, Cox. DP—Dodgers 3 (Cox to Gilliam to Hodges; Snider to Gilliam to Campanella; Labine to Gilliam to Hodges). LOB—Dodgers 6, Yankees 13. Scoring Position—Dodgers 0-for-4, Yankees 2-for-10. 2B—Furillo (2), Berra (1), Martin (1). HR—Furillo (1). GDP—Martin, McDougald. SB—Robinson (1).

Dodgers	IP	H	R	ER	BB	K	ERA
Carl Erskine	4.0	6	3	3	3	1	5.79
Bob Milliken	2.0	2	0	0	1	0	0.00
Clem Labine (L, 0-2)	2.1	5	1	1	1	1	3.60

Yankees	IP	H	R	ER	BB	K	ERA
Whitey Ford	7.0	6	1	1	1	7	4.50
Allie Reynolds (BS, 1; W, 1-0)	2.0	2	2	2	1	3	6.75

Time—2:55. Attendance—62,370. Umpires—HP, Stewart. 1B, Hurley. 2B, Gore. 3B, Grieve.

1953 World Series—Composite Statistics

Batting

Yankees	G	AB	R	H	RBI	2B	3B	HR	BB	SO	SB	CS	Avg	OBP	Slg
Hank Bauer	6	23	6	6	1	0	1	0	2	4	0	0	.261	.346	.348
Yogi Berra	6	21	3	9	4	1	0	1	3	3	0	1	.429	.538	.619
Don Bollweg	3	2	0	0	0	0	0	0	0	2	0	0	.000	.000	.000
Joe Collins	6	24	4	4	2	1	0	1	3	8	0	0	.167	.259	.333
Whitey Ford	2	3	0	1	0	0	0	0	0	0	0	0	.333	.333	.333
Tom Gorman	1	1	0	0	0	0	0	0	0	1	0	0	.000	.000	.000
Bob Kuzava	1	1	0	0	0	0	0	0	0	1	0	0	.000	.000	.000
Ed Lopat	1	3	0	0	0	0	0	0	0	2	0	0	.000	.000	.000
Mickey Mantle	6	24	3	5	7	0	0	2	3	8	0	1	.208	.296	.458
Billy Martin	6	24	5	12	8	1	2	2	1	2	1	2	.500	.520	.958
Jim McDonald	1	2	0	1	1	1	0	0	1	1	0	0	.500	.667	1.000
Gil McDougald	6	24	2	4	4	0	1	2	1	3	0	0	.167	.231	.500
Johnny Mize	3	3	0	0	0	0	0	0	0	0	0	0	.000	.000	.000
Irv Noren	2	1	0	0	0	0	0	0	1	0	0	0	.000	.500	.000
Vic Raschi	1	2	0	0	0	0	0	0	0	1	0	0	.000	.000	.000
Allie Reynolds	3	2	0	1	0	0	0	0	1	1	0	0	.500	.667	.500
Phil Rizzuto	6	19	4	6	0	1	0	0	3	2	1	0	.316	.409	.368
Johnny Sain	2	2	1	1	2	1	0	0	0	1	0	0	.500	.500	1.000
Gene Woodling	6	20	5	6	3	0	0	1	6	2	0	0	.300	.462	.450
Totals	6	201	33	56	32	6	4	9	25	43	2	4	.279	.370	.483

Batting

Dodgers	G	AB	R	H	RBI	2B	3B	HR	BB	SO	SB	CS	Avg	OBP	Slg
Wayne Belardi	2	2	0	0	0	0	0	0	0	1	0	0	.000	.000	.000
Roy Campanella	6	22	6	6	2	0	0	1	2	3	0	0	.273	.360	.409
Billy Cox	6	23	3	7	6	3	0	1	1	4	0	0	.304	.333	.565
Carl Erskine	3	4	0	1	0	0	0	0	0	1	0	0	.250	.250	.250
Carl Furillo	6	24	4	8	4	2	0	1	1	3	0	0	.333	.360	.542
Jim Gilliam	6	27	4	8	4	3	0	2	0	2	0	1	.296	.321	.630
Gil Hodges	6	22	3	8	1	0	0	1	3	3	1	0	.364	.440	.500
Jim Hughes	1	1	0	0	0	0	0	0	0	1	0	0	.000	.000	.000
Clem Labine	3	2	0	0	0	0	0	0	0	1	0	0	.000	.000	.000
Billy Loes	1	3	0	2	0	0	0	0	0	0	0	0	.667	.667	.667
Russ Meyer	1	1	0	0	0	0	0	0	0	1	0	0	.000	.000	.000
Bobby Morgan	1	1	0	0	0	0	0	0	0	0	0	0	.000	.000	.000
Johnny Podres	1	1	0	1	0	0	0	0	0	0	0	0	1.000	1.000	1.000
Pee Wee Reese	6	24	0	5	0	0	1	0	4	1	0	0	.208	.321	.292
Jackie Robinson	6	25	3	8	2	2	0	0	1	0	1	0	.320	.346	.400
Preacher Roe	1	3	0	0	0	0	0	0	0	2	0	0	.000	.000	.000
George Shuba	2	1	1	1	2	0	0	1	0	0	0	0	1.000	1.000	4.000
Duke Snider	6	25	3	8	5	3	0	1	2	6	0	0	.320	.370	.560
Dick Williams	3	2	0	1	0	0	0	0	0	1	1	0	.500	.667	.500
Totals	6	213	27	64	26	13	1	8	15	30	2	1	.300	.352	.484

Pitching

Yankees	G	GS	CG	IP	H	R	ER	BB	SO	W-L	Sv-Op	Hld	ERA
Whitey Ford	2	2	0	8.0	9	4	4	2	7	0-1	0-0	0	4.50
Tom Gorman	1	0	0	3.0	4	1	1	0	1	0-0	0-0	0	3.00
Bob Kuzava	1	0	0	0.2	2	1	1	0	1	0-0	0-0	0	13.50
Ed Lopat	1	1	1	9.0	9	2	2	4	3	1-0	0-0	0	2.00
Jim McDonald	1	1	0	7.2	12	6	5	0	3	1-0	0-0	0	5.87
Vic Raschi	1	1	1	8.0	9	3	3	3	4	0-1	0-0	0	3.38
Allie Reynolds	3	1	0	8.0	9	6	6	4	9	1-2	0-0	0	6.75
Johnny Sain	2	0	0	5.2	8	3	3	1	1	1-0	0-1	0	4.76
Art Schallock	1	0	0	2.0	2	1	1	1	1	0-0	0-0	0	4.50
Totals	6	6	2	52.0	64	27	26	15	30	4-2	1-3	0	4.50

Pitching

Dodgers	G	GS	CG	IP	H	R	ER	BB	SO	W-L	Sv-Op	Hld	ERA
Joe Black	1	0	0	1.0	1	1	1	0	2	0-0	0-0	0	9.00
Carl Erskine	3	3	1	14.0	14	9	9	9	16	1-0	0-0	0	5.79
Jim Hughes	1	0	0	4.0	3	1	1	1	3	0-0	0-0	0	2.25
Clem Labine	3	0	0	5.0	10	2	2	1	3	0-2	1-1	0	3.60
Billy Loes	1	1	0	8.0	8	3	3	2	8	1-0	0-0	0	3.38
Russ Meyer	1	0	0	4.1	8	4	3	4	5	0-0	0-0	0	6.23
Bob Milliken	1	0	0	2.0	2	0	0	1	0	0-0	0-0	0	0.00
Johnny Podres	1	1	0	2.2	1	5	1	2	0	0-1	0-0	0	3.38
Preacher Roe	1	1	1	8.0	5	4	4	4	4	0-1	0-0	0	4.50
Ben Wade	2	0	0	2.1	4	4	4	1	2	0-0	0-0	0	15.43
Totals	6	6	2	51.1	56	33	28	25	43	2-4	1-1	0	4.91

Fielding

Yankees	Pos	G	PO	Ast	E	DP	PB	FPct
Hank Bauer	rf	6	14	0	0	0	—	1.000
Yogi Berra	c	6	37	3	0	0	0	1.000
Don Bollweg	1b	1	0	0	0	0	—	—
Joe Collins	1b	6	50	4	0	3	—	1.000
Whitey Ford	p	2	0	1	0	0	—	1.000
Tom Gorman	p	1	1	0	0	0	—	1.000
Bob Kuzava	p	1	0	0	0	0	—	—
Ed Lopat	p	1	0	2	0	0	—	1.000
Mickey Mantle	cf	6	14	0	0	0	—	1.000
Billy Martin	2b	6	13	15	0	2	—	1.000
Jim McDonald	p	1	2	0	0	0	—	1.000
Gil McDougald	3b	6	4	14	0	0	—	1.000
Vic Raschi	p	1	1	1	0	0	—	1.000
Allie Reynolds	p	3	0	0	0	0	—	—
Phil Rizzuto	ss	6	11	19	1	3	—	.968
Johnny Sain	p	2	0	0	0	0	—	—
Art Schallock	p	1	0	1	0	0	—	1.000
Gene Woodling	lf	6	9	1	0	0	—	1.000
Totals		6	156	61	1	8	0	.995

Fielding

Dodgers	Pos	G	PO	Ast	E	DP	PB	FPct
Joe Black	p	1	0	0	0	0	—	—
Roy Campanella	c	6	47	9	0	1	0	1.000
Billy Cox	3b	6	1	10	1	1	—	.917
Carl Erskine	p	3	1	2	1	0	—	.750
Carl Furillo	rf	6	10	0	2	0	—	.833
Jim Gilliam	2b	6	15	16	1	3	—	.969
Gil Hodges	1b	6	47	4	1	2	—	.981
Jim Hughes	p	1	0	0	1	0	—	.000
Clem Labine	p	3	0	2	0	1	—	1.000
Billy Loes	p	1	0	0	0	0	—	—
Russ Meyer	p	1	0	1	0	0	—	1.000
Bob Milliken	p	1	0	0	0	0	—	—
Johnny Podres	p	1	0	1	0	0	—	1.000
Pee Wee Reese	ss	6	7	14	0	0	—	1.000
Jackie Robinson	lf	6	8	0	0	0	—	1.000
Preacher Roe	p	1	1	1	0	0	—	1.000
Duke Snider	cf	6	17	1	0	1	—	1.000
Don Thompson	lf	2	0	1	0	0	—	1.000
Ben Wade	p	2	0	0	0	0	—	—
Totals		6	154	62	7	9	0	.969

1954 New York Giants (NL) 4, Cleveland Indians (AL) 0

Willie Mays made Vic Wertz a household name, Dusty Rhodes provided key pinch-hits at every turn, and the New York Giants swept a four-game World Series from the Cleveland Indians. The opener was tied 2-2 in the top of the eighth when Cleveland put men on first and second with no one out. Wertz sent a 440-foot drive to center field, but Mays sprinted back and made an unforgettable over-the-shoulder catch to prevent Cleveland from taking the lead. Rhodes came off the bench to deliver a game-winning, pinch-hit, three-run homer in the bottom of the 10th. In Game 2, Rhodes tied the game in the fifth with a pinch-hit RBI single, and added a homer in the seventh as the Giants won, 3-1. In Game 3, Rhodes pinch-hit in the third with the bases loaded, and drilled a two-run single to send the Giants to a 6-2 victory. The Giants ran up a 7-0 lead before taking the fourth game, 7-4. Rhodes finished with two singles, two homers and seven RBI in six at-bats.

Game 1

Wednesday, September 29

Indians	AB	R	H	RBI	BB	K	Avg
Al Smith, lf	4	1	1	0	0	1	.250
Bobby Avila, 2b	5	1	1	0	0	0	.200
Larry Doby, cf	3	0	1	0	2	0	.333
Al Rosen, 3b	5	0	1	0	0	0	.200
Vic Wertz, 1b	5	0	4	2	0	0	.800
Rudy Regalado, pr	0	0	0	0	0	0	—
Mickey Grasso, c	0	0	0	0	0	0	—
Dave Philley, rf	3	0	0	0	0	0	.000
Hank Majeski, ph	0	0	0	0	0	0	—
Dale Mitchell, ph	0	0	0	0	1	0	—
Sam Dente, ss	0	0	0	0	0	0	—
George Strickland, ss	3	0	0	0	0	1	.000
Dave Pope, ph-rf	1	0	0	0	1	1	.000
Jim Hegan, c	4	0	0	0	0	0	.000
Bill Glynn, ph-1b	1	0	0	0	0	1	.000
Bob Lemon, p	4	0	0	0	1	0	.000
TOTALS	38	2	8	2	5	4	.211

Giants	AB	R	H	RBI	BB	K	Avg
Whitey Lockman, 1b	5	1	1	0	0	0	.200
Al Dark, ss	4	0	2	0	0	0	.500
Don Mueller, rf	5	1	2	1	0	1	.400
Willie Mays, cf	3	1	0	0	2	0	.000
Hank Thompson, 3b	3	1	1	1	2	1	.333
Monte Irvin, lf	3	0	0	0	1	0	.000
Dusty Rhodes, ph	1	1	1	3	0	0	1.000
Davey Williams, 2b	4	0	0	0	0	0	.000
Wes Westrum, c	4	0	2	0	0	0	.500
Sal Maglie, p	3	0	0	0	0	2	.000
Don Liddle, p	0	0	0	0	0	0	—
Marv Grissom, p	1	0	0	0	0	1	.000
TOTALS	36	5	9	5	5	6	.250

	1	2	3	4	5	6	7	8	9	10		R	H	E
Indians	2	0	0	0	0	0	0	0	0	0		2	8	0
Giants	0	0	2	0	0	0	0	0	0	3		5	9	3

E—Irvin, Mueller 2. LOB—Indians 13, Giants 9. Scoring Position—Indians 1-for-16, Giants 3-for-11. 2B—Wertz (1). 3B—Wertz (1). HR—Rhodes (1). S—Irvin, Dente. SB—Mays (1).

Indians	IP	H	R	ER	BB	K	ERA
Bob Lemon (L, 0-1)	9.1	9	5	5	5	6	4.82

Giants	IP	H	R	ER	BB	K	ERA
Sal Maglie	7.0	7	2	2	2	2	2.57
Don Liddle	0.1	0	0	0	0	0	0.00
Marv Grissom (W, 1-0)	2.2	1	0	0	3	2	0.00

Maglie pitched to two batters in the 8th.

WP—Lemon. HBP—Smith by Maglie. Time—3:11. Attendance—52,751. Umpires—HP, Barlick. 1B, Berry. 2B, Conlan. 3B, Stevens.

Game 2

Thursday, September 30

Indians	AB	R	H	RBI	BB	K	Avg
Al Smith, lf	4	1	2	1	1	1	.375
Bobby Avila, 2b	4	0	1	0	1	0	.222
Larry Doby, cf	5	0	0	0	0	3	.125
Al Rosen, 3b	3	0	1	0	1	0	.250
Rudy Regalado, pr-3b	1	0	0	0	0	0	.000
Vic Wertz, 1b	3	0	1	0	2	0	.625
Wally Westlake, rf	3	0	1	0	1	1	.333
George Strickland, ss	3	0	0	0	0	0	.000
Dave Philley, ph	1	0	0	0	0	1	.000
Sam Dente, ss	0	0	0	0	0	0	—
Jim Hegan, c	4	0	1	0	0	1	.125
Early Wynn, p	2	0	1	0	1	0	.500
Hank Majeski, ph	1	0	0	0	0	1	.000
Don Mossi, p	0	0	0	0	0	0	—
TOTALS	34	1	8	1	6	9	.242

Giants	AB	R	H	RBI	BB	K	Avg
Whitey Lockman, 1b	4	0	0	0	0	1	.111
Al Dark, ss	4	0	1	0	0	0	.375
Don Mueller, rf	4	0	0	0	0	0	.222
Willie Mays, cf	2	1	0	0	1	1	.000
Hank Thompson, 3b	3	1	1	0	0	0	.333
Monte Irvin, lf	1	0	0	0	0	1	.000
Dusty Rhodes, ph-lf	2	1	2	2	0	0	1.000
Davey Williams, 2b	3	0	0	0	0	2	.000
Wes Westrum, c	2	0	0	0	1	0	.333
Johnny Antonelli, p	3	0	0	1	0	0	.000
TOTALS	28	3	4	3	2	5	.217

	1	2	3	4	5	6	7	8	9		R	H	E
Indians	1	0	0	0	0	0	0	0	0		1	8	0
Giants	0	0	0	0	2	0	1	0	x		3	4	0

LOB—Indians 13, Giants 3. Scoring Position—Indians 1-for-11, Giants 1-for-7. 2B—Hegan (1), Wynn (1). HR—Smith (1), Rhodes (2). S—Wynn.

Indians	IP	H	R	ER	BB	K	ERA
Early Wynn (L, 0-1)	7.0	4	3	3	2	5	3.86
Don Mossi	1.0	0	0	0	0	0	0.00

Giants	IP	H	R	ER	BB	K	ERA
Johnny Antonelli (W, 1-0)	9.0	8	1	1	6	9	1.00

WP—Wynn. Time—2:50. Attendance—49,099. Umpires—HP, Berry. 1B, Conlan. 2B, Stevens. 3B, Barlick.

Game 3

Friday, October 1

Giants	AB	R	H	RBI	BB	K	Avg
Whitey Lockman, 1b	4	1	1	0	1	0	.154
Al Dark, ss	4	0	1	0	0	1	.333
Don Mueller, rf	5	2	2	0	0	0	.286
Willie Mays, cf	5	1	3	0	0	0	.300
Hank Thompson, 3b	3	2	1	0	2	0	.333
Monte Irvin, lf	1	0	0	0	0	0	.000
Dusty Rhodes, ph-lf	3	0	1	2	1	2	.667
Davey Williams, 2b	2	0	0	1	1	0	.000
Wes Westrum, c	4	0	1	1	0	2	.300
Ruben Gomez, p	4	0	0	0	0	2	.000
Hoyt Wilhelm, p	0	0	0	0	0	0	—
TOTALS	35	6	10	6	5	7	.250

Indians	AB	R	H	RBI	BB	K	Avg
Al Smith, lf	3	0	0	1	1	0	.273
Bobby Avila, 2b	2	0	0	0	1	0	.182
Larry Doby, cf	4	0	1	0	0	0	.167
Vic Wertz, 1b	4	1	1	1	0	1	.500
Hank Majeski, 3b	4	0	0	0	0	1	.000
Dave Philley, rf	3	0	1	0	1	1	.143
George Strickland, ss	3	0	0	0	0	0	.000
Dave Pope, ph	1	0	0	0	0	0	.000
Jim Hegan, c	2	0	0	0	0	0	.100
Bill Glynn, ph	1	1	1	0	0	0	.500
Hal Naragon, c	0	0	0	0	0	0	—
Mike Garcia, p	0	0	0	0	0	0	—
Bob Lemon, ph	1	0	0	0	0	1	.000
Art Houtteman, p	0	0	0	0	0	0	—
Rudy Regalado, ph	1	0	0	0	0	0	.000
Ray Narleski, p	0	0	0	0	0	0	—
Dale Mitchell, ph	1	0	0	0	0	0	—
Don Mossi, p	0	0	0	0	0	0	—
TOTALS	30	2	4	2	3	4	.180

	1	2	3	4	5	6	7	8	9		R	H	E
Giants	1	0	3	0	1	1	0	0	0		6	10	1
Indians	0	0	0	0	0	0	1	1	0		2	4	2

E—Strickland, Garcia, Dark. DP—Giants 1 (Dark to Williams to Lockman), Indians 1 (Strickland to Wertz). LOB—Giants 9, Indians 5. Scoring Position—Giants 4-for-16, Indians 0-for-6. 2B—Thompson (1), Glynn (1). HR—Wertz (1). S—Dark, Williams, Avila. GDP—Majeski.

Game 4

Saturday, October 2

Giants	AB	R	H	RBI	BB	K	Avg
Whitey Lockman, 1b	5	0	0	0	0	1	.111
Al Dark, ss	5	2	3	0	0	0	.412
Don Mueller, rf	4	1	3	0	0	0	.389
Willie Mays, cf	4	1	1	1	1	0	.286
Hank Thompson, 3b	2	2	1	1	3	0	.364
Monte Irvin, lf	4	1	2	2	0	1	.222
Davey Williams, 2b	2	0	0	1	0	0	.000
Wes Westrum, c	1	0	0	2	0	1	.273
Don Liddle, p	3	0	0	0	0	2	.000
Hoyt Wilhelm, p	1	0	0	0	0	1	.000
Johnny Antonelli, p	0	0	0	0	0	0	.000
TOTALS	31	7	10	6	5	6	.250

Indians	AB	R	H	RBI	BB	K	Avg
Al Smith, lf	3	0	0	0	0	0	.214
Dave Pope, ph-lf	1	0	0	0	0	0	.000
Dale Mitchell, ph	1	0	0	0	0	0	.000
Bobby Avila, 2b	4	0	0	0	0	1	.133
Larry Doby, cf	4	0	0	0	0	1	.125
Al Rosen, 3b	4	0	1	0	0	0	.250
Vic Wertz, 1b	4	1	2	0	0	1	.500
Wally Westlake, rf	4	0	0	0	0	2	.143
Sam Dente, ss	3	1	0	0	1	0	.000
Jim Hegan, c	3	1	1	0	1	0	.154
Bob Lemon, p	1	0	0	0	0	0	.000
Hal Newhouser, p	0	0	0	0	0	0	—
Ray Narleski, p	0	0	0	0	0	0	—
Hank Majeski, ph	1	1	1	3	0	0	.167
Don Mossi, p	0	0	0	0	0	0	—
Rudy Regalado, ph	1	0	1	1	0	0	.333
Mike Garcia, p	0	0	0	0	0	0	—
Dave Philley, ph	1	0	0	0	0	1	.125
TOTALS	35	4	6	4	2	6	.194

	1	2	3	4	5	6	7	8	9		R	H	E
Giants	0	2	1	0	4	0	0	0	0		7	10	3
Indians	0	0	0	0	3	0	1	0	0		4	6	2

E—Liddle, Wilhelm, Williams, Westlake, Wertz. DP—Giants 1 (Thompson to Williams to Lockman), Indians 1 (Dente to Avila to Wertz). LOB—Giants 7, Indians 6. Scoring Position—Giants 2-for-10, Indians 2-for-7. 2B—Mays (1), Irvin (1), Wertz (2). HR—Majeski (1). S—Mueller, Williams, Westrum. SF—Westrum 2. GDP—Irvin, Smith. CS—Westrum (1).

Giants	IP	H	R	ER	BB	K	ERA
Don Liddle (W, 1-0)	6.2	5	4	1	1	2	1.29
Hoyt Wilhelm (H, 1)	0.2	1	0	0	0	1	0.00
Johnny Antonelli (S, 1)	1.2	0	0	0	1	3	0.84

Indians	IP	H	R	ER	BB	K	ERA
Bob Lemon (L, 0-2)	4.0	7	6	5	3	5	6.75
Hal Newhouser	0.0	1	1	1	1	0	—
Ray Narleski	1.0	0	0	0	0	0	2.25
Don Mossi	2.0	1	0	0	0	0	0.00
Mike Garcia	2.0	1	0	0	1	1	5.40

Lemon pitched to three batters in the 5th. Newhouser pitched to two batters in the 5th.

WP—Liddle. Time—2:52. Attendance—78,102. Umpires—HP, Stevens. 1B, Barlick. 2B, Berry. 3B, Conlan.

1954 World Series—Composite Statistics

Batting

Giants	G	AB	R	H	RBI	2B	3B	HR	BB	SO	SB	CS	Avg	OBP	Slg
Johnny Antonelli	2	3	0	0	1	0	0	0	0	0	0	0	.000	.000	.000
Al Dark	4	17	2	7	0	0	0	0	1	1	0	0	.412	.444	.412
Ruben Gomez	1	4	0	0	0	0	0	0	0	2	0	0	.000	.000	.000
Marv Grissom	1	1	0	0	0	0	0	0	0	1	0	0	.000	.000	.000
Monte Irvin	4	9	1	2	2	1	0	0	0	3	0	0	.222	.222	.333
Don Liddle	2	3	0	0	0	0	0	0	0	2	0	0	.000	.000	.000
Whitey Lockman	4	18	2	2	0	0	0	0	1	2	0	0	.111	.158	.111
Sal Maglie	1	3	0	0	0	0	0	0	0	2	0	0	.000	.000	.000
Willie Mays	4	14	4	4	3	1	0	0	4	1	1	0	.286	.444	.357
Don Mueller	4	18	4	7	1	0	0	0	0	1	0	0	.389	.389	.389
Dusty Rhodes	3	6	2	4	7	0	0	2	1	2	0	0	.667	.714	1.667
Hank Thompson	4	11	6	4	2	1	0	0	7	1	0	0	.364	.611	.455
Wes Westrum	4	11	0	3	3	0	0	0	1	3	0	1	.273	.286	.273
Hoyt Wilhelm	2	1	0	0	0	0	0	0	0	1	0	0	.000	.000	.000
Davey Williams	4	11	0	0	1	0	0	0	2	2	0	0	.000	.154	.000
Totals	4	130	21	33	20	3	0	2	17	24	1	1	.254	.336	.323

Batting

Indians	G	AB	R	H	RBI	2B	3B	HR	BB	SO	SB	CS	Avg	OBP	Slg
Bobby Avila	4	15	1	2	0	0	0	0	2	1	0	0	.133	.235	.133
Sam Dente	3	3	1	0	0	0	0	0	1	0	0	0	.000	.250	.000
Larry Doby	4	16	0	2	0	0	0	0	2	4	0	0	.125	.222	.125
Bill Glynn	2	2	1	1	0	1	0	0	0	1	0	0	.500	.500	1.000
Jim Hegan	4	13	1	2	0	1	0	0	1	1	0	0	.154	.214	.231
Bob Lemon	3	6	0	0	0	0	0	0	1	1	0	0	.000	.143	.000
Hank Majeski	4	6	1	1	3	0	0	1	0	1	0	0	.167	.167	.667
Dale Mitchell	3	2	0	0	0	0	0	0	1	0	0	0	.000	.333	.000
Dave Philley	4	8	0	1	0	0	0	0	1	3	0	0	.125	.222	.125
Dave Pope	3	3	0	0	0	0	0	0	1	1	0	0	.000	.250	.000
Rudy Regalado	4	3	0	1	1	0	0	0	0	0	0	0	.333	.333	.333
Al Rosen	3	12	0	3	0	0	0	0	1	0	0	0	.250	.308	.250
Al Smith	4	14	2	3	0	0	0	1	2	2	0	0	.214	.353	.429
George Strickland	3	9	0	0	0	0	0	0	0	2	0	0	.000	.000	.000
Vic Wertz	4	16	2	8	3	2	1	1	2	2	0	0	.500	.556	.938
Wally Westlake	2	7	0	1	0	0	0	0	1	3	0	0	.143	.250	.143
Early Wynn	1	2	0	1	0	1	0	0	0	1	0	0	.500	.500	1.000
Totals	4	137	9	26	9	5	1	3	16	23	0	0	.190	.279	.307

Pitching

Giants	G	GS	CG	IP	H	R	ER	BB	SO	W-L	Sv-Op	Hld	ERA
Johnny Antonelli	2	1	1	10.2	8	1	1	7	12	1-0	1-1	0	0.84
Ruben Gomez	1	1	0	7.1	4	2	2	3	2	1-0	0-0	0	2.45
Marv Grissom	1	0	0	2.2	1	0	0	3	2	1-0	0-0	0	0.00
Don Liddle	2	1	0	7.0	5	4	1	1	2	1-0	0-0	0	1.29
Sal Maglie	1	1	0	7.0	7	2	2	2	2	0-0	0-0	0	2.57
Hoyt Wilhelm	2	0	0	2.1	1	0	0	0	3	0-0	1-1	1	0.00
Totals	4	4	1	37.0	26	9	6	16	23	4-0	2-2	1	1.46

Pitching

Indians	G	GS	CG	IP	H	R	ER	BB	SO	W-L	Sv-Op	Hld	ERA
Mike Garcia	2	1	0	5.0	6	4	3	4	4	0-1	0-0	0	5.40
Art Houtteman	1	0	0	2.0	2	1	1	1	1	0-0	0-0	0	4.50
Bob Lemon	2	2	1	13.1	16	11	10	8	11	0-2	0-0	0	6.75
Don Mossi	3	0	0	4.0	3	0	0	0	1	0-0	0-0	0	0.00
Ray Narleski	2	0	0	4.0	1	1	1	1	2	0-0	0-0	0	2.25
Hal Newhouser	1	0	0	0.0	1	1	1	1		0-0	0-0	0	—
Early Wynn	1	1	0	7.0	4	3	3	2	5	0-1	0-0	0	3.86
Totals	4	4	1	35.1	33	21	19	17	24	0-4	0-0	0	4.84

Fielding

Giants	Pos	G	PO	Ast	E	DP	PB	FPct
Johnny Antonelli	p	2	0	1	0	0	—	1.000
Al Dark	ss	4	7	11	1	1	—	.947
Ruben Gomez	p	1	1	2	0	0	—	1.000
Marv Grissom	p	1	0	0	0	0	—	—
Monte Irvin	lf	4	8	0	1	0	—	.889
Don Liddle	p	2	0	1	1	0	—	.500
Whitey Lockman	1b	4	40	1	0	2	—	1.000
Sal Maglie	p	1	0	2	0	0	—	1.000
Willie Mays	cf	4	10	0	0	0	—	1.000
Don Mueller	rf	4	3	0	2	0	—	.600
Dusty Rhodes	lf	2	4	0	0	0	—	1.000
Hank Thompson	3b	4	5	12	0	1	—	1.000
Wes Westrum	c	4	23	0	0	0	0	1.000
Hoyt Wilhelm	p	2	0	1	1	0	—	.500
Davey Williams	2b	4	10	9	1	2	—	.950
Totals		4	111	40	7	6	0	.956

Fielding

Indians	Pos	G	PO	Ast	E	DP	PB	FPct
Bobby Avila	2b	4	12	7	0	1	—	1.000
Sam Dente	ss	3	1	1	0	1	—	1.000
Larry Doby	cf	4	7	0	0	0	—	1.000
Mike Garcia	p	2	0	2	1	0	—	.667
Bill Glynn	1b	1	0	0	0	0	—	—
Mickey Grasso	c	1	1	0	0	0	0	1.000
Jim Hegan	c	4	27	2	0	0	0	1.000
Art Houtteman	p	1	0	0	0	0	—	—
Bob Lemon	p	2	2	2	0	0	—	1.000
Hank Majeski	3b	1	2	1	0	0	—	1.000
Don Mossi	p	3	0	2	0	0	—	1.000
Hal Naragon	c	1	1	0	0	0	0	1.000
Ray Narleski	p	2	0	1	0	0	—	1.000
Hal Newhouser	p	1	0	0	0	0	—	—
Dave Philley	rf	2	1	0	0	0	—	1.000
Dave Pope	lf	1	0	0	0	0	—	—
	rf	1	0	0	0	0	—	—
Rudy Regalado	3b	1	0	0	0	0	—	—
Al Rosen	3b	3	2	6	0	0	—	1.000
Al Smith	lf	4	4	0	0	0	—	1.000
George Strickland	ss	3	6	8	1	1	—	.933
Vic Wertz	1b	4	33	6	1	2	—	.975
Wally Westlake	rf	2	6	0	1	0	—	.857
Early Wynn	p	1	1	1	0	0	—	1.000
Totals		4	106	39	4	5	0	.973

1955 Brooklyn Dodgers (NL) 4, New York Yankees (AL) 3

"Next year" finally came for the Brooklyn Dodgers as they defeated the New York Yankees in seven games. Joe Collins drove in three runs with a pair of homers in Game 1 and the Yankees survived a steal of home by Jackie Robinson to win, 6-5. Tommy Byrne put the Dodgers in a deep hole when he drove in a pair of runs and tossed a complete-game victory in Game 2. Johnny Podres got Brooklyn on the board with an 8-3 victory in Game 3. Homers by Roy Campanella, Duke Snider and Gil Hodges gave the Dodgers an 8-5 win in the fourth game, and Snider added two more homers and a double as Brooklyn took Game 5, 5-3. The Yankees sent Karl Spooner to the showers with a five-run first inning in Game 6, and Whitey Ford went the route for a 5-1 win. Johnny Podres blanked the Yankees 2-0 in Game 7 to give the Brooklynites their first World Series triumph. Sandy Amoros saved the victory with a spectacular catch off Yogi Berra with two on in the sixth inning.

Game 1

Wednesday, September 28

Dodgers	AB	R	H	RBI	BB	K	Avg
Jim Gilliam, lf	3	0	0	2	0	0	.000
Pee Wee Reese, ss	5	0	1	0	0	1	.200
Duke Snider, cf	5	1	2	1	0	1	.400
Roy Campanella, c	5	0	0	0	0	0	.000
Carl Furillo, rf	4	2	3	1	1	1	.750
Gil Hodges, 1b	4	0	1	0	0	0	.250
Jackie Robinson, 3b	4	2	1	0	0	1	.250
Don Zimmer, 2b	2	0	1	2	1	0	.500
Don Newcombe, p	3	0	0	0	0	0	.000
Don Bessent, p	0	0	0	0	0	0	—
Frank Kellert, ph	1	0	1	0	0	0	1.000
Don Hoak, pr	0	0	0	0	0	0	—
Clem Labine, p	0	0	0	0	0	0	—
TOTALS	36	5	10	4	4	4	.278

Yankees	AB	R	H	RBI	BB	K	Avg
Hank Bauer, rf	4	0	2	0	0	0	.500
Gil McDougald, 3b	4	0	1	0	0	1	.250
Irv Noren, cf	4	0	0	1	0	0	.000
Yogi Berra, c	3	1	1	0	1	0	.333
Joe Collins, 1b	3	3	2	3	1	0	.667
Elston Howard, lf	3	1	1	2	0	1	.333
Billy Martin, 2b	3	0	2	0	0	0	.667
Phil Rizzuto, ss	2	0	0	0	0	1	.000
Eddie Robinson, ph	0	0	0	0	0	0	—
Jerry Coleman, ss	1	0	0	0	0	0	.000
Whitey Ford, p	2	1	0	0	1	1	.000
Bob Grim, p	0	0	0	0	0	0	—
TOTALS	29	6	9	6	3	4	.310

	1	2	3	4	5	6	7	8	9	R	H	E
Dodgers	0	2	1	0	0	0	0	2	0	5	10	0
Yankees	0	2	1	1	0	2	0	0	x	6	9	1

E—McDougald. DP—Dodgers 2 (Zimmer to Hodges; Hodges to Reese), Yankees 1 (Martin to Rizzuto to Collins). LOB—Dodgers 9, Yankees 2. Scoring Position—Dodgers 1-for-4, Yankees 0-for-3. 3B—JRobinson (1), Martin (1). HR—Snider (1), Furillo (1), Collins 2 (2), Howard (1). SF—Zimmer. GDP—Reese, Noren 2. SB—JRobinson (1). CS—Martin 2 (2).

Dodgers	IP	H	R	ER	BB	K	ERA
Don Newcombe (L, 0-1)	5.2	8	6	6	2	4	9.53
Don Bessent	1.1	0	0	0	0	0	0.00
Clem Labine	1.0	1	0	0	1	0	0.00

Yankees	IP	H	R	ER	BB	K	ERA
Whitey Ford (W, 1-0)	8.0	9	5	3	4	2	3.38
Bob Grim (S, 1)	1.0	1	0	0	0	2	0.00

Time—2:31. Attendance—63,869. Umpires—HP, Summers. 1B, Ballanfant. 2B, Honochick. 3B, Dascoli.

Game 2

Thursday, September 29

Dodgers	AB	R	H	RBI	BB	K	Avg
Jim Gilliam, lf	4	0	1	1	0	1	.143
Pee Wee Reese, ss	4	1	2	0	0	1	.333
Duke Snider, cf	4	0	1	1	0	1	.333
Roy Campanella, c	3	0	0	0	1	0	.000
Carl Furillo, rf	3	0	0	0	1	0	.429
Gil Hodges, 1b	3	0	0	0	1	1	.143
Jackie Robinson, 3b	2	1	0	0	1	0	.167
Don Zimmer, 2b	3	0	1	0	0	2	.400
Billy Loes, p	1	0	0	0	0	0	.000
Don Bessent, p	0	0	0	0	0	0	—
Frank Kellert, ph	1	0	0	0	0	0	.500
Karl Spooner, p	0	0	0	0	0	0	—
Don Hoak, ph	0	0	0	0	1	0	—
Clem Labine, p	0	0	0	0	0	0	—
TOTALS	28	2	5	2	5	6	.246

Yankees	AB	R	H	RBI	BB	K	Avg
Hank Bauer, rf	1	0	1	0	0	0	.600
Bob Cerv, cf	3	0	0	0	0	1	.000
Gil McDougald, 3b	4	0	1	0	0	3	.250
Irv Noren, cf-lf	3	0	0	1	0	0	.000
Yogi Berra, c	3	1	2	0	0	1	.500
Joe Collins, 1b	3	1	0	0	1	2	.333
Elston Howard, lf-rf	4	1	1	1	0	1	.286
Billy Martin, 2b	3	1	1	0	2	0	.500
Phil Rizzuto, ss	1	0	1	0	0	0	.333
Eddie Robinson, ph	0	0	0	0	0	0	—
Jerry Coleman, pr-ss	1	0	0	0	0	1	.000
Tommy Byrne, p	3	0	1	2	0	0	.333
TOTALS	29	4	8	4	2	11	.304

	1	2	3	4	5	6	7	8	9	R	H	E
Dodgers	0	0	0	1	1	0	0	0	0	2	5	2
Yankees	0	0	0	4	0	0	0	0	x	4	8	0

E—Zimmer 2. DP—Dodgers 3 (Campanella to Zimmer; Zimmer to Reese to Hodges; Hodges to Reese), Yankees 3 (Coleman to Martin to Collins; Berra to Martin; Martin to Coleman to Collins). LOB—Dodgers 4, Yankees 5. Scoring Position—Dodgers 2-for-3, Yankees 3-for-5. 2B—Reese (1). GDP—Gilliam, Noren, Byrne, Kellert. CS—Hodges (1), Bauer (1), Berra (1).

Dodgers	IP	H	R	ER	BB	K	ERA
Billy Loes (L, 0-1)	3.2	7	4	4	1	5	9.82
Don Bessent	0.1	0	0	0	0	0	0.00
Karl Spooner	3.0	1	0	0	1	5	0.00
Clem Labine	1.0	0	0	0	0	1	0.00

Yankees	IP	H	R	ER	BB	K	ERA
Tommy Byrne (W, 1-0)	9.0	5	2	2	5	6	2.00

HBP—Berra by Loes, ERobinson by Loes. Time—2:28. Attendance—64,707. Umpires—HP, Ballanfant. 1B, Honochick. 2B, Dascoli. 3B, Summers.

Game 3

Friday, September 30

Yankees	AB	R	H	RBI	BB	K	Avg
Bob Cerv, lf-cf	4	0	0	0	0	3	.000
Gil McDougald, 3b	4	0	1	0	0	0	.250
Yogi Berra, c	4	0	1	0	0	0	.400
Mickey Mantle, cf-rf	4	1	1	1	0	0	.250
Bill Skowron, 1b	4	1	2	0	0	1	.500
Elston Howard, rf-lf	4	0	0	0	0	1	.182
Billy Martin, 2b	4	0	0	0	0	1	.300
Phil Rizzuto, ss	2	1	1	0	2	0	.400
Bob Turley, p	1	0	0	0	0	0	.000
Tom Morgan, p	0	0	0	0	0	0	—
Hank Bauer, ph	1	0	0	0	0	0	.500
Johnny Kucks, p	0	0	0	0	0	0	—
Andy Carey, ph	1	0	1	1	0	0	1.000
Tom Sturdivant, p	0	0	0	0	0	0	—
TOTALS	33	3	7	2	2	6	.296

Dodgers	AB	R	H	RBI	BB	K	Avg
Jim Gilliam, 2b	3	1	1	1	2	0	.200
Pee Wee Reese, ss	3	1	1	2	2	0	.333
Duke Snider, cf	4	1	1	0	1	1	.308
Roy Campanella, c	5	1	3	3	0	0	.231
Carl Furillo, rf	4	0	1	0	0	0	.364
Gil Hodges, 1b	5	0	0	0	0	1	.083
Jackie Robinson, 3b	5	2	2	0	0	0	.273
Sandy Amoros, lf	1	1	1	1	2	0	1.000
Johnny Podres, p	3	1	1	0	0	1	.333
TOTALS	33	8	11	8	7	2	.267

	1	2	3	4	5	6	7	8	9	R	H	E
Yankees	0	2	0	0	0	0	1	0	0	3	7	0
Dodgers	2	2	0	2	0	0	2	0	x	8	11	1

E—Campanella. DP—Dodgers 1 (Reese to Gilliam to Hodges). LOB—Yankees 5, Dodgers 11. Scoring Position—Yankees 1-for-7, Dodgers 4-for-15. 2B—Skowron (1), Campanella (1), Furillo (1), Robinson (1). 3B—Carey (1). HR—Mantle (1), Campanella (1). S—Podres. SF—Furillo. GDP—Mantle.

Yankees	IP	H	R	ER	BB	K	ERA
Bob Turley (L, 0-1)	1.1	3	4	4	2	1	27.00
Tom Morgan	2.2	3	2	2	3	1	6.75
Johnny Kucks	2.0	1	0	0	1	0	0.00
Tom Sturdivant	2.0	4	2	2	1	0	9.00

Dodgers	IP	H	R	ER	BB	K	ERA
Johnny Podres (W, 1-0)	9.0	7	3	2	2	6	2.00

HBP—Amoros by Turley. Time—2:20. Attendance—34,209. Umpires—HP, Honochick. 1B, Dascoli. 2B, Summers. 3B, Ballanfant.

Game 4

Saturday, October 1

Yankees	AB	R	H	RBI	BB	K	Avg
Irv Noren, cf	5	0	1	0	0	1	.083
Gil McDougald, 3b	5	1	1	1	0	1	.235
Mickey Mantle, rf	5	0	1	0	0	2	.222
Yogi Berra, c	3	0	1	0	1	0	.385
Joe Collins, 1b	2	2	0	0	2	0	.250
Elston Howard, lf	3	1	1	0	0	0	.214
Billy Martin, 2b	4	1	2	2	0	0	.357
Phil Rizzuto, ss	3	0	1	1	1	0	.375
Don Larsen, p	2	0	0	0	0	0	.000
Johnny Kucks, p	0	0	0	0	0	0	—
Eddie Robinson, ph	1	0	1	1	0	0	1.000
Tom Carroll, pr	0	0	0	0	0	0	—
Rip Coleman, p	0	0	0	0	0	0	—
Tom Morgan, p	0	0	0	0	0	0	—
Bill Skowron, ph	1	0	0	0	0	0	.400
Tom Sturdivant, p	0	0	0	0	0	0	—
TOTALS	34	5	9	5	4	4	.272

Dodgers	AB	R	H	RBI	BB	K	Avg
Jim Gilliam, 2b	4	1	2	1	1	0	.286
Pee Wee Reese, ss	4	1	2	0	0	0	.375
Duke Snider, cf	4	1	1	3	1	0	.294
Roy Campanella, c	5	2	3	1	0	0	.333
Carl Furillo, rf	5	1	2	0	0	2	.375
Gil Hodges, 1b	4	1	3	3	0	0	.250
Jackie Robinson, 3b	4	0	0	0	0	0	.200
Sandy Amoros, lf	3	1	1	0	1	0	.500
Carl Erskine, p	1	0	0	0	0	0	.000
Don Bessent, p	1	0	0	0	0	1	.000
Clem Labine, p	2	0	0	0	0	1	.000
TOTALS	37	8	14	8	3	4	.300

	1	2	3	4	5	6	7	8	9	R	H	E
Yankees	1	1	0	1	0	2	0	0	0	5	9	0
Dodgers	0	0	1	3	3	0	1	0	x	8	14	0

DP—Dodgers 1 (JRobinson to Gilliam to Hodges). LOB—Yankees 7, Dodgers 9. Scoring Position—Yankees 3-for-9, Dodgers 4-for-15. 2B—Martin (1), Gilliam (1), Campanella (2). HR—McDougald (1), Snider (2), Campanella (2), Hodges (1). S—Howard, Reese. GDP—Rizzuto. SB—Collins (1), Rizzuto (1), Gilliam (1).

Yankees	IP	H	R	ER	BB	K	ERA
Don Larsen (L, 0-1)	4.0	5	5	5	2	2	11.25
Johnny Kucks	1.0	3	2	2	0	1	6.00
Rip Coleman	1.0	5	1	1	0	1	9.00
Tom Morgan	1.0	0	0	0	0	0	4.91
Tom Sturdivant	1.0	1	0	0	1	0	6.00

Dodgers	IP	H	R	ER	BB	K	ERA
Carl Erskine	3.0	3	3	3	2	3	9.00
Don Bessent	1.2	3	0	0	1	1	0.00
Clem Labine (W, 1-0)	4.1	3	2	2	1	0	2.84

Erskine pitched to two batters in the 4th. Larsen pitched to two batters in the 5th. Coleman pitched to three batters in the 7th.

Time—2:57. Attendance—36,242. Umpires—HP, Dascoli. 1B, Summers. 2B, Ballanfant. 3B, Honochick.

Game 5
Sunday, October 2

Yankees	AB	R	H	RBI	BB	K	Avg
Elston Howard, lf	4	0	1	0	1	2	.222
Irv Noren, cf	4	0	0	0	0	0	.063
Gil McDougald, 3b	3	0	0	0	1	0	.200
Yogi Berra, c	4	2	2	1	0	0	.412
Joe Collins, rf-1b	3	0	0	0	1	2	.182
Eddie Robinson, 1b	2	0	1	0	2	1	.667
Tom Carroll, pr	0	0	0	0	0	0	—
Hank Bauer, rf	0	0	0	0	0	0	.500
Billy Martin, 2b	4	0	1	1	0	0	.333
Phil Rizzuto, ss	1	0	0	0	0	0	.333
Bill Skowron, ph	1	0	0	0	0	0	.333
Jerry Coleman, ss	1	0	0	0	0	0	.000
Andy Carey, ph	1	0	0	0	0	0	.500
Bob Grim, p	2	0	0	0	0	0	.000
Bob Cerv, ph	1	1	1	1	0	0	.125
Bob Turley, p	0	0	0	0	0	0	.000
Tommy Byrne, ph	1	0	0	0	0	0	.250
TOTALS	32	3	6	3	5	5	.257

Dodgers	AB	R	H	RBI	BB	K	Avg
Jim Gilliam, 2b	3	0	1	0	1	0	.294
Pee Wee Reese, ss	3	0	0	0	1	1	.316
Duke Snider, cf	4	2	3	2	0	0	.381
Roy Campanella, c	3	0	0	0	1	2	.286
Carl Furillo, rf	4	1	1	0	0	1	.350
Gil Hodges, 1b	3	1	2	0	0	1	.316
Jackie Robinson, 3b	3	0	1	1	1	0	.222
Sandy Amoros, lf	4	1	1	2	0	3	.375
Roger Craig, p	0	0	0	0	1	0	—
Clem Labine, p	2	0	0	0	0	2	.000
TOTALS	29	5	9	5	5	10	.306

	1	2	3	4	5	6	7	8	9	R	H	E
Yankees	0	0	0	1	0	0	1	1	0	3	6	0
Dodgers	0	2	1	0	1	0	0	1	x	5	9	2

E—JRobinson, Reese. DP—Yankees 2 (Martin to ERobinson; Coleman to Martin to ERobinson), Dodgers 3 (Gilliam to Reese to Hodges; Hodges to Reese; JRobinson to Gilliam to Hodges). LOB—Yankees 7, Dodgers 7. Scoring Position—Yankees 1-for-6, Dodgers 1-for-4. 2B—Snider (1). HR—Berra (1), Snider 2 (4), Amoros (1), Cerv (1). S—Hodges, Craig. GDP—Noren 2, Martin, Furillo, JRobinson.

Yankees	IP	H	R	ER	BB	K	ERA
Bob Grim (L, 0-1)	6.0	6	4	4	4	5	5.14
Bob Turley	2.0	3	1	1	1	5	13.50

Dodgers	IP	H	R	ER	BB	K	ERA
Roger Craig (W, 1-0)	6.0	4	2	2	5	4	3.00
Clem Labine (S, 1)	3.0	2	1	1	0	1	2.89

Craig pitched to two batters in the 7th.

Time—2:40. Attendance—36,796. Umpires—HP, Summers. 1B, Ballanfant. 2B, Honochick. 3B, Dascoli.

Game 6
Monday, October 3

Dodgers	AB	R	H	RBI	BB	K	Avg
Jim Gilliam, 2b-lf	3	0	1	0	1	0	.300
Pee Wee Reese, ss	4	1	1	0	0	1	.304
Duke Snider, cf	1	0	0	0	0	1	.364
Don Zimmer, ph-2b	2	0	0	0	1	2	.286
Roy Campanella, c	3	0	0	0	1	1	.250
Carl Furillo, rf	3	0	1	1	0	1	.348
Gil Hodges, 1b	3	0	0	0	1	0	.273
Jackie Robinson, 3b	4	0	0	0	0	1	.182
Sandy Amoros, lf-cf	4	0	1	0	0	1	.333
Karl Spooner, p	0	0	0	0	0	0	—
Russ Meyer, p	2	0	0	0	0	1	.000
Frank Kellert, ph	1	0	0	0	0	0	.333
Ed Roebuck, p	0	0	0	0	0	0	—
TOTALS	30	1	4	1	4	8	.289

Yankees	AB	R	H	RBI	BB	K	Avg
Phil Rizzuto, ss	3	1	0	0	1	0	.250
Billy Martin, 2b	4	0	1	0	0	2	.318
Gil McDougald, 3b	3	1	0	0	1	0	.174
Yogi Berra, c	3	1	2	1	1	0	.450
Hank Bauer, rf	4	1	3	1	0	0	.600
Bill Skowron, 1b	2	1	1	3	0	0	.375
Joe Collins, ph-1b	1	0	0	0	1	0	.167
Bob Cerv, cf	4	0	1	0	0	0	.167
Elston Howard, lf	4	0	0	0	0	3	.182
Irv Noren, lf	0	0	0	0	0	0	.063
Whitey Ford, p	4	0	0	0	0	0	.000
TOTALS	32	5	8	5	4	5	.252

	1	2	3	4	5	6	7	8	9	R	H	E
Dodgers	0	0	0	1	0	0	0	0	0	1	4	1
Yankees	5	0	0	0	0	0	0	0	x	5	8	0

E—Robinson. DP—Dodgers 1 (Robinson to Hodges), Yankees 1 (McDougald to Martin to Skowron). LOB—Dodgers 7, Yankees 7. Scoring Position—Dodgers 1-for-6, Yankees 3-for-8. HR—Skowron (1). GDP—Robinson, Cerv. SB—Rizzuto (2).

Dodgers	IP	H	R	ER	BB	K	ERA
Karl Spooner (L, 0-1)	0.1	3	5	5	2	1	13.50
Russ Meyer	5.2	4	0	0	2	4	0.00
Ed Roebuck	2.0	1	0	0	0	0	0.00

Yankees	IP	H	R	ER	BB	K	ERA
Whitey Ford (W, 2-0)	9.0	4	1	1	4	8	2.12

WP—Ford. HBP—Furillo by Ford. Time—2:34. Attendance—64,022. Umpires—HP, Ballanfant. 1B, Honochick. 2B, Dascoli. 3B, Summers.

Game 7
Tuesday, October 4

Dodgers	AB	R	H	RBI	BB	K	Avg
Jim Gilliam, lf-2b	4	0	1	0	1	0	.292
Pee Wee Reese, ss	4	1	1	0	0	1	.296
Duke Snider, cf	3	0	0	0	0	2	.320
Roy Campanella, c	3	1	1	0	0	0	.259
Carl Furillo, rf	3	0	0	0	1	0	.308
Gil Hodges, 1b	2	0	1	2	1	0	.292
Don Hoak, 3b	3	0	1	0	1	0	.333
Don Zimmer, 2b	2	0	0	0	0	1	.222
George Shuba, ph	1	0	0	0	0	0	.000
Sandy Amoros, lf	0	0	0	0	1	0	.333
Johnny Podres, p	4	0	0	0	0	0	.143
TOTALS	29	2	5	2	5	4	.286

Yankees	AB	R	H	RBI	BB	K	Avg
Phil Rizzuto, ss	3	0	1	0	1	0	.267
Billy Martin, 2b	3	0	1	0	1	0	.320
Gil McDougald, 3b	4	0	3	0	0	1	.259
Yogi Berra, c	4	0	1	0	0	0	.417
Hank Bauer, rf	4	0	0	0	0	1	.429
Bill Skowron, 1b	4	0	1	0	0	0	.333
Bob Cerv, cf	4	0	0	0	0	0	.125
Elston Howard, lf	4	0	0	0	0	0	.192
Tommy Byrne, p	2	0	0	0	0	2	.167
Bob Grim, p	0	0	0	0	0	0	.000
Mickey Mantle, ph	1	0	0	0	0	0	.200
Bob Turley, p	0	0	0	0	0	0	.000
TOTALS	33	0	8	0	2	4	.275

	1	2	3	4	5	6	7	8	9	R	H	E
Dodgers	0	0	0	1	0	1	0	0	0	2	5	0
Yankees	0	0	0	0	0	0	0	0	0	0	8	1

E—Skowron. DP—Dodgers 1 (Amoros). LOB—Dodgers 8, Yankees 8. Scoring Position—Dodgers 1-for-5, Yankees 1-for-9. 2B—Campanella (3), Berra (1), Skowron (2). S—Snider, Campanella. SF—Hodges. CS—Gilliam (1).

Dodgers	IP	H	R	ER	BB	K	ERA
Johnny Podres (W, 2-0)	9.0	8	0	0	2	4	1.00

Yankees	IP	H	R	ER	BB	K	ERA
Tommy Byrne (L, 1-1)	5.1	3	2	1	3	2	1.88
Bob Grim	1.2	1	0	0	1	1	4.15
Bob Turley	2.0	1	0	0	1	1	8.44

WP—Grim. Time—2:44. Attendance—62,465. Umpires—HP, Honochick. 1B, Dascoli. 2B, Summers. 3B, Ballanfant.

1955 World Series—Composite Statistics

Batting

Dodgers	G	AB	R	H	RBI	2B	3B	HR	BB	SO	SB	CS	Avg	OBP	Slg
Sandy Amoros	5	12	3	4	3	0	0	1	4	4	0	0	.333	.529	.583
Don Bessent	3	1	0	0	0	0	0	0	0	1	0	0	.000	.000	.000
Roy Campanella	7	27	4	7	4	3	0	2	3	3	0	0	.259	.333	.593
Roger Craig	1	0	0	0	0	0	0	0	1	0	0	0	—	1.000	—
Carl Erskine	1	1	0	0	0	0	0	0	0	0	0	0	.000	.000	.000
Carl Furillo	7	26	4	8	3	1	0	1	3	5	0	0	.308	.387	.462
Jim Gilliam	7	24	2	7	3	1	0	0	8	1	1	1	.292	.469	.333
Don Hoak	3	3	0	1	0	0	0	0	2	0	0	0	.333	.600	.333
Gil Hodges	7	24	2	7	5	0	0	1	3	2	0	1	.292	.357	.417
Frank Kellert	3	3	0	1	0	0	0	0	0	0	0	0	.333	.333	.333
Clem Labine	4	4	0	0	0	0	0	0	0	3	0	0	.000	.000	.000
Billy Loes	1	1	0	0	0	0	0	0	0	0	0	0	.000	.000	.000
Russ Meyer	1	2	0	0	0	0	0	0	0	1	0	0	.000	.000	.000
Don Newcombe	1	3	0	0	0	0	0	0	0	0	0	0	.000	.000	.000
Johnny Podres	2	7	1	1	0	0	0	0	0	1	0	0	.143	.143	.143
Pee Wee Reese	7	27	5	8	2	1	0	0	3	5	0	0	.296	.367	.333
Jackie Robinson	6	22	5	4	1	1	1	0	2	1	1	0	.182	.250	.318
George Shuba	1	1	0	0	0	0	0	0	0	0	0	0	.000	.000	.000
Duke Snider	7	25	5	8	7	1	0	4	2	6	0	0	.320	.370	.840
Don Zimmer	4	9	0	2	2	0	0	0	2	5	0	0	.222	.333	.222
Totals	7	222	31	58	30	8	1	9	33	38	2	2	.261	.358	.428

Pitching

Dodgers	G	GS	CG	IP	H	R	ER	BB	SO	W-L	Sv-Op	Hld	ERA
Don Bessent	3	0	0	3.1	3	0	0	1	1	0-0	0-0	0	0.00
Roger Craig	1	1	0	6.0	4	2	2	5	4	1-0	0-0	0	3.00
Carl Erskine	1	1	0	3.0	3	3	3	2	3	0-0	0-0	0	9.00
Clem Labine	4	0	0	9.1	6	3	3	2	2	1-0	1-1	0	2.89
Billy Loes	1	1	0	3.2	7	4	4	1	5	0-1	0-0	0	9.82
Russ Meyer	1	0	0	5.2	4	0	0	2	4	0-0	0-0	0	0.00
Don Newcombe	1	1	0	5.2	8	6	6	2	4	0-1	0-0	0	9.53
Johnny Podres	2	2	2	18.0	15	3	2	4	10	2-0	0-0	0	1.00
Ed Roebuck	1	0	0	2.0	1	0	0	0	0	0-0	0-0	0	0.00
Karl Spooner	2	1	0	3.1	4	5	5	3	6	0-1	0-0	0	13.50
Totals	7	7	2	60.0	55	26	25	22	39	4-3	1-1	0	3.75

Fielding

Dodgers	Pos	G	PO	Ast	E	DP	PB	FPct
Sandy Amoros	lf	5	9	1	0	1	—	1.000
	cf	1	1	0	0	0	—	1.000
Don Bessent	p	3	0	1	0	0	—	1.000
Roy Campanella	c	7	42	3	1	1	0	.978
Roger Craig	p	1	0	1	0	0	—	1.000
Carl Erskine	p	1	0	1	0	0	—	1.000
Carl Furillo	rf	7	8	0	0	0	—	1.000
Jim Gilliam	2b	5	4	12	0	4	—	1.000
	lf	4	4	1	0	0	—	1.000
Don Hoak	3b	1	1	1	0	0	—	1.000
Gil Hodges	1b	7	73	4	0	10	—	1.000
Clem Labine	p	4	0	3	0	0	—	1.000
Billy Loes	p	1	0	0	0	0	—	—
Russ Meyer	p	1	0	1	0	0	—	1.000
Don Newcombe	p	1	0	1	0	0	—	1.000
Johnny Podres	p	2	0	2	0	0	—	1.000
Pee Wee Reese	ss	7	15	22	1	6	—	.974
Jackie Robinson	3b	6	4	18	2	3	—	.917
Ed Roebuck	p	1	2	0	0	0	—	1.000
Duke Snider	cf	7	13	0	0	0	—	1.000
Karl Spooner	p	2	0	1	0	0	—	1.000
Don Zimmer	2b	4	4	8	2	3	—	.857
Totals		7	180	81	6	28	0	.978

Batting

Yankees	G	AB	R	H	RBI	2B	3B	HR	BB	SO	SB	CS	Avg	OBP	Slg
Hank Bauer	6	14	1	6	1	0	0	0	0	1	0	1	.429	.429	.429
Yogi Berra	7	24	5	10	2	1	0	1	3	1	0	1	.417	.500	.583
Tommy Byrne	3	6	0	1	2	0	0	0	0	2	0	0	.167	.167	.167
Andy Carey	2	2	0	1	1	0	1	0	0	0	0	0	.500	.500	1.500
Tom Carroll	2	0	0	0	0	0	0	0	0	0	0	0	—	—	—
Bob Cerv	5	16	1	2	1	0	0	1	0	4	0	0	.125	.125	.313
Jerry Coleman	3	3	0	0	0	0	0	0	0	1	0	0	.000	.000	.000
Joe Collins	5	12	6	2	3	0	0	2	6	4	1	0	.167	.444	.667
Whitey Ford	2	6	1	0	0	0	0	0	1	1	0	0	.000	.143	.000
Bob Grim	3	2	0	0	0	0	0	0	0	0	0	0	.000	.000	.000
Elston Howard	7	26	3	5	3	0	0	1	1	8	0	0	.192	.222	.308
Don Larsen	1	2	0	0	0	0	0	0	0	0	0	0	.000	.000	.000
Mickey Mantle	3	10	1	2	1	0	0	1	0	2	0	0	.200	.200	.500
Billy Martin	7	25	2	8	4	1	1	0	1	5	0	2	.320	.346	.440
Gil McDougald	7	27	2	7	1	0	0	1	2	6	0	0	.259	.310	.370
Irv Noren	5	16	0	1	1	0	0	0	1	1	0	0	.063	.118	.063
Phil Rizzuto	7	15	2	4	1	0	0	0	5	1	2	0	.267	.450	.267
Eddie Robinson	4	3	0	2	1	0	0	0	2	1	0	0	.667	.833	.667
Bill Skowron	5	12	2	4	3	2	0	1	0	1	0	0	.333	.333	.750
Bob Turley	3	1	0	0	0	0	0	0	0	0	0	0	.000	.000	.000
Totals	7	222	26	55	25	4	2	8	22	39	3	4	.248	.321	.392

Pitching

Yankees	G	GS	CG	IP	H	R	ER	BB	SO	W-L	Sv-Op	Hld	ERA
Tommy Byrne	2	2	1	14.1	8	4	3	8	8	1-1	0-0	0	1.88
Rip Coleman	1	0	0	1.0	5	1	1	0	1	0-0	0-0	0	9.00
Whitey Ford	2	2	1	17.0	13	6	4	8	10	2-0	0-0	0	2.12
Bob Grim	3	1	0	8.2	8	4	4	5	8	0-1	1-1	0	4.15
Johnny Kucks	2	0	0	3.0	4	2	2	1	1	0-0	0-0	0	6.00
Don Larsen	1	1	0	4.0	5	5	5	2	2	0-1	0-0	0	11.25
Tom Morgan	2	0	0	3.2	3	2	2	3	1	0-0	0-0	0	4.91
Tom Sturdivant	2	0	0	3.0	5	2	2	2	0	0-0	0-0	0	6.00
Bob Turley	3	1	0	5.1	7	5	5	4	7	0-1	0-0	0	8.44
Totals	7	7	2	60.0	58	31	28	33	38	3-4	1-1	0	4.20

Fielding

Yankees	Pos	G	PO	Ast	E	DP	PB	FPct
Hank Bauer	rf	5	7	0	0	0	—	1.000
Yogi Berra	c	7	40	4	0	1	0	1.000
Tommy Byrne	p	2	0	2	0	0	—	1.000
Bob Cerv	cf	4	10	0	0	0	—	1.000
	lf	1	0	0	0	0	—	—
Jerry Coleman	ss	3	2	3	0	3	—	1.000
Rip Coleman	p	1	0	0	0	0	—	—
Joe Collins	1b	5	27	3	0	3	—	1.000
	rf	1	0	0	0	0	—	—
Whitey Ford	p	2	1	4	0	0	—	1.000
Bob Grim	p	3	1	1	0	0	—	1.000
Elston Howard	lf	7	9	0	0	0	—	1.000
	rf	2	2	1	0	0	—	1.000
Johnny Kucks	p	2	0	1	0	0	—	1.000
Don Larsen	p	1	0	1	0	0	—	1.000
Mickey Mantle	rf	2	2	0	0	0	—	1.000
	cf	1	2	0	0	0	—	1.000
Billy Martin	2b	7	17	20	0	7	—	1.000
Gil McDougald	3b	7	6	13	1	1	—	.950
Tom Morgan	p	2	0	0	0	0	—	—
Irv Noren	cf	4	9	0	0	0	—	1.000
	lf	2	4	0	0	0	—	1.000
Phil Rizzuto	ss	7	13	14	0	1	—	1.000
Eddie Robinson	1b	1	6	0	0	2	—	1.000
Bill Skowron	1b	3	22	3	1	1	—	.962
Tom Sturdivant	p	2	0	1	0	0	—	1.000
Bob Turley	p	3	0	1	0	0	—	1.000
Totals		7	180	72	2	19	0	.992

1956 New York Yankees (AL) 4, Brooklyn Dodgers (NL) 3

Don Larsen pitched a perfect game in Game 5, as the Yankees defeated the Brooklyn Dodgers in seven games. Sal Maglie bested Whitey Ford in the opener by the score of 6-3. In Game 2, the Yanks knocked out Don Newcombe with a five-run second inning, but the Dodgers came back to win, 13-8. Gil Hodges had two doubles and a single and drove in four runs. Ford came back on short rest to win Game 3, 5-3, on Enos Slaughter's three-run homer in the sixth. Tom Sturdivant won the fourth game, 6-2, to even the Series. Larsen made history in the fifth game, retiring 27 Dodgers in order using only 97 pitches. Dodger relief ace Clem Labine made his fourth start of the year in Game 6, pitching 10 shutout innings before Jackie Robinson singled in the winning run in the bottom of the 12th. Yogi Berra hit a pair of two-run homers in Game 7 as Johnny Kucks blanked the Dodgers 9-0 to clinch the flag.

Game 1

Wednesday, October 3

Yankees	AB	R	H	RBI	BB	K	Avg
Hank Bauer, rf	5	0	2	0	0	1	.400
Enos Slaughter, lf	5	1	3	0	0	0	.600
Mickey Mantle, cf	3	1	1	2	2	1	.333
Yogi Berra, c	3	0	0	0	1	0	.000
Bill Skowron, 1b	4	0	0	0	0	1	.000
Gil McDougald, ss	4	0	0	0	0	3	.000
Billy Martin, 2b-3b	3	1	1	1	1	0	.333
Andy Carey, 3b	3	0	1	0	0	1	.333
Joe Collins, ph	1	0	0	0	0	1	.000
Bob Turley, p	0	0	0	0	0	0	—
Whitey Ford, p	1	0	0	0	0	1	.000
George Wilson, ph	1	0	0	0	0	1	.000
Johnny Kucks, p	0	0	0	0	0	0	—
Bob Cerv, ph	1	0	1	0	0	0	1.000
Tom Morgan, p	0	0	0	0	0	0	—
Tommy Byrne, ph	1	0	0	0	0	0	.000
Jerry Coleman, 2b	0	0	0	0	0	0	—
TOTALS	35	3	9	3	4	10	.257

Dodgers	AB	R	H	RBI	BB	K	Avg
Jim Gilliam, 2b	3	0	0	0	1	0	.000
Pee Wee Reese, ss	4	1	2	0	0	1	.500
Duke Snider, cf	3	1	1	0	1	0	.333
Jackie Robinson, 3b	4	1	1	1	0	0	.250
Gil Hodges, 1b	4	2	2	3	0	1	.500
Carl Furillo, rf	4	0	1	1	0	0	.250
Roy Campanella, c	4	1	1	0	0	1	.250
Sandy Amoros, lf	3	0	1	1	0	0	.333
Sal Maglie, p	3	0	0	0	0	1	.000
TOTALS	32	6	9	6	2	4	.281

	1	2	3	4	5	6	7	8	9		R	H	E
Yankees	2	0	0	1	0	0	0	0	0		3	9	1
Dodgers	0	2	3	1	0	0	0	0	x		6	9	0

E—Skowron. DP—Yankees 1 (Skowron to McDougald to Martin). LOB—Yankees 9, Dodgers 4. Scoring Position—Yankees 0-for-6, Dodgers 2-for-8. 2B—Furillo (1), Campanella (1). HR—Mantle (1), Martin (1), Robinson (1), Hodges (1). GDP—Mantle, Maglie. SB—Gilliam (1).

Yankees	IP	H	R	ER	BB	K	ERA
Whitey Ford (L, 0-1)	3.0	6	5	5	0	1	15.00
Johnny Kucks	2.0	2	1	1	0	1	4.50
Tom Morgan	2.0	1	0	0	2	0	0.00
Bob Turley	1.0	0	0	0	0	2	0.00

Dodgers	IP	H	R	ER	BB	K	ERA
Sal Maglie (W, 1-0)	9.0	9	3	3	4	10	3.00

Time—2:32. Attendance—34,479. Umpires—HP, Pinelli. 1B, Soar. 2B, Boggess. 3B, Napp.

Game 2

Friday, October 5

Yankees	AB	R	H	RBI	BB	K	Avg
Gil McDougald, ss	3	0	1	0	1	0	.143
Enos Slaughter, lf	4	3	2	1	0	0	.556
Mickey Mantle, cf	4	1	1	0	1	1	.286
Yogi Berra, c	4	1	2	4	1	0	.286
Joe Collins, 1b	4	0	1	2	1	0	.200
Hank Bauer, rf	5	0	1	0	0	0	.300
Billy Martin, 3b-2b	4	1	1	0	0	2	.286
Jerry Coleman, 2b	2	0	0	0	0	0	.000
Bill Skowron, ph	1	0	0	0	0	1	.000
Andy Carey, 3b	0	0	0	0	0	0	.333
Don Larsen, p	1	1	1	1	0	0	1.000
Johnny Kucks, p	0	0	0	0	0	0	—
Tommy Byrne, p	0	0	0	0	0	0	.000
Tom Sturdivant, p	0	0	0	0	0	0	—
Tom Morgan, p	1	1	1	0	0	0	1.000
Bob Turley, p	0	0	0	0	0	0	—
Norm Siebern, ph	1	0	0	0	0	0	.000
Mickey McDermott, p	1	0	1	0	0	0	1.000
TOTALS	35	8	12	8	4	4	.299

Dodgers	AB	R	H	RBI	BB	K	Avg
Jim Gilliam, 2b	3	1	1	2	3	1	.167
Pee Wee Reese, ss	6	1	1	2	0	0	.300
Duke Snider, cf	4	3	2	3	2	2	.429
Jackie Robinson, 3b	4	2	2	0	1	1	.375
Gil Hodges, 1b	3	2	3	4	2	0	.714
Sandy Amoros, lf	4	1	0	0	0	3	.143
Randy Jackson, ph	1	0	0	0	0	0	.000
Gino Cimoli, lf	0	0	0	0	0	0	—
Carl Furillo, rf	4	2	2	0	1	0	.375
Roy Campanella, c	3	1	0	1	1	1	.143
Don Newcombe, p	0	0	0	0	0	0	—
Ed Roebuck, p	0	0	0	0	0	0	—
Dale Mitchell, ph	1	0	0	0	0	0	.000
Don Bessent, p	2	0	1	1	1	1	.500
TOTALS	35	13	12	13	11	10	.328

	1	2	3	4	5	6	7	8	9		R	H	E
Yankees	1	5	0	1	0	0	0	0	1		8	12	2
Dodgers	0	6	1	2	2	0	0	2	x		13	12	0

E—Collins, Bauer. DP—Yankees 1 (Martin to Collins), Dodgers 1 (Reese to Gilliam to Hodges). LOB—Yankees 7, Dodgers 11. Scoring Position—Yankees 3-for-6, Dodgers 6-for-15. 2B—Hodges 2 (2). HR—Berra (1), Snider (1). S—McDougald, Coleman, Bessent. SF—Slaughter, Campanella. GDP—Martin, Robinson.

Yankees	IP	H	R	ER	BB	K	ERA
Don Larsen	1.2	1	4	0	4	0	0.00
Johnny Kucks	0.0	1	1	0	0	0	4.50
Tommy Byrne	0.1	1	1	0	0	1	0.00
Tom Sturdivant	0.2	2	1	1	2	2	13.50
Tom Morgan (L, 0-1)	2.0	5	4	4	2	3	9.00
Bob Turley	0.1	0	0	0	0	1	0.00
Mickey McDermott	3.0	2	2	1	3	3	3.00

Dodgers	IP	H	R	ER	BB	K	ERA
Don Newcombe	1.2	6	6	6	2	0	32.40
Ed Roebuck	0.1	0	0	0	0	0	0.00
Don Bessent (W, 1-0)	7.0	6	2	2	2	4	2.57

Kucks pitched to one batter in the 2nd.

WP—Bessent. Time—3:26. Attendance—36,217. Umpires—HP, Soar. 1B, Boggess. 2B, Napp. 3B, Pinelli.

Game 3

Saturday, October 6

Dodgers	AB	R	H	RBI	BB	K	Avg
Jim Gilliam, lf	4	0	0	0	0	0	.100
Pee Wee Reese, ss	4	1	2	0	0	1	.357
Duke Snider, cf	3	0	0	1	0	3	.300
Jackie Robinson, 3b	3	1	1	0	1	0	.364
Gil Hodges, 1b	3	1	1	0	1	0	.600
Carl Furillo, rf	4	0	2	0	0	1	.417
Roy Campanella, c	3	0	1	1	0	1	.200
Charlie Neal, 2b	4	0	0	0	0	1	.000
Roger Craig, p	2	0	1	0	0	0	.500
Randy Jackson, ph	1	0	0	0	0	0	.000
Clem Labine, p	0	0	0	0	0	0	—
TOTALS	31	3	8	2	2	7	.318

Yankees	AB	R	H	RBI	BB	K	Avg
Hank Bauer, rf	4	1	1	0	0	1	.286
Joe Collins, 1b	4	1	0	0	0	0	.111
Mickey Mantle, cf	4	0	1	0	0	0	.273
Yogi Berra, c	4	1	2	1	0	0	.364
Enos Slaughter, lf	3	1	2	3	1	0	.583
Billy Martin, 2b	4	1	1	0	0	0	.273
Gil McDougald, ss	2	0	1	0	1	0	.222
Andy Carey, 3b	3	0	0	0	0	3	.167
Whitey Ford, p	3	0	0	0	0	2	.000
TOTALS	31	5	8	5	2	6	.287

	1	2	3	4	5	6	7	8	9		R	H	E
Dodgers	0	1	0	0	0	1	1	0	0		3	8	1
Yankees	0	1	0	0	0	3	0	1	x		5	8	1

E—Neal, Carey. DP—Dodgers 2 (Craig to Reese to Hodges; Neal to Reese to Hodges), Yankees 1 (Martin to McDougald to Collins). LOB—Dodgers 5, Yankees 4. Scoring Position—Dodgers 0-for-5, Yankees 1-for-2. 2B—Furillo (2), Berra (1). 3B—Reese (1). HR—Slaughter (1), Martin (2). SF—Snider, Campanella. GDP—Gilliam, Martin, Ford. CS—Campanella (1).

Dodgers	IP	H	R	ER	BB	K	ERA
Roger Craig (L, 0-1)	6.0	7	4	4	1	4	6.00
Clem Labine	2.0	1	1	0	1	2	0.00

Yankees	IP	H	R	ER	BB	K	ERA
Whitey Ford (W, 1-1)	9.0	8	3	2	2	7	5.25

Time—2:17. Attendance—73,977. Umpires—HP, Boggess. 1B, Napp. 2B, Pinelli. 3B, Soar.

Game 4

Sunday, October 7

Dodgers	AB	R	H	RBI	BB	K	Avg
Jim Gilliam, 2b	4	0	0	0	1	0	.071
Pee Wee Reese, ss	4	0	1	0	0	2	.333
Duke Snider, cf	4	1	1	0	0	1	.286
Jackie Robinson, 3b	3	1	1	0	1	0	.357
Gil Hodges, 1b	4	0	1	0	2	0	.500
Sandy Amoros, lf	3	0	0	0	0	1	.100
Carl Furillo, rf	3	0	0	0	1	0	.333
Roy Campanella, c	2	0	2	1	2	0	.333
Carl Erskine, p	1	0	0	0	0	1	.000
Rube Walker, ph	1	0	0	0	0	0	.000
Ed Roebuck, p	0	0	0	0	0	0	—
Dale Mitchell, ph	1	0	0	0	0	0	.000
Don Drysdale, p	0	0	0	0	0	0	—
Randy Jackson, ph	1	0	0	0	0	1	.000
TOTALS	31	2	6	2	6	7	.280

Yankees	AB	R	H	RBI	BB	K	Avg
Hank Bauer, rf	4	1	1	2	0	1	.278
Joe Collins, 1b	3	1	1	0	1	0	.167
Mickey Mantle, cf	3	2	1	1	1	0	.286
Yogi Berra, c	4	0	1	1	0	1	.333
Enos Slaughter, lf	3	1	0	0	1	0	.467
Billy Martin, 2b	4	0	1	1	0	1	.267
Gil McDougald, ss	2	0	0	1	0	0	.182
Andy Carey, 3b	3	1	1	0	0	1	.222
Tom Sturdivant, p	3	0	1	0	0	1	.333
TOTALS	29	6	7	6	3	5	.286

	1	2	3	4	5	6	7	8	9		R	H	E
Dodgers	0	0	0	1	0	0	0	0	1		2	6	0
Yankees	1	0	0	2	0	1	2	0	x		6	7	2

E—Carey, Collins. DP—Dodgers 1 (Gilliam to Reese to Hodges), Yankees 2 (Collins; Martin to McDougald to Collins). LOB—Dodgers 5, Yankees 3. Scoring Position—Dodgers 2-for-9, Yankees 2-for-3. 2B—Snider (1), Robinson (1), Collins (1). HR—Bauer (1), Mantle (2). SF—McDougald. GDP—Collins, Walker. SB—Mantle (1). CS—Gilliam (1).

Dodgers	IP	H	R	ER	BB	K	ERA
Carl Erskine (L, 0-1)	4.0	4	3	3	2	2	6.75
Ed Roebuck	2.0	1	1	1	0	2	3.86
Don Drysdale	2.0	2	2	2	1	1	9.00

Yankees	IP	H	R	ER	BB	K	ERA
Tom Sturdivant (W, 1-0)	9.0	6	2	2	6	7	2.79

Time—2:43. Attendance—69,705. Umpires—HP, Napp. 1B, Pinelli. 2B, Soar. 3B, Boggess.

Postseason: World Series

Game 5

Monday, October 8

Dodgers	AB	R	H	RBI	BB	K	Avg
Jim Gilliam, 2b	3	0	0	0	0	1	.059
Pee Wee Reese, ss	3	0	0	0	0	1	.286
Duke Snider, cf	3	0	0	0	0	1	.235
Jackie Robinson, 3b	3	0	0	0	0	0	.294
Gil Hodges, 1b	3	0	0	0	0	1	.412
Sandy Amoros, lf	3	0	0	0	0	0	.077
Carl Furillo, rf	3	0	0	0	0	0	.278
Roy Campanella, c	3	0	0	0	0	1	.267
Sal Maglie, p	2	0	0	0	0	1	.000
Dale Mitchell, ph	1	0	0	0	0	1	.000
TOTALS	27	0	0	0	0	7	.231

Yankees	AB	R	H	RBI	BB	K	Avg
Hank Bauer, rf	4	0	1	1	0	1	.273
Joe Collins, 1b	4	0	1	0	0	2	.188
Mickey Mantle, cf	3	1	1	1	0	0	.294
Yogi Berra, c	3	0	0	0	0	0	.278
Enos Slaughter, lf	2	0	0	0	1	0	.412
Billy Martin, 2b	3	0	1	0	0	1	.278
Gil McDougald, ss	2	0	0	0	1	0	.154
Andy Carey, 3b	3	1	1	0	0	0	.250
Don Larsen, p	2	0	0	0	0	1	.333
TOTALS	26	2	5	2	2	5	.272

	1	2	3	4	5	6	7	8	9		R	H	E
Dodgers	0	0	0	0	0	0	0	0	0		0	0	0
Yankees	0	0	0	1	0	1	0	0	x		2	5	0

DP—Dodgers 2 (Reese to Hodges; Hodges to Campanella to Robinson). LOB—Dodgers 0, Yankees 3. Scoring Position—Dodgers 0-for-0, Yankees 1-for-3. HR—Mantle (3). S—Larsen.

Dodgers	IP	H	R	ER	BB	K	ERA
Sal Maglie (L, 1-1)	8.0	5	2	2	2	5	2.65

Yankees	IP	H	R	ER	BB	K	ERA
Don Larsen (W, 1-0)	9.0	0	0	0	0	7	0.00

Time—2:06. Attendance—64,519. Umpires—HP, Pinelli. 1B, Soar. 2B, Boggess. 3B, Napp.

Game 6

Tuesday, October 9

Yankees	AB	R	H	RBI	BB	K	Avg
Hank Bauer, rf	5	0	2	0	0	1	.296
Joe Collins, 1b	5	0	2	0	0	0	.238
Mickey Mantle, cf	3	0	0	0	1	0	.250
Yogi Berra, c	4	0	2	0	0	0	.318
Enos Slaughter, lf	3	0	0	0	1	0	.350
Billy Martin, 2b	4	0	1	0	0	0	.273
Gil McDougald, ss	4	0	0	0	0	3	.118
Andy Carey, 3b	4	0	0	0	0	0	.188
Bob Turley, p	4	0	0	0	0	1	.000
TOTALS	36	0	7	0	2	5	.254

Dodgers	AB	R	H	RBI	BB	K	Avg
Jim Gilliam, 2b	3	1	1	0	2	1	.100
Pee Wee Reese, ss	4	0	0	0	0	1	.240
Duke Snider, cf	2	0	1	0	3	0	.263
Jackie Robinson, 3b	4	0	1	1	1	0	.286
Gil Hodges, 1b	3	0	0	0	1	0	.350
Sandy Amoros, lf	3	0	0	0	1	1	.063
Carl Furillo, rf	4	0	0	0	0	2	.227
Roy Campanella, c	4	0	0	0	0	3	.211
Clem Labine, p	4	0	1	0	0	2	.250
TOTALS	31	1	4	1	8	11	.223

	1	2	3	4	5	6	7	8	9	10		R	H	E
Yankees	0	0	0	0	0	0	0	0	0	0		0	7	0
Dodgers	0	0	0	0	0	0	0	0	0	1		1	4	0

DP—Dodgers 1 (Gilliam to Reese to Hodges). LOB—Yankees 8, Dodgers 10. Scoring Position—Yankees 0-for-4, Dodgers 1-for-6. 2B—Collins (2), Berra (2), Labine (1). S—Reese. GDP—Collins.

Yankees	IP	H	R	ER	BB	K	ERA
Bob Turley (L, 0-1)	9.2	4	1	1	8	11	0.82

Dodgers	IP	H	R	ER	BB	K	ERA
Clem Labine (W, 1-0)	10.0	7	0	0	2	5	0.00

Time—2:37. Attendance—33,224. Umpires—HP, Soar. 1B, Boggess. 2B, Napp. 3B, Pinelli.

Game 7

Wednesday, October 10

Yankees	AB	R	H	RBI	BB	K	Avg
Hank Bauer, rf	5	1	1	0	0	0	.281
Billy Martin, 2b	5	2	2	0	0	2	.296
Mickey Mantle, cf	4	1	1	0	1	3	.250
Yogi Berra, c	3	3	2	4	2	0	.360
Bill Skowron, 1b	5	1	1	4	0	1	.100
Elston Howard, lf	5	1	2	1	0	0	.400
Gil McDougald, ss	4	0	1	0	0	0	.143
Andy Carey, 3b	3	0	0	0	1	1	.158
Johnny Kucks, p	3	0	0	0	0	1	.000
TOTALS	37	9	10	9	4	8	.247

Dodgers	AB	R	H	RBI	BB	K	Avg
Jim Gilliam, 2b	4	0	0	0	0	0	.083
Pee Wee Reese, ss	2	0	0	0	2	0	.222
Duke Snider, cf	4	0	2	0	0	0	.304
Jackie Robinson, 3b	3	0	0	0	1	1	.250
Gil Hodges, 1b	3	0	0	0	0	0	.304
Sandy Amoros, lf	3	0	0	0	0	0	.053
Carl Furillo, rf	3	0	1	0	0	0	.240
Roy Campanella, c	3	0	0	0	0	0	.182
Don Newcombe, p	1	0	0	0	0	0	.000
Don Bessent, p	0	0	0	0	0	0	.500
Dale Mitchell, ph	1	0	0	0	0	0	.000
Roger Craig, p	0	0	0	0	0	0	.500
Ed Roebuck, p	0	0	0	0	0	0	—
Rube Walker, ph	1	0	0	0	0	0	.000
Carl Erskine, p	0	0	0	0	0	0	.000
TOTALS	28	0	3	0	3	1	.206

	1	2	3	4	5	6	7	8	9		R	H	E
Yankees	2	0	2	1	0	0	4	0	0		9	10	0
Dodgers	0	0	0	0	0	0	0	0	0		0	3	1

E—Reese. DP—Yankees 2 (Kucks to Martin to Skowron; McDougald to Skowron). LOB—Yankees 6, Dodgers 4. Scoring Position—Yankees 2-for-12, Dodgers 0-for-1. 2B—Mantle (1), Howard (1). HR—Berra 2 (3), Skowron (1), Howard (1). S—Kucks. GDP—Robinson. SB—Bauer (1).

Yankees	IP	H	R	ER	BB	K	ERA
Johnny Kucks (W, 1-0)	9.0	3	0	0	3	1	0.82

Dodgers	IP	H	R	ER	BB	K	ERA
Don Newcombe (L, 0-1)	3.0	5	5	5	1	4	21.21
Don Bessent	3.0	2	0	0	1	1	1.80
Roger Craig	0.0	3	4	4	2	0	12.00
Ed Roebuck	2.0	0	0	0	0	3	2.08
Carl Erskine	1.0	0	0	0	0	0	5.40

Newcombe pitched to one batter in the 4th. Craig pitched to six batters in the 7th.

WP—Craig. Time—2:19. Attendance—33,782. Umpires—HP, Boggess. 1B, Napp. 2B, Pinelli. 3B, Soar.

1956 World Series—Composite Statistics

Batting

Yankees	G	AB	R	H	RBI	2B	3B	HR	BB	SO	SB	CS	Avg	OBP	Slg
Hank Bauer	7	32	3	9	3	0	0	1	0	5	1	0	.281	.281	.375
Yogi Berra	7	25	5	9	10	2	0	3	4	1	0	0	.360	.448	.800
Tommy Byrne	2	1	0	0	0	0	0	0	0	0	0	0	.000	.000	.000
Andy Carey	7	19	2	3	0	0	0	0	1	6	0	0	.158	.200	.158
Bob Cerv	1	1	0	1	0	0	0	0	0	0	0	0	1.000	1.000	1.000
Jerry Coleman	2	2	0	0	0	0	0	0	0	0	0	0	.000	.000	.000
Joe Collins	6	21	2	5	2	2	0	0	2	3	0	0	.238	.304	.333
Whitey Ford	2	4	0	0	0	0	0	0	3	0	0	0	.000	.000	.000
Elston Howard	1	5	1	2	1	1	0	1	0	0	0	0	.400	.400	1.200
Johnny Kucks	3	3	0	0	0	0	0	0	0	1	0	0	.000	.000	.000
Don Larsen	2	3	1	1	1	0	0	0	0	1	0	0	.333	.333	.333
Mickey Mantle	7	24	6	6	4	1	0	3	6	5	1	0	.250	.400	.667
Billy Martin	7	27	5	8	3	0	0	2	1	6	0	0	.296	.321	.519
Mickey McDermott	1	1	0	1	0	0	0	0	0	0	0	0	1.000	1.000	1.000
Gil McDougald	7	21	0	3	1	0	0	0	3	6	0	0	.143	.240	.143
Tom Morgan	2	1	1	1	0	0	0	0	0	0	0	0	1.000	1.000	1.000
Norm Siebern	1	1	0	0	0	0	0	0	0	0	0	0	.000	.000	.000
Bill Skowron	3	10	1	1	4	0	0	1	0	3	0	0	.100	.100	.400
Enos Slaughter	6	20	6	7	4	0	0	1	4	0	0	0	.350	.440	.500
Tom Sturdivant	2	3	0	1	0	0	0	0	0	1	0	0	.333	.333	.333
Bob Turley	3	4	0	0	0	0	0	0	0	1	0	0	.000	.000	.000
George Wilson	1	1	0	0	0	0	0	0	0	1	0	0	.000	.000	.000
Totals	7	229	33	58	33	6	0	12	21	43	2	0	.253	.313	.437

Batting

Dodgers	G	AB	R	H	RBI	2B	3B	HR	BB	SO	SB	CS	Avg	OBP	Slg
Sandy Amoros	6	19	1	1	1	0	0	0	2	4	0	0	.053	.143	.053
Don Bessent	2	2	0	1	1	0	0	0	1	1	0	0	.500	.667	.500
Roy Campanella	7	22	2	4	3	1	0	0	3	7	0	1	.182	.259	.227
Roger Craig	2	2	0	1	0	0	0	0	0	0	0	0	.500	.500	.500
Carl Erskine	2	1	0	0	0	0	0	0	0	1	0	0	.000	.000	.000
Carl Furillo	7	25	2	6	1	2	0	0	2	3	0	0	.240	.296	.320
Jim Gilliam	7	24	2	2	2	0	0	0	7	3	1	1	.083	.290	.083
Gil Hodges	7	23	5	7	8	2	0	1	4	4	0	0	.304	.407	.522
Randy Jackson	3	3	0	0	0	0	0	0	0	2	0	0	.000	.000	.000
Clem Labine	2	4	0	1	0	1	0	0	0	2	0	0	.250	.250	.500
Sal Maglie	2	5	0	0	0	0	0	0	0	2	0	0	.000	.000	.000
Dale Mitchell	4	4	0	0	0	0	0	0	0	1	0	0	.000	.000	.000
Charlie Neal	1	4	0	0	0	0	0	0	0	1	0	0	.000	.000	.000
Don Newcombe	2	1	0	0	0	0	0	0	0	0	0	0	.000	.000	.000
Pee Wee Reese	7	27	3	6	2	0	1	0	2	6	0	0	.222	.276	.296
Jackie Robinson	7	24	5	6	2	1	0	1	5	2	0	0	.250	.379	.417
Duke Snider	7	23	5	7	4	1	0	1	6	8	0	0	.304	.433	.478
Rube Walker	2	2	0	0	0	0	0	0	0	0	0	0	.000	.000	.000
Totals	7	215	25	42	24	8	1	3	32	47	1	2	.195	.296	.284

Pitching

Yankees	G	GS	CG	IP	H	R	ER	BB	SO	W-L	Sv-Op	Hld	ERA
Tommy Byrne	1	0	0	0.1	1	1	0	0	1	0-0	0-0	0	0.00
Whitey Ford	2	2	1	12.0	14	8	7	2	8	1-1	0-0	0	5.25
Johnny Kucks	3	1	1	11.0	6	2	1	3	2	1-0	0-0	0	0.82
Don Larsen	2	2	1	10.2	1	4	0	4	7	1-0	0-0	0	0.00
Mickey McDermott	1	0	0	3.0	2	2	1	3	3	0-0	0-0	0	3.00
Tom Morgan	2	0	0	4.0	6	4	4	4	3	0-1	0-0	0	9.00
Tom Sturdivant	2	1	1	9.2	8	3	3	8	9	1-0	0-0	0	2.79
Bob Turley	3	1	1	11.0	4	1	1	8	14	0-1	0-0	0	0.82
Totals	7	7	5	61.2	42	25	17	32	47	4-3	0-0	0	2.48

Pitching

Dodgers	G	GS	CG	IP	H	R	ER	BB	SO	W-L	Sv-Op	Hld	ERA
Don Bessent	2	0	0	10.0	8	2	2	3	5	1-0	0-0	0	1.80
Roger Craig	2	1	0	6.0	10	8	8	3	4	0-1	0-0	0	12.00
Don Drysdale	1	0	0	2.0	2	2	2	1	1	0-0	0-0	0	9.00
Carl Erskine	2	1	0	5.0	4	3	3	2	2	0-1	0-0	0	5.40
Clem Labine	2	1	1	12.0	8	1	0	3	7	1-0	0-0	0	0.00
Sal Maglie	2	2	2	17.0	14	5	5	6	15	1-1	0-0	0	2.65
Don Newcombe	2	2	0	4.2	11	11	11	3	4	0-1	0-0	0	21.21
Ed Roebuck	3	0	0	4.1	1	1	1	0	5	0-0	0-0	0	2.08
Totals	7	7	3	61.0	58	33	32	21	43	3-4	0-0	0	4.72

Fielding

Yankees	Pos	G	PO	Ast	E	DP	PB	FPct
Hank Bauer	rf	7	14	1	1	0	—	.938
Yogi Berra	c	7	50	3	0	0	0	1.000
Tommy Byrne	p	1	0	0	0	0	—	—
Andy Carey	3b	7	7	10	2	0	—	.895
Jerry Coleman	2b	2	2	2	0	0	—	1.000
Joe Collins	1b	5	30	3	2	4	—	.943
Whitey Ford	p	2	1	0	0	0	—	1.000
Elston Howard	lf	1	2	0	0	0	—	1.000
Johnny Kucks	p	3	1	2	0	1	—	1.000
Don Larsen	p	2	0	1	0	0	—	1.000
Mickey Mantle	cf	7	18	1	0	0	—	1.000
Billy Martin	2b	7	12	18	0	4	—	1.000
	3b	2	2	2	0	1	—	1.000
Mickey McDermott	p	1	0	0	0	0	—	—
Gil McDougald	ss	7	15	16	0	4	—	1.000
Tom Morgan	p	2	0	0	0	0	—	—
Bill Skowron	1b	2	21	3	1	3	—	.960
Enos Slaughter	lf	6	8	1	0	0	—	1.000
Tom Sturdivant	p	2	2	0	0	0	—	1.000
Bob Turley	p	3	0	2	0	0	—	1.000
Totals		7	185	65	6	17	0	.977

Fielding

Dodgers	Pos	G	PO	Ast	E	DP	PB	FPct
Sandy Amoros	lf	6	10	0	0	0	—	1.000
Don Bessent	p	2	0	0	0	0	—	—
Roy Campanella	c	7	49	3	0	1	0	1.000
Gino Cimoli	lf	1	1	0	0	0	—	1.000
Roger Craig	p	2	1	1	0	1	—	1.000
Don Drysdale	p	1	0	0	0	0	—	—
Carl Erskine	p	2	1	2	0	0	—	1.000
Carl Furillo	rf	7	7	0	0	0	—	1.000
Jim Gilliam	2b	6	17	17	0	4	—	1.000
	lf	1	2	0	0	0	—	1.000
Gil Hodges	1b	7	54	5	0	8	—	1.000
Clem Labine	p	2	0	3	0	0	—	1.000
Sal Maglie	p	2	0	1	0	0	—	1.000
Charlie Neal	2b	1	2	2	1	1	—	.800
Don Newcombe	p	2	0	2	0	0	—	1.000
Pee Wee Reese	ss	7	14	21	1	7	—	.972
Jackie Robinson	3b	7	5	11	0	1	—	1.000
Ed Roebuck	p	3	0	0	0	0	—	—
Duke Snider	cf	7	20	0	0	0	—	1.000
Totals		7	183	68	2	23	0	.992

1957 Milwaukee Braves (NL) 4, New York Yankees (AL) 3

Milwaukee Braves righthander Lew Burdette notched three complete-game victories to give Milwaukee its first World Championship. Whitey Ford won the opener, 3-1, before Burdette evened it up with a 4-2 victory in the second game. Tony Kubek launched two home runs and drove in four runs as the Yankees routed the Braves in Game 3, 12-3. Warren Spahn was one strike away from a 4-1 victory in Game 4 when Elston Howard hit a game-tying three-run homer. Hank Bauer's RBI triple gave the Yanks the lead in the 10th, but the Braves tied it in the bottom of the inning and won it on Eddie Mathews' homer. Burdette blanked the Yanks on seven hits to win Game 5, 1-0. In Game 6, Hank Bauer's seventh-inning solo shot and Bob Turley's four-hit complete game gave the Yanks a 3-2 win. Spahn came down with the flu, so Burdette started the seventh game on two days' rest and stopped the Yanks 5-0 for his second shutout of the Series.

Game 1

Wednesday, October 2

Braves	AB	R	H	RBI	BB	K	Avg
Red Schoendienst, 2b	4	0	1	1	0	0	.250
Johnny Logan, ss	3	0	0	0	1	1	.000
Eddie Mathews, 3b	2	0	0	0	2	0	.000
Hank Aaron, cf	4	0	1	0	0	1	.250
Joe Adcock, 1b	4	0	0	0	0	0	.000
Frank Torre, 1b	0	0	0	0	0	0	—
Andy Pafko, rf	4	0	0	0	0	1	.000
Wes Covington, lf	4	1	2	0	0	2	.500
Del Crandall, c	4	0	1	0	0	0	.250
Warren Spahn, p	1	0	0	0	1	0	.000
Ernie Johnson, p	0	0	0	0	0	0	—
Nippy Jones, ph	1	0	0	0	0	0	.000
Don McMahon, p	0	0	0	0	0	0	—
TOTALS	31	1	5	1	4	5	.161

Yankees	AB	R	H	RBI	BB	K	Avg
Hank Bauer, rf	4	0	1	1	0	1	.250
Gil McDougald, ss	4	0	1	0	0	1	.250
Mickey Mantle, cf	4	0	2	0	0	0	.500
Bill Skowron, 1b	1	0	0	0	0	0	.000
Elston Howard, 1b	2	1	1	0	0	0	.500
Joe Collins, 1b	1	0	0	0	0	1	.000
Yogi Berra, c	3	1	1	0	1	0	.333
Andy Carey, 3b	3	0	1	1	1	0	.333
Jerry Coleman, 2b	3	1	2	1	0	0	.667
Tony Kubek, lf	3	0	0	0	0	1	.000
Whitey Ford, p	3	0	0	0	0	0	.000
TOTALS	31	3	9	3	2	4	.290

	1 2 3	4 5 6	7 8 9	R	H	E
Braves	0 0 0	0 0 0	1 0 0	1	5	0
Yankees	0 0 0	0 1 2	0 0 x	3	9	1

E—Howard. DP—Braves 1 (Crandall to Logan), Yankees 1 (McDougald to Coleman to Howard). LOB—Braves 7, Yankees 7. Scoring Position—Braves 1-for-8, Yankees 2-for-10. 2B—Covington (1), Bauer (1), Coleman (1). S—Coleman. GDP—Adcock. CS—Mantle (1).

Braves	IP	H	R	ER	BB	K	ERA
Warren Spahn (L, 0-1)	5.1	7	3	3	1	0	5.06
Ernie Johnson	0.2	0	0	0	0	1	0.00
Don McMahon	2.0	2	0	0	1	3	0.00

Yankees	IP	H	R	ER	BB	K	ERA
Whitey Ford (W, 1-0)	9.0	5	1	1	4	5	1.00

Time—2:10. Attendance—69,476. Umpires—HP, Paparella. 1B, Conlan. 2B, McKinley. 3B, Donatelli.

Game 2

Thursday, October 3

Braves	AB	R	H	RBI	BB	K	Avg
Red Schoendienst, 2b	4	0	0	0	0	1	.125
Johnny Logan, ss	3	1	1	1	0	1	.167
Eddie Mathews, 3b	4	0	0	0	0	2	.000
Hank Aaron, cf	4	1	1	0	0	1	.250
Joe Adcock, 1b	4	1	2	1	0	0	.250
Frank Torre, 1b	0	0	0	0	0	0	—
Andy Pafko, rf	4	1	1	0	0	0	.125
Wes Covington, lf	4	0	2	1	0	0	.500
Del Crandall, c	3	0	1	0	1	0	.286
Lew Burdette, p	3	0	0	0	0	0	.000
TOTALS	33	4	8	3	1	6	.210

Yankees	AB	R	H	RBI	BB	K	Avg
Hank Bauer, rf	5	1	1	1	0	1	.222
Gil McDougald, ss	4	0	0	0	0	0	.125
Mickey Mantle, cf	3	0	0	0	1	0	.286
Yogi Berra, c	4	0	0	0	0	0	.143
Enos Slaughter, lf	3	1	1	0	1	2	.333
Harry Simpson, 1b	4	0	0	0	0	1	.000
Tony Kubek, 3b	4	0	2	0	0	0	.286
Jerry Coleman, 2b	2	0	1	1	1	0	.600
Joe Collins, ph	1	0	0	0	0	0	.000
Bobby Shantz, p	1	0	0	0	0	0	.000
Art Ditmar, p	1	0	0	0	0	1	.000
Jerry Lumpe, ph	1	0	1	0	0	0	1.000
Bob Grim, p	0	0	0	0	0	0	—
Elston Howard, ph	1	0	1	0	0	0	.667
Bobby Richardson, pr	0	0	0	0	0	0	—
TOTALS	34	2	7	2	3	5	.259

	1 2 3	4 5 6	7 8 9	R	H	E
Braves	0 1 1	2 0 0	0 0 0	4	8	0
Yankees	0 1 1	0 0 0	0 0 0	2	7	2

E—Kubek, Mantle. DP—Yankees 1 (McDougald to Simpson). LOB—Braves 5, Yankees 8. Scoring Position—Braves 2-for-11, Yankees 1-for-6. 2B—Slaughter (1). 3B—Aaron (1). HR—Logan (1), Bauer (1). S—Burdette. GDP—Mathews.

Braves	IP	H	R	ER	BB	K	ERA
Lew Burdette (W, 1-0)	9.0	7	2	2	3	5	2.00

Yankees	IP	H	R	ER	BB	K	ERA
Bobby Shantz (L, 0-1)	3.0	6	4	3	1	3	9.00
Art Ditmar	4.0	1	0	0	0	1	0.00
Bob Grim	2.0	1	0	0	0	2	0.00

Shantz pitched to four batters in the 4th.

HBP—Logan by Ditmar. Time—2:26. Attendance—65,202. Umpires—HP, Conlan. 1B, McKinley. 2B, Donatelli. 3B, Paparella.

Game 3

Saturday, October 5

Yankees	AB	R	H	RBI	BB	K	Avg
Hank Bauer, rf	5	1	1	2	1	1	.214
Tony Kubek, lf	5	3	3	4	0	1	.417
Mickey Mantle, cf	3	2	2	2	2	0	.400
Yogi Berra, c	4	2	1	0	1	0	.182
Gil McDougald, ss	1	2	0	1	3	0	.111
Harry Simpson, 1b	1	0	1	1	0	0	.200
Elston Howard, ph-1b	2	0	0	0	1	1	.400
Joe Collins, 1b	1	0	0	0	0	1	.000
Jerry Lumpe, 3b	5	0	1	2	0	0	.333
Jerry Coleman, 2b	4	1	0	0	1	1	.333
Bob Turley, p	1	0	0	0	0	0	.000
Don Larsen, p	2	1	0	0	2	1	.000
TOTALS	34	12	9	12	11	6	.264

Braves	AB	R	H	RBI	BB	K	Avg
Red Schoendienst, 2b	5	0	3	1	0	0	.308
Johnny Logan, ss	4	1	2	0	1	1	.300
Eddie Mathews, 3b	2	0	0	0	3	0	.000
Hank Aaron, cf	5	1	2	2	0	0	.308
Wes Covington, lf	3	0	0	0	2	1	.364
Joe Adcock, 1b	3	0	0	0	0	2	.182
Bob Trowbridge, p	0	0	0	0	0	0	—
Nippy Jones, ph	1	0	0	0	0	0	.000
Don McMahon, p	0	0	0	0	0	0	—
Andy Pafko, ph	0	0	0	0	0	0	.125
Bob Hazle, rf	4	1	0	0	1	0	.000
Del Rice, c	3	0	1	0	1	0	.333
John DeMerit, pr	0	0	0	0	0	0	—
Del Crandall, c	1	0	0	0	0	1	.250
Bob Buhl, p	0	0	0	0	0	0	—
Juan Pizarro, p	1	0	0	0	0	0	.000
Gene Conley, p	0	0	0	0	0	0	—
Carl Sawatski, ph	1	0	0	0	0	1	.000
Ernie Johnson, p	0	0	0	0	0	0	—
Frank Torre, ph-1b	2	0	0	0	0	0	.000
TOTALS	35	3	8	3	8	6	.221

	1 2 3	4 5 6	7 8 9	R	H	E
Yankees	3 0 2	2 0 0	5 0 0	12	9	0
Braves	0 1 0	0 2 0	0 0 0	3	8	1

E—Buhl. DP—Braves 1 (Schoendienst to Torre). LOB—Yankees 7, Braves 14. Scoring Position—Yankees 4-for-11, Braves 1-for-11. HR—Kubek 2 (2), Mantle (1), Aaron (1). SF—McDougald. SB—McDougald (1).

Yankees	IP	H	R	ER	BB	K	ERA
Bob Turley	1.2	3	1	1	4	2	5.40
Don Larsen (W, 1-0)	7.1	5	2	2	4	4	2.45

Braves	IP	H	R	ER	BB	K	ERA
Bob Buhl (L, 0-1)	0.2	2	3	2	2	0	27.00
Juan Pizarro	1.2	3	2	2	2	1	10.80
Gene Conley	1.2	2	2	2	1	0	10.80
Ernie Johnson	2.0	0	0	0	1	2	0.00
Bob Trowbridge	1.0	2	5	5	3	1	45.00
Don McMahon	2.0	0	0	0	2	2	0.00

WP—Turley. PB—Rice. HBP—Pafko by Larsen. Time—3:18. Attendance—45,804. Umpires—HP, McKinley. 1B, Donatelli. 2B, Paparella. 3B, Conlan.

Game 4

Sunday, October 6

Yankees	AB	R	H	RBI	BB	K	Avg
Tony Kubek, lf-cf	5	1	2	0	0	0	.412
Hank Bauer, rf	5	0	1	1	0	0	.211
Mickey Mantle, cf	5	1	0	0	0	1	.267
Enos Slaughter, lf	0	0	0	0	0	0	.333
Yogi Berra, c	3	1	2	0	1	0	.286
Gil McDougald, ss	4	1	2	1	0	0	.231
Elston Howard, 1b	4	1	1	3	0	0	.333
Joe Collins, 1b	0	0	0	0	0	0	.000
Andy Carey, 3b	4	0	1	0	0	0	.286
Jerry Coleman, 2b	4	0	1	0	0	0	.308
Tom Sturdivant, p	1	0	0	0	0	0	.000
Harry Simpson, ph	1	0	0	0	0	0	.167
Bobby Shantz, p	0	0	0	0	0	0	.000
Jerry Lumpe, ph	1	0	1	0	0	0	.429
Johnny Kucks, p	0	0	0	0	0	0	—
Tommy Byrne, p	1	0	0	0	0	1	.000
Bob Grim, p	0	0	0	0	0	0	—
TOTALS	38	5	11	5	1	2	.279

Braves	AB	R	H	RBI	BB	K	Avg
Red Schoendienst, 2b	4	0	1	0	0	0	.294
Johnny Logan, ss	4	2	1	1	1	1	.286
Eddie Mathews, 3b	4	2	2	2	1	0	.167
Hank Aaron, cf	3	1	2	3	1	1	.375
Wes Covington, lf	4	0	0	0	0	2	.267
Frank Torre, 1b	3	1	1	1	0	0	.200
Joe Adcock, ph-1b	1	0	0	0	0	0	.167
Bob Hazle, rf	2	0	0	0	0	1	.000
Andy Pafko, rf	2	0	0	0	0	0	.100
Del Crandall, c	4	0	0	0	0	0	.167
Warren Spahn, p	3	0	0	0	0	2	.000
Nippy Jones, ph	0	0	0	0	0	0	.000
Felix Mantilla, pr	0	1	0	0	0	0	—
TOTALS	34	7	7	7	3	7	.216

	1 2 3	4 5 6	7 8 9	10	R	H	E
Yankees	1 0 0	0 0 0	0 0 3	1	5	11	0
Braves	0 0 0	4 0 0	0 0 0	3	7	7	0

DP—Braves 3 (Schoendienst to Torre; Logan to Schoendienst to Torre; Logan to Schoendienst to Torre). LOB—Yankees 4, Braves 4. Scoring Position—Yankees 3-for-8, Braves 3-for-8. 2B—Carey (1), Schoendienst (1), Logan (1), Mathews (1). 3B—Bauer (1). HR—Howard (1), Mathews (1), Aaron (2), Torre (1). S—Schoendienst. GDP—Kubek, Howard, Simpson. SB—Covington (1).

Yankees	IP	H	R	ER	BB	K	ERA
Tom Sturdivant	4.0	4	4	4	1	1	9.00
Bobby Shantz	3.0	0	0	0	1	4	4.50
Johnny Kucks	0.2	1	0	0	1	1	0.00
Tommy Byrne	1.1	0	1	1	0	1	6.75
Bob Grim (BS, 1; L, 0-1)	0.1	2	2	2	0	0	7.71

Braves	IP	H	R	ER	BB	K	ERA
Warren Spahn (W, 1-1)	10.0	11	5	5	1	2	4.70

Byrne pitched to one batter in the 10th.

HBP—Jones by Byrne. Time—2:31. Attendance—45,804. Umpires—HP, Donatelli. 1B, Paparella. 2B, Conlan. 3B, McKinley.

Game 5
Monday, October 7

Yankees	AB	R	H	RBI	BB	K	Avg
Hank Bauer, rf	4	0	2	0	0	1	.261
Tony Kubek, cf	3	0	0	0	0	1	.350
Gil McDougald, ss	4	0	1	0	0	0	.235
Yogi Berra, c	4	0	1	0	0	0	.278
Enos Slaughter, lf	3	0	2	0	0	0	.500
Harry Simpson, 1b	3	0	0	0	0	1	.111
Jerry Lumpe, 3b	3	0	0	0	0	0	.300
Jerry Coleman, 2b	3	0	1	0	0	0	.313
Mickey Mantle, pr	0	0	0	0	0	0	.267
Bob Turley, p	0	0	0	0	0	0	.000
Whitey Ford, p	2	0	0	0	0	1	.000
Elston Howard, ph	1	0	0	0	0	1	.300
Bobby Richardson, 2b	0	0	0	0	0	0	—
TOTALS	30	0	7	0	0	5	.273

Braves	AB	R	H	RBI	BB	K	Avg
Red Schoendienst, 2b	1	0	0	0	0	0	.278
Felix Mantilla, 2b	3	0	0	0	0	0	.000
Johnny Logan, ss	4	0	0	0	0	1	.222
Eddie Mathews, 3b	3	1	1	0	1	2	.200
Hank Aaron, cf	3	0	2	0	0	0	.421
Joe Adcock, 1b	3	0	1	1	0	0	.200
Frank Torre, 1b	0	0	0	0	0	0	.200
Andy Pafko, rf	3	0	2	0	0	0	.231
Wes Covington, lf	2	0	0	0	0	0	.235
Del Crandall, c	3	0	0	0	0	0	.133
Lew Burdette, p	3	0	0	0	0	1	.000
TOTALS	28	1	6	1	1	4	.229

	1 2 3	4 5 6	7 8 9	R	H	E
Yankees	0 0 0	0 0 0	0 0 0	0	7	0
Braves	0 0 0	0 0 1	0 0 x	1	6	1

E—Adcock. DP—Yankees 1 (McDougald to Coleman to Simpson), Braves 3 (Crandall to Logan; Mathews to Mantilla to Adcock; Logan to Adcock). LOB—Yankees 4, Braves 5. Scoring Position—Yankees 0-for-3, Braves 1-for-4. S—Kubek, Covington. GDP—Slaughter, Simpson, Adcock. CS—Slaughter (1), Mantle (2).

Yankees	IP	H	R	ER	BB	K	ERA
Whitey Ford (L, 1-1)	7.0	6	1	1	1	2	1.13
Bob Turley	1.0	0	0	0	0	2	3.38

Braves	IP	H	R	ER	BB	K	ERA
Lew Burdette (W, 2-0)	9.0	7	0	0	0	5	1.00

Time—2:00. Attendance—45,811. Umpires—HP, Paparella. 1B, Conlan. 2B, McKinley. 3B, Donatelli.

Game 6
Wednesday, October 9

Braves	AB	R	H	RBI	BB	K	Avg
Felix Mantilla, 2b	3	0	0	0	1	0	.000
Johnny Logan, ss	4	0	0	0	0	1	.182
Eddie Mathews, 3b	3	0	1	0	1	0	.222
Hank Aaron, cf	4	1	1	1	0	2	.391
Wes Covington, lf	4	0	0	0	0	0	.190
Frank Torre, 1b	3	1	2	1	0	0	.375
Bob Hazle, rf	3	0	0	0	0	0	.000
Del Rice, c	3	0	0	0	0	2	.167
Bob Buhl, p	1	0	0	0	0	1	.000
Ernie Johnson, p	1	0	0	0	0	1	.000
Carl Sawatski, ph	1	0	0	0	0	1	.000
Don McMahon, p	0	0	0	0	0	0	—
TOTALS	30	2	4	2	2	8	.214

Yankees	AB	R	H	RBI	BB	K	Avg
Hank Bauer, rf	4	1	1	1	0	2	.259
Tony Kubek, cf	4	0	0	0	0	1	.292
Enos Slaughter, lf	2	1	0	0	2	0	.375
Yogi Berra, c	4	1	3	2	0	0	.364
Gil McDougald, ss	3	0	1	0	0	2	.250
Jerry Lumpe, 3b	3	0	1	0	1	0	.308
Harry Simpson, 1b	3	0	0	0	0	2	.083
Joe Collins, 1b	0	0	0	0	0	0	.000
Jerry Coleman, 2b	2	0	1	0	1	0	.333
Bob Turley, p	3	0	0	0	0	2	.000
TOTALS	28	3	7	3	4	9	.272

	1 2 3	4 5 6	7 8 9	R	H	E
Braves	0 0 0	0 1 0	1 0 0	2	4	0
Yankees	0 0 2	0 0 0	1 0 x	3	7	0

DP—Braves 2 (Rice to Logan; Covington to Rice). LOB—Braves 3, Yankees 6. Scoring Position—Braves 0-for-2, Yankees 0-for-6. 2B—Mathews (2), Berra (1), Coleman (2). HR—Aaron (3), Torre (2), Bauer (2), Berra (1). S—McDougald. GDP—Covington. CS—Lumpe (1).

Braves	IP	H	R	ER	BB	K	ERA
Bob Buhl	2.2	4	2	2	4	4	10.80
Ernie Johnson (L, 0-1)	4.1	2	1	1	0	5	1.29
Don McMahon	1.0	1	0	0	0	0	0.00

Yankees	IP	H	R	ER	BB	K	ERA
Bob Turley (W, 1-0)	9.0	4	2	2	2	8	2.31

WP—Buhl. Time—2:09. Attendance—61,408. Umpires—HP, Conlan. 1B, McKinley. 2B, Donatelli. 3B, Paparella.

Game 7
Thursday, October 10

Braves	AB	R	H	RBI	BB	K	Avg
Bob Hazle, rf	4	1	2	0	0	1	.154
Andy Pafko, ph-rf	1	0	0	0	0	0	.214
Johnny Logan, ss	5	1	1	0	0	0	.185
Eddie Mathews, 3b	4	1	1	2	0	1	.227
Hank Aaron, cf	5	1	2	1	0	1	.393
Wes Covington, lf	3	0	1	0	0	0	.208
Frank Torre, 1b	2	0	0	1	2	0	.300
Felix Mantilla, 2b	4	0	0	0	0	0	.000
Del Crandall, c	4	1	2	1	0	0	.211
Lew Burdette, p	2	0	0	0	1	1	.000
TOTALS	34	5	9	5	3	4	.217

Yankees	AB	R	H	RBI	BB	K	Avg
Hank Bauer, rf	4	0	1	0	0	0	.258
Enos Slaughter, lf	4	0	0	0	0	0	.250
Mickey Mantle, cf	4	0	1	0	0	0	.263
Yogi Berra, c	3	0	0	0	1	0	.320
Gil McDougald, ss	4	0	1	0	0	0	.250
Tony Kubek, 3b	4	0	1	0	0	0	.286
Jerry Coleman, 2b	4	0	2	0	0	0	.364
Joe Collins, 1b	2	0	0	0	0	1	.000
Tom Sturdivant, p	0	0	0	0	0	0	.000
Elston Howard, ph	1	0	0	0	0	1	.273
Tommy Byrne, p	1	0	1	0	0	0	.500
Don Larsen, p	0	0	0	0	0	0	.000
Bobby Shantz, p	0	0	0	0	0	0	.000
Jerry Lumpe, ph	1	0	0	0	0	1	.286
Art Ditmar, p	0	0	0	0	0	0	.000
Bill Skowron, ph-1b	3	0	0	0	0	0	.000
TOTALS	35	0	7	0	1	3	.267

	1 2 3	4 5 6	7 8 9	R	H	E
Braves	0 0 4	0 0 0	0 1 0	5	9	1
Yankees	0 0 0	0 0 0	0 0 0	0	7	3

E—Kubek, Mathews, McDougald, Berra. DP—Yankees 1 (McDougald to Coleman to Skowron). LOB—Braves 8, Yankees 9. Scoring Position—Braves 2-for-10, Yankees 1-for-8. 2B—Mathews (3), Bauer (2). HR—Crandall (1). S—Mathews, Covington, Burdette. GDP—Mantilla. CS—Crandall (1).

Braves	IP	H	R	ER	BB	K	ERA
Lew Burdette (W, 3-0)	9.0	7	0	0	1	3	0.67

Yankees	IP	H	R	ER	BB	K	ERA
Don Larsen (L, 1-1)	2.1	3	3	2	1	2	3.72
Bobby Shantz	0.2	1	0	0	0	0	4.05
Art Ditmar	2.0	1	0	0	1	0	0.00
Tom Sturdivant	2.0	2	0	0	0	1	6.00
Tommy Byrne	2.0	1	1	1	2	0	5.40

Time—2:34. Attendance—61,207. Umpires—HP, McKinley. 1B, Donatelli. 2B, Paparella. 3B, Conlan.

1957 World Series—Composite Statistics

Batting

Braves	G	AB	R	H	RBI	2B	3B	HR	BB	SO	SB	CS	Avg	OBP	Slg
Hank Aaron	7	28	5	11	7	0	1	3	1	6	0	0	.393	.414	.786
Joe Adcock	5	15	1	3	2	0	0	0	2	0	0	0	.200	.200	.200
Bob Buhl	2	1	0	0	0	0	0	0	0	1	0	0	.000	.000	.000
Lew Burdette	3	8	0	0	0	0	0	0	1	2	0	0	.000	.111	.000
Wes Covington	7	24	1	5	1	1	0	0	2	6	1	0	.208	.269	.250
Del Crandall	6	19	1	4	1	0	0	1	1	1	0	1	.211	.250	.368
John DeMerit	1	0	0	0	0	0	0	0	0	0	0	0	—	—	—
Bob Hazle	4	13	2	2	0	0	0	0	1	2	0	0	.154	.214	.154
Ernie Johnson	3	1	0	0	0	0	0	0	0	1	0	0	.000	.000	.000
Nippy Jones	3	2	0	0	0	0	0	0	0	0	0	0	.000	.333	.000
Johnny Logan	7	27	5	5	2	1	0	1	3	6	0	0	.185	.290	.333
Felix Mantilla	4	10	1	0	0	0	0	0	1	0	0	0	.000	.091	.000
Eddie Mathews	7	22	4	5	4	3	0	1	8	5	0	0	.227	.433	.500
Andy Pafko	6	14	1	3	0	0	0	0	0	1	0	0	.214	.267	.214
Juan Pizarro	1	1	0	0	0	0	0	0	0	0	0	0	.000	.000	.000
Del Rice	2	6	0	1	0	0	0	0	1	2	0	0	.167	.286	.167
Carl Sawatski	2	2	0	0	0	0	0	0	0	2	0	0	.000	.000	.000
Red Schoendienst	5	18	0	5	2	1	0	0	0	1	0	0	.278	.278	.333
Warren Spahn	2	4	0	0	0	0	0	0	1	2	0	0	.000	.200	.000
Frank Torre	7	10	2	3	3	0	0	2	2	0	0	0	.300	.417	.900
Totals	7	225	23	47	22	6	1	8	22	40	1	1	.209	.288	.351

Yankees	G	AB	R	H	RBI	2B	3B	HR	BB	SO	SB	CS	Avg	OBP	Slg
Hank Bauer	7	31	3	8	6	2	1	2	1	6	0	0	.258	.281	.581
Yogi Berra	7	25	5	8	2	1	0	1	4	0	0	0	.320	.414	.480
Tommy Byrne	2	2	0	1	0	0	0	0	0	1	0	0	.500	.500	.500
Andy Carey	2	7	0	2	1	1	0	0	1	0	0	0	.286	.375	.429
Jerry Coleman	7	22	2	8	2	2	0	0	3	1	0	0	.364	.440	.455
Joe Collins	6	5	0	0	0	0	0	0	0	3	0	0	.000	.000	.000
Art Ditmar	2	1	0	0	0	0	0	0	0	1	0	0	.000	.000	.000
Whitey Ford	2	5	0	0	0	0	0	0	0	1	0	0	.000	.000	.000
Elston Howard	6	11	2	3	3	0	0	1	1	3	0	0	.273	.333	.545
Tony Kubek	7	28	4	8	4	0	0	2	0	4	0	0	.286	.286	.500
Don Larsen	2	2	1	0	0	0	0	0	2	1	0	0	.000	.500	.000
Jerry Lumpe	6	14	0	4	2	0	0	0	1	1	0	1	.286	.333	.286
Mickey Mantle	6	19	3	5	2	0	0	1	3	1	0	2	.263	.364	.421
Gil McDougald	7	24	3	6	2	0	0	0	3	3	1	0	.250	.321	.250
Bobby Shantz	3	1	0	0	0	0	0	0	0	0	0	0	.000	.000	.000
Harry Simpson	5	12	0	1	1	0	0	0	0	4	0	0	.083	.083	.083
Bill Skowron	2	4	0	0	0	0	0	0	0	0	0	0	.000	.000	.000
Enos Slaughter	5	12	2	3	0	1	0	0	3	2	0	1	.250	.400	.333
Tom Sturdivant	2	1	0	0	0	0	0	0	0	0	0	0	.000	.000	.000
Bob Turley	3	4	0	0	0	0	0	0	0	2	0	0	.000	.000	.000
Totals	7	230	25	57	25	7	1	7	22	34	1	4	.248	.312	.378

Pitching

Braves	G	GS	CG	IP	H	R	ER	BB	SO	W-L	Sv-Op	Hld	ERA
Bob Buhl	2	2	0	3.1	6	5	4	6	4	0-1	0-0	0	10.80
Lew Burdette	3	3	3	27.0	21	2	2	4	13	3-0	0-0	0	0.67
Gene Conley	1	0	0	1.2	2	2	2	1	0	0-0	0-0	0	10.80
Ernie Johnson	3	0	0	7.0	2	1	1	1	8	0-1	0-0	0	1.29
Don McMahon	3	0	0	5.0	3	0	0	3	5	0-0	0-0	0	0.00
Juan Pizarro	1	0	0	1.2	3	2	2	2	1	0-0	0-0	0	10.80
Warren Spahn	2	2	1	15.1	18	8	8	2	2	1-1	0-0	0	4.70
Bob Trowbridge	1	0	0	1.0	2	5	5	3	1	0-0	0-0	0	45.00
Totals	7	7	4	62.0	57	25	24	22	34	4-3	0-0	0	3.48

Yankees	G	GS	CG	IP	H	R	ER	BB	SO	W-L	Sv-Op	Hld	ERA
Tommy Byrne	2	0	0	3.1	1	2	2	2	1	0-0	0-0	0	5.40
Art Ditmar	2	0	0	6.0	2	0	0	0	2	0-0	0-0	0	0.00
Whitey Ford	2	2	1	16.0	11	2	2	5	7	1-1	0-0	0	1.13
Bob Grim	2	0	0	2.1	3	2	2	0	2	0-1	0-1	0	7.71
Johnny Kucks	1	0	0	0.2	1	0	0	1	1	0-0	0-0	0	0.00
Don Larsen	2	1	0	9.2	8	5	4	5	6	1-1	0-0	0	3.72
Bobby Shantz	3	1	0	6.2	8	5	3	2	7	0-1	0-0	0	4.05
Tom Sturdivant	2	1	0	6.0	6	4	4	1	2	0-0	0-0	0	6.00
Bob Turley	3	2	1	11.2	7	3	3	6	12	1-0	0-0	0	2.31
Totals	7	7	2	62.1	47	23	20	22	40	3-4	0-1	0	2.89

Fielding

Braves	Pos	G	PO	Ast	E	DP	PB	FPct
Hank Aaron	cf	7	11	0	0	0	—	1.000
Joe Adcock	1b	5	38	2	1	2	—	.976
Bob Buhl	p	2	0	2	1	0	—	.667
Lew Burdette	p	3	0	9	0	1	—	1.000
Gene Conley	p	1	1	0	0	0	—	1.000
Wes Covington	lf	7	13	1	0	1	—	1.000
Del Crandall	c	6	21	4	0	2	0	1.000
Bob Hazle	rf	4	6	0	0	0	—	1.000
Ernie Johnson	p	3	1	4	0	0	—	1.000
Johnny Logan	ss	7	13	24	0	7	—	1.000
Felix Mantilla	2b	3	6	8	0	1	—	1.000
Eddie Mathews	3b	7	9	18	1	2	—	.964
Don McMahon	p	3	0	2	0	0	—	1.000
Andy Pafko	rf	5	9	0	0	0	—	1.000
Juan Pizarro	p	1	0	0	0	0	—	—
Del Rice	c	2	15	2	0	2	1	1.000
Red Schoendienst	2b	5	5	10	0	4	—	1.000
Warren Spahn	p	2	1	3	0	0	—	1.000
Frank Torre	1b	7	37	2	0	4	—	1.000
Bob Trowbridge	p	1	0	0	0	0	—	—
Totals		7	186	91	3	26	1	.989

Yankees	Pos	G	PO	Ast	E	DP	PB	FPct
Hank Bauer	rf	7	10	0	0	0	—	1.000
Yogi Berra	c	7	45	2	1	0	0	.979
Tommy Byrne	p	2	0	0	0	0	—	—
Andy Carey	3b	2	3	6	0	0	—	1.000
Jerry Coleman	2b	7	16	17	0	3	—	1.000
Joe Collins	1b	5	12	2	0	1	—	1.000
Art Ditmar	p	2	0	0	0	0	—	—
Whitey Ford	p	2	1	1	0	0	—	1.000
Bob Grim	p	2	0	0	0	0	—	—
Elston Howard	1b	3	21	1	1	1	—	.957
Tony Kubek	cf	3	7	0	0	0	—	1.000
	lf	3	6	0	0	0	—	1.000
	3b	2	4	5	2	0	—	.818
Johnny Kucks	p	1	0	0	0	0	—	—
Don Larsen	p	2	0	1	0	0	—	1.000
Jerry Lumpe	3b	3	3	6	0	0	—	1.000
Mickey Mantle	cf	5	8	0	1	0	—	.889
Gil McDougald	ss	7	13	24	1	5	—	.974
Bobby Richardson	2b	1	0	0	0	0	—	—
Bobby Shantz	p	3	0	1	0	0	—	1.000
Harry Simpson	1b	4	24	1	0	2	—	1.000
Bill Skowron	1b	2	5	2	0	1	—	1.000
Enos Slaughter	lf	5	7	0	0	0	—	1.000
Tom Sturdivant	p	2	0	1	0	0	—	1.000
Bob Turley	p	3	2	2	0	1	—	1.000
Totals		7	187	72	6	14	0	.977

1958 New York Yankees (AL) 4, Milwaukee Braves (NL) 3

After dropping three of the first four games, the New York Yankees came back to defeat the Milwaukee Braves in seven games, avenging their World Series loss to the Braves the year before. The Braves pulled out the opener, 4-3 in 10 innings. Wes Covington's sacrifice fly tied it in the eighth and Bill Bruton's RBI single won it in the 10th. Lew Burdette socked a three-run homer and beat the Yanks 13-5 in Game 2. Don Larsen and Ryne Duren combined to beat Milwaukee 4-0 in Game 3, but the Braves took the fourth game 3-0 as Warren Spahn spun a two-hit shutout. Bob Turley kept the Yanks alive with a five-hit whitewash in Game 5, and Turley returned in Game 6 to record the final out as the Yanks stopped Milwaukee, 4-3 in 10 innings. The next day, Turley relieved Don Larsen in the third inning and allowed only two hits the rest of the way. Elston Howard's RBI single in the eighth put the Yanks ahead for good as they won 6-2 to wrap up the championship.

Game 1
Wednesday, October 1

Yankees	AB	R	H	RBI	BB	K	Avg
Hank Bauer, rf	5	1	2	2	0	1	.400
Gil McDougald, 2b	4	0	2	0	1	1	.500
Mickey Mantle, cf	3	0	0	0	2	0	.000
Elston Howard, lf	5	0	0	0	0	0	.000
Yogi Berra, c	4	0	2	0	0	0	.500
Bill Skowron, 1b	4	1	2	1	0	1	.500
Andy Carey, 3b	4	0	0	0	0	1	.000
Tony Kubek, ss	4	0	0	0	0	1	.000
Whitey Ford, p	2	1	0	0	1	1	.000
Ryne Duren, p	1	0	0	0	0	0	.000
TOTALS	36	3	8	3	4	6	.222

Braves	AB	R	H	RBI	BB	K	Avg
Red Schoendienst, 2b	4	0	0	0	1	1	.000
Johnny Logan, ss	4	0	1	0	0	2	.250
Frank Torre, ph	1	0	0	0	0	0	.000
Felix Mantilla, ss	0	0	0	0	0	0	—
Eddie Mathews, 3b	3	1	0	0	2	3	.000
Hank Aaron, rf	4	1	1	0	1	2	.250
Joe Adcock, 1b	5	1	2	0	0	1	.400
Wes Covington, lf	4	0	0	1	0	0	.000
Del Crandall, c	5	1	2	1	0	2	.400
Andy Pafko, cf	3	0	1	0	0	0	.333
Bill Bruton, ph-cf	2	0	1	1	0	1	.500
Warren Spahn, p	4	0	2	1	0	1	.500
TOTALS	39	4	10	4	4	13	.256

	1	2	3	4	5	6	7	8	9	10	R	H	E
Yankees	0	0	0	1	2	0	0	0	0	0	3	8	1
Braves	0	0	0	2	0	0	0	1	0	1	4	10	0

E—Kubek. LOB—Yankees 7, Braves 11. Scoring Position—Yankees 0-for-7, Braves 3-for-14. 2B—Berra (1), Logan (1), Aaron (1). HR—Bauer (1), Skowron (1). SF—Covington. CS—Bauer (1).

Yankees	IP	H	R	ER	BB	K	ERA
Whitey Ford	7.0	6	3	3	3	8	3.86
Ryne Duren (BS, 1; L, 0-1)	2.2	4	1	1	1	5	3.38

Braves	IP	H	R	ER	BB	K	ERA
Warren Spahn (W, 1-0)	10.0	8	3	3	4	6	2.70

Ford pitched to two batters in the 8th.

WP—Spahn, Ford. PB—Berra. Time—3:09. Attendance—46,367. Umpires—HP, Barlick. 1B, Berry. 2B, Gorman. 3B, Flaherty.

Game 2
Thursday, October 2

Yankees	AB	R	H	RBI	BB	K	Avg
Hank Bauer, rf	4	2	2	1	0	1	.444
Gil McDougald, 2b	4	1	1	0	0	0	.375
Mickey Mantle, cf	3	2	2	3	1	0	.333
Elston Howard, lf	1	0	0	1	0	0	.000
Norm Siebern, lf	3	0	1	0	0	0	.333
Yogi Berra, c	4	0	0	0	0	0	.250
Bill Skowron, 1b	4	0	0	0	0	1	.250
Andy Carey, 3b	2	0	0	0	0	1	.000
Enos Slaughter, ph	1	0	0	0	0	0	.000
Bobby Richardson, 3b	1	0	0	0	0	0	.000
Tony Kubek, ss	3	0	0	0	0	1	.000
Bob Turley, p	0	0	0	0	0	0	—
Duke Maas, p	0	0	0	0	0	0	—
Johnny Kucks, p	1	0	1	0	0	0	1.000
Jerry Lumpe, ph	1	0	0	0	0	0	.000
Murry Dickson, p	0	0	0	0	0	0	—
Marv Throneberry, ph	1	0	0	0	0	1	.000
Zack Monroe, p	0	0	0	0	0	0	—
TOTALS	33	5	7	5	1	5	.227

Braves	AB	R	H	RBI	BB	K	Avg
Bill Bruton, cf	4	2	3	1	1	0	.667
Red Schoendienst, 2b	5	2	2	0	0	0	.222
Eddie Mathews, 3b	5	2	2	0	1	1	.250
Hank Aaron, rf	4	2	2	0	1	0	.375
Wes Covington, lf	4	1	3	2	0	0	.375
Felix Mantilla, pr	0	1	0	0	0	0	—
Andy Pafko, lf	0	0	0	0	1	0	.333
Frank Torre, 1b	5	0	1	1	0	0	.167
Del Crandall, c	2	1	0	1	1	1	.286
Johnny Logan, ss	4	1	1	2	0	0	.250
Lew Burdette, p	4	1	1	3	0	1	.250
TOTALS	37	13	15	13	3	3	.313

	1	2	3	4	5	6	7	8	9	R	H	E
Yankees	1	0	0	1	0	0	0	0	3	5	7	0
Braves	7	1	0	0	0	0	2	3	x	13	15	1

E—Mathews. DP—Braves 2 (Schoendienst to Logan to Torre; Logan to Schoendienst to Torre). LOB—Yankees 2, Braves 8. Scoring Position—Yankees 0-for-2, Braves 6-for-10. 2B—Schoendienst 2 (2), Mathews (1). HR—Bauer (2), Mantle 2 (2), Bruton (1), Burdette (1). SF—Crandall, Pafko. GDP—Bauer, Berra (1). SB—Mathews (1).

Yankees	IP	H	R	ER	BB	K	ERA
Bob Turley (L, 0-1)	0.1	3	4	4	1	1	108.00
Duke Maas	0.1	2	3	3	1	0	81.00
Johnny Kucks	3.1	3	1	1	0	0	2.70
Murry Dickson	3.0	4	2	2	0	1	6.00
Zack Monroe	1.0	3	3	3	1	1	27.00

Braves	IP	H	R	ER	BB	K	ERA
Lew Burdette (W, 1-0)	9.0	7	5	4	1	5	4.00

Time—2:43. Attendance—46,367. Umpires—HP, Berry. 1B, Gorman. 2B, Flaherty. 3B, Barlick.

Game 3
Saturday, October 4

Braves	AB	R	H	RBI	BB	K	Avg
Bill Bruton, cf	3	0	0	0	2	0	.444
Red Schoendienst, 2b	4	0	2	0	0	0	.308
Eddie Mathews, 3b	3	0	0	0	1	3	.182
Hank Aaron, rf	3	0	0	0	1	1	.273
Wes Covington, lf	3	0	1	0	1	0	.364
Frank Torre, 1b	4	0	2	0	0	0	.300
Del Crandall, c	4	0	1	0	0	2	.273
Johnny Logan, ss	3	0	0	0	1	0	.182
Bob Rush, p	2	0	0	0	0	2	.000
Harry Hanebrink, ph	1	0	0	0	0	0	.000
Don McMahon, p	0	0	0	0	0	0	—
Casey Wise, ph	1	0	0	0	0	1	.000
TOTALS	31	0	6	0	6	9	.275

Yankees	AB	R	H	RBI	BB	K	Avg
Hank Bauer, rf	4	1	3	4	0	0	.538
Tony Kubek, ss	4	0	0	0	0	1	.000
Mickey Mantle, cf	2	0	0	0	2	1	.250
Yogi Berra, c	4	0	0	0	0	0	.167
Norm Siebern, lf	2	1	0	0	2	0	.200
Jerry Lumpe, 3b	3	0	1	0	0	0	.250
Bobby Richardson, 3b	1	0	0	0	0	0	.000
Bill Skowron, 1b	4	0	0	0	0	1	.167
Gil McDougald, 2b	2	1	0	0	1	1	.300
Don Larsen, p	1	0	0	0	0	0	.000
Enos Slaughter, ph	0	1	0	0	1	0	.000
Ryne Duren, p	0	0	0	0	0	0	.000
TOTALS	27	4	4	4	7	4	.225

	1	2	3	4	5	6	7	8	9	R	H	E
Braves	0	0	0	0	0	0	0	0	0	0	6	0
Yankees	0	0	0	2	0	0	2	0	x	4	4	0

DP—Braves 1 (Crandall to Torre). LOB—Braves 10, Yankees 6. Scoring Position—Braves 1-for-6, Yankees 1-for-3. HR—Bauer (3). GDP—Bruton.

Game 4
Sunday, October 5

Braves	AB	R	H	RBI	BB	K	Avg
Red Schoendienst, 2b	5	1	1	0	0	0	.278
Johnny Logan, ss	5	1	1	0	0	1	.188
Eddie Mathews, 3b	4	0	1	1	0	1	.200
Hank Aaron, cf-rf	4	0	2	0	0	1	.333
Joe Adcock, 1b	3	0	0	0	0	1	.250
Frank Torre, ph-1b	1	0	0	0	0	0	.273
Del Crandall, c	3	1	2	0	1	0	.357
Wes Covington, lf	3	0	0	0	1	1	.286
Bill Bruton, pr-cf	0	0	0	0	0	0	.444
Andy Pafko, rf-lf	4	0	1	0	0	0	.286
Warren Spahn, p	4	0	1	1	0	2	.375
TOTALS	36	3	9	2	2	6	.289

Yankees	AB	R	H	RBI	BB	K	Avg
Norm Siebern, lf	3	0	0	0	1	2	.125
Gil McDougald, 2b	4	0	0	0	0	1	.214
Hank Bauer, rf	4	0	0	0	0	1	.412
Mickey Mantle, cf	4	0	1	0	0	1	.250
Bill Skowron, 1b	3	0	1	0	0	0	.200
Yogi Berra, c	3	0	0	0	0	1	.133
Bobby Richardson, 3b	2	0	0	0	0	0	.000
Elston Howard, ph	1	0	0	0	0	1	.000
Andy Carey, 3b	0	0	0	0	0	0	.000
Tony Kubek, ss	2	0	0	0	0	0	.000
Enos Slaughter, ph	1	0	0	0	0	1	.000
Murry Dickson, p	0	0	0	0	0	0	—
Whitey Ford, p	1	0	0	0	0	1	.000
Johnny Kucks, p	0	0	0	0	0	0	1.000
Jerry Lumpe, ph-ss	1	0	0	0	0	0	.200
TOTALS	29	0	2	0	2	7	.172

	1	2	3	4	5	6	7	8	9	R	H	E
Braves	0	0	0	0	0	1	1	1	0	3	9	0
Yankees	0	0	0	0	0	0	0	0	0	0	2	1

E—Kubek. DP—Yankees 1 (McDougald to Kubek to Skowron). LOB—Braves 8, Yankees 4. Scoring Position—Braves 3-for-9, Yankees 0-for-2. 2B—Logan (2), Mathews (2), Aaron (2), Pafko (1). 3B—Schoendienst (1), Mantle (1). GDP—Schoendienst.

Braves	IP	H	R	ER	BB	K	ERA
Warren Spahn (W, 2-0)	9.0	2	0	0	2	7	1.42

Yankees	IP	H	R	ER	BB	K	ERA
Whitey Ford (L, 0-1)	7.0	8	3	2	1	6	3.21
Johnny Kucks	1.0	1	0	0	1	0	2.08
Murry Dickson	1.0	0	0	0	0	0	4.50

Ford pitched to two batters in the 8th.

WP—Ford. Time—2:17. Attendance—71,563. Umpires—HP, Flaherty. 1B, Barlick. 2B, Berry. 3B, Gorman.

Game 3 (pitching)

Braves	IP	H	R	ER	BB	K	ERA
Bob Rush (L, 0-1)	6.0	3	2	2	5	2	3.00
Don McMahon	2.0	1	2	2	2	2	9.00

Yankees	IP	H	R	ER	BB	K	ERA
Don Larsen (W, 1-0)	7.0	6	0	0	3	8	0.00
Ryne Duren (S, 1)	2.0	0	0	0	3	1	1.93

WP—Duren. Time—2:42. Attendance—71,599. Umpires—HP, Gorman. 1B, Flaherty. 2B, Barlick. 3B, Berry.

Game 5
Monday, October 6

Braves	AB	R	H	RBI	BB	K	Avg
Bill Bruton, cf	3	0	2	0	1	1	.500
Red Schoendienst, 2b	3	0	1	0	0	0	.286
Eddie Mathews, 3b	4	0	1	0	0	1	.211
Hank Aaron, rf	4	0	0	0	0	2	.263
Wes Covington, lf	4	0	1	0	0	2	.278
Casey Wise, pr	0	0	0	0	0	0	.000
Frank Torre, 1b	3	0	0	0	1	0	.214
Del Crandall, c	3	0	0	0	1	1	.294
Johnny Logan, ss	3	0	0	0	0	2	.158
Lew Burdette, p	2	0	0	0	0	1	.167
Juan Pizarro, p	0	0	0	0	0	0	—
Harry Hanebrink, ph	1	0	0	0	0	0	.000
Carl Willey, p	0	0	0	0	0	0	—
TOTALS	30	0	5	0	3	10	.257

Yankees	AB	R	H	RBI	BB	K	Avg
Hank Bauer, rf	4	1	1	0	0	2	.381
Jerry Lumpe, 3b	3	0	1	0	0	1	.250
Bobby Richardson, 3b	1	0	0	0	0	0	.000
Mickey Mantle, cf	3	1	2	0	1	1	.333
Yogi Berra, c	4	1	1	1	0	0	.158
Elston Howard, lf	3	1	0	0	1	1	.000
Bill Skowron, 1b	4	1	1	1	0	1	.211
Gil McDougald, 2b	4	2	2	3	0	1	.278
Tony Kubek, ss	4	0	1	0	0	2	.059
Bob Turley, p	3	0	1	2	0	0	.333
TOTALS	33	7	10	7	2	9	.215

	1	2	3	4	5	6	7	8	9		R	H	E
Braves	0	0	0	0	0	0	0	0	0		0	5	0
Yankees	0	0	1	0	0	6	0	0	x		7	10	0

DP—Braves 1 (Mathews to Torre), Yankees 1 (Howard to McDougald to Skowron). LOB—Braves 7, Yankees 4. Scoring Position—Braves 0-for-2, Yankees 4-for-9. 2B—Berra (2), McDougald (1). HR—McDougald (1). S—Schoendienst. GDP—Berra.

Braves	IP	H	R	ER	BB	K	ERA
Lew Burdette (L, 1-1)	5.1	8	6	6	1	4	6.28
Juan Pizarro	1.2	2	1	1	3		5.40
Carl Willey	1.0	0	0	0	0	2	0.00

Yankees	IP	H	R	ER	BB	K	ERA
Bob Turley (W, 1-1)	9.0	5	0	0	3	10	3.86

WP—Pizarro. Time—2:19. Attendance—65,279. Umpires—HP, Berry. 1B, Gorman. 2B, Flaherty. 3B, Jackowski.

Game 6
Wednesday, October 8

Yankees	AB	R	H	RBI	BB	K	Avg
Andy Carey, 3b	5	0	0	0	0	1	.000
Gil McDougald, 2b	5	1	2	1	0	0	.304
Hank Bauer, rf	5	1	2	1	0	0	.385
Mickey Mantle, cf	5	1	1	0	0	0	.300
Elston Howard, lf	5	1	2	0	0	1	.133
Yogi Berra, c	4	0	2	1	0	0	.217
Bill Skowron, 1b	4	0	1	1	1	0	.217
Tony Kubek, ss	2	0	0	0	0	1	.053
Enos Slaughter, ph	1	0	0	0	0	0	.000
Ryne Duren, p	2	0	0	0	0	2	.000
Bob Turley, p	0	0	0	0	0	0	.333
Whitey Ford, p	1	0	0	0	0	0	.000
Art Ditmar, p	1	0	0	0	0	0	.000
Jerry Lumpe, ph-ss	1	0	0	0	1	1	.222
TOTALS	41	4	10	4	2	6	.213

Braves	AB	R	H	RBI	BB	K	Avg
Red Schoendienst, 2b	4	1	2	0	1	0	.320
Johnny Logan, ss	2	1	0	0	1	0	.143
Eddie Mathews, 3b	5	0	0	0	0	2	.167
Hank Aaron, rf	5	0	3	2	0	0	.333
Joe Adcock, 1b	4	0	1	0	1	1	.250
Felix Mantilla, pr	0	0	0	0	0	0	—
Del Crandall, c	4	0	0	0	0	3	.238
Frank Torre, ph	1	0	0	0	0	0	.200
Wes Covington, lf	4	1	2	0	0	1	.318
Andy Pafko, cf	2	0	1	0	0	0	.333
Bill Bruton, cf	2	0	0	0	0	2	.429
Warren Spahn, p	4	0	1	1	0	3	.333
Don McMahon, p	0	0	0	0	0	0	—
TOTALS	37	3	10	3	3	12	.271

	1	2	3	4	5	6	7	8	9	10		R	H	E
Yankees	1	0	0	0	0	1	0	0	0	2		4	10	1
Braves	1	1	0	0	0	0	0	0	0	1		3	10	4

E—Ditmar, Bruton, Logan 2, Schoendienst. DP—Yankees 1 (Howard to Berra), Braves 1 (Crandall to Schoendienst). LOB—Yankees 10, Braves 9. Scoring Position—Yankees 1-for-4, Braves 3-for-10. 2B—Schoendienst (3). HR—McDougald (2), Bauer (4). S—Logan 2. SF—Berra. CS—Lumpe (1).

Yankees	IP	H	R	ER	BB	K	ERA
Whitey Ford	1.1	5	2	2	1	2	4.11
Art Ditmar	3.2	2	0	0	0	2	0.00
Ryne Duren (W, 1-1)	4.2	3	1	1	2	8	1.93
Bob Turley (S, 1)	0.1	0	0	0	0	0	3.72

Braves	IP	H	R	ER	BB	K	ERA
Warren Spahn (L, 2-1)	9.2	9	4	4	2	5	2.20
Don McMahon	0.1	1	0	0	0	1	7.71

Time—3:07. Attendance—46,367. Umpires—HP, Berry. 1B, Gorman. 2B, Flaherty. 3B, Barlick.

Game 7
Thursday, October 9

Yankees	AB	R	H	RBI	BB	K	Avg
Hank Bauer, rf	5	0	0	0	0	1	.323
Gil McDougald, 2b	5	0	2	0	0	0	.321
Mickey Mantle, cf	4	0	0	0	1	1	.250
Yogi Berra, c	4	2	1	0	1	0	.222
Elston Howard, lf	3	2	2	1	0	1	.222
Jerry Lumpe, 3b	3	0	0	0	0	0	.167
Andy Carey, 3b	1	1	1	0	0	0	.083
Bill Skowron, 1b	4	1	2	4	0	0	.259
Tony Kubek, ss	2	0	0	1	1	1	.048
Don Larsen, p	1	0	0	0	0	0	.000
Bob Turley, p	2	0	0	0	0	1	.200
TOTALS	34	6	8	6	3	5	.227

Braves	AB	R	H	RBI	BB	K	Avg
Red Schoendienst, 2b	5	1	1	0	0	0	.300
Bill Bruton, cf	3	0	1	0	1	1	.412
Frank Torre, 1b	2	0	0	0	0	0	.176
Hank Aaron, rf	3	0	1	0	1	0	.333
Wes Covington, lf	4	0	0	1	0	0	.269
Eddie Mathews, 3b	1	0	0	0	3	0	.160
Del Crandall, c	4	1	1	1	0	1	.240
Johnny Logan, ss	4	0	0	0	1	0	.120
Lew Burdette, p	3	0	0	0	0	1	.111
Don McMahon, p	0	0	0	0	0	0	—
Joe Adcock, ph	1	0	1	0	0	0	.308
Felix Mantilla, pr	0	0	0	0	0	0	—
TOTALS	30	2	5	2	6	3	.248

	1	2	3	4	5	6	7	8	9		R	H	E
Yankees	0	2	0	0	0	0	0	4	0		6	8	0
Braves	1	0	0	0	0	1	0	0	0		2	5	2

E—Torre 2. DP—Yankees 1 (McDougald to Skowron). LOB—Yankees 7, Braves 8. Scoring Position—Yankees 2-for-11, Braves 0-for-5. 2B—McDougald (2), Berra (3). HR—Skowron (2), Crandall (1). S—Howard, Torre, Turley. SF—Kubek. GDP—Aaron. SB—Howard (1).

Yankees	IP	H	R	ER	BB	K	ERA
Don Larsen	2.1	3	1	1	3	1	0.96
Bob Turley (W, 2-1)	6.2	2	1	1	3	2	2.76

Braves	IP	H	R	ER	BB	K	ERA
Lew Burdette (L, 1-2)	8.0	7	6	4	2	3	5.64
Don McMahon	1.0	1	0	0	1	2	5.40

Time—2:31. Attendance—46,367. Umpires—HP, Gorman. 1B, Flaherty. 2B, Barlick. 3B, Berry.

1958 World Series—Composite Statistics

Batting

Yankees	G	AB	R	H	RBI	2B	3B	HR	BB	SO	SB	CS	Avg	OBP	Slg
Hank Bauer	7	31	6	10	8	0	0	4	0	5	0	1	.323	.323	.710
Yogi Berra	7	27	3	6	2	3	0	0	1	0	0	0	.222	.241	.333
Andy Carey	5	12	1	1	0	0	0	0	0	3	0	0	.083	.083	.083
Art Ditmar	1	1	0	0	0	0	0	0	0	0	0	0	.000	.000	.000
Ryne Duren	3	3	0	0	0	0	0	0	0	2	0	0	.000	.000	.000
Whitey Ford	3	4	1	0	0	0	0	0	2	2	0	0	.000	.333	.000
Elston Howard	6	18	4	4	2	0	0	0	1	4	1	0	.222	.263	.222
Tony Kubek	7	21	0	1	1	0	0	0	1	7	0	0	.048	.087	.048
Johnny Kucks	2	1	0	1	0	0	0	0	0	0	0	0	1.000	1.000	1.000
Don Larsen	2	2	0	0	0	0	0	0	1	0	0	0	.000	.333	.000
Jerry Lumpe	6	12	0	2	0	0	0	0	1	2	0	1	.167	.231	.167
Mickey Mantle	7	24	4	6	3	0	1	2	7	4	0	0	.250	.419	.583
Gil McDougald	7	28	5	9	4	2	0	2	2	4	0	0	.321	.367	.607
Bobby Richardson	4	5	0	0	0	0	0	0	0	0	0	0	.000	.000	.000
Norm Siebern	3	8	1	1	0	0	0	0	3	2	0	0	.125	.364	.125
Bill Skowron	7	27	3	7	7	0	0	2	1	4	0	0	.259	.286	.481
Enos Slaughter	4	3	1	0	0	0	0	0	0	1	1	0	.000	.250	.000
Marv Throneberry	1	1	0	0	0	0	0	0	0	1	0	0	.000	.000	.000
Bob Turley	4	5	0	1	2	0	0	0	0	1	0	0	.200	.200	.200
Totals	7	233	29	49	29	5	1	10	21	42	1	2	.210	.273	.369

Batting

Braves	G	AB	R	H	RBI	2B	3B	HR	BB	SO	SB	CS	Avg	OBP	Slg
Hank Aaron	7	27	3	9	2	2	0	0	4	6	0	0	.333	.419	.407
Joe Adcock	4	13	1	4	0	0	0	0	1	3	0	0	.308	.357	.308
Bill Bruton	7	17	2	7	2	0	0	1	5	5	0	0	.412	.545	.588
Lew Burdette	3	9	1	1	3	0	0	1	0	3	0	0	.111	.111	.444
Wes Covington	7	26	2	7	4	0	0	0	2	4	0	0	.269	.310	.269
Del Crandall	7	25	4	6	3	0	0	1	3	10	0	0	.240	.310	.360
Harry Hanebrink	2	2	0	0	0	0	0	0	0	0	0	0	.000	.000	.000
Johnny Logan	7	25	3	3	2	2	0	0	2	4	0	0	.120	.185	.200
Felix Mantilla	4	0	1	0	0	0	0	0	0	0	0	0	—	—	—
Eddie Mathews	7	25	3	4	3	2	0	0	6	11	1	0	.160	.323	.240
Andy Pafko	4	9	0	3	1	1	0	0	0	0	0	0	.333	.300	.444
Bob Rush	1	2	0	0	0	0	0	0	0	2	0	0	.000	.000	.000
Red Schoendienst	7	30	5	9	0	3	1	0	2	1	0	0	.300	.344	.467
Warren Spahn	3	12	0	4	3	0	0	0	0	6	0	0	.333	.333	.333
Frank Torre	7	17	0	3	1	0	0	0	2	0	0	0	.176	.263	.176
Casey Wise	2	1	0	0	0	0	0	0	0	1	0	0	.000	.000	.000
Totals	7	240	25	60	24	10	1	3	27	56	1	0	.250	.322	.338

Pitching

Yankees	G	GS	CG	IP	H	R	ER	BB	SO	W-L	Sv-Op	Hld	ERA
Murry Dickson	2	0	0	4.0	4	2	2	0	1	0-0	0-0	0	4.50
Art Ditmar	1	0	0	3.2	2	0	0	0	2	0-0	0-0	0	0.00
Ryne Duren	3	0	0	9.1	7	2	2	6	14	1-1	1-2	0	1.93
Whitey Ford	3	3	0	15.1	19	8	7	5	16	0-1	0-0	0	4.11
Johnny Kucks	2	0	0	4.1	4	1	1	1	0	0-0	0-0	0	2.08
Don Larsen	2	2	0	9.1	9	1	1	6	9	1-0	0-0	0	0.96
Duke Maas	1	0	0	0.1	2	3	3	1	0	0-0	0-0	0	81.00
Zack Monroe	1	0	0	1.0	3	3	3	1	1	0-0	0-0	0	27.00
Bob Turley	4	2	1	16.1	10	5	5	7	13	2-1	1-1	0	2.76
Totals	7	7	1	63.2	60	25	24	27	56	4-3	2-3	0	3.39

Pitching

Braves	G	GS	CG	IP	H	R	ER	BB	SO	W-L	Sv-Op	Hld	ERA
Lew Burdette	3	3	1	22.1	22	17	14	4	12	1-2	0-0	0	5.64
Don McMahon	3	0	0	3.1	3	2	2	3	5	0-0	0-0	0	5.40
Juan Pizarro	1	0	0	1.2	2	1	1	1	3	0-0	0-0	0	5.40
Bob Rush	1	1	0	6.0	3	2	2	5	2	0-1	0-0	0	3.00
Warren Spahn	3	3	2	28.2	19	7	7	8	18	2-1	0-0	0	2.20
Carl Willey	1	0	0	1.0	0	0	0	0	2	0-0	0-0	0	0.00
Totals	7	7	3	63.0	49	29	26	21	42	3-4	0-0	0	3.71

Fielding

Yankees	Pos	G	PO	Ast	E	DP	PB	FPct
Hank Bauer	rf	7	7	0	0	0	—	1.000
Yogi Berra	c	7	60	6	0	1	1	1.000
Andy Carey	3b	5	2	6	0	0	—	1.000
Murry Dickson	p	2	0	0	0	0	—	—
Art Ditmar	p	1	1	0	1	0	—	.500
Ryne Duren	p	3	0	1	0	1	—	1.000
Whitey Ford	p	3	1	1	0	0	—	1.000
Elston Howard	lf	5	14	2	0	2	—	1.000
Tony Kubek	ss	7	8	15	2	2	—	.920
Johnny Kucks	p	2	0	0	0	0	—	—
Don Larsen	p	2	1	0	0	0	—	1.000
Jerry Lumpe	3b	3	2	4	0	0	—	1.000
	ss	2	0	1	0	0	—	1.000
Duke Maas	p	1	0	0	0	0	—	—
Mickey Mantle	cf	7	16	0	0	0	—	1.000
Gil McDougald	2b	7	20	22	0	3	—	1.000
Zack Monroe	p	1	0	0	0	0	—	—
Bobby Richardson	3b	4	0	1	0	0	—	1.000
Norm Siebern	lf	3	5	0	0	0	—	1.000
Bill Skowron	1b	7	54	4	0	4	—	1.000
Bob Turley	p	4	0	1	0	0	—	1.000
Totals		7	191	64	3	13	1	.988

Fielding

Braves	Pos	G	PO	Ast	E	DP	PB	FPct
Hank Aaron	rf	7	13	0	0	0	—	1.000
	cf	1	2	0	0	0	—	1.000
Joe Adcock	1b	3	23	2	0	0	—	1.000
Bill Bruton	cf	7	12	0	1	0	—	.923
Lew Burdette	p	3	2	2	0	0	—	1.000
Wes Covington	lf	7	10	1	0	0	—	1.000
Del Crandall	c	7	43	5	0	2	0	1.000
Johnny Logan	ss	7	10	24	2	2	—	.944
Felix Mantilla	ss	1	0	0	0	0	—	—
Eddie Mathews	3b	7	5	12	1	1	—	.944
Don McMahon	p	3	1	0	0	0	—	1.000
Andy Pafko	cf	2	7	0	0	0	—	1.000
	lf	2	1	0	0	0	—	1.000
	rf	1	0	0	0	0	—	—
Juan Pizarro	p	1	0	1	0	0	—	1.000
Bob Rush	p	1	0	3	0	0	—	1.000
Red Schoendienst	2b	7	19	19	1	3	—	.974
Warren Spahn	p	3	2	6	0	0	—	1.000
Frank Torre	1b	5	39	2	2	4	—	.953
Carl Willey	p	1	0	0	0	0	—	—
Totals		7	189	77	7	12	0	.974

1959 Los Angeles Dodgers (NL) 4, Chicago White Sox (AL) 2

The Los Angeles Dodgers were routed by the Chicago White Sox in the opener, but the Dodgers took three close games in a row and finished with a resounding win for a six-game World Series victory. Ted Kluszewski drove in five runs in Game 1 with a single and a pair of two-run homers as Early Wynn shut down the Dodgers for an 11-0 victory. Charlie Neal saved the Dodgers in Game 2, launching a solo homer in the fifth and adding a two-run shot in the seventh to plate the winning runs in the Dodgers' 4-3 win. A record 92,394 fans watched Don Drysdale pitch the Dodgers to a 3-1 victory in Game 3. Gil Hodges' eighth-inning solo homer was the difference in the Dodgers' 5-4 win in Game 4, but Bob Shaw kept the Chisox alive with a 1-0 win over Sandy Koufax in Game 5. The Dodgers erupted for three homers in Game 6, wrapping up the title with a 9-3 win.

Game 1

Thursday, October 1

Dodgers	AB	R	H	RBI	BB	K	Avg
Jim Gilliam, 3b	4	0	1	0	0	1	.250
Charlie Neal, 2b	4	0	2	0	0	0	.500
Wally Moon, lf	4	0	1	0	0	0	.250
Duke Snider, cf	2	0	0	0	1	0	.000
Don Demeter, cf	1	0	0	0	0	0	.000
Norm Larker, rf	4	0	1	0	0	1	.250
Gil Hodges, 1b	4	0	2	0	0	0	.500
John Roseboro, c	4	0	0	0	0	1	.000
Maury Wills, ss	3	0	1	0	0	1	.333
Carl Furillo, ph	1	0	0	0	0	0	.000
Roger Craig, p	1	0	0	0	0	1	.000
Chuck Churn, p	0	0	0	0	0	0	—
Clem Labine, p	0	0	0	0	0	0	—
Chuck Essegian, ph	1	0	0	0	0	1	.000
Sandy Koufax, p	0	0	0	0	0	0	—
Ron Fairly, ph	1	0	0	0	0	0	.000
Johnny Klippstein, p	0	0	0	0	0	0	—
TOTALS	34	0	8	0	1	7	.235

White Sox	AB	R	H	RBI	BB	K	Avg
Luis Aparicio, ss	5	0	0	0	0	0	.000
Nellie Fox, 2b	4	2	1	0	1	0	.250
Jim Landis, cf	4	3	3	1	0	0	.750
Ted Kluszewski, 1b	4	2	3	5	0	0	.750
Sherm Lollar, c	3	1	0	1	0	0	.000
Billy Goodman, 3b	2	1	1	1	0	0	.500
Sammy Esposito, 3b	2	0	0	0	0	1	.000
Al Smith, lf	4	1	2	0	0	1	.500
Jim Rivera, rf	4	1	0	0	0	1	.000
Early Wynn, p	3	0	1	1	0	1	.333
Gerry Staley, p	1	0	0	0	0	1	.000
TOTALS	36	11	11	9	1	5	.306

	1	2	3	4	5	6	7	8	9		R	H	E
Dodgers	0	0	0	0	0	0	0	0	0		0	8	3
White Sox	2	0	7	2	0	0	0	0	x		11	11	0

E—Neal, Snider 2. DP—White Sox 1 (Aparicio to Fox to Kluszewski). LOB—Dodgers 8, White Sox 3. Scoring Position—Dodgers 0-for-6, White Sox 4-for-8. 2B—Fox (1), Smith 2 (2), Wynn (1). HR—Kluszewski 2 (2). SF—Lollar. GDP—Neal. SB—Neal (1).

Dodgers	IP	H	R	ER	BB	K	ERA
Roger Craig (L, 0-1)	2.1	5	5	5	1	1	19.29
Chuck Churn	0.2	5	6	2	0	0	27.00
Clem Labine	1.0	0	0	0	0	1	0.00
Sandy Koufax	2.0	0	0	0	0	1	0.00
Johnny Klippstein	2.0	1	0	0	0	2	0.00

White Sox	IP	H	R	ER	BB	K	ERA
Early Wynn (W, 1-0)	7.0	6	0	0	1	6	0.00
Gerry Staley (S, 1)	2.0	2	0	0	0	1	0.00

Churn pitched to two batters in the 4th. Wynn pitched to one batter in the 8th.

Time—2:35. Attendance—48,013. Umpires—HP, Summers. 1B, Dascoli. 2B, Hurley. 3B, Secory.

Game 2

Friday, October 2

Dodgers	AB	R	H	RBI	BB	K	Avg
Jim Gilliam, 3b	4	1	1	0	1	0	.250
Charlie Neal, 2b	5	2	2	3	0	0	.444
Wally Moon, lf	3	0	1	0	1	0	.286
Duke Snider, cf	4	0	1	0	0	0	.167
Don Demeter, cf	0	0	0	0	0	0	.000
Norm Larker, rf	3	0	0	0	0	0	.143
Larry Sherry, p	1	0	0	0	0	1	.000
Gil Hodges, 1b	4	0	0	0	0	1	.250
John Roseboro, c	4	0	1	0	0	1	.125
Maury Wills, ss	4	0	1	0	0	0	.286
Johnny Podres, p	2	0	1	0	0	0	.500
Chuck Essegian, ph	1	1	1	1	0	0	.500
Ron Fairly, rf	1	0	0	0	0	0	.000
TOTALS	36	4	9	4	2	4	.250

White Sox	AB	R	H	RBI	BB	K	Avg
Luis Aparicio, ss	5	1	2	0	0	0	.200
Nellie Fox, 2b	4	0	0	0	1	0	.125
Jim Landis, cf	3	1	0	0	1	1	.429
Ted Kluszewski, 1b	4	0	1	1	0	0	.500
Earl Torgeson, pr-1b	0	1	0	0	0	0	—
Sherm Lollar, c	4	0	2	1	0	1	.286
Al Smith, lf	3	0	1	1	1	0	.429
Bubba Phillips, 3b	3	0	1	0	0	0	.333
Billy Goodman, ph-3b	1	0	0	0	0	1	.333
Jim McAnany, rf	3	0	0	0	0	0	.000
Jim Rivera, rf	1	0	0	0	0	0	.000
Bob Shaw, p	3	0	1	0	0	1	.333
Turk Lown, p	0	0	0	0	0	0	—
Norm Cash, ph	1	0	0	0	0	0	.000
TOTALS	35	3	8	3	3	4	.277

	1	2	3	4	5	6	7	8	9		R	H	E
Dodgers	0	0	0	0	1	0	3	0	0		4	9	1
White Sox	2	0	0	0	0	0	0	1	0		3	8	0

E—Wills. LOB—Dodgers 7, White Sox 8. Scoring Position—Dodgers 1-for-4, White Sox 2-for-10. 2B—Aparicio (1), Smith (3), Phillips (1). HR—Neal 2 (2), Essegian (1). SB—Gilliam (1), Moon (1).

Dodgers	IP	H	R	ER	BB	K	ERA
Johnny Podres (W, 1-0)	6.0	5	2	2	3	3	3.00
Larry Sherry (S, 1)	3.0	3	1	1	0	1	3.00

White Sox	IP	H	R	ER	BB	K	ERA
Bob Shaw (L, 0-1)	6.2	8	4	4	1	1	5.40
Turk Lown	2.1	1	0	0	1	3	0.00

Time—2:21. Attendance—47,368. Umpires—HP, Dascoli. 1B, Hurley. 2B, Secory. 3B, Summers.

Game 3

Sunday, October 4

White Sox	AB	R	H	RBI	BB	K	Avg
Luis Aparicio, ss	4	0	2	0	1	2	.286
Nellie Fox, 2b	4	0	3	0	1	0	.333
Jim Landis, cf	5	0	1	0	0	3	.333
Ted Kluszewski, 1b	3	1	1	0	1	0	.455
Sherm Lollar, c	4	0	2	0	0	0	.364
Billy Goodman, 3b	3	0	2	0	0	0	.500
Sammy Esposito, pr-3b	0	0	0	0	0	0	.000
Al Smith, lf	4	0	0	0	0	1	.273
Jim Rivera, rf	3	0	0	0	1	0	.000
Dick Donovan, p	3	0	1	0	0	1	.333
Gerry Staley, p	0	0	0	0	0	0	.000
Norm Cash, ph	1	0	0	0	0	1	.000
TOTALS	34	1	12	0	4	8	.301

Dodgers	AB	R	H	RBI	BB	K	Avg
Jim Gilliam, 3b	4	0	0	0	0	0	.167
Charlie Neal, 2b	4	1	2	1	0	0	.462
Wally Moon, rf	4	0	0	0	0	0	.182
Norm Larker, lf	2	1	0	0	1	1	.111
Gil Hodges, 1b	2	0	1	0	1	1	.300
Don Demeter, cf	2	0	0	0	0	0	.000
Carl Furillo, ph	1	0	1	2	0	0	.500
Ron Fairly, pr-cf	0	0	0	0	0	0	.000
John Roseboro, c	3	0	0	0	0	0	.091
Maury Wills, ss	3	1	1	0	0	1	.300
Don Drysdale, p	2	0	0	0	0	2	.000
Larry Sherry, p	0	0	0	0	0	0	.000
TOTALS	27	3	5	3	2	5	.221

	1	2	3	4	5	6	7	8	9		R	H	E
White Sox	0	0	0	0	0	0	1	0			1	12	0
Dodgers	0	0	0	0	0	0	2	1	x		3	5	0

DP—White Sox 1 (Aparicio to Fox to Kluszewski), Dodgers 3 (Roseboro to Neal; Gilliam to Neal to Hodges; Wills to Neal to Hodges). LOB—White Sox 11, Dodgers 3. Scoring Position—White Sox 0-for-7, Dodgers 2-for-5. 2B—Neal (1). S—Sherry. GDP—Smith 2, Demeter. CS—Aparicio (1), Fox (1), Rivera (1).

White Sox	IP	H	R	ER	BB	K	ERA
Dick Donovan (L, 0-1)	6.2	2	2	2	2	5	2.70
Gerry Staley	1.1	3	1	1	0	0	2.70

Dodgers	IP	H	R	ER	BB	K	ERA
Don Drysdale (W, 1-0)	7.0	11	1	1	4	5	1.29
Larry Sherry (S, 2)	2.0	1	0	0	0	3	1.80

Drysdale pitched to two batters in the 8th.

HBP—Goodman by Sherry. Time—2:33. Attendance—92,394. Umpires—HP, Hurley. 1B, Secory. 2B, Summers. 3B, Dascoli.

Game 4
Monday, October 5

White Sox	AB	R	H	RBI	BB	K	Avg
Jim Landis, cf	5	1	1	0	0	1	.294
Luis Aparicio, ss	3	0	1	0	1	0	.294
Nellie Fox, 2b	5	1	3	0	0	1	.412
Ted Kluszewski, 1b	4	1	2	1	1	0	.467
Sherm Lollar, c	4	1	1	3	0	1	.333
Billy Goodman, 3b	4	0	0	0	0	3	.300
Al Smith, lf	3	0	2	0	1	0	.357
Jim Rivera, rf	3	0	0	0	1	0	.000
Early Wynn, p	1	0	0	0	0	0	.250
Turk Lown, p	0	0	0	0	0	0	—
Norm Cash, ph	1	0	0	0	0	1	.000
Billy Pierce, p	0	0	0	0	0	0	—
Earl Torgeson, ph	1	0	0	0	0	0	.000
Gerry Staley, p	0	0	0	0	1	0	.000
TOTALS	34	4	10	4	5	7	.304

Dodgers	AB	R	H	RBI	BB	K	Avg
Jim Gilliam, 3b	4	0	0	0	0	0	.125
Charlie Neal, 2b	4	0	0	0	0	0	.353
Wally Moon, rf-lf	4	1	2	0	0	1	.267
Norm Larker, lf	2	1	1	0	0	1	.182
Carl Furillo, ph-rf	1	0	0	0	0	0	.333
Ron Fairly, rf	1	0	0	0	0	1	.000
Gil Hodges, 1b	4	2	2	2	0	0	.357
Don Demeter, cf	3	1	2	0	1	1	.333
John Roseboro, c	3	0	1	1	0	0	.143
Maury Wills, ss	4	0	1	0	0	0	.286
Roger Craig, p	2	0	0	0	0	1	.000
Larry Sherry, p	0	0	0	0	0	0	.000
TOTALS	32	5	9	3	1	6	.239

	1 2 3	4 5 6	7 8 9	R	H	E
White Sox	0 0 0	0 0 0	4 0 0	4	10	3
Dodgers	0 0 4	0 0 0	0 1 x	5	9	0

E—Landis, Aparicio, Pierce. DP—Dodgers 2 (Wills to Neal to Hodges; Neal to Wills to Hodges). LOB—White Sox 9, Dodgers 6. Scoring Position—White Sox 4-for-8, Dodgers 3-for-7. 2B—Fox (2). HR—Lollar (1), Hodges (1). S—Aparicio, Roseboro, Craig. GDP—Kluszewski, Lollar. SB—Aparicio (1), Wills (1).

White Sox	IP	H	R	ER	BB	K	ERA
Early Wynn	2.2	8	4	3	0	2	2.79
Turk Lown	0.1	0	0	0	0	0	0.00
Billy Pierce	3.0	0	0	0	1	2	0.00
Gerry Staley (L, 0-1)	2.0	1	1	1	0	2	3.38

Dodgers	IP	H	R	ER	BB	K	ERA
Roger Craig	7.0	10	4	4	4	7	8.68
Larry Sherry (W, 1-0)	2.0	0	0	0	1	0	1.29

PB—Lollar. Time—2:30. Attendance—92,650. Umpires—HP, Secory. 1B, Summers. 2B, Dascoli. 3B, Hurley.

Game 5
Tuesday, October 6

White Sox	AB	R	H	RBI	BB	K	Avg
Luis Aparicio, ss	4	0	2	0	0	1	.333
Nellie Fox, 2b	3	1	1	0	1	0	.400
Jim Landis, cf	4	0	1	0	0	2	.286
Sherm Lollar, c	4	0	0	0	0	1	.263
Ted Kluszewski, 1b	4	0	0	0	0	0	.368
Al Smith, rf-lf	4	0	0	0	0	2	.278
Bubba Phillips, 3b	3	0	1	0	0	0	.333
Jim McAnany, lf	1	0	0	0	1	0	.000
Jim Rivera, rf	0	0	0	0	1	0	.000
Bob Shaw, p	1	0	0	0	0	1	.250
Billy Pierce, p	0	0	0	0	0	0	—
Dick Donovan, p	0	0	0	0	0	0	.333
TOTALS	28	1	5	0	3	7	.288

Dodgers	AB	R	H	RBI	BB	K	Avg
Jim Gilliam, 3b	5	0	4	0	0	0	.286
Charlie Neal, 2b	5	0	1	0	0	0	.318
Wally Moon, rf-cf	4	0	1	0	0	0	.263
Norm Larker, lf	4	0	0	0	0	0	.133
Gil Hodges, 1b	4	0	3	0	0	0	.444
Don Demeter, cf	3	0	0	0	0	0	.222
Ron Fairly, rf	0	0	0	0	0	0	.000
Rip Repulski, ph-rf	0	0	0	0	1	0	—
John Roseboro, c	3	0	0	0	0	0	.118
Carl Furillo, ph	1	0	0	0	0	0	.250
Joe Pignatano, c	0	0	0	0	0	0	—
Maury Wills, ss	2	0	0	0	0	0	.250
Chuck Essegian, ph	0	0	0	0	1	0	.500
Don Zimmer, pr-ss	1	0	0	0	0	0	.000
Sandy Koufax, p	2	0	0	0	0	1	.000
Duke Snider, ph	1	0	0	0	0	0	.143
Johnny Podres, pr	0	0	0	0	0	0	.500
Stan Williams, p	0	0	0	0	0	0	—
Larry Sherry, ph	1	0	0	0	0	0	.000
TOTALS	36	0	9	0	2	1	.250

	1 2 3	4 5 6	7 8 9	R	H	E
White Sox	0 0 0	1 0 0	0 0 0	1	5	0
Dodgers	0 0 0	0 0 0	0 0 0	0	9	0

DP—Dodgers 1 (Neal to Hodges). LOB—White Sox 5, Dodgers 11. Scoring Position—White Sox 1-for-4, Dodgers 0-for-9. 3B—Hodges (1). S—Shaw 2. GDP—Lollar. SB—Gilliam (2).

White Sox	IP	H	R	ER	BB	K	ERA
Bob Shaw (W, 1-1)	7.1	9	0	0	1	1	2.57
Billy Pierce	0.0	0	0	0	1	0	0.00
Dick Donovan (S, 1)	1.2	0	0	0	0	0	2.16

Dodgers	IP	H	R	ER	BB	K	ERA
Sandy Koufax (L, 0-1)	7.0	5	1	1	1	6	1.00
Stan Williams	2.0	0	0	0	2	1	0.00

Pierce pitched to one batter in the 8th.

WP—Shaw. Time—2:28. Attendance—92,706. Umpires—HP, Summers. 1B, Dascoli. 2B, Hurley. 3B, Secori.

Game 6
Thursday, October 8

Dodgers	AB	R	H	RBI	BB	K	Avg
Jim Gilliam, 3b	4	1	0	0	1	1	.240
Charlie Neal, 2b	5	1	3	2	0	1	.370
Wally Moon, lf	4	2	1	2	1	1	.261
Duke Snider, cf-rf	3	1	1	2	1	0	.200
Chuck Essegian, ph	1	1	1	1	0	0	.667
Ron Fairly, rf	0	0	0	0	0	0	.000
Gil Hodges, 1b	5	0	1	0	0	0	.391
Norm Larker, rf	1	0	1	0	1	0	.188
Don Demeter, pr-cf	3	1	1	0	0	1	.250
John Roseboro, c	4	0	0	0	0	0	.095
Maury Wills, ss	4	1	1	1	0	0	.250
Johnny Podres, p	2	1	1	1	0	0	.500
Larry Sherry, p	2	0	2	0	0	0	.500
TOTALS	38	9	13	9	4	4	.272

White Sox	AB	R	H	RBI	BB	K	Avg
Luis Aparicio, ss	5	0	1	0	0	0	.308
Nellie Fox, 2b	4	0	1	0	0	0	.375
Jim Landis, cf	3	1	1	0	0	0	.292
Sherm Lollar, c	3	1	0	0	1	0	.227
Ted Kluszewski, 1b	4	1	2	3	0	0	.391
Al Smith, lf	2	0	0	2	0	0	.250
Bubba Phillips, 3b-rf	4	0	1	0	0	0	.300
Jim McAnany, rf	1	0	0	0	0	0	.000
Billy Goodman, ph-3b	3	0	0	0	0	1	.231
Early Wynn, p	1	0	0	0	1	0	.200
Dick Donovan, p	0	0	0	0	0	0	.333
Turk Lown, p	0	0	0	0	0	0	—
Earl Torgeson, ph	0	0	0	0	1	0	.000
Gerry Staley, p	0	0	0	0	0	0	.000
John Romano, c	1	0	0	0	0	0	.000
Billy Pierce, p	0	0	0	0	0	0	—
Ray Moore, p	0	0	0	0	0	0	—
Norm Cash, ph	1	0	0	0	0	0	.000
TOTALS	32	3	6	3	4	2	.280

	1 2 3	4 5 6	7 8 9	R	H	E
Dodgers	0 0 2	6 0 0	0 0 1	9	13	0
White Sox	0 0 0	3 0 0	0 0 0	3	6	1

E—Aparicio. DP—Dodgers 1 (Podres to Neal to Hodges). LOB—Dodgers 7, White Sox 7. Scoring Position—Dodgers 3-for-7, White Sox 1-for-8. 2B—Neal (2), Podres (1), Fox (3), Kluszewski (1). HR—Moon (1), Snider (1), Kluszewski (3), Essegian (2). S—Roseboro. GDP—Phillips. CS—Demeter (1).

Dodgers	IP	H	R	ER	BB	K	ERA
Johnny Podres	3.1	2	3	3	3	1	4.82
Larry Sherry (W, 2-0)	5.2	4	0	0	1	1	0.71

White Sox	IP	H	R	ER	BB	K	ERA
Early Wynn (L, 1-1)	3.1	5	5	5	3	2	5.54
Dick Donovan	0.0	2	3	3	1	0	5.40
Turk Lown	0.2	1	0	0	0	0	0.00
Gerry Staley	3.0	2	0	0	0	0	2.16
Billy Pierce	1.0	2	0	0	0	1	0.00
Ray Moore	1.0	1	1	1	0	1	9.00

Donovan pitched to three batters in the 4th.

HBP—Landis by Podres. Time—2:33. Attendance—47,653. Umpires—HP, Dascoli. 1B, Hurley. 2B, Secory. 3B, Summers.

1959 World Series—Composite Statistics

Batting

Dodgers	G	AB	R	H	RBI	2B	3B	HR	BB	SO	SB	CS	Avg	OBP	Slg
Roger Craig	2	3	0	0	0	0	0	0	0	2	0	0	.000	.000	.000
Don Demeter	6	12	2	3	0	0	0	0	1	3	0	1	.250	.308	.250
Don Drysdale	1	2	0	0	0	0	0	0	0	2	0	0	.000	.000	.000
Chuck Essegian	4	3	2	2	2	0	0	2	1	1	0	0	.667	.750	2.667
Ron Fairly	6	3	0	0	0	0	0	0	0	1	0	0	.000	.000	.000
Carl Furillo	4	4	0	1	2	0	0	0	0	1	0	0	.250	.250	.250
Jim Gilliam	6	25	2	6	0	0	0	0	2	2	2	0	.240	.296	.240
Gil Hodges	6	23	2	9	2	0	1	1	1	2	0	0	.391	.417	.609
Sandy Koufax	2	2	0	0	0	0	0	0	0	1	0	0	.000	.000	.000
Norm Larker	6	16	2	3	0	0	0	0	2	3	0	0	.188	.278	.188
Wally Moon	6	23	3	6	2	0	0	1	2	2	1	0	.261	.320	.391
Charlie Neal	6	27	4	10	6	2	0	2	0	1	1	0	.370	.370	.667
Johnny Podres	3	4	1	2	1	1	0	0	0	1	0	0	.500	.500	.750
Rip Repulski	1	0	0	0	0	0	0	0	1	0	0	0	—	1.000	—
John Roseboro	6	21	0	2	1	0	0	0	0	2	0	0	.095	.095	.095
Larry Sherry	5	4	0	2	0	0	0	0	0	1	0	0	.500	.500	.500
Duke Snider	4	10	1	2	2	0	0	1	2	0	0	0	.200	.333	.200
Maury Wills	6	20	2	5	1	0	0	0	0	3	1	0	.250	.250	.250
Don Zimmer	1	1	0	0	0	0	0	0	0	0	0	0	.000	.000	.000
Totals	6	203	21	53	19	3	1	7	12	27	5	1	.261	.302	.389

Batting

White Sox	G	AB	R	H	RBI	2B	3B	HR	BB	SO	SB	CS	Avg	OBP	Slg
Luis Aparicio	6	26	1	8	0	1	0	0	2	3	1	1	.308	.357	.346
Norm Cash	4	4	0	0	0	0	0	0	0	2	0	0	.000	.000	.000
Dick Donovan	3	3	0	1	0	0	0	0	0	1	0	0	.333	.333	.333
Sammy Esposito	2	2	0	0	0	0	0	0	0	1	0	0	.000	.000	.000
Nellie Fox	6	24	4	9	0	3	0	0	4	1	0	1	.375	.464	.500
Billy Goodman	5	13	1	3	1	0	0	0	0	5	0	0	.231	.286	.231
Ted Kluszewski	6	23	5	9	10	1	0	3	2	0	0	0	.391	.440	.826
Jim Landis	6	24	6	7	1	0	0	0	1	7	0	0	.292	.346	.292
Sherm Lollar	6	22	3	5	5	0	0	1	1	3	0	0	.227	.250	.364
Jim McAnany	3	5	0	0	0	0	0	0	1	0	0	0	.000	.167	.000
Bubba Phillips	3	10	0	3	0	1	0	0	0	0	0	0	.300	.300	.400
Jim Rivera	5	11	1	0	0	0	0	0	3	1	0	1	.000	.214	.000
John Romano	1	1	0	0	0	0	0	0	0	0	0	0	.000	.000	.000
Bob Shaw	2	4	0	1	0	0	0	0	0	2	0	0	.250	.250	.250
Al Smith	6	20	1	5	1	3	0	0	4	4	0	0	.250	.375	.400
Gerry Staley	4	1	0	0	0	0	0	0	0	1	0	0	.000	.500	.000
Earl Torgeson	3	1	1	0	0	0	0	0	1	0	0	0	.000	.500	.000
Early Wynn	3	5	0	1	1	1	0	0	0	2	0	0	.200	.200	.400
Totals	6	199	23	52	19	10	0	4	20	33	1	3	.261	.333	.372

Pitching

Dodgers	G	GS	CG	IP	H	R	ER	BB	SO	W-L	Sv-Op	Hld	ERA
Chuck Churn	1	0	0	0.2	5	6	2	0	0	0-0	0-0	0	27.00
Roger Craig	2	2	0	9.1	15	9	9	5	8	0-1	0-0	0	8.68
Don Drysdale	1	1	0	7.0	11	1	1	4	5	1-0	0-0	0	1.29
Johnny Klippstein	1	0	0	2.0	1	0	0	0	2	0-0	0-0	0	0.00
Sandy Koufax	2	1	0	9.0	5	1	1	1	7	0-1	0-0	0	1.00
Clem Labine	1	0	0	1.0	0	0	0	0	1	0-0	0-0	0	0.00
Johnny Podres	2	2	0	9.1	7	5	5	6	4	1-0	0-0	0	4.82
Larry Sherry	4	0	0	12.2	8	1	1	2	5	2-0	2-2	0	0.71
Stan Williams	1	0	0	2.0	0	0	0	2	1	0-0	0-0	0	0.00
Totals	6	6	0	53.0	52	23	19	20	33	4-2	2-2	0	3.23

Pitching

White Sox	G	GS	CG	IP	H	R	ER	BB	SO	W-L	Sv-Op	Hld	ERA
Dick Donovan	3	1	0	8.1	4	5	5	3	5	0-1	1-1	0	5.40
Turk Lown	3	0	0	3.1	2	0	0	1	3	0-0	0-0	0	0.00
Ray Moore	1	0	0	1.0	1	1	1	0	1	0-0	0-0	0	9.00
Billy Pierce	3	0	0	4.0	2	0	0	2	3	0-0	0-0	0	0.00
Bob Shaw	2	2	0	14.0	17	4	4	2	2	1-1	0-0	0	2.57
Gerry Staley	4	0	0	8.1	8	2	2	0	3	0-1	1-1	0	2.16
Early Wynn	3	3	0	13.0	19	9	8	4	10	1-1	0-0	0	5.54
Totals	6	6	0	52.0	53	21	20	12	27	2-4	2-2	0	3.46

Fielding

Dodgers	Pos	G	PO	Ast	E	DP	PB	FPct
Chuck Churn	p	1	0	1	0	0	—	1.000
Roger Craig	p	2	0	2	0	0	—	1.000
Don Demeter	cf	6	9	0	0	0	—	1.000
Don Drysdale	p	1	1	1	0	0	—	1.000
Ron Fairly	rf	3	0	0	0	0	—	—
	cf	1	0	0	0	0	—	—
Carl Furillo	rf	1	0	0	0	0	—	—
Jim Gilliam	3b	6	4	10	0	1	—	1.000
Gil Hodges	1b	6	53	3	0	6	—	1.000
Johnny Klippstein	p	1	0	1	0	0	—	1.000
Sandy Koufax	p	2	0	0	0	0	—	—
Clem Labine	p	1	0	0	0	0	—	—
Norm Larker	rf	3	8	0	0	0	—	1.000
	lf	3	4	1	0	0	—	1.000
Wally Moon	lf	4	8	1	0	0	—	1.000
	rf	3	2	0	0	0	—	1.000
	cf	1	0	0	0	0	—	—
Charlie Neal	2b	6	18	19	1	7	—	.974
Joe Pignatano	c	1	1	0	0	0	0	1.000
Johnny Podres	p	2	0	1	0	1	—	1.000
Rip Repulski	rf	1	0	0	0	0	—	—
John Roseboro	c	6	35	4	0	1	0	1.000
Larry Sherry	p	4	1	3	0	0	—	1.000
Duke Snider	cf	3	3	0	2	0	—	.600
	rf	1	2	0	0	0	—	1.000
Stan Williams	p	1	0	0	0	0	—	—
Maury Wills	ss	6	10	21	1	3	—	.969
Don Zimmer	ss	1	0	1	0	0	—	1.000
Totals		6	159	69	4	19	0	.983

Fielding

White Sox	Pos	G	PO	Ast	E	DP	PB	FPct
Luis Aparicio	ss	6	10	16	2	2	—	.929
Dick Donovan	p	3	1	1	0	0	—	1.000
Sammy Esposito	3b	2	1	0	0	0	—	1.000
Nellie Fox	2b	6	14	23	0	2	—	1.000
Billy Goodman	3b	5	1	2	0	0	—	1.000
Ted Kluszewski	1b	6	58	3	0	2	—	1.000
Jim Landis	cf	6	9	0	1	0	—	.900
Sherm Lollar	c	6	29	5	0	0	1	1.000
Turk Lown	p	3	0	0	0	0	—	—
Jim McAnany	rf	2	4	0	0	0	—	1.000
	lf	1	1	0	0	0	—	1.000
Ray Moore	p	1	0	0	0	0	—	—
Bubba Phillips	3b	3	3	3	0	0	—	1.000
	rf	1	3	0	0	0	—	1.000
Billy Pierce	p	3	0	0	1	0	—	.000
Jim Rivera	rf	5	10	0	0	0	—	1.000
Bob Shaw	p	2	0	4	0	0	—	1.000
Al Smith	lf	6	10	0	0	0	—	1.000
	rf	1	0	0	0	0	—	—
Gerry Staley	p	4	1	1	0	0	—	1.000
Earl Torgeson	1b	1	0	0	0	0	—	—
Early Wynn	p	3	1	3	0	0	—	1.000
Totals		6	156	61	4	6	1	.982

1960 Pittsburgh Pirates (NL) 4, New York Yankees (AL) 3

Bill Mazeroski won the seventh game of the World Series with a homer in the bottom of the ninth as the Pittsburgh Pirates squeaked by the New York Yankees in one of the most wild World Series ever played. Pittsburgh won the opener 6-4 behind Vern Law, but the Yankees took Game 2, 16-3, in one of the most lopsided contests in World Series history. Mickey Mantle homered twice and drove in five runs. In Game 3, Mantle singled twice, doubled and homered as Whitey Ford blanked the Bucs on four hits. Law won the fourth game, 3-2, doubling in the tying run himself. Harvey Haddix and Elroy Face stopped the Yanks in Game 5, 5-2, but New York came back to hand the Pirates a 12-0 drubbing in Game 6. Ford tossed his second straight shutout, and Bobby Richardson drove in three runs with a pair of triples. Game 7 was a classic see-saw battle that Mazeroski ultimately won with his leadoff home run in the bottom of the ninth.

Game 1

Wednesday, October 5

Yankees	AB	R	H	RBI	BB	K	Avg
Tony Kubek, ss	5	0	3	0	0	0	.600
Hector Lopez, lf	5	0	1	0	0	0	.200
Roger Maris, rf	4	2	3	1	0	0	.750
Mickey Mantle, cf	3	0	0	0	1	2	.000
Yogi Berra, c	4	0	1	0	0	0	.250
Bill Skowron, 1b	4	0	2	1	0	2	.500
Clete Boyer, 3b	0	0	0	0	0	0	—
Dale Long, ph	1	0	0	0	0	0	.000
Gil McDougald, 3b	3	0	1	0	0	0	.333
Bobby Richardson, 2b	4	1	0	0	0	0	.000
Art Ditmar, p	0	0	0	0	0	0	—
Jim Coates, p	1	0	0	0	0	1	.000
Johnny Blanchard, ph	1	0	0	0	0	0	.000
Duke Maas, p	0	0	0	0	0	0	—
Bob Cerv, ph	1	0	1	0	0	0	1.000
Ryne Duren, p	0	0	0	0	0	0	—
Elston Howard, ph	1	1	1	2	0	0	1.000
TOTALS	37	4	13	4	1	5	.351

Pirates	AB	R	H	RBI	BB	K	Avg
Bill Virdon, cf	3	1	1	1	1	1	.333
Dick Groat, ss	4	1	2	1	0	0	.500
Bob Skinner, lf	3	1	1	1	0	0	.333
Gino Cimoli, lf	0	0	0	0	0	0	—
Dick Stuart, 1b	4	0	1	0	0	1	.250
Roberto Clemente, rf	4	0	1	1	0	0	.250
Smoky Burgess, c	4	0	0	0	0	1	.000
Don Hoak, 3b	2	1	0	0	2	0	.000
Bill Mazeroski, 2b	4	2	2	2	0	1	.500
Vern Law, p	1	0	0	0	0	0	.000
Roy Face, p	1	0	0	0	0	0	.000
TOTALS	30	6	8	6	3	4	.267

	1 2 3	4 5 6	7 8 9	R H E
Yankees	1 0 0	1 0 0	0 0 2	4 13 2
Pirates	3 0 0	2 0 1	0 0 x	6 8 0

E—Kubek, Richardson. DP—Pirates 2 (Mazeroski to Stuart; Skinner to Mazeroski). LOB—Yankees 7, Pirates 6. Scoring Position—Yankees 1-for-10, Pirates 4-for-9. 2B—Virdon (1), Groat (1). HR—Maris (1), Mazeroski (1), Howard (1). S—Law. GDP—Lopez 2. SB—Virdon (1), Skinner (1). CS—Hoak (1).

Yankees	IP	H	R	ER	BB	K	ERA
Art Ditmar (L, 0-1)	0.1	3	3	3	1	0	81.00
Jim Coates	3.2	3	2	2	1	2	4.91
Duke Maas	2.0	2	1	1	0	1	4.50
Ryne Duren	2.0	0	0	0	1	1	0.00

Pirates	IP	H	R	ER	BB	K	ERA
Vern Law (W, 1-0)	7.0	10	2	2	1	3	2.57
Roy Face (S, 1)	2.0	3	2	2	0	2	9.00

Law pitched to two batters in the 8th.

WP—Law. HBP—Skinner by Duren, Law by Coates. Time—2:29. Attendance—36,676. Umpires—HP, Boggess. 1B, Stevens. 2B, Jackowski. 3B, Chylak.

Game 2

Thursday, October 6

Yankees	AB	R	H	RBI	BB	K	Avg
Tony Kubek, ss-lf	6	3	3	1	0	0	.545
Gil McDougald, 3b	3	1	2	2	1	1	.500
Joe DeMaestri, ss	2	1	1	0	0	1	.500
Roger Maris, rf	5	2	1	0	1	2	.444
Mickey Mantle, cf	4	3	2	5	2	2	.286
Yogi Berra, lf	4	1	1	2	0	0	.250
Clete Boyer, 3b	2	0	1	0	0	0	.500
Bill Skowron, 1b	6	1	2	1	0	2	.400
Elston Howard, c	5	1	2	1	0	2	.500
Bobby Richardson, 2b	4	3	3	2	1	0	.375
Bob Turley, p	4	0	1	1	0	1	.250
Bobby Shantz, p	0	0	0	0	0	0	—
TOTALS	45	16	19	15	5	11	.411

Pirates	AB	R	H	RBI	BB	K	Avg
Bill Virdon, cf	5	0	0	0	0	0	.125
Dick Groat, ss	4	0	1	0	0	0	.375
Joe Gibbon, p	0	0	0	0	0	0	—
Tom Cheney, p	0	0	0	0	0	0	—
Joe Christopher, ph	0	1	0	0	0	0	—
Roberto Clemente, rf	5	0	2	0	0	0	.333
Rocky Nelson, 1b	5	1	2	0	0	0	.400
Gino Cimoli, lf	4	1	2	1	0	0	.500
Smoky Burgess, c	4	0	2	0	1	0	.250
Don Hoak, 3b	5	0	2	1	0	0	.286
Bill Mazeroski, 2b	4	0	1	0	0	0	.375
Bob Friend, p	1	0	0	0	0	0	.000
Gene Baker, ph	1	0	0	0	0	0	.000
Fred Green, p	0	0	0	0	0	0	—
Clem Labine, p	0	0	0	0	0	0	—
George Witt, p	0	0	0	0	0	0	—
Dick Schofield, ph-ss	1	0	1	0	1	0	1.000
TOTALS	39	3	13	2	3	0	.317

	1 2 3	4 5 6	7 8 9	R H E
Yankees	0 0 2	1 2 7	3 0 1	16 19 1
Pirates	0 0 0	1 0 0	0 0 2	3 13 1

E—Richardson, Groat. LOB—Yankees 8, Pirates 13. Scoring Position—Yankees 9-for-17, Pirates 4-for-15. 2B—McDougald (1), Richardson (1), Hoak 2 (2), Mazeroski (1), Boyer (1). 3B—Howard (1). HR—Mantle 2 (2). S—Turley. GDP—Hoak. CS—Kubek (1).

Yankees	IP	H	R	ER	BB	K	ERA
Bob Turley (W, 1-0)	8.1	13	3	2	3	0	2.16
Bobby Shantz	0.2	0	0	0	0	0	0.00

Pirates	IP	H	R	ER	BB	K	ERA
Bob Friend (L, 0-1)	4.0	6	3	2	2	6	4.50
Fred Green	1.0	3	4	4	1	0	36.00
Clem Labine	0.2	3	5	0	1	1	0.00
George Witt	0.1	2	0	0	0	0	0.00
Joe Gibbon	2.0	4	3	3	0	2	13.50
Tom Cheney	1.0	1	1	1	1	2	9.00

Green pitched to two batters in the 6th.

WP—Cheney. PB—Burgess 2. HBP—Christopher by Turley. Time—3:14. Attendance—37,308. Umpires—HP, Stevens. 1B, Jackowski. 2B, Chylak. 3B, Boggess.

Game 3

Saturday, October 8

Pirates	AB	R	H	RBI	BB	K	Avg
Bill Virdon, cf	4	0	1	0	0	0	.167
Dick Groat, ss	4	0	0	0	0	0	.250
Roberto Clemente, rf	4	0	1	0	0	1	.308
Dick Stuart, 1b	4	0	1	0	0	1	.250
Gino Cimoli, lf	3	0	0	0	1	1	.286
Hal Smith, c	3	0	0	0	0	0	.000
Don Hoak, 3b	3	0	0	0	0	0	.200
Bill Mazeroski, 2b	3	0	1	0	0	0	.364
Vinegar Bend Mizell, p	0	0	0	0	0	0	—
Clem Labine, p	0	0	0	0	0	0	—
Fred Green, p	1	0	0	0	0	0	.000
George Witt, p	0	0	0	0	0	0	—
Gene Baker, ph	1	0	0	0	0	0	.000
Tom Cheney, p	0	0	0	0	0	0	—
Dick Schofield, ph	1	0	0	0	0	0	.500
Joe Gibbon, p	0	0	0	0	0	0	—
TOTALS	31	0	4	0	1	3	.247

Yankees	AB	R	H	RBI	BB	K	Avg
Bob Cerv, lf	5	1	2	0	0	1	.500
Roger Maris, rf	3	0	0	0	1	0	.333
Yogi Berra, rf	1	0	1	0	0	0	.333
Mickey Mantle, cf	5	2	4	2	0	1	.500
Bill Skowron, 1b	5	2	2	1	0	1	.400
Gil McDougald, 3b	4	2	1	0	1	1	.400
Elston Howard, c	4	1	2	1	1	1	.500
Bobby Richardson, 2b	5	1	2	6	0	1	.385
Tony Kubek, ss	3	0	1	0	1	0	.500
Whitey Ford, p	4	1	1	0	0	1	.250
TOTALS	39	10	16	10	4	7	.419

	1 2 3	4 5 6	7 8 9	R H E
Pirates	0 0 0	0 0 0	0 0 0	0 4 0
Yankees	6 0 0	4 0 0	0 0 x	10 16 1

E—Kubek. DP—Yankees 1 (Ford to Richardson to Skowron). LOB—Pirates 5, Yankees 9. Scoring Position—Pirates 0-for-7, Yankees 6-for-12. 2B—Virdon (2), Mantle (1). HR—Mantle (3), Richardson (1). GDP—Smith. CS—Mantle (1).

Pirates	IP	H	R	ER	BB	K	ERA
Vinegar Bend Mizell (L, 0-1)	0.1	3	4	4	1	0	108.00
Clem Labine	0.1	4	2	2	0	0	18.00
Fred Green	3.0	5	4	4	0	3	18.00
George Witt	1.1	3	0	0	2	1	0.00
Tom Cheney	2.0	1	0	0	0	3	3.00
Joe Gibbon	1.0	0	0	0	1	0	9.00

Yankees	IP	H	R	ER	BB	K	ERA
Whitey Ford (W, 1-0)	9.0	4	0	0	1	3	0.00

WP—Green, Witt. Time—2:41. Attendance—70,001. Umpires—HP, Jackowski. 1B, Chylak. 2B, Boggess. 3B, Stevens.

Game 4

Sunday, October 9

Pirates	AB	R	H	RBI	BB	K	Avg
Bill Virdon, cf	4	0	1	2	0	2	.188
Dick Groat, ss	4	0	0	0	0	0	.188
Roberto Clemente, rf	4	0	1	0	0	2	.294
Dick Stuart, 1b	4	0	0	0	0	0	.167
Gino Cimoli, lf	4	1	1	0	0	0	.273
Smoky Burgess, c	3	1	0	0	1	0	.182
Bob Oldis, c	0	0	0	0	0	0	—
Don Hoak, 3b	4	0	1	0	0	0	.214
Bill Mazeroski, 2b	3	0	1	0	0	1	.357
Vern Law, p	3	1	2	1	0	1	.500
Roy Face, p	1	0	0	0	0	1	.000
TOTALS	34	3	7	3	1	7	.239

Yankees	AB	R	H	RBI	BB	K	Avg
Bob Cerv, lf	4	0	1	0	0	1	.400
Tony Kubek, ss	4	0	1	0	0	1	.444
Roger Maris, rf	4	0	0	0	0	0	.250
Mickey Mantle, cf	3	0	0	0	1	2	.400
Yogi Berra, c	4	0	0	0	0	0	.231
Bill Skowron, 1b	4	2	2	1	0	0	.421
Gil McDougald, 3b	4	0	1	0	0	1	.357
Bobby Richardson, 2b	3	0	2	1	0	0	.438
Dale Long, ph	1	0	0	0	0	0	.000
Ralph Terry, p	2	0	0	0	0	1	.000
Bobby Shantz, p	0	0	0	0	0	0	—
Johnny Blanchard, ph	1	0	1	0	0	0	.500
Joe DeMaestri, pr	0	0	0	0	0	0	.500
Jim Coates, p	0	0	0	0	0	0	.000
TOTALS	34	2	8	2	1	6	.362

	1 2 3	4 5 6	7 8 9	R H E
Pirates	0 0 0	0 3 0	0 0 0	3 7 0
Yankees	0 0 0	1 0 0	1 0 0	2 8 0

DP—Pirates 1 (Hoak to Stuart). LOB—Pirates 6, Yankees 6. Scoring Position—Pirates 3-for-10, Yankees 1-for-7. 2B—Law (1), Kubek (1), Skowron (1), Richardson (2). HR—Skowron (1). S—Mazeroski. GDP—Berra.

Pirates	IP	H	R	ER	BB	K	ERA
Vern Law (W, 2-0)	6.1	8	2	2	1	5	2.70
Roy Face (S, 2)	2.2	0	0	0	0	1	3.86

Yankees	IP	H	R	ER	BB	K	ERA
Ralph Terry (L, 0-1)	6.1	6	3	3	1	5	4.26
Bobby Shantz	0.2	0	0	0	0	1	0.00
Jim Coates	2.0	1	0	0	0	1	3.18

Time—2:29. Attendance—67,812. Umpires—HP, Chylak. 1B, Boggess. 2B, Stevens. 3B, Jackowski.

Game 5
Monday, October 10

Pirates	AB	R	H	RBI	BB	K	Avg
Bill Virdon, cf	5	0	1	0	0	0	.190
Dick Groat, ss	4	1	1	0	0	0	.200
Roberto Clemente, rf	4	0	1	1	0	1	.286
Dick Stuart, 1b	4	0	1	0	0	0	.188
Rocky Nelson, 1b	0	0	0	0	0	0	.400
Gino Cimoli, lf	4	1	0	0	0	2	.200
Smoky Burgess, c	4	1	2	0	0	0	.267
Joe Christopher, pr	0	1	0	0	0	0	—
Bob Oldis, c	0	0	0	0	0	0	—
Don Hoak, 3b	4	1	2	2	0	1	.278
Bill Mazeroski, 2b	4	0	1	2	0	1	.333
Harvey Haddix, p	3	0	1	0	0	1	.333
Roy Face, p	1	0	0	0	0	1	.000
TOTALS	37	5	10	5	0	7	.245

Yankees	AB	R	H	RBI	BB	K	Avg
Gil McDougald, 3b	4	0	0	0	0	0	.278
Roger Maris, rf	4	1	1	1	0	1	.250
Bob Cerv, lf	4	0	1	0	0	1	.357
Mickey Mantle, cf	1	0	0	0	3	1	.375
Bill Skowron, 1b	4	0	0	0	0	1	.348
Elston Howard, c	3	1	1	0	0	1	.462
Yogi Berra, ph-c	1	0	0	0	0	0	.214
Bobby Richardson, 2b	4	0	0	0	0	0	.350
Tony Kubek, ss	4	0	1	1	0	1	.409
Art Ditmar, p	0	0	0	0	0	0	—
Luis Arroyo, p	1	0	0	0	0	0	.000
Bill Stafford, p	1	0	0	0	0	1	.000
Hector Lopez, ph	1	0	1	0	0	0	.333
Ryne Duren, p	0	0	0	0	0	0	—
Johnny Blanchard, ph	1	0	0	0	0	0	.333
TOTALS	33	2	5	2	3	7	.333

	1	2	3	4	5	6	7	8	9		R	H	E
Pirates	0	3	1	0	0	0	0	0	1		5	10	2
Yankees	0	1	1	0	0	0	0	0	0		2	5	2

E—Hoak, Groat, Cerv, McDougald. DP—Pirates 1 (Mazeroski to Stuart), Yankees 1 (Stafford to Kubek to Skowron). LOB—Pirates 5, Yankees 7. Scoring Position—Pirates 3-for-7, Yankees 0-for-5. 2B—Virdon (3), Groat (2), Burgess (1), Mazeroski (2), Howard (1). HR—Maris (2). GDP—Haddix.

Pirates	IP	H	R	ER	BB	K	ERA
Harvey Haddix (W, 1-0)	6.1	5	2	2	2	6	2.84
Roy Face (S, 3)	2.2	0	0	0	1	1	2.45

Yankees	IP	H	R	ER	BB	K	ERA
Art Ditmar (L, 0-2)	1.1	3	3	1	0	0	21.60
Luis Arroyo	0.2	2	1	1	0	1	13.50
Bill Stafford	5.0	3	0	0	0	2	0.00
Ryne Duren	2.0	2	1	1	0	4	2.25

Arroyo pitched to two batters in the 3rd.

WP—Duren. PB—Burgess. Time—2:32. Attendance—62,753. Umpires—HP, Boggess. 1B, Stevens. 2B, Jackowski. 3B, Chylak.

Game 6
Wednesday, October 12

Yankees	AB	R	H	RBI	BB	K	Avg
Clete Boyer, 3b	6	1	1	0	0	1	.250
Tony Kubek, ss-lf	5	2	1	1	0	0	.370
Roger Maris, rf	5	1	3	0	0	0	.320
Mickey Mantle, cf	4	2	1	2	1	1	.350
Yogi Berra, lf	4	3	3	2	1	0	.333
Joe DeMaestri, ss	0	0	0	0	0	0	.500
Bill Skowron, 1b	4	0	2	1	0	0	.370
Elston Howard, c	0	0	0	0	0	0	.462
Eli Grba, pr	0	0	0	0	0	0	—
Johnny Blanchard, c	4	2	3	1	0	0	.571
Bobby Richardson, 2b	5	1	2	3	0	0	.360
Whitey Ford, p	4	0	1	2	0	1	.250
TOTALS	41	12	17	12	2	4	.361

Pirates	AB	R	H	RBI	BB	K	Avg
Bill Virdon, cf	4	0	1	0	0	0	.200
Dick Groat, ss	4	0	1	0	0	1	.208
George Witt, p	0	0	0	0	0	0	—
Roberto Clemente, rf	4	0	2	0	0	0	.320
Dick Stuart, 1b	4	0	0	0	0	1	.150
Gino Cimoli, lf	4	0	1	0	0	1	.211
Hal Smith, c	4	0	2	0	0	0	.286
Don Hoak, 3b	2	0	0	0	1	0	.250
Bill Mazeroski, 2b	3	0	0	0	0	0	.286
Bob Friend, p	0	0	0	0	0	0	.000
Tom Cheney, p	0	0	0	0	0	0	—
Gene Baker, ph	1	0	0	0	0	1	.000
Vinegar Bend Mizell, p	0	0	0	0	0	0	—
Rocky Nelson, ph	1	0	0	0	0	1	.333
Fred Green, p	0	0	0	0	0	0	.000
Clem Labine, p	0	0	0	0	0	0	—
Dick Schofield, ph-ss	1	0	0	0	0	0	.333
TOTALS	32	0	7	0	1	5	.234

	1	2	3	4	5	6	7	8	9		R	H	E
Yankees	0	1	5	0	0	2	2	2	0		12	17	1
Pirates	0	0	0	0	0	0	0	0	0		0	7	1

E—Kubek, Virdon. DP—Yankees 2 (Richardson to Kubek to Skowron; Boyer to Richardson to Skowron), Pirates 2 (Groat to Mazeroski to Stuart; Hoak to Mazeroski to Stuart). LOB—Yankees 8, Pirates 6. Scoring Position—Yankees 8-for-19, Pirates 0-for-2. 2B—Maris (1), Skowron (2), Blanchard 2 (2). 3B—Boyer (1), Richardson 2 (2). S—Ford. SF—Skowron. GDP—Boyer, Skowron, Groat, Smith, Mazeroski.

Yankees	IP	H	R	ER	BB	K	ERA
Whitey Ford (W, 2-0)	9.0	7	0	0	1	5	0.00

Pirates	IP	H	R	ER	BB	K	ERA
Bob Friend (L, 0-2)	2.0	5	5	5	1	1	10.50
Tom Cheney	1.0	2	1	1	0	1	4.50
Vinegar Bend Mizell	2.0	1	0	0	1	1	15.43
Fred Green	0.0	3	2	2	0	0	22.50
Clem Labine	3.0	6	4	4	0	1	13.50
George Witt	1.0	0	0	0	0	0	0.00

Friend pitched to four batters in the 3rd. Green pitched to three batters in the 6th.

WP—Labine. HBP—Kubek by Friend, Howard by Friend. Time—2:38. Attendance—38,580. Umpires—HP, Stevens. 1B, Jackowski. 2B, Chylak. 3B, Boggess.

Game 7
Thursday, October 13

Yankees	AB	R	H	RBI	BB	K	Avg
Bobby Richardson, 2b	5	2	2	0	0	0	.367
Tony Kubek, ss	3	1	0	0	1	0	.333
Joe DeMaestri, ss	0	0	0	0	0	0	.500
Dale Long, ph	1	0	1	0	0	0	.333
Gil McDougald, pr-3b	0	1	0	0	0	0	.278
Roger Maris, rf	5	0	0	0	0	0	.267
Mickey Mantle, cf	5	1	3	2	0	0	.400
Yogi Berra, lf	4	2	1	4	1	0	.318
Bill Skowron, 1b	5	2	2	1	0	0	.375
Johnny Blanchard, c	4	0	1	1	0	0	.455
Clete Boyer, 3b-ss	4	0	1	1	0	0	.250
Bob Turley, p	0	0	0	0	0	0	.250
Bill Stafford, p	0	0	0	0	0	0	.000
Hector Lopez, ph	1	0	1	0	0	0	.429
Bobby Shantz, p	3	0	1	0	0	0	.333
Jim Coates, p	0	0	0	0	0	0	.000
Ralph Terry, p	0	0	0	0	0	0	.000
TOTALS	40	9	13	9	2	0	.335

Pirates	AB	R	H	RBI	BB	K	Avg
Bill Virdon, cf	4	1	2	2	0	0	.241
Dick Groat, ss	4	1	1	1	0	0	.214
Bob Skinner, lf	2	1	0	0	1	0	.200
Rocky Nelson, 1b	3	1	1	2	1	0	.333
Roberto Clemente, rf	4	1	1	1	0	0	.310
Smoky Burgess, c	3	0	2	0	0	0	.333
Joe Christopher, pr	0	0	0	0	0	0	—
Hal Smith, c	1	1	1	3	0	0	.375
Don Hoak, 3b	3	1	0	0	1	0	.217
Bill Mazeroski, 2b	4	2	2	1	0	0	.320
Vern Law, p	2	0	0	0	0	0	.333
Roy Face, p	0	0	0	0	0	0	.000
Gino Cimoli, ph	1	1	1	0	0	0	.250
Bob Friend, p	0	0	0	0	0	0	.000
Harvey Haddix, p	0	0	0	0	0	0	.333
TOTALS	31	10	11	10	3	0	.271

	1	2	3	4	5	6	7	8	9		R	H	E
Yankees	0	0	0	0	1	4	0	2	2		9	13	1
Pirates	2	2	0	0	0	0	0	5	1		10	11	0

E—Maris. DP—Yankees 3 (Stafford to Blanchard to Skowron; Richardson to Kubek to Skowron; Kubek to Richardson to Skowron). LOB—Yankees 6, Pirates 1. Scoring Position—Yankees 5-for-10, Pirates 5-for-8. 2B—Boyer (2). HR—Berra (1), Skowron (2), Nelson (1), Mazeroski (2), Smith (1). S—Skinner. GDP—Clemente, Mazeroski, Law.

Yankees	IP	H	R	ER	BB	K	ERA
Bob Turley	1.0	2	3	3	1	0	4.82
Bill Stafford	1.0	2	1	1	1	0	1.50
Bobby Shantz	5.0	4	3	3	1	0	4.26
Jim Coates (BS, 1)	0.2	2	2	2	0	0	5.68
Ralph Terry (L, 0-2)	0.1	1	1	1	1	0	5.40

Pirates	IP	H	R	ER	BB	K	ERA
Vern Law	5.0	4	3	3	1	0	3.44
Roy Face (BS, 1)	3.0	6	4	4	1	0	5.23
Bob Friend	0.0	2	2	2	0	0	13.50
Harvey Haddix (BS, 1; W, 2-0)	1.0	1	0	0	0	0	2.45

Turley pitched to one batter in the 2nd. Law pitched to two batters in the 6th. Shantz pitched to three batters in the 8th. Friend pitched to two batters in the 9th. Terry pitched to one batter in the 9th.

Time—2:36. Attendance—36,683. Umpires—HP, Jackowski. 1B, Chylak. 2B, Boggess. 3B, Stevens.

1960 World Series—Composite Statistics

Batting

Pirates

Pirates	G	AB	R	H	RBI	2B	3B	HR	BB	SO	SB	CS	Avg	OBP	Slg
Gene Baker	3	3	0	0	0	0	0	0	0	0	1	0	0	.000	.000
Smoky Burgess	5	18	2	6	0	1	0	0	2	1	0	0	.333	.400	.389
Joe Christopher	3	0	2	0	0	0	0	0	0	0	0	0	—	1.000	—
Gino Cimoli	7	20	4	5	1	0	0	0	2	4	0	0	.250	.318	.250
Roberto Clemente	7	29	1	9	3	0	0	0	4	0	0	0	.310	.310	.310
Roy Face	4	3	0	0	0	0	0	0	0	2	0	0	.000	.000	.000
Bob Friend	3	1	0	0	0	0	0	0	0	0	0	0	.000	.000	.000
Fred Green	3	1	0	0	0	0	0	0	0	0	0	0	.000	.000	.000
Dick Groat	7	28	3	6	2	2	0	0	1	0	0	0	.214	.214	.286
Harvey Haddix	2	3	0	1	0	0	0	0	0	1	0	0	.333	.333	.333
Don Hoak	7	23	3	5	3	2	0	0	4	1	0	1	.217	.333	.304
Vern Law	3	6	1	2	1	1	0	0	0	1	0	0	.333	.429	.500
Bill Mazeroski	7	25	4	8	5	2	0	2	0	3	0	0	.320	.320	.640
Rocky Nelson	4	9	2	3	2	0	0	1	1	1	0	0	.333	.400	.667
Dick Schofield	3	3	0	1	0	0	0	0	1	0	0	0	.333	.500	.333
Bob Skinner	2	5	2	1	1	0	0	0	1	0	1	0	.200	.429	.200
Hal Smith	3	8	1	3	3	0	0	1	0	0	0	0	.375	.375	.750
Dick Stuart	5	20	0	3	0	0	0	0	0	3	0	0	.150	.150	.150
Bill Virdon	7	29	2	7	5	3	0	0	1	3	1	0	.241	.267	.345
Totals	7	234	27	60	26	11	0	4	12	26	2	1	.256	.301	.355

Yankees

Yankees	G	AB	R	H	RBI	2B	3B	HR	BB	SO	SB	CS	Avg	OBP	Slg
Luis Arroyo	1	1	0	0	0	0	0	0	0	0	0	0	.000	.000	.000
Yogi Berra	7	22	6	7	8	0	0	1	2	0	0	0	.318	.375	.455
Johnny Blanchard	5	11	2	5	2	2	0	0	0	0	0	0	.455	.455	.636
Clete Boyer	4	12	1	3	1	2	1	0	0	1	0	0	.250	.250	.583
Bob Cerv	4	14	1	5	0	0	0	0	0	3	0	0	.357	.357	.357
Jim Coates	3	1	0	0	0	0	0	0	0	0	0	0	.000	.000	.000
Joe DeMaestri	4	2	1	1	0	0	0	0	0	1	0	0	.500	.500	.500
Whitey Ford	2	8	1	2	2	0	0	0	0	2	0	0	.250	.250	.250
Eli Grba	1	0	0	0	0	0	0	0	0	0	0	0	—	—	—
Elston Howard	5	13	4	6	4	1	1	1	1	4	0	0	.462	.533	.923
Tony Kubek	7	30	6	10	3	1	0	0	2	2	0	1	.333	.394	.367
Dale Long	3	3	0	1	0	0	0	0	0	0	0	0	.333	.333	.333
Hector Lopez	3	7	0	3	0	0	0	0	0	0	0	0	.429	.429	.429
Mickey Mantle	7	25	8	10	11	1	0	3	8	9	0	1	.400	.545	.800
Roger Maris	7	30	6	8	2	1	0	2	2	4	0	0	.267	.313	.500
Gil McDougald	6	18	4	5	2	0	0	0	2	3	0	0	.278	.350	.333
Bobby Richardson	7	30	8	11	12	2	2	1	1	1	0	0	.367	.387	.667
Bobby Shantz	3	3	0	1	0	0	0	0	0	0	0	0	.333	.333	.333
Bill Skowron	7	32	7	12	6	2	0	2	0	6	0	0	.375	.364	.625
Bill Stafford	2	1	0	0	0	0	0	0	0	1	0	0	.000	.000	.000
Ralph Terry	2	2	0	0	0	0	0	0	0	0	0	0	.000	.000	.000
Bob Turley	2	4	0	1	0	0	0	0	0	1	0	0	.250	.250	.250
Totals	7	269	55	91	54	13	4	10	18	40	0	2	.338	.383	.528

Pitching

Pirates

Pirates	G	GS	CG	IP	H	R	ER	BB	SO	W-L	Sv-Op	Hld	ERA
Tom Cheney	3	0	0	4.0	4	2	2	1	6	0-0	0-0	0	4.50
Roy Face	4	0	0	10.1	9	6	6	2	4	0-0	3-4	0	5.23
Bob Friend	3	2	0	6.0	13	10	9	3	7	0-2	0-0	0	13.50
Joe Gibbon	2	0	0	3.0	4	3	3	1	2	0-0	0-0	0	9.00
Fred Green	3	0	0	4.0	11	10	10	1	3	0-0	0-0	0	22.50
Harvey Haddix	2	1	0	7.1	6	2	2	2	6	2-0	0-1	0	2.45
Clem Labine	3	0	0	4.0	13	11	6	1	2	0-0	0-0	0	13.50
Vern Law	3	3	0	18.1	22	7	7	3	8	2-0	0-0	0	3.44
Vinegar Bend Mizell	2	1	0	2.1	4	4	4	2	1	0-1	0-0	0	15.43
George Witt	3	0	0	2.2	5	0	0	2	1	0-0	0-0	0	0.00
Totals	7	7	0	62.0	91	55	49	18	40	4-3	3-5	0	7.11

Yankees

Yankees	G	GS	CG	IP	H	R	ER	BB	SO	W-L	Sv-Op	Hld	ERA
Luis Arroyo	1	0	0	0.2	2	1	1	0	1	0-0	0-0	0	13.50
Jim Coates	3	0	0	6.1	6	4	4	1	3	0-0	0-1	0	5.68
Art Ditmar	2	2	0	1.2	6	6	4	1	0	0-2	0-0	0	21.60
Ryne Duren	2	0	0	4.0	2	1	1	1	5	0-0	0-0	0	2.25
Whitey Ford	2	2	2	18.0	11	0	0	2	8	2-0	0-0	0	0.00
Duke Maas	1	0	0	2.0	2	1	1	0	1	0-0	0-0	0	4.50
Bobby Shantz	3	0	0	6.1	4	3	3	1	1	0-0	0-0	0	4.26
Bill Stafford	2	0	0	6.0	5	1	1	1	2	0-0	0-0	0	1.50
Ralph Terry	2	1	0	6.2	7	4	4	1	5	0-2	0-0	0	5.40
Bob Turley	2	2	0	9.1	15	6	5	4	0	1-0	0-0	0	4.82
Totals	7	7	2	61.0	60	27	24	12	26	3-4	0-1	0	3.54

Fielding

Pirates

Pirates	Pos	G	PO	Ast	E	DP	PB	FPct
Smoky Burgess	c	5	27	2	0	0	3	1.000
Tom Cheney	p	3	0	1	0	0	—	1.000
Gino Cimoli	lf	6	5	0	0	0	—	1.000
Roberto Clemente	rf	7	19	0	0	0	—	1.000
Roy Face	p	4	0	2	0	0	—	1.000
Bob Friend	p	3	1	3	0	0	—	1.000
Joe Gibbon	p	2	1	0	0	0	—	1.000
Fred Green	p	3	0	0	0	0	—	—
Dick Groat	ss	7	12	12	2	2	—	.923
Harvey Haddix	p	2	1	1	0	0	—	1.000
Don Hoak	3b	7	8	10	1	2	—	.947
Clem Labine	p	3	0	2	0	0	—	1.000
Vern Law	p	3	0	6	0	0	—	1.000
Bill Mazeroski	2b	7	17	23	0	6	—	1.000
Vinegar Bend Mizell	p	2	0	0	0	0	—	—
Rocky Nelson	1b	3	13	3	0	0	—	1.000
Bob Oldis	c	2	0	0	0	0	0	—
Dick Schofield	ss	2	1	0	0	0	—	1.000
Bob Skinner	lf	2	4	1	0	1	—	1.000
Hal Smith	c	3	14	1	0	0	0	1.000
Dick Stuart	1b	5	45	0	0	6	—	1.000
Bill Virdon	cf	7	18	0	1	0	—	.947
George Witt	p	3	0	0	0	0	—	—
Totals		7	186	67	4	17	3	.984

Yankees

Yankees	Pos	G	PO	Ast	E	DP	PB	FPct
Luis Arroyo	p	1	0	0	0	0	—	—
Yogi Berra	c	3	13	1	0	0	0	1.000
	lf	3	4	0	0	0	—	1.000
	rf	1	1	0	0	0	—	1.000
Johnny Blanchard	c	2	5	2	0	1	0	1.000
Clete Boyer	3b	4	0	8	0	2	—	1.000
	ss	1	0	0	0	0	—	—
Bob Cerv	lf	3	8	0	1	0	—	.889
Jim Coates	p	3	1	1	0	0	—	1.000
Joe DeMaestri	ss	3	0	2	0	0	—	1.000
Art Ditmar	p	2	0	0	0	0	—	—
Ryne Duren	p	2	0	2	0	0	—	1.000
Whitey Ford	p	2	3	5	0	1	—	1.000
Elston Howard	c	4	11	0	0	0	0	1.000
Tony Kubek	ss	7	10	21	3	4	—	.912
	lf	2	2	0	0	0	—	1.000
Hector Lopez	lf	1	0	1	0	0	—	1.000
Duke Maas	p	1	0	0	0	0	—	—
Mickey Mantle	cf	7	14	0	0	0	—	1.000
Roger Maris	rf	7	12	0	1	0	—	.923
Gil McDougald	3b	6	5	7	1	0	—	.923
Bobby Richardson	2b	7	21	28	2	7	—	.961
Bobby Shantz	p	3	3	2	0	1	—	1.000
Bill Skowron	1b	7	70	6	0	9	—	1.000
Bill Stafford	p	2	0	2	0	2	—	1.000
Ralph Terry	p	2	0	3	0	0	—	1.000
Bob Turley	p	2	0	2	0	0	—	1.000
Totals		7	183	93	8	27	0	.972

1961 New York Yankees (AL) 4, Cincinnati Reds (NL) 1

The Cincinnati Reds were no match for the powerful New York Yankees, falling to the AL Champs in five games. Whitey Ford tossed a two-hit shutout to beat Jim O'Toole 2-0 in the opener, as New York won on solo shots from Elston Howard and Moose Skowron. Joey Jay four-hit the Yanks in Game 2 for a 6-2 victory and Elio Chacon scored the go-ahead run on a passed ball by Howard. The Yanks came back to take the third game, 3-2, on an eighth-inning homer by Johnny Blanchard and a ninth-inning shot from Roger Maris. Whitey Ford tossed five scoreless innings in Game 4 to extend his World Series-record scoreless-inning streak to 32. He left with an ankle injury in the bottom of the sixth, but Jim Coates closed out the 7-0 victory. Six Yankees notched muti-hit games in Game 5 as the Yanks buried the Reds with a 13-5 runaway win.

Game 1

Wednesday, October 4

Reds	AB	R	H	RBI	BB	K	Avg
Don Blasingame, 2b	3	0	0	0	0	2	.000
Jerry Lynch, ph	1	0	0	0	0	0	.000
Eddie Kasko, ss	4	0	1	0	0	0	.250
Vada Pinson, cf	4	0	0	0	0	0	.000
Frank Robinson, lf	2	0	0	0	1	2	.000
Wally Post, rf	3	0	1	0	0	0	.333
Gene Freese, 3b	3	0	0	0	0	0	.000
Gordy Coleman, 1b	3	0	0	0	0	0	.000
Darrell Johnson, c	2	0	0	0	0	0	.000
Leo Cardenas, ph	1	0	0	0	0	1	.000
Jerry Zimmerman, c	0	0	0	0	0	0	—
Jim O'Toole, p	2	0	0	0	0	1	.000
Dick Gernert, ph	1	0	0	0	0	0	.000
Jim Brosnan, p	0	0	0	0	0	0	—
TOTALS	29	0	2	0	1	6	.069

Yankees	AB	R	H	RBI	BB	K	Avg
Bobby Richardson, 2b	4	0	3	0	0	0	.750
Tony Kubek, ss	3	0	0	0	1	0	.000
Roger Maris, cf-rf	4	0	0	0	0	1	.000
Elston Howard, c	4	1	1	1	0	0	.250
Bill Skowron, 1b	3	1	1	1	1	1	.333
Yogi Berra, lf	2	0	0	0	2	0	.000
Hector Lopez, rf	2	0	0	0	1	1	.000
Johnny Blanchard, ph	1	0	0	0	0	0	.000
Jack Reed, cf	0	0	0	0	0	0	—
Clete Boyer, 3b	3	0	1	0	0	0	.333
Whitey Ford, p	3	0	0	0	0	0	.000
TOTALS	29	2	6	2	5	3	.207

	1	2	3	4	5	6	7	8	9		R	H	E
Reds	0	0	0	0	0	0	0	0	0		0	2	0
Yankees	0	0	0	1	0	1	0	0	x		2	6	0

DP—Reds 1 (Johnson to Kasko to Coleman). LOB—Reds 3, Yankees 8. Scoring Position—Reds 0-for-1, Yankees 0-for-4. HR—Howard (1), Skowron (1). CS—Richardson (1).

Reds	IP	H	R	ER	BB	K	ERA
Jim O'Toole (L, 0-1)	7.0	6	2	2	4	2	2.57
Jim Brosnan	1.0	0	0	0	1	1	0.00

Yankees	IP	H	R	ER	BB	K	ERA
Whitey Ford (W, 1-0)	9.0	2	0	0	1	6	0.00

Time—2:11. Attendance—62,397. Umpires—HP, Runge. 1B, Conlan. 2B, Umont. 3B, Donatelli.

Game 2

Thursday, October 5

Reds	AB	R	H	RBI	BB	K	Avg
Elio Chacon, 2b	4	1	1	0	1	0	.250
Eddie Kasko, ss	5	0	1	0	0	2	.222
Vada Pinson, cf	5	0	1	0	0	1	.111
Frank Robinson, lf	4	2	0	0	1	0	.000
Gordy Coleman, 1b	5	1	2	2	0	1	.250
Wally Post, rf	4	2	2	0	0	1	.429
Gene Freese, 3b	2	0	0	0	2	1	.000
Johnny Edwards, c	4	0	2	2	0	0	.500
Joey Jay, p	4	0	0	0	0	2	.000
TOTALS	37	6	9	4	4	8	.196

Yankees	AB	R	H	RBI	BB	K	Avg
Bobby Richardson, 2b	4	0	1	0	0	0	.500
Tony Kubek, ss	4	0	1	0	0	2	.143
Roger Maris, cf	3	1	0	0	1	2	.000
Yogi Berra, lf	4	1	2	2	0	0	.333
Johnny Blanchard, rf	4	0	0	0	0	0	.000
Elston Howard, c	3	0	0	0	1	0	.143
Bill Skowron, 1b	3	0	0	0	1	2	.167
Clete Boyer, 3b	2	0	0	0	2	0	.200
Ralph Terry, p	2	0	0	0	0	0	.000
Hector Lopez, ph	0	0	0	0	1	0	.000
Luis Arroyo, p	0	0	0	0	0	0	—
Billy Gardner, ph	1	0	0	0	0	0	.000
TOTALS	30	2	4	2	6	6	.179

	1	2	3	4	5	6	7	8	9		R	H	E
Reds	0	0	0	2	1	1	0	2	0		6	9	0
Yankees	0	0	0	2	0	0	0	0	0		2	4	3

E—Boyer, Arroyo, Berra. DP—Reds 2 (Chacon to Kasko to Coleman; Chacon to Kasko to Coleman). LOB—Reds 8, Yankees 7. Scoring Position—Reds 2-for-8, Yankees 0-for-2. 2B—Pinson (1), Post (1), Edwards (1). HR—Coleman (1), Berra (1). GDP—Howard, Skowron.

Reds	IP	H	R	ER	BB	K	ERA
Joey Jay (W, 1-0)	9.0	4	2	2	6	6	2.00

Yankees	IP	H	R	ER	BB	K	ERA
Ralph Terry (L, 0-1)	7.0	6	4	2	2	7	2.57
Luis Arroyo	2.0	3	2	1	2	1	4.50

PB—Howard. Time—2:43. Attendance—63,083. Umpires—HP, Conlan. 1B, Umont. 2B, Donatelli. 3B, Runge.

Game 3

Saturday, October 7

Yankees	AB	R	H	RBI	BB	K	Avg
Bobby Richardson, 2b	4	0	1	0	0	0	.417
Tony Kubek, ss	4	1	1	0	0	0	.182
Roger Maris, rf	4	1	1	1	0	0	.091
Mickey Mantle, cf	4	0	0	0	0	2	.000
Jack Reed, cf	0	0	0	0	0	0	—
Yogi Berra, lf	3	0	1	1	1	1	.333
Elston Howard, c	4	0	1	0	0	0	.182
Bill Skowron, 1b	3	0	0	0	0	0	.111
Clete Boyer, 3b	3	0	0	0	0	0	.125
Bill Stafford, p	2	0	0	0	0	0	.000
Bud Daley, p	0	0	0	0	0	0	—
Johnny Blanchard, ph	1	1	1	1	0	0	.167
Luis Arroyo, p	0	0	0	0	0	0	—
TOTALS	32	3	6	3	1	3	.193

Reds	AB	R	H	RBI	BB	K	Avg
Elio Chacon, 2b	3	1	1	0	0	1	.286
Jerry Lynch, ph	0	0	0	0	1	0	.000
Don Blasingame, pr-2b	0	0	0	0	0	0	.000
Gus Bell, ph	1	0	0	0	0	0	.000
Eddie Kasko, ss	4	0	2	1	0	0	.308
Vada Pinson, cf	4	0	0	0	0	0	.077
Frank Robinson, rf	4	0	1	1	0	2	.100
Gordy Coleman, 1b	4	0	2	0	0	0	.333
Wally Post, lf	4	0	0	0	0	0	.273
Gene Freese, 3b	3	0	0	0	1	1	.000
Johnny Edwards, c	3	1	1	0	0	0	.429
Leo Cardenas, ph	1	0	1	0	0	0	.500
Bob Purkey, p	3	0	0	0	0	3	.000
Dick Gernert, ph	1	0	0	0	0	0	.000
TOTALS	35	2	8	2	2	7	.204

	1	2	3	4	5	6	7	8	9		R	H	E
Yankees	0	0	0	0	0	0	1	1	1		3	6	1
Reds	0	0	1	0	0	0	1	0	0		2	8	0

E—Stafford. DP—Reds 1 (Kasko). LOB—Yankees 3, Reds 8. Scoring Position—Yankees 1-for-4, Reds 2-for-11. 2B—Howard (1), Robinson (1), Edwards (2), Cardenas (1). HR—Maris (1), Blanchard (1). SB—Richardson (1).

Yankees	IP	H	R	ER	BB	K	ERA
Bill Stafford	6.2	7	2	2	2	5	2.70
Bud Daley	0.1	0	0	0	0	0	0.00
Luis Arroyo (W, 1-0)	2.0	1	0	0	0	2	2.25

Reds	IP	H	R	ER	BB	K	ERA
Bob Purkey (L, 0-1)	9.0	6	3	2	1	3	2.00

PB—Edwards. Time—2:15. Attendance—32,589. Umpires—HP, Umont. 1B, Donatelli. 2B, Runge. 3B, Conlan.

Game 4
Sunday, October 8

Yankees	AB	R	H	RBI	BB	K	Avg
Bobby Richardson, 2b	5	1	3	0	0	0	.471
Tony Kubek, ss	5	0	1	1	0	2	.188
Roger Maris, rf-cf	3	2	0	0	2	1	.071
Mickey Mantle, cf	2	0	1	0	0	0	.167
Hector Lopez, pr-rf	3	1	1	2	0	1	.200
Elston Howard, c	4	1	1	0	0	2	.200
Yogi Berra, lf	2	1	0	0	2	0	.273
Bill Skowron, 1b	3	0	3	1	1	0	.333
Clete Boyer, 3b	4	0	1	2	0	0	.167
Whitey Ford, p	2	1	0	0	1	0	.000
Jim Coates, p	1	0	0	0	1	0	.000
TOTALS	34	7	11	6	6	7	.228

Reds	AB	R	H	RBI	BB	K	Avg
Elio Chacon, 2b	4	0	1	0	0	1	.273
Eddie Kasko, ss	4	0	1	0	0	0	.294
Vada Pinson, cf	4	0	0	0	0	0	.059
Frank Robinson, rf	1	0	0	0	1	0	.091
Wally Post, lf	4	0	1	0	0	0	.267
Gene Freese, 3b	4	0	0	0	0	1	.000
Gordy Coleman, 1b	4	0	0	0	0	0	.250
Darrell Johnson, c	2	0	2	0	0	0	.500
Gus Bell, ph	1	0	0	0	0	0	.000
Jerry Zimmerman, c	0	0	0	0	0	0	—
Jim O'Toole, p	1	0	0	0	0	0	.000
Dick Gernert, ph	1	0	0	0	0	0	.000
Jim Brosnan, p	0	0	0	0	0	0	—
Jerry Lynch, ph	1	0	0	0	0	1	.000
Bill Henry, p	0	0	0	0	0	0	—
TOTALS	31	0	5	0	1	3	.177

	1	2	3	4	5	6	7	8	9		R	H	E
Yankees	0	0	0	1	1	2	3	0	0		7	11	0
Reds	0	0	0	0	0	0	0	0	0		0	5	1

E—Pinson. DP—Yankees 1 (Kubek to Richardson to Skowron), Reds 3 (Kasko to Chacon to Coleman; Freese to Chacon to Coleman; Coleman). LOB—Yankees 6, Reds 7. Scoring Position—Yankees 5-for-11, Reds 0-for-4. 2B—Richardson (1), Howard (2), Boyer (1). GDP—Howard, Boyer, Post.

Yankees	IP	H	R	ER	BB	K	ERA
Whitey Ford (W, 2-0)	5.0	4	0	0	0	1	0.00
Jim Coates (S, 1)	4.0	1	0	0	1	2	0.00

Reds	IP	H	R	ER	BB	K	ERA
Jim O'Toole (L, 0-2)	5.0	5	2	2	3	2	3.00
Jim Brosnan	3.0	6	5	5	3	3	11.25
Bill Henry	1.0	0	0	0	0	2	0.00

Ford pitched to one batter in the 6th.

WP—Brosnan. HBP—Robinson by Ford, Robinson by Coates. Time—2:27. Attendance—32,589. Umpires—HP, Donatelli. 1B, Runge. 2B, Conlan. 3B, Umont.

Game 5
Monday, October 9

Yankees	AB	R	H	RBI	BB	K	Avg
Bobby Richardson, 2b	6	1	1	0	0	0	.391
Tony Kubek, ss	6	2	2	0	0	0	.227
Roger Maris, cf-rf	5	0	1	1	1	2	.105
Johnny Blanchard, rf	4	3	3	2	2	0	.400
Jack Reed, cf	0	0	0	0	0	0	—
Elston Howard, c	5	3	2	0	1	1	.250
Bill Skowron, 1b	5	2	2	3	0	1	.353
Hector Lopez, lf	4	2	2	5	0	1	.333
Clete Boyer, 3b	3	0	2	1	2	0	.267
Ralph Terry, p	1	0	0	0	0	1	.000
Bud Daley, p	1	0	0	1	0	0	.000
TOTALS	40	13	15	13	6	6	.273

Reds	AB	R	H	RBI	BB	K	Avg
Don Blasingame, 2b	4	1	1	0	0	1	.143
Elio Chacon, ph	1	0	0	0	0	0	.250
Eddie Kasko, ss	5	1	2	0	0	0	.318
Vada Pinson, cf	5	0	1	0	0	0	.091
Frank Robinson, rf	4	1	2	3	0	0	.200
Gordy Coleman, 1b	4	1	1	0	0	0	.250
Wally Post, lf	3	1	2	2	0	0	.333
Gene Freese, 3b	4	0	1	0	0	1	.063
Johnny Edwards, c	4	0	1	0	0	0	.364
Joey Jay, p	0	0	0	0	0	0	.000
Jim Maloney, p	0	0	0	0	0	0	—
Ken Johnson, p	0	0	0	0	0	0	—
Gus Bell, ph	1	0	0	0	0	0	.000
Bill Henry, p	0	0	0	0	0	0	—
Sherman Jones, p	0	0	0	0	0	0	—
Dick Gernert, ph	1	0	0	0	0	1	.000
Bob Purkey, p	0	0	0	0	0	0	.000
Leo Cardenas, ph	1	0	0	0	0	0	.333
Jim Brosnan, p	0	0	0	0	0	0	—
Jerry Lynch, ph	1	0	0	0	0	0	.000
Ken Hunt, p	0	0	0	0	0	0	—
TOTALS	38	5	11	5	0	3	.202

	1	2	3	4	5	6	7	8	9		R	H	E
Yankees	5	1	0	5	0	2	0	0	0		13	15	1
Reds	0	0	3	0	2	0	0	0	0		5	11	3

E—Coleman, Kasko, Daley, Purkey. LOB—Yankees 10, Reds 7. Scoring Position—Yankees 5-for-14, Reds 1-for-5. 2B—Maris (1), Blanchard (1), Howard (3), Boyer (2), Robinson (2), Freese (1). 3B—Lopez (1). HR—Blanchard (2), Lopez (1), Robinson (1), Post (1). S—Lopez, Terry, Daley. SF—Daley.

Yankees	IP	H	R	ER	BB	K	ERA
Ralph Terry	2.1	6	3	3	0	0	4.82
Bud Daley (W, 1-0)	6.2	5	2	0	0	3	0.00

Reds	IP	H	R	ER	BB	K	ERA
Joey Jay (L, 1-1)	0.2	4	4	4	0	0	5.59
Jim Maloney	0.2	4	2	2	1	1	27.00
Ken Johnson	0.2	0	0	0	0	0	0.00
Bill Henry	1.1	4	5	5	2	1	19.29
Sherman Jones	0.2	0	0	0	0	0	0.00
Bob Purkey	2.0	0	2	0	2	2	1.64
Jim Brosnan	2.0	3	0	0	1	1	7.50
Ken Hunt	1.0	0	0	0	1	1	0.00

WP—Brosnan. HBP—Post by Daley. Time—3:05. Attendance—32,589. Umpires—HP, Runge. 1B, Conlan. 2B, Umont. 3B, Donatelli.

1961 World Series—Composite Statistics

Batting

Yankees

Yankees	G	AB	R	H	RBI	2B	3B	HR	BB	SO	SB	CS	Avg	OBP	Slg
Yogi Berra	4	11	2	3	3	0	0	1	5	1	0	0	.273	.500	.545
Johnny Blanchard	4	10	4	4	3	1	0	2	2	0	0	0	.400	.500	1.100
Clete Boyer	5	15	0	4	3	2	0	0	4	0	0	0	.267	.421	.400
Jim Coates	1	1	0	0	0	0	0	0	0	1	0	0	.000	.000	.000
Bud Daley	2	1	0	0	1	0	0	0	0	0	0	0	.000	.000	.000
Whitey Ford	2	5	1	0	0	0	0	0	1	0	0	0	.000	.167	.000
Billy Gardner	1	1	0	0	0	0	0	0	0	0	0	0	.000	.000	.000
Elston Howard	5	20	5	5	1	3	0	1	2	3	0	0	.250	.318	.550
Tony Kubek	5	22	3	5	1	0	0	0	1	4	0	0	.227	.261	.227
Hector Lopez	4	9	3	3	7	0	1	1	2	3	0	0	.333	.455	.889
Mickey Mantle	2	6	0	1	0	0	0	0	0	2	0	0	.167	.167	.167
Roger Maris	5	19	4	2	2	1	0	1	4	6	0	0	.105	.261	.316
Bobby Richardson	5	23	2	9	0	1	0	0	0	1	1	1	.391	.391	.435
Bill Skowron	5	17	3	6	5	0	0	1	3	4	0	0	.353	.450	.529
Bill Stafford	1	2	0	0	0	0	0	0	0	0	0	0	.000	.000	.000
Ralph Terry	2	3	0	0	0	0	0	0	0	1	0	0	.000	.000	.000
Totals	5	165	27	42	26	8	1	7	24	25	1	1	.255	.347	.442

Reds

Reds	G	AB	R	H	RBI	2B	3B	HR	BB	SO	SB	CS	Avg	OBP	Slg
Gus Bell	3	3	0	0	0	0	0	0	0	0	0	0	.000	.000	.000
Don Blasingame	3	7	1	1	0	0	0	0	0	3	0	0	.143	.143	.143
Leo Cardenas	3	3	0	1	0	1	0	0	0	1	0	0	.333	.333	.667
Elio Chacon	4	12	2	3	0	0	0	0	1	2	0	0	.250	.308	.250
Gordy Coleman	5	20	2	5	2	0	0	1	0	1	0	0	.250	.250	.400
Johnny Edwards	3	11	1	4	2	2	0	0	0	0	0	0	.364	.364	.545
Gene Freese	5	16	0	1	0	1	0	0	3	4	0	0	.063	.211	.125
Dick Gernert	4	4	0	0	0	0	0	0	0	1	0	0	.000	.000	.000
Joey Jay	2	4	0	0	0	0	0	0	0	2	0	0	.000	.000	.000
Darrell Johnson	2	4	0	2	0	0	0	0	0	0	0	0	.500	.500	.500
Eddie Kasko	5	22	1	7	1	0	0	0	0	2	0	0	.318	.318	.318
Jerry Lynch	4	3	0	0	0	0	0	0	1	1	0	0	.000	.250	.000
Jim O'Toole	2	3	0	0	0	0	0	0	0	1	0	0	.000	.000	.000
Vada Pinson	5	22	0	2	0	1	0	0	0	1	0	0	.091	.091	.136
Wally Post	5	18	3	6	2	1	0	1	0	1	0	0	.333	.368	.556
Bob Purkey	2	3	0	0	0	0	0	0	0	3	0	0	.000	.000	.000
Frank Robinson	5	15	3	3	4	2	0	1	3	4	0	0	.200	.400	.533
Totals	5	170	13	35	11	8	0	3	8	27	0	0	.206	.254	.306

Pitching

Yankees

Yankees	G	GS	CG	IP	H	R	ER	BB	SO	W-L	Sv-Op	Hld	ERA
Luis Arroyo	2	0	0	4.0	4	2	1	2	3	1-0	0-0	0	2.25
Jim Coates	1	0	0	4.0	1	0	0	1	2	0-0	1-1	0	0.00
Bud Daley	2	0	0	7.0	5	2	0	0	3	1-0	0-0	0	0.00
Whitey Ford	2	2	1	14.0	6	0	0	1	7	2-0	0-0	0	0.00
Bill Stafford	1	1	0	6.2	7	2	2	2	5	0-0	0-0	0	2.70
Ralph Terry	2	2	0	9.1	12	7	5	2	7	0-1	0-0	0	4.82
Totals	5	5	1	45.0	35	13	8	8	27	4-1	1-1	0	1.60

Reds

Reds	G	GS	CG	IP	H	R	ER	BB	SO	W-L	Sv-Op	Hld	ERA
Jim Brosnan	3	0	0	6.0	9	5	5	4	5	0-0	0-0	0	7.50
Bill Henry	2	0	0	2.1	4	5	5	2	3	0-0	0-0	0	19.29
Ken Hunt	1	0	0	1.0	0	0	0	1	1	0-0	0-0	0	0.00
Joey Jay	2	2	1	9.2	8	6	6	6	6	1-1	0-0	0	5.59
Ken Johnson	1	0	0	0.2	0	0	0	0	0	0-0	0-0	0	0.00
Sherman Jones	1	0	0	0.2	0	0	0	0	0	0-0	0-0	0	0.00
Jim Maloney	1	0	0	0.2	4	2	2	1	1	0-0	0-0	0	27.00
Jim O'Toole	2	2	0	12.0	11	4	4	7	4	0-2	0-0	0	3.00
Bob Purkey	2	1	1	11.0	6	5	2	3	5	0-1	0-0	0	1.64
Totals	5	5	2	44.0	42	27	24	24	25	1-4	0-0	0	4.91

Fielding

Yankees

Yankees	Pos	G	PO	Ast	E	DP	PB	FPct
Luis Arroyo	p	2	1	1	1	0	—	.667
Yogi Berra	lf	4	11	0	1	0	—	.917
Johnny Blanchard	rf	2	2	1	0	0	—	1.000
Clete Boyer	3b	5	6	12	1	0	—	.947
Jim Coates	p	1	0	0	0	0	—	—
Bud Daley	p	2	0	0	1	0	—	.000
Whitey Ford	p	2	0	1	0	0	—	1.000
Elston Howard	c	5	31	0	0	0	1	1.000
Tony Kubek	ss	5	5	11	0	1	—	1.000
Hector Lopez	rf	2	3	0	0	0	—	1.000
	lf	1	5	0	0	0	—	1.000
Mickey Mantle	cf	2	2	0	0	0	—	1.000
Roger Maris	cf	4	6	1	0	0	—	1.000
	rf	4	5	0	0	0	—	1.000
Jack Reed	cf	3	0	0	0	0	—	—
Bobby Richardson	2b	5	10	16	0	1	—	1.000
Bill Skowron	1b	5	46	5	0	1	—	1.000
Bill Stafford	p	1	1	0	1	0	—	.500
Ralph Terry	p	2	1	2	0	0	—	1.000
Totals		5	135	50	5	3	1	.974

Reds

Reds	Pos	G	PO	Ast	E	DP	PB	FPct
Don Blasingame	2b	3	5	4	0	0	—	1.000
Jim Brosnan	p	3	0	0	0	0	—	—
Elio Chacon	2b	3	12	9	0	4	—	1.000
Gordy Coleman	1b	5	30	4	1	6	—	.971
Johnny Edwards	c	3	17	1	0	0	1	1.000
Gene Freese	3b	5	6	4	0	1	—	1.000
Bill Henry	p	2	0	1	0	0	—	1.000
Ken Hunt	p	1	0	1	0	0	—	1.000
Joey Jay	p	2	1	0	0	0	—	1.000
Darrell Johnson	c	2	8	1	0	1	0	1.000
Ken Johnson	p	1	0	0	0	0	—	—
Sherman Jones	p	1	0	0	0	0	—	—
Eddie Kasko	ss	5	13	13	1	5	—	.963
Jim Maloney	p	1	0	0	0	0	—	—
Jim O'Toole	p	2	1	0	0	0	—	1.000
Vada Pinson	cf	5	18	1	1	0	—	.950
Wally Post	lf	3	6	0	0	0	—	1.000
	rf	2	2	0	0	0	—	—
Bob Purkey	p	2	4	3	1	0	—	.875
Frank Robinson	rf	3	5	0	0	0	—	1.000
	lf	2	0	0	0	0	—	—
Jerry Zimmerman	c	2	4	0	0	0	0	1.000
Totals		5	132	42	4	17	1	.978

1962 New York Yankees (AL) 4, San Francisco Giants (NL) 3

The New York Yankees beat the San Francisco Giants in a seven-game Series that was in doubt until the final out. Whitey Ford won the opener, 6-2, with Clete Boyer breaking a 2-2 tie with a solo homer in the seventh. Jack Sanford tossed a three-hit shutout at the Yanks in Game 2. Roger Maris singled in a pair of runs in Game 3, and Bill Stafford came within one out of a shutout before settling for a 3-2 victory. Chuck Hiller's seventh-inning grand slam sent the Giants to a 7-3 win in the fourth game, but New York's Tom Tresh turned the tables the next day, socking a three-run homer in the eighth for a 5-3 New York victory. After three days of rain, Billy Pierce stopped the Yankees, 5-2. The Giants were down 1-0 in the bottom of the ninth in Game 7 when Willie McCovery came to the plate with the winning runs on second and third. McCovery lashed a vicious liner toward right, but second baseman Bobby Richardson speared it to save Ralph Terry's four-hit shutout and end the Series.

Game 1

Thursday, October 4

Yankees	AB	R	H	RBI	BB	K	Avg
Tony Kubek, ss	5	0	2	0	0	1	.400
Bobby Richardson, 2b	5	1	1	0	0	0	.200
Tom Tresh, lf	5	2	2	0	0	0	.400
Mickey Mantle, cf	4	0	0	0	1	2	.000
Roger Maris, rf	4	1	2	2	1	1	.500
Elston Howard, c	3	1	2	1	1	0	.667
Bill Skowron, 1b	2	0	0	0	1	1	.000
Dale Long, 1b	2	0	1	1	0	0	.500
Clete Boyer, 3b	3	1	1	2	0	1	.333
Whitey Ford, p	3	0	0	0	1	2	.000
TOTALS	36	6	11	6	5	8	.306

Giants	AB	R	H	RBI	BB	K	Avg
Harvey Kuenn, lf	5	0	0	0	0	1	.000
Chuck Hiller, 2b	4	1	1	0	0	1	.250
Felipe Alou, rf	4	0	1	0	0	2	.250
Willie Mays, cf	4	1	3	1	0	0	.750
Orlando Cepeda, 1b	4	0	0	0	0	1	.000
Jim Davenport, 3b	2	0	1	0	2	0	.500
Ed Bailey, c	4	0	0	0	0	0	.000
Stu Miller, p	0	0	0	0	0	0	—
Jose Pagan, ss	4	0	3	1	0	0	.750
Billy O'Dell, p	3	0	1	0	0	0	.333
Don Larsen, p	0	0	0	0	0	0	—
John Orsino, c	1	0	0	0	0	0	.000
TOTALS	35	2	10	2	2	6	.286

	1 2 3	4 5 6	7 8 9		R	H	E
Yankees	2 0 0	0 0 0	1 2 1		6	11	0
Giants	0 1 1	0 0 0	0 0 0		2	10	0

DP—Yankees 2 (Richardson to Kubek to Skowron; Boyer to Richardson to Long), Giants 1 (Davenport to Hiller to Cepeda). LOB—Yankees 10, Giants 8. Scoring Position—Yankees 3-for-9, Giants 3-for-7. 2B—Maris (1), Hiller (1). HR—Boyer (1). SF—Boyer. GDP—Skowron, Cepeda, Orsino. SB—Tresh (1), Mantle (1).

Yankees	IP	H	R	ER	BB	K	ERA
Whitey Ford (W, 1-0)	9.0	10	2	2	2	6	2.00

Giants	IP	H	R	ER	BB	K	ERA
Billy O'Dell (L, 0-1)	7.1	9	5	5	3	8	6.14
Don Larsen	1.0	1	1	1	0		9.00
Stu Miller	0.2	1	0	0	1	0	0.00

HBP—Howard by O'Dell. Time—2:43. Attendance—43,852. Umpires—HP, Barlick. 1B, Berry. 2B, Landes. 3B, Honochick.

Game 2

Friday, October 5

Yankees	AB	R	H	RBI	BB	K	Avg
Tony Kubek, ss	4	0	0	0	0	1	.222
Bobby Richardson, 2b	4	0	0	0	0	0	.111
Tom Tresh, lf	3	0	1	0	1	1	.375
Mickey Mantle, cf	4	0	1	0	0	0	.125
Roger Maris, rf	3	0	0	0	1	0	.286
Yogi Berra, c	2	0	0	0	1	0	.000
Dale Long, 1b	3	0	0	0	0	1	.200
Clete Boyer, 3b	3	0	1	0	0	1	.333
Ralph Terry, p	2	0	0	0	0	1	.000
Johnny Blanchard, ph	1	0	0	0	0	1	.000
Bud Daley, p	0	0	0	0	0	0	—
TOTALS	29	0	3	0	3	6	.211

Giants	AB	R	H	RBI	BB	K	Avg
Chuck Hiller, 2b	3	1	1	0	1	0	.286
Felipe Alou, rf	2	0	1	0	1	0	.333
Matty Alou, lf	4	0	1	1	0	0	.250
Willie Mays, cf	4	0	0	0	0	1	.375
Willie McCovey, 1b	4	1	1	1	0	1	.250
Tom Haller, c	3	0	1	0	0	0	.333
Jim Davenport, 3b	3	0	0	0	0	1	.200
Jose Pagan, ss	1	0	0	0	0	0	.600
Jack Sanford, p	3	0	1	0	0	2	.333
TOTALS	27	2	6	2	2	5	.333

	1 2 3	4 5 6	7 8 9		R	H	E
Yankees	0 0 0	0 0 0	0 0 0		0	3	1
Giants	1 0 0	0 0 0	1 0 x		2	6	0

E—Kubek. DP—Giants 1 (Hiller to Pagan to McCovey). LOB—Yankees 5, Giants 6. Scoring Position—Yankees 0-for-2, Giants 1-for-4. 2B—Mantle (1), Hiller (2). HR—McCovey (1). S—FAlou, Pagan. GDP—Berra. SB—Tresh (2). CS—Haller (1).

Yankees	IP	H	R	ER	BB	K	ERA
Ralph Terry (L, 0-1)	7.0	5	2	2	1	5	2.57
Bud Daley	1.0	1	0	0	1	0	0.00

Giants	IP	H	R	ER	BB	K	ERA
Jack Sanford (W, 1-0)	9.0	3	0	0	3	6	0.00

HBP—Pagan by Terry. Time—2:11. Attendance—43,910. Umpires—HP, Berry. 1B, Landes. 2B, Honochick. 3B, Barlick.

Game 3

Sunday, October 7

Giants	AB	R	H	RBI	BB	K	Avg
Felipe Alou, lf	4	0	0	0	0	0	.200
Chuck Hiller, 2b	3	0	0	0	1	1	.200
Willie Mays, cf	4	1	1	0	0	1	.333
Willie McCovey, rf	3	0	0	0	1	1	.143
Orlando Cepeda, 1b	4	0	0	0	0	0	.000
Ed Bailey, c	4	1	1	2	0	0	.125
Jim Davenport, 3b	4	0	1	0	0	1	.222
Jose Pagan, ss	3	0	1	0	0	0	.500
Billy Pierce, p	2	0	0	0	0	1	.000
Don Larsen, p	0	0	0	0	0	0	—
Matty Alou, ph	1	0	0	0	0	0	.200
Bobby Bolin, p	0	0	0	0	0	0	—
TOTALS	32	2	4	2	2	5	.215

Yankees	AB	R	H	RBI	BB	K	Avg
Tony Kubek, ss	4	0	1	0	0	0	.231
Bobby Richardson, 2b	4	0	0	0	0	0	.077
Tom Tresh, lf	4	1	1	0	0	2	.333
Mickey Mantle, cf	3	1	1	0	0	0	.182
Roger Maris, rf	3	1	1	2	0	0	.300
Elston Howard, c	3	0	1	0	0	0	.500
Bill Skowron, 1b	2	0	0	0	0	1	.000
Clete Boyer, 3b	3	0	0	1	0	0	.222
Bill Stafford, p	3	0	0	0	0	1	.000
TOTALS	29	3	5	3	0	4	.222

	1 2 3	4 5 6	7 8 9		R	H	E
Giants	0 0 0	0 0 0	0 0 2		2	4	3
Yankees	0 0 0	0 0 0	3 0 x		3	5	1

E—McCovey, FAlou, Davenport, Boyer. DP—Giants 1 (Davenport to Hiller). LOB—Giants 5, Yankees 3. Scoring Position—Giants 1-for-7, Yankees 1-for-5. 2B—Mays (1), Davenport (1), Kubek (1), Howard (1). HR—Bailey (1).

Giants	IP	H	R	ER	BB	K	ERA
Billy Pierce (L, 0-1)	6.0	5	3	2	0	3	3.00
Don Larsen	1.0	0	0	0	0	0	4.50
Bobby Bolin	1.0	0	0	0	0	1	0.00

Yankees	IP	H	R	ER	BB	K	ERA
Bill Stafford (W, 1-0)	9.0	4	2	2	2	5	2.00

Pierce pitched to five batters in the 7th.

HBP—Skowron by Larsen. Time—2:06. Attendance—71,434. Umpires—HP, Landes. 1B, Honochick. 2B, Barlick. 3B, Berry.

Game 4

Monday, October 8

Giants	AB	R	H	RBI	BB	K	Avg
Harvey Kuenn, rf	3	0	0	0	1	0	.000
Billy O'Dell, p	0	0	0	0	0	0	.333
Chuck Hiller, 2b	5	1	2	4	0	1	.267
Willie Mays, cf	5	0	1	0	0	1	.294
Felipe Alou, lf	4	1	1	0	0	0	.214
Orlando Cepeda, 1b	4	0	0	0	0	1	.000
Jim Davenport, 3b	2	1	0	0	2	1	.182
Tom Haller, c	4	1	2	2	0	2	.429
Jose Pagan, ss	2	0	1	0	0	0	.500
Matty Alou, ph-rf	2	2	2	0	0	0	.429
Juan Marichal, p	2	0	0	0	0	1	.000
Bobby Bolin, p	0	0	0	0	0	0	—
Don Larsen, p	0	0	0	0	0	0	—
Ed Bailey, ph	0	0	0	0	0	0	.125
Bob Nieman, ph	0	0	0	0	1	0	—
Ernie Bowman, pr-ss	1	1	0	0	0	0	.000
TOTALS	34	7	9	6	4	7	.235

Yankees	AB	R	H	RBI	BB	K	Avg
Tony Kubek, ss	4	1	1	0	1	0	.235
Bobby Richardson, 2b	4	0	1	0	1	1	.118
Tom Tresh, lf	5	0	2	1	0	1	.353
Mickey Mantle, cf	4	1	0	0	1	2	.133
Roger Maris, rf	3	1	0	0	0	0	.231
Elston Howard, c	4	0	0	0	0	1	.300
Bill Skowron, 1b	4	0	3	1	0	0	.375
Clete Boyer, 3b	4	0	2	1	0	0	.308
Whitey Ford, p	2	0	0	0	0	0	.000
Yogi Berra, ph	0	0	0	0	1	0	.000
Jim Coates, p	0	0	0	0	0	0	—
Marshall Bridges, p	0	0	0	0	0	0	—
Hector Lopez, ph	1	0	0	0	0	0	.000
TOTALS	35	3	9	3	5	5	.229

	1 2 3	4 5 6	7 8 9		R	H	E
Giants	0 2 0	0 0 0	4 0 1		7	9	1
Yankees	0 0 0	0 0 2	0 0 1		3	9	1

E—Davenport, Richardson. DP—Giants 2 (Haller to Hiller to Cepeda to Marichal; Hiller to Cepeda), Yankees 1 (Boyer to Richardson to Skowron). LOB—Giants 5, Yankees 10. Scoring Position—Giants 3-for-9, Yankees 3-for-10. 2B—FAlou (1), MAlou (1). 3B—Skowron (1). HR—Hiller (1), Haller (1). S—O'Dell. GDP—FAlou, Richardson. CS—Kubek (1).

Giants	IP	H	R	ER	BB	K	ERA
Juan Marichal	4.0	2	0	0	2	4	0.00
Bobby Bolin	1.2	4	2	2	2	1	6.75
Don Larsen (W, 1-0)	0.1	0	1	0	0	0	3.86
Billy O'Dell (S, 1)	3.0	3	1	1	0	0	5.23

Yankees	IP	H	R	ER	BB	K	ERA
Whitey Ford	6.0	5	2	2	1	3	2.40
Jim Coates (L, 0-1)	0.1	1	2	2	1	1	54.00
Marshall Bridges	2.2	3	3	2	2	3	6.75

Time—2:55. Attendance—66,607. Umpires—HP, Honochick. 1B, Barlick. 2B, Berry. 3B, Landes.

Game 5
Wednesday, October 10

Giants	AB	R	H	RBI	BB	K	Avg
Chuck Hiller, 2b	3	0	1	1	1	0	.278
Jim Davenport, 3b	4	0	0	0	0	3	.133
Matty Alou, rf	4	0	0	0	0	1	.273
Willie Mays, cf	4	0	0	0	0	1	.238
Willie McCovey, 1b	4	1	1	0	0	1	.182
Felipe Alou, lf	4	0	2	0	0	1	.278
Tom Haller, c	4	0	1	1	0	0	.364
Jose Pagan, ss	4	2	2	1	0	0	.500
Jack Sanford, p	2	0	1	0	0	0	.400
Stu Miller, p	0	0	0	0	0	0	—
Ed Bailey, ph	1	0	0	0	0	0	.111
TOTALS	34	3	8	3	1	7	.271

Yankees	AB	R	H	RBI	BB	K	Avg
Tony Kubek, ss	4	1	2	0	0	1	.286
Bobby Richardson, 2b	4	2	2	0	0	0	.190
Tom Tresh, lf	3	2	3	3	0	0	.400
Mickey Mantle, cf	3	0	0	0	1	0	.111
Roger Maris, rf	3	0	0	0	1	0	.188
Elston Howard, c	4	0	0	0	0	2	.214
Bill Skowron, 1b	3	0	0	0	0	3	.273
Clete Boyer, 3b	3	0	0	0	0	1	.250
Ralph Terry, p	3	0	0	0	0	3	.000
TOTALS	30	5	6	3	2	10	.232

	1	2	3	4	5	6	7	8	9	R	H	E
Giants	0	0	1	0	1	0	0	0	1	3	8	2
Yankees	0	0	0	1	0	1	0	3	x	5	6	0

E—McCovey, Hiller. DP—Giants 1 (Sanford to McCovey). LOB—Giants 6, Yankees 4. Scoring Position—Giants 1-for-7, Yankees 1-for-8. 2B—Hiller (3), Haller (1), Tresh (1). 3B—FAlou (1). HR—Pagan (1), Tresh (1). S—Sanford, Tresh. SB—Mantle (2).

Giants	IP	H	R	ER	BB	K	ERA
Jack Sanford (L, 1-1)	7.1	6	5	4	1	10	2.20
Stu Miller	0.2	0	0	0	1	0	0.00

Yankees	IP	H	R	ER	BB	K	ERA
Ralph Terry (W, 1-1)	9.0	8	3	3	1	7	2.81

WP—Sanford. PB—Haller. Time—2:42. Attendance—63,165. Umpires—HP, Barlick. 1B, Berry. 2B, Landes. 3B, Honochick.

Game 6
Monday, October 15

Yankees	AB	R	H	RBI	BB	K	Avg
Tony Kubek, ss	4	0	1	1	0	0	.280
Bobby Richardson, 2b	4	0	0	0	0	0	.160
Tom Tresh, lf	4	0	0	0	0	0	.333
Mickey Mantle, cf	4	0	0	0	0	0	.091
Roger Maris, rf	3	1	1	1	1	1	.211
Elston Howard, c	3	0	0	0	0	0	.176
Bill Skowron, 1b	3	0	0	0	0	0	.214
Clete Boyer, 3b	2	1	1	0	1	0	.278
Whitey Ford, p	2	0	0	0	0	1	.000
Jim Coates, p	0	0	0	0	0	0	—
Hector Lopez, ph	1	0	0	0	0	0	.000
Marshall Bridges, p	0	0	0	0	0	0	—
TOTALS	30	2	3	2	2	2	.208

Giants	AB	R	H	RBI	BB	K	Avg
Harvey Kuenn, lf	4	1	1	0	0	0	.083
Matty Alou, lf	0	0	0	0	0	0	.273
Chuck Hiller, 2b	4	1	2	0	0	0	.318
Felipe Alou, rf	4	1	2	1	0	0	.318
Willie Mays, cf	3	1	1	0	1	0	.250
Orlando Cepeda, 1b	4	1	3	2	0	0	.188
Jim Davenport, 3b	4	0	1	1	0	1	.158
Ed Bailey, c	4	0	0	0	0	3	.077
Jose Pagan, ss	3	0	0	0	0	1	.412
Billy Pierce, p	3	0	0	0	0	0	.000
TOTALS	33	5	10	4	1	5	.236

	1	2	3	4	5	6	7	8	9	R	H	E
Yankees	0	0	0	0	1	0	0	1	0	2	3	2
Giants	0	0	0	3	2	0	0	0	x	5	10	1

E—Davenport, Boyer, Ford. DP—Yankees 2 (Kubek to Richardson to Skowron; Howard to Kubek), Giants 1 (Davenport to Hiller to Cepeda). LOB—Yankees 3, Giants 5. Scoring Position—Yankees 1-for-4, Giants 4-for-9. 2B—Boyer (1), Cepeda (1). HR—Maris (1). GDP—Howard, Mays. SB—Mays (1). CS—Cepeda (1).

Yankees	IP	H	R	ER	BB	K	ERA
Whitey Ford (L, 1-1)	4.2	9	5	5	1	3	4.12
Jim Coates	2.1	0	0	0	0	2	6.75
Marshall Bridges	1.0	1	0	0	0	0	4.91

Giants	IP	H	R	ER	BB	K	ERA
Billy Pierce (W, 1-1)	9.0	3	2	2	2	2	2.40

Time—2:00. Attendance—43,948. Umpires—HP, Berry. 1B, Landes. 2B, Honochick. 3B, Barlick.

Game 7
Tuesday, October 16

Yankees	AB	R	H	RBI	BB	K	Avg
Tony Kubek, ss	4	0	1	0	0	0	.276
Bobby Richardson, 2b	2	0	0	0	2	0	.148
Tom Tresh, lf	4	0	1	0	0	0	.321
Mickey Mantle, cf	3	0	1	0	1	1	.120
Roger Maris, rf	4	0	0	0	0	0	.174
Elston Howard, c	4	0	0	0	0	1	.143
Bill Skowron, 1b	4	1	1	0	0	0	.222
Clete Boyer, 3b	4	0	2	0	0	0	.318
Ralph Terry, p	3	0	1	0	1	2	.125
TOTALS	32	1	7	0	4	4	.214

Giants	AB	R	H	RBI	BB	K	Avg
Felipe Alou, rf	4	0	0	0	0	1	.269
Chuck Hiller, 2b	4	0	0	0	0	1	.269
Willie Mays, cf	4	0	1	0	0	0	.250
Willie McCovey, lf	4	0	1	0	0	0	.200
Orlando Cepeda, 1b	3	0	0	0	0	2	.158
Tom Haller, c	3	0	0	0	0	0	.286
Jim Davenport, 3b	3	0	0	0	0	0	.136
Jose Pagan, ss	2	0	0	0	0	0	.368
Ed Bailey, ph	1	0	0	0	0	0	.071
Ernie Bowman, ss	0	0	0	0	0	0	.000
Jack Sanford, p	2	0	1	0	0	0	.429
Billy O'Dell, p	0	0	0	0	0	0	.333
Matty Alou, ph	1	0	1	0	0	0	.333
TOTALS	31	0	4	0	0	4	.243

	1	2	3	4	5	6	7	8	9	R	H	E
Yankees	0	0	0	0	1	0	0	0	0	1	7	0
Giants	0	0	0	0	0	0	0	0	0	0	4	1

E—Pagan. DP—Giants 2 (Pagan to Hiller to Cepeda; Davenport to Cepeda). LOB—Yankees 8, Giants 4. Scoring Position—Yankees 1-for-7, Giants 0-for-2. 2B—Mays (2). 3B—McCovey (1). GDP—Kubek, Howard.

Yankees	IP	H	R	ER	BB	K	ERA
Ralph Terry (W, 2-1)	9.0	4	0	0	0	4	1.80

Giants	IP	H	R	ER	BB	K	ERA
Jack Sanford (L, 1-2)	7.0	7	1	1	4	3	1.93
Billy O'Dell	2.0	0	0	0	0	1	4.38

Sanford pitched to three batters in the 8th.

Time—2:29. Attendance—43,948. Umpires—HP, Landes. 1B, Honochick. 2B, Barlick. 3B, Berry.

1962 World Series—Composite Statistics

Batting

Yankees	G	AB	R	H	RBI	2B	3B	HR	DB	SO	SB	CS	Avg	OBP	Slg
Yogi Berra	2	2	0	0	0	0	0	0	2	0	0	0	.000	.500	.000
Johnny Blanchard	1	1	0	0	0	0	0	0	0	1	0	0	.000	.000	.000
Clete Boyer	7	22	2	7	4	1	0	1	1	3	0	0	.318	.333	.500
Whitey Ford	3	7	0	0	0	0	0	0	1	3	0	0	.000	.125	.000
Elston Howard	6	21	1	3	1	1	0	0	1	4	0	0	.143	.217	.190
Tony Kubek	7	29	2	8	1	1	0	0	1	3	0	1	.276	.300	.310
Dale Long	2	5	0	1	1	0	0	0	0	1	0	0	.200	.200	.200
Hector Lopez	2	2	0	0	0	0	0	0	0	0	0	0	.000	.000	.000
Mickey Mantle	7	25	2	3	0	1	0	0	4	5	2	0	.120	.241	.160
Roger Maris	7	23	4	4	5	1	0	1	5	2	0	0	.174	.321	.348
Bobby Richardson	7	27	3	4	0	0	0	3	1	0	0	0	.148	.233	.148
Bill Skowron	6	18	1	4	1	0	1	0	1	5	0	0	.222	.300	.333
Bill Stafford	1	3	0	0	0	0	0	0	0	1	0	0	.000	.000	.000
Ralph Terry	3	8	0	1	0	0	0	0	1	6	0	0	.125	.222	.125
Tom Tresh	7	28	5	9	4	1	0	1	1	4	2	0	.321	.345	.464
Totals	7	221	20	44	17	6	1	3	21	39	4	1	.199	.273	.276

Giants	G	AB	R	H	RBI	2B	3B	HR	BB	SO	SB	CS	Avg	OBP	Slg
Felipe Alou	7	26	2	7	1	1	1	1	0	4	0	0	.269	.296	.385
Matty Alou	6	12	4	1	1	1	0	0	1	0	0	0	.333	.333	.417
Ed Bailey	6	14	1	1	2	0	0	1	0	3	0	0	.071	.071	.286
Ernie Bowman	2	1	1	0	0	0	0	0	0	0	0	0	.000	.000	.000
Orlando Cepeda	5	19	1	3	2	1	0	0	0	4	0	1	.158	.158	.211
Jim Davenport	7	22	1	3	1	1	0	0	4	7	0	0	.136	.269	.182
Tom Haller	4	14	1	4	3	0	0	1	0	2	0	1	.286	.286	.571
Chuck Hiller	7	26	4	7	5	3	0	1	3	4	0	0	.269	.345	.500
Harvey Kuenn	3	12	1	1	0	0	0	0	1	1	0	0	.083	.154	.083
Juan Marichal	1	2	0	0	0	0	0	0	0	1	0	0	.000	.000	.000
Willie Mays	7	28	3	7	1	2	0	0	1	5	1	0	.250	.276	.321
Willie McCovey	4	15	2	3	1	0	1	1	3	0	0	0	.200	.250	.533
Bob Nieman	1	0	0	0	0	0	0	0	1	0	0	0	—	1.000	—
Billy O'Dell	3	3	0	1	0	0	0	0	0	0	0	0	.333	.333	.333
John Orsino	1	1	0	0	0	0	0	0	0	0	0	0	.000	.000	.000
Jose Pagan	7	19	2	7	2	0	0	1	0	1	0	0	.368	.400	.526
Billy Pierce	2	5	0	0	0	0	0	0	0	0	0	0	.000	.000	.000
Jack Sanford	3	7	0	3	0	0	0	0	0	2	0	0	.429	.429	.429
Totals	7	226	21	51	19	10	2	5	12	39	1	2	.226	.268	.354

Pitching

Yankees	G	GS	CG	IP	H	R	ER	BB	SO	W-L	Sv-Op	Hld	ERA
Marshall Bridges	2	0	0	3.2	4	3	2	3	3	0-0	0-0	0	4.91
Jim Coates	2	0	0	2.2	1	2	2	1	3	0-1	0-0	0	6.75
Bud Daley	1	0	0	1.0	1	0	0	1	0	0-0	0-0	0	0.00
Whitey Ford	3	3	1	19.2	24	9	9	4	12	1-1	0-0	0	4.12
Bill Stafford	1	1	1	9.0	4	2	2	2	5	1-0	0-0	0	2.00
Ralph Terry	3	3	2	25.0	17	5	5	2	16	2-1	0-0	0	1.80
Totals	7	7	4	61.0	51	21	20	12	39	4-3	0-0	0	2.95

Giants	G	GS	CG	IP	H	R	ER	BB	SO	W-L	Sv-Op	Hld	ERA
Bobby Bolin	2	0	0	2.2	4	2	2	2	2	0-0	0-0	0	6.75
Don Larsen	3	0	0	2.1	1	1	1	2	0	1-0	0-0	0	3.86
Juan Marichal	1	1	0	4.0	2	0	0	2	4	0-0	0-0	0	0.00
Stu Miller	2	0	0	1.1	1	0	0	2	0	0-0	0-0	0	0.00
Billy O'Dell	3	1	0	12.1	12	6	6	3	9	0-1	1-1	0	4.38
Billy Pierce	2	2	1	15.0	8	5	4	2	5	1-1	0-0	0	2.40
Jack Sanford	3	3	1	23.1	16	6	5	8	19	1-2	0-0	0	1.93
Totals	7	7	2	61.0	44	20	18	21	39	3-4	1-1	0	2.66

Fielding

Yankees	Pos	G	PO	Ast	E	DP	PB	FPct
Yogi Berra	c	1	6	1	0	0	0	1.000
Clete Boyer	3b	7	9	16	2	2	—	.926
Marshall Bridges	p	2	0	1	0	0	—	1.000
Jim Coates	p	2	0	0	0	0	—	—
Bud Daley	p	1	0	0	0	0	—	—
Whitey Ford	p	3	0	4	1	0	—	.800
Elston Howard	c	6	37	1	0	1	0	1.000
Tony Kubek	ss	7	12	17	1	3	—	.967
Dale Long	1b	2	9	3	0	1	—	1.000
Mickey Mantle	cf	7	11	0	0	0	—	1.000
Roger Maris	rf	7	11	1	0	0	—	1.000
Bobby Richardson	2b	7	19	19	1	4	—	.974
Bill Skowron	1b	6	52	1	0	3	—	1.000
Bill Stafford	p	1	0	1	0	0	—	1.000
Ralph Terry	p	3	3	2	0	0	—	1.000
Tom Tresh	lf	7	14	0	0	0	—	1.000
Totals		7	183	67	5	14	0	.980

Giants	Pos	G	PO	Ast	E	DP	PB	FPct
Felipe Alou	rf	4	3	0	0	0	—	1.000
	lf	3	6	0	1	0	—	.857
Matty Alou	lf	2	2	0	0	0	—	1.000
	rf	2	0	0	0	0	—	—
Ed Bailey	c	3	15	0	0	0	0	1.000
Bobby Bolin	p	2	0	0	0	0	—	—
Ernie Bowman	ss	2	0	5	0	0	—	1.000
Orlando Cepeda	1b	5	39	4	0	6	—	1.000
Jim Davenport	3b	7	6	12	3	4	—	.857
Tom Haller	c	4	29	2	0	1	1	1.000
Chuck Hiller	2b	7	16	22	1	7	—	.974
Harvey Kuenn	lf	2	8	0	0	0	—	1.000
	rf	1	3	0	0	0	—	1.000
Don Larsen	p	3	1	0	0	0	—	1.000
Juan Marichal	p	1	1	0	0	1	—	1.000
Willie Mays	cf	7	19	0	0	0	—	1.000
Willie McCovey	1b	2	18	4	1	2	—	.957
	lf	1	3	0	0	0	—	1.000
	rf	1	2	0	1	0	—	.667
Stu Miller	p	2	0	1	0	0	—	1.000
Billy O'Dell	p	3	0	0	0	0	—	—
John Orsino	c	1	0	0	0	0	0	—
Jose Pagan	ss	7	8	14	1	2	—	.957
Billy Pierce	p	2	1	0	0	0	—	1.000
Jack Sanford	p	3	3	3	0	1	—	1.000
Totals		7	183	67	8	24	1	.969

1963 Los Angeles Dodgers (NL) 4, New York Yankees (AL) 0

Led by their incomparable pitching staff, the Los Angeles Dodgers took the World Series from the New York Yankees in four games straight. Sandy Koufax set a new World Series record with 15 strikeouts in the Dodgers' 5-2 victory over the Yankees in Game 1. Johnny Podres beat the Yanks 4-1 in Game 2, as Roger Maris had a tough day in the field. In the first inning, he fell down while chasing a drive off the bat of Willie Davis, with the ball going to the wall for a two-run double. In the third inning, he went into the right-field corner to field Tommy Davis' drive and banged into the railing, injuring his knee and elbow and sidelining him for the remainder of the Series. In Game 3, Tommy Davis' first-inning chopper over the mound plated the game's only run, and Don Drysdale tossed a three-hit shutout to beat the Yanks 1-0. Willie Davis' seventh-inning sacrifice fly brought home the decisive run in Game 4 as Koufax went the distance for a 2-1 victory.

Game 1

Wednesday, October 2

Dodgers	AB	R	H	RBI	BB	K	Avg
Maury Wills, ss	5	0	0	0	0	2	.000
Jim Gilliam, 3b	4	0	1	0	1	1	.250
Willie Davis, cf	3	1	0	0	0	2	.000
Tommy Davis, lf	4	0	3	0	0	0	.750
Frank Howard, rf	4	1	1	0	0	1	.250
Ron Fairly, rf	0	0	0	0	0	0	—
Bill Skowron, 1b	3	1	2	2	1	1	.667
Dick Tracewski, 2b	4	1	1	0	0	0	.250
John Roseboro, c	4	1	1	3	0	2	.250
Sandy Koufax, p	4	0	0	0	0	1	.000
TOTALS	35	5	9	5	2	10	.257

Yankees	AB	R	H	RBI	BB	K	Avg
Tony Kubek, ss	4	1	1	0	0	2	.250
Bobby Richardson, 2b	3	0	0	0	1	3	.000
Tom Tresh, lf	3	1	1	2	1	2	.333
Mickey Mantle, cf	3	0	0	0	1	2	.000
Roger Maris, rf	4	0	0	0	0	1	.000
Elston Howard, c	4	0	1	0	0	1	.250
Joe Pepitone, 1b	4	0	2	0	0	1	.500
Clete Boyer, 3b	4	0	1	0	0	0	.250
Whitey Ford, p	1	0	0	0	0	0	.000
Hector Lopez, ph	1	0	0	0	0	1	.000
Stan Williams, p	0	0	0	0	0	0	—
Phil Linz, ph	1	0	0	0	0	1	.000
Steve Hamilton, p	0	0	0	0	0	0	—
Harry Bright, ph	1	0	0	0	0	1	.000
TOTALS	33	2	6	2	3	15	.182

	1	2	3	4	5	6	7	8	9	R	H	E
Dodgers	0	4	1	0	0	0	0	0	0	5	9	0
Yankees	0	0	0	0	0	0	0	2	0	2	6	0

LOB—Dodgers 6, Yankees 7. Scoring Position—Dodgers 4-for-9, Yankees 1-for-4. 2B—FHoward (1). HR—Roseboro (1), Tresh (1). S—WDavis (1). SB—TDavis (1).

Dodgers	IP	H	R	ER	BB	K	ERA
Sandy Koufax (W, 1-0)	9.0	6	2	2	3	15	2.00

Yankees	IP	H	R	ER	BB	K	ERA
Whitey Ford (L, 0-1)	5.0	8	5	5	2	4	9.00
Stan Williams	3.0	1	0	0	0	5	0.00
Steve Hamilton	1.0	0	0	0	0	1	0.00

Time—2:09. Attendance—69,000. Umpires—HP, Paparella. 1B, Gorman. 2B, Napp. 3B, Crawford.

Game 2

Thursday, October 3

Dodgers	AB	R	H	RBI	BB	K	Avg
Maury Wills, ss	4	1	2	0	0	0	.222
Jim Gilliam, 3b	4	1	1	0	0	0	.250
Willie Davis, cf	4	1	2	2	0	2	.286
Tommy Davis, lf	4	0	2	1	0	0	.625
Frank Howard, rf	3	0	0	0	0	1	.143
Ron Fairly, ph-rf	0	0	0	0	1	0	—
Bill Skowron, 1b	4	1	2	1	0	1	.571
Dick Tracewski, 2b	3	0	0	0	1	1	.143
John Roseboro, c	4	0	0	0	0	1	.125
Johnny Podres, p	4	0	1	0	0	0	.250
Ron Perranoski, p	0	0	0	0	0	0	—
TOTALS	34	4	10	4	2	6	.292

Yankees	AB	R	H	RBI	BB	K	Avg
Tony Kubek, ss	4	0	0	0	0	0	.125
Bobby Richardson, 2b	4	0	1	0	0	0	.143
Tom Tresh, lf	4	0	2	0	0	0	.429
Mickey Mantle, cf	4	0	0	0	0	0	.000
Roger Maris, rf	1	0	0	0	0	0	.000
Hector Lopez, rf	3	1	2	0	0	0	.500
Elston Howard, c	4	0	2	1	0	0	.375
Joe Pepitone, 1b	3	0	0	0	1	0	.286
Clete Boyer, 3b	4	0	0	0	0	3	.125
Al Downing, p	1	0	0	0	0	1	.000
Harry Bright, ph	1	0	0	0	0	1	.000
Ralph Terry, p	0	0	0	0	0	0	—
Phil Linz, ph	1	0	0	0	0	0	.000
Hal Reniff, p	0	0	0	0	0	0	—
TOTALS	34	1	7	1	1	5	.197

	1	2	3	4	5	6	7	8	9	R	H	E
Dodgers	2	0	0	1	0	0	0	1	0	4	10	1
Yankees	0	0	0	0	0	0	0	0	1	1	7	0

E—Podres. DP—Yankees 3 (Richardson to Kubek to Pepitone; Kubek to Richardson to Pepitone; Terry to Richardson to Pepitone). LOB—Dodgers 5, Yankees 7. Scoring Position—Dodgers 3-for-8, Yankees 1-for-7. 2B—WDavis 2 (2), Lopez 2 (2). 3B—TDavis 2 (2). HR—Skowron (1). GDP—Gilliam, Skowron, Roseboro. SB—Wills (1).

Dodgers	IP	H	R	ER	BB	K	ERA
Johnny Podres (W, 1-0)	8.1	6	1	1	1	4	1.08
Ron Perranoski (S, 1)	0.2	1	0	0	0	1	0.00

Yankees	IP	H	R	ER	BB	K	ERA
Al Downing (L, 0-1)	5.0	7	3	3	1	6	5.40
Ralph Terry	3.0	3	1	1	1	0	3.00
Hal Reniff	1.0	0	0	0	0	0	0.00

Time—2:13. Attendance—66,455. Umpires—HP, Gorman. 1B, Napp. 2B, Crawford. 3B, Paparella.

Game 3

Saturday, October 5

Yankees	AB	R	H	RBI	BB	K	Avg
Tony Kubek, ss	4	0	2	0	0	0	.250
Bobby Richardson, 2b	3	0	0	0	0	0	.100
Tom Tresh, lf	4	0	0	0	0	2	.273
Mickey Mantle, cf	4	0	1	0	0	0	.091
Joe Pepitone, 1b	3	0	0	0	0	0	.200
Elston Howard, c	3	0	0	0	0	2	.273
Johnny Blanchard, rf	3	0	0	0	0	0	.000
Clete Boyer, 3b	2	0	0	0	1	1	.100
Jim Bouton, p	2	0	0	0	0	2	.000
Yogi Berra, ph	1	0	0	0	0	0	.000
Hal Reniff, p	0	0	0	0	0	0	—
TOTALS	29	0	3	0	1	9	.173

Dodgers	AB	R	H	RBI	BB	K	Avg
Maury Wills, ss	4	0	0	0	0	0	.154
Jim Gilliam, 3b	2	1	0	0	2	0	.200
Willie Davis, cf	3	0	0	0	0	1	.200
Tommy Davis, lf	4	0	1	1	0	2	.500
Ron Fairly, rf	1	0	0	0	2	0	.000
Bill Skowron, 1b	3	0	1	0	0	1	.500
John Roseboro, c	3	0	1	0	0	0	.182
Dick Tracewski, 2b	3	0	1	0	0	0	.200
Don Drysdale, p	1	0	0	0	2	0	.000
TOTALS	24	1	4	1	6	5	.269

	1	2	3	4	5	6	7	8	9	R	H	E
Yankees	0	0	0	0	0	0	0	0	0	0	3	0
Dodgers	1	0	0	0	0	0	0	0	x	1	4	1

Game 4

Sunday, October 6

Yankees	AB	R	H	RBI	BB	K	Avg
Tony Kubek, ss	4	0	0	0	0	1	.188
Bobby Richardson, 2b	4	0	2	0	0	0	.214
Tom Tresh, lf	4	0	0	0	0	2	.200
Mickey Mantle, cf	4	1	1	1	0	1	.133
Elston Howard, c	4	0	2	0	0	0	.333
Hector Lopez, rf	4	0	0	0	0	0	.250
Joe Pepitone, 1b	3	0	0	0	0	2	.154
Clete Boyer, 3b	3	0	0	0	0	2	.077
Whitey Ford, p	2	0	0	0	0	0	.000
Phil Linz, ph	1	0	1	0	0	0	.333
Hal Reniff, p	0	0	0	0	0	0	—
TOTALS	33	1	6	1	0	8	.191

Dodgers	AB	R	H	RBI	BB	K	Avg
Maury Wills, ss	2	0	0	0	1	1	.133
Jim Gilliam, 3b	3	1	0	0	0	0	.154
Willie Davis, cf	2	0	0	1	0	1	.167
Tommy Davis, lf	3	0	0	0	0	0	.400
Frank Howard, rf	3	1	2	1	0	0	.300
Ron Fairly, rf	0	0	0	0	0	0	.000
Bill Skowron, 1b	3	0	0	0	0	0	.385
John Roseboro, c	3	0	0	0	0	1	.143
Dick Tracewski, 2b	3	0	0	0	0	0	.154
Sandy Koufax, p	2	0	0	0	0	1	.000
TOTALS	24	2	2	2	1	4	.214

	1	2	3	4	5	6	7	8	9	R	H	E
Yankees	0	0	0	0	0	0	1	0	0	1	6	1
Dodgers	0	0	0	1	0	1	0	x		2	2	1

E—Tracewski, Pepitone. DP—Yankees 2 (EHoward to Pepitone; Kubek to Richardson to Pepitone), Dodgers 1 (Tracewski to Skowron). LOB—Yankees 5, Dodgers 0. Scoring Position—Yankees 0-for-3, Dodgers 0-for-0. 2B—Richardson (1). HR—Mantle (1), FHoward (1). SF—WDavis. GDP—Kubek, Skowron.

Yankees	IP	H	R	ER	BB	K	ERA
Whitey Ford (L, 0-2)	7.0	2	2	1	1	4	4.50
Hal Reniff	1.0	0	0	0	0	0	0.00

Dodgers	IP	H	R	ER	BB	K	ERA
Sandy Koufax (W, 2-0)	9.0	6	1	1	0	8	1.50

Time—1:50. Attendance—55,912. Umpires—HP, Crawford. 1B, Paparella. 2B, Gorman. 3B, Napp.

E—Wills. DP—Yankees 2 (Pepitone to Kubek; Richardson to Pepitone to Kubek). LOB—Yankees 5, Dodgers 6. Scoring Position—Yankees 0-for-5, Dodgers 1-for-6. S—Richardson, WDavis. GDP—Gilliam. CS—Kubek (1), Gilliam (1).

Yankees	IP	H	R	ER	BB	K	ERA
Jim Bouton (L, 0-1)	7.0	4	1	1	5	4	1.29
Hal Reniff	1.0	0	0	0	1	1	0.00

Dodgers	IP	H	R	ER	BB	K	ERA
Don Drysdale (W, 1-0)	9.0	3	0	0	1	9	0.00

WP—Bouton 2. HBP—Pepitone by Drysdale. Time—2:05. Attendance—55,912. Umpires—HP, Napp. 1B, Crawford. 2B, Paparella. 3B, Gorman.

1963 World Series—Composite Statistics

Batting

Dodgers	G	AB	R	H	RBI	2B	3B	HR	BB	SO	SB	CS	Avg	OBP	Slg
Tommy Davis	4	15	0	6	2	0	2	0	0	2	1	0	.400	.400	.667
Willie Davis	4	12	2	2	3	2	0	0	0	6	0	0	.167	.154	.333
Don Drysdale	1	1	0	0	0	0	0	0	2	0	0		.000	.667	.000
Ron Fairly	4	1	0	0	0	0	0	0	3	0	0	0	.000	.750	.000
Jim Gilliam	4	13	3	2	0	0	0	0	3	1	0	1	.154	.313	.154
Frank Howard	3	10	2	3	1	1	0	1	0	2	0	0	.300	.300	.700
Sandy Koufax	2	6	0	0	0	0	0	0	0	2	0	0	.000	.000	.000
Johnny Podres	1	4	0	1	0	0	0	0	0	0	0	0	.250	.250	.250
John Roseboro	4	14	1	2	3	0	0	1	0	4	0	0	.143	.143	.357
Bill Skowron	4	13	2	5	3	0	0	1	1	3	0	0	.385	.429	.615
Dick Tracewski	4	13	1	2	0	0	0	0	1	2	0	0	.154	.214	.154
Maury Wills	4	15	1	2	0	0	0	0	1	3	1	0	.133	.188	.133
Totals	**4**	**117**	**12**	**25**	**12**	**3**	**2**	**3**	**11**	**25**	**2**	**1**	**.214**	**.279**	**.350**

Yankees	G	AB	R	H	RBI	2B	3B	HR	BB	SO	SB	CS	Avg	OBP	Slg
Yogi Berra	1	1	0	0	0	0	0	0	0	0	0	0	.000	.000	.000
Johnny Blanchard	1	3	0	0	0	0	0	0	0	0	0	0	.000	.000	.000
Jim Bouton	1	2	0	0	0	0	0	0	0	2	0	0	.000	.000	.000
Clete Boyer	4	13	0	1	0	0	0	0	1	6	0	0	.077	.143	.077
Harry Bright	2	2	0	0	0	0	0	0	0	2	0	0	.000	.000	.000
Al Downing	1	1	0	0	0	0	0	0	0	1	0	0	.000	.000	.000
Whitey Ford	2	3	0	0	0	0	0	0	0	0	0	0	.000	.000	.000
Elston Howard	4	15	0	5	1	0	0	0	0	3	0	0	.333	.333	.333
Tony Kubek	4	16	1	3	0	0	0	0	0	3	0	1	.188	.188	.188
Phil Linz	3	3	0	1	0	0	0	0	0	1	0	0	.333	.333	.333
Hector Lopez	3	8	1	2	0	2	0	0	0	1	0	0	.250	.250	.500
Mickey Mantle	4	15	1	2	1	0	0	1	1	5	0	0	.133	.188	.333
Roger Maris	2	5	0	0	0	0	0	0	0	1	0	0	.000	.000	.000
Joe Pepitone	4	13	0	2	0	0	0	0	1	3	0	0	.154	.267	.154
Bobby Richardson	4	14	0	3	0	1	0	0	1	3	0	0	.214	.267	.286
Tom Tresh	4	15	1	3	2	0	0	1	1	6	0	0	.200	.250	.400
Totals	**4**	**129**	**4**	**22**	**4**	**3**	**0**	**2**	**5**	**37**	**0**	**1**	**.171**	**.207**	**.240**

Pitching

Dodgers	G	GS	CG	IP	H	R	ER	BB	SO	W-L	Sv-Op	Hld	ERA
Don Drysdale	1	1	1	9.0	3	0	0	1	9	1-0	0-0	0	0.00
Sandy Koufax	2	2	2	18.0	12	3	3	3	23	2-0	0-0	0	1.50
Ron Perranoski	1	0	0	0.2	1	0	0	0	1	0-0	1-1	0	0.00
Johnny Podres	1	1	0	8.1	6	1	1	1	4	1-0	0-0	0	1.08
Totals	**4**	**4**	**3**	**36.0**	**22**	**4**	**4**	**5**	**37**	**4-0**	**1-1**	**0**	**1.00**

Yankees	G	GS	CG	IP	H	R	ER	BB	SO	W-L	Sv-Op	Hld	ERA
Jim Bouton	1	1	0	7.0	4	1	1	5	4	0-1	0-0	0	1.29
Al Downing	1	1	0	5.0	7	3	3	1	6	0-1	0-0	0	5.40
Whitey Ford	2	2	0	12.0	10	7	6	3	8	0-2	0-0	0	4.50
Steve Hamilton	1	0	0	1.0	0	0	0	0	1	0-0	0-0	0	0.00
Hal Reniff	3	0	0	3.0	0	0	0	1	1	0-0	0-0	0	0.00
Ralph Terry	1	0	0	3.0	3	1	1	1	0	0-0	0-0	0	3.00
Stan Williams	1	0	0	3.0	1	0	0	0	5	0-0	0-0	0	0.00
Totals	**4**	**4**	**0**	**34.0**	**25**	**12**	**11**	**11**	**25**	**0-4**	**0-0**	**0**	**2.91**

Fielding

Dodgers	Pos	G	PO	Ast	E	DP	PB	FPct
Tommy Davis	lf	4	6	0	0	0	—	1.000
Willie Davis	cf	4	6	0	0	0	—	1.000
Don Drysdale	p	1	1	3	0	0	—	1.000
Ron Fairly	rf	4	3	0	0	0	—	1.000
Jim Gilliam	3b	4	2	2	0	0	—	1.000
Frank Howard	rf	3	4	0	0	0	—	1.000
Sandy Koufax	p	2	1	3	0	0	—	1.000
Ron Perranoski	p	1	0	0	0	0	—	—
Johnny Podres	p	1	0	2	1	0	—	.667
John Roseboro	c	4	43	0	0	0	0	1.000
Bill Skowron	1b	4	30	4	0	1	—	1.000
Dick Tracewski	2b	4	7	7	1	1	—	.933
Maury Wills	ss	4	5	10	1	0	—	.938
Totals		**4**	**108**	**31**	**3**	**2**	**0**	**.979**

Yankees	Pos	G	PO	Ast	E	DP	PB	FPct
Johnny Blanchard	rf	1	1	0	0	0	—	1.000
Jim Bouton	p	1	1	2	0	0	—	1.000
Clete Boyer	3b	4	2	8	0	0	—	1.000
Al Downing	p	1	0	1	0	0	—	1.000
Whitey Ford	p	2	3	2	0	0	—	1.000
Steve Hamilton	p	1	0	0	0	0	—	—
Elston Howard	c	4	30	2	0	1	0	1.000
Tony Kubek	ss	4	5	13	0	5	—	1.000
Hector Lopez	rf	2	2	0	0	0	—	1.000
Mickey Mantle	cf	4	6	0	0	0	—	1.000
Roger Maris	rf	2	3	0	0	0	—	1.000
Joe Pepitone	1b	4	37	6	1	7	—	.977
Hal Reniff	p	3	1	0	0	0	—	1.000
Bobby Richardson	2b	4	7	14	0	5	—	1.000
Ralph Terry	p	1	1	1	0	1	—	1.000
Tom Tresh	lf	4	3	0	0	0	—	1.000
Stan Williams	p	1	0	0	0	0	—	—
Totals		**4**	**102**	**49**	**1**	**19**	**0**	**.993**

1964 St. Louis Cardinals (NL) 4, New York Yankees (AL) 3

The St. Louis Cardinals beat the New York Yankees in an eventful seven-game Series. The Cardinals' Mike Shannon hit a two-run homer off the Busch Stadium scoreboard in Game 1, and the Cardinals bombed Whitey Ford, winning 9-5. New York's Mel Stottlemyre beat Bob Gibson, 8-3, in Game 2. Jim Bouton and Curt Simmons battled to a 1-1 tie after eight innings before Mickey Mantle's ninth-inning blast off Barney Schultz won Game 3 for New York, 2-1. Ken Boyer's grand slam gave the Cards a 4-3 win in the fourth game, and Tim McCarver's three-run shot in the 10th inning gave St. Louis a 5-2 win in Game 5. The sixth game went to the Yanks, 8-3, on a barrage of homers that included a grand slam by Joe Pepitone. In the seventh game, Bob Gibson went the distance and survived a pair of ninth-inning solo homers to win, 7-5. The day after the final game, New York manager Yogi Berra was fired, and St. Louis skipper Johnny Keane resigned. Several days later, Keane was hired to manage the Yankees.

Game 1

Wednesday, October 7

Yankees	AB	R	H	RBI	BB	K	Avg
Phil Linz, ss	4	0	0	0	1	0	.000
Bobby Richardson, 2b	5	0	2	1	0	0	.400
Roger Maris, cf	4	0	1	0	1	1	.250
Mickey Mantle, rf	5	1	2	0	0	1	.400
Elston Howard, c	4	1	2	0	1	0	.500
Tom Tresh, lf	4	1	2	3	1	0	.500
Joe Pepitone, 1b	5	0	0	0	0	1	.000
Clete Boyer, 3b	4	1	1	0	0	0	.250
Whitey Ford, p	1	0	1	1	2	0	1.000
Al Downing, p	0	0	0	0	0	0	—
Johnny Blanchard, ph	1	0	1	0	0	0	1.000
Mike Hegan, pr	0	1	0	0	0	0	—
Rollie Sheldon, p	0	0	0	0	0	0	—
Pete Mikkelsen, p	0	0	0	0	0	0	—
TOTALS	37	5	12	5	6	3	.324

Cardinals	AB	R	H	RBI	BB	K	Avg
Curt Flood, cf	5	1	2	2	0	0	.400
Lou Brock, lf	5	1	2	2	0	0	.400
Dick Groat, ss	4	0	1	0	1	0	.250
Ken Boyer, 3b	3	1	1	1	1	1	.333
Bill White, 1b	4	0	0	0	0	2	.000
Mike Shannon, rf	4	3	2	2	0	0	.500
Tim McCarver, c	3	1	2	0	1	0	.667
Dal Maxvill, 2b	2	0	0	0	0	1	.000
Charlie James, ph	1	0	0	0	0	0	.000
Barney Schultz, p	1	0	0	0	0	0	.000
Ray Sadecki, p	2	0	1	0	1	1	.500
Carl Warwick, ph	1	0	1	1	0	0	1.000
Julian Javier, pr-2b	0	1	0	0	0	0	—
Bob Skinner, ph	0	0	0	1	0	0	—
Jerry Buchek, pr-2b	0	1	0	0	0	0	—
TOTALS	35	9	12	9	4	5	.343

	1	2	3	4	5	6	7	8	9	R	H	E
Yankees	0	3	0	0	1	0	0	1	0	5	12	2
Cardinals	1	1	0	0	4	0	3	x		9	12	0

E—CBoyer, Mantle. DP—Yankees 1 (Sheldon to Pepitone), Cardinals 1 (Groat to Maxvill to White). LOB—Yankees 11, Cardinals 7. Scoring Position—Yankees 4-for-9, Cardinals 6-for-14. 2B—Tresh (1), Brock (1), Blanchard (1). 3B—Flood (1), McCarver (1). HR—Tresh (1), Shannon (1). SF—KBoyer. GDP—Tresh. SB—CBoyer (1).

Yankees	IP	H	R	ER	BB	K	ERA
Whitey Ford (L, 0-1)	5.1	8	5	5	1	4	8.44
Al Downing	1.2	2	1	1	0	1	5.40
Rollie Sheldon	0.2	0	2	0	2	0	0.00
Pete Mikkelsen	0.1	2	1	0	1	0	0.00

Cardinals	IP	H	R	ER	BB	K	ERA
Ray Sadecki (W, 1-0)	6.0	8	4	4	5	2	6.00
Barney Schultz (S, 1)	3.0	4	1	1	1	1	3.00

PB—Howard 2. Time—2:42. Attendance—30,805. Umpires—HP, Secory. 1B, McKinley. 2B, Burkhart. 3B, Soar.

Game 2

Thursday, October 8

Yankees	AB	R	H	RBI	BB	K	Avg
Phil Linz, ss	4	2	3	1	1	0	.375
Bobby Richardson, 2b	5	1	2	1	0	1	.400
Roger Maris, cf	5	1	2	0	0	1	.333
Mickey Mantle, rf	4	2	1	2	1	2	.333
Hector Lopez, rf	0	0	0	0	0	0	—
Elston Howard, c	4	2	1	0	1	1	.375
Joe Pepitone, 1b	4	0	2	1	0	0	.222
Tom Tresh, lf	3	0	1	2	1	1	.429
Clete Boyer, 3b	3	0	0	1	1	0	.143
Mel Stottlemyre, p	5	0	0	0	0	4	.000
TOTALS	37	8	12	8	5	10	.306

Cardinals	AB	R	H	RBI	BB	K	Avg
Curt Flood, cf	4	0	0	1	0	1	.222
Lou Brock, lf	4	0	0	0	1	0	.222
Bill White, 1b	3	0	0	0	1	1	.000
Ken Boyer, 3b	4	0	0	0	0	1	.143
Dick Groat, ss	3	1	1	0	1	0	.286
Tim McCarver, c	4	0	1	1	0	0	.429
Mike Shannon, rf	4	1	0	0	0	0	.375
Dal Maxvill, 2b	2	0	1	0	0	0	.250
Carl Warwick, ph	1	1	1	0	0	0	1.000
Barney Schultz, p	0	0	0	0	0	0	.000
Gordie Richardson, p	0	0	0	0	0	0	—
Roger Craig, p	0	0	0	0	0	0	—
Charlie James, ph	1	0	0	0	0	1	.000
Bob Gibson, p	1	0	1	0	0	0	1.000
Bob Skinner, ph	1	0	1	0	0	0	1.000
Jerry Buchek, pr-2b	0	0	0	0	0	0	—
TOTALS	32	3	7	3	2	4	.277

	1	2	3	4	5	6	7	8	9	R	H	E
Yankees	0	0	0	1	0	1	2	0	4	8	12	0
Cardinals	0	0	1	0	0	0	0	1	1	3	7	0

DP—Yankees 1 (Linz to BRichardson to Pepitone). LOB—Yankees 10, Cardinals 5. Scoring Position—Yankees 4-for-12, Cardinals 1-for-6. 2B—BRichardson (1), Mantle (1), Howard (1), Pepitone (1), Skinner (1). 3B—Groat (1). HR—Linz (1). S—Gibson. SF—Tresh, CBoyer. GDP—Shannon.

Yankees	IP	H	R	ER	BB	K	ERA
Mel Stottlemyre (W, 1-0)	9.0	7	3	3	2	4	3.00

Cardinals	IP	H	R	ER	BB	K	ERA
Bob Gibson (L, 0-1)	8.0	8	4	4	3	9	4.50
Barney Schultz	0.1	2	2	2	0	0	8.10
Gordie Richardson	0.1	2	2	2	2	0	54.00
Roger Craig	0.1	0	0	0	0	1	0.00

WP—Gibson. PB—Howard. HBP—Pepitone by Gibson. Time—2:29. Attendance—30,805. Umpires—HP, McKinley. 1B, Burkhart. 2B, Soar. 3B, VSmith.

Game 3

Saturday, October 10

Cardinals	AB	R	H	RBI	BB	K	Avg
Curt Flood, cf	5	0	0	0	0	0	.143
Lou Brock, lf	4	0	0	0	0	0	.154
Bill White, 1b	4	0	1	0	0	0	.091
Ken Boyer, 3b	4	0	0	0	0	0	.091
Dick Groat, ss	4	0	1	0	0	1	.273
Tim McCarver, c	2	1	1	0	2	0	.444
Mike Shannon, rf	3	0	1	0	0	0	.364
Dal Maxvill, 2b	3	0	1	0	0	0	.286
Carl Warwick, ph	0	0	0	0	1	0	1.000
Jerry Buchek, 2b	0	0	0	0	0	0	—
Curt Simmons, p	2	0	1	1	0	1	.500
Bob Skinner, ph	1	0	0	0	0	0	.500
Barney Schultz, p	0	0	0	0	0	0	.000
TOTALS	32	1	6	1	3	2	.245

Yankees	AB	R	H	RBI	BB	K	Avg
Phil Linz, ss	4	0	0	0	0	0	.250
Bobby Richardson, 2b	4	0	1	0	0	0	.357
Roger Maris, cf	4	0	0	0	0	1	.231
Mickey Mantle, rf	3	1	2	1	1	0	.417
Elston Howard, c	2	1	1	0	1	0	.400
Tom Tresh, lf	3	0	0	0	0	0	.300
Joe Pepitone, 1b	2	0	0	0	1	0	.182
Clete Boyer, 3b	3	0	1	1	0	1	.200
Jim Bouton, p	3	0	0	0	0	0	.000
TOTALS	28	2	5	2	3	2	.284

	1	2	3	4	5	6	7	8	9	R	H	E
Cardinals	0	0	0	0	1	0	0	0	0	1	6	0
Yankees	0	1	0	0	0	0	0	0	1	2	5	2

Game 4

Sunday, October 11

Cardinals	AB	R	H	RBI	BB	K	Avg
Curt Flood, cf	4	1	2	0	0	0	.222
Lou Brock, lf	4	0	0	0	0	1	.118
Dick Groat, ss	4	1	1	0	0	1	.267
Ken Boyer, 3b	4	1	1	4	0	1	.133
Bill White, 1b	4	0	0	0	0	0	.067
Mike Shannon, rf	4	0	0	0	0	2	.267
Tim McCarver, c	3	0	1	0	1	0	.417
Dal Maxvill, 2b	3	0	0	0	1	1	.200
Ray Sadecki, p	0	0	0	0	0	0	.500
Roger Craig, p	1	0	0	0	0	0	.000
Carl Warwick, ph	1	1	1	0	0	0	1.000
Ron Taylor, p	1	0	0	0	0	0	.000
TOTALS	33	4	6	4	2	8	.226

Yankees	AB	R	H	RBI	BB	K	Avg
Phil Linz, ss	4	1	1	0	0	2	.250
Bobby Richardson, 2b	4	1	1	1	0	0	.333
Roger Maris, cf	4	1	1	0	0	0	.235
Mickey Mantle, rf	2	0	1	1	2	1	.429
Elston Howard, c	3	0	1	1	1	1	.385
Tom Tresh, lf	4	0	0	0	0	3	.214
Joe Pepitone, 1b	3	0	0	0	1	0	.143
Clete Boyer, 3b	4	0	1	0	0	1	.214
Al Downing, p	2	0	0	0	0	2	.000
Pete Mikkelsen, p	0	0	0	0	0	0	—
Johnny Blanchard, ph	1	0	0	0	0	0	.500
Ralph Terry, p	0	0	0	0	0	0	—
TOTALS	31	3	6	3	4	10	.274

	1	2	3	4	5	6	7	8	9	R	H	E
Cardinals	0	0	0	0	0	4	0	0	0	4	6	1
Yankees	3	0	0	0	0	0	0	0	0	3	6	1

E—Richardson, KBoyer. DP—Yankees 1 (Linz to Richardson to Pepitone). LOB—Cardinals 4, Yankees 5. Scoring Position—Cardinals 1-for-6, Yankees 4-for-6. 2B—Linz (1), Richardson (2). HR—KBoyer (1). GDP—KBoyer. CS—Linz (1).

Cardinals	IP	H	R	ER	BB	K	ERA
Ray Sadecki	0.1	4	3	2	0	0	8.53
Roger Craig (W, 1-0)	4.2	2	0	0	0	0	0.00
Ron Taylor (S, 1)	4.0	0	0	0	1	2	0.00

Yankees	IP	H	R	ER	BB	K	ERA
Al Downing (L, 0-1)	6.0	4	4	4	2	4	4.70
Pete Mikkelsen	1.0	0	0	0	0	1	0.00
Ralph Terry	2.0	2	0	0	0	3	0.00

Downing pitched to one batter in the 7th.

Time—2:18. Attendance—66,312. Umpires—HP, Soar. 1B, VSmith. 2B, ASmith. 3B, Secory.

Game 5
Monday, October 12

Cardinals	AB	R	H	RBI	BB	K	Avg
Curt Flood, cf	4	1	1	0	1	0	.227
Lou Brock, lf	5	0	2	1	0	1	.182
Bill White, 1b	4	1	0	1	1	1	.053
Ken Boyer, 3b	4	1	0	0	0	0	.158
Dick Groat, ss	4	1	1	0	1	0	.263
Tim McCarver, c	5	1	3	3	0	1	.471
Mike Shannon, rf	5	0	0	0	0	2	.200
Dal Maxvill, 2b	5	0	1	0	0	1	.200
Bob Gibson, p	4	1	1	0	0	3	.400
TOTALS	40	5	10	5	3	9	.222

Yankees	AB	R	H	RBI	BB	K	Avg
Phil Linz, ss	5	0	0	0	0	2	.190
Bobby Richardson, 2b	5	0	3	0	0	0	.391
Roger Maris, cf	5	0	0	0	0	0	.182
Mickey Mantle, rf	3	1	0	0	1	2	.353
Elston Howard, c	3	0	0	0	0	2	.313
Joe Pepitone, 1b	4	0	1	0	0	1	.167
Tom Tresh, lf	3	1	1	2	1	1	.235
Clete Boyer, 3b	2	0	0	0	0	2	.188
Johnny Blanchard, ph	1	0	0	0	0	0	.333
Pedro Gonzalez, 3b	1	0	0	0	0	0	.000
Mel Stottlemyre, p	2	0	1	0	0	1	.143
Hector Lopez, ph	1	0	0	0	0	1	.000
Hal Reniff, p	0	0	0	0	0	0	—
Pete Mikkelsen, p	0	0	0	0	0	0	—
Mike Hegan, ph	1	0	0	0	0	1	.000
TOTALS	36	2	6	2	2	13	.245

	1	2	3	4	5	6	7	8	9	10	R	H	E
Cardinals	0	0	0	0	2	0	0	0	0	3	5	10	1
Yankees	0	0	0	0	0	0	0	2	0	0	2	6	2

E—Richardson, Howard, Groat. DP—Cardinals 1 (Maxvill to Groat to White), Yankees 1 (Linz to Richardson to Pepitone). LOB—Cardinals 9, Yankees 7. Scoring Position—Cardinals 2-for-8, Yankees 1-for-4. HR—McCarver (1), Tresh (2). GDP—Shannon, Maris. SB—White (1).

Cardinals	IP	H	R	ER	BB	K	ERA
Bob Gibson (W, 1-1)	10.0	6	2	0	2	13	2.00

Yankees	IP	H	R	ER	BB	K	ERA
Mel Stottlemyre	7.0	6	2	1	2	6	2.25
Hal Reniff	0.1	2	0	0	0	0	0.00
Pete Mikkelsen (L, 0-1)	2.2	2	3	3	1	3	6.75

Reached, Catcher's Interference—Cardinals 1, KBoyer by Howard. Yankees 0. HBP—Howard by Gibson. Time—2:37. Attendance—65,633. Umpires—HP, VSmith. 1B, ASmith. 2B, Secory. 3B, McKinley.

Game 6
Wednesday, October 14

Yankees	AB	R	H	RBI	BB	K	Avg
Phil Linz, ss	5	1	1	0	0	1	.192
Bobby Richardson, 2b	4	0	2	0	0	0	.407
Roger Maris, cf	4	1	1	1	0	1	.192
Mickey Mantle, rf	3	2	1	1	1	1	.350
Elston Howard, c	4	1	1	1	0	0	.300
Tom Tresh, lf	3	2	1	0	1	1	.250
Joe Pepitone, 1b	4	1	1	4	0	1	.182
Clete Boyer, 3b	4	0	1	0	0	0	.200
Jim Bouton, p	4	0	1	1	0	2	.143
Steve Hamilton, p	0	0	0	0	0	0	—
TOTALS	35	8	10	8	2	7	.255

Cardinals	AB	R	H	RBI	BB	K	Avg
Curt Flood, cf	3	2	1	0	2	0	.240
Lou Brock, lf	4	0	3	0	0	0	.269
Bill White, 1b	4	0	0	1	0	0	.043
Ken Boyer, 3b	4	0	0	0	0	1	.130
Dick Groat, ss	4	0	0	0	0	1	.217
Tim McCarver, c	4	0	2	0	0	0	.476
Mike Shannon, rf	4	1	1	0	0	3	.208
Dal Maxvill, 2b	2	0	0	0	0	0	.176
Carl Warwick, ph	1	0	0	0	0	0	.750
Jerry Buchek, 2b	1	0	1	0	0	0	1.000
Curt Simmons, p	2	0	1	0	0	0	.500
Ron Taylor, p	0	0	0	0	0	0	.000
Charlie James, ph	1	0	0	0	0	0	.000
Barney Schultz, p	0	0	0	0	0	0	.000
Gordie Richardson, p	0	0	0	0	0	0	—
Bob Humphreys, p	0	0	0	0	0	0	—
Bob Skinner, ph	1	0	1	1	0	0	.667
TOTALS	35	3	10	2	2	5	.241

	1	2	3	4	5	6	7	8	9	R	H	E
Yankees	0	0	0	0	1	2	0	5	0	8	10	0
Cardinals	1	0	0	0	0	0	0	1	1	3	10	1

E—Brock. DP—Yankees 1 (BRichardson to Linz to Pepitone), Cardinals 1 (Maxvill to Groat). LOB—Yankees 3, Cardinals 7. Scoring Position—Yankees 3-for-9, Cardinals 1-for-7. 2B—Tresh (2), Brock (2). HR—Maris (1), Mantle (2), Pepitone (1). S—BRichardson. GDP—Flood, White. SB—BRichardson (1).

Yankees	IP	H	R	ER	BB	K	ERA
Jim Bouton (W, 2-0)	8.1	9	3	3	2	5	1.56
Steve Hamilton (S, 1)	0.2	1	0	0	0	0	0.00

Cardinals	IP	H	R	ER	BB	K	ERA
Curt Simmons (L, 0-1)	6.1	7	3	3	0	6	2.51
Ron Taylor	0.2	0	0	0	0	0	0.00
Barney Schultz	0.2	2	4	4	2	0	18.00
Gordie Richardson	0.1	1	1	1	0	0	40.50
Bob Humphreys	1.0	0	0	0	0	1	0.00

Time—2:37. Attendance—30,805. Umpires—HP, ASmith. 1B, Secory. 2B, McKinley. 3B, Burkhart.

Game 7
Thursday, October 15

Yankees	AB	R	H	RBI	BB	K	Avg
Phil Linz, ss	5	1	2	1	0	0	.226
Bobby Richardson, 2b	5	1	2	0	0	1	.406
Roger Maris, cf	4	1	1	0	0	0	.200
Mickey Mantle, rf	4	1	1	3	0	1	.333
Elston Howard, c	4	0	1	0	0	2	.292
Joe Pepitone, 1b	4	0	0	0	0	0	.154
Tom Tresh, lf	2	0	1	0	2	1	.273
Clete Boyer, 3b	4	1	1	1	0	1	.208
Mel Stottlemyre, p	1	0	0	0	0	1	.125
Mike Hegan, ph	0	0	0	0	1	0	.000
Al Downing, p	0	0	0	0	0	0	.000
Rollie Sheldon, p	0	0	0	0	0	0	—
Hector Lopez, ph	1	0	0	0	0	1	.000
Steve Hamilton, p	0	0	0	0	0	0	—
Pete Mikkelsen, p	0	0	0	0	0	0	—
Johnny Blanchard, ph	1	0	0	0	0	1	.250
TOTALS	35	5	9	5	3	9	.252

Cardinals	AB	R	H	RBI	BB	K	Avg
Curt Flood, cf	5	0	0	0	0	0	.200
Lou Brock, lf	4	1	2	1	0	1	.300
Bill White, 1b	4	1	2	0	0	1	.111
Ken Boyer, 3b	4	3	3	1	0	1	.222
Dick Groat, ss	3	0	0	1	1	0	.192
Tim McCarver, c	2	1	1	1	1	0	.478
Mike Shannon, rf	4	1	1	0	0	2	.214
Dal Maxvill, 2b	3	0	1	0	1	0	.200
Bob Gibson, p	4	0	0	0	0	0	.222
TOTALS	33	7	10	5	2	6	.236

	1	2	3	4	5	6	7	8	9	R	H	E
Yankees	0	0	0	0	0	3	0	0	2	5	9	2
Cardinals	0	0	3	0	3	0	1	0	x	7	10	1

E—Linz, CBoyer, Groat. DP—Cardinals 2 (Groat to Maxvill to White; Shannon to Groat). LOB—Yankees 6, Cardinals 6. Scoring Position—Yankees 1-for-4, Cardinals 1-for-8. 2B—White (1), KBoyer (2). HR—Linz (2), Mantle (3), CBoyer (1), Brock (1), KBoyer (2). S—Maxvill. SF—McCarver. GDP—Richardson. SB—McCarver (1), Shannon (1).

Yankees	IP	H	R	ER	BB	K	ERA
Mel Stottlemyre (L, 1-1)	4.0	5	3	3	2	2	3.15
Al Downing	0.0	3	3	3	0	0	8.22
Rollie Sheldon	2.0	0	0	0	0	2	0.00
Steve Hamilton	1.1	2	1	1	0	2	4.50
Pete Mikkelsen	0.2	0	0	0	0	0	5.79

Cardinals	IP	H	R	ER	BB	K	ERA
Bob Gibson (W, 2-1)	9.0	9	5	5	3	9	3.00

Downing pitched to three batters in the 5th.

Time—2:40. Attendance—30,346. Umpires—HP, Secory. 1B, McKinley. 2B, Burkhart. 3B, Soar.

1964 World Series—Composite Statistics

Batting

Cardinals	G	AB	R	H	RBI	2B	3B	HR	BB	SO	SB	CS	Avg	OBP	Slg
Ken Boyer	7	27	5	6	6	1	0	2	1	5	0	0	.222	.241	.481
Lou Brock	7	30	2	9	5	2	0	1	0	3	0	0	.300	.300	.467
Jerry Buchek	4	1	1	1	0	0	0	0	0	0	0	0	1.000	1.000	1.000
Roger Craig	2	1	0	0	0	0	0	0	0	0	0	0	.000	.000	.000
Curt Flood	7	30	5	6	3	0	1	0	3	1	0	0	.200	.273	.267
Bob Gibson	3	9	1	2	0	0	0	0	0	3	0	0	.222	.222	.222
Dick Groat	7	26	3	5	1	1	1	0	4	3	0	0	.192	.300	.308
Charlie James	3	3	0	0	0	0	0	0	0	1	0	0	.000	.000	.000
Julian Javier	1	0	1	0	0	0	0	0	0	0	0	0	—	—	—
Dal Maxvill	7	20	0	4	1	1	0	0	1	4	0	0	.200	.238	.250
Tim McCarver	7	23	4	11	5	1	1	1	5	1	1	0	.478	.552	.739
Ray Sadecki	2	2	0	1	1	0	0	0	0	1	0	0	.500	.500	.500
Barney Schultz	4	1	0	0	0	0	0	0	0	0	0	0	.000	.000	.000
Mike Shannon	7	28	6	6	2	0	0	1	0	9	1	0	.214	.214	.321
Curt Simmons	2	4	0	2	1	0	0	0	0	1	0	0	.500	.500	.500
Bob Skinner	4	3	0	2	1	1	0	0	1	0	0	0	.667	.750	1.000
Ron Taylor	2	1	0	0	0	0	0	0	0	0	0	0	.000	.000	.000
Carl Warwick	5	4	2	3	1	0	0	0	1	0	0	0	.750	.800	.750
Bill White	7	27	2	3	2	1	0	0	2	6	1	0	.111	.172	.148
Totals	7	240	32	61	29	8	3	5	18	39	3	0	.254	.304	.375

Yankees	G	AB	R	H	RBI	2B	3B	HR	BB	SO	SB	CS	Avg	OBP	Slg
Johnny Blanchard	4	4	0	1	0	1	0	0	0	1	0	0	.250	.250	.500
Jim Bouton	2	7	0	1	1	0	0	0	0	2	0	0	.143	.143	.143
Clete Boyer	7	24	2	5	3	1	0	1	1	5	1	0	.208	.231	.375
Al Downing	3	2	0	0	0	0	0	0	0	2	0	0	.000	.000	.000
Whitey Ford	1	1	0	1	1	0	0	0	0	2	0	0	1.000	1.000	1.000
Pedro Gonzalez	1	1	0	0	0	0	0	0	0	0	0	0	.000	.000	.000
Mike Hegan	3	1	1	0	0	0	0	0	1	1	0	0	.000	.500	.000
Elston Howard	7	24	5	7	2	1	0	0	4	6	0	0	.292	.414	.333
Phil Linz	7	31	5	7	2	1	0	2	2	5	0	1	.226	.273	.452
Hector Lopez	3	2	0	0	0	0	0	0	0	2	0	0	.000	.000	.000
Mickey Mantle	7	24	8	8	8	2	0	3	6	8	0	0	.333	.467	.792
Roger Maris	7	30	4	6	1	0	0	1	1	4	0	0	.200	.226	.300
Joe Pepitone	7	26	1	4	5	1	0	1	2	3	0	0	.154	.241	.308
Bobby Richardson	7	32	3	13	3	2	0	0	0	2	1	0	.406	.406	.469
Mel Stottlemyre	3	8	0	1	0	0	0	0	0	6	0	0	.125	.125	.125
Tom Tresh	7	22	4	6	7	2	0	2	6	7	0	0	.273	.414	.636
Totals	7	239	33	60	33	11	0	10	25	54	2	1	.251	.325	.423

Pitching

Cardinals	G	GS	CG	IP	H	R	ER	BB	SO	W-L	Sv-Op	Hld	ERA
Roger Craig	2	0	0	5.0	2	0	0	3	9	1-0	0-0	0	0.00
Bob Gibson	3	3	2	27.0	23	11	9	8	31	2-1	0-0	0	3.00
Bob Humphreys	1	0	0	1.0	0	0	0	0	1	0-0	0-0	0	0.00
Gordie Richardson	2	0	0	0.2	3	3	3	2	0	0-0	0-0	0	40.50
Ray Sadecki	2	2	0	6.1	12	7	6	5	2	1-0	0-0	0	8.53
Barney Schultz	4	0	0	4.0	9	8	8	3	1	0-1	1-1	0	18.00
Curt Simmons	2	2	0	14.1	11	4	4	3	8	0-1	0-0	0	2.51
Ron Taylor	2	0	0	4.2	0	0	0	1	2	0-0	1-1	0	0.00
Totals	7	7	2	63.0	60	33	30	25	54	4-3	2-2	0	4.29

Yankees	G	GS	CG	IP	H	R	ER	BB	SO	W-L	Sv-Op	Hld	ERA
Jim Bouton	2	2	1	17.1	15	4	3	5	7	2-0	0-0	0	1.56
Al Downing	3	1	0	7.2	9	8	7	2	5	0-1	0-0	0	8.22
Whitey Ford	1	1	0	5.1	8	5	5	1	4	0-1	0-0	0	8.44
Steve Hamilton	2	0	0	2.0	3	1	1	0	2	0-0	1-1	0	4.50
Pete Mikkelsen	4	0	0	4.2	4	4	3	2	4	0-1	0-0	0	5.79
Hal Reniff	1	0	0	0.1	0	0	0	0	0	0-0	0-0	0	0.00
Rollie Sheldon	2	0	0	2.2	0	2	0	2	2	0-0	0-0	0	0.00
Mel Stottlemyre	3	3	1	20.0	18	8	7	6	12	1-1	0-0	0	3.15
Ralph Terry	1	0	0	2.0	2	0	0	0	3	0-0	0-0	0	0.00
Totals	7	7	2	62.0	61	32	26	18	39	3-4	1-1	0	3.77

Fielding

Cardinals	Pos	G	PO	Ast	E	DP	PB	FPct
Ken Boyer	3b	7	9	16	1	0	—	.962
Lou Brock	lf	7	8	1	1	0	—	.900
Jerry Buchek	2b	4	0	1	0	0	—	1.000
Roger Craig	p	2	0	2	0	0	—	1.000
Curt Flood	cf	7	13	0	0	0	—	1.000
Bob Gibson	p	3	1	2	0	0	—	1.000
Dick Groat	ss	7	11	16	2	6	—	.931
Bob Humphreys	p	1	0	0	0	0	—	—
Julian Javier	2b	1	0	1	0	0	—	1.000
Dal Maxvill	2b	7	13	15	0	5	—	1.000
Tim McCarver	c	7	57	1	0	0	0	1.000
Gordie Richardson	p	2	0	0	0	0	—	—
Ray Sadecki	p	2	0	1	0	0	—	1.000
Barney Schultz	p	4	0	0	0	0	—	—
Mike Shannon	rf	7	13	2	0	1	—	1.000
Curt Simmons	p	2	2	1	0	0	—	1.000
Ron Taylor	p	2	0	2	0	0	—	1.000
Bill White	1b	7	62	3	0	4	—	1.000
Totals		7	189	64	4	16	0	.984

Yankees	Pos	G	PO	Ast	E	DP	PB	FPct
Jim Bouton	p	2	4	0	0	0	—	1.000
Clete Boyer	3b	7	6	22	2	0	—	.933
Al Downing	p	3	0	1	0	0	—	1.000
Whitey Ford	p	1	0	1	0	0	—	1.000
Pedro Gonzalez	3b	1	1	3	0	0	—	1.000
Steve Hamilton	p	2	0	0	0	0	—	—
Elston Howard	c	7	40	2	1	0	3	.977
Phil Linz	ss	7	7	21	2	5	—	.933
Hector Lopez	rf	1	0	0	0	0	—	—
Mickey Mantle	rf	7	12	0	2	0	—	.857
Roger Maris	cf	7	20	0	0	0	—	1.000
Pete Mikkelsen	p	4	1	1	0	0	—	1.000
Joe Pepitone	1b	7	62	6	0	6	—	1.000
Hal Reniff	p	1	0	0	0	0	—	—
Bobby Richardson	2b	7	19	19	2	5	—	.950
Rollie Sheldon	p	2	1	1	0	1	—	1.000
Mel Stottlemyre	p	3	2	5	0	0	—	1.000
Ralph Terry	p	1	0	0	0	0	—	—
Tom Tresh	lf	7	11	0	0	0	—	1.000
Totals		7	186	82	9	17	3	.968

1965 Los Angeles Dodgers (NL) 4, Minnesota Twins (AL) 3

The Los Angeles Dodgers notched a seven-game victory over the Minnesota Twins on the strength of Sandy Koufax' left arm. Minnesota's Mudcat Grant beat Don Drysdale in the opener, 8-2, as Zoilo Versalles socked a three-run homer. Koufax and Jim Kaat pitched scoreless ball in Game 2 until Tony Oliva's RBI double and Harmon Killebrew's RBI single broke the ice in the bottom of the sixth. Kaat went the route for a 5-1 win. Los Angeles' Claude Osteen twirled a five-hit shutout in Game 3, and Drysdale evened the Series with an 11-strikeout, 7-2 victory in the fourth game. Koufax blanked the Twins on four hits while Maury Wills had four of his own in the Dodgers' 7-0 win in Game 5. When Mudcat Grant stopped the Dodgers 5-1 in Game 6, Dodgers manager Walter Alston had to choose between his two aces for the seventh-game assignment. Instead of going with Drysdale on three days' rest, he opted for Koufax on two. The move paid off, as the lefty spun a three-hit shutout to ice the championship.

Game 1

Wednesday, October 6

Dodgers	AB	R	H	RBI	BB	K	Avg
Maury Wills, ss	5	0	2	1	0	1	.400
Jim Gilliam, 3b	5	0	1	0	0	0	.200
Willie Davis, cf	4	0	1	0	0	1	.250
Ron Fairly, rf	4	1	1	1	0	0	.250
Lou Johnson, lf	4	0	1	0	0	1	.250
Jim Lefebvre, 2b	4	1	1	0	0	0	.250
Wes Parker, 1b	3	0	1	0	0	1	.333
John Roseboro, c	4	0	1	0	0	0	.250
Don Drysdale, p	1	0	0	0	0	0	.000
Howie Reed, p	0	0	0	0	0	0	—
Willie Crawford, ph	1	0	1	0	0	0	1.000
Jim Brewer, p	0	0	0	0	0	0	—
Wally Moon, ph	1	0	0	0	0	0	.000
Ron Perranoski, p	0	0	0	0	0	0	—
Don LeJohn, ph	1	0	0	0	0	1	.000
TOTALS	37	2	10	2	1	5	.270

Twins	AB	R	H	RBI	BB	K	Avg
Zoilo Versalles, ss	5	1	2	4	0	2	.400
Sandy Valdespino, lf	4	1	1	0	0	0	.250
Tony Oliva, rf	4	0	0	0	0	0	.000
Harmon Killebrew, 3b	3	1	1	0	1	2	.333
Jimmie Hall, cf	3	0	1	0	1	2	.333
Don Mincher, 1b	3	2	1	1	0	0	.333
Earl Battey, c	4	0	2	0	0	0	.250
Frank Quilici, 2b	4	1	2	1	0	0	.500
Mudcat Grant, p	3	2	1	0	0	0	.333
TOTALS	33	8	10	8	3	6	.303

	1	2	3	4	5	6	7	8	9	R	H	E
Dodgers	0	1	0	0	0	0	0	0	1	2	10	1
Twins	0	1	6	0	0	1	0	0	x	8	10	0

E—Lefebvre. DP—Dodgers 1 (Perranoski to Wills to Parker). LOB—Dodgers 9, Twins 5. Scoring Position—Dodgers 1-for-7, Twins 5-for-13. 2B—Valdespino (1), Quilici (1), Grant (1). HR—Fairly (1), Versalles (1), Mincher (1). S—Grant. GDP—Battey. SB—Versalles (1).

Dodgers	IP	H	R	ER	BB	K	ERA
Don Drysdale (L, 0-1)	2.2	7	7	3	1	4	10.13
Howie Reed	1.1	0	0	0	1	0	0.00
Jim Brewer	2.0	3	1	1	0	1	4.50
Ron Perranoski	2.0	0	0	0	2	0	0.00

Twins	IP	H	R	ER	BB	K	ERA
Mudcat Grant (W, 1-0)	9.0	10	2	2	1	5	2.00

WP—Brewer. Time—2:29. Attendance—47,797. Umpires—HP, Hurley. 1B, Venzon. 2B, Flaherty. 3B, Sudol.

Game 2

Thursday, October 7

Dodgers	AB	R	H	RBI	BB	K	Avg
Maury Wills, ss	4	0	1	0	0	0	.333
Jim Gilliam, 3b	4	0	0	0	0	0	.111
Willie Davis, cf	4	0	0	0	0	0	.125
Lou Johnson, lf	4	0	0	0	0	1	.125
Ron Fairly, rf	4	1	2	0	0	1	.375
Jim Lefebvre, 2b	4	0	2	0	0	0	.375
Wes Parker, 1b	1	0	1	0	1	0	.500
John Roseboro, c	4	0	1	1	0	0	.250
Sandy Koufax, p	2	0	0	0	0	0	—
Don Drysdale, ph	1	0	0	0	0	1	.000
Ron Perranoski, p	0	0	0	0	0	0	—
Bob Miller, p	0	0	0	0	0	0	—
Dick Tracewski, ph	1	0	0	0	0	0	.000
TOTALS	33	1	7	1	1	3	.239

Twins	AB	R	H	RBI	BB	K	Avg
Zoilo Versalles, ss	5	2	1	0	0	1	.300
Joe Nossek, cf	3	0	1	0	0	0	.333
Tony Oliva, rf	4	1	1	1	0	1	.125
Harmon Killebrew, 3b	3	0	2	1	1	0	.500
Earl Battey, c	4	0	1	0	0	1	.250
Bob Allison, lf	4	1	1	0	0	3	.250
Don Mincher, 1b	4	1	1	0	0	1	.286
Frank Quilici, 2b	2	0	0	0	2	0	.333
Jim Kaat, p	4	0	1	2	0	3	.250
TOTALS	33	5	9	4	3	10	.286

	1	2	3	4	5	6	7	8	9	R	H	E
Dodgers	0	0	0	0	0	0	1	0	0	1	7	3
Twins	0	0	0	0	0	2	1	2	x	5	9	0

E—Johnson, Gilliam 2. LOB—Dodgers 8, Twins 8. Scoring Position—Dodgers 1-for-10, Twins 3-for-9. 2B—Oliva (1), Allison (1). 3B—Versalles (1). S—Parker, Nossek. CS—Quilici (1).

Dodgers	IP	H	R	ER	BB	K	ERA
Sandy Koufax (L, 0-1)	6.0	6	2	1	1	9	1.50
Ron Perranoski	1.2	3	3	3	2	1	7.36
Bob Miller	0.1	0	0	0	0	0	0.00

Twins	IP	H	R	ER	BB	K	ERA
Jim Kaat (W, 1-0)	9.0	7	1	1	1	3	1.00

Balk—Perranoski. WP—Perranoski. HBP—Parker by Kaat. Time—2:13. Attendance—48,700. Umpires—HP, Venzon. 1B, Flaherty. 2B, Sudol. 3B, Stewart.

Game 3

Saturday, October 9

Twins	AB	R	H	RBI	BB	K	Avg
Zoilo Versalles, ss	3	0	2	0	1	0	.385
Joe Nossek, cf	4	0	1	0	0	0	.286
Tony Oliva, rf	4	0	1	0	0	1	.167
Harmon Killebrew, 3b	3	0	0	0	0	0	.333
Earl Battey, c	3	0	0	0	0	0	.182
Jerry Zimmerman, c	1	0	0	0	0	0	.000
Bob Allison, lf	3	0	0	0	0	1	.143
Don Mincher, 1b	3	0	1	0	0	0	.300
Frank Quilici, 2b	3	0	0	0	0	0	.222
Camilo Pascual, p	1	0	0	0	0	0	.000
Rich Rollins, ph	1	0	0	0	0	0	.000
Jim Merritt, p	0	0	0	0	0	0	—
Sandy Valdespino, ph	1	0	0	0	0	0	.200
Johnny Klippstein, p	0	0	0	0	0	0	—
TOTALS	30	0	5	0	2	2	.244

Dodgers	AB	R	H	RBI	BB	K	Avg
Maury Wills, ss	4	0	1	1	0	0	.308
Jim Gilliam, 3b	4	0	1	0	0	0	.154
John Kennedy, 3b	0	0	0	0	0	0	—
Willie Davis, cf	4	1	1	0	0	0	.167
Ron Fairly, rf	4	1	1	0	0	0	.333
Lou Johnson, lf	2	0	2	1	1	0	.300
Jim Lefebvre, 2b	2	1	1	0	0	0	.400
Dick Tracewski, 2b	2	0	0	0	0	1	.000
Wes Parker, 1b	3	1	1	0	1	0	.429
John Roseboro, c	3	0	1	2	0	0	.273
Claude Osteen, p	2	0	1	0	0	0	.500
TOTALS	30	4	10	4	2	1	.280

	1	2	3	4	5	6	7	8	9	R	H	E
Twins	0	0	0	0	0	0	0	0	0	0	5	0
Dodgers	0	0	0	2	1	1	0	0	x	4	10	1

E—Kennedy. DP—Twins 1 (Zimmerman to Versalles), Dodgers 1 (Tracewski to Parker). LOB—Twins 5, Dodgers 6. Scoring Position—Twins 0-for-4, Dodgers 4-for-14. 2B—Versalles (1), Wills (1), Gilliam (1), Fairly (1), Johnson 2 (2). S—Johnson, Osteen. GDP—Oliva, Zimmerman. SB—Wills (1), Parker (1), Roseboro (1). CS—Versalles (1), Johnson (1).

Game 4

Sunday, October 10

Twins	AB	R	H	RBI	BB	K	Avg
Zoilo Versalles, ss	4	0	1	0	0	1	.353
Sandy Valdespino, lf	4	0	0	0	0	1	.222
Tony Oliva, rf	4	1	1	1	0	0	.188
Harmon Killebrew, 3b	2	1	1	1	2	1	.364
Jimmie Hall, cf	4	0	0	0	0	3	.143
Don Mincher, 1b	4	0	0	0	0	3	.214
Earl Battey, c	3	0	0	0	0	2	.143
Jerry Zimmerman, c	1	0	0	0	0	0	.000
Frank Quilici, 2b	3	0	0	0	0	0	.167
Mudcat Grant, p	2	0	0	0	0	1	.200
Al Worthington, p	0	0	0	0	0	0	—
Joe Nossek, ph	1	0	1	0	0	0	.375
Bill Pleis, p	0	0	0	0	0	0	—
TOTALS	31	2	5	2	2	11	.237

Dodgers	AB	R	H	RBI	BB	K	Avg
Maury Wills, ss	4	1	2	0	0	0	.353
Jim Gilliam, 3b	2	1	0	0	1	0	.133
John Kennedy, pr-3b	0	0	0	0	0	0	—
Willie Davis, cf	4	1	2	0	0	0	.250
Ron Fairly, rf	4	1	1	3	0	0	.313
Lou Johnson, lf	4	1	2	1	0	0	.357
Wes Parker, 1b	4	2	2	1	0	1	.455
John Roseboro, c	3	0	1	0	1	0	.286
Dick Tracewski, 2b	4	0	0	0	0	0	.000
Don Drysdale, p	3	0	0	0	0	3	.000
TOTALS	32	7	10	5	2	4	.270

	1	2	3	4	5	6	7	8	9	R	H	E
Twins	0	0	0	1	0	1	0	0	0	2	5	2
Dodgers	1	1	0	1	0	3	0	1	x	7	10	0

E—Quilici, Worthington. DP—Twins 1 (Battey to Versalles). LOB—Twins 4, Dodgers 4. Scoring Position—Twins 0-for-0, Dodgers 3-for-5. HR—Oliva (1), Killebrew (1), Johnson (1), Parker (1). SB—Wills (2), Parker (2). CS—Wills (1), Roseboro (1).

Twins	IP	H	R	ER	BB	K	ERA
Mudcat Grant (L, 1-1)	5.0	6	5	4	1	2	3.86
Al Worthington	2.0	2	1	0	1	2	0.00
Bill Pleis	1.0	2	1	1	0	0	9.00

Dodgers	IP	H	R	ER	BB	K	ERA
Don Drysdale (W, 1-1)	9.0	5	2	2	2	11	3.86

Grant pitched to three batters in the 6th.

WP—Grant. HBP—Gilliam by Worthington. Time—2:15. Attendance—55,920. Umpires—HP, Sudol. 1B, Stewart. 2B, Vargo. 3B, Hurley.

Game 3 pitching (continued)

Twins	IP	H	R	ER	BB	K	ERA
Camilo Pascual (L, 0-1)	5.0	8	3	3	1	0	5.40
Jim Merritt	2.0	2	1	1	0	0	4.50
Johnny Klippstein	1.0	0	0	0	1	1	0.00

Dodgers	IP	H	R	ER	BB	K	ERA
Claude Osteen (W, 1-0)	9.0	5	0	0	2	2	0.00

Time—2:06. Attendance—55,934. Umpires—HP, Flaherty. 1B, Sudol. 2B, Stewart. 3B, Vargo.

Game 5

Monday, October 11

Twins	AB	R	H	RBI	BB	K	Avg
Zoilo Versalles, ss	4	0	0	0	0	2	.286
Joe Nossek, cf	4	0	1	0	0	0	.333
Tony Oliva, rf	3	0	0	0	0	2	.158
Harmon Killebrew, 3b	3	0	1	0	0	1	.357
Earl Battey, c	3	0	0	0	0	0	.118
Bob Allison, lf	2	0	0	0	1	2	.111
Don Mincher, 1b	3	0	0	0	0	1	.176
Frank Quilici, 2b	3	0	1	0	0	1	.200
Jim Kaat, p	1	0	0	0	0	1	.200
Dave Boswell, p	0	0	0	0	0	0	—
Rich Rollins, ph	1	0	0	0	0	0	.000
Jim Perry, p	0	0	0	0	0	0	—
Sandy Valdespino, ph	1	0	1	0	0	0	.300
TOTALS	28	0	4	0	1	10	.220

Dodgers	AB	R	H	RBI	BB	K	Avg
Maury Wills, ss	5	2	4	1	0	0	.455
Jim Gilliam, 3b	4	1	2	2	0	0	.211
John Kennedy, 3b	1	0	0	0	0	0	.000
Willie Davis, cf	4	1	2	0	0	1	.300
Lou Johnson, lf	5	1	1	1	0	0	.316
Ron Fairly, rf	5	1	3	1	0	0	.381
Wes Parker, 1b	4	0	0	0	0	1	.333
Dick Tracewski, 2b	3	0	1	0	1	1	.100
John Roseboro, c	2	1	0	0	2	1	.250
Sandy Koufax, p	4	0	1	1	0	3	.167
TOTALS	37	7	14	6	3	7	.302

	1	2	3	4	5	6	7	8	9		R	H	E
Twins	0	0	0	0	0	0	0	0	0		0	4	1
Dodgers	2	0	2	1	0	0	2	0	x		7	14	0

E—Quilici. DP—Dodgers 2 (Wills to Tracewski to Parker; Wills to Tracewski to Parker). LOB—Twins 2, Dodgers 11. Scoring Position—Twins 0-for-2, Dodgers 5-for-21. 2B—Wills 2 (3), Fairly (2). S—Davis, Parker. GDP—Battey, Mincher. SB—Wills (3), Davis 3 (3). CS—Tracewski (1).

Twins	IP	H	R	ER	BB	K	ERA
Jim Kaat (L, 1-1)	2.1	6	4	3	0	1	3.18
Dave Boswell	2.2	3	1	1	2	3	3.38
Jim Perry	3.0	5	2	2	1	3	6.00

Dodgers	IP	H	R	ER	BB	K	ERA
Sandy Koufax (W, 1-1)	9.0	4	0	0	1	10	0.60

Time—2:34. Attendance—55,801. Umpires—HP, Stewart. 1B, Vargo. 2B, Hurley. 3B, Venzon.

Game 6

Wednesday, October 13

Dodgers	AB	R	H	RBI	BB	K	Avg
Maury Wills, ss	4	0	1	0	0	1	.423
Jim Gilliam, 3b	4	0	0	0	0	0	.174
Willie Davis, cf	4	0	0	0	0	0	.250
Ron Fairly, rf	4	1	2	1	0	0	.400
Lou Johnson, lf	4	0	1	0	0	1	.304
Wes Parker, 1b	4	0	0	0	0	0	.263
John Roseboro, c	3	0	1	0	0	1	.263
Dick Tracewski, 2b	3	0	1	0	0	1	.154
Claude Osteen, p	1	0	0	0	0	0	.333
Willie Crawford, ph	1	0	0	0	0	1	.500
Howie Reed, p	0	0	0	0	0	0	—
Wally Moon, ph	1	0	0	0	0	0	.000
Bob Miller, p	0	0	0	0	0	0	—
TOTALS	33	1	6	1	0	5	.291

Twins	AB	R	H	RBI	BB	K	Avg
Zoilo Versalles, ss	3	0	1	0	1	1	.292
Joe Nossek, cf	4	0	0	0	0	1	.250
Tony Oliva, rf	4	0	2	0	0	0	.217
Harmon Killebrew, 3b	4	0	0	0	0	0	.278
Earl Battey, c	4	1	1	0	0	0	.143
Bob Allison, lf	3	2	1	2	1	1	.167
Don Mincher, 1b	3	0	0	0	1	1	.150
Frank Quilici, 2b	2	1	0	0	2	1	.176
Mudcat Grant, p	3	1	1	3	0	0	.250
TOTALS	30	5	6	5	5	5	.214

	1	2	3	4	5	6	7	8	9		R	H	E
Dodgers	0	0	0	0	0	0	1	0	0		1	6	1
Twins	0	0	0	2	0	3	0	0	x		5	6	1

E—Tracewski, Killebrew. DP—Dodgers 1 (Osteen to Wills to Parker), Twins 1 (Battey to Versalles). LOB—Dodgers 5, Twins 6. Scoring Position—Dodgers 0-for-3, Twins 1-for-7. 3B—Battey (1). HR—Fairly (2), Allison (1), Grant (1). GDP—Nossek. SB—Allison (1). CS—Roseboro (2).

Dodgers	IP	H	R	ER	BB	K	ERA
Claude Osteen (L, 1-1)	5.0	4	2	1	3	2	0.64
Howie Reed	2.0	2	3	3	2	3	8.10
Bob Miller	1.0	0	0	0	0	0	0.00

Twins	IP	H	R	ER	BB	K	ERA
Mudcat Grant (W, 2-1)	9.0	6	1	1	0	5	2.74

Time—2:16. Attendance—49,578. Umpires—HP, Vargo. 1B, Hurley. 2B, Venzon. 3B, Flaherty.

Game 7

Thursday, October 14

Dodgers	AB	R	H	RBI	BB	K	Avg
Maury Wills, ss	4	0	0	0	1	1	.367
Jim Gilliam, 3b	5	0	2	0	0	0	.214
John Kennedy, 3b	0	0	0	0	0	0	.000
Willie Davis, cf	2	0	0	0	0	0	.231
Lou Johnson, lf	4	1	1	1	0	0	.296
Ron Fairly, rf	4	1	1	0	0	0	.379
Wes Parker, 1b	4	0	2	1	0	0	.304
Dick Tracewski, 2b	4	0	0	0	0	2	.118
John Roseboro, c	2	0	1	0	2	1	.286
Sandy Koufax, p	3	0	0	0	1	2	.111
TOTALS	32	2	7	2	4	6	.275

Twins	AB	R	H	RBI	BB	K	Avg
Zoilo Versalles, ss	4	0	1	0	0	1	.286
Joe Nossek, cf	4	0	0	0	0	0	.200
Tony Oliva, rf	3	0	0	0	1	2	.192
Harmon Killebrew, 3b	3	0	1	0	1	0	.286
Earl Battey, c	4	0	0	0	0	2	.120
Bob Allison, lf	4	0	0	0	0	2	.125
Don Mincher, 1b	3	0	0	0	0	1	.130
Frank Quilici, 2b	3	0	1	0	0	1	.200
Jim Kaat, p	1	0	0	0	0	1	.167
Al Worthington, p	0	0	0	0	0	0	—
Rich Rollins, ph	0	0	0	0	1	0	.000
Johnny Klippstein, p	0	0	0	0	0	0	—
Jim Merritt, p	0	0	0	0	0	0	—
Sandy Valdespino, ph	1	0	0	0	0	0	.273
Jim Perry, p	0	0	0	0	0	0	—
TOTALS	30	0	3	0	3	10	.197

	1	2	3	4	5	6	7	8	9		R	H	E
Dodgers	0	0	0	2	0	0	0	0	0		2	7	0
Twins	0	0	0	0	0	0	0	0	0		0	3	1

E—Oliva. LOB—Dodgers 9, Twins 6. Scoring Position—Dodgers 1-for-12, Twins 0-for-3. 2B—Fairly (3), Roseboro (1), Quilici (2). 3B—Parker (1). HR—Johnson (2). S—Davis. CS—Wills (2).

Dodgers	IP	H	R	ER	BB	K	ERA
Sandy Koufax (W, 2-1)	9.0	3	0	0	3	10	0.38

Twins	IP	H	R	ER	BB	K	ERA
Jim Kaat (L, 1-2)	3.0	5	2	2	1	2	3.77
Al Worthington	2.0	0	0	0	1	0	0.00
Johnny Klippstein	1.2	2	0	0	1	2	0.00
Jim Merritt	1.1	0	0	0	0	1	2.70
Jim Perry	1.0	0	0	0	1	1	4.50

Kaat pitched to four batters in the 4th.

HBP—Davis by Klippstein. Time—2:27. Attendance—50,596. Umpires—HP, Hurley. 1B, Venzon. 2B, Flaherty. 3B, Sudol.

1965 World Series—Composite Statistics

Batting

Dodgers	G	AB	R	H	RBI	2B	3B	HR	BB	SO	SB	CS	Avg	OBP	Slg
Willie Crawford	2	2	0	1	0	0	0	0	0	1	0	0	.500	.500	.500
Willie Davis	7	26	3	6	0	0	0	0	0	2	3	0	.231	.259	.231
Don Drysdale	3	5	0	0	0	0	0	0	0	4	0	0	.000	.000	.000
Ron Fairly	7	29	7	11	6	3	0	2	0	1	0	0	.379	.379	.690
Jim Gilliam	7	28	2	6	2	1	0	0	1	0	0	0	.214	.267	.250
Lou Johnson	7	27	3	8	4	2	0	2	1	3	0	1	.296	.321	.593
John Kennedy	4	1	0	0	0	0	0	0	0	0	0	0	.000	.000	.000
Sandy Koufax	3	9	0	1	1	0	0	0	1	5	0	0	.111	.200	.111
Jim Lefebvre	3	10	2	4	0	0	0	0	0	0	0	0	.400	.400	.400
Don LeJohn	1	1	0	0	0	0	0	0	0	1	0	0	.000	.000	.000
Wally Moon	2	2	0	0	0	0	0	0	0	0	0	0	.000	.000	.000
Claude Osteen	2	3	0	1	0	0	0	0	0	0	0	0	.333	.333	.333
Wes Parker	7	23	3	7	2	0	1	1	3	3	2	0	.304	.407	.522
John Roseboro	7	21	1	6	3	1	0	0	5	3	1	2	.286	.423	.333
Dick Tracewski	6	17	0	2	0	0	0	0	1	5	0	1	.118	.167	.118
Maury Wills	7	30	3	11	3	3	0	0	1	3	3	2	.367	.387	.467
Totals	7	234	24	64	21	10	1	5	13	31	9	6	.274	.320	.389

Batting

Twins	G	AB	R	H	RBI	2B	3B	HR	BB	SO	SB	CS	Avg	OBP	Slg
Bob Allison	5	16	3	2	2	1	0	1	2	9	1	0	.125	.222	.375
Earl Battey	7	25	1	3	2	0	1	0	0	5	0	0	.120	.120	.200
Mudcat Grant	3	8	3	2	3	1	0	1	0	1	0	0	.250	.250	.750
Jimmie Hall	2	7	0	1	0	0	0	0	1	5	0	0	.143	.250	.143
Jim Kaat	3	6	0	1	2	0	0	0	0	5	0	0	.167	.167	.167
Harmon Killebrew	7	21	2	6	2	0	0	1	6	4	0	0	.286	.444	.429
Don Mincher	7	23	3	3	1	0	0	1	2	7	0	0	.130	.200	.261
Joe Nossek	6	20	0	4	0	0	0	0	0	1	0	0	.200	.200	.200
Tony Oliva	7	26	2	5	2	1	0	1	1	6	0	0	.192	.222	.346
Camilo Pascual	1	1	0	0	0	0	0	0	0	0	0	0	.000	.000	.000
Frank Quilici	7	20	2	4	1	2	0	0	4	3	0	1	.200	.333	.300
Rich Rollins	3	2	0	0	0	0	0	0	1	0	0	0	.000	.333	.000
Sandy Valdespino	5	11	1	3	0	1	0	0	0	1	0	0	.273	.273	.364
Zoilo Versalles	7	28	3	8	4	1	1	1	2	7	1	1	.286	.333	.500
Jerry Zimmerman	2	1	0	0	0	0	0	0	0	0	0	0	.000	.000	.000
Totals	7	215	20	42	19	7	2	6	19	54	2	2	.195	.261	.330

Pitching

Dodgers	G	GS	CG	IP	H	R	ER	BB	SO	W-L	Sv-Op	Hld	ERA
Jim Brewer	1	0	0	2.0	3	1	1	0	1	0-0	0-0	0	4.50
Don Drysdale	2	2	1	11.2	12	9	5	3	15	1-1	0-0	0	3.86
Sandy Koufax	3	3	2	24.0	13	2	1	5	29	2-1	0-0	0	0.38
Bob Miller	2	0	0	1.1	0	0	0	0	0	0-0	0-0	0	0.00
Claude Osteen	2	2	1	14.0	9	2	1	5	4	1-1	0-0	0	0.64
Ron Perranoski	2	0	0	3.2	3	3	3	4	1	0-0	0-0	0	7.36
Howie Reed	2	0	0	3.1	2	3	3	2	4	0-0	0-0	0	8.10
Totals	7	7	4	60.0	42	20	14	19	54	4-3	0-0	0	2.10

Pitching

Twins	G	GS	CG	IP	H	R	ER	BB	SO	W-L	Sv-Op	Hld	ERA
Dave Boswell	1	0	0	2.2	3	1	1	2	3	0-0	0-0	0	3.38
Mudcat Grant	3	3	2	23.0	22	8	7	2	12	2-1	0-0	0	2.74
Jim Kaat	3	3	1	14.1	18	7	6	2	6	1-2	0-0	0	3.77
Johnny Klippstein	2	0	0	2.2	2	0	0	2	3	0-0	0-0	0	0.00
Jim Merritt	2	0	0	3.1	2	1	1	0	1	0-0	0-0	0	2.70
Camilo Pascual	1	1	0	5.0	8	3	3	1	0	0-1	0-0	0	5.40
Jim Perry	2	0	0	4.0	5	2	2	2	4	0-0	0-0	0	4.50
Bill Pleis	1	0	0	1.0	2	1	1	0	0	0-0	0-0	0	9.00
Al Worthington	2	0	0	4.0	2	1	0	2	2	0-0	0-0	0	0.00
Totals	7	7	3	60.0	64	24	21	13	31	3-4	0-0	0	3.15

Fielding

Dodgers	Pos	G	PO	Ast	E	DP	PB	FPct
Jim Brewer	p	1	0	0	0	0	—	—
Willie Davis	cf	7	11	0	0	0	—	1.000
Don Drysdale	p	2	0	2	0	0	—	1.000
Ron Fairly	rf	7	8	0	0	0	—	1.000
Jim Gilliam	3b	7	4	6	2	0	—	.833
Lou Johnson	lf	7	13	1	1	0	—	.933
John Kennedy	3b	4	0	2	1	0	—	.667
Sandy Koufax	p	3	1	4	0	0	—	1.000
Jim Lefebvre	2b	3	3	7	1	0	—	.909
Bob Miller	p	2	0	0	0	0	—	—
Claude Osteen	p	2	2	3	0	1	—	1.000
Wes Parker	1b	7	55	4	0	6	—	1.000
Ron Perranoski	p	2	0	1	0	1	—	1.000
Howie Reed	p	2	1	0	0	0	—	1.000
John Roseboro	c	7	57	4	0	0	0	1.000
Dick Tracewski	2b	5	11	11	1	4	—	.957
Maury Wills	ss	7	14	27	0	6	—	1.000
Totals		7	180	72	6	18	0	.977

Fielding

Twins	Pos	G	PO	Ast	E	DP	PB	FPct
Bob Allison	lf	5	11	0	0	0	—	1.000
Earl Battey	c	7	31	6	0	2	0	1.000
Dave Boswell	p	1	0	0	0	0	—	—
Mudcat Grant	p	3	0	1	0	0	—	1.000
Jimmie Hall	cf	2	2	0	0	0	—	1.000
Jim Kaat	p	3	5	2	0	0	—	1.000
Harmon Killebrew	3b	7	11	7	1	0	—	.947
Johnny Klippstein	p	2	0	0	0	0	—	—
Jim Merritt	p	2	0	2	0	0	—	1.000
Don Mincher	1b	7	51	4	0	0	—	1.000
Joe Nossek	cf	5	13	0	0	0	—	1.000
Tony Oliva	rf	7	20	0	1	0	—	.952
Camilo Pascual	p	1	0	1	0	0	—	1.000
Jim Perry	p	2	0	1	0	0	—	1.000
Bill Pleis	p	1	0	1	0	0	—	1.000
Frank Quilici	2b	7	15	18	2	0	—	.943
Sandy Valdespino	lf	2	6	0	0	0	—	1.000
Zoilo Versalles	ss	7	12	12	0	3	—	1.000
Al Worthington	p	2	1	1	1	0	—	.667
Jerry Zimmerman	c	2	2	1	0	1	0	1.000
Totals		7	180	57	5	6	0	.979

1966 Baltimore Orioles (AL) 4, Los Angeles Dodgers (NL) 0

The Baltimore Orioles held the Los Angeles Dodgers scoreless over their final 33 innings en route to a four-game World Series sweep. In the first inning of the first game, Frank Robinson smacked a two-run homer, and Brooks Robinson followed with a solo shot to give the O's a 3-0 lead. The Dodgers knocked out Baltimore starter Dave McNally in the third inning, but Moe Drabowsky pitched 6.2 innings of scoreless relief, allowing one hit and striking out 11, and the Orioles prevailed, 5-2. The Dodgers committed six errors in Game 2 (three by Willie Davis) as Jim Palmer blanked the Dodgers 6-0 on four hits. Wally Bunker gave the O's their second straight shutout with a 1-0 whitewash of the Dodgers in Game 3. Paul Blair's fifth-inning home run was the difference. It was a virtual replay the next day, as McNally beat Don Drysdale 1-0 on Frank Robinson's fourth-inning homer.

Game 1
Wednesday, October 5

Orioles	AB	R	H	RBI	BB	K	Avg
Luis Aparicio, ss	5	0	0	1	0	0	.000
Russ Snyder, cf-lf	3	1	1	1	2	0	.333
Frank Robinson, rf	5	1	2	2	0	1	.400
Brooks Robinson, 3b	5	1	1	1	0	0	.200
Boog Powell, 1b	5	0	1	0	0	0	.200
Curt Blefary, lf	3	0	1	0	1	0	.333
Paul Blair, cf	0	0	0	0	0	0	—
Dave Johnson, 2b	4	1	2	0	0	1	.500
Andy Etchebarren, c	3	1	1	0	1	0	.333
Dave McNally, p	0	0	0	0	0	0	—
Moe Drabowsky, p	2	0	0	0	1	1	.000
TOTALS	35	5	9	5	5	3	.257

Dodgers	AB	R	H	RBI	BB	K	Avg
Maury Wills, ss	3	0	0	0	2	2	.000
Willie Davis, cf	4	0	1	0	0	1	.250
Lou Johnson, rf	3	1	0	0	1	1	.000
Tommy Davis, lf	3	0	0	0	1	1	.000
Jim Lefebvre, 2b	3	1	1	1	1	1	.333
Wes Parker, 1b	4	0	1	0	0	2	.250
Jim Gilliam, 3b	2	0	0	1	2	0	.000
John Roseboro, c	4	0	0	0	0	1	.000
Don Drysdale, p	0	0	0	0	0	0	—
Dick Stuart, ph	1	0	0	0	0	0	.000
Joe Moeller, p	0	0	0	0	0	0	—
Jim Barbieri, ph	1	0	0	0	0	1	.000
Bob Miller, p	0	0	0	0	0	0	—
Wes Covington, ph	1	0	0	0	0	1	.000
Ron Perranoski, p	0	0	0	0	0	0	—
Ron Fairly, ph	1	0	0	0	0	1	.000
TOTALS	30	2	3	2	7	12	.100

	1	2	3	4	5	6	7	8	9	R	H	E
Orioles	3	1	0	1	0	0	0	0	0	5	9	0
Dodgers	0	1	1	0	0	0	0	0	0	2	3	0

LOB—Orioles 9, Dodgers 8. Scoring Position—Orioles 1-for-7, Dodgers 0-for-10. 2B—Powell (1), DJohnson (1), Parker (1). HR—FRobinson (1), BRobinson (1), Lefebvre (1). S—McNally. SB—Wills (1).

Orioles	IP	H	R	ER	BB	K	ERA
Dave McNally	2.1	2	2	2	5	1	7.71
Moe Drabowsky (W, 1-0)	6.2	1	0	0	2	11	0.00

Dodgers	IP	H	R	ER	BB	K	ERA
Don Drysdale (L, 0-1)	2.0	4	4	4	2	1	18.00
Joe Moeller	2.0	1	1	1	1	0	4.50
Bob Miller	3.0	2	0	0	2	1	0.00
Ron Perranoski	2.0	2	0	0	0	1	0.00

Time—2:56. Attendance—55,941. Umpires—HP, Jackowski. 1B, Chylak. 2B, Pelekoudas. 3B, Rice.

Game 2
Thursday, October 6

Orioles	AB	R	H	RBI	BB	K	Avg
Luis Aparicio, ss	5	0	2	1	0	0	.200
Curt Blefary, lf	5	0	0	0	0	2	.125
Frank Robinson, rf	3	2	1	0	2	0	.375
Brooks Robinson, 3b	4	1	1	0	0	0	.222
Boog Powell, 1b	3	1	2	1	0	0	.375
Dave Johnson, 2b	4	0	2	1	0	0	.500
Paul Blair, cf	3	1	0	0	1	0	.000
Andy Etchebarren, c	3	1	0	0	1	1	.167
Jim Palmer, p	4	0	0	0	0	2	.000
TOTALS	34	6	8	3	4	5	.250

Dodgers	AB	R	H	RBI	BB	K	Avg
Maury Wills, ss	4	0	0	0	0	0	.000
Jim Gilliam, 3b	4	0	0	0	0	0	.000
Willie Davis, cf	4	0	0	0	0	2	.125
Ron Fairly, rf	3	0	0	0	1	2	.000
Jim Lefebvre, 2b	3	0	0	0	1	2	.167
Lou Johnson, lf	4	0	1	0	0	0	.143
John Roseboro, c	4	0	1	0	0	0	.125
Wes Parker, 1b	2	0	1	0	1	0	.333
Sandy Koufax, p	2	0	0	0	0	0	.000
Ron Perranoski, p	0	0	0	0	0	0	—
Phil Regan, p	0	0	0	0	0	0	—
Tommy Davis, ph	1	0	1	0	0	0	.250
Jim Brewer, p	0	0	0	0	0	0	—
TOTALS	31	0	4	0	3	6	.121

	1	2	3	4	5	6	7	8	9	R	H	E
Orioles	0	0	0	0	3	1	0	2	0	6	8	0
Dodgers	0	0	0	0	0	0	0	0	0	0	4	6

E—Perranoski, WDavis 3, Fairly, Gilliam. DP—Dodgers 1 (Gilliam to Roseboro to Parker). LOB—Orioles 6, Dodgers 7. Scoring Position—Orioles 3-for-10, Dodgers 0-for-4. 2B—Aparicio (1), LJohnson (1). 3B—FRobinson (1). S—Powell. GDP—Etchebarren. CS—Aparicio (1).

Orioles	IP	H	R	ER	BB	K	ERA
Jim Palmer (W, 1-0)	9.0	4	0	0	3	6	0.00

Dodgers	IP	H	R	ER	BB	K	ERA
Sandy Koufax (L, 0-1)	6.0	6	4	1	2	2	1.50
Ron Perranoski	1.1	2	2	1	1	0	5.40
Phil Regan	0.2	0	0	0	1	1	0.00
Jim Brewer	1.0	0	0	0	0	1	0.00

WP—Palmer, Regan. Time—2:26. Attendance—55,947. Umpires—HP, Chylak. 1B, Pelekoudas. 2B, Rice. 3B, Steiner.

Game 3
Saturday, October 8

Dodgers	AB	R	H	RBI	BB	K	Avg
Maury Wills, ss	3	0	1	0	0	1	.100
Wes Parker, 1b	4	0	1	0	0	1	.300
Phil Regan, p	0	0	0	0	0	0	—
Willie Davis, cf	4	0	0	0	0	0	.083
Ron Fairly, rf-1b	3	0	1	0	1	1	.143
Jim Lefebvre, 2b	4	0	0	0	0	1	.100
Lou Johnson, lf-rf	4	0	2	0	0	0	.273
John Roseboro, c	3	0	0	0	0	0	.091
John Kennedy, 3b	3	0	0	0	0	1	.000
Claude Osteen, p	2	0	0	0	0	1	.000
Tommy Davis, ph-lf	1	0	1	0	0	0	.400
TOTALS	31	0	6	0	1	6	.160

Orioles	AB	R	H	RBI	BB	K	Avg
Luis Aparicio, ss	3	0	1	0	0	0	.231
Curt Blefary, lf	3	0	0	0	0	1	.091
Russ Snyder, lf	0	0	0	0	0	0	.333
Frank Robinson, rf	3	0	0	0	0	1	.273
Brooks Robinson, 3b	2	0	0	0	1	0	.182
Boog Powell, 1b	3	0	1	0	0	0	.364
Dave Johnson, 2b	3	0	0	0	0	0	.364
Paul Blair, cf	3	1	1	1	0	0	.167
Andy Etchebarren, c	3	0	0	0	0	1	.111
Wally Bunker, p	2	0	0	0	0	1	.000
TOTALS	25	1	3	1	1	4	.227

	1	2	3	4	5	6	7	8	9	R	H	E
Dodgers	0	0	0	0	0	0	0	0	0	0	6	0
Orioles	0	0	0	0	1	0	0	0	x	1	3	0

DP—Dodgers 2 (Wills to Lefebvre to Parker; Lefebvre to Wills to Parker), Orioles 1 (Aparicio to DJohnson to Powell). LOB—Dodgers 6, Orioles 1. Scoring Position—Dodgers 0-for-6, Orioles 0-for-0. 2B—Parker (2). HR—Blair (1). S—Wills. GDP—LJohnson, Powell, DJohnson.

Game 4
Sunday, October 9

Dodgers	AB	R	H	RBI	BB	K	Avg
Maury Wills, ss	3	0	0	0	1	0	.077
Willie Davis, cf	4	0	0	0	0	1	.063
Lou Johnson, rf	4	0	1	0	0	0	.267
Tommy Davis, lf	3	0	0	0	0	0	.250
Jim Lefebvre, 2b	2	0	1	0	1	0	.167
Wes Parker, 1b	3	0	0	0	0	0	.231
John Roseboro, c	3	0	0	0	0	1	.071
John Kennedy, 3b	2	0	1	0	0	0	.200
Dick Stuart, ph	1	0	0	0	0	1	.000
Don Drysdale, p	2	0	0	0	0	1	.000
Al Ferrara, ph	1	0	1	0	0	0	1.000
Nate Oliver, pr	0	0	0	0	0	0	—
TOTALS	28	0	4	0	2	4	.158

Orioles	AB	R	H	RBI	BB	K	Avg
Luis Aparicio, ss	3	0	1	0	0	0	.250
Russ Snyder, cf-lf	3	0	0	0	0	0	.167
Frank Robinson, rf	3	1	1	1	0	1	.286
Brooks Robinson, 3b	3	0	1	0	0	0	.214
Boog Powell, 1b	3	0	1	0	0	0	.357
Curt Blefary, lf	2	0	0	0	1	0	.077
Paul Blair, cf	0	0	0	0	0	0	.167
Dave Johnson, 2b	3	0	0	0	0	0	.286
Andy Etchebarren, c	3	0	0	0	0	2	.083
Dave McNally, p	3	0	0	0	0	1	.000
TOTALS	26	1	4	1	1	5	.214

	1	2	3	4	5	6	7	8	9	R	H	E
Dodgers	0	0	0	0	0	0	0	0	0	0	4	0
Orioles	0	0	0	1	0	0	0	0	x	1	4	0

DP—Dodgers 1 (Lefebvre to Wills to Parker), Orioles 3 (Aparicio to DJohnson to Powell; BRobinson to DJohnson to Powell; Etchebarren to DJohnson). LOB—Dodgers 3, Orioles 2. Scoring Position—Dodgers 0-for-1, Orioles 0-for-1. HR—FRobinson (2). GDP—TDavis, Parker, DJohnson. CS—Kennedy (1), Aparicio (2).

Dodgers	IP	H	R	ER	BB	K	ERA
Don Drysdale (L, 0-2)	8.0	4	1	1	1	5	4.50

Orioles	IP	H	R	ER	BB	K	ERA
Dave McNally (W, 1-0)	9.0	4	0	0	2	4	1.59

Time—1:45. Attendance—54,458. Umpires—HP, Rice. 1B, Steiner. 2B, Drummond. 3B, Jackowski.

Game 3 (continued pitching)

Dodgers	IP	H	R	ER	BB	K	ERA
Claude Osteen (L, 0-1)	7.0	3	1	1	1	3	1.29
Phil Regan	1.0	0	0	0	0	1	0.00

Orioles	IP	H	R	ER	BB	K	ERA
Wally Bunker (W, 1-0)	9.0	6	0	0	1	6	0.00

Time—1:55. Attendance—54,445. Umpires—HP, Pelekoudas. 1B, Rice. 2B, Steiner. 3B, Drummond.

1966 World Series—Composite Statistics

Batting

Orioles	G	AB	R	H	RBI	2B	3B	HR	BB	SO	SB	CS	Avg	OBP	Slg
Luis Aparicio	4	16	0	4	2	1	0	0	0	0	0	2	.250	.250	.313
Paul Blair	4	6	2	1	1	0	0	1	1	0	0	0	.167	.286	.667
Curt Blefary	4	13	0	1	0	0	0	0	2	3	0	0	.077	.200	.077
Wally Bunker	1	2	0	0	0	0	0	0	0	1	0	0	.000	.000	.000
Moe Drabowsky	1	2	0	0	0	0	0	0	1	1	0	0	.000	.333	.000
Andy Etchebarren	4	12	2	1	0	0	0	0	2	4	0	0	.083	.214	.083
Dave Johnson	4	14	1	4	1	1	0	0	0	1	0	0	.286	.286	.357
Dave McNally	2	3	0	0	0	0	0	0	0	1	0	0	.000	.000	.000
Jim Palmer	1	4	0	0	0	0	0	0	0	2	0	0	.000	.000	.000
Boog Powell	4	14	1	5	1	1	0	0	0	1	0	0	.357	.357	.429
Brooks Robinson	4	14	2	3	1	0	0	1	1	0	0	0	.214	.267	.429
Frank Robinson	4	14	4	4	3	0	1	2	2	3	0	0	.286	.375	.857
Russ Snyder	3	6	1	1	1	0	0	0	2	0	0	0	.167	.375	.167
Totals	**4**	**120**	**13**	**24**	**10**	**3**	**1**	**4**	**11**	**17**	**0**	**2**	**.200**	**.267**	**.342**

Dodgers	G	AB	R	H	RBI	2B	3B	HR	BB	SO	SB	CS	Avg	OBP	Slg
Jim Barbieri	1	1	0	0	0	0	0	0	0	1	0	0	.000	.000	.000
Wes Covington	1	1	0	0	0	0	0	0	0	1	0	0	.000	.000	.000
Tommy Davis	4	8	0	2	0	0	0	0	1	1	0	0	.250	.333	.250
Willie Davis	4	16	0	1	0	0	0	0	0	4	0	0	.063	.063	.063
Don Drysdale	2	2	0	0	0	0	0	0	0	1	0	0	.000	.000	.000
Ron Fairly	3	7	0	1	0	0	0	0	2	4	0	0	.143	.333	.143
Al Ferrara	1	1	0	1	0	0	0	0	0	0	0	1	1.000	1.000	1.000
Jim Gilliam	2	6	0	0	1	0	0	0	2	0	0	0	.000	.250	.000
Lou Johnson	4	15	1	4	0	1	0	0	1	1	0	0	.267	.313	.333
John Kennedy	2	5	0	1	0	0	0	0	0	0	0	1	.200	.200	.200
Sandy Koufax	1	2	0	0	0	0	0	0	0	0	0	0	.000	.000	.000
Jim Lefebvre	4	12	1	2	1	0	0	1	3	4	0	0	.167	.333	.417
Nate Oliver	1	0	0	0	0	0	0	0	0	0	0	0	—	—	—
Claude Osteen	1	2	0	0	0	0	0	0	0	1	0	0	.000	.000	.000
Wes Parker	4	13	0	3	0	2	0	0	1	3	0	0	.231	.286	.385
John Roseboro	4	14	0	1	0	0	0	0	0	3	0	0	.071	.071	.071
Dick Stuart	2	2	0	0	0	0	0	0	0	1	0	0	.000	.000	.000
Maury Wills	4	13	0	1	0	0	0	0	3	3	1	0	.077	.250	.077
Totals	**4**	**120**	**2**	**17**	**2**	**3**	**0**	**1**	**13**	**28**	**1**	**1**	**.142**	**.226**	**.192**

Pitching

Orioles	G	GS	CG	IP	H	R	ER	BB	SO	W-L	Sv-Op	Hld	ERA
Wally Bunker	1	1	1	9.0	6	0	0	1	6	1-0	0-0	0	0.00
Moe Drabowsky	1	0	0	6.2	1	0	0	2	11	1-0	0-0	0	0.00
Dave McNally	2	2	1	11.1	6	2	2	7	5	1-0	0-0	0	1.59
Jim Palmer	1	1	1	9.0	4	0	0	3	6	1-0	0-0	0	0.00
Totals	**4**	**4**	**3**	**36.0**	**17**	**2**	**2**	**13**	**28**	**4-0**	**0-0**	**0**	**0.50**

Dodgers	G	GS	CG	IP	H	R	ER	BB	SO	W-L	Sv-Op	Hld	ERA
Jim Brewer	1	0	0	1.0	0	0	0	0	1	0-0	0-0	0	0.00
Don Drysdale	2	2	1	10.0	8	5	5	3	6	0-2	0-0	0	4.50
Sandy Koufax	1	1	0	6.0	6	4	1	2	2	0-1	0-0	0	1.50
Bob Miller	1	0	0	3.0	2	0	0	2	1	0-0	0-0	0	0.00
Joe Moeller	1	0	0	2.0	1	1	1	1	0	0-0	0-0	0	4.50
Claude Osteen	1	1	0	7.0	3	1	1	1	3	0-1	0-0	0	1.29
Ron Perranoski	2	0	0	3.1	4	2	2	1	2	0-0	0-0	0	5.40
Phil Regan	2	0	0	1.2	0	0	0	1	2	0-0	0-0	0	0.00
Totals	**4**	**4**	**1**	**34.0**	**24**	**13**	**10**	**11**	**17**	**0-4**	**0-0**	**0**	**2.65**

Fielding

Orioles	Pos	G	PO	Ast	E	DP	PB	FPct
Luis Aparicio	ss	4	9	8	0	2	—	1.000
Paul Blair	cf	4	9	0	0	0	—	1.000
Curt Blefary	lf	4	7	0	0	0	—	1.000
Wally Bunker	p	1	0	3	0	0	—	1.000
Moe Drabowsky	p	1	0	0	0	0	—	—
Andy Etchebarren	c	4	32	1	0	1	0	1.000
Dave Johnson	2b	4	12	12	0	4	—	1.000
Dave McNally	p	2	0	0	0	0	—	—
Jim Palmer	p	1	0	2	0	0	—	1.000
Boog Powell	1b	4	27	1	0	3	—	1.000
Brooks Robinson	3b	4	4	6	0	1	—	1.000
Frank Robinson	rf	4	6	0	0	0	—	1.000
Russ Snyder	lf	3	0	0	0	0	—	—
	cf	2	2	0	0	0	—	1.000
Totals		**4**	**108**	**33**	**0**	**11**	**0**	**1.000**

Dodgers	Pos	G	PO	Ast	E	DP	PB	FPct
Jim Brewer	p	1	0	0	0	0	—	—
Tommy Davis	lf	3	3	0	0	0	—	1.000
Willie Davis	cf	4	6	0	3	0	—	.667
Don Drysdale	p	2	0	3	0	0	—	1.000
Ron Fairly	rf	2	3	0	1	0	—	.750
	1b	1	2	0	0	0	—	1.000
Jim Gilliam	3b	2	3	4	1	1	—	.875
Lou Johnson	rf	3	7	0	0	0	—	1.000
	lf	2	2	0	0	0	—	1.000
John Kennedy	3b	2	0	3	0	0	—	1.000
Sandy Koufax	p	1	0	1	0	0	—	1.000
Jim Lefebvre	2b	4	11	11	0	3	—	1.000
Bob Miller	p	1	0	1	0	0	—	1.000
Joe Moeller	p	1	0	0	0	0	—	—
Claude Osteen	p	1	1	0	0	0	—	1.000
Wes Parker	1b	4	31	2	0	4	—	1.000
Ron Perranoski	p	2	0	2	1	0	—	.667
Phil Regan	p	2	0	1	0	0	—	1.000
John Roseboro	c	4	22	2	0	1	0	1.000
Maury Wills	ss	4	11	14	0	3	—	1.000
Totals		**4**	**102**	**44**	**6**	**12**	**0**	**.961**

1967 St. Louis Cardinals (NL) 4, Boston Red Sox (AL) 3

Bob Gibson recorded three complete-game victories as the St. Louis Cardinals beat the Boston Red Sox, four games to three. Gibson won the opener 2-1. Lou Brock had four hits and two stolen bases and scored both of the Cardinals' runs. Jim Lonborg answered with a one-hit shutout in Game 2 while Carl Yastrzemski homered twice and drove in four runs. Nelson Briles won the third game, 5-2, before Gibson tossed a five-hit shutout in Game 4. Lonborg beat the Cards 3-1 on a three-hitter in Game 5. The Sox ripped four homers in Game 6 as surprise starter Gary Waslewski held the Cards in check, with the Sox winning 8-4 to force a seventh game. Lonborg came back on two days' rest, but he was no match for Gibson, who pitched a three-hitter for a 7-2 win and the World Championship.

Game 1

Wednesday, October 4

Cardinals	AB	R	H	RBI	BB	K	Avg
Lou Brock, lf	4	2	4	0	1	0	1.000
Curt Flood, cf	5	0	1	0	0	1	.200
Roger Maris, rf	4	0	1	2	1	0	.250
Orlando Cepeda, 1b	4	0	0	0	0	1	.000
Tim McCarver, c	3	0	0	0	1	1	.000
Mike Shannon, 3b	4	0	2	0	0	0	.500
Julian Javier, 2b	4	0	2	0	0	2	.500
Dal Maxvill, ss	2	0	0	0	2	0	.000
Bob Gibson, p	4	0	0	0	0	1	.000
TOTALS	34	2	10	2	5	6	.294

Red Sox	AB	R	H	RBI	BB	K	Avg
Jerry Adair, 2b	4	0	0	0	0	2	.000
Dalton Jones, 3b	4	0	1	0	0	1	.250
Carl Yastrzemski, lf	4	0	0	0	0	0	.000
Ken Harrelson, rf	3	0	0	0	0	0	.000
John Wyatt, p	0	0	0	0	0	0	—
Joe Foy, ph	1	0	0	0	0	0	.000
George Scott, 1b	3	0	2	0	1	0	.667
Rico Petrocelli, ss	3	0	0	0	0	3	.000
Mike Andrews, ph	1	0	0	0	0	0	.000
Reggie Smith, cf	3	0	1	0	0	1	.333
Russ Gibson, c	2	0	0	0	0	2	.000
Norm Siebern, ph-rf	1	0	1	0	0	0	1.000
Jose Tartabull, pr-rf	0	0	0	0	0	0	—
Jose Santiago, p	2	1	1	1	0	1	.500
Elston Howard, c	0	0	0	0	0	0	—
TOTALS	31	1	6	1	1	10	.194

	1	2	3	4	5	6	7	8	9		R	H	E
Cardinals	0	0	1	0	0	0	1	0	0		2	10	0
Red Sox	0	0	1	0	0	0	0	0	0		1	6	0

DP—Red Sox 2 (Jones to Scott; Jones to Adair to Scott). LOB—Cardinals 10, Red Sox 5. Scoring Position—Cardinals 1-for-15, Red Sox 0-for-3. HR—Santiago (1). S—Howard. GDP—Cepeda, BGibson. SB—Brock 2 (2). CS—Smith (1).

Cardinals	IP	H	R	ER	BB	K	ERA
Bob Gibson (W, 1-0)	9.0	6	1	1	1	10	1.00

Red Sox	IP	H	R	ER	BB	K	ERA
Jose Santiago (L, 0-1)	7.0	10	2	2	3	5	2.57
John Wyatt	2.0	0	0	0	2	1	0.00

Balk—Wyatt. PB—RGibson. Time—2:22. Attendance—34,796. Umpires—HP, Stevens. 1B, Barlick. 2B, Umont. 3B, Donatelli.

Game 2

Thursday, October 5

Cardinals	AB	R	H	RBI	BB	K	Avg
Lou Brock, lf	4	0	0	0	0	0	.500
Curt Flood, cf	3	0	0	0	1	0	.125
Roger Maris, rf	3	0	0	0	0	0	.143
Orlando Cepeda, 1b	3	0	0	0	0	0	.000
Tim McCarver, c	3	0	0	0	0	0	.000
Mike Shannon, 3b	3	0	0	0	0	2	.286
Julian Javier, 2b	3	0	1	0	0	0	.429
Dal Maxvill, ss	2	0	0	0	0	0	.000
Bobby Tolan, ph	1	0	0	0	0	0	.000
Eddie Bressoud, ss	0	0	0	0	0	0	—
Dick Hughes, p	2	0	0	0	0	2	.000
Ron Willis, p	0	0	0	0	0	0	—
Joe Hoerner, p	0	0	0	0	0	0	—
Jack Lamabe, p	0	0	0	0	0	0	—
Dave Ricketts, ph	1	0	0	0	0	0	.000
TOTALS	28	0	1	0	1	4	.190

Red Sox	AB	R	H	RBI	BB	K	Avg
Jose Tartabull, rf	4	1	0	0	1	1	.000
Dalton Jones, 3b	5	1	2	0	0	1	.333
Carl Yastrzemski, lf	4	2	3	4	1	0	.375
George Scott, 1b	4	1	1	0	1	1	.429
Reggie Smith, cf	3	0	0	0	1	0	.167
Jerry Adair, 2b	4	0	2	0	0	0	.250
Rico Petrocelli, ss	2	0	1	1	1	1	.200
Elston Howard, c	3	0	0	0	1	1	.000
Jim Lonborg, p	4	0	0	0	0	3	.000
TOTALS	33	5	9	5	6	8	.241

	1	2	3	4	5	6	7	8	9		R	H	E
Cardinals	0	0	0	0	0	0	0	0	0		0	1	1
Red Sox	0	0	0	1	0	1	3	0	x		5	9	0

E—Shannon. LOB—Cardinals 2, Red Sox 11. Scoring Position—Cardinals 0-for-1, Red Sox 1-for-7. 2B—Javier (1). HR—Yastrzemski 2 (2). SF—Petrocelli. SB—Adair (1).

Cardinals	IP	H	R	ER	BB	K	ERA
Dick Hughes (L, 0-1)	5.1	4	2	1	3	5	1.69
Ron Willis	0.2	1	2	2	2	1	27.00
Joe Hoerner	0.2	2	1	1	1	0	13.50
Jack Lamabe	1.1	2	0	0	0	2	0.00

Red Sox	IP	H	R	ER	BB	K	ERA
Jim Lonborg (W, 1-0)	9.0	1	0	0	1	4	0.00

Willis pitched to two batters in the 7th.

Time—2:24. Attendance—35,188. Umpires—HP, Barlick. 1B, Umont. 2B, Donatelli. 3B, Runge.

Game 3

Saturday, October 7

Red Sox	AB	R	H	RBI	BB	K	Avg
Jose Tartabull, rf	4	0	0	0	0	0	.000
Dalton Jones, 3b	4	0	3	1	0	1	.462
Carl Yastrzemski, lf	3	0	0	0	0	0	.273
George Scott, 1b	4	0	0	0	0	1	.273
Reggie Smith, cf	4	1	2	1	0	0	.300
Jerry Adair, 2b	4	0	0	0	0	0	.167
Rico Petrocelli, ss	3	0	0	0	0	0	.125
Elston Howard, c	3	0	1	0	0	1	.167
Gary Bell, p	0	0	0	0	0	0	—
George Thomas, ph	1	0	0	0	0	1	.000
Gary Waslewski, p	0	0	0	0	0	0	—
Mike Andrews, ph	1	1	1	0	0	0	.500
Lee Stange, p	0	0	0	0	0	0	—
Joe Foy, ph	1	0	0	0	0	0	.000
Dan Osinski, p	0	0	0	0	0	0	—
TOTALS	32	2	7	2	0	4	.238

Cardinals	AB	R	H	RBI	BB	K	Avg
Lou Brock, lf	4	2	2	0	0	1	.500
Curt Flood, cf	4	0	1	1	0	0	.167
Roger Maris, rf	4	1	2	0	0	0	.273
Orlando Cepeda, 1b	4	0	1	1	0	1	.091
Tim McCarver, c	4	1	1	0	0	0	.100
Mike Shannon, 3b	3	1	2	2	0	0	.400
Julian Javier, 2b	3	0	1	0	0	1	.400
Dal Maxvill, ss	3	0	0	0	0	1	.000
Nelson Briles, p	3	0	0	0	0	0	.000
TOTALS	32	5	10	5	0	4	.244

	1	2	3	4	5	6	7	8	9		R	H	E
Red Sox	0	0	0	0	0	1	0	0	1		2	7	1
Cardinals	1	2	0	0	0	1	0	1	x		5	10	0

E—Stange. DP—Red Sox 1 (Bell to Petrocelli to Scott), Cardinals 1 (Javier to Maxvill to Cepeda). LOB—Red Sox 4, Cardinals 3. Scoring Position—Red Sox 1-for-2, Cardinals 2-for-6. 2B—Cepeda (1). 3B—Brock (1). HR—Smith (1), Shannon (1). GDP—Yastrzemski, Maris. CS—Yastrzemski (1).

Red Sox	IP	H	R	ER	BB	K	ERA
Gary Bell (L, 0-1)	2.0	5	3	3	0	1	13.50
Gary Waslewski	3.0	0	0	0	0	3	0.00
Lee Stange	2.0	3	1	0	0	0	0.00
Dan Osinski	1.0	2	1	1	0	0	9.00

Cardinals	IP	H	R	ER	BB	K	ERA
Nelson Briles (W, 1-0)	9.0	7	2	2	0	4	2.00

HBP—Yastrzemski by Briles. Time—2:15. Attendance—54,575. Umpires—HP, Umont. 1B, Donatelli. 2B, Runge. 3B, Pryor.

Game 4

Sunday, October 8

Red Sox	AB	R	H	RBI	BB	K	Avg
Jose Tartabull, rf	4	0	2	0	0	0	.167
Dalton Jones, 3b	4	0	0	0	0	0	.353
Carl Yastrzemski, lf	4	0	2	0	0	0	.333
George Scott, 1b	4	0	1	0	0	1	.267
Reggie Smith, cf	3	0	0	0	1	1	.231
Jerry Adair, 2b	4	0	0	0	0	1	.125
Rico Petrocelli, ss	3	0	0	0	0	1	.091
Elston Howard, c	2	0	0	0	0	1	.125
Dave Morehead, p	0	0	0	0	0	0	—
Norm Siebern, ph	1	0	0	0	0	0	.500
Ken Brett, p	0	0	0	0	0	0	—
Jose Santiago, p	0	0	0	0	0	0	.500
Gary Bell, p	0	0	0	0	0	0	—
Joe Foy, ph	1	0	0	0	0	1	.000
Jerry Stephenson, p	0	0	0	0	0	0	—
Mike Ryan, c	2	0	0	0	0	1	.000
TOTALS	32	0	5	0	1	6	.224

Cardinals	AB	R	H	RBI	BB	K	Avg
Lou Brock, lf	4	1	2	0	0	0	.500
Curt Flood, cf	4	1	1	0	0	0	.188
Roger Maris, rf	4	1	1	2	0	0	.267
Orlando Cepeda, 1b	4	1	1	0	0	0	.133
Tim McCarver, c	3	1	1	2	0	1	.154
Mike Shannon, 3b	3	1	1	0	1	0	.308
Julian Javier, 2b	4	0	2	1	0	2	.429
Dal Maxvill, ss	3	0	1	1	1	0	.100
Bob Gibson, p	3	0	0	0	1	0	.000
TOTALS	32	6	9	6	3	3	.252

	1	2	3	4	5	6	7	8	9		R	H	E
Red Sox	0	0	0	0	0	0	0	0	0		0	5	0
Cardinals	4	0	2	0	0	0	0	0	x		6	9	0

LOB—Red Sox 6, Cardinals 6. Scoring Position—Red Sox 0-for-3, Cardinals 3-for-11. 2B—Yastrzemski (1), Brock (1), Maris (1), Cepeda (2), Javier (2). SF—McCarver. SB—Brock (3).

Red Sox	IP	H	R	ER	BB	K	ERA
Jose Santiago (L, 0-2)	0.2	6	4	4	0	0	7.04
Gary Bell	1.1	0	0	0	0	0	8.10
Jerry Stephenson	2.0	3	2	2	1	0	9.00
Dave Morehead	3.0	0	0	0	1	2	9.00
Ken Brett	1.0	0	0	0	1	1	0.00

Cardinals	IP	H	R	ER	BB	K	ERA
Bob Gibson (W, 2-0)	9.0	5	0	0	1	6	0.50

WP—Stephenson. Time—2:05. Attendance—54,575. Umpires—HP, Donatelli. 1B, Runge. 2B, Pryor. 3B, Stevens.

Game 5
Monday, October 9

Red Sox	AB	R	H	RBI	BB	K	Avg
Joe Foy, 3b	5	1	1	0	0	3	.125
Mike Andrews, 2b	3	0	1	0	0	0	.400
Carl Yastrzemski, lf	3	0	1	0	1	1	.333
Ken Harrelson, rf	3	0	1	1	1	0	.167
Jose Tartabull, rf	0	0	0	0	0	0	.167
George Scott, 1b	3	1	0	0	1	1	.222
Reggie Smith, cf	4	1	1	0	0	0	.235
Rico Petrocelli, ss	3	0	0	0	1	1	.071
Elston Howard, c	4	0	1	1	0	0	.167
Jim Lonborg, p	4	0	0	0	0	3	.000
TOTALS	32	3	6	2	4	9	.195

Cardinals	AB	R	H	RBI	BB	K	Avg
Lou Brock, lf	4	0	0	0	0	1	.400
Curt Flood, cf	4	0	0	0	0	0	.150
Roger Maris, rf	4	1	2	1	0	0	.316
Orlando Cepeda, 1b	4	0	0	0	0	1	.105
Tim McCarver, c	3	0	0	0	0	0	.125
Mike Shannon, 3b	3	0	0	0	0	1	.250
Julian Javier, 2b	3	0	0	0	0	0	.353
Dal Maxvill, ss	2	0	1	0	0	0	.167
Dave Ricketts, ph	1	0	0	0	0	0	.000
Ron Willis, p	0	0	0	0	0	0	—
Jack Lamabe, p	0	0	0	0	0	0	—
Steve Carlton, p	1	0	0	0	0	0	.000
Bobby Tolan, ph	1	0	0	0	0	1	.000
Ray Washburn, p	0	0	0	0	0	0	—
Phil Gagliano, ph	1	0	0	0	0	0	.000
Eddie Bressoud, ss	0	0	0	0	0	0	—
TOTALS	31	1	3	1	0	4	.228

	1	2	3	4	5	6	7	8	9	R	H	E
Red Sox	0	0	1	0	0	0	0	0	2	3	6	1
Cardinals	0	0	0	0	0	0	0	0	1	1	3	2

E—Petrocelli, Shannon, Maris. DP—Cardinals 2 (Javier to Maxvill to Cepeda; McCarver to Javier to Shannon to Lamabe). LOB—Red Sox 7, Cardinals 3. Scoring Position—Red Sox 2-for-7, Cardinals 0-for-1. 2B—Yastrzemski (2), Smith (1). HR—Maris (1). S—Andrews. GDP—Scott. CS—Petrocelli (1).

Red Sox	IP	H	R	ER	BB	K	ERA
Jim Lonborg (W, 2-0)	9.0	3	1	1	0	4	0.50

Cardinals	IP	H	R	ER	BB	K	ERA
Steve Carlton (L, 0-1)	6.0	3	1	0	2	5	0.00
Ray Washburn	2.0	1	0	0	0	0	0.00
Ron Willis	0.0	1	2	1	2	0	40.50
Jack Lamabe	1.0	1	0	0	0	2	0.00

Willis pitched to three batters in the 9th.

WP—Carlton. Time—2:20. Attendance—54,575. Umpires—HP, Runge. 1B, Pryor. 2B, Stevens. 3B, Barlick.

Game 6
Wednesday, October 11

Cardinals	AB	R	H	RBI	BB	K	Avg
Lou Brock, lf	5	2	2	3	0	1	.400
Curt Flood, cf	5	0	1	1	0	1	.160
Roger Maris, rf	4	0	2	0	1	1	.348
Orlando Cepeda, 1b	5	0	1	0	0	0	.125
Tim McCarver, c	3	0	0	0	1	0	.105
Mike Shannon, 3b	4	0	1	0	0	0	.250
Julian Javier, 2b	4	1	1	0	0	0	.333
Dal Maxvill, ss	3	0	0	0	1	0	.133
Dick Hughes, p	1	0	0	0	0	1	.000
Ron Willis, p	0	0	0	0	0	0	—
Ed Spiezio, ph	1	0	0	0	0	0	.000
Nelson Briles, p	0	0	0	0	0	0	.000
Bobby Tolan, ph	0	1	0	0	1	0	.000
Jack Lamabe, p	0	0	0	0	0	0	—
Joe Hoerner, p	0	0	0	0	0	0	—
Larry Jaster, p	0	0	0	0	0	0	—
Ray Washburn, p	0	0	0	0	0	0	—
Dave Ricketts, ph	1	0	0	0	0	0	.000
Hal Woodeshick, p	0	0	0	0	0	0	—
TOTALS	36	4	8	4	4	4	.223

Red Sox	AB	R	H	RBI	BB	K	Avg
Joe Foy, 3b	4	1	1	0	0	0	.167
Mike Andrews, 2b	5	1	2	1	0	0	.400
Carl Yastrzemski, lf	4	2	3	1	1	0	.409
Ken Harrelson, rf	3	0	0	0	0	1	.111
Jose Tartabull, rf	0	0	0	0	0	0	.167
Jerry Adair, ph	0	0	0	1	0	0	.125
Gary Bell, p	0	0	0	0	0	0	—
George Scott, 1b	4	0	1	0	0	0	.227
Reggie Smith, cf	4	1	2	2	0	0	.286
Rico Petrocelli, ss	3	2	2	2	1	0	.176
Elston Howard, c	4	0	0	0	0	0	.125
Gary Waslewski, p	1	0	0	0	0	1	.000
John Wyatt, p	0	0	0	0	0	0	—
Dalton Jones, ph	1	1	1	0	0	0	.389
George Thomas, rf	1	0	0	0	0	0	.000
TOTALS	34	8	12	8	2	2	.242

	1	2	3	4	5	6	7	8	9	R	H	E
Cardinals	0	0	2	0	0	0	2	0	0	4	8	0
Red Sox	0	1	0	3	0	0	4	0	x	8	12	1

E—Petrocelli. LOB—Cardinals 9, Red Sox 7. Scoring Position—Cardinals 2-for-9, Red Sox 2-for-5. 2B—Shannon (1), Javier (3), Foy (1). HR—Brock (1), Yastrzemski (3), Smith (2), Petrocelli 2 (2). S—Foy. SF—Adair. SB—Brock (4).

Cardinals	IP	H	R	ER	BB	K	ERA
Dick Hughes	3.2	5	4	4	0	2	5.00
Ron Willis	0.1	0	0	0	0	0	27.00
Nelson Briles	2.0	0	0	0	1	0	1.64
Jack Lamabe (L, 0-1)	0.1	2	2	2	0	0	6.75
Joe Hoerner	0.0	2	2	2	0	0	40.50
Larry Jaster	0.1	2	0	0	0	0	0.00
Ray Washburn	0.1	0	0	0	1	0	0.00
Hal Woodeshick	1.0	1	0	0	0	0	0.00

Red Sox	IP	H	R	ER	BB	K	ERA
Gary Waslewski	5.1	4	2	2	4	4	2.16
John Wyatt (BS, 1; W, 1-0)	1.2	1	2	2	1	0	4.91
Gary Bell (S, 1)	2.0	3	0	0	1	0	5.06

Hoerner pitched to two batters in the 7th.

HBP—Waslewski by Briles. Time—2:48. Attendance—35,188. Umpires—HP, Pryor. 1B, Stevens. 2B, Barlick. 3B, Umont.

Game 7
Thursday, October 12

Cardinals	AB	R	H	RBI	BB	K	Avg
Lou Brock, lf	4	1	2	0	1	0	.414
Curt Flood, cf	3	1	1	1	2	1	.179
Roger Maris, rf	3	0	2	1	1	0	.385
Orlando Cepeda, 1b	5	0	0	0	0	1	.103
Tim McCarver, c	5	1	1	0	0	0	.125
Mike Shannon, 3b	4	1	0	0	0	1	.208
Julian Javier, 2b	4	1	2	3	0	1	.360
Dal Maxvill, ss	4	1	1	0	0	0	.158
Bob Gibson, p	4	1	1	1	0	1	.091
TOTALS	36	7	10	6	4	5	.237

Red Sox	AB	R	H	RBI	BB	K	Avg
Joe Foy, 3b	3	0	0	0	1	1	.133
Dave Morehead, p	0	0	0	0	0	0	—
Dan Osinski, p	0	0	0	0	0	0	—
Ken Brett, p	0	0	0	0	0	0	—
Mike Andrews, 2b	3	0	0	0	0	1	.308
Carl Yastrzemski, lf	3	0	1	0	1	0	.400
Ken Harrelson, rf	4	0	0	0	0	2	.077
George Scott, 1b	4	1	1	0	0	2	.231
Reggie Smith, cf	3	0	0	0	0	0	.250
Rico Petrocelli, ss	3	1	1	0	0	2	.200
Elston Howard, c	2	0	0	0	0	0	.111
Dalton Jones, ph-3b	0	0	0	0	1	0	.389
Jim Lonborg, p	1	0	0	0	0	1	.000
Jose Tartabull, ph	1	0	0	0	0	1	.154
Jose Santiago, p	0	0	0	0	0	0	.500
Norm Siebern, ph	1	0	1	1	0	0	.333
Russ Gibson, c	0	0	0	0	0	0	.000
TOTALS	28	2	3	1	3	10	.229

	1	2	3	4	5	6	7	8	9	R	H	E
Cardinals	0	0	2	0	2	3	0	0	0	7	10	1
Red Sox	0	0	0	0	1	0	0	1	0	2	3	1

E—Foy, Javier. DP—Cardinals 1 (Maxvill to Javier to Cepeda). LOB—Cardinals 7, Red Sox 3. Scoring Position—Cardinals 2-for-9, Red Sox 0-for-3. 2B—Brock (2), McCarver (1), Petrocelli (1). 3B—Maxvill (1), Scott (1). HR—Javier (1), BGibson (1). S—Andrews. SF—Maris. GDP—Harrelson. SB—Brock 3 (7). CS—Javier (1).

Cardinals	IP	H	R	ER	BB	K	ERA
Bob Gibson (W, 3-0)	9.0	3	2	2	3	10	1.00

Red Sox	IP	H	R	ER	BB	K	ERA
Jim Lonborg (L, 2-1)	6.0	10	7	6	1	3	2.63
Jose Santiago	2.0	0	0	0	0	1	5.59
Dave Morehead	0.1	0	0	0	3	1	0.00
Dan Osinski	0.1	0	0	0	0	0	6.75
Ken Brett	0.1	0	0	0	0	0	0.00

WP—Lonborg, BGibson. Time—2:23. Attendance—35,188. Umpires—HP, Stevens. 1B, Barlick. 2B, Umont. 3B, Donatelli.

1967 World Series—Composite Statistics

Batting

Cardinals	G	AB	R	H	RBI	2B	3B	HR	BB	SO	SB	CS	Avg	OBP	Slg
Nelson Briles	2	3	0	0	0	0	0	0	0	0	0	0	.000	.000	.000
Lou Brock	7	29	8	12	3	2	1	1	2	3	7	0	.414	.452	.655
Steve Carlton	1	1	0	0	0	0	0	0	0	0	0	0	.000	.000	.000
Orlando Cepeda	7	29	1	3	1	2	0	0	0	4	0	0	.103	.103	.172
Curt Flood	7	28	2	5	3	1	0	0	3	3	0	0	.179	.258	.214
Phil Gagliano	1	1	0	0	0	0	0	0	0	0	0	0	.000	.000	.000
Bob Gibson	3	11	1	1	1	0	0	1	1	2	0	0	.091	.167	.364
Dick Hughes	2	3	0	0	0	0	0	0	0	3	0	0	.000	.000	.000
Julian Javier	7	25	2	9	4	3	0	1	0	6	0	1	.360	.360	.600
Roger Maris	7	26	3	10	7	1	0	1	3	1	0	0	.385	.433	.538
Dal Maxvill	7	19	1	3	1	0	1	0	4	1	0	0	.158	.304	.263
Tim McCarver	7	24	3	3	2	1	0	0	2	2	0	0	.125	.185	.167
Dave Ricketts	3	3	0	0	0	0	0	0	0	0	0	0	.000	.000	.000
Mike Shannon	7	24	3	5	2	1	0	1	1	4	0	0	.208	.240	.375
Ed Spiezio	1	1	0	0	0	0	0	0	0	0	0	0	.000	.000	.000
Bobby Tolan	3	2	1	0	0	0	0	0	1	1	0	0	.000	.333	.000
Totals	7	229	25	51	24	11	2	5	17	30	7	1	.223	.274	.354

Red Sox	G	AB	R	H	RBI	2B	3B	HR	BB	SO	SB	CS	Avg	OBP	Slg
Jerry Adair	5	16	0	2	1	0	0	0	0	3	1	0	.125	.118	.125
Mike Andrews	5	13	2	4	1	0	0	0	1	0	0	0	.308	.308	.308
Joe Foy	6	15	2	2	1	1	0	0	1	5	0	0	.133	.188	.200
Russ Gibson	2	2	0	0	0	0	0	0	0	2	0	0	.000	.000	.000
Ken Harrelson	4	13	0	1	1	0	0	0	1	3	0	0	.077	.143	.077
Elston Howard	7	18	0	2	1	0	0	0	1	2	0	0	.111	.158	.111
Dalton Jones	6	18	2	7	1	0	0	0	1	3	0	0	.389	.421	.389
Jim Lonborg	3	9	0	0	0	0	0	0	0	7	0	0	.000	.000	.000
Rico Petrocelli	7	20	3	4	3	1	0	2	3	8	0	1	.200	.292	.550
Mike Ryan	1	2	0	0	0	0	0	0	0	1	0	0	.000	.000	.000
Jose Santiago	3	2	1	1	1	0	0	1	0	1	0	0	.500	.500	2.000
George Scott	7	26	3	6	0	1	1	0	3	6	0	0	.231	.310	.346
Norm Siebern	3	3	0	1	1	0	0	0	0	0	0	0	.333	.333	.333
Reggie Smith	7	24	3	6	3	1	0	2	2	2	0	1	.250	.308	.542
Jose Tartabull	7	13	1	2	0	0	0	0	1	2	0	0	.154	.214	.154
George Thomas	2	2	0	0	0	0	0	0	0	1	0	0	.000	.000	.000
Gary Waslewski	2	1	0	0	0	0	0	0	0	0	0	0	.000	.500	.000
Carl Yastrzemski	7	25	4	10	5	2	0	3	4	1	0	1	.400	.500	.840
Totals	7	222	21	48	19	6	1	8	17	49	1	3	.216	.276	.360

Pitching

Cardinals	G	GS	CG	IP	H	R	ER	BB	SO	W-L	Sv-Op	Hld	ERA
Nelson Briles	2	1	1	11.0	7	2	2	1	4	1-0	0-0	0	1.64
Steve Carlton	1	1	0	6.0	3	1	0	2	5	0-1	0-0	0	0.00
Bob Gibson	3	3	3	27.0	14	3	3	5	26	3-0	0-0	0	1.00
Joe Hoerner	2	0	0	0.2	4	3	3	1	0	0-0	0-0	0	40.50
Dick Hughes	2	2	0	9.0	9	6	5	3	7	0-1	0-0	0	5.00
Larry Jaster	1	0	0	0.1	2	0	0	0	0	0-0	0-0	0	0.00
Jack Lamabe	3	0	0	2.2	5	2	2	0	4	0-1	0-0	0	6.75
Ray Washburn	2	0	0	2.1	1	0	0	1	2	0-0	0-0	0	0.00
Ron Willis	3	0	0	1.0	2	4	3	4	1	0-0	0-0	0	27.00
Hal Woodeshick	1	0	0	1.0	1	0	0	0	0	0-0	0-0	0	0.00
Totals	7	7	4	61.0	48	21	18	17	49	4-3	0-0	0	2.66

Red Sox	G	GS	CG	IP	H	R	ER	BB	SO	W-L	Sv-Op	Hld	ERA
Gary Bell	3	1	0	5.1	8	3	3	1	1	0-1	1-1	0	5.06
Ken Brett	2	0	0	1.1	0	0	0	1	1	0-0	0-0	0	0.00
Jim Lonborg	3	3	2	24.0	14	8	7	2	11	2-1	0-0	0	2.63
Dave Morehead	2	0	0	3.1	0	0	0	4	3	0-0	0-0	0	0.00
Dan Osinski	2	0	0	1.1	2	1	1	0	0	0-0	0-0	0	6.75
Jose Santiago	3	2	0	9.2	16	6	6	3	6	0-2	0-0	0	5.59
Lee Stange	1	0	0	2.0	3	1	0	0	0	0-0	0-0	0	0.00
Jerry Stephenson	1	0	0	2.0	3	2	2	1	0	0-0	0-0	0	9.00
Gary Waslewski	2	1	0	8.1	4	2	2	2	7	0-0	0-0	0	2.16
John Wyatt	2	0	0	3.2	1	2	2	3	1	1-0	0-1	0	4.91
Totals	7	7	2	61.0	51	25	23	17	30	3-4	1-2	0	3.39

Fielding

Cardinals	Pos	G	PO	Ast	E	DP	PB	FPct
Eddie Bressoud	ss	2	0	0	0	0	—	—
Nelson Briles	p	2	0	4	0	0	—	1.000
Lou Brock	lf	7	13	0	0	0	—	1.000
Steve Carlton	p	1	0	0	0	0	—	—
Orlando Cepeda	1b	7	52	4	0	3	—	1.000
Curt Flood	cf	7	15	0	0	0	—	1.000
Bob Gibson	p	3	2	3	0	0	—	1.000
Joe Hoerner	p	2	0	0	0	0	—	—
Dick Hughes	p	2	1	0	0	0	—	1.000
Larry Jaster	p	1	0	0	0	0	—	—
Julian Javier	2b	7	12	20	1	4	—	.970
Jack Lamabe	p	3	0	1	0	1	—	1.000
Roger Maris	rf	7	15	0	1	0	—	.938
Dal Maxvill	ss	7	13	17	0	3	—	1.000
Tim McCarver	c	7	55	3	0	1	0	1.000
Mike Shannon	3b	7	5	13	2	1	—	.900
Ray Washburn	p	2	0	1	0	0	—	1.000
Ron Willis	p	3	0	0	0	0	—	—
Hal Woodeshick	p	1	0	1	0	0	—	1.000
Totals		7	183	67	4	13	0	.984

Red Sox	Pos	G	PO	Ast	E	DP	PB	FPct
Jerry Adair	2b	4	7	12	0	1	—	1.000
Mike Andrews	2b	3	2	6	0	0	—	1.000
Gary Bell	p	3	0	2	0	1	—	1.000
Ken Brett	p	2	0	0	0	0	—	—
Joe Foy	3b	3	7	10	1	0	—	.944
Russ Gibson	c	2	9	0	0	0	1	1.000
Ken Harrelson	rf	4	5	0	0	0	—	1.000
Elston Howard	c	7	23	1	0	0	0	1.000
Dalton Jones	3b	5	4	8	0	2	—	1.000
Jim Lonborg	p	3	1	2	0	0	—	1.000
Dave Morehead	p	2	0	0	0	0	—	—
Dan Osinski	p	2	0	0	0	0	—	—
Rico Petrocelli	ss	7	11	20	2	1	—	.939
Mike Ryan	c	1	4	0	0	0	0	1.000
Jose Santiago	p	3	0	0	0	0	—	—
George Scott	1b	7	70	3	0	3	—	1.000
Norm Siebern	rf	1	0	0	0	0	—	—
Reggie Smith	cf	7	14	0	0	0	—	1.000
Lee Stange	p	1	0	0	1	0	—	.000
Jerry Stephenson	p	1	0	0	0	0	—	—
Jose Tartabull	rf	6	7	0	0	0	—	1.000
George Thomas	rf	1	1	0	0	0	—	1.000
Gary Waslewski	p	2	2	0	0	0	—	1.000
John Wyatt	p	2	0	0	0	0	—	—
Carl Yastrzemski	lf	7	16	2	0	0	—	1.000
Totals		7	183	66	4	8	1	.984

1968 Detroit Tigers (AL) 4, St. Louis Cardinals (NL) 3

Mickey Lolich beat Bob Gibson in the seventh game of the World Series as the Detroit Tigers came back from a three-games-to-one deficit and slipped past the St. Louis Cardinals, four games to three. Gibson set a World Series record with 17 strikeouts in the opener, a 4-0 blanking of Detroit. Lolich countered by homering and going the distance to win Game 2, 8-1. Tim McCarver and Orlando Cepeda cracked three-run homers in Game 3, a 7-3 Cards triumph. In Game 4, Lou Brock drove in four runs with a double, a triple and a homer, and Gibson beat Denny McLain, 10-1. Lolich singled to right in the seventh inning of Game 5, starting a three-run rally that gave him a 5-3 win. Jim Northrup hit a grand slam and McLain went the distance in Game 6 as the Tigers rolled, 13-1. Lolich beat Gibson 4-1 in Game 7, with Curt Flood misplaying Northrup's triple for two crucial Detroit runs in the seventh. Detroit manager Mayo Smith used outfielder Mickey Stanley at shortstop in the Series, and the unconventional move paid off.

Game 1
Wednesday, October 2

Tigers	AB	R	H	RBI	BB	K	Avg
Dick McAuliffe, 2b	4	0	1	0	0	1	.250
Mickey Stanley, ss	4	0	2	0	0	1	.500
Al Kaline, rf	4	0	1	0	0	3	.250
Norm Cash, 1b	4	0	0	0	0	3	.000
Willie Horton, lf	4	0	0	0	0	2	.000
Jim Northrup, cf	3	0	0	0	0	2	.000
Bill Freehan, c	2	0	0	0	1	2	.000
Don Wert, 3b	2	0	1	0	0	1	.500
Eddie Mathews, ph	1	0	0	0	0	1	.000
Dick Tracewski, 3b	0	0	0	0	0	0	—
Denny McLain, p	1	0	0	0	0	1	.000
Tommy Matchick, ph	1	0	0	0	0	0	.000
Pat Dobson, p	0	0	0	0	0	0	—
Gates Brown, ph	1	0	0	0	0	0	.000
Don McMahon, p	0	0	0	0	0	0	—
TOTALS	31	0	5	0	1	17	.161

Cardinals	AB	R	H	RBI	BB	K	Avg
Lou Brock, lf	4	1	1	1	0	0	.250
Curt Flood, cf	4	0	1	0	0	0	.250
Roger Maris, rf	3	1	0	0	1	0	.000
Orlando Cepeda, 1b	4	0	0	0	0	0	.000
Tim McCarver, c	3	1	1	0	0	1	.333
Mike Shannon, 3b	4	1	2	1	0	1	.500
Julian Javier, 2b	3	0	1	2	1	1	.333
Dal Maxvill, ss	2	0	0	0	1	0	.000
Bob Gibson, p	2	0	0	0	0	1	.000
TOTALS	29	4	6	4	4	3	.207

```
          1 2 3  4 5 6  7 8 9        R H E
Tigers    0 0 0  0 0 0  0 0 0        0 5 3
Cardinals 0 0 0  3 0 0  1 0 x        4 6 0
```

E—Horton, Freehan, Cash. LOB—Tigers 5, Cardinals 6. Scoring Position—Tigers 0-for-1, Cardinals 2-for-9. 2B—Kaline (1). 3B—McCarver (1). HR—Brock (1). S—Gibson. SB—Brock (1), Flood (1), Javier (1). CS—Stanley (1), Javier (1).

Tigers	IP	H	R	ER	BB	K	ERA
Denny McLain (L, 0-1)	5.0	3	3	2	3	3	3.60
Pat Dobson	2.0	2	1	1	1	0	4.50
Don McMahon	1.0	1	0	0	0	0	0.00

Cardinals	IP	H	R	ER	BB	K	ERA
Bob Gibson (W, 1-0)	9.0	5	0	0	1	17	0.00

Time—2:29. Attendance—54,692. Umpires—HP, Gorman. 1B, Honochick. 2B, Landes. 3B, Kinnamon.

Game 2
Thursday, October 3

Tigers	AB	R	H	RBI	BB	K	Avg
Dick McAuliffe, 2b	5	0	2	2	1	0	.333
Mickey Stanley, ss-cf	5	0	1	0	0	1	.333
Al Kaline, rf	5	2	2	0	0	0	.333
Norm Cash, 1b	5	2	3	1	0	0	.333
Willie Horton, lf	3	2	2	1	1	0	.286
Ray Oyler, ss	0	0	0	0	0	0	—
Jim Northrup, cf-lf	5	1	1	0	0	1	.125
Bill Freehan, c	4	0	0	0	1	2	.000
Don Wert, 3b	2	0	0	1	3	1	.250
Mickey Lolich, p	4	1	2	2	1	1	.500
TOTALS	38	8	13	7	7	6	.277

Cardinals	AB	R	H	RBI	BB	K	Avg
Lou Brock, lf	3	1	1	0	1	2	.286
Julian Javier, 2b	4	0	2	0	0	1	.429
Curt Flood, cf	3	0	1	0	1	1	.286
Orlando Cepeda, 1b	4	0	2	1	0	0	.250
Mike Shannon, 3b	4	0	0	0	0	1	.250
Tim McCarver, c	4	0	0	0	0	0	.143
Ron Davis, rf	4	0	0	0	0	1	.000

Dal Maxvill, ss	3	0	0	0	0	1	.000
Nelson Briles, p	2	0	0	0	0	2	.000
Steve Carlton, p	0	0	0	0	0	0	—
Ron Willis, p	0	0	0	0	0	0	—
Phil Gagliano, ph	1	0	0	0	0	0	.000
Joe Hoerner, p	0	0	0	0	0	0	—
TOTALS	32	1	6	1	2	9	.214

```
          1 2 3  4 5 6  7 8 9        R H E
Tigers    0 1 1  0 0 3  1 0 2        8 13 1
Cardinals 0 0 0  0 0 1  0 0 0        1  6 1
```

E—Stanley, Shannon. DP—Tigers 1 (Stanley to McAuliffe to Cash), Cardinals 2 (Maxvill to Cepeda; Javier to Maxvill to Cepeda). LOB—Tigers 11, Cardinals 6. Scoring Position—Tigers 1-for-11, Cardinals 2-for-9. HR—Cash (1), Horton (1), Lolich (1). S—Oyler. GDP—Stanley, Northrup, Shannon. SB—Brock 2 (3).

Tigers	IP	H	R	ER	BB	K	ERA
Mickey Lolich (W, 1-0)	9.0	6	1	1	2	9	1.00

Cardinals	IP	H	R	ER	BB	K	ERA
Nelson Briles (L, 0-1)	5.0	7	4	4	1	2	7.20
Steve Carlton	1.0	4	2	2	1	0	18.00
Ron Willis	2.0	1	0	0	2	2	0.00
Joe Hoerner	1.0	1	2	0	3	1	0.00

Briles pitched to two batters in the 6th. Carlton pitched to two batters in the 7th.

Time—2:41. Attendance—54,692. Umpires—HP, Honochick. 1B, Landes. 2B, Kinnamon. 3B, Harvey.

Game 3
Saturday, October 5

Cardinals	AB	R	H	RBI	BB	K	Avg
Lou Brock, lf	4	1	3	0	1	1	.455
Curt Flood, cf	4	2	2	1	1	0	.364
Roger Maris, rf	3	2	1	0	2	1	.167
Orlando Cepeda, 1b	5	1	1	3	0	0	.231
Tim McCarver, c	5	1	2	3	0	0	.250
Mike Shannon, 3b	4	0	2	0	1	0	.333
Julian Javier, 2b	4	0	1	0	1	1	.364
Dal Maxvill, ss	4	0	0	0	1	0	.000
Ray Washburn, p	3	0	0	0	1	0	.000
Joe Hoerner, p	2	0	1	0	0	1	.500
TOTALS	38	7	13	7	7	5	.278

Tigers	AB	R	H	RBI	BB	K	Avg
Dick McAuliffe, 2b	4	2	2	1	0	0	.385
Mickey Stanley, ss	3	0	0	0	1	0	.250
Al Kaline, rf	4	1	1	2	0	0	.308
Norm Cash, 1b	3	0	0	0	1	1	.250
Willie Horton, lf	2	0	0	0	2	1	.222
Jim Northrup, cf	4	0	0	0	0	0	.083
Bill Freehan, c	3	0	0	0	1	0	.000
Don Wert, 3b	4	0	0	0	0	0	.125
Earl Wilson, p	1	0	0	0	0	1	.000
Pat Dobson, p	0	0	0	0	0	0	—
Tommy Matchick, ph	1	0	0	0	0	1	.000
Don McMahon, p	0	0	0	0	0	0	—
Daryl Patterson, p	0	0	0	0	0	0	—
Wayne Comer, ph	1	0	1	0	0	0	1.000
John Hiller, p	0	0	0	0	0	0	—
Jim Price, ph	1	0	0	0	0	0	.000
TOTALS	31	3	4	3	5	5	.215

```
          1 2 3  4 5 6  7 8 9        R H E
Cardinals 0 0 0  0 4 0  3 0 0        7 13 0
Tigers    0 0 2  0 1 0  0 0 0        3  4 0
```

DP—Tigers 2 (Freehan to Wert; Freehan to Wert). LOB—Cardinals 11, Tigers 6. Scoring Position—Cardinals 3-for-12, Tigers 1-for-5. 2B—Flood (1), Maris (1). HR—Cepeda (1), McCarver (1), McAuliffe (1), Kaline (1). SB—Brock 3 (6). CS—Brock (1), McCarver (1).

Cardinals	IP	H	R	ER	BB	K	ERA
Ray Washburn (W, 1-0)	5.1	3	3	3	4	3	5.06
Joe Hoerner (S, 1)	3.2	1	0	0	1	2	0.00

Tigers	IP	H	R	ER	BB	K	ERA
Earl Wilson (L, 0-1)	4.1	4	3	3	6	3	6.23
Pat Dobson	0.2	2	1	1	0	0	6.75
Don McMahon	1.0	3	3	3	0	1	13.50
Daryl Patterson	1.0	0	0	0	0	0	0.00
John Hiller	2.0	4	0	0	1	1	0.00

McMahon pitched to three batters in the 7th.

Time—3:17. Attendance—53,634. Umpires—HP, Landes. 1B, Kinnamon. 2B, Harvey. 3B, Haller.

Game 4
Sunday, October 6

Cardinals	AB	R	H	RBI	BB	K	Avg
Lou Brock, lf	5	2	3	4	0	0	.500
Curt Flood, cf	5	1	1	0	0	0	.313
Roger Maris, rf	5	1	0	1	0	0	.091
Orlando Cepeda, 1b	4	0	1	0	1	1	.235
Tim McCarver, c	5	1	3	1	0	0	.353
Mike Shannon, 3b	5	1	2	2	0	0	.353
Julian Javier, 2b	4	1	2	0	1	1	.400
Dal Maxvill, ss	4	1	0	0	1	2	.000
Bob Gibson, p	3	2	1	2	1	0	.200
TOTALS	40	10	13	10	4	4	.291

Tigers	AB	R	H	RBI	BB	K	Avg
Dick McAuliffe, 2b	4	0	0	0	0	2	.294
Mickey Stanley, ss	4	0	0	0	0	1	.188
Al Kaline, rf	4	0	2	0	0	0	.353
Norm Cash, 1b	4	0	1	0	0	1	.250
Willie Horton, lf	3	0	0	0	0	1	.167
Jim Northrup, cf	4	1	1	1	0	0	.125
Eddie Mathews, 3b	2	0	1	0	1	0	.333
Bill Freehan, c	3	0	0	0	0	3	.000
Denny McLain, p	1	0	0	0	0	0	.000
Joe Sparma, p	0	0	0	0	0	0	—
Daryl Patterson, p	0	0	0	0	0	0	—
Jim Price, ph	1	0	0	0	0	1	.000
Fred Lasher, p	0	0	0	0	0	0	—
Tommy Matchick, ph	1	0	0	0	0	0	.000
John Hiller, p	0	0	0	0	0	0	—
Pat Dobson, p	0	0	0	0	0	0	—
TOTALS	31	1	5	1	2	10	.198

```
          1 2 3  4 5 6  7 8 9        R H E
Cardinals 2 0 2  2 2 0  0 4 0        10 13 0
Tigers    0 0 0  1 0 0  0 0 0        1  5 4
```

E—Northrup, McLain, Freehan, Mathews. LOB—Cardinals 7, Tigers 5. Scoring Position—Cardinals 3-for-13, Tigers 0-for-3. 2B—Brock (1), Shannon (1), Javier (1), Kaline (2). 3B—Brock (1), McCarver (2). HR—Brock (2), Gibson (1), Northrup (1). GDP—Northrup. SB—Brock (7). CS—Cepeda (1), Javier (2).

Cardinals	IP	H	R	ER	BB	K	ERA
Bob Gibson (W, 2-0)	9.0	5	1	1	2	10	0.50

Tigers	IP	H	R	ER	BB	K	ERA
Denny McLain (L, 0-2)	2.2	6	4	3	1	3	5.87
Joe Sparma	0.1	2	2	2	0	0	54.00
Daryl Patterson	2.0	1	0	0	1	0	0.00
Fred Lasher	2.0	1	0	0	0	1	0.00
John Hiller	0.0	2	4	3	2	0	13.50
Pat Dobson	2.0	1	0	0	0	0	3.86

Sparma pitched to two batters in the 4th. Hiller pitched to five batters in the 8th.

Time—2:34. Attendance—53,634. Umpires—HP, Kinnamon. 1B, Harvey. 2B, Haller. 3B, Gorman.

Game 5
Monday, October 7

Cardinals	AB	R	H	RBI	BB	K	Avg
Lou Brock, lf	5	1	3	0	0	0	.524
Julian Javier, 2b	4	0	2	0	0	0	.421
Curt Flood, cf	4	1	1	1	0	0	.300
Orlando Cepeda, 1b	4	1	1	2	0	1	.238
Mike Shannon, 3b	4	0	0	0	0	1	.286
Tim McCarver, c	3	0	1	0	1	1	.350
Ron Davis, rf	3	0	0	0	0	1	.000
Phil Gagliano, ph	1	0	0	0	0	0	.000
Dal Maxvill, ss	3	0	0	0	0	1	.000
Ed Spiezio, ph	1	0	1	0	0	0	1.000
Dick Schofield, pr	0	0	0	0	0	0	—
Nelson Briles, p	2	0	0	0	0	2	.000
Joe Hoerner, p	0	0	0	0	0	0	.500
Ron Willis, p	0	0	0	0	0	0	—
Roger Maris, ph	1	0	0	0	0	1	.083
TOTALS	35	3	9	3	1	8	.277

Tigers	AB	R	H	RBI	BB	K	Avg
Dick McAuliffe, 2b	4	1	1	0	0	1	.286
Mickey Stanley, ss-cf	3	2	1	0	1	0	.211
Al Kaline, rf	4	0	2	2	0	1	.381
Norm Cash, 1b	2	0	2	2	1	0	.333
Willie Horton, lf	4	1	1	0	0	0	.188
Ray Oyler, ss	0	0	0	0	0	0	—
Jim Northrup, cf-lf	3	0	1	1	1	0	.158
Bill Freehan, c	4	0	0	0	0	1	.000
Don Wert, 3b	3	0	0	0	1	1	.091
Mickey Lolich, p	4	1	1	0	0	2	.375
TOTALS	31	5	9	5	4	6	.228

	1	2	3	4	5	6	7	8	9		R	H	E
Cardinals	3	0	0	0	0	0	0	0	0		3	9	0
Tigers	0	0	0	2	0	0	3	0	x		5	9	1

E—Cash. DP—Cardinals 1 (Shannon to Javier to Cepeda). LOB—Cardinals 7, Tigers 7. Scoring Position—Cardinals 3-for-8, Tigers 3-for-8. 2B—Brock 2 (3). 3B—Stanley (1), Horton (1). HR—Cepeda (2). SF—Cash. GDP—Horton. SB—Flood (2). CS—Brock (3).

Cardinals	IP	H	R	ER	BB	K	ERA
Nelson Briles	6.1	6	3	3	3	5	5.56
Joe Hoerner (BS, 1; L, 0-1)	0.0	3	2	2	1	0	3.86
Ron Willis	1.2	0	0	0	0	1	0.00

Tigers	IP	H	R	ER	BB	K	ERA
Mickey Lolich (W, 2-0)	9.0	9	3	3	1	8	2.00

Hoerner pitched to four batters in the 7th.

HBP—Briles by Lolich. Time—2:43. Attendance—53,634. Umpires—HP, Harvey. 1B, Haller. 2B, Gorman. 3B, Honochick.

Game 6
Wednesday, October 9

Tigers	AB	R	H	RBI	BB	K	Avg
Dick McAuliffe, 2b	2	2	0	0	3	2	.261
Mickey Stanley, ss-cf	5	2	1	0	0	0	.208
Al Kaline, rf	4	3	3	4	0	1	.440
Norm Cash, 1b	4	2	3	2	1	0	.409
Willie Horton, lf	3	2	2	2	1	0	.263
Jim Northrup, cf-lf	5	1	2	4	0	1	.208
Bill Freehan, c	4	0	1	1	1	0	.050
Don Wert, 3b	3	1	0	0	1	0	.071
Denny McLain, p	4	0	0	0	0	3	.000
TOTALS	34	13	12	13	7	7	.243

Cardinals	AB	R	H	RBI	BB	K	Avg
Lou Brock, lf	4	0	1	0	0	1	.480
Curt Flood, cf	4	0	0	0	0	1	.250
Roger Maris, rf	4	1	2	0	0	0	.188
Orlando Cepeda, 1b	4	0	2	0	0	0	.280
Tim McCarver, c	4	0	1	0	0	1	.333
Mike Shannon, 3b	4	0	1	0	0	1	.280
Julian Javier, 2b	4	0	1	1	0	0	.391
Dal Maxvill, ss	4	0	0	0	0	1	.000
Ray Washburn, p	0	0	0	0	0	0	.000
Larry Jaster, p	0	0	0	0	0	0	—
Ron Willis, p	0	0	0	0	0	0	—
Dick Hughes, p	0	0	0	0	0	0	—
Dave Ricketts, ph	1	0	1	0	0	0	1.000
Steve Carlton, p	0	0	0	0	0	0	—
Bobby Tolan, ph	1	0	0	0	0	1	.000
Wayne Granger, p	0	0	0	0	0	0	—
Johnny Edwards, ph	1	0	0	0	0	1	.000
Mel Nelson, p	0	0	0	0	0	0	—
TOTALS	35	1	9	1	0	7	.282

	1	2	3	4	5	6	7	8	9		R	H	E
Tigers	0	2	1	0	0	1	0	0	0		13	12	1
Cardinals	0	0	0	0	0	0	0	0	1		1	9	1

E—Stanley, Brock. DP—Tigers 1 (Stanley to McAuliffe to Cash), Cardinals 3 (Maxvill to Javier to Cepeda; Maxvill to Javier to Cepeda; Granger to Maxvill to Cepeda). LOB—Tigers 5, Cardinals 7. Scoring Position—Tigers 7-for-12, Cardinals 1-for-6. 2B—Horton (1). HR—Kaline (2), Northrup (2). S—McLain. GDP—Stanley, Northrup, McLain, Shannon. CS—Northrup (1).

Tigers	IP	H	R	ER	BB	K	ERA
Denny McLain (W, 1-2)	9.0	9	1	1	0	7	3.24

Cardinals	IP	H	R	ER	BB	K	ERA
Ray Washburn (L, 1-1)	2.0	4	5	5	3	3	9.82
Larry Jaster	0.0	2	3	3	1	0	—
Ron Willis	0.2	1	4	4	2	0	8.31
Dick Hughes	0.1	2	0	0	0	0	0.00
Steve Carlton	3.0	3	1	1	0	2	6.75
Wayne Granger	2.0	0	0	0	1	1	0.00
Mel Nelson	1.0	0	0	0	0	1	0.00

Washburn pitched to three batters in the 3rd. Jaster pitched to three batters in the 3rd.

HBP—Horton by Granger, Wert by Willis, Kaline by Granger. Time—2:26. Attendance—54,692. Umpires—HP, Haller. 1B, Gorman. 2B, Honochick. 3B, Landes.

Game 7
Thursday, October 10

Tigers	AB	R	H	RBI	BB	K	Avg
Dick McAuliffe, 2b	4	0	0	0	0	0	.222
Mickey Stanley, ss-cf	4	0	1	0	0	1	.214
Al Kaline, rf	4	0	0	0	0	2	.379
Norm Cash, 1b	4	1	1	0	0	0	.385
Willie Horton, lf	4	1	2	0	0	1	.304
Dick Tracewski, pr	0	1	0	0	0	0	—
Ray Oyler, ss	0	0	0	0	0	0	—
Jim Northrup, cf-lf	4	1	2	2	0	1	.250
Bill Freehan, c	4	0	1	1	0	0	.083
Don Wert, 3b	3	0	1	1	1	1	.118
Mickey Lolich, p	4	0	0	0	0	2	.250
TOTALS	35	4	8	4	1	8	.252

Cardinals	AB	R	H	RBI	BB	K	Avg
Lou Brock, lf	3	0	1	0	1	0	.464
Julian Javier, 2b	4	0	0	0	0	0	.333
Curt Flood, cf	4	0	2	0	0	0	.286
Orlando Cepeda, 1b	3	0	0	1	0	1	.250
Mike Shannon, 3b	4	1	1	1	0	1	.276
Tim McCarver, c	3	0	1	0	1	0	.333
Roger Maris, rf	3	0	0	0	0	1	.158
Dal Maxvill, ss	2	0	0	0	0	0	.000
Phil Gagliano, ph	1	0	0	0	0	0	.000
Dick Schofield, ss	0	0	0	0	0	0	—
Bob Gibson, p	3	0	0	0	0	1	.125
TOTALS	30	1	5	1	3	4	.265

	1	2	3	4	5	6	7	8	9		R	H	E
Tigers	0	0	0	0	0	0	3	0	1		4	8	1
Cardinals	0	0	0	0	0	0	0	0	1		1	5	0

E—Northrup. DP—Tigers 1 (Stanley to Cash). LOB—Tigers 5, Cardinals 5. Scoring Position—Tigers 3-for-6, Cardinals 0-for-3. 2B—Freehan (1). 3B—Northrup (1). HR—Shannon (1). GDP—Maris. SB—Flood (3). CS—Brock (3), Flood (1).

Tigers	IP	H	R	ER	BB	K	ERA
Mickey Lolich (W, 3-0)	9.0	5	1	1	3	4	1.67

Cardinals	IP	H	R	ER	BB	K	ERA
Bob Gibson (L, 2-1)	9.0	8	4	4	1	8	1.67

Time—2:07. Attendance—54,692. Umpires—HP, Gorman. 1B, Honochick. 2B, Landes. 3B, Kinnamon.

1968 World Series—Composite Statistics

Batting

Tigers

Tigers	G	AB	R	H	RBI	2B	3B	HR	BB	SO	SB	CS	Avg	OBP	Slg
Gates Brown	1	1	0	0	0	0	0	0	0	0	0	0	.000	.000	.000
Norm Cash	7	26	5	10	5	0	0	1	3	5	0	0	.385	.433	.500
Wayne Comer	1	1	0	1	0	0	0	0	0	0	0	0	1.000	1.000	1.000
Bill Freehan	7	24	0	2	2	1	0	0	4	8	0	0	.083	.214	.125
Willie Horton	7	23	6	7	3	1	1	1	5	6	0	0	.304	.448	.565
Al Kaline	7	29	6	11	8	2	0	2	0	7	0	0	.379	.400	.655
Mickey Lolich	3	12	2	3	2	0	0	1	1	5	0	0	.250	.308	.500
Tommy Matchick	3	3	0	0	0	0	0	0	0	1	0	0	.000	.000	.000
Eddie Mathews	2	3	0	1	0	0	0	0	1	1	0	0	.333	.500	.333
Dick McAuliffe	7	27	5	6	3	0	0	1	4	6	0	0	.222	.323	.333
Denny McLain	3	6	0	0	0	0	0	0	0	4	0	0	.000	.000	.000
Jim Northrup	7	28	4	7	8	0	1	2	1	5	0	1	.250	.276	.536
Ray Oyler	4	0	0	0	0	0	0	0	0	0	0	0	—	—	—
Jim Price	2	2	0	0	0	0	0	0	0	1	0	0	.000	.000	.000
Mickey Stanley	7	28	4	6	0	0	1	0	2	4	0	1	.214	.267	.286
Dick Tracewski	2	0	1	0	0	0	0	0	0	0	0	0	—	—	—
Don Wert	6	17	1	2	2	0	0	0	6	5	0	0	.118	.375	.118
Earl Wilson	1	1	0	0	0	0	0	0	0	1	0	0	.000	.000	.000
Totals	7	231	34	56	33	4	3	8	27	59	0	2	.242	.328	.390

Cardinals

Cardinals	G	AB	R	H	RBI	2B	3B	HR	BB	SO	SB	CS	Avg	OBP	Slg
Nelson Briles	2	4	0	0	0	0	0	0	0	4	0	0	.000	.200	.000
Lou Brock	7	28	6	13	5	3	1	2	3	4	7	3	.464	.516	.857
Orlando Cepeda	7	28	2	7	6	0	0	2	2	3	0	1	.250	.300	.464
Ron Davis	2	7	0	0	0	0	0	0	0	2	0	0	.000	.000	.000
Johnny Edwards	1	1	0	0	0	0	0	0	0	1	0	0	.000	.000	.000
Curt Flood	7	28	4	8	2	1	0	0	2	2	3	1	.286	.333	.321
Phil Gagliano	3	3	0	0	0	0	0	0	0	0	0	0	.000	.000	.000
Bob Gibson	3	8	2	1	2	0	0	1	1	2	0	0	.125	.222	.500
Joe Hoerner	3	2	0	1	0	0	0	0	0	1	0	0	.500	.500	.500
Julian Javier	7	27	1	9	3	1	0	0	3	4	1	2	.333	.400	.370
Roger Maris	6	19	5	3	1	1	0	0	3	3	0	0	.158	.273	.211
Dal Maxvill	7	22	1	0	0	0	0	0	3	5	0	0	.000	.120	.000
Tim McCarver	7	27	3	9	4	0	2	1	3	2	0	1	.333	.400	.593
Dave Ricketts	1	1	0	1	0	0	0	0	0	0	0	0	1.000	1.000	1.000
Mike Shannon	7	29	3	8	4	1	0	1	1	5	0	0	.276	.300	.414
Ed Spiezio	1	1	0	1	0	0	0	0	0	0	0	0	1.000	1.000	1.000
Bobby Tolan	1	1	0	0	0	0	0	0	0	0	0	0	.000	.000	.000
Ray Washburn	2	3	0	0	0	0	0	0	0	1	0	0	.000	.000	.000
Totals	7	239	27	61	27	7	3	7	21	40	11	8	.255	.318	.397

Pitching

Tigers

Tigers	G	GS	CG	IP	H	R	ER	BB	SO	W-L	Sv-Op	Hld	ERA
Pat Dobson	3	0	0	4.2	5	2	2	1	0	0-0	0-0	0	3.86
John Hiller	2	0	0	2.0	6	4	3	3	1	0-0	0-0	0	13.50
Fred Lasher	1	0	0	2.0	1	0	0	0	1	0-0	0-0	0	0.00
Mickey Lolich	3	3	3	27.0	20	5	5	6	21	3-0	0-0	0	1.67
Denny McLain	3	3	1	16.2	18	8	6	4	13	1-2	0-0	0	3.24
Don McMahon	2	0	0	2.0	4	3	3	0	1	0-0	0-0	0	13.50
Daryl Patterson	2	0	0	3.0	1	0	0	1	0	0-0	0-0	0	0.00
Joe Sparma	1	0	0	0.1	2	2	2	0	0	0-0	0-0	0	54.00
Earl Wilson	1	1	0	4.1	4	3	3	6	3	0-1	0-0	0	6.23
Totals	7	7	4	62.0	61	27	24	21	40	4-3	0-0	0	3.48

Cardinals

Cardinals	G	GS	CG	IP	H	R	ER	BB	SO	W-L	Sv-Op	Hld	ERA
Nelson Briles	2	2	0	11.1	13	7	7	4	7	0-1	0-0	0	5.56
Steve Carlton	2	0	0	4.2	3	3	3	1	3	0-0	0-0	0	6.75
Bob Gibson	3	3	3	27.0	18	5	5	4	35	2-1	0-0	0	1.67
Wayne Granger	1	0	0	2.0	0	0	0	1	1	0-0	0-0	0	0.00
Joe Hoerner	3	0	0	4.2	5	4	2	5	3	0-1	1-2	0	3.86
Dick Hughes	1	0	0	0.1	2	0	0	0	0	0-0	0-0	0	0.00
Larry Jaster	1	0	0	0.2	3	3	3	1	0	0-0	0-0	0	—
Mel Nelson	1	0	0	1.0	0	0	0	0	1	0-0	0-0	0	0.00
Ray Washburn	2	2	0	7.1	7	8	8	7	6	1-1	0-0	0	9.82
Ron Willis	3	0	0	4.1	2	4	4	4	3	0-0	0-0	0	8.31
Totals	7	7	3	62.0	56	34	32	27	59	3-4	1-2	0	4.65

Fielding

Tigers

Tigers	Pos	G	PO	Ast	E	DP	PB	FPct
Norm Cash	1b	7	58	7	2	3	—	.970
Pat Dobson	p	3	1	0	0	0	—	1.000
Bill Freehan	c	7	45	6	2	2	0	.962
John Hiller	p	2	1	0	0	0	—	1.000
Willie Horton	lf	7	5	1	1	0	—	.857
Al Kaline	rf	7	19	0	0	0	—	1.000
Fred Lasher	p	1	0	1	0	0	—	1.000
Mickey Lolich	p	3	1	4	0	0	—	1.000
Eddie Mathews	3b	1	0	1	1	0	—	.500
Dick McAuliffe	2b	7	12	16	0	2	—	1.000
Denny McLain	p	3	0	3	1	0	—	.750
Don McMahon	p	2	1	0	0	0	—	1.000
Jim Northrup	cf	7	19	0	2	0	—	.905
	lf	4	1	0	0	0	—	1.000
Ray Oyler	ss	4	2	0	0	0	—	1.000
Daryl Patterson	p	2	0	1	0	0	—	1.000
Joe Sparma	p	1	0	0	0	0	—	—
Mickey Stanley	ss	7	14	16	2	3	—	.938
	cf	4	2	0	0	0	—	1.000
Dick Tracewski	3b	1	0	0	0	0	—	—
Don Wert	3b	6	5	14	0	2	—	1.000
Earl Wilson	p	1	0	2	0	0	—	1.000
Totals		7	186	72	11	12	0	.959

Cardinals

Cardinals	Pos	G	PO	Ast	E	DP	PB	FPct
Nelson Briles	p	2	0	2	0	0	—	1.000
Lou Brock	lf	7	14	0	1	0	—	.933
Steve Carlton	p	2	1	0	0	0	—	1.000
Orlando Cepeda	1b	7	47	4	0	7	—	1.000
Ron Davis	rf	2	5	0	0	0	—	1.000
Curt Flood	cf	7	12	0	0	0	—	1.000
Bob Gibson	p	3	2	0	0	0	—	1.000
Wayne Granger	p	1	0	1	0	1	—	1.000
Joe Hoerner	p	3	0	0	0	0	—	—
Dick Hughes	p	1	0	0	0	0	—	—
Larry Jaster	p	1	0	0	0	0	—	—
Julian Javier	2b	7	15	13	0	4	—	1.000
Roger Maris	rf	5	8	0	0	0	—	1.000
Dal Maxvill	ss	7	15	15	0	6	—	1.000
Tim McCarver	c	7	61	1	0	0	0	1.000
Mel Nelson	p	1	0	0	0	0	—	—
Dick Schofield	ss	1	0	0	0	0	—	—
Mike Shannon	3b	7	5	10	1	1	—	.938
Ray Washburn	p	2	0	1	0	0	—	1.000
Ron Willis	p	3	1	0	0	0	—	1.000
Totals		7	186	47	2	19	0	.991

1969 New York Mets (NL) 4, Baltimore Orioles (AL) 1

The New York Mets stunned the Baltimore Orioles—and the rest of the world—with a five-game World Series victory. Mike Cuellar beat the Mets in Game 1, going the distance while singling in a run during a three-run rally in the fourth. In Game 2, Jerry Koosman pitched 8.2 two-hit innings, and light-hitting Al Weis drove in the decisive run with a two-out RBI single in the top of the ninth, as the Mets won, 2-1. Tommie Agee homered and made two circus catches in Game 3, and Gary Gentry and Nolan Ryan combined to blank the O's, 5-0. Tom Seaver took a 1-0 lead into the ninth inning of Game 4 before the Orioles put two runners on base. Ron Swoboda made a sliding catch in right field to prevent the Orioles from going ahead, but a run scored on the sacrifice fly and the game went into bonus frames. With men on first and second in the bottom of the 10th, J.C. Martin bunted to pitcher Pete Richert, whose throw to first hit Martin's wrist and rolled away as the winning run scored. Baltimore took a 3-0 lead in Game 5, but the Mets came back to win it 5-3 on eighth-inning RBI doubles by Cleon Jones and Swoboda.

Game 1

Saturday, October 11

Mets	AB	R	H	RBI	BB	K	Avg
Tommie Agee, cf	4	0	0	0	0	2	.000
Bud Harrelson, ss	3	0	1	0	1	0	.333
Cleon Jones, lf	4	0	1	0	0	0	.250
Donn Clendenon, 1b	4	1	2	0	0	2	.500
Ron Swoboda, rf	3	0	1	0	1	1	.333
Ed Charles, 3b	4	0	0	0	0	1	.000
Jerry Grote, c	4	0	1	0	0	1	.250
Al Weis, 2b	1	0	0	1	2	0	.000
Tom Seaver, p	1	0	0	0	0	1	.000
Duffy Dyer, ph	1	0	0	0	0	1	.000
Don Cardwell, p	0	0	0	0	0	0	—
Rod Gaspar, ph	1	0	0	0	0	0	.000
Ron Taylor, p	0	0	0	0	0	0	—
Art Shamsky, ph	1	0	0	0	0	0	.000
TOTALS	31	1	6	1	4	8	.194

Orioles	AB	R	H	RBI	BB	K	Avg
Don Buford, lf	4	1	2	2	0	0	.500
Paul Blair, cf	3	0	0	0	1	1	.000
Frank Robinson, rf	4	0	0	0	0	2	.000
Boog Powell, 1b	4	0	1	0	0	0	.250
Brooks Robinson, 3b	4	0	0	0	0	1	.000
Ellie Hendricks, c	3	1	1	0	0	0	.333
Dave Johnson, 2b	2	1	0	0	1	0	.000
Mark Belanger, ss	3	1	1	1	0	0	.333
Mike Cuellar, p	3	0	1	1	0	2	.333
TOTALS	30	4	6	4	2	6	.200

	1	2	3	4	5	6	7	8	9		R	H	E
Mets	0	0	0	0	0	0	0	1	0		1	6	1
Orioles	1	0	0	3	0	0	0	0	x		4	6	0

E—Weis. DP—Orioles 1 (Belanger to Johnson to Powell). LOB—Mets 8, Orioles 4. Scoring Position—Mets 1-for-5, Orioles 3-for-4. 2B—Clendenon (1), Buford (1). HR—Buford (1). SF—Weis. GDP—Agee. CS—Blair (1).

Mets	IP	H	R	ER	BB	K	ERA
Tom Seaver (L, 0-1)	5.0	6	4	4	1	3	7.20
Don Cardwell	1.0	0	0	0	0	0	0.00
Ron Taylor	2.0	0	0	0	1	3	0.00

Orioles	IP	H	R	ER	BB	K	ERA
Mike Cuellar (W, 1-0)	9.0	6	1	1	4	8	1.00

Time—2:13. Attendance—50,429. Umpires—HP, Soar. 1B, Secory. 2B, Napp. 3B, Crawford.

Game 2

Sunday, October 12

Mets	AB	R	H	RBI	BB	K	Avg
Tommie Agee, cf	4	0	0	0	0	2	.000
Bud Harrelson, ss	3	0	0	0	1	0	.167
Cleon Jones, lf	4	0	0	0	0	0	.125
Donn Clendenon, 1b	3	1	1	1	1	1	.429
Ron Swoboda, rf	4	0	0	0	0	1	.143
Ed Charles, 3b	4	1	2	0	0	0	.250
Jerry Grote, c	4	0	1	0	0	0	.250
Al Weis, 2b	3	0	2	1	1	1	.500
Jerry Koosman, p	4	0	0	0	0	2	.000
Ron Taylor, p	0	0	0	0	0	0	—
TOTALS	33	2	6	2	3	7	.200

Orioles	AB	R	H	RBI	BB	K	Avg
Don Buford, lf	4	0	0	0	0	1	.250
Paul Blair, cf	4	1	1	0	0	0	.143
Frank Robinson, rf	3	0	0	0	1	0	.000
Merv Rettenmund, pr	0	0	0	0	0	0	—
Boog Powell, 1b	3	0	0	0	1	1	.143
Brooks Robinson, 3b	4	0	1	1	0	0	.125
Dave Johnson, 2b	2	0	0	0	1	0	.000
Andy Etchebarren, c	3	0	0	0	0	0	.000
Mark Belanger, ss	3	0	0	0	0	1	.167
Dave McNally, p	3	0	0	0	0	1	.000
TOTALS	29	1	2	1	3	4	.113

	1	2	3	4	5	6	7	8	9		R	H	E
Mets	0	0	0	1	0	0	0	0	1		2	6	0
Orioles	0	0	0	0	0	0	1	0	0		1	2	0

LOB—Mets 7, Orioles 4. Scoring Position—Mets 1-for-6, Orioles 1-for-2. 2B—Charles (1). HR—Clendenon (1). SB—Blair (1).

Mets	IP	H	R	ER	BB	K	ERA
Jerry Koosman (W, 1-0)	8.2	2	1	1	3	4	1.04
Ron Taylor (S, 1)	0.1	0	0	0	0	0	0.00

Orioles	IP	H	R	ER	BB	K	ERA
Dave McNally (L, 0-1)	9.0	6	2	2	3	7	2.00

WP—McNally. Time—2:20. Attendance—50,850. Umpires—HP, Secory. 1B, Napp. 2B, Crawford. 3B, DiMuro.

Game 3

Tuesday, October 14

Orioles	AB	R	H	RBI	BB	K	Avg
Don Buford, lf	3	0	0	0	2	2	.182
Paul Blair, cf	5	0	0	0	0	2	.083
Frank Robinson, rf	2	0	1	0	2	0	.111
Boog Powell, 1b	4	0	2	0	0	1	.273
Brooks Robinson, 3b	4	0	0	0	0	2	.083
Ellie Hendricks, c	4	0	0	0	0	0	.143
Dave Johnson, 2b	4	0	0	0	0	0	.000
Mark Belanger, ss	2	0	0	0	2	0	.125
Jim Palmer, p	2	0	0	0	0	0	.000
Dave May, ph	0	0	0	0	1	0	—
Dave Leonhard, p	0	0	0	0	0	0	—
Clay Dalrymple, ph	1	0	1	0	0	0	1.000
Chico Salmon, pr	0	0	0	0	0	0	—
TOTALS	31	0	4	0	7	7	.136

Mets	AB	R	H	RBI	BB	K	Avg
Tommie Agee, cf	3	1	1	1	1	0	.091
Wayne Garrett, 3b	1	0	0	0	2	1	.000
Cleon Jones, lf	4	0	0	0	0	1	.083
Art Shamsky, rf	4	0	0	0	0	0	.000
Al Weis, 2b	0	0	0	0	0	0	.500
Ken Boswell, 2b	3	1	1	0	0	0	.333
Rod Gaspar, rf	1	0	0	0	0	0	.000
Ed Kranepool, 1b	4	1	1	1	0	0	.250
Jerry Grote, c	3	1	1	1	1	0	.273
Bud Harrelson, ss	3	1	1	0	1	2	.222
Gary Gentry, p	3	0	1	2	0	2	.333
Nolan Ryan, p	0	0	0	0	0	0	—
TOTALS	29	5	6	5	5	6	.185

	1	2	3	4	5	6	7	8	9		R	H	E
Orioles	0	0	0	0	0	0	0	0	0		0	4	1
Mets	1	2	0	0	0	1	0	1	x		5	6	0

E—Palmer. LOB—Orioles 11, Mets 6. Scoring Position—Orioles 0-for-5, Mets 2-for-9. 2B—Grote (1), Gentry (1). HR—Agee (1), Kranepool (1). S—Garrett.

Orioles	IP	H	R	ER	BB	K	ERA
Jim Palmer (L, 0-1)	6.0	5	4	4	4	5	6.00
Dave Leonhard	2.0	1	1	1	1	1	4.50

Mets	IP	H	R	ER	BB	K	ERA
Gary Gentry (W, 1-0)	6.2	3	0	0	5	4	0.00
Nolan Ryan (S, 1)	2.1	1	0	0	2	3	0.00

Time—2:23. Attendance—56,335. Umpires—HP, Napp. 1B, Crawford. 2B, DiMuro. 3B, Weyer.

Game 4
Wednesday, October 15

Orioles	AB	R	H	RBI	BB	K	Avg
Don Buford, lf	5	0	0	0	0	1	.125
Paul Blair, cf	4	0	1	0	1	1	.125
Frank Robinson, rf	4	1	1	0	0	0	.154
Boog Powell, 1b	4	0	1	0	0	1	.267
Brooks Robinson, 3b	3	0	0	1	0	0	.067
Ellie Hendricks, c	3	0	0	0	1	0	.100
Dave Johnson, 2b	4	0	0	0	0	1	.000
Mark Belanger, ss	4	0	1	0	0	0	.167
Mike Cuellar, p	2	0	1	0	0	1	.400
Dave May, ph	1	0	0	0	0	1	.000
Eddie Watt, p	0	0	0	0	0	0	—
Clay Dalrymple, ph	1	0	1	0	0	0	1.000
Dick Hall, p	0	0	0	0	0	0	—
Pete Richert, p	0	0	0	0	0	0	—
TOTALS	35	1	6	1	2	6	.154

Mets	AB	R	H	RBI	BB	K	Avg
Tommie Agee, cf	4	0	1	0	0	1	.133
Bud Harrelson, ss	4	0	1	0	0	0	.231
Cleon Jones, lf	4	0	1	0	0	0	.125
Donn Clendenon, 1b	4	1	1	1	0	2	.364
Ron Swoboda, rf	4	0	3	0	0	0	.364
Ed Charles, 3b	3	0	0	0	0	1	.182
Art Shamsky, ph	1	0	0	0	0	0	.000
Wayne Garrett, 3b	0	0	0	0	0	0	.000
Jerry Grote, c	4	0	1	0	0	2	.267
Rod Gaspar, pr	0	1	0	0	0	0	.000
Al Weis, 2b	3	0	2	0	1	0	.571
Tom Seaver, p	3	0	0	0	0	1	.000
J.C. Martin, ph	0	0	0	0	0	0	—
TOTALS	34	2	10	1	1	7	.223

	1	2	3	4	5	6	7	8	9	10		R	H	E
Orioles	0	0	0	0	0	0	0	0	1	0		1	6	1
Mets	0	1	0	0	0	0	0	0	0	1		2	10	1

E—Garrett, Richert. DP—Orioles 3 (Belanger to Johnson to Powell; Hendricks to Johnson; Belanger to Johnson to Powell). LOB—Orioles 7, Mets 7. Scoring Position—Orioles 0-for-5, Mets 0-for-3. 2B—Grote (2). HR—Clendenon (2). S—Martin. SF—BRobinson. GDP—Jones, Seaver. CS—Johnson (1), Swoboda (1).

Orioles	IP	H	R	ER	BB	K	ERA
Mike Cuellar	7.0	7	1	1	0	5	1.13
Eddie Watt	2.0	2	0	0	0	2	0.00
Dick Hall (L, 0-1)	0.0	1	1	0	1	0	—
Pete Richert	0.0	0	0	0	0	0	—

Mets	IP	H	R	ER	BB	K	ERA
Tom Seaver (W, 1-1)	10.0	6	1	1	2	6	3.00

Hall pitched to two batters in the 10th. Richert pitched to one batter in the 10th.

Time—2:33. Attendance—57,367. Umpires—HP, Crawford. 1B, DiMuro. 2B, Weyer. 3B, Soar.

Game 5
Thursday, October 16

Orioles	AB	R	H	RBI	BB	K	Avg
Don Buford, lf	4	0	0	0	0	0	.100
Paul Blair, cf	4	0	0	0	0	1	.100
Frank Robinson, rf	3	1	1	1	1	1	.188
Boog Powell, 1b	4	0	1	0	0	1	.263
Chico Salmon, pr	0	0	0	0	0	0	—
Brooks Robinson, 3b	4	0	0	0	0	0	.053
Dave Johnson, 2b	4	0	1	0	0	0	.063
Andy Etchebarren, c	3	0	0	0	0	1	.000
Mark Belanger, ss	3	1	1	0	0	0	.200
Dave McNally, p	2	1	1	2	0	1	.200
Curt Motton, ph	1	0	0	0	0	0	.000
Eddie Watt, p	0	0	0	0	0	0	—
TOTALS	32	3	5	3	1	5	.131

Mets	AB	R	H	RBI	BB	K	Avg
Tommie Agee, cf	3	0	1	0	1	0	.167
Bud Harrelson, ss	4	0	0	0	0	2	.176
Cleon Jones, lf	3	2	1	0	0	0	.158
Donn Clendenon, 1b	3	1	1	2	1	1	.357
Ron Swoboda, rf	4	1	2	1	0	1	.400
Ed Charles, 3b	4	0	0	0	0	0	.133
Jerry Grote, c	4	0	0	0	0	0	.211
Al Weis, 2b	4	1	1	1	0	1	.455
Jerry Koosman, p	3	0	1	0	0	2	.143
TOTALS	32	5	7	4	2	7	.237

	1	2	3	4	5	6	7	8	9		R	H	E
Orioles	0	0	3	0	0	0	0	0	0		3	5	2
Mets	0	0	0	0	0	2	1	2	x		5	7	0

E—Watt, Powell. LOB—Orioles 3, Mets 6. Scoring Position—Orioles 0-for-0, Mets 1-for-9. 2B—Jones (1), Swoboda (1), Koosman (1). HR—FRobinson (1), McNally (1), Clendenon (3), Weis (1). SB—Agee (1).

Orioles	IP	H	R	ER	BB	K	ERA
Dave McNally	7.0	5	3	3	2	6	2.81
Eddie Watt (L, 0-1)	1.0	2	2	1	0	1	3.00

Mets	IP	H	R	ER	BB	K	ERA
Jerry Koosman (W, 2-0)	9.0	5	3	3	1	5	2.04

HBP—Jones by McNally. Time—2:14. Attendance—57,397. Umpires—HP, DiMuro. 1B, Weyer. 2B, Soar. 3B, Secory.

1969 World Series—Composite Statistics

Batting

Mets	G	AB	R	H	RBI	2B	3B	HR	BB	SO	SB	CS	Avg	OBP	Slg
Tommie Agee	5	18	1	3	1	0	0	1	2	5	1	0	.167	.250	.333
Ken Boswell	1	3	1	1	0	0	0	0	0	0	0	0	.333	.333	.333
Ed Charles	4	15	1	2	0	1	0	0	0	2	0	0	.133	.133	.200
Donn Clendenon	4	14	4	5	4	1	0	3	2	6	0	0	.357	.438	1.071
Duffy Dyer	1	1	0	0	0	0	0	0	0	0	0	0	.000	.000	.000
Wayne Garrett	2	1	0	0	0	0	0	0	2	1	0	0	.000	.667	.000
Rod Gaspar	3	2	1	0	0	0	0	0	0	0	0	0	.000	.000	.000
Gary Gentry	1	3	0	1	2	1	0	0	0	2	0	0	.333	.333	.667
Jerry Grote	5	19	1	4	1	2	0	0	1	3	0	0	.211	.250	.316
Bud Harrelson	5	17	1	3	0	0	0	0	3	4	0	0	.176	.300	.176
Cleon Jones	5	19	2	3	0	1	0	0	0	1	0	0	.158	.200	.211
Jerry Koosman	2	7	0	1	0	1	0	0	4	0	0	0	.143	.143	.286
Ed Kranepool	1	4	1	1	1	0	0	1	0	0	0	0	.250	.250	1.000
J.C. Martin	1	0	0	0	0	0	0	0	0	0	0	0	—	—	—
Tom Seaver	2	4	0	0	0	0	0	0	0	2	0	0	.000	.000	.000
Art Shamsky	3	6	0	0	0	0	0	0	0	0	0	0	.000	.000	.000
Ron Swoboda	4	15	1	6	1	1	0	0	1	3	0	1	.400	.438	.467
Al Weis	5	11	1	5	3	0	0	1	4	2	0	0	.455	.563	.727
Totals	5	159	15	35	13	8	0	6	15	35	1	1	.220	.290	.384

Orioles	G	AB	R	H	RBI	2B	3B	HR	BB	SO	SB	CS	Avg	OBP	Slg
Mark Belanger	5	15	2	3	1	0	0	0	2	1	0	0	.200	.294	.200
Paul Blair	5	20	1	2	0	0	0	0	2	5	1	1	.100	.182	.100
Don Buford	5	20	1	2	2	1	0	1	2	4	0	0	.100	.182	.300
Mike Cuellar	2	5	0	2	1	0	0	0	0	3	0	0	.400	.400	.400
Clay Dalrymple	2	2	0	2	0	0	0	0	0	0	0	0	1.000	1.000	1.000
Andy Etchebarren	2	6	0	0	0	0	0	0	0	1	0	0	.000	.000	.000
Ellie Hendricks	3	10	1	1	0	0	0	0	1	0	0	0	.100	.182	.100
Dave Johnson	5	16	1	1	0	0	0	0	2	1	0	1	.063	.167	.063
Dave May	2	1	0	0	0	0	0	0	1	1	0	0	.000	.500	.000
Dave McNally	2	5	1	1	2	0	0	1	0	2	0	0	.200	.200	.800
Curt Motton	1	1	0	0	0	0	0	0	0	0	0	0	.000	.000	.000
Jim Palmer	1	2	0	0	0	0	0	0	0	0	0	0	.000	.000	.000
Boog Powell	5	19	0	5	0	0	0	0	1	4	0	0	.263	.300	.263
Merv Rettenmund	1	0	0	0	0	0	0	0	0	0	0	0	—	—	—
Brooks Robinson	5	19	0	1	2	0	0	0	3	0	0	0	.053	.050	.053
Frank Robinson	5	16	2	3	1	0	0	1	4	3	0	0	.188	.350	.375
Chico Salmon	2	0	0	0	0	0	0	0	0	0	0	0	—	—	—
Totals	5	157	9	23	9	1	0	3	15	28	1	2	.146	.220	.210

Pitching

Mets	G	GS	CG	IP	H	R	ER	BB	SO	W-L	Sv-Op	Hld	ERA
Don Cardwell	1	0	0	1.0	0	0	0	0	0	0-0	0-0	0	0.00
Gary Gentry	1	1	0	6.2	3	0	0	5	4	1-0	0-0	0	0.00
Jerry Koosman	2	2	1	17.2	7	4	4	4	9	2-0	0-0	0	2.04
Nolan Ryan	1	0	0	2.1	1	0	0	2	3	0-0	1-1	0	0.00
Tom Seaver	2	2	1	15.0	12	5	5	3	9	1-1	0-0	0	3.00
Ron Taylor	2	0	0	2.1	0	0	0	1	3	0-0	1-1	0	0.00
Totals	5	5	2	45.0	23	9	9	15	28	4-1	2-2	0	1.80

Orioles	G	GS	CG	IP	H	R	ER	BB	SO	W-L	Sv-Op	Hld	ERA
Mike Cuellar	2	2	1	16.0	13	2	2	4	13	1-0	0-0	0	1.13
Dick Hall	1	0	0	0.0	1	1	0	1	0	0-1	0-0	0	—
Dave Leonhard	1	0	0	2.0	1	1	1	1	1	0-0	0-0	0	4.50
Dave McNally	2	2	1	16.0	11	5	5	5	13	0-1	0-0	0	2.81
Jim Palmer	1	1	0	6.0	5	4	4	4	5	0-1	0-0	0	6.00
Pete Richert	1	0	0	0.0	0	0	0	0	0	0-0	0-0	0	—
Eddie Watt	2	0	0	3.0	4	2	1	0	3	0-1	0-0	0	3.00
Totals	5	5	2	43.0	35	15	13	15	35	1-4	0-0	0	2.72

Fielding

Mets	Pos	G	PO	Ast	E	DP	PB	FPct
Tommie Agee	cf	5	19	0	0	0	—	1.000
Ken Boswell	2b	1	0	1	0	0	—	1.000
Don Cardwell	p	1	0	0	0	0	—	—
Ed Charles	3b	4	3	9	0	0	—	1.000
Donn Clendenon	1b	4	30	4	0	0	—	1.000
Wayne Garrett	3b	2	1	0	1	0	—	.500
Rod Gaspar	rf	1	2	0	0	0	—	1.000
Gary Gentry	p	1	0	0	0	0	—	—
Jerry Grote	c	5	29	2	0	0	0	1.000
Bud Harrelson	ss	5	13	17	0	0	—	1.000
Cleon Jones	lf	5	7	0	0	0	—	1.000
Jerry Koosman	p	2	0	2	0	0	—	1.000
Ed Kranepool	1b	1	7	0	0	0	—	1.000
Nolan Ryan	p	1	0	0	0	0	—	—
Tom Seaver	p	2	2	1	0	0	—	1.000
Art Shamsky	rf	1	1	0	0	0	—	1.000
Ron Swoboda	rf	4	14	0	0	0	—	1.000
Ron Taylor	p	2	0	1	0	0	—	1.000
Al Weis	2b	5	7	5	1	0	—	.923
Totals		5	135	42	2	0	0	.989

Orioles	Pos	G	PO	Ast	E	DP	PB	FPct
Mark Belanger	ss	5	7	14	0	3	—	1.000
Paul Blair	cf	5	7	0	0	0	—	1.000
Don Buford	lf	5	8	0	0	0	—	1.000
Mike Cuellar	p	2	0	1	0	0	—	1.000
Andy Etchebarren	c	2	16	0	0	0	0	1.000
Dick Hall	p	1	0	0	0	0	—	—
Ellie Hendricks	c	3	21	1	0	1	0	1.000
Dave Johnson	2b	5	8	15	0	4	—	1.000
Dave Leonhard	p	1	0	1	0	0	—	1.000
Dave McNally	p	2	1	1	0	0	—	1.000
Jim Palmer	p	1	1	0	1	0	—	.500
Boog Powell	1b	5	46	2	1	3	—	.980
Pete Richert	p	1	0	0	1	0	—	.000
Brooks Robinson	3b	5	1	16	0	0	—	1.000
Frank Robinson	rf	5	13	0	0	0	—	1.000
Eddie Watt	p	2	0	0	1	0	—	.000
Totals		5	129	51	4	11	0	.978

1970 Baltimore Orioles (AL) 4, Cincinnati Reds (NL) 1

The Baltimore Orioles avenged their loss to the New York Mets in the previous season's World Series by defeating the Cincinnati Reds in five games. Brooks Robinson's seventh-inning solo homer was the difference in the opener as the Orioles' Jim Palmer beat the Reds' Gary Nolan, 4-3. In Game 2, Elrod Hendricks' two-run double capped a five-run fifth-inning rally that sent the Reds on the way to a 6-5 victory. Dave McNally hit a grand slam and pitched the O's to a 9-3 win in Game 3. Baltimore was six outs away from a sweep in Game 4 when Lee May cracked a three-run homer in the top of the eighth. The blast gave the Reds a 6-5 victory, but Mike Cuellar beat them 9-3 the next day to put the final nail in the coffin.

Game 1
Saturday, October 10

Orioles	AB	R	H	RBI	BB	K	Avg
Don Buford, lf	4	0	1	0	0	0	.250
Paul Blair, cf	4	1	1	0	0	1	.250
Boog Powell, 1b	3	1	1	2	1	1	.333
Frank Robinson, rf	4	0	0	0	0	1	.000
Brooks Robinson, 3b	4	1	1	1	0	1	.250
Ellie Hendricks, c	4	1	1	1	0	2	.250
Dave Johnson, 2b	3	0	1	0	1	1	.333
Mark Belanger, ss	3	0	1	0	1	2	.333
Jim Palmer, p	4	0	0	0	0	2	.000
Pete Richert, p	0	0	0	0	0	0	—
TOTALS	33	4	7	4	3	11	.212

Reds	AB	R	H	RBI	BB	K	Avg
Pete Rose, rf	3	0	0	0	1	0	.000
Bobby Tolan, cf	4	2	1	0	1	0	.250
Tony Perez, 3b	3	0	0	0	1	0	.000
Johnny Bench, c	4	0	1	1	0	0	.250
Lee May, 1b	4	1	2	2	0	0	.500
Bernie Carbo, lf	2	0	0	0	2	0	.000
Tommy Helms, 2b	4	0	1	0	0	0	.250
Woody Woodward, ss	2	0	0	0	0	0	.000
Ty Cline, ph	1	0	0	0	0	0	.000
Darrel Chaney, ss	0	0	0	0	0	0	—
Jimmy Stewart, ph	1	0	0	0	0	1	.000
Gary Nolan, p	2	0	0	0	0	0	.000
Clay Carroll, p	0	0	0	0	0	0	—
Angel Bravo, ph	1	0	0	0	0	1	.000
TOTALS	31	3	5	3	5	2	.161

	1	2	3	4	5	6	7	8	9		R	H	E
Orioles	0	0	0	2	1	0	1	0	0		4	7	2
Reds	1	0	2	0	0	0	0	0	0		3	5	0

E—Hendricks, BRobinson. DP—Reds 1 (May to Woodward). LOB—Orioles 5, Reds 8. Scoring Position—Orioles 0-for-2, Reds 2-for-10. 2B—Johnson (1), Tolan (1). HR—Powell (1), BRobinson (1), Hendricks (1), May (1). S—Nolan. GDP—Powell. SB—Tolan (1). CS—Carbo (1).

Orioles	IP	H	R	ER	BB	K	ERA
Jim Palmer (W, 1-0)	8.2	5	3	3	5	2	3.12
Pete Richert (S, 1)	0.1	0	0	0	0	0	0.00

Reds	IP	H	R	ER	BB	K	ERA
Gary Nolan (L, 0-1)	6.2	5	4	4	1	7	5.40
Clay Carroll	2.1	2	0	0	2	4	0.00

Reached, Catcher's Interference—Orioles 0. Reds 1, Rose by Hendricks. WP—Palmer. Time—2:24. Attendance—51,531. Umpires—HP, Burkhart. 1B, Flaherty. 2B, Venzon. 3B, Stewart.

Game 2
Sunday, October 11

Orioles	AB	R	H	RBI	BB	K	Avg
Don Buford, lf	4	1	2	0	1	0	.375
Paul Blair, cf	5	1	2	1	0	0	.333
Boog Powell, 1b	3	2	2	2	2	0	.500
Frank Robinson, rf	5	0	0	0	0	2	.000
Brooks Robinson, 3b	4	1	1	1	0	0	.250
Ellie Hendricks, c	3	0	1	2	1	0	.286
Dave Johnson, 2b	3	0	1	0	1	0	.333
Mark Belanger, ss	4	0	0	0	0	0	.143
Mike Cuellar, p	1	0	0	0	0	1	.000
Tom Phoebus, p	0	0	0	0	0	0	—
Chico Salmon, ph	1	1	1	0	0	0	1.000
Moe Drabowsky, p	1	0	0	0	0	1	.000
Marcelino Lopez, p	0	0	0	0	0	0	—
Dick Hall, p	1	0	0	0	0	1	.000
TOTALS	35	6	10	6	5	5	.266

Reds	AB	R	H	RBI	BB	K	Avg
Pete Rose, rf	3	0	0	0	1	0	.000
Bobby Tolan, cf	4	2	1	1	0	0	.250
Tony Perez, 3b	4	1	1	0	0	1	.143
Johnny Bench, c	3	1	1	1	1	0	.286
Lee May, 1b	4	1	1	2	0	0	.375
Hal McRae, lf	4	0	2	1	0	0	.500
Tommy Helms, 2b	4	0	0	0	0	0	.125
Woody Woodward, ss	2	0	0	0	0	0	.000
Ty Cline, ph	1	0	1	0	0	0	.500
Darrel Chaney, ss	0	0	0	0	0	0	—
Bernie Carbo, ph	1	0	0	0	0	0	.000
Jim McGlothlin, p	2	0	0	0	0	1	.000
Milt Wilcox, p	0	0	0	0	0	0	—
Clay Carroll, p	0	0	0	0	0	0	—
Angel Bravo, ph	0	0	0	0	0	0	.000
Don Gullett, p	0	0	0	0	0	0	—
Jimmy Stewart, ph	1	0	0	0	0	0	.000
TOTALS	33	5	7	5	2	2	.194

	1	2	3	4	5	6	7	8	9		R	H	E
Orioles	0	0	0	1	5	0	0	0	0		6	10	2
Reds	3	0	1	0	0	1	0	0	0		5	7	0

E—Belanger, Blair. DP—Orioles 1 (BRobinson to Johnson to Powell), Reds 2 (Woodward to Helms to May; May to Woodward). LOB—Orioles 7, Reds 4. Scoring Position—Orioles 4-for-7, Reds 2-for-8. 2B—Hendricks (1), May (1), McRae (1). HR—Powell (2), Tolan (1), Bench (1). S—Bravo. GDP—Blair, Powell, May.

Orioles	IP	H	R	ER	BB	K	ERA
Mike Cuellar	2.1	4	4	1	1	1	3.86
Tom Phoebus (W, 1-0)	1.2	1	0	0	0	0	0.00
Moe Drabowsky	2.1	2	1	1	1	1	3.86
Marcelino Lopez (H, 1)	0.1	0	0	0	0	0	0.00
Dick Hall (S, 1)	2.1	0	0	0	0	0	0.00

Reds	IP	H	R	ER	BB	K	ERA
Jim McGlothlin	4.1	6	4	4	2	2	8.31
Milt Wilcox (L, 0-1)	0.1	3	2	2	0	0	54.00
Clay Carroll	2.1	1	0	0	0	1	0.00
Don Gullett	2.0	0	0	0	3	2	0.00

Time—2:26. Attendance—51,531. Umpires—HP, Flaherty. 1B, Venzon. 2B, Stewart. 3B, Williams.

Game 3
Tuesday, October 13

Reds	AB	R	H	RBI	BB	K	Avg
Pete Rose, rf	5	0	2	1	0	0	.182
Bobby Tolan, cf	4	0	1	0	0	0	.250
Tony Perez, 3b	3	0	0	0	1	1	.100
Johnny Bench, c	4	0	0	0	0	1	.182
Lee May, 1b	3	1	1	0	1	1	.364
Hal McRae, lf	4	1	2	0	0	1	.500
Tommy Helms, 2b	4	1	1	0	0	0	.167
Dave Concepcion, ss	3	0	1	2	0	0	.333
Tony Cloninger, p	2	0	0	0	0	1	.000
Wayne Granger, p	0	0	0	0	0	0	—
Woody Woodward, ph	1	0	1	0	0	0	.200
Don Gullett, p	0	0	0	0	0	0	—
Ty Cline, ph	1	0	0	0	0	0	.333
TOTALS	34	3	9	3	2	5	.239

Orioles	AB	R	H	RBI	BB	K	Avg
Don Buford, lf	3	2	1	1	1	0	.364
Mark Belanger, ss	4	0	0	0	0	0	.091
Boog Powell, 1b	3	1	0	0	1	0	.333
Frank Robinson, rf	4	2	3	1	0	0	.231
Paul Blair, cf	3	1	3	1	1	0	.500
Brooks Robinson, 3b	4	1	2	2	0	0	.333
Dave Johnson, 2b	2	1	0	0	2	0	.250
Andy Etchebarren, c	4	0	0	0	0	2	.000
Dave McNally, p	4	1	1	4	0	2	.250
TOTALS	31	9	10	9	5	4	.286

	1	2	3	4	5	6	7	8	9		R	H	E
Reds	0	1	0	0	0	0	2	0	0		3	9	0
Orioles	2	0	1	0	1	4	1	0	x		9	10	1

E—Etchebarren. DP—Reds 1 (Bench to Helms), Orioles 1 (BRobinson to Powell). LOB—Reds 7, Orioles 3. Scoring Position—Reds 2-for-7, Orioles 3-for-6. 2B—Blair (1), BRobinson 2 (2). HR—Buford (1), FRobinson (1), McNally (1). SF—Concepcion. GDP—Perez. CS—Blair (1), Johnson (1).

Reds	IP	H	R	ER	BB	K	ERA
Tony Cloninger (L, 0-1)	5.1	6	5	5	3	3	8.44
Wayne Granger	0.2	2	3	3	1	1	40.50
Don Gullett	2.0	2	1	1	1	0	2.25

Orioles	IP	H	R	ER	BB	K	ERA
Dave McNally (W, 1-0)	9.0	9	3	3	2	5	3.00

Time—2:09. Attendance—51,773. Umpires—HP, Venzon. 1B, Stewart. 2B, Williams. 3B, Ashford.

Game 4
Wednesday, October 14

Reds	AB	R	H	RBI	BB	K	Avg
Bobby Tolan, cf	3	1	1	0	2	1	.267
Pete Rose, rf	5	1	2	1	0	0	.250
Tony Perez, 3b	4	1	0	0	1	2	.071
Johnny Bench, c	4	1	1	0	0	0	.200
Lee May, 1b	3	2	2	4	1	0	.429
Bernie Carbo, lf	4	0	0	0	0	3	.000
Tommy Helms, 2b	3	0	1	0	1	1	.200
Dave Concepcion, ss	3	0	1	1	0	0	.333
Clay Carroll, p	1	0	0	0	0	1	.000
Gary Nolan, p	1	0	0	0	0	0	.000
Don Gullett, p	1	0	0	0	0	1	.000
Woody Woodward, ss	0	0	0	0	0	0	.200
Angel Bravo, ph	1	0	0	0	0	0	.000
Darrel Chaney, ss	1	0	0	0	0	1	.000
TOTALS	34	6	8	6	5	10	.209

Orioles	AB	R	H	RBI	BB	K	Avg
Don Buford, lf	4	0	0	0	1	2	.267
Paul Blair, cf	3	0	0	0	2	0	.400
Boog Powell, 1b	3	1	0	0	1	1	.250
Frank Robinson, rf	4	1	1	1	0	1	.235
Brooks Robinson, 3b	4	2	4	2	0	0	.500
Ellie Hendricks, c	4	0	2	1	0	0	.364
Dave Johnson, 2b	4	0	0	0	0	1	.167
Mark Belanger, ss	3	0	0	0	0	0	.071
Terry Crowley, ph	1	0	0	0	0	0	.000
Jim Palmer, p	3	1	1	0	0	1	.143
Eddie Watt, p	0	0	0	0	0	0	—
Moe Drabowsky, p	0	0	0	0	0	0	.000
Merv Rettenmund, ph	1	0	0	0	0	0	.000
TOTALS	34	5	8	4	2	8	.270

	1	2	3	4	5	6	7	8	9	R	H	E
Reds	0	1	1	0	1	0	0	3	0	6	8	3
Orioles	0	1	3	0	0	1	0	0	0	5	8	0

E—Perez, Rose, Tolan. LOB—Reds 6, Orioles 5. Scoring Position—Reds 2-for-8, Orioles 3-for-8. 3B—Concepcion (1). HR—Rose (1), May (2), BRobinson (2). S—Blair. CS—Tolan (1).

Reds	IP	H	R	ER	BB	K	ERA
Gary Nolan	2.2	4	4	4	2	2	7.71
Don Gullett	2.2	3	1	0	0	2	1.35
Clay Carroll (W, 1-0)	3.2	1	0	0	0	4	0.00

Orioles	IP	H	R	ER	BB	K	ERA
Jim Palmer	7.0	6	5	5	4	7	4.60
Eddie Watt (BS, 1; L, 0-1)	1.0	2	1	1	1	3	9.00
Moe Drabowsky	1.0	0	0	0	0	0	2.70

Palmer pitched to two batters in the 8th. Watt pitched to one batter in the 9th.

Time—2:26. Attendance—53,007. Umpires—HP, Stewart. 1B, Williams. 2B, Ashford. 3B, Burkhart.

Game 5
Thursday, October 15

Reds	AB	R	H	RBI	BB	K	Avg
Bobby Tolan, cf	4	0	0	0	0	1	.211
Pete Rose, rf	4	1	1	0	0	0	.250
Tony Perez, 3b	4	0	0	0	0	0	.056
Johnny Bench, c	4	1	1	1	0	1	.211
Lee May, 1b	4	1	1	0	0	1	.389
Hal McRae, lf	3	0	1	2	0	0	.455
Pat Corrales, ph	1	0	0	0	0	0	.000
Tommy Helms, 2b	3	0	1	0	0	0	.222
Dave Concepcion, ss	3	0	1	0	0	0	.333
Jim Merritt, p	1	0	0	0	0	1	.000
Wayne Granger, p	0	0	0	0	0	0	—
Milt Wilcox, p	0	0	0	0	0	0	—
Angel Bravo, ph	0	0	0	0	1	0	.000
Tony Cloninger, p	0	0	0	0	0	0	.000
Bernie Carbo, ph	1	0	0	0	0	0	.000
Ray Washburn, p	0	0	0	0	0	0	—
Clay Carroll, p	0	0	0	0	0	0	.000
TOTALS	32	3	6	3	1	4	.224

Orioles	AB	R	H	RBI	BB	K	Avg
Mark Belanger, ss	5	0	1	1	0	0	.105
Paul Blair, cf	4	2	3	1	1	1	.474
Frank Robinson, rf	5	2	2	2	0	1	.273
Boog Powell, 1b	5	1	2	1	0	0	.294
Merv Rettenmund, lf	4	2	2	2	1	0	.400
Brooks Robinson, 3b	5	0	1	0	0	1	.429
Dave Johnson, 2b	4	1	3	2	1	0	.313
Andy Etchebarren, c	3	1	1	0	2	1	.143
Mike Cuellar, p	3	0	0	0	0	1	.000
TOTALS	38	9	15	9	5	5	.300

	1	2	3	4	5	6	7	8	9	R	H	E
Reds	3	0	0	0	0	0	0	0	0	3	6	0
Orioles	2	2	2	0	1	0	0	2	x	9	15	0

DP—Orioles 1 (Cuellar to Belanger to Powell). LOB—Reds 3, Orioles 11. Scoring Position—Reds 2-for-5, Orioles 5-for-16. 2B—Rose (1), May (2), McRae (2), Powell (1), Johnson (2). HR—FRobinson (2), Rettenmund (1). S—Cuellar. GDP—Carbo.

Reds	IP	H	R	ER	BB	K	ERA
Jim Merritt (L, 0-1)	1.2	3	4	4	1	0	21.60
Wayne Granger	0.2	5	2	2	0	0	33.75
Milt Wilcox	1.2	0	0	0	0	2	9.00
Tony Cloninger	2.0	4	1	1	2	1	7.36
Ray Washburn	1.1	2	2	2	2	0	13.50
Clay Carroll	0.2	1	0	0	0	2	0.00

Orioles	IP	H	R	ER	BB	K	ERA
Mike Cuellar (W, 1-0)	9.0	6	3	3	1	4	3.18

Time—2:35. Attendance—45,341. Umpires—HP, Williams. 1B, Ashford. 2B, Burkhart. 3B, Flaherty.

1970 World Series—Composite Statistics

Batting

Orioles	G	AB	R	H	RBI	2B	3B	HR	BB	SO	SB	CS	Avg	OBP	Slg
Mark Belanger	5	19	0	2	1	0	0	0	1	2	0	0	.105	.150	.105
Paul Blair	5	19	5	9	3	1	0	0	2	4	0	1	.474	.524	.526
Don Buford	4	15	3	4	1	0	0	1	3	2	0	0	.267	.389	.467
Terry Crowley	1	1	0	0	0	0	0	0	0	0	0	0	.000	.000	.000
Mike Cuellar	2	4	0	0	0	0	0	0	0	2	0	0	.000	.000	.000
Moe Drabowsky	2	1	0	0	0	0	0	0	0	1	0	0	.000	.000	.000
Andy Etchebarren	2	7	1	1	0	0	0	0	2	3	0	0	.143	.333	.143
Dick Hall	1	1	0	0	0	0	0	0	0	1	0	0	.000	.000	.000
Ellie Hendricks	3	11	1	4	4	1	0	1	1	2	0	0	.364	.417	.727
Dave Johnson	5	16	2	5	2	2	0	0	5	2	0	1	.313	.476	.438
Dave McNally	1	4	1	1	4	0	0	1	0	2	0	0	.250	.250	1.000
Jim Palmer	2	7	1	1	0	0	0	0	0	3	0	0	.143	.143	.143
Boog Powell	5	17	6	5	5	1	0	2	5	2	0	0	.294	.455	.706
Merv Rettenmund	2	5	2	2	2	0	0	1	1	0	0	0	.400	.500	1.000
Brooks Robinson	5	21	5	9	6	2	0	2	0	2	0	0	.429	.429	.810
Frank Robinson	5	22	5	6	4	0	0	2	0	5	0	0	.273	.273	.545
Chico Salmon	1	1	1	1	0	0	0	0	0	0	0	0	1.000	1.000	1.000
Totals	5	171	33	50	32	7	0	10	20	33	0	2	.292	.366	.509

Batting

Reds	G	AB	R	H	RBI	2B	3B	HR	BB	SO	SB	CS	Avg	OBP	Slg
Johnny Bench	5	19	3	4	3	0	0	1	1	2	0	0	.211	.250	.368
Angel Bravo	4	2	0	0	0	0	0	0	1	1	0	0	.000	.333	.000
Bernie Carbo	4	8	0	0	0	0	0	0	2	3	0	1	.000	.200	.000
Clay Carroll	4	1	0	0	0	0	0	0	0	1	0	0	.000	.000	.000
Darrel Chaney	3	1	0	0	0	0	0	0	0	1	0	0	.000	.000	.000
Ty Cline	3	3	0	1	0	0	0	0	0	0	0	0	.333	.333	.333
Tony Cloninger	2	2	0	0	0	0	0	0	0	1	0	0	.000	.000	.000
Dave Concepcion	3	9	0	3	3	0	1	0	0	0	0	0	.333	.300	.556
Pat Corrales	1	1	0	0	0	0	0	0	0	0	0	0	.000	.000	.000
Don Gullett	3	1	0	0	0	0	0	0	0	1	0	0	.000	.000	.000
Tommy Helms	5	18	1	4	0	0	0	0	1	1	0	0	.222	.263	.222
Lee May	5	18	6	7	8	2	0	2	2	2	0	0	.389	.450	.833
Jim McGlothlin	1	2	0	0	0	0	0	0	0	1	0	0	.000	.000	.000
Hal McRae	3	11	1	5	3	2	0	0	0	1	0	0	.455	.455	.636
Jim Merritt	1	1	0	0	0	0	0	0	0	1	0	0	.000	.000	.000
Gary Nolan	2	3	0	0	0	0	0	0	0	0	0	0	.000	.000	.000
Tony Perez	5	18	2	1	0	0	0	0	3	4	0	0	.056	.190	.056
Pete Rose	5	20	2	5	2	1	0	1	2	0	0	0	.250	.318	.450
Jimmy Stewart	2	2	0	0	0	0	0	0	0	1	0	0	.000	.000	.000
Bobby Tolan	5	19	5	4	1	1	0	1	3	2	1	1	.211	.318	.421
Woody Woodward	4	5	0	1	0	0	0	0	0	0	0	0	.200	.200	.200
Totals	5	164	20	35	20	6	1	5	15	23	1	2	.213	.278	.354

Pitching

Orioles	G	GS	CG	IP	H	R	ER	BB	SO	W-L	Sv-Op	Hld	ERA
Mike Cuellar	2	2	1	11.1	10	7	4	2	5	1-0	0-0	0	3.18
Moe Drabowsky	2	0	0	3.1	2	1	1	1	1	0-0	0-0	0	2.70
Dick Hall	1	0	0	2.1	0	0	0	0	0	0-0	1-1	0	0.00
Marcelino Lopez	1	0	0	0.1	0	0	0	0	0	0-0	0-0	1	0.00
Dave McNally	1	1	1	9.0	9	3	3	2	5	1-0	0-0	0	3.00
Jim Palmer	2	2	0	15.2	11	8	8	9	9	1-0	0-0	0	4.60
Tom Phoebus	1	0	0	1.2	1	0	0	0	0	1-0	0-0	0	0.00
Pete Richert	1	0	0	0.1	0	0	0	0	0	0-0	1-1	0	0.00
Eddie Watt	1	0	0	1.0	2	1	1	1	3	0-1	0-1	0	9.00
Totals	5	5	2	45.0	35	20	17	15	23	4-1	2-3	1	3.40

Pitching

Reds	G	GS	CG	IP	H	R	ER	BB	SO	W-L	Sv-Op	Hld	ERA
Clay Carroll	4	0	0	9.0	5	0	0	2	11	1-0	0-0	0	0.00
Tony Cloninger	2	1	0	7.1	10	6	6	5	4	0-1	0-0	0	7.36
Wayne Granger	2	0	0	1.1	7	5	5	1	1	0-0	0-0	0	33.75
Don Gullett	3	0	0	6.2	5	2	1	4	4	0-0	0-0	0	1.35
Jim McGlothlin	1	1	0	4.1	6	4	4	2	2	0-0	0-0	0	8.31
Jim Merritt	1	1	0	1.2	3	4	4	1	0	0-1	0-0	0	21.60
Gary Nolan	2	2	0	9.1	9	8	8	3	9	0-1	0-0	0	7.71
Ray Washburn	1	0	0	1.1	2	2	2	2	0	0-0	0-0	0	13.50
Milt Wilcox	2	0	0	2.0	3	2	2	0	2	0-1	0-0	0	9.00
Totals	5	5	0	43.0	50	33	32	20	33	1-4	0-0	0	6.70

Fielding

Orioles	Pos	G	PO	Ast	E	DP	PB	FPct
Mark Belanger	ss	5	11	14	1	1	—	.962
Paul Blair	cf	5	18	0	1	0	—	.947
Don Buford	lf	4	6	0	0	0	—	1.000
Mike Cuellar	p	2	0	1	0	1	—	1.000
Moe Drabowsky	p	2	1	0	0	0	—	1.000
Andy Etchebarren	c	2	10	0	1	0	0	.909
Dick Hall	p	1	0	0	0	0	—	—
Ellie Hendricks	c	3	17	2	1	0	0	.950
Dave Johnson	2b	5	15	9	0	1	—	1.000
Marcelino Lopez	p	1	0	0	0	0	—	—
Dave McNally	p	1	0	1	0	0	—	1.000
Jim Palmer	p	2	0	0	0	0	—	—
Tom Phoebus	p	1	0	0	0	0	—	—
Boog Powell	1b	5	38	2	0	3	—	1.000
Merv Rettenmund	lf	1	3	0	0	0	—	1.000
Pete Richert	p	1	0	0	0	0	—	—
Brooks Robinson	3b	5	9	14	1	2	—	.958
Frank Robinson	rf	5	7	0	0	0	—	1.000
Eddie Watt	p	1	0	0	0	0	—	—
Totals		5	135	43	5	8	0	.973

Fielding

Reds	Pos	G	PO	Ast	E	DP	PB	FPct
Johnny Bench	c	5	36	3	0	1	0	1.000
Bernie Carbo	lf	2	4	0	0	0	—	1.000
Clay Carroll	p	4	0	0	0	0	—	—
Darrel Chaney	ss	3	1	2	0	0	—	1.000
Tony Cloninger	p	2	0	1	0	0	—	1.000
Dave Concepcion	ss	3	2	2	0	0	—	1.000
Wayne Granger	p	2	0	1	0	0	—	1.000
Don Gullett	p	3	0	0	0	0	—	—
Tommy Helms	2b	5	10	13	0	2	—	1.000
Lee May	1b	5	48	2	0	3	—	1.000
Jim McGlothlin	p	1	0	0	0	0	—	—
Hal McRae	lf	3	2	1	0	0	—	1.000
Jim Merritt	p	1	0	0	0	0	—	—
Gary Nolan	p	2	0	1	0	0	—	1.000
Tony Perez	3b	5	3	14	1	0	—	.944
Pete Rose	rf	5	14	1	1	0	—	.938
Bobby Tolan	cf	5	4	0	1	0	—	.800
Ray Washburn	p	1	1	3	0	0	—	1.000
Milt Wilcox	p	2	0	1	0	0	—	1.000
Woody Woodward	ss	3	4	5	0	3	—	1.000
Totals		5	129	50	3	9	0	.984

1971 Pittsburgh Pirates (NL) 4, Baltimore Orioles (AL) 3

The Pittsburgh Pirates overcame a heavily-favored Baltimore Orioles club to take the World Series in seven games. Dave McNally got the O's off on the right foot with a three-hit, 5-3 victory in the opener. Both Frank and Brooks Robinson had three hits in Game 2 as the Orioles piled it on, winning 11-3. Steve Blass got Pittsburgh on the board with a three-hit, 5-1 victory in Game 3, aided by Bob Robertson's three-run blast. The Pirates evened the Series with a 4-3 win in Game 4, which was the first night contest in World Series history. Milt May's pinch-hit RBI single drove home the winning run in the bottom of the seventh. Nelson Briles spun a two-hit shutout in Game 5 to put the Pirates one game away from a championship, but Baltimore pulled out Game 6, 3-2 in 10 innings, as Brooks Robinson plated the winning run with a sacrifice fly. Steve Blass came up big in the finale, tossing a four-hitter for a 2-1 win and a World Championship for Pittsburgh.

Game 1

Saturday, October 9

Pirates	AB	R	H	RBI	BB	K	Avg
Dave Cash, 2b	4	0	1	1	0	0	.250
Gene Clines, cf	4	0	0	0	0	0	.000
Roberto Clemente, rf	4	0	2	0	0	0	.500
Willie Stargell, lf	3	0	0	0	1	2	.000
Bob Robertson, 1b	3	1	0	0	1	2	.000
Manny Sanguillen, c	4	1	0	0	1	1	.000
Jose Pagan, 3b	4	0	0	0	0	0	.000
Jackie Hernandez, ss	2	1	0	1	0	1	.000
Al Oliver, ph	1	0	0	0	0	1	.000
Dock Ellis, p	1	0	0	0	0	1	.000
Bob Moose, p	1	0	0	0	0	1	.000
Bill Mazeroski, ph	1	0	0	0	0	0	.000
Bob Miller, p	0	0	0	0	0	0	—
TOTALS	32	3	3	2	2	9	.094

Orioles	AB	R	H	RBI	BB	K	Avg
Don Buford, lf	4	2	2	1	0	0	.500
Paul Blair, cf	0	0	0	0	0	0	—
Merv Rettenmund, cf-lf	4	1	1	3	0	1	.250
Boog Powell, 1b	3	0	0	0	1	0	.000
Frank Robinson, rf	4	1	2	1	0	2	.500
Ellie Hendricks, c	4	0	1	0	0	0	.250
Brooks Robinson, 3b	4	0	1	0	0	0	.250
Dave Johnson, 2b	4	0	1	0	0	0	.250
Mark Belanger, ss	4	1	2	0	0	0	.500
Dave McNally, p	3	0	0	0	0	3	.000
TOTALS	34	5	10	5	1	6	.294

	1	2	3	4	5	6	7	8	9	R	H	E
Pirates	0	3	0	0	0	0	0	0	0	3	3	0
Orioles	0	1	3	0	1	0	0	0	x	5	10	3

E—Belanger 2, Hendricks. LOB—Pirates 5, Orioles 6. Scoring Position—Pirates 1-for-10, Orioles 2-for-6. 2B—Clemente (1). 3B—Belanger (1). HR—Buford (1), Rettenmund (1), FRobinson (1). S—Hernandez.

Pirates	IP	H	R	ER	BB	K	ERA
Dock Ellis (L, 0-1)	2.1	4	4	4	1	1	15.43
Bob Moose	3.2	3	1	1	0	4	2.45
Bob Miller	2.0	3	0	0	0	1	0.00

Orioles	IP	H	R	ER	BB	K	ERA
Dave McNally (W, 1-0)	9.0	3	3	0	2	9	0.00

WP—McNally, Moose. Time—2:06. Attendance—53,229. Umpires—HP, Chylak. 1B, Sudol. 2B, Rice. 3B, Vargo.

Game 2

Monday, October 11

Pirates	AB	R	H	RBI	BB	K	Avg
Dave Cash, 2b	5	0	0	0	0	0	.111
Richie Hebner, 3b	3	1	1	3	2	1	.333
Roberto Clemente, rf	5	0	2	0	0	0	.444
Willie Stargell, lf	3	0	1	0	2	1	.167
Dave Giusti, p	0	0	0	0	0	0	—
Al Oliver, cf	5	0	1	0	0	2	.167
Bob Robertson, 1b	3	0	0	0	2	2	.000
Manny Sanguillen, c	5	0	1	0	0	1	.111
Jackie Hernandez, ss	2	1	1	0	2	0	.250
Milt May, ph	1	0	0	0	0	0	.000
Bob Johnson, p	2	0	0	0	0	2	.000
Bruce Kison, p	0	0	0	0	0	0	—
Bob Moose, p	0	0	0	0	0	0	.000
Bob Veale, p	0	0	0	0	0	0	—
Charlie Sands, ph	1	0	0	0	0	1	.000
Bob Miller, p	0	0	0	0	0	0	—
Vic Davalillo, ph-lf	1	1	1	0	0	0	1.000
TOTALS	36	3	8	3	8	10	.190

Orioles	AB	R	H	RBI	BB	K	Avg
Don Buford, lf	5	0	0	1	0	1	.222
Merv Rettenmund, cf-rf	5	1	2	1	0	0	.333
Boog Powell, 1b	5	1	1	0	0	0	.125
Frank Robinson, rf	4	2	3	0	0	0	.625
Paul Blair, pr-cf	1	1	1	0	0	0	1.000
Ellie Hendricks, c	3	2	2	1	1	0	.429
Brooks Robinson, 3b	3	2	3	3	2	0	.571
Dave Johnson, 2b	5	1	2	2	0	1	.333
Mark Belanger, ss	3	1	0	0	2	0	.286
Jim Palmer, p	2	0	0	2	2	0	.000
Dick Hall, p	0	0	0	0	0	0	—
TOTALS	36	11	14	10	7	2	.358

	1	2	3	4	5	6	7	8	9	R	H	E
Pirates	0	0	0	0	0	0	0	3	0	3	8	1
Orioles	0	1	0	3	6	1	0	0	x	11	14	1

E—Belanger, Oliver. DP—Pirates 2 (Cash to Hernandez; Stargell to Sanguillen). LOB—Pirates 14, Orioles 9. Scoring Position—Pirates 1-for-13, Orioles 6-for-16. 2B—Clemente (2). HR—Hebner (1).

Pirates	IP	H	R	ER	BB	K	ERA
Bob Johnson (L, 0-1)	3.1	4	4	4	2	1	10.80
Bruce Kison	0.0	0	0	0	2	0	—
Bob Moose	1.0	5	5	5	0	0	11.57
Bob Veale	0.2	1	1	1	2	0	13.50
Bob Miller	2.0	3	1	1	0	1	2.25
Dave Giusti	1.0	1	0	0	1	0	0.00

Orioles	IP	H	R	ER	BB	K	ERA
Jim Palmer (W, 1-0)	8.0	7	3	3	8	10	3.38
Dick Hall	1.0	1	0	0	0	0	0.00

Kison pitched to two batters in the 4th.

HBP—Hendricks by BJohnson. Time—2:55. Attendance—53,239. Umpires—HP, Sudol. 1B, Rice. 2B, Vargo. 3B, Odom.

Game 3

Tuesday, October 12

Orioles	AB	R	H	RBI	BB	K	Avg
Don Buford, lf	4	0	0	0	0	1	.154
Merv Rettenmund, cf	4	0	0	0	0	1	.231
Boog Powell, 1b	4	0	0	0	0	1	.083
Frank Robinson, rf	4	1	2	1	0	1	.583
Ellie Hendricks, c	3	0	0	0	1	2	.300
Brooks Robinson, 3b	3	0	1	0	0	1	.500
Dave Johnson, 2b	3	0	0	0	0	0	.250
Mark Belanger, ss	3	0	0	0	0	0	.200
Mike Cuellar, p	1	0	0	0	1	0	.000
Tom Dukes, p	0	0	0	0	0	0	—
Tom Shopay, ph	1	0	0	0	0	0	.000
Eddie Watt, p	0	0	0	0	0	0	—
TOTALS	30	1	3	1	2	8	.277

Pirates	AB	R	H	RBI	BB	K	Avg
Dave Cash, 2b	4	1	1	0	1	0	.154
Al Oliver, cf	4	0	0	0	1	1	.100
Roberto Clemente, rf	4	1	1	1	0	0	.385
Willie Stargell, lf	1	1	0	0	3	1	.143
Bob Robertson, 1b	4	1	1	3	0	2	.100
Manny Sanguillen, c	4	1	2	0	0	0	.231
Jose Pagan, 3b	4	0	2	1	0	0	.250
Gene Alley, ss	2	0	0	0	1	0	.000
Jackie Hernandez, ss	1	0	0	0	0	0	.200
Steve Blass, p	4	0	0	0	0	1	.000
TOTALS	32	5	7	5	6	5	.188

	1	2	3	4	5	6	7	8	9	R	H	E
Orioles	0	0	0	0	0	0	1	0	0	1	3	3
Pirates	1	0	0	0	0	1	3	0	x	5	7	0

E—Powell, Cuellar, BRobinson. DP—Orioles 1 (BRobinson to Johnson). LOB—Orioles 4, Pirates 9. Scoring Position—Orioles 0-for-1, Pirates 2-for-13. 2B—Cash (1), Sanguillen (1), Pagan (1). HR—FRobinson (2), Robertson (1).

Game 4

Wednesday, October 13

Orioles	AB	R	H	RBI	BB	K	Avg
Paul Blair, cf	4	1	2	0	0	0	.600
Mark Belanger, ss	4	1	1	0	0	1	.214
Merv Rettenmund, lf	4	1	1	0	0	0	.235
Frank Robinson, rf	2	0	0	0	1	1	.500
Brooks Robinson, 3b	3	0	0	1	0	0	.385
Boog Powell, 1b	3	0	0	1	0	0	.067
Dave Johnson, 2b	3	0	0	0	0	0	.200
Andy Etchebarren, c	2	0	0	0	0	0	.000
Pat Dobson, p	2	0	0	0	0	2	.000
Grant Jackson, p	0	0	0	0	0	0	—
Tom Shopay, ph	1	0	0	0	0	0	.000
Eddie Watt, p	0	0	0	0	0	0	—
Pete Richert, p	0	0	0	0	0	0	—
TOTALS	28	3	4	2	1	4	.263

Pirates	AB	R	H	RBI	BB	K	Avg
Dave Cash, 2b	4	1	1	0	1	0	.176
Richie Hebner, 3b	5	1	1	0	0	1	.250
Roberto Clemente, rf	4	0	3	0	1	1	.471
Willie Stargell, lf	5	1	2	1	0	1	.250
Al Oliver, cf	4	0	2	2	1	1	.214
Bob Robertson, 1b	4	1	1	0	0	0	.143
Manny Sanguillen, c	4	0	2	0	0	0	.294
Jackie Hernandez, ss	3	0	1	0	0	0	.250
Vic Davalillo, ph	1	0	0	0	0	0	.500
Dave Giusti, p	0	0	0	0	0	0	—
Luke Walker, p	0	0	0	0	0	0	—
Bruce Kison, p	2	0	0	0	1	2	.000
Milt May, ph	1	0	1	1	0	0	.500
Gene Alley, pr-ss	0	0	0	0	0	0	.000
TOTALS	37	4	14	4	4	6	.261

	1	2	3	4	5	6	7	8	9	R	H	E
Orioles	3	0	0	0	0	0	0	0	0	3	4	1
Pirates	2	0	1	0	0	1	0	0	x	4	14	0

E—Blair. DP—Orioles 1 (Belanger to Johnson to Powell), Pirates 1 (Hernandez to Cash to Robertson). LOB—Orioles 4, Pirates 13. Scoring Position—Orioles 1-for-3, Pirates 4-for-15. 2B—Blair (1), Stargell (1), Oliver (1). SF—BRobinson, Powell. GDP—Etchebarren, Cash. SB—Sanguillen (1), Hernandez (1).

Orioles	IP	H	R	ER	BB	K	ERA
Pat Dobson	5.1	10	3	3	4	4	5.06
Grant Jackson	0.2	0	0	0	1	0	0.00
Eddie Watt (L, 0-1)	1.1	4	1	1	0	1	3.86
Pete Richert	0.2	0	0	0	0	1	0.00

Pirates	IP	H	R	ER	BB	K	ERA
Luke Walker	0.2	3	3	3	1	0	40.50
Bruce Kison (W, 1-0)	6.1	1	0	0	0	3	0.00
Dave Giusti (S, 1)	2.0	0	0	0	0	1	0.00

PB—Sanguillen. HBP—Johnson by Kison, Etchebarren by Kison, FRobinson by Kison. Time—2:48. Attendance—51,378. Umpires—HP, Vargo. 1B, Odom. 2B, Kibler. 3B, Chylak.

(Game 3 continued — pitching)

Orioles	IP	H	R	ER	BB	K	ERA
Mike Cuellar (L, 0-1)	6.0	7	5	4	6	4	6.00
Tom Dukes	1.0	0	0	0	0	0	0.00
Eddie Watt	1.0	0	0	0	0	1	0.00

Pirates	IP	H	R	ER	BB	K	ERA
Steve Blass (W, 1-0)	9.0	3	1	1	2	8	1.00

Cuellar pitched to three batters in the 7th.

Time—2:20. Attendance—50,403. Umpires—HP, Rice. 1B, Vargo. 2B, Odom. 3B, Kibler.

Game 5

Thursday, October 14

Orioles	AB	R	H	RBI	BB	K	Avg
Don Buford, lf	3	0	0	0	1	0	.125
Paul Blair, cf	4	0	0	0	0	1	.333
Boog Powell, 1b	3	0	1	0	0	0	.111
Frank Robinson, rf	3	0	0	0	0	1	.412
Ellie Hendricks, c	2	0	0	0	1	0	.250
Brooks Robinson, 3b	3	0	1	0	0	0	.375
Dave Johnson, 2b	3	0	0	0	0	0	.167
Mark Belanger, ss	3	0	0	0	0	0	.176
Dave McNally, p	1	0	0	0	0	0	.000
Dave Leonhard, p	0	0	0	0	0	0	—
Tom Shopay, ph	1	0	0	0	0	0	.000
Tom Dukes, p	0	0	0	0	0	0	—
Merv Rettenmund, ph	1	0	0	0	0	0	.222
TOTALS	27	0	2	0	2	2	.223

Pirates	AB	R	H	RBI	BB	K	Avg
Dave Cash, 2b	4	0	0	0	1	0	.143
Gene Clines, cf	3	2	1	0	1	0	.143
Roberto Clemente, rf	4	0	1	1	0	0	.429
Willie Stargell, lf	4	0	1	0	0	0	.250
Bob Robertson, 1b	3	1	1	1	1	0	.176
Manny Sanguillen, c	4	1	1	0	0	1	.286
Jose Pagan, 3b	4	0	1	0	0	1	.250
Jackie Hernandez, ss	3	0	2	0	0	1	.364
Nelson Briles, p	2	0	1	1	0	1	.500
TOTALS	31	4	9	3	3	4	.266

	1 2 3	4 5 6	7 8 9		R	H	E
Orioles	0 0 0	0 0 0	0 0 0		0	2	1
Pirates	0 2 1	0 1 0	0 0 x		4	9	0

E—BRobinson. DP—Pirates 2 (Hernandez to Cash to Robertson; Pagan to Cash to Robertson). LOB—Orioles 2, Pirates 9. Scoring Position—Orioles 0-for-0, Pirates 2-for-13. 3B—Clines (1). HR—Robertson (2). S—Briles 2. GDP—FRobinson, BRobinson. SB—Clines (1), Sanguillen (2).

Orioles	IP	H	R	ER	BB	K	ERA
Dave McNally (L, 1-1)	4.0	7	4	3	2	3	2.08
Dave Leonhard	1.0	0	0	0	1	0	0.00
Tom Dukes	3.0	2	0	0	0	1	0.00

Pirates	IP	H	R	ER	BB	K	ERA
Nelson Briles (W, 1-0)	9.0	2	0	0	2	2	0.00

McNally pitched to two batters in the 5th.

WP—McNally. HBP—Hernandez by Dukes. Time—2:16. Attendance—51,377. Umpires—HP, Odom. 1B, Kibler. 2B, Chylak. 3B, Sudol.

Game 6

Saturday, October 16

Pirates	AB	R	H	RBI	BB	K	Avg
Dave Cash, 2b	5	0	1	0	0	0	.154
Richie Hebner, 3b	4	0	0	0	1	1	.167
Roberto Clemente, rf	4	1	2	1	1	0	.440
Willie Stargell, lf	4	0	0	0	1	2	.200
Al Oliver, cf	5	1	1	0	0	0	.211
Bob Robertson, 1b	4	0	2	1	0	1	.238
Manny Sanguillen, c	4	0	3	0	0	0	.360
Jackie Hernandez, ss	4	0	0	0	0	2	.267
Bob Moose, p	1	0	0	0	0	0	.000
Bob Johnson, p	1	0	0	0	0	0	.000
Dave Giusti, p	0	0	0	0	0	0	—
Vic Davalillo, ph-cf	1	0	0	0	0	0	.333
TOTALS	37	2	9	2	3	6	.257

Orioles	AB	R	H	RBI	BB	K	Avg
Don Buford, lf	4	1	3	1	1	1	.250
Dave Johnson, 2b	5	0	1	1	0	0	.174
Boog Powell, 1b	5	0	1	0	0	0	.130
Frank Robinson, rf	4	1	0	0	1	2	.333
Merv Rettenmund, cf	5	0	1	0	0	2	.217
Brooks Robinson, 3b	4	0	1	1	0	0	.350
Mark Belanger, ss	1	1	1	0	3	0	.222
Jim Palmer, p	2	0	0	0	0	2	.000
Tom Shopay, ph	1	0	0	0	0	0	.000
Pat Dobson, p	0	0	0	0	0	0	.000
Dave McNally, p	0	0	0	0	0	0	.000
TOTALS	35	3	8	3	5	8	.213

	1 2 3	4 5 6	7 8 9 10	R	H	E
Pirates	0 1 1	0 0 0	0 0 0 0	2	9	1
Orioles	0 0 0	0 0 1	1 0 0 1	3	8	0

E—Hebner. DP—Pirates 1 (Hebner to Cash to Robertson). LOB—Pirates 9, Orioles 10. Scoring Position—Pirates 1-for-5, Orioles 1-for-8. 2B—Oliver (2), Buford (1). 3B—Clemente (1). HR—Clemente (1), Buford (2). S—Moose, Palmer. SF—BRobinson. GDP—DJohnson. SB—Cash (1), Belanger (1).

Pirates	IP	H	R	ER	BB	K	ERA
Bob Moose	5.0	4	1	1	2	3	6.52
Bob Johnson (H, 1)	1.2	1	1	1	1	2	9.00
Dave Giusti (BS, 1)	2.1	2	0	0	1	3	0.00
Bob Miller (L, 0-1)	0.2	1	1	1	1	0	3.86

Orioles	IP	H	R	ER	BB	K	ERA
Jim Palmer	9.0	8	2	2	1	5	2.65
Pat Dobson	0.2	1	0	0	1	1	4.50
Dave McNally (W, 2-1)	0.1	0	0	0	1	0	2.03

Moose pitched to three batters in the 6th.

Time—2:59. Attendance—44,174. Umpires—HP, Kibler. 1B, Chylak. 2B, Sudol. 3B, Rice.

Game 7

Sunday, October 17

Pirates	AB	R	H	RBI	BB	K	Avg
Dave Cash, 2b	4	0	0	0	0	1	.133
Gene Clines, cf	4	0	0	0	0	1	.091
Roberto Clemente, rf	4	1	1	1	0	1	.414
Bob Robertson, 1b	4	0	1	0	0	1	.240
Manny Sanguillen, c	4	0	2	0	0	0	.379
Willie Stargell, lf	4	1	1	0	0	2	.208
Jose Pagan, 3b	3	0	1	1	0	0	.267
Jackie Hernandez, ss	3	0	0	0	0	1	.222
Steve Blass, p	3	0	0	0	0	0	.000
TOTALS	33	2	6	2	0	7	.250

Orioles	AB	R	H	RBI	BB	K	Avg
Don Buford, lf	3	0	1	1	1	0	.261
Dave Johnson, 2b	4	0	0	0	0	0	.148
Boog Powell, 1b	4	0	0	0	0	2	.111
Frank Robinson, rf	4	0	0	0	0	1	.280
Merv Rettenmund, cf	4	0	0	0	0	0	.185
Brooks Robinson, 3b	2	0	0	0	1	0	.318
Ellie Hendricks, c	3	1	2	0	0	0	.263
Mark Belanger, ss	3	0	1	0	0	0	.238
Mike Cuellar, p	2	0	0	0	0	2	.000
Tom Shopay, ph	0	0	0	0	0	0	.000
Pat Dobson, p	0	0	0	0	0	0	.000
Dave McNally, p	0	0	0	0	0	0	.000
TOTALS	29	1	4	1	2	5	.206

	1 2 3	4 5 6	7 8 9		R	H	E
Pirates	0 0 0	1 0 0	0 1 0		2	6	1
Orioles	0 0 0	0 0 0	0 1 0		1	4	0

E—Robertson. DP—Pirates 1 (Cash to Robertson). LOB—Pirates 4, Orioles 4. Scoring Position—Pirates 0-for-4, Orioles 0-for-5. 2B—Pagan (2), Hendricks (1). HR—Clemente (2). S—Shopay. GDP—Belanger. CS—Buford (1).

Pirates	IP	H	R	ER	BB	K	ERA
Steve Blass (W, 2-0)	9.0	4	1	1	2	5	1.00

Orioles	IP	H	R	ER	BB	K	ERA
Mike Cuellar (L, 0-2)	8.0	4	2	2	0	6	3.86
Pat Dobson	0.2	2	0	0	0	0	4.05
Dave McNally	0.1	0	0	0	0	0	1.98

Time—2:10. Attendance—47,291. Umpires—HP, Chylak. 1B, Sudol. 2B, Rice. 3B, Vargo.

1971 World Series—Composite Statistics

Batting

Pirates	G	AB	R	H	RBI	2B	3B	HR	BB	SO	SB	CS	Avg	OBP	Slg
Gene Alley	2	2	0	0	0	0	0	0	1	0	0	0	.000	.333	.000
Steve Blass	2	7	0	0	0	0	0	0	0	1	0	0	.000	.000	.000
Nelson Briles	1	2	0	1	1	0	0	0	0	1	0	0	.500	.500	.500
Dave Cash	7	30	2	4	1	1	0	0	3	1	1	0	.133	.212	.167
Roberto Clemente	7	29	3	12	4	2	1	2	2	2	0	0	.414	.452	.759
Gene Clines	3	11	2	1	0	0	1	0	1	1	1	0	.091	.167	.273
Vic Davalillo	3	3	1	1	0	0	0	0	0	0	0	0	.333	.333	.333
Dock Ellis	1	1	0	0	0	0	0	0	0	1	0	0	.000	.000	.000
Richie Hebner	3	12	2	2	3	0	0	1	3	3	0	0	.167	.333	.417
Jackie Hernandez	7	18	2	4	1	0	0	0	2	5	1	0	.222	.333	.222
Bob Johnson	2	3	0	0	0	0	0	0	0	2	0	0	.000	.000	.000
Bruce Kison	2	2	0	0	0	0	0	0	1	2	0	0	.000	.333	.000
Milt May	2	2	0	1	1	0	0	0	0	0	0	0	.500	.500	.500
Bill Mazeroski	1	1	0	0	0	0	0	0	0	0	0	0	.000	.000	.000
Bob Moose	3	2	0	0	0	0	0	0	0	1	0	0	.000	.000	.000
Al Oliver	5	19	1	4	2	2	0	0	2	5	0	0	.211	.286	.316
Jose Pagan	4	15	0	4	2	2	0	0	0	1	0	0	.267	.267	.400
Bob Robertson	7	25	4	6	5	0	0	2	4	8	0	0	.240	.345	.480
Charlie Sands	1	1	0	0	0	0	0	0	1	0	0	0	.000	.000	.000
Manny Sanguillen	7	29	3	11	0	1	0	0	0	3	2	0	.379	.379	.414
Willie Stargell	7	24	3	5	1	1	0	0	7	9	0	0	.208	.387	.250
Totals	7	238	23	56	21	9	2	5	26	47	5	0	.235	.313	.353

Batting

Orioles	G	AB	R	H	RBI	2B	3B	HR	BB	SO	SB	CS	Avg	OBP	Slg
Mark Belanger	7	21	4	5	0	0	1	0	5	2	1	0	.238	.385	.333
Paul Blair	4	9	2	3	0	1	0	0	0	1	0	0	.333	.333	.444
Don Buford	6	23	3	6	4	1	0	2	3	3	0	1	.261	.346	.565
Mike Cuellar	2	3	0	0	0	0	0	0	1	2	0	0	.000	.250	.000
Pat Dobson	3	2	0	0	0	0	0	0	0	2	0	0	.000	.000	.000
Andy Etchebarren	1	2	0	0	0	0	0	0	0	0	0	0	.000	.333	.000
Ellie Hendricks	6	19	3	5	1	1	0	0	3	3	0	0	.263	.391	.316
Dave Johnson	7	27	1	4	3	0	0	0	1	0	0	0	.148	.179	.148
Dave McNally	4	4	0	0	0	0	0	0	0	3	0	0	.000	.000	.000
Jim Palmer	2	4	0	0	2	0	0	0	2	2	0	0	.000	.333	.000
Boog Powell	7	27	1	3	1	0	0	0	1	3	0	0	.111	.138	.111
Merv Rettenmund	7	27	3	5	4	0	1	0	4	0	0	0	.185	.185	.296
Brooks Robinson	7	22	2	7	5	0	0	3	1	0	0	0	.318	.370	.318
Frank Robinson	7	25	5	7	2	0	2	2	8	0	0	0	.280	.357	.520
Tom Shopay	5	4	0	0	0	0	0	0	0	0	0	0	.000	.000	.000
Totals	7	219	24	45	22	3	1	5	20	35	1	1	.205	.280	.297

Pitching

Pirates	G	GS	CG	IP	H	R	ER	BB	SO	W-L	Sv-Op	Hld	ERA
Steve Blass	2	2	2	18.0	7	2	2	4	13	2-0	0-0	0	1.00
Nelson Briles	1	1	1	9.0	2	0	0	2	2	1-0	0-0	0	0.00
Dock Ellis	1	1	0	2.1	4	4	4	1	1	0-1	0-0	0	15.43
Dave Giusti	3	0	0	5.1	3	0	0	2	4	0-0	1-2	0	0.00
Bob Johnson	2	1	0	5.0	5	5	5	3	3	0-1	0-0	1	9.00
Bruce Kison	2	0	0	6.1	1	0	0	2	3	1-0	0-0	0	0.00
Bob Miller	3	0	0	4.2	7	2	2	1	2	0-1	0-0	0	3.86
Bob Moose	3	1	0	9.2	12	7	7	2	7	0-0	0-0	0	6.52
Bob Veale	1	0	0	0.2	1	1	1	2	0	0-0	0-0	0	13.50
Luke Walker	1	1	0	0.2	3	3	3	1	0	0-0	0-0	0	40.50
Totals	7	7	3	61.2	45	24	24	20	35	4-3	1-2	1	3.50

Pitching

Orioles	G	GS	CG	IP	H	R	ER	BB	SO	W-L	Sv-Op	Hld	ERA
Mike Cuellar	2	2	0	14.0	11	7	6	6	10	0-2	0-0	0	3.86
Pat Dobson	3	1	0	6.2	13	3	3	4	6	0-0	0-0	0	4.05
Tom Dukes	2	0	0	4.0	2	0	0	0	1	0-0	0-0	0	0.00
Dick Hall	1	0	0	1.0	1	0	0	0	0	0-0	1-1	0	0.00
Grant Jackson	1	0	0	0.2	0	0	0	1	0	0-0	0-0	0	0.00
Dave Leonhard	1	0	0	1.0	0	0	0	1	0	0-0	0-0	0	0.00
Dave McNally	4	2	1	13.2	10	7	3	5	12	2-1	0-0	0	1.98
Jim Palmer	2	2	0	17.0	15	5	5	9	15	1-0	0-0	0	2.65
Pete Richert	1	0	0	0.2	0	0	0	0	1	0-0	0-0	0	0.00
Eddie Watt	2	0	0	2.1	4	1	1	0	2	0-1	0-0	0	3.86
Totals	7	7	1	61.0	56	23	18	26	47	3-4	1-1	0	2.66

Fielding

Pirates	Pos	G	PO	Ast	E	DP	PB	FPct
Gene Alley	ss	2	1	4	0	0	—	1.000
Steve Blass	p	2	2	4	0	0	—	1.000
Nelson Briles	p	1	0	1	0	0	—	1.000
Dave Cash	2b	7	20	23	0	6	—	1.000
Roberto Clemente	rf	7	15	0	0	0	—	1.000
Gene Clines	cf	3	6	0	0	0	—	1.000
Vic Davalillo	lf	1	1	0	0	0	—	1.000
	cf	1	1	0	0	0	—	1.000
Dock Ellis	p	1	1	0	0	0	—	1.000
Dave Giusti	p	3	0	0	0	0	—	—
Richie Hebner	3b	3	1	3	1	1	—	.800
Jackie Hernandez	ss	7	9	16	0	3	—	1.000
Bob Johnson	p	2	2	0	0	0	—	1.000
Bruce Kison	p	2	0	1	0	0	—	1.000
Bob Miller	p	3	1	1	0	0	—	1.000
Bob Moose	p	3	0	3	0	0	—	1.000
Al Oliver	cf	4	11	0	1	0	—	.917
Jose Pagan	3b	4	2	8	0	1	—	1.000
Bob Robertson	1b	7	64	4	1	5	—	.986
Manny Sanguillen	c	7	37	0	0	1	1	1.000
Willie Stargell	lf	7	11	1	0	1	—	1.000
Bob Veale	p	1	0	1	0	0	—	1.000
Luke Walker	p	1	0	0	0	0	—	—
Totals		7	185	70	3	18	1	.988

Fielding

Orioles	Pos	G	PO	Ast	E	DP	PB	FPct
Mark Belanger	ss	7	10	21	3	1	—	.912
Paul Blair	cf	4	6	2	1	0	—	.889
Don Buford	lf	6	13	1	0	0	—	1.000
Mike Cuellar	p	2	0	3	1	0	—	.750
Pat Dobson	p	3	0	3	0	0	—	1.000
Tom Dukes	p	2	0	0	0	0	—	—
Andy Etchebarren	c	1	6	0	0	0	0	1.000
Dick Hall	p	1	1	0	0	0	—	1.000
Ellie Hendricks	c	6	40	4	1	0	0	.978
Grant Jackson	p	1	0	0	0	0	—	—
Dave Johnson	2b	7	18	11	0	2	—	1.000
Dave Leonhard	p	1	0	0	0	0	—	—
Dave McNally	p	4	0	2	0	0	—	1.000
Jim Palmer	p	2	2	1	0	0	—	1.000
Boog Powell	1b	7	52	4	1	1	—	.982
Merv Rettenmund	cf	5	13	0	0	0	—	1.000
	lf	2	3	0	0	0	—	1.000
	rf	1	1	0	0	0	—	1.000
Pete Richert	p	1	0	0	0	0	—	—
Brooks Robinson	3b	7	6	17	2	1	—	.920
Frank Robinson	rf	7	12	0	0	0	—	1.000
Eddie Watt	p	2	0	0	0	0	—	—
Totals		7	183	69	9	5	0	.966

1972 Oakland Athletics (AL) 4, Cincinnati Reds (NL) 3

The Oakland A's edged the Cincinnati Reds in a seven-game World Series in which six of the contests were decided by a single run. Gene Tenace was the hero of Game 1, homering twice and driving in all three runs in the A's 3-2 victory. Catfish Hunter won Game 2, 2-1, with last-out relief help from Rollie Fingers. Jack Billingham got the Reds their first win with a 1-0 victory in Game 3, as Cesar Geronimo drove in the game's only run. The A's mounted a two-run rally in the bottom of the ninth inning to pull out Game 4, 3-2. Angel Mangual drove in the winning run with a single through the drawn-in infield. Cincinnati rallied in similar fashion to take Game 5, 5-4. After scoring the tying run in the eighth, the Reds got the eventual game-winner in the ninth on Pete Rose's RBI single. The Reds exploded for five runs in the bottom of the eighth to take Game 6, 8-1. Game 7 pitted Billingham against Blue Moon Odom. Each pitched well but was relieved early. In the sixth inning, RBI doubles by Tenace and Sal Bando off Pedro Borbon plated the eventual winning run for the A's.

Game 1

Saturday, October 14

Athletics	AB	R	H	RBI	BB	K	Avg
Bert Campaneris, ss	3	0	2	0	0	0	.667
Joe Rudi, lf	4	0	0	0	0	0	.000
Matty Alou, rf	3	0	0	0	1	0	.000
Mike Epstein, 1b	3	0	0	0	1	0	.000
Allan Lewis, pr	0	0	0	0	0	0	—
Mike Hegan, 1b	0	0	0	0	0	0	—
Sal Bando, 3b	4	0	0	0	0	1	.000
George Hendrick, cf	2	1	0	0	1	0	.000
Gene Tenace, c	3	2	2	3	0	0	.667
Dick Green, 2b	2	0	0	0	0	0	.000
Gonzalo Marquez, ph	1	0	0	0	0	0	.000
Ted Kubiak, 2b	0	0	0	0	0	0	—
Ken Holtzman, p	2	0	0	0	0	0	.000
Rollie Fingers, p	0	0	0	0	0	0	—
Vida Blue, p	0	0	0	0	1	0	—
TOTALS	27	3	4	3	4	1	.148

Reds	AB	R	H	RBI	BB	K	Avg
Pete Rose, lf	4	0	0	0	1	0	.000
Joe Morgan, 2b	3	0	0	0	1	1	.000
Bobby Tolan, cf	4	0	1	0	0	0	.250
Johnny Bench, c	3	2	2	0	1	0	.667
Tony Perez, 1b	4	0	2	0	0	1	.500
Denis Menke, 3b	3	0	0	1	1	2	.000
Cesar Geronimo, rf	3	0	0	0	0	0	.000
Hal McRae, ph	1	0	1	0	0	0	1.000
George Foster, pr	0	0	0	0	0	0	—
Dave Concepcion, ss	2	0	1	1	1	0	.500
Gary Nolan, p	2	0	0	0	0	2	.000
Pedro Borbon, p	0	0	0	0	0	0	—
Ted Uhlaender, ph	1	0	0	0	0	1	.000
Clay Carroll, p	0	0	0	0	0	0	—
Julian Javier, ph	1	0	0	0	0	0	.000
TOTALS	31	2	7	2	5	7	.226

	1 2 3	4 5 6	7 8 9	R	H	E
Athletics	0 2 0	0 1 0	0 0 0	3	4	0
Reds	0 1 0	1 0 0	0 0 0	2	7	0

DP—Reds 1 (Morgan to Perez). LOB—Athletics 2, Reds 8. Scoring Position—Athletics 0-for-1, Reds 0-for-11. 2B—Bench (1). HR—Tenace 2 (2). S—Campaneris, Concepcion. CS—Campaneris (1), Tolan (1), Concepcion (1), Lewis (1).

Athletics	IP	H	R	ER	BB	K	ERA
Ken Holtzman (W, 1-0)	5.0	5	2	2	3	3	3.60
Rollie Fingers (H, 1)	1.2	1	0	0	1	3	0.00
Vida Blue (S, 1)	2.1	1	0	0	1	1	0.00

Reds	IP	H	R	ER	BB	K	ERA
Gary Nolan (L, 0-1)	6.0	4	3	3	2	0	4.50
Pedro Borbon	1.0	0	0	0	0	0	0.00
Clay Carroll	2.0	0	0	0	2	1	0.00

Holtzman pitched to one batter in the 6th.

WP—Blue. Time—2:18. Attendance—52,918. Umpires—HP, Pelekoudas. 1B, Honochick. 2B, Steiner. 3B, Umont.

Game 2

Sunday, October 15

Athletics	AB	R	H	RBI	BB	K	Avg
Bert Campaneris, ss	5	0	1	0	0	1	.375
Matty Alou, rf	4	0	1	0	0	0	.143
Joe Rudi, lf	3	1	2	1	1	1	.286
Mike Epstein, 1b	2	0	0	0	1	1	.000
Allan Lewis, pr	0	0	0	0	0	0	—
Mike Hegan, 1b	1	0	0	0	0	1	.000
Sal Bando, 3b	4	0	1	0	0	1	.125
George Hendrick, cf	4	1	1	0	0	0	.167
Gene Tenace, c	4	0	0	0	0	1	.286
Dick Green, 2b	4	0	2	0	0	1	.333
Catfish Hunter, p	3	0	1	1	1	0	.333
Rollie Fingers, p	0	0	0	0	0	0	—
TOTALS	34	2	9	2	3	7	.224

Reds	AB	R	H	RBI	BB	K	Avg
Pete Rose, lf	4	0	1	0	0	1	.125
Joe Morgan, 2b	4	0	0	0	0	1	.000
Bobby Tolan, cf	4	0	0	0	0	1	.125
Johnny Bench, c	3	0	1	0	1	0	.500
Tony Perez, 1b	3	1	2	0	1	0	.571
Denis Menke, 3b	4	0	0	0	0	1	.000
Cesar Geronimo, rf	4	0	0	0	0	1	.000
Darrel Chaney, ss	2	0	0	0	1	0	.000
Hal McRae, ph	1	0	1	1	0	0	1.000
Dave Concepcion, pr	0	0	0	0	0	0	.500
Ross Grimsley, p	1	0	0	0	0	1	.000
Ted Uhlaender, ph	1	0	1	0	0	0	.500
Pedro Borbon, p	0	0	0	0	0	0	—
Joe Hague, ph	1	0	0	0	0	0	.000
Tom Hall, p	0	0	0	0	0	0	—
Julian Javier, ph	1	0	0	0	0	0	.000
TOTALS	33	1	6	1	3	6	.210

	1 2 3	4 5 6	7 8 9	R	H	E
Athletics	0 1 1	0 0 0	0 0 0	2	9	2
Reds	0 0 0	0 0 0	0 0 1	1	6	0

E—Hunter, Epstein. DP—Athletics 1 (Campaneris to Green to Epstein), Reds 1 (Bench to Chaney). LOB—Athletics 8, Reds 8. Scoring Position—Athletics 2-for-4, Reds 1-for-8. 2B—Uhlaender (1). HR—Rudi (1). GDP—Menke. SB—Alou (1), Morgan (1). CS—Lewis (2).

Athletics	IP	H	R	ER	BB	K	ERA
Catfish Hunter (W, 1-0)	8.2	6	1	1	3	6	1.04
Rollie Fingers (S, 1)	0.1	0	0	0	0	0	0.00

Reds	IP	H	R	ER	BB	K	ERA
Ross Grimsley (L, 0-1)	5.0	6	2	2	0	1	3.60
Pedro Borbon	2.0	0	0	0	1	4	0.00
Tom Hall	2.0	3	0	0	2	2	0.00

Time—2:26. Attendance—53,224. Umpires—HP, Honochick. 1B, Steiner. 2B, Umont. 3B, Engel.

Game 3

Wednesday, October 18

Reds	AB	R	H	RBI	BB	K	Avg
Pete Rose, lf	3	0	0	0	1	2	.091
Joe Morgan, 2b	3	0	0	0	1	1	.000
Bobby Tolan, cf	4	0	1	0	0	1	.167
Johnny Bench, c	4	0	0	0	0	3	.300
Tony Perez, 1b	3	1	1	0	1	1	.500
Denis Menke, 3b	2	0	1	0	1	0	.111
Cesar Geronimo, rf	4	0	1	1	0	1	.091
Darrel Chaney, ss	4	0	0	0	0	2	.000
Jack Billingham, p	4	0	0	0	0	3	.000
Clay Carroll, p	0	0	0	0	0	0	—
TOTALS	31	1	4	1	4	14	.157

Athletics	AB	R	H	RBI	BB	K	Avg
Bert Campaneris, ss	3	0	0	0	1	1	.273
Matty Alou, rf	3	0	0	0	0	0	.100
Joe Rudi, lf	4	0	1	0	0	1	.273
Mike Epstein, 1b	2	0	0	0	2	0	.000
Sal Bando, 3b	4	0	0	0	0	1	.083
George Hendrick, cf	4	0	0	0	0	1	.100
Gene Tenace, c	3	0	0	0	0	1	.200
Dick Green, 2b	2	0	1	0	0	0	.375
Gonzalo Marquez, ph	1	0	1	0	0	0	.500
Allan Lewis, pr	0	0	0	0	0	0	—
Ted Kubiak, 2b	0	0	0	0	0	0	—
Blue Moon Odom, p	2	0	0	0	0	2	.000
Mike Hegan, ph	1	0	0	0	0	0	.000
Vida Blue, p	0	0	0	0	0	0	—
Rollie Fingers, p	0	0	0	0	0	0	—
TOTALS	29	0	3	0	3	7	.176

	1 2 3	4 5 6	7 8 9	R	H	E
Reds	0 0 0	0 0 0	1 0 0	1	4	2
Athletics	0 0 0	0 0 0	0 0 0	0	3	2

E—Tenace, Morgan, Bench, Epstein. DP—Reds 1 (Morgan to Chaney to Perez). LOB—Reds 8, Athletics 6. Scoring Position—Reds 1-for-7, Athletics 0-for-2. S—Menke, Alou. GDP—Bando. SB—Rose (1), Tolan (1), Geronimo (1).

Reds	IP	H	R	ER	BB	K	ERA
Jack Billingham (W, 1-0)	8.0	3	0	0	3	7	0.00
Clay Carroll (S, 1)	1.0	0	0	0	0	0	0.00

Athletics	IP	H	R	ER	BB	K	ERA
Blue Moon Odom (L, 0-1)	7.0	3	1	1	2	11	1.29
Vida Blue	0.1	1	0	0	1	0	0.00
Rollie Fingers	1.2	0	0	0	1	3	0.00

Time—2:24. Attendance—49,410. Umpires—HP, Steiner. 1B, Umont. 2B, Engel. 3B, Haller.

Game 4

Thursday, October 19

Reds	AB	R	H	RBI	BB	K	Avg
Pete Rose, lf	4	0	0	0	0	0	.067
Joe Morgan, 2b	3	1	0	0	1	0	.000
Bobby Tolan, cf	4	0	1	2	0	0	.188
Johnny Bench, c	4	0	2	0	0	0	.357
Tony Perez, 1b	4	0	2	0	0	1	.500
Hal McRae, rf	4	0	1	0	0	1	.500
Denis Menke, 3b	4	0	0	0	0	0	.077
Dave Concepcion, ss	3	1	1	0	0	0	.400
Don Gullett, p	2	0	0	0	0	0	.000
Julian Javier, ph	0	0	0	0	0	0	.000
Pedro Borbon, p	0	0	0	0	0	0	—
Clay Carroll, p	0	0	0	0	0	0	—
TOTALS	32	2	7	2	1	2	.220

Athletics	AB	R	H	RBI	BB	K	Avg
Bert Campaneris, ss	4	0	0	0	0	0	.200
Matty Alou, rf	3	0	0	0	1	0	.077
Joe Rudi, lf	4	0	2	0	0	1	.333
Sal Bando, 3b	3	0	2	0	1	0	.200
Mike Epstein, 1b	3	0	0	0	0	0	.000
Mike Hegan, 1b	1	0	0	0	0	0	.000
George Hendrick, cf	3	0	0	0	0	1	.077
Gonzalo Marquez, ph	1	0	1	0	0	0	.667
Allan Lewis, pr	0	1	0	0	0	0	—
Gene Tenace, c	4	2	2	1	0	1	.286
Dick Green, 2b	3	0	1	0	0	1	.364
Don Mincher, ph	1	0	1	1	0	0	1.000
Blue Moon Odom, pr	0	0	0	0	0	0	.000
Ken Holtzman, p	3	0	0	0	0	0	.000
Vida Blue, p	0	0	0	0	0	0	—
Rollie Fingers, p	0	0	0	0	0	0	—
Angel Mangual, ph	1	0	1	1	0	0	1.000
TOTALS	34	3	10	3	2	4	.207

	1 2 3	4 5 6	7 8 9	R	H	E
Reds	0 0 0	0 0 0	0 2 0	2	7	1
Athletics	0 0 0	0 1 0	0 0 2	3	10	1

E—Perez, Holtzman. DP—Reds 1 (Concepcion to Perez), Athletics 1 (Holtzman to Green to Hegan). LOB—Reds 5, Athletics 8. Scoring Position—Reds 1-for-4, Athletics 2-for-6. 2B—Tolan (1), Green (1). HR—Tenace (3). S—Javier. GDP—Menke, Hendrick. SB—Bench (1). CS—Perez (1).

Reds	IP	H	R	ER	BB	K	ERA
Don Gullett	7.0	5	1	1	2	4	1.29
Pedro Borbon (H, 1)	1.1	2	1	1	0	0	2.08
Clay Carroll (BS, 1; L, 0-1)	0.0	3	1	1	0	0	3.00

Athletics	IP	H	R	ER	BB	K	ERA
Ken Holtzman	7.2	5	1	1	0	1	2.13
Vida Blue (BS, 1)	0.1	2	1	1	1	0	3.00
Rollie Fingers (W, 1-0)	1.0	0	0	0	0	1	0.00

Blue pitched to one batter in the 9th. Carroll pitched to three batters in the 9th.

Time—2:06. Attendance—49,410. Umpires—HP, Umont. 1B, Engel. 2B, Haller. 3B, Pelekoudas.

Game 5

Friday, October 20

Reds	AB	R	H	RBI	BB	K	Avg
Pete Rose, lf	5	1	3	2	0	0	.200
Joe Morgan, 2b	3	2	0	0	2	0	.000
Bobby Tolan, cf	4	0	2	2	0	0	.250
Johnny Bench, c	4	0	0	0	0	2	.278
Tony Perez, 1b	4	0	1	0	0	1	.444
Denis Menke, 3b	3	1	1	1	0	2	.125
Cesar Geronimo, rf	4	1	1	0	0	1	.133
Darrel Chaney, ss	1	0	0	0	1	0	.000
Joe Hague, ph	1	0	0	0	0	0	.000
Clay Carroll, p	0	0	0	0	0	0	—
Ross Grimsley, p	0	0	0	0	0	0	.000
Jack Billingham, p	0	0	0	0	0	0	.000
Jim McGlothlin, p	1	0	0	0	0	0	.000
Pedro Borbon, p	0	0	0	0	0	0	—
Ted Uhlaender, ph	1	0	0	0	0	0	.333
Tom Hall, p	0	0	0	0	0	0	—
Dave Concepcion, ph-ss	2	0	0	0	0	0	.286
TOTALS	33	5	8	5	3	6	.196

Athletics	AB	R	H	RBI	BB	K	Avg
Bert Campaneris, ss	5	0	0	0	0	2	.150
Matty Alou, rf	4	0	0	0	0	0	.059
Joe Rudi, lf	3	0	0	0	0	2	.278
Mike Epstein, 1b	2	1	0	0	1	0	.000
Mike Hegan, 1b	1	0	1	0	0	0	.250
Sal Bando, 3b	3	1	1	0	1	0	.222
George Hendrick, cf	2	1	1	0	0	0	.133
Don Mincher, ph	0	0	0	0	0	0	1.000
Angel Mangual, ph-cf	1	0	0	0	0	0	.500
Gene Tenace, c	2	1	1	3	2	0	.313
Blue Moon Odom, pr	0	0	0	0	0	0	.000
Dick Green, 2b	1	0	0	0	0	0	.333
Gonzalo Marquez, ph	1	0	1	1	0	0	.750
Allan Lewis, pr	0	0	0	0	0	0	—
Ted Kubiak, 2b	2	0	1	0	0	0	.500
Catfish Hunter, p	2	0	0	0	0	1	.200
Rollie Fingers, p	0	0	0	0	0	0	—
Dave Hamilton, p	0	0	0	0	0	0	—
Dave Duncan, ph	1	0	1	0	0	0	1.000
TOTALS	30	4	7	4	4	5	.221

	1	2	3	4	5	6	7	8	9		R	H	E
Reds	1	0	0	1	1	0	0	1	1		5	8	0
Athletics	0	3	0	1	0	0	0	0	0		4	7	2

E—Bando, Alou. DP—Athletics 1 (Alou to Tenace). LOB—Reds 6, Athletics 6. Scoring Position—Reds 2-for-10, Athletics 2-for-5. 2B—Perez (1). HR—Rose (1), Menke (1), Tenace (4). S—Menke, Hendrick, Fingers, Grimsley. SB—Morgan (2), Tolan 2 (3). CS—Tenace (1).

Reds	IP	H	R	ER	BB	K	ERA
Jim McGlothlin	3.0	2	4	4	2	3	12.00
Pedro Borbon	1.0	1	0	0	1	0	1.69
Tom Hall	2.0	0	0	0	0	1	0.00
Clay Carroll	1.2	3	0	0	0	1	1.93
Ross Grimsley (W, 1-1)	0.2	0	0	0	1	0	3.18
Jack Billingham (S, 1)	0.2	1	0	0	0	0	0.00

Athletics	IP	H	R	ER	BB	K	ERA
Catfish Hunter	4.2	5	3	3	2	2	2.70
Rollie Fingers (L, 1-1)	3.2	3	2	2	1	4	2.16
Dave Hamilton	0.2	0	0	0	0	0	0.00

McGlothlin pitched to one batter in the 4th.

WP—Fingers. HBP—Rudi by McGlothlin. Time—2:26. Attendance—49,410. Umpires—HP, Engel. 1B, Haller. 2B, Pelekoudas. 3B, Honochick.

Game 6

Saturday, October 21

Athletics	AB	R	H	RBI	BB	K	Avg
Bert Campaneris, ss	4	0	0	0	0	0	.125
Matty Alou, rf	4	0	0	0	0	0	.048
Joe Rudi, lf	4	0	1	0	0	0	.273
Mike Epstein, 1b	4	0	0	0	0	2	.000
Sal Bando, 3b	4	1	2	0	0	0	.273
Angel Mangual, cf	4	0	2	0	0	0	.500
Gene Tenace, c	4	0	1	0	0	0	.300
Dick Green, 2b	2	0	1	1	0	0	.357
Gonzalo Marquez, ph	1	0	0	0	0	0	.600
Ted Kubiak, 2b	1	0	0	0	0	0	.333
Vida Blue, p	1	0	0	0	1	1	.000
Bob Locker, p	0	0	0	0	0	0	—
Don Mincher, ph	0	0	0	0	0	0	1.000
Dave Duncan, ph	1	0	0	0	0	1	.500
Dave Hamilton, p	0	0	0	0	0	0	—
Joe Horlen, p	0	0	0	0	0	0	—
TOTALS	34	1	7	1	1	4	.229

Reds	AB	R	H	RBI	BB	K	Avg
Pete Rose, lf	3	1	0	0	2	1	.174
Joe Morgan, 2b	5	1	2	1	0	0	.095
Bobby Tolan, cf	4	2	2	2	0	1	.292
Johnny Bench, c	2	2	1	1	2	0	.300
Tony Perez, 1b	3	0	1	1	1	0	.429
Hal McRae, rf	3	1	1	0	0	0	.444
Cesar Geronimo, rf	1	0	1	2	0	0	.188
Denis Menke, 3b	4	0	0	0	0	0	.100
Dave Concepcion, ss	3	1	2	1	0	1	.400
Gary Nolan, p	1	0	0	0	0	1	.000
Ross Grimsley, p	1	0	0	0	0	1	.000
Pedro Borbon, p	0	0	0	0	0	0	—
Tom Hall, p	2	0	0	0	0	1	.000
TOTALS	32	8	10	8	5	6	.240

	1	2	3	4	5	6	7	8	9		R	H	E
Athletics	0	0	0	0	1	0	0	0	0		1	7	1
Reds	0	0	1	1	1	5	0	x			8	10	0

E—Mangual. LOB—Athletics 7, Reds 6. Scoring Position—Athletics 0-for-4, Reds 4-for-13. 2B—Green (2), Morgan (1), McRae (1). 3B—Concepcion (1). HR—Bench (1). SF—Concepcion. SB—Tolan 2 (5), Concepcion (1). CS—Rose (1).

Athletics	IP	H	R	ER	BB	K	ERA
Vida Blue (L, 0-1)	5.2	4	3	3	2	4	4.15
Bob Locker	0.1	1	0	0	0	0	0.00
Dave Hamilton	0.2	3	4	4	1	1	27.00
Joe Horlen	1.1	2	1	1	2	1	6.75

Reds	IP	H	R	ER	BB	K	ERA
Gary Nolan	4.2	3	1	1	0	3	3.38
Ross Grimsley (W, 2-1)	1.0	0	0	0	1	0	2.70
Pedro Borbon (H, 2)	1.0	1	0	0	0	0	1.42
Tom Hall (S, 1)	2.1	2	0	0	0	1	0.00

WP—Horlen. Time—2:21. Attendance—52,737. Umpires—HP, Haller. 1B, Pelekoudas. 2B, Honochick. 3B, Steiner.

Game 7

Sunday, October 22

Athletics	AB	R	H	RBI	BB	K	Avg
Bert Campaneris, ss	4	1	2	0	0	0	.179
Angel Mangual, cf	4	1	0	0	0	0	.300
Joe Rudi, lf	3	0	0	0	1	0	.240
Gene Tenace, 1b	3	0	2	2	0	1	.348
Allan Lewis, pr	0	1	0	0	0	0	—
Mike Hegan, 1b	1	0	0	0	0	1	.200
Sal Bando, 3b	4	0	1	1	0	2	.269
Matty Alou, rf	3	0	0	0	1	0	.042
Dave Duncan, c	3	0	0	0	1	2	.200
Dick Green, 2b	4	0	1	0	0	2	.333
Blue Moon Odom, p	2	0	0	0	0	1	.000
Catfish Hunter, p	0	0	0	0	1	0	.200
Ken Holtzman, p	0	0	0	0	0	0	.000
Rollie Fingers, p	1	0	0	0	0	0	.000
TOTALS	32	3	6	3	4	9	.218

Reds	AB	R	H	RBI	BB	K	Avg
Pete Rose, lf	5	1	2	0	0	0	.214
Joe Morgan, 2b	3	0	1	0	1	0	.125
Bobby Tolan, cf	2	0	0	0	1	1	.269
George Foster, rf	0	0	0	0	0	0	—
Julian Javier, ph	0	0	0	0	0	0	.000
Joe Hague, ph-rf	1	0	0	0	0	0	.000
Johnny Bench, c	3	0	0	0	1	0	.261
Tony Perez, 1b	2	1	1	1	1	0	.435
Denis Menke, 3b	4	0	0	0	0	1	.083
Cesar Geronimo, rf-cf	3	0	0	0	1	1	.158
Dave Concepcion, ss	3	0	0	0	1	1	.308
Jack Billingham, p	1	0	0	0	0	1	.000
Hal McRae, ph	0	0	0	1	0	0	.444
Pedro Borbon, p	0	0	0	0	0	0	—
Clay Carroll, p	0	0	0	0	0	0	—
Ross Grimsley, p	0	0	0	0	0	0	.000
Ted Uhlaender, ph	1	0	0	0	0	0	.250
Tom Hall, p	0	0	0	0	0	0	.000
Darrel Chaney, ph	0	0	0	0	0	0	.000
TOTALS	28	2	4	2	6	5	.215

	1	2	3	4	5	6	7	8	9		R	H	E
Athletics	1	0	0	0	0	2	0	0	0		3	6	1
Reds	0	0	0	0	1	0	0	1	0		2	4	2

E—Campaneris, Concepcion, Tolan. DP—Athletics 1 (Campaneris to Tenace). LOB—Athletics 8, Reds 8. Scoring Position—Athletics 3-for-9, Reds 0-for-5. 2B—Tenace (1), Bando (1), Morgan (2), Perez (2). S—Campaneris, Mangual. SF—Perez, McRae. GDP—Morgan. SB—Bench (2). CS—Duncan (1), Morgan (1).

Athletics	IP	H	R	ER	BB	K	ERA
Blue Moon Odom	4.1	2	1	1	4	2	1.59
Catfish Hunter (W, 2-0)	2.2	1	1	1	1	3	2.81
Ken Holtzman	0.0	1	0	0	0	0	2.13
Rollie Fingers (S, 2)	2.0	0	0	0	1	0	1.74

Reds	IP	H	R	ER	BB	K	ERA
Jack Billingham	5.0	2	1	0	1	4	0.00
Pedro Borbon (L, 0-1)	0.2	3	2	2	0	0	3.86
Clay Carroll	1.0	0	0	0	2	1	1.59
Ross Grimsley	0.1	0	0	0	1	1	2.57
Tom Hall	2.0	1	0	0	0	3	0.00

Hunter pitched to one batter in the 8th. Holtzman pitched to one batter in the 8th.

WP—Hunter. HBP—Chaney by Fingers. Time—2:50. Attendance—56,040. Umpires—HP, Pelekoudas. 1B, Honochick. 2B, Steiner. 3B, Umont.

1972 World Series—Composite Statistics

Batting

Athletics	G	AB	R	H	RBI	2B	3B	HR	BB	SO	SB	CS	Avg	OBP	Slg
Matty Alou	7	24	0	1	0	0	0	0	3	0	1	0	.042	.148	.042
Sal Bando	7	26	2	7	1	1	0	0	2	5	0	0	.269	.321	.308
Vida Blue	4	1	0	0	0	0	0	0	2	1	0	0	.000	.667	.000
Bert Campaneris	7	28	1	5	0	0	0	0	1	4	0	1	.179	.207	.179
Dave Duncan	3	5	0	1	0	0	0	0	1	3	0	1	.200	.333	.200
Mike Epstein	6	16	1	0	0	0	0	0	5	3	0	0	.000	.238	.000
Rollie Fingers	6	1	0	0	0	0	0	0	0	0	0	0	.000	.000	.000
Dick Green	7	18	0	6	1	2	0	0	4	0	0	0	.333	.333	.444
Mike Hegan	6	5	0	1	0	0	0	0	0	2	0	0	.200	.200	.200
George Hendrick	5	15	3	2	0	0	0	0	1	2	0	0	.133	.188	.133
Ken Holtzman	3	5	0	0	0	0	0	0	0	0	0	0	.000	.000	.000
Catfish Hunter	3	5	0	1	1	0	0	0	2	1	0	0	.200	.429	.200
Ted Kubiak	4	3	0	1	0	0	0	0	0	0	0	0	.333	.333	.333
Allan Lewis	6	0	2	0	0	0	0	0	0	0	0	2	—	—	—
Angel Mangual	4	10	1	3	1	0	0	0	0	0	0	0	.300	.300	.300
Gonzalo Marquez	5	5	0	3	1	0	0	0	0	0	0	0	.600	.600	.600
Don Mincher	3	1	0	1	1	0	0	0	0	0	0	0	1.000	1.000	1.000
Blue Moon Odom	4	4	0	0	0	0	0	0	0	3	0	0	.000	.000	.000
Joe Rudi	7	25	1	6	1	0	0	1	2	5	0	0	.240	.321	.360
Gene Tenace	7	23	5	8	9	1	0	4	2	4	0	1	.348	.400	.913
Totals	**7**	**220**	**16**	**46**	**16**	**4**	**0**	**5**	**21**	**37**	**1**	**5**	**.209**	**.281**	**.295**

Reds	G	AB	R	H	RBI	2B	3B	HR	BB	SO	SB	CS	Avg	OBP	Slg
Johnny Bench	7	23	4	6	1	1	0	1	5	5	2	0	.261	.393	.435
Jack Billingham	3	5	0	0	0	0	0	0	0	4	0	0	.000	.000	.000
Darrel Chaney	4	7	0	0	0	0	0	0	2	2	0	0	.000	.300	.000
Dave Concepcion	6	13	2	4	2	0	1	0	2	2	1	1	.308	.375	.462
Cesar Geronimo	6	19	1	3	3	0	0	1	4	1	0		.158	.200	.158
Ross Grimsley	4	2	0	0	0	0	0	0	0	2	0	0	.000	.000	.000
Don Gullett	1	2	0	0	0	0	0	0	0	0	0	0	.000	.000	.000
Joe Hague	3	3	0	0	0	0	0	0	0	0	0	0	.000	.000	.000
Tom Hall	4	2	0	0	0	0	0	0	0	1	0	0	.000	.000	.000
Julian Javier	4	2	0	0	0	0	0	0	0	0	0	0	.000	.000	.000
Jim McGlothlin	1	1	0	0	0	0	0	0	0	0	0	0	.000	.000	.000
Hal McRae	5	9	1	4	2	1	0	0	0	1	0	0	.444	.400	.556
Denis Menke	7	24	1	2	2	0	0	1	2	6	0	0	.083	.154	.208
Joe Morgan	7	24	4	3	1	2	0	0	6	3	2	1	.125	.300	.208
Gary Nolan	2	3	0	0	0	0	0	0	0	3	0	0	.000	.000	.000
Tony Perez	7	23	3	10	2	2	0	0	4	4	0	1	.435	.500	.522
Pete Rose	7	28	3	6	2	0	0	1	4	4	1	1	.214	.313	.321
Bobby Tolan	7	26	2	7	6	1	0	0	1	4	5	1	.269	.296	.308
Ted Uhlaender	4	4	0	1	0	1	0	0	0	1	0	0	.250	.250	.500
Totals	**7**	**220**	**21**	**46**	**21**	**8**	**1**	**3**	**27**	**46**	**12**	**5**	**.209**	**.295**	**.295**

Pitching

Athletics	G	GS	CG	IP	H	R	ER	BB	SO	W-L	Sv-Op	Hld	ERA
Vida Blue	4	1	0	8.2	8	4	4	5	5	0-1	1-2	0	4.15
Rollie Fingers	6	0	0	10.1	4	2	2	4	11	1-1	2-2	1	1.74
Dave Hamilton	2	0	0	1.1	3	4	4	1	1	0-0	0-0	0	27.00
Ken Holtzman	3	2	0	12.2	11	3	3	3	4	1-0	0-0	0	2.13
Joe Horlen	1	0	0	1.1	2	1	1	2	1	0-0	0-0	0	6.75
Catfish Hunter	3	2	0	16.0	12	5	5	6	11	2-0	0-0	0	2.81
Bob Locker	1	0	0	0.1	1	0	0	0	0	0-0	0-0	0	0.00
Blue Moon Odom	2	2	0	11.1	5	2	2	6	13	0-1	0-0	0	1.59
Totals	**7**	**7**	**0**	**62.0**	**46**	**21**	**21**	**27**	**46**	**4-3**	**3-4**	**1**	**3.05**

Reds	G	GS	CG	IP	H	R	ER	BB	SO	W-L	Sv-Op	Hld	ERA
Jack Billingham	3	2	0	13.2	6	1	0	4	11	1-0	1-1	0	0.00
Pedro Borbon	6	0	0	7.0	7	3	3	2	4	0-1	0-0	2	3.86
Clay Carroll	5	0	0	5.2	6	1	1	4	3	0-1	1-2	0	1.59
Ross Grimsley	4	1	0	7.0	7	2	2	3	2	2-1	0-0	0	2.57
Don Gullett	1	1	0	7.0	5	1	1	2	4	0-0	0-0	0	1.29
Tom Hall	4	0	0	8.1	6	0	0	2	7	0-0	1-1	0	0.00
Jim McGlothlin	1	1	0	3.0	2	4	4	2	3	0-0	0-0	0	12.00
Gary Nolan	2	2	0	10.2	7	4	4	2	3	0-1	0-0	0	3.38
Totals	**7**	**7**	**0**	**62.1**	**46**	**16**	**15**	**21**	**37**	**3-4**	**3-4**	**2**	**2.17**

Fielding

Athletics	Pos	G	PO	Ast	E	DP	PB	FPct
Matty Alou	rf	7	11	1	1	1	—	.923
Sal Bando	3b	7	3	13	1	0	—	.941
Vida Blue	p	4	0	1	0	0	—	1.000
Bert Campaneris	ss	7	17	15	1	2	—	.970
Dave Duncan	c	1	5	1	0	0	0	1.000
Mike Epstein	1b	6	35	2	2	1	—	.949
Rollie Fingers	p	6	0	2	0	0	—	1.000
Dick Green	2b	7	12	13	0	2	—	1.000
Dave Hamilton	p	2	0	0	0	0	—	—
Mike Hegan	1b	5	11	1	0	1	—	1.000
George Hendrick	cf	5	12	0	0	0	—	1.000
Ken Holtzman	p	3	0	3	1	1	—	.750
Joe Horlen	p	1	1	0	0	0	—	1.000
Catfish Hunter	p	3	0	3	1	0	—	.750
Ted Kubiak	2b	4	4	3	0	0	—	1.000
Bob Locker	p	1	0	0	0	0	—	—
Angel Mangual	cf	3	6	0	1	0	—	.857
Blue Moon Odom	p	2	1	3	0	0	—	1.000
Joe Rudi	lf	7	20	0	0	0	—	1.000
Gene Tenace	c	6	45	4	1	1	0	.980
	1b	1	3	1	0	1	—	1.000
Totals		**7**	**186**	**66**	**9**	**10**	**0**	**.966**

Reds	Pos	G	PO	Ast	E	DP	PB	FPct
Johnny Bench	c	7	41	7	1	2	0	.980
Jack Billingham	p	3	1	1	0	0	—	1.000
Pedro Borbon	p	6	0	3	0	0	—	1.000
Clay Carroll	p	5	1	3	0	0	—	1.000
Darrel Chaney	ss	3	5	11	0	2	—	1.000
Dave Concepcion	ss	5	4	11	1	1	—	.938
George Foster	rf	1	0	0	0	0	—	—
Cesar Geronimo	rf	6	8	0	0	0	—	1.000
	cf	1	1	0	0	0	—	1.000
Ross Grimsley	p	4	0	2	0	0	—	1.000
Don Gullett	p	1	0	1	0	0	—	1.000
Joe Hague	rf	1	0	0	0	0	—	—
Tom Hall	p	4	0	2	0	0	—	1.000
Jim McGlothlin	p	1	0	1	0	0	—	1.000
Hal McRae	rf	2	4	0	0	0	—	1.000
Denis Menke	3b	7	6	23	0	0	—	1.000
Joe Morgan	2b	7	18	18	1	3	—	.973
Gary Nolan	p	2	0	2	0	0	—	1.000
Tony Perez	1b	7	73	3	1	3	—	.987
Pete Rose	lf	7	14	1	0	0	—	1.000
Bobby Tolan	cf	7	11	0	1	0	—	.917
Totals		**7**	**187**	**89**	**5**	**11**	**0**	**.982**

1973 Oakland Athletics (AL) 4, New York Mets (NL) 3

The Oakland A's triumphed over the New York Mets in a seven-game Series in which there was never a dull moment. In Game 1, Felix Millan's error helped the A's score two in the bottom of the third. Rollie Fingers and Darold Knowles combined to throw four innings of shutout relief to give Oakland a 2-1 victory. The Mets won the second game 10-7 in 12 innings. Willie Mays drove in the go-ahead run with an RBI single in the top of the 12th, and two consecutive errors by second baseman Mike Andrews allowed three more runs to cross the plate. The next day, Oakland owner Charlie Finley forced Andrews to sign a false affidavit stating that he was injured, but Commissioner Bowie Kuhn ordered Andrews reinstated. The same day, Oakland manager Dick Williams announced he was resigning at the conclusion of the Series. Oakland won the third game, 3-2, on an RBI single by Bert Campaneris in the top of the 11th. Rusty Staub homered and notched four hits in Game 4 as Jon Matlack beat Oakland, 6-1. The next day, Jerry Koosman and Tug McGraw combined to blank the A's, 2-0. Catfish Hunter won Game 6, 3-1, to force a seventh game. The A's took the final contest, 5-2, with two-run homers from Campaneris and Reggie Jackson.

Game 1
Saturday, October 13

Mets	AB	R	H	RBI	BB	K	Avg
Wayne Garrett, 3b	5	0	0	0	0	0	.000
Felix Millan, 2b	4	0	1	0	0	0	.250
Willie Mays, cf	4	0	1	0	0	1	.250
Cleon Jones, lf	4	1	2	0	0	0	.500
John Milner, 1b	4	0	2	1	0	0	.500
Jerry Grote, c	4	0	0	0	0	0	.000
Don Hahn, rf	2	0	0	0	1	2	.000
Ed Kranepool, ph	1	0	0	0	0	0	.000
Bud Harrelson, ss	2	0	0	0	1	2	.000
Ron Hodges, ph	0	0	0	0	1	0	—
Ted Martinez, pr	0	0	0	0	0	0	—
Jon Matlack, p	0	0	0	0	1	0	—
Ken Boswell, ph	1	0	1	0	0	0	1.000
Tug McGraw, p	0	0	0	0	0	0	—
Rusty Staub, ph	0	0	0	0	0	0	—
Jim Beauchamp, ph	1	0	0	0	0	0	.000
TOTALS	32	1	7	1	4	5	.219

Athletics	AB	R	H	RBI	BB	K	Avg
Bert Campaneris, ss	4	1	1	0	0	1	.250
Joe Rudi, lf	3	0	1	1	0	0	.333
Sal Bando, 3b	3	0	1	0	1	0	.333
Reggie Jackson, cf-rf	3	0	0	0	1	0	.000
Gene Tenace, 1b	3	0	0	0	0	1	.000
Jesus Alou, rf	3	0	0	0	0	0	.000
Vic Davalillo, cf	0	0	0	0	0	0	—
Ray Fosse, c	3	0	0	0	0	0	.000
Dick Green, 2b	2	0	0	0	1	1	.000
Ken Holtzman, p	1	1	1	0	0	0	1.000
Angel Mangual, ph	1	0	0	0	0	0	.000
Rollie Fingers, p	1	0	0	0	0	1	.000
Darold Knowles, p	0	0	0	0	0	0	—
TOTALS	27	2	4	1	3	4	.148

	1	2	3	4	5	6	7	8	9		R	H	E
Mets	0	0	0	1	0	0	0	0	0		1	7	2
Athletics	0	0	2	0	0	0	0	0	x		2	4	0

E—Millan, Mays. DP—Athletics 2 (Holtzman to Tenace; Green to Campaneris to Tenace). LOB—Mets 9, Athletics 5. Scoring Position—Mets 1-for-9, Athletics 1-for-4. 2B—Jones (1), Holtzman (1). 3B—Millan (1). S—Matlack, Rudi. GDP—Garrett. SB—Campaneris (1). CS—Green (1).

Mets	IP	H	R	ER	BB	K	ERA
Jon Matlack (L, 0-1)	6.0	3	2	0	2	3	0.00
Tug McGraw	2.0	1	0	0	1	1	0.00

Athletics	IP	H	R	ER	BB	K	ERA
Ken Holtzman (W, 1-0)	5.0	4	1	1	3	2	1.80
Rollie Fingers (H, 1)	3.1	3	0	0	1	3	0.00
Darold Knowles (S, 1)	0.2	0	0	0	0	0	0.00

PB—Fosse. Time—2:26. Attendance—46,021. Umpires—HP, Springstead. 1B, Donatelli. 2B, Neudecker. 3B, Pryor.

Game 2
Sunday, October 14

Mets	AB	R	H	RBI	BB	K	Avg
Wayne Garrett, 3b	6	1	1	1	1	4	.091
Felix Millan, 2b	6	0	0	0	1	1	.100
Rusty Staub, rf	5	0	1	0	0	1	.200
Willie Mays, pr-cf	2	1	1	1	0	0	.333
Cleon Jones, lf	5	3	3	1	1	0	.556
John Milner, 1b	6	1	2	0	1	1	.400
Jerry Grote, c	6	1	2	0	0	0	.200
Don Hahn, cf-rf	7	1	1	1	0	1	.111
Bud Harrelson, ss	6	1	3	1	0	1	.375
Jerry Koosman, p	1	0	0	0	0	0	.000
Ray Sadecki, p	0	0	0	0	0	0	—
George Theodore, ph	1	0	0	0	0	0	.000
Harry Parker, p	0	0	0	0	0	0	—
Ed Kranepool, ph	0	0	0	0	0	0	.000
Jim Beauchamp, ph	1	0	0	0	0	0	.000
Tug McGraw, p	2	1	1	0	0	1	.500
George Stone, p	0	0	0	0	0	0	—
TOTALS	54	10	15	5	4	10	.247

Athletics	AB	R	H	RBI	BB	K	Avg
Bert Campaneris, ss	6	2	1	0	0	2	.200
Joe Rudi, lf	5	1	2	1	1	1	.375
Sal Bando, 3b	5	2	1	1	1	3	.250
Reggie Jackson, cf	6	1	4	2	0	1	.444
Gene Tenace, 1b	3	0	1	1	3	1	.167
Jesus Alou, rf	6	0	3	2	0	0	.333
Ray Fosse, c	5	0	0	0	1	1	.000
Dick Green, 2b	2	0	0	0	0	2	.000
Angel Mangual, ph	1	0	0	0	0	1	.000
Ted Kubiak, 2b	0	0	0	0	0	0	—
Mike Andrews, ph-2b	2	0	0	0	1	1	.000
Vida Blue, p	2	0	0	0	0	2	.000
Horacio Pina, p	0	0	0	0	0	0	—
Darold Knowles, p	0	0	0	0	0	0	—
Billy Conigliaro, ph	1	0	0	0	0	0	.000
Blue Moon Odom, p	0	0	0	0	0	0	—
Deron Johnson, ph	1	0	1	0	0	0	1.000
Allan Lewis, pr	0	1	0	0	0	0	—
Rollie Fingers, p	1	0	0	0	0	0	.000
Paul Lindblad, p	0	0	0	0	0	0	—
Vic Davalillo, ph	1	0	0	0	0	0	.000
TOTALS	47	7	13	7	7	15	.219

	1	2	3	4	5	6	7	8	9	10	11	12	R	H	E
Mets	0	1	1	0	0	4	0	0	0	0	0	4	10	15	1
Athletics	2	1	0	0	0	0	1	0	2	0	0	1	7	13	5

E—Bando, Tenace, Knowles, Koosman, Andrews 2. DP—Mets 1 (Garrett to Millan to Milner), Athletics 1 (Rudi to Fosse). LOB—Mets 15, Athletics 12. Scoring Position—Mets 5-for-21, Athletics 7-for-19. 2B—Harrelson (1), Rudi (1), Jackson (1), Alou (1), Johnson (1). 3B—Campaneris (1), Bando (1), Jackson (1). HR—Garrett (1), Jones (1). S—McGraw. GDP—Tenace. SB—Campaneris (2). CS—Rudi (1), Tenace (1).

Mets	IP	H	R	ER	BB	K	ERA
Jerry Koosman	2.1	6	3	3	3	4	11.57
Ray Sadecki	1.2	0	0	0	0	3	0.00
Harry Parker	1.0	1	0	0	0	0	0.00
Tug McGraw (BS, 1; W, 1-0)	6.0	5	4	4	3	8	4.50
George Stone (S, 1)	1.0	1	0	0	1	0	0.00

Athletics	IP	H	R	ER	BB	K	ERA
Vida Blue	5.1	4	4	4	2	4	6.75
Horacio Pina (BS, 1)	0.0	2	2	0	0	0	0.00
Darold Knowles	1.2	1	0	0	2	2	0.00
Blue Moon Odom	2.0	0	0	0	0	0	0.00
Rollie Fingers (L, 0-1)	2.2	6	4	1	0	2	1.50
Paul Lindblad	0.1	0	0	0	0	0	0.00

Pina pitched to three batters in the 6th. McGraw pitched to two batters in the 12th.

HBP—Grote by Pina, Jones by Fingers, Campaneris by McGraw. Time—4:13. Attendance—49,151. Umpires—HP, Donatelli. 1B, Neudecker. 2B, Pryor. 3B, Goetz.

Game 3
Tuesday, October 16

Athletics	AB	R	H	RBI	BB	K	Avg
Bert Campaneris, ss	6	1	3	1	0	1	.313
Joe Rudi, lf	5	0	2	1	0	0	.385
Sal Bando, 3b	4	1	2	0	0	1	.333
Reggie Jackson, rf	5	0	0	0	0	3	.286
Gene Tenace, 1b-c	3	0	1	1	2	2	.222
Vic Davalillo, cf-1b	5	0	1	0	0	1	.167
Ray Fosse, c	2	0	0	0	0	1	.000
Pat Bourque, ph-1b	2	0	1	0	0	0	.500
Allan Lewis, pr	0	0	0	0	0	0	—
Paul Lindblad, p	1	0	0	0	0	0	.000
Rollie Fingers, p	0	0	0	0	0	0	.000
Dick Green, 2b	2	0	0	0	0	1	.000
Jesus Alou, ph	1	0	0	0	0	0	.300
Ted Kubiak, 2b	1	1	0	0	1	0	.000
Catfish Hunter, p	2	0	0	0	0	1	.000
Deron Johnson, ph	1	0	0	0	0	1	.500
Darold Knowles, p	0	0	0	0	0	0	—
Angel Mangual, ph-cf	2	0	0	0	0	2	.000
TOTALS	42	3	10	3	3	14	.236

Mets	AB	R	H	RBI	BB	K	Avg
Wayne Garrett, 3b	4	1	2	1	2	1	.200
Felix Millan, 2b	5	1	2	0	0	0	.200
Rusty Staub, rf	6	0	2	0	0	0	.273
Cleon Jones, lf	5	0	0	0	1	1	.357
John Milner, 1b	3	0	1	0	2	0	.385
Jerry Grote, c	5	0	0	0	0	1	.133
Don Hahn, cf	5	0	1	0	0	0	.143
Bud Harrelson, ss	5	0	2	0	0	0	.385
Tom Seaver, p	3	0	0	0	0	2	.000
Jim Beauchamp, ph	1	0	0	0	0	0	.000
Ray Sadecki, p	0	0	0	0	0	0	—
Tug McGraw, p	0	0	0	0	0	0	.500
Willie Mays, ph	1	0	0	0	0	0	.286
Harry Parker, p	0	0	0	0	0	0	—
TOTALS	43	2	10	1	5	5	.248

	1	2	3	4	5	6	7	8	9	10	11	R	H	E
Athletics	0	0	0	0	0	1	0	1	0	0	1	3	10	1
Mets	2	0	0	0	0	0	0	0	0	0	0	2	10	2

E—Hunter, Millan 2. LOB—Athletics 10, Mets 14. Scoring Position—Athletics 3-for-15, Mets 1-for-11. 2B—Rudi (2), Bando (1), Tenace (1), Staub (1), Hahn (1). HR—Garrett (2). S—Bando, Millan. SB—Campaneris (3).

Athletics	IP	H	R	ER	BB	K	ERA
Catfish Hunter	6.0	7	2	2	3	5	3.00
Darold Knowles	2.0	0	0	0	1	0	0.00
Paul Lindblad (W, 1-0)	2.0	3	0	0	1	0	0.00
Rollie Fingers (S, 1)	1.0	0	0	0	0	0	1.29

Mets	IP	H	R	ER	BB	K	ERA
Tom Seaver	8.0	7	2	2	1	12	2.25
Ray Sadecki	0.0	1	0	0	0	0	0.00
Tug McGraw	2.0	1	0	0	1	1	3.60
Harry Parker (L, 0-1)	1.0	1	1	0	1	1	0.00

Sadecki pitched to two batters in the 9th. Lindblad pitched to one batter in the 11th.

WP—Hunter. PB—Grote. Time—3:15. Attendance—54,817. Umpires—HP, Neudecker. 1B, Pryor. 2B, Goetz. 3B, Wendelstedt.

Game 4
Wednesday, October 17

Athletics	AB	R	H	RBI	BB	K	Avg
Bert Campaneris, ss	4	0	0	0	0	1	.250
Joe Rudi, lf	4	0	1	0	0	1	.353
Sal Bando, 3b	3	1	0	0	1	0	.267
Reggie Jackson, cf	4	0	1	0	0	1	.278
Gene Tenace, 1b	3	0	1	1	1	0	.250
Jesus Alou, rf	4	0	0	0	0	0	.214
Ray Fosse, c	4	0	1	0	0	2	.071
Dick Green, 2b	1	0	0	0	0	1	.000
Angel Mangual, ph	1	0	0	0	0	0	.000
Ted Kubiak, 2b	1	0	0	0	0	0	.000
Deron Johnson, ph	1	0	1	0	0	0	.667
Ken Holtzman, p	0	0	0	0	0	0	1.000
Blue Moon Odom, p	1	0	0	0	0	1	.000
Darold Knowles, p	0	0	0	0	0	0	—
Billy Conigliaro, ph	1	0	0	0	0	0	.000
Horacio Pina, p	0	0	0	0	0	0	—
Mike Andrews, ph	1	0	0	0	0	0	.000
Paul Lindblad, p	0	0	0	0	0	0	.000
Vic Davalillo, ph	0	0	0	0	0	0	.167
TOTALS	33	1	5	1	3	7	.220

Mets	AB	R	H	RBI	BB	K	Avg
Wayne Garrett, 3b	4	2	1	0	0	1	.211
Felix Millan, 2b	5	1	1	0	0	0	.200
Rusty Staub, rf	4	1	4	5	1	0	.467
Cleon Jones, lf	3	0	1	0	1	0	.353
George Theodore, lf	1	0	0	0	0	0	.000
John Milner, 1b	3	0	0	0	1	0	.313
Jerry Grote, c	4	0	3	0	0	0	.263
Don Hahn, cf	4	1	1	0	0	0	.167
Bud Harrelson, ss	2	1	1	0	2	0	.400
Jon Matlack, p	3	0	1	0	1	1	.333
Ray Sadecki, p	0	0	0	0	0	0	—
TOTALS	33	6	13	5	6	2	.285

	1	2	3	4	5	6	7	8	9		R	H	E
Athletics	0	0	0	1	0	0	0	0	0		1	5	1
Mets	3	0	0	3	0	0	0	0	x		6	13	1

E—Garrett, Green. DP—Athletics 4 (Bando to Green to Tenace; Green to Campaneris to Tenace; Knowles to Fosse to Tenace; Kubiak to Tenace). LOB—Athletics 9, Mets 10. Scoring Position—Athletics 0-for-5, Mets 3-for-12. HR—Staub (1). GDP—Milner, Grote, Hahn, Matlack.

Athletics	IP	H	R	ER	BB	K	ERA
Ken Holtzman (L, 1-1)	0.1	4	3	3	1	0	6.75
Blue Moon Odom	2.2	3	2	2	2	0	3.86
Darold Knowles	1.0	1	1	0	1	1	0.00
Horacio Pina	3.0	4	0	0	2	0	0.00
Paul Lindblad	1.0	1	0	0	0	1	0.00

Mets	IP	H	R	ER	BB	K	ERA
Jon Matlack (W, 1-1)	8.0	3	1	0	2	5	0.00
Ray Sadecki (S, 1)	1.0	2	0	0	1	2	0.00

Odom pitched to two batters in the 4th.

WP—Odom. HBP—Campaneris by Matlack, Garrett by Knowles. Time—2:41. Attendance—54,817. Umpires—HP, Pryor. 1B, Goetz. 2B, Wendelstedt. 3B, Springstead.

Game 5
Thursday, October 18

Athletics	AB	R	H	RBI	BB	K	Avg
Bert Campaneris, ss	3	0	1	0	1	1	.261
Joe Rudi, lf	4	0	0	0	0	0	.286
Sal Bando, 3b	3	0	1	0	1	0	.278
Reggie Jackson, cf	3	0	0	0	1	1	.238
Gene Tenace, 1b	1	0	0	0	3	1	.231
Blue Moon Odom, pr	0	0	0	0	0	0	.000
Pat Bourque, 1b	0	0	0	0	0	0	.500
Jesus Alou, rf	4	0	0	0	0	0	.167
Ray Fosse, c	4	0	1	0	0	0	.111
Dick Green, 2b	2	0	0	0	0	0	.000
Deron Johnson, ph	0	0	0	0	1	0	.667
Allan Lewis, pr	0	0	0	0	0	0	—
Ted Kubiak, 2b	1	0	0	0	0	1	.000
Vida Blue, p	2	0	0	0	0	2	.000
Darold Knowles, p	0	0	0	0	0	0	—
Angel Mangual, ph	1	0	0	0	0	0	.000
Rollie Fingers, p	0	0	0	0	0	0	.000
Billy Conigliaro, ph	1	0	0	0	0	1	.000
TOTALS	29	0	3	0	7	7	.200

Mets	AB	R	H	RBI	BB	K	Avg
Wayne Garrett, 3b	3	0	0	0	1	2	.182
Felix Millan, 2b	4	0	0	0	0	0	.167
Rusty Staub, rf	3	0	1	0	1	0	.444
Cleon Jones, lf	4	1	2	0	0	0	.381
John Milner, 1b	4	0	2	1	0	0	.350
Jerry Grote, c	3	1	1	0	0	0	.273
Don Hahn, cf	4	0	1	0	0	1	.182
Bud Harrelson, ss	2	0	0	0	2	0	.353
Jerry Koosman, p	3	0	0	0	0	3	.000
Tug McGraw, p	1	0	0	0	0	0	.333
TOTALS	31	2	7	2	4	6	.277

	1	2	3	4	5	6	7	8	9		R	H	E
Athletics	0	0	0	0	0	0	0	0	0		0	3	1
Mets	0	1	0	0	0	1	0	0	x		2	7	1

E—Campaneris, Garrett. DP—Mets 1 (Millan to Harrelson to Milner). LOB—Athletics 9, Mets 10. Scoring Position—Athletics 0-for-4, Mets 1-for-10. 2B—Fosse (1), Jones (2). 3B—Hahn (1). S—Grote. GDP—Jackson.

Athletics	IP	H	R	ER	BB	K	ERA
Vida Blue (L, 0-1)	5.2	6	2	2	1	4	4.91
Darold Knowles	0.1	0	0	0	1	1	0.00
Rollie Fingers	2.0	1	0	0	2	1	1.00

Mets	IP	H	R	ER	BB	K	ERA
Jerry Koosman (W, 1-0)	6.1	3	0	0	4	4	3.12
Tug McGraw (S, 1)	2.2	0	0	0	3	3	2.84

WP—Blue. Time—2:39. Attendance—54,817. Umpires—HP, Goetz. 1B, Wendelstedt. 2B, Springstead. 3B, Donatelli.

Game 6
Saturday, October 20

Mets	AB	R	H	RBI	BB	K	Avg
Wayne Garrett, 3b	3	0	1	0	1	0	.200
Felix Millan, 2b	4	0	1	1	0	0	.179
Rusty Staub, rf	4	0	1	0	0	1	.409
Cleon Jones, lf	4	0	0	0	0	0	.320
John Milner, 1b	4	0	1	0	0	0	.333
Jerry Grote, c	4	0	1	0	0	0	.269
Don Hahn, cf	3	0	0	0	0	1	.160
Ed Kranepool, ph	1	0	0	0	0	0	.000
Bud Harrelson, ss	3	0	0	0	0	0	.300
Tom Seaver, p	2	0	0	0	0	0	.000
Ken Boswell, ph	1	1	1	0	0	0	1.000
Tug McGraw, p	0	0	0	0	0	0	.333
TOTALS	33	1	6	1	1	2	.266

Athletics	AB	R	H	RBI	BB	K	Avg
Bert Campaneris, ss	4	0	0	0	0	1	.222
Joe Rudi, lf	3	1	1	0	1	1	.292
Sal Bando, 3b	4	1	1	0	0	0	.273
Reggie Jackson, rf-cf	4	1	3	2	0	0	.320
Gene Tenace, c-1b	3	0	0	0	1	1	.188
Vic Davalillo, cf	2	0	0	0	1	0	.125
Jesus Alou, ph-rf	0	0	0	1	0	0	.167
Deron Johnson, 1b	4	0	1	0	0	1	.429
Ray Fosse, c	0	0	0	0	0	0	.111
Dick Green, 2b	3	0	1	0	0	0	.083
Catfish Hunter, p	3	0	0	0	0	2	.000
Darold Knowles, p	0	0	0	0	0	0	—
Rollie Fingers, p	0	0	0	0	0	0	.000
TOTALS	30	3	7	3	3	7	.217

	1	2	3	4	5	6	7	8	9		R	H	E
Mets	0	0	0	0	0	0	0	1	0		1	6	2
Athletics	1	0	1	0	0	0	0	1	x		3	7	0

E—Garrett, Hahn. DP—Mets 1 (Grote to Millan). LOB—Mets 6, Athletics 7. Scoring Position—Mets 1-for-5, Athletics 0-for-5. 2B—Jackson 2 (3). SF—Alou. CS—Tenace (2).

Mets	IP	H	R	ER	BB	K	ERA
Tom Seaver (L, 0-1)	7.0	6	2	2	2	6	2.40
Tug McGraw	1.0	1	1	0	1	1	2.63

Athletics	IP	H	R	ER	BB	K	ERA
Catfish Hunter (W, 1-0)	7.1	4	1	1	1	1	2.03
Darold Knowles (H, 1)	0.1	2	0	0	0	0	0.00
Rollie Fingers (S, 2)	1.1	0	0	0	0	0	0.87

WP—Seaver. Time—2:07. Attendance—49,333. Umpires—HP, Wendelstedt. 1B, Springstead. 2B, Donatelli. 3B, Neudecker.

Game 7
Sunday, October 21

Mets	AB	R	H	RBI	BB	K	Avg
Wayne Garrett, 3b	5	0	0	0	0	3	.167
Felix Millan, 2b	4	1	1	0	0	0	.188
Rusty Staub, rf	4	0	2	1	0	0	.423
Cleon Jones, lf	3	0	0	0	1	1	.286
John Milner, 1b	3	1	0	1	0	0	.296
Jerry Grote, c	4	0	1	0	0	0	.267
Don Hahn, cf	4	3	0	0	0	1	.241
Bud Harrelson, ss	4	0	0	0	0	0	.250
Jon Matlack, p	1	0	0	0	0	0	.250
Harry Parker, p	0	0	0	0	0	0	—
Jim Beauchamp, ph	1	0	0	0	0	1	.000
Ray Sadecki, p	0	0	0	0	0	0	—
Ken Boswell, ph	1	0	1	0	0	0	1.000
George Stone, p	0	0	0	0	0	0	—
Ed Kranepool, ph	1	0	0	0	0	0	.000
Ted Martinez, pr	0	0	0	0	0	0	—
TOTALS	35	2	8	1	2	6	.263

Athletics	AB	R	H	RBI	BB	K	Avg
Bert Campaneris, ss	4	2	3	2	0	0	.290
Joe Rudi, lf	3	1	2	1	1	1	.333
Sal Bando, 3b	4	0	0	0	0	2	.231
Reggie Jackson, cf-rf	4	1	1	2	0	1	.310
Gene Tenace, c-1b	3	0	0	0	1	1	.158
Jesus Alou, rf	1	0	0	0	0	0	.158
Vic Davalillo, ph-cf	3	0	0	0	0	0	.091
Deron Johnson, 1b	3	0	0	0	0	2	.300
Ray Fosse, c	1	0	1	0	0	0	.158
Dick Green, 2b	4	0	0	0	0	1	.063
Ken Holtzman, p	2	1	1	0	0	0	.667
Rollie Fingers, p	1	0	1	0	0	0	.333
Darold Knowles, p	0	0	0	0	0	0	—
TOTALS	33	5	9	5	2	8	.235

	1	2	3	4	5	6	7	8	9		R	H	E
Mets	0	0	0	0	0	1	0	0	1		2	8	1
Athletics	0	0	4	0	1	0	0	0	x		5	9	1

E—Tenace, Jones. DP—Athletics 1 (Bando to Campaneris to Green). LOB—Mets 8, Athletics 6. Scoring Position—Mets 1-for-8, Athletics 2-for-5. 2B—Millan (1), Staub (2), Holtzman (2). HR—Campaneris (1), Jackson (1). GDP—Matlack.

Mets	IP	H	R	ER	BB	K	ERA
Jon Matlack (L, 1-2)	2.2	4	4	4	1	3	2.16
Harry Parker	1.1	0	0	0	1	1	0.00
Ray Sadecki	2.0	2	1	1	0	1	1.93
George Stone	2.0	3	0	0	0	3	0.00

Athletics	IP	H	R	ER	BB	K	ERA
Ken Holtzman (W, 2-1)	5.1	5	1	1	1	4	4.22
Rollie Fingers	3.1	3	1	0	1	2	0.66
Darold Knowles (S, 2)	0.1	0	0	0	0	0	0.00

Time—2:37. Attendance—49,333. Umpires—HP, Springstead. 1B, Donatelli. 2B, Neudecker. 3B, Pryor.

1973 World Series—Composite Statistics

Batting

Athletics	G	AB	R	H	RBI	2B	3B	HR	BB	SO	SB	CS	Avg	OBP	Slg
Jesus Alou	7	19	0	3	3	1	0	0	0	0	0	0	.158	.150	.211
Mike Andrews	2	3	0	0	0	0	0	0	1	1	0	0	.000	.250	.000
Sal Bando	7	26	5	6	1	1	1	0	4	7	0	0	.231	.333	.346
Vida Blue	2	4	0	0	0	0	0	0	0	4	0	0	.000	.000	.000
Pat Bourque	2	2	0	1	0	0	0	0	0	0	0	0	.500	.500	.500
Bert Campaneris	7	31	6	9	3	0	1	1	1	7	3	0	.290	.353	.452
Billy Conigliaro	3	3	0	0	0	0	0	0	0	0	0	0	.000	.000	.000
Vic Davalillo	6	11	0	1	0	0	0	0	2	1	0	0	.091	.231	.091
Rollie Fingers	6	3	0	1	0	0	0	0	0	1	0	0	.333	.333	.333
Ray Fosse	7	19	0	3	0	1	0	0	1	4	0	0	.158	.200	.211
Dick Green	7	16	0	1	0	0	0	0	1	6	0	1	.063	.118	.063
Ken Holtzman	3	3	2	2	0	2	0	0	0	0	0	0	.667	.667	1.333
Catfish Hunter	2	5	0	0	0	0	0	0	0	3	0	0	.000	.000	.000
Reggie Jackson	7	29	3	9	6	3	1	1	2	7	0	0	.310	.355	.586
Deron Johnson	6	10	0	3	0	1	0	0	1	4	0	0	.300	.364	.400
Ted Kubiak	4	3	1	0	0	0	0	0	1	1	0	0	.000	.250	.000
Allan Lewis	3	0	1	0	0	0	0	0	0	0	0	0	—	—	—
Paul Lindblad	3	1	0	0	0	0	0	0	0	0	0	0	.000	.000	.000
Angel Mangual	5	6	0	0	0	0	0	0	0	3	0	0	.000	.000	.000
Blue Moon Odom	3	1	0	0	0	0	0	0	0	1	0	0	.000	.000	.000
Joe Rudi	7	27	3	9	4	2	0	0	3	4	0	1	.333	.400	.407
Gene Tenace	7	19	0	3	3	1	0	0	11	7	0	2	.158	.467	.211
Totals	7	241	21	51	20	12	3	2	28	62	3	4	.212	.298	.311

Batting

Mets	G	AB	R	H	RBI	2B	3B	HR	BB	SO	SB	CS	Avg	OBP	Slg
Jim Beauchamp	4	4	0	0	0	0	0	0	0	1	0	0	.000	.000	.000
Ken Boswell	3	3	1	3	0	0	0	0	0	0	0	0	1.000	1.000	1.000
Wayne Garrett	7	30	4	5	2	0	0	2	5	11	0	0	.167	.306	.367
Jerry Grote	7	30	2	8	0	0	0	0	1	0	0	0	.267	.290	.267
Don Hahn	7	29	2	7	2	1	1	0	1	6	0	0	.241	.267	.345
Bud Harrelson	7	24	2	6	1	1	0	0	5	3	0	0	.250	.379	.292
Ron Hodges	1	0	0	0	0	0	0	0	1	0	0	0	—	1.000	
Cleon Jones	7	28	5	8	1	2	0	1	4	2	0	0	.286	.394	.464
Jerry Koosman	2	4	0	0	0	0	0	0	0	3	0	0	.000	.000	.000
Ed Kranepool	4	3	0	0	0	0	0	0	0	0	0	0	.000	.000	.000
Ted Martinez	2	0	0	0	0	0	0	0	0	0	0	0	—	—	—
Jon Matlack	3	4	0	1	0	0	0	0	2	1	0	0	.250	.500	.250
Willie Mays	3	7	1	2	1	0	0	0	1	0	0	0	.286	.286	.286
Tug McGraw	5	3	1	1	0	0	0	0	0	1	0	0	.333	.333	.333
Felix Millan	7	32	3	6	1	1	1	0	1	1	0	0	.188	.212	.281
John Milner	7	27	2	8	2	0	0	0	5	1	0	0	.296	.406	.296
Tom Seaver	2	5	0	0	0	0	0	0	0	2	0	0	.000	.000	.000
Rusty Staub	7	26	1	11	6	2	0	1	2	2	0	0	.423	.464	.615
George Theodore	2	2	0	0	0	0	0	0	0	0	0	0	.000	.000	.000
Totals	7	261	24	66	16	7	2	4	26	36	0	0	.253	.328	.341

Pitching

Athletics	G	GS	CG	IP	H	R	ER	BB	SO	W-L	Sv-Op	Hld	ERA
Vida Blue	2	2	0	11.0	10	6	6	3	8	0-1	0-0	0	4.91
Rollie Fingers	6	0	0	13.2	13	5	1	4	8	0-1	2-2	1	0.66
Ken Holtzman	3	3	0	10.2	13	5	5	5	6	2-1	0-0	0	4.22
Catfish Hunter	2	2	0	13.1	11	3	3	4	6	1-0	0-0	0	2.03
Darold Knowles	7	0	0	6.1	4	1	0	5	5	0-0	2-2	1	0.00
Paul Lindblad	3	0	0	3.1	4	0	0	1	1	1-0	0-0	0	0.00
Blue Moon Odom	2	0	0	4.2	5	2	2	2	2	0-0	0-0	0	3.86
Horacio Pina	2	0	0	3.0	6	2	0	2	0	0-0	0-1	0	0.00
Totals	7	7	0	66.0	66	24	17	26	36	4-3	4-5	2	2.32

Pitching

Mets	G	GS	CG	IP	H	R	ER	BB	SO	W-L	Sv-Op	Hld	ERA
Jerry Koosman	2	2	0	8.2	9	3	3	7	8	1-0	0-0	0	3.12
Jon Matlack	3	3	0	16.2	10	7	4	5	11	1-2	0-0	0	2.16
Tug McGraw	5	0	0	13.2	8	5	4	9	14	1-0	1-2	0	2.63
Harry Parker	3	0	0	3.1	2	1	0	2	2	0-1	0-0	0	0.00
Ray Sadecki	4	0	0	4.2	5	1	1	1	6	0-0	1-1	0	1.93
Tom Seaver	2	2	0	15.0	13	4	4	3	18	0-1	0-0	0	2.40
George Stone	2	0	0	3.0	4	0	0	1	3	0-0	1-1	0	0.00
Totals	7	7	0	65.0	51	21	16	28	62	3-4	3-4	0	2.22

Fielding

Athletics	Pos	G	PO	Ast	E	DP	PB	FPct
Jesus Alou	rf	6	5	0	0	0	—	1.000
Mike Andrews	2b	1	1	0	2	0	—	.333
Sal Bando	3b	7	6	14	1	2	—	.952
Vida Blue	p	2	2	1	0	0	—	1.000
Pat Bourque	1b	2	3	1	0	0	—	1.000
Bert Campaneris	ss	7	10	28	1	3	—	.974
Vic Davalillo	cf	4	12	0	0	0	—	1.000
	1b	1	5	0	0	0	—	1.000
Rollie Fingers	p	6	0	2	0	0	—	1.000
Ray Fosse	c	7	32	3	0	2	1	1.000
Dick Green	2b	7	14	11	1	4	—	.962
Ken Holtzman	p	3	1	3	0	1	—	1.000
Catfish Hunter	p	2	1	2	1	0	—	.750
Reggie Jackson	cf	6	10	0	0	0	—	1.000
	rf	4	5	0	0	0	—	1.000
Deron Johnson	1b	2	8	1	0	0	—	1.000
Darold Knowles	p	7	0	1	1	1	—	.500
Ted Kubiak	2b	4	5	7	0	1	—	1.000
Paul Lindblad	p	3	0	0	0	0	—	—
Angel Mangual	cf	1	1	0	0	0	—	1.000
Blue Moon Odom	p	2	0	1	0	0	—	1.000
Horacio Pina	p	2	0	0	0	0	—	—
Joe Rudi	lf	7	20	2	0	1	—	1.000
Gene Tenace	1b	7	51	2	2	6	—	.964
	c	3	6	0	0	0	0	1.000
Totals		7	198	79	9	21	1	.969

Fielding

Mets	Pos	G	PO	Ast	E	DP	PB	FPct
Wayne Garrett	3b	7	4	19	3	1	—	.885
Jerry Grote	c	7	67	5	0	1	1	1.000
Don Hahn	cf	6	13	1	1	0	—	.933
	rf	2	0	0	0	0	—	—
Bud Harrelson	ss	7	11	24	0	1	—	1.000
Cleon Jones	lf	7	11	1	1	0	—	.923
Jerry Koosman	p	2	0	1	1	0	—	.500
Jon Matlack	p	3	0	1	0	0	—	1.000
Willie Mays	cf	2	1	0	1	0	—	.500
Tug McGraw	p	5	0	3	0	0	—	1.000
Felix Millan	2b	7	17	13	3	3	—	.909
John Milner	1b	7	65	1	0	2	—	1.000
Harry Parker	p	3	0	0	0	0	—	—
Ray Sadecki	p	4	0	1	0	0	—	1.000
Tom Seaver	p	2	0	2	0	0	—	1.000
Rusty Staub	rf	6	5	0	0	0	—	1.000
George Stone	p	2	0	0	0	0	—	—
George Theodore	lf	1	1	0	0	0	—	1.000
Totals		7	195	72	10	8	1	.964

1974 Oakland Athletics (AL) 4, Los Angeles Dodgers (NL) 1

The Oakland A's downed the Los Angeles Dodgers in five games to take their third straight championship. The A's took the opener 3-2, as Rollie Fingers tossed 4.1 innings of relief and Catfish Hunter recorded the final out for a save. The Dodgers got their only win in Game 2 as Don Sutton worked eight strong innings and Joe Ferguson smacked a two-run homer for a 3-2 Los Angeles victory. Hunter and Fingers combined to beat the Dodgers 3-2 in Game 3. Jim Holt ripped a pinch-hit, two-run single during a four-run Oakland uprising in the bottom of the sixth as the A's took Game 4, 5-2. In the sixth inning of the fifth game, Walter Alston sent up Tom Paciorek to pinch-hit for pitcher Don Sutton with the Dodgers trailing 2-0. Paciorek doubled to start a two-run rally that knotted the game at two apiece, but Joe Rudi ripped a solo homer off Mike Marshall in the bottom of the seventh, and Rollie Fingers worked the last two innings to seal Oakland's third straight World Series.

Game 1
Saturday, October 12

Athletics	AB	R	H	RBI	BB	K	Avg
Bert Campaneris, ss	2	1	1	1	0	0	.500
Bill North, cf	2	0	0	0	1	1	.000
Sal Bando, 3b	4	0	0	0	0	2	.000
Reggie Jackson, rf	3	1	1	1	1	0	.333
Claudell Washington, rf	0	0	0	0	0	0	—
Joe Rudi, lf	4	0	2	0	0	1	.500
Gene Tenace, 1b	3	0	1	0	0	1	.333
Ray Fosse, c	3	0	0	0	1	2	.000
Dick Green, 2b	3	0	0	0	0	1	.000
Jim Holt, ph	1	0	0	0	0	0	.000
Dal Maxvill, 2b	0	0	0	0	0	0	—
Ken Holtzman, p	1	1	1	0	1	0	1.000
Rollie Fingers, p	2	0	0	0	0	1	.000
Catfish Hunter, p	0	0	0	0	0	0	—
TOTALS	28	3	6	2	4	9	.214

Dodgers	AB	R	H	RBI	BB	K	Avg
Davey Lopes, 2b	5	1	0	0	0	1	.000
Bill Buckner, lf	5	0	2	0	0	0	.400
Jimmy Wynn, cf	4	1	1	1	1	0	.250
Steve Garvey, 1b	5	0	2	0	0	1	.400
Tom Paciorek, pr	0	0	0	0	0	0	—
Joe Ferguson, rf-c	3	0	0	0	1	2	.000
Ron Cey, 3b	3	0	1	0	1	0	.333
Bill Russell, ss	4	0	1	0	0	1	.250
Steve Yeager, c	3	0	1	0	0	1	.333
Willie Crawford, ph-rf	1	0	1	0	0	0	1.000
Andy Messersmith, p	3	0	2	0	0	1	.667
Von Joshua, ph	1	0	0	0	0	0	.000
Mike Marshall, p	0	0	0	0	0	0	—
TOTALS	37	2	11	1	3	7	.297

	1	2	3	4	5	6	7	8	9	R	H	E
Athletics	0	1	0	0	1	0	0	1	0	3	6	2
Dodgers	0	0	0	0	1	0	0	0	1	2	11	1

E—Campaneris, Cey, Jackson. DP—Athletics 1 (Campaneris to Green to Tenace), Dodgers 1 (Ferguson to Yeager). LOB—Athletics 6, Dodgers 12. Scoring Position—Athletics 0-for-6, Dodgers 0-for-9. 2B—Holtzman (1). HR—Jackson (1), Wynn (1). S—Campaneris 2, North, Tenace. GDP—Cey. CS—North (1), Buckner (1).

Athletics	IP	H	R	ER	BB	K	ERA
Ken Holtzman	4.1	7	1	0	2	3	0.00
Rollie Fingers (W, 1-0)	4.1	4	1	1	1	3	2.08
Catfish Hunter (S, 1)	0.1	0	0	0	0	1	0.00

Dodgers	IP	H	R	ER	BB	K	ERA
Andy Messersmith (L, 0-1)	8.0	5	3	2	3	8	2.25
Mike Marshall	1.0	1	0	0	1	1	0.00

WP—Messersmith. HBP—Ferguson by Fingers. Time—2:43. Attendance—55,974. Umpires—HP, Gorman. 1B, Kunkel. 2B, Harvey. 3B, Denkinger.

Game 2
Sunday, October 13

Athletics	AB	R	H	RBI	BB	K	Avg
Bert Campaneris, ss	4	0	1	0	0	2	.333
Bill North, cf	4	0	0	0	1	1	.000
Larry Haney, c	0	0	0	0	0	0	—
Sal Bando, 3b	3	1	0	0	0	0	.000
Reggie Jackson, rf	3	1	2	0	1	0	.500
Joe Rudi, lf	4	0	1	2	0	1	.375
Herb Washington, pr	0	0	0	0	0	0	—
Gene Tenace, 1b	3	0	0	0	1	1	.167
Ray Fosse, c	2	0	0	0	0	1	.000
Jesus Alou, ph	1	0	0	0	0	0	.000
Blue Moon Odom, p	0	0	0	0	0	0	—
Angel Mangual, ph	1	0	0	0	0	1	.000
Dick Green, 2b	2	0	0	0	0	1	.000
Jim Holt, ph	1	0	1	0	0	0	.500
Dal Maxvill, pr-2b	0	0	0	0	0	0	—
Vida Blue, p	2	0	0	0	0	2	.000
Claudell Washington, ph-cf	1	0	1	0	0	0	1.000
TOTALS	31	2	6	2	2	11	.196

Dodgers	AB	R	H	RBI	BB	K	Avg
Davey Lopes, 2b	4	0	0	0	0	1	.000
Bill Buckner, lf	4	0	0	0	0	1	.222
Jimmy Wynn, cf	3	0	0	0	1	3	.143
Steve Garvey, 1b	4	1	2	0	0	1	.444
Joe Ferguson, rf	3	1	1	2	1	0	.167
Ron Cey, 3b	3	1	0	0	1	0	.167
Bill Russell, ss	3	0	1	0	0	0	.286
Steve Yeager, c	3	0	2	1	0	0	.500
Don Sutton, p	2	0	0	0	0	1	.000
Mike Marshall, p	0	0	0	0	0	0	—
TOTALS	29	3	6	3	3	7	.230

	1	2	3	4	5	6	7	8	9	R	H	E
Athletics	0	0	0	0	0	0	0	0	2	2	6	0
Dodgers	0	1	0	0	2	0	0	x		3	6	1

E—Russell. DP—Dodgers 2 (Sutton to Lopes to Garvey; Russell to Garvey). LOB—Athletics 5, Dodgers 6. Scoring Position—Athletics 1-for-5, Dodgers 1-for-6. 2B—Campaneris (1), Jackson (1). HR—Ferguson (1). S—Sutton. GDP—North, Tenace. SB—Ferguson (1).

Athletics	IP	H	R	ER	BB	K	ERA
Vida Blue (L, 0-1)	7.0	6	3	3	2	5	3.86
Blue Moon Odom	1.0	0	0	0	1	2	0.00

Dodgers	IP	H	R	ER	BB	K	ERA
Don Sutton (W, 1-0)	8.0	5	2	2	2	9	2.25
Mike Marshall (S, 1)	1.0	1	0	0	0	2	0.00

Sutton pitched to two batters in the 9th.

WP—Sutton. HBP—Bando by Sutton. Time—2:40. Attendance—55,989. Umpires—HP, Kunkel. 1B, Harvey. 2B, Denkinger. 3B, Olsen.

Game 3
Tuesday, October 15

Dodgers	AB	R	H	RBI	BB	K	Avg
Davey Lopes, 2b	3	0	2	0	1	0	.167
Bill Buckner, lf	4	1	1	1	0	0	.231
Jimmy Wynn, cf	4	0	1	0	0	0	.182
Steve Garvey, 1b	4	0	1	0	0	0	.385
Willie Crawford, rf	4	1	1	1	0	0	.400
Joe Ferguson, c	3	0	0	0	1	2	.111
Rick Auerbach, pr	0	0	0	0	0	0	—
Ron Cey, 3b	4	0	0	0	0	2	.100
Bill Russell, ss	4	0	1	0	0	0	.273
Al Downing, p	1	0	0	0	0	0	.000
Jim Brewer, p	0	0	0	0	0	0	—
Lee Lacy, ph	1	0	0	0	0	1	.000
Charlie Hough, p	0	0	0	0	0	0	—
Von Joshua, ph	1	0	0	0	0	0	.000
Mike Marshall, p	0	0	0	0	0	0	—
TOTALS	33	2	7	2	2	5	.216

Athletics	AB	R	H	RBI	BB	K	Avg
Bill North, cf	4	1	1	0	0	2	.100
Bert Campaneris, ss	4	0	2	1	0	0	.400
Sal Bando, 3b	3	1	0	0	1	1	.000
Reggie Jackson, rf	3	0	0	1	1	1	.333
Claudell Washington, rf	0	0	0	0	0	0	1.000
Joe Rudi, lf	4	0	1	0	1	1	.333
Gene Tenace, 1b	2	0	1	0	2	1	.250
Herb Washington, pr	0	0	0	0	0	0	—
Jim Holt, 1b	0	0	0	0	0	0	.500
Ray Fosse, c	4	0	0	0	0	0	.000
Dick Green, 2b	3	1	0	0	1	1	.000
Catfish Hunter, p	2	0	0	0	0	2	.000
Rollie Fingers, p	0	0	0	0	0	0	.000
TOTALS	29	3	5	2	5	9	.193

	1	2	3	4	5	6	7	8	9	R	H	E
Dodgers	0	0	0	0	0	0	0	1	1	2	7	2
Athletics	0	0	2	1	0	0	0	0	x	3	5	2

E—Campaneris, Ferguson 2, Green. DP—Athletics 2 (Green to Campaneris; Campaneris; Green to Tenace). Scoring Position—Dodgers 0-for-4, Athletics 2-for-11. 2B—Campaneris (2). HR—Buckner (1), Crawford (1). S—Hunter. GDP—Russell. SB—Lopes 2 (2), Jackson (1).

Dodgers	IP	H	R	ER	BB	K	ERA
Al Downing (L, 0-1)	3.2	4	3	1	4	3	2.45
Jim Brewer	0.1	0	0	0	0	1	0.00
Charlie Hough	2.0	0	0	0	1	4	0.00
Mike Marshall	2.0	1	0	0	0	1	0.00

Athletics	IP	H	R	ER	BB	K	ERA
Catfish Hunter (W, 1-0)	7.1	5	1	1	2	4	1.17
Rollie Fingers (BS, 1)	1.2	2	1	1	0	1	3.00

WP—Hough. Time—2:35. Attendance—49,347. Umpires—HP, Harvey. 1B, Denkinger. 2B, Olsen. 3B, Luciano.

Game 4

Wednesday, October 16

Dodgers	AB	R	H	RBI	BB	K	Avg
Davey Lopes, 2b	4	0	0	0	0	2	.125
Bill Buckner, lf	4	0	1	0	0	0	.235
Jimmy Wynn, cf	3	0	1	0	1	1	.214
Steve Garvey, 1b	4	1	2	0	0	1	.412
Joe Ferguson, rf	3	1	0	0	1	0	.083
Ron Cey, 3b	4	0	1	0	0	1	.143
Bill Russell, ss	4	0	1	2	0	1	.267
Steve Yeager, c	3	0	1	0	0	1	.444
Von Joshua, ph	1	0	0	0	0	0	.000
Andy Messersmith, p	1	0	0	0	0	1	.500
Tom Paciorek, ph	1	0	0	0	0	0	.000
Mike Marshall, p	0	0	0	0	0	0	—
TOTALS	32	2	7	2	2	9	.238

Athletics	AB	R	H	RBI	BB	K	Avg
Bert Campaneris, ss	3	0	0	0	0	0	.308
Bill North, cf	3	1	0	0	1	1	.077
Sal Bando, 3b	3	1	1	1	1	1	.077
Reggie Jackson, rf	3	1	1	0	1	1	.333
Joe Rudi, 1b-lf	3	0	0	0	0	0	.267
Claudell Washington, lf	3	1	2	0	1	1	.750
Gene Tenace, 1b	0	0	0	0	0	0	.250
Ray Fosse, c	2	0	1	0	0	1	.091
Jim Holt, ph	1	0	1	2	0	0	.667
Herb Washington, pr	0	0	0	0	0	0	—
Larry Haney, c	0	0	0	0	0	0	—
Dick Green, 2b	2	0	0	1	0	0	.000
Ken Holtzman, p	3	1	1	1	0	1	.500
Rollie Fingers, p	0	0	0	0	0	0	.000
TOTALS	26	5	7	5	4	6	.222

	1	2	3	4	5	6	7	8	9		R	H	E
Dodgers	0	0	0	2	0	0	0	0	0		2	7	1
Athletics	0	0	1	0	0	4	0	0	x		5	7	0

E—Messersmith. DP—Dodgers 2 (Lopes to Garvey; Russell to Lopes to Garvey). LOB—Dodgers 6, Athletics 4. Scoring Position—Dodgers 1-for-11, Athletics 2-for-5. 2B—Buckner (1), Wynn (1), Yeager (1). 3B—Russell (1). HR—Holtzman (1). S—Messersmith, Rudi, Green. GDP—Rudi, Joshua. CS—Campaneris (1).

Dodgers	IP	H	R	ER	BB	K	ERA
Andy Messersmith (L, 0-2)	6.0	6	5	5	4	4	4.50
Mike Marshall	2.0	1	0	0	0	2	0.00

Athletics	IP	H	R	ER	BB	K	ERA
Ken Holtzman (W, 1-0)	7.2	6	2	2	2	7	1.50
Rollie Fingers (S, 1)	1.1	1	0	0	0	2	2.45

WP—Holtzman. HBP—Campaneris by Messersmith. Time—2:17. Attendance—49,347. Umpires—HP, Denkinger. 1B, Olsen. 2B, Luciano. 3B, Gorman.

Game 5

Thursday, October 17

Dodgers	AB	R	H	RBI	BB	K	Avg
Davey Lopes, 2b	2	1	0	0	2	0	.111
Bill Buckner, lf	3	0	1	0	0	0	.250
Jimmy Wynn, cf	2	0	0	1	1	0	.188
Steve Garvey, 1b	4	0	1	1	0	0	.381
Joe Ferguson, rf	4	0	1	0	0	1	.125
Ron Cey, 3b	3	0	1	0	1	0	.176
Bill Russell, ss	3	0	0	0	0	0	.222
Willie Crawford, ph	1	0	0	0	0	0	.333
Steve Yeager, c	2	0	0	0	1	2	.364
Von Joshua, ph	1	0	0	0	0	0	.000
Don Sutton, p	1	0	0	0	0	1	.000
Tom Paciorek, ph	1	1	1	0	0	0	.500
Mike Marshall, p	0	0	0	0	1	0	—
TOTALS	27	2	5	2	6	4	.224

Athletics	AB	R	H	RBI	BB	K	Avg
Bert Campaneris, ss	4	0	2	0	0	0	.353
Bill North, cf	4	1	0	0	0	0	.059
Sal Bando, 3b	3	0	0	1	0	0	.063
Reggie Jackson, rf	2	0	0	0	1	1	.286
Joe Rudi, 1b-lf	3	1	2	1	0	0	.333
Claudell Washington, lf	3	0	1	0	0	0	.571
Rollie Fingers, p	0	0	0	0	0	0	.000
Ray Fosse, c	3	1	1	1	0	1	.143
Dick Green, 2b	3	0	0	0	0	1	.000
Vida Blue, p	2	0	0	0	0	2	.000
Blue Moon Odom, p	0	0	0	0	0	0	—
Gene Tenace, 1b	1	0	0	0	0	1	.222
TOTALS	28	3	6	3	1	7	.198

	1	2	3	4	5	6	7	8	9		R	H	E
Dodgers	0	0	0	0	0	2	0	0	0		2	5	1
Athletics	1	1	0	0	0	0	1	0	x		3	6	1

E—Yeager, North. DP—Athletics 1 (Campaneris to Green to Rudi). LOB—Dodgers 6, Athletics 3. Scoring Position—Dodgers 1-for-4, Athletics 0-for-3. 2B—Paciorek (1). HR—Rudi (1), Fosse (1). S—Buckner. SF—Wynn, Bando. GDP—Russell. SB—Campaneris (1), North (1). CS—Lopes (1), Washington (1).

Dodgers	IP	H	R	ER	BB	K	ERA
Don Sutton	5.0	4	2	2	1	3	2.77
Mike Marshall (L, 0-1)	3.0	2	1	1	0	4	1.00

Athletics	IP	H	R	ER	BB	K	ERA
Vida Blue	6.2	4	2	2	5	4	3.29
Blue Moon Odom (W, 1-0)	0.1	0	0	0	0	0	0.00
Rollie Fingers (S, 2)	2.0	1	0	0	1	0	1.93

Time—2:23. Attendance—49,347. Umpires—HP, Olsen. 1B, Luciano. 2B, Gorman. 3B, Kunkel.

1974 World Series—Composite Statistics

Batting

Athletics	G	AB	R	H	RBI	2B	3B	HR	BB	SO	SB	CS	Avg	OBP	Slg
Jesus Alou	1	1	0	0	0	0	0	0	0	1	0	0	.000	.000	.000
Sal Bando	5	16	3	1	2	0	0	0	2	5	0	0	.063	.200	.063
Vida Blue	2	4	0	0	0	0	0	0	0	4	0	0	.000	.000	.000
Bert Campaneris	5	17	1	6	2	2	0	0	2	1	1	1	.353	.389	.471
Rollie Fingers	4	2	0	0	0	0	0	0	0	1	0	0	.000	.000	.000
Ray Fosse	5	14	1	2	1	0	0	1	1	5	0	0	.143	.200	.357
Dick Green	5	13	1	0	1	0	0	0	1	4	0	0	.000	.071	.000
Jim Holt	4	3	0	2	2	0	0	0	0	0	0	0	.667	.667	.667
Ken Holtzman	2	4	2	2	1	1	0	1	1	1	0	0	.500	.600	1.500
Catfish Hunter	2	2	0	0	0	0	0	0	0	2	0	0	.000	.000	.000
Reggie Jackson	5	14	3	4	1	1	0	1	5	3	1	0	.286	.474	.571
Angel Mangual	1	1	0	0	0	0	0	0	0	1	0	0	.000	.000	.000
Bill North	5	17	3	1	0	0	0	0	2	5	1	1	.059	.158	.059
Joe Rudi	5	18	1	6	4	0	0	1	0	3	0	0	.333	.333	.500
Gene Tenace	5	9	0	2	0	0	0	0	3	4	0	0	.222	.417	.222
Claudell Washington	5	7	1	4	0	0	0	0	1	1	0	1	.571	.625	.571
Herb Washington	3	0	0	0	0	0	0	0	0	0	0	0	—	—	—
Totals	5	142	16	30	14	4	0	4	16	42	3	3	.211	.298	.324

Batting

Dodgers	G	AB	R	H	RBI	2B	3B	HR	BB	SO	SB	CS	Avg	OBP	Slg
Rick Auerbach	1	0	0	0	0	0	0	0	0	0	0	0	—	—	—
Bill Buckner	5	20	1	5	1	1	0	1	0	1	0	1	.250	.250	.450
Ron Cey	5	17	1	3	0	0	0	0	3	3	0	0	.176	.300	.176
Willie Crawford	3	6	1	2	1	0	0	1	0	0	0	0	.333	.333	.833
Al Downing	1	1	0	0	0	0	0	0	0	0	0	0	.000	.000	.000
Joe Ferguson	5	16	2	2	2	0	0	1	4	6	1	0	.125	.333	.313
Steve Garvey	5	21	2	8	1	0	0	0	0	3	0	0	.381	.381	.381
Von Joshua	4	4	0	0	0	0	0	0	0	0	0	0	.000	.000	.000
Lee Lacy	1	1	0	0	0	0	0	0	0	1	0	0	.000	.000	.000
Davey Lopes	5	18	2	2	0	0	0	0	3	4	2	1	.111	.238	.111
Mike Marshall	5	0	0	0	0	0	0	0	1	0	0	0	—	1.000	—
Andy Messersmith	2	4	0	2	0	0	0	0	0	2	0	0	.500	.500	.500
Tom Paciorek	3	2	1	1	0	1	0	0	0	0	0	0	.500	.500	1.000
Bill Russell	5	18	0	4	2	0	1	0	0	2	0	0	.222	.222	.333
Don Sutton	2	3	0	0	0	0	0	0	0	2	0	0	.000	.000	.000
Jimmy Wynn	5	16	1	3	2	1	0	1	4	4	0	0	.188	.333	.438
Steve Yeager	4	11	0	4	1	1	0	0	1	4	0	0	.364	.417	.455
Totals	5	158	11	36	10	4	1	4	16	32	3	2	.228	.301	.342

Pitching

Athletics	G	GS	CG	IP	H	R	ER	BB	SO	W-L	Sv-Op	Hld	ERA
Vida Blue	2	2	0	13.2	10	5	5	7	9	0-1	0-0	0	3.29
Rollie Fingers	4	0	0	9.1	8	2	2	2	6	1-0	2-3	0	1.93
Ken Holtzman	2	2	0	12.0	13	3	2	4	10	1-0	0-0	0	1.50
Catfish Hunter	2	1	0	7.2	5	1	1	2	5	1-0	1-1	0	1.17
Blue Moon Odom	2	0	0	1.1	0	0	0	1	2	1-0	0-0	0	0.00
Totals	5	5	0	44.0	36	11	10	16	32	4-1	3-4	0	2.05

Pitching

Dodgers	G	GS	CG	IP	H	R	ER	BB	SO	W-L	Sv-Op	Hld	ERA
Jim Brewer	1	0	0	0.1	0	0	0	0	1	0-0	0-0	0	0.00
Al Downing	1	1	0	3.2	4	3	1	4	3	0-1	0-0	0	2.45
Charlie Hough	1	0	0	2.0	0	0	0	1	4	0-0	0-0	0	0.00
Mike Marshall	5	0	0	9.0	6	1	1	1	10	0-1	1-1	0	1.00
Andy Messersmith	2	2	0	14.0	11	8	7	7	12	0-2	0-0	0	4.50
Don Sutton	2	2	0	13.0	9	4	4	3	12	1-0	0-0	0	2.77
Totals	5	5	0	42.0	30	16	13	16	42	1-4	1-1	0	2.79

Fielding

Athletics	Pos	G	PO	Ast	E	DP	PB	FPct
Sal Bando	3b	5	2	10	0	0	—	1.000
Vida Blue	p	2	0	3	0	0	—	1.000
Bert Campaneris	ss	5	6	16	2	5	—	.917
Rollie Fingers	p	4	0	1	0	0	—	1.000
Ray Fosse	c	5	27	1	0	0	0	1.000
Dick Green	2b	5	15	14	1	6	—	.967
Larry Haney	c	2	6	0	0	0	0	1.000
Jim Holt	1b	1	1	0	0	1	—	1.000
Ken Holtzman	p	2	0	3	0	0	—	1.000
Catfish Hunter	p	2	1	2	0	0	—	1.000
Reggie Jackson	rf	5	8	1	1	0	—	.900
Dal Maxvill	2b	2	0	0	0	0	—	—
Bill North	cf	5	17	0	1	0	—	.944
Blue Moon Odom	p	2	0	0	0	0	—	—
Joe Rudi	lf	5	11	0	0	0	—	1.000
	1b	2	17	0	0	1	—	1.000
Gene Tenace	1b	5	20	1	0	3	—	1.000
Claudell Washington	lf	2	1	0	0	0	—	1.000
	rf	2	0	0	0	0	—	—
	cf	1	0	0	0	0	—	—
Totals		5	132	52	5	16	0	.974

Fielding

Dodgers	Pos	G	PO	Ast	E	DP	PB	FPct
Jim Brewer	p	1	0	0	0	0	—	—
Bill Buckner	lf	5	10	0	0	0	—	1.000
Ron Cey	3b	5	5	9	1	0	—	.933
Willie Crawford	rf	2	1	0	0	0	—	1.000
Al Downing	p	1	0	3	0	0	—	1.000
Joe Ferguson	rf	4	5	1	0	1	—	1.000
	c	2	10	0	2	0	0	.833
Steve Garvey	1b	5	34	3	0	4	—	1.000
Charlie Hough	p	1	0	0	0	0	—	—
Davey Lopes	2b	5	19	9	0	3	—	1.000
Mike Marshall	p	5	0	4	0	0	—	1.000
Andy Messersmith	p	2	1	4	1	0	—	.833
Bill Russell	ss	5	4	11	1	2	—	.938
Don Sutton	p	2	0	2	0	1	—	1.000
Jimmy Wynn	cf	5	5	0	0	0	—	1.000
Steve Yeager	c	4	32	4	1	1	0	.973
Totals		5	126	50	6	12	0	.967

1975 Cincinnati Reds (NL) 4, Boston Red Sox (AL) 3

The Cincinnati Reds defeated the Boston Red Sox in seven games in the most thrilling World Series in modern memory. Luis Tiant threw a five-hit shutout in the opener, matching goose eggs with Don Gullett for six innings before starting the winning rally himself with a seventh-inning single. The Red Sox came within an out of taking the second game before Dave Concepcion tied the game with an RBI single and Ken Griffey doubled in the eventual winning run. Dwight Evans blasted a game-tying, two-run homer in the top of the ninth to send Game 3 into extra innings. In the bottom of the 10th, Ed Armbrister laid down a bunt and collided with catcher Carlton Fisk, who threw the ball away. No interference was called on the highly controversial play. Moments later, Joe Morgan drove in the winning run. Tiant gave a gutty performance in Game 4, using 163 pitches to down the Reds, 5-4. Tony Perez homered twice as Don Gullett won Game 5, 6-2. Three days of rain enabled the Sox to send Tiant back to the hill for Game 6. Fred Lynn's three-run homer in the first gave Boston an early lead, but the Reds came back to take a 6-3 lead into the bottom of the eighth. Then Bernie Carbo saved the Sox with a game-tying, pinch-hit, three-run homer. Denny Doyle was thrown out at the plate to end the ninth when he mistakenly tried to score on a fly ball. In the top of the 11th, Dwight Evans made a spectacular catch in deep right field to rob Morgan of a potential home run. Fisk brought the action to a climax in the bottom of the 12th when he lined a shot down the left field line. Fisk frantically waved the ball fair, and it cooperated, banging off the foul pole for a game-winning homer. Game 7 went into the ninth tied 3-3 before Morgan drove in the winning run with an RBI single.

Game 1
Saturday, October 11

Reds	AB	R	H	RBI	BB	K	Avg
Pete Rose, 3b	4	0	0	0	0	0	.000
Joe Morgan, 2b	4	0	2	0	0	0	.500
Johnny Bench, c	4	0	0	0	0	0	.000
Tony Perez, 1b	4	0	0	0	0	2	.000
George Foster, lf	4	0	2	0	0	0	.500
Dave Concepcion, ss	4	0	0	0	0	1	.000
Ken Griffey Sr., rf	3	0	1	0	0	0	.333
Cesar Geronimo, cf	1	0	0	0	2	0	.000
Don Gullett, p	3	0	0	0	0	0	.000
Clay Carroll, p	0	0	0	0	0	0	—
Will McEnaney, p	0	0	0	0	0	0	—
TOTALS	31	0	5	0	2	3	.161

Red Sox	AB	R	H	RBI	BB	K	Avg
Dwight Evans, rf	4	1	1	0	0	0	.250
Denny Doyle, 2b	3	1	2	0	1	0	.667
Carl Yastrzemski, lf	4	1	1	1	1	0	.250
Carlton Fisk, c	3	1	0	1	1	0	.000
Fred Lynn, cf	4	0	2	0	0	1	.500
Rico Petrocelli, 3b	3	1	2	2	1	0	.667
Rick Burleson, ss	3	0	3	1	1	0	1.000
Cecil Cooper, 1b	3	0	0	1	0	2	.000
Luis Tiant, p	3	1	1	0	1	1	.333
TOTALS	30	6	12	6	6	4	.400

	1	2	3	4	5	6	7	8	9		R	H	E
Reds	0	0	0	0	0	0	0	0	0		0	5	0
Red Sox	0	0	0	0	0	0	6	0	x		6	12	0

DP—Reds 2 (Geronimo to Bench; Perez). LOB—Reds 6, Red Sox 9. Scoring Position—Reds 0-for-6, Red Sox 5-for-13. 2B—Morgan (1), Griffey Sr. (1), Petrocelli (1). S—Evans, Doyle. SF—Cooper. CS—Foster (1), Burleson (1).

Reds	IP	H	R	ER	BB	K	ERA
Don Gullett (L, 0-1)	6.0	10	4	4	4	3	6.00
Clay Carroll	0.0	0	1	1	1	0	—
Will McEnaney	2.0	2	1	1	1	1	4.50

Red Sox	IP	H	R	ER	BB	K	ERA
Luis Tiant (W, 1-0)	9.0	5	0	0	2	3	0.00

Gullett pitched to four batters in the 7th. Carroll pitched to one batter in the 7th.

Balk—Tiant. Time—2:27. Attendance—35,205. Umpires—HP, Frantz. 1B, Colosi. 2B, Barnett. 3B, Stello.

Game 2
Sunday, October 12

Reds	AB	R	H	RBI	BB	K	Avg
Pete Rose, 3b	4	0	2	0	0	1	.250
Joe Morgan, 2b	3	1	0	0	1	0	.286
Johnny Bench, c	4	1	2	0	0	0	.250
Tony Perez, 1b	3	0	0	1	1	1	.000
George Foster, lf	4	0	1	0	0	1	.375
Dave Concepcion, ss	4	1	1	1	0	0	.125
Ken Griffey Sr., rf	4	0	1	1	0	0	.286
Cesar Geronimo, cf	3	0	0	0	0	1	.000
Jack Billingham, p	2	0	0	0	0	0	.000
Pedro Borbon, p	0	0	0	0	0	0	—
Will McEnaney, p	0	0	0	0	0	0	—
Merv Rettenmund, ph	1	0	0	0	0	0	.000
Rawly Eastwick, p	1	0	0	0	0	0	.000
TOTALS	33	3	7	3	3	5	.197

Red Sox	AB	R	H	RBI	BB	K	Avg
Cecil Cooper, 1b	5	0	1	0	0	0	.125
Denny Doyle, 2b	4	0	1	0	0	1	.429
Carl Yastrzemski, lf	3	2	1	0	1	0	.286
Carlton Fisk, c	3	0	1	1	1	1	.167
Fred Lynn, cf	4	0	0	0	0	0	.250
Rico Petrocelli, 3b	4	0	2	1	0	1	.571
Dwight Evans, rf	2	0	0	0	1	2	.167
Rick Burleson, ss	4	0	1	0	0	1	.571
Bill Lee, p	3	0	0	0	0	2	.000
Dick Drago, p	0	0	0	0	0	0	—
Bernie Carbo, ph	1	0	0	0	0	0	.000
TOTALS	33	2	7	2	3	8	.300

	1	2	3	4	5	6	7	8	9		R	H	E
Reds	0	0	0	1	0	0	0	0	2		3	7	1
Red Sox	1	0	0	0	0	0	1	0	0		2	7	0

E—Concepcion. DP—Reds 1 (Billingham to Concepcion to Bench to Rose). LOB—Reds 6, Red Sox 8. Scoring Position—Reds 2-for-7, Red Sox 3-for-8. 2B—Bench (1), Griffey Sr. (2), Cooper (1). SB—Concepcion (1). CS—Morgan (1), Evans (1).

Reds	IP	H	R	ER	BB	K	ERA
Jack Billingham	5.2	6	2	1	2	5	1.59
Pedro Borbon	0.1	0	0	0	0	0	0.00
Will McEnaney	1.0	0	0	0	0	2	3.00
Rawly Eastwick (W, 1-0)	2.0	1	0	0	1	1	0.00

Red Sox	IP	H	R	ER	BB	K	ERA
Bill Lee	8.0	5	2	2	2	5	2.25
Dick Drago (BS, 1; L, 0-1)	1.0	2	1	1	1	0	9.00

Lee pitched to one batter in the 9th.

HBP—Evans by Billingham. Time—2:38. Attendance—35,205. Umpires—HP, Colosi. 1B, Barnett. 2B, Stello. 3B, Maloney.

Game 3
Tuesday, October 14

Red Sox	AB	R	H	RBI	BB	K	Avg
Cecil Cooper, 1b	5	0	0	0	0	0	.077
Denny Doyle, 2b	5	0	1	0	0	0	.333
Carl Yastrzemski, lf	4	1	0	0	1	1	.182
Carlton Fisk, c	3	1	1	1	2	0	.222
Fred Lynn, cf	3	0	1	1	0	1	.273
Rico Petrocelli, 3b	4	1	2	0	0	0	.545
Dwight Evans, rf	4	1	2	2	0	0	.300
Rick Burleson, ss	4	0	2	0	0	0	.545
Rick Wise, p	2	0	0	0	0	0	.000
Jim Burton, p	0	0	0	0	0	0	—
Reggie Cleveland, p	0	0	0	0	0	0	—
Bernie Carbo, ph	1	1	1	1	0	0	.500
Jim Willoughby, p	0	0	0	0	0	0	—
Roger Moret, p	0	0	0	0	0	0	—
TOTALS	35	5	10	5	3	2	.304

Reds	AB	R	H	RBI	BB	K	Avg
Pete Rose, 3b	4	1	1	0	1	0	.250
Ken Griffey Sr., rf	3	0	0	0	1	0	.200
Merv Rettenmund, ph	1	0	0	0	0	1	.000
Joe Morgan, 2b	4	0	1	2	0	0	.273
Tony Perez, 1b	3	1	0	0	1	2	.000
Johnny Bench, c	4	1	1	2	0	1	.250
George Foster, lf	3	0	0	0	1	0	.273
Dave Concepcion, ss	4	1	1	1	0	0	.167
Cesar Geronimo, cf	4	2	2	1	0	0	.250
Gary Nolan, p	1	0	0	0	0	0	.000
Pat Darcy, p	1	0	0	0	0	1	.000
Clay Carroll, p	0	0	0	0	0	0	—
Will McEnaney, p	1	0	1	0	0	0	1.000
Rawly Eastwick, p	0	0	0	0	0	0	.000
Ed Armbrister, ph	1	0	0	0	0	0	.000
TOTALS	34	6	7	6	4	5	.204

	1	2	3	4	5	6	7	8	9	10		R	H	E
Red Sox	0	1	0	0	0	1	1	0	2	0		5	10	2
Reds	0	0	0	2	3	0	0	0	0	1		6	7	0

E—Fisk 2. DP—Red Sox 1 (Petrocelli to Cooper), Reds 2 (Morgan to Concepcion to Perez; Morgan to Perez). LOB—Red Sox 5, Reds 5. Scoring Position—Red Sox 0-for-3, Reds 2-for-5. 3B—Rose (1). HR—Fisk (1), Evans (1), Bench (1), Concepcion (1), Geronimo (1), Carbo (1). S—Willoughby. SF—Lynn, Morgan. GDP—Fisk, Burleson. SB—Griffey Sr. (1), Perez (1), Foster (1).

Red Sox	IP	H	R	ER	BB	K	ERA
Rick Wise	4.1	4	5	5	2	1	10.38
Jim Burton	0.1	0	0	0	1	0	0.00
Reggie Cleveland	1.1	0	0	0	0	2	0.00
Jim Willoughby (L, 0-1)	3.0	2	1	0	0	1	0.00
Roger Moret	0.1	1	0	0	1	1	0.00

Reds	IP	H	R	ER	BB	K	ERA
Gary Nolan	4.0	3	1	1	1	0	2.25
Pat Darcy	2.0	2	1	1	2	0	4.50
Clay Carroll (H, 1)	0.2	1	1	1	0	0	27.00
Will McEnaney (H, 1)	1.2	1	1	1	0	2	3.86
Rawly Eastwick (BS, 1; W, 2-0)	1.2	3	1	1	0	0	2.45

Darcy pitched to one batter in the 7th. Willoughby pitched to two batters in the 10th.

WP—Darcy. Time—3:03. Attendance—55,392. Umpires—HP, Barnett. 1B, Stello. 2B, Maloney. 3B, Davidson.

Game 4

Wednesday, October 15

Red Sox	AB	R	H	RBI	BB	K	Avg
Juan Beniquez, lf	4	0	1	1	0	0	.250
Rick Miller, lf	1	0	0	0	0	0	.000
Denny Doyle, 2b	5	0	1	0	0	0	.294
Carl Yastrzemski, 1b	4	0	2	1	1	0	.267
Carlton Fisk, c	5	1	1	0	0	1	.214
Fred Lynn, cf	4	1	1	0	0	1	.267
Rico Petrocelli, 3b	4	0	1	0	0	1	.467
Dwight Evans, rf	4	1	2	2	0	0	.357
Rick Burleson, ss	4	1	1	1	0	0	.467
Luis Tiant, p	3	1	1	0	1	1	.333
TOTALS	38	5	11	5	2	4	.328

Reds	AB	R	H	RBI	BB	K	Avg
Pete Rose, 3b	3	1	1	0	2	0	.267
Ken Griffey Sr., rf	5	0	1	1	0	0	.200
Joe Morgan, 2b	3	1	0	0	2	0	.214
Tony Perez, 1b	4	0	0	0	0	1	.000
Johnny Bench, c	4	0	1	1	0	1	.250
George Foster, lf	4	1	2	0	0	0	.333
Dave Concepcion, ss	4	1	1	1	0	0	.188
Cesar Geronimo, cf	4	0	3	1	0	0	.417
Fred Norman, p	1	0	0	0	0	0	.000
Pedro Borbon, p	0	0	0	0	0	0	—
Terry Crowley, ph	1	0	0	0	0	1	.000
Clay Carroll, p	0	0	0	0	0	0	—
Darrel Chaney, ph	1	0	0	0	0	1	.000
Rawly Eastwick, p	0	0	0	0	0	0	—
Ed Armbrister, ph	0	0	0	0	0	0	—
TOTALS	34	4	9	4	4	4	.221

	1 2 3	4 5 6	7 8 9		R	H	E
Red Sox	0 0 0	5 0 0	0 0 0		5	11	1
Reds	2 0 0	2 0 0	0 0 0		4	9	1

E—Perez, Doyle. DP—Reds 1 (Morgan to Concepcion to Perez). LOB—Red Sox 8, Reds 8. Scoring Position—Red Sox 4-for-10, Reds 3-for-9. 2B—Burleson (1), Griffey Sr. (3), Bench (2), Concepcion (1). 3B—Evans (1), Geronimo (1). S—Armbrister. GDP—Yastrzemski.

Red Sox	IP	H	R	ER	BB	K	ERA
Luis Tiant (W, 2-0)	9.0	9	4	4	4	4	2.00

Reds	IP	H	R	ER	BB	K	ERA
Fred Norman (L, 0-1)	3.1	7	4	4	1	2	10.80
Pedro Borbon	0.2	2	1	0	0	0	0.00
Clay Carroll	2.0	2	0	0	0	2	6.75
Rawly Eastwick	3.0	0	0	0	1	0	1.35

WP—Norman. Time—2:52. Attendance—55,667. Umpires—HP, Stello. 1B, Maloney. 2B, Davidson. 3B, Frantz.

Game 5

Thursday, October 16

Red Sox	AB	R	H	RBI	BB	K	Avg
Juan Beniquez, lf	3	0	0	0	1	1	.143
Denny Doyle, 2b	4	1	1	0	0	0	.286
Carl Yastrzemski, 1b	3	1	1	1	0	0	.278
Carlton Fisk, c	4	0	1	0	0	2	.222
Fred Lynn, cf	4	0	1	1	0	1	.263
Rico Petrocelli, 3b	4	0	0	0	0	2	.368
Dwight Evans, rf	3	0	1	0	0	0	.353
Rick Burleson, ss	3	0	0	0	0	0	.389
Reggie Cleveland, p	2	0	0	0	0	0	.000
Jim Willoughby, p	0	0	0	0	0	0	—
Doug Griffin, ph	1	0	0	0	0	0	.000
Dick Pole, p	0	0	0	0	0	0	—
Diego Segui, p	0	0	0	0	0	0	—
TOTALS	31	2	5	2	1	8	.293

Reds	AB	R	H	RBI	BB	K	Avg
Pete Rose, 3b	3	0	2	1	1	0	.333
Ken Griffey Sr., rf	4	0	1	0	0	1	.211
Joe Morgan, 2b	3	1	1	0	1	0	.235
Johnny Bench, c	3	2	1	0	1	0	.263
Tony Perez, 1b	3	2	2	4	1	1	.118
George Foster, lf	4	0	0	0	0	1	.263
Dave Concepcion, ss	2	0	0	1	0	0	.167
Cesar Geronimo, cf	4	0	0	0	0	0	.313
Don Gullett, p	3	1	1	0	0	2	.167
Rawly Eastwick, p	0	0	0	0	0	0	.000
TOTALS	29	6	8	6	4	4	.233

	1 2 3	4 5 6	7 8 9		R	H	E
Red Sox	1 0 0	0 0 0	0 0 1		2	5	0
Reds	0 0 0	1 1 3	0 1 x		6	8	0

DP—Red Sox 2 (Beniquez to Fisk; Burleson to Yastrzemski). LOB—Red Sox 4, Reds 5. Scoring Position—Red Sox 1-for-2, Reds 1-for-6. 2B—Lynn (1), Rose (1). 3B—Doyle (1). HR—Perez 2 (2). SF—Yastrzemski, Concepcion. SB—Morgan (1), Concepcion (2).

Red Sox	IP	H	R	ER	BB	K	ERA
Reggie Cleveland (L, 0-1)	5.0	7	5	5	2	3	7.11
Jim Willoughby	2.0	1	0	0	0	1	0.00
Dick Pole	0.0	0	1	1	2	0	—
Diego Segui	1.0	0	0	0	0	0	0.00

Reds	IP	H	R	ER	BB	K	ERA
Don Gullett (W, 1-1)	8.2	5	2	2	1	7	3.68
Rawly Eastwick (S, 1)	0.1	0	0	0	0	1	1.29

Cleveland pitched to four batters in the 6th. Pole pitched to two batters in the 8th.

HBP—Concepcion by Willoughby. Time—2:23. Attendance—56,393. Umpires—HP, Maloney. 1B, Davidson. 2B, Frantz. 3B, Colosi.

Game 6

Tuesday, October 21

Reds	AB	R	H	RBI	BB	K	Avg
Pete Rose, 3b	5	1	2	0	0	0	.348
Ken Griffey Sr., rf	5	2	2	2	1	0	.250
Joe Morgan, 2b	6	1	1	0	0	0	.217
Johnny Bench, c	6	0	1	1	0	2	.240
Tony Perez, 1b	6	0	2	0	0	2	.174
George Foster, lf	6	0	2	2	0	0	.280
Dave Concepcion, ss	6	1	0	0	0	0	.167
Cesar Geronimo, cf	6	1	2	1	0	3	.318
Gary Nolan, p	0	0	0	0	0	0	.000
Darrel Chaney, ph	1	0	0	0	0	0	.000
Fred Norman, p	0	0	0	0	0	0	.000
Jack Billingham, p	0	0	0	0	0	0	.000
Ed Armbrister, ph	0	1	0	0	1	0	.000
Clay Carroll, p	0	0	0	0	0	0	—
Terry Crowley, ph	1	0	1	0	0	0	.500
Pedro Borbon, p	1	0	0	0	0	0	.000
Rawly Eastwick, p	0	0	0	0	0	0	.000
Will McEnaney, p	0	0	0	0	0	0	1.000
Dan Driessen, ph	1	0	0	0	0	0	.000
Pat Darcy, p	0	0	0	0	0	0	.000
TOTALS	50	6	14	6	2	7	.241

Red Sox	AB	R	H	RBI	BB	K	Avg
Cecil Cooper, 1b	5	0	0	0	0	1	.056
Dick Drago, p	0	0	0	0	0	0	.000
Rick Miller, ph	1	0	0	0	0	0	.000
Rick Wise, p	0	0	0	0	0	0	.000
Denny Doyle, 2b	5	0	1	0	1	0	.269
Carl Yastrzemski, lf-1b	6	1	3	0	0	0	.333
Carlton Fisk, c	4	2	2	1	2	0	.273
Fred Lynn, cf	4	2	2	3	1	0	.304
Rico Petrocelli, 3b	4	1	0	0	1	1	.304
Dwight Evans, rf	5	0	1	0	0	2	.318
Rick Burleson, ss	3	0	0	0	2	0	.333
Luis Tiant, p	2	0	0	0	0	2	.250
Roger Moret, p	0	0	0	0	0	0	—
Bernie Carbo, ph-lf	2	1	1	3	0	1	.500
TOTALS	41	7	10	7	7	7	.277

	1 2 3	4 5 6	7 8 9	10 11 12		R	H	E
Reds	0 0 0	0 3 0	2 1 0	0 0 0		6	14	0
Red Sox	3 0 0	0 0 0	0 3 0	0 0 1		7	10	1

E—Burleson. DP—Reds 1 (Foster to Bench), Red Sox 1 (Evans). LOB—Reds 11, Red Sox 9. Scoring Position—Reds 3-for-13, Red Sox 2-for-10. 2B—Foster (1), Doyle (1), Evans (1). 3B—Griffey Sr. (1). HR—Geronimo (2), Fisk (2), Lynn (1), Carbo (2). S—Tiant. SB—Concepcion (3).

Reds	IP	H	R	ER	BB	K	ERA
Gary Nolan	2.0	3	3	3	0	2	6.00
Fred Norman	0.2	1	0	0	2	0	9.00
Jack Billingham	1.1	1	0	0	1	1	1.29
Clay Carroll	1.0	1	0	0	0	0	4.91
Pedro Borbon	2.0	1	2	2	2	1	6.00
Rawly Eastwick (BS, 2)	1.0	2	1	1	1	2	2.25
Will McEnaney	1.0	0	0	0	1	0	3.18
Pat Darcy (L, 0-1)	2.0	1	1	1	0	1	4.50

Red Sox	IP	H	R	ER	BB	K	ERA
Luis Tiant	7.0	11	6	6	2	5	3.60
Roger Moret	1.0	0	0	0	0	0	0.00
Dick Drago	3.0	1	0	0	0	1	2.25
Rick Wise (W, 1-0)	1.0	2	0	0	0	1	8.44

Tiant pitched to one batter in the 8th. Borbon pitched to two batters in the 8th. Eastwick pitched to two batters in the 9th. Darcy pitched to one batter in the 12th.

HBP—Rose by Drago. Time—4:01. Attendance—35,205. Umpires—HP, Davidson. 1B, Frantz. 2B, Colosi. 3B, Barnett.

Game 7

Wednesday, October 22

Reds	AB	R	H	RBI	BB	K	Avg
Pete Rose, 3b	4	0	2	1	1	0	.370
Joe Morgan, 2b	4	0	1	1	1	1	.259
Johnny Bench, c	4	1	0	0	1	0	.207
Tony Perez, 1b	5	1	1	2	0	0	.179
George Foster, lf	4	0	1	0	0	0	.276
Ken Griffey Sr., rf	2	2	1	0	2	0	.269
Cesar Geronimo, cf	3	0	0	0	0	1	.280
Don Gullett, p	1	0	1	0	0	0	.286
Merv Rettenmund, ph	1	0	0	0	0	0	.000
Jack Billingham, p	0	0	0	0	0	0	.000
Ed Armbrister, ph	0	0	0	0	1	0	.000
Clay Carroll, p	0	0	0	0	0	0	—
Dan Driessen, ph	1	0	0	0	0	0	.000
Will McEnaney, p	0	0	0	0	0	0	1.000
TOTALS	33	4	9	4	6	2	.247

Red Sox	AB	R	H	RBI	BB	K	Avg
Bernie Carbo, lf	3	1	1	0	1	0	.429
Rick Miller, lf	0	0	0	0	0	0	.000
Juan Beniquez, ph	1	0	0	0	0	0	.125
Denny Doyle, 2b	4	1	1	0	0	0	.267
Bob Montgomery, ph	1	0	0	0	0	0	.000
Carl Yastrzemski, 1b	5	1	1	1	0	0	.310
Carlton Fisk, c	3	0	0	0	1	3	.240
Fred Lynn, cf	2	0	0	0	2	1	.280
Rico Petrocelli, 3b	3	0	1	1	1	1	.308
Dwight Evans, rf	2	0	1	0	2	0	.292
Rick Burleson, ss	3	0	0	0	1	1	.292
Bill Lee, p	3	0	1	0	0	1	.167
Roger Moret, p	0	0	0	0	0	0	—
Jim Willoughby, p	0	0	0	0	0	0	—
Cecil Cooper, ph	1	0	0	0	0	0	.053
Jim Burton, p	0	0	0	0	0	0	—
Reggie Cleveland, p	0	0	0	0	0	0	.000
TOTALS	31	3	5	3	8	7	.254

	1 2 3	4 5 6	7 8 9		R	H	E
Reds	0 0 0	0 0 2	1 0 1		4	9	0
Red Sox	0 0 3	0 0 0	0 0 0		3	5	2

E—Doyle 2. DP—Reds 1 (Concepcion to Morgan to Perez), Red Sox 2 (Doyle to Burleson to Yastrzemski; Burleson to Doyle to Yastrzemski). LOB—Reds 9, Red Sox 9. Scoring Position—Reds 3-for-10, Red Sox 1-for-11. 2B—Carbo (1). HR—Perez (3). S—Geronimo. GDP—Geronimo, Burleson, Rettenmund. SB—Morgan (2), Griffey Sr. (2).

Reds	IP	H	R	ER	BB	K	ERA
Don Gullett	4.0	4	3	3	5	5	4.34
Jack Billingham	2.0	1	0	0	2	1	1.00
Clay Carroll (W, 1-0)	2.0	0	0	0	1	1	3.18
Will McEnaney (S, 1)	1.0	0	0	0	1	0	2.70

Red Sox	IP	H	R	ER	BB	K	ERA
Bill Lee	6.1	7	3	3	1	2	3.14
Roger Moret (BS, 1)	0.1	1	0	0	2	0	0.00
Jim Willoughby	1.1	0	0	0	0	0	0.00
Jim Burton (L, 0-1)	0.2	1	1	1	2	0	9.00
Reggie Cleveland	0.1	0	0	0	1	0	6.75

WP—Gullett. Time—2:52. Attendance—35,205. Umpires—HP, Frantz. 1B, Colosi. 2B, Barnett. 3B, Stello.

1975 World Series—Composite Statistics

Batting

Reds	G	AB	R	H	RBI	2B	3B	HR	BB	SO	SB	CS	Avg	OBP	Slg
Ed Armbrister	4	1	1	0	0	0	0	0	2	0	0	0	.000	.667	.000
Johnny Bench	7	29	5	6	4	2	0	1	2	4	0	0	.207	.258	.379
Jack Billingham	3	2	0	0	0	0	0	0	0	0	0	0	.000	.000	.000
Pedro Borbon	3	1	0	0	0	0	0	0	0	0	0	0	.000	.000	.000
Darrel Chaney	2	2	0	0	0	0	0	0	0	1	0	0	.000	.000	.000
Dave Concepcion	7	28	3	5	4	1	0	1	0	1	3	0	.179	.200	.321
Terry Crowley	2	2	0	1	0	0	0	0	0	0	0	0	.500	.500	.500
Pat Darcy	2	1	0	0	0	0	0	0	0	1	0	0	.000	.000	.000
Dan Driessen	2	2	0	0	0	0	0	0	0	0	0	0	.000	.000	.000
Rawly Eastwick	5	1	0	0	0	0	0	0	0	0	0	0	.000	.000	.000
George Foster	7	29	1	8	2	1	0	0	1	1	1	1	.276	.300	.310
Cesar Geronimo	7	25	3	7	3	0	1	2	3	5	0	0	.280	.357	.600
Ken Griffey Sr.	7	26	4	7	4	3	1	0	4	2	2	0	.269	.367	.462
Don Gullett	3	7	1	2	0	0	0	0	0	2	0	0	.286	.286	.286
Will McEnaney	5	1	0	1	0	0	0	0	0	0	0	0	1.000	1.000	1.000
Joe Morgan	7	27	4	7	3	1	0	0	5	1	2	1	.259	.364	.296
Gary Nolan	2	1	0	0	0	0	0	0	0	0	0	0	.000	.000	.000
Fred Norman	2	1	0	0	0	0	0	0	0	0	0	0	.000	.000	.000
Tony Perez	7	28	4	5	7	0	0	3	3	9	1	0	.179	.258	.500
Merv Rettenmund	3	3	0	0	0	0	0	0	0	1	0	0	.000	.000	.000
Pete Rose	7	27	3	10	2	1	1	0	5	1	0	0	.370	.485	.481
Totals	**7**	**244**	**29**	**59**	**29**	**9**	**3**	**7**	**25**	**30**	**9**	**2**	**.242**	**.315**	**.389**

Red Sox	G	AB	R	H	RBI	2B	3B	HR	BB	SO	SB	CS	Avg	OBP	Slg
Juan Beniquez	3	8	0	1	1	0	0	0	1	1	0	0	.125	.222	.125
Rick Burleson	7	24	1	7	2	1	0	0	4	2	0	1	.292	.393	.333
Bernie Carbo	4	7	3	3	4	1	0	2	1	1	0	0	.429	.500	1.429
Reggie Cleveland	3	2	0	0	0	0	0	0	0	2	0	0	.000	.000	.000
Cecil Cooper	5	19	0	1	1	1	0	0	0	3	0	0	.053	.050	.105
Denny Doyle	7	30	3	8	0	1	1	0	2	1	0	0	.267	.313	.367
Dwight Evans	7	24	3	7	5	1	1	1	3	4	0	1	.292	.393	.542
Carlton Fisk	7	25	5	6	4	0	0	2	7	7	0	0	.240	.406	.480
Doug Griffin	1	1	0	0	0	0	0	0	0	0	0	0	.000	.000	.000
Bill Lee	2	6	0	1	0	0	0	0	0	3	0	0	.167	.167	.167
Fred Lynn	7	25	3	7	5	1	0	1	3	5	0	0	.280	.345	.440
Rick Miller	3	2	0	0	0	0	0	0	0	0	0	0	.000	.000	.000
Bob Montgomery	1	1	0	0	0	0	0	0	0	0	0	0	.000	.000	.000
Rico Petrocelli	7	26	3	8	4	1	0	0	3	6	0	0	.308	.379	.346
Luis Tiant	3	8	2	2	0	0	0	0	2	4	0	0	.250	.400	.250
Jim Willoughby	3	0	0	0	0	0	0	0	0	0	0	0	—	—	—
Rick Wise	2	2	0	0	0	0	0	0	0	0	0	0	.000	.000	.000
Carl Yastrzemski	7	29	7	9	4	0	0	0	4	1	0	0	.310	.382	.310
Totals	**7**	**239**	**30**	**60**	**30**	**7**	**2**	**6**	**30**	**40**	**0**	**2**	**.251**	**.333**	**.372**

Pitching

Reds	G	GS	CG	IP	H	R	ER	BB	SO	W-L	Sv-Op	Hld	ERA
Jack Billingham	3	1	0	9.0	8	2	1	5	7	0-0	0-0	0	1.00
Pedro Borbon	3	0	0	3.0	3	3	2	2	1	0-0	0-0	0	6.00
Clay Carroll	5	0	0	5.2	4	2	2	2	3	1-0	0-0	1	3.18
Pat Darcy	2	0	0	4.0	3	2	2	2	1	0-1	0-0	0	4.50
Rawly Eastwick	5	0	0	8.0	6	2	2	3	4	2-0	1-3	0	2.25
Don Gullett	3	3	0	18.2	19	9	9	10	15	1-1	0-0	0	4.34
Will McEnaney	5	0	0	6.2	3	2	2	2	5	0-0	1-1	1	2.70
Gary Nolan	2	2	0	6.0	6	4	4	1	2	0-0	0-0	0	6.00
Fred Norman	2	1	0	4.0	8	4	4	3	2	0-1	0-0	0	9.00
Totals	**7**	**7**	**0**	**65.0**	**60**	**30**	**28**	**30**	**40**	**4-3**	**2-4**	**2**	**3.88**

Red Sox	G	GS	CG	IP	H	R	ER	BB	SO	W-L	Sv-Op	Hld	ERA
Jim Burton	2	0	0	1.0	1	1	1	3	0	0-1	0-0	0	9.00
Reggie Cleveland	3	1	0	6.2	7	5	5	3	5	0-1	0-0	0	6.75
Dick Drago	2	0	0	4.0	3	1	1	1	1	0-1	0-1	0	2.25
Bill Lee	2	2	0	14.1	12	5	5	3	7	0-0	0-0	0	3.14
Roger Moret	3	0	0	1.2	0	0	0	3	1	0-0	0-1	0	0.00
Dick Pole	1	0	0	0.0	0	1	1	2	0	0-0	0-0	0	—
Diego Segui	1	0	0	1.0	0	0	0	0	0	0-0	0-0	0	0.00
Luis Tiant	3	3	2	25.0	25	10	10	8	12	2-0	0-0	0	3.60
Jim Willoughby	3	0	0	6.1	3	1	0	0	2	0-1	0-0	0	0.00
Rick Wise	2	1	0	5.1	6	5	5	2	2	1-0	0-0	0	8.44
Totals	**7**	**7**	**2**	**65.1**	**59**	**29**	**28**	**25**	**30**	**3-4**	**0-2**	**0**	**3.86**

Fielding

Reds	Pos	G	PO	Ast	E	DP	PB	FPct
Johnny Bench	c	7	44	5	0	3	0	1.000
Jack Billingham	p	3	0	2	0	1	—	1.000
Pedro Borbon	p	3	0	0	0	0	—	—
Clay Carroll	p	5	2	0	0	0	—	1.000
Dave Concepcion	ss	7	12	23	1	4	—	.972
Pat Darcy	p	2	0	1	0	0	—	1.000
Rawly Eastwick	p	5	0	0	0	0	—	—
George Foster	lf	7	14	1	0	1	—	1.000
Cesar Geronimo	cf	7	23	1	0	1	—	1.000
Ken Griffey Sr.	rf	7	10	1	0	0	—	1.000
Don Gullett	p	3	0	0	0	0	—	—
Will McEnaney	p	5	0	0	0	0	—	—
Joe Morgan	2b	7	16	27	0	4	—	1.000
Gary Nolan	p	2	1	0	0	0	—	1.000
Fred Norman	p	2	0	0	0	0	—	—
Tony Perez	1b	7	66	5	1	5	—	.986
Pete Rose	3b	7	7	9	0	1	—	1.000
Totals		**7**	**195**	**75**	**2**	**20**	**0**	**.993**

Red Sox	Pos	G	PO	Ast	E	DP	PB	FPct
Juan Beniquez	lf	2	5	1	0	1	—	1.000
Rick Burleson	ss	7	8	20	1	3	—	.966
Jim Burton	p	2	0	0	0	0	—	—
Bernie Carbo	lf	2	1	1	0	0	—	1.000
Reggie Cleveland	p	3	0	0	0	0	—	—
Cecil Cooper	1b	4	40	1	0	1	—	1.000
Denny Doyle	2b	7	12	23	3	2	—	.921
Dick Drago	p	2	0	0	0	0	—	—
Dwight Evans	rf	7	25	0	0	1	—	1.000
Carlton Fisk	c	7	37	3	2	1	0	.952
Bill Lee	p	2	0	1	0	0	—	1.000
Fred Lynn	cf	7	23	1	0	0	—	1.000
Rick Miller	lf	2	1	0	0	0	—	1.000
Roger Moret	p	3	0	1	0	0	—	1.000
Rico Petrocelli	3b	7	7	14	0	1	—	1.000
Dick Pole	p	1	0	0	0	0	—	—
Diego Segui	p	1	0	0	0	0	—	—
Luis Tiant	p	3	0	4	0	0	—	1.000
Jim Willoughby	p	3	1	0	0	0	—	1.000
Rick Wise	p	2	0	0	0	0	—	—
Carl Yastrzemski	1b	4	28	0	0	3	—	1.000
	lf	4	8	0	0	0	—	1.000
Totals		**7**	**196**	**70**	**6**	**13**	**0**	**.978**

1976 Cincinnati Reds (NL) 4, New York Yankees (AL) 0

The Cincinnati Reds made short work of the New York Yankees, winning the World Series in four games to complete a clean sweep of the postseason. Don Gullett was sharp in the opener, combining with Pedro Borbon to stymie the Yankees, 5-1. Game 2 was much closer. With the score tied and two outs in the bottom of the ninth, Fred Stanley's throwing error put Ken Griffey on second base. After an intentional walk to Joe Morgan, Tony Perez reached Catfish Hunter for a game-winning RBI single. Pat Zachry and Will McEnaney teamed up to down the Yanks 6-2 in the third game. The Reds took a 3-2 lead into the ninth in the fourth game before Johnny Bench blasted a three-run homer to all but seal it. The Reds went on to win 7-2, and Bench ended the Series with a .533 batting average and six RBI.

Game 1

Saturday, October 16 (N)

Yankees	AB	R	H	RBI	BB	K	Avg
Mickey Rivers, cf	4	0	0	0	0	1	.000
Roy White, lf	4	0	1	0	0	1	.250
Thurman Munson, c	4	0	1	0	0	1	.250
Lou Piniella, dh	3	1	1	0	0	0	.333
Carlos May, ph-dh	1	0	0	0	0	0	.000
Chris Chambliss, 1b	3	0	1	0	0	0	.333
Graig Nettles, 3b	3	0	0	1	0	0	.000
Elliott Maddox, rf	2	0	1	0	1	0	.500
Oscar Gamble, ph	1	0	0	0	0	0	.000
Willie Randolph, 2b	2	0	0	1	0	0	.000
Fred Stanley, ss	1	0	0	0	1	1	.000
Otto Velez, ph	1	0	0	0	0	1	.000
Jim Mason, ss	0	0	0	0	0	0	—
TOTALS	29	1	5	1	3	4	.172

Reds	AB	R	H	RBI	BB	K	Avg
Pete Rose, 3b	2	0	0	1	1	0	.000
Ken Griffey Sr., rf	4	1	0	0	0	1	.000
Joe Morgan, 2b	4	1	1	1	0	1	.250
Tony Perez, 1b	4	0	3	1	0	1	.750
Dan Driessen, dh	4	0	0	0	0	0	.000
George Foster, lf	3	1	2	0	1	0	.667
Johnny Bench, c	3	1	2	1	0	0	.667
Cesar Geronimo, cf	3	0	1	0	0	0	.333
Dave Concepcion, ss	3	1	1	0	0	1	.333
TOTALS	30	5	10	4	2	4	.333

	1	2	3	4	5	6	7	8	9	R	H	E
Yankees	0	1	0	0	0	0	0	0	0	1	5	1
Reds	1	0	1	0	0	1	2	0	x	5	10	1

E—Chambliss, Geronimo. DP—Yankees 2 (Alexander to Randolph to Chambliss; Randolph to Stanley to Chambliss), Reds 2 (Morgan to Concepcion to Perez; Morgan to Perez). LOB—Yankees 6, Reds 4. Scoring Position—Yankees 1-for-6, Reds 2-for-6. 2B—Piniella (1), Perez (1), Geronimo (1). 3B—Maddox (1), Bench (1), Concepcion (1). HR—Morgan (1). SF—Nettles, Rose. GDP—Nettles 2, Bench, Geronimo. SB—Griffey Sr. (1). CS—Rivers (1), Perez (1).

Yankees	IP	H	R	ER	BB	K	ERA
Doyle Alexander (L, 0-1)	6.0	9	5	5	2	1	7.50
Sparky Lyle	2.0	1	0	0	0	3	0.00

Reds	IP	H	R	ER	BB	K	ERA
Don Gullett (W, 1-0)	7.1	5	1	1	3	4	1.23
Pedro Borbon	1.2	0	0	0	0	0	0.00

Alexander pitched to two batters in the 7th.

WP—Lyle. HBP—Chambliss by Gullett. Time—2:18. Attendance—54,826. Umpires—HP, Weyer. 1B, DiMuro. 2B, Williams. 3B, Deegun.

Game 2

Sunday, October 17

Yankees	AB	R	H	RBI	BB	K	Avg
Mickey Rivers, cf	5	0	0	0	0	0	.000
Roy White, lf	3	0	1	0	1	0	.286
Thurman Munson, c	4	1	1	1	0	0	.250
Lou Piniella, rf	4	0	2	0	0	0	.429
Chris Chambliss, 1b	4	0	2	0	0	0	.429
Graig Nettles, 3b	4	0	1	1	0	0	.143
Elliott Maddox, dh	3	0	0	0	0	2	.200
Carlos May, ph-dh	1	0	0	0	0	0	.000
Willie Randolph, 2b	4	1	1	0	0	1	.167
Fred Stanley, ss	3	1	1	1	1	0	.250
TOTALS	35	3	9	3	2	3	.226

Reds	AB	R	H	RBI	BB	K	Avg
Pete Rose, 3b	4	0	0	0	1	1	.000
Ken Griffey Sr., rf	4	1	0	1	0	0	.000
Joe Morgan, 2b	4	0	2	0	1	0	.375
Tony Perez, 1b	5	0	2	1	0	0	.556
Dan Driessen, dh	4	1	2	0	0	0	.250
George Foster, lf	4	0	1	1	0	2	.429
Johnny Bench, c	4	1	2	0	0	1	.571
Cesar Geronimo, cf	2	1	0	0	2	0	.200
Dave Concepcion, ss	4	0	1	1	0	1	.286
TOTALS	35	4	10	4	4	5	.308

	1	2	3	4	5	6	7	8	9	R	H	E
Yankees	0	0	0	1	0	0	2	0	0	3	9	1
Reds	0	3	0	0	0	0	0	0	1	4	10	0

E—Stanley. DP—Reds 1 (Concepcion to Morgan to Perez). LOB—Yankees 7, Reds 10. Scoring Position—Yankees 2-for-9, Reds 3-for-9. 2B—Stanley (1), Driessen (1), Bench (1). 3B—Morgan (1). SF—Griffey Sr. GDP—Maddox (1). SB—Morgan (1), Concepcion (1). CS—Foster (1).

Yankees	IP	H	R	ER	BB	K	ERA
Catfish Hunter (L, 0-1)	8.2	10	4	3	4	5	3.12

Reds	IP	H	R	ER	BB	K	ERA
Fred Norman	6.1	9	3	3	2	2	4.26
Jack Billingham (BS, 1; W, 1-0)	2.2	0	0	0	0	1	0.00

Time—2:33. Attendance—54,816. Umpires—HP, DiMuro. 1B, Williams. 2B, Deegan. 3B, Froemming.

Game 3

Tuesday, October 19

Reds	AB	R	H	RBI	BB	K	Avg
Pete Rose, 3b	5	1	2	0	0	1	.182
Ken Griffey Sr., rf	4	0	1	0	0	0	.083
Joe Morgan, 2b	4	1	1	1	0	1	.333
Tony Perez, 1b	4	0	0	0	0	1	.385
Dan Driessen, dh	3	2	3	1	1	0	.455
George Foster, lf	4	1	2	2	0	0	.455
Johnny Bench, c	4	0	2	0	0	0	.545
Cesar Geronimo, cf	4	1	1	1	0	1	.222
Dave Concepcion, ss	4	0	1	1	0	1	.273
TOTALS	36	6	13	6	1	5	.327

Yankees	AB	R	H	RBI	BB	K	Avg
Mickey Rivers, cf	4	0	2	0	1	1	.154
Roy White, lf	3	0	0	0	2	0	.200
Thurman Munson, c	5	0	3	0	0	0	.385
Chris Chambliss, 1b	5	1	1	0	0	2	.333
Carlos May, dh	4	0	0	0	0	1	.000
Graig Nettles, 3b	2	0	0	0	2	1	.111
Oscar Gamble, rf	3	0	1	1	0	0	.250
Lou Piniella, ph-rf	1	0	0	0	0	0	.375
Willie Randolph, 2b	4	0	0	0	0	1	.100
Fred Stanley, ss	1	0	0	0	0	0	.200
Ellie Hendricks, ph	1	0	0	0	0	0	.000
Jim Mason, ss	1	1	1	1	0	0	1.000
Otto Velez, ph	1	0	0	0	0	1	.000
TOTALS	35	2	8	2	5	7	.223

	1	2	3	4	5	6	7	8	9	R	H	E
Reds	0	3	0	1	0	0	0	2	0	6	13	2
Yankees	0	0	0	1	0	0	1	0	0	2	8	0

E—Morgan, Zachry. DP—Reds 1 (Perez to Concepcion), Yankees 3 (Stanley to Randolph to Chambliss; Nettles to Chambliss; Nettles to Randolph to Chambliss). LOB—Reds 4, Yankees 11. Scoring Position—Reds 5-for-11, Yankees 1-for-8. 2B—Morgan (1), Driessen (2), Foster (1). HR—Driessen (1), Mason (1). GDP—Rose, Bench, Concepcion. SB—Driessen (1), Geronimo (1). CS—Bench (1).

Reds	IP	H	R	ER	BB	K	ERA
Pat Zachry (W, 1-0)	6.2	6	2	2	5	6	2.70
Will McEnaney (S, 1)	2.1	2	0	0	0	1	0.00

Yankees	IP	H	R	ER	BB	K	ERA
Dock Ellis (L, 0-1)	3.1	7	4	4	0	1	10.80
Grant Jackson	3.2	4	2	2	0	3	4.91
Dick Tidrow	2.0	2	0	0	1	1	0.00

Jackson pitched to three batters in the 8th.

Time—2:40. Attendance—56,667. Umpires—HP, Williams. 1B, Deegan. 2B, Froemming. 3B, Phillips.

Game 4

Thursday, October 21

Reds	AB	R	H	RBI	BB	K	Avg
Pete Rose, 3b	5	0	1	0	0	0	.188
Ken Griffey Sr., rf	5	0	0	0	0	0	.059
Joe Morgan, 2b	3	1	1	0	1	0	.333
Tony Perez, 1b	3	1	0	0	1	0	.313
Dan Driessen, dh	3	1	0	0	1	0	.357
George Foster, lf	3	1	1	1	1	1	.429
Johnny Bench, c	4	2	2	5	0	0	.533
Cesar Geronimo, cf	4	1	2	0	0	1	.308
Dave Concepcion, ss	3	0	2	1	1	0	.357
TOTALS	33	7	9	7	5	2	.313

Yankees	AB	R	H	RBI	BB	K	Avg
Mickey Rivers, cf	5	1	1	0	0	0	.167
Roy White, lf	5	0	0	0	0	0	.133
Thurman Munson, c	4	1	4	1	0	0	.529
Chris Chambliss, 1b	4	0	1	1	0	0	.313
Carlos May, dh	3	0	0	0	0	0	.000
Lou Piniella, ph-dh	1	0	0	0	0	0	.333
Graig Nettles, 3b	3	0	2	0	1	0	.250
Oscar Gamble, rf	4	0	0	0	0	0	.125
Willie Randolph, 2b	4	0	0	0	0	1	.071
Fred Stanley, ss	1	0	0	0	1	0	.167
Ellie Hendricks, ph	1	0	0	0	0	0	.000
Jim Mason, ss	0	0	0	0	0	0	1.000
Otto Velez, ph	1	0	0	0	0	1	.000
TOTALS	36	2	8	2	2	2	.223

	1	2	3	4	5	6	7	8	9	R	H	E
Reds	0	0	0	3	0	0	0	0	4	7	9	2
Yankees	1	0	0	0	1	0	0	0	0	2	8	0

E—Concepcion, Morgan. DP—Yankees 1 (Stanley to Nettles to Chambliss to Randolph). LOB—Reds 4, Yankees 9. Scoring Position—Reds 3-for-12, Yankees 1-for-4. 2B—Rose (1), Geronimo (2), Concepcion (1), Chambliss (1). HR—Bench 2 (2). SB—Morgan (2), Geronimo (2), Rivers (1). CS—Foster (2), Concepcion (1), Nettles (1).

Reds	IP	H	R	ER	BB	K	ERA
Gary Nolan (W, 1-0)	6.2	8	2	2	1	1	2.70
Will McEnaney (S, 2)	2.1	0	0	0	1	1	0.00

Yankees	IP	H	R	ER	BB	K	ERA
Ed Figueroa (L, 0-1)	8.0	6	5	5	5	2	5.63
Dick Tidrow	0.1	3	2	2	0	0	7.71
Sparky Lyle	0.2	0	0	0	0	0	0.00

Figueroa pitched to three batters in the 9th.

WP—Figueroa. Time—2:36. Attendance—56,700. Umpires—HP, Deegan. 1B, Froemming. 2B, Phillips. 3B, Weyer.

1976 World Series—Composite Statistics

Batting

Reds	G	AB	R	H	RBI	2B	3B	HR	BB	SO	SB	CS	Avg	OBP	Slg
Johnny Bench	4	15	4	8	6	1	1	2	0	1	0	1	.533	.533	1.133
Dave Concepcion	4	14	1	5	3	1	1	0	1	3	1	1	.357	.400	.571
Dan Driessen	4	14	4	5	1	2	0	1	2	0	1	0	.357	.438	.714
George Foster	4	14	3	6	4	1	0	0	2	3	0	2	.429	.500	.500
Cesar Geronimo	4	13	3	4	1	2	0	0	2	2	2	0	.308	.400	.462
Ken Griffey Sr.	4	17	2	1	1	0	0	0	0	1	1	0	.059	.056	.059
Joe Morgan	4	15	3	5	2	1	1	1	2	2	2	0	.333	.412	.733
Tony Perez	4	16	1	5	2	1	0	0	1	2	0	1	.313	.353	.375
Pete Rose	4	16	1	3	1	1	0	0	2	2	0	0	.188	.263	.250
Totals	4	134	22	42	21	10	3	4	12	16	7	5	.313	.365	.522

Batting

Yankees	G	AB	R	H	RBI	2B	3B	HR	BB	SO	SB	CS	Avg	OBP	Slg
Chris Chambliss	4	16	1	5	1	1	0	0	0	2	0	0	.313	.353	.375
Oscar Gamble	3	8	0	1	1	0	0	0	0	0	0	0	.125	.125	.125
Ellie Hendricks	2	2	0	0	0	0	0	0	0	0	0	0	.000	.000	.000
Elliott Maddox	2	5	0	1	0	0	1	0	1	2	0	0	.200	.333	.600
Jim Mason	3	1	1	1	1	0	0	1	0	0	0	0	1.000	1.000	4.000
Carlos May	4	9	0	0	0	0	0	0	0	1	0	0	.000	.000	.000
Thurman Munson	4	17	2	9	2	0	0	0	1	0	0	0	.529	.529	.529
Graig Nettles	4	12	0	3	2	0	0	0	3	1	0	1	.250	.375	.250
Lou Piniella	4	9	1	3	0	1	0	0	0	0	0	0	.333	.333	.444
Willie Randolph	4	14	1	1	0	0	0	0	1	3	0	0	.071	.133	.071
Mickey Rivers	4	18	1	3	0	0	0	0	1	2	1	1	.167	.211	.167
Fred Stanley	4	6	1	1	1	1	0	0	3	1	0	0	.167	.444	.333
Otto Velez	3	3	0	0	0	0	0	0	0	3	0	0	.000	.000	.000
Roy White	4	15	0	2	0	0	0	0	3	0	0	0	.133	.278	.133
Totals	4	135	8	30	8	3	1	1	12	16	1	2	.222	.289	.281

Pitching

Reds	G	GS	CG	IP	H	R	ER	BB	SO	W-L	Sv-Op	Hld	ERA
Jack Billingham	1	0	0	2.2	0	0	0	0	1	1-0	0-1	0	0.00
Pedro Borbon	1	0	0	1.2	0	0	0	0	0	0-0	0-1	0	0.00
Don Gullett	1	1	0	7.1	5	1	1	3	4	1-0	0-0	0	1.23
Will McEnaney	2	0	0	4.2	2	0	0	1	2	0-0	2-2	0	0.00
Gary Nolan	1	1	0	6.2	8	2	2	1	1	1-0	0-0	0	2.70
Fred Norman	1	1	0	6.1	9	3	3	2	2	0-0	0-0	0	4.26
Pat Zachry	1	1	0	6.2	6	2	2	5	6	1-0	0-0	0	2.70
Totals	4	4	0	36.0	30	8	8	12	16	4-0	2-3	0	2.00

Pitching

Yankees	G	GS	CG	IP	H	R	ER	BB	SO	W-L	Sv-Op	Hld	ERA
Doyle Alexander	1	1	0	6.0	9	5	5	2	1	0-0	0-0	0	7.50
Dock Ellis	1	1	0	3.1	7	4	4	0	1	0-1	0-0	0	10.80
Ed Figueroa	1	1	0	8.0	6	5	5	5	2	0-1	0-0	0	5.63
Catfish Hunter	1	1	1	8.2	10	4	3	4	5	0-1	0-0	0	3.12
Grant Jackson	1	0	0	3.2	4	2	2	0	3	0-0	0-0	0	4.91
Sparky Lyle	2	0	0	2.2	1	0	0	0	3	0-0	0-0	0	0.00
Dick Tidrow	2	0	0	2.1	5	2	2	1	1	0-0	0-0	0	7.71
Totals	4	4	1	34.2	42	22	21	12	16	0-4	0-0	0	5.45

Fielding

Reds	Pos	G	PO	Ast	E	DP	PB	FPct
Johnny Bench	c	4	18	2	0	0	0	1.000
Jack Billingham	p	1	1	0	0	0	—	1.000
Pedro Borbon	p	1	0	1	0	0	—	1.000
Dave Concepcion	ss	4	6	11	1	3	—	.944
George Foster	lf	4	14	0	0	0	—	1.000
Cesar Geronimo	cf	4	12	0	1	0	—	.923
Ken Griffey Sr.	rf	4	5	0	0	0	—	1.000
Don Gullett	p	1	0	1	0	0	—	1.000
Will McEnaney	p	2	1	0	0	0	—	1.000
Joe Morgan	2b	4	13	10	2	3	—	.920
Gary Nolan	p	1	0	1	0	0	—	1.000
Fred Norman	p	1	0	1	0	0	—	1.000
Tony Perez	1b	4	32	4	0	4	—	1.000
Pete Rose	3b	4	6	3	0	0	—	1.000
Pat Zachry	p	1	0	2	1	0	—	.667
Totals		4	108	36	5	10	0	.966

Fielding

Yankees	Pos	G	PO	Ast	E	DP	PB	FPct
Doyle Alexander	p	1	0	1	0	1	—	1.000
Chris Chambliss	1b	4	26	3	1	6	—	.967
Dock Ellis	p	1	0	0	0	0	—	—
Ed Figueroa	p	1	0	1	0	0	—	1.000
Oscar Gamble	rf	2	3	0	0	0	—	1.000
Catfish Hunter	p	1	0	1	0	0	—	1.000
Grant Jackson	p	1	0	3	0	0	—	1.000
Sparky Lyle	p	2	0	0	0	0	—	—
Elliott Maddox	rf	1	0	0	0	0	—	—
Jim Mason	ss	3	1	2	0	0	—	1.000
Thurman Munson	c	4	21	6	0	0	0	1.000
Graig Nettles	3b	4	8	8	0	3	—	1.000
Lou Piniella	rf	2	0	0	0	0	—	—
Willie Randolph	2b	4	13	8	0	5	—	1.000
Mickey Rivers	cf	4	14	0	0	0	—	1.000
Fred Stanley	ss	4	4	7	1	3	—	.917
Dick Tidrow	p	2	0	0	0	0	—	—
Roy White	lf	4	14	0	0	0	—	1.000
Totals		4	104	40	2	18	0	.986

1977 New York Yankees (AL) 4, Los Angeles Dodgers (NL) 2

Reggie Jackson hit a World Series-record five home runs, including three in the final game, as the New York Yankees defeated the Los Angeles Dodgers in six games. Paul Blair's RBI single in the bottom of the 12th gave the Yanks a 4-3 victory in Game 1. Burt Hooton tossed a five-hitter for a 6-1 Los Angeles victory in Game 2. Mike Torrez stepped up for the Yankees in Game 3, going the distance for a 5-3 win. Ron Guidry put the Yankees up three games to one with a four-hit, 4-2 win in Game 4, but the Dodgers fought back for a 10-4 win in the fifth game. That set the stage for Jackson's heroics. He lined a two-run homer in the bottom of the fourth to put the Yankees ahead 4-3. He followed with another two-run homer in the next frame, and yet another circuit shot in the eighth as the Yankees wrapped up the World Championship, 8-4.

Game 1
Tuesday, October 11

Dodgers	AB	R	H	RBI	BB	K	Avg
Davey Lopes, 2b	5	1	0	0	1	2	.000
Bill Russell, ss	6	1	1	1	0	0	.167
Reggie Smith, rf	4	0	1	0	1	1	.250
Ron Cey, 3b	3	0	0	1	1	1	.000
Steve Garvey, 1b	4	0	1	0	1	1	.250
Dusty Baker, lf	4	1	1	0	0	0	.250
Glenn Burke, cf	3	0	1	0	0	1	.333
Manny Mota, ph	1	0	0	0	0	0	.000
Rick Monday, cf	1	0	0	0	0	1	.000
Steve Yeager, c	3	0	0	0	1	0	.000
Rafael Landestoy, pr	0	0	0	0	0	0	—
Jerry Grote, c	1	0	0	0	0	0	.000
Don Sutton, p	2	0	0	0	1	1	.000
Lance Rautzhan, p	0	0	0	0	0	0	—
Elias Sosa, p	0	0	0	0	0	0	—
Lee Lacy, ph	1	0	1	1	0	0	1.000
Mike Garman, p	0	0	0	0	0	0	—
Vic Davalillo, ph	1	0	0	0	0	0	.000
Rick Rhoden, p	0	0	0	0	0	0	—
TOTALS	39	3	6	3	6	8	.154

Yankees	AB	R	H	RBI	BB	K	Avg
Mickey Rivers, cf	6	0	0	0	0	1	.000
Willie Randolph, 2b	5	3	2	1	1	1	.400
Thurman Munson, c	4	1	2	1	2	1	.500
Reggie Jackson, rf	2	0	1	0	1	0	.500
Paul Blair, rf	2	0	1	1	0	0	.500
Chris Chambliss, 1b	5	0	1	1	0	0	.200
Graig Nettles, 3b	4	0	0	0	1	0	.000
Lou Piniella, lf	5	0	2	0	0	2	.400
Bucky Dent, ss	5	0	2	0	0	0	.400
Don Gullett, p	1	0	0	0	0	1	.000
Sparky Lyle, p	2	0	0	0	0	2	.000
TOTALS	41	4	11	4	5	8	.268

	1	2	3	4	5	6	7	8	9	10	11	12	R	H	E
Dodgers	2	0	0	0	0	0	0	0	1	0	0	0	3	6	0
Yankees	1	0	0	0	1	0	1	0	0	0	0	1	4	11	0

LOB—Dodgers 8, Yankees 12. Scoring Position—Dodgers 1-for-5, Yankees 2-for-8. 2B—Randolph (1), Munson (1). 3B—Russell (1). HR—Randolph (1). S—Gullett 2. SF—Cey. CS—Smith (1).

Dodgers	IP	H	R	ER	BB	K	ERA
Don Sutton	7.0	8	3	3	1	4	3.86
Lance Rautzhan	0.1	0	0	0	2	0	0.00
Elias Sosa	0.2	0	0	0	0	1	0.00
Mike Garman	3.0	1	0	0	1	3	0.00
Rick Rhoden (L, 0-1)	0.0	2	1	1	1	0	—

Yankees	IP	H	R	ER	BB	K	ERA
Don Gullett	8.1	5	3	3	6	6	3.24
Sparky Lyle (BS, 1; W, 1-0)	3.2	1	0	0	0	2	0.00

Sutton pitched to two batters in the 8th. Rhoden pitched to three batters in the 12th.

HBP—Baker by Gullett, Jackson by Sutton. Time—3:24. Attendance—56,668. Umpires—HP, Chylak. 1B, Sudol. 2B, McCoy. 3B, Dale.

Game 2
Wednesday, October 12

Dodgers	AB	R	H	RBI	BB	K	Avg
Davey Lopes, 2b	4	0	0	0	0	0	.000
Bill Russell, ss	4	1	1	0	0	0	.167
Reggie Smith, rf	3	2	2	2	1	0	.429
Ron Cey, 3b	4	1	1	2	0	0	.143
Steve Garvey, 1b	4	1	2	1	0	0	.375
Dusty Baker, lf	4	0	0	0	0	0	.125
Rick Monday, cf	3	0	1	0	0	0	.250
Glenn Burke, cf	1	0	0	0	0	0	.250
Steve Yeager, c	4	1	2	1	0	0	.286
Burt Hooton, p	3	0	0	0	0	1	.000
TOTALS	34	6	9	6	1	1	.209

Yankees	AB	R	H	RBI	BB	K	Avg
Mickey Rivers, cf	4	0	0	0	0	0	.000
Willie Randolph, 2b	4	1	1	0	0	1	.333
Thurman Munson, c	4	0	1	0	0	1	.375
Reggie Jackson, rf	4	0	0	0	0	2	.167
Chris Chambliss, 1b	4	0	0	0	0	1	.111
Graig Nettles, 3b	2	0	1	0	1	0	.167
Lou Piniella, lf	3	0	1	0	0	0	.375
Bucky Dent, ss	2	0	1	0	0	1	.429
Cliff Johnson, ph	1	0	0	0	0	0	.000
Fred Stanley, ss	0	0	0	0	0	0	—
Catfish Hunter, p	0	0	0	0	0	0	—
Dick Tidrow, p	1	0	0	0	0	1	.000
George Zeber, ph	1	0	0	0	0	1	.000
Ken Clay, p	0	0	0	0	0	0	—
Roy White, ph	1	0	0	0	0	0	.000
Sparky Lyle, p	0	0	0	0	0	0	.000
TOTALS	31	1	5	0	1	8	.217

	1	2	3	4	5	6	7	8	9		R	H	E
Dodgers	2	1	2	0	0	0	0	0	1		6	9	0
Yankees	0	0	0	1	0	0	0	0	0		1	5	0

DP—Dodgers 1 (Garvey to Russell). LOB—Dodgers 2, Yankees 4. Scoring Position—Dodgers 1-for-1, Yankees 0-for-3. 2B—Smith (1). HR—Smith (1), Cey (1), Garvey (1), Yeager (1). CS—Garvey (1), Monday (1).

Dodgers	IP	H	R	ER	BB	K	ERA
Burt Hooton (W, 1-0)	9.0	5	1	1	1	8	1.00

Yankees	IP	H	R	ER	BB	K	ERA
Catfish Hunter (L, 0-1)	2.1	5	5	5	0	0	19.29
Dick Tidrow	2.2	3	0	0	0	1	0.00
Ken Clay	3.0	0	0	0	1	0	0.00
Sparky Lyle	1.0	1	1	1	0	0	1.93

Time—2:27. Attendance—56,691. Umpires—HP, Sudol. 1B, McCoy. 2B, Dale. 3B, Evans.

Game 3
Friday, October 14

Yankees	AB	R	H	RBI	BB	K	Avg
Mickey Rivers, cf	5	1	3	1	0	0	.200
Willie Randolph, 2b	4	0	0	0	1	0	.231
Thurman Munson, c	5	1	1	1	0	3	.308
Reggie Jackson, rf	3	2	1	1	1	2	.222
Paul Blair, rf	1	0	0	0	0	0	.333
Lou Piniella, lf	3	0	2	1	0	0	.455
Chris Chambliss, 1b	4	0	1	0	0	1	.154
Graig Nettles, 3b	4	1	1	0	0	1	.200
Bucky Dent, ss	3	0	1	0	1	0	.400
Mike Torrez, p	3	0	0	0	0	2	.000
TOTALS	35	5	10	5	3	9	.260

Dodgers	AB	R	H	RBI	BB	K	Avg
Davey Lopes, 2b	4	0	0	0	1	1	.000
Bill Russell, ss	4	0	0	0	0	1	.143
Reggie Smith, rf	3	1	1	0	1	1	.400
Ron Cey, 3b	3	0	0	0	1	0	.100
Steve Garvey, 1b	4	1	2	0	0	0	.417
Dusty Baker, lf	4	1	2	3	0	1	.250
Rick Monday, cf	4	0	0	0	0	2	.125
Steve Yeager, c	4	0	2	0	0	0	.364
Tommy John, p	2	0	0	0	0	2	.000
Vic Davalillo, ph	1	0	0	0	0	0	.000
Charlie Hough, p	0	0	0	0	0	0	—
Manny Mota, ph	1	0	0	0	0	1	.000
TOTALS	34	3	7	3	3	9	.208

	1	2	3	4	5	6	7	8	9		R	H	E
Yankees	3	0	0	1	1	0	0	0	0		5	10	0
Dodgers	0	0	3	0	0	0	0	0	0		3	7	1

E—Baker. DP—Dodgers 1 (Garvey to Russell). LOB—Yankees 8, Dodgers 7. Scoring Position—Yankees 4-for-12, Dodgers 1-for-7. 2B—Rivers 2 (2), Munson (2), Yeager (1). HR—Baker (1). S—Torrez. GDP—Chambliss. SB—Rivers (1), Lopes (1).

Yankees	IP	H	R	ER	BB	K	ERA
Mike Torrez (W, 1-0)	9.0	7	3	3	3	9	3.00

Dodgers	IP	H	R	ER	BB	K	ERA
Tommy John (L, 0-1)	6.0	9	5	4	3	7	6.00
Charlie Hough	3.0	1	0	0	0	2	0.00

HBP—Piniella by John. Time—2:31. Attendance—55,992. Umpires—HP, McCoy. 1B, Dale. 2B, Evans. 3B, McSherry.

Game 4
Saturday, October 15

Yankees	AB	R	H	RBI	BB	K	Avg
Mickey Rivers, cf	4	0	1	0	0	1	.211
Willie Randolph, 2b	4	0	0	0	0	0	.176
Thurman Munson, c	4	0	1	0	0	2	.294
Reggie Jackson, rf	4	2	2	1	0	0	.308
Paul Blair, rf	0	0	0	0	0	0	.333
Lou Piniella, lf	4	1	1	1	0	1	.400
Chris Chambliss, 1b	3	1	1	0	0	0	.188
Graig Nettles, 3b	3	0	0	1	0	0	.154
Bucky Dent, ss	3	0	1	1	0	0	.385
Ron Guidry, p	2	0	0	0	0	1	.000
TOTALS	31	4	7	4	0	5	.258

Dodgers	AB	R	H	RBI	BB	K	Avg
Davey Lopes, 2b	2	1	1	2	2	0	.067
Bill Russell, ss	4	0	0	0	0	2	.111
Reggie Smith, cf	4	0	0	0	0	1	.286
Ron Cey, 3b	4	0	2	0	0	1	.214
Steve Garvey, 1b	4	0	0	0	0	2	.313
Dusty Baker, lf	4	0	0	0	0	0	.188
Lee Lacy, rf	2	0	0	0	1	1	.333
Steve Yeager, c	3	0	0	0	0	0	.286
Doug Rau, p	0	0	0	0	0	0	—
Rick Rhoden, p	2	1	1	0	0	0	.500
Manny Mota, ph	1	0	0	0	0	0	.000
Mike Garman, p	0	0	0	0	0	0	—
TOTALS	30	2	4	2	3	7	.209

	1	2	3	4	5	6	7	8	9		R	H	E
Yankees	0	3	0	0	0	1	0	0	0		4	7	0
Dodgers	0	0	2	0	0	0	0	0	0		2	4	0

DP—Dodgers 2 (Russell to Lopes to Garvey; Lopes to Russell to Garvey). LOB—Yankees 1, Dodgers 4. Scoring Position—Yankees 2-for-4, Dodgers 1-for-7. 2B—Jackson (1), Chambliss (1), Cey (1), Rhoden (1). HR—Jackson (1), Lopes (1). S—Guidry. GDP—Munson, Piniella. SB—Lopes (2). CS—Lopes (1).

Yankees	IP	H	R	ER	BB	K	ERA
Ron Guidry (W, 1-0)	9.0	4	2	2	3	7	2.00

Dodgers	IP	H	R	ER	BB	K	ERA
Doug Rau (L, 0-1)	1.0	4	3	3	0	0	27.00
Rick Rhoden	7.0	2	1	1	0	5	2.57
Mike Garman	1.0	1	0	0	0	0	0.00

Rau pitched to three batters in the 2nd.

Time—2:07. Attendance—55,995. Umpires—HP, Dale. 1B, Evans. 2B, McSherry. 3B, Chylak.

Game 5
Sunday, October 16

Yankees	AB	R	H	RBI	BB	K	Avg
Mickey Rivers, cf	4	0	0	0	0	0	.174
Willie Randolph, 2b	4	0	1	0	0	0	.190
Thurman Munson, c	4	1	2	1	0	0	.333
Reggie Jackson, rf	4	2	2	1	0	0	.353
Chris Chambliss, 1b	4	1	2	0	0	0	.250
Graig Nettles, 3b	4	0	2	1	0	0	.235
Lou Piniella, lf	4	0	0	0	0	0	.316
Bucky Dent, ss	4	0	0	1	0	0	.294
Don Gullett, p	1	0	0	0	0	1	.000
Ken Clay, p	0	0	0	0	0	0	—
George Zeber, ph	1	0	0	0	0	1	.000
Dick Tidrow, p	0	0	0	0	0	0	.000
Roy White, ph	1	0	0	0	0	0	.000
Catfish Hunter, p	0	0	0	0	0	0	—
Paul Blair, ph	1	0	0	0	0	0	.250
TOTALS	36	4	9	4	0	2	.253

Dodgers	AB	R	H	RBI	BB	K	Avg
Davey Lopes, 2b	5	1	2	0	0	0	.150
Bill Russell, ss	5	1	2	1	0	0	.174
Reggie Smith, cf-rf	4	2	1	2	1	0	.278
Ron Cey, 3b	4	0	0	0	0	1	.167
Steve Garvey, 1b	4	2	2	0	0	1	.350
Dusty Baker, lf	4	2	3	2	0	0	.300
Lee Lacy, rf	3	1	2	1	0	0	.500
Glenn Burke, cf	1	0	0	0	0	0	.200
Steve Yeager, c	2	1	1	4	0	0	.313
Johnny Oates, ph-c	1	0	0	0	0	0	.000
Don Sutton, p	4	0	0	0	0	3	.000
TOTALS	37	10	13	10	1	5	.242

	1	2	3	4	5	6	7	8	9		R	H	E
Yankees	0	0	0	0	0	0	2	2	0		4	9	2
Dodgers	1	0	0	4	3	2	0	0	x		10	13	0

E—Piniella, Nettles. LOB—Yankees 5, Dodgers 5. Scoring Position—Yankees 1-for-6, Dodgers 5-for-8. 2B—Randolph (2), Nettles (1), Garvey (1). 3B—Lopes (1). HR—Munson (1), Jackson (2), Smith (2), Yeager (2). SF—Yeager.

Yankees	IP	H	R	ER	BB	K	ERA
Don Gullett (L, 0-1)	4.1	8	7	6	1	4	6.39
Ken Clay	0.2	2	1	1	0	0	2.45
Dick Tidrow	1.0	2	2	2	0	0	4.91
Catfish Hunter	2.0	1	0	0	0	1	10.38

Dodgers	IP	H	R	ER	BB	K	ERA
Don Sutton (W, 1-0)	9.0	9	4	4	0	2	3.94

Time—2:29. Attendance—55,955. Umpires—HP, Evans. 1B, McSherry. 2B, Chylak. 3B, Sudol.

Game 6
Tuesday, October 18

Dodgers	AB	R	H	RBI	BB	K	Avg
Davey Lopes, 2b	4	0	1	0	0	0	.167
Bill Russell, ss	3	0	0	0	1	0	.154
Reggie Smith, rf	4	2	1	1	0	0	.273
Ron Cey, 3b	3	1	1	0	1	2	.190
Steve Garvey, 1b	4	1	2	0	0	0	.375
Dusty Baker, lf	4	0	1	0	0	1	.292
Rick Monday, cf	4	0	1	0	0	0	.167
Steve Yeager, c	3	0	1	0	0	1	.316
Vic Davalillo, ph	1	0	1	1	0	0	.333
Burt Hooton, p	2	0	0	0	0	1	.000
Elias Sosa, p	0	0	0	0	0	0	—
Doug Rau, p	0	0	0	0	0	0	—
Ed Goodson, ph	1	0	0	0	0	1	.000
Charlie Hough, p	0	0	0	0	0	0	—
Lee Lacy, ph	1	0	0	0	0	0	.429
TOTALS	34	4	9	4	2	6	.245

Yankees	AB	R	H	RBI	BB	K	Avg
Mickey Rivers, cf	4	0	2	0	0	0	.222
Willie Randolph, 2b	4	1	0	0	0	0	.160
Thurman Munson, c	4	1	1	0	0	1	.320
Reggie Jackson, rf	3	4	3	5	1	0	.450
Chris Chambliss, 1b	4	2	2	2	0	0	.292
Graig Nettles, 3b	4	0	0	0	0	2	.190
Lou Piniella, lf	3	0	0	1	0	0	.273
Bucky Dent, ss	2	0	0	0	1	0	.263
Mike Torrez, p	3	0	0	0	0	2	.000
TOTALS	31	8	8	8	2	5	.259

	1	2	3	4	5	6	7	8	9		R	H	E
Dodgers	2	0	1	0	0	0	0	0	1		4	9	0
Yankees	0	2	0	3	2	0	0	1	x		8	8	1

E—Dent. DP—Yankees 2 (Dent to Randolph to Chambliss; Chambliss to Dent). LOB—Dodgers 5, Yankees 2. Scoring Position—Dodgers 2-for-6, Yankees 0-for-2. 2B—Chambliss (2). 3B—Garvey (1). HR—Smith (3), Jackson 3 (5), Chambliss (1). SF—Piniella. GDP—Smith 2.

Dodgers	IP	H	R	ER	BB	K	ERA
Burt Hooton (L, 1-1)	3.0	3	4	4	1	1	3.75
Elias Sosa	1.2	3	3	3	1	0	11.57
Doug Rau	1.1	0	0	0	0	1	11.57
Charlie Hough	2.0	2	1	1	0	3	1.80

Yankees	IP	H	R	ER	BB	K	ERA
Mike Torrez (W, 2-0)	9.0	9	4	2	2	6	2.50

Hooton pitched to two batters in the 4th.

PB—Munson. Time—2:18. Attendance—56,407. Umpires—HP, McSherry. 1B, Chylak. 2B, Sudol. 3B, McCoy.

1977 World Series—Composite Statistics

Batting

Yankees	G	AB	R	H	RBI	2B	3B	HR	BB	SO	SB	CS	Avg	OBP	Slg
Paul Blair	4	4	0	1	1	0	0	0	0	0	0	0	.250	.250	.250
Chris Chambliss	6	24	4	7	4	2	0	1	0	2	0	0	.292	.292	.500
Bucky Dent	6	19	0	5	2	0	0	0	2	1	0	0	.263	.333	.263
Ron Guidry	1	2	0	0	0	0	0	0	0	1	0	0	.000	.000	.000
Don Gullett	2	2	0	0	0	0	0	0	0	2	0	0	.000	.000	.000
Reggie Jackson	6	20	10	9	8	1	0	5	3	4	0	0	.450	.542	1.250
Cliff Johnson	1	1	0	0	0	0	0	0	0	0	0	0	.000	.000	.000
Sparky Lyle	2	2	0	0	0	0	0	0	0	2	0	0	.000	.000	.000
Thurman Munson	6	25	4	8	3	2	0	1	2	8	0	0	.320	.370	.520
Graig Nettles	6	21	1	4	2	1	0	0	2	3	0	0	.190	.261	.238
Lou Piniella	6	22	1	6	3	0	0	0	0	3	0	0	.273	.292	.273
Willie Randolph	6	25	5	4	1	2	0	1	2	2	0	0	.160	.222	.360
Mickey Rivers	6	27	1	6	1	2	0	0	0	2	1	0	.222	.222	.296
Dick Tidrow	2	1	0	0	0	0	0	0	0	1	0	0	.000	.000	.000
Mike Torrez	2	6	0	0	0	0	0	0	0	4	0	0	.000	.000	.000
Roy White	2	2	0	0	0	0	0	0	0	0	0	0	.000	.000	.000
George Zeber	2	2	0	0	0	0	0	0	0	2	0	0	.000	.000	.000
Totals	6	205	26	50	25	10	0	8	11	37	1	0	.244	.288	.410

Batting

Dodgers	G	AB	R	H	RBI	2B	3B	HR	BB	SO	SB	CS	Avg	OBP	Slg
Dusty Baker	6	24	4	7	5	0	0	1	0	2	0	0	.292	.320	.417
Glenn Burke	3	5	0	1	0	0	0	0	0	1	0	0	.200	.200	.200
Ron Cey	6	21	2	4	3	1	0	1	3	5	0	0	.190	.280	.381
Vic Davalillo	3	3	0	1	1	0	0	0	0	0	0	0	.333	.333	.333
Steve Garvey	6	24	5	9	3	1	1	1	1	4	0	1	.375	.400	.625
Ed Goodson	1	1	0	0	0	0	0	0	0	1	0	0	.000	.000	.000
Jerry Grote	1	1	0	0	0	0	0	0	0	0	0	0	.000	.000	.000
Burt Hooton	2	5	0	0	0	0	0	0	0	2	0	0	.000	.000	.000
Tommy John	1	2	0	0	0	0	0	0	0	2	0	0	.000	.000	.000
Lee Lacy	4	7	1	3	2	0	0	0	1	1	0	0	.429	.500	.429
Rafael Landestoy	1	0	0	0	0	0	0	0	0	0	0	0	—	—	—
Davey Lopes	6	24	3	4	2	0	1	1	4	3	2	1	.167	.286	.375
Rick Monday	4	12	0	2	0	0	0	0	0	3	0	1	.167	.167	.167
Manny Mota	3	3	0	0	0	0	0	0	0	1	0	0	.000	.000	.000
Johnny Oates	1	1	0	0	0	0	0	0	0	0	0	0	.000	.000	.000
Rick Rhoden	2	2	1	1	0	1	0	0	0	0	0	0	.500	.500	1.000
Bill Russell	6	26	3	4	2	0	1	0	1	3	0	0	.154	.185	.231
Reggie Smith	6	22	7	6	5	1	0	3	4	3	0	1	.273	.385	.727
Don Sutton	2	6	0	0	0	0	0	0	1	4	0	0	.000	.143	.000
Steve Yeager	6	19	2	6	5	1	0	2	1	1	0	0	.316	.333	.684
Totals	6	208	28	48	28	5	3	9	16	36	2	4	.231	.286	.413

Pitching

Yankees	G	GS	CG	IP	H	R	ER	BB	SO	W-L	Sv-Op	Hld	ERA
Ken Clay	2	0	0	3.2	2	1	1	1	1	0-0	0-0	0	2.45
Ron Guidry	1	1	1	9.0	4	2	2	3	7	1-0	0-0	0	2.00
Don Gullett	2	2	0	12.2	13	10	9	7	10	0-1	0-0	0	6.39
Catfish Hunter	2	1	0	4.1	6	5	5	0	1	0-1	0-0	0	10.38
Sparky Lyle	2	0	0	4.2	2	1	1	0	2	1-0	0-1	0	1.93
Dick Tidrow	2	0	0	3.2	5	2	2	0	1	0-0	0-0	0	4.91
Mike Torrez	2	2	2	18.0	16	7	5	5	15	2-0	0-0	0	2.50
Totals	6	6	3	56.0	48	28	25	16	36	4-2	0-1	0	4.02

Pitching

Dodgers	G	GS	CG	IP	H	R	ER	BB	SO	W-L	Sv-Op	Hld	ERA
Mike Garman	2	0	0	4.0	2	0	0	1	3	0-0	0-0	0	0.00
Burt Hooton	2	2	1	12.0	8	5	5	2	9	1-1	0-0	0	3.75
Charlie Hough	2	0	0	5.0	3	1	1	0	5	0-0	0-0	0	1.80
Tommy John	1	1	0	6.0	9	5	4	3	7	0-1	0-0	0	6.00
Doug Rau	2	1	0	2.1	4	3	3	0	1	0-1	0-0	0	11.57
Lance Rautzhan	1	0	0	0.1	0	0	0	0	0	0-0	0-0	0	0.00
Rick Rhoden	2	0	0	7.0	4	2	2	1	5	0-1	0-0	0	2.57
Elias Sosa	2	0	0	2.1	3	3	3	1	1	0-0	0-0	0	11.57
Don Sutton	2	2	1	16.0	17	7	7	1	6	1-0	0-0	0	3.94
Totals	6	6	2	55.0	50	26	25	11	37	2-4	0-0	0	4.09

Fielding

Yankees	Pos	G	PO	Ast	E	DP	PB	FPct
Paul Blair	rf	3	1	0	0	0	—	1.000
Chris Chambliss	1b	6	55	5	0	2	—	1.000
Ken Clay	p	2	1	1	0	0	—	1.000
Bucky Dent	ss	6	2	15	1	2	—	.944
Ron Guidry	p	1	0	0	0	0	—	—
Don Gullett	p	2	1	2	0	0	—	1.000
Catfish Hunter	p	2	1	0	0	0	—	1.000
Reggie Jackson	rf	6	9	0	0	0	—	1.000
Sparky Lyle	p	2	0	0	0	0	—	—
Thurman Munson	c	6	40	4	0	0	1	1.000
Graig Nettles	3b	6	2	20	1	0	—	.957
Lou Piniella	lf	6	16	1	1	0	—	.944
Willie Randolph	2b	6	13	14	0	1	—	1.000
Mickey Rivers	cf	6	24	1	0	0	—	1.000
Fred Stanley	ss	1	1	0	0	0	—	1.000
Dick Tidrow	p	2	0	1	0	0	—	1.000
Mike Torrez	p	2	2	3	0	0	—	1.000
Totals		6	168	67	3	5	1	.987

Fielding

Dodgers	Pos	G	PO	Ast	E	DP	PB	FPct
Dusty Baker	lf	6	12	0	1	0	—	.923
Glenn Burke	cf	3	9	0	0	0	—	1.000
Ron Cey	3b	6	5	7	0	0	—	1.000
Mike Garman	p	2	0	0	0	0	—	—
Steve Garvey	1b	6	59	5	0	4	—	1.000
Jerry Grote	c	1	3	3	0	0	0	1.000
Burt Hooton	p	2	0	0	0	0	—	—
Charlie Hough	p	2	0	0	0	0	—	—
Tommy John	p	1	0	0	0	0	—	—
Lee Lacy	rf	2	2	0	0	0	—	1.000
Davey Lopes	2b	6	12	22	0	2	—	1.000
Rick Monday	cf	4	5	0	0	0	—	1.000
Johnny Oates	c	1	1	0	0	0	0	1.000
Doug Rau	p	2	0	0	0	0	—	—
Lance Rautzhan	p	1	0	1	0	0	—	1.000
Rick Rhoden	p	2	1	1	0	0	—	1.000
Bill Russell	ss	6	9	21	0	4	—	1.000
Reggie Smith	rf	5	8	1	0	0	—	1.000
	cf	2	6	0	0	0	—	1.000
Elias Sosa	p	2	0	0	0	0	—	—
Don Sutton	p	2	1	1	0	0	—	1.000
Steve Yeager	c	6	32	6	0	0	0	1.000
Totals		6	165	68	1	10	0	.996

1978 New York Yankees (AL) 4, Los Angeles Dodgers (NL) 2

The New York Yankees dropped the first two games to the Los Angeles Dodgers before sweeping the next four to take the World Championship in six games. Davey Lopes homered twice and drove in five runs as the Dodgers drew first blood with an 11-5 victory. Ron Cey's three-run homer gave the Dodgers a 4-3 lead in the second game, and rookie Bob Welch fanned Reggie Jackson with the go-ahead runs on base to end the game. Ron Guidry started the Yanks' comeback with a complete-game 5-1 victory in Game 3, as Graig Nettles saved the day with several stellar defensive plays. The Yankees scored an important run in the sixth inning of Game 4 when Bill Russell's potentially inning-ending throw to first hit Jackson in the leg and skidded into right field. The Dodgers argued, unsuccessfully, that Jackson had committed interference. The Yanks ultimately won in 10 innings on a single by Lou Piniella. Thurman Munson drove in five runs, and Jim Beattie went the distance as the Yankees blasted the Dodgers 12-2 in Game 5. Catfish Hunter sealed it with a 7-2 win in the sixth game.

Game 1

Tuesday, October 10

Yankees	AB	R	H	RBI	BB	K	Avg
Mickey Rivers, cf	4	0	0	0	0	0	.000
Paul Blair, cf	1	0	0	0	0	1	.000
Roy White, lf	4	0	1	0	1	3	.250
Thurman Munson, c	4	1	0	0	0	1	.000
Reggie Jackson, dh	4	1	3	1	0	0	.750
Lou Piniella, rf	4	2	1	0	0	0	.250
Graig Nettles, 3b	4	0	1	1	0	1	.250
Chris Chambliss, 1b	4	1	1	0	0	0	.250
Fred Stanley, 2b	2	0	1	0	1	0	.500
Cliff Johnson, ph	1	0	0	0	0	1	.000
Brian Doyle, 2b	0	0	0	0	0	0	—
Bucky Dent, ss	4	0	1	2	0	0	.250
TOTALS	36	5	9	5	2	7	.250

Dodgers	AB	R	H	RBI	BB	K	Avg
Davey Lopes, 2b	5	2	2	5	0	0	.400
Bill Russell, ss	5	1	3	0	0	0	.600
Reggie Smith, rf	5	0	1	1	0	1	.200
Steve Garvey, 1b	5	1	2	0	0	2	.400
Ron Cey, 3b	4	1	1	0	1	0	.250
Dusty Baker, lf	4	2	3	1	0	0	.750
Rick Monday, cf	2	2	1	0	1	1	.500
Bill North, ph-cf	1	1	1	2	0	0	1.000
Lee Lacy, dh	3	0	1	1	0	0	.333
Steve Yeager, c	4	1	0	0	0	0	.000
TOTALS	38	11	15	10	3	4	.395

	1	2	3	4	5	6	7	8	9		R	H	E
Yankees	0	0	0	0	0	0	3	2	0		5	9	1
Dodgers	0	3	0	3	1	0	3	1	x		11	15	2

E—Dent, Lopes, Russell. DP—Yankees 2 (Dent to Stanley to Chambliss; Munson to Doyle), Dodgers 1 (Lopes to Russell to Garvey). LOB—Yankees 6, Dodgers 6. Scoring Position—Yankees 2-for-9, Dodgers 5-for-11. 2B—Stanley (1), Russell (1), Monday (1), North (1). HR—Jackson (1), Lopes 2 (2), Baker (1). GDP—Munson, Yeager. CS—Smith (1).

Yankees	IP	H	R	ER	BB	K	ERA
Ed Figueroa (L, 0-1)	1.2	5	3	3	1	0	16.20
Ken Clay	2.1	4	4	3	2	2	11.57
Paul Lindblad	2.1	4	3	3	0	1	11.57
Dick Tidrow	1.2	2	1	1	0	1	5.40

Dodgers	IP	H	R	ER	BB	K	ERA
Tommy John (W, 1-0)	7.2	8	5	3	2	4	3.52
Terry Forster	1.1	1	0	0	0	3	0.00

Clay pitched to three batters in the 5th.

WP—Clay. Time—2:48. Attendance—55,997. Umpires—HP, Vargo. 1B, Haller. 2B, Kibler. 3B, Springstead.

Game 2

Wednesday, October 11

Yankees	AB	R	H	RBI	BB	K	Avg
Roy White, lf	5	2	2	0	0	0	.333
Gary Thomasson, cf	3	0	1	0	0	0	.333
Paul Blair, ph-cf	1	0	1	0	1	0	.500
Thurman Munson, c	4	1	1	0	1	2	.125
Reggie Jackson, dh	4	0	1	3	0	2	.500
Graig Nettles, 3b	4	0	0	0	0	3	.125
Lou Piniella, rf	4	0	2	0	0	0	.375
Jim Spencer, 1b	4	0	1	0	0	1	.250
Brian Doyle, 2b	3	0	1	0	0	0	.333
Cliff Johnson, ph	1	0	0	0	0	0	.000
Fred Stanley, 2b	0	0	0	0	0	0	.500
Bucky Dent, ss	4	0	1	0	0	1	.250
TOTALS	37	3	11	3	2	9	.292

Dodgers	AB	R	H	RBI	BB	K	Avg
Davey Lopes, 2b	4	1	1	0	0	0	.333
Bill Russell, ss	4	0	1	0	0	0	.444
Reggie Smith, rf	4	2	1	0	0	0	.222
Steve Garvey, 1b	3	0	1	0	0	0	.375
Ron Cey, 3b	3	1	2	4	0	0	.429
Dusty Baker, lf	3	0	0	0	0	0	.429
Rick Monday, cf	3	0	0	0	0	1	.200
Bill North, cf	0	0	0	0	0	0	1.000
Lee Lacy, dh	3	0	0	0	0	0	.167
Steve Yeager, c	3	0	1	0	0	1	.143
TOTALS	30	4	7	4	0	2	.324

	1	2	3	4	5	6	7	8	9		R	H	E
Yankees	0	0	2	0	0	0	1	0	0		3	11	0
Dodgers	0	0	0	1	0	3	0	0	x		4	7	0

DP—Yankees 1 (Nettles to Spencer), Dodgers 1 (Cey to Lopes to Garvey). LOB—Yankees 10, Dodgers 2. Scoring Position—Yankees 1-for-10, Dodgers 2-for-4. 2B—Munson (1), Jackson (1), Blair (1). HR—Cey (1). GDP—Baker, Johnson. SB—White (1). CS—Thomasson (1).

Yankees	IP	H	R	ER	BB	K	ERA
Catfish Hunter (L, 0-1)	6.0	7	4	4	0	2	6.00
Goose Gossage	2.0	0	0	0	0	0	0.00

Dodgers	IP	H	R	ER	BB	K	ERA
Burt Hooton (W, 1-0)	6.0	8	3	3	1	5	4.50
Terry Forster (H, 1)	2.1	3	0	0	1	3	0.00
Bob Welch (S, 1)	0.2	0	0	0	0	1	0.00

Hooton pitched to one batter in the 7th.

WP—Hooton. HBP—Jackson by Hooton. Time—2:37. Attendance—55,982. Umpires—HP, Haller. 1B, Kibler. 2B, Springstead. 3B, Pulli.

Game 3

Friday, October 13

Dodgers	AB	R	H	RBI	BB	K	Avg
Davey Lopes, 2b	5	0	1	0	0	0	.286
Bill Russell, ss	4	0	2	1	1	0	.462
Reggie Smith, rf	4	0	1	0	1	1	.231
Steve Garvey, 1b	4	0	1	0	0	0	.333
Ron Cey, 3b	3	0	0	0	1	1	.300
Dusty Baker, lf	3	0	2	0	1	0	.500
Lee Lacy, dh	4	0	1	0	0	1	.200
Bill North, cf	3	1	0	0	1	0	.250
Steve Yeager, c	1	0	0	0	1	0	.125
Manny Mota, ph	0	0	0	0	1	0	—
Jerry Grote, c	0	0	0	0	0	0	—
Joe Ferguson, c	1	0	0	0	0	1	.000
TOTALS	32	1	8	1	7	4	.305

Yankees	AB	R	H	RBI	BB	K	Avg
Mickey Rivers, cf	4	0	3	0	0	0	.375
Paul Blair, pr-cf	0	0	0	0	0	0	.500
Roy White, lf	3	2	1	1	1	0	.333
Thurman Munson, c	4	1	1	1	0	2	.167
Reggie Jackson, dh	3	0	1	1	1	0	.455
Lou Piniella, rf	4	0	1	1	0	0	.333
Graig Nettles, 3b	4	1	1	0	0	0	.167
Chris Chambliss, 1b	3	0	1	0	0	0	.286
Brian Doyle, 2b	4	0	0	0	0	0	.143
Bucky Dent, ss	4	1	1	1	0	0	.250
TOTALS	33	5	10	5	3	2	.284

	1	2	3	4	5	6	7	8	9		R	H	E
Dodgers	0	0	1	0	0	0	0	0	0		1	8	0
Yankees	1	1	0	0	0	0	3	0	x		5	10	1

E—Dent. DP—Yankees 2 (Nettles to Doyle to Chambliss; Dent to Doyle to Chambliss). LOB—Dodgers 11, Yankees 7. Scoring Position—Dodgers 2-for-9, Yankees 2-for-10. 2B—Garvey (1). HR—White (1). GDP—Lacy 2. SB—North (1), Piniella (1). CS—Russell (1), Rivers (1).

Dodgers	IP	H	R	ER	BB	K	ERA
Don Sutton (L, 0-1)	6.1	9	5	5	3	2	7.11
Lance Rautzhan	0.2	1	0	0	0	0	0.00
Charlie Hough	1.0	0	0	0	0	0	0.00

Yankees	IP	H	R	ER	BB	K	ERA
Ron Guidry (W, 1-0)	9.0	8	1	1	7	4	1.00

Time—2:27. Attendance—56,447. Umpires—HP, Kibler. 1B, Springstead. 2B, Pulli. 3B, Brinkman.

Game 4
Saturday, October 14

Dodgers	AB	R	H	RBI	BB	K	Avg
Davey Lopes, 2b	4	1	0	0	1	0	.222
Bill Russell, ss	5	0	2	0	0	1	.444
Reggie Smith, rf	4	1	1	3	1	2	.235
Steve Garvey, 1b	4	0	0	0	1	1	.250
Ron Cey, 3b	4	0	1	0	0	1	.286
Dusty Baker, lf	4	0	0	0	0	2	.357
Rick Monday, dh	2	0	1	0	2	0	.286
Bill North, cf	4	0	0	0	0	0	.125
Steve Yeager, c	3	1	1	0	0	1	.182
Vic Davalillo, ph	1	0	0	0	0	0	.000
Jerry Grote, c	0	0	0	0	0	0	—
TOTALS	35	3	6	3	5	8	.274

Yankees	AB	R	H	RBI	BB	K	Avg
Paul Blair, cf	4	1	2	0	0	1	.500
Mickey Rivers, ph	1	0	0	0	0	0	.333
Roy White, lf	3	2	1	0	1	0	.333
Thurman Munson, c	3	1	2	1	2	0	.267
Reggie Jackson, dh	4	0	2	1	0	1	.467
Lou Piniella, rf	5	0	1	1	0	0	.294
Graig Nettles, 3b	4	0	0	0	0	1	.125
Chris Chambliss, 1b	4	0	0	0	0	1	.182
Fred Stanley, 2b	3	0	0	0	0	0	.200
Jim Spencer, ph	1	0	0	0	0	0	.200
Brian Doyle, 2b	0	0	0	0	0	0	.143
Bucky Dent, ss	4	0	1	0	0	0	.250
TOTALS	36	4	9	3	3	5	.277

	1	2	3	4	5	6	7	8	9	10		R	H	E
Dodgers	0	0	0	0	3	0	0	0	0	0		3	6	1
Yankees	0	0	0	0	0	2	0	1	0	1		4	9	0

E—Russell. DP—Yankees 1 (Piniella to Chambliss to Dent). LOB—Dodgers 7, Yankees 8. Scoring Position—Dodgers 1-for-8, Yankees 4-for-9. 2B—Yeager (1), Munson (2). HR—Smith (1). S—White. SB—Garvey (1), Munson (1).

Dodgers	IP	H	R	ER	BB	K	ERA
Tommy John	7.0	6	3	2	2	2	3.07
Terry Forster (BS, 1)	0.1	1	0	0	0	0	0.00
Bob Welch (L, 0-1)	2.1	2	1	1	1	3	3.00

Yankees	IP	H	R	ER	BB	K	ERA
Ed Figueroa	5.0	4	3	3	4	2	8.10
Dick Tidrow	3.0	2	0	0	0	4	1.93
Goose Gossage (W, 1-0)	2.0	0	0	0	1	2	0.00

John pitched to one batter in the 8th.

HBP—Jackson by Forster. Time—3:17. Attendance—56,445. Umpires—HP, Springstead. 1B, Pulli. 2B, Brinkman. 3B, Vargo.

Game 5
Sunday, October 15

Dodgers	AB	R	H	RBI	BB	K	Avg
Davey Lopes, 2b	4	2	2	0	1	0	.273
Bill Russell, ss	5	0	2	1	0	1	.435
Reggie Smith, rf	4	0	1	1	0	1	.238
Steve Garvey, 1b	4	0	1	0	0	2	.250
Ron Cey, 3b	3	0	1	0	1	1	.294
Dusty Baker, lf	4	0	0	0	0	1	.278
Rick Monday, cf	3	0	0	0	1	0	.200
Lee Lacy, dh	4	0	0	0	0	2	.143
Steve Yeager, c	2	0	1	0	0	0	.231
Johnny Oates, ph-c	1	0	1	0	1	0	1.000
TOTALS	34	2	9	2	4	8	.277

Yankees	AB	R	H	RBI	BB	K	Avg
Mickey Rivers, cf	5	2	3	1	0	1	.429
Paul Blair, pr-cf	1	1	0	0	0	1	.429
Roy White, lf	5	2	2	3	0	0	.350
Jay Johnstone, rf	0	0	0	0	0	0	—
Thurman Munson, c	5	1	3	5	0	0	.350
Mike Heath, c	0	0	0	0	0	0	—
Reggie Jackson, dh	3	0	1	0	2	1	.444
Lou Piniella, rf	4	0	1	1	0	0	.286
Gary Thomasson, lf	1	0	0	0	0	1	.250
Graig Nettles, 3b	5	0	1	0	1	1	.143
Jim Spencer, 1b	4	2	1	0	1	0	.222
Brian Doyle, 2b	5	2	3	0	0	0	.333
Bucky Dent, ss	4	2	3	1	1	1	.350
TOTALS	42	12	18	11	4	6	.325

	1	2	3	4	5	6	7	8	9		R	H	E
Dodgers	1	0	1	0	0	0	0	0	0		2	9	3
Yankees	0	0	4	3	0	0	4	1	x		12	18	0

E—Garvey, Russell, Smith. DP—Dodgers 2 (Russell to Lopes to Garvey; Lopes to Russell to Garvey), Yankees 1 (Nettles to Doyle to Spencer). LOB—Dodgers 9, Yankees 10. Scoring Position—Dodgers 2-for-13, Yankees 9-for-20. 2B—Russell (2), Munson (3), Dent (1). GDP—Lopes, Piniella, Nettles. SB—Lopes (2), Russell (1), Rivers (1), White (2). CS—Monday (1).

Dodgers	IP	H	R	ER	BB	K	ERA
Burt Hooton (L, 1-1)	2.1	5	4	3	2	1	6.48
Lance Rautzhan	1.1	3	3	3	0	0	13.50
Charlie Hough	4.1	10	5	5	2	5	8.44

Yankees	IP	H	R	ER	BB	K	ERA
Jim Beattie (W, 1-0)	9.0	9	2	2	4	8	2.00

WP—Hough 2. PB—Yeager. Time—2:56. Attendance—56,448. Umpires—HP, Pulli. 1B, Brinkman. 2B, Vargo. 3B, Haller.

Game 6
Tuesday, October 17

Yankees	AB	R	H	RBI	BB	K	Avg
Mickey Rivers, cf	4	0	0	0	0	1	.333
Paul Blair, cf	1	0	0	0	0	1	.375
Roy White, lf	4	1	1	0	1	2	.333
Gary Thomasson, lf	0	0	0	0	0	0	.250
Thurman Munson, c	5	0	1	0	0	2	.320
Reggie Jackson, dh	5	1	1	2	0	3	.391
Lou Piniella, rf	4	1	1	0	0	0	.280
Jay Johnstone, rf	0	0	0	0	0	0	—
Graig Nettles, 3b	4	1	1	0	0	0	.160
Jim Spencer, 1b	3	1	0	0	1	2	.167
Brian Doyle, 2b	4	2	3	2	0	0	.438
Bucky Dent, ss	4	0	3	3	0	0	.417
TOTALS	38	7	11	7	2	11	.319

Dodgers	AB	R	H	RBI	BB	K	Avg
Davey Lopes, 2b	4	1	2	2	0	1	.308
Bill Russell, ss	3	0	1	0	1	0	.423
Reggie Smith, rf	4	0	0	0	0	1	.200
Steve Garvey, 1b	4	0	0	0	0	2	.208
Ron Cey, 3b	4	0	1	0	0	0	.286
Dusty Baker, lf	3	0	0	0	0	0	.238
Rick Monday, cf	3	0	0	0	0	1	.154
Joe Ferguson, c	3	1	2	0	0	0	.500
Vic Davalillo, dh	2	0	1	0	0	0	.333
TOTALS	30	2	7	2	1	5	.276

	1	2	3	4	5	6	7	8	9		R	H	E
Yankees	0	3	0	0	0	2	2	0	0		7	11	0
Dodgers	1	0	1	0	0	0	0	0	0		2	7	1

E—Ferguson. DP—Yankees 2 (Doyle to Dent to Spencer; Nettles to Doyle to Spencer). LOB—Yankees 6, Dodgers 3. Scoring Position—Yankees 4-for-9, Dodgers 2-for-5. 2B—Doyle (1), Ferguson 2 (2). HR—Jackson (2), Lopes (3). S—Davalillo. GDP—Russell, Smith. SB—Lopes (2). CS—Russell (2).

Yankees	IP	H	R	ER	BB	K	ERA
Catfish Hunter (W, 1-1)	7.0	6	2	2	1	3	4.15
Goose Gossage	2.0	1	0	0	0	2	0.00

Dodgers	IP	H	R	ER	BB	K	ERA
Don Sutton (L, 0-2)	5.2	8	5	5	1	6	7.50
Bob Welch	1.1	2	2	2	1	2	6.23
Doug Rau	2.0	1	0	0	0	3	0.00

Hunter pitched to one batter in the 8th.

WP—Sutton. Time—2:34. Attendance—55,985. Umpires—HP, Brinkman. 1B, Vargo. 2B, Haller. 3B, Kibler.

1978 World Series—Composite Statistics

Batting

Yankees	G	AB	R	H	RBI	2B	3B	HR	BB	SO	SB	CS	Avg	OBP	Slg
Paul Blair	6	8	2	3	0	1	0	0	1	4	0	0	.375	.444	.500
Chris Chambliss	3	11	1	2	0	0	0	0	1	1	0	0	.182	.250	.182
Bucky Dent	6	24	3	10	7	1	0	0	1	2	0	0	.417	.440	.458
Brian Doyle	6	16	4	7	2	1	0	0	0	0	0	0	.438	.438	.500
Reggie Jackson	6	23	2	9	8	1	0	2	3	7	0	0	.391	.500	.696
Cliff Johnson	2	2	0	0	0	0	0	0	0	0	0	0	.000	.000	.000
Thurman Munson	6	25	5	8	7	3	0	0	3	7	1	0	.320	.393	.440
Graig Nettles	6	25	2	4	1	0	0	0	0	6	0	0	.160	.160	.160
Lou Piniella	6	25	3	7	4	0	0	0	0	0	1	0	.280	.280	.280
Mickey Rivers	5	18	2	6	1	0	0	0	0	2	1	1	.333	.333	.333
Jim Spencer	4	12	3	2	0	0	0	0	2	4	0	0	.167	.286	.167
Fred Stanley	3	5	0	1	0	1	0	0	1	0	0	0	.200	.333	.400
Gary Thomasson	3	4	0	1	0	0	0	0	0	1	0	0	.250	.250	.250
Roy White	6	24	9	8	4	0	0	1	4	5	2	0	.333	.429	.458
Totals	**6**	**222**	**36**	**68**	**34**	**8**	**0**	**3**	**16**	**40**	**5**	**2**	**.306**	**.358**	**.383**

Dodgers	G	AB	R	H	RBI	2B	3B	HR	BB	SO	SB	CS	Avg	OBP	Slg
Dusty Baker	6	21	2	5	1	0	0	1	1	3	0	0	.238	.273	.381
Ron Cey	6	21	2	6	4	0	0	1	3	3	0	0	.286	.375	.429
Vic Davalillo	2	3	0	1	0	0	0	0	0	0	0	0	.333	.333	.333
Joe Ferguson	2	4	1	2	0	2	0	0	0	1	0	0	.500	.500	1.000
Steve Garvey	6	24	1	5	0	1	0	0	1	7	1	0	.208	.240	.250
Lee Lacy	4	14	0	2	1	0	0	0	1	3	0	0	.143	.200	.143
Davey Lopes	6	26	7	8	7	0	0	3	2	1	2	0	.308	.357	.654
Rick Monday	5	13	2	2	0	1	0	0	4	3	0	1	.154	.353	.231
Manny Mota	1	0	0	0	0	0	0	0	1	0	0	0	—	1.000	—
Bill North	4	8	2	1	2	1	0	0	1	0	1	0	.125	.222	.250
Johnny Oates	1	1	0	1	0	0	0	0	0	1	0	0	1.000	1.000	1.000
Bill Russell	6	26	1	11	2	2	0	0	2	2	1	2	.423	.464	.500
Reggie Smith	6	25	3	5	5	0	0	1	2	6	0	1	.200	.259	.320
Steve Yeager	5	13	2	3	0	1	0	0	1	2	0	0	.231	.286	.308
Totals	**6**	**199**	**23**	**52**	**22**	**8**	**0**	**6**	**20**	**31**	**5**	**4**	**.261**	**.329**	**.392**

Pitching

Yankees	G	GS	CG	IP	H	R	ER	BB	SO	W-L	Sv-Op	Hld	ERA
Jim Beattie	1	1	1	9.0	9	2	2	4	8	1-0	0-0	0	2.00
Ken Clay	1	0	0	2.1	4	4	3	2	2	0-0	0-0	0	11.57
Ed Figueroa	2	2	0	6.2	9	6	6	5	2	0-1	0-0	0	8.10
Goose Gossage	3	0	0	6.0	1	0	0	1	4	1-0	0-0	0	0.00
Ron Guidry	1	1	1	9.0	8	1	1	7	4	1-0	0-0	0	1.00
Catfish Hunter	2	2	0	13.0	13	6	6	1	5	1-1	0-0	0	4.15
Paul Lindblad	1	0	0	2.1	4	3	3	0	1	0-0	0-0	0	11.57
Dick Tidrow	2	0	0	4.2	4	1	1	0	5	0-0	0-0	0	1.93
Totals	**6**	**6**	**2**	**53.0**	**52**	**23**	**22**	**20**	**31**	**4-2**	**0-0**	**0**	**3.74**

Dodgers	G	GS	CG	IP	H	R	ER	BB	SO	W-L	Sv-Op	Hld	ERA
Terry Forster	3	0	0	4.0	5	0	0	1	6	0-0	0-1	1	0.00
Burt Hooton	2	2	0	8.1	13	7	6	3	6	1-1	0-0	0	6.48
Charlie Hough	2	0	0	5.1	10	5	5	2	5	0-0	0-0	0	8.44
Tommy John	2	2	0	14.2	14	8	5	4	6	1-0	0-0	0	3.07
Doug Rau	1	0	0	2.0	1	0	0	0	3	0-0	0-0	0	0.00
Lance Rautzhan	2	0	0	2.0	4	3	3	0	0	0-0	0-0	0	13.50
Don Sutton	2	2	0	12.0	17	10	10	4	8	0-2	0-0	0	7.50
Bob Welch	3	0	0	4.1	4	3	3	2	6	0-1	1-1	0	6.23
Totals	**6**	**6**	**0**	**52.2**	**68**	**36**	**32**	**16**	**40**	**2-4**	**1-2**	**1**	**5.47**

Fielding

Yankees	Pos	G	PO	Ast	E	DP	PB	FPct
Jim Beattie	p	1	0	1	0	0	—	1.000
Paul Blair	cf	6	5	0	0	0	—	1.000
Chris Chambliss	1b	3	17	1	0	4	—	1.000
Ken Clay	p	1	0	0	0	0	—	—
Bucky Dent	ss	6	8	16	2	4	—	.923
Brian Doyle	2b	6	17	7	0	6	—	1.000
Ed Figueroa	p	2	0	0	0	0	—	—
Goose Gossage	p	3	0	0	0	0	—	—
Ron Guidry	p	1	1	1	0	0	—	1.000
Mike Heath	c	1	0	0	0	0	0	—
Catfish Hunter	p	2	2	0	0	0	—	1.000
Jay Johnstone	rf	2	1	0	0	0	—	1.000
Paul Lindblad	p	1	0	0	0	0	—	—
Thurman Munson	c	6	33	5	0	1	0	1.000
Graig Nettles	3b	6	8	18	0	4	—	1.000
Lou Piniella	rf	6	14	1	0	1	—	1.000
Mickey Rivers	cf	4	7	0	0	0	—	1.000
Jim Spencer	1b	3	23	2	0	4	—	1.000
Fred Stanley	2b	3	5	2	0	1	—	1.000
Gary Thomasson	lf	2	1	0	0	0	—	1.000
	cf	1	2	0	0	0	—	1.000
Dick Tidrow	p	2	0	0	0	0	—	—
Roy White	lf	6	15	0	0	0	—	1.000
Totals		**6**	**159**	**54**	**2**	**25**	**0**	**.991**

Dodgers	Pos	G	PO	Ast	E	DP	PB	FPct
Dusty Baker	lf	6	12	0	0	0	—	1.000
Ron Cey	3b	6	2	12	0	1	—	1.000
Joe Ferguson	c	2	11	0	1	0	0	.917
Terry Forster	p	3	0	1	0	0	—	1.000
Steve Garvey	1b	6	58	3	1	4	—	.984
Jerry Grote	c	2	3	0	0	0	—	1.000
Burt Hooton	p	2	1	0	0	0	—	1.000
Charlie Hough	p	2	1	0	0	0	—	1.000
Tommy John	p	2	0	4	0	0	—	1.000
Davey Lopes	2b	6	10	19	1	4	—	.967
Rick Monday	cf	4	5	0	0	0	—	1.000
Bill North	cf	4	7	0	0	0	—	1.000
Johnny Oates	c	1	3	1	0	0	0	1.000
Doug Rau	p	1	0	1	0	0	—	1.000
Lance Rautzhan	p	2	0	0	0	0	—	—
Bill Russell	ss	6	11	20	3	3	—	.912
Reggie Smith	rf	6	11	1	1	0	—	.923
Don Sutton	p	2	0	0	0	0	—	—
Bob Welch	p	3	0	0	0	0	—	—
Steve Yeager	c	5	23	2	0	0	1	1.000
Totals		**6**	**158**	**64**	**7**	**12**	**1**	**.969**

1979 Pittsburgh Pirates (NL) 4, Baltimore Orioles (AL) 3

Just as they had eight years before, the Pittsburgh Pirates fell behind the Baltimore Orioles by two games before rallying to take the World Series in seven. The O's scored five runs in the first inning of Game 1, and Mike Flanagan took it the rest of the way for a 5-4 win. Manny Sanguillen's pinch-hit RBI single in the top of the ninth gave the Pirates a 3-2 victory in Game 2. Scott McGregor fell behind 3-0 in Game 3, but the O's rallied for an 8-4 win as Kiko Garcia notched four hits and four RBI. Baltimore took the fourth game, 9-6, with pinch-hit doubles by John Lowenstein and Terry Crowley highlighting a six-run rally in the top of the eighth. Pittsburgh stayed alive with a 7-1 win in Game 5 behind Tim Foli's two hits and three RBI. John Candelaria and Kent Tekulve combined to blank Baltimore 4-0 in Game 6, and the Pirates completed the comeback with a 4-1 win in Game 7. Willie Stargell put the Pirates ahead to stay in the deciding game with a two-run homer in the top of the sixth. He batted .400 for the Series with three home runs and seven RBI.

Game 1

Wednesday, October 10

Pirates	AB	R	H	RBI	BB	K	Avg
Omar Moreno, cf	5	0	0	0	0	2	.000
Tim Foli, ss	5	1	1	0	0	0	.200
Dave Parker, rf	5	1	4	0	0	0	.800
Bill Robinson, lf	5	1	1	0	0	1	.200
Willie Stargell, 1b	5	1	1	2	0	2	.200
Bill Madlock, 3b	3	0	0	0	1	0	.000
Steve Nicosia, c	4	0	0	0	0	1	.000
Phil Garner, 2b	4	0	3	2	0	1	.750
Bruce Kison, p	0	0	0	0	0	0	—
Jim Rooker, p	1	0	0	0	0	0	.000
Manny Sanguillen, ph	1	0	0	0	0	0	.000
Enrique Romo, p	0	0	0	0	0	0	—
Lee Lacy, ph	1	0	0	0	0	0	.000
Don Robinson, p	0	0	0	0	0	0	—
Rennie Stennett, ph	1	0	1	0	0	0	1.000
Grant Jackson, p	0	0	0	0	0	0	—
TOTALS	40	4	11	4	1	7	.275

Orioles	AB	R	H	RBI	BB	K	Avg
Al Bumbry, cf	4	1	1	0	0	0	.250
Mark Belanger, ss	3	1	0	0	1	1	.000
Ken Singleton, rf	3	0	1	0	1	0	.333
Eddie Murray, 1b	2	1	1	0	2	0	.500
John Lowenstein, lf	4	1	0	1	0	1	.000
Gary Roenicke, lf	0	0	0	0	0	0	—
Doug DeCinces, 3b	3	1	1	2	1	0	.333
Billy Smith, 2b	2	0	1	0	1	0	.500
Rich Dauer, ph-2b	1	0	1	0	0	0	1.000
Rick Dempsey, c	4	0	0	0	0	0	.000
Mike Flanagan, p	4	0	0	0	0	2	.000
TOTALS	30	5	6	3	6	4	.200

	1	2	3	4	5	6	7	8	9	R	H	E
Pirates	0	0	0	1	0	2	0	1	0	4	11	3
Orioles	5	0	0	0	0	0	0	0	x	5	6	3

E—Belanger, DeCinces 2, Foli, Stargell, Garner. DP—Pirates 1 (Madlock to Garner to Stargell). LOB—Pirates 10, Orioles 8. Scoring Position—Pirates 1-for-16, Orioles 1-for-8. 2B—Parker (1), Garner (1). HR—Stargell (1), DeCinces (1). S—Bumbry. GDP—Smith. SB—Murray (1). CS—Parker (1).

Pirates	IP	H	R	ER	BB	K	ERA
Bruce Kison (L, 0-1)	0.1	3	5	4	2	0	108.00
Jim Rooker	3.2	2	0	0	1	2	0.00
Enrique Romo	1.0	0	0	0	2	0	0.00
Don Robinson	2.0	0	0	0	1	1	0.00
Grant Jackson	1.0	1	0	0	0	1	0.00

Orioles	IP	H	R	ER	BB	K	ERA
Mike Flanagan (W, 1-0)	9.0	11	4	2	1	7	2.00

WP—Kison. Time—3:18. Attendance—53,735. Umpires—HP, Neudecker. 1B, Engel. 2B, Goetz. 3B, Tata.

Game 2

Thursday, October 11

Pirates	AB	R	H	RBI	BB	K	Avg
Omar Moreno, cf	5	0	1	0	0	2	.100
Tim Foli, ss	4	0	1	0	0	0	.222
Dave Parker, rf	4	0	1	0	0	0	.556
Willie Stargell, 1b	4	1	1	0	0	1	.222
John Milner, lf	3	1	1	0	0	0	.333
Bill Robinson, ph	1	0	1	0	0	0	.333
Matt Alexander, pr-lf	0	0	0	0	0	0	—
Bill Madlock, 3b	4	0	2	1	0	0	.286
Ed Ott, c	3	1	1	1	0	1	.333
Phil Garner, 2b	2	0	1	0	2	0	.667
Bert Blyleven, p	2	0	0	0	0	0	.000
Mike Easler, ph	0	0	0	0	1	0	—
Don Robinson, p	0	0	0	0	0	0	—
Manny Sanguillen, ph	1	0	1	1	0	0	.500
Kent Tekulve, p	0	0	0	0	0	0	—
TOTALS	33	3	11	3	3	4	.318

Orioles	AB	R	H	RBI	BB	K	Avg
Al Bumbry, cf	5	0	0	0	0	1	.111
Mark Belanger, ss	3	0	0	0	1	0	.000
Terry Crowley, ph	0	0	0	0	1	0	—
Tippy Martinez, p	0	0	0	0	0	0	—
Don Stanhouse, p	0	0	0	0	0	0	—
Ken Singleton, rf	4	1	1	0	0	0	.286
Eddie Murray, 1b	3	1	3	2	1	0	.800
Doug DeCinces, 3b	4	0	0	0	0	0	.143
John Lowenstein, lf	3	0	1	0	1	0	.143
Billy Smith, 2b	4	0	0	0	0	1	.167
Rick Dempsey, c	3	0	1	0	1	1	.143
Jim Palmer, p	2	0	0	0	0	1	.000
Pat Kelly, ph	0	0	0	0	1	0	—
Kiko Garcia, ss	1	0	0	0	0	1	.000
TOTALS	32	2	6	2	5	5	.193

	1	2	3	4	5	6	7	8	9	R	H	E
Pirates	0	2	0	0	0	0	0	0	1	3	11	2
Orioles	0	1	0	0	0	1	0	0	0	2	6	1

E—DeCinces, Foli, Parker. DP—Pirates 3 (Madlock to Garner to Stargell; Parker to Ott; Foli to Garner to Madlock), Orioles 2 (Murray to Palmer; Murray to Belanger to Smith). LOB—Pirates 7, Orioles 8. Scoring Position—Pirates 2-for-6, Orioles 0-for-8. 2B—Murray (1). HR—Murray (1). SF—Ott. GDP—Blyleven, Smith. CS—Madlock (1), Alexander (1).

Pirates	IP	H	R	ER	BB	K	ERA
Bert Blyleven	6.0	5	2	2	2	1	3.00
Don Robinson (W, 1-0)	2.0	1	0	0	3	2	0.00
Kent Tekulve (S, 1)	1.0	0	0	0	0	2	0.00

Orioles	IP	H	R	ER	BB	K	ERA
Jim Palmer	7.0	8	2	2	3	3	2.57
Tippy Martinez	1.0	1	0	0	0	1	0.00
Don Stanhouse (L, 0-1)	1.0	2	1	1	1	0	9.00

Martinez pitched to one batter in the 9th.

WP—Palmer. Time—3:13. Attendance—53,739. Umpires—HP, Engel. 1B, Goetz. 2B, Tata. 3B, McKean.

Game 3

Friday, October 12

Orioles	AB	R	H	RBI	BB	K	Avg
Kiko Garcia, ss	4	2	4	4	1	0	.800
Bennie Ayala, lf	2	1	2	2	0	0	1.000
Al Bumbry, ph-cf	2	1	1	0	0	0	.182
Ken Singleton, rf	5	0	2	1	0	1	.333
Eddie Murray, 1b	4	0	0	0	1	0	.444
Doug DeCinces, 3b	5	0	0	1	0	1	.083
Gary Roenicke, cf-lf	5	0	1	0	0	2	.200
Rich Dauer, 2b	5	1	1	0	0	1	.333
Rick Dempsey, c	5	2	2	0	0	1	.250
Scott McGregor, p	3	1	0	0	1	1	.000
TOTALS	40	8	13	8	3	7	.299

Pirates	AB	R	H	RBI	BB	K	Avg
Omar Moreno, cf	4	1	2	0	0	1	.214
Tim Foli, ss	4	0	0	0	0	0	.154
Dave Parker, rf	3	0	0	1	0	1	.417
Bill Robinson, lf	4	0	1	0	0	2	.300
Willie Stargell, 1b	4	2	2	0	0	0	.308
Bill Madlock, 3b	4	0	1	0	1	0	.273
Steve Nicosia, c	4	1	1	0	0	0	.125
Phil Garner, 2b	4	0	1	2	0	0	.500
John Candelaria, p	1	0	1	0	0	0	1.000
Enrique Romo, p	1	0	0	0	0	0	.000
Grant Jackson, p	0	0	0	0	0	0	—
Lee Lacy, ph	1	0	0	0	0	0	.000
Kent Tekulve, p	0	0	0	0	0	0	—
TOTALS	34	4	9	4	0	6	.284

	1	2	3	4	5	6	7	8	9	R	H	E
Orioles	0	0	2	5	0	0	1	0	0	8	13	0
Pirates	1	2	0	0	0	1	0	0	0	4	9	2

E—Foli, Stargell. LOB—Orioles 9, Pirates 4. Scoring Position—Orioles 7-for-18, Pirates 2-for-5. 2B—Garcia (1), Dauer (1), Dempsey (1), Moreno 2 (2), Stargell (1), Garner (2). 3B—Garcia (1). HR—Ayala (1). SF—Parker.

Orioles	IP	H	R	ER	BB	K	ERA
Scott McGregor (W, 1-0)	9.0	9	4	4	0	6	4.00

Pirates	IP	H	R	ER	BB	K	ERA
John Candelaria (L, 0-1)	3.0	8	6	5	2	2	15.00
Enrique Romo	3.2	5	2	2	1	4	3.86
Grant Jackson	0.1	0	0	0	0	0	0.00
Kent Tekulve	2.0	0	0	0	0	1	0.00

Candelaria pitched to four batters in the 4th.

Balk—McGregor. WP—Romo. HBP—Bumbry by Romo. Time—2:51. Attendance—50,848. Umpires—HP, Goetz. 1B, Tata. 2B, McKean. 3B, Runge.

Game 4
Saturday, October 13

Orioles	AB	R	H	RBI	BB	K	Avg
Al Bumbry, cf	5	1	1	1	0	0	.188
Kiko Garcia, ss	5	2	2	2	0	2	.600
Mark Belanger, ss	0	0	0	0	0	0	.000
Ken Singleton, rf	5	0	3	1	0	1	.412
Eddie Murray, 1b	5	1	0	0	0	2	.286
Doug DeCinces, 3b	1	1	0	0	4	0	.077
Gary Roenicke, lf	3	0	0	0	0	1	.125
John Lowenstein, ph-lf	2	1	1	2	0	0	.222
Rich Dauer, 2b	3	0	1	0	0	0	.333
Billy Smith, ph-2b	0	1	0	0	1	0	.167
Dave Skaggs, c	3	1	1	0	0	0	.333
Terry Crowley, ph	1	0	1	2	0	0	1.000
Rick Dempsey, pr-c	0	1	0	0	0	0	.250
Dennis Martinez, p	0	0	0	0	0	0	—
Sammy Stewart, p	1	0	0	0	0	1	.000
Lee May, ph	1	0	0	0	0	1	.000
Steve Stone, p	0	0	0	0	0	0	—
Pat Kelly, p	1	0	1	0	0	0	1.000
Tim Stoddard, p	1	0	1	1	0	0	1.000
TOTALS	37	9	12	9	5	8	.273

Pirates	AB	R	H	RBI	BB	K	Avg
Omar Moreno, cf	5	0	2	1	0	0	.263
Tim Foli, ss	4	2	3	0	1	0	.294
Dave Parker, rf	5	0	2	1	0	1	.412
Willie Stargell, 1b	5	1	3	1	0	1	.389
John Milner, lf	3	1	2	1	1	0	.500
Don Robinson, p	0	0	0	0	0	0	—
Kent Tekulve, p	0	0	0	0	0	0	—
Mike Easler, ph	1	0	0	0	0	0	.000
Bill Madlock, 3b	3	1	2	0	2	0	.357
Ed Ott, c	5	0	1	2	0	1	.250
Phil Garner, 2b	4	1	2	0	0	0	.500
Jim Bibby, p	3	0	0	0	0	1	.000
Grant Jackson, p	0	0	0	0	0	0	—
Bill Robinson, lf	1	0	0	0	0	1	.273
TOTALS	39	6	17	6	4	5	.344

	1	2	3	4	5	6	7	8	9		R	H	E
Orioles	0	0	3	0	0	0	0	6	0		9	12	0
Pirates	0	4	0	0	1	1	0	0	0		6	17	1

E—Madlock. DP—Orioles 2 (Martinez to Garcia to Murray; Dauer to Garcia to Murray), Pirates 3 (Foli to Garner to Stargell; Garner to Foli to Stargell; Foli to Garner to Stargell). LOB—Orioles 6, Pirates 10. Scoring Position—Orioles 5-for-11, Pirates 4-for-11. 2B—Garcia (2), Singleton (1), Parker (2), Stargell (2), Milner (1), Madlock (1), Ott (1), Lowenstein (1), Crowley (1). HR—Stargell (2). GDP—Bumbry, Murray, Skaggs, Parker, Madlock. SB—DeCinces (1). CS—Madlock (2).

Orioles	IP	H	R	ER	BB	K	ERA
Dennis Martinez	1.1	6	4	4	0	0	27.00
Sammy Stewart	2.2	4	0	0	1	0	0.00
Steve Stone	2.0	4	2	2	2	2	9.00
Tim Stoddard (W, 1-0)	3.0	3	0	0	1	3	0.00

Pirates	IP	H	R	ER	BB	K	ERA
Jim Bibby	6.1	7	3	2	2	7	2.84
Grant Jackson (H, 1)	0.2	0	0	0	0	0	0.00
Don Robinson (H, 1)	0.1	2	3	3	1	0	6.23
Kent Tekulve (BS, 1; L, 0-1)	1.2	3	3	3	2	1	5.79

Time—3:48. Attendance—50,883. Umpires—HP, Tata. 1B, McKean. 2B, Runge. 3B, Neudecker.

Game 5
Sunday, October 14

Orioles	AB	R	H	RBI	BB	K	Avg
Kiko Garcia, ss	4	0	0	0	0	0	.429
Bennie Ayala, lf	1	0	0	0	1	0	.667
Al Bumbry, ph-cf	1	0	0	0	1	0	.176
Ken Singleton, rf	4	0	0	0	0	1	.333
Eddie Murray, 1b	4	0	0	0	0	0	.222
Gary Roenicke, cf-lf	4	1	1	0	0	1	.167
Doug DeCinces, 3b	4	0	2	0	0	2	.176
Rich Dauer, 2b	3	0	0	0	0	0	.250
John Lowenstein, ph	1	0	1	0	0	0	.300
Rick Dempsey, c	3	0	2	0	0	0	.333
Terry Crowley, ph	1	0	0	0	0	0	.500
Mike Flanagan, p	1	0	0	0	0	1	.000
Pat Kelly, ph	1	0	0	0	0	1	.500
Tim Stoddard, p	0	0	0	0	0	0	1.000
Tippy Martinez, p	0	0	0	0	0	0	—
Don Stanhouse, p	0	0	0	0	0	0	—
TOTALS	32	1	6	0	3	5	.275

Game 6
Tuesday, October 16

Pirates	AB	R	H	RBI	BB	K	Avg
Omar Moreno, cf	5	1	3	1	0	0	.286
Tim Foli, ss	5	1	2	0	0	0	.346
Dave Parker, rf	4	0	1	1	1	1	.400
Willie Stargell, 1b	4	0	0	1	0	1	.320
John Milner, lf	3	0	0	0	1	0	.333
Kent Tekulve, p	1	0	0	0	0	0	.000
Bill Madlock, 3b	3	0	0	0	0	0	.429
Ed Ott, c	4	1	2	0	0	0	.333
Phil Garner, 2b	3	1	2	0	0	0	.524
John Candelaria, p	2	0	0	0	0	2	.333
Lee Lacy, ph	1	0	0	0	0	1	.250
Bill Robinson, lf	0	0	0	0	1	0	.267
TOTALS	35	4	10	4	3	5	.358

Orioles	AB	R	H	RBI	BB	K	Avg
Kiko Garcia, ss	3	0	1	0	0	0	.412
Pat Kelly, ph	1	0	0	0	0	0	.333
Mark Belanger, ss	0	0	0	0	0	0	.000
Bennie Ayala, lf	3	0	0	0	0	0	.333
Terry Crowley, ph	1	0	0	0	0	0	.333
Tim Stoddard, p	0	0	0	0	0	0	1.000
Ken Singleton, rf	4	0	3	0	0	0	.400
Eddie Murray, 1b	4	0	0	0	0	0	.182
Doug DeCinces, 3b	4	0	0	0	0	1	.143
Gary Roenicke, cf	2	0	0	0	0	0	.143
Al Bumbry, ph-cf	1	0	0	0	0	0	.167
Rich Dauer, 2b	2	0	1	0	0	0	.286
Billy Smith, ph-2b	1	0	1	0	0	0	.286
Rick Dempsey, c	3	0	1	0	0	1	.333
Jim Palmer, p	2	0	0	0	0	2	.000
John Lowenstein, ph-lf	1	0	0	0	0	1	.273
TOTALS	32	0	7	0	0	6	.258

	1	2	3	4	5	6	7	8	9		R	H	E
Pirates	0	0	0	0	0	0	2	2	0		4	10	0
Orioles	0	0	0	0	0	0	0	0	0		0	7	1

E—Bumbry. DP—Pirates 2 (Madlock to Stargell; Foli to Garner to Stargell). LOB—Pirates 10, Orioles 5. Scoring Position—Pirates 2-for-9, Orioles 0-for-3. 2B—Foli (1), Garner (3). SF—Stargell, Robinson. GDP—Murray, Dempsey.

Pirates	IP	H	R	ER	BB	K	ERA
John Candelaria (W, 1-1)	6.0	6	0	0	0	2	5.00
Kent Tekulve (S, 2)	3.0	1	0	0	0	4	3.52

Orioles	IP	H	R	ER	BB	K	ERA
Jim Palmer (L, 0-1)	8.0	10	4	4	3	5	3.60
Tim Stoddard	1.0	0	0	0	0	0	3.86

HBP—Garner by Palmer. Time—2:30. Attendance—53,739. Umpires—HP, Runge. 1B, Neudecker. 2B, Engel. 3B, Goetz.

Game 7
Wednesday, October 17

Pirates	AB	R	H	RBI	BB	K	Avg
Omar Moreno, cf	5	1	3	1	0	0	.333
Tim Foli, ss	4	0	1	0	0	0	.333
Dave Parker, rf	4	0	0	0	0	2	.345
Bill Robinson, lf	4	1	1	1	0	0	.263
Willie Stargell, 1b	5	1	4	2	0	0	.400
Bill Madlock, 3b	3	0	0	0	1	0	.375
Steve Nicosia, c	4	0	0	0	0	0	.063
Phil Garner, 2b	3	1	1	0	1	0	.500
Jim Bibby, p	1	0	0	0	0	0	.000
Manny Sanguillen, ph	1	0	0	0	0	0	.333
Don Robinson, p	0	0	0	0	0	0	—
Grant Jackson, p	1	0	0	0	0	0	.000
Kent Tekulve, p	1	0	0	0	0	0	.000
TOTALS	36	4	10	4	2	2	.330

Orioles	AB	R	H	RBI	BB	K	Avg
Al Bumbry, cf	3	0	0	0	1	0	.143
Kiko Garcia, ss	3	0	1	0	0	0	.400
Bennie Ayala, lf	0	0	0	0	0	0	.333
Terry Crowley, ph	1	0	0	0	0	0	.250
Tim Stoddard, p	0	0	0	0	0	0	1.000
Mike Flanagan, p	0	0	0	0	0	0	.000
Don Stanhouse, p	0	0	0	0	0	0	—
Tippy Martinez, p	0	0	0	0	0	0	—
Dennis Martinez, p	0	0	0	0	0	0	—
Ken Singleton, rf	3	0	0	0	1	0	.357
Eddie Murray, 1b	4	0	0	0	0	2	.154
John Lowenstein, lf	2	0	0	0	0	1	.231
Gary Roenicke, ph-lf	2	0	0	0	0	2	.125
Doug DeCinces, 3b	4	0	2	0	0	1	.200
Rick Dempsey, c	3	0	0	0	0	0	.286
Pat Kelly, ph	1	0	0	0	0	0	.250
Rich Dauer, 2b	3	1	1	1	0	0	.294
Scott McGregor, p	1	0	0	0	0	1	.000
Lee May, ph	0	0	0	0	1	0	.000
Mark Belanger, pr-ss	0	0	0	0	0	0	.000
TOTALS	30	1	4	1	4	6	.234

	1	2	3	4	5	6	7	8	9		R	H	E
Pirates	0	0	0	0	0	2	0	0	2		4	10	0
Orioles	0	0	1	0	0	0	0	0	0		1	4	2

E—Lowenstein, Garcia. DP—Orioles 1 (Belanger to Murray). LOB—Pirates 10, Orioles 6. Scoring Position—Pirates 1-for-12, Orioles 0-for-3. 2B—Stargell 2 (4), Garner (4). HR—Stargell (3), Dauer (1). S—Foli. GDP—Stargell. CS—Garcia (1).

Pirates	IP	H	R	ER	BB	K	ERA
Jim Bibby	4.0	3	1	1	0	3	2.61
Don Robinson	0.2	0	0	0	1	0	5.40
Grant Jackson (W, 1-0)	2.2	0	0	0	2	1	0.00
Kent Tekulve (S, 3)	1.2	0	0	0	1	2	2.89

Orioles	IP	H	R	ER	BB	K	ERA
Scott McGregor (L, 1-1)	8.0	7	2	2	2	2	3.18
Tim Stoddard	0.1	1	0	0	0	0	5.40
Mike Flanagan	0.0	1	1	1	0	0	3.00
Don Stanhouse	0.0	1	0	0	0	0	13.50
Tippy Martinez	0.0	0	0	0	1	0	6.75
Dennis Martinez	0.2	0	1	1	1	0	18.00

Flanagan pitched to one batter in the 9th. Stanhouse pitched to one batter in the 9th. TMartinez pitched to one batter in the 9th.

HBP—BRobinson by DMartinez, Parker by TMartinez. Time—2:54. Attendance—53,733. Umpires—HP, Neudecker. 1B, Engel. 2B, Goetz. 3B, Tata.

1979 World Series—Composite Statistics

Batting

Pirates	G	AB	R	H	RBI	2B	3B	HR	BB	SO	SB	CS	Avg	OBP	Slg
Matt Alexander	1	0	0	0	0	0	0	0	0	0	0	1	—	—	—
Jim Bibby	2	4	0	0	0	0	0	0	0	1	0	0	.000	.000	.000
Bert Blyleven	2	3	0	0	0	0	0	0	0	0	0	0	.000	.000	.000
John Candelaria	2	3	0	1	0	0	0	0	0	2	0	0	.333	.333	.333
Mike Easler	2	1	0	0	0	0	0	0	1	0	0	0	.000	.500	.000
Tim Foli	7	30	6	10	3	1	0	0	2	0	0	0	.333	.375	.433
Phil Garner	7	24	4	12	5	4	0	0	3	1	0	0	.500	.571	.667
Grant Jackson	4	1	0	0	0	0	0	0	0	0	0	0	.000	.000	.000
Lee Lacy	4	4	0	1	0	0	0	0	0	1	0	0	.250	.250	.250
Bill Madlock	7	24	2	9	3	1	0	0	5	1	0	2	.375	.483	.417
John Milner	3	9	2	3	1	1	0	0	2	0	0	0	.333	.455	.444
Omar Moreno	7	33	4	11	3	2	0	0	1	7	0	0	.333	.353	.394
Steve Nicosia	4	16	1	1	0	0	0	0	0	2	0	0	.063	.063	.063
Ed Ott	3	12	2	4	3	1	0	0	0	2	0	0	.333	.308	.417
Dave Parker	7	29	2	10	4	3	0	0	2	7	0	1	.345	.394	.448
Bill Robinson	7	19	2	5	2	1	0	0	4	0	0	0	.263	.286	.316
Enrique Romo	2	1	0	0	0	0	0	0	0	0	0	0	.000	.000	.000
Jim Rooker	2	2	0	0	0	0	0	0	0	1	0	0	.000	.000	.000
Manny Sanguillen	3	3	0	1	1	0	0	0	0	0	0	0	.333	.333	.333
Willie Stargell	7	30	7	12	7	4	0	3	0	6	0	0	.400	.375	.833
Rennie Stennett	1	1	0	1	0	0	0	0	0	0	0	0	1.000	1.000	1.000
Kent Tekulve	5	2	0	0	0	0	0	0	0	0	0	0	.000	.000	.000
Totals	7	251	32	81	32	18	1	3	16	35	0	4	.323	.364	.438

Orioles	G	AB	R	H	RBI	2B	3B	HR	BB	SO	SB	CS	Avg	OBP	Slg
Bennie Ayala	4	6	1	2	2	0	0	1	1	0	0	0	.333	.429	.833
Mark Belanger	5	6	1	0	0	0	0	0	1	1	0	0	.000	.143	.000
Al Bumbry	7	21	3	3	1	0	0	0	2	1	0	0	.143	.250	.143
Terry Crowley	5	4	0	1	2	1	0	0	1	0	0	0	.250	.400	.500
Rich Dauer	6	17	2	5	1	1	0	1	0	1	0	0	.294	.294	.529
Doug DeCinces	7	25	2	5	3	0	0	1	5	5	1	0	.200	.333	.320
Rick Dempsey	7	21	3	6	0	2	0	0	1	3	0	0	.286	.318	.381
Mike Flanagan	3	5	0	0	0	0	0	0	1	2	0	0	.000	.167	.000
Kiko Garcia	6	20	4	8	6	2	1	0	1	3	0	1	.400	.429	.600
Pat Kelly	5	4	0	1	0	0	0	0	1	1	0	0	.250	.400	.250
John Lowenstein	6	13	2	3	3	1	0	0	1	3	0	0	.231	.286	.308
Lee May	2	1	0	0	0	0	0	0	0	1	0	0	.000	.500	.000
Scott McGregor	2	4	1	0	0	0	0	0	0	2	0	0	.000	.333	.000
Eddie Murray	7	26	3	4	2	1	0	1	4	4	1	0	.154	.267	.308
Jim Palmer	2	4	0	0	0	0	0	0	0	3	0	0	.000	.000	.000
Gary Roenicke	6	16	1	2	0	1	0	0	0	6	0	0	.125	.125	.188
Ken Singleton	7	28	1	10	2	1	0	0	2	5	0	0	.357	.400	.393
Dave Skaggs	1	3	1	1	0	0	0	0	0	0	0	0	.333	.333	.333
Billy Smith	4	7	1	2	0	0	0	0	2	0	0	0	.286	.444	.286
Sammy Stewart	1	1	0	0	0	0	0	0	0	1	0	0	.000	.000	.000
Tim Stoddard	4	1	0	1	1	0	0	0	0	0	0	0	1.000	1.000	1.000
Totals	7	233	26	54	23	10	1	4	26	41	2	1	.232	.312	.335

Pitching

Pirates	G	GS	CG	IP	H	R	ER	BB	SO	W-L	Sv-Op	Hld	ERA
Jim Bibby	2	2	0	10.1	10	4	3	2	10	0-0	0-0	0	2.61
Bert Blyleven	2	1	0	10.0	8	2	2	3	4	1-0	0-0	0	1.80
John Candelaria	2	2	0	9.0	14	6	5	2	4	1-1	0-0	0	5.00
Grant Jackson	4	0	0	4.2	1	0	0	2	2	1-0	0-0	1	0.00
Bruce Kison	1	1	0	0.1	3	5	4	2	0	0-1	0-0	0	108.00
Don Robinson	4	0	0	5.0	4	3	3	6	3	1-0	0-0	1	5.40
Enrique Romo	2	0	0	4.2	5	2	2	3	4	0-0	0-0	0	3.86
Jim Rooker	2	1	0	8.2	5	1	1	3	4	0-0	0-0	0	1.04
Kent Tekulve	5	0	0	9.1	4	3	3	3	10	0-1	3-4	0	2.89
Totals	7	7	0	62.0	54	26	22	26	41	4-3	3-4	2	3.19

Orioles	G	GS	CG	IP	H	R	ER	BB	SO	W-L	Sv-Op	Hld	ERA
Mike Flanagan	3	2	1	15.0	18	7	5	2	13	1-1	0-0	0	3.00
Dennis Martinez	2	1	0	2.0	6	4	4	0	0	0-0	0-0	0	18.00
Tippy Martinez	3	0	0	1.1	3	1	1	0	1	0-0	0-0	0	6.75
Scott McGregor	2	2	1	17.0	16	6	6	2	8	1-1	0-0	0	3.18
Jim Palmer	2	2	0	15.0	18	6	6	5	8	0-1	0-0	0	3.60
Don Stanhouse	3	0	0	2.0	6	3	3	3	0	0-1	0-0	0	13.50
Sammy Stewart	1	0	0	2.2	4	0	1	1	0	0-0	0-0	0	0.00
Tim Stoddard	4	0	0	5.0	6	3	3	1	3	1-0	0-0	0	5.40
Steve Stone	1	0	0	2.0	4	2	2	2	2	0-0	0-0	0	9.00
Totals	7	7	2	62.0	81	32	30	16	35	3-4	0-0	0	4.35

Fielding

Pirates	Pos	G	PO	Ast	E	DP	PB	FPct
Matt Alexander	lf	1	0	0	0	0	—	—
Jim Bibby	p	2	1	0	0	0	—	1.000
Bert Blyleven	p	2	0	1	0	1	—	1.000
John Candelaria	p	2	0	1	0	0	—	1.000
Tim Foli	ss	7	8	32	3	7	—	.930
Phil Garner	2b	7	21	22	2	9	—	.956
Grant Jackson	p	4	0	0	0	0	—	—
Bruce Kison	p	1	0	1	0	0	—	1.000
Bill Madlock	3b	7	3	10	1	4	—	.929
John Milner	lf	3	5	0	0	0	—	1.000
Omar Moreno	cf	7	20	1	0	0	—	1.000
Steve Nicosia	c	4	23	2	0	0	0	1.000
Ed Ott	c	3	20	0	0	1	0	1.000
Dave Parker	rf	7	13	1	1	1	—	.933
Bill Robinson	lf	6	11	1	0	0	—	1.000
Don Robinson	p	4	0	1	0	0	—	1.000
Enrique Romo	p	2	0	1	0	0	—	1.000
Jim Rooker	p	2	1	2	0	0	—	1.000
Willie Stargell	1b	7	59	2	2	9	—	.968
Kent Tekulve	p	5	1	0	0	0	—	1.000
Totals		7	186	78	9	32	0	.967

Orioles	Pos	G	PO	Ast	E	DP	PB	FPct
Bennie Ayala	lf	3	4	0	0	0	—	1.000
Mark Belanger	ss	5	3	7	1	2	—	.909
Al Bumbry	cf	7	14	1	1	0	—	.938
Rich Dauer	2b	6	10	10	0	1	—	1.000
Doug DeCinces	3b	7	7	21	3	0	—	.903
Rick Dempsey	c	7	38	2	0	0	0	1.000
Mike Flanagan	p	3	0	4	0	0	—	1.000
Kiko Garcia	ss	6	10	17	1	2	—	.964
John Lowenstein	lf	5	6	0	1	0	—	.857
Dennis Martinez	p	2	0	1	0	1	—	1.000
Tippy Martinez	p	3	0	0	0	0	—	—
Scott McGregor	p	2	1	2	0	0	—	1.000
Eddie Murray	1b	7	60	7	0	5	—	1.000
Jim Palmer	p	2	2	1	0	1	—	1.000
Gary Roenicke	lf	5	6	0	0	0	—	1.000
	cf	3	8	1	0	0	—	1.000
Ken Singleton	rf	7	9	0	0	0	—	1.000
Dave Skaggs	c	1	2	2	0	0	0	1.000
Billy Smith	2b	4	4	3	0	1	—	1.000
Don Stanhouse	p	3	0	0	1	0	—	.000
Sammy Stewart	p	1	1	2	0	0	—	1.000
Tim Stoddard	p	4	1	4	1	0	—	.833
Steve Stone	p	1	0	0	0	0	—	—
Totals		7	186	85	9	13	0	.968

1980 Philadelphia Phillies (NL) 4, Kansas City Royals (AL) 2

The Philadelphia Phillies downed the Kansas City Royals in six games to claim their first World Championship after 97 years. Rookie Bob Walk started the opener for the Phillies, and won 7-6 thanks to a three-run homer from Bake McBride and two innings of scoreless relief from Tug McGraw. Mike Schmidt doubled in the go-ahead run off Dan Quisenberry in the bottom of the eighth inning of Game 2, as the Phils rallied for four runs to take a 6-4 decision. In Game 3, Willie Aikens singled in the winning run in the bottom of the 10th to give the Royals their first win. The next day, Aikens blasted two homers, his second two-homer game in the Series, and the Royals chased Larry Christenson after only one-third of an inning, as Kansas City evened the Series with a 5-3 win. Quisenberry and the Royals took a 3-2 lead into the ninth inning of Game 5, but Del Unser doubled in the tying run and Manny Trillo singled in the eventual game-winner. In the sixth and final game, Steve Carlton and McGraw teamed up to finish off the Royals, 4-1.

Game 1

Tuesday, October 14

Royals	AB	R	H	RBI	BB	K	Avg
Willie Wilson, lf	5	0	0	0	0	2	.000
Hal McRae, dh	3	1	1	0	1	0	.333
George Brett, 3b	4	1	1	0	0	1	.250
Willie Aikens, 1b	4	2	2	4	0	1	.500
Darrell Porter, c	2	1	0	0	2	0	.000
Amos Otis, cf	4	1	3	2	0	0	.750
Clint Hurdle, rf	3	0	1	0	0	0	.333
John Wathan, ph-rf	1	0	0	0	0	0	.000
Frank White, 2b	4	0	1	0	0	0	.250
U.L. Washington, ss	4	0	0	0	0	1	.000
TOTALS	34	6	9	6	3	5	.265

Phillies	AB	R	H	RBI	BB	K	Avg
Lonnie Smith, lf	4	0	2	0	0	0	.500
Greg Gross, lf	1	0	0	0	0	0	.000
Pete Rose, 1b	3	1	0	0	0	0	.000
Mike Schmidt, 3b	2	2	1	0	2	1	.500
Bake McBride, rf	4	1	3	3	0	0	.750
Greg Luzinski, dh	3	0	0	0	0	2	.000
Garry Maddox, cf	3	0	1	0	1	0	.000
Manny Trillo, 2b	4	1	1	0	0	0	.250
Larry Bowa, ss	4	1	1	0	0	0	.250
Bob Boone, c	4	1	3	2	0	0	.750
TOTALS	32	7	11	6	2	4	.344

	1	2	3	4	5	6	7	8	9		R	H	E
Royals	0	2	2	0	0	0	0	2	0		6	9	1
Phillies	0	0	5	1	1	0	0	0	x		7	11	0

E—Leonard. DP—Phillies 1 (Bowa to Trillo to Rose). LOB—Royals 4, Phillies 6. Scoring Position—Royals 2-for-4, Phillies 4-for-9. 2B—Brett (1), Boone 2 (2). HR—Aikens 2 (2), Otis (1), McBride (1). SF—Maddox. GDP—Wathan. SB—White (1), Bowa (1). CS—Smith (1).

Royals	IP	H	R	ER	BB	K	ERA
Dennis Leonard (L, 0-1)	3.2	6	6	6	1	3	14.73
Renie Martin	4.0	5	1	1	1	1	2.25
Dan Quisenberry	0.1	0	0	0	0	0	0.00

Phillies	IP	H	R	ER	BB	K	ERA
Bob Walk (W, 1-0)	7.0	8	6	6	3	3	7.71
Tug McGraw (S, 1)	2.0	1	0	0	0	2	0.00

Walk pitched to three batters in the 8th.

WP—Walk. HBP—Luzinski by Martin, Rose by Leonard. Time—3:01. Attendance—65,791. Umpires—HP, Wendelstedt. 1B, Kunkel. 2B, Pryor. 3B, Denkinger.

Game 2

Wednesday, October 15

Royals	AB	R	H	RBI	BB	K	Avg
Willie Wilson, lf	4	1	1	0	1	3	.111
U.L. Washington, ss	4	0	1	0	0	2	.125
George Brett, 3b	2	0	2	0	1	0	.500
Dave Chalk, 3b	0	1	0	0	1	0	—
Darrell Porter, ph	1	0	0	0	0	1	.000
Hal McRae, dh	4	1	3	0	1	1	.571
Amos Otis, cf	5	1	2	2	0	0	.556
John Wathan, c	3	0	0	0	1	1	.000
Willie Aikens, 1b	3	0	1	0	1	1	.429
Pete LaCock, 1b	0	0	0	0	0	0	—
Jose Cardenal, rf	4	0	0	0	0	2	.000
Frank White, 2b	4	0	1	0	0	1	.250
TOTALS	34	4	11	2	6	12	.292

Phillies	AB	R	H	RBI	BB	K	Avg
Lonnie Smith, lf	3	0	0	0	0	1	.286
Del Unser, ph-lf	1	1	1	1	0	0	1.000
Pete Rose, 1b	4	0	0	0	0	0	.000
Bake McBride, rf	3	1	1	1	1	0	.571
Mike Schmidt, 3b	4	1	2	1	0	0	.500
Keith Moreland, dh	4	1	2	1	0	0	.500
Garry Maddox, cf	3	1	1	0	0	1	.167
Greg Gross, ph-cf	1	0	0	0	0	0	.000
Manny Trillo, 2b	2	0	1	0	1	0	.167
Larry Bowa, ss	3	0	1	0	0	0	.286
Bob Boone, c	1	1	0	0	2	0	.600
TOTALS	29	6	8	6	3	2	.328

	1	2	3	4	5	6	7	8	9		R	H	E
Royals	0	0	0	0	1	0	3	0	0		4	11	0
Phillies	0	0	0	2	0	0	0	4	x		6	8	1

E—Trillo. DP—Royals 2 (Washington to White to Aikens; Washington to White to LaCock), Phillies 4 (Bowa to Trillo to Rose; Bowa to Trillo to Rose; Bowa to Trillo to Rose; Maddox to Rose to Schmidt). LOB—Royals 11, Phillies 3. Scoring Position—Royals 1-for-9, Phillies 3-for-6. 2B—Otis (1), Schmidt (1), Maddox (1), Unser (1). S—Washington. SF—Wathan, Trillo. GDP—Otis, Cardenal, White, Moreland, Gross. SB—Wilson (1), Chalk (1).

Royals	IP	H	R	ER	BB	K	ERA
Larry Gura	6.0	4	2	2	2	2	3.00
Dan Quisenberry (BS, 1; L, 0-1)	2.0	4	4	4	1	0	15.43

Phillies	IP	H	R	ER	BB	K	ERA
Steve Carlton (W, 1-0)	8.0	10	4	3	6	10	3.38
Ron Reed (S, 1)	1.0	1	0	0	0	2	0.00

WP—Carlton. Time—3:01. Attendance—65,775. Umpires—HP, Kunkel. 1B, Pryor. 2B, Denkinger. 3B, Rennert.

Game 3

Friday, October 17

Phillies	AB	R	H	RBI	BB	K	Avg
Lonnie Smith, lf	4	0	2	1	1	0	.364
Greg Gross, ph-lf	0	0	0	0	0	0	.000
Pete Rose, 1b	4	0	1	1	2	2	.091
Mike Schmidt, 3b	5	1	1	1	1	0	.364
Bake McBride, rf	5	0	2	0	0	1	.500
Keith Moreland, dh	5	0	0	0	0	1	.333
Garry Maddox, cf	4	0	1	0	1	0	.200
Manny Trillo, 2b	5	1	2	0	0	0	.273
Larry Bowa, ss	5	1	3	0	0	0	.417
Bob Boone, c	4	0	1	0	1	0	.444
TOTALS	41	3	14	3	6	4	.327

Royals	AB	R	H	RBI	BB	K	Avg
Willie Wilson, lf	4	1	0	0	1	2	.077
Frank White, 2b	5	0	0	0	0	3	.154
George Brett, 3b	4	1	2	1	0	0	.500
Willie Aikens, 1b	5	1	2	1	0	2	.417
Hal McRae, dh	4	0	2	1	0	0	.545
Amos Otis, cf	4	1	2	1	0	0	.538
Clint Hurdle, rf	4	0	2	0	0	0	.429
Onix Concepcion, pr	0	0	0	0	0	0	—
Jose Cardenal, rf	0	0	0	0	0	0	.000
Darrell Porter, c	4	0	0	0	0	1	.000
U.L. Washington, ss	4	0	1	0	0	0	.167
TOTALS	38	4	11	4	2	8	.304

	1	2	3	4	5	6	7	8	9	10		R	H	E
Phillies	0	1	0	0	1	0	0	1	0	0		3	14	0
Royals	1	0	0	1	0	0	1	0	0	1		4	11	0

DP—Phillies 1 (Bowa to Trillo to Rose), Royals 2 (White to Washington to Aikens; White). LOB—Phillies 15, Royals 7. Scoring Position—Phillies 1-for-13, Royals 2-for-5. 2B—Trillo (1), Brett (2). 3B—Aikens (1). HR—Schmidt (1), Brett (1), Otis (2). S—Gross. GDP—Trillo, Otis. SB—Bowa (2), Wilson (2), Hurdle (1). CS—Washington (1).

Phillies	IP	H	R	ER	BB	K	ERA
Dick Ruthven	9.0	9	3	3	0	7	3.00
Tug McGraw (L, 0-1)	0.2	2	1	1	2	1	3.38

Royals	IP	H	R	ER	BB	K	ERA
Rich Gale	4.1	7	2	2	3	3	4.15
Renie Martin	3.1	5	1	1	1	1	2.45
Dan Quisenberry (W, 1-1)	2.1	2	0	0	2	0	7.71

Time—3:19. Attendance—42,380. Umpires—HP, Pryor. 1B, Denkinger. 2B, Rennert. 3B, Bremigan.

Game 4

Saturday, October 18

Phillies	AB	R	H	RBI	BB	K	Avg
Lonnie Smith, dh	4	0	0	0	0	0	.267
Pete Rose, 1b	4	1	2	0	0	0	.200
Bake McBride, rf	3	0	1	0	1	0	.467
Mike Schmidt, 3b	3	0	1	1	0	1	.357
Del Unser, lf	4	0	1	0	0	1	.400
Garry Maddox, cf	4	0	1	0	0	0	.214
Manny Trillo, 2b	4	2	1	0	0	0	.267
Larry Bowa, ss	4	0	2	1	0	0	.438
Bob Boone, c	3	0	1	1	0	0	.417
TOTALS	33	3	10	3	1	2	.331

Royals	AB	R	H	RBI	BB	K	Avg
Willie Wilson, lf	4	1	1	0	1	1	.118
Frank White, 2b	5	0	0	0	0	0	.111
George Brett, 3b	5	1	1	1	0	1	.400
Willie Aikens, 1b	3	2	2	3	1	1	.467
Hal McRae, dh	4	1	2	0	0	1	.533
Amos Otis, cf	4	0	2	1	0	0	.529
Clint Hurdle, rf	2	0	1	0	2	0	.444
Darrell Porter, c	3	0	0	0	1	2	.000
U.L. Washington, ss	4	0	1	0	0	0	.188
TOTALS	34	5	10	5	5	6	.311

	1	2	3	4	5	6	7	8	9		R	H	E
Phillies	0	1	0	0	0	0	1	1	0		3	10	1
Royals	4	1	0	0	0	0	0	0	x		5	10	2

E—Washington, White, Christenson. DP—Royals 1 (Brett to White to Aikens). LOB—Phillies 6, Royals 10. Scoring Position—Phillies 2-for-10, Royals 4-for-14. 2B—Rose (1), McBride (1), Trillo (2), McRae 2 (2), Otis (2), Hurdle (1). 3B—Brett (1). HR—Aikens 2 (4). SF—Schmidt, Boone. GDP—Smith. SB—Bowa (3). CS—McBride (1).

Phillies	IP	H	R	ER	BB	K	ERA
Larry Christenson (L, 0-1)	0.1	5	4	4	0	0	108.00
Dickie Noles	4.2	5	1	1	2	6	1.93
Kevin Saucier	0.2	0	0	0	2	0	0.00
Warren Brusstar	2.1	0	0	0	1	0	0.00

Royals	IP	H	R	ER	BB	K	ERA
Dennis Leonard (W, 1-1)	7.0	9	3	2	1	2	6.75
Dan Quisenberry (S, 1)	2.0	1	0	0	0	0	5.40

Leonard pitched to one batter in the 8th.

WP—Leonard, Saucier. Time—2:37. Attendance—42,363. Umpires—HP, Denkinger. 1B, Rennert. 2B, Bremigan. 3B, Wendelstedt.

Game 5

Sunday, October 19

Phillies	AB	R	H	RBI	BB	K	Avg
Pete Rose, 1b	4	0	0	0	0	0	.158
Bake McBride, rf	4	1	0	0	0	0	.368
Mike Schmidt, 3b	4	2	2	2	0	0	.389
Greg Luzinski, lf	2	0	0	0	1	1	.000
Lonnie Smith, pr-lf	0	0	0	0	0	0	.267
Del Unser, ph-lf	1	1	1	1	0	0	.500
Keith Moreland, dh	3	0	1	0	0	0	.333
Garry Maddox, cf	4	0	0	0	0	1	.167
Manny Trillo, 2b	4	0	1	1	0	0	.263
Larry Bowa, ss	4	0	1	0	0	0	.400
Bob Boone, c	3	0	1	0	0	0	.400
TOTALS	33	4	7	4	1	2	.301

Royals	AB	R	H	RBI	BB	K	Avg
Willie Wilson, lf	5	0	2	0	0	1	.182
Frank White, 2b	3	0	0	0	1	0	.095
George Brett, 3b	5	0	1	1	0	2	.350
Willie Aikens, 1b	3	0	1	0	2	2	.444
Onix Concepcion, pr	0	0	0	0	0	0	—
Hal McRae, dh	5	0	1	0	0	0	.450
Amos Otis, cf	3	1	2	1	2	1	.550
Clint Hurdle, rf	3	1	1	0	0	1	.417
Jose Cardenal, ph-rf	2	0	0	0	0	1	.000
Darrell Porter, c	4	0	2	0	0	0	.143
U.L. Washington, ss	3	1	2	1	0	1	.263
TOTALS	36	3	12	3	5	9	.308

	1	2	3	4	5	6	7	8	9		R	H	E
Phillies	0	0	0	2	0	0	0	0	2		4	7	0
Royals	0	0	0	1	2	0	0	0			3	12	2

E—Aikens, Brett. DP—Royals 2 (White to Aikens to Gura; Gura to Aikens). LOB—Phillies 4, Royals 13. Scoring Position—Phillies 1-for-6, Royals 0-for-12. 2B—Wilson (1), McRae (3), Unser (2). HR—Schmidt (2), Otis (3). S—Moreland, White. SF—Washington. SB—Brett (1).

Phillies	IP	H	R	ER	BB	K	ERA
Marty Bystrom	5.0	10	3	3	1	4	5.40
Ron Reed	1.0	1	0	0	0	0	0.00
Tug McGraw (W, 1-1)	3.0	1	0	0	4	5	1.59

Royals	IP	H	R	ER	BB	K	ERA
Larry Gura	6.1	4	2	1	1	2	2.19
Dan Quisenberry (BS, 2; L, 1-2)	2.2	3	2	2	0	0	5.79

Bystrom pitched to three batters in the 6th.

Time—2:51. Attendance—42,369. Umpires—HP, Rennert. 1B, Bremigan. 2B, Wendelstedt. 3B, Kunkel.

Game 6

Tuesday, October 21

Royals	AB	R	H	RBI	BB	K	Avg
Willie Wilson, lf	4	0	0	0	1	3	.154
U.L. Washington, ss	3	0	1	1	0	2	.273
George Brett, 3b	4	0	2	0	0	0	.375
Hal McRae, dh	4	0	0	0	0	0	.375
Amos Otis, cf	3	0	0	0	1	2	.478
Willie Aikens, 1b	2	0	0	0	2	1	.400
Onix Concepcion, pr	0	0	0	0	0	0	—
John Wathan, c	3	1	2	0	1	0	.286
Jose Cardenal, rf	4	0	2	0	0	0	.200
Frank White, 2b	4	0	0	0	0	1	.080
TOTALS	31	1	7	1	5	9	.293

Phillies	AB	R	H	RBI	BB	K	Avg
Lonnie Smith, lf	4	2	1	0	0	0	.263
Greg Gross, lf	0	0	0	0	0	0	.000
Pete Rose, 1b	4	0	3	0	0	0	.261
Mike Schmidt, 3b	3	0	1	2	1	1	.381
Bake McBride, rf	4	0	0	1	0	0	.304
Greg Luzinski, dh	4	0	0	0	0	2	.000
Garry Maddox, cf	4	0	2	0	0	0	.227
Manny Trillo, 2b	4	0	0	0	0	0	.217
Larry Bowa, ss	4	1	1	0	0	0	.375
Bob Boone, c	2	1	1	1	1	0	.412
TOTALS	33	4	9	4	2	3	.284

	1	2	3	4	5	6	7	8	9		R	H	E
Royals	0	0	0	0	0	0	0	1	0		1	7	2
Phillies	0	0	2	0	1	1	0	0	x		4	9	0

E—Aikens, White. DP—Royals 1 (Splittorff to Washington to Aikens), Phillies 2 (Bowa to Trillo to Rose; Bowa to Rose). LOB—Royals 9, Phillies 7. Scoring Position—Royals 2-for-7, Phillies 3-for-11. 2B—Smith (1), Maddox (2), Bowa (1). SF—Washington. GDP—Brett, Wathan, Trillo. CS—Rose (1).

Royals	IP	H	R	ER	BB	K	ERA
Rich Gale (L, 0-1)	2.0	4	2	1	1	0	4.26
Renie Martin	2.1	1	1	1	1	0	2.79
Paul Splittorff	1.2	4	1	1	0	0	5.40
Marty Pattin	1.0	0	0	0	0	2	0.00
Dan Quisenberry	1.0	0	0	0	0	0	5.23

Phillies	IP	H	R	ER	BB	K	ERA
Steve Carlton (W, 2-0)	7.0	4	1	1	3	7	2.40
Tug McGraw (S, 2)	2.0	3	0	0	2	2	1.17

Carlton pitched to two batters in the 8th. Gale pitched to four batters in the 3rd. Splittorff pitched to one batter in the 7th.

Time—3:00. Attendance—65,838. Umpires—HP, Bremigan. 1B, Wendelstedt. 2B, Kunkel. 3B, Pryor.

1980 World Series—Composite Statistics

Batting

Phillies	G	AB	R	H	RBI	2B	3B	HR	BB	SO	SB	CS	Avg	OBP	Slg
Bob Boone	6	17	3	7	4	2	0	0	4	0	0	0	.412	.500	.529
Larry Bowa	6	24	3	9	2	1	0	0	0	0	3	0	.375	.375	.417
Greg Gross	4	2	0	0	0	0	0	0	0	0	0	0	.000	.000	.000
Greg Luzinski	3	9	0	0	0	0	0	0	1	5	0	0	.000	.182	.000
Garry Maddox	6	22	1	5	1	2	0	0	1	3	0	0	.227	.250	.318
Bake McBride	6	23	3	7	5	1	0	1	2	1	0	1	.304	.360	.478
Keith Moreland	3	12	1	4	1	0	0	0	0	1	0	0	.333	.333	.333
Pete Rose	6	23	2	6	1	1	0	0	2	2	0	1	.261	.346	.304
Mike Schmidt	6	21	6	8	7	1	0	2	4	3	0	0	.381	.462	.714
Lonnie Smith	6	19	2	5	1	1	0	0	1	1	0	1	.263	.300	.316
Manny Trillo	6	23	4	5	2	2	0	0	0	0	0	0	.217	.208	.304
Del Unser	3	6	2	3	2	2	0	0	1	0	0	0	.500	.500	.833
Totals	**6**	**201**	**27**	**59**	**26**	**13**	**0**	**3**	**15**	**17**	**3**	**3**	**.294**	**.342**	**.403**

Royals	G	AB	R	H	RBI	2B	3B	HR	BB	SO	SB	CS	Avg	OBP	Slg
Willie Aikens	6	20	5	8	8	0	1	4	6	8	0	0	.400	.538	1.100
George Brett	6	24	3	9	3	2	1	1	2	4	1	0	.375	.423	.667
Jose Cardenal	4	10	0	2	0	0	0	0	0	3	0	0	.200	.200	.200
Dave Chalk	1	0	1	0	0	0	0	0	0	1	0	1	—	1.000	—
Onix Concepcion	3	0	0	0	0	0	0	0	0	0	0	0	—	—	—
Clint Hurdle	4	12	1	5	0	1	0	0	2	1	1	0	.417	.500	.500
Hal McRae	6	24	3	9	1	3	0	0	2	2	0	0	.375	.423	.500
Amos Otis	6	23	4	11	7	2	0	3	3	3	0	0	.478	.538	.957
Darrell Porter	5	14	1	2	0	0	0	0	3	4	0	0	.143	.294	.143
U.L. Washington	6	22	1	6	2	0	0	0	0	6	0	1	.273	.250	.273
John Wathan	3	7	1	2	0	0	0	0	2	1	0	0	.286	.400	.286
Frank White	6	25	0	2	0	0	0	0	1	5	1	0	.080	.115	.080
Willie Wilson	6	26	3	4	0	1	0	0	4	12	2	0	.154	.267	.192
Totals	**6**	**207**	**23**	**60**	**21**	**9**	**2**	**8**	**26**	**49**	**6**	**1**	**.290**	**.364**	**.469**

Pitching

Phillies	G	GS	CG	IP	H	R	ER	BB	SO	W-L	Sv-Op	Hld	ERA
Warren Brusstar	1	0	0	2.1	0	0	0	1	0	0-0	0-0	0	0.00
Marty Bystrom	1	1	0	5.0	10	3	3	1	4	0-0	0-0	0	5.40
Steve Carlton	2	2	0	15.0	14	5	4	9	17	2-0	0-0	0	2.40
Larry Christenson	1	1	0	0.1	5	4	4	0	0	0-1	0-0	0	108.00
Tug McGraw	4	0	0	7.2	7	1	1	8	10	1-1	2-2	0	1.17
Dickie Noles	1	0	0	4.2	5	1	1	2	6	0-0	0-0	0	1.93
Ron Reed	2	0	0	2.0	2	0	0	0	2	1-1	0-0	0	0.00
Dick Ruthven	1	1	0	9.0	9	3	3	0	7	0-0	0-0	0	3.00
Kevin Saucier	1	0	0	0.2	0	0	0	2	0	0-0	0-0	0	0.00
Bob Walk	1	1	0	7.0	8	6	6	3	3	1-0	0-0	0	7.71
Totals	**6**	**6**	**0**	**53.2**	**60**	**23**	**22**	**26**	**49**	**4-2**	**3-3**	**0**	**3.69**

Royals	G	GS	CG	IP	H	R	ER	BB	SO	W-L	Sv-Op	Hld	ERA
Rich Gale	2	2	0	6.1	11	4	3	4	4	0-1	0-0	0	4.26
Larry Gura	2	2	0	12.1	8	4	3	3	4	0-0	0-0	0	2.19
Dennis Leonard	2	2	0	10.2	15	9	8	2	5	1-1	0-0	0	6.75
Renie Martin	3	0	0	9.2	11	3	3	3	2	0-0	0-0	0	2.79
Marty Pattin	1	0	0	1.0	0	0	0	0	2	0-0	0-0	0	0.00
Dan Quisenberry	6	0	0	10.1	10	6	6	3	0	1-2	1-3	0	5.23
Paul Splittorff	1	0	0	1.2	4	1	1	0	0	0-0	0-0	0	5.40
Totals	**6**	**6**	**0**	**52.0**	**59**	**27**	**24**	**15**	**17**	**2-4**	**1-3**	**0**	**4.15**

Fielding

Phillies	Pos	G	PO	Ast	E	DP	PB	FPct
Bob Boone	c	6	49	3	0	0	0	1.000
Larry Bowa	ss	6	5	18	0	7	—	1.000
Warren Brusstar	p	1	0	0	0	0	—	—
Marty Bystrom	p	1	1	1	0	0	—	1.000
Steve Carlton	p	2	0	3	0	0	—	1.000
Larry Christenson	p	1	0	0	1	0	—	.000
Greg Gross	lf	3	1	0	0	0	—	1.000
	cf	1	0	0	0	0	—	—
Greg Luzinski	lf	1	1	0	0	0	—	1.000
Garry Maddox	cf	6	11	1	0	1	—	1.000
Bake McBride	rf	6	13	1	0	0	—	1.000
Tug McGraw	p	4	0	1	0	0	—	1.000
Dickie Noles	p	1	1	0	0	0	—	1.000
Ron Reed	p	2	0	0	0	0	—	—
Pete Rose	1b	6	49	6	0	8	—	1.000
Dick Ruthven	p	1	0	0	0	0	—	—
Kevin Saucier	p	1	0	0	0	0	—	—
Mike Schmidt	3b	6	9	8	0	1	—	1.000
Lonnie Smith	lf	5	4	1	0	0	—	1.000
Manny Trillo	2b	6	14	25	1	6	—	.975
Del Unser	lf	3	1	0	0	0	—	1.000
Bob Walk	p	1	2	0	0	0	—	1.000
Totals		**6**	**161**	**68**	**2**	**23**	**0**	**.991**

Royals	Pos	G	PO	Ast	E	DP	PB	FPct
Willie Aikens	1b	6	55	2	2	6	—	.966
George Brett	3b	6	4	17	1	1	—	.955
Jose Cardenal	rf	4	7	0	0	0	—	1.000
Dave Chalk	3b	1	0	1	0	0	—	1.000
Rich Gale	p	2	0	1	0	0	—	1.000
Larry Gura	p	2	2	4	0	2	—	1.000
Clint Hurdle	rf	4	8	0	0	0	—	1.000
Pete LaCock	1b	1	2	0	0	1	—	1.000
Dennis Leonard	p	2	0	0	1	0	—	.000
Renie Martin	p	3	0	0	0	0	—	—
Amos Otis	cf	6	21	0	0	0	—	1.000
Marty Pattin	p	1	0	0	0	0	—	—
Darrell Porter	c	4	13	2	0	0	0	1.000
Dan Quisenberry	p	6	1	1	0	0	—	1.000
Paul Splittorff	p	1	0	1	0	1	—	1.000
U.L. Washington	ss	6	8	21	1	4	—	.967
John Wathan	c	2	6	1	0	0	0	1.000
	rf	1	1	0	0	0	—	1.000
Frank White	2b	6	13	20	2	6	—	.943
Willie Wilson	lf	6	15	1	0	0	—	1.000
Totals		**6**	**156**	**72**	**7**	**21**	**0**	**.970**

1981 Los Angeles Dodgers (NL) 4, New York Yankees (AL) 2

It looked like another typical Yankees-Dodgers World Series after New York took the first two games, but the Dodgers broke character, taking the last four games to claim the World Championship. Bob Watson hit a three-run homer in the first inning of Game 1, and Ron Guidry went seven innings for a 5-3 victory. Tommy John threw seven shutout innings in Game 2 as the Yanks prevailed, 3-0. Fernando Valenzuela survived nine hits and seven walks in Game 3, going the distance for a 5-4 win. The Yankees jumped out to a 4-0 lead in Game 4, but the Dodgers battled back, tying the game on an RBI single by Bill Russell after Reggie Jackson had dropped a flyball, and going on to win, 8-7. Southpaws Ron Guidry and Jerry Reuss squared off in Game 5. Guidry held a 1-0 lead until the bottom of the seventh, when Pedro Guerrero and Steve Yeager hit consecutive home runs to give the Dodgers a one-run lead. Reuss completed the five-hitter for a 2-1 win. The sixth game was tied 1-1 in the bottom of the fourth when Yankees manager Bob Lemon pinch-hit for starter John. In the very next inning, the Dodgers got three runs off reliever George Frazier and ran away with a 9-2 title-clinching victory.

Game 1

Tuesday, October 20

Dodgers	AB	R	H	RBI	BB	K	Avg
Davey Lopes, 2b	3	1	0	0	1	0	.000
Bill Russell, ss	3	0	0	0	0	0	.000
Jay Johnstone, ph	1	0	1	1	0	0	1.000
Dave Stewart, p	0	0	0	0	0	0	—
Dusty Baker, lf	2	0	1	1	1	0	.500
Steve Garvey, 1b	4	0	1	0	0	1	.250
Ron Cey, 3b	4	0	1	0	0	0	.250
Pedro Guerrero, cf	3	0	0	0	1	2	.000
Rick Monday, rf	4	0	0	0	0	3	.000
Steve Yeager, c	3	1	1	1	0	1	.333
Ken Landreaux, ph	1	0	0	0	0	0	.000
Jerry Reuss, p	1	0	0	0	0	1	.000
Bobby Castillo, p	0	0	0	0	0	0	—
Dave Goltz, p	0	0	0	0	0	0	—
Steve Sax, ph	1	0	0	0	0	0	.000
Tom Niedenfuer, p	0	0	0	0	0	0	—
Derrel Thomas, ph-ss	0	1	0	1	0	0	—
TOTALS	30	3	5	3	4	8	.167

Yankees	AB	R	H	RBI	BB	K	Avg
Willie Randolph, 2b	3	0	0	0	1	0	.000
Jerry Mumphrey, cf	3	2	2	0	1	0	.667
Dave Winfield, lf	3	0	0	1	1	1	.000
Lou Piniella, rf	4	1	2	1	0	0	.500
Bob Watson, 1b	3	1	2	3	1	0	.667
Graig Nettles, 3b	3	0	0	0	1	0	.000
Rick Cerone, c	3	0	0	0	1	0	.000
Larry Milbourne, ss	4	1	0	0	0	0	.000
Ron Guidry, p	2	0	0	0	0	1	.000
Ron Davis, p	0	0	0	0	0	0	—
Goose Gossage, p	0	0	0	0	0	0	—
TOTALS	28	5	6	5	6	2	.214

	1	2	3	4	5	6	7	8	9		R	H	E
Dodgers	0	0	0	0	1	0	0	2	0		3	5	0
Yankees	5	0	1	1	0	0	0	0	x		5	6	0

DP—Dodgers 1 (Thomas to Garvey). LOB—Dodgers 5, Yankees 6. Scoring Position—Dodgers 1-for-1, Yankees 2-for-4. 2B—Piniella (1). HR—Yeager (1), Watson (1). S—Guidry. SF—Baker. GDP—Milbourne. SB—Mumphrey (1), Piniella (1).

Dodgers	IP	H	R	ER	BB	K	ERA
Jerry Reuss (L, 0-1)	2.2	5	4	0	2	1	13.50
Bobby Castillo	1.0	0	0	1	5	0	9.00
Dave Goltz	0.1	0	0	0	0	0	0.00
Tom Niedenfuer	3.0	1	0	0	0	0	0.00
Dave Stewart	1.0	0	0	0	1	0	0.00

Yankees	IP	H	R	ER	BB	K	ERA
Ron Guidry (W, 1-0)	7.0	4	1	1	2	6	1.29
Ron Davis	0.0	0	2	2	2	0	—
Goose Gossage (S, 1)	2.0	1	0	0	2	0	0.00

Davis pitched to three batters in the 8th.

PB—Cerone. Time—2:32. Attendance—56,470. Umpires—HP, Barnett. 1B, Colosi. 2B, Cooney. 3B, Harvey.

Game 2

Wednesday, October 21

Dodgers	AB	R	H	RBI	BB	K	Avg
Davey Lopes, 2b	3	0	0	0	0	0	.000
Rick Monday, ph	1	0	0	0	0	1	.000
Steve Howe, p	0	0	0	0	0	0	—
Dave Stewart, p	0	0	0	0	0	0	—
Bill Russell, ss	4	0	1	0	0	0	.143
Dusty Baker, lf	4	0	0	0	0	1	.167
Steve Garvey, 1b	3	0	2	0	1	0	.429
Ron Cey, 3b	4	0	0	0	0	1	.125
Pedro Guerrero, rf	4	0	0	0	0	0	.000
Ken Landreaux, cf	3	0	0	0	0	1	.000
Steve Yeager, c	2	0	0	0	0	0	.200
Jay Johnstone, ph	1	0	0	0	0	0	.500
Mike Scioscia, c	0	0	0	0	0	0	—
Burt Hooton, p	2	0	0	0	0	2	.000
Terry Forster, p	0	0	0	0	0	0	—
Reggie Smith, ph	1	0	1	0	0	0	1.000
Steve Sax, pr-2b	0	0	0	0	0	0	.000
TOTALS	32	0	4	0	1	7	.148

Yankees	AB	R	H	RBI	BB	K	Avg
Jerry Mumphrey, cf	2	0	0	0	2	0	.400
Larry Milbourne, ss	4	0	1	1	0	0	.125
Dave Winfield, lf	4	0	0	0	0	0	.000
Oscar Gamble, rf	2	0	0	0	1	0	.000
Lou Piniella, ph	1	0	1	0	0	0	.600
Bobby Brown, pr-rf	0	1	0	0	0	0	—
Graig Nettles, 3b	4	1	2	0	0	1	.286
Bob Watson, 1b	4	0	2	1	0	0	.571
Rick Cerone, c	2	0	0	0	2	0	.000
Willie Randolph, 2b	2	1	0	1	1	0	.000
Tommy John, p	1	0	0	0	0	0	.000
Bobby Murcer, ph	0	0	0	0	0	0	—
Goose Gossage, p	1	0	0	0	0	1	.000
TOTALS	27	3	6	3	6	2	.226

	1	2	3	4	5	6	7	8	9		R	H	E
Dodgers	0	0	0	0	0	0	0	0	0		0	4	2
Yankees	0	0	0	1	0	0	2	x			3	6	1

E—Lopes, Milbourne, Stewart. DP—Dodgers 1 (Russell to Lopes to Garvey). LOB—Dodgers 6, Yankees 9. Scoring Position—Dodgers 0-for-3, Yankees 2-for-7. 2B—Milbourne (1). S—John, Murcer. SF—Randolph. GDP—Milbourne.

Dodgers	IP	H	R	ER	BB	K	ERA
Burt Hooton (L, 0-1)	6.0	3	1	0	4	1	0.00
Terry Forster	1.0	0	0	0	1	0	0.00
Steve Howe	0.1	2	2	2	0	0	54.00
Dave Stewart	0.2	1	0	0	1	1	0.00

Yankees	IP	H	R	ER	BB	K	ERA
Tommy John (W, 1-0)	7.0	3	0	0	0	4	0.00
Goose Gossage (S, 2)	2.0	1	0	0	1	3	0.00

Hooton pitched to two batters in the 7th.

Time—2:29. Attendance—56,505. Umpires—HP, Colosi. 1B, Cooney. 2B, Harvey. 3B, Garcia.

Game 3

Friday, October 23

Yankees	AB	R	H	RBI	BB	K	Avg
Willie Randolph, 2b	2	0	0	0	3	0	.000
Jerry Mumphrey, cf	5	0	0	0	0	1	.200
Dave Winfield, lf	3	0	0	0	2	1	.000
Lou Piniella, rf	5	1	1	0	0	1	.400
Bob Watson, 1b	4	1	2	1	0	0	.545
Rick Cerone, c	4	2	2	2	0	1	.222
Aurelio Rodriguez, 3b	4	0	2	0	0	0	.500
Larry Milbourne, ss	2	0	1	2	2	0	.300
Dave Righetti, p	1	0	0	0	0	1	.000
George Frazier, p	1	0	0	0	0	1	.000
Rudy May, p	0	0	0	0	0	0	—
Bobby Murcer, ph	1	0	0	0	0	0	.000
Ron Davis, p	0	0	0	0	0	0	—
TOTALS	32	4	9	4	7	6	.257

Dodgers	AB	R	H	RBI	BB	K	Avg
Davey Lopes, 2b	4	1	2	0	0	1	.200
Bill Russell, ss	5	1	2	0	0	0	.250
Dusty Baker, lf	4	0	0	0	0	1	.100
Steve Garvey, 1b	4	1	2	0	0	1	.455
Ron Cey, 3b	2	2	2	3	2	0	.300
Pedro Guerrero, cf-rf	3	0	1	1	0	2	.100
Rick Monday, rf	2	0	1	0	1	0	.143
Derrel Thomas, ph-cf	1	0	0	0	0	0	.000
Steve Yeager, c	1	0	0	0	0	0	.167
Mike Scioscia, ph-c	3	0	1	0	0	0	.333
Fernando Valenzuela, p	3	0	0	0	0	0	.000
TOTALS	32	5	11	4	4	5	.217

	1	2	3	4	5	6	7	8	9		R	H	E
Yankees	0	2	2	0	0	0	0	0	0		4	9	0
Dodgers	3	0	0	0	2	0	0	0	x		5	11	1

E—Lopes. DP—Yankees 2 (Randolph to Watson; Milbourne to Randolph to Watson), Dodgers 2 (Russell to Lopes to Garvey; Cey to Garvey). LOB—Yankees 9, Dodgers 9. Scoring Position—Yankees 1-for-10, Dodgers 3-for-13. 2B—Watson (1), Cerone (1), Lopes (1), Guerrero (1). HR—Watson (2), Cerone (1), Cey (1). S—Righetti, Lopes. GDP—Piniella, Scioscia, Thomas. CS—Randolph (1).

Yankees	IP	H	R	ER	BB	K	ERA
Dave Righetti	2.0	5	3	3	2	1	13.50
George Frazier (L, 0-1)	2.0	3	2	2	1	1	9.00
Rudy May	3.0	2	0	0	0	2	0.00
Ron Davis	1.0	1	0	0	0	1	18.00

Dodgers	IP	H	R	ER	BB	K	ERA
Fernando Valenzuela (W, 1-0)	9.0	9	4	4	7	6	4.00

Righetti pitched to two batters in the 3rd. Frazier pitched to four batters in the 5th.

HBP—Guerrero by Righetti. Time—3:04. Attendance—56,236. Umpires—HP, Cooney. 1B, Harvey. 2B, Garcia. 3B, Stello.

Game 4
Saturday, October 24

Yankees	AB	R	H	RBI	BB	K	Avg
Willie Randolph, 2b	5	3	2	1	1	0	.167
Larry Milbourne, ss	4	1	1	1	0	0	.286
Dave Winfield, cf-lf-cf	4	0	0	0	1	0	.000
Reggie Jackson, rf	3	2	3	1	2	0	1.000
Oscar Gamble, lf	4	1	2	1	0	0	.333
Bobby Brown, pr-cf	0	0	0	0	0	0	—
Lou Piniella, ph-lf	1	0	0	0	0	0	.364
Bob Watson, 1b	3	0	1	2	1	0	.500
Rick Cerone, c	5	0	2	1	0	0	.286
Andre Robertson, pr	0	0	0	0	0	0	—
Aurelio Rodriguez, 3b	4	0	2	0	0	1	.500
Barry Foote, ph	1	0	0	0	0	1	.000
Rick Reuschel, p	2	0	0	0	0	1	.000
Rudy May, p	1	0	0	0	0	0	.000
Ron Davis, p	0	0	0	0	0	0	—
George Frazier, p	1	0	0	0	0	0	.000
Tommy John, p	0	0	0	0	0	0	—
Bobby Murcer, ph	1	0	0	0	0	0	.000
TOTALS	39	7	13	7	5	3	.286

Dodgers	AB	R	H	RBI	BB	K	Avg
Davey Lopes, 2b	5	2	2	2	0	0	.267
Bill Russell, ss	5	0	1	1	0	1	.235
Steve Garvey, 1b	5	1	3	0	0	1	.500
Ron Cey, 3b	5	0	2	2	0	0	.333
Dusty Baker, lf	5	1	1	0	0	2	.133
Rick Monday, rf	3	1	1	0	1	1	.200
Derrel Thomas, cf	1	0	0	0	0	0	.000
Pedro Guerrero, cf-rf	3	0	2	0	1	0	.231
Mike Scioscia, c	1	1	0	0	1	0	.250
Steve Yeager, ph-c	0	0	0	1	0	0	.167
Bob Welch, p	0	0	0	0	0	0	—
Dave Goltz, p	0	0	0	0	0	0	—
Ken Landreaux, ph	1	1	1	0	0	0	.200
Terry Forster, p	0	0	0	0	0	0	—
Reggie Smith, ph	1	0	0	0	0	1	.500
Tom Niedenfuer, p	0	0	0	0	0	0	—
Jay Johnstone, ph	1	1	1	2	0	0	.667
Steve Howe, p	0	0	0	0	0	0	—
TOTALS	36	8	14	8	3	7	.276

	1	2	3	4	5	6	7	8	9		R	H	E
Yankees	2	1	1	0	0	2	0	1	0		7	13	1
Dodgers	0	0	2	0	1	3	2	0	x		8	14	2

E—Jackson, Russell, Howe. LOB—Yankees 12, Dodgers 10. Scoring Position—Yankees 7-for-14, Dodgers 5-for-11. 2B—Milbourne (2), Garvey (1), Monday (1), Landreaux (1). 3B—Randolph (1). HR—Randolph (1), Jackson (1), Johnstone (1). S—Milbourne, Scioscia, Howe. SF—Watson, Yeager. SB—Winfield (1), Lopes 2 (2).

Yankees	IP	H	R	ER	BB	K	ERA
Rick Reuschel	3.0	6	2	2	1	2	6.00
Rudy May	1.1	2	1	1	0	1	2.08
Ron Davis	1.0	2	3	2	1	2	18.00
George Frazier (L, 0-2)	0.2	2	2	2	1	0	13.50
Tommy John	2.0	2	0	0	0	2	0.00

Dodgers	IP	H	R	ER	BB	K	ERA
Bob Welch	0.0	3	2	2	1	0	—
Dave Goltz	3.0	4	2	2	1	2	5.40
Terry Forster	1.0	1	0	0	2	0	0.00
Tom Niedenfuer	2.0	2	2	0	1	0	0.00
Steve Howe (W, 1-0)	3.0	3	1	1	0	1	8.10

Welch pitched to four batters in the 1st. Reuschel pitched to two batters in the 4th. Frazier pitched to three batters in the 7th.

Time—3:32. Attendance—56,242. Umpires—HP, Harvey. 1B, Garcia. 2B, Stello. 3B, Barnett.

Game 5
Sunday, October 25

Yankees	AB	R	H	RBI	BB	K	Avg
Willie Randolph, 2b	3	0	0	0	1	0	.133
Larry Milbourne, ss	4	0	1	0	0	0	.278
Dave Winfield, cf-lf	4	0	1	0	0	2	.056
Reggie Jackson, rf	4	1	1	0	0	1	.571
Goose Gossage, p	0	0	0	0	0	0	—
Bob Watson, 1b	3	0	0	0	1	0	.412
Lou Piniella, lf-rf	4	0	2	1	0	0	.400
Bobby Brown, pr	0	0	0	0	0	0	—
Rick Cerone, c	4	0	0	0	0	0	.222
Aurelio Rodriguez, 3b	3	0	0	0	1	1	.364
Ron Guidry, p	3	0	0	0	0	2	.000
Jerry Mumphrey, cf	0	0	0	0	0	0	.200
TOTALS	32	1	5	1	3	6	.259

Dodgers	AB	R	H	RBI	BB	K	Avg
Davey Lopes, 2b	3	0	0	0	1	1	.222
Bill Russell, ss	4	0	0	0	0	0	.190
Steve Garvey, 1b	4	0	1	0	0	2	.450
Ron Cey, 3b	2	0	0	0	1	1	.294
Ken Landreaux, pr-cf	0	0	0	0	0	0	.200
Dusty Baker, lf	4	0	0	0	0	2	.105
Pedro Guerrero, rf	3	1	1	1	0	1	.250
Steve Yeager, c	3	1	2	1	0	0	.333
Derrel Thomas, cf-3b	3	0	0	0	0	1	.000
Jerry Reuss, p	2	0	0	0	1	1	.000
TOTALS	28	2	4	2	3	9	.241

	1	2	3	4	5	6	7	8	9		R	H	E
Yankees	0	1	0	0	0	0	0	0	0		1	5	0
Dodgers	0	0	0	0	0	0	2	0	x		2	4	3

E—Lopes 3. DP—Dodgers 2 (Russell to Lopes to Garvey; Lopes to Garvey). LOB—Yankees 7, Dodgers 6. Scoring Position—Yankees 1-for-9, Dodgers 0-for-4. 2B—Jackson (1), Yeager (1). HR—Guerrero (1), Yeager (2). GDP—Jackson, Cerone. SB—Lopes (3), Landreaux (1).

Yankees	IP	H	R	ER	BB	K	ERA
Ron Guidry (L, 1-1)	7.0	4	2	2	2	9	1.93
Goose Gossage	1.0	0	0	0	1	0	0.00

Dodgers	IP	H	R	ER	BB	K	ERA
Jerry Reuss (W, 1-1)	9.0	5	1	1	3	6	3.86

HBP—Cey by Gossage. Time—2:19. Attendance—56,115. Umpires—HP, Garcia. 1B, Stello. 2B, Barnett. 3B, Colosi.

Game 6
Wednesday, October 28

Dodgers	AB	R	H	RBI	BB	K	Avg
Davey Lopes, 2b	4	2	1	0	2	1	.227
Bill Russell, ss	4	0	2	1	0	0	.240
Steve Garvey, 1b	4	1	1	0	1	0	.417
Ron Cey, 3b	3	1	2	1	0	1	.350
Derrel Thomas, ph-3b	2	1	0	1	0	0	.000
Dusty Baker, lf	5	2	2	0	0	0	.167
Pedro Guerrero, cf-rf	5	1	3	5	0	0	.333
Rick Monday, rf	3	0	1	0	1	1	.231
Ken Landreaux, cf	1	0	0	0	0	1	.167
Steve Yeager, c	5	0	1	1	0	1	.286
Burt Hooton, p	2	1	0	0	1	1	.000
Steve Howe, p	2	0	0	0	0	2	.000
TOTALS	40	9	13	9	5	8	.258

Yankees	AB	R	H	RBI	BB	K	Avg
Willie Randolph, 2b	3	1	2	1	2	0	.222
Jerry Mumphrey, cf	5	0	1	0	0	1	.200
Dave Winfield, lf	4	0	0	0	1	0	.045
Reggie Jackson, rf	5	0	0	0	0	2	.333
Bob Watson, 1b	5	0	0	0	0	2	.318
Graig Nettles, 3b	3	0	2	0	0	0	.400
Aurelio Rodriguez, pr-3b	1	1	1	0	0	0	.417
Rick Cerone, c	3	0	0	0	1	1	.190
Larry Milbourne, ss	2	0	0	0	2	0	.250
Tommy John, p	1	0	0	0	0	0	.000
Bobby Murcer, ph	1	0	0	0	0	0	.000
George Frazier, p	0	0	0	0	0	0	.000
Ron Davis, p	0	0	0	0	0	0	—
Rick Reuschel, p	0	0	0	0	0	0	.000
Oscar Gamble, ph	0	0	0	0	0	0	.333
Lou Piniella, ph	1	0	1	1	0	0	.438
Rudy May, p	0	0	0	0	0	0	.000
Bobby Brown, ph	1	0	0	0	0	1	.000
Dave LaRoche, p	0	0	0	0	0	0	—
TOTALS	35	2	7	2	6	5	.249

	1	2	3	4	5	6	7	8	9		R	H	E
Dodgers	0	0	0	1	3	4	0	1	0		9	13	1
Yankees	0	0	1	0	0	1	0	0	0		2	7	2

E—Lopes, Milbourne, Nettles. LOB—Dodgers 10, Yankees 12. Scoring Position—Dodgers 5-for-13, Yankees 1-for-13. 2B—Randolph (1), Nettles (1). 3B—Guerrero (1). HR—Guerrero (2), Randolph (2). S—Russell. SB—Lopes (4), Russell (1), Randolph (1). CS—Russell (1).

Dodgers	IP	H	R	ER	BB	K	ERA
Burt Hooton (W, 1-1)	5.1	5	2	2	5	2	1.59
Steve Howe (S, 1)	3.2	2	0	0	1	3	3.86

Yankees	IP	H	R	ER	BB	K	ERA
Tommy John	4.0	6	1	1	0	2	0.69
George Frazier (L, 0-3)	1.0	4	3	3	0	1	17.18
Ron Davis	0.1	1	3	2	2	1	23.14
Rick Reuschel	0.2	1	1	0	2	0	4.91
Rudy May	2.0	1	1	1	1	2	2.84
Dave LaRoche	1.0	0	0	0	0	2	0.00

Time—3:09. Attendance—56,513. Umpires—HP, Stello. 1B, Barnett. 2B, Colosi. 3B, Cooney.

1981 World Series—Composite Statistics

Batting

Dodgers	G	AB	R	H	RBI	2B	3B	HR	BB	SO	SB	CS	Avg	OBP	Slg
Dusty Baker	6	24	3	4	1	0	0	0	1	6	0	0	.167	.192	.167
Ron Cey	6	20	3	7	6	0	0	1	3	3	0	0	.350	.458	.500
Steve Garvey	6	24	3	10	0	1	0	0	2	5	0	0	.417	.462	.458
Pedro Guerrero	6	21	2	7	7	1	1	2	2	6	0	0	.333	.417	.762
Burt Hooton	2	4	1	0	0	0	0	0	1	3	0	0	.000	.200	.000
Steve Howe	3	2	0	0	0	0	0	0	0	2	0	0	.000	.000	.000
Jay Johnstone	3	3	1	2	3	0	0	1	0	0	0	0	.667	.667	1.667
Ken Landreaux	5	6	1	1	0	1	0	0	0	2	1	0	.167	.167	.333
Davey Lopes	6	22	6	5	2	1	0	0	4	3	4	0	.227	.346	.273
Rick Monday	5	13	1	3	0	1	0	0	3	6	0	0	.231	.375	.308
Jerry Reuss	2	3	0	0	0	0	0	0	1	2	0	0	.000	.250	.000
Bill Russell	6	25	1	6	2	0	0	0	1	1	1	1	.240	.240	.240
Steve Sax	2	1	0	0	0	0	0	0	0	0	0	0	.000	.000	.000
Mike Scioscia	3	4	1	1	0	0	0	0	1	0	0	0	.250	.400	.250
Reggie Smith	2	2	0	1	0	0	0	0	0	1	0	0	.500	.500	.500
Derrel Thomas	5	7	2	0	1	0	0	0	1	2	0	0	.000	.125	.000
Fernando Valenzuela	1	3	0	0	0	0	0	0	1	0	0	0	.000	.250	.000
Steve Yeager	6	14	2	4	4	1	0	2	0	2	0	0	.286	.267	.786
Totals	6	198	27	51	26	6	1	6	20	44	6	1	.258	.329	.389

Batting

Yankees	G	AB	R	H	RBI	2B	3B	HR	BB	SO	SB	CS	Avg	OBP	Slg
Bobby Brown	4	1	1	0	0	0	0	0	0	1	0	0	.000	.000	.000
Rick Cerone	6	21	2	4	3	1	0	1	4	2	0	0	.190	.320	.381
Barry Foote	1	1	0	0	0	0	0	0	0	1	0	0	.000	.000	.000
George Frazier	3	2	0	0	0	0	0	0	0	1	0	0	.000	.000	.000
Oscar Gamble	3	6	1	2	1	0	0	0	1	0	0	0	.333	.429	.333
Goose Gossage	3	1	0	0	0	0	0	0	0	1	0	0	.000	.000	.000
Ron Guidry	2	5	0	0	0	0	0	0	0	3	0	0	.000	.000	.000
Reggie Jackson	3	12	3	4	1	1	0	1	2	3	0	0	.333	.429	.667
Tommy John	3	2	0	0	0	0	0	0	0	0	0	0	.000	.000	.000
Rudy May	3	1	0	0	0	0	0	0	0	0	0	0	.000	.000	.000
Larry Milbourne	6	20	2	5	3	2	0	0	4	0	0	0	.250	.375	.350
Jerry Mumphrey	5	15	2	3	0	0	0	0	3	2	1	0	.200	.333	.200
Bobby Murcer	4	3	0	0	0	0	0	0	0	0	0	0	.000	.000	.000
Graig Nettles	3	10	1	4	0	1	0	0	1	1	0	0	.400	.455	.500
Lou Piniella	6	16	2	7	3	1	0	0	0	1	1	0	.438	.438	.500
Willie Randolph	6	18	5	4	3	1	1	2	9	0	1	1	.222	.464	.722
Rick Reuschel	2	0	0	0	0	0	0	0	0	1	0	0	.000	.000	.000
Dave Righetti	1	1	0	0	0	0	0	0	0	1	0	0	.000	.000	.000
Andre Robertson	1	0	0	0	0	0	0	0	0	0	0	0	—	—	—
Aurelio Rodriguez	4	12	1	5	0	0	0	0	1	2	0	0	.417	.462	.417
Bob Watson	6	22	2	7	7	1	0	2	3	0	0	0	.318	.385	.636
Dave Winfield	6	22	0	1	1	0	0	0	5	4	1	0	.045	.222	.045
Totals	6	193	22	46	22	8	1	6	33	24	4	1	.238	.346	.383

Pitching

Dodgers	G	GS	CG	IP	H	R	ER	BB	SO	W-L	Sv-Op	Hld	ERA
Bobby Castillo	1	0	0	1.0	0	0	1	5	0	0-0	0-0	0	9.00
Terry Forster	2	0	0	2.0	1	0	0	3	0	0-0	0-0	0	0.00
Dave Goltz	2	0	0	3.1	4	2	2	1	2	0-0	0-0	0	5.40
Burt Hooton	2	2	0	11.1	8	3	2	9	3	1-1	0-0	0	1.59
Steve Howe	3	0	0	7.0	7	3	3	1	4	1-0	1-1	0	3.86
Tom Niedenfuer	2	0	0	5.0	3	2	0	1	0	0-0	0-0	0	0.00
Jerry Reuss	2	2	1	11.2	10	6	5	3	8	1-1	0-0	0	3.86
Dave Stewart	2	0	0	1.2	1	0	0	2	1	0-0	0-0	0	0.00
Fernando Valenzuela	1	1	1	9.0	9	4	4	7	6	1-0	0-0	0	4.00
Bob Welch	1	1	0	0.0	3	2	2	1	0	0-0	0-0	0	—
Totals	6	6	2	52.0	46	22	19	33	24	4-2	1-1	0	3.29

Pitching

Yankees	G	GS	CG	IP	H	R	ER	BB	SO	W-L	Sv-Op	Hld	ERA
Ron Davis	4	0	0	2.1	4	8	6	5	4	0-0	0-0	0	23.14
George Frazier	3	0	0	3.2	9	7	7	3	2	0-3	0-0	0	17.18
Goose Gossage	3	0	0	5.0	2	0	0	2	5	0-0	2-2	0	0.00
Ron Guidry	2	2	0	14.0	8	3	3	4	15	1-1	0-0	0	1.93
Tommy John	3	2	0	13.0	11	1	1	0	8	1-0	0-0	0	0.69
Dave LaRoche	1	0	0	1.0	0	0	0	0	2	0-0	0-0	0	0.00
Rudy May	3	0	0	6.1	5	2	2	1	5	0-0	0-0	0	2.84
Rick Reuschel	2	1	0	3.2	7	3	2	3	2	0-0	0-0	0	4.91
Dave Righetti	1	1	0	2.0	5	3	3	2	1	0-0	0-0	0	13.50
Totals	6	6	0	51.0	51	27	24	20	44	2-4	2-2	0	4.24

Fielding

Dodgers	Pos	G	PO	Ast	E	DP	PB	FPct
Dusty Baker	lf	6	13	0	0	0	—	1.000
Bobby Castillo	p	1	0	2	0	0	—	1.000
Ron Cey	3b	6	4	11	0	1	—	1.000
Terry Forster	p	2	0	1	0	0	—	1.000
Steve Garvey	1b	6	45	3	0	6	—	1.000
Dave Goltz	p	2	0	0	0	0	—	—
Pedro Guerrero	rf	5	10	0	0	0	—	1.000
	cf	4	7	1	0	0	—	1.000
Burt Hooton	p	2	1	0	0	0	—	1.000
Steve Howe	p	3	0	1	1	0	—	.500
Ken Landreaux	cf	3	6	0	0	0	—	1.000
Davey Lopes	2b	6	25	14	6	4	—	.867
Rick Monday	rf	4	9	0	0	0	—	1.000
Tom Niedenfuer	p	2	0	0	0	0	—	—
Jerry Reuss	p	2	1	3	0	0	—	1.000
Bill Russell	ss	6	4	26	1	3	—	.968
Steve Sax	2b	1	0	0	0	0	—	—
Mike Scioscia	c	3	7	1	0	0	0	1.000
Dave Stewart	p	2	0	0	1	0	—	.000
Derrel Thomas	cf	3	3	0	0	0	—	1.000
	3b	2	0	0	0	0	—	—
	ss	1	1	1	0	1	—	1.000
Fernando Valenzuela	p	1	0	1	0	0	—	1.000
Bob Welch	p	1	0	0	0	0	—	—
Steve Yeager	c	6	20	0	0	0	0	1.000
Totals		6	156	65	9	15	0	.961

Fielding

Yankees	Pos	G	PO	Ast	E	DP	PB	FPct
Bobby Brown	cf	1	1	0	0	0	—	1.000
	rf	1	0	0	0	0	—	—
Rick Cerone	c	6	42	4	0	0	1	1.000
Ron Davis	p	4	0	0	0	0	—	—
George Frazier	p	3	0	0	0	0	—	—
Oscar Gamble	lf	1	2	0	0	0	—	1.000
	rf	1	2	0	0	0	—	1.000
Goose Gossage	p	3	0	0	0	0	—	—
Ron Guidry	p	2	0	0	0	0	—	—
Reggie Jackson	rf	3	5	0	1	0	—	.833
Tommy John	p	3	0	3	0	0	—	1.000
Dave LaRoche	p	1	0	0	0	0	—	—
Rudy May	p	3	0	1	0	0	—	1.000
Larry Milbourne	ss	6	5	16	2	1	—	.913
Jerry Mumphrey	cf	5	6	0	0	0	—	1.000
Graig Nettles	3b	3	3	10	1	0	—	.929
Lou Piniella	rf	3	5	1	0	0	—	1.000
	lf	2	2	0	0	0	—	1.000
Willie Randolph	2b	6	13	11	0	2	—	1.000
Rick Reuschel	p	2	0	0	0	0	—	—
Dave Righetti	p	1	0	0	0	0	—	—
Aurelio Rodriguez	3b	4	3	9	0	0	—	1.000
Bob Watson	1b	6	51	0	0	2	—	1.000
Dave Winfield	lf	6	7	0	0	0	—	1.000
	cf	2	6	0	0	0	—	1.000
Totals		6	153	55	4	5	1	.981

1982 St. Louis Cardinals (NL) 4, Milwaukee Brewers (AL) 3

The one player who might have had the biggest impact on the 1982 Series was a player who wasn't even able to play—Rollie Fingers. Sidelined with a torn muscle in his forearm, the Milwaukee Brewers' relief ace wasn't needed in Game 1, as the Brewers drubbed the Cardinals 10-0. Paul Molitor enjoyed a five-hit game, Robin Yount smacked four hits, and Mike Caldwell tossed a three-hit shutout. Fingers' absence was felt in Game 2 when Pete Ladd walked in the winning run in the bottom of the eighth, a 5-4 St. Louis win. Willie McGee starred in Game 3, clouting two home runs and making a pair of spectacular leaping catches in center field, and the Cardinals won again, 6-2. The Brewers trailed 5-1 in Game 4 before a six-run uprising in the bottom of the seventh gave Milwaukee a 7-5 victory. Mike Caldwell got his second win of the Series in Game 5, allowing 14 hits but surviving to win, 6-4. The Cardinals won a rain-drenched Game 6, 13-1, to force a seventh game. The Brewers took a 3-1 lead into the bottom of the sixth, but the Cardinals tied the score on a two-run single by Keith Hernandez and went ahead 4-3 on an RBI single by George Hendrick. Without Fingers available to keep the game within reach, the Cardinals got two more runs in the bottom of the eighth, and Bruce Sutter closed out the 6-3 win to clinch the World Championship for St. Louis.

Game 1

Tuesday, October 12

Brewers	AB	R	H	RBI	BB	K	Avg
Paul Molitor, 3b	6	1	5	2	0	0	.833
Robin Yount, ss	6	1	4	2	0	1	.667
Cecil Cooper, 1b	4	1	0	0	1	1	.000
Ted Simmons, c	5	1	2	1	0	1	.400
Ben Oglivie, lf	4	1	0	0	0	0	.000
Gorman Thomas, cf	4	0	1	1	1	0	.250
Roy Howell, dh	2	0	0	0	0	0	.000
Don Money, ph-dh	2	1	1	1	0	0	.500
Charlie Moore, rf	5	2	2	0	0	0	.400
Jim Gantner, 2b	4	2	2	2	0	0	.500
TOTALS	42	10	17	9	3	3	.405

Cardinals	AB	R	H	RBI	BB	K	Avg
Tom Herr, 2b	3	0	0	0	1	0	.000
Lonnie Smith, lf	4	0	0	0	0	2	.000
Keith Hernandez, 1b	4	0	0	0	0	0	.000
George Hendrick, rf	4	0	0	0	0	0	.000
Gene Tenace, dh	3	0	0	0	0	1	.000
Darrell Porter, c	3	0	2	0	0	0	.667
David Green, cf	3	0	0	0	0	0	.000
Ken Oberkfell, 3b	3	0	1	0	0	0	.333
Ozzie Smith, ss	3	0	0	0	0	0	.000
TOTALS	30	0	3	0	1	3	.100

	1 2 3	4 5 6	7 8 9	R	H	E
Brewers	2 0 0	1 1 2	0 0 4	10	17	0
Cardinals	0 0 0	0 0 0	0 0 0	0	3	1

E—Hernandez. DP—Cardinals 1 (Hernandez to OSmith). LOB—Brewers 10, Cardinals 4. Scoring Position—Brewers 6-for-13, Cardinals 0-for-3. 2B—Yount (1), Moore (1), Porter (1). 3B—Gantner (1). HR—Simmons (1). S—Gantner. GDP—Oglivie.

Brewers	IP	H	R	ER	BB	K	ERA
Mike Caldwell (W, 1-0)	9.0	3	0	0	1	3	0.00

Cardinals	IP	H	R	ER	BB	K	ERA
Bob Forsch (L, 0-1)	5.2	10	6	4	1	1	6.35
Jim Kaat	1.1	1	0	0	1	1	0.00
Dave LaPoint	1.2	3	2	2	1	0	10.80
Jeff Lahti	0.1	3	2	2	0	1	54.00

HBP—Howell by Forsch. Time—2:30. Attendance—53,723. Umpires—HP, Weyer. 1B, Haller. 2B, Kibler. 3B, Phillips.

Game 2

Wednesday, October 13

Brewers	AB	R	H	RBI	BB	K	Avg
Paul Molitor, 3b	5	1	2	0	0	2	.636
Robin Yount, ss	4	1	1	1	1	0	.500
Cecil Cooper, 1b	5	0	3	1	0	0	.333
Ted Simmons, c	3	1	1	1	1	0	.375
Ben Oglivie, lf	4	0	1	0	0	1	.125
Gorman Thomas, cf	3	0	0	0	1	1	.143
Roy Howell, dh	4	1	0	0	0	3	.000
Charlie Moore, rf	4	0	2	1	0	0	.444
Jim Gantner, 2b	3	0	0	0	1	0	.286
TOTALS	35	4	10	4	4	7	.347

Cardinals	AB	R	H	RBI	BB	K	Avg
Tom Herr, 2b	3	1	1	1	1	1	.167
Ken Oberkfell, 3b	3	1	2	1	0	0	.500
Gene Tenace, ph	1	0	0	0	0	0	.000
Mike Ramsey, 3b	0	0	0	0	0	0	—
Keith Hernandez, 1b	3	0	0	0	1	0	.000
George Hendrick, rf	3	2	0	0	1	1	.000
Darrell Porter, c	4	0	2	2	0	0	.571
Lonnie Smith, lf	3	0	0	0	1	1	.000
Dane Iorg, dh	2	0	1	0	0	0	.500
David Green, ph-dh	1	0	0	0	0	1	.000
Steve Braun, ph-dh	0	0	0	1	1	0	—
Willie McGee, cf	4	1	0	0	0	1	.000
Ozzie Smith, ss	4	0	2	0	0	0	.286
TOTALS	31	5	8	5	5	5	.180

	1 2 3	4 5 6	7 8 9	R	H	E
Brewers	0 1 2	0 1 0	0 0 0	4	10	1
Cardinals	0 0 2	0 0 2	0 1 x	5	8	0

E—Oglivie. DP—Cardinals 1 (Hernandez to OSmith). LOB—Brewers 8, Cardinals 7. Scoring Position—Brewers 2-for-6, Cardinals 4-for-9. 2B—Yount (2), Cooper (1), Moore (2), Herr (1), Porter (2). HR—Simmons (2). GDP—Simmons. SB—Molitor (1), Oberkfell (1), McGee (1), OSmith (1). CS—Molitor (1).

Brewers	IP	H	R	ER	BB	K	ERA
Don Sutton	6.0	5	4	4	1	3	6.00
Bob McClure (L, 0-1)	1.1	2	1	1	2	2	6.75
Peter Ladd	0.2	1	0	0	2	0	0.00

Cardinals	IP	H	R	ER	BB	K	ERA
John Stuper	4.0	6	4	4	3	3	9.00
Jim Kaat	0.2	1	0	0	0	0	0.00
Doug Bair	2.0	1	0	0	0	3	0.00
Bruce Sutter (W, 1-0)	2.1	2	0	0	1	1	0.00

Stuper pitched to one batter in the 5th.

WP—Stuper 2. Time—2:54. Attendance—53,723. Umpires—HP, Haller. 1B, Kibler. 2B, Phillips. 3B, Davidson.

Game 3

Friday, October 15

Cardinals	AB	R	H	RBI	BB	K	Avg
Tom Herr, 2b	5	0	0	0	0	0	.091
Ken Oberkfell, 3b	4	0	0	0	0	0	.300
Keith Hernandez, 1b	4	0	0	0	0	0	.000
George Hendrick, rf	2	1	1	0	1	0	.111
Darrell Porter, c	4	0	0	0	0	1	.364
Lonnie Smith, lf	4	2	2	0	0	0	.182
David Green, lf	0	0	0	0	0	0	.000
Dane Iorg, dh	4	1	1	0	0	0	.333
Willie McGee, cf	3	2	2	4	1	0	.286
Ozzie Smith, ss	3	0	0	1	1	0	.200
TOTALS	33	6	6	5	3	1	.189

Brewers	AB	R	H	RBI	BB	K	Avg
Paul Molitor, 3b	4	0	0	0	0	1	.467
Robin Yount, ss	3	1	0	0	1	0	.385
Cecil Cooper, 1b	4	1	1	2	0	0	.308
Ted Simmons, c	4	0	1	0	0	0	.333
Ben Oglivie, lf	4	0	0	0	0	2	.083
Gorman Thomas, cf	4	0	1	0	0	1	.182
Roy Howell, dh	2	0	0	0	0	0	.000
Don Money, ph-dh	1	0	0	0	0	1	.333
Charlie Moore, rf	3	0	0	0	1	0	.333
Jim Gantner, 2b	3	0	2	0	0	0	.400
TOTALS	32	2	5	2	3	5	.294

	1 2 3	4 5 6	7 8 9	R	H	E
Cardinals	0 0 0	0 3 0	2 0 1	6	6	1
Brewers	0 0 0	0 0 0	0 2 0	2	5	3

E—Cooper, Hernandez, Simmons, Gantner. DP—Cardinals 1 (Herr to OSmith to Hernandez). LOB—Cardinals 4, Brewers 6. Scoring Position—Cardinals 1-for-5, Brewers 0-for-3. 2B—LSmith (1), Iorg (1), Gantner (1). 3B—LSmith (1). HR—McGee 2 (2), Cooper (1). GDP—Yount (1). CS—Hendrick (1).

Game 4

Saturday, October 16

Cardinals	AB	R	H	RBI	BB	K	Avg
Tom Herr, 2b	4	0	0	2	0	2	.067
Ken Oberkfell, 3b	2	2	1	0	2	0	.333
Gene Tenace, ph	1	0	0	0	0	1	.000
Keith Hernandez, 1b	4	0	0	0	0	1	.000
George Hendrick, rf	4	0	1	1	0	0	.154
Darrell Porter, c	3	0	1	0	1	1	.357
Lonnie Smith, lf	4	1	1	0	0	1	.200
Dane Iorg, dh	4	0	2	1	0	0	.400
David Green, pr-dh	0	0	0	0	0	0	.000
Willie McGee, cf	4	1	1	0	0	0	.273
Ozzie Smith, ss	3	1	1	0	1	0	.231
TOTALS	33	5	8	4	4	6	.197

Brewers	AB	R	H	RBI	BB	K	Avg
Paul Molitor, 3b	4	1	0	0	1	1	.368
Robin Yount, ss	4	1	2	2	0	0	.412
Cecil Cooper, 1b	4	1	2	1	0	0	.353
Ted Simmons, c	2	0	0	0	2	1	.286
Gorman Thomas, cf	4	0	1	2	0	0	.200
Ben Oglivie, lf	3	1	1	0	0	1	.133
Don Money, dh	4	2	2	0	0	1	.429
Charlie Moore, rf	4	0	1	0	0	0	.313
Jim Gantner, 2b	4	1	1	1	0	0	.357
TOTALS	33	7	10	6	4	3	.313

	1 2 3	4 5 6	7 8 9	R	H	E
Cardinals	1 3 0	0 0 1	0 0 0	5	8	1
Brewers	0 0 0	0 1 0	6 0 x	7	10	2

E—Yount, Gantner, LaPoint. DP—Cardinals 2 (Herr to Hernandez; OSmith to Hernandez), Brewers 2 (Gantner to Yount to Cooper; Gantner to Cooper). LOB—Cardinals 6, Brewers 6. Scoring Position—Cardinals 2-for-10, Brewers 5-for-11. 2B—Oberkfell (2), LSmith (2), Money (1), Gantner (2). 3B—Oglivie (1). SF—Herr. GDP—Hernandez, McGee, Gantner. SB—Oberkfell (2), McGee (2).

Cardinals	IP	H	R	ER	BB	K	ERA
Dave LaPoint	6.2	7	4	1	1	3	3.24
Doug Bair (BS, 1; L, 0-1)	0.0	1	2	2	1	0	9.00
Jim Kaat (BS, 1)	0.1	1	1	1	1	0	3.86
Jeff Lahti	1.1	1	0	0	1	0	10.80

Brewers	IP	H	R	ER	BB	K	ERA
Moose Haas	5.1	7	5	4	2	3	6.75
Jim Slaton (W, 1-0)	2.0	1	0	0	2	1	0.00
Bob McClure (S, 1)	1.2	0	0	0	0	2	2.70

Bair pitched to two batters in the 7th. Kaat pitched to three batters in the 7th.

WP—Haas, Kaat. Time—3:04. Attendance—56,560. Umpires—HP, Phillips. 1B, Davidson. 2B, Evans. 3B, Weyer.

Continued from Game 2 (Cardinals):

Cardinals	AB	R	H	RBI	BB	K	Avg
Dane Iorg, dh	2	0	1	0	0	0	.500
David Green, ph-dh	1	0	0	0	0	1	.000
Steve Braun, ph-dh	0	0	0	1	1	0	—
Willie McGee, cf	4	1	0	0	0	1	.000
Ozzie Smith, ss	4	0	2	0	0	0	.286
TOTALS	31	5	8	5	5	5	.180

Cardinals (Game 2 pitching)	IP	H	R	ER	BB	K	ERA
Joaquin Andujar (W, 1-0)	6.1	3	0	0	1	3	0.00
Jim Kaat	0.1	1	0	0	0	1	0.00
Doug Bair	0.0	0	0	0	0	0	0.00
Bruce Sutter (S, 1)	2.1	1	2	2	1	1	3.86

Brewers (Game 2 pitching)	IP	H	R	ER	BB	K	ERA
Pete Vuckovich (L, 0-1)	8.2	6	6	4	3	1	4.15
Bob McClure	0.1	0	0	0	0	0	5.40

Bair pitched to one batter in the 7th.

Reached, Catcher's Interference—Cardinals 1, Hendrick by Simmons. Brewers 0. Time—2:53. Attendance—56,556. Umpires—HP, Kibler. 1B, Phillips. 2B, Davidson. 3B, Evans.

Sunday, October 17

Cardinals	AB	R	H	RBI	BB	K	Avg
Lonnie Smith, dh	5	0	2	0	0	0	.250
David Green, lf	5	2	2	0	0	1	.222
Keith Hernandez, 1b	4	1	3	2	1	0	.158
George Hendrick, rf	5	0	3	2	0	0	.278
Darrell Porter, c	5	0	1	0	0	1	.316
Mike Ramsey, pr	0	0	0	0	0	0	—
Willie McGee, cf	5	0	1	0	0	2	.250
Ken Oberkfell, 3b	4	0	3	0	0	0	.438
Gene Tenace, ph	1	0	0	0	0	0	.000
Tom Herr, 2b	4	0	0	0	0	0	.053
Ozzie Smith, ss	3	1	0	0	1	0	.188
TOTALS	41	4	15	4	2	4	.228

Brewers	AB	R	H	RBI	BB	K	Avg
Paul Molitor, 3b	4	1	1	1	1	0	.348
Robin Yount, ss	4	2	4	1	0	0	.524
Cecil Cooper, 1b	4	0	1	0	0	0	.333
Ted Simmons, c	3	0	0	1	1	1	.235
Ben Oglivie, lf	4	1	2	0	0	1	.211
Gorman Thomas, cf	4	0	0	0	0	2	.158
Don Money, dh	3	1	0	0	1	1	.300
Charlie Moore, rf	4	1	2	1	0	0	.350
Jim Gantner, 2b	4	0	1	1	0	0	.333
TOTALS	34	6	11	6	3	5	.315

	1	2	3	4	5	6	7	8	9		R	H	E
Cardinals	0	0	1	0	0	0	1	0	2		4	15	2
Brewers	1	0	1	0	1	0	1	2	x		6	11	1

E—Gantner, Forsch, Herr. DP—Cardinals 2 (Porter to Herr; Oberkfell to Herr to Hernandez), Brewers 1 (Molitor to Cooper). LOB—Cardinals 12, Brewers 7. Scoring Position—Cardinals 5-for-12, Brewers 3-for-11. 2B—Green (1), Hernandez 2 (2), Yount (3), Moore (3). 3B—Green (1). HR—Yount (1). GDP—OSmith, Money. SB—LSmith (1). CS—LSmith (1), Oglivie (1).

Cardinals	IP	H	R	ER	BB	K	ERA
Bob Forsch (L, 0-2)	7.0	8	4	3	2	3	4.97
Bruce Sutter	1.0	3	2	2	1	2	6.35

Brewers	IP	H	R	ER	BB	K	ERA
Mike Caldwell (W, 2-0)	8.1	14	4	4	2	3	2.08
Bob McClure (S, 2)	0.2	1	0	0	0	1	2.25

Time—3:02. Attendance—56,562. Umpires—HP, Davidson. 1B, Evans. 2B, Weyer. 3B, Haller.

Tuesday, October 19

Brewers	AB	R	H	RBI	BB	K	Avg
Paul Molitor, 3b	4	0	1	0	0	0	.333
Robin Yount, ss	4	0	0	0	0	0	.440
Cecil Cooper, 1b	4	0	0	0	0	0	.280
Ted Simmons, c	2	0	0	0	1	0	.211
Ned Yost, c	0	0	0	0	1	0	—
Ben Oglivie, lf	4	0	1	0	0	0	.217
Gorman Thomas, cf	3	0	0	0	0	1	.136
Marshall Edwards, pr-cf	0	0	0	0	0	0	—
Don Money, dh	3	0	0	0	0	0	.231
Charlie Moore, rf	3	0	1	0	0	0	.348
Jim Gantner, 2b	3	1	1	0	0	1	.333
TOTALS	30	1	4	0	2	2	.288

Cardinals	AB	R	H	RBI	BB	K	Avg
Lonnie Smith, lf	3	1	1	0	0	1	.261
David Green, lf	1	1	0	0	1	1	.200
Ken Oberkfell, 3b	5	1	0	0	0	0	.333
Keith Hernandez, 1b	5	2	2	4	0	0	.208
George Hendrick, rf	5	2	2	1	0	1	.304
Darrell Porter, c	4	1	1	2	0	0	.304
Glenn Brummer, c	0	0	0	0	0	0	—
Dane Iorg, dh	4	3	3	0	0	0	.500
Willie McGee, cf	4	1	1	1	0	0	.250
Tom Herr, 2b	3	1	2	2	0	0	.136
Ozzie Smith, ss	4	0	0	0	0	0	.150
TOTALS	38	13	12	10	1	3	.260

	1	2	3	4	5	6	7	8	9		R	H	E
Brewers	0	0	0	0	0	0	0	0	1		1	4	4
Cardinals	0	2	0	3	2	6	0	0	x		13	12	1

E—Yount 2, Gantner 2, Oberkfell. DP—Cardinals 2 (Oberkfell to Herr to Hernandez; Herr to OSmith to Hernandez). LOB—Brewers 4, Cardinals 3. Scoring Position—Brewers 1-for-6, Cardinals 5-for-13. 2B—Gantner (3), Iorg 2 (4), Herr (2). 3B—Iorg (1). HR—Hernandez (1), Porter (1). S—Herr. GDP—Molitor, Money. SB—LSmith (2). CS—LSmith (2).

Brewers	IP	H	R	ER	BB	K	ERA
Don Sutton (L, 0-1)	4.1	7	7	5	0	2	7.84
Jim Slaton	0.2	0	0	0	0	0	
Doc Medich	2.0	5	6	4	1	0	18.00
Dwight Bernard	1.0	0	0	0	0	1	0.00

Cardinals	IP	H	R	ER	BB	K	ERA
John Stuper (W, 1-0)	9.0	4	1	1	2	2	3.46

Balk—Sutton. WP—Stuper, Medich 2. Time—2:21. Attendance—53,723. Umpires—HP, Evans. 1B, Weyer. 2B, Haller. 3B, Kibler.

Wednesday, October 20

Brewers	AB	R	H	RBI	BB	K	Avg
Paul Molitor, 3b	4	1	2	0	0	0	.355
Robin Yount, ss	4	0	1	0	0	1	.414
Cecil Cooper, 1b	3	0	1	1	0	0	.286
Ted Simmons, c	4	0	0	0	0	0	.174
Ben Oglivie, lf	4	1	1	1	0	0	.222
Gorman Thomas, cf	4	0	0	0	0	2	.115
Roy Howell, dh	3	0	0	0	0	0	.000
Charlie Moore, rf	3	0	1	0	0	0	.346
Jim Gantner, 2b	3	1	1	0	0	0	.333
TOTALS	32	3	7	2	0	3	.271

Cardinals	AB	R	H	RBI	BB	K	Avg
Lonnie Smith, lf	5	2	3	1	0	0	.321
Ken Oberkfell, 3b	3	0	0	0	0	1	.292
Gene Tenace, ph	0	0	0	0	1	0	.000
Mike Ramsey, pr-3b	1	1	0	0	0	0	.000
Keith Hernandez, 1b	3	1	2	2	2	1	.259
George Hendrick, rf	5	0	2	1	0	0	.321
Darrell Porter, c	5	0	1	0	0	1	.286
Dane Iorg, dh	3	0	2	0	0	0	.529
David Green, ph	0	0	0	0	0	0	.200
Steve Braun, ph-dh	2	0	1	1	0	0	.500
Willie McGee, cf	5	1	1	0	0	0	.240
Tom Herr, 2b	3	0	1	0	1	0	.160
Ozzie Smith, ss	4	1	2	0	0	0	.208
TOTALS	39	6	15	6	4	4	.273

	1	2	3	4	5	6	7	8	9		R	H	E
Brewers	0	0	0	0	1	2	0	0	0		3	7	0
Cardinals	0	0	0	1	0	3	0	2	x		6	15	1

E—Andujar. LOB—Brewers 3, Cardinals 13. Scoring Position—Brewers 2-for-2, Cardinals 6-for-17. 2B—Gantner (4), LSmith 2 (4). HR—Oglivie (1). SF—Cooper.

Brewers	IP	H	R	ER	BB	K	ERA
Pete Vuckovich	5.1	10	3	3	2	3	4.50
Bob McClure (BS, 1; L, 0-2)	0.1	2	1	1	1	0	4.15
Moose Haas	2.0	1	2	2	1	1	7.36
Mike Caldwell	0.1	2	0	0	0	0	2.04

Cardinals	IP	H	R	ER	BB	K	ERA
Joaquin Andujar (W, 2-0)	7.0	7	3	2	0	1	1.35
Bruce Sutter (S, 2)	2.0	0	0	0	0	2	4.70

Time—2:50. Attendance—53,723. Umpires—HP, Weyer. 1B, Haller. 2B, Kibler. 3B, Phillips.

1982 World Series—Composite Statistics

Batting

Cardinals	G	AB	R	H	RBI	2B	3B	HR	BB	SO	SB	CS	Avg	OBP	Slg
Steve Braun	2	2	0	1	2	0	0	0	1	0	0	0	.500	.667	.500
David Green	7	10	3	2	0	1	1	0	1	3	0	0	.200	.273	.500
George Hendrick	7	28	5	9	5	0	0	0	2	2	0	1	.321	.367	.321
Keith Hernandez	7	27	4	7	8	2	0	1	4	2	0	0	.259	.355	.444
Tom Herr	7	25	2	4	5	2	0	0	3	3	0	0	.160	.241	.240
Dane Iorg	5	17	4	9	1	4	1	0	0	0	0	0	.529	.529	.882
Willie McGee	6	25	6	6	5	0	0	2	1	3	2	0	.240	.269	.480
Ken Oberkfell	7	24	4	7	1	1	0	0	2	1	2	0	.292	.346	.333
Darrell Porter	7	28	1	8	5	2	0	1	1	4	0	0	.286	.310	.464
Mike Ramsey	3	1	1	0	0	0	0	0	0	1	0	0	.000	.000	.000
Lonnie Smith	7	28	6	9	1	4	1	0	1	5	2	2	.321	.345	.536
Ozzie Smith	7	24	3	5	1	0	0	0	3	0	1	0	.208	.296	.208
Gene Tenace	5	6	0	0	0	0	0	0	1	2	0	0	.000	.143	.000
Totals	**7**	**245**	**39**	**67**	**34**	**16**	**3**	**4**	**20**	**26**	**7**	**3**	**.273**	**.327**	**.412**

Brewers	G	AB	R	H	RBI	2B	3B	HR	BB	SO	SB	CS	Avg	OBP	Slg
Cecil Cooper	7	28	3	8	6	1	0	1	1	1	0	0	.286	.300	.429
Jim Gantner	7	24	5	8	4	4	1	0	1	1	0	0	.333	.360	.583
Roy Howell	4	11	1	0	0	0	0	0	0	3	0	0	.000	.083	.000
Paul Molitor	7	31	5	11	3	0	0	0	2	4	1	1	.355	.394	.355
Don Money	5	13	4	3	1	1	0	0	2	3	0	0	.231	.333	.308
Charlie Moore	7	26	3	9	2	3	0	0	1	0	0	0	.346	.370	.462
Ben Oglivie	7	27	4	6	1	0	1	1	2	4	0	1	.222	.276	.407
Ted Simmons	7	23	2	4	3	0	0	2	5	3	0	0	.174	.321	.435
Gorman Thomas	7	26	0	3	3	0	0	0	2	7	0	0	.115	.179	.115
Ned Yost	1	0	0	0	0	0	0	0	1	0	0	0	—	1.000	—
Robin Yount	7	29	6	12	6	3	0	1	2	2	0	0	.414	.452	.621
Totals	**7**	**238**	**33**	**64**	**29**	**12**	**2**	**5**	**19**	**28**	**1**	**2**	**.269**	**.324**	**.399**

Pitching

Cardinals	G	GS	CG	IP	H	R	ER	BB	SO	W-L	Sv-Op	Hld	ERA
Joaquin Andujar	2	2	0	13.1	10	3	2	1	4	2-0	0-0	0	1.35
Doug Bair	3	0	0	2.0	2	2	2	2	3	0-1	0-1	0	9.00
Bob Forsch	2	2	0	12.2	18	10	7	3	4	0-2	0-0	0	4.97
Jim Kaat	4	0	0	2.1	4	1	1	2	2	0-0	0-1	0	3.86
Jeff Lahti	2	0	0	1.2	4	2	2	1	1	0-0	0-0	0	10.80
Dave LaPoint	2	1	0	8.1	10	6	3	2	3	0-0	0-0	0	3.24
John Stuper	2	2	1	13.0	10	5	5	5	5	1-0	0-0	0	3.46
Bruce Sutter	4	0	0	7.2	6	4	4	3	6	1-0	2-2	0	4.70
Totals	**7**	**7**	**1**	**61.0**	**64**	**33**	**23**	**19**	**28**	**4-3**	**2-4**	**0**	**3.39**

Brewers	G	GS	CG	IP	H	R	ER	BB	SO	W-L	Sv-Op	Hld	ERA
Dwight Bernard	1	0	0	1.0	0	0	0	0	1	0-0	0-0	0	0.00
Mike Caldwell	3	2	1	17.2	19	4	4	3	6	2-0	0-0	0	2.04
Moose Haas	2	1	0	7.1	8	7	6	3	4	0-0	0-0	0	7.36
Peter Ladd	1	0	0	0.2	1	0	0	2	0	0-0	0-0	0	0.00
Bob McClure	5	0	0	4.1	5	2	2	3	5	0-2	2-3	0	4.15
Doc Medich	1	0	0	2.0	5	6	4	1	0	0-0	0-0	0	18.00
Jim Slaton	2	0	0	2.2	1	0	0	2	1	1-0	0-0	0	0.00
Don Sutton	2	2	0	10.1	12	11	9	1	5	0-1	0-0	0	7.84
Pete Vuckovich	2	2	0	14.0	16	9	7	5	4	0-1	0-0	0	4.50
Totals	**7**	**7**	**1**	**60.0**	**67**	**39**	**32**	**20**	**26**	**3-4**	**2-3**	**0**	**4.80**

Fielding

Cardinals	Pos	G	PO	Ast	E	DP	PB	FPct
Joaquin Andujar	p	2	1	2	1	0	—	.750
Doug Bair	p	3	0	0	0	0	—	—
Glenn Brummer	c	1	0	0	0	0	0	—
Bob Forsch	p	2	1	0	1	0	—	.500
David Green	lf	3	2	0	0	0	—	1.000
	cf	1	2	0	0	0	—	1.000
George Hendrick	rf	7	10	1	0	0	—	1.000
Keith Hernandez	1b	7	62	7	2	8	—	.972
Tom Herr	2b	7	11	19	1	6	—	.968
Jim Kaat	p	4	0	0	0	0	—	—
Jeff Lahti	p	2	0	1	0	0	—	1.000
Dave LaPoint	p	2	0	2	1	0	—	.667
Willie McGee	cf	6	24	0	0	0	—	1.000
Ken Oberkfell	3b	7	3	21	1	2	—	.960
Darrell Porter	c	7	33	2	0	1	0	1.000
Mike Ramsey	3b	2	0	0	0	0	—	—
Lonnie Smith	lf	6	11	0	0	0	—	1.000
Ozzie Smith	ss	7	22	17	0	5	—	1.000
John Stuper	p	2	1	1	0	0	—	1.000
Bruce Sutter	p	4	0	1	0	0	—	1.000
Totals		**7**	**183**	**74**	**7**	**22**	**0**	**.973**

Brewers	Pos	G	PO	Ast	E	DP	PB	FPct
Dwight Bernard	p	1	0	0	0	0	—	—
Mike Caldwell	p	3	4	2	0	0	—	1.000
Cecil Cooper	1b	7	71	10	1	3	—	.988
Marshall Edwards	cf	1	0	0	0	0	—	—
Jim Gantner	2b	7	9	33	5	2	—	.894
Moose Haas	p	2	1	2	0	0	—	1.000
Peter Ladd	p	1	0	0	0	0	—	—
Bob McClure	p	5	0	0	0	0	—	—
Doc Medich	p	1	0	0	0	0	—	—
Paul Molitor	3b	7	4	9	0	1	—	1.000
Charlie Moore	rf	7	13	0	0	0	—	1.000
Ben Oglivie	lf	7	13	0	1	0	—	.929
Ted Simmons	c	7	28	2	1	0	0	.968
Jim Slaton	p	2	0	0	0	0	—	—
Don Sutton	p	2	1	3	0	0	—	1.000
Gorman Thomas	cf	7	15	0	0	0	—	1.000
Pete Vuckovich	p	2	0	2	0	0	—	1.000
Ned Yost	c	1	1	0	0	0	0	1.000
Robin Yount	ss	7	20	19	3	1	—	.929
Totals		**7**	**180**	**82**	**11**	**7**	**0**	**.960**

1983 Baltimore Orioles (AL) 4, Philadelphia Phillies (NL) 1

In their first season after Earl Weaver's retirement, the Orioles won their first World Series in 13 years, defeating the Philadelphia Phillies in five games. Philadelphia got its only win in the opener, when Garry Maddox' eighth-inning home run broke a 1-1 tie and gave John Denny a 2-1 victory over Scott McGregor. Mike Boddicker came back with a three-hit 4-1 win in Game 2 to even the Series at one game apiece. The O's took the third game 3-2 by scoring twice in the top of the seventh. Benny Ayala drove in the tying run with an RBI single off Steve Carlton. The go-ahead run scored when shortstop Ivan DeJesus booted Dan Ford's grounder. Rich Dauer had three hits and drove in three runs in Game 4, as the Orioles won 5-4 to go up three games to one. They had blown a similar lead in the 1979 World Series, but this time, Scott McGregor tossed a five-hit shutout to wrap up the World Championship.

Game 1
Tuesday, October 11

Phillies	AB	R	H	RBI	BB	K	Avg
Joe Morgan, 2b	4	1	2	1	0	0	.500
Pete Rose, 1b	4	0	1	0	0	1	.250
Mike Schmidt, 3b	4	0	0	0	0	2	.000
Sixto Lezcano, rf	3	0	0	0	0	1	.000
Von Hayes, ph-rf	1	0	0	0	0	0	.000
Gary Matthews, lf	3	0	1	0	0	0	.333
Garry Maddox, cf	3	1	1	1	0	1	.333
Bo Diaz, c	3	0	0	0	0	0	.000
Ivan DeJesus, ss	3	0	0	0	0	1	.000
John Denny, p	3	0	0	0	0	1	.000
Al Holland, p	0	0	0	0	0	0	—
TOTALS	31	2	5	2	0	7	.161

Orioles	AB	R	H	RBI	BB	K	Avg
Al Bumbry, cf	4	0	1	0	0	0	.250
Sammy Stewart, p	0	0	0	0	0	0	—
Tippy Martinez, p	0	0	0	0	0	0	—
Jim Dwyer, rf	3	1	1	1	0	0	.333
Dan Ford, ph-rf	1	0	0	0	0	0	.000
Cal Ripken Jr., ss	4	0	1	0	0	1	.250
Eddie Murray, 1b	4	0	1	0	0	1	.250
John Lowenstein, lf	3	0	1	0	0	1	.333
Gary Roenicke, ph	1	0	0	0	0	0	.000
Rich Dauer, 2b	3	0	0	0	0	1	.000
Todd Cruz, 3b	3	0	0	0	0	1	.000
Rick Dempsey, c	2	0	0	0	0	0	.000
John Shelby, ph-cf	1	0	0	0	0	1	.000
Scott McGregor, p	2	0	0	0	0	0	.000
Joe Nolan, ph-c	1	0	0	0	0	0	.000
TOTALS	32	1	5	1	0	6	.156

	1	2	3	4	5	6	7	8	9		R	H	E
Phillies	0	0	0	0	0	1	0	1	0		2	5	0
Orioles	1	0	0	0	0	0	0	0	0		1	5	1

E—Cruz. DP—Orioles 1 (Ripken Jr. to Dauer to Murray). LOB—Phillies 2, Orioles 4. Scoring Position—Phillies 0-for-0, Orioles 0-for-1. 2B—Bumbry (1). HR—Morgan (1), Maddox (1), Dwyer (1). GDP—Maddox. CS—Morgan (1).

Phillies	IP	H	R	ER	BB	K	ERA
John Denny (W, 1-0)	7.2	5	1	1	0	5	1.17
Al Holland (S, 1)	1.1	0	0	0	0	1	0.00

Orioles	IP	H	R	ER	BB	K	ERA
Scott McGregor (L, 0-1)	8.0	4	2	2	0	6	2.25
Sammy Stewart	0.2	1	0	0	0	1	0.00
Tippy Martinez	0.1	0	0	0	0	0	0.00

Time—2:22. Attendance—52,204. Umpires—HP, Springstead. 1B, Vargo. 2B, Clark. 3B, Pulli.

Game 2
Wednesday, October 12

Phillies	AB	R	H	RBI	BB	K	Avg
Joe Morgan, 2b	4	1	1	0	0	1	.375
Pete Rose, 1b	4	0	0	0	0	1	.125
Mike Schmidt, 3b	4	0	0	0	0	1	.000
Joe Lefebvre, rf	2	0	0	1	0	1	.000
Gary Matthews, lf	3	0	1	0	0	0	.333
Greg Gross, cf	3	0	0	0	0	0	.000
Bo Diaz, c	3	0	1	0	0	1	.167
Juan Samuel, pr	0	0	0	0	0	0	—
Ozzie Virgil, c	0	0	0	0	0	0	—
Ivan DeJesus, ss	3	0	0	0	0	0	.000
Charles Hudson, p	1	0	0	0	0	0	.000
Willie Hernandez, p	0	0	0	0	0	0	—
Von Hayes, ph	1	0	0	0	0	1	.000
Larry Andersen, p	0	0	0	0	0	0	—
Tony Perez, ph	1	0	0	0	0	0	.000
Ron Reed, p	0	0	0	0	0	0	—
TOTALS	29	1	3	1	0	6	.137

Orioles	AB	R	H	RBI	BB	K	Avg
Al Bumbry, cf	2	0	0	0	0	1	.167
John Shelby, ph-cf	2	1	1	0	0	1	.333
Dan Ford, rf	3	0	1	0	0	1	.250
Cal Ripken Jr., ss	3	0	1	1	1	0	.286
Eddie Murray, 1b	4	0	0	0	0	0	.125
John Lowenstein, lf	4	1	3	1	0	0	.571
Tito Landrum, pr-lf	0	0	0	0	0	0	—
Rich Dauer, 2b	4	1	1	0	0	1	.143
Todd Cruz, 3b	4	1	1	0	0	0	.143
Rick Dempsey, c	3	0	1	1	1	1	.200
Mike Boddicker, p	3	0	0	1	0	1	.000
TOTALS	32	4	9	4	2	6	.228

	1	2	3	4	5	6	7	8	9		R	H	E
Phillies	0	0	0	1	0	0	0	0	0		1	3	0
Orioles	0	0	0	3	0	1	0	x			4	9	1

E—Murray. DP—Orioles 1 (Dauer to Ripken Jr. to Murray). LOB—Phillies 2, Orioles 8. Scoring Position—Phillies 0-for-3, Orioles 2-for-9. 2B—Lowenstein (1), Dempsey (1). HR—Lowenstein (1). SF—Lefebvre, Boddicker. GDP—Perez. SB—Morgan (1), Landrum (1).

Phillies	IP	H	R	ER	BB	K	ERA
Charles Hudson (L, 0-1)	4.1	5	3	3	0	3	6.23
Willie Hernandez	0.2	0	0	0	1	1	0.00
Larry Andersen	2.0	3	1	1	0	1	4.50
Ron Reed	1.0	1	0	0	1	1	0.00

Orioles	IP	H	R	ER	BB	K	ERA
Mike Boddicker (W, 1-0)	9.0	3	1	0	0	6	0.00

HBP—Ford by Hernandez. Time—2:27. Attendance—52,132. Umpires—HP, Vargo. 1B, Clark. 2B, Pulli. 3B, Palermo.

Game 3
Friday, October 14

Orioles	AB	R	H	RBI	BB	K	Avg
John Shelby, cf	4	0	2	0	0	2	.429
Dan Ford, rf	3	1	1	1	1	0	.286
Cal Ripken Jr., ss	3	0	0	0	1	1	.200
Eddie Murray, 1b	4	0	0	0	0	2	.083
Gary Roenicke, lf	4	0	0	0	0	1	.000
Rich Dauer, 2b	4	0	0	0	0	1	.091
Todd Cruz, 3b	3	0	0	0	1	0	.100
Rick Dempsey, c	4	1	2	0	0	1	.333
Mike Flanagan, p	1	0	0	0	0	1	.000
Ken Singleton, ph	1	0	0	0	0	1	.000
Jim Palmer, p	0	0	0	0	0	0	—
Bennie Ayala, ph	1	1	1	1	0	0	1.000
Sammy Stewart, p	1	0	0	0	0	0	.000
Tippy Martinez, p	0	0	0	0	0	0	—
TOTALS	33	3	6	2	3	11	.187

Phillies	AB	R	H	RBI	BB	K	Avg
Joe Morgan, 2b	3	1	1	1	1	0	.364
Sixto Lezcano, rf	4	0	1	0	0	1	.143
Von Hayes, rf	0	0	0	0	0	0	.000
Mike Schmidt, 3b	4	0	0	0	0	1	.000
Gary Matthews, lf	3	1	1	1	1	1	.333
Tony Perez, 1b	4	0	1	0	0	0	.200
Garry Maddox, cf	4	0	0	0	0	1	.143
Bo Diaz, c	3	0	2	0	0	0	.333
Joe Lefebvre, ph	0	0	0	0	0	0	.000
Pete Rose, ph	1	0	0	0	0	0	.111
Ivan DeJesus, ss	3	0	2	0	0	0	.222
Steve Carlton, p	3	0	0	0	0	1	.000
Al Holland, p	0	0	0	0	0	0	—
Ozzie Virgil, ph	1	0	0	0	0	0	.000
TOTALS	33	2	8	2	3	5	.186

	1	2	3	4	5	6	7	8	9		R	H	E
Orioles	0	0	0	0	0	1	2	0	0		3	6	1
Phillies	0	1	1	0	0	0	0	0	0		2	8	2

E—Cruz, DeJesus, Schmidt. DP—Phillies 2 (DeJesus to Morgan to Perez; Schmidt to Morgan to Perez). LOB—Orioles 6, Phillies 7. Scoring Position—Orioles 1-for-6, Phillies 0-for-2. 2B—Dempsey 2 (3). HR—Ford (1), Morgan (2), Matthews (1). GDP—Roenicke, Dempsey. CS—Morgan (2).

Orioles	IP	H	R	ER	BB	K	ERA
Mike Flanagan	4.0	6	2	2	1	1	4.50
Jim Palmer (W, 1-0)	2.0	2	0	0	1	1	0.00
Sammy Stewart (H, 1)	2.0	0	0	0	1	3	0.00
Tippy Martinez (S, 1)	1.0	0	0	0	0	0	0.00

Phillies	IP	H	R	ER	BB	K	ERA
Steve Carlton (L, 0-1)	6.2	5	3	2	3	7	2.70
Al Holland	2.1	1	0	0	0	4	0.00

WP—Carlton, Palmer. Time—2:35. Attendance—65,792. Umpires—HP, Clark. 1B, Pulli. 2B, Palermo. 3B, Rennert.

Game 4

Saturday, October 15

Orioles	AB	R	H	RBI	BB	K	Avg
Al Bumbry, cf	3	0	0	0	0	0	.111
Dan Ford, ph	1	0	0	0	0	1	.250
Sammy Stewart, p	1	0	0	0	0	0	.000
Tippy Martinez, p	0	0	0	0	0	0	—
Jim Dwyer, rf	5	2	2	0	0	0	.375
Tito Landrum, rf	0	0	0	0	0	0	—
Cal Ripken Jr., ss	5	1	1	0	0	1	.200
Eddie Murray, 1b	4	0	1	0	1	0	.125
John Lowenstein, lf	4	1	1	0	0	2	.455
Rich Dauer, 2b-3b	4	1	3	3	0	0	.267
Todd Cruz, 3b	2	0	1	0	0	1	.167
Joe Nolan, ph-c	1	0	0	0	1	0	.000
Rick Dempsey, c	1	0	0	0	1	0	.300
Ken Singleton, ph	0	0	0	1	1	0	.000
Lenn Sakata, pr-2b	1	0	0	0	0	0	.000
Storm Davis, p	2	0	0	0	0	2	.000
John Shelby, ph-cf	1	0	1	1	0	0	.500
TOTALS	35	5	10	5	4	7	.242

Phillies	AB	R	H	RBI	BB	K	Avg
Joe Morgan, 2b	5	0	0	0	0	1	.250
Pete Rose, 1b	3	1	2	1	1	1	.250
Mike Schmidt, 3b	4	0	1	0	0	1	.063
Joe Lefebvre, rf	3	0	1	1	0	0	.200
Tony Perez, ph	1	0	1	0	0	0	.333
Juan Samuel, pr	0	0	0	0	0	0	—
Sixto Lezcano, rf	0	0	0	0	0	0	.143
Gary Matthews, lf	3	0	1	0	1	0	.333
Greg Gross, cf	3	0	0	0	0	0	.000
Garry Maddox, ph	1	0	0	0	0	0	.125
Bo Diaz, c	4	1	2	0	0	1	.385
Bob Dernier, pr	0	1	0	0	0	0	—
Ivan DeJesus, ss	4	0	0	0	0	1	.154
John Denny, p	2	1	1	1	0	0	.200
Willie Hernandez, p	0	0	0	0	0	0	—
Ron Reed, p	0	0	0	0	0	0	—
Von Hayes, ph	1	0	0	0	0	0	.000
Larry Andersen, p	0	0	0	0	0	0	—
Ozzie Virgil, ph	1	0	1	1	0	0	.500
TOTALS	35	4	10	4	2	5	.210

	1	2	3	4	5	6	7	8	9		R	H	E
Orioles	0	0	0	2	0	2	0	1	0		5	10	1
Phillies	0	0	0	1	2	0	0	0	1		4	10	0

E—Lowenstein. DP—Orioles 2 (Dauer to Murray; Ripken Jr. to Sakata to Murray), Phillies 1 (Andersen to DeJesus to Morgan). LOB—Orioles 8, Phillies 6. Scoring Position—Orioles 3-for-10, Phillies 4-for-10. 2B—Dwyer (1), Dauer (1), Rose (1), Lefebvre (1), Diaz (1). SF—Shelby. GDP—Matthews, Gross, Stewart.

Orioles	IP	H	R	ER	BB	K	ERA
Storm Davis (W, 1-0)	5.0	6	3	3	1	3	5.40
Sammy Stewart (H, 2)	2.1	1	0	0	1	2	0.00
Tippy Martinez (S, 2)	1.2	3	1	1	0	0	3.00

Phillies	IP	H	R	ER	BB	K	ERA
John Denny (L, 1-1)	5.1	7	4	4	3	4	3.46
Willie Hernandez	0.1	0	0	0	0	0	0.00
Ron Reed	1.1	2	1	1	1	3	3.86
Larry Andersen	2.0	1	0	0	0	0	2.25

Balk—Stewart. WP—Davis. Time—2:50. Attendance—66,947. Umpires—HP, Pulli. 1B, Palermo. 2B, Rennert. 3B, Springstead.

Game 5

Sunday, October 16

Orioles	AB	R	H	RBI	BB	K	Avg
Al Bumbry, cf	2	0	0	1	0	0	.091
John Shelby, ph-cf	1	0	0	0	0	0	.444
Dan Ford, rf	4	0	0	0	0	3	.167
Tito Landrum, rf	0	0	0	0	0	0	—
Cal Ripken Jr., ss	3	1	0	0	1	1	.167
Eddie Murray, 1b	4	2	3	3	0	1	.250
John Lowenstein, lf	2	0	0	0	0	0	.385
Gary Roenicke, ph-lf	2	0	0	0	0	1	.000
Rich Dauer, 2b	4	0	0	0	0	0	.211
Todd Cruz, 3b	4	0	0	0	0	1	.125
Rick Dempsey, c	3	2	2	1	0	0	.385
Scott McGregor, p	3	0	0	0	0	0	.000
TOTALS	32	5	5	5	1	7	.217

Phillies	AB	R	H	RBI	BB	K	Avg
Joe Morgan, 2b	3	0	1	0	1	1	.263
Pete Rose, rf	4	0	2	0	0	0	.313
Mike Schmidt, 3b	4	0	0	0	0	1	.050
Gary Matthews, lf	4	0	0	0	0	1	.250
Tony Perez, 1b	4	0	0	0	0	2	.200
Garry Maddox, cf	4	0	2	0	0	0	.250
Bo Diaz, c	2	0	0	0	1	0	.333
Ivan DeJesus, ss	3	0	0	0	0	0	.125
Charles Hudson, p	1	0	0	0	0	1	.000
Marty Bystrom, p	0	0	0	0	0	0	—
Juan Samuel, ph	1	0	0	0	0	0	.000
Willie Hernandez, p	0	0	0	0	0	0	—
Sixto Lezcano, ph	1	0	0	0	0	0	.125
Ron Reed, p	0	0	0	0	0	0	—
TOTALS	31	0	5	0	2	6	.207

	1	2	3	4	5	6	7	8	9		R	H	E
Orioles	0	1	1	2	1	0	0	0	0		5	5	0
Phillies	0	0	0	0	0	0	0	0	0		0	5	1

E—Diaz. DP—Orioles 1 (Cruz to Dauer to Murray). LOB—Orioles 2, Phillies 6. Scoring Position—Orioles 0-for-3, Phillies 0-for-6. 2B—Dempsey (4), Maddox (1). 3B—Morgan (1). HR—Murray 2 (2), Dempsey (1). SF—Bumbry. GDP—DeJesus.

Orioles	IP	H	R	ER	BB	K	ERA
Scott McGregor (W, 1-1)	9.0	5	0	0	2	6	1.06

Phillies	IP	H	R	ER	BB	K	ERA
Charles Hudson (L, 0-2)	4.0	4	5	5	1	3	8.64
Marty Bystrom	1.0	0	0	0	0	1	0.00
Willie Hernandez	3.0	0	0	0	0	3	0.00
Ron Reed	1.0	1	0	0	0	0	2.70

Hudson pitched to one batter in the 5th.

WP—Bystrom. Time—2:21. Attendance—67,064. Umpires—HP, Palermo. 1B, Rennert. 2B, Springstead. 3B, Vargo.

1983 World Series—Composite Statistics

Batting

Orioles

Orioles	G	AB	R	H	RBI	2B	3B	HR	BB	SO	SB	CS	Avg	OBP	Slg
Bennie Ayala	1	1	1	1	1	0	0	0	0	0	0	0	1.000	1.000	1.000
Mike Boddicker	1	3	0	0	1	0	0	0	0	1	0	0	.000	.000	.000
Al Bumbry	4	11	0	1	1	1	0	0	0	1	0	0	.091	.083	.182
Todd Cruz	5	16	1	2	0	0	0	0	1	3	0	0	.125	.176	.125
Rich Dauer	5	19	2	4	3	1	0	0	0	3	0	0	.211	.211	.263
Storm Davis	1	2	0	0	0	0	0	0	0	2	0	0	.000	.000	.000
Rick Dempsey	5	13	3	5	2	4	0	1	2	2	0	0	.385	.467	.923
Jim Dwyer	2	8	3	3	1	1	0	1	0	0	0	0	.375	.375	.875
Mike Flanagan	1	1	0	0	0	0	0	0	0	1	0	0	.000	.000	.000
Dan Ford	5	12	1	2	1	0	0	1	1	5	0	0	.167	.286	.417
Tito Landrum	3	0	0	0	0	0	0	0	0	0	1	0	—	—	—
John Lowenstein	4	13	2	5	1	1	0	1	0	3	0	0	.385	.385	.692
Scott McGregor	2	5	0	0	0	0	0	0	0	0	0	0	.000	.000	.000
Eddie Murray	5	20	2	5	3	0	0	2	1	4	0	0	.250	.286	.550
Joe Nolan	2	2	0	0	0	0	0	0	1	0	0	0	.000	.333	.000
Cal Ripken Jr.	5	18	2	3	1	0	0	0	3	4	0	0	.167	.286	.167
Gary Roenicke	3	7	0	0	0	0	0	0	0	2	0	0	.000	.000	.000
Lenn Sakata	1	1	0	0	0	0	0	0	0	0	0	0	.000	.000	.000
John Shelby	5	9	1	4	1	0	0	0	0	4	0	0	.444	.400	.444
Ken Singleton	2	1	0	0	1	0	0	0	1	1	0	0	.000	.500	.000
Sammy Stewart	3	2	0	0	0	0	0	0	0	1	0	0	.000	.000	.000
Totals	5	164	18	35	17	8	0	6	10	37	1	0	.213	.258	.372

Phillies

Phillies	G	AB	R	H	RBI	2B	3B	HR	BB	SO	SB	CS	Avg	OBP	Slg
Steve Carlton	1	3	0	0	0	0	0	0	1	0	0	0	.000	.000	.000
Ivan DeJesus	5	16	0	2	0	0	0	0	1	2	0	0	.125	.176	.125
John Denny	2	5	1	1	1	0	0	0	0	1	0	0	.200	.200	.200
Bob Dernier	1	0	1	0	0	0	0	0	0	0	0	0	—	—	—
Bo Diaz	5	15	1	5	0	1	0	0	1	2	0	0	.333	.375	.400
Greg Gross	2	6	0	0	0	0	0	0	0	0	0	0	.000	.000	.000
Von Hayes	4	3	0	0	0	0	0	0	0	1	0	0	.000	.000	.000
Charles Hudson	2	2	0	0	0	0	0	0	0	1	0	0	.000	.000	.000
Joe Lefebvre	3	5	0	1	2	1	0	0	0	1	0	0	.200	.167	.400
Sixto Lezcano	4	8	0	1	0	0	0	0	0	2	0	0	.125	.125	.125
Garry Maddox	4	12	1	3	1	1	0	1	0	2	0	0	.250	.250	.583
Gary Matthews	5	16	1	4	1	0	0	1	2	2	0	0	.250	.333	.438
Joe Morgan	5	19	3	5	2	0	1	2	2	3	1	2	.263	.333	.684
Tony Perez	4	10	0	2	0	0	0	0	0	2	0	0	.200	.200	.200
Pete Rose	5	16	1	5	1	1	0	0	1	3	0	0	.313	.353	.375
Juan Samuel	3	1	0	0	0	0	0	0	0	0	0	0	.000	.000	.000
Mike Schmidt	5	20	0	1	0	0	0	0	0	6	0	0	.050	.050	.050
Ozzie Virgil	3	2	0	1	1	0	0	0	0	0	0	0	.500	.500	.500
Totals	5	159	9	31	9	4	1	4	7	29	1	2	.195	.228	.308

Pitching

Orioles

Orioles	G	GS	CG	IP	H	R	ER	BB	SO	W-L	Sv-Op	Hld	ERA
Mike Boddicker	1	1	1	9.0	3	1	0	0	6	1-0	0-0	0	0.00
Storm Davis	1	1	0	5.0	6	3	3	1	3	1-0	0-0	0	5.40
Mike Flanagan	1	1	0	4.0	6	2	2	1	1	0-0	0-0	0	4.50
Tippy Martinez	3	0	0	3.0	3	1	1	0	0	0-0	2-2	0	3.00
Scott McGregor	2	2	1	17.0	9	2	2	2	12	1-1	0-0	0	1.06
Jim Palmer	1	0	0	2.0	2	0	0	1	1	1-0	0-0	0	0.00
Sammy Stewart	3	0	0	5.0	2	0	0	2	6	0-0	0-0	2	2.00
Totals	5	5	2	45.0	31	9	8	7	29	4-1	2-2	2	1.60

Phillies

Phillies	G	GS	CG	IP	H	R	ER	BB	SO	W-L	Sv-Op	Hld	ERA
Larry Andersen	2	0	0	4.0	4	1	1	0	1	0-0	0-0	0	2.25
Marty Bystrom	1	0	0	1.0	0	0	0	0	1	0-0	0-0	0	0.00
Steve Carlton	1	1	0	6.2	5	3	2	3	7	0-1	0-0	0	2.70
John Denny	2	2	0	13.0	12	5	5	3	9	1-1	0-0	0	3.46
Willie Hernandez	3	0	0	4.0	0	0	0	1	4	0-0	0-0	0	0.00
Al Holland	2	0	0	3.2	1	0	0	0	5	0-0	1-1	0	0.00
Charles Hudson	2	2	0	8.1	9	8	8	1	6	0-2	0-0	0	8.64
Ron Reed	3	0	0	3.1	4	1	1	2	4	0-0	0-0	0	2.70
Totals	5	5	0	44.0	35	18	17	10	37	1-4	1-1	0	3.48

Fielding

Orioles

Orioles	Pos	G	PO	Ast	E	DP	PB	FPct
Mike Boddicker	p	1	1	2	0	0	—	1.000
Al Bumbry	cf	4	12	0	0	0	—	1.000
Todd Cruz	3b	5	1	18	2	1	—	.905
Rich Dauer	2b	5	13	7	0	4	—	1.000
	3b	1	1	1	0	0	—	1.000
Storm Davis	p	1	0	1	0	0	—	1.000
Rick Dempsey	c	5	27	4	0	0	0	1.000
Jim Dwyer	rf	2	2	0	0	0	—	1.000
Mike Flanagan	p	1	0	0	0	0	—	—
Dan Ford	rf	4	5	1	0	0	—	1.000
Tito Landrum	rf	2	1	0	0	0	—	1.000
	lf	1	0	0	0	0	—	—
John Lowenstein	lf	4	4	0	1	0	—	.800
Tippy Martinez	p	3	0	0	0	0	—	—
Scott McGregor	p	2	0	0	0	0	—	—
Eddie Murray	1b	5	45	1	1	5	—	.979
Joe Nolan	c	2	3	0	0	0	0	1.000
Jim Palmer	p	1	0	0	0	0	—	—
Cal Ripken Jr.	ss	5	6	14	0	3	—	1.000
Gary Roenicke	lf	2	2	1	0	0	—	1.000
Lenn Sakata	2b	1	2	2	0	1	—	1.000
John Shelby	cf	5	10	0	0	0	—	1.000
Sammy Stewart	p	3	0	0	0	0	—	—
Totals		5	135	52	4	14	0	.979

Phillies

Phillies	Pos	G	PO	Ast	E	DP	PB	FPct
Larry Andersen	p	2	1	1	0	1	—	1.000
Marty Bystrom	p	1	0	0	0	0	—	—
Steve Carlton	p	1	0	0	0	0	—	—
Ivan DeJesus	ss	5	5	14	1	2	—	.950
John Denny	p	2	3	1	0	0	—	1.000
Bo Diaz	c	5	37	1	1	0	0	.974
Greg Gross	cf	2	8	0	0	0	—	1.000
Von Hayes	rf	2	1	0	0	0	—	1.000
Willie Hernandez	p	3	1	0	0	0	—	1.000
Al Holland	p	2	0	0	0	0	—	—
Charles Hudson	p	2	0	0	0	0	—	—
Joe Lefebvre	rf	2	3	0	0	0	—	1.000
Sixto Lezcano	rf	3	2	0	0	0	—	1.000
Garry Maddox	cf	3	7	0	0	0	—	1.000
Gary Matthews	lf	5	15	0	0	0	—	1.000
Joe Morgan	2b	5	8	10	0	3	—	1.000
Tony Perez	1b	2	13	1	0	2	—	1.000
Ron Reed	p	3	0	0	0	0	—	—
Pete Rose	1b	3	23	4	0	0	—	1.000
	rf	1	3	0	0	0	—	1.000
Mike Schmidt	3b	5	1	10	1	1	—	.917
Ozzie Virgil	c	1	1	0	0	0	0	1.000
Totals		5	132	42	3	9	0	.983

1984 Detroit Tigers (AL) 4, San Diego Padres (NL) 1

The Detroit Tigers shelled the San Diego Padres' starting pitchers without mercy, dispatching with them and the rest of their team in five short games. Mark Thurmond last all of five innings in Game 1. Although it was the longest outing of the Series for a San Diego starter, he left the game trailing 3-2 after Larry Herndon's two-run homer put the Tigers on top. Jack Morris shut down San Diego the rest of the way for the win. Although the Tigers knocked out Ed Whitson in the first inning of Game 2, Kurt Bevacqua's three-run homer enabled the Padres to come back for a 5-3 victory. Tim Lollar was the Tigers' next victim, lasting only 1.2 innings in the third game before being driven from the mound by a Marty Castillo two-run homer and Alan Trammell's RBI double. Milt Wilcox went six innings to pick up the 5-2 victory. Jack Morris hurled another complete game in Game 4, winning 4-2 on the strength of Trammell's pair of two-run circuit shots. Detroit made it a wrap in Game 5, as Mark Thurmond exited after allowing hits to five of the six hitters he faced. Detroit's 8-4 win capped a season in which the Tigers led wire-to-wire and were never seriously challenged.

Game 1

Tuesday, October 9

Tigers	AB	R	H	RBI	BB	K	Avg
Lou Whitaker, 2b	4	1	1	0	1	1	.250
Alan Trammell, ss	5	0	2	1	0	0	.400
Kirk Gibson, rf	4	0	0	0	1	1	.000
Lance Parrish, c	3	1	2	0	1	0	.667
Larry Herndon, lf	3	1	2	2	1	0	.667
Barbaro Garbey, dh	4	0	0	0	0	1	.000
Chet Lemon, cf	4	0	1	0	0	0	.250
Darrell Evans, 1b	3	0	0	0	1	0	.000
Dave Bergman, pr-1b	0	0	0	0	0	0	—
Marty Castillo, 3b	2	0	0	0	1	0	.000
John Grubb, ph	0	0	0	0	0	0	—
Tom Brookens, ph-3b	1	0	0	0	0	0	.000
TOTALS	33	3	8	3	6	3	.242

Padres	AB	R	H	RBI	BB	K	Avg
Alan Wiggins, 2b	4	0	1	0	0	1	.250
Tony Gwynn, rf	2	0	1	0	2	0	.500
Steve Garvey, 1b	4	1	1	0	0	1	.250
Graig Nettles, 3b	2	1	2	0	1	0	1.000
Luis Salazar, pr-3b	1	0	0	0	0	0	.000
Terry Kennedy, c	4	0	2	2	0	1	.500
Bobby Brown, cf	4	0	0	0	0	2	.000
Carmelo Martinez, lf	4	0	0	0	0	2	.000
Garry Templeton, ss	4	0	0	0	0	2	.000
Kurt Bevacqua, dh	3	0	1	0	0	0	.333
TOTALS	32	2	8	2	3	9	.250

	1	2	3	4	5	6	7	8	9		R	H	E
Tigers	1	0	0	0	2	0	0	0	0		3	8	0
Padres	2	0	0	0	0	0	0	0	0		2	8	1

E—Martinez. DP—Tigers 1 (Whitaker to Evans), Padres 1 (Garvey). LOB—Tigers 9, Padres 6. Scoring Position—Tigers 2-for-8, Padres 1-for-8. 2B—Whitaker (1), Parrish (1), Kennedy (1), Bevacqua (1). HR—Herndon (1). GDP—Garvey. SB—Trammell (1), Gwynn (1). CS—Trammell (1), Gibson (1), Gwynn (1).

Tigers	IP	H	R	ER	BB	K	ERA
Jack Morris (W, 1-0)	9.0	8	2	2	3	9	2.00

Padres	IP	H	R	ER	BB	K	ERA
Mark Thurmond (L, 0-1)	5.0	7	3	3	3	2	5.40
Andy Hawkins	2.2	1	0	0	3	0	0.00
Dave Dravecky	1.1	0	0	0	0	1	0.00

Time—3:18. Attendance—57,908. Umpires—HP, Harvey. 1B, Barnett. 2B, Froemming. 3B, Garcia.

Game 2

Wednesday, October 10

Tigers	AB	R	H	RBI	BB	K	Avg
Lou Whitaker, 2b	4	1	1	0	0	1	.250
Alan Trammell, ss	4	1	2	0	0	2	.444
Kirk Gibson, rf	4	1	2	1	0	1	.250
Lance Parrish, c	3	0	0	1	0	1	.333
Darrell Evans, 3b-1b	4	0	1	1	0	1	.143
Ruppert Jones, lf	2	0	0	0	0	0	.000
Larry Herndon, ph-lf	2	0	0	0	0	0	.400
John Grubb, dh	2	0	1	0	0	0	.500
Rusty Kuntz, ph-dh	1	0	0	0	0	1	.000
Chet Lemon, cf	3	0	0	0	0	0	.143
Dave Bergman, 1b	2	0	0	0	0	0	.000
Tom Brookens, ph-3b	1	0	0	0	0	1	.000
TOTALS	32	3	7	3	0	8	.254

Padres	AB	R	H	RBI	BB	K	Avg
Alan Wiggins, 2b	5	1	3	0	0	0	.444
Tony Gwynn, rf	3	0	1	0	1	0	.400
Steve Garvey, 1b	3	0	0	0	0	0	.143
Graig Nettles, 3b	1	1	0	1	2	0	.667
Terry Kennedy, c	4	1	1	0	0	0	.375
Kurt Bevacqua, dh	4	2	3	3	0	0	.571
Carmelo Martinez, lf	3	0	0	0	1	2	.000
Garry Templeton, ss	4	0	3	0	0	0	.375
Bobby Brown, cf	3	0	0	1	0	1	.000
Luis Salazar, cf	1	0	0	0	0	0	.000
TOTALS	31	5	11	5	4	3	.302

	1	2	3	4	5	6	7	8	9		R	H	E
Tigers	3	0	0	0	0	0	0	0	0		3	7	3
Padres	1	0	0	1	3	0	0	0	x		5	11	0

E—Trammell, Gibson 2. DP—Tigers 1 (Parrish to Whitaker), Padres 1 (Gwynn to Garvey). LOB—Tigers 3, Padres 8. Scoring Position—Tigers 2-for-3, Padres 1-for-8. HR—Bevacqua (1). S—Garvey. SF—Parrish, Nettles. SB—Gibson (1). CS—Wiggins (1), Gwynn (2), Bevacqua (1).

Tigers	IP	H	R	ER	BB	K	ERA
Dan Petry (L, 0-1)	4.1	8	5	5	3	2	10.38
Aurelio Lopez	0.2	1	0	0	1	0	0.00
Bill Scherrer	1.1	2	0	0	0	0	0.00
Doug Bair	0.2	0	0	0	0	1	0.00
Willie Hernandez	1.0	0	0	0	0	0	0.00

Padres	IP	H	R	ER	BB	K	ERA
Ed Whitson	0.2	5	3	3	0	0	40.50
Andy Hawkins (W, 1-0)	5.1	1	0	0	0	3	0.00
Craig Lefferts (S, 1)	3.0	1	0	0	0	5	0.00

Balk—Petry. Time—2:44. Attendance—57,911. Umpires—HP, Barnett. 1B, Froemming. 2B, Garcia. 3B, Runge.

Game 3

Friday, October 12

Padres	AB	R	H	RBI	BB	K	Avg
Alan Wiggins, 2b	5	1	2	0	0	0	.429
Tony Gwynn, rf	5	1	2	0	0	1	.400
Steve Garvey, 1b	5	0	1	1	0	1	.167
Graig Nettles, 3b	2	0	0	1	1	0	.400
Terry Kennedy, c	3	0	0	0	1	0	.273
Kurt Bevacqua, dh	4	0	1	0	0	0	.455
Carmelo Martinez, lf	4	0	1	0	0	2	.091
Garry Templeton, ss	4	0	2	0	0	0	.417
Bobby Brown, cf	3	0	0	0	0	0	.000
Luis Salazar, ph	1	0	1	0	0	0	.333
TOTALS	36	2	10	2	2	4	.293

Tigers	AB	R	H	RBI	BB	K	Avg
Lou Whitaker, 2b	3	1	0	0	2	2	.182
Alan Trammell, ss	3	1	2	1	2	0	.500
Kirk Gibson, rf	2	0	0	1	2	0	.200
Lance Parrish, c	3	0	1	0	2	0	.333
Larry Herndon, lf	4	0	1	1	1	0	.333
Barbaro Garbey, dh	5	0	0	0	0	1	.000
Chet Lemon, cf	5	1	2	0	0	1	.250
Darrell Evans, 1b	2	1	0	0	2	1	.111
Dave Bergman, 1b	0	0	0	0	0	0	.000
Marty Castillo, 3b	4	1	1	2	0	0	.167
TOTALS	31	5	7	5	11	5	.236

	1	2	3	4	5	6	7	8	9		R	H	E
Padres	0	0	1	0	0	0	1	0	0		2	10	0
Tigers	0	4	1	0	0	0	0	0	x		5	7	0

LOB—Padres 10, Tigers 14. Scoring Position—Padres 0-for-9, Tigers 2-for-9. 2B—Wiggins (1), Garvey (1), Trammell (1). HR—Castillo (1). SF—Nettles. SB—Gibson (2).

Padres	IP	H	R	ER	BB	K	ERA
Tim Lollar (L, 0-1)	1.2	4	4	4	4	0	21.60
Greg Booker	1.0	0	1	1	4	0	9.00
Greg Harris	5.1	3	0	0	3	5	0.00

Tigers	IP	H	R	ER	BB	K	ERA
Milt Wilcox (W, 1-0)	6.0	7	1	1	2	4	1.50
Bill Scherrer	0.2	2	1	1	0	0	4.50
Willie Hernandez (S, 1)	2.1	1	0	0	0	0	0.00

WP—Lollar. HBP—Gibson by Harris. Time—3:11. Attendance—51,970. Umpires—HP, Froemming. 1B, Garcia. 2B, Runge. 3B, Reilly.

Game 4
Saturday, October 13

Padres	AB	R	H	RBI	BB	K	Avg
Alan Wiggins, 2b	3	0	0	0	0	0	.353
Champ Summers, ph	1	0	0	0	0	1	.000
Ron Roenicke, lf	0	0	0	0	0	0	—
Tony Gwynn, rf	4	0	1	0	0	0	.357
Steve Garvey, 1b	4	1	1	0	0	0	.188
Graig Nettles, 3b	4	0	0	0	0	0	.222
Terry Kennedy, c	4	1	1	1	0	0	.267
Kurt Bevacqua, dh	3	0	1	0	0	1	.429
Carmelo Martinez, lf	2	0	0	0	0	1	.077
Tim Flannery, ph-2b	1	0	1	0	0	0	1.000
Garry Templeton, ss	3	0	0	0	0	1	.333
Bobby Brown, cf	3	0	0	0	0	0	.000
TOTALS	32	2	5	1	0	4	.258

Tigers	AB	R	H	RBI	BB	K	Avg
Lou Whitaker, 2b	4	2	2	0	0	0	.267
Alan Trammell, ss	4	2	3	4	0	0	.563
Kirk Gibson, rf	4	0	1	0	0	1	.214
Lance Parrish, c	4	0	0	0	0	0	.231
Darrell Evans, 3b	2	0	0	0	1	1	.091
Tom Brookens, 3b	1	0	0	0	0	0	.000
John Grubb, dh	1	0	0	0	0	0	.333
Barbaro Garbey, ph-dh	2	0	0	0	0	0	.000
Ruppert Jones, lf	1	0	0	0	0	1	.000
Larry Herndon, ph-lf	2	0	1	0	0	1	.364
Chet Lemon, cf	2	0	0	0	1	1	.214
Dave Bergman, 1b	3	0	0	0	0	1	.000
TOTALS	30	4	7	4	2	6	.235

	1	2	3	4	5	6	7	8	9		R	H	E
Padres	0	1	0	0	0	0	0	0	1		2	5	2
Tigers	2	0	2	0	0	0	0	0	x		4	7	0

E—Wiggins, Gwynn. DP—Padres 2 (Kennedy to Nettles; Templeton to Wiggins to Garvey). LOB—Padres 3, Tigers 4. Scoring Position—Padres 0-for-4, Tigers 2-for-7. 2B—Garvey (2), Bevacqua (2), Whitaker (2). HR—Kennedy (1), Trammell 2 (2). GDP—Lemon. SB—Gibson (3), Lemon (1). CS—Lemon (1).

Padres	IP	H	R	ER	BB	K	ERA
Eric Show (L, 0-1)	2.2	4	4	3	1	2	10.13
Dave Dravecky	3.1	3	0	0	1	4	0.00
Craig Lefferts	1.0	0	0	0	0	0	0.00
Goose Gossage	1.0	0	0	0	0	0	0.00

Tigers	IP	H	R	ER	BB	K	ERA
Jack Morris (W, 2-0)	9.0	5	2	2	0	4	2.00

WP—Morris 2. Time—2:20. Attendance—52,130. Umpires—HP, Garcia. 1B, Runge. 2B, Reilly. 3B, Harvey.

Game 5
Sunday, October 14

Padres	AB	R	H	RBI	BB	K	Avg
Alan Wiggins, 2b	5	0	2	1	0	1	.364
Tony Gwynn, rf	5	0	0	0	0	1	.263
Steve Garvey, 1b	4	0	1	1	0	0	.200
Graig Nettles, 3b	3	0	1	0	1	0	.250
Terry Kennedy, c	4	0	0	0	0	0	.211
Kurt Bevacqua, dh	3	2	1	1	1	1	.412
Carmelo Martinez, lf	4	0	2	0	0	2	.176
Luis Salazar, pr-cf	0	0	0	0	0	0	.333
Garry Templeton, ss	4	1	1	0	0	0	.316
Bobby Brown, cf-lf	2	1	1	1	0	1	.067
Bruce Bochy, ph	1	0	1	0	0	0	1.000
Ron Roenicke, pr	0	0	0	0	0	0	—
TOTALS	35	4	10	4	2	6	.262

Tigers	AB	R	H	RBI	BB	K	Avg
Lou Whitaker, 2b	3	1	1	0	1	0	.278
Alan Trammell, ss	4	1	0	0	0	0	.450
Kirk Gibson, rf	4	3	3	5	1	1	.333
Lance Parrish, c	5	2	2	1	0	1	.278
Larry Herndon, lf	4	0	1	0	1	1	.333
Chet Lemon, cf	3	0	2	1	1	0	.294
Barbaro Garbey, dh	1	0	0	0	0	0	.000
John Grubb, ph-dh	0	0	0	0	0	0	.333
Rusty Kuntz, ph-dh	0	0	0	1	0	0	.000
Howard Johnson, ph-dh	1	0	0	0	0	0	.000
Darrell Evans, 1b	4	0	0	0	0	1	.067
Dave Bergman, 1b	0	0	0	0	0	0	.000
Marty Castillo, 3b	3	1	2	0	1	1	.333
TOTALS	32	8	11	8	5	5	.263

	1	2	3	4	5	6	7	8	9		R	H	E
Padres	0	0	1	2	0	0	0	1	0		4	10	1
Tigers	3	0	0	0	1	0	1	3	x		8	11	1

E—Parrish, Wiggins. DP—Padres 1 (Garvey to Templeton). LOB—Padres 7, Tigers 9. Scoring Position—Padres 2-for-7, Tigers 3-for-8. 2B—Templeton (1). HR—Bevacqua (2), Gibson 2 (2), Parrish (1). S—Whitaker, Kuntz. SF—Brown, Kuntz. GDP—Whitaker. SB—Wiggins (1), Parrish (1), Lemon (2). CS—Herndon (1), Salazar (1).

Padres	IP	H	R	ER	BB	K	ERA
Mark Thurmond	0.1	5	3	3	0	0	10.13
Andy Hawkins (L, 1-1)	4.0	2	1	1	3	1	0.75
Craig Lefferts	2.0	1	0	0	1	2	0.00
Goose Gossage	1.2	3	4	4	1	2	13.50

Tigers	IP	H	R	ER	BB	K	ERA
Dan Petry	3.2	6	3	3	2	2	9.00
Bill Scherrer	1.0	1	0	0	0	0	3.00
Aurelio Lopez (W, 1-0)	2.1	0	0	0	0	4	0.00
Willie Hernandez (S, 2)	2.0	3	1	1	0	0	1.69

WP—Hawkins. HBP—Grubb by Hawkins. Time—2:55. Attendance—51,901. Umpires—HP, Runge. 1B, Reilly. 2B, Harvey. 3B, Barnett.

1984 World Series—Composite Statistics

Batting

Tigers	G	AB	R	H	RBI	2B	3B	HR	BB	SO	SB	CS	Avg	OBP	Slg
Dave Bergman	5	5	0	0	0	0	0	0	0	0	1	0	.000	.000	.000
Tom Brookens	3	3	0	0	0	0	0	0	0	1	0	0	.000	.000	.000
Marty Castillo	3	9	2	3	2	0	0	1	2	1	0	0	.333	.455	.667
Darrell Evans	5	15	1	1	1	0	0	0	4	4	0	0	.067	.263	.067
Barbaro Garbey	4	12	0	0	0	0	0	0	0	2	0	0	.000	.000	.000
Kirk Gibson	5	18	4	6	7	0	0	2	4	4	3	1	.333	.478	.667
John Grubb	4	3	0	1	0	0	0	0	0	0	0	0	.333	.500	.333
Larry Herndon	5	15	1	5	3	0	0	1	3	2	0	1	.333	.444	.533
Howard Johnson	1	1	0	0	0	0	0	0	0	0	0	0	.000	.000	.000
Ruppert Jones	2	3	0	0	0	0	0	0	0	1	0	0	.000	.000	.000
Rusty Kuntz	2	1	0	0	1	0	0	0	0	1	0	0	.000	.000	.000
Chet Lemon	5	17	1	5	1	0	0	0	2	2	2	1	.294	.368	.294
Lance Parrish	5	18	3	5	2	1	0	1	3	2	1	0	.278	.364	.500
Alan Trammell	5	20	5	9	6	1	0	2	2	2	1	1	.450	.500	.800
Lou Whitaker	5	18	6	5	0	2	0	0	4	4	0	0	.278	.409	.389
Totals	**5**	**158**	**23**	**40**	**23**	**4**	**0**	**7**	**24**	**27**	**7**	**4**	**.253**	**.355**	**.411**

Padres	G	AB	R	H	RBI	2B	3B	HR	BB	SO	SB	CS	Avg	OBP	Slg
Kurt Bevacqua	5	17	4	7	4	2	0	2	1	2	0	1	.412	.444	.882
Bruce Bochy	1	1	0	1	0	0	0	0	0	0	0	0	1.000	1.000	1.000
Bobby Brown	5	15	1	1	2	0	0	0	0	4	0	0	.067	.063	.067
Tim Flannery	1	1	0	1	0	0	0	0	0	0	0	0	1.000	1.000	1.000
Steve Garvey	5	20	2	4	2	2	0	0	0	2	0	0	.200	.200	.300
Tony Gwynn	5	19	1	5	0	0	0	0	3	2	1	2	.263	.364	.263
Terry Kennedy	5	19	2	4	3	1	0	1	1	1	0	0	.211	.250	.421
Carmelo Martinez	5	17	0	3	0	0	0	0	1	9	0	0	.176	.222	.176
Graig Nettles	5	12	2	3	2	0	0	0	5	0	0	0	.250	.421	.250
Luis Salazar	4	3	0	1	0	0	0	0	0	0	0	1	.333	.333	.333
Champ Summers	1	1	0	0	0	0	0	0	0	1	0	0	.000	.000	.000
Garry Templeton	5	19	1	6	0	1	0	0	0	3	0	0	.316	.316	.368
Alan Wiggins	5	22	2	8	1	1	0	0	0	2	1	1	.364	.364	.409
Totals	**5**	**166**	**15**	**44**	**14**	**7**	**0**	**3**	**11**	**26**	**2**	**5**	**.265**	**.306**	**.361**

Pitching

Tigers	G	GS	CG	IP	H	R	ER	BB	SO	W-L	Sv-Op	Hld	ERA
Doug Bair	1	0	0	0.2	0	0	0	0	1	0-0	0-0	0	0.00
Willie Hernandez	3	0	0	5.1	4	1	1	0	0	0-0	2-2	0	1.69
Aurelio Lopez	2	0	0	3.0	1	0	0	1	4	1-0	0-0	0	0.00
Jack Morris	2	2	2	18.0	13	4	4	3	13	2-0	0-0	0	2.00
Dan Petry	2	2	0	8.0	14	8	8	5	4	0-1	0-0	0	9.00
Bill Scherrer	3	0	0	3.0	5	1	1	0	0	0-0	0-0	0	3.00
Milt Wilcox	1	1	0	6.0	7	1	1	2	4	1-0	0-0	0	1.50
Totals	**5**	**5**	**2**	**44.0**	**44**	**15**	**15**	**11**	**26**	**4-1**	**2-2**	**0**	**3.07**

Padres	G	GS	CG	IP	H	R	ER	BB	SO	W-L	Sv-Op	Hld	ERA
Greg Booker	1	0	0	1.0	0	1	1	4	0	0-0	0-0	0	9.00
Dave Dravecky	2	0	0	4.2	3	0	0	1	5	0-0	0-0	0	0.00
Goose Gossage	2	0	0	2.2	3	4	4	1	2	0-0	0-0	0	13.50
Greg Harris	1	0	0	5.1	3	0	0	3	5	0-0	0-0	0	0.00
Andy Hawkins	3	0	0	12.0	4	1	1	6	4	1-1	0-0	0	0.75
Craig Lefferts	3	0	0	6.0	2	0	0	1	7	0-0	1-1	0	0.00
Tim Lollar	1	1	0	1.2	4	4	4	4	0	0-1	0-0	0	21.60
Eric Show	1	1	0	2.2	4	4	3	1	2	0-1	0-0	0	10.13
Mark Thurmond	2	2	0	5.1	12	6	6	3	2	0-1	0-0	0	10.13
Ed Whitson	1	1	0	0.2	5	3	3	0	0	0-0	0-0	0	40.50
Totals	**5**	**5**	**0**	**42.0**	**40**	**23**	**22**	**24**	**27**	**1-4**	**1-1**	**0**	**4.71**

Fielding

Tigers	Pos	G	PO	Ast	E	DP	PB	FPct
Doug Bair	p	1	0	0	0	0	—	—
Dave Bergman	1b	5	22	4	0	0	—	1.000
Tom Brookens	3b	3	0	3	0	0	—	1.000
Marty Castillo	3b	3	3	3	0	0	—	1.000
Darrell Evans	1b	4	15	3	0	1	—	1.000
	3b	2	3	2	0	0	—	1.000
Kirk Gibson	rf	5	5	1	2	0	—	.750
Willie Hernandez	p	3	0	1	0	0	—	1.000
Larry Herndon	lf	5	6	0	0	0	—	1.000
Ruppert Jones	lf	2	3	0	0	0	—	1.000
Chet Lemon	cf	5	15	0	0	0	—	1.000
Aurelio Lopez	p	2	0	0	0	0	—	—
Jack Morris	p	2	5	1	0	0	—	1.000
Lance Parrish	c	5	30	3	1	1	0	.971
Dan Petry	p	2	1	1	0	0	—	1.000
Bill Scherrer	p	3	0	2	0	0	—	1.000
Alan Trammell	ss	5	8	9	1	0	—	.944
Lou Whitaker	2b	5	15	18	0	2	—	1.000
Milt Wilcox	p	1	1	1	0	0	—	1.000
Totals		**5**	**132**	**52**	**4**	**4**	**0**	**.979**

Padres	Pos	G	PO	Ast	E	DP	PB	FPct
Greg Booker	p	1	0	1	0	0	—	1.000
Bobby Brown	cf	5	13	0	0	0	—	1.000
	lf	1	0	0	0	0	—	—
Dave Dravecky	p	2	0	0	0	0	—	—
Tim Flannery	2b	1	1	0	0	0	—	1.000
Steve Garvey	1b	5	34	3	0	4	—	1.000
Goose Gossage	p	2	0	1	0	0	—	1.000
Tony Gwynn	rf	5	12	1	1	1	—	.929
Greg Harris	p	1	0	0	0	0	—	—
Andy Hawkins	p	3	0	1	0	0	—	1.000
Terry Kennedy	c	5	30	2	0	1	0	1.000
Craig Lefferts	p	3	0	0	0	0	—	—
Tim Lollar	p	1	0	0	0	0	—	—
Carmelo Martinez	lf	5	7	0	1	0	—	.875
Graig Nettles	3b	5	7	12	0	1	—	1.000
Ron Roenicke	lf	1	0	0	0	0	—	—
Luis Salazar	cf	2	1	0	0	0	—	1.000
	3b	1	0	0	0	0	—	—
Eric Show	p	1	0	0	0	0	—	—
Garry Templeton	ss	5	8	11	0	2	—	1.000
Mark Thurmond	p	2	0	2	0	0	—	1.000
Ed Whitson	p	1	0	0	0	0	—	—
Alan Wiggins	2b	5	13	6	2	1	—	.905
Totals		**5**	**126**	**40**	**4**	**10**	**0**	**.976**

1985 Kansas City Royals (AL) 4, St. Louis Cardinals (NL) 3

After coming back from a three-games-to-one deficit in the ALCS, the Kansas City Royals spotted the St. Louis Cardinals an identical advantage in the World Series before mounting an equally successful comeback. John Tudor outdueled Danny Jackson in the opener, 3-1. St. Louis took the second game when Terry Pendleton doubled in three runs with the Cardinals trailing by a run with two outs in the ninth. Bret Saberhagen got the Royals a 6-1 win in the third game, but John Tudor tossed a five-hit shutout in Game 4 to put the Cardinals on the brink of a championship. Jackson came through with a clutch 6-1 win in Game 5. Then the Cardinals came within three outs of victory in Game 6, taking a 1-0 shutout into the ninth. Jorge Orta opened with a much-disputed single; the replay showed him to be out at first base, but umpire Don Denkinger called him safe. After a single and an intentional walk loaded the bases, Dane Iorg hit a two-run single to win it for Kansas City and force a seventh game. Tudor wasn't sharp, and the Royals knocked him out early. Cardinals manager Whitey Herzog and pitcher Joaquin Andujar were both ejected during an ugly fifth inning in which the Royals scored six runs to blow the game wide open. Bret Saberhagen finished up a five-hit shutout to cap the 11-0 victory for the World Champion Kansas City Royals.

Game 1
Saturday, October 19

Cardinals	AB	R	H	RBI	BB	K	Avg
Willie McGee, cf	4	0	1	1	0	1	.250
Ozzie Smith, ss	3	0	0	0	1	0	.000
Tom Herr, 2b	4	1	1	0	0	0	.250
Jack Clark, 1b	4	0	1	1	0	1	.250
Tito Landrum, lf	4	1	2	0	0	0	.500
Cesar Cedeno, rf	3	0	1	1	0	1	.333
Todd Worrell, p	1	0	0	0	0	0	.000
Terry Pendleton, 3b	2	1	0	0	2	1	.000
Darrell Porter, c	3	0	1	0	1	2	.333
John Tudor, p	1	0	0	0	0	1	.000
Andy Van Slyke, rf	2	0	0	0	0	2	.000
TOTALS	31	3	7	3	4	10	.226

Royals	AB	R	H	RBI	BB	K	Avg
Lonnie Smith, lf	3	0	1	0	1	1	.333
Willie Wilson, cf	4	0	1	0	0	0	.250
George Brett, 3b	4	0	1	0	0	1	.250
Frank White, 2b	4	0	0	0	0	0	.000
Jim Sundberg, c	3	1	1	0	1	0	.333
Darryl Motley, rf	3	0	1	0	0	0	.333
Pat Sheridan, ph	1	0	1	0	0	0	1.000
Steve Balboni, 1b	4	0	1	1	0	1	.250
Buddy Biancalana, ss	1	0	0	0	1	0	.000
Lynn Jones, ph	1	0	1	0	0	0	1.000
Dan Quisenberry, p	0	0	0	0	0	0	—
Bud Black, p	0	0	0	0	0	0	—
Jorge Orta, ph	1	0	0	0	0	0	.000
Danny Jackson, p	2	0	0	0	0	2	.000
Hal McRae, ph	0	0	0	0	0	0	—
Onix Concepcion, pr-ss	0	0	0	0	0	0	—
Dane Iorg, ph	1	0	0	0	0	0	.000
TOTALS	32	1	8	1	3	5	.250

	1	2	3	4	5	6	7	8	9	R	H	E
Cardinals	0	0	1	1	0	0	0	0	1	3	7	1
Royals	0	1	0	0	0	0	0	0	0	1	8	0

E—Pendleton. DP—Cardinals 1 (Pendleton to Porter). LOB—Cardinals 6, Royals 8. Scoring Position—Cardinals 1-for-6, Royals 1-for-8. 2B—McGee (1), Clark (1), Landrum (1), Cedeno (1), Sundberg (1), Sheridan (1), Jones (1). S—Tudor. SB—OSmith (1). CS—LSmith (1), Motley (1).

Cardinals	IP	H	R	ER	BB	K	ERA
John Tudor (W, 1-0)	6.2	7	1	1	2	5	1.35
Todd Worrell (S, 1)	2.1	1	0	0	1	0	0.00

Royals	IP	H	R	ER	BB	K	ERA
Danny Jackson (L, 0-1)	7.0	4	2	2	2	7	2.57
Dan Quisenberry	1.2	3	1	1	0	0	5.40
Bud Black	0.1	0	0	0	2	1	0.00

PB—Sundberg. HBP—McRae by Tudor. Time—2:48. Attendance—41,650. Umpires—HP, Denkinger. 1B, Williams. 2B, McKean. 3B, Engel.

Game 2
Sunday, October 20

Cardinals	AB	R	H	RBI	BB	K	Avg
Willie McGee, cf	4	1	1	0	0	0	.250
Ozzie Smith, ss	4	0	0	0	0	0	.000
Tom Herr, 2b	4	0	0	0	0	0	.125
Jack Clark, 1b	3	1	1	1	1	1	.286
Tito Landrum, lf	4	1	2	0	0	1	.500
Cesar Cedeno, rf	3	1	0	0	1	0	.167
Jeff Lahti, p	0	0	0	0	0	0	—
Terry Pendleton, 3b	4	0	2	3	0	0	.333
Darrell Porter, c	3	0	0	0	1	2	.167
Danny Cox, p	2	0	0	0	0	2	.000
Brian Harper, ph	1	0	0	0	0	0	.000
Ken Dayley, p	0	0	0	0	0	0	—
Andy Van Slyke, ph-rf	1	0	0	0	0	0	.000
TOTALS	33	4	6	4	3	6	.210

Royals	AB	R	H	RBI	BB	K	Avg
Lonnie Smith, lf	4	0	2	0	0	0	.429
Lynn Jones, lf	0	0	0	0	0	0	1.000
Willie Wilson, cf	4	1	2	0	0	0	.375
George Brett, 3b	4	1	1	1	0	1	.250
Frank White, 2b	3	0	3	1	1	0	.429
Pat Sheridan, rf	4	0	0	0	0	2	.200
Dan Quisenberry, p	0	0	0	0	0	0	—
Jim Sundberg, c	4	0	0	0	0	2	.143
Steve Balboni, 1b	4	0	1	0	0	1	.250
Buddy Biancalana, ss	1	0	0	0	2	0	.000
Jorge Orta, ph	1	0	0	0	0	0	.000
Charlie Leibrandt, p	2	0	0	0	0	0	.000
Darryl Motley, rf	0	0	0	0	0	0	.333
TOTALS	31	2	9	2	3	6	.283

	1	2	3	4	5	6	7	8	9	R	H	E
Cardinals	0	0	0	0	0	0	0	0	4	4	6	0
Royals	0	0	2	0	0	0	0	0	0	2	9	0

DP—Cardinals 2 (Herr to OSmith to Clark; Cox to OSmith to Herr). LOB—Cardinals 5, Royals 6. Scoring Position—Cardinals 2-for-6, Royals 2-for-11. 2B—McGee (2), Landrum (2), Pendleton (1), Brett (1), White 2 (2). S—Leibrandt. GDP—Wilson, Leibrandt, Orta. SB—Wilson (1), White (1).

Cardinals	IP	H	R	ER	BB	K	ERA
Danny Cox	7.0	7	2	2	3	5	2.57
Ken Dayley (W, 1-0)	1.0	1	0	0	0	1	0.00
Jeff Lahti (S, 1)	1.0	1	0	0	0	0	0.00

Royals	IP	H	R	ER	BB	K	ERA
Charlie Leibrandt (L, 0-1)	8.2	6	4	4	2	6	4.15
Dan Quisenberry	0.1	0	0	0	1	0	4.50

Time—2:44. Attendance—41,656. Umpires—HP, Williams. 1B, McKean. 2B, Engel. 3B, Shulock.

Game 3
Tuesday, October 22

Royals	AB	R	H	RBI	BB	K	Avg
Lonnie Smith, lf	5	0	2	2	0	2	.417
Lynn Jones, lf	0	0	0	0	0	0	1.000
Willie Wilson, cf	5	0	2	0	0	2	.385
George Brett, 3b	2	2	2	0	3	0	.400
Frank White, 2b	4	2	2	3	1	0	.455
Pat Sheridan, rf	5	0	0	0	0	1	.100
Jim Sundberg, c	2	1	1	0	3	0	.222
Steve Balboni, 1b	4	0	0	0	1	1	.167
Buddy Biancalana, ss	5	1	2	1	0	1	.286
Bret Saberhagen, p	3	0	0	0	0	1	.000
TOTALS	35	6	11	6	8	8	.307

Cardinals	AB	R	H	RBI	BB	K	Avg
Willie McGee, cf	4	0	1	0	0	1	.250
Ozzie Smith, ss	4	1	1	0	0	0	.091
Tom Herr, 2b	3	0	1	0	1	0	.182
Jack Clark, 1b	4	0	1	1	0	3	.273
Andy Van Slyke, rf	4	0	0	0	0	2	.000
Terry Pendleton, 3b	4	0	1	0	0	0	.300
Darrell Porter, c	3	0	0	0	0	0	.111
Tito Landrum, lf	3	0	1	0	0	1	.455
Joaquin Andujar, p	1	0	1	0	0	1	.000
Bill Campbell, p	0	0	0	0	0	0	—
Mike Jorgensen, ph	1	0	0	0	0	0	.000
Ricky Horton, p	0	0	0	0	0	0	—
Brian Harper, ph	1	0	0	0	0	0	.000
Ken Dayley, p	0	0	0	0	0	0	—
TOTALS	32	1	6	1	1	8	.209

	1	2	3	4	5	6	7	8	9	R	H	E
Royals	0	0	0	2	2	0	2	0	0	6	11	0
Cardinals	0	0	0	0	0	1	0	0	0	1	6	0

DP—Royals 1 (Sundberg to Brett), Cardinals 1 (Herr to Clark). LOB—Royals 11, Cardinals 5. Scoring Position—Royals 3-for-9, Cardinals 1-for-4. 2B—LSmith (1), White (3). HR—White (1). S—Saberhagen. GDP—White. SB—Wilson (2), McGee (1). CS—LSmith (2), McGee (1).

Royals	IP	H	R	ER	BB	K	ERA
Bret Saberhagen (W, 1-0)	9.0	6	1	1	1	8	1.00

Cardinals	IP	H	R	ER	BB	K	ERA
Joaquin Andujar (L, 0-1)	4.0	9	4	4	3	3	9.00
Bill Campbell	1.0	0	0	0	1	2	0.00
Ricky Horton	2.0	2	2	2	2	1	9.00
Ken Dayley	2.0	0	0	0	2	2	0.00

Andujar pitched to two batters in the 5th.

Balk—Horton. Time—3:00. Attendance—53,634. Umpires—HP, McKean. 1B, Engel. 2B, Shulock. 3B, Quick.

Game 4
Wednesday, October 23

Royals	AB	R	H	RBI	BB	K	Avg
Lonnie Smith, lf	4	0	0	0	0	2	.313
Willie Wilson, cf	4	0	1	0	0	0	.353
George Brett, 3b	4	0	1	0	0	2	.357
Frank White, 2b	4	0	0	0	0	0	.333
Jim Sundberg, c	4	0	1	0	0	0	.231
Darryl Motley, rf	4	0	0	0	0	1	.143
Steve Balboni, 1b	2	0	1	0	1	0	.214
Buddy Biancalana, ss	2	0	0	0	0	1	.222
Hal McRae, ph	1	0	0	0	0	0	.000
Onix Concepcion, ss	0	0	0	0	0	0	—
Bud Black, p	1	0	0	0	0	1	.000
John Wathan, ph	1	0	0	0	0	1	.000
Joe Beckwith, p	0	0	0	0	0	0	—
Lynn Jones, ph	1	0	1	0	0	0	1.000
Dan Quisenberry, p	0	0	0	0	0	0	—
TOTALS	32	0	5	0	1	8	.291

Cardinals	AB	R	H	RBI	BB	K	Avg
Willie McGee, cf	3	1	2	1	1	0	.333
Ozzie Smith, ss	2	0	0	0	1	0	.077
Tom Herr, 2b	3	0	1	0	1	1	.214
Jack Clark, 1b	3	0	1	0	1	2	.286
Tito Landrum, lf	4	1	1	1	0	0	.400
Cesar Cedeno, rf	3	0	0	0	0	0	.111
Andy Van Slyke, rf	0	0	0	0	0	0	.000
Terry Pendleton, 3b	3	1	1	0	0	0	.308
Tom Nieto, c	1	0	0	1	1	1	.000
John Tudor, p	3	0	0	0	0	2	.000
TOTALS	25	3	6	3	5	6	.229

	1	2	3	4	5	6	7	8	9	R	H	E
Royals	0	0	0	0	0	0	0	0	0	0	5	1
Cardinals	0	1	1	0	1	0	0	0	x	3	6	0

E—Black. DP—Royals 1 (Black to White). LOB—Royals 6, Cardinals 5. Scoring Position—Royals 0-for-6, Cardinals 0-for-6. 2B—Herr (1), Jones (1). 3B—Pendleton (1). HR—McGee (1), Landrum (1). S—OSmith, Nieto. CS—OSmith (1).

Royals	IP	H	R	ER	BB	K	ERA
Bud Black (L, 0-1)	5.0	4	3	3	3	3	5.06
Joe Beckwith	2.0	1	0	0	0	3	0.00
Dan Quisenberry	1.0	1	0	0	2	0	3.00

Cardinals	IP	H	R	ER	BB	K	ERA
John Tudor (W, 2-0)	9.0	5	0	0	1	8	0.57

WP—Quisenberry. Time—2:19. Attendance—53,634. Umpires—HP, Engel. 1B, Shulock. 2B, Quick. 3B, Denkinger.

Game 5
Thursday, October 24

Royals	AB	R	H	RBI	BB	K	Avg
Lonnie Smith, lf	4	2	2	0	1	2	.350
Lynn Jones, lf	0	0	0	0	0	0	1.000
Willie Wilson, cf	5	0	2	2	0	2	.364
George Brett, 3b	4	0	1	0	1	1	.333
Greg Pryor, 3b	0	0	0	0	0	0	—
Frank White, 2b	5	1	0	1	0	3	.250
Pat Sheridan, rf	5	0	2	1	0	2	.200
Steve Balboni, 1b	4	0	1	0	1	1	.222
Jim Sundberg, c	4	2	1	0	0	0	.235
Buddy Biancalana, ss	3	1	2	1	1	1	.333
Danny Jackson, p	4	0	0	0	0	3	.000
TOTALS	38	6	11	5	4	15	.287

Cardinals	AB	R	H	RBI	BB	K	Avg
Willie McGee, cf	4	0	2	0	0	1	.368
Ozzie Smith, ss	3	0	0	0	1	0	.063
Tom Herr, 2b	4	1	1	0	0	0	.222
Jack Clark, 1b	3	0	1	1	1	0	.294
Tito Landrum, lf	4	0	1	0	0	0	.368
Cesar Cedeno, rf	4	0	0	0	0	0	.077
Terry Pendleton, 3b	3	0	0	0	1	1	.250
Tom Nieto, c	4	0	0	0	0	1	.000
Bob Forsch, p	0	0	0	0	0	0	—
Ricky Horton, p	1	0	0	0	0	1	.000
Bill Campbell, p	0	0	0	0	0	0	—
Ivan DeJesus, ph	1	0	0	0	0	0	.000
Todd Worrell, p	0	0	0	0	0	0	.000
Brian Harper, ph	1	0	0	0	0	1	.000
Jeff Lahti, p	0	0	0	0	0	0	—
TOTALS	32	1	5	1	3	5	.225

	1	2	3	4	5	6	7	8	9		R	H	E
Royals	1	3	0	0	0	0	0	1	1		6	11	2
Cardinals	1	0	0	0	0	0	0	0	0		1	5	1

E—Brett, OSmith, Jackson. DP—Cardinals 1 (Pendleton to Herr). LOB—Royals 9, Cardinals 7. Scoring Position—Royals 2-for-13, Cardinals 1-for-6. 2B—Sheridan (2), Sundberg (2), Herr (2), Clark (2). 3B—Wilson (1). GDP—Sundberg. SB—LSmith (1). CS—McGee (2).

Royals	IP	H	R	ER	BB	K	ERA
Danny Jackson (W, 1-1)	9.0	5	1	1	3	5	1.69

Cardinals	IP	H	R	ER	BB	K	ERA
Bob Forsch (L, 0-1)	1.2	5	4	4	1	2	21.60
Ricky Horton	2.0	1	0	0	3	4	4.50
Bill Campbell	1.1	0	0	0	0	2	0.00
Todd Worrell	2.0	0	0	0	0	6	0.00
Jeff Lahti	2.0	5	2	1	0	1	3.00

Time—2:52. Attendance—53,634. Umpires—HP, Shulock. 1B, Quick. 2B, Denkinger. 3B, Williams.

Game 6
Saturday, October 26

Cardinals	AB	R	H	RBI	BB	K	Avg
Ozzie Smith, ss	3	0	0	0	1	0	.053
Willie McGee, cf	4	0	0	0	0	0	.304
Tom Herr, 2b	4	0	0	0	0	1	.182
Jack Clark, 1b	4	0	0	0	0	2	.238
Tito Landrum, lf	4	0	1	0	0	0	.348
Terry Pendleton, 3b	4	1	1	0	0	0	.250
Cesar Cedeno, rf	2	0	1	0	1	1	.133
Andy Van Slyke, pr-rf	0	0	0	0	0	0	.000
Darrell Porter, c	3	0	1	0	0	1	.167
Danny Cox, p	2	0	0	0	0	0	.000
Brian Harper, ph	1	0	1	1	0	0	.250
Ken Dayley, p	0	0	0	0	0	0	—
Todd Worrell, p	0	0	0	0	0	0	.000
TOTALS	31	1	5	1	2	5	.205

Royals	AB	R	H	RBI	BB	K	Avg
Lonnie Smith, lf	4	0	1	0	0	1	.333
Willie Wilson, cf	3	0	1	0	1	0	.360
George Brett, 3b	4	0	0	0	0	2	.273
Frank White, 2b	4	0	1	0	0	1	.250
Pat Sheridan, rf	3	0	1	0	0	2	.222
Darryl Motley, ph	0	0	0	0	0	0	.143
Jorge Orta, ph	1	0	1	0	0	0	.333
Steve Balboni, 1b	3	0	2	0	1	0	.286
Onix Concepcion, pr	0	1	0	0	0	0	—
Jim Sundberg, c	4	1	1	0	0	2	.238
Buddy Biancalana, ss	3	0	1	0	0	0	.333
Hal McRae, ph	0	0	0	0	1	0	.000
John Wathan, pr	0	0	0	0	0	0	.000
Charlie Leibrandt, p	2	0	0	0	0	2	.000
Dan Quisenberry, p	0	0	0	0	0	0	—
Dane Iorg, ph	1	0	1	2	0	0	.500
TOTALS	32	2	10	2	3	10	.277

	1	2	3	4	5	6	7	8	9		R	H	E
Cardinals	0	0	0	0	0	0	1	0			1	5	0
Royals	0	0	0	0	0	0	0	2			2	10	0

DP—Cardinals 1 (Herr to OSmith to Clark), Royals 1 (Biancalana to White to Balboni). LOB—Cardinals 5, Royals 9. Scoring Position—Cardinals 1-for-5, Royals 1-for-7. 2B—LSmith (2). S—Leibrandt. GDP—OSmith, Brett. CS—White (1).

Cardinals	IP	H	R	ER	BB	K	ERA
Danny Cox	7.0	7	0	0	1	8	1.29
Ken Dayley (H, 1)	1.0	0	0	0	1	2	0.00
Todd Worrell (BS, 1; L, 0-1)	0.1	3	2	2	1	0	3.86

Royals	IP	H	R	ER	BB	K	ERA
Charlie Leibrandt	7.2	4	1	1	2	4	2.76
Dan Quisenberry (W, 1-0)	1.1	1	0	0	0	1	2.08

PB—Porter. Time—2:48. Attendance—41,628. Umpires—HP, Quick. 1B, Denkinger. 2B, Williams. 3B, McKean.

Game 7
Sunday, October 27

Cardinals	AB	R	H	RBI	BB	K	Avg
Ozzie Smith, ss	4	0	1	0	0	0	.087
Willie McGee, cf	4	0	0	0	0	0	.259
Tom Herr, 2b	4	0	0	0	0	0	.154
Jack Clark, 1b	4	0	1	0	0	0	.240
Andy Van Slyke, rf	4	0	1	0	0	1	.091
Terry Pendleton, 3b	3	0	1	0	0	0	.261
Tito Landrum, lf	2	0	1	0	0	0	.360
Joaquin Andujar, p	0	0	0	0	0	0	.000
Bob Forsch, p	0	0	0	0	0	0	—
Steve Braun, ph	1	0	0	0	0	0	.000
Ken Dayley, p	0	0	0	0	0	0	—
Darrell Porter, c	3	0	0	0	0	0	.133
John Tudor, p	1	0	0	0	0	1	.000
Bill Campbell, p	0	0	0	0	0	0	—
Jeff Lahti, p	0	0	0	0	0	0	—
Ricky Horton, p	0	0	0	0	0	0	.000
Mike Jorgensen, lf	2	0	0	0	0	0	.000
TOTALS	32	0	5	0	0	2	.199

Royals	AB	R	H	RBI	BB	K	Avg
Lonnie Smith, lf	3	2	1	2	1	0	.333
Lynn Jones, lf	1	0	0	0	0	0	.667
Willie Wilson, cf	5	1	2	1	0	0	.367
George Brett, 3b	5	2	4	0	0	0	.370
Frank White, 2b	4	1	1	1	1	0	.250
Jim Sundberg, c	3	1	1	2	2	0	.250
Steve Balboni, 1b	4	2	2	2	1	0	.320
Darryl Motley, rf	4	1	3	3	0	0	.364
Buddy Biancalana, ss	3	0	0	0	1	1	.278
Bret Saberhagen, p	4	1	0	0	0	3	.000
TOTALS	36	11	14	10	6	4	.310

	1	2	3	4	5	6	7	8	9		R	H	E
Cardinals	0	0	0	0	0	0	0	0	0		0	5	0
Royals	0	2	3	0	6	0	0	0	x		11	14	0

DP—Cardinals 2 (Pendleton to Herr to Clark; Herr to OSmith to Clark). LOB—Cardinals 5, Royals 7. Scoring Position—Cardinals 0-for-2, Royals 5-for-11. 2B—LSmith (3). HR—Motley (1). GDP—White, Biancalana. SB—LSmith (2), Brett (1).

Cardinals	IP	H	R	ER	BB	K	ERA
John Tudor (L, 2-1)	2.1	3	5	5	4	1	3.00
Bill Campbell	1.2	4	1	1	1	1	2.25
Jeff Lahti	0.2	4	4	4	0	1	12.27
Ricky Horton	0.0	1	1	1	0	0	6.75
Joaquin Andujar	0.0	1	0	0	1	0	9.00
Bob Forsch	1.1	1	0	0	0	1	12.00
Ken Dayley	2.0	0	0	0	0	0	0.00

Royals	IP	H	R	ER	BB	K	ERA
Bret Saberhagen (W, 2-0)	9.0	5	0	0	0	2	0.50

Campbell pitched to one batter in the 5th. Horton pitched to one batter in the 5th. Andujar pitched to two batters in the 5th.

WP—Forsch. Time—2:46. Attendance—41,658. Umpires—HP, Denkinger. 1B, Williams. 2B, McKean. 3B, Engel.

1985 World Series—Composite Statistics

Batting

Royals	G	AB	R	H	RBI	2B	3B	HR	BB	SO	SB	CS	Avg	OBP	Slg
Steve Balboni	7	25	2	8	3	0	0	0	5	4	0	0	.320	.433	.320
Buddy Biancalana	7	18	2	5	2	0	0	0	5	4	0	0	.278	.435	.278
Bud Black	2	1	0	0	0	0	0	0	0	1	0	0	.000	.000	.000
George Brett	7	27	5	10	1	1	0	0	4	7	1	0	.370	.452	.407
Onix Concepcion	3	0	1	0	0	0	0	0	0	0	0	0	—	—	—
Dane Iorg	2	2	0	1	2	0	0	0	0	0	0	0	.500	.500	.500
Danny Jackson	2	6	0	0	0	0	0	0	0	5	0	0	.000	.000	.000
Lynn Jones	6	3	0	2	0	1	1	0	0	0	0	0	.667	.667	1.667
Charlie Leibrandt	2	4	0	0	0	0	0	0	0	2	0	0	.000	.000	.000
Hal McRae	3	1	0	0	0	0	0	0	1	0	0	0	.000	.667	.000
Darryl Motley	5	11	1	4	3	0	0	1	0	1	0	1	.364	.364	.636
Jorge Orta	3	3	0	1	0	0	0	0	0	0	0	0	.333	.333	.333
Bret Saberhagen	2	7	1	0	0	0	0	0	0	4	0	0	.000	.000	.000
Pat Sheridan	5	18	0	4	1	2	0	0	0	7	0	0	.222	.222	.333
Lonnie Smith	7	27	4	9	4	3	0	0	3	8	2	2	.333	.400	.444
Jim Sundberg	7	24	6	6	1	2	0	0	6	4	0	0	.250	.400	.333
John Wathan	2	1	0	0	0	0	0	0	0	1	0	0	.000	.000	.000
Frank White	7	28	4	7	6	3	0	1	3	4	1	1	.250	.323	.464
Willie Wilson	7	30	2	11	3	0	1	0	1	4	2	0	.367	.387	.433
Totals	**7**	**236**	**28**	**68**	**26**	**12**	**2**	**2**	**28**	**56**	**6**	**4**	**.288**	**.366**	**.381**

Cardinals	G	AB	R	H	RBI	2B	3B	HR	BB	SO	SB	CS	Avg	OBP	Slg
Joaquin Andujar	2	1	0	0	0	0	0	0	0	1	0	0	.000	.000	.000
Steve Braun	1	1	0	0	0	0	0	0	0	0	0	0	.000	.000	.000
Cesar Cedeno	5	15	1	2	1	1	0	0	2	2	0	0	.133	.235	.200
Jack Clark	7	25	1	6	4	2	0	0	3	9	0	0	.240	.321	.320
Danny Cox	2	4	0	0	0	0	0	0	0	2	0	0	.000	.000	.000
Ivan DeJesus	1	1	0	0	0	0	0	0	0	0	0	0	.000	.000	.000
Brian Harper	4	4	0	1	1	0	0	0	0	1	0	0	.250	.250	.250
Tom Herr	7	26	2	4	0	2	0	0	2	2	0	0	.154	.214	.231
Ricky Horton	3	1	0	0	0	0	0	0	0	1	0	0	.000	.000	.000
Mike Jorgensen	2	3	0	0	0	0	0	0	0	0	0	0	.000	.000	.000
Tito Landrum	7	25	3	9	1	2	0	1	0	2	0	0	.360	.360	.560
Tom Lawless	1	0	0	0	0	0	0	0	0	0	0	0	—	—	—
Willie McGee	7	27	2	7	2	2	0	1	1	3	1	2	.259	.286	.444
Tom Nieto	2	5	0	0	0	0	0	0	1	2	0	0	.000	.167	.000
Terry Pendleton	7	23	3	6	3	1	1	0	3	2	0	0	.261	.346	.391
Darrell Porter	5	15	0	2	0	0	0	0	2	5	0	0	.133	.235	.133
Ozzie Smith	7	23	1	2	0	0	0	0	4	0	1	1	.087	.222	.087
John Tudor	3	5	0	0	0	0	0	0	0	4	0	0	.000	.000	.000
Andy Van Slyke	6	11	0	1	0	0	0	0	0	5	0	0	.091	.091	.091
Todd Worrell	3	1	0	0	0	0	0	0	0	1	0	0	.000	.000	.000
Totals	**7**	**216**	**13**	**40**	**13**	**10**	**1**	**2**	**18**	**42**	**2**	**3**	**.185**	**.248**	**.269**

Pitching

Royals	G	GS	CG	IP	H	R	ER	BB	SO	W-L	Sv-Op	Hld	ERA
Joe Beckwith	1	0	0	2.0	1	0	0	0	3	0-0	0-0	0	0.00
Bud Black	2	1	0	5.1	4	3	3	5	4	0-1	0-0	0	5.06
Danny Jackson	2	2	1	16.0	9	3	3	5	12	1-1	0-0	0	1.69
Charlie Leibrandt	2	2	0	16.1	10	5	5	4	10	0-1	0-0	0	2.76
Dan Quisenberry	4	0	0	4.1	5	1	1	3	3	1-0	0-0	0	2.08
Bret Saberhagen	2	2	2	18.0	11	1	1	1	10	2-0	0-0	0	0.50
Totals	**7**	**7**	**3**	**62.0**	**40**	**13**	**13**	**18**	**42**	**4-3**	**0-0**	**0**	**1.89**

Cardinals	G	GS	CG	IP	H	R	ER	BB	SO	W-L	Sv-Op	Hld	ERA
Joaquin Andujar	2	1	0	4.0	10	4	4	4	3	0-1	0-0	0	9.00
Bill Campbell	3	0	0	4.0	4	1	1	2	5	0-0	0-0	0	2.25
Danny Cox	2	2	0	14.0	14	2	2	4	13	0-0	0-0	0	1.29
Ken Dayley	4	0	0	6.0	1	0	0	3	5	1-0	0-0	1	0.00
Bob Forsch	2	1	0	3.0	6	4	4	1	3	0-1	0-0	0	12.00
Ricky Horton	3	0	0	4.0	4	3	3	5	5	0-0	0-0	0	6.75
Jeff Lahti	3	0	0	3.2	10	6	5	0	2	0-0	1-1	0	12.27
John Tudor	3	3	1	18.0	15	6	6	7	14	2-1	0-0	0	3.00
Todd Worrell	3	0	0	4.2	4	2	2	2	6	0-1	1-2	0	3.86
Totals	**7**	**7**	**1**	**61.1**	**68**	**28**	**27**	**28**	**56**	**3-4**	**2-3**	**1**	**3.96**

Fielding

Royals	Pos	G	PO	Ast	E	DP	PB	FPct
Steve Balboni	1b	7	70	3	0	1	—	1.000
Joe Beckwith	p	1	0	0	0	0	—	—
Buddy Biancalana	ss	7	6	20	0	1	—	1.000
Bud Black	p	2	1	2	1	1	—	.750
George Brett	3b	7	10	19	1	1	—	.967
Onix Concepcion	ss	2	0	2	0	0	—	1.000
Danny Jackson	p	2	0	4	1	0	—	.800
Lynn Jones	lf	4	4	0	0	0	—	1.000
Charlie Leibrandt	p	2	1	2	0	0	—	1.000
Darryl Motley	rf	4	4	0	0	0	—	1.000
Greg Pryor	3b	1	0	1	0	0	—	1.000
Dan Quisenberry	p	4	1	1	0	0	—	1.000
Bret Saberhagen	p	2	0	0	0	0	—	—
Pat Sheridan	rf	4	6	0	0	0	—	1.000
Lonnie Smith	lf	7	7	2	0	0	—	1.000
Jim Sundberg	c	7	47	3	0	1	1	1.000
Frank White	2b	7	10	20	0	2	—	1.000
Willie Wilson	cf	7	19	1	0	0	—	1.000
Totals		**7**	**186**	**80**	**3**	**7**	**1**	**.989**

Cardinals	Pos	G	PO	Ast	E	DP	PB	FPct
Joaquin Andujar	p	2	0	1	0	0	—	1.000
Bill Campbell	p	3	1	0	0	0	—	1.000
Cesar Cedeno	rf	5	9	0	0	0	—	1.000
Jack Clark	1b	7	49	4	0	6	—	1.000
Danny Cox	p	2	1	2	0	1	—	1.000
Ken Dayley	p	4	0	0	0	0	—	—
Bob Forsch	p	2	0	0	0	0	—	—
Tom Herr	2b	7	11	13	0	8	—	1.000
Ricky Horton	p	3	2	0	0	0	—	1.000
Mike Jorgensen	lf	1	1	0	0	0	—	1.000
Jeff Lahti	p	3	0	0	0	0	—	—
Tito Landrum	lf	7	12	1	0	0	—	1.000
Willie McGee	cf	7	15	0	0	0	—	1.000
Tom Nieto	c	2	23	1	0	0	0	1.000
Terry Pendleton	3b	7	6	14	1	3	—	.952
Darrell Porter	c	5	36	4	0	1	1	1.000
Ozzie Smith	ss	7	10	16	1	5	—	.963
John Tudor	p	3	0	3	0	0	—	1.000
Andy Van Slyke	rf	6	8	0	0	0	—	1.000
Todd Worrell	p	3	0	1	0	0	—	1.000
Totals		**7**	**184**	**60**	**2**	**24**	**1**	**.992**

1986 New York Mets (NL) 4, Boston Red Sox (AL) 3

One strike away from their first World Series victory since selling Babe Ruth to the Yankees, the curse struck the Red Sox once again. The Sox took the first two games from the New York Mets, as Bruce Hurst beat Ron Darling 1-0 in the opener and Boston's bats exploded for a 9-3 win in Game 2. But the Mets evened it up with a 7-1 win from Bobby Ojeda in Game 3 and a 6-2 win from Darling in Game 4. Bruce Hurst got his second win of the Series in Game 5, going the distance to beat the Mets, 4-2. Roger Clemens took a 3-2 lead into the bottom of the eighth in Game 6, but left with a blister in favor of Calvin Schiraldi, who allowed the tying run to score on a Gary Carter sacrifice fly. In the top of the 10th, Dave Henderson lined a solo homer to give Boston the lead, and Marty Barrett poked an RBI single to bring home another run. Schiraldi got two quick outs in the bottom of the 10th, but the Mets refused to die, lining three straight hits—the last coming from Ray Knight on an 0-2 count, scoring a run to make it a one-run game. Bob Stanley relieved Schiraldi and allowed the tying run to score when he threw a wild pitch with Mookie Wilson at the plate. Wilson eventually tapped a cue-shot roller to first baseman Bill Buckner, who watched the ball skip under his glove into right field as Knight scored the winning run. In the deciding game, Hurst held a 3-0 lead going into the bottom of the sixth, but the Mets rallied to tie it. Schiraldi came in to pitch the seventh, and was immediately greeted by a Knight home run. The Mets scored three runs in the inning, and won 8-5 to complete their incredible comeback. Schiraldi took the loss in each of the final two games.

Game 1

Saturday, October 18

Red Sox	AB	R	H	RBI	BB	K	Avg
Wade Boggs, 3b	4	0	0	0	0	1	.000
Marty Barrett, 2b	4	0	1	0	0	1	.250
Bill Buckner, 1b	4	0	1	0	0	1	.250
Dave Stapleton, 1b	0	0	0	0	0	0	—
Jim Rice, lf	2	1	1	0	2	0	.500
Dwight Evans, rf	3	0	0	0	1	0	.000
Rich Gedman, c	4	0	0	0	0	1	.000
Dave Henderson, cf	4	0	2	0	0	0	.500
Spike Owen, ss	2	0	0	0	2	1	.000
Bruce Hurst, p	3	0	0	0	0	3	.000
Mike Greenwell, ph	1	0	0	0	0	0	.000
Calvin Schiraldi, p	0	0	0	0	0	0	—
TOTALS	31	1	5	0	5	8	.161

Mets	AB	R	H	RBI	BB	K	Avg
Mookie Wilson, lf	4	0	1	0	0	1	.250
Roger McDowell, p	0	0	0	0	0	0	—
Lenny Dykstra, cf	3	0	0	0	1	2	.000
Keith Hernandez, 1b	3	0	0	0	1	0	.000
Gary Carter, c	4	0	1	0	0	0	.250
Darryl Strawberry, rf	2	0	0	0	2	2	.000
Ray Knight, 3b	3	0	0	0	1	0	.000
Tim Teufel, 2b	3	0	2	0	0	1	.667
Wally Backman, pr-2b	1	0	0	0	0	0	.000
Rafael Santana, ss	2	0	0	0	0	0	.000
Danny Heep, ph	1	0	0	0	0	1	.000
Ron Darling, p	2	0	0	0	0	1	.000
Kevin Mitchell, ph-lf	1	0	0	0	0	1	.000
TOTALS	29	0	4	0	5	9	.138

	1 2 3	4 5 6	7 8 9	R	H	E
Red Sox	0 0 0	0 0 0	1 0 0	1	5	0
Mets	0 0 0	0 0 0	0 0 0	0	4	1

E—Teufel. DP—Red Sox 1 (Boggs to Barrett to Buckner), Mets 1 (Teufel to Santana to Hernandez). LOB—Red Sox 8, Mets 8. Scoring Position—Red Sox 1-for-8, Mets 0-for-8. S—Santana. GDP—Buckner, Knight. SB—Wilson (1), Strawberry (1).

Red Sox	IP	H	R	ER	BB	K	ERA
Bruce Hurst (W, 1-0)	8.0	4	0	0	4	8	0.00
Calvin Schiraldi (S, 1)	1.0	0	0	0	1	1	0.00

Mets	IP	H	R	ER	BB	K	ERA
Ron Darling (L, 0-1)	7.0	3	1	0	3	8	0.00
Roger McDowell	2.0	2	0	0	2	0	0.00

WP—Darling 2. Time—2:59. Attendance—55,076. Umpires—HP, Kibler. 1B, Evans. 2B, Wendelstedt. 3B, Brinkman.

Game 2

Sunday, October 19

Red Sox	AB	R	H	RBI	BB	K	Avg
Wade Boggs, 3b	5	1	2	2	1	1	.222
Marty Barrett, 2b	5	0	2	1	1	0	.333
Bill Buckner, 1b	5	0	2	1	0	1	.333
Dave Stapleton, pr-1b	1	0	0	0	0	0	.000
Jim Rice, lf	6	2	3	0	0	2	.500
Dwight Evans, rf	4	2	2	2	1	1	.286
Rich Gedman, c	5	0	1	0	0	3	.111
Dave Henderson, cf	5	2	3	2	0	1	.556
Spike Owen, ss	4	1	3	1	1	1	.500
Ed Romero, pr-ss	0	0	0	0	0	0	—
Roger Clemens, p	1	1	0	0	0	0	.000
Steve Crawford, p	1	0	0	0	0	0	.000
Mike Greenwell, ph	1	0	0	0	0	1	.000
Bob Stanley, p	1	0	0	0	0	1	.000
TOTALS	44	9	18	9	4	12	.319

Mets	AB	R	H	RBI	BB	K	Avg
Lenny Dykstra, cf	3	0	1	0	1	1	.167
Wally Backman, 2b	3	1	2	1	2	0	.500
Keith Hernandez, 1b	4	0	1	1	1	1	.143
Gary Carter, c	4	0	1	1	0	1	.250
Darryl Strawberry, rf	4	0	0	0	0	2	.000
Danny Heep, lf	2	0	0	0	1	0	.000
Rick Aguilera, p	0	0	0	0	0	0	—
Jesse Orosco, p	0	0	0	0	0	0	—
Lee Mazzilli, ph	1	0	0	0	0	0	.000
Sid Fernandez, p	0	0	0	0	0	0	—
Doug Sisk, p	0	0	0	0	0	0	—
Howard Johnson, 3b	4	0	0	0	0	1	.000
Rafael Santana, ss	4	1	2	0	0	1	.333
Dwight Gooden, p	2	1	1	0	0	0	.500
Mookie Wilson, lf	2	0	0	0	0	1	.167
TOTALS	33	3	8	3	5	8	.189

	1 2 3	4 5 6	7 8 9	R	H	E
Red Sox	0 0 3	1 2 0	2 0 1	9	18	0
Mets	0 0 2	0 1 0	0 0 0	3	8	1

E—Hernandez. DP—Mets 1 (Santana to Backman to Hernandez). LOB—Red Sox 13, Mets 9. Scoring Position—Red Sox 7-for-22, Mets 2-for-11. 2B—Boggs 2 (2). HR—Evans (1), Henderson (1). S—Clemens, Dykstra. GDP—Evans. CS—Backman (1).

Red Sox	IP	H	R	ER	BB	K	ERA
Roger Clemens	4.1	5	3	3	4	3	6.23
Steve Crawford (W, 1-0)	1.2	1	0	0	0	2	0.00
Bob Stanley (S, 1)	3.0	2	0	0	1	3	0.00

Mets	IP	H	R	ER	BB	K	ERA
Dwight Gooden (L, 0-1)	5.0	8	6	5	2	6	9.00
Rick Aguilera	1.0	5	2	2	1	1	18.00
Jesse Orosco	2.0	2	0	0	0	3	0.00
Sid Fernandez	0.1	3	1	1	0	1	27.00
Doug Sisk	0.2	0	0	0	1	1	0.00

Aguilera pitched to five batters in the 7th.

Time—3:36. Attendance—55,063. Umpires—HP, Evans. 1B, Wendelstedt. 2B, Brinkman. 3B, Montague.

Game 3

Tuesday, October 21

Mets	AB	R	H	RBI	BB	K	Avg
Lenny Dykstra, cf	5	2	4	1	0	0	.455
Wally Backman, 2b	5	1	1	0	0	1	.333
Keith Hernandez, 1b	4	1	2	0	1	0	.273
Gary Carter, c	5	1	2	3	0	0	.308
Darryl Strawberry, rf	4	1	1	0	0	1	.100
Ray Knight, 3b	4	0	1	1	0	0	.143
Danny Heep, dh	3	0	1	2	0	0	.167
Kevin Mitchell, ph	0	0	0	0	0	0	.000
Lee Mazzilli, ph-dh	1	0	0	0	0	0	.000
Mookie Wilson, lf	4	0	0	0	0	2	.100
Rafael Santana, ss	4	1	1	0	0	0	.300
TOTALS	39	7	13	7	1	4	.244

Red Sox	AB	R	H	RBI	BB	K	Avg
Wade Boggs, 3b	3	0	1	0	1	0	.250
Marty Barrett, 2b	4	0	2	1	0	0	.385
Bill Buckner, 1b	4	0	0	0	0	0	.231
Jim Rice, lf	3	0	0	0	1	1	.364
Don Baylor, dh	4	0	1	0	0	0	.250
Dwight Evans, rf	4	0	0	0	0	1	.182
Rich Gedman, c	4	0	0	0	0	2	.077
Dave Henderson, cf	2	1	1	0	1	1	.545
Spike Owen, ss	3	0	0	0	0	1	.333
TOTALS	31	1	5	1	3	6	.289

	1 2 3	4 5 6	7 8 9	R	H	E
Mets	4 0 0	0 0 0	2 1 0	7	13	0
Red Sox	0 0 1	0 0 0	0 0 0	1	5	0

DP—Mets 1 (Backman to Santana to Hernandez), Red Sox 1 (Owen to Barrett to Buckner). LOB—Mets 6, Red Sox 6. Scoring Position—Mets 4-for-15, Red Sox 1-for-7. 2B—Carter (1), Knight (1), Baylor (1). HR—Dykstra (1). GDP—Carter, Owen.

Mets	IP	H	R	ER	BB	K	ERA
Bobby Ojeda (W, 1-0)	7.0	5	1	1	3	6	1.29
Roger McDowell	2.0	0	0	0	0	0	0.00

Red Sox	IP	H	R	ER	BB	K	ERA
Oil Can Boyd (L, 0-1)	7.0	9	6	6	1	3	7.71
Joe Sambito	0.0	2	1	1	0	0	—
Bob Stanley	2.0	2	0	0	0	1	0.00

Sambito pitched to four batters in the 8th.

WP—Ojeda, Sambito. PB—Gedman. Time—2:58. Attendance—33,595. Umpires—HP, Wendelstedt. 1B, Brinkman. 2B, Montague. 3B, Ford.

Game 4

Wednesday, October 22

Mets	AB	R	H	RBI	BB	K	Avg
Lenny Dykstra, cf	5	1	1	2	0	0	.375
Wally Backman, 2b	4	1	2	0	0	0	.385
Keith Hernandez, 1b	3	0	0	0	1	0	.214
Gary Carter, c	4	2	3	3	0	1	.412
Darryl Strawberry, rf	4	1	2	0	0	0	.214
Ray Knight, 3b	4	0	2	1	0	1	.273
Danny Heep, dh	4	0	0	0	0	0	.100
Mookie Wilson, lf	4	1	2	0	0	0	.214
Rafael Santana, ss	4	0	0	0	0	2	.214
TOTALS	36	6	12	6	1	4	.276

Red Sox	AB	R	H	RBI	BB	K	Avg
Wade Boggs, 3b	5	0	0	0	0	0	.176
Marty Barrett, 2b	4	0	2	0	1	0	.412
Bill Buckner, 1b	5	0	0	0	0	0	.167
Jim Rice, lf	4	1	1	0	1	2	.333
Don Baylor, dh	3	0	0	0	1	1	.143
Dwight Evans, rf	3	1	1	1	1	0	.214
Rich Gedman, c	4	0	3	0	0	0	.235
Dave Henderson, cf	3	0	0	1	0	2	.429
Spike Owen, ss	1	0	0	0	2	0	.300
Mike Greenwell, ph	0	0	0	0	1	0	.000
Ed Romero, pr-ss	0	0	0	0	0	0	—
TOTALS	32	2	7	2	7	5	.267

	1 2 3	4 5 6	7 8 9	R	H	E
Mets	0 0 0	3 0 0	2 1 0	6	12	0
Red Sox	0 0 0	0 0 0	0 2 0	2	7	1

E—Gedman. DP—Red Sox 3 (Buckner to Owen; Rice to Gedman; Gedman to Barrett). LOB—Mets 4, Red Sox 11. Scoring Position—Mets 2-for-7, Red Sox 1-for-10. 2B—Carter (2), Strawberry (1), Barrett (1), Rice (1), Gedman (1). HR—Dykstra (2), Carter 2 (2). SF—Henderson. GDP—Heep. SB—Backman (1), Wilson 2 (3). CS—Strawberry (1).

Mets	IP	H	R	ER	BB	K	ERA
Ron Darling (W, 1-1)	7.0	4	0	0	6	4	0.00
Roger McDowell	0.2	3	2	2	1	0	3.86
Jesse Orosco (S, 1)	1.1	0	0	0	0	1	0.00

Red Sox	IP	H	R	ER	BB	K	ERA
Al Nipper (L, 0-1)	6.0	7	3	3	1	2	4.50
Steve Crawford	2.0	4	3	3	0	2	7.36
Bob Stanley	1.0	1	0	0	0	0	0.00

Time—3:22. Attendance—33,920. Umpires—HP, Brinkman. 1B, Montague. 2B, Ford. 3B, Kibler.

Game 5
Thursday, October 23

Mets	AB	R	H	RBI	BB	K	Avg
Lenny Dykstra, cf	5	0	1	0	0	2	.333
Tim Teufel, 2b	4	1	2	1	0	0	.571
Keith Hernandez, 1b	4	0	1	0	0	0	.222
Gary Carter, c	4	0	0	0	0	1	.333
Darryl Strawberry, rf	4	0	1	0	0	1	.222
Ray Knight, 3b	4	0	1	0	0	0	.267
Kevin Mitchell, dh	4	0	1	0	0	1	.200
Mookie Wilson, lf	4	1	2	0	0	1	.278
Rafael Santana, ss	2	0	1	1	1	0	.250
TOTALS	35	2	10	2	1	6	.288

Red Sox	AB	R	H	RBI	BB	K	Avg
Wade Boggs, 3b	5	0	2	0	0	0	.227
Marty Barrett, 2b	4	0	2	0	1	0	.429
Bill Buckner, 1b	5	1	1	0	0	0	.174
Dave Stapleton, 1b	0	0	0	0	0	0	.000
Jim Rice, lf	3	1	2	0	1	1	.389
Don Baylor, dh	3	1	1	1	0	2	.200
Dwight Evans, rf	4	0	2	1	0	0	.278
Rich Gedman, c	4	0	0	0	0	2	.190
Dave Henderson, cf	4	1	2	1	0	1	.444
Spike Owen, ss	3	0	0	1	0	2	.231
TOTALS	35	4	12	4	2	8	.285

```
        1 2 3 4 5 6 7 8 9   R  H  E
Mets    0 0 0 0 0 0 0 1 1   2  10 1
Red Sox 0 1 1 0 2 0 0 0 x   4  12 0
```

E—Santana. DP—Red Sox 1 (Boggs to Barrett to Buckner). LOB—Mets 8, Red Sox 11. Scoring Position—Mets 1-for-8, Red Sox 3-for-11. 2B—Teufel (1), Wilson (1), Barrett (2), Henderson (1). 3B—Rice (1), Henderson (1). HR—Teufel (1). S—Santana. SF—Owen. GDP—Knight.

Mets	IP	H	R	ER	BB	K	ERA
Dwight Gooden (L, 0-2)	4.0	9	4	3	2	3	8.00
Sid Fernandez	4.0	3	0	0	0	5	2.08

Red Sox	IP	H	R	ER	BB	K	ERA
Bruce Hurst (W, 2-0)	9.0	10	2	2	1	6	1.06

Gooden pitched to three batters in the 5th.

HBP—Baylor by Gooden. Time—3:09. Attendance—34,010. Umpires—HP, Montague. 1B, Ford. 2B, Kibler. 3B, Wendelstedt.

Game 6
Saturday, October 25

Red Sox	AB	R	H	RBI	BB	K	Avg
Wade Boggs, 3b	5	2	3	0	1	0	.296
Marty Barrett, 2b	4	1	3	2	2	0	.480
Bill Buckner, 1b	5	0	0	0	0	0	.143
Jim Rice, lf	5	0	0	0	1	2	.304
Dwight Evans, rf	4	0	1	2	0	1	.273
Rich Gedman, c	5	0	1	0	0	1	.192
Dave Henderson, cf	5	1	2	1	0	0	.435
Spike Owen, ss	4	1	3	0	0	1	.353
Roger Clemens, p	3	0	0	0	0	1	.000
Mike Greenwell, ph	1	0	0	0	0	1	.000
Calvin Schiraldi, p	1	0	0	0	0	1	.000
Bob Stanley, p	0	0	0	0	0	0	.000
TOTALS	42	5	13	5	5	7	.290

Mets	AB	R	H	RBI	BB	K	Avg
Lenny Dykstra, cf	4	0	0	0	0	2	.280
Wally Backman, 2b	4	0	1	0	0	1	.353
Keith Hernandez, 1b	4	0	1	0	1	0	.227
Gary Carter, c	4	1	1	1	0	1	.320
Darryl Strawberry, rf	2	1	0	0	2	0	.200
Rick Aguilera, p	0	0	0	0	0	0	—
Kevin Mitchell, ph	1	1	1	0	0	0	.333
Ray Knight, 3b	4	2	2	2	1	1	.316
Mookie Wilson, lf	5	0	1	0	0	1	.261
Rafael Santana, ss	1	0	0	0	0	1	.235
Danny Heep, ph	1	0	0	0	0	0	.091
Kevin Elster, ss	1	0	0	0	0	0	.000
Howard Johnson, ph-ss	1	0	0	0	0	1	.000
Bobby Ojeda, p	2	0	0	0	0	1	.000
Roger McDowell, p	0	0	0	0	0	0	—
Jesse Orosco, p	0	0	0	0	0	0	—
Lee Mazzilli, ph-rf	2	1	1	0	0	0	.250
TOTALS	36	6	8	3	4	9	.254

```
        1 2 3 4 5 6 7 8 9 10   R  H  E
Red Sox 1 1 0 0 0 0 1 0 0 2    5  13 3
Mets    0 0 0 2 0 0 1 0 3      6  8  2
```

E—Knight, Buckner, Evans, Gedman, Elster. DP—Red Sox 1 (Barrett to Owen to Buckner), Mets 1 (Backman to Elster to Hernandez). LOB—Red Sox 14, Mets 8. Scoring Position—Red Sox 4-for-12, Mets 2-for-11. 2B—Boggs (3), Evans (1). HR—Henderson (2). S—Owen, Dykstra, Backman. SF—Carter. GDP—Gedman, Heep. SB—Strawberry 2 (3).

Red Sox	IP	H	R	ER	BB	K	ERA
Roger Clemens	7.0	4	2	1	2	8	3.18
Calvin Schiraldi (BS, 1; L, 0-1)	2.2	4	4	3	2	1	7.36
Bob Stanley (BS, 1)	0.0	0	0	0	0	0	0.00

Mets	IP	H	R	ER	BB	K	ERA
Bobby Ojeda	6.0	8	2	2	2	3	2.08
Roger McDowell	1.2	2	1	0	3	1	2.84
Jesse Orosco	0.1	0	0	0	0	0	0.00
Rick Aguilera (W, 1-0)	2.0	3	2	2	0	3	12.00

Stanley pitched to two batters in the 10th.

WP—Stanley. HBP—Buckner by Aguilera. Time—4:02. Attendance—55,078. Umpires—HP, Ford. 1B, Kibler. 2B, Evans. 3B, Wendelstedt.

Game 7
Monday, October 27

Red Sox	AB	R	H	RBI	BB	K	Avg
Wade Boggs, 3b	4	0	1	1	1	0	.290
Marty Barrett, 2b	5	0	1	0	0	1	.433
Bill Buckner, 1b	4	1	2	0	0	0	.188
Jim Rice, lf	4	1	2	0	0	1	.333
Dwight Evans, rf	4	1	2	3	0	1	.308
Rich Gedman, c	4	1	1	1	0	1	.200
Dave Henderson, cf	2	1	0	0	1	1	.400
Spike Owen, ss	3	0	0	0	0	1	.300
Don Baylor, ph	1	0	0	0	0	0	.182
Al Nipper, p	0	0	0	0	0	0	.000
Steve Crawford, p	0	0	0	0	0	0	.000
Bruce Hurst, p	0	0	0	0	0	0	.000
Tony Armas, ph	1	0	0	0	0	1	.000
Calvin Schiraldi, p	0	0	0	0	0	0	.000
Joe Sambito, p	0	0	0	0	0	0	—
Bob Stanley, p	0	0	0	0	0	0	.000
Ed Romero, ss	1	0	0	0	0	0	.000
TOTALS	33	5	9	5	2	7	.288

Mets	AB	R	H	RBI	BB	K	Avg
Mookie Wilson, cf-lf	3	1	1	0	1	0	.269
Tim Teufel, 2b	2	0	0	0	1	1	.444
Wally Backman, pr-2b	1	1	0	1	0	0	.333
Keith Hernandez, 1b	4	0	1	3	0	0	.231
Gary Carter, c	4	0	0	1	0	0	.276
Darryl Strawberry, rf	4	1	1	1	0	0	.208
Ray Knight, 3b	4	2	3	1	0	0	.391
Kevin Mitchell, lf	2	0	0	0	0	1	.250
Lenny Dykstra, ph-cf	2	1	1	0	0	0	.296
Rafael Santana, ss	3	1	1	1	1	1	.250
Ron Darling, p	1	0	0	0	0	0	.000
Sid Fernandez, p	0	0	0	0	0	0	—
Lee Mazzilli, ph	1	1	1	0	0	0	.400
Roger McDowell, p	0	0	0	0	0	0	—
Jesse Orosco, p	1	0	1	0	0	0	1.000
TOTALS	32	8	10	8	4	3	.288

```
        1 2 3 4 5 6 7 8 9   R  H  E
Red Sox 0 3 0 0 0 0 2 0     5  9  0
Mets    0 0 0 0 0 3 3 2 x   8  10 0
```

LOB—Red Sox 6, Mets 7. Scoring Position—Red Sox 2-for-7, Mets 3-for-7. 2B—Evans (2). HR—Evans (2), Gedman (1), Strawberry (1), Knight (1). S—Hurst 2, McDowell. SF—Hernandez.

Red Sox	IP	H	R	ER	BB	K	ERA
Bruce Hurst	6.0	4	3	3	1	3	1.96
Calvin Schiraldi (L, 0-2)	0.1	3	3	3	0	0	13.50
Joe Sambito	0.1	0	0	0	2	0	27.00
Bob Stanley	0.1	0	0	0	0	0	0.00
Al Nipper	0.1	3	2	2	1	0	7.11
Steve Crawford	0.2	0	0	0	0	0	6.23

Mets	IP	H	R	ER	BB	K	ERA
Ron Darling	3.2	6	3	3	1	0	1.53
Sid Fernandez	2.1	0	0	0	1	4	1.35
Roger McDowell (W, 1-0)	1.0	3	2	2	0	1	4.91
Jesse Orosco (S, 2)	2.0	0	0	0	0	2	0.00

McDowell pitched to three batters in the 8th.

WP—Schiraldi. HBP—Henderson by Darling, Wilson by Crawford. Time—3:11. Attendance—55,032. Umpires—HP, Kibler. 1B, Evans. 2B, Wendelstedt. 3B, Brinkman.

1986 World Series—Composite Statistics

Batting

Mets	G	AB	R	H	RBI	2B	3B	HR	BB	SO	SB	CS	Avg	OBP	Slg
Wally Backman	6	18	4	6	1	0	0	0	3	2	1	1	.333	.429	.333
Gary Carter	7	29	4	8	9	2	0	2	0	4	0	0	.276	.267	.552
Ron Darling	3	3	0	0	0	0	0	0	0	1	0	0	.000	.000	.000
Lenny Dykstra	7	27	4	8	3	0	0	2	2	7	0	0	.296	.345	.519
Kevin Elster	1	1	0	0	0	0	0	0	0	0	0	0	.000	.000	.000
Dwight Gooden	2	2	1	1	0	0	0	0	0	0	0	0	.500	.500	.500
Danny Heep	5	11	0	1	2	0	0	0	1	1	0	0	.091	.167	.091
Keith Hernandez	7	26	1	6	4	0	0	0	5	1	0	0	.231	.344	.231
Howard Johnson	2	5	0	0	0	0	0	0	0	2	0	0	.000	.000	.000
Ray Knight	6	23	4	9	5	1	0	1	2	2	0	0	.391	.440	.565
Lee Mazzilli	4	5	2	2	0	0	0	0	0	0	0	0	.400	.400	.400
Roger McDowell	5	0	0	0	0	0	0	0	0	0	0	0	—	—	—
Kevin Mitchell	5	8	1	2	0	0	0	0	0	3	0	0	.250	.250	.250
Bobby Ojeda	2	2	0	0	0	0	0	0	0	1	0	0	.000	.000	.000
Jesse Orosco	4	1	0	1	1	0	0	0	0	0	0	0	1.000	1.000	1.000
Rafael Santana	7	20	3	5	2	0	0	0	2	5	0	0	.250	.318	.250
Darryl Strawberry	7	24	4	5	1	1	0	1	4	6	3	1	.208	.321	.375
Tim Teufel	3	9	1	4	1	1	0	1	1	2	0	0	.444	.500	.889
Mookie Wilson	7	26	3	7	0	1	0	0	1	6	3	0	.269	.321	.308
Totals	7	240	32	65	29	6	0	7	21	43	7	2	.271	.330	.383

Red Sox	G	AB	R	H	RBI	2B	3B	HR	BB	SO	SB	CS	Avg	OBP	Slg
Tony Armas	1	1	0	0	0	0	0	0	0	1	0	0	.000	.000	.000
Marty Barrett	7	30	1	13	4	2	0	0	5	2	0	0	.433	.514	.500
Don Baylor	4	11	1	2	1	1	0	0	1	3	0	0	.182	.308	.273
Wade Boggs	7	31	3	9	3	3	0	0	4	2	0	0	.290	.371	.387
Bill Buckner	7	32	2	6	1	0	0	0	0	3	0	0	.188	.212	.188
Roger Clemens	2	4	1	0	0	0	0	0	0	1	0	0	.000	.000	.000
Steve Crawford	3	1	0	0	0	0	0	0	0	0	0	0	.000	.000	.000
Dwight Evans	7	26	4	8	9	2	0	2	4	3	0	0	.308	.400	.615
Rich Gedman	7	30	1	6	1	1	0	1	0	10	0	0	.200	.200	.333
Mike Greenwell	4	3	0	0	0	0	0	0	1	2	0	0	.000	.250	.000
Dave Henderson	7	25	6	10	5	1	1	2	2	6	0	0	.400	.448	.760
Bruce Hurst	3	3	0	0	0	0	0	0	0	3	0	0	.000	.000	.000
Spike Owen	7	20	2	6	2	0	0	0	5	6	0	0	.300	.423	.300
Jim Rice	7	27	6	9	0	1	1	0	6	9	0	0	.333	.455	.444
Ed Romero	3	1	0	0	0	0	0	0	0	0	0	0	.000	.000	.000
Calvin Schiraldi	3	1	0	0	0	0	0	0	0	1	0	0	.000	.000	.000
Bob Stanley	5	1	0	0	0	0	0	0	0	1	0	0	.000	.000	.000
Dave Stapleton	3	1	0	0	0	0	0	0	0	0	0	0	.000	.000	.000
Totals	7	248	27	69	26	11	2	5	28	53	0	0	.278	.356	.399

Pitching

Mets	G	GS	CG	IP	H	R	ER	BB	SO	W-L	Sv-Op	Hld	ERA
Rick Aguilera	2	0	0	3.0	8	4	4	1	4	1-0	0-0	0	12.00
Ron Darling	3	3	0	17.2	13	4	3	10	12	1-1	0-0	0	1.53
Sid Fernandez	3	0	0	6.2	6	1	1	1	10	0-0	0-0	0	1.35
Dwight Gooden	2	2	0	9.0	17	10	8	4	9	0-2	0-0	0	8.00
Roger McDowell	5	0	0	7.1	10	5	4	6	2	1-0	0-0	0	4.91
Bobby Ojeda	2	2	0	13.0	13	3	3	5	9	1-0	0-0	0	2.08
Jesse Orosco	4	0	0	5.2	2	0	0	0	6	0-0	2-2	0	0.00
Doug Sisk	1	0	0	0.2	0	0	0	1	0	0-0	0-0	0	0.00
Totals	7	7	0	63.0	69	27	23	28	53	4-3	2-2	0	3.29

Red Sox	G	GS	CG	IP	H	R	ER	BB	SO	W-L	Sv-Op	Hld	ERA
Oil Can Boyd	1	1	0	7.0	9	6	6	1	3	0-1	0-0	0	7.71
Roger Clemens	2	2	0	11.1	9	5	4	6	11	0-0	0-0	0	3.18
Steve Crawford	3	0	0	4.1	5	3	3	0	4	1-0	0-0	0	6.23
Bruce Hurst	3	3	1	23.0	18	5	5	6	17	2-0	0-0	0	1.96
Al Nipper	2	1	0	6.1	10	5	5	2	2	0-1	0-0	0	7.11
Joe Sambito	2	0	0	0.1	2	1	1	2	0	0-0	0-0	0	27.00
Calvin Schiraldi	3	0	0	4.0	7	7	6	3	2	0-2	1-2	0	13.50
Bob Stanley	5	0	0	6.1	5	0	0	1	4	0-0	1-2	0	0.00
Totals	7	7	1	62.2	65	32	30	21	43	3-4	2-4	0	4.31

Fielding

Mets	Pos	G	PO	Ast	E	DP	PB	FPct
Rick Aguilera	p	2	0	0	0	0	—	—
Wally Backman	2b	6	9	13	0	3	—	1.000
Gary Carter	c	7	57	1	0	0	0	1.000
Ron Darling	p	3	0	4	0	0	—	1.000
Lenny Dykstra	cf	7	15	0	0	0	—	1.000
Kevin Elster	ss	1	3	3	1	1	—	.857
Sid Fernandez	p	3	0	0	0	0	—	—
Dwight Gooden	p	2	1	2	0	0	—	1.000
Danny Heep	lf	1	1	0	0	0	—	1.000
Keith Hernandez	1b	7	48	4	1	4	—	.981
Howard Johnson	3b	1	1	0	0	0	—	1.000
	ss	1	0	0	0	0	—	—
Ray Knight	3b	6	5	6	1	0	—	.917
Lee Mazzilli	rf	1	1	0	0	0	—	1.000
Roger McDowell	p	5	1	4	0	0	—	1.000
Kevin Mitchell	lf	2	1	2	0	0	—	1.000
Bobby Ojeda	p	2	0	2	0	0	—	1.000
Jesse Orosco	p	4	0	0	0	0	—	—
Rafael Santana	ss	7	11	17	1	3	—	.966
Doug Sisk	p	1	0	0	0	0	—	—
Darryl Strawberry	rf	7	19	0	0	0	—	1.000
Tim Teufel	2b	3	3	3	1	1	—	.857
Mookie Wilson	lf	7	11	2	0	0	—	1.000
	cf	1	2	0	0	0	—	1.000
Totals		7	189	63	5	12	0	.981

Red Sox	Pos	G	PO	Ast	E	DP	PB	FPct
Marty Barrett	2b	7	14	25	0	5	—	1.000
Wade Boggs	3b	7	4	15	0	2	—	1.000
Oil Can Boyd	p	1	1	0	0	0	—	1.000
Bill Buckner	1b	7	53	7	1	5	—	.984
Roger Clemens	p	2	1	2	0	0	—	1.000
Steve Crawford	p	3	0	0	0	0	—	—
Dwight Evans	rf	7	16	1	1	0	—	.944
Rich Gedman	c	7	46	3	2	2	1	.961
Dave Henderson	cf	7	22	0	0	0	—	1.000
Bruce Hurst	p	3	1	3	0	0	—	1.000
Al Nipper	p	2	1	2	0	0	—	1.000
Spike Owen	ss	7	9	13	0	3	—	1.000
Jim Rice	lf	7	16	2	0	1	—	1.000
Ed Romero	ss	3	0	1	0	0	—	1.000
Joe Sambito	p	2	0	0	0	0	—	—
Calvin Schiraldi	p	3	0	1	0	0	—	1.000
Bob Stanley	p	5	1	2	0	0	—	1.000
Dave Stapleton	1b	3	3	2	0	0	—	1.000
Totals		7	188	79	4	18	1	.985

1987 Minnesota Twins (AL) 4, St. Louis Cardinals (NL) 3

The Minnesota Twins rode their home-field advantage to a seven-game victory over the St. Louis Cardinals. After fashioning a 56-25 record at the Metrodome during the regular season, the Twins dropped all three World Series games at St. Louis' Busch Stadium but swept all four home games to take the World Championship. Dan Gladden hit a grand slam in Game 1 as Frank Viola pitched the Twins to a 10-1 victory. The next day, Bert Blyleven put the Twins up two games to none with an 8-4 victory. As the Series shifted to St. Louis, John Tudor got one back with a 3-1 win, as Vince Coleman doubled in the go-ahead runs in the bottom of the seventh. Tom Lawless's three-run homer led the Cards to a 7-2 win in Game 4, and Danny Cox bested Blyleven in Game 5 by the score of 4-2, putting the Cardinals up three games to two. But the Twins took the battle back to Minnesota, where Kent Hrbek belted a grand slam during the Twins' 11-5 victory in Game 6. Game 7 belonged to Viola, who went eight strong innings for his second win of the Series, giving Minnesota a 4-2 victory and the World Championship.

Game 1

Saturday, October 17

Cardinals	AB	R	H	RBI	BB	K	Avg
Vince Coleman, lf	4	0	0	0	0	1	.000
Ozzie Smith, ss	4	0	0	0	0	1	.000
Tom Herr, 2b	4	0	0	0	0	0	.000
Jim Lindeman, 1b	4	1	2	0	0	0	.500
Willie McGee, cf	3	0	2	0	0	0	.667
Tony Pena, c	3	0	0	1	0	0	.000
Steve Lake, c	0	0	0	0	0	0	—
Jose Oquendo, rf	3	0	0	0	0	1	.000
Tom Pagnozzi, dh	3	0	1	0	0	0	.333
Tom Lawless, 3b	3	0	0	0	0	2	.000
TOTALS	31	1	5	1	0	5	.161

Twins	AB	R	H	RBI	BB	K	Avg
Dan Gladden, lf	4	1	2	5	1	0	.500
Greg Gagne, ss	5	0	0	0	0	1	.000
Kirby Puckett, cf	5	0	1	0	0	0	.200
Gary Gaetti, 3b	5	1	2	0	0	0	.400
Don Baylor, dh	5	1	1	0	0	0	.200
Tom Brunansky, rf	3	1	1	0	1	0	.333
Mark Davidson, rf	0	0	0	0	0	0	—
Kent Hrbek, 1b	2	2	1	2	2	0	.500
Gene Larkin, 1b	0	0	0	0	0	0	—
Steve Lombardozzi, 2b	3	3	2	2	1	0	.667
Tim Laudner, c	3	1	1	1	1	1	.333
TOTALS	35	10	11	10	6	2	.314

	1	2	3	4	5	6	7	8	9		R	H	E
Cardinals	0	1	0	0	0	0	0	0	0		1	5	1
Twins	0	0	0	7	2	0	1	0	x		10	11	0

E—Lawless. DP—Twins 1 (Gaetti to Lombardozzi to Hrbek), Cardinals 1 (Lawless to Herr to Lindeman). LOB—Twins 7, Cardinals 3. Scoring Position—Twins 4-for-9, Cardinals 0-for-3. 2B—Lindeman (1), Gladden (1), Gaetti (1). HR—Gladden (1), Lombardozzi (1). GDP—Pena, Baylor. SB—Gladden (1).

Cardinals	IP	H	R	ER	BB	K	ERA
Joe Magrane (L, 0-1)	3.0	4	5	5	4	1	15.00
Bob Forsch	3.0	4	4	4	2	0	12.00
Ricky Horton	2.0	3	1	1	0	1	4.50

Twins	IP	H	R	ER	BB	K	ERA
Frank Viola (W, 1-0)	8.0	5	1	1	0	5	1.13
Keith Atherton	1.0	0	0	0	0	0	0.00

Magrane pitched to six batters in the 4th.

Time—2:39. Attendance—55,171. Umpires—HP, Phillips. 1B, Weyer. 2B, Kosc. 3B, McSherry.

Game 2

Sunday, October 18

Cardinals	AB	R	H	RBI	BB	K	Avg
Vince Coleman, lf	4	1	1	0	0	2	.125
Ozzie Smith, ss	4	0	1	0	0	1	.125
Tom Herr, 2b	4	0	0	0	0	0	.000
Dan Driessen, 1b	4	1	1	1	0	0	.250
Willie McGee, cf	4	0	1	1	0	2	.429
Terry Pendleton, dh	4	1	1	0	0	0	.250
Curt Ford, rf	3	1	2	0	1	0	.667
Jose Oquendo, 3b	4	0	1	0	0	1	.143
Tony Pena, c	4	0	1	2	0	1	.143
TOTALS	35	4	9	4	1	8	.196

Twins	AB	R	H	RBI	BB	K	Avg
Dan Gladden, lf	5	0	1	1	0	0	.333
Greg Gagne, ss	4	0	1	1	0	0	.111
Kirby Puckett, cf	4	1	1	0	0	0	.222
Kent Hrbek, 1b	3	1	1	0	1	0	.400
Gary Gaetti, 3b	3	2	2	1	1	1	.500
Randy Bush, dh	3	1	1	2	0	1	.333
Gene Larkin, ph-dh	1	0	0	0	0	0	.000

Tom Brunansky, rf	3	1	0	0	1	1	.167
Steve Lombardozzi, 2b	3	0	0	0	0	1	.333
Roy Smalley, ph	1	0	1	0	0	0	1.000
Al Newman, pr-2b	0	0	0	0	0	0	—
Tim Laudner, c	3	2	2	3	1	1	.500
TOTALS	33	8	10	8	4	5	.317

	1	2	3	4	5	6	7	8	9		R	H	E
Cardinals	0	0	0	0	1	0	1	2	0		4	9	0
Twins	0	1	0	6	0	1	0	0	x		8	10	0

LOB—Twins 5, Cardinals 5. Scoring Position—Twins 4-for-9, Cardinals 3-for-9. 2B—Driessen (1), Gagne (1), Bush (1), Smalley (1). HR—Gaetti (1), Laudner (1). SB—Coleman (1).

Cardinals	IP	H	R	ER	BB	K	ERA
Danny Cox (L, 0-1)	3.2	6	7	7	2	3	17.18
Lee Tunnell	2.1	3	1	1	1	1	3.86
Ken Dayley	1.1	0	0	0	0	1	0.00
Todd Worrell	0.2	1	0	0	1	0	0.00

Twins	IP	H	R	ER	BB	K	ERA
Bert Blyleven (W, 1-0)	7.0	6	2	2	1	8	2.57
Juan Berenguer	1.0	3	2	2	0	0	18.00
Jeff Reardon	1.0	0	0	0	0	0	0.00

WP—Cox. Time—2:42. Attendance—55,257. Umpires—HP, Weyer. 1B, Kosc. 2B, McSherry. 3B, Kaiser.

Game 3

Tuesday, October 20

Twins	AB	R	H	RBI	BB	K	Avg
Dan Gladden, lf	4	0	1	0	0	1	.308
Greg Gagne, ss	3	1	0	0	1	0	.083
Kirby Puckett, cf	3	0	1	0	1	0	.250
Gary Gaetti, 3b	4	0	0	0	0	1	.333
Tom Brunansky, rf	4	0	1	1	0	1	.200
Kent Hrbek, 1b	4	0	0	0	0	1	.222
Tim Laudner, c	3	0	2	0	0	1	.556
Randy Bush, ph	1	0	0	0	0	0	.250
Steve Lombardozzi, 2b	3	0	0	0	0	1	.222
Les Straker, p	2	0	0	0	0	2	.000
Gene Larkin, ph	1	0	0	0	0	0	.000
Juan Berenguer, p	0	0	0	0	0	0	—
Dan Schatzeder, p	0	0	0	0	0	0	—
TOTALS	32	1	5	1	2	8	.255

Cardinals	AB	R	H	RBI	BB	K	Avg
Vince Coleman, lf	4	1	1	2	0	1	.167
Ozzie Smith, ss	4	0	2	1	0	0	.250
Tom Herr, 2b	4	0	1	0	0	0	.083
Dan Driessen, 1b	4	0	0	0	0	0	.125
Todd Worrell, p	0	0	0	0	0	0	—
Willie McGee, cf	4	0	2	0	0	1	.455
Curt Ford, rf	4	0	1	0	0	1	.429
Jose Oquendo, 3b	3	1	1	0	1	0	.200
Tony Pena, c	2	1	1	0	1	0	.222
John Tudor, p	2	0	0	0	0	2	.000
Terry Pendleton, ph	0	0	0	0	0	0	.250
Jim Lindeman, 1b	0	0	0	0	0	0	.500
TOTALS	31	3	9	3	2	5	.242

	1	2	3	4	5	6	7	8	9		R	H	E
Twins	0	0	0	0	0	1	0	0	0		1	5	1
Cardinals	0	0	0	0	0	0	3	0	x		3	9	1

E—Pena, Gagne. DP—Twins 1 (Gagne to Lombardozzi to Hrbek). LOB—Cardinals 7, Twins 6. Scoring Position—Cardinals 2-for-9, Twins 1-for-7. 2B—Laudner (1), Coleman (1), McGee (1). 3B—Puckett (1). S—Pendleton. GDP—Herr. SB—Coleman 2 (3). CS—Ford (1).

Game 4

Wednesday, October 21

Twins	AB	R	H	RBI	BB	K	Avg
Dan Gladden, lf	5	0	1	0	0	2	.278
Al Newman, 2b	3	0	1	0	1	1	.333
Don Baylor, ph	1	0	1	0	0	0	.333
Kirby Puckett, cf	4	0	1	0	0	0	.250
Gary Gaetti, 3b	3	0	0	0	0	1	.333
Tom Brunansky, rf	4	0	0	0	0	0	.143
Kent Hrbek, 1b	4	0	1	0	0	1	.231
Tim Laudner, c	3	0	0	0	1	0	.417
Sal Butera, c	0	0	0	0	0	0	—
Greg Gagne, ss	4	1	1	1	0	2	.125
Frank Viola, p	1	0	0	0	0	1	.000
Dan Schatzeder, p	0	0	0	0	0	0	—
Gene Larkin, ph	0	1	0	0	1	0	.000
Joe Niekro, p	0	0	0	0	0	0	—
Roy Smalley, ph	1	0	0	0	0	0	.500
George Frazier, p	0	0	0	0	0	0	—
Mark Davidson, ph	1	0	0	0	0	0	.000
TOTALS	34	2	7	2	3	8	.252

Cardinals	AB	R	H	RBI	BB	K	Avg
Vince Coleman, lf	4	1	1	0	1	1	.188
Ozzie Smith, ss	4	1	0	0	1	1	.188
Tom Herr, 2b	3	1	2	0	2	0	.200
Jim Lindeman, 1b	4	1	2	2	0	1	.500
Willie McGee, cf	4	0	2	2	0	2	.467
Tony Pena, c	3	1	1	0	1	0	.250
Jose Oquendo, rf	4	1	1	0	0	0	.214
Tom Lawless, 3b	4	1	1	3	0	2	.143
Greg Mathews, p	1	0	0	0	0	0	.000
Bob Forsch, p	2	0	0	0	0	0	.000
Ken Dayley, p	1	0	0	0	0	1	.000
TOTALS	34	7	10	7	5	8	.252

	1	2	3	4	5	6	7	8	9		R	H	E
Twins	0	0	1	0	1	0	0	0	0		2	7	1
Cardinals	0	0	1	6	0	0	0	x			7	10	1

E—Puckett, Lindeman. DP—Cardinals 1 (Lindeman to Forsch). LOB—Cardinals 9, Twins 10. Scoring Position—Cardinals 4-for-11, Twins 2-for-11. 2B—Coleman (2), McGee (2). HR—Gagne (1), Lawless (1). GDP—Laudner. SB—Gaetti (1), Brunansky (1), Coleman (4).

Twins	IP	H	R	ER	BB	K	ERA
Frank Viola (L, 1-1)	3.1	6	5	5	3	4	4.76
Dan Schatzeder	0.2	2	2	2	1	1	7.71
Joe Niekro	2.0	1	0	0	1	1	0.00
George Frazier	2.0	1	0	0	0	2	0.00

Cardinals	IP	H	R	ER	BB	K	ERA
Greg Mathews	3.2	2	1	1	2	3	2.45
Bob Forsch (W, 1-0)	2.2	4	1	1	1	3	7.94
Ken Dayley (S, 1)	2.2	1	0	0	0	2	0.00

WP—Mathews. HBP—Lindeman by Niekro, Gaetti by Mathews, Puckett by Forsch. Time—3:11. Attendance—55,347. Umpires—HP, McSherry. 1B, Kaiser. 2B, Tata. 3B, Phillips.

Game 5
Thursday, October 22

Twins	AB	R	H	RBI	BB	K	Avg
Dan Gladden, lf	3	1	1	0	2	0	.286
Greg Gagne, ss	4	1	1	0	0	1	.150
Don Baylor, ph	1	0	0	0	0	0	.286
Kirby Puckett, cf	4	0	0	0	0	0	.200
Kent Hrbek, 1b	4	0	1	0	0	0	.235
Gary Gaetti, 3b	4	0	1	2	0	2	.316
Tom Brunansky, rf	4	0	1	0	0	1	.167
Tim Laudner, c	2	0	0	0	1	1	.357
Al Newman, ph	1	0	0	0	0	0	.250
Steve Lombardozzi, 2b	2	0	1	0	1	0	.273
Roy Smalley, ph	0	0	0	0	1	0	.500
Bert Blyleven, p	1	0	0	0	0	1	.000
Gene Larkin, ph	1	0	0	0	0	0	.000
Keith Atherton, p	0	0	0	0	0	0	—
Jeff Reardon, p	0	0	0	0	0	0	—
Randy Bush, ph	1	0	0	0	0	0	.200
TOTALS	32	2	6	2	5	6	.241

Cardinals	AB	R	H	RBI	BB	K	Avg
Vince Coleman, lf	3	2	1	0	1	1	.211
Ozzie Smith, ss	4	1	2	1	0	0	.250
Tom Herr, 2b	4	0	0	0	0	0	.158
Dan Driessen, 1b	3	1	1	0	1	0	.182
Ken Dayley, p	0	0	0	0	0	0	.000
Todd Worrell, p	0	0	0	0	0	0	—
Willie McGee, cf	4	0	0	0	0	3	.368
Curt Ford, rf	4	0	1	2	0	0	.364
Jose Oquendo, 3b	4	0	2	0	0	1	.278
Tony Pena, c	4	0	3	0	0	0	.375
Lance Johnson, ph	0	0	0	0	0	0	.000
Steve Lake, c	0	0	0	0	0	0	—
Danny Cox, p	2	0	0	0	0	1	.000
Jim Lindeman, 1b	1	0	0	0	0	1	.444
TOTALS	33	4	10	3	2	7	.276

	1 2 3	4 5 6	7 8 9		R	H	E
Twins	0 0 0	0 0 0	0 2 0		2	6	1
Cardinals	0 0 0	0 3 1	0 x		4	10	0

E—Gagne. DP—Twins 1 (Laudner to Gaetti). LOB—Cardinals 8, Twins 9. Scoring Position—Cardinals 3-for-13, Twins 1-for-9. 3B—Gaetti (1). S—Blyleven, Cox. SB—Gladden (2), Coleman 2 (6), Smith 2 (2), Johnson (1). CS—Oquendo (1).

Twins	IP	H	R	ER	BB	K	ERA
Bert Blyleven (L, 1-1)	6.0	7	3	2	1	4	2.77
Keith Atherton	0.1	0	1	1	1	0	6.75
Jeff Reardon	1.2	3	0	0	0	3	0.00

Cardinals	IP	H	R	ER	BB	K	ERA
Danny Cox (W, 1-1)	7.1	5	2	2	3	6	7.36
Ken Dayley (H, 1)	0.1	0	0	0	0	0	0.00
Todd Worrell (S, 2)	1.1	1	0	0	2	0	0.00

Balk—Atherton. Time—3:21. Attendance—55,347. Umpires—HP, Kaiser. 1B, Tata. 2B, Phillips. 3B, Weyer.

Game 6
Saturday, October 24

Cardinals	AB	R	H	RBI	BB	K	Avg
Vince Coleman, lf	5	0	0	0	0	2	.167
Ozzie Smith, ss	4	1	1	0	1	0	.250
Tom Herr, 2b	5	1	3	1	0	1	.250
Dan Driessen, 1b	2	1	1	0	0	0	.231
Tom Pagnozzi, ph	1	0	0	0	0	0	.250
John Morris, rf	2	0	0	0	0	0	.000
Willie McGee, cf	4	1	2	1	0	0	.391
Terry Pendleton, dh	3	1	2	1	1	1	.429
Curt Ford, rf	1	0	0	0	0	0	.333
Jim Lindeman, ph-rf-1b	3	0	0	0	0	0	.333
Jose Oquendo, 3b	3	0	1	2	0	0	.286
Tony Pena, c	3	0	1	0	1	0	.368
TOTALS	36	5	11	5	3	4	.286

Twins	AB	R	H	RBI	BB	K	Avg
Dan Gladden, lf	5	1	2	0	0	0	.308
Greg Gagne, ss	5	1	1	0	0	0	.160
Kirby Puckett, cf	4	4	4	1	1	0	.333
Gary Gaetti, 3b	5	1	1	1	0	0	.292
Don Baylor, dh	3	2	2	3	1	0	.400
Randy Bush, ph-dh	1	0	0	0	0	0	.167
Tom Brunansky, rf	4	1	1	1	1	1	.182
Kent Hrbek, 1b	4	1	1	4	1	0	.238
Tim Laudner, c	5	0	0	0	0	0	.263
Steve Lombardozzi, 2b	4	0	3	1	0	0	.400
TOTALS	40	11	15	11	4	1	.271

	1 2 3	4 5 6	7 8 9		R	H	E
Cardinals	1 1 0	2 1 0	0 0 0		5	11	2
Twins	2 0 0	4 4 0	1 x		11	15	0

E—McGee, Lindeman. DP—Twins 1 (Lombardozzi to Gagne to Hrbek). LOB—Twins 9, Cardinals 8. Scoring Position—Twins 5-for-14, Cardinals 4-for-10. 2B—Driessen (2), Gaetti (2), Lombardozzi (1). 3B—Gladden (1). HR—Herr (1), Baylor (1), Hrbek (1). SF—Oquendo. GDP—Morris. SB—Pendleton 2 (2), Puckett (1).

Cardinals	IP	H	R	ER	BB	K	ERA
John Tudor (L, 1-1)	4.0	11	6	6	1	1	5.73
Ricky Horton	1.0	2	1	1	0	0	6.00
Bob Forsch	0.2	0	2	2	2	0	9.95
Ken Dayley	0.1	1	1	1	0	0	1.93
Lee Tunnell	2.0	1	1	0	1	0	2.08

Twins	IP	H	R	ER	BB	K	ERA
Les Straker	3.0	5	4	4	1	2	4.00
Dan Schatzeder (W, 1-0)	2.0	1	1	1	2	1	6.23
Juan Berenguer (H, 1)	3.0	3	0	0	0	1	10.38
Jeff Reardon	1.0	2	0	0	0	0	0.00

Straker pitched to four batters in the 4th. Tudor pitched to four batters in the 5th. Horton pitched to one batter in the 6th.

PB—Pena. Time—3:22. Attendance—55,293. Umpires—HP, Tata. 1B, Phillips. 2B, Weyer. 3B, Kosc.

Game 7
Sunday, October 25

Cardinals	AB	R	H	RBI	BB	K	Avg
Vince Coleman, lf	4	0	0	0	0	2	.143
Ozzie Smith, ss	4	0	0	0	0	0	.214
Tom Herr, 2b	4	0	1	0	0	1	.250
Jim Lindeman, 1b	3	1	1	0	0	1	.333
Curt Ford, ph	1	0	0	0	0	0	.308
Willie McGee, cf	4	1	1	0	0	1	.370
Tony Pena, dh	3	0	2	1	0	1	.409
Jose Oquendo, rf	3	0	0	0	0	1	.250
Tom Lawless, 3b	3	0	0	0	0	0	.100
Steve Lake, c	3	0	1	1	0	0	.333
TOTALS	32	2	6	2	0	7	.268

Twins	AB	R	H	RBI	BB	K	Avg
Dan Gladden, lf	5	0	1	1	0	1	.290
Greg Gagne, ss	5	1	2	1	0	2	.200
Kirby Puckett, cf	4	0	2	1	0	1	.357
Gary Gaetti, 3b	3	0	0	0	1	0	.259
Don Baylor, dh	3	0	1	0	0	1	.385
Tom Brunansky, rf	3	2	1	0	1	0	.200
Kent Hrbek, 1b	3	0	0	1	1	1	.208
Tim Laudner, c	3	1	2	0	1	0	.318
Steve Lombardozzi, 2b	2	0	1	1	0	0	.412
Roy Smalley, ph	0	0	0	0	1	0	.500
Al Newman, pr-2b	1	0	0	0	0	0	.200
TOTALS	32	4	10	4	5	6	.281

	1 2 3	4 5 6	7 8 9		R	H	E
Cardinals	0 2 0	0 0 0	0 0 0		2	6	1
Twins	0 1 0	0 1 1	0 1 x		4	10	0

E—Lindeman. LOB—Twins 10, Cardinals 3. Scoring Position—Twins 4-for-11, Cardinals 2-for-7. 2B—Pena (1), Gladden (2), Puckett (1). SB—Pena (1), Gaetti (2). CS—Herr (1), Puckett (1).

Cardinals	IP	H	R	ER	BB	K	ERA
Joe Magrane	4.1	5	2	2	1	4	8.59
Danny Cox (L, 1-2)	0.2	2	1	1	3	0	7.71
Todd Worrell	3.0	3	1	1	1	2	1.29

Twins	IP	H	R	ER	BB	K	ERA
Frank Viola (W, 2-1)	8.0	6	2	2	0	7	3.72
Jeff Reardon (S, 1)	1.0	0	0	0	0	0	0.00

Cox pitched to two batters in the 6th.

HBP—Baylor by Magrane. Time—3:04. Attendance—55,376. Umpires—HP, Phillips. 1B, Weyer. 2B, Kosc. 3B, McSherry.

1987 World Series—Composite Statistics

Batting

Twins	G	AB	R	H	RBI	2B	3B	HR	BB	SO	SB	CS	Avg	OBP	Slg
Don Baylor	5	13	3	5	3	0	0	1	1	1	0	0	.385	.467	.615
Bert Blyleven	2	1	0	0	0	0	0	0	0	1	0	0	.000	.000	.000
Tom Brunansky	7	25	5	5	2	0	0	4	4	1	0	0	.200	.310	.200
Randy Bush	4	6	1	1	2	1	0	0	1	0	0	0	.167	.167	.333
Mark Davidson	2	1	0	0	0	0	0	0	0	0	0	0	.000	.000	.000
Gary Gaetti	7	27	4	7	4	2	1	1	2	5	2	0	.259	.333	.519
Greg Gagne	7	30	5	6	3	1	0	1	1	6	0	0	.200	.226	.333
Dan Gladden	7	31	3	9	7	2	1	1	3	4	2	0	.290	.353	.516
Kent Hrbek	7	24	4	5	6	0	0	1	5	3	0	0	.208	.345	.333
Gene Larkin	5	3	1	0	0	0	0	0	1	0	0	0	.000	.250	.000
Tim Laudner	7	22	4	7	4	1	0	1	5	4	0	0	.318	.444	.500
Steve Lombardozzi	6	17	3	7	4	1	0	1	2	2	0	0	.412	.474	.647
Al Newman	4	5	0	1	0	0	0	0	1	1	0	0	.200	.333	.200
Kirby Puckett	7	28	5	10	3	1	1	0	2	1	1	1	.357	.419	.464
Roy Smalley	4	2	0	1	0	1	0	0	2	0	0	0	.500	.750	1.000
Les Straker	2	2	0	0	0	0	0	0	0	2	0	0	.000	.000	.000
Frank Viola	3	1	0	0	0	0	0	0	0	1	0	0	.000	.000	.000
Totals	**7**	**238**	**38**	**64**	**38**	**10**	**3**	**7**	**29**	**36**	**6**	**1**	**.269**	**.356**	**.424**

Cardinals	G	AB	R	H	RBI	2B	3B	HR	BB	SO	SB	CS	Avg	OBP	Slg
Vince Coleman	7	28	5	4	2	2	0	0	2	10	6	0	.143	.200	.214
Danny Cox	3	2	0	0	0	0	0	0	0	1	0	0	.000	.000	.000
Ken Dayley	4	1	0	0	0	0	0	0	0	0	0	0	.000	.000	.000
Dan Driessen	4	13	3	3	1	2	0	0	1	1	0	0	.231	.286	.385
Curt Ford	5	13	1	4	2	0	0	0	1	1	0	1	.308	.357	.308
Bob Forsch	3	2	0	0	0	0	0	0	0	0	0	0	.000	.000	.000
Tom Herr	7	28	2	7	1	0	0	1	2	2	0	1	.250	.300	.357
Lance Johnson	1	0	0	0	0	0	0	0	0	0	1	0	—	—	—
Steve Lake	3	3	0	1	1	0	0	0	0	0	0	0	.333	.333	.333
Tom Lawless	3	10	1	1	3	0	0	1	0	4	0	0	.100	.100	.400
Jim Lindeman	6	15	3	5	2	1	0	0	0	3	0	0	.333	.375	.400
Greg Mathews	1	1	0	0	0	0	0	0	0	0	0	0	.000	.000	.000
Willie McGee	7	27	2	10	4	2	0	0	0	9	0	0	.370	.370	.444
John Morris	1	2	0	0	0	0	0	0	0	0	0	0	.000	.000	.000
Jose Oquendo	7	24	2	6	2	0	0	0	1	4	0	1	.250	.269	.250
Tom Pagnozzi	2	4	0	1	0	0	0	0	0	0	0	0	.250	.250	.250
Tony Pena	7	22	2	9	4	1	0	0	3	2	1	0	.409	.480	.455
Terry Pendleton	3	7	2	3	1	0	0	0	1	1	2	0	.429	.500	.429
Ozzie Smith	7	28	3	6	2	0	0	0	2	3	2	0	.214	.267	.214
John Tudor	2	2	0	0	0	0	0	0	0	2	0	0	.000	.000	.000
Totals	**7**	**232**	**26**	**60**	**25**	**8**	**0**	**2**	**13**	**44**	**12**	**3**	**.259**	**.300**	**.319**

Pitching

Twins	G	GS	CG	IP	H	R	ER	BB	SO	W-L	Sv-Op	Hld	ERA
Keith Atherton	2	0	0	1.1	0	1	1	1	0	0-0	0-0	0	6.75
Juan Berenguer	3	0	0	4.1	10	5	5	0	1	0-1	0-1	1	10.38
Bert Blyleven	2	2	0	13.0	13	5	4	2	12	1-1	0-0	0	2.77
George Frazier	1	0	0	2.0	1	0	0	0	2	0-0	0-0	0	0.00
Joe Niekro	1	0	0	2.0	1	0	0	1	1	0-0	0-0	0	0.00
Jeff Reardon	4	0	0	4.2	5	0	0	0	3	0-0	1-1	0	0.00
Dan Schatzeder	3	0	0	4.1	4	3	3	3	3	1-0	0-0	0	6.23
Les Straker	2	2	0	9.0	9	4	4	3	6	0-0	0-0	0	4.00
Frank Viola	3	3	0	19.1	17	8	8	3	16	2-1	0-0	0	3.72
Totals	**7**	**7**	**0**	**60.0**	**60**	**26**	**25**	**13**	**44**	**4-3**	**1-2**	**1**	**3.75**

Cardinals	G	GS	CG	IP	H	R	ER	BB	SO	W-L	Sv-Op	Hld	ERA
Danny Cox	3	2	0	11.2	13	10	10	8	9	1-2	0-0	0	7.71
Ken Dayley	4	0	0	4.2	2	1	1	0	3	0-0	1-1	0	1.93
Bob Forsch	3	0	0	6.1	8	7	7	5	3	1-0	0-0	0	9.95
Ricky Horton	2	0	0	3.0	5	2	2	0	1	0-0	0-0	0	6.00
Joe Magrane	2	2	0	7.1	9	7	7	5	5	0-1	0-0	0	8.59
Greg Mathews	1	1	0	3.2	2	1	1	2	3	0-0	0-0	0	2.45
John Tudor	2	2	0	11.0	15	7	7	3	8	1-1	0-0	0	5.73
Lee Tunnell	2	0	0	4.1	4	2	1	2	1	0-0	0-0	0	2.08
Todd Worrell	4	0	0	7.0	6	1	1	4	3	0-0	2-2	0	1.29
Totals	**7**	**7**	**0**	**59.0**	**64**	**38**	**37**	**29**	**36**	**3-4**	**3-3**	**1**	**5.64**

Fielding

Twins	Pos	G	PO	Ast	E	DP	PB	FPct
Keith Atherton	p	2	0	0	0	0	—	—
Juan Berenguer	p	3	0	0	0	0	—	—
Bert Blyleven	p	2	0	1	0	0	—	1.000
Tom Brunansky	rf	7	14	0	0	0	—	1.000
Sal Butera	c	1	0	0	0	0	0	—
Mark Davidson	rf	1	0	0	0	0	—	—
George Frazier	p	1	0	1	0	0	—	1.000
Gary Gaetti	3b	7	6	15	0	2	—	1.000
Greg Gagne	ss	7	6	20	2	2	—	.929
Dan Gladden	lf	7	12	0	0	0	—	1.000
Kent Hrbek	1b	7	68	2	0	3	—	1.000
Gene Larkin	1b	1	1	0	0	0	—	1.000
Tim Laudner	c	7	46	2	0	1	0	1.000
Steve Lombardozzi	2b	6	9	24	0	3	—	1.000
Al Newman	2b	3	1	2	0	0	—	1.000
Joe Niekro	p	1	0	1	0	0	—	1.000
Kirby Puckett	cf	7	15	1	1	0	—	.941
Jeff Reardon	p	4	0	0	0	0	—	—
Dan Schatzeder	p	3	0	0	0	0	—	—
Les Straker	p	2	1	0	0	0	—	1.000
Frank Viola	p	3	1	4	0	0	—	1.000
Totals		**7**	**180**	**73**	**3**	**11**	**0**	**.988**

Cardinals	Pos	G	PO	Ast	E	DP	PB	FPct
Vince Coleman	lf	7	10	2	0	0	—	1.000
Danny Cox	p	3	1	1	0	0	—	1.000
Ken Dayley	p	4	0	0	0	0	—	—
Dan Driessen	1b	4	27	1	0	0	—	1.000
Curt Ford	rf	4	5	0	0	0	—	1.000
Bob Forsch	p	3	1	0	0	1	—	1.000
Tom Herr	2b	7	24	17	0	1	—	1.000
Ricky Horton	p	2	0	1	0	0	—	1.000
Steve Lake	c	3	8	1	0	0	0	1.000
Tom Lawless	3b	3	3	6	1	1	—	.900
Jim Lindeman	1b	6	28	2	3	2	—	.909
	rf	1	0	0	0	0	—	—
Joe Magrane	p	2	1	1	0	0	—	1.000
Greg Mathews	p	1	0	1	0	0	—	1.000
Willie McGee	cf	7	21	1	1	0	—	.957
John Morris	rf	1	2	0	0	0	—	1.000
Jose Oquendo	3b	4	1	10	0	0	—	1.000
	rf	3	7	0	0	0	—	1.000
Tony Pena	c	6	32	1	1	0	1	.971
Ozzie Smith	ss	7	6	19	0	1	—	1.000
John Tudor	p	2	0	4	0	0	—	1.000
Lee Tunnell	p	2	0	1	0	0	—	1.000
Todd Worrell	p	4	0	0	0	0	—	—
Totals		**7**	**177**	**69**	**6**	**6**	**1**	**.976**

1988 Los Angeles Dodgers (NL) 4, Oakland Athletics (AL) 1

After stunning the Mets in the NLCS, the Los Angeles Dodgers did the same to the Oakland A's in the World Series. The Dodgers prevailed in five games, beating the AL champs at their own game—power and pitching. The A's appeared poised to take the opener when Dennis Eckersley was called upon to protect a one-run lead in the bottom of the ninth. With two outs and the tying run on second base, Kirk Gibson fought off pain and several two-strike pitches to hit the home run for which he will always be remembered, a game-winning two-run blast. Orel Hershiser followed with a three-hit shutout in Game 2 to put the Dodgers in the driver's seat. The A's got a badly-needed victory in Game 3 when Mark McGwire hit a game-winning solo homer in the bottom of the ninth for a 2-1 Oakland win. But the Dodgers held on for a 4-3 victory the next day, as Jay Howell threw 2.1 innings of scoreless relief. With Hershiser coming back to start Game 5, it soon was all over. Mike Davis and Mickey Hatcher each hit two-run homers, and Hershiser went the route for a 5-2 victory and a Los Angeles World Championship.

Game 1

Saturday, October 15

Athletics	AB	R	H	RBI	BB	K	Avg
Carney Lansford, 3b	4	1	0	0	1	1	.000
Dave Henderson, cf	5	0	2	0	0	2	.400
Jose Canseco, rf	4	1	1	4	0	1	.250
Dave Parker, lf	2	0	0	0	2	0	.000
Stan Javier, pr-lf	1	0	1	0	0	0	1.000
Mark McGwire, 1b	3	0	0	0	2	0	.000
Terry Steinbach, c	4	0	1	0	0	1	.250
Ron Hassey, c	0	0	0	0	0	0	—
Glenn Hubbard, 2b	4	1	2	0	0	0	.500
Walt Weiss, ss	4	0	0	0	0	1	.000
Dave Stewart, p	3	1	0	0	1	3	.000
Dennis Eckersley, p	0	0	0	0	0	0	—
TOTALS	34	4	7	4	6	9	.206

Dodgers	AB	R	H	RBI	BB	K	Avg
Steve Sax, 2b	3	1	1	0	0	0	.333
Franklin Stubbs, 1b	4	0	0	0	0	0	.000
Mickey Hatcher, lf	3	1	1	2	1	1	.333
Mike Marshall, rf	4	1	1	0	0	1	.250
John Shelby, cf	4	0	1	0	0	1	.250
Mike Scioscia, c	4	0	1	1	0	0	.250
Jeff Hamilton, 3b	4	0	0	0	0	2	.000
Alfredo Griffin, ss	2	0	1	0	1	0	.500
Mike Davis, ph	0	1	0	0	1	0	—
Tim Belcher, p	0	0	0	0	0	0	—
Danny Heep, ph	1	0	0	0	0	0	.000
Tim Leary, p	0	0	0	0	0	0	—
Tracy Woodson, ph	1	0	0	0	0	0	.000
Brian Holton, p	0	0	0	0	0	0	—
Jose Gonzalez, ph	1	0	0	0	0	1	.000
Alejandro Pena, p	0	0	0	0	0	0	—
Kirk Gibson, ph	1	1	1	2	0	0	1.000
TOTALS	32	5	7	5	3	6	.219

	1	2	3	4	5	6	7	8	9		R	H	E
Athletics	0	4	0	0	0	0	0	0	0		4	7	0
Dodgers	2	0	0	0	0	1	0	0	2		5	7	0

DP—Athletics 1 (Lansford to McGwire). LOB—Athletics 10, Dodgers 5. Scoring Position—Athletics 1-for-11, Dodgers 3-for-6. 2B—Henderson (1). HR—Canseco (1), Hatcher (1), Gibson (1). GDP—Hamilton. SB—Canseco (1), Sax (1), Davis (1).

Athletics	IP	H	R	ER	BB	K	ERA
Dave Stewart	8.0	6	3	3	2	5	3.38
Dennis Eckersley (BS, 1; L, 0-1)	0.2	1	2	2	1	1	27.00

Dodgers	IP	H	R	ER	BB	K	ERA
Tim Belcher	2.0	3	4	4	4	3	18.00
Tim Leary	3.0	3	0	0	1	3	0.00
Brian Holton	2.0	0	0	0	1	0	0.00
Alejandro Pena (W, 1-0)	2.0	1	0	0	0	3	0.00

Balk—Stewart. WP—Stewart. HBP—Canseco by Belcher, Sax by Stewart. Time—3:04. Attendance—55,983. Umpires—HP, Harvey. 1B, Merrill. 2B, Froemming. 3B, Cousins.

Game 2

Sunday, October 16

Athletics	AB	R	H	RBI	BB	K	Avg
Carney Lansford, 3b	3	0	0	0	1	1	.000
Dave Henderson, cf	4	0	0	0	0	2	.222
Jose Canseco, rf	4	0	0	0	0	1	.125
Dave Parker, lf	4	0	3	0	0	1	.500
Mark McGwire, 1b	3	0	0	0	0	0	.000
Ron Hassey, c	3	0	0	0	0	1	.000
Glenn Hubbard, 2b	2	0	0	0	1	0	.333
Walt Weiss, ss	3	0	0	0	0	0	.000
Storm Davis, p	1	0	0	0	0	1	.000
Gene Nelson, p	0	0	0	0	0	0	—
Luis Polonia, ph	1	0	0	0	0	0	.000
Matt Young, p	0	0	0	0	0	0	—
Eric Plunk, p	0	0	0	0	0	0	—
Don Baylor, ph	1	0	0	0	0	1	.000
Rick Honeycutt, p	0	0	0	0	0	0	—
TOTALS	29	0	3	0	2	8	.145

Dodgers	AB	R	H	RBI	BB	K	Avg
Steve Sax, 2b	4	1	1	0	0	0	.286
Franklin Stubbs, 1b	2	1	1	1	1	0	.167
Tracy Woodson, ph-1b	1	0	0	0	0	0	.000
Mickey Hatcher, lf	4	1	2	1	0	1	.429
Mike Marshall, rf	4	1	2	3	0	2	.375
Jose Gonzalez, rf	0	0	0	0	0	0	.000
John Shelby, cf	4	0	0	0	0	2	.125
Mike Scioscia, c	4	0	0	0	0	1	.125
Jeff Hamilton, 3b	4	0	0	0	0	1	.000
Alfredo Griffin, ss	4	1	1	0	0	1	.333
Orel Hershiser, p	3	1	3	1	0	0	1.000
TOTALS	34	6	10	6	1	8	.250

	1	2	3	4	5	6	7	8	9		R	H	E
Athletics	0	0	0	0	0	0	0	0	0		0	3	0
Dodgers	0	0	5	1	0	0	0	0	x		6	10	1

E—Hamilton. DP—Dodgers 2 (Griffin to Sax to Stubbs; Hamilton to Sax to Stubbs). LOB—Athletics 4, Dodgers 5. Scoring Position—Athletics 0-for-5, Dodgers 3-for-10. 2B—Hershiser 2 (2). 3B—Marshall (1). HR—Marshall (1). GDP—McGwire 2. SB—Weiss (1).

Athletics	IP	H	R	ER	BB	K	ERA
Storm Davis (L, 0-1)	3.1	8	6	6	0	2	16.20
Gene Nelson	1.2	1	0	0	1	1	0.00
Matt Young	1.0	1	0	0	0	0	0.00
Eric Plunk	1.0	0	0	0	0	3	0.00
Rick Honeycutt	1.0	0	0	0	0	2	0.00

Dodgers	IP	H	R	ER	BB	K	ERA
Orel Hershiser (W, 1-0)	9.0	3	0	0	2	8	0.00

Time—2:30. Attendance—56,051. Umpires—HP, Merrill. 1B, Froemming. 2B, Cousins. 3B, Crawford.

Game 3

Tuesday, October 18

Dodgers	AB	R	H	RBI	BB	K	Avg
Steve Sax, 2b	5	0	1	0	0	0	.250
Franklin Stubbs, 1b	4	0	1	1	0	3	.200
Tracy Woodson, ph-1b	1	0	0	0	0	0	.000
Mickey Hatcher, lf-rf	4	0	1	0	0	1	.364
Mike Marshall, rf	1	0	0	0	0	0	.333
Danny Heep, ph-lf	3	0	1	0	0	1	.250
John Shelby, cf	3	0	2	0	1	1	.273
Mike Davis, dh	2	0	0	0	1	0	.000
Dave Anderson, ph-dh	1	0	0	0	0	0	.000
Mike Scioscia, c	4	0	1	0	0	1	.167
Jeff Hamilton, 3b	3	1	1	0	1	1	.091
Alfredo Griffin, ss	3	0	0	0	0	2	.222
TOTALS	34	1	8	1	3	12	.221

Athletics	AB	R	H	RBI	BB	K	Avg
Tony Phillips, lf	1	0	0	0	0	0	.000
Luis Polonia, ph-lf	3	0	0	0	0	1	.000
Dave Henderson, cf	4	0	0	0	0	2	.154
Jose Canseco, rf	4	0	0	0	0	1	.083
Mark McGwire, 1b	4	1	1	1	0	2	.100
Terry Steinbach, dh	3	0	2	0	0	0	.429
Carney Lansford, 3b	3	0	0	0	0	0	.000
Glenn Hubbard, 2b	3	1	1	0	0	0	.333
Ron Hassey, c	1	0	1	1	2	0	.250
Walt Weiss, ss	3	0	0	0	0	0	.000
TOTALS	29	2	5	2	2	6	.138

	1	2	3	4	5	6	7	8	9		R	H	E
Dodgers	0	0	0	1	0	0	0	0	0		1	8	1
Athletics	0	0	1	0	0	0	0	0	1		2	5	0

E—Scioscia. DP—Dodgers 1 (Leary to Stubbs). LOB—Dodgers 10, Athletics 4. Scoring Position—Dodgers 2-for-11, Athletics 1-for-5. 2B—Stubbs (1), Hatcher (1), Steinbach (1), Heep (1). HR—McGwire (1). S—Griffin. SB—Shelby (1), Hubbard (1).

Dodgers	IP	H	R	ER	BB	K	ERA
John Tudor	1.1	0	0	0	0	1	0.00
Tim Leary	3.2	3	1	1	1	1	1.35
Alejandro Pena	3.0	1	0	0	1	4	0.00
Jay Howell (L, 0-1)	0.1	1	1	1	0	0	27.00

Athletics	IP	H	R	ER	BB	K	ERA
Bob Welch	5.0	6	1	1	3	8	1.80
Greg Cadaret	0.1	0	0	0	0	0	0.00
Gene Nelson	1.2	2	0	0	0	1	0.00
Rick Honeycutt (W, 1-0)	2.0	0	0	0	0	3	0.00

Welch pitched to four batters in the 6th. Nelson pitched to one batter in the 8th.

Balk—Leary. Time—3:21. Attendance—49,316. Umpires—HP, Froemming. 1B, Cousins. 2B, Crawford. 3B, McCoy.

Game 4

Wednesday, October 19

Dodgers	AB	R	H	RBI	BB	K	Avg
Steve Sax, 2b	4	1	1	0	1	1	.250
Franklin Stubbs, 1b	3	1	1	0	0	0	.231
Tracy Woodson, ph-1b	1	0	0	1	0	0	.000
Mickey Hatcher, lf	4	1	1	0	0	0	.333
Mike Marshall, rf	0	0	0	0	0	0	.333
Mike Davis, rf	3	0	0	0	0	0	.000
Jose Gonzalez, ph-rf-lf	1	0	0	0	0	1	.000
John Shelby, cf	4	0	1	1	0	0	.267
Mike Scioscia, c	2	0	1	0	0	0	.214
Rick Dempsey, c	1	0	0	0	1	1	.000
Danny Heep, dh	4	0	1	0	0	1	.250
Jeff Hamilton, 3b	4	0	1	0	0	0	.133
Alfredo Griffin, ss	3	1	1	0	1	0	.250
TOTALS	34	4	8	2	3	4	.225

Athletics	AB	R	H	RBI	BB	K	Avg
Luis Polonia, lf	5	1	1	0	0	1	.111
Dave Henderson, cf	5	1	4	1	0	0	.333
Stan Javier, pr	0	0	0	0	0	0	1.000
Jose Canseco, rf	3	0	0	1	2	1	.067
Dave Parker, dh	5	0	0	0	0	2	.273
Mark McGwire, 1b	3	0	0	0	1	1	.077
Carney Lansford, 3b	4	0	1	1	0	0	.071
Terry Steinbach, c	4	0	1	0	0	1	.364
Glenn Hubbard, 2b	3	0	0	0	0	2	.250
Ron Hassey, ph	1	0	1	0	0	0	.400
Mike Gallego, pr-2b	0	0	0	0	0	0	—
Walt Weiss, ss	4	1	1	0	0	1	.071
TOTALS	37	3	9	3	3	9	.195

	1	2	3	4	5	6	7	8	9		R	H	E
Dodgers	2	0	1	0	0	0	1	0	0		4	8	1
Athletics	1	0	0	0	0	1	1	0	0		3	9	2

E—Hubbard, Griffin, Weiss. LOB—Dodgers 6, Athletics 10. Scoring Position—Dodgers 0-for-9, Athletics 2-for-10. 2B—Stubbs (2), Shelby (1), Henderson (2). SB—Davis (2). CS—Scioscia (1), Heep (1), Griffin (1).

Dodgers	IP	H	R	ER	BB	K	ERA
Tim Belcher (W, 1-0)	6.2	7	3	2	2	7	6.23
Jay Howell (S, 1)	2.1	2	0	0	1	2	3.38

Athletics	IP	H	R	ER	BB	K	ERA
Dave Stewart (L, 0-1)	6.1	6	4	2	3	0	3.14
Greg Cadaret	1.2	1	0	0	0	3	0.00
Dennis Eckersley	1.0	1	0	0	0	1	10.80

PB—Scioscia, Steinbach. Time—3:05. Attendance—49,317. Umpires—HP, Cousins. 1B, Crawford. 2B, McCoy. 3B, Harvey.

Game 5

Thursday, October 20

Dodgers	AB	R	H	RBI	BB	K	Avg
Steve Sax, 2b	4	0	2	0	0	0	.300
Franklin Stubbs, 1b	4	1	2	0	0	0	.294
Mickey Hatcher, lf	4	2	2	2	0	0	.368
Jose Gonzalez, lf	0	0	0	0	0	0	.000
Mike Marshall, rf	4	0	0	0	0	1	.231
John Shelby, cf	3	0	0	0	1	3	.222
Mike Davis, dh	2	2	1	2	2	0	.143
Rick Dempsey, c	4	0	1	1	0	1	.200
Jeff Hamilton, 3b	4	0	0	0	0	0	.105
Alfredo Griffin, ss	4	0	0	0	0	1	.188
TOTALS	33	5	8	5	3	6	.235

Athletics	AB	R	H	RBI	BB	K	Avg
Stan Javier, lf	3	0	1	2	0	1	.500
Dave Henderson, cf	2	0	0	0	2	1	.300
Jose Canseco, rf	4	0	0	0	0	1	.053
Dave Parker, dh	4	0	0	0	0	1	.200
Mark McGwire, 1b	4	0	0	0	0	1	.059
Ron Hassey, c	3	0	0	0	1	2	.250
Carney Lansford, 3b	4	1	2	0	0	0	.167
Tony Phillips, 2b	3	1	1	0	1	2	.250
Walt Weiss, ss	2	0	0	0	0	0	.063
TOTALS	29	2	4	2	4	9	.165

	1	2	3	4	5	6	7	8	9		R	H	E
Dodgers	2	0	0	2	0	1	0	0	0		5	8	0
Athletics	0	0	1	0	0	0	0	1	0		2	4	0

DP—Athletics 1 (Weiss to Phillips to McGwire). LOB—Dodgers 4, Athletics 6. Scoring Position—Dodgers 0-for-2, Athletics 1-for-5. 2B—Dempsey (1). HR—Hatcher (2), MDavis (1). S—Weiss. SF—Javier. GDP—Dempsey. CS—Sax (1).

Dodgers	IP	H	R	ER	BB	K	ERA
Orel Hershiser (W, 2-0)	9.0	4	2	2	4	9	1.00

Athletics	IP	H	R	ER	BB	K	ERA
Storm Davis (L, 0-2)	4.2	6	4	4	1	5	11.25
Greg Cadaret	0.0	1	0	0	0	0	0.00
Gene Nelson	3.0	1	1	1	2	1	1.42
Rick Honeycutt	0.1	0	0	0	0	0	0.00
Eric Plunk	0.2	0	0	0	0	0	0.00
Todd Burns	0.1	0	0	0	0	0	0.00

Cadaret pitched to one batter in the 5th.

WP—Hershiser. Time—2:51. Attendance—49,317. Umpires—HP, Crawford. 1B, McCoy. 2B, Harvey. 3B, Merrill.

1988 World Series—Composite Statistics

Batting

Dodgers	G	AB	R	H	RBI	2B	3B	HR	BB	SO	SB	CS	Avg	OBP	Slg
Dave Anderson	1	1	0	0	0	0	0	0	0	1	0	0	.000	.000	.000
Mike Davis	4	7	3	1	2	0	0	1	4	0	2	0	.143	.455	.571
Rick Dempsey	2	5	0	1	1	1	0	0	1	2	0	0	.200	.333	.400
Kirk Gibson	1	1	1	1	2	0	0	1	0	0	0	0	1.000	1.000	4.000
Jose Gonzalez	4	2	0	0	0	0	0	0	0	2	0	0	.000	.000	.000
Alfredo Griffin	5	16	2	3	0	0	0	0	2	4	0	1	.188	.278	.188
Jeff Hamilton	5	19	1	2	0	0	0	0	1	4	0	0	.105	.150	.105
Mickey Hatcher	5	19	5	7	5	1	0	2	1	3	0	0	.368	.400	.737
Danny Heep	3	8	0	2	0	1	0	0	0	2	0	1	.250	.250	.375
Orel Hershiser	2	3	1	3	1	2	0	0	0	0	0	0	1.000	1.000	1.667
Mike Marshall	5	13	2	3	3	0	1	1	0	5	0	0	.231	.231	.615
Steve Sax	5	20	3	6	0	0	0	0	1	1	1	0	.300	.364	.300
Mike Scioscia	4	14	0	3	1	0	0	0	0	2	0	1	.214	.214	.214
John Shelby	5	18	0	4	1	1	0	0	2	7	1	0	.222	.300	.278
Franklin Stubbs	5	17	3	5	2	2	0	0	1	3	0	0	.294	.333	.412
Tracy Woodson	4	4	0	0	1	0	0	0	0	0	0	0	.000	.000	.000
Totals	5	167	21	41	19	8	1	5	13	36	4	4	.246	.304	.395

Batting

Athletics	G	AB	R	H	RBI	2B	3B	HR	BB	SO	SB	CS	Avg	OBP	Slg
Don Baylor	1	1	0	0	0	0	0	0	0	1	0	0	.000	.000	.000
Jose Canseco	5	19	1	1	5	0	0	1	2	5	1	0	.053	.182	.211
Storm Davis	2	1	0	0	0	0	0	0	0	1	0	0	.000	.000	.000
Ron Hassey	5	8	0	2	1	0	0	0	3	3	0	0	.250	.455	.250
Dave Henderson	5	20	1	6	1	2	0	0	2	7	0	0	.300	.364	.400
Glenn Hubbard	4	12	2	3	0	0	0	0	1	2	1	0	.250	.308	.250
Stan Javier	3	4	0	2	2	0	0	0	0	1	0	0	.500	.400	.500
Carney Lansford	5	18	2	3	1	0	0	0	2	2	0	0	.167	.250	.167
Mark McGwire	5	17	1	1	1	0	0	1	3	4	0	0	.059	.200	.235
Dave Parker	4	15	0	3	0	0	0	0	2	4	0	0	.200	.294	.200
Tony Phillips	2	4	1	1	0	0	0	0	1	2	0	0	.250	.400	.250
Luis Polonia	3	9	1	1	0	0	0	0	0	2	0	0	.111	.111	.111
Terry Steinbach	3	11	0	4	0	1	0	0	0	2	0	0	.364	.364	.455
Dave Stewart	2	3	1	0	0	0	0	0	1	3	0	0	.000	.250	.000
Walt Weiss	5	16	1	1	0	0	0	0	0	2	1	0	.063	.063	.063
Totals	5	158	11	28	11	3	0	2	17	41	3	0	.177	.260	.234

Pitching

Dodgers	G	GS	CG	IP	H	R	ER	BB	SO	W-L	Sv-Op	Hld	ERA
Tim Belcher	2	2	0	8.2	10	7	6	6	10	1-0	0-0	0	6.23
Orel Hershiser	2	2	2	18.0	7	2	2	6	17	2-0	0-0	0	1.00
Brian Holton	1	0	0	2.0	0	0	0	1	0	0-0	0-0	0	0.00
Jay Howell	2	0	0	2.2	3	1	1	1	2	0-1	1-1	0	3.38
Tim Leary	2	0	0	6.2	6	1	1	2	4	0-0	0-0	0	1.35
Alejandro Pena	2	0	0	5.0	2	0	0	1	7	1-0	0-0	0	0.00
John Tudor	1	1	0	1.1	0	0	0	0	1	0-0	0-0	0	0.00
Totals	5	5	2	44.1	28	11	10	17	41	4-1	1-1	0	2.03

Pitching

Athletics	G	GS	CG	IP	H	R	ER	BB	SO	W-L	Sv-Op	Hld	ERA
Todd Burns	1	0	0	0.1	0	0	0	0	0	0-0	0-0	0	0.00
Greg Cadaret	3	0	0	2.0	2	0	0	0	3	0-0	0-0	0	0.00
Storm Davis	2	2	0	8.0	14	10	10	1	7	0-2	0-0	0	11.25
Dennis Eckersley	2	0	0	1.2	2	2	2	1	2	0-1	0-1	0	10.80
Rick Honeycutt	3	0	0	3.1	0	0	0	0	5	1-0	0-0	0	0.00
Gene Nelson	3	0	0	6.1	4	1	1	3	3	0-0	0-0	0	1.42
Eric Plunk	2	0	0	1.2	0	0	0	0	3	0-0	0-0	0	0.00
Dave Stewart	2	2	0	14.1	12	7	5	5	5	0-1	0-0	0	3.14
Bob Welch	1	1	0	5.0	6	1	1	3	8	0-0	0-0	0	1.80
Matt Young	1	0	0	1.0	1	0	0	0	0	0-0	0-0	0	0.00
Totals	5	5	0	43.2	41	21	19	13	36	1-4	0-1	0	3.92

Fielding

Dodgers	Pos	G	PO	Ast	E	DP	PB	FPct
Tim Belcher	p	2	0	0	0	0	—	—
Mike Davis	rf	1	0	0	0	0	—	—
Rick Dempsey	c	2	13	1	0	0	0	1.000
Jose Gonzalez	lf	2	1	0	0	0	—	1.000
	rf	2	1	0	0	0	—	1.000
Alfredo Griffin	ss	5	7	12	1	1	—	.950
Jeff Hamilton	3b	5	2	6	1	1	—	.889
Mickey Hatcher	lf	5	6	0	0	0	—	1.000
	rf	1	2	0	0	0	—	1.000
Danny Heep	lf	1	0	0	0	0	—	—
Orel Hershiser	p	2	1	1	0	0	—	1.000
Brian Holton	p	1	0	1	0	0	—	1.000
Jay Howell	p	2	0	0	0	0	—	—
Tim Leary	p	2	1	3	0	1	—	1.000
Mike Marshall	rf	5	6	0	0	0	—	1.000
Alejandro Pena	p	2	0	0	0	0	—	—
Steve Sax	2b	5	11	11	0	2	—	1.000
Mike Scioscia	c	4	28	0	1	0	1	.966
John Shelby	cf	5	14	0	0	0	—	1.000
Franklin Stubbs	1b	5	34	0	0	3	—	1.000
John Tudor	p	1	0	0	0	0	—	—
Tracy Woodson	1b	3	6	1	0	0	—	1.000
Totals		5	133	36	3	8	1	.983

Fielding

Athletics	Pos	G	PO	Ast	E	DP	PB	FPct
Todd Burns	p	1	0	0	0	0	—	—
Greg Cadaret	p	3	0	0	0	0	—	—
Jose Canseco	rf	5	7	0	0	0	—	1.000
Storm Davis	p	2	2	1	0	0	—	1.000
Dennis Eckersley	p	2	0	0	0	0	—	—
Mike Gallego	2b	1	0	0	0	0	—	—
Ron Hassey	c	4	28	1	0	0	0	1.000
Dave Henderson	cf	5	13	0	0	0	—	1.000
Rick Honeycutt	p	3	0	0	0	0	—	—
Glenn Hubbard	2b	4	5	7	1	0	—	.923
Stan Javier	lf	2	1	0	0	0	—	1.000
Carney Lansford	3b	5	8	7	0	1	—	1.000
Mark McGwire	1b	5	40	3	0	2	—	1.000
Gene Nelson	p	3	1	2	0	0	—	1.000
Dave Parker	lf	2	4	0	0	0	—	1.000
Tony Phillips	2b	1	3	5	0	1	—	1.000
	lf	1	0	0	0	0	—	—
Eric Plunk	p	2	0	0	0	0	—	—
Luis Polonia	lf	2	2	0	0	0	—	1.000
Terry Steinbach	c	2	11	3	0	0	1	1.000
Dave Stewart	p	2	0	1	0	0	—	1.000
Walt Weiss	ss	5	5	11	1	1	—	.941
Bob Welch	p	1	1	1	0	0	—	1.000
Matt Young	p	1	0	1	0	0	—	1.000
Totals		5	131	43	2	5	1	.989

1989 Oakland Athletics (AL) 4, San Francisco Giants (NL) 0

Nothing could stop the Oakland A's—not even an earthquake. In a showdown of the two San Francisco Bay-area teams, Dave Stewart blanked the San Francisco Giants on five hits in the opener for a 5-0 victory. Game 2 was a virtual replay, as Terry Steinbach crunched a three-run homer and Mike Moore tossed seven strong innings for a 5-1 Oakland victory. Minutes before the start of Game 3, a serious earthquake hit the Bay area, inflicting widespread damage and casting doubt on the completion of the Series. The games eventually resumed 10 days later, and Oakland never missed a beat. They smashed five home runs in Game 3, cruising to a 13-7 win as Dave Stewart won his second game of the Series. Rickey Henderson had three hits and two RBI in the fourth game, and the A's held on for a 9-6 triumph to complete their somewhat delayed World Series sweep.

Game 1

Saturday, October 14

Giants	AB	R	H	RBI	BB	K	Avg
Brett Butler, cf	4	0	0	0	0	0	.000
Robby Thompson, 2b	4	0	0	0	0	1	.000
Will Clark, 1b	4	0	2	0	0	0	.500
Kevin Mitchell, lf	4	0	2	0	0	1	.500
Matt Williams, 3b-ss	4	0	0	0	0	2	.000
Ernest Riles, dh	4	0	0	0	0	1	.000
Candy Maldonado, rf	4	0	0	0	0	1	.000
Terry Kennedy, c	3	0	0	0	0	0	.000
Jose Uribe, ss	2	0	1	0	0	0	.500
Ken Oberkfell, ph-3b	0	0	0	0	1	0	—
TOTALS	33	0	5	0	1	6	.152

Athletics	AB	R	H	RBI	BB	K	Avg
Rickey Henderson, lf	5	0	2	1	0	2	.400
Carney Lansford, 3b	5	0	1	0	0	0	.200
Mike Gallego, 2b	0	0	0	0	0	0	—
Jose Canseco, rf	3	0	0	0	1	2	.000
Dave Parker, dh	4	1	1	1	0	1	.250
Dave Henderson, cf	3	1	0	0	1	0	.000
Mark McGwire, 1b	4	0	3	0	0	0	.750
Terry Steinbach, c	4	1	1	0	0	1	.250
Tony Phillips, 2b-3b	4	1	2	1	0	1	.500
Walt Weiss, ss	4	1	1	1	0	1	.250
TOTALS	36	5	11	4	2	8	.306

	1 2 3	4 5 6	7 8 9	R	H	E
Giants	0 0 0	0 0 0	0 0 0	0	5	1
Athletics	0 3 1	1 0 0	0 0 x	5	11	1

E—Kennedy, Stewart. LOB—Giants 7, Athletics 9. Scoring Position—Giants 0-for-6, Athletics 2-for-7. 2B—Clark (1). HR—Parker (1), Weiss (1).

Giants	IP	H	R	ER	BB	K	ERA
Scott Garrelts (L, 0-1)	4.0	7	5	4	1	5	9.00
Atlee Hammaker	1.2	3	0	0	0	2	0.00
Jeff Brantley	1.1	1	0	0	1	0	0.00
Mike LaCoss	1.0	0	0	0	0	1	0.00

Athletics	IP	H	R	ER	BB	K	ERA
Dave Stewart (W, 1-0)	9.0	5	0	0	1	6	0.00

PB—Steinbach. Time—2:45. Attendance—49,385. Umpires—HP, Garcia. 1B, Runge. 2B, Voltaggio. 3B, Rennert.

Game 2

Sunday, October 15

Giants	AB	R	H	RBI	BB	K	Avg
Brett Butler, cf	2	0	1	0	2	1	.167
Robby Thompson, 2b	3	0	0	1	0	1	.000
Will Clark, 1b	4	0	0	0	0	1	.250
Kevin Mitchell, lf	4	0	1	0	0	0	.375
Matt Williams, 3b-ss	4	0	0	0	0	2	.000
Ernest Riles, dh	3	0	0	0	0	0	.000
Candy Maldonado, rf	3	0	0	0	0	1	.000
Terry Kennedy, c	3	0	1	0	0	2	.167
Jose Uribe, ss	2	1	0	0	0	0	.250
Ken Oberkfell, ph-3b	1	0	1	0	0	0	1.000
TOTALS	29	1	4	1	2	8	.145

Athletics	AB	R	H	RBI	BB	K	Avg
Rickey Henderson, lf	3	1	3	0	1	0	.625
Carney Lansford, 3b	3	0	1	1	1	0	.250
Jose Canseco, rf	2	1	0	0	2	1	.000
Dave Parker, dh	4	1	1	1	0	1	.250
Dave Henderson, cf	3	1	0	0	1	2	.000
Mark McGwire, 1b	4	0	1	0	0	2	.500
Terry Steinbach, c	4	1	1	3	0	0	.250
Tony Phillips, 2b	3	0	0	0	0	0	.286
Walt Weiss, ss	3	0	0	0	0	1	.143
TOTALS	29	5	7	5	5	7	.277

	1 2 3	4 5 6	7 8 9	R	H	E
Giants	0 0 1	0 0 0	0 0 0	1	4	0
Athletics	1 0 0	4 0 0	0 0 x	5	7	0

DP—Giants 2 (Williams to Thompson to Clark; Kennedy to Williams), Athletics 1 (Weiss to Phillips to McGwire). LOB—Giants 4, Athletics 5. Scoring Position—Giants 0-for-5, Athletics 2-for-12. 2B—Lansford (1), Parker (1), McGwire (1). 3B—RHenderson (1). HR—Steinbach (1). SF—Thompson. GDP—Thompson, Lansford. SB—Butler 2 (2), RHenderson (1). CS—RHenderson (1).

Giants	IP	H	R	ER	BB	K	ERA
Rick Reuschel (L, 0-1)	4.0	5	5	5	4	2	11.25
Kelly Downs	2.0	1	0	0	0	2	0.00
Craig Lefferts	1.0	1	0	0	1	1	0.00
Steve Bedrosian	1.0	0	0	0	0	2	0.00

Athletics	IP	H	R	ER	BB	K	ERA
Mike Moore (W, 1-0)	7.0	4	1	1	2	7	1.29
Rick Honeycutt	1.1	0	0	0	0	1	0.00
Dennis Eckersley	0.2	0	0	0	0	0	0.00

Reuschel pitched to two batters in the 5th. Moore pitched to one batter in the 8th.

WP—Moore 2. Time—2:47. Attendance—49,388. Umpires—HP, Runge. 1B, Voltaggio. 2B, Rennert. 3B, Clark.

Game 3

Friday, October 27

Athletics	AB	R	H	RBI	BB	K	Avg
Rickey Henderson, lf	5	1	1	0	1	0	.462
Gene Nelson, p	0	0	0	0	0	0	—
Todd Burns, p	0	0	0	0	0	0	—
Carney Lansford, 3b	4	4	3	2	1	1	.417
Rick Honeycutt, p	0	0	0	0	0	0	—
Mike Gallego, ph-3b	1	0	0	0	0	0	.000
Jose Canseco, rf	5	3	3	3	0	0	.300
Stan Javier, rf	0	0	0	0	0	0	—
Mark McGwire, 1b	4	0	0	1	1	1	.333
Dave Henderson, cf	4	2	3	4	0	0	.300
Terry Steinbach, c	4	0	1	1	1	0	.250
Tony Phillips, 2b-3b-lf	5	1	1	1	0	2	.250
Walt Weiss, ss	5	1	1	0	0	0	.167
Dave Stewart, p	3	0	0	0	0	1	.000
Lance Blankenship, ph-2b	2	1	1	0	0	0	.500
TOTALS	42	13	14	12	4	5	.303

Giants	AB	R	H	RBI	BB	K	Avg
Brett Butler, cf	3	0	0	0	0	0	.111
Donell Nixon, ph-cf	2	1	1	0	0	0	.500
Robby Thompson, 2b	3	0	0	0	0	2	.000
Greg Litton, ph-2b	2	0	2	1	0	0	1.000
Will Clark, 1b	4	1	1	0	1	2	.250
Kevin Mitchell, lf	5	1	1	0	0	1	.308
Ken Oberkfell, 3b	2	1	1	0	2	0	.667
Matt Williams, ss	4	1	1	1	0	1	.083
Terry Kennedy, c	3	0	1	2	0	1	.222
Kirt Manwaring, c	1	1	1	0	0	0	1.000
Pat Sheridan, rf	2	0	0	0	0	0	.000
Jeff Brantley, p	0	0	0	0	0	0	—
Ernest Riles, ph	1	0	0	0	0	0	.000
Atlee Hammaker, p	0	0	0	0	0	0	—
Craig Lefferts, p	0	0	0	0	0	0	—
Bill Bathe, ph	1	1	1	3	0	0	1.000
Scott Garrelts, p	1	0	0	0	0	1	.000
Kelly Downs, p	0	0	0	0	0	0	—
Candy Maldonado, rf	3	0	0	0	0	2	.000
TOTALS	37	7	10	7	3	10	.189

	1 2 3	4 5 6	7 8 9	R	H	E
Athletics	2 0 0	2 4 1	0 4 0	13	14	0
Giants	0 1 0	2 0 0	0 0 4	7	10	3

E—Oberkfell, Lefferts, Mitchell. DP—Giants 1 (Oberkfell to Thompson to Clark). LOB—Athletics 7, Giants 6. Scoring Position—Athletics 5-for-15, Giants 2-for-5. 2B—RHenderson (1), DHenderson (1), Litton (1), Manwaring (1). HR—Lansford (1), Canseco (1), DHenderson 2 (2), Phillips (1), Williams (1), Bathe (1). GDP—DHenderson. SB—RHenderson 2 (3).

Athletics	IP	H	R	ER	BB	K	ERA
Dave Stewart (W, 2-0)	7.0	5	3	3	1	8	1.69
Rick Honeycutt	1.0	1	0	0	0	1	0.00
Gene Nelson	0.2	3	4	4	1	1	54.00
Todd Burns	0.1	1	0	0	1	0	0.00

Giants	IP	H	R	ER	BB	K	ERA
Scott Garrelts (L, 0-2)	3.1	6	4	4	0	3	9.82
Kelly Downs	1.0	2	4	4	2	1	12.00
Jeff Brantley	2.2	1	1	1	2	1	2.25
Atlee Hammaker	0.2	5	4	4	0	0	15.43
Craig Lefferts	1.1	0	0	0	0	0	0.00

Balk—Brantley. HBP—DHenderson by Hammaker. Time—3:30. Attendance—62,038. Umpires—HP, Voltaggio. 1B, Rennert. 2B, Clark. 3B, Gregg.

Game 4

Saturday, October 28

Athletics	AB	R	H	RBI	BB	K	Avg
Rickey Henderson, lf	6	2	3	2	0	0	.474
Carney Lansford, 3b	4	1	2	1	1	0	.438
Jose Canseco, rf	4	1	2	0	1	0	.357
Mark McGwire, 1b	5	0	1	0	0	0	.294
Dave Henderson, cf	3	2	1	0	2	1	.308
Terry Steinbach, c	4	1	1	3	1	0	.250
Tony Phillips, 2b	5	0	1	1	0	0	.235
Walt Weiss, ss	3	1	0	0	2	0	.133
Mike Moore, p	3	1	1	2	0	1	.333
Ken Phelps, ph	1	0	0	0	0	0	.000
Gene Nelson, p	0	0	0	0	0	0	—
Rick Honeycutt, p	0	0	0	0	0	0	—
Todd Burns, p	0	0	0	0	0	0	—
Dave Parker, ph	1	0	0	0	0	0	.222
Dennis Eckersley, p	0	0	0	0	0	0	—
TOTALS	39	9	12	9	7	2	.307

Giants	AB	R	H	RBI	BB	K	Avg
Brett Butler, cf	5	1	3	1	0	0	.286
Ken Oberkfell, 3b	3	0	0	0	0	0	.333
Robby Thompson, ph-2b	1	0	1	1	0	0	.091
Steve Bedrosian, p	0	0	0	0	0	0	—
Will Clark, 1b	4	1	1	0	0	0	.250
Kevin Mitchell, lf	4	1	1	2	0	1	.294
Matt Williams, ss-3b	4	0	1	0	0	1	.125
Terry Kennedy, c	3	1	0	0	1	0	.167
Greg Litton, 2b-3b-2b	4	1	1	2	0	0	.500
Donell Nixon, rf	3	0	0	0	1	1	.200
Don Robinson, p	0	0	0	0	0	0	—
Mike LaCoss, p	1	0	0	0	0	0	.000
Bill Bathe, ph	1	0	0	0	0	0	.500
Jeff Brantley, p	0	0	0	0	0	0	—
Kelly Downs, p	0	0	0	0	0	0	—
Ernest Riles, ph	0	0	0	0	0	0	.000
Candy Maldonado, ph	1	1	1	0	0	0	.091
Craig Lefferts, p	0	0	0	0	0	0	—
Jose Uribe, ss	1	0	0	0	0	0	.200
TOTALS	35	6	9	6	2	3	.208

	1 2 3	4 5 6	7 8 9	R	H	E
Athletics	1 3 0	0 3 1	0 1 0	9	12	0
Giants	0 0 0	0 0 2	4 0 0	6	9	0

LOB—Athletics 10, Giants 4. Scoring Position—Athletics 6-for-14, Giants 2-for-4. 2B—DHenderson (2), Phillips (1), Moore (1), Butler (1). 3B—RHenderson (2), Steinbach (1), Maldonado (1). HR—RHenderson (1), Mitchell (1), Litton (1). SB—Canseco (1). CS—Butler (1).

Athletics	IP	H	R	ER	BB	K	ERA
Mike Moore (W, 2-0)	6.0	5	2	2	1	3	2.08
Gene Nelson	0.1	1	2	2	1	0	54.00
Rick Honeycutt	0.1	3	2	2	0	0	6.75
Todd Burns (H, 1)	1.1	0	0	0	0	0	0.00
Dennis Eckersley (S, 1)	1.0	0	0	0	0	0	0.00

Giants	IP	H	R	ER	BB	K	ERA
Don Robinson (L, 0-1)	1.2	4	4	4	1	0	21.60
Mike LaCoss	3.1	4	3	3	3	1	6.23
Jeff Brantley	0.1	3	1	1	0	0	4.15
Kelly Downs	1.2	0	0	0	0	1	7.71
Craig Lefferts	0.1	1	1	1	1	0	3.38
Steve Bedrosian	1.2	0	0	0	2	0	0.00

Time—3:07. Attendance—62,032. Umpires—HP, Rennert. 1B, Clark. 2B, Gregg. 3B, Garcia.

1989 World Series—Composite Statistics

Batting

Athletics	G	AB	R	H	RBI	2B	3B	HR	BB	SO	SB	CS	Avg	OBP	Slg
Lance Blankenship	1	2	1	1	0	0	0	0	0	0	0	0	.500	.500	.500
Jose Canseco	4	14	5	5	3	0	0	1	4	3	1	0	.357	.500	.571
Mike Gallego	2	1	0	0	0	0	0	0	0	0	0	0	.000	.000	.000
Dave Henderson	4	13	6	4	4	2	0	2	4	3	0	0	.308	.500	.923
Rickey Henderson	4	19	4	9	3	1	2	1	2	2	3	1	.474	.524	.895
Carney Lansford	4	16	5	7	4	1	0	1	3	1	0	0	.438	.526	.688
Mark McGwire	4	17	0	5	1	1	0	0	1	3	0	0	.294	.333	.353
Mike Moore	2	3	1	1	2	1	0	0	0	1	0	0	.333	.333	.667
Dave Parker	3	9	2	2	2	1	0	1	0	2	0	0	.222	.222	.667
Ken Phelps	1	1	0	0	0	0	0	0	0	0	0	0	.000	.000	.000
Tony Phillips	4	17	2	4	3	1	0	1	0	3	0	0	.235	.235	.471
Terry Steinbach	4	16	3	4	7	0	1	1	2	1	0	0	.250	.333	.563
Dave Stewart	2	3	0	0	0	0	0	0	0	0	1	0	.000	.000	.000
Walt Weiss	4	15	3	2	1	0	0	1	2	2	0	0	.133	.235	.333
Totals	4	146	32	44	30	8	3	9	18	22	4	1	.301	.382	.582

Giants	G	AB	R	H	RBI	2B	3B	HR	BB	SO	SB	CS	Avg	OBP	Slg
Bill Bathe	2	2	1	1	3	0	0	1	0	0	0	0	.500	.500	2.000
Brett Butler	4	14	1	4	1	1	0	0	2	1	2	1	.286	.375	.357
Will Clark	4	16	2	4	0	1	0	0	1	3	0	0	.250	.294	.313
Scott Garrelts	2	1	0	0	0	0	0	0	0	1	0	0	.000	.000	.000
Terry Kennedy	4	12	1	2	2	0	0	0	1	3	0	0	.167	.231	.167
Mike LaCoss	2	1	0	0	0	0	0	0	0	0	0	0	.000	.000	.000
Greg Litton	2	6	1	3	3	1	0	1	0	0	0	0	.500	.500	1.167
Candy Maldonado	4	11	1	1	0	0	1	0	0	4	0	0	.091	.091	.273
Kirt Manwaring	1	1	1	1	0	1	0	0	0	0	0	0	1.000	1.000	2.000
Kevin Mitchell	4	17	2	5	2	0	0	1	0	3	0	0	.294	.294	.471
Donell Nixon	2	5	1	1	0	0	0	0	1	1	0	0	.200	.333	.200
Ken Oberkfell	4	6	1	2	0	0	0	0	3	0	0	0	.333	.556	.333
Ernest Riles	4	8	0	0	0	0	0	0	0	1	0	0	.000	.000	.000
Pat Sheridan	1	2	0	0	0	0	0	0	0	0	0	0	.000	.000	.000
Robby Thompson	4	11	0	1	2	0	0	0	0	4	0	0	.091	.083	.091
Jose Uribe	3	5	1	1	0	0	0	0	0	0	0	0	.200	.200	.200
Matt Williams	4	16	1	2	1	0	0	1	0	6	0	0	.125	.125	.313
Totals	4	134	14	28	14	4	1	4	8	27	2	1	.209	.252	.343

Pitching

Athletics	G	GS	CG	IP	H	R	ER	BB	SO	W-L	Sv-Op	Hld	ERA
Todd Burns	2	0	0	1.2	1	0	0	1	0	0-0	0-0	1	0.00
Dennis Eckersley	2	0	0	1.2	0	0	0	0	0	0-0	1-1	0	0.00
Rick Honeycutt	3	0	0	2.2	4	2	2	0	2	0-0	0-0	0	6.75
Mike Moore	2	2	0	13.0	9	3	3	3	10	2-0	0-0	0	2.08
Gene Nelson	2	0	0	1.0	4	6	6	2	1	0-0	0-0	0	54.00
Dave Stewart	2	2	1	16.0	10	3	3	2	14	2-0	0-0	0	1.69
Totals	4	4	1	36.0	28	14	14	8	27	4-0	1-1	1	3.50

Giants	G	GS	CG	IP	H	R	ER	BB	SO	W-L	Sv-Op	Hld	ERA
Steve Bedrosian	2	0	0	2.2	0	0	0	2	2	0-0	0-0	0	0.00
Jeff Brantley	3	0	0	4.1	5	2	2	3	1	0-0	0-0	0	4.15
Kelly Downs	3	0	0	4.2	3	4	4	2	4	0-0	0-0	0	7.71
Scott Garrelts	2	2	0	7.1	13	9	8	1	8	0-2	0-0	0	9.82
Atlee Hammaker	2	0	0	2.1	8	4	4	0	2	0-0	0-0	0	15.43
Mike LaCoss	2	0	0	4.1	4	3	3	3	2	0-0	0-0	0	6.23
Craig Lefferts	3	0	0	2.2	2	1	1	2	1	0-0	0-0	0	3.38
Rick Reuschel	1	1	0	4.0	5	5	5	4	2	0-1	0-0	0	11.25
Don Robinson	1	1	0	1.2	4	4	4	1	0	0-1	0-0	0	21.60
Totals	4	4	0	34.0	44	32	31	18	22	0-4	0-0	0	8.21

Fielding

Athletics	Pos	G	PO	Ast	E	DP	PB	FPct
Lance Blankenship	2b	1	1	0	0	0	—	1.000
Todd Burns	p	2	0	0	0	0	—	—
Jose Canseco	rf	4	6	0	0	0	—	1.000
Dennis Eckersley	p	2	1	0	0	0	—	1.000
Mike Gallego	2b	1	0	0	0	0	—	—
	3b	1	0	0	0	0	—	—
Dave Henderson	cf	4	13	0	0	0	—	1.000
Rickey Henderson	lf	4	9	0	0	0	—	1.000
Rick Honeycutt	p	3	0	0	0	0	—	—
Stan Javier	rf	1	0	0	0	0	—	—
Carney Lansford	3b	4	5	5	0	0	—	1.000
Mark McGwire	1b	4	28	2	0	1	—	1.000
Mike Moore	p	2	0	3	0	0	—	1.000
Gene Nelson	p	2	0	0	0	0	—	—
Tony Phillips	2b	4	7	13	0	1	—	1.000
	3b	2	0	2	0	0	—	1.000
	lf	1	1	0	0	0	—	1.000
Terry Steinbach	c	4	27	2	0	0	1	1.000
Dave Stewart	p	2	3	0	1	0	—	.750
Walt Weiss	ss	4	7	8	0	1	—	1.000
Totals		4	108	35	1	3	1	.993

Giants	Pos	G	PO	Ast	E	DP	PB	FPct
Steve Bedrosian	p	2	0	0	0	0	—	—
Jeff Brantley	p	3	1	0	0	0	—	1.000
Brett Butler	cf	4	9	0	0	0	—	1.000
Will Clark	1b	4	40	2	0	2	—	1.000
Kelly Downs	p	3	0	0	0	0	—	—
Scott Garrelts	p	2	0	2	0	0	—	1.000
Atlee Hammaker	p	2	0	1	0	0	—	1.000
Terry Kennedy	c	4	23	1	1	1	0	.960
Mike LaCoss	p	2	1	0	0	0	—	1.000
Craig Lefferts	p	3	0	1	1	0	—	.500
Greg Litton	2b	2	2	3	0	0	—	1.000
	3b	1	0	0	0	0	—	—
Candy Maldonado	rf	3	5	0	0	0	—	1.000
Kirt Manwaring	c	1	0	0	0	0	0	—
Kevin Mitchell	lf	4	10	0	1	0	—	.909
Donell Nixon	rf	1	2	0	0	0	—	1.000
	cf	1	0	0	0	0	—	—
Ken Oberkfell	3b	4	0	5	1	1	—	.833
Rick Reuschel	p	1	0	0	0	0	—	—
Don Robinson	p	1	0	0	0	0	—	—
Pat Sheridan	rf	1	0	0	0	0	—	—
Robby Thompson	2b	4	4	10	0	2	—	1.000
Jose Uribe	ss	3	1	3	0	0	—	1.000
Matt Williams	ss	4	2	6	0	0	—	1.000
	3b	3	2	6	0	2	—	1.000
Totals		4	102	40	4	8	0	.973

1990 Cincinnati Reds (NL) 4, Oakland Athletics (AL) 0

For the second time in three years, the Oakland A's were upset in the World Series by a team that was considered far inferior. This time it was the Cincinnati Reds. The A's might have known they were in trouble when their best big-game pitcher, Dave Stewart, was shelled for four runs in four innings in Game 1. Jose Rijo threw seven shutout innings for a 7-0 Reds victory. In the second game, Bob Welch took a 4-3 lead into the eighth inning, until Billy Hatcher ended up with a leadoff triple on a ball that some thought Jose Canseco should have caught. Hatcher went on to score the tying run, and Cincinnati beat Dennis Eckersley in the 10th to win, 5-4. Chris Sabo hit a pair of home runs in Game 3, as the Reds exploded for seven runs in the third inning and won, 8-3. Dave Stewart was sharp in Game 4, but not sharp enough. The Reds pushed across two runs in the top of the eighth to take the game 2-1, completing their sweep. Jose Rijo allowed two hits and one run in eight-plus innings for his second win of the Series.

Game 1

Tuesday, October 16

Athletics	AB	R	H	RBI	BB	K	Avg
Rickey Henderson, lf	5	0	3	0	0	1	.600
Willie McGee, cf	5	0	1	0	0	0	.200
Jose Canseco, rf	2	0	0	0	2	1	.000
Mark McGwire, 1b	3	0	0	0	1	0	.000
Carney Lansford, 3b	4	0	2	0	0	0	.500
Terry Steinbach, c	4	0	1	0	0	1	.250
Willie Randolph, 2b	4	0	1	0	0	0	.250
Mike Gallego, ss	4	0	0	0	0	2	.000
Dave Stewart, p	1	0	0	0	0	1	.000
Doug Jennings, ph	1	0	1	0	0	0	1.000
Todd Burns, p	0	0	0	0	0	0	—
Gene Nelson, p	0	0	0	0	0	0	—
Ron Hassey, ph	1	0	0	0	0	0	.000
Scott Sanderson, p	0	0	0	0	0	0	—
Dennis Eckersley, p	0	0	0	0	0	0	—
Dave Henderson, ph	1	0	0	0	0	1	.000
TOTALS	35	0	9	0	3	7	.257

Reds	AB	R	H	RBI	BB	K	Avg
Barry Larkin, ss	4	1	0	0	1	0	.000
Billy Hatcher, cf	3	3	3	1	1	0	1.000
Paul O'Neill, rf	2	1	0	1	2	1	.000
Eric Davis, lf	4	2	2	3	0	0	.500
Hal Morris, 1b	4	0	1	0	0	1	.250
Chris Sabo, 3b	3	0	1	2	1	1	.333
Joe Oliver, c	4	0	1	0	0	0	.250
Mariano Duncan, 2b	3	0	1	0	1	1	.333
Jose Rijo, p	3	0	1	0	0	0	.333
Rob Dibble, p	0	0	0	0	0	0	—
Todd Benzinger, ph	1	0	0	0	0	0	.000
Randy Myers, p	0	0	0	0	0	0	—
TOTALS	31	7	10	7	6	4	.323

	1 2 3	4 5 6	7 8 9	R H E
Athletics	0 0 0	0 0 0	0 0 0	0 9 1
Reds	2 0 2	0 3 0	0 0 x	7 10 0

E—Gallego. DP—Athletics 2 (Randolph to McGwire; Gallego to Randolph to McGwire), Reds 1 (Duncan to Larkin to Morris). LOB—Athletics 11, Reds 6. Scoring Position—Athletics 0-for-9, Reds 2-for-6. 2B—RHenderson 2 (2), Hatcher 2 (2). HR—Davis (1). GDP—McGee, Larkin, Oliver. SB—McGee (1), Lansford (1). CS—Sabo (1).

Athletics	IP	H	R	ER	BB	K	ERA
Dave Stewart (L, 0-1)	4.0	3	4	3	4	3	6.75
Todd Burns	0.2	4	3	3	1	0	40.50
Gene Nelson	1.1	2	0	0	1	0	0.00
Scott Sanderson	1.0	1	0	0	0	0	0.00
Dennis Eckersley	1.0	0	0	0	0	1	0.00

Reds	IP	H	R	ER	BB	K	ERA
Jose Rijo (W, 1-0)	7.0	7	0	0	2	5	0.00
Rob Dibble	1.0	1	0	0	1	0	0.00
Randy Myers	1.0	1	0	0	0	2	0.00

WP—Dibble. Time—2:38. Attendance—55,830. Umpires—HP, Pulli. 1B, Roe. 2B, Quick. 3B, Hendry.

Game 2

Wednesday, October 17

Athletics	AB	R	H	RBI	BB	K	Avg
Rickey Henderson, lf	4	1	1	0	1	0	.444
Carney Lansford, 3b	4	0	1	0	0	0	.375
Jose Canseco, rf	5	1	1	2	0	2	.143
Mark McGwire, 1b	4	1	2	0	1	2	.286
Dave Henderson, cf	4	1	2	0	1	0	.400
Terry Steinbach, c	0	0	0	0	0	0	.250
Willie Randolph, 2b	4	0	0	0	1	0	.125
Ron Hassey, c	4	0	2	1	0	0	.400
Mike Bordick, pr-ss	0	0	0	0	0	0	—
Mike Gallego, ss	4	0	1	1	0	0	.125
Harold Baines, ph	1	0	0	0	0	1	.000
Dennis Eckersley, p	0	0	0	0	0	0	—
Bob Welch, p	3	0	0	0	0	2	.000
Rick Honeycutt, p	0	0	0	0	0	0	—
Willie McGee, cf	0	0	0	0	0	0	.200
TOTALS	37	4	10	4	4	7	.257

Reds	AB	R	H	RBI	BB	K	Avg
Barry Larkin, ss	5	1	3	0	0	0	.333
Billy Hatcher, cf	4	2	4	1	1	0	1.000
Paul O'Neill, rf	4	0	0	0	1	0	.000
Eric Davis, lf	5	0	0	1	0	0	.222
Hal Morris, 1b	3	0	0	0	0	0	.143
Glenn Braggs, ph	1	0	0	1	0	0	.000
Rob Dibble, p	0	0	0	0	0	0	—
Billy Bates, ph	1	1	1	0	0	0	1.000
Chris Sabo, 3b	5	0	3	0	0	1	.500
Joe Oliver, c	5	1	2	1	0	0	.333
Mariano Duncan, 2b	3	0	0	0	1	0	.167
Danny Jackson, p	1	0	0	0	0	1	.000
Scott Scudder, p	0	0	0	0	0	0	—
Ron Oester, ph	1	0	1	1	0	0	1.000
Jack Armstrong, p	0	0	0	0	0	0	—
Herm Winningham, ph	1	0	0	0	0	0	.000
Norm Charlton, p	0	0	0	0	0	0	—
Todd Benzinger, 1b	1	0	0	0	0	0	.000
TOTALS	40	5	14	5	3	2	.338

	1 2 3	4 5 6	7 8 9 10	R H E
Athletics	1 0 3	0 0 0	0 0 0 0	4 10 2
Reds	2 0 0	1 0 0	0 1 0 1	5 14 2

E—Hassey, Jackson, McGwire, Oliver. DP—Reds 1 (Larkin to Duncan to Benzinger). LOB—Athletics 10, Reds 10. Scoring Position—Athletics 1-for-10, Reds 3-for-14. 2B—Larkin (1), Hatcher 2 (4), Oliver (1). 3B—Hatcher (1). HR—Canseco (1). S—Lansford, Welch. SF—Hassey. GDP—Canseco. SB—RHenderson (1).

Athletics	IP	H	R	ER	BB	K	ERA
Bob Welch	7.1	9	4	4	2	2	4.91
Rick Honeycutt (BS, 1)	1.2	2	0	0	1	0	0.00
Dennis Eckersley (L, 0-1)	0.1	3	1	1	0	0	6.75

Reds	IP	H	R	ER	BB	K	ERA
Danny Jackson	2.2	6	4	3	2	0	10.13
Scott Scudder	1.1	0	0	0	2	2	0.00
Jack Armstrong	3.0	1	0	0	0	3	0.00
Norm Charlton	1.0	1	0	0	0	0	0.00
Rob Dibble (W, 1-0)	2.0	2	0	0	0	2	0.00

Time—3:31. Attendance—55,832. Umpires—HP, Roe. 1B, Quick. 2B, Hendry. 3B, Marsh.

Game 3

Friday, October 19

Reds	AB	R	H	RBI	BB	K	Avg
Barry Larkin, ss	5	0	2	1	0	0	.357
Billy Hatcher, cf	5	1	2	0	0	0	.750
Paul O'Neill, rf	3	1	1	0	2	0	.111
Eric Davis, lf	5	1	2	1	0	0	.286
Hal Morris, dh	4	0	0	1	1	0	.091
Chris Sabo, 3b	4	2	2	3	1	0	.500
Todd Benzinger, 1b	5	1	2	0	0	0	.286
Joe Oliver, c	5	1	2	1	0	1	.357
Mariano Duncan, 2b	4	1	1	1	0	0	.200
TOTALS	40	8	14	8	4	1	.340

Athletics	AB	R	H	RBI	BB	K	Avg
Rickey Henderson, lf	3	1	1	1	1	1	.417
Carney Lansford, 3b	3	0	0	0	1	0	.273
Jose Canseco, rf	4	0	0	0	0	1	.091
Dave Henderson, cf	4	1	1	0	0	0	.333
Harold Baines, dh	4	1	1	2	0	1	.200
Mark McGwire, 1b	4	0	1	0	0	1	.273
Terry Steinbach, c	4	0	0	0	0	0	.125
Willie Randolph, 2b	4	0	3	0	0	0	.333
Mike Gallego, ss	2	0	0	0	0	0	.100
Willie McGee, ph	1	0	0	0	0	1	.167
Mike Bordick, ss	0	0	0	0	0	0	—
Lance Blankenship, ph	1	0	0	0	0	1	.000
TOTALS	34	3	7	3	2	5	.240

	1 2 3	4 5 6	7 8 9	R H E
Reds	0 1 7	0 0 0	0 0 0	8 14 1
Athletics	0 2 1	0 0 0	0 0 0	3 7 1

E—McGwire, Oliver. DP—Athletics 2 (Gallego to Randolph to McGwire; Randolph to McGwire). LOB—Reds 9, Athletics 6. Scoring Position—Reds 5-for-12, Athletics 1-for-4. 2B—Oliver (2), DHenderson (1). 3B—Larkin (1). HR—Sabo 2 (2), RHenderson (1), Baines (1). GDP—Hatcher, Benzinger. SB—O'Neill (1), Duncan (1), RHenderson (2), Randolph (1).

Reds	IP	H	R	ER	BB	K	ERA
Tom Browning (W, 1-0)	6.0	6	3	3	2	2	4.50
Rob Dibble	1.2	0	0	0	0	2	0.00
Randy Myers	1.1	1	0	0	0	1	0.00

Athletics	IP	H	R	ER	BB	K	ERA
Mike Moore (L, 0-1)	2.2	8	6	2	0	1	6.75
Scott Sanderson	0.2	3	2	2	1	0	10.80
Joe Klink	0.0	0	0	0	1	0	—
Gene Nelson	3.2	1	0	0	1	0	0.00
Todd Burns	1.0	1	0	0	1	0	16.20
Curt Young	1.0	1	0	0	0	0	0.00

Klink pitched to one batter in the 4th. Browning pitched to one batter in the 7th.

WP—Sanderson, Burns. Time—3:01. Attendance—48,269. Umpires—HP, Quick. 1B, Hendry. 2B, Marsh. 3B, Froemming.

Game 4

Saturday, October 20

Reds	AB	R	H	RBI	BB	K	Avg
Barry Larkin, ss	3	1	1	0	1	0	.353
Billy Hatcher, cf	0	0	0	0	0	0	.750
Herm Winningham, cf	3	1	2	0	0	0	.500
Paul O'Neill, rf	3	0	0	0	0	1	.083
Eric Davis, lf	0	0	0	0	0	0	.286
Glenn Braggs, ph-lf	3	0	0	1	1	0	.000
Hal Morris, dh	3	0	0	1	0	0	.071
Chris Sabo, 3b	4	0	3	0	0	0	.563
Todd Benzinger, 1b	4	0	0	0	0	0	.182
Joe Oliver, c	4	0	1	0	0	0	.333
Mariano Duncan, 2b	4	0	0	0	0	1	.143
TOTALS	31	2	7	2	2	2	.309

Athletics	AB	R	H	RBI	BB	K	Avg
Rickey Henderson, lf	3	0	0	0	1	2	.333
Willie McGee, rf	4	1	1	0	0	1	.200
Dave Henderson, cf	4	0	0	0	0	2	.231
Harold Baines, dh	2	0	0	0	1	0	.143
Jose Canseco, ph-dh	1	0	0	0	0	0	.083
Carney Lansford, 3b	4	0	1	1	0	0	.267
Jamie Quirk, c	3	0	0	0	0	2	.000
Mark McGwire, 1b	3	0	0	0	0	1	.214
Willie Randolph, 2b	3	0	0	0	0	0	.267
Mike Gallego, ss	1	0	0	0	1	1	.091
Ron Hassey, ph	1	0	0	0	0	0	.333
Mike Bordick, ss	0	0	0	0	0	0	—
TOTALS	29	1	2	1	3	9	.215

	1 2 3	4 5 6	7 8 9	R H E
Reds	0 0 0	0 0 0	0 2 0	2 7 1
Athletics	1 0 0	0 0 0	0 0 0	1 2 1

E—Stewart, Oliver. DP—Athletics 1 (Randolph to Gallego to McGwire). LOB—Reds 7, Athletics 4. Scoring Position—Reds 0-for-9, Athletics 1-for-4. 2B—Sabo (1), Oliver (3), McGee (1). S—O'Neill. SF—Morris. GDP—Morris. SB—RHenderson (3), Gallego (1). CS—Hatcher (1).

Reds	IP	H	R	ER	BB	K	ERA
Jose Rijo (W, 2-0)	8.1	2	1	1	3	9	0.59
Randy Myers (S, 1)	0.2	0	0	0	0	0	0.00

Athletics	IP	H	R	ER	BB	K	ERA
Dave Stewart (L, 0-2)	9.0	7	2	1	2	2	2.77

HBP—Hatcher by Stewart. Time—2:48. Attendance—48,613. Umpires—HP, Hendry. 1B, Marsh. 2B, Froemming. 3B, Pulli.

1990 World Series—Composite Statistics

Batting

Reds	G	AB	R	H	RBI	2B	3B	HR	BB	SO	SB	CS	Avg	OBP	Slg
Billy Bates	1	1	1	1	0	0	0	0	0	0	0	0	1.000	1.000	1.000
Todd Benzinger	4	11	1	2	0	0	0	0	0	0	0	0	.182	.182	.182
Glenn Braggs	2	4	0	0	2	0	0	0	1	0	0	0	.000	.200	.000
Eric Davis	4	14	3	4	5	0	0	1	0	0	0	0	.286	.286	.500
Mariano Duncan	4	14	1	2	1	0	0	0	2	2	1	0	.143	.250	.143
Billy Hatcher	4	12	6	9	2	4	1	0	2	0	0	1	.750	.800	1.250
Danny Jackson	1	1	0	0	0	0	0	0	0	1	0	0	.000	.000	.000
Barry Larkin	4	17	3	6	1	1	1	0	2	0	0	0	.353	.421	.529
Hal Morris	4	14	0	1	2	0	0	0	1	1	0	0	.071	.125	.071
Paul O'Neill	4	12	2	1	1	0	0	0	5	2	1	0	.083	.353	.083
Ron Oester	1	1	0	1	1	0	0	0	0	0	0	0	1.000	1.000	1.000
Joe Oliver	4	18	2	6	2	3	0	0	0	1	0	0	.333	.333	.333
Jose Rijo	2	3	0	1	0	0	0	0	0	0	0	0	.333	.333	.333
Chris Sabo	4	16	2	9	5	1	0	2	2	2	0	1	.563	.611	1.000
Herm Winningham	2	4	1	2	0	0	0	0	0	0	0	0	.500	.500	.500
Totals	4	142	22	45	22	9	2	3	15	9	2	2	.317	.384	.472

Batting

Athletics	G	AB	R	H	RBI	2B	3B	HR	BB	SO	SB	CS	Avg	OBP	Slg
Harold Baines	3	7	1	1	2	0	0	1	1	2	0	0	.143	.250	.571
Lance Blankenship	1	1	0	0	0	0	0	0	0	1	0	0	.000	.000	.000
Jose Canseco	4	12	1	1	2	0	0	1	2	3	0	0	.083	.214	.333
Mike Gallego	4	11	0	1	1	0	0	0	1	3	1	0	.091	.167	.091
Ron Hassey	3	6	0	2	1	0	0	0	0	0	0	0	.333	.286	.333
Dave Henderson	4	13	2	3	0	1	0	0	1	3	0	0	.231	.286	.308
Rickey Henderson	4	15	2	5	1	2	0	1	3	4	3	0	.333	.444	.667
Rick Honeycutt	1	0	0	0	0	0	0	0	0	0	0	0	.000	.000	.000
Doug Jennings	1	1	0	1	0	0	0	0	0	0	0	0	1.000	1.000	1.000
Carney Lansford	4	15	0	4	1	0	0	0	1	0	1	0	.267	.313	.267
Willie McGee	4	10	1	2	0	1	0	0	0	2	1	0	.200	.200	.300
Mark McGwire	4	14	1	3	0	0	0	0	2	4	0	0	.214	.313	.214
Jamie Quirk	1	3	0	0	0	0	0	0	0	2	0	0	.000	.000	.000
Willie Randolph	4	15	0	4	0	0	0	0	1	0	1	0	.267	.313	.267
Terry Steinbach	3	8	0	1	0	0	0	0	0	1	0	0	.125	.125	.125
Dave Stewart	2	1	0	0	0	0	0	0	0	1	0	0	.000	.000	.000
Bob Welch	1	3	0	0	0	0	0	0	0	2	0	0	.000	.000	.000
Totals	4	135	8	28	8	4	0	3	12	28	7	0	.207	.270	.304

Pitching

Reds	G	GS	CG	IP	H	R	ER	BB	SO	W-L	Sv-Op	Hld	ERA
Jack Armstrong	1	0	0	3.0	1	0	0	0	3	0-0	0-0	0	0.00
Tom Browning	1	1	0	6.0	6	3	3	2	2	1-0	0-0	0	4.50
Norm Charlton	1	0	0	1.0	1	0	0	0	0	0-0	0-0	0	0.00
Rob Dibble	3	0	0	4.2	3	0	0	1	4	1-0	0-0	0	0.00
Danny Jackson	1	1	0	2.2	6	4	3	2	0	0-0	0-0	0	10.13
Randy Myers	3	0	0	3.0	2	0	0	0	3	0-0	1-1	0	0.00
Jose Rijo	2	2	0	15.1	9	1	1	5	14	2-0	0-0	0	0.59
Scott Scudder	1	0	0	1.1	0	0	0	2	2	0-0	0-0	0	0.00
Totals	4	4	0	37.0	28	8	7	12	28	4-0	1-1	0	1.70

Pitching

Athletics	G	GS	CG	IP	H	R	ER	BB	SO	W-L	Sv-Op	Hld	ERA
Todd Burns	2	0	0	1.2	5	3	3	2	0	0-0	0-0	0	16.20
Dennis Eckersley	2	0	0	1.1	3	1	1	0	1	0-1	0-0	0	6.75
Rick Honeycutt	1	0	0	1.2	2	0	0	1	0	0-0	0-1	0	0.00
Joe Klink	1	0	0	0.0	0	0	0	1	0	0-0	0-0	0	—
Mike Moore	1	1	0	2.2	8	6	2	0	1	0-1	0-0	0	6.75
Gene Nelson	2	0	0	5.0	3	0	0	2	0	0-0	0-0	0	0.00
Scott Sanderson	2	0	0	1.2	4	2	2	1	0	0-0	0-0	0	10.80
Dave Stewart	2	2	1	13.0	10	6	4	6	5	0-2	0-0	0	2.77
Bob Welch	1	1	0	7.1	9	4	4	2	0	0-0	0-0	0	4.91
Curt Young	1	0	0	1.0	1	0	0	0	0	0-0	0-0	0	0.00
Totals	4	4	1	35.1	45	22	14	15	9	0-4	0-1	0	3.57

Fielding

Reds	Pos	G	PO	Ast	E	DP	PB	FPct
Jack Armstrong	p	1	0	0	0	0	—	—
Todd Benzinger	1b	3	24	0	0	1	—	1.000
Glenn Braggs	lf	1	0	0	0	0	—	—
Tom Browning	p	1	0	0	0	0	—	—
Norm Charlton	p	1	0	0	0	0	—	—
Eric Davis	lf	4	4	0	0	0	—	1.000
Rob Dibble	p	3	0	0	0	0	—	—
Mariano Duncan	2b	4	9	9	0	2	—	1.000
Billy Hatcher	cf	4	11	0	0	0	—	1.000
Danny Jackson	p	1	0	1	1	0	—	.500
Barry Larkin	ss	4	1	14	0	2	—	1.000
Hal Morris	1b	2	18	1	0	1	—	1.000
Randy Myers	p	3	0	0	0	0	—	—
Paul O'Neill	rf	4	11	0	0	0	—	1.000
Joe Oliver	c	4	27	1	3	0	0	.903
Jose Rijo	p	2	0	2	0	0	—	1.000
Chris Sabo	3b	4	3	14	0	0	—	1.000
Scott Scudder	p	1	0	0	0	0	—	—
Herm Winningham	cf	1	3	0	0	0	—	1.000
Totals		4	111	42	4	6	0	.975

Fielding

Athletics	Pos	G	PO	Ast	E	DP	PB	FPct
Mike Bordick	ss	3	0	2	0	0	—	1.000
Todd Burns	p	2	0	0	0	0	—	—
Jose Canseco	rf	3	4	0	0	0	—	1.000
Dennis Eckersley	p	3	0	0	0	0	—	—
Mike Gallego	ss	4	7	10	1	3	—	.944
Ron Hassey	c	1	2	0	1	0	0	.667
Dave Henderson	cf	3	7	0	0	0	—	1.000
Rickey Henderson	lf	4	12	1	0	0	—	1.000
Joe Klink	p	1	0	0	0	0	—	—
Carney Lansford	3b	4	1	14	0	0	—	1.000
Willie McGee	cf	2	3	0	0	0	—	1.000
	rf	1	2	0	0	0	—	1.000
Mark McGwire	1b	4	42	1	2	5	—	.956
Mike Moore	p	1	0	0	0	0	—	—
Gene Nelson	p	2	0	0	0	0	—	—
Jamie Quirk	c	1	2	2	0	0	0	1.000
Willie Randolph	2b	4	14	12	0	5	—	1.000
Scott Sanderson	p	2	0	0	0	0	—	—
Terry Steinbach	c	3	8	1	0	0	0	1.000
Dave Stewart	p	2	2	1	1	0	—	.750
Bob Welch	p	1	0	2	0	0	—	1.000
Curt Young	p	1	0	0	0	0	—	—
Totals		4	106	46	5	13	0	.968

1991 Minnesota Twins (AL) 4, Atlanta Braves (NL) 3

The Minnesota Twins and Atlanta Braves each finished last in 1990, but this year they played for the World Championship. Greg Gagne hit a three-run homer in the opener as Minnesota's Jack Morris beat Atlanta's Charlie Leibrandt, 5-2. The Twins used the same formula to take a 2-0 lead in the Series, as Chili Davis homered and Kevin Tapani beat Tom Glavine, 3-2, in the second game. Mark Lemke rapped a 12th-inning RBI single to give the Braves a 5-4 victory in Game 3, and he tripled and scored the winning run in the bottom of the the ninth of Game 4 to help the Braves even the Series with a 3-2 victory. David Justice had a homer and five RBI in the Braves' 14-5 win in Game 5. Charlie Liebrandt was brought in to pitch the bottom of the 11th in Game 6 with the game knotted at three apiece. Kirby Puckett led off with a game-winning homer, his third hit and third RBI of the game. In Game 7, John Smoltz and Morris matched zeroes for the first seven innings. In the eighth, Terry Pendleton lashed a double to the wall on a hit-and-run, but Lonnie Smith hesitated rounding second base when he lost track of the ball. He was only able to advance to third base, where he was ultimately stranded. In the bottom of the 10th, Dan Gladden doubled, moved to third on a sacrifice, and scored the winning run on Gene Larkin's sacrifice fly. Morris pitched all 10 innings for the victory.

Game 1

Saturday, October 19

Braves	AB	R	H	RBI	BB	K	Avg
Lonnie Smith, dh	3	1	0	0	1	0	.000
Jeff Treadway, 2b	3	1	1	0	1	2	.333
Terry Pendleton, 3b	4	0	0	0	0	0	.000
David Justice, rf	2	0	1	0	2	0	.500
Ron Gant, cf	4	0	3	2	0	0	.750
Sid Bream, 1b	4	0	0	0	0	1	.000
Brian Hunter, lf	4	0	0	0	0	0	.000
Greg Olson, c	3	0	1	0	1	0	.333
Rafael Belliard, ss	1	0	0	0	0	0	.000
Jeff Blauser, ph-ss	2	0	0	0	0	0	.000
TOTALS	30	2	6	2	5	3	.200

Twins	AB	R	H	RBI	BB	K	Avg
Dan Gladden, lf	2	1	0	0	2	0	.000
Chuck Knoblauch, 2b	3	0	3	1	1	0	1.000
Kirby Puckett, cf	4	0	0	0	0	2	.000
Chili Davis, dh	3	0	0	0	1	1	.000
Brian Harper, c	4	0	2	0	0	0	.500
Shane Mack, rf	4	0	0	0	0	1	.000
Kent Hrbek, 1b	4	2	2	1	0	1	.500
Scott Leius, 3b	2	1	1	0	0	0	.500
Mike Pagliarulo, ph-3b	1	0	0	0	0	0	.000
Greg Gagne, ss	3	1	1	3	0	1	.333
TOTALS	30	5	9	5	4	6	.300

	1	2	3	4	5	6	7	8	9		R	H	E
Braves	0	0	0	0	0	1	0	1	0		2	6	1
Twins	0	0	1	0	3	1	0	0	x		5	9	1

E—Gladden, Treadway. DP—Braves 2 (Belliard to Treadway; Hunter to Pendleton to Olson), Twins 2 (Gagne to Hrbek; Knoblauch to Gagne to Hrbek). LOB—Braves 7, Twins 5. Scoring Position—Braves 2-for-7, Twins 3-for-7. 2B—Harper (1), Hrbek (1). HR—Hrbek (1), Gagne (1). S—Belliard. GDP—Pendleton, Belliard. SB—Gladden (1), Knoblauch 2 (2). CS—Gladden (1).

Braves	IP	H	R	ER	BB	K	ERA
Charlie Leibrandt (L, 0-1)	4.0	7	4	4	1	3	9.00
Jim Clancy	2.0	1	1	1	2	0	4.50
Mark Wohlers	1.0	1	0	0	1	1	0.00
Mike Stanton	1.0	0	0	0	0	2	0.00

Twins	IP	H	R	ER	BB	K	ERA
Jack Morris (W, 1-0)	7.0	5	2	2	4	3	2.57
Mark Guthrie (H, 1)	0.2	0	0	0	1	0	0.00
Rick Aguilera (S, 1)	1.1	1	0	0	0	0	0.00

Leibrandt pitched to three batters in the 5th. Morris pitched to two batters in the 8th.

Time—3:00. Attendance—55,108. Umpires—HP, Denkinger. 1B, Wendelstedt. 2B, Coble. 3B, Tata.

Game 2

Sunday, October 20

Braves	AB	R	H	RBI	BB	K	Avg
Lonnie Smith, dh	3	0	0	0	0	0	.000
Terry Pendleton, 3b	4	0	2	0	0	1	.250
Ron Gant, cf	4	0	1	0	0	0	.500
David Justice, rf	4	1	1	0	0	0	.333
Sid Bream, 1b	4	0	1	0	0	1	.125
Brian Hunter, lf	3	0	1	1	0	1	.143
Greg Olson, c	4	1	1	0	0	1	.286
Mark Lemke, 2b	3	0	0	0	0	1	.000
Tommy Gregg, ph	1	0	0	0	1	0	.000
Rafael Belliard, ss	2	0	1	0	0	0	.333
TOTALS	32	2	8	2	0	6	.228

Twins	AB	R	H	RBI	BB	K	Avg
Dan Gladden, lf	4	0	0	0	0	1	.000
Chuck Knoblauch, 2b	3	1	0	0	1	0	.500
Kirby Puckett, cf	4	0	0	0	0	1	.000
Chili Davis, dh	3	1	1	2	0	0	.167
Brian Harper, c	2	0	1	0	1	0	.500
Shane Mack, rf	3	0	0	0	0	2	.000
Kent Hrbek, 1b	2	0	0	0	1	1	.333
Scott Leius, 3b	3	1	1	1	0	0	.400
Greg Gagne, ss	3	0	1	0	0	1	.333
TOTALS	27	3	4	3	3	6	.232

	1	2	3	4	5	6	7	8	9		R	H	E
Braves	0	1	0	0	1	0	0	0	0		2	8	1
Twins	2	0	0	0	0	0	0	1	x		3	4	1

E—Justice, Leius. DP—Braves 2 (Pendleton to Bream; Glavine to Lemke to Bream). LOB—Braves 6, Twins 3. Scoring Position—Braves 1-for-6, Twins 1-for-4. 2B—Bream (1), Olson (1). HR—Davis (1), Leius (1). S—Smith. SF—Hunter, Belliard. GDP—Puckett, Leius.

Braves	IP	H	R	ER	BB	K	ERA
Tom Glavine (L, 0-1)	8.0	4	3	1	3	6	1.13

Twins	IP	H	R	ER	BB	K	ERA
Kevin Tapani (W, 1-0)	8.0	7	2	2	0	3	2.25
Rick Aguilera (S, 2)	1.0	1	0	0	0	3	0.00

Balk—Glavine. Time—2:37. Attendance—55,145. Umpires—HP, Wendelstedt. 1B, Coble. 2B, Tata. 3B, Reed.

Game 3

Tuesday, October 22

Twins	AB	R	H	RBI	BB	K	Avg
Dan Gladden, lf	6	1	3	0	0	1	.250
Chuck Knoblauch, 2b	5	0	1	1	0	0	.364
Kent Hrbek, 1b	6	0	1	0	0	2	.250
Kirby Puckett, cf	4	1	1	1	2	2	.083
Shane Mack, rf	4	0	0	0	0	2	.000
Carl Willis, p	0	0	0	0	0	0	—
Paul Sorrento, ph	1	0	0	0	0	1	.000
Mark Guthrie, p	0	0	0	0	0	0	—
Rick Aguilera, ph-p	1	0	0	0	0	0	.000
Scott Leius, 3b	3	0	0	0	0	0	.250
Mike Pagliarulo, ph-3b	1	0	0	0	0	1	.000
Al Newman, ph-3b	1	0	0	0	0	0	.000
Greg Gagne, ss	5	0	0	0	0	1	.182
Junior Ortiz, c	2	0	1	0	0	0	.500
Brian Harper, ph-c	3	1	1	0	0	0	.444
Scott Erickson, p	1	0	0	0	0	1	.000
David West, p	0	0	0	0	0	0	—
Terry Leach, p	0	0	0	0	0	0	—
Gene Larkin, ph	1	0	1	0	0	0	1.000
Steve Bedrosian, p	0	0	0	0	0	0	—
Chili Davis, ph	1	1	1	2	0	0	.286
Jarvis Brown, rf	0	0	0	0	0	0	—
Randy Bush, ph-rf	2	0	0	0	0	0	.000
TOTALS	47	4	10	4	2	13	.221

Braves	AB	R	H	RBI	BB	K	Avg
Lonnie Smith, lf	4	1	1	1	0	1	.100
Keith Mitchell, lf	2	0	0	0	0	1	.000
Terry Pendleton, 3b	4	1	0	0	2	0	.167
Ron Gant, cf	6	0	0	0	0	0	.286
David Justice, rf	6	2	2	1	0	1	.333
Sid Bream, 1b	3	0	1	0	1	0	.182
Brian Hunter, ph-1b	2	0	0	0	0	0	.111
Greg Olson, c	3	1	1	1	0	0	.300
Mark Lemke, 2b	5	0	2	1	1	1	.250
Rafael Belliard, ss	3	0	1	1	1	0	.333
Jeff Blauser, ph-ss	1	0	0	0	0	0	.000
Steve Avery, p	3	0	0	0	0	2	.000
Alejandro Pena, p	0	0	0	0	0	0	—
Jeff Treadway, ph	0	0	0	0	0	0	.333
Mike Stanton, p	0	0	0	0	0	0	—
Francisco Cabrera, ph	1	0	0	0	0	0	.000
Mark Wohlers, p	0	0	0	0	0	0	—
Kent Mercker, p	0	0	0	0	0	0	—
Jim Clancy, p	0	0	0	0	0	0	—
TOTALS	43	5	8	5	8	6	.212

	1	2	3	4	5	6	7	8	9	10	11	12		R	H	E
Twins	1	0	0	0	0	0	1	2	0	0	0	0		4	10	1
Braves	0	1	0	1	2	0	0	0	0	0	0	1		5	8	2

E—Pendleton, Lemke, Knoblauch. LOB—Twins 10, Braves 12. Scoring Position—Twins 0-for-10, Braves 2-for-11. 2B—Bream (2), Olson (2). 3B—Gladden (1). HR—Puckett (1), Smith (1), Justice (1), Davis (2). S—Treadway. SF—Knoblauch. SB—Knoblauch (3), Justice (1).

Twins	IP	H	R	ER	BB	K	ERA
Scott Erickson	4.2	5	4	3	2	3	5.79
David West	0.0	0	0	0	2	0	—
Terry Leach	0.1	0	0	0	0	1	0.00
Steve Bedrosian	2.0	0	0	0	0	1	0.00
Carl Willis	2.0	0	0	0	2	0	0.00
Mark Guthrie	2.0	1	0	0	1	1	0.00
Rick Aguilera (L, 0-1)	0.2	2	1	1	1	0	3.00

Braves	IP	H	R	ER	BB	K	ERA
Steve Avery	7.0	4	3	2	0	5	2.57
Alejandro Pena (BS, 1)	2.0	4	1	1	0	4	4.50
Mike Stanton	2.0	1	0	0	1	3	0.00
Mark Wohlers	0.1	1	0	0	0	0	0.00
Kent Mercker	0.1	0	0	0	0	1	0.00
Jim Clancy (W, 1-0)	0.1	0	0	0	1	0	3.86

West pitched to two batters in the 5th. Avery pitched to one batter in the 8th.

WP—Erickson, Pena. Time—4:04. Attendance—50,878. Umpires—HP, Coble. 1B, Tata. 2B, Reed. 3B, Montague.

Game 4

Wednesday, October 23

Twins	AB	R	H	RBI	BB	K	Avg
Dan Gladden, lf	4	0	0	0	0	0	.188
Chuck Knoblauch, 2b	3	0	1	0	1	1	.357
Kirby Puckett, cf	4	0	1	0	0	0	.125
Kent Hrbek, 1b	4	0	0	0	0	1	.188
Brian Harper, c	4	1	2	0	0	0	.462
Shane Mack, rf	4	0	0	0	0	2	.000
Mike Pagliarulo, 3b	3	1	3	2	0	0	.600
Scott Leius, ph-3b	1	0	0	0	0	0	.222
Steve Bedrosian, p	0	0	0	0	0	0	—
Greg Gagne, ss	3	0	0	0	0	3	.143
Jack Morris, p	2	0	0	0	0	1	.000
Gene Larkin, ph	1	0	0	0	0	0	.500
Carl Willis, p	0	0	0	0	0	0	—
Mark Guthrie, p	0	0	0	0	0	0	—
Al Newman, 3b	0	0	0	0	0	0	.000
TOTALS	33	2	7	2	1	8	.220

Braves	AB	R	H	RBI	BB	K	Avg
Lonnie Smith, lf	4	1	2	1	0	1	.214
Terry Pendleton, 3b	4	1	2	1	0	0	.250
Ron Gant, cf	3	0	1	0	1	0	.294
David Justice, rf	3	0	0	0	1	1	.267
Sid Bream, 1b	3	0	0	0	1	1	.143
Brian Hunter, ph-1b	1	0	0	0	0	0	.100
Greg Olson, c	3	0	0	1	0	1	.231
Mark Lemke, 2b	4	1	3	0	0	0	.417
Rafael Belliard, ss	2	0	0	0	0	0	.250
Jeff Treadway, ph	1	0	0	0	0	0	.250
Jeff Blauser, ss	0	0	0	0	0	1	.000

	AB	R	H	RBI	BB	K	Avg
John Smoltz, p	2	0	0	0	0	1	.000
Tommy Gregg, ph	1	0	0	0	0	1	.000
Mark Wohlers, p	0	0	0	0	0	0	—
Mike Stanton, p	0	0	0	0	0	0	—
Francisco Cabrera, ph	0	0	0	0	0	0	.000
Jerry Willard, ph	0	0	0	1	0	0	—
TOTALS	31	3	8	3	4	6	.229

	1	2	3	4	5	6	7	8	9		R	H	E
Twins	0	1	0	0	0	0	1	0	0		2	7	0
Braves	0	0	1	0	0	0	1	0	1		3	8	0

LOB—Twins 5, Braves 7. Scoring Position—Twins 1-for-8, Braves 1-for-6. 2B—Knoblauch (1), Harper (2), Pendleton (1), Lemke (1). 3B—Lemke (1). HR—Pagliarulo (1), Smith (2), Pendleton (1). SF—Willard. SB—Knoblauch (4), Smith (1), Gant (1). CS—Mack (1).

Twins	IP	H	R	ER	BB	K	ERA
Jack Morris	6.0	6	1	1	3	4	2.08
Carl Willis (BS, 1)	1.1	1	1	1	0	1	2.70
Mark Guthrie (L, 0-1)	1.0	1	1	1	1	1	2.45
Steve Bedrosian	0.1	0	0	0	0	0	0.00

Braves	IP	H	R	ER	BB	K	ERA
John Smoltz	7.0	7	2	2	0	7	2.57
Mark Wohlers	0.1	0	0	0	1	0	0.00
Mike Stanton (W, 1-0)	1.2	0	0	0	0	0	1.00

WP—Morris. Time—2:57. Attendance—50,878. Umpires—HP, Tata. 1B, Reed. 2B, Montague. 3B, Denkinger.

Game 5

Thursday, October 24

Twins	AB	R	H	RBI	BB	K	Avg
Dan Gladden, lf	5	1	1	0	0	1	.190
Chuck Knoblauch, 2b	3	1	1	0	1	1	.353
Steve Bedrosian, p	0	0	0	0	0	0	—
Junior Ortiz, c	1	0	0	1	0	0	.333
Kirby Puckett, cf	2	1	1	0	0	0	.167
Jarvis Brown, ph-cf	2	0	0	0	0	0	.000
Chili Davis, rf	3	2	1	0	1	0	.300
Carl Willis, p	0	0	0	0	0	0	—
Brian Harper, c	2	0	1	1	1	0	.400
Randy Bush, ph-rf	1	0	0	0	0	0	.000
Scott Leius, 3b	2	0	1	1	1	1	.273
David West, p	0	0	0	0	0	0	—
Al Newman, 2b	1	0	1	1	0	0	.500
Kent Hrbek, 1b	3	0	0	1	0	0	.158
Paul Sorrento, ph-1b	0	0	0	0	1	0	.000
Greg Gagne, ss	4	0	1	0	0	0	.167
Kevin Tapani, p	1	0	0	0	0	0	.000
Gene Larkin, ph	1	0	0	0	0	0	.333
Terry Leach, p	0	0	0	0	0	0	—
Mike Pagliarulo, ph-3b	2	0	0	0	0	0	.429
TOTALS	33	5	7	5	5	4	.245

Braves	AB	R	H	RBI	BB	K	Avg
Lonnie Smith, lf	5	1	1	1	0	1	.211
Keith Mitchell, lf	0	0	0	0	0	0	.000
Terry Pendleton, 3b	4	3	2	0	1	0	.300
Ron Gant, cf	4	3	3	1	1	1	.381
David Justice, rf	5	2	2	5	0	1	.300
Sid Bream, 1b	2	0	0	1	1	0	.125
Brian Hunter, ph-1b	2	2	2	2	0	0	.250
Greg Olson, c	5	1	3	0	0	0	.333
Randy St. Claire, p	0	0	0	0	0	0	—
Mark Lemke, 2b	4	2	2	3	1	1	.438
Rafael Belliard, ss	4	0	2	2	0	0	.333
Tom Glavine, p	2	0	0	0	0	0	.000
Kent Mercker, p	0	0	0	0	0	0	—
Tommy Gregg, ph	1	0	0	0	0	0	.000
Jim Clancy, p	1	0	0	0	0	1	.000
Francisco Cabrera, c	0	0	0	0	0	0	.000
TOTALS	39	14	17	14	4	6	.282

	1	2	3	4	5	6	7	8	9		R	H	E
Twins	0	0	0	0	0	3	0	1	1		5	7	1
Braves	0	0	0	4	1	0	6	3	x		14	17	1

E—Harper, Pendleton. DP—Twins 1 (Newman to Gagne to

Sorrento). LOB—Twins 7, Braves 5. Scoring Position—Twins 1-for-9, Braves 6-for-15. 2B—Gagne (1), Pendleton (2), Belliard (1). 3B—Gladden (2), Gant (1), Lemke 2 (3), Newman (1). HR—Smith (3), Justice (2), Hunter (1). S—Puckett. GDP—Lemke. SB—Justice (2), Olson (1). CS—Leius (1).

Twins	IP	H	R	ER	BB	K	ERA
Kevin Tapani (L, 1-1)	4.0	6	4	4	2	4	4.50
Terry Leach	2.0	2	1	1	0	1	3.86
David West	0.0	2	4	4	2	0	—
Steve Bedrosian	1.0	3	2	2	0	1	5.40
Carl Willis	1.0	4	3	3	0	0	8.31

Braves	IP	H	R	ER	BB	K	ERA
Tom Glavine (W, 1-1)	5.1	4	3	3	4	2	2.70
Kent Mercker (H, 1)	0.2	0	0	0	0	0	1.00
Jim Clancy (H, 1)	2.0	2	1	1	1	2	4.15
Randy St. Claire	1.0	1	1	1	0	0	9.00

West pitched to four batters in the 7th.

WP—Bedrosian. Time—2:59. Attendance—50,878. Umpires—HP, Reed. 1B, Montague. 2B, Denkinger. 3B, Wendelstedt.

Game 6

Saturday, October 26

Braves	AB	R	H	RBI	BB	K	Avg
Lonnie Smith, dh	3	1	0	0	1	0	.182
Terry Pendleton, 3b	5	1	4	2	0	0	.400
Ron Gant, cf	5	0	0	1	0	0	.308
David Justice, rf	4	0	0	0	1	1	.250
Sid Bream, 1b	4	0	1	0	1	0	.150
Keith Mitchell, pr-lf	0	0	0	0	0	0	.000
Brian Hunter, lf-1b	5	0	0	0	0	0	.176
Greg Olson, c	5	0	0	0	0	1	.261
Mark Lemke, 2b	4	1	2	0	0	0	.450
Rafael Belliard, ss	2	0	1	0	0	1	.357
Tommy Gregg, ph	0	0	0	0	0	0	.000
Jeff Blauser, ph-ss	2	0	1	0	0	1	.200
TOTALS	39	3	9	3	3	4	.274

Twins	AB	R	H	RBI	BB	K	Avg
Dan Gladden, lf	4	1	0	0	1	0	.160
Chuck Knoblauch, 2b	5	1	1	0	0	0	.318
Kirby Puckett, cf	4	2	3	3	0	1	.273
Chili Davis, dh	4	0	0	0	0	1	.214
Shane Mack, rf	4	0	2	1	0	0	.105
Scott Leius, 3b	3	0	2	0	0	0	.357
Mike Pagliarulo, ph-3b	1	0	0	0	0	1	.375
Kent Hrbek, 1b	4	0	0	0	0	1	.130
Junior Ortiz, c	2	0	0	0	0	1	.200
Brian Harper, ph-c	2	0	0	0	0	1	.353
Greg Gagne, ss	4	0	1	0	0	0	.182
TOTALS	37	4	9	4	1	6	.230

	1	2	3	4	5	6	7	8	9	10	11		R	H	E
Braves	0	0	0	0	2	0	1	0	0	0	0		3	9	1
Twins	2	0	0	0	1	0	0	0	0	0	1		4	9	0

E—Hunter. DP—Braves 2 (Bream to Belliard; Blauser to Lemke to Bream), Twins 2 (Gagne to Hrbek; Gagne). LOB—Braves 7, Twins 5. Scoring Position—Braves 1-for-4, Twins 1-for-9. 2B—Mack (1). 3B—Puckett (1). HR—Pendleton (2), Puckett (2). SF—Puckett. GDP—Smith, Gladden, Hrbek. SB—Gladden (2), Puckett (1). CS—Mitchell (1).

Braves	IP	H	R	ER	BB	K	ERA
Steve Avery	6.0	6	3	3	1	3	3.46
Mike Stanton	2.0	2	0	0	0	1	0.00
Alejandro Pena	2.0	0	0	0	0	2	2.25
Charlie Leibrandt (L, 0-2)	0.0	1	1	1	0	0	11.25

Twins	IP	H	R	ER	BB	K	ERA
Scott Erickson	6.0	5	3	3	2	2	5.06
Mark Guthrie (H, 2)	0.1	1	0	0	1	1	2.25
Carl Willis (BS, 2)	2.2	1	0	0	1	1	5.14
Rick Aguilera (W, 1-1)	2.0	2	0	0	0	0	1.80

Erickson pitched to one batter in the 7th. Leibrandt pitched to one batter in the 11th.

WP—Guthrie. HBP—Smith by Erickson. Time—3:36. Attendance—55,155. Umpires—HP, Montague. 1B, Denkinger. 2B, Wendelstedt. 3B, Coble.

Game 7

Sunday, October 27

Braves	AB	R	H	RBI	BB	K	Avg
Lonnie Smith, dh	4	0	2	0	1	1	.231
Terry Pendleton, 3b	5	0	1	0	0	0	.367
Ron Gant, cf	4	0	0	0	0	2	.267
David Justice, rf	3	0	1	0	1	1	.259
Sid Bream, 1b	4	0	0	0	0	0	.125
Brian Hunter, lf	4	0	1	0	0	1	.190
Greg Olson, c	4	0	0	0	0	1	.222
Mark Lemke, 2b	4	0	1	0	0	1	.417
Rafael Belliard, ss	2	0	1	0	0	1	.375
Jeff Blauser, ph-ss	1	0	0	0	0	0	.167
TOTALS	35	0	7	0	2	8	.268

Twins	AB	R	H	RBI	BB	K	Avg
Dan Gladden, lf	5	1	3	0	0	1	.233
Chuck Knoblauch, 2b	4	0	1	0	0	0	.308
Kirby Puckett, cf	2	0	0	0	3	1	.250
Kent Hrbek, 1b	3	0	0	0	1	0	.115
Chili Davis, dh	4	0	1	0	0	1	.222
Jarvis Brown, pr-dh	0	0	0	0	0	0	.000
Gene Larkin, ph	1	0	1	1	0	0	.500
Brian Harper, c	4	0	2	0	0	0	.381
Shane Mack, rf	4	0	1	0	0	0	.130
Mike Pagliarulo, 3b	3	0	0	0	1	0	.273
Greg Gagne, ss	2	0	0	0	0	1	.167
Randy Bush, ph	1	0	1	0	0	0	.250
Al Newman, pr-ss	0	0	0	0	0	0	.500
Paul Sorrento, ph	1	0	0	0	0	1	.000
Scott Leius, ss	0	0	0	0	0	0	.357
TOTALS	34	1	10	1	5	5	.238

	1	2	3	4	5	6	7	8	9	10		R	H	E
Braves	0	0	0	0	0	0	0	0	0	0		0	7	0
Twins	0	0	0	0	0	0	0	0	0	1		1	10	0

DP—Braves 3 (Bream to Belliard; Lemke; Lemke to Belliard to Bream), Twins 1 (Hrbek to Harper). LOB—Braves 8, Twins 12. Scoring Position—Braves 1-for-10, Twins 1-for-7. 2B—Pendleton (1), Hunter (1), Gladden 2 (2). S—Belliard, Knoblauch. GDP—Bream, Davis, Mack.

Braves	IP	H	R	ER	BB	K	ERA
John Smoltz	7.1	6	0	0	1	4	1.26
Mike Stanton	0.2	2	0	0	1	0	0.00
Alejandro Pena (L, 0-1)	1.1	2	1	1	3	1	3.38

Twins	IP	H	R	ER	BB	K	ERA
Jack Morris (W, 2-0)	10.0	7	0	0	2	8	1.17

Stanton pitched to two batters in the 9th.

PB—Harper. HBP—Hrbek by Smoltz. Time—3:23. Attendance—55,118. Umpires—HP, Denkinger. 1B, Wendelstedt. 2B, Coble. 3B, Tata.

1991 World Series—Composite Statistics

Batting

Batting (Twins)

Twins	G	AB	R	H	RBI	2B	3B	HR	BB	SO	SB	CS	Avg	OBP	Slg
Rick Aguilera	4	1	0	0	0	0	0	0	0	0	0	0	.000	.000	.000
Jarvis Brown	3	2	0	0	0	0	0	0	0	0	0	0	.000	.000	.000
Randy Bush	3	4	0	1	0	0	0	0	0	1	0	0	.250	.250	.250
Chili Davis	6	18	4	4	4	0	0	2	2	3	0	0	.222	.300	.556
Scott Erickson	2	1	0	0	0	0	0	0	0	1	0	0	.000	.000	.000
Greg Gagne	7	24	1	4	3	1	0	1	0	7	0	0	.167	.167	.333
Dan Gladden	7	30	5	7	0	2	2	0	3	4	2	1	.233	.303	.433
Brian Harper	7	21	2	8	1	2	0	0	2	2	0	0	.381	.435	.476
Kent Hrbek	7	26	2	3	2	1	0	1	2	6	0	0	.115	.207	.269
Chuck Knoblauch	7	26	3	8	2	1	0	0	4	2	4	0	.308	.387	.346
Gene Larkin	4	4	0	2	1	0	0	0	0	0	0	0	.500	.500	.500
Scott Leius	7	14	2	5	2	0	0	1	1	2	0	1	.357	.400	.571
Shane Mack	6	23	0	3	1	1	0	0	0	7	0	1	.130	.130	.174
Jack Morris	3	2	0	0	0	0	0	0	0	1	0	0	.000	.000	.000
Al Newman	4	2	0	1	1	0	1	0	0	0	0	0	.500	.500	1.500
Junior Ortiz	3	5	0	1	1	0	0	0	0	1	0	0	.200	.200	.200
Mike Pagliarulo	6	11	1	3	2	0	0	1	1	2	0	0	.273	.333	.545
Kirby Puckett	7	24	4	6	4	0	1	2	5	7	1	0	.250	.367	.583
Paul Sorrento	3	2	0	0	0	0	0	0	1	2	0	0	.000	.333	.000
Kevin Tapani	2	1	0	0	0	0	0	0	0	0	0	0	.000	.000	.000
Totals	7	241	24	56	24	8	4	8	21	48	7	3	.232	.294	.398

Batting (Braves)

Braves	G	AB	R	H	RBI	2B	3B	HR	BB	SO	SB	CS	Avg	OBP	Slg
Steve Avery	2	3	0	0	0	0	0	0	0	2	0	0	.000	.000	.000
Rafael Belliard	7	16	0	6	4	1	0	0	1	2	0	0	.375	.389	.438
Jeff Blauser	5	6	0	1	0	0	0	0	1	1	0	0	.167	.286	.167
Sid Bream	7	24	0	3	0	2	0	0	3	4	0	0	.125	.222	.208
Francisco Cabrera	3	1	0	0	0	0	0	0	0	0	0	0	.000	.000	.000
Jim Clancy	3	1	0	0	0	0	0	0	0	0	0	0	.000	.000	.000
Ron Gant	7	30	3	8	4	0	1	0	2	3	1	0	.267	.313	.333
Tom Glavine	2	2	0	0	0	0	0	0	0	0	0	0	.000	.000	.000
Tommy Gregg	4	3	0	0	0	0	0	0	0	2	0	0	.000	.000	.000
Brian Hunter	7	21	2	4	3	1	0	1	0	2	0	0	.190	.182	.381
David Justice	7	27	5	7	6	0	0	2	5	5	2	0	.259	.375	.481
Mark Lemke	6	24	4	10	4	1	3	0	2	4	0	0	.417	.462	.708
Keith Mitchell	3	2	0	0	0	0	0	0	0	1	0	1	.000	.000	.000
Greg Olson	7	27	3	6	1	2	0	0	5	4	1	0	.222	.344	.296
Terry Pendleton	7	30	6	11	3	3	0	2	3	1	0	0	.367	.424	.667
Lonnie Smith	7	26	5	6	3	0	0	3	3	4	1	0	.231	.333	.577
John Smoltz	2	2	0	0	0	0	0	0	0	1	0	0	.000	.000	.000
Jeff Treadway	3	4	1	1	0	0	0	0	1	2	0	0	.250	.400	.250
Jerry Willard	1	0	0	0	1	0	0	0	0	0	0	0	—	.000	—
Totals	7	249	29	63	29	10	4	8	26	39	5	1	.253	.323	.422

Pitching

Pitching (Twins)

Twins	G	GS	CG	IP	H	R	ER	BB	SO	W-L	Sv-Op	Hld	ERA
Rick Aguilera	4	0	0	5.0	6	1	1	1	3	1-1	2-2	0	1.80
Steve Bedrosian	3	0	0	3.1	3	2	2	0	2	0-0	0-0	0	5.40
Scott Erickson	2	2	0	10.2	10	7	6	4	5	0-0	0-0	0	5.06
Mark Guthrie	4	0	0	4.0	3	1	1	4	3	0-1	0-0	2	2.25
Terry Leach	2	0	0	2.1	2	1	1	0	2	0-0	0-0	0	3.86
Jack Morris	3	3	1	23.0	18	3	3	9	15	2-0	0-0	0	1.17
Kevin Tapani	2	2	0	12.0	13	6	6	2	7	1-1	0-0	0	4.50
David West	2	0	0	0.0	2	4	4	4	0	0-0	0-0	0	—
Carl Willis	4	0	0	7.0	6	4	4	2	2	0-0	0-2	0	5.14
Totals	7	7	1	67.1	63	29	28	26	39	4-3	2-4	2	3.74

Pitching (Braves)

Braves	G	GS	CG	IP	H	R	ER	BB	SO	W-L	Sv-Op	Hld	ERA
Steve Avery	2	2	0	13.0	10	6	5	1	8	0-0	0-0	0	3.46
Jim Clancy	3	0	0	4.1	3	2	2	4	2	1-0	0-0	1	4.15
Tom Glavine	2	2	1	13.1	8	6	4	7	8	1-1	0-0	0	2.70
Charlie Leibrandt	2	1	0	4.0	8	5	5	1	3	0-2	0-0	0	11.25
Kent Mercker	2	0	0	1.0	0	0	0	0	1	0-0	0-0	1	0.00
Alejandro Pena	3	0	0	5.1	6	2	2	3	7	0-1	0-1	0	3.38
John Smoltz	2	2	0	14.1	13	2	2	1	11	0-0	0-0	0	1.26
Randy St. Claire	1	0	0	1.0	1	1	1	0	0	0-0	0-0	0	9.00
Mike Stanton	5	0	0	7.1	5	0	0	2	7	1-0	0-0	0	0.00
Mark Wohlers	3	0	0	1.2	2	0	0	2	1	0-0	0-0	0	0.00
Totals	7	7	1	65.1	56	24	21	21	48	3-4	0-1	2	2.89

Fielding

Fielding (Twins)

Twins	Pos	G	PO	Ast	E	DP	PB	FPct
Rick Aguilera	p	4	0	0	0	0	—	—
Steve Bedrosian	p	3	0	1	0	0	—	1.000
Jarvis Brown	cf	1	0	0	0	0	—	—
	rf	1	0	0	0	0	—	—
Randy Bush	rf	2	0	0	0	0	—	—
Chili Davis	rf	1	1	0	0	0	—	1.000
Scott Erickson	p	2	1	0	0	0	—	1.000
Greg Gagne	ss	7	13	24	0	5	—	1.000
Dan Gladden	lf	7	25	1	1	0	—	.963
Mark Guthrie	p	4	0	1	0	0	—	1.000
Brian Harper	c	7	33	5	1	1	1	.974
Kent Hrbek	1b	7	65	8	0	4	—	1.000
Chuck Knoblauch	2b	7	15	14	1	1	—	.967
Terry Leach	p	2	0	0	0	0	—	—
Scott Leius	3b	6	5	7	1	0	—	.923
	ss	1	0	1	0	0	—	1.000
Shane Mack	rf	6	11	0	0	0	—	1.000
Jack Morris	p	3	3	3	0	0	—	1.000
Al Newman	3b	2	0	0	0	0	—	—
	2b	1	0	1	0	1	—	1.000
	ss	1	0	1	0	0	—	1.000
Junior Ortiz	c	3	9	0	0	0	0	1.000
Mike Pagliarulo	3b	6	3	3	0	0	—	1.000
Kirby Puckett	cf	7	16	1	0	0	—	1.000
Paul Sorrento	1b	1	1	1	0	1	—	1.000
Kevin Tapani	p	2	0	2	0	0	—	1.000
David West	p	2	0	0	0	0	—	—
Carl Willis	p	4	1	0	0	0	—	1.000
Totals		7	202	74	4	13	1	.986

Fielding (Braves)

Braves	Pos	G	PO	Ast	E	DP	PB	FPct
Steve Avery	p	2	1	0	0	0	—	1.000
Rafael Belliard	ss	7	8	21	0	4	—	1.000
Jeff Blauser	ss	5	3	3	0	1	—	1.000
Sid Bream	1b	7	69	7	0	6	—	1.000
Francisco Cabrera	c	1	0	0	0	0	0	—
Jim Clancy	p	3	0	0	0	0	—	—
Ron Gant	cf	7	19	0	0	0	—	1.000
Tom Glavine	p	2	0	3	0	1	—	1.000
Brian Hunter	1b	4	3	0	0	0	—	1.000
	lf	4	3	1	1	1	—	.800
David Justice	rf	7	21	1	1	0	—	.957
Charlie Leibrandt	p	2	0	1	0	0	—	1.000
Mark Lemke	2b	6	14	19	1	4	—	.971
Kent Mercker	p	2	0	0	0	0	—	—
Keith Mitchell	lf	3	0	0	0	0	—	—
Greg Olson	c	7	47	6	0	1	0	1.000
Alejandro Pena	p	3	0	0	0	0	—	—
Terry Pendleton	3b	7	3	20	2	2	—	.920
Lonnie Smith	lf	3	2	0	0	0	—	1.000
John Smoltz	p	2	2	1	0	0	—	1.000
Randy St. Claire	p	1	0	0	0	0	—	—
Mike Stanton	p	5	0	0	0	0	—	—
Jeff Treadway	2b	1	1	3	1	1	—	.800
Mark Wohlers	p	3	0	0	0	0	—	—
Totals		7	196	86	6	21	0	.979

1992 Toronto Blue Jays (AL) 4, Atlanta Braves (NL) 2

The Toronto Blue Jays finally shook off their choke-artists label, downing the Atlanta Braves in six games. Tom Glavine went the route in the opener for a 3-1 Atlanta victory, but the Blue Jays staged a late-inning comeback to take Game 2. Trailing 4-3 in the top of the ninth, Ed Sprague clouted a two-run homer off Atlanta stopper Jeff Reardon, giving Toronto a 5-4 win. The Jays got to Reardon again in the third game, as Candy Maldonado lined a bases-loaded single to break up a 2-2 deadlock in the bottom of the ninth. Jimmy Key bested Glavine in Game 4 for a 2-1 victory, giving Toronto a three-games-to-one lead. Lonnie Smith saved Atlanta's hopes in Game 5 with a grand slam off Jack Morris, leading to a 7-2 Atlanta victory. The final game was the wildest: Toronto took a one-run lead into the ninth, but slap-hitting Otis Nixon lined an RBI single off Toronto stopper Tom Henke to send the game into extra innings. Dave Winfield bounced a two-run double down the third-base line in the top of the 11th, but the Braves staged yet another last-gasp rally in the bottom of the inning. Brian Hunter's groundout scored one run and put the tying run on third base, but Nixon was unable to play the hero a second time. Mike Timlin fielded his bunt attempt and threw him out at first to clinch Toronto's first World Championship.

Game 1
Saturday, October 17

Blue Jays	AB	R	H	RBI	BB	K	Avg
Devon White, cf	4	0	0	0	0	0	.000
Roberto Alomar, 2b	4	0	0	0	0	1	.000
Joe Carter, 1b	4	1	1	1	0	0	.250
Dave Winfield, rf	3	0	1	0	0	0	.333
Candy Maldonado, lf	3	0	0	0	0	2	.000
Kelly Gruber, 3b	3	0	0	0	0	1	.000
Pat Borders, c	3	0	2	0	0	0	.667
Manuel Lee, ss	3	0	0	0	0	0	.000
Jack Morris, p	2	0	0	0	0	2	.000
Todd Stottlemyre, p	0	0	0	0	0	0	—
Pat Tabler, ph	1	0	0	0	0	0	.000
David Wells, p	0	0	0	0	0	0	—
TOTALS	30	1	4	1	0	6	.133

Braves	AB	R	H	RBI	BB	K	Avg
Otis Nixon, cf	3	0	1	0	1	1	.333
Jeff Blauser, ss	4	0	0	0	0	2	.000
Rafael Belliard, ss	0	0	0	0	0	0	—
Terry Pendleton, 3b	4	0	0	0	1	0	.000
David Justice, rf	2	1	0	2	2	1	.000
Sid Bream, 1b	3	0	1	0	1	0	.333
Ron Gant, lf	3	1	0	0	1	2	.000
Damon Berryhill, c	4	1	1	3	0	2	.250
Mark Lemke, 2b	3	0	1	0	0	1	.333
Tom Glavine, p	2	0	0	0	1	0	.000
TOTALS	28	3	4	3	6	10	.143

	1 2 3	4 5 6	7 8 9		R	H	E
Blue Jays	0 0 0	1 0 0	0 0 0		1	4	0
Braves	0 0 0	0 3 0	0 x		3	4	0

DP—Braves 1 (Belliard to Bream). LOB—Blue Jays 2, Braves 7. Scoring Position—Blue Jays 0-for-1, Braves 1-for-7. HR—Carter (1), Berryhill (1). GDP—Lee. SB—Nixon (1), Gant (1).

Blue Jays	IP	H	R	ER	BB	K	ERA
Jack Morris (L, 0-1)	6.0	4	3	3	5	7	4.50
Todd Stottlemyre	1.0	0	0	0	0	2	0.00
David Wells	1.0	0	0	0	1	1	0.00

Braves	IP	H	R	ER	BB	K	ERA
Tom Glavine (W, 1-0)	9.0	4	1	1	0	6	1.00

WP—Morris. Time—2:37. Attendance—51,763. Umpires—HP, Crawford. 1B, Reilly. 2B, West. 3B, Morrison.

Game 2
Sunday, October 18

Blue Jays	AB	R	H	RBI	BB	K	Avg
Devon White, cf	5	0	1	1	0	1	.111
Roberto Alomar, 2b	4	1	1	0	1	0	.125
Joe Carter, lf	3	0	1	0	1	1	.286
Dave Winfield, rf	4	0	1	1	0	1	.286
John Olerud, 1b	4	0	0	0	0	1	.000
Kelly Gruber, 3b	4	0	0	0	0	3	.000
Pat Borders, c	3	1	1	0	1	0	.500
Manuel Lee, ss	3	1	1	0	0	1	.167
Derek Bell, ph	0	1	0	0	1	0	—
Alfredo Griffin, ss	0	0	0	0	0	0	—
David Cone, p	2	0	2	1	0	0	1.000
David Wells, p	0	0	0	0	0	0	—
Candy Maldonado, ph	1	0	0	0	0	1	.000
Todd Stottlemyre, p	0	0	0	0	0	0	—
Duane Ward, p	0	0	0	0	0	0	—
Ed Sprague, ph	1	1	1	2	0	0	1.000
Tom Henke, p	0	0	0	0	0	0	—
TOTALS	34	5	9	5	4	9	.213

Braves	AB	R	H	RBI	BB	K	Avg
Otis Nixon, cf	5	0	0	0	0	1	.125
Deion Sanders, lf	3	1	1	0	2	0	.333
Terry Pendleton, 3b	4	1	1	0	1	0	.125
David Justice, rf	3	1	1	1	1	0	.200
Sid Bream, 1b	1	1	0	0	1	0	.250
Brian Hunter, ph-1b	1	0	0	1	0	0	.000
Jeff Blauser, ss	3	0	1	0	1	1	.143
Rafael Belliard, ss	0	0	0	0	0	0	—
Damon Berryhill, c	3	0	0	0	1	2	.143
Mark Lemke, 2b	4	0	1	1	0	0	.286
John Smoltz, p	3	0	0	0	0	2	.000
Mike Stanton, p	0	0	0	0	0	0	—
Jeff Reardon, p	0	0	0	0	0	0	—
Lonnie Smith, ph	0	0	0	0	0	0	—
Ron Gant, pr	0	0	0	0	0	0	.000
TOTALS	30	4	5	3	7	6	.161

	1 2 3	4 5 6	7 8 9		R	H	E
Blue Jays	0 0 0	0 2 0	0 1 2		5	9	2
Braves	0 1 0	1 2 0	0 0 0		4	5	1

E—Bream, Lee, Borders. DP—Blue Jays 2 (Lee to Olerud; Lee to Olerud), Braves 1 (Blauser to Hunter). LOB—Blue Jays 6, Braves 8. Scoring Position—Blue Jays 4-for-11, Braves 3-for-10. 2B—Alomar (1), Borders (1). HR—Sprague (1). SF—Hunter. GDP—Lemke, Smoltz. SB—Sanders 2 (2), Justice (1), Blauser (1), Gant (2).

Blue Jays	IP	H	R	ER	BB	K	ERA
David Cone	4.1	5	4	3	5	2	6.23
David Wells	1.2	0	0	0	1	2	0.00
Todd Stottlemyre	1.0	0	0	0	0	0	0.00
Duane Ward (W, 1-0)	1.0	0	0	0	0	2	0.00
Tom Henke (S, 1)	1.0	0	0	0	1	0	0.00

Braves	IP	H	R	ER	BB	K	ERA
John Smoltz	7.1	8	3	2	3	8	2.45
Mike Stanton (H, 1)	0.1	0	0	0	0	0	0.00
Jeff Reardon (BS, 1; L, 0-1)	1.1	1	2	2	1	1	13.50

WP—Smoltz 2, Cone. HBP—Smith by Henke. Time—3:30. Attendance—51,763. Umpires—HP, Reilly. 1B, West. 2B, Morrison. 3B, Davidson.

Game 3
Tuesday, October 20

Braves	AB	R	H	RBI	BB	K	Avg
Otis Nixon, cf	4	1	0	0	0	0	.083
Deion Sanders, lf	4	1	3	0	0	0	.571
Terry Pendleton, 3b	4	0	2	0	0	0	.250
David Justice, rf	3	0	1	1	1	1	.250
Lonnie Smith, dh	4	0	1	1	0	2	.250
Sid Bream, 1b	4	0	2	0	0	0	.375
Brian Hunter, pr-1b	0	0	0	0	0	0	.000
Jeff Blauser, ss	4	0	0	0	0	3	.091
Damon Berryhill, c	4	0	0	0	0	3	.091
Mark Lemke, 2b	3	0	0	0	0	0	.200
TOTALS	34	2	9	2	1	9	.214

Blue Jays	AB	R	H	RBI	BB	K	Avg
Devon White, cf	4	0	0	0	0	2	.077
Roberto Alomar, 2b	4	1	1	0	0	0	.167
Joe Carter, rf	3	1	1	1	1	0	.300
Dave Winfield, dh	3	0	1	0	0	1	.300
John Olerud, 1b	3	0	0	0	0	2	.000
Ed Sprague, ph	0	0	0	0	1	0	1.000
Candy Maldonado, lf	4	0	1	0	1	0	.125
Kelly Gruber, 3b	2	1	1	1	1	0	.111
Pat Borders, c	3	0	1	0	0	1	.444
Manuel Lee, ss	3	0	0	0	0	0	.111
TOTALS	29	3	6	3	3	9	.193

	1 2 3	4 5 6	7 8 9		R	H	E
Braves	0 0 0	0 0 1	0 1 0		2	9	0
Blue Jays	0 0 0	1 0 0	0 1 1		3	6	1

E—Gruber. DP—Braves 1 (Pendleton to Lemke to Bream), Blue Jays 2 (White to Lee; Borders to Lee). LOB—Braves 6, Blue Jays 5. Scoring Position—Braves 3-for-11, Blue Jays 1-for-3. 2B—Sanders (1). HR—Carter (2), Gruber (1). S—Winfield. GDP—Maldonado. SB—Nixon (2), Sanders (3), Alomar (1), Gruber (1). CS—Hunter (1).

Braves	IP	H	R	ER	BB	K	ERA
Steve Avery (L, 0-1)	8.0	5	3	3	1	9	3.38
Mark Wohlers	0.1	0	0	0	1	0	0.00
Mike Stanton	0.0	0	0	0	1	0	0.00
Jeff Reardon	0.0	1	0	0	0	0	13.50

Blue Jays	IP	H	R	ER	BB	K	ERA
Juan Guzman	8.0	8	2	1	1	7	1.13
Duane Ward (W, 2-0)	1.0	1	0	0	0	2	0.00

Avery pitched to one batter in the 9th. Stanton pitched to one batter in the 9th. Reardon pitched to one batter in the 9th.

Time—2:49. Attendance—51,813. Umpires—HP, West. 1B, Morrison. 2B, Davidson. 3B, Shulock.

Game 4
Wednesday, October 21

Braves

	AB	R	H	RBI	BB	K	Avg
Otis Nixon, cf	4	0	2	0	0	1	.188
Jeff Blauser, ss	4	0	1	0	0	1	.133
Terry Pendleton, 3b	4	0	0	0	0	1	.188
Lonnie Smith, dh	4	0	0	0	0	1	.125
David Justice, rf	4	0	0	0	0	1	.167
Ron Gant, lf	3	1	1	0	0	0	.167
Brian Hunter, 1b	3	0	1	0	0	1	.250
Damon Berryhill, c	3	0	0	0	0	1	.071
Mark Lemke, 2b	3	0	0	1	0	1	.154
TOTALS	32	1	5	1	0	8	.154

Blue Jays

	AB	R	H	RBI	BB	K	Avg
Devon White, cf	4	0	3	1	0	0	.235
Roberto Alomar, 2b	3	0	0	0	1	0	.133
Joe Carter, rf	3	0	0	0	1	0	.231
Dave Winfield, dh	3	0	0	0	1	0	.231
John Olerud, 1b	3	0	2	0	0	1	.200
Candy Maldonado, lf	3	0	0	0	0	1	.091
Kelly Gruber, 3b	2	1	0	0	1	0	.091
Pat Borders, c	3	1	1	1	0	0	.417
Manuel Lee, ss	3	0	0	0	0	0	.083
TOTALS	27	2	6	2	4	2	.193

	1	2	3	4	5	6	7	8	9		R	H	E
Braves	0	0	0	0	0	0	0	1	0		1	5	0
Blue Jays	0	0	1	0	0	0	1	0	x		2	6	0

DP—Braves 2 (Blauser to Lemke; Blauser to Lemke to Hunter). LOB—Braves 4, Blue Jays 5. Scoring Position—Braves 1-for-7, Blue Jays 1-for-6. 2B—Gant (1), White (1). HR—Borders (1). GDP—Gruber. SB—Nixon (3), Blauser (2), Alomar (2).

Braves

	IP	H	R	ER	BB	K	ERA
Tom Glavine (L, 1-1)	8.0	6	2	2	4	2	1.59

Blue Jays

	IP	H	R	ER	BB	K	ERA
Jimmy Key (W, 1-0)	7.2	5	1	1	0	6	1.17
Duane Ward (H, 1)	0.1	0	0	0	0	1	0.00
Tom Henke (S, 2)	1.0	0	0	0	0	1	0.00

WP—Ward. Time—2:21. Attendance—52,090. Umpires—HP, Morrison. 1B, Davidson. 2B, Shulock. 3B, Crawford.

Game 5
Thursday, October 22

Braves

	AB	R	H	RBI	BB	K	Avg
Otis Nixon, cf	5	2	3	0	0	0	.286
Deion Sanders, lf	5	1	2	1	0	1	.500
Terry Pendleton, 3b	5	1	2	1	0	1	.238
David Justice, rf	3	2	1	1	1	1	.200
Lonnie Smith, dh	4	1	1	4	0	1	.167
Sid Bream, 1b	4	0	0	0	0	0	.250
Jeff Blauser, ss	4	0	1	0	0	1	.158
Rafael Belliard, ss	0	0	0	0	0	0	—
Damon Berryhill, c	4	0	1	0	0	2	.111
Mark Lemke, 2b	4	0	2	0	0	0	.235
TOTALS	38	7	13	7	1	7	.231

Blue Jays

	AB	R	H	RBI	BB	K	Avg
Devon White, cf	4	0	0	0	0	2	.190
Roberto Alomar, 2b	3	0	0	0	1	0	.111
Joe Carter, rf	4	0	1	0	0	1	.235
Dave Winfield, dh	4	0	1	0	0	1	.235
John Olerud, 1b	3	2	2	0	0	0	.308
Ed Sprague, ph-1b	1	0	0	0	0	0	.500
Candy Maldonado, lf	2	0	0	2	2	0	.077
Kelly Gruber, 3b	4	0	0	0	0	1	.067
Pat Borders, c	4	0	2	2	0	0	.438
Manuel Lee, ss	3	0	0	0	1	0	.067
TOTALS	32	2	6	2	4	5	.197

	1	2	3	4	5	6	7	8	9		R	H	E
Braves	1	0	0	1	5	0	0	0	0		7	13	0
Blue Jays	0	1	0	1	0	0	0	0	0		2	6	0

DP—Braves 1 (Lemke to Blauser to Bream), Blue Jays 1 (Maldonado to Borders). LOB—Braves 5, Blue Jays 7. Scoring Position—Braves 4-for-10, Blue Jays 2-for-10. 2B—Nixon (1), Pendleton 2 (2), Borders (2). HR—Justice (1), Smith (1). GDP—Alomar. SB—Nixon 2 (5). CS—Blauser (1).

Braves

	IP	H	R	ER	BB	K	ERA
John Smoltz (W, 1-0)	6.0	5	2	2	4	4	2.70
Mike Stanton (S, 1)	3.0	1	0	0	0	1	0.00

Blue Jays

	IP	H	R	ER	BB	K	ERA
Jack Morris (L, 0-2)	4.2	9	7	7	1	5	8.44
David Wells	1.1	1	0	0	0	0	0.00
Mike Timlin	1.0	0	0	0	0	0	0.00
Mark Eichhorn	1.0	0	0	0	0	1	0.00
Todd Stottlemyre	1.0	3	0	0	0	1	0.00

Smoltz pitched to one batter in the 7th.

Time—3:05. Attendance—52,268. Umpires—HP, Davidson. 1B, Shulock. 2B, Crawford. 3B, Reilly.

Game 6
Saturday, October 24

Blue Jays

	AB	R	H	RBI	BB	K	Avg
Devon White, cf	5	2	2	0	0	1	.231
Roberto Alomar, 2b	6	1	3	0	0	1	.208
Joe Carter, 1b	5	0	2	1	0	0	.273
Dave Winfield, rf	5	0	1	2	1	0	.227
Candy Maldonado, lf	6	1	2	1	0	0	.158
Kelly Gruber, 3b	4	0	1	0	0	0	.105
Pat Borders, c	4	0	2	0	1	0	.450
Manuel Lee, ss	4	0	1	0	0	1	.105
Pat Tabler, ph	1	0	0	0	0	0	.000
Alfredo Griffin, ss	0	0	0	0	0	0	—
David Cone, p	2	0	0	0	1	0	.500
Todd Stottlemyre, p	0	0	0	0	0	0	—
David Wells, p	0	0	0	0	0	0	—
Derek Bell, ph	1	0	0	0	0	0	.000
Duane Ward, p	0	0	0	0	0	0	—
Tom Henke, p	0	0	0	0	0	0	—
Jimmy Key, p	1	0	0	0	0	0	.000
Mike Timlin, p	0	0	0	0	0	0	—
TOTALS	44	4	14	4	3	2	.223

Braves

	AB	R	H	RBI	BB	K	Avg
Otis Nixon, cf	6	0	2	1	0	0	.296
Deion Sanders, lf	3	1	2	0	0	0	.533
Ron Gant, ph-lf	2	0	0	0	0	0	.125
Terry Pendleton, 3b	4	0	1	1	0	2	.240
David Justice, rf	4	0	0	0	1	1	.158
Sid Bream, 1b	3	0	0	0	2	0	.200
Jeff Blauser, ss	5	2	3	0	0	0	.250
Damon Berryhill, c	4	0	0	0	0	1	.091
John Smoltz, pr	0	0	0	0	0	0	.000
Mark Lemke, 2b	2	0	0	1	1	1	.211
Lonnie Smith, ph	0	0	0	0	0	0	.167
Rafael Belliard, 2b	0	0	0	0	0	0	—
Steve Avery, p	1	0	0	0	0	1	.000
Pete Smith, p	1	0	0	0	0	1	.000
Jeff Treadway, ph	1	0	0	0	0	0	—
Mike Stanton, p	0	0	0	0	0	0	—
Mark Wohlers, p	0	0	0	0	0	0	—
Francisco Cabrera, ph	1	0	0	0	0	0	.000
Charlie Leibrandt, p	0	0	0	0	0	0	—
Brian Hunter, ph	1	0	0	1	0	0	.200
TOTALS	38	3	8	3	5	8	.222

	1	2	3	4	5	6	7	8	9	10	11		R	H	E
Blue Jays	1	0	0	1	0	0	0	0	0	0	2		4	14	1
Braves	0	0	1	0	0	0	0	0	1	0	1		3	8	1

E—Griffin, Justice. DP—Braves 1 (Lemke to Blauser to Bream). LOB—Blue Jays 13, Braves 10. Scoring Position—Blue Jays 2-for-15, Braves 1-for-9. 2B—Carter 2 (2), Winfield (1), Borders (3), Sanders (2). HR—Maldonado (1). S—Gruber, Berryhill, Belliard. SF—Carter, Pendleton. GDP—Cone. SB—White (1), Alomar (3), Sanders 2 (5). CS—Nixon (1).

Blue Jays

	IP	H	R	ER	BB	K	ERA
David Cone	6.0	4	1	1	3	6	3.48
Todd Stottlemyre (H, 1)	0.2	1	0	0	0	1	0.00
David Wells (H, 1)	0.1	0	0	0	0	0	0.00
Duane Ward (H, 2)	1.0	0	0	0	1	1	0.00
Tom Henke (BS, 1)	1.1	2	1	1	1	0	2.70
Jimmy Key (W, 2-0)	1.1	1	1	1	0	0	1.00
Mike Timlin (S, 1)	0.1	0	0	0	0	0	0.00

Braves

	IP	H	R	ER	BB	K	ERA
Steve Avery	4.0	6	2	2	2	2	3.75
Pete Smith	3.0	3	0	0	0	0	0.00
Mike Stanton	1.2	0	0	0	1	0	0.00
Mark Wohlers	0.1	0	0	0	0	0	0.00
Charlie Leibrandt (L, 0-1)	2.0	3	2	2	0	0	9.00

HBP—White by Leibrandt. Time—4:07. Attendance—51,763. Umpires—HP, Shulock. 1B, Crawford. 2B, Reilly. 3B, West.

1992 World Series—Composite Statistics

Batting

Blue Jays

Blue Jays	G	AB	R	H	RBI	2B	3B	HR	BB	SO	SB	CS	Avg	OBP	Slg
Roberto Alomar	6	24	3	5	0	1	0	0	3	3	3	0	.208	.296	.250
Derek Bell	2	1	1	0	0	0	0	0	1	0	0	0	.000	.500	.000
Pat Borders	6	20	2	9	3	3	0	1	2	1	0	0	.450	.500	.750
Joe Carter	6	22	2	6	3	2	0	2	3	2	0	0	.273	.346	.636
David Cone	2	4	0	2	1	0	0	0	1	0	0	0	.500	.600	.500
Kelly Gruber	6	19	2	2	1	0	0	1	2	5	1	0	.105	.190	.263
Jimmy Key	2	1	0	0	0	0	0	0	0	0	0	0	.000	.000	.000
Manuel Lee	6	19	1	2	0	0	0	0	1	2	0	0	.105	.150	.105
Candy Maldonado	6	19	1	3	2	0	0	1	2	5	0	0	.158	.238	.316
Jack Morris	2	2	0	0	0	0	0	0	0	2	0	0	.000	.000	.000
John Olerud	4	13	2	4	0	0	0	0	4	0	0	0	.308	.308	.308
Ed Sprague	3	2	1	1	2	0	0	1	1	0	0	0	.500	.667	2.000
Pat Tabler	2	2	0	0	0	0	0	0	0	0	0	0	.000	.000	.000
Devon White	6	26	2	6	2	1	0	0	0	6	1	0	.231	.259	.269
Dave Winfield	6	22	0	5	3	1	0	0	2	3	0	0	.227	.292	.273
Totals	6	196	17	45	17	8	0	6	18	33	5	0	.230	.296	.362

Braves

Braves	G	AB	R	H	RBI	2B	3B	HR	BB	SO	SB	CS	Avg	OBP	Slg
Steve Avery	2	1	0	0	0	0	0	0	0	1	0	0	.000	.000	.000
Rafael Belliard	4	0	0	0	0	0	0	0	0	0	0	0	—	—	—
Damon Berryhill	6	22	1	2	3	0	0	1	1	11	0	0	.091	.130	.227
Jeff Blauser	6	24	2	6	0	0	0	0	1	9	2	1	.250	.280	.250
Sid Bream	5	15	1	3	0	0	0	0	4	0	0	0	.200	.368	.200
Francisco Cabrera	1	1	0	0	0	0	0	0	0	0	0	0	.000	.000	.000
Ron Gant	4	8	2	1	0	1	0	0	1	2	2	0	.125	.222	.250
Tom Glavine	2	2	0	0	0	0	0	0	1	0	0	0	.000	.333	.000
Brian Hunter	4	5	0	1	2	0	0	0	0	1	0	1	.200	.167	.200
David Justice	6	19	4	3	3	0	0	1	6	5	1	0	.158	.360	.316
Mark Lemke	6	19	0	4	2	0	0	0	1	3	0	0	.211	.250	.211
Otis Nixon	6	27	3	8	1	1	0	0	1	3	5	1	.296	.321	.333
Terry Pendleton	6	25	2	6	2	2	0	0	1	5	0	0	.240	.259	.320
Deion Sanders	4	15	4	8	1	2	0	0	2	1	5	0	.533	.588	.667
Lonnie Smith	5	12	1	2	5	0	0	1	1	4	0	0	.167	.286	.417
Pete Smith	1	1	0	0	0	0	0	0	0	1	0	0	.000	.000	.000
John Smoltz	3	3	0	0	0	0	0	0	0	2	0	0	.000	.000	.000
Jeff Treadway	1	1	0	0	0	0	0	0	0	0	0	0	.000	.000	.000
Totals	6	200	20	44	19	6	0	3	20	48	15	3	.220	.291	.295

Pitching

Blue Jays

Blue Jays	G	GS	CG	IP	H	R	ER	BB	SO	W-L	Sv-Op	Hld	ERA
David Cone	2	2	0	10.1	9	5	4	8	8	0-0	0-0	0	3.48
Mark Eichhorn	1	0	0	1.0	0	0	0	0	1	0-0	0-0	0	0.00
Juan Guzman	1	1	0	8.0	8	2	1	1	7	0-0	0-0	0	1.13
Tom Henke	3	0	0	3.1	2	1	1	2	1	0-0	2-3	0	2.70
Jimmy Key	2	1	0	9.0	6	2	1	0	6	2-0	0-0	0	1.00
Jack Morris	2	2	0	10.2	13	10	10	6	12	0-2	0-0	0	8.44
Todd Stottlemyre	4	0	0	3.2	4	0	0	0	4	0-0	0-0	1	0.00
Mike Timlin	2	0	0	1.1	0	0	0	0	0	1-1	0-0	0	0.00
Duane Ward	4	0	0	3.1	1	0	0	1	6	2-0	0-0	2	0.00
David Wells	4	0	0	4.1	1	0	0	2	3	0-0	0-0	1	0.00
Totals	6	6	0	55.0	44	20	17	20	48	4-2	3-4	4	2.78

Braves

Braves	G	GS	CG	IP	H	R	ER	BB	SO	W-L	Sv-Op	Hld	ERA
Steve Avery	2	2	0	12.0	11	5	5	3	11	0-1	0-0	0	3.75
Tom Glavine	2	2	2	17.0	10	3	3	4	8	1-1	0-0	0	1.59
Charlie Leibrandt	1	0	0	2.0	3	2	2	0	0	0-1	0-0	0	9.00
Jeff Reardon	2	0	0	1.1	2	2	2	1	1	0-1	0-1	0	13.50
Pete Smith	1	0	0	3.0	3	0	0	0	0	0-0	0-0	0	0.00
John Smoltz	2	2	0	13.1	13	5	4	7	12	1-0	0-0	0	2.70
Mike Stanton	4	0	0	5.0	3	0	0	2	1	0-0	1-1	1	0.00
Mark Wohlers	2	0	0	0.2	0	0	0	1	0	0-0	0-0	0	0.00
Totals	6	6	2	54.1	45	17	16	18	33	2-4	1-2	1	2.65

Fielding

Blue Jays

Blue Jays	Pos	G	PO	Ast	E	DP	PB	FPct
Roberto Alomar	2b	6	5	12	0	0	—	1.000
Pat Borders	c	6	48	5	1	2	0	.981
Joe Carter	rf	3	5	0	0	0	—	1.000
	1b	2	20	1	0	0	—	1.000
	lf	1	2	0	0	0	—	1.000
David Cone	p	2	0	0	0	0	—	—
Mark Eichhorn	p	1	0	0	0	0	—	—
Alfredo Griffin	ss	2	0	1	1	0	—	.500
Kelly Gruber	3b	6	5	5	1	0	—	.909
Juan Guzman	p	1	2	0	0	0	—	1.000
Tom Henke	p	3	0	2	0	0	—	1.000
Jimmy Key	p	2	2	4	0	0	—	1.000
Manuel Lee	ss	6	14	10	1	4	—	.960
Candy Maldonado	lf	5	8	2	0	1	—	1.000
Jack Morris	p	2	0	1	0	0	—	1.000
John Olerud	1b	4	25	3	0	2	—	1.000
Ed Sprague	1b	1	0	0	0	0	—	—
Todd Stottlemyre	p	4	0	0	0	0	—	—
Mike Timlin	p	2	0	1	0	0	—	1.000
Duane Ward	p	4	0	0	0	0	—	—
David Wells	p	4	0	0	0	0	—	—
Devon White	cf	6	22	1	0	1	—	1.000
Dave Winfield	rf	3	7	0	0	0	—	1.000
Totals		6	165	48	4	10	0	.982

Braves

Braves	Pos	G	PO	Ast	E	DP	PB	FPct
Steve Avery	p	2	0	2	0	0	—	1.000
Rafael Belliard	ss	3	1	2	0	1	—	1.000
	2b	1	1	0	0	0	—	1.000
Damon Berryhill	c	6	33	2	0	0	0	1.000
Jeff Blauser	ss	6	7	22	0	5	—	1.000
Sid Bream	1b	5	41	1	1	4	—	.977
Ron Gant	lf	3	3	1	0	0	—	1.000
Tom Glavine	p	2	0	2	0	0	—	1.000
Brian Hunter	1b	3	14	1	0	2	—	1.000
David Justice	rf	6	15	0	1	0	—	.938
Charlie Leibrandt	p	1	1	0	0	0	—	1.000
Mark Lemke	2b	6	19	12	0	5	—	1.000
Otis Nixon	cf	6	18	0	0	0	—	1.000
Terry Pendleton	3b	6	4	19	0	1	—	1.000
Jeff Reardon	p	2	0	0	0	0	—	—
Deion Sanders	lf	4	5	1	0	0	—	1.000
Pete Smith	p	1	1	0	0	0	—	—
John Smoltz	p	2	1	2	0	0	—	1.000
Mike Stanton	p	4	0	0	0	0	—	—
Mark Wohlers	p	2	0	0	0	0	—	—
Totals		6	163	67	2	18	0	.991

1993 Toronto Blue Jays (AL) 4, Philadelphia Phillies (NL) 2

For those who weren't alive to witness Bobby Thomson's homer off Ralph Branca, Joe Carter and Mitch Williams re-created the event. It all started with the Toronto Blue Jays taking the opening game from the Philadelphia Phillies and Curt Schilling, 8-5. The Phils came back to win Game 2, 6-4, as Jim Eisenreich launched a three-run homer off Dave Stewart. Paul Molitor singled, tripled and homered, while Roberto Alomar notched four hits in Toronto's 10-3 win in the third game. Game 4 was one of the wildest on record. The Phils took a 14-9 lead into the top of the eighth, but Williams couldn't hold it, allowing the Jays to rally for six runs. Toronto won 15-14 to go up three games to one. Schilling turned in a clutch mound performance in Game 5, blanking the Jays on five hits and going the route for a 2-0 victory. Then came historic Game 6. The Phillies rallied for five runs in the top of the seventh to take a 6-5 lead. As the lead held into the bottom of the ninth, Jim Fregosi called on Williams to get the last three outs. He put two runners on with one out, bringing up Carter. Carter lit into a slider down and in, sending it over the left field fence for the only come-from-behind, Series-winning home run in World Series history.

Game 1

Saturday, October 16

Phillies	AB	R	H	RBI	BB	K	Avg
Lenny Dykstra, cf	4	1	1	0	1	0	.250
Mariano Duncan, 2b	5	2	3	0	0	2	.600
John Kruk, 1b	4	2	3	2	1	1	.750
Dave Hollins, 3b	4	0	0	0	1	1	.000
Darren Daulton, c	4	0	1	1	1	2	.250
Jim Eisenreich, rf	5	0	1	0	2	2	.200
Ricky Jordan, dh	5	0	1	0	0	2	.200
Milt Thompson, lf	3	0	0	0	1	0	.000
Pete Incaviglia, ph-lf	1	0	0	0	0	0	.000
Kevin Stocker, ss	3	0	1	0	1	0	.333
TOTALS	38	5	11	4	5	11	.289

Blue Jays	AB	R	H	RBI	BB	K	Avg
Rickey Henderson, lf	3	1	1	0	1	0	.333
Devon White, cf	4	3	2	0	0	0	.500
Roberto Alomar, 2b	4	0	1	2	0	1	.250
Joe Carter, rf	3	1	1	1	0	1	.333
John Olerud, 1b	3	2	2	1	1	0	.667
Paul Molitor, dh	4	0	1	0	0	0	.250
Tony Fernandez, ss	3	0	0	1	1	0	.000
Ed Sprague, 3b	4	0	1	0	0	2	.250
Pat Borders, c	4	1	1	0	0	1	.250
TOTALS	32	8	10	8	3	5	.313

	1	2	3	4	5	6	7	8	9		R	H	E
Phillies	2	0	1	0	1	0	0	0	1		5	11	1
Blue Jays	0	2	1	0	1	1	3	0	x		8	10	3

E—Carter, Thompson, Alomar, Sprague. DP—Phillies 1 (Stocker to Duncan to Kruk), Blue Jays 1 (Fernandez to Olerud). LOB—Phillies 11, Blue Jays 4. Scoring Position—Phillies 5-for-13, Blue Jays 3-for-9. 2B—White (1), Alomar (1). 3B—Duncan (1). HR—White (1), Olerud (1). SF—Carter. GDP—Thompson, White. SB—Dykstra (1), Duncan (1), Alomar (1). CS—Fernandez (1).

Phillies	IP	H	R	ER	BB	K	ERA
Curt Schilling (L, 0-1)	6.1	8	7	6	2	3	8.53
David West	0.0	2	1	1	0	0	—
Larry Andersen	0.2	0	0	0	1	1	0.00
Roger Mason	1.0	0	0	0	0	1	0.00

Blue Jays	IP	H	R	ER	BB	K	ERA
Juan Guzman	5.0	5	4	4	4	6	7.20
Al Leiter (W, 1-0)	2.2	4	0	0	1	2	0.00
Duane Ward (S, 1)	1.1	2	1	0	0	3	0.00

West pitched to two batters in the 7th.

WP—Guzman. PB—Daulton. Time—3:27. Attendance—52,011. Umpires—HP, Phillips. 1B, Runge. 2B, Johnson. 3B, Williams.

Game 2

Sunday, October 17

Phillies	AB	R	H	RBI	BB	K	Avg
Lenny Dykstra, cf	4	2	2	1	1	0	.375
Mariano Duncan, 2b	4	1	1	0	1	2	.444
John Kruk, 1b	5	1	2	1	0	1	.556
Dave Hollins, 3b	4	1	2	1	1	2	.250
Kim Batiste, 3b	0	0	0	0	0	0	—
Darren Daulton, c	5	0	1	0	0	0	.222
Jim Eisenreich, rf	4	1	1	3	1	1	.222
Pete Incaviglia, lf	4	0	1	0	0	2	.200
Milt Thompson, pr-lf	0	0	0	0	0	0	.000
Ricky Jordan, dh	4	0	1	0	0	0	.222
Kevin Stocker, ss	3	0	1	0	1	0	.333
TOTALS	37	6	12	6	5	8	.307

Blue Jays	AB	R	H	RBI	BB	K	Avg
Rickey Henderson, lf	3	0	0	0	1	1	.167
Devon White, cf	4	0	1	0	0	2	.375
Paul Molitor, dh	3	2	2	0	1	0	.429
Joe Carter, rf	4	1	1	2	0	1	.286
John Olerud, 1b	3	0	0	1	0	0	.333
Roberto Alomar, 2b	3	1	1	0	1	1	.286
Tony Fernandez, ss	3	0	2	1	1	0	.333
Ed Sprague, 3b	4	0	0	0	0	1	.125
Alfredo Griffin, pr	0	0	0	0	0	0	—
Pat Borders, c	4	0	1	0	0	0	.250
TOTALS	31	4	8	4	4	6	.286

	1	2	3	4	5	6	7	8	9		R	H	E
Phillies	0	0	5	0	0	0	1	0	0		6	12	0
Blue Jays	0	0	0	2	0	1	0	1	0		4	8	0

DP—Blue Jays 1 (Sprague to Alomar to Olerud). LOB—Phillies 9, Blue Jays 5. Scoring Position—Phillies 4-for-12, Blue Jays 0-for-3. 2B—White (2), Molitor (1), Fernandez (1). HR—Dykstra (1), Eisenreich (1), Carter (1). SF—Olerud. GDP—Eisenreich, Borders. SB—Molitor (1), Alomar (2). CS—Stocker (1), Henderson (1), Alomar (1).

Phillies	IP	H	R	ER	BB	K	ERA
Terry Mulholland (W, 1-0)	5.2	7	3	3	2	4	4.76
Roger Mason (H, 1)	1.2	1	1	1	0	2	3.38
Mitch Williams (S, 1)	1.2	0	0	0	2	0	0.00

Blue Jays	IP	H	R	ER	BB	K	ERA
Dave Stewart (L, 0-1)	6.0	6	5	5	4	6	7.50
Tony Castillo	1.0	3	1	1	0	0	9.00
Mark Eichhorn	0.1	1	0	0	1	0	0.00
Mike Timlin	1.2	2	0	0	0	2	0.00

Balk—Stewart. WP—Stewart. Time—3:35. Attendance—52,062. Umpires—HP, Runge. 1B, Johnson. 2B, Williams. 3B, McClelland.

Game 3

Tuesday, October 19

Blue Jays	AB	R	H	RBI	BB	K	Avg
Rickey Henderson, lf	4	2	2	0	0	0	.300
Devon White, cf	4	2	1	1	1	0	.333
Paul Molitor, 1b	4	3	3	3	1	0	.545
Joe Carter, rf	4	1	1	1	0	1	.273
Roberto Alomar, 2b	5	2	4	2	0	0	.500
Tony Fernandez, ss	3	0	2	2	1	0	.444
Ed Sprague, 3b	4	0	0	1	0	2	.083
Pat Borders, c	4	0	0	0	1	0	.167
Pat Hentgen, p	3	0	0	0	0	1	.000
Danny Cox, p	1	0	0	0	0	0	.000
Duane Ward, p	0	0	0	0	0	0	—
TOTALS	36	10	13	10	4	4	.312

Phillies	AB	R	H	RBI	BB	K	Avg
Lenny Dykstra, cf	5	0	1	0	0	1	.308
Mariano Duncan, 2b	5	0	2	1	0	1	.429
John Kruk, 1b	3	1	2	0	2	1	.583
Dave Hollins, 3b	3	0	0	0	1	1	.182
Darren Daulton, c	3	0	0	0	1	1	.167
Jim Eisenreich, rf	4	0	1	1	0	0	.231
Pete Incaviglia, lf	3	0	0	0	0	2	.125
Bobby Thigpen, p	0	0	0	0	0	0	—
Mickey Morandini, ph	0	0	0	0	1	0	—
Larry Andersen, p	0	0	0	0	0	0	—
Kevin Stocker, ss	4	0	1	0	0	2	.300
Danny Jackson, p	1	0	0	0	0	1	.000
Wes Chamberlain, ph	1	0	0	0	0	0	.000
Ben Rivera, p	0	0	0	0	0	0	—
Milt Thompson, lf	2	2	2	1	0	0	.400
TOTALS	34	3	9	3	5	10	.300

	1	2	3	4	5	6	7	8	9		R	H	E
Blue Jays	3	0	1	0	0	1	3	0	2		10	13	1
Phillies	0	0	0	0	0	1	1	0	1		3	9	0

E—Carter. DP—Blue Jays 2 (Alomar to Fernandez to Molitor; Molitor to Fernandez to Cox). LOB—Blue Jays 7, Phillies 9. Scoring Position—Blue Jays 5-for-8, Phillies 2-for-9. 2B—Henderson (1), Kruk (1). 3B—White (1), Molitor (1), Alomar (1). HR—Molitor (1), Thompson (1). SF—Carter, Fernandez, Sprague. GDP—Hollins, Chamberlain. SB—Alomar 2 (4).

Blue Jays	IP	H	R	ER	BB	K	ERA
Pat Hentgen (W, 1-0)	6.0	5	1	1	3	6	1.50
Danny Cox	2.0	3	1	1	2	2	4.50
Duane Ward	1.0	1	1	1	0	2	3.86

Phillies	IP	H	R	ER	BB	K	ERA
Danny Jackson (L, 0-1)	5.0	6	4	4	1	1	7.20
Ben Rivera	1.1	4	4	4	2	3	27.00
Bobby Thigpen	1.2	0	0	0	1	0	0.00
Larry Andersen	1.0	3	2	2	0	0	10.80

HBP—Henderson by Thigpen. Time—3:16. Attendance—62,689. Umpires—HP, Johnson. 1B, Williams. 2B, McClelland. 3B, DeMuth.

Game 4
Wednesday, October 20

Blue Jays	AB	R	H	RBI	BB	K	Avg
Rickey Henderson, lf	5	2	2	2	1	1	.333
Devon White, cf	5	2	3	4	1	1	.412
Roberto Alomar, 2b	6	1	2	1	0	1	.444
Joe Carter, rf	6	2	3	0	0	0	.353
John Olerud, 1b	4	2	1	0	2	0	.300
Paul Molitor, 3b	4	2	2	2	1	0	.533
Alfredo Griffin, 3b	0	0	0	0	0	0	—
Tony Fernandez, ss	6	2	3	5	0	1	.467
Pat Borders, c	4	1	1	1	1	0	.188
Todd Stottlemyre, p	0	0	0	0	0	1	—
Rob Butler, ph	1	1	0	0	0	0	.000
Al Leiter, p	1	0	1	0	0	0	1.000
Tony Castillo, p	1	0	0	0	0	1	.000
Ed Sprague, ph	1	0	0	0	1	1	.077
Mike Timlin, p	0	0	0	0	0	0	—
Duane Ward, p	0	0	0	0	0	0	—
TOTALS	44	15	18	15	7	6	.353

Phillies	AB	R	H	RBI	BB	K	Avg
Lenny Dykstra, cf	5	4	3	4	1	1	.389
Mariano Duncan, 2b	6	1	3	1	0	0	.450
John Kruk, 1b	5	0	0	0	1	2	.412
Dave Hollins, 3b	4	3	2	0	2	0	.267
Darren Daulton, c	3	2	1	3	1	0	.200
Jim Eisenreich, rf	4	2	1	1	1	0	.235
Milt Thompson, lf	5	1	3	5	0	0	.500
Kevin Stocker, ss	4	0	0	0	1	1	.214
Tommy Greene, p	1	1	1	0	0	0	1.000
Roger Mason, p	1	0	0	0	0	0	—
Ricky Jordan, ph	1	0	0	0	0	0	.200
David West, p	0	0	0	0	0	0	—
Wes Chamberlain, ph	1	0	0	0	0	1	.000
Larry Andersen, p	0	0	0	0	0	0	—
Mitch Williams, p	0	0	0	0	0	0	—
Mickey Morandini, ph	1	0	0	0	0	1	.000
Bobby Thigpen, p	0	0	0	0	0	0	—
TOTALS	41	14	14	14	7	7	.319

	1	2	3	4	5	6	7	8	9	R	H	E
Blue Jays	3	0	4	0	0	2	0	6	0	15	18	0
Phillies	4	2	0	1	5	1	1	0	0	14	14	0

LOB—Blue Jays 10, Phillies 8. Scoring Position—Blue Jays 10-for-23, Phillies 4-for-14. 2B—Henderson (2), White (3), Carter (1), Molitor (2), Dykstra (1), Hollins (1), Thompson (1), Leiter (1). 3B—White (2), Thompson (1). HR—Dykstra 2 (3), Daulton (1). SB—Henderson (1), White (1), Dykstra (2), Duncan (2).

Blue Jays	IP	H	R	ER	BB	K	ERA
Todd Stottlemyre	2.0	3	6	6	4	1	27.00
Al Leiter	2.2	8	6	6	0	1	10.13
Tony Castillo (W, 1-0)	2.1	3	2	2	3	1	8.10
Mike Timlin (H, 1)	0.2	0	0	0	0	2	0.00
Duane Ward (S, 2)	1.1	0	0	0	0	2	2.45

Phillies	IP	H	R	ER	BB	K	ERA
Tommy Greene	2.1	7	7	7	4	1	27.00
Roger Mason	2.2	2	0	0	1	2	1.69
David West	1.0	3	2	2	0	0	27.00
Larry Andersen	1.1	2	3	3	1	2	15.00
Mitch Williams (BS, 1; L, 0-1)	0.2	3	3	3	1	1	11.57
Bobby Thigpen	1.0	1	0	0	0	0	0.00

HBP—Molitor by West, Daulton by Castillo. Time—4:14. Attendance—62,731. Umpires—HP, Williams. 1B, McClelland. 2B, DeMuth. 3B, Phillips.

Game 5
Thursday, October 21

Blue Jays	AB	R	H	RBI	BB	K	Avg
Rickey Henderson, lf	3	0	0	0	1	0	.278
Devon White, cf	3	0	0	0	1	2	.350
Roberto Alomar, 2b	3	0	1	0	1	0	.429
Joe Carter, rf	4	0	0	0	0	1	.286
John Olerud, 1b	4	0	0	0	0	1	.214
Paul Molitor, 3b	4	0	1	0	0	0	.474
Tony Fernandez, ss	3	0	0	0	0	1	.389
Pat Borders, c	3	0	2	0	0	0	.263
Willie Canate, pr	0	0	0	0	0	0	—
Randy Knorr, c	0	0	0	0	0	0	—
Juan Guzman, p	2	0	0	0	0	1	.000
Rob Butler, ph	1	0	1	0	0	0	.500
Danny Cox, p	0	0	0	0	0	0	.000
TOTALS	30	0	5	0	3	6	.335

Phillies	AB	R	H	RBI	BB	K	Avg
Lenny Dykstra, cf	2	1	0	0	2	1	.350
Mariano Duncan, 2b	4	0	0	0	0	1	.375
John Kruk, 1b	3	0	1	1	1	0	.400
Dave Hollins, 3b	3	0	1	0	1	1	.278
Kim Batiste, 3b	0	0	0	0	0	0	—
Darren Daulton, c	4	1	1	0	0	1	.211
Jim Eisenreich, rf	4	0	0	0	0	1	.190
Milt Thompson, lf	3	0	0	0	1	1	.385
Kevin Stocker, ss	2	0	1	1	1	1	.250
Curt Schilling, p	2	0	1	0	0	1	.500
TOTALS	27	2	5	2	6	9	.307

	1	2	3	4	5	6	7	8	9	R	H	E
Blue Jays	0	0	0	0	0	0	0	0	0	0	5	1
Phillies	1	1	0	0	0	0	0	0	x	2	5	1

E—Duncan, Borders. DP—Blue Jays 1 (Fernandez to Olerud), Phillies 3 (Kruk to Stocker to Duncan; Daulton to Duncan; Duncan to Stocker to Kruk). LOB—Blue Jays 6, Phillies 8. Scoring Position—Blue Jays 0-for-4, Phillies 1-for-11. 2B—Daulton (1), Stocker (1). S—Schilling. GDP—Alomar, Guzman, Duncan. SB—Dykstra (3). CS—Alomar (2).

Blue Jays	IP	H	R	ER	BB	K	ERA
Juan Guzman (L, 0-1)	7.0	5	2	1	4	6	3.75
Danny Cox	1.0	0	0	0	2	3	3.00

Phillies	IP	H	R	ER	BB	K	ERA
Curt Schilling (W, 1-1)	9.0	5	0	0	3	6	3.52

Time—2:53. Attendance—62,706. Umpires—HP, McClelland. 1B, DeMuth. 2B, Phillips. 3B, Runge.

Game 6
Saturday, October 23

Phillies	AB	R	H	RBI	BB	K	Avg
Lenny Dykstra, cf	3	1	1	3	2	1	.348
Mariano Duncan, dh	5	1	1	0	0	1	.345
John Kruk, 1b	3	0	0	0	2	1	.348
Dave Hollins, 3b	5	1	1	1	0	0	.261
Kim Batiste, 3b	0	0	0	0	0	0	—
Darren Daulton, c	4	1	1	0	1	0	.217
Jim Eisenreich, rf	5	0	2	1	0	0	.231
Milt Thompson, lf	3	0	0	0	0	0	.313
Pete Incaviglia, ph-lf	0	0	0	1	0	0	.125
Kevin Stocker, ss	3	1	0	0	1	1	.211
Mickey Morandini, 2b	4	1	1	0	0	1	.200
TOTALS	35	6	7	6	6	5	.277

Blue Jays	AB	R	H	RBI	BB	K	Avg
Rickey Henderson, lf	4	1	0	0	1	0	.227
Devon White, cf	4	1	0	0	1	2	.292
Paul Molitor, dh	5	3	3	2	0	0	.500
Joe Carter, rf	4	1	1	4	0	0	.280
John Olerud, 1b	3	1	1	0	1	0	.235
Alfredo Griffin, pr-3b	0	0	0	0	0	0	—
Roberto Alomar, 2b	4	1	3	1	0	0	.480
Tony Fernandez, ss	3	0	0	0	0	1	.333
Ed Sprague, 3b-1b	2	0	0	1	1	0	.067
Pat Borders, c	4	0	2	0	0	0	.304
TOTALS	33	8	10	8	4	3	.316

	1	2	3	4	5	6	7	8	9	R	H	E
Phillies	0	0	0	1	0	0	5	0	0	6	7	0
Blue Jays	3	0	0	1	1	0	0	0	3	8	10	2

E—Alomar, Sprague. LOB—Phillies 9, Blue Jays 7. Scoring Position—Phillies 4-for-7, Blue Jays 2-for-4. 2B—Daulton (2), Olerud (1), Alomar (2). 3B—Molitor (2). HR—Dykstra (4), Molitor (2), Carter (2). SF—Carter, Sprague, Incaviglia. SB—Dykstra (4), Duncan (3).

Phillies	IP	H	R	ER	BB	K	ERA
Terry Mulholland	5.0	7	5	5	1	1	6.75
Roger Mason	2.1	1	0	0	0	2	1.17
David West	0.0	0	0	0	1	0	27.00
Larry Andersen (H, 1)	0.2	0	0	0	1	0	12.27
Mitch Williams (BS, 2; L, 0-2)	0.1	2	3	3	1	0	20.25

Blue Jays	IP	H	R	ER	BB	K	ERA
Dave Stewart	6.0	4	4	4	4	2	6.75
Danny Cox (BS, 1)	0.1	3	2	2	1	1	8.10
Al Leiter	1.2	0	0	0	1	2	7.71
Duane Ward (W, 1-0)	1.0	0	0	0	0	0	1.93

Stewart pitched to three batters in the 7th. West pitched to one batter in the 8th.

HBP—Fernandez by Andersen. Time—3:27. Attendance—52,195. Umpires—HP, DeMuth. 1B, Phillips. 2B, Runge. 3B, Johnson.

1993 World Series—Composite Statistics

Batting

Blue Jays	G	AB	R	H	RBI	2B	3B	HR	BB	SO	SB	CS	Avg	OBP	Slg
Roberto Alomar	6	25	5	12	6	2	1	0	2	3	4	2	.480	.519	.640
Pat Borders	6	23	2	7	1	0	0	0	2	1	0	0	.304	.360	.304
Rob Butler	2	2	1	1	0	0	0	0	0	0	0	0	.500	.500	.500
Willie Canate	1	0	0	0	0	0	0	0	0	0	0	0	—	—	—
Joe Carter	6	25	6	7	8	1	0	2	0	4	0	0	.280	.250	.560
Tony Castillo	2	1	0	0	0	0	0	0	0	1	0	0	.000	.000	.000
Danny Cox	3	1	0	0	0	0	0	0	0	0	0	0	.000	.000	.000
Tony Fernandez	6	21	2	7	9	1	0	0	3	3	0	1	.333	.423	.381
Juan Guzman	2	2	0	0	0	0	0	0	0	1	0	0	.000	.000	.000
Rickey Henderson	6	22	6	5	2	2	0	0	5	2	1	1	.227	.393	.318
Pat Hentgen	1	3	0	0	0	0	0	0	0	1	0	0	.000	.000	.000
Al Leiter	3	1	0	1	0	1	0	0	0	0	0	0	1.000	1.000	2.000
Paul Molitor	6	24	10	12	8	2	2	2	3	0	1	0	.500	.571	1.000
John Olerud	5	17	5	4	2	1	0	1	4	1	0	0	.235	.364	.471
Ed Sprague	5	15	0	1	2	0	0	0	1	6	0	0	.067	.111	.067
Todd Stottlemyre	1	0	0	0	0	0	0	0	1	0	0	0	—	1.000	—
Devon White	6	24	8	7	3	2	1	0	2	7	3	0	.292	.393	.708
Totals	6	206	45	64	45	13	5	6	25	30	7	4	.311	.382	.510

Batting

Phillies	G	AB	R	H	RBI	2B	3B	HR	BB	SO	SB	CS	Avg	OBP	Slg
Wes Chamberlain	2	2	0	0	0	0	0	0	0	0	1	0	.000	.000	.000
Darren Daulton	6	23	4	5	4	2	0	1	4	5	0	0	.217	.357	.435
Mariano Duncan	6	29	5	10	2	0	1	0	1	7	3	0	.345	.367	.414
Lenny Dykstra	6	23	9	8	8	1	0	4	7	4	4	0	.348	.500	.913
Jim Eisenreich	6	26	3	6	7	0	0	1	2	4	0	0	.231	.286	.346
Tommy Greene	1	1	1	1	0	0	0	0	0	0	0	0	1.000	1.000	1.000
Dave Hollins	6	23	5	6	2	1	0	0	6	5	0	0	.261	.414	.304
Pete Incaviglia	4	8	0	1	0	0	0	0	0	4	0	0	.125	.111	.125
Danny Jackson	1	1	0	0	0	0	0	0	0	1	0	0	.000	.000	.000
Ricky Jordan	3	10	0	2	0	0	0	0	0	2	0	0	.200	.200	.200
John Kruk	6	23	4	8	4	1	0	0	7	7	0	0	.348	.500	.391
Roger Mason	4	1	0	0	0	0	0	0	0	0	0	0	.000	.000	.000
Mickey Morandini	3	5	1	1	0	0	0	0	1	2	0	0	.200	.333	.200
Curt Schilling	2	2	0	1	0	0	0	0	0	1	0	0	.500	.500	.500
Kevin Stocker	6	19	1	4	1	1	0	0	5	5	0	1	.211	.375	.263
Milt Thompson	6	16	3	5	6	1	1	1	1	2	0	0	.313	.353	.688
Totals	6	212	36	58	35	7	2	7	34	50	7	1	.274	.375	.425

Pitching

Blue Jays	G	GS	CG	IP	H	R	ER	BB	SO	W-L	Sv-Op	Hld	ERA
Tony Castillo	2	0	0	3.1	6	3	3	3	1	1-0	0-0	0	8.10
Danny Cox	3	0	0	3.1	6	3	3	5	6	0-0	0-1	0	8.10
Mark Eichhorn	1	0	0	0.1	1	0	0	1	0	0-0	0-0	0	0.00
Juan Guzman	2	2	0	12.0	10	6	5	8	12	0-1	0-0	0	3.75
Pat Hentgen	1	1	0	6.0	5	1	1	3	6	1-0	0-0	0	1.50
Al Leiter	3	0	0	7.0	12	6	6	2	5	1-0	0-0	0	7.71
Dave Stewart	2	2	0	12.0	10	9	9	8	8	0-1	0-0	0	6.75
Todd Stottlemyre	1	1	0	2.0	3	6	4	1	0	0-0	0-0	0	27.00
Mike Timlin	2	0	0	2.1	2	0	0	0	4	0-0	0-0	1	0.00
Duane Ward	4	0	0	4.2	3	2	1	0	7	1-0	2-2	0	1.93
Totals	6	6	0	53.0	58	36	34	34	50	4-2	2-3	1	5.77

Pitching

Phillies	G	GS	CG	IP	H	R	ER	BB	SO	W-L	Sv-Op	Hld	ERA
Larry Andersen	4	0	0	3.2	5	5	5	3	3	0-0	0-0	1	12.27
Tommy Greene	1	1	0	2.1	7	7	7	4	1	0-0	0-0	0	27.00
Danny Jackson	1	1	0	5.0	6	4	4	1	1	0-1	0-0	0	7.20
Roger Mason	4	0	0	7.2	4	1	1	1	7	0-0	0-0	0	1.17
Terry Mulholland	2	2	0	10.2	14	8	8	3	5	1-0	0-0	0	6.75
Ben Rivera	1	0	0	1.1	4	4	4	2	3	0-0	0-0	0	27.00
Curt Schilling	2	2	1	15.1	13	7	6	5	9	1-1	0-0	0	3.52
Bobby Thigpen	2	0	0	2.2	1	0	0	1	0	0-0	0-0	0	0.00
David West	3	0	0	1.0	5	3	3	1	0	0-0	0-0	0	27.00
Mitch Williams	3	0	0	2.2	5	6	6	4	1	0-2	1-3	0	20.25
Totals	6	6	1	52.1	64	45	44	25	30	2-4	1-3	2	7.57

Fielding

Blue Jays	Pos	G	PO	Ast	E	DP	PB	FPct
Roberto Alomar	2b	6	9	21	2	2	—	.938
Pat Borders	c	6	50	2	1	0	0	.981
Joe Carter	rf	6	13	0	2	0	—	.867
Tony Castillo	p	2	0	0	0	0	—	—
Danny Cox	p	3	1	0	0	1	—	1.000
Mark Eichhorn	p	1	0	0	0	0	—	—
Tony Fernandez	ss	6	11	8	0	4	—	1.000
Alfredo Griffin	3b	2	0	0	0	0	—	—
Juan Guzman	p	2	0	1	0	0	—	1.000
Rickey Henderson	lf	6	8	0	0	0	—	1.000
Pat Hentgen	p	1	0	0	0	0	—	—
Randy Knorr	c	1	3	0	0	0	0	1.000
Al Leiter	p	3	0	0	0	0	—	—
Paul Molitor	3b	2	0	2	0	0	—	1.000
	1b	1	7	1	0	2	—	1.000
John Olerud	1b	5	36	0	0	3	—	1.000
Ed Sprague	3b	4	3	9	2	1	—	.857
	1b	1	1	0	0	0	—	1.000
Dave Stewart	p	2	1	1	0	0	—	1.000
Todd Stottlemyre	p	1	0	0	0	0	—	—
Mike Timlin	p	2	0	0	0	0	—	—
Duane Ward	p	4	0	0	0	0	—	—
Devon White	cf	6	16	0	0	0	—	1.000
Totals		6	159	45	7	13	0	.967

Fielding

Phillies	Pos	G	PO	Ast	E	DP	PB	FPct
Larry Andersen	p	4	0	0	0	0	—	—
Kim Batiste	3b	3	0	1	0	0	—	1.000
Darren Daulton	c	6	31	4	0	1	1	1.000
Mariano Duncan	2b	5	11	17	1	5	—	.966
Lenny Dykstra	cf	6	18	1	0	0	—	1.000
Jim Eisenreich	rf	6	18	0	0	0	—	1.000
Tommy Greene	p	1	0	0	0	0	—	—
Dave Hollins	3b	6	9	9	0	0	—	1.000
Pete Incaviglia	lf	4	7	0	0	0	—	1.000
Danny Jackson	p	1	0	0	0	0	—	—
John Kruk	1b	6	42	3	0	4	—	1.000
Roger Mason	p	4	0	0	0	0	—	—
Mickey Morandini	2b	1	2	0	0	0	—	1.000
Terry Mulholland	p	2	1	1	0	0	—	1.000
Ben Rivera	p	1	0	0	0	0	—	—
Curt Schilling	p	2	0	3	0	0	—	1.000
Kevin Stocker	ss	6	8	13	0	4	—	1.000
Bobby Thigpen	p	2	0	1	0	0	—	1.000
Milt Thompson	lf	6	10	0	1	0	—	.909
David West	p	3	0	0	0	0	—	—
Mitch Williams	p	3	0	1	0	0	—	1.000
Totals		6	157	54	2	14	1	.991

1995 Atlanta Braves (NL) 4, Cleveland Indians (AL) 2

After losing the 1991 and 1992 World Series, as well as the 1993 NLCS, the Braves finally won the big one, taking down the upstart Cleveland Indians in six games. Greg Maddux was at his best in Game 1, crafting a two-hitter to beat Orel Hershiser, 3-2. Tom Glavine wasn't nearly as brilliant in Game 2, but Javy Lopez hit a two-run homer and picked the potential tying run off first base in the top of the eighth. Cleveland rebounded in Game 3, knocking out John Smoltz after only 2.1 innings, and later tying the score in the bottom of the eighth after Atlanta had rallied to go ahead 6-5. It remained tied until the bottom of the 11th, when Eddie Murray lined an RBI single to win the game. Rather than go back to Maddux in Game 4, Bobby Cox went with his fourth starter, Steve Avery. The decision paid off as Avery allowed only one run over six innings while the Braves won 5-2 to take a 3-to-1 lead in the Series. In Game 5, Hershiser beat Maddux 5-4 to keep Cleveland's hopes alive, but Glavine sealed it with an eight-inning, one-hit masterpiece in the sixth game. David Justice homered for the game's only run, and the Braves were champions at last.

Game 1
Saturday, October 21

Indians	AB	R	H	RBI	BB	K	Avg
Kenny Lofton, cf	4	2	1	0	0	0	.250
Omar Vizquel, ss	4	0	0	0	0	1	.000
Carlos Baerga, 2b	4	0	0	1	0	1	.000
Albert Belle, lf	3	0	0	0	0	0	.000
Eddie Murray, 1b	3	0	0	0	0	0	.000
Julian Tavarez, p	0	0	0	0	0	0	—
Alan Embree, p	0	0	0	0	0	0	—
Jim Thome, 3b	3	0	1	0	0	0	.333
Manny Ramirez, rf	3	0	0	0	0	2	.000
Sandy Alomar Jr., c	3	0	0	0	0	0	.000
Orel Hershiser, p	2	0	0	0	0	0	.000
Paul Assenmacher, p	0	0	0	0	0	0	—
Paul Sorrento, 1b	1	0	0	0	0	0	.000
TOTALS	30	2	2	1	0	4	.067

Braves	AB	R	H	RBI	BB	K	Avg
Marquis Grissom, cf	4	0	1	0	0	1	.250
Mark Lemke, 2b	3	0	1	0	1	1	.333
Chipper Jones, 3b	4	0	0	0	0	2	.000
Fred McGriff, 1b	3	2	1	1	1	1	.333
David Justice, rf	1	1	0	0	2	0	.000
Ryan Klesko, lf	2	0	0	0	2	2	.000
Mike Devereaux, ph-lf	0	0	0	0	1	0	—
Charlie O'Brien, c	2	0	0	0	0	1	.000
Luis Polonia, ph	1	0	0	1	0	0	.000
Javy Lopez, c	0	0	0	0	0	0	—
Rafael Belliard, ss	2	0	0	1	0	0	.000
Greg Maddux, p	3	0	0	0	0	1	.000
TOTALS	25	3	3	3	5	9	.120

	1	2	3	4	5	6	7	8	9		R	H	E
Indians	1	0	0	0	0	0	0	0	1		2	2	0
Braves	0	1	0	0	0	0	2	0	x		3	3	2

E—Belliard, McGriff. DP—Indians 1 (Vizquel to Baerga). LOB—Indians 1, Braves 4. Scoring Position—Indians 0-for-1, Braves 0-for-3. HR—McGriff (1). S—Belliard. SB—Lofton 2 (2).

Indians	IP	H	R	ER	BB	K	ERA
Orel Hershiser (L, 0-1)	6.0	3	3	3	3	7	4.50
Paul Assenmacher	0.0	0	0	0	1	0	—
Julian Tavarez	1.1	0	0	0	1	0	0.00
Alan Embree	0.2	0	0	0	0	2	0.00

Braves	IP	H	R	ER	BB	K	ERA
Greg Maddux (W, 1-0)	9.0	2	2	0	0	4	0.00

Hershiser pitched to two batters in the 7th. Assenmacher pitched to one batter in the 7th.

Time—2:37. Attendance—51,876. Umpires—HP, Wendelstedt. 1B, McKean. 2B, Froemming. 3B, Hirshbeck.

Game 2
Sunday, October 22

Indians	AB	R	H	RBI	BB	K	Avg
Kenny Lofton, cf	5	1	1	0	0	0	.222
Omar Vizquel, ss	4	0	1	0	1	0	.125
Carlos Baerga, 2b	4	0	0	0	1	0	.000
Albert Belle, lf	3	1	1	0	1	1	.167
Eddie Murray, 1b	3	1	1	2	1	0	.167
Manny Ramirez, rf	4	0	2	0	0	1	.286
Jim Thome, 3b	3	0	0	0	1	1	.167
Tony Pena, c	3	0	0	0	0	0	.000
Paul Sorrento, ph	1	0	0	0	0	0	.000
Sandy Alomar Jr., c	0	0	0	0	0	0	.000
Dennis Martinez, p	2	0	0	0	0	0	.000
Alan Embree, p	0	0	0	0	0	0	—
Wayne Kirby, ph	1	0	0	0	0	1	.000
Jim Poole, p	0	0	0	0	0	0	—
Julian Tavarez, p	0	0	0	0	0	0	—
Ruben Amaro, ph	1	0	0	0	0	1	.000
TOTALS	34	3	6	2	5	5	.129

Braves	AB	R	H	RBI	BB	K	Avg
Marquis Grissom, cf	3	1	1	0	0	0	.286
Mark Lemke, 2b	3	1	1	0	1	0	.333
Chipper Jones, 3b	3	0	2	1	0	0	.286
Fred McGriff, 1b	4	0	0	0	0	0	.143
David Justice, rf	3	1	2	1	1	0	.500
Mark Wohlers, p	0	0	0	0	0	0	—
Ryan Klesko, lf	3	0	0	0	0	1	.000
Mike Devereaux, lf-rf	0	0	0	0	0	0	.000
Javy Lopez, c	3	1	1	2	0	0	.333
Rafael Belliard, ss	4	0	0	0	0	1	.000
Tom Glavine, p	1	0	0	0	0	1	.000
Dwight Smith, ph	1	0	1	0	0	0	1.000
Greg McMichael, p	0	0	0	0	0	0	—
Alejandro Pena, p	0	0	0	0	0	0	—
Luis Polonia, lf	0	0	0	0	0	0	.000
TOTALS	29	4	8	4	3	3	.224

	1	2	3	4	5	6	7	8	9		R	H	E
Indians	0	2	0	0	0	0	0	1	0		3	6	2
Braves	0	0	2	0	0	2	0	0	x		4	8	2

E—Martinez, Devereaux, Belle, Jones. DP—Indians 2 (Baerga to Vizquel to Murray; Vizquel to Baerga to Murray). LOB—Indians 9, Braves 7. Scoring Position—Indians 0-for-5, Braves 2-for-6. 2B—Jones (1). HR—Murray (1), Lopez (1). SF—Jones. GDP—McGriff, Belliard. SB—Lofton 2 (4), Vizquel (1).

Indians	IP	H	R	ER	BB	K	ERA
Dennis Martinez (L, 0-1)	5.2	8	4	4	3	3	6.35
Alan Embree	0.1	0	0	0	0	0	0.00
Jim Poole	1.0	0	0	0	0	0	0.00
Julian Tavarez	1.0	0	0	0	0	0	0.00

Braves	IP	H	R	ER	BB	K	ERA
Tom Glavine (W, 1-0)	6.0	3	2	2	3	3	3.00
Greg McMichael (H, 1)	0.2	1	1	0	1	1	0.00
Alejandro Pena (H, 1)	1.0	1	0	0	0	1	0.00
Mark Wohlers (S, 1)	1.1	1	0	0	0	1	0.00

WP—Glavine, McMichael. HBP—Grissom by Martinez, Lopez by Tavarez. Time—3:17. Attendance—51,877. Umpires—HP, McKean. 1B, Froemming. 2B, Hirshbeck. 3B, Pulli.

Game 3
Tuesday, October 24

Braves	AB	R	H	RBI	BB	K	Avg
Marquis Grissom, cf	6	1	2	0	0	2	.308
Luis Polonia, lf	4	1	1	1	1	1	.200
Chipper Jones, 3b	3	2	1	0	2	0	.300
Fred McGriff, 1b	5	1	3	2	0	1	.333
David Justice, rf	5	0	1	0	0	0	.222
Ryan Klesko, dh	3	1	2	1	0	0	.250
Mike Devereaux, ph-dh	2	0	1	1	0	1	.333
Javy Lopez, c	5	0	0	0	0	0	.125
Mark Lemke, 2b	5	0	2	0	0	0	.364
Rafael Belliard, ss	2	0	0	0	0	1	.000
Dwight Smith, ph	1	0	0	0	0	0	.500
Mike Mordecai, ss	1	0	0	0	0	0	.000
TOTALS	42	6	12	6	3	7	.256

Indians	AB	R	H	RBI	BB	K	Avg
Kenny Lofton, cf	3	3	3	0	3	0	.417
Omar Vizquel, ss	6	2	2	1	0	1	.214
Carlos Baerga, 2b	6	0	3	3	0	0	.214
Alvaro Espinoza, pr	0	1	0	0	0	0	—
Albert Belle, lf	4	0	1	1	2	0	.200
Eddie Murray, dh	6	0	1	1	0	3	.167
Jim Thome, 3b	4	0	0	0	1	1	.100
Manny Ramirez, rf	2	1	0	0	3	0	.222
Paul Sorrento, 1b	4	0	1	0	0	3	.167
Wayne Kirby, pr	0	0	0	0	0	0	.000
Herbert Perry, 1b	1	0	0	0	0	1	.000
Sandy Alomar Jr., c	5	0	1	0	1	0	.125
TOTALS	41	7	12	7	9	10	.206

	1	2	3	4	5	6	7	8	9	10	11		R	H	E
Braves	1	0	0	0	0	1	1	3	0	0	0		6	12	1
Indians	2	0	2	0	0	0	1	1	0	0	1		7	12	2

E—Belliard, Sorrento, Baerga. DP—Braves 1 (Lemke to McGriff), Indians 2 (Baerga to Vizquel to Sorrento; Baerga to Vizquel to Perry). LOB—Braves 7, Indians 13. Scoring Position—Braves 3-for-10, Indians 6-for-14. 2B—Grissom (1), Jones (2), Lofton (1), Baerga (1), Alomar Jr. (1). 3B—Vizquel (1). HR—McGriff (2), Klesko (1). S—Mordecai. GDP—Grissom, Lopez, Ramirez. SB—Polonia (1), McGriff (1), Lofton (5), Ramirez (1). CS—Grissom (1), Lofton (1).

Braves	IP	H	R	ER	BB	K	ERA
John Smoltz	2.1	6	4	4	2	4	15.43
Brad Clontz	2.1	1	0	0	0	1	0.00
Kent Mercker	2.0	1	1	1	2	2	4.50
Greg McMichael	0.2	1	1	1	1	1	6.75
Mark Wohlers (BS, 1)	2.2	1	0	0	3	2	0.00
Alejandro Pena (L, 0-1)	0.0	2	1	1	1	0	9.00

Indians	IP	H	R	ER	BB	K	ERA
Charles Nagy	7.0	8	5	5	1	4	6.43
Paul Assenmacher (BS, 1)	0.1	0	1	1	1	0	27.00
Julian Tavarez	0.2	1	0	0	0	0	0.00
Jose Mesa (W, 1-0)	3.0	3	0	0	1	3	0.00

Nagy pitched to two batters in the 8th. Pena pitched to three batters in the 11th.

Time—4:09. Attendance—43,584. Umpires—HP, Froemming. 1B, Hirshbeck. 2B, Pulli. 3B, Brinkman.

Game 4
Wednesday, October 25

Braves

	AB	R	H	RBI	BB	K	Avg
Marquis Grissom, cf	4	1	3	0	1	0	.412
Luis Polonia, lf	4	1	2	1	0	0	.333
Mike Devereaux, lf	0	0	0	0	1	0	.333
Chipper Jones, 3b	4	1	0	0	1	0	.214
Fred McGriff, 1b	3	1	1	0	2	1	.333
David Justice, rf	5	0	1	2	0	0	.214
Ryan Klesko, dh	3	1	1	1	1	1	.273
Mike Mordecai, ph-dh	1	0	0	0	0	0	.000
Javy Lopez, c	5	0	2	1	0	1	.231
Mark Lemke, 2b	5	0	1	0	0	0	.313
Rafael Belliard, ss	3	0	0	0	0	1	.000
TOTALS	37	5	11	5	6	4	.264

Indians

	AB	R	H	RBI	BB	K	Avg
Kenny Lofton, cf	5	0	0	0	0	1	.294
Omar Vizquel, ss	3	0	0	0	1	0	.176
Carlos Baerga, 2b	4	0	1	0	0	0	.222
Albert Belle, lf	3	1	1	1	1	1	.231
Eddie Murray, dh	2	0	0	0	2	0	.143
Manny Ramirez, rf	3	1	1	1	0	0	.250
Herbert Perry, 1b	3	0	0	0	0	1	.000
Paul Sorrento, ph	1	0	1	0	0	0	.286
Alvaro Espinoza, 3b	2	0	1	0	0	0	.500
Jim Thome, ph-3b	2	0	1	0	0	1	.167
Sandy Alomar Jr., c	4	0	0	0	1	1	.083
TOTALS	32	2	6	2	5	5	.203

	1	2	3	4	5	6	7	8	9		R	H	E
Braves	0	0	0	0	0	1	3	0	1		5	11	1
Indians	0	0	0	0	0	1	0	0	1		2	6	0

E—Lemke. DP—Braves 1 (Jones to Lemke to McGriff). LOB—Braves 12, Indians 8. Scoring Position—Braves 3-for-16, Indians 0-for-8. 2B—Polonia (1), McGriff (1), Lopez 2 (2), Thome (1), Sorrento (1). HR—Klesko (2), Belle (1), Ramirez (1). S—Belliard. GDP—Baerga. SB—Grissom 2 (2). CS—Espinoza (1).

Braves

	IP	H	R	ER	BB	K	ERA
Steve Avery (W, 1-0)	6.0	3	1	1	5	3	1.50
Greg McMichael (H, 2)	2.0	1	0	0	0	0	2.70
Mark Wohlers	0.0	2	1	1	0	0	2.25
Pedro Borbon (S, 1)	1.0	0	0	0	0	2	0.00

Indians

	IP	H	R	ER	BB	K	ERA
Ken Hill (L, 0-1)	6.1	6	3	3	4	1	4.26
Paul Assenmacher	0.2	1	1	0	1	2	9.00
Julian Tavarez	0.2	2	0	0	1	1	0.00
Alan Embree	1.1	2	1	1	0	0	3.86

Wohlers pitched to two batters in the 9th.

Balk—Avery. PB—Alomar Jr. Time—3:14. Attendance—43,578. Umpires—HP, Hirschbeck. 1B, Polli. 2B, Brinkman. 3B, Wendelstedt.

Game 5
Thursday, October 26

Braves

	AB	R	H	RBI	BB	K	Avg
Marquis Grissom, cf	4	0	1	1	0	0	.381
Luis Polonia, lf	4	1	1	1	0	1	.308
Chipper Jones, 3b	4	0	1	0	0	1	.222
Fred McGriff, 1b	4	1	1	0	0	2	.316
David Justice, rf	4	0	0	0	0	1	.167
Ryan Klesko, dh	4	2	2	2	0	0	.333
Mark Lemke, 2b	4	0	0	0	0	1	.250
Charlie O'Brien, c	1	0	0	0	0	0	.000
Javy Lopez, ph-c	1	0	0	0	0	0	.214
Rafael Belliard, ss	1	0	0	0	0	1	.000
Dwight Smith, ph	0	0	0	0	1	0	.500
Mike Mordecai, ss	1	0	1	0	0	0	.333
TOTALS	32	4	7	4	1	7	.253

Indians

	AB	R	H	RBI	BB	K	Avg
Kenny Lofton, cf	4	0	0	0	0	0	.238
Omar Vizquel, ss	3	1	1	0	1	1	.200
Carlos Baerga, 2b	4	1	1	0	0	0	.227
Albert Belle, lf	3	2	1	2	1	2	.250
Eddie Murray, dh	3	0	0	0	1	0	.118
Jim Thome, 3b	4	1	2	2	0	0	.250
Manny Ramirez, rf	3	0	1	1	0	1	.267
Herbert Perry, 1b	1	0	0	0	0	0	.000
Paul Sorrento, 1b	3	0	0	0	0	1	.200
Wayne Kirby, rf	0	0	0	0	0	0	.000
Sandy Alomar Jr., c	3	0	2	0	0	0	.200
TOTALS	31	5	8	5	3	5	.209

	1	2	3	4	5	6	7	8	9		R	H	E
Braves	0	0	0	1	1	0	0	0	2		4	7	0
Indians	2	0	0	0	0	2	0	1	x		5	8	1

E—Hershiser. DP—Indians 2 (Vizquel to Baerga to Sorrento; Hershiser to Perry). LOB—Braves 3, Indians 5. Scoring Position—Braves 2-for-5, Indians 3-for-6. 2B—Jones (3), McGriff (2), Baerga (2), Alomar Jr. (2). HR—Polonia (1), Klesko (3), Belle (2), Thome (1). S—O'Brien. GDP—Polonia.

Braves

	IP	H	R	ER	BB	K	ERA
Greg Maddux (L, 1-1)	7.0	7	4	4	3	4	2.25
Brad Clontz	1.0	1	1	1	0	1	2.70

Indians

	IP	H	R	ER	BB	K	ERA
Orel Hershiser (W, 1-1)	8.0	5	2	1	1	6	2.57
Jose Mesa (S, 1)	1.0	2	2	2	0	1	4.50

Time—2:33. Attendance—43,595. Umpires—HP, Pulli. 1B, Brinkman. 2B, Wendelstedt. 3B, McKean.

Game 6
Saturday, October 28

Indians

	AB	R	H	RBI	BB	K	Avg
Kenny Lofton, cf	4	0	0	0	0	0	.200
Omar Vizquel, ss	3	0	0	0	0	2	.174
Paul Sorrento, ph	1	0	0	0	0	0	.182
Carlos Baerga, 2b	4	0	0	0	0	0	.192
Albert Belle, lf	1	0	0	0	2	1	.235
Eddie Murray, 1b	2	0	0	0	1	1	.105
Manny Ramirez, rf	3	0	0	0	0	1	.222
Alan Embree, p	0	0	0	0	0	0	—
Julian Tavarez, p	0	0	0	0	0	0	—
Paul Assenmacher, p	0	0	0	0	0	0	—
Jim Thome, 3b	3	0	0	0	0	2	.211
Tony Pena, c	3	0	1	0	0	0	.167
Dennis Martinez, p	1	0	0	0	0	1	.000
Jim Poole, p	1	0	0	0	0	0	.000
Ken Hill, p	0	0	0	0	0	0	—
Ruben Amaro, rf	1	0	0	0	0	0	.000
TOTALS	27	0	1	0	3	8	.182

Braves

	AB	R	H	RBI	BB	K	Avg
Marquis Grissom, cf	4	0	1	0	0	0	.360
Mark Lemke, 2b	2	0	1	0	1	0	.273
Chipper Jones, 3b	3	0	2	0	1	0	.286
Fred McGriff, 1b	4	0	0	0	0	2	.261
David Justice, rf	2	1	2	1	2	0	.250
Ryan Klesko, lf	1	0	0	0	2	0	.313
Mike Devereaux, lf	1	0	0	0	0	0	.250
Javy Lopez, c	3	0	0	0	1	0	.176
Rafael Belliard, ss	4	0	0	0	0	0	.000
Tom Glavine, p	3	0	0	0	0	1	.000
Luis Polonia, ph	1	0	0	0	0	1	.286
Mark Wohlers, p	0	0	0	0	0	0	—
TOTALS	28	1	6	1	7	4	.247

	1	2	3	4	5	6	7	8	9		R	H	E
Indians	0	0	0	0	0	0	0	0	0		0	1	1
Braves	0	0	0	0	0	1	0	0	x		1	6	0

E—Thome. DP—Indians 1 (Vizquel to Baerga to Murray). LOB—Indians 3, Braves 11. Scoring Position—Indians 0-for-1, Braves 0-for-6. 2B—Justice (1). HR—Justice (1). S—Lemke. GDP—Belliard. SB—Lofton (6), Grissom (3). CS—Belle (1), Lemke (1).

Indians

	IP	H	R	ER	BB	K	ERA
Dennis Martinez	4.2	4	0	0	5	2	3.48
Jim Poole (L, 0-1)	1.1	1	1	1	0	1	3.86
Ken Hill	0.0	1	0	0	0	0	4.26
Alan Embree	1.0	0	0	0	2	0	2.70
Julian Tavarez	0.2	0	0	0	0	0	0.00
Paul Assenmacher	0.1	0	0	0	0	1	6.75

Braves

	IP	H	R	ER	BB	K	ERA
Tom Glavine (W, 2-0)	8.0	1	0	0	3	8	1.29
Mark Wohlers (S, 2)	1.0	0	0	0	0	0	1.80

Hill pitched to one batter in the 7th.

Time—3:02. Attendance—51,875. Umpires—HP, Brinkman. 1B, Wendelstedt. 2B, McKean. 3B, Froemming.

1995 World Series—Composite Statistics

Batting

Braves	G	AB	R	H	RBI	2B	3B	HR	BB	SO	SB	CS	Avg	OBP	Slg
Rafael Belliard	6	16	0	0	1	0	0	0	0	4	0	0	.000	.000	.000
Mike Devereaux	5	4	0	1	1	0	0	0	2	1	0	0	.250	.500	.250
Tom Glavine	2	4	0	0	0	0	0	0	0	1	0	0	.000	.000	.000
Marquis Grissom	6	25	3	9	1	1	0	0	1	3	3	1	.360	.407	.400
Chipper Jones	6	21	3	6	1	3	0	0	4	3	0	0	.286	.385	.429
David Justice	6	20	3	5	5	1	0	1	5	1	0	0	.250	.400	.450
Ryan Klesko	6	16	4	5	4	0	0	3	3	4	0	0	.313	.421	.875
Mark Lemke	6	22	1	6	0	0	0	0	3	2	0	1	.273	.360	.273
Javy Lopez	6	17	1	3	3	2	0	1	1	1	0	0	.176	.263	.471
Greg Maddux	2	3	0	0	0	0	0	0	0	1	0	0	.000	.000	.000
Fred McGriff	6	23	5	6	3	2	0	2	3	7	1	0	.261	.346	.609
Mike Mordecai	3	3	0	1	0	0	0	0	0	1	0	0	.333	.333	.333
Charlie O'Brien	2	3	0	0	0	0	0	0	0	0	0	0	.000	.000	.000
Luis Polonia	6	14	3	4	4	1	0	1	1	3	1	0	.286	.333	.571
Dwight Smith	3	2	0	1	0	0	0	0	0	1	0	0	.500	.667	.500
Totals	6	193	23	47	23	10	0	8	25	34	5	2	.244	.335	.420

Indians	G	AB	R	H	RBI	2B	3B	HR	BB	SO	SB	CS	Avg	OBP	Slg
Sandy Alomar Jr.	5	15	0	3	1	2	0	0	0	2	0	0	.200	.200	.333
Ruben Amaro	2	2	0	0	0	0	0	0	0	1	0	0	.000	.000	.000
Carlos Baerga	6	26	1	5	4	2	0	0	1	1	0	0	.192	.222	.269
Albert Belle	6	17	4	4	4	0	0	2	7	5	0	1	.235	.458	.588
Alvaro Espinoza	2	2	1	1	0	0	0	0	0	0	0	1	.500	.500	.500
Orel Hershiser	2	2	0	0	0	0	0	0	0	0	0	0	.000	.000	.000
Wayne Kirby	3	1	0	0	0	0	0	0	0	0	0	0	.000	.000	.000
Kenny Lofton	6	25	6	5	0	1	0	0	3	1	6	1	.200	.286	.240
Dennis Martinez	2	3	0	0	0	0	0	0	0	1	0	0	.000	.000	.000
Eddie Murray	6	19	1	2	3	0	0	1	5	4	0	0	.105	.292	.263
Tony Pena	2	6	0	1	0	0	0	0	0	0	0	0	.167	.167	.167
Herbert Perry	3	5	0	0	0	0	0	0	0	2	0	0	.000	.000	.000
Jim Poole	2	1	0	0	0	0	0	0	0	0	0	0	.000	.000	.000
Manny Ramirez	6	18	2	4	2	0	0	1	4	5	1	0	.222	.364	.389
Paul Sorrento	6	11	0	2	0	1	0	0	0	4	0	0	.182	.182	.273
Jim Thome	6	19	1	4	2	1	0	1	2	5	0	0	.211	.286	.421
Omar Vizquel	6	23	3	4	1	0	1	0	3	5	1	0	.174	.269	.261
Totals	6	195	19	35	17	7	1	5	25	37	8	3	.179	.273	.303

Pitching

Braves	G	GS	CG	IP	H	R	ER	BB	SO	W-L	Sv-Op	Hld	ERA
Steve Avery	1	1	0	6.0	3	1	1	5	3	1-0	0-0	0	1.50
Pedro Borbon	1	0	0	1.0	0	0	0	0	2	0-0	1-1	0	0.00
Brad Clontz	2	0	0	3.1	2	1	1	0	2	0-0	0-0	0	2.70
Tom Glavine	2	2	0	14.0	4	2	2	6	11	2-0	0-0	0	1.29
Greg Maddux	2	2	1	16.0	9	6	4	3	8	1-1	0-0	0	2.25
Greg McMichael	3	0	0	3.1	3	2	1	2	2	0-0	0-0	2	2.70
Kent Mercker	1	0	0	2.0	1	1	1	2	2	0-0	0-0	0	4.50
Alejandro Pena	2	0	0	1.0	3	1	1	2	0	0-1	0-0	1	9.00
John Smoltz	1	1	0	2.1	6	4	4	2	4	0-0	0-0	0	15.43
Mark Wohlers	4	0	0	5.0	4	1	1	3	3	0-0	2-3	0	1.80
Totals	6	6	1	54.0	35	19	16	25	37	4-2	3-4	3	2.67

Indians	G	GS	CG	IP	H	R	ER	BB	SO	W-L	Sv-Op	Hld	ERA
Paul Assenmacher	4	0	0	1.1	1	2	1	3	3	0-0	0-1	0	6.75
Alan Embree	4	0	0	3.1	2	1	1	2	2	0-0	0-0	0	2.70
Orel Hershiser	2	2	0	14.0	8	5	4	4	13	1-1	0-0	0	2.57
Ken Hill	2	1	0	6.1	7	3	3	4	1	0-1	0-0	0	4.26
Dennis Martinez	2	2	0	10.1	12	4	4	8	5	0-1	0-0	0	3.48
Jose Mesa	2	0	0	4.0	5	2	2	1	4	1-0	1-1	0	4.50
Charles Nagy	1	1	0	7.0	8	5	5	1	4	0-0	0-0	0	6.43
Jim Poole	2	0	0	2.1	1	1	1	0	1	0-1	0-0	0	3.86
Julian Tavarez	5	0	0	4.1	3	0	0	2	1	0-0	0-0	0	0.00
Totals	6	6	0	53.0	47	23	21	25	34	2-4	1-2	0	3.57

Fielding

Braves	Pos	G	PO	Ast	E	DP	PB	FPct
Steve Avery	p	1	0	0	0	0	—	—
Rafael Belliard	ss	6	3	11	2	0	—	.875
Pedro Borbon	p	1	0	0	0	0	—	—
Brad Clontz	p	2	0	0	0	0	—	—
Mike Devereaux	lf	4	0	0	1	0	—	.000
	rf	1	0	0	0	0	—	—
Tom Glavine	p	2	1	3	0	0	—	1.000
Marquis Grissom	cf	6	13	0	0	0	—	1.000
Chipper Jones	3b	6	6	12	1	1	—	.947
David Justice	rf	6	16	0	0	0	—	1.000
Ryan Klesko	lf	3	1	0	0	0	—	1.000
Mark Lemke	2b	6	10	24	1	2	—	.971
Javy Lopez	c	6	32	4	0	0	0	1.000
Greg Maddux	p	2	2	4	0	0	—	1.000
Fred McGriff	1b	6	68	2	1	2	—	.986
Greg McMichael	p	3	0	1	0	0	—	1.000
Kent Mercker	p	1	0	0	0	0	—	—
Mike Mordecai	ss	2	0	6	0	0	—	1.000
Charlie O'Brien	c	2	7	2	0	0	0	1.000
Alejandro Pena	p	2	0	0	0	0	—	—
Luis Polonia	lf	4	3	0	0	0	—	1.000
John Smoltz	p	1	0	0	0	0	—	—
Mark Wohlers	p	4	0	0	0	0	—	—
Totals		6	162	69	6	5	0	.975

Indians	Pos	G	PO	Ast	E	DP	PB	FPct
Sandy Alomar Jr.	c	5	28	0	0	0	1	1.000
Ruben Amaro	rf	1	0	0	0	0	—	—
Paul Assenmacher	p	4	0	0	0	0	—	—
Carlos Baerga	2b	6	15	24	1	7	—	.975
Albert Belle	lf	6	10	0	1	0	—	.909
Alan Embree	p	4	0	1	0	0	—	1.000
Alvaro Espinoza	3b	1	1	1	0	0	—	1.000
Orel Hershiser	p	2	1	7	1	1	—	.889
Ken Hill	p	2	1	2	0	0	—	1.000
Wayne Kirby	rf	1	1	0	0	0	—	1.000
Kenny Lofton	cf	6	12	0	0	0	—	1.000
Dennis Martinez	p	2	0	3	1	0	—	.750
Jose Mesa	p	2	0	0	0	0	—	—
Eddie Murray	1b	3	27	0	0	3	—	1.000
Charles Nagy	p	1	1	1	0	0	—	1.000
Tony Pena	c	2	7	1	0	0	0	1.000
Herbert Perry	1b	3	13	2	0	2	—	1.000
Jim Poole	p	2	0	0	0	0	—	—
Manny Ramirez	rf	6	8	0	0	0	—	1.000
Paul Sorrento	1b	3	19	2	1	2	—	.955
Julian Tavarez	p	5	0	2	0	0	—	1.000
Jim Thome	3b	6	3	5	1	0	—	.889
Omar Vizquel	ss	6	12	22	0	7	—	1.000
Totals		6	159	73	6	22	1	.975

1996 New York Yankees (AL) 4, Atlanta Braves (NL) 2

The Yankees went in as heavy underdogs to unseat the defending-champion Atlanta Braves, and things looked even bleaker for Joe Torre's crew after they dropped the first two games—at home, no less—by a combined score of 16-1. David Cone came through with a gutty performance in Game 3, however, and the Yankees torched middle reliever Greg McMichael en route to a 5-2 victory. The Braves rebounded to take a 6-3 lead into the late innings of Game 4. Now only six outs away from taking a 3-1 lead in the Series, Atlanta manager Bobby Cox made an uncharacteristic decision, bringing in closer Mark Wohlers to start the eighth inning, instead of saving the fireballer for the ninth. Wohlers hung a slider to Jim Leyritz, who hit it out for a game-tying homer. Steve Avery walked Wade Boggs to force in the winning run in the top of the 10th, and the Yankees won, 8-6. New York took a 3-2 lead the next day when Andy Pettitte outdueled John Smoltz, 1-0. Back in New York for Game 6, the Yankees put together a three-run rally against Greg Maddux and made the runs stand up for a 3-2 victory and a most improbable World Series comeback.

Game 1

Sunday, October 20

Braves	AB	R	H	RBI	BB	K	Avg
Marquis Grissom, cf	5	2	2	1	0	0	.400
Mark Lemke, 2b	4	0	2	1	0	0	.500
Chipper Jones, 3b	4	1	1	3	0	0	.250
Fred McGriff, 1b	5	2	2	2	0	2	.400
Javy Lopez, c	4	2	1	0	1	1	.250
Eddie Perez, c	0	0	0	0	0	0	—
Jermaine Dye, rf	5	0	1	0	0	1	.200
Andruw Jones, lf	4	3	3	5	0	0	.750
Ryan Klesko, dh	4	1	0	0	0	1	.000
Jeff Blauser, ss	3	1	1	0	0	0	.333
Luis Polonia, ph	1	0	0	0	0	1	.000
Rafael Belliard, ss	0	0	0	0	0	0	—
TOTALS	39	12	13	12	1	6	.333

Yankees	AB	R	H	RBI	BB	K	Avg
Derek Jeter, ss	3	1	0	0	1	1	.000
Wade Boggs, 3b	4	0	2	1	0	0	.500
Bernie Williams, cf	3	0	0	0	1	1	.000
Tino Martinez, 1b	3	0	1	0	1	1	.333
Cecil Fielder, dh	4	0	0	0	0	1	.000
Darryl Strawberry, lf	3	0	0	0	0	0	.000
Tim Raines, lf	1	0	0	0	0	0	.000
Paul O'Neill, rf	2	0	0	0	1	0	.000
Mike Aldrete, rf	0	0	0	0	0	0	—
Charlie Hayes, ph	1	0	0	0	0	0	.000
Mariano Duncan, 2b	3	0	0	0	0	0	.000
Andy Fox, 2b	0	0	0	0	0	0	—
Luis Sojo, ph	1	0	0	0	0	0	.000
Jim Leyritz, c	3	0	1	0	1	1	.333
TOTALS	31	1	4	1	5	5	.129

	1	2	3	4	5	6	7	8	9		R	H	E
Braves	0	2	6	0	1	3	0	0	0		12	13	0
Yankees	0	0	0	0	1	0	0	0	0		1	4	1

E—Duncan. LOB—Braves 3, Yankees 8. Scoring Position—Braves 5-for-7, Yankees 0-for-4. 2B—Boggs (1). HR—McGriff (1), AJones 2 (2). S—Lemke. SF—CJones. SB—CJones.

Braves	IP	H	R	ER	BB	K	ERA
John Smoltz (W, 1-0)	6.0	2	1	1	5	4	1.50
Greg McMichael	1.0	2	0	0	0	1	0.00
Denny Neagle	1.0	0	0	0	0	0	0.00
Terrell Wade	0.2	0	0	0	0	0	0.00
Brad Clontz	0.1	0	0	0	0	0	0.00

Yankees	IP	H	R	ER	BB	K	ERA
Andy Pettitte (L, 0-1)	2.1	6	7	7	1	1	27.00
Brian Boehringer	3.0	5	5	3	0	2	9.00
Dave Weathers	1.2	1	0	0	0	0	0.00
Jeff Nelson	1.0	1	0	0	0	1	0.00
John Wetteland	1.0	0	0	0	0	2	0.00

Time—3:02. Attendance—56,365. Umpires—HP, Evans. 1B, Tata. 2B, Welke. 3B, Rippley.

Game 2

Monday, October 21

Braves	AB	R	H	RBI	BB	K	Avg
Marquis Grissom, cf	5	1	2	1	0	1	.400
Mark Lemke, 2b	4	2	2	0	0	0	.500
Chipper Jones, 3b	3	0	1	0	1	1	.286
Fred McGriff, 1b	3	0	2	3	0	1	.500
Javy Lopez, c	4	0	1	0	0	0	.250
Jermaine Dye, rf	4	0	1	0	0	0	.222
Andruw Jones, lf	3	0	0	0	0	1	.429
Terry Pendleton, dh	4	1	1	0	0	1	.250
Jeff Blauser, ss	2	0	0	0	1	0	.200
Luis Polonia, ph	1	0	0	0	0	0	.000
Rafael Belliard, ss	0	0	0	0	0	0	—
TOTALS	33	4	10	4	2	5	.338

Yankees	AB	R	H	RBI	BB	K	Avg
Tim Raines, lf	4	0	2	0	0	0	.400
Wade Boggs, 3b	4	0	1	0	0	0	.375
Bernie Williams, cf	4	0	0	0	0	1	.000
Tino Martinez, 1b	4	0	0	0	0	2	.143
Cecil Fielder, dh	4	0	2	0	0	0	.250
Andy Fox, pr	0	0	0	0	0	0	—
Paul O'Neill, rf	4	0	1	0	0	1	.167
Mariano Duncan, 2b	3	0	0	0	0	1	.000
Joe Girardi, c	3	0	0	0	0	0	.000
Derek Jeter, ss	2	0	1	0	0	0	.200
TOTALS	32	0	7	0	0	5	.182

	1	2	3	4	5	6	7	8	9		R	H	E
Braves	1	0	1	0	1	1	0	0	0		4	10	0
Yankees	0	0	0	0	0	0	0	0	0		0	7	1

E—Raines. DP—Braves 1 (Lemke to Blauser to McGriff), Yankees 2 (Duncan to Jeter to Martinez; Key to Duncan to Martinez). LOB—Braves 7, Yankees 6. Scoring Position—Braves 3-for-12, Yankees 0-for-5. 2B—Grissom (1), Lemke (1), CJones (1), Pendleton (1), O'Neill (1). S—Lemke. SF—McGriff. GDP—Lopez, Blauser, Boggs. CS—Raines (1).

Braves	IP	H	R	ER	BB	K	ERA
Greg Maddux (W, 1-0)	8.0	6	0	0	0	2	0.00
Mark Wohlers	1.0	1	0	0	0	3	0.00

Yankees	IP	H	R	ER	BB	K	ERA
Jimmy Key (L, 0-1)	6.0	10	4	4	2	0	6.00
Graeme Lloyd	0.2	0	0	0	0	2	0.00
Jeff Nelson	1.1	0	0	0	0	2	0.00
Mariano Rivera	1.0	0	0	0	0	1	0.00

HBP—AJones by Key, Jeter by Maddux. Time—2:44. Attendance—56,340. Umpires—HP, Tata. 1B, Welke. 2B, Rippley. 3B, Young.

Game 3

Tuesday, October 22

Yankees	AB	R	H	RBI	BB	K	Avg
Tim Raines, lf	4	1	1	0	1	0	.333
Derek Jeter, ss	3	1	1	0	1	1	.250
Bernie Williams, cf	5	2	2	3	0	1	.167
Cecil Fielder, 1b	3	0	1	0	1	0	.273
Andy Fox, pr	0	1	0	0	0	0	—
Tino Martinez, 1b	0	0	0	0	1	0	.143
Charlie Hayes, 3b	5	0	0	0	0	3	.000
Darryl Strawberry, rf	3	0	1	1	1	2	.167
Mariano Duncan, 2b	3	0	1	0	0	1	.111
Luis Sojo, 2b	1	0	1	1	0	0	.500
Joe Girardi, c	2	0	0	0	1	2	.000
David Cone, p	2	0	0	0	0	1	.000
Jim Leyritz, ph	1	0	0	0	0	0	.250
Mariano Rivera, p	1	0	0	0	0	0	.000
Graeme Lloyd, p	0	0	0	0	0	0	—
John Wetteland, p	0	0	0	0	0	0	—
TOTALS	33	5	8	5	6	11	.183

Braves	AB	R	H	RBI	BB	K	Avg
Marquis Grissom, cf	4	1	3	0	0	0	.500
Mark Lemke, 2b	4	0	1	1	0	0	.417
Chipper Jones, 3b	3	0	1	0	1	1	.300
Fred McGriff, 1b	3	0	0	0	1	0	.364
Ryan Klesko, lf	3	0	1	1	1	2	.000
Javy Lopez, c	4	0	1	0	0	0	.250
Andruw Jones, rf	4	0	0	0	0	2	.273
Jeff Blauser, ss	4	0	0	0	0	2	.111
Tom Glavine, p	1	1	0	0	0	0	.000
Luis Polonia, ph	0	0	0	0	1	0	.000
Greg McMichael, p	0	0	0	0	0	0	—
Brad Clontz, p	0	0	0	0	0	0	—
Mike Bielecki, p	0	0	0	0	0	0	—
Terry Pendleton, ph	1	0	0	0	0	0	.200
TOTALS	31	2	6	2	5	7	.287

	1	2	3	4	5	6	7	8	9		R	H	E
Yankees	1	0	0	1	0	0	0	3	0		5	8	1
Braves	0	0	0	0	0	1	0	0			2	6	1

E—Blauser, Jeter. DP—Yankees 1 (Fielder to Jeter), Braves 1 (AJones to McGriff). LOB—Yankees 9, Braves 7. Scoring Position—Yankees 3-for-13, Braves 1-for-4. 2B—Fielder (1). 3B—Grissom (1). HR—Williams (1). S—Jeter, Girardi. GDP—Lemke. CS—AJones (1), Polonia (1).

Yankees	IP	H	R	ER	BB	K	ERA
David Cone (W, 1-0)	6.0	4	1	1	4	3	1.50
Mariano Rivera (H, 1)	1.1	2	1	1	1	1	3.86
Graeme Lloyd (H, 1)	0.2	0	0	0	0	1	0.00
John Wetteland (S, 1)	1.0	0	0	0	0	2	0.00

Braves	IP	H	R	ER	BB	K	ERA
Tom Glavine (L, 0-1)	7.0	4	2	1	3	8	1.29
Greg McMichael	0.0	3	3	3	0	0	27.00
Brad Clontz	1.0	1	0	0	1	1	0.00
Mike Bielecki	1.0	0	0	0	2	2	0.00

McMichael pitched to three batters in the 8th.

Time—3:22. Attendance—51,843. Umpires—HP, Welke. 1B, Rippley. 2B, Young. 3B, Davis.

Game 4
Wednesday, October 23

Yankees	AB	R	H	RBI	BB	K	Avg
Tim Raines, lf	5	1	0	0	1	1	.214
Derek Jeter, ss	4	2	2	0	2	2	.333
Bernie Williams, cf	4	1	0	0	2	1	.125
Cecil Fielder, 1b	4	1	2	1	1	0	.333
Andy Fox, pr-3b	0	0	0	0	0	0	—
Wade Boggs, ph-3b	0	0	0	1	1	0	.375
Charlie Hayes, 3b-1b	5	1	3	1	1	0	.273
Darryl Strawberry, rf	5	0	2	0	1	2	.273
Mariano Duncan, 2b	5	1	0	0	0	1	.071
Joe Girardi, c	2	0	0	0	0	0	.000
Paul O'Neill, ph	1	0	0	0	0	1	.143
Jim Leyritz, c	2	1	1	3	0	0	.333
Kenny Rogers, p	1	0	1	0	0	0	1.000
Brian Boehringer, p	0	0	0	0	0	0	—
Luis Sojo, ph	1	0	1	0	0	0	.667
Dave Weathers, p	0	0	0	0	0	0	—
Tino Martinez, ph	1	0	0	0	0	1	.125
Jeff Nelson, p	0	0	0	0	0	0	—
Mike Aldrete, ph	1	0	0	0	0	0	.000
Mariano Rivera, p	0	0	0	0	0	0	.000
Graeme Lloyd, p	1	0	0	0	0	0	.000
John Wetteland, p	0	0	0	0	0	0	—
TOTALS	42	8	12	6	9	9	.228

Braves	AB	R	H	RBI	BB	K	Avg
Marquis Grissom, cf	5	0	1	2	0	0	.421
Mark Lemke, 2b	5	0	1	0	0	1	.353
Chipper Jones, 3b-ss	3	2	1	0	2	0	.308
Fred McGriff, 1b	3	1	2	1	2	0	.429
Brad Clontz, p	0	0	0	0	0	0	—
Javy Lopez, c	2	1	0	1	1	1	.214
Mark Wohlers, p	0	0	0	0	0	0	—
Steve Avery, p	0	0	0	0	0	0	—
Ryan Klesko, 1b	1	0	0	0	0	1	.000
Andruw Jones, lf	4	1	3	1	1	1	.400
Jermaine Dye, rf	4	0	0	0	0	0	.154
Jeff Blauser, ss	3	1	1	1	0	2	.167
Rafael Belliard, ss	0	0	0	0	0	0	—
Luis Polonia, ph	1	0	0	0	0	1	.000
Terry Pendleton, 3b	1	0	0	0	0	0	.167
Denny Neagle, p	1	0	0	0	0	1	.000
Terrell Wade, p	0	0	0	0	0	0	—
Mike Bielecki, p	1	0	0	0	0	1	.000
Eddie Perez, c	1	0	0	0	0	0	.000
TOTALS	35	6	9	6	6	9	.277

	1	2	3	4	5	6	7	8	9	10		R	H	E
Yankees	0	0	0	0	0	3	0	3	0	2		8	12	0
Braves	0	4	1	0	1	0	0	0	0	0		6	9	2

E—Klesko, Dye. DP—Yankees 1 (Jeter to Duncan to Hayes), Braves 1 (Blauser to Lemke to McGriff). LOB—Yankees 13, Braves 8. Scoring Position—Yankees 4-for-12, Braves 3-for-12. 2B—Grissom (2), AJones (1). HR—McGriff (2), Leyritz (1). S—Dye, Neagle. SF—Lopez. GDP—Williams, McGriff.

Yankees	IP	H	R	ER	BB	K	ERA
Kenny Rogers	2.0	5	5	5	2	0	22.50
Brian Boehringer	2.0	0	0	0	0	3	5.40
Dave Weathers	1.0	1	1	1	2	2	3.38
Jeff Nelson	2.0	0	0	0	1	2	0.00
Mariano Rivera	1.1	2	0	0	1	1	2.45
Graeme Lloyd (W, 1-0)	1.0	0	0	0	0	1	0.00
John Wetteland (S, 2)	0.2	1	0	0	0	0	0.00

Braves	IP	H	R	ER	BB	K	ERA
Denny Neagle	5.0	5	3	2	4	3	3.00
Terrell Wade	0.0	0	0	0	1	0	0.00
Mike Bielecki (H, 1)	2.0	0	0	0	1	4	0.00
Mark Wohlers (BS, 1)	2.0	6	3	3	0	1	9.00
Steve Avery (L, 0-1)	0.2	1	2	1	3	0	13.50
Brad Clontz	0.1	0	0	0	0	1	0.00

Rogers pitched to two batters in the 3rd. Neagle pitched to five batters in the 6th. Wade pitched to one batter in the 6th.

Balk—Weathers. Time—4:17. Attendance—51,881. Umpires—HP, Rippley. 1B, Young. 2B, Davis. 3B, Evans.

Game 5
Thursday, October 24

Yankees	AB	R	H	RBI	BB	K	Avg
Derek Jeter, ss	4	0	0	0	0	1	.250
Charlie Hayes, 3b	4	1	0	0	0	2	.200
Bernie Williams, cf	4	0	0	0	0	2	.100
Cecil Fielder, 1b	4	0	3	1	0	1	.421
Tino Martinez, 1b	0	0	0	0	0	0	.125
Darryl Strawberry, lf	3	0	0	0	1	1	.214
Paul O'Neill, rf	2	0	0	0	2	0	.111
Mariano Duncan, 2b	4	0	0	0	0	1	.056
Luis Sojo, 2b	0	0	0	0	0	0	.667
Jim Leyritz, c	2	0	1	0	2	1	.375
Andy Pettitte, p	4	0	0	0	0	1	.000
John Wetteland, p	0	0	0	0	0	0	—
TOTALS	31	1	4	1	5	10	.209

Braves	AB	R	H	RBI	BB	K	Avg
Marquis Grissom, cf	3	0	2	0	1	1	.455
Mark Lemke, 2b	4	0	0	0	0	2	.286
Chipper Jones, 3b	4	0	1	0	0	0	.294
Fred McGriff, 1b	3	0	0	0	1	1	.353
Javy Lopez, c	4	0	0	0	0	0	.167
Andruw Jones, lf	2	0	1	0	1	0	.412
Ryan Klesko, ph	0	0	0	0	1	0	.000
Jermaine Dye, rf	3	0	0	0	0	0	.125
Luis Polonia, ph	1	0	0	0	0	0	.000
Jeff Blauser, ss	3	0	0	0	0	0	.133
John Smoltz, p	2	0	1	0	0	0	.500
Mike Mordecai, ph	1	0	0	0	0	0	.000
Mark Wohlers, p	0	0	0	0	0	0	—
TOTALS	30	0	5	0	4	4	.266

	1	2	3	4	5	6	7	8	9		R	H	E
Yankees	0	0	0	1	0	0	0	0	0		1	4	1
Braves	0	0	0	0	0	0	0	0	0		0	5	1

E—Grissom, Jeter. DP—Yankees 2 (Duncan to Jeter to Fielder; Pettitte to Duncan to Fielder), Braves 1 (McGriff). LOB—Yankees 8, Braves 7. Scoring Position—Yankees 1-for-8, Braves 0-for-7. 2B—Fielder (2), CJones (2). GDP—CJones, Lopez. SB—Duncan (1), Leyritz (1), Grissom (1), AJones (1). CS—AJones (2).

Yankees	IP	H	R	ER	BB	K	ERA
Andy Pettitte (W, 1-1)	8.1	5	0	0	3	4	5.91
John Wetteland (S, 3)	0.2	0	0	0	1	0	0.00

Braves	IP	H	R	ER	BB	K	ERA
John Smoltz (L, 1-1)	8.0	4	1	0	3	10	0.64
Mark Wohlers	1.0	0	0	0	2	0	6.75

WP—Wohlers. Time—2:54. Attendance—51,881. Umpires—HP, Young. 1B, Davis. 2B, Evans. 3B, Tata.

Game 6
Saturday, October 26

Braves	AB	R	H	RBI	BB	K	Avg
Marquis Grissom, cf	5	0	2	1	0	0	.444
Mark Lemke, 2b	5	0	0	0	0	0	.231
Chipper Jones, 3b	4	0	1	0	0	0	.286
Fred McGriff, 1b	3	1	0	0	1	0	.300
Javy Lopez, c	3	0	1	0	1	2	.190
Andruw Jones, lf-rf	3	0	1	0	1	2	.400
Jermaine Dye, rf	1	0	0	1	1	0	.118
Ryan Klesko, ph-lf	2	1	1	0	0	0	.100
Terry Pendleton, dh	3	0	1	0	1	0	.222
Rafael Belliard, pr	0	0	0	0	0	0	—
Jeff Blauser, ss	3	0	1	0	0	0	.167
Luis Polonia, ph	1	0	0	0	0	0	.000
TOTALS	33	2	8	2	5	5	.258

Yankees	AB	R	H	RBI	BB	K	Avg
Derek Jeter, ss	4	1	1	1	0	1	.250
Wade Boggs, 3b	3	0	0	0	0	0	.273
Charlie Hayes, 3b	1	0	0	0	0	0	.188
Bernie Williams, cf	4	0	2	1	0	0	.167
Cecil Fielder, dh	4	0	1	0	0	1	.391
Tino Martinez, 1b	3	0	0	0	0	1	.091
Darryl Strawberry, lf	2	0	0	0	1	1	.188
Paul O'Neill, rf	3	1	1	0	0	0	.167
Mariano Duncan, 2b	1	0	0	0	0	0	.053
Luis Sojo, 2b	2	0	1	0	0	0	.600
Joe Girardi, c	3	1	2	1	0	0	.200
TOTALS	30	3	8	3	1	3	.216

	1	2	3	4	5	6	7	8	9		R	H	E
Braves	0	0	0	1	0	0	0	0	1		2	8	0
Yankees	0	0	3	0	0	0	0	0	x		3	8	1

E—Duncan. DP—Braves 2 (CJones to Lemke to McGriff; McGriff to Blauser), Yankees 1 (Jeter to Martinez). LOB—Braves 9, Yankees 4. Scoring Position—Braves 2-for-10, Yankees 3-for-8. 2B—CJones (3), Blauser (1), O'Neill (2), Sojo (1). 3B—Girardi (1). GDP—Pendleton, Jeter, O'Neill. SB—Jeter (1), Williams (1). CS—Pendleton (1).

Braves	IP	H	R	ER	BB	K	ERA
Greg Maddux (L, 1-1)	7.2	8	3	3	1	3	1.72
Mark Wohlers	0.1	0	0	0	0	0	6.23

Yankees	IP	H	R	ER	BB	K	ERA
Jimmy Key (W, 1-1)	5.1	5	1	1	3	1	3.97
Dave Weathers (H, 1)	0.1	0	0	0	1	1	3.00
Graeme Lloyd (H, 2)	0.1	0	0	0	1	1	0.00
Mariano Rivera (H, 2)	2.0	0	0	0	1	1	1.59
John Wetteland (S, 4)	1.0	3	1	1	0	2	2.08

Time—2:53. Attendance—56,375. Umpires—HP, Davis. 1B, Evans. 2B, Tata. 3B, Welke.

1996 World Series—Composite Statistics

Batting

Yankees	G	AB	R	H	RBI	2B	3B	HR	BB	SO	SB	CS	Avg	OBP	Slg
Mike Aldrete	2	1	0	0	0	0	0	0	0	0	0	0	.000	.000	.000
Wade Boggs	4	11	0	3	2	1	0	0	1	0	0	0	.273	.333	.364
David Cone	1	2	0	0	0	0	0	0	0	1	0	0	.000	.000	.000
Mariano Duncan	6	19	1	1	0	0	0	0	0	4	1	0	.053	.053	.053
Cecil Fielder	6	23	1	9	2	2	0	0	2	2	0	0	.391	.440	.478
Andy Fox	4	0	1	0	0	0	0	0	0	0	0	0	—	—	—
Joe Girardi	4	10	1	2	1	0	1	0	1	2	0	0	.200	.273	.400
Charlie Hayes	5	16	2	3	1	0	0	1	5	0	0	.188	.235	.188
Derek Jeter	6	20	5	5	1	0	0	4	6	1	0	.250	.400	.250
Jim Leyritz	4	8	1	3	3	0	0	1	3	2	1	0	.375	.545	.750
Graeme Lloyd	4	1	0	0	0	0	0	0	0	0	0	0	.000	.000	.000
Tino Martinez	6	11	0	1	0	0	0	0	2	5	0	0	.091	.231	.091
Paul O'Neill	5	12	1	2	0	2	0	0	3	2	0	0	.167	.333	.333
Andy Pettitte	2	4	0	0	0	0	0	0	0	1	0	0	.000	.000	.000
Tim Raines	4	14	2	3	0	0	0	0	2	1	0	1	.214	.313	.214
Mariano Rivera	4	1	0	0	0	0	0	0	0	0	0	0	.000	.000	.000
Kenny Rogers	1	1	0	1	0	0	0	0	0	0	0	0	1.000	1.000	1.000
Luis Sojo	5	5	0	3	1	1	0	0	0	0	0	0	.600	.600	.800
Darryl Strawberry	5	16	0	3	1	0	0	0	4	6	0	0	.188	.350	.188
Bernie Williams	6	24	3	4	4	0	0	1	3	6	1	0	.167	.259	.292
Totals	6	199	18	43	16	6	1	2	26	43	4	1	.216	.310	.286

Batting

Braves	G	AB	R	H	RBI	2B	3B	HR	BB	SO	SB	CS	Avg	OBP	Slg
Mike Bielecki	2	1	0	0	0	0	0	0	0	1	0	0	.000	.000	.000
Jeff Blauser	6	18	2	3	1	1	0	0	1	4	0	0	.167	.211	.222
Jermaine Dye	5	17	0	2	1	0	0	0	1	1	0	0	.118	.167	.118
Tom Glavine	1	1	1	0	0	0	0	0	1	0	0	0	.000	.500	.000
Marquis Grissom	6	27	4	12	5	2	1	0	1	2	1	0	.444	.464	.593
Andruw Jones	6	20	4	8	6	1	0	2	3	6	1	2	.400	.500	.750
Chipper Jones	6	21	3	6	3	3	0	0	4	2	1	0	.286	.385	.429
Ryan Klesko	5	10	2	1	1	0	0	0	2	4	0	0	.100	.250	.100
Mark Lemke	6	26	2	6	2	1	0	0	3	0	0	0	.231	.231	.269
Javy Lopez	6	21	3	4	1	0	0	0	3	4	0	0	.190	.280	.190
Fred McGriff	6	20	4	6	6	0	0	2	5	4	0	0	.300	.423	.600
Mike Mordecai	1	1	0	0	0	0	0	0	0	0	0	0	.000	.000	.000
Denny Neagle	2	1	0	0	0	0	0	0	0	0	0	0	.000	.000	.000
Terry Pendleton	4	9	1	2	0	1	0	0	1	1	0	1	.222	.300	.333
Eddie Perez	2	1	0	0	0	0	0	0	0	0	0	0	.000	.000	.000
Luis Polonia	6	5	0	0	0	0	0	0	1	3	0	1	.000	.167	.000
John Smoltz	2	2	0	1	0	0	0	0	0	0	0	0	.500	.500	.500
Totals	6	201	26	51	26	9	1	4	23	36	3	4	.254	.329	.368

Pitching

Yankees	G	GS	CG	IP	H	R	ER	BB	SO	W-L	Sv-Op	Hld	ERA
Brian Boehringer	2	0	0	5.0	5	5	3	0	3	0-0	0-0	0	5.40
David Cone	1	1	0	6.0	4	1	1	4	3	1-0	0-0	0	1.50
Jimmy Key	2	2	0	11.1	15	5	5	5	1	1-1	0-0	0	3.97
Graeme Lloyd	4	0	0	2.2	0	0	0	0	4	1-0	0-0	2	0.00
Jeff Nelson	3	0	0	4.1	1	0	0	1	5	0-0	0-0	0	0.00
Andy Pettitte	2	2	0	10.2	11	7	7	4	5	1-1	0-0	0	5.91
Mariano Rivera	4	0	0	5.2	4	1	1	3	4	0-0	0-0	2	1.59
Kenny Rogers	1	1	0	2.0	5	5	5	2	0	0-0	0-0	0	22.50
Dave Weathers	3	0	0	3.0	2	1	1	3	3	0-0	0-0	1	3.00
John Wetteland	5	0	0	4.1	4	1	1	1	6	0-0	4-4	0	2.08
Totals	6	6	0	55.0	51	26	24	23	36	4-2	4-4	5	3.93

Pitching

Braves	G	GS	CG	IP	H	R	ER	BB	SO	W-L	Sv-Op	Hld	ERA
Steve Avery	1	0	0	0.2	1	2	1	3	0	0-1	0-0	0	13.50
Mike Bielecki	2	0	0	3.0	0	0	0	3	6	0-0	0-0	1	0.00
Brad Clontz	3	0	0	1.2	1	0	0	1	2	0-0	0-0	0	0.00
Tom Glavine	1	1	0	7.0	4	2	1	3	8	0-1	0-0	0	1.29
Greg Maddux	2	2	0	15.2	14	3	3	1	5	1-1	0-0	0	1.72
Greg McMichael	2	0	0	1.0	5	3	3	0	1	0-0	0-0	0	27.00
Denny Neagle	2	1	0	6.0	5	3	2	4	3	0-0	0-0	0	3.00
John Smoltz	2	2	0	14.0	6	2	1	8	14	1-1	0-0	0	0.64
Terrell Wade	2	0	0	0.2	0	0	0	1	0	0-0	0-0	0	0.00
Mark Wohlers	4	0	0	4.1	7	3	3	2	4	0-0	0-1	0	6.23
Totals	6	6	0	54.0	43	18	14	26	43	2-4	0-1	1	2.33

Fielding

Yankees	Pos	G	PO	Ast	E	DP	PB	FPct
Mike Aldrete	rf	1	0	0	0	0	—	—
Brian Boehringer	p	2	0	0	0	0	—	—
Wade Boggs	3b	4	0	0	0	0	—	—
David Cone	p	1	2	1	0	0	—	1.000
Mariano Duncan	2b	6	9	14	2	5	—	.920
Cecil Fielder	1b	3	21	5	0	3	—	1.000
Andy Fox	2b	1	1	0	0	0	—	1.000
	3b	1	0	0	0	0	—	—
Joe Girardi	c	4	23	4	0	0	0	1.000
Charlie Hayes	3b	4	2	6	0	0	—	1.000
	1b	1	1	0	0	1	—	1.000
Derek Jeter	ss	6	14	22	2	5	—	.947
Jimmy Key	p	2	0	3	0	1	—	1.000
Jim Leyritz	c	3	15	0	0	0	0	1.000
Graeme Lloyd	p	4	0	0	0	0	—	—
Tino Martinez	1b	5	27	0	0	3	—	1.000
Jeff Nelson	p	3	2	0	0	0	—	1.000
Paul O'Neill	rf	4	12	0	0	0	—	1.000
Andy Pettitte	p	2	0	5	0	1	—	1.000
Tim Raines	lf	4	5	0	1	0	—	.833
Mariano Rivera	p	4	0	2	0	0	—	1.000
Kenny Rogers	p	1	0	0	0	0	—	—
Luis Sojo	2b	3	5	2	0	0	—	1.000
Darryl Strawberry	lf	3	10	0	0	0	—	1.000
	rf	2	1	0	0	0	—	1.000
Dave Weathers	p	3	0	0	0	0	—	—
John Wetteland	p	5	0	0	0	0	—	—
Bernie Williams	cf	6	15	0	0	0	—	1.000
Totals		6	165	64	5	19	0	.979

Fielding

Braves	Pos	G	PO	Ast	E	DP	PB	FPct
Steve Avery	p	1	0	0	0	0	—	—
Rafael Belliard	ss	3	0	3	0	0	—	1.000
Mike Bielecki	p	2	1	0	0	0	—	1.000
Jeff Blauser	ss	6	9	15	1	3	—	.960
Brad Clontz	p	3	0	0	0	0	—	—
Jermaine Dye	rf	5	15	0	1	0	—	.938
Tom Glavine	p	1	0	2	0	0	—	1.000
Marquis Grissom	cf	6	7	0	1	0	—	.875
Andruw Jones	lf	5	4	0	0	0	—	1.000
	rf	2	3	1	0	1	—	1.000
Chipper Jones	3b	6	4	6	0	1	—	1.000
	ss	1	0	1	0	0	—	1.000
Ryan Klesko	lf	2	1	0	0	0	—	1.000
	1b	1	0	0	1	0	—	.000
Mark Lemke	2b	6	11	24	0	3	—	1.000
Javy Lopez	c	6	41	4	0	0	0	1.000
Greg Maddux	p	2	2	7	0	0	—	1.000
Fred McGriff	1b	6	62	5	0	6	—	1.000
Greg McMichael	p	2	0	0	0	0	—	—
Denny Neagle	p	2	0	1	0	0	—	1.000
Terry Pendleton	3b	1	0	2	0	0	—	1.000
Eddie Perez	c	2	2	0	0	0	0	1.000
John Smoltz	p	2	0	1	0	0	—	1.000
Terrell Wade	p	2	0	0	0	0	—	—
Mark Wohlers	p	4	0	1	0	0	—	1.000
Totals		6	162	73	4	14	0	.983

1997 Florida Marlins (NL) 4, Cleveland Indians (AL) 3

The Florida Marlins captured the World Championship in only their fifth season of existence by defeating the Cleveland Indians with an extra-inning comeback victory in Game 7 of the World Series. Postseason veteran Orel Hershiser started the opener for Cleveland, but the Marlins took the lead on back-to-back home runs by Moises Alou and Charles Johnson in the fourth inning, and won 7-4. Cleveland's Chad Ogea beat Florida ace Kevin Brown 6-1 in Game 2 to even the Series. Cleveland jumped out to a 7-3 lead in Game 3, but Florida battled back to tie it before srtiking for seven runs in the top of the ninth. The Marlins held on to win, 14-11. In a battle of rookies, Cleveland's Jaret Wright beat Florida's Tony Saunders in Game 4, 10-3. Alou hit another critical home run off Hershiser in Game 5. The three-run blast in the sixth inning put the Marlins ahead 5-4 in a game they ultimately would win, 8-7. Cleveland pitcher Ogea laced a two-run single and held the Marlins in check for five innings in Game 6 as the Indians pulled off several spectacular defensive plays en route to a 4-1 victory. Wright and three Cleveland relievers limited the Marlins to two hits over the first eight innings in Game 7 as the Tribe took a 2-1 lead into the bottom of the ninth. But Alou led off the frame with a base hit, and then moved to third on a single and scored the tying run on Craig Counsell's sacrifice fly. In the bottom of the 11th, the Marlins loaded the bases with help from Tony Fernandez' error, and Edgar Renteria singled to center to win the game and the World Series.

Game 1
Saturday, October 18

Indians	AB	R	H	RBI	BB	K	Avg
Bip Roberts, 2b	4	1	2	0	1	0	.500
Omar Vizquel, ss	4	0	0	0	0	2	.000
Manny Ramirez, rf	3	1	1	1	2	0	.333
David Justice, lf	4	0	2	1	1	0	.500
Matt Williams, 3b	5	0	1	0	0	1	.200
Jim Thome, 1b	5	1	1	1	0	2	.200
Sandy Alomar Jr., c	5	0	1	0	0	2	.200
Marquis Grissom, cf	3	1	2	0	1	1	.667
Orel Hershiser, p	2	0	0	0	0	0	.000
Jeff Juden, p	0	0	0	0	0	0	—
Jeff Branson, ph	1	0	0	0	0	1	.000
Eric Plunk, p	0	0	0	0	0	0	—
Brian Giles, ph	1	0	1	1	0	0	1.000
Paul Assenmacher, p	0	0	0	0	0	0	—
TOTALS	37	4	11	4	5	10	.297

Marlins	AB	R	H	RBI	BB	K	Avg
Devon White, cf	4	0	0	0	1	1	.000
Edgar Renteria, ss	4	0	1	0	0	0	.000
Gary Sheffield, rf	2	1	0	0	2	1	.000
Bobby Bonilla, 3b	3	2	2	0	1	1	.667
Darren Daulton, 1b	2	1	1	0	0	0	.500
Jeff Conine, 1b	2	0	1	0	0	0	.500
Moises Alou, lf	3	1	1	3	1	1	.333
Charles Johnson, c	3	1	1	1	1	0	.333
Craig Counsell, 2b	3	1	1	0	1	0	.333
Livan Hernandez, p	2	0	0	0	0	0	.000
Dennis Cook, p	0	0	0	0	0	0	—
Jay Powell, p	0	0	0	0	0	0	—
John Cangelosi, ph	1	0	0	0	0	1	.000
Robb Nen, p	0	0	0	0	0	0	—
TOTALS	29	7	7	6	7	5	.241

	1	2	3	4	5	6	7	8	9	R	H	E
Indians	1	0	0	0	1	1	0	1	0	4	11	0
Marlins	0	0	1	4	2	0	0	0	x	7	7	1

E—Sheffield. DP—Indians 1 (Roberts to Vizquel to Thome). LOB—Indians 12, Marlins 6. Scoring Position—Indians 1-for-12, Marlins 2-for-6. 2B—Roberts 2 (2), Grissom (1), Counsell (1), Giles (1). HR—Ramirez (1), Thome (1), Alou (1), Johnson (1). S—Vizquel, Hernandez. GDP—Conine.

Indians	IP	H	R	ER	BB	K	ERA
Orel Hershiser (L, 0-1)	4.1	6	7	7	4	2	14.54
Jeff Juden	0.2	0	0	0	2	0	0.00
Eric Plunk	2.0	1	0	0	1	1	0.00
Paul Assenmacher	1.0	0	0	0	0	2	0.00

Marlins	IP	H	R	ER	BB	K	ERA
Livan Hernandez (W, 1-0)	5.2	8	3	3	2	5	4.76
Dennis Cook (H, 1)	1.2	0	0	0	1	2	0.00
Jay Powell	0.2	1	1	1	2	1	13.50
Robb Nen (S, 1)	1.0	2	0	0	2	2	0.00

WP—Juden. Time—3:19. Attendance—67,245. Umpires—HP, Montague. 1B, Ford. 2B, West. 3B, Kosc.

Game 2
Sunday, October 19

Indians	AB	R	H	RBI	BB	K	Avg
Bip Roberts, 2b	3	0	1	2	0	1	.429
Tony Fernandez, ph-2b	2	0	2	0	0	0	1.000
Omar Vizquel, ss	4	1	2	0	1	0	.250
Manny Ramirez, rf	5	0	0	0	0	1	.125
David Justice, lf	3	0	1	1	1	1	.429
Matt Williams, 3b	4	2	2	0	0	0	.333
Jim Thome, 1b	4	0	1	0	0	1	.222
Sandy Alomar Jr., c	4	2	2	0	0	0	.333
Marquis Grissom, cf	4	1	3	1	0	0	.714
Chad Ogea, p	2	0	0	0	0	1	.000
Mike Jackson, p	1	0	0	0	0	0	.000
Jose Mesa, p	0	0	0	0	0	0	—
TOTALS	36	6	14	6	2	5	.348

Marlins	AB	R	H	RBI	BB	K	Avg
Devon White, cf	5	0	2	0	0	1	.222
Edgar Renteria, ss	4	1	2	0	0	1	.250
Gary Sheffield, rf	2	0	1	0	1	0	.250
Bobby Bonilla, 3b	4	0	0	0	0	1	.286
Jeff Conine, 1b	3	0	1	1	0	0	.400
Darren Daulton, ph-1b	1	0	0	0	0	0	.333
Moises Alou, lf	4	0	2	0	0	0	.429
Charles Johnson, c	3	0	0	0	0	1	.167
Greg Zaun, ph	1	0	0	0	0	0	.000
Craig Counsell, 2b	3	0	0	0	1	0	.167
Kevin Brown, p	2	0	0	0	0	1	.000
Felix Heredia, p	0	0	0	0	0	0	—
Jim Eisenreich, ph	1	0	0	0	0	0	.000
Antonio Alfonseca, p	0	0	0	0	0	0	—
Cliff Floyd, ph	1	0	0	0	0	0	.000
TOTALS	34	1	8	1	2	6	.250

	1	2	3	4	5	6	7	8	9	R	H	E
Indians	1	0	0	0	3	2	0	0	0	6	14	0
Marlins	1	0	0	0	0	0	0	0	0	1	8	0

DP—Indians 1 (Williams to Roberts to Thome), Marlins 3 (Bonilla to Counsell to Conine; Counsell to Renteria to Conine; Bonilla to Counsell to Daulton). LOB—Indians 6, Marlins 9. Scoring Position—Indians 3-for-9, Marlins 1-for-8. 2B—Vizquel (1), White (1), Renteria (1), Alou 2 (2), Fernandez (1). HR—Alomar Jr. (1). S—Ogea. GDP—Ramirez 2, Alomar Jr., Sheffield. CS—Justice (1).

Indians	IP	H	R	ER	BB	K	ERA
Chad Ogea (W, 1-0)	6.2	7	1	1	1	4	1.35
Mike Jackson	1.1	1	0	0	0	1	0.00
Jose Mesa	1.0	0	0	0	1	1	0.00

Marlins	IP	H	R	ER	BB	K	ERA
Kevin Brown (L, 0-1)	6.0	10	6	6	2	4	9.00
Felix Heredia	1.0	1	0	0	0	1	0.00
Antonio Alfonseca	2.0	3	0	0	0	0	0.00

HBP—Sheffield by Ogea. Time—2:48. Attendance—67,025. Umpires—HP, Ford. 1B, West. 2B, Kosc. 3B, Marsh.

Game 3
Tuesday, October 21

Marlins	AB	R	H	RBI	BB	K	Avg
Devon White, cf	5	0	1	0	1	1	.214
Edgar Renteria, ss	4	2	2	1	2	0	.333
Gary Sheffield, rf	5	2	3	5	1	0	.444
Bobby Bonilla, 3b	5	1	1	2	1	1	.250
Darren Daulton, 1b	4	3	2	1	2	0	.429
Jeff Conine, 1b	0	0	0	0	0	0	.400
Moises Alou, lf	5	0	0	0	0	3	.250
Jim Eisenreich, dh	3	1	2	2	0	0	.500
Kurt Abbott, ph-dh	1	0	0	0	0	1	.000
Cliff Floyd, ph-dh	0	1	0	1	0	0	.000
Charles Johnson, c	5	2	3	0	0	0	.364
Craig Counsell, 2b	5	2	2	1	2	2	.273
TOTALS	42	14	16	12	8	8	.313

Indians	AB	R	H	RBI	BB	K	Avg
Bip Roberts, lf	5	1	1	2	0	1	.333
Omar Vizquel, ss	4	0	0	1	2	1	.167
Manny Ramirez, rf	5	0	1	1	0	0	.154
David Justice, lf	3	2	0	0	2	0	.300
Matt Williams, 3b	5	0	1	0	0	2	.286
Sandy Alomar Jr., c	3	2	2	1	1	0	.417
Brian Giles, ph	0	1	0	0	1	0	1.000
Jim Thome, 1b	4	3	2	1	1	0	.308
Tony Fernandez, 2b	4	0	1	1	0	0	.500
Marquis Grissom, cf	3	2	2	1	2	0	.700
TOTALS	36	11	10	10	9	5	.340

	1	2	3	4	5	6	7	8	9	R	H	E
Marlins	1	0	1	1	0	2	2	0	7	14	16	3
Indians	2	0	0	3	2	0	0	0	4	11	10	3

E—Fernandez, Bonilla 2, Leiter, Grissom, Thome. DP—Marlins 1 (Counsell to Renteria to Daulton), Indians 2 (Thome to Nagy; Vizquel to Fernandez to Thome). LOB—Marlins 9, Indians 9. Scoring Position—Marlins 4-for-12, Indians 6-for-15. 2B—Sheffield (1), Roberts (3). HR—Sheffield (1), Daulton (1), Eisenreich (1), Thome (2). S—Roberts. SF—Fernandez. GDP—Sheffield, Bonilla, Grissom.

Marlins	IP	H	R	ER	BB	K	ERA
Al Leiter	4.2	6	7	4	6	3	7.71
Felix Heredia	2.1	0	0	0	1	0	0.00
Dennis Cook (W, 1-0)	1.0	1	0	0	0	1	0.00
Robb Nen	1.0	3	4	4	2	1	18.00

Indians	IP	H	R	ER	BB	K	ERA
Charles Nagy	6.0	6	5	5	4	5	7.50
Brian Anderson (H, 1)	0.1	1	1	1	0	0	27.00
Mike Jackson (BS, 1)	0.2	2	1	1	1	0	4.50
Paul Assenmacher	0.2	3	0	0	0	1	0.00
Eric Plunk (L, 0-1)	0.2	4	3	2	1	0	10.13
Alvin Morman	0.1	0	2	0	1	1	0.00
Jose Mesa	0.1	2	1	1	0	0	6.75

WP—Mesa. Time—4:12. Attendance—44,880. Umpires—HP, West. 1B, Kosc. 2B, Marsh. 3B, Kaiser.

Game 4
Wednesday, October 22

Marlins	AB	R	H	RBI	BB	K	Avg
Devon White, cf	4	0	0	0	0	4	.167
Edgar Renteria, ss	4	0	1	0	0	0	.313
Gary Sheffield, rf	3	0	0	0	1	2	.333
Bobby Bonilla, 3b	4	0	0	0	0	0	.188
Darren Daulton, 1b	3	2	2	0	1	0	.500
Moises Alou, lf	3	1	1	2	1	0	.267
Jim Eisenreich, dh	2	0	2	1	1	0	.667
Alex Arias, ph	1	0	0	0	0	0	.000
Charles Johnson, c	4	0	0	0	0	1	.267
Craig Counsell, 2b	2	0	0	0	1	0	.231
Kurt Abbott, ph	1	0	0	0	0	0	.000
TOTALS	31	3	6	3	5	7	.282

Indians	AB	R	H	RBI	BB	K	Avg
Bip Roberts, lf	4	0	1	0	0	2	.313
Brian Giles, lf	1	0	1	1	0	0	1.000
Omar Vizquel, ss	5	2	2	0	0	0	.235
Manny Ramirez, rf	4	2	1	2	1	1	.176
David Justice, dh	3	2	1	0	2	2	.308
Matt Williams, 3b	3	3	3	2	2	0	.412
Sandy Alomar Jr., c	5	0	3	3	0	0	.471
Jim Thome, 1b	4	0	1	0	1	1	.294
Tony Fernandez, 2b	5	1	2	1	0	0	.455
Marquis Grissom, cf	4	0	0	0	0	1	.355
TOTALS	38	10	15	9	6	7	.355

	1	2	3	4	5	6	7	8	9	R	H	E
Marlins	0	0	0	1	0	2	0	0	0	3	6	2
Indians	3	0	3	0	0	1	1	2	x	10	15	0

E—Renteria, Saunders. DP—Indians 2 (Fernandez to Vizquel to Thome; Thome). LOB—Marlins 6, Indians 10. Scoring Position—Marlins 1-for-7, Indians 4-for-12. 2B—Daulton (1), Roberts (4), Alomar Jr. (1). HR—Alou (2), Ramirez (2), Williams (1). GDP—Bonilla. SB—Counsell (1), Vizquel (1). CS—Giles (1).

Marlins	IP	H	R	ER	BB	K	ERA
Tony Saunders (L, 0-1)	2.0	7	6	6	3	2	27.00
Antonio Alfonseca	3.0	0	0	0	0	4	0.00
Ed Vosberg	2.0	3	2	2	2	1	9.00
Jay Powell	1.0	2	2	2	1	0	16.20

Indians	IP	H	R	ER	BB	K	ERA
Jaret Wright (W, 1-0)	6.0	5	3	3	5	5	4.50
Brian Anderson (S, 1)	3.0	1	0	0	0	2	2.70

Saunders pitched to seven batters in the 3rd.

WP—Wright. Time—3:15. Attendance—44,877. Umpires—HP, Kosc. 1B, Marsh. 2B, Kaiser. 3B, Montague.

Game 5
Thursday, October 23

Marlins	AB	R	H	RBI	BB	K	Avg
Devon White, cf	4	0	2	2	1	0	.227
Edgar Renteria, ss	5	0	1	0	0	2	.286
Gary Sheffield, rf	5	1	2	0	0	2	.353
Bobby Bonilla, 3b	4	1	1	0	1	0	.200
Alex Arias, pr-3b	0	1	0	0	0	0	.000
Darren Daulton, dh	5	1	2	0	0	1	.467
Moises Alou, lf	5	2	3	4	0	1	.350
Jeff Conine, 1b	5	1	1	0	0	0	.300
Charles Johnson, c	5	1	3	2	0	2	.350
Craig Counsell, 2b	2	0	0	0	2	1	.200
TOTALS	40	8	15	8	4	6	.298

Indians	AB	R	H	RBI	BB	K	Avg
Bip Roberts, 2b	3	1	0	0	2	0	.263
Omar Vizquel, ss	4	1	1	0	0	0	.238
Manny Ramirez, rf	5	0	1	0	0	1	.182
David Justice, dh	5	0	1	2	0	1	.278
Matt Williams, 3b	3	2	1	0	2	0	.400
Jim Thome, 1b	4	2	2	1	1	0	.333
Sandy Alomar Jr., c	5	1	2	4	0	0	.455
Brian Giles, lf	1	0	0	0	3	1	.667
Marquis Grissom, cf	4	0	1	0	0	0	.444
TOTALS	34	7	9	7	8	3	.329

	1	2	3	4	5	6	7	8	9	R	H	E
Marlins	0	2	0	0	0	4	0	1	1	8	15	2
Indians	0	1	3	0	0	0	0	0	3	7	9	0

E—Counsell, Hernandez. DP—Marlins 2 (Renteria to Counsell to Conine; Hernandez to Renteria to Conine), Indians 1 (Roberts to Vizquel to Thome). LOB—Marlins 9, Indians 9. Scoring Position—Marlins 6-for-15, Indians 4-for-11. 2B—White 2 (3), Bonilla (1), Daulton (2). 3B—Thome (1). HR—Alou (3), Alomar Jr. (2). S—Vizquel. GDP—Bonilla, Justice, Alomar Jr. SB—Daulton (1), Alou (1).

Marlins	IP	H	R	ER	BB	K	ERA
Livan Hernandez (W, 2-0)	8.0	7	6	5	8	2	5.27
Robb Nen (S, 2)	1.0	2	1	0	0	1	12.00

Indians	IP	H	R	ER	BB	K	ERA
Orel Hershiser (L, 0-2)	5.2	9	6	6	2	3	11.70
Alvin Morman	0.0	0	0	0	0	0	0.00
Eric Plunk	0.1	0	0	0	1	1	9.00
Jeff Juden	1.1	2	1	1	1	0	4.50
Paul Assenmacher	0.2	1	0	0	0	1	0.00
Jose Mesa	1.0	3	1	1	0	1	7.71

Morman pitched to one batter in the 6th. Hernandez pitched to two batters in the 9th.

WP—Hernandez. Time—3:39. Attendance—44,888. Umpires—HP, Marsh. 1B, Kaiser. 2B, Montague. 3B, Ford.

Game 6
Saturday, October 25

Indians	AB	R	H	RBI	BB	K	Avg
Bip Roberts, 2b	3	0	1	0	0	1	.273
Tony Fernandez, 2b	1	0	1	0	0	0	.500
Omar Vizquel, ss	4	1	1	0	0	0	.240
Manny Ramirez, rf	1	0	0	2	1	0	.174
David Justice, lf	4	0	0	0	0	1	.227
Matt Williams, 3b	4	1	2	0	0	1	.417
Jim Thome, 1b	3	1	0	0	1	2	.292
Sandy Alomar Jr., c	3	0	0	0	1	1	.400
Marquis Grissom, cf	3	0	0	0	1	1	.381
Chad Ogea, p	2	1	2	2	0	0	.500
Mike Jackson, p	1	0	0	0	0	1	.000
Paul Assenmacher, p	0	0	0	0	0	0	—
Kevin Seitzer, ph	1	0	0	0	0	0	.000
Jose Mesa, p	0	0	0	0	0	0	—
TOTALS	30	4	7	4	4	8	.312

Marlins	AB	R	H	RBI	BB	K	Avg
Devon White, cf	5	0	3	0	0	1	.296
Edgar Renteria, ss	5	0	0	0	0	2	.231
Gary Sheffield, rf	3	0	0	0	2	0	.300
Bobby Bonilla, 3b	4	0	0	0	0	0	.167
Jeff Conine, 1b	2	0	0	0	0	0	.250
Jim Eisenreich, ph-1b	1	0	0	0	1	1	.571
Moises Alou, lf	3	1	1	0	1	0	.348
Charles Johnson, c	4	0	2	0	0	0	.375
Craig Counsell, 2b	4	0	1	0	0	1	.211
Kevin Brown, p	1	0	0	0	0	0	.000
Darren Daulton, ph	0	0	0	0	1	0	.467
Felix Heredia, p	0	0	0	0	0	0	—
John Cangelosi, ph	1	0	1	0	0	0	.500
Jay Powell, p	0	0	0	0	0	0	—
Ed Vosberg, p	0	0	0	0	0	0	—
Cliff Floyd, ph	1	0	0	0	0	0	.000
TOTALS	34	1	8	1	4	5	.294

	1	2	3	4	5	6	7	8	9	R	H	E
Indians	0	2	1	0	1	0	0	0	0	4	7	0
Marlins	0	0	0	0	1	0	0	0	0	1	8	0

DP—Marlins 1 (Counsell to Renteria to Conine). LOB—Indians 5, Marlins 11. Scoring Position—Indians 2-for-9, Marlins 0-for-10. 2B—Vizquel (2), Williams (1), Ogea (1). 3B—White (1). SF—Ramirez 2, Daulton. GDP—Roberts. SB—Vizquel 2 (3), White (1). CS—Roberts (1).

Indians	IP	H	R	ER	BB	K	ERA
Chad Ogea (W, 2-0)	5.0	4	1	1	2	1	1.54
Mike Jackson (H, 1)	2.0	2	0	0	2	2	2.25
Paul Assenmacher (H, 1)	1.0	1	0	0	0	1	0.00
Jose Mesa (S, 1)	1.0	1	0	0	0	1	5.40

Marlins	IP	H	R	ER	BB	K	ERA
Kevin Brown (L, 0-2)	5.0	5	4	4	3	2	8.18
Felix Heredia	2.0	0	0	0	0	4	0.00
Jay Powell	1.0	2	0	0	0	1	10.13
Ed Vosberg	1.0	0	0	0	0	1	6.00

Ogea pitched to one batter in the 6th. Powell pitched to one batter in the 9th.

Time—3:15. Attendance—67,498. Umpires—HP, Kaiser. 1B, Montague. 2B, Ford. 3B, West.

Game 7
Sunday, October 26

Indians	AB	R	H	RBI	BB	K	Avg
Omar Vizquel, ss	5	0	1	0	0	2	.233
Tony Fernandez, 2b	5	0	2	2	0	1	.471
Manny Ramirez, rf	3	0	0	0	2	2	.154
David Justice, lf	5	0	0	0	0	3	.185
Matt Williams, 3b	2	0	0	0	3	2	.385
Sandy Alomar Jr., c	5	0	1	0	0	0	.367
Jim Thome, 1b	4	1	1	0	1	0	.286
Marquis Grissom, cf	4	1	1	0	0	1	.360
Jaret Wright, p	2	0	0	0	0	2	.000
Paul Assenmacher, p	0	0	0	0	0	0	—
Mike Jackson, p	0	0	0	0	0	0	.000
Brian Anderson, p	0	0	0	0	0	0	—
Brian Giles, ph	1	0	0	0	0	0	.500
Jose Mesa, p	0	0	0	0	0	0	—
Charles Nagy, p	0	0	0	0	0	0	—
TOTALS	36	2	6	2	6	13	.295

Marlins	AB	R	H	RBI	BB	K	Avg
Devon White, cf	6	0	0	0	0	2	.242
Edgar Renteria, ss	5	0	3	1	1	0	.290
Gary Sheffield, rf	4	0	1	0	1	2	.292
Darren Daulton, 1b	3	0	0	0	0	0	.389
Jeff Conine, ph-1b	1	0	0	0	0	0	.231
Robb Nen, p	0	0	0	0	0	0	—
John Cangelosi, ph	1	0	0	0	0	1	.333
Jay Powell, p	0	0	0	0	0	0	—
Moises Alou, lf	5	1	1	0	0	1	.321
Bobby Bonilla, 3b	5	1	2	1	0	2	.207
Charles Johnson, c	4	0	1	0	0	0	.357
Greg Zaun, pr-c	1	0	0	0	0	0	.000
Craig Counsell, 2b	3	1	0	1	1	1	.182
Al Leiter, p	0	0	0	0	2	0	—
Dennis Cook, p	0	0	0	0	0	0	—
Cliff Floyd, ph	0	0	0	0	0	0	.000
Kurt Abbott, ph	1	0	0	0	0	0	.000
Antonio Alfonseca, p	0	0	0	0	0	0	—
Felix Heredia, p	0	0	0	0	0	0	—
Jim Eisenreich, 1b	1	0	0	0	1	0	.500
TOTALS	40	3	8	3	6	11	.279

	1	2	3	4	5	6	7	8	9	10	11	R	H	E
Indians	0	0	2	0	0	0	0	0	0	0	0	2	6	2
Marlins	0	0	0	0	0	0	1	0	1	0	1	3	8	0

E—Fernandez, Ramirez. DP—Indians 1 (Fernandez to Vizquel to Thome), Marlins 2 (Daulton to Renteria; Counsell to Renteria to Eisenreich). LOB—Indians 8, Marlins 12. Scoring Position—Indians 1-for-7, Marlins 1-for-7. 2B—Renteria (2). HR—Bonilla (1). S—Wright. SF—Counsell. GDP—Thome 2, Daulton. SB—Vizquel 2 (5).

Indians	IP	H	R	ER	BB	K	ERA
Jaret Wright	6.1	2	1	1	5	7	2.92
Paul Assenmacher (H, 2)	0.2	0	0	0	0	1	0.00
Mike Jackson (H, 2)	0.2	0	0	0	0	1	1.93
Brian Anderson (H, 2)	0.1	0	0	0	0	0	2.45
Jose Mesa (BS, 1)	1.2	4	1	1	0	2	5.40
Charles Nagy (L, 0-1)	1.0	2	1	0	1	0	6.43

Marlins	IP	H	R	ER	BB	K	ERA
Al Leiter	6.0	4	2	2	4	7	5.06
Dennis Cook	1.0	0	0	0	0	2	0.00
Antonio Alfonseca	1.1	0	0	0	1	1	0.00
Felix Heredia	0.0	1	0	0	0	0	—
Robb Nen	1.2	1	0	0	0	3	7.71
Jay Powell (W, 1-0)	1.0	0	0	0	1	0	7.36

Heredia pitched to one batter in the 9th.

Time—4:10. Attendance—67,204. Umpires—HP, Montague. 1B, Ford. 2B, West. 3B, Kosc.

1997 World Series—Composite Statistics

Batting

Marlins	G	AB	R	H	RBI	2B	3B	HR	BB	SO	SB	CS	Avg	OBP	Slg
Kurt Abbott	3	3	0	0	0	0	0	0	0	0	1	0	0	.000	.000
Moises Alou	7	28	6	9	9	2	0	3	3	6	1	0	.321	.387	.714
Alex Arias	2	1	1	0	0	0	0	0	0	0	0	0	.000	.000	.000
Bobby Bonilla	7	29	5	6	3	1	0	1	3	5	0	0	.207	.281	.345
Kevin Brown	2	3	0	0	0	0	0	0	0	1	0	0	.000	.000	.000
John Cangelosi	3	3	0	1	0	0	0	0	0	2	0	0	.333	.333	.333
Jeff Conine	6	13	1	3	2	0	0	0	0	0	0	0	.231	.231	.231
Craig Counsell	7	22	4	4	2	1	0	0	6	5	1	0	.182	.345	.227
Darren Daulton	7	18	7	7	2	2	0	1	3	0	1	0	.389	.455	.667
Jim Eisenreich	5	8	1	4	3	0	1	3	1	0	0	0	.500	.636	.875
Cliff Floyd	4	2	1	0	0	0	0	0	1	1	0	0	.000	.333	.000
Livan Hernandez	2	2	0	0	0	0	0	0	0	0	0	0	.000	.000	.000
Charles Johnson	7	28	4	10	3	0	0	1	1	6	0	0	.357	.379	.464
Al Leiter	2	0	0	0	0	0	0	0	0	2	0	0	—	1.000	
Edgar Renteria	7	31	3	9	3	2	0	0	3	5	0	0	.290	.353	.355
Gary Sheffield	7	24	4	7	5	1	0	1	8	5	0	0	.292	.485	.458
Devon White	7	33	0	8	2	3	1	0	3	10	1	0	.242	.306	.394
Greg Zaun	2	2	0	0	0	0	0	0	0	0	0	0	.000	.000	.000
Totals	7	250	37	68	34	12	1	8	36	48	4	0	.272	.363	.424

Batting

Indians	G	AB	R	H	RBI	2B	3B	HR	BB	SO	SB	CS	Avg	OBP	Slg
Sandy Alomar Jr.	7	30	5	11	10	1	0	2	2	3	0	0	.367	.406	.600
Jeff Branson	1	1	0	0	0	0	0	0	0	0	1	0	.000	.000	.000
Tony Fernandez	5	17	1	8	4	1	0	0	1	0	1	0	.471	.444	.529
Brian Giles	5	4	1	2	2	1	0	0	4	1	0	1	.500	.750	.750
Marquis Grissom	7	25	5	9	2	1	0	0	4	4	0	0	.360	.448	.400
Orel Hershiser	2	2	0	0	0	0	0	0	0	1	0	0	.000	.000	.000
Mike Jackson	4	2	0	0	0	0	0	0	0	1	0	0	.000	.000	.000
David Justice	7	27	4	5	4	0	0	0	6	8	0	1	.185	.333	.185
Chad Ogea	2	4	1	2	2	1	0	0	0	1	0	0	.500	.500	.750
Manny Ramirez	7	26	3	4	6	0	0	2	6	5	0	0	.154	.294	.385
Bip Roberts	6	22	3	6	4	4	0	0	3	5	0	1	.273	.360	.455
Kevin Seitzer	1	1	0	0	0	0	0	0	0	0	0	0	.000	.000	.000
Jim Thome	7	28	8	8	4	0	1	2	5	7	0	0	.286	.394	.571
Omar Vizquel	7	30	5	7	1	2	0	0	3	5	5	0	.233	.303	.300
Matt Williams	7	26	8	10	3	1	0	1	7	6	0	0	.385	.515	.538
Jaret Wright	2	2	0	0	0	0	0	0	0	2	0	0	.000	.000	.000
Totals	7	247	44	72	42	12	1	7	40	51	5	3	.291	.386	.433

Pitching

Marlins	G	GS	CG	IP	H	R	ER	BB	SO	W-L	Sv-Op	Hld	ERA
Antonio Alfonseca	3	0	0	6.1	6	0	0	1	5	0-0	0-0	0	0.00
Kevin Brown	2	2	0	11.0	15	10	10	5	6	0-2	0-0	0	8.18
Dennis Cook	3	0	0	3.2	1	0	0	1	5	1-0	0-0	1	0.00
Felix Heredia	4	0	0	5.1	2	0	0	1	5	0-0	0-0	0	0.00
Livan Hernandez	2	2	0	13.2	15	9	8	10	7	2-0	0-0	0	5.27
Al Leiter	2	2	0	10.2	10	9	6	10	10	0-0	0-0	0	5.06
Robb Nen	4	0	0	4.2	8	5	4	2	7	0-0	2-2	0	7.71
Jay Powell	4	0	0	3.2	5	3	3	4	2	1-0	0-0	0	7.36
Tony Saunders	1	1	0	2.0	7	6	6	3	2	0-1	0-0	0	27.00
Ed Vosberg	2	0	0	3.0	3	2	2	3	2	0-0	0-0	0	6.00
Totals	7	7	0	64.0	72	44	39	40	51	4-3	2-2	1	5.48

Pitching

Indians	G	GS	CG	IP	H	R	ER	BB	SO	W-L	Sv-Op	Hld	ERA
Brian Anderson	3	0	0	3.2	2	1	1	0	2	0-0	1-1	2	2.45
Paul Assenmacher	5	0	0	4.0	5	0	0	0	6	0-0	0-0	2	0.00
Orel Hershiser	2	2	0	10.0	15	13	13	6	5	0-2	0-0	0	11.70
Mike Jackson	4	0	0	4.2	5	1	1	3	4	0-0	0-1	2	1.93
Jeff Juden	2	0	0	2.0	2	1	1	2	0	0-0	0-0	0	4.50
Jose Mesa	5	0	0	5.0	10	3	3	1	5	0-0	1-2	0	5.40
Alvin Morman	2	0	0	0.1	0	2	0	2	1	0-0	0-0	0	0.00
Charles Nagy	2	1	0	7.0	8	6	5	5	5	0-1	0-0	0	6.43
Chad Ogea	2	2	0	11.2	11	2	2	3	5	2-0	0-0	0	1.54
Eric Plunk	3	0	0	3.0	3	4	3	4	3	0-1	0-0	0	9.00
Jaret Wright	2	2	0	12.1	7	4	4	10	12	1-0	0-0	0	2.92
Totals	7	7	0	63.2	68	37	32	36	48	3-4	2-4	6	4.52

Fielding

Marlins	Pos	G	PO	Ast	E	DP	PB	FPct
Antonio Alfonseca	p	3	1	1	0	0	—	1.000
Moises Alou	lf	7	11	0	0	0	—	1.000
Alex Arias	3b	1	0	0	0	0	—	—
Bobby Bonilla	3b	7	3	20	2	2	—	.920
Kevin Brown	p	2	0	3	0	0	—	1.000
Jeff Conine	1b	6	30	2	0	5	—	1.000
Dennis Cook	p	3	0	0	0	0	—	—
Craig Counsell	2b	7	18	15	1	7	—	.971
Darren Daulton	1b	5	28	4	0	3	—	1.000
Jim Eisenreich	1b	2	3	1	0	1	—	1.000
Felix Heredia	p	4	1	0	0	0	—	1.000
Livan Hernandez	p	2	0	4	1	1	—	.800
Charles Johnson	c	7	49	2	0	0	0	1.000
Al Leiter	p	2	1	0	1	0	—	.500
Robb Nen	p	4	0	0	0	0	—	—
Jay Powell	p	4	0	2	0	0	—	1.000
Edgar Renteria	ss	7	12	26	1	7	—	.974
Tony Saunders	p	1	0	1	1	0	—	.500
Gary Sheffield	rf	7	16	0	1	0	—	.941
Ed Vosberg	p	2	0	1	0	0	—	1.000
Devon White	cf	7	16	0	0	0	—	1.000
Greg Zaun	c	1	3	0	0	0	0	1.000
Totals		7	192	82	8	26	0	.972

Fielding

Indians	Pos	G	PO	Ast	E	DP	PB	FPct
Sandy Alomar Jr.	c	7	49	3	0	0	0	1.000
Brian Anderson	p	3	0	1	0	0	—	1.000
Paul Assenmacher	p	5	0	0	0	0	—	—
Tony Fernandez	2b	5	9	14	2	3	—	.920
Brian Giles	lf	2	2	0	0	0	—	1.000
Marquis Grissom	cf	7	19	0	1	0	—	.950
Orel Hershiser	p	2	1	1	0	0	—	1.000
Mike Jackson	p	4	1	1	0	0	—	1.000
Jeff Juden	p	2	0	0	0	0	—	—
David Justice	lf	4	9	0	0	0	—	1.000
Jose Mesa	p	5	1	1	0	0	—	1.000
Alvin Morman	p	2	0	0	0	0	—	—
Charles Nagy	p	2	2	1	0	1	—	1.000
Chad Ogea	p	2	0	2	0	0	—	1.000
Eric Plunk	p	3	0	0	0	0	—	—
Manny Ramirez	rf	7	16	1	1	0	—	.944
Bip Roberts	2b	4	7	8	0	3	—	1.000
	lf	2	1	0	0	0	—	1.000
Jim Thome	1b	7	57	5	1	8	—	.984
Omar Vizquel	ss	7	12	17	0	6	—	1.000
Matt Williams	3b	7	5	9	0	1	—	1.000
Jaret Wright	p	2	0	1	0	0	—	1.000
Totals		7	191	65	5	22	0	.981

1969 Baltimore Orioles (AL) 3, Minnesota Twins (AL) 0

The Baltimore Orioles won two squeakers and a blowout to sweep the Minnesota Twins in the first Championship Series in American League history. Minnesota's Jim Perry took a 3-2 lead into the bottom of the ninth in Game 1 before Boog Powell lined a solo homer to send the game into extra innings. In the last of the 12th, Paul Blair's surprise bunt single brought home Mark Belanger with the winning run. Dave Boswell and Dave McNally battled for 10 scoreless frames in Game 2 before Baltimore's Curt Motton won it with a pinch-hit RBI single in the bottom of the 11th. McNally went the distance and fanned 11. In Game 3, Paul Blair hit two singles, two doubles and a homer and drove in five runs in Baltimore's pennant-clinching 11-2 victory.

Game 1

Saturday, October 4

Twins	AB	R	H	RBI	BB	K	Avg
Cesar Tovar, cf	4	0	0	0	1	2	.000
Rod Carew, 2b	5	0	1	0	0	3	.200
Harmon Killebrew, 3b	2	1	0	0	3	0	.000
Tony Oliva, rf	5	2	2	2	0	1	.400
Bob Allison, lf	3	0	0	1	0	0	.000
Ted Uhlaender, lf	1	0	1	0	0	0	1.000
Rich Reese, 1b	4	0	0	0	1	1	.000
Leo Cardenas, ss	5	0	0	0	0	2	.000
George Mitterwald, c	4	0	0	0	0	2	.000
John Roseboro, ph-c	1	0	0	0	0	0	.000
Jim Perry, p	3	0	0	0	0	1	.000
Ron Perranoski, p	1	0	0	0	0	0	.000
TOTALS	38	3	4	3	5	12	.105

Orioles	AB	R	H	RBI	BB	K	Avg
Don Buford, lf	6	0	0	0	0	0	.000
Paul Blair, cf	5	0	1	1	1	0	.200
Frank Robinson, rf	3	1	1	1	2	2	.333
Boog Powell, 1b	5	1	2	1	0	0	.400
Brooks Robinson, 3b	5	0	4	0	0	0	.800
Ellie Hendricks, c	3	0	0	0	0	0	.000
Curt Motton, ph	1	0	0	0	0	0	.000
Eddie Watt, p	0	0	0	0	0	0	—
Chico Salmon, ph	1	0	0	0	0	0	.000
Marcelino Lopez, p	0	0	0	0	0	0	—
Dick Hall, p	0	0	0	0	0	0	—
Dave Johnson, 2b	5	0	0	0	0	1	.000
Mark Belanger, ss	5	2	1	0	0	0	.400
Mike Cuellar, p	2	0	0	0	0	1	.000
Dave May, ph	1	0	0	0	0	0	.000
Pete Richert, p	0	0	0	0	0	0	—
Merv Rettenmund, ph	0	0	0	0	0	0	—
Andy Etchebarren, c	1	0	0	0	0	0	.000
TOTALS	43	4	10	4	3	4	.233

	1 2 3	4 5 6	7 8 9	10 11 12	R	H	E
Twins	0 0 0	0 1 0	2 0 0	0 0 0	3	4	2
Orioles	0 0 0	1 1 0	0 0 1	0 0 1	4	10	1

E—Carew, Uhlaender, FRobinson. DP—Orioles 1 (Johnson to Powell). LOB—Twins 5, Orioles 8. Scoring Position—Twins 0-for-5, Orioles 1-for-7. 2B—Oliva (1). HR—Oliva (1), FRobinson (1), Powell (1), Belanger (1). S—Etchebarren. SF—Allison. GDP—Killebrew. SB—Tovar (1). CS—BRobinson 2 (2).

Twins	IP	H	R	ER	BB	K	ERA
Jim Perry	8.0	6	3	3	3	3	3.38
Ron Perranoski (L, 0-1)	3.2	4	1	1	0	1	2.45

Orioles	IP	H	R	ER	BB	K	ERA
Mike Cuellar	8.0	3	3	2	1	7	2.25
Pete Richert	1.0	0	0	0	2	2	0.00
Eddie Watt	2.0	0	0	0	0	0	0.00
Marcelino Lopez	0.1	1	0	0	2	0	0.00
Dick Hall (W, 1-0)	0.2	0	0	0	0	1	0.00

Perry pitched to three batters in the 9th.

WP—Lopez. Time—3:29. Attendance—39,324. Umpires—HP, Chylak. 1B, Runge. 2B, Umont. 3B, Stewart.

Game 2

Sunday, October 5

Twins	AB	R	H	RBI	BB	K	Avg
Cesar Tovar, cf	5	0	1	0	0	0	.111
Rod Carew, 2b	4	0	0	0	1	1	.111
Harmon Killebrew, 3b	3	0	0	0	2	1	.000
Tony Oliva, rf	4	0	1	0	1	1	.333
Bob Allison, lf	5	0	0	0	0	0	.000
Rich Reese, 1b	4	0	0	0	0	0	.000
George Mitterwald, c	3	0	1	0	1	1	.143
Leo Cardenas, ss	4	0	0	0	0	3	.000
Dave Boswell, p	4	0	0	0	0	4	.000
Ron Perranoski, p	0	0	0	0	0	0	.000
TOTALS	36	0	3	0	5	11	.087

Orioles	AB	R	H	RBI	BB	K	Avg
Don Buford, lf	3	0	0	0	2	0	.000
Paul Blair, cf	4	0	0	0	1	1	.111
Frank Robinson, rf	5	0	2	0	0	1	.375
Boog Powell, 1b	3	1	1	0	2	0	.375
Brooks Robinson, 3b	4	0	2	0	0	0	.667
Dave Johnson, 2b	4	0	2	0	1	0	.222
Mark Belanger, ss	5	0	0	0	0	0	.200
Andy Etchebarren, c	3	0	0	0	0	0	.000
Ellie Hendricks, ph-c	0	0	0	0	1	0	.000
Curt Motton, ph	1	0	1	1	0	0	.500
Dave McNally, p	4	0	0	0	0	2	.000
TOTALS	36	1	8	1	7	4	.240

	1 2 3	4 5 6	7 8 9	10 11	R	H	E
Twins	0 0 0	0 0 0	0 0 0	0 0	0	3	1
Orioles	0 0 0	0 0 0	0 0 0	0 1	1	8	0

E—Cardenas. DP—Twins 2 (Cardenas to Reese; Boswell to Cardenas to Reese). LOB—Twins 8, Orioles 11. Scoring Position—Twins 0-for-3, Orioles 2-for-10. 2B—FRobinson 2 (2). S—BRobinson. GDP—Blair, Etchebarren. SB—Oliva (1). CS—Buford (1), Blair (1).

Twins	IP	H	R	ER	BB	K	ERA
Dave Boswell (L, 0-1)	10.2	7	1	1	7	4	0.84
Ron Perranoski	0.0	1	0	0	0	0	2.45

Orioles	IP	H	R	ER	BB	K	ERA
Dave McNally (W, 1-0)	11.0	3	0	0	5	11	0.00

Perranoski pitched to one batter in the 11th.

WP—Boswell. Time—3:17. Attendance—41,704. Umpires—HP, Runge. 1B, Umont. 2B, Stewart. 3B, Rice.

Game 3

Monday, October 6

Orioles	AB	R	H	RBI	BB	K	Avg
Don Buford, lf	5	3	4	1	1	0	.286
Paul Blair, cf	6	1	5	5	0	1	.400
Frank Robinson, rf	4	0	1	1	1	0	.333
Boog Powell, 1b	5	0	2	0	0	1	.385
Brooks Robinson, 3b	5	1	1	0	0	0	.500
Dave Johnson, 2b	4	2	1	0	1	0	.231
Ellie Hendricks, c	5	2	2	3	0	2	.250
Mark Belanger, ss	5	2	2	0	0	0	.267
Jim Palmer, p	5	0	0	0	0	3	.000
TOTALS	44	11	18	10	3	6	.321

Twins	AB	R	H	RBI	BB	K	Avg
Ted Uhlaender, lf	5	0	0	0	0	0	.167
Rod Carew, 2b	5	0	0	0	0	0	.071
Tony Oliva, rf	4	1	2	0	0	1	.385
Harmon Killebrew, 3b	3	1	1	0	1	1	.125
Rich Reese, 1b	4	0	2	2	0	0	.167
Cesar Tovar, cf	4	0	0	0	0	0	.077
John Roseboro, c	4	0	1	0	0	0	.200
Leo Cardenas, ss	4	0	2	0	0	2	.154
Bob Miller, p	0	0	0	0	0	0	—
Dick Woodson, p	1	0	1	0	0	0	1.000
Tom Hall, p	0	0	0	0	0	0	—
Charlie Manuel, ph	0	0	0	0	1	0	—
Al Worthington, p	0	0	0	0	0	0	—
Joe Grzenda, p	0	0	0	0	0	0	—
Rick Renick, ph	1	0	0	0	0	0	.000
Dean Chance, p	0	0	0	0	0	0	—
Ron Perranoski, p	0	0	0	0	0	0	.000
Graig Nettles, ph	1	0	1	0	0	0	1.000
TOTALS	36	2	10	2	2	4	.182

	1 2 3	4 5 6	7 8 9	R	H	E
Orioles	0 3 0	2 0 1	0 2 3	11	18	0
Twins	0 0 0	0 1 0	0 0 0	2	10	2

E—Oliva 2. DP—Orioles 1 (Belanger to Johnson to Powell), Twins 1 (Carew to Cardenas to Reese). LOB—Orioles 9, Twins 9. Scoring Position—Orioles 6-for-17, Twins 2-for-6. 2B—Buford (1), Blair 2 (2), BRobinson (1), Hendricks 2 (2), Oliva (2), Killebrew (1). 3B—Belanger (1), Cardenas (1). HR—Blair (1). GDP—Powell, Renick.

Orioles	IP	H	R	ER	BB	K	ERA
Jim Palmer (W, 1-0)	9.0	10	2	2	2	4	2.00

Twins	IP	H	R	ER	BB	K	ERA
Bob Miller (L, 0-1)	1.2	5	3	1	0	0	5.40
Dick Woodson	1.2	3	2	2	3	2	10.80
Tom Hall	0.2	0	0	0	0	0	0.00
Al Worthington	1.1	3	1	1	0	1	6.75
Joe Grzenda	0.2	0	0	0	0	0	0.00
Dean Chance	2.0	4	3	3	0	2	13.50
Ron Perranoski	1.0	3	2	2	0	1	5.79

Chance pitched to one batter in the 9th.

WP—Palmer. Time—2:48. Attendance—32,735. Umpires—HP, Umont. 1B, Stewart. 2B, Rice. 3B, Flaherty.

1969 AL Championship Series—Composite Statistics

Batting

Orioles	G	AB	R	H	RBI	2B	3B	HR	BB	SO	SB	CS	Avg	OBP	Slg
Mark Belanger	3	15	4	4	1	0	1	1	0	0	0	0	.267	.267	.600
Paul Blair	3	15	1	6	6	2	0	1	2	2	0	1	.400	.471	.733
Don Buford	3	14	3	4	1	1	0	0	3	0	1	1	.286	.412	.357
Mike Cuellar	1	2	0	0	0	0	0	0	0	1	0	0	.000	.000	.000
Andy Etchebarren	2	4	0	0	0	0	0	0	0	0	0	0	.000	.000	.000
Ellie Hendricks	3	8	2	2	3	2	0	0	1	2	0	0	.250	.333	.500
Dave Johnson	3	13	2	3	0	0	0	0	2	1	0	0	.231	.333	.231
Dave May	1	1	0	0	0	0	0	0	0	0	0	0	.000	.000	.000
Dave McNally	1	4	0	0	0	0	0	0	0	2	0	0	.000	.000	.000
Curt Motton	2	2	0	1	1	0	0	0	0	0	0	0	.500	.500	.500
Jim Palmer	1	5	0	0	0	0	0	0	0	3	0	0	.000	.000	.000
Boog Powell	3	13	2	5	1	0	0	1	2	0	0	0	.385	.467	.615
Merv Rettenmund	1	0	0	0	0	0	0	0	0	0	0	0	—	—	—
Brooks Robinson	3	14	1	7	0	1	0	0	0	0	0	2	.500	.500	.571
Frank Robinson	3	12	1	4	2	2	0	1	3	3	0	0	.333	.467	.750
Chico Salmon	1	1	0	0	0	0	0	0	0	0	0	0	.000	.000	.000
Totals	3	123	16	36	15	8	1	4	13	14	0	4	.293	.360	.472

Batting

Twins	G	AB	R	H	RBI	2B	3B	HR	BB	SO	SB	CS	Avg	OBP	Slg
Bob Allison	2	8	0	0	1	0	0	0	0	0	0	0	.000	.000	.000
Dave Boswell	1	4	0	0	0	0	0	0	0	4	0	0	.000	.000	.000
Leo Cardenas	3	13	0	2	0	0	1	0	0	7	0	0	.154	.154	.308
Rod Carew	3	14	0	1	0	0	0	0	1	4	0	0	.071	.133	.071
Harmon Killebrew	3	8	2	1	0	1	0	0	6	2	0	0	.125	.500	.250
Charlie Manuel	1	0	0	0	0	0	0	0	1	0	0	0	—	1.000	—
George Mitterwald	2	7	0	1	0	0	0	0	1	3	0	0	.143	.250	.143
Graig Nettles	1	1	0	1	0	0	0	0	0	0	0	0	1.000	1.000	1.000
Tony Oliva	3	13	3	5	2	2	0	1	1	3	1	0	.385	.429	.769
Ron Perranoski	3	1	0	0	0	0	0	0	0	0	0	0	.000	.000	.000
Jim Perry	1	3	0	0	0	0	0	0	0	1	0	0	.000	.000	.000
Rich Reese	3	12	0	2	2	0	0	0	1	1	0	0	.167	.231	.167
Rick Renick	1	1	0	0	0	0	0	0	0	0	0	0	.000	.000	.000
John Roseboro	2	5	0	1	0	0	0	0	0	0	0	0	.200	.200	.200
Cesar Tovar	3	13	0	1	0	0	0	0	1	2	1	0	.077	.143	.077
Ted Uhlaender	2	6	0	1	0	0	0	0	0	0	0	0	.167	.167	.167
Dick Woodson	1	1	0	1	0	0	0	0	0	0	0	0	1.000	1.000	1.000
Totals	3	110	5	17	5	3	1	1	12	27	2	0	.155	.236	.227

Pitching

Orioles	G	GS	CG	IP	H	R	ER	BB	SO	W-L	Sv-Op	Hld	ERA
Mike Cuellar	1	1	0	8.0	3	3	2	1	7	0-0	0-0	0	2.25
Dick Hall	1	0	0	0.2	0	0	0	0	1	1-0	0-0	0	0.00
Marcelino Lopez	1	0	0	0.1	1	0	0	2	0	0-0	0-0	0	0.00
Dave McNally	1	1	1	11.0	3	0	0	5	11	1-0	0-0	0	0.00
Jim Palmer	1	1	1	9.0	10	2	2	2	4	1-0	0-0	0	2.00
Pete Richert	1	0	0	1.0	0	0	0	2	2	0-0	0-0	0	0.00
Eddie Watt	1	0	0	2.0	0	0	0	0	2	0-0	0-0	0	0.00
Totals	3	3	2	32.0	17	5	4	12	27	3-0	0-0	0	1.13

Pitching

Twins	G	GS	CG	IP	H	R	ER	BB	SO	W-L	Sv-Op	Hld	ERA
Dave Boswell	1	1	0	10.2	7	1	1	7	4	0-1	0-0	0	0.84
Dean Chance	1	0	0	2.0	4	3	3	0	2	0-0	0-0	0	13.50
Joe Grzenda	1	0	0	0.2	0	0	0	0	0	0-0	0-0	0	0.00
Tom Hall	1	0	0	0.2	0	0	0	0	0	0-0	0-0	0	0.00
Bob Miller	1	1	0	1.2	5	3	1	0	0	0-1	0-0	0	5.40
Ron Perranoski	3	0	0	4.2	8	3	3	0	2	0-1	0-0	0	5.79
Jim Perry	1	1	0	8.0	6	3	3	3	3	0-0	0-0	0	3.38
Dick Woodson	1	0	0	1.2	3	2	2	3	2	0-0	0-0	0	10.80
Al Worthington	1	0	0	1.1	3	1	1	0	1	0-0	0-0	0	6.75
Totals	3	3	0	31.1	36	16	14	13	14	0-3	0-0	0	4.02

Fielding

Orioles	Pos	G	PO	Ast	E	DP	PB	FPct
Mark Belanger	ss	3	4	9	0	1	—	1.000
Paul Blair	cf	3	8	0	0	0	—	1.000
Don Buford	lf	3	7	0	0	0	—	1.000
Mike Cuellar	p	1	0	0	0	0	—	—
Andy Etchebarren	c	2	11	0	0	0	0	1.000
Dick Hall	p	1	0	0	0	0	—	—
Ellie Hendricks	c	3	18	0	0	0	0	1.000
Dave Johnson	2b	3	5	11	0	2	—	1.000
Marcelino Lopez	p	1	0	0	0	0	—	—
Dave McNally	p	1	0	0	0	0	—	—
Jim Palmer	p	1	0	1	0	0	—	1.000
Boog Powell	1b	3	34	0	0	2	—	1.000
Pete Richert	p	1	0	0	0	0	—	—
Brooks Robinson	3b	3	6	10	0	0	—	1.000
Frank Robinson	rf	3	3	0	1	0	—	.750
Eddie Watt	p	1	0	0	0	0	—	—
Totals		3	96	31	1	5	0	.992

Fielding

Twins	Pos	G	PO	Ast	E	DP	PB	FPct
Bob Allison	lf	2	6	0	0	0	—	1.000
Dave Boswell	p	1	1	4	0	1	—	1.000
Leo Cardenas	ss	3	13	12	1	3	—	.962
Rod Carew	2b	3	6	3	1	1	—	.900
Dean Chance	p	1	0	0	0	0	—	—
Joe Grzenda	p	1	0	0	0	0	—	—
Tom Hall	p	1	0	0	0	0	—	—
Harmon Killebrew	3b	3	6	3	0	0	—	1.000
Bob Miller	p	1	0	0	0	0	—	—
George Mitterwald	c	2	10	4	0	0	0	1.000
Tony Oliva	rf	3	6	1	2	0	—	.778
Ron Perranoski	p	3	0	0	0	0	—	—
Jim Perry	p	1	0	1	0	0	—	1.000
Rich Reese	1b	3	26	4	0	3	—	1.000
John Roseboro	c	2	6	1	0	0	0	1.000
Cesar Tovar	cf	3	10	0	0	0	—	1.000
Ted Uhlaender	lf	2	4	0	1	0	—	.800
Dick Woodson	p	1	0	0	0	0	—	—
Al Worthington	p	1	0	0	0	0	—	—
Totals		3	94	33	5	8	0	.962

1969 New York Mets (NL) 3, Atlanta Braves (NL) 0

The New York Mets prevailed over the Atlanta Braves, winning the first-ever NLCS in three straight games. Phil Niekro and the Braves led Game 1 by a run going into the top of the eighth, but the Mets rallied for five runs to take a 9-5 decision. J.C. Martin's two-run pinch-hit single was the biggest blow. Cleon Jones had a homer, three hits and three RBI in Game 2 as the Mets shelled the Braves, 11-6. Nolan Ryan pitched seven innings of three-hit relief in Game 3, and Wayne Garrett put the Mets ahead with his first homer in five months, as the Mets won 7-4 to advance to the World Series.

Game 1
Saturday, October 4

Mets	AB	R	H	RBI	BB	K	Avg
Tommie Agee, cf	5	0	0	0	0	3	.000
Wayne Garrett, 3b	4	1	2	0	1	0	.500
Cleon Jones, lf	5	1	1	1	0	0	.200
Art Shamsky, rf	4	1	3	0	0	0	.750
Al Weis, pr-2b	0	0	0	0	0	0	—
Ken Boswell, 2b	3	2	0	0	1	0	.000
Rod Gaspar, rf	0	0	0	0	0	0	
Ed Kranepool, 1b	4	2	1	0	0	1	.250
Jerry Grote, c	3	1	1	1	1	0	.333
Bud Harrelson, ss	3	1	1	2	1	1	.333
Tom Seaver, p	3	0	0	0	0	0	.000
J.C. Martin, ph	1	0	1	2	0	0	1.000
Ron Taylor, p	0	0	0	0	0	0	
TOTALS	35	9	10	6	4	5	.286

Braves	AB	R	H	RBI	BB	K	Avg
Felix Millan, 2b	5	1	2	0	0	0	.400
Tony Gonzalez, cf	5	2	2	2	0	1	.400
Hank Aaron, rf	5	1	2	2	0	0	.400
Rico Carty, lf	3	1	1	0	1	0	.333
Mike Lum, lf	1	0	1	0	0	0	1.000
Orlando Cepeda, 1b	4	0	1	0	0	0	.250
Clete Boyer, 3b	1	0	0	1	2	0	.000
Bob Didier, c	4	0	0	0	0	1	.000
Gil Garrido, ss	4	0	1	0	0	1	.250
Phil Niekro, p	3	0	0	0	1	1	.000
Bob Aspromonte, ph	1	0	0	0	0	0	.000
Cecil Upshaw, p	0	0	0	0	0	0	—
TOTALS	36	5	10	5	3	4	.278

	1	2	3	4	5	6	7	8	9		R	H	E
Mets	0	2	0	2	0	0	0	5	0		9	10	1
Braves	0	1	2	0	1	0	1	0	0		5	10	2

E—Boswell, Gonzalez, Cepeda. DP—Braves 2 (Garrido to Millan to Cepeda; Upshaw to Garrido to Cepeda). LOB—Mets 3, Braves 9. Scoring Position—Mets 4-for-10, Braves 2-for-7. 2B—Garrett (1), Millan (1), Gonzalez (1), Aaron (1), Carty (1), Lum (1). HR—Gonzalez (1), Aaron (1). 3B—Harrelson (1). SF—Boyer. GDP—Jones 2. SB—Jones (1), Cepeda (1). CS—Garrido (1).

Mets	IP	H	R	ER	BB	K	ERA
Tom Seaver (W, 1-0)	7.0	8	5	5	3	2	6.43
Ron Taylor (S, 1)	2.0	2	0	0	0	2	0.00

Braves	IP	H	R	ER	BB	K	ERA
Phil Niekro (L, 0-1)	8.0	9	9	4	4	4	4.50
Cecil Upshaw	1.0	1	0	0	0	1	0.00

PB—Didier, Grote. HBP—Cepeda by Seaver. Time—2:37. Attendance—50,122. Umpires—HP, Barlick. 1B, Donatelli. 2B, Sudol. 3B, Vargo.

Game 2
Sunday, October 5

Mets	AB	R	H	RBI	BB	K	Avg
Tommie Agee, cf	4	3	2	2	2	1	.222
Wayne Garrett, 3b	5	1	1	1	1	1	.444
Cleon Jones, lf	5	2	3	3	1	1	.400
Art Shamsky, rf	5	1	3	1	0	2	.667
Rod Gaspar, pr-rf	0	0	0	0	0	0	—
Ken Boswell, 2b	5	1	1	2	0	1	.125
Tug McGraw, p	0	0	0	0	0	0	
Ed Kranepool, 1b	4	0	1	1	1	0	.250
Jerry Grote, c	5	1	0	0	0	1	.125
Bud Harrelson, ss	5	1	1	1	0	1	.250
Jerry Koosman, p	2	1	0	0	1	2	.000
Ron Taylor, p	0	0	0	0	0	0	—
J.C. Martin, ph	1	0	0	0	0	0	.500
Al Weis, 2b	1	0	0	0	0	0	.000
TOTALS	42	11	13	11	6	12	.311

Braves	AB	R	H	RBI	BB	K	Avg
Felix Millan, 2b	2	1	2	0	3	0	.571
Tony Gonzalez, cf	4	1	1	0	1	2	.333
Hank Aaron, rf	5	1	3	3	0	1	.300
Rico Carty, lf	4	2	1	0	1	0	.286
Orlando Cepeda, 1b	4	1	2	1	0	1	.375
Clete Boyer, 3b	4	0	1	2	0	1	.200
Bob Didier, c	4	0	0	0	0	1	.000
Gil Garrido, ss	4	0	1	0	0	0	.250
Ron Reed, p	0	0	0	0	0	0	—
Paul Doyle, p	0	0	0	0	0	0	
Milt Pappas, p	1	0	0	0	0	1	.000
Tommie Aaron, ph	1	0	0	0	0	0	.000
Jim Britton, p	0	0	0	0	0	0	—
Cecil Upshaw, p	1	0	0	0	0	1	.000
Bob Aspromonte, ph	1	0	0	0	0	0	.000
Gary Neibauer, p	0	0	0	0	0	0	—
TOTALS	35	6	9	6	5	8	.269

	1	2	3	4	5	6	7	8	9		R	H	E
Mets	1	3	2	2	1	0	2	0	0		11	13	1
Braves	0	0	0	1	5	0	0	0	0		6	9	3

E—Harrelson, Cepeda, Boyer, HAaron. DP—Mets 1 (Harrelson to Boswell to Kranepool), Braves 1 (Didier to Boyer). LOB—Mets 10, Braves 7. Scoring Position—Mets 5-for-16, Braves 3-for-8. 2B—Garrett (2), Jones (1), Harrelson (1), Carty (2), Cepeda (1). HR—Agee (1), Jones (1), Boswell (1), HAaron (2). GDP—HAaron, Carty. SB—Agee 2 (2), Garrett (1), Jones (2). CS—Kranepool (1).

Mets	IP	H	R	ER	BB	K	ERA
Jerry Koosman	4.2	7	6	6	4	5	11.57
Ron Taylor (W, 1-0)	1.1	1	0	0	0	2	0.00
Tug McGraw (S, 1)	3.0	1	0	0	1	1	0.00

Braves	IP	H	R	ER	BB	K	ERA
Ron Reed (L, 0-1)	1.2	5	4	4	3	3	21.60
Paul Doyle	1.0	2	2	0	1	3	0.00
Milt Pappas	2.1	4	3	3	0	4	11.57
Jim Britton	0.1	0	0	0	1	0	0.00
Cecil Upshaw	2.2	2	2	2	1	1	4.91
Gary Neibauer	1.0	0	0	0	0	1	0.00

Time—3:10. Attendance—50,270. Umpires—HP, Donatelli. 1B, Sudol. 2B, Vargo. 3B, Pelekoudas.

Game 3
Monday, October 6

Braves	AB	R	H	RBI	BB	K	Avg
Felix Millan, 2b	5	0	0	0	0	0	.333
Tony Gonzalez, cf	5	1	2	0	0	1	.357
Hank Aaron, rf	4	1	2	2	0	0	.357
Rico Carty, lf	3	1	1	0	1	1	.300
Orlando Cepeda, 1b	3	1	2	2	1	1	.455
Clete Boyer, 3b	4	0	0	0	0	2	.111
Bob Didier, c	3	0	0	0	0	0	.000
Mike Lum, ph	1	0	1	0	0	0	1.000
Sonny Jackson, ss	0	0	0	0	0	0	—
Gil Garrido, ss	2	0	0	0	1	0	.200
Felipe Alou, ph	1	0	0	0	0	0	.000
Bob Tillman, c	0	0	0	0	0	0	—
Pat Jarvis, p	2	0	0	0	0	2	.000
George Stone, p	1	0	0	0	0	1	.000
Cecil Upshaw, p	0	0	0	0	0	0	.000
Bob Aspromonte, ph	1	0	0	0	0	0	.000
TOTALS	35	4	8	4	3	8	.267

Mets	AB	R	H	RBI	BB	K	Avg
Tommie Agee, cf	5	1	3	2	0	1	.357
Wayne Garrett, 3b	4	1	1	2	0	1	.385
Cleon Jones, lf	4	1	2	0	0	1	.429
Art Shamsky, rf	4	1	1	0	0	1	.538
Rod Gaspar, pr-rf	0	0	0	0	0	0	—
Ken Boswell, 2b	4	1	3	3	0	0	.333
Al Weis, 2b	0	0	0	0	0	0	.000
Ed Kranepool, 1b	4	0	1	0	0	0	.250
Jerry Grote, c	4	1	1	0	0	3	.167
Bud Harrelson, ss	3	0	0	0	0	0	.182
Gary Gentry, p	0	0	0	0	0	0	—
Nolan Ryan, p	4	1	2	0	0	1	.500
TOTALS	36	7	14	7	0	8	.340

	1	2	3	4	5	6	7	8	9		R	H	E
Braves	2	0	0	2	0	0	0	0	0		4	8	1
Mets	0	0	1	2	3	1	0	0	x		7	14	0

E—Millan. DP—Braves 1 (Jarvis to Garrido). LOB—Braves 7, Mets 6. Scoring Position—Braves 0-for-5, Mets 2-for-5. 2B—Aaron (2), Cepeda (2), Agee (1), Jones (2), Kranepool (1), Grote (1). HR—Aaron (3), Cepeda (1), Agee (2), Garrett (1), Boswell (2). S—Harrelson.

Braves	IP	H	R	ER	BB	K	ERA
Pat Jarvis (L, 0-1)	4.1	10	6	6	0	6	12.46
George Stone	1.0	2	1	1	0	0	9.00
Cecil Upshaw	2.2	2	0	0	0	2	2.84

Mets	IP	H	R	ER	BB	K	ERA
Gary Gentry	2.0	5	2	2	1	1	9.00
Nolan Ryan (W, 1-0)	7.0	3	2	2	2	7	2.57

Gentry pitched to two batters in the 3rd.

Time—2:24. Attendance—53,195. Umpires—HP, Sudol. 1B, Vargo. 2B, Pelekoudas. 3B, Steiner.

1969 NL Championship Series—Composite Statistics

Batting

Mets	G	AB	R	H	RBI	2B	3B	HR	BB	SO	SB	CS	Avg	OBP	Slg
Tommie Agee	3	14	4	5	4	1	0	2	2	5	2	0	.357	.438	.857
Ken Boswell	3	12	4	4	5	0	0	2	1	2	0	0	.333	.385	.833
Wayne Garrett	3	13	3	5	3	2	0	1	2	2	1	0	.385	.467	.769
Jerry Grote	3	12	3	2	1	1	0	0	1	4	0	0	.167	.231	.250
Bud Harrelson	3	11	2	2	3	1	1	0	1	2	0	0	.182	.250	.455
Cleon Jones	3	14	4	6	4	2	0	1	1	2	2	0	.429	.467	.786
Jerry Koosman	1	2	1	0	0	0	0	0	1	2	0	0	.000	.333	.000
Ed Kranepool	3	12	2	3	1	1	0	0	1	2	0	1	.250	.308	.333
J.C. Martin	2	2	0	1	2	0	0	0	0	0	0	0	.500	.500	.500
Nolan Ryan	1	4	1	2	0	0	0	0	0	1	0	0	.500	.500	.500
Tom Seaver	1	3	0	0	0	0	0	0	0	0	0	0	.000	.000	.000
Art Shamsky	3	13	3	7	1	0	0	0	0	3	0	0	.538	.538	.538
Al Weis	3	1	0	0	0	0	0	0	0	0	0	0	.000	.000	.000
Totals	3	113	27	37	24	8	1	6	10	25	5	1	.327	.382	.575

Braves	G	AB	R	H	RBI	2B	3B	HR	BB	SO	SB	CS	Avg	OBP	Slg
Hank Aaron	3	14	3	5	7	2	0	3	0	1	0	0	.357	.357	1.143
Tommie Aaron	1	1	0	0	0	0	0	0	0	0	0	0	.000	.000	.000
Felipe Alou	1	1	0	0	0	0	0	0	0	0	0	0	.000	.000	.000
Bob Aspromonte	3	3	0	0	0	0	0	0	0	0	0	0	.000	.000	.000
Clete Boyer	3	9	0	1	3	0	0	0	2	3	0	0	.111	.250	.111
Rico Carty	3	10	4	3	0	2	0	0	3	1	0	0	.300	.462	.500
Orlando Cepeda	3	11	2	5	3	2	0	1	1	2	1	0	.455	.538	.909
Bob Didier	3	11	0	0	0	0	0	0	0	2	0	0	.000	.000	.000
Gil Garrido	3	10	0	2	0	0	0	0	1	1	0	1	.200	.273	.200
Tony Gonzalez	3	14	4	5	2	1	0	1	1	4	0	0	.357	.400	.643
Pat Jarvis	1	2	0	0	0	0	0	0	0	2	0	0	.000	.000	.000
Mike Lum	2	2	0	2	0	1	0	0	0	0	0	0	1.000	1.000	1.500
Felix Millan	3	12	2	4	0	1	0	0	3	0	0	0	.333	.467	.417
Phil Niekro	1	3	0	0	0	0	0	0	0	1	0	0	.000	.000	.000
Milt Pappas	1	1	0	0	0	0	0	0	0	1	0	0	.000	.000	.000
George Stone	1	1	0	0	0	0	0	0	0	1	0	0	.000	.000	.000
Cecil Upshaw	3	1	0	0	0	0	0	0	0	1	0	0	.000	.000	.000
Totals	3	106	15	27	15	9	0	5	11	20	1	1	.255	.328	.481

Pitching

Mets	G	GS	CG	IP	H	R	ER	BB	SO	W-L	Sv-Op	Hld	ERA
Gary Gentry	1	1	0	2.0	5	2	2	1	1	0-0	0-0	0	9.00
Jerry Koosman	1	1	0	4.2	7	6	6	4	5	0-0	0-0	0	11.57
Tug McGraw	1	0	0	3.0	1	0	0	1	1	0-0	1-1	0	0.00
Nolan Ryan	1	0	0	7.0	3	2	2	2	7	1-0	0-0	0	2.57
Tom Seaver	1	1	0	7.0	8	5	5	3	2	0-0	0-0	0	6.43
Ron Taylor	2	0	0	3.1	3	0	0	0	4	1-0	1-1	0	0.00
Totals	3	3	0	27.0	27	15	15	11	20	3-0	2-2	0	5.00

Braves	G	GS	CG	IP	H	R	ER	BB	SO	W-L	Sv-Op	Hld	ERA
Jim Britton	1	0	0	0.1	0	0	0	1	0	0-0	0-0	0	0.00
Paul Doyle	1	0	0	1.0	2	2	0	1	3	0-0	0-0	0	0.00
Pat Jarvis	1	1	0	4.1	10	6	6	0	6	0-1	0-0	0	12.46
Gary Neibauer	1	0	0	1.0	0	0	0	0	1	0-0	0-0	0	0.00
Phil Niekro	1	1	0	8.0	9	9	4	4	4	0-1	0-0	0	4.50
Milt Pappas	1	0	0	2.1	4	3	3	0	4	0-0	0-0	0	11.57
Ron Reed	1	1	0	1.2	5	4	4	3	3	0-1	0-0	0	21.60
George Stone	1	0	0	1.0	2	1	1	0	0	0-0	0-0	0	9.00
Cecil Upshaw	3	0	0	6.1	5	2	2	1	4	0-0	0-0	0	2.84
Totals	3	3	0	26.0	37	27	20	10	25	0-3	0-0	0	6.92

Fielding

Mets	Pos	G	PO	Ast	E	DP	PB	FPct
Tommie Agee	cf	3	9	0	0	0	—	1.000
Ken Boswell	2b	3	3	2	1	1	—	.833
Wayne Garrett	3b	3	1	6	0	0	—	1.000
Rod Gaspar	rf	3	2	0	0	0	—	1.000
Gary Gentry	p	1	0	0	0	0	—	—
Jerry Grote	c	3	22	1	0	0	1	1.000
Bud Harrelson	ss	3	6	6	1	2	—	.923
Cleon Jones	lf	3	11	0	0	0	—	1.000
Jerry Koosman	p	1	0	1	0	0	—	1.000
Ed Kranepool	1b	3	20	3	0	2	—	1.000
Tug McGraw	p	1	0	0	0	0	—	—
Nolan Ryan	p	1	1	0	0	0	—	1.000
Tom Seaver	p	1	1	1	0	0	—	1.000
Art Shamsky	rf	3	3	0	0	0	—	1.000
Ron Taylor	p	2	1	0	0	0	—	1.000
Al Weis	2b	3	1	3	0	1	—	1.000
Totals		3	81	23	2	6	1	.981

Braves	Pos	G	PO	Ast	E	DP	PB	FPct
Hank Aaron	rf	3	5	1	1	0	—	.857
Clete Boyer	3b	3	4	8	1	1	—	.923
Jim Britton	p	1	0	0	0	0	—	—
Rico Carty	lf	3	2	0	0	0	—	1.000
Orlando Cepeda	1b	3	29	1	2	2	—	.938
Bob Didier	c	3	24	1	0	1	1	1.000
Paul Doyle	p	1	0	0	0	0	—	—
Gil Garrido	ss	3	4	8	0	3	—	1.000
Tony Gonzalez	cf	3	3	0	1	0	—	.750
Sonny Jackson	ss	1	0	0	0	0	—	—
Pat Jarvis	p	1	1	2	0	1	—	1.000
Mike Lum	lf	1	0	0	0	0	—	—
Felix Millan	2b	3	3	8	1	1	—	.917
Gary Neibauer	p	1	0	0	0	0	—	—
Phil Niekro	p	1	0	3	0	0	—	1.000
Milt Pappas	p	1	0	0	0	0	—	—
Ron Reed	p	1	0	1	0	0	—	1.000
George Stone	p	1	1	1	0	0	—	1.000
Bob Tillman	c	1	2	0	0	0	0	1.000
Cecil Upshaw	p	3	0	1	0	1	—	1.000
Totals		3	78	35	6	10	1	.950

1970 Baltimore Orioles (AL) 3, Minnesota Twins (AL) 0

For the second straight season, the Baltimore Orioles swept the Minnesota Twins, knocking the Twins from the postseason race. Baltimore starter Mike Cuellar lifted a wind-aided grand slam in the opener, and Tom Hall pitched 4.2 innings of one-hit relief to pick up the victory in the O's 10-6 win. In Game 2, Dave McNally took a 4-3 lead into the ninth before igniting a seven-run Baltimore rally with a double. McNally went the distance for an 11-3 victory. Jim Palmer clinched it with a complete-game, 12-strikeout performance in the Orioles' 6-1 win in the third game. Brooks Robinson batted .583, while the O's used only four pitchers in the series.

Game 1
Saturday, October 3

Orioles	AB	R	H	RBI	BB	K	Avg
Don Buford, lf	3	1	1	1	2	0	.294
Paul Blair, cf	5	0	0	0	0	1	.300
Boog Powell, 1b	5	1	2	2	0	1	.389
Frank Robinson, rf	4	1	1	0	1	1	.313
Ellie Hendricks, c	5	2	2	0	0	1	.308
Brooks Robinson, 3b	3	1	3	1	0	0	.588
Dave Johnson, 2b	3	1	1	0	0	0	.250
Mark Belanger, ss	4	1	1	1	0	0	.263
Mike Cuellar, p	2	1	1	4	0	1	.250
Dick Hall, p	2	1	1	0	0	1	.500
TOTALS	36	10	13	9	3	6	.338

Twins	AB	R	H	RBI	BB	K	Avg
Cesar Tovar, cf-2b	5	1	2	1	0	0	.167
Leo Cardenas, ss	4	0	0	0	0	0	.118
Harmon Killebrew, 3b	5	1	2	2	0	1	.231
Tony Oliva, rf	4	1	3	0	0	1	.471
Brant Alyea, lf	3	1	0	0	1	1	.000
Rich Reese, 1b	4	0	0	0	0	0	.125
George Mitterwald, c	4	2	3	2	0	1	.364
Danny Thompson, 2b	3	0	1	0	0	0	.333
Stan Williams, p	0	0	0	0	0	0	—
Jim Holt, ph-cf	1	0	0	0	0	0	.000
Jim Perry, p	1	0	0	1	0	0	.000
Bill Zepp, p	0	0	0	0	0	0	—
Bob Allison, ph	1	0	0	0	0	1	.000
Dick Woodson, p	0	0	0	0	0	0	1.000
Frank Quilici, 2b	1	0	0	0	0	1	.000
Rod Carew, ph	1	0	0	0	0	1	.067
Ron Perranoski, p	0	0	0	0	0	0	.000
TOTALS	37	6	11	6	1	5	.192

	1	2	3	4	5	6	7	8	9		R	H	E
Orioles	0	2	0	7	0	1	0	0	0		10	13	0
Twins	1	1	0	1	3	0	0	0	0		6	11	2

E—Thompson, Killebrew. DP—Orioles 1 (Johnson to Belanger to Powell), Twins 3 (Cardenas to Reese; Reese to Mitterwald; Cardenas to Quilici to Reese). LOB—Orioles 4, Twins 6. Scoring Position—Orioles 3-for-9, Twins 3-for-11. 2B—BRobinson (2), Oliva 2 (4), Thompson (1). HR—Buford (1), Powell (2), Cuellar (1), Killebrew (1). S—Cardenas. SF—BRobinson. GDP—Powell, Hendricks, Johnson, Thompson.

Orioles	IP	H	R	ER	BB	K	ERA
Mike Cuellar	4.1	10	6	6	1	2	5.84
Dick Hall (W, 2-0)	4.2	1	0	0	0	3	0.00

Twins	IP	H	R	ER	BB	K	ERA
Jim Perry (L, 0-1)	3.1	8	8	7	1	1	7.94
Bill Zepp	0.2	1	1	1	0	2	13.50
Dick Woodson	1.0	2	1	1	1	0	10.13
Stan Williams	3.0	2	0	0	1	1	0.00
Ron Perranoski	1.0	0	0	0	0	2	4.76

Woodson pitched to two batters in the 6th.

HBP—Johnson by Perry. Time—2:36. Attendance—26,847. Umpires—HP, Stevens. 1B, Deegan. 2B, Satchell. 3B, Berry.

Game 2
Sunday, October 4

Orioles	AB	R	H	RBI	BB	K	Avg
Mark Belanger, ss	4	3	3	0	1	0	.348
Paul Blair, cf	4	0	0	0	1	1	.250
Frank Robinson, rf	3	2	1	2	2	0	.316
Boog Powell, 1b	5	1	3	3	0	1	.435
Merv Rettenmund, lf	3	1	1	1	2	1	.333
Brooks Robinson, 3b	5	1	1	0	0	0	.500
Dave Johnson, 2b	5	1	1	3	0	0	.238
Andy Etchebarren, c	5	1	1	0	0	2	.111
Dave McNally, p	5	1	2	1	0	1	.222
TOTALS	39	11	13	10	6	6	.327

Twins	AB	R	H	RBI	BB	K	Avg
Cesar Tovar, cf-lf	4	0	1	0	0	0	.182
Leo Cardenas, ss	3	1	1	0	1	0	.150
Harmon Killebrew, 1b	3	1	1	2	1	1	.250
Tony Oliva, rf	4	1	1	1	0	0	.429
Brant Alyea, lf	3	0	0	0	1	1	.000
Jim Holt, pr-cf	0	0	0	0	0	0	.000
George Mitterwald, c	4	0	1	0	0	1	.333
Rick Renick, 3b	4	0	1	0	0	1	.200
Danny Thompson, 2b	4	0	0	0	0	0	.143
Tom Hall, p	1	0	0	0	0	1	.000
Bill Zepp, p	0	0	0	0	0	0	—
Stan Williams, p	0	0	0	0	1	0	—
Bob Allison, ph	0	0	0	0	1	0	.000
Ron Perranoski, p	0	0	0	0	0	0	.000
Luis Tiant, p	0	0	0	0	0	0	—
Frank Quilici, ph	1	0	0	0	0	0	.000
TOTALS	31	3	6	3	5	5	.214

	1	2	3	4	5	6	7	8	9		R	H	E
Orioles	1	0	2	1	0	0	0	0	7		11	13	0
Twins	0	0	0	3	0	0	0	0	0		3	6	2

E—Cardenas 2. DP—Orioles 1 (Johnson to Belanger to Powell), Twins 2 (Oliva to Mitterwald; Perranoski to Cardenas to Killebrew). LOB—Orioles 7, Twins 6. Scoring Position—Orioles 6-for-15, Twins 1-for-3. 2B—Powell 2 (2), McNally (1), Mitterwald (1). HR—FRobinson (2), Johnson (1), Killebrew (2), Oliva (2). GDP—Etchebarren, Thompson. SB—Rettenmund (1).

Orioles	IP	H	R	ER	BB	K	ERA
Dave McNally (W, 2-0)	9.0	6	3	3	5	5	1.35

Twins	IP	H	R	ER	BB	K	ERA
Tom Hall (L, 0-1)	3.1	6	4	4	3	4	9.00
Bill Zepp	0.2	1	0	0	2	0	6.75
Stan Williams	3.0	0	0	0	0	1	0.00
Ron Perranoski	1.1	5	5	5	1	1	10.29
Luis Tiant	0.2	1	2	1	0	0	13.50

Zepp pitched to three batters in the 5th.

Time—2:59. Attendance—27,490. Umpires—HP, Haller. 1B, Odom. 2B, Neudecker. 3B, Honochick.

Game 3
Monday, October 5

Twins	AB	R	H	RBI	BB	K	Avg
Cesar Tovar, lf	4	1	2	0	0	0	.231
Leo Cardenas, ss	4	0	1	1	0	1	.167
Tony Oliva, rf	4	0	2	0	0	1	.440
Harmon Killebrew, 3b	3	0	0	0	1	2	.211
Jim Holt, cf	4	0	0	0	0	2	.000
Paul Ratliff, c	4	0	1	0	0	1	.250
Rich Reese, 1b	3	0	1	0	1	1	.158
Luis Tiant, pr	0	0	0	0	0	0	—
Danny Thompson, 2b	1	0	0	0	1	0	.125
Bob Allison, ph	1	0	0	0	0	0	.000
Frank Quilici, 2b	0	0	0	0	0	0	.000
Brant Alyea, ph	1	0	0	0	0	1	.000
Jim Kaat, p	1	0	0	0	0	1	.000
Bert Blyleven, p	0	0	0	0	0	0	—
Charlie Manuel, ph	1	0	0	0	0	1	.000
Tom Hall, p	0	0	0	0	0	0	.000
Rod Carew, ph	1	0	0	0	0	1	.063
Jim Perry, p	0	0	0	0	0	0	.000
Rick Renick, ph	1	0	0	0	0	0	.167
TOTALS	33	1	7	1	3	12	.180

Orioles	AB	R	H	RBI	BB	K	Avg
Don Buford, lf	4	1	2	2	0	0	.333
Paul Blair, cf	4	0	1	0	0	2	.250
Frank Robinson, rf	3	0	0	0	2	1	.273
Boog Powell, 1b	4	0	1	1	0	1	.407
Brooks Robinson, 3b	4	1	3	0	0	1	.538
Dave Johnson, 2b	3	2	2	1	1	1	.292
Andy Etchebarren, c	4	0	0	0	0	1	.077
Mark Belanger, ss	4	1	0	0	0	0	.296
Jim Palmer, p	4	1	1	1	0	0	.111
TOTALS	34	6	10	5	3	7	.315

	1	2	3	4	5	6	7	8	9		R	H	E
Twins	0	0	0	0	1	0	0	0	0		1	7	2
Orioles	1	1	3	0	0	0	1	0	x		6	10	0

E—Holt, Ratliff. DP—Orioles 1 (Belanger to Johnson to Powell). LOB—Twins 8, Orioles 9. Scoring Position—Twins 1-for-6, Orioles 4-for-11. 2B—Buford (2), BRobinson (3), Palmer (1). 3B—Tovar (1). HR—Johnson (2). S—Blair. SF—Buford. GDP—Cardenas.

Twins	IP	H	R	ER	BB	K	ERA
Jim Kaat (L, 0-1)	2.0	6	4	2	2	1	9.00
Bert Blyleven	2.0	2	1	0	0	2	0.00
Tom Hall	2.0	0	0	0	1	2	6.00
Jim Perry	2.0	2	1	1	0	2	7.43

Orioles	IP	H	R	ER	BB	K	ERA
Jim Palmer (W, 2-0)	9.0	7	1	1	3	12	1.50

Kaat pitched to two batters in the 3rd.

Time—2:20. Attendance—27,608. Umpires—HP, Odom. 1B, Neudecker. 2B, Springstead. 3B, Honochick.

Postseason: League Championship Series

1970 AL Championship Series—Composite Statistics

Batting

Orioles	G	AB	R	H	RBI	2B	3B	HR	BB	SO	SB	CS	Avg	OBP	Slg
Mark Belanger	3	12	5	4	1	0	0	0	1	0	0	0	.333	.385	.333
Paul Blair	3	13	0	1	0	0	0	0	1	4	0	0	.077	.143	.077
Don Buford	2	7	2	3	3	1	0	1	2	0	0	0	.429	.500	1.000
Mike Cuellar	1	2	1	1	4	0	0	1	0	1	0	0	.500	.500	2.000
Andy Etchebarren	2	9	1	1	0	0	0	0	0	3	0	0	.111	.111	.111
Dick Hall	1	2	1	1	0	0	0	0	0	1	0	0	.500	.500	.500
Ellie Hendricks	1	5	2	2	0	0	0	0	0	1	0	0	.400	.400	.400
Dave Johnson	3	11	4	4	4	0	0	2	1	1	0	0	.364	.462	.909
Dave McNally	1	5	1	2	1	1	0	0	1	0	0	0	.400	.400	.600
Jim Palmer	1	4	1	1	1	1	0	0	0	0	0	0	.250	.250	.500
Boog Powell	3	14	2	6	6	2	0	1	0	3	0	0	.429	.429	.786
Merv Rettenmund	1	3	1	1	1	0	0	0	2	1	1	0	.333	.600	.333
Brooks Robinson	3	12	3	7	1	2	0	0	0	1	0	0	.583	.538	.750
Frank Robinson	3	10	3	2	2	0	0	1	5	2	0	0	.200	.467	.500
Totals	3	109	27	36	24	7	0	6	12	19	1	0	.330	.395	.560

Batting

Twins	G	AB	R	H	RBI	2B	3B	HR	BB	SO	SB	CS	Avg	OBP	Slg
Bob Allison	3	2	0	0	0	0	0	0	1	1	0	0	.000	.333	.000
Brant Alyea	3	7	1	0	0	0	0	0	2	3	0	0	.000	.222	.000
Leo Cardenas	3	11	1	2	1	0	0	0	1	1	0	0	.182	.250	.182
Rod Carew	2	2	0	0	0	0	0	0	0	1	0	0	.000	.000	.000
Tom Hall	2	1	0	0	0	0	0	0	0	1	0	0	.000	.000	.000
Jim Holt	3	5	0	0	0	0	0	0	0	2	0	0	.000	.000	.000
Jim Kaat	1	1	0	0	0	0	0	0	0	1	0	0	.000	.000	.000
Harmon Killebrew	3	11	2	3	4	0	0	2	2	4	0	0	.273	.385	.818
Charlie Manuel	1	1	0	0	0	0	0	0	0	1	0	0	.000	.000	.000
George Mitterwald	2	8	2	4	2	1	0	0	0	2	0	0	.500	.500	.625
Tony Oliva	3	12	2	6	1	2	0	1	0	1	0	0	.500	.500	.917
Jim Perry	2	1	0	0	1	0	0	0	0	0	0	0	.000	.000	.000
Frank Quilici	3	2	0	0	0	0	0	0	0	1	0	0	.000	.000	.000
Paul Ratliff	1	4	0	1	0	0	0	0	0	1	0	0	.250	.250	.250
Rich Reese	2	7	0	1	0	0	0	0	1	1	0	0	.143	.250	.143
Rick Renick	2	5	0	1	0	0	0	0	0	1	0	0	.200	.200	.200
Danny Thompson	3	8	0	1	0	1	0	0	1	0	0	0	.125	.222	.250
Cesar Tovar	3	13	2	5	1	0	1	0	0	0	0	0	.385	.385	.538
Stan Williams	2	0	0	0	0	0	0	0	0	1	0	0	—	1.000	—
Totals	3	101	10	24	10	4	1	3	9	22	0	0	.238	.300	.386

Pitching

Orioles	G	GS	CG	IP	H	R	ER	BB	SO	W-L	Sv-Op	Hld	ERA
Mike Cuellar	1	1	0	4.1	10	6	6	1	2	0-0	0-0	0	12.46
Dick Hall	1	0	0	4.2	1	0	0	0	3	1-0	0-0	0	0.00
Dave McNally	1	1	1	9.0	6	3	3	5	5	1-0	0-0	0	3.00
Jim Palmer	1	1	1	9.0	7	1	1	3	12	1-0	0-0	0	1.00
Totals	3	3	2	27.0	24	10	10	9	22	3-0	0-0	0	3.33

Pitching

Twins	G	GS	CG	IP	H	R	ER	BB	SO	W-L	Sv-Op	Hld	ERA
Bert Blyleven	1	0	0	2.0	2	1	0	0	2	0-0	0-0	0	0.00
Tom Hall	2	1	0	5.1	6	4	4	4	6	0-1	0-0	0	6.75
Jim Kaat	1	1	0	2.0	6	4	2	2	1	0-1	0-0	0	9.00
Ron Perranoski	2	0	0	2.1	5	5	5	1	3	0-0	0-0	0	19.29
Jim Perry	2	1	0	5.1	10	9	8	1	3	0-1	0-0	0	13.50
Luis Tiant	1	0	0	0.2	1	2	1	0	0	0-0	0-0	0	13.50
Stan Williams	2	0	0	6.0	2	0	0	1	2	0-0	0-0	0	0.00
Dick Woodson	1	0	0	1.0	2	1	1	1	0	0-0	0-0	0	9.00
Bill Zepp	2	0	0	1.1	2	1	1	2	2	0-0	0-0	0	6.75
Totals	3	3	0	26.0	36	27	22	12	19	0-3	0-0	0	7.62

Fielding

Orioles	Pos	G	PO	Ast	E	DP	PB	FPct
Mark Belanger	ss	3	7	13	0	3	—	1.000
Paul Blair	cf	3	4	0	0	0	—	1.000
Don Buford	lf	2	1	0	0	0	—	1.000
Mike Cuellar	p	1	1	3	0	0	—	1.000
Andy Etchebarren	c	2	19	0	0	0	0	1.000
Dick Hall	p	1	0	0	0	0	—	—
Ellie Hendricks	c	1	5	0	0	0	0	1.000
Dave Johnson	2b	3	9	4	0	3	—	1.000
Dave McNally	p	1	0	0	0	0	—	—
Jim Palmer	p	1	1	1	0	0	—	1.000
Boog Powell	1b	3	24	1	0	3	—	1.000
Merv Rettenmund	lf	1	3	1	0	0	—	1.000
Brooks Robinson	3b	3	4	5	0	0	—	1.000
Frank Robinson	rf	3	3	0	0	0	—	1.000
Totals		3	81	28	0	9	0	1.000

Fielding

Twins	Pos	G	PO	Ast	E	DP	PB	FPct
Brant Alyea	lf	2	0	0	0	0	—	—
Bert Blyleven	p	1	1	0	0	0	—	1.000
Leo Cardenas	ss	3	6	12	2	3	—	.900
Tom Hall	p	2	0	0	0	0	—	—
Jim Holt	cf	3	3	0	1	0	—	.750
Jim Kaat	p	1	0	0	0	0	—	—
Harmon Killebrew	3b	2	0	4	1	0	—	.800
	1b	1	7	0	0	1	—	1.000
George Mitterwald	c	2	16	1	0	2	0	1.000
Tony Oliva	rf	3	10	1	0	1	—	1.000
Ron Perranoski	p	2	0	1	0	1	—	1.000
Jim Perry	p	2	1	0	0	0	—	1.000
Frank Quilici	2b	2	1	1	0	1	—	1.000
Paul Ratliff	c	1	7	0	1	0	0	.875
Rich Reese	1b	2	17	2	0	3	—	1.000
Rick Renick	3b	1	1	3	0	0	—	1.000
Danny Thompson	2b	3	2	3	1	0	—	.833
Luis Tiant	p	1	0	0	0	0	—	—
Cesar Tovar	lf	2	3	0	0	0	—	1.000
	cf	2	3	0	0	0	—	1.000
	2b	1	0	0	0	0	—	—
Stan Williams	p	2	0	0	0	0	—	—
Dick Woodson	p	1	0	0	0	0	—	—
Bill Zepp	p	2	0	0	0	0	—	—
Totals		3	78	28	6	12	0	.946

1970 Cincinnati Reds (NL) 3, Pittsburgh Pirates (NL) 0

The Cincinnati Reds silenced the Pittsburgh Pirates' offense en route to a three-game sweep in the NLCS. Dock Ellis and Gary Nolan matched zeroes for nine innings in the opener before the Reds finally got to Ellis. Pete Rose singled in the first run of the game in the top of the 10th, and Lee May added a two-run double to give the Reds a 3-0 win. Bobby Tolan had three hits, including a homer, and scored all three runs in Cincinnati's 3-1 victory in Game 2. Tolan went on to drive in the decisive run in Game 3, singling in Ty Cline in the bottom of the eighth to break a 2-2 deadlock and give the Reds a pennant-clinching 3-2 victory. The Reds' staff posted a stellar 0.96 ERA in the series.

Game 1
Saturday, October 3

Reds	AB	R	H	RBI	BB	K	Avg
Pete Rose, rf	5	1	2	1	0	0	.400
Bobby Tolan, cf	5	0	1	0	0	0	.200
Tony Perez, 3b-1b	4	0	1	0	1	0	.250
Johnny Bench, c	3	1	0	0	2	0	.000
Lee May, 1b	5	0	1	2	0	1	.200
Dave Concepcion, pr-ss	0	0	0	0	0	0	—
Bernie Carbo, lf	3	0	0	0	1	0	.000
Hal McRae, ph	1	0	0	0	0	0	.000
Clay Carroll, p	0	0	0	0	0	0	—
Tommy Helms, 2b	4	0	2	0	0	0	.500
Woody Woodward, ss-3b	4	0	0	0	0	0	.000
Gary Nolan, p	3	0	1	0	0	0	.333
Ty Cline, ph-lf	1	1	1	0	0	0	1.000
TOTALS	38	3	9	3	4	2	.237

Pirates	AB	R	H	RBI	BB	K	Avg
Matty Alou, cf	3	0	2	0	2	0	.667
Dave Cash, 2b	5	0	0	0	0	1	.000
Roberto Clemente, rf	5	0	0	0	0	3	.000
Willie Stargell, lf	4	0	3	0	0	0	.750
Johnny Jeter, pr-lf	1	0	0	0	0	1	.000
Al Oliver, 1b	3	0	0	0	1	0	.000
Manny Sanguillen, c	4	0	1	0	0	1	.250
Richie Hebner, 3b	4	0	2	0	0	1	.500
Gene Alley, ss	3	0	0	0	1	0	.000
Dock Ellis, p	2	0	0	0	0	1	.000
Joe Gibbon, p	0	0	0	0	0	0	—
TOTALS	34	0	8	0	4	8	.235

	1	2	3	4	5	6	7	8	9	10		R	H	E
Reds	0	0	0	0	0	0	0	0	0	3		3	9	0
Pirates	0	0	0	0	0	0	0	0	0	0		0	8	0

DP—Pirates 1 (Alley to Cash to Oliver). LOB—Reds 9, Pirates 10. Scoring Position—Reds 2-for-8, Pirates 0-for-7. 2B—Perez (1), May (1), Alou (1), Stargell (1). 3B—Cline (1). S—Ellis 2. GDP—Bench. CS—Alou (1).

Reds	IP	H	R	ER	BB	K	ERA
Gary Nolan (W, 1-0)	9.0	8	0	0	4	6	0.00
Clay Carroll (S, 1)	1.0	0	0	0	0	2	0.00

Pirates	IP	H	R	ER	BB	K	ERA
Dock Ellis (L, 0-1)	9.2	9	3	3	4	1	2.79
Joe Gibbon	0.1	0	0	0	0	1	0.00

Time—2:23. Attendance—33,088. Umpires—HP, Grimsley. 1B, Blandford. 2B, Morganweck. 3B, Grygiel.

Game 2
Sunday, October 4

Reds	AB	R	H	RBI	BB	K	Avg
Pete Rose, rf	4	0	0	0	0	0	.222
Bobby Tolan, cf	4	3	3	1	0	1	.444
Tony Perez, 3b	4	0	2	1	0	0	.375
Dave Concepcion, pr-ss	0	0	0	0	0	0	—
Johnny Bench, c	3	0	0	0	1	1	.000
Lee May, 1b	4	0	1	0	0	0	.222
Hal McRae, lf	3	0	0	0	0	1	.000
Clay Carroll, p	0	0	0	0	0	0	—
Don Gullett, p	1	0	0	0	0	0	.000
Tommy Helms, 2b	4	0	1	0	0	0	.375
Woody Woodward, ss-3b	3	0	1	0	1	0	.143
Jim Merritt, p	2	0	0	0	0	2	.000
Jimmy Stewart, lf	2	0	0	0	0	0	.000
TOTALS	34	3	8	2	2	5	.231

Pirates	AB	R	H	RBI	BB	K	Avg
Matty Alou, cf	4	0	0	0	0	0	.286
Dave Cash, 2b	3	1	1	0	1	0	.125
Roberto Clemente, rf	4	0	1	1	0	0	.111
Manny Sanguillen, c	4	0	1	0	0	0	.250
Bob Robertson, 1b	4	0	1	0	0	0	.250
Willie Stargell, lf	4	0	0	0	0	0	.375
Jose Pagan, 3b	3	0	1	0	1	1	.333
Gene Alley, ss	4	0	0	0	0	2	.000
Luke Walker, p	2	0	0	0	0	1	.000
Johnny Jeter, ph	1	0	0	0	0	1	.000
Dave Giusti, p	0	0	0	0	0	0	—
TOTALS	33	1	5	1	2	5	.190

	1	2	3	4	5	6	7	8	9		R	H	E
Reds	0	0	1	0	1	0	0	1	0		3	8	1
Pirates	0	0	0	0	0	1	0	0	0		1	5	2

E—Perez, Sanguillen, Walker. DP—Pirates 2 (Alley to Cash; Alley to Cash to Robertson). LOB—Reds 6, Pirates 7. Scoring Position—Reds 0-for-3, Pirates 1-for-6. 2B—Perez (2), Cash (1), Robertson (1). HR—Tolan (1). GDP—May. SB—Tolan (1).

Reds	IP	H	R	ER	BB	K	ERA
Jim Merritt (W, 1-0)	5.1	3	1	1	0	2	1.69
Clay Carroll (H, 1)	0.1	2	0	0	0	0	0.00
Don Gullett (S, 1)	3.1	0	0	0	2	3	0.00

Pirates	IP	H	R	ER	BB	K	ERA
Luke Walker (L, 0-1)	7.0	5	2	1	1	5	1.29
Dave Giusti	2.0	3	1	1	1	0	4.50

WP—Walker. Time—2:10. Attendance—39,317. Umpires—HP, Landes. 1B, Pryor. 2B, Harvey. 3B, Engel.

Game 3
Monday, October 5

Pirates	AB	R	H	RBI	BB	K	Avg
Freddie Patek, ss	3	0	0	0	1	2	.000
Bob Robertson, ph	1	0	0	0	0	0	.200
Matty Alou, cf	5	1	1	0	0	1	.250
Roberto Clemente, rf	5	1	2	0	0	1	.214
Willie Stargell, lf	4	0	3	1	1	1	.500
Johnny Jeter, pr	0	0	0	0	0	0	.000
Al Oliver, 1b	5	0	2	1	0	0	.250
Manny Sanguillen, c	4	0	0	0	0	0	.167
Richie Hebner, 3b	2	0	2	0	2	0	.667
Bill Mazeroski, 2b	2	0	0	0	2	0	.000
Bob Moose, p	4	0	0	0	0	1	.000
Joe Gibbon, p	0	0	0	0	0	0	—
Dave Giusti, p	0	0	0	0	0	0	—
TOTALS	35	2	10	2	6	6	.263

Reds	AB	R	H	RBI	BB	K	Avg
Pete Rose, rf	4	0	1	0	0	0	.231
Bobby Tolan, cf	3	0	1	1	1	0	.417
Tony Perez, 3b	4	1	1	1	0	1	.333
Wayne Granger, p	0	0	0	0	0	0	—
Don Gullett, p	0	0	0	0	0	0	.000
Johnny Bench, c	3	1	2	1	0	0	.222
Lee May, 1b	3	0	0	0	0	1	.167
Bernie Carbo, lf	3	0	0	0	0	2	.000
Tommy Helms, 2b	3	0	0	0	0	1	.273
Woody Woodward, ss-3b	3	0	0	0	0	0	.100
Tony Cloninger, p	1	0	0	0	0	0	.000
Angel Bravo, ph	1	0	0	0	0	0	.000
Milt Wilcox, p	0	0	0	0	0	0	—
Ty Cline, ph	0	1	0	0	1	0	1.000
Dave Concepcion, ss	0	0	0	0	0	0	—
TOTALS	28	3	5	3	2	5	.236

	1	2	3	4	5	6	7	8	9		R	H	E
Pirates	1	0	0	0	1	0	0	0	0		2	10	0
Reds	2	0	0	0	0	0	0	1	x		3	5	0

DP—Reds 1 (Perez to Helms to May). LOB—Pirates 12, Reds 3. Scoring Position—Pirates 2-for-13, Reds 1-for-2. 2B—Hebner 2 (2). HR—Perez (1), Bench (1). GDP—Patek. CS—Patek (1), Tolan (1).

Pirates	IP	H	R	ER	BB	K	ERA
Bob Moose (L, 0-1)	7.2	4	3	3	2	4	3.52
Joe Gibbon	0.0	1	0	0	0	0	0.00
Dave Giusti	0.1	0	0	0	0	1	3.86

Reds	IP	H	R	ER	BB	K	ERA
Tony Cloninger	5.0	7	2	2	4	1	3.60
Milt Wilcox (W, 1-0)	3.0	1	0	0	2	5	0.00
Wayne Granger (H, 1)	0.2	1	0	0	0	0	0.00
Don Gullett (S, 2)	0.1	1	0	0	0	0	0.00

Gibbon pitched to one batter in the 8th.

WP—Cloninger. Time—2:38. Attendance—40,538. Umpires—HP, Pryor. 1B. Harvey. 2B, Engel. 3B, Wendelstedt.

1970 NL Championship Series—Composite Statistics

Batting

Reds	G	AB	R	H	RBI	2B	3B	HR	BB	SO	SB	CS	Avg	OBP	Slg
Johnny Bench	3	9	2	2	1	0	0	1	3	1	0	0	.222	.417	.556
Angel Bravo	1	1	0	0	0	0	0	0	0	0	0	0	.000	.000	.000
Bernie Carbo	2	6	0	0	0	0	0	0	1	2	0	0	.000	.143	.000
Ty Cline	2	1	2	1	0	0	1	0	1	0	0	0	1.000	1.000	3.000
Tony Cloninger	1	1	0	0	0	0	0	0	0	0	0	0	.000	.000	.000
Don Gullett	2	1	0	0	0	0	0	0	0	0	0	0	.000	.000	.000
Tommy Helms	3	11	0	3	0	0	0	0	0	1	0	0	.273	.273	.273
Lee May	3	12	0	2	2	1	0	0	0	2	0	0	.167	.167	.250
Hal McRae	2	4	0	0	0	0	0	0	0	2	0	0	.000	.000	.000
Jim Merritt	1	2	0	0	0	0	0	0	0	2	0	0	.000	.000	.000
Gary Nolan	1	3	0	1	0	0	0	0	0	0	0	0	.333	.333	.333
Tony Perez	3	12	1	4	2	2	0	1	1	1	0	0	.333	.385	.750
Pete Rose	3	13	1	3	1	0	0	0	0	0	0	0	.231	.231	.231
Jimmy Stewart	1	2	0	0	0	0	0	0	0	0	0	0	.000	.000	.000
Bobby Tolan	3	12	3	5	2	0	0	1	1	1	1	1	.417	.462	.667
Woody Woodward	3	10	0	1	0	0	0	0	1	0	0	0	.100	.182	.100
Totals	3	100	9	22	8	3	1	3	8	12	1	1	.220	.278	.360

Batting

Pirates	G	AB	R	H	RBI	2B	3B	HR	BB	SO	SB	CS	Avg	OBP	Slg
Gene Alley	2	7	0	0	0	0	0	0	1	2	0	0	.000	.125	.000
Matty Alou	3	12	1	3	0	1	0	0	2	1	0	1	.250	.357	.333
Dave Cash	2	8	1	1	0	1	0	0	1	1	0	0	.125	.222	.250
Roberto Clemente	3	14	1	3	1	0	0	0	0	4	0	0	.214	.214	.214
Dock Ellis	1	2	0	0	0	0	0	0	0	1	0	0	.000	.000	.000
Richie Hebner	2	6	0	4	0	2	0	0	2	1	0	0	.667	.750	1.000
Johnny Jeter	3	2	0	0	0	0	0	0	0	2	0	0	.000	.000	.000
Bill Mazeroski	1	2	0	0	0	0	0	0	0	2	0	0	.000	.500	.000
Bob Moose	1	4	0	0	0	0	0	0	0	1	0	0	.000	.000	.000
Al Oliver	2	8	0	2	1	0	0	0	1	0	0	0	.250	.333	.250
Jose Pagan	1	3	0	1	0	0	0	0	1	1	0	0	.333	.500	.333
Freddie Patek	1	3	0	0	0	0	0	0	1	2	0	1	.000	.250	.000
Bob Robertson	2	5	0	1	0	1	0	0	0	0	0	0	.200	.200	.400
Manny Sanguillen	3	12	0	2	0	0	0	0	0	1	0	0	.167	.167	.167
Willie Stargell	3	12	0	6	1	1	0	0	1	1	0	0	.500	.538	.583
Luke Walker	1	2	0	0	0	0	0	0	0	1	0	0	.000	.000	.000
Totals	3	102	3	23	3	6	0	0	12	19	0	2	.225	.307	.284

Pitching

Reds	G	GS	CG	IP	H	R	ER	BB	SO	W-L	Sv-Op	Hld	ERA
Clay Carroll	2	0	0	1.1	2	0	0	0	2	0-0	1-1	1	0.00
Tony Cloninger	1	1	0	5.0	7	2	2	4	1	0-0	0-0	0	3.60
Wayne Granger	1	0	0	0.2	1	0	0	0	0	0-0	0-0	1	0.00
Don Gullett	2	0	0	3.2	1	0	0	2	3	0-0	2-2	0	0.00
Jim Merritt	1	1	0	5.1	3	1	1	0	2	1-0	0-0	0	1.69
Gary Nolan	1	1	0	9.0	8	0	0	4	6	1-0	0-0	0	0.00
Milt Wilcox	1	0	0	3.0	1	0	0	2	5	1-0	0-0	0	0.00
Totals	3	3	0	28.0	23	3	3	12	19	3-0	3-3	2	0.96

Pitching

Pirates	G	GS	CG	IP	H	R	ER	BB	SO	W-L	Sv-Op	Hld	ERA
Dock Ellis	1	1	0	9.2	9	3	3	4	1	0-1	0-0	0	2.79
Joe Gibbon	2	0	0	0.1	1	0	0	0	1	0-0	0-0	0	0.00
Dave Giusti	2	0	0	2.1	3	1	1	1	1	0-0	0-0	0	3.86
Bob Moose	1	1	0	7.2	4	3	3	2	4	0-1	0-0	0	3.52
Luke Walker	1	1	0	7.0	5	2	1	1	5	0-1	0-0	0	1.29
Totals	3	3	0	27.0	22	9	8	8	12	0-3	0-0	0	2.67

Fielding

Reds	Pos	G	PO	Ast	E	DP	PB	FPct
Johnny Bench	c	3	20	2	0	0	0	1.000
Bernie Carbo	lf	2	0	0	0	0	—	—
Clay Carroll	p	2	0	0	0	0	—	—
Ty Cline	lf	1	0	0	0	0	—	—
Tony Cloninger	p	1	0	2	0	0	—	1.000
Dave Concepcion	ss	3	1	1	0	0	—	1.000
Wayne Granger	p	1	0	0	0	0	—	—
Don Gullett	p	2	0	0	0	0	—	—
Tommy Helms	2b	3	11	12	0	1	—	1.000
Lee May	1b	3	31	1	0	1	—	1.000
Hal McRae	lf	1	2	0	0	0	—	1.000
Jim Merritt	p	1	0	2	0	0	—	1.000
Gary Nolan	p	1	0	3	0	0	—	1.000
Tony Perez	3b	3	5	6	1	1	—	.917
	1b	1	1	0	0	0	—	1.000
Pete Rose	rf	3	3	0	0	0	—	1.000
Jimmy Stewart	lf	1	0	0	0	0	—	—
Bobby Tolan	cf	3	5	0	0	0	—	1.000
Milt Wilcox	p	1	0	1	0	0	—	1.000
Woody Woodward	ss	3	5	8	0	0	—	1.000
	3b	3	0	1	0	0	—	1.000
Totals		3	84	39	1	3	0	.992

Fielding

Pirates	Pos	G	PO	Ast	E	DP	PB	FPct
Gene Alley	ss	2	6	7	0	3	—	1.000
Matty Alou	cf	3	6	0	0	0	—	1.000
Dave Cash	2b	2	6	8	0	3	—	1.000
Roberto Clemente	rf	3	7	0	0	0	—	1.000
Dock Ellis	p	1	0	3	0	0	—	1.000
Joe Gibbon	p	2	0	0	0	0	—	—
Dave Giusti	p	2	1	0	0	0	—	1.000
Richie Hebner	3b	2	0	4	0	0	—	1.000
Johnny Jeter	lf	1	2	0	0	0	—	1.000
Bill Mazeroski	2b	1	1	4	0	0	—	1.000
Bob Moose	p	1	0	3	0	0	—	1.000
Al Oliver	1b	2	23	0	0	1	—	1.000
Jose Pagan	3b	1	0	4	0	0	—	1.000
Freddie Patek	ss	1	1	2	0	0	—	1.000
Bob Robertson	1b	1	11	1	0	1	—	1.000
Manny Sanguillen	c	3	13	1	1	0	0	.933
Willie Stargell	lf	3	4	0	0	0	—	1.000
Luke Walker	p	1	0	0	1	0	—	.000
Totals		3	81	37	2	8	0	.983

1971 Baltimore Orioles (AL) 3, Oakland Athletics (AL) 0

The Baltimore Orioles swept the Oakland Athletics, and it was as easy as one-two-three. "One" was Dave McNally, who went seven innings to beat Vida Blue 5-3 in Game 1; "Two" was Mike Cuellar, who beat Catfish Hunter, 5-1, in Game 2; and "Three" was Jim Palmer, who went the distance for a 5-3 pennant-clinching victory in Game 3. Pat Dobson, the Orioles' fourth 20-game winner, didn't even get to pitch. Boog Powell notched two homers in the series and Brooks Robinson batted .364. The sweep gave Baltimore a perfect 9-0 record in LCS play since its adoption in 1969.

Game 1
Sunday, October 3

Athletics	AB	R	H	RBI	BB	K	Avg
Bert Campaneris, ss	4	0	1	0	0	0	.250
Joe Rudi, lf	4	0	1	0	0	0	.250
Reggie Jackson, rf	4	0	0	0	0	1	.000
Tommy Davis, 1b	4	1	1	0	0	0	.250
Sal Bando, 3b	4	1	2	0	0	0	.500
Angel Mangual, cf	4	1	2	2	0	1	.500
Dave Duncan, c	3	0	2	1	0	0	.667
Mike Epstein, ph	1	0	0	0	0	1	.000
Dick Green, 2b	1	0	0	0	1	0	.000
Vida Blue, p	3	0	0	0	0	3	—
Rollie Fingers, p	0	0	0	0	0	0	—
TOTALS	32	3	9	3	1	6	.281

Orioles	AB	R	H	RBI	BB	K	Avg
Paul Blair, cf	4	0	1	2	0	1	.250
Dave Johnson, 2b	4	1	1	0	0	0	.250
Merv Rettenmund, lf	4	0	1	0	1	2	.250
Frank Robinson, rf	3	1	0	0	1	3	.000
Boog Powell, 1b	4	0	1	0	0	2	.250
Brooks Robinson, 3b	3	1	1	0	0	0	.333
Andy Etchebarren, c	3	0	0	0	0	0	.000
Mark Belanger, ss	2	1	1	1	1	1	.500
Dave McNally, p	2	0	0	0	0	0	.000
Curt Motton, ph	1	0	1	1	0	0	1.000
Jim Palmer, pr	0	1	0	0	0	0	—
Eddie Watt, p	0	0	0	0	0	0	—
TOTALS	30	5	7	5	2	9	.233

	1	2	3	4	5	6	7	8	9		R	H	E
Athletics	0	2	0	1	0	0	0	0	0		3	9	0
Orioles	0	0	0	1	0	0	4	0	x		5	7	1

E—Johnson. DP—Athletics 1 (Bando to Green to Davis), Orioles 3 (McNally to Powell to Etchebarren; Belanger to Johnson to Powell; Johnson to Belanger to Powell). LOB—Athletics 4, Orioles 3. Scoring Position—Athletics 2-for-9, Orioles 5-for-9. 2B—Campaneris (1), Rudi (1), Bando (1), Mangual (1), Duncan (1), Blair (1), Johnson (1), Rettenmund (1), Motton (1). 3B—Mangual (1). S—Green. GDP—Mangual, Green, BRobinson. CS—Davis (1), Duncan (1).

Athletics	IP	H	R	ER	BB	K	ERA
Vida Blue (L, 0-1)	7.0	7	5	5	2	8	6.43
Rollie Fingers	1.0	0	0	0	0	1	0.00

Orioles	IP	H	R	ER	BB	K	ERA
Dave McNally (W, 1-0)	7.0	7	3	3	1	5	3.86
Eddie Watt (S, 1)	2.0	2	0	0	0	1	0.00

Time—2:23. Attendance—42,621. Umpires—HP, Chylak. 1B, Sudol. 2B, Rice. 3B, Vargo.

Game 2
Monday, October 4

Athletics	AB	R	H	RBI	BB	K	Avg
Bert Campaneris, ss	4	0	1	0	0	0	.250
Joe Rudi, lf	3	0	0	0	1	0	.143
Reggie Jackson, rf	4	0	1	0	0	0	.125
Tommy Davis, 1b	3	0	1	0	0	0	.286
Sal Bando, 3b	4	1	1	0	0	0	.375
Angel Mangual, cf	4	0	0	0	0	0	.250
Dave Duncan, c	3	0	1	1	0	0	.500
Dick Green, 2b	3	0	1	0	0	1	.250
Catfish Hunter, p	3	0	0	0	0	1	.000
TOTALS	31	1	6	1	1	2	.254

Orioles	AB	R	H	RBI	BB	K	Avg
Don Buford, lf	3	0	0	0	1	1	.000
Paul Blair, cf	0	0	0	0	0	0	.250
Dave Johnson, 2b	3	1	0	0	1	1	.143
Boog Powell, 1b	4	2	2	3	0	0	.375
Frank Robinson, rf	4	0	0	0	0	0	.000
Merv Rettenmund, cf-lf	4	0	1	0	0	1	.250
Brooks Robinson, 3b	3	1	1	1	0	0	.333
Ellie Hendricks, c	3	1	2	1	0	0	.667
Mark Belanger, ss	3	0	0	0	0	1	.200
Mike Cuellar, p	3	0	1	0	0	2	.333
TOTALS	30	5	7	5	2	6	.241

	1	2	3	4	5	6	7	8	9		R	H	E
Athletics	0	0	0	1	0	0	0	0	0		1	6	0
Orioles	0	1	1	0	0	0	1	2	x		5	7	0

LOB—Athletics 5, Orioles 3. Scoring Position—Athletics 1-for-8, Orioles 0-for-1. 2B—Jackson (1), Davis (1), Bando (2). HR—Powell 2 (2), BRobinson (1), Hendricks (1). S—Davis. CS—Campaneris (1).

Athletics	IP	H	R	ER	BB	K	ERA
Catfish Hunter (L, 0-1)	8.0	7	5	5	2	6	5.63

Orioles	IP	H	R	ER	BB	K	ERA
Mike Cuellar (W, 1-0)	9.0	6	1	1	1	2	1.00

Time—2:04. Attendance—35,003. Umpires—HP, Napp. 1B, O'Donnell. 2B, Luciano. 3B, DiMuro.

Game 3
Tuesday, October 5

Orioles	AB	R	H	RBI	BB	K	Avg
Don Buford, lf	4	1	3	0	1	0	.429
Merv Rettenmund, pr-lf	0	0	0	0	0	0	.250
Paul Blair, cf	5	1	2	0	0	2	.333
Boog Powell, 1b	2	2	0	0	3	1	.300
Frank Robinson, rf	5	1	1	1	0	1	.083
Ellie Hendricks, c	1	0	1	1	1	1	.500
Andy Etchebarren, ph-c	2	0	0	0	0	0	.000
Brooks Robinson, 3b	5	0	2	2	0	1	.364
Dave Johnson, 2b	3	0	2	0	2	0	.300
Mark Belanger, ss	3	0	1	0	2	0	.250
Jim Palmer, p	5	0	1	0	0	1	.200
TOTALS	35	5	12	4	9	7	.270

Athletics	AB	R	H	RBI	BB	K	Avg
Bert Campaneris, ss	4	0	0	0	0	1	.167
Rick Monday, cf	3	0	0	0	1	2	.000
Reggie Jackson, rf	4	2	3	2	0	0	.333
Mike Epstein, 1b	4	0	1	0	0	2	.200
Sal Bando, 3b	3	1	1	1	1	0	.364
Angel Mangual, lf	4	0	0	0	0	0	.167
Gene Tenace, c	3	0	0	0	1	1	.000
Dick Green, 2b	3	0	1	0	0	0	.286
Mike Hegan, ph	1	0	0	0	0	1	.000
Diego Segui, p	2	0	0	0	0	0	.000
Rollie Fingers, p	0	0	0	0	0	0	—
Darold Knowles, p	0	0	0	0	0	0	—
Bob Locker, p	0	0	0	0	0	0	—
Tommy Davis, ph	1	0	1	0	0	0	.375
Mudcat Grant, p	0	0	0	0	0	0	—
Curt Blefary, ph	1	0	0	0	0	1	.000
TOTALS	33	3	7	3	3	8	.234

	1	2	3	4	5	6	7	8	9		R	H	E
Orioles	1	0	0	0	2	0	2	0	0		5	12	0
Athletics	0	0	1	0	0	1	0	1	0		3	7	0

DP—Orioles 1 (Belanger to Johnson to Powell), Athletics 3 (Campaneris to Green; Green to Epstein; Bando to Epstein). LOB—Orioles 13, Athletics 6. Scoring Position—Orioles 1-for-14, Athletics 0-for-5. 2B—FRobinson (1), BRobinson (1), Johnson (2). 3B—Buford (1). HR—Jackson 2 (2), Bando (1). SF—Hendricks. GDP—Palmer, Bando.

Orioles	IP	H	R	ER	BB	K	ERA
Jim Palmer (W, 1-0)	9.0	7	3	3	3	8	3.00

Athletics	IP	H	R	ER	BB	K	ERA
Diego Segui (L, 0-1)	4.2	6	3	3	6	4	5.79
Rollie Fingers	1.1	2	2	2	1	1	7.71
Darold Knowles	0.1	1	0	0	0	0	0.00
Bob Locker	0.2	0	0	0	2	0	0.00
Mudcat Grant	2.0	3	0	0	0	2	0.00

Fingers pitched to two batters in the 7th.

WP—Palmer, Knowles. Time—2:49. Attendance—33,176. Umpires—HP, DiMuro. 1B, Luciano. 2B, Soar. 3B, Kunkel.

Postseason: League Championship Series

1971 AL Championship Series—Composite Statistics

Batting

Orioles	G	AB	R	H	RBI	2B	3B	HR	BB	SO	SB	CS	Avg	OBP	Slg
Mark Belanger	3	8	1	2	1	0	0	0	3	2	0	0	.250	.455	.250
Paul Blair	3	9	1	3	2	1	0	0	0	3	0	0	.333	.333	.444
Don Buford	2	7	1	3	0	0	1	0	2	1	0	0	.429	.556	.714
Mike Cuellar	1	3	0	1	0	0	0	0	0	2	0	0	.333	.333	.333
Andy Etchebarren	2	5	0	0	0	0	0	0	0	0	0	0	.000	.000	.000
Ellie Hendricks	2	4	1	2	2	0	0	1	1	1	0	0	.500	.500	1.250
Dave Johnson	3	10	2	3	0	2	0	0	3	1	0	0	.300	.462	.500
Dave McNally	1	2	0	0	0	0	0	0	0	0	0	0	.000	.000	.000
Curt Motton	1	1	0	1	1	1	0	0	0	0	0	0	1.000	1.000	2.000
Jim Palmer	2	5	1	1	0	0	0	0	0	1	0	0	.200	.200	.200
Boog Powell	3	10	4	3	3	0	0	2	3	3	0	0	.300	.462	.900
Merv Rettenmund	3	8	0	2	1	1	0	0	0	3	0	0	.250	.250	.375
Brooks Robinson	3	11	2	4	3	1	0	1	0	1	0	0	.364	.364	.727
Frank Robinson	3	12	2	1	1	1	0	0	1	4	0	0	.083	.154	.167
Totals	3	95	15	26	14	7	1	4	13	22	0	0	.274	.358	.495

Batting

Athletics	G	AB	R	H	RBI	2B	3B	HR	BB	SO	SB	CS	Avg	OBP	Slg
Sal Bando	3	11	3	4	1	2	0	1	1	0	0	0	.364	.417	.818
Curt Blefary	1	1	0	0	0	0	0	0	0	1	0	0	.000	.000	.000
Vida Blue	1	3	0	0	0	0	0	0	0	3	0	0	.000	.000	.000
Bert Campaneris	3	12	0	2	0	1	0	0	0	1	0	1	.167	.167	.250
Tommy Davis	3	8	1	3	0	1	0	0	0	0	0	1	.375	.375	.500
Dave Duncan	2	6	0	3	2	1	0	0	0	0	0	1	.500	.500	.667
Mike Epstein	2	5	0	1	0	0	0	0	0	3	0	0	.200	.200	.200
Dick Green	3	7	0	2	0	0	0	0	1	1	0	0	.286	.375	.286
Mike Hegan	1	1	0	0	0	0	0	0	0	1	0	0	.000	.000	.000
Catfish Hunter	1	3	0	0	0	0	0	0	0	1	0	0	.000	.000	.000
Reggie Jackson	3	12	2	4	2	1	0	2	0	1	0	0	.333	.333	.917
Angel Mangual	3	12	1	2	2	1	1	0	0	1	0	0	.167	.167	.417
Rick Monday	1	3	0	0	0	0	0	0	1	2	0	0	.000	.250	.000
Joe Rudi	2	7	0	1	0	1	0	0	1	0	0	0	.143	.250	.286
Diego Segui	1	2	0	0	0	0	0	0	0	0	0	0	.000	.000	.000
Gene Tenace	1	3	0	0	0	0	0	0	1	1	0	0	.000	.250	.000
Totals	3	96	7	22	7	8	1	3	5	16	0	3	.229	.267	.427

Pitching

Orioles	G	GS	CG	IP	H	R	ER	BB	SO	W-L	Sv-Op	Hld	ERA
Mike Cuellar	1	1	1	9.0	6	1	1	1	2	1-0	0-0	0	1.00
Dave McNally	1	1	0	7.0	7	3	3	1	5	1-0	0-0	0	3.86
Jim Palmer	1	1	1	9.0	7	3	3	3	8	1-0	0-0	0	3.00
Eddie Watt	1	0	0	2.0	2	0	0	0	1	0-0	1-1	0	0.00
Totals	3	3	2	27.0	22	7	7	5	16	3-0	1-1	0	2.33

Pitching

Athletics	G	GS	CG	IP	H	R	ER	BB	SO	W-L	Sv-Op	Hld	ERA
Vida Blue	1	1	0	7.0	7	5	5	2	8	0-1	0-0	0	6.43
Rollie Fingers	2	0	0	2.1	2	2	2	1	2	0-0	0-0	0	7.71
Mudcat Grant	1	0	0	2.0	3	0	0	0	2	0-0	0-0	0	0.00
Catfish Hunter	1	1	1	8.0	7	5	5	2	6	0-1	0-0	0	5.63
Darold Knowles	1	0	0	0.1	1	0	0	0	0	0-0	0-0	0	0.00
Bob Locker	1	0	0	0.2	1	0	0	0	2	0-0	0-0	0	0.00
Diego Segui	1	1	0	4.2	6	3	3	6	4	0-1	0-0	0	5.79
Totals	3	3	1	25.0	26	15	15	13	22	0-3	0-0	0	5.40

Fielding

Orioles	Pos	G	PO	Ast	E	DP	PB	FPct
Mark Belanger	ss	3	6	11	0	3	—	1.000
Paul Blair	cf	3	5	0	0	0	—	1.000
Don Buford	lf	2	1	0	0	0	—	1.000
Mike Cuellar	p	1	0	2	0	0	—	1.000
Andy Etchebarren	c	2	11	0	0	1	0	1.000
Ellie Hendricks	c	2	6	0	0	0	0	1.000
Dave Johnson	2b	3	5	6	1	3	—	.917
Dave McNally	p	1	0	2	0	1	—	1.000
Jim Palmer	p	1	1	0	0	0	—	1.000
Boog Powell	1b	3	28	2	0	4	—	1.000
Merv Rettenmund	lf	3	3	0	0	0	—	1.000
	cf	1	3	0	0	0	—	1.000
Brooks Robinson	3b	3	4	7	0	0	—	1.000
Frank Robinson	rf	3	8	0	0	0	—	1.000
Eddie Watt	p	1	0	1	0	0	—	1.000
Totals		3	81	31	1	12	0	.991

Fielding

Athletics	Pos	G	PO	Ast	E	DP	PB	FPct
Sal Bando	3b	3	6	2	0	2	—	1.000
Vida Blue	p	1	0	1	0	0	—	1.000
Bert Campaneris	ss	3	3	6	0	1	—	1.000
Tommy Davis	1b	2	8	0	0	1	—	1.000
Dave Duncan	c	2	15	0	0	0	0	1.000
Mike Epstein	1b	1	4	0	0	2	—	1.000
Rollie Fingers	p	2	0	0	0	0	—	—
Mudcat Grant	p	1	0	1	0	0	—	1.000
Dick Green	2b	3	8	4	0	3	—	1.000
Catfish Hunter	p	1	0	0	0	0	—	—
Reggie Jackson	rf	3	10	1	0	0	—	1.000
Darold Knowles	p	1	0	0	0	0	—	—
Bob Locker	p	1	0	0	0	0	—	—
Angel Mangual	cf	2	4	0	0	0	—	1.000
	lf	1	2	0	0	0	—	1.000
Rick Monday	cf	1	4	0	0	0	—	1.000
Joe Rudi	lf	2	3	0	0	0	—	—
Diego Segui	p	1	0	0	0	0	—	—
Gene Tenace	c	1	8	0	0	0	0	1.000
Totals		3	75	15	0	9	0	1.000

1971 Pittsburgh Pirates (NL) 3, San Francisco Giants (NL) 1

The Pittsburgh Pirates topped the San Francisco Giants in a war of longballs, taking the NL pennant in four games. The Giants held the Pirates homeless in Game 1, a 5-4 San Francisco victory for Gaylord Perry. The Giants did their damage with two-run homers from Tito Fuentes and Willie McCovey. Bob Robertson had the day of his life in Game 2, cracking three home runs and a double while driving in five runs, as Pittsburgh won 9-4 to even the Series. Richie Hebner's eighth-inning homer was the difference in Game 3, and Bob Johnson beat Juan Marichal, 2-1. The fourth game was tied at five after only two innings, but it was Al Oliver's three-run homer in the bottom of the sixth that iced the 9-5 victory for the Pirates, who moved on to the World Series.

Game 1

Saturday, October 2

Pirates	AB	R	H	RBI	BB	K	Avg
Dave Cash, 2b	5	2	2	1	0	0	.400
Richie Hebner, 3b	5	0	1	0	0	0	.200
Roberto Clemente, rf	4	0	0	0	1	1	.000
Willie Stargell, lf	4	0	0	0	0	1	.000
Al Oliver, cf	4	0	1	2	0	2	.250
Bob Robertson, 1b	4	0	2	0	0	0	.500
Manny Sanguillen, c	4	0	1	0	0	0	.250
Jackie Hernandez, ss	2	1	1	0	0	0	.500
Vic Davalillo, ph	1	0	0	0	0	0	.000
Bob Moose, p	0	0	0	0	0	0	—
Milt May, ph	1	0	0	0	0	0	.000
Dave Giusti, p	0	0	0	0	0	0	—
Steve Blass, p	1	0	0	0	0	1	.000
Gene Alley, ss	2	1	1	0	0	0	.500
TOTALS	37	4	9	3	1	5	.243

Giants	AB	R	H	RBI	BB	K	Avg
Ken Henderson, lf	4	0	2	1	0	0	.500
Tito Fuentes, 2b	4	1	1	2	0	2	.250
Willie Mays, cf	2	1	1	0	2	1	.500
Willie McCovey, 1b	3	1	1	2	1	0	.333
Dave Kingman, rf	3	0	0	0	0	2	.000
Bobby Bonds, rf	1	0	0	0	0	0	.000
Dick Dietz, c	4	0	0	0	0	1	.000
Al Gallagher, 3b	2	0	0	0	0	2	.000
Hal Lanier, 3b	1	0	0	0	0	0	.000
Chris Speier, ss	3	2	2	0	0	0	.667
Gaylord Perry, p	1	0	0	0	0	0	.000
TOTALS	28	5	7	5	3	10	.250

	1	2	3	4	5	6	7	8	9	R	H	E
Pirates	0	0	2	0	0	0	2	0	0	4	9	0
Giants	0	0	1	0	4	0	0	0	x	5	7	2

E—McCovey, Speier. DP—Pirates 1 (Alley to Cash to Robertson). LOB—Pirates 9, Giants 4. Scoring Position—Pirates 2-for-11, Giants 2-for-7. 2B—Cash (1), Henderson (1), Mays (1). HR—Fuentes (1), McCovey (1). S—Blass, Perry 2. GDP—Dietz.

Pirates	IP	H	R	ER	BB	K	ERA
Steve Blass (L, 0-1)	5.0	6	5	5	2	9	9.00
Bob Moose	2.0	0	0	0	0	0	0.00
Dave Giusti	1.0	1	0	0	1	1	0.00

Giants	IP	H	R	ER	BB	K	ERA
Gaylord Perry (W, 1-0)	9.0	9	4	3	1	5	3.00

HBP—Stargell by Perry. Time—2:44. Attendance—40,977. Umpires—HP, Gorman. 1B, Crawford. 2B, Weyer. 3B, Olson.

Game 2

Sunday, October 3

Pirates	AB	R	H	RBI	BB	K	Avg
Dave Cash, 2b	5	1	1	0	0	0	.500
Gene Clines, cf	3	1	1	1	0	1	.333
Al Oliver, ph-cf	1	1	1	0	1	0	.400
Roberto Clemente, rf	5	1	3	1	0	1	.333
Willie Stargell, lf	5	0	0	0	0	3	.000
Bob Robertson, 1b	5	4	4	5	0	1	.667
Manny Sanguillen, c	5	1	2	1	0	1	.333
Jose Pagan, 3b	1	0	0	0	0	0	.000
Richie Hebner, ph-3b	3	0	0	0	0	3	.125
Jackie Hernandez, ss	4	0	1	1	0	1	.333
Dock Ellis, p	3	0	0	0	0	2	.000
Bob Miller, p	1	0	0	0	0	0	.000
Dave Giusti, p	0	0	0	0	0	0	—
TOTALS	41	9	15	9	1	13	.315

Giants	AB	R	H	RBI	BB	K	Avg
Ken Henderson, lf	3	0	1	1	2	0	.429
Tito Fuentes, 2b	5	2	2	0	0	1	.333
Willie Mays, cf	5	1	2	3	0	0	.429
Willie McCovey, 1b	3	0	1	0	2	0	.333
Jimmy Rosario, pr	0	0	0	0	0	0	—
Dave Kingman, rf	4	0	1	0	1	1	.143
Dick Dietz, c	4	0	0	0	1	1	.000
Al Gallagher, 3b	4	0	0	0	0	0	.000
Chris Speier, ss	3	1	2	1	0	0	.667
John Cumberland, p	0	0	0	0	0	0	—
Jim Barr, p	1	0	0	0	0	0	.000
Don McMahon, p	0	0	0	0	0	0	—
Frank Duffy, ph	1	0	0	0	0	1	.000
Don Carrithers, p	0	0	0	0	0	0	—
Ron Bryant, p	0	0	0	0	0	0	—
Jim Ray Hart, ph	1	0	0	0	0	0	.000
Steve Hamilton, p	0	0	0	0	0	0	—
TOTALS	34	4	9	4	7	4	.271

	1	2	3	4	5	6	7	8	9	R	H	E
Pirates	0	1	0	2	1	0	4	0	1	9	15	0
Giants	1	1	0	0	0	0	0	0	2	4	9	0

DP—Pirates 1 (Hernandez to Cash to Robertson), Giants 1 (Dietz to Fuentes). LOB—Pirates 7, Giants 12. Scoring Position—Pirates 5-for-6, Giants 4-for-11. 2B—Cash (2), Robertson (1), Fuentes (1), Mays (2), Speier (1). HR—Clines (1), Robertson 3 (3), Mays (1). S—Cumberland. GDP—Hart. SB—Sanguillen (1), Henderson (1). CS—Cash (1).

Pirates	IP	H	R	ER	BB	K	ERA
Dock Ellis (W, 1-0)	5.0	6	2	2	4	1	3.60
Bob Miller (H, 1)	3.0	3	2	2	3	3	6.00
Dave Giusti (S, 1)	1.0	0	0	0	0	0	0.00

Giants	IP	H	R	ER	BB	K	ERA
John Cumberland (L, 0-1)	3.0	7	3	3	0	4	9.00
Jim Barr	1.0	3	1	1	0	2	9.00
Don McMahon	2.0	0	0	0	0	2	0.00
Don Carrithers	0.0	3	3	3	0	0	—
Ron Bryant	2.0	1	1	1	1	2	4.50
Steve Hamilton	1.0	1	1	1	3	3	9.00

Cumberland pitched to two batters in the 4th. Barr pitched to two batters in the 5th. Ellis pitched to two batters in the 6th. Carrithers pitched to three batters in the 7th. Miller pitched to three batters in the 9th.

PB—Sanguillen. HBP—Hebner by Bryant, Gallagher by Ellis. Time—3:23. Attendance—42,562. Umpires—HP, Crawford. 1B, Weyer. 2B, Olsen. 3B, Stello.

Game 3

Tuesday, October 5

Giants	AB	R	H	RBI	BB	K	Avg
Ken Henderson, lf	4	1	1	0	0	1	.364
Tito Fuentes, 2b	3	0	0	0	0	0	.250
Willie Mays, cf	4	0	1	0	0	1	.364
Willie McCovey, 1b	3	0	1	0	1	0	.333
Bobby Bonds, rf	3	0	1	0	1	2	.250
Dick Dietz, c	3	0	0	0	1	1	.000
Al Gallagher, 3b	3	0	1	0	0	0	.111
Jim Ray Hart, ph	1	0	0	0	0	0	.000
Chris Speier, ss	4	0	0	0	0	1	.400
Juan Marichal, p	3	0	0	0	0	0	.000
Dave Kingman, ph	1	0	0	0	0	0	.125
TOTALS	32	1	5	0	3	7	.233

Pirates	AB	R	H	RBI	BB	K	Avg
Dave Cash, 2b	4	0	0	0	0	0	.357
Richie Hebner, 3b	4	1	2	1	0	1	.250
Roberto Clemente, rf	4	0	1	0	0	1	.308
Willie Stargell, lf	3	0	0	0	0	0	.000
Al Oliver, cf	3	0	0	0	0	0	.250
Bob Robertson, 1b	3	1	1	1	0	0	.583
Manny Sanguillen, c	3	0	0	0	0	0	.250
Jackie Hernandez, ss	3	0	0	0	0	1	.222
Bob Johnson, p	2	0	0	0	0	1	.000
Vic Davalillo, ph	1	0	0	0	0	1	.000
Dave Giusti, p	0	0	0	0	0	0	—
TOTALS	30	2	4	2	0	6	.271

Game 4

Wednesday, October 6

Giants	AB	R	H	RBI	BB	K	Avg
Ken Henderson, lf	5	2	1	0	0	0	.313
Tito Fuentes, 2b	4	1	2	0	1	0	.313
Willie Mays, cf	4	0	0	0	1	1	.267
Willie McCovey, 1b	5	1	3	4	0	1	.429
Bobby Bonds, rf	4	0	1	0	1	1	.250
Dick Dietz, c	4	0	1	0	0	2	.067
Jim Ray Hart, 3b	3	0	0	0	0	2	.000
Al Gallagher, 3b	1	0	0	0	0	0	.100
Chris Speier, ss	4	1	1	1	0	0	.357
Gaylord Perry, p	3	0	1	0	0	0	.250
Jerry Johnson, p	0	0	0	0	0	0	—
Dave Kingman, ph	1	0	0	0	0	0	.111
Don McMahon, p	0	0	0	0	0	0	—
TOTALS	38	5	10	5	3	7	.246

Pirates	AB	R	H	RBI	BB	K	Avg
Dave Cash, 2b	5	2	3	0	0	1	.421
Richie Hebner, 3b	5	2	3	0	0	0	.294
Roberto Clemente, rf	5	1	2	3	0	3	.333
Willie Stargell, lf	2	1	0	0	2	1	.000
Al Oliver, cf	4	1	1	3	0	1	.250
Bob Robertson, 1b	4	0	0	0	0	1	.438
Manny Sanguillen, c	3	0	1	0	1	0	.267
Jackie Hernandez, ss	4	1	1	0	0	2	.231
Steve Blass, p	1	0	0	0	0	0	.000
Bill Mazeroski, ph	1	1	0	0	0	0	1.000
Bruce Kison, p	2	0	0	0	0	0	.000
Dave Giusti, p	1	0	0	0	0	0	.000
TOTALS	36	9	11	9	3	9	.287

	1	2	3	4	5	6	7	8	9	R	H	E
Giants	1	4	0	0	0	0	0	0	0	5	10	0
Pirates	2	3	0	0	0	4	0	0	x	9	11	2

E—Cash, Hernandez. DP—Pirates 1 (Cash to Hernandez to Robertson). LOB—Giants 9, Pirates 6. Scoring Position—Giants 3-for-10, Pirates 5-for-8. 2B—Hebner (1). HR—McCovey (2), Speier (1), Hebner (2), Oliver (1). GDP—McCovey. SB—Cash (1).

Giants	IP	H	R	ER	BB	K	ERA
Gaylord Perry (L, 1-1)	5.2	10	7	7	2	6	6.14
Jerry Johnson	1.1	1	2	2	1	0	13.50
Don McMahon	1.0	0	0	0	0	1	0.00

Pirates	IP	H	R	ER	BB	K	ERA
Steve Blass	2.0	8	5	4	0	2	11.57
Bruce Kison (W, 1-0)	4.2	2	0	0	2	3	0.00
Dave Giusti (S, 3)	2.1	0	0	0	0	0	0.00

WP—Perry, Kison. PB—Dietz. Time—3:00. Attendance—35,487. Umpires—HP, Olsen. 1B, Stello. 2B, Davidson. 3B, Gorman.

(Game 3 line score and pitching — continued)

	1	2	3	4	5	6	7	8	9	R	H	E
Giants	0	0	0	0	0	1	0	0	0	1	5	2
Pirates	0	1	0	0	0	0	0	1	x	2	4	1

E—Bonds, Hebner, Fuentes. LOB—Giants 8, Pirates 4. Scoring Position—Giants 0-for-8, Pirates 0-for-5. HR—Hebner (1), Robertson (4). S—Fuentes. SB—Mays (1).

Giants	IP	H	R	ER	BB	K	ERA
Juan Marichal (L, 0-1)	8.0	4	2	2	0	6	2.25

Pirates	IP	H	R	ER	BB	K	ERA
Bob Johnson (W, 1-0)	8.0	5	1	0	3	7	0.00
Dave Giusti (S, 2)	1.0	0	0	0	0	0	0.00

WP—Marichal 2. Time—2:26. Attendance—38,322. Umpires—HP, Weyer. 1B, Olsen. 2B, Stello. 3B, Davidson.

1971 NL Championship Series—Composite Statistics

Batting

Pirates	G	AB	R	H	RBI	2B	3B	HR	BB	SO	SB	CS	Avg	OBP	Slg
Gene Alley	1	2	1	1	0	0	0	0	0	0	0	0	.500	.500	.500
Steve Blass	2	1	0	0	0	0	0	0	0	1	0	0	.000	.000	.000
Dave Cash	4	19	5	8	1	2	0	0	1	1	1	1	.421	.421	.526
Roberto Clemente	4	18	2	6	4	0	0	0	1	6	0	0	.333	.368	.333
Gene Clines	1	3	1	1	1	0	0	1	0	1	0	0	.333	.333	1.333
Vic Davalillo	2	2	0	0	0	0	0	0	0	1	0	0	.000	.000	.000
Dock Ellis	1	3	0	0	0	0	0	0	0	2	0	0	.000	.000	.000
Dave Giusti	4	1	0	0	0	0	0	0	0	0	0	0	.000	.000	.000
Richie Hebner	4	17	3	5	4	1	0	2	0	4	0	0	.294	.333	.706
Jackie Hernandez	4	13	2	3	1	0	0	0	0	4	0	0	.231	.231	.231
Bob Johnson	1	2	0	0	0	0	0	0	0	1	0	0	.000	.000	.000
Bruce Kison	1	2	0	0	0	0	0	0	0	0	0	0	.000	.000	.000
Milt May	1	1	0	0	0	0	0	0	0	0	0	0	.000	.000	.000
Bill Mazeroski	1	1	1	1	0	0	0	0	0	0	0	0	1.000	1.000	1.000
Bob Miller	1	1	0	0	0	0	0	0	0	0	0	0	.000	.000	.000
Al Oliver	4	12	2	3	5	0	0	1	1	3	0	0	.250	.308	.500
Jose Pagan	1	1	0	0	0	0	0	0	0	0	0	0	.000	.000	.000
Bob Robertson	4	16	5	7	6	1	0	4	0	2	0	0	.438	.438	1.250
Manny Sanguillen	4	15	1	4	1	0	0	0	1	1	1	0	.267	.313	.267
Willie Stargell	4	14	1	0	0	0	0	0	2	6	0	0	.000	.176	.000
Totals	4	144	24	39	23	4	0	8	5	33	2	1	.271	.305	.465

Batting

Giants	G	AB	R	H	RBI	2B	3B	HR	BB	SO	SB	CS	Avg	OBP	Slg
Jim Barr	1	1	0	0	0	0	0	0	0	0	0	0	.000	.000	.000
Bobby Bonds	3	8	0	2	0	0	0	0	2	4	0	0	.250	.400	.250
John Cumberland	1	0	0	0	0	0	0	0	0	0	0	0	.000	.000	.000
Dick Dietz	4	15	0	1	0	0	0	0	2	5	0	0	.067	.176	.067
Frank Duffy	1	1	0	0	0	0	0	0	0	1	0	0	.000	.000	.000
Tito Fuentes	4	16	4	5	2	1	0	1	1	3	0	0	.313	.353	.563
Al Gallagher	4	10	0	1	0	0	0	0	0	2	0	0	.100	.182	.100
Jim Ray Hart	3	5	0	0	0	0	0	0	0	2	0	0	.000	.000	.000
Ken Henderson	4	16	3	5	2	1	0	0	2	1	1	0	.313	.389	.375
Dave Kingman	4	9	0	1	0	0	0	0	1	3	0	0	.111	.200	.111
Hal Lanier	1	1	0	0	0	0	0	0	0	0	0	0	.000	.000	.000
Juan Marichal	1	3	0	0	0	0	0	0	0	1	0	0	.000	.000	.000
Willie Mays	4	15	2	4	3	2	0	1	3	3	1	0	.267	.389	.600
Willie McCovey	4	14	2	6	6	0	0	2	4	2	0	0	.429	.556	.857
Gaylord Perry	2	4	0	1	0	0	0	0	0	0	0	0	.250	.250	.250
Jimmy Rosario	1	0	0	0	0	0	0	0	0	0	0	0	—	—	—
Chris Speier	4	14	4	5	1	1	1	0	1	1	1	0	.357	.400	.643
Totals	4	132	15	31	14	5	0	5	16	28	2	0	.235	.322	.386

Pitching

Pirates	G	GS	CG	IP	H	R	ER	BB	SO	W-L	Sv-Op	Hld	ERA
Steve Blass	2	2	0	7.0	14	10	9	2	11	0-1	0-0	0	11.57
Dock Ellis	1	1	0	5.0	6	2	2	4	1	1-0	0-0	0	3.60
Dave Giusti	4	0	0	5.1	1	0	0	2	3	0-0	3-3	0	0.00
Bob Johnson	1	1	0	8.0	5	1	0	3	7	1-0	0-0	0	0.00
Bruce Kison	1	0	0	4.2	2	0	0	2	3	1-0	0-0	0	0.00
Bob Miller	1	0	0	3.0	3	2	2	3	3	0-0	0-0	1	6.00
Bob Moose	1	0	0	2.0	0	0	0	0	0	0-0	0-0	0	0.00
Totals	4	4	0	35.0	31	15	13	16	28	3-1	3-3	1	3.34

Pitching

Giants	G	GS	CG	IP	H	R	ER	BB	SO	W-L	Sv-Op	Hld	ERA
Jim Barr	1	0	0	1.0	3	1	1	0	2	0-0	0-0	0	9.00
Ron Bryant	1	0	0	2.0	1	1	1	1	2	0-0	0-0	0	4.50
Don Carrithers	1	0	0	3.0	3	3	3	0	0	0-0	0-0	0	—
John Cumberland	1	1	0	3.0	7	3	3	0	4	0-1	0-0	0	9.00
Steve Hamilton	1	0	0	1.0	1	1	1	0	3	0-0	0-0	0	9.00
Jerry Johnson	1	0	0	1.1	2	2	2	1	2	0-0	0-0	0	13.50
Juan Marichal	1	1	1	8.0	4	2	2	0	6	0-1	0-0	0	2.25
Don McMahon	2	0	0	3.0	0	0	0	0	3	0-0	0-0	0	0.00
Gaylord Perry	2	2	1	14.2	19	11	10	3	11	1-1	0-0	0	6.14
Totals	4	4	2	34.0	39	24	23	5	33	1-3	0-0	0	6.09

Fielding

Pirates	Pos	G	PO	Ast	E	DP	PB	FPct
Gene Alley	ss	1	1	1	0	1	—	1.000
Steve Blass	p	2	1	1	0	0	—	1.000
Dave Cash	2b	4	12	11	1	3	—	.958
Roberto Clemente	rf	4	12	0	0	0	—	1.000
Gene Clines	cf	1	1	0	0	0	—	1.000
Dock Ellis	p	1	0	0	0	0	—	—
Dave Giusti	p	4	0	1	0	0	—	1.000
Richie Hebner	3b	4	4	3	1	0	—	.875
Jackie Hernandez	ss	4	7	9	1	2	—	.941
Bob Johnson	p	1	0	0	0	0	—	—
Bruce Kison	p	1	0	1	0	0	—	1.000
Bob Miller	p	1	1	0	0	0	—	1.000
Bob Moose	p	1	0	0	0	0	—	—
Al Oliver	cf	4	5	0	0	0	—	1.000
Jose Pagan	3b	1	1	2	0	0	—	1.000
Bob Robertson	1b	4	24	2	0	3	—	1.000
Manny Sanguillen	c	4	30	1	0	0	1	1.000
Willie Stargell	lf	4	6	0	0	0	—	1.000
Totals		4	105	32	3	9	1	.979

Fielding

Giants	Pos	G	PO	Ast	E	DP	PB	FPct
Jim Barr	p	1	0	0	0	0	—	—
Bobby Bonds	rf	3	3	0	1	0	—	.750
Ron Bryant	p	1	0	0	0	0	—	—
Don Carrithers	p	1	0	0	0	0	—	—
John Cumberland	p	1	0	0	0	0	—	—
Dick Dietz	c	4	34	2	0	1	1	1.000
Tito Fuentes	2b	4	9	4	1	1	—	.929
Al Gallagher	3b	4	0	4	0	0	—	1.000
Steve Hamilton	p	1	0	0	0	0	—	—
Jim Ray Hart	3b	1	0	2	0	0	—	1.000
Ken Henderson	lf	4	4	0	0	0	—	1.000
Jerry Johnson	p	1	0	0	0	0	—	—
Dave Kingman	rf	2	5	0	0	0	—	1.000
Hal Lanier	3b	1	1	0	0	0	—	1.000
Juan Marichal	p	1	2	4	0	0	—	1.000
Willie Mays	cf	4	5	0	0	0	—	1.000
Willie McCovey	1b	4	34	3	1	0	—	.974
Don McMahon	p	2	1	1	0	0	—	1.000
Gaylord Perry	p	2	1	1	0	0	—	1.000
Chris Speier	ss	4	3	14	1	0	—	.944
Totals		4	102	35	4	2	1	.972

1972 Oakland Athletics (AL) 3, Detroit Tigers (AL) 2

The Oakland A's topped the Detroit Tigers in a hard-fought five-game ALCS. Mickey Lolich took a 2-1 lead into the bottom of the 11th inning in Game 1, but Gonzalo Marquez drove in the tying run with a pinch-hit RBI single, and the game-winning run scored when right fielder Al Kaline's throw skipped past third baseman Aurelio Rodriguez. Blue Moon Odom spun a three-hit shutout for a 5-0 Oakland win in Game 2. Bert Campaneris was suspended for the rest of the series after throwing his bat at pitcher Lerrin LaGrow, who'd hit Campaneris on the ankle with a pitch. Detroit's Joe Coleman fanned 14 batters in Game 3, winning 3-0 for Detroit's first win. Game 4 went into extra innings, and the A's appeared to have the AL title wrapped up when they scored two runs in the top of the 10th, but the Tigers came back in the bottom of the frame. Jim Northrup's RBI single capped a three-run comeback that gave Detroit a 4-3 win and forced a fifth game. Odom teamed with Vida Blue to outduel Woodie Fryman for a 2-1 Oakland win to send the A's to the World Series.

Game 1
Saturday, October 7

Tigers	AB	R	H	RBI	BB	K	Avg
Dick McAuliffe, 2b	5	0	0	0	0	3	.000
Al Kaline, rf	5	1	1	1	0	0	.200
Duke Sims, c	5	0	2	0	0	0	.400
Norm Cash, 1b	3	1	1	1	1	0	.333
Willie Horton, lf	3	0	0	0	0	1	.000
Gates Brown, ph	1	0	0	0	0	0	.000
Mickey Stanley, cf	1	0	0	0	0	0	.000
Jim Northrup, cf-lf	3	0	1	0	1	0	.333
Aurelio Rodriguez, 3b	4	0	0	0	0	0	.000
Ed Brinkman, ss	4	0	1	0	0	0	.250
Mickey Lolich, p	4	0	0	0	0	1	.000
Chuck Seelbach, p	0	0	0	0	0	0	—
TOTALS	38	2	6	2	2	5	.158

Athletics	AB	R	H	RBI	BB	K	Avg
Bert Campaneris, ss	4	1	0	0	1	0	.000
Matty Alou, rf	5	0	1	0	0	0	.200
Joe Rudi, lf	4	0	0	1	0	2	.000
Reggie Jackson, cf	5	0	2	0	0	1	.400
Sal Bando, 3b	4	0	2	0	0	0	.500
Blue Moon Odom, pr	0	0	0	0	0	0	—
Mike Epstein, 1b	3	0	2	0	2	0	.667
Mike Hegan, pr	0	1	0	0	0	0	—
Gene Tenace, c	5	1	0	0	0	1	.000
Dick Green, 2b	0	0	0	0	0	0	.
Angel Mangual, ph	1	0	0	0	0	0	.000
Ted Kubiak, 2b	2	0	1	0	0	0	.500
George Hendrick, ph	1	0	0	0	0	0	.000
Dal Maxvill, 2b	0	0	0	0	0	0	—
Gonzalo Marquez, ph	1	0	1	1	0	0	1.000
Catfish Hunter, p	3	0	1	0	0	0	.333
Vida Blue, p	0	0	0	0	0	0	—
Rollie Fingers, p	1	0	0	0	0	0	.000
TOTALS	39	3	10	2	3	4	.256

	1	2	3	4	5	6	7	8	9	10	11	R	H	E
Tigers	0	1	0	0	0	0	0	0	0	0	1	2	6	2
Athletics	0	0	1	0	0	0	0	0	0	0	2	3	10	1

E—Kubiak, McAuliffe, Kaline. DP—Tigers 1 (Rodriguez to McAuliffe), Athletics 1 (Campaneris to Epstein). LOB—Tigers 6, Athletics 10. Scoring Position—Tigers 0-for-8, Athletics 1-for-7. 2B—Sims (1), Brinkman (1). 3B—Sims (1). HR—Kaline (1), Cash (1). S—Cash, Bando. SF—Rudi.

Tigers	IP	H	R	ER	BB	K	ERA
Mickey Lolich (L, 0-1)	10.0	9	3	2	3	4	1.80
Chuck Seelbach (BS, 1)	0.1	1	0	0	0	0	0.00

Athletics	IP	H	R	ER	BB	K	ERA
Catfish Hunter	8.0	4	1	1	2	4	1.13
Vida Blue	0.0	0	0	0	0	0	
Rollie Fingers (W, 1-0)	3.0	2	1	1	0	1	3.00

Hunter pitched to one batter in the 9th. Blue pitched to one batter in the 9th. Lolich pitched to two batters in the 11th.

Time—3:09. Attendance—29,536. Umpires—HP, Flaherty. 1B, Chylak. 2B, Rice. 3B, Denkinger.

Game 2
Sunday, October 8

Tigers	AB	R	H	RBI	BB	K	Avg
Dick McAuliffe, ss	4	0	0	0	0	0	.000
Al Kaline, rf	4	0	1	0	0	0	.222
Duke Sims, c	3	0	0	0	0	1	.250
Norm Cash, 1b	3	0	1	0	0	0	.333
Willie Horton, lf	3	0	0	0	0	0	.000
Jim Northrup, cf	3	0	1	0	0	1	.333
Tony Taylor, 2b	3	0	0	0	0	0	.000
Aurelio Rodriguez, 3b	3	0	0	0	0	0	.000
Woodie Fryman, p	1	0	0	0	0	0	.000
Chris Zachary, p	0	0	0	0	0	0	—
Fred Scherman, p	0	0	0	0	0	0	—
Tom Haller, ph	1	0	0	0	0	0	.000
Lerrin LaGrow, p	0	0	0	0	0	0	—
John Hiller, p	0	0	0	0	0	0	—
Gates Brown, ph	1	0	0	0	0	0	.000
TOTALS	29	0	3	0	0	2	.138

Athletics	AB	R	H	RBI	BB	K	Avg
Bert Campaneris, ss	3	2	3	0	0	0	.429
Dal Maxvill, pr-ss	0	0	0	0	0	0	—
Matty Alou, rf	4	1	1	1	0	0	.222
Joe Rudi, lf	3	1	2	1	1	0	.286
Reggie Jackson, cf	4	0	1	2	0	2	.333
Sal Bando, 3b	4	0	0	0	0	2	.250
Mike Epstein, 1b	3	0	0	0	1	1	.333
Mike Hegan, 1b	0	0	0	0	0	0	—
Gene Tenace, c	3	0	0	0	0	2	.000
Dick Green, 2b	1	0	0	0	0	0	.000
George Hendrick, ph	1	1	1	0	0	0	.500
Ted Kubiak, 2b	1	0	0	0	0	0	.333
Blue Moon Odom, p	2	0	0	0	1	0	.000
TOTALS	29	5	8	4	2	8	.258

	1	2	3	4	5	6	7	8	9	R	H	E
Tigers	0	0	0	0	0	0	0	0	0	0	3	1
Athletics	1	0	0	0	4	0	0	0	x	5	8	0

E—McAuliffe. DP—Tigers 2 (Cash to McAuliffe to Fryman; Taylor to McAuliffe to Cash). LOB—Tigers 2, Athletics 4. Scoring Position—Tigers 0-for-1, Athletics 4-for-8. 2B—Rudi (1), Jackson (1). S—Odom. GDP—Alou. SB—Campaneris 2 (2). CS—Northrup (1), Alou (1).

Tigers	IP	H	R	ER	BB	K	ERA
Woodie Fryman (L, 0-1)	4.1	7	4	4	1	5	8.31
Chris Zachary	0.0	0	1	1	1	0	
Fred Scherman	0.2	1	0	0	0	1	0.00
Lerrin LaGrow	1.0	0	0	0	0	1	0.00
John Hiller	2.0	0	0	0	0	1	0.00

Athletics	IP	H	R	ER	BB	K	ERA
Blue Moon Odom (W, 1-0)	9.0	3	0	0	0	2	0.00

Zachary pitched to three batters in the 5th. LaGrow pitched to one batter in the 7th.

WP—Zachary 2. HBP—Campaneris by LaGrow. Time—2:37. Attendance—31,088. Umpires—HP, Chylak. 1B, Rice. 2B, Frantz. 3B, Barnett.

Game 3
Tuesday, October 10

Athletics	AB	R	H	RBI	BB	K	Avg
Matty Alou, rf	5	0	3	0	0	2	.357
Dal Maxvill, ss	2	0	0	0	1	2	.000
Dave Duncan, ph-c	1	0	0	0	0	1	.000
Joe Rudi, lf	4	0	3	0	0	1	.455
Reggie Jackson, cf	4	0	0	0	0	1	.231
Mike Epstein, 1b	4	0	0	0	0	2	.200
Sal Bando, 3b	4	0	1	0	0	1	.250
Gene Tenace, c-2b	2	0	0	0	2	0	.000
Dick Green, 2b	1	0	0	0	0	0	.000
Don Mincher, ph	1	0	0	0	0	1	.000
Ted Kubiak, 2b	0	0	0	0	0	0	.333
Gonzalo Marquez, ph	1	0	0	0	0	0	.500
Tim Cullen, ss	1	0	0	0	0	0	.000
Ken Holtzman, p	1	0	0	0	0	1	.000
Angel Mangual, ph	1	0	0	0	0	1	.000
Rollie Fingers, p	0	0	0	0	0	0	.000
Vida Blue, p	0	0	0	0	0	0	
Mike Hegan, ph	1	0	0	0	0	0	.000
Bob Locker, p	0	0	0	0	0	0	—
George Hendrick, ph	1	0	0	0	0	1	.333
TOTALS	34	0	7	0	3	14	.233

Tigers	AB	R	H	RBI	BB	K	Avg
Tony Taylor, 2b	4	0	0	0	0	0	.000
Aurelio Rodriguez, 3b	4	0	0	0	0	1	.000
Al Kaline, rf	3	1	2	0	1	0	.333
Bill Freehan, c	3	2	2	1	0	0	.667
Willie Horton, lf	2	0	0	0	1	2	.000
Jim Northrup, ph-lf	1	0	0	0	0	0	.286
Mickey Stanley, cf	3	0	1	0	0	0	.250
Ike Brown, 1b	2	0	1	2	0	1	.500
Norm Cash, ph-1b	1	0	0	0	0	0	.286
Dick McAuliffe, ss	3	0	1	0	0	0	.083
Joe Coleman, p	2	0	1	0	1	0	.500
TOTALS	28	3	8	3	3	4	.187

	1	2	3	4	5	6	7	8	9	R	H	E
Athletics	0	0	0	0	0	0	0	0	0	0	7	0
Tigers	0	0	0	2	0	0	0	1	x	3	8	1

E—McAuliffe. DP—Athletics 3 (Maxvill to Epstein; Maxvill to Kubiak to Epstein; Bando to Tenace to Epstein). LOB—Athletics 10, Tigers 5. Scoring Position—Athletics 0-for-6, Tigers 2-for-6. 2B—Alou 2 (2), Freehan (1). HR—Freehan (1). S—Freehan. GDP—Taylor 2. SB—Alou (1), Maxvill (1). CS—Tenace (1).

Athletics	IP	H	R	ER	BB	K	ERA
Ken Holtzman (L, 0-1)	4.0	4	2	2	2	2	4.50
Rollie Fingers	1.2	2	0	0	1	1	1.93
Vida Blue	0.1	0	0	0	0	0	0.00
Bob Locker	2.0	2	1	1	0	1	4.50

Tigers	IP	H	R	ER	BB	K	ERA
Joe Coleman (W, 1-0)	9.0	7	0	0	3	14	0.00

Time—2:27. Attendance—41,156. Umpires—HP, Rice. 1B, Denkinger. 2B, Chylak. 3B, Frantz.

Game 4

Wednesday, October 11

Athletics	AB	R	H	RBI	BB	K	Avg
Matty Alou, rf	5	1	2	1	0	0	.368
Dal Maxvill, ss	2	0	1	0	0	0	.250
George Hendrick, ph	1	0	0	0	0	0	.250
Tim Cullen, ss	0	0	0	0	0	0	.000
Angel Mangual, ph	1	0	0	0	0	0	.000
Ted Kubiak, ss	1	0	1	1	0	0	.500
Joe Rudi, lf	5	0	0	0	0	0	.313
Reggie Jackson, cf	5	0	2	0	0	2	.278
Sal Bando, 3b	5	0	0	0	0	0	.176
Mike Epstein, 1b	3	1	1	1	1	1	.231
Gene Tenace, c-2b	4	0	0	0	0	1	.000
Dick Green, 2b	2	0	1	0	0	0	.250
Dave Duncan, ph-c	1	0	0	0	1	0	.000
Catfish Hunter, p	3	0	0	0	0	2	.167
Rollie Fingers, p	0	0	0	0	0	0	.000
Vida Blue, p	0	0	0	0	0	0	—
Gonzalo Marquez, ph	1	1	1	0	0	0	.667
Bob Locker, p	0	0	0	0	0	0	—
Joe Horlen, p	0	0	0	0	0	0	—
Dave Hamilton, p	0	0	0	0	0	0	—
TOTALS	39	3	9	3	2	6	.240

Tigers	AB	R	H	RBI	BB	K	Avg
Dick McAuliffe, ss	4	2	2	1	1	1	.188
Al Kaline, rf	3	1	1	0	1	1	.333
Duke Sims, lf	3	0	1	0	0	0	.273
Mickey Stanley, cf	1	0	1	0	0	0	.400
Gates Brown, ph	0	1	0	0	1	0	.000
Bill Freehan, c	5	0	1	1	0	1	.375
Norm Cash, 1b	4	0	1	1	1	2	.273
Jim Northrup, cf-lf	5	0	1	1	0	2	.250
Tony Taylor, 2b	4	0	2	0	0	0	.182
Aurelio Rodriguez, 3b	2	0	0	0	2	0	.000
Mickey Lolich, p	3	0	0	0	0	1	.000
Willie Horton, ph	1	0	0	0	0	0	.000
Chuck Seelbach, p	0	0	0	0	0	0	—
John Hiller, p	0	0	0	0	0	0	—
TOTALS	35	4	10	4	6	8	.200

	1	2	3	4	5	6	7	8	9	10		R	H	E
Athletics	0	0	0	0	0	0	1	0	0	2		3	9	2
Tigers	0	0	1	0	0	0	0	0	0	3		4	10	1

E—Jackson, Rodriguez, Tenace. DP—Athletics 1 (Cullen to Green to Epstein). LOB—Athletics 8, Tigers 11. Scoring Position—Athletics 2-for-7, Tigers 2-for-8. 2B—Alou 2 (4), Green (1), Sims (2), Taylor 2 (2). HR—Epstein (1), McAuliffe (1). S—Kaline. GDP—Northrup. CS—McAuliffe (1).

Athletics	IP	H	R	ER	BB	K	ERA
Catfish Hunter	7.1	6	1	1	3	5	1.17
Rollie Fingers	0.2	0	0	0	0	1	1.69
Vida Blue	1.0	1	0	0	1	2	0.00
Bob Locker	0.0	2	2	2	0	0	13.50
Joe Horlen (L, 0-1)	0.0	0	1	1	1	0	—
Dave Hamilton (BS, 1)	0.0	1	0	0	1	0	—

Tigers	IP	H	R	ER	BB	K	ERA
Mickey Lolich	9.0	5	1	1	2	6	1.42
Chuck Seelbach	0.2	3	2	2	0	0	18.00
John Hiller (W, 1-0)	0.1	1	0	0	0	0	0.00

Locker pitched to two batters in the 10th. Horlen pitched to three batters in the 10th. Hamilton pitched to two batters in the 10th.

WP—Horlen. Time—3:04. Attendance—37,615. Umpires—HP, Denkinger. 1B, Chylak. 2B, Rice. 3B, Flaherty.

Game 5

Thursday, October 12

Athletics	AB	R	H	RBI	BB	K	Avg
Matty Alou, rf	2	0	1	0	0	0	.381
Dal Maxvill, ss	4	0	0	0	0	0	.125
Joe Rudi, lf	4	0	0	0	0	1	.250
Reggie Jackson, cf	0	1	0	0	1	0	.278
George Hendrick, cf	3	1	0	0	0	0	.143
Sal Bando, 3b	3	0	1	0	0	0	.200
Mike Epstein, 1b	3	0	0	0	0	1	.188
Gene Tenace, c	3	0	1	1	1	1	.059
Dick Green, 2b	4	0	0	0	0	0	.125
Blue Moon Odom, p	2	0	1	0	0	0	.250
Vida Blue, p	1	0	0	0	0	0	.000
TOTALS	29	2	4	1	2	3	.214

Tigers	AB	R	H	RBI	BB	K	Avg
Dick McAuliffe, ss	4	1	1	0	0	0	.200
Al Kaline, rf	4	0	0	0	0	1	.263
Duke Sims, lf	3	0	0	0	1	1	.214
Bill Freehan, c	4	0	0	1	0	0	.250
Norm Cash, 1b	4	0	1	0	0	1	.267
Joe Niekro, pr	0	0	0	0	0	0	—
Jim Northrup, cf	2	0	2	0	1	0	.357
Mickey Stanley, ph	1	0	0	0	0	0	.333
Tony Taylor, 2b	4	0	0	0	0	2	.133
Aurelio Rodriguez, 3b	3	0	0	0	0	1	.000
Woodie Fryman, p	2	0	0	0	0	0	.000
Willie Horton, ph	1	0	1	0	0	0	.100
John Knox, pr	0	0	0	0	0	0	—
John Hiller, p	0	0	0	0	0	0	—
TOTALS	32	1	5	1	2	6	.201

	1	2	3	4	5	6	7	8	9		R	H	E
Athletics	0	1	0	1	0	0	0	0	0		2	4	0
Tigers	1	0	0	0	0	0	0	0	0		1	5	2

E—Sims, McAuliffe. DP—Tigers 1 (Rodriguez to Taylor to Cash). LOB—Athletics 6, Tigers 6. Scoring Position—Athletics 1-for-10, Tigers 0-for-4. 2B—Odom (1). S—Alou, Bando. GDP—Green. SB—Jackson 2 (2), Epstein (1).

Athletics	IP	H	R	ER	BB	K	ERA
Blue Moon Odom (W, 2-0)	5.0	2	1	0	2	3	0.00
Vida Blue (S, 1)	4.0	3	0	0	0	3	0.00

Tigers	IP	H	R	ER	BB	K	ERA
Woodie Fryman (L, 0-2)	8.0	4	2	1	1	3	3.65
John Hiller	1.0	0	0	0	1	0	0.00

Balk—Fryman. WP—Odom. PB—Tenace. HBP—Epstein by Fryman, Alou by Fryman. Time—2:48. Attendance—50,276. Umpires—HP, Chylak. 1B, Rice. 2B, Barnett. 3B, Flaherty.

1972 AL Championship Series—Composite Statistics

Batting

Athletics	G	AB	R	H	RBI	2B	3B	HR	BB	SO	SB	CS	Avg	OBP	Slg
Matty Alou	5	21	2	8	2	4	0	0	0	2	1	1	.381	.409	.571
Sal Bando	5	20	0	4	0	0	0	0	0	3	0	0	.200	.200	.200
Vida Blue	4	1	0	0	0	0	0	0	0	0	0	0	.000	.000	.000
Bert Campaneris	2	7	3	3	0	0	0	0	1	0	2	0	.429	.556	.429
Tim Cullen	2	1	0	0	0	0	0	0	0	0	0	0	.000	.000	.000
Dave Duncan	2	2	0	0	0	0	0	0	1	1	0	0	.000	.333	.000
Mike Epstein	5	16	1	3	1	0	0	1	4	5	1	0	.188	.381	.375
Rollie Fingers	3	1	0	0	0	0	0	0	0	0	0	0	.000	.000	.000
Dick Green	5	8	0	1	0	1	0	0	0	0	0	0	.125	.125	.250
Mike Hegan	3	1	1	0	0	0	0	0	0	0	0	0	.000	.000	.000
George Hendrick	5	7	2	1	0	0	0	0	0	1	0	0	.143	.143	.143
Ken Holtzman	1	1	0	0	0	0	0	0	0	1	0	0	.000	.000	.000
Catfish Hunter	2	6	0	1	0	0	0	0	0	2	0	0	.167	.167	.167
Reggie Jackson	5	18	1	5	2	1	0	0	1	6	2	0	.278	.316	.333
Ted Kubiak	4	4	0	2	1	0	0	0	0	1	0	0	.500	.500	.500
Angel Mangual	3	3	0	0	0	0	0	0	0	1	0	0	.000	.000	.000
Gonzalo Marquez	3	3	1	2	1	0	0	0	0	0	0	0	.667	.667	.667
Dal Maxvill	5	8	0	1	0	0	0	0	1	2	1	0	.125	.222	.125
Don Mincher	1	1	0	0	0	0	0	0	0	1	0	0	.000	.000	.000
Blue Moon Odom	3	4	0	1	0	1	0	0	0	1	0	0	.250	.250	.500
Joe Rudi	5	20	1	5	2	1	0	0	1	4	0	0	.250	.273	.300
Gene Tenace	5	17	1	1	1	0	0	0	3	5	0	1	.059	.200	.059
Totals	5	170	13	38	10	8	0	1	12	35	7	2	.224	.285	.288

Batting

Tigers	G	AB	R	H	RBI	2B	3B	HR	BB	SO	SB	CS	Avg	OBP	Slg
Ed Brinkman	1	4	0	1	0	1	0	0	0	0	0	0	.250	.250	.500
Gates Brown	3	2	1	0	0	0	0	0	1	0	0	0	.000	.333	.000
Ike Brown	1	2	0	1	2	0	0	0	0	1	0	0	.500	.500	.500
Norm Cash	5	15	1	4	2	0	0	1	2	3	0	0	.267	.353	.467
Joe Coleman	1	2	0	1	0	0	0	0	1	0	0	0	.500	.667	.500
Bill Freehan	3	12	2	3	3	1	0	1	0	1	0	0	.250	.250	.583
Woodie Fryman	2	3	0	0	0	0	0	0	0	0	0	0	.000	.000	.000
Tom Haller	1	1	0	0	0	0	0	0	0	0	0	0	.000	.000	.000
Willie Horton	5	10	0	1	0	0	0	0	1	3	0	0	.100	.182	.100
Al Kaline	5	19	3	5	1	0	0	1	2	2	0	0	.263	.333	.421
John Knox	1	0	0	0	0	0	0	0	0	0	0	0	—	—	—
Mickey Lolich	2	7	0	0	0	0	0	0	0	2	0	0	.000	.000	.000
Dick McAuliffe	5	20	3	4	1	0	0	1	1	4	0	1	.200	.238	.350
Joe Niekro	1	0	0	0	0	0	0	0	0	0	0	0	—	—	—
Jim Northrup	5	14	0	5	1	0	0	0	2	3	0	1	.357	.438	.357
Aurelio Rodriguez	5	16	0	0	0	0	0	0	0	2	2	0	.000	.111	.000
Duke Sims	4	14	0	3	0	2	1	0	1	2	0	0	.214	.267	.500
Mickey Stanley	4	6	0	2	0	0	0	0	0	0	0	0	.333	.333	.333
Tony Taylor	4	15	0	2	0	2	0	0	0	2	0	0	.133	.133	.267
Totals	5	162	10	32	10	6	1	4	13	25	0	2	.198	.257	.321

Pitching

Athletics	G	GS	CG	IP	H	R	ER	BB	SO	W-L	Sv-Op	Hld	ERA
Vida Blue	4	0	0	5.1	4	0	0	1	5	0-0	1-1	0	0.00
Rollie Fingers	3	0	0	5.1	4	1	1	1	3	1-0	0-0	0	1.69
Dave Hamilton	1	0	0	0.0	1	0	0	1	0	0-0	0-1	0	—
Ken Holtzman	1	1	0	4.0	4	2	2	2	2	0-1	0-0	0	4.50
Joe Horlen	1	0	0	0.0	0	1	1	1	0	0-0	0-0	0	—
Catfish Hunter	2	2	0	15.1	10	2	2	5	9	0-0	0-0	0	1.17
Bob Locker	2	0	0	2.0	4	3	3	0	1	0-0	0-0	0	13.50
Blue Moon Odom	2	2	1	14.0	5	1	0	2	5	2-0	0-0	0	0.00
Totals	5	5	1	46.0	32	10	9	13	25	3-2	1-2	0	1.76

Pitching

Tigers	G	GS	CG	IP	H	R	ER	BB	SO	W-L	Sv-Op	Hld	ERA
Joe Coleman	1	1	1	9.0	7	0	0	3	14	1-0	0-0	0	0.00
Woodie Fryman	2	2	0	12.1	11	6	5	2	8	0-2	0-0	0	3.65
John Hiller	3	0	0	3.1	1	0	0	1	1	1-0	0-0	0	0.00
Lerrin LaGrow	1	0	0	1.0	0	0	0	0	1	0-0	0-0	0	0.00
Mickey Lolich	2	2	0	19.0	14	4	3	5	10	0-1	0-0	0	1.42
Fred Scherman	1	0	0	0.2	1	0	0	0	1	0-0	0-0	0	0.00
Chuck Seelbach	2	0	0	1.0	4	2	2	0	0	0-0	0-1	0	18.00
Chris Zachary	1	0	0	0.0	0	1	1	1	0	0-0	0-0	0	—
Totals	5	5	1	46.1	38	13	11	12	35	2-3	0-1	0	2.14

Fielding

Athletics	Pos	G	PO	Ast	E	DP	PB	FPct
Matty Alou	rf	5	8	0	0	0	—	1.000
Sal Bando	3b	5	6	14	0	1	—	1.000
Vida Blue	p	4	0	1	0	0	—	1.000
Bert Campaneris	ss	2	3	7	0	1	—	1.000
Tim Cullen	ss	2	0	2	0	1	—	1.000
Dave Duncan	c	2	5	1	0	0	0	1.000
Mike Epstein	1b	5	55	2	0	5	—	1.000
Rollie Fingers	p	3	0	0	0	0	—	—
Dick Green	2b	5	5	7	0	1	—	1.000
Dave Hamilton	p	1	0	0	0	0	—	—
Mike Hegan	1b	1	1	0	0	0	—	1.000
George Hendrick	cf	1	1	0	0	0	—	1.000
Ken Holtzman	p	1	0	1	0	0	—	1.000
Joe Horlen	p	1	0	0	0	0	—	—
Catfish Hunter	p	2	0	0	0	0	—	—
Reggie Jackson	cf	5	14	0	1	0	—	.933
Ted Kubiak	2b	3	3	7	1	1	—	.909
	ss	1	0	0	0	0	—	—
Bob Locker	p	2	0	0	0	0	—	—
Dal Maxvill	ss	4	3	7	0	2	—	1.000
	2b	1	0	1	0	0	—	1.000
Blue Moon Odom	p	2	2	2	0	0	—	1.000
Joe Rudi	lf	5	11	0	0	0	—	1.000
Gene Tenace	c	5	19	3	0	0	1	1.000
	2b	2	2	2	1	1	—	.800
Totals		5	138	57	3	13	1	.985

Fielding

Tigers	Pos	G	PO	Ast	E	DP	PB	FPct
Ed Brinkman	ss	1	1	5	0	0	—	1.000
Ike Brown	1b	1	2	0	0	0	—	1.000
Norm Cash	1b	5	39	2	0	3	—	1.000
Joe Coleman	p	1	0	1	0	0	—	1.000
Bill Freehan	c	3	24	3	0	0	0	1.000
Woodie Fryman	p	2	0	3	0	1	—	1.000
John Hiller	p	3	0	0	0	0	—	—
Willie Horton	lf	3	7	0	0	0	—	1.000
Al Kaline	rf	5	13	0	1	0	—	.929
Lerrin LaGrow	p	1	0	0	0	0	—	—
Mickey Lolich	p	2	1	4	0	0	—	1.000
Dick McAuliffe	ss	4	10	7	3	2	—	.850
	2b	1	2	0	1	1	—	.667
Jim Northrup	cf	4	8	0	0	0	—	1.000
	lf	3	2	0	0	0	—	1.000
Aurelio Rodriguez	3b	5	2	13	1	2	—	.938
Fred Scherman	p	1	0	0	0	0	—	—
Chuck Seelbach	p	2	0	0	0	0	—	—
Duke Sims	c	2	13	1	0	0	0	1.000
	lf	2	3	0	1	0	—	.750
Mickey Stanley	cf	3	7	0	0	0	—	1.000
Tony Taylor	2b	4	5	9	0	2	—	1.000
Chris Zachary	p	1	0	0	0	0	—	—
Totals		5	139	48	7	11	0	.964

1972 Cincinnati Reds (NL) 3, Pittsburgh Pirates (NL) 2

The Cincinnati Reds beat the Pittsburgh Pirates in the NLCS on, of all things, a wild pitch. The Pirates took a one-run lead into the ninth inning of the fifth game, and relief ace Dave Giusti was summoned to get the final three outs. The first batter he faced, Johnny Bench, thwarted that plan with a game-tying homer. After the next two batters singled, Bob Moose was brought in. He got the next two outs, but George Foster moved to third on a fly ball. Then Moose bounced a pitch to the backstop, bringing home Foster with the run that sent Cincinnati to the World Series. Steve Blass beat the Reds 5-1 in the opener before Cincinnati bombed Moose and took a 5-3 victory in Game 2. Manny Sanguillen plated the winning run with an eighth-inning RBI groundout as the Pirates took the third game, 3-2. Ross Grimsley two-hit the Bucs for a 7-1 win in Game 4, setting the stage for Game 5. Blass tossed 7.1 strong innings and exited with a 3-2 lead, but his bullpen came up short at the end.

Game 1
Saturday, October 7

Reds	AB	R	H	RBI	BB	K	Avg
Pete Rose, lf	5	0	2	0	0	0	.400
Joe Morgan, 2b	4	1	1	1	1	0	.250
Bobby Tolan, cf	5	0	1	0	0	1	.200
Johnny Bench, c	3	0	0	0	1	0	.000
Tony Perez, 1b	4	0	1	0	0	1	.250
Denis Menke, 3b	3	0	1	0	1	0	.333
Cesar Geronimo, rf	4	0	0	0	0	0	.000
Darrel Chaney, ss	4	0	0	0	0	0	.000
Don Gullett, p	2	0	1	0	0	0	.500
Ted Uhlaender, ph	1	0	1	0	0	0	1.000
Pedro Borbon, p	0	0	0	0	0	0	—
Joe Hague, ph	0	0	0	0	1	0	—
TOTALS	35	1	8	1	4	2	.229

Pirates	AB	R	H	RBI	BB	K	Avg
Rennie Stennett, lf	4	2	2	0	0	0	.500
Al Oliver, cf	4	2	2	3	0	0	.500
Roberto Clemente, rf	4	0	0	0	0	1	.000
Willie Stargell, 1b	3	1	1	1	0	1	.333
Bob Robertson, 1b	0	0	0	0	0	0	—
Manny Sanguillen, c	3	0	0	0	0	0	.000
Richie Hebner, 3b	3	0	1	1	0	0	.333
Dave Cash, 2b	3	0	0	0	0	0	.000
Gene Alley, ss	3	0	0	0	0	0	.000
Steve Blass, p	3	0	0	0	0	1	.000
Ramon Hernandez, p	0	0	0	0	0	0	—
TOTALS	30	5	6	5	0	3	.200

	1	2	3	4	5	6	7	8	9		R	H	E
Reds	1	0	0	0	0	0	0	0	0		1	8	0
Pirates	3	0	0	0	2	0	0	0	x		5	6	0

LOB—Reds 11, Pirates 1. Scoring Position—Reds 0-for-7, Pirates 3-for-5. 2B—Rose (1), Stargell (1). 3B—Oliver (1). HR—Morgan (1), Oliver (1).

Reds	IP	H	R	ER	BB	K	ERA
Don Gullett (L, 0-1)	6.0	6	5	5	0	3	7.50
Pedro Borbon	2.0	0	0	0	0	0	0.00

Pirates	IP	H	R	ER	BB	K	ERA
Steve Blass (W, 1-0)	8.1	8	1	1	4	1	1.08
Ramon Hernandez (S, 1)	0.2	0	0	0	0	1	0.00

PB—Bench. Time—1:57. Attendance—50,476. Umpires—HP, Donatelli. 1B, Burkhart. 2B, Harvey. 3B, Williams.

Game 2
Sunday, October 8

Reds	AB	R	H	RBI	BB	K	Avg
Pete Rose, lf	4	1	1	0	0	1	.333
Joe Morgan, 2b	4	2	2	1	0	0	.375
Bobby Tolan, cf	4	1	2	2	0	1	.333
Johnny Bench, c	4	1	1	0	0	2	.143
Tony Perez, 1b	4	0	1	2	0	2	.250
Denis Menke, 3b	3	0	0	0	1	1	.167
Cesar Geronimo, rf	4	0	1	0	0	2	.125
Darrel Chaney, ss	2	0	0	0	0	0	.000
Dave Concepcion, ph-ss	2	0	0	0	0	0	.000
Jack Billingham, p	2	0	0	0	0	1	.000
Tom Hall, p	1	0	0	0	0	0	.000
TOTALS	34	5	8	5	1	10	.212

Pirates	AB	R	H	RBI	BB	K	Avg
Rennie Stennett, lf-2b	4	0	1	0	1	0	.375
Al Oliver, cf	5	1	2	0	0	2	.444
Roberto Clemente, rf	3	0	0	1	1	0	.000
Willie Stargell, 1b-lf	3	0	0	0	1	1	.167
Richie Hebner, 3b	4	0	0	0	0	2	.143
Milt May, c	2	0	1	1	0	0	.500
Manny Sanguillen, ph-c	2	1	1	0	0	0	.200
Dave Cash, 2b	4	0	1	1	0	0	.143
Dave Giusti, p	0	0	0	0	0	0	—
Gene Alley, ss	3	1	0	0	0	0	.000
Bob Moose, p	0	0	0	0	0	0	—
Bob Johnson, p	1	0	0	0	0	1	.000
Bill Mazeroski, ph	1	0	1	0	0	0	1.000
Dock Ellis, pr	0	0	0	0	0	0	—
Bruce Kison, p	0	0	0	0	0	0	—
Gene Clines, ph	1	0	0	0	0	1	.000
Ramon Hernandez, p	0	0	0	0	0	0	—
Bob Robertson, 1b	0	0	0	0	1	0	.000
TOTALS	33	3	7	3	4	8	.217

	1	2	3	4	5	6	7	8	9		R	H	E
Reds	4	0	0	0	0	0	0	1	0		5	8	1
Pirates	0	0	0	1	1	1	0	0	0		3	7	1

E—Cash, Bench. DP—Reds 1 (Morgan to Chaney to Perez), Pirates 2 (Hebner to Stargell; May to Cash). LOB—Reds 3, Pirates 8. Scoring Position—Reds 3-for-6, Pirates 3-for-10. 2B—Tolan (1), Bench (1), Perez (1), Oliver (1), Sanguillen (1). HR—Morgan (2). GDP—Menke, Stargell. CS—Tolan (1).

Reds	IP	H	R	ER	BB	K	ERA
Jack Billingham	4.2	5	2	2	4	4	3.86
Tom Hall (W, 1-0)	4.1	2	1	2	4	2.08

Pirates	IP	H	R	ER	BB	K	ERA
Bob Moose (L, 0-1)	0.0	5	4	4	0	0	—
Bob Johnson	5.0	1	0	0	1	6	0.00
Bruce Kison	1.0	0	0	0	0	2	0.00
Ramon Hernandez	2.0	1	1	1	0	1	3.38
Dave Giusti	1.0	1	0	0	0	1	0.00

Moose pitched to five batters in the 1st.

WP—Johnson. HBP—Alley by Billingham. Time—2:43. Attendance—50,584. Umpires—HP, Burkhart. 1B, Harvey. 2B, Williams. 3B, Kibler.

Game 3
Monday, October 9

Pirates	AB	R	H	RBI	BB	K	Avg
Rennie Stennett, lf	5	0	2	1	0	0	.385
Dave Cash, 2b	5	0	1	0	0	0	.167
Roberto Clemente, rf	3	0	1	0	1	1	.100
Willie Stargell, 1b	3	0	0	0	1	1	.111
Gene Clines, pr	0	1	0	0	0	0	.000
Bob Robertson, 1b	0	0	0	0	0	0	.000
Al Oliver, cf	4	0	1	0	0	1	.385
Richie Hebner, 3b	2	1	0	0	1	0	.111
Manny Sanguillen, c	4	1	2	2	0	0	.333
Gene Alley, ss	3	0	0	0	0	0	.000
Nelson Briles, p	2	0	0	0	0	1	.000
Vic Davalillo, ph	0	0	0	0	1	0	—
Bruce Kison, p	0	0	0	0	0	0	—
Dave Giusti, p	1	0	0	0	0	0	.000
TOTALS	32	3	7	3	4	4	.205

Reds	AB	R	H	RBI	BB	K	Avg
Pete Rose, lf	4	0	3	0	0	0	.462
Joe Morgan, 2b	4	1	1	1	0	1	.333
Bobby Tolan, cf	4	0	1	1	0	1	.308
Johnny Bench, c	4	0	1	0	1	0	.182
Tony Perez, 1b	4	0	1	0	0	1	.250
Dave Concepcion, pr	0	0	0	0	0	0	.000
Denis Menke, 3b	3	0	0	0	1	0	.111
Cesar Geronimo, rf	4	0	0	0	0	0	.083
Darrel Chaney, ss	3	1	1	0	0	0	.111
Gary Nolan, p	2	0	0	0	0	1	.000
Pedro Borbon, p	0	0	0	0	0	0	—
Clay Carroll, p	0	0	0	0	0	0	—
Joe Hague, ph	1	0	0	0	0	1	.000
Jim McGlothlin, p	0	0	0	0	0	0	—
TOTALS	33	2	8	2	1	6	.229

	1	2	3	4	5	6	7	8	9		R	H	E
Pirates	0	0	0	1	0	0	1	1	0		3	7	0
Reds	0	0	2	0	0	0	0	0	0		2	8	1

E—Chaney. DP—Pirates 1 (Stennett to Sanguillen), Reds 1 (Geronimo to Bench to Morgan). LOB—Pirates 8, Reds 5. Scoring Position—Pirates 1-for-9, Reds 2-for-9. 2B—Clemente (1), Oliver (2), Rose 2 (3). 3B—Bench (1). HR—Sanguillen (1). S—Alley. SB—Morgan (1). CS—Stennett (1).

Pirates	IP	H	R	ER	BB	K	ERA
Nelson Briles	6.0	6	2	2	1	3	3.00
Bruce Kison (W, 1-0)	1.1	1	0	0	0	1	0.00
Dave Giusti (S, 1)	1.2	1	0	0	0	2	0.00

Reds	IP	H	R	ER	BB	K	ERA
Gary Nolan	6.0	4	1	1	1	4	1.50
Pedro Borbon (H, 1)	0.1	1	1	1	0	0	3.86
Clay Carroll (BS, 1; L, 0-1)	1.2	2	1	1	3	0	5.40
Jim McGlothlin	1.0	0	0	0	0	0	0.00

WP—Nolan. HBP—Hebner by Borbon. Time—2:33. Attendance—52,420. Umpires—HP, Harvey. 1B, Williams. 2B, Kibler. 3B, Wendelstedt.

Game 4
Tuesday, October 10

Pirates	AB	R	H	RBI	BB	K	Avg
Rennie Stennett, lf	4	0	0	0	0	0	.294
Al Oliver, cf	4	0	0	0	0	0	.294
Roberto Clemente, rf	4	1	2	1	0	1	.214
Willie Stargell, 1b	3	0	0	0	0	0	.083
Manny Sanguillen, c	3	0	0	0	0	0	.250
Dave Cash, 2b	3	0	0	0	0	0	.133
Richie Hebner, 3b	3	0	0	0	0	1	.083
Gene Alley, ss	3	0	0	0	0	2	.000
Dock Ellis, p	1	0	0	0	0	0	.000
Bill Mazeroski, ph	1	0	0	0	0	1	.500
Bob Johnson, p	0	0	0	0	0	0	.000
Luke Walker, p	0	0	0	0	0	0	—
Gene Clines, ph	1	0	0	0	0	0	.000
Bob Miller, p	0	0	0	0	0	0	—
TOTALS	30	1	2	1	0	5	.179

Reds	AB	R	H	RBI	BB	K	Avg
Pete Rose, lf	4	0	2	1	1	0	.471
Joe Morgan, 2b	3	1	1	0	0	1	.333
Bobby Tolan, cf	4	2	1	1	0	0	.294
Johnny Bench, c	3	1	2	1	0	0	.286
Tony Perez, 1b	4	0	0	0	0	1	.188
Denis Menke, 3b	4	1	2	0	0	2	.231
Cesar Geronimo, rf	4	1	0	0	0	0	.063
Darrel Chaney, ss	3	1	1	1	1	0	.167
Ross Grimsley, p	4	0	2	1	0	1	.500
TOTALS	33	7	11	5	2	5	.266

	1	2	3	4	5	6	7	8	9		R	H	E
Pirates	0	0	0	0	0	0	1	0	0		1	2	3
Reds	1	0	0	2	0	2	2	0	x		7	11	1

E—Sanguillen, Chaney, Alley 2. LOB—Pirates 2, Reds 6. Scoring Position—Pirates 0-for-0, Reds 3-for-9. 2B—Menke (1), Grimsley (1). 3B—Tolan (1). HR—Clemente (1). S—Morgan. SF—Bench. SB—Bench 2 (2), Chaney (1).

Pirates	IP	H	R	ER	BB	K	ERA
Dock Ellis (L, 0-1)	5.0	5	3	0	1	3	0.00
Bob Johnson	1.0	3	2	2	1	1	3.00
Luke Walker	1.0	3	2	2	0	0	18.00
Bob Miller	1.0	0	0	0	0	1	0.00

Reds	IP	H	R	ER	BB	K	ERA
Ross Grimsley (W, 1-0)	9.0	2	1	1	0	5	1.00

Time—1:58. Attendance—39,447. Umpires—HP, Williams. 1B, Kibler. 2B, Wendelstedt. 3B, Donatelli.

Game 5
Wednesday, October 11

Pirates	AB	R	H	RBI	BB	K	Avg
Rennie Stennett, lf	4	0	1	0	0	0	.286
Al Oliver, cf	3	0	0	0	0	1	.250
Roberto Clemente, rf	3	0	1	0	1	1	.235
Willie Stargell, 1b	4	0	0	0	0	2	.063
Bob Robertson, 1b	0	0	0	0	0	0	—
Manny Sanguillen, c	4	2	2	0	0	0	.313
Richie Hebner, 3b	4	1	2	0	0	0	.188
Dave Cash, 2b	4	0	2	2	0	0	.211
Gene Alley, ss	4	0	0	0	0	1	.000
Steve Blass, p	3	0	0	0	0	2	.000
Ramon Hernandez, p	0	0	0	0	0	0	—
Dave Giusti, p	0	0	0	0	0	0	.000
Bob Moose, p	0	0	0	0	0	0	—
TOTALS	33	3	8	2	1	7	.189

Reds	AB	R	H	RBI	BB	K	Avg
Pete Rose, lf	3	0	1	1	0	1	.450
Joe Morgan, 2b	4	0	0	0	0	0	.263
Bobby Tolan, cf	4	0	0	0	0	1	.238
Johnny Bench, c	4	1	2	1	0	0	.333
Tony Perez, 1b	4	0	1	0	0	2	.200
George Foster, pr	0	1	0	0	0	0	—
Denis Menke, 3b	3	0	1	0	1	0	.250
Cesar Geronimo, rf	4	1	1	1	0	0	.100
Darrel Chaney, ss	4	1	1	0	0	1	.188
Don Gullett, p	0	0	0	0	0	0	.500
Pedro Borbon, p	0	0	0	0	0	0	—
Ted Uhlaender, ph	1	0	0	0	0	0	.500
Tom Hall, p	0	0	0	0	0	0	.000
Joe Hague, ph	0	0	0	0	1	0	.000
Dave Concepcion, pr	0	0	0	0	0	0	.000
Clay Carroll, p	0	0	0	0	0	0	—
Hal McRae, ph	0	0	0	0	0	0	—
TOTALS	31	4	7	3	2	5	.253

	1	2	3	4	5	6	7	8	9		R	H	E
Pirates	0	2	0	1	0	0	0	0	0		3	8	0
Reds	0	0	1	0	1	0	0	0	2		4	7	1

E—Chaney. DP—Reds 1 (Morgan to Chaney to Perez). LOB—Pirates 5, Reds 5. Scoring Position—Pirates 2-for-9, Reds 1-for-7. 2B—Hebner (1), Rose (4). HR—Bench (1), Geronimo (1). S—Oliver, Rose, Gullett. GDP—Blass.

Pirates	IP	H	R	ER	BB	K	ERA
Steve Blass	7.1	4	2	2	2	4	1.72
Ramon Hernandez (H, 1)	0.2	0	0	0	0	1	2.70
Dave Giusti (BS, 1; L, 0-1)	0.0	3	2	2	0	0	6.75
Bob Moose	0.2	0	0	0	0	0	54.00

Reds	IP	H	R	ER	BB	K	ERA
Don Gullett	3.0	6	3	3	0	2	8.00
Pedro Borbon	2.0	1	0	0	0	1	2.08
Tom Hall	3.0	1	0	0	1	4	1.23
Clay Carroll (W, 1-1)	1.0	0	0	0	0	0	3.38

Gullett pitched to two batters in the 4th. Giusti pitched to three batters in the 9th.

WP—Gullett, Moose. Time—2:19. Attendance—41,887. Umpires—HP, Donatelli. 1B, Williams. 2B, Kibler. 3B, Wendelstedt.

Postseason: League Championship Series

1972 NL Championship Series—Composite Statistics

Batting

Reds	G	AB	R	H	RBI	2B	3B	HR	BB	SO	SB	CS	Avg	OBP	Slg
Johnny Bench	5	18	3	6	2	1	1	1	1	3	2	0	.333	.350	.667
Jack Billingham	1	2	0	0	0	0	0	0	0	1	0	0	.000	.000	.000
Darrel Chaney	5	16	3	3	1	0	0	0	1	1	1	0	.188	.235	.188
Dave Concepcion	3	2	0	0	0	0	0	0	0	0	0	0	.000	.000	.000
George Foster	1	0	1	0	0	0	0	0	0	0	0	0	—	—	—
Cesar Geronimo	5	20	2	2	1	0	0	1	0	2	0	0	.100	.100	.250
Ross Grimsley	1	4	0	2	1	1	0	0	0	1	0	0	.500	.500	.750
Don Gullett	2	2	0	1	0	0	0	0	0	0	0	0	.500	.500	.500
Joe Hague	3	1	0	0	0	0	0	0	2	1	0	0	.000	.667	.000
Tom Hall	2	1	0	0	0	0	0	0	0	0	0	0	.000	.000	.000
Hal McRae	1	0	0	0	0	0	0	0	0	0	0	0	—	—	—
Denis Menke	5	16	1	4	0	1	0	0	4	3	0	0	.250	.400	.313
Joe Morgan	5	19	5	5	3	0	0	2	1	2	1	0	.263	.300	.579
Gary Nolan	1	2	0	0	0	0	0	0	0	1	0	0	.000	.000	.000
Tony Perez	5	20	0	4	2	1	0	0	0	7	0	0	.200	.200	.250
Pete Rose	5	20	1	9	2	4	0	0	1	2	0	0	.450	.476	.650
Bobby Tolan	5	21	3	5	4	1	1	0	0	4	0	1	.238	.238	.381
Ted Uhlaender	2	2	0	1	0	0	0	0	0	0	0	0	.500	.500	.500
Totals	5	166	19	42	16	9	2	4	10	28	4	1	.253	.294	.404

Batting

Pirates	G	AB	R	H	RBI	2B	3B	HR	BB	SO	SB	CS	Avg	OBP	Slg
Gene Alley	5	16	1	0	0	0	0	0	0	3	0	0	.000	.059	.000
Steve Blass	2	6	0	0	0	0	0	0	0	3	0	0	.000	.000	.000
Nelson Briles	1	2	0	0	0	0	0	0	0	1	0	0	.000	.000	.000
Dave Cash	5	19	0	4	3	0	0	0	0	0	0	0	.211	.211	.211
Roberto Clemente	5	17	1	4	2	1	0	1	3	5	0	0	.235	.350	.471
Gene Clines	3	2	1	0	0	0	0	0	0	1	0	0	.000	.000	.000
Vic Davalillo	1	0	0	0	0	0	0	0	1	0	0	0	—	1.000	—
Dock Ellis	2	1	0	0	0	0	0	0	0	0	0	0	.000	.000	.000
Dave Giusti	3	1	0	0	0	0	0	0	0	0	0	0	.000	.000	.000
Richie Hebner	5	16	2	3	1	1	0	0	1	3	0	0	.188	.278	.250
Bob Johnson	2	1	0	0	0	0	0	0	0	1	0	0	.000	.000	.000
Milt May	1	2	0	1	1	0	0	0	0	0	0	0	.500	.500	.500
Bill Mazeroski	2	2	0	1	0	0	0	0	0	1	0	0	.500	.500	.500
Al Oliver	5	20	3	5	3	2	1	1	0	4	0	0	.250	.250	.600
Bob Robertson	4	0	0	0	0	0	0	0	1	0	0	0	—	1.000	—
Manny Sanguillen	5	16	4	5	2	1	0	1	0	0	0	0	.313	.313	.563
Willie Stargell	5	16	1	1	1	0	0	0	2	5	0	0	.063	.167	.125
Rennie Stennett	5	21	2	6	1	0	0	0	1	0	0	1	.286	.318	.286
Totals	5	158	15	30	14	6	1	3	9	27	0	1	.190	.243	.297

Pitching

Reds	G	GS	CG	IP	H	R	ER	BB	SO	W-L	Sv-Op	Hld	ERA
Jack Billingham	1	1	0	4.2	5	2	2	2	4	0-0	0-0	0	3.86
Pedro Borbon	3	0	0	4.1	2	1	1	0	1	0-0	0-0	1	2.08
Clay Carroll	2	0	0	2.2	2	1	1	3	0	1-1	0-1	0	3.38
Ross Grimsley	1	1	1	9.0	2	1	1	0	5	1-0	0-0	0	1.00
Don Gullett	2	2	0	9.0	12	8	8	0	5	0-1	0-0	0	8.00
Tom Hall	2	0	0	7.1	3	1	1	3	8	1-0	0-0	0	1.23
Jim McGlothlin	1	0	0	1.0	0	0	0	0	0	0-0	0-0	0	0.00
Gary Nolan	1	1	0	6.0	4	1	1	1	4	0-0	0-0	0	1.50
Totals	5	5	1	44.0	30	15	15	9	27	3-2	0-1	1	3.07

Pitching

Pirates	G	GS	CG	IP	H	R	ER	BB	SO	W-L	Sv-Op	Hld	ERA
Steve Blass	2	2	0	15.2	12	3	3	6	5	1-0	0-0	0	1.72
Nelson Briles	1	1	0	6.0	6	2	2	1	3	0-0	0-0	0	3.00
Dock Ellis	1	1	0	5.0	5	3	0	1	3	0-1	0-0	0	0.00
Dave Giusti	3	0	0	2.2	5	2	2	0	3	0-1	1-2	0	6.75
Ramon Hernandez	3	0	0	3.1	1	1	1	0	3	0-0	1-1	1	2.70
Bob Johnson	2	0	0	6.0	4	2	2	2	7	0-0	0-0	0	3.00
Bruce Kison	2	0	0	2.1	1	0	0	0	3	1-0	0-0	0	0.00
Bob Miller	1	0	0	1.0	0	0	0	0	1	0-0	0-0	0	0.00
Bob Moose	2	1	0	0.2	5	4	4	0	0	0-1	0-0	0	54.00
Luke Walker	1	0	0	1.0	3	2	2	0	0	0-0	0-0	0	18.00
Totals	5	5	0	43.2	42	19	16	10	28	2-3	2-3	1	3.30

Fielding

Reds	Pos	G	PO	Ast	E	DP	PB	FPct
Johnny Bench	c	5	29	3	1	1	1	.970
Jack Billingham	p	1	1	0	0	0	—	1.000
Pedro Borbon	p	3	1	0	0	0	—	1.000
Clay Carroll	p	2	0	1	0	0	—	1.000
Darrel Chaney	ss	5	8	16	3	2	—	.889
Dave Concepcion	ss	1	0	0	0	0	—	—
Cesar Geronimo	rf	5	9	1	0	1	—	1.000
Ross Grimsley	p	1	0	0	0	0	—	—
Don Gullett	p	2	0	0	0	0	—	—
Tom Hall	p	2	1	0	0	0	—	1.000
Jim McGlothlin	p	1	0	0	0	0	—	—
Denis Menke	3b	5	3	11	0	0	—	1.000
Joe Morgan	2b	5	12	18	0	3	—	1.000
Gary Nolan	p	1	0	0	0	0	—	—
Tony Perez	1b	5	45	3	0	2	—	1.000
Pete Rose	lf	5	10	0	0	0	—	1.000
Bobby Tolan	cf	5	13	0	0	0	—	1.000
Totals		5	132	53	4	9	1	.979

Fielding

Pirates	Pos	G	PO	Ast	E	DP	PB	FPct
Gene Alley	ss	5	10	4	2	0	—	.875
Steve Blass	p	2	1	3	0	0	—	1.000
Nelson Briles	p	1	1	1	0	0	—	1.000
Dave Cash	2b	5	5	10	1	1	—	.938
Roberto Clemente	rf	5	9	0	0	0	—	1.000
Dock Ellis	p	1	0	0	0	0	—	—
Dave Giusti	p	3	0	1	0	0	—	1.000
Richie Hebner	3b	5	5	11	0	1	—	1.000
Ramon Hernandez	p	3	0	0	0	0	—	—
Bob Johnson	p	2	0	0	0	0	—	—
Bruce Kison	p	2	0	0	0	0	—	—
Milt May	c	1	8	1	0	1	0	1.000
Bob Miller	p	1	0	0	0	0	—	—
Bob Moose	p	2	0	0	0	0	—	—
Al Oliver	cf	5	17	1	0	0	—	1.000
Bob Robertson	1b	4	3	0	0	0	—	1.000
Manny Sanguillen	c	5	22	0	1	1	0	.957
Willie Stargell	1b	5	31	3	0	1	—	1.000
	lf	1	0	0	0	0	—	—
Rennie Stennett	lf	5	18	1	0	1	—	1.000
	2b	1	1	0	0	0	—	1.000
Luke Walker	p	1	0	0	0	0	—	—
Totals		5	131	36	4	6	0	.977

1973 Oakland Athletics (AL) 3, Baltimore Orioles (AL) 2

The Oakland A's wrested the AL flag from the Baltimore Orioles in the full five games. Baltimore knocked out Vida Blue in the first inning of Game 1 and Jim Palmer spun a five-hit shutout for a 6-0 win. The next day, Sal Bando blasted a pair of homers, and Joe Rudi and Bert Campaneris also went deep as the A's beat Baltimore, 6-3. Campaneris won Game 3 with a solo shot off Mike Cuellar in the bottom of the 11th. Ken Holtzman pitched all 11 innings for the win, while Cuellar tossed 10 four-hit innings but wound up with the loss. Vida Blue took a 4-0 lead into the seventh inning of Game 4 when the O's began to rally. Andy Etchebarren's three-run shot tied the score, and Bobby Grich homered off Rollie Fingers in the eighth for a 5-4 Baltimore win. Catfish Hunter was magnificent in Game 5, tossing a five-hit shutout to put the A's back in the World Series.

Game 1

Saturday, October 6

Athletics	AB	R	H	RBI	BB	K	Avg
Bert Campaneris, ss	3	0	1	0	1	0	.333
Joe Rudi, lf	2	0	0	0	2	0	.000
Sal Bando, 3b	3	0	0	0	1	1	.000
Reggie Jackson, rf	4	0	1	0	0	2	.250
Deron Johnson, dh	2	0	0	0	0	2	.000
Pat Bourque, ph-dh	1	0	0	0	1	1	.000
Gene Tenace, 1b-c	4	0	1	0	0	0	.250
Angel Mangual, cf	4	0	0	0	0	2	.000
Ray Fosse, c	2	0	0	0	0	1	.000
Vic Davalillo, ph-1b	2	0	2	0	0	0	1.000
Dick Green, 2b	2	0	0	0	0	0	.000
Jesus Alou, ph	1	0	0	0	0	1	.000
Ted Kubiak, 2b	1	0	0	0	0	0	.000
TOTALS	31	0	5	0	5	12	.161

Orioles	AB	R	H	RBI	BB	K	Avg
Merv Rettenmund, rf	4	1	1	0	1	0	.250
Bobby Grich, 2b	5	0	0	0	0	2	.000
Paul Blair, cf	4	2	1	0	1	2	.250
Tommy Davis, dh	5	1	3	1	0	0	.600
Don Baylor, lf	3	2	2	1	2	1	.667
Brooks Robinson, 3b	5	0	0	0	0	1	.000
Earl Williams, 1b	4	0	2	2	0	0	.500
Andy Etchebarren, c	3	0	2	1	0	1	.667
Mark Belanger, ss	3	0	1	1	1	0	.333
TOTALS	36	6	12	6	5	7	.333

	1	2	3	4	5	6	7	8	9		R	H	E
Athletics	0	0	0	0	0	0	0	0	0		0	5	1
Orioles	4	0	0	0	0	0	1	1	x		6	12	0

E—Campaneris. DP—Athletics 1 (Fosse to Green). LOB—Athletics 9, Orioles 12. Scoring Position—Athletics 0-for-9, Orioles 6-for-14. 2B—Davis (1), Williams (1), Davalillo (1). GDP—Kubiak. SB—Campaneris (1). CS—Rettenmund (1).

Athletics	IP	H	R	ER	BB	K	ERA
Vida Blue (L, 0-1)	0.2	3	4	4	2	2	54.00
Horacio Pina	2.0	3	0	0	1	0	0.00
Blue Moon Odom	5.0	6	2	1	2	4	1.80
Rollie Fingers	0.1	0	0	0	0	0	0.00

Orioles	IP	H	R	ER	BB	K	ERA
Jim Palmer (W, 1-0)	9.0	5	0	0	5	12	0.00

WP—Blue. HBP—Etchebarren by Pina. Time—2:51. Attendance—41,279. Umpires—HP, Chylak. 1B, Haller. 2B, Maloney. 3B, Odom.

Game 2

Sunday, October 7

Athletics	AB	R	H	RBI	BB	K	Avg
Bert Campaneris, ss	5	2	3	2	0	0	.500
Joe Rudi, lf	4	1	2	1	1	0	.333
Sal Bando, 3b	4	2	2	3	1	1	.286
Reggie Jackson, rf	5	0	0	0	0	2	.111
Gene Tenace, 1b	3	0	0	0	1	2	.143
Deron Johnson, dh	4	0	1	0	0	1	.167
Angel Mangual, cf	4	1	1	0	0	1	.125
Ray Fosse, c	3	0	0	0	0	0	.000
Dick Green, 2b	4	0	0	0	0	2	.000
TOTALS	36	6	9	6	3	9	.194

Orioles	AB	R	H	RBI	BB	K	Avg
Al Bumbry, lf	4	1	0	0	1	2	.000
Rich Coggins, rf-cf	5	1	2	0	0	0	.400
Tommy Davis, dh	5	0	2	1	0	0	.500
Boog Powell, 1b	4	1	0	0	0	1	.000
Earl Williams, c	4	0	2	1	0	1	.500
Paul Blair, cf	3	0	0	0	0	1	.143
Terry Crowley, ph-rf	1	0	0	0	0	0	.000
Brooks Robinson, 3b	3	0	1	1	1	0	.125
Don Hood, pr	0	0	0	0	0	0	—
Frank Baker, ss	0	0	0	0	0	0	—
Bobby Grich, 2b	2	0	0	0	2	1	.000
Mark Belanger, ss	3	0	1	0	0	0	.333
Don Baylor, ph	1	0	0	0	0	0	.500
Larry Brown, 3b	0	0	0	0	0	0	—
TOTALS	35	3	8	3	4	6	.266

	1	2	3	4	5	6	7	8	9		R	H	E
Athletics	1	0	0	0	0	2	0	2	1		6	9	0
Orioles	1	0	0	0	0	1	0	1	0		3	8	0

LOB—Athletics 7, Orioles 9. Scoring Position—Athletics 2-for-7, Orioles 2-for-9. 2B—Williams (2). HR—Campaneris (1), Rudi (1), Bando 2 (2). S—Fosse. SB—Campaneris 2 (3).

Athletics	IP	H	R	ER	BB	K	ERA
Catfish Hunter (W, 1-0)	7.1	7	3	3	3	5	3.68
Rollie Fingers (S, 1)	1.2	1	0	0	1	1	0.00

Orioles	IP	H	R	ER	BB	K	ERA
Dave McNally (L, 0-1)	7.2	7	5	5	2	7	5.87
Bob Reynolds	1.0	2	1	1	1	2	9.00
Grant Jackson	0.1	0	0	0	0	0	0.00

WP—McNally. PB—Williams. Time—2:42. Attendance—48,425. Umpires—HP, Haller. 1B, Chylak. 2B, Maloney. 3B, Odom.

Game 3

Tuesday, October 9

Orioles	AB	R	H	RBI	BB	K	Avg
Merv Rettenmund, rf	5	0	0	0	0	2	.111
Bobby Grich, 2b	5	0	1	0	0	0	.083
Paul Blair, cf	4	0	1	0	0	1	.182
Tommy Davis, dh	3	0	0	0	1	0	.385
Don Baylor, lf	4	0	0	0	0	3	.250
Brooks Robinson, 3b	4	0	0	0	0	0	.083
Earl Williams, 1b	4	1	1	1	0	0	.417
Andy Etchebarren, c	4	0	0	0	0	0	.286
Mark Belanger, ss	4	0	0	0	0	1	.200
TOTALS	37	1	3	1	1	7	.223

Athletics	AB	R	H	RBI	BB	K	Avg
Bert Campaneris, ss	5	1	1	1	0	1	.385
Joe Rudi, lf	4	0	1	0	0	0	.300
Sal Bando, 3b	4	0	0	0	0	2	.182
Reggie Jackson, rf	4	0	0	0	0	2	.077
Gene Tenace, 1b-c	4	0	1	0	0	1	.182
Deron Johnson, dh	2	0	0	0	2	1	.125
Billy Conigliaro, cf	4	0	0	0	0	2	.000
Ray Fosse, c	1	0	0	0	1	1	.000
Jesus Alou, ph	1	0	1	0	0	0	.500
Allan Lewis, pr	0	1	0	0	0	0	—
Vic Davalillo, 1b	1	0	0	0	0	0	.667
Dick Green, 2b	2	0	0	0	0	0	.000
Mike Andrews, ph	0	0	0	0	0	0	—
Ted Kubiak, 2b	1	0	0	0	0	1	.000
TOTALS	33	2	4	2	3	11	.187

	1	2	3	4	5	6	7	8	9	10	11		R	H	E
Orioles	0	1	0	0	0	0	0	0	0	0	0		1	3	0
Athletics	0	0	0	0	0	0	0	1	0	0	1		2	4	3

E—Campaneris, Davalillo, Green. DP—Athletics 1 (Holtzman to Green to Tenace). LOB—Orioles 4, Athletics 5. Scoring Position—Orioles 0-for-2, Athletics 1-for-3. HR—Williams (1), Campaneris (2). S—Andrews. GDP—Baylor.

Orioles	IP	H	R	ER	BB	K	ERA
Mike Cuellar (L, 0-1)	10.0	4	2	2	3	11	1.80

Athletics	IP	H	R	ER	BB	K	ERA
Ken Holtzman (W, 1-0)	11.0	3	1	1	1	7	0.82

Cuellar pitched to one batter in the 11th.

Time—2:23. Attendance—34,367. Umpires—HP, Maloney. 1B, Haller. 2B, Anthony. 3B, Chylak.

Postseason: League Championship Series

Game 4

Wednesday, October 10

Orioles	AB	R	H	RBI	BB	K	Avg
Merv Rettenmund, rf	2	0	0	0	2	0	.091
Bobby Grich, 2b	4	1	1	1	0	1	.125
Paul Blair, cf	4	0	1	0	0	1	.200
Tommy Davis, dh	4	0	1	0	0	0	.353
Earl Williams, 1b	3	1	0	0	1	1	.333
Don Baylor, lf	3	1	1	0	1	1	.273
Brooks Robinson, 3b	4	1	2	1	0	0	.188
Andy Etchebarren, c	4	1	2	3	0	0	.364
Mark Belanger, ss	4	0	0	0	0	0	.143
TOTALS	32	5	8	5	4	4	.230

Athletics	AB	R	H	RBI	BB	K	Avg
Bert Campaneris, ss	4	0	1	0	1	0	.353
Joe Rudi, lf	4	0	0	0	0	1	.214
Sal Bando, 3b	3	0	0	0	1	2	.143
Reggie Jackson, rf	4	0	1	0	0	0	.118
Gene Tenace, 1b-c	3	2	1	0	1	0	.214
Vic Davalillo, cf	3	1	2	0	0	0	.667
Angel Mangual, ph-cf	1	0	0	0	0	0	.111
Deron Johnson, dh	2	0	0	0	0	2	.100
Pat Bourque, ph-dh	0	0	0	0	1	0	.000
Mike Andrews, ph-1b	1	0	0	0	0	0	.000
Ray Fosse, c	2	1	1	3	1	0	.125
Allan Lewis, pr	0	0	0	0	0	0	—
Ted Kubiak, 2b	0	0	0	0	0	0	.000
Dick Green, 2b	3	0	1	1	0	0	.091
Jesus Alou, ph	1	0	0	0	0	0	.333
Rollie Fingers, p	0	0	0	0	0	0	—
TOTALS	31	4	7	4	5	5	.197

	1 2 3	4 5 6	7 8 9	R	H	E
Orioles	0 0 0	0 0 0	4 1 0	5	8	0
Athletics	0 3 0	0 0 1	0 0 0	4	7	0

DP—Athletics 2 (Campaneris to Green to Tenace; Fosse to Green). LOB—Orioles 4, Athletics 8. Scoring Position—Orioles 2-for-6, Athletics 3-for-9. 2B—Robinson (1), Tenace (1), Fosse (1), Green (1). HR—Grich (1), Etchebarren (1). S—Rudi. SF—Fosse. GDP—Davis. CS—Rettenmund (2), Davis (1), RJackson (1).

Orioles	IP	H	R	ER	BB	K	ERA
Jim Palmer	1.1	4	3	3	2	2	2.61
Bob Reynolds	4.2	3	1	1	2	3	3.18
Eddie Watt	0.1	0	0	0	0	0	0.00
Grant Jackson (W, 1-0)	2.2	0	0	0	1	0	0.00

Athletics	IP	H	R	ER	BB	K	ERA
Vida Blue	6.1	5	4	4	3	1	10.29
Rollie Fingers (L, 0-1)	2.2	3	1	1	1	3	1.93

Reynolds pitched to one batter in the 7th.

HBP—Bando by Watt. Time—2:31. Attendance—27,497. Umpires—HP, Chylak. 1B, Haller. 2B, Maloney. 3B, Odom.

Game 5

Thursday, October 11

Orioles	AB	R	H	RBI	BB	K	Avg
Al Bumbry, lf	3	0	0	0	1	0	.000
Rich Coggins, rf	4	0	2	0	0	0	.444
Tommy Davis, dh	4	0	0	0	0	0	.286
Earl Williams, 1b	3	0	0	0	1	0	.278
Paul Blair, cf	3	0	0	0	0	0	.167
Brooks Robinson, 3b	4	0	2	0	0	0	.250
Bobby Grich, 2b	4	0	0	0	0	1	.100
Andy Etchebarren, c	3	0	1	0	0	0	.357
Mark Belanger, ss	2	0	0	0	0	0	.125
Terry Crowley, ph	1	0	0	0	0	0	.000
Frank Baker, ss	0	0	0	0	0	0	—
TOTALS	31	0	5	0	2	1	.221

Athletics	AB	R	H	RBI	BB	K	Avg
Bert Campaneris, ss	4	0	1	0	0	1	.333
Joe Rudi, lf	4	0	1	1	0	0	.222
Sal Bando, 3b	4	0	1	0	0	0	.167
Reggie Jackson, rf	4	0	1	0	0	0	.143
Gene Tenace, 1b	3	1	1	0	0	1	.235
Vic Davalillo, cf	2	1	1	1	1	0	.625
Jesus Alou, dh	3	0	1	1	0	0	.333
Ray Fosse, c	3	1	0	0	0	0	.091
Dick Green, 2b	2	0	0	0	0	0	.077
TOTALS	29	3	7	3	1	2	.226

	1 2 3	4 5 6	7 8 9	R	H	E
Orioles	0 0 0	0 0 0	0 0 0	0	5	2
Athletics	0 0 1	2 0 0	0 0 x	3	7	0

E—Bumbry, Robinson. DP—Orioles 1 (Alexander to Grich to Williams). LOB—Orioles 7, Athletics 5. Scoring Position—Orioles 0-for-7, Athletics 2-for-6. 2B—Coggins (1), Robinson (2), Etchebarren (1), Campaneris (1). 3B—Davalillo (1). S—Green. GDP—Davalillo. SB—Bumbry (1). CS—Blair (1).

Orioles	IP	H	R	ER	BB	K	ERA
Doyle Alexander (L, 0-1)	3.2	5	3	2	0	1	4.91
Jim Palmer	4.1	2	0	0	1	1	1.84

Athletics	IP	H	R	ER	BB	K	ERA
Catfish Hunter (W, 2-0)	9.0	5	0	0	2	1	1.65

HBP—Blair by Hunter, Tenace by Alexander. Time—2:11. Attendance—24,265. Umpires—HP, Haller. 1B, Chylak. 2B, Maloney. 3B, Odom.

1973 AL Championship Series—Composite Statistics

Batting

Athletics	G	AB	R	H	RBI	2B	3B	HR	BB	SO	SB	CS	Avg	OBP	Slg
Jesus Alou	4	6	0	2	1	0	0	0	0	1	0	0	.333	.333	.333
Mike Andrews	2	1	0	0	0	0	0	0	0	0	0	0	.000	.000	.000
Sal Bando	5	18	2	3	3	0	0	2	3	6	0	0	.167	.318	.500
Pat Bourque	2	1	0	0	0	0	0	0	2	1	0	0	.000	.667	.000
Bert Campaneris	5	21	3	7	3	1	0	2	2	2	3	0	.333	.391	.667
Billy Conigliaro	1	4	0	0	0	0	0	0	0	2	0	0	.000	.000	.000
Vic Davalillo	4	8	2	5	1	1	1	1	0	1	0	0	.625	.667	1.000
Ray Fosse	5	11	2	1	3	1	0	0	2	2	0	0	.091	.214	.182
Dick Green	5	13	0	1	1	1	0	0	0	4	0	0	.077	.077	.154
Reggie Jackson	5	21	0	3	0	0	0	0	0	6	0	1	.143	.143	.143
Deron Johnson	4	10	0	1	0	0	0	0	2	6	0	0	.100	.250	.100
Ted Kubiak	3	2	0	0	0	0	0	0	0	1	0	0	.000	.000	.000
Allan Lewis	2	0	1	0	0	0	0	0	0	0	0	0	—	—	—
Angel Mangual	3	9	1	1	0	0	0	0	0	3	0	0	.111	.111	.111
Joe Rudi	5	18	1	4	3	0	0	1	3	1	0	0	.222	.333	.389
Gene Tenace	5	17	3	4	0	1	0	0	2	4	0	0	.235	.350	.294
Totals	5	160	15	32	15	5	1	5	17	39	3	1	.200	.283	.338

Batting

Orioles	G	AB	R	H	RBI	2B	3B	HR	BB	SO	SB	CS	Avg	OBP	Slg
Don Baylor	4	11	3	3	1	0	0	0	3	5	0	0	.273	.429	.273
Mark Belanger	5	16	0	2	1	0	0	1	1	1	0	0	.125	.176	.125
Paul Blair	5	18	2	3	0	0	0	0	1	5	0	1	.167	.250	.167
Al Bumbry	2	7	1	0	0	0	0	0	2	2	1	0	.000	.222	.000
Rich Coggins	2	9	1	4	0	1	0	0	0	0	0	0	.444	.444	.556
Terry Crowley	2	2	0	0	0	0	0	0	0	0	0	0	.000	.000	.000
Tommy Davis	5	21	1	6	2	1	0	0	1	0	0	1	.286	.318	.333
Andy Etchebarren	4	14	1	5	4	1	0	1	0	1	0	0	.357	.400	.643
Bobby Grich	5	20	1	2	1	0	0	1	2	5	0	0	.100	.182	.250
Don Hood	1	0	0	0	0	0	0	0	0	0	0	0	—	—	—
Boog Powell	1	4	1	0	0	0	0	0	0	1	0	0	.000	.000	.000
Merv Rettenmund	3	11	1	1	0	0	0	0	3	2	0	2	.091	.286	.091
Brooks Robinson	5	20	1	5	3	2	0	0	1	1	0	0	.250	.286	.350
Earl Williams	5	18	2	5	4	2	0	1	2	2	0	0	.278	.350	.556
Totals	5	171	15	36	15	7	0	3	16	25	1	4	.211	.286	.304

Pitching

Athletics	G	GS	CG	IP	H	R	ER	BB	SO	W-L	Sv-Op	Hld	ERA
Vida Blue	2	2	0	7.0	8	8	8	5	3	0-1	0-0	0	10.29
Rollie Fingers	3	0	0	4.2	4	1	1	2	4	0-1	1-1	0	1.93
Ken Holtzman	1	1	1	11.0	3	1	1	1	7	1-0	0-0	0	0.82
Catfish Hunter	2	2	1	16.1	12	3	3	5	6	2-0	0-0	0	1.65
Blue Moon Odom	1	0	0	5.0	6	2	1	2	4	0-0	0-0	0	1.80
Horacio Pina	1	0	0	2.0	3	0	0	1	1	0-0	0-0	0	0.00
Totals	5	5	2	46.0	36	15	14	16	25	3-2	1-1	0	2.74

Pitching

Orioles	G	GS	CG	IP	H	R	ER	BB	SO	W-L	Sv-Op	Hld	ERA
Doyle Alexander	1	1	0	3.2	5	3	2	0	1	0-1	0-0	0	4.91
Mike Cuellar	1	1	1	10.0	4	2	2	3	11	0-1	0-0	0	1.80
Grant Jackson	2	0	0	3.0	0	0	0	1	0	1-0	0-0	0	0.00
Dave McNally	1	1	0	7.2	7	5	5	5	7	0-1	0-0	0	5.87
Jim Palmer	3	2	1	14.2	11	3	3	8	15	1-0	0-0	0	1.84
Bob Reynolds	2	0	0	5.2	5	2	2	3	5	0-0	0-0	0	3.18
Eddie Watt	1	0	0	0.1	0	0	0	0	0	0-0	0-0	0	0.00
Totals	5	5	2	45.0	32	15	14	17	39	2-3	0-0	0	2.80

Fielding

Athletics	Pos	G	PO	Ast	E	DP	PB	FPct
Mike Andrews	1b	1	1	0	0	0	—	1.000
Sal Bando	3b	5	7	11	0	0	—	1.000
Vida Blue	p	2	1	0	0	0	—	1.000
Bert Campaneris	ss	5	6	14	2	1	—	.909
Billy Conigliaro	cf	1	5	0	0	0	—	1.000
Vic Davalillo	cf	2	4	0	0	0	—	1.000
	1b	2	3	0	1	0	—	.750
Rollie Fingers	p	3	0	0	0	0	—	—
Ray Fosse	c	5	25	4	0	2	0	1.000
Dick Green	2b	5	12	11	1	4	—	.958
Ken Holtzman	p	1	1	2	0	1	—	1.000
Catfish Hunter	p	2	1	0	0	0	—	1.000
Reggie Jackson	rf	5	19	0	0	0	—	1.000
Ted Kubiak	2b	3	0	1	0	0	—	1.000
Angel Mangual	cf	3	2	0	0	0	—	1.000
Blue Moon Odom	p	1	0	1	0	0	—	1.000
Horacio Pina	p	1	0	0	0	0	—	—
Joe Rudi	lf	5	11	0	0	0	—	1.000
Gene Tenace	1b	5	38	3	0	2	—	1.000
	c	3	2	0	0	0	0	1.000
Totals		5	138	47	4	10	0	.979

Fielding

Orioles	Pos	G	PO	Ast	E	DP	PB	FPct
Doyle Alexander	p	1	0	2	0	1	—	1.000
Frank Baker	ss	2	0	0	0	0	—	—
Don Baylor	lf	3	7	0	0	0	—	1.000
Mark Belanger	ss	5	8	17	0	1	—	1.000
Paul Blair	cf	5	8	0	0	0	—	1.000
Larry Brown	3b	1	0	0	0	0	—	—
Al Bumbry	lf	2	4	1	1	0	—	.833
Rich Coggins	rf	2	4	0	0	0	—	1.000
	cf	1	0	0	0	0	—	—
Terry Crowley	rf	1	1	0	0	0	—	1.000
Mike Cuellar	p	1	0	2	0	0	—	1.000
Andy Etchebarren	c	4	30	2	0	0	0	1.000
Bobby Grich	2b	5	17	9	0	1	—	1.000
Grant Jackson	p	2	0	0	0	0	—	—
Dave McNally	p	1	0	0	0	0	—	—
Jim Palmer	p	3	1	1	0	1	—	1.000
Boog Powell	1b	1	7	0	0	0	—	1.000
Merv Rettenmund	rf	3	2	0	0	0	—	1.000
Bob Reynolds	p	2	1	0	0	0	—	1.000
Brooks Robinson	3b	5	2	14	1	0	—	.941
Eddie Watt	p	1	0	1	0	0	—	1.000
Earl Williams	1b	4	35	2	0	2	—	1.000
	c	1	8	0	0	0	1	1.000
Totals		5	135	51	2	6	1	.989

1973 New York Mets (NL) 3, Cincinnati Reds (NL) 2

On the strength of their starting pitching, the New York Mets defeated the heavily-favored Cincinnati Reds in five games. Tom Seaver nearly won the opener himself when he doubled in a run and took a 1-0 lead into the bottom of the eighth. The Reds turned it around, though, tying it in the eighth on a home run by Pete Rose and winning it in the ninth on another by Johnny Bench. Jon Matlack evened the series with a two-hit shutout in Game 2. Rusty Staub hit a pair of homers in Game 3, and Jerry Koosman went the distance for a 9-2 Mets victory in a game that featured a brawl involving Rose and Met shortstop Bud Harrelson. Rose homered in the bottom of the 12th inning of Game 4 to give the Reds a 2-1 win and force a fifth game. This time, Seaver was not to be denied, and he teamed with Tug McGraw for a 7-2 victory to clinch the NL title.

Game 1

Saturday, October 6

Mets	AB	R	H	RBI	BB	K	Avg
Wayne Garrett, 3b	4	0	1	0	0	0	.250
Felix Millan, 2b	3	0	0	0	0	0	.000
Rusty Staub, rf	2	0	0	0	2	0	.000
John Milner, 1b	3	0	1	0	1	1	.333
Cleon Jones, lf	4	0	0	0	0	1	.000
Jerry Grote, c	4	0	0	0	0	1	.000
Don Hahn, cf	3	0	0	0	0	2	.000
Bud Harrelson, ss	2	1	0	0	1	0	.000
Tom Seaver, p	3	0	1	1	0	1	.333
TOTALS	28	1	3	1	4	6	.107

Reds	AB	R	H	RBI	BB	K	Avg
Pete Rose, lf	4	1	1	1	0	1	.250
Joe Morgan, 2b	4	0	0	0	0	1	.000
Dan Driessen, 3b	4	0	1	0	0	1	.250
Tony Perez, 1b	4	0	0	0	0	1	.000
Johnny Bench, c	4	1	3	1	0	1	.750
Ken Griffey Sr., rf	2	0	0	0	0	1	.000
Cesar Geronimo, cf	3	0	1	0	0	2	.333
Darrel Chaney, ss	2	0	0	0	0	2	.000
Larry Stahl, ph	1	0	0	0	0	1	.000
Ed Crosby, ss	0	0	0	0	0	0	—
Jack Billingham, p	1	0	0	0	0	1	.000
Hal King, ph	1	0	0	0	0	1	.000
Tom Hall, p	0	0	0	0	0	0	—
Pedro Borbon, p	0	0	0	0	0	0	—
TOTALS	30	2	6	2	0	13	.200

	1	2	3	4	5	6	7	8	9		R	H	E
Mets	0	1	0	0	0	0	0	0	0		1	3	0
Reds	0	0	0	0	0	0	0	1	1		2	6	0

DP—Reds 1 (Chaney to Morgan to Perez). LOB—Mets 5, Reds 5. Scoring Position—Mets 1-for-3, Reds 0-for-6. 2B—Seaver (1), Driessen (1), Bench (1). HR—Rose (1), Bench (1). S—Millan, Billingham. GDP—Jones.

Mets	IP	H	R	ER	BB	K	ERA
Tom Seaver (L, 0-1)	8.1	6	2	2	0	13	2.16

Reds	IP	H	R	ER	BB	K	ERA
Jack Billingham	8.0	3	1	1	3	6	1.13
Tom Hall	0.0	0	0	0	1	0	—
Pedro Borbon (W, 1-0)	1.0	0	0	0	0	0	0.00

Hall pitched to one batter in the 9th.

HBP—Griffey Sr. by Seaver. Time—2:00. Attendance—53,431. Umpires—HP, Sudol. 1B, Vargo. 2B, Pelekoudas. 3B, Engel.

Game 2

Sunday, October 7

Mets	AB	R	H	RBI	BB	K	Avg
Wayne Garrett, 3b	5	0	0	0	0	2	.111
Felix Millan, 2b	4	1	1	0	0	1	.143
Rusty Staub, rf	3	2	1	1	1	0	.200
Cleon Jones, lf	3	1	1	1	0	0	.143
John Milner, 1b	3	1	0	0	1	0	.167
Jerry Grote, c	4	0	1	2	0	0	.125
Don Hahn, cf	3	0	2	0	1	1	.333
Bud Harrelson, ss	4	0	1	1	0	0	.167
Jon Matlack, p	2	0	0	0	1	2	.000
TOTALS	31	5	7	5	5	6	.161

Reds	AB	R	H	RBI	BB	K	Avg
Pete Rose, lf	4	0	0	0	0	1	.125
Joe Morgan, 2b	4	0	0	0	0	0	.000
Tony Perez, 1b	4	0	0	0	0	0	.000
Johnny Bench, c	4	0	0	0	0	1	.375
Andy Kosco, rf	2	0	2	0	1	0	1.000
Dan Driessen, 3b	3	0	0	0	0	1	.143
Cesar Geronimo, cf	3	0	0	0	0	3	.167
Darrel Chaney, ss	0	0	0	0	2	0	.000
Ed Armbrister, ph	1	0	0	0	0	1	.000
Tom Hall, p	0	0	0	0	0	0	—
Pedro Borbon, p	0	0	0	0	0	0	—
Don Gullett, p	0	0	0	0	0	0	—
Phil Gagliano, ph	1	0	0	0	0	1	.000
Clay Carroll, p	0	0	0	0	0	0	—
Denis Menke, ph-ss	1	0	0	0	0	1	.000
TOTALS	27	0	2	0	3	9	.154

	1	2	3	4	5	6	7	8	9		R	H	E
Mets	0	0	0	1	0	0	0	0	4		5	7	0
Reds	0	0	0	0	0	0	0	0	0		0	2	0

DP—Mets 1 (Milner to Harrelson to Matlack to Millan), Reds 2 (Morgan to Chaney to Perez; Bench to Morgan to Driessen). LOB—Mets 5, Reds 4. Scoring Position—Mets 4-for-6, Reds 0-for-2. HR—Staub (1). S—Matlack, Gullett. GDP—Milner. CS—Driessen (1).

Mets	IP	H	R	ER	BB	K	ERA
Jon Matlack (W, 1-0)	9.0	2	0	0	3	9	0.00

Reds	IP	H	R	ER	BB	K	ERA
Don Gullett (L, 0-1)	5.0	2	1	1	2	3	1.80
Clay Carroll	3.0	0	0	0	1	2	0.00
Tom Hall	0.1	2	4	4	2	0	108.00
Pedro Borbon	0.2	3	0	0	0	1	0.00

Time—2:19. Attendance—54,041. Umpires—HP, Sudol. 1B, Vargo. 2B, Pelekoudas. 3B, Engel.

Game 3

Monday, October 8

Reds	AB	R	H	RBI	BB	K	Avg
Pete Rose, lf	4	0	2	0	0	0	.250
Joe Morgan, 2b	4	0	1	1	0	1	.083
Tony Perez, 1b	4	0	0	0	0	1	.000
Johnny Bench, c	4	0	1	0	0	1	.333
Andy Kosco, rf	4	0	0	0	0	1	.333
Ed Armbrister, cf	4	0	1	0	0	3	.200
Denis Menke, 3b	4	1	1	1	0	1	.200
Darrel Chaney, ss	3	0	0	0	0	0	.000
Phil Gagliano, ph	1	0	0	0	0	0	.000
Ross Grimsley, p	0	0	0	0	0	0	—
Tom Hall, p	0	0	0	0	0	0	—
Larry Stahl, ph	1	1	1	0	0	0	.500
Dave Tomlin, p	0	0	0	0	0	0	—
Roger Nelson, p	1	0	0	0	0	1	.000
Hal King, ph	1	0	1	0	0	0	.500
Pedro Borbon, p	0	0	0	0	0	0	—
TOTALS	35	2	8	2	0	9	.184

Mets	AB	R	H	RBI	BB	K	Avg
Wayne Garrett, 3b	4	0	0	1	0	3	.077
Felix Millan, 2b	3	2	1	1	2	0	.200
Rusty Staub, rf	5	2	2	4	0	0	.300
Cleon Jones, lf	3	1	2	0	1	0	.300
John Milner, 1b	4	0	1	1	0	2	.200
Jerry Grote, c	3	2	1	0	1	0	.182
Don Hahn, cf	4	1	2	0	0	0	.400
Bud Harrelson, ss	4	0	0	0	0	1	.100
Jerry Koosman, p	4	1	2	1	0	0	.500
TOTALS	34	9	11	8	4	6	.227

	1	2	3	4	5	6	7	8	9		R	H	E
Reds	0	0	2	0	0	0	0	0	0		2	8	1
Mets	1	5	1	2	0	0	0	0	x		9	11	1

E—Garrett, Kosco. DP—Mets 1 (Milner to Harrelson). LOB—Reds 6, Mets 6. Scoring Position—Reds 1-for-4, Mets 5-for-8. 2B—Bench (2), Jones (1). HR—Menke (1), Staub 2 (3). SF—Garrett. GDP—Morgan.

Reds	IP	H	R	ER	BB	K	ERA
Ross Grimsley (L, 0-1)	1.2	5	5	5	1	2	27.00
Tom Hall	0.1	1	1	1	1	1	67.50
Dave Tomlin	1.2	5	3	3	1	1	16.20
Roger Nelson	2.1	0	0	0	1	0	0.00
Pedro Borbon	2.0	0	0	0	0	2	0.00

Mets	IP	H	R	ER	BB	K	ERA
Jerry Koosman (W, 1-0)	9.0	8	2	2	0	9	2.00

Time—2:48. Attendance—53,967. Umpires—HP, Pelekoudas. 1B, Engel. 2B, Froemming. 3B, Dale.

Game 4
Tuesday, October 9

Reds	AB	R	H	RBI	BB	K	Avg
Pete Rose, lf	5	1	3	1	1	0	.353
Joe Morgan, 2b	4	0	0	0	1	0	.063
Tony Perez, 1b	6	1	1	1	0	0	.056
Johnny Bench, c	4	0	1	0	1	0	.313
Andy Kosco, rf	4	0	1	0	1	2	.300
Denis Menke, 3b-ss	4	0	1	0	1	0	.222
Cesar Geronimo, cf	5	0	0	0	0	2	.091
Darrel Chaney, ss	2	0	0	0	0	1	.000
Ed Armbrister, ph	1	0	0	0	0	1	.167
Ed Crosby, ss	1	0	1	0	0	0	1.000
Dan Driessen, pr-3b	1	0	0	0	0	0	.125
Fred Norman, p	1	0	0	0	0	1	.000
Larry Stahl, ph	1	0	0	0	0	0	.333
Don Gullett, p	1	0	0	0	0	0	.000
Phil Gagliano, ph	1	0	0	0	0	0	.000
Clay Carroll, p	0	0	0	0	0	0	—
Ken Griffey Sr., ph	1	0	0	0	0	0	.000
Pedro Borbon, p	0	0	0	0	0	0	—
TOTALS	42	2	8	2	5	7	.177

Mets	AB	R	H	RBI	BB	K	Avg
Wayne Garrett, 3b	5	0	0	0	0	0	.056
Felix Millan, 2b	5	0	2	1	0	0	.267
Rusty Staub, rf	5	0	0	0	2	0	.200
Cleon Jones, lf	5	0	0	0	0	1	.200
John Milner, 1b	4	0	0	0	1	0	.143
Jerry Grote, c	4	0	1	0	0	1	.200
Don Hahn, cf	3	1	0	0	0	0	.308
Bud Harrelson, ss	4	0	0	0	0	0	.071
George Stone, p	1	0	0	0	1	1	.000
Tug McGraw, p	1	0	0	0	0	1	.000
Ken Boswell, ph	1	0	0	0	0	0	.000
Harry Parker, p	0	0	0	0	0	0	—
TOTALS	38	1	3	1	3	6	.172

	1	2	3	4	5	6	7	8	9	10	11	12	R	H	E
Reds	0	0	0	0	0	0	1	0	0	0	0	1	2	8	0
Mets	0	0	1	0	0	0	0	0	0	0	0	0	1	3	2

E—Grote, McGraw. DP—Reds 1 (Chaney to Morgan to Perez), Mets 2 (Millan to Harrelson to Milner; Harrelson to Millan to Milner). LOB—Reds 10, Mets 4. Scoring Position—Reds 0-for-7, Mets 1-for-3. HR—Rose (2), Perez (1). S—Morgan. GDP—Perez, Kosco, Grote.

Reds	IP	H	R	ER	BB	K	ERA
Fred Norman	5.0	1	1	1	3	3	1.80
Don Gullett	4.0	2	0	0	0	3	1.00
Clay Carroll (W, 1-0)	2.0	0	0	0	0	1	0.00
Pedro Borbon (S, 1)	1.0	0	0	0	0	0	0.00

Mets	IP	H	R	ER	BB	K	ERA
George Stone	6.2	3	1	1	2	4	1.35
Tug McGraw	4.1	4	0	0	3	3	0.00
Harry Parker (L, 0-1)	1.0	1	1	1	0	0	9.00

WP—McGraw. Time—3:07. Attendance—50,786. Umpires—HP, Engel. 1B, Froemming. 2B, Dale. 3B, Sudol.

Game 5
Wednesday, October 10

Reds	AB	R	H	RBI	BB	K	Avg
Pete Rose, lf	4	1	2	0	1	0	.381
Joe Morgan, 2b	4	1	1	0	1	0	.100
Dan Driessen, 3b	4	0	1	1	0	0	.167
Tony Perez, 1b	4	0	1	1	0	2	.091
Johnny Bench, c	3	0	0	0	1	0	.263
Ken Griffey Sr., rf	4	0	1	0	0	0	.143
Cesar Geronimo, cf	4	0	0	0	0	0	.067
Darrel Chaney, ss	2	0	0	0	1	1	.000
Larry Stahl, ph	1	0	1	0	0	0	.500
Jack Billingham, p	2	0	0	0	0	0	.000
Don Gullett, p	0	0	0	0	0	0	.000
Clay Carroll, p	0	0	0	0	0	0	—
Ed Crosby, ph	1	0	0	0	0	1	.500
Ross Grimsley, p	0	0	0	0	0	0	—
Hal King, ph	0	0	0	0	1	0	.500
TOTALS	33	2	7	2	5	4	.182

Mets	AB	R	H	RBI	BB	K	Avg
Wayne Garrett, 3b	5	1	1	0	0	0	.087
Felix Millan, 2b	4	2	2	0	0	0	.316
Cleon Jones, rf-lf	5	1	3	2	0	2	.300
John Milner, 1b	3	1	1	0	2	0	.176
Ed Kranepool, lf	2	0	1	2	0	0	.500
Willie Mays, ph-cf	3	1	1	0	0	0	.333
Jerry Grote, c	4	0	1	0	0	1	.211
Don Hahn, cf-rf	4	0	0	1	0	1	.235
Bud Harrelson, ss	4	0	2	1	0	0	.167
Tom Seaver, p	3	1	1	0	1	0	.333
Tug McGraw, p	0	0	0	0	0	0	.000
TOTALS	37	7	13	7	3	4	.221

	1	2	3	4	5	6	7	8	9	R	H	E
Reds	0	0	1	0	1	0	0	0	0	2	7	1
Mets	2	0	0	0	4	1	0	0	x	7	13	1

E—Driessen, Jones. LOB—Reds 10, Mets 10. Scoring Position—Reds 1-for-9, Mets 5-for-14. 2B—Rose (1), Morgan (1), Griffey Sr. (1), Garrett (1), Jones (2), Seaver (2). S—Millan. SF—Driessen.

Reds	IP	H	R	ER	BB	K	ERA
Jack Billingham (L, 0-1)	4.0	6	5	5	1	3	4.50
Don Gullett	0.0	0	1	1	1	0	2.00
Clay Carroll	2.0	5	1	1	0	0	1.29
Ross Grimsley	2.0	2	0	0	1	1	12.27

Mets	IP	H	R	ER	BB	K	ERA
Tom Seaver (W, 1-1)	8.1	7	2	1	5	4	1.62
Tug McGraw (S, 1)	0.2	0	0	0	0	0	0.00

Billingham pitched to three batters in the 5th. Gullett pitched to one batter in the 5th.

WP—Seaver. Time—2:40. Attendance—50,323. Umpires—HP, Froemming. 1B, Dale. 2B, Sudol. 3B, Vargo.

1973 NL Championship Series—Composite Statistics

Batting

Mets	G	AB	R	H	RBI	2B	3B	HR	BB	SO	SB	CS	Avg	OBP	Slg
Ken Boswell	1	1	0	0	0	0	0	0	0	0	0	0	.000	.000	.000
Wayne Garrett	5	23	1	2	1	1	0	0	0	5	0	0	.087	.083	.130
Jerry Grote	5	19	2	4	2	0	0	0	1	3	0	0	.211	.250	.211
Don Hahn	5	17	2	4	1	0	0	0	2	4	0	0	.235	.316	.235
Bud Harrelson	5	18	1	3	2	0	0	0	1	1	0	0	.167	.211	.167
Cleon Jones	5	20	3	6	3	2	0	0	2	4	0	0	.300	.364	.400
Jerry Koosman	1	4	1	2	1	0	0	0	0	0	0	0	.500	.500	.500
Ed Kranepool	1	2	0	1	2	0	0	0	0	0	0	0	.500	.500	.500
Jon Matlack	1	2	0	0	0	0	0	0	1	2	0	0	.000	.333	.000
Willie Mays	1	3	1	1	1	0	0	0	0	0	0	0	.333	.333	.333
Tug McGraw	2	1	0	0	0	0	0	0	0	1	0	0	.000	.000	.000
Felix Millan	5	19	5	6	2	0	0	0	2	1	0	0	.316	.381	.316
John Milner	5	17	2	3	1	0	0	0	5	3	0	0	.176	.364	.176
Tom Seaver	2	6	1	2	1	2	0	0	1	0	0	0	.333	.429	.667
Rusty Staub	4	15	4	3	5	0	0	3	3	2	0	0	.200	.333	.800
George Stone	1	1	0	0	0	0	0	0	0	1	1	0	.000	.500	.000
Totals	5	168	23	37	22	5	0	3	19	28	0	0	.220	.298	.304

Reds	G	AB	R	H	RBI	2B	3B	HR	BB	SO	SB	CS	Avg	OBP	Slg
Ed Armbrister	3	6	0	1	0	0	0	0	0	5	0	0	.167	.167	.167
Johnny Bench	5	19	1	5	1	2	0	1	2	3	0	0	.263	.333	.526
Jack Billingham	2	3	0	0	0	0	0	0	0	1	0	0	.000	.000	.000
Darrel Chaney	5	9	0	0	0	0	0	0	3	4	0	0	.000	.250	.000
Ed Crosby	3	2	0	1	0	0	0	0	0	1	0	0	.500	.500	.500
Dan Driessen	4	12	0	2	1	1	0	0	0	2	0	1	.167	.154	.250
Phil Gagliano	3	3	0	0	0	0	0	0	0	1	0	0	.000	.000	.000
Cesar Geronimo	4	15	0	1	0	0	0	0	0	7	0	0	.067	.067	.067
Ken Griffey Sr.	3	7	0	1	0	1	0	0	1	0	0	0	.143	.250	.286
Don Gullett	3	1	0	0	0	0	0	0	0	0	0	0	.000	.000	.000
Hal King	3	2	0	1	0	0	0	0	1	1	0	0	.500	.667	.500
Andy Kosco	3	10	0	3	0	0	0	0	2	3	0	0	.300	.417	.300
Denis Menke	3	9	1	2	1	0	0	1	1	2	0	0	.222	.300	.556
Joe Morgan	5	20	1	2	1	1	0	0	2	2	0	0	.100	.182	.150
Roger Nelson	1	1	0	0	0	0	0	0	0	1	0	0	.000	.000	.000
Fred Norman	1	1	0	0	0	0	0	0	0	1	0	0	.000	.000	.000
Tony Perez	5	22	1	2	2	0	0	1	0	4	0	0	.091	.091	.227
Pete Rose	5	21	3	8	2	1	0	2	2	2	0	0	.381	.435	.714
Larry Stahl	4	4	1	2	0	0	0	0	0	1	0	0	.500	.500	.500
Totals	5	167	8	31	8	6	0	5	13	42	0	1	.186	.247	.311

Pitching

Mets	G	GS	CG	IP	H	R	ER	BB	SO	W-L	Sv-Op	Hld	ERA
Jerry Koosman	1	1	1	9.0	8	2	2	0	9	1-0	0-0	0	2.00
Jon Matlack	1	1	1	9.0	2	0	0	3	9	1-0	0-0	0	0.00
Tug McGraw	2	0	0	5.0	4	0	0	3	3	0-0	1-1	0	0.00
Harry Parker	1	0	0	1.0	1	1	1	0	0	0-1	0-0	0	9.00
Tom Seaver	2	2	1	16.2	13	4	3	5	17	1-1	0-0	0	1.62
George Stone	1	1	0	6.2	3	1	1	2	4	0-0	0-0	0	1.35
Totals	5	5	3	47.1	31	8	7	13	42	3-2	1-1	0	1.33

Reds	G	GS	CG	IP	H	R	ER	BB	SO	W-L	Sv-Op	Hld	ERA
Jack Billingham	2	2	0	12.0	9	6	6	4	9	0-1	0-0	0	4.50
Pedro Borbon	4	0	0	4.2	3	0	0	0	3	1-0	1-1	0	0.00
Clay Carroll	3	0	0	7.0	5	1	1	1	2	1-0	0-0	0	1.29
Ross Grimsley	2	1	0	3.2	7	5	5	2	3	0-1	0-0	0	12.27
Don Gullett	3	1	0	9.0	4	2	2	3	6	0-1	0-0	0	2.00
Tom Hall	3	0	0	0.2	3	5	5	4	1	0-0	0-0	0	67.50
Roger Nelson	1	0	0	2.1	0	0	0	1	0	0-0	0-0	0	0.00
Fred Norman	1	1	0	5.0	1	1	1	3	3	0-0	0-0	0	1.80
Dave Tomlin	1	0	0	1.2	5	3	3	1	1	0-0	0-0	0	16.20
Totals	5	5	0	46.0	37	23	23	19	28	2-3	1-1	0	4.50

Fielding

Mets	Pos	G	PO	Ast	E	DP	PB	FPct
Wayne Garrett	3b	5	4	6	1	0	—	.909
Jerry Grote	c	5	42	1	1	0	0	.977
Don Hahn	cf	5	12	0	0	0	—	1.000
	rf	1	0	0	0	0	—	—
Bud Harrelson	ss	5	11	14	0	4	—	1.000
Cleon Jones	lf	5	9	0	0	0	—	1.000
	rf	1	0	0	1	0	—	.000
Jerry Koosman	p	1	0	0	0	0	—	—
Ed Kranepool	lf	1	2	0	0	0	—	1.000
Jon Matlack	p	1	0	1	0	1	—	1.000
Willie Mays	cf	1	1	0	0	0	—	1.000
Tug McGraw	p	2	2	0	1	0	—	.667
Felix Millan	2b	5	10	11	0	3	—	1.000
John Milner	1b	5	37	5	0	4	—	1.000
Harry Parker	p	1	0	0	0	0	—	—
Tom Seaver	p	2	0	4	0	0	—	1.000
Rusty Staub	rf	4	11	0	0	0	—	1.000
George Stone	p	1	1	2	0	0	—	1.000
Totals		5	142	44	4	12	0	.979

Reds	Pos	G	PO	Ast	E	DP	PB	FPct
Ed Armbrister	cf	1	3	0	0	0	—	1.000
Johnny Bench	c	5	31	3	0	1	0	1.000
Jack Billingham	p	2	0	2	0	0	—	1.000
Pedro Borbon	p	4	0	2	0	0	—	1.000
Clay Carroll	p	3	0	1	0	0	—	1.000
Darrel Chaney	ss	5	2	11	0	3	—	1.000
Ed Crosby	ss	2	1	2	0	0	—	1.000
Dan Driessen	3b	4	3	4	1	1	—	.875
Cesar Geronimo	cf	4	12	1	0	0	—	1.000
Ken Griffey Sr.	rf	2	1	0	0	0	—	1.000
Ross Grimsley	p	2	1	0	0	0	—	1.000
Don Gullett	p	3	1	0	0	0	—	1.000
Tom Hall	p	3	1	0	0	0	—	1.000
Andy Kosco	rf	3	12	0	1	0	—	.923
Denis Menke	3b	2	0	2	0	0	—	1.000
	ss	2	0	0	0	0	—	—
Joe Morgan	2b	5	12	25	0	4	—	1.000
Roger Nelson	p	1	0	0	0	0	—	—
Fred Norman	p	1	1	0	0	0	—	1.000
Tony Perez	1b	5	47	4	0	3	—	1.000
Pete Rose	lf	5	10	1	0	0	—	1.000
Dave Tomlin	p	1	0	0	0	0	—	—
Totals		5	138	58	2	12	0	.990

1974 Oakland Athletics (AL) 3, Baltimore Orioles (AL) 1

The Oakland A's wrapped up their third straight AL title with a four-game victory over the Baltimore Orioles in the ALCS. Baltimore beat Catfish Hunter 6-3 in the opener, thanks to homers from Paul Blair, Brooks Robinson and Bobby Grich. But that was it for the Orioles as the A's hurlers shut the O's down over the final three games. Ken Holtzman tossed a five-hit shutout in Game 2, and Vida Blue pitched a two-hit masterpiece in Game 3, winning 1-0 on a Sal Bando home run. Catfish Hunter tossed seven shutout innings in Game 4, and Rollie Fingers saved the pennant-clinching 2-1 win.

Game 1

Saturday, October 5

Orioles	AB	R	H	RBI	BB	K	Avg
Rich Coggins, rf	4	0	0	0	0	1	.000
Paul Blair, cf	4	2	2	2	0	0	.500
Bobby Grich, 2b	4	2	2	2	0	0	.500
Tommy Davis, dh	4	0	2	1	0	0	.500
Boog Powell, 1b	4	0	0	0	0	0	.000
Don Baylor, lf	4	0	2	0	0	0	.500
Brooks Robinson, 3b	4	1	1	1	0	0	.250
Ellie Hendricks, c	4	1	1	0	0	2	.250
Mark Belanger, ss	3	0	0	0	0	2	.000
TOTALS	35	6	10	6	0	5	.286

Athletics	AB	R	H	RBI	BB	K	Avg
Bill North, cf	5	2	1	0	0	0	.200
Bert Campaneris, ss	4	0	3	3	0	0	.750
Reggie Jackson, rf	4	0	0	0	1	2	.000
Sal Bando, 3b	4	0	1	0	0	0	.250
Joe Rudi, lf	4	0	0	0	0	0	.000
Gene Tenace, 1b	3	0	0	0	1	2	.000
Angel Mangual, dh	4	0	1	0	0	0	.250
Ray Fosse, c	2	0	1	0	1	0	.500
Jesus Alou, ph	1	0	1	0	0	0	1.000
Manny Trillo, pr	0	1	0	0	0	0	—
Dick Green, 2b	2	0	0	0	1	0	.000
Claudell Washington, ph	1	0	1	0	0	0	1.000
TOTALS	34	3	9	3	4	4	.265

	1	2	3	4	5	6	7	8	9		R	H	E
Orioles	1	0	0	1	4	0	0	0	0		6	10	0
Athletics	0	0	1	0	1	0	0	0	1		3	9	0

DP—Athletics 1 (Bando to Green to Tenace). LOB—Orioles 3, Athletics 9. Scoring Position—Orioles 2-for-5, Athletics 2-for-8. 2B—Grich (1), North (1), Washington (1). HR—Blair (1), Grich (1), Robinson (1). S—Belanger. SF—Campaneris. GDP—Robinson. SB—North (1), Campaneris (1). CS—Campaneris (1).

Orioles	IP	H	R	ER	BB	K	ERA
Mike Cuellar (W, 1-0)	8.0	9	3	3	4	4	3.38
Ross Grimsley (BS, 1)	1.0	0	0	0	0	0	0.00

Athletics	IP	H	R	ER	BB	K	ERA
Catfish Hunter (L, 0-1)	4.2	8	6	6	0	3	11.57
Blue Moon Odom	3.1	1	0	0	0	1	0.00
Rollie Fingers	1.0	1	0	0	0	1	0.00

Cuellar pitched to two batters in the 9th.

PB—Fosse. Time—2:29. Attendance—41,609. Umpires—HP, Napp. 1B, Neudecker. 2B, Goetz. 3B, Phillips.

Game 2

Sunday, October 6

Orioles	AB	R	H	RBI	BB	K	Avg
Mark Belanger, ss	3	0	0	0	0	0	.000
Curt Motton, ph	1	0	0	0	0	0	.000
Frank Baker, ss	0	0	0	0	0	0	—
Paul Blair, cf	3	0	1	0	1	1	.429
Bobby Grich, 2b	4	0	0	0	0	1	.250
Tommy Davis, dh	4	0	1	0	0	0	.375
Don Baylor, lf	4	0	0	0	0	0	.250
Brooks Robinson, 3b	2	0	0	0	1	0	.167
Earl Williams, 1b	3	0	0	0	0	0	.000
Enos Cabell, rf	3	0	1	0	0	1	.333
Andy Etchebarren, c	3	0	2	0	0	0	.667
Al Bumbry, pr	0	0	0	0	0	0	—
Ellie Hendricks, c	0	0	0	0	0	0	.250
TOTALS	30	0	5	0	2	3	.263

Athletics	AB	R	H	RBI	BB	K	Avg
Bert Campaneris, ss	4	0	0	0	0	2	.375
Bill North, cf	2	1	0	0	2	0	.143
Sal Bando, 3b	3	1	1	1	1	0	.286
Reggie Jackson, dh	3	0	0	0	1	0	.000
Herb Washington, pr-dh	0	0	0	0	0	0	—
Joe Rudi, lf	4	0	2	1	0	0	.250
Gene Tenace, 1b	3	1	0	0	1	1	.000
Claudell Washington, rf	4	1	1	0	0	0	.400
Ray Fosse, c	4	1	3	3	0	0	.667
Dick Green, 2b	1	0	1	0	0	0	.333
Jim Holt, ph	0	0	0	0	1	0	—
Blue Moon Odom, pr	0	0	0	0	0	0	—
Dal Maxvill, 2b	1	0	0	0	0	1	.000
TOTALS	29	5	8	5	6	4	.259

	1	2	3	4	5	6	7	8	9		R	H	E
Orioles	0	0	0	0	0	0	0	0	0		0	5	2
Athletics	0	0	0	1	0	1	0	3	x		5	8	0

E—Grich, Baker. DP—Orioles 2 (Grich to Williams; Belanger to Grich to Williams), Athletics 2 (Fosse to Green; Bando to Maxvill to Tenace). LOB—Orioles 5, Athletics 7. Scoring Position—Orioles 0-for-1, Athletics 2-for-10. 2B—Fosse (1). 3B—Rudi (1). HR—Bando (1), Fosse (1). S—Green. GDP—Grich, Campaneris, CWashington. SB—Tenace (1). CS—Blair (1), HWashington (1).

Orioles	IP	H	R	ER	BB	K	ERA
Dave McNally (L, 0-1)	5.2	6	2	1	2	2	1.59
Wayne Garland	0.2	0	0	1	0	0	0.00
Bob Reynolds	1.1	0	1	0	3	1	0.00
Grant Jackson	0.1	1	2	0	0	1	0.00

Athletics	IP	H	R	ER	BB	K	ERA
Ken Holtzman (W, 1-0)	9.0	5	0	0	2	3	0.00

WP—McNally. Time—2:23. Attendance—42,810. Umpires—HP, Neudecker. 1B, Goetz. 2B, Phillips. 3B, Springstead.

Game 3

Tuesday, October 8

Athletics	AB	R	H	RBI	BB	K	Avg
Bert Campaneris, ss	4	0	0	0	0	0	.250
Bill North, cf	4	0	0	0	0	1	.091
Sal Bando, 3b	4	1	1	1	0	0	.273
Reggie Jackson, dh	4	0	1	0	0	0	.091
Joe Rudi, lf	4	0	0	0	0	0	.167
Gene Tenace, 1b	2	0	0	0	1	0	.000
Herb Washington, pr	0	0	0	0	0	0	—
Jim Holt, 1b	0	0	0	0	0	0	—
Claudell Washington, rf	2	0	1	0	0	0	.429
Ray Fosse, c	2	0	0	0	0	0	.500
Dick Green, 2b	3	0	1	0	0	1	.333
TOTALS	29	1	4	1	1	4	.221

Orioles	AB	R	H	RBI	BB	K	Avg
Rich Coggins, rf	3	0	0	0	0	2	.000
Enos Cabell, ph	1	0	0	0	0	1	.250
Paul Blair, cf	4	0	0	0	0	0	.273
Bobby Grich, 2b	4	0	1	0	0	0	.250
Tommy Davis, dh	3	0	0	0	0	0	.273
Don Baylor, lf	3	0	1	0	0	0	.273
Brooks Robinson, 3b	3	0	0	0	0	0	.111
Earl Williams, 1b	3	0	0	0	0	2	.000
Andy Etchebarren, c	3	0	0	0	0	0	.333
Mark Belanger, ss	3	0	0	0	0	1	.000
TOTALS	30	0	2	0	0	7	.186

	1	2	3	4	5	6	7	8	9		R	H	E
Athletics	0	0	0	1	0	0	0	0	0		1	4	2
Orioles	0	0	0	0	0	0	0	0	0		0	2	1

E—Williams, Green 2. DP—Orioles 1 (Robinson to Williams). LOB—Athletics 4, Orioles 3. Scoring Position—Athletics 0-for-2, Orioles 0-for-0. HR—Bando (2). S—Fosse. CS—Baylor (1), HWashington (2).

Athletics	IP	H	R	ER	BB	K	ERA
Vida Blue (W, 1-0)	9.0	2	0	0	0	7	0.00

Orioles	IP	H	R	ER	BB	K	ERA
Jim Palmer (L, 0-1)	9.0	4	1	1	1	4	1.00

HBP—CWashington by Palmer. Time—1:57. Attendance—32,060. Umpires—HP, Goetz. 1B, Phillips. 2B, Springstead. 3B, Deegan.

Game 4

Wednesday, October 9

Athletics	AB	R	H	RBI	BB	K	Avg
Bert Campaneris, ss	5	0	0	0	0	1	.176
Bill North, cf	5	0	0	0	0	0	.063
Sal Bando, 3b	2	2	0	0	3	0	.231
Reggie Jackson, dh	1	0	1	1	3	0	.167
Blue Moon Odom, pr-dh	0	0	0	0	0	0	—
Joe Rudi, lf	1	0	0	0	3	0	.154
Gene Tenace, 1b	3	0	1	1	1	0	.000
Claudell Washington, rf	4	0	0	0	0	0	.273
Ray Fosse, c	4	0	0	0	0	2	.333
Dick Green, 2b	3	0	0	0	1	0	.222
TOTALS	28	2	1	2	11	4	.175

Orioles	AB	R	H	RBI	BB	K	Avg
Rich Coggins, rf	4	0	0	0	0	0	.000
Paul Blair, cf	3	1	1	0	1	1	.286
Bobby Grich, 2b	4	0	1	0	0	0	.250
Tommy Davis, dh	4	0	1	0	0	0	.267
Enos Cabell, rr	0	0	0	0	0	0	.250
Boog Powell, 1b	4	0	1	1	0	0	.125
Jim Palmer, pr	0	0	0	0	0	0	—
Don Baylor, lf	4	0	1	0	0	2	.267
Brooks Robinson, 3b	3	0	0	0	0	0	.083
Ellie Hendricks, c	2	0	0	0	1	1	.167
Mark Belanger, ss	0	0	0	0	1	0	.000
Al Bumbry, ph	1	0	0	0	0	1	.000
Frank Baker, ss	0	0	0	0	0	0	—
TOTALS	29	1	5	1	3	5	.180

	1	2	3	4	5	6	7	8	9		R	H	E
Athletics	0	0	0	0	1	0	1	0	0		2	1	0
Orioles	0	0	0	0	0	0	0	0	1		1	5	1

E—Belanger. DP—Athletics 1 (Green to Campaneris to Tenace), Orioles 1 (Belanger to Grich to Powell). LOB—Athletics 10, Orioles 5. Scoring Position—Athletics 0-for-5, Orioles 1-for-6. 2B—Jackson (1). S—Belanger. GDP—Tenace, Powell. CS—Blair (2).

Athletics	IP	H	R	ER	BB	K	ERA
Catfish Hunter (W, 1-1)	7.0	3	0	0	2	3	4.63
Rollie Fingers (S, 1)	2.0	2	1	1	1	2	3.00

Orioles	IP	H	R	ER	BB	K	ERA
Mike Cuellar (L, 1-1)	4.2	0	1	1	9	2	2.84
Ross Grimsley	4.1	1	1	1	2	2	1.69

Hunter pitched to one batter in the 8th.

WP—Cuellar. Time—2:46. Attendance—28,136. Umpires—HP, Phillips. 1B, Springstead. 2B, Deegan. 3B, Napp.

Postseason: League Championship Series

1974 AL Championship Series—Composite Statistics

Batting

Athletics	G	AB	R	H	RBI	2B	3B	HR	BB	SO	SB	CS	Avg	OBP	Slg
Jesus Alou	1	1	0	1	0	0	0	0	0	0	0	0	1.000	1.000	1.000
Sal Bando	4	13	4	3	2	0	0	2	4	0	0	0	.231	.412	.692
Bert Campaneris	4	17	0	3	3	0	0	0	3	1	1	1	.176	.167	.176
Ray Fosse	4	12	1	4	3	1	0	1	1	2	0	0	.333	.385	.667
Dick Green	4	9	0	2	0	0	0	0	2	1	0	0	.222	.364	.222
Jim Holt	2	0	0	0	0	0	0	0	1	0	0	0	—	1.000	—
Reggie Jackson	4	12	0	2	1	1	0	0	5	2	0	0	.167	.412	.250
Angel Mangual	1	4	0	1	0	0	0	0	0	0	0	0	.250	.250	.250
Dal Maxvill	1	1	0	0	0	0	0	0	0	1	0	0	.000	.000	.000
Bill North	4	16	3	1	0	1	0	0	2	1	1	0	.063	.167	.125
Joe Rudi	4	13	0	2	1	0	1	0	3	2	0	0	.154	.313	.308
Gene Tenace	4	11	1	0	1	0	0	0	4	4	1	0	.000	.267	.000
Manny Trillo	1	0	1	0	0	0	0	0	0	0	0	0	—	—	—
Claudell Washington	4	11	1	3	0	1	0	0	0	0	0	0	.273	.333	.364
Herb Washington	2	0	0	0	0	0	0	0	0	0	0	2	—	—	—
Totals	4	120	11	22	11	4	1	3	22	16	3	3	.183	.313	.308

Orioles	G	AB	R	H	RBI	2B	3B	HR	BB	SO	SB	CS	Avg	OBP	Slg
Don Baylor	4	15	0	4	0	0	0	0	0	2	0	1	.267	.267	.267
Mark Belanger	4	9	0	0	0	0	0	0	1	3	0	0	.000	.100	.000
Paul Blair	4	14	3	4	2	0	0	1	2	2	0	2	.286	.375	.500
Al Bumbry	2	1	0	0	0	0	0	0	0	1	0	0	.000	.000	.000
Enos Cabell	3	4	0	1	0	0	0	0	0	2	0	0	.250	.250	.250
Rich Coggins	3	11	0	0	0	0	0	0	0	3	0	0	.000	.000	.000
Tommy Davis	4	15	0	4	1	0	0	0	0	1	0	0	.267	.267	.267
Andy Etchebarren	2	6	0	2	0	0	0	0	0	0	0	0	.333	.333	.333
Bobby Grich	4	16	2	4	2	1	0	1	0	1	0	0	.250	.250	.500
Ellie Hendricks	3	6	1	1	0	0	0	0	1	3	0	0	.167	.286	.167
Curt Motton	1	1	0	0	0	0	0	0	0	0	0	0	.000	.000	.000
Boog Powell	2	8	0	1	1	0	0	0	0	0	0	0	.125	.125	.125
Brooks Robinson	4	12	1	1	1	0	0	1	1	0	0	0	.083	.154	.333
Earl Williams	2	6	0	0	0	0	0	0	0	2	0	0	.000	.000	.000
Totals	4	124	7	22	7	1	0	3	5	20	0	3	.177	.209	.258

Pitching

Athletics	G	GS	CG	IP	H	R	ER	BB	SO	W-L	Sv-Op	Hld	ERA
Vida Blue	1	1	1	9.0	2	0	0	0	7	1-0	0-0	0	0.00
Rollie Fingers	2	0	0	3.0	3	1	1	1	3	0-0	1-1	0	3.00
Ken Holtzman	1	1	1	9.0	5	0	0	2	3	1-0	0-0	0	0.00
Catfish Hunter	2	2	0	11.2	11	6	6	2	6	1-1	0-0	0	4.63
Blue Moon Odom	1	0	0	3.1	1	0	0	0	1	0-0	0-0	0	0.00
Totals	4	4	2	36.0	22	7	7	5	20	3-1	1-1	0	1.75

Orioles	G	GS	CG	IP	H	R	ER	BB	SO	W-L	Sv-Op	Hld	ERA
Mike Cuellar	2	2	0	12.2	9	4	4	13	6	1-1	0-0	0	2.84
Wayne Garland	1	0	0	0.2	1	0	0	1	0	0-0	0-0	0	0.00
Ross Grimsley	2	0	0	5.1	1	1	1	2	2	0-0	0-1	0	1.69
Grant Jackson	1	0	0	0.1	1	2	0	0	1	0-0	0-0	0	0.00
Dave McNally	1	1	0	5.2	6	2	1	2	2	0-1	0-0	0	1.59
Jim Palmer	1	1	1	9.0	4	1	1	1	4	0-1	0-0	0	1.00
Bob Reynolds	1	0	0	1.1	0	1	0	3	1	0-0	0-0	0	0.00
Totals	4	4	1	35.0	22	11	7	22	16	1-3	0-1	0	1.80

Fielding

Athletics	Pos	G	PO	Ast	E	DP	PB	FPct
Sal Bando	3b	4	3	8	0	2	—	1.000
Vida Blue	p	1	0	1	0	0	—	1.000
Bert Campaneris	ss	4	3	17	0	1	—	1.000
Rollie Fingers	p	2	0	0	0	0	—	—
Ray Fosse	c	4	21	3	0	1	1	1.000
Dick Green	2b	4	10	8	2	3	—	.900
Jim Holt	1b	1	1	0	0	0	—	1.000
Ken Holtzman	p	1	0	1	0	0	—	1.000
Catfish Hunter	p	2	3	2	0	0	—	1.000
Reggie Jackson	rf	1	0	0	0	0	—	—
Dal Maxvill	2b	1	2	1	0	1	—	1.000
Bill North	cf	4	14	0	0	0	—	1.000
Blue Moon Odom	p	1	0	0	0	0	—	—
Joe Rudi	lf	4	5	0	0	0	—	1.000
Gene Tenace	1b	4	35	2	0	3	—	1.000
Claudell Washington	rf	3	11	0	0	0	—	1.000
Totals		4	108	43	2	11	1	.987

Orioles	Pos	G	PO	Ast	E	DP	PB	FPct
Frank Baker	ss	2	1	1	1	0	—	.667
Don Baylor	lf	4	9	0	0	0	—	1.000
Mark Belanger	ss	4	7	12	1	2	—	.950
Paul Blair	cf	4	7	0	0	0	—	1.000
Enos Cabell	rf	1	2	0	0	0	—	1.000
Rich Coggins	rf	3	6	0	0	0	—	1.000
Mike Cuellar	p	2	0	5	0	0	—	1.000
Andy Etchebarren	c	2	7	1	0	0	0	1.000
Wayne Garland	p	1	0	0	0	0	—	—
Bobby Grich	2b	4	13	12	1	3	—	.962
Ross Grimsley	p	2	0	1	0	0	—	1.000
Ellie Hendricks	c	3	11	1	0	0	0	1.000
Grant Jackson	p	1	0	0	0	0	—	—
Dave McNally	p	1	0	0	0	0	—	—
Jim Palmer	p	1	0	2	0	0	—	1.000
Boog Powell	1b	2	22	1	0	1	—	1.000
Bob Reynolds	p	1	0	0	0	0	—	—
Brooks Robinson	3b	4	4	13	0	1	—	1.000
Earl Williams	1b	2	16	1	1	3	—	.944
Totals		4	105	50	4	10	0	.975

1974 Los Angeles Dodgers (NL) 3, Pittsburgh Pirates (NL) 1

Don Sutton pitched two great games, leading the Dodgers to a four-game victory over the Pittsburgh Pirates. Sutton tossed a four-hit shutout in the opener to outduel Jerry Reuss by the score of 3-0. Reuss allowed only one run in seven innings in a losing cause. With the score tied 2-2 in the eighth inning of the second game, the Dodgers broke through for three runs against Pirates ace reliever Dave Giusti. Ron Cey had four hits in the Dodgers' 5-2 victory. The Pirates came back to win the third game 7-0, blasting Doug Rau out of the box with a five-run first inning. Willie Stargell and Richie Hebner each homered and drove in three runs. The Dodgers ended it the next day, however, winning 12-1 behind Sutton's eight strong innings. Steve Garvey has two singles and two homers and drove in four runs in the clincher.

Game 1

Saturday, October 5

Dodgers	AB	R	H	RBI	BB	K	Avg
Davey Lopes, 2b	4	1	0	1	1	0	.000
Bill Buckner, lf	5	0	1	0	0	0	.200
Jimmy Wynn, cf	3	1	1	1	2	0	.333
Steve Garvey, 1b	4	0	2	0	1	0	.500
Joe Ferguson, rf	4	1	2	1	0	0	.500
Ron Cey, 3b	3	0	0	0	2	0	.000
Bill Russell, ss	5	0	2	0	0	0	.400
Steve Yeager, c	4	0	0	0	0	1	.000
Don Sutton, p	3	0	1	0	1	2	.333
TOTALS	35	3	9	3	7	3	.257

Pirates	AB	R	H	RBI	BB	K	Avg
Rennie Stennett, 2b	4	0	0	0	0	1	.000
Richie Hebner, 3b	3	0	0	0	0	0	.000
Al Oliver, cf	4	0	0	0	0	1	.000
Willie Stargell, lf	4	0	2	0	0	0	.500
Richie Zisk, rf	4	0	0	0	0	3	.000
Manny Sanguillen, c	4	0	1	0	0	0	.250
Ed Kirkpatrick, 1b	3	0	0	0	1	0	.000
Frank Taveras, ss	2	0	0	0	0	0	.000
Paul Popovich, ph-ss	1	0	1	0	0	0	1.000
Jerry Reuss, p	2	0	0	0	0	0	.000
Dave Parker, ph	1	0	0	0	0	0	.000
Dave Giusti, p	0	0	0	0	0	0	—
TOTALS	32	0	4	0	1	6	.125

	1	2	3	4	5	6	7	8	9		R	H	E
Dodgers	0	1	0	0	0	0	0	0	2		3	9	2
Pirates	0	0	0	0	0	0	0	0	0		0	4	0

E—Cey 2. DP—Dodgers 1 (Cey to Lopes to Garvey). LOB—Dodgers 13, Pirates 7. Scoring Position—Dodgers 2-for-11, Pirates 0-for-1. 2B—Buckner (1), Wynn (1), Garvey (1). S—Ferguson. GDP—Stennett. SB—Lopes (1).

Dodgers	IP	H	R	ER	BB	K	ERA
Don Sutton (W, 1-0)	9.0	4	0	0	1	6	0.00

Pirates	IP	H	R	ER	BB	K	ERA
Jerry Reuss (L, 0-1)	7.0	5	1	1	4	3	1.29
Dave Giusti	2.0	4	2	2	3	0	9.00

HBP—Hebner by Sutton. Time—2:25. Attendance—40,638. Umpires—HP, Colosi. 1B, Pryor. 2B, Weyer. 3B, McSherry.

Game 2

Sunday, October 6

Dodgers	AB	R	H	RBI	BB	K	Avg
Davey Lopes, 2b	4	1	2	1	1	0	.250
Bill Buckner, lf	5	0	2	0	0	1	.300
Jimmy Wynn, cf	2	0	0	0	3	0	.200
Steve Garvey, 1b	5	0	1	1	0	1	.333
Joe Ferguson, rf-c	4	0	0	0	0	0	.250
Ron Cey, 3b	5	2	4	1	0	0	.500
Bill Russell, ss	4	1	1	0	1	0	.333
Steve Yeager, c	3	0	0	0	0	1	.000
Willie Crawford, ph-rf	2	1	1	1	0	0	.500
Andy Messersmith, p	3	0	0	0	0	1	.000
Manny Mota, ph	1	0	1	1	0	0	1.000
Lee Lacy, pr	0	0	0	0	0	0	—
Mike Marshall, p	0	0	0	0	0	0	—
TOTALS	38	5	12	5	6	5	.286

Pirates	AB	R	H	RBI	BB	K	Avg
Rennie Stennett, 2b	3	0	0	0	1	0	.000
Richie Hebner, 3b	3	0	1	1	1	0	.167
Al Oliver, cf	4	0	1	1	0	0	.125
Willie Stargell, lf	3	0	1	0	1	0	.429
Dave Giusti, p	0	0	0	0	0	0	—
Larry Demery, p	0	0	0	0	0	0	—
Ramon Hernandez, p	0	0	0	0	0	0	—
Dave Parker, rf	4	0	0	0	0	0	.000
Manny Sanguillen, c	4	0	2	0	0	0	.375
Ed Kirkpatrick, 1b	4	0	0	0	0	0	.000
Frank Taveras, ss	0	0	0	0	0	0	.000
Mario Mendoza, ss	1	0	0	0	0	0	.000
Paul Popovich, ph-ss	2	1	1	0	0	0	.667
Jim Rooker, p	2	0	1	0	0	0	.500
Richie Zisk, ph	1	0	1	0	0	0	.200
Gene Clines, pr-lf	1	1	0	0	0	0	.000
TOTALS	32	2	8	2	3	0	.194

	1	2	3	4	5	6	7	8	9		R	H	E
Dodgers	1	0	0	1	0	0	0	3	0		5	12	0
Pirates	0	0	0	0	0	0	2	0	0		2	8	3

E—Sanguillen 2, Rooker. DP—Dodgers 2 (Messersmith to Russell to Garvey; Lopes to Russell to Garvey), Pirates 1 (Hernandez to Sanguillen to Kirkpatrick). LOB—Dodgers 12, Pirates 8. Scoring Position—Dodgers 5-for-17, Pirates 1-for-5. 2B—Cey 2 (2). HR—Cey (1). S—Stennett. GDP—Garvey, Hebner, Kirkpatrick. SB—Lopes (2), Wynn (1), Taveras (1).

Dodgers	IP	H	R	ER	BB	K	ERA
Andy Messersmith (W, 1-0)	7.0	8	2	2	3	0	2.57
Mike Marshall (BS, 1)	2.0	0	0	0	0	0	0.00

Pirates	IP	H	R	ER	BB	K	ERA
Jim Rooker	7.0	6	2	2	5	4	2.57
Dave Giusti (L, 0-1)	0.0	4	3	3	0	0	22.50
Larry Demery	0.0	1	0	0	0	0	—
Ramon Hernandez	2.0	1	0	0	1	1	0.00

Giusti pitched to five batters in the 8th. Demery pitched to two batters in the 8th.

WP—Demery. HBP—Taveras by Messersmith. Time—2:44. Attendance—49,247. Umpires—HP, Pryor. 1B, Weyer. 2B, McSherry. 3B, Crawford.

Game 3

Tuesday, October 8

Pirates	AB	R	H	RBI	BB	K	Avg
Rennie Stennett, 2b	5	1	1	0	0	0	.083
Manny Sanguillen, c	5	0	1	0	0	0	.308
Al Oliver, cf	3	1	1	0	2	0	.182
Willie Stargell, lf	5	2	2	3	0	0	.417
Richie Zisk, rf	5	1	2	0	0	0	.300
Gene Clines, rf	0	0	0	0	0	0	.000
Bob Robertson, 1b	5	1	0	0	0	0	.000
Richie Hebner, 3b	3	1	2	3	0	0	.333
Mario Mendoza, ss	3	0	1	1	1	0	.250
Bruce Kison, p	3	0	0	0	0	0	.000
Ramon Hernandez, p	1	0	0	0	0	1	.000
TOTALS	38	7	10	7	3	3	.235

Dodgers	AB	R	H	RBI	BB	K	Avg
Davey Lopes, 2b	3	0	0	0	2	1	.182
Bill Buckner, lf	3	0	0	0	0	0	.231
Manny Mota, ph-lf	1	0	0	0	0	0	.500
Jimmy Wynn, cf	3	0	0	0	1	1	.125
Steve Garvey, 1b	4	0	0	0	0	0	.231
Willie Crawford, rf	2	0	0	0	0	0	.250
Tom Paciorek, ph-rf	1	0	1	0	0	0	1.000
Ron Cey, 3b	4	0	0	0	0	2	.333
Joe Ferguson, c	3	0	0	0	1	1	.182
Bill Russell, ss	4	0	2	0	0	0	.385
Doug Rau, p	0	0	0	0	0	0	—
Charlie Hough, p	0	0	0	0	0	0	—
Von Joshua, ph	0	0	0	0	1	0	—
Al Downing, p	1	0	0	0	0	0	.000
Ken McMullen, ph	1	0	0	0	0	1	.000
Eddie Solomon, p	0	0	0	0	0	0	—
Rick Auerbach, ph	1	0	1	0	0	0	1.000
TOTALS	31	0	4	0	6	6	.264

	1	2	3	4	5	6	7	8	9		R	H	E
Pirates	5	0	2	0	0	0	0	0	0		7	10	0
Dodgers	0	0	0	0	0	0	0	0	0		0	4	4

E—Garvey, Lopes, Hough, Downing. DP—Dodgers 3 (Russell to Lopes; Lopes to Russell to Garvey; Russell). LOB—Pirates 8, Dodgers 10. Scoring Position—Pirates 3-for-10, Dodgers 0-for-7. 2B—Sanguillen (1), Auerbach (1). HR—Stargell (1), Hebner (1). GDP—Stargell.

Pirates	IP	H	R	ER	BB	K	ERA
Bruce Kison (W, 1-0)	6.2	2	0	0	6	5	0.00
Ramon Hernandez	2.1	2	0	0	0	1	0.00

Dodgers	IP	H	R	ER	BB	K	ERA
Doug Rau (L, 0-1)	0.2	3	5	3	1	0	40.50
Charlie Hough	2.1	4	2	2	0	2	7.71
Al Downing	4.0	1	0	0	1	0	0.00
Eddie Solomon	2.0	2	0	0	1	1	0.00

Reached, Catcher's Interference—Pirates 1, Hebner by Ferguson. Dodgers 0. PB—Ferguson, Sanguillen. Time—2:41. Attendance—55,953. Umpires—HP, Weyer. 1B, McSherry. 2B, Crawford. 3B, Davidson.

Game 4

Wednesday, October 9

Pirates	AB	R	H	RBI	BB	K	Avg
Rennie Stennett, 2b	4	0	0	0	0	0	.063
Richie Hebner, 3b	4	0	0	0	0	3	.231
Al Oliver, cf	3	0	0	0	1	0	.143
Willie Stargell, lf	3	1	1	1	0	2	.400
Dave Parker, rf	3	0	1	0	0	1	.125
Manny Sanguillen, c	3	0	0	0	0	0	.250
Ed Kirkpatrick, 1b	2	0	0	0	1	0	.000
Mario Mendoza, ss	1	0	0	0	0	0	.200
Paul Popovich, ph-ss	2	0	1	0	0	0	.600
Jerry Reuss, p	0	0	0	0	0	0	.000
Ken Brett, p	1	0	0	0	0	1	.000
Larry Demery, p	0	0	0	0	0	0	—
Dave Giusti, p	0	0	0	0	0	0	—
Juan Pizarro, p	0	0	0	0	0	0	—
Art Howe, ph	1	0	0	0	0	0	.000
TOTALS	27	1	3	1	1	8	.200

Dodgers	AB	R	H	RBI	BB	K	Avg
Davey Lopes, 2b	4	2	2	1	1	0	.267
Bill Buckner, lf	5	0	0	0	0	1	.167
Jimmy Wynn, cf	2	3	1	1	3	0	.200
Steve Garvey, 1b	5	4	4	4	0	0	.389
Joe Ferguson, rf	2	2	1	1	3	0	.231
Ron Cey, 3b	4	0	1	0	1	0	.313
Bill Russell, ss	5	0	2	3	0	0	.389
Steve Yeager, c	2	1	0	0	3	1	.000
Don Sutton, p	4	0	1	1	0	0	.286
Manny Mota, ph	1	0	0	0	0	0	.333
Mike Marshall, p	0	0	0	0	0	0	—
TOTALS	34	12	12	11	11	2	.268

	1	2	3	4	5	6	7	8	9		R	H	E
Pirates	0	0	0	0	0	0	1	0	0		1	3	0
Dodgers	1	0	2	0	2	2	2	3	x		12	12	0

DP—Pirates 1 (Hebner to Stennett to Kirkpatrick), Dodgers 2 (Russell to Garvey; Sutton to Garvey). LOB—Pirates 1, Dodgers 9. Scoring Position—Pirates 0-for-1, Dodgers 6-for-15. 2B—Wynn (2), Cey (3). 3B—Lopes (1). HR—Stargell (2), Garvey 2 (2). S—Reuss. GDP—Sanguillen, Mota. SB—Lopes (3), Yeager (1).

Pirates	IP	H	R	ER	BB	K	ERA
Jerry Reuss (L, 0-2)	2.2	2	3	3	4	0	3.72
Ken Brett	2.1	3	2	2	1	1	7.71
Larry Demery	1.0	2	4	4	2	0	36.00
Dave Giusti	1.1	5	3	3	2	1	21.60
Juan Pizarro	0.2	0	0	0	1	0	0.00

Dodgers	IP	H	R	ER	BB	K	ERA
Don Sutton (W, 2-0)	8.0	3	1	1	1	7	0.53
Mike Marshall	1.0	0	0	0	0	1	0.00

Demery pitched to two batters in the 7th.

Time—2:36. Attendance—54,424. Umpires—HP, McSherry. 1B, Crawford. 2B, Davidson. 3B, Colosi.

1974 NL Championship Series—Composite Statistics

Batting

Dodgers	G	AB	R	H	RBI	2B	3B	HR	BB	SO	SB	CS	Avg	OBP	Slg
Rick Auerbach	1	1	0	1	0	1	0	0	0	0	0	0	1.000	1.000	2.000
Bill Buckner	4	18	0	3	0	1	0	0	0	2	0	0	.167	.167	.222
Ron Cey	4	16	2	5	1	3	0	1	3	2	0	0	.313	.421	.688
Willie Crawford	2	4	1	1	1	0	0	0	1	1	0	0	.250	.400	.250
Al Downing	1	1	0	0	0	0	0	0	0	0	0	0	.000	.000	.000
Joe Ferguson	4	13	3	3	2	0	0	0	5	1	0	0	.231	.444	.231
Steve Garvey	4	18	4	7	5	1	0	2	1	1	0	0	.389	.421	.778
Von Joshua	1	0	0	0	0	0	0	0	1	0	0	0	—	1.000	—
Lee Lacy	1	0	0	0	0	0	0	0	0	0	0	0	—	—	—
Davey Lopes	4	15	4	4	3	0	1	0	5	1	3	0	.267	.450	.400
Ken McMullen	1	1	0	0	0	0	0	0	0	1	0	0	.000	.000	.000
Andy Messersmith	1	3	0	0	0	0	0	0	0	1	0	0	.000	.000	.000
Manny Mota	3	3	0	1	1	0	0	0	0	0	0	0	.333	.333	.333
Tom Paciorek	1	1	0	1	0	0	0	0	0	0	0	0	1.000	1.000	1.000
Bill Russell	4	18	1	7	3	0	0	0	1	0	0	0	.389	.421	.389
Don Sutton	2	7	0	2	1	0	0	0	1	2	0	0	.286	.375	.286
Jimmy Wynn	4	10	4	2	2	2	0	0	9	1	1	0	.200	.579	.400
Steve Yeager	3	9	1	0	0	0	0	0	3	3	1	0	.000	.250	.000
Totals	4	138	20	37	19	8	1	3	30	16	5	0	.268	.399	.406

Pirates	G	AB	R	H	RBI	2B	3B	HR	BB	SO	SB	CS	Avg	OBP	Slg
Ken Brett	1	1	0	0	0	0	0	0	0	0	1	0	.000	.000	.000
Gene Clines	2	1	1	0	0	0	0	0	0	0	0	0	.000	.000	.000
Richie Hebner	4	13	1	3	4	0	0	1	1	4	0	0	.231	.333	.462
Ramon Hernandez	2	1	0	0	0	0	0	0	0	1	0	0	.000	.000	.000
Art Howe	1	1	0	0	0	0	0	0	0	0	0	0	.000	.000	.000
Ed Kirkpatrick	3	9	0	0	0	0	0	0	2	0	0	0	.000	.182	.000
Bruce Kison	1	3	0	0	0	0	0	0	0	2	0	0	.000	.000	.000
Mario Mendoza	3	5	0	1	1	0	0	0	1	0	0	0	.200	.333	.200
Al Oliver	4	14	1	2	1	0	0	0	2	2	0	0	.143	.250	.143
Dave Parker	3	8	0	1	0	0	0	0	0	1	0	0	.125	.125	.125
Paul Popovich	3	5	1	3	0	0	0	0	0	1	0	0	.600	.600	.600
Jerry Reuss	2	2	0	0	0	0	0	0	0	0	0	0	.000	.000	.000
Bob Robertson	1	5	1	0	0	0	0	0	0	0	0	0	.000	.000	.000
Jim Rooker	1	2	0	1	0	0	0	0	0	0	0	0	.500	.500	.500
Manny Sanguillen	4	16	0	4	0	1	0	0	0	0	0	0	.250	.250	.313
Willie Stargell	4	15	3	6	4	0	0	2	1	2	0	0	.400	.438	.800
Rennie Stennett	4	16	1	1	0	0	0	0	1	1	0	0	.063	.118	.063
Frank Taveras	2	2	0	0	0	0	0	0	0	0	1	0	.000	.333	.000
Richie Zisk	3	10	1	3	0	0	0	0	0	3	0	0	.300	.300	.300
Totals	4	129	10	25	10	1	0	3	8	17	1	0	.194	.252	.271

Pitching

Dodgers	G	GS	CG	IP	H	R	ER	BB	SO	W-L	Sv-Op	Hld	ERA
Al Downing	1	0	0	4.0	1	0	0	1	0	0-0	0-0	0	0.00
Charlie Hough	1	0	0	2.1	4	2	2	0	2	0-0	0-0	0	7.71
Mike Marshall	2	0	0	3.0	0	0	0	0	1	1-0	0-1	0	0.00
Andy Messersmith	1	1	0	7.0	8	2	2	3	1	1-0	0-0	0	2.57
Doug Rau	1	1	0	0.2	3	5	3	1	0	0-1	0-0	0	40.50
Eddie Solomon	1	0	0	2.0	2	0	0	1	1	0-0	0-0	0	0.00
Don Sutton	2	2	1	17.0	7	1	1	2	13	2-0	0-0	0	0.53
Totals	4	4	1	36.0	25	10	8	8	17	3-1	0-1	0	2.00

Pirates	G	GS	CG	IP	H	R	ER	BB	SO	W-L	Sv-Op	Hld	ERA
Ken Brett	1	0	0	2.1	3	2	2	2	1	0-0	0-0	0	7.71
Larry Demery	2	0	0	1.0	3	4	4	2	0	0-0	0-0	0	36.00
Dave Giusti	3	0	0	3.1	13	8	8	5	1	0-1	0-0	0	21.60
Ramon Hernandez	2	0	0	4.1	3	0	0	1	2	0-0	0-0	0	0.00
Bruce Kison	1	1	0	6.2	2	0	0	6	5	1-0	0-0	0	0.00
Juan Pizarro	1	0	0	0.2	0	0	0	1	0	0-0	0-0	0	0.00
Jerry Reuss	2	2	0	9.2	7	4	4	8	3	0-2	0-0	0	3.72
Jim Rooker	1	1	0	7.0	6	2	2	5	4	0-0	0-0	0	2.57
Totals	4	4	0	35.0	37	20	20	30	16	1-3	0-0	0	5.14

Fielding

Dodgers	Pos	G	PO	Ast	E	DP	PB	FPct
Bill Buckner	lf	4	6	0	0	0	—	1.000
Ron Cey	3b	4	2	5	2	1	—	.778
Willie Crawford	rf	2	0	0	0	0	—	—
Al Downing	p	1	0	0	1	0	—	.000
Joe Ferguson	rf	3	6	0	0	0	—	1.000
	c	2	3	0	0	0	1	1.000
Steve Garvey	1b	4	41	2	1	6	—	.977
Charlie Hough	p	1	0	0	1	0	—	.000
Davey Lopes	2b	4	9	18	1	4	—	.964
Mike Marshall	p	2	0	0	0	0	—	—
Andy Messersmith	p	1	1	2	0	1	—	1.000
Manny Mota	lf	1	1	0	0	0	—	1.000
Tom Paciorek	rf	1	0	0	0	0	—	—
Doug Rau	p	1	0	0	0	0	—	—
Bill Russell	ss	4	13	15	0	6	—	1.000
Eddie Solomon	p	1	0	0	0	0	—	—
Don Sutton	p	2	2	3	0	1	—	1.000
Jimmy Wynn	cf	4	10	0	0	0	—	1.000
Steve Yeager	c	3	14	1	0	0	0	1.000
Totals		4	108	46	6	19	1	.963

Pirates	Pos	G	PO	Ast	E	DP	PB	FPct
Ken Brett	p	1	0	1	0	0	—	1.000
Gene Clines	lf	1	0	0	0	0	—	—
	rf	1	0	0	0	0	—	—
Larry Demery	p	2	0	1	0	0	—	1.000
Dave Giusti	p	3	1	2	0	0	—	1.000
Richie Hebner	3b	4	5	7	0	1	—	1.000
Ramon Hernandez	p	2	0	1	0	1	—	1.000
Ed Kirkpatrick	1b	3	22	0	0	0	—	1.000
Bruce Kison	p	1	1	1	0	0	—	1.000
Mario Mendoza	ss	3	4	7	0	0	—	1.000
Al Oliver	cf	4	9	0	0	0	—	1.000
Dave Parker	rf	2	4	1	0	0	—	1.000
Juan Pizarro	p	1	0	0	0	0	—	—
Paul Popovich	ss	3	2	0	0	0	—	1.000
Jerry Reuss	p	2	0	0	0	0	—	—
Bob Robertson	1b	1	11	0	0	0	—	1.000
Jim Rooker	p	1	0	3	1	0	—	.750
Manny Sanguillen	c	4	19	2	2	1	1	.913
Willie Stargell	lf	4	13	0	0	0	—	1.000
Rennie Stennett	2b	4	10	10	0	1	—	1.000
Frank Taveras	ss	2	2	1	0	0	—	1.000
Richie Zisk	rf	2	2	0	0	0	—	1.000
Totals		4	105	37	3	6	1	.979

1975 Boston Red Sox (AL) 3, Oakland Athletics (AL) 0

The Boston Red Sox ended the Oakland A's three-year reign as American League Champions, sweeping them out of the ALCS in three straight games. Four Oakland errors helped the Red Sox take the first game, 7-1, as Luis Tiant tossed a complete-game three-hitter. The Red Sox cuffed around Vida Blue in Game 2, and gave the same rude treatment to Rollie Fingers later in the game, emerging with a 6-3 win. Ken Holtzman came back on two days' rest to pitch Game 3, but he had nothing, and the Red Sox won 5-3 to move on to the World Series. Carl Yastrzemski batted .455 and made several fine plays in left field.

Game 1
Saturday, October 4

Athletics	AB	R	H	RBI	BB	K	Avg
Bill North, cf	3	0	0	1	1	0	.000
Claudell Washington, lf	4	0	0	0	0	2	.000
Sal Bando, 3b	4	0	0	0	0	3	.000
Reggie Jackson, rf	4	0	1	0	0	0	.250
Gene Tenace, c	3	0	0	0	1	1	.000
Joe Rudi, 1b	4	0	1	0	0	1	.250
Billy Williams, dh	3	0	0	0	1	0	.000
Don Hopkins, pr	0	0	0	0	0	0	—
Bert Campaneris, ss	4	1	0	0	0	0	.000
Phil Garner, 2b	2	0	0	0	0	1	.000
Jim Holt, ph	1	0	1	0	0	0	1.000
Ted Martinez, pr-2b	0	0	0	0	0	0	—
TOTALS	32	1	3	1	3	8	.094

Red Sox	AB	R	H	RBI	BB	K	Avg
Juan Beniquez, dh	4	1	2	1	0	0	.500
Denny Doyle, 2b	3	1	0	1	0	1	.000
Carl Yastrzemski, lf	4	1	1	0	0	1	.250
Carlton Fisk, c	4	2	1	0	0	0	.250
Fred Lynn, cf	4	0	1	2	0	0	.250
Rico Petrocelli, 3b	4	0	0	0	0	0	.000
Dwight Evans, rf	4	1	1	0	0	1	.250
Cecil Cooper, 1b	3	0	1	0	0	1	.333
Rick Burleson, ss	3	1	1	1	1	0	.333
TOTALS	33	7	8	5	1	4	.242

	1	2	3	4	5	6	7	8	9		R	H	E
Athletics	0	0	0	0	0	0	0	1	0		1	3	4
Red Sox	2	0	0	0	0	5	0	x			7	8	3

E—Bando, Burleson, Cooper, Lynn, Washington, North, Garner. LOB—Athletics 7, Red Sox 5. Scoring Position—Athletics 0-for-8, Red Sox 3-for-6. 2B—Lynn (1), Evans (1), Burleson (1), Holt (1). S—Cooper. SF—Doyle. SB—Beniquez 2 (2).

Athletics	IP	H	R	ER	BB	K	ERA
Ken Holtzman (L, 0-1)	6.1	5	4	2	1	4	2.84
Jim Todd	0.0	1	1	1	0	0	—
Paul Lindblad	0.1	2	2	0	0	0	0.00
Dick Bosman	0.1	0	0	0	0	0	0.00
Glenn Abbott	1.0	0	0	0	0	0	0.00

Red Sox	IP	H	R	ER	BB	K	ERA
Luis Tiant (W, 1-0)	9.0	3	1	0	3	8	0.00

Todd pitched to one batter in the 7th.

Time—2:40. Attendance—35,578. Umpires—HP, Denkinger. 1B, DiMuro. 2B, Kunkel. 3B, Luciano.

Game 2
Sunday, October 5

Athletics	AB	R	H	RBI	BB	K	Avg
Bill North, cf	4	0	0	0	0	0	.000
Bert Campaneris, ss	3	0	0	0	1	0	.000
Sal Bando, 3b	4	1	4	0	0	0	.500
Reggie Jackson, rf	4	1	2	2	0	1	.375
Gene Tenace, 1b-c	4	0	0	0	0	1	.000
Joe Rudi, lf	4	1	2	0	0	0	.375
Claudell Washington, dh	4	0	2	1	0	0	.250
Phil Garner, 2b	2	0	0	0	0	0	.000
Tommy Harper, ph	0	0	0	0	1	0	—
Jim Holt, 1b	1	0	0	0	0	0	.500
Ray Fosse, c	2	0	0	0	0	1	.000
Billy Williams, ph	1	0	0	0	0	0	.000
Ted Martinez, 2b	0	0	0	0	0	0	—
Cesar Tovar, ph	1	0	0	0	0	0	.000
TOTALS	34	3	10	3	2	4	.197

Red Sox	AB	R	H	RBI	BB	K	Avg
Juan Beniquez, dh	4	1	1	0	0	0	.375
Denny Doyle, 2b	3	1	1	0	0	0	.167
Carl Yastrzemski, lf	3	2	2	2	1	0	.429
Carlton Fisk, c	4	1	2	1	0	2	.375
Fred Lynn, cf	4	0	2	1	0	0	.375
Rico Petrocelli, 3b	4	1	1	1	0	0	.125
Dwight Evans, rf	3	0	0	0	0	1	.143
Cecil Cooper, 1b	3	0	2	0	0	0	.500
Rick Burleson, ss	2	0	1	0	1	0	.400
TOTALS	30	6	12	5	1	5	.317

	1	2	3	4	5	6	7	8	9		R	H	E
Athletics	2	0	0	1	0	0	0	0	0		3	10	0
Red Sox	0	0	0	3	0	1	1	1	x		6	12	0

DP—Athletics 4 (Campaneris to Garner to Tenace; Campaneris to Garner to Tenace; Jackson to Fosse; Tenace to Campaneris), Red Sox 2 (Petrocelli to Doyle to Cooper; Lynn to Cooper). LOB—Athletics 6, Red Sox 3. Scoring Position—Athletics 2-for-6, Red Sox 4-for-9. 2B—Bando (2), Rudi 2 (2), Washington (1), Yastrzemski (1), Fisk (1), Cooper 2 (2). HR—Jackson (1), Yastrzemski (1), Petrocelli (1). S—Doyle, Burleson. GDP—Tenace, Beniquez, Lynn, Petrocelli.

Athletics	IP	H	R	ER	BB	K	ERA
Vida Blue	3.0	6	3	3	0	2	9.00
Jim Todd	1.0	1	0	0	0	0	9.00
Rollie Fingers (L, 0-1)	4.0	5	3	3	1	3	6.75

Red Sox	IP	H	R	ER	BB	K	ERA
Reggie Cleveland	5.0	7	3	3	1	2	5.40
Roger Moret (W, 1-0)	1.0	1	0	0	1	0	0.00
Dick Drago (S, 1)	3.0	2	0	0	0	2	0.00

Blue pitched to four batters in the 4th. Todd pitched to one batter in the 5th. Cleveland pitched to one batter in the 6th. Moret pitched to one batter in the 7th.

WP—Drago. Time—2:27. Attendance—35,578. Umpires—HP, DiMuro. 1B, Kunkel. 2B, Luciano. 3B, Evans.

Game 3
Tuesday, October 7

Red Sox	AB	R	H	RBI	BB	K	Avg
Juan Beniquez, dh	4	0	0	0	0	1	.250
Denny Doyle, 2b	5	1	2	1	0	0	.273
Carl Yastrzemski, lf	4	1	2	0	0	0	.455
Carlton Fisk, c	4	1	2	1	0	0	.417
Fred Lynn, cf	3	1	1	0	0	0	.364
Rico Petrocelli, 3b	4	0	1	1	0	1	.167
Dwight Evans, rf	3	0	0	1	0	1	.100
Cecil Cooper, 1b	4	0	1	1	0	0	.400
Rick Burleson, ss	4	1	2	0	0	0	.444
TOTALS	35	5	11	4	1	3	.316

Athletics	AB	R	H	RBI	BB	K	Avg
Bert Campaneris, ss	4	0	0	0	0	1	.000
Claudell Washington, lf	4	1	1	0	0	0	.250
Sal Bando, 3b	4	0	2	2	0	0	.500
Reggie Jackson, rf	4	0	2	1	0	1	.417
Joe Rudi, 1b	4	0	0	0	0	0	.250
Billy Williams, dh	4	0	0	0	0	0	.000
Gene Tenace, c	2	0	0	0	2	0	.000
Bill North, cf	3	0	0	0	1	0	.000
Phil Garner, 2b	1	0	0	0	0	0	.000
Cesar Tovar, ph-2b	1	2	1	0	1	0	.500
Ted Martinez, 2b	0	0	0	0	0	0	—
Jim Holt, ph	1	0	0	0	0	0	.333
TOTALS	32	3	6	3	4	2	.198

	1	2	3	4	5	6	7	8	9		R	H	E
Red Sox	0	0	0	1	3	0	0	1	0		5	11	1
Athletics	0	0	0	0	0	1	0	2	0		3	6	2

E—Washington, Doyle, Tovar. DP—Red Sox 1 (Burleson to Doyle to Cooper). LOB—Red Sox 6, Athletics 6. Scoring Position—Red Sox 4-for-10, Athletics 2-for-5. 2B—Burleson (2). S—Beniquez, Lynn. GDP—Rudi. SB—Fisk (1).

Red Sox	IP	H	R	ER	BB	K	ERA
Rick Wise (W, 1-0)	7.1	6	3	2	3	2	2.45
Dick Drago (S, 2)	1.2	0	0	0	1	0	0.00

Athletics	IP	H	R	ER	BB	K	ERA
Ken Holtzman (L, 0-2)	4.2	7	4	3	0	3	4.09
Jim Todd	0.0	1	1	1	0	0	9.00
Paul Lindblad	4.1	3	1	0	1	0	0.00

Todd pitched to one batter in the 5th.

WP—Lindblad. Time—2:30. Attendance—49,358. Umpires—HP, Kunkel. 1B, Luciano. 2B, Evans. 3B, Morganweck.

1975 AL Championship Series—Composite Statistics

Batting

Red Sox	G	AB	R	H	RBI	2B	3B	HR	BB	SO	SB	CS	Avg	OBP	Slg
Juan Beniquez	3	12	2	3	1	0	0	0	0	1	2	0	.250	.250	.250
Rick Burleson	3	9	2	4	1	2	0	0	1	0	0	0	.444	.500	.667
Cecil Cooper	3	10	0	4	1	2	0	0	0	2	0	0	.400	.400	.600
Denny Doyle	3	11	3	3	2	0	0	0	0	1	0	0	.273	.250	.273
Dwight Evans	3	10	1	1	0	1	0	0	1	2	0	0	.100	.182	.200
Carlton Fisk	3	12	4	5	2	1	0	0	0	2	1	0	.417	.417	.500
Fred Lynn	3	11	1	4	3	1	0	0	0	0	0	0	.364	.364	.455
Rico Petrocelli	3	12	1	2	2	0	0	1	0	3	0	0	.167	.167	.417
Carl Yastrzemski	3	11	4	5	2	1	0	1	1	1	0	0	.455	.500	.818
Totals	**3**	**98**	**18**	**31**	**14**	**8**	**0**	**2**	**3**	**12**	**3**	**0**	**.316**	**.333**	**.459**

Batting

Athletics	G	AB	R	H	RBI	2B	3B	HR	BB	SO	SB	CS	Avg	OBP	Slg
Sal Bando	3	12	1	6	2	2	0	0	0	3	0	0	.500	.500	.667
Bert Campaneris	3	11	1	0	0	0	0	0	1	1	0	0	.000	.083	.000
Ray Fosse	1	2	0	0	0	0	0	0	0	1	0	0	.000	.000	.000
Phil Garner	3	5	0	0	0	0	0	0	0	1	0	0	.000	.000	.000
Tommy Harper	1	0	0	0	0	0	0	0	1	0	0	0	—	1.000	—
Jim Holt	3	3	0	1	0	1	0	0	0	0	0	0	.333	.333	.667
Don Hopkins	1	0	0	0	0	0	0	0	0	0	0	0	—	—	—
Reggie Jackson	3	12	1	5	3	0	0	1	0	2	0	0	.417	.417	.667
Bill North	3	10	0	0	1	0	0	0	2	0	0	0	.000	.167	.000
Joe Rudi	3	12	1	3	0	2	0	0	0	1	0	0	.250	.250	.417
Gene Tenace	3	9	0	0	0	0	0	0	3	2	0	0	.000	.250	.000
Cesar Tovar	2	2	2	1	0	0	0	0	1	0	0	0	.500	.667	.500
Claudell Washington	3	12	1	3	1	1	0	0	0	2	0	0	.250	.250	.333
Billy Williams	3	8	0	0	0	0	0	0	1	1	0	0	.000	.111	.000
Totals	**3**	**98**	**7**	**19**	**7**	**6**	**0**	**1**	**9**	**14**	**0**	**0**	**.194**	**.262**	**.286**

Pitching

Red Sox	G	GS	CG	IP	H	R	ER	BB	SO	W-L	Sv-Op	Hld	ERA
Reggie Cleveland	1	1	0	5.0	7	3	3	1	2	0-0	0-0	0	5.40
Dick Drago	2	0	0	4.2	2	0	0	1	2	0-0	2-2	0	0.00
Roger Moret	1	0	0	1.0	1	0	0	1	0	1-0	0-0	0	0.00
Luis Tiant	1	1	1	9.0	3	1	0	3	8	1-0	0-0	0	0.00
Rick Wise	1	1	0	7.1	6	3	2	3	2	1-0	0-0	0	2.45
Totals	**3**	**3**	**1**	**27.0**	**19**	**7**	**5**	**9**	**14**	**3-0**	**2-2**	**0**	**1.67**

Pitching

Athletics	G	GS	CG	IP	H	R	ER	BB	SO	W-L	Sv-Op	Hld	ERA
Glenn Abbott	1	0	0	1.0	0	0	0	0	0	0-0	0-0	0	0.00
Vida Blue	1	1	0	3.0	6	3	3	0	2	0-0	0-0	0	9.00
Dick Bosman	1	0	0	0.1	0	0	0	0	0	0-0	0-0	0	0.00
Rollie Fingers	1	0	0	4.0	5	3	3	1	3	0-1	0-0	0	6.75
Ken Holtzman	2	2	0	11.0	12	8	5	1	7	0-2	0-0	0	4.09
Paul Lindblad	2	0	0	4.2	5	3	0	1	0	0-0	0-0	0	0.00
Jim Todd	3	0	0	1.0	3	1	1	0	0	0-0	0-0	0	9.00
Totals	**3**	**3**	**0**	**25.0**	**31**	**18**	**12**	**3**	**12**	**0-3**	**0-0**	**0**	**4.32**

Fielding

Red Sox	Pos	G	PO	Ast	E	DP	PB	FPct
Rick Burleson	ss	3	3	12	1	1	—	.938
Reggie Cleveland	p	1	0	1	0	0	—	1.000
Cecil Cooper	1b	3	24	1	1	3	—	.962
Denny Doyle	2b	3	6	8	1	2	—	.933
Dick Drago	p	2	1	0	0	0	—	1.000
Dwight Evans	rf	3	7	0	0	0	—	1.000
Carlton Fisk	c	3	15	0	0	0	0	1.000
Fred Lynn	cf	3	12	1	1	1	—	.929
Roger Moret	p	1	0	0	0	0	—	—
Rico Petrocelli	3b	3	4	3	0	1	—	1.000
Luis Tiant	p	1	0	1	0	0	—	1.000
Rick Wise	p	1	2	3	0	0	—	1.000
Carl Yastrzemski	lf	3	7	2	0	0	—	1.000
Totals		**3**	**81**	**32**	**4**	**8**	**0**	**.966**

Fielding

Athletics	Pos	G	PO	Ast	E	DP	PB	FPct
Glenn Abbott	p	1	0	0	0	0	—	—
Sal Bando	3b	3	3	11	1	0	—	.933
Vida Blue	p	1	0	0	0	0	—	—
Dick Bosman	p	1	0	0	0	0	—	—
Bert Campaneris	ss	3	2	10	0	3	—	1.000
Rollie Fingers	p	1	1	0	0	0	—	1.000
Ray Fosse	c	1	3	0	0	1	0	1.000
Phil Garner	2b	3	7	4	1	2	—	.917
Jim Holt	1b	1	1	2	0	0	—	1.000
Ken Holtzman	p	2	1	1	0	0	—	1.000
Reggie Jackson	rf	3	5	1	0	1	—	1.000
Paul Lindblad	p	2	1	4	0	0	—	1.000
Ted Martinez	2b	3	1	1	0	0	—	1.000
Bill North	cf	3	6	1	1	0	—	.875
Joe Rudi	1b	2	21	2	0	0	—	1.000
	lf	1	1	0	0	0	—	1.000
Gene Tenace	c	3	11	0	0	0	0	1.000
	1b	1	8	1	0	3	—	1.000
Jim Todd	p	3	0	0	0	0	—	—
Cesar Tovar	2b	1	2	2	1	0	—	.800
Claudell Washington	lf	2	1	0	2	0	—	.333
Totals		**3**	**75**	**40**	**6**	**10**	**0**	**.950**

1975 Cincinnati Reds (NL) 3, Pittsburgh Pirates (NL) 0

The Cincinnati Reds chewed up and spat out the Pittsburgh Pirates with efficiency, defeating Pittsburgh in three straight games before entering the World Series. Don Gullett was a one-man gang in the opener, tossing a complete-game 8-3 victory while singling, homering and driving in three runs at the plate. The Reds shelled Jim Rooker in Game 2, winning 6-1 on the strength of Tony Perez' homer, three hits and three RBI. In Game 3, it seemed that the Pirates had finally found the hurler who could quiet the Reds' big bats: young lefthander John Candelaria. He took a 2-1 lead into the eighth, and fanned the first two batters of the inning to run his strikeout total to 14. But after a two-out walk to Merv Rettenmund, Pete Rose blasted a two-run homer to give the Reds the lead. Cincinnati reliever Rawly Eastwick walked in the tying run in the bottom of the ninth, but the Reds broke through in the top of the 10th with a pair of runs and a 5-3 win.

Game 1

Saturday, October 4

Pirates	AB	R	H	RBI	BB	K	Avg
Rennie Stennett, 2b	5	0	1	0	0	1	.200
Manny Sanguillen, c	4	0	1	0	0	0	.250
Al Olivor, cf	4	0	1	0	0	0	.250
Willie Stargell, 1b	4	0	0	0	0	0	.000
Richie Zisk, lf	4	0	1	0	0	1	.250
Dave Parker, rf	2	0	0	0	1	0	.000
Richie Hebner, 3b	4	1	2	1	0	0	.500
Frank Taveras, ss	3	0	1	1	1	1	.333
Jerry Reuss, p	1	0	0	0	0	0	.000
Ken Brett, p	0	0	0	0	0	0	—
Bill Robinson, ph	1	0	0	0	0	1	.000
Larry Demery, p	0	0	0	0	0	0	—
Willie Randolph, ph	1	0	0	0	0	1	.000
Dock Ellis, p	0	0	0	0	0	0	—
Bob Robertson, ph	1	0	1	1	0	0	1.000
Craig Reynolds, pr	0	0	0	0	0	0	—
TOTALS	34	3	8	3	2	5	.235

Reds	AB	R	H	RBI	BB	K	Avg
Pete Rose, 3b	5	0	2	0	0	0	.400
Joe Morgan, 2b	3	1	0	2	1	0	.000
Johnny Bench, c	4	1	1	0	1	0	.250
Tony Perez, 1b	4	2	2	1	1	0	.500
George Foster, lf	4	2	2	0	0	0	.500
Dave Concepcion, ss	3	0	1	0	1	1	.333
Ken Griffey Sr., rf	4	1	1	3	0	1	.250
Cesar Geronimo, cf	3	0	0	1	0	1	.000
Don Gullett, p	4	1	2	3	0	0	.500
TOTALS	34	8	11	8	5	5	.324

	1	2	3	4	5	6	7	8	9		R	H	E
Pirates	0	2	0	0	0	0	0	0	1		3	8	0
Reds	0	1	3	0	4	0	0	0	x		8	11	0

LOB—Pirates 7, Reds 8. Scoring Position—Pirates 2-for-6, Reds 4-for-16. 2B—Hebner (1), Griffey Sr. (1). HR—Gullett (1). SF—Geronimo. SB—Morgan 3 (3).

Pirates	IP	H	R	ER	BB	K	ERA
Jerry Reuss (L, 0-1)	2.2	4	4	4	4	1	13.50
Ken Brett	1.1	1	0	0	0	1	0.00
Larry Demery	2.0	4	4	4	1	1	18.00
Dock Ellis	2.0	2	0	0	0	2	0.00

Reds	IP	H	R	ER	BB	K	ERA
Don Gullett (W, 1-0)	9.0	8	3	3	2	5	3.00

WP—Gullett. PB—Sanguillen 2. HBP—Parker by Gullett. Time—3:00. Attendance—54,633. Umpires—HP, Kibler. 1B, Olsen. 2B, Pulli. 3B, Williams.

Game 2

Sunday, October 5

Pirates	AB	R	H	RBI	BB	K	Avg
Rennie Stennett, 2b	4	0	2	0	0	0	.333
Manny Sanguillen, c	4	0	0	0	0	0	.125
Al Oliver, cf	2	0	0	0	2	0	.167
Willie Stargell, 1b	3	1	1	0	1	1	.143
Richie Zisk, lf	3	0	2	0	1	0	.429
Dave Parker, rf	4	0	0	0	0	2	.000
Richie Hebner, 3b	3	0	1	1	1	0	.286
Frank Taveras, ss	3	0	0	0	0	1	.167
Bob Robertson, ph	1	0	0	0	0	0	.500
Jim Rooker, p	1	0	0	0	0	1	.000
Bill Robinson, ph	1	0	0	0	0	0	.000
Kent Tekulve, p	0	0	0	0	0	0	—
Ken Brett, p	0	0	0	0	0	0	—
Ed Kirkpatrick, ph	1	0	0	0	0	0	.000
Bruce Kison, p	0	0	0	0	0	0	—
TOTALS	30	1	5	1	5	5	.210

Reds	AB	R	H	RBI	BB	K	Avg
Pete Rose, 3b	4	1	1	0	0	1	.333
Joe Morgan, 2b	3	1	1	0	1	0	.167
Johnny Bench, c	4	0	0	0	0	3	.125
Tony Perez, 1b	4	1	3	3	0	0	.625
George Foster, lf	4	1	2	0	0	1	.500
Dave Concepcion, ss	4	1	3	0	0	0	.571
Ken Griffey Sr., rf	4	1	2	1	0	0	.375
Cesar Geronimo, cf	3	0	0	0	1	3	.000
Fred Norman, p	1	0	0	0	0	0	.000
Ed Armbrister, ph	0	0	0	0	0	0	—
Terry Crowley, ph	0	0	0	0	0	0	—
Merv Rettenmund, ph	1	0	0	0	0	0	.000
Rawly Eastwick, p	0	0	0	0	0	0	—
TOTALS	32	6	12	5	2	8	.339

	1	2	3	4	5	6	7	8	9		R	H	E
Pirates	0	0	0	1	0	0	0	0	0		1	5	0
Reds	2	0	0	2	0	1	1	0	x		6	12	1

E—Concepcion. DP—Pirates 3 (Parker to Sanguillen; Stennett to Taveras to Stargell; Stennett to Taveras to Stargell), Reds 2 (Concepcion to Perez; Morgan to Concepcion to Perez). LOB—Pirates 7, Reds 5. Scoring Position—Pirates 0-for-8, Reds 4-for-12. 2B—Stargell (1), Zisk (1), Morgan (1). HR—Perez (1). SF—Norman. GDP—Sanguillen, Parker, Foster, Griffey Sr. SB—Morgan (4), Foster (1), Concepcion 2 (2), Griffey Sr. 3 (3).

Pirates	IP	H	R	ER	BB	K	ERA
Jim Rooker (L, 0-1)	4.0	7	4	4	0	5	9.00
Kent Tekulve	1.0	3	1	1	1	2	9.00
Ken Brett	1.0	0	0	0	0	0	0.00
Bruce Kison	2.0	2	1	1	1	1	4.50

Reds	IP	H	R	ER	BB	K	ERA
Fred Norman (W, 1-0)	6.0	4	1	1	5	4	1.50
Rawly Eastwick (S, 1)	3.0	1	0	0	0	1	0.00

Tekulve pitched to four batters in the 6th.

Balk—Brett. WP—Norman. Time—2:51. Attendance—54,752. Umpires—HP, Olsen. 1B, Pulli. 2B, Williams. 3B, Gorman.

Game 3

Tuesday, October 7

Reds	AB	R	H	RBI	BB	K	Avg
Pete Rose, 3b	5	2	2	2	0	1	.357
Joe Morgan, 2b	5	0	2	1	0	1	.273
Johnny Bench, c	5	0	0	0	0	2	.077
Tony Perez, 1b	4	0	0	0	0	2	.417
George Foster, lf	3	0	0	0	1	1	.364
Dave Concepcion, ss	4	1	1	1	0	1	.455
Ken Griffey Sr., rf	4	1	1	0	0	2	.333
Cesar Geronimo, cf	4	0	0	0	0	3	.000
Gary Nolan, p	2	0	0	0	0	2	.000
Clay Carroll, p	0	0	0	0	0	0	—
Merv Rettenmund, ph	0	1	0	0	1	0	.000
Will McEnaney, p	0	0	0	0	0	0	—
Rawly Eastwick, p	0	0	0	0	0	0	—
Ed Armbrister, ph	0	0	0	1	0	0	—
Pedro Borbon, p	0	0	0	0	0	0	—
TOTALS	36	5	6	5	2	15	.278

Pirates	AB	R	H	RBI	BB	K	Avg
Rennie Stennett, 2b-ss	5	0	0	0	0	0	.214
Richie Hebner, 3b	5	1	2	0	0	1	.333
Al Oliver, cf	5	1	1	2	0	0	.182
Willie Stargell, 1b	4	0	1	0	0	2	.182
Willie Randolph, pr-2b	1	1	0	0	0	0	.000
Dave Parker, rf	4	0	0	0	0	1	.000
Richie Zisk, lf	3	0	2	0	1	1	.500
Manny Sanguillen, c	4	0	1	0	0	0	.167
Frank Taveras, ss	1	0	0	0	0	0	.143
Ed Kirkpatrick, ph	1	0	0	0	0	0	.000
Craig Reynolds, ss	1	0	0	0	0	0	.000
Bob Robertson, ph-1b	0	0	0	0	1	0	.500
John Candelaria, p	3	0	0	0	0	3	.000
Dave Giusti, p	0	0	0	0	0	0	—
Duffy Dyer, ph	0	0	0	1	1	0	—
Ramon Hernandez, p	0	0	0	0	0	0	—
Kent Tekulve, p	0	0	0	0	0	0	—
TOTALS	37	3	7	3	3	8	.206

	1	2	3	4	5	6	7	8	9	10		R	H	E
Reds	0	1	0	0	0	0	0	2	0	2		5	6	0
Pirates	0	0	0	0	0	2	0	0	1	0		3	7	2

E—Reynolds, Sanguillen. LOB—Reds 4, Pirates 7. Scoring Position—Reds 0-for-5, Pirates 0-for-6. 2B—Morgan 2 (3). HR—Rose (1), Concepcion (1), Oliver (1). SF—Armbrister. SB—Bench (1).

Reds	IP	H	R	ER	BB	K	ERA
Gary Nolan	6.0	5	2	2	0	5	3.00
Clay Carroll	1.0	0	0	0	1	1	0.00
Will McEnaney (H, 1)	1.1	1	1	1	0	1	6.75
Rawly Eastwick (BS, 1; W, 1-0)	0.2	1	0	0	2	0	0.00
Pedro Borbon (S, 1)	1.0	0	0	0	0	1	0.00

Pirates	IP	H	R	ER	BB	K	ERA
John Candelaria	7.2	3	3	3	2	14	3.52
Dave Giusti	1.1	0	0	0	0	1	0.00
Ramon Hernandez (L, 0-1)	0.2	3	2	2	0	0	27.00
Kent Tekulve	0.1	0	0	0	0	0	6.75

Balk—Hernandez. Time—2:47. Attendance—46,355. Umpires—HP, Pulli. 1B, Williams. 2B, Gorman. 3B, Williams.

1975 NL Championship Series—Composite Statistics

Batting

Reds	G	AB	R	H	RBI	2B	3B	HR	BB	SO	SB	CS	Avg	OBP	Slg
Ed Armbrister	2	0	0	0	1	0	0	0	0	0	0	0	—	.000	—
Johnny Bench	3	13	1	1	0	0	0	0	1	6	1	0	.077	.143	.077
Dave Concepcion	3	11	2	5	1	0	0	1	1	2	2	0	.455	.500	.727
Terry Crowley	1	0	0	0	0	0	0	0	0	0	0	0	—	—	—
George Foster	3	11	3	4	0	0	0	0	1	2	1	0	.364	.417	.364
Cesar Geronimo	3	10	0	0	1	0	0	0	1	7	0	0	.000	.083	.000
Ken Griffey Sr.	3	12	3	4	4	1	0	0	3	3	0	.333	.333	.417
Don Gullett	1	4	1	2	3	0	0	1	0	0	0	0	.500	.500	1.250
Joe Morgan	3	11	2	3	1	3	0	0	3	2	4	0	.273	.429	.545
Gary Nolan	1	2	0	0	0	0	0	0	0	2	0	0	.000	.000	.000
Fred Norman	1	1	0	0	1	0	0	0	0	0	0	0	.000	.000	.000
Tony Perez	3	12	3	5	4	0	0	1	1	2	0	0	.417	.462	.667
Merv Rettenmund	2	1	1	0	0	0	0	0	1	0	0	0	.000	.500	.000
Pete Rose	3	14	3	5	2	0	0	1	0	2	0	0	.357	.357	.571
Totals	**3**	**102**	**19**	**29**	**18**	**4**	**0**	**4**	**9**	**28**	**11**	**0**	**.284**	**.333**	**.441**

Pirates	G	AB	R	H	RBI	2B	3B	HR	BB	SO	SB	CS	Avg	OBP	Slg
John Candelaria	1	3	0	0	0	0	0	0	0	3	0	0	.000	.000	.000
Duffy Dyer	1	0	0	0	1	0	0	0	1	0	0	0	—	1.000	—
Richie Hebner	3	12	2	4	2	1	0	1	1	1	0	0	.333	.385	.417
Ed Kirkpatrick	2	2	0	0	0	0	0	0	0	0	0	0	.000	.000	.000
Al Oliver	3	11	1	2	2	0	0	1	2	0	0	0	.182	.308	.455
Dave Parker	3	10	2	0	0	0	0	0	1	3	0	0	.000	.167	.000
Willie Randolph	2	2	1	0	0	0	0	0	0	1	0	0	.000	.000	.000
Jerry Reuss	1	1	0	0	0	0	0	0	0	0	0	0	.000	.000	.000
Craig Reynolds	2	1	0	0	0	0	0	0	0	0	0	0	.000	.000	.000
Bob Robertson	3	2	0	1	1	0	0	0	1	0	0	0	.500	.667	.500
Bill Robinson	2	2	0	0	0	0	0	0	0	1	0	0	.000	.000	.000
Jim Rooker	1	1	0	0	0	0	0	0	0	1	0	0	.000	.000	.000
Manny Sanguillen	3	12	0	2	0	0	0	0	0	0	0	0	.167	.167	.167
Willie Stargell	3	11	1	2	0	1	0	0	1	3	0	0	.182	.250	.273
Rennie Stennett	3	14	0	3	0	0	0	0	0	1	0	0	.214	.214	.214
Frank Taveras	3	7	0	1	1	0	0	0	1	2	0	0	.143	.250	.143
Richie Zisk	3	10	0	5	0	1	0	0	2	2	0	0	.500	.583	.600
Totals	**3**	**101**	**7**	**20**	**7**	**3**	**0**	**1**	**10**	**18**	**0**	**0**	**.198**	**.277**	**.257**

Pitching

Reds	G	GS	CG	IP	H	R	ER	BB	SO	W-L	Sv-Op	Hld	ERA
Pedro Borbon	1	0	0	1.0	0	0	0	0	1	0-0	1-1	0	0.00
Clay Carroll	1	0	0	1.0	0	0	0	1	1	0-0	0-0	0	0.00
Rawly Eastwick	2	0	0	3.2	2	0	0	2	1	1-0	1-2	0	0.00
Don Gullett	1	1	1	9.0	8	3	3	2	5	1-0	0-0	0	3.00
Will McEnaney	1	0	0	1.1	1	1	1	0	1	0-0	0-0	1	6.75
Gary Nolan	1	1	0	6.0	5	2	2	0	5	0-0	0-0	0	3.00
Fred Norman	1	1	0	6.0	4	1	1	5	4	1-0	0-0	0	1.50
Totals	**3**	**3**	**1**	**28.0**	**20**	**7**	**7**	**10**	**18**	**3-0**	**2-3**	**1**	**2.25**

Pirates	G	GS	CG	IP	H	R	ER	BB	SO	W-L	Sv-Op	Hld	ERA
Ken Brett	2	0	0	2.1	1	0	0	0	1	0-0	0-0	0	0.00
John Candelaria	1	1	0	7.2	3	3	3	2	14	0-0	0-0	0	3.52
Larry Demery	1	0	0	2.0	4	4	4	1	1	0-0	0-0	0	18.00
Dock Ellis	1	0	0	2.0	2	0	0	0	2	0-0	0-0	0	0.00
Dave Giusti	1	0	0	1.1	0	0	0	0	1	0-0	0-0	0	0.00
Ramon Hernandez	1	0	0	0.2	3	2	2	0	0	0-1	0-0	0	27.00
Bruce Kison	1	0	0	2.0	2	1	1	1	1	0-0	0-0	0	4.50
Jerry Reuss	1	1	0	2.2	4	4	4	4	1	0-1	0-0	0	13.50
Jim Rooker	1	1	0	4.0	7	4	4	0	5	0-1	0-0	0	9.00
Kent Tekulve	2	0	0	1.1	3	1	1	1	2	0-0	0-0	0	6.75
Totals	**3**	**3**	**0**	**26.0**	**29**	**19**	**19**	**9**	**28**	**0-3**	**0-0**	**0**	**6.58**

Fielding

Reds	Pos	G	PO	Ast	E	DP	PB	FPct
Johnny Bench	c	3	18	4	0	0	0	1.000
Pedro Borbon	p	1	0	0	0	0		—
Clay Carroll	p	1	0	1	0	0	—	1.000
Dave Concepcion	ss	3	6	8	1	2	—	.933
Rawly Eastwick	p	2	1	0	0	0	—	1.000
George Foster	lf	3	7	0	0	0	—	1.000
Cesar Geronimo	cf	3	13	0	0	0	—	1.000
Ken Griffey Sr.	rf	3	4	1	0	0	—	1.000
Don Gullett	p	1	4	1	0	0	—	1.000
Will McEnaney	p	1	0	0	0	0	—	—
Joe Morgan	2b	3	2	9	0	1	—	1.000
Gary Nolan	p	1	0	0	0	0	—	—
Fred Norman	p	1	0	1	0	0	—	1.000
Tony Perez	1b	3	27	5	0	2	—	1.000
Pete Rose	3b	3	2	1	0	0	—	1.000
Totals		**3**	**84**	**31**	**1**	**5**	**0**	**.991**

Pirates	Pos	G	PO	Ast	E	DP	PB	FPct
Ken Brett	p	2	0	0	0	0	—	—
John Candelaria	p	1	0	0	0	0	—	—
Larry Demery	p	1	0	0	0	0	—	—
Dock Ellis	p	1	0	0	0	0	—	—
Dave Giusti	p	1	0	0	0	0	—	—
Richie Hebner	3b	3	0	2	0	0	—	1.000
Ramon Hernandez	p	1	0	0	0	0	—	—
Bruce Kison	p	1	0	0	0	0	—	—
Al Oliver	cf	3	5	0	0	0	—	1.000
Dave Parker	rf	3	13	1	0	1	—	1.000
Willie Randolph	2b	1	0	1	0	0	—	1.000
Jerry Reuss	p	1	0	1	0	0	—	1.000
Craig Reynolds	ss	1	0	0	1	0	—	.000
Bob Robertson	1b	1	1	0	0	0	—	1.000
Jim Rooker	p	1	0	0	0	0	—	—
Manny Sanguillen	c	3	29	1	1	1	2	.968
Willie Stargell	1b	3	15	0	0	2	—	1.000
Rennie Stennett	2b	3	3	8	0	2	—	1.000
	ss	1	0	0	0	0		
Frank Taveras	ss	3	4	6	0	2	—	1.000
Kent Tekulve	p	2	0	0	0	0	—	—
Richie Zisk	lf	3	8	0	0	0	—	1.000
Totals		**3**	**78**	**20**	**2**	**8**	**2**	**.980**

1976 New York Yankees (AL) 3, Kansas City Royals (AL) 2

Chris Chambliss put the New York Yankees in the World Series with a home run off Kansas City Royals reliever Mark Littell in the bottom of the ninth inning of the fifth and final game of the ALCS. This came after the two clubs traded wins for the first four games. The Yanks won the opener 4-1 behind Catfish Hunter, but Paul Splittorff tossed 5.2 innings of shutout relief and the Royals took Game 2, 7-3. Chambliss singled, homered and drove in three runs as the Yanks took the third game, 5-3. Diminutive Kansas City shortstop Fred Patek came up big in Game 4 with a single, two doubles and three RBI. That set the stage for Chambliss' game-winning blast in the fifth game. Chambliss batted .524 in the Series, homering twice and driving in eight runs.

Game 1

Saturday, October 9

Yankees	AB	R	H	RBI	BB	K	Avg
Mickey Rivers, cf	5	2	2	0	0	1	.400
Roy White, lf	4	0	1	2	1	0	.250
Thurman Munson, c	5	1	1	0	0	1	.200
Lou Piniella, dh	4	0	2	0	0	1	.500
Chris Chambliss, 1b	4	0	2	1	0	1	.500
Graig Nettles, 3b	4	0	0	0	0	1	.000
Elliott Maddox, rf	4	0	1	0	0	0	.250
Willie Randolph, 2b	4	0	0	0	0	0	.000
Fred Stanley, ss	4	1	3	0	0	0	.750
TOTALS	38	4	12	3	1	4	.316

Royals	AB	R	H	RBI	BB	K	Avg
Amos Otis, cf	1	0	0	0	0	0	.000
Jim Wohlford, lf	3	0	0	0	0	1	.000
George Brett, 3b	4	0	3	0	0	0	.750
Hal McRae, dh	4	0	0	0	0	2	.000
John Mayberry, 1b	3	0	0	0	0	0	.000
Al Cowens, rf-cf	3	1	1	0	0	0	.333
Tom Poquette, lf-rf	3	0	0	1	0	0	.000
Frank White, 2b	2	0	0	0	0	0	.000
Cookie Rojas, ph-2b	1	0	0	0	0	0	.000
Freddie Patek, ss	3	0	1	0	0	0	.333
Buck Martinez, c	2	0	0	0	0	2	.000
Jamie Quirk, ph	0	0	0	0	0	0	—
John Wathan, c	0	0	0	0	0	0	—
Bob Stinson, ph	1	0	0	0	0	0	.000
TOTALS	30	1	5	1	0	5	.167

	1	2	3	4	5	6	7	8	9	R	H	E
Yankees	2	0	0	0	0	0	0	0	2	4	12	0
Royals	0	0	0	0	0	0	0	1	0	1	5	2

E—Brett 2. DP—Royals 1 (Brett to FWhite to Mayberry). LOB—Yankees 8, Royals 2. Scoring Position—Yankees 2-for-9, Royals 0-for-1. 2B—RWhite (1), Stanley (1). 3B—Chambliss (1), Cowens (1). GDP—Randolph. CS—Brett (1), Patek (1).

Yankees	IP	H	R	ER	BB	K	ERA
Catfish Hunter (W, 1-0)	9.0	5	1	1	0	5	1.00

Royals	IP	H	R	ER	BB	K	ERA
Larry Gura (L, 0-1)	8.2	12	4	3	1	4	3.12
Mark Littell	0.1	0	0	0	0	0	0.00

Time—2:06. Attendance—41,077. Umpires—HP, Brinkman. 1B, Haller. 2B, Maloney. 3B, Barnett.

Game 2

Sunday, October 10

Yankees	AB	R	H	RBI	BB	K	Avg
Mickey Rivers, cf	4	0	0	0	1	0	.222
Roy White, lf	4	1	2	0	1	0	.375
Thurman Munson, c	5	1	2	1	0	0	.300
Chris Chambliss, 1b	5	0	3	1	0	0	.556
Carlos May, dh	5	1	2	0	0	2	.400
Graig Nettles, 3b	3	0	1	0	1	0	.143
Oscar Gamble, rf	4	0	1	1	0	0	.250
Willie Randolph, 2b	3	0	0	0	1	0	.000
Fred Stanley, ss	3	0	1	0	0	0	.571
Lou Piniella, ph	1	0	0	0	0	0	.400
Jim Mason, ss	0	0	0	0	0	0	—
TOTALS	37	3	12	3	4	2	.324

Royals	AB	R	H	RBI	BB	K	Avg
Jim Wohlford, lf	4	1	1	0	1	0	.143
Al Cowens, cf	5	1	1	0	0	0	.250
George Brett, 3b	3	1	1	1	0	0	.571
John Mayberry, 1b	4	1	1	0	0	0	.143
Hal McRae, dh	3	0	0	0	1	1	.000
Tom Poquette, rf	3	1	2	2	1	0	.333
Frank White, 2b	4	1	1	0	0	1	.167
Freddie Patek, ss	4	1	1	1	0	0	.286
Buck Martinez, c	4	0	1	2	0	0	.167
TOTALS	34	7	9	7	3	2	.230

	1	2	3	4	5	6	7	8	9	R	H	E
Yankees	0	1	2	0	0	0	0	0	0	3	12	5
Royals	2	0	0	0	0	2	0	3	x	7	9	0

E—Chambliss, Stanley, Gamble, Munson 2. DP—Royals 2 (Patek to FWhite to Mayberry; Patek to Mayberry). LOB—Yankees 11, Royals 7. Scoring Position—Yankees 3-for-13, Royals 4-for-11. 2B—RWhite (2), Munson (1), May (1), Nettles (1), Stanley (2), Poquette (1). 3B—Brett (1). SF—Brett. GDP—Munson, Randolph. SB—Wohlford (1), Cowens 2 (2).

Yankees	IP	H	R	ER	BB	K	ERA
Ed Figueroa (L, 0-1)	5.1	4	4	2	2	0	6.75
Dick Tidrow	2.2	3	3	2	1	0	6.75

Royals	IP	H	R	ER	BB	K	ERA
Dennis Leonard	2.1	6	3	3	2	0	11.57
Paul Splittorff (W, 1-0)	5.2	4	0	0	2	1	0.00
Steve Mingori	1.0	2	0	0	0	1	0.00

Time—2:45. Attendance—41,091. Umpires—HP, Barnett. 1B, Maloney. 2B, Haller. 3B, Frantz.

Game 3

Tuesday, October 12

Royals	AB	R	H	RBI	BB	K	Avg
Jim Wohlford, lf	2	1	0	0	2	0	.111
Al Cowens, cf	4	0	1	0	0	1	.250
George Brett, 3b	3	1	2	1	1	0	.600
John Mayberry, 1b	4	1	1	0	0	0	.182
Hal McRae, dh	2	0	0	1	0	0	.000
Tom Poquette, rf	3	0	1	1	0	2	.333
Dave Nelson, ph	1	0	0	0	0	0	.000
Frank White, 2b	2	0	0	0	0	0	.125
Cookie Rojas, ph-2b	1	0	0	0	0	0	.000
Freddie Patek, ss	3	0	1	0	0	0	.300
Buck Martinez, c	2	0	0	0	0	1	.125
Jamie Quirk, ph	1	0	0	0	0	1	.000
Bob Stinson, c	0	0	0	0	0	0	.000
TOTALS	28	3	6	3	3	5	.220

Yankees	AB	R	H	RBI	BB	K	Avg
Mickey Rivers, cf	5	0	1	0	0	0	.214
Roy White, lf	3	1	0	0	1	1	.273
Thurman Munson, c	4	1	2	0	0	0	.357
Lou Piniella, dh	2	1	1	0	0	0	.429
Carlos May, ph-dh	1	0	0	0	1	1	.333
Chris Chambliss, 1b	4	2	2	3	0	0	.538
Graig Nettles, 3b	3	0	1	1	1	0	.200
Elliott Maddox, rf	4	0	1	1	0	1	.250
Willie Randolph, 2b	3	0	0	0	1	1	.100
Fred Stanley, ss	3	0	1	0	1	0	.400
TOTALS	32	5	9	5	5	5	.311

	1	2	3	4	5	6	7	8	9	R	H	E
Royals	3	0	0	0	0	0	0	0	0	3	6	0
Yankees	0	0	0	2	0	3	0	0	x	5	9	0

DP—Royals 1 (Martinez to FWhite), Yankees 2 (Randolph to Chambliss; Chambliss to Stanley to Randolph). LOB—Royals 3, Yankees 8. Scoring Position—Royals 2-for-4, Yankees 3-for-10. 2B—Poquette (2), Munson (2), Piniella (1), Maddox (1). HR—Chambliss (1). SF—McRae. GDP—Brett. SB—Wohlford (2), Chambliss (1), Randolph (1). CS—McRae (1), Patek (2), Rivers (1).

Royals	IP	H	R	ER	BB	K	ERA
Andy Hassler (L, 0-1)	5.0	4	4	4	3	3	7.20
Marty Pattin	0.0	0	1	1	1	0	—
Tom Hall (BS, 1)	0.1	1	0	0	0	0	0.00
Steve Mingori	0.0	1	0	0	0	0	0.00
Mark Littell	2.2	3	0	0	1	2	0.00

Yankees	IP	H	R	ER	BB	K	ERA
Dock Ellis (W, 1-0)	8.0	6	3	3	2	5	3.38
Sparky Lyle (S, 1)	1.0	0	0	0	1	0	0.00

Hassler pitched to two batters in the 6th. Pattin pitched to one batter in the 6th. Mingori pitched to one batter in the 6th.

PB—Munson. HBP—McRae by Ellis. Time—3:00. Attendance—56,808. Umpires—HP, Maloney. 1B, Haller. 2B, Frantz. 3B, McCoy.

Game 4
Wednesday, October 13

Royals	AB	R	H	RBI	BB	K	Avg
Al Cowens, cf	5	0	0	0	0	0	.176
Tom Poquette, lf-rf	4	0	0	0	1	0	.231
George Brett, 3b	4	0	0	0	1	1	.429
John Mayberry, 1b	3	1	0	0	1	0	.143
Hal McRae, rf	4	2	2	0	0	0	.154
Jim Wohlford, lf	0	0	0	0	0	0	.111
Jamie Quirk, dh	2	1	1	2	0	0	.333
Dave Nelson, ph-dh	1	0	0	0	0	1	.000
Cookie Rojas, 2b	3	1	2	1	0	0	.400
Frank White, pr-2b	0	1	0	0	0	0	.125
Freddie Patek, ss	4	1	3	3	0	0	.429
Buck Martinez, c	3	0	1	1	1	0	.182
TOTALS	33	7	9	7	4	2	.236

Yankees	AB	R	H	RBI	BB	K	Avg
Mickey Rivers, cf	4	0	1	0	0	0	.222
Roy White, lf	4	0	1	0	0	0	.267
Thurman Munson, c	4	0	2	0	0	0	.389
Lou Piniella, dh	4	0	0	0	0	0	.273
Chris Chambliss, 1b	4	1	1	0	0	0	.471
Graig Nettles, 3b	4	2	2	3	0	1	.286
Elliott Maddox, rf	1	0	0	0	0	0	.222
Oscar Gamble, ph-rf	2	1	1	0	0	0	.333
Otto Velez, ph	1	0	0	0	0	0	.000
Willie Randolph, 2b	4	0	1	1	0	0	.143
Fred Stanley, ss	2	0	1	0	0	0	.417
Ellie Hendricks, ph	1	0	1	0	0	0	1.000
Ron Guidry, pr	0	0	0	0	0	0	—
Jim Mason, ss	0	0	0	0	0	0	—
Sandy Alomar, ph	1	0	0	0	0	0	.000
TOTALS	36	4	11	4	0	1	.307

	1	2	3	4	5	6	7	8	9		R	H	E
Royals	0	3	0	2	0	1	0	1	0		7	9	1
Yankees	0	2	0	0	0	0	1	0	1		4	11	0

E—Bird. DP—Royals 1 (Rojas to Patek to Mayberry). LOB—Royals 5, Yankees 5. Scoring Position—Royals 3-for-5, Yankees 0-for-6. 2B—McRae (1), Patek 2 (2), RWhite (3), Gamble (1). 3B—McRae (1), Quirk (1). HR—Nettles 2 (2). SF—Quirk, Rojas. GDP—Chambliss. CS—Patek (3), Munson (1).

Royals	IP	H	R	ER	BB	K	ERA
Larry Gura	2.0	6	2	2	0	0	4.22
Doug Bird (W, 1-0)	4.2	4	1	1	0	1	1.93
Steve Mingori (S, 1)	2.1	1	1	1	0	0	2.70

Yankees	IP	H	R	ER	BB	K	ERA
Catfish Hunter (L, 1-1)	3.0	5	5	5	1	0	4.50
Dick Tidrow	3.2	2	1	1	2	0	4.26
Grant Jackson	2.1	2	1	1	1	2	3.86

Gura pitched to one batter in the 3rd. Hunter pitched to two batters in the 4th.

Time—2:50. Attendance—56,355. Umpires—HP, Haller. 1B, Frantz. 2B, McCoy. 3B, Brinkman.

Game 5
Thursday, October 14

Royals	AB	R	H	RBI	BB	K	Avg
Al Cowens, cf	4	1	1	0	1	0	.190
Tom Poquette, lf	3	0	0	0	0	1	.188
Jim Wohlford, ph-lf	2	1	1	0	0	0	.182
George Brett, 3b	4	2	2	3	0	0	.444
John Mayberry, 1b	4	1	2	2	0	0	.222
Hal McRae, rf	4	0	0	0	0	1	.118
Jamie Quirk, dh	4	0	0	0	0	1	.143
Cookie Rojas, 2b	4	1	1	0	0	0	.333
Freddie Patek, ss	4	0	1	0	0	1	.389
Buck Martinez, c	4	0	3	1	0	0	.333
TOTALS	37	6	11	6	1	4	.260

Yankees	AB	R	H	RBI	BB	K	Avg
Mickey Rivers, cf	5	3	4	0	0	0	.348
Roy White, lf	2	2	1	1	2	0	.294
Thurman Munson, c	5	0	3	2	0	1	.435
Chris Chambliss, 1b	4	2	3	3	0	0	.524
Carlos May, dh	4	0	0	0	0	1	.200
Sandy Alomar, pr-dh	0	0	0	0	0	0	.000
Graig Nettles, 3b	3	0	0	0	1	0	.235
Oscar Gamble, rf	2	0	0	0	1	1	.250
Willie Randolph, 2b	3	0	0	0	1	0	.118
Fred Stanley, ss	3	0	0	0	1	0	.333
TOTALS	31	7	11	6	6	3	.322

	1	2	3	4	5	6	7	8	9		R	H	E
Royals	2	1	0	0	0	0	0	3	0		6	11	1
Yankees	2	0	2	0	0	2	0	0	1		7	11	1

E—Brett, Gamble. DP—Yankees 1 (Stanley to Chambliss). LOB—Royals 5, Yankees 9. Scoring Position—Royals 3-for-6, Yankees 4-for-14. 2B—Brett (1), Chambliss (1). 3B—Rivers (1). HR—Brett (1), Mayberry (1), Chambliss (2). S—White, Gamble. SF—Chambliss. GDP—Cowens. SB—Rojas (1), White (1), Chambliss (2). CS—Alomar (1).

Royals	IP	H	R	ER	BB	K	ERA
Dennis Leonard	0.0	3	2	2	0	0	19.29
Paul Splittorff	3.2	3	2	2	3	1	1.93
Marty Pattin	0.1	0	0	0	0	0	27.00
Andy Hassler	2.1	4	2	1	3	1	6.14
Mark Littell (L, 0-1)	1.2	1	1	1	0	1	1.93

Yankees	IP	H	R	ER	BB	K	ERA
Ed Figueroa	7.0	8	4	4	0	3	5.84
Grant Jackson (BS, 1)	1.0	2	2	2	0	1	8.10
Dick Tidrow (W, 1-0)	1.0	1	0	0	1	0	3.68

Leonard pitched to four batters in the 1st. Figueroa pitched to one batter in the 8th. Littell pitched to one batter in the 9th.

Time—3:13. Attendance—56,821. Umpires—HP, Frantz. 1B, McCoy. 2B, Brinkman. 3B, Barnett.

1976 AL Championship Series—Composite Statistics

Batting

Yankees	G	AB	R	H	RBI	2B	3B	HR	BB	SO	SB	CS	Avg	OBP	Slg
Sandy Alomar	2	1	0	0	0	0	0	0	0	0	0	1	.000	.000	.000
Chris Chambliss	5	21	5	11	8	1	1	2	0	1	2	0	.524	.500	.952
Oscar Gamble	3	8	1	2	1	1	0	0	1	1	0	0	.250	.333	.375
Ron Guidry	1	0	0	0	0	0	0	0	0	0	0	0	—	—	—
Ellie Hendricks	1	1	0	1	0	0	0	0	0	0	0	0	1.000	1.000	1.000
Elliott Maddox	3	9	0	2	1	1	0	0	0	1	0	0	.222	.222	.333
Carlos May	3	10	1	2	0	1	0	0	1	4	0	0	.200	.273	.300
Thurman Munson	5	23	3	10	3	2	0	0	0	1	0	1	.435	.435	.522
Graig Nettles	5	17	2	4	4	1	0	2	3	3	0	0	.235	.350	.647
Lou Piniella	4	11	1	3	0	1	0	0	0	1	0	0	.273	.273	.364
Willie Randolph	5	17	0	2	1	0	0	0	3	1	1	0	.118	.250	.118
Mickey Rivers	5	23	5	8	0	0	1	0	1	1	0	1	.348	.375	.435
Fred Stanley	5	15	1	5	0	2	0	0	2	0	0	0	.333	.412	.467
Otto Velez	1	1	0	0	0	0	0	0	0	0	0	0	.000	.000	.000
Roy White	5	17	4	5	3	3	0	0	5	1	1	0	.294	.455	.471
Totals	**5**	**174**	**23**	**55**	**21**	**13**	**2**	**4**	**16**	**15**	**4**	**3**	**.316**	**.372**	**.483**

Batting

Royals	G	AB	R	H	RBI	2B	3B	HR	BB	SO	SB	CS	Avg	OBP	Slg
George Brett	5	18	4	8	5	1	1	1	2	1	0	1	.444	.476	.778
Al Cowens	5	21	3	4	0	0	1	0	1	1	2	0	.190	.227	.286
Buck Martinez	5	15	0	5	4	0	0	0	1	3	0	0	.333	.375	.333
John Mayberry	5	18	4	4	3	0	0	1	1	0	0	0	.222	.263	.389
Hal McRae	5	17	2	2	1	1	1	0	1	4	0	1	.118	.200	.294
Dave Nelson	2	2	0	0	0	0	0	0	0	1	0	0	.000	.000	.000
Amos Otis	1	1	0	0	0	0	0	0	0	0	0	0	.000	.000	.000
Freddie Patek	5	18	2	7	4	2	0	0	1	0	3	3	.389	.389	.500
Tom Poquette	5	16	1	3	4	2	0	0	2	3	0	0	.188	.278	.313
Jamie Quirk	4	7	1	1	2	0	1	0	0	2	0	0	.143	.125	.429
Cookie Rojas	4	9	2	3	1	0	0	0	0	0	1	0	.333	.300	.333
Bob Stinson	2	1	0	0	0	0	0	0	0	0	0	0	.000	.000	.000
Frank White	4	8	2	1	0	0	0	0	0	1	0	0	.125	.125	.125
Jim Wohlford	5	11	3	2	0	0	0	0	3	1	2	0	.182	.357	.182
Totals	**5**	**162**	**24**	**40**	**24**	**6**	**4**	**2**	**11**	**18**	**5**	**5**	**.247**	**.292**	**.370**

Pitching

Yankees	G	GS	CG	IP	H	R	ER	BB	SO	W-L	Sv-Op	Hld	ERA
Dock Ellis	1	1	0	8.0	6	3	3	2	5	1-0	0-0	0	3.38
Ed Figueroa	2	2	0	12.1	14	8	8	2	5	0-1	0-0	0	5.84
Catfish Hunter	2	2	1	12.0	10	6	6	1	5	1-1	0-0	0	4.50
Grant Jackson	2	0	0	3.1	4	3	3	1	3	0-0	0-1	0	8.10
Sparky Lyle	1	0	0	1.0	0	0	0	1	0	0-0	1-1	0	0.00
Dick Tidrow	3	0	0	7.1	6	4	3	4	0	1-0	0-0	0	3.68
Totals	**5**	**5**	**1**	**44.0**	**40**	**24**	**23**	**11**	**18**	**3-2**	**1-2**	**0**	**4.70**

Pitching

Royals	G	GS	CG	IP	H	R	ER	BB	SO	W-L	Sv-Op	Hld	ERA
Doug Bird	1	0	0	4.2	4	1	1	0	1	1-0	0-0	0	1.93
Larry Gura	2	2	0	10.2	18	6	5	1	4	0-1	0-0	0	4.22
Tom Hall	1	0	0	0.1	1	0	0	0	0	0-0	0-1	0	0.00
Andy Hassler	2	1	0	7.1	8	6	5	6	4	0-1	0-0	0	6.14
Dennis Leonard	2	2	0	2.1	9	5	5	2	0	0-0	0-0	0	19.29
Mark Littell	3	0	0	4.2	4	1	1	1	3	0-1	0-0	0	1.93
Steve Mingori	3	0	0	3.1	1	1	1	0	1	0-0	1-1	0	2.70
Marty Pattin	2	0	0	0.1	0	1	1	1	0	0-0	0-0	0	27.00
Paul Splittorff	2	0	0	9.1	7	2	2	5	2	1-0	0-0	0	1.93
Totals	**5**	**5**	**0**	**43.0**	**55**	**23**	**21**	**16**	**15**	**2-3**	**1-2**	**0**	**4.40**

Fielding

Yankees	Pos	G	PO	Ast	E	DP	PB	FPct
Chris Chambliss	1b	5	50	3	1	3	—	.981
Dock Ellis	p	1	1	0	0	0	—	1.000
Ed Figueroa	p	2	0	2	0	0	—	1.000
Oscar Gamble	rf	3	4	0	2	0	—	.667
Catfish Hunter	p	2	0	3	0	0	—	1.000
Grant Jackson	p	2	0	1	0	0	—	1.000
Sparky Lyle	p	1	0	0	0	0	—	—
Elliott Maddox	rf	3	9	0	0	0	—	1.000
Jim Mason	ss	2	1	2	0	0	—	1.000
Thurman Munson	c	5	18	6	2	0	1	.923
Graig Nettles	3b	5	5	14	0	0	—	1.000
Willie Randolph	2b	5	8	14	0	2	—	1.000
Mickey Rivers	cf	5	11	0	0	0	—	1.000
Fred Stanley	ss	5	7	15	1	2	—	.957
Dick Tidrow	p	3	1	0	0	0	—	1.000
Roy White	lf	5	17	0	0	0	—	1.000
Totals		**5**	**132**	**60**	**6**	**7**	**1**	**.970**

Fielding

Royals	Pos	G	PO	Ast	E	DP	PB	FPct
Doug Bird	p	1	0	1	1	0	—	.500
George Brett	3b	5	3	7	3	1	—	.769
Al Cowens	cf	5	15	0	0	0	—	1.000
	rf	1	0	0	0	0	—	—
Larry Gura	p	2	0	0	0	0	—	—
Tom Hall	p	1	0	0	0	0	—	—
Andy Hassler	p	2	0	0	0	0	—	—
Dennis Leonard	p	2	0	0	0	0	—	—
Mark Littell	p	3	0	1	0	0	—	1.000
Buck Martinez	c	5	15	4	0	1	0	1.000
John Mayberry	1b	5	48	1	0	4	—	1.000
Hal McRae	rf	2	5	1	0	0	—	1.000
Steve Mingori	p	3	0	0	0	0	—	—
Amos Otis	cf	1	0	0	0	0	—	—
Freddie Patek	ss	5	13	18	0	3	—	1.000
Marty Pattin	p	2	0	0	0	0	—	—
Tom Poquette	rf	4	8	0	0	0	—	1.000
	lf	3	5	0	0	0	—	1.000
Cookie Rojas	2b	4	4	6	0	1	—	1.000
Paul Splittorff	p	2	0	1	0	0	—	1.000
Bob Stinson	c	1	0	0	0	0	0	—
John Wathan	c	1	0	0	0	0	0	—
Frank White	2b	4	6	11	0	3	—	1.000
Jim Wohlford	lf	5	7	0	0	0	—	1.000
Totals		**5**	**129**	**51**	**4**	**13**	**0**	**.978**

1976 Cincinnati Reds (NL) 3, Philadelphia Phillies (NL) 0

The Cincinnati Reds captured their second straight NL title with a three-game sweep of the Philadelphia Phillies in the NLCS. In the opener, Don Gullett not only outpitched Steve Carlton, but drove in three runs with a single and a double in a 6-3 Reds win. The Phillies stranded 10 runners in Game 2 as the Reds prevailed, 6-2. The Phils took a 6-4 lead into the bottom of the ninth in Game 3, but the first two Cincinnati batters of the inning, George Foster and Johnny Bench, each homered off Ron Reed, tying the game at six apiece. The Reds then loaded the bases before Ken Griffey singled off first baseman Bobby Tolan's glove to bring home the winning run.

Game 1

Saturday, October 9

Reds	AB	R	H	RBI	BB	K	Avg
Pete Rose, 3b	5	1	3	1	0	0	.600
Ken Griffey Sr., rf	4	0	1	0	1	1	.250
Joe Morgan, 2b	2	0	0	0	3	0	.000
Rawly Eastwick, p	0	0	0	0	0	0	—
Tony Perez, 1b	3	0	0	1	1	2	.000
George Foster, lf	5	1	1	1	0	3	.200
Johnny Bench, c	5	1	2	0	0	1	.400
Dave Concepcion, ss	3	2	1	0	1	1	.333
Cesar Geronimo, cf	4	0	0	0	0	2	.000
Don Gullett, p	4	1	2	3	0	0	.500
Doug Flynn, 2b	0	0	0	0	0	0	—
TOTALS	35	6	10	6	6	10	.286

Phillies	AB	R	H	RBI	BB	K	Avg
Dave Cash, 2b	4	1	1	0	0	0	.250
Garry Maddox, cf	4	1	2	0	0	0	.500
Mike Schmidt, 3b	3	0	0	1	0	0	.000
Greg Luzinski, lf	3	1	1	1	1	2	.333
Dick Allen, 1b	3	0	1	0	1	0	.333
Ollie Brown, rf	2	0	0	0	1	1	.000
Jay Johnstone, ph	1	0	1	1	0	0	1.000
Tim McCarver, c	3	0	0	0	0	1	.000
Tug McGraw, p	0	0	0	0	0	0	—
Bobby Tolan, ph	1	0	0	0	0	0	.000
Larry Bowa, ss	3	0	0	0	0	0	.000
Tom Hutton, ph	1	0	0	0	0	0	.000
Steve Carlton, p	2	0	0	0	0	0	.000
Bob Boone, c	1	0	0	0	0	0	.000
TOTALS	31	3	6	3	3	4	.194

	1	2	3	4	5	6	7	8	9	R	H	E
Reds	0	0	1	0	0	2	0	3	0	6	10	0
Phillies	1	0	0	0	0	0	0	0	2	3	6	1

E—Schmidt. DP—Phillies 2 (Schmidt; Schmidt to Cash). LOB—Reds 9, Phillies 5. Scoring Position—Reds 3-for-21, Phillies 3-for-8. 2B—Rose 2 (2), Bench (1), Concepcion (1), Gullett (1), Cash (1), Luzinski (1). 3B—Rose (1), Griffey Sr. (1). HR—Foster (1). SF—Perez, Schmidt. SB—Griffey Sr. (1), Morgan 2 (2), Bench (1). CS—Maddox (1).

Reds	IP	H	R	ER	BB	K	ERA
Don Gullett (W, 1-0)	8.0	2	1	1	3	4	1.13
Rawly Eastwick	1.0	4	2	2	0	0	18.00

Phillies	IP	H	R	ER	BB	K	ERA
Steve Carlton (L, 0-1)	7.0	8	5	4	5	6	5.14
Tug McGraw	2.0	2	1	1	1	4	4.50

Carlton pitched to two batters in the 8th.

WP—McGraw, Eastwick. Time—2:39. Attendance—62,640. Umpires—HP, Sudol. 1B, Dale. 2B, Stello. 3B, Vargo.

Game 2

Sunday, October 10

Reds	AB	R	H	RBI	BB	K	Avg
Pete Rose, 3b	5	2	2	1	0	0	.500
Ken Griffey Sr., rf	4	1	2	1	1	0	.375
Joe Morgan, 2b	2	1	0	0	2	0	.000
Tony Perez, 1b	3	0	0	1	0	0	.000
George Foster, lf	4	0	0	1	0	1	.111
Johnny Bench, c	4	0	1	0	0	1	.333
Cesar Geronimo, cf	4	0	1	0	0	0	.125
Dave Concepcion, ss	3	1	0	0	1	0	.167
Pat Zachry, p	1	0	0	0	0	0	.000
Dan Driessen, ph	1	0	0	0	0	0	.000
Pedro Borbon, p	2	1	0	0	0	2	.000
TOTALS	33	6	6	4	4	4	.219

Phillies	AB	R	H	RBI	BB	K	Avg
Dave Cash, 2b	5	0	2	0	0	0	.333
Garry Maddox, cf	4	0	0	0	1	0	.250
Mike Schmidt, 3b	5	0	1	0	0	1	.125
Greg Luzinski, lf	4	1	1	1	0	1	.286
Dick Allen, 1b	3	1	1	0	1	1	.333
Jay Johnstone, rf	4	0	3	0	0	0	.800
Bob Boone, c	3	0	2	1	0	0	.500
Larry Bowa, ss	2	0	0	0	2	0	.000
Jim Lonborg, p	1	0	0	0	0	0	.000
Gene Garber, p	0	0	0	0	0	0	—
Bobby Tolan, ph	1	0	0	0	0	0	.000
Tug McGraw, p	0	0	0	0	0	0	—
Ron Reed, p	0	0	0	0	0	0	—
Tim McCarver, ph	1	0	0	0	0	0	.000
TOTALS	33	2	10	2	4	3	.271

	1	2	3	4	5	6	7	8	9	R	H	E
Reds	0	0	0	0	0	4	2	0	0	6	6	0
Phillies	0	1	0	0	1	0	0	0	0	2	10	1

E—Allen. DP—Reds 2 (Rose to Bench to Perez; Morgan). LOB—Reds 5, Phillies 10. Scoring Position—Reds 3-for-9, Phillies 1-for-6. HR—Luzinski (1). S—Boone, Lonborg. SF—Perez. GDP—Lonborg. SB—Griffey Sr. (2). CS—Geronimo (1).

Reds	IP	H	R	ER	BB	K	ERA
Pat Zachry (W, 1-0)	5.0	6	2	2	3	3	3.60
Pedro Borbon (S, 1)	4.0	4	0	0	1	0	0.00

Phillies	IP	H	R	ER	BB	K	ERA
Jim Lonborg (L, 0-1)	5.1	2	3	1	2	2	1.69
Gene Garber (BS, 1)	0.2	1	1	0	1	0	0.00
Tug McGraw	0.1	2	2	2	0	1	11.57
Ron Reed	2.2	1	0	0	1	1	0.00

WP—McGraw. Time—2:24. Attendance—62,651. Umpires—HP, Dale. 1B, Stello. 2B, Vargo. 3B, Harvey.

Game 3

Tuesday, October 12

Phillies	AB	R	H	RBI	BB	K	Avg
Dave Cash, 2b	4	0	1	1	0	0	.308
Garry Maddox, cf	5	1	1	1	0	0	.231
Mike Schmidt, 3b	5	1	3	1	0	0	.308
Greg Luzinski, lf	4	0	1	1	0	1	.273
Ron Reed, p	1	0	0	0	0	0	.000
Gene Garber, p	0	0	0	0	0	0	—
Tom Underwood, p	0	0	0	0	0	0	—
Dick Allen, 1b	3	0	0	0	1	1	.222
Jerry Martin, lf	1	1	0	0	0	0	.000
Jay Johnstone, rf	4	1	3	1	1	0	.778
Bob Boone, c	3	0	0	0	1	0	.286
Terry Harmon, pr	0	1	0	0	0	0	—
Johnny Oates, c	1	0	0	0	0	0	.000
Larry Bowa, ss	3	1	1	1	1	0	.125
Jim Kaat, p	2	0	1	0	0	0	.500
Bobby Tolan, lf-1b	0	0	0	0	1	0	.000
TOTALS	36	6	11	6	5	2	.300

Reds	AB	R	H	RBI	BB	K	Avg
Pete Rose, 3b	4	0	1	0	1	0	.429
Ken Griffey Sr., rf	5	1	2	1	0	0	.385
Joe Morgan, 2b	3	1	0	0	1	1	.000
Tony Perez, 1b	4	1	2	1	0	0	.200
George Foster, lf	3	1	1	2	0	0	.167
Johnny Bench, c	3	2	1	1	1	0	.333
Dave Concepcion, ss	4	1	1	0	0	0	.200
Cesar Geronimo, cf	3	0	1	2	1	1	.182
Gary Nolan, p	1	0	0	0	1	0	.000
Manny Sarmiento, p	1	0	0	0	0	0	.000
Pedro Borbon, p	0	0	0	0	0	0	.000
Mike Lum, ph	1	0	0	0	0	0	.000
Rawly Eastwick, p	0	0	0	0	0	0	—
Ed Armbrister, ph	0	0	0	0	0	0	—
TOTALS	31	7	9	7	5	2	.247

	1	2	3	4	5	6	7	8	9	R	H	E
Phillies	0	0	0	1	0	0	2	2	1	6	11	0
Reds	0	0	0	0	0	0	4	0	3	7	9	2

E—Perez, Rose. DP—Phillies 1 (Bowa to Cash to Allen), Reds 1 (Concepcion to Morgan to Perez). LOB—Phillies 10, Reds 6. Scoring Position—Phillies 4-for-12, Reds 3-for-5. 2B—Maddox (1), Schmidt 2 (2), Luzinski (2). 3B—Johnstone (1), Geronimo (1). HR—Foster (2), Bench (1). S—Kaat, Armbrister. SF—Cash, Foster. GDP—Cash, Bench.

Phillies	IP	H	R	ER	BB	K	ERA
Jim Kaat	6.0	2	2	2	2	1	3.00
Ron Reed (BS, 1)	2.0	5	4	4	1	1	7.71
Gene Garber (L, 0-1)	0.0	1	1	1	0	0	13.50
Tom Underwood	0.1	1	0	0	2	0	0.00

Reds	IP	H	R	ER	BB	K	ERA
Gary Nolan	5.2	6	1	1	2	1	1.59
Manny Sarmiento	1.0	2	2	2	1	0	18.00
Pedro Borbon	0.1	0	0	0	0	0	0.00
Rawly Eastwick (BS, 1; W, 1-0)	2.0	3	3	2	2	1	12.00

Kaat pitched to two batters in the 7th. Reed pitched to two batters in the 9th. Garber pitched to one batter in the 9th.

WP—Eastwick. Time—2:43. Attendance—55,047. Umpires—HP, Stello. 1B, Vargo. 2B, Harvey. 3B, Tata.

1976 NL Championship Series—Composite Statistics

Batting

Reds	G	AB	R	H	RBI	2B	3B	HR	BB	SO	SB	CS	Avg	OBP	Slg
Ed Armbrister	1	0	0	0	0	0	0	0	0	0	0	0	—	—	—
Johnny Bench	3	12	3	4	1	1	0	1	1	2	1	0	.333	.385	.667
Pedro Borbon	2	2	1	0	0	0	0	0	0	2	0	0	.000	.000	.000
Dave Concepcion	3	10	4	2	0	1	0	0	2	1	0	0	.200	.333	.300
Dan Driessen	1	1	0	0	0	0	0	0	0	0	0	0	.000	.000	.000
George Foster	3	12	2	2	4	0	0	2	0	4	0	0	.167	.154	.667
Cesar Geronimo	3	11	0	2	2	0	1	0	1	3	0	1	.182	.250	.364
Ken Griffey Sr.	3	13	2	5	2	0	1	0	2	1	2	0	.385	.467	.538
Don Gullett	1	4	1	2	3	1	0	0	0	0	0	0	.500	.500	.750
Mike Lum	1	1	0	0	0	0	0	0	0	0	0	0	.000	.000	.000
Joe Morgan	3	7	2	0	0	0	0	0	6	1	2	0	.000	.462	.000
Gary Nolan	1	0	0	0	0	0	0	0	1	0	0	0	—	1.000	—
Tony Perez	3	10	1	2	3	0	0	1	2	0	0	0	.200	.231	.200
Pete Rose	3	14	3	6	2	2	1	0	1	0	0	0	.429	.467	.714
Manny Sarmiento	1	1	0	0	0	0	0	0	0	0	0	0	.000	.000	.000
Pat Zachry	1	1	0	0	0	0	0	0	0	0	0	0	.000	.000	.000
Totals	**3**	**99**	**19**	**25**	**17**	**5**	**3**	**3**	**15**	**16**	**5**	**1**	**.253**	**.342**	**.455**

Batting

Phillies	G	AB	R	H	RBI	2B	3B	HR	BB	SO	SB	CS	Avg	OBP	Slg
Dick Allen	3	9	1	2	0	0	0	0	3	2	0	0	.222	.417	.222
Bob Boone	3	7	0	2	1	0	0	0	1	0	0	0	.286	.375	.286
Larry Bowa	3	8	1	1	1	1	0	0	3	0	0	0	.125	.364	.250
Ollie Brown	1	2	0	0	0	0	0	0	1	1	0	0	.000	.333	.000
Steve Carlton	1	2	0	0	0	0	0	0	0	0	0	0	.000	.000	.000
Dave Cash	3	13	1	4	1	1	0	0	0	0	0	0	.308	.286	.385
Terry Harmon	1	0	1	0	0	0	0	0	0	0	0	0	—	—	—
Tom Hutton	1	1	0	0	0	0	0	0	0	0	0	0	.000	.000	.000
Jay Johnstone	3	9	1	7	2	1	1	0	1	0	0	0	.778	.800	1.111
Jim Kaat	1	2	0	1	0	0	0	0	0	0	0	0	.500	.500	.500
Jim Lonborg	1	1	0	0	0	0	0	0	0	0	0	0	.000	.000	.000
Greg Luzinski	3	11	2	3	3	2	0	1	1	4	0	0	.273	.333	.727
Garry Maddox	3	13	2	3	1	1	0	0	1	0	0	1	.231	.286	.308
Jerry Martin	1	1	1	0	0	0	0	0	0	0	0	0	.000	.000	.000
Tim McCarver	2	4	0	0	0	0	0	0	1	0	0	0	.000	.000	.000
Johnny Oates	1	1	0	0	0	0	0	0	0	0	0	0	.000	.000	.000
Ron Reed	2	1	0	0	0	0	0	0	0	0	0	0	.000	.000	.000
Mike Schmidt	3	13	1	4	2	2	0	0	1	0	0	0	.308	.286	.462
Bobby Tolan	3	2	0	0	0	0	0	0	1	0	0	0	.000	.333	.000
Totals	**3**	**100**	**11**	**27**	**11**	**8**	**1**	**1**	**12**	**9**	**0**	**1**	**.270**	**.342**	**.400**

Pitching

Reds	G	GS	CG	IP	H	R	ER	BB	SO	W-L	Sv-Op	Hld	ERA
Pedro Borbon	2	0	0	4.1	4	0	0	1	0	0-0	1-1	0	0.00
Rawly Eastwick	2	0	0	3.0	7	5	4	2	1	1-0	0-1	0	12.00
Don Gullett	1	1	0	8.0	2	1	1	3	4	1-0	0-0	0	1.13
Gary Nolan	1	1	0	5.2	6	1	1	2	1	0-0	0-0	0	1.59
Manny Sarmiento	1	0	0	1.0	2	2	2	1	0	0-0	0-0	0	18.00
Pat Zachry	1	1	0	5.0	6	2	2	3	3	1-0	0-0	0	3.60
Totals	**3**	**3**	**0**	**27.0**	**27**	**11**	**10**	**12**	**9**	**3-0**	**1-2**	**0**	**3.33**

Pitching

Phillies	G	GS	CG	IP	H	R	ER	BB	SO	W-L	Sv-Op	Hld	ERA
Steve Carlton	1	1	0	7.0	8	5	4	5	6	0-1	0-0	0	5.14
Gene Garber	2	0	0	2.2	2	1	1	0	0	0-1	0-0	0	13.50
Jim Kaat	1	1	0	6.0	2	2	2	1	0	1-0	0-0	0	3.00
Jim Lonborg	1	1	0	5.1	2	3	1	2	2	0-1	0-0	0	1.69
Tug McGraw	2	0	0	2.1	4	3	3	1	5	0-0	0-0	0	11.57
Ron Reed	2	0	0	4.2	6	4	4	2	2	0-0	0-1	0	7.71
Tom Underwood	1	0	0	0.1	1	0	0	2	0	0-0	0-0	0	0.00
Totals	**3**	**3**	**0**	**26.1**	**25**	**19**	**15**	**15**	**16**	**0-3**	**0-2**	**0**	**5.13**

Fielding

Reds	Pos	G	PO	Ast	E	DP	PB	FPct
Johnny Bench	c	3	11	4	0	1	0	1.000
Pedro Borbon	p	2	0	0	0	0	—	—
Dave Concepcion	ss	3	2	12	0	1	—	1.000
Rawly Eastwick	p	2	0	1	0	0	—	1.000
Doug Flynn	2b	1	0	0	0	0	—	—
George Foster	lf	3	7	0	0	0	—	1.000
Cesar Geronimo	cf	3	10	0	0	0	—	1.000
Ken Griffey Sr.	rf	3	11	0	0	0	—	1.000
Don Gullett	p	1	0	0	0	0	—	—
Joe Morgan	2b	3	9	5	0	2	—	1.000
Gary Nolan	p	1	1	0	0	0	—	1.000
Tony Perez	1b	3	27	2	1	2	—	.967
Pete Rose	3b	3	2	5	1	1	—	.875
Manny Sarmiento	p	1	0	0	0	0	—	—
Pat Zachry	p	1	1	3	0	0	—	1.000
Totals		**3**	**81**	**32**	**2**	**7**	**0**	**.983**

Fielding

Phillies	Pos	G	PO	Ast	E	DP	PB	FPct
Dick Allen	1b	3	28	0	1	1	—	.966
Bob Boone	c	3	8	2	0	0	0	1.000
Larry Bowa	ss	3	2	11	0	1	—	1.000
Ollie Brown	rf	1	2	0	0	0	—	1.000
Steve Carlton	p	1	0	0	0	0	—	—
Dave Cash	2b	3	8	8	0	2	—	1.000
Gene Garber	p	2	0	0	0	0	—	—
Jay Johnstone	rf	3	3	0	0	0	—	1.000
Jim Kaat	p	1	0	1	0	0	—	1.000
Jim Lonborg	p	1	0	2	0	0	—	1.000
Greg Luzinski	lf	3	6	0	0	0	—	1.000
Garry Maddox	cf	3	9	0	0	0	—	1.000
Jerry Martin	lf	1	1	0	0	0	—	1.000
Tim McCarver	c	1	6	0	0	0	0	1.000
Tug McGraw	p	2	0	1	0	0	—	1.000
Johnny Oates	c	1	1	0	0	0	0	1.000
Ron Reed	p	2	0	0	0	0	—	—
Mike Schmidt	3b	3	4	9	1	2	—	.929
Bobby Tolan	lf	1	1	0	0	0	—	1.000
	1b	1	0	0	0	0	—	—
Tom Underwood	p	1	0	0	0	0	—	—
Totals		**3**	**79**	**34**	**2**	**6**	**0**	**.983**

1977 New York Yankees (AL) 3, Kansas City Royals (AL) 2

Kansas City Royals manager Whitey Herzog emptied his bullpen, but couldn't preserve a one-run lead in the ninth inning of the ALCS finale. The New York Yankees came up with three runs to win the game 5-3 and take the AL flag. The Royals took Game 1, 7-2, behind Paul Splittorff, but Ron Guidry tossed a three-hitter for a 6-2 Yankees victory in Game 2. Dennis Leonard answered for Kansas City with a four-hit, 6-2 victory in Game 3. Mickey Rivers had four hits in Game 4 and Sparky Lyle tossed 5.1 innings of shutout relief as the Yankees prevailed, 6-4. Needing only three more outs to complete a 3-2 win in Game 5, Herzog summoned Game 3 starter Dennis Leonard. When Paul Blair singled and Roy White walked, Herzog called for Game 4 starter Larry Gura. And when Mickey Rivers singled to tie the score, Herzog turned to Mark Littell, the goat of the 1976 ALCS. This time, Littell surrendered a sacrifice fly to Willie Randolph, putting the Yanks ahead to stay.

Game 1

Wednesday, October 5

Royals	AB	R	H	RBI	BB	K	Avg
Freddie Patek, ss	4	1	2	2	1	2	.500
Hal McRae, dh	5	1	1	2	0	0	.200
George Brett, 3b	5	0	0	0	0	0	.000
Al Cowens, rf	4	2	3	1	0	0	.750
Amos Otis, cf	4	0	0	0	0	1	.000
John Mayberry, 1b	3	1	1	2	1	0	.333
Joe Zdeb, lf	4	0	0	0	0	0	.000
Darrell Porter, c	2	1	1	0	2	0	.500
Frank White, 2b	4	1	1	0	0	0	.250
TOTALS	35	7	9	7	4	3	.257

Yankees	AB	R	H	RBI	BB	K	Avg
Mickey Rivers, cf	4	1	3	0	0	0	.750
Graig Nettles, 3b	4	0	0	0	0	0	.000
Thurman Munson, c	4	1	1	2	0	0	.250
Reggie Jackson, rf	4	0	0	0	0	1	.000
Lou Piniella, lf	4	0	1	0	0	0	.250
Chris Chambliss, 1b	3	0	1	0	1	1	.333
Cliff Johnson, dh	4	0	2	0	0	0	.500
Willie Randolph, 2b	4	0	1	0	0	0	.250
Bucky Dent, ss	3	0	0	0	0	0	.000
Roy White, ph	1	0	0	0	0	0	.000
TOTALS	35	2	9	2	1	2	.257

	1	2	3	4	5	6	7	8	9		R	H	E
Royals	2	2	2	0	0	0	0	1	0		7	9	0
Yankees	0	0	2	0	0	0	0	0	0		2	9	0

DP—Royals 1 (Brett to FWhite). LOB—Royals 5, Yankees 7. Scoring Position—Royals 1-for-6, Yankees 0-for-5. 2B—Patek (1), Rivers (1), Randolph (1). HR—McRae (1), Cowens (1), Mayberry (1), Munson (1). GDP—Randolph. SB—Zdeb (1). CS—Cowens (1).

Royals	IP	H	R	ER	BB	K	ERA
Paul Splittorff (W, 1-0)	8.0	8	2	2	1	2	2.25
Doug Bird	1.0	1	0	0	0	0	0.00

Yankees	IP	H	R	ER	BB	K	ERA
Don Gullett (L, 0-1)	2.0	4	4	4	2	0	18.00
Dick Tidrow	6.2	5	3	2	3	3	4.05
Sparky Lyle	0.1	0	0	0	0	0	0.00

Splittorff pitched to one batter in the 9th.

Time—2:40. Attendance—54,930. Umpires—HP, Neudecker. 1B, Goetz. 2B, McKean. 3B, Springstead.

Game 2

Thursday, October 6

Royals	AB	R	H	RBI	BB	K	Avg
Freddie Patek, ss	3	1	1	1	0	0	.429
Hal McRae, dh	2	0	0	0	2	1	.143
George Brett, 3b	4	0	1	0	0	0	.111
Al Cowens, rf	4	0	0	0	0	2	.375
Amos Otis, cf	4	0	0	0	0	0	.000
John Mayberry, 1b	3	0	0	0	0	0	.167
Joe Zdeb, lf	3	0	0	0	0	2	.000
Darrell Porter, c	1	1	0	0	1	0	.333
John Wathan, ph-c	1	0	0	0	0	1	.000
Frank White, 2b	3	0	1	0	0	1	.286
TOTALS	28	2	3	1	3	7	.190

Yankees	AB	R	H	RBI	BB	K	Avg
Mickey Rivers, cf	5	0	0	0	0	1	.333
Graig Nettles, 3b	4	0	0	0	0	1	.000
Thurman Munson, c	4	1	3	0	0	1	.500
Reggie Jackson, rf	4	1	1	0	0	0	.125
Paul Blair, rf	0	0	0	0	0	0	—
Lou Piniella, lf	4	1	1	0	0	0	.250
Cliff Johnson, dh	4	2	2	2	0	1	.500
Chris Chambliss, 1b	2	0	0	0	2	1	.200
Willie Randolph, 2b	4	1	2	1	0	0	.375
Bucky Dent, ss	3	0	1	1	1	0	.167
TOTALS	34	6	10	4	3	5	.279

	1	2	3	4	5	6	7	8	9		R	H	E
Royals	0	0	1	0	0	1	0	0	0		2	3	1
Yankees	0	0	0	0	2	3	0	1	x		6	10	1

E—Brett, Dent. LOB—Royals 3, Yankees 7. Scoring Position—Royals 0-for-3, Yankees 3-for-8. 2B—Patek (2), Johnson (1). HR—Johnson (1). SF—Patek. SB—Jackson (1). CS—McRae (1), White (1).

Royals	IP	H	R	ER	BB	K	ERA
Andy Hassler (L, 0-1)	5.2	5	3	3	0	3	4.76
Mark Littell	2.0	5	3	1	3	1	4.50
Steve Mingori	0.1	0	0	0	0	1	0.00

Yankees	IP	H	R	ER	BB	K	ERA
Ron Guidry (W, 1-0)	9.0	3	2	2	3	7	2.00

Balk—Hassler. Time—2:58. Attendance—56,230. Umpires—HP, Goetz. 1B, McKean. 2B, Springstead. 3B, Bremigan.

Game 3

Friday, October 7

Yankees	AB	R	H	RBI	BB	K	Avg
Mickey Rivers, cf	4	0	0	0	0	0	.231
Roy White, lf	4	1	2	0	0	0	.400
Thurman Munson, c	4	0	0	0	0	0	.333
Reggie Jackson, rf	3	0	0	1	0	0	.091
Chris Chambliss, 1b	4	0	0	0	0	1	.111
Graig Nettles, 3b	3	1	1	0	0	1	.091
Lou Piniella, dh	3	0	1	1	0	1	.273
Willie Randolph, 2b	3	0	0	0	0	0	.273
Bucky Dent, ss	2	0	0	0	0	0	.125
Cliff Johnson, ph	1	0	0	0	0	1	.444
Fred Stanley, ss	0	0	0	0	0	0	—
TOTALS	31	2	4	1	1	4	.230

Royals	AB	R	H	RBI	BB	K	Avg
Tom Poquette, rf	3	0	1	0	0	0	.333
Amos Otis, ph-cf	2	0	1	0	2	0	.100
Hal McRae, lf	4	2	2	0	0	0	.273
Joe Zdeb, lf	0	0	0	0	0	0	.000
George Brett, 3b	4	1	2	0	0	0	.231
Al Cowens, cf-rf	4	0	0	2	0	1	.250
John Mayberry, 1b	4	0	1	1	0	0	.200
Joe Lahoud, dh	1	2	0	0	2	0	.000
John Wathan, ph-dh	1	0	0	0	0	0	.000
Darrell Porter, c	4	1	3	0	0	0	.571
Freddie Patek, ss	2	0	1	1	0	0	.444
Frank White, 2b	4	0	1	0	0	1	.273
TOTALS	33	6	12	6	2	2	.250

	1	2	3	4	5	6	7	8	9		R	H	E
Yankees	0	0	0	0	1	0	0	0	1		2	4	1
Royals	0	1	1	0	1	2	1	0	x		6	12	1

E—Mayberry, RWhite. LOB—Yankees 3, Royals 7. Scoring Position—Yankees 0-for-4, Royals 3-for-16. 2B—RWhite 2 (2), Piniella (1), McRae 2 (2), Mayberry (1), Otis (1). S—Patek 2. SB—FWhite (1), Otis (1).

Yankees	IP	H	R	ER	BB	K	ERA
Mike Torrez (L, 0-1)	5.2	8	5	5	2	1	7.94
Sparky Lyle	2.1	4	1	1	0	1	3.38

Royals	IP	H	R	ER	BB	K	ERA
Dennis Leonard (W, 1-0)	9.0	4	2	1	1	4	1.00

Time—2:19. Attendance—41,285. Umpires—HP, McKean. 1B, Springstead. 2B, Bremigan. 3B, Deegan.

Game 4

Saturday, October 8

Yankees	AB	R	H	RBI	BB	K	Avg
Mickey Rivers, cf	5	2	4	1	0	0	.389
Graig Nettles, 3b	5	0	2	1	0	0	.188
Thurman Munson, c	4	1	1	2	0	0	.313
Reggie Jackson, rf	3	0	0	0	1	1	.071
Paul Blair, rf	1	0	1	0	0	0	1.000
Lou Piniella, lf	5	0	2	1	0	0	.313
Cliff Johnson, dh	4	0	1	0	0	0	.385
Roy White, pr-dh	0	0	0	0	0	0	.400
Chris Chambliss, 1b	4	0	0	0	0	1	.077
Willie Randolph, 2b	4	2	1	0	0	0	.267
Bucky Dent, ss	3	1	1	1	0	0	.182
TOTALS	38	6	13	6	1	2	.261

Royals	AB	R	H	RBI	BB	K	Avg
Tom Poquette, lf	3	0	0	0	0	0	.167
Joe Zdeb, ph-lf	2	0	0	0	0	0	.000
Hal McRae, dh	3	1	2	0	1	0	.357
George Brett, 3b	4	0	2	1	0	0	.294
Al Cowens, rf	3	0	0	0	1	0	.200
John Mayberry, 1b	2	0	0	0	0	2	.167
John Wathan, 1b	2	0	0	0	0	0	.000
Darrell Porter, c	4	0	0	0	0	0	.364
Amos Otis, cf	3	1	0	0	1	1	.077
Freddie Patek, ss	4	2	3	1	0	0	.538
Frank White, 2b	3	0	1	2	0	1	.286
TOTALS	33	4	8	4	3	4	.250

	1	2	3	4	5	6	7	8	9	R	H	E
Yankees	1	2	1	1	0	0	0	0	1	6	13	0
Royals	0	0	2	2	0	0	0	0	0	4	8	2

E—Mayberry, Patek. DP—Yankees 1 (Nettles to Randolph to Chambliss), Royals 1 (Pattin to Brett). LOB—Yankees 8, Royals 6. Scoring Position—Yankees 4-for-13, Royals 1-for-5. 2B—Rivers (2), Munson (1), Piniella (2), Dent (1), Patek (3), FWhite (1). 3B—Brett (1), Patek (1). S—Dent. SF—Munson, FWhite. GDP—Cowens.

Yankees	IP	H	R	ER	BB	K	ERA
Ed Figueroa	3.1	5	4	4	2	3	10.80
Dick Tidrow	0.1	1	0	0	1	0	3.86
Sparky Lyle (W, 1-0)	5.1	2	0	0	0	1	1.13

Royals	IP	H	R	ER	BB	K	ERA
Larry Gura (L, 0-1)	2.0	6	4	4	1	2	18.00
Marty Pattin	6.0	6	2	1	0	0	1.50
Steve Mingori	0.1	0	0	0	0	0	0.00
Doug Bird	0.2	1	0	0	0	0	0.00

Gura pitched to two batters in the 3rd. Pattin pitched to one batter in the 9th.

WP—Mingori. Time—3:08. Attendance—41,135. Umpires—HP, Springstead. 1B, Bremigan. 2B, Deegan. 3B, Neudecker.

Game 5

Sunday, October 9

Yankees	AB	R	H	RBI	BB	K	Avg
Mickey Rivers, cf	5	2	2	1	0	1	.391
Willie Randolph, 2b	3	1	1	1	1	0	.278
Thurman Munson, c	5	0	1	1	0	1	.286
Lou Piniella, lf	5	0	2	0	0	0	.333
Cliff Johnson, dh	2	0	1	0	1	0	.400
Reggie Jackson, ph-dh	2	0	1	1	0	0	.125
Graig Nettles, 3b	4	0	0	0	0	1	.150
Chris Chambliss, 1b	4	0	0	0	0	0	.059
Paul Blair, rf	4	1	1	0	0	0	.400
Bucky Dent, ss	3	0	1	0	0	0	.214
Roy White, ph	0	1	0	0	1	0	.400
Fred Stanley, ss	0	0	0	0	0	0	—
TOTALS	37	5	10	4	3	3	.263

Royals	AB	R	H	RBI	BB	K	Avg
Freddie Patek, ss	5	0	0	0	0	0	.389
Hal McRae, lf	4	2	3	0	0	0	.444
George Brett, 3b	3	1	1	1	1	0	.300
Al Cowens, rf	4	0	2	0	0	0	.263
Amos Otis, cf	3	0	1	0	1	1	.125
John Wathan, 1b	2	0	0	0	0	2	.000
Pete LaCock, ph-1b	1	0	0	0	1	1	.000
Cookie Rojas, dh	4	0	1	0	0	1	.250
Darrell Porter, c	4	0	1	0	0	0	.333
Frank White, 2b	4	0	1	0	0	1	.278
TOTALS	34	3	10	3	3	6	.289

	1	2	3	4	5	6	7	8	9	R	H	E
Yankees	0	0	1	0	0	0	0	1	3	5	10	0
Royals	2	0	1	0	0	0	0	0	0	3	10	1

E—Brett. LOB—Yankees 9, Royals 7. Scoring Position—Yankees 3-for-16, Royals 1-for-6. 2B—Piniella (3), Johnson (2), McRae (3). 3B—Brett (2). SF—Randolph. GDP—Patek. SB—Rivers (1), Otis (2), Rojas (1). CS—Brett (1).

Yankees	IP	H	R	ER	BB	K	ERA
Ron Guidry	2.1	6	3	3	0	1	3.97
Mike Torrez	5.1	3	0	0	3	4	4.09
Sparky Lyle (W, 2-0)	1.1	1	0	0	0	1	0.96

Royals	IP	H	R	ER	BB	K	ERA
Paul Splittorff	7.0	6	2	2	2	2	2.40
Doug Bird (H, 1)	0.1	2	0	0	0	1	0.00
Steve Mingori (H, 1)	0.2	0	0	0	0	0	0.00
Dennis Leonard (L, 1-1)	0.0	1	2	2	1	0	3.00
Larry Gura (BS, 1)	0.0	1	1	0	0	0	18.00
Mark Littell	1.0	0	0	0	0	0	3.00

Splittorff pitched to one batter in the 8th. Leonard pitched to two batters in the 9th. Gura pitched to one batter in the 9th.

Time—3:04. Attendance—41,133. Umpires—HP, Bremigan. 1B, Deegan. 2B, Neudecker. 3B, Springstead.

1977 AL Championship Series—Composite Statistics

Batting

Yankees	G	AB	R	H	RBI	2B	3B	HR	BB	SO	SB	CS	Avg	OBP	Slg
Paul Blair	3	5	1	2	0	0	0	0	0	0	0	0	.400	.400	.400
Chris Chambliss	5	17	0	1	0	0	0	0	3	4	0	0	.059	.200	.059
Bucky Dent	5	14	1	3	2	1	0	0	1	0	0	0	.214	.267	.286
Reggie Jackson	5	16	1	2	1	0	0	0	2	2	1	0	.125	.222	.125
Cliff Johnson	5	15	2	6	2	2	0	1	1	2	0	0	.400	.438	.733
Thurman Munson	5	21	3	6	5	1	0	1	0	2	0	0	.286	.273	.476
Graig Nettles	5	20	1	3	1	0	0	0	3	0	0	0	.150	.150	.150
Lou Piniella	5	21	1	7	2	3	0	0	0	1	0	0	.333	.333	.476
Willie Randolph	5	18	4	5	2	1	0	0	1	0	0	0	.278	.300	.333
Mickey Rivers	5	23	5	9	2	2	0	0	0	2	1	0	.391	.391	.478
Roy White	4	5	2	2	0	2	0	0	1	0	0	0	.400	.500	.800
Totals	5	175	21	46	17	12	0	2	9	16	2	0	.263	.296	.366

Royals	G	AB	R	H	RBI	2B	3B	HR	BB	SO	SB	CS	Avg	OBP	Slg
George Brett	5	20	2	6	2	0	2	0	1	0	0	1	.300	.333	.500
Al Cowens	5	19	2	5	5	0	0	1	1	3	0	1	.263	.300	.421
Pete LaCock	1	1	0	0	0	0	0	0	1	1	0	0	.000	.500	.000
Joe Lahoud	1	1	2	0	0	0	0	0	2	0	0	0	.000	.667	.000
John Mayberry	4	12	1	2	3	1	0	1	1	2	0	0	.167	.231	.500
Hal McRae	5	18	6	8	2	3	0	1	3	1	0	1	.444	.524	.778
Amos Otis	5	16	1	2	2	1	0	0	2	3	2	0	.125	.222	.188
Freddie Patek	5	18	4	7	5	3	1	0	1	2	0	0	.389	.400	.667
Tom Poquette	2	6	0	1	0	0	0	0	0	0	0	0	.167	.167	.167
Darrell Porter	5	15	3	5	0	0	0	0	3	0	0	0	.333	.444	.333
Cookie Rojas	1	4	0	1	0	0	0	0	0	1	1	0	.250	.250	.250
John Wathan	4	6	0	0	0	0	0	0	0	2	1	0	.000	.000	.000
Frank White	5	18	1	5	2	1	0	0	0	4	1	1	.278	.263	.333
Joe Zdeb	4	9	0	0	0	0	0	0	0	2	1	0	.000	.000	.000
Totals	5	163	22	42	21	9	3	3	15	22	5	4	.258	.317	.405

Pitching

Yankees	G	GS	CG	IP	H	R	ER	BB	SO	W-L	Sv-Op	Hld	ERA
Ed Figueroa	1	1	0	3.1	5	4	4	2	3	0-0	0-0	0	10.80
Ron Guidry	2	2	1	11.1	9	5	5	3	8	1-0	0-0	0	3.97
Don Gullett	1	1	0	2.0	4	4	4	2	0	0-1	0-0	0	18.00
Sparky Lyle	4	0	0	9.1	7	1	1	0	3	2-0	0-0	0	0.96
Dick Tidrow	2	0	0	7.0	6	3	3	3	3	0-0	0-0	0	3.86
Mike Torrez	2	1	0	11.0	11	5	5	5	5	0-1	0-0	0	4.09
Totals	5	5	1	44.0	42	22	22	15	22	3-2	0-0	0	4.50

Royals	G	GS	CG	IP	H	R	ER	BB	SO	W-L	Sv-Op	Hld	ERA
Doug Bird	3	0	0	2.0	4	0	0	0	1	0-0	0-0	1	0.00
Larry Gura	2	1	0	2.0	7	5	4	1	2	0-1	0-1	0	18.00
Andy Hassler	1	1	0	5.2	5	3	3	0	3	0-1	0-0	0	4.76
Dennis Leonard	2	1	1	9.0	5	4	3	2	4	1-1	0-0	0	3.00
Mark Littell	2	0	0	3.0	5	3	1	3	1	0-0	0-0	0	3.00
Steve Mingori	3	0	0	1.1	0	0	0	0	1	0-0	0-0	1	0.00
Marty Pattin	1	0	0	6.0	6	2	1	0	0	0-0	0-0	0	1.50
Paul Splittorff	2	2	0	15.0	14	4	4	3	4	1-0	0-0	0	2.40
Totals	5	5	1	44.0	46	21	16	9	16	2-3	0-1	2	3.27

Fielding

Yankees	Pos	G	PO	Ast	E	DP	PB	FPct
Paul Blair	rf	3	2	0	0	0	—	1.000
Chris Chambliss	1b	5	35	7	0	2	—	1.000
Bucky Dent	ss	5	10	14	1	0	—	.960
Ed Figueroa	p	1	0	0	0	0	—	—
Ron Guidry	p	2	2	0	0	0	—	1.000
Don Gullett	p	1	0	0	0	0	—	—
Reggie Jackson	rf	4	10	1	0	0	—	1.000
Sparky Lyle	p	4	0	0	0	0	—	—
Thurman Munson	c	5	24	4	0	0	0	1.000
Graig Nettles	3b	5	2	12	0	2	—	1.000
Lou Piniella	lf	4	9	1	0	0	—	1.000
Willie Randolph	2b	5	13	9	0	2	—	1.000
Mickey Rivers	cf	5	19	0	0	0	—	1.000
Fred Stanley	ss	2	1	0	0	0	—	1.000
Dick Tidrow	p	2	1	2	0	0	—	1.000
Mike Torrez	p	2	2	1	0	0	—	1.000
Roy White	lf	1	2	0	1	0	—	.667
Totals		5	132	51	2	6	0	.989

Royals	Pos	G	PO	Ast	E	DP	PB	FPct
Doug Bird	p	3	0	0	0	0	—	
George Brett	3b	5	5	12	2	2	—	.895
Al Cowens	rf	5	14	0	0	0	—	1.000
	cf	1	0	0	0	0	—	—
Larry Gura	p	2	0	0	0	0	—	—
Andy Hassler	p	1	1	0	0	0	—	1.000
Pete LaCock	1b	1	4	0	0	0	—	1.000
Dennis Leonard	p	2	0	0	0	0	—	—
Mark Littell	p	2	0	0	0	0	—	—
John Mayberry	1b	4	29	1	2	0	—	.938
Hal McRae	lf	2	2	1	0	0	—	1.000
Steve Mingori	p	3	0	0	0	0	—	—
Amos Otis	cf	5	11	1	0	0	—	1.000
Freddie Patek	ss	5	8	18	1	0	—	.963
Marty Pattin	p	1	1	2	0	1	—	1.000
Tom Poquette	rf	1	3	0	0	0	—	1.000
	lf	1	0	0	0	0	—	—
Darrell Porter	c	5	18	0	0	0	0	1.000
Paul Splittorff	p	2	0	3	0	0	—	1.000
John Wathan	1b	2	17	0	0	0	—	1.000
	c	1	2	0	0	0	0	1.000
Frank White	2b	5	13	16	0	1	—	1.000
Joe Zdeb	lf	4	4	0	0	0	—	1.000
Totals		5	132	54	5	4	0	.974

1977 Los Angeles Dodgers (NL) 3, Philadelphia Phillies (NL) 1

After coming within a hair's breadth of falling behind two games to one, the Dodgers rallied to win the NLCS in four games. Philadelphia jumped ahead 5-1 in Game 1. Ron Cey tied it up with a grand slam in the bottom of the seventh, but the Phils came back with two in the ninth to win, 7-5. Don Sutton evened the series with a complete-game, 7-1 win in Game 2. The Phillies held a 5-3 lead with two outs in the ninth inning of the third game, but the Dodgers rallied for three runs. The key hit was a double by pinch-hitter Manny Mota that Phils left fielder Greg Luzinski dropped as he hit the wall. Davey Lopes scored the go-ahead run on Bill Russell's single over the middle. The next day, Tommy John went the distance to down Philly, 4-1, in a game that was played in a steady downpour. Dusty Baker batted .357 with two homers and eight RBI in the series.

Game 1

Tuesday, October 4

Phillies	AB	R	H	RBI	BB	K	Avg
Bake McBride, cf	5	1	2	0	0	0	.400
Larry Bowa, ss	5	2	1	0	0	0	.200
Mike Schmidt, 3b	5	2	1	1	0	2	.200
Greg Luzinski, lf	3	1	1	2	2	1	.333
Dave Johnson, 1b	4	0	1	2	0	1	.250
Tom Hutton, 1b	1	0	0	0	0	0	.000
Jerry Martin, rf	3	0	0	0	0	2	.000
Jay Johnstone, ph-rf	1	0	0	0	0	0	.000
Tim McCarver, c	3	1	1	0	1	1	.333
Bob Boone, c	0	0	0	0	0	0	—
Ted Sizemore, 2b	3	0	0	0	0	0	.000
Steve Carlton, p	2	0	2	1	0	0	1.000
Gene Garber, p	0	0	0	0	0	0	—
Richie Hebner, ph	1	0	0	0	0	0	.000
Tug McGraw, p	0	0	0	0	0	0	—
TOTALS	36	7	9	6	3	7	.250

Dodgers	AB	R	H	RBI	BB	K	Avg
Davey Lopes, 2b	5	1	2	1	0	0	.400
Bill Russell, ss	5	1	0	0	0	0	.000
Reggie Smith, rf	4	1	0	0	1	1	.000
Ron Cey, 3b	4	1	2	4	0	1	.500
Steve Garvey, 1b	4	0	3	0	0	0	.750
Dusty Baker, lf	3	0	1	0	1	1	.333
Glenn Burke, cf	3	0	0	0	0	0	.000
Rick Monday, ph-cf	1	0	0	0	0	1	.000
Steve Yeager, c	4	0	0	0	0	1	.000
Tommy John, p	1	0	0	0	0	0	.000
Mike Garman, p	0	0	0	0	0	0	—
Lee Lacy, ph	1	1	1	0	0	0	1.000
Charlie Hough, p	0	0	0	0	0	0	—
Jerry Grote, ph	0	0	0	0	1	0	—
Elias Sosa, p	1	0	0	0	0	0	.000
TOTALS	36	5	9	5	3	5	.250

	1 2 3	4 5 6	7 8 9	R	H	E
Phillies	2 0 0	0 2 1	0 0 2	7	9	0
Dodgers	0 0 0	0 1 0	4 0 0	5	9	2

E—Russell 2. DP—Dodgers 1 (Russell to Lopes to Garvey). LOB—Phillies 7, Dodgers 7. Scoring Position—Phillies 3-for-10, Dodgers 2-for-10. HR—Luzinski (1), Cey (1). S—Sizemore. GDP—Bowa. SB—Luzinski (1), Garvey (1).

Phillies	IP	H	R	ER	BB	K	ERA
Steve Carlton	6.2	9	5	5	3	3	6.75
Gene Garber (W, 1-0)	1.1	0	0	0	0	2	0.00
Tug McGraw (S, 1)	1.0	0	0	0	0	0	0.00

Dodgers	IP	H	R	ER	BB	K	ERA
Tommy John	4.2	4	4	0	3	3	0.00
Mike Garman	0.1	0	0	0	0	1	0.00
Charlie Hough	2.0	2	1	1	0	3	4.50
Elias Sosa (L, 0-1)	2.0	3	2	2	0	0	9.00

Balk—Carlton, Sosa. HBP—Carlton by John. Time—2:35. Attendance—55,968. Umpires—HP, Pryor. 1B, Engel. 2B, Wendelstedt. 3B, Froemming.

Game 2

Wednesday, October 5

Phillies	AB	R	H	RBI	BB	K	Avg
Bake McBride, cf	4	1	2	1	0	0	.444
Larry Bowa, ss	4	0	1	0	0	0	.222
Mike Schmidt, 3b	4	0	0	0	0	1	.111
Greg Luzinski, lf	4	0	1	0	0	0	.286
Richie Hebner, 1b	4	0	2	0	0	0	.400
Jay Johnstone, rf	4	0	1	0	0	1	.200
Bob Boone, c	4	0	1	0	0	0	.250
Ted Sizemore, 2b	4	0	1	0	0	0	.143
Jim Lonborg, p	1	0	0	0	0	1	.000
Tom Hutton, ph	1	0	0	0	0	0	.000
Ron Reed, p	0	0	0	0	0	0	—
Ollie Brown, ph	1	0	0	0	0	1	.000
Warren Brusstar, p	0	0	0	0	0	0	—
TOTALS	35	1	9	1	0	4	.237

Dodgers	AB	R	H	RBI	BB	K	Avg
Davey Lopes, 2b	4	0	1	1	0	0	.333
Bill Russell, ss	4	2	2	0	0	0	.222
Reggie Smith, rf	4	1	2	1	0	1	.250
Ron Cey, 3b	3	1	1	0	0	1	.429
Steve Garvey, 1b	3	1	0	0	1	1	.429
Dusty Baker, lf	4	1	1	4	0	2	.286
Rick Monday, cf	3	1	1	0	1	0	.250
Glenn Burke, cf	0	0	0	0	0	0	.000
Steve Yeager, c	3	0	1	1	0	0	.143
Don Sutton, p	3	0	0	0	0	0	.000
TOTALS	31	7	9	7	2	5	.266

	1 2 3	4 5 6	7 8 9	R	H	E
Phillies	0 0 1	0 0 0	0 0 0	1	9	1
Dodgers	0 0 1	4 0 1	1 0 x	7	9	1

E—Lopes, Sizemore. DP—Dodgers 1 (Garvey to Russell). LOB—Phillies 7, Dodgers 3. Scoring Position—Phillies 0-for-3, Dodgers 3-for-8. 2B—Luzinski (1), Monday (1). 3B—Smith (1). HR—McBride (1), Baker (1). S—Cey. GDP—Sizemore. SB—Cey (1). CS—Lopes (1).

Phillies	IP	H	R	ER	BB	K	ERA
Jim Lonborg (L, 0-1)	4.0	5	5	5	1	1	11.25
Ron Reed	2.0	2	1	1	1	2	4.50
Warren Brusstar	2.0	2	1	1	0	2	4.50

Dodgers	IP	H	R	ER	BB	K	ERA
Don Sutton (W, 1-0)	9.0	9	1	1	0	4	1.00

Time—2:14. Attendance—55,973. Umpires—HP, Engel. 1B, Wendelstedt. 2B, Froemming. 3B, Rennert.

Game 3

Friday, October 7

Dodgers	AB	R	H	RBI	BB	K	Avg
Davey Lopes, 2b	5	1	1	1	0	0	.286
Bill Russell, ss	5	0	2	1	0	0	.286
Reggie Smith, rf	5	0	0	0	0	3	.154
Ron Cey, 3b	4	1	1	0	0	1	.364
Steve Garvey, 1b	4	1	1	0	0	0	.364
Dusty Baker, lf	4	1	2	2	0	0	.364
Rick Monday, cf	3	0	1	0	1	0	.286
Jerry Grote, c	0	0	0	0	0	0	—
Steve Yeager, c	2	0	1	1	1	0	.222
Vic Davalillo, ph	1	1	1	0	0	0	1.000
Glenn Burke, cf	0	0	0	0	0	0	.000
Burt Hooton, p	1	0	1	0	0	0	1.000
Rick Rhoden, p	1	0	0	0	0	0	.000
Ed Goodson, ph	1	0	0	0	0	0	.000
Doug Rau, p	0	0	0	0	0	0	—
Elias Sosa, p	0	0	0	0	0	0	.000
Lance Rautzhan, p	0	0	0	0	0	0	—
Manny Mota, ph	1	1	1	0	0	0	1.000
Mike Garman, p	0	0	0	0	0	0	—
TOTALS	37	6	12	5	2	4	.293

Phillies	AB	R	H	RBI	BB	K	Avg
Bake McBride, rf	4	0	0	1	1	0	.308
Larry Bowa, ss	4	0	0	1	1	0	.154
Mike Schmidt, 3b	4	0	0	0	1	0	.077
Greg Luzinski, lf	3	0	1	0	1	1	.300
Jerry Martin, pr	0	0	0	0	0	0	.000
Richie Hebner, 1b	5	2	1	0	0	0	.300
Garry Maddox, cf	4	1	1	1	0	1	.250
Bob Boone, c	4	1	2	0	0	0	.375
Ted Sizemore, 2b	3	1	1	0	1	0	.200
Larry Christenson, p	0	0	0	1	1	0	—
Warren Brusstar, p	0	0	0	0	0	0	—
Tom Hutton, ph	1	0	0	0	0	0	.000
Ron Reed, p	0	0	0	0	0	0	—
Tim McCarver, ph	1	0	0	0	0	0	.250
Gene Garber, p	0	0	0	0	0	0	—
TOTALS	33	5	6	4	6	2	.220

	1 2 3	4 5 6	7 8 9	R	H	E
Dodgers	0 2 0	1 0 0	0 0 3	6	12	2
Phillies	0 3 0	0 0 0	0 2 0	5	6	2

E—Cey, Sizemore, Garber, Smith. DP—Phillies 1 (McBride to Boone). LOB—Dodgers 6, Phillies 9. Scoring Position—Dodgers 4-for-9, Phillies 1-for-6. 2B—Russell (1), Cey (1), Baker (1), Hooton (1), Hebner (1), Mota (1). S—Garber.

Dodgers	IP	H	R	ER	BB	K	ERA
Burt Hooton	1.2	2	3	3	4	1	16.20
Rick Rhoden	4.1	2	0	0	2	0	0.00
Doug Rau	1.0	0	0	0	0	1	0.00
Elias Sosa	0.2	2	2	1	0	0	10.13
Lance Rautzhan (W, 1-0)	0.1	0	0	0	0	0	0.00
Mike Garman (S, 1)	1.0	0	0	0	0	0	0.00

Phillies	IP	H	R	ER	BB	K	ERA
Larry Christenson	3.1	7	3	3	0	2	8.10
Warren Brusstar	0.2	0	0	0	1	0	3.38
Ron Reed	2.0	1	0	0	1	2	2.25
Gene Garber (L, 1-1)	3.0	4	3	2	0	0	4.15

PB—Boone. HBP—Luzinski by Garman. Time—2:51. Attendance—63,719. Umpires—HP, Wendelstedt. 1B, Froemming. 2B, Rennert. 3B, Runge.

Game 4

Saturday, October 8

Dodgers	AB	R	H	RBI	BB	K	Avg
Davey Lopes, 2b	3	0	0	0	2	0	.235
Bill Russell, ss	4	0	1	1	0	0	.278
Reggie Smith, rf	3	0	1	0	1	0	.188
Ron Cey, 3b	2	1	0	0	2	1	.308
Steve Garvey, 1b	2	0	0	0	1	0	.308
Dusty Baker, lf	3	2	1	2	1	0	.357
Glenn Burke, cf	4	0	0	0	0	3	.000
Steve Yeager, c	4	1	1	0	0	2	.231
Tommy John, p	4	0	1	0	0	2	.200
TOTALS	29	4	5	3	7	8	.250

Phillies	AB	R	H	RBI	BB	K	Avg
Bake McBride, rf	5	0	0	0	0	2	.222
Larry Bowa, ss	4	0	0	0	0	0	.118
Mike Schmidt, 3b	3	0	0	0	1	0	.063
Greg Luzinski, lf	4	1	1	0	0	1	.286
Richie Hebner, 1b	4	0	2	0	0	1	.357
Garry Maddox, cf	3	0	2	1	0	0	.429
Tim McCarver, c	2	0	0	0	0	2	.167
Ron Reed, p	0	0	0	0	0	0	—
Ollie Brown, ph	1	0	0	0	0	0	.000
Tug McGraw, p	0	0	0	0	0	0	—
Jerry Martin, ph	1	0	0	0	0	0	.000
Gene Garber, p	0	0	0	0	0	0	—
Ted Sizemore, 2b	3	0	1	0	1	0	.231
Steve Carlton, p	2	0	0	0	0	2	.500
Bob Boone, c	2	0	1	0	0	0	.400
TOTALS	34	1	7	1	2	8	.232

	1 2 3	4 5 6	7 8 9	R	H	E
Dodgers	0 2 0	0 2 0	0 0 0	4	5	0
Phillies	0 0 0	1 0 0	0 0 0	1	7	0

DP—Phillies 2 (Bowa to Sizemore to Hebner; Bowa to Sizemore to Hebner). LOB—Dodgers 6, Phillies 9. Scoring Position—Dodgers 1-for-7, Phillies 1-for-7. 2B—Hebner (2). HR—Baker (2). S—Garvey. GDP—Russell, Cey. SB—Smith (1).

Dodgers	IP	H	R	ER	BB	K	ERA
Tommy John (W, 1-0)	9.0	7	1	1	2	8	0.66

Phillies	IP	H	R	ER	BB	K	ERA
Steve Carlton (L, 0-1)	5.0	4	4	4	5	3	6.94
Ron Reed	1.0	0	0	0	0	1	1.80
Tug McGraw	2.0	1	0	0	2	3	0.00
Gene Garber	1.0	0	0	0	0	1	3.38

Carlton pitched to one batter in the 6th.

WP—Carlton. HBP—Maddox by John. Time—2:39. Attendance—64,924. Umpires—HP, Froemming. 1B, Rennert. 2B, Runge. 3B, Pryor.

1977 NL Championship Series—Composite Statistics

Batting

Dodgers	G	AB	R	H	RBI	2B	3B	HR	BB	SO	SB	CS	Avg	OBP	Slg
Dusty Baker	4	14	4	5	8	1	0	2	2	3	0	0	.357	.438	.857
Glenn Burke	4	7	0	0	0	0	0	0	0	3	0	0	.000	.000	.000
Ron Cey	4	13	4	4	4	1	0	1	2	4	1	0	.308	.400	.615
Vic Davalillo	1	1	1	1	0	0	0	0	0	0	0	0	1.000	1.000	1.000
Steve Garvey	4	13	2	4	0	0	0	0	2	1	1	0	.308	.400	.308
Ed Goodson	1	1	0	0	0	0	0	0	0	0	0	0	.000	.000	.000
Jerry Grote	2	0	0	0	0	0	0	0	1	0	0	0	—	1.000	—
Burt Hooton	1	1	0	1	0	1	0	0	0	0	0	0	1.000	1.000	2.000
Tommy John	2	5	0	1	0	0	0	0	0	2	0	0	.200	.200	.200
Lee Lacy	1	1	1	1	0	0	0	0	0	0	0	0	1.000	1.000	1.000
Davey Lopes	4	17	2	4	3	0	0	0	2	0	0	1	.235	.316	.235
Rick Monday	3	7	1	2	0	1	0	0	2	1	0	0	.286	.444	.429
Manny Mota	1	1	1	1	0	1	0	0	0	0	0	0	1.000	1.000	2.000
Rick Rhoden	1	1	0	0	0	0	0	0	0	0	0	0	.000	.000	.000
Bill Russell	4	18	3	5	2	1	0	0	0	0	0	0	.278	.278	.333
Reggie Smith	4	16	2	3	1	0	1	0	2	5	1	0	.188	.278	.313
Elias Sosa	2	1	0	0	0	0	0	0	0	0	0	0	.000	.000	.000
Don Sutton	1	3	0	0	0	0	0	0	0	0	0	0	.000	.000	.000
Steve Yeager	4	13	1	3	2	0	0	0	1	3	0	0	.231	.286	.231
Totals	4	133	22	35	20	6	1	3	14	22	3	1	.263	.333	.391

Batting

Phillies	G	AB	R	H	RBI	2B	3B	HR	BB	SO	SB	CS	Avg	OBP	Slg
Bob Boone	4	10	1	4	0	0	0	0	0	0	0	0	.400	.400	.400
Larry Bowa	4	17	2	2	1	0	0	1	0	0	0	0	.118	.167	.118
Ollie Brown	2	2	0	0	0	0	0	0	0	1	0	0	.000	.000	.000
Steve Carlton	2	4	0	2	1	0	0	0	0	2	0	0	.500	.600	.500
Larry Christenson	1	0	0	0	1	0	0	0	1	0	0	0	—	1.000	—
Gene Garber	3	0	0	0	0	0	0	0	0	0	0	0	—	—	—
Richie Hebner	4	14	2	5	0	2	0	0	0	1	0	0	.357	.357	.500
Tom Hutton	3	3	0	0	0	0	0	0	0	0	0	0	.000	.000	.000
Dave Johnson	1	4	0	1	2	0	0	0	0	1	0	0	.250	.250	.250
Jay Johnstone	2	5	0	1	0	0	0	0	0	1	0	0	.200	.200	.200
Jim Lonborg	1	1	0	0	0	0	0	0	0	1	0	0	.000	.000	.000
Greg Luzinski	4	14	2	4	2	1	0	1	3	3	1	0	.286	.444	.571
Garry Maddox	2	7	1	3	2	0	0	0	0	1	0	0	.429	.500	.429
Jerry Martin	3	4	0	0	0	0	0	0	0	2	0	0	.000	.000	.000
Bake McBride	4	18	2	4	2	0	0	1	1	2	0	0	.222	.263	.389
Tim McCarver	3	6	1	1	0	0	0	0	1	3	0	0	.167	.286	.167
Mike Schmidt	4	16	2	1	1	0	0	0	2	3	0	0	.063	.167	.063
Ted Sizemore	4	13	1	3	0	0	0	0	2	0	0	0	.231	.333	.231
Totals	4	138	14	31	12	3	0	2	11	21	1	0	.225	.296	.290

Pitching

Dodgers	G	GS	CG	IP	H	R	ER	BB	SO	W-L	Sv-Op	Hld	ERA
Mike Garman	2	0	0	1.1	0	0	0	0	1	0-0	1-1	0	0.00
Burt Hooton	1	1	0	1.2	2	3	3	4	1	0-0	0-0	0	16.20
Charlie Hough	1	0	0	2.0	2	1	1	0	3	0-0	0-0	0	4.50
Tommy John	2	2	1	13.2	11	5	1	5	11	1-0	0-0	0	0.66
Doug Rau	1	0	0	1.0	0	0	0	0	1	0-0	0-0	0	0.00
Lance Rautzhan	1	0	0	0.1	0	0	0	0	0	1-0	0-0	0	0.00
Rick Rhoden	1	0	0	4.1	2	0	0	2	0	0-0	0-0	0	0.00
Elias Sosa	2	0	0	2.2	5	4	3	0	0	0-1	0-0	0	10.13
Don Sutton	1	1	1	9.0	9	1	1	0	4	1-0	0-0	0	1.00
Totals	4	4	2	36.0	31	14	9	11	21	3-1	1-1	0	2.25

Pitching

Phillies	G	GS	CG	IP	H	R	ER	BB	SO	W-L	Sv-Op	Hld	ERA
Warren Brusstar	2	0	0	2.2	2	1	1	1	2	0-0	0-0	0	3.38
Steve Carlton	2	2	0	11.2	13	9	9	8	6	0-1	0-0	0	6.94
Larry Christenson	1	1	0	3.1	7	3	3	0	2	0-0	0-0	0	8.10
Gene Garber	3	0	0	5.1	4	3	2	0	3	1-1	0-0	0	3.38
Jim Lonborg	1	1	0	4.0	5	5	5	1	1	0-1	0-0	0	11.25
Tug McGraw	2	0	0	3.0	1	0	0	2	3	0-0	1-1	0	0.00
Ron Reed	3	0	0	5.0	3	1	1	2	5	0-0	0-0	0	1.80
Totals	4	4	0	35.0	35	22	21	14	22	1-3	1-1	0	5.40

Fielding

Dodgers	Pos	G	PO	Ast	E	DP	PB	FPct
Dusty Baker	lf	4	3	0	0	0	—	1.000
Glenn Burke	cf	4	3	0	0	0	—	1.000
Ron Cey	3b	4	7	15	1	0	—	.957
Mike Garman	p	2	0	0	0	0	—	—
Steve Garvey	1b	4	40	1	0	3	—	1.000
Jerry Grote	c	1	0	0	0	0	0	—
Burt Hooton	p	1	0	1	0	0	—	1.000
Charlie Hough	p	1	0	1	0	0	—	1.000
Tommy John	p	2	0	1	0	0	—	1.000
Davey Lopes	2b	4	9	9	1	1	—	.947
Rick Monday	cf	3	6	0	0	0	—	1.000
Doug Rau	p	1	0	0	0	0	—	—
Lance Rautzhan	p	1	0	0	0	0	—	—
Rick Rhoden	p	1	0	0	0	0	—	—
Bill Russell	ss	4	11	12	2	3	—	.920
Reggie Smith	rf	4	7	0	1	0	—	.875
Elias Sosa	p	2	0	1	0	0	—	1.000
Don Sutton	p	1	0	2	0	0	—	1.000
Steve Yeager	c	4	22	1	0	0	0	1.000
Totals		4	108	44	5	7	0	.968

Fielding

Phillies	Pos	G	PO	Ast	E	DP	PB	FPct
Bob Boone	c	4	18	2	0	1	1	1.000
Larry Bowa	ss	4	0	17	0	2	—	1.000
Warren Brusstar	p	2	0	0	0	0	—	—
Steve Carlton	p	2	0	0	0	0	—	—
Larry Christenson	p	1	0	0	0	0	—	—
Gene Garber	p	3	0	2	1	0	—	.667
Richie Hebner	1b	3	32	0	0	2	—	1.000
Tom Hutton	1b	1	5	0	0	0	—	1.000
Dave Johnson	1b	1	8	0	0	0	—	1.000
Jay Johnstone	rf	2	4	0	0	0	—	1.000
Jim Lonborg	p	1	0	2	0	0	—	1.000
Greg Luzinski	lf	4	4	1	0	0	—	1.000
Garry Maddox	cf	2	6	0	0	0	—	1.000
Jerry Martin	rf	1	1	0	0	0	—	1.000
Bake McBride	cf	2	3	1	0	0	—	1.000
	rf	2	3	1	0	1	—	1.000
Tim McCarver	c	2	7	0	0	0	0	1.000
Tug McGraw	p	2	0	0	0	0	—	—
Ron Reed	p	3	0	0	0	0	—	—
Mike Schmidt	3b	4	4	15	0	0	—	1.000
Ted Sizemore	2b	4	10	8	2	2	—	.900
Totals		4	105	49	3	8	1	.981

1978 New York Yankees (AL) 3, Kansas City Royals (AL) 1

For the third straight year, the Kansas City Royals came up short against the New York Yankees, dropping the ALCS in four games. Reggie Jackson homered and drove in three runs in the opener as Jim Beattie and Ken Clay combined to stifle the Royals, 7-1. Kansas City repaid the favor the next day, winning 10-4 behind a 16-hit attack. George Brett launched solo homers in each of his first three at-bats of Game 3, but the Yanks won the back-and-forth affair on Thurman Munson's two-run homer in the bottom of the eighth. Dennis Leonard and Ron Guidry were tough in Game 4, but the Yanks won 2-1 on Roy White's solo homer in the bottom of the sixth. Jackson batted .462 with a pair of home runs and six RBI.

Game 1
Tuesday, October 3

Yankees	AB	R	H	RBI	BB	K	Avg
Mickey Rivers, cf	5	0	2	0	0	0	.400
Paul Blair, pr-cf	1	1	0	0	0	1	1.000
Thurman Munson, c	5	0	1	0	0	0	.200
Lou Piniella, rf	5	2	2	0	0	0	.400
Reggie Jackson, dh	3	2	3	3	2	0	1.000
Graig Nettles, 3b	5	1	2	1	0	0	.400
Chris Chambliss, 1b	5	0	2	1	0	2	.400
Roy White, lf	4	1	1	0	1	0	.250
Brian Doyle, 2b	5	0	2	1	0	0	.400
Bucky Dent, ss	5	0	1	0	0	0	.200
TOTALS	43	7	16	7	3	3	.372

Royals	AB	R	H	RBI	BB	K	Avg
Steve Braun, lf	4	0	0	0	1	0	.000
George Brett, 3b	4	1	1	0	0	0	.250
Amos Otis, cf	2	0	0	0	2	2	.000
Darrell Porter, c	3	0	0	1	0	0	.000
Pete LaCock, 1b	2	0	0	0	2	0	.000
Hal McRae, dh	2	0	0	1	1	0	.000
Al Cowens, rf	4	0	1	0	0	1	.250
Freddie Patek, ss	3	0	0	0	0	2	.000
Clint Hurdle, ph	0	0	0	0	1	0	—
Frank White, 2b	3	0	0	0	0	0	.000
Tom Poquette, ph	1	0	0	0	0	0	.000
TOTALS	28	1	2	1	8	5	.071

	1	2	3	4	5	6	7	8	9	R	H	E
Yankees	0	1	1	0	2	0	0	3	0	7	16	0
Royals	0	0	0	0	0	1	0	0	0	1	2	2

E—Brett, Otis. LOB—Yankees 12, Royals 9. Scoring Position—Yankees 5-for-17, Royals 0-for-7. 2B—Jackson (1), RWhite (1), Brett (1). 3B—Nettles (1). HR—Jackson (1). SF—McRae. SB—Otis (1), LaCock (1).

Yankees	IP	H	R	ER	BB	K	ERA
Jim Beattie (W, 1-0)	5.1	2	1	1	5	3	1.69
Ken Clay (S, 1)	3.2	0	0	0	3	2	0.00

Royals	IP	H	R	ER	BB	K	ERA
Dennis Leonard (L, 0-1)	4.0	9	3	3	0	2	6.75
Steve Mingori	3.2	5	3	3	0	0	7.36
Al Hrabosky	0.1	1	1	1	0	0	27.00
Doug Bird	1.0	1	0	0	0	1	0.00

Leonard pitched to one batter in the 5th.

PB—Porter. Time—2:57. Attendance—41,143. Umpires—HP, MDiMuro. 1B, Garcia. 2B, Luciano. 3B, Kunkel.

Game 2
Wednesday, October 4

Yankees	AB	R	H	RBI	BB	K	Avg
Mickey Rivers, cf	3	0	2	0	1	0	.500
Gary Thomasson, ph-cf	1	0	0	0	0	0	.000
Thurman Munson, c	5	0	0	0	0	0	.100
Lou Piniella, lf	5	0	0	0	0	1	.200
Reggie Jackson, rf	4	1	1	0	1	1	.571
Graig Nettles, 3b	4	1	1	0	0	0	.333
Chris Chambliss, 1b	4	1	4	1	0	0	.667
Roy White, dh	4	1	1	0	0	1	.250
Fred Stanley, 2b	2	0	1	0	0	0	.500
Cliff Johnson, ph	1	0	0	0	0	0	.000
Brian Doyle, 2b	0	0	0	0	0	0	.400
Paul Blair, ph-2b	1	0	0	0	0	0	.000
Bucky Dent, ss	4	0	2	3	0	0	.333
TOTALS	38	4	12	4	2	3	.346

Game 3
Friday, October 6

Royals	AB	R	H	RBI	BB	K	Avg
George Brett, 3b	5	3	3	3	0	0	.429
Hal McRae, dh	5	0	0	0	0	1	.200
Amos Otis, cf	3	1	2	0	1	1	.500
Darrell Porter, c	4	1	2	1	0	0	.364
Pete LaCock, 1b	3	0	2	0	1	1	.400
Clint Hurdle, lf	4	0	1	0	0	2	.429
Willie Wilson, pr-lf	0	0	0	0	0	0	.000
Al Cowens, rf	4	0	0	1	0	0	.167
Freddie Patek, ss	3	0	0	0	1	1	.100
Frank White, 2b	3	0	0	0	1	0	.100
Steve Braun, ph	1	0	0	0	0	1	.000
TOTALS	35	5	10	5	3	7	.280

Yankees	AB	R	H	RBI	BB	K	Avg
Mickey Rivers, cf	1	0	1	0	0	0	.556
Paul Blair, ph-cf	3	0	0	0	0	0	.000
Roy White, lf	4	2	2	0	0	0	.333
Gary Thomasson, lf	0	0	0	0	0	0	.000
Thurman Munson, c	4	2	3	2	0	0	.286
Reggie Jackson, dh	3	2	2	3	0	0	.600
Lou Piniella, rf	4	0	2	0	0	1	.286
Graig Nettles, 3b	3	0	0	0	0	0	.250
Chris Chambliss, 1b	3	0	0	0	0	0	.500
Fred Stanley, 2b	3	0	0	0	0	2	.200
Bucky Dent, ss	3	0	0	0	0	0	.250
TOTALS	31	6	10	5	0	3	.340

	1	2	3	4	5	6	7	8	9	R	H	E
Royals	1	0	1	0	1	0	0	2	0	5	10	1
Yankees	0	1	0	2	0	1	0	2	x	6	10	0

E—Patek. DP—Royals 2 (FWhite to Patek to LaCock; Hurdle to Porter), Yankees 1 (Rivers to Nettles). LOB—Royals 6, Yankees 2. Scoring Position—Royals 1-for-11, Yankees 1-for-3. 2B—Otis (1), Porter (1), LaCock (2), Munson (1). 3B—LaCock (1). HR—Brett 3 (3), Munson (1), Jackson (2). SF—Jackson. GDP—RWhite. SB—Otis (4). CS—Patek (1).

Royals	IP	H	R	ER	BB	K	ERA
Paul Splittorff	7.1	9	5	4	0	2	4.91
Doug Bird (BS, 1; L, 0-1)	0.0	1	1	1	0	0	9.00
Al Hrabosky	0.2	0	0	0	0	1	3.00

Yankees	IP	H	R	ER	BB	K	ERA
Catfish Hunter	6.0	7	3	3	3	5	4.50
Goose Gossage (BS, 1; W, 1-0)	3.0	3	2	2	0	2	6.00

Bird pitched to one batter in the 8th.

PB—Munson. Time—2:13. Attendance—55,535. Umpires—HP, Luciano. 1B, Kunkel. 2B, Phillips. 3B, Cooney.

Game 4
Saturday, October 7

Royals	AB	R	H	RBI	BB	K	Avg
George Brett, 3b	4	1	1	0	0	1	.389
Hal McRae, dh	4	0	1	1	0	1	.214
Amos Otis, cf	4	0	0	0	0	1	.429
Al Cowens, rf	3	0	0	0	0	1	.133
Clint Hurdle, ph	1	0	0	0	0	1	.375
Darrell Porter, c	3	0	1	0	1	0	.357
John Wathan, 1b	3	0	0	0	0	0	.000
Pete LaCock, ph	1	0	0	0	0	0	.364
Frank White, 2b	3	0	2	0	0	0	.231
Freddie Patek, ss	3	0	0	0	0	1	.077
Willie Wilson, lf	3	0	1	0	0	2	.250
TOTALS	32	1	7	1	1	8	.276

Yankees	AB	R	H	RBI	BB	K	Avg
Mickey Rivers, cf	2	0	0	0	1	0	.455
Paul Blair, cf	1	0	0	0	0	0	.000
Roy White, lf	4	1	1	1	0	1	.313
Gary Thomasson, lf	0	0	0	0	0	0	.000
Thurman Munson, c	4	0	1	0	0	0	.278
Reggie Jackson, dh	3	0	0	0	0	3	.462
Lou Piniella, rf	3	0	0	0	0	1	.235
Graig Nettles, 3b	3	1	2	0	0	1	.333
Chris Chambliss, 1b	3	0	0	0	0	2	.400
Brian Doyle, 2b	2	0	0	0	1	1	.286
Bucky Dent, ss	3	0	0	0	0	0	.200
TOTALS	28	2	4	2	2	9	.306

	1	2	3	4	5	6	7	8	9	R	H	E
Royals	1	0	0	0	0	0	0	0	0	1	7	0
Yankees	0	1	0	0	0	1	0	0	x	2	4	0

DP—Yankees 1 (Nettles to Chambliss). LOB—Royals 5, Yankees 4. Scoring Position—Royals 1-for-8, Yankees 0-for-3. 2B—Otis (2). 3B—Brett (1). HR—RWhite (1), Nettles (1). SB—McRae (1). CS—Wilson (1).

Royals	IP	H	R	ER	BB	K	ERA
Dennis Leonard (L, 0-2)	8.0	4	2	2	2	9	3.75

Yankees	IP	H	R	ER	BB	K	ERA
Ron Guidry (W, 1-0)	8.0	7	1	1	1	7	1.13
Goose Gossage (S, 1)	1.0	0	0	0	0	1	4.50

Guidry pitched to one batter in the 9th.

WP—Leonard. Time—2:20. Attendance—56,356. Umpires—HP, Kunkel. 1B, Phillips. 2B, Cooney. 3B, DiMuro.

1978 AL Championship Series—Composite Statistics

Batting

Yankees	G	AB	R	H	RBI	2B	3B	HR	BB	SO	SB	CS	Avg	OBP	Slg
Paul Blair	4	6	1	0	0	0	0	0	1	0	0	0	.000	.000	.000
Chris Chambliss	4	15	1	6	2	0	0	0	0	4	0	0	.400	.400	.400
Bucky Dent	4	15	0	3	4	0	0	0	0	0	0	0	.200	.200	.200
Brian Doyle	3	7	0	2	1	0	0	0	1	1	0	0	.286	.375	.286
Reggie Jackson	4	13	5	6	6	1	0	2	3	4	0	0	.462	.529	1.000
Cliff Johnson	1	1	0	0	0	0	0	0	0	0	0	0	.000	.000	.000
Thurman Munson	4	18	2	5	2	1	0	1	0	0	0	0	.278	.278	.500
Graig Nettles	4	15	3	5	2	0	1	1	0	1	0	0	.333	.333	.667
Lou Piniella	4	17	2	4	0	0	0	0	0	3	0	0	.235	.235	.235
Mickey Rivers	4	11	0	5	0	0	0	0	2	0	0	0	.455	.538	.455
Fred Stanley	2	5	0	1	0	0	0	0	0	2	0	0	.200	.200	.200
Gary Thomasson	3	1	0	0	0	0	0	0	0	0	0	0	.000	.000	.000
Roy White	4	16	5	5	1	1	0	1	1	2	0	0	.313	.353	.563
Totals	4	140	19	42	18	3	1	5	7	18	0	0	.300	.331	.443

Royals	G	AB	R	H	RBI	2B	3B	HR	BB	SO	SB	CS	Avg	OBP	Slg
Steve Braun	2	5	0	0	0	0	0	0	1	1	0	0	.000	.167	.000
George Brett	4	18	7	7	3	1	1	3	0	1	0	0	.389	.389	1.056
Al Cowens	4	15	2	2	1	0	0	0	2	0	0	0	.133	.133	.133
Clint Hurdle	4	8	1	3	1	0	1	0	2	3	0	0	.375	.500	.625
Pete LaCock	4	11	1	4	1	2	1	0	3	1	1	0	.364	.500	.727
Hal McRae	4	14	0	3	2	0	0	0	2	2	1	1	.214	.294	.214
Amos Otis	4	14	2	6	1	2	0	0	3	5	4	0	.429	.529	.571
Freddie Patek	4	13	2	1	2	0	0	1	1	4	0	1	.077	.143	.308
Tom Poquette	1	1	0	0	0	0	0	0	0	0	0	0	.000	.000	.000
Darrell Porter	4	14	1	5	3	1	0	0	2	0	0	0	.357	.412	.429
John Wathan	1	3	0	0	0	0	0	0	0	0	0	0	.000	.000	.000
Frank White	4	13	1	3	2	0	0	0	0	0	0	0	.231	.231	.231
Willie Wilson	3	4	0	1	0	0	0	0	0	2	0	1	.250	.250	.250
Totals	4	133	17	35	16	6	3	4	14	21	6	3	.263	.329	.444

Pitching

Yankees	G	GS	CG	IP	H	R	ER	BB	SO	W-L	Sv-Op	Hld	ERA
Jim Beattie	1	1	0	5.1	2	1	1	5	3	1-0	0-0	0	1.69
Ken Clay	1	0	0	3.2	0	0	0	3	2	0-0	1-1	0	0.00
Ed Figueroa	1	1	0	1.0	5	5	3	0	0	0-1	0-0	0	27.00
Goose Gossage	2	0	0	4.0	3	2	2	0	3	1-0	1-2	0	4.50
Ron Guidry	1	1	0	8.0	7	1	1	1	7	1-0	0-0	0	1.13
Catfish Hunter	1	1	0	6.0	7	3	3	3	5	0-0	0-0	0	4.50
Sparky Lyle	1	0	0	1.1	3	2	2	0	0	0-0	0-0	0	13.50
Dick Tidrow	1	0	0	5.2	8	3	3	2	1	0-0	0-0	0	4.76
Totals	4	4	0	35.0	35	17	15	14	21	3-1	2-3	0	3.86

Royals	G	GS	CG	IP	H	R	ER	BB	SO	W-L	Sv-Op	Hld	ERA
Doug Bird	2	0	0	1.0	2	1	1	0	1	0-1	0-1	0	9.00
Larry Gura	1	1	0	6.1	8	2	2	2	2	1-0	0-0	0	2.84
Al Hrabosky	3	0	0	3.0	3	1	1	0	2	0-0	0-0	0	3.00
Dennis Leonard	2	2	1	12.0	13	5	5	2	11	0-2	0-0	0	3.75
Steve Mingori	1	0	0	3.2	5	3	3	3	0	0-0	0-0	0	7.36
Marty Pattin	1	0	0	0.2	2	2	2	0	0	0-0	0-0	1	27.00
Paul Splittorff	1	1	0	7.1	9	5	4	0	2	0-0	0-0	0	4.91
Totals	4	4	1	34.0	42	19	18	7	18	1-3	0-1	1	4.76

Fielding

Yankees	Pos	G	PO	Ast	E	DP	PB	FPct
Jim Beattie	p	1	2	0	0	0	—	1.000
Paul Blair	cf	3	7	0	0	0	—	1.000
	2b	1	1	0	0	0	—	1.000
Chris Chambliss	1b	4	28	1	0	1	—	1.000
Ken Clay	p	1	0	0	0	0	—	—
Bucky Dent	ss	4	2	7	1	0	—	.900
Brian Doyle	2b	3	3	6	0	0	—	1.000
Ed Figueroa	p	1	0	0	0	0	—	—
Goose Gossage	p	2	0	1	0	0	—	1.000
Ron Guidry	p	1	0	0	0	0	—	—
Catfish Hunter	p	1	0	1	0	0	—	1.000
Reggie Jackson	rf	1	4	0	0	0	—	1.000
Sparky Lyle	p	1	1	1	0	0	—	1.000
Thurman Munson	c	4	22	4	0	0	1	1.000
Graig Nettles	3b	4	6	8	0	2	—	1.000
Lou Piniella	rf	3	10	0	0	0	—	1.000
	lf	1	3	0	0	0	—	1.000
Mickey Rivers	cf	4	8	1	0	1	—	1.000
Fred Stanley	2b	2	3	3	0	0	—	1.000
Gary Thomasson	lf	2	2	0	0	0	—	1.000
	cf	1	0	0	0	0	—	—
Dick Tidrow	p	1	0	2	0	0	—	1.000
Roy White	lf	3	3	0	0	0	—	1.000
Totals		4	105	35	1	4	1	.993

Royals	Pos	G	PO	Ast	E	DP	PB	FPct
Doug Bird	p	2	0	1	0	0	—	1.000
Steve Braun	lf	1	5	0	0	0	—	1.000
George Brett	3b	4	3	8	1	1	—	.917
Al Cowens	rf	4	5	0	0	0	—	1.000
Larry Gura	p	1	1	4	0	0	—	1.000
Al Hrabosky	p	3	0	0	0	0	—	—
Clint Hurdle	lf	2	6	1	0	1	—	1.000
Pete LaCock	1b	3	26	1	0	3	—	1.000
Dennis Leonard	p	2	1	0	0	0	—	1.000
Steve Mingori	p	1	0	0	0	0	—	—
Amos Otis	cf	4	8	0	1	0	—	.889
Freddie Patek	ss	4	9	8	2	2	—	.895
Marty Pattin	p	1	0	0	0	0	—	—
Darrell Porter	c	4	21	1	0	1	1	1.000
Paul Splittorff	p	1	0	0	0	0	—	—
John Wathan	1b	1	7	0	0	0	—	1.000
Frank White	2b	4	8	12	0	3	—	1.000
Willie Wilson	lf	3	2	0	0	0	—	1.000
Totals		4	102	36	4	11	1	.972

1978 Los Angeles Dodgers (NL) 3, Philadelphia Phillies (NL) 1

The Dodgers downed the Phillies in the NLCS for the third straight year, taking the NL flag in four games. Steve Garvey homered twice and drove in four runs in the Dodgers' 9-5 opening-game victory. Los Angeles took Game 2, 4-0, as Tommy John tossed a four-hit shutout and Davey Lopes tripled, homered and drove in three runs. Game 3 belonged to Steve Carlton. The Philadelphia lefty blasted a three-run homer and added an RBI single, going the distance to beat the Dodgers, 9-4. Garry Maddox wore the goat horns in Game 4. With two out in the bottom of the 10th, Dusty Baker lifted a liner to center that Maddox dropped for an error. Bill Russell followed with an RBI single to give Los Angeles a 4-3 win and the NL title.

Game 1

Wednesday, October 4

Dodgers	AB	R	H	RBI	BB	K	Avg
Davey Lopes, 2b	5	2	3	2	0	0	.600
Bill Russell, ss	5	1	1	0	0	0	.200
Reggie Smith, rf	3	1	1	1	0	1	.333
Bill North, cf	1	0	0	0	0	0	.000
Steve Garvey, 1b	5	3	3	4	0	1	.600
Ron Cey, 3b	5	0	2	1	0	1	.400
Dusty Baker, lf	3	0	1	0	2	0	.333
Rick Monday, cf-rf	4	1	1	0	1	2	.250
Steve Yeager, c	4	1	1	1	1	0	.250
Burt Hooton, p	2	0	0	0	0	1	.000
Bob Welch, p	2	0	0	0	0	1	.000
TOTALS	39	9	13	9	4	7	.333

Phillies	AB	R	H	RBI	BB	K	Avg
Bake McBride, rf	5	1	1	0	0	2	.200
Larry Bowa, ss	5	1	3	0	0	1	.600
Garry Maddox, cf	5	0	2	2	0	2	.400
Greg Luzinski, lf	4	1	1	0	0	1	.250
Richie Hebner, 1b	4	0	1	1	0	0	.250
Mike Schmidt, 3b	3	0	0	1	0	1	.000
Bob Boone, c	4	0	1	0	0	1	.250
Ted Sizemore, 2b	4	1	2	0	0	0	.500
Larry Christenson, p	1	0	0	0	0	1	.000
Warren Brusstar, p	0	0	0	0	0	0	—
Orlando Gonzalez, ph	1	0	0	0	0	1	.000
Rawly Eastwick, p	0	0	0	0	0	0	—
Tim McCarver, ph	1	0	0	0	0	0	.000
Tug McGraw, p	0	0	0	0	0	0	—
Jerry Martin, ph	1	1	1	1	0	0	1.000
TOTALS	38	5	12	5	0	10	.316

	1	2	3	4	5	6	7	8	9	R	H	E
Dodgers	0	0	4	2	1	1	0	0	1	9	13	1
Phillies	0	1	0	0	3	0	0	0	1	5	12	1

E—Lopes, Schmidt. DP—Dodgers 1 (Russell to Garvey), Phillies 1 (Bowa to Sizemore to Hebner). LOB—Dodgers 8, Phillies 7. Scoring Position—Dodgers 3-for-8. 2B—Lopes (1). 3B—Garvey (1), Monday (1), Luzinski (1). HR—Lopes (1), Garvey 2 (2), Yeager (1), Martin (1). SF—Schmidt. GDP—Baker, Luzinski.

Dodgers	IP	H	R	ER	BB	K	ERA
Burt Hooton	4.2	10	4	4	0	5	7.71
Bob Welch (W, 1-0)	4.1	2	1	1	0	5	2.08

Phillies	IP	H	R	ER	BB	K	ERA
Larry Christenson (L, 0-1)	4.1	7	7	6	1	3	12.46
Warren Brusstar	0.2	1	0	0	0	0	0.00
Rawly Eastwick	1.0	3	1	1	0	1	9.00
Tug McGraw	3.0	2	1	1	3	3	3.00

HBP—Smith by Eastwick. Time—2:37. Attendance—63,460. Umpires—HP, Weyer. 1B, Colosi. 2B, Olsen. 3B, Davidson.

Game 2

Thursday, October 5

Dodgers	AB	R	H	RBI	BB	K	Avg
Davey Lopes, 2b	4	1	3	3	0	0	.667
Bill Russell, ss	4	0	1	0	0	1	.222
Reggie Smith, rf	4	0	1	0	0	0	.286
Bill North, cf	0	0	0	0	0	0	.000
Steve Garvey, 1b	4	0	0	0	0	0	.333
Ron Cey, 3b	4	0	0	0	0	2	.222
Dusty Baker, lf	4	1	1	0	0	0	.286
Rick Monday, cf-rf	4	1	1	0	0	1	.250
Steve Yeager, c	3	1	1	1	1	0	.286
Tommy John, p	3	0	0	0	0	0	.000
TOTALS	34	4	8	4	1	4	.304

Phillies	AB	R	H	RBI	BB	K	Avg
Mike Schmidt, 3b	4	0	1	0	0	0	.143
Larry Bowa, ss	4	0	0	0	0	1	.333
Garry Maddox, cf	4	0	1	0	0	0	.333
Greg Luzinski, lf	3	0	1	0	0	0	.286
Jose Cardenal, 1b	2	0	0	0	1	0	.000
Bob Boone, c	3	0	1	0	0	0	.286
Jerry Martin, rf	2	0	0	0	1	0	.333
Ted Sizemore, 2b	3	0	0	0	0	0	.286
Dick Ruthven, p	1	0	0	0	0	1	.000
Warren Brusstar, p	0	0	0	0	0	0	—
Jim Morrison, ph	1	0	0	0	0	1	.000
Ron Reed, p	0	0	0	0	0	0	—
Barry Foote, ph	1	0	0	0	0	1	.000
Tug McGraw, p	0	0	0	0	0	0	—
TOTALS	28	0	4	0	2	4	.259

	1	2	3	4	5	6	7	8	9	R	H	E
Dodgers	0	0	0	1	2	0	1	0	0	4	8	0
Phillies	0	0	0	0	0	0	0	0	0	0	4	0

DP—Dodgers 3 (Russell to Lopes to Garvey; Lopes to Russell to Garvey; Cey to Lopes to Garvey). LOB—Dodgers 5, Phillies 3. Scoring Position—Dodgers 3-for-9, Phillies 0-for-4. 2B—Smith (1), Baker (1). 3B—Lopes (1). HR—Lopes (2). S—John. GDP—Boone, Martin, Sizemore. SB—Yeager (1).

Dodgers	IP	H	R	ER	BB	K	ERA
Tommy John (W, 1-0)	9.0	4	0	0	2	4	0.00

Phillies	IP	H	R	ER	BB	K	ERA
Dick Ruthven (L, 0-1)	4.2	6	3	3	0	3	5.79
Warren Brusstar	1.1	0	0	0	0	0	0.00
Ron Reed	2.0	2	1	1	0	1	4.50
Tug McGraw	1.0	0	0	0	1	0	2.25

Time—2:06. Attendance—60,642. Umpires—HP, Colosi. 1B, Olsen. 2B, Davidson. 3B, Williams.

Game 3

Friday, October 6

Phillies	AB	R	H	RBI	BB	K	Avg
Bake McBride, rf	3	0	0	0	0	0	.125
Jerry Martin, ph-rf	2	0	1	1	0	1	.400
Larry Bowa, ss	5	0	1	0	0	0	.286
Garry Maddox, cf	5	1	1	0	0	0	.286
Greg Luzinski, lf	5	1	3	1	0	0	.417
Richie Hebner, 1b	4	0	0	0	0	0	.125
Mike Schmidt, 3b	4	1	1	0	1	0	.182
Tim McCarver, c	3	2	1	2	0	0	.000
Ted Sizemore, 2b	2	2	1	1	1	0	.444
Steve Carlton, p	4	2	2	4	0	0	.500
TOTALS	37	9	11	8	4	1	.281

Dodgers	AB	R	H	RBI	BB	K	Avg
Davey Lopes, 2b	4	0	0	0	0	1	.462
Bill North, cf	4	0	0	0	0	1	.000
Reggie Smith, rf	4	1	1	0	0	1	.273
Steve Garvey, 1b	4	2	2	2	0	0	.385
Ron Cey, 3b	3	1	1	1	1	1	.250
Dusty Baker, lf	3	0	1	0	1	0	.300
Bill Russell, ss	4	0	2	1	0	0	.308
Steve Yeager, c	3	0	0	0	0	2	.200
Lee Lacy, ph	1	0	0	0	0	0	.000
Don Sutton, p	2	0	0	0	0	2	.000
Lance Rautzhan, p	0	0	0	0	0	0	—
Manny Mota, ph	1	0	1	0	0	0	1.000
Charlie Hough, p	0	0	0	0	0	0	—
Joe Ferguson, ph	1	0	0	0	0	0	.000
TOTALS	34	4	8	4	2	8	.293

	1	2	3	4	5	6	7	8	9	R	H	E
Phillies	0	4	0	0	0	3	1	0	1	9	11	1
Dodgers	0	1	2	0	0	0	0	1	0	4	8	2

E—Lopes, Schmidt, Smith. DP—Phillies 1 (Sizemore to Bowa to Hebner). LOB—Phillies 7, Dodgers 5. Scoring Position—Phillies 4-for-11, Dodgers 2-for-7. 2B—Schmidt (1), Garvey (1), Russell (1), Martin (1), Mota (1). HR—Luzinski (1), Carlton (1), Garvey (3). S—Hebner, Sizemore. GDP—North, Ferguson.

Game 4

Saturday, October 7

Phillies	AB	R	H	RBI	BB	K	Avg
Mike Schmidt, 3b	4	0	1	0	1	1	.200
Larry Bowa, ss	4	1	2	0	0	1	.333
Garry Maddox, cf	5	0	1	0	0	1	.263
Greg Luzinski, lf	4	1	1	2	1	1	.375
Jose Cardenal, 1b	4	0	1	0	0	1	.167
Jerry Martin, rf	4	0	0	0	0	2	.222
Ted Sizemore, 2b	4	0	1	0	0	0	.385
Randy Lerch, p	2	0	0	0	0	0	.000
Warren Brusstar, p	0	0	0	0	0	0	—
Bake McBride, ph	1	1	1	1	0	0	.222
Ron Reed, p	0	0	0	0	0	0	—
Richie Hebner, ph	1	0	0	0	0	0	.111
Tug McGraw, p	0	0	0	0	0	0	—
TOTALS	37	3	8	3	3	6	.260

Dodgers	AB	R	H	RBI	BB	K	Avg
Davey Lopes, 2b	5	0	1	0	0	0	.389
Bill North, cf	3	0	0	0	0	0	.000
Rick Monday, ph-cf	2	0	0	0	0	2	.200
Reggie Smith, rf	5	0	0	0	0	0	.188
Steve Garvey, 1b	5	1	2	1	0	0	.389
Ron Cey, 3b	4	3	2	1	1	0	.313
Dusty Baker, lf	5	0	4	1	0	0	.467
Bill Russell, ss	4	0	3	1	1	0	.412
Steve Yeager, c	3	0	1	0	0	0	.231
Lee Lacy, ph	1	0	0	0	0	0	.000
Jerry Grote, c	0	0	0	0	0	0	—
Doug Rau, p	1	0	0	0	0	0	.000
Manny Mota, ph	0	0	0	0	0	0	1.000
Rick Rhoden, p	0	0	0	0	0	0	.000
Joe Ferguson, ph	1	0	0	0	0	1	.000
Terry Forster, p	0	0	0	0	0	0	—
TOTALS	40	4	13	4	2	3	.304

	1	2	3	4	5	6	7	8	9	10	R	H	E
Phillies	0	0	2	0	0	0	1	0	0	0	3	8	2
Dodgers	4	1	3	0							4	13	0

E—Maddox, Boone. DP—Phillies 1 (Sizemore to Bowa to Cardenal). LOB—Phillies 7, Dodgers 10. Scoring Position—Phillies 1-for-6, Dodgers 2-for-9. 2B—Schmidt (2), Cey (1), Baker (2). 3B—Sizemore (1). HR—Luzinski (2), Garvey (4), Cey (1), McBride (1). S—Mota. GDP—Russell (1). SB—Lopes (1). CS—Schmidt (1), Garvey (1).

Phillies	IP	H	R	ER	BB	K	ERA
Randy Lerch	5.1	7	3	3	0	0	5.06
Warren Brusstar	0.2	1	0	0	0	0	0.00
Ron Reed	2.0	4	0	0	0	1	2.25
Tug McGraw (L, 0-1)	1.2	1	1	0	1	2	1.59

Dodgers	IP	H	R	ER	BB	K	ERA
Doug Rau	5.0	5	2	2	2	1	3.60
Rick Rhoden	4.0	2	1	1	1	3	2.25
Terry Forster (W, 1-0)	1.0	1	0	0	0	0	0.00

Time—2:53. Attendance—55,124. Umpires—HP, Davidson. 1B, Williams. 2B, McSherry. 3B, Weyer.

(Game 3 pitching, bottom of middle column)

Phillies	IP	H	R	ER	BB	K	ERA
Steve Carlton (W, 1-0)	9.0	8	4	4	2	8	4.00

Dodgers	IP	H	R	ER	BB	K	ERA
Don Sutton (L, 0-1)	5.2	7	7	4	2	0	6.35
Lance Rautzhan	1.1	3	1	1	2	0	6.75
Charlie Hough	2.0	1	1	1	0	1	4.50

Time—2:18. Attendance—55,043. Umpires—HP, Olsen. 1B, Davidson. 2B, Williams. 3B, McSherry.

1978 NL Championship Series—Composite Statistics

Batting

Dodgers	G	AB	R	H	RBI	2B	3B	HR	BB	SO	SB	CS	Avg	OBP	Slg
Dusty Baker	4	15	1	7	1	2	0	0	3	0	0	0	.467	.556	.600
Ron Cey	4	16	4	5	3	1	0	1	2	4	0	0	.313	.389	.563
Joe Ferguson	2	2	0	0	0	0	0	0	0	1	0	0	.000	.000	.000
Steve Garvey	4	18	6	7	7	1	1	4	0	1	0	1	.389	.389	1.222
Burt Hooton	1	2	0	0	0	0	0	0	0	1	0	0	.000	.000	.000
Tommy John	1	3	0	0	0	0	0	0	0	0	0	0	.000	.000	.000
Lee Lacy	2	2	0	0	0	0	0	0	0	0	0	0	.000	.000	.000
Davey Lopes	4	18	3	7	5	1	1	2	0	1	1	0	.389	.389	.889
Rick Monday	3	10	2	2	0	0	1	0	1	5	0	0	.200	.273	.400
Manny Mota	2	1	0	1	0	1	0	0	0	0	0	0	1.000	1.000	2.000
Bill North	4	8	0	0	0	0	0	0	0	1	0	0	.000	.000	.000
Doug Rau	1	1	0	0	0	0	0	0	0	0	0	0	.000	.000	.000
Rick Rhoden	1	1	0	0	0	0	0	0	0	0	0	0	.000	.000	.000
Bill Russell	4	17	1	7	2	1	0	0	1	1	0	0	.412	.444	.471
Reggie Smith	4	16	2	3	1	1	0	0	0	2	0	0	.188	.235	.250
Don Sutton	1	2	0	0	0	0	0	0	0	2	0	0	.000	.000	.000
Bob Welch	1	2	0	0	0	0	0	0	0	0	0	0	.000	.000	.000
Steve Yeager	4	13	2	3	2	0	0	1	2	2	1	0	.231	.333	.462
Totals	4	147	21	42	21	8	3	8	9	22	2	1	.286	.331	.544

Phillies	G	AB	R	H	RBI	2B	3B	HR	BB	SO	SB	CS	Avg	OBP	Slg
Bob Boone	3	11	0	2	0	0	0	0	0	0	1	0	.182	.182	.182
Larry Bowa	4	18	2	6	0	0	0	0	1	2	0	0	.333	.368	.333
Jose Cardenal	2	6	0	1	0	0	0	0	1	1	0	0	.167	.286	.167
Steve Carlton	1	4	2	2	4	0	0	1	0	0	0	0	.500	.500	1.250
Larry Christenson	1	1	0	0	0	0	0	0	0	1	0	0	.000	.000	.000
Barry Foote	1	1	0	0	0	0	0	0	0	1	0	0	.000	.000	.000
Orlando Gonzalez	1	1	0	0	0	0	0	0	0	1	0	0	.000	.000	.000
Richie Hebner	3	9	0	1	1	0	0	0	0	0	0	0	.111	.111	.111
Randy Lerch	1	2	0	0	0	0	0	0	0	0	0	0	.000	.000	.000
Greg Luzinski	4	16	3	6	3	0	1	2	1	2	0	0	.375	.412	.875
Garry Maddox	4	19	1	5	2	0	0	0	0	3	0	0	.263	.263	.263
Jerry Martin	4	9	1	2	2	1	0	1	1	3	0	0	.222	.300	.667
Bake McBride	3	9	2	2	1	0	0	1	0	2	0	0	.222	.222	.556
Tim McCarver	2	4	2	0	1	0	0	0	2	0	0	0	.000	.333	.000
Jim Morrison	1	1	0	0	0	0	0	0	0	1	0	0	.000	.000	.000
Dick Ruthven	1	1	0	0	0	0	0	0	0	1	0	0	.000	.000	.000
Mike Schmidt	4	15	1	3	1	2	0	0	2	2	0	1	.200	.278	.333
Ted Sizemore	4	13	3	5	1	0	1	0	1	0	0	0	.385	.429	.538
Totals	4	140	17	35	16	3	2	5	9	21	0	1	.250	.293	.407

Pitching

Dodgers	G	GS	CG	IP	H	R	ER	BB	SO	W-L	Sv-Op	Hld	ERA
Terry Forster	1	0	0	1.0	1	0	0	0	2	1-0	0-0	0	0.00
Burt Hooton	1	1	0	4.2	10	4	4	0	5	0-0	0-0	0	7.71
Charlie Hough	1	0	0	2.0	1	1	1	0	1	0-0	0-0	0	4.50
Tommy John	1	1	1	9.0	4	0	0	2	4	1-0	0-0	0	0.00
Doug Rau	1	1	0	5.0	5	2	2	2	1	0-0	0-0	0	3.60
Lance Rautzhan	1	0	0	1.1	3	1	1	2	0	0-0	0-0	0	6.75
Rick Rhoden	1	0	0	4.0	2	1	1	1	3	0-0	0-0	0	2.25
Don Sutton	1	1	0	5.2	7	7	4	2	0	0-1	0-0	0	6.35
Bob Welch	1	0	0	4.1	2	1	1	0	5	1-0	0-0	0	2.08
Totals	4	4	1	37.0	35	17	14	9	21	3-1	0-0	0	3.41

Phillies	G	GS	CG	IP	H	R	ER	BB	SO	W-L	Sv-Op	Hld	ERA
Warren Brusstar	3	0	0	2.2	2	0	0	1	0	0-0	0-0	0	0.00
Steve Carlton	1	1	1	9.0	8	4	4	2	8	1-0	0-0	0	4.00
Larry Christenson	1	1	0	4.1	7	7	6	1	3	0-1	0-0	0	12.46
Rawly Eastwick	1	0	0	1.0	3	1	1	0	1	0-0	0-0	0	9.00
Randy Lerch	1	1	0	5.1	7	3	3	0	0	0-0	0-0	0	5.06
Tug McGraw	3	0	0	5.2	3	2	1	5	5	0-1	0-0	0	1.59
Ron Reed	2	0	0	4.0	6	1	1	0	2	0-0	0-0	0	2.25
Dick Ruthven	1	1	0	4.2	6	3	3	0	3	0-1	0-0	0	5.79
Totals	4	4	1	36.2	42	21	19	9	22	1-3	0-0	0	4.66

Fielding

Dodgers	Pos	G	PO	Ast	E	DP	PB	FPct
Dusty Baker	lf	4	5	0	0	0	—	1.000
Ron Cey	3b	4	2	15	0	1	—	1.000
Terry Forster	p	1	0	0	0	0	—	—
Steve Garvey	1b	4	44	4	0	4	—	1.000
Jerry Grote	c	1	2	0	0	0	0	1.000
Burt Hooton	p	1	1	0	0	0	—	1.000
Charlie Hough	p	1	1	1	0	0	—	1.000
Tommy John	p	1	0	0	0	0	—	—
Davey Lopes	2b	4	10	10	2	3	—	.909
Rick Monday	cf	3	4	0	0	0	—	1.000
	rf	2	2	0	0	0	—	1.000
Bill North	cf	4	9	0	0	0	—	1.000
Doug Rau	p	1	1	0	0	0	—	1.000
Lance Rautzhan	p	1	0	1	0	0	—	1.000
Rick Rhoden	p	1	0	2	0	0	—	1.000
Bill Russell	ss	4	4	13	0	3	—	1.000
Reggie Smith	rf	4	5	0	1	0	—	.833
Don Sutton	p	1	0	1	0	0	—	1.000
Bob Welch	p	1	0	1	0	0	—	1.000
Steve Yeager	c	4	21	2	0	0	0	1.000
Totals		4	111	50	3	11	0	.982

Phillies	Pos	G	PO	Ast	E	DP	PB	FPct
Bob Boone	c	3	16	2	1	0	0	.947
Larry Bowa	ss	4	5	16	0	4	—	1.000
Warren Brusstar	p	3	0	0	0	0	—	—
Jose Cardenal	1b	2	21	0	0	1	—	1.000
Steve Carlton	p	1	0	0	0	0	—	—
Larry Christenson	p	1	0	0	0	0	—	—
Rawly Eastwick	p	1	0	0	0	0	—	—
Richie Hebner	1b	2	21	0	0	3	—	1.000
Randy Lerch	p	1	0	1	0	0	—	1.000
Greg Luzinski	lf	4	5	1	0	0	—	1.000
Garry Maddox	cf	4	16	0	1	0	—	.941
Jerry Martin	rf	3	7	0	0	0	—	1.000
Bake McBride	rf	2	1	0	0	0	—	1.000
Tim McCarver	c	1	8	0	0	0	0	1.000
Tug McGraw	p	3	0	0	0	0	—	—
Ron Reed	p	2	0	0	0	0	—	—
Dick Ruthven	p	1	0	0	0	0	—	—
Mike Schmidt	3b	4	3	18	2	0	—	.913
Ted Sizemore	2b	4	7	8	0	4	—	1.000
Totals		4	110	46	4	12	0	.975

1979 Baltimore Orioles (AL) 3, California Angels (AL) 1

Earl Weaver's Baltimore Orioles came within two outs of sweeping the California Angels and ultimately prevailed in four games. The opener featured a classic matchup: Baltimore's Jim Palmer versus California's Nolan Ryan. Each was impressive, and the game went into the bottom of the 10th knotted at three. With two out and two on, John Lowenstein sliced an opposite-field three-run homer off John Montague for a 6-3 Baltimore victory. Eddie Murray homered and drove in four runs in Game 2, staking Mike Flanagan to a 9-1 lead, but the Angels kept pecking away. Don Stanhouse allowed California to cut it to 9-8 as they loaded the bases with two outs in the ninth, but Stanhouse got Brian Downing to ground out to end the threat and the game. In Game 3, Stanhouse came on to protect a one-run lead with a man on second in the ninth. After walking Downing, he induced Bobby Grich to line to center field. Al Bumbry dropped it for an error and the tying run scored; Larry Harlow followed with a double to plate the game-winner. The Orioles wrapped it up in Game 4, however, as Scott McGregor tossed a six-hit shutout for an 8-0 victory.

Game 1

Wednesday, October 3

Angels	AB	R	H	RBI	BB	K	Avg
Rick Miller, cf	5	1	1	0	0	0	.200
Carney Lansford, 3b	4	0	0	0	1	1	.000
Dan Ford, rf	4	1	2	2	0	0	.500
Don Baylor, dh	4	0	0	0	0	0	.000
Rod Carew, 1b	4	1	3	0	0	0	.750
Brian Downing, c	4	0	0	0	0	0	.000
Bobby Grich, 2b	3	0	1	1	1	0	.333
Larry Harlow, lf	4	0	0	0	0	2	.000
Jim Anderson, ss	3	0	0	0	0	0	.000
Willie Davis, ph	1	0	0	0	0	0	.000
Bert Campaneris, ss	0	0	0	0	0	0	—
TOTALS	36	3	7	3	2	3	.194

Orioles	AB	R	H	RBI	BB	K	Avg
Al Bumbry, cf	4	1	0	0	1	2	.000
Mark Belanger, ss	4	0	1	1	0	1	.250
John Lowenstein, ph	1	1	1	3	0	1	1.000
Ken Singleton, rf	3	0	0	0	1	1	.000
Eddie Murray, 1b	2	0	0	0	2	2	.000
Pat Kelly, lf	3	1	1	0	1	1	.333
Lee May, dh	4	0	0	0	0	2	.000
Doug DeCinces, 3b	3	2	1	0	0	0	.333
Rich Dauer, 2b	3	0	1	0	0	0	.333
Rick Dempsey, c	3	1	1	0	0	0	.333
Terry Crowley, ph	1	0	0	0	0	0	.000
TOTALS	31	6	6	6	5	9	.194

	1	2	3	4	5	6	7	8	9	10		R	H	E
Angels	1	0	1	0	0	1	0	0	0	0		3	7	1
Orioles	0	0	2	1	0	0	0	0	0	3		6	6	1

E—Grich. DP—Angels 2 (Lansford to Grich to Carew; Miller to Carew). LOB—Angels 5, Orioles 3. Scoring Position—Angels 1-for-6, Orioles 2-for-6. 2B—Ford (1), Carew (1), Grich (1), Dempsey (1). HR—Ford (1), Lowenstein (1). S—Dauer. SF—DeCinces. GDP—May. SB—Kelly (1). CS—Carew (1), Murray (1).

Angels	IP	H	R	ER	BB	K	ERA
Nolan Ryan	7.0	4	3	1	3	8	1.29
John Montague (L, 0-1)	2.2	2	3	2	1	1	10.13

Orioles	IP	H	R	ER	BB	K	ERA
Jim Palmer	9.0	7	3	3	2	3	3.00
Don Stanhouse (W, 1-0)	1.0	0	0	0	0	0	0.00

WP—Ryan. PB—Dempsey. Time—3:10. Attendance—52,787. Umpires—HP, Barnett. 1B, Ford. 2B, Evans. 3B, Denkinger.

Game 2

Thursday, October 4

Angels	AB	R	H	RBI	BB	K	Avg
Rod Carew, 1b	5	2	1	1	0	0	.444
Carney Lansford, 3b	5	1	3	3	0	0	.333
Dan Ford, rf	5	1	2	1	0	0	.444
Don Baylor, dh	4	1	2	1	1	0	.250
Brian Downing, c	4	0	1	1	0	0	.125
Bobby Grich, 2b	3	0	0	1	0	0	.167
Bobby Clark, lf	3	0	0	0	0	2	.000
Larry Harlow, ph	0	0	0	0	1	0	.000
Rick Miller, cf	4	1	0	0	0	0	.111
Jim Anderson, ss	2	0	0	0	0	0	.000
Merv Rettenmund, ph	0	0	0	0	1	0	.000
Dickie Thon, pr-ss	0	1	0	0	0	0	—
Willie Davis, ph	1	1	1	0	0	0	.500
TOTALS	36	8	10	8	3	2	.236

Orioles	AB	R	H	RBI	BB	K	Avg
Al Bumbry, cf	4	2	3	0	1	0	.375
Kiko Garcia, ss	3	1	2	2	2	1	.667
Ken Singleton, rf	5	1	1	0	0	1	.125
Eddie Murray, 1b	4	2	2	4	0	0	.333
John Lowenstein, lf	3	1	0	0	1	2	.250
Pat Kelly, dh	4	1	1	1	0	1	.286
Doug DeCinces, 3b	3	1	1	1	1	0	.333
Rich Dauer, 2b	4	0	0	0	0	0	.143
Rick Dempsey, c	4	0	1	0	0	0	.286
TOTALS	34	9	11	8	5	5	.286

	1	2	3	4	5	6	7	8	9		R	H	E
Angels	1	0	0	0	0	1	1	3	2		8	10	1
Orioles	4	4	1	0	0	0	0	0	x		9	11	1

E—Grich, Murray. DP—Angels 1 (Anderson to Grich to Carew). LOB—Angels 6, Orioles 6. Scoring Position—Angels 4-for-7, Orioles 6-for-12. 2B—Carew (2), Davis (1). HR—Ford (2), Murray (1). SF—Downing, Grich. GDP—Singleton. SB—Bumbry 2 (2).

Angels	IP	H	R	ER	BB	K	ERA
Dave Frost (L, 0-1)	1.1	5	6	5	3	0	33.75
Mark Clear	5.2	4	3	3	2	3	4.76
Don Aase	1.0	2	0	0	0	2	0.00

Orioles	IP	H	R	ER	BB	K	ERA
Mike Flanagan (W, 1-0)	7.0	6	6	4	1	2	5.14
Don Stanhouse	2.0	4	2	2	2	0	6.00

Flanagan pitched to three batters in the 8th.

WP—Clear. Time—2:51. Attendance—52,108. Umpires—HP, Ford. 1B, Evans. 2B, Denkinger. 3B, Clark.

Game 3

Friday, October 5

Orioles	AB	R	H	RBI	BB	K	Avg
Al Bumbry, cf	5	1	1	0	0	1	.308
Kiko Garcia, ss	3	0	0	0	0	2	.333
Terry Crowley, ph	1	0	1	1	0	0	.500
Mark Belanger, pr-ss	1	0	0	0	0	0	.200
Ken Singleton, rf	4	2	2	0	0	0	.250
Eddie Murray, 1b	2	0	2	0	2	0	.500
Lee May, dh	3	0	1	1	1	1	.143
Doug DeCinces, 3b	3	0	0	0	0	1	.222
Gary Roenicke, lf	1	0	0	0	0	0	.000
John Lowenstein, ph-lf	1	0	0	0	1	0	.200
Rich Dauer, 2b	4	0	1	0	0	1	.182
Dave Skaggs, c	4	0	0	0	0	1	.000
TOTALS	32	3	8	3	4	7	.253

Angels	AB	R	H	RBI	BB	K	Avg
Rick Miller, cf	4	0	1	0	0	1	.154
Carney Lansford, 3b	4	1	1	0	0	1	.308
Dan Ford, rf	4	0	1	0	0	0	.385
Don Baylor, dh	4	1	1	1	0	0	.250
Rod Carew, 1b	4	1	2	0	0	0	.462
Brian Downing, c	3	1	1	0	1	0	.182
Bobby Grich, 2b	4	0	0	0	0	1	.100
Larry Harlow, lf	4	0	1	1	0	0	.125
Jim Anderson, ss	3	0	1	0	0	1	.125
TOTALS	34	4	9	3	1	4	.248

	1	2	3	4	5	6	7	8	9		R	H	E
Orioles	0	0	0	1	0	1	1	0	0		3	8	3
Angels	1	0	0	1	0	0	0	0	2		4	9	0

E—Bumbry, Garcia, Murray. DP—Orioles 2 (Roenicke to Garcia to Dauer; Dauer to Murray), Angels 2 (Lansford to Grich to Carew; Miller to Downing). LOB—Orioles 8, Angels 6. Scoring Position—Orioles 3-for-7, Angels 2-for-7. 2B—Singleton (1), Carew (3), Harlow (1). 3B—Bumbry (1). HR—Baylor (1). SF—DeCinces. GDP—DeCinces, Ford. SB—Lansford (1), Carew (1).

Orioles	IP	H	R	ER	BB	K	ERA
Dennis Martinez	8.1	8	3	3	0	4	3.24
Don Stanhouse (BS, 1; L, 1-1)	0.0	1	1	0	1	0	6.00

Angels	IP	H	R	ER	BB	K	ERA
Frank Tanana	5.0	6	2	2	2	3	3.60
Don Aase (BS, 1; W, 1-0)	4.0	2	1	1	2	4	1.80

Tanana pitched to three batters in the 6th. Stanhouse pitched to three batters in the 9th.

HBP—Roenicke by Tanana. Time—2:59. Attendance—43,199. Umpires—HP, Evans. 1B, Denkinger. 2B, Clark. 3B, Kosc.

Game 4

Saturday, October 6

Orioles	AB	R	H	RBI	BB	K	Avg
Al Bumbry, cf	3	1	0	0	2	0	.250
Kiko Garcia, ss	5	0	1	0	0	1	.273
Mark Belanger, ss	0	0	0	0	0	0	.200
Ken Singleton, rf	4	1	3	2	0	0	.375
Eddie Murray, 1b	4	1	1	1	1	0	.417
John Lowenstein, lf	1	0	0	0	0	0	.167
Gary Roenicke, ph-lf	4	1	1	1	0	0	.200
Pat Kelly, dh	4	1	2	3	0	1	.364
Doug DeCinces, 3b	4	1	2	0	0	0	.308
Billy Smith, 2b	4	0	0	0	0	1	.000
Rich Dauer, 2b	0	0	0	0	0	0	.182
Rick Dempsey, c	3	2	2	1	1	0	.400
TOTALS	36	8	12	8	4	3	.292

Angels	AB	R	H	RBI	BB	K	Avg
Rod Carew, 1b	4	0	1	0	0	0	.412
Carney Lansford, 3b	4	0	1	0	0	0	.294
Dan Ford, rf	4	0	0	0	0	0	.294
Don Baylor, lf	4	0	0	0	0	2	.188
Brian Downing, c	4	0	1	0	0	1	.200
Bobby Grich, 2b	3	0	1	0	0	0	.154
Merv Rettenmund, dh	2	0	0	0	1	1	.000
Rick Miller, cf	3	0	2	0	0	0	.250
Jim Anderson, ss	3	0	0	0	0	0	.091
TOTALS	31	0	6	0	1	4	.242

	1	2	3	4	5	6	7	8	9		R	H	E
Orioles	0	0	2	1	0	0	5	0	0		8	12	1
Angels	0	0	0	0	0	0	0	0	0		0	6	0

E—Garcia. DP—Orioles 3 (Smith to Garcia to Murray; DeCinces to Murray; Garcia to Smith to Murray), Angels 2 (Anderson to Grich to Carew; Lansford to Carew). LOB—Orioles 6, Angels 5. Scoring Position—Orioles 6-for-13, Angels 0-for-4. 2B—Singleton (2), DeCinces (1), Dempsey (2). HR—Kelly (1). SF—Singleton. GDP—Lansford, Anderson 2, Roenicke. SB—Kelly (2), Dempsey (1).

Orioles	IP	H	R	ER	BB	K	ERA
Scott McGregor (W, 1-0)	9.0	6	0	0	1	4	0.00

Angels	IP	H	R	ER	BB	K	ERA
Chris Knapp (L, 0-1)	2.1	5	2	2	1	0	7.71
Dave LaRoche	1.1	1	1	1	1	1	6.75
Dave Frost	3.0	3	4	4	2	1	18.69
John Montague	1.1	2	1	1	0	1	9.00
Mike Barlow	1.0	0	0	0	0	0	0.00

WP—Frost. Time—2:56. Attendance—43,199. Umpires—HP, Denkinger. 1B, Clark. 2B, Kosc. 3B, Barnett.

1979 AL Championship Series—Composite Statistics

Batting

Orioles	G	AB	R	H	RBI	2B	3B	HR	BB	SO	SB	CS	Avg	OBP	Slg
Mark Belanger	3	5	0	1	1	0	0	0	0	2	0	0	.200	.200	.200
Al Bumbry	4	16	5	4	0	0	1	0	4	3	2	0	.250	.400	.375
Terry Crowley	2	2	0	1	1	0	0	0	0	0	0	0	.500	.500	.500
Rich Dauer	4	11	0	2	0	0	0	0	0	1	0	0	.182	.182	.182
Doug DeCinces	4	13	4	4	3	1	0	0	1	1	0	0	.308	.313	.385
Rick Dempsey	3	10	3	4	2	2	0	0	1	0	1	0	.400	.455	.600
Kiko Garcia	3	11	1	3	2	0	0	0	2	4	0	0	.273	.385	.273
Pat Kelly	3	11	3	4	4	0	0	1	1	3	2	0	.364	.417	.636
John Lowenstein	4	6	2	1	3	0	0	1	2	2	0	0	.167	.375	.667
Lee May	2	7	0	1	1	0	0	0	1	3	0	0	.143	.250	.143
Eddie Murray	4	12	3	5	5	0	0	1	5	2	0	1	.417	.588	.667
Gary Roenicke	2	5	1	1	1	0	0	0	0	0	0	0	.200	.333	.200
Ken Singleton	4	16	4	6	2	2	0	0	1	2	0	0	.375	.389	.500
Dave Skaggs	1	4	0	0	0	0	0	0	0	0	0	0	.000	.000	.000
Billy Smith	1	4	0	0	0	0	0	0	0	1	0	0	.000	.000	.000
Totals	4	133	26	37	25	5	1	3	18	24	5	1	.278	.361	.398

Batting

Angels	G	AB	R	H	RBI	2B	3B	HR	BB	SO	SB	CS	Avg	OBP	Slg
Jim Anderson	4	11	0	1	0	0	0	0	0	1	0	0	.091	.091	.091
Don Baylor	4	16	2	3	2	0	0	1	1	2	0	0	.188	.235	.375
Rod Carew	4	17	4	7	1	3	0	0	0	0	1	1	.412	.412	.588
Bobby Clark	1	3	0	0	0	0	0	0	0	2	0	0	.000	.000	.000
Willie Davis	2	2	1	1	0	1	0	0	0	0	0	0	.500	.500	1.000
Brian Downing	4	15	1	3	1	0	0	0	1	1	0	0	.200	.235	.200
Dan Ford	4	17	2	5	4	1	0	2	0	0	0	0	.294	.294	.706
Bobby Grich	4	13	0	2	2	1	0	0	1	1	0	0	.154	.200	.231
Larry Harlow	3	8	0	1	1	1	0	0	1	2	0	0	.125	.222	.250
Carney Lansford	4	17	2	5	3	0	0	0	1	2	1	0	.294	.333	.294
Rick Miller	4	16	2	4	0	0	0	0	0	1	0	0	.250	.250	.250
Merv Rettenmund	2	2	0	0	0	0	0	0	2	1	0	0	.000	.500	.000
Dickie Thon	1	0	1	0	0	0	0	0	0	0	0	0	—	—	—
Totals	4	137	15	32	14	7	0	3	7	13	2	1	.234	.267	.350

Pitching

Orioles	G	GS	CG	IP	H	R	ER	BB	SO	W-L	Sv-Op	Hld	ERA
Mike Flanagan	1	1	0	7.0	6	6	4	1	2	1-0	0-0	0	5.14
Dennis Martinez	1	1	0	8.1	8	3	3	0	4	0-0	0-0	0	3.24
Scott McGregor	1	1	1	9.0	6	0	0	1	4	1-0	0-0	0	0.00
Jim Palmer	1	1	0	9.0	7	3	3	2	3	0-0	0-0	0	3.00
Don Stanhouse	3	0	0	3.0	5	3	2	3	0	1-1	0-1	0	6.00
Totals	4	4	1	36.1	32	15	12	7	13	3-1	0-1	0	2.97

Pitching

Angels	G	GS	CG	IP	H	R	ER	BB	SO	W-L	Sv-Op	Hld	ERA
Don Aase	2	0	0	5.0	4	1	1	2	6	1-0	0-1	0	1.80
Mike Barlow	1	0	0	1.0	0	0	0	0	0	0-0	0-0	0	0.00
Mark Clear	1	0	0	5.2	4	3	3	2	3	0-0	0-0	0	4.76
Dave Frost	2	1	0	4.1	8	10	9	5	1	0-1	0-0	0	18.69
Chris Knapp	1	1	0	2.1	5	2	2	1	0	0-1	0-0	0	7.71
Dave LaRoche	1	0	0	1.1	2	1	1	1	1	0-0	0-0	0	6.75
John Montague	2	0	0	4.0	4	4	4	2	2	0-1	0-0	0	9.00
Nolan Ryan	1	1	0	7.0	4	3	1	3	8	0-0	0-0	0	1.29
Frank Tanana	1	1	0	5.0	6	2	2	2	3	0-0	0-0	0	3.60
Totals	4	4	0	35.2	37	26	23	18	24	1-3	0-1	0	5.80

Fielding

Orioles	Pos	G	PO	Ast	E	DP	PB	FPct
Mark Belanger	ss	3	0	6	0	0	—	1.000
Al Bumbry	cf	4	10	0	1	0	—	.909
Rich Dauer	2b	4	11	12	0	2	—	1.000
Doug DeCinces	3b	4	5	8	0	1	—	1.000
Rick Dempsey	c	3	10	1	0	0	1	1.000
Mike Flanagan	p	1	0	0	0	0	—	—
Kiko Garcia	ss	3	7	17	2	3	—	.923
Pat Kelly	lf	1	3	0	0	0	—	1.000
John Lowenstein	lf	3	6	0	0	0	—	1.000
Dennis Martinez	p	1	2	0	0	0	—	1.000
Scott McGregor	p	1	0	0	0	0	—	—
Eddie Murray	1b	4	44	3	2	4	—	.959
Jim Palmer	p	1	1	1	0	0	—	1.000
Gary Roenicke	lf	2	2	1	0	1	—	1.000
Ken Singleton	rf	4	4	1	0	0	—	1.000
Dave Skaggs	c	1	3	1	0	0	0	1.000
Billy Smith	2b	1	1	2	0	2	—	1.000
Don Stanhouse	p	3	0	0	0	0	—	—
Totals		4	109	53	5	13	1	.970

Fielding

Angels	Pos	G	PO	Ast	E	DP	PB	FPct
Don Aase	p	2	0	1	0	0	—	1.000
Jim Anderson	ss	4	3	11	0	2	—	1.000
Mike Barlow	p	1	0	0	0	0	—	—
Don Baylor	lf	1	4	0	0	0	—	1.000
Bert Campaneris	ss	1	0	0	0	0	—	—
Rod Carew	1b	4	34	1	0	6	—	1.000
Bobby Clark	lf	1	4	0	0	0	—	1.000
Mark Clear	p	1	0	0	0	0	—	—
Brian Downing	c	4	27	0	0	1	0	1.000
Dan Ford	rf	4	6	0	0	0	—	1.000
Dave Frost	p	2	0	0	0	0	—	—
Bobby Grich	2b	4	4	12	2	4	—	.889
Larry Harlow	lf	2	6	0	0	0	—	1.000
Chris Knapp	p	1	0	0	0	0	—	—
Carney Lansford	3b	4	4	8	0	3	—	1.000
Dave LaRoche	p	1	0	0	0	0	—	—
Rick Miller	cf	4	14	2	0	2	—	1.000
John Montague	p	2	1	1	0	0	—	1.000
Nolan Ryan	p	1	0	0	0	0	—	—
Frank Tanana	p	1	0	0	0	0	—	—
Dickie Thon	ss	1	0	0	0	0	—	—
Totals		4	107	36	2	18	0	.986

1979 Pittsburgh Pirates (NL) 3, Cincinnati Reds (NL) 0

Pittsburgh Pirates first baseman Willie Stargell starred in the 1979 NLCS, leading Pittsburgh to a three-game sweep of the Cincinnati Reds. Starters John Candelaria and Tom Seaver were sharp in Game 1, and the contest went into the top of the 11th inning tied, 2-2. That's when Stargell first made his presence felt, coming up with two men on base and blasting a three-run homer for a 5-2 Pittsburgh victory. In Game 2, the Pirates took a 2-1 lead into the ninth before the Reds tied it up with doubles from Heity Cruz and Dave Collins. The Pirates came back to win in the top of the 10th as Dave Parker singled in Omar Moreno. Stargell doubled, homered and drove in three runs in Game 3, and the Pirates finished off the Reds with a 7-1 triumph.

Game 1

Tuesday, October 2

Pirates	AB	R	H	RBI	BB	K	Avg
Omar Moreno, cf	5	1	1	0	0	2	.200
Tim Foli, ss	4	0	2	1	0	0	.500
Matt Alexander, pr	0	1	0	0	0	0	—
Bill Robinson, lf	0	0	0	0	0	0	—
Dave Parker, rf	4	1	1	0	1	0	.250
Willie Stargell, 1b	4	1	1	3	1	1	.250
John Milner, lf	5	0	0	0	0	0	.000
Rennie Stennett, 2b	0	0	0	0	0	0	—
Bill Madlock, 3b	5	0	2	0	0	0	.400
Ed Ott, c	5	0	1	0	0	0	.200
Phil Garner, 2b-ss	4	1	2	1	1	0	.500
John Candelaria, p	3	0	0	0	0	2	.000
Enrique Romo, p	0	0	0	0	0	0	—
Kent Tekulve, p	0	0	0	0	0	0	—
Mike Easler, ph	1	0	0	0	0	0	.000
Grant Jackson, p	1	0	0	0	0	0	.000
Don Robinson, p	0	0	0	0	0	0	—
TOTALS	41	5	10	5	3	7	.244

Reds	AB	R	H	RBI	BB	K	Avg
Dave Collins, rf	5	0	2	0	0	0	.400
Joe Morgan, 2b	4	0	0	0	1	0	.000
Dave Concepcion, ss	5	1	2	0	0	0	.400
George Foster, lf	3	1	1	2	2	0	.333
Johnny Bench, c	3	0	2	0	2	0	.667
Ray Knight, 3b	5	0	0	0	0	2	.000
Dan Driessen, 1b	4	0	0	0	0	2	.000
Heity Cruz, cf	4	0	0	0	0	1	.000
Tom Seaver, p	2	0	0	0	0	1	.000
Rick Auerbach, ph	1	0	0	0	0	1	.000
Tom Hume, p	1	0	0	0	0	1	.000
Dave Tomlin, p	0	0	0	0	0	0	—
TOTALS	37	2	7	2	5	8	.189

	1	2	3	4	5	6	7	8	9	10	11		R	H	E
Pirates	0	0	2	0	0	0	0	0	0	0	3		5	10	0
Reds	0	0	0	2	0	0	0	0	0	0	0		2	7	0

DP—Pirates 2 (Garner to Foli to Stargell; Madlock to Garner to Stargell), Reds 1 (Concepcion to Morgan to Driessen). LOB—Pirates 7, Reds 7. Scoring Position—Pirates 1-for-5, Reds 0-for-4. 3B—Moreno (1), Bench (1). HR—Stargell (1), Garner (1), Foster (1). SF—Foli. GDP—Parker, Concepcion, Knight. SB—Madlock 2 (2), Collins (1). CS—Bench (1).

Pirates	IP	H	R	ER	BB	K	ERA
John Candelaria	7.0	5	2	2	1	4	2.57
Enrique Romo	0.1	1	0	0	1	1	0.00
Kent Tekulve	1.2	0	0	0	1	0	0.00
Grant Jackson (W, 1-0)	1.2	1	0	0	1	2	0.00
Don Robinson (S, 1)	0.1	0	0	0	1	1	0.00

Reds	IP	H	R	ER	BB	K	ERA
Tom Seaver	8.0	5	2	2	2	5	2.25
Tom Hume (L, 0-1)	2.1	5	3	3	0	1	11.57
Dave Tomlin	0.2	0	0	0	1	1	0.00

Time—3:14. Attendance—55,006. Umpires—HP, Kibler. 1B, Montague. 2B, Dale. 3B, Pulli.

Game 2

Wednesday, October 3

Pirates	AB	R	H	RBI	BB	K	Avg
Omar Moreno, cf	5	1	2	0	0	0	.300
Tim Foli, ss	4	1	2	1	0	0	.500
Dave Parker, rf	5	0	2	1	0	2	.333
Willie Stargell, 1b	3	0	2	0	2	0	.429
John Milner, lf	2	0	0	0	1	0	.000
Bill Robinson, lf	2	0	0	0	0	0	.000
Bill Madlock, 3b	5	0	1	0	0	0	.200
Ed Ott, c	4	0	2	0	0	0	.333
Phil Garner, 2b	4	1	1	0	0	0	.375
Jim Bibby, p	0	0	0	0	1	0	—
Grant Jackson, p	0	0	0	0	0	0	.000
Enrique Romo, p	0	0	0	0	0	0	—
Kent Tekulve, p	1	0	0	0	0	1	.000
Dave Roberts, p	0	0	0	0	0	0	—
Don Robinson, p	0	0	0	0	0	0	—
TOTALS	35	3	11	3	4	3	.292

Reds	AB	R	H	RBI	BB	K	Avg
Dave Collins, rf	5	0	1	1	0	2	.300
Joe Morgan, 2b	3	0	0	0	2	0	.000
Dave Concepcion, ss	5	0	2	0	0	1	.400
George Foster, lf	3	0	1	0	2	1	.333
Johnny Bench, c	5	0	0	0	0	2	.250
Dan Driessen, 1b	4	1	1	0	1	0	.125
Ray Knight, 3b	5	0	2	0	0	0	.200
Cesar Geronimo, cf	3	0	0	0	0	3	.000
Frank Pastore, p	0	0	0	1	1	0	—
Harry Spilman, ph	1	0	0	0	0	0	.000
Dave Tomlin, p	0	0	0	0	0	0	—
Tom Hume, p	0	0	0	0	0	0	.000
Heity Cruz, ph	1	1	1	0	0	0	.200
Doug Bair, p	0	0	0	0	0	0	—
TOTALS	35	2	8	2	6	9	.217

	1	2	3	4	5	6	7	8	9	10		R	H	E
Pirates	0	0	0	1	1	0	0	0	0	1		3	11	0
Reds	0	1	0	0	0	0	0	0	1	0		2	8	0

DP—Reds 1 (Concepcion to Morgan to Driessen). LOB—Pirates 9, Reds 11. Scoring Position—Pirates 4-for-11, Reds 1-for-12. 2B—Foli (1), Stargell (1), Collins (1), Concepcion (1), Cruz (1). S—Foli, Bibby 2, Geronimo. SF—Pastore. GDP—Madlock (1). SB—Collins (2), Morgan (1), Knight (1). CS—Concepcion (1).

Pirates	IP	H	R	ER	BB	K	ERA
Jim Bibby	7.0	4	1	1	4	5	1.29
Grant Jackson (H, 1)	0.1	0	0	0	0	0	0.00
Enrique Romo	0.2	0	0	0	0	0	0.00
Kent Tekulve (BS, 1)	1.0	2	1	1	1	2	3.38
Dave Roberts	0.0	0	0	0	0	1	—
Don Robinson (W, 0-1)	1.2	0	0	0	0	2	0.00

Reds	IP	H	R	ER	BB	K	ERA
Frank Pastore	7.0	7	2	2	3	1	2.57
Dave Tomlin	0.2	1	0	0	0	1	0.00
Tom Hume	1.1	1	0	0	0	1	7.36
Doug Bair (L, 0-1)	1.0	2	1	1	1	0	9.00

Romo pitched to two batters in the 8th. Roberts pitched to one batter in the 9th.

WP—Tekulve. Time—3:24. Attendance—55,000. Umpires—HP, Montague. 1B, Dale. 2B, Pulli. 3B, Stello.

Game 3

Friday, October 5

Reds	AB	R	H	RBI	BB	K	Avg
Dave Collins, rf	4	0	2	0	0	0	.357
Joe Morgan, 2b	4	0	0	0	0	1	.000
Dave Concepcion, ss	4	0	2	0	0	2	.429
George Foster, lf	4	0	0	0	0	2	.200
Johnny Bench, c	4	1	1	1	0	0	.250
Dan Driessen, 1b	4	0	0	0	0	1	.083
Ray Knight, 3b	4	0	2	0	0	0	.286
Cesar Geronimo, cf	4	0	1	0	0	2	.143
Mike LaCoss, p	0	0	0	0	0	0	—
Fred Norman, p	1	0	0	0	0	1	.000
Charlie Leibrandt, p	0	0	0	0	0	0	—
Rick Auerbach, ph	1	0	0	0	0	0	.000
Mario Soto, p	0	0	0	0	0	0	—
Harry Spilman, ph	1	0	0	0	0	0	.000
Dave Tomlin, p	0	0	0	0	0	0	—
Tom Hume, p	0	0	0	0	0	0	.000
TOTALS	35	1	8	1	0	9	.220

Pirates	AB	R	H	RBI	BB	K	Avg
Omar Moreno, cf	2	1	0	0	2	0	.250
Tim Foli, ss	4	0	1	0	0	0	.333
Dave Parker, rf	3	1	1	1	1	1	.333
Willie Stargell, 1b	4	1	2	3	0	1	.455
John Milner, lf	2	0	0	0	1	0	.000
Bill Robinson, lf	1	0	0	0	0	0	.000
Bill Madlock, 3b	2	1	1	1	2	0	.250
Ed Ott, c	4	0	0	0	0	0	.231
Phil Garner, 2b	4	2	2	0	0	0	.417
Bert Blyleven, p	3	1	1	0	0	1	.333
TOTALS	29	7	7	6	6	3	.283

	1	2	3	4	5	6	7	8	9		R	H	E
Reds	0	0	0	0	0	1	0	0	0		1	8	1
Pirates	1	1	2	2	0	0	0	1	x		7	7	0

E—Geronimo. LOB—Reds 7, Pirates 8. Scoring Position—Reds 1-for-3, Pirates 1-for-12. 2B—Knight (1), Stargell (2). 3B—Garner (1). HR—Bench (1), Stargell (2), Madlock (1). S—Moreno, Blyleven. SF—Foli, Parker. SB—Moreno (1), Parker (1).

Reds	IP	H	R	ER	BB	K	ERA
Mike LaCoss (L, 0-1)	1.2	1	2	2	4	0	10.80
Fred Norman	2.0	4	4	4	1	1	18.00
Charlie Leibrandt	0.1	0	0	0	0	0	0.00
Mario Soto	2.0	0	0	0	0	1	0.00
Dave Tomlin	1.2	2	1	0	1	1	0.00
Tom Hume	0.1	0	0	0	0	0	6.75

Pirates	IP	H	R	ER	BB	K	ERA
Bert Blyleven (W, 1-0)	9.0	8	1	1	0	9	1.00

Balk—Leibrandt. Time—2:45. Attendance—42,240. Umpires—HP, Dale. 1B, Pulli. 2B, Stello. 3B, Quick.

1979 NL Championship Series—Composite Statistics

Batting

Pirates	G	AB	R	H	RBI	2B	3B	HR	BB	SO	SB	CS	Avg	OBP	Slg
Matt Alexander	1	0	1	0	0	0	0	0	0	0	0	0	—	—	—
Jim Bibby	1	0	0	0	0	0	0	0	1	0	0	0	—	1.000	—
Bert Blyleven	1	3	1	1	0	0	0	0	0	1	0	0	.333	.333	.333
John Candelaria	1	3	0	0	0	0	0	0	0	2	0	0	.000	.000	.000
Mike Easler	1	1	0	0	0	0	0	0	0	0	0	0	.000	.000	.000
Tim Foli	3	12	1	4	3	1	0	0	0	0	0	0	.333	.286	.417
Phil Garner	3	12	4	5	1	0	1	1	1	0	0	0	.417	.462	.833
Grant Jackson	2	1	0	0	0	0	0	0	0	0	0	0	.000	.000	.000
Bill Madlock	3	12	1	3	2	0	0	1	2	0	2	0	.250	.357	.500
John Milner	3	9	0	0	0	0	0	0	2	0	0	0	.000	.182	.000
Omar Moreno	3	12	3	3	0	0	1	0	2	2	1	0	.250	.357	.417
Ed Ott	3	13	0	3	0	0	0	0	0	2	0	0	.231	.231	.231
Dave Parker	3	12	2	4	2	0	0	0	2	3	1	0	.333	.400	.333
Bill Robinson	3	3	0	0	0	0	0	0	0	0	0	0	.000	.000	.000
Willie Stargell	3	11	2	5	6	2	0	2	3	2	0	0	.455	.571	1.182
Kent Tekulve	2	1	0	0	0	0	0	0	0	1	0	0	.000	.000	.000
Totals	3	105	15	28	14	3	2	4	13	13	4	0	.267	.339	.448

Batting

Reds	G	AB	R	H	RBI	2B	3B	HR	BB	SO	SB	CS	Avg	OBP	Slg
Rick Auerbach	2	2	0	0	0	0	0	0	0	1	0	0	.000	.000	.000
Johnny Bench	3	12	1	3	1	0	1	1	2	2	0	1	.250	.357	.667
Dave Collins	3	14	0	5	1	1	0	0	0	2	2	0	.357	.357	.429
Dave Concepcion	3	14	1	6	0	1	0	0	0	3	0	1	.429	.429	.500
Heity Cruz	2	5	1	1	0	1	0	0	0	1	0	0	.200	.200	.400
Dan Driessen	3	12	1	1	0	0	0	0	1	3	0	0	.083	.154	.083
George Foster	3	10	1	2	2	0	0	1	4	3	0	0	.200	.429	.500
Cesar Geronimo	2	7	0	1	0	0	0	0	0	5	0	0	.143	.143	.143
Tom Hume	3	1	0	0	0	0	0	0	0	1	0	0	.000	.000	.000
Ray Knight	3	14	0	4	0	1	0	0	0	2	1	0	.286	.286	.357
Joe Morgan	3	11	0	0	0	0	0	0	3	1	1	0	.000	.214	.000
Fred Norman	1	1	0	0	0	0	0	0	0	1	0	0	.000	.000	.000
Frank Pastore	1	0	0	0	0	0	0	0	1	0	0	0	—	.500	—
Tom Seaver	1	2	0	0	0	0	0	0	0	1	0	0	.000	.000	.000
Harry Spilman	2	2	0	0	0	0	0	0	0	0	0	0	.000	.000	.000
Totals	3	107	5	23	5	4	1	2	11	26	4	2	.215	.286	.327

Pitching

Pirates	G	GS	CG	IP	H	R	ER	BB	SO	W-L	Sv-Op	Hld	ERA
Jim Bibby	1	1	0	7.0	4	1	1	4	5	0-0	0-0	0	1.29
Bert Blyleven	1	1	1	9.0	8	1	1	0	9	1-0	0-0	0	1.00
John Candelaria	1	1	0	7.0	5	2	2	1	4	0-0	0-0	0	2.57
Grant Jackson	2	0	0	2.0	1	0	0	1	2	1-0	0-0	1	0.00
Dave Roberts	1	0	0	0.0	0	0	0	1	0	0-0	0-0	0	—
Don Robinson	2	0	0	2.0	0	0	0	1	3	1-0	1-1	0	0.00
Enrique Romo	2	0	0	0.1	3	0	0	1	1	0-0	0-0	0	0.00
Kent Tekulve	2	0	0	2.2	2	1	1	2	2	0-0	0-1	0	3.38
Totals	3	3	1	30.0	23	5	5	11	26	3-0	1-2	1	1.50

Pitching

Reds	G	GS	CG	IP	H	R	ER	BB	SO	W-L	Sv-Op	Hld	ERA
Doug Bair	1	0	0	1.0	2	1	1	1	0	0-1	0-0	0	9.00
Tom Hume	3	0	0	4.0	6	3	3	0	2	0-1	0-0	0	6.75
Mike LaCoss	1	1	0	1.2	1	2	2	4	0	0-1	0-0	0	10.80
Charlie Leibrandt	1	0	0	0.1	0	0	0	0	0	0-0	0-0	0	0.00
Fred Norman	1	0	0	2.0	4	4	4	1	1	0-0	0-0	0	18.00
Frank Pastore	1	1	0	7.0	7	2	2	3	1	0-0	0-0	0	2.57
Tom Seaver	1	1	0	8.0	5	2	2	2	5	0-0	0-0	0	2.25
Mario Soto	1	0	0	2.0	0	0	0	0	1	0-0	0-0	0	0.00
Dave Tomlin	3	0	0	3.0	3	1	0	2	3	0-0	0-0	0	0.00
Totals	3	3	0	29.0	28	15	14	13	13	0-3	0-0	0	4.34

Fielding

Pirates	Pos	G	PO	Ast	E	DP	PB	FPct
Jim Bibby	p	1	0	1	0	0	—	1.000
Bert Blyleven	p	1	1	1	0	0	—	1.000
John Candelaria	p	1	0	0	0	0	—	—
Tim Foli	ss	3	3	9	0	1	—	1.000
Phil Garner	2b	3	8	9	0	2	—	1.000
	ss	1	0	0	0	0	—	—
Grant Jackson	p	2	0	0	0	0	—	—
Bill Madlock	3b	3	1	7	0	1	—	1.000
John Milner	lf	3	1	0	0	0	—	1.000
Omar Moreno	cf	3	7	0	0	0	—	1.000
Ed Ott	c	3	25	3	0	0	0	1.000
Dave Parker	rf	3	9	0	0	0	—	1.000
Dave Roberts	p	1	0	0	0	0	—	—
Bill Robinson	lf	3	3	0	0	0	—	1.000
Don Robinson	p	2	0	0	0	0	—	—
Enrique Romo	p	2	0	0	0	0	—	—
Willie Stargell	1b	3	32	2	0	2	—	1.000
Rennie Stennett	2b	1	0	1	0	0	—	1.000
Kent Tekulve	p	2	0	1	0	0	—	1.000
Totals		3	90	34	0	6	0	1.000

Fielding

Reds	Pos	G	PO	Ast	E	DP	PB	FPct
Doug Bair	p	1	0	1	0	0	—	1.000
Johnny Bench	c	3	17	2	0	0	0	1.000
Dave Collins	rf	3	5	0	0	0	—	1.000
Dave Concepcion	ss	3	4	14	0	2	—	1.000
Heity Cruz	cf	1	2	0	0	0	—	1.000
Dan Driessen	1b	3	32	0	0	2	—	1.000
George Foster	lf	3	6	2	0	0	—	1.000
Cesar Geronimo	cf	2	8	0	1	0	—	.889
Tom Hume	p	3	0	2	0	0	—	1.000
Ray Knight	3b	3	0	5	0	0	—	1.000
Mike LaCoss	p	1	0	1	0	0	—	1.000
Charlie Leibrandt	p	1	0	0	0	0	—	—
Joe Morgan	2b	3	12	11	0	2	—	1.000
Fred Norman	p	1	0	0	0	0	—	—
Frank Pastore	p	1	0	0	0	0	—	—
Tom Seaver	p	1	0	0	0	0	—	—
Mario Soto	p	1	0	0	0	0	—	—
Dave Tomlin	p	3	1	1	0	0	—	1.000
Totals		3	87	39	1	6	0	.992

1980 Kansas City Royals (AL) 3, New York Yankees (AL) 0

George Brett put the Kansas City Royals in the World Series with a three-run homer off New York Yankees relief ace Goose Gossage in Game 3. The Royals, who'd lost three straight ALCS showdowns to the Yankees from 1976 to 1978, took the first two games behind strong efforts from their starting pitchers. Larry Gura allowed 10 hits in Game 1 but stranded nine baserunners on the way to a 7-2 victory. Dennis Leonard won the second game 3-2 with relief help from Dan Quisenberry. Willie Wilson provided the offense, lacing a two-run triple and scoring the third run on a double by U.L. Washington. In Game 3, the Yanks held a 2-1 lead when Tommy John allowed a two-out double in the top of the seventh. Gossage entered and allowed an infield single to bring up Brett, who blasted a Gossage fastball into the Yankee Stadium upper deck. Quisenberry pitched the final 3.2 innings for the pennant-clinching win.

Game 1
Wednesday, October 8

Yankees	AB	R	H	RBI	BB	K	Avg
Willie Randolph, 2b	5	0	2	0	0	1	.400
Bucky Dent, ss	4	0	2	0	0	0	.500
Bob Watson, 1b	4	0	2	0	0	0	.500
Reggie Jackson, rf	4	0	0	0	0	1	.000
Eric Soderholm, dh	4	0	1	0	0	0	.250
Rick Cerone, c	4	1	1	1	0	0	.250
Lou Piniella, lf	3	1	1	1	1	1	.333
Aurelio Rodriguez, 3b	4	0	1	0	0	0	.250
Bobby Brown, cf	4	0	0	0	0	1	.000
TOTALS	36	2	10	2	1	4	.278

Royals	AB	R	H	RBI	BB	K	Avg
Willie Wilson, lf	5	0	1	2	0	1	.222
U.L. Washington, ss	4	0	1	0	1	2	.250
George Brett, 3b	3	2	2	1	1	0	.667
Hal McRae, dh	3	0	0	0	0	2	.000
Amos Otis, cf	4	2	2	0	0	0	.500
John Wathan, rf	1	1	0	0	3	1	.000
Clint Hurdle, rf	0	0	0	0	0	0	—
Willie Aikens, 1b	4	0	1	2	0	1	.250
Pete LaCock, 1b	0	0	0	0	0	0	—
Darrell Porter, c	4	1	0	0	0	0	.000
Frank White, 2b	4	1	3	2	0	0	.750
TOTALS	32	7	10	7	5	7	.313

	1	2	3	4	5	6	7	8	9	R	H	E
Yankees	0	2	0	0	0	0	0	0	0	2	10	1
Royals	0	2	2	0	0	0	1	2	x	7	10	0

E—Watson. DP—Yankees 1 (Randolph to Dent to Watson). LOB—Yankees 9, Royals 7. Scoring Position—Yankees 0-for-7, Royals 4-for-12. 2B—Randolph (1), Watson (1), Rodriguez (1), Wilson (1), Brett (1), Otis (1), White (1). HR—Cerone (1), Piniella (1), Brett (1). S—Dent. GDP—Brett. SB—Otis (1), White (1). CS—Washington (1), McRae (1).

Yankees	IP	H	R	ER	BB	K	ERA
Ron Guidry (L, 0-1)	3.0	5	4	4	4	2	12.00
Ron Davis	4.0	3	1	1	1	3	2.25
Tom Underwood	1.0	2	2	0	0	2	0.00

Royals	IP	H	R	ER	BB	K	ERA
Larry Gura (W, 1-0)	9.0	10	2	2	1	4	2.00

HBP—McRae by Davis. Time—3:00. Attendance—42,598. Umpires—HP, Palermo. 1B, Brinkman. 2B, McCoy. 3B, Haller.

Game 2
Thursday, October 9

Yankees	AB	R	H	RBI	BB	K	Avg
Willie Randolph, 2b	4	0	2	1	0	1	.444
Bobby Murcer, dh	4	0	0	0	0	2	.000
Bob Watson, 1b	4	0	1	0	0	0	.375
Reggie Jackson, rf	4	0	2	0	0	1	.250
Oscar Gamble, lf	4	0	0	0	0	1	.000
Rick Cerone, c	4	0	2	0	0	0	.375
Graig Nettles, 3b	4	1	1	1	0	1	.250
Bucky Dent, ss	3	0	0	0	0	1	.286
Bobby Brown, cf	2	1	0	0	1	1	.000
TOTALS	33	2	8	2	1	8	.259

Royals	AB	R	H	RBI	BB	K	Avg
Willie Wilson, lf	3	1	1	2	1	0	.250
U.L. Washington, ss	3	0	1	1	1	1	.286
George Brett, 3b	4	0	0	0	0	0	.286
Hal McRae, dh	3	0	0	1	1	0	.000
Amos Otis, cf	4	0	1	0	0	2	.375
John Wathan, rf	3	0	0	0	0	0	.000
Clint Hurdle, rf	0	0	0	0	0	0	—
Willie Aikens, 1b	3	0	0	0	0	0	.143
Darrell Porter, c	3	1	1	0	0	0	.143
Frank White, 2b	3	1	2	0	0	0	.714
TOTALS	29	3	6	3	3	4	.262

	1	2	3	4	5	6	7	8	9	R	H	E
Yankees	0	0	0	2	0	0	0	0	0	2	8	0
Royals	0	0	3	0	0	0	0	0	x	3	6	0

LOB—Yankees 5, Royals 5. Scoring Position—Yankees 0-for-4, Royals 2-for-7. 2B—Randolph (2), Watson (2), Washington (1). 3B—Wilson (1). HR—Nettles (1). GDP—Nettles. SB—Otis (2). CS—McRae (2).

Yankees	IP	H	R	ER	BB	K	ERA
Rudy May (L, 0-1)	8.0	6	3	3	3	4	3.38

Royals	IP	H	R	ER	BB	K	ERA
Dennis Leonard (W, 1-0)	8.0	7	2	2	1	8	2.25
Dan Quisenberry (S, 1)	1.0	1	0	0	0	0	0.00

Leonard pitched to one batter in the 9th.

Time—2:51. Attendance—42,633. Umpires—HP, Brinkman. 1B, McCoy. 2B, Haller. 3B, Kaiser.

Game 3
Friday, October 10

Royals	AB	R	H	RBI	BB	K	Avg
Willie Wilson, lf	5	1	2	0	0	1	.286
U.L. Washington, ss	4	1	2	0	0	0	.364
George Brett, 3b	4	1	1	3	0	0	.273
Hal McRae, dh	4	0	2	0	0	0	.200
Amos Otis, cf	4	0	1	0	0	1	.333
Willie Aikens, 1b	4	0	3	0	0	0	.364
Darrell Porter, c	3	0	0	0	1	0	.100
Clint Hurdle, rf	2	0	0	0	0	1	.000
John Wathan, ph-rf	2	0	0	0	0	0	.000
Frank White, 2b	4	1	1	1	0	1	.545
TOTALS	36	4	12	4	1	4	.289

Yankees	AB	R	H	RBI	BB	K	Avg
Willie Randolph, 2b	4	0	1	0	1	1	.385
Bucky Dent, ss	4	0	0	0	0	0	.182
Bob Watson, 1b	4	0	3	0	0	0	.500
Reggie Jackson, rf	3	1	1	0	1	2	.273
Eric Soderholm, dh	2	0	0	0	0	0	.167
Oscar Gamble, ph-dh	1	1	1	0	1	0	.200
Rick Cerone, c	4	0	1	0	1	1	.333
Lou Piniella, lf	2	0	0	0	1	0	.200
Jim Spencer, ph	1	0	0	0	0	0	.000
Joe Lefebvre, lf	0	0	0	0	0	0	—
Aurelio Rodriguez, 3b	2	0	1	0	0	0	.333
Graig Nettles, ph-3b	2	0	0	0	0	0	.167
Bobby Brown, cf	4	0	0	0	0	0	.000
TOTALS	33	2	8	1	4	4	.265

	1	2	3	4	5	6	7	8	9	R	H	E
Royals	0	0	0	1	0	0	3	0	0	4	12	1
Yankees	0	0	0	0	0	2	0	0	0	2	8	0

E—White. DP—Royals 2 (Splittorff to White to Aikens; Washington to White), Yankees 1 (Randolph to Dent to Watson). LOB—Royals 6, Yankees 8. Scoring Position—Royals 2-for-6, Yankees 2-for-8. 2B—Wilson (3), Watson (3), Jackson (1). 3B—Watson (1). HR—Brett (2), White (1). GDP—Hurdle, Dent. CS—McRae (3), Otis (1).

Royals	IP	H	R	ER	BB	K	ERA
Paul Splittorff	5.1	5	1	1	2	3	1.69
Dan Quisenberry (BS, 1; W, 1-0)	3.2	3	1	0	2	1	0.00

Yankees	IP	H	R	ER	BB	K	ERA
Tommy John	6.2	8	2	2	1	3	2.70
Goose Gossage (BS, 1; L, 0-1)	0.1	3	2	2	0	0	54.00
Tom Underwood	2.0	1	0	0	0	1	0.00

Balk—Splittorff. WP—John. Time—2:59. Attendance—56,588. Umpires—HP, McCoy. 1B, Haller. 2B, Kaiser. 3B, Maloney.

1980 AL Championship Series—Composite Statistics

Batting

Royals	G	AB	R	H	RBI	2B	3B	HR	BB	SO	SB	CS	Avg	OBP	Slg
Willie Aikens	3	11	0	4	2	0	0	0	0	1	0	0	.364	.364	.364
George Brett	3	11	3	3	4	1	0	2	1	0	0	0	.273	.333	.909
Clint Hurdle	3	2	0	0	0	0	0	0	0	1	0	0	.000	.000	.000
Hal McRae	3	10	0	2	0	0	0	0	1	3	0	3	.200	.333	.200
Amos Otis	3	12	2	4	0	1	0	0	0	3	2	1	.333	.333	.417
Darrell Porter	3	10	2	1	0	0	0	0	1	0	0	0	.100	.182	.100
U.L. Washington	3	11	1	4	1	1	0	0	2	3	0	1	.364	.462	.455
John Wathan	3	6	1	0	0	0	0	0	3	1	0	0	.000	.333	.000
Frank White	3	11	3	6	3	1	0	1	0	1	1	0	.545	.545	.909
Willie Wilson	3	13	2	4	4	2	1	0	1	2	0	0	.308	.357	.615
Totals	3	97	14	28	14	6	1	3	9	15	3	5	.289	.355	.464

Yankees	G	AB	R	H	RBI	2B	3B	HR	BB	SO	SB	CS	Avg	OBP	Slg
Bobby Brown	3	10	1	0	0	0	0	0	1	2	0	0	.000	.091	.000
Rick Cerone	3	12	1	4	2	0	0	1	0	1	0	0	.333	.333	.583
Bucky Dent	3	11	0	2	0	0	0	0	0	1	0	0	.182	.182	.182
Oscar Gamble	2	5	1	1	0	0	0	0	1	1	0	0	.200	.333	.200
Reggie Jackson	3	11	1	3	0	1	0	0	1	4	0	0	.273	.333	.364
Bobby Murcer	1	4	0	0	0	0	0	0	0	2	0	0	.000	.000	.000
Graig Nettles	2	6	1	1	1	0	0	1	0	1	0	0	.167	.167	.667
Lou Piniella	2	5	1	1	1	0	0	1	2	1	0	0	.200	.429	.800
Willie Randolph	3	13	0	5	1	2	0	0	1	3	0	0	.385	.429	.538
Aurelio Rodriguez	2	6	0	2	0	1	0	0	0	0	0	0	.333	.333	.500
Eric Soderholm	2	6	0	1	0	0	0	0	0	0	0	0	.167	.167	.167
Jim Spencer	1	1	0	0	0	0	0	0	0	0	0	0	.000	.000	.000
Bob Watson	3	12	0	6	0	3	1	0	0	0	0	0	.500	.500	.917
Totals	3	102	6	26	5	7	1	3	6	16	0	0	.255	.296	.431

Pitching

Royals	G	GS	CG	IP	H	R	ER	BB	SO	W-L	Sv-Op	Hld	ERA
Larry Gura	1	1	1	9.0	10	2	2	1	4	1-0	0-0	0	2.00
Dennis Leonard	1	1	0	8.0	7	2	2	1	8	1-0	0-0	0	2.25
Dan Quisenberry	2	0	0	4.2	4	1	0	2	1	1-0	1-2	0	0.00
Paul Splittorff	1	1	0	5.1	5	1	1	2	3	0-0	0-0	0	1.69
Totals	3	3	1	27.0	26	6	5	6	16	3-0	1-2	0	1.67

Yankees	G	GS	CG	IP	H	R	ER	BB	SO	W-L	Sv-Op	Hld	ERA
Ron Davis	1	0	0	4.0	3	1	1	1	3	0-0	0-0	0	2.25
Goose Gossage	1	0	0	0.1	3	2	2	0	0	0-1	0-1	0	54.00
Ron Guidry	1	1	0	3.0	5	4	4	4	2	0-1	0-0	0	12.00
Tommy John	1	1	0	6.2	8	2	2	1	3	0-0	0-0	0	2.70
Rudy May	1	1	1	8.0	6	3	3	3	4	0-1	0-0	0	3.38
Tom Underwood	2	0	0	3.0	3	2	0	0	3	0-0	0-0	0	0.00
Totals	3	3	1	25.0	28	14	12	9	15	0-3	0-1	0	4.32

Fielding

Royals	Pos	G	PO	Ast	E	DP	PB	FPct
Willie Aikens	1b	3	22	1	0	2	—	1.000
George Brett	3b	3	2	7	0	0	—	1.000
Larry Gura	p	1	0	1	0	0	—	1.000
Clint Hurdle	rf	3	1	0	0	0	—	1.000
Pete LaCock	1b	1	0	0	0	0	—	—
Dennis Leonard	p	1	0	0	0	0	—	—
Amos Otis	cf	3	11	0	0	0	—	1.000
Darrell Porter	c	3	17	1	0	0	0	1.000
Dan Quisenberry	p	2	1	0	0	0	—	1.000
Paul Splittorff	p	1	0	1	0	1	—	1.000
U.L. Washington	ss	3	5	7	0	2	—	1.000
John Wathan	rf	3	7	0	0	0	—	1.000
Frank White	2b	3	9	10	1	3	—	.950
Willie Wilson	lf	3	6	1	0	0	—	1.000
Totals		3	81	29	1	8	0	.991

Yankees	Pos	G	PO	Ast	E	DP	PB	FPct
Bobby Brown	cf	3	7	0	0	0	—	1.000
Rick Cerone	c	3	14	4	0	0	0	1.000
Ron Davis	p	1	0	2	0	0	—	1.000
Bucky Dent	ss	3	10	12	0	2	—	1.000
Oscar Gamble	lf	1	1	0	0	0	—	1.000
Goose Gossage	p	1	0	0	0	0	—	—
Ron Guidry	p	1	0	1	0	0	—	1.000
Reggie Jackson	rf	3	5	0	0	0	—	1.000
Tommy John	p	1	0	1	0	0	—	1.000
Joe Lefebvre	lf	1	0	0	0	0	—	—
Rudy May	p	1	2	2	0	0	—	1.000
Graig Nettles	3b	2	0	2	0	0	—	1.000
Lou Piniella	lf	2	5	0	0	0	—	1.000
Willie Randolph	2b	3	1	9	0	2	—	1.000
Aurelio Rodriguez	3b	2	2	2	0	0	—	1.000
Tom Underwood	p	2	0	2	0	0	—	1.000
Bob Watson	1b	3	28	5	1	2	—	.971
Totals		3	75	42	1	6	0	.992

1980 Philadelphia Phillies (NL) 3, Houston Astros (NL) 2

The Philadelphia Phillies edged the Houston Astros in five games in one of the most thrilling postseason series of all time. Steve Calton beat Ken Forsch 3-1 in the opener, the only game of the series that was settled without extra innings. The second game went 10 innings before Jose Cruz put the Astros up to stay with an RBI single in the top of the 10th. Houston got three more runs in the inning and held on to win, 7-4. Joe Niekro spun 10 scoreless innings in the third game, but neither side was able to push across a run until Denny Walling brought home the game-winner with a bases-loaded sacrifice fly in the bottom of the 11th. Game 4 erupted in controversy when it was ruled that Houston pitcher Vern Ruhle had caught (and not trapped) Garry Maddox' fourth-inning pop up. Ruhle was able to turn it into a double play, but the Phils took a 3-2 lead into the bottom of the ninth. Terry Puhl rapped an RBI single to send the game into extra innings. Pete Rose bowled over catcher Bruce Bochy to tally the go-ahead run in the top of the 10th, as the Phillies pulled it out, 5-3. The finale went into extra innings as well before Garry Maddox doubled in the game-winner in the top of the 10th to put Philadelphia in the World Series.

Game 1

Tuesday, October 7

Astros	AB	R	H	RBI	BB	K	Avg
Rafael Landestoy, 2b	5	0	0	0	0	0	.000
Enos Cabell, 3b	4	0	1	0	0	0	.250
Jose Cruz, lf	3	1	1	0	1	0	.333
Cesar Cedeno, cf	3	0	1	0	1	0	.333
Art Howe, 1b	4	0	0	0	0	0	.000
Gary Woods, rf	4	0	2	1	0	1	.500
Luis Pujols, c	3	0	0	0	1	0	.000
Dave Bergman, pr	0	0	0	0	0	0	—
Craig Reynolds, ss	2	0	0	1	1	1	.000
Terry Puhl, ph	1	0	0	0	0	0	.000
Ken Forsch, p	2	0	2	0	0	1	1.000
Jeffrey Leonard, ph	1	0	0	0	0	1	.000
TOTALS	32	1	7	1	4	4	.219

Phillies	AB	R	H	RBI	BB	K	Avg
Pete Rose, 1b	4	1	2	0	0	0	.500
Bake McBride, rf	4	0	1	0	0	1	.250
Mike Schmidt, 3b	3	0	0	0	1	1	.000
Greg Luzinski, lf	4	1	1	2	0	1	.250
Del Unser, lf	0	0	0	0	0	0	—
Manny Trillo, 2b	4	0	0	0	0	1	.000
Garry Maddox, cf	3	1	1	0	0	0	.333
Larry Bowa, ss	2	0	1	0	0	0	.500
Bob Boone, c	3	0	1	0	0	0	.333
Steve Carlton, p	2	0	0	0	0	1	.000
Greg Gross, ph	1	0	1	1	0	0	1.000
Tug McGraw, p	0	0	0	0	0	0	—
TOTALS	30	3	8	3	1	5	.267

	1	2	3	4	5	6	7	8	9		R	H	E
Astros	0	0	1	0	0	0	0	0	0		1	7	0
Phillies	0	0	0	0	2	1	0	x			3	8	1

E—Bowa. DP—Phillies 1 (Trillo to Bowa to Rose). LOB—Astros 9, Phillies 5. Scoring Position—Astros 1-for-7, Phillies 1-for-5. HR—Luzinski (1). S—Forsch, Bowa. GDP—Cedeno. SB—McBride (1), Maddox (1). CS—Rose (1).

Astros	IP	H	R	ER	BB	K	ERA
Ken Forsch (L, 0-1)	8.0	8	3	3	1	5	3.38

Phillies	IP	H	R	ER	BB	K	ERA
Steve Carlton (W, 1-0)	7.0	7	1	1	3	3	1.29
Tug McGraw (S, 1)	2.0	0	0	0	1	1	0.00

Time—2:35. Attendance—65,277. Umpires—HP, Engel. 1B, Tata. 2B, Froemming. 3B, Harvey.

Game 2

Wednesday, October 8

Astros	AB	R	H	RBI	BB	K	Avg
Terry Puhl, rf	5	1	3	2	0	0	.500
Enos Cabell, 3b	4	0	0	0	0	2	.125
Joe Morgan, 2b	2	1	1	0	3	0	.500
Rafael Landestoy, pr-2b	0	1	0	0	0	0	.000
Jose Cruz, lf	4	1	2	2	1	0	.429
Cesar Cedeno, cf	5	1	1	1	0	0	.250
Art Howe, 1b	4	0	0	0	0	1	.000
Dave Bergman, 1b	1	0	1	2	0	0	1.000
Alan Ashby, c	5	0	0	0	0	0	.000
Craig Reynolds, ss	3	1	0	0	2	0	.000
Nolan Ryan, p	1	1	0	0	1	1	.000
Joe Sambito, p	0	0	0	0	0	0	—
Dave Smith, p	0	0	0	0	0	0	—
Jeffrey Leonard, ph	1	0	0	0	0	1	.000
Frank LaCorte, p	1	0	0	0	0	0	.000
Joaquin Andujar, p	0	0	0	0	0	0	—
TOTALS	36	7	8	7	7	5	.186

Phillies	AB	R	H	RBI	BB	K	Avg
Pete Rose, 1b	4	0	2	0	2	0	.500
Bake McBride, rf	5	0	1	0	1	1	.222
Mike Schmidt, 3b	6	1	2	0	0	1	.222
Greg Luzinski, lf	4	1	2	1	0	2	.375
Lonnie Smith, pr-lf	1	1	1	0	0	0	.333
Manny Trillo, 2b	3	0	1	0	0	1	.143
Garry Maddox, cf	5	0	2	2	0	1	.375
Larry Bowa, ss	4	1	2	0	1	1	.500
Bob Boone, c	4	0	1	0	1	1	.286
Dick Ruthven, p	2	0	0	0	0	2	.000
Greg Gross, ph	0	0	0	0	0	0	1.000
Tug McGraw, p	0	0	0	0	0	0	—
Del Unser, ph	1	0	0	0	0	0	.000
Ron Reed, p	0	0	0	0	0	0	—
Kevin Saucier, p	0	0	0	0	0	0	—
George Vukovich, ph	1	0	0	0	0	0	.000
TOTALS	40	4	14	3	5	10	.324

	1	2	3	4	5	6	7	8	9	10		R	H	E
Astros	0	0	1	0	0	0	1	1	0	4		7	8	1
Phillies	0	0	0	2	0	0	0	1	0	1		4	14	2

E—McBride, Reynolds, Schmidt. DP—Phillies 1 (Bowa to Trillo to Rose). LOB—Astros 8, Phillies 14. Scoring Position—Astros 5-for-11, Phillies 4-for-13. 2B—Puhl (1), Morgan (1), Schmidt (1), Luzinski (1). 3B—Bergman (1). S—Cabell, Ryan, Trillo 2, Gross. GDP—Cedeno. CS—Maddox (1).

Astros	IP	H	R	ER	BB	K	ERA
Nolan Ryan	6.1	8	2	2	1	6	2.84
Joe Sambito	0.1	0	0	0	1	1	0.00
Dave Smith	1.1	2	1	1	1	2	6.75
Frank LaCorte (W, 1-0)	1.0	4	1	0	1	0	0.00
Joaquin Andujar (S, 1)	1.0	0	0	0	1	0	0.00

Phillies	IP	H	R	ER	BB	K	ERA
Dick Ruthven	7.0	3	2	2	5	4	2.57
Tug McGraw	1.0	2	1	1	0	0	3.00
Ron Reed (L, 0-1)	1.1	2	4	4	1	1	27.00
Kevin Saucier	0.2	1	0	0	1	0	0.00

LaCorte pitched to two batters in the 10th.

Time—3:34. Attendance—65,476. Umpires—HP, Tata. 1B, Froemming. 2B, Harvey. 3B, Vargo.

Game 3

Friday, October 10

Phillies	AB	R	H	RBI	BB	K	Avg
Pete Rose, 1b	5	0	1	0	0	1	.385
Bake McBride, rf	5	0	1	0	0	0	.214
Mike Schmidt, 3b	5	0	1	0	0	0	.214
Greg Luzinski, lf	5	0	0	0	0	1	.231
Manny Trillo, 2b	5	0	2	0	0	0	.250
Garry Maddox, cf	4	0	2	0	0	0	.417
Larry Bowa, ss	3	0	0	0	2	0	.333
Bob Boone, c	4	0	0	0	0	0	.182
Del Unser, ph	1	0	0	0	0	1	.000
Keith Moreland, c	0	0	0	0	0	0	—
Larry Christenson, p	2	0	0	0	0	1	.000
George Vukovich, ph	1	0	0	0	0	0	.000
Dickie Noles, p	0	0	0	0	0	0	—
Tug McGraw, p	1	0	0	0	0	0	.000
TOTALS	41	0	7	0	2	4	.257

Astros	AB	R	H	RBI	BB	K	Avg
Terry Puhl, rf-cf	4	0	2	0	1	1	.500
Enos Cabell, 3b	4	0	2	0	0	0	.250
Joe Morgan, 2b	4	0	1	0	1	0	.333
Rafael Landestoy, pr	0	1	0	0	0	0	.000
Jose Cruz, lf	2	0	1	0	3	0	.444
Cesar Cedeno, cf	3	0	0	0	0	0	.182
Dave Bergman, 1b	1	0	0	0	0	0	.500
Art Howe, ph	0	0	0	0	1	0	.000
Denny Walling, 1b-rf	3	0	0	1	1	0	.000
Luis Pujols, c	3	0	0	0	1	0	.000
Craig Reynolds, ss	3	0	0	0	0	0	.000
Joe Niekro, p	3	0	0	0	0	1	.000
Gary Woods, ph	1	0	0	0	0	1	.400
Dave Smith, p	0	0	0	0	0	0	—
TOTALS	31	1	6	1	8	3	.216

	1	2	3	4	5	6	7	8	9	10	11		R	H	E
Phillies	0	0	0	0	0	0	0	0	0	0	0		0	7	1
Astros	0	0	0	0	0	0	0	0	0	0	1		1	6	1

E—Bergman, Christenson. DP—Phillies 2 (Bowa to Trillo to Rose; Bowa to Trillo to Rose). LOB—Phillies 11, Astros 10. Scoring Position—Phillies 0-for-8, Astros 0-for-9. 2B—Trillo (1), Maddox (1), Puhl (2). 3B—Morgan (1), Cruz (1). S—Cabell, Reynolds. SF—Walling. GDP—Cruz, Cedeno. SB—Schmidt (1), Maddox (2). CS—Cabell (1).

Phillies	IP	H	R	ER	BB	K	ERA
Larry Christenson	6.0	3	0	0	4	2	0.00
Dickie Noles	1.1	1	0	0	1	0	0.00
Tug McGraw (L, 0-1)	3.0	2	1	1	3	1	3.00

Astros	IP	H	R	ER	BB	K	ERA
Joe Niekro	10.0	6	0	0	1	2	0.00
Dave Smith (W, 1-0)	1.0	1	0	0	1	2	3.86

PB—Pujols. HBP—Maddox by Niekro. Time—3:22. Attendance—44,443. Umpires—HP, Froemming. 1B, Harvey. 2B, Vargo. 3B, Crawford.

Game 4

Saturday, October 11

Phillies	AB	R	H	RBI	BB	K	Avg
Lonnie Smith, lf	4	1	2	0	0	0	.375
Del Unser, lf-rf	1	0	0	0	0	1	.000
Pete Rose, 1b	4	2	2	1	1	1	.412
Mike Schmidt, 3b	5	0	2	1	0	1	.263
Bake McBride, rf	4	0	2	0	0	1	.278
Greg Luzinski, ph	1	1	1	1	0	0	.286
Tug McGraw, p	0	0	0	0	0	0	.000
Manny Trillo, 2b	4	0	2	2	0	0	.313
Garry Maddox, cf	4	0	0	0	1	1	.313
Larry Bowa, ss	5	0	1	0	0	1	.286
Bob Boone, c	4	0	0	0	0	1	.133
Steve Carlton, p	2	0	0	0	0	0	.000
Dickie Noles, p	0	0	0	0	0	0	—
Kevin Saucier, p	0	0	0	0	0	0	—
Ron Reed, p	0	0	0	0	0	0	—
Greg Gross, ph	1	1	1	0	0	0	1.000
Warren Brusstar, p	1	0	0	0	0	1	.000
George Vukovich, lf	0	0	0	0	0	0	.000
TOTALS	40	5	13	5	2	8	.286

Astros	AB	R	H	RBI	BB	K	Avg
Terry Puhl, cf	3	0	1	1	2	1	.462
Enos Cabell, 3b	4	1	1	0	1	0	.250
Joe Morgan, 2b	3	0	0	0	2	1	.222
Gary Woods, rf	2	0	0	0	1	0	.286
Denny Walling, ph	1	0	0	0	0	0	.000
Jeffrey Leonard, rf	1	0	0	0	0	0	.000
Art Howe, 1b	3	0	1	1	1	0	.091
Jose Cruz, lf	3	0	0	0	1	1	.333
Luis Pujols, c	3	1	1	0	0	0	.111
Bruce Bochy, c	1	0	0	0	0	0	.000
Rafael Landestoy, ss	3	1	1	1	1	0	.125
Vern Ruhle, p	3	0	0	0	0	1	.000
Dave Smith, p	0	0	0	0	0	0	—
Joe Sambito, p	0	0	0	0	0	0	—
TOTALS	30	3	5	3	9	4	.219

	1	2	3	4	5	6	7	8	9	10	R	H	E
Phillies	0	0	0	0	0	0	0	3	0	2	5	13	0
Astros	0	0	0	1	1	0	0	0	1	0	3	5	1

E—Landestoy. DP—Phillies 3 (LSmith to Schmidt; McBride to Boone to Noles to Schmidt; McBride to Rose), Astros 2 (Ruhle to Howe; Leonard to Bochy to Morgan). LOB—Phillies 8, Astros 8. Scoring Position—Phillies 3-for-14, Astros 2-for-8. 2B—Trillo (2), Cabell (1), Howe (1), Luzinski (2). 3B—Pujols (1). S—Sambito. SF—Trillo, Howe. SB—LSmith (1), McBride (2), Bowa (1), Puhl (1), Woods (1), Landestoy (1).

Phillies	IP	H	R	ER	BB	K	ERA
Steve Carlton	5.1	4	2	2	5	3	2.19
Dickie Noles	1.1	0	0	0	2	0	0.00
Kevin Saucier	0.0	0	0	0	1	0	0.00
Ron Reed	0.1	0	0	0	0	0	21.60
Warren Brusstar (BS, 1; W, 1-0)	2.0	1	1	1	1	0	4.50
Tug McGraw (S, 2)	1.0	0	0	0	0	1	2.57

Astros	IP	H	R	ER	BB	K	ERA
Vern Ruhle	7.0	8	3	3	1	3	3.86
Dave Smith (BS, 1)	0.0	1	0	0	0	0	3.86
Joe Sambito (L, 0-1)	3.0	4	2	2	1	5	5.40

Saucier pitched to one batter in the 7th. Ruhle pitched to four batters in the 8th. DSmith pitched to one batter in the 8th.

Time—3:55. Attendance—44,952. Umpires—HP, Harvey. 1B, Vargo. 2B, Crawford. 3B, Engel.

Game 5

Sunday, October 12

Phillies	AB	R	H	RBI	BB	K	Avg
Pete Rose, 1b	3	0	1	1	2	1	.400
Bake McBride, rf	3	0	0	0	0	2	.238
Keith Moreland, ph	1	0	0	1	0	0	.000
Ramon Aviles, pr	0	1	0	0	0	0	—
Tug McGraw, p	0	0	0	0	0	0	.000
George Vukovich, ph	1	0	0	0	0	0	.000
Dick Ruthven, p	0	0	0	0	0	0	.000
Mike Schmidt, 3b	5	0	0	0	0	3	.208
Greg Luzinski, lf	3	0	1	0	0	2	.294
Lonnie Smith, pr	0	0	0	0	0	0	.444
Larry Christenson, p	0	0	0	0	0	0	.000
Ron Reed, p	0	0	0	0	0	0	—
Del Unser, ph-rf	2	2	2	1	0	0	.400
Manny Trillo, 2b	5	1	3	2	0	0	.381
Garry Maddox, cf	4	1	1	1	1	0	.300
Larry Bowa, ss	5	1	2	0	0	1	.316
Bob Boone, c	3	1	2	2	0	0	.222
Marty Bystrom, p	2	0	0	0	0	1	.000
Warren Brusstar, p	0	0	0	0	0	0	.000
Greg Gross, lf	2	1	1	0	0	0	.750
TOTALS	39	8	13	8	3	10	.296

Astros	AB	R	H	RBI	BB	K	Avg
Terry Puhl, cf	6	3	4	0	0	0	.526
Enos Cabell, 3b	5	0	1	0	0	1	.238
Joe Morgan, 2b	4	0	0	0	0	0	.154
Rafael Landestoy, 2b	1	0	1	1	0	0	.222
Jose Cruz, lf	3	1	2	2	2	0	.400
Frank LaCorte, p	0	0	0	0	0	0	.000
Denny Walling, rf	5	2	1	1	0	0	.111
Art Howe, 1b	4	0	2	1	0	0	.200
Dave Bergman, pr-1b	1	0	0	0	0	0	.333
Luis Pujols, c	1	0	0	0	1	0	.100
Alan Ashby, ph-c	3	0	1	1	0	0	.125
Craig Reynolds, ss	5	1	2	0	0	0	.154
Nolan Ryan, p	3	0	0	0	0	1	.000
Joe Sambito, p	0	0	0	0	0	0	—
Ken Forsch, p	0	0	0	0	0	0	1.000
Gary Woods, ph-rf	1	0	0	0	0	1	.250
Danny Heep, ph	1	0	0	0	0	0	.000
TOTALS	43	7	14	6	3	3	.252

	1	2	3	4	5	6	7	8	9	10	R	H	E
Phillies	0	2	0	0	0	0	0	5	0	1	8	13	2
Astros	1	0	0	0	0	1	3	2	0	0	7	14	0

E—Luzinski, Trillo. DP—Astros 2 (Reynolds to Morgan to Howe; Cabell to Morgan to Howe). LOB—Phillies 5, Astros 10. Scoring Position—Phillies 5-for-13, Astros 5-for-16. 2B—Maddox (2), Cruz (1), Reynolds (1), Unser (1). 3B—Trillo (1), Howe (1). S—Boone, Cabell. GDP—Maddox 2. SB—Puhl (2). CS—Rose (2).

Phillies	IP	H	R	ER	BB	K	ERA
Marty Bystrom	5.1	7	2	1	2	1	1.69
Warren Brusstar	0.2	0	0	0	0	0	3.38
Larry Christenson	0.2	2	3	3	1	0	4.05
Ron Reed	0.1	1	0	0	0	0	18.00
Tug McGraw (BS, 1)	1.0	4	2	2	0	2	4.50
Dick Ruthven (W, 1-0)	2.0	0	0	0	0	0	2.00

Astros	IP	H	R	ER	BB	K	ERA
Nolan Ryan	7.0	8	6	6	2	8	5.40
Joe Sambito (H, 1)	0.1	0	0	0	0	0	4.91
Ken Forsch (BS, 1)	0.2	2	1	1	0	1	4.15
Frank LaCorte (L, 1-1)	2.0	3	1	1	1	1	3.00

Ryan pitched to four batters in the 8th.

WP—Christenson. Time—3:38. Attendance—44,802. Umpires—HP, Vargo. 1B, Crawford. 2B, Engel. 3B, Tata.

1980 NL Championship Series—Composite Statistics

Batting

Phillies	G	AB	R	H	RBI	2B	3B	HR	BB	SO	SB	CS	Avg	OBP	Slg
Ramon Aviles	1	0	1	0	0	0	0	0	0	0	0	0	—	—	—
Bob Boone	5	18	1	4	2	0	0	1	2	0	0		.222	.263	.222
Larry Bowa	5	19	2	6	0	0	0	0	3	3	1	0	.316	.409	.316
Warren Brusstar	2	1	0	0	0	0	0	0	0	1	0	0	.000	.000	.000
Marty Bystrom	1	2	0	0	0	0	0	0	0	1	0	0	.000	.000	.000
Steve Carlton	2	4	0	0	0	0	0	0	0	1	0	0	.000	.000	.000
Larry Christenson	2	2	0	0	0	0	0	0	0	1	0	0	.000	.000	.000
Greg Gross	4	4	2	3	1	0	0	0	0	0	0	0	.750	.750	.750
Greg Luzinski	5	17	3	5	4	2	0	1	0	6	0	0	.294	.294	.588
Garry Maddox	5	20	2	6	3	2	0	0	2	2	2	1	.300	.391	.400
Bake McBride	5	21	0	5	0	0	0	0	1	5	2	0	.238	.273	.238
Tug McGraw	5	1	0	0	0	0	0	0	0	0	0	0	.000	.000	.000
Keith Moreland	2	1	0	0	1	0	0	0	0	0	0	0	.000	.000	.000
Pete Rose	5	20	3	8	2	0	0	0	5	3	0	2	.400	.520	.400
Dick Ruthven	2	2	0	0	0	0	0	0	0	2	0	0	.000	.000	.000
Mike Schmidt	5	24	1	5	1	1	0	0	1	6	1	0	.208	.240	.250
Lonnie Smith	3	5	2	3	0	0	0	0	0	0	1	0	.600	.600	.600
Manny Trillo	5	21	1	8	4	2	1	0	0	2	0	0	.381	.364	.571
Del Unser	5	5	2	2	1	1	0	0	0	2	0	0	.400	.400	.600
George Vukovich	4	3	0	0	0	0	0	0	0	0	0	0	.000	.000	.000
Totals	5	190	20	55	19	8	1	1	13	37	7	3	.289	.337	.358

Astros	G	AB	R	H	RBI	2B	3B	HR	BB	SO	SB	CS	Avg	OBP	Slg
Alan Ashby	2	8	0	1	1	0	0	0	0	0	0	0	.125	.125	.125
Dave Bergman	4	3	0	1	2	0	1	0	0	0	0	0	.333	.333	1.000
Bruce Bochy	1	1	0	0	0	0	0	0	0	0	0	0	.000	.000	.000
Enos Cabell	5	21	1	5	0	1	0	0	1	3	0	1	.238	.273	.286
Cesar Cedeno	3	11	1	2	1	0	0	0	1	0	0	0	.182	.250	.182
Jose Cruz	5	15	3	6	4	1	1	0	8	1	0	0	.400	.609	.600
Ken Forsch	2	2	0	2	0	0	0	0	0	0	0	1	1.000	1.000	1.000
Danny Heep	1	1	0	0	0	0	0	0	0	0	0	0	.000	.000	.000
Art Howe	5	15	0	3	2	1	1	0	2	2	0	0	.200	.278	.400
Frank LaCorte	2	1	0	0	0	0	0	0	0	0	0	0	.000	.000	.000
Rafael Landestoy	5	9	3	2	2	0	0	0	1	0	1	0	.222	.300	.222
Jeffrey Leonard	3	3	0	0	0	0	0	0	0	2	0	0	.000	.000	.000
Joe Morgan	4	13	1	2	0	1	1	0	6	1	0	0	.154	.421	.385
Joe Niekro	1	3	0	0	0	0	0	0	0	0	0	0	.000	.000	.000
Terry Puhl	5	19	4	10	3	2	0	0	3	2	2	0	.526	.591	.632
Luis Pujols	4	10	1	1	0	0	1	0	3	0	0	0	.100	.308	.300
Craig Reynolds	4	13	2	2	0	1	0	0	3	1	0	0	.154	.313	.231
Vern Ruhle	1	3	0	0	0	0	0	0	0	1	0	0	.000	.000	.000
Nolan Ryan	2	4	1	0	0	0	0	0	1	2	0	0	.000	.200	.000
Joe Sambito	3	0	0	0	0	0	0	0	0	0	0	0	—	—	—
Denny Walling	3	9	2	1	2	0	0	0	1	0	0	0	.111	.182	.111
Gary Woods	4	8	0	2	1	0	0	0	1	3	1	0	.250	.333	.250
Totals	5	172	19	40	18	7	5	0	31	19	4	1	.233	.346	.331

Pitching

Phillies	G	GS	CG	IP	H	R	ER	BB	SO	W-L	Sv-Op	Hld	ERA
Warren Brusstar	2	0	0	2.2	1	1	1	1	0	1-0	0-1	0	3.38
Marty Bystrom	1	1	0	5.1	7	2	1	2	1	0-0	0-0	0	1.69
Steve Carlton	2	2	0	12.1	11	3	3	8	6	1-0	0-0	0	2.19
Larry Christenson	2	1	0	6.2	5	3	3	5	2	0-0	0-0	0	4.05
Tug McGraw	5	0	0	8.0	8	4	4	4	5	0-1	2-3	0	4.50
Dickie Noles	2	0	0	2.2	1	0	0	3	0	0-0	0-0	0	0.00
Ron Reed	3	0	0	2.0	3	4	4	1	1	0-1	0-0	0	18.00
Dick Ruthven	2	1	0	9.0	3	2	2	5	4	1-0	0-0	0	2.00
Kevin Saucier	2	0	0	0.2	1	0	0	2	0	0-0	0-0	0	0.00
Totals	5	5	0	49.1	40	19	18	31	19	3-2	2-4	0	3.28

Astros	G	GS	CG	IP	H	R	ER	BB	SO	W-L	Sv-Op	Hld	ERA
Joaquin Andujar	1	0	0	1.0	0	0	0	1	0	0-0	1-1	0	0.00
Ken Forsch	2	1	1	8.2	10	4	4	1	6	0-1	0-1	0	4.15
Frank LaCorte	2	0	0	3.0	7	2	1	2	2	1-1	0-0	0	3.00
Joe Niekro	1	1	0	10.0	6	0	0	1	2	0-0	0-0	0	0.00
Vern Ruhle	1	1	0	7.0	8	3	3	1	3	0-0	0-0	0	3.86
Nolan Ryan	2	2	0	13.1	16	8	8	3	14	0-0	0-0	0	5.40
Joe Sambito	3	0	0	3.2	4	2	2	2	6	0-1	0-0	1	4.91
Dave Smith	3	0	0	2.1	4	1	1	2	4	1-0	0-1	0	3.86
Totals	5	5	1	49.0	55	20	19	13	37	2-3	1-3	1	3.49

Fielding

Phillies	Pos	G	PO	Ast	E	DP	PB	FPct
Bob Boone	c	5	22	3	0	1	0	1.000
Larry Bowa	ss	5	4	11	1	4	—	.938
Warren Brusstar	p	2	0	0	0	0	—	—
Marty Bystrom	p	1	0	0	0	0	—	—
Steve Carlton	p	2	0	1	0	0	—	1.000
Larry Christenson	p	2	0	1	1	0	—	.500
Greg Gross	lf	1	1	0	0	0	—	1.000
Greg Luzinski	lf	4	5	0	1	0	—	.833
Garry Maddox	cf	5	23	0	0	0	—	1.000
Bake McBride	rf	5	11	3	1	2	—	.933
Tug McGraw	p	5	0	0	0	0	—	—
Keith Moreland	c	1	0	0	0	0	0	—
Dickie Noles	p	2	1	2	0	1	—	1.000
Ron Reed	p	3	1	0	0	0	—	1.000
Pete Rose	1b	5	53	7	0	5	—	1.000
Dick Ruthven	p	2	2	0	0	0	—	1.000
Kevin Saucier	p	2	0	0	0	0	—	—
Mike Schmidt	3b	5	3	17	1	2	—	.952
Lonnie Smith	lf	2	2	1	0	1	—	1.000
Manny Trillo	2b	5	18	25	1	4	—	.977
Del Unser	lf	2	1	0	0	0	—	1.000
	rf	2	1	0	0	0	—	1.000
George Vukovich	lf	1	0	0	0	0	—	—
Totals		5	148	71	6	20	0	.973

Astros	Pos	G	PO	Ast	E	DP	PB	FPct
Joaquin Andujar	p	1	0	0	0	0	—	—
Alan Ashby	c	2	11	2	0	0	0	1.000
Dave Bergman	1b	3	8	2	1	0	—	.909
Bruce Bochy	c	1	5	1	0	1	0	1.000
Enos Cabell	3b	5	1	9	0	1	—	1.000
Cesar Cedeno	cf	3	5	0	0	0	—	1.000
Jose Cruz	lf	5	19	0	0	0	—	1.000
Ken Forsch	p	2	1	0	0	0	—	1.000
Art Howe	1b	4	29	3	0	3	—	1.000
Frank LaCorte	p	2	0	0	0	0	—	—
Rafael Landestoy	2b	3	3	4	0	0	—	1.000
	ss	1	2	4	1	0	—	.857
Jeffrey Leonard	rf	1	2	1	0	1	—	1.000
Joe Morgan	2b	4	9	8	0	3	—	1.000
Joe Niekro	p	1	1	0	0	0	—	1.000
Terry Puhl	cf	3	8	0	0	0	—	1.000
	rf	2	5	0	0	0	—	1.000
Luis Pujols	c	4	21	2	0	0	1	1.000
Craig Reynolds	ss	4	8	12	1	1	—	.952
Vern Ruhle	p	1	1	1	0	1	—	1.000
Nolan Ryan	p	2	1	3	0	0	—	1.000
Joe Sambito	p	3	0	0	0	0	—	—
Dave Smith	p	3	0	0	0	0	—	—
Denny Walling	rf	2	1	0	0	0	—	1.000
	1b	1	5	0	0	0	—	1.000
Gary Woods	rf	3	1	0	0	0	—	1.000
Totals		5	147	52	3	11	1	.985

1981 New York Yankees (AL) 3, Oakland Athletics (AL) 0

Graig Nettles drove in nine runs as the New York Yankees swept the Oakland Athletics in three straight games. His first at-bat of the series was a three-run double that provided the margin of victory in Game 1. Tommy John went six innings and got relief help from Ron Davis and Goose Gossage in a 3-1 New York victory. Oakland took a 3-1 lead in Game 2 before the Yankees exploded for a seven-run fourth inning, keyed by Dave Winfield's two-run double and Lou Piniella's three-run homer. Ron Davis relieved Dave Righetti in the top of the seventh inning of Game 3 and held onto a 1-0 lead until Nettles could come up with some more runs. He did, stroking a three-run double in the top of the ninth as the Yanks wrapped up the AL title with a 4-0 victory at the expense of their own ex-manager, Billy Martin.

Game 1

Tuesday, October 13

Athletics	AB	R	H	RBI	BB	K	Avg
Rickey Henderson, lf	4	0	2	0	0	1	.172
Dwayne Murphy, cf	2	0	0	1	2	0	.000
Cliff Johnson, dh	3	0	0	0	1	1	.000
Tony Armas, rf	4	0	1	0	0	1	.250
Mickey Klutts, 3b	3	0	2	0	0	0	.667
Wayne Gross, ph-3b	1	0	0	0	0	0	.000
Kelvin Moore, 1b	4	0	0	0	0	0	.000
Jeff Newman, c	2	0	0	0	0	0	.000
Keith Drumright, ph	1	0	0	0	0	0	.000
Mike Heath, c	1	0	0	0	0	0	.000
Dave McKay, 2b	4	0	0	0	0	1	.000
Rob Picciolo, ss	3	1	1	0	0	2	.333
TOTALS	32	1	6	1	3	6	.188

Yankees	AB	R	H	RBI	BB	K	Avg
Jerry Mumphrey, cf	4	0	1	0	0	1	.250
Larry Milbourne, ss	4	1	3	0	0	0	.750
Dave Winfield, lf	3	0	0	0	1	0	.000
Reggie Jackson, rf	3	1	0	0	1	0	.000
Oscar Gamble, dh	2	1	0	0	1	2	.000
Lou Piniella, ph-dh	1	0	1	0	0	0	1.000
Graig Nettles, 3b	3	0	1	3	1	0	.333
Bob Watson, 1b	3	0	1	0	0	0	.333
Bobby Brown, pr	0	0	0	0	0	0	—
Dave Revering, 1b	1	0	0	0	0	0	.000
Rick Cerone, c	2	0	0	0	0	0	.000
Willie Randolph, 2b	3	0	0	0	0	1	.000
TOTALS	29	3	7	3	4	4	.241

	1	2	3	4	5	6	7	8	9	R	H	E
Athletics	0	0	0	0	1	0	0	0	0	1	6	1
Yankees	3	0	0	0	0	0	0	0	x	3	7	1

E—Nettles, Henderson. DP—Yankees 2 (Nettles to Randolph to Watson; Milbourne to Randolph to Watson). LOB—Athletics 7, Yankees 7. Scoring Position—Athletics 0-for-8, Yankees 2-for-6. 2B—Henderson 2 (4), Nettles (1). S—Cerone. GDP—Moore, Newman. SB—Jackson (1). CS—Mumphrey (1).

Athletics	IP	H	R	ER	BB	K	ERA
Mike Norris (L, 0-1)	7.1	6	3	3	2	4	3.68
Tom Underwood	0.2	1	0	0	2	0	0.00

Yankees	IP	H	R	ER	BB	K	ERA
Tommy John (W, 1-0)	6.0	6	1	1	1	3	1.50
Ron Davis (H, 1)	1.1	0	0	0	2	3	0.00
Goose Gossage (S, 1)	1.2	0	0	0	0	0	0.00

Time—2:52. Attendance—55,740. Umpires—HP, Bremigan. 1B, Goetz. 2B, Neudecker. 3B, Springstead.

Game 2

Wednesday, October 14

Athletics	AB	R	H	RBI	BB	K	Avg
Rickey Henderson, lf	5	0	1	1	0	0	.176
Dwayne Murphy, cf	5	0	2	0	0	2	.286
Kelvin Moore, 1b	2	0	0	0	0	1	.000
Jim Spencer, ph-1b	2	0	0	0	0	0	.000
Tony Armas, rf	4	0	0	0	0	3	.125
Mickey Klutts, 3b	2	1	1	0	0	1	.600
Wayne Gross, ph-3b	2	0	0	0	0	0	.000
Mike Heath, c	4	1	2	0	0	1	.400
Dave McKay, 2b	4	0	2	1	0	1	.250
Rick Bosetti, dh	1	1	1	0	0	0	1.000
Keith Drumright, ph-dh	2	0	0	0	1	0	.000
Fred Stanley, ss	3	0	1	1	0	1	.333
Mike Davis, ph	1	0	1	0	0	0	1.000
TOTALS	37	3	11	3	1	10	.262

Yankees	AB	R	H	RBI	BB	K	Avg
Jerry Mumphrey, cf	5	2	4	0	1	0	.556
Larry Milbourne, ss	5	2	2	1	0	0	.556
Andre Robertson, ph-ss	1	0	0	0	0	0	.000
Dave Winfield, lf	5	2	2	2	1	0	.250
Reggie Jackson, rf	1	0	0	1	0	0	.000
Lou Piniella, rf	3	1	1	3	0	0	.500
Bobby Brown, rf	1	1	1	0	0	0	1.000
Oscar Gamble, dh	3	1	1	1	1	1	.200
Graig Nettles, 3b	4	2	4	3	0	0	.714
Aurelio Rodriguez, 3b	0	0	0	0	0	0	—
Bob Watson, 1b	4	0	1	1	0	1	.286
Dave Revering, 1b	1	0	0	0	0	0	.500
Rick Cerone, c	4	1	0	0	0	0	.000
Barry Foote, c	0	0	0	0	0	0	—
Willie Randolph, 2b	5	1	2	1	0	0	.250
TOTALS	42	13	19	13	3	2	.366

	1	2	3	4	5	6	7	8	9	R	H	E
Athletics	0	0	1	2	0	0	0	0	0	3	11	1
Yankees	1	0	0	7	0	1	4	0	x	13	19	0

E—Klutts. DP—Yankees 1 (Frazier to Cerone to Watson). LOB—Athletics 8, Yankees 11. Scoring Position—Athletics 3-for-13, Yankees 8-for-17. 2B—Murphy (1), Bosetti (1), Mumphrey (1), Winfield (1). 3B—Henderson (1). HR—Nettles (1), Piniella (1). SF—Gamble. GDP—Henderson, Murphy. SB—Winfield (1).

Athletics	IP	H	R	ER	BB	K	ERA
Steve McCatty (L, 0-1)	3.1	6	5	5	2	2	13.50
Dave Beard	0.2	5	3	3	0	0	40.50
Jeff Jones	2.0	2	1	1	1	0	4.50
Brian Kingman	0.1	3	3	3	0	0	81.00
Bob Owchinko	1.2	3	1	1	0	0	5.40

Yankees	IP	H	R	ER	BB	K	ERA
Rudy May	3.1	6	3	3	0	5	8.10
George Frazier (W, 1-0)	5.2	5	0	0	1	5	0.00

WP—Frazier. PB—Cerone. HBP—Cerone by McCatty, Nettles by Jones. Time—3:08. Attendance—48,497. Umpires—HP, Goetz. 1B, Neudecker. 2B, Springstead. 3B, Merrill.

Game 3

Thursday, October 15

Yankees	AB	R	H	RBI	BB	K	Avg
Jerry Mumphrey, cf	3	0	1	0	2	1	.500
Larry Milbourne, ss	4	1	1	0	0	0	.462
Dave Winfield, lf	5	0	0	0	0	2	.154
Bobby Murcer, dh	3	0	1	0	1	1	.333
Lou Piniella, ph-dh	1	1	1	0	0	0	.600
Oscar Gamble, rf	1	0	0	0	3	0	.167
Barry Foote, ph	1	0	1	0	0	0	1.000
Bobby Brown, pr-rf	0	1	0	0	0	0	1.000
Graig Nettles, 3b	5	0	1	3	0	0	.500
Bob Watson, 1b	5	0	1	0	0	0	.250
Rick Cerone, c	4	0	1	0	0	0	.100
Willie Randolph, 2b	4	1	2	1	0	0	.333
TOTALS	36	4	10	4	6	4	.350

Athletics	AB	R	H	RBI	BB	K	Avg
Rickey Henderson, lf	2	0	1	0	1	1	.194
Mike Heath, lf	1	0	0	0	0	0	.333
Dwayne Murphy, cf	1	0	0	0	0	1	.250
Rick Bosetti, ph-cf	3	0	0	0	0	0	.250
Cliff Johnson, dh	3	0	0	0	1	1	.000
Tony Armas, rf	4	0	1	0	0	1	.167
Mickey Klutts, 3b	2	0	0	0	0	0	.429
Wayne Gross, ph-3b	2	0	0	0	0	0	.000
Kelvin Moore, 1b	2	0	2	0	0	0	.250
Jim Spencer, ph-1b	1	0	0	0	0	0	.000
Dave McKay, 2b	3	0	1	0	0	0	.273
Jeff Newman, c	3	0	0	0	0	2	.000
Rob Picciolo, ss	2	0	0	0	0	0	.200
Keith Drumright, ph	1	0	0	0	0	0	.000
Fred Stanley, ss	0	0	0	0	0	0	.333
TOTALS	30	0	5	0	2	7	.214

	1	2	3	4	5	6	7	8	9	R	H	E
Yankees	0	0	0	0	0	1	0	0	3	4	10	0
Athletics	0	0	0	0	0	0	0	0	0	0	5	2

E—McKay, Picciolo. DP—Yankees 2 (Milbourne to Randolph to Watson; Nettles to Randolph to Watson), Athletics 1 (Picciolo to Spencer). LOB—Yankees 12, Athletics 5. Scoring Position—Yankees 3-for-12, Athletics 0-for-7. 2B—Nettles (2). HR—Randolph (1). S—Milbourne. GDP—Randolph, Armas, McKay. SB—Henderson 2 (4).

Yankees	IP	H	R	ER	BB	K	ERA
Dave Righetti (W, 1-0)	6.0	4	0	0	2	4	0.00
Ron Davis (H, 2)	2.0	0	0	0	0	1	0.00
Goose Gossage	1.0	1	0	0	0	2	0.00

Athletics	IP	H	R	ER	BB	K	ERA
Matt Keough (L, 0-1)	8.1	7	2	1	6	4	1.08
Tom Underwood	0.2	3	2	2	0	0	13.50

WP—Keough. Time—3:19. Attendance—47,302. Umpires—HP, Neudecker. 1B, Springstead. 2B, Merrill. 3B, Voltaggio.

1981 AL Championship Series—Composite Statistics

Batting

Yankees	G	AB	R	H	RBI	2B	3B	HR	BB	SO	SB	CS	Avg	OBP	Slg
Bobby Brown	3	1	2	1	0	0	0	0	0	0	0	0	1.000	1.000	1.000
Rick Cerone	3	10	1	1	0	0	0	0	0	0	0	0	.100	.182	.100
Barry Foote	2	1	0	1	0	0	0	0	0	0	0	0	1.000	1.000	1.000
Oscar Gamble	3	6	2	1	1	0	0	0	5	3	0	0	.167	.500	.167
Reggie Jackson	2	4	1	0	1	0	0	0	1	0	1	0	.000	.200	.000
Larry Milbourne	3	13	4	6	1	0	0	0	0	0	0	0	.462	.462	.462
Jerry Mumphrey	3	12	2	6	0	1	0	0	3	2	0	1	.500	.600	.583
Bobby Murcer	1	3	0	1	0	0	0	0	0	1	1	0	.333	.500	.333
Graig Nettles	3	12	2	6	9	2	0	1	1	0	0	0	.500	.571	.917
Lou Piniella	3	5	2	3	3	0	0	1	0	0	0	0	.600	.600	1.200
Willie Randolph	3	12	2	4	2	0	0	1	0	1	0	0	.333	.333	.583
Dave Revering	2	2	0	1	0	0	0	0	0	0	0	0	.500	.500	.500
Andre Robertson	1	1	0	0	0	0	0	0	0	0	0	0	.000	.000	.000
Bob Watson	3	12	0	3	1	0	0	0	0	1	0	0	.250	.250	.250
Dave Winfield	3	13	2	2	2	1	0	0	2	2	1	0	.154	.267	.231
Totals	3	107	20	36	20	4	0	3	13	10	2	1	.336	.415	.458

Batting

Athletics	G	AB	R	H	RBI	2B	3B	HR	BB	SO	SB	CS	Avg	OBP	Slg
Tony Armas	3	12	0	2	0	0	0	0	0	5	0	0	.167	.167	.167
Rick Bosetti	2	4	1	1	0	1	0	0	0	1	0	0	.250	.250	.500
Mike Davis	1	1	0	1	0	0	0	0	0	0	0	0	1.000	1.000	1.000
Keith Drumright	3	4	0	0	0	0	0	0	1	0	0	0	.000	.200	.000
Wayne Gross	3	5	0	0	0	0	0	0	0	0	0	0	.000	.000	.000
Mike Heath	3	6	1	2	0	0	0	0	0	1	0	0	.333	.333	.333
Rickey Henderson	3	11	0	4	1	2	1	0	1	2	2	0	.364	.417	.727
Cliff Johnson	2	6	0	0	0	0	0	0	2	2	0	0	.000	.250	.000
Mickey Klutts	3	7	1	3	0	0	0	0	0	1	0	0	.429	.429	.429
Dave McKay	3	11	0	3	1	0	0	0	0	2	0	0	.273	.273	.273
Kelvin Moore	3	8	0	2	0	0	0	0	0	1	0	0	.250	.250	.250
Dwayne Murphy	3	8	0	2	1	1	0	0	2	3	0	0	.250	.400	.375
Jeff Newman	2	5	0	0	0	0	0	0	0	2	0	0	.000	.000	.000
Rob Picciolo	2	5	1	1	0	0	0	0	0	2	0	0	.200	.200	.200
Jim Spencer	2	3	0	0	0	0	0	0	0	0	0	0	.000	.000	.000
Fred Stanley	2	3	0	1	1	0	0	0	0	1	0	0	.333	.333	.333
Totals	3	99	4	22	4	4	1	0	6	23	2	0	.222	.267	.283

Pitching

Yankees	G	GS	CG	IP	H	R	ER	BB	SO	W-L	Sv-Op	Hld	ERA
Ron Davis	2	0	0	3.1	0	0	0	2	4	0-0	0-0	2	0.00
George Frazier	1	0	0	5.2	5	0	0	1	5	1-0	0-0	0	0.00
Goose Gossage	2	0	0	2.2	1	0	0	0	2	0-0	1-1	0	0.00
Tommy John	1	1	0	6.0	6	1	1	1	3	1-0	0-0	0	1.50
Rudy May	1	1	0	3.1	6	3	3	0	5	0-0	0-0	0	8.10
Dave Righetti	1	1	0	6.0	4	0	0	2	4	1-0	0-0	0	0.00
Totals	3	3	0	27.0	22	4	4	6	23	3-0	1-1	2	1.33

Pitching

Athletics	G	GS	CG	IP	H	R	ER	BB	SO	W-L	Sv-Op	Hld	ERA
Dave Beard	1	0	0	0.2	5	3	3	0	0	0-0	0-0	0	40.50
Jeff Jones	1	0	0	2.0	2	1	1	1	0	0-0	0-0	0	4.50
Matt Keough	1	1	0	8.1	7	2	1	6	4	0-1	0-0	0	1.08
Brian Kingman	1	0	0	0.1	3	3	3	0	0	0-0	0-0	0	81.00
Steve McCatty	1	1	0	3.1	6	5	5	2	2	0-1	0-0	0	13.50
Mike Norris	1	1	0	7.1	6	3	3	2	4	0-1	0-0	0	3.68
Bob Owchinko	1	0	0	1.2	3	1	1	0	0	0-0	0-0	0	5.40
Tom Underwood	2	0	0	1.1	4	2	2	2	0	0-0	0-0	0	13.50
Totals	3	3	0	25.0	36	20	19	13	10	0-3	0-0	0	6.84

Fielding

Yankees	Pos	G	PO	Ast	E	DP	PB	FPct
Bobby Brown	rf	2	0	0	0	0	—	—
Rick Cerone	c	3	23	2	0	1	1	1.000
Ron Davis	p	2	0	0	0	0	—	—
Barry Foote	c	1	0	0	0	0	0	—
George Frazier	p	1	0	2	0	1	—	1.000
Oscar Gamble	rf	1	4	0	0	0	—	1.000
Goose Gossage	p	2	0	0	0	0	—	—
Reggie Jackson	rf	2	1	0	0	0	—	1.000
Tommy John	p	1	0	1	0	0	—	1.000
Rudy May	p	1	0	0	0	0	—	—
Larry Milbourne	ss	3	2	7	0	2	—	1.000
Jerry Mumphrey	cf	3	4	0	0	0	—	1.000
Graig Nettles	3b	3	4	4	1	2	—	.889
Lou Piniella	rf	1	0	0	0	0	—	—
Willie Randolph	2b	3	12	12	0	4	—	1.000
Dave Revering	1b	2	6	1	0	1	—	1.000
Dave Righetti	p	1	0	1	0	0	—	1.000
Andre Robertson	ss	1	2	1	0	1	—	1.000
Aurelio Rodriguez	3b	1	0	0	0	0	—	—
Bob Watson	1b	3	17	0	0	5	—	1.000
Dave Winfield	lf	3	6	0	0	0	—	1.000
Totals		3	81	31	1	17	1	.991

Fielding

Athletics	Pos	G	PO	Ast	E	DP	PB	FPct
Tony Armas	rf	3	5	2	0	0	—	1.000
Dave Beard	p	1	0	1	0	0	—	1.000
Rick Bosetti	cf	1	2	0	0	0	—	1.000
Wayne Gross	3b	3	2	0	0	0	—	1.000
Mike Heath	c	2	3	0	0	0	0	1.000
	lf	1	0	1	0	0	—	1.000
Rickey Henderson	lf	3	6	0	1	0	—	.857
Jeff Jones	p	1	1	0	0	0	—	1.000
Matt Keough	p	1	0	0	0	0	—	—
Brian Kingman	p	1	0	0	0	0	—	—
Mickey Klutts	3b	3	3	4	1	0	—	.875
Steve McCatty	p	1	1	1	0	0	—	1.000
Dave McKay	2b	3	7	6	1	0	—	.929
Kelvin Moore	1b	3	13	3	0	0	—	1.000
Dwayne Murphy	cf	3	9	0	0	0	—	1.000
Jeff Newman	c	2	9	1	0	0	0	1.000
Mike Norris	p	1	1	2	0	0	—	1.000
Bob Owchinko	p	1	0	1	0	0	—	1.000
Rob Picciolo	ss	2	5	6	1	1	—	.917
Jim Spencer	1b	2	4	2	0	1	—	1.000
Fred Stanley	ss	2	4	2	0	0	—	1.000
Tom Underwood	p	2	0	0	0	0	—	—
Totals		3	75	32	4	2	0	.964

1981 Los Angeles Dodgers (NL) 3, Montreal Expos (NL) 2

Thirty years after the fact, Rick Monday provided the Dodgers' answer to Bobby Thomson. With two out and the score tied in the top of the ninth inning in the last game of the NLCS, Monday ripped a Steve Rogers pitch over the center field fence to give the Dodgers a 2-1 win and the NL pennant. Burt Hooton won the opening game 5-1, but Ray Burris blanked the Dodgers 3-0 in Game 2. The third game also went to the Expos, as Rogers won 4-1 on a three-run homer from Jerry White. Game 4 was tied 1-1 going into the eighth inning, but the Dodgers exploded for six runs in the last two frames for a 7-1 win. In Game 5, Burris battled Fernando Valenzuela for eight innings before Montreal manager Jim Fanning summoned his ace starting pitcher, Rogers, to pitch the ninth. Rogers got two outs before Monday went deep for the Dodgers' eventual winning run.

Game 1

Tuesday, October 13

Expos	AB	R	H	RBI	BB	K	Avg
Tim Raines, lf	4	0	1	0	0	0	.419
Rodney Scott, 2b	3	0	2	0	1	1	.667
Andre Dawson, cf	4	0	0	0	0	1	.000
Gary Carter, c	3	1	2	0	1	0	.667
Larry Parrish, 3b	4	0	1	1	0	0	.250
Warren Cromartie, 1b	4	0	1	0	0	0	.250
Jerry White, rf	4	0	2	0	0	0	.500
Chris Speier, ss	4	0	0	0	0	0	.000
Bill Gullickson, p	1	0	0	0	1	0	.000
Terry Francona, ph	1	0	0	0	0	1	.000
Jeff Reardon, p	0	0	0	0	0	0	—
TOTALS	32	1	9	1	3	3	.281

Dodgers	AB	R	H	RBI	BB	K	Avg
Davey Lopes, 2b	3	0	1	0	1	1	.333
Ken Landreaux, cf	4	0	1	0	0	1	.250
Dusty Baker, lf	3	0	0	0	0	0	.000
Steve Garvey, 1b	4	1	1	0	0	1	.250
Ron Cey, 3b	4	1	2	1	0	1	.500
Derrel Thomas, pr-3b	0	1	0	0	0	0	—
Pedro Guerrero, rf	4	1	1	2	0	1	.250
Mike Scioscia, c	3	1	2	1	1	0	.667
Bill Russell, ss	3	0	0	1	0	0	.000
Burt Hooton, p	3	0	0	0	1	0	.000
Bob Welch, p	0	0	0	0	0	0	—
Steve Howe, p	0	0	0	0	0	0	—
TOTALS	31	5	8	5	2	6	.258

	1	2	3	4	5	6	7	8	9		R	H	E
Expos	0	0	0	0	0	0	0	0	1		1	9	0
Dodgers	0	2	0	0	0	0	0	3	x		5	8	0

DP—Dodgers 3 (Cey to Lopes to Garvey; Lopes to Russell to Garvey; Guerrero to Lopes). LOB—Expos 7, Dodgers 6. Scoring Position—Expos 2-for-9, Dodgers 1-for-7. 2B—Carter (1), Parrish (1), White (1), Landreaux (1), Cey (1). HR—Guerrero (1), Scioscia (1). S—Russell. GDP—Dawson, Cromartie, Speier. SB—Scott (1), White (1), Lopes 2 (2).

Expos	IP	H	R	ER	BB	K	ERA
Bill Gullickson (L, 0-1)	7.0	5	2	2	2	6	2.57
Jeff Reardon	1.0	3	3	3	0	0	27.00

Dodgers	IP	H	R	ER	BB	K	ERA
Burt Hooton (W, 1-0)	7.1	6	0	0	3	2	0.00
Bob Welch (H, 1)	0.2	2	1	1	0	1	13.50
Steve Howe	1.0	1	0	0	0	0	0.00

Welch pitched to two batters in the 9th.

HBP—Baker by Gullickson. Time—2:47. Attendance—51,273. Umpires—HP, Pryor. 1B, Gregg. 2B, Runge. 3B, Rennert.

Game 2

Wednesday, October 14

Expos	AB	R	H	RBI	BB	K	Avg
Tim Raines, lf	5	0	3	1	0	0	.444
Terry Francona, lf	0	0	0	0	0	0	.000
Rodney Scott, 2b	4	0	0	0	0	2	.286
Andre Dawson, cf	4	1	1	0	0	0	.125
Gary Carter, c	4	0	2	0	0	1	.571
Larry Parrish, 3b	4	1	1	0	0	0	.250
Jerry White, rf	3	1	1	0	1	0	.429
Warren Cromartie, 1b	4	0	1	1	0	0	.250
Chris Speier, ss	3	0	1	0	1	0	.143
Ray Burris, p	4	0	0	0	0	3	.000
TOTALS	35	3	10	2	2	6	.288

Dodgers	AB	R	H	RBI	BB	K	Avg
Davey Lopes, 2b	3	0	0	0	0	0	.167
Rick Monday, ph	1	0	0	0	0	1	.000
Bobby Castillo, p	0	0	0	0	0	0	—
Ken Landreaux, cf	3	0	0	0	1	0	.143
Dusty Baker, lf	4	0	2	0	0	0	.286
Steve Garvey, 1b	4	0	1	0	0	1	.250
Ron Cey, 3b	4	0	0	0	0	1	.250
Pedro Guerrero, rf	3	0	0	0	1	0	.143
Mike Scioscia, c	3	0	0	0	0	0	.333
Bill Russell, ss	3	0	2	0	0	0	.333
Fernando Valenzuela, p	2	0	0	0	0	0	.000
Tom Niedenfuer, p	0	0	0	0	0	0	—
Terry Forster, p	0	0	0	0	0	0	—
Alejandro Pena, p	0	0	0	0	0	0	—
Jay Johnstone, ph	1	0	0	0	0	0	.000
Steve Sax, 2b	0	0	0	0	0	0	—
TOTALS	31	0	5	0	2	3	.220

	1	2	3	4	5	6	7	8	9		R	H	E
Expos	0	2	0	0	0	1	0	0	0		3	10	1
Dodgers	0	0	0	0	0	0	0	0	0		0	5	1

E—Baker, Speier. DP—Expos 1 (Parrish to Scott to Cromartie). LOB—Expos 7, Dodgers 6. Scoring Position—Expos 2-for-7, Dodgers 0-for-2. 2B—Raines (3), Cromartie (1). GDP—Garvey. CS—Raines (2).

Expos	IP	H	R	ER	BB	K	ERA
Ray Burris (W, 1-0)	9.0	5	0	0	2	3	0.00

Dodgers	IP	H	R	ER	BB	K	ERA
Fernando Valenzuela (L, 0-1)	6.0	7	3	3	2	4	4.50
Tom Niedenfuer	0.1	2	0	0	0	0	0.00
Terry Forster	0.1	0	0	0	0	1	0.00
Alejandro Pena	1.1	1	0	0	0	0	0.00
Bobby Castillo	1.0	0	0	0	0	1	0.00

WP—Valenzuela. Time—2:48. Attendance—53,463. Umpires—HP, Gregg. 1B, Runge. 2B, Rennert. 3B, Wendelstedt.

Game 3

Friday, October 16

Dodgers	AB	R	H	RBI	BB	K	Avg
Davey Lopes, 2b	4	0	2	0	0	1	.300
Ken Landreaux, cf	3	0	0	0	1	1	.100
Dusty Baker, lf	4	1	1	0	0	0	.273
Steve Garvey, 1b	4	0	2	0	0	1	.333
Ron Cey, 3b	4	0	1	1	0	0	.250
Pedro Guerrero, rf	4	0	0	0	0	1	.091
Mike Scioscia, c	4	0	0	0	0	1	.200
Bill Russell, ss	3	0	1	0	0	0	.333
Jerry Reuss, p	2	0	0	0	0	0	.000
Jay Johnstone, ph	1	0	0	0	0	0	.000
Alejandro Pena, p	0	0	0	0	0	0	—
TOTALS	33	1	7	1	1	5	.225

Expos	AB	R	H	RBI	BB	K	Avg
Tim Raines, lf	4	0	0	0	0	1	.400
Rodney Scott, 2b	4	0	0	0	0	0	.182
Andre Dawson, cf	4	1	2	0	0	0	.250
Gary Carter, c	3	1	1	0	1	0	.500
Larry Parrish, 3b	4	1	2	1	0	0	.333
Jerry White, rf	3	1	1	3	0	0	.400
Warren Cromartie, 1b	3	0	0	0	0	0	.182
Chris Speier, ss	3	0	1	0	0	0	.200
Steve Rogers, p	2	0	0	0	0	1	.000
TOTALS	30	4	7	4	1	2	.286

	1	2	3	4	5	6	7	8	9		R	H	E
Dodgers	0	0	0	1	0	0	0	0	0		1	7	0
Expos	0	0	0	0	0	4	0	0	x		4	7	1

E—Scott. DP—Expos 3 (Speier to Scott to Cromartie; Parrish to Speier to Scott; Parrish to Scott). LOB—Dodgers 6, Expos 4. Scoring Position—Dodgers 0-for-8, Expos 2-for-6. HR—White (1). S—Rogers. GDP—Guerrero 2, Reuss. SB—Lopes (3).

Dodgers	IP	H	R	ER	BB	K	ERA
Jerry Reuss (L, 0-1)	7.0	7	4	4	1	2	5.14
Alejandro Pena	1.0	0	0	0	0	0	0.00

Expos	IP	H	R	ER	BB	K	ERA
Steve Rogers (W, 1-0)	9.0	7	1	1	1	5	1.00

WP—Rogers. PB—Scioscia. Time—2:27. Attendance—54,372. Umpires—HP, Runge. 1B, Rennert. 2B, Wendelstedt. 3B, West.

Game 4

Saturday, October 17

Dodgers	AB	R	H	RBI	BB	K	Avg
Davey Lopes, 2b	4	0	1	0	0	1	.286
Bill Russell, ss	3	2	0	0	1	1	.250
Dusty Baker, lf	4	2	3	3	1	0	.400
Steve Garvey, 1b	5	1	2	2	0	1	.353
Ron Cey, 3b	3	0	2	1	2	0	.333
Rick Monday, rf	4	0	1	0	0	2	.200
Ken Landreaux, cf	0	0	0	0	1	0	.100
Pedro Guerrero, cf-rf	4	0	0	0	0	1	.067
Bob Welch, p	0	0	0	0	0	0	—
Reggie Smith, ph	1	0	1	1	0	0	1.000
Steve Howe, p	0	0	0	0	0	0	—
Mike Scioscia, c	2	0	0	0	1	0	.167
Steve Yeager, ph-c	2	1	1	0	0	0	.500
Burt Hooton, p	2	0	0	0	0	1	.000
Derrel Thomas, rf	1	1	1	0	0	0	1.000
TOTALS	35	7	12	7	6	7	.258

Expos	AB	R	H	RBI	BB	K	Avg
Tim Raines, lf	4	0	0	0	0	1	.364
Rodney Scott, 2b	4	0	1	0	0	0	.200
Andre Dawson, cf	4	0	0	0	0	2	.188
Gary Carter, c	3	1	1	0	1	0	.462
Larry Parrish, 3b	4	0	0	0	0	1	.250
Jerry White, rf	3	0	1	0	1	0	.385
Warren Cromartie, 1b	4	0	1	1	0	1	.200
Chris Speier, ss	3	0	1	0	1	0	.231
Bill Gullickson, p	2	0	0	0	0	2	.000
Woodie Fryman, p	0	0	0	0	0	0	—
Elias Sosa, p	0	0	0	0	0	0	—
Bill Lee, p	0	0	0	0	0	0	—
John Milner, ph	1	0	0	0	0	1	.000
TOTALS	32	1	5	1	3	8	.254

	1 2 3	4 5 6	7 8 9	R	H	E
Dodgers	0 0 1	0 0 0	0 2 4	7	12	1
Expos	0 0 0	1 0 0	0 0 0	1	5	1

E—Cey, Parrish. DP—Expos 2 (Scott to Speier to Cromartie; Scott to Speier to Cromartie). LOB—Dodgers 10, Expos 8. Scoring Position—Dodgers 3-for-15, Expos 1-for-6. 2B—Baker (1). HR—Garvey (1). S—Lopes, Russell, Hooton, Gullickson. GDP—Guerrero, Scioscia. SB—Lopes (4).

Dodgers	IP	H	R	ER	BB	K	ERA
Burt Hooton (W, 2-0)	7.1	5	1	0	3	5	0.00
Bob Welch (H, 2)	0.2	0	0	0	0	1	6.75
Steve Howe	1.0	0	0	0	0	2	0.00

Expos	IP	H	R	ER	BB	K	ERA
Bill Gullickson (L, 0-2)	7.1	7	3	2	4	6	2.51
Woodie Fryman	1.0	3	4	4	1	1	36.00
Elias Sosa	0.1	1	0	0	1	0	0.00
Bill Lee	0.1	1	0	0	0	0	0.00

Time—3:14. Attendance—54,499. Umpires—HP, Rennert. 1B, Wendelstedt. 2B, West. 3B, Pryor.

Game 5

Monday, October 19

Dodgers	AB	R	H	RBI	BB	K	Avg
Davey Lopes, 2b	4	0	1	0	0	0	.278
Bill Russell, ss	4	0	2	0	0	0	.313
Dusty Baker, lf	4	0	0	0	0	0	.316
Steve Garvey, 1b	4	0	0	0	0	0	.286
Ron Cey, 3b	3	0	0	0	1	0	.278
Rick Monday, rf	4	2	2	1	0	1	.333
Ken Landreaux, cf	0	0	0	0	0	0	.100
Pedro Guerrero, cf-rf	4	0	1	0	0	1	.105
Mike Scioscia, c	3	0	0	0	0	0	.133
Fernando Valenzuela, p	3	0	0	1	0	0	.000
Bob Welch, p	0	0	0	0	0	0	—
TOTALS	33	2	6	2	1	2	.233

Expos	AB	R	H	RBI	BB	K	Avg
Tim Raines, lf	4	1	1	0	0	1	.354
Rodney Scott, 2b	3	0	0	0	0	0	.167
Andre Dawson, cf	4	0	0	0	0	1	.150
Gary Carter, c	3	0	1	0	1	1	.438
Jerry Manuel, pr	0	0	0	0	0	0	—
Larry Parrish, 3b	3	0	1	0	1	0	.263
Jerry White, rf	3	0	0	0	1	1	.313
Warren Cromartie, 1b	3	0	0	0	0	1	.167
Chris Speier, ss	3	0	0	0	0	0	.188
Ray Burris, p	2	0	0	0	0	1	.000
Tim Wallach, ph	1	0	0	0	0	0	.000
Steve Rogers, p	0	0	0	0	0	0	.000
TOTALS	29	1	3	0	3	6	.222

	1 2 3	4 5 6	7 8 9	R	H	E
Dodgers	0 0 0	0 1 0	0 0 1	2	6	0
Expos	1 0 0	0 0 0	0 0 0	1	3	1

E—Speier. DP—Dodgers 1 (Lopes to Russell to Garvey), Expos 1 (Speier to Scott to Cromartie). LOB—Dodgers 5, Expos 5. Scoring Position—Dodgers 0-for-9, Expos 0-for-3. 2B—Raines (4), Parrish (2). 3B—Russell (1). HR—Monday (1). S—Scott. GDP—Guerrero, Dawson. SB—Lopes (5).

Dodgers	IP	H	R	ER	BB	K	ERA
Fernando Valenzuela (W, 1-1)	8.2	3	1	1	3	6	2.45
Bob Welch (S, 1)	0.1	0	0	0	0	0	5.40

Expos	IP	H	R	ER	BB	K	ERA
Ray Burris	8.0	5	1	1	1	1	0.53
Steve Rogers (L, 1-1)	1.0	1	1	1	0	1	1.80

WP—Burris. Time—2:41. Attendance—36,491. Umpires—HP, Wendelstedt. 1B, West. 2B, Pryor. 3B, Gregg.

1981 NL Championship Series—Composite Statistics

Batting

Dodgers	G	AB	R	H	RBI	2B	3B	HR	BB	SO	SB	CS	Avg	OBP	Slg
Dusty Baker	5	19	3	6	3	1	0	0	1	0	0	0	.316	.381	.368
Ron Cey	5	18	1	5	3	1	0	0	3	2	0	0	.278	.381	.333
Steve Garvey	5	21	2	6	2	0	0	1	0	4	0	0	.286	.286	.429
Pedro Guerrero	5	19	1	2	2	0	0	1	1	4	0	0	.105	.150	.263
Burt Hooton	2	5	0	0	0	0	0	0	0	2	0	0	.000	.000	.000
Jay Johnstone	2	2	0	0	0	0	0	0	0	0	0	0	.000	.000	.000
Ken Landreaux	5	10	0	1	0	1	0	0	3	2	0	0	.100	.308	.200
Davey Lopes	5	18	0	5	0	0	0	0	1	3	5	0	.278	.316	.278
Rick Monday	3	9	2	3	1	0	0	1	0	4	0	0	.333	.333	.667
Jerry Reuss	1	2	0	0	0	0	0	0	0	0	0	0	.000	.000	.000
Bill Russell	5	16	2	5	1	0	1	0	1	1	0	0	.313	.353	.438
Mike Scioscia	5	15	1	2	1	0	0	1	2	1	0	0	.133	.235	.333
Reggie Smith	1	1	0	1	1	0	0	0	0	0	0	0	1.000	1.000	1.000
Derrel Thomas	2	1	2	1	0	0	0	0	0	0	0	0	1.000	1.000	1.000
Fernando Valenzuela	2	5	0	0	1	0	0	0	0	0	0	0	.000	.000	.000
Steve Yeager	1	2	1	1	0	0	0	0	0	0	0	0	.500	.500	.500
Totals	5	163	15	38	15	3	1	4	12	23	5	0	.233	.290	.337

Batting

Expos	G	AB	R	H	RBI	2B	3B	HR	BB	SO	SB	CS	Avg	OBP	Slg
Ray Burris	2	6	0	0	0	0	0	0	0	4	0	0	.000	.000	.000
Gary Carter	5	16	3	7	0	1	0	0	4	2	0	0	.438	.550	.500
Warren Cromartie	5	18	0	3	2	1	0	0	0	2	0	0	.167	.167	.222
Andre Dawson	5	20	2	3	0	0	0	0	0	4	0	0	.150	.150	.150
Terry Francona	2	1	0	0	0	0	0	0	0	1	0	0	.000	.000	.000
Bill Gullickson	2	3	0	0	0	0	0	0	1	2	0	0	.000	.250	.000
Jerry Manuel	1	0	0	0	0	0	0	0	0	0	0	0	—	—	—
John Milner	1	1	0	0	0	0	0	0	0	1	0	0	.000	.000	.000
Larry Parrish	5	19	2	5	2	2	0	0	1	1	0	0	.263	.300	.368
Tim Raines	5	21	1	5	1	2	0	0	3	0	1		.238	.238	.333
Steve Rogers	2	2	0	0	0	0	0	0	0	1	0	0	.000	.000	.000
Rodney Scott	5	18	0	3	0	0	0	0	1	3	1	0	.167	.211	.167
Chris Speier	5	16	0	3	0	0	0	0	2	0	0	0	.188	.278	.188
Tim Wallach	1	1	0	0	0	0	0	0	0	0	0	0	.000	.000	.000
Jerry White	5	16	2	5	3	1	0	1	3	1	1	0	.313	.421	.563
Totals	5	158	10	34	8	7	0	1	12	25	2	1	.215	.271	.278

Pitching

Dodgers	G	GS	CG	IP	H	R	ER	BB	SO	W-L	Sv-Op	Hld	ERA
Bobby Castillo	1	0	0	1.0	0	0	0	0	1	0-0	0-0	0	0.00
Terry Forster	1	0	0	0.1	0	0	0	0	1	0-0	0-0	0	0.00
Burt Hooton	2	2	0	14.2	11	1	0	6	7	2-0	0-0	0	0.00
Steve Howe	2	0	0	2.0	1	0	0	0	2	0-0	0-0	0	0.00
Tom Niedenfuer	1	0	0	0.1	2	0	0	0	0	0-0	0-0	0	0.00
Alejandro Pena	2	0	0	2.1	1	0	0	0	0	0-0	0-0	0	0.00
Jerry Reuss	1	1	0	7.0	7	4	4	1	2	0-1	0-0	0	5.14
Fernando Valenzuela	2	2	0	14.2	10	4	4	5	10	1-1	0-0	0	2.45
Bob Welch	3	0	0	1.2	2	1	1	0	2	0-0	1-1	2	5.40
Totals	5	5	0	44.0	34	10	9	12	25	3-2	1-1	2	1.84

Pitching

Expos	G	GS	CG	IP	H	R	ER	BB	SO	W-L	Sv-Op	Hld	ERA
Ray Burris	2	2	1	17.0	10	1	1	3	4	1-0	0-0	0	0.53
Woodie Fryman	1	0	0	1.0	3	4	4	1	1	0-0	0-0	0	36.00
Bill Gullickson	2	2	0	14.1	12	5	4	6	12	0-2	0-0	0	2.51
Bill Lee	1	0	0	0.1	1	0	0	0	0	0-0	0-0	0	0.00
Jeff Reardon	1	0	0	1.0	3	3	3	0	0	0-0	0-0	0	27.00
Steve Rogers	2	1	1	10.0	8	2	2	1	6	1-1	0-0	0	1.80
Elias Sosa	1	0	0	0.1	1	0	0	1	0	0-0	0-0	0	0.00
Totals	5	5	2	44.0	38	15	14	12	23	2-3	0-0	0	2.86

Fielding

Dodgers	Pos	G	PO	Ast	E	DP	PB	FPct
Dusty Baker	lf	5	10	0	1	0	—	.909
Bobby Castillo	p	1	0	1	0	0	—	1.000
Ron Cey	3b	5	5	16	1	1	—	.955
Terry Forster	p	1	0	0	0	0	—	—
Steve Garvey	1b	5	49	2	0	4	—	1.000
Pedro Guerrero	rf	5	4	2	0	1	—	1.000
	cf	2	5	0	0	0	—	1.000
Burt Hooton	p	2	0	1	0	0	—	1.000
Steve Howe	p	2	0	0	0	0	—	—
Ken Landreaux	cf	5	4	0	0	0	—	1.000
Davey Lopes	2b	5	13	13	0	5	—	1.000
Rick Monday	rf	2	2	0	0	0	—	1.000
Tom Niedenfuer	p	1	0	1	0	0	—	1.000
Alejandro Pena	p	2	0	0	0	0	—	—
Jerry Reuss	p	1	0	0	0	0	—	—
Bill Russell	ss	5	10	13	0	3	—	1.000
Steve Sax	2b	1	0	1	0	0	—	1.000
Mike Scioscia	c	5	27	1	0	0	1	1.000
Derrel Thomas	rf	1	1	0	0	0	—	1.000
	3b	1	0	0	0	0	—	—
Fernando Valenzuela	p	2	0	2	0	0	—	1.000
Bob Welch	p	3	0	0	0	0	—	—
Steve Yeager	c	1	2	0	0	0	0	1.000
Totals		5	132	53	2	14	1	.989

Fielding

Expos	Pos	G	PO	Ast	E	DP	PB	FPct
Ray Burris	p	2	0	1	0	0	—	1.000
Gary Carter	c	5	27	3	0	0	0	1.000
Warren Cromartie	1b	5	48	2	0	6	—	1.000
Andre Dawson	cf	5	12	0	0	0	—	1.000
Terry Francona	lf	1	0	0	0	0	—	—
Woodie Fryman	p	1	0	0	0	0	—	—
Bill Gullickson	p	2	0	2	0	0	—	1.000
Bill Lee	p	1	0	0	0	0	—	—
Larry Parrish	3b	5	3	13	1	3	—	.941
Tim Raines	lf	5	9	0	0	0	—	1.000
Jeff Reardon	p	1	0	0	0	0	—	—
Steve Rogers	p	2	0	1	0	0	—	1.000
Rodney Scott	2b	5	12	14	1	7	—	.963
Elias Sosa	p	1	0	0	0	0	—	—
Chris Speier	ss	5	15	16	2	6	—	.939
Jerry White	rf	5	6	0	0	0	—	1.000
Totals		5	132	52	4	22	0	.979

1982 Milwaukee Brewers (AL) 3, California Angels (AL) 2

The Milwaukee Brewers became the first team to come back from a two-games-to-none deficit to win a League Championship Series, taking the last three games to defeat the California Angels in the full five games. Tommy John went the route in the opener and Don Baylor drove in five runs for an 8-3 Angels victory. The next day, Bruce Kison gave the Angels their second straight complete game, tossing a five-hitter to win 4-2. Don Sutton finally got the Brewers a win with a 5-3 victory in the third game. Paul Molitor socked a two-run homer and Pete Ladd got the last four outs for a save. Mark Brouhard, a backup outfielder, was the hero of Game 4, doubling, homering and driving in three runs in the Brewers' 9-5 win. In the finale, Gene Mauch's Angels took a 3-2 lead into the bottom of the seventh, when the Brewers mounted a rally, loading the bases with two outs. With lefthanded-hitting Cecil Cooper due to hit, Mauch decided not to bring in lefthander Andy Hassler, and stuck with righthander Luis Sanchez instead. Cooper lined a 1-1 pitch into left field, scoring Charlie Moore and Jim Gantner with the go-ahead runs. The Brewers held off the Angels after that, winning 4-3 to capture the AL title.

Game 1

Tuesday, October 5

Brewers	AB	R	H	RBI	BB	K	Avg
Paul Molitor, 3b	4	1	1	0	0	2	.250
Robin Yount, ss	4	0	1	0	0	0	.250
Cecil Cooper, 1b	4	0	1	1	0	0	.250
Ted Simmons, c	4	1	2	0	0	1	.500
Gorman Thomas, cf	4	1	1	2	0	1	.250
Ben Oglivie, lf	4	0	0	0	0	1	.000
Don Money, dh	3	0	0	0	1	0	.000
Charlie Moore, rf	3	0	1	0	0	0	.333
Jim Gantner, 2b	4	0	0	0	0	0	.000
TOTALS	34	3	7	3	1	5	.206

Angels	AB	R	H	RBI	BB	K	Avg
Brian Downing, lf	4	2	1	0	1	0	.250
Juan Beniquez, lf	0	0	0	0	0	0	—
Doug DeCinces, 3b	4	2	1	0	0	1	.250
Bobby Grich, 2b	3	1	2	1	1	1	.667
Don Baylor, dh	3	1	2	5	0	0	.667
Reggie Jackson, rf	4	0	0	1	0	1	.000
Bobby Clark, rf	0	0	0	0	0	0	—
Fred Lynn, cf	4	1	3	1	0	1	.750
Rod Carew, 1b	4	0	0	0	0	3	.000
Tim Foli, ss	4	0	0	0	0	0	.000
Bob Boone, c	4	1	1	0	0	0	.250
TOTALS	34	8	10	8	2	7	.294

	1	2	3	4	5	6	7	8	9		R	H	E
Brewers	0	2	1	0	0	0	0	0	0		3	7	2
Angels	1	0	4	2	1	0	0	0	x		8	10	0

E—Molitor, Caldwell. DP—Brewers 1 (Yount). LOB—Brewers 6, Angels 5. Scoring Position—Brewers 0-for-3, Angels 3-for-10. 2B—Cooper (1), Grich (1). 3B—Baylor (1). HR—Thomas (1), Lynn (1). SF—Baylor.

Brewers	IP	H	R	ER	BB	K	ERA
Mike Caldwell (L, 0-1)	3.0	7	6	5	1	2	15.00
Jim Slaton	3.0	3	2	1	1	2	3.00
Peter Ladd	1.0	0	0	0	0	3	0.00
Dwight Bernard	1.0	0	0	0	0	0	0.00

Angels	IP	H	R	ER	BB	K	ERA
Tommy John (W, 1-0)	9.0	7	3	3	1	5	3.00

Caldwell pitched to one batter in the 4th.

WP—Caldwell. HBP—Moore by John. Time—2:31. Attendance—64,406. Umpires—HP, Barnett. 1B, Kunkel. 2B, Garcia. 3B, Palermo.

Game 2

Wednesday, October 6

Brewers	AB	R	H	RBI	BB	K	Avg
Paul Molitor, 3b	4	1	2	2	0	1	.375
Robin Yount, ss	4	0	1	0	0	0	.250
Cecil Cooper, 1b	4	0	0	0	0	1	.125
Ted Simmons, c	4	0	0	0	0	1	.250
Ben Oglivie, lf	4	0	0	0	0	1	.000
Gorman Thomas, cf	3	0	0	0	0	2	.143
Roy Howell, dh	3	0	0	0	0	1	.000
Charlie Moore, rf	3	1	2	0	0	1	.500
Jim Gantner, 2b	3	0	0	0	0	0	.000
TOTALS	32	2	5	2	0	8	.190

Angels	AB	R	H	RBI	BB	K	Avg
Brian Downing, lf	3	0	0	0	1	1	.143
Juan Beniquez, lf	0	0	0	0	0	0	—
Rod Carew, 1b	4	0	0	0	0	1	.000
Reggie Jackson, rf	3	1	1	1	1	0	.143
Bobby Clark, rf	0	0	0	0	0	0	—
Fred Lynn, cf	4	1	2	0	0	0	.625
Don Baylor, dh	3	0	0	0	1	0	.333
Doug DeCinces, 3b	3	2	1	0	1	1	.286
Bobby Grich, 2b	2	0	1	0	0	1	.600
Tim Foli, ss	2	0	1	1	0	0	.167
Bob Boone, c	1	0	0	2	0	0	.200
TOTALS	25	4	6	4	4	4	.271

	1	2	3	4	5	6	7	8	9		R	H	E
Brewers	0	0	0	0	2	0	0	0	0		2	5	0
Angels	0	2	1	1	0	0	0	0	x		4	6	0

DP—Brewers 2 (Yount to Gantner to Cooper; Gantner to Yount to Cooper). LOB—Brewers 3, Angels 5. Scoring Position—Brewers 1-for-3, Angels 1-for-3. 2B—DeCinces (1). HR—Molitor (1), Jackson (1). S—Foli, Boone. SF—Boone. GDP—Lynn, Baylor.

Brewers	IP	H	R	ER	BB	K	ERA
Pete Vuckovich (L, 0-1)	8.0	6	4	4	4	4	4.50

Angels	IP	H	R	ER	BB	K	ERA
Bruce Kison (W, 1-0)	9.0	5	2	2	0	8	2.00

HBP—Grich by Vuckovich. Time—2:06. Attendance—64,179. Umpires—HP, Kunkel. 1B, Garcia. 2B, Palermo. 3B, Denkinger.

Game 3

Friday, October 8

Angels	AB	R	H	RBI	BB	K	Avg
Brian Downing, lf	4	0	0	0	0	0	.091
Rod Carew, 1b	4	1	2	0	0	0	.167
Reggie Jackson, rf	4	0	1	0	0	3	.182
Fred Lynn, cf	3	1	2	1	1	1	.636
Don Baylor, dh	3	0	1	1	1	0	.333
Doug DeCinces, 3b	4	0	1	0	0	1	.273
Bobby Grich, 2b	4	0	0	0	0	3	.333
Tim Foli, ss	3	0	0	0	0	1	.111
Rob Wilfong, ph	1	0	0	0	0	1	.000
Bob Boone, c	4	1	1	1	0	1	.222
TOTALS	34	3	8	3	2	11	.258

Brewers	AB	R	H	RBI	BB	K	Avg
Paul Molitor, 3b	4	1	1	2	0	0	.333
Robin Yount, ss	2	1	1	0	2	0	.300
Cecil Cooper, 1b	4	1	1	1	0	3	.167
Ted Simmons, c	4	1	1	0	0	0	.250
Gorman Thomas, cf	3	0	0	1	0	1	.100
Ben Oglivie, lf	3	0	1	0	0	0	.091
Don Money, dh	1	0	0	1	1	0	.000
Marshall Edwards, pr-dh	0	1	0	0	0	0	—
Charlie Moore, rf	2	0	1	0	0	1	.500
Jim Gantner, 2b	3	0	0	0	0	1	.000
TOTALS	26	5	6	5	3	6	.202

	1	2	3	4	5	6	7	8	9		R	H	E
Angels	0	0	0	0	0	0	3	0			3	8	0
Brewers	0	0	0	3	0	0	2	0	x		5	6	0

DP—Angels 1 (DeCinces to Grich to Carew), Brewers 1 (Molitor to Cooper). LOB—Angels 6, Brewers 4. Scoring Position—Angels 1-for-4, Brewers 2-for-3. 2B—Lynn (1), Baylor (1), Cooper (2). HR—Boone (1), Molitor (2). S—Moore. SF—Thomas, Money. GDP—Molitor. SB—Carew (1).

Angels	IP	H	R	ER	BB	K	ERA
Geoff Zahn (L, 0-1)	3.2	4	3	3	1	2	7.36
Mike Witt	3.0	2	2	2	2	3	6.00
Andy Hassler	1.1	0	0	0	0	1	0.00

Brewers	IP	H	R	ER	BB	K	ERA
Don Sutton (W, 1-0)	7.2	8	3	3	2	9	3.52
Peter Ladd (S, 1)	1.1	0	0	0	0	2	0.00

HBP—Oglivie by Zahn. Time—2:41. Attendance—50,135. Umpires—HP, Garcia. 1B, Palermo. 2B, Denkinger. 3B, Clark.

Game 4

Saturday, October 9

Angels	AB	R	H	RBI	BB	K	Avg
Brian Downing, lf	4	1	1	0	1	1	.133
Rod Carew, 1b	2	1	1	0	2	0	.214
Reggie Jackson, rf	4	1	0	0	0	2	.133
Fred Lynn, cf	3	1	1	1	1	1	.571
Don Baylor, dh	4	1	1	4	0	0	.308
Doug DeCinces, 3b	4	0	0	0	0	1	.200
Bobby Grich, 2b	3	0	0	0	1	1	.250
Tim Foli, ss	4	0	1	0	0	1	.154
Bob Boone, c	4	0	0	0	0	1	.154
TOTALS	32	5	5	5	5	8	.234

Brewers	AB	R	H	RBI	BB	K	Avg
Paul Molitor, 3b	4	0	0	1	1	0	.250
Robin Yount, ss	4	0	1	0	1	0	.286
Cecil Cooper, 1b	4	0	0	0	0	0	.125
Ted Simmons, c	3	1	0	0	1	1	.200
Gorman Thomas, cf	2	0	0	0	2	2	.083
Don Money, dh	3	2	2	0	1	0	.286
Marshall Edwards, pr-dh	0	1	0	0	0	0	—
Mark Brouhard, lf	4	4	3	3	0	0	.750
Charlie Moore, rf	2	1	1	0	1	0	.500
Jim Gantner, 2b	4	0	2	2	0	0	.143
TOTALS	30	9	9	6	7	3	.241

	1	2	3	4	5	6	7	8	9		R	H	E
Angels	0	0	0	0	0	1	0	4	0		5	5	3
Brewers	0	3	0	3	0	1	0	2	x		9	9	2

E—Cooper, DeCinces 2, Lynn, Yount. DP—Angels 1 (Grich to Carew). LOB—Angels 5, Brewers 5. Scoring Position—Angels 2-for-6, Brewers 4-for-11. 2B—Carew (1), Lynn (2), Brouhard (1). HR—Baylor (1), Brouhard (1). S—Moore. GDP—Yount. SB—Edwards (1). CS—Carew (1), Molitor (1), Thomas (1).

Angels	IP	H	R	ER	BB	K	ERA
Tommy John (L, 1-1)	3.1	4	6	4	5	1	5.11
Dave Goltz	3.2	4	3	3	2	2	7.36
Luis Sanchez	1.0	1	0	0	0	0	0.00

Brewers	IP	H	R	ER	BB	K	ERA
Moose Haas (W, 1-0)	7.1	5	5	4	5	7	4.91
Jim Slaton (S, 1)	1.2	0	0	0	0	1	1.93

Goltz pitched to three batters in the 8th.

WP—John 3. PB—Boone. Time—3:10. Attendance—51,003. Umpires—HP, Palermo. 1B, Denkinger. 2B, Clark. 3B, Barnett.

Game 5

Sunday, October 10

Angels	AB	R	H	RBI	BB	K	Avg
Brian Downing, lf	4	1	1	0	0	0	.158
Rod Carew, 1b	3	0	0	0	2	0	.176
Reggie Jackson, rf	3	0	0	0	1	1	.111
Fred Lynn, cf	4	0	3	2	0	0	.611
Don Baylor, dh	4	0	1	0	0	0	.294
Doug DeCinces, 3b	4	1	3	0	0	1	.316
Bobby Grich, 2b	3	0	0	0	0	1	.200
Tim Foli, ss	3	0	0	0	0	1	.125
Ron Jackson, ph	1	0	1	0	0	0	1.000
Rob Wilfong, pr	0	0	0	0	0	0	.000
Bob Boone, c	3	1	2	1	0	0	.250
TOTALS	32	3	11	3	3	4	.255

Brewers	AB	R	H	RBI	BB	K	Avg
Paul Molitor, 3b	3	1	2	0	1	0	.316
Robin Yount, ss	2	0	0	0	2	0	.250
Cecil Cooper, 1b	4	0	1	2	0	2	.150
Ted Simmons, c	3	0	0	1	0	1	.167
Ben Oglivie, lf	4	1	1	1	0	1	.133
Gorman Thomas, cf	3	0	0	0	0	1	.067
Marshall Edwards, cf	1	0	0	0	0	0	.000
Don Money, dh	4	0	0	0	0	1	.182
Charlie Moore, rf	3	1	1	0	0	0	.462
Jim Gantner, 2b	2	1	1	0	1	0	.188
TOTALS	29	4	6	4	4	6	.208

	1	2	3	4	5	6	7	8	9		R	H	E
Angels	1	0	1	1	0	0	0	0	0		3	11	1
Brewers	1	0	0	1	0	0	2	0	x		4	6	3

E—Cooper, DeCinces, Oglivie 2. DP—Angels 1 (DeCinces to Grich), Brewers 2 (Molitor to Gantner to Cooper; Gantner to Yount to Cooper). LOB—Angels 8, Brewers 6. Scoring Position—Angels 3-for-13, Brewers 1-for-7. 2B—Downing (1), DeCinces (2), Molitor (1). HR—Oglivie (1). S—Downing, Grich, Boone. SF—Simmons. GDP—Downing, ReJackson, Yount. SB—Molitor (1). CS—DeCinces (1).

Angels	IP	H	R	ER	BB	K	ERA
Bruce Kison	5.0	3	2	1	3	4	1.93
Luis Sanchez (BS, 1; L, 0-1)	1.2	3	2	2	1	1	6.75
Andy Hassler	1.1	0	0	0	0	1	0.00

Brewers	IP	H	R	ER	BB	K	ERA
Pete Vuckovich	6.1	9	3	3	3	4	4.40
Bob McClure (W, 1-0)	1.2	2	0	0	0	0	0.00
Peter Ladd (S, 2)	1.0	0	0	0	0	0	0.00

McClure pitched to one batter in the 9th.

Time—3:01. Attendance—54,968. Umpires—HP, Denkinger. 1B, Clark. 2B, Barnett. 3B, Kunkel.

1982 AL Championship Series—Composite Statistics

Batting

Brewers	G	AB	R	H	RBI	2B	3B	HR	BB	SO	SB	CS	Avg	OBP	Slg
Mark Brouhard	1	4	4	3	3	1	0	1	0	0	0	0	.750	.750	1.750
Cecil Cooper	5	20	1	3	4	2	0	0	0	6	0	0	.150	.150	.250
Marshall Edwards	3	1	2	0	0	0	0	0	0	0	1	0	.000	.000	.000
Jim Gantner	5	16	1	3	2	0	0	0	1	1	0	0	.188	.235	.188
Roy Howell	1	3	0	0	0	0	0	0	0	1	0	0	.000	.000	.000
Paul Molitor	5	19	4	6	5	1	0	2	2	3	1	1	.316	.381	.684
Don Money	4	11	2	2	1	0	0	0	3	1	0	0	.182	.333	.182
Charlie Moore	5	13	3	6	0	0	0	0	1	2	0	0	.462	.533	.462
Ben Oglivie	4	15	1	2	1	0	0	1	0	3	0	0	.133	.188	.333
Ted Simmons	5	18	3	3	1	0	0	0	1	4	0	0	.167	.200	.167
Gorman Thomas	5	15	1	1	3	0	0	1	2	7	0	1	.067	.167	.267
Robin Yount	5	16	1	4	0	0	0	0	5	2	0	0	.250	.429	.250
Totals	5	151	23	33	20	4	0	5	15	28	2	2	.219	.292	.344

Batting

Angels	G	AB	R	H	RBI	2B	3B	HR	BB	SO	SB	CS	Avg	OBP	Slg
Don Baylor	5	17	2	5	10	1	1	1	2	0	0	0	.294	.350	.647
Bob Boone	5	16	3	4	4	0	0	1	0	2	0	0	.250	.235	.438
Rod Carew	5	17	2	3	0	1	0	0	4	4	1	1	.176	.333	.235
Doug DeCinces	5	19	5	6	0	2	0	0	1	5	0	1	.316	.350	.421
Brian Downing	5	19	4	3	0	1	0	0	3	2	0	0	.158	.273	.211
Tim Foli	5	16	0	2	1	0	0	0	0	3	0	0	.125	.125	.125
Bobby Grich	5	15	1	3	1	1	0	0	2	7	0	0	.200	.333	.267
Reggie Jackson	5	18	2	2	2	0	0	1	2	7	0	0	.111	.200	.278
Ron Jackson	1	1	0	1	0	0	0	0	0	0	0	1	1.000	1.000	1.000
Fred Lynn	5	18	4	11	5	2	0	1	2	3	0	0	.611	.650	.889
Rob Wilfong	2	1	0	0	0	0	0	0	0	1	0	0	.000	.000	.000
Totals	5	157	23	40	23	8	1	4	16	34	1	2	.255	.324	.395

Pitching

Brewers	G	GS	CG	IP	H	R	ER	BB	SO	W-L	Sv-Op	Hld	ERA
Dwight Bernard	1	0	0	1.0	0	0	0	0	0	0-0	0-0	0	0.00
Mike Caldwell	1	1	0	3.0	7	6	5	1	2	0-1	0-0	0	15.00
Moose Haas	1	1	0	7.1	5	5	4	5	7	1-0	0-0	0	4.91
Peter Ladd	3	0	0	3.1	0	0	0	0	5	0-0	2-2	0	0.00
Bob McClure	1	0	0	1.2	2	0	0	0	0	1-0	0-0	0	0.00
Jim Slaton	2	0	0	4.2	3	2	1	1	3	0-0	1-1	0	1.93
Don Sutton	1	1	0	7.2	8	3	3	2	9	1-0	0-0	0	3.52
Pete Vuckovich	2	2	1	14.1	15	7	7	7	8	0-1	0-0	0	4.40
Totals	5	5	1	43.0	40	23	20	16	34	3-2	3-3	0	4.19

Pitching

Angels	G	GS	CG	IP	H	R	ER	BB	SO	W-L	Sv-Op	Hld	ERA
Dave Goltz	1	0	0	3.2	4	3	3	2	2	0-0	0-0	0	7.36
Andy Hassler	2	0	0	2.2	0	0	0	0	2	0-0	0-0	0	0.00
Tommy John	2	2	1	12.1	11	9	7	6	6	1-1	0-0	0	5.11
Bruce Kison	2	2	1	14.0	8	4	3	3	12	1-0	0-0	0	1.93
Luis Sanchez	2	0	0	2.2	4	2	2	1	1	0-1	0-1	0	6.75
Mike Witt	1	0	0	3.0	2	2	2	2	3	0-0	0-0	0	6.00
Geoff Zahn	1	1	0	3.2	4	3	3	1	2	0-1	0-0	0	7.36
Totals	5	5	2	42.0	33	23	20	15	28	2-3	0-1	0	4.29

Fielding

Brewers	Pos	G	PO	Ast	E	DP	PB	FPct
Dwight Bernard	p	1	0	0	0	0	—	—
Mark Brouhard	lf	1	1	0	0	0	—	1.000
Mike Caldwell	p	1	0	2	1	0	—	.667
Cecil Cooper	1b	5	37	3	2	5	—	.952
Marshall Edwards	cf	1	2	0	0	0	—	1.000
Jim Gantner	2b	5	12	8	0	4	—	1.000
Moose Haas	p	1	0	0	0	0	—	—
Peter Ladd	p	3	0	1	0	0	—	1.000
Bob McClure	p	1	0	0	0	0	—	—
Paul Molitor	3b	5	4	11	1	2	—	.938
Charlie Moore	rf	5	7	1	0	0	—	1.000
Ben Oglivie	lf	4	5	0	2	0	—	.714
Ted Simmons	c	5	36	3	0	0	0	1.000
Jim Slaton	p	2	1	0	0	0	—	1.000
Don Sutton	p	1	0	1	0	0	—	1.000
Gorman Thomas	cf	5	13	0	0	0	—	1.000
Pete Vuckovich	p	2	0	3	0	0	—	1.000
Robin Yount	ss	5	11	12	1	4	—	.958
Totals		5	129	45	7	15	0	.961

Fielding

Angels	Pos	G	PO	Ast	E	DP	PB	FPct
Juan Beniquez	lf	2	1	0	0	0	—	1.000
Bob Boone	c	5	30	3	0	0	1	1.000
Rod Carew	1b	5	42	3	0	2	—	1.000
Bobby Clark	rf	2	1	0	0	0	—	1.000
Doug DeCinces	3b	5	8	12	3	2	—	.870
Brian Downing	lf	5	5	0	0	0	—	1.000
Tim Foli	ss	5	6	6	0	0	—	1.000
Dave Goltz	p	1	0	0	0	0	—	—
Bobby Grich	2b	5	11	17	0	3	—	1.000
Andy Hassler	p	2	0	1	0	0	—	1.000
Reggie Jackson	rf	5	3	0	0	0	—	1.000
Tommy John	p	2	3	1	0	0	—	1.000
Bruce Kison	p	2	0	0	0	0	—	—
Fred Lynn	cf	5	16	0	1	0	—	.941
Luis Sanchez	p	2	0	0	0	0	—	—
Mike Witt	p	1	0	1	0	0	—	1.000
Geoff Zahn	p	1	0	0	0	0	—	—
Totals		5	126	44	4	7	1	.977

1982 St. Louis Cardinals (NL) 3, Atlanta Braves (NL) 0

In the opening game of the 1982 NLCS, the Braves led the Cardinals 1-0 after four-and-one-half innings. Then the rains came, washing out the game. Given a fresh start, the Cardinals blanked the Braves in the real Game 1, 7-0. St. Louis starter Bob Forsch starred both on the mound and at the plate. He tossed a three-hitter, contributed two hits himself and knocked in a run with a sacrifice fly. The Braves took a 3-1 lead into the sixth inning of the second game behind Phil Niekro, but the Cardinals fought back and pushed across the tying run in the bottom of the eighth against Gene Garber. With one out and a man on second in the bottom of the ninth, Ken Oberkfell lined a shot over the head of center fielder Brett Butler to bring home the game-winner. Willie McGee tripled, homered and drove in three runs in Game 3, and the Cardinals completed their sweep by the score of 6-2.

Game 1

Thursday, October 7

Braves	AB	R	H	RBI	BB	K	Avg
Claudell Washington, rf	4	0	2	0	0	0	.500
Rafael Ramirez, ss	4	0	0	0	0	0	.000
Dale Murphy, cf	4	0	0	0	0	0	.000
Chris Chambliss, 1b	3	0	0	0	0	0	.000
Bob Horner, 3b	3	0	0	0	0	0	.000
Jerry Royster, lf	3	0	0	0	0	2	.000
Glenn Hubbard, 2b	3	0	0	0	0	1	.000
Bruce Benedict, c	3	0	1	0	0	1	.333
Pascual Perez, p	2	0	0	0	0	1	.000
Steve Bedrosian, p	0	0	0	0	0	0	—
Donnie Moore, p	0	0	0	0	0	0	—
Larry Whisenton, ph	1	0	0	0	0	1	.000
Bob Walk, p	0	0	0	0	0	0	—
TOTALS	30	0	3	0	0	6	.100

Cardinals	AB	R	H	RBI	BB	K	Avg
Tom Herr, 2b	5	0	2	0	0	1	.400
Ken Oberkfell, 3b	5	0	1	1	0	0	.200
Lonnie Smith, lf	3	1	1	1	0	0	.333
David Green, lf	0	0	0	0	0	0	—
Keith Hernandez, 1b	4	1	1	0	1	1	.250
George Hendrick, rf	4	1	1	1	1	1	.250
Darrell Porter, c	4	1	2	0	1	0	.500
Willie McGee, cf	4	2	2	0	0	2	.500
Ozzie Smith, ss	3	0	1	2	0	0	.333
Bob Forsch, p	3	1	2	1	0	0	.667
TOTALS	35	7	13	7	3	5	.371

	1	2	3	4	5	6	7	8	9		R	H	E
Braves	0	0	0	0	0	0	0	0	0		0	3	0
Cardinals	0	0	1	0	0	5	0	1	x		7	13	1

E—Oberkfell. LOB—Braves 3, Cardinals 11. Scoring Position—Braves 0-for-1, Cardinals 4-for-12. 2B—Porter (1). 3B—McGee (1). SF—LSmith, OSmith, Forsch. CS—Washington (1).

Braves	IP	H	R	ER	BB	K	ERA
Pascual Perez (L, 0-1)	5.0	7	4	4	1	2	7.20
Steve Bedrosian	0.2	3	2	2	1	0	27.00
Donnie Moore	1.1	1	0	0	0	1	0.00
Bob Walk	1.0	2	1	1	1	1	9.00

Cardinals	IP	H	R	ER	BB	K	ERA
Bob Forsch (W, 1-0)	9.0	3	0	0	0	6	0.00

Perez pitched to three batters in the 6th.

WP—Bedrosian. HBP—LSmith by Moore. Time—2:25. Attendance—53,008. Umpires—HP, CWilliams. 1B, Engel. 2B, Wendelstedt. 3B, Froemming.

Game 2

Saturday, October 9

Braves	AB	R	H	RBI	BB	K	Avg
Claudell Washington, rf	3	0	0	0	1	1	.286
Rafael Ramirez, ss	4	1	1	1	0	1	.125
Dale Murphy, cf-lf	4	0	1	0	0	1	.125
Chris Chambliss, 1b	3	0	0	0	1	0	.000
Bob Horner, 3b	4	0	0	0	0	2	.000
Brett Butler, cf	0	0	0	0	0	0	—
Jerry Royster, lf-3b	4	0	2	0	0	0	.286
Glenn Hubbard, 2b	3	1	1	0	0	0	.167
Bruce Benedict, c	2	1	1	0	2	0	.400
Phil Niekro, p	0	0	0	0	1	0	—
Biff Pocoroba, ph	1	0	0	0	0	0	.000
Gene Garber, p	1	0	0	0	0	0	.000
TOTALS	29	3	6	2	4	5	.161

Cardinals	AB	R	H	RBI	BB	K	Avg
Tom Herr, 2b	3	0	0	0	1	1	.250
Ken Oberkfell, 3b	5	1	1	1	0	0	.200
Lonnie Smith, lf	4	0	1	0	0	1	.286
Bruce Sutter, p	0	0	0	0	0	0	—
Keith Hernandez, 1b	4	1	1	0	0	1	.250
Darrell Porter, c	2	1	2	1	2	0	.667
George Hendrick, rf	4	0	2	0	0	1	.375
Willie McGee, cf	4	0	0	1	0	3	.250
Ozzie Smith, ss	2	0	1	0	2	0	.400
John Stuper, p	1	0	0	0	0	0	.000
Steve Braun, ph	1	0	0	0	0	0	.000
Doug Bair, p	0	0	0	0	0	0	—
David Green, lf	1	1	1	0	0	0	1.000
TOTALS	31	4	9	3	5	7	.317

	1	2	3	4	5	6	7	8	9		R	H	E
Braves	0	0	2	0	1	0	0	0	0		3	6	0
Cardinals	1	0	0	0	0	1	0	1	1		4	9	1

E—McGee. DP—Cardinals 1 (Porter to Oberkfell). LOB—Braves 6, Cardinals 9. Scoring Position—Braves 1-for-7, Cardinals 1-for-9. 2B—Benedict (1), Porter 2 (3). S—Hubbard, Niekro, Herr, Stuper. SF—Niekro. SB—Murphy (1), OSmith (1). CS—Murphy (1).

Braves	IP	H	R	ER	BB	K	ERA
Phil Niekro	6.0	6	2	2	4	5	3.00
Gene Garber (BS, 1; L, 0-1)	2.1	3	2	2	1	2	7.71

Cardinals	IP	H	R	ER	BB	K	ERA
John Stuper	6.0	4	3	2	1	4	3.00
Doug Bair	1.0	2	0	0	3	0	0.00
Bruce Sutter (W, 1-0)	2.0	0	0	0	0	1	0.00

Bair pitched to three batters in the 8th.

WP—Niekro. PB—Benedict. Time—2:46. Attendance—53,408. Umpires—HP, Engel. 1B, Wendelstedt. 2B, Froemming. 3B, Rennert.

Game 3

Sunday, October 10

Cardinals	AB	R	H	RBI	BB	K	Avg
Tom Herr, 2b	5	1	1	0	0	0	.231
Ken Oberkfell, 3b	5	0	1	0	0	0	.200
Lonnie Smith, lf	4	0	1	0	0	0	.273
Keith Hernandez, 1b	4	1	2	1	1	1	.333
Darrell Porter, c	3	1	1	0	2	2	.556
George Hendrick, rf	5	1	1	1	0	0	.308
Willie McGee, cf	5	2	2	3	0	0	.308
Ozzie Smith, ss	4	0	3	1	1	0	.556
Joaquin Andujar, p	1	0	0	0	0	1	.000
Bruce Sutter, p	1	0	0	0	0	0	.000
TOTALS	37	6	12	6	4	4	.320

Braves	AB	R	H	RBI	BB	K	Avg
Rafael Ramirez, ss	3	0	1	0	1	0	.182
Jerry Royster, lf	4	0	0	0	0	0	.182
Claudell Washington, rf	2	0	1	0	1	1	.333
Terry Harper, pr-rf	1	1	0	0	0	0	.000
Bob Horner, 3b	4	0	1	0	0	0	.091
Chris Chambliss, 1b	4	0	0	0	0	0	.000
Dale Murphy, cf	3	1	2	0	0	1	.273
Glenn Hubbard, 2b	3	0	1	1	0	2	.222
Bruce Benedict, c	3	0	0	0	0	0	.250
Rick Camp, p	0	0	0	0	0	0	—
Pascual Perez, p	1	0	0	0	0	0	.000
Donnie Moore, p	0	0	0	0	0	0	—
Larry Whisenton, ph	1	0	0	0	0	0	.000
Rick Mahler, p	0	0	0	0	0	0	—
Steve Bedrosian, p	0	0	0	0	0	0	—
Brett Butler, ph	1	0	0	0	0	0	.000
Gene Garber, p	0	0	0	0	0	0	.000
TOTALS	30	2	6	1	2	4	.170

	1	2	3	4	5	6	7	8	9		R	H	E
Cardinals	0	4	0	0	1	0	0	0	1		6	12	0
Braves	0	0	0	0	0	0	2	0	0		2	6	1

E—Ramirez. DP—Cardinals 3 (Oberkfell to Herr to Hernandez; Herr to Hernandez; Herr to OSmith to Hernandez). LOB—Cardinals 11, Braves 3. Scoring Position—Cardinals 5-for-14, Braves 1-for-4. 2B—Herr (1). 3B—McGee (2). HR—McGee (1). S—LSmith, Andujar 2. GDP—Royster 2, Chambliss.

Cardinals	IP	H	R	ER	BB	K	ERA
Joaquin Andujar (W, 1-0)	6.2	6	2	2	2	4	2.70
Bruce Sutter (S, 1)	2.1	0	0	0	0	0	0.00

Braves	IP	H	R	ER	BB	K	ERA
Rick Camp (L, 0-1)	1.0	4	4	4	1	0	36.00
Pascual Perez	3.2	4	1	1	1	2	5.19
Donnie Moore	1.1	1	0	0	0	0	0.00
Rick Mahler	1.2	3	0	0	2	0	0.00
Steve Bedrosian	0.1	0	0	0	0	1	18.00
Gene Garber	1.0	1	1	1	0	1	8.10

Camp pitched to five batters in the 2nd.

Balk—Andujar. WP—Andujar 2. Time—2:51. Attendance—52,173. Umpires—HP, Wendelstedt. 1B, Froemming. 2B, Rennert. 3B, Runge.

1982 NL Championship Series—Composite Statistics

Batting

Cardinals	G	AB	R	H	RBI	2B	3B	HR	BB	SO	SB	CS	Avg	OBP	Slg
Joaquin Andujar	1	1	0	0	0	0	0	0	0	1	0	0	.000	.000	.000
Steve Braun	1	1	0	0	0	0	0	0	0	0	0	0	.000	.000	.000
Bob Forsch	1	3	1	2	1	0	0	0	0	0	0	0	.667	.500	.667
David Green	2	1	1	1	0	0	0	0	0	0	0	0	1.000	1.000	1.000
George Hendrick	3	13	2	4	2	0	0	0	1	2	0	0	.308	.357	.308
Keith Hernandez	3	12	3	4	1	0	0	0	2	3	0	0	.333	.429	.333
Tom Herr	3	13	1	3	0	1	0	0	1	2	0	0	.231	.286	.308
Willie McGee	3	13	4	4	5	0	2	1	0	5	0	0	.308	.308	.846
Ken Oberkfell	3	15	1	3	2	0	0	0	0	0	0	0	.200	.200	.200
Darrell Porter	3	9	3	5	1	3	0	0	5	2	0	0	.556	.714	.889
Lonnie Smith	3	11	1	3	1	0	0	0	0	1	0	0	.273	.308	.273
Ozzie Smith	3	9	0	5	3	0	0	0	3	0	1	0	.556	.615	.556
John Stuper	1	1	0	0	0	0	0	0	0	0	0	0	.000	.000	.000
Bruce Sutter	2	1	0	0	0	0	0	0	0	0	0	0	.000	.000	.000
Totals	3	103	17	34	16	4	2	1	12	16	1	0	.330	.395	.437

Braves	G	AB	R	H	RBI	2B	3B	HR	BB	SO	SB	CS	Avg	OBP	Slg
Bruce Benedict	3	8	1	2	0	1	0	0	2	1	0	0	.250	.400	.375
Brett Butler	2	1	0	0	0	0	0	0	0	0	0	0	.000	.000	.000
Chris Chambliss	3	10	0	0	0	0	0	0	1	0	0	0	.000	.091	.000
Gene Garber	2	1	0	0	0	0	0	0	0	0	0	0	.000	.000	.000
Terry Harper	1	1	1	0	0	0	0	0	0	0	0	0	.000	.000	.000
Bob Horner	3	11	0	1	0	0	0	0	0	2	0	0	.091	.091	.091
Glenn Hubbard	3	9	1	2	1	0	0	0	0	3	0	0	.222	.222	.222
Dale Murphy	3	11	1	3	0	0	0	0	0	2	1	1	.273	.273	.273
Phil Niekro	1	0	0	0	1	0	0	0	0	0	0	0	—	.000	.000
Pascual Perez	2	3	0	0	0	0	0	0	1	0	0	0	.000	.000	.000
Biff Pocoroba	1	1	0	0	0	0	0	0	0	0	0	0	.000	.000	.000
Rafael Ramirez	3	11	1	2	1	0	0	0	1	1	0	0	.182	.250	.182
Jerry Royster	3	11	0	2	0	0	0	0	0	2	0	0	.182	.182	.182
Claudell Washington	3	9	3	3	0	0	0	0	2	2	0	1	.333	.455	.333
Larry Whisenton	2	2	0	0	0	0	0	0	0	1	0	0	.000	.000	.000
Totals	3	89	5	15	3	1	0	0	6	15	1	2	.169	.219	.180

Pitching

Cardinals	G	GS	CG	IP	H	R	ER	BB	SO	W-L	Sv-Op	Hld	ERA
Joaquin Andujar	1	1	0	6.2	6	2	2	2	4	1-0	0-0	0	2.70
Doug Bair	1	0	0	1.0	2	0	0	3	0	0-0	0-0	0	0.00
Bob Forsch	1	1	1	9.0	3	0	0	0	6	1-0	0-0	0	0.00
John Stuper	1	1	0	6.0	4	3	2	1	4	0-0	0-0	0	3.00
Bruce Sutter	2	0	0	4.1	0	0	0	0	1	1-0	1-1	0	0.00
Totals	3	3	1	27.0	15	5	4	6	15	3-0	1-1	0	1.33

Braves	G	GS	CG	IP	H	R	ER	BB	SO	W-L	Sv-Op	Hld	ERA
Steve Bedrosian	2	0	0	1.0	3	2	2	1	2	0-0	0-0	0	18.00
Rick Camp	1	1	0	1.0	4	4	4	1	0	0-1	0-0	0	36.00
Gene Garber	2	0	0	3.1	4	3	3	1	3	0-1	0-1	0	8.10
Rick Mahler	1	0	0	1.2	3	0	0	2	0	0-0	0-0	0	0.00
Donnie Moore	2	0	0	2.2	2	0	0	0	1	0-0	0-0	0	0.00
Phil Niekro	1	1	0	6.0	6	2	2	4	5	0-0	0-0	0	3.00
Pascual Perez	2	1	0	8.2	10	5	5	2	4	0-1	0-0	0	5.19
Bob Walk	1	0	0	1.0	2	1	1	1	1	0-0	0-0	0	9.00
Totals	3	3	0	25.1	34	17	17	12	16	0-3	0-1	0	6.04

Fielding

Cardinals	Pos	G	PO	Ast	E	DP	PB	FPct
Joaquin Andujar	p	1	0	1	0	0	—	1.000
Doug Bair	p	1	0	1	0	0	—	1.000
Bob Forsch	p	1	0	2	0	0	—	1.000
David Green	lf	2	0	0	0	0	—	—
George Hendrick	rf	3	5	0	0	0	—	1.000
Keith Hernandez	1b	3	35	1	0	3	—	1.000
Tom Herr	2b	3	6	10	0	3	—	1.000
Willie McGee	cf	3	12	0	1	0	—	.923
Ken Oberkfell	3b	3	2	4	1	2	—	.857
Darrell Porter	c	3	15	3	0	1	0	1.000
Lonnie Smith	lf	3	2	0	0	0	—	1.000
Ozzie Smith	ss	3	4	11	0	1	—	1.000
John Stuper	p	1	0	0	0	0	—	—
Bruce Sutter	p	2	0	2	0	0	—	1.000
Totals		3	81	35	2	10	0	.983

Braves	Pos	G	PO	Ast	E	DP	PB	FPct
Steve Bedrosian	p	2	0	0	0	0	—	—
Bruce Benedict	c	3	16	2	0	0	1	1.000
Brett Butler	cf	1	0	0	0	0	—	—
Rick Camp	p	1	0	0	0	0	—	—
Chris Chambliss	1b	3	31	5	0	0	—	1.000
Gene Garber	p	2	0	1	0	0	—	1.000
Terry Harper	rf	1	0	0	0	0	—	—
Bob Horner	3b	3	2	5	0	0	—	1.000
Glenn Hubbard	2b	3	4	13	0	0	—	1.000
Rick Mahler	p	1	0	1	0	0	—	1.000
Donnie Moore	p	2	1	0	0	0	—	1.000
Dale Murphy	cf	3	7	0	0	0	—	1.000
	lf	1	0	0	0	0	—	—
Phil Niekro	p	1	1	1	0	0	—	1.000
Pascual Perez	p	2	0	1	0	0	—	1.000
Rafael Ramirez	ss	3	5	11	1	0	—	.941
Jerry Royster	lf	3	4	0	0	0	—	1.000
	3b	1	0	0	0	0	—	—
Bob Walk	p	1	0	0	0	0	—	—
Claudell Washington	rf	3	5	0	0	0	—	1.000
Totals		3	76	40	1	0	1	.991

1983 Baltimore Orioles (AL) 3, Chicago White Sox (AL) 1

The Baltimore Orioles held the Chicago White Sox to a total of just three runs while winning the ALCS in four games. LaMarr Hoyt gave the White Sox their only win when he outdueled Scott McGregor 2-1 in the opener. Baltimore's Mike Boddicker was masterful in Game 2, tossing a five-hit shutout while striking out 14. The O's bombed the Sox 11-1 in the third game with help from the White Sox hurlers, who issued a total of nine walks. Eddie Murray slugged a three-run homer, walked three times, and scored four runs. Britt Burns and Storm Davis hooked up in Game 4. Davis exited after six scoreless innings, but Tippy Martinez held the fort as the game went into bonus frames. Seldom-used outfielder Tito Landrum finally broke the deadlock with a home run in the top of the 10th. The O's added two more runs in the inning for a 3-0 victory and the AL title.

Game 1

Wednesday, October 5

White Sox	AB	R	H	RBI	BB	K	Avg
Rudy Law, cf	5	1	3	0	0	0	.600
Carlton Fisk, c	5	0	1	0	0	1	.200
Tom Paciorek, 1b-lf	4	1	2	1	1	0	.500
Greg Luzinski, dh	3	0	1	0	1	0	.333
Ron Kittle, lf	3	0	0	0	0	2	.000
Mike Squires, 1b	1	0	0	0	0	0	.000
Harold Baines, rf	4	0	0	0	0	0	.000
Vance Law, 3b	3	0	0	0	1	1	.000
Scott Fletcher, ss	2	0	0	0	1	0	.000
Julio Cruz, 2b	2	0	0	0	2	0	.000
TOTALS	32	2	7	1	6	4	.219

Orioles	AB	R	H	RBI	BB	K	Avg
Al Bumbry, cf	4	0	0	0	0	1	.000
Dan Ford, rf	4	0	1	0	0	1	.250
Tito Landrum, pr	0	1	0	0	0	0	—
Cal Ripken Jr., ss	4	0	1	1	0	1	.250
Eddie Murray, 1b	4	0	0	0	0	0	.000
John Lowenstein, lf	3	0	0	0	0	1	.000
Ken Singleton, dh	3	0	1	0	0	0	.333
Rich Dauer, 2b	3	0	0	0	0	0	.000
Todd Cruz, 3b	3	0	1	0	0	0	.333
Rick Dempsey, c	2	0	1	0	0	0	.500
Jim Dwyer, ph	1	0	0	0	0	0	.000
TOTALS	31	1	5	1	0	4	.161

	1	2	3	4	5	6	7	8	9	R	H	E
White Sox	0	0	1	0	0	1	0	0	0	2	7	0
Orioles	0	0	0	0	0	0	0	0	1	1	5	1

E—Murray. DP—White Sox 1 (Fletcher to JCruz to Paciorek), Orioles 2 (Ripken Jr. to Dauer to Murray; McGregor to Dauer to Dempsey). LOB—White Sox 10, Orioles 3. Scoring Position—White Sox 1-for-13, Orioles 1-for-3. 2B—RLaw (1), Luzinski (1), Ford (1), Singleton (1). S—Fletcher. GDP—Kittle, Ford.

White Sox	IP	H	R	ER	BB	K	ERA
LaMarr Hoyt (W, 1-0)	9.0	5	1	1	0	4	1.00

Orioles	IP	H	R	ER	BB	K	ERA
Scott McGregor (L, 0-1)	6.2	6	2	1	3	2	1.35
Sammy Stewart	0.1	1	0	0	1	1	0.00
Tippy Martinez	2.0	0	0	0	2	1	0.00

Stewart pitched to two batters in the 8th.

Balk—McGregor. WP—Martinez. Time—2:38. Attendance—51,289. Umpires—HP, McKean. 1B, Merrill. 2B, Bremigan. 3B, Evans.

Game 2

Thursday, October 6

White Sox	AB	R	H	RBI	BB	K	Avg
Rudy Law, cf	4	0	2	0	0	0	.556
Carlton Fisk, c	3	0	0	0	1	2	.125
Harold Baines, rf	4	0	0	0	0	3	.000
Jerry Dybzinski, ss	0	0	0	0	0	0	—
Greg Luzinski, dh	3	0	0	0	0	1	.167
Tom Paciorek, 1b	3	0	1	0	0	1	.429
Ron Kittle, lf	3	0	1	0	1	0	.167
Vance Law, 3b	2	0	0	0	0	2	.000
Greg Walker, ph	1	0	0	0	0	1	.000
Aurelio Rodriguez, 3b	0	0	0	0	0	0	—
Mike Squires, ph	1	0	0	0	0	0	.000
Scott Fletcher, ss	2	0	0	0	0	0	.000
Jerry Hairston, ph-rf	1	0	0	0	1	1	.000
Julio Cruz, 2b	4	0	1	0	0	3	.167
TOTALS	31	0	5	0	3	14	.190

Orioles	AB	R	H	RBI	BB	K	Avg
John Shelby, cf	4	0	1	0	0	1	.250
Tito Landrum, rf	4	0	0	0	0	1	.000
Cal Ripken Jr., ss	4	1	2	0	0	0	.375
Eddie Murray, 1b	4	0	0	0	0	2	.000
Gary Roenicke, lf	2	3	2	2	2	0	1.000
Ken Singleton, dh	4	0	1	1	0	0	.286
Rich Dauer, 2b	3	0	0	0	0	0	.000
Todd Cruz, 3b	3	0	0	0	0	0	.167
Rick Dempsey, c	3	0	0	0	0	1	.200
TOTALS	31	4	6	3	2	5	.200

	1	2	3	4	5	6	7	8	9	R	H	E
White Sox	0	0	0	0	0	0	0	0	0	0	5	2
Orioles	0	1	0	1	0	2	0	0	x	4	6	0

E—Rodriguez, VLaw. DP—White Sox 1 (Dybzinski to Paciorek), Orioles 1 (Dempsey to TCruz). LOB—White Sox 9, Orioles 5. Scoring Position—White Sox 0-for-7, Orioles 1-for-10. 2B—Ripken Jr. (1), Roenicke (1), Singleton (2). HR—Roenicke (1). GDP—Singleton. SB—RLaw 2 (2), Shelby (1). CS—Paciorek (1).

White Sox	IP	H	R	ER	BB	K	ERA
Floyd Bannister (L, 0-1)	6.0	5	4	3	1	5	4.50
Salome Barojas	1.0	1	0	0	0	0	0.00
Dennis Lamp	1.0	0	0	0	1	0	0.00

Orioles	IP	H	R	ER	BB	K	ERA
Mike Boddicker (W, 1-0)	9.0	5	0	0	3	14	0.00

HBP—Luzinski by Boddicker, Paciorek by Boddicker. Time—2:51. Attendance—52,347. Umpires—HP, Merrill. 1B, Bremigan. 2B, Evans. 3B, Phillips.

Game 3

Friday, October 7

Orioles	AB	R	H	RBI	BB	K	Avg
Al Bumbry, cf	4	0	1	1	0	1	.125
John Shelby, ph-cf	0	1	0	0	1	0	.250
Jim Dwyer, rf	3	1	1	0	1	0	.250
Tito Landrum, ph-rf	1	0	0	0	0	0	.000
Cal Ripken Jr., ss	4	3	2	0	0	1	.417
Eddie Murray, 1b	2	4	1	3	3	0	.100
John Lowenstein, lf	3	0	1	2	1	0	.167
Gary Roenicke, ph-lf	0	1	0	1	1	0	1.000
Ken Singleton, dh	3	0	1	0	1	1	.300
Jim Palmer, pr-dh	0	0	0	0	0	0	—
Joe Nolan, ph-dh	0	0	0	1	0	0	—
Rich Dauer, 2b	4	0	0	1	0	0	.000
Todd Cruz, 3b	5	0	1	1	0	3	.182
Rick Dempsey, c	3	1	0	0	1	0	.125
TOTALS	32	11	8	10	9	7	.200

White Sox	AB	R	H	RBI	BB	K	Avg
Rudy Law, cf	4	0	2	0	0	0	.538
Carlton Fisk, c	4	0	1	0	0	0	.167
Tom Paciorek, 1b	4	0	0	0	0	0	.273
Greg Luzinski, dh	4	0	1	0	0	1	.200
Ron Kittle, lf	1	1	1	0	0	0	.286
Jerry Hairston, ph-lf	2	0	0	0	0	0	.000
Harold Baines, rf	4	0	0	0	0	0	.000
Vance Law, 3b	2	0	1	1	0	0	.143
Mike Squires, ph	1	0	0	0	0	0	.000
Aurelio Rodriguez, 3b	0	0	0	0	0	0	—
Scott Fletcher, ss	3	0	0	0	0	0	.000
Julio Cruz, 2b	3	0	0	0	0	1	.111
TOTALS	32	1	6	1	0	2	.191

	1	2	3	4	5	6	7	8	9	R	H	E
Orioles	3	1	0	0	2	0	0	1	4	11	8	1
White Sox	0	1	0	0	0	0	0	0	0	1	6	1

E—Dempsey, Hairston. DP—Orioles 1 (Dauer to Ripken Jr. to Murray), White Sox 1 (Fletcher to JCruz to Paciorek). LOB—

Game 4

Saturday, October 8

Orioles	AB	R	H	RBI	BB	K	Avg
John Shelby, cf	5	0	1	0	0	2	.222
Tito Landrum, rf	5	1	2	1	0	1	.200
Cal Ripken Jr., ss	3	1	1	0	2	1	.400
Eddie Murray, 1b	5	1	3	0	0	1	.267
Gary Roenicke, lf	2	0	1	1	2	0	.750
Ken Singleton, dh	2	0	0	0	1	1	.250
Al Bumbry, pr-dh	0	0	0	0	0	0	.125
Dan Ford, ph-dh	1	0	0	0	0	0	.200
John Lowenstein, ph	0	0	0	0	0	0	.167
Bennie Ayala, ph-dh	0	0	0	1	0	0	—
Rich Dauer, 2b	4	0	0	0	0	0	.000
Todd Cruz, 3b	4	0	0	0	0	2	.133
Rick Dempsey, c	4	0	1	0	0	0	.167
TOTALS	35	3	9	3	5	8	.216

White Sox	AB	R	H	RBI	BB	K	Avg
Rudy Law, cf	5	0	0	0	0	1	.389
Carlton Fisk, c	5	0	1	0	0	0	.176
Harold Baines, rf	4	0	2	0	1	0	.125
Greg Luzinski, dh	5	0	0	0	0	3	.133
Tom Paciorek, lf	5	0	1	0	0	0	.250
Greg Walker, 1b	2	0	1	0	1	1	.333
Mike Squires, pr-1b	1	0	0	0	0	0	.000
Vance Law, 3b	4	0	1	0	0	0	.182
Jerry Dybzinski, ss	4	0	1	0	1	0	.250
Julio Cruz, 2b	3	0	3	0	1	0	.333
TOTALS	38	0	10	0	3	6	.224

	1	2	3	4	5	6	7	8	9	10	R	H	E
Orioles	0	0	0	0	0	0	0	0	0	3	3	9	0
White Sox	0	0	0	0	0	0	0	0	0	0	0	10	0

DP—Orioles 1 (Ripken Jr. to Murray), White Sox 2 (Dybzinski to Walker; VLaw to JCruz to Walker). LOB—Orioles 10, White Sox 11. Scoring Position—Orioles 1-for-10, White Sox 1-for-7. HR—Landrum (1). S—Dauer. SF—Ayala. GDP—Ripken Jr., Roenicke, Baines. SB—JCruz 2 (2).

Orioles	IP	H	R	ER	BB	K	ERA
Storm Davis	6.0	5	0	0	2	2	0.00
Tippy Martinez (W, 1-0)	4.0	5	0	0	1	4	0.00

White Sox	IP	H	R	ER	BB	K	ERA
Britt Burns (L, 0-1)	9.1	6	1	1	5	8	0.96
Salome Barojas	0.0	3	2	2	0	0	18.00
Juan Agosto	0.1	0	0	0	0	0	0.00
Dennis Lamp	0.1	0	0	0	0	0	0.00

Davis pitched to one batter in the 7th. Barojas pitched to three batters in the 10th.

HBP—Roenicke by Burns. Time—3:41. Attendance—45,477. Umpires—HP, Evans. 1B, Phillips. 2B, Reilly. 3B, McKean.

Orioles 6, White Sox 5. Scoring Position—Orioles 4-for-10, White Sox 1-for-5. 2B—Bumbry (1), Dwyer (1), Ripken Jr. (2), Lowenstein (1), Fisk (1), Kittle (1). HR—Murray (1). SF—Dauer, Nolan. GDP—Singleton, Baines. SB—Murray (1).

Orioles	IP	H	R	ER	BB	K	ERA
Mike Flanagan (W, 1-0)	5.0	5	1	1	0	1	1.80
Sammy Stewart (S, 1)	4.0	1	0	0	0	1	0.00

White Sox	IP	H	R	ER	BB	K	ERA
Rich Dotson (L, 0-1)	5.0	6	6	6	3	3	10.80
Dick Tidrow	3.0	1	1	1	3	3	3.00
Jerry Koosman	0.1	1	3	2	2	0	54.00
Dennis Lamp	0.2	0	1	0	1	1	0.00

HBP—Ripken Jr. by Dotson, Kittle by Flanagan. Time—2:58. Attendance—46,635. Umpires—HP, Bremigan. 1B, Evans. 2B, Phillips. 3B, Reilly.

1983 AL Championship Series—Composite Statistics

Batting

Orioles	G	AB	R	H	RBI	2B	3B	HR	BB	SO	SB	CS	Avg	OBP	Slg
Bennie Ayala	1	0	0	0	1	0	0	0	0	0	0	0	—	.000	—
Al Bumbry	3	8	0	1	1	1	0	0	0	2	0	0	.125	.125	.250
Todd Cruz	4	15	0	2	1	0	0	0	0	5	0	0	.133	.133	.133
Rich Dauer	4	14	0	0	1	0	0	0	0	0	0	0	.000	.000	.000
Rick Dempsey	4	12	1	2	0	0	0	0	1	1	0	0	.167	.231	.167
Jim Dwyer	2	4	1	1	0	0	0	0	1	0	0	0	.250	.400	.500
Dan Ford	2	5	0	1	0	1	0	0	0	1	0	0	.200	.200	.400
Tito Landrum	4	10	2	2	1	0	0	1	0	2	0	0	.200	.200	.500
John Lowenstein	3	6	0	1	2	1	0	0	1	2	0	0	.167	.286	.333
Eddie Murray	4	15	5	4	3	0	0	1	3	3	1	0	.267	.389	.467
Joe Nolan	1	0	0	0	1	0	0	0	0	0	0	0	—	.000	—
Jim Palmer	1	0	0	0	0	0	0	0	0	0	0	0	—	—	—
Cal Ripken Jr.	4	15	5	6	1	2	0	0	2	3	0	0	.400	.500	.533
Gary Roenicke	3	4	4	3	4	1	0	1	5	0	0	0	.750	.900	1.750
John Shelby	3	9	1	2	0	0	0	0	1	3	1	0	.222	.300	.222
Ken Singleton	4	12	0	3	1	2	0	0	2	2	0	0	.250	.357	.417
Totals	**4**	**129**	**19**	**28**	**17**	**9**	**0**	**3**	**16**	**24**	**2**	**0**	**.217**	**.307**	**.357**

Batting

White Sox	G	AB	R	H	RBI	2B	3B	HR	BB	SO	SB	CS	Avg	OBP	Slg
Harold Baines	4	16	0	2	0	0	0	0	1	3	0	0	.125	.176	.125
Julio Cruz	4	12	0	4	0	0	0	0	3	4	2	0	.333	.467	.333
Jerry Dybzinski	2	4	1	0	0	0	0	0	0	0	0	0	.250	.250	.250
Carlton Fisk	4	17	0	3	0	1	0	0	1	3	0	0	.176	.222	.235
Scott Fletcher	3	7	0	0	0	0	0	0	1	0	0	0	.000	.125	.000
Jerry Hairston	2	3	0	0	0	0	0	0	1	1	0	0	.000	.250	.000
Ron Kittle	3	7	1	2	0	1	0	0	1	2	0	0	.286	.444	.429
Rudy Law	4	18	1	7	0	1	0	0	0	1	2	0	.389	.389	.444
Vance Law	4	11	0	2	1	0	0	0	1	3	0	0	.182	.250	.182
Greg Luzinski	4	15	0	2	0	1	0	0	1	5	0	0	.133	.235	.200
Tom Paciorek	4	16	1	4	1	0	0	0	1	2	0	1	.250	.333	.250
Mike Squires	4	4	0	0	0	0	0	0	0	0	0	0	.000	.000	.000
Greg Walker	2	3	0	1	0	0	0	0	1	2	0	0	.333	.500	.333
Totals	**4**	**133**	**3**	**28**	**2**	**4**	**0**	**0**	**12**	**26**	**4**	**1**	**.211**	**.291**	**.241**

Pitching

Orioles	G	GS	CG	IP	H	R	ER	BB	SO	W-L	Sv-Op	Hld	ERA
Mike Boddicker	1	1	1	9.0	5	0	0	3	14	1-0	0-0	0	0.00
Storm Davis	1	1	0	6.0	5	0	0	2	2	0-0	0-0	0	0.00
Mike Flanagan	1	1	0	5.0	5	1	1	0	1	1-0	0-0	0	1.80
Tippy Martinez	2	0	0	6.0	5	0	0	3	5	1-0	0-0	0	0.00
Scott McGregor	1	1	0	6.2	6	2	1	3	2	0-1	0-0	0	1.35
Sammy Stewart	2	0	0	4.1	2	0	0	1	2	0-0	1-1	0	0.00
Totals	**4**	**4**	**1**	**37.0**	**28**	**3**	**2**	**12**	**26**	**3-1**	**1-1**	**0**	**0.49**

Pitching

White Sox	G	GS	CG	IP	H	R	ER	BB	SO	W-L	Sv-Op	Hld	ERA
Juan Agosto	1	0	0	0.1	0	0	0	0	0	0-0	0-0	0	0.00
Floyd Bannister	1	1	0	6.0	5	4	3	1	5	0-1	0-0	0	4.50
Salome Barojas	2	0	0	1.0	4	2	2	0	0	0-0	0-0	0	18.00
Britt Burns	1	1	0	9.1	6	1	1	5	8	0-1	0-0	0	0.96
Rich Dotson	1	1	0	5.0	6	6	6	3	4	0-0	0-0	0	10.80
LaMarr Hoyt	1	1	1	9.0	5	1	1	0	4	1-0	0-0	0	1.00
Jerry Koosman	1	0	0	0.1	1	3	2	2	0	0-0	0-0	0	54.00
Dennis Lamp	3	0	0	2.0	0	1	0	2	1	0-0	0-0	0	0.00
Dick Tidrow	1	0	0	3.0	1	1	1	3	3	0-0	0-0	0	3.00
Totals	**4**	**4**	**1**	**36.0**	**28**	**19**	**16**	**16**	**24**	**1-3**	**0-0**	**0**	**4.00**

Fielding

Orioles	Pos	G	PO	Ast	E	DP	PB	FPct
Mike Boddicker	p	1	0	1	0	0	—	1.000
Al Bumbry	cf	2	3	0	0	0	—	1.000
Todd Cruz	3b	4	6	13	0	1	—	1.000
Rich Dauer	2b	4	8	12	0	3	—	1.000
Storm Davis	p	1	0	0	0	0	—	—
Rick Dempsey	c	4	29	5	1	2	0	.971
Jim Dwyer	rf	1	4	0	0	0	—	1.000
Mike Flanagan	p	1	0	0	0	0	—	—
Dan Ford	rf	1	1	0	0	0	—	1.000
Tito Landrum	rf	3	5	0	0	0	—	1.000
John Lowenstein	lf	2	4	0	0	0	—	1.000
Tippy Martinez	p	2	0	2	0	0	—	1.000
Scott McGregor	p	1	1	1	0	1	—	1.000
Eddie Murray	1b	4	34	3	1	3	—	.974
Cal Ripken Jr.	ss	4	7	11	0	3	—	1.000
Gary Roenicke	lf	3	5	1	0	0	—	1.000
John Shelby	cf	3	2	0	0	0	—	1.000
Sammy Stewart	p	2	2	0	0	0	—	1.000
Totals		**4**	**111**	**49**	**2**	**13**	**0**	**.988**

Fielding

White Sox	Pos	G	PO	Ast	E	DP	PB	FPct
Juan Agosto	p	1	0	0	0	0	—	—
Harold Baines	rf	4	5	1	0	0	—	1.000
Floyd Bannister	p	1	0	0	0	0	—	—
Salome Barojas	p	2	0	1	0	0	—	1.000
Britt Burns	p	1	0	1	0	0	—	1.000
Julio Cruz	2b	4	10	14	0	3	—	1.000
Rich Dotson	p	1	1	1	0	0	—	1.000
Jerry Dybzinski	ss	2	3	8	0	2	—	1.000
Carlton Fisk	c	4	27	3	0	0	0	1.000
Scott Fletcher	ss	3	3	8	0	2	—	1.000
Jerry Hairston	lf	1	0	0	1	0	—	.000
	rf	1	0	0	0	0	—	—
LaMarr Hoyt	p	1	2	1	0	0	—	1.000
Ron Kittle	lf	3	3	0	0	0	—	1.000
Jerry Koosman	p	1	0	0	0	0	—	—
Dennis Lamp	p	3	0	0	0	0	—	—
Rudy Law	cf	4	10	0	0	0	—	1.000
Vance Law	3b	4	1	9	1	1	—	.909
Tom Paciorek	1b	3	29	3	0	3	—	1.000
	lf	2	1	0	0	0	—	1.000
Aurelio Rodriguez	3b	2	0	0	1	0	—	.000
Mike Squires	1b	2	6	0	0	0	—	1.000
Dick Tidrow	p	1	0	0	0	0	—	—
Greg Walker	1b	1	7	1	0	2	—	1.000
Totals		**4**	**108**	**51**	**3**	**13**	**0**	**.981**

1983 Philadelphia Phillies (NL) 3, Los Angeles Dodgers (NL) 1

The Los Angeles Dodgers had beaten the Philadelphia Phillies in 11 of 12 contests during the regular season, but the Phillies won when it counted, downing the Dodgers in a four-game NLCS. Mike Schmidt socked a first-inning homer off Jerry Reuss in Game 1, and Steve Carlton and Al Holland combined to blank the Dodgers, 1-0. Fernando Valenzuela won the second game 4-1, with Pedro Guerrero suppling the offense with a two-run triple. Gary Matthews got the Phillies back on track in Game 3, driving in four runs with two singles and a homer, as Charles Hudson tossed a four-hitter for a 7-2 victory. Matthews came through with a three-run homer in the first inning of the fourth game, and the Phils cruised to another 7-2 decision to advance to the World Series.

Game 1

Tuesday, October 4

Phillies	AB	R	H	RBI	BB	K	Avg
Joe Morgan, 2b	4	0	0	0	0	0	.000
Pete Rose, 1b	4	0	1	0	0	0	.250
Mike Schmidt, 3b	3	1	2	1	1	0	.667
Sixto Lezcano, rf	3	0	1	0	1	0	.333
Gary Matthews, lf	4	0	0	0	0	0	.000
Al Holland, p	0	0	0	0	0	0	—
Garry Maddox, cf	4	0	1	0	0	0	.250
Bo Diaz, c	3	0	0	0	1	0	.000
Ivan DeJesus, ss	3	0	0	0	1	2	.000
Steve Carlton, p	3	0	0	0	0	2	.000
Greg Gross, lf	1	0	0	0	0	0	.000
TOTALS	32	1	5	1	4	4	.156

Dodgers	AB	R	H	RBI	BB	K	Avg
Steve Sax, 2b	4	0	3	0	0	0	.750
Bill Russell, ss	3	0	1	0	0	1	.333
Dusty Baker, lf	4	0	1	0	0	0	.250
Pedro Guerrero, 3b	2	0	0	0	2	1	.000
Mike Marshall, 1b	4	0	0	0	0	1	.000
Tom Niedenfuer, p	0	0	0	0	0	0	—
Steve Yeager, c	4	0	0	0	0	0	.000
Ken Landreaux, cf	3	0	0	0	0	1	.000
Jose Morales, ph	1	0	0	0	0	0	.000
Derrel Thomas, rf	4	0	2	0	0	1	.500
Jerry Reuss, p	1	0	0	0	0	1	.000
Candy Maldonado, ph	1	0	0	0	0	0	.000
Greg Brock, 1b	1	0	0	0	0	0	.000
TOTALS	32	0	7	0	2	6	.219

	1	2	3	4	5	6	7	8	9		R	H	E
Phillies	1	0	0	0	0	0	0	0	0		1	5	1
Dodgers	0	0	0	0	0	0	0	0	0		0	7	0

E—Schmidt. LOB—Phillies 8, Dodgers 9. Scoring Position—Phillies 0-for-4, Dodgers 0-for-5. HR—Schmidt (1). S—Russell, Reuss. SB—Thomas (1). CS—Sax (1).

Phillies	IP	H	R	ER	BB	K	ERA
Steve Carlton (W, 1-0)	7.2	7	0	0	2	6	0.00
Al Holland (S, 1)	1.1	0	0	0	0	0	0.00

Dodgers	IP	H	R	ER	BB	K	ERA
Jerry Reuss (L, 0-1)	8.0	5	1	1	3	3	1.13
Tom Niedenfuer	1.0	0	0	0	1	1	0.00

WP—Reuss, Carlton. Time—2:17. Attendance—49,963. Umpires—HP, Tata. 1B, Stello. 2B, McSherry. 3B, Weyer.

Game 2

Wednesday, October 5

Phillies	AB	R	H	RBI	BB	K	Avg
Joe Morgan, 2b	3	0	0	0	1	1	.000
Pete Rose, 1b	3	0	0	0	1	1	.143
Mike Schmidt, 3b	4	0	1	0	0	2	.429
Sixto Lezcano, rf	4	0	0	0	0	0	.143
Gary Matthews, lf	4	1	2	1	0	0	.250
Garry Maddox, cf	3	0	2	0	0	0	.429
Greg Gross, ph	0	0	0	0	1	0	.000
Bo Diaz, c	3	0	0	0	0	0	.000
Joe Lefebvre, ph	1	0	0	0	0	1	.000
Ivan DeJesus, ss	2	0	1	0	1	1	.200
Von Hayes, ph	1	0	0	0	0	0	.000
John Denny, p	1	0	0	0	0	0	.000
Tony Perez, ph	1	0	1	0	0	0	1.000
Juan Samuel, pr	0	0	0	0	0	0	—
Ron Reed, p	0	0	0	0	0	0	—
Ozzie Virgil, ph	1	0	0	0	0	1	.000
TOTALS	31	1	7	1	4	7	.200

Dodgers	AB	R	H	RBI	BB	K	Avg
Steve Sax, 2b	4	0	0	0	0	0	.375
Greg Brock, 1b	4	1	0	0	0	1	.000
Derrel Thomas, rf	0	0	0	0	0	0	.500
Dusty Baker, lf	3	2	0	0	1	0	.143
Pedro Guerrero, 3b	3	0	1	2	0	0	.200
Ken Landreaux, cf	3	0	2	1	1	0	.333
Mike Marshall, rf-1b	4	0	0	0	0	1	.000
Bill Russell, ss	3	1	2	0	1	1	.500
Jack Fimple, c	4	0	1	1	0	1	.250
Fernando Valenzuela, p	3	0	0	0	1	0	.000
Tom Niedenfuer, p	0	0	0	0	0	0	—
TOTALS	31	4	6	4	4	4	.232

	1	2	3	4	5	6	7	8	9		R	H	E
Phillies	0	1	0	0	0	0	0	0	0		1	7	2
Dodgers	1	0	0	0	2	0	0	1	x		4	6	1

E—DeJesus, Maddox, Russell. DP—Dodgers 3 (Russell to Sax to Brock; Russell to Sax to Brock; Russell to Sax to Marshall). LOB—Phillies 8, Dodgers 8. Scoring Position—Phillies 0-for-8, Dodgers 3-for-9. 2B—Maddox (1). 3B—Guerrero (1). HR—Matthews (1). S—Denny. GDP—Rose, Lezcano, Diaz. SB—Rose (1), Russell (1).

Phillies	IP	H	R	ER	BB	K	ERA
John Denny (L, 0-1)	6.0	5	3	3	3	3	0.00
Ron Reed	2.0	1	1	1	1	1	4.50

Dodgers	IP	H	R	ER	BB	K	ERA
Fernando Valenzuela (W, 1-0)	8.0	7	1	1	4	5	1.13
Tom Niedenfuer (S, 1)	1.0	0	0	0	0	2	0.00

Valenzuela pitched to three batters in the 9th.

WP—Valenzuela. HBP—Guerrero by Denny. Time—2:51. Attendance—53,490. Umpires—HP, Stello. 1B, McSherry. 2B, Weyer. 3B, Harvey.

Game 3

Friday, October 7

Dodgers	AB	R	H	RBI	BB	K	Avg
Steve Sax, 2b	3	0	0	0	1	0	.273
Greg Brock, 1b	4	0	0	0	0	2	.000
Dusty Baker, lf	4	1	2	0	0	0	.273
Pedro Guerrero, 3b	4	0	0	0	0	2	.111
Ken Landreaux, cf	4	0	0	0	0	0	.200
Mike Marshall, rf	3	1	1	2	1	2	.091
Bill Russell, ss	4	0	0	0	0	0	.300
Jack Fimple, c	3	0	0	0	0	2	.143
Bob Welch, p	0	0	0	0	0	0	.000
Alejandro Pena, p	1	0	1	0	0	0	1.000
Rafael Landestoy, ph	1	0	0	0	0	0	.000
Rick Honeycutt, p	0	0	0	0	0	0	—
Joe Beckwith, p	0	0	0	0	0	0	—
Derrel Thomas, ph	1	0	0	0	0	1	.400
Pat Zachry, p	0	0	0	0	0	0	—
TOTALS	32	2	4	2	2	9	.200

Phillies	AB	R	H	RBI	BB	K	Avg
Joe Morgan, 2b	4	1	1	0	0	0	.091
Pete Rose, 1b	4	2	3	0	0	0	.364
Mike Schmidt, 3b	3	1	1	0	1	0	.400
Joe Lefebvre, rf	1	0	0	1	0	0	.000
Sixto Lezcano, ph-rf	2	0	0	0	0	1	.111
Gary Matthews, lf	3	2	3	4	1	0	.455
Bob Dernier, cf	0	0	0	0	0	0	—
Greg Gross, cf-lf	3	1	0	0	1	2	.000
Bo Diaz, c	3	0	0	1	0	2	.000
Ivan DeJesus, ss	4	0	1	1	0	0	.222
Charles Hudson, p	4	0	0	0	0	2	.000
TOTALS	31	7	9	6	4	7	.213

	1	2	3	4	5	6	7	8	9		R	H	E
Dodgers	0	0	0	0	0	0	0	0	0		2	4	0
Phillies	0	2	1	1	2	0	1	0	x		7	9	1

E—DeJesus. DP—Dodgers 1 (Baker to Fimple to Sax). LOB—Dodgers 5, Phillies 5. Scoring Position—Dodgers 0-for-2, Phillies 2-for-10. 2B—Baker (1), Schmidt (1). HR—Marshall (1), Matthews (2). SF—Lefebvre. SB—Sax (1), Matthews (1). CS—Rose (1).

Game 4

Saturday, October 8

Dodgers	AB	R	H	RBI	BB	K	Avg
Steve Sax, 2b	5	0	1	0	0	0	.250
Bill Russell, ss	4	0	1	0	1	2	.286
Pedro Guerrero, 3b	3	1	2	1	0	0	.250
Dusty Baker, lf	3	1	2	1	1	0	.357
Mike Marshall, 1b	4	0	1	0	0	2	.133
Steve Yeager, c	2	0	1	0	0	0	.167
Rick Monday, ph	0	0	0	0	0	0	—
Jose Morales, ph	1	0	0	0	0	1	.000
Jack Fimple, c	0	0	0	0	0	0	.143
Ken Landreaux, cf	4	0	0	0	0	2	.143
Derrel Thomas, rf	4	0	2	0	0	1	.444
Jerry Reuss, p	2	0	0	0	0	0	.000
Joe Beckwith, p	0	0	0	0	0	0	—
Rick Honeycutt, p	0	0	0	0	0	0	—
Rafael Landestoy, ph	1	0	0	0	0	1	.000
Pat Zachry, p	0	0	0	0	0	0	—
Candy Maldonado, ph	1	0	0	0	0	1	.000
TOTALS	34	2	10	1	3	12	.224

Phillies	AB	R	H	RBI	BB	K	Avg
Joe Morgan, 2b	4	0	0	0	1	0	.067
Pete Rose, 1b	5	1	2	0	0	0	.375
Mike Schmidt, 3b	5	3	3	1	0	1	.467
Sixto Lezcano, rf-lf	4	2	3	2	0	0	.308
Gary Matthews, lf	3	1	1	3	1	1	.429
Ron Reed, p	0	0	0	0	0	0	—
Von Hayes, rf	1	0	0	0	0	0	.000
Garry Maddox, cf	4	0	1	0	1	0	.273
Bo Diaz, c	4	0	2	0	0	0	.154
Ivan DeJesus, ss	3	0	1	0	1	0	.250
Steve Carlton, p	2	0	1	0	0	1	.200
Greg Gross, lf	1	0	0	0	0	0	.000
Al Holland, p	0	0	0	0	0	0	—
TOTALS	36	7	13	7	3	4	.273

	1	2	3	4	5	6	7	8	9		R	H	E
Dodgers	0	0	0	1	0	0	0	1	0		2	10	0
Phillies	3	0	0	0	2	2	0	0	x		7	13	1

E—Lezcano. LOB—Dodgers 9, Phillies 10. Scoring Position—Dodgers 0-for-12, Phillies 1-for-9. 2B—Guerrero (1), Marshall (1), Yeager (1), Thomas (1), Schmidt (2), Diaz (1). HR—Baker (1), Lezcano (1), Matthews (3). S—Lezcano, Carlton. CS—Sax (2), Marshall (1).

Dodgers	IP	H	R	ER	BB	K	ERA
Jerry Reuss (L, 0-2)	4.0	9	5	5	0	1	4.50
Joe Beckwith	0.2	0	0	0	2	0	0.00
Rick Honeycutt	1.1	2	2	2	0	2	21.60
Pat Zachry	2.0	2	0	0	1	1	2.25

Phillies	IP	H	R	ER	BB	K	ERA
Steve Carlton (W, 2-0)	6.0	6	1	1	3	7	0.66
Ron Reed	1.1	2	1	1	0	2	2.70
Al Holland	1.2	1	0	0	0	3	0.00

Reuss pitched to two batters in the 5th.

HBP—Yeager by Carlton. Time—2:50. Attendance—64,494. Umpires—HP, Weyer. 1B, Harvey. 2B, Crawford. 3B, Tata.

The Game 3 "Dodgers" pitching lines follow:

Dodgers	IP	H	R	ER	BB	K	ERA
Bob Welch (L, 0-1)	1.1	2	2	2	1	0	6.75
Alejandro Pena	2.2	4	2	2	1	3	6.75
Rick Honeycutt	0.1	2	2	2	0	0	54.00
Joe Beckwith	1.2	1	0	0	0	3	0.00
Pat Zachry	2.0	2	1	1	1	1	4.50

Phillies	IP	H	R	ER	BB	K	ERA
Charles Hudson (W, 1-0)	9.0	4	2	2	2	9	2.00

WP—Welch, Pena. PB—Fimple. Time—2:51. Attendance—53,490. Umpires—HP, McSherry. 1B, Weyer. 2B, Harvey. 3B, Crawford.

1983 NL Championship Series—Composite Statistics

Batting

Phillies	G	AB	R	H	RBI	2B	3B	HR	BB	SO	SB	CS	Avg	OBP	Slg
Steve Carlton	2	5	0	1	0	0	0	0	0	3	0	0	.200	.200	.200
Ivan DeJesus	4	12	0	3	1	0	0	0	3	3	0	0	.250	.400	.250
John Denny	1	1	0	0	0	0	0	0	0	0	0	0	.000	.000	.000
Bo Diaz	4	13	0	2	0	1	0	0	2	2	0	0	.154	.267	.231
Greg Gross	4	5	1	0	0	0	0	0	2	2	0	0	.000	.286	.000
Von Hayes	2	2	0	0	0	0	0	0	0	0	0	0	.000	.000	.000
Charles Hudson	1	4	0	0	0	0	0	0	0	2	0	0	.000	.000	.000
Joe Lefebvre	2	2	0	0	1	0	0	0	1	0	0	0	.000	.000	.000
Sixto Lezcano	4	13	2	4	2	0	0	1	1	1	0	0	.308	.357	.538
Garry Maddox	3	11	0	3	1	1	0	0	0	1	0	0	.273	.273	.364
Gary Matthews	4	14	4	6	8	0	0	3	2	1	1	0	.429	.500	1.071
Joe Morgan	4	15	1	1	0	0	0	0	2	1	0	0	.067	.176	.067
Tony Perez	1	1	0	1	0	0	0	0	0	0	0	0	1.000	1.000	1.000
Pete Rose	4	16	3	6	0	0	0	0	1	1	1	1	.375	.412	.375
Juan Samuel	1	0	0	0	0	0	0	0	0	0	0	0	—	—	—
Mike Schmidt	4	15	5	7	2	2	0	1	2	3	0	0	.467	.529	.800
Ozzie Virgil	1	1	0	0	0	0	0	0	0	1	0	0	.000	.000	.000
Totals	4	130	16	34	15	4	0	5	15	22	2	1	.262	.336	.408

Batting

Dodgers	G	AB	R	H	RBI	2B	3B	HR	BB	SO	SB	CS	Avg	OBP	Slg
Dusty Baker	4	14	4	5	1	1	0	1	2	0	0	0	.357	.438	.643
Greg Brock	3	9	1	0	0	0	0	0	0	3	0	0	.000	.000	.000
Jack Fimple	3	7	0	1	1	0	0	0	0	3	0	0	.143	.143	.143
Pedro Guerrero	4	12	1	3	2	1	1	0	3	3	0	0	.250	.438	.500
Rafael Landestoy	2	2	0	0	0	0	0	0	0	1	0	0	.000	.000	.000
Ken Landreaux	4	14	0	2	1	0	0	0	1	3	0	0	.143	.200	.143
Candy Maldonado	2	2	0	0	0	0	0	0	0	1	0	0	.000	.000	.000
Mike Marshall	4	15	1	2	2	1	0	1	1	6	0	1	.133	.188	.400
Rick Monday	1	0	0	0	0	0	0	0	0	0	0	0	—	—	—
Jose Morales	2	2	0	0	0	0	0	0	0	1	0	0	.000	.000	.000
Alejandro Pena	1	1	0	1	0	0	0	0	0	0	0	0	1.000	1.000	1.000
Jerry Reuss	2	3	0	0	0	0	0	0	0	3	0	0	.000	.000	.000
Bill Russell	4	14	1	4	0	0	0	0	2	4	1	0	.286	.375	.286
Steve Sax	4	16	0	4	0	0	0	0	1	0	1	2	.250	.294	.250
Derrel Thomas	4	9	0	4	0	1	0	0	0	3	1	0	.444	.444	.556
Fernando Valenzuela	1	3	0	0	0	0	0	0	1	0	0	0	.000	.250	.000
Steve Yeager	2	6	0	1	0	1	0	0	0	0	0	0	.167	.286	.333
Totals	4	129	8	27	7	5	1	2	11	31	3	3	.209	.282	.310

Pitching

Phillies	G	GS	CG	IP	H	R	ER	BB	SO	W-L	Sv-Op	Hld	ERA
Steve Carlton	2	2	0	13.2	13	1	1	5	13	2-0	0-0	0	0.66
John Denny	1	1	0	6.0	5	3	0	3	3	0-1	0-0	0	0.00
Al Holland	2	0	0	3.0	1	0	0	0	3	0-0	1-1	0	0.00
Charles Hudson	1	1	1	9.0	4	2	2	2	9	1-0	0-0	0	2.00
Ron Reed	2	0	0	3.1	4	2	1	1	3	0-0	0-0	0	2.70
Totals	4	4	1	35.0	27	8	4	11	31	3-1	1-1	0	1.03

Pitching

Dodgers	G	GS	CG	IP	H	R	ER	BB	SO	W-L	Sv-Op	Hld	ERA
Joe Beckwith	2	0	0	2.1	1	0	0	2	3	0-0	0-0	0	0.00
Rick Honeycutt	2	0	0	1.2	4	4	4	0	2	0-0	0-0	0	21.60
Tom Niedenfuer	2	0	0	2.0	0	0	0	1	3	0-0	1-1	0	0.00
Alejandro Pena	1	0	0	2.2	4	2	2	1	3	0-0	0-0	0	6.75
Jerry Reuss	2	2	0	12.0	14	6	6	3	4	0-2	0-0	0	4.50
Fernando Valenzuela	1	1	0	8.0	7	1	1	4	5	1-0	0-0	0	1.13
Bob Welch	1	1	0	1.1	0	2	1	2	0	0-1	0-0	0	6.75
Pat Zachry	2	0	0	4.0	4	1	1	2	2	0-0	0-0	0	2.25
Totals	4	4	0	34.0	34	16	15	15	22	1-3	1-1	0	3.97

Fielding

Phillies	Pos	G	PO	Ast	E	DP	PB	FPct
Steve Carlton	p	2	1	5	0	0	—	1.000
Ivan DeJesus	ss	4	4	12	2	0	—	.889
John Denny	p	1	0	0	0	0	—	—
Bob Dernier	cf	1	0	0	0	0	—	—
Bo Diaz	c	4	32	2	0	0	0	1.000
Greg Gross	lf	3	1	0	0	0	—	1.000
	cf	1	3	0	0	0	—	1.000
Von Hayes	rf	1	0	0	0	0	—	—
Al Holland	p	2	0	0	0	0	—	—
Charles Hudson	p	1	0	0	0	0	—	—
Joe Lefebvre	rf	1	2	0	0	0	—	1.000
Sixto Lezcano	rf	4	5	1	1	0	—	.857
	lf	1	0	0	0	0	—	—
Garry Maddox	cf	3	8	0	1	0	—	.889
Gary Matthews	lf	4	6	0	0	0	—	1.000
Joe Morgan	2b	4	8	7	0	0	—	1.000
Ron Reed	p	2	0	1	0	0	—	1.000
Pete Rose	1b	4	30	2	0	0	—	1.000
Mike Schmidt	3b	4	5	7	1	0	—	.923
Totals		4	105	37	5	0	0	.966

Fielding

Dodgers	Pos	G	PO	Ast	E	DP	PB	FPct
Dusty Baker	lf	4	9	0	0	1	—	1.000
Joe Beckwith	p	2	0	0	0	0	—	—
Greg Brock	1b	3	13	0	0	2	—	1.000
Jack Fimple	c	3	14	2	0	1	1	1.000
Pedro Guerrero	3b	4	1	9	0	0	—	1.000
Rick Honeycutt	p	2	1	0	0	0	—	1.000
Ken Landreaux	cf	4	12	0	0	0	—	1.000
Mike Marshall	1b	3	17	2	0	1	—	1.000
	rf	2	4	0	0	0	—	1.000
Tom Niedenfuer	p	2	0	1	0	0	—	1.000
Alejandro Pena	p	1	0	0	0	0	—	—
Jerry Reuss	p	2	0	1	0	0	—	1.000
Bill Russell	ss	4	4	10	1	3	—	.933
Steve Sax	2b	4	11	12	0	4	—	1.000
Derrel Thomas	rf	3	7	0	0	0	—	1.000
Fernando Valenzuela	p	1	1	0	0	0	—	1.000
Bob Welch	p	1	0	0	0	0	—	—
Steve Yeager	c	2	7	1	0	0	0	1.000
Pat Zachry	p	2	1	0	0	0	—	1.000
Totals		4	102	38	1	12	1	.993

1984 Detroit Tigers (AL) 3, Kansas City Royals (AL) 0

The Detroit Tigers, who won 20 more games than the Kansas City Royals during the regular season, proved their superiority with a convincing three-game sweep of the Royals in the ALCS. Jack Morris won the opener as Alan Trammell drove in three runs with a single, triple and homer. Detroit jumped out to a 3-0 lead in the second game, but the Royals battled back and eventually tied it in the bottom of the eighth on a pinch-hit RBI double by Hal McRae. The game went into extra innings before Johnny Grubb reached Dan Quisenberry for a two-run double in the top of the 11th. Aurelio Lopez tossed three scoreless innings of relief for the Tigers to pick up the win, 5-3. The third game was a nail-biter, but Milt Wilcox protected a 1-0 lead for six innings and Willie Hernandez worked a scoreless ninth to advance the Tigers to the World Series. The Tigers held the Royals to only four runs in three games.

Game 1
Tuesday, October 2

Tigers	AB	R	H	RBI	BB	K	Avg
Lou Whitaker, 2b	5	2	1	0	0	0	.200
Tom Brookens, 2b	0	0	0	0	0	0	—
Alan Trammell, ss	3	2	3	3	2	0	1.000
Doug Baker, ss	0	0	0	0	0	0	—
Kirk Gibson, rf	5	0	2	0	0	0	.400
Lance Parrish, c	4	1	1	2	0	1	.250
Larry Herndon, lf	3	1	1	1	0	1	.333
Ruppert Jones, ph-lf	1	0	0	0	0	0	.000
Rusty Kuntz, ph-lf	1	0	0	0	0	0	.000
Barbaro Garbey, dh	5	1	2	0	0	0	.400
Chet Lemon, cf	5	0	0	0	0	1	.000
Darrell Evans, 1b	4	0	2	1	0	0	.500
Dave Bergman, pr-1b	0	1	0	0	0	0	—
Marty Castillo, 3b	4	0	2	1	0	2	.500
TOTALS	40	8	14	8	2	5	.350

Royals	AB	R	H	RBI	BB	K	Avg
Willie Wilson, cf	4	0	1	0	0	0	.250
Pat Sheridan, rf	2	0	0	0	1	2	.000
Lynn Jones, ph-rf	1	0	0	0	0	0	.000
George Brett, 3b	4	0	0	0	0	1	.000
Jorge Orta, dh	4	1	1	0	0	1	.250
Darryl Motley, lf	4	0	0	1	0	1	.000
Steve Balboni, 1b	4	0	0	0	0	1	.000
Frank White, 2b	3	0	1	0	0	0	.333
Don Slaught, c	3	0	2	0	0	0	.667
Onix Concepcion, ss	3	0	0	0	0	0	.000
TOTALS	32	1	5	1	1	6	.156

	1	2	3	4	5	6	7	8	9		R	H	E
Tigers	2	0	0	1	1	0	1	2	1		8	14	0
Royals	0	0	0	0	0	0	1	0	0		1	5	1

E—Sheridan. DP—Royals 1 (Concepcion to White to Balboni). LOB—Tigers 8, Royals 5. Scoring Position—Tigers 2-for-9, Royals 0-for-3. 2B—Evans (1). 3B—Trammell (1), Orta (1). HR—Trammell (1), Parrish (1), Herndon (1). SF—Parrish. GDP—Lemon.

Tigers	IP	H	R	ER	BB	K	ERA
Jack Morris (W, 1-0)	7.0	5	1	1	1	4	1.29
Willie Hernandez	2.0	0	0	0	0	2	0.00

Royals	IP	H	R	ER	BB	K	ERA
Bud Black (L, 0-1)	5.0	7	4	4	1	3	7.20
Mark Huismann	2.2	6	3	2	1	2	6.75
Mike Jones	1.1	1	1	1	0	0	6.75

WP—Huismann. Time—2:42. Attendance—41,973. Umpires—HP, Deegan. 1B, Bible. 2B, Christal. 3B, Zirbel.

Game 2
Wednesday, October 3

Tigers	AB	R	H	RBI	BB	K	Avg
Lou Whitaker, 2b	5	1	1	0	0	2	.200
Alan Trammell, ss	5	0	1	0	0	1	.500
Kirk Gibson, rf	4	2	2	2	1	0	.444
Lance Parrish, c	5	0	2	1	0	1	.333
Darrell Evans, 3b-1b	4	1	0	0	0	0	.250
Ruppert Jones, lf	4	1	0	0	1	1	.000
John Grubb, dh	4	0	1	2	0	0	.250
Chet Lemon, cf	5	0	0	0	0	0	.000
Dave Bergman, 1b	1	0	1	0	0	1	1.000
Tom Brookens, 3b	2	0	0	0	0	1	.000
Barbaro Garbey, ph	1	0	0	0	0	0	.333
Marty Castillo, 3b	1	0	0	0	0	0	.400
TOTALS	41	5	8	5	2	6	.273

Royals	AB	R	H	RBI	BB	K	Avg
Willie Wilson, cf	5	0	1	0	1	1	.222
Pat Sheridan, rf	2	1	0	0	1	0	.000
Lynn Jones, ph-rf	3	1	1	0	0	0	.250
George Brett, 3b	5	0	2	0	0	1	.222
Greg Pryor, pr-3b	0	0	0	0	0	0	—
Jorge Orta, dh	3	0	0	1	0	0	.143
Hal McRae, ph	1	0	1	1	0	0	1.000
John Wathan, pr-dh	1	0	0	0	0	0	.000
Darryl Motley, lf	4	0	2	0	1	0	.250
Steve Balboni, 1b	5	0	1	0	0	2	.111
Frank White, 2b	5	1	0	0	0	1	.125
Don Slaught, c	5	0	1	0	0	0	.375
Onix Concepcion, ss	2	0	0	0	0	0	.000
Dane Iorg, ph	1	0	1	1	0	0	1.000
Buddy Biancalana, pr-ss	1	0	0	0	0	1	.000
U.L. Washington, ph	1	0	0	0	0	1	.000
TOTALS	44	3	10	3	3	7	.197

	1	2	3	4	5	6	7	8	9	10	11		R	H	E
Tigers	2	0	1	0	0	0	0	0	0	0	2		5	8	1
Royals	0	0	0	1	0	0	1	1	0	0	0		3	10	3

E—Brookens, Concepcion, Slaught, Saberhagen. LOB—Tigers 7, Royals 11. Scoring Position—Tigers 3-for-12, Royals 1-for-9. 2B—Gibson (1), Parrish (1), Grubb (1), McRae (1). HR—Gibson (1). S—Evans, Grubb. SB—Bergman (1). CS—Wilson (1).

Tigers	IP	H	R	ER	BB	K	ERA
Dan Petry	7.0	4	2	2	1	4	2.57
Willie Hernandez (BS, 1)	1.0	2	1	1	1	1	3.00
Aurelio Lopez (W, 1-0)	3.0	4	0	0	1	2	0.00

Royals	IP	H	R	ER	BB	K	ERA
Bret Saberhagen	8.0	6	3	2	1	5	2.25
Dan Quisenberry (L, 0-1)	3.0	2	2	1	1	1	3.00

Time—3:37. Attendance—42,019. Umpires—HP, Deegan. 1B, Bible. 2B, Christal. 3B, Jones.

Game 3
Friday, October 5

Royals	AB	R	H	RBI	BB	K	Avg
Willie Wilson, cf	4	0	0	0	0	1	.154
Pat Sheridan, rf	2	0	0	0	1	1	.000
Lynn Jones, ph	1	0	0	0	0	0	.200
George Brett, 3b	4	0	1	0	0	0	.231
Jorge Orta, dh	3	0	0	0	0	1	.100
Hal McRae, ph	1	0	1	0	0	0	1.000
U.L. Washington, pr	0	0	0	0	0	0	.000
Darryl Motley, lf	4	0	0	0	0	2	.167
Steve Balboni, 1b	2	0	0	0	1	1	.091
Frank White, 2b	3	0	0	0	0	2	.091
Don Slaught, c	3	0	1	0	0	0	.364
Onix Concepcion, ss	2	0	0	0	0	0	.000
Dane Iorg, ph	1	0	0	0	0	0	.500
Buddy Biancalana, ss	0	0	0	0	0	0	.000
TOTALS	30	0	3	0	2	8	.171

Tigers	AB	R	H	RBI	BB	K	Avg
Lou Whitaker, 2b	4	0	0	0	0	1	.143
Alan Trammell, ss	3	0	0	0	1	0	.364
Kirk Gibson, rf	3	0	1	0	1	1	.417
Lance Parrish, c	3	0	0	0	1	0	.250
Larry Herndon, lf	2	0	0	0	1	1	.200
Barbaro Garbey, dh	3	0	1	0	0	1	.333
Chet Lemon, cf	3	1	0	0	0	0	.000
Darrell Evans, 1b	2	0	1	0	1	0	.300
Marty Castillo, 3b	3	0	0	1	0	1	.250
TOTALS	26	1	3	1	4	6	.245

	1	2	3	4	5	6	7	8	9		R	H	E
Royals	0	0	0	0	0	0	0	0	0		0	3	3
Tigers	0	1	0	0	0	0	0	0	x		1	3	0

E—Balboni, Slaught 2. DP—Royals 1 (Brett to White to Balboni). LOB—Royals 5, Tigers 5. Scoring Position—Royals 0-for-0, Tigers 0-for-7. GDP—Garbey. SB—Gibson (1), Evans (1), Castillo (1).

Royals	IP	H	R	ER	BB	K	ERA
Charlie Leibrandt (L, 0-1)	8.0	3	1	1	4	6	1.13

Tigers	IP	H	R	ER	BB	K	ERA
Milt Wilcox (W, 1-0)	8.0	2	0	0	2	8	0.00
Willie Hernandez (S, 1)	1.0	1	0	0	0	0	2.25

Time—2:39. Attendance—52,168. Umpires—HP, Deegan. 1B, Bible. 2B, Christal. 3B, Cossey.

1984 AL Championship Series—Composite Statistics

Batting

Tigers	G	AB	R	H	RBI	2B	3B	HR	BB	SO	SB	CS	Avg	OBP	Slg
Dave Bergman	2	1	1	1	0	0	0	0	0	0	1	0	1.000	1.000	1.000
Tom Brookens	2	2	0	0	0	0	0	0	0	1	0	0	.000	.000	.000
Marty Castillo	3	8	0	2	2	0	0	0	0	3	1	0	.250	.250	.250
Darrell Evans	3	10	1	3	1	1	0	0	1	0	1	0	.300	.364	.400
Barbaro Garbey	3	9	1	3	0	0	0	0	0	1	0	0	.333	.333	.333
Kirk Gibson	3	12	2	5	2	1	0	1	2	1	1	0	.417	.500	.750
John Grubb	1	4	0	1	2	1	0	0	0	0	0	0	.250	.250	.500
Larry Herndon	2	5	1	1	1	0	0	1	1	2	0	0	.200	.333	.800
Ruppert Jones	2	5	1	0	0	0	0	0	1	1	0	0	.000	.167	.000
Rusty Kuntz	1	1	0	0	0	0	0	0	0	0	0	0	.000	.000	.000
Chet Lemon	3	13	1	0	0	0	0	0	0	1	0	0	.000	.000	.000
Lance Parrish	3	12	1	3	3	1	0	1	0	3	0	0	.250	.231	.583
Alan Trammell	3	11	2	4	3	0	1	1	3	1	0	0	.364	.500	.818
Lou Whitaker	3	14	3	2	0	0	0	0	0	3	0	0	.143	.143	.143
Totals	3	107	14	25	14	4	1	4	8	17	4	0	.234	.284	.402

Royals	G	AB	R	H	RBI	2B	3B	HR	BB	SO	SB	CS	Avg	OBP	Slg
Steve Balboni	3	11	0	1	0	0	0	0	0	1	4	0	0	.091	.167	.091
Buddy Biancalana	2	1	0	0	0	0	0	0	0	1	0	0	.000	.000	.000
George Brett	3	13	0	3	0	0	0	0	0	2	0	0	.231	.231	.231
Onix Concepcion	3	7	0	0	0	0	0	0	0	0	0	0	.000	.000	.000
Dane Iorg	2	2	0	1	1	0	0	0	0	0	0	0	.500	.500	.500
Lynn Jones	3	5	1	1	0	0	0	0	0	0	0	0	.200	.200	.200
Hal McRae	2	2	0	2	1	1	0	0	0	0	0	1	1.000	1.000	1.500
Darryl Motley	3	12	0	2	1	0	0	0	1	3	0	0	.167	.231	.167
Jorge Orta	3	10	1	1	1	0	1	0	0	2	0	0	.100	.100	.300
Pat Sheridan	3	6	1	0	0	0	0	0	0	3	3	0	.000	.333	.000
Don Slaught	3	11	0	4	0	0	0	0	0	0	0	0	.364	.364	.364
U.L. Washington	2	1	0	0	0	0	0	0	0	1	0	0	.000	.000	.000
John Wathan	1	1	0	0	0	0	0	0	0	0	0	0	.000	.000	.000
Frank White	3	11	1	1	0	0	0	0	0	3	0	0	.091	.091	.091
Willie Wilson	3	13	0	2	0	0	0	0	1	2	0	1	.154	.214	.154
Totals	3	106	4	18	4	1	1	0	6	21	0	1	.170	.214	.198

Pitching

Tigers	G	GS	CG	IP	H	R	ER	BB	SO	W-L	Sv-Op	Hld	ERA
Willie Hernandez	3	0	0	4.0	3	1	1	1	3	0-0	1-2	0	2.25
Aurelio Lopez	1	0	0	3.0	4	0	0	1	2	1-0	0-0	0	0.00
Jack Morris	1	1	0	7.0	5	1	1	1	4	1-0	0-0	0	1.29
Dan Petry	1	1	0	7.0	4	2	2	1	4	0-0	0-0	0	2.57
Milt Wilcox	1	1	0	8.0	2	0	0	2	8	1-0	0-0	0	0.00
Totals	3	3	0	29.0	18	4	4	6	21	3-0	1-2	0	1.24

Royals	G	GS	CG	IP	H	R	ER	BB	SO	W-L	Sv-Op	Hld	ERA
Bud Black	1	1	0	5.0	7	4	4	1	3	0-1	0-0	0	7.20
Mark Huismann	1	0	0	2.2	3	2	2	1	2	0-0	0-0	0	6.75
Mike Jones	1	0	0	1.1	1	1	1	0	0	0-0	0-0	0	6.75
Charlie Leibrandt	1	1	1	8.0	3	1	1	4	6	0-1	0-0	0	1.13
Dan Quisenberry	1	0	0	3.0	2	2	1	1	1	0-1	0-0	0	3.00
Bret Saberhagen	1	1	0	8.0	6	3	2	1	5	0-0	0-0	0	2.25
Totals	3	3	1	28.0	25	14	11	8	17	0-3	0-0	0	3.54

Fielding

Tigers	Pos	G	PO	Ast	E	DP	PB	FPct
Doug Baker	ss	1	0	0	0	0	—	—
Dave Bergman	1b	2	5	0	0	0	—	1.000
Tom Brookens	2b	1	0	0	0	0	—	—
	3b	1	0	2	1	0	—	.667
Marty Castillo	3b	3	3	4	0	0	—	1.000
Darrell Evans	1b	3	22	3	0	0	—	1.000
	3b	1	0	1	0	0	—	1.000
Kirk Gibson	rf	3	7	0	0	0	—	1.000
Willie Hernandez	p	3	0	0	0	0	—	—
Larry Herndon	lf	2	6	0	0	0	—	1.000
Ruppert Jones	lf	2	5	0	0	0	—	1.000
Rusty Kuntz	lf	1	0	0	0	0	—	—
Chet Lemon	cf	3	9	0	0	0	—	1.000
Aurelio Lopez	p	1	0	0	0	0	—	—
Jack Morris	p	1	1	1	0	0	—	1.000
Lance Parrish	c	3	21	2	0	0	0	1.000
Dan Petry	p	1	0	0	0	0	—	—
Alan Trammell	ss	3	1	8	0	0	—	1.000
Lou Whitaker	2b	3	5	6	0	0	—	1.000
Milt Wilcox	p	1	2	0	0	0	—	1.000
Totals		3	87	27	1	0	0	.991

Royals	Pos	G	PO	Ast	E	DP	PB	FPct
Steve Balboni	1b	3	20	3	1	2	—	.958
Buddy Biancalana	ss	2	1	2	0	0	—	1.000
Bud Black	p	1	1	1	0	0	—	1.000
George Brett	3b	3	2	7	0	1	—	1.000
Onix Concepcion	ss	3	0	6	1	1	—	.857
Mark Huismann	p	1	0	0	0	0	—	—
Lynn Jones	rf	2	2	0	0	0	—	1.000
Mike Jones	p	1	0	0	0	0	—	—
Charlie Leibrandt	p	1	1	2	0	0	—	1.000
Darryl Motley	lf	3	11	0	0	0	—	1.000
Greg Pryor	3b	1	1	0	0	0	—	1.000
Dan Quisenberry	p	1	1	1	0	0	—	1.000
Bret Saberhagen	p	1	1	1	1	0	—	.667
Pat Sheridan	rf	3	9	0	1	0	—	.900
Don Slaught	c	3	17	0	3	0	0	.850
Frank White	2b	3	7	3	0	2	—	1.000
Willie Wilson	cf	3	10	0	0	0	—	1.000
Totals		3	84	26	7	6	0	.940

1984 San Diego Padres (NL) 3, Chicago Cubs (NL) 2

The Cubs were only a game away from the World Series when reality struck. Chicago's crushing 13-0 victory over San Diego in the opener and solid 4-2 win in Game 2 put them on the brink of the NL pennant. Rick Sutcliffe tossed seven shutout innings and homered in the first game, while Steve Trout tossed 8.1 innings of five-hit ball in the second. The Padres got back on track with a 7-1 win in Game 3. Kevin McReynolds hit a three-run homer and Ed Whitson went eight innings for the win. Game 4 was the Steve Garvey show. The Padres' veteran first sacker doubled in a run in the third to give San Diego a 2-0 lead. When they fell behind 3-2, Garvey singled in a run in the fifth to tie it up. In the seventh, he drove in the go-ahead run, but the Cubs tied it back up as the game went into the bottom of the ninth. With one out and one on, Lee Smith grooved a fastball that Garvey launched into the right-center-field seats for a game-winning home run. In the fifth game, the Cubs took an early 3-0 lead before the Padres got two back in the bottom of the sixth. In the following inning, Cubs first baseman Leon Durham let Tim Flannery's roller skip under his glove, allowing the tying run to come around to score. After Alan Wiggins chipped a single, Tony Gwynn hit a hard smash at second baseman Ryne Sandberg. The ball took an odd hop and sailed over Sandberg's shoulder into right field for a two-run double, plating the eventual winning runs as the Padres completed their comeback with a 6-3 victory.

Game 1

Tuesday, October 2

Padres	AB	R	H	RBI	BB	K	Avg
Alan Wiggins, 2b	5	0	0	0	0	1	.000
Tony Gwynn, rf	4	0	0	0	0	0	.000
Steve Garvey, 1b	4	0	2	0	0	1	.500
Graig Nettles, 3b	4	0	1	0	0	1	.250
Terry Kennedy, c	3	0	0	0	1	1	.000
Kevin McReynolds, cf	2	0	0	0	2	1	.000
Carmelo Martinez, lf	3	0	1	0	1	1	.333
Garry Templeton, ss	3	0	2	0	1	0	.667
Eric Show, p	1	0	0	0	0	1	.000
Tim Flannery, ph	0	0	0	0	0	0	—
Greg Harris, p	0	0	0	0	0	0	—
Bobby Brown, ph	1	0	0	0	0	1	.000
Greg Booker, p	0	0	0	0	0	0	—
Champ Summers, ph	1	0	0	0	0	0	.000
TOTALS	31	0	6	0	5	8	.194

Cubs	AB	R	H	RBI	BB	K	Avg
Bob Dernier, cf	3	3	2	1	2	1	.667
Ryne Sandberg, 2b	4	2	1	1	1	1	.500
Gary Matthews, lf	4	2	2	4	0	1	.500
Henry Cotto, lf	1	0	1	0	0	0	1.000
Leon Durham, 1b	5	0	1	1	0	0	.200
Keith Moreland, rf	3	1	1	1	0	0	.333
Gary Woods, ph-rf	1	0	0	0	0	1	.000
Ron Cey, 3b	3	2	1	1	2	1	.333
Tom Veryzer, 3b	0	0	0	0	0	0	—
Jody Davis, c	4	1	2	1	0	0	.500
Steve Lake, c	1	0	1	0	0	0	1.000
Larry Bowa, ss	4	1	1	1	1	0	.250
Rick Sutcliffe, p	4	1	2	1	0	1	.500
Warren Brusstar, p	1	0	0	0	0	0	.000
TOTALS	38	13	16	12	6	6	.421

	1	2	3	4	5	6	7	8	9		R	H	E
Padres	0	0	0	0	0	0	0	0	0		0	6	1
Cubs	2	0	3	0	6	2	0	0	x		13	16	0

E—Templeton. DP—Padres 1 (Templeton to Garvey), Cubs 2 (Sandberg to Bowa to Durham; Sandberg to Bowa to Durham). LOB—Padres 10, Cubs 8. Scoring Position—Padres 0-for-7, Cubs 5-for-10. 2B—Dernier (1), Davis (1), Lake (1). HR—Dernier (1), Matthews 2 (2), Cey (1), Sutcliffe (1). SF—Moreland. GDP—Wiggins, Kennedy, Bowa.

Padres	IP	H	R	ER	BB	K	ERA
Eric Show (L, 0-1)	4.0	5	5	5	2	2	11.25
Greg Harris	2.0	9	8	7	3	2	31.50
Greg Booker	2.0	2	0	0	1	2	0.00

Cubs	IP	H	R	ER	BB	K	ERA
Rick Sutcliffe (W, 1-0)	7.0	2	0	0	5	8	0.00
Warren Brusstar	2.0	4	0	0	0	0	0.00

HBP—Flannery by Sutcliffe. Time—2:49. Attendance—36,282. Umpires—HP, Cavanaugh. 1B, Schlickenmeyer. 2B, Pomponi. 3B, Maher.

Game 2

Wednesday, October 3

Padres	AB	R	H	RBI	BB	K	Avg
Alan Wiggins, 2b	3	1	1	0	1	0	.125
Tony Gwynn, rf	4	1	1	0	0	1	.125
Steve Garvey, 1b	4	0	1	1	0	0	.375
Kevin McReynolds, cf	2	0	0	1	1	0	.000
Carmelo Martinez, lf	4	0	1	0	0	1	.286
Terry Kennedy, c	4	0	0	0	0	0	.000
Luis Salazar, 3b	3	0	0	0	0	1	.000
Garry Templeton, ss	2	0	0	0	1	0	.400
Mark Thurmond, p	1	0	1	0	0	0	1.000
Andy Hawkins, p	0	0	0	0	0	0	—
Mario Ramirez, ph	1	0	0	0	0	0	.000
Dave Dravecky, p	0	0	0	0	0	0	—
Kurt Bevacqua, ph	1	0	0	0	0	0	.000
Craig Lefferts, p	0	0	0	0	0	0	—
TOTALS	29	2	5	2	3	3	.189

Cubs	AB	R	H	RBI	BB	K	Avg
Bob Dernier, cf	3	2	1	0	1	1	.500
Ryne Sandberg, 2b	4	0	2	1	0	0	.500
Gary Matthews, lf	3	0	0	1	1	0	.286
Henry Cotto, lf	0	0	0	0	0	0	1.000
Keith Moreland, rf	4	1	2	0	0	0	.429
Lee Smith, p	0	0	0	0	0	0	—
Ron Cey, 3b	3	1	1	1	1	0	.333
Jody Davis, c	3	0	0	1	0	1	.286
Leon Durham, 1b	4	0	0	0	0	0	.111
Larry Bowa, ss	3	0	1	0	0	0	.286
Steve Trout, p	2	0	1	0	0	0	.500
Davey Lopes, rf	0	0	0	0	0	0	—
TOTALS	29	4	8	4	3	2	.350

	1	2	3	4	5	6	7	8	9		R	H	E
Padres	0	0	0	1	0	1	0	0	0		2	5	0
Cubs	1	0	2	1	0	0	0	0	x		4	8	1

E—Trout. DP—Cubs 2 (Bowa to Sandberg to Durham; Sandberg to Bowa to Durham). LOB—Padres 4, Cubs 6. Scoring Position—Padres 1-for-3, Cubs 1-for-5. 2B—Gwynn (1), Sandberg (1), Moreland (1), Cey (1). S—Trout. SF—McReynolds, Davis. GDP—Wiggins, Bevacqua. SB—Dernier (1). CS—Sandberg (1).

Padres	IP	H	R	ER	BB	K	ERA
Mark Thurmond (L, 0-1)	3.2	7	4	4	2	1	9.82
Andy Hawkins	1.1	0	0	0	1	0	0.00
Dave Dravecky	2.0	1	0	0	0	1	0.00
Craig Lefferts	1.0	0	0	0	0	0	0.00

Cubs	IP	H	R	ER	BB	K	ERA
Steve Trout (W, 1-0)	8.1	5	2	2	3	2	2.16
Lee Smith (S, 1)	0.2	0	0	0	0	1	0.00

Time—2:18. Attendance—36,282. Umpires—HP, Schlickenmeyer. 1B, Pomponi. 2B, Maher. 3B, Cavanaugh.

Game 3

Thursday, October 4

Cubs	AB	R	H	RBI	BB	K	Avg
Bob Dernier, cf	3	0	0	0	1	0	.333
Ryne Sandberg, 2b	4	0	1	0	0	1	.417
Gary Matthews, lf	3	0	1	0	1	1	.300
Leon Durham, 1b	4	0	0	0	0	1	.077
Keith Moreland, rf	4	1	1	0	0	1	.364
Ron Cey, 3b	4	0	1	1	0	1	.300
Jody Davis, c	3	0	1	0	0	1	.300
Larry Bowa, ss	3	0	0	0	0	0	.200
Dennis Eckersley, p	2	0	0	0	0	1	.000
George Frazier, p	0	0	0	0	0	0	—
Thad Bosley, ph	1	0	0	0	0	1	.000
Tim Stoddard, p	0	0	0	0	0	0	—
TOTALS	31	1	5	1	2	8	.273

Padres	AB	R	H	RBI	BB	K	Avg
Alan Wiggins, 2b	4	0	2	1	0	0	.250
Tony Gwynn, rf	4	1	3	0	0	0	.333
Steve Garvey, 1b	4	0	0	0	0	0	.250
Graig Nettles, 3b	4	1	1	1	0	0	.250
Terry Kennedy, c	4	2	2	0	0	1	.182
Kevin McReynolds, cf	3	2	2	3	0	0	.286
Carmelo Martinez, lf	3	0	0	0	0	0	.200
Garry Templeton, ss	3	1	1	2	0	0	.375
Ed Whitson, p	3	0	0	0	0	1	.000
Goose Gossage, p	0	0	0	0	0	0	—
TOTALS	32	7	11	7	0	3	.253

	1	2	3	4	5	6	7	8	9		R	H	E
Cubs	0	1	0	0	0	0	0	0	0		1	5	0
Padres	0	0	0	0	3	4	0	0	x		7	11	0

DP—Cubs 1 (Bowa to Sandberg to Durham), Padres 1 (Wiggins to Templeton to Garvey). LOB—Cubs 5, Padres 1. Scoring Position—Cubs 1-for-7, Padres 4-for-8. 2B—Moreland (2), Gwynn (2), Templeton (1). HR—McReynolds (1). GDP—Durham, Garvey. SB—Sandberg (1). CS—Wiggins (1).

Cubs	IP	H	R	ER	BB	K	ERA
Dennis Eckersley (L, 0-1)	5.1	9	5	5	0	0	8.44
George Frazier	1.2	2	2	2	0	1	10.80
Tim Stoddard	1.0	0	0	0	0	2	0.00

Padres	IP	H	R	ER	BB	K	ERA
Ed Whitson (W, 1-0)	8.0	5	1	1	2	6	1.13
Goose Gossage	1.0	0	0	0	0	2	0.00

Time—2:19. Attendance—58,346. Umpires—HP, Bovey. 1B, Campagna. 2B, Fisher. 3B, Stewart.

Game 4

Saturday, October 6

Cubs	AB	R	H	RBI	BB	K	Avg
Bob Dernier, cf	4	0	1	0	1	2	.308
Ryne Sandberg, 2b	3	1	1	0	2	0	.400
Gary Matthews, lf	3	1	0	0	2	1	.231
Keith Moreland, rf	4	0	1	1	0	0	.333
Henry Cotto, pr-rf	0	1	0	0	0	0	1.000
Ron Cey, 3b	5	0	0	0	0	0	.200
Jody Davis, c	4	1	3	3	0	1	.429
Leon Durham, 1b	3	1	1	1	1	1	.125
Larry Bowa, ss	3	0	1	0	0	0	.231
Richie Hebner, ph	1	0	0	0	0	0	.000
Lee Smith, p	0	0	0	0	0	0	—
Scott Sanderson, p	2	0	0	0	0	1	.000
Warren Brusstar, p	0	0	0	0	0	0	.000
Davey Lopes, ph	1	0	0	0	0	0	.000
Tim Stoddard, p	0	0	0	0	0	0	—
Tom Veryzer, ss	1	0	0	0	0	0	.000
TOTALS	34	5	8	5	6	6	.273

Padres	AB	R	H	RBI	BB	K	Avg
Alan Wiggins, 2b	4	1	1	0	0	1	.250
Tony Gwynn, rf	3	2	1	1	1	0	.333
Steve Garvey, 1b	5	1	4	5	0	0	.412
Graig Nettles, 3b	3	0	0	0	1	0	.182
Terry Kennedy, c	4	0	1	0	0	0	.200
Kevin McReynolds, cf	3	0	1	0	0	0	.300
Luis Salazar, ph-cf	1	0	0	0	0	0	.000
Carmelo Martinez, lf	4	0	1	0	0	1	.214
Garry Templeton, ss	4	1	1	0	0	0	.333
Tim Lollar, p	1	0	0	0	0	1	.000
Andy Hawkins, p	0	0	0	0	0	0	—
Tim Flannery, ph	1	1	1	0	0	0	1.000
Dave Dravecky, p	0	0	0	0	0	0	—
Bobby Brown, ph	0	1	0	0	1	0	.000
Goose Gossage, p	0	0	0	0	0	0	—
Champ Summers, ph	1	0	0	0	0	1	.000
Craig Lefferts, p	0	0	0	0	0	0	—
TOTALS	34	7	11	6	3	4	.269

	1	2	3	4	5	6	7	8	9		R	H	E
Cubs	0	0	0	3	0	0	0	2	0		5	8	1
Padres	0	0	2	0	1	0	2	0	2		7	11	0

E—Sandberg. DP—Cubs 1 (Bowa to Sandberg to Durham), Padres 1 (Hawkins to Templeton to Garvey). LOB—Cubs 9, Padres 7. Scoring Position—Cubs 1-for-9, Padres 3-for-8. 2B—Dernier (2), Davis (2), Bowa (1), Garvey (1). HR—Davis (1), Durham (1), Garvey (1). S—Wiggins. SF—Gwynn. GDP—Matthews, Martinez. SB—Dernier (2), Sandberg (2), Templeton (1), Brown (1).

Cubs	IP	H	R	ER	BB	K	ERA
Scott Sanderson	4.2	6	3	3	1	2	5.79
Warren Brusstar	1.1	1	0	0	0	0	0.00
Tim Stoddard	1.0	1	2	1	2	0	4.50
Lee Smith (L, 0-1)	1.1	3	2	2	0	2	9.00

Padres	IP	H	R	ER	BB	K	ERA
Tim Lollar	4.1	3	3	3	4	3	6.23
Andy Hawkins	0.2	0	0	0	0	0	0.00
Dave Dravecky	2.0	1	0	0	0	2	0.00
Goose Gossage (BS, 1)	1.0	3	2	2	1	1	9.00
Craig Lefferts (W, 1-0)	1.0	1	0	0	1	0	0.00

PB—Davis. HBP—Cotto by Lefferts. Time—3:13. Attendance—58,354. Umpires—HP, Bovey. 1B, Campagna. 2B, Fisher. 3B, Stewart.

Game 5

Sunday, October 7

Cubs	AB	R	H	RBI	BB	K	Avg
Bob Dernier, cf	4	0	0	0	0	0	.235
Ryne Sandberg, 2b	4	0	1	0	0	0	.368
Gary Matthews, lf	2	1	0	0	2	1	.200
Leon Durham, 1b	4	1	1	2	0	2	.150
Keith Moreland, rf	3	0	1	0	1	0	.333
Ron Cey, 3b	4	0	0	0	0	1	.158
Jody Davis, c	4	1	1	1	0	0	.389
Larry Bowa, ss	2	0	0	0	0	0	.200
Thad Bosley, ph	1	0	0	0	0	1	.000
Tom Veryzer, ss	0	0	0	0	0	0	.000
Rick Sutcliffe, p	2	0	1	0	0	1	.500
Steve Trout, p	0	0	0	0	0	0	.500
Richie Hebner, ph	0	0	0	0	1	0	.000
Warren Brusstar, p	0	0	0	0	0	0	.000
TOTALS	30	3	5	3	3	6	.260

Padres	AB	R	H	RBI	BB	K	Avg
Alan Wiggins, 2b	3	2	2	0	1	0	.316
Tony Gwynn, rf	4	2	2	2	0	1	.368
Steve Garvey, 1b	3	0	1	1	1	0	.400
Graig Nettles, 3b	3	0	0	1	0	0	.143
Terry Kennedy, c	3	0	1	1	0	1	.222
Bobby Brown, cf	3	0	0	0	0	1	.000
Luis Salazar, cf	1	0	1	0	0	0	.200
Carmelo Martinez, lf	3	1	0	0	1	1	.176
Garry Templeton, ss	3	0	1	0	0	0	.333
Eric Show, p	0	0	0	0	0	0	.000
Andy Hawkins, p	0	0	0	0	0	0	—
Mario Ramirez, ph	1	0	0	0	0	0	.000
Dave Dravecky, p	0	0	0	0	0	0	—
Kurt Bevacqua, ph	1	0	0	0	0	0	.000
Craig Lefferts, p	0	0	0	0	0	0	—
Tim Flannery, ph	1	1	0	0	0	0	.500
Goose Gossage, p	0	0	0	0	0	0	—
TOTALS	29	6	8	5	3	4	.268

	1	2	3	4	5	6	7	8	9		R	H	E
Cubs	2	1	0	0	0	0	0	0	0		3	5	1
Padres	0	0	0	0	2	4	0	x			6	8	0

E—Durham. DP—Padres 2 (Wiggins to Templeton to Kennedy; Kennedy to Templeton to Garvey to Wiggins). LOB—Cubs 4, Padres 5. Scoring Position—Cubs 1-for-2, Padres 2-for-3. 2B—Gwynn (3). 3B—Salazar (1). HR—Durham (2), Davis (2). S—Templeton. SF—Nettles, Kennedy. SB—Sandberg (3), Matthews (1). CS—Dernier (1), Matthews (1), Salazar (1).

Cubs	IP	H	R	ER	BB	K	ERA
Rick Sutcliffe (L, 1-1)	6.1	7	6	5	3	2	3.38
Steve Trout	0.2	0	0	0	0	1	2.00
Warren Brusstar	1.0	1	0	0	0	1	0.00

Padres	IP	H	R	ER	BB	K	ERA
Eric Show	1.1	3	3	3	2	0	13.50
Andy Hawkins	1.2	0	0	0	1	1	0.00
Dave Dravecky	2.0	0	0	0	0	2	0.00
Craig Lefferts (W, 2-0)	2.0	0	0	0	0	1	0.00
Goose Gossage (S, 1)	2.0	2	0	0	0	2	4.50

HBP—Hebner by Gossage. Time—2:41. Attendance—58,359. Umpires—HP, Kibler. 1B, Runge. 2B, McSherry. 3B, Harvey.

1984 NL Championship Series—Composite Statistics

Batting

Padres	G	AB	R	H	RBI	2B	3B	HR	BB	SO	SB	CS	Avg	OBP	Slg
Kurt Bevacqua	2	2	0	0	0	0	0	0	0	0	0	0	.000	.000	.000
Bobby Brown	3	4	1	0	0	0	0	0	1	2	1	0	.000	.200	.000
Tim Flannery	3	2	2	1	0	0	0	0	0	0	0	0	.500	.667	.500
Steve Garvey	5	20	1	8	7	1	0	1	1	2	0	0	.400	.429	.600
Tony Gwynn	5	19	6	7	3	3	0	0	1	2	0	0	.368	.381	.526
Terry Kennedy	5	18	2	4	1	0	0	0	1	3	0	0	.222	.250	.222
Tim Lollar	1	1	0	0	0	0	0	0	0	0	1	0	.000	.000	.000
Carmelo Martinez	5	17	1	3	0	0	0	0	2	4	0	0	.176	.263	.176
Kevin McReynolds	4	10	2	3	4	0	0	1	3	1	0	0	.300	.429	.600
Graig Nettles	4	14	1	2	2	0	0	0	1	1	0	0	.143	.188	.143
Mario Ramirez	2	2	0	0	0	0	0	0	0	0	0	0	.000	.000	.000
Luis Salazar	3	5	0	1	0	0	1	0	0	1	0	1	.200	.200	.600
Eric Show	2	1	0	0	0	0	0	0	0	0	0	0	.000	.000	.000
Champ Summers	2	2	0	0	0	0	0	0	0	1	0	0	.000	.000	.000
Garry Templeton	5	15	2	5	2	1	0	0	2	0	1	0	.333	.412	.400
Mark Thurmond	1	1	0	1	0	0	0	0	0	0	0	0	1.000	1.000	1.000
Ed Whitson	1	3	0	0	0	0	0	0	0	1	0	0	.000	.000	.000
Alan Wiggins	5	19	4	6	1	0	0	0	2	2	0	1	.316	.381	.316
Totals	5	155	22	41	20	5	1	2	14	22	2	2	.265	.322	.348

Cubs	G	AB	R	H	RBI	2B	3B	HR	BB	SO	SB	CS	Avg	OBP	Slg
Thad Bosley	2	2	0	0	0	0	0	0	0	2	0	0	.000	.000	.000
Larry Bowa	5	15	1	3	1	1	0	0	1	0	0	0	.200	.250	.267
Warren Brusstar	3	1	0	0	0	0	0	0	0	0	0	0	.000	.000	.000
Ron Cey	5	19	3	3	3	1	0	1	3	3	0	0	.158	.273	.368
Henry Cotto	3	1	1	1	0	0	0	0	0	0	0	0	1.000	1.000	1.000
Jody Davis	5	18	3	7	6	2	0	2	0	3	0	0	.389	.368	.833
Bob Dernier	5	17	5	4	1	2	0	1	5	4	2	1	.235	.409	.529
Leon Durham	5	20	3	4	4	0	0	2	1	4	0	0	.150	.190	.450
Dennis Eckersley	1	2	0	0	0	0	0	0	0	1	0	0	.000	.000	.000
Richie Hebner	2	1	0	0	0	0	0	0	0	0	0	0	.000	.500	.000
Steve Lake	1	1	0	1	0	1	0	0	0	0	0	0	1.000	1.000	2.000
Davey Lopes	2	1	0	0	0	0	0	0	0	0	0	0	.000	.000	.000
Gary Matthews	5	15	4	3	5	0	0	2	6	4	1	1	.200	.429	.600
Keith Moreland	5	18	3	6	2	2	0	0	1	1	0	0	.333	.350	.444
Ryne Sandberg	5	19	3	7	2	2	0	0	3	2	3	1	.368	.455	.474
Scott Sanderson	1	2	0	0	0	0	0	0	0	1	0	0	.000	.000	.000
Rick Sutcliffe	2	6	1	3	1	0	0	1	0	2	0	0	.500	.500	1.000
Steve Trout	2	2	0	1	0	0	0	0	0	0	0	0	.500	.500	.500
Tom Veryzer	3	1	0	0	0	0	0	0	0	0	0	0	.000	.000	.000
Gary Woods	1	1	0	0	0	0	0	0	0	1	0	0	.000	.000	.000
Totals	5	162	26	42	25	11	0	9	20	28	6	3	.259	.344	.494

Pitching

Padres	G	GS	CG	IP	H	R	ER	BB	SO	W-L	Sv-Op	Hld	ERA
Greg Booker	1	0	0	2.0	2	0	0	1	2	0-0	0-0	0	0.00
Dave Dravecky	3	0	0	6.0	2	0	0	0	5	0-0	0-0	0	0.00
Goose Gossage	3	0	0	4.0	5	2	2	1	5	0-0	1-2	0	4.50
Greg Harris	1	0	0	2.0	9	8	7	3	2	0-0	0-0	0	31.50
Andy Hawkins	3	0	0	3.2	0	0	0	2	1	0-0	0-0	0	0.00
Craig Lefferts	3	0	0	4.0	1	0	0	1	1	2-0	0-0	0	0.00
Tim Lollar	1	1	0	4.1	3	3	3	4	3	0-0	0-0	0	6.23
Eric Show	2	2	0	5.1	8	8	8	4	2	0-1	0-0	0	13.50
Mark Thurmond	1	1	0	3.2	7	4	4	2	1	0-1	0-0	0	9.82
Ed Whitson	1	1	0	8.0	5	1	1	2	6	1-0	0-0	0	1.13
Totals	5	5	0	43.0	42	26	25	20	28	3-2	1-2	0	5.23

Cubs	G	GS	CG	IP	H	R	ER	BB	SO	W-L	Sv-Op	Hld	ERA
Warren Brusstar	3	0	0	4.1	6	0	0	0	1	0-0	0-0	0	0.00
Dennis Eckersley	1	1	0	5.1	9	5	5	0	0	0-1	0-0	0	8.44
George Frazier	1	0	0	1.2	2	2	2	0	1	0-0	0-0	0	10.80
Scott Sanderson	1	1	0	4.2	6	3	3	1	2	0-0	0-0	0	5.79
Lee Smith	2	0	0	2.0	3	2	2	0	3	0-1	1-1	0	9.00
Tim Stoddard	2	0	0	2.0	1	2	1	2	2	0-0	0-0	0	4.50
Rick Sutcliffe	2	2	0	13.1	9	6	5	8	10	1-1	0-0	0	3.38
Steve Trout	2	1	0	9.0	5	2	2	3	3	1-0	0-0	0	2.00
Totals	5	5	0	42.1	41	22	20	14	22	2-3	1-1	0	4.25

Fielding

Padres	Pos	G	PO	Ast	E	DP	PB	FPct
Greg Booker	p	1	0	0	0	0	—	—
Bobby Brown	cf	1	3	0	0	0	—	1.000
Dave Dravecky	p	3	1	1	0	0	—	1.000
Steve Garvey	1b	5	35	3	0	4	—	1.000
Goose Gossage	p	3	0	0	0	0	—	—
Tony Gwynn	rf	5	9	0	0	0	—	1.000
Greg Harris	p	1	0	0	0	0	—	—
Andy Hawkins	p	3	0	1	0	1	—	1.000
Terry Kennedy	c	5	29	3	0	2	0	1.000
Craig Lefferts	p	3	0	0	0	0	—	—
Tim Lollar	p	1	0	0	0	0	—	—
Carmelo Martinez	lf	5	6	0	0	0	—	1.000
Kevin McReynolds	cf	4	10	0	0	0	—	1.000
Graig Nettles	3b	4	5	8	0	0	—	1.000
Luis Salazar	cf	2	0	0	0	0	—	—
	3b	1	1	3	0	0	—	1.000
Eric Show	p	2	0	0	0	0	—	—
Garry Templeton	ss	5	18	12	1	5	—	.968
Mark Thurmond	p	1	0	1	0	0	—	1.000
Ed Whitson	p	1	1	0	0	0	—	1.000
Alan Wiggins	2b	5	11	11	0	3	—	1.000
Totals		5	129	43	1	15	0	.994

Cubs	Pos	G	PO	Ast	E	DP	PB	FPct
Larry Bowa	ss	5	8	14	0	6	—	1.000
Warren Brusstar	p	3	0	1	0	0	—	1.000
Ron Cey	3b	5	1	6	0	0	—	1.000
Henry Cotto	lf	2	2	0	0	0	—	1.000
	rf	1	0	0	0	0	—	—
Jody Davis	c	5	24	1	0	0	1	1.000
Bob Dernier	cf	5	12	1	0	0	—	1.000
Leon Durham	1b	5	45	3	1	6	—	.980
Dennis Eckersley	p	1	0	0	0	0	—	—
George Frazier	p	1	0	0	0	0	—	—
Steve Lake	c	1	0	0	0	0	0	—
Davey Lopes	rf	1	0	0	0	0	—	—
Gary Matthews	lf	5	11	0	0	0	—	1.000
Keith Moreland	rf	5	9	0	0	0	—	1.000
Ryne Sandberg	2b	5	13	18	1	6	—	.969
Scott Sanderson	p	1	0	1	0	0	—	1.000
Lee Smith	p	2	0	0	0	0	—	—
Tim Stoddard	p	2	1	1	0	0	—	1.000
Rick Sutcliffe	p	2	0	0	0	0	—	—
Steve Trout	p	2	0	1	1	0	—	.500
Tom Veryzer	ss	2	0	0	0	0	—	—
	3b	1	0	0	0	0	—	—
Gary Woods	rf	1	1	0	0	0	—	1.000
Totals		5	127	47	3	18	1	.983

1985 Kansas City Royals (AL) 4, Toronto Blue Jays (AL) 3

The Championship Series was expanded to a seven-game format in 1985, and the Kansas City Royals must have been glad of that. After losing three of the first four games to the Toronto Blue Jays, they would have been eliminated under the old system. But they took full advantage of the expanded playoff series, winning the last three games to take the AL title in seven games. Dave Stieb won the first game for Toronto, 6-1, and Al Oliver's 10th-inning RBI single beat Dan Quisenberry in Game 2, 6-5. The Royals won Game 3, 6-5, thanks to George Brett's 4-for-4, two-homer performance, but Oliver logged another game-winning hit in Game 4 for a 3-1 win and a three-games-to-one Toronto lead. Then the Royals mounted their comeback. Danny Jackson blanked the Jays 2-0 in Game 5, and in Game 6, George Brett's home run led the Royals to a 5-3 victory. Jim Sundberg was the hero of Game 7, breaking the game open with a bases-loaded triple off the top of the right field wall in the top of the sixth. The Royals won 6-2 to advance to the World Series.

Game 1

Tuesday, October 8

Royals	AB	R	H	RBI	BB	K	Avg
Lonnie Smith, lf	4	0	0	0	0	0	.000
Willie Wilson, cf	4	1	1	0	0	1	.250
George Brett, 3b	4	0	3	0	0	1	.750
Jorge Orta, dh	4	0	0	0	0	1	.000
Pat Sheridan, rf	3	0	0	1	1	1	.000
Frank White, 2b	4	0	0	0	0	1	.000
Steve Balboni, 1b	3	0	0	0	0	1	.000
Jim Sundberg, c	3	0	0	0	0	1	.000
Buddy Biancalana, ss	2	0	0	0	0	1	.000
Dane Iorg, ph	1	0	1	0	0	0	1.000
Onix Concepcion, ss	0	0	0	0	0	0	—
TOTALS	32	1	5	1	1	8	.156

Blue Jays	AB	R	H	RBI	BB	K	Avg
Damaso Garcia, 2b	5	0	2	0	0	0	.400
Manuel Lee, pr-2b	0	0	0	0	0	0	—
Lloyd Moseby, cf	5	0	0	0	0	1	.000
George Bell, lf	5	1	2	0	0	0	.400
Cliff Johnson, dh	4	1	1	0	0	1	.250
Jesse Barfield, rf	2	1	1	0	2	0	.500
Willie Upshaw, 1b	3	2	1	0	0	1	.333
Garth Iorg, 3b	1	1	0	0	0	0	.000
Rance Mulliniks, ph-3b	3	0	1	1	0	0	.333
Ernie Whitt, c	3	0	1	2	1	0	.333
Tony Fernandez, ss	3	0	2	2	0	0	.667
TOTALS	34	6	11	5	3	3	.324

	1	2	3	4	5	6	7	8	9		R	H	E
Royals	0	0	0	0	0	0	0	0	1		1	5	1
Blue Jays	0	2	3	1	0	0	0	0	x		6	11	0

E—Balboni. LOB—Royals 5, Blue Jays 9. Scoring Position—Royals 0-for-5, Blue Jays 5-for-15. 2B—Brett (1), Bell (1), Johnson (1), DIorg (1). SF—Fernandez. SB—Barfield (1).

Royals	IP	H	R	ER	BB	K	ERA
Charlie Leibrandt (L, 0-1)	2.0	7	5	5	1	0	22.50
Steve Farr	2.0	2	1	1	1	0	4.50
Mark Gubicza	3.0	0	0	0	1	2	0.00
Danny Jackson	1.0	2	0	0	0	1	0.00

Blue Jays	IP	H	R	ER	BB	K	ERA
Dave Stieb (W, 1-0)	8.0	3	0	0	1	8	0.00
Tom Henke	1.0	2	1	1	0	0	9.00

Leibrandt pitched to three batters in the 3rd.

HBP—Upshaw by Leibrandt. Time—2:24. Attendance—39,115. Umpires—HP, Phillips. 1B, Ford. 2B, Evans. 3B, Hendry.

Game 2

Wednesday, October 9

Royals	AB	R	H	RBI	BB	K	Avg
Lonnie Smith, lf	5	0	0	0	0	2	.000
Willie Wilson, cf	5	2	3	2	0	0	.444
George Brett, 3b	4	0	0	0	1	1	.375
Hal McRae, dh	5	0	2	0	0	1	.400
Frank White, 2b	4	0	2	1	1	0	.250
Steve Balboni, 1b	5	0	0	0	0	2	.000
Darryl Motley, rf	2	1	0	0	1	2	.000
Pat Sheridan, ph-rf	1	1	1	1	0	0	.250
Jim Sundberg, c	4	0	1	1	0	1	.143
Buddy Biancalana, ss	2	1	1	0	0	0	.200
Dane Iorg, ph	0	0	0	0	1	0	1.000
Onix Concepcion, pr-ss	0	0	0	0	0	0	—
TOTALS	37	5	10	5	4	9	.231

Blue Jays	AB	R	H	RBI	BB	K	Avg
Damaso Garcia, 2b	5	0	0	0	0	2	.200
Lloyd Moseby, cf	5	2	2	1	0	0	.200
George Bell, lf	3	2	0	1	0	1	.250
Cliff Johnson, dh	3	0	2	1	0	0	.429
Lou Thornton, pr	0	1	0	0	0	0	—
Al Oliver, dh	2	0	1	1	0	0	.500
Jesse Barfield, rf	4	0	1	2	0	1	.333
Willie Upshaw, 1b	4	0	1	0	0	0	.286
Garth Iorg, 3b	3	0	1	0	0	1	.250
Rance Mulliniks, ph-3b	1	0	0	0	0	0	.500
Ernie Whitt, c	4	0	0	0	0	1	.143
Tony Fernandez, ss	3	1	1	0	1	1	.375
TOTALS	37	6	10	6	1	7	.296

	1	2	3	4	5	6	7	8	9	10		R	H	E
Royals	0	0	2	1	0	0	0	0	1	1		5	10	3
Blue Jays	0	0	0	1	0	2	0	1	0	2		6	10	0

E—Brett, Sundberg, Balboni. DP—Royals 1 (Black to Balboni), Blue Jays 1 (Whitt to Fernandez). LOB—Royals 7, Blue Jays 5. Scoring Position—Royals 2-for-8, Blue Jays 4-for-5. 2B—Sundberg (1), Johnson (2). HR—Wilson (1), Sheridan (1). S—Biancalana. SB—Wilson (1), Moseby (1). CS—Brett (1), Concepcion (1).

Royals	IP	H	R	ER	BB	K	ERA
Bud Black	7.0	5	3	2	1	5	2.57
Dan Quisenberry (L, 0-1)	2.2	5	3	1	0	2	3.38

Blue Jays	IP	H	R	ER	BB	K	ERA
Jimmy Key	3.1	7	3	3	1	2	6.14
Dennis Lamp	3.2	0	0	0	0	3	0.00
Gary Lavelle	0.0	0	0	0	1	0	—
Tom Henke (W, 1-0)	3.0	3	2	2	4	4	6.75

Lavelle pitched to one batter in the 8th.

WP—Black. HBP—Bell by Black. Time—3:39. Attendance—34,029. Umpires—HP, Ford. 1B, Evans. 2B, Voltaggio. 3B, Hendry.

Game 3

Friday, October 11

Blue Jays	AB	R	H	RBI	BB	K	Avg
Damaso Garcia, 2b	5	1	2	0	0	0	.267
Lloyd Moseby, cf	4	1	1	1	1	0	.214
Rance Mulliniks, 3b	4	1	1	2	0	2	.375
Willie Upshaw, 1b	4	0	1	0	0	0	.273
Al Oliver, dh	2	0	1	0	0	0	.500
Cliff Johnson, ph-dh	2	0	1	0	0	1	.444
George Bell, lf	4	0	3	0	0	0	.417
Ernie Whitt, c	3	1	1	0	1	2	.200
Jesse Barfield, rf	4	1	1	2	0	1	.300
Tony Fernandez, ss	4	0	1	0	0	1	.333
TOTALS	36	5	13	5	2	7	.320

Royals	AB	R	H	RBI	BB	K	Avg
Lonnie Smith, lf	4	0	1	0	0	1	.077
Lynn Jones, lf	0	0	0	0	0	0	—
Willie Wilson, cf	4	1	2	0	0	0	.462
George Brett, 3b	4	4	4	3	0	0	.583
Hal McRae, dh	3	0	1	0	0	1	.375
Frank White, 2b	3	0	0	1	0	0	.182
Pat Sheridan, rf	3	0	0	0	1	0	.143
Steve Balboni, 1b	4	0	1	0	0	1	.083
Jim Sundberg, c	4	1	1	1	0	1	.182
Buddy Biancalana, ss	1	0	0	0	0	1	.200
Dane Iorg, ph	1	0	0	0	0	0	.500
Onix Concepcion, ss	1	0	0	0	0	0	.000
TOTALS	32	6	10	6	1	5	.263

	1	2	3	4	5	6	7	8	9		R	H	E
Blue Jays	0	0	0	0	5	0	0	0	0		5	13	1
Royals	1	0	0	1	1	2	0	1	x		6	10	1

E—Smith, Upshaw. DP—Royals 4 (White to Biancalana to Balboni; Brett to Sundberg to Saberhagen to Balboni; Farr to Concepcion to Balboni; Sundberg to Concepcion). LOB—Blue Jays 6, Royals 5. Scoring Position—Blue Jays 1-for-7, Royals 1-for-7. 2B—Garcia 2 (2), Upshaw (1), Brett (2), McRae (1). HR—Mulliniks (1), Barfield (1), Brett 2 (2), Sundberg (1). S—

McRae. SF—White. GDP—Moseby. CS—Moseby (1), Bell (1), Wilson (1).

Blue Jays	IP	H	R	ER	BB	K	ERA
Doyle Alexander	5.0	7	5	5	0	3	9.00
Dennis Lamp	2.0	1	0	0	2	0	0.00
Jim Clancy (L, 0-1)	1.0	2	1	1	1	0	9.00

Royals	IP	H	R	ER	BB	K	ERA
Bret Saberhagen	4.1	9	5	5	1	4	10.38
Bud Black	0.1	2	0	0	1	0	2.45
Steve Farr (W, 1-0)	4.1	2	0	0	0	3	1.42

Alexander pitched to three batters in the 6th.

Time—2:51. Attendance—40,224. Umpires—HP, Evans. 1B, Hendry. 2B, Voltaggio. 3B, Cousins.

Game 4

Saturday, October 12

Blue Jays	AB	R	H	RBI	BB	K	Avg
Damaso Garcia, 2b	3	1	1	0	1	0	.278
Lloyd Moseby, cf	4	1	1	0	0	0	.222
George Bell, lf	4	1	1	0	0	0	.375
Cliff Johnson, dh	2	0	0	0	1	0	.364
Al Oliver, dh	1	0	1	2	0	0	.600
Jesse Barfield, rf	4	0	2	0	0	1	.357
Willie Upshaw, 1b	4	0	0	0	0	0	.200
Garth Iorg, 3b	4	0	0	0	0	0	.125
Ernie Whitt, c	2	0	0	0	0	0	.167
Cecil Fielder, ph	1	0	1	0	0	0	1.000
Lou Thornton, pr	0	0	0	0	0	0	—
Jeff Hearron, c	0	0	0	0	0	0	—
Tony Fernandez, ss	3	0	0	1	0	0	.300
TOTALS	32	3	7	3	2	1	.290

Royals	AB	R	H	RBI	BB	K	Avg
Lonnie Smith, lf	1	1	0	0	3	0	.071
Lynn Jones, lf	0	0	0	0	0	0	—
Jamie Quirk, ph	1	0	0	0	0	0	.000
Willie Wilson, cf	3	0	2	0	0	0	.500
George Brett, 3b	2	0	0	0	2	0	.500
Hal McRae, dh	3	0	0	1	1	1	.273
Pat Sheridan, rf	4	0	0	0	0	1	.091
Frank White, 2b	4	0	0	0	0	0	.133
Steve Balboni, 1b	3	0	0	0	1	2	.067
Jim Sundberg, c	3	0	0	0	0	1	.143
Jorge Orta, ph	1	0	0	0	0	0	.000
Buddy Biancalana, ss	2	0	0	0	1	1	.143
Dane Iorg, ph	0	0	0	0	1	0	.500
Onix Concepcion, pr	0	0	0	0	0	0	.000
TOTALS	27	1	2	1	9	6	.214

	1	2	3	4	5	6	7	8	9		R	H	E
Blue Jays	0	0	0	0	0	0	0	0	3		3	7	0
Royals	0	0	0	0	0	1	0	0	0		1	2	0

DP—Blue Jays 1 (Fernandez to Garcia to Upshaw), Royals 1 (Biancalana). LOB—Blue Jays 4, Royals 9. Scoring Position—Blue Jays 2-for-10, Royals 0-for-6. 2B—Garcia (3), Moseby (1), Barfield (1), Fielder (1), Oliver (1). S—Wilson. GDP—White. CS—Barfield (1).

Blue Jays	IP	H	R	ER	BB	K	ERA
Dave Stieb	6.2	2	1	1	7	6	0.61
Tom Henke (W, 2-0)	2.1	0	0	0	2	0	4.26

Royals	IP	H	R	ER	BB	K	ERA
Charlie Leibrandt (L, 0-2)	8.0	5	2	2	2	1	6.30
Dan Quisenberry	1.0	2	1	1	0	0	4.91

Leibrandt pitched to two batters in the 9th.

Time—3:02. Attendance—41,112. Umpires—HP, Hendry. 1B, Voltaggio. 2B, Cousins. 3B, Phillips.

Game 5
Sunday, October 13

Blue Jays	AB	R	H	RBI	BB	K	Avg
Damaso Garcia, 2b	4	0	0	0	0	1	.227
Lloyd Moseby, cf	4	0	0	0	0	1	.182
George Bell, lf	4	0	2	0	0	0	.400
Cliff Johnson, dh	4	0	1	0	0	1	.333
Jesse Barfield, rf	4	0	1	0	0	1	.333
Willie Upshaw, 1b	4	0	1	0	0	1	.211
Garth Iorg, 3b	3	0	1	0	1	1	.182
Ernie Whitt, c	3	0	1	0	0	0	.200
Cecil Fielder, ph	1	0	0	0	0	0	.500
Tony Fernandez, ss	3	0	1	0	0	0	.320
TOTALS	34	0	8	0	1	6	.269

Royals	AB	R	H	RBI	BB	K	Avg
Lonnie Smith, lf	4	1	3	0	0	0	.222
Lynn Jones, lf	0	0	0	0	0	0	—
Willie Wilson, cf	4	0	0	0	0	2	.400
George Brett, 3b	3	0	0	1	1	0	.412
Hal McRae, dh	4	0	0	0	0	1	.200
Frank White, 2b	3	1	2	0	0	0	.222
Steve Balboni, 1b	3	0	2	0	0	0	.167
Darryl Motley, rf	1	0	1	1	0	0	.333
Pat Sheridan, ph-rf	1	0	0	0	0	0	.083
Jim Sundberg, c	3	0	0	0	0	2	.118
Buddy Biancalana, ss	3	0	0	0	0	0	.100
TOTALS	29	2	8	2	1	5	.230

	1	2	3	4	5	6	7	8	9		R	H	E
Blue Jays	0	0	0	0	0	0	0	0	0		0	8	0
Royals	1	1	0	0	0	0	0	0	x		2	8	0

DP—Blue Jays 1 (Garcia to Upshaw). LOB—Blue Jays 8, Royals 5. Scoring Position—Blue Jays 0-for-6, Royals 0-for-7. 2B—Bell (2), Whitt (1), Smith (1). SF—Motley (1). SB—Smith (1). CS—Smith (1).

Blue Jays	IP	H	R	ER	BB	K	ERA
Jimmy Key (L, 0-1)	5.1	8	2	2	1	3	4.02
Jim Acker	2.2	0	0	0	0	2	0.00

Royals	IP	H	R	ER	BB	K	ERA
Danny Jackson (W, 1-0)	9.0	8	0	0	1	6	0.00

Time—2:21. Attendance—40,046. Umpires—HP, Voltaggio. 1B, Cousins. 2B, Phillips. 3B, Ford.

Game 6
Tuesday, October 15

Royals	AB	R	H	RBI	BB	K	Avg
Lonnie Smith, lf	5	0	1	1	0	2	.217
Lynn Jones, lf	0	0	0	0	0	0	—
Willie Wilson, cf	4	1	1	0	1	1	.375
George Brett, 3b	3	2	1	1	2	1	.400
Hal McRae, dh	5	0	3	2	0	1	.300
Pat Sheridan, rf	4	0	0	0	0	0	.063
Steve Balboni, 1b	4	0	0	0	0	1	.136
Jim Sundberg, c	3	1	0	0	1	1	.100
Frank White, 2b	3	0	0	0	0	1	.190
Buddy Biancalana, ss	4	1	2	1	0	2	.214
TOTALS	35	5	8	5	4	11	.228

Blue Jays	AB	R	H	RBI	BB	K	Avg
Damaso Garcia, 2b	3	1	1	0	2	0	.240
Lloyd Moseby, cf	4	1	3	1	1	0	.269
Rance Mulliniks, 3b	2	0	0	0	1	0	.300
Garth Iorg, ph-3b	2	0	0	0	0	1	.154
Willie Upshaw, 1b	3	0	0	0	1	1	.182
Al Oliver, dh	2	0	0	0	0	0	.429
Cliff Johnson, ph-dh	2	0	2	1	0	0	.412
George Bell, lf	4	0	0	0	0	1	.333
Ernie Whitt, c	3	0	0	0	0	0	.167
Cecil Fielder, ph	1	0	0	0	0	1	.333
Jeff Hearron, c	0	0	0	0	0	0	—
Jesse Barfield, rf	4	0	0	0	0	2	.273
Tony Fernandez, ss	4	1	2	0	0	0	.353
TOTALS	34	3	8	2	5	6	.275

	1	2	3	4	5	6	7	8	9		R	H	E
Royals	1	0	1	0	1	2	0	0	0		5	8	1
Blue Jays	1	0	1	0	0	1	0	0	0		3	8	2

E—Brett, Barfield, Fernandez. DP—Royals 2 (Gubicza to Biancalana to Balboni; White to Biancalana to Balboni). LOB—Royals 8, Blue Jays 9. Scoring Position—Royals 3-for-9, Blue Jays 2-for-9. 2B—Smith (2), McRae (2), Biancalana (1), Garcia (4), Fernandez (2). HR—Brett (3). S—White. GDP—Mulliniks, Fernandez.

Royals	IP	H	R	ER	BB	K	ERA
Mark Gubicza (W, 1-0)	5.1	4	3	3	3	2	3.24
Bud Black (H, 1)	3.1	4	0	0	2	3	1.69
Dan Quisenberry (S, 1)	0.1	0	0	0	0	1	4.50

Blue Jays	IP	H	R	ER	BB	K	ERA
Doyle Alexander (L, 0-1)	5.1	7	5	5	3	6	8.71
Dennis Lamp	3.2	1	0	0	1	5	0.00

WP—Alexander, Gubicza, Black. Time—3:12. Attendance—37,557. Umpires—HP, Cousins. 1B, Phillips. 2B, Ford. 3B, Evans.

Game 7
Wednesday, October 16

Royals	AB	R	H	RBI	BB	K	Avg
Lonnie Smith, lf	5	0	2	0	0	1	.250
Lynn Jones, lf	0	0	0	0	0	0	—
Willie Wilson, cf	5	0	0	0	0	1	.310
George Brett, 3b	3	0	0	0	1	2	.348
Hal McRae, dh	3	1	0	0	0	0	.261
Pat Sheridan, rf	4	3	2	1	0	0	.150
Steve Balboni, 1b	3	1	0	0	1	1	.120
Jim Sundberg, c	4	1	2	4	0	0	.167
Frank White, 2b	4	0	1	1	0	0	.200
Buddy Biancalana, ss	4	0	1	0	0	1	.222
TOTALS	35	6	8	6	2	7	.228

Blue Jays	AB	R	H	RBI	BB	K	Avg
Damaso Garcia, 2b	5	1	1	1	0	0	.233
Lloyd Moseby, cf	5	0	0	0	0	1	.226
Rance Mulliniks, 3b	1	0	1	0	1	0	.364
Garth Iorg, ph-3b	2	0	0	0	0	0	.133
Willie Upshaw, 1b	4	0	2	1	0	1	.231
Al Oliver, dh	1	0	0	0	0	0	.375
Cliff Johnson, ph-dh	2	0	0	0	0	1	.368
George Bell, lf	4	0	1	0	0	1	.321
Ernie Whitt, c	3	0	1	0	0	1	.190
Jeff Burroughs, ph	1	0	0	0	0	0	.000
Jesse Barfield, rf	3	1	1	0	1	1	.280
Tony Fernandez, ss	4	0	1	0	0	1	.342
TOTALS	35	2	8	2	2	7	.268

	1	2	3	4	5	6	7	8	9		R	H	E
Royals	0	1	0	1	0	4	0	0	0		6	8	0
Blue Jays	0	0	0	0	1	0	0	0	1		2	8	1

E—Fernandez. DP—Blue Jays 1 (Garcia to Upshaw). LOB—Royals 5, Blue Jays 9. Scoring Position—Royals 3-for-5, Blue Jays 1-for-11. 2B—Mulliniks (1), Upshaw (2), Bell (3), Fernandez (3). 3B—Sundberg (1). HR—Sheridan (2). GDP—Wilson.

Royals	IP	H	R	ER	BB	K	ERA
Bret Saberhagen	3.0	3	0	0	1	2	6.14
Charlie Leibrandt (W, 1-2)	5.1	5	2	2	1	5	5.28
Dan Quisenberry	0.2	0	0	0	0	0	3.86

Blue Jays	IP	H	R	ER	BB	K	ERA
Dave Stieb (L, 1-1)	5.2	6	6	6	2	4	3.10
Jim Acker	3.1	2	0	0	0	3	0.00

HBP—McRae by Stieb, Oliver by Saberhagen. Time—2:49. Attendance—32,084. Umpires—HP, Phillips. 1B, Ford. 2B, Evans. 3B, Hendry.

1985 AL Championship Series—Composite Statistics

Batting

Royals	G	AB	R	H	RBI	2B	3B	HR	BB	SO	SB	CS	Avg	OBP	Slg
Steve Balboni	7	25	1	3	1	0	0	0	2	8	0	0	.120	.185	.120
Buddy Biancalana	7	18	2	4	1	1	0	0	1	6	0	0	.222	.263	.278
George Brett	7	23	6	8	5	2	0	3	7	5	0	1	.348	.500	.826
Onix Concepcion	4	1	0	0	0	0	0	0	0	0	0	1	.000	.000	.000
Dane Iorg	4	2	0	1	0	1	0	0	2	0	0	0	.500	.750	1.000
Hal McRae	6	23	1	6	3	2	0	1	6	0	0	0	.261	.320	.348
Darryl Motley	2	3	1	1	1	0	0	0	1	2	0	0	.333	.400	.333
Jorge Orta	2	5	0	0	0	0	0	0	0	1	0	0	.000	.000	.000
Jamie Quirk	1	1	0	0	0	0	0	0	0	0	0	0	.000	.000	.000
Pat Sheridan	7	20	4	3	3	0	0	2	2	3	0	0	.150	.227	.450
Lonnie Smith	7	28	2	7	1	2	0	3	6	1	1	1	.250	.323	.321
Jim Sundberg	7	24	3	4	6	1	1	1	7	0	0	0	.167	.200	.417
Frank White	7	25	1	5	3	0	0	1	2	0	0	0	.200	.222	.200
Willie Wilson	7	29	5	9	2	0	0	1	5	1	1	1	.310	.333	.414
Totals	**7**	**227**	**26**	**51**	**26**	**9**	**1**	**7**	**22**	**51**	**2**	**4**	**.225**	**.294**	**.366**

Batting

Blue Jays	G	AB	R	H	RBI	2B	3B	HR	BB	SO	SB	CS	Avg	OBP	Slg
Jesse Barfield	7	25	3	7	4	1	0	1	3	7	1	1	.280	.357	.440
George Bell	7	28	4	9	1	3	0	0	4	0	0	1	.321	.333	.429
Jeff Burroughs	1	1	0	0	0	0	0	0	0	0	0	0	.000	.000	.000
Tony Fernandez	7	24	2	8	2	2	0	1	2	0	0	0	.333	.346	.417
Cecil Fielder	3	3	0	1	0	1	0	0	0	1	0	0	.333	.333	.667
Damaso Garcia	7	30	4	7	1	4	0	0	3	3	0	0	.233	.303	.367
Garth Iorg	6	15	1	2	0	0	0	0	1	3	0	0	.133	.188	.133
Cliff Johnson	7	19	1	7	2	2	0	1	4	0	0	0	.368	.400	.474
Lloyd Moseby	7	31	5	7	4	1	0	0	2	3	1	1	.226	.273	.258
Rance Mulliniks	5	11	1	4	3	1	0	1	2	2	0	0	.364	.462	.727
Al Oliver	5	8	0	3	3	1	0	0	0	0	0	0	.375	.444	.500
Lou Thornton	2	0	1	0	0	0	0	0	0	0	0	0	—	—	—
Willie Upshaw	7	26	2	6	1	2	0	0	1	4	0	0	.231	.286	.308
Ernie Whitt	7	21	1	4	2	1	0	0	2	4	0	0	.190	.261	.238
Totals	**7**	**242**	**25**	**65**	**23**	**19**	**0**	**2**	**16**	**37**	**2**	**3**	**.269**	**.319**	**.372**

Pitching

Royals	G	GS	CG	IP	H	R	ER	BB	SO	W-L	Sv-Op	Hld	ERA
Bud Black	3	1	0	10.2	11	3	2	4	8	0-0	0-0	1	1.69
Steve Farr	2	0	0	6.1	4	1	1	1	3	1-0	0-0	0	1.42
Mark Gubicza	2	1	0	8.1	4	3	3	4	1	1-0	0-0	0	3.24
Danny Jackson	2	1	1	10.0	10	0	0	1	7	1-0	0-0	0	0.00
Charlie Leibrandt	3	2	0	15.1	17	9	9	4	6	1-2	0-0	0	5.28
Dan Quisenberry	4	0	0	4.2	7	4	2	0	3	0-1	1-1	0	3.86
Bret Saberhagen	2	2	0	7.1	12	5	5	2	6	0-0	0-0	0	6.14
Totals	**7**	**7**	**1**	**62.2**	**65**	**25**	**22**	**16**	**37**	**4-3**	**1-1**	**1**	**3.16**

Pitching

Blue Jays	G	GS	CG	IP	H	R	ER	BB	SO	W-L	Sv-Op	Hld	ERA
Jim Acker	2	0	0	6.0	2	0	0	5	0-0		0-0	0	0.00
Doyle Alexander	2	2	0	10.1	14	10	10	3	9	0-1	0-0	0	8.71
Jim Clancy	1	0	0	1.0	2	1	1	1	0	0-1	0-0	0	9.00
Tom Henke	3	0	0	6.1	5	3	3	4	4	2-0	0-0	0	4.26
Jimmy Key	2	2	0	8.2	15	5	5	2	5	0-1	0-0	0	5.19
Dennis Lamp	3	0	0	9.1	2	0	0	1	10	0-0	0-0	0	0.00
Gary Lavelle	1	0	0	0.0	0	0	0	1	0	0-0	0-0	0	—
Dave Stieb	3	3	0	20.1	11	7	7	10	18	1-1	0-0	0	3.10
Totals	**7**	**7**	**0**	**62.0**	**51**	**26**	**26**	**22**	**51**	**3-4**	**0-0**	**0**	**3.77**

Fielding

Royals	Pos	G	PO	Ast	E	DP	PB	FPct
Steve Balboni	1b	7	72	7	2	6	—	.975
Buddy Biancalana	ss	7	9	20	0	4	—	1.000
Bud Black	p	3	2	3	0	1	—	1.000
George Brett	3b	7	7	8	2	1	—	.882
Onix Concepcion	ss	3	2	4	0	2	—	1.000
Steve Farr	p	2	0	1	0	1	—	1.000
Mark Gubicza	p	2	0	1	0	1	—	1.000
Danny Jackson	p	2	1	1	0	0	—	1.000
Lynn Jones	lf	5	2	0	0	0	—	1.000
Charlie Leibrandt	p	3	3	8	0	0	—	1.000
Darryl Motley	rf	2	4	0	0	0	—	1.000
Dan Quisenberry	p	4	1	1	0	0	—	1.000
Bret Saberhagen	p	2	2	1	0	1	—	1.000
Pat Sheridan	rf	7	13	0	0	0	—	1.000
Lonnie Smith	lf	7	8	2	1	0	—	.909
Jim Sundberg	c	7	41	2	1	2	0	.977
Frank White	2b	7	9	28	0	2	—	1.000
Willie Wilson	cf	7	12	0	0	0	—	1.000
Totals		**7**	**188**	**87**	**6**	**21**	**0**	**.979**

Fielding

Blue Jays	Pos	G	PO	Ast	E	DP	PB	FPct
Jim Acker	p	2	0	1	0	0	—	1.000
Doyle Alexander	p	2	1	0	0	0	—	1.000
Jesse Barfield	rf	7	21	0	1	0	—	.955
George Bell	lf	7	13	0	0	0	—	1.000
Jim Clancy	p	1	0	1	0	0	—	1.000
Tony Fernandez	ss	7	11	15	2	2	—	.929
Damaso Garcia	2b	7	10	12	0	3	—	1.000
Jeff Hearron	c	2	2	0	0	0	0	1.000
Tom Henke	p	3	1	0	0	0	—	1.000
Garth Iorg	3b	6	5	10	0	0	—	1.000
Jimmy Key	p	2	0	3	0	0	—	1.000
Dennis Lamp	p	3	1	2	0	0	—	1.000
Gary Lavelle	p	1	0	0	0	0	—	—
Manuel Lee	2b	1	0	0	0	0	—	—
Lloyd Moseby	cf	7	16	0	0	0	—	1.000
Rance Mulliniks	3b	5	1	4	0	0	—	1.000
Dave Stieb	p	3	1	3	0	0	—	1.000
Willie Upshaw	1b	7	53	7	1	3	—	.984
Ernie Whitt	c	7	50	3	0	1	0	1.000
Totals		**7**	**186**	**61**	**4**	**9**	**0**	**.984**

1985 St. Louis Cardinals (NL) 4, Los Angeles Dodgers (NL) 2

The most second-guessed move of Tommy Lasorda's managerial career was his decision to pitch to Jack Clark in Game 6 of the 1985 NLCS. The Cardinals were up three games to two at the time. The Dodgers took the first two games of the Series behind Fernando Valenzuela and Orel Hershiser, but the Cardinals evened the Series by beating Bob Welch 4-2 and bombing Jerry Reuss 12-2. In Game 5, the Dodgers brought in Tom Niedenfuer to pitch the ninth inning of a tie game. Ozzie Smith connected for a game-winning homer off Niedenfuer, the first lefthanded home run of the switch-hitter's career. That set the stage for Game 6. The Dodgers had a one-run lead going into the ninth, and once again, Niedenfuer was on the mound. A walk, a single and a sacrifice put runners on second and third with two outs and Jack Clark due to hit. With Andy Van Slyke on deck, an intentional walk was an option, but Lasorda elected to let Niedenfuer pitch to Clark, who ripped the first pitch into the left-field seats for a 7-5 St. Louis lead. The Dodgers went quietly in their half of the ninth, and the Cardinals were NL Champions.

Game 1

Wednesday, October 9

Cardinals	AB	R	H	RBI	BB	K	Avg
Vince Coleman, lf	4	0	0	0	0	1	.000
Willie McGee, cf	4	0	0	0	0	3	.000
Tom Herr, 2b	3	0	1	0	1	0	.333
Jack Clark, 1b	3	0	1	0	1	1	.333
Cesar Cedeno, rf	4	0	0	0	0	0	.000
Todd Worrell, p	0	0	0	0	0	0	—
Terry Pendleton, 3b	4	1	2	0	0	1	.500
Darrell Porter, c	4	0	1	0	0	1	.250
Ozzie Smith, ss	4	0	2	0	0	0	.500
John Tudor, p	2	0	0	0	0	1	.000
Ken Dayley, p	0	0	0	0	0	0	—
Tito Landrum, ph	1	0	1	1	0	0	1.000
Bill Campbell, p	0	0	0	0	0	0	—
Andy Van Slyke, rf	0	0	0	0	0	0	—
TOTALS	33	1	8	1	2	8	.242

Dodgers	AB	R	H	RBI	BB	K	Avg
Mariano Duncan, ss	4	0	0	0	0	0	.000
Enos Cabell, 1b	4	0	0	0	0	1	.000
Bill Madlock, 3b	4	2	1	0	0	0	.250
Pedro Guerrero, lf	3	1	2	1	1	0	.667
Mike Marshall, rf	4	0	0	0	0	0	.000
Mike Scioscia, c	4	1	1	1	0	0	.250
Candy Maldonado, cf	3	0	1	1	0	1	.333
Ken Landreaux, ph-cf	1	0	0	0	0	0	.000
Steve Sax, 2b	3	0	2	1	0	0	.667
Fernando Valenzuela, p	2	0	1	0	0	0	.500
Tom Niedenfuer, p	0	0	0	0	0	0	—
TOTALS	32	4	8	4	1	3	.250

	1	2	3	4	5	6	7	8	9		R	H	E
Cardinals	0	0	0	0	0	0	1	0	0		1	8	1
Dodgers	0	0	0	1	0	3	0	0	x		4	8	0

E—Pendleton. DP—Dodgers 1 (Duncan to Cabell). LOB—Cardinals 7, Dodgers 6. Scoring Position—Cardinals 2-for-5, Dodgers 4-for-11. 2B—Herr (1), Madlock (1), Sax (1). S—Valenzuela. GDP—Coleman. SB—Smith (1), Madlock (1), Guerrero 2 (2). CS—Pendleton (1).

Cardinals	IP	H	R	ER	BB	K	ERA
John Tudor (L, 0-1)	5.2	7	4	3	1	3	4.76
Ken Dayley	0.1	0	0	0	0	0	0.00
Bill Campbell	1.0	1	0	0	0	0	0.00
Todd Worrell	1.0	0	0	0	0	0	0.00

Dodgers	IP	H	R	ER	BB	K	ERA
Fernando Valenzuela (W, 1-0)	6.1	7	1	1	2	6	1.42
Tom Niedenfuer (S, 1)	2.2	1	0	0	0	2	0.00

Campbell pitched to one batter in the 8th.

WP—Worrell. Time—2:42. Attendance—55,270. Umpires—HP, Stello. 1B, Froemming. 2B, McSherry. 3B, Tata.

Game 2

Thursday, October 10

Cardinals	AB	R	H	RBI	BB	K	Avg
Vince Coleman, lf	5	0	2	1	0	0	.222
Willie McGee, cf	5	1	1	0	0	0	.111
Tom Herr, 2b	3	0	1	0	1	0	.333
Jack Clark, 1b	3	0	1	0	1	1	.333
Andy Van Slyke, rf	3	0	0	0	1	0	.000
Terry Pendleton, 3b	4	1	1	0	0	0	.375
Darrell Porter, c	2	0	0	0	2	1	.167
Ozzie Smith, ss	4	0	2	0	0	0	.500
Joaquin Andujar, p	2	0	0	0	0	1	.000
Ricky Horton, p	0	0	0	0	0	0	—
Bill Campbell, p	0	0	0	0	0	0	—
Steve Braun, ph	1	0	0	0	0	0	.000
Ken Dayley, p	0	0	0	0	0	0	—
Jeff Lahti, p	0	0	0	0	0	0	—
Mike Jorgensen, ph	1	0	0	0	0	0	.000
TOTALS	33	2	8	1	5	4	.254

Dodgers	AB	R	H	RBI	BB	K	Avg
Mariano Duncan, ss	4	0	1	0	0	1	.125
Dave Anderson, pr-ss	1	1	0	0	0	0	.000
Ken Landreaux, cf	4	3	3	1	1	1	.600
Bill Madlock, 3b	5	0	3	2	0	1	.444
Bob Bailor, pr-3b	0	0	0	0	0	0	—
Pedro Guerrero, lf	3	0	1	1	2	1	.500
Candy Maldonado, lf	0	0	0	0	0	0	.333
Mike Marshall, rf	4	0	1	1	0	2	.125
Mike Scioscia, c	3	1	1	0	1	0	.286
Greg Brock, 1b	4	1	1	2	0	0	.250
Steve Sax, 2b	4	1	1	0	0	1	.429
Orel Hershiser, p	4	1	1	1	0	1	.250
TOTALS	36	8	13	8	4	8	.323

	1	2	3	4	5	6	7	8	9		R	H	E
Cardinals	0	0	1	0	0	0	0	0	1		2	8	1
Dodgers	0	0	3	2	1	2	0	0	x		8	13	1

E—Andujar, Duncan. DP—Cardinals 1 (Horton to Pendleton), Dodgers 1 (Hershiser to Duncan to Sax). LOB—Cardinals 9, Dodgers 8. Scoring Position—Cardinals 1-for-9, Dodgers 5-for-10. 2B—Herr (2), Duncan (1), Landreaux 2 (2). HR—Brock (1). GDP—Andujar. CS—Coleman (1), McGee (1).

Cardinals	IP	H	R	ER	BB	K	ERA
Joaquin Andujar (L, 0-1)	4.1	8	6	6	2	6	12.46
Ricky Horton	1.1	1	2	2	2	0	13.50
Bill Campbell	0.1	2	0	0	0	1	0.00
Ken Dayley	1.0	0	0	0	0	0	0.00
Jeff Lahti	1.0	2	0	0	0	1	0.00

Dodgers	IP	H	R	ER	BB	K	ERA
Orel Hershiser (W, 1-0)	9.0	8	2	2	5	4	2.00

WP—Hershiser. PB—Porter. Time—3:04. Attendance—55,222. Umpires—HP, Froemming. 1B, McSherry. 2B, Tata. 3B, Runge.

Game 3

Saturday, October 12

Dodgers	AB	R	H	RBI	BB	K	Avg
Dave Anderson, ss	3	0	0	0	2	1	.000
Ken Landreaux, cf	5	0	2	1	0	0	.500
Bill Madlock, 3b	4	0	0	0	0	0	.308
Pedro Guerrero, lf	3	1	1	0	1	0	.444
Mike Marshall, rf	4	0	2	1	0	0	.250
Mike Scioscia, c	3	0	0	0	1	0	.200
Greg Brock, 1b	4	0	0	0	0	2	.125
Steve Sax, 2b	3	0	2	0	1	0	.500
Bob Welch, p	1	0	0	0	0	1	.000
Rick Honeycutt, p	0	0	0	0	0	0	—
Jay Johnstone, ph	1	0	0	0	0	0	.000
Carlos Diaz, p	0	0	0	0	0	0	—
Len Matuszek, ph	0	0	0	0	0	0	—
Enos Cabell, ph	1	1	0	0	0	0	.000
Ken Howell, p	0	0	0	0	0	0	—
Terry Whitfield, ph	0	0	0	0	0	0	—
Candy Maldonado, ph	1	0	0	0	0	0	.250
TOTALS	33	2	7	2	5	4	.287

Cardinals	AB	R	H	RBI	BB	K	Avg
Vince Coleman, lf	5	2	2	0	0	1	.286
Willie McGee, cf	4	1	2	1	1	1	.231
Tom Herr, 2b	4	1	2	1	1	1	.400
Jack Clark, 1b	2	0	0	2	1	0	.250
Andy Van Slyke, rf	1	0	0	1	0	0	.000
Cesar Cedeno, ph-rf	2	0	0	0	0	1	.000
Todd Worrell, p	0	0	0	0	0	0	—
Ken Dayley, p	0	0	0	0	0	0	—
Terry Pendleton, 3b	4	0	0	1	0	0	.250
Darrell Porter, c	3	0	1	0	1	0	.222
Ozzie Smith, ss	3	0	1	0	1	0	.455
Danny Cox, p	2	0	0	0	1	1	.000
Ricky Horton, p	0	0	0	0	0	0	—
Tito Landrum, rf	1	0	0	0	0	0	.500
TOTALS	31	4	8	3	8	6	.264

	1	2	3	4	5	6	7	8	9		R	H	E
Dodgers	0	0	0	1	0	0	1	0	0		2	7	2
Cardinals	2	2	0	0	0	0	0	0	x		4	8	0

E—Welch, Scioscia. LOB—Dodgers 9, Cardinals 11. Scoring Position—Dodgers 2-for-13, Cardinals 1-for-12. 2B—Landreaux (3), Guerrero (1), Marshall 2 (2), Sax (2), Herr (3), Porter (1), Smith (1). HR—Herr (1). SB—Coleman (1), McGee (1), Herr (1). CS—Sax (1), Coleman (2), McGee (2).

Dodgers	IP	H	R	ER	BB	K	ERA
Bob Welch (L, 0-1)	2.2	5	4	2	6	2	6.75
Rick Honeycutt	1.1	1	0	0	1	0	0.00
Carlos Diaz	2.0	2	0	0	1	1	0.00
Ken Howell	2.0	0	0	0	0	2	0.00

Cardinals	IP	H	R	ER	BB	K	ERA
Danny Cox (W, 1-0)	6.0	4	2	2	5	4	3.00
Ricky Horton (H, 1)	0.2	1	0	0	0	0	9.00
Todd Worrell (H, 1)	1.1	2	0	0	0	0	0.00
Ken Dayley (S, 1)	1.0	0	0	0	0	0	0.00

Cox pitched to one batter in the 7th. Worrell pitched to one batter in the 9th.

Time—3:21. Attendance—53,708. Umpires—HP, McSherry. 1B, Tata. 2B, Runge. 3B, Crawford.

Game 4
Sunday, October 13

Dodgers	AB	R	H	RBI	BB	K	Avg
Mariano Duncan, ss	2	0	0	0	0	1	.100
Dave Anderson, ss	1	0	0	0	1	0	.000
Enos Cabell, 1b	4	0	0	0	0	1	.000
Pedro Guerrero, lf	4	0	1	1	0	0	.385
Carlos Diaz, p	0	0	0	0	0	0	
Bill Madlock, 3b	3	1	1	1	0	0	.313
Bob Bailor, 3b	1	0	0	0	0	0	.000
Mike Marshall, rf	4	0	1	0	0	0	.250
Mike Scioscia, c	1	0	0	0	0	0	.182
Steve Yeager, ph-c	2	0	0	0	1	1	.000
Candy Maldonado, cf	3	0	0	0	0	2	.143
Greg Brock, ph	1	0	0	0	0	0	.111
Steve Sax, 2b	3	0	1	0	0	0	.462
Jerry Reuss, p	0	0	0	0	0	0	
Rick Honeycutt, p	0	0	0	0	0	0	
Bobby Castillo, p	2	0	0	0	0	1	.000
Len Matuszek, ph-lf	1	1	1	0	0	0	1.000
TOTALS	32	2	5	2	2	7	.226

Cardinals	AB	R	H	RBI	BB	K	Avg
Willie McGee, cf	5	1	1	0	0	0	.222
Ozzie Smith, ss	5	1	2	1	0	0	.438
Tom Herr, 2b	4	1	1	2	0	1	.357
Jack Clark, 1b	5	3	3	1	0	0	.385
Cesar Cedeno, rf	2	2	2	0	1	0	.250
Andy Van Slyke, pr-rf	2	1	1	1	0	0	.167
Tito Landrum, lf	5	1	4	3	0	1	.714
Terry Pendleton, 3b	4	0	1	3	1	0	.250
Tom Nieto, c	3	1	0	0	1	2	.000
John Tudor, p	2	1	0	0	1	0	.000
Mike Jorgensen, ph	1	0	0	0	0	1	.000
Ricky Horton, p	0	0	0	0	0	0	
Bill Campbell, p	0	0	0	0	0	0	
TOTALS	38	12	15	11	4	5	.308

	1	2	3	4	5	6	7	8	9	R	H	E
Dodgers	0	0	0	0	0	0	1	1	0	2	5	2
Cardinals	0	9	0	1	1	0	0	1	x	12	15	0

E—Reuss, Maldonado. DP—Dodgers 1 (Castillo to Anderson to Cabell). LOB—Dodgers 5, Cardinals 7. Scoring Position—Dodgers 1-for-5, Cardinals 8-for-18. 2B—Sax (3), McGee (1), Cedeno (1). HR—Madlock (1). SF—Herr. GDP—Tudor.

Dodgers	IP	H	R	ER	BB	K	ERA
Jerry Reuss (L, 0-1)	1.2	5	7	2	1	0	10.80
Rick Honeycutt	0.0	3	2	2	1	0	13.50
Bobby Castillo	5.1	4	2	2	2	4	3.38
Carlos Diaz	1.0	3	1	1	0	1	3.00

Cardinals	IP	H	R	ER	BB	K	ERA
John Tudor (W, 1-1)	7.0	3	1	1	2	5	2.84
Ricky Horton	1.0	2	1	1	0	1	9.00
Bill Campbell	1.0	0	0	0	0	1	0.00

Honeycutt pitched to four batters in the 2nd.

Time—2:47. Attendance—53,708. Umpires—HP, Tata. 1B, Runge. 2B, Crawford. 3B, Stello.

Game 5
Monday, October 14

Dodgers	AB	R	H	RBI	BB	K	Avg
Mariano Duncan, ss	3	0	0	0	1	0	.077
Ken Landreaux, cf	4	1	2	0	0	0	.500
Pedro Guerrero, lf	4	0	0	0	0	0	.294
Bill Madlock, 3b	4	1	1	2	0	0	.300
Mike Marshall, rf	3	0	0	0	1	0	.211
Mike Scioscia, c	2	0	1	0	1	0	.231
Greg Brock, 1b	1	0	0	0	0	0	.100
Enos Cabell, ph-1b	3	0	1	0	0	0	.083
Tom Niedenfuer, p	0	0	0	0	0	0	
Steve Sax, 2b	3	0	0	0	0	2	.375
Fernando Valenzuela, p	3	0	0	0	0	0	.200
Len Matuszek, 1b	0	0	0	0	0	0	1.000
TOTALS	30	2	5	2	3	2	.257

Cardinals	AB	R	H	RBI	BB	K	Avg
Willie McGee, cf	3	1	0	0	2	2	.190
Ozzie Smith, ss	3	2	1	1	1	0	.421
Tom Herr, 2b	4	0	1	2	0	0	.333
Jack Clark, 1b	3	0	1	0	1	1	.375
Cesar Cedeno, rf	3	0	0	0	1	1	.182
Tito Landrum, lf	3	0	0	0	1	0	.500
Terry Pendleton, 3b	4	0	1	0	0	1	.250
Darrell Porter, c	2	0	0	0	2	2	.182
Bob Forsch, p	0	0	0	0	0	0	
Ken Dayley, p	2	0	1	0	0	0	.500
Todd Worrell, p	0	0	0	0	0	0	
Brian Harper, ph	1	0	0	0	0	0	.000
Jeff Lahti, p	0	0	0	0	0	0	
TOTALS	28	3	5	3	8	7	.302

	1	2	3	4	5	6	7	8	9	R	H	E
Dodgers	0	0	0	2	0	0	0	0	0	2	5	1
Cardinals	2	0	0	0	0	0	0	0	1	3	5	0

E—Valenzuela. DP—Cardinals 2 (Smith to Herr to Clark; Pendleton to Herr to Clark). LOB—Dodgers 5, Cardinals 10. Scoring Position—Dodgers 0-for-4, Cardinals 1-for-11. 2B—Herr (4), Pendleton (1). HR—Madlock (2), Smith (1). S—Smith, Forsch. GDP—Guerrero, Cabell. SB—Landrum (1).

Dodgers	IP	H	R	ER	BB	K	ERA
Fernando Valenzuela	8.0	4	2	2	8	7	1.88
Tom Niedenfuer (L, 0-1)	0.1	1	1	1	0	0	3.00

Cardinals	IP	H	R	ER	BB	K	ERA
Bob Forsch	3.1	3	2	2	2	0	5.40
Ken Dayley	2.2	2	0	0	1	1	0.00
Todd Worrell	2.0	0	0	0	0	1	0.00
Jeff Lahti (W, 1-0)	1.0	0	0	0	0	0	0.00

Dayley pitched to two batters in the 7th.

Reached, Catcher's Interference—Dodgers 1, Scioscia by Porter. Cardinals 0. WP—Valenzuela. Time—2:56. Attendance—53,708. Umpires—HP, Runge. 1B, Crawford. 2B, Stello. 3B, Froemming.

Game 6
Wednesday, October 16

Cardinals	AB	R	H	RBI	BB	K	Avg
Willie McGee, cf	5	2	3	2	0	0	.269
Ozzie Smith, ss	4	1	2	1	1	1	.435
Tom Herr, 2b	3	0	1	1	2	0	.333
Jack Clark, 1b	5	1	2	3	0	1	.381
Andy Van Slyke, rf	5	0	0	0	0	1	.091
Terry Pendleton, 3b	4	0	0	0	2	0	.208
Darrell Porter, c	4	1	2	0	0	0	.267
Tito Landrum, lf	4	1	1	0	0	0	.429
Joaquin Andujar, p	2	1	1	0	0	0	.250
Steve Braun, ph	1	0	0	0	0	0	.000
Todd Worrell, p	0	0	0	0	0	0	
Cesar Cedeno, ph	1	0	0	0	0	1	.167
Ken Dayley, p	0	0	0	0	0	0	.500
TOTALS	38	7	12	7	3	4	.297

Dodgers	AB	R	H	RBI	BB	K	Avg
Mariano Duncan, ss	5	2	3	1	0	1	.222
Ken Landreaux, cf	4	0	0	0	0	0	.389
Enos Cabell, 1b	1	0	0	0	0	0	.077
Pedro Guerrero, lf	3	0	0	1	1	0	.250
Bill Madlock, 3b	4	1	2	2	0	1	.333
Dave Anderson, 3b	0	0	0	0	0	0	.000
Mike Marshall, rf	4	1	1	1	0	1	.217
Mike Scioscia, c	3	0	1	0	1	0	.250
Greg Brock, 1b	2	1	0	0	2	0	.083
Steve Sax, 2b	4	0	0	0	0	1	.300
Orel Hershiser, p	3	0	1	0	0	1	.286
Tom Niedenfuer, p	1	0	0	0	0	1	.000
TOTALS	34	5	8	5	4	7	.243

	1	2	3	4	5	6	7	8	9	R	H	E
Cardinals	0	0	1	0	0	0	3	0	3	7	12	1
Dodgers	1	1	0	0	2	0	0	1	0	5	8	0

E—Andujar. DP—Cardinals 1 (Smith to Herr to Clark). LOB—Cardinals 7, Dodgers 7. Scoring Position—Cardinals 3-for-11, Dodgers 2-for-9. 2B—Andujar (1), Duncan (2). 3B—Smith (1), Duncan (1). HR—Clark (1), Madlock (3), Marshall (1). SF—Guerrero. GDP—Madlock. SB—McGee (2), Duncan (1). CS—McGee (3).

Cardinals	IP	H	R	ER	BB	K	ERA
Joaquin Andujar	6.0	6	4	2	2	3	6.97
Todd Worrell (W, 1-0)	2.0	2	1	1	2	2	1.42
Ken Dayley (S, 2)	1.0	0	0	0	0	2	0.00

Dodgers	IP	H	R	ER	BB	K	ERA
Orel Hershiser	6.1	9	4	4	1	1	2.42
Tom Niedenfuer (BS, 1; L, 0-2)	2.2	3	3	3	2	3	6.35

Time—3:32. Attendance—55,208. Umpires—HP, Crawford. 1B, Stello. 2B, Froemming. 3B, McSherry.

Postseason: League Championship Series

1985 NL Championship Series—Composite Statistics

Batting

Cardinals	G	AB	R	H	RBI	2B	3B	HR	BB	SO	SB	CS	Avg	OBP	Slg
Joaquin Andujar	2	4	1	1	0	1	0	0	0	1	0	0	.250	.250	.500
Steve Braun	2	2	0	0	0	0	0	0	0	0	0	0	.000	.000	.000
Cesar Cedeno	5	12	2	2	0	1	0	0	2	3	0	0	.167	.286	.250
Jack Clark	6	21	4	8	4	0	0	1	5	5	0	0	.381	.500	.524
Vince Coleman	3	14	2	4	1	0	0	0	0	2	1	2	.286	.286	.286
Danny Cox	1	2	0	0	0	0	0	0	1	1	0	0	.000	.333	.000
Ken Dayley	5	2	0	1	0	0	0	0	0	0	0	0	.500	.500	.500
Bob Forsch	1	0	0	0	0	0	0	0	0	0	0	0	—	—	—
Brian Harper	1	1	0	0	0	0	0	0	0	0	0	0	.000	.000	.000
Tom Herr	6	21	2	7	6	4	0	1	5	2	1	0	.333	.444	.667
Mike Jorgensen	2	2	0	0	0	0	0	0	0	1	0	0	.000	.000	.000
Tito Landrum	5	14	2	6	4	0	0	0	1	1	1	0	.429	.467	.429
Willie McGee	6	26	6	7	3	1	0	0	3	6	2	3	.269	.345	.308
Tom Nieto	1	3	1	0	0	0	0	0	1	2	0	0	.000	.250	.000
Terry Pendleton	6	24	2	5	4	1	0	0	1	3	0	1	.208	.240	.250
Darrell Porter	5	15	1	4	0	1	0	0	5	4	0	0	.267	.450	.333
Ozzie Smith	6	23	4	10	3	1	1	1	3	1	1	0	.435	.500	.696
John Tudor	2	4	1	0	0	0	0	0	1	1	0	0	.000	.200	.000
Andy Van Slyke	5	11	1	1	1	0	0	0	2	1	0	0	.091	.231	.091
Totals	6	201	29	56	26	10	1	3	30	34	6	6	.279	.371	.383

Batting

Dodgers	G	AB	R	H	RBI	2B	3B	HR	BB	SO	SB	CS	Avg	OBP	Slg
Dave Anderson	4	5	1	0	0	0	0	0	3	1	0	0	.000	.375	.000
Bob Bailor	2	1	0	0	0	0	0	0	0	0	0	0	.000	.000	.000
Greg Brock	5	12	2	1	2	0	0	1	2	2	0	0	.083	.214	.333
Enos Cabell	5	13	1	1	0	0	0	0	0	3	0	0	.077	.077	.077
Bobby Castillo	1	2	0	0	0	0	0	0	0	1	0	0	.000	.000	.000
Mariano Duncan	5	18	2	4	1	2	1	0	1	3	1	0	.222	.263	.444
Pedro Guerrero	6	20	2	5	4	1	0	0	5	2	2	0	.250	.385	.300
Orel Hershiser	2	7	1	2	1	0	0	0	0	2	0	0	.286	.286	.286
Jay Johnstone	1	1	0	0	0	0	0	0	0	0	0	0	.000	.000	.000
Ken Landreaux	5	18	4	7	2	3	0	0	1	1	0	0	.389	.421	.556
Bill Madlock	6	24	5	8	7	1	0	3	0	2	1	0	.333	.333	.750
Candy Maldonado	4	7	0	1	1	0	0	0	0	3	0	0	.143	.143	.143
Mike Marshall	6	23	1	5	3	2	0	1	3	3	0	0	.217	.250	.435
Len Matuszek	3	1	1	1	0	0	0	0	0	0	0	0	1.000	1.000	1.000
Tom Niedenfuer	3	1	0	0	0	0	0	0	0	1	0	0	.000	.000	.000
Steve Sax	6	20	1	6	1	3	0	0	1	5	0	1	.300	.333	.450
Mike Scioscia	6	16	2	4	1	0	0	0	4	0	0	0	.250	.400	.250
Fernando Valenzuela	2	5	0	1	0	0	0	0	0	0	0	0	.200	.200	.200
Bob Welch	1	1	0	0	0	0	0	0	0	0	0	0	.000	.000	.000
Terry Whitfield	1	0	0	0	0	0	0	0	0	0	0	0	—	—	—
Steve Yeager	1	2	0	0	0	0	0	0	1	1	0	0	.000	.333	.000
Totals	6	197	23	46	23	12	1	5	19	31	4	1	.234	.300	.381

Pitching

Cardinals	G	GS	CG	IP	H	R	ER	BB	SO	W-L	Sv-Op	Hld	ERA
Joaquin Andujar	2	2	0	10.1	14	10	8	4	9	0-1	0-0	0	6.97
Bill Campbell	3	0	0	2.1	3	0	0	0	2	0-0	0-0	0	0.00
Danny Cox	1	1	0	6.0	4	2	2	5	4	1-0	0-0	0	3.00
Ken Dayley	5	0	0	6.0	2	0	0	1	3	0-0	2-2	0	0.00
Bob Forsch	1	1	0	3.1	3	2	2	2	0	0-0	0-0	0	5.40
Ricky Horton	3	0	0	3.0	4	3	3	2	1	0-0	0-0	1	9.00
Jeff Lahti	2	0	0	2.0	2	0	0	0	1	1-0	0-0	0	0.00
John Tudor	2	2	0	12.2	10	5	4	3	8	1-1	0-0	0	2.84
Todd Worrell	4	0	0	6.1	4	1	1	2	3	1-0	0-0	1	1.42
Totals	6	6	0	52.0	46	23	20	19	31	4-2	2-2	2	3.46

Pitching

Dodgers	G	GS	CG	IP	H	R	ER	BB	SO	W-L	Sv-Op	Hld	ERA
Bobby Castillo	1	0	0	5.1	4	2	2	2	4	0-0	0-0	0	3.38
Carlos Diaz	2	0	0	3.0	5	1	1	1	2	0-0	0-0	0	3.00
Orel Hershiser	2	2	1	15.1	17	6	6	6	5	1-0	0-0	0	3.52
Rick Honeycutt	2	0	0	1.1	4	2	2	2	1	0-0	0-0	0	13.50
Ken Howell	1	0	0	2.0	0	0	0	0	2	0-0	0-0	0	0.00
Tom Niedenfuer	3	0	0	5.2	5	4	4	2	5	0-2	1-2	0	6.35
Jerry Reuss	1	1	0	1.2	5	7	2	1	0	0-1	0-0	0	10.80
Fernando Valenzuela	2	2	0	14.1	11	3	3	10	13	1-0	0-0	0	1.88
Bob Welch	1	1	0	2.2	5	4	2	6	2	0-1	0-0	0	6.75
Totals	6	6	1	51.1	56	29	20	30	34	2-4	1-2	0	3.51

Fielding

Cardinals	Pos	G	PO	Ast	E	DP	PB	FPct
Joaquin Andujar	p	2	0	0	2	0	—	.000
Bill Campbell	p	3	0	0	0	0	—	—
Cesar Cedeno	rf	4	5	0	0	0	—	1.000
Jack Clark	1b	6	55	0	0	3	—	1.000
Vince Coleman	lf	3	8	0	0	0	—	1.000
Danny Cox	p	1	0	0	0	0	—	—
Ken Dayley	p	5	0	1	0	0	—	1.000
Bob Forsch	p	1	0	1	0	0	—	1.000
Tom Herr	2b	6	13	12	0	3	—	1.000
Ricky Horton	p	3	1	2	0	1	—	1.000
Jeff Lahti	p	2	0	0	0	0	—	—
Tito Landrum	lf	3	6	0	0	0	—	1.000
	rf	1	0	0	0	0	—	—
Willie McGee	cf	6	18	0	0	0	—	1.000
Tom Nieto	c	1	7	0	0	0	0	1.000
Terry Pendleton	3b	6	6	18	1	2	—	.960
Darrell Porter	c	5	25	2	0	0	1	1.000
Ozzie Smith	ss	6	6	16	0	2	—	1.000
John Tudor	p	2	0	1	0	0	—	1.000
Andy Van Slyke	rf	5	6	0	0	0	—	1.000
Todd Worrell	p	4	0	1	0	0	—	1.000
Totals		6	156	54	3	11	1	.986

Fielding

Dodgers	Pos	G	PO	Ast	E	DP	PB	FPct
Dave Anderson	ss	3	3	4	0	1	—	1.000
	3b	1	0	0	0	0	—	—
Bob Bailor	3b	2	0	1	0	0	—	1.000
Greg Brock	1b	4	35	4	0	0	—	1.000
Enos Cabell	1b	3	20	2	0	2	—	1.000
Bobby Castillo	p	1	1	3	0	1	—	1.000
Carlos Diaz	p	2	1	0	0	0	—	1.000
Mariano Duncan	ss	5	7	16	1	2	—	.958
Pedro Guerrero	lf	6	11	0	0	0	—	1.000
Orel Hershiser	p	2	2	2	0	1	—	1.000
Rick Honeycutt	p	2	0	1	0	0	—	1.000
Ken Howell	p	1	0	1	0	0	—	1.000
Ken Landreaux	cf	5	7	0	0	0	—	1.000
Bill Madlock	3b	6	6	9	0	0	—	1.000
Candy Maldonado	cf	2	4	0	1	0	—	.800
	lf	1	0	0	0	0	—	—
Mike Marshall	rf	6	8	0	0	0	—	1.000
Len Matuszek	1b	1	0	0	0	0	—	—
	lf	1	0	0	0	0	—	—
Tom Niedenfuer	p	3	2	0	0	0	—	1.000
Jerry Reuss	p	1	0	0	1	0	—	.000
Steve Sax	2b	6	11	21	0	1	—	1.000
Mike Scioscia	c	6	31	4	1	0	0	.972
Fernando Valenzuela	p	2	1	3	1	0	—	.800
Bob Welch	p	1	0	0	1	0	—	.000
Steve Yeager	c	1	4	0	0	0	0	1.000
Totals		6	154	71	6	8	0	.974

1986 Boston Red Sox (AL) 4, California Angels (AL) 3

For once, destiny was on the side of the Boston Red Sox. When the California Angels took a three-games-to-one lead in the ALCS, it looked like just another postseason disappointment for the Red Sox. Mike Witt was dominant in the opener; Bruce Hurst returned the favor in Game 2, John Candelaria put the Angels back in front with a solid effort in Game 3. Disaster struck the Sox in Game 4, when Roger Clemens was unable to close out a 3-0 game. Only one out away from victory, Calvin Schiraldi hit Brian Downing to force in the tying run, and the Angels went on to win in extra innings. The next day, it looked like it was all over when the Angels took a 5-2 lead into the ninth inning. But Don Baylor hit a two-run homer to make it a one-run game, and later in the inning, Dave Henderson took Donnie Moore deep for one of the most famous home runs in Red Sox history. The two-run shot put Boston ahead 6-5, but the Angels sent the game into extra innings with a run in the ninth. Henderson beat Moore once again, lifting a sacrifice fly in the top of the 11th to drive in the eventual winning run. Reinvigorated by their momentous comeback, the Sox rolled to 10-4 and 8-1 victories in the sixth and seventh games to take the AL flag.

Game 1

Tuesday, October 7

Angels	AB	R	H	RBI	BB	K	Avg
Ruppert Jones, rf	4	1	1	1	0	1	.250
Rick Burleson, ph	1	0	0	0	0	0	.000
Devon White, rf	0	0	0	0	0	0	—
Wally Joyner, 1b	4	1	2	1	1	0	.500
Brian Downing, lf	5	0	2	4	0	0	.400
Reggie Jackson, dh	4	0	0	0	1	1	.000
Doug DeCinces, 3b	5	0	1	0	0	0	.200
Rob Wilfong, 2b	5	1	0	0	0	1	.000
Dick Schofield, ss	5	1	1	0	0	2	.200
Bob Boone, c	3	2	2	1	1	0	.667
Gary Pettis, cf	3	2	2	1	1	0	.667
TOTALS	39	8	11	8	4	5	.282

Red Sox	AB	R	H	RBI	BB	K	Avg
Wade Boggs, 3b	3	0	1	0	1	0	.333
Marty Barrett, 2b	4	0	2	1	0	0	.500
Bill Buckner, 1b	4	0	0	0	0	0	.000
Jim Rice, lf	4	0	0	0	0	1	.000
Don Baylor, dh	4	0	1	0	0	0	.250
Dwight Evans, rf	4	0	0	0	0	1	.000
Rich Gedman, c	3	0	0	0	0	0	.000
Tony Armas, cf	3	0	0	0	0	0	.000
Spike Owen, ss	2	1	1	0	1	1	.500
TOTALS	31	1	5	1	2	3	.161

	1	2	3	4	5	6	7	8	9	R	H	E
Angels	0	4	1	0	0	0	0	3	0	8	11	0
Red Sox	0	0	0	0	0	1	0	0	0	1	5	1

E—Owen. DP—Angels 1 (DeCinces to Wilfong to Joyner). LOB—Angels 8, Red Sox 5. Scoring Position—Angels 6-for-11, Red Sox 2-for-6. 2B—Joyner 2 (2), Baylor (1). GDP—Barrett. SB—Schofield (1).

Angels	IP	H	R	ER	BB	K	ERA
Mike Witt (W, 1-0)	9.0	5	1	1	2	3	1.00

Red Sox	IP	H	R	ER	BB	K	ERA
Roger Clemens (L, 0-1)	7.1	10	8	7	3	5	8.59
Joe Sambito	0.1	0	0	0	1	0	0.00
Bob Stanley	1.1	1	0	0	0	0	0.00

Time—2:52. Attendance—32,993. Umpires—HP, Barnett. 1B, McCoy. 2B, Cooney. 3B, Bremigan.

Game 2

Wednesday, October 8

Angels	AB	R	H	RBI	BB	K	Avg
Rick Burleson, dh	5	0	1	0	0	0	.167
Wally Joyner, 1b	4	1	2	1	0	0	.500
Brian Downing, lf	4	1	1	0	0	1	.333
Doug DeCinces, 3b	4	0	1	0	0	0	.222
George Hendrick, rf	4	0	0	0	0	1	.000
Bobby Grich, 2b	4	0	2	0	0	0	.500
Dick Schofield, ss	4	0	2	1	0	0	.333
Bob Boone, c	4	0	1	0	0	1	.429
Gary Pettis, cf	4	0	1	0	0	1	.429
TOTALS	37	2	11	2	0	4	.333

Red Sox	AB	R	H	RBI	BB	K	Avg
Wade Boggs, 3b	4	1	2	0	0	0	.429
Marty Barrett, 2b	5	1	3	2	0	2	.556
Bill Buckner, 1b	4	2	1	1	0	0	.125
Dave Stapleton, 1b	0	0	0	0	0	0	—
Jim Rice, lf	5	2	2	2	0	2	.222
Don Baylor, dh	2	1	2	0	3	0	.500
Dwight Evans, rf	5	0	1	2	0	0	.111
Rich Gedman, c	4	1	1	1	0	1	.143
Tony Armas, cf	4	0	0	0	1	0	.000
Dave Henderson, cf	0	0	0	0	0	0	—
Spike Owen, ss	3	1	1	0	1	0	.400
TOTALS	36	9	13	8	4	6	.269

	1	2	3	4	5	6	7	8	9	R	H	E
Angels	0	0	0	1	1	0	0	0	0	2	11	3
Red Sox	1	1	0	0	1	0	3	3	x	9	13	2

E—DeCinces, Grich, Boggs, Owen, Schofield. DP—Angels 1 (Joyner to Schofield to McCaskill), Red Sox 1 (Barrett to Owen to Buckner). LOB—Angels 8, Red Sox 9. Scoring Position—Angels 2-for-7, Red Sox 5-for-12. 2B—Barrett (1), Evans (1). 3B—Boggs (1). HR—Joyner (1), Rice (1). S—Boggs. SF—Buckner. GDP—Joyner, Buckner.

Angels	IP	H	R	ER	BB	K	ERA
Kirk McCaskill (L, 0-1)	7.0	10	6	3	3	6	3.86
Gary Lucas	0.2	1	2	2	1	0	27.00
Doug Corbett	0.1	2	1	1	0	0	27.00

Red Sox	IP	H	R	ER	BB	K	ERA
Bruce Hurst (W, 1-0)	9.0	11	2	1	0	4	1.00

Time—2:47. Attendance—32,786. Umpires—HP, McCoy. 1B, Cooney. 2B, Bremigan. 3B, Roe.

Game 3

Friday, October 10

Red Sox	AB	R	H	RBI	BB	K	Avg
Wade Boggs, 3b	4	0	0	0	1	0	.273
Marty Barrett, 2b	5	1	2	0	0	0	.500
Bill Buckner, 1b	5	0	0	0	0	2	.077
Jim Rice, lf	3	2	1	0	1	2	.250
Don Baylor, dh	3	0	1	0	1	0	.444
Dwight Evans, rf	3	0	1	0	1	0	.167
Rich Gedman, c	4	0	3	2	0	0	.364
Tony Armas, cf	4	0	1	0	0	0	.091
Spike Owen, ss	3	0	0	0	0	1	.250
Mike Greenwell, ph	1	0	0	0	0	0	.000
TOTALS	35	3	9	2	4	5	.265

Angels	AB	R	H	RBI	BB	K	Avg
Gary Pettis, cf	3	1	1	2	1	1	.400
Wally Joyner, 1b	3	1	1	0	0	0	.455
Brian Downing, lf	4	0	1	0	0	1	.308
Reggie Jackson, dh	3	1	1	1	1	0	.143
Doug DeCinces, 3b	4	0	1	0	0	0	.231
Ruppert Jones, rf	3	0	0	1	0	0	.143
Devon White, rf	0	0	0	0	0	0	—
Bobby Grich, 2b	4	0	0	0	0	1	.250
Dick Schofield, ss	3	1	2	1	0	0	.417
Bob Boone, c	3	1	1	0	0	0	.400
TOTALS	30	5	8	5	3	3	.319

	1	2	3	4	5	6	7	8	9	R	H	E
Red Sox	0	1	0	0	0	0	0	2	0	3	9	1
Angels	0	0	0	0	0	1	3	1	x	5	8	0

E—Boggs. DP—Red Sox 1 (Boggs to Barrett to Buckner). LOB—Red Sox 9, Angels 5. Scoring Position—Red Sox 3-for-10, Angels 2-for-5. 2B—Rice (1), Armas (1), Schofield (1). HR—Pettis (1), Schofield (1). SF—Jones. GDP—DeCinces. CS—Pettis (1).

Red Sox	IP	H	R	ER	BB	K	ERA
Oil Can Boyd (L, 0-1)	6.2	8	4	4	2	3	5.40
Joe Sambito	0.1	0	0	0	0	0	0.00
Calvin Schiraldi	1.0	0	1	0	1	0	0.00

Angels	IP	H	R	ER	BB	K	ERA
John Candelaria (W, 1-0)	7.0	5	1	1	3	5	1.29
Donnie Moore (S, 1)	2.0	4	2	2	1	0	9.00

Balk—Moore. Time—2:48. Attendance—64,206. Umpires—HP, Cooney. 1B, Bremigan. 2B, Roe. 3B, Garcia.

Game 4

Saturday, October 11

Red Sox	AB	R	H	RBI	BB	K	Avg
Wade Boggs, 3b	5	0	1	0	0	0	.250
Marty Barrett, 2b	3	1	1	1	1	0	.471
Bill Buckner, 1b	5	0	1	0	0	0	.111
Jim Rice, lf	5	0	0	0	0	0	.176
Don Baylor, dh	5	0	1	0	0	2	.357
Dwight Evans, rf	4	0	0	0	1	0	.125
Rich Gedman, c	5	0	0	0	0	1	.250
Tony Armas, cf	3	1	1	0	0	1	.143
Dave Henderson, cf	1	0	0	0	0	0	.000
Spike Owen, ss	3	1	1	0	0	0	.273
TOTALS	39	3	6	2	2	4	.236

Angels	AB	R	H	RBI	BB	K	Avg
Ruppert Jones, rf	2	0	1	0	4	1	.222
Bobby Grich, 2b	6	0	1	0	3	0	.214
Brian Downing, lf	3	0	0	1	1	1	.250
Reggie Jackson, dh	5	0	0	0	1	0	.083
Doug DeCinces, 3b	5	1	2	1	0	0	.278
George Hendrick, 1b	5	0	0	0	0	1	.000
Dick Schofield, ss	5	1	1	0	0	2	.353
Bob Boone, c	4	0	2	0	0	1	.429
Devon White, pr	0	1	0	0	0	0	.000
Jerry Narron, c	1	1	1	0	0	0	1.000
Gary Pettis, cf	4	0	3	1	0	1	.500
TOTALS	40	4	11	4	5	11	.282

	1	2	3	4	5	6	7	8	9	10	11	R	H	E
Red Sox	0	0	0	0	0	1	0	2	0	0	0	3	6	1
Angels	0	0	0	0	0	0	0	0	3	0	1	4	11	2

E—DeCinces, Grich, Owen. DP—Red Sox 1 (Owen to Buckner). LOB—Red Sox 7, Angels 12. Scoring Position—Red Sox 2-for-12, Angels 2-for-10. 2B—Boggs (1), Buckner (1), Baylor (2), Jones (1), Pettis (1). HR—DeCinces (1). S—Barrett, Owen, Pettis. GDP—Hendrick. CS—Pettis (2).

Red Sox	IP	H	R	ER	BB	K	ERA
Roger Clemens	8.1	8	3	3	3	9	5.74
Calvin Schiraldi (BS, 1; L, 0-1)	2.0	3	1	1	2	2	3.00

Angels	IP	H	R	ER	BB	K	ERA
Don Sutton	6.1	4	1	1	1	2	1.42
Gary Lucas	0.1	0	0	0	0	1	18.00
Vern Ruhle	0.2	2	2	1	0	0	13.50
Chuck Finley	0.0	0	0	0	0	0	—
Doug Corbett (W, 1-0)	3.2	0	0	0	1	1	2.25

Finley pitched to two batters in the 8th.

WP—Ruhle. PB—Boone. HBP—Downing by Schiraldi. Time—3:50. Attendance—64,223. Umpires—HP, Bremigan. 1B, Roe. 2B, Garcia. 3B, Barnett.

Postseason: League Championship Series

Game 5
Sunday, October 12

Red Sox	AB	R	H	RBI	BB	K	Avg
Wade Boggs, 3b	5	0	1	0	1	0	.238
Marty Barrett, 2b	5	0	0	0	0	0	.364
Bill Buckner, 1b	4	0	1	0	0	0	.136
Dave Stapleton, pr-1b	1	1	1	0	0	0	1.000
Jim Rice, lf	5	1	1	0	0	2	.182
Don Baylor, dh	4	2	1	2	0	1	.333
Dwight Evans, rf	5	0	1	0	0	1	.143
Rich Gedman, c	4	2	4	2	0	0	.400
Tony Armas, cf	2	0	0	0	0	0	.125
Dave Henderson, cf	2	1	1	3	0	1	.333
Spike Owen, ss	2	0	0	0	0	0	.231
Mike Greenwell, ph	1	0	1	0	0	0	.500
Ed Romero, pr-ss	2	0	0	0	0	0	.000
TOTALS	42	7	12	7	1	5	.246

Angels	AB	R	H	RBI	BB	K	Avg
Rick Burleson, 2b	2	0	0	0	0	0	.125
Rob Wilfong, ph-2b	3	0	2	2	0	1	.250
Dick Schofield, ss	5	0	1	0	1	1	.318
Brian Downing, lf	3	0	0	1	2	0	.211
Doug DeCinces, 3b	5	1	2	0	0	0	.304
Bobby Grich, 1b	5	1	1	2	0	2	.211
Reggie Jackson, dh	5	0	1	0	0	3	.118
George Hendrick, rf	3	0	1	0	0	0	.083
Devon White, pr-rf	2	1	1	0	0	1	.500
Bob Boone, c	3	1	3	1	0	0	.529
Ruppert Jones, pr	0	1	0	0	0	0	.222
Jerry Narron, c	0	0	0	0	1	0	1.000
Gary Pettis, cf	3	1	1	0	1	0	.471
TOTALS	39	6	13	6	5	8	.282

	1	2	3	4	5	6	7	8	9	10	11	R	H	E
Red Sox	0	2	0	0	0	0	0	0	4	0	1	7	12	0
Angels	0	0	1	0	0	2	2	0	1	0	0	6	13	0

DP—Angels 2 (Schofield to Wilfong to Grich; Schofield to Wilfong to Grich). LOB—Red Sox 6, Angels 9. Scoring Position—Red Sox 1-for-6, Angels 3-for-11. 2B—Gedman (1), DeCinces 2 (2), Wilfong (1). HR—Baylor (1), Gedman (1), Grich (1), Boone (1), Henderson (1). S—Burleson, Boone, Pettis. SF—Downing, Henderson. GDP—Boggs, Rice. CS—Downing (1), White (1).

Red Sox	IP	H	R	ER	BB	K	ERA
Bruce Hurst	6.0	7	3	3	1	4	2.40
Bob Stanley	2.1	4	3	3	2	1	7.36
Joe Sambito (BS, 1)	0.0	1	0	0	0	0	0.00
Steve Crawford (W, 1-0)	1.2	1	0	0	2	1	0.00
Calvin Schiraldi (S, 1)	1.0	0	0	0	0	2	2.25

Angels	IP	H	R	ER	BB	K	ERA
Mike Witt	8.2	8	4	4	0	5	2.55
Gary Lucas	0.0	0	1	1	0	0	27.00
Donnie Moore (BS, 1; L, 0-1)	2.0	4	2	2	1	0	9.00
Chuck Finley	0.1	0	0	0	0	0	0.00

Lucas pitched to one batter in the 9th. Sambito pitched to one batter in the 9th.

HBP—Baylor by Moore, Gedman by Lucas. Time—3:54. Attendance—64,223. Umpires—HP, Roe. 1B, Garcia. 2B, Barnett. 3B, McCoy.

Game 6
Tuesday, October 14

Angels	AB	R	H	RBI	BB	K	Avg
Gary Pettis, cf	5	0	1	0	0	1	.409
Ruppert Jones, rf	4	1	0	0	1	0	.154
Brian Downing, lf	5	1	1	1	0	1	.208
Reggie Jackson, dh	5	1	3	1	0	1	.227
Doug DeCinces, 3b	5	0	1	0	1	1	.286
Dick Schofield, ss	4	1	2	0	0	0	.346
Bobby Grich, 1b	3	0	1	0	0	0	.227
Rob Wilfong, 2b	4	0	2	0	0	0	.333
Bob Boone, c	3	0	0	0	0	1	.450
Jack Howell, ph	0	0	0	0	1	0	—
Jerry Narron, c	0	0	0	0	0	0	1.000
TOTALS	38	4	11	3	2	5	.300

Red Sox	AB	R	H	RBI	BB	K	Avg
Wade Boggs, 3b	4	2	1	0	1	0	.240
Marty Barrett, 2b	4	1	3	1	1	0	.423
Bill Buckner, 1b	4	1	2	1	0	0	.192
Dave Stapleton, pr-1b	1	0	1	0	0	0	1.000
Jim Rice, lf	5	1	0	1	0	1	.148
Don Baylor, dh	4	2	1	0	0	0	.318
Dwight Evans, rf	4	0	2	1	0	0	.200
Rich Gedman, c	4	1	2	0	0	0	.417
Dave Henderson, cf	3	1	0	1	1	1	.167
Spike Owen, ss	4	1	4	2	0	0	.412
TOTALS	37	10	16	7	3	4	.290

	1	2	3	4	5	6	7	8	9	R	H	E
Angels	2	0	0	0	0	0	1	1	0	4	11	1
Red Sox	2	0	5	0	1	0	2	0	x	10	16	1

E—Grich, Owen. DP—Angels 3 (Schofield to Wilfong to Grich; DeCinces to Wilfong to Grich; DeCinces to Wilfong to Grich), Red Sox 1 (Barrett to Buckner). LOB—Angels 10, Red Sox 7. Scoring Position—Angels 2-for-10, Red Sox 7-for-18. 2B—Jackson 2 (2), DeCinces (3), Barrett (2). 3B—Owen (1). HR—Downing (1). GDP—DeCinces, Boggs, Rice, Baylor.

Red Sox	IP	H	R	ER	BB	K	ERA
Oil Can Boyd (W, 1-1)	7.0	9	3	3	1	5	4.61
Bob Stanley	2.0	2	1	0	1	0	4.76

Angels	IP	H	R	ER	BB	K	ERA
Kirk McCaskill (L, 0-2)	2.1	6	7	5	2	1	7.71
Gary Lucas	1.1	2	0	0	0	1	11.57
Doug Corbett	2.2	7	3	3	1	1	5.40
Chuck Finley	1.2	1	0	0	0	1	0.00

PB—Boone. HBP—Grich by Boyd, Baylor by Corbett. Time—3:23. Attendance—32,998. Umpires—HP, Garcia. 1B, Barnett. 2B, McCoy. 3B, Cooney.

Game 7
Wednesday, October 15

Angels	AB	R	H	RBI	BB	K	Avg
Ruppert Jones, rf	4	1	1	0	0	0	.176
Rob Wilfong, 2b	1	0	0	0	0	0	.308
Rick Burleson, 2b	3	0	2	0	0	0	.273
Brian Downing, lf	3	0	1	0	1	1	.222
Reggie Jackson, dh	4	0	0	0	0	1	.192
Doug DeCinces, 3b	4	0	1	1	0	1	.281
Dick Schofield, ss	4	0	0	0	0	0	.300
Gary Pettis, cf	4	0	0	0	0	1	.346
Bobby Grich, 1b	2	0	0	0	0	2	.208
Jack Howell, ph	1	0	0	0	0	0	.000
Bob Boone, c	2	0	1	0	0	0	.455
Jerry Narron, ph	1	0	0	0	0	1	.500
TOTALS	33	1	6	1	1	8	.277

Red Sox	AB	R	H	RBI	BB	K	Avg
Wade Boggs, 3b	5	0	1	2	0	1	.233
Marty Barrett, 2b	4	0	0	0	0	1	.367
Bill Buckner, 1b	2	0	1	0	0	0	.214
Dave Stapleton, pr-1b	1	1	0	0	0	0	.667
Jim Rice, lf	4	2	1	3	0	0	.161
Don Baylor, dh	4	1	2	0	0	1	.346
Dwight Evans, rf	3	2	1	1	1	0	.214
Rich Gedman, c	4	0	0	1	0	1	.357
Dave Henderson, cf	3	1	0	0	1	0	.111
Spike Owen, ss	4	1	2	1	0	0	.429
TOTALS	34	8	8	8	3	4	.282

	1	2	3	4	5	6	7	8	9	R	H	E
Angels	0	0	0	0	0	0	0	1	0	1	6	2
Red Sox	0	3	0	4	0	0	1	0	x	8	8	1

E—Pettis, Owen, Schofield. DP—Red Sox 1 (Clemens to Barrett to Stapleton). LOB—Angels 8, Red Sox 5. Scoring Position—Angels 1-for-7, Red Sox 4-for-10. 2B—Baylor (3). HR—Rice (2), Evans (1). GDP—DeCinces. SB—Owen (1).

Angels	IP	H	R	ER	BB	K	ERA
John Candelaria (L, 1-1)	3.2	6	7	0	3	2	0.84
Don Sutton	3.1	2	1	1	0	2	1.86
Donnie Moore	1.0	0	0	0	0	0	7.20

Red Sox	IP	H	R	ER	BB	K	ERA
Roger Clemens (W, 1-1)	7.0	4	1	1	1	3	4.37
Calvin Schiraldi	2.0	2	0	0	0	5	1.50

Clemens pitched to one batter in the 8th.

HBP—Grich by Clemens, Boone by Clemens. Time—2:39. Attendance—33,001. Umpires—HP, Barnett. 1B, McCoy. 2B, Garcia. 3B, Bremigan.

1986 AL Championship Series—Composite Statistics

Batting

Red Sox	G	AB	R	H	RBI	2B	3B	HR	BB	SO	SB	CS	Avg	OBP	Slg
Tony Armas	5	16	1	2	0	1	0	0	0	2	0	0	.125	.125	.188
Marty Barrett	7	30	4	11	5	2	0	0	2	2	0	0	.367	.406	.433
Don Baylor	7	26	6	9	2	3	0	1	4	5	0	0	.346	.469	.577
Wade Boggs	7	30	3	7	2	1	1	0	4	1	0	0	.233	.324	.333
Bill Buckner	7	28	3	6	3	1	0	0	0	2	0	0	.214	.207	.250
Dwight Evans	7	28	2	6	4	1	0	1	3	3	0	0	.214	.290	.357
Rich Gedman	7	28	4	10	6	1	0	1	0	4	0	0	.357	.379	.500
Mike Greenwell	2	2	0	1	0	0	0	0	0	0	0	0	.500	.500	.500
Dave Henderson	5	9	3	1	4	0	0	1	2	2	0	0	.111	.250	.444
Spike Owen	7	21	5	9	3	0	1	0	2	2	1	0	.429	.478	.524
Jim Rice	7	31	8	5	6	1	0	2	1	8	0	0	.161	.188	.387
Ed Romero	1	2	0	0	0	0	0	0	0	0	0	0	.000	.000	.000
Dave Stapleton	4	3	2	2	0	0	0	0	1	0	0	0	.667	.750	.667
Totals	**7**	**254**	**41**	**69**	**35**	**11**	**2**	**6**	**19**	**31**	**1**	**0**	**.272**	**.327**	**.402**

Angels	G	AB	R	H	RBI	2B	3B	HR	BB	SO	SB	CS	Avg	OBP	Slg
Bob Boone	7	22	4	10	2	0	0	1	1	3	0	0	.455	.500	.591
Rick Burleson	4	11	0	3	0	0	0	0	0	0	0	0	.273	.273	.273
Doug DeCinces	7	32	2	9	3	3	0	1	2	0	0	0	.281	.281	.469
Brian Downing	7	27	2	6	7	0	0	1	4	5	0	1	.222	.333	.333
Bobby Grich	6	24	1	5	3	0	0	1	0	8	0	0	.208	.269	.333
George Hendrick	3	12	0	1	0	0	0	0	0	2	0	0	.083	.083	.083
Jack Howell	2	1	0	0	0	0	0	0	1	1	0	0	.000	.500	.000
Reggie Jackson	6	26	2	5	2	2	0	0	2	7	0	0	.192	.250	.269
Ruppert Jones	6	17	4	3	2	1	0	0	5	2	0	0	.176	.348	.235
Wally Joyner	3	11	3	5	2	2	0	1	2	0	0	0	.455	.538	.909
Jerry Narron	4	2	1	1	0	0	0	0	1	1	0	0	.500	.667	.500
Gary Pettis	7	26	4	9	4	1	0	1	3	5	0	2	.346	.414	.500
Dick Schofield	7	30	4	9	2	1	0	1	1	5	1	0	.300	.323	.433
Devon White	4	2	2	1	0	0	0	0	0	1	0	1	.500	.500	.500
Rob Wilfong	4	13	1	4	2	1	0	0	0	2	0	0	.308	.308	.385
Totals	**7**	**256**	**30**	**71**	**29**	**11**	**0**	**7**	**20**	**44**	**1**	**4**	**.277**	**.337**	**.402**

Pitching

Red Sox	G	GS	CG	IP	H	R	ER	BB	SO	W-L	Sv-Op	Hld	ERA
Oil Can Boyd	2	2	0	13.2	17	7	7	3	8	1-1	0-0	0	4.61
Roger Clemens	3	3	0	22.2	22	12	11	7	17	1-1	0-0	0	4.37
Steve Crawford	1	0	0	1.2	1	0	0	2	1	1-0	0-0	0	0.00
Bruce Hurst	2	2	1	15.0	18	5	4	1	8	1-0	0-0	0	2.40
Joe Sambito	3	0	0	0.2	1	0	0	1	0	0-0	0-1	0	0.00
Calvin Schiraldi	4	0	0	6.0	5	2	1	3	9	0-1	1-2	0	1.50
Bob Stanley	3	0	0	5.2	7	4	3	3	1	0-0	0-0	0	4.76
Totals	**7**	**7**	**1**	**65.1**	**71**	**30**	**26**	**20**	**44**	**4-3**	**1-3**	**0**	**3.58**

Angels	G	GS	CG	IP	H	R	ER	BB	SO	W-L	Sv-Op	Hld	ERA
John Candelaria	2	2	0	10.2	11	8	1	6	7	1-1	0-0	0	0.84
Doug Corbett	3	0	0	6.2	9	4	4	2	2	1-0	0-0	0	5.40
Chuck Finley	3	0	0	2.0	1	0	0	0	1	0-0	0-0	0	0.00
Gary Lucas	4	0	0	2.1	3	3	3	1	2	0-0	0-0	0	11.57
Kirk McCaskill	2	0	0	9.1	16	13	8	5	7	0-2	0-0	0	7.71
Donnie Moore	3	0	0	5.0	8	4	4	2	0	0-1	1-2	0	7.20
Vern Ruhle	1	0	0	0.2	2	2	1	0	0	0-0	0-0	0	13.50
Don Sutton	2	1	0	9.2	6	2	2	1	4	0-0	0-0	0	1.86
Mike Witt	2	2	1	17.2	13	5	5	2	8	1-0	0-0	0	2.55
Totals	**7**	**7**	**1**	**64.0**	**69**	**41**	**28**	**19**	**31**	**3-4**	**1-2**	**0**	**3.94**

Fielding

Red Sox	Pos	G	PO	Ast	E	DP	PB	FPct
Tony Armas	cf	5	12	0	0	0	—	1.000
Marty Barrett	2b	7	19	21	0	4	—	1.000
Wade Boggs	3b	7	7	13	2	1	—	.909
Oil Can Boyd	p	2	2	2	0	0	—	1.000
Bill Buckner	1b	7	49	5	0	4	—	1.000
Roger Clemens	p	3	1	2	0	1	—	1.000
Steve Crawford	p	1	1	0	0	0	—	1.000
Dwight Evans	rf	7	11	0	0	0	—	1.000
Rich Gedman	c	7	45	4	0	0	0	1.000
Dave Henderson	cf	5	11	0	0	0	—	1.000
Bruce Hurst	p	2	1	2	0	0	—	1.000
Spike Owen	ss	7	12	21	5	2	—	.868
Jim Rice	lf	7	13	1	0	0	—	1.000
Ed Romero	ss	1	0	0	0	0	—	—
Joe Sambito	p	3	0	0	0	0	—	—
Calvin Schiraldi	p	4	0	0	0	0	—	—
Bob Stanley	p	3	0	1	0	0	—	1.000
Dave Stapleton	1b	4	12	1	0	1	—	1.000
Totals		**7**	**196**	**73**	**7**	**13**	**0**	**.975**

Angels	Pos	G	PO	Ast	E	DP	PB	FPct
Bob Boone	c	7	33	2	0	0	2	1.000
Rick Burleson	2b	2	3	5	0	0	—	1.000
John Candelaria	p	2	0	1	0	0	—	1.000
Doug Corbett	p	3	0	1	0	0	—	1.000
Doug DeCinces	3b	7	6	18	2	3	—	.923
Brian Downing	lf	7	18	0	0	0	—	1.000
Chuck Finley	p	3	0	0	0	0	—	—
Bobby Grich	1b	3	26	2	1	5	—	.966
	2b	3	3	7	2	0	—	.833
George Hendrick	rf	2	2	0	0	0	—	1.000
	1b	1	14	2	0	0	—	1.000
Ruppert Jones	rf	5	6	0	0	0	—	1.000
Wally Joyner	1b	3	24	1	0	2	—	1.000
Gary Lucas	p	4	0	0	0	0	—	—
Kirk McCaskill	p	2	1	0	0	1	—	1.000
Donnie Moore	p	3	0	0	0	0	—	—
Jerry Narron	c	3	1	0	0	0	0	1.000
Gary Pettis	cf	7	28	0	1	0	—	.966
Vern Ruhle	p	1	0	0	0	0	—	—
Dick Schofield	ss	7	13	23	2	4	—	.947
Don Sutton	p	2	1	1	0	0	—	1.000
Devon White	rf	3	3	0	0	0	—	1.000
Rob Wilfong	2b	4	8	10	0	6	—	1.000
Mike Witt	p	2	2	4	0	0	—	1.000
Totals		**7**	**192**	**77**	**8**	**21**	**2**	**.971**

1986 New York Mets (NL) 4, Houston Astros (NL) 2

Everyone knew that Mike Scott would have won it for the Houston Astros in Game 7, and the New York Mets barely escaped that fate when they pulled out an extra-inning win in Game 6 for an exhausting six-game victory in the NLCS. Scott had been overpowering in both Game 1 and Game 4, tossing a five-hit shutout and striking out 14 for a 1-0 victory in the former, while authoring a three-hitter for a 3-1 win in the latter. In between, Bobby Ojeda won Game 2 for the Mets, 5-1, and Lenny Dykstra crushed a game-winning two-run homer in the ninth inning for a 6-5 New York victory in Game 3. With the series tied at two games apiece, the Mets knew they had to win the next two games to avoid facing Scott in Game 7. In the fifth game, Houston starter Nolan Ryan allowed two hits and one run over nine innings, but Mets starter Dwight Gooden allowed nine hits and one run over 10 innings. Gary Carter finally won it for New York with an RBI single in the bottom of the 12th. In Game 6, Houston's Bob Knepper took a 3-0 lead into the ninth before faltering. The Mets scored two runs before he was replaced by closer Dave Smith, who allowed a game-tying sacrifice fly to Ray Knight. The Mets finally broke through for a run in the top of the 14th, but Billy Hatcher homered in the bottom of the frame to keep the game going. The Mets mounted a three-run rally in the top of the 16th and barely held off Houston in the bottom of the inning, winning 7-6 to advance to the World Series.

Game 1

Wednesday, October 8

Mets	AB	R	H	RBI	BB	K	Avg
Lenny Dykstra, cf	3	0	1	0	1	0	.333
Wally Backman, 2b	4	0	0	0	0	1	.000
Keith Hernandez, 1b	4	0	1	0	0	3	.250
Gary Carter, c	4	0	0	0	0	3	.000
Darryl Strawberry, rf	4	0	1	0	0	2	.250
Mookie Wilson, lf	4	0	0	0	0	1	.000
Ray Knight, 3b	4	0	0	0	0	2	.000
Rafael Santana, ss	2	0	1	0	0	0	.500
Lee Mazzilli, ph	1	0	0	0	0	1	.000
Jesse Orosco, p	0	0	0	0	0	0	—
Dwight Gooden, p	2	0	0	0	0	1	.000
Danny Heep, ph	1	0	1	0	0	0	1.000
Kevin Elster, pr-ss	0	0	0	0	0	0	—
TOTALS	33	0	5	0	1	14	.152

Astros	AB	R	H	RBI	BB	K	Avg
Billy Hatcher, cf	3	0	0	0	1	1	.000
Bill Doran, 2b	4	0	0	0	0	0	.000
Denny Walling, 3b	4	0	0	0	0	1	.000
Glenn Davis, 1b	4	1	1	1	0	0	.250
Kevin Bass, rf	4	0	2	0	0	0	.500
Jose Cruz, lf	4	0	1	0	0	2	.250
Alan Ashby, c	1	0	1	0	2	0	1.000
Craig Reynolds, ss	3	0	2	0	0	0	.667
Dickie Thon, ss	0	0	0	0	0	0	—
Mike Scott, p	3	0	0	0	0	2	.000
TOTALS	30	1	7	1	3	6	.233

	1	2	3	4	5	6	7	8	9	R	H	E
Mets	0	0	0	0	0	0	0	0	0	0	5	0
Astros	0	1	0	0	0	0	0	0	x	1	7	1

E—Reynolds. DP—Mets 1 (Santana to Backman to Hernandez). LOB—Mets 7, Astros 8. Scoring Position—Mets 0-for-5, Astros 2-for-10. 2B—Bass (1). HR—Davis (1). GDP—Scott. SB—Dykstra (1), Strawberry (1), Hatcher (1), Bass (1).

Mets	IP	H	R	ER	BB	K	ERA
Dwight Gooden (L, 0-1)	7.0	7	1	1	3	5	1.29
Jesse Orosco	1.0	0	0	0	0	1	0.00

Astros	IP	H	R	ER	BB	K	ERA
Mike Scott (W, 1-0)	9.0	5	0	0	1	14	0.00

Time—2:56. Attendance—44,131. Umpires—HP, Harvey. 1B, Weyer. 2B, Pulli. 3B, Rennert.

Game 2

Thursday, October 9

Mets	AB	R	H	RBI	BB	K	Avg
Lenny Dykstra, cf	5	1	2	0	0	0	.375
Wally Backman, 2b	5	2	2	1	0	0	.222
Keith Hernandez, 1b	3	1	2	2	2	0	.429
Gary Carter, c	5	0	1	1	0	1	.111
Darryl Strawberry, rf	3	0	0	1	0	2	.143
Mookie Wilson, lf	4	0	1	0	0	0	.125
Ray Knight, 3b	3	0	1	0	1	1	.143
Rafael Santana, ss	4	0	1	0	0	2	.333
Bobby Ojeda, p	4	1	0	0	0	2	.000
TOTALS	36	5	10	5	3	8	.215

Astros	AB	R	H	RBI	BB	K	Avg
Billy Hatcher, cf	5	1	1	0	0	1	.125
Bill Doran, 2b	4	0	1	0	0	1	.125
Phil Garner, 3b	3	0	1	1	1	0	.333
Glenn Davis, 1b	4	0	1	0	0	0	.250
Kevin Bass, rf	3	0	2	0	1	0	.571
Jose Cruz, lf	4	0	1	0	0	1	.250
Alan Ashby, c	4	0	0	0	0	0	.200
Dickie Thon, ss	4	0	2	0	0	1	.500
Nolan Ryan, p	1	0	0	0	0	0	.000
Jim Pankovits, ph	1	0	0	0	0	1	.000
Larry Andersen, p	0	0	0	0	0	0	—
Terry Puhl, ph	1	0	1	0	0	0	1.000
Aurelio Lopez, p	0	0	0	0	0	0	—
Charlie Kerfeld, p	0	0	0	0	0	0	—
Davey Lopes, ph	1	0	0	0	0	0	.000
TOTALS	35	1	10	1	2	5	.273

	1	2	3	4	5	6	7	8	9	R	H	E
Mets	0	0	0	2	3	0	0	0	0	5	10	0
Astros	0	0	0	0	0	0	1	0	0	1	10	2

E—Davis, Hatcher. DP—Mets 2 (Backman to Hernandez; Santana to Backman to Hernandez), Astros 1 (Thon to Doran to Davis). LOB—Mets 8, Astros 9. Scoring Position—Mets 3-for-10, Astros 3-for-11. 2B—Dykstra (1), Carter (1), Bass (2). 3B—Hernandez (1). SF—Strawberry (1). GDP—Carter, Lopes. SB—Wilson (1).

Mets	IP	H	R	ER	BB	K	ERA
Bobby Ojeda (W, 1-0)	9.0	10	1	1	2	5	1.00

Astros	IP	H	R	ER	BB	K	ERA
Nolan Ryan (L, 0-1)	5.0	7	5	5	0	5	9.00
Larry Andersen	2.0	1	0	0	1	2	0.00
Aurelio Lopez	1.1	2	0	0	2	1	0.00
Charlie Kerfeld	0.2	0	0	0	0	0	0.00

Time—2:40. Attendance—44,391. Umpires—HP, Weyer. 1B, Pulli. 2B, Rennert. 3B, West.

Game 3

Saturday, October 11

Astros	AB	R	H	RBI	BB	K	Avg
Bill Doran, 2b	4	2	2	2	1	0	.250
Billy Hatcher, cf	3	1	2	0	1	0	.273
Denny Walling, 3b	5	1	1	2	0	2	.111
Glenn Davis, 1b	3	0	1	0	0	1	.273
Kevin Bass, rf	3	0	0	0	1	1	.400
Jose Cruz, lf	3	0	1	1	1	2	.273
Alan Ashby, c	4	0	0	0	0	0	.111
Craig Reynolds, ss	2	1	1	0	1	1	.600
Davey Lopes, ph	1	0	0	0	0	0	.000
Charlie Kerfeld, p	0	0	0	0	0	0	—
Dave Smith, p	0	0	0	0	0	0	—
Bob Knepper, p	3	0	0	0	0	1	.000
Dickie Thon, ss	1	0	0	0	0	0	.400
TOTALS	32	5	8	5	5	8	.261

Mets	AB	R	H	RBI	BB	K	Avg
Mookie Wilson, cf-lf	4	0	0	0	0	1	.083
Kevin Mitchell, lf	4	1	2	0	0	0	.500
Jesse Orosco, p	0	0	0	0	0	0	—
Keith Hernandez, 1b	4	1	2	0	0	0	.455
Gary Carter, c	4	1	0	0	0	0	.077
Darryl Strawberry, rf	4	1	2	3	0	2	.273
Ray Knight, 3b	4	0	1	0	0	0	.182
Tim Teufel, 2b	3	0	0	0	0	0	.000
Wally Backman, 2b	1	1	1	0	0	0	.300
Rafael Santana, ss	3	0	0	0	0	0	.222
Danny Heep, ph	1	0	0	0	0	0	.500
Ron Darling, p	1	0	0	0	0	0	.000
Lee Mazzilli, ph	1	0	1	0	0	0	.500
Rick Aguilera, p	0	0	0	0	0	0	—
Lenny Dykstra, ph-cf	2	1	1	2	0	1	.400
TOTALS	36	6	10	5	0	4	.253

	1	2	3	4	5	6	7	8	9	R	H	E
Astros	2	2	0	0	0	0	1	0	0	5	8	1
Mets	0	0	0	4	0	0	0	0	2	6	10	1

E—Knight, Reynolds. DP—Mets 1 (Knight to Teufel to Hernandez). LOB—Astros 7, Mets 5. Scoring Position—Astros 2-for-7, Mets 2-for-6. HR—Doran (1), Strawberry (1), Dykstra (1). S—Hatcher. GDP—Ashby. SB—Hatcher 2 (3), Bass (2).

Astros	IP	H	R	ER	BB	K	ERA
Bob Knepper	7.0	8	4	3	0	3	3.86
Charlie Kerfeld (H, 1)	1.0	0	0	0	0	1	0.00
Dave Smith (BS, 1; L, 0-1)	0.1	2	2	2	0	0	54.00

Mets	IP	H	R	ER	BB	K	ERA
Ron Darling	5.0	6	4	4	2	5	7.20
Rick Aguilera	2.0	1	1	0	2	1	0.00
Jesse Orosco (W, 1-0)	2.0	1	0	0	1	2	0.00

WP—Darling. PB—Ashby 2. HBP—Davis by Darling. Time—2:55. Attendance—55,052. Umpires—HP, Pulli. 1B, Rennert. 2B, West. 3B, Brocklander.

Game 4
Sunday, October 12

Astros	AB	R	H	RBI	BB	K	Avg
Bill Doran, 2b	4	0	0	0	0	0	.188
Billy Hatcher, cf	4	0	0	0	0	0	.200
Phil Garner, 3b	3	0	0	0	0	1	.167
Denny Walling, ph-3b	1	0	1	0	0	0	.200
Glenn Davis, 1b	3	1	1	0	1	0	.286
Kevin Bass, rf	3	0	0	0	1	1	.308
Jose Cruz, lf	4	0	0	0	0	1	.200
Alan Ashby, c	3	1	1	2	0	0	.167
Dickie Thon, ss	3	1	1	1	0	0	.375
Mike Scott, p	3	0	0	0	0	3	.000
TOTALS	31	3	4	3	2	6	.217

Mets	AB	R	H	RBI	BB	K	Avg
Lenny Dykstra, cf	4	0	1	0	0	1	.357
Wally Backman, 2b	4	0	0	0	0	0	.214
Keith Hernandez, 1b	4	0	0	0	0	0	.333
Gary Carter, c	4	0	0	0	0	1	.059
Darryl Strawberry, rf	3	0	0	0	0	2	.214
Mookie Wilson, lf	3	1	1	0	0	0	.133
Ray Knight, 3b	3	0	1	0	0	0	.214
Rafael Santana, ss	2	0	0	0	0	0	.182
Danny Heep, ph	0	0	0	1	0	0	.500
Doug Sisk, p	0	0	0	0	0	0	—
Sid Fernandez, p	1	0	0	0	0	0	.000
Lee Mazzilli, ph	1	0	0	0	0	1	.333
Roger McDowell, p	0	0	0	0	0	0	—
Howard Johnson, ph	1	0	0	0	0	0	.000
Kevin Elster, ss	0	0	0	0	1	0	—
TOTALS	30	1	3	1	0	5	.215

	1	2	3	4	5	6	7	8	9	R	H	E
Astros	0	2	0	0	1	0	0	0	0	3	4	1
Mets	0	0	0	0	0	0	0	1	0	1	3	0

E—Scott. LOB—Astros 3, Mets 3. Scoring Position—Astros 0-for-2, Mets 0-for-4. 2B—Walling (1). HR—Ashby (1), Thon (1). SF—Heep. SB—Backman (1).

Astros	IP	H	R	ER	BB	K	ERA
Mike Scott (W, 2-0)	9.0	3	1	1	0	5	0.50

Mets	IP	H	R	ER	BB	K	ERA
Sid Fernandez (L, 0-1)	6.0	3	3	3	1	5	4.50
Roger McDowell	2.0	0	0	0	0	1	0.00
Doug Sisk	1.0	1	0	0	1	0	0.00

Time—2:23. Attendance—55,038. Umpires—HP, Rennert. 1B, West. 2B, Brocklander. 3B, Harvey.

Game 5
Tuesday, October 14

Astros	AB	R	H	RBI	BB	K	Avg
Bill Doran, 2b	4	0	1	1	1	0	.200
Billy Hatcher, cf	3	0	1	0	1	0	.222
Denny Walling, 3b	5	0	1	0	0	1	.200
Glenn Davis, 1b	5	0	0	0	0	1	.211
Kevin Bass, rf	5	0	2	0	0	0	.333
Jose Cruz, lf	5	0	1	0	0	1	.200
Alan Ashby, c	5	1	1	0	0	1	.176
Craig Reynolds, ss	4	0	1	0	0	0	.444
Dickie Thon, ph-ss	1	0	0	0	0	0	.333
Nolan Ryan, p	3	0	0	0	0	2	.000
Terry Puhl, ph	1	0	1	0	0	0	1.000
Charlie Kerfeld, p	0	0	0	0	0	0	—
TOTALS	41	1	9	1	2	6	.245

Mets	AB	R	H	RBI	BB	K	Avg
Lenny Dykstra, cf	5	0	0	0	0	2	.263
Wally Backman, 2b	5	1	1	0	0	3	.211
Keith Hernandez, 1b	4	0	1	0	1	1	.316
Gary Carter, c	5	0	1	0	0	0	.091
Darryl Strawberry, rf	3	1	1	1	1	2	.235
Mookie Wilson, lf	4	0	0	0	0	3	.105
Jesse Orosco, p	0	0	0	0	0	0	—
Ray Knight, 3b	4	0	0	0	0	1	.167
Rafael Santana, ss	3	0	0	0	0	1	.143
Lee Mazzilli, ph	1	0	0	0	0	1	.250
Kevin Elster, ss	0	0	0	0	0	0	—
Dwight Gooden, p	3	0	0	0	0	1	.000
Danny Heep, lf	1	0	0	0	0	1	.333
TOTALS	38	2	4	2	2	15	.189

	1	2	3	4	5	6	7	8	9	10	11	12	R	H	E
Astros	0	0	0	0	1	0	0	0	0	0	0	0	1	9	1
Mets	0	0	0	1	0	0	0	0	0	0	0	1	2	4	0

E—Kerfeld. DP—Mets 2 (Backman to Santana to Hernandez; Wilson to Santana). LOB—Astros 7, Mets 4. Scoring Position—Astros 1-for-8, Mets 1-for-2. 2B—Ashby (1). HR—Strawberry (2). S—Hatcher. GDP—Reynolds. SB—Doran (1), Puhl (1). CS—Bass (1).

Astros	IP	H	R	ER	BB	K	ERA
Nolan Ryan	9.0	2	1	1	1	12	3.86
Charlie Kerfeld (L, 0-1)	2.1	2	1	1	1	3	2.25

Mets	IP	H	R	ER	BB	K	ERA
Dwight Gooden	10.0	9	1	1	2	4	1.06
Jesse Orosco (W, 2-0)	2.0	0	0	0	0	2	0.00

Time—3:45. Attendance—54,986. Umpires—HP, West. 1B, Brocklander. 2B, Harvey. 3B, Weyer.

Game 6
Wednesday, October 15

Mets	AB	R	H	RBI	BB	K	Avg
Mookie Wilson, cf-lf	7	1	1	1	1	2	.115
Kevin Mitchell, lf	4	0	0	0	0	1	.250
Kevin Elster, ss	3	0	0	0	0	1	.000
Keith Hernandez, 1b	7	1	1	1	0	2	.269
Gary Carter, c	5	0	2	0	2	0	.148
Darryl Strawberry, rf	5	2	1	0	2	2	.227
Ray Knight, 3b	6	1	1	2	0	1	.167
Tim Teufel, 2b	3	0	1	0	0	0	.167
Wally Backman, ph-2b	2	1	1	1	2	0	.238
Rafael Santana, ss	3	0	1	0	0	0	.176
Danny Heep, ph	1	0	0	0	0	1	.250
Roger McDowell, p	1	0	0	0	0	0	.000
Howard Johnson, ph	1	0	0	0	0	0	.000
Jesse Orosco, p	0	0	0	0	0	0	—
Bobby Ojeda, p	1	0	0	0	0	0	.000
Lee Mazzilli, ph	1	0	0	0	0	1	.200
Rick Aguilera, p	0	0	0	0	0	0	—
Lenny Dykstra, ph-cf	4	1	2	1	1	0	.304
TOTALS	54	7	11	6	8	11	.195

Astros	AB	R	H	RBI	BB	K	Avg
Bill Doran, 2b	7	1	2	0	0	1	.222
Billy Hatcher, cf	7	2	3	2	0	0	.280
Phil Garner, 3b	3	1	1	1	0	1	.222
Denny Walling, ph-3b	4	0	0	0	0	0	.158
Glenn Davis, 1b	7	1	3	2	0	1	.269
Kevin Bass, rf	6	0	1	0	1	2	.292
Jose Cruz, lf	6	0	1	1	0	1	.192
Alan Ashby, c	6	0	0	0	0	0	.130
Dickie Thon, ss	3	0	0	0	0	0	.250
Craig Reynolds, ph-ss	3	0	0	0	0	2	.333
Bob Knepper, p	2	0	0	0	1	1	.000
Dave Smith, p	0	0	0	0	0	0	—
Terry Puhl, ph	1	0	0	0	0	0	.667
Larry Andersen, p	0	0	0	0	0	0	—
Jim Pankovits, ph	1	0	0	0	0	0	.000
Aurelio Lopez, p	0	0	0	0	0	0	—
Jeff Calhoun, p	0	0	0	0	0	0	—
Davey Lopes, ph	0	1	0	0	1	0	.000
TOTALS	56	6	11	6	3	9	.228

	1	2	3	4	5	6	7	8	9	10	11	12	13	14	15	16	R	H	E
Mets	0	0	0	0	0	0	0	3	0	0	0	0	0	1	0	3	7	11	0
Astros	3	0	0	0	0	0	0	0	0	0	0	0	1	0	2	6	11	1

E—Bass. DP—Astros 2 (Thon to Davis; Doran to Reynolds to Davis). LOB—Mets 9, Astros 5. Scoring Position—Mets 5-for-10, Astros 5-for-10. 2B—Hernandez (1), Strawberry (1), Garner (1), Davis (1). 3B—Dykstra (1). HR—Hatcher (1). S—Orosco. SF—Knight. GDP—Wilson, Santana. SB—Doran (2). CS—Bass 2 (3).

Mets	IP	H	R	ER	BB	K	ERA
Bobby Ojeda	5.0	5	3	3	2	1	2.57
Rick Aguilera	3.0	1	0	0	0	1	0.00
Roger McDowell	5.0	1	0	0	0	2	0.00
Jesse Orosco (BS, 1; W, 3-0)	3.0	4	3	3	1	5	3.38

Astros	IP	H	R	ER	BB	K	ERA
Bob Knepper	8.1	5	3	3	1	6	3.52
Dave Smith (BS, 2)	1.2	0	0	0	3	2	9.00
Larry Andersen	3.0	0	0	0	1	1	0.00
Aurelio Lopez (L, 0-1)	2.0	5	3	3	2	2	8.10
Jeff Calhoun	1.0	1	1	1	1	0	9.00

Lopez pitched to three batters in the 16th.

WP—Calhoun 2. Time—4:42. Attendance—45,718. Umpires—HP, Brocklander. 1B, Harvey. 2B, Weyer. 3B, Pulli.

Postseason: League Championship Series

1986 NL Championship Series—Composite Statistics

Batting

Mets	G	AB	R	H	RBI	2B	3B	HR	BB	SO	SB	CS	Avg	OBP	Slg
Wally Backman	6	21	5	5	2	0	0	0	2	4	1	0	.238	.304	.238
Gary Carter	6	27	1	4	2	1	0	0	2	5	0	0	.148	.207	.185
Ron Darling	1	1	0	0	0	0	0	0	0	0	0	0	.000	.000	.000
Lenny Dykstra	6	23	3	7	3	1	1	1	2	4	1	0	.304	.360	.565
Kevin Elster	4	3	0	0	0	0	0	0	0	1	0	0	.000	.000	.000
Sid Fernandez	1	1	0	0	0	0	0	0	0	0	0	0	.000	.000	.000
Dwight Gooden	2	5	0	0	0	0	0	0	0	2	0	0	.000	.000	.000
Danny Heep	5	4	0	1	1	0	0	0	0	2	0	0	.250	.200	.250
Keith Hernandez	6	26	3	7	3	1	1	0	3	6	0	0	.269	.345	.385
Howard Johnson	2	2	0	0	0	0	0	0	0	0	0	0	.000	.000	.000
Ray Knight	6	24	1	4	2	0	0	0	1	5	0	0	.167	.192	.167
Lee Mazzilli	5	5	0	1	0	0	0	0	0	3	0	0	.200	.200	.200
Roger McDowell	2	1	0	0	0	0	0	0	0	0	0	0	.000	.000	.000
Kevin Mitchell	2	8	1	2	0	0	0	0	0	1	0	0	.250	.250	.250
Bobby Ojeda	2	5	1	0	0	0	0	0	0	2	0	0	.000	.000	.000
Jesse Orosco	4	0	0	0	0	0	0	0	0	0	0	0	—	—	—
Rafael Santana	6	17	0	3	0	0	0	0	0	3	0	0	.176	.176	.176
Darryl Strawberry	6	22	4	5	5	1	0	2	3	12	1	0	.227	.308	.545
Tim Teufel	2	6	0	1	0	0	0	0	0	0	0	0	.167	.167	.167
Mookie Wilson	6	26	2	3	1	0	0	0	1	7	1	0	.115	.148	.115
Totals	6	227	21	43	19	4	2	3	14	57	4	0	.189	.234	.264

Batting

Astros	G	AB	R	H	RBI	2B	3B	HR	BB	SO	SB	CS	Avg	OBP	Slg
Alan Ashby	6	23	2	3	2	1	0	1	2	1	0	0	.130	.200	.304
Kevin Bass	6	24	0	7	0	2	0	0	4	4	2	3	.292	.393	.375
Jose Cruz	6	26	0	5	2	0	0	0	1	8	0	0	.192	.222	.192
Glenn Davis	6	26	3	7	3	1	0	1	1	3	0	0	.269	.321	.423
Bill Doran	6	27	3	6	3	0	0	1	2	2	2	0	.222	.276	.333
Phil Garner	3	9	1	2	2	1	0	0	1	2	0	0	.222	.300	.333
Billy Hatcher	6	25	4	7	2	0	0	1	3	2	3	0	.280	.357	.400
Bob Knepper	2	5	0	0	0	0	0	0	1	2	0	0	.000	.167	.000
Davey Lopes	3	2	1	0	0	0	0	0	1	0	0	0	.000	.333	.000
Jim Pankovits	2	2	0	0	0	0	0	0	0	1	0	0	.000	.000	.000
Terry Puhl	3	3	0	2	0	0	0	0	0	0	1	0	.667	.667	.667
Craig Reynolds	4	12	1	4	0	0	0	0	1	3	0	0	.333	.385	.333
Nolan Ryan	2	4	0	0	0	0	0	0	0	2	0	0	.000	.000	.000
Mike Scott	2	6	0	0	0	0	0	0	0	5	0	0	.000	.000	.000
Dickie Thon	6	12	1	3	1	0	0	1	0	1	0	0	.250	.250	.500
Denny Walling	5	19	1	3	2	1	0	0	0	4	0	0	.158	.158	.211
Totals	6	225	17	49	17	6	0	5	17	40	8	3	.218	.276	.311

Pitching

Mets	G	GS	CG	IP	H	R	ER	BB	SO	W-L	Sv-Op	Hld	ERA
Rick Aguilera	2	0	0	5.0	2	1	0	2	2	0-0	0-0	0	0.00
Ron Darling	1	1	0	5.0	6	4	4	2	5	0-0	0-0	0	7.20
Sid Fernandez	1	1	0	6.0	3	3	3	1	5	0-1	0-0	0	4.50
Dwight Gooden	2	2	0	17.0	16	2	2	5	9	0-1	0-0	0	1.06
Roger McDowell	2	0	0	7.0	1	0	0	0	3	0-0	0-0	0	0.00
Bobby Ojeda	2	2	1	14.0	15	4	4	4	6	1-0	0-0	0	2.57
Jesse Orosco	4	0	0	8.0	5	3	3	2	10	3-0	0-1	0	3.38
Doug Sisk	1	0	0	1.0	1	0	0	1	0	0-0	0-0	0	0.00
Totals	6	6	1	63.0	49	17	16	17	40	4-2	0-1	0	2.29

Pitching

Astros	G	GS	CG	IP	H	R	ER	BB	SO	W-L	Sv-Op	Hld	ERA
Larry Andersen	2	0	0	5.0	1	0	0	2	3	0-0	0-0	0	0.00
Jeff Calhoun	1	0	0	1.0	1	1	1	1	0	0-0	0-0	0	9.00
Charlie Kerfeld	3	0	0	4.0	2	1	1	1	4	0-1	0-0	1	2.25
Bob Knepper	2	2	0	15.1	13	7	6	1	9	0-0	0-0	0	3.52
Aurelio Lopez	2	0	0	3.1	7	3	3	4	3	0-1	0-0	0	8.10
Nolan Ryan	2	2	0	14.0	9	6	6	1	17	0-1	0-0	0	3.86
Mike Scott	2	2	2	18.0	8	1	1	1	19	2-0	0-0	0	0.50
Dave Smith	2	0	0	2.0	2	2	2	3	2	0-1	0-2	0	9.00
Totals	6	6	2	62.2	43	21	20	14	57	2-4	0-2	1	2.87

Fielding

Mets	Pos	G	PO	Ast	E	DP	PB	FPct
Rick Aguilera	p	2	1	1	0	0	—	1.000
Wally Backman	2b	6	9	17	0	4	—	1.000
Gary Carter	c	6	43	4	0	0	0	1.000
Ron Darling	p	1	1	2	0	0	—	1.000
Lenny Dykstra	cf	6	10	0	0	0	—	1.000
Kevin Elster	ss	4	2	3	0	0	—	1.000
Sid Fernandez	p	1	0	0	0	0	—	—
Dwight Gooden	p	2	3	2	0	0	—	1.000
Danny Heep	lf	1	0	0	0	0	—	—
Keith Hernandez	1b	6	66	11	0	5	—	1.000
Ray Knight	3b	6	5	19	1	1	—	.960
Roger McDowell	p	2	3	1	0	0	—	1.000
Kevin Mitchell	lf	2	3	0	0	0	—	1.000
Bobby Ojeda	p	2	2	4	0	0	—	1.000
Jesse Orosco	p	4	1	1	0	0	—	1.000
Rafael Santana	ss	6	13	18	0	4	—	1.000
Doug Sisk	p	1	0	0	0	0	—	—
Darryl Strawberry	rf	6	9	0	0	0	—	1.000
Tim Teufel	2b	2	2	8	0	1	—	1.000
Mookie Wilson	lf	6	13	1	0	1	—	1.000
	cf	2	3	0	0	0	—	1.000
Totals		6	189	92	1	16	0	.996

Fielding

Astros	Pos	G	PO	Ast	E	DP	PB	FPct
Larry Andersen	p	2	1	1	0	0	—	1.000
Alan Ashby	c	6	59	1	0	0	2	1.000
Kevin Bass	rf	6	16	0	1	0	—	.941
Jeff Calhoun	p	1	0	0	0	0	—	—
Jose Cruz	lf	6	10	0	0	0	—	1.000
Glenn Davis	1b	6	62	3	1	3	—	.985
Bill Doran	2b	6	10	17	0	2	—	1.000
Phil Garner	3b	3	1	8	0	0	—	1.000
Billy Hatcher	cf	6	12	0	1	0	—	.923
Charlie Kerfeld	p	3	0	1	1	0	—	.500
Bob Knepper	p	2	0	3	0	0	—	1.000
Aurelio Lopez	p	2	0	1	0	0	—	1.000
Craig Reynolds	ss	4	7	8	2	1	—	.882
Nolan Ryan	p	2	0	2	0	0	—	1.000
Mike Scott	p	2	2	4	1	0	—	.857
Dave Smith	p	2	0	0	0	0	—	—
Dickie Thon	ss	6	5	10	0	2	—	1.000
Denny Walling	3b	5	3	6	0	0	—	1.000
Totals		6	188	65	7	8	2	.973

1987 Minnesota Twins (AL) 4, Detroit Tigers (AL) 1

The AL East champion Detroit Tigers had baseball's best record during the regular season, but the Minnesota Twins upended them in only five games in the ALCS. The Tigers took a 5-4 lead into the bottom of the eighth in Game 1, but Don Baylor singled in the go-ahead run as the Twins rallied for four runs to take the game 8-5. Bert Blyleven outpitched Jack Morris in Game 2, putting the Twins ahead two games to none with a 6-3 victory. The Tigers came back to win the third game on a dramatic two-run homer by Pat Sheridan in the bottom of the eighth, but the Twins took Game 4, 5-3, as Greg Gagne and Kirby Puckett each homered. Tom Brunansky's two-run double gave the Twins an early lead in Game 5, and they came away with a 9-5 victory to wrap up the AL title. Brunansky finished the series with a .412 batting average and nine RBI.

Game 1

Wednesday, October 7

Tigers	AB	R	H	RBI	BB	K	Avg
Lou Whitaker, 2b	4	0	0	0	1	0	.000
Bill Madlock, dh	5	0	0	0	0	3	.000
Kirk Gibson, lf	4	2	1	1	1	2	.250
Alan Trammell, ss	4	1	1	0	0	0	.250
Larry Herndon, rf	3	1	1	0	0	0	.333
Dave Bergman, ph	0	0	0	0	1	0	—
Pat Sheridan, rf	0	0	0	0	0	0	—
Chet Lemon, cf	3	0	2	1	0	0	.667
Darrell Evans, 1b	4	0	2	0	0	1	.500
Tom Brookens, 3b	3	0	0	0	0	2	.000
John Grubb, ph	1	0	1	0	0	0	1.000
Mike Heath, c	3	1	2	2	0	0	.667
Matt Nokes, ph	1	0	0	0	0	1	.000
TOTALS	35	5	10	5	2	9	.286

Twins	AB	R	H	RBI	BB	K	Avg
Dan Gladden, lf	4	1	2	1	0	0	.500
Greg Gagne, ss	4	0	0	0	2	0	.000
Kirby Puckett, cf	4	1	1	1	0	1	.250
Kent Hrbek, 1b	3	1	0	1	0	0	.000
Gary Gaetti, 3b	3	3	2	2	1	0	.667
Randy Bush, dh	3	1	1	0	0	0	.333
Don Baylor, ph-dh	1	0	1	1	0	0	1.000
Tom Brunansky, rf	4	1	2	3	0	0	.500
Steve Lombardozzi, 2b	3	0	1	0	0	0	.333
Tim Laudner, c	3	0	0	0	0	2	.000
TOTALS	32	8	10	8	2	5	.313

	1	2	3	4	5	6	7	8	9	R	H	E
Tigers	0	0	1	0	0	1	1	2	0	5	10	0
Twins	0	1	0	0	3	0	4	x		8	10	0

LOB—Tigers 7, Twins 3. Scoring Position—Tigers 2-for-7, Twins 4-for-6. 2B—Trammell (1), Puckett (1), Brunansky 2 (2). 3B—Bush (1). HR—Gibson (1), Heath (1), Gaetti 2 (2). S—Lombardozzi. SF—Lemon, Bergman.

Tigers	IP	H	R	ER	BB	K	ERA
Doyle Alexander (L, 0-1)	7.1	8	6	6	0	5	7.36
Mike Henneman	0.0	0	2	2	2	0	—
Willie Hernandez	0.1	2	0	0	0	0	0.00
Eric King	0.1	0	0	0	0	0	0.00

Twins	IP	H	R	ER	BB	K	ERA
Frank Viola	7.0	9	5	5	1	6	6.43
Jeff Reardon (BS, 1; W, 1-0)	2.0	1	0	0	1	3	0.00

Viola pitched to two batters in the 8th. Henneman pitched to two batters in the 8th.

Time—2:46. Attendance—53,269. Umpires—HP, Brinkman. 1B, Merrill. 2B, Coble. 3B, Clark.

Game 2

Thursday, October 8

Tigers	AB	R	H	RBI	BB	K	Avg
Lou Whitaker, 2b	3	1	2	1	1	0	.286
Darrell Evans, 1b	4	0	2	0	0	1	.500
Kirk Gibson, lf	4	0	0	0	0	3	.125
Alan Trammell, ss	4	0	0	0	0	1	.125
Matt Nokes, dh-c	4	1	1	0	0	1	.200
Chet Lemon, cf	4	1	1	2	0	2	.429
Pat Sheridan, rf	4	0	1	0	2	0	.250
Tom Brookens, 3b	2	0	0	0	0	0	.000
Mike Heath, c	2	0	0	0	0	0	.400
John Grubb, ph	1	0	0	0	0	1	.500
Jack Morris, p	0	0	0	0	0	0	—
TOTALS	32	3	7	3	1	10	.271

Twins	AB	R	H	RBI	BB	K	Avg
Dan Gladden, lf	4	0	1	2	0	0	.375
Steve Lombardozzi, 2b	4	0	0	0	0	1	.143
Kirby Puckett, cf	4	0	0	0	0	1	.125
Kent Hrbek, 1b	4	1	1	1	0	0	.143
Gary Gaetti, 3b	4	1	1	0	0	2	.429
Randy Bush, dh	4	1	1	0	0	1	.286
Tom Brunansky, rf	2	2	1	1	1	0	.500
Greg Gagne, ss	1	1	0	0	2	1	.000
Tim Laudner, c	3	0	1	2	0	1	.167
TOTALS	30	6	6	6	3	7	.246

	1	2	3	4	5	6	7	8	9	R	H	E
Tigers	0	2	0	0	0	0	0	1	0	3	7	1
Twins	0	3	0	2	1	0	0	0	x	6	6	0

E—Trammell. DP—Tigers 1 (Whitaker to Trammell to Evans), Twins 1 (Gagne to Lombardozzi to Hrbek). LOB—Tigers 4, Twins 3. Scoring Position—Tigers 0-for-5, Twins 3-for-7. 2B—Gaetti (1), Brunansky (3), Laudner (1). HR—Whitaker (1), Lemon (1), Hrbek (1). S—Brookens. GDP—Trammell, Hrbek. SB—Whitaker (1), Sheridan (1), Bush 2 (2).

Twins	IP	H	R	ER	BB	K	ERA
Jack Morris (L, 0-1)	8.0	6	6	6	3	7	6.75

Twins	IP	H	R	ER	BB	K	ERA
Bert Blyleven (W, 1-0)	7.1	7	3	3	1	6	3.68
Juan Berenguer (S, 1)	1.2	0	0	0	0	4	0.00

Time—2:54. Attendance—55,245. Umpires—HP, Merrill. 1B, Coble. 2B, Clark. 3B, Reilly.

Game 3

Saturday, October 10

Twins	AB	R	H	RBI	BB	K	Avg
Dan Gladden, lf	3	1	1	0	2	0	.364
Greg Gagne, ss	5	2	1	1	0	1	.100
Kirby Puckett, cf	5	0	0	0	0	2	.077
Kent Hrbek, 1b	3	1	0	0	2	0	.100
Gary Gaetti, 3b	5	0	2	2	0	1	.417
Randy Bush, dh	3	1	1	1	1	0	.300
Tom Brunansky, rf	3	1	1	2	1	0	.444
Steve Lombardozzi, 2b	3	0	0	0	1	0	.100
Sal Butera, c	3	0	2	0	0	0	.667
Mark Davidson, pr	0	0	0	0	0	0	—
Tim Laudner, c	1	0	0	0	0	0	.143
TOTALS	34	6	8	6	7	5	.242

Tigers	AB	R	H	RBI	BB	K	Avg
Lou Whitaker, 2b	4	1	1	0	1	1	.273
Darrell Evans, 1b	1	0	0	0	3	0	.444
Kirk Gibson, lf	5	1	1	1	0	1	.154
Alan Trammell, ss	4	1	1	0	1	0	.167
Matt Nokes, c	3	0	0	0	1	1	.125
Chet Lemon, cf	3	1	0	0	1	1	.300
Dave Bergman, dh	1	0	0	0	0	0	.000
Larry Herndon, ph-dh	3	0	2	2	0	0	.500
Jack Morris, pr-dh	0	1	0	0	0	0	—
Tom Brookens, 3b	4	0	0	0	0	1	.000
Pat Sheridan, rf	4	2	2	2	0	0	.375
TOTALS	32	7	7	6	6	7	.241

	1	2	3	4	5	6	7	8	9	R	H	E
Twins	0	0	0	2	0	2	2	0	0	6	8	1
Tigers	0	0	5	0	0	0	0	2	x	7	7	0

E—Lombardozzi. LOB—Twins 8, Tigers 8. Scoring Position—Twins 2-for-9, Tigers 3-for-12. 2B—Sheridan (1), Herndon (1). HR—Gagne (1), Brunansky (1), Sheridan (1). SB—Gibson 2 (2). CS—Gladden (1).

Twins	IP	H	R	ER	BB	K	ERA
Les Straker	2.2	5	5	4	1	1	16.88
Dan Schatzeder	3.1	2	0	0	0	5	0.00
Juan Berenguer (H, 1)	1.0	0	0	0	1	1	0.00
Jeff Reardon (BS, 2; L, 1-1)	1.0	2	2	2	1	0	6.00

Tigers	IP	H	R	ER	BB	K	ERA
Walt Terrell	6.0	7	6	6	4	4	9.00
Mike Henneman (BS, 1; W, 1-0)	3.0	1	0	0	3	1	6.00

Terrell pitched to two batters in the 7th. Schatzeder pitched to one batter in the 7th.

Balk—Straker. HBP—Evans by Schatzeder. Time—3:29. Attendance—49,730. Umpires—HP, Coble. 1B, Clark. 2B, Reilly. 3B, McKean.

Game 4

Sunday, October 11

Twins	AB	R	H	RBI	BB	K	Avg
Dan Gladden, lf	3	0	0	0	0	1	.286
Al Newman, 2b	2	0	0	0	0	0	.000
Gene Larkin, ph	1	0	1	1	0	0	1.000
Steve Lombardozzi, pr-2b	1	0	1	1	0	0	.182
Kirby Puckett, cf	5	2	2	1	0	0	.167
Gary Gaetti, 3b	4	0	0	1	0	0	.313
Don Baylor, dh	4	0	1	0	0	0	.400
Tom Brunansky, rf	3	0	0	0	2	1	.333
Kent Hrbek, 1b	5	0	0	0	0	0	.067
Greg Gagne, ss	4	2	2	1	0	0	.214
Tim Laudner, c	2	1	0	0	2	0	.111
TOTALS	34	5	7	5	4	2	.222

Tigers	AB	R	H	RBI	BB	K	Avg
Lou Whitaker, 2b	2	2	0	0	3	1	.231
Jim Morrison, dh	4	0	1	0	0	1	.250
Matt Nokes, ph	1	0	0	0	0	1	.111
Kirk Gibson, lf	4	0	1	1	1	2	.176
Alan Trammell, ss	3	0	1	0	1	0	.200
Larry Herndon, rf	3	0	0	0	1	0	.333
Chet Lemon, cf	4	1	1	0	0	0	.286
Darrell Evans, 1b-3b	4	0	1	0	0	0	.385
Tom Brookens, 3b	2	0	0	0	0	0	.000
Dave Bergman, ph-1b	2	0	1	1	0	1	.333
Mike Heath, c	2	0	0	0	0	0	.286
John Grubb, ph	1	0	1	0	0	0	.667
Pat Sheridan, pr	0	0	0	0	0	0	.375
TOTALS	32	3	7	2	6	6	.246

	1	2	3	4	5	6	7	8	9	R	H	E
Twins	0	0	1	1	1	1	1	0	1	0	5	7	1
Tigers	1	0	0	0	1	1	0	0	0	3	7	3

E—Evans 2, Herndon, Gagne. DP—Twins 1 (Gaetti to Lombardozzi to Hrbek). LOB—Twins 11, Tigers 9. Scoring Position—Twins 2-for-11, Tigers 2-for-6. 2B—Gagne (1), Larkin (1). HR—Puckett (1), Gagne (2). S—Newman, Heath. SF—Gaetti. GDP—Trammell.

Twins	IP	H	R	ER	BB	K	ERA
Frank Viola (W, 1-0)	5.0	5	3	2	4	3	5.25
Keith Atherton (H, 1)	0.1	1	0	0	0	0	0.00
Juan Berenguer (H, 2)	2.2	0	0	0	2	1	0.00
Jeff Reardon (S, 1)	1.0	1	0	0	0	2	4.50

Tigers	IP	H	R	ER	BB	K	ERA
Frank Tanana (L, 0-1)	5.1	6	4	3	4	1	5.06
Dan Petry	3.1	1	1	0	0	1	0.00
Mark Thurmond	0.1	0	0	0	0	0	0.00

Viola pitched to two batters in the 6th.

WP—Tanana, Petry, Berenguer. HBP—Baylor by Tanana, Gladden by Tanana, Gladden by Tanana. Time—3:24. Attendance—51,939. Umpires—HP, Clark. 1B, Reilly. 2B, McKean. 3B, Brinkman.

Game 5

Monday, October 12

Twins	AB	R	H	RBI	BB	K	Avg
Dan Gladden, lf	6	3	3	2	0	0	.350
Greg Gagne, ss	4	0	2	1	1	0	.278
Kirby Puckett, cf	6	0	2	1	0	1	.208
Kent Hrbek, 1b	5	1	2	0	0	0	.150
Gary Gaetti, 3b	4	1	1	0	0	0	.300
Randy Bush, dh	2	1	0	1	2	0	.250
Tom Brunansky, rf	5	1	3	3	0	2	.412
Steve Lombardozzi, 2b	4	2	2	0	1	1	.267
Tim Laudner, c	5	0	0	0	0	2	.071
TOTALS	41	9	15	8	4	6	.256

Tigers	AB	R	H	RBI	BB	K	Avg
Lou Whitaker, 2b	4	0	0	0	1	1	.176
Darrell Evans, 1b	4	0	0	0	1	0	.294
Kirk Gibson, lf	4	1	3	1	1	0	.286
Alan Trammell, ss	5	1	1	0	0	0	.200
Matt Nokes, c	5	1	1	2	0	0	.143
Chet Lemon, cf	4	1	1	1	0	1	.278
John Grubb, dh	4	0	2	0	0	1	.571
Pat Sheridan, rf	2	0	0	0	0	0	.300
Tom Brookens, 3b	2	0	0	0	0	0	.000
Dave Bergman, ph	1	0	0	0	0	0	.250
Jim Morrison, 3b	1	1	1	0	0	0	.400
TOTALS	36	5	9	5	3	3	.240

	1	2	3	4	5	6	7	8	9	R	H	E
Twins	0	4	0	0	0	0	1	1	3	9	15	1
Tigers	0	0	0	3	0	0	0	1	1	5	9	1

E—Evans, Gagne. DP—Twins 1 (Lombardozzi to Gagne to Hrbek). LOB—Twins 12, Tigers 9. Scoring Position—Twins 5-for-17, Tigers 2-for-10. 2B—Gladden 2 (2), Gagne 2 (3), Brunansky (4), Gibson (1). HR—Brunansky (2), Nokes (1), Lemon (2). SF—Bush. GDP—Evans. SB—Puckett (1), Bush (3), Gibson (3).

Twins	IP	H	R	ER	BB	K	ERA
Bert Blyleven (W, 2-0)	6.0	5	3	3	2	3	4.05
Dan Schatzeder (H, 1)	1.0	0	0	0	0	0	0.00
Juan Berenguer (H, 3)	0.2	1	1	1	0	0	1.50
Jeff Reardon (S, 2)	1.1	3	1	1	1	0	5.06

Tigers	IP	H	R	ER	BB	K	ERA
Doyle Alexander (L, 0-2)	1.2	6	4	4	1	0	10.00
Eric King	5.0	3	1	1	2	4	1.69
Mike Henneman	2.0	5	4	4	1	2	10.80
Jeff Robinson	0.1	1	0	0	0	0	0.00

WP—King, Reardon. PB—Nokes. HBP—Gaetti by King, Gagne by Alexander, Sheridan by Blyleven, Sheridan by Blyleven. Time—3:14. Attendance—47,448. Umpires—HP, Reilly. 1B, McKean. 2B, Brinkman. 3B, Merrill.

1987 AL Championship Series—Composite Statistics

Batting

Twins	G	AB	R	H	RBI	2B	3B	HR	BB	SO	SB	CS	Avg	OBP	Slg
Don Baylor	2	5	0	2	1	0	0	0	0	0	0	0	.400	.500	.400
Tom Brunansky	5	17	5	7	9	4	0	2	4	3	0	0	.412	.524	1.000
Randy Bush	4	12	4	3	2	0	1	0	3	2	3	0	.250	.375	.417
Sal Butera	1	3	0	2	0	0	0	0	0	0	0	0	.667	.667	.667
Mark Davidson	1	0	0	0	0	0	0	0	0	0	0	0	—	—	—
Gary Gaetti	5	20	5	6	5	1	0	2	1	3	0	0	.300	.348	.650
Greg Gagne	5	18	5	5	3	2	0	2	3	4	0	0	.278	.409	.778
Dan Gladden	5	20	5	7	5	2	0	0	2	1	0	1	.350	.458	.450
Kent Hrbek	5	20	4	3	1	0	0	1	3	0	0	0	.150	.261	.300
Gene Larkin	1	1	0	1	1	1	0	0	0	0	0	0	1.000	1.000	2.000
Tim Laudner	5	14	1	1	2	1	0	0	2	5	0	0	.071	.188	.143
Steve Lombardozzi	5	15	2	4	1	0	0	0	2	3	0	0	.267	.353	.267
Al Newman	1	2	0	0	0	0	0	0	0	0	0	0	.000	.000	.000
Kirby Puckett	5	24	3	5	3	1	0	1	0	5	1	0	.208	.208	.375
Totals	5	171	34	46	33	13	1	8	20	25	4	1	.269	.359	.497

Tigers	G	AB	R	H	RBI	2B	3B	HR	BB	SO	SB	CS	Avg	OBP	Slg
Dave Bergman	4	4	0	1	2	0	0	0	0	1	0	0	.250	.200	.250
Tom Brookens	5	13	0	0	0	0	0	0	0	3	0	0	.000	.000	.000
Darrell Evans	5	17	0	5	0	0	0	0	4	2	0	0	.294	.455	.294
Kirk Gibson	5	21	4	6	4	1	0	1	3	8	3	0	.286	.375	.476
John Grubb	4	7	0	4	0	0	0	0	0	1	0	0	.571	.571	.571
Mike Heath	3	7	1	2	2	0	0	1	0	0	0	0	.286	.286	.714
Larry Herndon	3	9	1	3	2	1	0	0	1	1	0	0	.333	.400	.444
Chet Lemon	5	18	4	5	4	0	0	2	1	4	0	0	.278	.300	.611
Bill Madlock	1	5	0	0	0	0	0	0	0	3	0	0	.000	.000	.000
Jack Morris	2	0	1	0	0	0	0	0	0	0	0	0	—	—	—
Jim Morrison	2	5	1	2	0	0	0	0	1	0	0	0	.400	.400	.400
Matt Nokes	5	14	2	2	2	0	1	1	4	0	0	0	.143	.200	.357
Pat Sheridan	5	10	2	3	2	1	0	1	0	2	1	0	.300	.417	.700
Alan Trammell	5	20	3	4	2	1	0	0	1	0	0	0	.200	.238	.250
Lou Whitaker	5	17	4	3	1	0	0	1	7	3	1	0	.176	.417	.353
Totals	5	167	23	40	21	4	0	7	18	35	5	0	.240	.321	.389

Pitching

Twins	G	GS	CG	IP	H	R	ER	BB	SO	W-L	Sv-Op	Hld	ERA
Keith Atherton	1	0	0	0.1	1	0	0	0	0	0-0	0-0	1	0.00
Juan Berenguer	4	0	0	6.0	1	1	1	3	6	0-0	1-1	3	1.50
Bert Blyleven	2	2	0	13.1	12	6	6	3	9	2-0	0-0	0	4.05
Jeff Reardon	4	0	0	5.1	7	3	3	3	5	1-1	2-4	0	5.06
Dan Schatzeder	2	0	0	4.1	2	0	0	0	5	0-0	0-0	1	0.00
Les Straker	1	1	0	2.2	3	5	5	4	1	0-0	0-0	0	16.88
Frank Viola	2	2	0	12.0	14	8	7	5	9	1-0	0-0	0	5.25
Totals	5	5	0	44.0	40	23	22	18	35	4-1	3-5	5	4.50

Tigers	G	GS	CG	IP	H	R	ER	BB	SO	W-L	Sv-Op	Hld	ERA
Doyle Alexander	2	2	0	9.0	14	10	10	1	5	0-2	0-0	0	10.00
Mike Henneman	3	0	0	5.0	6	6	6	6	3	1-0	0-1	0	10.80
Willie Hernandez	1	0	0	0.1	2	0	0	0	0	0-0	0-0	0	0.00
Eric King	2	0	0	5.1	3	1	1	2	4	0-0	0-0	0	1.69
Jack Morris	1	1	1	8.0	6	6	6	3	7	0-1	0-0	0	6.75
Dan Petry	1	0	0	3.1	1	1	0	0	1	0-0	0-0	0	0.00
Jeff Robinson	1	0	0	0.1	0	0	0	0	0	0-0	0-0	0	0.00
Frank Tanana	1	1	0	5.1	6	4	3	4	1	0-1	0-0	0	5.06
Walt Terrell	1	1	0	6.0	7	6	6	4	4	0-0	0-0	0	9.00
Mark Thurmond	1	0	0	0.1	0	0	0	0	0	0-0	0-0	0	0.00
Totals	5	5	1	43.0	46	34	32	20	25	1-4	0-1	0	6.70

Fielding

Twins	Pos	G	PO	Ast	E	DP	PB	FPct
Keith Atherton	p	1	0	0	0	0	—	—
Juan Berenguer	p	4	0	0	0	0	—	—
Bert Blyleven	p	2	0	1	0	0	—	1.000
Tom Brunansky	rf	5	10	0	0	0	—	1.000
Sal Butera	c	1	6	0	0	0	0	1.000
Gary Gaetti	3b	5	8	7	0	1	—	1.000
Greg Gagne	ss	5	9	13	2	2	—	.917
Dan Gladden	lf	5	12	0	0	0	—	1.000
Kent Hrbek	1b	5	40	3	0	3	—	1.000
Tim Laudner	c	5	31	2	0	0	0	1.000
Steve Lombardozzi	2b	5	8	9	1	3	—	.944
Al Newman	2b	1	0	1	0	0	—	1.000
Kirby Puckett	cf	5	7	0	0	0	—	1.000
Jeff Reardon	p	4	0	1	0	0	—	1.000
Dan Schatzeder	p	2	1	1	0	0	—	1.000
Les Straker	p	1	0	2	0	0	—	1.000
Frank Viola	p	2	0	2	0	0	—	1.000
Totals		5	132	42	3	9	0	.983

Tigers	Pos	G	PO	Ast	E	DP	PB	FPct
Doyle Alexander	p	2	1	1	0	0	—	1.000
Dave Bergman	1b	1	6	0	0	0	—	1.000
Tom Brookens	3b	5	3	15	0	0	—	1.000
Darrell Evans	1b	5	43	3	1	1	—	.979
	3b	1	0	1	2	0	—	.333
Kirk Gibson	lf	5	10	1	0	0	—	1.000
Mike Heath	c	3	14	0	0	0	0	1.000
Mike Henneman	p	3	0	2	0	0	—	1.000
Willie Hernandez	p	1	0	0	0	0	—	—
Larry Herndon	rf	2	2	0	1	0	—	.667
Eric King	p	2	1	1	0	0	—	1.000
Chet Lemon	cf	5	13	0	0	0	—	1.000
Jack Morris	p	1	0	0	0	0	—	—
Jim Morrison	3b	1	1	2	0	0	—	1.000
Matt Nokes	c	3	11	2	0	0	1	1.000
Dan Petry	p	1	0	1	0	0	—	1.000
Jeff Robinson	p	1	0	1	0	0	—	1.000
Pat Sheridan	rf	4	7	1	0	0	—	1.000
Frank Tanana	p	1	0	1	0	0	—	1.000
Walt Terrell	p	1	0	1	0	0	—	1.000
Mark Thurmond	p	1	0	0	0	0	—	—
Alan Trammell	ss	5	6	9	1	1	—	.938
Lou Whitaker	2b	5	11	14	0	1	—	1.000
Totals		5	129	56	5	3	1	.974

1987 St. Louis Cardinals (NL) 4, San Francisco Giants (NL) 3

Down three games to two, the St. Louis Cardinals strung together two straight shutouts to down the San Francisco Giants in seven games. Emergency starter Greg Mathews won the opener for St. Louis, 5-3, but Dave Dravecky evened the score with a two-hit shutout for the Giants in Game 2. After the Cardinals pulled out a 6-5 comeback victory in Game 3, Mike Krukow outdueled Danny Cox in Game 4 to tie up the series once again. Joe Price tossed five innings of one-hit relief in Game 5 as the Giants won 6-3 to move to within a game of the NL title. With their backs to the wall, the Cardinals came up with two clutch pitching performances. In Game 6, John Tudor and two relievers combined to beat San Francisco, 1-0. Jose Oquendo drove in the only run of the game with a sacrifice fly. In Game 7, Oquendo launched a three-run homer and Danny Cox went the distance for a 6-0 victory. Jeffrey Leonard batted .417 with four home runs in a losing cause for the Giants.

Game 1

Tuesday, October 6

Giants	AB	R	H	RBI	BB	K	Avg
Robby Thompson, 2b	3	2	0	0	1	1	.000
Kevin Mitchell, 3b	4	0	1	0	0	0	.250
Jeffrey Leonard, lf	4	1	2	1	0	0	.500
Candy Maldonado, rf	4	0	1	2	0	0	.250
Chili Davis, cf	3	0	0	0	1	2	.000
Will Clark, 1b	4	0	1	0	0	0	.250
Bob Brenly, c	4	0	0	0	0	3	.000
Jose Uribe, ss	4	0	2	0	0	0	.500
Rick Reuschel, p	1	0	0	0	0	0	.000
Craig Lefferts, p	0	0	0	0	0	0	—
Chris Speier, ph	1	0	0	0	0	0	.000
Scott Garrelts, p	0	0	0	0	0	0	—
Bob Melvin, ph	1	0	0	0	0	0	.000
TOTALS	33	3	7	3	2	8	.212

Cardinals	AB	R	H	RBI	BB	K	Avg
Vince Coleman, lf	3	0	1	1	1	0	.333
Ozzie Smith, ss	3	1	1	0	1	0	.333
Tom Herr, 2b	4	0	0	0	0	0	.000
Dan Driessen, 1b	4	1	2	0	0	0	.500
Willie McGee, cf	4	1	2	1	0	0	.500
Terry Pendleton, 3b	4	1	1	1	0	2	.250
Curt Ford, rf	4	0	1	0	0	0	.250
Tony Pena, c	3	1	1	0	1	1	.333
Greg Mathews, p	1	0	1	2	0	0	1.000
Todd Worrell, p	0	0	0	0	0	0	—
Ken Dayley, p	0	0	0	0	0	0	—
TOTALS	30	5	10	5	3	3	.333

	1	2	3	4	5	6	7	8	9		R	H	E
Giants	1	0	0	1	0	0	0	1	0		3	7	1
Cardinals	0	0	1	1	0	3	0	0	x		5	10	1

E—Driessen, Uribe. DP—Giants 1 (Lefferts to Thompson to Uribe to Clark). LOB—Giants 6, Cardinals 6. Scoring Position—Giants 1-for-8, Cardinals 6-for-12. 2B—Maldonado (1), Driessen 2 (2). 3B—Smith (1). HR—Leonard (1). S—Reuschel, Mathews 2. GDP—Herr, Melvin. SB—Clark (1). CS—Coleman (1).

Giants	IP	H	R	ER	BB	K	ERA
Rick Reuschel (L, 0-1)	6.0	9	5	5	2	1	7.50
Craig Lefferts	1.0	1	0	0	1	0	0.00
Scott Garrelts	1.0	0	0	0	0	2	0.00

Cardinals	IP	H	R	ER	BB	K	ERA
Greg Mathews (W, 1-0)	7.1	4	3	2	1	7	2.45
Todd Worrell (H, 1)	0.1	2	0	0	1	0	0.00
Ken Dayley (S, 1)	1.1	1	0	0	0	1	0.00

Time—2:34. Attendance—55,331. Umpires—HP, Kibler. 1B, Montague. 2B, Pallone. 3B, Gregg.

Game 2

Wednesday, October 7

Giants	AB	R	H	RBI	BB	K	Avg
Robby Thompson, 2b	5	0	0	0	0	2	.000
Kevin Mitchell, 3b	5	0	0	0	0	1	.111
Jeffrey Leonard, lf	4	2	3	1	0	0	.625
Candy Maldonado, rf	4	2	2	0	0	2	.375
Chili Davis, cf	3	0	1	0	0	0	.167
Eddie Milner, pr-cf	0	0	0	0	0	0	—
Will Clark, 1b	3	1	2	2	1	0	.429
Bob Melvin, c	3	0	0	0	1	1	.000
Jose Uribe, ss	4	0	1	0	0	1	.375
Dave Dravecky, p	4	0	1	0	0	1	.250
TOTALS	35	5	10	3	2	8	.274

Cardinals	AB	R	H	RBI	BB	K	Avg
Vince Coleman, lf	3	0	0	0	1	1	.167
Ozzie Smith, ss	3	0	0	1	0	0	.167
Tom Herr, 2b	4	0	1	0	0	0	.125
Terry Pendleton, 3b	3	0	0	0	0	1	.143
Willie McGee, cf	3	0	0	0	0	1	.286
Jim Lindeman, 1b	3	0	1	0	0	0	.333
Jose Oquendo, rf	2	0	0	0	1	0	.000
Tony Pena, c	2	0	0	0	1	1	.200
John Tudor, p	2	0	0	0	0	2	.000
Tom Pagnozzi, ph	1	0	0	0	0	0	.000
Bob Forsch, p	0	0	0	0	0	0	—
TOTALS	26	0	2	0	4	6	.170

	1	2	3	4	5	6	7	8	9		R	H	E
Giants	0	2	0	1	0	0	0	2	0		5	10	0
Cardinals	0	0	0	0	0	0	0	0	0		0	2	1

E—Smith. DP—Giants 2 (Uribe to Clark; Mitchell to Thompson to Clark). LOB—Giants 6, Cardinals 3. Scoring Position—Giants 1-for-7, Cardinals 0-for-3. 2B—Uribe (1). HR—Leonard (2), Clark (1). S—Milner. GDP—Smith, Pagnozzi. CS—Uribe (1), Pena (1).

Giants	IP	H	R	ER	BB	K	ERA
Dave Dravecky (W, 1-0)	9.0	2	0	0	4	6	0.00

Cardinals	IP	H	R	ER	BB	K	ERA
John Tudor (L, 0-1)	8.0	10	5	3	2	6	3.38
Bob Forsch	1.0	0	0	0	0	2	0.00

Time—2:33. Attendance—55,331. Umpires—HP, Montague. 1B, Pallone. 2B, Gregg. 3B, Quick.

Game 3

Friday, October 9

Cardinals	AB	R	H	RBI	BB	K	Avg
Vince Coleman, lf	4	1	1	2	1	0	.200
Ozzie Smith, ss	5	1	3	0	0	0	.364
Tom Herr, 2b	4	0	0	0	0	0	.083
Jim Lindeman, 1b	3	1	1	3	0	1	.333
Willie McGee, cf	4	0	1	0	0	2	.273
Tony Pena, c	4	0	1	0	0	0	.222
Jose Oquendo, rf-3b	4	1	1	0	0	0	.167
Tom Lawless, 3b	2	0	1	0	0	0	.500
Curt Ford, ph-rf	1	1	1	0	1	0	.400
Joe Magrane, p	1	0	0	0	0	0	.000
Jack Clark, ph	1	0	0	0	0	1	.000
Bob Forsch, p	0	0	0	0	0	0	—
Dan Driessen, ph	1	0	1	0	0	0	.600
Lance Johnson, pr	0	1	0	0	0	0	—
Todd Worrell, p	1	0	0	0	0	1	.000
TOTALS	35	6	11	6	2	5	.263

Giants	AB	R	H	RBI	BB	K	Avg
Robby Thompson, 2b	2	0	0	0	2	1	.000
Harry Spilman, ph	1	1	1	1	0	0	1.000
Kevin Mitchell, 3b	5	0	1	0	0	0	.143
Jeffrey Leonard, lf	3	1	1	1	0	0	.545
Candy Maldonado, rf	4	0	0	0	0	0	.250
Chili Davis, cf	3	1	1	0	0	0	.222
Eddie Milner, cf	1	0	0	0	0	1	.000
Will Clark, 1b	4	1	2	1	0	1	.455
Bob Brenly, c	4	1	1	1	0	2	.125
Jose Uribe, ss	4	0	0	0	0	0	.250
Atlee Hammaker, p	3	0	0	0	0	2	.000
Don Robinson, p	0	0	0	0	0	0	—
Craig Lefferts, p	0	0	0	0	0	0	—
Mike LaCoss, p	0	0	0	0	0	0	—
Mike Aldrete, ph	1	0	0	0	0	1	.000
TOTALS	35	5	7	4	2	8	.247

	1	2	3	4	5	6	7	8	9		R	H	E
Cardinals	0	0	0	0	0	2	4	0	0		6	11	1
Giants	0	3	1	0	0	0	0	0	1		5	7	1

E—Herr, Mitchell. DP—Giants 2 (Davis to WClark; Uribe to Thompson to WClark). LOB—Cardinals 6, Giants 6. Scoring Position—Cardinals 2-for-6, Giants 1-for-7. 2B—Davis (1), WClark (1), Brenly (1). 3B—McGee (1). HR—Lindeman (1), Leonard (3), Spilman (1). S—Herr. SF—Lindeman. GDP—Herr. SB—Herr (1), Thompson (1), Johnson (1).

Game 4

Saturday, October 10

Cardinals	AB	R	H	RBI	BB	K	Avg
Vince Coleman, lf	4	0	2	1	0	0	.286
Ozzie Smith, ss	4	0	0	0	0	0	.267
Tom Herr, 2b	4	0	1	0	0	0	.125
Dan Driessen, 1b	3	0	0	0	1	1	.375
Willie McGee, cf	4	0	1	0	0	0	.267
Terry Pendleton, 3b	4	0	1	0	0	0	.182
Curt Ford, rf	4	1	1	0	0	1	.333
Tony Pena, c	3	1	2	0	0	0	.333
Danny Cox, p	3	0	1	1	0	1	.333
TOTALS	33	2	9	2	1	3	.262

Giants	AB	R	H	RBI	BB	K	Avg
Eddie Milner, cf	4	0	0	0	0	1	.000
Kevin Mitchell, 3b	4	1	2	0	0	0	.222
Jeffrey Leonard, lf	2	1	1	2	2	1	.538
Will Clark, 1b	4	0	2	0	0	1	.467
Mike Aldrete, rf	4	0	1	0	0	0	.200
Bob Brenly, c	4	1	2	1	0	0	.250
Robby Thompson, 2b	4	1	1	1	0	1	.071
Jose Uribe, ss	4	0	0	0	0	1	.188
Mike Krukow, p	2	0	0	0	1	0	.000
TOTALS	32	4	9	4	3	6	.260

	1	2	3	4	5	6	7	8	9		R	H	E
Cardinals	0	2	0	0	0	0	0	0	0		2	9	0
Giants	0	0	0	1	2	0	0	1	x		4	9	2

E—Clark, Thompson. DP—Giants 3 (Thompson to Clark; Krukow to Uribe to Clark; Clark to Uribe). LOB—Cardinals 5, Giants 7. Scoring Position—Cardinals 2-for-7, Giants 1-for-4. 2B—Mitchell (1), Clark (2). HR—Leonard (4), Brenly (1), Thompson (1). GDP—Coleman, Driessen, Ford.

Cardinals	IP	H	R	ER	BB	K	ERA
Danny Cox (L, 0-1)	8.0	9	4	4	3	6	4.50

Giants	IP	H	R	ER	BB	K	ERA
Mike Krukow (W, 1-0)	9.0	9	2	2	1	3	2.00

Time—2:23. Attendance—57,997. Umpires—HP, Gregg. 1B, Quick. 2B, Engel. 3B, Kibler.

Game 5

Sunday, October 11

Cardinals	AB	R	H	RBI	BB	K	Avg
Vince Coleman, lf	4	1	2	0	0	1	.333
Ozzie Smith, ss	2	0	0	0	0	1	.235
Tom Herr, 2b	3	0	0	1	0	0	.105
Dan Driessen, 1b	3	0	0	0	0	0	.273
Jim Lindeman, ph-1b	1	0	0	0	0	1	.286
Willie McGee, cf	4	0	2	0	0	1	.316
Terry Pendleton, 3b	4	1	1	0	0	1	.200
John Morris, rf	2	0	0	0	0	0	.000
Bob Forsch, p	0	0	0	0	0	0	—
Ricky Horton, p	0	0	0	0	0	0	—
Tom Lawless, ph-rf	2	0	0	0	0	0	.250

	AB	R	H	RBI	BB	K	Avg
Tony Pena, c	2	1	1	0	1	1	.357
Greg Mathews, p	1	0	1	0	0	0	1.000
Curt Ford, rf	0	0	0	0	0	0	.333
Jose Oquendo, ph-rf	2	0	0	0	0	1	.125
Ken Dayley, p	0	0	0	0	0	0	—
TOTALS	30	3	7	2	1	7	.262

Giants	AB	R	H	RBI	BB	K	Avg
Robby Thompson, 2b	2	1	1	1	1	0	.125
Kevin Mitchell, 3b	4	1	2	2	0	0	.273
Jeffrey Leonard, lf	4	0	0	0	0	1	.412
Candy Maldonado, rf	4	0	1	0	0	1	.250
Chili Davis, cf	3	1	1	0	0	0	.250
Eddie Milner, cf	1	0	0	0	0	1	.000
Will Clark, 1b	3	1	1	0	1	1	.444
Bob Brenly, c	1	1	0	0	3	0	.231
Jose Uribe, ss	4	1	1	2	0	1	.200
Rick Reuschel, p	1	0	0	0	0	1	.000
Mike Aldrete, ph	0	0	0	1	0	0	.200
Joe Price, p	1	0	0	0	0	1	.000
TOTALS	28	6	7	6	5	7	.257

	1	2	3	4	5	6	7	8	9		R	H	E
Cardinals	1	0	1	1	0	0	0	0	0		3	7	0
Giants	1	0	1	4	0	0	0	0	x		6	7	1

E—Reuschel. DP—Cardinals 1 (Pendleton to Herr to Driessen), Giants 1 (Thompson to Uribe to Clark). LOB—Cardinals 4, Giants 5. Scoring Position—Cardinals 1-for-4, Giants 3-for-9. 2B—Coleman (1). 3B—Pendleton (1), Thompson (1). HR—Mitchell (1). S—Smith. SF—Smith, Herr, Aldrete. GDP—Herr, Davis. SB—Thompson (2), Mitchell (1), Uribe (1). CS—McGee (1), Thompson (1).

Cardinals	IP	H	R	ER	BB	K	ERA
Greg Mathews	3.0	2	2	2	2	3	3.48
Bob Forsch (L, 1-1)	0.0	3	4	4	1	0	12.00
Ricky Horton	3.0	2	0	0	0	2	0.00
Ken Dayley	2.0	0	0	0	2	2	0.00

Giants	IP	H	R	ER	BB	K	ERA
Rick Reuschel	4.0	6	3	2	0	1	6.30
Joe Price (W, 1-0)	5.0	1	0	0	1	6	0.00

Forsch pitched to four batters in the 4th.

WP—Reuschel. HBP—Thompson by Dayley. Time—2:48. Attendance—59,363. Umpires—HP, Quick. 1B, Engel. 2B, Kibler. 3B, Montague.

Game 6
Tuesday, October 13

Giants	AB	R	H	RBI	BB	K	Avg
Robby Thompson, 2b	3	0	0	0	1	2	.105
Kevin Mitchell, 3b	4	0	1	0	0	0	.269
Jeffrey Leonard, lf	3	0	1	0	1	2	.400
Candy Maldonado, rf	3	0	0	0	0	0	.211
Mike Aldrete, ph-rf	1	0	0	0	0	1	.167
Chili Davis, cf	4	0	0	0	0	0	.188
Will Clark, 1b	3	0	0	0	1	2	.381
Bob Melvin, c	3	0	3	0	0	0	.429
Eddie Milner, pr	0	0	0	0	0	0	.000
Don Robinson, p	0	0	0	0	0	0	—
Harry Spilman, ph	0	0	0	0	0	0	1.000
Chris Speier, ph	1	0	0	0	0	1	.000
Jose Uribe, ss	3	0	1	0	0	0	.217
Dave Dravecky, p	2	0	0	0	0	1	.167
Bob Brenly, ph-c	1	0	0	0	0	0	.214
TOTALS	31	0	6	0	3	9	.247

Cardinals	AB	R	H	RBI	BB	K	Avg
Vince Coleman, lf	4	0	0	0	0	2	.273
Ozzie Smith, ss	4	0	0	0	0	1	.190
Tom Herr, 2b	3	0	2	0	0	0	.182
Jim Lindeman, 1b	3	0	2	0	0	0	.400
Terry Pendleton, 3b	3	0	0	0	0	2	.167
Tony Pena, c	3	1	1	0	0	0	.353
Willie McGee, cf	3	0	0	0	0	1	.273
Jose Oquendo, rf	2	0	0	1	0	1	.100
Todd Worrell, p-rf	0	0	0	0	0	0	.000
John Tudor, p	2	0	0	0	0	2	.000
John Morris, rf	1	0	0	0	0	0	.000
Ken Dayley, p	0	0	0	0	0	0	—
TOTALS	28	1	5	1	0	9	.227

	1	2	3	4	5	6	7	8	9		R	H	E
Giants	0	0	0	0	0	0	0	0	0		0	6	0
Cardinals	0	1	0	0	0	0	0	0	x		1	5	0

LOB—Giants 8, Cardinals 4. Scoring Position—Giants 0-for-7, Cardinals 0-for-2. 3B—Pena (1). S—Uribe. SF—Oquendo. CS—Thompson (2).

Giants	IP	H	R	ER	BB	K	ERA
Dave Dravecky (L, 1-1)	6.0	5	1	1	0	8	0.60
Don Robinson	2.0	0	0	0	0	1	13.50

Cardinals	IP	H	R	ER	BB	K	ERA
John Tudor (W, 1-1)	7.1	6	0	0	3	6	1.76
Todd Worrell (H, 2)	1.0	0	0	0	0	2	2.08
Ken Dayley (S, 2)	0.2	0	0	0	0	1	0.00

Time—3:09. Attendance—55,431. Umpires—HP, Engel. 1B, Kibler. 2B, Montague. 3B, Pallone.

Game 7
Wednesday, October 14

Giants	AB	R	H	RBI	BB	K	Avg
Mike Aldrete, rf	4	0	0	0	0	0	.100
Kevin Mitchell, 3b	4	0	1	0	0	2	.267
Jeffrey Leonard, lf	4	0	2	0	0	0	.417
Will Clark, 1b	4	0	1	0	0	1	.360
Chili Davis, cf	4	0	0	0	0	0	.150
Bob Brenly, c	3	0	1	0	0	1	.235
Chris Speier, 2b	3	0	0	0	0	1	.000
Jose Uribe, ss	3	0	2	0	0	0	.269
Atlee Hammaker, p	0	0	0	0	0	0	.000
Eddie Milner, ph	1	0	1	0	0	0	.143
Joe Price, p	0	0	0	0	0	0	.000
Kelly Downs, p	0	0	0	0	0	0	—
Robby Thompson, ph	1	0	0	0	0	0	.100
Scott Garrelts, p	0	0	0	0	0	0	—
Craig Lefferts, p	0	0	0	0	0	0	—
Mike LaCoss, p	0	0	0	0	0	0	—
Harry Spilman, ph	0	0	0	0	0	0	.500
Don Robinson, p	0	0	0	0	0	0	—
TOTALS	32	0	8	0	0	5	.242

Cardinals	AB	R	H	RBI	BB	K	Avg
Vince Coleman, lf	4	1	1	0	1	2	.269
Ozzie Smith, ss	4	0	1	0	1	2	.200
Tom Herr, 2b	5	0	2	2	0	1	.222
Jim Lindeman, 1b	3	0	0	0	0	1	.308
Dan Driessen, ph-1b	1	0	0	0	0	0	.250
Terry Pendleton, 3b	1	1	1	0	0	0	.211
Tom Lawless, ph-3b	2	0	1	0	1	1	.333
Tony Pena, c	4	1	2	0	0	1	.381
Willie McGee, cf	4	1	2	1	0	0	.308
Jose Oquendo, rf	2	2	1	3	2	0	.167
Danny Cox, p	3	0	1	0	0	1	.333
TOTALS	33	6	12	6	5	9	.264

	1	2	3	4	5	6	7	8	9		R	H	E
Giants	0	0	0	0	0	0	0	0	0		0	8	1
Cardinals	0	4	0	0	0	2	0	0	x		6	12	0

E—Davis. DP—Cardinals 3 (Lindeman to Smith to Cox; Cox to Smith to Lindeman; Herr to Smith to Lindeman). LOB—Giants 5, Cardinals 9. Scoring Position—Giants 0-for-4, Cardinals 3-for-8. 2B—McGee (1). HR—Oquendo (1). S—Cox. GDP—Aldrete, Clark, Speier. SB—Coleman (1), Pena (1). CS—Coleman (2).

Giants	IP	H	R	ER	BB	K	ERA
Atlee Hammaker (L, 0-1)	2.0	5	4	4	0	3	7.88
Joe Price	0.2	2	0	0	0	1	0.00
Kelly Downs	1.1	1	0	0	0	0	0.00
Scott Garrelts	1.2	2	2	2	4	2	6.75
Craig Lefferts	0.0	1	0	0	0	0	0.00
Mike LaCoss	1.1	1	0	0	1	1	0.00
Don Robinson	1.0	0	0	0	0	2	9.00

Cardinals	IP	H	R	ER	BB	K	ERA
Danny Cox (W, 1-1)	9.0	8	0	0	0	5	2.12

Lefferts pitched to one batter in the 6th.

WP—Garrelts. PB—Brenly. Time—2:59. Attendance—55,331. Umpires—HP, Kibler. 1B, Montague. 2B, Pallone. 3B, Gregg.

1987 NL Championship Series—Composite Statistics

Batting

Cardinals	G	AB	R	H	RBI	2B	3B	HR	BB	SO	SB	CS	Avg	OBP	Slg
Jack Clark	1	1	0	0	0	0	0	0	0	1	0	0	.000	.000	.000
Vince Coleman	7	26	3	7	4	1	0	0	4	6	1	2	.269	.367	.308
Danny Cox	2	6	0	2	1	0	0	0	2	0	0	0	.333	.333	.333
Dan Driessen	5	12	1	3	1	2	0	0	1	1	0	0	.250	.308	.417
Curt Ford	4	9	2	3	0	0	0	0	1	1	0	0	.333	.400	.333
Tom Herr	7	27	0	6	3	0	0	0	0	1	1	0	.222	.214	.222
Lance Johnson	1	0	1	0	0	0	0	0	0	0	1	0	—	—	—
Tom Lawless	3	6	2	2	0	0	0	0	1	1	0	0	.333	.429	.333
Jim Lindeman	5	13	1	4	3	0	0	1	0	3	0	0	.308	.286	.538
Joe Magrane	1	1	0	0	0	0	0	0	0	0	0	0	.000	.000	.000
Greg Mathews	2	2	0	2	2	0	0	0	0	0	0	0	1.000	1.000	1.000
Willie McGee	7	26	2	8	2	1	1	0	0	5	0	1	.308	.308	.423
John Morris	2	3	0	0	0	0	0	0	0	0	0	0	.000	.000	.000
Jose Oquendo	5	12	3	2	4	0	0	1	3	2	0	0	.167	.313	.417
Tom Pagnozzi	1	1	0	0	0	0	0	0	0	0	0	0	.000	.000	.000
Tony Pena	7	21	5	8	0	0	1	0	3	4	1	1	.381	.458	.476
Terry Pendleton	6	19	3	4	1	0	1	0	0	6	0	0	.211	.211	.316
Ozzie Smith	7	25	2	5	1	0	1	0	3	4	0	0	.200	.276	.280
John Tudor	2	4	0	0	0	0	0	0	0	4	0	0	.000	.000	.000
Todd Worrell	3	1	0	0	0	0	0	0	0	1	0	0	.000	.000	.000
Totals	7	215	23	56	22	4	4	2	16	42	4	4	.260	.306	.344

Batting

Giants	G	AB	R	H	RBI	2B	3B	HR	BB	SO	SB	CS	Avg	OBP	Slg
Mike Aldrete	5	10	0	1	1	0	0	0	0	2	0	0	.100	.091	.100
Bob Brenly	6	17	3	4	2	1	0	1	3	7	0	0	.235	.350	.471
Will Clark	7	25	3	9	3	2	0	1	3	6	1	0	.360	.429	.560
Chili Davis	6	20	2	3	0	1	0	0	1	4	0	0	.150	.190	.200
Dave Dravecky	2	6	0	1	0	0	0	0	0	1	0	0	.167	.167	.167
Atlee Hammaker	2	3	0	0	0	0	0	0	0	2	0	0	.000	.000	.000
Mike Krukow	1	2	0	0	0	0	0	0	0	1	0	0	.000	.333	.000
Jeffrey Leonard	7	24	5	10	5	0	0	4	3	4	0	0	.417	.500	.917
Candy Maldonado	5	19	2	4	2	1	0	0	0	3	0	0	.211	.211	.263
Bob Melvin	3	7	0	3	0	0	0	0	0	1	1	0	.429	.500	.429
Eddie Milner	6	7	0	1	0	0	0	0	0	3	0	0	.143	.143	.143
Kevin Mitchell	7	30	2	8	2	1	0	1	0	3	1	0	.267	.267	.400
Joe Price	2	1	0	0	0	0	0	0	0	0	0	0	.000	.000	.000
Rick Reuschel	2	2	0	0	0	0	0	0	0	1	0	0	.000	.000	.000
Chris Speier	3	5	0	0	0	0	0	0	0	2	0	0	.000	.000	.000
Harry Spilman	3	2	1	1	1	0	0	1	0	0	0	0	.500	.500	2.000
Robby Thompson	7	20	4	2	2	0	1	1	5	7	2	2	.100	.308	.350
Jose Uribe	7	26	1	7	2	1	0	0	0	4	1	1	.269	.269	.308
Totals	7	226	23	54	20	7	1	9	17	51	5	3	.239	.297	.398

Pitching

Cardinals	G	GS	CG	IP	H	R	ER	BB	SO	W-L	Sv-Op	Hld	ERA
Danny Cox	2	2	2	17.0	17	4	4	3	11	1-1	0-0	0	2.12
Ken Dayley	3	0	0	4.0	1	0	0	2	4	0-0	2-2	0	0.00
Bob Forsch	3	0	0	3.0	4	4	4	1	3	1-1	0-0	0	12.00
Ricky Horton	1	0	0	3.0	2	0	0	0	2	0-0	0-0	0	0.00
Joe Magrane	1	1	0	4.0	4	4	4	2	3	0-0	0-0	0	9.00
Greg Mathews	2	2	0	10.1	5	4	3	10	10	1-0	0-0	0	3.48
John Tudor	2	2	0	15.1	16	5	3	5	12	1-1	0-0	0	1.76
Todd Worrell	3	0	0	4.1	4	1	1	1	6	0-0	1-1	2	2.08
Totals	7	7	2	61.0	54	23	20	17	51	4-3	3-3	2	2.95

Pitching

Giants	G	GS	CG	IP	H	R	ER	BB	SO	W-L	Sv-Op	Hld	ERA
Kelly Downs	1	0	0	1.1	1	0	0	0	0	0-0	0-0	0	0.00
Dave Dravecky	2	2	1	15.0	7	1	1	4	14	1-1	0-0	0	0.60
Scott Garrelts	2	0	0	2.2	2	2	2	4	4	0-0	0-0	0	6.75
Atlee Hammaker	2	2	0	8.0	12	7	7	0	7	0-1	0-0	0	7.88
Mike Krukow	1	1	1	9.0	9	2	2	1	3	1-0	0-0	0	2.00
Mike LaCoss	2	0	0	3.1	1	0	0	3	2	0-0	0-0	0	0.00
Craig Lefferts	3	0	0	2.0	3	0	0	1	0	0-0	0-0	0	0.00
Joe Price	2	0	0	5.2	3	0	0	1	7	1-0	0-0	0	0.00
Rick Reuschel	2	2	0	10.0	15	8	7	2	2	0-1	0-0	0	6.30
Don Robinson	3	0	0	3.0	3	3	3	0	3	0-1	0-1	0	9.00
Totals	7	7	2	60.0	56	23	22	16	42	3-4	0-1	0	3.30

Fielding

Cardinals	Pos	G	PO	Ast	E	DP	PB	FPct
Vince Coleman	lf	7	8	1	0	0	—	1.000
Danny Cox	p	2	4	5	0	2	—	1.000
Ken Dayley	p	3	0	0	0	0	—	—
Dan Driessen	1b	4	26	3	1	2	—	.967
Curt Ford	rf	4	6	0	0	0	—	1.000
Bob Forsch	p	3	0	1	0	0	—	1.000
Tom Herr	2b	7	12	11	1	3	—	.958
Ricky Horton	p	1	0	0	0	0	—	—
Tom Lawless	3b	2	0	4	0	0	—	1.000
	rf	1	1	0	0	0	—	1.000
Jim Lindeman	1b	5	33	2	0	3	—	1.000
Joe Magrane	p	1	0	1	0	0	—	1.000
Greg Mathews	p	2	0	0	0	0	—	—
Willie McGee	cf	7	17	0	0	0	—	1.000
John Morris	rf	2	1	0	0	0	—	1.000
Jose Oquendo	rf	5	7	0	0	0	—	1.000
	3b	1	0	0	0	0	—	—
Tony Pena	c	7	55	5	0	0	0	1.000
Terry Pendleton	3b	6	3	11	0	1	—	1.000
Ozzie Smith	ss	7	10	19	1	4	—	.967
John Tudor	p	2	0	4	0	0	—	1.000
Todd Worrell	p	3	0	0	0	0	—	—
	rf	1	0	0	0	0	—	—
Totals		7	183	67	3	15	0	.988

Fielding

Giants	Pos	G	PO	Ast	E	DP	PB	FPct
Mike Aldrete	rf	3	5	0	0	0	—	1.000
Bob Brenly	c	6	28	2	0	0	1	1.000
Will Clark	1b	7	62	8	1	10	—	.986
Chili Davis	cf	6	11	1	1	1	—	.923
Kelly Downs	p	1	0	0	0	0	—	—
Dave Dravecky	p	2	0	2	0	0	—	1.000
Scott Garrelts	p	2	2	0	0	0	—	1.000
Atlee Hammaker	p	2	0	1	0	0	—	1.000
Mike Krukow	p	1	2	2	0	1	—	1.000
Mike LaCoss	p	2	0	2	0	0	—	1.000
Craig Lefferts	p	3	0	2	0	1	—	1.000
Jeffrey Leonard	lf	7	14	1	0	0	—	1.000
Candy Maldonado	rf	5	7	0	0	0	—	1.000
Bob Melvin	c	2	14	1	0	0	0	1.000
Eddie Milner	cf	4	8	0	0	0	—	1.000
Kevin Mitchell	3b	7	4	11	1	1	—	.938
Joe Price	p	2	0	0	0	0	—	—
Rick Reuschel	p	2	0	3	1	0	—	.750
Don Robinson	p	3	0	0	0	0	—	—
Chris Speier	2b	1	1	3	0	0	—	1.000
Robby Thompson	2b	6	11	19	1	6	—	.968
Jose Uribe	ss	7	11	20	1	7	—	.969
Totals		7	180	78	6	27	1	.977

1988 Oakland Athletics (AL) 4, Boston Red Sox (AL) 0

The Oakland A's swept past the Boston Red Sox in four straight games, getting timely hitting and solid pitching every step of the way. Dave Henderson's eighth-inning RBI single was the difference in Oakland's 2-1 victory in the opener. Walt Weiss was the next day's hero, driving in the go-ahead run in the top of the ninth for a 4-3 Oakland win. The Red Sox jumped out to a 5-0 lead in Game 3, but the A's came back to launch four home runs and bury the Sox, 10-6. Dave Stewart wrapped it up with a 4-1 victory in the fourth game. Dennis Eckersley saved all four games for the A's, and Jose Canseco hit three of Oakland's seven longballs.

Game 1

Wednesday, October 5

Athletics	AB	R	H	RBI	BB	K	Avg
Carney Lansford, 3b	4	1	1	0	0	1	.250
Dave Henderson, cf	4	0	2	1	0	1	.500
Jose Canseco, rf	4	1	1	1	0	1	.250
Mark McGwire, 1b	4	0	0	0	0	1	.000
Terry Steinbach, c	2	0	1	0	1	0	.500
Ron Hassey, c	1	0	0	0	0	0	.000
Don Baylor, dh	3	0	0	0	1	1	.000
Luis Polonia, pr-dh	0	0	0	0	0	0	—
Tony Phillips, lf	3	0	0	0	1	2	.000
Mike Gallego, 2b	4	0	0	0	0	0	.000
Walt Weiss, ss	3	0	1	0	0	0	.333
TOTALS	32	2	6	2	3	7	.188

Red Sox	AB	R	H	RBI	BB	K	Avg
Wade Boggs, 3b	4	0	1	1	0	2	.250
Marty Barrett, 2b	4	0	0	0	0	0	.000
Dwight Evans, rf	4	0	1	0	0	3	.250
Mike Greenwell, lf	3	0	0	0	1	0	.000
Todd Benzinger, 1b	4	0	0	0	0	1	.000
Ellis Burks, cf	4	0	0	0	0	1	.000
Jim Rice, dh	2	0	1	0	1	1	.500
Kevin Romine, pr-dh	0	1	0	0	0	0	—
Larry Parrish, ph	1	0	0	0	0	1	.000
Jody Reed, ss	2	0	1	0	1	0	.500
Rich Gedman, c	3	0	2	0	1	0	.667
Ed Romero, pr	0	0	0	0	0	0	—
TOTALS	31	1	6	1	4	9	.194

	1 2 3	4 5 6	7 8 9	R	H	E
Athletics	0 0 0	1 0 0	0 1 0	2	6	0
Red Sox	0 0 0	0 0 0	1 0 0	1	6	0

DP—Athletics 1 (Weiss to Gallego to McGwire), Red Sox 1 (Reed to Barrett to Benzinger). LOB—Athletics 6, Red Sox 9. Scoring Position—Athletics 1-for-5, Red Sox 2-for-8. 2B—Lansford (1), Weiss (1), Evans (1), Reed (1). HR—Canseco (1). SF—Boggs. GDP—Canseco, Benzinger.

Athletics	IP	H	R	ER	BB	K	ERA
Dave Stewart	6.1	5	1	1	3	6	1.42
Rick Honeycutt (BS, 1; W, 1-0)	0.2	0	0	0	0	0	0.00
Dennis Eckersley (S, 1)	2.0	1	0	0	1	3	0.00

Red Sox	IP	H	R	ER	BB	K	ERA
Bruce Hurst (L, 0-1)	9.0	6	2	2	3	7	2.00

PB—Steinbach. HBP—Reed by Stewart. Time—2:44. Attendance—34,104. Umpires—HP, Denkinger. 1B, Hendry. 2B, McClelland. 3B, Kosc.

Game 2

Thursday, October 6

Athletics	AB	R	H	RBI	BB	K	Avg
Luis Polonia, lf	5	0	2	0	0	2	.400
Mike Gallego, 2b	0	0	0	0	0	0	.000
Dave Henderson, cf	3	1	1	0	1	1	.429
Jose Canseco, rf	4	1	1	2	0	0	.250
Dave Parker, dh	4	0	1	0	0	0	.250
Carney Lansford, 3b	4	1	0	0	0	1	.125
Ron Hassey, c	4	1	1	0	0	1	.200
Mark McGwire, 1b	4	0	1	1	0	2	.125
Tony Phillips, 2b-lf	4	0	2	0	0	1	.286
Walt Weiss, ss	4	0	1	1	0	1	.286
TOTALS	36	4	10	4	1	9	.238

Red Sox	AB	R	H	RBI	BB	K	Avg
Wade Boggs, 3b	3	0	0	0	1	1	.143
Marty Barrett, 2b	4	0	0	0	0	0	.000
Dwight Evans, rf	3	1	0	0	1	0	.143
Mike Greenwell, lf	2	1	0	0	2	0	.000
Jim Rice, dh	4	0	1	0	0	0	.333
Kevin Romine, pr-dh	0	0	0	0	0	0	—
Ellis Burks, cf	4	0	1	1	0	0	.125
Todd Benzinger, 1b	3	0	1	0	1	1	.143
Jody Reed, ss	2	0	0	0	0	1	.250
Larry Parrish, ph	1	0	0	0	0	0	.000
Rich Gedman, c	4	1	1	1	0	1	.429
TOTALS	30	3	4	2	5	4	.164

	1 2 3	4 5 6	7 8 9	R	H	E
Athletics	0 0 0	0 0 0	3 0 1	4	10	1
Red Sox	0 0 0	0 0 2	1 0 0	3	4	1

E—Henderson, Clemens. DP—Athletics 1 (Weiss to Phillips). LOB—Athletics 6, Red Sox 6. Scoring Position—Athletics 2-for-8, Red Sox 1-for-4. 2B—Phillips (1). HR—Canseco (2), Gedman (1). S—Reed. CS—Polonia (1).

Athletics	IP	H	R	ER	BB	K	ERA
Storm Davis	6.1	2	2	0	5	4	0.00
Greg Cadaret (BS, 1)	0.1	1	1	1	0	0	27.00
Gene Nelson (W, 1-0)	1.1	1	0	0	0	0	0.00
Dennis Eckersley (S, 2)	1.0	0	0	0	0	0	0.00

Red Sox	IP	H	R	ER	BB	K	ERA
Roger Clemens	7.0	6	3	3	0	8	3.86
Bob Stanley	0.1	1	0	0	1	0	0.00
Lee Smith (L, 0-1)	1.2	3	1	1	0	1	5.40

Balk—Clemens. WP—Clemens, Davis. PB—Gedman. Time—3:14. Attendance—34,605. Umpires—HP, Hendry. 1B, McClelland. 2B, Kosc. 3B, Kaiser.

Game 3

Saturday, October 8

Red Sox	AB	R	H	RBI	BB	K	Avg
Ellis Burks, cf	5	2	2	0	0	1	.231
Marty Barrett, 2b	4	1	1	0	0	0	.083
Wade Boggs, 3b	4	2	3	2	0	0	.364
Mike Greenwell, lf	5	1	2	3	0	0	.200
Jim Rice, dh	5	0	0	0	0	2	.182
Dwight Evans, rf	2	0	1	1	2	0	.222
Rich Gedman, c	3	0	2	0	1	0	.500
Jody Reed, ss	3	0	1	0	1	0	.286
Todd Benzinger, 1b	3	0	0	0	0	1	.100
Larry Parrish, ph-1b	1	0	0	0	0	1	.000
TOTALS	35	6	12	6	4	5	.229

Athletics	AB	R	H	RBI	BB	K	Avg
Carney Lansford, 3b	5	2	3	2	0	0	.308
Dave Henderson, cf	5	1	2	2	0	3	.417
Jose Canseco, rf	4	0	0	0	1	1	.167
Dave Parker, dh	5	1	1	0	0	2	.222
Mark McGwire, 1b	4	3	3	1	0	1	.333
Ron Hassey, c	3	1	3	3	1	0	.500
Stan Javier, lf	3	0	1	1	1	0	.333
Mike Gallego, 2b	4	1	1	0	0	2	.125
Walt Weiss, ss	4	1	1	1	0	1	.273
TOTALS	37	10	15	10	3	10	.295

	1 2 3	4 5 6	7 8 9	R	H	E
Red Sox	3 2 0	0 0 0	1 0 0	6	12	0
Athletics	0 4 2	0 1 0	1 2 x	10	15	1

E—Henderson. DP—Red Sox 1 (Benzinger to Reed to Gedman to Boggs), Athletics 2 (Gallego to Weiss to McGwire; Lansford to Gallego to McGwire). LOB—Red Sox 8, Athletics 6. Scoring Position—Red Sox 4-for-10, Athletics 2-for-6. 2B—Burks (1), Greenwell (1), Parker (1), Hassey (1), Weiss (2). HR—Greenwell (1), Lansford (1), Henderson (1), McGwire (1), Hassey (1). S—Barrett. SF—Boggs. GDP—Reed, Benzinger. CS—Lansford (1).

Red Sox	IP	H	R	ER	BB	K	ERA
Mike Boddicker (L, 0-1)	2.2	8	6	6	1	2	20.25
Wes Gardner	4.2	6	3	3	2	8	5.79
Bob Stanley	0.2	1	1	1	0	0	9.00

Athletics	IP	H	R	ER	BB	K	ERA
Bob Welch	1.2	6	5	5	2	0	27.00
Gene Nelson (W, 2-0)	3.1	4	0	0	1	0	0.00
Curt Young (H, 1)	1.1	1	1	0	0	2	0.00
Eric Plunk (H, 1)	0.1	1	0	0	0	1	0.00
Rick Honeycutt (H, 1)	0.1	0	0	0	1	0	0.00
Dennis Eckersley (S, 3)	2.0	0	0	0	0	2	0.00

Honeycutt pitched to one batter in the 8th.

Balk—Welch. Time—3:14. Attendance—49,261. Umpires—HP, McClelland. 1B, Kosc. 2B, Kaiser. 3B, Shulock.

Game 4

Sunday, October 9

Red Sox	AB	R	H	RBI	BB	K	Avg
Ellis Burks, cf	4	0	1	0	0	1	.235
Marty Barrett, 2b	3	1	0	0	1	0	.067
Wade Boggs, 3b	2	0	1	0	2	1	.385
Mike Greenwell, lf	4	0	1	0	0	0	.214
Jim Rice, dh	2	0	0	1	1	1	.154
Spike Owen, ph	0	0	0	0	1	0	—
Dwight Evans, rf	3	0	0	0	0	2	.167
Todd Benzinger, ph	1	0	0	0	0	0	.091
Rich Gedman, c	4	0	0	0	0	0	.357
Jody Reed, ss	4	0	1	0	0	0	.273
Larry Parrish, 1b	3	0	0	0	0	0	.000
TOTALS	30	1	4	1	5	5	.206

Athletics	AB	R	H	RBI	BB	K	Avg
Carney Lansford, 3b	4	0	1	0	0	0	.294
Dave Henderson, cf	4	0	1	1	0	2	.375
Jose Canseco, rf	4	2	3	1	0	0	.313
Mark McGwire, 1b	3	1	1	1	1	1	.333
Dave Parker, lf	3	0	1	0	0	2	.250
Stan Javier, pr-lf	1	0	1	0	0	0	.500
Terry Steinbach, c	2	0	0	0	1	0	.250
Luis Polonia, ph	0	0	0	0	1	0	.400
Ron Hassey, c	0	0	0	0	0	0	.500
Don Baylor, dh	3	0	0	1	0	1	.000
Mike Gallego, 2b	4	0	0	0	0	1	.083
Walt Weiss, ss	4	1	2	0	0	2	.333
TOTALS	32	4	10	4	3	9	.300

	1 2 3	4 5 6	7 8 9	R	H	E
Red Sox	0 0 0	0 0 1	0 0 0	1	4	0
Athletics	1 0 1	0 0 0	0 2 x	4	10	1

E—Parker. DP—Athletics 1 (Lansford to Gallego to McGwire). LOB—Red Sox 7, Athletics 8. Scoring Position—Red Sox 0-for-4, Athletics 2-for-7. 2B—Henderson (1), Canseco (1). HR—Canseco (3). SF—Baylor. GDP—Barrett. SB—Canseco (1). CS—Canseco (1).

Red Sox	IP	H	R	ER	BB	K	ERA
Bruce Hurst (L, 0-2)	4.0	4	2	2	2	5	2.77
Mike Smithson	2.1	3	0	0	0	1	0.00
Lee Smith	1.2	3	2	2	1	3	8.10

Athletics	IP	H	R	ER	BB	K	ERA
Dave Stewart (W, 1-0)	7.0	4	1	1	3	5	1.35
Rick Honeycutt (H, 2)	1.0	0	0	0	1	0	0.00
Dennis Eckersley (S, 4)	1.0	0	0	0	1	0	0.00

Stewart pitched to one batter in the 8th.

Time—2:55. Attendance—49,406. Umpires—HP, Kosc. 1B, Kaiser. 2B, Shulock. 3B, Denkinger.

1988 AL Championship Series—Composite Statistics

Batting

Athletics	G	AB	R	H	RBI	2B	3B	HR	BB	SO	SB	CS	Avg	OBP	Slg
Don Baylor	2	6	0	0	1	0	0	0	1	2	0	0	.000	.125	.000
Jose Canseco	4	16	4	5	4	1	0	3	1	2	1	1	.313	.353	.938
Mike Gallego	4	12	1	1	0	0	0	0	0	3	0	0	.083	.083	.083
Ron Hassey	4	8	2	4	3	1	0	1	1	1	0	0	.500	.556	1.000
Dave Henderson	4	16	2	6	4	1	0	1	1	7	0	0	.375	.412	.625
Stan Javier	2	4	0	2	1	0	0	0	1	0	0	0	.500	.600	.500
Carney Lansford	4	17	4	5	2	1	0	1	0	2	0	1	.294	.294	.529
Mark McGwire	4	15	4	5	3	0	0	1	1	5	0	0	.333	.375	.533
Dave Parker	3	12	1	3	0	1	0	0	0	4	0	0	.250	.250	.333
Tony Phillips	2	7	0	2	0	1	0	0	1	3	0	0	.286	.375	.429
Luis Polonia	3	5	0	2	0	0	0	0	1	2	0	1	.400	.500	.400
Terry Steinbach	2	4	0	1	0	0	0	0	2	0	0	0	.250	.500	.250
Walt Weiss	4	15	2	5	2	2	0	0	4	0	0	0	.333	.333	.467
Totals	4	137	20	41	20	8	0	7	10	35	1	3	.299	.345	.511

Batting

Red Sox	G	AB	R	H	RBI	2B	3B	HR	BB	SO	SB	CS	Avg	OBP	Slg
Marty Barrett	4	15	2	1	0	0	0	0	1	0	0	0	.067	.125	.067
Todd Benzinger	4	11	0	1	0	0	0	0	1	3	0	0	.091	.167	.091
Wade Boggs	4	13	2	5	3	0	0	0	3	4	0	0	.385	.444	.385
Ellis Burks	4	17	2	4	1	1	0	0	3	0	0	0	.235	.235	.294
Dwight Evans	4	12	1	2	1	1	0	0	3	5	0	0	.167	.333	.250
Rich Gedman	4	14	1	5	1	0	0	1	2	1	0	0	.357	.438	.571
Mike Greenwell	4	14	2	3	3	1	0	1	3	0	0	0	.214	.353	.500
Spike Owen	1	0	0	0	0	0	0	0	0	1	0	0	—	1.000	—
Larry Parrish	4	6	0	0	0	0	0	0	0	2	0	0	.000	.000	.000
Jody Reed	4	11	0	3	0	1	0	0	2	1	0	0	.273	.429	.364
Jim Rice	4	13	0	2	1	0	0	0	2	4	0	0	.154	.267	.154
Ed Romero	1	0	0	0	0	0	0	0	0	0	0	0	—	—	—
Kevin Romine	2	0	1	0	0	0	0	0	0	0	0	0	—	—	—
Totals	4	126	11	26	10	4	0	2	18	23	0	0	.206	.306	.286

Pitching

Athletics	G	GS	CG	IP	H	R	ER	BB	SO	W-L	Sv-Op	Hld	ERA
Greg Cadaret	1	0	0	0.1	1	1	1	0	0	0-0	0-1	0	27.00
Storm Davis	1	1	0	6.1	2	2	0	5	4	0-0	0-0	0	0.00
Dennis Eckersley	4	0	0	6.0	1	0	0	2	5	0-0	4-4	0	0.00
Rick Honeycutt	3	0	0	2.0	0	0	0	2	0	1-0	0-1	2	0.00
Gene Nelson	2	0	0	4.2	5	0	0	1	0	2-0	0-0	0	0.00
Eric Plunk	1	0	0	0.1	1	0	0	0	1	0-0	0-0	1	0.00
Dave Stewart	2	2	0	13.1	9	2	2	6	11	1-0	0-0	0	1.35
Bob Welch	1	1	0	1.2	6	5	5	2	0	0-0	0-0	0	27.00
Curt Young	1	0	0	1.1	1	1	0	0	2	0-0	0-0	1	0.00
Totals	4	4	0	36.0	26	11	8	18	23	4-0	4-6	4	2.00

Pitching

Red Sox	G	GS	CG	IP	H	R	ER	BB	SO	W-L	Sv-Op	Hld	ERA
Mike Boddicker	1	1	0	2.2	8	6	6	1	2	0-1	0-0	0	20.25
Roger Clemens	1	1	0	7.0	6	3	3	0	8	0-0	0-0	0	3.86
Wes Gardner	1	0	0	4.2	6	3	3	2	8	0-0	0-0	0	5.79
Bruce Hurst	2	2	1	13.0	10	4	4	5	12	0-2	0-0	0	2.77
Lee Smith	2	0	0	3.1	6	3	3	1	4	0-1	0-0	0	8.10
Mike Smithson	1	0	0	2.1	3	0	0	0	1	0-0	0-0	0	0.00
Bob Stanley	2	0	0	1.0	2	1	1	1	0	0-0	0-0	0	9.00
Totals	4	4	1	34.0	41	20	20	10	35	0-4	0-0	0	5.29

Fielding

Athletics	Pos	G	PO	Ast	E	DP	PB	FPct
Greg Cadaret	p	1	0	0	0	0	—	—
Jose Canseco	rf	4	6	0	0	0	—	1.000
Storm Davis	p	1	0	2	0	0	—	1.000
Dennis Eckersley	p	4	2	0	0	0	—	1.000
Mike Gallego	2b	4	7	6	0	4	—	1.000
Ron Hassey	c	4	13	0	0	0	0	1.000
Dave Henderson	cf	4	11	0	2	0	—	.846
Rick Honeycutt	p	3	0	0	0	0	—	—
Stan Javier	lf	2	5	0	0	0	—	1.000
Carney Lansford	3b	4	7	8	0	2	—	1.000
Mark McGwire	1b	4	24	2	0	4	—	1.000
Gene Nelson	p	2	0	0	0	0	—	—
Dave Parker	lf	1	1	0	1	0	—	.500
Tony Phillips	lf	2	6	0	0	0	—	1.000
	2b	1	4	0	0	1	—	1.000
Eric Plunk	p	1	0	0	0	0	—	—
Luis Polonia	lf	1	2	0	0	0	—	1.000
Terry Steinbach	c	2	12	0	0	0	1	1.000
Dave Stewart	p	2	0	2	0	0	—	1.000
Walt Weiss	ss	4	7	10	0	3	—	1.000
Bob Welch	p	1	1	0	0	0	—	1.000
Curt Young	p	1	0	0	0	0	—	—
Totals		4	108	30	3	14	1	.979

Fielding

Red Sox	Pos	G	PO	Ast	E	DP	PB	FPct
Marty Barrett	2b	4	6	9	0	1	—	1.000
Todd Benzinger	1b	3	21	1	0	2	—	1.000
Mike Boddicker	p	1	0	0	0	0	—	—
Wade Boggs	3b	4	6	6	0	1	—	1.000
Ellis Burks	cf	4	10	0	0	0	—	1.000
Roger Clemens	p	1	0	0	1	0	—	.000
Dwight Evans	rf	4	11	0	0	0	—	1.000
Wes Gardner	p	1	0	0	0	0	—	—
Rich Gedman	c	4	34	5	0	1	1	1.000
Mike Greenwell	lf	4	4	0	0	0	—	1.000
Bruce Hurst	p	2	0	3	0	0	—	1.000
Larry Parrish	1b	2	7	0	0	0	—	1.000
Jody Reed	ss	4	3	10	0	2	—	1.000
Lee Smith	p	2	0	0	0	0	—	—
Mike Smithson	p	1	0	0	0	0	—	—
Bob Stanley	p	2	0	0	0	0	—	—
Totals		4	102	34	1	7	1	.993

1988 Los Angeles Dodgers (NL) 4, New York Mets (NL) 3

The Dodgers pulled one of the biggest upsets in the history of the NLCS, defeating a formidable New York Mets team that had beaten Los Angeles 10 times in 11 regular-season meetings. Orel Hershiser took a 2-0 shutout into the ninth inning in the opener, but Gary Carter doubled just in front of diving center fielder John Shelby, giving the Mets a 3-2 win. In Game 2, the Dodgers knocked out Mets starter David Cone, who'd disparaged them in a newspaper column. Los Angeles' 6-3 victory knotted the series. New York rallied for five runs in the bottom of the eighth in Game 3 to take an 8-4 victory—all after Dodgers reliever Jay Howell was ejected and suspended for having pine tar on his glove. The Mets came three outs away from taking a three-games-to-one lead when Dwight Gooden took a 4-2 lead into the ninth in Game 4. But Mike Scioscia hit a game-tying two-run homer, and Kirk Gibson won it for the Dodgers with a solo shot in the 12th. Gibson's three-run homer helped the Dodgers take Game 5 by the score of 7-4, but Cone came back to pitch the Mets to a 5-1 victory in Game 6. In the finale, Hershiser put the Dodgers in the World Series with a complete-game, five-hit, 6-0 victory.

Game 1
Tuesday, October 4

Mets	AB	R	H	RBI	BB	K	Avg
Mookie Wilson, cf	4	0	1	0	0	0	.250
Randy Myers, p	0	0	0	0	0	0	—
Gregg Jefferies, 3b	4	1	3	0	0	0	.750
Keith Hernandez, 1b	4	0	1	0	0	1	.250
Darryl Strawberry, rf	4	1	1	1	0	0	.250
Kevin McReynolds, lf	3	1	0	0	1	1	.000
Howard Johnson, ss	4	0	0	0	0	1	.000
Kevin Elster, ss	0	0	0	0	0	0	—
Gary Carter, c	4	0	2	2	0	1	.500
Wally Backman, 2b	3	0	0	0	0	1	.000
Dwight Gooden, p	2	0	0	0	0	2	.000
Lenny Dykstra, ph-cf	0	0	0	0	0	0	—
TOTALS	32	3	8	3	2	7	.250

Dodgers	AB	R	H	RBI	BB	K	Avg
Steve Sax, 2b	3	1	1	0	0	1	.333
Franklin Stubbs, 1b	3	0	0	0	0	2	.000
Tracy Woodson, ph-1b	1	0	0	0	0	0	.000
Kirk Gibson, lf	4	0	0	0	0	2	.000
Jay Howell, p	0	0	0	0	0	0	—
Mike Marshall, rf	4	0	1	1	0	2	.250
John Shelby, cf	4	0	0	0	0	1	.000
Mike Scioscia, c	3	1	1	0	0	1	.333
Rick Dempsey, ph	1	0	0	0	0	0	.000
Jeff Hamilton, 3b	3	0	0	0	0	0	.000
Alfredo Griffin, ss	3	0	1	0	0	0	.333
Orel Hershiser, p	2	0	0	0	1	1	.000
Jose Gonzalez, lf	0	0	0	0	0	0	—
TOTALS	31	2	4	2	1	10	.129

	1	2	3	4	5	6	7	8	9		R	H	E
Mets	0	0	0	0	0	0	0	0	3		3	8	1
Dodgers	1	0	0	0	0	0	1	0	0		2	4	0

E—Backman. DP—Dodgers 2 (Sax to Stubbs; Griffin to Stubbs). LOB—Mets 5, Dodgers 4. Scoring Position—Mets 3-for-8, Dodgers 2-for-8. 2B—Strawberry (1), Carter (1), Scioscia (1). S—Backman. GDP—Wilson. SB—Sax (1). CS—Griffin (1).

Mets	IP	H	R	ER	BB	K	ERA
Dwight Gooden	7.0	4	2	2	1	10	2.57
Randy Myers (W, 1-0)	2.0	0	0	0	0	0	0.00

Dodgers	IP	H	R	ER	BB	K	ERA
Orel Hershiser	8.1	7	2	2	1	6	2.16
Jay Howell (BS, 1; L, 0-1)	0.2	1	1	1	1	1	13.50

HBP—Sax by Gooden. Time—2:45. Attendance—55,582. Umpires—HP, Wendelstedt. 1B, McSherry. 2B, West. 3B, Rennert.

Game 2
Wednesday, October 5

Mets	AB	R	H	RBI	BB	K	Avg
Lenny Dykstra, cf	3	1	1	0	1	0	.333
Gregg Jefferies, 3b	3	1	1	0	1	0	.571
Keith Hernandez, 1b	3	1	2	3	1	1	.429
Darryl Strawberry, rf	4	0	2	0	0	0	.375
Kevin McReynolds, lf	4	0	0	0	0	2	.000
Howard Johnson, ss	3	0	0	0	1	2	.000
Gary Carter, c	4	0	0	0	0	0	.250
Wally Backman, 2b	3	0	0	0	0	2	.000
David Cone, p	0	0	0	0	0	0	—
Mackey Sasser, ph	1	0	0	0	0	1	.000
Rick Aguilera, p	1	0	0	0	0	1	.000
Terry Leach, p	0	0	0	0	0	0	—
Mookie Wilson, ph	1	0	0	0	0	1	.200
Roger McDowell, p	0	0	0	0	0	0	—
TOTALS	30	3	6	3	4	10	.233

Dodgers	AB	R	H	RBI	BB	K	Avg
Steve Sax, 2b	5	1	1	1	0	0	.250
Mickey Hatcher, 1b	3	2	1	2	1	0	.333
Kirk Gibson, lf	2	0	0	0	2	0	.000
Mike Marshall, rf	4	1	3	2	0	0	.500
John Shelby, cf	4	0	0	0	0	2	.000
Mike Scioscia, c	4	0	1	0	0	0	.286
Jeff Hamilton, 3b	1	1	0	0	2	1	.000
Alfredo Griffin, ss	4	0	0	1	0	1	.143
Tim Belcher, p	4	1	1	0	0	1	.250
Jesse Orosco, p	0	0	0	0	0	0	—
Alejandro Pena, p	0	0	0	0	0	0	—
TOTALS	31	6	7	6	5	5	.200

	1	2	3	4	5	6	7	8	9		R	H	E
Mets	0	0	0	2	0	0	0	0	1		3	6	0
Dodgers	1	4	0	0	1	0	0	0	x		6	7	0

DP—Dodgers 2 (Griffin; Sax to Griffin to Hatcher). LOB—Mets 4, Dodgers 7. Scoring Position—Mets 1-for-5, Dodgers 4-for-10. 2B—Dykstra (1), Jefferies (1), Hatcher (1). HR—Hernandez (1). GDP—Jefferies. SB—Gibson (1). CS—Strawberry (1).

Mets	IP	H	R	ER	BB	K	ERA
David Cone (L, 0-1)	2.0	5	5	5	2	2	22.50
Rick Aguilera	3.0	2	1	1	2	0	3.00
Terry Leach	2.0	0	0	0	1	2	0.00
Roger McDowell	1.0	0	0	0	0	1	0.00

Dodgers	IP	H	R	ER	BB	K	ERA
Tim Belcher (W, 1-0)	8.1	5	3	3	3	10	3.24
Jesse Orosco	0.0	1	0	0	0	0	—
Alejandro Pena (S, 1)	0.2	0	0	0	1	0	0.00

Orosco pitched to one batter in the 9th.

Balk—Cone. HBP—Hamilton by Cone. Time—3:10. Attendance—55,780. Umpires—HP, McSherry. 1B, West. 2B, Rennert. 3B, Davidson.

Game 3
Saturday, October 8

Dodgers	AB	R	H	RBI	BB	K	Avg
Steve Sax, 2b	5	1	1	0	0	1	.231
Mickey Hatcher, 1b	4	0	1	0	0	0	.286
Tracy Woodson, 1b	1	0	0	0	0	0	.000
Kirk Gibson, lf	5	0	1	1	0	1	.091
Mike Marshall, rf	4	1	0	0	1	1	.333
John Shelby, cf	2	1	1	0	2	1	.100
Mike Scioscia, c	4	0	2	0	0	0	.364
Jose Gonzalez, pr	0	1	0	0	0	0	—
Rick Dempsey, c	0	0	0	0	0	0	.000
Jeff Hamilton, 3b	3	0	1	1	1	0	.143
Alfredo Griffin, ss	3	0	0	0	0	3	.100
Mike Davis, ph	0	0	0	0	1	0	—
Jay Howell, p	0	0	0	0	0	0	—
Alejandro Pena, p	0	0	0	0	0	0	—
Jesse Orosco, p	0	0	0	0	0	0	—
Ricky Horton, p	0	0	0	0	0	0	—
Orel Hershiser, p	3	0	0	0	0	1	.000
Danny Heep, ph	0	0	0	0	0	0	—
Mike Sharperson, ph-ss	0	0	0	1	1	0	—
TOTALS	34	4	7	3	6	9	.191

Mets	AB	R	H	RBI	BB	K	Avg
Mookie Wilson, cf	4	2	1	1	1	1	.222
David Cone, p	0	0	0	0	0	0	—
Gregg Jefferies, 3b	3	0	1	0	1	0	.500
Kevin Elster, pr-ss	0	1	0	0	0	0	—
Keith Hernandez, 1b	2	0	1	1	3	0	.444
Darryl Strawberry, rf	5	1	3	3	0	0	.462
Kevin McReynolds, lf	4	0	0	0	1	1	.000
Howard Johnson, ss-3b	4	2	0	0	0	0	.000
Gary Carter, c	4	0	1	1	0	0	.250
Wally Backman, 2b	4	1	2	2	0	0	.200

Game 4
Sunday, October 9

Dodgers	AB	R	H	RBI	BB	K	Avg
Steve Sax, 2b	5	1	1	0	1	0	.222
Mickey Hatcher, 1b	4	1	0	0	1	0	.182
Alejandro Pena, p	0	0	0	0	0	0	—
Franklin Stubbs, ph	1	0	0	0	0	1	.000
Tim Leary, p	0	0	0	0	0	0	—
Jesse Orosco, p	0	0	0	0	0	0	—
Orel Hershiser, p	0	0	0	0	0	0	.000
Kirk Gibson, lf	6	1	1	1	0	2	.118
Mike Marshall, rf	5	0	0	0	0	1	.235
John Shelby, cf	4	1	2	2	1	1	.214
Mike Scioscia, c	4	1	1	2	0	1	.333
Rick Dempsey, ph-c	0	0	0	0	0	0	.000
Jeff Hamilton, 3b	4	0	0	0	0	1	.091
Mike Sharperson, ph-3b	1	0	0	0	0	0	—
Alfredo Griffin, ss	4	0	1	0	0	0	.143
John Tudor, p	2	0	0	0	0	2	.000
Brian Holton, p	0	0	0	0	0	0	—
Danny Heep, ph	0	0	0	0	1	0	—
Ricky Horton, p	0	0	0	0	0	0	—
Mike Davis, ph	0	0	0	0	0	0	—
Tracy Woodson, ph-1b	2	0	1	0	0	0	.250
TOTALS	42	5	7	5	6	10	.179

Mets	AB	R	H	RBI	BB	K	Avg
Mookie Wilson, cf	4	0	0	0	1	0	.154
Roger McDowell, p	0	0	0	0	0	0	—
Lee Mazzilli, ph	1	0	1	0	0	0	1.000
Gregg Jefferies, 3b	5	0	0	0	0	0	.333
Keith Hernandez, 1b	5	1	2	0	1	1	.429
Darryl Strawberry, rf	6	1	1	2	0	2	.368
Kevin McReynolds, lf	5	2	2	1	1	0	.125
Gary Carter, c	4	0	2	1	0	1	.313
Randy Myers, p	0	0	0	0	0	0	—
Lenny Dykstra, cf	1	0	0	0	0	0	.250
Tim Teufel, 2b	3	0	0	0	0	1	.000

Dodgers	AB	R	H	RBI	BB	K	Avg
Ron Darling, p	2	0	0	0	0	2	.000
Dave Magadan, ph	1	0	0	0	0	0	.000
Roger McDowell, p	0	0	0	0	0	0	—
Randy Myers, p	0	0	0	0	0	0	—
Lenny Dykstra, ph-cf	0	1	0	0	1	0	.333
TOTALS	33	8	9	8	7	4	.253

	1	2	3	4	5	6	7	8	9		R	H	E
Dodgers	0	2	1	0	0	0	0	1	0		4	7	2
Mets	0	0	1	0	0	2	0	5	x		8	9	2

E—Hernandez, Gibson, McDowell, Hamilton. DP—Dodgers 1 (Sax to Griffin to Hatcher). LOB—Dodgers 9, Mets 9. Scoring Position—Dodgers 2-for-13, Mets 6-for-16. 2B—Strawberry (2), Backman (1). GDP—Strawberry. SB—Sax (2), Shelby (1), Johnson (1).

Dodgers	IP	H	R	ER	BB	K	ERA
Orel Hershiser	7.0	6	3	1	4	4	1.76
Jay Howell	0.0	0	1	1	1	0	27.00
Alejandro Pena (BS, 1; L, 0-1)	0.2	1	2	2	1	0	13.50
Jesse Orosco	0.0	1	2	2	1	0	—
Ricky Horton	0.1	1	0	0	0	0	0.00

Mets	IP	H	R	ER	BB	K	ERA
Ron Darling	6.0	5	3	2	4	5	3.00
Roger McDowell	1.2	2	1	1	1	3	3.38
Randy Myers (W, 2-0)	0.1	0	0	0	1	0	0.00
David Cone	1.0	0	0	0	0	1	15.00

Howell pitched to one batter in the 8th. Orosco pitched to three batters in the 8th.

WP—Hershiser. HBP—Jefferies by Orosco. Time—3:44. Attendance—44,672. Umpires—HP, West. 1B, Rennert. 2B, Davidson. 3B, Runge.

	AB	R	H	RBI	BB	K	Avg
Wally Backman, 2b	1	0	0	0	1	0	.182
Kevin Elster, ss	2	0	0	0	1	0	.000
Howard Johnson, ph-ss	2	0	0	0	1	0	.000
Dwight Gooden, p	3	0	1	0	0	0	.200
Mackey Sasser, c	2	0	1	0	0	0	.333
Ron Darling, pr	0	0	0	0	0	0	.000
TOTALS	44	4	10	4	6	4	.241

	1	2	3	4	5	6	7	8	9	10	11	12	R	H	E
Dodgers	2	0	0	0	0	0	0	0	2	0	0	1	5	7	1
Mets	0	0	0	3	0	1	0	0	0	0	0	0	4	10	2

E—Hatcher, Elster 2. DP—Dodgers 1 (Griffin to Sax to Hatcher), Mets 1 (Hernandez to Elster). LOB—Dodgers 8, Mets 10. Scoring Position—Dodgers 1-for-14, Mets 1-for-11. 2B—McReynolds (1). 3B—Carter (1). HR—Gibson (1), Scioscia (1), Strawberry (1), McReynolds (1). S—Griffin. GDP—Scioscia, Gooden. SB—Sax 3 (5), Shelby (2), McReynolds (1). CS—Wilson (1).

Dodgers	IP	H	R	ER	BB	K	ERA
John Tudor	5.0	8	4	4	1	1	7.20
Brian Holton	1.0	0	0	0	1	1	0.00
Ricky Horton	2.0	0	0	0	0	1	0.00
Alejandro Pena (W, 1-1)	3.0	0	0	0	3	1	4.15
Tim Leary (H, 1)	0.1	2	0	0	0	0	0.00
Jesse Orosco (H, 1)	0.1	0	0	0	1	0	54.00
Orel Hershiser (S, 1)	0.1	0	0	0	0	0	1.72

Mets	IP	H	R	ER	BB	K	ERA
Dwight Gooden	8.1	5	4	4	5	9	3.52
Randy Myers	2.1	1	0	0	1	0	0.00
Roger McDowell (L, 0-1)	1.1	1	1	1	0	1	4.50

Tudor pitched to two batters in the 6th.

Balk—Gooden. WP—Gooden 2. Time—4:29. Attendance—54,014. Umpires—HP, Rennert. 1B, Davidson. 2B, Runge. 3B, Wendelstedt.

Game 5

Monday, October 10

Dodgers	AB	R	H	RBI	BB	K	Avg
Steve Sax, 2b	5	1	1	0	0	1	.217
Mickey Hatcher, 1b	3	1	1	0	0	0	.214
Franklin Stubbs, ph-1b	2	0	0	0	0	1	.000
Kirk Gibson, lf	5	1	2	3	0	1	.182
Jose Gonzalez, pr-lf	0	1	0	0	0	0	—
Mike Marshall, rf	5	1	3	1	0	1	.318
John Shelby, cf	3	1	1	0	2	1	.235
Rick Dempsey, c	4	1	2	2	0	0	.400
Mike Davis, ph	1	0	0	0	0	0	.000
Mike Scioscia, c	0	0	0	0	0	0	.333
Jeff Hamilton, 3b	4	0	1	0	0	1	.133
Alfredo Griffin, ss	4	0	1	1	0	1	.167
Tim Belcher, p	4	0	0	0	0	2	.125
Ricky Horton, p	0	0	0	0	0	0	—
Brian Holton, p	0	0	0	0	0	0	—
TOTALS	40	7	12	7	2	9	.217

Mets	AB	R	H	RBI	BB	K	Avg
Lenny Dykstra, cf	3	2	2	3	1	0	.429
Gregg Jefferies, 3b	4	0	2	1	0	0	.368
Keith Hernandez, 1b	4	0	0	0	0	2	.333
Darryl Strawberry, rf	4	0	1	0	0	1	.348
Kevin McReynolds, lf	4	0	1	0	0	0	.150
Gary Carter, c	4	0	1	0	0	1	.300
Howard Johnson, ss	4	1	1	0	0	2	.059
Wally Backman, 2b	4	1	1	0	0	1	.200
Sid Fernandez, p	1	0	0	0	0	0	.000
Terry Leach, p	0	0	0	0	0	0	—
Dave Magadan, ph	1	0	0	0	0	1	.000
Rick Aguilera, p	0	0	0	0	0	0	.000
Mackey Sasser, ph	1	0	0	0	0	0	.250
Roger McDowell, p	0	0	0	0	0	0	—
Lee Mazzilli, ph	1	0	0	0	0	0	.500
TOTALS	35	4	9	4	1	8	.262

	1	2	3	4	5	6	7	8	9	R	H	E
Dodgers	0	0	0	3	3	0	0	0	1	7	12	0
Mets	0	0	0	3	0	0	1	0		4	9	1

E—Johnson. LOB—Dodgers 8, Mets 5. Scoring Position—Dodgers 4-for-13, Mets 3-for-8. 2B—Marshall (1), Dempsey 2 (2), Griffin (1), Dykstra (2). 3B—Marshall (1). HR—Gibson (2), Dykstra (1). SB—Gibson (2).

Game 6

Tuesday, October 11

Mets	AB	R	H	RBI	BB	K	Avg
Lenny Dykstra, cf	4	2	2	0	0	0	.455
Wally Backman, 2b	4	0	2	0	0	0	.263
Keith Hernandez, 1b	5	0	1	1	0	1	.304
Darryl Strawberry, rf	3	2	1	0	2	1	.346
Kevin McReynolds, lf	4	1	4	3	0	0	.292
Gregg Jefferies, 3b	4	0	0	0	1	0	.304
Gary Carter, c	4	0	0	0	1	1	.250
Kevin Elster, ss	3	0	1	1	2	0	.200
David Cone, p	4	0	0	0	0	0	.000
TOTALS	35	5	11	5	6	4	.296

Dodgers	AB	R	H	RBI	BB	K	Avg
Steve Sax, 2b	2	0	0	0	2	0	.200
Mickey Hatcher, 1b	3	0	1	1	1	0	.235
Kirk Gibson, lf	4	0	0	0	0	0	.154
Jose Gonzalez, lf	0	0	0	0	0	0	—
Mike Marshall, rf	4	0	0	0	0	2	.269
John Shelby, cf	4	0	0	0	0	3	.190
Mike Scioscia, c	4	0	1	0	0	0	.316
Jeff Hamilton, 3b	4	0	2	0	0	0	.211
Alfredo Griffin, ss	3	0	0	0	0	0	.143
Mike Davis, ph	1	0	0	0	0	0	.000
Tim Leary, p	1	0	0	0	0	0	.000
Brian Holton, p	1	1	1	0	0	0	1.000
Ricky Horton, p	0	0	0	0	0	0	—
Danny Heep, ph	1	0	0	0	0	1	.000
Jesse Orosco, p	0	0	0	0	0	0	—
TOTALS	32	1	5	1	3	6	.212

	1	2	3	4	5	6	7	8	9	R	H	E
Mets	1	0	1	0	2	1	0	0	0	5	11	0
Dodgers	0	0	0	0	1	0	0	0	0	1	5	2

E—Hatcher, Hamilton. DP—Dodgers 2 (Sax to Griffin to Hatcher; Horton to Scioscia to Hatcher). LOB—Mets 13, Dodgers 7. Scoring Position—Mets 2-for-17, Dodgers 1-for-6. 2B—Dykstra (3), McReynolds (2), Elster (1). HR—McReynolds (2). S—Backman, Cone. SF—McReynolds. GDP—Hernandez, Cone. SB—Backman (1), Hernandez (1), McReynolds (2).

Mets	IP	H	R	ER	BB	K	ERA
David Cone (W, 1-1)	9.0	5	1	1	3	6	4.50

Dodgers	IP	H	R	ER	BB	K	ERA
Tim Leary (L, 0-1)	4.0	6	4	3	3	3	6.23
Brian Holton	1.1	1	1	1	0	0	2.25
Ricky Horton	1.2	2	0	0	2	1	0.00
Jesse Orosco	2.0	2	0	0	1	0	7.71

Leary pitched to two batters in the 5th.

WP—Cone. PB—Scioscia. HBP—Dykstra by Leary. Time—3:16. Attendance—55,885. Umpires—HP, Runge. 1B, Wendelstedt. 2B, McSherry. 3B, West.

Game 7

Wednesday, October 12

Mets	AB	R	H	RBI	BB	K	Avg
Lenny Dykstra, cf	3	0	1	0	0	0	.429
Wally Backman, 2b	3	0	1	0	1	0	.273
Keith Hernandez, 1b	3	0	0	0	1	1	.269
Darryl Strawberry, rf	4	0	0	0	0	1	.300
Kevin McReynolds, lf	4	0	0	0	0	1	.250
Gregg Jefferies, 3b	4	0	2	0	0	0	.333
Gary Carter, c	3	0	0	0	0	0	.222
Rick Aguilera, p	0	0	0	0	0	0	.000
Lee Mazzilli, ph	0	0	0	0	0	0	.500
Kevin Elster, ss	3	0	1	0	0	0	.250
Howard Johnson, ph	1	0	0	0	0	1	.056
Ron Darling, p	1	0	0	0	0	0	.000
Dwight Gooden, p	0	0	0	0	0	0	.200
Dave Magadan, ph	1	0	0	0	0	1	.000
Terry Leach, p	0	0	0	0	0	0	—
Mackey Sasser, c	1	0	0	0	0	0	.200
TOTALS	31	0	5	0	2	5	.256

Dodgers	AB	R	H	RBI	BB	K	Avg
Steve Sax, 2b	5	2	3	2	0	0	.267
Mickey Hatcher, 1b-lf	4	0	1	0	0	0	.238
Jose Gonzalez, lf	0	0	0	0	0	0	—
Kirk Gibson, lf	0	0	0	1	1	0	.154
Franklin Stubbs, 1b	2	0	2	0	0	0	.250
Mike Marshall, rf	4	0	0	1	0	1	.233
John Shelby, cf	3	0	0	1	0	3	.167
Mike Scioscia, c	3	1	2	0	1	0	.364
Jeff Hamilton, 3b	4	1	1	0	0	1	.217
Alfredo Griffin, ss	4	1	1	0	0	0	.160
Orel Hershiser, p	4	1	0	1	0	0	.000
TOTALS	33	6	10	6	2	5	.216

	1	2	3	4	5	6	7	8	9	R	H	E
Mets	0	0	0	0	0	0	0	0	0	0	5	2
Dodgers	1	5	0	0	0	0	0	0	x	6	10	0

E—Backman, Jefferies. DP—Mets 1 (Backman to Elster to Hernandez), Dodgers 1 (Sax to Griffin to Hatcher). LOB—Mets 8, Dodgers 7. Scoring Position—Mets 0-for-7, Dodgers 2-for-9. 2B—Jefferies (2), Hatcher (2). SF—Gibson, Shelby. GDP—Hernandez, Marshall. SB—Mazzilli (1).

Mets	IP	H	R	ER	BB	K	ERA
Ron Darling (L, 0-1)	1.0	6	6	4	0	2	7.71
Dwight Gooden	3.0	1	0	0	2	1	2.95
Terry Leach	2.0	3	0	0	0	1	0.00
Rick Aguilera	2.0	0	0	0	0	1	1.29

Dodgers	IP	H	R	ER	BB	K	ERA
Orel Hershiser (W, 1-0)	9.0	5	0	0	2	5	1.09

Darling pitched to five batters in the 2nd.

WP—Hershiser. HBP—Mazzilli by Hershiser, Dykstra by Hershiser. Time—2:51. Attendance—55,693. Umpires—HP, Wendelstedt. 1B, McSherry. 2B, West. 3B, Rennert.

1988 NL Championship Series—Composite Statistics

Batting

Dodgers	G	AB	R	H	RBI	2B	3B	HR	BB	SO	SB	CS	Avg	OBP	Slg
Tim Belcher	2	8	1	1	0	0	0	0	0	3	0	0	.125	.125	.125
Mike Davis	4	2	0	0	0	0	0	0	1	0	0	0	.000	.333	.000
Rick Dempsey	4	5	1	2	2	2	0	0	1	0	0	0	.400	.500	.800
Kirk Gibson	7	26	2	4	6	0	0	2	3	6	2	0	.154	.233	.385
Jose Gonzalez	5	0	2	0	0	0	0	0	0	0	0	0	—	—	—
Alfredo Griffin	7	25	1	4	3	1	0	0	0	5	0	1	.160	.160	.200
Jeff Hamilton	7	23	2	5	1	0	0	0	3	4	0	0	.217	.333	.217
Mickey Hatcher	6	21	4	5	3	2	0	0	3	0	0	0	.238	.333	.333
Danny Heep	3	1	0	0	0	0	0	0	1	1	0	0	.000	.500	.000
Orel Hershiser	4	9	1	0	1	0	0	0	1	2	0	0	.000	.100	.000
Brian Holton	3	1	1	1	0	0	0	0	0	0	0	0	1.000	1.000	1.000
Tim Leary	2	1	0	0	0	0	0	0	0	0	0	0	.000	.000	.000
Mike Marshall	7	30	3	7	5	1	1	0	2	9	0	0	.233	.281	.333
Steve Sax	7	30	7	8	3	0	0	0	3	5	0	0	.267	.353	.267
Mike Scioscia	7	22	3	8	2	1	0	1	1	2	0	0	.364	.391	.545
Mike Sharperson	2	1	0	0	1	0	0	0	1	0	0	0	.000	.500	.000
John Shelby	7	24	3	4	3	0	0	0	5	12	2	0	.167	.300	.167
Franklin Stubbs	4	8	0	2	0	0	0	0	0	4	0	0	.250	.250	.250
John Tudor	1	2	0	0	0	0	0	0	0	1	0	0	.000	.000	.000
Tracy Woodson	3	4	0	1	0	0	0	0	0	1	0	0	.250	.250	.250
Totals	7	243	31	52	30	7	1	3	25	54	9	1	.214	.290	.288

Batting

Mets	G	AB	R	H	RBI	2B	3B	HR	BB	SO	SB	CS	Avg	OBP	Slg
Rick Aguilera	3	1	0	0	0	0	0	0	0	1	0	0	.000	.000	.000
Wally Backman	7	22	2	6	2	1	0	0	2	5	1	0	.273	.333	.318
Gary Carter	7	27	0	6	4	1	1	0	1	3	0	0	.222	.250	.333
David Cone	3	4	0	0	0	0	0	0	0	0	0	0	.000	.000	.000
Ron Darling	3	3	0	0	0	0	0	0	0	2	0	0	.000	.000	.000
Lenny Dykstra	7	14	6	6	3	3	0	1	4	0	0	0	.429	.600	.857
Kevin Elster	5	8	1	2	1	1	0	0	3	0	0	0	.250	.455	.375
Sid Fernandez	1	1	0	0	0	0	0	0	0	0	0	0	.000	.000	.000
Dwight Gooden	3	5	0	1	0	0	0	0	0	2	0	0	.200	.200	.200
Keith Hernandez	7	26	2	7	5	0	0	1	6	7	1	0	.269	.406	.385
Gregg Jefferies	7	27	2	9	1	2	0	0	4	0	0	0	.333	.438	.407
Howard Johnson	6	18	3	1	0	0	0	0	1	6	1	0	.056	.105	.056
Dave Magadan	3	4	0	0	0	0	0	0	0	2	0	0	.000	.000	.000
Lee Mazzilli	3	2	1	0	0	0	0	0	0	1	1	0	.500	.667	.500
Kevin McReynolds	7	28	4	7	4	2	0	2	3	5	0	0	.250	.313	.536
Mackey Sasser	4	5	0	1	0	0	0	0	0	1	0	0	.200	.200	.200
Darryl Strawberry	7	30	5	9	6	2	0	1	2	5	0	1	.300	.344	.467
Tim Teufel	1	3	0	0	0	0	0	0	0	1	0	0	.000	.000	.000
Mookie Wilson	4	13	2	2	1	0	0	0	2	2	0	1	.154	.267	.154
Totals	7	240	27	58	27	12	1	5	28	42	6	2	.242	.330	.363

Pitching

Dodgers	G	GS	CG	IP	H	R	ER	BB	SO	W-L	Sv-Op	Hld	ERA
Tim Belcher	2	2	0	15.1	12	7	7	4	16	2-0	0-0	0	4.11
Orel Hershiser	4	3	1	24.2	18	5	3	7	15	1-0	1-1	0	1.09
Brian Holton	3	0	0	4.0	2	1	1	1	2	0-0	1-1	0	2.25
Ricky Horton	4	0	0	4.1	4	0	0	2	3	0-0	0-0	1	0.00
Jay Howell	2	0	0	0.2	1	2	2	2	1	0-1	0-1	0	27.00
Tim Leary	2	1	0	4.1	8	4	3	3	3	0-1	0-0	1	6.23
Jesse Orosco	4	0	0	2.1	4	2	2	3	0	0-0	0-0	1	7.71
Alejandro Pena	3	0	0	4.1	1	2	2	5	1	1-1	1-2	0	4.15
John Tudor	1	1	0	5.0	8	4	4	1	1	0-0	0-0	0	7.20
Totals	7	7	1	65.0	58	27	24	28	42	4-3	3-5	3	3.32

Pitching

Mets	G	GS	CG	IP	H	R	ER	BB	SO	W-L	Sv-Op	Hld	ERA
Rick Aguilera	3	0	0	7.0	3	1	1	2	4	0-0	0-0	0	1.29
David Cone	3	2	1	12.0	10	6	6	5	9	1-1	0-0	0	4.50
Ron Darling	2	2	0	7.0	11	9	6	4	7	0-1	0-0	0	7.71
Sid Fernandez	1	1	0	4.0	7	6	6	1	5	0-1	0-0	0	13.50
Dwight Gooden	3	2	0	18.1	10	6	6	8	20	0-0	0-0	0	2.95
Terry Leach	3	0	0	5.0	4	0	0	1	4	0-0	0-0	0	0.00
Roger McDowell	4	0	0	6.0	6	3	3	2	5	0-1	0-0	0	4.50
Randy Myers	3	0	0	4.2	1	0	0	2	0	2-0	0-0	0	0.00
Totals	7	7	1	64.0	52	31	28	25	54	3-4	0-0	0	3.94

Fielding

Dodgers	Pos	G	PO	Ast	E	DP	PB	FPct
Tim Belcher	p	2	1	0	0	0	—	1.000
Rick Dempsey	c	3	7	0	0	0	0	1.000
Kirk Gibson	lf	7	17	1	1	0	—	.947
Jose Gonzalez	lf	4	3	0	0	0	—	1.000
Alfredo Griffin	ss	7	17	13	0	7	—	1.000
Jeff Hamilton	3b	7	9	10	2	0	—	.905
Mickey Hatcher	1b	6	33	1	2	6	—	.944
	lf	1	1	0	0	0	—	1.000
Orel Hershiser	p	4	3	3	0	0	—	1.000
Brian Holton	p	3	0	1	0	0	—	1.000
Ricky Horton	p	4	0	1	0	1	—	1.000
Jay Howell	p	2	0	0	0	0	—	—
Tim Leary	p	2	0	1	0	0	—	1.000
Mike Marshall	rf	7	14	0	0	0	—	1.000
Jesse Orosco	p	4	1	0	0	0	—	1.000
Alejandro Pena	p	3	0	0	0	0	—	—
Steve Sax	2b	7	12	22	0	6	—	1.000
Mike Scioscia	c	7	37	4	0	1	1	1.000
Mike Sharperson	3b	1	1	0	0	0	—	1.000
	ss	1	0	0	0	0	—	—
John Shelby	cf	7	19	0	0	0	—	1.000
Franklin Stubbs	1b	3	16	2	0	2	—	1.000
John Tudor	p	1	1	2	0	0	—	1.000
Tracy Woodson	1b	3	3	0	0	0	—	1.000
Totals		7	195	61	5	23	1	.981

Fielding

Mets	Pos	G	PO	Ast	E	DP	PB	FPct
Rick Aguilera	p	3	0	1	0	0	—	1.000
Wally Backman	2b	7	7	19	2	1	—	.929
Gary Carter	c	7	58	1	0	0	0	1.000
David Cone	p	3	1	0	0	0	—	1.000
Ron Darling	p	2	1	3	0	0	—	1.000
Lenny Dykstra	cf	7	9	0	0	0	—	1.000
Kevin Elster	ss	5	7	7	2	2	—	.875
Sid Fernandez	p	1	0	0	0	0	—	—
Dwight Gooden	p	3	1	3	0	0	—	1.000
Keith Hernandez	1b	7	57	4	1	2	—	.984
Gregg Jefferies	3b	7	5	8	1	0	—	.929
Howard Johnson	ss	5	6	9	1	0	—	.938
	3b	1	0	0	0	0	—	—
Terry Leach	p	3	1	0	0	0	—	1.000
Roger McDowell	p	4	0	3	1	0	—	.750
Kevin McReynolds	lf	7	19	0	0	0	—	1.000
Randy Myers	p	3	0	1	0	0	—	1.000
Mackey Sasser	c	2	2	0	0	0	—	1.000
Darryl Strawberry	rf	7	11	0	0	0	—	1.000
Tim Teufel	2b	1	1	3	0	0	—	1.000
Mookie Wilson	cf	3	6	0	0	0	—	1.000
Totals		7	192	62	8	5	0	.969

1989 Oakland Athletics (AL) 4, Toronto Blue Jays (AL) 1

The Oakland A's made short work of the Toronto Blue Jays, wrapping up the AL title in five games. Dave Stewart pitched the A's to a 7-3 victory in Game 1, and Mike Moore put them two games up with a 6-3 decision in Game 2. Jimmy Key got Toronto their first win in Game 3, but Rickey Henderson hit a pair of two-run homers to give Oakland a 6-5 victory in Game 4. Dave Stewart went eight solid innings to win the clincher, 4-3. Henderson dominated the series, scoring eight runs, driving in five and stealing eight bases. Dennis Eckersley finished off all four of Oakland's wins, earning three saves.

Game 1

Tuesday, October 3

Blue Jays	AB	R	H	RBI	BB	K	Avg
Lloyd Moseby, cf	4	0	0	0	0	0	.000
Mookie Wilson, rf	3	0	1	0	1	2	.333
Fred McGriff, 1b	4	0	0	0	0	1	.000
George Bell, lf	4	1	1	0	0	1	.250
Tony Fernandez, ss	4	1	1	0	0	0	.250
Ernie Whitt, c	3	1	1	2	0	0	.333
Kelly Gruber, 3b	3	0	0	1	0	0	.000
Lee Mazzilli, dh	3	0	0	0	0	2	.000
Nelson Liriano, 2b	2	0	1	1	1	0	.500
TOTALS	30	3	5	3	3	6	.167

Athletics	AB	R	H	RBI	BB	K	Avg
Rickey Henderson, lf	2	1	0	0	2	0	.000
Carney Lansford, 3b	5	1	2	2	0	1	.400
Jose Canseco, rf	4	0	0	0	1	3	.000
Dave Parker, dh	4	0	1	1	0	0	.250
Dave Henderson, cf	4	1	2	1	0	1	.500
Mark McGwire, 1b	4	1	1	1	0	1	.250
Terry Steinbach, c	4	0	1	0	0	3	.250
Tony Phillips, 2b	3	1	2	0	1	0	.667
Mike Gallego, ss	4	2	2	0	0	0	.500
TOTALS	34	7	11	5	4	9	.324

	1	2	3	4	5	6	7	8	9		R	H	E
Blue Jays	0	2	0	1	0	0	0	0	0		3	5	1
Athletics	0	1	0	0	1	3	0	2	x		7	11	0

E—Liriano. DP—Athletics 1 (Phillips to McGwire). LOB—Blue Jays 4, Athletics 8. Scoring Position—Blue Jays 1-for-5, Athletics 3-for-12. 2B—Phillips (1), Gallego (1). HR—Whitt (1), DHenderson (1), McGwire (1). SF—Whitt. SB—Wilson (1), Fernandez (1), Liriano (1), RHenderson 2 (2), Lansford (1), Phillips (1).

Blue Jays	IP	H	R	ER	BB	K	ERA
Dave Stieb (L, 0-1)	5.1	8	4	4	2	6	6.75
Jim Acker	1.2	1	1	0	0	1	0.00
Duane Ward	1.0	2	2	2	2	2	18.00

Athletics	IP	H	R	ER	BB	K	ERA
Dave Stewart (W, 1-0)	8.0	5	3	3	3	6	3.38
Dennis Eckersley	1.0	0	0	0	0	0	0.00

WP—Ward. PB—Whitt. HBP—RHenderson by Acker. Time—2:52. Attendance—49,435. Umpires—HP, Phillips. 1B, Morrison. 2B, Ford. 3B, Cousins.

Game 2

Wednesday, October 4

Blue Jays	AB	R	H	RBI	BB	K	Avg
Lloyd Moseby, cf	3	2	1	0	1	0	.143
Mookie Wilson, rf	3	0	1	0	1	0	.333
Fred McGriff, 1b	4	0	1	2	0	1	.125
George Bell, lf	4	0	1	0	0	0	.250
Tony Fernandez, ss	3	0	0	0	1	0	.143
Ernie Whitt, c	4	0	0	0	0	1	.143
Kelly Gruber, 3b	4	0	0	0	0	1	.000
Lee Mazzilli, dh	4	0	0	0	0	1	.000
Nelson Liriano, 2b	2	1	1	0	1	0	.500
TOTALS	31	3	5	2	4	3	.164

Athletics	AB	R	H	RBI	BB	K	Avg
Rickey Henderson, lf	2	2	2	0	2	0	.500
Carney Lansford, 3b	3	1	1	1	1	0	.375
Dave Parker, dh	4	1	1	0	0	0	.250
Mark McGwire, 1b	4	1	3	1	0	0	.500
Dave Henderson, cf	4	1	1	0	0	2	.375
Ron Hassey, c	2	0	0	1	1	0	.000
Tony Phillips, 2b	4	0	1	1	0	1	.429
Stan Javier, rf	2	0	0	0	0	1	.000
Jose Canseco, ph-rf	1	0	0	0	1	0	.000
Walt Weiss, ss	3	0	0	0	0	0	.000
TOTALS	29	6	9	5	5	5	.309

	1	2	3	4	5	6	7	8	9		R	H	E
Blue Jays	0	0	1	0	0	0	0	2	0		3	5	1
Athletics	0	0	0	2	0	3	1	0	x		6	9	1

E—McGriff, McGwire. DP—Blue Jays 2 (Fernandez; Liriano to Fernandez to McGriff), Athletics 1 (Phillips to Weiss to McGwire). LOB—Blue Jays 5, Athletics 5. Scoring Position—Blue Jays 1-for-10, Athletics 3-for-10. 2B—McGwire (1), DHenderson (1). HR—Parker (1). SF—Hassey. GDP—Bell, Hassey. SB—Fernandez (2), Liriano (2), RHenderson 4 (6), Lansford (2), Phillips (2). CS—Canseco (1).

Blue Jays	IP	H	R	ER	BB	K	ERA
Todd Stottlemyre (L, 0-1)	5.0	7	4	4	2	3	7.20
Jim Acker	0.1	2	1	1	0	0	4.50
David Wells	1.0	0	1	0	2	1	0.00
Tom Henke	0.2	0	0	0	0	1	0.00
John Cerutti	1.0	0	0	0	1	0	0.00

Athletics	IP	H	R	ER	BB	K	ERA
Mike Moore (W, 1-0)	7.0	4	3	3	2	3	0.00
Rick Honeycutt	0.0	1	2	2	2	0	—
Dennis Eckersley (S, 1)	2.0	0	0	0	0	0	0.00

Stottlemyre pitched to two batters in the 6th. Honeycutt pitched to three batters in the 8th.

Time—3:20. Attendance—49,444. Umpires—HP, Morrison. 1B, Ford. 2B, Cousins. 3B, Palermo.

Game 3

Friday, October 6

Athletics	AB	R	H	RBI	BB	K	Avg
Rickey Henderson, lf	4	2	1	0	1	0	.375
Carney Lansford, 3b	3	0	2	1	1	0	.455
Lance Blankenship, 2b	0	0	0	0	0	0	—
Jose Canseco, rf	4	0	2	0	0	1	.222
Mark McGwire, 1b	2	0	0	1	1	0	.400
Dave Henderson, cf	4	0	1	0	0	1	.333
Terry Steinbach, c	4	0	0	0	0	0	.125
Dave Parker, dh	4	1	1	1	0	0	.250
Tony Phillips, 2b-3b	4	0	0	0	0	0	.273
Mike Gallego, ss	2	0	0	0	0	1	.333
Ken Phelps, ph	1	0	1	0	0	0	1.000
Walt Weiss, pr-ss	1	0	0	0	0	1	.000
TOTALS	33	3	8	3	3	4	.304

Blue Jays	AB	R	H	RBI	BB	K	Avg
Lloyd Moseby, cf	2	1	0	1	2	0	.111
Mookie Wilson, lf	4	1	2	1	0	0	.400
Fred McGriff, 1b	4	1	1	0	0	0	.167
George Bell, dh	3	0	0	1	0	2	.182
Tony Fernandez, ss	4	2	2	1	0	1	.273
Ernie Whitt, c	3	0	1	1	1	1	.200
Kelly Gruber, 3b	2	1	0	2	0	0	.000
Manuel Lee, 2b	4	1	1	0	0	0	.250
Junior Felix, rf	3	0	1	0	1	0	.333
TOTALS	29	7	8	6	5	5	.203

	1	2	3	4	5	6	7	8	9		R	H	E
Athletics	1	0	1	1	0	0	0	0	0		3	8	1
Blue Jays	0	0	0	4	0	0	3	0	x		7	8	0

E—Canseco. DP—Athletics 1 (Gallego to McGwire), Blue Jays 1 (Gruber to Lee to McGriff). LOB—Athletics 7, Blue Jays 4. Scoring Position—Athletics 1-for-12, Blue Jays 6-for-9. 2B—RHenderson (1), DHenderson (2), Fernandez 2 (2), Phelps (1). HR—Parker (2). SF—McGwire, Bell. GDP—McGwire, Gruber. SB—RHenderson (7).

Athletics	IP	H	R	ER	BB	K	ERA
Storm Davis (L, 0-1)	6.1	5	6	5	2	3	7.11
Rick Honeycutt	0.0	2	1	1	1	0	—
Gene Nelson	1.1	1	0	0	0	2	0.00
Matt Young	0.1	0	0	0	2	0	0.00

Blue Jays	IP	H	R	ER	BB	K	ERA
Jimmy Key (W, 1-0)	6.0	7	3	3	2	2	4.50
Jim Acker (H, 1)	2.0	1	0	0	1	1	2.25
Tom Henke	1.0	0	0	0	0	1	0.00

Honeycutt pitched to three batters in the 7th.

Time—2:54. Attendance—50,268. Umpires—HP, Ford. 1B, Cousins. 2B, Palermo. 3B, Reed.

Game 4
Saturday, October 7

Athletics	AB	R	H	RBI	BB	K	Avg
Rickey Henderson, lf	4	2	2	4	1	0	.417
Dave Henderson, cf	4	1	1	0	1	0	.313
Jose Canseco, rf	5	1	2	2	0	1	.286
Mark McGwire, 1b	4	0	2	0	0	2	.429
Terry Steinbach, dh	3	0	1	0	1	1	.182
Tony Phillips, 3b	3	0	0	0	1	1	.214
Ron Hassey, c	4	0	1	0	0	2	.167
Mike Gallego, 2b	4	1	1	0	0	0	.300
Walt Weiss, ss	3	1	1	0	0	0	.143
TOTALS	34	6	11	6	4	7	.288

Blue Jays	AB	R	H	RBI	BB	K	Avg
Lloyd Moseby, cf	3	0	2	0	2	1	.250
Mookie Wilson, lf	5	1	1	1	0	0	.333
Fred McGriff, 1b	5	0	1	1	0	2	.176
George Bell, dh	5	0	0	0	0	1	.125
Tony Fernandez, ss	5	2	2	0	0	0	.313
Ernie Whitt, c	2	0	0	0	1	1	.167
Pat Borders, ph-c	1	0	1	1	0	0	1.000
Rance Mulliniks, ph	1	0	0	0	0	1	.000
Kelly Gruber, 3b	5	1	4	0	0	0	.286
Manuel Lee, 2b	4	1	1	0	0	1	.250
Lee Mazzilli, ph	1	0	0	0	0	0	.000
Junior Felix, rf	4	0	1	2	0	0	.286
TOTALS	41	5	13	5	3	6	.228

	1	2	3	4	5	6	7	8	9	R	H	E
Athletics	0	0	3	0	2	0	1	0	0	6	11	1
Blue Jays	0	0	0	1	0	1	1	2	0	5	13	0

E—RHenderson. DP—Blue Jays 2 (Flanagan to Fernandez; Flanagan to McGriff). LOB—Athletics 6, Blue Jays 12. Scoring Position—Athletics 3-for-6, Blue Jays 2-for-13. 2B—DHenderson (3), Weiss (1), Fernandez (3), Felix (1). HR—RHenderson 2 (2), Canseco (1). S—Weiss. SB—Weiss (1), Moseby (1), Fernandez (3), Gruber (1). CS—RHenderson (1).

Athletics	IP	H	R	ER	BB	K	ERA
Bob Welch (W, 1-0)	5.2	8	2	2	1	4	3.18
Rick Honeycutt (H, 1)	1.2	3	3	3	2	1	32.40
Dennis Eckersley (S, 2)	1.2	2	0	0	0	1	0.00

Blue Jays	IP	H	R	ER	BB	K	ERA
Mike Flanagan (L, 0-1)	4.1	7	5	5	1	3	10.38
Duane Ward	2.2	4	1	1	1	3	7.36
John Cerutti	1.2	0	0	0	2	1	0.00
Jim Acker	0.1	0	0	0	0	0	2.08

WP—Honeycutt. Time—3:29. Attendance—50,076. Umpires—HP, Cousins. 1B, Palermo. 2B, Reed. 3B, Phillips.

Game 5
Sunday, October 8

Athletics	AB	R	H	RBI	BB	K	Avg
Rickey Henderson, lf	3	1	1	1	1	0	.400
Tony Phillips, 3b	4	0	0	0	0	2	.167
Jose Canseco, rf	3	0	1	1	1	1	.294
Dave Parker, dh	4	0	0	0	0	0	.188
Dave Henderson, cf	3	1	0	0	1	0	.263
Mark McGwire, 1b	4	1	1	0	0	1	.389
Terry Steinbach, c	4	0	1	1	0	1	.200
Walt Weiss, ss	2	1	0	0	1	0	.111
Mike Gallego, 2b	1	0	0	1	0	1	.273
TOTALS	28	4	4	4	4	7	.261

Blue Jays	AB	R	H	RBI	BB	K	Avg
Lloyd Moseby, cf	4	1	2	1	0	1	.313
Mookie Wilson, lf	4	0	0	0	0	0	.263
Fred McGriff, 1b	4	0	0	0	0	0	.143
George Bell, dh	4	1	2	1	0	0	.200
Tony Fernandez, ss	4	1	2	0	0	1	.350
Ernie Whitt, c	4	0	0	0	0	0	.125
Kelly Gruber, 3b	3	0	1	1	0	1	.294
Junior Felix, rf	4	0	1	0	0	1	.273
Nelson Liriano, 2b	3	0	1	0	0	0	.429
TOTALS	34	3	9	3	0	4	.252

	1	2	3	4	5	6	7	8	9	R	H	E
Athletics	1	0	1	0	0	0	2	0	0	4	4	0
Blue Jays	0	0	0	0	0	0	0	1	2	3	9	0

DP—Athletics 1 (McGwire to Weiss to Gallego). LOB—Athletics 3, Blue Jays 5. Scoring Position—Athletics 3-for-8, Blue Jays 0-for-7. 2B—Gruber (1). 3B—RHenderson (1). HR—Moseby (1), Bell (1). S—Gallego 2. SF—Gruber. GDP—Liriano. SB—RHenderson (8), Fernandez 2 (5), Liriano (3). CS—Canseco (2).

Athletics	IP	H	R	ER	BB	K	ERA
Dave Stewart (W, 2-0)	8.0	8	2	2	0	3	2.81
Dennis Eckersley (S, 3)	1.0	1	1	1	0	1	1.59

Blue Jays	IP	H	R	ER	BB	K	ERA
Dave Stieb (L, 0-2)	6.0	4	4	4	4	4	6.35
Jim Acker	2.0	0	0	0	0	2	1.42
Tom Henke	1.0	0	0	0	0	1	0.00

Stieb pitched to three batters in the 7th. Stewart pitched to one batter in the 9th.

Time—2:52. Attendance—50,024. Umpires—HP, Palermo. 1B, Reed. 2B, Phillips. 3B, Morrison.

1989 AL Championship Series—Composite Statistics

Batting

Athletics	G	AB	R	H	RBI	2B	3B	HR	BB	SO	SB	CS	Avg	OBP	Slg
Jose Canseco	5	17	1	5	3	0	0	1	3	7	0	2	.294	.400	.471
Mike Gallego	4	11	3	3	1	1	0	0	0	2	0	0	.273	.273	.364
Ron Hassey	2	6	0	1	1	0	0	0	1	2	0	0	.167	.250	.167
Dave Henderson	5	19	4	5	1	3	0	1	2	5	0	0	.263	.333	.579
Rickey Henderson	5	15	8	6	5	1	1	2	7	0	8	1	.400	.609	1.000
Stan Javier	1	2	0	0	0	0	0	0	0	1	0	0	.000	.000	.000
Carney Lansford	3	11	2	5	4	0	0	0	2	1	2	0	.455	.538	.455
Mark McGwire	5	18	3	7	3	1	0	1	1	4	0	0	.389	.400	.611
Dave Parker	4	16	2	3	0	0	0	2	0	0	0	0	.188	.188	.563
Ken Phelps	1	1	0	1	0	1	0	0	0	0	0	0	1.000	1.000	2.000
Tony Phillips	5	18	1	3	1	1	0	0	2	4	2	0	.167	.250	.222
Terry Steinbach	4	15	0	3	1	0	0	0	1	5	0	0	.200	.250	.200
Walt Weiss	4	9	2	1	0	1	0	0	1	1	1	0	.111	.200	.222
Totals	5	158	26	43	23	9	1	7	20	32	13	3	.272	.354	.475

Batting

Blue Jays	G	AB	R	H	RBI	2B	3B	HR	BB	SO	SB	CS	Avg	OBP	Slg
George Bell	5	20	2	4	2	0	0	1	0	3	0	0	.200	.190	.350
Pat Borders	1	1	0	1	1	0	0	0	0	0	0	0	1.000	1.000	1.000
Junior Felix	3	11	0	3	3	1	0	0	0	2	0	0	.273	.273	.364
Tony Fernandez	5	20	6	7	1	3	0	0	1	2	5	0	.350	.381	.500
Kelly Gruber	5	17	2	5	1	1	0	0	3	2	1	0	.294	.381	.353
Manuel Lee	2	8	2	2	0	0	0	0	0	1	0	0	.250	.250	.250
Nelson Liriano	3	7	1	3	1	0	0	0	2	0	3	0	.429	.556	.429
Lee Mazzilli	3	8	0	0	0	0	0	0	0	2	0	0	.000	.000	.000
Fred McGriff	5	21	1	3	3	0	0	0	4	0	0	0	.143	.143	.143
Lloyd Moseby	5	16	4	5	2	0	0	1	5	2	1	0	.313	.476	.500
Rance Mulliniks	1	1	0	0	0	0	0	0	0	1	0	0	.000	.000	.000
Ernie Whitt	5	16	1	2	3	0	0	1	2	3	0	0	.125	.211	.313
Mookie Wilson	5	19	2	5	2	0	0	0	2	2	1	0	.263	.333	.263
Totals	5	165	21	40	19	5	0	3	15	24	11	0	.242	.301	.327

Pitching

Athletics	G	GS	CG	IP	H	R	ER	BB	SO	W-L	Sv-Op	Hld	ERA
Storm Davis	1	1	0	6.1	5	6	5	2	3	0-1	0-0	0	7.11
Dennis Eckersley	4	0	0	5.2	4	1	1	0	2	0-0	3-3	0	1.59
Rick Honeycutt	3	0	0	1.2	6	6	6	5	1	0-0	0-0	1	32.40
Mike Moore	1	1	0	7.0	3	1	0	2	3	1-0	0-0	0	0.00
Gene Nelson	1	0	0	1.1	1	0	0	0	2	0-0	0-0	0	0.00
Dave Stewart	2	2	0	16.0	13	5	5	3	9	2-0	0-0	0	2.81
Bob Welch	1	1	0	5.2	8	2	2	1	4	1-0	0-0	0	3.18
Matt Young	1	0	0	0.1	0	0	0	2	0	0-0	0-0	0	0.00
Totals	5	5	0	44.0	40	21	19	15	24	4-1	3-3	1	3.89

Pitching

Blue Jays	G	GS	CG	IP	H	R	ER	BB	SO	W-L	Sv-Op	Hld	ERA
Jim Acker	5	0	0	6.1	4	2	1	1	4	0-0	0-0	1	1.42
John Cerutti	2	0	0	2.2	0	0	0	3	1	0-0	0-0	0	0.00
Mike Flanagan	1	1	0	4.1	7	5	5	1	3	0-1	0-0	0	10.38
Tom Henke	3	0	0	2.2	0	0	0	0	3	0-0	0-0	0	0.00
Jimmy Key	1	1	0	6.0	7	3	3	2	2	1-0	0-0	0	4.50
Dave Stieb	2	2	0	11.1	12	8	8	6	10	0-2	0-0	0	6.35
Todd Stottlemyre	1	1	0	5.0	7	4	4	2	3	0-1	0-0	0	7.20
Duane Ward	2	0	0	3.2	6	3	3	5	5	0-0	0-0	0	7.36
David Wells	1	0	0	1.0	0	1	0	2	1	0-0	0-0	0	0.00
Totals	5	5	0	43.0	43	26	24	20	32	1-4	0-0	1	5.02

Fielding

Athletics	Pos	G	PO	Ast	E	DP	PB	FPct
Lance Blankenship	2b	1	0	1	0	0	—	1.000
Jose Canseco	rf	5	6	1	1	0	—	.875
Storm Davis	p	1	0	0	0	0	—	—
Dennis Eckersley	p	4	0	1	0	0	—	1.000
Mike Gallego	2b	2	3	9	0	1	—	1.000
	ss	2	3	5	0	1	—	1.000
Ron Hassey	c	2	10	0	0	0	0	1.000
Dave Henderson	cf	5	22	0	0	0	—	1.000
Rickey Henderson	lf	5	13	0	1	0	—	.929
Rick Honeycutt	p	3	0	0	0	0	—	—
Stan Javier	rf	1	1	0	0	0	—	1.000
Carney Lansford	3b	3	1	2	0	0	—	1.000
Mark McGwire	1b	5	46	1	1	4	—	.979
Mike Moore	p	1	0	1	0	0	—	1.000
Gene Nelson	p	1	0	0	0	0	—	—
Tony Phillips	2b	3	2	11	0	2	—	1.000
	3b	3	2	3	0	0	—	1.000
Terry Steinbach	c	3	17	0	0	0	0	1.000
Dave Stewart	p	2	0	1	0	0	—	1.000
Walt Weiss	ss	4	5	10	0	2	—	1.000
Bob Welch	p	1	1	0	0	0	—	1.000
Matt Young	p	1	0	0	0	0	—	—
Totals		5	132	46	3	10	0	.983

Fielding

Blue Jays	Pos	G	PO	Ast	E	DP	PB	FPct
Jim Acker	p	5	1	1	0	0	—	1.000
George Bell	lf	2	3	1	0	0	—	1.000
Pat Borders	c	1	1	0	0	0	0	1.000
John Cerutti	p	2	0	2	0	0	—	1.000
Junior Felix	rf	3	8	0	0	0	—	1.000
Tony Fernandez	ss	5	9	15	0	3	—	1.000
Mike Flanagan	p	1	2	3	0	2	—	1.000
Kelly Gruber	3b	5	4	8	0	1	—	1.000
Tom Henke	p	3	0	1	0	0	—	1.000
Jimmy Key	p	1	0	0	0	0	—	—
Manuel Lee	2b	2	4	1	0	1	—	1.000
Nelson Liriano	2b	3	4	3	1	1	—	.875
Fred McGriff	1b	5	35	2	1	3	—	.974
Lloyd Moseby	cf	5	15	0	0	0	—	1.000
Dave Stieb	p	2	0	1	0	0	—	1.000
Todd Stottlemyre	p	1	0	0	0	0	—	—
Duane Ward	p	2	1	0	0	0	—	1.000
David Wells	p	1	0	0	0	0	—	—
Ernie Whitt	c	5	32	2	0	0	1	1.000
Mookie Wilson	lf	3	7	0	0	0	—	1.000
	rf	2	3	0	0	0	—	1.000
Totals		5	129	40	2	11	1	.988

1989 San Francisco Giants (NL) 4, Chicago Cubs (NL) 1

The San Francisco Giants simply overpowered the Chicago Cubs, raining eight longballs on them en route to a five-game NLCS victory. Will Clark led the charge from start to finish. He blasted a grand slam and drove in six runs to propel the Giants to an 11-3 romp in the opener. The Cubs came back to knock out Rick Reuschel in the first inning of Game 2, evening the series with a 9-5 victory. Robbie Thompson hit a two-run homer off reliever Les Lancaster to give the Giants a 5-4 win in the third game. In Game 4, Clark had three hits and Matt Williams contributed a homer and four RBI as the Giants came out on top, 6-4. Game 5 was tied 1-1 in the bottom of the eighth when the Cubs brought in Mitch Williams to face Clark with two outs and the bases loaded. Williams got ahead 0-and-2, but Clark fought off several pitches and then lined a two-run single to bring home the eventual winning runs. He ended the series with a .650 batting average and eight RBI.

Game 1
Wednesday, October 4

Giants	AB	R	H	RBI	BB	K	Avg
Brett Butler, cf	4	2	1	0	1	1	.250
Robby Thompson, 2b	4	1	1	0	0	0	.250
Will Clark, 1b	4	4	4	6	1	0	1.000
Kevin Mitchell, lf	5	2	2	3	0	1	.400
Matt Williams, 3b	4	0	1	2	0	0	.250
Terry Kennedy, c	4	0	1	0	0	0	.250
Kirt Manwaring, ph-c	1	0	0	0	0	0	.000
Pat Sheridan, rf	4	1	2	0	0	0	.500
Candy Maldonado, ph-rf	1	0	0	0	0	0	.000
Jose Uribe, ss	4	1	1	0	1	2	.250
Scott Garrelts, p	3	0	0	0	0	1	.000
Bill Bathe, ph	1	0	0	0	0	1	.000
Jeff Brantley, p	0	0	0	0	0	0	—
Atlee Hammaker, p	0	0	0	0	0	0	—
TOTALS	39	11	13	11	3	6	.333

Cubs	AB	R	H	RBI	BB	K	Avg
Jerome Walton, cf	4	0	1	0	0	1	.250
Steve Wilson, p	0	0	0	0	0	0	—
Domingo Ramos, ph	1	0	0	0	0	0	.000
Ryne Sandberg, 2b	5	2	3	1	0	0	.600
Dwight Smith, lf	4	0	0	0	0	1	.000
Mark Grace, 1b	4	1	3	2	0	0	.750
Andre Dawson, rf	3	0	0	1	1	1	.000
Luis Salazar, 3b	4	0	2	0	0	0	.500
Shawon Dunston, ss	4	0	0	0	0	1	.000
Rick Wrona, c	4	0	0	0	0	2	.000
Greg Maddux, p	1	0	0	0	0	1	.000
Vance Law, ph	1	0	0	0	0	1	.000
Paul Kilgus, p	0	0	0	0	0	0	—
Marvell Wynne, ph-cf	1	0	0	0	0	0	.000
Lloyd McClendon, ph	1	0	1	0	0	0	1.000
TOTALS	37	3	10	3	1	7	.270

	1	2	3	4	5	6	7	8	9		R	H	E
Giants	3	0	1	4	0	0	0	3	0		11	13	0
Cubs	2	0	1	0	0	0	0	0	0		3	10	1

E—Salazar. LOB—Giants 6, Cubs 8. Scoring Position—Giants 5-for-10, Cubs 1-for-9. 2B—Clark (1), Williams (1), Sandberg (1). 3B—Sheridan (1), Salazar (1). HR—Clark 2 (2), Mitchell (1), Sandberg (1), Grace (1). S—Thompson. SB—Uribe (1), Grace (1). CS—Sheridan (1).

Giants	IP	H	R	ER	BB	K	ERA
Scott Garrelts (W, 1-0)	7.0	8	3	3	1	6	3.86
Jeff Brantley	1.0	1	0	0	0	1	0.00
Atlee Hammaker	1.0	1	0	0	0	0	0.00

Cubs	IP	H	R	ER	BB	K	ERA
Greg Maddux (L, 0-1)	4.0	8	8	8	1	3	18.00
Paul Kilgus	3.0	4	0	0	1	1	0.00
Steve Wilson	2.0	1	3	0	1	2	0.00

WP—Wilson. HBP—Williams by Maddux. Time—2:51. Attendance—39,195. Umpires—HP, Harvey. 1B, Froemming. 2B, Tata. 3B, Quick.

Game 2
Thursday, October 5

Giants	AB	R	H	RBI	BB	K	Avg
Brett Butler, cf	4	0	0	0	1	0	.125
Robby Thompson, 2b	4	1	1	1	0	0	.250
Will Clark, 1b	4	1	1	0	1	0	.625
Kevin Mitchell, lf	4	2	3	2	0	0	.556
Matt Williams, 3b-ss	4	1	2	2	0	0	.375
Terry Kennedy, c	2	0	1	0	0	1	.333
Bill Bathe, ph	0	0	0	0	0	0	.000
Ken Oberkfell, ph-3b	2	0	0	0	0	0	.000
Steve Bedrosian, p	0	0	0	0	0	0	—
Pat Sheridan, rf	3	0	0	0	0	2	.286
Craig Lefferts, p	0	0	0	0	0	0	—
Jeff Brantley, p	0	0	0	0	0	0	—
Greg Litton, ph-3b	1	0	1	0	0	0	1.000
Jose Uribe, ss	2	0	1	0	0	1	.333
Ernest Riles, ph	1	0	0	0	0	0	.000
Kirt Manwaring, c	1	0	0	0	0	0	.000
Rick Reuschel, p	0	0	0	0	0	0	—
Kelly Downs, p	1	0	0	0	0	0	.000
Donell Nixon, rf	2	0	0	0	0	1	.000
TOTALS	35	5	10	5	3	5	.329

Cubs	AB	R	H	RBI	BB	K	Avg
Jerome Walton, cf	4	2	3	1	1	0	.500
Ryne Sandberg, 2b	3	2	1	2	1	0	.500
Dwight Smith, lf	4	1	1	0	0	1	.125
Mark Grace, 1b	4	1	3	4	1	1	.750
Andre Dawson, rf	4	0	0	0	1	3	.000
Luis Salazar, 3b	3	1	1	1	0	0	.429
Les Lancaster, p	1	0	0	0	0	1	.000
Shawon Dunston, ss	3	1	1	0	1	0	.143
Joe Girardi, c	3	1	0	0	0	0	.000
Mike Bielecki, p	2	0	1	0	2	0	.500
Paul Assenmacher, p	0	0	0	0	0	0	—
Vance Law, 3b	2	0	0	0	0	2	.000
TOTALS	33	9	11	9	8	9	.323

	1	2	3	4	5	6	7	8	9		R	H	E
Giants	0	0	0	2	0	0	2	0	1		5	10	0
Cubs	6	0	0	0	0	3	0	0	x		9	11	0

DP—Giants 2 (Thompson to Clark to Williams; Downs to Kennedy). LOB—Giants 7, Cubs 8. Scoring Position—Giants 0-for-7, Cubs 5-for-14. 2B—Kennedy (1), Smith (1), Grace 2 (2). 3B—Sandberg (1). HR—Thompson (1), Mitchell (2), Williams (1). S—Downs. GDP—Salazar, Bielecki. SB—Dunston (1). CS—Butler (1).

Giants	IP	H	R	ER	BB	K	ERA
Rick Reuschel (L, 0-1)	0.2	5	5	5	0	1	67.50
Kelly Downs	4.2	5	3	3	5	5	5.79
Craig Lefferts	0.2	1	1	1	2	1	13.50
Jeff Brantley	1.0	0	0	0	1	1	0.00
Steve Bedrosian	1.0	0	0	0	0	1	0.00

Cubs	IP	H	R	ER	BB	K	ERA
Mike Bielecki	4.2	4	2	2	3	3	3.86
Paul Assenmacher	0.1	2	0	0	0	0	0.00
Les Lancaster (BS, 1; W, 1-0)	4.0	4	3	3	0	2	6.75

Assenmacher pitched to two batters in the 6th.

PB—Manwaring. Time—3:08. Attendance—39,195. Umpires—HP, Froemming. 1B, Tata. 2B, Quick. 3B, CWilliams.

Game 3
Saturday, October 7

Cubs	AB	R	H	RBI	BB	K	Avg
Jerome Walton, cf	5	0	0	0	0	1	.308
Ryne Sandberg, 2b	3	1	1	1	1	1	.455
Dwight Smith, lf	5	1	1	0	0	1	.154
Mark Grace, 1b	3	0	2	0	1	0	.727
Andre Dawson, rf	4	0	1	2	0	0	.091
Luis Salazar, 3b	4	0	1	0	0	0	.364
Curtis Wilkerson, pr-3b	0	0	0	0	0	0	—
Shawon Dunston, ss	4	1	2	0	0	0	.273
Joe Girardi, c	2	0	1	0	0	0	.200
Marvell Wynne, ph	1	0	0	0	0	0	.000
Lloyd McClendon, ph-c	1	0	0	0	0	0	.500
Rick Sutcliffe, p	2	0	1	0	0	0	.500
Greg Maddux, pr	0	1	0	0	0	0	.000
Paul Assenmacher, p	0	0	0	0	0	0	—
Les Lancaster, p	0	0	0	0	0	0	.000
Mitch Webster, ph	1	0	0	0	0	0	.000
TOTALS	34	4	10	3	2	3	.319

Giants	AB	R	H	RBI	BB	K	Avg
Brett Butler, cf	4	2	2	0	0	0	.250
Robby Thompson, 2b	4	2	2	2	0	1	.333
Will Clark, 1b	4	0	2	0	0	1	.583
Kevin Mitchell, lf	3	1	1	0	1	0	.500
Matt Williams, 3b	4	0	1	0	0	0	.250
Terry Kennedy, c	3	0	0	0	1	1	.222
Candy Maldonado, rf	2	0	0	1	1	0	.000
Don Robinson, p	0	0	0	0	0	0	—
Craig Lefferts, p	0	0	0	0	0	0	—
Ken Oberkfell, ph	1	0	0	0	0	0	.000
Steve Bedrosian, p	0	0	0	0	0	0	—
Jose Uribe, ss	4	0	1	1	0	0	.300
Mike LaCoss, p	1	0	0	0	0	0	.000
Jeff Brantley, p	0	0	0	0	1	0	—
Donell Nixon, rf	1	0	0	0	0	0	.000
Pat Sheridan, rf	0	0	0	0	0	0	.286
TOTALS	31	5	8	5	4	3	.313

	1	2	3	4	5	6	7	8	9		R	H	E
Cubs	2	0	0	1	0	0	1	0	0		4	10	0
Giants	3	0	0	0	0	0	2	0	x		5	8	3

E—LaCoss, Sheridan, Uribe. DP—Cubs 1 (Sandberg to Dunston to Grace), Giants 2 (Clark to Kennedy; Mitchell to Thompson). LOB—Cubs 8, Giants 6. Scoring Position—Cubs 1-for-8, Giants 1-for-5. 2B—Grace (3), Sutcliffe (1). HR—Thompson (2). S—Girardi, Sutcliffe. SF—Sandberg. GDP—Sutcliffe, Mitchell.

Cubs	IP	H	R	ER	BB	K	ERA
Rick Sutcliffe	6.0	5	3	3	4	2	4.50
Paul Assenmacher (H, 1)	0.1	1	1	1	0	0	13.50
Les Lancaster (BS, 2; L, 1-1)	1.2	2	1	1	0	1	6.35

Giants	IP	H	R	ER	BB	K	ERA
Mike LaCoss	3.0	7	3	3	0	2	9.00
Jeff Brantley	3.0	0	0	0	1	1	0.00
Don Robinson (W, 1-0)	1.2	3	1	0	0	0	0.00
Craig Lefferts (H, 1)	0.1	0	0	0	0	0	9.00
Steve Bedrosian (S, 1)	1.0	0	0	0	0	1	0.00

LaCoss pitched to three batters in the 4th.

Balk—Sutcliffe. WP—LaCoss, Brantley. Time—2:48. Attendance—62,065. Umpires—HP, Tata. 1B, Quick. 2B, CWilliams. 3B, Marsh.

Game 4
Sunday, October 8

Cubs	AB	R	H	RBI	BB	K	Avg
Jerome Walton, cf	5	1	2	0	0	0	.333
Ryne Sandberg, 2b	5	1	2	0	0	1	.438
Dwight Smith, lf	2	0	1	0	1	0	.200
Lloyd McClendon, lf-c	1	0	1	0	1	0	.667
Mark Grace, 1b	3	1	1	2	1	0	.643
Andre Dawson, rf	5	0	1	1	0	1	.125
Luis Salazar, 3b	4	1	2	1	0	0	.400
Shawon Dunston, ss	4	0	2	0	0	0	.333
Rick Wrona, c	1	0	0	0	0	1	.000
Marvell Wynne, ph	1	0	0	0	0	0	.000
Joe Girardi, c	2	0	0	0	0	1	.143
Mitch Williams, p	0	0	0	0	0	0	—
Greg Maddux, p	2	0	0	0	0	0	.000
Steve Wilson, p	0	0	0	0	0	0	—
Curtis Wilkerson, ph	1	0	0	0	0	0	.000
Scott Sanderson, p	0	0	0	0	0	0	—
Mitch Webster, lf	1	0	0	0	0	0	.000
TOTALS	37	4	12	4	3	4	.311

Giants	AB	R	H	RBI	BB	K	Avg
Brett Butler, cf	4	1	1	0	0	1	.250
Robby Thompson, 2b	3	1	1	0	1	1	.333
Will Clark, 1b	4	2	3	0	0	0	.625
Kevin Mitchell, lf	3	0	0	1	1	0	.400
Matt Williams, 3b	4	1	2	4	0	1	.313
Terry Kennedy, c	4	0	1	0	0	2	.231
Donell Nixon, pr	0	0	0	0	0	0	.000
Kirt Manwaring, c	0	0	0	0	0	0	.000
Pat Sheridan, rf	4	0	0	0	0	0	.182
Jose Uribe, ss	4	1	1	0	0	1	.286
Scott Garrelts, p	1	0	0	0	1	0	.000
Kelly Downs, p	2	0	0	0	0	1	.000
Steve Bedrosian, p	0	0	0	0	0	0	—
TOTALS	33	6	9	5	3	7	.305

	1	2	3	4	5	6	7	8	9		R	H	E
Cubs	1	1	0	0	2	0	0	0	0		4	12	1
Giants	1	0	2	1	2	0	0	0	x		6	9	1

E—Uribe, Maddux. DP—Giants 1 (MaWilliams to Thompson to Clark). LOB—Cubs 10, Giants 6. Scoring Position—Cubs 3-for-11, Giants 2-for-8. 2B—Sandberg (2), Dawson (1), Clark 2 (3), Uribe (1). 3B—Grace (1). HR—Salazar (1), MaWilliams (2). SF—Grace. GDP—Dawson. SB—Smith (1), Nixon (1).

Cubs	IP	H	R	ER	BB	K	ERA
Greg Maddux	3.1	5	4	3	3	2	13.50
Steve Wilson (L, 0-1)	1.2	2	2	2	0	2	4.91
Scott Sanderson	2.0	2	0	0	0	1	0.00
Mitch Williams	1.0	0	0	0	0	2	0.00

Giants	IP	H	R	ER	BB	K	ERA
Scott Garrelts	4.2	8	4	4	1	2	5.40
Kelly Downs (W, 1-0)	4.0	3	0	0	1	1	3.12
Steve Bedrosian (S, 2)	0.1	1	0	0	1	1	0.00

Sanderson pitched to one batter in the 8th.

WP—Garrelts, Maddux. Time—3:13. Attendance—62,078. Umpires—HP, Quick. 1B, CWilliams. 2B, Marsh. 3B, Harvey.

Game 5
Monday, October 9

Cubs	AB	R	H	RBI	BB	K	Avg
Jerome Walton, cf	4	1	2	1	1	0	.364
Ryne Sandberg, 2b	4	0	1	1	0	1	.400
Marvell Wynne, lf	4	0	1	0	0	0	.167
Mark Grace, 1b	3	0	2	0	1	0	.647
Andre Dawson, rf	3	0	0	0	0	1	.105
Mitch Williams, p	0	0	0	0	0	0	—
Les Lancaster, p	0	0	0	0	0	0	.000
Luis Salazar, 3b	4	0	1	0	0	0	.368
Shawon Dunston, ss	4	0	1	0	0	0	.316
Joe Girardi, c	3	0	0	0	0	0	.100
Curtis Wilkerson, ph	1	1	1	0	0	0	.500
Mike Bielecki, p	3	0	0	0	0	2	.200
Mitch Webster, rf	1	0	1	0	0	0	.333
TOTALS	34	2	10	2	2	4	.329

Giants	AB	R	H	RBI	BB	K	Avg
Brett Butler, cf	3	1	0	0	1	1	.211
Robby Thompson, 2b	3	0	0	0	1	0	.278
Will Clark, 1b	4	1	3	2	0	1	.650
Kevin Mitchell, lf	2	0	0	1	1	2	.353
Matt Williams, 3b	4	0	1	0	0	1	.300
Terry Kennedy, c	3	0	0	0	0	0	.188
Pat Sheridan, rf	2	0	0	0	0	2	.154
Ken Oberkfell, ph	1	0	0	0	0	0	.000
Steve Bedrosian, p	0	0	0	0	0	0	—
Jose Uribe, ss	3	0	0	0	0	1	.235
Rick Reuschel, p	2	0	0	0	0	0	.000
Candy Maldonado, ph-rf	0	1	0	0	1	0	.000
TOTALS	27	3	4	3	4	8	.289

	1	2	3	4	5	6	7	8	9		R	H	E
Cubs	0	0	1	0	0	0	0	0	1		2	10	1
Giants	0	0	0	0	0	0	1	2	x		3	4	1

E—Mitchell, Dunston. DP—Giants 2 (Thompson to Uribe to Clark; Uribe to Clark). LOB—Cubs 9, Giants 5. Scoring Position—Cubs 2-for-9, Giants 1-for-5. 2B—Sandberg (3). 3B—Clark (1). S—Sandberg. SF—Mitchell. GDP—Dunston, Girardi.

Cubs	IP	H	R	ER	BB	K	ERA
Mike Bielecki (L, 0-1)	7.2	3	3	3	3	8	3.65
Mitch Williams	0.0	1	0	0	0	0	0.00
Les Lancaster	0.1	0	0	0	1	0	6.00

Giants	IP	H	R	ER	BB	K	ERA
Rick Reuschel (W, 1-1)	8.0	7	1	0	2	4	5.19
Steve Bedrosian (S, 3)	1.0	3	1	1	0	0	2.70

MiWilliams pitched to one batter in the 8th.

PB—Girardi. HBP—Dawson by Reuschel. Time—2:47. Attendance—62,084. Umpires—HP, CWilliams. 1B, Marsh. 2B, Harvey. 3B, Froemming.

1989 NL Championship Series—Composite Statistics

Batting

Giants	G	AB	R	H	RBI	2B	3B	HR	BB	SO	SB	CS	Avg	OBP	Slg
Bill Bathe	2	1	0	0	0	0	0	0	0	1	0	0	.000	.000	.000
Jeff Brantley	3	0	0	0	0	0	0	0	1	0	0	0	—	1.000	—
Brett Butler	5	19	6	4	0	0	0	0	3	3	0	1	.211	.318	.211
Will Clark	5	20	8	13	8	3	1	2	2	2	0	0	.650	.682	1.200
Kelly Downs	2	3	0	0	0	0	0	0	0	1	0	0	.000	.000	.000
Scott Garrelts	2	4	0	0	0	0	0	0	1	1	0	0	.000	.200	.000
Terry Kennedy	5	16	0	3	0	1	0	0	1	4	0	0	.188	.235	.250
Mike LaCoss	1	1	0	0	0	0	0	0	0	0	0	0	.000	.000	.000
Greg Litton	1	1	0	1	0	0	0	0	0	0	0	0	1.000	1.000	1.000
Candy Maldonado	3	3	1	0	1	0	0	0	2	0	0	0	.000	.400	.000
Kirt Manwaring	3	2	0	0	0	0	0	0	0	0	0	0	.000	.000	.000
Kevin Mitchell	5	17	5	6	7	0	0	2	3	3	0	0	.353	.429	.706
Donell Nixon	3	3	0	0	0	0	0	0	0	1	1	0	.000	.000	.000
Ken Oberkfell	3	4	0	0	0	0	0	0	0	0	0	0	.000	.000	.000
Rick Reuschel	2	2	0	0	0	0	0	0	0	0	0	0	.000	.000	.000
Ernest Riles	1	1	0	0	0	0	0	0	0	0	0	0	.000	.000	.000
Pat Sheridan	5	13	1	2	0	0	1	0	0	4	0	1	.154	.154	.308
Robby Thompson	5	18	5	5	3	0	0	2	3	2	0	0	.278	.381	.611
Jose Uribe	5	17	2	4	1	1	0	0	1	5	1	0	.235	.278	.294
Matt Williams	5	20	2	6	9	1	0	2	0	2	0	0	.300	.333	.650
Totals	5	165	30	44	29	6	2	8	17	29	2	2	.267	.337	.473

Cubs	G	AB	R	H	RBI	2B	3B	HR	BB	SO	SB	CS	Avg	OBP	Slg
Mike Bielecki	2	5	0	1	2	0	0	0	0	2	0	0	.200	.200	.200
Andre Dawson	5	19	0	2	3	1	0	0	2	6	0	0	.105	.227	.158
Shawon Dunston	5	19	2	6	0	0	0	0	1	1	1	0	.316	.350	.316
Joe Girardi	4	10	1	1	0	0	0	0	1	2	0	0	.100	.182	.100
Mark Grace	5	17	3	11	8	3	1	1	4	1	1	0	.647	.682	1.118
Les Lancaster	3	1	0	0	0	0	0	0	0	1	0	0	.000	.000	.000
Vance Law	2	5	0	0	0	0	0	0	0	3	0	0	.000	.000	.000
Greg Maddux	3	1	0	0	0	0	0	0	0	0	0	0	.000	.000	.000
Lloyd McClendon	3	3	0	2	0	0	0	0	1	0	0	0	.667	.750	.667
Domingo Ramos	1	1	0	0	0	0	0	0	0	0	0	0	.000	.000	.000
Luis Salazar	5	19	2	7	2	0	1	1	0	4	0	0	.368	.368	.632
Ryne Sandberg	5	20	6	8	4	3	1	1	3	4	0	0	.400	.458	.800
Dwight Smith	4	15	2	3	0	1	0	0	2	2	1	0	.200	.294	.267
Rick Sutcliffe	1	2	0	1	0	1	0	0	0	0	0	0	.500	.500	1.000
Jerome Walton	5	22	4	8	2	0	0	0	2	2	0	0	.364	.417	.364
Mitch Webster	3	3	0	1	0	0	0	0	0	0	0	0	.333	.333	.333
Curtis Wilkerson	3	2	1	1	0	0	0	0	0	0	0	0	.500	.500	.500
Rick Wrona	2	5	0	0	0	0	0	0	0	3	0	0	.000	.000	.000
Marvell Wynne	4	6	0	1	0	0	0	0	0	0	0	0	.167	.167	.167
Totals	5	175	22	53	21	9	3	3	16	27	3	0	.303	.361	.440

Pitching

Giants	G	GS	CG	IP	H	R	ER	BB	SO	W-L	Sv-Op	Hld	ERA
Steve Bedrosian	4	0	0	3.1	4	1	1	2	2	0-0	3-3	0	2.70
Jeff Brantley	3	0	0	5.0	1	0	0	2	3	0-0	0-0	0	0.00
Kelly Downs	2	0	0	8.2	8	3	3	6	6	1-0	0-0	0	3.12
Scott Garrelts	2	2	0	11.2	16	7	7	2	8	1-0	0-0	0	5.40
Atlee Hammaker	1	0	0	1.0	1	0	0	0	0	0-0	0-0	0	0.00
Mike LaCoss	1	1	0	3.0	7	3	3	0	2	0-0	0-0	0	9.00
Craig Lefferts	2	0	0	1.0	1	1	1	2	1	0-0	0-0	1	9.00
Rick Reuschel	2	2	0	8.2	12	6	5	2	5	1-1	0-0	0	5.19
Don Robinson	1	0	0	1.2	3	1	0	0	0	1-0	0-0	0	0.00
Totals	5	5	0	44.0	53	22	20	16	27	4-1	3-3	1	4.09

Cubs	G	GS	CG	IP	H	R	ER	BB	SO	W-L	Sv-Op	Hld	ERA
Paul Assenmacher	2	0	0	0.2	3	1	1	0	0	0-0	0-0	1	13.50
Mike Bielecki	2	2	0	12.1	7	5	5	6	11	0-1	0-0	0	3.65
Paul Kilgus	1	0	0	3.0	4	0	0	1	1	0-0	0-0	0	0.00
Les Lancaster	3	0	0	6.0	6	4	4	1	3	1-1	0-2	0	6.00
Greg Maddux	2	2	0	7.1	13	12	11	4	5	0-1	0-0	0	13.50
Scott Sanderson	1	0	0	2.0	2	0	0	0	1	0-0	0-0	0	0.00
Rick Sutcliffe	1	1	0	6.0	5	3	3	4	2	0-0	0-0	0	4.50
Mitch Williams	2	0	0	1.0	1	0	0	2	0	0-0	0-0	0	0.00
Steve Wilson	2	0	0	3.2	3	5	2	1	4	0-1	0-0	0	4.91
Totals	5	5	0	42.0	44	30	26	17	29	1-4	0-2	1	5.57

Fielding

Giants	Pos	G	PO	Ast	E	DP	PB	FPct
Steve Bedrosian	p	4	0	0	0	0	—	—
Jeff Brantley	p	3	0	0	0	0	—	—
Brett Butler	cf	5	9	0	0	0	—	1.000
Will Clark	1b	5	43	5	0	6	—	1.000
Kelly Downs	p	2	0	1	0	1	—	1.000
Scott Garrelts	p	2	0	1	0	0	—	1.000
Atlee Hammaker	p	1	0	0	0	0	—	—
Terry Kennedy	c	5	26	1	0	2	0	1.000
Mike LaCoss	p	1	0	0	1	0	—	.000
Craig Lefferts	p	2	0	0	0	0	—	—
Greg Litton	3b	1	0	0	0	0	—	—
Candy Maldonado	rf	3	2	0	0	0	—	1.000
Kirt Manwaring	c	3	5	0	0	0	1	1.000
Kevin Mitchell	lf	5	15	1	1	1	—	.941
Donell Nixon	rf	2	2	0	0	0	—	1.000
Ken Oberkfell	3b	1	0	1	0	0	—	1.000
Rick Reuschel	p	2	0	3	0	0	—	1.000
Don Robinson	p	1	0	0	0	0	—	—
Pat Sheridan	rf	5	9	1	1	0	—	.909
Robby Thompson	2b	5	10	13	0	4	—	1.000
Jose Uribe	ss	5	6	9	2	2	—	.882
Matt Williams	3b	5	5	12	0	2	—	1.000
	ss	1	0	0	0	0	—	—
Totals		5	132	48	5	18	1	.973

Cubs	Pos	G	PO	Ast	E	DP	PB	FPct
Paul Assenmacher	p	2	0	0	0	0	—	—
Mike Bielecki	p	2	1	2	0	0	—	1.000
Andre Dawson	rf	5	4	0	0	0	—	1.000
Shawon Dunston	ss	5	10	14	1	1	—	.960
Joe Girardi	c	4	20	0	0	0	1	1.000
Mark Grace	1b	5	44	3	0	0	—	1.000
Paul Kilgus	p	1	0	0	0	0	—	—
Les Lancaster	p	3	0	1	0	0	—	1.000
Vance Law	3b	1	0	0	0	0	—	—
Greg Maddux	p	2	0	1	0	0	—	.000
Lloyd McClendon	c	2	3	0	0	0	0	1.000
	lf	1	1	0	0	0	—	1.000
Luis Salazar	3b	5	4	5	1	0	—	.900
Ryne Sandberg	2b	5	7	11	0	1	—	1.000
Scott Sanderson	p	1	0	0	0	0	—	—
Dwight Smith	lf	4	9	0	0	0	—	1.000
Rick Sutcliffe	p	1	0	2	0	0	—	1.000
Jerome Walton	cf	5	11	0	0	0	—	1.000
Mitch Webster	lf	1	0	0	0	0	—	—
	rf	1	0	0	0	0	—	—
Curtis Wilkerson	3b	1	0	0	0	0	—	—
Mitch Williams	p	2	0	0	0	0	—	—
Steve Wilson	p	2	0	1	0	0	—	1.000
Rick Wrona	c	2	9	1	0	0	0	1.000
Marvell Wynne	lf	1	3	0	0	0	—	1.000
	cf	1	0	0	0	0	—	—
Totals		5	126	40	3	3	1	.982

Postseason: League Championship Series

1990 Oakland Athletics (AL) 4, Boston Red Sox (AL) 0

In one of the most lopsided playoff series of all time, the Oakland A's rolled over the Boston Red Sox in four straight games. In the opener, Wade Boggs launched a fourth-inning solo shot off Dave Stewart to give Roger Clemens and the Red Sox a 1-0 lead. Clemens left after six innings with the lead intact, but the Boston bullpen allowed nine runs in three innings and Boston lost, 9-1. Game 2 was not unlike the opener; Boston's Dana Kiecker left with two out in the sixth and the game tied 1-1, and the bullpen allowed three runs as Oakland won 4-1 to go up two games to nothing. Mike Moore outdueled Mike Boddicker for a 4-1 Oakland win in the third game, and then things got strange. Oakland led Game 4 1-0 in the bottom of the second when Clemens issued a two-out walk to Willie Randolph. Clemens began yelling at home plate umpire Terry Cooney. By the time he finished, he was gone, and so were the last remnants of Boston's hopes. Stewart worked eight strong innings to complete the sweep. The A's outscored the Red Sox 20-4 in the four games without hitting a single home run.

Game 1

Saturday, October 6

Athletics	AB	R	H	RBI	BB	K	Avg
Rickey Henderson, lf	5	1	2	3	0	0	.400
Willie McGee, cf	4	1	0	0	1	2	.000
Jose Canseco, rf	2	1	1	1	2	0	.500
Harold Baines, dh	3	0	1	0	1	0	.333
Lance Blankenship, pr-dh	0	1	0	0	0	0	—
Carney Lansford, 3b	5	1	3	2	0	0	.600
Terry Steinbach, c	5	1	3	1	0	1	.600
Mark McGwire, 1b	3	1	0	0	2	0	.000
Walt Weiss, ss	3	2	0	0	2	1	.000
Mike Gallego, 2b	1	0	1	0	1	0	1.000
Jamie Quirk, ph	1	0	1	0	0	0	1.000
Willie Randolph, pr-2b	2	0	1	1	0	0	.500
TOTALS	34	9	13	8	9	4	.382

Red Sox	AB	R	H	RBI	BB	K	Avg
Jody Reed, 2b-ss	3	0	0	0	0	0	.000
Carlos Quintana, 1b	4	0	0	0	0	0	.000
Wade Boggs, 3b	4	1	1	1	0	2	.250
Ellis Burks, cf	4	0	1	0	0	1	.250
Mike Greenwell, lf	4	0	0	0	0	0	.000
Dwight Evans, dh	2	0	0	0	1	0	.000
Tom Brunansky, rf	3	0	1	0	0	0	.333
Tony Pena, c	3	0	0	0	0	0	.000
Luis Rivera, ss	2	0	1	0	0	0	.500
Mike Marshall, ph	1	0	1	0	0	0	1.000
Randy Kutcher, pr	0	0	0	0	0	0	—
Marty Barrett, 2b	0	0	0	0	0	0	—
TOTALS	30	1	5	1	1	3	.167

	1 2 3	4 5 6	7 8 9	R H E
Athletics	0 0 0	0 0 0	1 1 7	9 13 0
Red Sox	0 0 0	1 0 0	0 0 0	1 5 1

E—Gray. DP—Athletics 1 (Lansford to Gallego to McGwire), Red Sox 1 (Reed to Rivera). LOB—Athletics 11, Red Sox 4. Scoring Position—Athletics 5-for-13, Red Sox 0-for-3. 2B—Lansford (1), Burks (1). HR—Boggs (1). S—McGee, Baines, Reed. SF—Henderson, Canseco. GDP—Pena. SB—Henderson (1), McGee (1), Canseco (1). CS—Gallego (1).

Athletics	IP	H	R	ER	BB	K	ERA
Dave Stewart (W, 1-0)	8.0	4	1	1	1	3	1.13
Dennis Eckersley	1.0	1	0	0	0	0	0.00

Red Sox	IP	H	R	ER	BB	K	ERA
Roger Clemens	6.0	4	0	0	4	4	0.00
Larry Andersen (BS, 1; L, 0-1)	1.0	2	2	2	1	0	18.00
Tom Bolton	0.1	0	0	0	0	0	0.00
Jeff Gray	0.2	3	2	1	1	0	13.50
Dennis Lamp	0.1	2	4	4	2	0	108.00
Rob Murphy	0.2	2	1	1	1	0	13.50

Andersen pitched to one batter in the 8th. Gray pitched to two batters in the 9th.

WP—Clemens. PB—Pena. Time—3:26. Attendance—35,192. Umpires—HP, Garcia. 1B, Hirschbeck. 2B, Evans. 3B, Cooney.

Game 2

Sunday, October 7

Athletics	AB	R	H	RBI	BB	K	Avg
Rickey Henderson, lf	5	0	1	0	0	0	.300
Willie McGee, cf	5	2	2	0	0	0	.222
Jose Canseco, rf	3	1	1	0	2	1	.400
Harold Baines, dh	5	0	2	3	0	0	.375
Lance Blankenship, pr-dh	0	0	0	0	0	0	—
Mark McGwire, 1b	5	0	2	1	0	1	.250
Carney Lansford, 3b	5	0	3	0	0	0	.600
Ron Hassey, c	3	0	1	0	1	0	.333
Walt Weiss, ss	4	0	0	0	0	1	.000
Willie Randolph, 2b	0	0	0	0	0	0	.500
Mike Gallego, 2b-ss	3	1	1	0	0	0	.500
TOTALS	38	4	13	4	3	3	.333

Red Sox	AB	R	H	RBI	BB	K	Avg
Jody Reed, 2b-ss	4	0	1	0	0	1	.143
Carlos Quintana, 1b	3	0	0	1	0	0	.000
Wade Boggs, 3b	4	0	2	0	0	1	.375
Ellis Burks, cf	3	0	1	0	1	0	.286
Mike Greenwell, lf	3	0	0	0	1	1	.000
Dwight Evans, dh	4	0	1	0	0	1	.167
Tom Brunansky, rf	3	0	0	0	1	1	.167
Tony Pena, c	4	0	0	0	0	0	.000
Luis Rivera, ss	2	1	1	0	0	1	.500
Mike Marshall, ph	1	0	0	0	0	0	.500
Marty Barrett, 2b	0	0	0	0	0	0	—
Danny Heep, ph	1	0	0	0	0	0	.000
TOTALS	32	1	6	1	3	6	.177

	1 2 3	4 5 6	7 8 9	R H E
Athletics	0 0 0	1 0 0	1 0 2	4 13 1
Red Sox	0 0 1	0 0 0	0 0 0	1 6 0

E—Weiss. DP—Athletics 1 (Weiss to Gallego to McGwire), Red Sox 2 (Reed to Rivera to Quintana; Quintana to Pena). LOB—Athletics 12, Red Sox 8. Scoring Position—Athletics 4-for-16, Red Sox 0-for-11. 2B—McGee (1), Baines (1), Evans (1), Rivera (1). SF—Quintana. GDP—Baines, Hassey, Pena. SB—McGee (2), Burks (1).

Athletics	IP	H	R	ER	BB	K	ERA
Bob Welch (W, 1-0)	7.1	6	1	1	3	4	1.23
Rick Honeycutt (H, 1)	0.1	0	0	0	0	0	0.00
Dennis Eckersley (S, 1)	1.1	0	0	0	0	2	0.00

Red Sox	IP	H	R	ER	BB	K	ERA
Dana Kiecker	5.2	6	1	1	1	2	1.59
Greg Harris (L, 0-1)	0.1	3	1	1	0	0	27.00
Larry Andersen	1.0	1	0	0	1	1	9.00
Jeff Reardon	2.0	3	2	2	1	0	9.00

Harris pitched to two batters in the 7th. Andersen pitched to one batter in the 8th.

HBP—Hassey by Reardon, Gallego by Kiecker. Time—3:42. Attendance—35,070. Umpires—HP, Hirschbeck. 1B, Evans. 2B, Cooney. 3B, Voltaggio.

Game 3

Tuesday, October 9

Red Sox	AB	R	H	RBI	BB	K	Avg
Jody Reed, 2b-ss	4	0	0	0	0	1	.091
Carlos Quintana, 1b	4	0	0	0	0	0	.000
Wade Boggs, 3b	4	0	2	0	0	0	.417
Ellis Burks, cf	4	0	1	0	0	0	.273
Mike Greenwell, lf	3	1	0	0	1	1	.000
Dwight Evans, dh	4	0	2	0	0	2	.300
Tom Brunansky, rf	3	0	0	1	0	1	.111
Tony Pena, c	4	0	3	0	0	0	.273
Randy Kutcher, pr	0	0	0	0	0	0	—
Luis Rivera, ss	2	0	0	0	0	1	.333
Mike Marshall, ph	1	0	0	0	0	0	.333
Marty Barrett, 2b	0	0	0	0	0	0	—
Danny Heep, ph	1	0	0	0	0	0	.000
TOTALS	34	1	8	1	1	6	.198

Athletics	AB	R	H	RBI	BB	K	Avg
Rickey Henderson, lf	4	0	1	0	0	0	.286
Carney Lansford, 3b	3	0	0	0	0	0	.462
Jose Canseco, rf	3	1	0	0	1	2	.250
Harold Baines, dh	3	2	1	0	1	0	.364
Mark McGwire, 1b	3	0	0	0	0	2	.182
Dave Henderson, cf	2	0	1	1	0	1	.500
Terry Steinbach, c	3	1	0	0	1	1	.375
Willie Randolph, 2b	4	0	2	2	0	0	.500
Mike Gallego, ss	3	0	1	0	0	1	.429
TOTALS	28	4	6	3	3	7	.350

	1 2 3	4 5 6	7 8 9	R H E
Red Sox	0 1 0	0 0 0	0 0 0	1 8 3
Athletics	0 0 0	2 0 2	0 0 x	4 6 0

E—Pena, Boddicker, Rivera. DP—Red Sox 1 (Boggs to Reed to Quintana). LOB—Red Sox 8, Athletics 7. Scoring Position—Red Sox 0-for-4, Athletics 2-for-10. 2B—Boggs (1). S—Lansford. SF—Brunansky, DHenderson. GDP—Steinbach. SB—Canseco (2), Baines (1), DHenderson (1). CS—RHenderson (1), Steinbach (1).

Red Sox	IP	H	R	ER	BB	K	ERA
Mike Boddicker (L, 0-1)	8.0	6	4	2	3	7	2.25

Athletics	IP	H	R	ER	BB	K	ERA
Mike Moore (W, 1-0)	6.0	4	1	1	1	5	1.50
Gene Nelson (H, 1)	1.2	3	0	0	0	0	0.00
Rick Honeycutt (H, 2)	0.1	0	0	0	0	0	0.00
Dennis Eckersley (S, 2)	1.0	1	0	0	0	1	0.00

HBP—DHenderson by Boddicker, McGwire by Boddicker. Time—2:47. Attendance—49,026. Umpires—HP, Evans. 1B, Cooney. 2B, Voltaggio. 3B, McCoy.

Game 4

Wednesday, October 10

Red Sox	AB	R	H	RBI	BB	K	Avg
Ellis Burks, cf	4	1	1	0	0	0	.267
Jody Reed, 2b	4	0	1	1	0	0	.133
Wade Boggs, 3b	4	0	2	0	0	0	.438
Mike Greenwell, lf	4	0	0	0	0	0	.000
Tony Pena, c	3	0	0	0	0	0	.214
Dwight Evans, dh	3	0	0	0	0	0	.231
Tom Brunansky, rf	3	0	0	0	0	1	.083
Carlos Quintana, 1b	2	0	0	0	1	0	.000
Luis Rivera, ss	3	0	0	0	0	0	.222
TOTALS	30	1	4	1	1	1	.182

Athletics	AB	R	H	RBI	BB	K	Avg
Rickey Henderson, lf	3	0	1	0	1	2	.294
Dave Henderson, cf	4	0	0	0	0	1	.167
Jose Canseco, rf	3	0	0	0	0	2	.182
Doug Jennings, rf	1	0	0	0	0	0	.000
Harold Baines, dh	3	0	1	0	0	1	.357
Willie McGee, pr-dh	0	0	0	0	0	0	.222
Ron Hassey, dh	0	0	0	0	1	0	.333
Lance Blankenship, pr-dh	0	0	0	0	0	0	—
Carney Lansford, 3b	3	1	1	0	0	1	.438
Terry Steinbach, c	3	0	2	0	0	0	.455
Mark McGwire, 1b	2	1	0	1	1	0	.154
Willie Randolph, 2b	2	1	0	0	1	0	.375
Mike Gallego, ss	3	0	1	2	0	0	.400
TOTALS	27	3	6	3	4	7	.311

	1 2 3	4 5 6	7 8 9	R H E
Red Sox	0 0 0	0 0 0	0 0 1	1 4 1
Athletics	0 3 0	0 0 0	0 0 x	3 6 0

E—Greenwell. DP—Red Sox 2 (Reed to Rivera to Quintana; Boggs to Quintana), Athletics 1 (Randolph to McGwire). LOB—Red Sox 3, Athletics 5. Scoring Position—Red Sox 1-for-1, Athletics 1-for-8. 2B—Burks (2), Gallego (1). S—Lansford. GDP—Boggs, DHenderson, Randolph. SB—RHenderson (2), Blankenship (1).

Red Sox	IP	H	R	ER	BB	K	ERA
Roger Clemens (L, 0-1)	1.2	3	3	3	1	0	3.52
Tom Bolton	2.2	2	0	0	2	3	0.00
Jeff Gray	2.2	1	0	0	0	2	2.70
Larry Andersen	1.0	0	0	0	1	2	6.00

Athletics	IP	H	R	ER	BB	K	ERA
Dave Stewart (W, 2-0)	8.0	4	1	1	1	1	1.13
Rick Honeycutt (S, 1)	1.0	0	0	0	0	0	0.00

Stewart pitched to two batters in the 9th.

Time—3:02. Attendance—49,052. Umpires—HP, Cooney. 1B, Voltaggio. 2B, McCoy. 3B, Garcia.

1990 AL Championship Series—Composite Statistics

Batting

Athletics	G	AB	R	H	RBI	2B	3B	HR	BB	SO	SB	CS	Avg	OBP	Slg
Harold Baines	4	14	2	5	3	1	0	0	2	1	1	0	.357	.438	.429
Lance Blankenship	3	0	1	0	0	0	0	0	0	0	1	0	—	—	—
Jose Canseco	4	11	3	2	1	0	0	0	5	5	2	0	.182	.412	.182
Mike Gallego	4	10	1	4	2	1	0	0	1	1	0	1	.400	.500	.500
Ron Hassey	2	3	0	1	0	0	0	0	2	0	0	0	.333	.667	.333
Dave Henderson	2	6	0	1	1	0	0	0	0	2	1	0	.167	.250	.167
Rickey Henderson	4	17	1	5	3	0	0	0	1	2	2	1	.294	.316	.294
Doug Jennings	1	1	0	0	0	0	0	0	0	0	0	0	.000	.000	.000
Carney Lansford	4	16	2	7	2	1	0	0	1	0	0	0	.438	.438	.500
Willie McGee	3	9	3	2	0	1	0	0	1	2	2	0	.222	.300	.333
Mark McGwire	4	13	2	2	2	0	0	0	3	3	0	0	.154	.353	.154
Jamie Quirk	1	1	0	1	0	0	0	0	0	0	0	1	1.000	1.000	1.000
Willie Randolph	4	8	1	3	3	0	0	0	1	0	0	0	.375	.444	.375
Terry Steinbach	3	11	2	5	1	0	0	0	1	2	0	1	.455	.500	.455
Walt Weiss	2	7	2	0	0	0	0	0	2	2	0	0	.000	.222	.000
Totals	4	127	20	38	18	4	0	0	19	21	9	3	.299	.399	.331

Red Sox	G	AB	R	H	RBI	2B	3B	HR	BB	SO	SB	CS	Avg	OBP	Slg
Wade Boggs	4	16	1	7	1	1	0	1	0	3	0	0	.438	.438	.688
Tom Brunansky	4	12	0	1	1	0	0	0	1	3	0	0	.083	.143	.083
Ellis Burks	4	15	1	4	0	2	0	0	1	1	1	0	.267	.313	.400
Dwight Evans	4	13	0	3	0	1	0	0	1	3	0	0	.231	.286	.308
Mike Greenwell	4	14	1	0	0	0	0	0	2	2	0	0	.000	.125	.000
Danny Heep	2	2	0	0	0	0	0	0	0	0	0	0	.000	.000	.000
Randy Kutcher	2	0	0	0	0	0	0	0	0	0	0	0	—	—	—
Mike Marshall	3	3	0	1	0	0	0	0	0	0	0	0	.333	.333	.333
Tony Pena	4	14	0	3	0	0	0	0	0	0	0	0	.214	.214	.214
Carlos Quintana	4	13	0	0	1	0	0	0	1	0	0	0	.000	.067	.000
Jody Reed	4	15	0	2	1	0	0	0	0	2	0	0	.133	.133	.133
Luis Rivera	4	9	1	2	0	0	0	0	0	2	0	0	.222	.222	.333
Totals	4	126	4	23	4	5	0	1	6	16	1	0	.183	.216	.246

Pitching

Athletics	G	GS	CG	IP	H	R	ER	BB	SO	W-L	Sv-Op	Hld	ERA
Dennis Eckersley	3	0	0	3.1	2	0	0	0	3	0-0	2-2	0	0.00
Rick Honeycutt	3	0	0	1.2	0	0	0	0	0	0-0	1-1	2	0.00
Mike Moore	1	1	0	6.0	4	1	1	1	5	1-0	0-0	0	1.50
Gene Nelson	1	0	0	1.2	3	0	0	0	0	0-0	0-0	1	0.00
Dave Stewart	2	2	0	16.0	8	2	2	2	4	2-0	0-0	0	1.13
Bob Welch	1	1	0	7.1	6	1	1	3	4	1-0	0-0	0	1.23
Totals	4	4	0	36.0	23	4	4	6	16	4-0	3-3	3	1.00

Red Sox	G	GS	CG	IP	H	R	ER	BB	SO	W-L	Sv-Op	Hld	ERA
Larry Andersen	3	0	0	3.0	3	2	2	3	3	0-1	0-1	0	6.00
Mike Boddicker	1	1	1	8.0	6	4	2	3	7	0-1	0-0	0	2.25
Tom Bolton	2	0	0	3.0	2	0	0	2	3	0-0	0-0	0	0.00
Roger Clemens	2	2	0	7.2	7	3	3	5	4	0-1	0-0	0	3.52
Jeff Gray	2	0	0	3.1	4	2	1	1	2	0-0	0-0	0	2.70
Greg Harris	1	0	0	0.1	3	1	1	0	0	0-1	0-0	0	27.00
Dana Kiecker	1	0	0	5.2	6	1	1	1	2	0-0	0-0	0	1.59
Dennis Lamp	1	0	0	0.1	2	4	4	2	0	0-0	0-0	0	108.00
Rob Murphy	1	0	0	0.2	2	1	1	1	0	0-0	0-0	0	13.50
Jeff Reardon	1	0	0	2.0	3	2	2	1	0	0-0	0-0	0	9.00
Totals	4	4	1	34.0	38	20	17	19	21	0-4	0-1	0	4.50

Fielding

Athletics	Pos	G	PO	Ast	E	DP	PB	FPct
Jose Canseco	rf	4	14	0	0	0	—	1.000
Dennis Eckersley	p	3	0	0	0	0	—	—
Mike Gallego	ss	3	3	5	0	0	—	1.000
	2b	2	5	4	0	2	—	1.000
Ron Hassey	c	1	6	0	0	0	0	1.000
Dave Henderson	cf	2	7	0	0	0	—	1.000
Rickey Henderson	lf	4	10	0	0	0	—	1.000
Rick Honeycutt	p	3	0	1	0	0	—	1.000
Doug Jennings	rf	1	0	0	0	0	—	—
Carney Lansford	3b	4	3	11	0	1	—	1.000
Willie McGee	cf	2	2	0	0	0	—	1.000
Mark McGwire	1b	4	40	0	0	3	—	1.000
Mike Moore	p	1	1	0	0	0	—	—
Gene Nelson	p	1	0	0	0	0	—	—
Willie Randolph	2b	4	5	9	0	1	—	1.000
Terry Steinbach	c	3	11	0	0	0	0	1.000
Dave Stewart	p	2	0	3	0	0	—	1.000
Walt Weiss	ss	2	2	7	1	1	—	.900
Bob Welch	p	1	0	3	0	0	—	1.000
Totals		4	108	43	1	8	0	.993

Red Sox	Pos	G	PO	Ast	E	DP	PB	FPct
Larry Andersen	p	3	1	0	0	0	—	1.000
Marty Barrett	2b	3	2	0	0	0	—	1.000
Mike Boddicker	p	1	0	2	1	0	—	.667
Wade Boggs	3b	4	6	10	0	2	—	1.000
Tom Bolton	p	2	0	0	0	0	—	—
Tom Brunansky	rf	4	13	0	0	0	—	1.000
Ellis Burks	cf	4	9	1	0	0	—	1.000
Roger Clemens	p	2	0	1	0	0	—	1.000
Jeff Gray	p	2	0	0	0	0	—	.000
Mike Greenwell	lf	4	3	0	1	0	—	.750
Greg Harris	p	1	0	0	0	0	—	—
Dana Kiecker	p	1	0	0	0	0	—	—
Dennis Lamp	p	1	0	0	0	0	—	—
Rob Murphy	p	1	0	0	0	0	—	—
Tony Pena	c	4	22	4	1	1	1	.963
Carlos Quintana	1b	4	29	2	0	5	—	1.000
Jeff Reardon	p	1	0	0	0	0	—	—
Jody Reed	2b	4	11	11	0	4	—	1.000
	ss	3	0	0	0	0	—	—
Luis Rivera	ss	4	6	16	1	3	—	.957
Totals		4	102	47	5	15	1	.968

1990 Cincinnati Reds (NL) 4, Pittsburgh Pirates (NL) 2

The Cincinnati Reds shut down the Pittsburgh Pirates' bats, earning a six-game victory in the NLCS. The Reds' bullpen blew it in Game 1, as Norm Charlton permitted the winning run to score in Pittsburgh's 4-3 victory. However, the Reds' bullpen would not allow another earned run for the remainder of the series. Paul O'Neill drove in both Reds runs in Game 2 and Tom Browning edged Doug Drabek, 2-1. Mariano Duncan hit a three-run homer and drove in four runs in Cincinnati's 6-3 win in Game 3. The Reds went up three games to one with a 5-3 win in Game 4, as Chris Sabo homered and drove in three runs. Drabek kept Pittsburgh alive with a gutty 3-2 win in the fifth game, but Danny Jackson and two relievers combined to one-hit the Pirates in Cincinnati's pennant-clinching 2-1 win in the sixth game.

Game 1

Thursday, October 4

Pirates	AB	R	H	RBI	BB	K	Avg
Wally Backman, 3b	2	0	0	0	1	1	.000
Jeff King, ph-3b	2	0	0	0	0	1	.000
Jay Bell, ss	3	0	0	0	1	1	.000
Andy Van Slyke, cf	4	0	1	1	0	2	.250
Bobby Bonilla, rf	4	0	1	0	0	1	.250
Barry Bonds, lf	3	1	1	0	1	0	.333
Sid Bream, 1b	3	1	2	2	1	1	.667
Mike LaValliere, c	3	1	0	0	1	1	.000
Jose Lind, 2b	4	0	1	1	0	1	.250
Bob Walk, p	2	0	0	0	0	2	.000
Gary Redus, ph	1	1	1	0	0	0	1.000
Stan Belinda, p	0	0	0	0	0	0	—
R.J. Reynolds, ph	1	0	0	0	0	1	.000
Bob Patterson, p	0	0	0	0	0	0	—
Ted Power, p	0	0	0	0	0	0	—
TOTALS	32	4	7	4	5	12	.219

Reds	AB	R	H	RBI	BB	K	Avg
Barry Larkin, ss	2	1	0	0	2	0	.000
Billy Hatcher, cf	3	0	0	0	0	2	.000
Hal Morris, 1b	3	1	1	1	0	0	.333
Todd Benzinger, ph	1	0	1	0	0	0	1.000
Eric Davis, lf	3	1	1	1	1	1	.333
Paul O'Neill, rf	3	0	1	1	0	0	.333
Ron Oester, ph	1	0	0	0	0	0	.000
Billy Bates, pr	0	0	0	0	0	0	—
Chris Sabo, 3b	4	0	1	0	0	2	.250
Jeff Reed, c	3	0	0	0	0	1	.000
Mariano Duncan, 2b	3	0	0	0	0	2	.000
Jose Rijo, p	2	0	0	0	0	1	.000
Norm Charlton, p	0	0	0	0	0	0	—
Herm Winningham, ph	1	0	0	0	0	0	.000
Rob Dibble, p	0	0	0	0	0	0	—
TOTALS	29	3	5	3	3	9	.172

	1	2	3	4	5	6	7	8	9	R	H	E
Pirates	0	0	1	2	0	0	1	0	0	4	7	1
Reds	3	0	0	0	0	0	0	0	0	3	5	0

E—Bonilla. DP—Reds 1 (Morris to Larkin to Charlton). LOB—Pirates 6, Reds 3. Scoring Position—Pirates 1-for-7, Reds 2-for-7. 2B—Van Slyke (1), Davis (1), O'Neill (1). 3B—Lind (1). HR—Bream (1). S—Hatcher. GDP—LaValliere. SB—Larkin (1), Redus (1). CS—Bates (1).

Pirates	IP	H	R	ER	BB	K	ERA
Bob Walk (W, 1-0)	6.0	4	3	3	2	5	4.50
Stan Belinda (H, 1)	2.0	0	0	0	0	3	0.00
Bob Patterson (H, 1)	0.1	1	0	0	1	0	0.00
Ted Power (S, 1)	0.2	0	0	0	0	1	0.00

Reds	IP	H	R	ER	BB	K	ERA
Jose Rijo	5.1	4	3	3	3	8	5.06
Norm Charlton (L, 0-1)	2.2	3	1	1	2	1	3.38
Rob Dibble	1.0	0	0	0	0	3	0.00

Time—2:51. Attendance—55,700. Umpires—HP, Wendelstedt. 1B, McSherry. 2B, Runge. 3B, Rennert.

Game 2

Friday, October 5

Pirates	AB	R	H	RBI	BB	K	Avg
Gary Redus, 1b	2	0	1	0	1	0	.667
Sid Bream, ph-1b	1	0	0	0	0	1	.500
Jay Bell, ss	3	0	2	0	1	0	.333
Andy Van Slyke, cf	4	0	1	0	0	0	.250
Bobby Bonilla, rf-3b	4	0	1	0	0	0	.250
Barry Bonds, lf	4	0	0	0	0	1	.143
Jeff King, 3b	0	0	0	0	1	0	.000
R.J. Reynolds, rf	3	0	0	0	0	1	.000
Don Slaught, c	2	0	0	0	0	0	.000
Wally Backman, ph	1	0	0	0	0	1	.000
Mike LaValliere, c	0	0	0	0	1	0	.000
Jose Lind, 2b	3	1	1	1	1	0	.286
Doug Drabek, p	3	0	0	0	0	1	.000
TOTALS	30	1	6	1	5	5	.217

Reds	AB	R	H	RBI	BB	K	Avg
Barry Larkin, ss	3	1	1	0	1	0	.200
Herm Winningham, cf	4	1	2	0	0	1	.400
Paul O'Neill, rf	4	0	2	2	0	1	.429
Eric Davis, lf	4	0	0	0	0	2	.143
Hal Morris, 1b	1	0	0	0	1	0	.250
Chris Sabo, 3b	3	0	0	0	0	0	.143
Joe Oliver, c	3	0	0	0	0	1	.000
Mariano Duncan, 2b	3	0	0	0	0	1	.000
Tom Browning, p	2	0	0	0	0	1	.000
Rob Dibble, p	1	0	0	0	0	1	.000
Randy Myers, p	0	0	0	0	0	0	—
TOTALS	28	2	5	2	2	8	.191

	1	2	3	4	5	6	7	8	9	R	H	E
Pirates	0	0	0	0	1	0	0	0	0	1	6	0
Reds	1	0	0	0	1	0	0	0	x	2	5	0

DP—Reds 1 (O'Neill to Sabo). LOB—Pirates 7, Reds 5. Scoring Position—Pirates 0-for-4, Reds 3-for-8. 2B—Winningham (1), O'Neill (2). HR—Lind (1). SB—Larkin (2), Winningham (1), O'Neill (1). CS—Redus (1), Winningham (1).

Pirates	IP	H	R	ER	BB	K	ERA
Doug Drabek (L, 0-1)	8.0	5	2	2	2	8	2.25

Reds	IP	H	R	ER	BB	K	ERA
Tom Browning (W, 1-0)	6.0	6	1	1	3	3	1.50
Rob Dibble (H, 1)	1.1	0	0	0	1	2	0.00
Randy Myers (S, 1)	1.2	0	0	0	1	0	0.00

HBP—Morris by Drabek. Time—2:38. Attendance—54,456. Umpires—HP, McSherry. 1B, Runge. 2B, Rennert. 3B, Crawford.

Game 3

Monday, October 8

Reds	AB	R	H	RBI	BB	K	Avg
Barry Larkin, ss	5	1	1	0	0	0	.200
Mariano Duncan, 2b	5	1	3	4	0	1	.273
Chris Sabo, 3b	5	0	1	0	0	2	.167
Eric Davis, lf	4	0	0	0	0	2	.091
Glenn Braggs, rf	4	0	1	0	0	1	.250
Todd Benzinger, 1b	4	0	1	0	0	0	.400
Joe Oliver, c	4	1	2	0	0	0	.286
Billy Bates, pr	0	1	0	0	0	0	—
Jeff Reed, c	0	0	0	0	0	0	.000
Billy Hatcher, cf	4	2	3	2	0	0	.429
Danny Jackson, p	1	0	0	0	0	1	.000
Rob Dibble, p	1	0	0	0	0	0	.000
Norm Charlton, p	0	0	0	0	0	0	—
Hal Morris, ph	1	0	1	0	0	0	.400
Randy Myers, p	0	0	0	0	0	0	—
TOTALS	38	6	13	6	0	7	.231

Pirates	AB	R	H	RBI	BB	K	Avg
Jeff King, 3b	5	0	1	0	0	3	.143
Jay Bell, ss	5	1	2	0	0	1	.364
Andy Van Slyke, cf	4	1	0	0	1	2	.167
Bobby Bonilla, rf	4	0	1	1	0	0	.250
Barry Bonds, lf	3	1	1	0	1	1	.200
Carmelo Martinez, 1b	4	0	1	1	0	1	.250
Don Slaught, c	2	0	1	0	2	0	.250
Jose Lind, 2b	4	0	1	0	0	1	.273
Zane Smith, p	2	0	0	0	0	1	.000
Bill Landrum, p	0	0	0	0	0	0	—
Gary Redus, ph	1	0	0	0	0	1	.500
John Smiley, p	0	0	0	0	0	0	—
R.J. Reynolds, ph	1	0	0	0	0	0	.000
Stan Belinda, p	0	0	0	0	0	0	—
TOTALS	35	3	8	2	4	11	.232

	1	2	3	4	5	6	7	8	9	R	H	E
Reds	0	2	0	0	3	0	0	0	1	6	13	1
Pirates	0	0	0	2	0	0	0	1	0	3	8	0

E—Duncan. DP—Pirates 1 (Bell to Lind to Martinez). LOB—Reds 6, Pirates 9. Scoring Position—Reds 3-for-7, Pirates 2-for-14. 2B—Hatcher (1), Bell (1), Martinez (1), Slaught (1), Lind (1). HR—Duncan (1), Hatcher (1). S—Jackson. GDP—Oliver.

Reds	IP	H	R	ER	BB	K	ERA
Danny Jackson (W, 1-0)	5.1	7	2	2	3	4	3.38
Rob Dibble (H, 2)	1.2	0	0	0	0	3	0.00
Norm Charlton (H, 1)	1.0	1	1	0	1	1	2.45
Randy Myers (S, 2)	1.0	0	0	0	0	3	0.00

Pirates	IP	H	R	ER	BB	K	ERA
Zane Smith (L, 0-1)	5.0	8	5	5	0	5	9.00
Bill Landrum	1.0	0	0	0	0	1	0.00
John Smiley	2.0	2	0	0	0	0	0.00
Stan Belinda	1.0	3	1	1	0	1	3.00

Time—2:51. Attendance—45,611. Umpires—HP, Runge. 1B, Rennert. 2B, Crawford. 3B, Davis.

Game 4
Tuesday, October 9

Reds	AB	R	H	RBI	BB	K	Avg
Barry Larkin, ss	5	0	0	0	0	1	.133
Billy Hatcher, cf	4	0	0	0	0	0	.273
Paul O'Neill, rf	4	1	3	1	0	0	.545
Eric Davis, lf	4	1	1	0	0	1	.133
Hal Morris, 1b	4	2	3	0	0	0	.556
Chris Sabo, 3b	3	1	2	3	0	0	.267
Jeff Reed, c	3	0	0	0	0	1	.000
Joe Oliver, c	1	0	0	0	0	0	.250
Mariano Duncan, 2b	3	0	1	0	0	2	.286
Todd Benzinger, ph	0	0	0	0	1	0	.400
Ron Oester, 2b	0	0	0	0	0	0	.000
Jose Rijo, p	3	0	0	0	0	0	.000
Randy Myers, p	0	0	0	0	0	0	—
Luis Quinones, ph	0	0	0	1	0	0	—
Rob Dibble, p	0	0	0	0	0	0	.000
TOTALS	34	5	10	5	1	5	.256

Pirates	AB	R	H	RBI	BB	K	Avg
Wally Backman, 3b	4	1	1	0	0	1	.143
Jay Bell, ss	4	1	1	1	0	1	.333
Andy Van Slyke, cf	4	1	1	1	0	1	.188
Bobby Bonilla, rf	3	0	1	0	1	0	.267
Barry Bonds, lf	4	0	1	0	0	2	.214
Sid Bream, 1b	3	0	1	1	1	1	.429
Mike LaValliere, c	3	0	0	0	1	0	.000
Jose Lind, 2b	4	0	2	0	0	1	.333
Bob Walk, p	2	0	0	0	0	2	.000
R.J. Reynolds, ph	0	0	0	0	1	0	.000
Ted Power, p	0	0	0	0	0	0	—
Jeff King, ph	1	0	0	0	0	1	.125
TOTALS	32	3	8	3	4	10	.223

	1	2	3	4	5	6	7	8	9	R	H	E
Reds	0	0	0	2	0	0	2	0	1	5	10	1
Pirates	1	0	0	1	0	0	0	1	0	3	8	0

E—Larkin. DP—Reds 1 (Larkin to Morris), Pirates 1 (Lind to Bream). LOB—Reds 5, Pirates 6. Scoring Position—Reds 1-for-4, Pirates 2-for-7. 2B—O'Neill (3), Morris (1), Backman (1), Bonilla (1), Bream (1). HR—O'Neill (1), Sabo (1), Bell (1). SF—Sabo, Quinones. GDP—Rijo, LaValliere. SB—Backman (1), Van Slyke (1), Bonds (1). CS—Bonilla (1).

Reds	IP	H	R	ER	BB	K	ERA
Jose Rijo (W, 1-0)	7.0	6	3	3	4	7	4.38
Randy Myers (H, 1)	1.0	2	0	0	0	1	0.00
Rob Dibble (S, 1)	1.0	0	0	0	0	2	0.00

Pirates	IP	H	R	ER	BB	K	ERA
Bob Walk (L, 1-1)	7.0	7	4	4	0	3	4.85
Ted Power	2.0	3	1	1	1	2	3.38

Rijo pitched to one batter in the 8th.

Time—3:00. Attendance—50,461. Umpires—HP, Rennert. 1B, Crawford. 2B. Davis. 3B, Wendelstedt.

Game 5
Wednesday, October 10

Reds	AB	R	H	RBI	BB	K	Avg
Barry Larkin, ss	4	1	2	1	0	0	.211
Herm Winningham, cf	2	0	0	1	1	0	.286
Paul O'Neill, rf	4	0	1	0	0	0	.467
Eric Davis, lf	4	0	1	0	0	3	.158
Hal Morris, 1b	3	0	0	0	0	0	.417
Chris Sabo, 3b	3	0	1	0	1	0	.278
Joe Oliver, c	2	0	0	0	0	0	.200
Ron Oester, ph	1	0	0	0	0	1	.000
Jeff Reed, c	1	0	0	0	0	0	.000
Mariano Duncan, 2b	3	0	1	0	0	1	.294
Tom Browning, p	1	0	0	0	0	0	.000
Todd Benzinger, ph	1	0	1	0	0	0	.500
Rick Mahler, p	0	0	0	0	0	0	—
Norm Charlton, p	0	0	0	0	0	0	—
Luis Quinones, ph	1	1	0	0	0	0	.000
Scott Scudder, p	0	0	0	0	0	0	—
TOTALS	30	2	7	2	2	5	.265

Pirates	AB	R	H	RBI	BB	K	Avg
Gary Redus, 1b	3	0	0	0	0	1	.286
Sid Bream, 1b	1	0	1	0	0	0	.500
Jay Bell, ss	2	1	0	0	1	0	.294
Andy Van Slyke, cf	4	1	2	1	0	1	.250
Bobby Bonilla, 3b	3	0	0	0	1	0	.222
Barry Bonds, lf	3	1	0	1	1	0	.176
R.J. Reynolds, rf	4	0	2	0	0	0	.222
Don Slaught, c	3	0	1	0	1	1	.143
Jose Lind, 2b	3	0	0	0	0	0	.278
Doug Drabek, p	3	0	1	0	0	1	.167
Bob Patterson, p	0	0	0	0	0	0	—
TOTALS	29	3	6	3	3	4	.252

	1	2	3	4	5	6	7	8	9	R	H	E
Reds	1	0	0	0	0	0	0	1	0	2	7	0
Pirates	2	0	0	1	0	0	0	0	x	3	6	1

E—Drabek. DP—Pirates 1 (Lind to Bell to Bream). LOB—Reds 5, Pirates 7. Scoring Position—Reds 1-for-3, Pirates 0-for-5. 2B—Larkin 2 (2). 3B—Van Slyke (1). S—Morris. SF—Winningham, Slaught. GDP—Larkin, Reed. SB—Bonds (2), Reynolds (1).

Reds	IP	H	R	ER	BB	K	ERA
Tom Browning (L, 1-1)	5.0	3	3	3	2		3.27
Rick Mahler	1.2	2	0	0	0	0	2.00
Norm Charlton	0.1	0	0	0	0	1	2.25
Scott Scudder	1.0	1	0	0	0	1	0.00

Pirates	IP	H	R	ER	BB	K	ERA
Doug Drabek (W, 1-1)	8.1	7	2	1	1	5	1.65
Bob Patterson (S, 1)	0.2	0	0	0	0	0	0.00

WP—Drabek. HBP—Bell by Browning. Time—2:48. Attendance—48,221. Umpires—HP, Crawford. 1B, Davis. 2B, Wendelstedt. 3B, McSherry.

Game 6
Friday, October 12

Pirates	AB	R	H	RBI	BB	K	Avg
Jeff King, 3b	2	0	0	0	0	0	.100
R.J. Reynolds, ph-rf	1	0	0	0	1	0	.200
Jay Bell, ss	3	0	0	0	1	0	.250
Andy Van Slyke, cf	4	0	0	0	0	1	.208
Bobby Bonilla, rf-3b	3	0	0	0	1	0	.190
Barry Bonds, lf	1	1	0	0	3	1	.167
Carmelo Martinez, 1b	4	0	1	1	0	0	.250
Don Slaught, c	4	0	0	0	0	2	.091
Jose Lind, 2b	3	0	0	0	0	1	.238
Ted Power, p	1	0	0	0	0	1	.000
Zane Smith, p	1	0	0	0	0	0	.000
Stan Belinda, p	0	0	0	0	0	0	—
Gary Redus, ph	1	0	0	0	0	1	.250
Bill Landrum, p	0	0	0	0	0	0	—
TOTALS	28	1	1	1	6	7	.194

Reds	AB	R	H	RBI	BB	K	Avg
Barry Larkin, ss	4	1	2	0	0	0	.261
Billy Hatcher, cf	4	0	2	0	0	0	.333
Paul O'Neill, rf	2	0	1	0	1	0	.471
Luis Quinones, ph	1	0	1	1	0	0	.500
Randy Myers, p	0	0	0	0	0	0	—
Eric Davis, lf	4	1	1	0	0	0	.174
Chris Sabo, 3b	4	0	0	0	0	0	.227
Todd Benzinger, 1b	3	0	0	0	1	0	.333
Mariano Duncan, 2b	3	0	1	0	0	1	.300
Norm Charlton, p	0	0	0	0	0	0	—
Glenn Braggs, rf	1	0	0	0	0	0	.200
Joe Oliver, c	4	0	0	0	0	1	.143
Danny Jackson, p	2	0	0	0	0	1	.000
Ron Oester, 2b	1	1	1	0	0	0	.333
TOTALS	33	2	9	2	2	3	.269

	1	2	3	4	5	6	7	8	9	R	H	E
Pirates	0	0	0	0	1	0	0	0	0	1	1	3
Reds	1	0	0	0	0	0	1	0	x	2	9	0

E—Slaught, Reynolds, Bell. LOB—Pirates 6, Reds 9. Scoring Position—Pirates 0-for-6, Reds 1-for-11. 2B—Martinez (2). SB—Larkin (3), Quinones (1). CS—Davis (1).

Pirates	IP	H	R	ER	BB	K	ERA
Ted Power	2.1	3	1	1	1	0	3.60
Zane Smith (L, 0-2)	4.0	6	1	1	1	3	6.00
Stan Belinda	0.2	0	0	0	0	0	2.45
Bill Landrum	1.0	0	0	0	0	0	0.00

Reds	IP	H	R	ER	BB	K	ERA
Danny Jackson	6.0	1	1	1	4	4	2.38
Norm Charlton (W, 1-1)	1.0	0	0	0	0	0	1.80
Randy Myers (S, 3)	2.0	0	0	0	2	3	0.00

Jackson pitched to two batters in the 7th.

Time—2:57. Attendance—56,079. Umpires—HP, Davis. 1B, Wendelstedt. 2B, McSherry. 3B, Runge.

1990 NL Championship Series—Composite Statistics

Batting

Reds	G	AB	R	H	RBI	2B	3B	HR	BB	SO	SB	CS	Avg	OBP	Slg
Billy Bates	2	0	1	0	0	0	0	0	0	0	0	1	—	—	—
Todd Benzinger	5	9	0	3	0	0	0	0	2	0	0	0	.333	.455	.333
Glenn Braggs	2	5	0	1	0	0	0	0	1	0	0	0	.200	.200	.200
Tom Browning	2	3	0	0	0	0	0	0	0	1	0	0	.000	.000	.000
Eric Davis	6	23	2	4	2	1	0	0	1	9	0	1	.174	.208	.217
Rob Dibble	4	2	0	0	0	0	0	0	0	1	0	0	.000	.000	.000
Mariano Duncan	6	20	1	6	4	0	0	1	0	8	0	0	.300	.300	.450
Billy Hatcher	4	15	2	5	2	1	0	1	0	2	0	0	.333	.333	.600
Danny Jackson	2	3	0	0	0	0	0	0	0	2	0	0	.000	.000	.000
Barry Larkin	6	23	5	6	1	2	0	0	3	1	3	0	.261	.346	.348
Hal Morris	5	12	3	5	1	1	0	0	1	0	0	0	.417	.500	.500
Paul O'Neill	5	17	1	8	4	3	0	1	1	1	1	0	.471	.500	.824
Ron Oester	4	3	1	1	0	0	0	0	0	1	0	0	.333	.333	.333
Joe Oliver	5	14	1	2	0	0	0	0	0	2	0	0	.143	.143	.143
Luis Quinones	3	2	1	1	2	0	0	0	0	0	1	0	.500	.333	.500
Jeff Reed	4	7	0	0	0	0	0	0	0	2	0	0	.000	.000	.000
Jose Rijo	2	5	0	0	0	0	0	0	0	1	0	0	.000	.000	.000
Chris Sabo	6	22	1	5	3	0	0	1	1	4	0	0	.227	.250	.364
Herm Winningham	3	7	1	2	1	1	0	0	1	1	1	1	.286	.333	.429
Totals	6	192	20	49	20	9	0	4	10	37	6	3	.255	.291	.365

Batting

Pirates	G	AB	R	H	RBI	2B	3B	HR	BB	SO	SB	CS	Avg	OBP	Slg
Wally Backman	3	7	1	1	0	1	0	0	1	3	1	0	.143	.250	.286
Jay Bell	6	20	3	5	1	1	0	1	4	3	0	0	.250	.400	.450
Barry Bonds	6	18	4	3	1	0	0	0	6	5	2	0	.167	.375	.167
Bobby Bonilla	6	21	0	4	1	1	0	0	3	1	0	1	.190	.292	.238
Sid Bream	4	8	1	4	3	1	0	1	2	3	0	0	.500	.600	1.000
Doug Drabek	2	6	0	1	0	0	0	0	0	2	0	0	.167	.167	.167
Jeff King	5	10	1	1	0	0	0	0	1	5	0	0	.100	.182	.100
Mike LaValliere	3	6	1	0	0	0	0	0	3	1	0	0	.000	.333	.000
Jose Lind	6	21	1	5	2	1	1	1	1	4	0	0	.238	.273	.524
Carmelo Martinez	2	8	0	2	2	2	0	0	0	1	0	0	.250	.250	.500
Ted Power	3	1	0	0	0	0	0	0	0	1	0	0	.000	.000	.000
Gary Redus	5	8	1	2	0	0	0	0	1	3	1	1	.250	.333	.250
R.J. Reynolds	6	10	0	2	0	0	0	0	2	2	1	0	.200	.333	.200
Don Slaught	4	11	0	1	1	1	0	0	2	3	0	0	.091	.214	.182
Zane Smith	2	3	0	0	0	0	0	0	0	1	0	0	.000	.000	.000
Andy Van Slyke	6	24	3	5	3	1	1	0	1	7	1	0	.208	.240	.333
Bob Walk	2	4	0	0	0	0	0	0	0	4	0	0	.000	.000	.000
Totals	6	186	15	36	14	9	2	3	27	49	6	2	.194	.298	.312

Pitching

Reds	G	GS	CG	IP	H	R	ER	BB	SO	W-L	Sv-Op	Hld	ERA
Tom Browning	2	2	0	11.0	9	4	4	6	5	1-1	0-0	0	3.27
Norm Charlton	4	0	0	5.0	4	2	1	3	3	1-1	0-0	1	1.80
Rob Dibble	4	0	0	5.0	0	0	0	1	10	0-0	1-1	2	0.00
Danny Jackson	2	2	0	11.1	8	3	3	7	8	1-0	0-0	0	2.38
Rick Mahler	1	0	0	1.2	2	0	0	0	0	0-0	0-0	0	0.00
Randy Myers	4	0	0	5.2	2	0	0	3	7	0-0	3-3	1	0.00
Jose Rijo	2	2	0	12.1	10	6	6	7	15	1-0	0-0	0	4.38
Scott Scudder	1	0	0	1.0	1	0	0	0	0	0-0	0-0	0	0.00
Totals	6	6	0	53.0	36	15	14	27	49	4-2	4-4	4	2.38

Pitching

Pirates	G	GS	CG	IP	H	R	ER	BB	SO	W-L	Sv-Op	Hld	ERA
Stan Belinda	3	0	0	3.2	3	1	1	0	4	0-0	0-0	1	2.45
Doug Drabek	2	2	1	16.1	12	4	3	3	13	1-1	0-0	0	1.65
Bill Landrum	2	0	0	2.0	0	0	0	0	1	0-0	0-0	0	0.00
Bob Patterson	2	0	0	1.0	1	0	0	2	0	0-0	1-1	1	0.00
Ted Power	3	1	0	5.0	6	2	2	2	3	0-0	1-1	0	3.60
John Smiley	1	0	0	2.0	2	0	0	0	0	0-0	0-0	0	0.00
Zane Smith	2	1	0	9.0	14	6	6	1	8	0-2	0-0	0	6.00
Bob Walk	2	2	0	13.0	11	7	7	2	8	1-1	0-0	0	4.85
Totals	6	6	1	52.0	49	20	19	10	37	2-4	2-2	2	3.29

Fielding

Reds	Pos	G	PO	Ast	E	DP	PB	FPct
Todd Benzinger	1b	2	17	0	0	0	—	1.000
Glenn Braggs	rf	2	2	0	0	0	—	1.000
Tom Browning	p	2	1	1	0	0	—	1.000
Norm Charlton	p	4	1	0	0	1	—	1.000
Eric Davis	lf	6	12	1	0	0	—	1.000
Rob Dibble	p	4	0	0	0	0	—	—
Mariano Duncan	2b	6	6	11	1	0	—	.944
Billy Hatcher	cf	4	5	1	0	0	—	1.000
Danny Jackson	p	2	0	2	0	0	—	1.000
Barry Larkin	ss	6	21	15	1	2	—	.973
Rick Mahler	p	1	0	0	0	0	—	—
Hal Morris	1b	4	20	2	0	2	—	1.000
Randy Myers	p	4	0	0	0	0	—	—
Paul O'Neill	rf	5	9	2	0	1	—	1.000
Ron Oester	2b	2	0	1	0	0	—	1.000
Joe Oliver	c	5	27	1	0	0	0	1.000
Jeff Reed	c	4	24	1	0	0	0	1.000
Jose Rijo	p	2	0	0	0	0	—	—
Chris Sabo	3b	6	7	7	0	1	—	1.000
Scott Scudder	p	1	0	0	0	0	—	—
Herm Winningham	cf	2	7	0	0	0	—	1.000
Totals		6	159	45	2	7	0	.990

Fielding

Pirates	Pos	G	PO	Ast	E	DP	PB	FPct
Wally Backman	3b	2	1	3	0	0	—	1.000
Stan Belinda	p	3	0	0	0	0	—	—
Jay Bell	ss	6	4	22	1	2	—	.963
Barry Bonds	lf	6	13	0	0	0	—	1.000
Bobby Bonilla	rf	5	3	0	1	0	—	.750
	3b	3	1	5	0	1	—	1.000
Sid Bream	1b	4	26	3	0	3	—	1.000
Doug Drabek	p	2	1	6	1	0	—	.875
Jeff King	3b	4	1	4	0	0	—	1.000
Bill Landrum	p	2	0	0	0	0	—	—
Mike LaValliere	c	3	17	2	0	0	0	1.000
Jose Lind	2b	6	19	19	0	4	—	1.000
Carmelo Martinez	1b	2	15	1	0	0	—	1.000
Bob Patterson	p	2	0	1	0	0	—	1.000
Ted Power	p	3	0	1	0	0	—	1.000
Gary Redus	1b	2	16	0	0	0	—	1.000
R.J. Reynolds	rf	3	2	0	1	0	—	.667
Don Slaught	c	4	22	1	1	0	0	.958
John Smiley	p	1	0	0	0	0	—	—
Zane Smith	p	2	0	1	0	0	—	1.000
Andy Van Slyke	cf	6	13	1	0	0	—	1.000
Bob Walk	p	2	2	1	0	0	—	1.000
Totals		6	156	71	5	11	0	.978

1991 Minnesota Twins (AL) 4, Toronto Blue Jays (AL) 1

The Minnesota Twins rolled to a surprisingly easy five-game victory over the Toronto Blue Jays in the ALCS. Toronto started knuckleballer Tom Candiotti in Game 1, but the Twins got to him early and held on for a 5-4 victory. The Blue Jays took Game 2 by the score of 5-2 behind rookie Juan Guzman, and things looked promising for Toronto when they took an early 2-0 lead in the third game. The Twins eventually tied it up, however, and Mike Pagliarulo won it for Minnesota with a pinch-hit home run in the top of the 10th. The Twins' bats came to life in the final two games, as they finished off Toronto, winning 9-3 and 8-5. Kirby Puckett went 6-for-9 in the final two games to finish with a .429 batting average, two home runs and six RBI.

Game 1

Tuesday, October 8

Blue Jays	AB	R	H	RBI	BB	K	Avg
Devon White, cf	4	1	1	0	0	1	.250
Roberto Alomar, 2b	4	1	2	0	0	1	.500
Joe Carter, rf	4	2	2	0	0	1	.500
John Olerud, 1b	4	0	2	2	0	0	.500
Rene Gonzales, pr-1b	0	0	0	0	0	0	—
Kelly Gruber, 3b	4	0	2	2	0	2	.500
Candy Maldonado, lf	4	0	0	0	0	2	.000
Rance Mulliniks, dh	4	0	0	0	0	0	.000
Pat Borders, c	4	0	0	0	0	0	.000
Manuel Lee, ss	3	0	0	0	0	2	.000
TOTALS	35	4	9	4	0	8	.257

Twins	AB	R	H	RBI	BB	K	Avg
Dan Gladden, lf	5	1	2	0	0	1	.400
Chuck Knoblauch, 2b	3	1	2	1	1	0	.667
Kirby Puckett, cf	4	0	0	0	0	1	.000
Kent Hrbek, 1b	4	0	1	0	0	0	.250
Chili Davis, dh	2	1	1	2	2	0	.500
Brian Harper, c	4	0	2	0	0	1	.500
Junior Ortiz, c	0	0	0	0	0	0	—
Shane Mack, rf	3	1	2	1	1	1	.667
Mike Pagliarulo, 3b	2	0	0	0	0	0	.000
Scott Leius, ph-3b	1	0	0	0	0	1	.000
Gene Larkin, ph	1	0	0	0	0	0	.000
Al Newman, 3b	0	0	0	0	0	0	—
Greg Gagne, ss	4	1	1	1	0	1	.250
TOTALS	33	5	11	5	4	6	.333

	1	2	3	4	5	6	7	8	9		R	H	E
Blue Jays	0	0	0	1	0	3	0	0	0		4	9	3
Twins	2	2	1	0	0	0	0	0	x		5	11	0

E—Gruber 2, Borders. DP—Blue Jays 1 (Alomar to Olerud). LOB—Blue Jays 4, Twins 8. Scoring Position—Blue Jays 3-for-8, Twins 4-for-12. 2B—Carter (1), Harper (1), Mack (1). GDP—Hrbek. SB—Gruber (1), Knoblauch 2 (2), Davis (1), Mack (1). CS—Knoblauch (1), Mack (1).

Blue Jays	IP	H	R	ER	BB	K	ERA
Tom Candiotti (L, 0-1)	2.2	8	5	5	1	2	16.88
David Wells	3.0	2	0	0	2	2	0.00
Mike Timlin	2.1	1	0	0	1	2	0.00

Twins	IP	H	R	ER	BB	K	ERA
Jack Morris (W, 1-0)	5.1	8	4	4	0	4	6.75
Carl Willis (H, 1)	2.1	0	0	0	0	2	0.00
Rick Aguilera (S, 1)	1.1	1	0	0	0	2	0.00

Time—3:17. Attendance—54,766. Umpires—HP, Barnett. 1B, Johnson. 2B, Roe. 3B, Welke.

Game 2

Wednesday, October 9

Blue Jays	AB	R	H	RBI	BB	K	Avg
Devon White, cf	4	3	2	0	1	1	.375
Roberto Alomar, 2b	3	1	2	0	0	0	.571
Joe Carter, rf	3	0	1	2	0	0	.429
John Olerud, 1b	4	0	0	0	0	1	.250
Kelly Gruber, 3b	4	0	2	2	0	1	.500
Candy Maldonado, lf	4	0	0	0	0	1	.000
Rance Mulliniks, dh	2	0	1	0	1	0	.167
Pat Tabler, ph-dh	1	0	0	0	0	1	.000
Pat Borders, c	4	0	1	0	0	0	.125
Manuel Lee, ss	3	1	0	0	1	1	.000
TOTALS	32	5	9	4	3	5	.269

Twins	AB	R	H	RBI	BB	K	Avg
Dan Gladden, lf	3	0	0	0	1	0	.250
Chuck Knoblauch, 2b	3	2	2	0	1	1	.667
Kirby Puckett, cf	3	0	1	1	1	0	.143
Kent Hrbek, 1b	4	0	0	0	0	1	.125
Chili Davis, dh	3	0	0	0	1	2	.200
Brian Harper, c	4	0	1	1	0	0	.375
Shane Mack, rf	3	0	0	0	0	1	.333
Gene Larkin, ph	1	0	0	0	0	1	.000
Mike Pagliarulo, 3b	4	0	0	0	0	1	.000
Greg Gagne, ss	3	0	1	0	0	1	.286
TOTALS	31	2	5	2	4	8	.254

	1	2	3	4	5	6	7	8	9		R	H	E
Blue Jays	1	0	2	0	0	0	2	0	0		5	9	0
Twins	0	0	1	0	0	1	0	0	0		2	5	1

E—Mack. DP—Blue Jays 1 (Lee to Olerud), Twins 1 (Pagliarulo to Knoblauch to Hrbek). LOB—Blue Jays 5, Twins 6. Scoring Position—Blue Jays 4-for-9, Twins 2-for-6. 2B—White (1). S—Alomar. SF—Carter. GDP—Borders, Gladden. SB—White (1), Alomar (1), Gladden (1). CS—Carter (1).

Blue Jays	IP	H	R	ER	BB	K	ERA
Juan Guzman (W, 1-0)	5.2	4	2	2	4	2	3.18
Tom Henke (H, 1)	1.1	0	0	0	0	2	0.00
Duane Ward (S, 1)	2.0	1	0	0	0	4	0.00

Twins	IP	H	R	ER	BB	K	ERA
Kevin Tapani (L, 0-1)	6.1	8	4	4	2	5	5.68
Steve Bedrosian	0.1	1	1	0	1	0	0.00
Mark Guthrie	2.1	0	0	0	0	0	0.00

WP—Guzman. Time—3:02. Attendance—54,816. Umpires—HP, Johnson. 1B, Roe. 2B, Welke. 3B, Reilly.

Game 3

Friday, October 11

Twins	AB	R	H	RBI	BB	K	Avg
Dan Gladden, lf	5	0	0	0	0	0	.154
Chuck Knoblauch, 2b	5	1	2	0	0	0	.545
Kirby Puckett, cf	5	0	2	1	0	1	.250
Chili Davis, dh	4	0	1	0	0	2	.222
Shane Mack, rf	4	1	1	0	0	1	.300
Kent Hrbek, 1b	3	0	0	1	1	1	.091
Greg Gagne, ss	2	0	0	0	1	1	.222
Paul Sorrento, ph	1	0	0	0	0	1	.000
Al Newman, ss	0	0	0	0	0	0	—
Junior Ortiz, c	3	0	0	0	0	0	.000
Gene Larkin, ph	1	0	0	0	0	0	.000
Brian Harper, c	0	0	0	0	0	0	.375
Scott Leius, 3b	3	0	0	0	0	0	.000
Mike Pagliarulo, ph-3b	1	1	1	1	0	0	.143
TOTALS	37	3	7	3	2	7	.228

Blue Jays	AB	R	H	RBI	BB	K	Avg
Devon White, cf	5	0	1	0	0	0	.308
Roberto Alomar, 2b	3	0	1	0	1	1	.500
Joe Carter, rf	3	1	1	1	1	2	.400
Rob Ducey, pr-rf	1	0	0	0	0	0	.000
John Olerud, 1b	2	1	0	0	3	0	.200
Kelly Gruber, 3b	5	0	1	0	0	1	.385
Candy Maldonado, lf	4	0	1	1	1	1	.083
Rance Mulliniks, dh	1	0	0	1	1	0	.143
Pat Tabler, ph	0	0	0	0	1	0	.000
Mookie Wilson, pr-dh	1	0	0	0	0	0	.000
Pat Borders, c	3	0	0	0	0	0	.091
Manuel Lee, ss	4	0	0	0	0	0	.000
TOTALS	32	2	5	2	8	6	.232

	1	2	3	4	5	6	7	8	9	10		R	H	E
Twins	0	0	0	0	1	1	0	0	0	1		3	7	0
Blue Jays	2	0	0	0	0	0	0	0	0	0		2	5	1

E—Timlin. DP—Twins 1 (Leius to Knoblauch to Hrbek), Blue Jays 2 (Key to Lee to Olerud; Alomar to Olerud). LOB—Twins 6, Blue Jays 10. Scoring Position—Twins 1-for-7, Blue Jays 1-for-9. 2B—Knoblauch (1), Puckett (1), Maldonado (1). 3B—Mack (1). HR—Carter (1), Pagliarulo (1). S—Alomar, Borders. GDP—Ortiz, Borders.

Twins	IP	H	R	ER	BB	K	ERA
Scott Erickson	4.0	3	2	2	5	2	4.50
David West	2.2	1	0	0	3	3	0.00
Carl Willis	2.0	1	0	0	0	1	0.00
Mark Guthrie (W, 1-0)	0.1	0	0	0	0	0	0.00
Rick Aguilera (S, 2)	1.0	0	0	0	0	0	0.00

Blue Jays	IP	H	R	ER	BB	K	ERA
Jimmy Key	6.0	5	2	2	1	1	3.00
David Wells	1.2	1	0	0	0	2	0.00
Tom Henke	1.1	0	0	0	1	3	0.00
Mike Timlin (L, 0-1)	1.0	1	1	1	1	0	2.70

Erickson pitched to one batter in the 5th.

WP—West 2. Time—3:36. Attendance—51,454. Umpires—HP, Roe. 1B, Welke. 2B, Reilly. 3B, McKean.

Postseason: League Championship Series

Game 4

Saturday, October 12

Twins	AB	R	H	RBI	BB	K	Avg
Dan Gladden, lf	5	1	3	3	0	1	.278
Chuck Knoblauch, 2b	5	0	0	0	0	2	.375
Kirby Puckett, cf	4	2	3	2	0	0	.375
Kent Hrbek, 1b	5	0	0	0	0	1	.063
Chili Davis, dh	4	1	2	0	1	2	.308
Jarvis Brown, pr-dh	0	1	0	0	0	0	—
Brian Harper, c	5	1	1	0	0	0	.308
Shane Mack, rf	3	1	1	1	1	1	.308
Mike Pagliarulo, 3b	4	2	2	2	0	0	.273
Scott Leius, ph-3b	0	0	0	0	1	0	.000
Greg Gagne, ss	4	0	1	0	0	2	.231
TOTALS	39	9	13	8	3	9	.271

Blue Jays	AB	R	H	RBI	BB	K	Avg
Devon White, cf	5	0	2	0	0	0	.333
Roberto Alomar, 2b	5	0	2	1	0	0	.467
Joe Carter, dh	5	0	0	0	0	3	.267
John Olerud, 1b	5	0	1	0	0	0	.200
Kelly Gruber, 3b	4	1	1	0	0	0	.353
Candy Maldonado, rf	4	1	1	0	0	0	.125
Pat Borders, c	4	0	3	2	0	0	.267
Manuel Lee, ss	3	0	0	0	0	1	.000
Rance Mulliniks, ph	0	1	0	0	1	0	.143
Mookie Wilson, lf	3	0	1	0	1	1	.250
TOTALS	38	3	11	3	2	5	.252

	1	2	3	4	5	6	7	8	9		R	H	E
Twins	0	0	0	4	0	2	1	1	1		9	13	1
Blue Jays	0	1	0	0	0	1	0	0	1		3	11	2

E—Gagne, Gruber, Lee. LOB—Twins 9, Blue Jays 10. Scoring Position—Twins 4-for-13, Blue Jays 3-for-16. 2B—Davis 2 (2), Harper (2), Pagliarulo (1), Gruber (1), Borders (1). HR—Puckett (1). SF—Puckett, Mack. SB—Gladden (2), White (2), Alomar (2). CS—Gagne (1).

Twins	IP	H	R	ER	BB	K	ERA
Jack Morris (W, 2-0)	8.0	9	2	2	1	3	4.05
Steve Bedrosian	1.0	2	1	0	1	2	0.00

Blue Jays	IP	H	R	ER	BB	K	ERA
Todd Stottlemyre (L, 0-1)	3.2	7	4	4	1	3	9.82
David Wells	1.2	2	2	2	0	3	2.84
Jim Acker	0.2	1	0	0	0	1	0.00
Mike Timlin	2.0	2	2	0	1	2	1.69
Bob MacDonald	1.0	1	1	1	1	0	9.00

WP—Morris 2. HBP—Gagne by Stottlemyre. Time—3:15. Attendance—51,526. Umpires—HP, Welke. 1B, Reilly. 2B, McKean. 3B, Barnett.

Game 5

Sunday, October 13

Twins	AB	R	H	RBI	BB	K	Avg
Dan Gladden, lf	5	2	1	0	0	1	.261
Chuck Knoblauch, 2b	4	1	1	2	1	0	.350
Kirby Puckett, cf	5	2	3	2	0	2	.429
Kent Hrbek, 1b	5	0	2	2	0	0	.143
Chili Davis, dh	4	1	1	0	1	2	.294
Brian Harper, c	5	0	1	0	0	1	.278
Junior Ortiz, c	0	0	0	0	0	0	.000
Shane Mack, rf	5	1	2	1	0	1	.333
Mike Pagliarulo, 3b	4	1	2	0	0	0	.333
Greg Gagne, ss	4	0	1	0	0	0	.235
TOTALS	41	8	14	7	2	7	.289

Blue Jays	AB	R	H	RBI	BB	K	Avg
Devon White, cf	4	1	2	0	1	1	.364
Roberto Alomar, 2b	4	1	2	3	1	1	.474
Joe Carter, dh	4	0	1	1	0	0	.263
John Olerud, 1b	4	0	0	1	0	0	.158
Kelly Gruber, 3b	4	0	0	0	0	0	.286
Candy Maldonado, rf	4	0	0	0	0	2	.100
Pat Borders, c	4	0	1	0	0	0	.263
Manuel Lee, ss	3	2	2	0	0	0	.125
Rance Mulliniks, ph	1	0	0	0	0	0	.125
Rene Gonzales, ss	0	0	0	0	0	0	—
Mookie Wilson, lf	4	1	1	0	0	2	.250
TOTALS	36	5	9	5	2	6	.251

	1	2	3	4	5	6	7	8	9		R	H	E
Twins	1	1	0	0	0	3	0	3	0		8	14	2
Blue Jays	0	0	3	2	0	0	0	0	0		5	9	1

E—Harper, Gagne, Borders. DP—Twins 1 (Knoblauch to Gagne to Hrbek), Blue Jays 1 (Candiotti to Lee to Olerud). LOB—Twins 9, Blue Jays 6. Scoring Position—Twins 5-for-14, Blue Jays 3-for-9. 2B—Knoblauch (2), Carter (2). HR—Puckett (2). S—Pagliarulo. GDP—Gagne, Mulliniks. SB—Gladden (3), Mack (2), White (3), Wilson (1). CS—Gagne (2).

Twins	IP	H	R	ER	BB	K	ERA
Kevin Tapani	4.0	8	5	5	1	4	7.84
David West (W, 1-0)	3.0	0	0	0	1	1	0.00
Carl Willis (H, 2)	1.0	1	0	0	0	0	0.00
Rick Aguilera (S, 3)	1.0	0	0	0	0	1	0.00

Blue Jays	IP	H	R	ER	BB	K	ERA
Tom Candiotti	5.0	9	4	2	1	3	8.22
Mike Timlin (BS, 1)	0.1	1	1	1	0	0	3.18
Duane Ward (L, 0-1)	2.1	3	3	3	1	2	6.23
David Wells	1.1	1	0	0	0	2	2.35

Candiotti pitched to three batters in the 6th.

WP—Candiotti. PB—Borders 2. Time—3:29. Attendance—51,425. Umpires—HP, Reilly. 1B, McKean. 2B, Barnett. 3B, Johnson.

1991 AL Championship Series—Composite Statistics

Batting

Twins	G	AB	R	H	RBI	2B	3B	HR	BB	SO	SB	CS	Avg	OBP	Slg
Jarvis Brown	1	0	1	0	0	0	0	0	0	0	0	0	—	—	—
Chili Davis	5	17	3	5	2	2	0	0	5	8	1	0	.294	.455	.412
Greg Gagne	5	17	1	4	1	0	0	0	1	5	0	2	.235	.316	.235
Dan Gladden	5	23	4	6	3	0	0	0	1	3	3	0	.261	.292	.261
Brian Harper	5	18	1	5	1	2	0	0	0	2	0	0	.278	.278	.389
Kent Hrbek	5	21	0	3	3	0	0	0	1	3	0	0	.143	.182	.143
Chuck Knoblauch	5	20	5	7	3	2	0	0	3	3	2	1	.350	.435	.450
Gene Larkin	3	3	0	0	0	0	0	0	1	0	0	0	.000	.000	.000
Scott Leius	3	4	0	0	0	0	0	0	1	1	0	0	.000	.200	.000
Shane Mack	5	18	4	6	3	1	1	0	2	4	2	1	.333	.381	.500
Junior Ortiz	3	3	0	0	0	0	0	0	0	0	0	0	.000	.000	.000
Mike Pagliarulo	5	15	4	5	3	1	0	1	0	2	0	0	.333	.333	.600
Kirby Puckett	5	21	4	9	6	1	0	2	1	4	0	0	.429	.435	.762
Paul Sorrento	1	1	0	0	0	0	0	0	0	1	0	0	.000	.000	.000
Totals	5	181	27	50	25	9	1	3	15	37	8	4	.276	.332	.387

Batting

Blue Jays	G	AB	R	H	RBI	2B	3B	HR	BB	SO	SB	CS	Avg	OBP	Slg
Roberto Alomar	5	19	3	9	4	0	0	0	2	3	2	0	.474	.524	.474
Pat Borders	5	19	0	5	2	1	0	0	0	0	0	0	.263	.263	.316
Joe Carter	5	19	3	5	4	2	0	1	1	5	0	1	.263	.286	.526
Rob Ducey	1	1	0	0	0	0	0	0	0	0	0	0	.000	.000	.000
Kelly Gruber	5	21	1	6	4	1	0	0	0	4	1	0	.286	.286	.333
Manuel Lee	5	16	3	2	0	0	0	0	1	5	0	0	.125	.176	.125
Candy Maldonado	5	20	1	2	1	1	0	0	1	6	0	0	.100	.143	.150
Rance Mulliniks	5	8	1	1	0	0	0	0	3	0	0	0	.125	.364	.125
John Olerud	5	19	1	3	3	0	0	0	3	1	0	0	.158	.273	.158
Pat Tabler	2	1	0	0	0	0	0	0	1	0	0	0	.000	.500	.000
Devon White	5	22	5	8	0	1	0	0	2	3	3	0	.364	.417	.409
Mookie Wilson	3	8	1	2	0	0	0	0	1	3	1	0	.250	.333	.250
Totals	5	173	19	43	18	6	0	1	15	30	7	1	.249	.307	.301

Pitching

Twins	G	GS	CG	IP	H	R	ER	BB	SO	W-L	Sv-Op	Hld	ERA
Rick Aguilera	3	0	0	3.1	1	0	0	0	3	0-0	3-3	0	0.00
Steve Bedrosian	2	0	0	1.1	3	2	0	2	0	0-0	0-0	0	0.00
Scott Erickson	1	1	0	4.0	3	2	2	5	2	0-0	0-0	0	4.50
Mark Guthrie	2	0	0	2.2	0	0	0	0	0	1-0	0-0	0	0.00
Jack Morris	2	2	0	13.1	17	6	6	1	7	2-0	0-0	0	4.05
Kevin Tapani	2	2	0	10.1	16	9	9	3	9	0-1	0-0	0	7.84
David West	2	0	0	5.2	1	0	0	4	4	1-0	0-0	0	0.00
Carl Willis	3	0	0	5.1	2	0	0	0	3	0-0	0-0	2	0.00
Totals	5	5	0	46.0	43	19	17	15	30	4-1	3-3	2	3.33

Pitching

Blue Jays	G	GS	CG	IP	H	R	ER	BB	SO	W-L	Sv-Op	Hld	ERA
Jim Acker	1	0	0	0.2	1	0	0	0	1	0-0	0-0	0	0.00
Tom Candiotti	2	2	0	7.2	17	9	7	2	5	0-1	0-0	0	8.22
Juan Guzman	1	1	0	5.2	4	2	2	4	2	1-0	0-0	0	3.18
Tom Henke	2	0	0	2.2	0	0	0	1	5	0-0	0-0	1	0.00
Jimmy Key	1	1	0	6.0	5	2	2	1	1	0-0	0-0	0	3.00
Bob MacDonald	1	0	0	1.0	1	1	1	1	0	0-0	0-0	0	9.00
Todd Stottlemyre	1	1	0	3.2	7	4	4	1	3	0-1	0-0	0	9.82
Mike Timlin	4	0	0	5.2	5	4	2	2	5	0-1	0-1	0	3.18
Duane Ward	2	0	0	4.1	4	3	3	1	6	0-1	1-1	0	6.23
David Wells	4	0	0	7.2	6	2	2	2	9	0-0	0-0	0	2.35
Totals	5	5	0	45.0	50	27	23	15	37	1-4	1-2	1	4.60

Fielding

Twins	Pos	G	PO	Ast	E	DP	PB	FPct
Rick Aguilera	p	3	0	0	0	0	—	—
Steve Bedrosian	p	2	0	0	0	0	—	—
Scott Erickson	p	1	1	1	0	0	—	1.000
Greg Gagne	ss	5	9	9	2	1	—	.900
Dan Gladden	lf	5	20	0	0	0	—	1.000
Mark Guthrie	p	2	0	1	0	0	—	1.000
Brian Harper	c	5	23	1	1	0	0	.960
Kent Hrbek	1b	5	40	7	0	3	—	1.000
Chuck Knoblauch	2b	5	8	14	0	3	—	1.000
Scott Leius	3b	3	1	4	0	1	—	1.000
Shane Mack	rf	5	3	0	1	0	—	.750
Jack Morris	p	2	3	2	0	0	—	1.000
Al Newman	3b	1	0	0	0	0	—	—
	ss	1	0	0	0	0	—	—
Junior Ortiz	c	3	10	0	0	0	0	1.000
Mike Pagliarulo	3b	5	4	10	0	1	—	1.000
Kirby Puckett	cf	5	13	1	0	0	—	1.000
Kevin Tapani	p	2	3	0	0	0	—	1.000
David West	p	2	0	0	0	0	—	—
Carl Willis	p	3	0	0	0	0	—	—
Totals		5	138	50	4	9	0	.979

Fielding

Blue Jays	Pos	G	PO	Ast	E	DP	PB	FPct
Jim Acker	p	1	0	0	0	0	—	—
Roberto Alomar	2b	5	14	9	0	2	—	1.000
Pat Borders	c	5	38	3	2	0	2	.953
Tom Candiotti	p	2	0	2	0	1	—	1.000
Joe Carter	rf	3	4	1	0	0	—	1.000
Rob Ducey	rf	1	0	0	0	0	—	—
Rene Gonzales	1b	1	2	0	0	0	—	1.000
	ss	1	0	0	0	0	—	—
Kelly Gruber	3b	5	3	6	3	0	—	.750
Juan Guzman	p	1	0	0	0	0	—	—
Tom Henke	p	2	0	2	0	0	—	1.000
Jimmy Key	p	1	0	3	0	1	—	1.000
Manuel Lee	ss	5	8	16	1	3	—	.960
Bob MacDonald	p	1	0	0	0	0	—	—
Candy Maldonado	lf	3	1	0	0	0	—	1.000
	rf	2	3	0	0	0	—	1.000
John Olerud	1b	5	40	3	0	5	—	1.000
Todd Stottlemyre	p	1	1	0	0	0	—	1.000
Mike Timlin	p	4	0	2	1	0	—	.667
Duane Ward	p	2	0	0	0	0	—	—
David Wells	p	4	1	1	0	0	—	1.000
Devon White	cf	5	16	0	0	0	—	1.000
Mookie Wilson	lf	2	4	0	0	0	—	1.000
Totals		5	135	48	7	12	2	.963

1991 Atlanta Braves (NL) 4, Pittsburgh Pirates (NL) 3

In a hard-fought series that featured many dramatic moments, the Atlanta Braves edged the Pittsburgh Pirates, four games to three, for the NL pennant (the two teams would meet in the following year's NLCS with eerily similar results). Jim Leyland selected Doug Drabek to pitch the opener, and the unflappable righthander tossed six shutout innings before leaving with a hamstring pull. Pittsburgh won, 5-1. In Game 2, Mark Lemke's sixth-inning bad-hop RBI double provided the only run, as Steve Avery bested Zane Smith. The Braves blasted starter John Smiley in Game 3, pounding him for five runs in two innings en route to a 10-3 victory. The Pirates came back to take the fourth game, 3-2, when Mike LaValliere came off the bench to drive in the go-ahead run in the top of the 10th. Smith came back on short rest to pitch Game 5, and this time, he ended up on the right end of a 1-0 game, putting the Pirates only one win away from the World Series. Avery and Drabek matched zeroes for eight innings in Game 6, until Greg Olson doubled in a run in the top of the ninth for a 1-0 Atlanta victory. Smiley took the hill in Game 7 and didn't make it out of the first inning, while John Smoltz pitched a six-hit shutout to give Atlanta a 4-0 victory and the NL pennant.

Game 1

Wednesday, October 9

Braves	AB	R	H	RBI	BB	K	Avg
Lonnie Smith, lf	4	0	0	0	0	1	.000
Mark Lemke, 2b	4	0	0	0	0	0	.000
Terry Pendleton, 3b	3	0	0	0	1	1	.000
David Justice, rf	3	1	2	1	1	1	.667
Ron Gant, cf	4	0	0	0	0	1	.000
Sid Bream, 1b	4	0	2	0	0	0	.500
Greg Olson, c	4	0	0	0	0	0	.000
Rafael Belliard, ss	2	0	0	0	0	1	.000
Jerry Willard, ph	1	0	0	0	0	1	.000
Jeff Blauser, ss	0	0	0	0	0	0	.000
Tom Glavine, p	2	0	1	0	0	0	.500
Tommy Gregg, ph	1	0	0	0	0	1	.000
Mark Wohlers, p	0	0	0	0	0	0	—
Mike Stanton, p	0	0	0	0	0	0	—
TOTALS	32	1	5	1	2	7	.156

Pirates	AB	R	H	RBI	BB	K	Avg
Gary Redus, 1b	4	0	1	0	0	0	.250
Jay Bell, ss	3	1	1	0	0	1	.333
Andy Van Slyke, cf	4	2	2	0	0	0	.500
Bobby Bonilla, rf	3	1	2	1	1	0	.667
Barry Bonds, lf	2	0	0	0	2	0	.000
Steve Buechele, 3b	3	1	1	0	1	1	.333
Don Slaught, c	3	0	0	0	1	1	.000
Jose Lind, 2b	3	0	0	1	0	0	.000
Doug Drabek, p	3	0	1	1	0	1	.333
Bob Walk, p	1	0	0	0	0	1	.000
TOTALS	29	5	8	5	5	5	.276

	1	2	3	4	5	6	7	8	9	R	H	E
Braves	0	0	0	0	0	0	0	0	1	1	5	1
Pirates	1	0	2	0	0	1	0	1	x	5	8	1

E—Belliard, Redus. DP—Braves 1 (Smith to Olson). LOB—Braves 6, Pirates 7. Scoring Position—Braves 0-for-2, Pirates 2-for-11. 2B—Van Slyke (1), Buechele (1), Drabek (1). HR—Justice (1), Van Slyke (1). S—Bell. SF—Lind. SB—Redus (1).

Braves	IP	H	R	ER	BB	K	ERA
Tom Glavine (L, 0-1)	6.0	6	4	4	3	4	6.00
Mark Wohlers	1.0	1	0	0	0	0	0.00
Mike Stanton	1.0	1	1	1	2	1	9.00

Pirates	IP	H	R	ER	BB	K	ERA
Doug Drabek (W, 1-0)	6.0	3	0	0	2	5	0.00
Bob Walk (S, 1)	3.0	2	1	1	0	2	3.00

Time—2:52. Attendance—57,347. Umpires—HP, Harvey. 1B, Pulli. 2B, DeMuth. 3B, Gregg.

Game 2

Thursday, October 10

Braves	AB	R	H	RBI	BB	K	Avg
Lonnie Smith, lf	3	0	0	0	1	0	.000
Keith Mitchell, pr-lf	1	0	0	0	0	0	.000
Terry Pendleton, 3b	4	0	0	0	0	0	.000
Ron Gant, cf	3	0	2	0	0	0	.286
David Justice, rf	4	1	1	0	0	2	.429
Brian Hunter, 1b	4	0	1	0	0	1	.250
Greg Olson, c	4	0	2	0	0	1	.250
Mark Lemke, 2b	4	0	2	1	0	0	.250
Rafael Belliard, ss	3	0	0	0	1	0	.000
Steve Avery, p	4	0	0	0	0	3	.000
Alejandro Pena, p	0	0	0	0	0	0	—
TOTALS	34	1	8	1	2	7	.172

Pirates	AB	R	H	RBI	BB	K	Avg
Gary Redus, 1b	3	0	1	0	1	1	.286
Jay Bell, ss	4	0	1	0	0	2	.286
Andy Van Slyke, cf	4	0	0	0	0	1	.250
Bobby Bonilla, rf	4	2	4	0	0	1	.571
Barry Bonds, lf	4	0	1	0	0	1	.167
Steve Buechele, 3b	3	0	0	0	1	1	.167
Don Slaught, c	3	0	0	0	0	1	.000
Curtis Wilkerson, ph	1	0	0	0	0	1	.000
Jose Lind, 2b	3	0	1	0	0	0	.167
Zane Smith, p	2	0	0	0	0	1	.000
Roger Mason, p	0	0	0	0	0	0	—
Lloyd McClendon, ph	1	0	0	0	0	0	.000
Stan Belinda, p	0	0	0	0	0	0	—
TOTALS	32	0	6	0	2	10	.228

	1	2	3	4	5	6	7	8	9	R	H	E
Braves	0	0	0	0	0	1	0	0	0	1	8	0
Pirates	0	0	0	0	0	0	0	0	0	0	6	0

DP—Braves 1 (Lemke to Belliard to Hunter), Pirates 1 (Lind to Bell to Redus). LOB—Braves 9, Pirates 7. Scoring Position—Braves 2-for-10, Pirates 1-for-7. 2B—Lemke (1), Bonilla (1). GDP—Pendleton, Bonds. SB—Gant 3 (3), Redus (2), Bonds 2 (2).

Braves	IP	H	R	ER	BB	K	ERA
Steve Avery (W, 1-0)	8.1	6	0	0	2	9	0.00
Alejandro Pena (S, 1)	0.2	0	0	0	0	1	0.00

Pirates	IP	H	R	ER	BB	K	ERA
Zane Smith (L, 0-1)	7.0	8	1	1	2	5	1.29
Roger Mason	1.0	0	0	0	0	1	0.00
Stan Belinda	1.0	0	0	0	0	0	0.00

WP—Pena. HBP—Gant by ZSmith. Time—2:46. Attendance—57,533. Umpires—HP, Pulli. 1B, DeMuth. 2B, Gregg. 3B, Davidson.

Game 3

Saturday, October 12

Pirates	AB	R	H	RBI	BB	K	Avg
Orlando Merced, 1b	5	1	1	1	0	1	.200
Rosario Rodriguez, p	0	0	0	0	0	0	—
Jay Bell, ss	5	1	3	1	0	2	.417
Andy Van Slyke, cf	3	0	1	0	2	0	.273
Bobby Bonilla, rf	5	0	0	0	0	1	.333
Barry Bonds, lf	5	1	1	0	0	0	.182
Steve Buechele, 3b	4	0	2	0	0	0	.300
Mike LaValliere, c	2	0	0	0	1	0	.000
Don Slaught, ph-c	1	0	1	0	0	0	.143
Jose Lind, 2b	4	0	1	1	0	3	.200
John Smiley, p	0	0	0	0	0	0	—
Cecil Espy, ph	1	0	0	0	0	1	.000
Bill Landrum, p	0	0	0	0	0	0	—
Gary Varsho, ph	1	0	0	0	0	1	.000
Bob Patterson, p	0	0	0	0	0	0	—
Curtis Wilkerson, ph	1	0	0	0	0	0	.000
Bob Kipper, p	0	0	0	0	0	0	—
Lloyd McClendon, ph-1b	0	0	0	0	1	0	.000
TOTALS	37	3	10	3	4	9	.247

Braves	AB	R	H	RBI	BB	K	Avg
Lonnie Smith, lf	3	1	0	0	0	2	.000
Keith Mitchell, lf	1	0	0	0	0	0	.000
Terry Pendleton, 3b	5	0	2	1	0	0	.167
Ron Gant, cf	5	2	2	1	0	2	.333
David Justice, rf	3	1	1	1	1	1	.400
Brian Hunter, 1b	4	1	1	1	0	1	.250
Alejandro Pena, p	0	0	0	0	0	0	—
Greg Olson, c	3	2	2	2	1	0	.364
Mark Lemke, 2b	2	1	0	0	1	0	.200
Rafael Belliard, ss	3	0	1	1	0	1	.125
John Smoltz, p	3	0	1	0	0	2	.333
Mike Stanton, p	0	0	0	0	0	0	—
Mark Wohlers, p	0	0	0	0	0	0	—
Sid Bream, 1b	1	1	1	3	0	0	.600
TOTALS	33	10	11	10	4	9	.253

	1	2	3	4	5	6	7	8	9	R	H	E
Pirates	1	0	0	1	0	0	1	0	0	3	10	2
Braves	4	1	1	0	0	0	1	3	x	10	11	0

E—Bell, Merced. LOB—Pirates 11, Braves 5. Scoring Position—Pirates 1-for-12, Braves 6-for-8. 2B—Bell (1), Buechele (2), Pendleton (1), Gant (1), Justice (1), Hunter (1). HR—Merced (1), Bell (1), Gant (1), Olson (1), Bream (1). S—Belliard. SB—Bonds (3), Olson (1), Smoltz (1). CS—Smith (1), Justice (1).

Pirates	IP	H	R	ER	BB	K	ERA
John Smiley (L, 0-1)	2.0	5	5	4	0	2	18.00
Bill Landrum	1.0	2	1	1	2	2	9.00
Bob Patterson	2.0	1	0	0	0	3	0.00
Bob Kipper	2.0	2	1	1	0	1	4.50
Rosario Rodriguez	1.0	1	3	3	2	1	27.00

Braves	IP	H	R	ER	BB	K	ERA
John Smoltz (W, 1-0)	6.1	8	3	3	2	7	4.26
Mike Stanton (H, 1)	0.2	1	0	0	1	0	5.40
Mark Wohlers	0.1	1	0	0	1	1	0.00
Alejandro Pena (S, 2)	1.2	0	0	0	0	1	0.00

Stanton pitched to one batter in the 8th.

WP—Stanton. HBP—Smith by Smiley. Time—3:21. Attendance—50,905. Umpires—HP, DeMuth. 1B, Gregg. 2B, Davidson. 3B, Froemming.

Game 4

Sunday, October 13

Pirates	AB	R	H	RBI	BB	K	Avg
Gary Redus, 1b	5	1	1	0	0	1	.250
Jay Bell, ss	5	0	3	0	0	1	.471
Andy Van Slyke, cf	3	1	0	0	2	1	.214
Bobby Bonilla, rf	3	1	1	0	2	0	.333
Barry Bonds, lf	5	0	1	0	0	1	.188
Steve Buechele, 3b	3	0	3	0	1	0	.462
Don Slaught, c	4	0	1	1	0	1	.182
Mike LaValliere, ph-c	1	0	1	1	0	0	.333
Jose Lind, 2b	4	0	0	0	0	2	.143
Randy Tomlin, p	2	0	0	0	0	0	.000
Curtis Wilkerson, ph	1	0	0	0	0	1	.000
Bob Walk, p	0	0	0	0	0	0	.000
Lloyd McClendon, ph	1	0	0	0	0	0	.000
Stan Belinda, p	0	0	0	0	0	0	—
TOTALS	37	3	11	2	5	8	.268

Braves	AB	R	H	RBI	BB	K	Avg
Lonnie Smith, lf	4	1	2	0	1	0	.143
Terry Pendleton, 3b	5	0	1	0	0	1	.176
Ron Gant, cf	5	0	0	1	0	1	.235
David Justice, rf	4	1	1	0	0	0	.357
Brian Hunter, 1b	3	0	1	0	0	0	.273
Sid Bream, ph-1b	1	0	0	0	0	0	.500
Greg Olson, c	3	0	1	1	1	0	.357
Mark Lemke, 2b	3	0	0	0	1	0	.154
Rafael Belliard, ss	3	0	1	0	0	0	.182
Charlie Leibrandt, p	1	0	0	0	0	0	.000
Jim Clancy, p	0	0	0	0	0	0	—
Tommy Gregg, ph	1	0	0	0	0	0	.000
Mike Stanton, p	0	0	0	0	0	0	—
Jerry Willard, ph	1	0	0	0	0	0	.000
Kent Mercker, p	0	0	0	0	0	0	—
Mark Wohlers, p	0	0	0	0	0	0	—
TOTALS	34	2	7	2	3	2	.238

	1	2	3	4	5	6	7	8	9	10	R	H	E
Pirates	0	1	0	0	1	0	0	0	0	1	3	11	1
Braves	2	0	0	0	0	0	0	0	0	0	2	7	1

E—Bonds, Justice. DP—Braves 1 (Olson to Belliard to Hunter). LOB—Pirates 10, Braves 7. Scoring Position—Pirates 2-for-10, Braves 1-for-8. 2B—Smith (1). S—Buechele, Belliard, Leibrandt. SB—Van Slyke (1). CS—Bell (1), Bonilla (1).

Pirates	IP	H	R	ER	BB	K	ERA
Randy Tomlin	6.0	6	2	2	2	1	3.00
Bob Walk	2.0	1	0	0	0	0	1.80
Stan Belinda (W, 1-0)	2.0	0	0	0	1	1	0.00

Braves	IP	H	R	ER	BB	K	ERA
Charlie Leibrandt	6.2	8	2	1	3	6	1.35
Jim Clancy	0.1	0	0	0	0	0	0.00
Mike Stanton	2.0	2	0	0	0	2	2.45
Kent Mercker (L, 0-1)	0.2	0	1	1	2	0	13.50
Mark Wohlers	0.1	1	0	0	0	0	0.00

Time—3:43. Attendance—51,109. Umpires—HP, Gregg. 1B, Davidson. 2B, Froemming. 3B, Harvey.

Game 5

Monday, October 14

Pirates	AB	R	H	RBI	BB	K	Avg
Gary Redus, 1b	4	0	0	0	0	1	.188
Jay Bell, ss	4	0	2	0	0	0	.476
Andy Van Slyke, cf	4	0	1	0	0	0	.222
Bobby Bonilla, rf	2	0	1	0	2	0	.353
Barry Bonds, lf	4	0	0	0	1	0	.150
Steve Buechele, 3b	3	1	0	0	1	1	.375
Don Slaught, c	3	0	1	0	0	0	.214
Jose Lind, 2b	4	0	1	1	0	1	.167
Zane Smith, p	3	0	0	0	0	3	.000
Roger Mason, p	1	0	0	0	0	1	.000
TOTALS	32	1	6	1	3	8	.260

Braves	AB	R	H	RBI	BB	K	Avg
Lonnie Smith, lf	4	0	2	0	0	1	.222
Alejandro Pena, p	0	0	0	0	0	0	—
Terry Pendleton, 3b	4	0	1	0	0	0	.190
Ron Gant, cf	4	0	1	0	0	0	.238
David Justice, rf	4	0	0	0	0	2	.278
Brian Hunter, 1b	3	0	1	0	0	0	.286
Tommy Gregg, ph	1	0	1	0	0	0	.333
Greg Olson, c	3	0	1	0	1	0	.353
Mark Lemke, 2b	4	0	2	0	0	0	.235
Rafael Belliard, ss	2	0	0	0	0	1	.154
Jeff Blauser, ph-ss	2	0	0	0	0	0	.000
Tom Glavine, p	2	0	0	0	0	2	.000
Keith Mitchell, ph-lf	1	0	0	0	0	0	.000
TOTALS	34	0	9	0	1	6	.238

	1	2	3	4	5	6	7	8	9	R	H	E
Pirates	0	0	0	0	1	0	0	0	0	1	6	2
Braves	0	0	0	0	0	0	0	0	0	0	9	1

E—Redus, Blauser, Lind. DP—Pirates 2 (Bell to Redus; Slaught to Buechele), Braves 1 (Belliard to Lemke to Hunter). LOB—Pirates 8, Braves 8. Scoring Position—Pirates 1-for-12, Braves 2-for-11. 2B—Bell (2), Van Slyke (2), Bonilla (2). 3B—Pendleton (1). S—Slaught. GDP—Bonilla, Pendleton. SB—LSmith (1), Gant (4). CS—Hunter (1).

Pirates	IP	H	R	ER	BB	K	ERA
Zane Smith (W, 1-1)	7.2	7	0	0	1	5	0.61
Roger Mason (S, 1)	1.1	2	0	0	0	1	0.00

Braves	IP	H	R	ER	BB	K	ERA
Tom Glavine (L, 0-2)	8.0	6	1	1	3	7	3.21
Alejandro Pena	1.0	0	0	0	0	1	0.00

Time—2:51. Attendance—51,109. Umpires—HP, Davidson. 1B, Froemming. 2B, Harvey. 3B, Pulli.

Game 6

Wednesday, October 16

Braves	AB	R	H	RBI	BB	K	Avg
Lonnie Smith, lf	3	0	2	0	1	0	.286
Keith Mitchell, lf	0	0	0	0	0	0	.000
Jeff Treadway, 2b	3	0	1	0	0	0	.333
Mark Lemke, 2b	0	0	0	0	0	0	.235
Terry Pendleton, 3b	4	0	0	0	0	1	.160
David Justice, rf	4	0	0	0	0	0	.227
Ron Gant, cf	3	1	1	0	1	0	.250
Sid Bream, 1b	4	0	0	0	0	1	.300
Greg Olson, c	4	0	1	0	1	0	.333
Rafael Belliard, ss	3	0	1	0	1	0	.188
Steve Avery, p	3	0	1	0	0	1	.143
Tommy Gregg, ph	1	0	0	0	0	1	.250
Alejandro Pena, p	0	0	0	0	0	0	—
TOTALS	32	1	7	1	3	5	.237

Pirates	AB	R	H	RBI	BB	K	Avg
Gary Redus, 1b	3	0	0	0	0	1	.158
Orlando Merced, ph	0	0	0	0	0	0	.200
Jay Bell, ss	4	0	0	0	0	2	.400
Andy Van Slyke, cf	3	0	0	0	1	2	.190
Bobby Bonilla, rf	2	0	0	0	1	0	.316
Barry Bonds, lf	3	0	0	0	0	1	.130
Steve Buechele, 3b	3	0	1	0	0	0	.368
Don Slaught, c	3	0	1	0	0	1	.235
Jose Lind, 2b	3	0	1	0	0	0	.190
Doug Drabek, p	2	0	0	0	0	1	.200
Gary Varsho, ph	1	0	1	0	0	0	.500
TOTALS	27	0	4	0	2	9	.250

	1	2	3	4	5	6	7	8	9	R	H	E
Braves	0	0	0	0	0	0	0	0	1	1	7	0
Pirates	0	0	0	0	0	0	0	0	0	0	4	0

DP—Braves 2 (Bream to Belliard; Pendleton to Treadway to Bream). LOB—Braves 8, Pirates 3. Scoring Position—Braves 1-for-12, Pirates 0-for-2. 2B—Smith (3), Olson (2). S—Treadway, Merced. GDP—Redus, Bonilla. SB—Gant 2 (6). CS—Smith (2).

Braves	IP	H	R	ER	BB	K	ERA
Steve Avery (W, 2-0)	8.0	3	0	0	2	8	0.00
Alejandro Pena (S, 3)	1.0	1	0	0	0	1	0.00

Pirates	IP	H	R	ER	BB	K	ERA
Doug Drabek (L, 1-1)	9.0	7	1	1	3	5	0.60

WP—Pena. Time—3:09. Attendance—54,508. Umpires—HP, Froemming. 1B, Harvey. 2B, Pulli. 3B, DeMuth.

Game 7

Thursday, October 17

Braves	AB	R	H	RBI	BB	K	Avg
Lonnie Smith, lf	3	1	0	0	1	1	.250
Keith Mitchell, lf	1	0	0	0	0	1	.000
Terry Pendleton, 3b	5	1	1	0	0	0	.167
Ron Gant, cf	3	1	1	1	1	0	.259
David Justice, rf	3	0	0	0	1	1	.200
Brian Hunter, 1b	4	1	2	3	0	0	.333
Greg Olson, c	3	0	1	0	1	1	.333
Mark Lemke, 2b	3	0	0	0	1	0	.200
Rafael Belliard, ss	3	0	1	0	0	0	.211
John Smoltz, p	2	0	0	0	1	2	.200
TOTALS	30	4	6	4	7	6	.235

Pirates	AB	R	H	RBI	BB	K	Avg
Orlando Merced, 1b	4	0	1	0	0	0	.222
Jay Bell, ss	4	0	2	0	0	2	.414
Andy Van Slyke, cf	4	0	0	0	0	1	.160
Bobby Bonilla, rf	4	0	1	0	0	0	.304
Barry Bonds, lf	4	0	1	0	0	0	.148
Steve Buechele, 3b	4	0	0	0	0	2	.304
Mike LaValliere, c	3	0	1	0	1	0	.333
Jose Lind, 2b	4	0	0	0	0	0	.160
John Smiley, p	0	0	0	0	0	0	—
Bob Walk, p	1	0	0	0	0	1	.000
Cecil Espy, ph	1	0	0	0	0	1	.000
Roger Mason, p	0	0	0	0	0	0	.000
Curtis Wilkerson, ph	1	0	0	0	0	1	.000
Stan Belinda, p	0	0	0	0	0	0	—
TOTALS	34	0	6	0	1	8	.239

	1	2	3	4	5	6	7	8	9	R	H	E
Braves	3	0	0	0	1	0	0	0	0	4	6	1
Pirates	0	0	0	0	0	0	0	0	0	0	6	0

E—Lemke. LOB—Braves 8, Pirates 8. Scoring Position—Braves 1-for-8, Pirates 0-for-8. 2B—Hunter (2), Bonds (1). HR—Hunter (1). S—Smoltz. SF—Gant. SB—Gant (7).

Braves	IP	H	R	ER	BB	K	ERA
John Smoltz (W, 2-0)	9.0	6	0	0	1	8	1.76

Pirates	IP	H	R	ER	BB	K	ERA
John Smiley (L, 0-2)	0.2	3	3	3	1	1	23.63
Bob Walk	4.1	2	1	1	3	3	1.93
Roger Mason	2.0	1	0	0	1	0	0.00
Stan Belinda	2.0	0	0	0	2	2	0.00

Balk—Walk. Time—3:04. Attendance—46,932. Umpires—HP, Harvey. 1B, Pulli. 2B, DeMuth. 3B, Gregg.

Postseason: League Championship Series

1991 NL Championship Series—Composite Statistics

Batting

Braves	G	AB	R	H	RBI	2B	3B	HR	BB	SO	SB	CS	Avg	OBP	Slg
Steve Avery	2	7	0	1	0	0	0	0	0	4	0	0	.143	.143	.143
Rafael Belliard	7	19	0	4	1	0	0	0	3	3	0	0	.211	.318	.211
Jeff Blauser	2	2	0	0	0	0	0	0	0	0	0	0	.000	.000	.000
Sid Bream	4	10	1	3	3	0	0	1	0	1	0	0	.300	.300	.600
Ron Gant	7	27	4	7	3	1	0	1	2	4	7	0	.259	.323	.407
Tom Glavine	2	4	0	1	0	0	0	0	0	2	0	0	.250	.250	.250
Tommy Gregg	4	4	0	1	0	0	0	0	0	2	0	0	.250	.250	.250
Brian Hunter	5	18	2	6	4	2	0	1	0	2	0	1	.333	.333	.611
David Justice	7	25	4	5	2	1	0	1	3	7	0	1	.200	.286	.360
Charlie Leibrandt	1	1	0	0	0	0	0	0	0	0	0	0	.000	.000	.000
Mark Lemke	7	20	1	4	1	1	0	0	4	0	0	0	.200	.333	.250
Keith Mitchell	5	4	0	0	0	0	0	0	0	1	0	0	.000	.000	.000
Greg Olson	7	24	3	8	4	1	0	1	4	3	1	0	.333	.429	.500
Terry Pendleton	7	30	1	5	1	1	1	0	1	3	0	0	.167	.194	.267
Lonnie Smith	7	24	3	6	0	3	0	4	5	1	2	0	.250	.379	.375
John Smoltz	2	5	0	1	0	0	0	0	1	4	1	0	.200	.333	.200
Jeff Treadway	1	3	0	1	0	0	0	0	0	0	0	0	.333	.333	.333
Jerry Willard	2	2	0	0	0	0	0	0	0	1	0	0	.000	.000	.000
Totals	**7**	**229**	**19**	**53**	**19**	**10**	**1**	**5**	**22**	**42**	**10**	**4**	**.231**	**.303**	**.349**

Pitching

Braves	G	GS	CG	IP	H	R	ER	BB	SO	W-L	Sv-Op	Hld	ERA
Steve Avery	2	2	0	16.1	9	0	0	4	17	2-0	0-0	0	0.00
Jim Clancy	1	0	0	0.1	0	0	0	0	0	0-0	0-0	0	0.00
Tom Glavine	2	2	0	14.0	12	5	5	6	11	0-2	0-0	0	3.21
Charlie Leibrandt	1	1	0	6.2	8	2	1	3	6	0-0	0-0	0	1.35
Kent Mercker	1	0	0	0.2	0	1	1	2	0	0-1	0-0	0	13.50
Alejandro Pena	4	0	0	4.1	1	0	0	0	4	0-0	3-3	0	0.00
John Smoltz	2	2	1	15.1	14	3	3	3	15	2-0	0-0	0	1.76
Mike Stanton	3	0	0	3.2	4	1	1	3	3	0-0	0-0	1	2.45
Mark Wohlers	3	0	0	1.2	3	0	0	1	1	0-0	0-0	0	0.00
Totals	**7**	**7**	**1**	**63.0**	**51**	**12**	**11**	**22**	**57**	**4-3**	**3-3**	**1**	**1.57**

Fielding

Braves	Pos	G	PO	Ast	E	DP	PB	FPct
Steve Avery	p	2	1	2	0	0	—	1.000
Rafael Belliard	ss	7	9	15	1	4	—	.960
Jeff Blauser	ss	2	0	1	1	0	—	.500
Sid Bream	1b	4	19	3	0	2	—	1.000
Jim Clancy	p	1	0	0	0	0	—	—
Ron Gant	cf	7	15	2	0	0	—	1.000
Tom Glavine	p	2	1	3	0	0	—	1.000
Brian Hunter	1b	5	30	4	0	3	—	1.000
David Justice	rf	7	17	0	1	0	—	.944
Charlie Leibrandt	p	1	0	1	0	0	—	1.000
Mark Lemke	2b	7	12	10	1	2	—	.957
Kent Mercker	p	1	0	0	0	0	—	—
Keith Mitchell	lf	5	2	0	0	0	—	1.000
Greg Olson	c	7	62	1	0	2	0	1.000
Alejandro Pena	p	4	1	2	0	0	—	1.000
Terry Pendleton	3b	7	5	11	0	1	—	1.000
Lonnie Smith	lf	7	10	2	0	1	—	1.000
John Smoltz	p	2	3	0	0	0	—	1.000
Mike Stanton	p	3	0	2	0	0	—	1.000
Jeff Treadway	2b	1	2	2	0	1	—	1.000
Mark Wohlers	p	3	0	0	0	0	—	—
Totals		**7**	**189**	**61**	**4**	**16**	**0**	**.984**

Batting

Pirates	G	AB	R	H	RBI	2B	3B	HR	BB	SO	SB	CS	Avg	OBP	Slg
Jay Bell	7	29	2	12	1	2	0	1	0	10	0	1	.414	.414	.586
Barry Bonds	7	27	1	4	0	1	0	0	2	4	3	0	.148	.207	.185
Bobby Bonilla	7	23	2	7	1	2	0	0	6	2	0	1	.304	.448	.391
Steve Buechele	7	23	2	7	0	2	0	0	4	6	0	0	.304	.407	.391
Doug Drabek	2	5	0	1	1	1	0	0	0	2	0	0	.200	.200	.400
Cecil Espy	2	2	0	0	0	0	0	0	0	2	0	0	.000	.000	.000
Mike LaValliere	3	6	0	2	1	0	0	0	2	0	0	0	.333	.500	.333
Jose Lind	7	25	0	4	3	0	0	0	0	6	0	0	.160	.154	.160
Roger Mason	3	1	0	0	0	0	0	0	0	1	0	0	.000	.000	.000
Lloyd McClendon	3	2	0	0	0	0	0	0	1	0	0	0	.000	.333	.000
Orlando Merced	3	9	1	2	1	0	0	1	0	1	0	0	.222	.222	.556
Gary Redus	5	19	1	3	0	0	0	0	1	4	2	0	.158	.200	.158
Don Slaught	6	17	0	4	1	0	0	0	1	4	0	0	.235	.278	.235
Zane Smith	2	5	0	0	0	0	0	0	0	4	0	0	.000	.000	.000
Randy Tomlin	1	2	0	0	0	0	0	0	0	0	0	0	.000	.000	.000
Andy Van Slyke	7	25	3	4	2	2	0	1	5	5	1	0	.160	.300	.360
Gary Varsho	2	2	0	1	0	0	0	0	0	1	0	0	.500	.500	.500
Bob Walk	3	2	0	0	0	0	0	0	0	2	0	0	.000	.000	.000
Curtis Wilkerson	4	4	0	0	0	0	0	0	0	3	0	0	.000	.000	.000
Totals	**7**	**228**	**12**	**51**	**11**	**10**	**0**	**3**	**22**	**57**	**6**	**2**	**.224**	**.291**	**.307**

Pitching

Pirates	G	GS	CG	IP	H	R	ER	BB	SO	W-L	Sv-Op	Hld	ERA
Stan Belinda	3	0	0	5.0	0	0	0	3	4	1-0	0-0	0	0.00
Doug Drabek	2	2	1	15.0	10	1	1	5	10	1-1	0-0	0	0.60
Bob Kipper	1	0	0	2.0	2	1	1	0	1	0-0	0-0	0	4.50
Bill Landrum	1	0	0	1.0	2	1	1	2	0	0-0	0-0	0	9.00
Roger Mason	3	0	0	4.1	3	0	0	1	2	0-0	1-1	0	0.00
Bob Patterson	1	0	0	2.0	1	0	0	0	3	0-0	0-0	0	0.00
Rosario Rodriguez	1	0	0	1.0	1	3	3	2	1	0-0	0-0	0	27.00
John Smiley	2	2	0	2.2	8	8	7	1	2	0-2	0-0	0	23.63
Zane Smith	2	2	0	14.2	15	1	1	3	10	1-1	0-0	0	0.61
Randy Tomlin	1	1	0	6.0	6	2	2	2	1	1-0	0-0	0	3.00
Bob Walk	3	0	0	9.1	5	2	2	3	5	0-0	1-1	0	1.93
Totals	**7**	**7**	**1**	**63.0**	**53**	**19**	**18**	**22**	**42**	**3-4**	**2-2**	**0**	**2.57**

Fielding

Pirates	Pos	G	PO	Ast	E	DP	PB	FPct
Stan Belinda	p	3	0	2	0	0	—	1.000
Jay Bell	ss	7	13	19	1	2	—	.970
Barry Bonds	lf	7	14	1	1	0	—	.938
Bobby Bonilla	rf	7	12	1	0	0	—	1.000
Steve Buechele	3b	7	8	14	0	1	—	1.000
Doug Drabek	p	2	3	0	0	0	—	1.000
Bob Kipper	p	1	0	1	0	0	—	1.000
Bill Landrum	p	1	0	0	0	0	—	—
Mike LaValliere	c	3	14	3	0	0	0	1.000
Jose Lind	2b	7	12	24	1	1	—	.973
Roger Mason	p	3	0	0	0	0	—	—
Lloyd McClendon	1b	1	0	0	0	0	—	—
Orlando Merced	1b	2	13	0	1	0	—	.929
Bob Patterson	p	1	0	0	0	0	—	—
Gary Redus	1b	5	51	0	2	2	—	.962
Rosario Rodriguez	p	1	0	0	0	0	—	—
Don Slaught	c	6	30	5	0	1	0	1.000
John Smiley	p	2	0	1	0	0	—	1.000
Zane Smith	p	2	0	3	0	0	—	1.000
Randy Tomlin	p	1	1	0	0	0	—	1.000
Andy Van Slyke	cf	7	18	1	0	0	—	1.000
Bob Walk	p	3	0	0	0	0	—	—
Totals		**7**	**189**	**75**	**6**	**7**	**0**	**.978**

1992 Toronto Blue Jays (AL) 4, Oakland Athletics (AL) 2

The Toronto Blue Jays took advantage of the Oakland A's vulnerable bullpen on the way to a six-game victory in the ALCS. Harold Baines hit a ninth-inning home run off Jack Morris to give the A's a 4-3 victory in Game 1. David Cone threw eight strong innings and Kelly Gruber socked a two-run homer in Game 2 as the Blue Jays evened things up with a 3-1 win. The A's were forever a run out of reach in Game 3, committing several blunders on the way to a 7-5 loss. Oakland closer Dennis Eckersley was brought into the fourth game with a four-run lead, no outs and two on in the top of the eighth. He allowed both inherited runners to score that inning, and Roberto Alomar hit a game-tying, two-run homer off Eckersley in the following frame. Toronto ultimately won it 7-6 in 11 innings. Dave Stewart kept Oakland alive with a complete-game 6-2 win in Game 5, but Toronto came out swinging in Game 6, and pummelled the A's 9-2 to take the AL crown.

Game 1

Wednesday, October 7

Athletics	AB	R	H	RBI	BB	K	Avg
Rickey Henderson, lf	2	0	0	0	2	0	.000
Carney Lansford, 3b	4	0	0	0	0	0	.000
Ruben Sierra, rf	4	0	0	0	0	0	.000
Harold Baines, dh	4	2	3	1	0	0	.750
Mark McGwire, 1b	3	1	1	2	1	1	.333
Terry Steinbach, c	4	1	1	1	0	0	.250
Willie Wilson, cf	4	0	1	0	0	1	.250
Mike Bordick, ss	4	0	0	0	0	1	.000
Lance Blankenship, 2b	2	0	0	0	1	1	.000
TOTALS	31	4	6	4	4	4	.194

Blue Jays	AB	R	H	RBI	BB	K	Avg
Devon White, cf	3	0	1	0	2	0	.333
Roberto Alomar, 2b	4	0	1	0	0	0	.250
Joe Carter, rf-1b	4	0	1	0	0	0	.250
Dave Winfield, dh	4	2	2	0	0	0	.500
John Olerud, 1b	3	0	1	1	1	0	.333
Derek Bell, pr-rf	0	0	0	0	0	0	—
Candy Maldonado, lf	4	0	0	0	0	2	.000
Kelly Gruber, 3b	4	0	0	0	0	0	.000
Pat Borders, c	4	1	1	1	0	0	.250
Manuel Lee, ss	3	0	1	0	0	0	.333
Ed Sprague, ph	1	0	1	0	0	0	1.000
Alfredo Griffin, pr	0	0	0	0	0	0	—
TOTALS	34	3	9	3	3	2	.265

	1	2	3	4	5	6	7	8	9		R	H	E
Athletics	0	3	0	0	0	0	0	0	1		4	6	1
Blue Jays	0	0	0	0	1	1	0	1	0		3	9	0

E—Henderson. DP—Athletics 2 (Bordick to Blankenship to McGwire; Bordick to Blankenship to McGwire), Blue Jays 2 (Morris to Lee to Olerud; Lee to Alomar to Olerud). LOB—Athletics 4, Blue Jays 7. Scoring Position—Athletics 0-for-5, Blue Jays 1-for-3. 2B—Winfield (1). HR—Baines (1), McGwire (1), Steinbach (1), Winfield (1), Borders (1). GDP—Lansford, Steinbach, Alomar, Gruber. SB—Wilson (1), Alomar (1).

Athletics	IP	H	R	ER	BB	K	ERA
Dave Stewart	7.2	7	3	3	3	2	3.52
Jeff Russell (BS, 1; W, 1-0)	0.1	1	0	0	0	0	0.00
Dennis Eckersley (S, 1)	1.0	1	0	0	0	0	0.00

Blue Jays	IP	H	R	ER	BB	K	ERA
Jack Morris (L, 0-1)	9.0	6	4	4	4	4	4.00

WP—Morris. Time—2:47. Attendance—51,039. Umpires—HP, Denkinger. 1B, Young. 2B, Clark. 3B, Merrill.

Game 2

Thursday, October 8

Athletics	AB	R	H	RBI	BB	K	Avg
Rickey Henderson, lf	4	0	0	0	0	2	.000
Carney Lansford, 3b	4	0	0	0	0	1	.000
Ruben Sierra, rf	3	1	1	0	1	0	.143
Harold Baines, dh	4	0	2	1	0	0	.625
Eric Fox, pr	0	0	0	0	0	0	—
Mark McGwire, 1b	4	0	0	0	0	1	.143
Terry Steinbach, c	4	0	1	0	0	3	.250
Willie Wilson, cf	4	0	1	0	0	0	.250
Mike Bordick, 2b	2	0	0	0	1	0	.000
Walt Weiss, ss	2	0	1	0	1	1	.500
TOTALS	31	1	6	1	3	7	.200

Blue Jays	AB	R	H	RBI	BB	K	Avg
Devon White, cf	3	0	0	0	1	2	.167
Roberto Alomar, 2b	3	0	1	0	1	0	.286
Joe Carter, rf	3	0	0	0	1	1	.143
Dave Winfield, dh	3	0	0	0	1	0	.286
John Olerud, 1b	3	0	0	0	0	0	.167
Candy Maldonado, lf	2	1	0	0	1	0	.000
Kelly Gruber, 3b	3	2	2	2	0	0	.286
Pat Borders, c	3	0	1	0	0	0	.286
Manuel Lee, ss	2	0	0	1	0	0	.200
TOTALS	25	3	4	3	5	3	.207

	1	2	3	4	5	6	7	8	9		R	H	E
Athletics	0	0	0	0	0	0	0	0	1		1	6	0
Blue Jays	0	0	0	0	2	0	1	0	x		3	4	0

DP—Athletics 1 (Lansford to Bordick to McGwire), Blue Jays 1 (Maldonado to Gruber). LOB—Athletics 6, Blue Jays 4. Scoring Position—Athletics 1-for-7, Blue Jays 0-for-5. 2B—Wilson (1), Gruber (1). 3B—Sierra (1). HR—Gruber (1). SF—Lee. GDP—Carter. SB—Wilson 3 (4), Bordick (1), Weiss 2 (2), Alomar (2), Carter (2). CS—Sierra (1), White (1).

Athletics	IP	H	R	ER	BB	K	ERA
Mike Moore (L, 0-1)	7.0	4	3	3	4	3	3.86
Jim Corsi	0.2	0	0	0	1	0	0.00
Jeff Parrett	0.1	0	0	0	0	0	0.00

Blue Jays	IP	H	R	ER	BB	K	ERA
David Cone (W, 1-0)	8.0	5	1	1	3	6	1.13
Tom Henke (S, 1)	1.0	1	0	0	0	1	0.00

Cone pitched to one batter in the 9th.

Time—2:58. Attendance—51,114. Umpires—HP, Young. 1B, Clark. 2B, Merrill. 3B, Brinkman.

Game 3

Saturday, October 10

Blue Jays	AB	R	H	RBI	BB	K	Avg
Devon White, cf	3	0	1	0	2	0	.222
Roberto Alomar, 2b	5	1	1	1	0	0	.250
Joe Carter, rf	5	0	1	0	0	1	.167
Dave Winfield, dh	4	2	1	1	1	0	.273
John Olerud, 1b	5	1	1	0	0	1	.182
Candy Maldonado, lf	3	1	2	2	1	0	.222
Kelly Gruber, 3b	4	0	0	0	0	1	.182
Pat Borders, c	4	1	1	0	0	1	.273
Manuel Lee, ss	3	1	1	2	1	0	.250
TOTALS	36	7	9	6	5	4	.223

Athletics	AB	R	H	RBI	BB	K	Avg
Rickey Henderson, lf	4	1	1	0	1	0	.100
Carney Lansford, 3b	5	0	1	0	0	0	.077
Ruben Sierra, rf	4	1	2	2	0	0	.273
Harold Baines, dh	5	2	2	1	0	2	.538
Mark McGwire, 1b	4	0	1	0	0	1	.182
Terry Steinbach, c	4	0	3	2	1	0	.417
Willie Wilson, cf	4	0	2	0	1	1	.333
Mike Bordick, 2b	2	0	0	0	0	0	.000
Jerry Browne, ph	0	0	0	0	1	0	—
Lance Blankenship, pr-2b	1	0	1	0	0	0	.333
Walt Weiss, ss	4	1	0	0	0	0	.167
TOTALS	37	5	13	5	4	4	.253

	1	2	3	4	5	6	7	8	9		R	H	E
Blue Jays	0	1	0	1	1	0	2	1	1		7	9	1
Athletics	0	0	0	2	0	0	2	1	0		5	13	3

E—Lansford, Lee, Blankenship 2. DP—Blue Jays 2 (Alomar to Lee to Olerud; Carter to Borders), Athletics 1 (Weiss to Bordick to McGwire). LOB—Blue Jays 7, Athletics 11. Scoring Position—Blue Jays 3-for-10, Athletics 4-for-12. 2B—White (1), Sierra (1). 3B—Lee (1). HR—Alomar (1), Maldonado (1). SF—Sierra. GDP—Alomar, Sierra. SB—Carter (2), Henderson (1), Wilson 2 (6). CS—White (2), Maldonado (1).

Blue Jays	IP	H	R	ER	BB	K	ERA
Juan Guzman (W, 1-0)	6.0	7	2	2	3	3	3.00
Duane Ward (H, 1)	1.0	3	2	2	1	1	18.00
Mike Timlin (H, 1)	0.1	2	1	1	0	0	27.00
Tom Henke (S, 2)	1.2	1	0	0	0	0	0.00

Athletics	IP	H	R	ER	BB	K	ERA
Ron Darling (L, 0-1)	6.0	4	3	2	2	3	3.00
Kelly Downs	1.0	2	2	0	0	0	0.00
Jim Corsi	0.1	0	0	0	0	0	0.00
Jeff Russell	0.2	1	2	2	3	0	18.00
Rick Honeycutt	0.2	0	0	0	0	0	0.00
Dennis Eckersley	0.1	2	0	0	0	1	0.00

Russell pitched to one batter in the 9th.

WP—Darling 2, Russell. HBP—McGwire by Guzman. Time—3:40. Attendance—46,911. Umpires—HP, Clark. 1B, Merrill. 2B, Brinkman. 3B, Coble.

Postseason: League Championship Series

Game 4
Sunday, October 11

Blue Jays	AB	R	H	RBI	BB	K	Avg
Devon White, cf	6	1	2	0	0	3	.267
Roberto Alomar, 2b	5	2	4	2	1	0	.412
Joe Carter, rf-1b	6	1	2	1	0	0	.222
Dave Winfield, dh	6	1	1	0	0	0	.235
John Olerud, 1b	5	1	4	2	0	1	.375
Derek Bell, pr-rf	0	1	0	0	1	0	—
Candy Maldonado, lf	5	0	2	1	1	1	.286
Kelly Gruber, 3b	5	0	0	0	1	1	.125
Pat Borders, c	5	0	1	1	0	0	.250
Manuel Lee, ss	3	0	1	0	0	1	.273
Ed Sprague, ph	1	0	0	0	0	1	.500
Alfredo Griffin, ss	2	0	0	0	0	0	.000
TOTALS	49	7	17	7	4	8	.271

Athletics	AB	R	H	RBI	BB	K	Avg
Rickey Henderson, lf	6	2	3	1	0	0	.250
Jerry Browne, cf	2	1	0	0	1	0	.000
Willie Wilson, cf	2	0	0	0	0	0	.286
Ruben Sierra, rf	4	0	2	2	1	1	.333
Harold Baines, dh	5	1	2	1	0	0	.500
Eric Fox, pr-dh	1	0	0	0	0	0	.000
Mark McGwire, 1b	4	0	0	0	1	1	.133
Terry Steinbach, c	4	0	0	1	1	1	.313
Carney Lansford, 3b	5	0	2	1	0	0	.167
Mike Bordick, ss	5	1	1	0	0	0	.077
Lance Blankenship, 2b	4	1	2	0	1	1	.429
TOTALS	42	6	12	6	5	4	.267

	1	2	3	4	5	6	7	8	9	10	11		R	H	E
Blue Jays	0	1	0	0	0	0	0	3	2	0	1		7	17	4
Athletics	0	0	5	0	0	1	0	0	0	0	0		6	12	2

E—Henderson, Lee 2, White, McGwire, Borders. DP—Blue Jays 2 (Lee to Alomar to Olerud; Lee to Alomar to Olerud). LOB—Blue Jays 14, Athletics 11. Scoring Position—Blue Jays 4-for-14, Athletics 4-for-16. 2B—Alomar (1), Olerud (1), Sierra (2), Baines (1). HR—Alomar (2), Olerud (1). S—Browne, McGwire. SF—Borders, Sierra. GDP—Baines, Bordick. SB—Alomar (3), Henderson (2), Blankenship (1), Fox (1).

Blue Jays	IP	H	R	ER	BB	K	ERA
Jack Morris	3.1	5	5	5	5	2	6.57
Todd Stottlemyre	3.2	3	1	1	0	1	2.45
Mike Timlin	1.2	2	0	0	0	1	6.75
Duane Ward (W, 1-0)	2.0	1	0	0	0	0	6.00
Tom Henke (S, 3)	1.0	1	0	0	0	0	0.00

Athletics	IP	H	R	ER	BB	K	ERA
Bob Welch	7.0	7	2	2	1	7	2.57
Jeff Parrett	0.0	2	2	2	0	0	54.00
Dennis Eckersley (BS, 1)	1.2	5	2	2	0	1	6.00
Jim Corsi	1.0	2	0	0	0	0	0.00
Kelly Downs (L, 0-1)	1.1	1	1	1	1	0	3.86

Welch pitched to one batter in the 8th. Parrett pitched to three batters in the 8th.

Time—4:25. Attendance—47,732. Umpires—HP, Merrill. 1B, Brinkman. 2B, Coble. 3B, Denkinger.

Game 5
Monday, October 12

Blue Jays	AB	R	H	RBI	BB	K	Avg
Devon White, cf	4	0	3	1	0	0	.368
Roberto Alomar, 2b	4	0	1	0	0	0	.381
Joe Carter, rf	3	0	0	0	1	1	.190
Dave Winfield, dh	3	1	2	1	1	0	.300
John Olerud, 1b	4	0	0	0	0	3	.300
Candy Maldonado, lf	4	0	0	0	0	0	.222
Kelly Gruber, 3b	3	1	0	0	1	0	.105
Pat Borders, c	4	0	1	0	0	0	.250
Manuel Lee, ss	3	0	0	0	0	1	.214
TOTALS	32	2	7	2	3	5	.262

Athletics	AB	R	H	RBI	BB	K	Avg
Rickey Henderson, lf	3	2	2	0	1	0	.316
Eric Fox, pr-lf	0	0	0	0	0	0	.000
Jerry Browne, 3b	4	2	4	2	0	0	.667
Ruben Sierra, rf	4	1	2	3	0	0	.368
Harold Baines, dh	3	0	0	0	0	1	.429
Mark McGwire, 1b	1	0	0	0	3	1	.125
Terry Steinbach, c	4	0	0	0	0	1	.250
Willie Wilson, cf	4	0	0	0	0	0	.222
Mike Bordick, ss	4	0	0	0	0	0	.059
Lance Blankenship, 2b	4	1	0	0	0	1	.273
TOTALS	31	6	8	5	4	4	.277

	1	2	3	4	5	6	7	8	9		R	H	E
Blue Jays	0	0	0	1	0	0	1	0	0		2	7	3
Athletics	2	0	1	0	3	0	0	0	x		6	8	0

E—Carter, Gruber, Cone. DP—Athletics 1 (Blankenship to Bordick). LOB—Blue Jays 6, Athletics 6. Scoring Position—Blue Jays 1-for-5, Athletics 4-for-10. 2B—White (2). HR—Winfield (2), Sierra (1). S—Baines. CS—White (3), Sierra (2).

Blue Jays	IP	H	R	ER	BB	K	ERA
David Cone (L, 1-1)	4.0	6	6	3	2	3	3.00
Jimmy Key	3.0	2	0	0	2	1	0.00
Mark Eichhorn	1.0	0	0	0	0	0	0.00

Athletics	IP	H	R	ER	BB	K	ERA
Dave Stewart (W, 1-0)	9.0	7	2	2	3	5	2.70

Cone pitched to five batters in the 5th.

PB—Borders. Time—2:51. Attendance—44,955. Umpires—HP, Brinkman. 1B, Coble. 2B, Denkinger. 3B, Young.

Game 6
Wednesday, October 14

Athletics	AB	R	H	RBI	BB	K	Avg
Rickey Henderson, lf	4	0	0	0	0	2	.261
Jamie Quirk, ph	1	0	0	0	0	0	.000
Jerry Browne, 3b	4	0	0	0	0	0	.400
Carney Lansford, 3b	0	0	0	0	0	1	.167
Ruben Sierra, rf	5	1	1	0	0	0	.333
Harold Baines, dh	4	1	2	0	0	0	.440
Mark McGwire, 1b	4	0	1	1	0	0	.150
Terry Steinbach, c	4	0	2	1	0	2	.292
Willie Wilson, cf	4	0	1	0	0	3	.227
Mike Bordick, ss	2	0	0	0	0	1	.053
Eric Fox, ph	0	0	0	0	1	0	.000
Walt Weiss, ss	0	0	0	0	1	0	.167
Lance Blankenship, 2b	2	0	0	0	1	1	.231
Randy Ready, ph	1	0	0	0	0	1	.000
TOTALS	35	2	7	2	4	10	.251

Blue Jays	AB	R	H	RBI	BB	K	Avg
Devon White, cf	4	1	1	1	0	1	.348
Roberto Alomar, 2b	5	1	3	1	0	1	.423
Joe Carter, rf	5	1	1	2	0	1	.192
Dave Winfield, dh	4	1	0	0	1	2	.250
John Olerud, 1b	3	2	2	1	1	0	.348
Candy Maldonado, lf	4	1	2	3	0	1	.273
Kelly Gruber, 3b	3	0	0	0	0	1	.091
Pat Borders, c	2	1	2	1	1	0	.318
Manuel Lee, ss	4	1	2	0	0	0	.278
TOTALS	34	9	13	9	3	7	.282

	1	2	3	4	5	6	7	8	9		R	H	E
Athletics	0	0	0	0	0	1	0	1	0		2	7	1
Blue Jays	2	0	4	0	1	0	0	2	x		9	13	0

E—Henderson. LOB—Athletics 10, Blue Jays 7. Scoring Position—Athletics 3-for-13, Blue Jays 4-for-9. 2B—Baines (2), Olerud (2), Lee (1). HR—Carter (1), Maldonado (2). S—Gruber. SF—White, Borders. SB—Sierra (1), Wilson (7), Alomar 2 (5), Fox (2). CS—White (4).

Athletics	IP	H	R	ER	BB	K	ERA
Mike Moore (L, 0-2)	2.2	7	6	5	1	4	7.45
Jeff Parrett	2.0	4	1	1	0	1	11.57
Rick Honeycutt	1.1	0	0	0	0	1	0.00
Jeff Russell	1.0	0	0	0	1	0	9.00
Bobby Witt	1.0	2	2	2	1	1	18.00

Blue Jays	IP	H	R	ER	BB	K	ERA
Juan Guzman (W, 2-0)	7.0	5	1	1	2	8	2.08
Duane Ward	1.0	2	1	1	0	1	6.75
Tom Henke	1.0	0	0	0	2	1	0.00

PB—Borders 2. Time—3:15. Attendance—51,335. Umpires—HP, Coble. 1B, Denkinger. 2B, Young. 3B, Clark.

1992 AL Championship Series—Composite Statistics

Batting

Blue Jays	G	AB	R	H	RBI	2B	3B	HR	BB	SO	SB	CS	Avg	OBP	Slg
Roberto Alomar	6	26	4	11	4	1	0	2	2	1	5	0	.423	.464	.692
Derek Bell	2	0	1	0	0	0	0	0	1	0	0	0	—	1.000	—
Pat Borders	6	22	3	7	3	0	0	1	1	1	0	0	.318	.320	.455
Joe Carter	6	26	2	5	3	0	0	1	2	4	2	0	.192	.250	.308
Alfredo Griffin	2	2	0	0	0	0	0	0	0	0	0	0	.000	.000	.000
Kelly Gruber	6	22	3	2	2	1	0	1	2	3	0	0	.091	.167	.273
Manuel Lee	6	18	2	5	3	1	1	0	1	2	0	0	.278	.300	.444
Candy Maldonado	6	22	3	6	6	0	0	2	3	4	0	1	.273	.360	.545
John Olerud	6	23	4	8	4	2	0	1	2	5	0	0	.348	.400	.565
Ed Sprague	2	2	0	1	0	0	0	0	0	1	0	0	.500	.500	.500
Devon White	6	23	2	8	2	2	0	0	5	6	0	4	.348	.448	.435
Dave Winfield	6	24	7	6	3	1	0	2	4	2	0	0	.250	.357	.542
Totals	6	210	31	59	30	8	1	10	23	29	7	5	.281	.346	.471

Batting

Athletics	G	AB	R	H	RBI	2B	3B	HR	BB	SO	SB	CS	Avg	OBP	Slg
Harold Baines	6	25	6	11	4	2	0	1	0	3	0	0	.440	.440	.640
Lance Blankenship	5	13	2	3	0	0	0	0	3	4	1	0	.231	.375	.231
Mike Bordick	6	19	1	1	0	0	0	0	1	2	1	0	.053	.100	.053
Jerry Browne	4	10	3	4	2	0	0	0	2	0	0	0	.400	.500	.400
Eric Fox	4	1	0	0	0	0	0	0	1	0	2	0	.000	.500	.000
Rickey Henderson	6	23	5	6	1	0	0	0	4	4	2	0	.261	.370	.261
Carney Lansford	5	18	0	3	1	0	0	0	1	1	0	0	.167	.211	.167
Mark McGwire	6	20	1	3	3	0	0	1	5	4	0	0	.150	.346	.300
Jamie Quirk	1	1	0	0	0	0	0	0	0	0	0	0	.000	.000	.000
Randy Ready	1	1	0	0	0	0	0	0	1	0	0	0	.000	.000	.000
Ruben Sierra	6	24	4	8	7	2	1	1	2	1	1	2	.333	.357	.625
Terry Steinbach	6	24	1	7	5	0	0	1	2	7	0	0	.292	.346	.417
Walt Weiss	3	6	1	1	0	0	0	0	2	1	0	0	.167	.375	.167
Willie Wilson	6	22	0	5	0	1	0	0	1	5	7	0	.227	.261	.273
Totals	6	207	24	52	23	5	1	4	24	33	16	2	.251	.329	.343

Pitching

Blue Jays	G	GS	CG	IP	H	R	ER	BB	SO	W-L	Sv-Op	Hld	ERA
David Cone	2	2	0	12.0	11	7	4	5	9	1-1	0-0	0	3.00
Mark Eichhorn	1	0	0	1.0	0	0	0	0	0	0-0	0-0	0	0.00
Juan Guzman	2	2	0	13.0	12	3	3	5	11	2-0	0-0	0	2.08
Tom Henke	4	0	0	4.2	3	0	0	2	2	0-0	3-3	0	0.00
Jimmy Key	1	0	0	3.0	2	0	0	2	1	0-0	0-0	0	0.00
Jack Morris	2	2	1	12.1	11	9	9	9	6	0-1	0-0	0	6.57
Todd Stottlemyre	1	0	0	3.2	4	1	1	0	1	0-0	0-0	0	2.45
Mike Timlin	2	0	0	1.1	4	1	1	0	1	0-0	0-0	1	6.75
Duane Ward	3	0	0	4.0	6	3	3	1	2	1-0	0-0	0	6.75
Totals	6	6	1	55.0	52	24	21	24	33	4-2	3-3	2	3.44

Pitching

Athletics	G	GS	CG	IP	H	R	ER	BB	SO	W-L	Sv-Op	Hld	ERA
Jim Corsi	3	0	0	2.0	2	0	0	3	0	0-0	0-0	0	0.00
Ron Darling	1	1	0	6.0	4	3	2	2	3	0-1	0-0	0	3.00
Kelly Downs	2	0	0	2.1	3	3	1	1	0	0-1	0-0	0	3.86
Dennis Eckersley	3	0	0	3.0	8	2	2	0	2	0-0	1-2	0	6.00
Rick Honeycutt	2	0	0	2.0	0	0	0	0	1	0-0	0-0	0	0.00
Mike Moore	2	0	0	9.2	11	9	8	5	7	0-2	0-0	0	7.45
Jeff Parrett	3	0	0	2.1	6	3	3	0	1	0-0	0-0	0	11.57
Jeff Russell	3	0	0	2.0	2	2	2	4	0	0-1	0-1	0	9.00
Dave Stewart	2	2	1	16.2	14	5	5	6	7	1-0	0-0	0	2.70
Bob Welch	1	1	0	7.0	7	2	2	1	7	0-0	0-0	0	2.57
Bobby Witt	1	0	0	1.0	2	2	2	1	1	0-0	0-0	0	18.00
Totals	6	6	1	54.0	59	31	27	23	29	2-4	1-3	0	4.50

Fielding

Blue Jays	Pos	G	PO	Ast	E	DP	PB	FPct
Roberto Alomar	2b	6	16	15	0	5	—	1.000
Derek Bell	rf	2	1	0	0	0	—	1.000
Pat Borders	c	6	38	3	1	1	3	.976
Joe Carter	rf	6	14	1	1	1	—	.938
	1b	2	2	0	0	0	—	1.000
David Cone	p	2	0	1	1	0	—	.500
Mark Eichhorn	p	1	0	0	0	0	—	—
Alfredo Griffin	ss	1	0	3	0	0	—	1.000
Kelly Gruber	3b	6	5	16	1	2	—	.955
Juan Guzman	p	2	0	0	0	0	—	—
Tom Henke	p	4	0	0	0	0	—	—
Jimmy Key	p	1	0	0	0	0	—	—
Manuel Lee	ss	6	12	15	3	5	—	.900
Candy Maldonado	lf	6	9	1	0	1	—	1.000
Jack Morris	p	2	0	4	0	1	—	1.000
John Olerud	1b	6	51	1	0	6	—	1.000
Todd Stottlemyre	p	1	0	0	0	0	—	—
Mike Timlin	p	2	0	0	0	0	—	—
Duane Ward	p	3	1	0	0	0	—	1.000
Devon White	cf	6	16	0	1	0	—	.941
Totals		6	165	60	8	22	3	.966

Fielding

Athletics	Pos	G	PO	Ast	E	DP	PB	FPct
Lance Blankenship	2b	5	11	13	2	3	—	.923
Mike Bordick	ss	4	10	10	0	3	—	1.000
	2b	2	5	4	0	1	—	1.000
Jerry Browne	3b	2	3	0	0	0	—	1.000
	cf	1	3	0	0	0	—	1.000
Jim Corsi	p	3	0	0	0	0	—	—
Ron Darling	p	1	1	0	0	0	—	1.000
Kelly Downs	p	2	0	0	0	0	—	—
Dennis Eckersley	p	3	0	0	0	0	—	—
Eric Fox	lf	1	1	0	0	0	—	1.000
Rickey Henderson	lf	6	15	0	3	0	—	.833
Rick Honeycutt	p	2	0	0	0	0	—	—
Carney Lansford	3b	5	2	9	1	0	—	.917
Mark McGwire	1b	6	46	2	1	3	—	.980
Mike Moore	p	2	1	1	0	0	—	1.000
Jeff Parrett	p	3	0	1	0	0	—	1.000
Jeff Russell	p	3	0	0	0	0	—	—
Ruben Sierra	rf	6	12	0	0	0	—	1.000
Terry Steinbach	c	6	30	7	0	0	0	1.000
Dave Stewart	p	2	1	1	0	0	—	1.000
Walt Weiss	ss	3	5	6	0	1	—	1.000
Bob Welch	p	1	0	1	0	0	—	1.000
Willie Wilson	cf	6	16	0	0	0	—	1.000
Bobby Witt	p	1	0	0	0	0	—	—
Totals		6	162	55	7	11	0	.969

1992 Atlanta Braves (NL) 4, Pittsburgh Pirates (NL) 3

After taking a 3-1 lead in the Series, the Braves almost blew it, but they survived thanks to a miracle. John Smoltz gave Atlanta eight strong innings in Game 1 for a 5-1 Atlanta victory. Braves hitters mounted a group attack in Game 2, running away with a 13-5 win. Rookie knuckleballer Tim Wakefield stopped the Braves in Game 3, 3-2, but the Braves took the fourth game, 6-4, to go up three games to one. Braves manager Bobby Cox elected to skip fourth starter Charlie Liebrandt, and brought back Steve Avery on short rest for Game 5. Avery never made it out of the first inning, and the Braves fell, 7-1. It was the same story the next day, as Tom Glavine came back on three days' rest and was pounded for eight runs before being lifted in the second inning. Wakefield pitched up another complete game in Pittsburgh's 13-4 win. In the seventh game, Doug Drabek outdueled Smoltz, taking a 2-0 lead into the bottom of the ninth. He couldn't close it out, though, loading the bases with none out before being lifted. After a sacrifice fly cut the lead to one run, Damon Berryhill walked and Brian Hunter popped out. With two out and the bases again loaded, pinch-hitter Orlando Cabrera singled to left. The tying run scored, and Sid Bream summoned every bit of his nearly nonexistent speed to barely beat Barry Bonds' throw to the plate, scoring the winning run and sending the Braves to their second straight World Series.

Game 1

Tuesday, October 6

Pirates	AB	R	H	RBI	BB	K	Avg
Alex Cole, rf	4	0	1	0	0	0	.250
Jay Bell, ss	3	0	0	0	1	0	.000
Andy Van Slyke, cf	4	0	1	0	0	2	.250
Barry Bonds, lf	3	0	0	0	1	1	.000
Jeff King, 3b	4	0	1	0	0	0	.250
Orlando Merced, 1b	3	0	0	0	1	2	.000
Mike LaValliere, c	3	0	0	0	0	1	.000
Jose Lind, 2b	3	1	2	1	0	0	.667
Doug Drabek, p	2	0	0	0	0	2	.000
Bob Patterson, p	0	0	0	0	0	0	—
Denny Neagle, p	0	0	0	0	0	0	—
Gary Varsho, ph	1	0	0	0	0	0	.000
Danny Cox, p	0	0	0	0	0	0	—
TOTALS	30	1	5	1	3	8	.167

Braves	AB	R	H	RBI	BB	K	Avg
Otis Nixon, cf	5	1	1	0	0	1	.200
Jeff Blauser, ss	3	1	1	1	1	0	.333
Rafael Belliard, pr-ss	0	0	0	0	0	0	—
Terry Pendleton, 3b	4	0	1	1	0	0	.250
David Justice, rf	3	1	1	0	1	0	.333
Sid Bream, 1b	4	2	2	1	0	0	.500
Ron Gant, lf	3	0	0	0	0	1	.000
Damon Berryhill, c	3	0	0	0	0	2	.000
Mark Lemke, 2b	3	0	2	1	1	0	.667
John Smoltz, p	3	0	0	0	0	2	.000
Lonnie Smith, ph	1	0	0	0	0	0	.000
Mike Stanton, p	0	0	0	0	0	0	—
TOTALS	32	5	8	4	4	6	.250

	1	2	3	4	5	6	7	8	9	R	H	E
Pirates	0	0	0	0	0	0	0	1	0	1	5	1
Braves	0	1	0	2	1	0	1	0	x	5	8	0

E—Merced. DP—Braves 1 (Pendleton to Lemke to Bream). LOB—Pirates 5, Braves 8. Scoring Position—Pirates 0-for-2, Braves 2-for-9. 2B—King (1), Justice (1), Bream (1). HR—Lind (1), Blauser (1). S—Gant. GDP—Bell. SB—Nixon (1), Gant (1). CS—Merced (1).

Pirates	IP	H	R	ER	BB	K	ERA
Doug Drabek (L, 0-1)	4.2	5	4	3	2	4	5.79
Bob Patterson	1.1	3	1	1	1	1	6.75
Denny Neagle	1.0	0	0	0	0	0	0.00
Danny Cox	1.0	0	0	0	1	1	0.00

Braves	IP	H	R	ER	BB	K	ERA
John Smoltz (W, 1-0)	8.0	4	1	1	3	6	1.13
Mike Stanton	1.0	1	0	0	0	2	0.00

Patterson pitched to four batters in the 7th.

WP—Smoltz. Time—3:00. Attendance—51,971. Umpires—HP, McSherry. 1B, Marsh. 2B, Ripley. 3B, Darling.

Game 2

Wednesday, October 7

Pirates	AB	R	H	RBI	BB	K	Avg
Gary Redus, 1b	3	0	0	0	0	0	.000
Orlando Merced, ph-1b	1	0	0	0	1	1	.000
Jay Bell, ss	4	0	1	0	1	0	.143
Andy Van Slyke, cf	5	0	0	0	0	1	.111
Barry Bonds, lf	3	2	1	0	1	1	.167
Jeff King, 3b	4	0	0	0	0	0	.125
Lloyd McClendon, rf	3	1	2	1	0	0	.667
Alex Cole, ph-rf	0	0	0	0	1	0	.250
Don Slaught, c	3	1	1	1	1	0	.333
Jose Lind, 2b	4	1	1	2	0	1	.429
Stan Belinda, p	0	0	0	0	0	0	—
Danny Jackson, p	0	0	0	0	0	0	—
Roger Mason, p	0	0	0	0	0	0	—
John Wehner, ph	1	0	0	0	0	1	.000
Bob Walk, p	1	0	0	0	0	0	.000
Randy Tomlin, p	0	0	0	0	0	0	—
Cecil Espy, ph	1	0	1	0	0	0	1.000
Denny Neagle, p	0	0	0	0	0	0	—
Bob Patterson, p	0	0	0	0	0	0	—
Carlos Garcia, 2b	1	0	0	0	0	0	.000
TOTALS	34	5	7	4	5	4	.207

Braves	AB	R	H	RBI	BB	K	Avg
Otis Nixon, cf	4	2	1	0	2	1	.222
Jeff Blauser, ss	2	1	1	1	1	0	.400
Rafael Belliard, ss	1	1	0	1	0	0	.000
Terry Pendleton, 3b	5	1	2	2	0	0	.333
David Justice, rf	3	1	1	2	2	1	.333
Brian Hunter, 1b	2	1	1	0	0	1	.500
Lonnie Smith, ph	1	0	0	0	0	0	.000
Sid Bream, 1b	1	0	0	0	0	0	.400
Ron Gant, lf	4	3	2	4	1	0	.286
Jeff Reardon, p	0	0	0	0	0	0	—
Damon Berryhill, c	5	1	2	1	0	0	.250
Mark Lemke, 2b	5	1	3	1	0	1	.625
Steve Avery, p	2	0	0	1	0	1	.000
Marvin Freeman, p	0	0	0	0	0	0	—
Mike Stanton, p	1	1	1	1	0	0	1.000
Mark Wohlers, p	0	0	0	0	0	0	—
Deion Sanders, ph-lf	1	0	0	0	0	0	.000
TOTALS	37	13	14	13	8	6	.333

	1	2	3	4	5	6	7	8	9	R	H	E
Pirates	0	0	0	0	0	0	4	1	0	5	7	0
Braves	0	4	0	0	4	0	5	0	x	13	14	0

LOB—Pirates 7, Braves 9. Scoring Position—Pirates 1-for-5, Braves 5-for-12. 2B—McClendon (1), Pendleton (1), Stanton (1). 3B—Lind (1). HR—Gant (1). SF—Avery. SB—Nixon (2).

Pirates	IP	H	R	ER	BB	K	ERA
Danny Jackson (L, 0-1)	1.2	4	4	4	2	0	21.60
Roger Mason	0.1	0	0	0	0	0	0.00
Bob Walk	2.2	3	4	4	2	4	13.50
Randy Tomlin	1.1	2	0	0	1	0	0.00
Denny Neagle	0.2	4	5	5	3	0	27.00
Bob Patterson	0.1	0	0	0	0	0	5.40
Stan Belinda	1.0	1	0	0	0	2	0.00

Braves	IP	H	R	ER	BB	K	ERA
Steve Avery (W, 1-0)	6.1	6	4	4	2	3	5.68
Marvin Freeman	0.1	1	0	0	0	1	0.00
Mike Stanton (H, 1)	0.1	0	1	0	1	0	0.00
Mark Wohlers	1.0	0	0	0	0	0	0.00
Jeff Reardon	1.0	0	0	0	1	0	0.00

Stanton pitched to one batter in the 8th.

WP—Avery. PB—Berryhill. Time—3:20. Attendance—51,975. Umpires—HP, Marsh. 1B, Ripley. 2B, Darling. 3B, Davis.

Game 3

Friday, October 9

Braves	AB	R	H	RBI	BB	K	Avg
Otis Nixon, cf	3	0	1	0	1	1	.250
Jeff Blauser, ss	4	0	0	0	0	1	.222
Terry Pendleton, 3b	4	0	0	0	0	1	.231
David Justice, rf	4	0	1	0	0	0	.300
Sid Bream, 1b	4	1	1	1	0	0	.333
Ron Gant, lf	3	1	1	1	0	0	.300
Damon Berryhill, c	3	0	0	0	0	0	.182
Mark Lemke, 2b	3	0	1	0	0	1	.545
Tom Glavine, p	2	0	0	0	0	0	.000
Mike Stanton, p	0	0	0	0	0	0	1.000
Lonnie Smith, ph	1	0	0	0	0	0	.000

Mark Wohlers, p	0	0	0	0	0	0	—
TOTALS	31	2	5	2	1	3	.286

Pirates	AB	R	H	RBI	BB	K	Avg
Gary Redus, 1b	3	1	3	0	1	0	.500
Jay Bell, ss	4	0	1	0	0	0	.182
Andy Van Slyke, cf	3	1	1	1	0	0	.167
Barry Bonds, lf	3	0	0	0	0	0	.111
Jeff King, 3b	4	0	1	1	0	0	.167
Lloyd McClendon, rf	2	0	0	0	1	1	.400
Cecil Espy, ph-rf	1	0	1	0	0	0	1.000
Don Slaught, c	3	1	1	1	1	0	.333
Jose Lind, 2b	4	0	0	0	0	1	.273
Tim Wakefield, p	3	0	0	0	0	0	.000
TOTALS	30	3	8	3	3	2	.247

	1	2	3	4	5	6	7	8	9	R	H	E
Braves	0	0	0	1	0	0	1	0	0	2	5	0
Pirates	0	0	0	0	1	1	1	0	x	3	8	1

E—Lind. DP—Braves 1 (Pendleton to Lemke to Bream), Pirates 2 (King to Lind; King to Lind to Redus). LOB—Braves 3, Pirates 8. Scoring Position—Braves 0-for-4, Pirates 1-for-10. 2B—Nixon (1), Lemke (1), Redus (1), Bell (1), Van Slyke (1), King (2). 3B—Redus (1). HR—Bream (1), Gant (2), Slaught (1). SF—Van Slyke. GDP—Blauser, Gant, Slaught.

Braves	IP	H	R	ER	BB	K	ERA
Tom Glavine (L, 0-1)	6.1	7	3	3	3	2	4.26
Mike Stanton	0.2	0	0	0	0	0	0.00
Mark Wohlers	1.0	1	0	0	0	0	0.00

Pirates	IP	H	R	ER	BB	K	ERA
Tim Wakefield (W, 1-0)	9.0	5	2	2	1	3	2.00

HBP—Bonds by Glavine. Time—2:37. Attendance—56,610. Umpires—HP, Ripley. 1B, Darling. 2B, Davis. 3B, Montague.

Game 4

Saturday, October 10

Braves	AB	R	H	RBI	BB	K	Avg
Otis Nixon, cf	5	2	4	0	0	0	.412
Jeff Blauser, ss	3	1	2	1	0	0	.333
Rafael Belliard, ss	1	0	0	0	0	0	.000
Terry Pendleton, 3b	5	0	0	0	0	1	.167
David Justice, rf	4	0	1	1	1	0	.286
Sid Bream, 1b	2	0	0	0	0	0	.273
Brian Hunter, ph-1b	2	0	0	0	0	0	.250
Ron Gant, lf	4	1	1	0	0	0	.286
Mike Stanton, p	0	0	0	0	0	0	1.000
Jeff Reardon, p	0	0	0	0	0	0	—
Damon Berryhill, c	3	0	1	0	1	0	.214
Mark Lemke, 2b	2	1	0	0	2	0	.462
John Smoltz, p	3	1	2	1	0	0	.333
Deion Sanders, lf	1	0	0	0	0	1	.000
TOTALS	35	6	11	5	4	2	.297

Pirates	AB	R	H	RBI	BB	K	Avg
Alex Cole, rf	4	1	1	1	1	2	.250
Jay Bell, ss	5	0	0	0	0	2	.125
Andy Van Slyke, cf	4	0	2	1	0	2	.250
Barry Bonds, lf	2	0	0	0	2	2	.091
Jeff King, 3b	4	1	0	0	0	1	.125
Orlando Merced, 1b	3	0	1	1	0	1	.143
Gary Redus, ph-1b	1	0	0	0	0	1	.429
Mike LaValliere, c	3	1	1	0	0	1	.167
Don Slaught, ph-c	1	0	0	0	0	0	.286
Jose Lind, 2b	3	1	1	1	0	0	.286
Doug Drabek, p	1	0	0	0	0	0	.000
Randy Tomlin, p	0	0	0	0	0	0	—
Danny Cox, p	0	0	0	0	0	0	—
John Wehner, ph	1	0	0	0	0	1	.000
Roger Mason, p	0	0	0	0	0	0	—
Cecil Espy, ph	1	0	0	0	0	1	.667
TOTALS	33	4	6	3	5	14	.207

	1 2 3 4 5 6 7 8 9	R	H	E
Braves	0 2 0 0 2 2 0 0 0	6	11	1
Pirates	0 2 1 0 0 0 1 0 0	4	6	1

E—Blauser, King. DP—Pirates 3 (King to Lind to Merced; Cole to Merced; King to Merced). LOB—Braves 7, Pirates 7. Scoring Position—Braves 5-for-12, Pirates 1-for-8. 2B—Nixon (2), Van Slyke (2), Merced (1). 3B—Van Slyke (1). S—Blauser. GDP—Gant. SB—Nixon (3), Smoltz (1).

Braves	IP	H	R	ER	BB	K	ERA
John Smoltz (W, 2-0)	6.1	6	4	3	5	9	2.51
Mike Stanton (H, 2)	1.2	0	0	0	0	3	0.00
Jeff Reardon (S, 1)	1.0	0	0	0	0	2	0.00

Pirates	IP	H	R	ER	BB	K	ERA
Doug Drabek (L, 0-2)	4.1	7	4	3	2	1	6.00
Randy Tomlin	1.1	3	2	2	0	0	6.75
Danny Cox	0.1	1	0	0	0	0	0.00
Roger Mason	3.0	0	0	0	2	1	0.00

Time—3:10. Attendance—57,164. Umpires—HP, Darling. 1B, Davis. 2B, Montague. 3B, McSherry.

Game 5
Sunday, October 11

Braves	AB	R	H	RBI	BB	K	Avg
Otis Nixon, cf	4	0	0	0	0	0	.333
Jeff Blauser, ss	3	0	0	1	1	0	.267
Terry Pendleton, 3b	4	0	1	0	0	0	.182
David Justice, rf	2	0	0	0	2	0	.250
Sid Bream, 1b	4	0	1	0	0	0	.267
Ron Gant, lf	3	0	0	0	1	1	.235
Damon Berryhill, c	4	0	0	0	0	0	.167
Mark Lemke, 2b	3	0	0	0	1	0	.375
Steve Avery, p	0	0	0	0	0	0	.000
Pete Smith, p	1	0	0	0	0	0	.000
Jeff Treadway, ph	1	0	0	0	0	1	.000
Charlie Leibrandt, p	0	0	0	0	0	0	—
Marvin Freeman, p	0	0	0	0	0	0	—
Lonnie Smith, ph	1	1	1	0	0	0	.250
Kent Mercker, p	0	0	0	0	0	0	—
TOTALS	30	1	3	1	5	2	.250

Pirates	AB	R	H	RBI	BB	K	Avg
Gary Redus, 1b	4	1	2	1	1	1	.455
Jay Bell, ss	5	1	1	0	0	0	.143
Andy Van Slyke, cf	5	0	1	0	0	0	.238
Barry Bonds, lf	5	2	2	1	0	0	.188
Jeff King, 3b	4	2	3	1	0	0	.250
Lloyd McClendon, rf	3	0	3	2	0	0	.625
Don Slaught, c	1	1	1	1	3	0	.375
Jose Lind, 2b	4	0	0	0	0	1	.222
Bob Walk, p	4	0	0	0	0	1	.000
TOTALS	35	7	13	7	4	3	.258

	1 2 3 4 5 6 7 8 9	R	H	E
Braves	0 0 0 0 0 0 0 1 0	1	3	0
Pirates	4 0 1 0 0 1 1 0 x	7	13	0

LOB—Braves 7, Pirates 9. Scoring Position—Braves 0-for-5, Pirates 7-for-14. 2B—Bream (2), Redus (3), Bonds (1), King (3), McClendon (2). 3B—LSmith (1). SF—McClendon. SB—Bonds (1). CS—King (1).

Braves	IP	H	R	ER	BB	K	ERA
Steve Avery (L, 1-1)	0.1	5	4	4	0	0	10.80
Pete Smith	3.2	2	1	1	2	3	2.45
Charlie Leibrandt	1.2	2	1	1	1	0	5.40
Marvin Freeman	1.1	3	1	1	0	0	5.40
Kent Mercker	1.0	1	0	0	1	0	0.00

Pirates	IP	H	R	ER	BB	K	ERA
Bob Walk (W, 1-0)	9.0	3	1	1	5	2	3.86

Time—2:52. Attendance—52,929. Umpires—HP, Davis. 1B, Montague. 2B, McSherry. 3B, Marsh.

Game 6
Tuesday, October 13

Pirates	AB	R	H	RBI	BB	K	Avg
Gary Redus, 1b	5	2	2	2	0	1	.438
Jay Bell, ss	4	1	1	3	0	1	.160
Andy Van Slyke, cf	4	0	1	1	1	1	.240
Barry Bonds, lf	4	1	2	1	1	0	.250
Jeff King, 3b	5	1	1	0	0	0	.240
Lloyd McClendon, rf	3	3	3	1	1	0	.727
Gary Varsho, ph-rf	1	0	1	0	0	0	.500
Don Slaught, c	4	2	1	2	1	2	.333
Jose Lind, 2b	5	2	1	2	0	1	.217
Tim Wakefield, p	3	1	0	0	0	0	.000
TOTALS	38	13	13	12	4	6	.279

Braves	AB	R	H	RBI	BB	K	Avg
Otis Nixon, cf	3	0	0	0	1	1	.292
Kent Mercker, p	0	0	0	0	0	0	—
Mark Wohlers, p	0	0	0	0	0	0	—
Francisco Cabrera, ph	1	0	0	0	0	0	.000
Jeff Blauser, ss	5	0	1	0	0	0	.250
Terry Pendleton, 3b	4	0	2	0	0	0	.231
Jeff Treadway, 2b	1	1	1	0	0	0	.500
David Justice, rf	5	2	3	3	0	0	.333
Sid Bream, 1b	4	1	1	0	1	0	.263
Ron Gant, lf	3	0	0	0	1	1	.200
Damon Berryhill, c	3	0	0	0	0	0	.143
Javy Lopez, c	1	0	0	0	0	0	.000
Mark Lemke, 2b-3b	3	0	0	0	1	1	.316
Tom Glavine, p	0	0	0	0	0	0	.000
Charlie Leibrandt, p	1	0	0	0	0	1	.000
Lonnie Smith, ph	1	0	1	1	0	0	.400
Marvin Freeman, p	0	0	0	0	0	0	—
Deion Sanders, ph-cf	2	0	0	0	0	0	.000
TOTALS	37	4	9	4	4	4	.247

	1 2 3 4 5 6 7 8 9	R	H	E
Pirates	0 8 0 0 4 1 0 0 0	13	13	1
Braves	0 0 0 1 0 0 1 0 2	4	9	1

E—Bell, Blauser. DP—Braves 1 (Lemke to Blauser to Bream). LOB—Pirates 5, Braves 10. Scoring Position—Pirates 6-for-8, Braves 1-for-9. 2B—Redus (4), Slaught (1), Lind (1). HR—Bell (1), Bonds (1), McClendon (1), Justice 2 (2). S—Wakefield 2. GDP—Van Slyke.

Pirates	IP	H	R	ER	BB	K	ERA
Tim Wakefield (W, 2-0)	9.0	9	4	4	4	4	3.00

Braves	IP	H	R	ER	BB	K	ERA
Tom Glavine (L, 0-2)	1.0	6	8	7	0	0	12.27
Charlie Leibrandt	3.0	2	0	0	2	3	1.93
Marvin Freeman	2.0	4	5	5	2	0	14.73
Kent Mercker	2.0	0	0	0	0	1	0.00
Mark Wohlers	1.0	1	0	0	0	2	0.00

Glavine pitched to nine batters in the 2nd.

WP—Wakefield. PB—Slaught 2. HBP—Bell by Glavine. Time—2:50. Attendance—51,975. Umpires—HP, Montague. 1B, McSherry. 2B, Marsh. 3B, Rippley.

Game 7
Wednesday, October 14

Pirates	AB	R	H	RBI	BB	K	Avg
Alex Cole, rf	2	1	0	0	1	0	.200
Lloyd McClendon, ph-rf	0	0	0	0	2	0	.727
Cecil Espy, pr-rf	0	0	0	0	0	0	.667
Jay Bell, ss	4	1	1	0	1	1	.172
Andy Van Slyke, cf	4	0	2	1	0	0	.276
Barry Bonds, lf	3	0	1	0	1	0	.261
Orlando Merced, 1b	3	0	0	1	0	0	.100
Jeff King, 3b	4	0	1	0	0	0	.241
Mike LaValliere, c	4	0	1	0	0	2	.200
Jose Lind, 2b	4	0	1	0	0	0	.222
Doug Drabek, p	3	0	0	0	0	2	.000
Stan Belinda, p	0	0	0	0	0	0	—
TOTALS	31	2	7	2	5	5	.251

Braves	AB	R	H	RBI	BB	K	Avg
Otis Nixon, cf	4	0	1	0	0	0	.286
Jeff Blauser, ss	4	0	0	0	0	2	.208
Terry Pendleton, 3b	4	1	1	0	0	0	.233
David Justice, rf	4	1	0	0	0	1	.280
Sid Bream, 1b	3	1	1	0	1	0	.273
Ron Gant, lf	2	0	1	1	1	1	.182
Damon Berryhill, c	3	0	1	0	0	0	.167
Mark Lemke, 2b	2	0	1	0	0	0	.333
Lonnie Smith, ph	1	0	0	0	0	0	.333
Rafael Belliard, 2b	0	0	0	0	0	0	.000
Brian Hunter, ph	1	0	0	0	0	0	.200
John Smoltz, p	1	0	0	0	0	0	.286
Jeff Treadway, ph	1	0	1	0	0	0	.667
Mike Stanton, p	0	0	0	0	0	0	1.000
Pete Smith, p	0	0	0	0	0	0	.000
Steve Avery, p	0	0	0	0	0	0	.000
Deion Sanders, ph	0	0	0	0	0	1	.000
Jeff Reardon, p	0	0	0	0	0	0	—
Francisco Cabrera, ph	1	0	1	2	0	0	.500
TOTALS	32	3	7	3	3	5	.248

	1 2 3 4 5 6 7 8 9	R	H	E
Pirates	1 0 0 0 0 1 0 0 0	2	7	1
Braves	0 0 0 0 0 0 0 0 3	3	7	0

E—Lind. DP—Pirates 1 (King). LOB—Pirates 9, Braves 7. Scoring Position—Pirates 1-for-7, Braves 2-for-11. 2B—Bell (2), Van Slyke (3), King (4), Lind (2), Pendleton (2), Bream (3), Berryhill (1). S—Drabek. SF—Merced, Gant.

Pirates	IP	H	R	ER	BB	K	ERA
Doug Drabek (L, 0-3)	8.0	6	3	1	2	5	3.71
Stan Belinda (BS, 1)	0.2	1	0	0	1	0	0.00

Braves	IP	H	R	ER	BB	K	ERA
John Smoltz	6.0	4	2	2	2	4	2.66
Mike Stanton	0.2	1	0	0	1	0	0.00
Pete Smith	0.0	0	0	0	0	0	2.45
Steve Avery	1.1	2	0	0	0	0	9.00
Jeff Reardon (W, 1-0)	1.0	0	0	0	1	1	0.00

P.Smith pitched to one batter in the 7th. Drabek pitched to three batters in the 9th.

WP—Reardon. Time—3:22. Attendance—51,975. Umpires—HP, McSherry/Marsh. 1B, Marsh/Montague. 2B, Rippley. 3B, Darling.

1992 NL Championship Series—Composite Statistics

Batting

Braves	G	AB	R	H	RBI	2B	3B	HR	BB	SO	SB	CS	Avg	OBP	Slg
Steve Avery	3	2	0	0	1	0	0	0	0	1	0	0	.000	.000	.000
Rafael Belliard	4	2	1	0	0	0	0	0	1	0	0	0	.000	.333	.000
Damon Berryhill	7	24	1	4	1	1	0	0	3	2	0	0	.167	.259	.208
Jeff Blauser	7	24	3	5	4	0	1	1	3	2	0	0	.208	.296	.417
Sid Bream	7	22	5	6	2	3	0	1	3	0	0	0	.273	.360	.545
Francisco Cabrera	2	2	0	1	2	0	0	0	0	0	0	0	.500	.500	.500
Ron Gant	7	22	5	4	6	0	0	2	4	4	1	0	.182	.296	.455
Tom Glavine	2	2	0	0	0	0	0	0	0	0	0	0	.000	.000	.000
Brian Hunter	3	5	1	1	0	0	0	0	0	1	0	0	.200	.200	.200
David Justice	7	25	5	7	6	1	0	2	6	2	0	0	.280	.419	.560
Charlie Leibrandt	2	1	0	0	0	0	0	0	0	1	0	0	.000	.000	.000
Mark Lemke	7	21	2	7	2	1	0	0	5	3	0	0	.333	.462	.381
Javy Lopez	1	1	0	0	0	0	0	0	0	0	0	0	.000	.000	.000
Otis Nixon	7	28	5	8	2	2	0	0	4	4	3	0	.286	.375	.357
Terry Pendleton	7	30	2	7	3	2	0	0	0	2	0	0	.233	.233	.300
Deion Sanders	4	5	0	0	0	0	0	0	0	3	0	0	.000	.000	.000
Lonnie Smith	6	6	1	2	1	0	1	0	0	0	0	0	.333	.333	.667
Pete Smith	2	1	0	0	0	0	0	0	0	0	0	0	.000	.000	.000
John Smoltz	3	7	1	2	1	0	0	0	0	2	1	0	.286	.286	.286
Mike Stanton	5	1	1	1	1	1	0	0	0	0	0	0	1.000	1.000	2.000
Jeff Treadway	3	3	1	2	0	0	0	0	0	1	0	0	.667	.667	.667
Totals	7	234	34	57	32	11	2	6	29	28	5	0	.244	.325	.385

Batting

Pirates	G	AB	R	H	RBI	2B	3B	HR	BB	SO	SB	CS	Avg	OBP	Slg
Jay Bell	7	29	3	5	4	2	0	1	3	4	0	0	.172	.273	.345
Barry Bonds	7	23	5	6	2	1	0	1	6	4	1	0	.261	.433	.435
Alex Cole	4	10	2	2	1	0	0	0	3	2	0	0	.200	.385	.200
Doug Drabek	3	6	0	0	0	0	0	0	1	4	0	0	.000	.143	.000
Cecil Espy	4	3	2	2	0	0	0	0	0	1	0	0	.667	.667	.667
Carlos Garcia	1	1	0	0	0	0	0	0	0	0	0	0	.000	.000	.000
Jeff King	7	29	4	7	2	4	0	0	1	0	1	1	.241	.241	.379
Mike LaValliere	3	10	1	2	0	0	0	0	3	0	0	0	.200	.200	.200
Jose Lind	7	27	5	6	5	2	1	1	1	4	0	0	.222	.250	.481
Lloyd McClendon	5	11	4	8	4	2	0	1	4	1	0	0	.727	.750	1.182
Orlando Merced	4	10	0	1	2	1	0	0	2	4	0	1	.100	.231	.200
Gary Redus	5	16	4	7	3	4	1	0	2	3	0	0	.438	.500	.813
Don Slaught	5	12	5	4	5	1	0	1	6	3	0	0	.333	.556	.667
Andy Van Slyke	7	29	1	8	4	3	1	0	1	5	0	0	.276	.290	.448
Gary Varsho	2	2	0	1	0	0	0	0	0	0	0	0	.500	.500	.500
Tim Wakefield	2	6	1	0	0	0	0	0	0	0	0	0	.000	.000	.000
Bob Walk	2	5	0	0	0	0	0	0	0	1	0	0	.000	.000	.000
John Wehner	2	2	0	0	0	0	0	0	0	2	0	0	.000	.000	.000
Totals	7	231	35	59	32	20	3	5	29	42	1	2	.255	.340	.433

Pitching

Braves	G	GS	CG	IP	H	R	ER	BB	SO	W-L	Sv-Op	Hld	ERA
Steve Avery	3	2	0	8.0	13	8	8	2	3	1-1	0-0	0	9.00
Marvin Freeman	3	0	0	3.2	8	6	6	2	1	0-0	0-0	0	14.73
Tom Glavine	2	2	0	7.1	13	11	10	3	2	0-2	0-0	0	12.27
Charlie Leibrandt	2	0	0	4.2	4	1	1	3	3	0-0	0-0	0	1.93
Kent Mercker	2	0	0	3.0	1	0	0	1	1	0-0	0-0	0	0.00
Jeff Reardon	3	0	0	3.0	0	0	2	3	1	1-0	1-1	0	0.00
Pete Smith	2	0	0	3.2	2	1	1	3	3	0-0	0-0	0	2.45
John Smoltz	3	3	0	20.1	14	7	6	10	19	2-0	0-0	0	2.66
Mike Stanton	5	0	0	4.1	2	1	0	2	5	0-0	0-0	2	0.00
Mark Wohlers	3	0	0	3.0	2	0	0	1	2	0-0	0-0	0	0.00
Totals	7	7	0	61.0	59	35	32	29	42	4-3	1-1	2	4.72

Pitching

Pirates	G	GS	CG	IP	H	R	ER	BB	SO	W-L	Sv-Op	Hld	ERA
Stan Belinda	2	0	0	1.2	2	0	0	1	2	0-0	0-1	0	0.00
Danny Cox	2	0	0	1.1	1	0	0	1	1	0-0	0-0	0	0.00
Doug Drabek	3	3	0	17.0	18	11	7	6	10	0-3	0-0	0	3.71
Danny Jackson	1	1	0	1.2	4	4	4	2	0	0-1	0-0	0	21.60
Roger Mason	2	0	0	3.1	0	0	0	2	1	0-0	0-0	0	0.00
Denny Neagle	2	0	0	1.2	4	5	5	3	0	0-0	0-0	0	27.00
Bob Patterson	2	0	0	1.2	3	1	1	1	1	0-0	0-0	0	5.40
Randy Tomlin	2	0	0	2.2	5	2	2	1	0	0-0	0-0	0	6.75
Tim Wakefield	2	2	2	18.0	14	6	6	5	7	2-0	0-0	0	3.00
Bob Walk	2	1	1	11.2	6	5	5	7	6	1-0	0-0	0	3.86
Totals	7	7	3	60.2	57	34	30	29	28	3-4	0-1	0	4.45

Fielding

Braves	Pos	G	PO	Ast	E	DP	PB	FPct
Steve Avery	p	3	0	0	0	0	—	—
Rafael Belliard	ss	3	1	3	0	0	—	1.000
	2b	1	1	0	0	0	—	1.000
Damon Berryhill	c	7	43	5	0	0	1	1.000
Jeff Blauser	ss	7	7	15	2	1	—	.917
Sid Bream	1b	7	53	3	0	3	—	1.000
Marvin Freeman	p	3	0	2	0	0	—	1.000
Ron Gant	lf	7	16	0	0	0	—	1.000
Tom Glavine	p	2	1	2	0	0	—	1.000
Brian Hunter	1b	2	7	0	0	0	—	1.000
David Justice	rf	7	19	3	0	0	—	1.000
Charlie Leibrandt	p	2	0	1	0	0	—	1.000
Mark Lemke	2b	7	11	16	0	3	—	1.000
	3b	1	0	0	0	0	—	—
Javy Lopez	c	1	2	0	0	0	0	1.000
Kent Mercker	p	2	0	0	0	0	—	—
Otis Nixon	cf	7	16	0	0	0	—	1.000
Terry Pendleton	3b	7	4	18	0	2	—	1.000
Jeff Reardon	p	3	0	0	0	0	—	—
Deion Sanders	lf	2	1	0	0	0	—	1.000
	cf	1	0	0	0	0	—	—
Pete Smith	p	2	0	1	0	0	—	1.000
John Smoltz	p	3	0	1	0	0	—	1.000
Mike Stanton	p	5	0	1	0	0	—	1.000
Jeff Treadway	2b	1	0	1	0	0	—	1.000
Mark Wohlers	p	3	1	0	0	0	—	1.000
Totals		7	183	72	2	9	1	.992

Fielding

Pirates	Pos	G	PO	Ast	E	DP	PB	FPct
Stan Belinda	p	2	0	0	0	0	—	—
Jay Bell	ss	7	6	8	1	0	—	.933
Barry Bonds	lf	7	17	0	0	0	—	1.000
Alex Cole	rf	4	7	1	0	1	—	1.000
Danny Cox	p	2	0	0	0	0	—	—
Doug Drabek	p	3	0	0	0	0	—	—
Cecil Espy	rf	2	0	0	0	0	—	—
Carlos Garcia	2b	1	0	0	0	0	—	—
Danny Jackson	p	1	0	0	0	0	—	—
Jeff King	3b	7	11	19	1	5	—	.968
Mike LaValliere	c	3	14	0	0	0	0	1.000
Jose Lind	2b	7	16	23	2	3	—	.951
Roger Mason	p	2	2	0	0	0	—	1.000
Lloyd McClendon	rf	5	10	0	0	0	—	1.000
Orlando Merced	1b	4	27	2	1	3	—	.967
Denny Neagle	p	2	0	0	0	0	—	—
Bob Patterson	p	2	0	0	0	0	—	—
Gary Redus	1b	5	31	4	0	1	—	1.000
Don Slaught	c	5	17	1	0	0	2	1.000
Randy Tomlin	p	2	0	1	0	0	—	1.000
Andy Van Slyke	cf	7	20	0	0	0	—	1.000
Gary Varsho	rf	1	0	0	0	0	—	—
Tim Wakefield	p	2	3	2	0	0	—	1.000
Bob Walk	p	2	1	2	0	0	—	1.000
Totals		7	182	63	5	13	2	.980

1993 Toronto Blue Jays (AL) 4, Chicago White Sox (AL) 2

The Toronto Blue Jays beat the Chicago White Sox in six games by pitching around Frank Thomas and blasting Jack McDowell. In the opener, Toronto torched McDowell for 13 hits and seven runs en route to a 7-3 victory. The Sox wasted several scoring opportunities in Game 2 as Dave Stewart beat Alex Fernandez, 3-1. Southpaw Wilson Alvarez got the Sox back in it with a 6-1 victory in the third game, and Lance Johnson helped even up the series with a two-run homer and a two-run triple in Chicago's 7-4 Game 4 win. The Jays knocked McDowell out of the box by the bottom of the third inning in Game 5, and Juan Guzman pitched Toronto to a 5-3 victory. Toronto had the ultimate big-game pitcher ready for Game 6, Stewart, and he wrapped up the AL pennant with a 6-3 win, upping his lifetime ALCS record to 8-0.

Game 1

Tuesday, October 5

Blue Jays	AB	R	H	RBI	BB	K	Avg
Rickey Henderson, lf	6	0	0	0	0	0	.000
Devon White, cf	5	0	2	0	0	2	.400
Roberto Alomar, 2b	4	1	0	0	1	1	.000
Joe Carter, rf	5	1	2	0	0	0	.400
John Olerud, 1b	4	3	3	2	1	1	.750
Paul Molitor, dh	5	2	4	3	0	0	.800
Tony Fernandez, ss	5	0	1	0	0	2	.200
Ed Sprague, 3b	5	0	4	2	0	1	.800
Pat Borders, c	5	0	1	0	0	1	.200
TOTALS	44	7	17	7	2	8	.386

White Sox	AB	R	H	RBI	BB	K	Avg
Tim Raines, lf	5	0	2	1	0	0	.400
Joey Cora, 2b	3	0	0	0	2	1	.000
Frank Thomas, dh	1	0	1	0	4	0	1.000
Robin Ventura, 3b	3	0	0	0	2	2	.000
Ellis Burks, rf	5	0	1	0	0	1	.200
Dan Pasqua, 1b	3	1	0	0	1	1	.000
Lance Johnson, cf	4	1	0	0	1	1	.000
Ron Karkovice, c	3	0	0	0	1	0	.000
Ozzie Guillen, ss	4	1	2	2	0	0	.500
TOTALS	31	3	6	3	10	7	.194

	1	2	3	4	5	6	7	8	9	R	H	E
Blue Jays	0	0	0	2	3	0	2	0	0	7	17	1
White Sox	0	0	0	3	0	0	0	0	0	3	6	1

E—Cora, Olerud. DP—Blue Jays 1 (Fernandez to Alomar to Olerud). LOB—Blue Jays 12, White Sox 13. Scoring Position—Blue Jays 4-for-10, White Sox 2-for-14. 2B—Olerud (1), Burks (1). 3B—Sprague (1). HR—Molitor (1). S—Karkovice. GDP—Cora. SB—Raines (1), Guillen (1). CS—Raines (1).

Blue Jays	IP	H	R	ER	BB	K	ERA
Juan Guzman (W, 1-0)	6.0	5	3	2	8	3	3.00
Danny Cox	2.0	1	0	0	2	2	0.00
Duane Ward	1.0	0	0	0	2	2	0.00

White Sox	IP	H	R	ER	BB	K	ERA
Jack McDowell (L, 0-1)	6.2	13	7	7	2	4	9.45
Jose DeLeon	1.0	2	0	0	0	1	0.00
Scott Radinsky	0.1	0	0	0	0	1	0.00
Kirk McCaskill	1.0	2	0	0	0	2	0.00

WP—Guzman 3. HBP—Pasqua by Guzman. Time—3:38. Attendance—46,246. Umpires—HP, Evans. 1B, Kosc. 2B, Shulock. 3B, Hendry.

Game 2

Wednesday, October 6

Blue Jays	AB	R	H	RBI	BB	K	Avg
Rickey Henderson, lf	3	1	0	0	1	1	.000
Devon White, cf	4	0	2	0	0	1	.444
Roberto Alomar, 2b	4	0	0	1	0	1	.000
Joe Carter, rf	4	0	1	0	0	0	.333
John Olerud, 1b	4	0	1	0	0	0	.500
Paul Molitor, dh	4	1	2	0	0	1	.667
Tony Fernandez, ss	3	1	1	1	1	0	.250
Ed Sprague, 3b	3	0	0	0	1	0	.500
Pat Borders, c	4	0	1	0	0	0	.222
TOTALS	33	3	8	2	3	5	.325

White Sox	AB	R	H	RBI	BB	K	Avg
Tim Raines, lf	4	1	1	0	1	1	.333
Joey Cora, 2b	5	0	0	0	0	2	.000
Frank Thomas, dh	3	0	2	0	1	0	.750
Robin Ventura, 3b-1b	3	0	1	0	1	2	.167
Ellis Burks, rf	2	0	0	0	2	0	.143
Dan Pasqua, 1b	3	0	0	0	0	1	.000
Craig Grebeck, ph-3b	1	0	1	0	0	0	1.000
Lance Johnson, cf	4	0	1	0	0	0	.125
Ron Karkovice, c	1	0	0	0	0	1	.000
Warren Newson, ph	1	0	0	0	0	0	.000
Mike LaValliere, c	1	0	1	0	0	0	1.000
Ozzie Guillen, ss	4	0	0	0	0	0	.250
TOTALS	32	1	7	0	5	7	.206

	1	2	3	4	5	6	7	8	9	R	H	E
Blue Jays	1	0	0	2	0	0	0	0	0	3	8	0
White Sox	1	0	0	0	0	0	0	0	0	1	7	2

E—Pasqua, Cora. DP—Blue Jays 1 (Alomar to TFernandez to Olerud), White Sox 2 (Pasqua to Guillen to AFernandez; Cora to Guillen to Pasqua). LOB—Blue Jays 6, White Sox 10. Scoring Position—Blue Jays 2-for-7, White Sox 0-for-7. 2B—Molitor (1), Johnson (1). S—Karkovice. GDP—Alomar, Sprague, Johnson.

Blue Jays	IP	H	R	ER	BB	K	ERA
Dave Stewart (W, 1-0)	6.0	4	1	1	4	5	1.50
Al Leiter (H, 1)	2.0	2	0	0	1	2	0.00
Duane Ward (S, 1)	1.0	1	0	0	0	0	0.00

White Sox	IP	H	R	ER	BB	K	ERA
Alex Fernandez (L, 0-1)	8.0	8	3	1	3	5	1.13
Roberto Hernandez	1.0	0	0	0	0	0	0.00

WP—Stewart. Time—3:00. Attendance—46,101. Umpires—HP, Kosc. 1B, Shulock. 2B, Hendry. 3B, Tschida.

Game 3

Friday, October 8

White Sox	AB	R	H	RBI	BB	K	Avg
Tim Raines, lf	5	1	4	0	0	0	.500
Joey Cora, 2b	3	1	2	0	0	0	.182
Frank Thomas, 1b	3	1	1	1	2	0	.571
Robin Ventura, 3b	2	1	0	1	2	1	.125
Ellis Burks, rf	5	1	2	2	0	1	.250
Bo Jackson, dh	4	0	0	0	1	3	.000
Lance Johnson, cf	5	0	2	2	0	0	.231
Ron Karkovice, c	4	0	0	0	0	3	.000
Ozzie Guillen, ss	4	1	1	0	0	0	.250
TOTALS	35	6	12	6	5	8	.258

Blue Jays	AB	R	H	RBI	BB	K	Avg
Rickey Henderson, lf	3	1	1	0	1	1	.083
Devon White, cf	4	0	1	1	0	0	.385
Paul Molitor, dh	4	0	1	0	0	1	.538
Joe Carter, rf	4	0	0	0	0	1	.231
John Olerud, 1b	4	0	2	0	0	0	.500
Roberto Alomar, 2b	3	0	1	0	1	0	.091
Tony Fernandez, ss	3	0	1	0	0	1	.273
Ed Sprague, 3b	3	0	0	0	0	0	.364
Pat Borders, c	3	0	0	0	0	2	.167
TOTALS	31	1	7	1	2	6	.296

	1	2	3	4	5	6	7	8	9	R	H	E
White Sox	0	0	5	1	0	0	0	0	0	6	12	0
Blue Jays	0	0	1	0	0	0	0	0	0	1	7	1

E—Henderson. DP—White Sox 2 (Guillen to Thomas; Alvarez to Cora to Thomas), Blue Jays 1 (Borders to Fernandez). LOB—White Sox 10, Blue Jays 5. Scoring Position—White Sox 3-for-11, Blue Jays 1-for-4. 2B—Raines 2 (2), Henderson (1). S—Cora 2. SF—Ventura. GDP—Fernandez, Sprague. SB—Johnson (1), Henderson (1). CS—Burks (1), White (1).

White Sox	IP	H	R	ER	BB	K	ERA
Wilson Alvarez (W, 1-0)	9.0	7	1	1	2	6	1.00

Blue Jays	IP	H	R	ER	BB	K	ERA
Pat Hentgen (L, 0-1)	3.0	9	6	6	2	3	18.00
Danny Cox	3.0	2	0	0	2	3	0.00
Mark Eichhorn	2.0	1	0	0	1	1	0.00
Tony Castillo	1.0	0	0	0	0	1	0.00

Hentgen pitched to two batters in the 4th.

Time—2:56. Attendance—51,783. Umpires—HP, Shulock. 1B, Hendry. 2B, Tschida. 3B, Kaiser.

Postseason: League Championship Series

Game 4
Saturday, October 9

White Sox	AB	R	H	RBI	BB	K	Avg
Tim Raines, lf	5	1	3	0	0	0	.526
Joey Cora, 2b	5	0	1	1	0	1	.188
Frank Thomas, 1b	3	1	1	1	2	1	.500
Robin Ventura, 3b	5	0	2	1	0	0	.231
Ellis Burks, rf	4	2	1	0	1	1	.250
Bo Jackson, dh	2	1	0	0	2	1	.000
Lance Johnson, cf	4	1	2	4	0	0	.294
Ron Karkovice, c	4	0	0	0	0	0	.000
Ozzie Guillen, ss	4	1	1	0	0	2	.250
TOTALS	36	7	11	7	5	6	.272

Blue Jays	AB	R	H	RBI	BB	K	Avg
Rickey Henderson, lf	3	1	0	0	2	1	.067
Devon White, cf	4	1	2	0	1	0	.412
Roberto Alomar, 2b	5	1	2	2	0	1	.188
Joe Carter, rf	4	0	2	2	1	0	.294
John Olerud, 1b	4	0	0	0	0	0	.375
Paul Molitor, dh	4	0	0	0	1	0	.412
Tony Fernandez, ss	3	0	2	0	1	1	.357
Ed Sprague, 3b	4	0	0	0	0	1	.267
Pat Borders, c	4	1	1	0	0	1	.188
TOTALS	35	4	9	4	6	5	.287

	1	2	3	4	5	6	7	8	9		R	H	E
White Sox	0	2	0	0	0	3	1	0	1		7	11	0
Blue Jays	0	0	3	0	0	1	0	0	0		4	9	0

DP—Blue Jays 1 (Sprague to Alomar to Olerud). LOB—White Sox 7, Blue Jays 11. Scoring Position—White Sox 3-for-10, Blue Jays 4-for-9. 2B—Alomar (1). 3B—Johnson (1), White (1). HR—Thomas (1), Johnson (1). GDP—Burks.

White Sox	IP	H	R	ER	BB	K	ERA
Jason Bere	2.1	5	3	3	2	3	11.57
Tim Belcher (W, 1-0)	3.2	3	1	1	3	1	2.45
Kirk McCaskill (H, 1)	1.1	1	0	0	1	1	0.00
Scott Radinsky (H, 1)	0.2	0	0	0	0	0	0.00
Roberto Hernandez (S, 1)	1.0	0	0	0	0	0	0.00

Blue Jays	IP	H	R	ER	BB	K	ERA
Todd Stottlemyre (L, 0-1)	6.0	6	5	5	4	4	7.50
Al Leiter	0.2	2	1	1	1	0	3.38
Mike Timlin	2.1	3	1	1	0	2	3.86

Balk—Stottlemyre. WP—Belcher. HBP—Olerud by Bere. Time—3:30. Attendance—51,889. Umpires—HP, Hendry. 1B, Tschida. 2B, Kaiser. 3B, Evans.

Game 5
Sunday, October 10

White Sox	AB	R	H	RBI	BB	K	Avg
Tim Raines, lf	4	1	1	0	0	1	.478
Joey Cora, 2b	3	0	0	0	1	1	.158
Frank Thomas, 1b	4	0	0	0	0	3	.357
Robin Ventura, 3b	4	1	1	2	0	0	.235
Ellis Burks, rf	3	1	2	1	0	1	.316
Bo Jackson, dh	4	0	0	0	0	2	.000
Lance Johnson, cf	3	0	0	0	0	0	.250
Ron Karkovice, c	2	0	0	0	1	1	.000
Ozzie Guillen, ss	3	0	1	0	0	0	.263
TOTALS	30	3	5	3	2	9	.252

Blue Jays	AB	R	H	RBI	BB	K	Avg
Rickey Henderson, lf	5	1	2	0	0	1	.150
Devon White, cf	5	1	2	0	0	1	.409
Roberto Alomar, 2b	3	1	3	1	2	0	.316
Joe Carter, rf	5	0	1	0	0	2	.273
John Olerud, 1b	3	0	1	0	2	0	.368
Paul Molitor, dh	3	2	1	0	1	0	.400
Tony Fernandez, ss	4	0	2	0	0	0	.389
Ed Sprague, 3b	3	0	1	2	0	1	.278
Pat Borders, c	4	0	1	0	0	2	.200
TOTALS	35	5	14	4	5	7	.309

	1	2	3	4	5	6	7	8	9		R	H	E
White Sox	0	0	0	0	1	0	0	0	2		3	5	1
Blue Jays	1	1	1	0	0	1	0	x			5	14	0

E—McDowell. DP—White Sox 1 (Guillen to Thomas), Blue Jays 2 (Alomar to Olerud; Olerud to Fernandez). LOB—White Sox 3, Blue Jays 12. Scoring Position—White Sox 0-for-1, Blue Jays 4-for-17. 2B—Henderson (2), White (1), Molitor (2). HR—Ventura (1), Burks (1). SF—Sprague. GDP—Guillen, Olerud. SB—Henderson (2), Alomar 3 (3), Borders (1). CS—Henderson (1).

White Sox	IP	H	R	ER	BB	K	ERA
Jack McDowell (L, 0-2)	2.1	5	3	3	3	1	10.00
Jose DeLeon	3.2	5	1	1	5	1.93
Scott Radinsky	0.1	1	1	1	1	0	6.75
Roberto Hernandez	1.2	3	0	0	0	1	0.00

Blue Jays	IP	H	R	ER	BB	K	ERA
Juan Guzman (W, 2-0)	7.0	3	1	1	1	6	2.08
Tony Castillo	1.0	0	0	0	1	0	0.00
Duane Ward	1.0	2	2	2	0	3	6.00

WP—McDowell. HBP—Burks by Ward. Time—3:09. Attendance—51,375. Umpires—HP, Tschida. 1B, Kaiser. 2B, Evans. 3B, Kosc.

Game 6
Tuesday, October 12

Blue Jays	AB	R	H	RBI	BB	K	Avg
Rickey Henderson, lf	5	0	0	0	0	1	.120
Devon White, cf	5	1	3	1	0	1	.444
Roberto Alomar, 2b	5	0	1	0	0	0	.292
Joe Carter, rf	5	1	1	0	0	1	.259
John Olerud, 1b	4	2	1	0	1	0	.348
Paul Molitor, dh	3	2	1	2	1	1	.391
Tony Fernandez, ss	4	0	0	0	0	0	.318
Ed Sprague, 3b	3	0	1	0	1	1	.286
Pat Borders, c	4	0	2	3	0	0	.301
TOTALS	38	6	10	6	3	5	.301

White Sox	AB	R	H	RBI	BB	K	Avg
Tim Raines, lf	4	1	1	0	1	0	.444
Joey Cora, 2b	3	0	0	0	0	1	.136
Frank Thomas, 1b	3	0	1	1	1	1	.353
Robin Ventura, 3b	3	0	0	1	1	1	.200
Ellis Burks, rf	4	0	1	0	0	1	.304
Warren Newson, dh	4	1	1	1	0	1	.200
Lance Johnson, cf	3	0	0	0	1	0	.217
Mike LaValliere, c	2	0	0	0	0	1	.333
Ron Karkovice, pr-c	1	0	0	0	0	1	.000
Ozzie Guillen, ss	3	1	1	0	0	0	.273
TOTALS	30	3	5	3	5	6	.254

	1	2	3	4	5	6	7	8	9		R	H	E
Blue Jays	0	2	0	1	0	0	0	0	3		6	10	0
White Sox	0	0	2	0	0	0	0	0	1		3	5	3

E—Cora, Ventura, Radinsky. DP—Blue Jays 1 (Alomar to TFernandez). LOB—Blue Jays 10, White Sox 7. Scoring Position—Blue Jays 2-for-12, White Sox 1-for-7. 2B—Borders (1), Guillen (1). 3B—Molitor (1). HR—White (1), Newson (1). S—TFernandez, Guillen. SB—Alomar (4).

Blue Jays	IP	H	R	ER	BB	K	ERA
Dave Stewart (W, 2-0)	7.1	4	2	2	4	3	2.03
Duane Ward (S, 2)	1.2	1	1	1	1	3	5.79

White Sox	IP	H	R	ER	BB	K	ERA
Alex Fernandez (L, 0-2)	7.0	7	3	2	3	5	1.80
Kirk McCaskill	1.1	0	0	0	0	0	0.00
Scott Radinsky	0.1	2	3	1	0	0	10.80
Roberto Hernandez	0.1	1	0	0	0	0	0.00

WP—Stewart. HBP—Molitor by AFernandez, Cora by Stewart. Time—3:31. Attendance—45,527. Umpires—HP, Kaiser. 1B, Evans. 2B, Kosc. 3B, Shulock.

1993 AL Championship Series—Composite Statistics

Batting

Blue Jays	G	AB	R	H	RBI	2B	3B	HR	BB	SO	SB	CS	Avg	OBP	Slg
Roberto Alomar	6	24	3	7	4	1	0	0	4	3	4	0	.292	.393	.333
Pat Borders	6	24	1	6	3	1	0	0	0	6	1	0	.250	.250	.292
Joe Carter	6	27	2	7	2	0	0	0	1	5	0	0	.259	.286	.259
Tony Fernandez	6	22	1	7	1	0	0	0	2	4	0	0	.318	.375	.318
Rickey Henderson	6	25	4	3	0	2	0	0	4	5	2	1	.120	.241	.200
Paul Molitor	6	23	7	9	5	2	1	1	3	3	0	0	.391	.481	.696
John Olerud	6	23	5	8	3	1	0	0	4	1	0	0	.348	.464	.391
Ed Sprague	6	21	0	6	4	0	1	0	2	4	0	0	.286	.333	.381
Devon White	6	27	3	12	2	1	1	1	1	5	0	1	.444	.464	.667
Totals	**6**	**216**	**26**	**65**	**24**	**8**	**3**	**2**	**21**	**36**	**7**	**2**	**.301**	**.367**	**.394**

Batting

White Sox	G	AB	R	H	RBI	2B	3B	HR	BB	SO	SB	CS	Avg	OBP	Slg
Ellis Burks	6	23	4	7	3	1	0	1	3	5	0	1	.304	.407	.478
Joey Cora	6	22	1	3	1	0	0	0	3	6	0	0	.136	.269	.136
Craig Grebeck	1	1	0	1	0	0	0	0	0	0	0	0	1.000	1.000	1.000
Ozzie Guillen	6	22	4	6	2	1	0	0	0	2	1	0	.273	.273	.318
Bo Jackson	3	10	1	0	0	0	0	0	3	6	0	0	.000	.231	.000
Lance Johnson	6	23	2	5	6	1	1	1	2	1	1	0	.217	.280	.478
Ron Karkovice	6	15	0	0	0	0	0	0	1	7	0	0	.000	.063	.000
Mike LaValliere	2	3	0	1	0	0	0	0	1	0	0	0	.333	.500	.333
Warren Newson	2	5	1	1	1	0	0	1	0	1	0	0	.200	.200	.800
Dan Pasqua	2	6	1	0	0	0	0	0	1	2	0	0	.000	.250	.000
Tim Raines	6	27	5	12	1	2	0	0	2	2	1	1	.444	.483	.519
Frank Thomas	6	17	2	6	3	0	0	1	10	5	0	0	.353	.593	.529
Robin Ventura	6	20	2	4	5	0	0	1	6	6	0	0	.200	.370	.350
Totals	**6**	**194**	**23**	**46**	**22**	**5**	**1**	**5**	**32**	**43**	**3**	**2**	**.237**	**.352**	**.351**

Pitching

Blue Jays	G	GS	CG	IP	H	R	ER	BB	SO	W-L	Sv-Op	Hld	ERA
Tony Castillo	2	0	0	2.0	0	0	0	1	1	0-0	0-0	0	0.00
Danny Cox	2	0	0	5.0	3	0	0	2	5	0-0	0-0	0	0.00
Mark Eichhorn	1	0	0	1.0	1	0	0	1	1	0-0	0-0	0	0.00
Juan Guzman	2	2	0	13.0	8	4	3	9	9	2-0	0-0	0	2.08
Pat Hentgen	1	1	0	3.0	9	6	6	2	3	0-1	0-0	0	18.00
Al Leiter	2	0	0	2.2	4	1	1	2	2	0-0	0-0	1	3.38
Dave Stewart	2	2	0	13.1	8	3	3	8	8	2-0	0-0	0	2.03
Todd Stottlemyre	1	1	0	6.0	6	5	5	4	4	0-1	0-0	0	7.50
Mike Timlin	1	0	0	2.1	3	1	1	0	2	0-0	0-0	0	3.86
Duane Ward	4	0	0	4.2	4	3	3	3	8	0-0	2-2	1	5.79
Totals	**6**	**6**	**0**	**54.0**	**46**	**23**	**22**	**32**	**43**	**4-2**	**2-2**	**1**	**3.67**

Pitching

White Sox	G	GS	CG	IP	H	R	ER	BB	SO	W-L	Sv-Op	Hld	ERA
Wilson Alvarez	1	1	1	9.0	7	1	1	2	6	1-0	0-0	0	1.00
Tim Belcher	1	0	0	3.2	3	1	1	3	1	1-0	0-0	0	2.45
Jason Bere	1	1	0	2.1	5	3	3	2	3	0-0	0-0	0	11.57
Jose DeLeon	2	0	0	4.2	7	1	1	1	6	0-0	0-0	0	1.93
Alex Fernandez	2	2	0	15.0	15	6	3	6	10	0-2	0-0	0	1.80
Roberto Hernandez	4	0	0	4.0	4	0	0	0	1	0-0	1-1	0	0.00
Kirk McCaskill	3	0	0	3.2	3	0	0	1	3	0-0	0-0	1	0.00
Jack McDowell	2	2	0	9.0	18	10	10	5	5	0-2	0-0	0	10.00
Scott Radinsky	4	0	0	1.2	3	4	2	1	1	0-0	0-0	1	10.80
Totals	**6**	**6**	**1**	**53.0**	**65**	**26**	**21**	**21**	**36**	**2-4**	**1-1**	**2**	**3.57**

Fielding

Blue Jays	Pos	G	PO	Ast	E	DP	PB	FPct
Roberto Alomar	2b	6	14	19	0	5	—	1.000
Pat Borders	c	6	41	4	0	1	0	1.000
Joe Carter	rf	6	12	1	0	0	—	1.000
Tony Castillo	p	2	0	1	0	0	—	1.000
Danny Cox	p	2	0	1	0	0	—	1.000
Mark Eichhorn	p	1	0	0	0	0	—	—
Tony Fernandez	ss	6	12	8	0	5	—	1.000
Juan Guzman	p	2	0	4	0	0	—	1.000
Rickey Henderson	lf	6	9	0	1	0	—	.900
Pat Hentgen	p	1	1	0	0	0	—	1.000
Al Leiter	p	2	0	0	0	0	—	—
John Olerud	1b	6	48	9	1	5	—	.983
Ed Sprague	3b	6	5	9	0	1	—	1.000
Dave Stewart	p	2	2	0	0	0	—	1.000
Todd Stottlemyre	p	1	2	0	0	0	—	1.000
Mike Timlin	p	1	1	1	0	0	—	1.000
Duane Ward	p	4	0	0	0	0	—	—
Devon White	cf	6	15	0	0	0	—	1.000
Totals		**6**	**162**	**57**	**2**	**17**	**0**	**.991**

Fielding

White Sox	Pos	G	PO	Ast	E	DP	PB	FPct
Wilson Alvarez	p	1	0	2	0	1	—	1.000
Tim Belcher	p	1	1	1	0	0	—	1.000
Jason Bere	p	1	0	0	0	0	—	—
Ellis Burks	rf	6	15	0	0	0	—	1.000
Joey Cora	2b	6	18	20	3	2	—	.927
Jose DeLeon	p	2	0	0	0	0	—	—
Alex Fernandez	p	2	2	1	0	1	—	1.000
Craig Grebeck	3b	1	0	0	0	0	—	—
Ozzie Guillen	ss	6	12	14	0	4	—	1.000
Roberto Hernandez	p	4	0	0	0	0	—	—
Lance Johnson	cf	6	15	0	0	0	—	1.000
Ron Karkovice	c	6	30	2	0	0	0	1.000
Mike LaValliere	c	2	8	0	0	0	0	1.000
Kirk McCaskill	p	3	0	2	0	0	—	1.000
Jack McDowell	p	2	0	1	1	0	—	.500
Dan Pasqua	1b	2	13	2	1	2	—	.938
Scott Radinsky	p	4	0	1	1	0	—	.000
Tim Raines	lf	6	12	2	0	0	—	1.000
Frank Thomas	1b	4	24	3	0	3	—	1.000
Robin Ventura	3b	6	6	6	1	0	—	.923
	1b	1	3	0	0	0	—	1.000
Totals		**6**	**159**	**56**	**7**	**13**	**0**	**.968**

1993 Philadelphia Phillies (NL) 4, Atlanta Braves (NL) 2

The Philadelphia Phillies might not have outplayed the Atlanta Braves, but they got all the big hits and made all the big plays. In the opener, defensive replacement Kim Batiste's ninth-inning error helped the Braves score the tying run, but Batiste redeemed himself with a game-winning RBI single in the bottom of the 10th. The Braves blasted Tommy Greene in Game 2, winning 14-3 behind Greg Maddux. The third game brought more of the same, as the Braves went quietly for five innings before exploding for a 9-4 win. Danny Jackson outdueled John Smoltz, 2-1, in Game 4 to even the series. Curt Schilling took a 3-0 lead into the bottom of the ninth in Game 5 but he and reliever Mitch Williams couldn't hold it. The Braves rallied to tie the score but couldn't get the winning run past third base. Lenny Dykstra homered in the top of the 10th for what proved to be the winning run. Atlanta had confidence in Game 6 starter Maddux, but the Atlanta ace struggled after taking a line drive off the leg in the first inning. Greene tossed seven solid innings, and the Phillies downed the stunned Braves 6-3 to advance to the World Series.

Game 1

Wednesday, October 6

Braves	AB	R	H	RBI	BB	K	Avg
Otis Nixon, cf	4	0	2	2	1	1	.500
Jeff Blauser, ss	4	0	0	0	1	3	.000
Ron Gant, lf	4	1	1	0	1	3	.250
Greg McMichael, p	0	0	0	0	0	0	—
Fred McGriff, 1b	5	0	1	0	0	2	.200
David Justice, rf	4	0	0	1	0	1	.000
Terry Pendleton, 3b	5	0	1	0	0	0	.200
Damon Berryhill, c	3	0	0	0	0	1	.000
Bill Pecota, ph	0	1	0	0	1	0	—
Greg Olson, c	1	0	1	0	0	0	1.000
Mark Lemke, 2b	4	0	1	0	0	0	.250
Tony Tarasco, pr-lf	1	0	0	0	0	1	.000
Steve Avery, p	2	1	2	0	0	0	1.000
Deion Sanders, ph	1	0	0	0	0	0	.000
Kent Mercker, p	0	0	0	0	0	0	—
Rafael Belliard, ph-2b	0	0	0	0	0	0	—
TOTALS	38	3	9	3	4	12	.237

Phillies	AB	R	H	RBI	BB	K	Avg
Lenny Dykstra, cf	4	1	1	0	1	1	.250
Mariano Duncan, 2b	5	0	1	0	0	2	.200
John Kruk, 1b	4	2	1	1	1	0	.250
Dave Hollins, 3b	4	0	1	0	0	0	.250
Kim Batiste, 3b	1	0	1	1	0	0	1.000
Darren Daulton, c	3	0	0	1	1	1	.000
Pete Incaviglia, lf	4	1	2	1	0	1	.500
Milt Thompson, pr-lf	0	0	0	0	0	0	—
Wes Chamberlain, rf	3	0	2	0	1	1	.667
Mitch Williams, p	0	0	0	0	0	0	—
Kevin Stocker, ss	3	0	0	0	1	0	.000
Curt Schilling, p	3	0	0	0	1	1	.000
Jim Eisenreich, rf	1	0	0	0	0	0	.000
TOTALS	35	4	9	3	5	7	.257

	1	2	3	4	5	6	7	8	9	10	R	H	E
Braves	0	0	1	1	0	0	0	0	1	0	3	9	0
Phillies	1	0	0	1	0	1	0	0	0	1	4	9	1

E—Batiste. DP—Braves 1 (Pendleton to Lemke to McGriff). LOB—Braves 11, Phillies 8. Scoring Position—Braves 1-for-8, Phillies 2-for-6. 2B—Nixon (1), Avery (1), Dykstra (1), Kruk (1), Hollins (1), Chamberlain 2 (2), Olson (1). HR—Incaviglia (1). S—Belliard. SF—Justice. GDP—Hollins.

Braves	IP	H	R	ER	BB	K	ERA
Steve Avery	6.0	5	3	3	4	5	4.50
Kent Mercker	2.0	2	0	0	1	2	0.00
Greg McMichael (L, 0-1)	1.1	2	1	1	0	0	6.75

Phillies	IP	H	R	ER	BB	K	ERA
Curt Schilling	8.0	7	2	2	2	10	2.25
Mitch Williams (BS, 1; W, 1-0)	2.0	2	1	0	2	2	0.00

WP—Avery. Time—3:33. Attendance—62,012. Umpires—HP, Froemming. 1B, Pulli. 2B, Tata. 3B, Quick.

Game 2

Thursday, October 7

Braves	AB	R	H	RBI	BB	K	Avg
Otis Nixon, cf	4	2	3	2	2	0	.625
Mark Wohlers, p	0	0	0	0	0	0	—
Jeff Blauser, ss	5	1	2	1	0	1	.222
Rafael Belliard, pr-ss	1	1	0	0	0	1	.000
Ron Gant, lf	5	1	2	3	0	1	.333
Fred McGriff, 1b	5	2	3	2	0	1	.400
Mike Stanton, p	0	0	0	0	0	0	—
Tony Tarasco, rf	0	0	0	0	0	0	.000
David Justice, rf	3	1	0	0	2	0	.000
Deion Sanders, cf	0	0	0	0	0	0	.000
Terry Pendleton, 3b	5	2	3	3	0	1	.400
Damon Berryhill, c	5	1	1	3	0	2	.125
Mark Lemke, 2b	5	1	0	0	0	1	.111
Greg Maddux, p	4	1	1	0	0	1	.250
Sid Bream, 1b	1	1	1	0	0	0	1.000
TOTALS	43	14	16	14	4	9	.282

Phillies	AB	R	H	RBI	BB	K	Avg
Lenny Dykstra, cf	4	1	1	1	1	2	.250
Mickey Morandini, 2b	5	0	1	0	0	2	.200
John Kruk, 1b	3	1	2	0	1	0	.429
Dave Hollins, 3b	3	1	1	2	1	0	.286
Darren Daulton, c	4	0	1	0	0	1	.143
Larry Andersen, p	0	0	0	0	0	0	—
Jim Eisenreich, rf	4	0	0	0	1	0	.000
Milt Thompson, lf	4	0	0	0	0	0	.000
Kevin Stocker, ss	4	0	1	0	0	2	.143
Tommy Greene, p	0	0	0	0	0	0	—
Bobby Thigpen, p	0	0	0	0	0	0	—
Tony Longmire, ph	1	0	0	0	0	1	.000
Ben Rivera, p	0	0	0	0	0	0	—
Wes Chamberlain, ph	1	0	0	0	0	1	.500
Roger Mason, p	0	0	0	0	0	0	—
Ricky Jordan, ph	1	0	0	0	1	0	—
David West, p	0	0	0	0	0	0	—
Todd Pratt, c	1	0	0	0	0	1	.000
TOTALS	34	3	7	3	4	11	.214

	1	2	3	4	5	6	7	8	9	R	H	E
Braves	2	0	6	0	1	0	0	4	1	14	16	0
Phillies	0	0	0	2	0	0	0	0	1	3	7	2

E—Morandini, Stocker. LOB—Braves 6, Phillies 8. Scoring Position—Braves 7-for-14, Phillies 0-for-7. 2B—Nixon (2), Gant 2 (2). HR—Blauser (1), McGriff (1), Pendleton (1), Berryhill (1), Dykstra (1), Hollins (1). SB—Morandini (1). CS—Nixon (1).

Braves	IP	H	R	ER	BB	K	ERA
Greg Maddux (W, 1-0)	7.0	5	2	2	3	8	2.57
Mike Stanton	1.0	1	0	0	1	0	0.00
Mark Wohlers	1.0	1	1	1	0	3	9.00

Phillies	IP	H	R	ER	BB	K	ERA
Tommy Greene (L, 0-1)	2.1	7	7	7	2	2	27.00
Bobby Thigpen	0.2	1	1	1	0	1	13.50
Ben Rivera	2.0	1	1	1	1	2	4.50
Roger Mason	2.0	1	0	0	0	1	0.00
David West	1.0	4	4	3	1	2	27.00
Larry Andersen	1.0	2	1	1	0	1	9.00

PB—Daulton. Time—3:14. Attendance—62,436. Umpires—HP, Pulli. 1B, Tata. 2B, Quick. 3B, Crawford.

Game 3

Saturday, October 9

Phillies	AB	R	H	RBI	BB	K	Avg
Lenny Dykstra, cf	5	0	1	0	0	2	.231
Mariano Duncan, 2b	5	2	2	0	0	1	.300
John Kruk, 1b	4	1	2	3	0	0	.455
Dave Hollins, 3b	3	0	0	0	1	0	.200
Darren Daulton, c	4	0	0	0	0	0	.091
Pete Incaviglia, lf	4	0	0	0	0	1	.250
Wes Chamberlain, rf	4	1	1	0	0	0	.375
Kevin Stocker, ss	4	0	3	0	0	0	.364
Terry Mulholland, p	2	0	0	0	0	1	.000
Roger Mason, p	0	0	0	0	0	0	—
Milt Thompson, ph	1	0	0	0	0	1	.000
Larry Andersen, p	0	0	0	0	0	0	—
David West, p	0	0	0	0	0	0	—
Bobby Thigpen, p	0	0	0	0	0	0	—
Jim Eisenreich, ph	1	0	1	1	0	0	.167
TOTALS	37	4	10	4	1	6	.253

Braves	AB	R	H	RBI	BB	K	Avg
Otis Nixon, cf	5	0	1	0	0	2	.462
Jeff Blauser, ss	4	2	2	0	1	0	.308
Ron Gant, lf	4	1	1	0	1	1	.308
Fred McGriff, 1b	4	2	2	1	1	0	.429
Terry Pendleton, 3b	4	2	2	2	0	0	.429
David Justice, rf	4	1	1	2	0	1	.091
Damon Berryhill, c	3	1	1	0	1	0	.182
Mark Lemke, 2b	4	0	2	3	0	1	.231
Tom Glavine, p	3	0	0	0	0	0	.000
Francisco Cabrera, ph	1	0	0	0	0	1	.000
Kent Mercker, p	0	0	0	0	0	0	—
Greg McMichael, p	0	0	0	0	0	0	—
TOTALS	36	9	12	8	4	7	.302

	1	2	3	4	5	6	7	8	9	R	H	E
Phillies	0	0	0	1	0	1	0	1	1	4	10	1
Braves	0	0	0	0	0	5	4	0	x	9	12	0

E—Duncan. LOB—Phillies 7, Braves 7. Scoring Position—Phillies 3-for-13, Braves 5-for-16. 2B—Chamberlain (3), Stocker (1), Blauser (1), Gant (3), McGriff (1), Justice (1), Lemke (1), Eisenreich (1). 3B—Duncan 2 (2), Kruk (1). HR—Kruk (1). SB—Hollins (1). CS—Nixon (2).

Phillies	IP	H	R	ER	BB	K	ERA
Terry Mulholland (L, 0-1)	5.0	9	5	4	1	2	7.20
Roger Mason	1.0	0	0	0	0	1	0.00
Larry Andersen	0.1	2	3	3	1	0	27.00
David West	0.2	1	1	1	1	2	21.60
Bobby Thigpen	1.0	0	0	0	1	2	5.40

Braves	IP	H	R	ER	BB	K	ERA
Tom Glavine (W, 1-0)	7.0	6	2	2	0	5	2.57
Kent Mercker	1.0	1	1	1	1	0	3.00
Greg McMichael	1.0	3	1	1	0	1	7.71

Mulholland pitched to five batters in the 6th.

Time—2:44. Attendance—52,032. Umpires—HP, Tata. 1B, Quick. 2B, Crawford. 3B, West.

Game 4
Sunday, October 10

Phillies	AB	R	H	RBI	BB	K	Avg
Lenny Dykstra, cf	3	0	2	0	2	1	.313
Mickey Morandini, 2b	5	0	2	0	0	1	.300
John Kruk, 1b	5	0	0	0	0	4	.313
Dave Hollins, 3b	4	0	1	0	1	3	.214
Kim Batiste, 3b	0	0	0	0	0	0	1.000
Darren Daulton, c	1	1	0	0	4	0	.083
Jim Eisenreich, rf	5	0	1	0	0	1	.182
Milt Thompson, lf	4	1	1	0	1	1	.111
Kevin Stocker, ss	4	0	0	1	0	1	.267
Danny Jackson, p	4	0	1	1	0	3	.250
Mitch Williams, p	0	0	0	0	0	0	—
TOTALS	35	2	8	2	8	15	.241

Braves	AB	R	H	RBI	BB	K	Avg
Otis Nixon, cf	3	0	1	0	0	1	.438
Jeff Blauser, ss	4	0	0	0	1	0	.235
Ron Gant, lf	5	0	0	0	0	2	.222
Fred McGriff, 1b	4	1	2	0	0	1	.444
Terry Pendleton, 3b	4	0	1	0	0	0	.389
David Justice, rf	4	0	2	0	0	0	.200
Greg Olson, c	2	0	0	0	0	1	.333
Damon Berryhill, c	1	0	1	0	0	0	.250
Mark Lemke, 2b	4	0	1	1	0	0	.235
John Smoltz, p	1	0	0	0	1	1	.000
Kent Mercker, p	0	0	0	0	0	0	—
Francisco Cabrera, ph	1	0	1	0	0	0	.500
Deion Sanders, pr	0	0	0	0	0	0	.000
Mark Wohlers, p	0	0	0	0	0	0	—
Bill Pecota, ph	1	0	1	0	0	0	1.000
TOTALS	34	1	10	1	2	6	.309

	1 2 3	4 5 6	7 8 9	R	H	E
Phillies	0 0 0	2 0 0	0 0 0	2	8	1
Braves	0 1 0	0 0 0	0 0 0	1	10	1

E—Williams, Lemke. LOB—Phillies 15, Braves 11. Scoring Position—Phillies 1-for-11, Braves 1-for-15. 2B—Thompson (1), McGriff (2), Pendleton (1), Lemke (2). S—Nixon 2. SF—Stocker. GDP—Gant. CS—Gant (1).

Phillies	IP	H	R	ER	BB	K	ERA
Danny Jackson (W, 1-0)	7.2	9	1	1	2	6	1.17
Mitch Williams (S, 1)	1.1	1	0	0	0	0	0.00

Braves	IP	H	R	ER	BB	K	ERA
John Smoltz (L, 0-1)	6.1	8	2	0	5	10	0.00
Kent Mercker	0.2	0	0	0	0	0	2.45
Mark Wohlers	2.0	0	0	0	3	5	3.00

WP—Wohlers. HBP—Olson by Jackson. Time—3:33. Attendance—52,032. Umpires—HP, Quick. 1B, Crawford. 2B, West. 3B, Froemming.

Game 5
Monday, October 11

Phillies	AB	R	H	RBI	BB	K	Avg
Lenny Dykstra, cf	5	1	1	1	0	0	.286
Mariano Duncan, 2b	5	1	1	0	0	2	.267
Larry Andersen, p	0	0	0	0	0	0	—
John Kruk, 1b	4	0	1	1	1	1	.300
Dave Hollins, 3b	4	0	0	0	0	1	.167
Kim Batiste, 3b	0	0	0	0	0	0	1.000
Darren Daulton, c	3	1	2	1	1	1	.200
Pete Incaviglia, lf	4	1	0	0	0	1	.167
Milt Thompson, lf	0	0	0	0	0	0	.111
Wes Chamberlain, rf	3	0	1	1	0	1	.364
Jim Eisenreich, rf	0	0	0	0	0	0	.182
Kevin Stocker, ss	4	0	0	0	0	0	.211
Curt Schilling, p	2	0	0	0	0	1	.000
Mitch Williams, p	0	0	0	0	0	0	—
Mickey Morandini, ph-2b	1	0	0	0	0	0	.273
TOTALS	35	4	6	4	2	8	.232

Braves	AB	R	H	RBI	BB	K	Avg
Otis Nixon, cf	4	0	0	0	1	1	.350
Jeff Blauser, ss	4	1	1	0	1	2	.238
Ron Gant, lf	5	1	1	0	0	1	.217
Fred McGriff, 1b	4	1	2	1	0	1	.455
David Justice, rf	2	0	0	1	1	1	.176
Terry Pendleton, 3b	4	0	1	0	0	1	.364
Damon Berryhill, c	3	0	1	0	0	1	.267
Francisco Cabrera, ph-c	1	0	1	1	0	0	.667
Mark Lemke, 2b	4	0	0	0	0	3	.190
Steve Avery, p	2	0	0	0	0	1	.500
Kent Mercker, p	0	0	0	0	0	0	—
Deion Sanders, ph	1	0	0	0	0	0	.000
Greg McMichael, p	0	0	0	0	0	0	—
Bill Pecota, ph	1	0	0	0	0	0	.500
Mark Wohlers, p	0	0	0	0	0	0	—
TOTALS	35	3	7	3	3	12	.297

	1 2 3	4 5 6	7 8 9 10	R	H	E
Phillies	1 0 0	1 0 0	0 0 1 1	4	6	1
Braves	0 0 0	0 0 0	0 3 0	3	7	1

E—Gant, Batiste. LOB—Phillies 5, Braves 6. Scoring Position—Phillies 0-for-3, Braves 2-for-5. 2B—Kruk (2). HR—Dykstra (2), Daulton (1). S—Schilling. SF—Chamberlain, Justice.

Phillies	IP	H	R	ER	BB	K	ERA
Curt Schilling	8.0	4	2	1	3	9	1.69
Mitch Williams (BS, 2; W, 2-0)	1.0	3	1	1	0	1	2.08
Larry Andersen (S, 1)	1.0	0	0	0	0	2	15.43

Braves	IP	H	R	ER	BB	K	ERA
Steve Avery	7.0	4	2	1	2	5	2.77
Kent Mercker	1.0	0	0	0	0	2	1.93
Greg McMichael	1.0	1	1	1	0	0	8.10
Mark Wohlers (L, 0-1)	1.0	1	1	1	0	1	4.50

Schilling pitched to two batters in the 9th.

WP—Avery. Time—3:21. Attendance—52,032. Umpires—HP, Crawford. 1B, West. 2B, Froemming. 3B, Pulli.

Game 6
Wednesday, October 13

Braves	AB	R	H	RBI	BB	K	Avg
Otis Nixon, cf	3	1	1	0	1	1	.348
Jeff Blauser, ss	4	1	2	3	0	1	.280
Ron Gant, lf	4	0	0	0	0	1	.185
Fred McGriff, 1b	1	0	0	0	3	1	.435
David Justice, rf	4	0	0	0	0	0	.143
Terry Pendleton, 3b	4	0	1	0	0	0	.346
Damon Berryhill, c	4	0	0	0	0	0	.211
Mark Lemke, 2b	3	1	1	0	1	1	.208
Greg Maddux, p	0	0	0	0	0	0	.250
Kent Mercker, p	0	0	0	0	0	0	—
Deion Sanders, ph	1	0	0	0	0	1	.000
Greg McMichael, p	0	0	0	0	0	0	—
Mark Wohlers, p	0	0	0	0	0	0	—
Bill Pecota, ph	1	0	0	0	0	1	.333
TOTALS	29	3	5	3	5	8	.268

Phillies	AB	R	H	RBI	BB	K	Avg
Lenny Dykstra, cf	4	2	1	0	1	2	.280
Mickey Morandini, 2b	5	1	1	2	0	0	.250
John Kruk, 1b	4	0	0	0	1	0	.250
Dave Hollins, 3b	2	1	1	2	2	0	.200
Kim Batiste, 3b	0	0	0	0	0	0	1.000
Darren Daulton, c	4	0	2	2	0	0	.263
Jim Eisenreich, rf	4	0	0	0	0	0	.133
Milt Thompson, lf	4	1	2	0	0	0	.231
Kevin Stocker, ss	3	0	0	0	1	2	.182
Tommy Greene, p	0	1	0	0	1	0	—
Ricky Jordan, ph	1	0	0	0	0	0	.000
David West, p	0	0	0	0	0	0	—
Mitch Williams, p	0	0	0	0	0	0	—
TOTALS	31	6	7	6	6	4	.231

	1 2 3	4 5 6	7 8 9	R	H	E
Braves	0 0 0	0 1 0	2 0 0	3	5	3
Phillies	0 0 2	0 2 2	0 0 x	6	7	1

E—Thompson, Maddux, Lemke, Justice. DP—Phillies 1 (Morandini to Stocker to Kruk). LOB—Braves 6, Phillies 9. Scoring Position—Braves 1-for-5, Phillies 3-for-12. 2B—Daulton (1). 3B—Morandini (1). HR—Blauser (2), Hollins (2). S—Maddux 2, Greene 2. GDP—Berryhill.

Braves	IP	H	R	ER	BB	K	ERA
Greg Maddux (L, 1-1)	5.2	6	6	5	4	3	4.97
Kent Mercker	0.1	0	0	0	0	0	1.80
Greg McMichael	0.2	1	0	0	2	0	6.75
Mark Wohlers	1.1	0	0	0	0	1	3.38

Phillies	IP	H	R	ER	BB	K	ERA
Tommy Greene (W, 1-1)	7.0	5	3	3	5	5	9.64
David West (H, 1)	1.0	0	0	0	0	1	13.50
Mitch Williams (S, 2)	1.0	0	0	0	0	2	1.69

PB—Daulton. Time—3:04. Attendance—62,502. Umpires—HP, West. 1B, Froemming. 2B, Pulli. 3B, Tata.

Postseason: League Championship Series

1993 NL Championship Series—Composite Statistics

Batting

Phillies	G	AB	R	H	RBI	2B	3B	HR	BB	SO	SB	CS	Avg	OBP	Slg
Kim Batiste	4	1	0	1	1	0	0	0	0	0	0	0	1.000	1.000	1.000
Wes Chamberlain	4	11	1	4	1	3	0	0	1	3	0	0	.364	.385	.636
Darren Daulton	6	19	2	5	3	1	0	1	6	3	0	0	.263	.440	.474
Mariano Duncan	3	15	3	4	0	0	2	0	0	5	0	0	.267	.267	.533
Lenny Dykstra	6	25	5	7	2	1	0	2	5	8	0	0	.280	.400	.560
Jim Eisenreich	6	15	0	2	1	1	0	0	0	2	0	0	.133	.133	.200
Tommy Greene	2	0	1	0	0	0	0	0	1	0	0	0	—	1.000	—
Dave Hollins	6	20	2	4	4	1	0	2	5	4	1	0	.200	.360	.550
Pete Incaviglia	3	12	2	2	1	0	0	1	0	3	0	0	.167	.167	.417
Danny Jackson	1	4	0	1	1	0	0	0	0	3	0	0	.250	.250	.250
Ricky Jordan	2	1	0	0	0	0	0	0	1	0	0	0	.000	.500	.000
John Kruk	6	24	4	6	5	2	1	1	4	5	0	0	.250	.357	.542
Tony Longmire	1	1	0	0	0	0	0	0	0	1	0	0	.000	.000	.000
Mickey Morandini	4	16	1	4	2	0	1	0	0	3	1	0	.250	.250	.375
Terry Mulholland	1	2	0	0	0	0	0	0	0	1	0	0	.000	.000	.000
Todd Pratt	1	1	0	0	0	0	0	0	0	1	0	0	.000	.000	.000
Curt Schilling	2	5	0	0	0	0	0	0	0	2	0	0	.000	.000	.000
Kevin Stocker	6	22	0	4	1	1	0	0	2	5	0	0	.182	.240	.227
Milt Thompson	6	13	2	3	0	1	0	0	1	2	0	0	.231	.286	.308
Totals	**6**	**207**	**23**	**47**	**22**	**11**	**4**	**7**	**26**	**51**	**2**	**0**	**.227**	**.311**	**.420**

Braves	G	AB	R	H	RBI	2B	3B	HR	BB	SO	SB	CS	Avg	OBP	Slg
Steve Avery	2	4	1	2	0	1	0	0	0	1	0	0	.500	.500	.750
Rafael Belliard	2	1	1	0	0	0	0	0	0	1	0	0	.000	.000	.000
Damon Berryhill	6	19	2	4	3	0	0	1	1	5	0	0	.211	.250	.368
Jeff Blauser	6	25	5	7	4	1	0	2	4	7	0	0	.280	.379	.560
Sid Bream	1	1	1	1	0	0	0	0	0	0	0	0	1.000	1.000	1.000
Francisco Cabrera	3	3	0	2	1	0	0	0	0	1	0	0	.667	.667	.667
Ron Gant	6	27	4	5	3	3	0	0	2	9	0	1	.185	.241	.296
Tom Glavine	1	3	0	0	0	0	0	0	0	0	0	0	.000	.000	.000
David Justice	6	21	2	3	4	1	0	0	3	3	0	0	.143	.231	.190
Mark Lemke	6	24	2	5	4	2	0	0	1	6	0	0	.208	.240	.292
Greg Maddux	2	4	1	1	0	0	0	0	0	1	0	0	.250	.250	.250
Fred McGriff	6	23	6	10	4	2	0	1	4	7	0	0	.435	.519	.652
Otis Nixon	6	23	3	8	4	2	0	0	5	6	0	2	.348	.464	.435
Greg Olson	2	3	0	1	0	1	0	0	0	1	0	0	.333	.500	.667
Bill Pecota	4	3	1	1	0	0	0	0	1	1	0	0	.333	.500	.333
Terry Pendleton	6	26	4	9	5	1	0	1	0	2	0	0	.346	.346	.500
Deion Sanders	5	3	0	0	0	0	0	0	0	0	1	0	.000	.000	.000
John Smoltz	1	1	0	0	0	0	0	0	0	1	0	0	.000	.500	.000
Tony Tarasco	2	1	0	0	0	0	0	0	0	0	0	0	.000	.000	.000
Totals	**6**	**215**	**33**	**59**	**32**	**14**	**0**	**5**	**22**	**54**	**0**	**3**	**.274**	**.342**	**.409**

Pitching

Phillies	G	GS	CG	IP	H	R	ER	BB	SO	W-L	Sv-Op	Hld	ERA
Larry Andersen	3	0	0	2.1	4	4	4	1	3	0-0	1-1	0	15.43
Tommy Greene	2	2	0	9.1	12	10	10	7	7	1-1	0-0	0	9.64
Danny Jackson	1	1	0	7.2	9	1	1	2	6	1-0	0-0	0	1.17
Roger Mason	2	0	0	3.0	1	0	0	0	2	0-0	0-0	0	0.00
Terry Mulholland	1	1	0	5.0	9	5	4	1	2	0-1	0-0	0	7.20
Ben Rivera	1	0	0	2.0	1	1	1	1	2	0-0	0-0	0	4.50
Curt Schilling	2	2	0	16.0	11	4	3	5	19	0-0	0-0	0	1.69
Bobby Thigpen	2	0	0	1.2	1	1	1	1	3	0-0	0-0	0	5.40
David West	3	0	0	2.2	5	5	4	2	5	0-0	0-0	1	13.50
Mitch Williams	4	0	0	5.1	6	2	1	2	5	2-0	2-4	0	1.69
Totals	**6**	**6**	**0**	**55.0**	**59**	**33**	**29**	**22**	**54**	**4-2**	**3-5**	**1**	**4.75**

Braves	G	GS	CG	IP	H	R	ER	BB	SO	W-L	Sv-Op	Hld	ERA
Steve Avery	2	2	0	13.0	9	5	4	6	10	0-0	0-0	0	2.77
Tom Glavine	1	1	0	7.0	6	2	2	0	5	1-0	0-0	0	2.57
Greg Maddux	2	2	0	12.2	11	8	7	7	11	1-1	0-0	0	4.97
Greg McMichael	4	0	0	4.0	7	3	3	2	1	0-1	0-0	0	6.75
Kent Mercker	5	0	0	5.0	3	1	1	2	4	0-0	0-0	0	1.80
John Smoltz	1	1	0	6.1	8	2	0	5	10	0-1	0-0	0	0.00
Mike Stanton	1	0	0	1.0	1	0	0	1	0	0-0	0-0	0	0.00
Mark Wohlers	4	0	0	5.1	2	2	2	3	10	0-1	0-0	0	3.38
Totals	**6**	**6**	**0**	**54.1**	**47**	**23**	**19**	**26**	**51**	**2-4**	**0-0**	**0**	**3.15**

Fielding

Phillies	Pos	G	PO	Ast	E	DP	PB	FPct
Larry Andersen	p	3	0	1	0	0	—	1.000
Kim Batiste	3b	4	2	0	2	0	—	.500
Wes Chamberlain	rf	3	2	2	0	0	—	1.000
Darren Daulton	c	6	54	3	0	0	2	1.000
Mariano Duncan	2b	3	5	6	1	0	—	.917
Lenny Dykstra	cf	6	13	0	0	0	—	1.000
Jim Eisenreich	rf	5	6	0	0	0	—	1.000
Tommy Greene	p	2	0	3	0	0	—	1.000
Dave Hollins	3b	6	5	4	0	0	—	1.000
Pete Incaviglia	lf	3	8	0	0	0	—	1.000
Danny Jackson	p	1	0	0	0	0	—	—
John Kruk	1b	6	44	2	0	2	—	1.000
Roger Mason	p	2	0	0	0	0	—	—
Mickey Morandini	2b	4	8	9	1	2	—	.944
Terry Mulholland	p	1	0	2	0	0	—	1.000
Todd Pratt	c	1	1	0	0	0	0	1.000
Ben Rivera	p	1	0	0	0	0	—	—
Curt Schilling	p	2	0	0	0	0	—	—
Kevin Stocker	ss	6	9	14	1	1	—	.958
Bobby Thigpen	p	2	0	0	0	0	—	—
Milt Thompson	lf	5	8	0	1	0	—	.889
David West	p	3	0	1	0	0	—	1.000
Mitch Williams	p	4	0	1	1	0	—	.500
Totals		**6**	**165**	**48**	**7**	**5**	**2**	**.968**

Braves	Pos	G	PO	Ast	E	DP	PB	FPct
Steve Avery	p	2	0	2	0	0	—	1.000
Rafael Belliard	2b	1	0	0	0	0	—	—
	ss	1	0	0	0	0	—	—
Damon Berryhill	c	6	42	0	0	0	0	1.000
Jeff Blauser	ss	6	6	14	0	0	—	1.000
Sid Bream	1b	1	1	0	0	0	—	1.000
Francisco Cabrera	c	1	1	0	0	0	0	1.000
Ron Gant	lf	6	10	1	1	0	—	.917
Tom Glavine	p	1	0	3	0	0	—	1.000
David Justice	rf	6	14	0	1	0	—	.933
Mark Lemke	2b	6	6	19	2	1	—	.926
Greg Maddux	p	2	3	5	1	0	—	.889
Fred McGriff	1b	6	50	3	0	1	—	1.000
Greg McMichael	p	4	0	1	0	0	—	1.000
Kent Mercker	p	5	0	0	0	0	—	—
Otis Nixon	cf	6	13	0	0	0	—	1.000
Greg Olson	c	2	10	0	0	0	0	1.000
Terry Pendleton	3b	6	7	5	0	1	—	1.000
Deion Sanders	cf	1	0	0	0	0	—	—
John Smoltz	p	1	0	0	0	0	—	—
Mike Stanton	p	1	0	0	0	0	—	—
Tony Tarasco	lf	1	0	0	0	0	—	—
	rf	1	0	0	0	0	—	—
Mark Wohlers	p	4	0	0	0	0	—	—
Totals		**6**	**163**	**53**	**5**	**3**	**0**	**.977**

1995 Cleveland Indians (AL) 4, Seattle Mariners (AL) 2

The Seattle Mariners finally ran out of miracles, while the Cleveland Indians took a giant step toward erasing their image as hapless losers. The Mariners' rotation was spent after their exhausting win in the Division Series, and Lou Piniella was forced to open with rookie Bob Wolcott. To everyone's surprise, he tossed seven solid innings to beat Cleveland's Dennis Martinez, 3-2. Orel Hershiser continued his postseason mastery in Game 2, beating Seattle 5-2 with help from Manny Ramirez, who homered twice and recorded four hits. Randy Johnson made his return in Game 3, taking a 2-1 lead into the eighth until Jay Buhner's error allowed Cleveland to score the tying run. Buhner atoned for his miscue with a game-winning homer in the top of the 11th. Cleveland came back with a 7-0 win in Game 4 behind Ken Hill, and took a 3-2 lead in the Series when Hershiser won Game 5. That put Johnson back on the mound for Game 6, his fourth must-win game in 15 days. Martinez both outpitched and outlasted Johnson, who kept it close until tiring in the eighth, as the Indians won 4-0 to move on to the World Series.

Game 1
Tuesday, October 10

Indians	AB	R	H	RBI	BB	K	Avg
Kenny Lofton, cf	3	0	3	0	2	0	1.000
Omar Vizquel, ss	4	0	0	0	1	0	.000
Carlos Baerga, 2b	4	1	1	0	1	1	.250
Albert Belle, lf	4	1	1	1	1	2	.250
Eddie Murray, dh	5	0	0	0	0	1	.000
Jim Thome, 3b	4	0	2	1	0	0	.500
Manny Ramirez, rf	4	0	1	0	0	0	.250
Paul Sorrento, 1b	4	0	1	0	0	1	.250
Sandy Alomar Jr., c	4	0	1	0	0	0	.250
Ruben Amaro, pr	0	0	0	0	0	0	.000
Tony Pena, c	0	0	0	0	0	0	—
TOTALS	36	2	10	2	5	5	.278

Mariners	AB	R	H	RBI	BB	K	Avg
Vince Coleman, lf	4	0	0	0	0	2	.000
Joey Cora, 2b	4	0	2	0	0	0	.500
Ken Griffey Jr., cf	3	2	2	0	1	1	.667
Edgar Martinez, dh	3	0	0	0	1	0	.000
Tino Martinez, 1b	3	0	0	0	1	0	.000
Jay Buhner, rf	3	2	1	0	1	2	.333
Mike Blowers, 3b	4	1	1	2	0	0	.250
Luis Sojo, ss	3	0	1	1	0	0	.333
Dan Wilson, c	3	0	0	0	0	1	.000
TOTALS	30	3	7	3	4	6	.233

	1	2	3	4	5	6	7	8	9	R	H	E
Indians	0	0	1	0	0	0	1	0	0	2	10	1
Mariners	0	2	0	0	0	0	1	0	x	3	7	0

E—Thome. DP—Indians 1 (Vizquel to Baerga to Sorrento), Mariners 1 (Sojo to TMartinez). LOB—Indians 12, Mariners 7. Scoring Position—Indians 2-for-11, Mariners 1-for-8. 2B—Sorrento (1), Cora (1), Griffey Jr. (1), Buhner (1), Sojo (1). 3B—Lofton (1). HR—Belle (1), Blowers (1). GDP—Sorrento, EMartinez. CS—Griffey Jr. (1).

Indians	IP	H	R	ER	BB	K	ERA
Dennis Martinez (L, 0-1)	6.1	6	3	3	2	4	4.26
Julian Tavarez	1.0	1	0	0	1	1	0.00
Paul Assenmacher	0.0	0	0	0	1	0	—
Eric Plunk	0.2	0	0	0	0	1	0.00

Mariners	IP	H	R	ER	BB	K	ERA
Bob Wolcott (W, 1-0)	7.0	8	2	2	5	2	2.57
Jeff Nelson (H, 1)	0.2	1	0	0	0	1	0.00
Norm Charlton (S, 1)	1.1	1	0	0	0	2	0.00

Assenmacher pitched to one batter in the 8th.

Time—3:07. Attendance—57,065. Umpires—HP, Phillips. 1B, Cousins. 2B, Reed. 3B, Ford.

Game 2
Wednesday, October 11

Indians	AB	R	H	RBI	BB	K	Avg
Kenny Lofton, cf	4	1	1	0	1	1	.571
Omar Vizquel, ss	3	0	0	0	2	0	.000
Carlos Baerga, 2b	5	0	2	2	0	0	.333
Albert Belle, lf	3	0	1	0	2	0	.286
Eddie Murray, dh	5	0	2	0	0	0	.200
Jim Thome, 3b	4	0	0	0	0	1	.250
Alvaro Espinoza, 3b	1	0	0	0	0	0	.000
Manny Ramirez, rf	4	2	4	2	0	0	.625
Wayne Kirby, rf	0	0	0	0	0	0	—
Paul Sorrento, 1b	4	2	1	0	0	0	.250
Sandy Alomar Jr., c	4	0	1	1	0	1	.250
TOTALS	37	5	12	5	5	3	.301

Mariners	AB	R	H	RBI	BB	K	Avg
Vince Coleman, lf	4	0	1	0	0	3	.125
Joey Cora, 2b	3	0	0	0	0	0	.286
Ken Griffey Jr., cf	4	1	2	1	0	0	.571
Edgar Martinez, dh	3	0	0	0	1	0	.000
Tino Martinez, 1b	4	0	0	0	0	2	.000
Jay Buhner, rf	4	1	1	1	0	1	.286
Mike Blowers, 3b	4	0	1	0	0	1	.250
Luis Sojo, ss	3	0	0	0	0	0	.167
Alex Diaz, ph	1	0	1	0	0	0	1.000
Dan Wilson, c	3	0	0	0	0	0	.000
Doug Strange, ph	1	0	0	0	0	0	.000
TOTALS	34	2	6	2	1	7	.203

	1	2	3	4	5	6	7	8	9	R	H	E
Indians	0	0	0	0	2	2	0	1	0	5	12	0
Mariners	0	0	0	0	0	1	0	0	1	2	6	1

E—Sojo. DP—Mariners 2 (TMartinez to Sojo; Ayala to Sojo to TMartinez). LOB—Indians 10, Mariners 7. Scoring Position—Indians 2-for-7, Mariners 0-for-3. 3B—Alomar Jr. (1). HR—Ramirez 2 (2), Griffey Jr. (1), Buhner (1). GDP—Thome, Sorrento. SB—Vizquel (1), Coleman (1).

Indians	IP	H	R	ER	BB	K	ERA
Orel Hershiser (W, 1-0)	8.0	4	1	1	1	7	1.13
Jose Mesa	1.0	2	1	1	0	0	9.00

Mariners	IP	H	R	ER	BB	K	ERA
Tim Belcher (L, 0-1)	5.2	9	4	4	2	1	6.35
Bobby Ayala	2.2	2	1	1	3	2	3.38
Bill Risley	0.2	1	0	0	0	0	0.00

WP—Hershiser. HBP—Cora by Hershiser. Time—3:14. Attendance—58,144. Umpires—HP, Cousins. 1B, Reed. 2B, Ford. 3B, McClelland.

Game 3
Friday, October 13

Mariners	AB	R	H	RBI	BB	K	Avg
Vince Coleman, lf	5	0	0	0	0	0	.077
Chris Widger, c	0	0	0	0	0	0	—
Joey Cora, 2b	4	1	1	0	0	0	.273
Felix Fermin, 2b	0	0	0	0	0	0	—
Ken Griffey Jr., cf	5	1	2	0	0	1	.500
Edgar Martinez, dh	5	0	0	0	0	1	.000
Tino Martinez, 1b	4	1	1	0	1	1	.091
Jay Buhner, rf	5	2	2	4	0	1	.333
Mike Blowers, 3b	3	0	1	0	0	0	.273
Alex Diaz, ph-lf	2	0	0	0	0	1	.333
Luis Sojo, ss	4	0	2	0	0	0	.300
Dan Wilson, c	3	0	0	0	0	2	.000
Doug Strange, ph-3b	1	0	0	0	0	0	.000
TOTALS	41	5	9	4	1	7	.210

Indians	AB	R	H	RBI	BB	K	Avg
Kenny Lofton, cf	5	1	2	1	0	2	.500
Omar Vizquel, ss	4	0	1	0	0	0	.000
Carlos Baerga, 2b	5	0	1	0	0	1	.286
Albert Belle, lf	4	0	0	0	0	0	.182
Eddie Murray, dh	4	0	0	0	0	1	.143
Ruben Amaro, pr-dh	1	0	0	0	0	0	.000
Manny Ramirez, rf	3	0	0	0	1	2	.455
Herbert Perry, 1b	3	0	0	0	1	1	.000
Sandy Alomar Jr., c	3	0	0	0	0	0	.182
Alvaro Espinoza, 3b	3	0	1	0	0	1	.250
Wayne Kirby, pr	0	1	0	0	0	0	—
Jim Thome, 3b	1	0	0	0	0	0	.222
TOTALS	36	2	4	2	3	8	.238

	1	2	3	4	5	6	7	8	9	10	11	R	H	E
Mariners	0	1	1	0	0	0	0	0	0	0	3	5	9	1
Indians	0	0	0	1	0	0	0	1	0	0	0	2	4	2

E—Espinoza, Buhner, Alomar Jr. DP—Indians 1 (Mesa to Perry). LOB—Mariners 5, Indians 6. Scoring Position—Mariners 1-for-4, Indians 1-for-6. 3B—Lofton (2). HR—Buhner 2 (3). SF—Vizquel. SB—Cora (1), Griffey Jr. (1), Lofton (1). CS—EMartinez (1), Perry (1).

Mariners	IP	H	R	ER	BB	K	ERA
Randy Johnson	8.0	4	2	1	2	6	1.13
Norm Charlton (W, 1-0)	3.0	0	0	0	1	2	0.00

Indians	IP	H	R	ER	BB	K	ERA
Charles Nagy	8.0	5	2	1	0	6	1.13
Jose Mesa	1.0	1	0	0	0	0	4.50
Julian Tavarez (L, 0-1)	1.0	2	1	1	0	0	4.50
Paul Assenmacher	0.1	0	0	0	0	0	0.00
Eric Plunk	0.2	1	2	2	1	1	13.50

Tavarez pitched to one batter in the 11th.

HBP—Cora by Nagy, Belle by Charlton. Time—3:18. Attendance—43,643. Umpires—HP, Reed. 1B, Ford. 2B, McClelland. 3B, Coble.

Postseason: League Championship Series

Game 4
Saturday, October 14

Mariners	AB	R	H	RBI	BB	K	Avg
Vince Coleman, lf	3	0	0	0	1	0	.063
Joey Cora, 2b	4	0	0	0	0	0	.200
Ken Griffey Jr., cf	3	0	0	0	1	1	.400
Edgar Martinez, dh	4	0	1	0	0	1	.067
Tino Martinez, 1b	4	0	1	0	0	2	.133
Jay Buhner, rf	3	0	3	0	1	0	.467
Mike Blowers, 3b	4	0	0	0	0	3	.200
Luis Sojo, ss	3	0	1	0	0	1	.308
Rich Amaral, ph	1	0	0	0	0	1	.000
Dan Wilson, c	2	0	0	0	0	0	.000
Chris Widger, c	1	0	0	0	0	1	.000
Doug Strange, ph	0	0	0	0	0	0	.000
Alex Rodriguez, ph	1	0	0	0	0	1	.000
TOTALS	33	0	6	0	3	11	.200

Indians	AB	R	H	RBI	BB	K	Avg
Kenny Lofton, cf	3	1	1	1	1	0	.467
Omar Vizquel, ss	4	1	1	1	1	2	.067
Carlos Baerga, 2b	4	1	2	1	0	0	.333
Eddie Murray, dh	3	1	1	2	1	1	.176
Jim Thome, 3b	3	1	1	2	1	1	.250
Manny Ramirez, rf	3	0	1	0	1	1	.429
Paul Sorrento, 1b	3	0	0	0	1	1	.182
Tony Pena, c	3	1	1	0	1	0	.333
Wayne Kirby, lf	4	1	1	0	0	0	.250
TOTALS	30	7	9	7	7	6	.275

	1	2	3	4	5	6	7	8	9		R	H	E
Mariners	0	0	0	0	0	0	0	0	0		0	6	1
Indians	3	1	2	0	0	1	0	0	x		7	9	0

E—Wilson. DP—Mariners 2 (Nelson to Sojo to TMartinez; Nelson to Sojo to TMartinez). LOB—Mariners 9, Indians 7. Scoring Position—Mariners 0-for-8, Indians 2-for-8. 2B—Buhner (2), Vizquel (1). HR—Murray (1), Thome (1). SF—Lofton. GDP—Sorrento, Kirby. SB—Coleman (2), Griffey Jr. (2), Lofton (2), Kirby (1).

Mariners	IP	H	R	ER	BB	K	ERA
Andy Benes (L, 0-1)	2.1	6	6	6	2	3	23.14
Bob Wells	3.0	2	1	1	2	2	3.00
Bobby Ayala	1.0	1	0	0	0	1	2.45
Jeff Nelson	1.1	0	0	0	2	0	0.00
Bill Risley	0.1	0	0	0	1	0	0.00

Indians	IP	H	R	ER	BB	K	ERA
Ken Hill (W, 1-0)	7.0	5	0	0	3	6	0.00
Jim Poole	1.0	0	0	0	0	2	0.00
Chad Ogea	0.2	1	0	0	0	2	0.00
Alan Embree	0.1	0	0	0	0	1	0.00

WP—Ogea. Time—3:30. Attendance—43,686. Umpires—HP, Ford. 1B, McClelland. 2B, Coble. 3B, Phillips.

Game 5
Sunday, October 15

Mariners	AB	R	H	RBI	BB	K	Avg
Joey Cora, 2b	4	2	1	0	1	0	.211
Edgar Martinez, dh	5	0	0	0	0	2	.050
Ken Griffey Jr., cf	3	0	1	1	1	1	.389
Jay Buhner, rf	4	0	0	0	0	3	.368
Tino Martinez, 1b	4	0	1	0	0	1	.158
Doug Strange, 3b	2	0	0	0	0	0	.000
Vince Coleman, ph	0	0	0	0	1	0	.063
Mike Blowers, 3b	0	0	0	0	0	0	.200
Alex Diaz, lf	3	0	2	0	1	0	.500
Luis Sojo, ss	4	0	0	0	0	0	.235
Dan Wilson, c	3	0	0	0	0	1	.000
Rich Amaral, ph	1	0	0	0	0	0	.000
TOTALS	33	2	5	1	4	10	.195

Indians	AB	R	H	RBI	BB	K	Avg
Kenny Lofton, cf	5	0	2	0	0	1	.450
Omar Vizquel, ss	4	1	1	0	1	0	.105
Carlos Baerga, 2b	3	0	1	0	1	0	.333
Albert Belle, lf	3	0	0	0	0	2	.143
Wayne Kirby, lf	0	0	0	0	0	0	.250
Eddie Murray, dh	3	1	3	1	1	0	.300
Jim Thome, 3b	3	1	1	2	1	1	.267
Alvaro Espinoza, 3b	0	0	0	0	0	0	.250
Manny Ramirez, rf	4	0	0	0	0	1	.333
Paul Sorrento, 1b	2	0	0	0	1	1	.154
Herbert Perry, 1b	1	0	0	0	0	1	.000
Sandy Alomar Jr., c	4	0	2	0	0	0	.267
Tony Pena, c	0	0	0	0	0	0	.333
TOTALS	32	3	10	3	5	7	.265

	1	2	3	4	5	6	7	8	9		R	H	E
Mariners	0	0	1	0	1	0	0	0	0		2	5	2
Indians	1	0	0	0	0	2	0	0	x		3	10	4

E—Griffey Jr., Belle 2, Sorrento 2, TMartinez. DP—Mariners 2 (Cora to Sojo; Sojo to Cora to TMartinez), Indians 1 (Vizquel). LOB—Mariners 9, Indians 11. Scoring Position—Mariners 1-for-10, Indians 2-for-10. 2B—Griffey Jr. (2), Diaz (1), Murray (1), Alomar (1). HR—Thome (2). S—Strange, Kirby. GDP—Ramirez. SB—Cora (2), Lofton 2 (4), Vizquel 2 (3), Coleman (3).

Mariners	IP	H	R	ER	BB	K	ERA
Chris Bosio (L, 0-1)	5.1	7	3	2	2	3	3.38
Jeff Nelson	1.0	2	0	0	3	2	0.00
Bill Risley	1.2	1	0	0	0	2	0.00

Indians	IP	H	R	ER	BB	K	ERA
Orel Hershiser (W, 2-0)	6.0	5	2	1	2	8	1.29
Julian Tavarez (H, 1)	0.1	0	0	0	0	0	3.86
Paul Assenmacher (H, 1)	1.0	0	0	0	0	2	0.00
Eric Plunk (H, 1)	0.2	0	0	0	2	0	9.00
Jose Mesa (S, 1)	1.0	0	0	0	0	0	3.00

Time—3:37. Attendance—43,607. Umpires—HP, McClelland. 1B, Coble. 2B, Cousins. 3B, Reed.

Game 6
Tuesday, October 17

Indians	AB	R	H	RBI	BB	K	Avg
Kenny Lofton, cf	4	1	2	1	0	2	.458
Omar Vizquel, ss	4	0	0	0	0	0	.087
Carlos Baerga, 2b	4	1	3	1	0	1	.400
Albert Belle, lf	4	0	2	0	0	1	.222
Eddie Murray, dh	4	0	0	0	0	0	.250
Manny Ramirez, rf	3	0	0	0	0	1	.286
Wayne Kirby, rf	1	0	0	0	0	0	.200
Herbert Perry, 1b	4	0	0	0	0	1	.000
Alvaro Espinoza, 3b	4	1	0	0	0	2	.125
Tony Pena, c	3	0	1	0	0	0	.333
Ruben Amaro, pr	0	1	0	0	0	0	.000
Sandy Alomar Jr., c	0	0	0	0	0	0	.267
TOTALS	35	4	8	2	0	8	.264

Mariners	AB	R	H	RBI	BB	K	Avg
Vince Coleman, lf	4	0	1	0	0	1	.100
Chris Widger, c	0	0	0	0	0	0	.000
Joey Cora, 2b	4	0	0	0	0	0	.174
Ken Griffey Jr., cf	3	0	0	0	1	0	.333
Edgar Martinez, dh	3	0	1	0	0	1	.087
Tino Martinez, 1b	3	0	0	0	1	1	.136
Jay Buhner, rf	4	0	0	0	0	1	.304
Mike Blowers, 3b	3	0	1	0	0	0	.222
Luis Sojo, ss	3	0	1	0	0	1	.250
Felix Fermin, ss	0	0	0	0	0	0	—
Dan Wilson, c	2	0	0	0	0	0	.000
Alex Diaz, ph-lf	1	0	0	0	0	0	.429
TOTALS	30	0	4	0	2	5	.191

	1	2	3	4	5	6	7	8	9		R	H	E
Indians	0	0	0	1	0	0	3	0			4	8	0
Mariners	0	0	0	0	0	0	0	0	0		0	4	1

E—Cora. DP—Indians 1 (Vizquel to Baerga to Perry). LOB—Indians 4, Mariners 6. Scoring Position—Indians 0-for-7, Mariners 0-for-6. 2B—Belle (1), Pena (1), Sojo (2). HR—Baerga (1). GDP—Sojo. SB—Lofton (5), Coleman (4), EMartinez (1).

Indians	IP	H	R	ER	BB	K	ERA
Dennis Martinez (W, 1-1)	7.0	4	0	0	1	3	2.03
Julian Tavarez	1.0	0	0	0	0	1	2.70
Jose Mesa	1.0	0	0	0	1	1	2.25

Mariners	IP	H	R	ER	BB	K	ERA
Randy Johnson (L, 0-1)	7.1	8	4	3	0	7	2.35
Norm Charlton	1.2	0	0	0	0	1	0.00

PB—Wilson. HBP—EMartinez by DMartinez. Time—2:54. Attendance—58,489. Umpires—HP, Coble. 1B, Kaiser. 2B, Cousins. 3B, Reed.

1995 AL Championship Series—Composite Statistics

Batting

Indians	G	AB	R	H	RBI	2B	3B	HR	BB	SO	SB	CS	Avg	OBP	Slg
Sandy Alomar Jr.	5	15	0	4	1	1	1	0	1	1	0	0	.267	.313	.467
Ruben Amaro	3	1	1	0	0	0	0	0	0	0	0	0	.000	.000	.000
Carlos Baerga	6	25	3	10	4	0	0	1	2	3	0	0	.400	.444	.520
Albert Belle	5	18	1	4	1	1	0	1	3	5	0	0	.222	.364	.444
Alvaro Espinoza	4	8	1	1	0	0	0	0	0	3	0	0	.125	.125	.125
Wayne Kirby	5	5	2	1	0	0	0	0	0	1	0	0	.200	.200	.200
Kenny Lofton	6	24	4	11	3	0	2	0	4	6	5	0	.458	.517	.625
Eddie Murray	6	24	2	6	3	1	0	1	2	3	0	0	.250	.308	.417
Tony Pena	4	6	1	2	0	1	0	0	1	0	0	0	.333	.429	.500
Herbert Perry	3	8	0	0	0	0	0	0	1	3	0	1	.000	.111	.000
Manny Ramirez	6	21	2	6	2	0	0	2	2	5	0	0	.286	.348	.571
Paul Sorrento	4	13	2	2	0	1	0	0	2	3	0	0	.154	.267	.231
Jim Thome	5	15	4	4	5	0	0	2	2	3	0	0	.267	.353	.667
Omar Vizquel	6	23	2	2	2	1	0	0	5	2	3	0	.087	.241	.130
Totals	**6**	**206**	**23**	**53**	**21**	**6**	**3**	**7**	**25**	**37**	**9**	**1**	**.257**	**.338**	**.417**

Batting

Mariners	G	AB	R	H	RBI	2B	3B	HR	BB	SO	SB	CS	Avg	OBP	Slg
Rich Amaral	2	2	0	0	0	0	0	0	0	1	0	0	.000	.000	.000
Mike Blowers	6	18	1	4	2	0	0	1	0	4	0	0	.222	.222	.389
Jay Buhner	6	23	5	7	5	2	0	3	2	8	0	0	.304	.360	.783
Vince Coleman	6	20	0	2	0	0	0	0	2	6	4	0	.100	.182	.100
Joey Cora	6	23	3	4	0	1	0	0	1	0	2	0	.174	.269	.217
Alex Diaz	4	7	0	3	0	1	0	0	1	1	0	0	.429	.500	.571
Ken Griffey Jr.	6	21	2	7	2	2	0	1	4	4	2	1	.333	.440	.571
Edgar Martinez	6	23	0	2	0	0	0	0	2	5	1	1	.087	.192	.087
Tino Martinez	6	22	1	3	0	0	0	0	3	7	0	0	.136	.240	.136
Alex Rodriguez	1	1	0	0	0	0	0	0	0	1	0	0	.000	.000	.000
Luis Sojo	6	20	0	5	1	2	0	0	0	2	0	0	.250	.250	.350
Doug Strange	4	4	0	0	0	0	0	0	0	2	0	0	.000	.000	.000
Chris Widger	3	1	0	0	0	0	0	0	0	1	0	0	.000	.000	.000
Dan Wilson	6	16	0	0	0	0	0	0	0	4	0	0	.000	.000	.000
Totals	**6**	**201**	**12**	**37**	**10**	**8**	**0**	**5**	**15**	**46**	**9**	**2**	**.184**	**.251**	**.299**

Pitching

Indians	G	GS	CG	IP	H	R	ER	BB	SO	W-L	Sv-Op	Hld	ERA
Paul Assenmacher	3	0	0	1.1	0	0	0	1	2	0-0	0-0	1	0.00
Alan Embree	1	0	0	0.1	0	0	0	0	1	0-0	0-0	0	0.00
Orel Hershiser	2	2	0	14.0	9	3	2	3	15	2-0	0-0	0	1.29
Ken Hill	1	1	0	7.0	5	0	0	3	6	1-0	0-0	0	0.00
Dennis Martinez	2	2	0	13.1	10	3	3	3	7	1-1	0-0	0	2.03
Jose Mesa	4	0	0	4.0	3	1	1	1	1	0-0	1-1	0	2.25
Charles Nagy	1	1	0	8.0	5	2	1	0	6	0-0	0-0	0	1.13
Chad Ogea	1	0	0	0.2	1	0	0	0	0	0-0	0-0	0	0.00
Eric Plunk	3	0	0	2.0	1	2	2	3	2	0-0	0-0	1	9.00
Jim Poole	1	0	0	1.0	0	0	0	0	2	0-0	0-0	0	0.00
Julian Tavarez	4	0	0	3.1	3	1	1	1	2	0-1	0-0	1	2.70
Totals	**6**	**6**	**0**	**55.0**	**37**	**12**	**10**	**15**	**46**	**4-2**	**1-1**	**3**	**1.64**

Pitching

Mariners	G	GS	CG	IP	H	R	ER	BB	SO	W-L	Sv-Op	Hld	ERA
Bobby Ayala	2	0	0	3.2	3	1	1	3	3	0-0	0-0	0	2.45
Tim Belcher	1	1	0	5.2	9	4	4	2	1	0-1	0-0	0	6.35
Andy Benes	1	1	0	2.1	6	6	6	2	3	0-1	0-0	0	23.14
Chris Bosio	1	1	0	5.1	7	3	2	2	3	0-1	0-0	0	3.38
Norm Charlton	3	0	0	6.0	1	0	0	1	5	1-0	1-1	0	0.00
Randy Johnson	2	2	0	15.1	12	6	4	4	13	0-1	0-0	0	2.35
Jeff Nelson	3	0	0	3.0	3	0	0	5	3	0-0	0-0	1	0.00
Bill Risley	3	0	0	2.2	2	0	0	1	3	0-0	0-0	0	0.00
Bob Wells	1	0	0	3.0	2	1	1	2	2	0-0	0-0	0	3.00
Bob Wolcott	1	1	0	7.0	8	2	2	5	2	1-0	0-0	0	2.57
Totals	**6**	**6**	**0**	**54.0**	**53**	**23**	**20**	**25**	**37**	**2-4**	**1-1**	**1**	**3.33**

Fielding

Indians	Pos	G	PO	Ast	E	DP	PB	FPct
Sandy Alomar Jr.	c	5	30	3	1	0	0	.971
Paul Assenmacher	p	3	0	0	0	0	—	—
Carlos Baerga	2b	6	12	22	0	2	—	1.000
Albert Belle	lf	5	4	0	2	0	—	.667
Alan Embree	p	1	0	0	0	0	—	—
Alvaro Espinoza	3b	4	0	3	1	0	—	.750
Orel Hershiser	p	2	0	4	0	0	—	1.000
Ken Hill	p	1	1	1	0	0	—	1.000
Wayne Kirby	lf	2	3	0	0	0	—	1.000
	rf	2	0	0	0	0	—	—
Kenny Lofton	cf	6	15	0	0	0	—	1.000
Dennis Martinez	p	2	1	1	0	0	—	1.000
Jose Mesa	p	4	1	2	0	1	—	1.000
Charles Nagy	p	1	0	1	0	0	—	1.000
Chad Ogea	p	1	0	0	0	0	—	—
Tony Pena	c	4	15	1	0	0	0	1.000
Herbert Perry	1b	3	30	0	0	2	—	1.000
Eric Plunk	p	3	0	0	0	0	—	—
Jim Poole	p	1	0	0	0	0	—	—
Manny Ramirez	rf	6	9	0	0	0	—	1.000
Paul Sorrento	1b	4	34	1	2	1	—	.946
Julian Tavarez	p	4	0	1	0	0	—	1.000
Jim Thome	3b	5	1	5	1	0	—	.857
Omar Vizquel	ss	6	9	21	0	3	—	1.000
Totals		**6**	**165**	**66**	**7**	**9**	**0**	**.971**

Fielding

Mariners	Pos	G	PO	Ast	E	DP	PB	FPct
Bobby Ayala	p	2	0	1	0	1	—	1.000
Tim Belcher	p	1	1	0	0	0	—	1.000
Andy Benes	p	1	0	0	0	0	—	—
Mike Blowers	3b	6	5	9	0	0	—	1.000
Chris Bosio	p	1	0	2	0	0	—	1.000
Jay Buhner	rf	6	15	0	1	0	—	.938
Norm Charlton	p	3	0	0	0	0	—	—
Vince Coleman	lf	5	12	0	0	0	—	1.000
Joey Cora	2b	6	15	12	1	3	—	.964
Alex Diaz	lf	3	1	0	0	0	—	1.000
Felix Fermin	2b	1	0	0	0	0	—	—
	ss	1	0	0	0	0	—	—
Ken Griffey Jr.	cf	6	13	0	1	0	—	.929
Randy Johnson	p	2	1	1	0	0	—	1.000
Tino Martinez	1b	6	45	5	1	6	—	.980
Jeff Nelson	p	3	0	3	0	1	—	1.000
Bill Risley	p	3	0	0	0	1	—	—
Luis Sojo	ss	6	9	18	1	7	—	.964
Doug Strange	3b	2	2	3	0	0	—	1.000
Bob Wells	p	1	0	1	0	0	—	1.000
Chris Widger	c	3	7	0	0	0	0	1.000
Dan Wilson	c	6	35	3	1	0	1	.974
Bob Wolcott	p	1	1	1	0	0	—	1.000
Totals		**6**	**162**	**59**	**6**	**19**	**1**	**.974**

1995 Atlanta Braves (NL) 4, Cincinnati Reds (NL) 0

The Atlanta Braves swept the Cincinnati Reds four straight, limiting the Reds to only five runs in the four contests. Cincy's Pete Schourek took a 1-0 lead into the ninth inning of the opener, but the Braves managed to get a a run to send the game into extra innings, and Mike Devereaux won it for Atlanta with an RBI single in the top of the 11th. Game 2 was another extra-inning affair, but Davey Johnson exhausted his bullpen. Starter Mark Portugal was pressed into service in the top of the 10th, and Javy Lopez reached him for a three-run homer, sending the Braves to a 6-2 win. Greg Maddux was on his game in the third contest, putting the Braves ahead three games to none with a 5-2 victory. Steve Avery outpitched Schourek in Game 4, and the Braves broke it open with a five-run rally in the seventh for a 6-0 win. Reggie Sanders personified the Reds' inability to solve the Braves' pitching, going 2-for-16 with 10 strikeouts and zero RBI.

Game 1
Tuesday, October 10

Braves	AB	R	H	RBI	BB	K	Avg
Marquis Grissom, cf	5	0	1	0	0	3	.200
Mark Lemke, 2b	5	0	0	0	0	0	.000
Chipper Jones, 3b	5	1	2	0	0	0	.400
Fred McGriff, 1b	4	1	1	0	1	0	.250
David Justice, rf	4	0	1	1	0	1	.250
Luis Polonia, pr-lf	0	0	0	0	0	0	—
Javy Lopez, c	5	0	1	0	0	0	.200
Ryan Klesko, lf	2	0	0	0	2	2	.000
Mike Devereaux, rf	1	0	1	1	0	0	1.000
Jeff Blauser, ss	4	0	0	0	1	2	.000
Brad Clontz, p	0	0	0	0	0	0	—
Steve Avery, p	0	0	0	0	0	0	—
Greg McMichael, p	0	0	0	0	0	0	—
Tom Glavine, p	1	0	0	0	1	0	.000
Mike Mordecai, ph	1	0	0	0	0	1	.000
Alejandro Pena, p	0	0	0	0	0	0	—
Dwight Smith, ph	1	0	0	0	0	0	.000
Mark Wohlers, p	0	0	0	0	0	0	—
Rafael Belliard, ss	0	0	0	0	0	0	—
TOTALS	38	2	7	2	5	9	.184

Reds	AB	R	H	RBI	BB	K	Avg
Jerome Walton, cf-lf	4	0	0	0	0	0	.000
Thomas Howard, ph	1	0	1	0	0	0	1.000
Barry Larkin, ss	5	1	2	0	0	0	.400
Ron Gant, lf	4	0	2	1	0	2	.500
Darren Lewis, cf	0	0	0	0	0	0	—
Lenny Harris, ph	0	0	0	0	0	0	—
Mariano Duncan, ph	0	0	0	0	1	0	—
Reggie Sanders, rf	4	0	0	0	1	1	.000
Benito Santiago, c	3	0	1	0	1	0	.333
Hal Morris, 1b	3	0	1	0	0	0	.333
Bret Boone, 2b	4	0	0	0	0	1	.000
Mark Lewis, 3b	3	0	1	0	0	1	.333
Jeff Branson, ph-3b	1	0	0	0	0	1	.000
Pete Schourek, p	3	0	0	0	0	3	.000
Jeff Brantley, p	0	0	0	0	0	0	—
Eric Anthony, ph	1	0	0	0	0	1	.000
Mike Jackson, p	0	0	0	0	0	0	—
TOTALS	36	1	8	1	3	10	.222

	1	2	3	4	5	6	7	8	9	10	11		R	H	E
Braves	0	0	0	0	0	0	0	0	1	0	1		2	7	0
Reds	0	0	0	1	0	0	0	0	0	0			1	8	0

DP—Braves 4 (Glavine to Blauser to McGriff; Blauser to McGriff; Lemke to Blauser to McGriff; Jones to Lemke to McGriff), Reds 1 (Santiago to Boone). LOB—Braves 9, Reds 6. Scoring Position—Braves 1-for-6, Reds 1-for-9. 2B—Larkin (1), Morris (1), Howard (1). 3B—Larkin (1). S—Polonia. GDP—Walton, Sanders, Santiago, Boone 2. CS—Klesko (1).

Braves	IP	H	R	ER	BB	K	ERA
Tom Glavine	7.0	7	1	1	2	5	1.29
Alejandro Pena	1.0	0	0	0	0	1	0.00
Mark Wohlers (W, 1-0)	2.0	0	0	0	0	4	0.00
Brad Clontz (H, 1)	0.1	1	0	0	0	0	0.00
Steve Avery	0.0	0	0	0	1	0	—
Greg McMichael (S, 1)	0.2	0	0	0	0	0	0.00

Reds	IP	H	R	ER	BB	K	ERA
Pete Schourek	8.1	6	1	1	2	8	1.08
Jeff Brantley	1.2	0	0	0	2	1	0.00
Mike Jackson (L, 0-1)	1.0	1	1	1	1	0	9.00

Avery pitched to one batter in the 11th.

WP—Schourek. HBP—Morris by Glavine. Time—3:18. Attendance—40,382. Umpires—HP, Runge. 1B, Quick. 2B, DeMuth. 3B, Davis.

Game 2
Wednesday, October 11

Braves	AB	R	H	RBI	BB	K	Avg
Marquis Grissom, cf	4	1	1	0	1	0	.222
Mark Lemke, 2b	4	1	1	0	1	0	.111
Chipper Jones, 3b	5	0	1	0	0	0	.300
Fred McGriff, 1b	4	2	3	0	1	0	.500
David Justice, rf	4	1	1	0	1	0	.250
Mike Devereaux, lf	4	0	1	1	0	0	.400
Ryan Klesko, ph-lf	1	0	0	0	0	0	.000
Javy Lopez, c	5	1	1	3	0	1	.200
Rafael Belliard, ss	3	0	1	0	0	0	.333
Luis Polonia, ph	1	0	0	0	0	0	.000
Mike Mordecai, ss	1	0	0	0	0	0	.000
John Smoltz, p	3	0	1	0	0	1	.333
Alejandro Pena, p	0	0	0	0	0	0	—
Dwight Smith, ph	1	0	0	0	0	0	.000
Greg McMichael, p	0	0	0	0	0	0	—
Mark Wohlers, p	0	0	0	0	0	0	—
TOTALS	40	6	11	5	4	2	.247

Reds	AB	R	H	RBI	BB	K	Avg
Thomas Howard, cf	3	0	1	0	1	0	.500
Mike Jackson, p	0	0	0	0	0	0	—
Jeff Brantley, p	0	0	0	0	0	0	—
Mariano Duncan, ph	1	0	0	0	0	0	.000
Mark Portugal, p	0	0	0	0	0	0	—
Barry Larkin, ss	5	0	3	0	0	0	.500
Ron Gant, lf	5	0	0	0	0	0	.222
Reggie Sanders, rf	5	0	1	0	0	4	.111
Hal Morris, 1b	4	0	0	0	1	1	.143
Benito Santiago, c	4	0	1	0	0	1	.286
Bret Boone, 2b	3	1	2	0	1	0	.286
Jeff Branson, 3b	3	1	0	0	0	0	.000
John Smiley, p	1	0	0	0	0	0	.000
Lenny Harris, ph	1	0	1	1	0	0	1.000
Dave Burba, p	0	0	0	0	0	0	—
Eric Anthony, ph	0	0	0	0	1	0	.000
Darren Lewis, pr-cf	1	0	0	0	0	0	.000
TOTALS	36	2	9	1	4	6	.258

	1	2	3	4	5	6	7	8	9	10		R	H	E
Braves	1	0	0	1	0	0	0	0	0	4		6	11	1
Reds	0	0	0	2	0	0	0	0	0			2	9	1

E—Smoltz, Sanders. DP—Reds 1 (Larkin to Boone to Morris). LOB—Braves 8, Reds 9. Scoring Position—Braves 4-for-15, Reds 1-for-10. 2B—McGriff (3), Devereaux (1), Larkin (2). HR—Lopez (1). S—Branson. GDP—Devereaux. SB—Smoltz (1), Larkin (1), Morris (1), Branson (1), Harris (1). CS—Howard (1), Sanders (1).

Braves	IP	H	R	ER	BB	K	ERA
John Smoltz	7.0	7	2	2	2	2	2.57
Alejandro Pena	1.0	1	0	0	1	2	0.00
Greg McMichael (W, 1-0)	1.0	0	0	0	1	0	0.00
Mark Wohlers	1.0	1	0	0	0	2	0.00

Reds	IP	H	R	ER	BB	K	ERA
John Smiley	5.0	5	2	2	0	1	3.60
Dave Burba	2.0	2	0	0	3	0	0.00
Mike Jackson	1.0	1	0	0	0	1	4.50
Jeff Brantley	1.0	0	0	0	0	0	0.00
Mark Portugal (L, 0-1)	1.0	3	4	4	1	0	36.00

Balk—Jackson. WP—Burba, Portugal. Time—3:26. Attendance—44,624. Umpires—HP, Quick. 1B, DeMuth. 2B, Davis. 3B, Marsh.

Game 3
Friday, October 13

Reds	AB	R	H	RBI	BB	K	Avg
Thomas Howard, cf	3	0	0	1	1	0	.286
Barry Larkin, ss	5	0	1	0	0	0	.400
Ron Gant, lf	3	1	1	0	0	0	.250
Reggie Sanders, rf	4	0	1	0	0	3	.154
Hal Morris, 1b	4	0	1	1	0	0	.182
Benito Santiago, c	3	0	0	0	1	0	.200
Bret Boone, 2b	4	0	1	0	0	1	.273
Jeff Branson, 3b	4	1	1	0	0	0	.125
David Wells, p	2	0	1	0	0	0	.500
Lenny Harris, ph	1	0	1	0	0	0	1.000
Xavier Hernandez, p	0	0	0	0	0	0	—
Hector Carrasco, p	0	0	0	0	0	0	—
Eddie Taubensee, ph	1	0	0	0	0	0	.000
TOTALS	34	2	8	2	2	4	.261

Braves	AB	R	H	RBI	BB	K	Avg
Marquis Grissom, cf	5	0	1	0	0	1	.214
Mark Lemke, 2b	4	1	1	0	0	0	.154
Chipper Jones, 3b	4	1	3	2	0	0	.429
Fred McGriff, 1b	4	1	2	0	0	0	.500
David Justice, rf	3	0	1	0	1	0	.273
Mike Devereaux, lf	3	1	1	0	1	1	.375
Charlie O'Brien, c	4	1	2	3	0	1	.500
Rafael Belliard, ss	4	0	1	0	0	1	.286
Greg Maddux, p	3	0	0	0	0	1	.000
Ryan Klesko, ph	1	0	0	0	0	1	.000
Mark Wohlers, p	0	0	0	0	0	0	—
TOTALS	35	5	12	5	2	6	.300

	1	2	3	4	5	6	7	8	9		R	H	E
Reds	0	0	0	0	0	0	0	1	1		2	8	0
Braves	0	0	0	0	0	3	2	0	x		5	12	1

E—Grissom. DP—Reds 1 (Branson to Boone to Morris). LOB—Reds 9, Braves 8. Scoring Position—Reds 1-for-8, Braves 1-for-7. 2B—Branson (1), McGriff (4). HR—Jones (1), O'Brien (1). SF—Howard. GDP—Lemke. SB—Jones (1). CS—Larkin (1).

Reds	IP	H	R	ER	BB	K	ERA
David Wells (L, 0-1)	6.0	8	3	3	2	3	4.50
Xavier Hernandez	0.2	3	2	2	0	0	27.00
Hector Carrasco	1.1	1	0	0	0	3	0.00

Braves	IP	H	R	ER	BB	K	ERA
Greg Maddux (W, 1-0)	8.0	7	1	1	2	4	1.13
Mark Wohlers	1.0	1	1	1	0	0	2.25

WP—Maddux. HBP—Gant by Maddux. Time—2:42. Attendance—51,424. Umpires—HP, DeMuth. 1B, Davis. 2B, Marsh. 3B, Crawford.

Game 4

Saturday, October 14

Reds	AB	R	H	RBI	BB	K	Avg
Jerome Walton, cf	3	0	0	0	0	2	.000
Thomas Howard, ph-cf	1	0	0	0	0	0	.250
Barry Larkin, ss	3	0	1	0	1	1	.389
Ron Gant, lf	4	0	0	0	0	1	.188
Reggie Sanders, rf	3	0	0	0	1	2	.125
Mariano Duncan, 1b	2	0	0	0	0	1	.000
Hal Morris, ph-1b	1	0	0	0	0	0	.167
Benito Santiago, c	3	0	1	0	0	2	.231
Mike Jackson, p	0	0	0	0	0	0	—
Dave Burba, p	0	0	0	0	0	0	—
Bret Boone, 2b	3	0	0	0	0	0	.214
Mark Lewis, 3b	1	0	0	0	1	0	.250
Jeff Branson, ph-3b	1	0	0	0	0	1	.111
Pete Schourek, p	2	0	0	0	0	1	.000
Eddie Taubensee, c	1	0	1	0	0	0	.500
TOTALS	28	0	3	0	3	11	.197

Braves	AB	R	H	RBI	BB	K	Avg
Marquis Grissom, cf	5	1	2	0	0	0	.263
Mark Lemke, 2b	5	0	1	1	0	0	.167
Chipper Jones, 3b	2	1	1	0	3	1	.438
Fred McGriff, 1b	4	1	1	0	1	0	.438
Mike Devereaux, rf	5	1	1	3	0	1	.308
Javy Lopez, c	4	1	3	0	0	0	.357
Ryan Klesko, lf	3	0	0	0	1	1	.000
Rafael Belliard, ss	4	1	1	0	0	2	.273
Steve Avery, p	2	0	1	0	0	0	.500
Charlie O'Brien, ph	1	0	0	0	0	0	.400
Greg McMichael, p	0	0	0	0	0	0	—
Luis Polonia, ph	1	0	1	1	0	0	.500
Alejandro Pena, p	0	0	0	0	0	0	—
Mark Wohlers, p	0	0	0	0	0	0	—
TOTALS	36	6	12	5	5	5	.309

	1	2	3	4	5	6	7	8	9		R	H	E
Reds	0	0	0	0	0	0	0	0	0		0	3	1
Braves	0	0	1	0	0	0	5	0	x		6	12	1

E—Belliard, Larkin. DP—Reds 1 (Schourek to Larkin to Duncan), Braves 3 (Jones to Lemke to McGriff; Belliard to Lemke to McGriff; Belliard to Lemke to McGriff). LOB—Reds 4, Braves 11. Scoring Position—Reds 0-for-2, Braves 3-for-12. 2B—Lopez (1). 3B—Grissom (1). HR—Devereaux (1). GDP—Gant, Sanders, Duncan, Devereaux.

Reds	IP	H	R	ER	BB	K	ERA
Pete Schourek (L, 0-1)	6.0	8	1	1	1	5	1.26
Mike Jackson	0.1	3	5	5	3	0	23.14
Dave Burba	1.2	1	0	0	1	0	0.00

Braves	IP	H	R	ER	BB	K	ERA
Steve Avery (W, 1-0)	6.0	2	0	0	3	6	0.00
Greg McMichael (H, 1)	1.0	0	0	0	0	2	0.00
Alejandro Pena	1.0	1	0	0	0	1	0.00
Mark Wohlers	1.0	0	0	0	0	2	1.80

PB—Taubensee. Time—2:54. Attendance—52,067. Umpires—HP, Davis. 1B, Marsh. 2B, Crawford. 3B, Runge.

1995 NL Championship Series—Composite Statistics

Batting

Braves	G	AB	R	H	RBI	2B	3B	HR	BB	SO	SB	CS	Avg	OBP	Slg
Steve Avery	2	2	0	1	0	0	0	0	0	0	0	0	.500	.500	.500
Rafael Belliard	4	11	1	3	0	0	0	0	0	3	0	0	.273	.273	.273
Jeff Blauser	1	4	0	0	0	0	0	0	0	2	0	0	.000	.200	.000
Mike Devereaux	4	13	2	4	5	1	0	1	1	2	0	0	.308	.357	.615
Tom Glavine	1	1	0	0	0	0	0	0	0	1	0	0	.000	.500	.000
Marquis Grissom	4	19	2	5	0	0	1	0	1	4	0	0	.263	.300	.368
Chipper Jones	4	16	3	7	3	0	0	1	3	1	1	0	.438	.526	.625
David Justice	3	11	1	3	1	0	0	0	2	1	0	0	.273	.385	.273
Ryan Klesko	4	7	0	0	0	0	0	0	3	4	0	1	.000	.300	.000
Mark Lemke	4	18	2	3	1	0	0	0	1	0	0	0	.167	.211	.167
Javy Lopez	3	14	2	5	3	1	0	1	0	1	0	0	.357	.357	.643
Greg Maddux	1	3	0	0	0	0	0	0	0	1	0	0	.000	.000	.000
Fred McGriff	4	16	5	7	0	4	0	0	3	0	0	0	.438	.526	.688
Mike Mordecai	2	2	0	0	0	0	0	0	0	1	0	0	.000	.000	.000
Charlie O'Brien	2	5	1	2	3	0	0	1	0	1	0	0	.400	.400	1.000
Luis Polonia	3	2	0	1	1	0	0	0	0	0	0	0	.500	.500	.500
Dwight Smith	2	2	0	0	0	0	0	0	0	0	0	0	.000	.000	.000
John Smoltz	1	3	0	1	0	0	0	0	0	1	1	0	.333	.333	.333
Totals	**4**	**149**	**19**	**42**	**17**	**6**	**1**	**4**	**16**	**22**	**2**	**1**	**.282**	**.352**	**.416**

Batting

Reds	G	AB	R	H	RBI	2B	3B	HR	BB	SO	SB	CS	Avg	OBP	Slg
Eric Anthony	2	1	0	0	0	0	0	0	1	1	0	0	.000	.500	.000
Bret Boone	4	14	1	3	0	0	0	0	1	2	0	0	.214	.267	.214
Jeff Branson	4	9	2	1	0	1	0	0	0	2	1	0	.111	.111	.222
Mariano Duncan	3	3	0	0	0	0	0	0	1	1	0	0	.000	.250	.000
Ron Gant	4	16	1	3	1	0	0	0	0	3	0	0	.188	.235	.188
Lenny Harris	3	2	0	2	1	0	0	0	0	0	1	0	1.000	1.000	1.000
Thomas Howard	4	8	0	2	1	1	0	0	2	0	0	1	.250	.364	.375
Barry Larkin	4	18	1	7	0	2	1	0	1	1	1	1	.389	.421	.611
Darren Lewis	2	1	0	0	0	0	0	0	0	0	0	0	.000	.000	.000
Mark Lewis	2	4	0	1	0	0	0	0	1	1	0	0	.250	.400	.250
Hal Morris	4	12	0	2	1	1	0	0	1	1	1	0	.167	.286	.250
Reggie Sanders	4	16	0	2	0	0	0	0	2	10	0	1	.125	.222	.125
Benito Santiago	4	13	0	3	0	0	0	0	2	3	0	0	.231	.333	.231
Pete Schourek	2	5	0	0	0	0	0	0	0	4	0	0	.000	.000	.000
John Smiley	1	1	0	0	0	0	0	0	0	0	0	0	.000	.000	.000
Eddie Taubensee	2	2	0	1	0	0	0	0	0	0	0	0	.500	.500	.500
Jerome Walton	2	7	0	0	0	0	0	0	0	2	0	0	.000	.000	.000
David Wells	1	2	0	1	0	0	0	0	0	0	0	0	.500	.500	.500
Totals	**4**	**134**	**5**	**28**	**4**	**5**	**1**	**0**	**12**	**31**	**4**	**3**	**.209**	**.282**	**.261**

Pitching

Braves	G	GS	CG	IP	H	R	ER	BB	SO	W-L	Sv-Op	Hld	ERA
Steve Avery	2	1	0	6.0	2	0	0	4	6	1-0	0-0	0	0.00
Brad Clontz	1	0	0	0.1	1	0	0	0	0	0-0	0-0	1	0.00
Tom Glavine	1	1	0	7.0	7	1	1	2	5	0-0	0-0	0	1.29
Greg Maddux	1	1	0	8.0	7	1	1	2	4	1-0	0-0	0	1.13
Greg McMichael	3	0	0	2.2	0	0	0	1	2	1-0	1-1	1	0.00
Alejandro Pena	3	0	0	3.0	2	0	0	1	4	0-0	0-0	0	0.00
John Smoltz	1	1	0	7.0	7	2	2	2	2	0-0	0-0	0	2.57
Mark Wohlers	4	0	0	5.0	2	1	1	0	8	1-0	0-0	0	1.80
Totals	**4**	**4**	**0**	**39.0**	**28**	**5**	**5**	**12**	**31**	**4-0**	**1-1**	**2**	**1.15**

Pitching

Reds	G	GS	CG	IP	H	R	ER	BB	SO	W-L	Sv-Op	Hld	ERA
Jeff Brantley	2	0	0	2.2	0	0	0	2	1	0-0	0-0	0	0.00
Dave Burba	2	0	0	3.2	3	0	0	4	0	0-0	0-0	0	0.00
Hector Carrasco	1	0	0	1.1	1	0	0	0	3	0-0	0-0	0	0.00
Xavier Hernandez	1	0	0	0.2	3	2	2	0	0	0-0	0-0	0	27.00
Mike Jackson	3	0	0	2.1	5	6	6	4	1	0-1	0-0	0	23.14
Mark Portugal	1	0	0	1.0	3	4	4	1	0	0-1	0-0	0	36.00
Pete Schourek	2	2	0	14.1	14	2	2	3	13	0-1	0-0	0	1.26
John Smiley	1	1	0	5.0	5	2	2	0	1	0-0	0-0	0	3.60
David Wells	1	1	0	6.0	8	3	3	2	3	0-1	0-0	0	4.50
Totals	**4**	**4**	**0**	**37.0**	**42**	**19**	**19**	**16**	**22**	**0-4**	**0-0**	**0**	**4.62**

Fielding

Braves	Pos	G	PO	Ast	E	DP	PB	FPct
Steve Avery	p	2	0	2	0	0	—	1.000
Rafael Belliard	ss	4	6	7	1	3	—	.929
Jeff Blauser	ss	1	4	6	0	3	—	1.000
Brad Clontz	p	1	0	0	0	0	—	—
Mike Devereaux	lf	2	2	0	0	0	—	1.000
	rf	2	0	0	0	0	—	—
Tom Glavine	p	1	0	1	0	1	—	1.000
Marquis Grissom	cf	4	8	0	1	0	—	.889
Chipper Jones	3b	4	4	13	0	2	—	1.000
David Justice	rf	3	4	0	0	0	—	1.000
Ryan Klesko	lf	3	1	0	0	0	—	1.000
Mark Lemke	2b	4	13	16	0	5	—	1.000
Javy Lopez	c	3	28	2	0	0	0	1.000
Greg Maddux	p	1	1	1	0	0	—	1.000
Fred McGriff	1b	4	42	4	0	8	—	1.000
Greg McMichael	p	3	0	0	0	0	—	—
Mike Mordecai	ss	1	0	0	0	0	—	—
Charlie O'Brien	c	1	3	1	0	0	0	1.000
Alejandro Pena	p	3	0	0	0	0	—	—
Luis Polonia	lf	1	0	0	0	0	—	—
John Smoltz	p	1	0	1	1	0	—	.500
Mark Wohlers	p	4	1	0	0	0	—	1.000
Totals		**4**	**117**	**54**	**3**	**22**	**0**	**.983**

Fielding

Reds	Pos	G	PO	Ast	E	DP	PB	FPct
Bret Boone	2b	4	9	13	0	3	—	1.000
Jeff Branson	3b	4	1	3	0	1	—	1.000
Jeff Brantley	p	2	2	0	0	0	—	1.000
Dave Burba	p	2	0	0	0	0	—	—
Hector Carrasco	p	1	0	0	0	0	—	—
Mariano Duncan	1b	1	9	0	0	1	—	1.000
Ron Gant	lf	4	9	0	0	0	—	1.000
Xavier Hernandez	p	1	0	0	0	0	—	—
Thomas Howard	cf	3	2	0	0	0	—	1.000
Mike Jackson	p	3	0	1	0	0	—	1.000
Barry Larkin	ss	4	10	15	1	2	—	.962
Darren Lewis	cf	2	2	0	0	0	—	1.000
Mark Lewis	3b	2	2	3	0	0	—	1.000
Hal Morris	1b	4	27	3	0	2	—	1.000
Mark Portugal	p	1	0	0	0	0	—	—
Reggie Sanders	rf	4	7	0	1	0	—	.875
Benito Santiago	c	4	23	1	0	1	0	1.000
Pete Schourek	p	2	1	3	0	1	—	1.000
John Smiley	p	1	1	1	0	0	—	1.000
Eddie Taubensee	c	1	0	0	0	0	1	—
Jerome Walton	cf	2	4	0	0	0	—	1.000
	lf	1	2	0	0	0	—	1.000
David Wells	p	1	0	0	0	0	—	—
Totals		**4**	**111**	**43**	**2**	**11**	**1**	**.987**

1996 New York Yankees (AL) 4, Baltimore Orioles (AL) 1

The Yankees downed the Orioles in a five-game series in which the Orioles appeared to be hopelessly cursed. In the opener, the O's led 4-3 in the eighth when Derek Jeter lifted a fly to right field. Tony Tarasco drifted to the wall and settled under it, but 12-year-old Jeffrey Maier reached out of the stands and caught it. Umpire Rich Garcia erroneously ruled it a game-tying home run, and Bernie Williams hit an 11th-inning homer to give the Yanks a 5-4 victory. After evening the series with a 5-3 win in Game 2, the O's dropped the third game when the ball slipped out of Todd Zeile's hand on a pump-fake late in the game, allowing Williams to score the go-ahead run. Darryl Strawberry helped the Yankees take a 3-to-1 lead in the series, going 3-for-4 with a pair of homers in their 8-4 victory in the fourth game. With one out and two on in the third inning of Game 5, Williams tapped a routine double-play ball to Roberto Alomar. The ball rolled under his glove and into right field. The Orioles, who trailed by one run at the time of Alomar's error, allowed a total of six runs before the third out was made. The Yankees won 6-4 to earn a trip to the World Series.

Game 1
Wednesday, October 9

Orioles	AB	R	H	RBI	BB	K	Avg
Brady Anderson, cf	5	1	2	1	1	1	.400
Todd Zeile, 3b	6	0	1	0	0	1	.167
Roberto Alomar, 2b	6	0	1	0	0	3	.167
Rafael Palmeiro, 1b	3	3	3	1	2	0	1.000
Bobby Bonilla, rf	4	0	0	0	0	0	.000
Tony Tarasco, rf	1	0	0	0	0	1	.000
Cal Ripken Jr., ss	5	0	2	0	0	1	.400
Eddie Murray, dh	4	0	1	1	1	0	.250
B.J. Surhoff, lf	3	0	0	1	0	1	.000
Mike Devereaux, lf	1	0	0	0	0	1	.000
Mark Parent, c	5	0	1	0	0	2	.200
TOTALS	43	4	11	4	4	10	.256

Yankees	AB	R	H	RBI	BB	K	Avg
Tim Raines, lf	6	1	2	0	0	0	.333
Wade Boggs, 3b	5	1	0	0	1	1	.000
Bernie Williams, cf	4	1	2	2	2	1	.500
Tino Martinez, 1b	5	0	1	0	0	1	.200
Cecil Fielder, dh	2	1	0	0	3	0	.000
Andy Fox, pr-dh	0	0	0	0	0	0	—
Paul O'Neill, rf	3	0	0	0	0	0	.000
Charlie Hayes, ph	0	0	0	0	0	0	—
Darryl Strawberry, ph-rf	1	0	0	1	1	0	.000
Mariano Duncan, 2b	4	0	1	0	0	1	.250
Jim Leyritz, c	4	0	1	1	0	2	.250
Mike Aldrete, ph	0	0	0	0	0	0	—
Joe Girardi, ph-c	1	0	0	0	0	0	.000
Derek Jeter, ss	5	1	4	1	0	0	.800
TOTALS	40	5	11	5	7	6	.275

	1	2	3	4	5	6	7	8	9	10	11	R	H	E
Orioles	0	1	1	1	0	1	0	0	0	0	0	4	11	1
Yankees	1	1	0	0	0	1	1	0	0	0	1	5	11	0

E—Alomar. DP—Orioles 2 (Ripken Jr. to Alomar; Zeile to Alomar to Palmeiro). LOB—Orioles 11, Yankees 13. Scoring Position—Orioles 0-for-9, Yankees 1-for-14. 2B—Anderson (1), Ripken Jr. (1), Raines (1), Williams (1), Jeter (1). HR—Anderson (1), Palmeiro (1), Williams (1), Jeter (1). SF—Surhoff. GDP—Raines. SB—Jeter (1).

Orioles	IP	H	R	ER	BB	K	ERA
Scott Erickson	6.1	7	3	2	3	3	2.84
Jesse Orosco (H, 1)	0.1	0	0	0	1	1	0.00
Armando Benitez (BS, 1)	1.0	2	1	1	2	2	9.00
Arthur Rhodes	0.1	0	0	0	0	0	0.00
Terry Mathews	0.1	0	0	0	1	0	0.00
Randy Myers (L, 0-1)	1.2	2	1	1	0	0	5.40

Yankees	IP	H	R	ER	BB	K	ERA
Andy Pettitte	7.0	7	4	4	4	4	5.14
Jeff Nelson	1.0	0	0	0	0	1	0.00
John Wetteland	1.0	1	0	0	0	2	0.00
Mariano Rivera (W, 1-0)	2.0	3	0	0	0	3	0.00

Myers pitched to one batter in the 11th.

Balk—Pettitte. HBP—Duncan by Mathews. Time—4:23. Attendance—56,495. Umpires—HP, Barnett. 1B, Scott. 2B, Reilly. 3B, Morrison.

Game 2
Thursday, October 10

Orioles	AB	R	H	RBI	BB	K	Avg
Brady Anderson, cf	4	2	1	0	1	1	.333
Todd Zeile, 3b	4	1	2	2	1	0	.300
Roberto Alomar, 2b	4	1	2	1	0	0	.300
Rafael Palmeiro, 1b	4	1	1	2	1	1	.571
Bobby Bonilla, rf	4	0	0	0	1	4	.000
Tony Tarasco, rf	0	0	0	0	0	0	.000
Cal Ripken Jr., ss	5	0	2	0	0	0	.400
Eddie Murray, dh	4	0	1	0	0	1	.250
B.J. Surhoff, lf	4	0	1	0	0	0	.143
Mike Devereaux, lf	0	0	0	0	0	0	.000
Chris Hoiles, c	3	0	0	0	1	0	.000
TOTALS	36	5	10	5	5	7	.270

Yankees	AB	R	H	RBI	BB	K	Avg
Derek Jeter, ss	5	1	2	0	0	2	.600
Tim Raines, lf	4	1	1	0	1	0	.300
Bernie Williams, cf	3	0	2	1	2	1	.571
Cecil Fielder, dh	5	0	1	1	0	0	.143
Tino Martinez, 1b	4	0	0	0	0	0	.111
Mariano Duncan, 2b	4	0	1	0	0	1	.250
Paul O'Neill, rf	2	0	1	0	1	1	.200
Jim Leyritz, ph-rf	1	0	0	0	0	0	.200
Charlie Hayes, 3b	4	0	1	0	0	2	.250
Joe Girardi, c	4	1	2	0	0	0	.400
TOTALS	36	3	11	2	4	8	.314

	1	2	3	4	5	6	7	8	9	R	H	E
Orioles	0	0	2	0	0	0	2	1	0	5	10	0
Yankees	2	0	0	0	0	0	1	0	0	3	11	1

E—Duncan. DP—Orioles 2 (Alomar to Ripken Jr. to Palmeiro; Zeile to Alomar to Palmeiro), Yankees 1 (O'Neill to Martinez). LOB—Orioles 10, Yankees 11. Scoring Position—Orioles 1-for-6, Yankees 2-for-11. 2B—Alomar (1), Duncan (1). 3B—Girardi (1). HR—Zeile (1), Palmeiro (2). SF—Alomar. GDP—Fielder, Duncan.

Orioles	IP	H	R	ER	BB	K	ERA
David Wells (W, 1-0)	6.2	8	3	3	3	6	4.05
Alan Mills	0.0	1	0	0	0	0	
Jesse Orosco (H, 2)	1.1	1	0	0	0	1	0.00
Randy Myers (H, 1)	0.1	1	0	0	1	1	4.50
Armando Benitez (S, 1)	0.2	0	0	0	0	0	5.40

Yankees	IP	H	R	ER	BB	K	ERA
David Cone	6.0	5	2	2	5	5	3.00
Jeff Nelson (L, 0-1)	1.1	5	3	3	0	1	11.57
Graeme Lloyd	1.1	0	0	0	0	1	0.00
Dave Weathers	0.1	0	0	0	0	0	0.00

Mills pitched to one batter in the 7th.

WP—Cone. HBP—Martinez by Wells. Time—4:13. Attendance—56,432. Umpires—HP, Scott. 1B, Reilly. 2B, Morrison. 3B, Roe.

Game 3
Friday, October 11

Yankees	AB	R	H	RBI	BB	K	Avg
Tim Raines, lf	5	0	1	0	0	0	.267
Derek Jeter, ss	4	1	1	0	0	0	.500
Bernie Williams, cf	3	2	1	1	1	1	.500
Tino Martinez, 1b	4	1	2	0	0	0	.231
Cecil Fielder, dh	4	1	1	3	0	2	.182
Darryl Strawberry, rf	4	0	1	0	0	1	.200
Mariano Duncan, 2b	4	0	0	0	0	1	.167
Luis Sojo, 2b	0	0	0	0	0	0	—
Charlie Hayes, 3b	2	0	0	2	0	0	.167
Joe Girardi, c	4	0	1	0	0	1	.333
TOTALS	34	5	8	4	3	7	.295

Orioles	AB	R	H	RBI	BB	K	Avg
Brady Anderson, cf	4	1	1	0	0	2	.308
Todd Zeile, 3b	4	1	1	2	0	0	.286
Roberto Alomar, 2b	4	0	0	0	0	0	.214
Rafael Palmeiro, 1b	3	0	0	0	0	0	.400
Bobby Bonilla, rf	3	0	0	0	0	0	.000
Cal Ripken Jr., ss	3	0	0	0	0	1	.308
Eddie Murray, dh	2	0	0	0	1	1	.200
B.J. Surhoff, lf	3	0	1	0	0	1	.200
Chris Hoiles, c	3	0	0	0	0	1	.000
TOTALS	29	2	3	2	1	6	.228

	1	2	3	4	5	6	7	8	9	R	H	E
Yankees	0	0	0	1	0	0	0	4	0	5	8	0
Orioles	2	0	0	0	0	0	0	0	0	2	3	2

E—Ripken Jr., Zeile. DP—Yankees 1 (Martinez), Orioles 2 (Ripken Jr. to Alomar to Palmeiro; Ripken Jr. to Alomar to Palmeiro). LOB—Yankees 5, Orioles 1. Scoring Position—Yankees 2-for-5, Orioles 0-for-0. 2B—Jeter (1), Martinez (1). HR—Fielder (1), Zeile (2). GDP—Duncan, Girardi, Surhoff.

Yankees	IP	H	R	ER	BB	K	ERA
Jimmy Key (W, 1-0)	8.0	3	2	2	1	5	2.25
John Wetteland (S, 1)	1.0	0	0	0	0	1	0.00

Orioles	IP	H	R	ER	BB	K	ERA
Mike Mussina (L, 0-1)	7.2	8	5	5	2	6	5.87
Jesse Orosco	0.1	0	0	0	0	0	0.00
Terry Mathews	1.0	0	0	0	1	1	0.00

Time—2:50. Attendance—48,635. Umpires—HP, Reilly. 1B, Morrison. 2B, Roe. 3B, Garcia.

Game 4
Saturday, October 12

Yankees	AB	R	H	RBI	BB	K	Avg
Derek Jeter, ss	5	1	1	0	0	2	.421
Wade Boggs, 3b	5	0	0	0	0	1	.000
Bernie Williams, cf	4	2	2	2	0	0	.500
Tino Martinez, 1b	4	1	1	0	0	0	.235
Cecil Fielder, dh	4	0	0	1	0	1	.133
Darryl Strawberry, lf	4	3	3	3	0	1	.444
Tim Raines, lf	0	0	0	0	0	0	.267
Paul O'Neill, rf	3	1	1	2	1	1	.250
Mariano Duncan, 2b	3	0	1	0	0	0	.200
Luis Sojo, 2b	1	0	0	0	0	0	.000
Joe Girardi, c	3	0	0	0	1	2	.250
TOTALS	36	8	9	8	2	8	.274

Orioles	AB	R	H	RBI	BB	K	Avg
Brady Anderson, cf	4	1	0	0	1	1	.235
Todd Zeile, 3b	5	0	2	0	0	0	.316
Roberto Alomar, 2b	5	0	2	0	0	1	.263
Rafael Palmeiro, 1b	3	0	0	1	1	2	.308
Bobby Bonilla, rf	5	0	0	0	0	0	.000
Cal Ripken Jr., ss	3	1	1	0	1	0	.313
Pete Incaviglia, dh	2	1	1	0	0	1	.500
Eddie Murray, ph-dh	2	0	1	0	0	0	.250
Mike Devereaux, lf	1	0	0	0	0	1	.000
B.J. Surhoff, ph-lf	3	0	2	1	0	0	.308
Chris Hoiles, c	4	1	2	2	0	1	.200
TOTALS	37	4	11	4	3	6	.245

	1	2	3	4	5	6	7	8	9		R	H	E
Yankees	2	1	0	2	0	0	0	3	0		8	9	0
Orioles	1	0	1	2	0	0	0	0	0		4	11	0

LOB—Yankees 3, Orioles 10. Scoring Position—Yankees 3-for-6, Orioles 3-for-15. 2B—Jeter (2), Williams (2), Duncan (2), Alomar (2). HR—Williams (2), Strawberry 2 (2), O'Neill (1), Hoiles (1). SF—Palmeiro.

Yankees	IP	H	R	ER	BB	K	ERA
Kenny Rogers	3.0	5	4	4	2	3	12.00
Dave Weathers (W, 1-0)	2.2	3	0	0	0	0	0.00
Graeme Lloyd (H, 1)	0.1	0	0	0	0	0	0.00
Mariano Rivera (H, 1)	2.0	3	0	0	1	2	0.00
John Wetteland	1.0	0	0	0	0	1	0.00

Orioles	IP	H	R	ER	BB	K	ERA
Rocky Coppinger (L, 0-1)	5.1	6	5	5	1	3	8.44
Arthur Rhodes	0.2	0	0	0	0	1	0.00
Alan Mills	1.1	1	1	1	0	2	6.75
Jesse Orosco	0.0	1	1	1	0	0	4.50
Armando Benitez	0.2	1	1	1	1	0	7.71
Terry Mathews	1.0	0	0	0	0	2	0.00

Rogers pitched to three batters in the 4th. Orosco pitched to one batter in the 8th.

WP—Rogers. Time—3:45. Attendance—48,974. Umpires—HP, Morrison. 1B, Roe. 2B, Garcia. 3B, Barnett.

Game 5
Sunday, October 13

Yankees	AB	R	H	RBI	BB	K	Avg
Derek Jeter, ss	5	1	2	0	0	0	.417
Wade Boggs, 3b	5	0	2	0	0	1	.133
Bernie Williams, cf	5	1	2	0	0	1	.474
Tino Martinez, 1b	5	1	0	0	0	1	.182
Cecil Fielder, dh	3	1	1	3	1	2	.167
Andy Fox, pr-dh	0	0	0	0	0	0	—
Charlie Hayes, ph-dh	1	0	0	0	0	0	.143
Darryl Strawberry, lf	3	1	1	1	1	0	.417
Tim Raines, lf	0	0	0	0	0	0	.267
Paul O'Neill, rf	3	0	1	0	1	0	.273
Jim Leyritz, c	3	1	1	1	1	2	.250
Luis Sojo, 2b	4	0	1	0	0	1	.200
TOTALS	37	6	11	5	4	8	.282

Orioles	AB	R	H	RBI	BB	K	Avg
Brady Anderson, cf	4	0	0	0	0	0	.190
Todd Zeile, 3b	3	1	2	1	1	0	.364
Roberto Alomar, 2b	4	1	0	0	0	0	.217
Rafael Palmeiro, 1b	4	0	0	0	0	1	.235
Bobby Bonilla, rf	4	1	1	2	0	0	.050
Cal Ripken Jr., ss	4	0	0	0	0	2	.250
Eddie Murray, dh	3	1	1	1	0	0	.267
B.J. Surhoff, lf	2	0	0	0	1	0	.267
Mark Parent, c	1	0	0	0	0	0	.167
Chris Hoiles, ph-c	2	0	0	0	0	1	.167
TOTALS	31	4	4	4	2	4	.222

	1	2	3	4	5	6	7	8	9		R	H	E
Yankees	0	0	6	0	0	0	0	0	0		6	11	0
Orioles	0	0	0	0	0	1	0	1	2		4	4	1

E—Alomar. DP—Orioles 1 (Ripken Jr. to Alomar to Palmeiro). LOB—Yankees 8, Orioles 2. Scoring Position—Yankees 2-for-10, Orioles 1-for-1. 2B—Williams (3). HR—Fielder (2), Strawberry (3), Leyritz (1), Zeile (3), Bonilla (1), Murray (1). GDP—O'Neill. SB—Jeter (2), Williams (2).

Yankees	IP	H	R	ER	BB	K	ERA
Andy Pettitte (W, 1-0)	8.0	3	2	2	1	3	3.60
John Wetteland	1.0	1	2	2	1	1	4.50

Orioles	IP	H	R	ER	BB	K	ERA
Scott Erickson (L, 0-1)	5.0	7	6	1	1	5	2.38
Arthur Rhodes	1.0	2	0	0	1	0	0.00
Alan Mills	1.0	1	0	0	1	1	3.86
Randy Myers	2.0	1	0	0	2	1	2.25

Mills pitched to one batter in the 8th.

WP—Rhodes. Time—2:57. Attendance—48,718. Umpires—HP, Roe. 1B, Garcia. 2B, Barnett. 3B, Scott.

1996 AL Championship Series—Composite Statistics

Batting

Yankees	G	AB	R	H	RBI	2B	3B	HR	BB	SO	SB	CS	Avg	OBP	Slg
Mike Aldrete	1	0	0	0	0	0	0	0	0	0	0	0	—	—	—
Wade Boggs	3	15	1	2	0	0	0	0	1	3	0	0	.133	.188	.133
Mariano Duncan	4	15	0	3	0	2	0	0	0	3	0	0	.200	.250	.333
Cecil Fielder	5	18	3	3	8	0	0	2	4	5	0	0	.167	.318	.500
Andy Fox	2	0	0	0	0	0	0	0	0	0	0	0	—	—	—
Joe Girardi	4	12	1	3	0	0	1	0	1	3	0	0	.250	.308	.417
Charlie Hayes	4	7	0	1	0	0	0	0	2	2	0	0	.143	.333	.143
Derek Jeter	5	24	5	10	1	2	0	1	0	5	2	0	.417	.417	.625
Jim Leyritz	3	8	1	2	2	0	0	1	1	4	0	0	.250	.333	.625
Tino Martinez	5	22	3	4	0	1	0	0	0	2	0	0	.182	.217	.227
Paul O'Neill	4	11	1	3	2	0	0	1	3	2	0	0	.273	.429	.545
Tim Raines	5	15	2	4	0	1	0	0	1	1	0	0	.267	.313	.333
Luis Sojo	3	5	0	1	0	0	0	0	0	1	0	0	.200	.200	.200
Darryl Strawberry	4	12	4	5	5	0	0	3	2	2	0	0	.417	.500	1.167
Bernie Williams	5	19	6	9	6	3	0	2	5	4	1	0	.474	.583	.947
Totals	5	183	27	50	24	9	1	10	20	37	3	0	.273	.351	.497

Batting

Orioles	G	AB	R	H	RBI	2B	3B	HR	BB	SO	SB	CS	Avg	OBP	Slg
Roberto Alomar	5	23	2	5	1	2	0	0	0	4	0	0	.217	.208	.304
Brady Anderson	5	21	5	4	1	1	0	1	3	5	0	0	.190	.292	.381
Bobby Bonilla	5	20	1	1	2	0	0	1	1	4	0	0	.050	.095	.200
Mike Devereaux	3	2	0	0	0	0	0	0	0	1	0	0	.000	.000	.000
Chris Hoiles	4	12	1	2	2	0	0	1	1	3	0	0	.167	.231	.417
Pete Incaviglia	1	2	1	1	0	0	0	0	0	0	0	0	.500	.500	.500
Eddie Murray	5	15	1	4	2	0	0	1	2	2	0	0	.267	.353	.467
Rafael Palmeiro	5	17	4	4	4	0	0	2	4	4	0	0	.235	.364	.588
Mark Parent	2	6	0	1	0	0	0	0	0	2	0	0	.167	.167	.167
Cal Ripken Jr.	5	20	1	5	0	1	0	0	1	4	0	0	.250	.286	.300
B.J. Surhoff	5	15	0	4	2	0	0	0	1	2	0	0	.267	.294	.267
Tony Tarasco	2	1	0	0	0	0	0	0	0	1	0	0	.000	.000	.000
Todd Zeile	5	22	3	8	5	0	0	3	2	1	0	0	.364	.417	.773
Totals	5	176	19	39	19	4	0	9	15	33	0	0	.222	.278	.398

Pitching

Yankees	G	GS	CG	IP	H	R	ER	BB	SO	W-L	Sv-Op	Hld	ERA
David Cone	1	1	0	6.0	5	2	2	5	5	0-0	0-0	0	3.00
Jimmy Key	1	1	0	8.0	3	2	2	1	5	1-0	0-0	0	2.25
Graeme Lloyd	2	0	0	1.2	0	0	0	0	1	0-0	0-0	1	0.00
Jeff Nelson	2	0	0	2.1	5	3	3	0	2	0-1	0-0	0	11.57
Andy Pettitte	2	2	0	15.0	10	6	6	5	7	1-0	0-0	0	3.60
Mariano Rivera	2	0	0	4.0	6	0	0	1	5	1-0	0-0	1	0.00
Kenny Rogers	1	1	0	3.0	5	4	4	2	3	0-0	0-0	0	12.00
Dave Weathers	2	0	0	3.0	3	0	0	0	1	1-0	0-0	0	0.00
John Wetteland	4	0	0	4.0	2	2	2	1	5	0-0	1-1	0	4.50
Totals	5	5	0	47.0	39	19	19	15	33	4-1	1-1	2	3.64

Pitching

Orioles	G	GS	CG	IP	H	R	ER	BB	SO	W-L	Sv-Op	Hld	ERA
Armando Benitez	3	0	0	2.1	3	2	2	3	2	0-0	1-2	0	7.71
Rocky Coppinger	1	1	0	5.1	6	5	5	1	3	0-1	0-0	0	8.44
Scott Erickson	2	2	0	11.1	14	9	3	4	8	0-1	0-0	0	2.38
Terry Mathews	3	0	0	2.1	0	0	0	2	3	0-0	0-0	0	0.00
Alan Mills	3	0	0	2.1	3	1	1	1	3	0-0	0-0	0	3.86
Mike Mussina	1	1	0	7.2	8	5	5	2	6	0-1	0-0	0	5.87
Randy Myers	3	0	0	4.0	4	1	1	3	2	0-1	0-0	1	2.25
Jesse Orosco	4	0	0	2.0	2	1	1	1	2	0-0	0-0	2	4.50
Arthur Rhodes	3	0	0	2.0	2	0	0	0	2	0-0	0-0	0	0.00
David Wells	1	1	0	6.2	8	3	3	3	6	1-0	0-0	0	4.05
Totals	5	5	0	46.0	50	27	21	20	37	1-4	1-2	3	4.11

Fielding

Yankees	Pos	G	PO	Ast	E	DP	PB	FPct
Wade Boggs	3b	3	2	11	0	0	—	1.000
David Cone	p	1	0	1	0	0	—	1.000
Mariano Duncan	2b	4	5	7	1	0	—	.923
Joe Girardi	c	4	22	0	0	0	0	1.000
Charlie Hayes	3b	2	0	3	0	0	—	1.000
Derek Jeter	ss	5	6	13	0	0	—	1.000
Jimmy Key	p	1	1	0	0	0	—	1.000
Jim Leyritz	c	2	11	2	0	0	0	1.000
	rf	1	0	0	0	0	—	—
Graeme Lloyd	p	2	0	0	0	0	—	—
Tino Martinez	1b	5	49	2	0	1	—	1.000
Jeff Nelson	p	2	0	0	0	0	—	—
Paul O'Neill	rf	4	9	1	0	0	—	1.000
Andy Pettitte	p	2	2	0	0	0	—	1.000
Tim Raines	lf	5	5	0	0	0	—	1.000
Mariano Rivera	p	2	0	0	0	0	—	—
Kenny Rogers	p	1	0	0	0	0	—	—
Luis Sojo	2b	3	4	4	0	0	—	1.000
Darryl Strawberry	rf	2	3	0	0	0	—	1.000
	lf	2	2	0	0	0	—	1.000
Dave Weathers	p	2	0	0	0	0	—	—
John Wetteland	p	4	0	0	0	0	—	—
Bernie Williams	cf	5	20	0	0	0	—	1.000
Totals		5	141	44	1	1	0	.995

Fielding

Orioles	Pos	G	PO	Ast	E	DP	PB	FPct
Roberto Alomar	2b	5	15	26	2	7	—	.953
Brady Anderson	cf	5	8	0	0	0	—	1.000
Armando Benitez	p	3	0	0	0	0	—	—
Bobby Bonilla	rf	5	11	0	0	0	—	1.000
Rocky Coppinger	p	1	1	1	0	0	—	1.000
Mike Devereaux	lf	3	1	0	0	0	—	1.000
Scott Erickson	p	2	0	2	0	0	—	1.000
Chris Hoiles	c	4	23	2	0	0	0	1.000
Terry Mathews	p	3	0	1	0	0	—	1.000
Alan Mills	p	3	0	0	0	0	—	—
Mike Mussina	p	1	0	0	0	0	—	—
Randy Myers	p	3	0	0	0	0	—	—
Jesse Orosco	p	4	0	1	0	0	—	1.000
Rafael Palmeiro	1b	5	44	3	0	6	—	1.000
Mark Parent	c	2	14	0	0	0	0	1.000
Arthur Rhodes	p	3	0	0	0	0	—	—
Cal Ripken Jr.	ss	5	4	14	1	5	—	.947
B.J. Surhoff	lf	5	11	1	0	0	—	1.000
Tony Tarasco	rf	2	2	0	0	0	—	1.000
David Wells	p	1	1	0	0	0	—	1.000
Todd Zeile	3b	5	3	7	1	2	—	.909
Totals		5	138	58	4	20	0	.980

1996 Atlanta Braves (NL) 4, St. Louis Cardinals (NL) 3

The St. Louis Cardinals almost unseated the mighty Atlanta Braves. Atlanta won Game 1 behind John Smoltz, 4-2, but Greg Maddux had an uncharacteristically poor outing in Game 2. Gary Gaetti hit a grand slam off him as the Cardinals evened the series with an 8-3 victory. Ron Gant hit a pair of homers as St. Louis took the third game, 3-2. Tony La Russa brought back ace Andy Benes on three days' rest in Game 4. The Cardinals staged a three-run rally against Atlanta starter Denny Neagle and reliever Greg McMichael, and Brian Jordan broke up a 3-3 tie with a solo homer in the bottom of the eighth, giving St. Louis a three-games-to-one lead. La Russa brought back Todd Stottlemyre on short rest in Game 5, but the Braves shelled him for seven runs in one-plus innings and rolled to a 14-0 victory. Maddux was back to his old self in Game 6, pitching the Braves to a 3-1 victory to even the series. It all came down to the seventh game, and La Russa was pressed for a starter. He could either use Benes on short rest again or go with a rested Donovan Osborne. He chose the latter, and the Braves shelled the lefthander for six runs in two-thirds of an inning, nailing down a 15-0 victory and a chance to defend their championship.

Game 1

Wednesday, October 9

Cardinals	AB	R	H	RBI	BB	K	Avg
Ozzie Smith, ss	4	0	0	0	0	0	.000
Ray Lankford, cf	4	0	0	0	0	1	.000
Ron Gant, lf	4	0	0	0	0	1	.000
Brian Jordan, rf	4	1	1	0	0	1	.250
Gary Gaetti, 3b	3	0	1	0	0	1	.333
Miguel Mejia, pr	0	1	0	0	0	0	—
Mike Gallego, 3b	0	0	0	0	0	0	—
Mark Sweeney, ph	1	0	0	0	0	1	.000
John Mabry, 1b	4	0	1	0	0	1	.250
Tom Pagnozzi, c	4	0	1	1	0	1	.250
Luis Alicea, 2b	2	0	0	1	0	.000
Andy Benes, p	1	0	1	0	1	0	1.000
Willie McGee, ph	1	0	0	0	0	1	.000
Mark Petkovsek, p	0	0	0	0	0	0	—
Tony Fossas, p	0	0	0	0	0	0	—
T.J. Mathews, p	0	0	0	0	0	0	—
TOTALS	32	2	5	1	2	7	.156

Braves	AB	R	H	RBI	BB	K	Avg
Marquis Grissom, cf	4	1	1	0	0	2	.250
Mark Lemke, 2b	3	0	1	2	1	0	.333
Andruw Jones, pr-lf	0	1	0	0	0	0	—
Chipper Jones, 3b	4	1	4	0	0	0	1.000
Fred McGriff, 1b	4	0	0	0	0	1	.000
Ryan Klesko, lf	3	0	1	0	0	1	.333
Terry Pendleton, ph	0	0	0	0	1	0	—
Rafael Belliard, 2b	0	0	0	0	0	0	—
Javy Lopez, c	4	0	1	2	0	0	.250
Jermaine Dye, rf	4	0	0	0	0	2	.000
Jeff Blauser, ss	4	1	1	0	0	2	.250
John Smoltz, p	3	0	0	0	0	3	.000
Mark Wohlers, p	0	0	0	0	0	0	—
TOTALS	33	4	9	4	2	11	.273

	1	2	3	4	5	6	7	8	9		R	H	E
Cardinals	0	1	0	0	0	0	1	0	0		2	5	1
Braves	0	0	0	2	0	0	2	x			4	9	0

E—Alicea. LOB—Cardinals 5, Braves 7. Scoring Position—Cardinals 1-for-7, Braves 2-for-7. 2B—Benes (1), Grissom (1). 3B—Jordan (1). SB—CJones (1).

Cardinals	IP	H	R	ER	BB	K	ERA
Andy Benes	6.0	7	2	2	0	7	3.00
Mark Petkovsek (L, 0-1)	1.0	1	2	2	1	2	18.00
Tony Fossas	0.1	0	0	0	0	0	0.00
T.J. Mathews	0.2	1	0	0	1	2	0.00

Braves	IP	H	R	ER	BB	K	ERA
John Smoltz (W, 1-0)	8.0	5	2	2	2	6	2.25
Mark Wohlers (S, 1)	1.0	0	0	0	0	1	0.00

Petkovsek pitched to three batters in the 8th.

WP—Smoltz 2. Time—2:35. Attendance—48,686. Umpires—HP, Runge. 1B, Hirschbeck. 2B, Davidson. 3B, West.

Game 2

Thursday, October 10

Cardinals	AB	R	H	RBI	BB	K	Avg
Royce Clayton, ss	4	2	2	0	1	1	.500
Ray Lankford, cf	3	1	0	1	1	1	.000
Ron Gant, lf	5	1	3	1	0	2	.333
Brian Jordan, rf	4	1	2	1	1	0	.375
Gary Gaetti, 3b	5	1	1	4	0	1	.250
John Mabry, 1b	4	0	1	0	0	1	.250
Tom Pagnozzi, c	4	0	1	0	0	1	.250
Mike Gallego, 2b	4	1	1	0	0	1	.250
Todd Stottlemyre, p	2	0	0	0	0	1	.000
Mark Sweeney, ph	0	1	0	0	1	0	.000
Mark Petkovsek, p	0	0	0	0	0	0	—

Dmitri Young, ph	1	0	0	0	0	0	.000
Rick Honeycutt, p	0	0	0	0	0	0	—
Dennis Eckersley, p	0	0	0	0	0	0	—
TOTALS	36	8	11	7	3	7	.250

Braves	AB	R	H	RBI	BB	K	Avg
Marquis Grissom, cf	5	2	2	2	0	0	.333
Mark Lemke, 2b	3	0	1	0	1	1	.333
Chipper Jones, 3b	4	0	0	0	0	0	.500
Steve Avery, p	0	0	0	0	0	0	—
Fred McGriff, 1b	3	0	0	1	0	1	.000
Ryan Klesko, lf	4	0	1	0	1	0	.286
Jermaine Dye, rf	4	0	0	0	0	1	.000
Eddie Perez, c	1	0	0	0	1	0	.000
Terry Pendleton, ph	1	0	0	0	0	1	.000
Javy Lopez, c	1	0	1	0	0	0	.400
Jeff Blauser, ss	4	1	0	0	0	1	.125
Greg Maddux, p	2	0	0	0	0	2	.000
Greg McMichael, p	0	0	0	0	0	0	—
Luis Polonia, ph	1	0	0	0	0	0	.000
Denny Neagle, p	0	0	0	0	0	0	—
Mike Mordecai, 3b	1	0	0	0	0	1	.000
TOTALS	34	3	5	3	3	10	.219

	1	2	3	4	5	6	7	8	9		R	H	E
Cardinals	1	0	2	0	0	0	5	0	0		8	11	2
Braves	0	0	2	0	0	1	0	0	0		3	5	2

E—Gallego, Grissom, Clayton, Jones. DP—Braves 1 (Lemke to McGriff). LOB—Cardinals 6, Braves 7. Scoring Position—Cardinals 3-for-11, Braves 1-for-6. 2B—Gant (1), Jordan (1), Pagnozzi (1). HR—Gaetti (1), Grissom (1). S—Sweeney. SF—Lankford. GDP—Gaetti. SB—Clayton (1), Grissom (1).

Cardinals	IP	H	R	ER	BB	K	ERA
Todd Stottlemyre (W, 1-0)	6.0	4	3	3	3	8	4.50
Mark Petkovsek	1.0	0	0	0	0	0	9.00
Rick Honeycutt	0.2	0	0	0	0	1	0.00
Dennis Eckersley	1.1	1	0	0	0	1	0.00

Braves	IP	H	R	ER	BB	K	ERA
Greg Maddux (L, 0-1)	6.2	9	8	3	2	3	4.05
Greg McMichael	0.1	1	0	0	0	1	0.00
Denny Neagle	1.0	0	0	0	2	0	0.00
Steve Avery	1.0	1	0	0	1	1	0.00

WP—Maddux. Time—2:53. Attendance—52,067. Umpires—HP, Hirschbeck. 1B, Davidson. 2B, West. 3B, Crawford.

Game 3

Saturday, October 12

Braves	AB	R	H	RBI	BB	K	Avg
Marquis Grissom, cf	5	1	2	0	0	2	.357
Mark Lemke, 2b	4	0	1	0	1	0	.300
Chipper Jones, 3b	3	1	1	1	0	0	.455
Fred McGriff, 1b	3	0	1	0	1	1	.100
Javy Lopez, c	4	0	3	0	0	0	.556
Jermaine Dye, rf	3	0	0	1	0	1	.000
Andruw Jones, lf	2	0	0	0	1	1	.000
Terry Pendleton, ph	1	0	0	0	0	0	.000
Greg McMichael, p	0	0	0	0	0	0	—
Jeff Blauser, ss	4	0	0	0	0	2	.083
Tom Glavine, p	2	0	0	0	0	0	.000
Mike Mordecai, ph	1	0	0	0	0	0	.000
Mike Bielecki, p	0	0	0	0	0	0	—
Ryan Klesko, lf	1	0	0	0	0	0	.250
TOTALS	33	2	8	2	3	8	.237

Cardinals	AB	R	H	RBI	BB	K	Avg
Royce Clayton, ss	4	1	2	0	0	0	.500
Ray Lankford, cf	4	0	0	0	0	1	.000
Rick Honeycutt, p	0	0	0	0	0	0	—
Dennis Eckersley, p	0	0	0	0	0	0	—
Ron Gant, lf	4	2	2	3	0	1	.385
Brian Jordan, rf	4	0	0	0	0	1	.250

Gary Gaetti, 3b	3	0	2	0	0	1	.364
John Mabry, 1b	2	0	1	0	0	0	.300
Tom Pagnozzi, c	3	0	0	0	0	1	.182
Mike Gallego, 2b	3	0	0	0	0	0	.143
Donovan Osborne, p	3	0	0	0	0	3	.000
Mark Petkovsek, p	0	0	0	0	0	0	—
Willie McGee, cf	0	0	0	0	0	0	.000
TOTALS	30	3	7	3	0	8	.253

	1	2	3	4	5	6	7	8	9		R	H	E
Braves	1	0	0	0	0	0	0	1	0		2	8	1
Cardinals	2	0	0	0	0	1	0	0	x		3	7	0

E—Blauser. DP—Braves 1 (Glavine to Blauser to McGriff). LOB—Braves 9, Cardinals 4. Scoring Position—Braves 1-for-6, Cardinals 0-for-3. 2B—Lopez (1). HR—Gant 2 (2). SF—CJones, Dye. GDP—Gallego.

Braves	IP	H	R	ER	BB	K	ERA
Tom Glavine (L, 0-1)	6.0	7	3	3	0	5	4.50
Mike Bielecki	1.0	0	0	0	0	1	0.00
Greg McMichael	1.0	0	0	0	0	2	0.00

Cardinals	IP	H	R	ER	BB	K	ERA
Donovan Osborne (W, 1-0)	7.0	7	2	2	3	6	2.57
Mark Petkovsek (H, 1)	1.0	1	0	0	0	1	6.00
Rick Honeycutt (H, 1)	0.1	0	0	0	0	0	0.00
Dennis Eckersley (S, 1)	0.2	0	0	0	0	0	0.00

Osborne pitched to two batters in the 8th.

WP—Osborne. HBP—Mabry by Glavine. Time—2:46. Attendance—56,769. Umpires—HP, Davidson. 1B, West. 2B, Crawford. 3B, Montague.

Game 4

Sunday, October 13

Braves	AB	R	H	RBI	BB	K	Avg
Marquis Grissom, cf	5	0	0	0	0	1	.263
Mark Lemke, 2b	4	1	1	1	0	0	.286
Chipper Jones, 3b	3	1	2	0	1	0	.500
Fred McGriff, 1b	3	0	0	0	1	0	.077
Ryan Klesko, lf	3	1	1	1	1	0	.273
Javy Lopez, c	3	0	0	0	0	0	.417
Mark Wohlers, p	0	0	0	0	0	0	—
Jermaine Dye, rf	4	0	3	1	0	0	.200
Jeff Blauser, ss	3	0	1	0	0	1	.133
Luis Polonia, ph	1	0	0	0	0	0	.000
Denny Neagle, p	2	0	1	0	0	0	.500
Greg McMichael, p	0	0	0	0	0	0	—
Eddie Perez, c	0	0	0	0	0	0	.000
Terry Pendleton, ph	1	0	0	0	0	1	.000
TOTALS	32	3	9	3	4	3	.256

Cardinals	AB	R	H	RBI	BB	K	Avg
Royce Clayton, ss	4	0	1	1	0	2	.417
Willie McGee, cf	4	0	1	0	0	0	.200
Ron Gant, lf	2	0	0	0	2	0	.333
Brian Jordan, rf	4	1	1	1	0	0	.250
Gary Gaetti, 3b	4	0	0	0	0	2	.267
John Mabry, 1b	4	1	0	0	0	1	.286
Tom Pagnozzi, c	2	1	0	0	1	1	.154
Mike Gallego, 2b	2	0	0	0	0	1	.111
Dmitri Young, ph	1	1	1	2	0	0	.500
Rick Honeycutt, p	0	0	0	0	0	0	—
Dennis Eckersley, p	0	0	0	0	0	0	—
Andy Benes, p	2	0	0	0	0	1	.333
Tony Fossas, p	0	0	0	0	0	0	—
T.J. Mathews, p	0	0	0	0	0	0	—
Alan Benes, p	0	0	0	0	0	0	—
Luis Alicea, ph-2b	0	0	0	0	1	0	.000
TOTALS	29	4	5	4	4	8	.264

	1	2	3	4	5	6	7	8	9	R	H	E
Braves	0	1	0	0	0	2	0	0	0	3	9	1
Cardinals	0	0	0	0	0	0	3	1	x	4	5	0

E—McGriff. DP—Braves 1 (Jones to Lemke to McGriff), Cardinals 2 (Gallego to Clayton to Mabry; Gallego to Clayton to Mabry). LOB—Braves 7, Cardinals 5. Scoring Position—Braves 1-for-7, Cardinals 2-for-6. 2B—Jones (1), Dye (1). 3B—Young (1). HR—Lemke (1), Klesko (1), Jordan (1). S—Neagle. GDP—McGriff, Klesko, Pagnozzi. CS—Dye (1).

Braves	IP	H	R	ER	BB	K	ERA
Denny Neagle	6.2	2	2	2	3	6	2.35
Greg McMichael (BS, 1; L, 0-1)	0.2	3	2	2	1	0	9.00
Mark Wohlers	0.2	0	0	0	0	2	0.00

Cardinals	IP	H	R	ER	BB	K	ERA
Andy Benes	5.0	7	3	3	1	0	4.09
Tony Fossas	0.2	0	0	0	2	0	0.00
T.J. Mathews	0.0	1	0	0	0	0	0.00
Alan Benes	1.1	0	0	0	0	1	0.00
Rick Honeycutt	0.2	0	0	0	1	0	0.00
Dennis Eckersley (W, 1-0)	1.1	1	0	0	0	2	0.00

AnBenes pitched to two batters in the 6th. Mathews pitched to one batter in the 6th.

Time—3:17. Attendance—56,764. Umpires—HP, West. 1B, Crawford. 2B, Montague. 3B, Runge.

Game 5
Monday, October 14

Braves	AB	R	H	RBI	BB	K	Avg
Marquis Grissom, cf	6	2	3	1	0	0	.320
Mark Lemke, 2b	5	2	4	1	0	0	.421
Mike Mordecai, 2b	1	1	1	0	0	0	.333
Chipper Jones, 3b	3	1	2	3	1	0	.529
Terry Pendleton, ph-3b	2	0	0	0	0	1	.000
Fred McGriff, 1b	6	1	2	3	0	1	.158
Ryan Klesko, lf	4	0	1	1	0	3	.267
Andruw Jones, ph-lf	1	0	0	0	1	0	.000
Javy Lopez, c	5	4	4	1	1	0	.529
Terrell Wade, p	0	0	0	0	0	0	—
Brad Clontz, p	0	0	0	0	0	0	—
Jermaine Dye, rf	6	1	1	0	0	2	.190
Jeff Blauser, ss	2	1	1	2	2	0	.176
Rafael Belliard, pr-ss	1	0	1	1	0	0	1.000
John Smoltz, p	4	1	2	1	0	0	.286
Luis Polonia, ph	1	0	0	0	0	0	.000
Mike Bielecki, p	0	0	0	0	0	0	—
Eddie Perez, c	0	0	0	0	0	0	.000
TOTALS	47	14	22	14	5	7	.301

Cardinals	AB	R	H	RBI	BB	K	Avg
Ozzie Smith, ss	4	0	0	0	0	1	.000
Willie McGee, cf	3	0	1	0	0	2	.250
Miguel Mejia, cf	1	0	0	0	0	0	.000
Ron Gant, lf	3	0	1	0	0	0	.333
Mike Gallego, 3b	0	0	0	0	1	0	.111
Brian Jordan, rf	2	0	1	0	0	0	.278
Tony Fossas, p	0	0	0	0	0	0	—
Dmitri Young, ph-1b	2	0	1	0	0	0	.500
Gary Gaetti, 3b	2	0	2	0	1	0	.353
Mark Petkovsek, p	0	0	0	0	0	0	—
Ray Lankford, ph	1	0	0	0	0	1	.000
Rick Honeycutt, p	0	0	0	0	0	0	—
John Mabry, 1b-rf	4	0	1	0	0	1	.278
Tom Pagnozzi, c	1	0	0	0	0	0	.143
Danny Sheaffer, ph-c	3	0	0	0	0	1	.000
Luis Alicea, 2b	4	0	0	0	0	0	.000
Todd Stottlemyre, p	0	0	0	0	0	0	.000
Danny Jackson, p	1	0	0	0	0	1	.000
Mark Sweeney, rf-lf	2	0	0	0	0	1	.000
TOTALS	33	0	7	0	2	9	.204

	1	2	3	4	5	6	7	8	9	R	H	E
Braves	5	2	0	3	1	0	0	1	2	14	22	0
Cardinals	0	0	0	0	0	0	0	0	0	0	7	0

DP—Braves 1 (Blauser to McGriff), Cardinals 2 (Mabry; Smith to Alicea to Mabry). LOB—Braves 11, Cardinals 8. Scoring Position—Braves 9-for-16, Cardinals 1-for-6. 2B—Lemke (1), CJones (2), Lopez 2 (3). 3B—Blauser (1), Lopez (1). HR—McGriff (1), Lopez (1). GDP—Smoltz. SB—Grissom (2).

Braves	IP	H	R	ER	BB	K	ERA
John Smoltz (W, 2-0)	7.0	7	0	0	1	6	1.20
Mike Bielecki	1.0	0	0	0	1	2	0.00
Terrell Wade	0.1	0	0	0	0	1	0.00
Brad Clontz	0.2	0	0	0	0	0	0.00

Cardinals	IP	H	R	ER	BB	K	ERA
Todd Stottlemyre (L, 1-1)	1.0	9	7	7	0	1	12.86
Danny Jackson	3.0	7	3	3	3	3	9.00
Tony Fossas	2.0	1	1	1	1	1	3.00
Mark Petkovsek	2.0	2	1	1	0	1	5.40
Rick Honeycutt	1.0	3	2	2	1	1	6.75

Stottlmyre pitched to three batters in the 2nd.

Time—2:57. Attendance—56,782. Umpires—HP, Crawford. 1B, Montague. 2B, Runge. 3B, Hirschbeck.

Game 6
Wednesday, October 16

Cardinals	AB	R	H	RBI	BB	K	Avg
Royce Clayton, ss	4	1	1	0	0	1	.375
Willie McGee, rf	4	0	2	0	0	0	.333
Ron Gant, lf	4	0	0	0	0	2	.273
Brian Jordan, cf	4	0	1	0	0	0	.273
Gary Gaetti, 3b	4	0	1	0	0	0	.333
John Mabry, 1b	4	0	1	0	0	0	.273
Tom Pagnozzi, c	3	0	0	0	0	0	.118
Mike Gallego, 2b	2	0	0	0	0	0	.091
Mark Sweeney, ph	1	0	0	0	0	0	.000
Todd Stottlemyre, p	0	0	0	0	0	0	.000
Alan Benes, p	1	0	0	0	0	0	.000
Ray Lankford, ph	1	0	0	0	0	0	.000
Tony Fossas, p	0	0	0	0	0	0	—
Mark Petkovsek, p	0	0	0	0	0	0	—
Luis Alicea, ph-2b	1	0	0	0	0	1	.000
TOTALS	33	1	6	0	0	8	.224

Braves	AB	R	H	RBI	BB	K	Avg
Marquis Grissom, cf	4	0	0	0	0	3	.276
Mark Lemke, 2b	4	0	2	1	0	0	.435
Chipper Jones, 3b	4	0	0	0	0	0	.429
Fred McGriff, 1b	4	1	1	0	0	0	.174
Ryan Klesko, lf	1	0	0	0	0	1	.250
Andruw Jones, ph-lf	2	0	0	0	0	1	.000
Javy Lopez, c	3	1	2	0	0	1	.550
Jermaine Dye, rf	2	0	1	1	1	0	.217
Jeff Blauser, ss	0	1	0	0	2	0	.176
Rafael Belliard, ss	1	0	1	1	0	0	1.000
Greg Maddux, p	2	0	0	0	0	0	.000
Mark Wohlers, p	1	0	0	0	0	1	.000
TOTALS	28	3	7	3	4	8	.304

	1	2	3	4	5	6	7	8	9	R	H	E
Cardinals	0	0	0	0	0	0	0	1	0	1	6	1
Braves	0	1	0	0	1	0	0	1	x	3	7	0

E—Petkovsek. DP—Cardinals 1 (Jordan to Petkovsek to Gaetti). LOB—Cardinals 5, Braves 9. Scoring Position—Cardinals 0-for-3, Braves 2-for-8. 2B—Lopez (4). S—Maddux. SF—Dye. SB—Lopez (1).

Cardinals	IP	H	R	ER	BB	K	ERA
Alan Benes (L, 0-1)	5.0	3	2	2	2	4	2.84
Tony Fossas	0.1	0	0	0	0	0	2.70
Mark Petkovsek	1.2	2	0	0	2	2	4.05
Todd Stottlemyre	1.0	2	1	1	0	2	12.38

Braves	IP	H	R	ER	BB	K	ERA
Greg Maddux (W, 1-1)	7.2	6	1	1	0	7	2.51
Mark Wohlers (S, 2)	1.1	0	0	0	0	1	

WP—Petkovsek, Wohlers. HBP—Blauser by Benes, Lopez by Stottlemyre. Time—2:41. Attendance—52,067. Umpires—HP, Montague. 1B, Runge. 2B, Hirschbeck. 3B, Davidson.

Game 7
Thursday, October 17

Cardinals	AB	R	H	RBI	BB	K	Avg
Royce Clayton, ss	4	0	1	0	0	0	.350
Willie McGee, rf	3	0	1	0	0	1	.333
Mark Sweeney, lf	0	0	0	0	0	0	.000
Ron Gant, lf	3	0	0	0	0	0	.240
Danny Sheaffer, c	0	0	0	0	0	0	.000
Brian Jordan, cf	3	0	0	0	0	0	.240
Miguel Mejia, cf	0	0	0	0	0	0	.000
Gary Gaetti, 3b	3	0	0	0	0	0	.292
Dmitri Young, 1b	3	0	0	0	0	2	.286
Tom Pagnozzi, c	2	0	0	0	0	0	.158
John Mabry, rf	1	0	0	0	0	1	.261
Mike Gallego, 2b	3	0	1	0	0	1	.143
Donovan Osborne, p	0	0	0	0	0	0	.000
Andy Benes, p	1	0	0	0	0	1	.250
Ozzie Smith, ph	1	0	0	0	0	0	.000
Mark Petkovsek, p	0	0	0	0	0	0	—
Rick Honeycutt, p	0	0	0	0	0	0	—
Tony Fossas, p	0	0	0	0	0	0	—
Luis Alicea, ph	1	0	0	0	0	0	.000
TOTALS	28	0	4	0	0	6	.221

Braves	AB	R	H	RBI	BB	K	Avg
Marquis Grissom, cf	6	1	2	0	0	0	.286
Mark Lemke, 2b	4	1	2	0	1	1	.444
Mike Mordecai, ph-2b	1	0	0	0	0	0	.250
Chipper Jones, 3b	4	2	2	0	1	0	.440
Eddie Perez, 1b	0	0	0	0	0	0	.000
Fred McGriff, 1b	5	4	3	4	0	0	.250
Mike Bielecki, p	0	0	0	0	0	0	.000
Steve Avery, p	0	0	0	0	0	0	—
Javy Lopez, c	4	3	2	3	1	0	.542
Jermaine Dye, rf	5	1	1	1	0	1	.214
Andruw Jones, lf	4	2	2	3	1	0	.222
Jeff Blauser, ss	0	1	0	0	1	0	.176
Rafael Belliard, ss	4	0	2	0	0	0	.667
Tom Glavine, p	4	0	1	3	0	2	.167
Terry Pendleton, 3b	1	0	0	0	0	0	.000
TOTALS	42	15	17	14	4	4	.324

	1	2	3	4	5	6	7	8	9	R	H	E
Cardinals	0	0	0	0	0	0	0	0	0	0	4	2
Braves	6	0	0	4	0	3	2	0	x	15	17	0

E—McGee, Clayton. DP—Braves 2 (CJones to Lemke to McGriff; Pendleton to Mordecai to Perez). LOB—Cardinals 1, Braves 8. Scoring Position—Cardinals 0-for-0, Braves 7-for-12. 2B—Lemke (2), Lopez (5). 3B—McGriff (1), Glavine (1). HR—McGriff (2), Lopez (2), AJones (1). GDP—Jordan, Alicea. CS—Clayton (1).

Cardinals	IP	H	R	ER	BB	K	ERA
Donovan Osborne (L, 1-1)	0.2	5	6	6	1	0	9.39
Andy Benes	4.1	5	4	4	2	2	5.28
Mark Petkovsek	0.2	5	3	3	0	1	7.36
Rick Honeycutt	1.1	2	2	2	1	1	9.00
Tony Fossas	1.0	0	0	0	0	0	2.08

Braves	IP	H	R	ER	BB	K	ERA
Tom Glavine (W, 1-1)	7.0	3	0	0	0	4	2.08
Mike Bielecki	1.0	0	0	0	0	0	0.00
Steve Avery	1.0	1	0	0	0	0	0.00

HBP—Blauser by Osborne. Time—2:25. Attendance—52,067. Umpires—HP, Runge. 1B, Hirschbeck. 2B, Davidson. 3B, West.

Postseason: League Championship Series

1996 NL Championship Series—Composite Statistics

Batting

Braves	G	AB	R	H	RBI	2B	3B	HR	BB	SO	SB	CS	Avg	OBP	Slg
Rafael Belliard	4	6	0	4	2	0	0	0	0	0	0	0	.667	.667	.667
Jeff Blauser	7	17	5	3	2	0	1	0	4	6	0	0	.176	.391	.294
Jermaine Dye	7	28	2	6	4	1	0	0	1	7	0	1	.214	.226	.250
Tom Glavine	2	6	0	1	3	0	1	0	0	3	0	0	.167	.167	.500
Marquis Grissom	7	35	7	10	3	1	0	1	0	8	2	0	.286	.286	.400
Andruw Jones	5	9	3	2	3	0	0	1	3	2	0	0	.222	.417	.556
Chipper Jones	7	25	6	11	4	2	0	0	3	1	1	0	.440	.483	.520
Ryan Klesko	6	16	1	4	3	0	0	1	2	6	0	0	.250	.333	.438
Mark Lemke	7	27	4	12	5	2	0	1	4	2	0	0	.444	.516	.630
Javy Lopez	7	24	8	13	6	5	0	2	3	1	1	0	.542	.607	1.000
Greg Maddux	2	4	0	0	0	0	0	0	0	2	0	0	.000	.000	.000
Fred McGriff	7	28	6	7	7	0	1	2	3	5	0	0	.250	.323	.536
Mike Mordecai	4	4	1	1	0	0	0	0	0	1	0	0	.250	.250	.250
Denny Neagle	2	2	0	1	0	0	0	0	0	0	0	0	.500	.500	.500
Terry Pendleton	6	6	0	0	0	0	0	0	1	3	0	0	.000	.143	.000
Eddie Perez	4	1	0	0	0	0	0	0	1	0	0	0	.000	.500	.000
Luis Polonia	3	3	0	0	0	0	0	0	0	0	0	0	.000	.000	.000
John Smoltz	2	7	1	2	1	0	0	0	0	3	0	0	.286	.286	.286
Mark Wohlers	3	1	0	0	0	0	0	0	0	1	0	0	.000	.000	.000
Totals	7	249	44	77	43	11	3	8	25	51	4	1	.309	.375	.474

Cardinals	G	AB	R	H	RBI	2B	3B	HR	BB	SO	SB	CS	Avg	OBP	Slg
Luis Alicea	5	8	0	0	0	0	0	0	2	1	0	0	.000	.200	.000
Alan Benes	2	1	0	0	0	0	0	0	0	1	0	0	.000	.000	.000
Andy Benes	3	4	0	1	0	1	0	0	1	2	0	0	.250	.400	.500
Royce Clayton	5	20	4	7	1	0	0	0	1	4	1	1	.350	.381	.350
Gary Gaetti	7	24	1	7	4	0	0	1	1	5	0	0	.292	.320	.417
Mike Gallego	7	14	1	2	0	0	0	0	1	3	0	0	.143	.200	.143
Ron Gant	7	25	3	6	4	1	0	2	2	6	0	0	.240	.296	.520
Danny Jackson	1	1	0	0	0	0	0	0	0	1	0	0	.000	.000	.000
Brian Jordan	7	25	3	6	2	1	1	1	1	3	0	0	.240	.269	.480
Ray Lankford	5	13	1	0	1	0	0	0	1	4	0	0	.000	.067	.000
John Mabry	7	23	1	6	0	0	0	0	0	6	0	0	.261	.292	.261
Willie McGee	6	15	0	5	0	0	0	0	0	3	0	0	.333	.333	.333
Miguel Mejia	3	1	1	0	0	0	0	0	0	0	0	0	.000	.000	.000
Donovan Osborne	2	3	0	0	0	0	0	0	0	3	0	0	.000	.000	.000
Tom Pagnozzi	7	19	1	3	1	1	0	0	1	4	0	0	.158	.200	.211
Danny Sheaffer	2	3	0	0	0	0	0	0	0	1	0	0	.000	.000	.000
Ozzie Smith	3	9	0	0	0	0	0	0	0	1	0	0	.000	.000	.000
Todd Stottlemyre	3	2	0	0	0	0	0	0	0	0	0	0	.000	.000	.000
Mark Sweeney	5	4	1	0	0	0	0	0	0	2	0	0	.000	.000	.000
Dmitri Young	4	7	1	2	2	0	1	0	0	2	0	0	.286	.286	.571
Totals	7	221	18	45	15	4	2	4	11	53	1	1	.204	.244	.294

Pitching

Braves	G	GS	CG	IP	H	R	ER	BB	SO	W-L	Sv-Op	Hld	ERA
Steve Avery	2	0	0	2.0	2	0	0	1	1	0-0	0-0	0	0.00
Mike Bielecki	3	0	0	3.0	0	0	0	1	5	0-0	0-0	0	0.00
Brad Clontz	1	0	0	0.2	0	0	0	0	0	0-0	0-0	0	0.00
Tom Glavine	2	2	0	13.0	10	3	3	0	9	1-1	0-0	0	2.08
Greg Maddux	2	2	0	14.1	15	9	4	2	10	1-1	0-0	0	2.51
Greg McMichael	3	0	0	2.0	4	2	2	1	3	0-1	0-1	0	9.00
Denny Neagle	2	1	0	7.2	2	2	2	3	8	0-0	0-0	0	2.35
John Smoltz	2	2	0	15.0	12	2	2	3	12	2-0	0-0	0	1.20
Terrell Wade	1	0	0	0.1	0	0	0	1	0	0-0	0-0	0	0.00
Mark Wohlers	3	0	0	3.0	0	0	0	0	4	0-0	2-2	0	0.00
Totals	7	7	0	61.0	45	18	13	11	53	4-3	2-3	0	1.92

Cardinals	G	GS	CG	IP	H	R	ER	BB	SO	W-L	Sv-Op	Hld	ERA
Alan Benes	2	1	0	6.1	3	2	2	2	5	0-1	0-0	0	2.84
Andy Benes	3	2	0	15.1	19	9	9	3	9	0-0	0-0	0	5.28
Dennis Eckersley	3	0	0	3.1	2	0	0	0	4	1-0	1-1	0	0.00
Tony Fossas	5	0	0	4.1	1	1	1	3	1	0-0	0-0	0	2.08
Rick Honeycutt	5	0	0	4.0	5	4	4	3	3	0-0	0-0	1	9.00
Danny Jackson	1	0	0	3.0	7	3	3	3	3	0-0	0-0	0	9.00
T.J. Mathews	2	0	0	0.2	0	0	0	1	2	0-0	0-0	0	0.00
Donovan Osborne	2	2	0	7.2	12	8	8	4	6	1-1	0-0	0	9.39
Mark Petkovsek	6	0	0	7.1	11	6	6	3	7	0-1	0-0	1	7.36
Todd Stottlemyre	3	2	0	8.0	15	11	11	3	11	1-1	0-0	0	12.38
Totals	7	7	0	60.0	77	44	44	25	51	3-4	1-1	2	6.60

Fielding

Braves	Pos	G	PO	Ast	E	DP	PB	FPct
Steve Avery	p	2	0	0	0	0	—	—
Rafael Belliard	ss	3	2	4	0	0	—	1.000
	2b	1	0	1	0	0	—	1.000
Mike Bielecki	p	3	0	0	0	0	—	—
Jeff Blauser	ss	7	5	9	1	2	—	.933
Brad Clontz	p	1	0	0	0	0	—	—
Jermaine Dye	rf	7	14	0	0	0	—	1.000
Tom Glavine	p	2	0	3	0	1	—	1.000
Marquis Grissom	cf	7	17	0	1	0	—	.944
Andruw Jones	lf	5	5	0	0	0	—	1.000
Chipper Jones	3b	7	5	7	1	2	—	.923
Ryan Klesko	lf	6	13	0	0	0	—	1.000
Mark Lemke	2b	7	9	18	0	3	—	1.000
Javy Lopez	c	7	48	3	0	0	0	1.000
Greg Maddux	p	2	1	4	0	0	—	1.000
Fred McGriff	1b	7	55	2	1	5	—	.983
Greg McMichael	p	3	1	0	0	0	—	1.000
Mike Mordecai	2b	2	1	1	0	1	—	1.000
	3b	1	0	0	0	0	—	—
Denny Neagle	p	2	0	1	0	0	—	1.000
Terry Pendleton	3b	2	0	1	0	1	—	1.000
Eddie Perez	c	3	5	0	0	0	0	1.000
	1b	1	2	0	0	1	—	1.000
John Smoltz	p	2	0	1	0	0	—	1.000
Terrell Wade	p	1	0	0	0	0	—	—
Mark Wohlers	p	3	0	0	0	0	—	—
Totals		7	183	55	4	16	0	.983

Cardinals	Pos	G	PO	Ast	E	DP	PB	FPct
Luis Alicea	2b	4	5	7	1	1	—	.923
Alan Benes	p	2	0	1	0	0	—	1.000
Andy Benes	p	3	1	4	0	0	—	1.000
Royce Clayton	ss	5	5	16	2	2	—	.913
Dennis Eckersley	p	3	0	1	0	0	—	1.000
Tony Fossas	p	5	0	0	0	0	—	—
Gary Gaetti	3b	7	4	12	0	1	—	1.000
Mike Gallego	2b	5	8	12	1	2	—	.952
	3b	2	0	0	0	0	—	—
Ron Gant	lf	7	12	0	0	0	—	1.000
Rick Honeycutt	p	5	0	0	0	0	—	—
Danny Jackson	p	1	0	0	0	0	—	—
Brian Jordan	rf	5	10	0	0	0	—	1.000
	cf	2	3	0	0	1	—	1.000
Ray Lankford	cf	3	7	0	0	0	—	1.000
John Mabry	1b	6	43	1	0	4	—	1.000
	rf	2	2	0	0	0	—	1.000
T.J. Mathews	p	2	0	0	0	0	—	—
Willie McGee	cf	3	2	0	0	0	—	1.000
	rf	2	3	0	1	0	—	.750
Miguel Mejia	cf	2	2	0	0	0	—	1.000
Donovan Osborne	p	2	0	1	0	0	—	1.000
Tom Pagnozzi	c	7	49	1	0	0	0	1.000
Mark Petkovsek	p	6	1	2	1	1	—	.750
Danny Sheaffer	c	2	3	0	0	0	0	1.000
Ozzie Smith	ss	2	7	2	0	1	—	1.000
Todd Stottlemyre	p	3	0	0	0	0	—	—
Mark Sweeney	lf	2	1	0	0	0	—	1.000
	rf	1	1	0	0	0	—	1.000
Dmitri Young	1b	2	11	1	0	0	—	1.000
Totals		7	180	61	6	13	0	.976

1997 Cleveland Indians (AL) 4, Baltimore Orioles (AL) 2

The Cleveland Indians downed the Baltimore Orioles in six games in one of the most tension-filled Championship Series in history. In the opener, Baltimore outfielder Brady Anderson leaped high above the fence to take away a home run in the top of the first, and hit one out to lead off the bottom of the inning. Scott Erickson went eight innings for a 3-0 victory. Cleveland's Marquis Grissom hit a three-run homer in the top of the eighth to give the Tribe a 5-4 victory in the second game. Baltimore's Mike Mussina fanned an LCS-record 15 batters in Game 3, but the game went into extra innings. The Indians won it in the bottom of the 12th when Omar Vizquel tried to lay down a suicide squeeze bunt. He missed the ball, but so did catcher Lenny Webster, and Grissom scored the winning run. Sandy Alomar Jr. won Game 4 with a ninth-inning RBI single, his fourth RBI of the game, as Cleveland slipped by the O's, 8-7. Baltimore held on to win Game 5, 4-2, as Orioles second baseman Roberto Alomar's brilliant stop converted a potentially game-tying ground ball into a game-ending groundout. Mussina struck out 10 and allowed only one hit in eight shutout innings in Game 6, but the scoreless game went into extra innings before Cleveland's Tony Fernandez won it with a solo homer in the top of the 11th to send the Indians to the World Series.

Game 1
Wednesday, October 8

Indians	AB	R	H	RBI	BB	K	Avg
Bip Roberts, 2b	4	0	1	0	0	1	.250
Omar Vizquel, ss	4	0	0	0	0	2	.000
Manny Ramirez, rf	3	0	0	0	0	0	.000
Jim Thome, 1b	3	0	0	0	0	1	.000
David Justice, dh	3	0	1	0	0	0	.333
Matt Williams, 3b	3	0	1	0	0	0	.333
Sandy Alomar Jr., c	3	0	0	0	0	0	.000
Brian Giles, lf	3	0	0	0	0	1	.000
Marquis Grissom, cf	3	0	1	0	0	0	.333
TOTALS	29	0	4	0	0	5	.138

Orioles	AB	R	H	RBI	BB	K	Avg
Brady Anderson, cf	4	2	2	1	0	1	.500
Roberto Alomar, 2b	3	1	1	2	1	0	.333
Geronimo Berroa, rf	3	0	0	0	0	0	.000
Eric Davis, rf	0	0	0	0	1	0	—
Rafael Palmeiro, 1b	4	0	0	0	0	1	.000
B.J. Surhoff, lf	3	0	1	0	1	0	.333
Cal Ripken Jr., 3b	3	0	1	0	1	0	.333
Harold Baines, dh	4	0	1	0	0	0	.250
Lenny Webster, c	3	0	0	0	0	0	.000
Mike Bordick, ss	3	0	0	0	0	1	.000
TOTALS	30	3	6	3	4	4	.200

	1	2	3	4	5	6	7	8	9	R	H	E
Indians	0	0	0	0	0	0	0	0	0	0	4	1
Orioles	1	0	2	0	0	0	0	0	x	3	6	1

E—Williams, Webster. DP—Indians 1 (Roberts to Vizquel to Thome), Orioles 2 (Ripken Jr. to Palmeiro; Erickson to Bordick to Palmeiro). LOB—Indians 2, Orioles 7. Scoring Position—Indians 0-for-1, Orioles 1-for-7. 2B—BraAnderson (1), Ripken Jr. (1). HR—BraAnderson (1), Alomar (1). GDP—Alomar Jr., Baines. SB—Roberts (1).

Indians	IP	H	R	ER	BB	K	ERA
Chad Ogea (L, 0-1)	6.0	6	3	3	3	3	4.50
Brian Anderson	2.0	0	0	0	1	1	0.00

Orioles	IP	H	R	ER	BB	K	ERA
Scott Erickson (W, 1-0)	8.0	4	0	0	0	3	0.00
Randy Myers (S, 1)	1.0	0	0	0	0	2	0.00

Time—2:33. Attendance—49,029. Umpires—HP, Brinkman. 1B, Joyce. 2B, Hirschbeck. 3B, Merrill.

Game 2
Thursday, October 9

Indians	AB	R	H	RBI	BB	K	Avg
Bip Roberts, lf	5	0	0	0	0	2	.111
Brian Giles, lf	0	0	0	0	0	0	.000
Omar Vizquel, ss	3	1	0	0	1	2	.000
Manny Ramirez, rf	4	1	1	2	1	1	.143
Matt Williams, 3b	5	0	1	0	0	1	.250
David Justice, dh	2	0	1	0	0	0	.400
Jeff Branson, ph-dh	2	0	0	0	0	2	.000
Sandy Alomar Jr., c	3	1	0	0	1	0	.000
Tony Fernandez, 2b	2	0	0	0	1	1	.000
Kevin Seitzer, 1b	2	0	0	0	1	1	.000
Jim Thome, ph-1b	0	1	0	0	1	0	.000
Marquis Grissom, cf	4	1	3	3	0	0	.571
TOTALS	32	5	6	5	6	10	.164

Orioles	AB	R	H	RBI	BB	K	Avg
Brady Anderson, cf	4	0	0	0	1	0	.250
Roberto Alomar, 2b	5	0	0	0	0	1	.125
Eric Davis, rf	5	0	1	0	0	0	.200
Rafael Palmeiro, 1b	4	1	2	0	0	2	.250
B.J. Surhoff, lf	3	1	1	0	1	0	.333
Cal Ripken Jr., 3b	4	2	2	2	0	1	.429
Harold Baines, dh	3	0	1	0	0	0	.286
Geronimo Berroa, ph-dh	1	0	0	0	0	0	.000
Chris Hoiles, c	3	0	0	0	1	1	.000
Mike Bordick, ss	3	0	1	2	0	0	.167
Jeffrey Hammonds, ph	0	0	0	0	1	0	—
TOTALS	35	4	8	4	4	5	.226

	1	2	3	4	5	6	7	8	9	R	H	E
Indians	2	0	0	0	0	0	0	3	0	5	6	3
Orioles	0	2	0	0	0	2	0	0	0	4	8	1

E—Fernandez, Roberts, Alomar, Ramirez. DP—Indians 1 (Williams to Seitzer), Orioles 1 (Ripken Jr. to Alomar to Palmeiro). LOB—Indians 9, Orioles 8. Scoring Position—Indians 1-for-9, Orioles 2-for-8. 2B—Palmeiro (1). HR—Ramirez (1), Grissom (1), Ripken Jr. (1). GDP—Ramirez, Hoiles. SB—Williams (1), Grissom (1).

Indians	IP	H	R	ER	BB	K	ERA
Charles Nagy	5.2	8	4	4	2	1	6.35
Alvin Morman	0.2	0	0	0	0	0	0.00
Jeff Juden	0.1	0	0	0	0	0	0.00
Paul Assenmacher (W, 1-0)	0.2	0	0	0	1	2	0.00
Mike Jackson (H, 1)	0.2	0	0	0	0	1	0.00
Jose Mesa (S, 1)	1.0	0	0	0	1	1	0.00

Orioles	IP	H	R	ER	BB	K	ERA
Jimmy Key	4.0	5	2	2	2	4	4.50
Scott Kamieniecki	3.0	0	0	0	1	1	0.00
Armando Benitez (BS, 1; L, 0-1)	1.0	1	3	3	2	3	27.00
Alan Mills	1.0	0	0	0	1	2	0.00

HBP—Fernandez by Key, Vizquel by Key, Justice by Key. Time—3:53. Attendance—49,131. Umpires—HP, Joyce. 1B, Hirschbeck. 2B, Merrill. 3B, McCoy.

Game 3
Saturday, October 11

Orioles	AB	R	H	RBI	BB	K	Avg
Brady Anderson, cf	4	0	2	1	1	0	.333
Roberto Alomar, 2b	3	0	1	0	2	0	.182
Eric Davis, rf	4	0	0	0	0	1	.111
Lenny Webster, c	1	0	1	0	0	0	.250
Rafael Palmeiro, 1b	5	0	1	0	0	4	.231
B.J. Surhoff, lf	5	0	0	0	0	0	.182
Cal Ripken Jr., 3b	5	0	0	0	0	2	.250
Harold Baines, dh	1	0	1	0	1	0	.375
Geronimo Berroa, ph-dh	3	0	1	0	0	0	.143
Chris Hoiles, c	3	0	1	0	0	1	.167
Jeff Reboulet, pr-ss	2	1	0	0	0	1	.000
Mike Bordick, ss	2	0	0	0	0	1	.125
Jeffrey Hammonds, ph-rf	2	0	0	0	1	0	.000
TOTALS	40	1	8	1	4	12	.210

Indians	AB	R	H	RBI	BB	K	Avg
Bip Roberts, 2b	3	0	0	0	0	3	.083
Tony Fernandez, 2b	3	0	1	0	0	1	.200
Omar Vizquel, ss	4	0	0	0	1	3	.000
Manny Ramirez, rf	4	0	2	0	1	2	.273
Jim Thome, 1b	1	1	0	0	3	1	.000
Kevin Seitzer, ph-1b	1	0	0	0	0	0	.000
David Justice, dh	5	0	0	0	0	2	.300
Matt Williams, 3b	4	0	2	1	1	1	.333
Sandy Alomar Jr., c	5	0	0	0	0	1	.000
Brian Giles, lf	5	0	0	0	0	3	.000
Marquis Grissom, cf	4	1	0	0	1	4	.364
TOTALS	39	2	6	1	7	21	.163

	1	2	3	4	5	6	7	8	9	10	11	12	R	H	E
Orioles	0	0	0	0	0	0	0	0	1	0	0	0	1	8	1
Indians	0	0	0	0	0	0	1	0	0	0	0	1	2	6	0

E—Alomar. DP—Indians 4 (Alomar Jr. to Vizquel; Roberts to Vizquel to Thome; Vizquel to Roberts to Thome; Williams to Roberts to Thome). LOB—Orioles 7, Indians 10. Scoring Position—Orioles 2-for-6, Indians 1-for-8. 2B—Anderson (2), Berroa (1). GDP—Alomar, Surhoff, Hoiles. SB—Anderson (1), Grissom (2). CS—Baines (1).

Orioles	IP	H	R	ER	BB	K	ERA
Mike Mussina	7.0	3	1	1	2	15	1.29
Armando Benitez	1.0	0	0	0	1	1	13.50
Jesse Orosco	0.2	0	0	0	1	1	0.00
Alan Mills	0.1	1	0	0	0	0	0.00
Arthur Rhodes	1.0	1	0	0	1	2	0.00
Randy Myers (L, 0-1)	1.1	1	1	1	2	2	3.86

Indians	IP	H	R	ER	BB	K	ERA
Orel Hershiser	7.0	4	0	0	1	7	0.00
Paul Assenmacher (H, 1)	0.2	0	0	0	0	1	0.00
Mike Jackson (H, 2)	0.1	0	0	0	0	0	0.00
Jose Mesa (BS, 1)	2.0	2	1	1	1	1	3.00
Jeff Juden	0.2	1	0	0	2	2	0.00
Alvin Morman	0.2	0	0	0	0	1	0.00
Eric Plunk (W, 1-0)	0.2	1	0	0	0	0	0.00

Benitez pitched to one batter in the 9th. Rhodes pitched to three batters in the 11th.

WP—Rhodes. Time—4:51. Attendance—45,047. Umpires—HP, Hirschbeck. 1B, Merrill. 2B, McCoy. 3B, Reilly.

Postseason: League Championship Series

Game 4
Sunday, October 12

Orioles	AB	R	H	RBI	BB	K	Avg
Brady Anderson, cf	4	2	2	1	1	0	.375
Roberto Alomar, 2b	3	1	0	0	2	1	.143
Geronimo Berroa, rf	5	1	2	1	0	1	.250
Jeffrey Hammonds, pr-rf	0	0	0	0	0	0	.000
Harold Baines, dh	3	1	1	2	0	0	.364
Eric Davis, ph-dh	2	0	0	0	0	1	.091
Rafael Palmeiro, 1b	5	1	3	2	0	2	.333
Cal Ripken Jr., 3b	4	1	1	0	1	1	.250
B.J. Surhoff, lf	5	0	2	1	0	1	.250
Lenny Webster, c	4	0	1	0	0	1	.250
Mike Bordick, ss	4	0	0	0	0	2	.083
TOTALS	39	7	12	7	4	10	.243

Indians	AB	R	H	RBI	BB	K	Avg
Bip Roberts, 2b	3	0	0	0	0	0	.067
Tony Fernandez, 2b	2	0	1	0	0	4	.286
Omar Vizquel, ss	4	0	0	0	0	1	.000
Manny Ramirez, rf	3	2	3	1	2	0	.429
Jim Thome, 1b	3	1	1	0	1	0	.143
Kevin Seitzer, ph	0	0	0	0	0	0	.000
David Justice, dh	5	2	2	0	0	0	.333
Matt Williams, 3b	4	0	0	0	1	1	.250
Sandy Alomar Jr., c	5	2	3	4	0	1	.188
Brian Giles, lf	3	1	2	0	1	0	.182
Marquis Grissom, cf	4	0	1	1	0	1	.333
TOTALS	36	8	13	6	5	4	.216

	1	2	3	4	5	6	7	8	9	R	H	E
Orioles	0	1	4	0	0	0	1	0	1	7	12	2
Indians	0	2	0	1	4	0	0	0	1	8	13	0

E—Anderson, Webster. DP—Orioles 1 (Ripken Jr. to Alomar to Palmeiro). LOB—Orioles 9, Indians 9. Scoring Position—Orioles 2-for-8, Indians 3-for-12. 2B—Surhoff 2 (2), Ramirez (1), Giles 2 (2). HR—BraAnderson (2), Baines (1), Palmeiro (2), Ramirez (2), Alomar Jr. (1). S—Vizquel, Seitzer. GDP—Justice. SB—BraAnderson (2).

Orioles	IP	H	R	ER	BB	K	ERA
Scott Erickson	4.2	11	7	6	1	3	4.26
Arthur Rhodes	1.1	0	0	0	2	0	0.00
Alan Mills (L, 0-1)	2.0	0	1	1	1	1	2.70
Jesse Orosco	0.2	0	0	0	0	0	0.00
Armando Benitez	0.0	1	0	0	1	0	13.50

Indians	IP	H	R	ER	BB	K	ERA
Jaret Wright	3.0	6	5	5	2	3	15.00
Brian Anderson	3.1	1	1	1	1	4	1.69
Jeff Juden	0.0	1	0	0	0	0	0.00
Paul Assenmacher (H, 2)	0.1	1	0	0	0	0	0.00
Mike Jackson (H, 3)	1.0	0	0	0	0	2	0.00
Jose Mesa (BS, 2; W, 1-0)	1.1	2	1	1	1	1	4.15

Juden pitched to two batters in the 7th. Mills pitched to one batter in the 9th. Benitez pitched to two batters in the 9th.

WP—Rhodes. Time—3:32. Attendance—45,081. Umpires—HP, Merrill. 1B, McCoy. 2B, Reilly. 3B, Brinkman.

Game 5
Monday, October 13

Orioles	AB	R	H	RBI	BB	K	Avg
Brady Anderson, cf	4	1	1	0	0	1	.350
Roberto Alomar, 2b	3	0	1	0	1	0	.176
Geronimo Berroa, rf	4	0	1	2	0	0	.250
Jeffrey Hammonds, pr-rf	0	0	0	0	0	0	.000
Harold Baines, dh	3	0	1	0	0	0	.357
Eric Davis, ph-dh	1	1	1	1	0	0	.167
Rafael Palmeiro, 1b	4	1	1	0	0	0	.318
Cal Ripken Jr., 3b	4	0	2	1	0	1	.300
B.J. Surhoff, lf	4	0	1	0	0	0	.250
Chris Hoiles, c	3	1	1	0	1	2	.222
Mike Bordick, ss	3	0	0	0	0	0	.067
TOTALS	33	4	10	4	2	5	.251

Indians	AB	R	H	RBI	BB	K	Avg
Bip Roberts, 2b-lf	5	0	2	0	0	2	.150
Omar Vizquel, ss	5	0	1	0	0	2	.050
Manny Ramirez, rf	3	0	0	0	0	1	.353
Jim Thome, 1b	3	0	0	0	0	0	.100
Kevin Seitzer, ph-1b	1	0	0	0	0	0	.000
David Justice, dh	3	1	1	0	1	1	.333
Matt Williams, 3b	3	1	1	1	1	1	.263
Sandy Alomar Jr., c	4	0	0	0	0	0	.150
Brian Giles, lf	2	0	1	0	0	0	.231
Tony Fernandez, ph-2b	2	0	1	1	0	0	.333
Marquis Grissom, cf	4	0	1	0	0	0	.316
TOTALS	35	2	8	2	2	8	.219

	1	2	3	4	5	6	7	8	9	R	H	E
Orioles	0	0	2	0	0	0	0	0	2	4	10	0
Indians	0	0	0	0	0	0	0	0	2	2	8	1

E—Williams. DP—Indians 3 (Vizquel to Roberts to Thome; Vizquel to Thome; Vizquel to Fernandez to Seitzer). LOB—Orioles 5, Indians 9. Scoring Position—Orioles 2-for-6, Indians 2-for-11. 2B—Palmeiro (2), Roberts (1), Williams (1), Giles (3), Fernandez (1). HR—Davis (1). S—Bordick. GDP—Berroa, Palmeiro, Bordick. SB—Grissom (3).

Orioles	IP	H	R	ER	BB	K	ERA
Scott Kamieniecki (W, 1-0)	5.0	4	0	0	1	4	0.00
Jimmy Key (H, 1)	3.0	0	0	0	1	3	2.57
Randy Myers	1.0	4	2	2	0	1	8.10

Indians	IP	H	R	ER	BB	K	ERA
Chad Ogea (L, 0-2)	8.0	6	2	2	4		3.21
Paul Assenmacher	0.0	4	2	2	0	0	10.80
Mike Jackson	1.0	0	0	0	0	1	0.00

Assenmacher pitched to four batters in the 9th.

HBP—Ramirez by Kamieniecki. Time—3:08. Attendance—45,068. Umpires—HP, McCoy. 1B, Reilly. 2B, Brinkman. 3B, Joyce.

Game 6
Wednesday, October 15

Indians	AB	R	H	RBI	BB	K	Avg
Omar Vizquel, ss	5	0	0	0	0	0	.040
Tony Fernandez, 2b	5	1	2	1	0	0	.357
Manny Ramirez, rf	4	0	0	0	1	1	.286
David Justice, dh	3	0	1	0	1	1	.333
Matt Williams, 3b	4	0	0	0	0	3	.217
Jim Thome, 1b	4	0	0	0	0	2	.071
Sandy Alomar Jr., c	4	0	0	0	0	1	.125
Brian Giles, lf	3	0	0	0	1	2	.188
Marquis Grissom, cf	4	0	0	0	0	4	.261
TOTALS	36	1	3	1	3	14	.204

Orioles	AB	R	H	RBI	BB	K	Avg
Brady Anderson, cf	5	0	2	0	1	2	.360
Roberto Alomar, 2b	5	0	1	0	1	1	.182
Geronimo Berroa, rf	5	0	2	0	0	1	.286
Jerome Walton, rf	0	0	0	0	0	0	—
Harold Baines, dh	3	0	1	0	1	1	.353
Eric Davis, ph-dh	1	0	0	0	0	1	.154
Rafael Palmeiro, 1b	3	0	0	0	0	1	.280
Jeffrey Hammonds, pr-lf	1	0	0	0	0	0	.000
Cal Ripken Jr., 3b	3	0	2	0	2	1	.348
B.J. Surhoff, lf-1b	5	0	0	0	0	0	.200
Chris Hoiles, c	5	0	2	0	0	1	.143
Mike Bordick, ss	4	0	2	0	0	1	.158
Lenny Webster, ph	1	0	0	0	0	0	.222
TOTALS	41	0	10	0	5	11	.250

	1	2	3	4	5	6	7	8	9	10	11	R	H	E
Indians	0	0	0	0	0	0	0	0	0	0	1	1	3	0
Orioles	0	0	0	0	0	0	0	0	0	0	0	0	10	0

DP—Indians 2 (Vizquel to Thome; Williams to Fernandez to Thome). LOB—Indians 5, Orioles 14. Scoring Position—Indians 0-for-5, Orioles 0-for-12. 2B—Justice (1), Berroa (2), Ripken Jr. (2), Bordick (1). HR—Fernandez (1). GDP—Alomar, Berroa. SB—Hammonds (1).

Indians	IP	H	R	ER	BB	K	ERA
Charles Nagy	7.1	9	0	0	3	4	2.77
Paul Assenmacher	0.1	0	0	0	0	0	9.00
Mike Jackson	1.1	0	0	0	1	3	0.00
Brian Anderson (W, 1-0)	1.0	0	0	0	1	2	1.42
Jose Mesa (S, 2)	1.0	1	0	0	0	2	3.38

Orioles	IP	H	R	ER	BB	K	ERA
Mike Mussina	8.0	1	0	0	2	10	0.60
Randy Myers	2.0	0	0	0	1	2	5.06
Armando Benitez (L, 0-2)	1.0	1	1	1	0	2	12.00

HBP—Palmeiro by Nagy. Time—3:52. Attendance—49,075. Umpires—HP, Reilly. 1B, Brinkman. 2B, Joyce. 3B, Hirschbeck.

1997 AL Championship Series—Composite Statistics

Batting

Indians	G	AB	R	H	RBI	2B	3B	HR	BB	SO	SB	CS	Avg	OBP	Slg
Sandy Alomar Jr.	6	24	3	3	4	0	0	1	1	3	0	0	.125	.160	.250
Jeff Branson	1	2	0	0	0	0	0	0	0	2	0	0	.000	.000	.000
Tony Fernandez	5	14	1	5	2	1	0	1	1	2	0	0	.357	.438	.643
Brian Giles	6	16	1	3	0	3	0	0	2	6	0	0	.188	.278	.375
Marquis Grissom	6	23	2	6	4	0	0	1	1	9	3	0	.261	.292	.391
David Justice	6	21	3	7	0	1	0	0	2	4	0	0	.333	.417	.381
Manny Ramirez	6	21	3	6	3	1	0	2	5	5	0	0	.286	.444	.619
Bip Roberts	5	20	0	3	0	1	0	0	0	8	1	0	.150	.150	.200
Kevin Seitzer	4	4	0	0	0	0	0	0	1	2	0	0	.000	.200	.000
Jim Thome	6	14	3	1	0	0	0	0	5	4	0	0	.071	.316	.071
Omar Vizquel	6	25	1	1	0	0	0	0	2	10	0	0	.040	.143	.040
Matt Williams	6	23	1	5	2	1	0	0	3	7	1	0	.217	.308	.261
Totals	6	207	18	40	15	8	0	5	23	62	5	0	.193	.286	.304

Orioles	G	AB	R	H	RBI	2B	3B	HR	BB	SO	SB	CS	Avg	OBP	Slg
Roberto Alomar	6	22	2	4	2	0	0	1	7	3	0	0	.182	.379	.318
Brady Anderson	6	25	5	9	3	2	0	2	4	4	2	0	.360	.448	.680
Harold Baines	6	17	1	6	2	0	0	1	2	1	0	1	.353	.421	.529
Geronimo Berroa	6	21	1	6	3	2	0	0	3	0	0	0	.286	.286	.381
Mike Bordick	6	19	0	3	2	1	0	0	0	6	0	0	.158	.158	.211
Eric Davis	6	13	1	2	1	0	0	1	1	3	0	0	.154	.214	.385
Jeffrey Hammonds	5	3	0	0	0	0	0	0	1	2	1	0	.000	.250	.000
Chris Hoiles	4	14	1	2	0	0	0	0	2	5	0	0	.143	.250	.143
Rafael Palmeiro	6	25	3	7	2	2	0	1	0	10	0	0	.280	.308	.480
Jeff Reboulet	1	2	1	0	0	0	0	0	0	1	0	0	.000	.000	.000
Cal Ripken Jr.	6	23	3	8	3	2	0	1	4	6	0	0	.348	.444	.565
B.J. Surhoff	6	25	1	5	1	2	0	0	2	2	0	0	.200	.259	.280
Lenny Webster	4	9	2	2	0	0	0	0	0	1	0	0	.222	.222	.222
Totals	6	218	19	54	19	11	0	7	23	47	3	1	.248	.322	.394

Pitching

Indians	G	GS	CG	IP	H	R	ER	BB	SO	W-L	Sv-Op	Hld	ERA
Brian Anderson	3	0	0	6.1	1	1	1	3	7	1-0	0-0	0	1.42
Paul Assenmacher	5	0	0	2.0	5	2	2	1	3	1-0	0-0	2	9.00
Orel Hershiser	1	1	0	7.0	4	0	0	1	7	0-0	0-0	0	0.00
Mike Jackson	5	0	0	4.1	1	0	0	1	7	0-0	0-0	3	0.00
Jeff Juden	3	0	0	1.0	2	0	0	2	2	0-0	0-0	0	0.00
Jose Mesa	4	0	0	5.1	5	2	2	3	5	1-0	2-4	0	3.38
Alvin Morman	2	0	0	1.1	0	0	0	1	0	0-0	0-0	0	0.00
Charles Nagy	2	2	0	13.0	17	4	4	5	5	0-0	0-0	0	2.77
Chad Ogea	2	2	0	14.0	12	5	5	5	7	0-2	0-0	0	3.21
Eric Plunk	1	0	0	0.2	1	0	0	0	0	1-0	0-0	0	0.00
Jaret Wright	1	1	0	3.0	6	5	5	2	3	0-0	0-0	0	15.00
Totals	6	6	0	58.0	54	19	19	23	47	4-2	2-4	5	2.95

Orioles	G	GS	CG	IP	H	R	ER	BB	SO	W-L	Sv-Op	Hld	ERA
Armando Benitez	4	0	0	3.0	3	4	4	4	6	0-2	0-1	0	12.00
Scott Erickson	2	2	0	12.2	15	7	6	1	6	1-0	0-0	0	4.26
Scott Kamieniecki	2	1	0	8.0	4	0	0	2	5	1-0	0-0	0	0.00
Jimmy Key	2	1	0	7.0	5	2	2	3	7	0-0	0-0	1	2.57
Alan Mills	3	0	0	3.1	1	1	1	2	3	0-1	0-0	0	2.70
Mike Mussina	2	2	0	15.0	4	1	1	4	25	0-0	0-0	0	0.60
Randy Myers	4	0	0	5.1	6	3	3	3	7	0-1	1-1	0	5.06
Jesse Orosco	2	0	0	1.1	0	0	0	1	1	0-0	0-0	0	0.00
Arthur Rhodes	2	0	0	2.1	2	0	0	3	2	0-0	0-0	0	0.00
Totals	6	6	0	58.0	40	18	17	23	62	2-4	1-2	1	2.64

Fielding

Indians	Pos	G	PO	Ast	E	DP	PB	FPct
Sandy Alomar Jr.	c	6	49	1	0	1	0	1.000
Brian Anderson	p	3	1	2	0	0	—	1.000
Paul Assenmacher	p	5	0	0	0	0	—	—
Tony Fernandez	2b	5	9	10	1	2	—	.950
Brian Giles	lf	6	9	0	0	0	—	1.000
Marquis Grissom	cf	6	13	1	0	0	—	1.000
Orel Hershiser	p	1	0	0	0	0	—	—
Mike Jackson	p	5	0	0	0	0	—	—
Jeff Juden	p	3	0	0	0	0	—	—
Jose Mesa	p	4	0	1	0	0	—	1.000
Alvin Morman	p	2	0	0	0	0	—	—
Charles Nagy	p	2	0	2	0	0	—	1.000
Chad Ogea	p	2	0	1	0	0	—	1.000
Eric Plunk	p	1	0	0	0	0	—	—
Manny Ramirez	rf	6	14	0	1	0	—	.933
Bip Roberts	2b	4	8	7	0	5	—	1.000
	lf	2	3	0	1	0	—	.750
Kevin Seitzer	1b	3	11	1	0	2	—	1.000
Jim Thome	1b	6	35	2	0	8	—	1.000
Omar Vizquel	ss	6	16	15	0	8	—	1.000
Matt Williams	3b	6	6	18	2	3	—	.923
Jaret Wright	p	1	0	0	0	0	—	—
Totals		6	174	61	5	29	0	.979

Orioles	Pos	G	PO	Ast	E	DP	PB	FPct
Roberto Alomar	2b	6	10	17	2	2	—	.931
Brady Anderson	cf	6	13	0	1	0	—	.929
Armando Benitez	p	4	0	1	0	0	—	1.000
Geronimo Berroa	rf	4	9	0	0	0	—	1.000
Mike Bordick	ss	6	5	14	0	1	—	1.000
Eric Davis	rf	3	3	0	0	0	—	1.000
Scott Erickson	p	2	0	5	0	1	—	1.000
Jeffrey Hammonds	rf	3	1	0	0	0	—	1.000
	lf	1	1	0	0	0	—	1.000
Chris Hoiles	c	4	47	2	0	0	0	1.000
Scott Kamieniecki	p	2	0	2	0	0	—	1.000
Jimmy Key	p	2	0	0	0	0	—	—
Alan Mills	p	3	0	0	0	0	—	—
Mike Mussina	p	2	2	1	0	0	—	1.000
Randy Myers	p	4	0	0	0	0	—	—
Jesse Orosco	p	2	0	2	0	0	—	1.000
Rafael Palmeiro	1b	6	55	0	0	4	—	1.000
Jeff Reboulet	ss	1	0	0	0	0	—	—
Arthur Rhodes	p	2	0	0	0	0	—	—
Cal Ripken Jr.	3b	6	1	14	0	3	—	1.000
B.J. Surhoff	lf	6	10	0	0	0	—	1.000
	1b	1	3	0	0	0	—	1.000
Jerome Walton	rf	1	0	0	0	0	—	—
Lenny Webster	c	3	14	0	2	0	0	.875
Totals		6	174	60	5	11	0	.979

1997 Florida Marlins (NL) 4, Atlanta Braves (NL) 2

The Florida Marlins upset the Atlanta Braves, winning the NLCS in six games. Several key fielding lapses by the Braves helped the Marlins get five unearned runs to defeat Greg Maddux in Game 1, 5-3. Tom Glavine pitched the Braves to a 7-1 win in the second game. In Game 3, Florida catcher Charles Johnson came up in the bottom of the sixth with the game tied, two out and the bases loaded, and delivered a three-run double to send Florida to a 5-2 victory. Atlanta's Denny Neagle tossed a four-hit shutout in Game 4 to even the series. In Game 5, rookie Livan Hernandez outshone Maddux, tying the LCS record with 15 strikeouts en route to a 2-1 victory. Glavine's command evaporated in Game 6, and Kevin Brown bested him 7-4 to wrap up the NL pennant for Florida.

Game 1
Tuesday, October 7

Marlins	AB	R	H	RBI	BB	K	Avg
Devon White, cf	5	0	0	0	0	2	.000
Edgar Renteria, ss	4	1	1	0	0	1	.250
Gary Sheffield, rf	3	2	1	0	1	0	.333
Bobby Bonilla, 3b	3	1	0	0	1	2	.000
Jeff Conine, 1b	4	1	0	0	0	0	.000
Moises Alou, lf	4	0	1	4	0	0	.250
Charles Johnson, c	4	0	1	1	0	2	.250
Craig Counsell, 2b	3	0	2	0	1	0	.667
Kevin Brown, p	2	0	0	0	0	1	.000
Dennis Cook, p	0	0	0	0	0	0	—
Jay Powell, p	0	0	0	0	0	0	—
Darren Daulton, ph	1	0	0	0	0	1	.000
Robb Nen, p	0	0	0	0	0	0	—
TOTALS	33	5	6	5	3	9	.182

Braves	AB	R	H	RBI	BB	K	Avg
Kenny Lofton, cf	5	0	0	0	0	0	.000
Keith Lockhart, 2b	3	1	1	0	0	0	.333
Chipper Jones, 3b	4	1	1	1	0	0	.250
Fred McGriff, 1b	4	0	1	0	0	0	.250
Ryan Klesko, lf	3	1	1	1	1	1	.333
Michael Tucker, rf	0	0	0	0	3	0	—
Andruw Jones, ph-rf	1	0	0	0	0	1	.000
Eddie Perez, c	0	0	0	0	0	0	—
Javy Lopez, ph-c	4	0	0	0	0	1	.000
Jeff Blauser, ss	3	0	1	0	0	0	.333
Greg Maddux, p	1	0	0	0	0	1	.000
Tommy Gregg, ph	1	0	0	0	0	0	.000
Denny Neagle, p	0	0	0	0	0	0	—
Greg Colbrunn, ph	1	0	0	0	0	0	.000
TOTALS	30	3	5	3	4	4	.167

	1	2	3	4	5	6	7	8	9		R	H	E
Marlins	3	0	2	0	0	0	0	0	0		5	6	0
Braves	1	0	1	0	0	1	0	0	0		3	5	2

E—McGriff, Lofton. DP—Marlins 1 (Conine to Renteria), Braves 1 (Tucker to Lopez). LOB—Marlins 6, Braves 7. Scoring Position—Marlins 2-for-12, Braves 1-for-5. 2B—Alou (1), Johnson (1), Lockhart (1). HR—CJones (1), Klesko (1). S—Brown, Maddux. SB—Renteria (1).

Marlins	IP	H	R	ER	BB	K	ERA
Kevin Brown (W, 1-0)	6.0	5	3	3	4	3	4.50
Dennis Cook (H, 1)	1.1	0	0	0	0	0	0.00
Jay Powell (H, 1)	0.2	0	0	0	0	1	0.00
Robb Nen (S, 1)	1.0	0	0	0	0	0	0.00

Braves	IP	H	R	ER	BB	K	ERA
Greg Maddux (L, 0-1)	6.0	5	5	0	3	7	0.00
Denny Neagle	3.0	1	0	0	0	2	0.00

HBP—Renteria by Neagle, Blauser by Brown, Lockhart by Cook. Time—3:04. Attendance—49,244. Umpires—HP, Froemming. 1B, CWilliams. 2B, Winters. 3B, Layne.

Game 2
Wednesday, October 8

Marlins	AB	R	H	RBI	BB	K	Avg
Kurt Abbott, 2b	4	0	2	0	0	1	.500
Edgar Renteria, ss	3	0	0	0	1	0	.143
Gary Sheffield, rf	3	0	0	0	1	1	.167
Bobby Bonilla, 3b	4	0	0	0	0	2	.000
Jeff Conine, 1b	2	0	0	0	1	1	.000
Ed Vosberg, p	0	0	0	0	0	0	—
Craig Counsell, ph	1	0	0	0	0	0	.500
Jim Eisenreich, lf	3	0	0	0	0	0	.000
Charles Johnson, c	2	1	0	0	1	0	.167
Greg Zaun, c	0	0	0	0	0	0	—
Devon White, cf	3	0	1	1	0	1	.125
Alex Fernandez, p	1	0	0	0	0	1	.000
Al Leiter, p	0	0	0	0	0	0	—
John Cangelosi, ph	1	0	0	0	0	0	.000
Felix Heredia, p	0	0	0	0	0	0	—
Darren Daulton, 1b	0	0	0	0	1	0	.000
TOTALS	27	1	3	1	5	7	.148

Braves	AB	R	H	RBI	BB	K	Avg
Kenny Lofton, cf	5	1	1	0	0	3	.100
Keith Lockhart, 2b	3	2	2	1	0	0	.500
Tony Graffanino, 2b	2	1	1	0	0	1	.500
Chipper Jones, 3b	5	2	3	3	0	1	.444
Fred McGriff, 1b	3	0	1	0	1	1	.286
Ryan Klesko, lf	3	1	1	2	1	0	.333
Danny Bautista, lf	0	0	0	0	0	0	—
Javy Lopez, c	2	0	1	1	1	0	.167
Michael Tucker, rf	2	0	0	0	0	0	.000
Andruw Jones, ph-rf	2	0	1	0	0	0	.333
Jeff Blauser, ss	4	0	1	0	0	0	.286
Tom Glavine, p	2	0	0	0	0	2	.000
Mike Cather, p	0	0	0	0	0	0	—
Greg Colbrunn, ph	1	0	1	0	0	0	.500
Mark Wohlers, p	0	0	0	0	0	0	—
TOTALS	34	7	13	7	3	8	.290

	1	2	3	4	5	6	7	8	9		R	H	E
Marlins	0	0	0	0	0	0	0	1	0		1	3	1
Braves	3	0	2	0	0	0	2	0	x		7	13	0

E—Johnson. DP—Marlins 1 (Bonilla to Johnson to Daulton), Braves 2 (Blauser to Lockhart to McGriff; Blauser to Lockhart to McGriff). LOB—Marlins 4, Braves 8. Scoring Position—Marlins 0-for-2, Braves 4-for-13. 2B—Abbott (1), White (1), Lopez (1), Graffanino (1). 3B—Lockhart (1). HR—CJones (2), Klesko (2). S—Glavine. SF—Lopez. GDP—Renteria, Eisenreich, Blauser.

Marlins	IP	H	R	ER	BB	K	ERA
Alex Fernandez (L, 0-1)	2.2	6	5	5	1	3	16.88
Al Leiter	2.1	3	0	0	0	1	0.00
Felix Heredia	1.1	3	2	2	2	2	13.50
Ed Vosberg	1.2	1	0	0	0	2	0.00

Braves	IP	H	R	ER	BB	K	ERA
Tom Glavine (W, 1-0)	7.2	3	1	1	4	5	1.17
Mike Cather	0.1	0	0	0	0	1	0.00
Mark Wohlers	1.0	0	0	0	1	1	0.00

Time—2:51. Attendance—48,933. Umpires—HP, CWilliams. 1B, Winters. 2B, Layne. 3B, Gregg.

Game 3
Friday, October 10

Braves	AB	R	H	RBI	BB	K	Avg
Kenny Lofton, cf	4	1	1	0	0	0	.143
Jeff Blauser, ss	3	1	1	0	1	2	.300
Chipper Jones, 3b	2	0	0	1	0	0	.364
Fred McGriff, 1b	3	0	1	1	0	1	.300
Javy Lopez, c	3	0	0	1	0	2	.111
Andruw Jones, rf	2	0	1	0	1	0	.400
Michael Tucker, ph	1	0	0	0	0	0	.000
Ryan Klesko, lf	4	0	1	0	0	0	.300
Tony Graffanino, 2b	2	0	0	0	0	0	.250
Keith Lockhart, ph-2b	2	0	1	0	0	0	.500
John Smoltz, p	2	0	0	0	0	1	.000
Tommy Gregg, ph	1	0	0	0	0	0	.000
Mike Cather, p	0	0	0	0	0	0	—
Kerry Ligtenberg, p	0	0	0	0	0	0	—
TOTALS	29	2	6	2	3	6	.261

Marlins	AB	R	H	RBI	BB	K	Avg
John Cangelosi, lf	3	0	0	0	1	0	.000
Edgar Renteria, ss	4	1	1	0	0	1	.182
Gary Sheffield, rf	3	2	2	1	1	0	.333
Bobby Bonilla, 3b	4	0	0	0	0	1	.091
Alex Arias, 3b	0	0	0	0	0	0	—
Darren Daulton, 1b	3	1	1	1	0	1	.250
Jeff Conine, 1b	1	0	0	0	0	0	.000
Devon White, cf	2	1	1	0	2	0	.200
Charles Johnson, c	3	0	1	3	0	2	.222
Craig Counsell, 2b	3	0	1	0	1	1	.429
Tony Saunders, p	2	0	0	0	0	2	.000
Livan Hernandez, p	1	0	0	0	0	1	.000
Dennis Cook, p	0	0	0	0	0	0	—
Moises Alou, ph	1	0	0	0	0	1	.200
Robb Nen, p	0	0	0	0	0	0	—
TOTALS	30	5	8	5	5	10	.188

	1	2	3	4	5	6	7	8	9		R	H	E
Braves	0	0	0	1	0	1	0	0	0		2	6	1
Marlins	0	0	0	1	0	4	0	0	x		5	8	1

E—Lofton, Counsell. DP—Braves 1 (AJones to McGriff), Marlins 1 (Renteria to Counsell to Daulton). LOB—Braves 6, Marlins 7. Scoring Position—Braves 1-for-4, Marlins 2-for-8. 2B—Renteria (1), Daulton (1), Johnson (2). HR—Sheffield (1). S—CJones, Johnson. SF—McGriff, Lopez. GDP—Graffanino.

Braves	IP	H	R	ER	BB	K	ERA
John Smoltz (L, 0-1)	6.0	5	5	5	5	9	7.50
Mike Cather	1.0	2	0	0	0	0	0.00
Kerry Ligtenberg	1.0	1	0	0	0	1	0.00

Marlins	IP	H	R	ER	BB	K	ERA
Tony Saunders	5.1	4	2	2	3	3	3.38
Livan Hernandez (W, 1-0)	1.2	2	0	0	0	1	0.00
Dennis Cook (H, 2)	1.0	0	0	0	0	2	0.00
Robb Nen (S, 2)	1.0	0	0	0	0	0	0.00

Time—2:59. Attendance—53,857. Umpires—HP, Winters. 1B, Layne. 2B, Gregg. 3B, Pulli.

Game 4
Saturday, October 11

Braves	AB	R	H	RBI	BB	K	Avg
Kenny Lofton, cf	5	0	1	0	0	1	.158
Jeff Blauser, ss	3	2	1	1	2	1	.308
Chipper Jones, 3b	5	2	3	0	0	0	.438
Fred McGriff, 1b	3	0	2	2	1	1	.385
Javy Lopez, c	4	0	0	0	0	2	.077
Andruw Jones, rf	4	0	2	1	0	0	.444
Danny Bautista, lf	4	0	1	0	0	0	.250
Tony Graffanino, 2b	4	0	1	0	0	2	.250
Denny Neagle, p	3	0	0	0	0	0	.000
TOTALS	35	4	11	4	3	8	.276

Marlins	AB	R	H	RBI	BB	K	Avg
Kurt Abbott, 2b	4	0	1	0	0	1	.375
Edgar Renteria, ss	4	0	1	0	0	1	.200
Gary Sheffield, rf	3	0	0	0	1	0	.250
Bobby Bonilla, 3b	4	0	0	0	0	1	.067
Jeff Conine, 1b	4	0	0	0	0	0	.000
Moises Alou, lf	3	0	0	0	0	0	.125
Charles Johnson, c	3	0	0	0	0	2	.167
Devon White, cf	3	0	0	0	0	0	.154
Al Leiter, p	1	0	0	0	0	0	.000
Alex Arias, ph	1	0	1	0	0	0	1.000
Felix Heredia, p	0	0	0	0	0	0	—
John Cangelosi, ph	1	0	1	0	0	0	.200
Ed Vosberg, p	0	0	0	0	0	0	—
TOTALS	31	0	4	0	1	7	.168

	1	2	3	4	5	6	7	8	9		R	H	E
Braves	1	0	1	0	2	0	0	0	0		4	11	0
Marlins	0	0	0	0	0	0	0	0	0		0	4	0

DP—Marlins 1 (Leiter to Renteria to Conine). LOB—Braves 8, Marlins 5. Scoring Position—Braves 2-for-10, Marlins 0-for-1. 2B—CJones (1), McGriff (1). HR—Blauser (1). S—Neagle. GDP—Lofton.

Braves	IP	H	R	ER	BB	K	ERA
Denny Neagle (W, 1-0)	9.0	4	0	0	1	7	

Marlins	IP	H	R	ER	BB	K	ERA
Al Leiter (L, 0-1)	6.0	10	4	4	2	5	4.32
Felix Heredia	2.0	0	0	0	0	2	5.40
Ed Vosberg	1.0	1	0	0	1	1	0.00

Time—2:48. Attendance—54,890. Umpires—HP, Layne. 1B, Gregg. 2B, Pulli. 3B, Froemming.

Game 5
Sunday, October 12

Braves	AB	R	H	RBI	BB	K	Avg
Kenny Lofton, cf	3	0	1	0	1	1	.182
Keith Lockhart, 2b	3	0	0	0	1	1	.364
Chipper Jones, 3b	4	0	0	0	0	2	.350
Fred McGriff, 1b	4	0	1	0	0	3	.353
Ryan Klesko, lf	3	0	0	0	0	2	.231
Michael Tucker, rf	3	1	1	1	0	2	.167
Andruw Jones, rf	0	0	0	0	0	0	.444
Eddie Perez, c	3	0	0	0	0	0	.000
Jeff Blauser, ss	3	0	0	0	0	2	.250
Greg Maddux, p	2	0	0	0	0	0	.000
Tommy Gregg, ph	1	0	0	0	0	1	.000
Mike Cather, p	0	0	0	0	0	0	—
TOTALS	29	1	3	1	2	15	.268

Marlins	AB	R	H	RBI	BB	K	Avg
Devon White, cf	3	1	0	0	0	2	.125
Edgar Renteria, ss	4	0	0	0	0	2	.158
Gary Sheffield, rf	2	0	0	0	1	1	.214
Bobby Bonilla, 3b	3	1	3	1	0	0	.222
Jeff Conine, 1b	3	0	1	1	0	0	.071
Moises Alou, lf	3	0	0	0	0	2	.091
Charles Johnson, c	3	0	0	0	0	2	.133
Craig Counsell, 2b	3	0	1	0	0	1	.400
Livan Hernandez, p	2	0	0	0	0	0	.000
TOTALS	26	2	5	2	1	10	.167

	1	2	3	4	5	6	7	8	9		R	H	E
Braves	0	1	0	0	0	0	0	0	0		1	3	0
Marlins	1	0	0	0	0	0	1	0	x		2	5	0

DP—Braves 1 (Maddux to Blauser to McGriff). LOB—Braves 3, Marlins 3. Scoring Position—Braves 0-for-3, Marlins 2-for-7. 2B—Bonilla (1). 3B—Lofton (1). HR—Tucker (1). S—Hernandez. GDP—Conine. SB—White (1). CS—Lofton (1).

Braves	IP	H	R	ER	BB	K	ERA
Greg Maddux (L, 0-2)	7.0	4	2	2	1	9	1.38
Mike Cather	1.0	1	0	0	0	1	0.00

Marlins	IP	H	R	ER	BB	K	ERA
Livan Hernandez (W, 2-0)	9.0	3	1	1	2	15	0.84

HBP—White by Maddux. Time—2:27. Attendance—51,982. Umpires—HP, Gregg. 1B, Pulli. 2B, Froemming. 3B, CWilliams.

Game 6
Tuesday, October 14

Marlins	AB	R	H	RBI	BB	K	Avg
Devon White, cf	5	2	2	0	0	2	.190
Edgar Renteria, ss	3	2	2	0	2	1	.227
Gary Sheffield, rf	3	2	1	0	2	1	.235
Bobby Bonilla, 3b	5	1	2	3	0	0	.261
Alex Arias, 3b	0	0	0	0	0	0	1.000
Jeff Conine, 1b	4	0	1	0	0	1	.111
Moises Alou, lf	4	0	0	1	1	0	.067
Charles Johnson, c	2	0	0	1	2	0	.118
Craig Counsell, 2b	4	0	2	2	1	1	.429
Kevin Brown, p	4	0	0	0	0	2	.000
TOTALS	34	7	10	7	8	9	.201

Braves	AB	R	H	RBI	BB	K	Avg
Kenny Lofton, cf	5	1	1	1	0	2	.185
Keith Lockhart, 2b	5	1	4	2	0	0	.500
Chipper Jones, 3b	4	0	0	1	0	1	.292
Fred McGriff, 1b	4	0	1	0	0	1	.333
Ryan Klesko, lf	4	0	1	1	0	0	.235
Javy Lopez, c	4	0	0	0	0	2	.059
Michael Tucker, rf	4	0	0	0	0	2	.100
Jeff Blauser, ss	4	2	2	0	0	1	.300
Tom Glavine, p	1	0	1	0	0	0	.333
Mike Cather, p	0	0	0	0	0	0	—
Tommy Gregg, ph	1	0	0	0	0	0	.000
Kerry Ligtenberg, p	0	0	0	0	0	0	—
Alan Embree, p	0	0	0	0	0	0	—
Greg Colbrunn, ph	1	0	1	0	0	0	.667
TOTALS	37	4	11	4	1	8	.259

	1	2	3	4	5	6	7	8	9		R	H	E
Marlins	4	0	0	0	0	3	0	0	0		7	10	1
Braves	1	2	0	0	0	0	0	0	1		4	11	1

E—Blauser, Johnson. DP—Braves 2 (Ligtenberg to Blauser to McGriff; Lopez to Lockhart). LOB—Marlins 11, Braves 8. Scoring Position—Marlins 4-for-13, Braves 4-for-9. S—Conine, Brown, Glavine. GDP—Alou. SB—Lofton (1). CS—Johnson (1).

Marlins	IP	H	R	ER	BB	K	ERA
Kevin Brown (W, 2-0)	9.0	11	4	4	1	8	4.20

Braves	IP	H	R	ER	BB	K	ERA
Tom Glavine (L, 1-1)	5.2	10	7	7	4		5.40
Mike Cather	0.1	0	0	0	0	1	0.00
Kerry Ligtenberg	2.0	0	0	0	0	3	0.00
Alan Embree	1.0	0	0	0	1	1	0.00

HBP—Johnson by Glavine. Time—3:10. Attendance—50,446. Umpires—HP, Pulli. 1B, Froemming. 2B, Winters. 3B, Layne.

Postseason: League Championship Series

1997 NL Championship Series—Composite Statistics

Batting

Marlins	G	AB	R	H	RBI	2B	3B	HR	BB	SO	SB	CS	Avg	OBP	Slg
Kurt Abbott	2	8	0	3	0	1	0	0	0	2	0	0	.375	.375	.500
Moises Alou	5	15	0	1	5	1	0	0	1	3	0	0	.067	.125	.133
Alex Arias	3	1	0	1	0	0	0	0	0	0	0	0	1.000	1.000	1.000
Bobby Bonilla	6	23	3	6	4	1	0	0	1	6	0	0	.261	.292	.304
Kevin Brown	2	6	0	0	0	0	0	0	0	3	0	0	.000	.000	.000
John Cangelosi	3	5	0	1	0	0	0	0	1	0	0	0	.200	.333	.200
Jeff Conine	6	18	1	2	1	0	0	0	1	4	0	0	.111	.158	.111
Craig Counsell	5	14	0	6	2	0	0	0	3	3	0	0	.429	.529	.429
Darren Daulton	3	4	1	1	1	1	0	0	1	2	0	0	.250	.400	.500
Jim Eisenreich	1	3	0	0	0	0	0	0	0	0	0	0	.000	.000	.000
Alex Fernandez	1	1	0	0	0	0	0	0	0	1	0	0	.000	.000	.000
Livan Hernandez	2	3	0	0	0	0	0	0	0	1	0	0	.000	.000	.000
Charles Johnson	6	17	1	2	5	2	0	0	3	8	0	1	.118	.286	.235
Al Leiter	2	1	0	0	0	0	0	0	0	1	0	0	.000	.000	.000
Edgar Renteria	6	22	4	5	0	1	0	0	3	6	1	0	.227	.346	.273
Tony Saunders	1	2	0	0	0	0	0	0	0	2	0	0	.000	.000	.000
Gary Sheffield	6	17	6	4	1	0	0	1	7	3	0	0	.235	.458	.412
Devon White	6	21	4	4	1	1	0	0	2	7	1	0	.190	.292	.238
Totals	6	181	20	36	20	8	0	1	23	52	2	1	.199	.300	.260

Braves	G	AB	R	H	RBI	2B	3B	HR	BB	SO	SB	CS	Avg	OBP	Slg
Danny Bautista	2	4	0	1	0	0	0	0	0	0	0	0	.250	.250	.250
Jeff Blauser	6	20	5	6	1	0	0	1	3	6	0	0	.300	.417	.450
Greg Colbrunn	3	3	0	2	0	0	0	0	0	0	0	0	.667	.667	.667
Tom Glavine	2	3	0	1	0	0	0	0	0	2	0	0	.333	.333	.333
Tony Graffanino	3	8	1	2	0	1	0	0	0	3	0	0	.250	.250	.375
Tommy Gregg	4	4	0	0	0	0	0	0	0	1	0	0	.000	.000	.000
Andruw Jones	5	9	0	4	1	0	0	0	1	1	0	0	.444	.500	.444
Chipper Jones	6	24	5	7	4	1	0	2	2	3	0	0	.292	.346	.583
Ryan Klesko	5	17	2	4	4	0	0	2	2	3	0	0	.235	.316	.588
Keith Lockhart	5	16	4	8	3	1	1	0	1	1	0	0	.500	.556	.688
Kenny Lofton	6	27	3	5	1	0	1	0	1	7	1	1	.185	.214	.259
Javy Lopez	5	17	0	1	2	1	0	0	1	7	0	0	.059	.100	.118
Greg Maddux	2	3	0	0	0	0	0	0	0	2	0	0	.000	.000	.000
Fred McGriff	6	21	0	7	4	1	0	0	2	7	0	0	.333	.375	.381
Denny Neagle	2	3	0	0	0	0	0	0	0	1	0	0	.000	.000	.000
Eddie Perez	2	3	0	0	0	0	0	0	0	0	0	0	.000	.000	.000
John Smoltz	1	2	0	0	0	0	0	0	0	1	0	0	.000	.000	.000
Michael Tucker	5	10	1	1	1	0	0	1	3	4	0	0	.100	.308	.400
Totals	6	194	21	49	21	5	2	6	16	49	1	1	.253	.312	.392

Pitching

Marlins	G	GS	CG	IP	H	R	ER	BB	SO	W-L	Sv-Op	Hld	ERA
Kevin Brown	2	2	1	15.0	16	7	7	5	11	2-0	0-0	0	4.20
Dennis Cook	2	0	0	2.1	0	0	0	0	2	0-0	0-0	2	0.00
Alex Fernandez	1	1	0	2.2	6	5	5	1	3	0-1	0-0	0	16.88
Felix Heredia	2	0	0	3.1	3	2	2	2	4	0-0	0-0	0	5.40
Livan Hernandez	2	1	1	10.2	5	1	1	2	16	2-0	0-0	0	0.84
Al Leiter	2	1	0	8.1	13	4	4	2	6	0-1	0-0	0	4.32
Robb Nen	2	0	0	2.0	0	0	0	0	0	0-0	2-2	0	0.00
Jay Powell	1	0	0	0.2	0	0	0	0	1	0-0	0-0	1	0.00
Tony Saunders	1	1	0	5.1	4	2	2	3	3	0-0	0-0	0	3.38
Ed Vosberg	2	0	0	2.2	2	0	0	1	3	0-0	0-0	0	0.00
Totals	6	6	2	53.0	49	21	21	16	49	4-2	2-2	3	3.57

Braves	G	GS	CG	IP	H	R	ER	BB	SO	W-L	Sv-Op	Hld	ERA
Mike Cather	4	0	0	2.2	3	0	0	0	3	0-0	0-0	0	0.00
Alan Embree	1	0	0	1.0	0	0	0	1	1	0-0	0-0	0	0.00
Tom Glavine	2	2	0	13.1	13	8	8	11	9	1-1	0-0	0	5.40
Kerry Ligtenberg	2	0	0	3.0	1	0	0	0	4	0-0	0-0	0	0.00
Greg Maddux	2	2	0	13.0	9	7	2	4	16	0-2	0-0	0	1.38
Denny Neagle	2	1	1	12.0	5	0	0	1	9	1-0	0-0	0	0.00
John Smoltz	1	1	0	6.0	5	5	5	5	9	0-1	0-0	0	7.50
Mark Wohlers	1	0	0	1.0	0	0	0	1	1	0-0	0-0	0	0.00
Totals	6	6	1	52.0	36	20	15	23	52	2-4	0-0	0	2.60

Fielding

Marlins	Pos	G	PO	Ast	E	DP	PB	FPct
Kurt Abbott	2b	2	4	1	0	0	—	1.000
Moises Alou	lf	4	3	0	0	0	—	1.000
Alex Arias	3b	2	0	0	0	0	—	—
Bobby Bonilla	3b	6	5	13	0	1	—	1.000
Kevin Brown	p	2	3	2	0	0	—	1.000
John Cangelosi	lf	1	2	0	0	0	—	1.000
Jeff Conine	1b	6	34	5	0	2	—	1.000
Dennis Cook	p	2	0	1	0	0	—	1.000
Craig Counsell	2b	4	7	9	1	1	—	.941
Darren Daulton	1b	2	8	1	0	2	—	1.000
Jim Eisenreich	lf	1	2	0	0	0	—	1.000
Alex Fernandez	p	1	0	0	0	0	—	—
Felix Heredia	p	2	0	0	0	0	—	—
Livan Hernandez	p	2	1	0	0	0	—	1.000
Charles Johnson	c	6	52	3	2	1	0	.965
Al Leiter	p	2	1	3	0	1	—	1.000
Robb Nen	p	2	0	1	0	0	—	1.000
Jay Powell	p	1	0	0	0	0	—	—
Edgar Renteria	ss	6	14	15	0	3	—	1.000
Tony Saunders	p	1	0	1	0	0	—	1.000
Gary Sheffield	rf	6	5	2	0	0	—	1.000
Ed Vosberg	p	2	0	0	0	0	—	—
Devon White	cf	6	16	0	0	0	—	1.000
Greg Zaun	c	1	2	0	0	0	0	1.000
Totals		6	159	57	3	11	0	.986

Braves	Pos	G	PO	Ast	E	DP	PB	FPct
Danny Bautista	lf	2	4	0	0	0	—	1.000
Jeff Blauser	ss	6	6	19	1	4	—	.962
Mike Cather	p	4	0	0	0	0	—	—
Alan Embree	p	1	0	0	0	0	—	—
Tom Glavine	p	2	0	5	0	0	—	1.000
Tony Graffanino	2b	3	4	2	0	0	—	1.000
Andruw Jones	rf	5	12	1	0	1	—	1.000
Chipper Jones	3b	6	1	8	0	0	—	1.000
Ryan Klesko	lf	5	5	0	0	0	—	1.000
Kerry Ligtenberg	p	2	0	2	0	1	—	1.000
Keith Lockhart	2b	5	14	5	0	3	—	1.000
Kenny Lofton	cf	6	9	1	2	0	—	.833
Javy Lopez	c	5	40	3	0	2	0	1.000
Greg Maddux	p	2	0	7	0	1	—	1.000
Fred McGriff	1b	6	41	2	1	5	—	.977
Denny Neagle	p	2	1	0	0	0	—	1.000
Eddie Perez	c	2	14	0	0	0	—	1.000
John Smoltz	p	1	0	1	0	0	—	1.000
Michael Tucker	rf	4	5	1	0	1	—	1.000
Mark Wohlers	p	1	0	0	0	0	—	—
Totals		6	156	57	4	18	0	.982

1981 New York Yankees (AL) 3, Milwaukee Brewers (AL) 2

After losing the first two games at home to the New York Yankees, the Milwaukee Brewers nearly came back to win the AL East Division Series, but came up just short. The Yankees won the opener 5-3 as Ron Davis and Goose Gossage combined to toss 4.2 innings of shutout relief. In Game 2, the Yanks downed longtime nemesis Mike Caldwell 3-0 on home runs by Lou Piniella and Reggie Jackson. Rollie Fingers blew a 3-1 lead in Game 3, but Paul Molitor's solo homer in the top of the eighth put the Brewers back on top. They went on to win, 5-3. The Brewers' bullpen successfully defended a 2-1 lead for the last four innings of Game 4, evening the series at two games apiece. The Brewers took a 2-0 lead in Game 5, but the Yankees came back to take the lead on homers by Jackson and Oscar Gamble, and won 7-3 to advance to the ALCS.

Game 1
Wednesday, October 7

Yankees	AB	R	H	RBI	BB	K	Avg
Willie Randolph, 2b	5	0	0	0	0	1	.000
Jerry Mumphrey, cf	5	1	2	0	0	0	.400
Dave Winfield, lf	5	0	1	0	0	1	.200
Reggie Jackson, rf	4	1	1	0	1	1	.250
Graig Nettles, 3b	5	0	0	0	0	0	.000
Oscar Gamble, dh	4	1	3	2	0	0	.750
Bob Watson, 1b	4	1	3	0	0	0	.750
Larry Milbourne, ss	4	1	1	0	0	0	.250
Rick Cerone, c	4	0	2	2	0	0	.500
TOTALS	40	5	13	4	1	3	.325

Brewers	AB	R	H	RBI	BB	K	Avg
Paul Molitor, rf	4	0	0	0	0	2	.000
Robin Yount, ss	2	1	1	1	1	0	.500
Cecil Cooper, 1b	3	0	1	0	1	1	.333
Ted Simmons, c	4	0	1	1	0	1	.250
Gorman Thomas, cf	4	0	0	0	0	2	.000
Ben Oglivie, lf	4	0	0	0	0	3	.000
Sal Bando, 3b	4	1	1	0	0	1	.250
Charlie Moore, dh	2	0	2	1	0	0	1.000
Roy Howell, ph-dh	2	0	1	0	0	1	.500
Jim Gantner, 2b	4	1	1	0	0	1	.250
TOTALS	33	3	8	3	2	12	.242

	1	2	3	4	5	6	7	8	9		R	H	E
Yankees	0	0	0	4	0	0	0	0	1		5	13	0
Brewers	0	1	1	0	1	0	0	0	0		3	8	2

E—Yount, Gantner. DP—Brewers 1 (Gantner to Cooper). LOB—Yankees 9, Brewers 7. Scoring Position—Yankees 1-for-11, Brewers 2-for-7. 2B—Gamble (1), Cerone 2 (2), Bando (1), Gantner (1). HR—Gamble (1). S—Molitor. SF—Yount. GDP—Nettles. SB—Mumphrey (1), Yount (1). CS—Mumphrey (1).

Yankees	IP	H	R	ER	BB	K	ERA
Ron Guidry	4.1	7	3	3	2	5	6.23
Ron Davis (W, 1-0)	2.2	0	0	0	0	4	0.00
Goose Gossage (S, 1)	2.0	1	0	0	0	3	0.00

Brewers	IP	H	R	ER	BB	K	ERA
Moose Haas (L, 0-1)	3.1	8	4	4	1	1	10.80
Dwight Bernard	0.2	0	0	0	0	0	0.00
Bob McClure	1.1	3	0	0	0	0	0.00
Jim Slaton	2.1	1	0	0	0	1	0.00
Rollie Fingers	1.1	1	1	0	0	1	0.00

Time—2:57. Attendance—35,064. Umpires—HP, McCoy. 1B, Ford. 2B, Kaiser. 3B, Phillips.

Game 2
Thursday, October 8

Yankees	AB	R	H	RBI	BB	K	Avg
Willie Randolph, 2b	4	0	2	0	0	0	.222
Jerry Mumphrey, cf	4	0	0	0	0	1	.222
Dave Winfield, lf	4	1	3	0	0	1	.444
Reggie Jackson, rf	4	1	1	2	0	0	.250
Lou Piniella, dh	4	1	1	1	0	0	.250
Graig Nettles, 3b	4	0	0	0	0	1	.000
Bob Watson, 1b	3	0	0	0	0	0	.429
Larry Milbourne, ss	3	0	0	0	0	0	.143
Rick Cerone, c	3	0	0	0	0	1	.286
TOTALS	33	3	7	3	0	4	.246

Brewers	AB	R	H	RBI	BB	K	Avg
Paul Molitor, rf	4	0	1	0	1	2	.125
Robin Yount, ss	5	0	0	0	0	2	.143
Cecil Cooper, 1b	4	0	1	0	0	1	.286
Ted Simmons, c	3	0	1	0	1	0	.286
Gorman Thomas, cf	3	0	0	0	1	3	.000
Ben Oglivie, lf	4	0	0	0	0	3	.000
Sal Bando, 3b	4	0	3	0	0	0	.500
Charlie Moore, dh	2	0	0	0	0	2	.500
Roy Howell, ph	0	0	0	0	1	0	.500
Thad Bosley, pr-dh	0	0	0	0	0	0	—
Don Money, ph	1	0	0	0	0	0	.000
Jim Gantner, 2b	4	0	1	0	0	1	.250
TOTALS	34	0	7	0	4	14	.224

	1	2	3	4	5	6	7	8	9		R	H	E
Yankees	0	0	0	1	0	0	0	0	2		3	7	0
Brewers	0	0	0	0	0	0	0	0	0		0	7	0

DP—Brewers 1 (Gantner to Yount to Cooper). LOB—Yankees 3, Brewers 11. Scoring Position—Yankees 1-for-2, Brewers 0-for-10. 2B—Winfield (1), Bando 2 (3). HR—Jackson (1), Piniella (1). GDP—Jackson.

Yankees	IP	H	R	ER	BB	K	ERA
Dave Righetti (W, 1-0)	6.0	4	0	0	2	10	0.00
Ron Davis (H, 1)	0.1	1	0	0	2	0	0.00
Goose Gossage (S, 2)	2.2	2	0	0	0	4	0.00

Brewers	IP	H	R	ER	BB	K	ERA
Mike Caldwell (L, 0-1)	8.1	7	3	3	0	4	3.24
Jim Slaton	0.2	0	0	0	0	0	0.00

WP—Davis. Time—2:35. Attendance—26,395. Umpires—HP, Ford. 1B, Kaiser. 2B, Phillips. 3B, Clark.

Game 3
Friday, October 9

Brewers	AB	R	H	RBI	BB	K	Avg
Paul Molitor, cf	4	1	3	1	0	0	.333
Robin Yount, ss	4	1	1	0	0	0	.182
Cecil Cooper, 1b	4	1	1	0	0	0	.273
Ted Simmons, c	3	1	2	3	1	0	.400
Gorman Thomas, dh	4	1	1	0	0	0	.091
Ben Oglivie, lf	3	0	0	0	0	0	.000
Sal Bando, 3b	4	0	1	1	0	0	.417
Charlie Moore, rf	2	0	0	0	1	0	.333
Marshall Edwards, pr-rf	1	0	0	0	0	1	.000
Jim Gantner, 2b	3	0	0	0	0	0	.182
TOTALS	32	5	9	5	2	1	.240

Yankees	AB	R	H	RBI	BB	K	Avg
Willie Randolph, 2b	5	0	1	1	0	2	.214
Jerry Mumphrey, cf	4	0	0	0	0	0	.154
Dave Winfield, lf	3	1	2	0	1	1	.500
Reggie Jackson, rf	4	0	0	0	0	2	.167
Lou Piniella, dh	3	0	0	0	0	0	.143
Oscar Gamble, ph-dh	1	0	1	0	0	0	.800
Graig Nettles, 3b	2	0	0	2	0	0	.000
Bob Watson, 1b	2	1	2	1	1	0	.556
Bobby Murcer, ph	1	0	0	0	0	0	.000
Dave Revering, 1b	0	0	0	0	0	0	—
Larry Milbourne, ss	4	1	1	0	0	1	.182
Rick Cerone, c	4	0	1	1	0	0	.273
TOTALS	33	3	8	3	4	6	.264

	1	2	3	4	5	6	7	8	9		R	H	E
Brewers	0	0	0	0	0	0	3	2	0		5	9	0
Yankees	0	0	0	1	0	0	2	0	0		3	8	2

E—Watson, May. DP—Brewers 1 (Lerch to Cooper to Yount), Yankees 1 (Randolph to Milbourne to Watson). LOB—Brewers 3, Yankees 7. Scoring Position—Brewers 2-for-5, Yankees 3-for-7. 2B—Simmons (1), Winfield (2). HR—Molitor (1), Simmons (1). S—Oglivie. GDP—Cooper, Piniella. CS—Bando (1), Nettles (1).

Brewers	IP	H	R	ER	BB	K	ERA
Randy Lerch	6.0	3	1	1	4	3	1.50
Rollie Fingers (BS, 1; W, 1-0)	3.0	5	2	2	0	3	4.15

Yankees	IP	H	R	ER	BB	K	ERA
Tommy John (L, 0-1)	7.0	8	5	5	2	0	6.43
Rudy May	2.0	1	0	0	0	1	0.00

John pitched to two batters in the 8th.

WP—May. Time—2:39. Attendance—54,171. Umpires—HP, Kaiser. 1B, Phillips. 2B, Clark. 3B, Reilly.

Game 4
Saturday, October 10

Brewers	AB	R	H	RBI	BB	K	Avg
Paul Molitor, rf	4	1	1	0	0	0	.313
Robin Yount, ss	3	1	1	0	1	0	.214
Cecil Cooper, 1b	3	0	0	1	0	1	.214
Ted Simmons, c	4	0	0	0	0	0	.286
Ben Oglivie, lf	3	0	1	1	0	0	.071
Gorman Thomas, cf	3	0	0	0	0	2	.071
Roy Howell, dh	3	0	1	0	0	1	.400
Sal Bando, 3b	3	0	0	0	0	1	.333
Jim Gantner, 2b	3	0	0	0	0	0	.143
TOTALS	29	2	4	2	1	5	.217

Yankees	AB	R	H	RBI	BB	K	Avg
Willie Randolph, 2b	3	0	0	0	1	1	.176
Jerry Mumphrey, cf	4	1	0	0	0	0	.118
Dave Winfield, lf	4	0	1	0	0	2	.438
Reggie Jackson, rf	4	0	1	0	0	2	.188
Oscar Gamble, dh	1	0	0	0	1	1	.667
Lou Piniella, ph-dh	2	0	0	1	0	0	.111
Graig Nettles, 3b	3	0	0	0	1	0	.000
Bob Watson, 1b	3	0	1	0	0	1	.500
Bobby Brown, pr	0	0	0	0	0	0	—
Dave Revering, 1b	0	0	0	0	0	0	—
Barry Foote, ph	0	0	0	0	0	0	—
Bobby Murcer, ph	0	0	0	0	1	0	.000
Larry Milbourne, ss	4	0	1	0	0	0	.200
Rick Cerone, c	4	0	1	0	0	1	.267
TOTALS	32	1	5	1	4	8	.239

	1	2	3	4	5	6	7	8	9		R	H	E
Brewers	0	0	0	2	0	0	0	0	0		2	4	2
Yankees	0	0	0	0	0	1	0	0	0		1	5	0

E—Cooper, Gantner. LOB—Brewers 2, Yankees 8. Scoring Position—Brewers 1-for-4, Yankees 0-for-7. 2B—Oglivie (1), Winfield (3). S—Cooper. CS—Howell (1).

Brewers	IP	H	R	ER	BB	K	ERA
Pete Vuckovich (W, 1-0)	5.0	2	1	0	3	4	0.00
Jamie Easterly (H, 1)	1.0	0	0	0	0	1	0.00
Jim Slaton (H, 1)	1.2	2	0	0	0	1	0.00
Bob McClure (H, 1)	1.0	0	0	0	0	1	0.00
Rollie Fingers (S, 1)	0.1	1	0	0	1	1	3.86

Yankees	IP	H	R	ER	BB	K	ERA
Rick Reuschel (L, 0-1)	6.0	4	2	2	1	3	3.00
Ron Davis	3.0	0	0	0	0	2	0.00

Vuckovich pitched to two batters in the 6th.

WP—Vuckovich. Time—2:34. Attendance—52,077. Umpires—HP, Phillips. 1B, Clark. 2B, Reilly. 3B, McCoy.

Game 5
Sunday, October 11

Brewers	AB	R	H	RBI	BB	K	Avg
Paul Molitor, cf	4	0	0	0	1	1	.250
Robin Yount, ss	5	1	3	0	0	0	.316
Cecil Cooper, 1b	4	0	1	2	0	0	.222
Ted Simmons, c	4	0	0	0	0	1	.222
Gorman Thomas, dh	4	1	1	1	0	2	.111
Ben Oglivie, lf	4	0	2	0	0	1	.167
Sal Bando, 3b	2	0	0	0	2	1	.294
Charlie Moore, rf	3	0	0	0	0	0	.222
Roy Howell, ph	0	0	0	0	1	0	.400
Marshall Edwards, pr-rf	0	0	0	0	0	0	.000
Ed Romero, 2b	2	1	1	0	0	1	.500
Don Money, ph-2b	2	0	0	0	0	0	.000
TOTALS	34	3	8	3	4	7	.230

Yankees	AB	R	H	RBI	BB	K	Avg
Jerry Mumphrey, cf	4	0	0	0	0	0	.095
Larry Milbourne, ss	4	2	3	0	0	0	.316
Dave Winfield, lf	4	0	0	0	0	0	.350
Reggie Jackson, rf	4	2	3	2	0	0	.300
Oscar Gamble, dh	3	1	1	1	0	1	.556
Lou Piniella, ph-dh	1	0	1	1	0	0	.200
Graig Nettles, 3b	3	1	1	1	0	0	.059
Bob Watson, 1b	4	0	1	0	0	0	.438
Rick Cerone, c	3	1	2	2	0	0	.333
Willie Randolph, 2b	3	0	1	0	0	0	.200
TOTALS	33	7	13	7	0	1	.271

	1	2	3	4	5	6	7	8	9		R	H	E
Brewers	0	1	1	0	0	0	1	0	0		3	8	0
Yankees	0	0	0	4	0	0	1	2	x		7	13	0

DP—Brewers 3 (Yount to Cooper; McClure to Cooper; Money to Cooper). LOB—Brewers 9, Yankees 3. Scoring Position—Brewers 2-for-5, Yankees 1-for-5. 2B—Milbourne (1), Piniella (1). 3B—Yount (1). HR—Thomas (1), Jackson (2), Gamble (2), Cerone (1). SF—Cooper, Nettles. GDP—Mumphrey.

Brewers	IP	H	R	ER	BB	K	ERA
Moose Haas (L, 0-2)	3.1	5	3	3	0	0	9.45
Mike Caldwell	0.0	2	1	1	0	0	4.32
Dwight Bernard	1.2	0	0	0	0	0	0.00
Bob McClure	1.0	1	0	0	0	1	0.00
Jim Slaton	1.1	3	2	2	0	0	3.00
Jamie Easterly	0.1	2	1	1	0	0	6.75
Pete Vuckovich	0.1	0	0	0	0	0	0.00

Yankees	IP	H	R	ER	BB	K	ERA
Ron Guidry	4.0	4	2	2	1	3	5.40
Dave Righetti (W, 2-0)	3.0	4	1	1	1	3	1.00
Goose Gossage (S, 3)	2.0	0	0	0	2	1	0.00

Caldwell pitched to two batters in the 4th.

Time—2:47. Attendance—47,505. Umpires—HP, Clark. 1B, Reilly. 2B, McCoy. 3B, Phillips.

1981 AL Eastern Division Series—Composite Statistics

Batting

Yankees	G	AB	R	H	RBI	2B	3B	HR	BB	SO	SB	CS	Avg	OBP	Slg
Bobby Brown	1	0	0	0	0	0	0	0	0	0	0	0	—	—	—
Rick Cerone	5	18	1	6	5	2	0	1	0	2	0	0	.333	.333	.611
Barry Foote	1	0	0	0	0	0	0	0	0	0	0	0	—	—	—
Oscar Gamble	4	9	2	5	3	1	0	2	1	2	0	0	.556	.600	1.333
Reggie Jackson	5	20	4	6	4	0	0	2	1	5	0	0	.300	.333	.600
Larry Milbourne	5	19	4	6	0	1	0	0	0	1	0	0	.316	.316	.368
Jerry Mumphrey	5	21	2	2	0	0	0	0	0	1	1	1	.095	.095	.095
Bobby Murcer	2	1	0	0	0	0	0	0	1	0	0	0	.000	.500	.000
Graig Nettles	5	17	1	1	1	0	0	0	3	1	0	1	.059	.190	.059
Lou Piniella	4	10	1	2	3	1	0	1	0	0	0	0	.200	.200	.600
Willie Randolph	5	20	0	4	1	0	0	0	4	0	0	0	.200	.238	.200
Bob Watson	5	16	2	7	1	0	0	0	1	0	0	0	.438	.471	.438
Dave Winfield	5	20	2	7	0	3	0	0	1	5	0	0	.350	.381	.500
Totals	5	171	19	46	18	8	0	6	9	22	1	2	.269	.304	.421

Brewers	G	AB	R	H	RBI	2B	3B	HR	BB	SO	SB	CS	Avg	OBP	Slg
Sal Bando	5	17	1	5	1	3	0	0	2	3	0	1	.294	.368	.471
Thad Bosley	1	0	0	0	0	0	0	0	0	0	0	0	—	—	—
Cecil Cooper	5	18	1	4	3	0	0	0	1	3	0	0	.222	.250	.222
Marshall Edwards	2	1	0	0	0	0	0	0	0	1	0	0	.000	.000	.000
Jim Gantner	4	14	1	2	0	1	0	0	0	2	0	0	.143	.143	.214
Roy Howell	4	5	0	2	0	0	0	0	2	2	0	1	.400	.571	.400
Paul Molitor	5	20	2	5	1	0	0	1	2	5	0	0	.250	.318	.400
Don Money	2	3	0	0	0	0	0	0	0	0	0	0	.000	.000	.000
Charlie Moore	4	9	0	2	1	0	0	0	1	2	0	0	.222	.300	.222
Ben Oglivie	5	18	0	3	1	1	0	0	0	7	0	0	.167	.167	.222
Ed Romero	1	2	1	1	0	0	0	0	0	1	0	0	.500	.500	.500
Ted Simmons	5	18	1	4	4	1	0	1	2	2	0	0	.222	.300	.444
Gorman Thomas	5	18	2	2	1	0	0	1	1	9	0	0	.111	.158	.278
Robin Yount	5	19	4	6	1	0	1	0	2	2	1	0	.316	.364	.421
Totals	5	162	13	36	13	6	1	3	13	39	1	2	.222	.277	.327

Pitching

Yankees	G	GS	CG	IP	H	R	ER	BB	SO	W-L	Sv-Op	Hld	ERA
Ron Davis	3	0	0	6.0	1	0	0	2	6	1-0	0-0	1	0.00
Goose Gossage	3	0	0	6.2	3	0	0	2	8	0-0	3-3	0	0.00
Ron Guidry	2	2	0	8.1	11	5	5	3	8	0-0	0-0	0	5.40
Tommy John	1	1	0	7.0	8	5	5	2	0	0-1	0-0	0	6.43
Rudy May	1	0	0	2.0	1	0	0	0	1	0-0	0-0	0	0.00
Rick Reuschel	1	1	0	6.0	4	2	2	1	3	0-1	0-0	0	3.00
Dave Righetti	2	1	0	9.0	8	1	1	3	13	2-0	0-0	0	1.00
Totals	5	5	0	45.0	36	13	13	13	39	3-2	3-3	1	2.60

Brewers	G	GS	CG	IP	H	R	ER	BB	SO	W-L	Sv-Op	Hld	ERA
Dwight Bernard	2	0	0	2.1	0	0	0	0	0	0-0	0-0	0	0.00
Mike Caldwell	2	1	0	8.1	9	4	4	0	4	0-1	0-0	0	4.32
Jamie Easterly	2	0	0	1.1	2	1	1	0	1	0-0	0-0	1	6.75
Rollie Fingers	3	0	0	4.2	7	3	2	1	5	1-0	1-2	0	3.86
Moose Haas	2	2	0	6.2	13	7	7	1	1	0-2	0-0	0	9.45
Randy Lerch	1	1	0	6.0	3	1	1	4	3	0-0	0-0	0	1.50
Bob McClure	3	0	0	3.1	4	0	0	0	2	0-0	0-0	1	0.00
Jim Slaton	4	0	0	6.0	6	2	2	0	2	0-0	0-0	1	3.00
Pete Vuckovich	2	1	0	5.1	2	1	0	3	4	1-0	0-0	0	0.00
Totals	5	5	0	44.0	46	19	17	9	22	2-3	1-2	3	3.48

Fielding

Yankees	Pos	G	PO	Ast	E	DP	PB	FPct
Rick Cerone	c	5	42	1	0	0	0	1.000
Ron Davis	p	3	1	0	0	0	—	1.000
Goose Gossage	p	3	0	0	0	0	—	—
Ron Guidry	p	2	0	0	0	0	—	—
Reggie Jackson	rf	5	7	0	0	0	—	1.000
Tommy John	p	1	0	3	0	0	—	1.000
Rudy May	p	1	1	0	1	0	—	.500
Larry Milbourne	ss	5	5	14	0	1	—	1.000
Jerry Mumphrey	cf	5	15	1	0	0	—	1.000
Graig Nettles	3b	5	8	7	0	0	—	1.000
Willie Randolph	2b	5	9	9	0	1	—	1.000
Rick Reuschel	p	1	1	2	0	0	—	1.000
Dave Revering	1b	2	3	0	0	0	—	1.000
Dave Righetti	p	2	0	1	0	0	—	1.000
Bob Watson	1b	5	34	4	1	1	—	.974
Dave Winfield	lf	5	9	1	0	0	—	1.000
Totals		5	135	43	2	3	0	.989

Brewers	Pos	G	PO	Ast	E	DP	PB	FPct
Sal Bando	3b	5	3	5	0	0	—	1.000
Dwight Bernard	p	2	0	0	0	0	—	—
Mike Caldwell	p	2	0	3	0	0	—	1.000
Cecil Cooper	1b	5	47	4	1	6	—	.981
Jamie Easterly	p	2	0	0	0	0	—	—
Marshall Edwards	rf	2	0	0	0	0	—	—
Rollie Fingers	p	3	0	0	0	0	—	—
Jim Gantner	2b	4	3	14	2	2	—	.895
Moose Haas	p	2	2	0	0	0	—	1.000
Randy Lerch	p	1	0	1	0	1	—	1.000
Bob McClure	p	3	1	1	0	1	—	1.000
Paul Molitor	rf	3	6	0	0	0	—	1.000
	cf	2	5	0	0	0	—	1.000
Don Money	2b	1	1	1	0	1	—	1.000
Charlie Moore	rf	2	7	0	0	0	—	1.000
Ben Oglivie	lf	5	13	1	0	0	—	1.000
Ed Romero	2b	1	2	2	0	0	—	1.000
Ted Simmons	c	5	23	2	0	0	0	1.000
Jim Slaton	p	4	0	0	0	0	—	—
Gorman Thomas	cf	3	12	0	0	0	—	1.000
Pete Vuckovich	p	2	0	1	0	0	—	1.000
Robin Yount	ss	5	7	23	1	3	—	.968
Totals		5	132	58	4	14	0	.979

1981 Oakland Athletics (AL) 3, Kansas City Royals (AL) 0

The Oakland A's, a team built around excellent starting pitching, got three superb performances from their starters en route to a three-game sweep of the Kansas City Royals. Mike Norris tossed a four-hit shutout in Game 1, as Wayne Gross blasted a three-run homer in the A's 4-0 win. Steve McCatty went the distance in Game 2, beating Mike Jones 2-1. Tony Armas doubled in the A's first run in the top of the first, and plated the eventual winning run in the top of the eighth with another RBI double. It was Rick Langford's turn in Game 3. He allowed 10 hits in 7.1 innings, but held the Royals to one run for a 4-1 victory. Rickey Henderson went 2-for-2 and scored three of Oakland's runs in the clincher.

Game 1
Tuesday, October 6

Athletics	AB	R	H	RBI	BB	K	Avg
Rickey Henderson, lf	4	0	0	0	0	0	.000
Dwayne Murphy, cf	3	2	2	1	1	0	.667
Keith Drumright, dh	4	0	1	0	0	0	.250
Tony Armas, rf	4	1	1	0	0	1	.250
Wayne Gross, 3b	4	1	2	3	0	0	.500
Jim Spencer, 1b	4	0	1	0	0	0	.250
Mike Heath, c	4	0	0	0	0	1	.000
Dave McKay, 2b	4	0	1	0	0	0	.250
Fred Stanley, ss	4	0	0	0	0	1	.000
TOTALS	35	4	8	4	1	3	.229

Royals	AB	R	H	RBI	BB	K	Avg
Willie Wilson, lf	4	0	1	0	0	0	.250
Frank White, 2b	3	0	0	0	1	0	.000
George Brett, 3b	4	0	0	0	0	0	.000
Willie Aikens, 1b	4	0	1	0	0	1	.250
Amos Otis, cf	4	0	0	0	0	1	.000
Hal McRae, dh	4	0	0	0	0	0	.000
Clint Hurdle, rf	3	0	1	0	1	0	.333
John Wathan, c	2	0	0	0	1	0	.000
U.L. Washington, ss	3	0	1	0	0	0	.333
TOTALS	31	0	4	0	3	2	.129

	1	2	3	4	5	6	7	8	9	R	H	E
Athletics	0	0	0	3	0	0	0	1	0	4	8	2
Royals	0	0	0	0	0	0	0	0	0	0	4	1

E—Brett, McKay, Norris. DP—Athletics 2 (Gross to McKay to Spencer; Gross to McKay), Royals 1 (White to Washington to Aikens). LOB—Athletics 5, Royals 7. Scoring Position—Athletics 1-for-5, Royals 2-for-9. 2B—Spencer (1). HR—Murphy (1), Gross (1). GDP—Drumright, Otis.

Athletics	IP	H	R	ER	BB	K	ERA
Mike Norris (W, 1-0)	9.0	4	0	0	3	2	0.00

Royals	IP	H	R	ER	BB	K	ERA
Dennis Leonard (L, 0-1)	8.0	7	4	1	1	3	1.13
Renie Martin	1.0	1	0	0	0	0	0.00

Time—2:35. Attendance—40,592. Umpires—HP, Maloney. 1B, Brinkman. 2B, Palermo. 3B, Denkinger.

Game 2
Wednesday, October 7

Athletics	AB	R	H	RBI	BB	K	Avg
Rickey Henderson, lf	5	0	0	0	0	0	.000
Dwayne Murphy, cf	4	2	2	0	0	0	.571
Cliff Johnson, dh	3	0	1	0	0	0	.333
Tony Armas, rf	4	0	4	2	0	0	.625
Rick Bosetti, pr-rf	0	0	0	0	0	0	—
Mickey Klutts, 3b	3	0	1	0	0	0	.333
Kelvin Moore, 1b	4	0	0	0	0	1	.000
Dave McKay, 2b	4	0	1	0	0	0	.250
Jeff Newman, c	3	0	0	0	0	1	.000
Rob Picciolo, ss	3	0	1	0	0	0	.333
Wayne Gross, ph	1	0	0	0	0	0	.400
Fred Stanley, ss	0	0	0	0	0	0	.000
TOTALS	34	2	10	2	0	2	.281

Royals	AB	R	H	RBI	BB	K	Avg
Willie Wilson, lf	5	0	1	1	0	0	.222
Frank White, 2b	4	0	0	0	0	0	.000
George Brett, 3b	4	0	1	0	0	0	.125
Willie Aikens, 1b	1	0	0	0	3	0	.200
Cesar Geronimo, pr	0	0	0	0	0	0	—
Lee May, 1b	0	0	0	0	0	0	—
Amos Otis, cf	4	0	0	0	0	2	.000
Hal McRae, dh	3	0	0	0	1	0	.000
Clint Hurdle, rf	4	0	1	0	0	0	.286
John Wathan, c	4	1	2	0	0	0	.333
U.L. Washington, ss	3	0	1	0	0	1	.333
TOTALS	32	1	6	1	4	3	.159

	1	2	3	4	5	6	7	8	9	R	H	E
Athletics	1	0	0	0	0	0	0	1	0	2	10	1
Royals	0	0	0	0	1	0	0	0	0	1	6	0

E—Armas. LOB—Athletics 8, Royals 9. Scoring Position—Athletics 2-for-13, Royals 1-for-10. 2B—Johnson (1), Armas 2 (2). S—Johnson, Klutts, Newman, Washington. SB—Henderson (1).

Athletics	IP	H	R	ER	BB	K	ERA
Steve McCatty (W, 1-0)	9.0	6	1	1	4	3	1.00

Royals	IP	H	R	ER	BB	K	ERA
Mike Jones (L, 0-1)	8.0	9	2	2	0	2	2.25
Dan Quisenberry	1.0	1	0	0	0	0	0.00

Time—2:50. Attendance—40,274. Umpires—HP, Brinkman. 1B, Palermo. 2B, Denkinger. 3B, Evans.

Game 3
Friday, October 9

Royals	AB	R	H	RBI	BB	K	Avg
Willie Wilson, lf	4	0	2	0	0	0	.308
Frank White, 2b	4	1	2	0	0	1	.182
George Brett, 3b	4	0	1	0	0	0	.167
Willie Aikens, 1b	4	0	2	0	0	1	.333
Amos Otis, cf	4	0	0	1	0	1	.000
Hal McRae, dh	4	0	1	0	0	1	.091
Clint Hurdle, rf	4	0	1	0	0	1	.273
John Wathan, c	4	0	1	0	0	1	.300
U.L. Washington, ss	3	0	0	0	0	0	.222
TOTALS	35	1	10	1	0	6	.204

Athletics	AB	R	H	RBI	BB	K	Avg
Rickey Henderson, lf	2	3	2	0	2	0	.182
Dwayne Murphy, cf	4	0	2	1	0	1	.545
Cliff Johnson, dh	4	0	1	0	0	1	.286
Tony Armas, rf	3	0	1	1	1	0	.545
Mickey Klutts, 3b	4	0	0	0	0	1	.143
Kelvin Moore, 1b	4	0	0	0	0	1	.000
Mike Heath, c	4	0	0	0	0	0	.000
Dave McKay, 2b	3	1	1	1	1	1	.273
Fred Stanley, ss	2	0	0	0	1	0	.000
TOTALS	30	4	7	3	5	5	.250

	1	2	3	4	5	6	7	8	9	R	H	E
Royals	0	0	0	1	0	0	0	0	0	1	10	3
Athletics	1	0	1	2	0	0	0	0	x	4	7	0

E—Washington, Wathan, White. DP—Athletics 1 (Klutts to McKay to Moore). LOB—Royals 7, Athletics 7. Scoring Position—Royals 1-for-6, Athletics 3-for-7. 2B—McRae (1), Murphy (1). HR—McKay (1). GDP—Otis. SB—Henderson (2). CS—Hurdle (1), Murphy (1).

Royals	IP	H	R	ER	BB	K	ERA
Larry Gura (L, 0-1)	3.2	7	4	3	3	3	7.36
Renie Martin	4.1	0	0	0	2	2	0.00

Athletics	IP	H	R	ER	BB	K	ERA
Rick Langford (W, 1-0)	7.1	10	1	1	0	3	1.23
Tom Underwood (H, 1)	0.1	0	0	0	0	1	0.00
Dave Beard (S, 1)	1.1	0	0	0	0	2	0.00

Time—2:59. Attendance—40,002. Umpires—HP, Palermo. 1B, Denkinger. 2B, Evans. 3B, McKean.

1981 AL Western Division Series—Composite Statistics

Batting

Athletics	G	AB	R	H	RBI	2B	3B	HR	BB	SO	SB	CS	Avg	OBP	Slg
Tony Armas	3	11	1	6	3	2	0	0	1	1	0	0	.545	.583	.727
Keith Drumright	1	4	0	1	0	0	0	0	0	0	0	0	.250	.250	.250
Wayne Gross	2	5	1	2	3	0	0	1	0	0	0	0	.400	.400	1.000
Mike Heath	2	8	0	0	0	0	0	0	0	1	0	0	.000	.000	.000
Rickey Henderson	3	11	3	2	0	0	0	0	2	0	2	0	.182	.308	.182
Cliff Johnson	2	7	0	2	0	1	0	0	0	1	0	0	.286	.286	.429
Mickey Klutts	2	7	0	1	0	0	0	0	0	1	0	0	.143	.143	.143
Dave McKay	3	11	1	3	1	0	0	1	1	1	0	0	.273	.333	.545
Kelvin Moore	2	8	0	0	0	0	0	0	0	2	0	0	.000	.000	.000
Dwayne Murphy	3	11	4	6	2	1	0	1	1	1	0	1	.545	.583	.909
Jeff Newman	1	3	0	0	0	0	0	0	0	1	0	0	.000	.000	.000
Rob Picciolo	1	3	0	1	0	0	0	0	0	0	0	0	.333	.333	.333
Jim Spencer	1	4	0	1	0	1	0	0	0	0	0	0	.250	.250	.500
Fred Stanley	3	6	0	0	0	0	0	0	1	1	0	0	.000	.143	.000
Totals	**3**	**99**	**10**	**25**	**9**	**5**	**0**	**3**	**6**	**10**	**2**	**1**	**.253**	**.295**	**.394**

Batting

Royals	G	AB	R	H	RBI	2B	3B	HR	BB	SO	SB	CS	Avg	OBP	Slg
Willie Aikens	3	9	0	3	0	0	0	0	3	2	0	0	.333	.500	.333
George Brett	3	12	0	2	0	0	0	0	0	0	0	0	.167	.167	.167
Cesar Geronimo	1	0	0	0	0	0	0	0	0	0	0	0	—	—	—
Clint Hurdle	3	11	0	3	0	0	0	0	1	1	0	1	.273	.333	.273
Hal McRae	3	11	0	1	0	1	0	0	1	1	0	0	.091	.167	.182
Amos Otis	3	12	0	0	1	0	0	0	0	4	0	0	.000	.000	.000
U.L. Washington	3	9	0	2	0	0	0	0	0	1	0	0	.222	.222	.222
John Wathan	3	10	1	3	0	0	0	0	1	1	0	0	.300	.364	.300
Frank White	3	11	1	2	0	0	0	0	1	1	0	0	.182	.250	.182
Willie Wilson	3	13	0	4	1	0	0	0	0	0	0	0	.308	.308	.308
Totals	**3**	**98**	**2**	**20**	**2**	**1**	**0**	**0**	**7**	**11**	**0**	**1**	**.204**	**.257**	**.214**

Pitching

Athletics	G	GS	CG	IP	H	R	ER	BB	SO	W-L	Sv-Op	Hld	ERA
Dave Beard	1	0	0	1.1	0	0	0	0	2	0-0	1-1	0	0.00
Rick Langford	1	1	0	7.1	10	1	1	0	3	1-0	0-0	0	1.23
Steve McCatty	1	1	1	9.0	6	1	1	4	3	1-0	0-0	0	1.00
Mike Norris	1	1	1	9.0	4	0	0	3	2	1-0	0-0	0	1.00
Tom Underwood	1	0	0	0.1	0	0	0	0	1	0-0	0-0	1	0.00
Totals	**3**	**3**	**2**	**27.0**	**20**	**2**	**2**	**7**	**11**	**3-0**	**1-1**	**1**	**0.67**

Pitching

Royals	G	GS	CG	IP	H	R	ER	BB	SO	W-L	Sv-Op	Hld	ERA
Larry Gura	1	1	0	3.2	7	4	3	3	3	0-1	0-0	0	7.36
Mike Jones	1	1	0	8.0	9	2	2	0	2	0-1	0-0	0	2.25
Dennis Leonard	1	1	0	8.0	7	4	1	1	3	0-1	0-0	0	1.13
Renie Martin	2	0	0	5.1	1	0	0	2	2	0-0	0-0	0	0.00
Dan Quisenberry	1	0	0	1.0	1	0	0	0	0	0-0	0-0	0	0.00
Totals	**3**	**3**	**0**	**26.0**	**25**	**10**	**6**	**6**	**10**	**0-3**	**0-0**	**0**	**2.08**

Fielding

Athletics	Pos	G	PO	Ast	E	DP	PB	FPct
Tony Armas	rf	3	6	0	1	0	—	.857
Dave Beard	p	1	0	0	0	0	—	—
Rick Bosetti	rf	1	0	0	0	0	—	—
Wayne Gross	3b	1	1	4	0	2	—	1.000
Mike Heath	c	2	9	1	0	0	0	1.000
Rickey Henderson	lf	3	8	0	0	0	—	1.000
Mickey Klutts	3b	2	0	2	0	1	—	1.000
Rick Langford	p	1	2	2	0	0	—	1.000
Steve McCatty	p	1	0	4	0	0	—	1.000
Dave McKay	2b	3	8	6	1	3	—	.933
Kelvin Moore	1b	2	14	1	0	1	—	1.000
Dwayne Murphy	cf	3	13	0	0	0	—	1.000
Jeff Newman	c	1	4	0	0	0	0	1.000
Mike Norris	p	1	2	1	1	0	—	.750
Rob Picciolo	ss	1	1	2	0	0	—	1.000
Jim Spencer	1b	1	6	2	0	1	—	1.000
Fred Stanley	ss	3	7	4	0	0	—	1.000
Tom Underwood	p	1	0	0	0	0	—	—
Totals		**3**	**81**	**29**	**3**	**8**	**0**	**.973**

Fielding

Royals	Pos	G	PO	Ast	E	DP	PB	FPct
Willie Aikens	1b	3	28	1	0	1	—	1.000
George Brett	3b	3	1	6	1	0	—	.875
Larry Gura	p	1	0	0	0	0	—	—
Clint Hurdle	rf	3	6	0	0	0	—	1.000
Mike Jones	p	1	0	0	0	0	—	—
Dennis Leonard	p	1	0	1	0	0	—	1.000
Renie Martin	p	2	1	0	0	0	—	1.000
Lee May	1b	1	2	0	0	0	—	1.000
Amos Otis	cf	3	12	0	0	0	—	1.000
Dan Quisenberry	p	1	0	0	0	0	—	—
U.L. Washington	ss	3	6	11	1	1	—	.944
John Wathan	c	3	11	3	1	0	0	.933
Frank White	2b	3	5	6	1	1	—	.917
Willie Wilson	lf	3	6	0	0	0	—	1.000
Totals		**3**	**78**	**28**	**4**	**3**	**0**	**.964**

1981 Montreal Expos (NL) 3, Philadelphia Phillies (NL) 2

The Montreal Expos beat Steve Carlton in Games 1 and 5, taking the NL East title from the Philadelphia Phillies in five games. Steve Rogers defeated Carlton 3-1 in Game 1, and Bill Gullickson downed Dick Ruthven by the same score in Game 2. The Phillies battled back to take the third game, 6-2, and won Game 4, 6-5, on a pinch-hit home run by George Vuckovich in the bottom of the 10th off Jeff Reardon. Rogers and Carlton were back on the hill for the fifth and deciding game. Once again, Rogers came out on top, tossing a six-hit shutout and driving in two runs in Montreal's 3-0 victory. Gary Carter batted .421 with six RBI in the series.

Game 1

Wednesday, October 7

Phillies	AB	R	H	RBI	BB	K	Avg
Lonnie Smith, cf	4	0	2	0	0	1	.500
Pete Rose, 1b	4	0	2	0	0	0	.500
Gary Matthews, lf	4	0	1	0	0	1	.250
Mike Schmidt, 3b	3	0	0	0	1	1	.000
Bake McBride, rf	4	0	0	0	0	1	.000
Keith Moreland, c	4	1	3	1	0	0	.750
Luis Aguayo, pr	0	0	0	0	0	0	—
Larry Bowa, ss	3	0	0	0	0	0	.000
George Vukovich, ph	1	0	1	0	0	0	1.000
Manny Trillo, 2b	3	0	0	0	1	0	.000
Steve Carlton, p	2	0	1	0	0	0	.500
Greg Gross, ph	1	0	0	0	0	0	.000
Ron Reed, p	0	0	0	0	0	0	—
TOTALS	33	1	10	1	2	3	.303

Expos	AB	R	H	RBI	BB	K	Avg
Warren Cromartie, 1b	5	0	2	1	0	2	.400
Jerry White, lf-rf	4	1	1	0	0	0	.250
Andre Dawson, cf	4	0	2	0	0	0	.500
Gary Carter, c	3	0	1	1	1	0	.333
Larry Parrish, 3b	3	0	0	0	1	2	.000
Tim Wallach, rf	2	1	1	0	1	0	.500
Terry Francona, lf	0	0	0	0	1	0	—
Jerry Manuel, 2b	4	0	0	0	0	2	.000
Chris Speier, ss	1	1	1	1	3	0	1.000
Steve Rogers, p	2	0	0	0	0	1	.000
Jeff Reardon, p	0	0	0	0	0	0	—
TOTALS	28	3	8	3	7	9	.286

	1	2	3	4	5	6	7	8	9		R	H	E
Phillies	0	1	0	0	0	0	0	0	0		1	10	1
Expos	1	1	0	1	0	0	0	0	x		3	8	0

E—Moreland. DP—Expos 2 (Manuel to Speier to Cromartie; Speier to Manuel to Cromartie). LOB—Phillies 7, Expos 10. Scoring Position—Phillies 1-for-5, Expos 3-for-19. 2B—Rose (1), Cromartie (1), Carter (1), Wallach (1), Speier (1). 3B—Matthews (1), Dawson (1). HR—Moreland (1). S—Rogers 2. GDP—Rose, Matthews. SB—White 2 (2), Dawson (1), Francona (1). CS—Smith (1), White (1), Rogers (1).

Phillies	IP	H	R	ER	BB	K	ERA
Steve Carlton (L, 0-1)	6.0	7	3	3	5	6	4.50
Ron Reed	2.0	1	0	0	2	3	0.00

Expos	IP	H	R	ER	BB	K	ERA
Steve Rogers (W, 1-0)	8.2	10	1	1	2	3	1.04
Jeff Reardon (S, 1)	0.1	0	0	0	0	0	0.00

WP—Carlton, Reed. Time—2:30. Attendance—34,327. Umpires—HP, Tata. 1B, Pulli. 2B, Froemming. 3B, CWilliams.

Game 2

Thursday, October 8

Phillies	AB	R	H	RBI	BB	K	Avg
Lonnie Smith, cf	4	1	2	0	0	1	.500
Pete Rose, 1b	4	0	1	1	0	0	.375
Bake McBride, rf	4	0	2	0	0	0	.250
Mike Schmidt, 3b	3	0	0	0	1	0	.000
Gary Matthews, lf	4	0	1	0	0	1	.250
Tug McGraw, p	0	0	0	0	0	0	—
Keith Moreland, c	3	0	0	0	1	1	.429
Larry Bowa, ss	4	0	0	0	0	0	.000
Manny Trillo, 2b	4	0	0	0	0	0	.000
Dick Ruthven, p	1	0	0	0	0	0	.000
Greg Gross, ph	1	0	0	0	0	0	.000
Warren Brusstar, p	0	0	0	0	0	0	—
Sparky Lyle, p	0	0	0	0	0	0	—
George Vukovich, ph-lf	1	0	0	0	0	1	.500
TOTALS	33	1	6	1	2	4	.234

Expos	AB	R	H	RBI	BB	K	Avg
Warren Cromartie, 1b	4	1	2	0	0	1	.444
Jerry White, rf	3	0	0	0	1	0	.143
Andre Dawson, cf	4	0	1	0	0	0	.375
Gary Carter, c	4	1	1	2	0	0	.286
Larry Parrish, 3b	4	1	0	0	0	0	.000
Terry Francona, lf	3	0	2	0	1	0	.667
Chris Speier, ss	2	0	1	1	1	0	.667
Jerry Manuel, 2b	3	0	0	0	0	0	.000
Bill Gullickson, p	3	0	0	0	1	1	.000
Jeff Reardon, p	0	0	0	0	0	0	—
TOTALS	30	3	7	3	3	2	.259

	1	2	3	4	5	6	7	8	9		R	H	E
Phillies	0	0	0	0	0	0	0	1	0		1	6	2
Expos	0	1	2	0	0	0	0	0	x		3	7	0

E—Bowa, Schmidt. LOB—Phillies 7, Expos 6. Scoring Position—Phillies 1-for-2, Expos 3-for-8. 2B—Smith (1), McBride (1), Cromartie (2). HR—Carter (1). SB—White (3), Francona (2). CS—Cromartie (1).

Phillies	IP	H	R	ER	BB	K	ERA
Dick Ruthven (L, 0-1)	4.0	3	3	2	1	0	4.50
Warren Brusstar	2.0	2	0	0	1	2	0.00
Sparky Lyle	1.0	1	0	0	1	0	0.00
Tug McGraw	1.0	1	0	0	0	0	0.00

Expos	IP	H	R	ER	BB	K	ERA
Bill Gullickson (W, 1-0)	7.2	6	1	1	1	3	1.17
Jeff Reardon (S, 2)	1.1	0	0	0	1	1	0.00

Time—2:31. Attendance—45,896. Umpires—HP, Pulli. 1B, Froemming. 2B, CWilliams. 3B, Kibler.

Game 3

Friday, October 9

Expos	AB	R	H	RBI	BB	K	Avg
Warren Cromartie, 1b	4	0	1	0	0	1	.385
Jerry White, rf	4	1	1	0	0	1	.182
Andre Dawson, cf	3	0	1	0	1	1	.364
Gary Carter, c	3	1	2	1	0	0	.400
Larry Parrish, 3b	4	0	0	0	0	0	.000
Terry Francona, lf	4	0	1	0	0	1	.429
Chris Speier, ss	4	0	2	1	0	1	.571
Jerry Manuel, 2b	3	0	0	0	0	1	.000
Wallace Johnson, ph	1	0	0	0	0	0	.000
Ray Burris, p	2	0	0	0	0	2	.000
Bill Lee, p	0	0	0	0	0	0	—
Tim Wallach, ph	0	0	0	0	1	0	.500
Elias Sosa, p	0	0	0	0	0	0	—
John Milner, ph	1	0	0	0	0	0	.000
TOTALS	33	2	8	2	2	8	.267

Phillies	AB	R	H	RBI	BB	K	Avg
Lonnie Smith, cf	4	0	0	0	0	0	.333
Bob Boone, c	1	0	0	0	0	0	.000
Pete Rose, 1b	4	0	1	1	1	0	.333
Bake McBride, rf	4	0	0	0	0	3	.167
Sparky Lyle, p	0	0	0	0	0	0	—
Greg Gross, lf	1	0	0	0	0	0	.000
Mike Schmidt, 3b	3	1	2	0	1	0	.222
Gary Matthews, lf	4	2	3	0	0	1	.417
Ron Reed, p	0	0	0	0	0	0	—
Keith Moreland, c	3	1	2	0	0	0	.500
Luis Aguayo, pr	0	1	0	0	0	0	—
Garry Maddox, cf	1	0	0	0	0	0	.000
Larry Bowa, ss	3	0	2	1	0	0	.200
Manny Trillo, 2b	2	1	1	1	2	0	.111
Larry Christenson, p	2	0	0	0	0	1	.000
George Vukovich, ph-rf	2	0	2	1	0	0	.750
TOTALS	34	6	13	4	4	5	.289

	1	2	3	4	5	6	7	8	9		R	H	E
Expos	0	1	0	0	0	0	0	1	0		2	8	4
Phillies	0	2	0	0	0	2	2	0	x		6	13	0

E—Cromartie, Dawson, Manuel, Sosa. DP—Expos 2 (Parrish to Manuel; Manuel to Speier to Cromartie), Phillies 1 (Schmidt to Trillo). LOB—Expos 7, Phillies 9. Scoring Position—Expos 2-for-7, Phillies 5-for-15. 2B—White (1), Carter (2), Schmidt (1), Bowa (1). S—Bowa. SF—Carter. GDP—Manuel, Gross. CS—Bowa (1), Boone (1).

Expos	IP	H	R	ER	BB	K	ERA
Ray Burris (L, 0-1)	5.1	7	4	3	4	4	5.06
Bill Lee	0.2	2	0	0	0	1	0.00
Elias Sosa	2.0	4	2	1	0	0	4.50

Phillies	IP	H	R	ER	BB	K	ERA
Larry Christenson (W, 1-0)	6.0	4	1	1	1	8	1.50
Sparky Lyle (H, 1)	1.0	2	0	0	0	1	0.00
Ron Reed	2.0	2	1	1	0	0	2.25

Time—2:45. Attendance—36,835. Umpires—HP, Froemming. 1B, CWilliams. 2B, Kibler. 3B, Crawford.

Game 4
Saturday, October 10

Expos	AB	R	H	RBI	BB	K	Avg
Warren Cromartie, 1b	5	0	0	0	0	2	.278
Jerry White, rf-lf	3	1	0	1	1	0	.143
Andre Dawson, cf	5	0	1	0	0	1	.313
Gary Carter, c	5	1	3	2	0	1	.467
Larry Parrish, 3b	5	1	1	0	0	1	.063
Terry Francona, lf	4	0	0	0	0	1	.273
Jeff Reardon, p	1	0	0	0	0	1	.000
Chris Speier, ss	4	2	2	0	0	1	.545
Jerry Manuel, 2b	1	0	1	0	1	0	.091
John Milner, ph	1	0	1	1	0	0	.500
Mike Phillips, pr-2b	1	0	0	0	0	0	.000
Scott Sanderson, p	1	0	0	0	0	1	.000
Stan Bahnsen, p	0	0	0	0	0	0	—
Brad Mills, ph	0	0	0	0	1	0	—
Elias Sosa, p	0	0	0	0	0	0	—
Wallace Johnson, ph	1	0	1	1	0	0	.500
Woodie Fryman, p	0	0	0	0	0	0	—
Tim Wallach, rf	1	0	0	0	0	0	.333
TOTALS	38	5	10	5	3	9	.270

Phillies	AB	R	H	RBI	BB	K	Avg
Lonnie Smith, cf	3	0	0	0	0	2	.267
Garry Maddox, cf	2	0	1	0	0	0	.333
Pete Rose, 1b	5	1	1	0	0	0	.294
Bake McBride, rf	3	1	1	0	0	1	.200
Ron Reed, p	0	0	0	0	0	0	—
Ramon Aviles, ph	0	0	0	0	1	0	—
Tug McGraw, p	0	0	0	0	0	0	—
George Vukovich, ph	1	1	1	1	0	0	.800
Mike Schmidt, 3b	3	2	1	2	1	1	.250
Gary Matthews, lf	4	1	2	1	0	0	.438
Keith Moreland, c	3	0	1	2	0	0	.462
Bob Boone, c	1	0	0	0	0	0	.000
Larry Bowa, ss	4	0	1	0	0	0	.214
Manny Trillo, 2b	3	0	0	0	1	0	.083
Dickie Noles, p	0	0	0	0	1	0	—
Warren Brusstar, p	0	0	0	0	0	0	—
Sparky Lyle, p	0	0	0	0	0	0	—
Dick Davis, ph-rf	2	0	0	0	0	1	.000
TOTALS	34	6	9	6	4	5	.294

	1	2	3	4	5	6	7	8	9	10		R	H	E
Expos	0	0	0	1	1	2	1	0	0	0		5	10	1
Phillies	2	0	2	0	0	1	0	0	0	1		6	9	0

E—Manuel. DP—Phillies 1 (McGraw to Trillo to Bowa). LOB—Expos 7, Phillies 6. Scoring Position—Expos 2-for-8, Phillies 1-for-6. 2B—Carter (3), Speier (2), Maddox (1). HR—Carter (2), Schmidt (1), Matthews (1), Vukovich (1). S—Noles. SF—White. SB—Dawson (2). CS—Moreland (1).

Expos	IP	H	R	ER	BB	K	ERA
Scott Sanderson	2.2	4	4	2	2	2	6.75
Stan Bahnsen	1.1	1	0	0	1	1	0.00
Elias Sosa	1.0	0	0	0	0	1	3.00
Woodie Fryman	1.1	3	1	1	1	0	6.75
Jeff Reardon (L, 0-1)	2.2	1	1	1	0	1	2.08

Phillies	IP	H	R	ER	BB	K	ERA
Dickie Noles	4.0	4	2	2	2	5	4.50
Warren Brusstar	1.2	3	2	2	0	1	4.91
Sparky Lyle (BS, 1)	0.1	1	0	0	0	1	0.00
Ron Reed (BS, 1)	1.0	1	1	1	1	0	3.60
Tug McGraw (W, 1-0)	3.0	1	0	0	0	2	0.00

Noles pitched to three batters in the 5th. Reardon pitched to one batter in the 10th.

Time—2:48. Attendance—38,818. Umpires—HP, CWilliams. 1B, Kibler. 2B, Crawford. 3B, Tata.

Game 5
Sunday, October 11

Expos	AB	R	H	RBI	BB	K	Avg
Warren Cromartie, 1b	4	0	0	0	0	3	.227
Jerry White, lf-rf	4	0	1	0	0	1	.167
Andre Dawson, cf	4	1	1	0	0	2	.300
Gary Carter, c	4	0	1	0	0	0	.421
Larry Parrish, 3b	4	1	2	1	0	0	.150
Tim Wallach, rf	1	0	0	0	2	0	.250
Terry Francona, lf	1	0	1	0	0	0	.333
Chris Speier, ss	4	1	0	0	0	0	.400
Jerry Manuel, 2b	3	0	0	0	1	2	.071
Steve Rogers, p	3	0	2	2	0	0	.400
TOTALS	32	3	8	3	3	8	.262

Phillies	AB	R	H	RBI	BB	K	Avg
Lonnie Smith, cf	4	0	1	0	0	0	.263
Pete Rose, 1b	3	0	1	0	1	0	.300
George Vukovich, rf	4	0	0	0	0	2	.444
Ron Reed, p	0	0	0	0	0	0	—
Mike Schmidt, 3b	4	0	1	0	0	0	.250
Gary Matthews, lf	4	0	1	0	0	0	.400
Manny Trillo, 2b	4	0	2	0	0	0	.188
Larry Bowa, ss	3	0	0	0	0	0	.176
Bob Boone, c	3	0	0	0	0	0	.000
Steve Carlton, p	2	0	0	0	0	0	.250
Greg Gross, ph-rf	1	0	0	0	0	0	.000
TOTALS	32	0	6	0	1	2	.262

	1	2	3	4	5	6	7	8	9		R	H	E
Expos	0	0	0	0	2	1	0	0	0		3	8	1
Phillies	0	0	0	0	0	0	0	0	0		0	6	0

E—Manuel. DP—Expos 1 (Manuel to Speier to Cromartie). LOB—Expos 5, Phillies 6. Scoring Position—Expos 1-for-4, Phillies 0-for-3. 2B—Parrish (1). GDP—Schmidt. CS—White (2).

Expos	IP	H	R	ER	BB	K	ERA
Steve Rogers (W, 2-0)	9.0	6	0	0	1	2	0.51

Phillies	IP	H	R	ER	BB	K	ERA
Steve Carlton (L, 0-2)	8.0	7	3	3	3	7	3.86
Ron Reed	1.0	1	0	0	0	1	3.00

Time—2:15. Attendance—47,384. Umpires—HP, Kibler. 1B, Crawford. 2B, Pulli. 3B, Tata.

Postseason: Division Series

1981 NL Eastern Division Series—Composite Statistics

Batting

Expos	G	AB	R	H	RBI	2B	3B	HR	BB	SO	SB	CS	Avg	OBP	Slg
Ray Burris	1	2	0	0	0	0	0	0	0	2	0	0	.000	.000	.000
Gary Carter	5	19	3	8	6	3	0	2	1	1	0	0	.421	.429	.895
Warren Cromartie	5	22	1	5	1	2	0	0	0	9	0	1	.227	.227	.318
Andre Dawson	5	20	1	6	0	0	1	0	1	6	2	0	.300	.333	.400
Terry Francona	5	12	0	4	0	0	0	0	2	2	2	0	.333	.429	.333
Bill Gullickson	1	3	0	0	0	0	0	0	0	1	0	0	.000	.000	.000
Wallace Johnson	2	2	0	1	1	0	0	0	0	0	0	0	.500	.500	.500
Jerry Manuel	5	14	0	1	0	0	0	0	2	5	0	0	.071	.188	.071
Brad Mills	1	0	0	0	0	0	0	0	1	0	0	0	—	1.000	—
John Milner	2	2	0	1	1	0	0	0	0	0	0	0	.500	.500	.500
Larry Parrish	5	20	3	3	1	1	0	0	1	3	0	0	.150	.190	.200
Mike Phillips	1	1	0	0	0	0	0	0	0	0	0	0	.000	.000	.000
Jeff Reardon	3	1	0	0	0	0	0	0	0	1	0	0	.000	.000	.000
Steve Rogers	2	5	0	2	2	0	0	0	0	1	0	1	.400	.400	.400
Scott Sanderson	1	1	0	0	0	0	0	0	0	1	0	0	.000	.000	.000
Chris Speier	5	15	4	6	3	2	0	0	4	2	0	0	.400	.526	.533
Tim Wallach	4	4	1	1	0	1	0	0	4	0	0	0	.250	.625	.500
Jerry White	5	18	3	3	1	1	0	0	2	2	3	2	.167	.238	.222
Totals	**5**	**161**	**16**	**41**	**16**	**10**	**1**	**2**	**18**	**36**	**7**	**4**	**.255**	**.326**	**.366**

Phillies	G	AB	R	H	RBI	2B	3B	HR	BB	SO	SB	CS	Avg	OBP	Slg
Luis Aguayo	2	0	1	0	0	0	0	0	0	0	0	0	—	—	—
Ramon Aviles	1	0	0	0	0	0	0	0	1	0	0	0	—	1.000	—
Bob Boone	3	5	0	0	0	0	0	0	0	0	0	1	.000	.000	.000
Larry Bowa	5	17	0	3	1	1	0	0	0	0	0	1	.176	.176	.235
Steve Carlton	2	4	0	1	0	0	0	0	0	0	0	0	.250	.250	.250
Larry Christenson	1	2	0	0	0	0	0	0	0	1	0	0	.000	.000	.000
Dick Davis	1	2	0	0	0	0	0	0	0	1	0	0	.000	.000	.000
Greg Gross	4	4	0	0	0	0	0	0	0	0	0	0	.000	.000	.000
Garry Maddox	2	3	0	1	0	1	0	0	0	0	0	0	.333	.333	.667
Gary Matthews	5	20	3	8	1	0	1	1	0	2	0	0	.400	.400	.650
Bake McBride	4	15	1	3	0	1	0	0	0	5	0	0	.200	.200	.267
Keith Moreland	4	13	2	6	3	0	0	1	1	1	0	1	.462	.500	.692
Dickie Noles	1	0	0	0	0	0	0	0	1	0	0	0	—	1.000	—
Pete Rose	5	20	1	6	2	1	0	0	2	0	0	0	.300	.364	.350
Dick Ruthven	1	1	0	0	0	0	0	0	0	0	0	0	.000	.000	.000
Mike Schmidt	5	16	3	4	2	1	0	1	4	2	0	0	.250	.400	.500
Lonnie Smith	5	19	1	5	0	1	0	0	0	4	0	1	.263	.263	.316
Manny Trillo	5	16	1	3	1	0	0	0	4	0	0	0	.188	.350	.188
George Vukovich	5	9	1	4	2	0	0	1	0	3	0	0	.444	.444	.778
Totals	**5**	**166**	**14**	**44**	**12**	**6**	**1**	**4**	**13**	**19**	**0**	**4**	**.265**	**.318**	**.386**

Pitching

Expos	G	GS	CG	IP	H	R	ER	BB	SO	W-L	Sv-Op	Hld	ERA
Stan Bahnsen	1	0	0	1.1	1	0	0	1	1	0-0	0-0	0	0.00
Ray Burris	1	1	0	5.1	7	4	3	4	4	0-1	0-0	0	5.06
Woodie Fryman	1	0	0	1.1	3	1	1	1	0	0-0	0-0	0	6.75
Bill Gullickson	1	1	0	7.2	6	1	1	1	3	1-0	0-0	0	1.17
Bill Lee	1	0	0	0.2	2	0	0	0	1	0-0	0-0	0	0.00
Jeff Reardon	3	0	0	4.1	1	1	1	1	2	0-1	2-2	0	2.08
Steve Rogers	2	2	1	17.2	16	1	1	3	5	2-0	0-0	0	0.51
Scott Sanderson	1	1	0	2.2	4	4	2	2	0	0-0	0-0	0	6.75
Elias Sosa	2	0	0	3.0	4	2	1	0	1	0-0	0-0	0	3.00
Totals	**5**	**5**	**1**	**44.0**	**44**	**14**	**10**	**13**	**19**	**3-2**	**2-2**	**0**	**2.05**

Phillies	G	GS	CG	IP	H	R	ER	BB	SO	W-L	Sv-Op	Hld	ERA
Warren Brusstar	2	0	0	3.2	5	2	2	1	3	0-0	0-0	0	4.91
Steve Carlton	2	2	0	14.0	14	6	6	8	13	0-2	0-0	0	3.86
Larry Christenson	1	1	0	6.0	4	1	1	1	8	1-0	0-0	0	1.50
Sparky Lyle	3	0	0	2.1	4	0	0	2	1	0-0	0-1	1	0.00
Tug McGraw	2	0	0	4.0	2	0	0	0	2	1-0	0-0	0	0.00
Dickie Noles	1	1	0	4.0	4	2	2	2	5	0-0	0-0	0	4.50
Ron Reed	4	0	0	6.0	5	2	2	3	4	0-0	0-1	0	3.00
Dick Ruthven	1	1	0	4.0	3	3	2	1	0	0-1	0-0	0	4.50
Totals	**5**	**5**	**0**	**44.0**	**41**	**16**	**15**	**18**	**36**	**2-3**	**0-2**	**1**	**3.07**

Fielding

Expos	Pos	G	PO	Ast	E	DP	PB	FPct
Stan Bahnsen	p	1	0	1	0	0	—	1.000
Ray Burris	p	1	0	0	0	0	—	—
Gary Carter	c	5	19	4	0	0	0	1.000
Warren Cromartie	1b	5	38	2	1	4	—	.976
Andre Dawson	cf	5	12	1	1	0	—	.929
Terry Francona	lf	5	8	0	0	0	—	1.000
Woodie Fryman	p	1	0	1	0	0	—	1.000
Bill Gullickson	p	1	0	1	0	0	—	1.000
Bill Lee	p	1	0	0	0	0	—	—
Jerry Manuel	2b	5	14	17	3	5	—	.912
Larry Parrish	3b	5	8	6	0	1	—	1.000
Mike Phillips	2b	1	0	1	0	0	—	1.000
Jeff Reardon	p	3	0	1	0	0	—	1.000
Steve Rogers	p	2	2	1	0	0	—	1.000
Scott Sanderson	p	1	0	1	0	0	—	1.000
Elias Sosa	p	2	0	2	1	0	—	.667
Chris Speier	ss	5	16	16	0	4	—	1.000
Tim Wallach	rf	3	3	0	0	0	—	1.000
Jerry White	rf	5	8	0	0	0	—	1.000
	lf	3	4	0	0	0	—	1.000
Totals		**5**	**132**	**55**	**6**	**14**	**0**	**.969**

Phillies	Pos	G	PO	Ast	E	DP	PB	FPct
Bob Boone	c	3	10	2	0	0	0	1.000
Larry Bowa	ss	5	13	8	1	1	—	.955
Warren Brusstar	p	2	0	0	0	0	—	—
Steve Carlton	p	2	0	4	0	0	—	1.000
Larry Christenson	p	1	0	0	0	0	—	—
Dick Davis	rf	1	2	0	0	0	—	1.000
Greg Gross	lf	1	0	0	0	0	—	—
	rf	1	0	0	0	0	—	—
Sparky Lyle	p	3	0	0	0	0	—	—
Garry Maddox	cf	2	3	0	0	0	—	1.000
Gary Matthews	lf	5	7	0	0	0	—	1.000
Bake McBride	rf	4	7	0	0	0	—	1.000
Tug McGraw	p	2	0	2	0	1	—	1.000
Keith Moreland	c	4	29	2	1	0	0	.969
Dickie Noles	p	1	0	1	0	0	—	1.000
Ron Reed	p	4	0	0	0	0	—	—
Pete Rose	1b	5	29	7	0	0	—	1.000
Dick Ruthven	p	1	1	1	0	0	—	1.000
Mike Schmidt	3b	5	6	11	1	1	—	.944
Lonnie Smith	cf	5	5	0	0	0	—	1.000
Manny Trillo	2b	5	14	9	0	2	—	1.000
George Vukovich	rf	2	6	1	0	0	—	1.000
	lf	1	0	0	0	0	—	—
Totals		**5**	**132**	**48**	**3**	**5**	**0**	**.984**

1981 Los Angeles Dodgers (NL) 3, Houston Astros (NL) 2

In the strike-torn 1981 baseball season, the Los Angeles were the NL West champions in the first half, and the Houston Astros were tops in the second half. When the two teams met in the NL West Division Series, the result was exactly the opposite: the Astros won the first two games, but the Dodgers rallied to take the last three and the Division title. In the opener, Nolan Ryan tossed a two-hitter and Alan Ashby broke up a tie game with a two-run homer in the bottom of the ninth for a 3-1 Houston victory. In Game 2, Denny Walling came off the bench in the bottom of the 10th to single in the only run of the game. But the Dodgers came back to win Game 3 behind Burt Hooton, 6-1, and Fernando Valenzuela beat Vern Ruhle 2-1 in Game 4 to force a fifth game. Jerry Reuss came through with a five-hit shutout, beating Ryan 4-0 to put the Dodgers in the NLCS.

Game 1

Tuesday, October 6

Dodgers	AB	R	H	RBI	BB	K	Avg
Davey Lopes, 2b	4	0	0	0	0	2	.000
Ken Landreaux, cf	4	0	1	0	0	1	.250
Dusty Baker, lf	3	0	0	0	0	0	.000
Steve Garvey, 1b	3	1	1	1	0	0	.333
Rick Monday, rf	2	0	0	0	1	1	.000
Pedro Guerrero, 3b	3	0	0	0	0	1	.000
Mike Scioscia, c	3	0	0	0	0	1	.000
Bill Russell, ss	3	0	0	0	0	0	.000
Fernando Valenzuela, p	2	0	0	0	0	1	.000
Jay Johnstone, ph	1	0	0	0	0	0	.000
Dave Stewart, p	0	0	0	0	0	0	—
TOTALS	28	1	2	1	1	7	.071

Astros	AB	R	H	RBI	BB	K	Avg
Terry Puhl, rf	4	1	2	0	0	0	.500
Phil Garner, 2b	3	0	0	0	1	1	.000
Tony Scott, cf	4	0	1	0	1	1	.250
Jose Cruz, lf	4	0	0	0	0	2	.000
Cesar Cedeno, 1b	4	0	2	0	0	1	.500
Art Howe, 3b	4	0	1	0	0	0	.250
Kiko Garcia, ss	3	0	0	0	0	1	.000
Craig Reynolds, ph	1	1	1	0	0	0	1.000
Alan Ashby, c	3	1	1	2	1	0	.333
Nolan Ryan, p	3	0	0	0	0	1	.000
TOTALS	33	3	8	3	2	7	.242

	1	2	3	4	5	6	7	8	9		R	H	E
Dodgers	0	0	0	0	0	0	1	0	0		1	2	0
Astros	0	0	0	0	0	1	0	0	2		3	8	0

DP—Astros 1 (Ryan to Garcia to Cedeno). LOB—Dodgers 1, Astros 6. Scoring Position—Dodgers 0-for-0, Astros 1-for-6. 2B—Cedeno (1). HR—Garvey (1), Ashby (1). GDP—Baker. SB—Cedeno 2 (2).

Dodgers	IP	H	R	ER	BB	K	ERA
Fernando Valenzuela	8.0	6	1	1	2	6	1.13
Dave Stewart (L, 0-1)	0.2	2	2	2	0	1	27.00

Astros	IP	H	R	ER	BB	K	ERA
Nolan Ryan (W, 1-0)	9.0	2	1	1	1	7	1.00

Time—2:22. Attendance—44,836. Umpires—HP, Dale. 1B, Quick. 2B, Davidson. 3B, McSherry.

Game 2

Wednesday, October 7

Dodgers	AB	R	H	RBI	BB	K	Avg
Davey Lopes, 2b	5	0	2	0	0	2	.222
Mike Marshall, ph	1	0	0	0	0	1	.000
Dave Stewart, p	0	0	0	0	0	0	—
Terry Forster, p	0	0	0	0	0	0	—
Tom Niedenfuer, p	0	0	0	0	0	0	—
Ken Landreaux, cf	4	0	1	0	0	0	.250
Dusty Baker, lf	4	0	1	0	1	0	.143
Steve Garvey, 1b	5	0	1	0	0	0	.250
Rick Monday, rf	4	0	1	0	0	0	.167
Derrel Thomas, rf	1	0	0	0	0	1	.000
Pedro Guerrero, 3b	5	0	1	0	0	0	.125
Mike Scioscia, c	4	0	1	0	0	0	.143
Steve Yeager, ph-c	1	0	1	0	0	0	1.000
Bill Russell, ss	2	0	0	0	3	0	.000
Jerry Reuss, p	4	0	0	0	0	4	.000
Steve Howe, p	0	0	0	0	0	0	—
Reggie Smith, ph	1	0	0	0	0	1	.000
Steve Sax, 2b	0	0	0	0	0	0	—
TOTALS	41	0	9	0	4	9	.167

Astros	AB	R	H	RBI	BB	K	Avg
Terry Puhl, rf	5	0	1	0	0	0	.333
Phil Garner, 2b	5	1	2	0	0	0	.250
Tony Scott, cf	5	0	1	0	0	1	.222
Jose Cruz, lf	5	0	2	0	0	0	.222
Cesar Cedeno, 1b	3	0	0	0	2	1	.286
Art Howe, 3b	4	0	0	0	1	1	.125
Dickie Thon, ss	4	0	2	0	0	0	.500
Denny Walling, ph	1	0	1	1	0	0	1.000
Luis Pujols, c	3	0	0	0	0	1	.000
Joe Niekro, p	2	0	0	0	0	0	.000
Gary Woods, ph	1	0	0	0	0	0	.000
Dave Smith, p	0	0	0	0	0	0	—
Joe Pittman, ph	1	0	0	0	0	0	.000
Joe Sambito, p	0	0	0	0	0	0	—
TOTALS	39	1	9	1	3	4	.242

	1	2	3	4	5	6	7	8	9	10	11		R	H	E
Dodgers	0	0	0	0	0	0	0	0	0	0	0		0	9	1
Astros	0	0	0	0	0	0	0	0	0	0	1		1	9	0

E—Russell. LOB—Dodgers 13, Astros 10. Scoring Position—Dodgers 0-for-9, Astros 2-for-10. 2B—Lopes (1), Yeager (1). S—Landreaux, Pujols. SB—Cruz (1). CS—Cedeno (1).

Dodgers	IP	H	R	ER	BB	K	ERA
Jerry Reuss	9.0	5	0	0	2	3	0.00
Steve Howe	1.0	1	0	0	0	0	0.00
Dave Stewart (L, 0-2)	0.0	2	1	1	0	0	40.50
Terry Forster	0.1	0	0	0	0	0	0.00
Tom Niedenfuer	0.1	1	0	0	1	1	0.00

Astros	IP	H	R	ER	BB	K	ERA
Joe Niekro	8.0	7	0	0	3	4	0.00
Dave Smith	2.0	1	0	0	0	3	0.00
Joe Sambito (W, 1-0)	1.0	1	0	0	1	2	0.00

Stewart pitched to two batters in the 11th.

Time—3:39. Attendance—42,398. Umpires—HP, Quick. 1B, Davidson. 2B, McSherry. 3B, Weyer.

Game 3

Friday, October 9

Astros	AB	R	H	RBI	BB	K	Avg
Terry Puhl, rf	4	0	0	0	0	1	.231
Phil Garner, 2b	2	0	0	0	2	1	.200
Tony Scott, cf	4	0	0	0	0	1	.154
Jose Cruz, lf	4	0	2	0	0	0	.308
Cesar Cedeno, 1b	4	0	0	0	0	0	.182
Alan Ashby, c	2	0	0	0	1	0	.200
Art Howe, 3b	2	1	1	1	1	0	.200
Craig Reynolds, ss	2	0	0	0	0	1	.333
Dickie Thon, ph-ss	1	0	0	0	0	0	.400
Bob Knepper, p	1	0	0	0	0	0	.000
Harry Spilman, ph	1	0	0	0	0	0	.000
Frank LaCorte, p	0	0	0	0	0	0	—
Gary Woods, ph	1	0	0	0	0	1	.000
Joe Sambito, p	0	0	0	0	0	0	—
Billy Smith, p	0	0	0	0	0	0	—
TOTALS	28	1	3	1	4	5	.218

Dodgers	AB	R	H	RBI	BB	K	Avg
Davey Lopes, 2b	3	1	1	0	2	0	.250
Ken Landreaux, cf	4	0	1	0	0	0	.250
Dusty Baker, lf	5	1	2	1	0	0	.250
Steve Garvey, 1b	4	1	2	2	0	2	.333
Pedro Guerrero, 3b	3	0	1	0	1	1	.182
Rick Monday, rf	3	0	1	0	0	1	.222
Derrel Thomas, ph-rf	1	1	0	0	0	0	.000
Steve Yeager, c	4	1	1	0	0	1	.400
Bill Russell, ss	4	1	1	1	0	1	.111
Burt Hooton, p	3	0	0	0	0	0	.000
Steve Howe, p	0	0	0	0	0	0	—
Reggie Smith, ph	0	0	0	1	0	0	.000
Bob Welch, p	0	0	0	0	0	0	—
TOTALS	34	6	10	6	3	6	.227

	1	2	3	4	5	6	7	8	9		R	H	E
Astros	0	0	1	0	0	0	0	0	0		1	3	2
Dodgers	3	0	0	0	0	0	0	3	x		6	10	0

E—Cruz, Cedeno. DP—Dodgers 2 (Garvey to Russell; Guerrero to Lopes to Garvey). LOB—Astros 4, Dodgers 9. Scoring Position—Astros 0-for-4, Dodgers 4-for-10. 2B—Cruz (1), Baker (1), Guerrero (1). HR—AHowe (1), Garvey (2). S—Landreaux. SF—RSmith. GDP—Cedeno.

Astros	IP	H	R	ER	BB	K	ERA
Bob Knepper (L, 0-1)	5.0	6	3	3	2	4	5.40
Frank LaCorte	2.0	0	0	0	0	2	0.00
Joe Sambito	0.2	4	3	3	1	0	16.20
Billy Smith	0.1	0	0	0	0	0	0.00

Dodgers	IP	H	R	ER	BB	K	ERA
Burt Hooton (W, 1-0)	7.0	3	1	1	3	2	1.29
Steve Howe (H, 1)	1.0	0	0	0	0	2	0.00
Bob Welch	1.0	0	0	0	1	1	0.00

Hooton pitched to one batter in the 8th.

WP—Knepper. Time—2:35. Attendance—46,820. Umpires—HP, Davidson. 1B, McSherry. 2B, Weyer. 3B, Montague.

Game 4

Saturday, October 10

Astros	AB	R	H	RBI	BB	K	Avg
Terry Puhl, rf	4	1	1	0	0	0	.235
Phil Garner, 2b	4	0	0	0	0	1	.143
Tony Scott, cf	4	0	1	1	0	2	.176
Jose Cruz, lf	4	0	0	0	0	0	.235
Cesar Cedeno, 1b	2	0	1	0	0	0	.231
Denny Walling, 1b	1	0	0	0	0	0	.500
Art Howe, 3b	3	0	1	0	0	0	.231
Dickie Thon, ss	2	0	0	0	1	0	.286
Luis Pujols, c	3	0	0	0	0	0	.000
Vern Ruhle, p	1	0	0	0	0	1	.000
Kiko Garcia, ph	1	0	0	0	0	0	.000
TOTALS	29	1	4	1	1	4	.198

Dodgers	AB	R	H	RBI	BB	K	Avg
Davey Lopes, 2b	3	0	0	0	1	0	.200
Ken Landreaux, cf	4	0	0	0	0	0	.188
Dusty Baker, lf	3	0	0	0	0	0	.200
Steve Garvey, 1b	3	1	1	0	0	0	.333
Rick Monday, rf	2	0	0	0	0	1	.182
Derrel Thomas, rf	0	0	0	0	0	0	.000
Pedro Guerrero, 3b	3	1	1	1	0	0	.214
Mike Scioscia, c	2	0	0	0	1	0	.111
Bill Russell, ss	3	0	2	1	0	0	.250
Fernando Valenzuela, p	2	0	0	0	0	0	.000
TOTALS	25	2	4	2	2	1	.204

	1	2	3	4	5	6	7	8	9		R	H	E
Astros	0	0	0	0	0	0	0	0	1		1	4	0
Dodgers	0	0	0	1	0	1	0	x			2	4	0

LOB—Astros 3, Dodgers 3. Scoring Position—Astros 1-for-4,
Dodgers 1-for-4. 2B—Puhl (1). HR—Guerrero (1). S—Ruhle,
Monday, Valenzuela. CS—Cedeno (2).

Astros	IP	H	R	ER	BB	K	ERA
Vern Ruhle (L, 0-1)	8.0	4	2	2	1	4	2.25

Dodgers	IP	H	R	ER	BB	K	ERA
Fernando Valenzuela (W, 1-0)	9.0	4	1	1	1	4	1.06

Time—2:00. Attendance—55,983. Umpires—HP, McSherry.
1B, Weyer. 2B, Montague. 3B, Dale.

Game 5

Sunday, October 11

Astros	AB	R	H	RBI	BB	K	Avg
Terry Puhl, rf	4	0	0	0	0	0	.190
Phil Garner, 2b	4	0	0	0	0	0	.111
Tony Scott, cf	3	0	0	0	1	1	.150
Art Howe, 3b	4	0	1	0	0	0	.235
Jose Cruz, lf	3	0	2	0	1	1	.300
Denny Walling, 1b	4	0	1	0	0	1	.333
Dickie Thon, ss	4	0	0	0	0	0	.182
Alan Ashby, c	4	0	0	0	0	0	.111
Nolan Ryan, p	1	0	1	0	1	0	.250
Joe Pittman, ph	1	0	0	0	0	0	.000
Dave Smith, p	0	0	0	0	0	0	—
Frank LaCorte, p	0	0	0	0	0	0	—
Dave Roberts, ph	1	0	0	0	0	1	.000
TOTALS	33	0	5	0	3	4	.194

Dodgers	AB	R	H	RBI	BB	K	Avg
Davey Lopes, 2b	5	0	1	0	0	3	.200
Ken Landreaux, cf	4	1	1	0	0	0	.200
Dusty Baker, lf	3	1	0	0	1	0	.167
Steve Garvey, 1b	4	1	2	1	0	0	.368
Rick Monday, rf	3	1	1	1	1	1	.214
Derrel Thomas, pr-rf	0	0	0	0	0	0	.000
Pedro Guerrero, 3b	3	0	0	0	1	2	.176
Mike Scioscia, c	4	0	1	1	0	1	.154
Bill Russell, ss	4	0	1	0	0	0	.250
Jerry Reuss, p	4	0	0	0	0	4	.000
TOTALS	34	4	7	3	3	11	.204

	1	2	3	4	5	6	7	8	9		R	H	E
Astros	0	0	0	0	0	0	0	0	0		0	5	3
Dodgers	0	0	0	0	0	3	1	0	x		4	7	2

E—Guerrero, Walling, Garner, Russell, Thon. LOB—Astros 9,
Dodgers 9. Scoring Position—Astros 0-for-7, Dodgers 3-for-15.
2B—Landreaux (1), Russell (1). 3B—Garvey (1). SB—Puhl (1),
Lopes (1), Guerrero (1). CS—Scott (1).

Astros	IP	H	R	ER	BB	K	ERA
Nolan Ryan (L, 1-1)	6.0	4	3	2	2	7	1.80
Dave Smith	0.1	1	1	1	0	1	3.86
Frank LaCorte	1.2	2	0	0	1	3	0.00

Dodgers	IP	H	R	ER	BB	K	ERA
Jerry Reuss (W, 1-0)	9.0	5	0	0	3	4	0.00

Time—2:52. Attendance—55,979. Umpires—HP, Weyer. 1B,
Montague. 2B, Dale. 3B, Quick.

1981 NL Western Division Series—Composite Statistics

Batting

Dodgers	G	AB	R	H	RBI	2B	3B	HR	BB	SO	SB	CS	Avg	OBP	Slg
Dusty Baker	5	18	2	3	1	1	0	0	2	0	0	0	.167	.250	.222
Steve Garvey	5	19	4	7	4	0	1	2	0	2	0	0	.368	.368	.789
Pedro Guerrero	5	17	1	3	1	1	0	1	2	4	1	0	.176	.263	.412
Burt Hooton	1	3	0	0	0	0	0	0	0	0	0	0	.000	.000	.000
Jay Johnstone	1	1	0	0	0	0	0	0	0	0	0	0	.000	.000	.000
Ken Landreaux	5	20	1	4	1	1	0	0	0	1	0	0	.200	.200	.250
Davey Lopes	5	20	1	4	0	1	0	0	3	7	1	0	.200	.304	.250
Mike Marshall	1	1	0	0	0	0	0	0	0	1	0	0	.000	.000	.000
Rick Monday	5	14	1	3	1	0	0	0	2	4	0	0	.214	.313	.214
Jerry Reuss	2	8	0	0	0	0	0	0	0	8	0	0	.000	.000	.000
Bill Russell	5	16	1	4	2	1	0	0	3	1	0	0	.250	.368	.313
Mike Scioscia	4	13	0	2	1	0	0	0	1	2	0	0	.154	.214	.154
Reggie Smith	2	1	0	0	0	0	0	0	0	1	0	0	.000	.000	.000
Derrel Thomas	4	2	1	0	0	0	0	0	0	0	0	0	.000	.000	.000
Fernando Valenzuela	2	4	0	0	0	0	0	0	0	1	0	0	.000	.000	.000
Steve Yeager	2	5	1	2	0	1	0	0	0	1	0	0	.400	.400	.600
Totals	5	162	13	32	12	6	1	3	13	34	2	0	.198	.256	.302

Astros	G	AB	R	H	RBI	2B	3B	HR	BB	SO	SB	CS	Avg	OBP	Slg
Alan Ashby	3	9	1	1	2	0	0	1	2	0	0	0	.111	.273	.444
Cesar Cedeno	4	13	0	3	0	1	0	0	2	2	2	2	.231	.333	.308
Jose Cruz	5	20	0	6	1	0	1	0	1	3	1	0	.300	.333	.350
Kiko Garcia	2	4	0	0	0	0	0	0	0	1	0	0	.000	.000	.000
Phil Garner	5	18	1	2	0	0	0	0	3	3	0	0	.111	.238	.111
Art Howe	5	17	1	4	1	0	0	1	2	1	0	0	.235	.316	.412
Bob Knepper	1	1	0	0	0	0	0	0	0	0	0	0	.000	.000	.000
Joe Niekro	1	2	0	0	0	0	0	0	0	0	0	0	.000	.000	.000
Joe Pittman	2	2	0	0	0	0	0	0	0	0	0	0	.000	.000	.000
Terry Puhl	5	21	2	4	0	1	0	0	0	1	1	0	.190	.190	.238
Luis Pujols	2	6	0	0	0	0	0	0	0	1	0	0	.000	.000	.000
Craig Reynolds	2	3	1	1	0	0	0	0	0	1	0	0	.333	.333	.333
Dave Roberts	1	1	0	0	0	0	0	0	0	1	0	0	.000	.000	.000
Vern Ruhle	1	1	0	0	0	0	0	0	0	1	0	0	.000	.000	.000
Nolan Ryan	2	4	1	0	0	0	0	0	1	1	0	0	.250	.400	.250
Tony Scott	5	20	0	3	2	0	0	0	1	6	0	1	.150	.190	.150
Harry Spilman	1	1	0	0	0	0	0	0	0	0	0	0	.000	.000	.000
Dickie Thon	4	11	0	2	0	0	0	0	1	0	0	0	.182	.250	.182
Denny Walling	3	6	2	1	0	0	0	0	1	0	0	0	.333	.333	.333
Gary Woods	2	2	0	0	0	0	0	0	0	1	0	0	.000	.000	.000
Totals	5	162	6	29	6	3	0	2	13	24	4	3	.179	.240	.235

Pitching

Dodgers	G	GS	CG	IP	H	R	ER	BB	SO	W-L	Sv-Op	Hld	ERA
Terry Forster	1	0	0	0.1	0	0	0	0	0	0-0	0-0	0	0.00
Burt Hooton	1	1	0	7.0	3	1	1	3	2	1-0	0-0	0	1.29
Steve Howe	2	0	0	2.0	1	0	0	0	2	0-0	0-0	1	0.00
Tom Niedenfuer	1	0	0	0.1	1	0	0	1	1	0-0	0-0	0	0.00
Jerry Reuss	2	2	1	18.0	10	0	0	5	7	1-0	0-0	0	0.00
Dave Stewart	2	0	0	0.2	4	3	3	0	1	0-2	0-0	0	40.50
Fernando Valenzuela	2	2	1	17.0	10	2	2	3	10	1-0	0-0	0	1.06
Bob Welch	1	0	0	1.0	0	0	0	1	1	0-0	0-0	0	0.00
Totals	5	5	2	46.1	29	6	6	13	24	3-2	0-0	1	1.17

Astros	G	GS	CG	IP	H	R	ER	BB	SO	W-L	Sv-Op	Hld	ERA
Bob Knepper	1	1	0	5.0	6	3	3	2	4	0-1	0-0	0	5.40
Frank LaCorte	2	0	0	3.2	2	0	0	1	5	0-0	0-0	0	0.00
Joe Niekro	1	1	0	8.0	7	0	0	3	4	0-0	0-0	0	0.00
Vern Ruhle	1	1	1	8.0	4	2	2	2	1	0-1	0-0	0	2.25
Nolan Ryan	2	2	1	15.0	6	4	3	3	14	1-1	0-0	0	1.80
Joe Sambito	2	0	0	1.2	5	3	3	2	2	1-0	0-0	0	16.20
Billy Smith	1	0	0	0.1	0	0	0	0	0	0-0	0-0	0	0.00
Dave Smith	2	0	0	2.1	2	1	1	0	4	0-0	0-0	0	3.86
Totals	5	5	2	44.0	32	13	12	13	34	2-3	0-0	0	2.45

Fielding

Dodgers	Pos	G	PO	Ast	E	DP	PB	FPct
Dusty Baker	lf	5	12	0	0	0	—	1.000
Terry Forster	p	1	0	0	0	0	—	—
Steve Garvey	1b	5	49	5	0	2	—	1.000
Pedro Guerrero	3b	5	3	14	1	1	—	.944
Burt Hooton	p	1	1	0	0	0	—	1.000
Steve Howe	p	2	0	1	0	0	—	1.000
Ken Landreaux	cf	5	16	0	0	0	—	1.000
Davey Lopes	2b	5	7	12	0	1	—	1.000
Rick Monday	rf	5	12	0	0	0	—	1.000
Tom Niedenfuer	p	1	0	0	0	0	—	—
Jerry Reuss	p	2	1	1	0	0	—	1.000
Bill Russell	ss	5	10	15	2	1	—	.926
Steve Sax	2b	1	0	0	0	0	—	—
Mike Scioscia	c	4	21	4	0	0	0	1.000
Dave Stewart	p	2	0	0	0	0	—	—
Derrel Thomas	rf	4	0	0	0	0	—	—
Fernando Valenzuela	p	2	0	5	0	0	—	1.000
Bob Welch	p	1	1	0	0	0	—	1.000
Steve Yeager	c	2	6	0	0	0	0	1.000
Totals		5	139	57	3	5	0	.985

Astros	Pos	G	PO	Ast	E	DP	PB	FPct
Alan Ashby	c	3	24	2	0	0	0	1.000
Cesar Cedeno	1b	4	36	1	1	1	—	.974
Jose Cruz	lf	5	16	0	1	0	—	.941
Kiko Garcia	ss	1	2	4	0	1	—	1.000
Phil Garner	2b	5	4	8	1	0	—	.923
Art Howe	3b	5	5	8	0	0	—	1.000
Bob Knepper	p	1	0	1	0	0	—	1.000
Frank LaCorte	p	2	0	0	0	0	—	—
Joe Niekro	p	1	0	1	0	0	—	1.000
Terry Puhl	rf	5	7	1	0	0	—	1.000
Luis Pujols	c	2	12	0	0	0	0	1.000
Craig Reynolds	ss	1	1	1	0	0	—	1.000
Vern Ruhle	p	1	2	3	0	0	—	1.000
Nolan Ryan	p	2	1	4	0	1	—	1.000
Joe Sambito	p	2	0	1	0	0	—	1.000
Tony Scott	cf	5	10	0	0	0	—	1.000
Billy Smith	p	1	0	0	0	0	—	—
Dave Smith	p	2	0	0	0	0	—	—
Dickie Thon	ss	4	6	11	1	0	—	.944
Denny Walling	1b	2	6	2	1	0	—	.889
Totals		5	132	48	5	3	0	.973

1995 Seattle Mariners (AL) 3, New York Yankees (AL) 2

It was simply one of the most thrilling playoff series of all time. The New York Yankees made their first postseason appearance in 14 years, while the Seattle Mariners reached the playoffs for the first time in franchise history, thanks to their tremendous September stretch run. David Cone fought his control but won the opener, 9-6. The two teams traded leads in Game 2 before reaching a 4-4 stalemate that sent the game into extra innings. Ken Griffey Jr. homered in the top of the 12th to give the Mariners a 5-4 lead. In the bottom of the frame, Ruben Sierra doubled in the tying run, but the winning run was thrown out at the plate on a perfect relay. Jim Leyritz' homer in the bottom of the 15th won it for New York. The Mariners returned home trailing two games to none, but Randy Johnson threw seven strong innings to win Game 3, 7-4. The fourth game was the Edgar Martinez show. He brought the M's back from an early five-run deficit with a three-run homer, and with the game tied in the eighth, he hit a game-breaking grand slam off John Wetteland. Seattle's 11-8 victory evened the series. Game 5 was one for the ages. Cone took a 4-2 lead into the bottom of the eighth. Obviously tiring, he allowed a solo homer to Griffey before loading the bases and walking Doug Strange to force in the tying run. When the Yankees put two men on base in the top of the ninth, Lou Piniella summoned Johnson, who'd pitched just two days before. Johnson pitched out of the jam and struck out the side in the 10th. The Yankees had lost faith in closer Wetteland and brought in Johnson's Game 3 opponent, Jack McDowell. Johnson, running on empty, blinked first, giving up an RBI single to long-time nemesis Randy Velarde in the 11th. The M's refused to lose, though, putting runners on first and third in the bottom of the inning. Edgar Martinez lined a shot into the left-field corner, bringing in the tying run, and Griffey raced around from first to score the game-winner.

Game 1

Tuesday, October 3

Mariners	AB	R	H	RBI	BB	K	Avg
Vince Coleman, lf	4	1	0	0	1	1	.000
Joey Cora, 2b	4	1	0	0	1	0	.000
Ken Griffey Jr., cf	5	3	3	3	0	0	.600
Edgar Martinez, dh	4	1	3	1	1	0	.750
Tino Martinez, 1b	3	0	1	1	2	1	.333
Jay Buhner, rf	5	0	1	0	0	0	.200
Mike Blowers, 3b	4	0	0	0	1	3	.000
Dan Wilson, c	3	0	0	1	1	1	.000
Luis Sojo, ss	4	0	1	0	0	0	.250
TOTALS	36	6	9	6	7	6	.250

Yankees	AB	R	H	RBI	BB	K	Avg
Wade Boggs, 3b	5	2	3	2	0	0	.600
Pat Kelly, pr-2b	0	1	0	0	0	0	—
Bernie Williams, cf	5	2	3	2	0	0	.600
Paul O'Neill, rf	3	0	1	1	1	0	.333
Ruben Sierra, dh	5	1	1	2	0	1	.200
Don Mattingly, 1b	4	1	2	1	0	0	.500
Dion James, lf	3	0	1	0	0	0	.333
Gerald Williams, pr-lf	1	0	0	0	0	1	.000
Mike Stanley, c	4	0	1	1	0	0	.250
Tony Fernandez, ss	3	0	0	0	1	0	.000
Randy Velarde, 2b-3b	3	2	1	0	0	0	.333
TOTALS	36	9	13	9	2	2	.361

	1	2	3	4	5	6	7	8	9		R	H	E
Mariners	0	0	0	1	0	1	2	0	2		6	9	0
Yankees	0	0	2	0	0	2	4	1	x		9	13	0

LOB—Mariners 10, Yankees 7. Scoring Position—Mariners 3-for-12, Yankees 5-for-10. 2B—Boggs (1), BWilliams (1), Mattingly (1). HR—Griffey Jr. 2 (2), Boggs (1), Sierra (1). SF—O'Neill.

Mariners	IP	H	R	ER	BB	K	ERA
Chris Bosio	5.2	6	4	4	1	1	6.35
Jeff Nelson (L, 0-1)	0.1	1	1	1	0	0	27.00
Bobby Ayala	0.1	4	3	3	0	0	81.00
Bill Risley	0.2	0	0	0	0	1	0.00
Bob Wells	1.0	2	1	1	1	0	9.00

Yankees	IP	H	R	ER	BB	K	ERA
David Cone (W, 1-0)	8.0	6	4	4	6	5	4.50
John Wetteland	1.0	3	2	2	1	1	18.00

Nelson pitched to one batter in the 7th.

HBP—Velarde by Nelson. Time—3:39. Attendance—57,178. Umpires—HP, Reilly. 1B, Scott. 2B, McKean. 3B, McCoy.

Game 2

Wednesday, October 4

Mariners	AB	R	H	RBI	BB	K	Avg
Vince Coleman, lf	5	2	2	1	0	1	.222
Chris Widger, c	2	0	0	0	0	2	.000
Luis Sojo, ss	7	0	1	1	0	2	.182
Ken Griffey Jr., cf	6	1	2	2	0	0	.455
Edgar Martinez, dh	6	1	3	0	1	1	.600
Jay Buhner, rf	6	0	3	0	1	1	.364
Mike Blowers, 3b	3	0	0	0	1	0	.000
Doug Strange, ph-3b	3	0	0	0	0	1	.000
Tino Martinez, 1b	7	0	2	1	0	1	.300
Dan Wilson, c	3	0	0	0	0	0	.000
Alex Diaz, ph-lf	3	0	1	0	0	1	.333
Joey Cora, 2b	4	1	2	0	0	0	.250
Felix Fermin, 2b	1	0	0	0	0	1	.000
TOTALS	56	5	16	5	3	11	.272

Yankees	AB	R	H	RBI	BB	K	Avg
Wade Boggs, 3b	4	1	1	0	2	1	.333
Jorge Posada, pr	0	1	0	0	0	0	—
Russ Davis, 3b	1	0	1	0	0	0	1.000
Bernie Williams, cf	6	0	1	1	1	1	.364
Paul O'Neill, rf	6	1	2	1	1	2	.333
Ruben Sierra, dh	7	1	2	2	0	2	.250
Don Mattingly, 1b	6	1	3	1	1	1	.500
Dion James, lf	3	0	0	0	0	1	.167
Gerald Williams, lf	1	0	0	0	0	0	.000
Darryl Strawberry, ph	1	0	0	0	0	1	.000
Pat Kelly, 2b	0	1	0	0	1	0	—
Jim Leyritz, c	6	1	1	2	0	0	.167
Tony Fernandez, ss	5	0	1	0	1	1	.125
Randy Velarde, 2b-lf	5	0	0	0	1	1	.125
TOTALS	51	7	11	7	8	11	.277

	1	2	3	4	5	6	7	8	9	10	11	12	13	14	15	R	H	E
Mariners	0	0	1	0	0	1	2	0	0	0	0	1	0	0	0	5	16	2
Yankees	0	0	0	0	1	2	1	0	0	0	0	1	0	0	2	7	11	0

E—Cora, Sojo. DP—Mariners 2 (TMartinez to Sojo; Fermin to TMartinez), Yankees 1 (GWilliams to Boggs to Velarde). LOB—Mariners 11, Yankees 11. Scoring Position—Mariners 3-for-12, Yankees 1-for-7. 2B—EMartinez (1), Buhner (1), Cora (1), BWilliams (2), Sierra (1). HR—Coleman (1), Griffey Jr. (3), O'Neill (1), Sierra (2), Mattingly (1), Leyritz (1). S—Cora, Kelly. SF—Griffey Jr. GDP—Mattingly. CS—Buhner (1), TMartinez (1).

Mariners	IP	H	R	ER	BB	K	ERA
Andy Benes	5.0	6	3	3	3	3	5.40
Bill Risley	1.0	0	0	0	0	0	0.00
Norm Charlton (BS, 1)	4.0	1	1	1	0	5	2.25
Jeff Nelson	1.1	0	1	1	1	3	10.80
Tim Belcher (BS, 1; L, 0-1)	3.0	4	2	2	4	0	6.00

Yankees	IP	H	R	ER	BB	K	ERA
Andy Pettitte	7.0	9	4	4	3	0	5.14
Bob Wickman	1.1	2	0	0	0	2	0.00
John Wetteland	3.1	3	1	1	0	4	6.23
Mariano Rivera (W, 1-0)	3.1	2	0	0	0	5	0.00

Benes pitched to two batters in the 6th.

HBP—Leyritz by Risley. Time—5:13. Attendance—57,126. Umpires—HP, Scott. 1B, McKean. 2B, McCoy. 3B, Garcia.

Game 3

Friday, October 6

Yankees	AB	R	H	RBI	BB	K	Avg
Randy Velarde, lf	3	0	0	0	1	1	.091
Bernie Williams, cf	3	2	3	2	1	0	.500
Mike Stanley, c	4	1	2	1	0	0	.375
Ruben Sierra, dh	3	0	0	0	1	0	.200
Don Mattingly, 1b	4	0	0	0	0	3	.357
Gerald Williams, rf	2	1	0	0	1	1	.000
Paul O'Neill, ph-rf	1	0	0	0	0	1	.300
Russ Davis, 3b	4	0	0	0	0	2	.200
Tony Fernandez, ss	4	0	1	0	0	1	.167
Pat Kelly, 2b	3	0	0	1	0	3	.000
TOTALS	31	4	6	4	4	12	.260

Mariners	AB	R	H	RBI	BB	K	Avg
Vince Coleman, lf	4	2	2	0	0	1	.308
Joey Cora, 2b	2	1	0	0	1	0	.200
Ken Griffey Jr., cf	3	0	0	0	1	1	.357
Edgar Martinez, dh	1	2	0	0	5	0	.545
Tino Martinez, 1b	4	2	3	3	0	0	.429
Jay Buhner, rf	4	0	1	0	0	1	.333
Mike Blowers, 3b	2	0	1	1	1	1	.111
Luis Sojo, ss	3	0	0	1	0	0	.143
Dan Wilson, c	4	0	0	0	0	3	.000
TOTALS	27	7	7	6	6	7	.282

	1	2	3	4	5	6	7	8	9		R	H	E
Yankees	0	0	0	1	0	0	1	2	0		4	6	2
Mariners	0	0	0	2	4	1	0	x			7	7	0

E—Stanley, Velarde. DP—Yankees 2 (Fernandez to Kelly to Mattingly; Kelly to Fernandez to Mattingly). LOB—Yankees 5, Mariners 5. Scoring Position—Yankees 0-for-2, Mariners 3-for-8. 3B—Coleman (1). HR—BWilliams (2), Stanley (1), TMartinez (1). S—Cora. SF—Kelly, Sojo. GDP—Buhner, Sojo. SB—BWilliams (1), Coleman (1), Cora (1), Griffey Jr. (1).

Yankees	IP	H	R	ER	BB	K	ERA
Jack McDowell (L, 0-1)	5.1	3	5	5	4	4	8.44
Steve Howe	0.0	1	1	1	0	0	—
Bob Wickman	0.2	2	0	0	0	1	0.00
Sterling Hitchcock	0.2	1	1	0	2	0	0.00
Mariano Rivera	1.1	0	0	0	0	2	0.00

Mariners	IP	H	R	ER	BB	K	ERA
Randy Johnson (W, 1-0)	7.0	4	2	2	4	10	2.57
Bill Risley	0.2	2	2	2	0	0	7.71
Norm Charlton (S, 1)	1.1	0	0	0	0	2	1.69

Howe pitched to one batter in the 6th.

WP—McDowell. HBP—Blowers by McDowell. Time—3:04. Attendance—57,944. Umpires—HP, Brinkman. 1B, Roe. 2B, Evans. 3B, Morrison.

Game 4
Saturday, October 7

Yankees	AB	R	H	RBI	BB	K	Avg
Wade Boggs, 3b	5	1	2	1	1	1	.357
Pat Kelly, pr	0	0	0	0	0	0	.000
Bernie Williams, cf	5	2	2	0	1	1	.474
Paul O'Neill, rf	3	2	2	2	2	1	.385
Ruben Sierra, dh	4	0	1	1	0	2	.211
Don Mattingly, 1b	5	1	4	2	0	0	.474
Dion James, lf	4	0	0	0	0	0	.100
Gerald Williams, lf	0	0	0	0	0	0	.000
Darryl Strawberry, ph	1	0	0	0	0	0	.000
Mike Stanley, c	4	1	1	1	1	1	.333
Tony Fernandez, ss	5	0	1	0	0	0	.176
Randy Velarde, 2b	2	1	1	0	3	0	.154
TOTALS	38	8	14	7	8	6	.290

Mariners	AB	R	H	RBI	BB	K	Avg
Vince Coleman, lf	4	1	0	0	1	1	.235
Joey Cora, 2b	4	2	2	0	1	0	.286
Ken Griffey Jr., cf	4	3	2	1	0	2	.389
Edgar Martinez, dh	4	2	3	7	1	0	.600
Tino Martinez, 1b	5	1	1	0	0	1	.368
Jay Buhner, rf	4	2	3	1	1	0	.421
Mike Blowers, 3b	4	0	1	0	0	1	.154
Luis Sojo, ss	4	0	3	1	0	0	.278
Felix Fermin, ss	0	0	0	0	0	0	.000
Dan Wilson, c	4	0	1	0	1	0	.071
TOTALS	37	11	16	10	5	5	.318

	1	2	3	4	5	6	7	8	9		R	H	E
Yankees	3	0	2	0	0	0	0	1	2		8	14	1
Mariners	0	0	4	0	1	1	0	5	x		11	16	0

E—Mattingly. DP—Yankees 1 (Boggs to Velarde to Mattingly), Mariners 2 (Cora to Sojo to TMartinez; Wilson to Cora). LOB—Yankees 12, Mariners 10. Scoring Position—Yankees 3-for-16, Mariners 2-for-8. 2B—Boggs (2), Sierra (2), Mattingly 2 (3). HR—O'Neill (2), Griffey Jr. (4), EMartinez 2 (2), Buhner (1). S—Blowers. SF—Sierra, Sojo. GDP—Boggs, Wilson. CS—Velarde (1).

Yankees	IP	H	R	ER	BB	K	ERA
Scott Kamieniecki	5.0	9	5	4	4	4	7.20
Sterling Hitchcock	1.0	1	1	1	0	1	5.40
Bob Wickman	1.0	1	0	0	0	0	0.00
John Wetteland (L, 0-1)	0.0	2	4	4	1	0	14.54
Steve Howe	1.0	3	1	1	0	0	18.00

Mariners	IP	H	R	ER	BB	K	ERA
Chris Bosio	2.0	4	5	5	3	1	10.57
Jeff Nelson	4.0	6	0	0	2	4	3.18
Tim Belcher (H, 1)	1.1	0	1	1	1	0	6.23
Norm Charlton (BS, 2; W, 1-0)	0.2	2	1	1	1	1	3.00
Bobby Ayala	0.1	2	1	1	1	0	54.00
Bill Risley (S, 1)	0.2	0	0	0	0	0	6.00

Bosio pitched to two batters in the 3rd. Nelson pitched to one batter in the 7th. Wetteland pitched to four batters in the 8th. Charlton pitched to one batter in the 9th.

WP—Charlton. HBP—Griffey Jr. by Wetteland. Time—4:08. Attendance—57,180. Umpires—HP, Roe. 1B, Evans. 2B, Morrison. 3B, Welke.

Game 5
Sunday, October 8

Yankees	AB	R	H	RBI	BB	K	Avg
Wade Boggs, 3b	5	0	0	0	0	3	.263
Jim Leyritz, ph-c	1	0	0	0	0	1	.143
Bernie Williams, cf	2	2	0	0	4	1	.429
Paul O'Neill, rf	5	2	1	2	1	1	.333
Ruben Sierra, dh	4	0	0	0	1	2	.174
Don Mattingly, 1b	5	0	1	2	0	1	.417
Dion James, lf	2	0	0	0	1	0	.083
Gerald Williams, pr-lf	1	0	0	0	1	1	.000
Mike Stanley, c	4	0	1	0	1	0	.313
Pat Kelly, pr-2b	0	1	0	0	0	0	.000
Tony Fernandez, ss	4	0	2	0	0	0	.238
Randy Velarde, 2b-3b	4	0	1	1	1	2	.176
TOTALS	37	5	6	5	10	12	.263

Mariners	AB	R	H	RBI	BB	K	Avg
Vince Coleman, lf	6	0	1	0	0	0	.217
Joey Cora, 2b	5	2	2	1	0	0	.316
Ken Griffey Jr., cf	5	2	2	1	1	1	.391
Edgar Martinez, dh	6	0	3	2	0	1	.571
Tino Martinez, 1b	3	1	2	0	1	1	.409
Alex Rodriguez, pr-ss	1	1	0	0	0	0	.000
Jay Buhner, rf	5	0	3	1	0	2	.458
Luis Sojo, ss	2	0	0	0	0	1	.250
Warren Newson, ph	1	0	0	0	0	1	.000
Felix Fermin, ss	0	0	0	0	0	0	.000
Alex Diaz, ph	0	0	0	0	1	0	.333
Chris Widger, c	1	0	0	0	0	1	.000
Dan Wilson, c	3	0	1	0	0	0	.118
Doug Strange, ph-3b	1	0	0	1	1	0	.000
Mike Blowers, 3b-1b	5	0	1	0	0	2	.167
TOTALS	44	6	15	6	4	12	.315

	1	2	3	4	5	6	7	8	9	10	11		R	H	E
Yankees	0	0	0	2	0	2	0	0	0		1		5	6	0
Mariners	0	0	1	1	0	0	0	2	0		2		6	15	0

DP—Mariners 1 (Sojo to TMartinez). LOB—Yankees 10, Mariners 13. Scoring Position—Yankees 2-for-10, Mariners 2-for-13. 2B—Mattingly (4), Fernandez 2 (2), EMartinez 2 (3), TMartinez (1). HR—O'Neill (3), Cora (1), Griffey Jr. (5). S—Fernandez, Cora. GDP—Fernandez.

Yankees	IP	H	R	ER	BB	K	ERA
David Cone	7.2	9	4	4	3	9	4.60
Mariano Rivera	0.2	1	0	0	1	1	0.00
Jack McDowell (L, 0-2)	1.2	5	2	2	0	2	9.00

Mariners	IP	H	R	ER	BB	K	ERA
Andy Benes	6.2	4	4	4	6	5	5.40
Norm Charlton	1.1	1	0	0	2	1	2.45
Randy Johnson (W, 2-0)	3.0	1	1	1	2	6	2.70

Charlton pitched to two batters in the 9th. McDowell pitched to three batters in the 11th.

WP—Cone 2. Time—4:19. Attendance—57,411. Umpires—HP, Evans. 1B, Morrison. 2B, Welke. 3B, Hirschbeck.

1995 AL Division Series—Composite Statistics

Batting

Mariners	G	AB	R	H	RBI	2B	3B	HR	BB	SO	SB	CS	Avg	OBP	Slg
Mike Blowers	5	18	0	3	1	0	0	0	3	7	0	0	.167	.318	.167
Jay Buhner	5	24	2	11	3	1	0	1	2	4	0	1	.458	.500	.625
Vince Coleman	5	23	6	5	1	0	1	1	2	4	1	0	.217	.280	.435
Joey Cora	5	19	7	6	1	1	0	1	3	0	1	0	.316	.409	.526
Alex Diaz	2	3	0	1	0	0	0	0	1	1	0	0	.333	.500	.333
Felix Fermin	3	1	0	0	0	0	0	0	0	1	0	0	.000	.000	.000
Ken Griffey Jr.	5	23	9	9	7	0	0	5	2	4	1	0	.391	.444	1.043
Edgar Martinez	5	21	6	12	10	3	0	2	6	2	0	0	.571	.667	1.000
Tino Martinez	5	22	4	9	5	1	0	1	3	4	0	1	.409	.480	.591
Warren Newson	1	1	0	0	0	0	0	0	0	1	0	0	.000	.000	.000
Alex Rodriguez	1	1	1	0	0	0	0	0	0	0	0	0	.000	.000	.000
Luis Sojo	5	20	0	5	3	0	0	0	0	3	0	0	.250	.227	.250
Doug Strange	2	4	0	0	1	0	0	0	1	1	0	0	.000	.200	.000
Chris Widger	2	3	0	0	0	0	0	0	0	3	0	0	.000	.000	.000
Dan Wilson	5	17	0	2	1	0	0	0	2	6	0	0	.118	.211	.118
Totals	5	200	35	63	33	6	1	11	25	41	3	2	.315	.391	.520

Yankees	G	AB	R	H	RBI	2B	3B	HR	BB	SO	SB	CS	Avg	OBP	Slg
Wade Boggs	4	19	4	5	3	2	0	1	3	5	0	0	.263	.364	.526
Russ Davis	2	5	0	1	0	0	0	0	0	2	0	0	.200	.200	.200
Tony Fernandez	5	21	0	5	0	2	0	0	2	2	0	0	.238	.304	.333
Dion James	4	12	0	1	0	0	0	0	1	1	0	0	.083	.154	.083
Pat Kelly	5	3	3	0	1	0	0	0	1	3	0	0	.000	.200	.000
Jim Leyritz	2	7	1	1	2	0	0	1	0	1	0	0	.143	.250	.571
Don Mattingly	5	24	3	10	6	4	0	1	5	6	0	0	.417	.440	.708
Paul O'Neill	5	18	5	6	6	0	0	3	5	5	0	0	.333	.458	.833
Jorge Posada	1	0	1	0	0	0	0	0	0	0	0	0	—	—	—
Ruben Sierra	5	23	2	4	5	2	0	2	2	7	0	0	.174	.231	.522
Mike Stanley	4	16	2	5	3	0	0	1	2	1	0	0	.313	.389	.500
Darryl Strawberry	2	2	0	0	0	0	0	0	0	1	0	0	.000	.000	.000
Randy Velarde	5	17	3	3	1	0	0	0	6	4	0	1	.176	.417	.176
Bernie Williams	5	21	8	9	5	2	0	2	7	3	1	0	.429	.571	.810
Gerald Williams	5	5	1	0	0	0	0	0	0	2	3	0	.000	.286	.000
Totals	5	193	33	50	32	12	0	11	32	43	1	1	.259	.365	.492

Pitching

Mariners	G	GS	CG	IP	H	R	ER	BB	SO	W-L	Sv-Op	Hld	ERA
Bobby Ayala	2	0	0	0.2	6	4	4	1	0	0-0	0-0	0	54.00
Tim Belcher	2	0	0	4.1	4	3	3	5	0	0-1	0-1	1	6.23
Andy Benes	2	2	0	11.2	10	7	7	9	8	0-0	0-0	0	5.40
Chris Bosio	2	2	0	7.2	10	9	9	4	2	0-0	0-0	0	10.57
Norm Charlton	4	0	0	7.1	4	2	2	3	9	1-0	1-3	0	2.45
Randy Johnson	2	1	0	10.0	5	3	3	6	16	2-0	0-0	0	2.70
Jeff Nelson	3	0	0	5.2	7	2	2	3	7	0-1	0-0	0	3.18
Bill Risley	4	0	0	3.0	2	2	2	0	1	0-0	1-1	0	6.00
Bob Wells	1	0	0	1.0	2	1	1	1	0	0-0	0-0	0	9.00
Totals	5	5	0	51.1	50	33	33	32	43	3-2	2-5	1	5.79

Yankees	G	GS	CG	IP	H	R	ER	BB	SO	W-L	Sv-Op	Hld	ERA
David Cone	2	2	0	15.2	15	8	8	9	14	1-0	0-0	0	4.60
Sterling Hitchcock	2	0	0	1.2	2	2	1	2	1	0-0	0-0	0	5.40
Steve Howe	2	0	0	1.0	4	2	2	0	0	0-0	0-0	0	18.00
Scott Kamieniecki	1	1	0	5.0	9	5	4	4	4	0-0	0-0	0	7.20
Jack McDowell	2	1	0	7.0	8	7	7	4	6	0-2	0-0	0	9.00
Andy Pettitte	1	1	0	7.0	9	4	4	3	0	0-0	0-0	0	5.14
Mariano Rivera	3	0	0	5.1	3	0	0	1	8	1-0	0-0	0	0.00
John Wetteland	3	0	0	4.1	8	7	7	2	5	0-1	0-0	0	14.54
Bob Wickman	3	0	0	3.0	5	0	0	0	3	0-0	0-0	0	0.00
Totals	5	5	0	50.0	63	35	33	25	41	2-3	0-0	0	5.94

Fielding

Mariners	Pos	G	PO	Ast	E	DP	PB	FPct
Bobby Ayala	p	2	0	0	0	0	—	—
Tim Belcher	p	2	0	1	0	0	—	1.000
Andy Benes	p	2	1	0	0	0	—	1.000
Mike Blowers	3b	5	2	5	0	0	—	1.000
	1b	1	0	1	0	0	—	1.000
Chris Bosio	p	2	1	0	0	0	—	1.000
Jay Buhner	rf	5	11	1	0	0	—	1.000
Norm Charlton	p	4	0	0	0	0	—	—
Vince Coleman	lf	5	14	0	0	0	—	1.000
Joey Cora	2b	5	10	12	1	2	—	.957
Alex Diaz	lf	1	1	1	0	0	—	1.000
Felix Fermin	ss	2	1	1	0	0	—	1.000
	2b	1	2	2	0	1	—	1.000
Ken Griffey Jr.	cf	5	15	1	0	0	—	1.000
Randy Johnson	p	2	0	0	0	0	—	—
Tino Martinez	1b	5	39	5	0	4	—	1.000
Jeff Nelson	p	3	0	1	0	0	—	1.000
Bill Risley	p	4	0	0	0	0	—	—
Alex Rodriguez	ss	1	0	0	0	0	—	—
Luis Sojo	ss	5	9	15	1	3	—	.960
Doug Strange	3b	2	0	0	0	0	—	—
Bob Wells	p	1	0	0	0	0	—	—
Chris Widger	c	2	14	0	0	0	0	1.000
Dan Wilson	c	5	34	1	0	1	0	1.000
Totals		5	154	47	2	11	0	.990

Yankees	Pos	G	PO	Ast	E	DP	PB	FPct
Wade Boggs	3b	4	4	8	0	2	—	1.000
David Cone	p	2	1	0	0	0	—	1.000
Russ Davis	3b	2	0	1	0	0	—	1.000
Tony Fernandez	ss	5	9	15	0	2	—	1.000
Sterling Hitchcock	p	2	0	1	0	0	—	1.000
Steve Howe	p	2	0	0	0	0	—	—
Dion James	lf	4	6	0	0	0	—	1.000
Scott Kamieniecki	p	1	0	0	0	0	—	—
Pat Kelly	2b	4	2	4	0	2	—	1.000
Jim Leyritz	c	2	13	0	0	0	0	1.000
Don Mattingly	1b	5	36	4	1	3	—	.976
Jack McDowell	p	2	0	0	0	0	—	—
Paul O'Neill	rf	5	13	0	0	0	—	1.000
Andy Pettitte	p	1	0	3	0	0	—	1.000
Mariano Rivera	p	3	0	0	0	0	—	—
Mike Stanley	c	4	30	0	1	0	—	.968
Randy Velarde	2b	4	13	11	0	2	—	1.000
	3b	2	1	0	0	0	—	1.000
	lf	2	1	0	1	0	—	.500
John Wetteland	p	3	1	0	0	0	—	1.000
Bob Wickman	p	3	0	1	0	0	—	1.000
Bernie Williams	cf	5	13	0	0	0	—	1.000
Gerald Williams	lf	4	5	1	0	1	—	1.000
	rf	1	2	0	0	0	—	1.000
Totals		5	150	49	3	12	0	.985

1995 Cleveland Indians (AL) 3, Boston Red Sox (AL) 0

The Boston Red Sox' postseason frustration continued as the Cleveland Indians swept them in three straight games. Cleveland got to Roger Clemens in the sixth inning of the first game, when Albert Belle lined a two-run double to help give the Indians a 3-2 lead. Luis Alicea tied it up with a solo homer in the eighth, and the game went into extra innings. Boston went ahead 4-3 on Tim Naehring's solo shot in the top of the 11th, but Belle tied it back up with a homer of his own in the bottom of the frame. Tony Pena finally won it for Cleveland with a homer in the bottom of the 13th. Orel Hershiser outdueled Erik Hanson in Game 2, 4-0. Back home at Fenway, the Sox were forced to send slumping knuckleballer Tim Wakefield to the mound. He gave up a two-run homer to Jim Thome in the second, and walked Thome with the bases loaded in the third to force in another run. The Red Sox trailed by only two runs going into the top of the sixth, but Cleveland exploded for five more and rolled to an 8-2 victory to advance to the ALCS. Boston's No.3 and No.4 hitters, Mo Vaughn and Jose Canseco, went 0-for-27 with nine strikeouts in the series.

Game 1
Tuesday, October 3

Red Sox	AB	R	H	RBI	BB	K	Avg
Dwayne Hosey, rf	5	1	0	0	1	1	.000
John Valentin, ss	4	1	2	2	2	0	.500
Mo Vaughn, 1b	6	0	0	0	0	3	.000
Jose Canseco, dh	6	0	0	0	0	1	.000
Mike Greenwell, lf	6	0	3	0	0	0	.500
Tim Naehring, 3b	5	1	2	1	0	1	.400
Lee Tinsley, cf	5	0	0	0	1	2	.000
Mike Macfarlane, c	3	0	0	0	0	1	.000
Matt Stairs, ph	1	0	0	0	0	1	.000
Bill Haselman, c	2	0	0	0	0	0	.000
Luis Alicea, 2b	5	1	4	1	0	0	.800
TOTALS	48	4	11	4	4	10	.229

Indians	AB	R	H	RBI	BB	K	Avg
Kenny Lofton, cf	5	0	1	0	0	2	.200
Omar Vizquel, ss	3	1	0	0	2	1	.000
Carlos Baerga, 2b	5	1	2	0	0	1	.400
Albert Belle, lf	5	2	2	3	1	1	.400
Eddie Murray, dh	6	0	1	0	0	0	.167
Jim Thome, 3b	6	0	1	0	0	3	.167
Manny Ramirez, rf	6	0	0	0	0	1	.000
Paul Sorrento, 1b	5	0	1	0	0	2	.200
Herbert Perry, ph	1	0	0	0	0	0	.000
Sandy Alomar Jr., c	4	0	1	0	0	0	.250
Wayne Kirby, pr	0	0	0	0	0	0	—
Tony Pena, c	2	1	1	1	0	0	.500
TOTALS	48	5	10	5	3	11	.208

	1	2	3	4	5	6	7	8	9	10	11	12	13	R	H	E
Red Sox	0	0	2	0	0	0	0	1	0	0	1	0	0	4	11	2
Indians	0	0	0	0	0	3	0	0	0	0	1	0	1	5	10	2

E—Macfarlane, Alicea, Sorrento, Lofton. DP—Indians 1 (Thome to Baerga). LOB—Red Sox 10, Indians 11. Scoring Position—Red Sox 0-for-11, Indians 2-for-11. 2B—Alicea (1), Belle (1). HR—Valentin (1), Naehring (1), Alicea (1), Belle (1), Pena (1). S—Naehring, Vizquel. SB—Alicea (1), Vizquel (1). CS—Valentin (1).

Red Sox	IP	H	R	ER	BB	K	ERA
Roger Clemens	7.0	5	3	3	1	5	3.86
Rheal Cormier	0.1	0	0	0	1	1	0.00
Stan Belinda	0.1	0	0	0	0	0	0.00
Mike Stanton	2.1	1	0	0	0	4	0.00
Rick Aguilera (BS, 1)	0.2	3	1	1	0	1	13.50
Mike Maddux	0.2	0	0	0	1	0	0.00
Zane Smith (L, 0-1)	1.1	1	1	1	0	0	6.75

Indians	IP	H	R	ER	BB	K	ERA
Dennis Martinez	6.0	5	2	2	0	2	3.00
Julian Tavarez (BS, 1)	1.1	2	1	1	0	2	6.75
Paul Assenmacher	0.1	0	0	0	0	1	0.00
Eric Plunk	1.1	1	0	0	1	1	0.00
Jose Mesa	1.0	0	0	0	2	0	0.00
Jim Poole	1.2	2	1	1	1	2	5.40
Ken Hill (W, 1-0)	1.1	1	0	0	0	2	0.00

HBP—Baerga by Cormier, Lofton by Maddux. Time—5:01. Attendance—44,218. Umpires—HP, Welke. 1B, Hirschbeck. 2B, Brinkman. 3B, Roe.

Game 2
Wednesday, October 4

Red Sox	AB	R	H	RBI	BB	K	Avg
Dwayne Hosey, cf	4	0	0	0	0	0	.000
John Valentin, ss	4	0	0	0	0	1	.250
Mo Vaughn, 1b	4	0	0	0	0	2	.000
Jose Canseco, dh	4	0	0	0	0	1	.000
Mike Greenwell, lf	4	0	0	0	0	0	.300
Tim Naehring, 3b	4	0	0	0	0	0	.222
Willie McGee, rf	3	0	1	0	0	2	.333
Mike Macfarlane, c	3	0	2	0	0	1	.333
Luis Alicea, 2b	1	0	0	0	2	1	.667
TOTALS	31	0	3	0	2	8	.197

Indians	AB	R	H	RBI	BB	K	Avg
Kenny Lofton, cf	3	1	0	0	1	0	.125
Omar Vizquel, ss	4	0	1	2	0	0	.143
Carlos Baerga, 2b	4	0	0	0	0	0	.222
Albert Belle, lf	2	1	1	0	2	0	.429
Eddie Murray, dh	4	1	2	2	0	1	.300
Jim Thome, 3b	4	0	0	0	0	3	.100
Manny Ramirez, rf	4	0	0	0	0	1	.000
Wayne Kirby, rf	0	0	0	0	0	0	—
Paul Sorrento, 1b	1	1	0	0	1	0	.167
Sandy Alomar Jr., c	2	0	0	0	0	0	.167
TOTALS	28	4	4	4	4	5	.178

	1	2	3	4	5	6	7	8	9	R	H	E
Red Sox	0	0	0	0	0	0	0	0	0	0	3	1
Indians	0	0	0	2	0	0	2	0	x	4	4	2

E—Belle, Sorrento, Valentin. LOB—Red Sox 6, Indians 6. Scoring Position—Red Sox 0-for-5, Indians 1-for-6. 2B—Vizquel (1). 3B—Murray (1). HR—Murray (1). S—Alomar Jr. SB—Hosey (1).

Red Sox	IP	H	R	ER	BB	K	ERA
Erik Hanson (L, 0-1)	8.0	4	4	4	4	5	4.50

Indians	IP	H	R	ER	BB	K	ERA
Orel Hershiser (W, 1-0)	7.1	3	0	0	2	7	0.00
Julian Tavarez (H, 1)	0.1	0	0	0	0	0	5.40
Paul Assenmacher (H, 1)	0.1	0	0	0	0	1	0.00
Jose Mesa	1.0	0	0	0	0	0	0.00

WP—Hershiser. PB—Macfarlane. HBP—Sorrento by Hanson. Time—2:33. Attendance—44,264. Umpires—HP, Hirschbeck. 1B, Brinkman. 2B, Roe. 3B, Denkinger.

Game 3
Friday, October 6

Indians	AB	R	H	RBI	BB	K	Avg
Kenny Lofton, cf	5	0	1	0	0	1	.154
Omar Vizquel, ss	5	1	1	2	0	1	.167
Carlos Baerga, 2b	5	1	2	1	0	0	.286
Albert Belle, lf	4	0	0	0	1	2	.273
Eddie Murray, dh	3	2	2	0	2	0	.385
Jim Thome, 3b	3	1	1	3	1	0	.154
Alvaro Espinoza, 3b	1	0	0	0	0	0	.000
Manny Ramirez, rf	2	1	0	0	1	0	.000
Wayne Kirby, rf	1	0	1	0	0	0	1.000
Paul Sorrento, 1b	4	1	2	1	1	1	.300
Sandy Alomar Jr., c	5	1	1	1	0	1	.182
Tony Pena, c	0	0	0	0	0	0	.500
TOTALS	38	8	11	8	6	6	.221

Red Sox	AB	R	H	RBI	BB	K	Avg
Dwayne Hosey, cf	3	0	0	0	1	2	.000
Willie McGee, ph-cf	1	0	0	0	1	0	.250
John Valentin, ss	4	0	1	0	1	0	.250
Mo Vaughn, 1b	4	0	0	0	1	2	.000
Jose Canseco, rf	3	0	0	2	0	0	.000
Mike Greenwell, lf	5	0	0	0	0	1	.200
Reggie Jefferson, dh	4	1	1	0	0	1	.250
Tim Naehring, 3b	4	1	2	0	0	0	.308
Luis Alicea, 2b	4	0	2	0	0	0	.600
Mike Macfarlane, c	3	0	1	0	1	1	.333
TOTALS	35	2	7	2	5	8	.198

	1	2	3	4	5	6	7	8	9	R	H	E
Indians	0	2	1	0	0	5	0	0	0	8	11	2
Red Sox	0	0	0	1	0	0	0	1	0	2	7	1

E—Macfarlane, Baerga, Lofton. LOB—Indians 10, Red Sox 12. Scoring Position—Indians 3-for-9, Red Sox 2-for-12. 2B—Baerga (1), Alomar Jr. (1), Valentin (1). HR—Thome (1). SF—Macfarlane.

Indians	IP	H	R	ER	BB	K	ERA
Charles Nagy (W, 1-0)	7.0	4	1	1	5	6	1.29
Julian Tavarez	1.0	3	1	1	0	1	6.75
Paul Assenmacher	1.0	0	0	0	0	1	0.00

Red Sox	IP	H	R	ER	BB	K	ERA
Tim Wakefield (L, 0-1)	5.1	5	7	7	5	4	11.81
Rheal Cormier	0.1	2	1	1	0	1	13.50
Mike Maddux	2.1	2	0	0	0	0	0.00
Joe Hudson	1.0	2	0	0	1	0	0.00

WP—Hudson. PB—Macfarlane. HBP—Ramirez by Wakefield. Time—3:18. Attendance—34,211. Umpires—HP, McKean. 1B, McCoy. 2B, Garcia. 3B, Joyce.

1995 AL Division Series—Composite Statistics

Batting

Indians	G	AB	R	H	RBI	2B	3B	HR	BB	SO	SB	CS	Avg	OBP	Slg
Sandy Alomar Jr.	3	11	1	2	1	1	0	0	0	1	0	0	.182	.182	.273
Carlos Baerga	3	14	2	4	1	1	0	0	1	0	0	0	.286	.333	.357
Albert Belle	3	11	3	3	3	1	0	1	4	3	0	0	.273	.467	.636
Alvaro Espinoza	1	1	0	0	0	0	0	0	0	0	0	0	.000	.000	.000
Wayne Kirby	3	1	0	1	0	0	0	0	0	0	0	0	1.000	1.000	1.000
Kenny Lofton	3	13	1	2	0	0	0	0	1	3	0	0	.154	.267	.154
Eddie Murray	3	13	3	5	3	0	1	1	2	1	0	0	.385	.467	.769
Tony Pena	2	2	1	1	0	0	0	1	0	0	0	0	.500	.500	2.000
Herbert Perry	1	1	0	0	0	0	0	0	0	0	0	0	.000	.000	.000
Manny Ramirez	3	12	1	0	0	0	0	0	1	2	0	0	.000	.143	.000
Paul Sorrento	3	10	2	3	1	0	0	0	2	3	0	0	.300	.462	.300
Jim Thome	3	13	1	2	3	0	0	1	1	6	0	0	.154	.214	.385
Omar Vizquel	3	12	2	2	4	1	0	0	2	2	1	0	.167	.286	.250
Totals	**3**	**114**	**17**	**25**	**17**	**4**	**1**	**4**	**13**	**22**	**1**	**0**	**.219**	**.321**	**.377**

Batting

Red Sox	G	AB	R	H	RBI	2B	3B	HR	BB	SO	SB	CS	Avg	OBP	Slg
Luis Alicea	3	10	1	6	1	1	0	1	2	2	1	0	.600	.667	1.000
Jose Canseco	3	13	0	0	0	0	0	0	2	2	0	0	.000	.133	.000
Mike Greenwell	3	15	0	3	0	0	0	0	0	1	0	0	.200	.200	.200
Bill Haselman	1	2	0	0	0	0	0	0	0	0	0	0	.000	.000	.000
Dwayne Hosey	3	12	1	0	0	0	0	0	2	3	1	0	.000	.143	.000
Reggie Jefferson	1	4	1	1	0	0	0	0	0	1	0	0	.250	.250	.250
Mike Macfarlane	3	9	0	3	1	0	0	0	0	3	0	0	.333	.300	.333
Willie McGee	2	4	0	1	0	0	0	0	0	2	0	0	.250	.250	.250
Tim Naehring	3	13	2	4	1	0	0	1	0	1	0	0	.308	.308	.538
Matt Stairs	1	1	0	0	0	0	0	0	0	1	0	0	.000	.000	.000
Lee Tinsley	1	5	0	0	0	0	0	0	1	2	0	0	.000	.167	.000
John Valentin	3	12	1	3	2	1	0	1	3	1	0	1	.250	.400	.583
Mo Vaughn	3	14	0	0	0	0	0	0	1	7	0	0	.000	.067	.000
Totals	**3**	**114**	**6**	**21**	**6**	**2**	**0**	**3**	**11**	**26**	**2**	**1**	**.184**	**.254**	**.281**

Pitching

Indians	G	GS	CG	IP	H	R	ER	BB	SO	W-L	Sv-Op	Hld	ERA
Paul Assenmacher	3	0	0	1.2	0	0	0	0	3	0-0	0-0	1	0.00
Orel Hershiser	1	1	0	7.1	3	0	0	2	7	1-0	0-0	0	0.00
Ken Hill	1	0	0	1.1	1	0	0	0	2	1-0	0-0	0	0.00
Dennis Martinez	1	1	0	6.0	5	2	2	0	2	0-0	0-0	0	3.00
Jose Mesa	2	0	0	2.0	0	0	0	2	0	0-0	0-0	0	0.00
Charles Nagy	1	1	0	7.0	4	1	1	5	6	1-0	0-0	0	1.29
Eric Plunk	1	0	0	1.1	1	0	0	1	1	0-0	0-0	0	0.00
Jim Poole	1	0	0	1.2	2	1	1	1	2	0-0	0-0	0	5.40
Julian Tavarez	3	0	0	2.2	5	2	2	0	3	0-0	0-1	1	6.75
Totals	**3**	**3**	**0**	**31.0**	**21**	**6**	**6**	**11**	**26**	**3-0**	**0-1**	**2**	**1.74**

Pitching

Red Sox	G	GS	CG	IP	H	R	ER	BB	SO	W-L	Sv-Op	Hld	ERA
Rick Aguilera	1	0	0	0.2	3	1	1	0	1	0-0	0-1	0	13.50
Stan Belinda	1	0	0	0.1	0	0	0	0	0	0-0	0-0	0	0.00
Roger Clemens	1	1	0	7.0	5	3	3	1	5	0-0	0-0	0	3.86
Rheal Cormier	2	0	0	0.2	2	1	1	1	2	0-0	0-0	0	13.50
Erik Hanson	1	1	1	8.0	4	4	4	4	5	0-1	0-0	0	4.50
Joe Hudson	1	0	0	1.0	2	0	0	1	0	0-0	0-0	0	0.00
Mike Maddux	2	0	0	3.0	2	0	0	0	1	0-0	0-0	0	0.00
Zane Smith	1	0	0	1.1	1	1	1	0	0	0-1	0-0	0	6.75
Mike Stanton	1	0	0	2.1	1	0	0	4	0	0-0	0-0	0	0.00
Tim Wakefield	1	1	0	5.1	5	7	7	5	4	0-1	0-0	0	11.81
Totals	**3**	**3**	**1**	**29.2**	**25**	**17**	**17**	**13**	**22**	**0-3**	**0-1**	**0**	**5.16**

Fielding

Indians	Pos	G	PO	Ast	E	DP	PB	FPct
Sandy Alomar Jr.	c	3	22	1	0	0	0	1.000
Paul Assenmacher	p	3	0	0	0	0	—	—
Carlos Baerga	2b	3	8	5	1	1	—	.929
Albert Belle	lf	3	7	0	1	0	—	.875
Alvaro Espinoza	3b	1	0	0	0	0	—	—
Orel Hershiser	p	1	0	0	0	0	—	—
Ken Hill	p	1	0	2	0	0	—	1.000
Wayne Kirby	rf	2	0	0	0	0	—	—
Kenny Lofton	cf	3	9	0	2	0	—	.818
Dennis Martinez	p	1	0	1	0	0	—	1.000
Jose Mesa	p	2	0	0	0	0	—	—
Charles Nagy	p	1	2	1	0	0	—	1.000
Tony Pena	c	2	5	0	0	0	0	1.000
Eric Plunk	p	1	0	1	0	0	—	1.000
Jim Poole	p	1	0	1	0	0	—	1.000
Manny Ramirez	rf	3	3	0	0	0	—	1.000
Paul Sorrento	1b	3	27	5	2	0	—	.941
Julian Tavarez	p	3	0	0	0	0	—	—
Jim Thome	3b	3	6	6	0	0	1	1.000
Omar Vizquel	ss	3	4	11	0	0	—	1.000
Totals		**3**	**93**	**34**	**6**	**2**	**0**	**.955**

Fielding

Red Sox	Pos	G	PO	Ast	E	DP	PB	FPct
Rick Aguilera	p	1	0	0	0	0	—	—
Luis Alicea	2b	3	6	11	1	0	—	.944
Stan Belinda	p	1	0	0	0	0	—	—
Jose Canseco	rf	1	4	0	0	0	—	1.000
Roger Clemens	p	1	0	0	0	0	—	—
Rheal Cormier	p	2	0	0	0	0	—	—
Mike Greenwell	lf	3	8	0	0	0	—	1.000
Erik Hanson	p	1	1	3	0	0	—	1.000
Bill Haselman	c	1	6	0	0	0	0	1.000
Dwayne Hosey	cf	2	4	0	0	0	—	1.000
	rf	1	3	0	0	0	—	1.000
Joe Hudson	p	1	0	0	0	0	—	—
Mike Macfarlane	c	3	18	0	2	0	2	.900
Mike Maddux	p	2	1	2	0	0	—	1.000
Willie McGee	cf	1	0	0	0	0	—	—
	rf	1	0	0	0	0	—	—
Tim Naehring	3b	3	5	5	0	0	—	1.000
Zane Smith	p	1	0	0	0	0	—	—
Mike Stanton	p	1	0	1	0	0	—	1.000
Lee Tinsley	cf	1	1	0	0	0	—	1.000
John Valentin	ss	3	5	5	1	0	—	.909
Mo Vaughn	1b	3	27	0	0	0	—	1.000
Tim Wakefield	p	1	0	0	0	0	—	—
Totals		**3**	**89**	**29**	**4**	**0**	**2**	**.967**

1995 Cincinnati Reds (NL) 3, Los Angeles Dodgers (NL) 0

The Los Angeles Dodgers couldn't stop the Reds' offense and couldn't buy a hit of their own when it counted. The result was a three-game sweep by the Reds, who dented Ramon Martinez for four runs in Game 1 before the Dodgers had even come to bat. That was all Pete Schourek needed, and the lefty tossed seven strong innings for a 7-2 win. Eric Karros notched a double and a pair of home runs in Game 2, but his teammates blew numerous opportunities and committed a pair of errors, losing 5-4 despite out-hitting the Reds 14-6. The Reds took a 3-1 lead against Hideo Nomo in Game 3 before loading the bases in the bottom of the sixth. With lefthanded reliever Mark Guthrie set to face Jeff Branson, Davey Johnson countered with pinch-hitter Mark Lewis. Lewis launched a grand slam to blow the game wide open, and the Reds rolled into the NLCS with a 10-1 victory.

Game 1

Tuesday, October 3

Reds	AB	R	H	RBI	BB	K	Avg
Thomas Howard, cf	3	0	1	0	0	1	.333
Jerome Walton, ph-cf-lf	2	0	0	0	0	1	.000
Barry Larkin, ss	4	1	2	0	1	1	.500
Ron Gant, lf	5	1	1	0	0	1	.200
Darren Lewis, cf	0	0	0	0	0	0	—
Reggie Sanders, rf	5	1	1	0	0	2	.200
Hal Morris, 1b	4	2	3	2	1	0	.750
Benito Santiago, c	3	1	1	3	1	1	.333
Bret Boone, 2b	4	1	1	0	0	2	.250
Jeff Branson, 3b	3	0	2	2	1	0	.667
Pete Schourek, p	2	0	0	0	0	1	.000
Mariano Duncan, ph	1	0	0	0	0	0	.000
Mike Jackson, p	0	0	0	0	0	0	—
Jeff Brantley, p	0	0	0	0	0	0	—
TOTALS	36	7	12	7	4	10	.333

Dodgers	AB	R	H	RBI	BB	K	Avg
Brett Butler, cf	5	0	1	1	0	1	.200
Chad Fonville, ss	4	0	1	0	0	1	.250
Mike Piazza, c	4	1	2	1	0	0	.500
Eric Karros, 1b	4	0	1	0	0	0	.250
Tim Wallach, 3b	3	0	0	0	1	1	.000
Raul Mondesi, rf	4	0	0	0	0	2	.000
Delino DeShields, 2b	3	1	2	0	1	0	.667
Roberto Kelly, lf	4	0	1	0	0	0	.250
Ramon Martinez, p	1	0	0	0	0	0	.000
John Cummings, p	0	0	0	0	0	0	—
Billy Ashley, ph	0	0	0	0	1	0	—
Pedro Astacio, p	0	0	0	0	0	0	—
Mitch Webster, ph	1	0	0	0	0	0	.000
Mark Guthrie, p	0	0	0	0	0	0	—
Antonio Osuna, p	0	0	0	0	0	0	—
Dave Hansen, ph	1	0	0	0	0	0	.000
TOTALS	34	2	8	2	3	5	.235

	1	2	3	4	5	6	7	8	9	R	H	E
Reds	4	0	0	0	3	0	0	0	0	7	12	0
Dodgers	0	0	0	0	1	1	0	0	0	2	8	0

DP—Reds 1 (Schourek to Larkin to Morris), Dodgers 1 (Fonville to DeShields to Karros). LOB—Reds 8, Dodgers 8. Scoring Position—Reds 4-for-14, Dodgers 1-for-6. 2B—Howard (1), Sanders (1), Morris (1), Boone (1), Branson (1). HR—Santiago (1), Piazza (1). S—Schourek. SF—Santiago. GDP—Fonville, Duncan. SB—Larkin 2 (2).

Reds	IP	H	R	ER	BB	K	ERA
Pete Schourek (W, 1-0)	7.0	5	2	2	3	5	2.57
Mike Jackson	1.0	2	0	0	0	0	0.00
Jeff Brantley	1.0	1	0	0	0	0	0.00

Dodgers	IP	H	R	ER	BB	K	ERA
Ramon Martinez (L, 0-1)	4.1	10	7	7	2	3	14.54
John Cummings	0.2	1	0	0	0	1	0.00
Pedro Astacio	2.0	0	0	0	0	4	0.00
Mark Guthrie	1.0	0	0	0	1	1	0.00
Antonio Osuna	1.0	1	0	0	1	1	0.00

Time—3:15. Attendance—44,199. Umpires—HP, Montague. 1B, Davidson. 2B, Gregg. 3B, Pulli.

Game 2

Wednesday, October 4

Reds	AB	R	H	RBI	BB	K	Avg
Thomas Howard, cf	4	0	0	0	0	0	.143
Darren Lewis, cf	1	0	0	0	0	0	.000
Barry Larkin, ss	4	0	1	1	0	1	.375
Ron Gant, lf	4	1	0	0	0	1	.111
Mike Jackson, p	0	0	0	0	0	0	—
Jeff Brantley, p	0	0	0	0	0	0	—
Reggie Sanders, rf	3	2	1	2	1	2	.250
Hal Morris, 1b	3	1	1	0	1	0	.571
Benito Santiago, c	3	0	1	0	1	1	.333
Bret Boone, 2b	3	0	0	0	1	1	.143
Dave Burba, p	0	0	0	0	0	0	—
Jerome Walton, lf	0	0	0	0	1	0	.000
Jeff Branson, 3b	3	0	0	0	0	1	.333
Mark Lewis, ph-3b	1	0	1	0	0	0	.000
John Smiley, p	2	0	0	0	0	1	.000
Mariano Duncan, 2b	2	1	2	1	0	0	.667
TOTALS	33	5	6	5	4	7	.269

Dodgers	AB	R	H	RBI	BB	K	Avg
Brett Butler, cf	5	1	3	0	0	0	.400
Chad Fonville, ss	4	1	4	0	0	0	.625
Mike Piazza, c	5	0	0	0	0	1	.222
Eric Karros, 1b	4	2	3	4	1	0	.500
Tim Wallach, 3b	5	0	1	0	0	1	.125
Delino DeShields, 2b	5	0	0	0	0	0	.250
Raul Mondesi, rf	3	0	1	0	0	0	.143
Todd Hollandsworth, rf	1	0	0	0	0	0	.000
Roberto Kelly, lf	4	0	1	0	0	0	.250
Ismael Valdes, p	3	0	0	0	0	0	.000
Antonio Osuna, p	0	0	0	0	0	0	—
Dave Hansen, ph	1	0	1	0	0	0	.500
Jose Offerman, pr	0	0	0	0	0	0	—
Kevin Tapani, p	0	0	0	0	0	0	—
Mark Guthrie, p	0	0	0	0	0	0	—
Pedro Astacio, p	0	0	0	0	0	0	—
TOTALS	40	4	14	4	1	2	.306

	1	2	3	4	5	6	7	8	9	R	H	E
Reds	0	0	0	2	0	0	0	1	2	5	6	0
Dodgers	1	0	0	1	0	0	0	0	2	4	14	2

E—Osuna, Fonville. DP—Dodgers 1 (Fonville to DeShields to Karros). LOB—Reds 5, Dodgers 11. Scoring Position—Reds 3-for-8, Dodgers 2-for-9. 2B—Karros (1). HR—Sanders (1), Karros 2 (2). S—Fonville. GDP—Branson. SB—Sanders 2 (2), Morris (1), Duncan (1).

Reds	IP	H	R	ER	BB	K	ERA
John Smiley	6.0	9	2	2	0	1	3.00
Dave Burba (W, 1-0)	1.0	2	0	0	1	0	0.00
Mike Jackson (H, 1)	1.0	1	0	0	0	0	0.00
Jeff Brantley (S, 1)	1.0	2	2	2	0	1	9.00

Dodgers	IP	H	R	ER	BB	K	ERA
Ismael Valdes	7.0	3	2	0	1	6	0.00
Antonio Osuna (L, 0-1)	1.0	2	1	1	0	0	4.50
Kevin Tapani	0.1	0	2	2	3	1	54.00
Mark Guthrie	0.1	0	0	0	0	0	0.00
Pedro Astacio	0.1	1	0	0	0	0	0.00

Time—3:21. Attendance—46,051. Umpires—HP, Davidson. 1B, Gregg. 2B, Pulli. 3B, Froemming.

Game 3

Friday, October 6

Dodgers	AB	R	H	RBI	BB	K	Avg
Brett Butler, cf	5	0	0	0	0	2	.267
Chad Fonville, ss	4	0	1	0	0	0	.500
Chris Gwynn, ph	1	0	0	0	0	1	.000
Mike Piazza, c	5	0	1	0	0	1	.214
Eric Karros, 1b	4	1	2	0	0	0	.500
Tim Wallach, 3b	4	0	0	0	0	1	.083
Delino DeShields, 2b	4	0	1	0	0	3	.250
Raul Mondesi, rf	2	0	1	1	0	0	.222
Todd Hollandsworth, ph-rf	1	0	0	0	0	0	.000
Roberto Kelly, lf	3	0	2	1	0	0	.364
Hideo Nomo, p	2	0	0	0	0	2	.000
Kevin Tapani, p	0	0	0	0	0	0	—
Mark Guthrie, p	0	0	0	0	0	0	—
Pedro Astacio, p	0	0	0	0	0	0	—
Mitch Webster, ph	1	0	0	0	0	0	.000
John Cummings, p	0	0	0	0	0	0	—
Antonio Osuna, p	0	0	0	0	0	0	—
Dave Hansen, ph	1	0	1	0	0	0	.667
TOTALS	37	1	9	1	1	10	.290

Reds	AB	R	H	RBI	BB	K	Avg
Thomas Howard, cf	3	0	0	0	0	1	.100
Darren Lewis, ph-cf	2	0	0	0	0	1	.000
Barry Larkin, ss	5	1	2	0	0	0	.385
Ron Gant, lf	4	1	2	2	0	1	.231
Jerome Walton, lf	1	0	0	0	0	0	.000
Reggie Sanders, rf	5	0	0	0	0	5	.154
Hal Morris, 1b	3	2	1	0	1	1	.500
Benito Santiago, c	3	1	1	0	1	1	.333
Bret Boone, 2b	3	3	2	1	1	0	.300
Jeff Branson, 3b	1	0	0	0	1	0	.286
Mark Lewis, ph-3b	1	2	1	4	1	0	.500
David Wells, p	3	0	1	0	0	1	.333
Mike Jackson, p	1	0	1	3	0	0	1.000
Jeff Brantley, p	0	0	0	0	0	0	—
TOTALS	35	10	11	10	5	11	.278

	1	2	3	4	5	6	7	8	9	R	H	E
Dodgers	0	0	0	1	0	0	0	0	0	1	9	1
Reds	0	0	2	0	1	0	4	3	0	x	10	11	2

E—Kelly, MLewis, Sanders. LOB—Dodgers 11, Reds 6. Scoring Position—Dodgers 1-for-11, Reds 3-for-7. 2B—Piazza (1), Jackson (1). HR—Gant (1), Boone (1), MLewis (1). SB—Larkin 2 (4), Boone (1).

Dodgers	IP	H	R	ER	BB	K	ERA
Hideo Nomo (L, 0-1)	5.0	7	5	5	2	6	9.00
Kevin Tapani	0.0	0	1	1	1	0	81.00
Mark Guthrie	0.0	2	1	1	0	0	6.75
Pedro Astacio	1.0	0	0	0	0	1	0.00
John Cummings	0.2	2	3	3	2	2	20.25
Antonio Osuna	1.1	0	0	0	0	2	2.70

Reds	IP	H	R	ER	BB	K	ERA
David Wells (W, 1-0)	6.1	6	1	0	1	8	0.00
Mike Jackson	1.2	1	0	0	0	0	0.00
Jeff Brantley	1.0	2	0	0	0	1	6.00

Nomo pitched to three batters in the 6th. Tapani pitched to one batter in the 6th. Guthrie pitched to two batters in the 6th.

WP—Nomo. HBP—Mondesi by Wells. Time—3:27. Attendance—53,276. Umpires—HP, West. 1B, Tata. 2B, Wendelstedt. 3B, Reliford.

1995 NL Division Series—Composite Statistics

Batting

Reds	G	AB	R	H	RBI	2B	3B	HR	BB	SO	SB	CS	Avg	OBP	Slg
Bret Boone	3	10	4	3	1	1	0	1	1	3	1	0	.300	.364	.700
Jeff Branson	3	7	0	2	2	1	0	0	2	0	0	0	.286	.444	.429
Mariano Duncan	2	3	1	2	1	0	0	0	0	1	0	0	.667	.667	.667
Ron Gant	3	13	3	3	2	0	0	1	0	3	1	0	.231	.231	.462
Thomas Howard	3	10	0	1	0	1	0	0	0	2	0	0	.100	.100	.200
Mike Jackson	3	1	0	1	3	1	0	0	0	0	0	0	1.000	1.000	2.000
Barry Larkin	3	13	2	5	1	0	0	0	1	2	4	0	.385	.429	.385
Darren Lewis	3	3	0	0	0	0	0	0	0	1	0	0	.000	.000	.000
Mark Lewis	2	2	1	5	0	0	1	1	0	0	0	0	.500	.667	2.000
Hal Morris	3	10	5	5	2	1	0	3	1	1	1	0	.500	.615	.600
Reggie Sanders	3	13	3	2	2	1	0	1	1	9	2	0	.154	.214	.462
Benito Santiago	3	9	2	3	3	0	0	1	3	3	0	0	.333	.462	.667
Pete Schourek	1	2	0	0	0	0	0	0	0	1	0	0	.000	.000	.000
John Smiley	1	2	0	0	0	0	0	0	0	1	0	0	.000	.000	.000
Jerome Walton	3	3	0	0	0	0	0	0	1	1	0	0	.000	.250	.000
David Wells	1	3	0	1	0	0	0	0	0	1	0	0	.333	.333	.333
Totals	**3**	**104**	**22**	**29**	**22**	**6**	**0**	**5**	**13**	**28**	**9**	**0**	**.279**	**.356**	**.481**

Batting

Dodgers	G	AB	R	H	RBI	2B	3B	HR	BB	SO	SB	CS	Avg	OBP	Slg
Billy Ashley	1	0	0	0	0	0	0	0	1	0	0	0	—	1.000	—
Brett Butler	3	15	1	4	1	0	0	0	3	0	0	0	.267	.267	.267
Delino DeShields	3	12	1	3	0	0	0	0	1	3	0	0	.250	.308	.250
Chad Fonville	3	12	1	6	0	0	0	0	0	1	0	0	.500	.500	.500
Chris Gwynn	1	1	0	0	0	0	0	0	0	1	0	0	.000	.000	.000
Dave Hansen	3	3	0	2	0	0	0	0	0	0	0	0	.667	.667	.667
Todd Hollandsworth	2	2	0	0	0	0	0	0	0	0	0	0	.000	.000	.000
Eric Karros	3	12	3	6	4	1	0	2	1	0	0	0	.500	.538	1.083
Roberto Kelly	3	11	0	4	0	0	0	0	1	0	0	0	.364	.417	.364
Ramon Martinez	1	1	0	0	0	0	0	0	0	0	0	0	.000	.000	.000
Raul Mondesi	3	9	0	2	1	0	0	0	0	2	0	0	.222	.300	.222
Hideo Nomo	1	2	0	0	0	0	0	0	0	2	0	0	.000	.000	.000
Jose Offerman	1	0	0	0	0	0	0	0	0	0	0	0	—	—	—
Mike Piazza	3	14	1	3	0	1	1	0	1	2	0	0	.214	.214	.500
Ismael Valdes	1	3	0	0	0	0	0	0	0	0	0	0	.000	.000	.000
Tim Wallach	3	12	0	1	0	0	0	0	1	3	0	0	.083	.154	.083
Mitch Webster	2	2	0	0	0	0	0	0	0	0	0	0	.000	.000	.000
Totals	**3**	**111**	**7**	**31**	**7**	**2**	**0**	**3**	**5**	**17**	**0**	**0**	**.279**	**.316**	**.378**

Pitching

Reds	G	GS	CG	IP	H	R	ER	BB	SO	W-L	Sv-Op	Hld	ERA
Jeff Brantley	3	0	0	3.0	5	2	2	0	2	0-0	1-1	0	6.00
Dave Burba	1	0	0	1.0	2	0	0	1	0	1-0	0-0	0	0.00
Mike Jackson	3	0	0	3.2	4	0	0	0	1	0-0	0-0	1	0.00
Pete Schourek	1	1	0	7.0	5	2	2	3	5	1-0	0-0	0	2.57
John Smiley	1	1	0	6.0	9	2	2	0	4	0-0	0-0	0	3.00
David Wells	1	1	0	6.1	6	1	0	1	8	1-0	0-0	0	0.00
Totals	**3**	**3**	**0**	**27.0**	**31**	**7**	**6**	**5**	**17**	**3-0**	**1-1**	**1**	**2.00**

Pitching

Dodgers	G	GS	CG	IP	H	R	ER	BB	SO	W-L	Sv-Op	Hld	ERA
Pedro Astacio	3	0	0	3.1	1	0	0	0	5	0-0	0-0	0	0.00
John Cummings	2	0	0	1.1	3	3	3	2	3	0-0	0-0	0	20.25
Mark Guthrie	3	0	0	1.1	2	1	1	1	1	0-0	0-0	0	6.75
Ramon Martinez	1	1	0	4.1	10	7	7	2	3	0-1	0-0	0	14.54
Hideo Nomo	1	1	0	5.0	7	5	5	2	6	0-1	0-0	0	9.00
Antonio Osuna	3	0	0	3.1	3	1	1	1	4	0-1	0-0	0	2.70
Kevin Tapani	2	0	0	0.1	0	3	3	4	1	0-0	0-0	0	81.00
Ismael Valdes	1	1	0	7.0	3	2	0	1	6	0-0	0-0	0	0.00
Totals	**3**	**3**	**0**	**26.0**	**29**	**22**	**20**	**13**	**28**	**0-3**	**0-0**	**0**	**6.92**

Fielding

Reds	Pos	G	PO	Ast	E	DP	PB	FPct
Bret Boone	2b	3	7	5	0	0	—	1.000
Jeff Branson	3b	3	1	8	0	0	—	1.000
Jeff Brantley	p	3	0	0	0	0	—	—
Dave Burba	p	1	0	0	0	0	—	—
Mariano Duncan	2b	1	0	1	0	0	—	1.000
Ron Gant	lf	3	8	1	0	0	—	1.000
Thomas Howard	cf	3	5	0	0	0	—	1.000
Mike Jackson	p	3	1	1	0	0	—	1.000
Barry Larkin	ss	3	3	8	0	1	—	1.000
Darren Lewis	cf	3	3	0	0	0	—	1.000
Mark Lewis	3b	2	0	0	1	0	—	.000
Hal Morris	1b	3	22	2	0	1	—	1.000
Reggie Sanders	rf	3	7	0	1	0	—	.875
Benito Santiago	c	3	20	0	0	0	0	1.000
Pete Schourek	p	1	0	2	0	1	—	1.000
John Smiley	p	1	0	1	0	0	—	1.000
Jerome Walton	lf	3	2	0	0	0	—	1.000
	cf	1	1	0	0	0	—	1.000
David Wells	p	1	1	1	0	0	—	1.000
Totals		**3**	**81**	**30**	**2**	**3**	**0**	**.982**

Fielding

Dodgers	Pos	G	PO	Ast	E	DP	PB	FPct
Pedro Astacio	p	3	0	2	0	0	—	1.000
Brett Butler	cf	3	7	0	0	0	—	1.000
John Cummings	p	2	0	0	0	0	—	—
Delino DeShields	2b	3	8	7	0	2	—	1.000
Chad Fonville	ss	3	1	7	1	2	—	.889
Mark Guthrie	p	3	0	0	0	0	—	—
Todd Hollandsworth	rf	2	0	0	0	0	—	—
Eric Karros	1b	3	14	0	0	2	—	1.000
Roberto Kelly	lf	3	8	0	1	0	—	.889
Ramon Martinez	p	1	0	1	0	0	—	1.000
Raul Mondesi	rf	3	8	0	0	0	—	1.000
Hideo Nomo	p	1	0	0	0	0	—	—
Antonio Osuna	p	3	0	0	1	0	—	.000
Mike Piazza	c	3	31	0	0	0	0	1.000
Kevin Tapani	p	2	0	0	0	0	—	—
Ismael Valdes	p	1	0	0	0	0	—	—
Tim Wallach	3b	3	1	2	0	0	—	1.000
Totals		**3**	**78**	**19**	**3**	**6**	**0**	**.970**

1995 Atlanta Braves (NL) 3, Colorado Rockies (NL) 1

The Colorado Rockies gave the Atlanta Braves more than they bargained for, although the Braves ultimately prevailed in four games. The Braves won the opener 5-4, thanks to their bend-but-don't-break bullpen. The Rockies loaded the bases in each of the last three innings, but came away with only one run. Chipper Jones hit a solo homer with two out in the top of the ninth—his second circuit shot of the game—to plate the eventual winning run. Don Baylor ran out of bench players and was forced to use pitcher Lance Painter to pinch-hit in the ninth. Painter fanned with the bases full to end the game. In the second game, the Braves entered the top of the ninth trailing by a run, but rallied to take the lead on RBI singles by Fred McGriff and Mike Mordecai. Eric Young's throwing error allowed two more runs to score, and the Braves won 7-4. The Braves mounted yet another ninth-inning rally in Game 3, pushing across a run to send the game into extra innings, but the Rockies scored twice in the 10th to stave off elimination. Atlanta made it a wrap in the fourth game, as McGriff homered twice and drove in five runs in Atlanta's 10-4 win.

Game 1

Tuesday, October 3

Braves	AB	R	H	RBI	BB	K	Avg
Marquis Grissom, cf	5	1	2	1	0	0	.400
Mark Lemke, 2b	5	0	1	0	0	1	.200
Chipper Jones, 3b	5	2	2	2	0	0	.400
Fred McGriff, 1b	5	0	1	0	0	1	.200
David Justice, rf	2	1	1	0	2	1	.500
Ryan Klesko, lf	4	1	3	0	0	1	.750
Greg McMichael, p	0	0	0	0	0	0	—
Alejandro Pena, p	0	0	0	0	0	0	—
Mark Wohlers, p	0	0	0	0	0	0	—
Charlie O'Brien, c	2	0	0	0	0	1	.000
Luis Polonia, ph	1	0	0	1	0	0	.000
Javy Lopez, c	1	0	1	0	0	0	1.000
Jeff Blauser, ss	2	0	0	0	1	1	.000
Dwight Smith, ph	1	0	1	1	0	0	1.000
Rafael Belliard, ss	0	0	0	0	0	0	—
Greg Maddux, p	3	0	0	0	0	1	.000
Mike Devereaux, ph-lf	1	0	0	0	0	0	.000
TOTALS	37	5	12	5	3	7	.324

Rockies	AB	R	H	RBI	BB	K	Avg
Eric Young, 2b	4	0	2	0	1	0	.500
Joe Girardi, c	3	0	1	0	0	0	.333
John VanderWal, ph	1	0	0	0	0	0	.000
Mike Munoz, p	0	0	0	0	0	0	—
Darren Holmes, p	0	0	0	0	0	0	—
Mike Kingery, cf	1	0	1	0	0	0	1.000
Dante Bichette, lf	4	1	2	0	1	0	.500
Larry Walker, rf	3	1	1	0	2	0	.333
Andres Galarraga, 1b	5	1	2	0	0	1	.400
Ellis Burks, cf	3	0	2	2	0	0	.667
Curt Leskanic, p	0	0	0	0	0	0	—
Lance Painter, ph	1	0	0	0	0	1	.000
Vinny Castilla, 3b	3	1	2	2	0	0	.667
Trent Hubbard, pr	0	0	0	0	0	0	—
Jayhawk Owens, c	1	0	0	0	0	1	.000
Walt Weiss, ss	2	0	0	0	1	0	.000
Kevin Ritz, p	2	0	0	0	0	0	.000
Steve Reed, p	0	0	0	0	0	0	—
Bruce Ruffin, p	0	0	0	0	0	0	—
Jason Bates, ph-3b	1	0	0	0	0	0	.000
TOTALS	34	4	13	4	5	3	.382

	1	2	3	4	5	6	7	8	9	R	H	E
Braves	0	0	1	0	0	2	0	1	1	5	12	1
Rockies	0	0	0	3	0	0	0	1	0	4	13	4

E—Burks, Girardi, Justice, Ritz, Castilla. DP—Braves 4 (Lemke to Blauser to McGriff; Blauser to Lemke to McGriff; Lemke to Blauser to McGriff; Maddux to Lopez to McGriff), Rockies 2 (Galarraga to Weiss; Castilla to Young to Galarraga). LOB—Braves 8, Rockies 11. Scoring Position—Braves 1-for-8, Rockies 1-for-9. 2B—Grissom (1), Young (1), Burks (1), Castilla (1). HR—Grissom (1), Jones 2 (2), Castilla (1). S—Bates. SF—Burks. GDP—Jones 2, Girardi, Walker, Castilla, VanderWal. SB—Polonia (1).

Braves	IP	H	R	ER	BB	K	ERA
Greg Maddux	7.0	9	3	3	2	0	3.86
Greg McMichael (H, 1)	0.1	1	1	1	1	0	27.00
Alejandro Pena (BS, 1; W, 1-0)	0.2	1	0	0	1	1	0.00
Mark Wohlers (S, 1)	1.0	2	0	0	1	2	0.00

Rockies	IP	H	R	ER	BB	K	ERA
Kevin Ritz	5.1	7	3	2	2	4	3.38
Steve Reed (BS, 1)	1.0	1	0	0	1	1	0.00
Bruce Ruffin	0.2	0	0	0	0	0	0.00
Mike Munoz	0.2	1	1	1	0	1	13.50
Darren Holmes	0.1	2	0	0	0	0	0.00
Curt Leskanic (L, 0-1)	1.0	1	1	1	0	1	9.00

HBP—Weiss by Maddux. Time—3:19. Attendance—50,040. Umpires—HP, McSherry. 1B, Layne. 2B, West. 3B, Tata.

Game 2

Wednesday, October 4

Braves	AB	R	H	RBI	BB	K	Avg
Marquis Grissom, cf	6	2	2	2	0	2	.364
Mark Lemke, 2b	4	1	1	0	1	0	.222
Chipper Jones, 3b	5	1	3	0	0	0	.500
Fred McGriff, 1b	4	1	1	1	1	2	.222
David Justice, rf	4	0	1	0	1	0	.333
Javy Lopez, c	4	0	1	1	0	2	.400
Ryan Klesko, lf	3	0	0	0	0	1	.429
Mike Devereaux, ph-lf	2	1	1	0	0	0	.333
Jeff Blauser, ss	2	0	0	0	0	1	.000
Luis Polonia, ph	1	0	0	0	0	1	.000
Steve Avery, p	0	0	0	0	0	0	—
Alejandro Pena, p	0	0	0	0	0	0	—
Mike Mordecai, ph	1	1	1	1	0	0	1.000
Mark Wohlers, p	0	0	0	0	0	0	—
Tom Glavine, p	3	0	1	0	0	1	.333
Dwight Smith, ph	1	0	1	0	0	0	1.000
Rafael Belliard, ss	1	0	0	0	0	0	.000
TOTALS	41	7	13	5	3	10	.342

Rockies	AB	R	H	RBI	BB	K	Avg
Eric Young, 2b	5	0	1	0	0	1	.333
Ellis Burks, cf	3	1	0	0	0	1	.333
Mike Kingery, cf	2	0	0	0	0	0	.333
Dante Bichette, lf	4	2	3	0	0	0	.625
Larry Walker, rf	4	1	1	3	0	1	.286
Andres Galarraga, 1b	4	0	1	1	0	1	.333
Vinny Castilla, 3b	3	0	0	0	0	0	.333
Joe Girardi, c	4	0	0	0	0	0	.143
Walt Weiss, ss	3	0	1	0	1	1	.200
Lance Painter, p	1	0	0	0	0	0	.000
Trent Hubbard, ph	1	0	0	0	0	0	.000
Steve Reed, p	0	0	0	0	0	0	—
Bruce Ruffin, p	0	0	0	0	0	0	—
Jason Bates, ph	1	0	1	0	0	0	.500
Curt Leskanic, p	0	0	0	0	0	0	—
Mike Munoz, p	0	0	0	0	0	0	—
Darren Holmes, p	0	0	0	0	0	0	—
John VanderWal, ph	1	0	0	0	0	1	.000
TOTALS	36	4	8	4	1	6	.313

	1	2	3	4	5	6	7	8	9	R	H	E
Braves	1	0	1	1	0	0	0	0	4	7	13	1
Rockies	0	0	0	0	0	3	0	1	0	4	8	2

E—Blauser, Young 2. LOB—Braves 12, Rockies 7. Scoring Position—Braves 3-for-14, Rockies 3-for-6. 2B—Jones (1), Bichette 2 (2), Galarraga (1), Smith (1). HR—Grissom 2 (3), Walker (1). SF—Lopez.

Braves	IP	H	R	ER	BB	K	ERA
Tom Glavine	7.0	5	3	2	1	3	2.57
Steve Avery	0.2	1	1	1	0	1	13.50
Alejandro Pena (W, 2-0)	0.1	1	0	0	0	0	0.00
Mark Wohlers (S, 2)	1.0	1	0	0	0	2	0.00

Rockies	IP	H	R	ER	BB	K	ERA
Lance Painter	5.0	5	3	3	2	4	5.40
Steve Reed	1.1	1	0	0	0	1	0.00
Bruce Ruffin	0.2	2	0	0	1	1	0.00
Curt Leskanic	1.0	2	1	1	0	2	9.00
Mike Munoz (BS, 1; L, 0-1)	0.1	1	1	1	0	0	18.00
Darren Holmes	0.2	2	2	0	0	2	0.00

Leskanic pitched to one batter in the 9th.

HBP—Blauser by Reed, Castilla by Pena. Time—3:08. Attendance—50,063. Umpires—HP, Layne. 1B, West. 2B, Tata. 3B, Wendelstedt.

Game 3

Friday, October 6

Rockies	AB	R	H	RBI	BB	K	Avg
Eric Young, 2b	3	2	1	2	1	0	.333
Steve Reed, p	0	0	0	0	0	0	—
Mike Munoz, p	0	0	0	0	0	0	—
Curt Leskanic, p	0	0	0	0	0	0	—
Bruce Ruffin, p	0	0	0	0	0	0	—
Darren Holmes, p	0	0	0	0	0	0	—
John VanderWal, ph	1	0	0	0	0	0	.000
Mark Thompson, p	0	0	0	0	0	0	—
Mike Kingery, cf	4	0	0	0	0	1	.143
Dante Bichette, lf	5	2	3	0	0	2	.615
Larry Walker, rf	3	1	1	0	1	1	.300
Andres Galarraga, 1b	5	0	1	1	0	3	.286
Vinny Castilla, 3b	5	1	2	3	0	1	.364
Joe Girardi, c	5	0	0	0	0	1	.083
Walt Weiss, ss	3	1	1	0	1	1	.250
Bill Swift, p	3	0	0	0	0	2	.000
Jason Bates, 2b	1	0	0	0	0	0	.333
TOTALS	38	7	9	6	3	12	.292

Braves	AB	R	H	RBI	BB	K	Avg
Marquis Grissom, cf	5	0	2	0	0	1	.375
Mark Lemke, 2b	5	0	0	0	0	1	.143
Chipper Jones, 3b	5	0	1	0	0	1	.400
Fred McGriff, 1b	4	1	1	0	1	0	.231
David Justice, rf	3	1	0	0	1	0	.222
Ryan Klesko, lf	4	3	3	1	0	1	.545
Javy Lopez, c	4	0	2	2	0	1	.444
Jeff Blauser, ss	2	0	0	0	0	1	.000
Rafael Belliard, ss	0	0	0	0	0	0	.000
Dwight Smith, ph	0	0	0	0	0	0	1.000
Mike Mordecai, ph-ss	2	0	1	1	0	0	.667
John Smoltz, p	2	0	0	0	0	0	.000
Brad Clontz, p	0	0	0	0	0	0	—
Mike Devereaux, ph	1	0	0	0	0	0	.250
Pedro Borbon, p	0	0	0	0	0	0	—
Greg McMichael, p	0	0	0	0	0	0	—
Luis Polonia, ph	1	0	1	1	0	0	.333
Mark Wohlers, p	0	0	0	0	0	0	—
Kent Mercker, p	0	0	0	0	0	0	—
TOTALS	38	5	11	5	2	6	.324

	1	2	3	4	5	6	7	8	9	10	R	H	E
Rockies	1	0	2	0	0	2	0	0	0	2	7	9	0
Braves	0	0	0	3	0	0	1	0	1	0	5	11	0

DP—Rockies 3 (Girardi to Young; Girardi to Weiss; Weiss to Galarraga). LOB—Rockies 6, Braves 5. Scoring Position—Rockies 3-for-8, Braves 3-for-9. 2B—Bichette (3), Klesko (1), Mordecai (1). HR—Young (1), Castilla (2). S—Kingery. GDP—McGriff. SB—Walker (1), Weiss (1), Grissom (1). CS—Grissom (1), Lopez (1).

Rockies	IP	H	R	ER	BB	K	ERA
Bill Swift	6.0	7	4	4	2	3	6.00
Steve Reed (H, 1)	0.1	0	0	0	0	1	0.00
Mike Munoz	0.0	1	0	0	0	0	18.00
Curt Leskanic (H, 1)	1.0	0	0	0	0	1	6.00
Bruce Ruffin (H, 1)	1.0	1	1	1	0	1	3.86
Darren Holmes (BS, 1; W, 1-0)	0.2	2	0	0	0	0	0.00
Mark Thompson (S, 1)	1.0	0	0	0	0	0	0.00

Braves	IP	H	R	ER	BB	K	ERA
John Smoltz	5.2	5	5	5	1	6	7.94
Brad Clontz	1.1	0	0	0	0	2	0.00
Pedro Borbon	1.0	1	0	0	0	3	0.00
Greg McMichael	1.0	0	0	0	1	1	6.75
Mark Wohlers (L, 0-1)	0.2	3	2	2	1	0	6.75
Kent Mercker	0.1	0	0	0	0	0	0.00

Swift pitched to one batter in the 7th. Munoz pitched to one batter in the 7th.

WP—Smoltz. HBP—Walker by Smoltz. Time—3:16. Attendance—51,300. Umpires—HP, Gregg. 1B, Pulli. 2B, Froemming. 3B, Darling.

Game 4

Rockies	AB	R	H	RBI	BB	K	Avg
Eric Young, 2b	4	1	3	0	0	1	.438
Mike Kingery, cf	3	1	1	0	0	0	.200
Dante Bichette, lf	4	1	2	3	0	1	.588
Larry Walker, rf	4	0	0	0	0	2	.214
Andres Galarraga, 1b	4	0	1	0	0	1	.278
Vinny Castilla, 3b	4	1	3	1	0	0	.467
Joe Girardi, c	4	0	1	0	0	1	.125
Walt Weiss, ss	4	0	0	0	0	1	.167
Bret Saberhagen, p	1	0	0	0	0	0	.000
Trent Hubbard, ph	1	0	0	0	0	0	.000
Kevin Ritz, p	0	0	0	0	0	0	.000
Mike Munoz, p	0	0	0	0	0	0	—
Jason Bates, ph	1	0	0	0	0	0	.250
Armando Reynoso, p	0	0	0	0	0	0	—
Bruce Ruffin, p	0	0	0	0	0	0	—
John VanderWal, ph	1	0	0	0	0	1	.000
TOTALS	35	4	11	4	0	8	.298

Braves	AB	R	H	RBI	BB	K	Avg
Marquis Grissom, cf	5	2	5	1	0	0	.524
Mark Lemke, 2b	5	2	2	1	0	1	.211
Chipper Jones, 3b	3	1	1	2	2	1	.389
Fred McGriff, 1b	5	2	3	5	0	0	.333
David Justice, rf	4	0	1	0	1	1	.231
Ryan Klesko, lf	4	1	1	0	0	0	.467
Mike Devereaux, lf	1	0	0	0	0	0	.200
Charlie O'Brien, c	3	0	1	0	1	0	.200
Rafael Belliard, ss	4	1	0	0	0	1	.000
Greg Maddux, p	3	1	1	0	0	0	.167
Dwight Smith, ph	1	0	0	0	0	0	.667
Alejandro Pena, p	0	0	0	0	0	0	—
TOTALS	38	10	15	9	4	4	.336

	1	2	3	4	5	6	7	8	9		R	H	E
Rockies	0	0	3	0	0	1	0	0	0		4	11	1
Braves	0	0	4	2	1	3	0	0	x		10	15	0

E—Young. DP—Rockies 1 (Young to Weiss to Galarraga), Braves 1 (Belliard to McGriff). LOB—Rockies 5, Braves 8. Scoring Position—Rockies 1-for-4, Braves 5-for-12. 2B—Grissom (2), Lemke (1), Jones (2). HR—Bichette (1), Castilla (3), McGriff 2 (2). S—Kingery. GDP—Girardi, Klesko. SB—Young (1), Grissom (2).

Rockies	IP	H	R	ER	BB	K	ERA
Bret Saberhagen (L, 0-1)	4.0	7	6	5	1	3	11.25
Kevin Ritz	1.2	5	4	4	1	1	7.71
Mike Munoz	0.1	1	0	0	1	0	13.50
Armando Reynoso	1.0	2	0	0	0	0	0.00
Bruce Ruffin	1.0	0	0	0	1	0	2.70

Braves	IP	H	R	ER	BB	K	ERA
Greg Maddux (W, 1-0)	7.0	10	4	4	0	7	4.50
Alejandro Pena	2.0	1	0	0	0	1	0.00

Time—2:38. Attendance—50,027. Umpires—HP, Pulli. 1B, Froemming. 2B, Darling. 3B, Montague.

1995 NL Division Series—Composite Statistics

Batting

Braves

Braves	G	AB	R	H	RBI	2B	3B	HR	BB	SO	SB	CS	Avg	OBP	Slg
Rafael Belliard	4	5	1	0	0	0	0	0	0	0	1	0	0	.000	.000	.000
Jeff Blauser	3	6	0	0	0	0	0	0	1	3	0	0	.000	.250	.000
Mike Devereaux	4	5	1	1	0	0	0	0	0	0	0	0	.200	.200	.200
Tom Glavine	1	3	0	1	0	0	0	0	0	1	0	0	.333	.333	.333
Marquis Grissom	4	21	5	11	4	2	0	3	0	3	2	1	.524	.524	1.048
Chipper Jones	4	18	4	7	4	2	0	2	2	2	0	0	.389	.450	.833
David Justice	4	13	2	3	0	0	0	0	5	2	0	0	.231	.444	.231
Ryan Klesko	4	15	5	7	1	1	0	0	0	3	0	0	.467	.467	.533
Mark Lemke	4	19	3	4	1	1	0	0	1	3	0	0	.211	.250	.263
Javy Lopez	3	9	0	4	3	0	0	0	0	3	0	1	.444	.400	.444
Greg Maddux	2	6	1	1	0	0	0	0	0	1	0	0	.167	.167	.167
Fred McGriff	4	18	4	6	6	0	0	2	2	3	0	0	.333	.400	.667
Mike Mordecai	2	3	1	2	1	0	0	0	0	0	0	0	.667	.667	1.000
Charlie O'Brien	2	5	0	1	0	0	0	0	1	1	0	0	.200	.333	.200
Luis Polonia	3	3	0	1	2	0	0	0	0	1	1	0	.333	.333	.333
Dwight Smith	4	3	0	2	1	1	0	0	0	0	0	0	.667	.667	1.000
John Smoltz	1	2	0	0	0	0	0	0	0	0	0	0	.000	.000	.000
Totals	**4**	**154**	**27**	**51**	**24**	**8**	**0**	**7**	**12**	**27**	**3**	**2**	**.331**	**.381**	**.519**

Rockies

Rockies	G	AB	R	H	RBI	2B	3B	HR	BB	SO	SB	CS	Avg	OBP	Slg
Jason Bates	4	4	0	1	0	0	0	0	0	0	0	0	.250	.250	.250
Dante Bichette	4	17	6	10	3	3	0	1	1	3	0	0	.588	.611	.941
Ellis Burks	2	6	1	2	2	1	0	0	0	1	0	0	.333	.286	.500
Vinny Castilla	4	15	3	7	6	1	0	3	0	1	0	0	.467	.500	1.133
Andres Galarraga	4	18	1	5	2	1	0	0	0	6	0	0	.278	.278	.333
Joe Girardi	4	16	0	2	0	0	0	0	0	2	0	0	.125	.125	.125
Trent Hubbard	3	2	0	0	0	0	0	0	0	0	0	0	.000	.000	.000
Mike Kingery	4	10	1	2	0	0	0	0	0	1	0	0	.200	.200	.200
Jayhawk Owens	1	1	0	0	0	0	0	0	0	0	0	0	.000	.000	.000
Lance Painter	2	2	0	0	0	0	0	0	0	1	0	0	.000	.000	.000
Kevin Ritz	2	2	0	0	0	0	0	0	0	0	0	0	.000	.000	.000
Bret Saberhagen	1	1	0	0	0	0	0	0	0	0	0	0	.000	.000	.000
Bill Swift	1	3	0	0	0	0	0	0	0	2	0	0	.000	.000	.000
John VanderWal	4	4	0	0	0	0	0	0	0	2	0	0	.000	.000	.000
Larry Walker	4	14	3	3	3	0	0	1	3	4	1	0	.214	.389	.429
Walt Weiss	4	12	1	2	0	0	0	0	3	3	1	0	.167	.375	.167
Eric Young	4	16	3	7	2	1	0	1	2	2	1	0	.438	.500	.688
Totals	**4**	**143**	**19**	**41**	**18**	**7**	**0**	**6**	**9**	**29**	**3**	**0**	**.287**	**.340**	**.462**

Pitching

Braves

Braves	G	GS	CG	IP	H	R	ER	BB	SO	W-L	Sv-Op	Hld	ERA
Steve Avery	1	0	0	0.2	1	1	1	0	1	0-0	0-0	0	13.50
Pedro Borbon	1	0	0	1.0	1	0	0	0	3	0-0	0-0	0	0.00
Brad Clontz	1	0	0	1.1	0	0	0	0	2	0-0	0-0	0	0.00
Tom Glavine	1	1	0	7.0	5	3	2	1	3	0-0	0-0	0	2.57
Greg Maddux	2	2	0	14.0	19	7	7	2	7	1-0	0-0	0	4.50
Greg McMichael	2	0	0	1.1	1	1	1	2	1	0-0	0-0	1	6.75
Kent Mercker	1	0	0	0.1	0	0	0	0	0	0-0	0-0	0	0.00
Alejandro Pena	3	0	0	3.0	3	0	0	1	2	2-0	0-1	0	0.00
John Smoltz	1	1	0	5.2	5	5	5	1	6	0-0	0-0	0	7.94
Mark Wohlers	3	0	0	2.2	6	2	2	4	4	0-1	2-2	0	6.75
Totals	**4**	**4**	**0**	**37.0**	**41**	**19**	**18**	**9**	**29**	**3-1**	**2-3**	**1**	**4.38**

Rockies

Rockies	G	GS	CG	IP	H	R	ER	BB	SO	W-L	Sv-Op	Hld	ERA
Darren Holmes	3	0	0	1.2	6	2	0	0	2	1-0	0-1	0	0.00
Curt Leskanic	3	0	0	3.0	3	2	2	0	4	0-1	0-0	1	6.00
Mike Munoz	4	0	0	1.1	4	2	2	1	1	0-1	0-1	0	13.50
Lance Painter	1	1	0	5.0	5	3	3	2	4	0-0	0-0	0	5.40
Steve Reed	3	0	0	2.2	2	0	0	1	3	0-0	0-1	1	0.00
Armando Reynoso	1	0	0	1.0	2	0	0	0	0	0-0	0-0	0	0.00
Kevin Ritz	2	1	0	7.0	12	7	6	3	5	0-0	0-0	0	7.71
Bruce Ruffin	4	0	0	3.1	3	1	1	2	2	0-0	0-0	1	2.70
Bret Saberhagen	1	1	0	4.0	7	6	5	1	3	0-1	0-0	0	11.25
Bill Swift	1	1	0	6.0	7	4	4	2	3	0-0	0-0	0	6.00
Mark Thompson	1	0	0	1.0	0	0	0	0	0	0-0	1-1	0	0.00
Totals	**4**	**4**	**0**	**36.0**	**51**	**27**	**23**	**12**	**27**	**1-3**	**1-4**	**3**	**5.75**

Fielding

Braves

Braves	Pos	G	PO	Ast	E	DP	PB	FPct
Steve Avery	p	1	0	0	0	0	—	—
Rafael Belliard	ss	4	2	5	0	1	—	1.000
Jeff Blauser	ss	3	5	11	1	3	—	.941
Pedro Borbon	p	1	0	0	0	0	—	—
Brad Clontz	p	1	0	1	0	0	—	1.000
Mike Devereaux	lf	3	2	0	0	0	—	1.000
Tom Glavine	p	1	1	1	0	0	—	1.000
Marquis Grissom	cf	4	9	0	0	0	—	1.000
Chipper Jones	3b	4	3	4	0	0	—	1.000
David Justice	rf	4	6	0	1	0	—	.857
Ryan Klesko	lf	4	3	0	0	0	—	1.000
Mark Lemke	2b	4	8	16	0	3	—	1.000
Javy Lopez	c	3	22	3	0	1	0	1.000
Greg Maddux	p	2	1	4	0	1	—	1.000
Fred McGriff	1b	4	39	2	0	5	—	1.000
Greg McMichael	p	2	0	0	0	0	—	—
Kent Mercker	p	1	0	0	0	0	—	—
Mike Mordecai	ss	1	1	0	0	0	—	1.000
Charlie O'Brien	c	2	8	1	0	0	0	1.000
Alejandro Pena	p	3	0	0	0	0	—	—
John Smoltz	p	1	1	1	0	0	—	1.000
Mark Wohlers	p	3	0	0	0	0	—	—
Totals		**4**	**111**	**49**	**2**	**14**	**0**	**.988**

Rockies

Rockies	Pos	G	PO	Ast	E	DP	PB	FPct
Jason Bates	2b	1	1	2	0	0	—	1.000
	3b	1	0	1	0	0	—	1.000
Dante Bichette	lf	4	9	0	0	0	—	1.000
Ellis Burks	cf	2	4	0	1	0	—	.800
Vinny Castilla	3b	4	3	13	1	1	—	.941
Andres Galarraga	1b	4	41	2	0	4	—	1.000
Joe Girardi	c	4	25	3	1	2	0	.966
Darren Holmes	p	3	0	0	0	0	—	—
Mike Kingery	cf	4	5	0	0	0	—	1.000
Curt Leskanic	p	3	0	0	0	0	—	—
Mike Munoz	p	4	0	0	0	0	—	—
Jayhawk Owens	c	1	2	1	0	0	—	1.000
Lance Painter	p	1	0	0	0	0	—	—
Steve Reed	p	3	0	1	0	0	—	1.000
Armando Reynoso	p	1	0	0	0	0	—	—
Kevin Ritz	p	2	0	1	1	0	—	.500
Bruce Ruffin	p	4	0	0	0	0	—	—
Bret Saberhagen	p	1	0	1	0	0	—	1.000
Bill Swift	p	1	0	0	0	0	—	—
Mark Thompson	p	1	1	0	0	0	—	1.000
Larry Walker	rf	4	3	0	0	0	—	1.000
Walt Weiss	ss	4	6	12	0	4	—	1.000
Eric Young	2b	4	8	13	3	3	—	.875
Totals		**4**	**108**	**50**	**7**	**14**	**0**	**.958**

1996 Baltimore Orioles (AL) 3, Cleveland Indians (AL) 1

Baltimore stunned the defending American League champion Cleveland Indians, downing Cleveland in four games. The O's blasted four home runs—including two by B.J. Surhoff and a grand slam by Bobby Bonilla—on the way to a 10-4 victory in the opener. In Game 2, Baltimore's Armando Benitez kept the game tied by pitching out of a bases-loaded jam in the top of the eighth, and the Orioles went ahead to stay in the bottom of the frame on Sandy Alomar's throwing error. Cleveland got one back by winning the third game, 9-4, as Albert Belle broken open a tie game with a grand slam in the bottom of the seventh. The umpires threatened to strike Game 4 after it was announced that Roberto Alomar (who had spit in the face of umpire John Hirschbeck the week before) would not have to serve his suspension until the start of the 1997 season. The umpires ultimately showed up, and so did Alomar, who stroked a game-tying RBI single in the top of the ninth to send the game into extra innings, and delivered a game-winning homer in the 12th to put the O's in the American League Championship Series.

Game 1
Tuesday, October 1

Indians	AB	R	H	RBI	BB	K	Avg
Kenny Lofton, cf	5	0	1	1	0	1	.200
Kevin Seitzer, dh	5	0	1	0	0	2	.200
Jim Thome, 3b	4	0	1	0	0	2	.250
Albert Belle, lf	4	0	0	0	0	0	.000
Julio Franco, 1b	4	0	1	0	0	0	.250
Manny Ramirez, rf	4	2	3	1	0	0	.750
Jeff Kent, 2b	4	1	1	0	0	0	.250
Sandy Alomar Jr., c	3	0	1	1	0	0	.333
Brian Giles, ph	1	0	0	0	0	1	.000
Tony Pena, c	0	0	0	0	0	0	—
Omar Vizquel, ss	2	1	1	1	1	0	.500
TOTALS	36	4	10	4	1	6	.278

Orioles	AB	R	H	RBI	BB	K	Avg
Brady Anderson, cf	5	2	2	1	0	0	.400
Todd Zeile, 3b	4	2	2	0	1	1	.500
Roberto Alomar, 2b	4	0	1	0	1	0	.250
Rafael Palmeiro, 1b	4	2	1	0	1	1	.250
Bobby Bonilla, rf	3	1	1	4	2	1	.333
Mike Devereaux, pr-rf	0	0	0	0	0	0	—
Cal Ripken Jr., ss	5	0	3	1	0	0	.600
Eddie Murray, dh	4	0	0	0	0	1	.000
B.J. Surhoff, lf	4	2	2	2	0	0	.500
Chris Hoiles, c	2	1	0	0	1	0	.000
Mark Parent, c	0	0	0	0	0	0	—
TOTALS	35	10	12	10	4	4	.343

	1	2	3	4	5	6	7	8	9	R	H	E
Indians	0	1	0	2	0	0	1	0	0	4	10	0
Orioles	1	1	2	0	0	5	1	0	x	10	12	1

E—Zeile. LOB—Indians 8, Orioles 8. Scoring Position—Indians 2-for-8, Orioles 3-for-7. 2B—Kent (1), Vizquel (1), Palmeiro (1), Ripken Jr. (1). HR—Ramirez (1), Anderson (1), Bonilla (1), Surhoff 2 (2). SF—Vizquel, Alomar. SB—Vizquel (1). CS—Vizquel (1).

Indians	IP	H	R	ER	BB	K	ERA
Charles Nagy (L, 0-1)	5.1	9	7	7	3	1	11.81
Alan Embree	0.1	0	1	1	0	0	27.00
Paul Shuey	1.1	3	2	2	0	2	13.50
Julian Tavarez	1.0	0	0	0	1	1	0.00

Orioles	IP	H	R	ER	BB	K	ERA
David Wells (W, 1-0)	6.2	8	4	4	1	3	5.40
Jesse Orosco	0.0	0	0	0	0	0	—
Terry Mathews	0.2	2	0	0	0	0	0.00
Arthur Rhodes	0.2	0	0	0	0	1	0.00
Randy Myers	1.0	0	0	0	0	2	0.00

Orosco pitched to one batter in the 7th.

WP—Mathews. HBP—Thome by Orosco, Palmeiro by Embree, Hoiles by Nagy. Time—3:25. Attendance—47,644. Umpires—HP, Coble. 1B, Kosc. 2B, Tschida. 3B, Welke.

Game 2
Wednesday, October 2

Indians	AB	R	H	RBI	BB	K	Avg
Kenny Lofton, cf	5	1	2	0	0	1	.300
Kevin Seitzer, 1b	4	0	2	1	0	0	.333
Jeff Kent, pr-1b	0	1	0	0	0	0	.250
Jim Thome, 3b	4	1	2	0	0	2	.375
Albert Belle, lf	3	1	1	2	1	0	.143
Julio Franco, dh	3	0	0	1	0	2	.143
Manny Ramirez, rf	4	0	0	0	0	2	.375
Sandy Alomar Jr., c	4	0	0	0	0	0	.143
Omar Vizquel, ss	3	0	0	0	1	0	.200
Jose Vizcaino, 2b	3	0	1	0	1	1	.333
TOTALS	33	4	8	4	3	8	.265

Orioles	AB	R	H	RBI	BB	K	Avg
Brady Anderson, cf	4	1	2	2	0	2	.444
Todd Zeile, 3b	4	0	0	0	1	0	.250
Roberto Alomar, 2b	4	1	1	1	0	1	.250
Rafael Palmeiro, 1b	3	1	1	0	1	1	.286
Bobby Bonilla, rf	2	1	0	0	2	0	.200
Mike Devereaux, pr-rf	0	0	0	0	0	0	—
Cal Ripken Jr., ss	3	1	2	1	0	0	.625
Eddie Murray, dh	3	0	2	1	1	1	.286
Manny Alexander, pr-dh	0	1	0	0	0	0	—
B.J. Surhoff, lf	4	0	0	0	0	0	.250
Pete Incaviglia, pr-lf	0	1	0	0	0	0	—
Mark Parent, c	3	0	1	0	0	1	.333
Chris Hoiles, ph-c	0	0	0	0	1	0	.000
TOTALS	30	7	9	5	7	5	.323

	1	2	3	4	5	6	7	8	9	R	H	E
Indians	0	0	0	0	0	3	0	1	0	4	8	2
Orioles	1	0	0	3	0	0	3	x		7	9	0

E—Seitzer, Alomar Jr. DP—Indians 1 (Hershiser to Vizquel to Seitzer), Orioles 1 (Erickson to Alomar to Palmeiro). LOB—Indians 6, Orioles 8. Scoring Position—Indians 0-for-7, Orioles 3-for-7. 2B—Seitzer (1), Ripken Jr. (2). HR—Belle (1), Anderson (2). SF—Franco, Anderson. GDP—Seitzer, Zeile. SB—Lofton 2 (2), Vizquel (2).

Indians	IP	H	R	ER	BB	K	ERA
Orel Hershiser	5.0	7	4	3	3	3	5.40
Eric Plunk (L, 0-1)	2.0	1	3	3	2	2	13.50
Paul Assenmacher	0.2	0	0	0	1	0	0.00
Julian Tavarez	0.1	1	0	0	1	0	0.00

Orioles	IP	H	R	ER	BB	K	ERA
Scott Erickson	6.2	6	3	3	2	6	4.05
Jesse Orosco (H, 1)	0.1	2	1	1	0	1	27.00
Armando Benitez (BS, 1; W, 1-0)	1.0	0	0	0	1	1	0.00
Randy Myers (S, 1)	1.0	0	0	0	0	0	0.00

Orosco pitched to two batters in the 8th. Plunk pitched to three batters in the 8th.

HBP—Ripken Jr. by Hershiser. Time—3:27. Attendance—48,970. Umpires—HP, Kosc. 1B, Tschida. 2B, Welke. 3B, Shulock.

Game 3
Friday, October 4

Orioles	AB	R	H	RBI	BB	K	Avg
Brady Anderson, cf	3	0	0	1	1	0	.333
Todd Zeile, 3b	5	0	1	0	0	3	.231
Roberto Alomar, 2b	3	0	0	0	1	2	.182
Rafael Palmeiro, 1b	4	0	0	0	0	0	.182
Bobby Bonilla, rf	4	1	1	0	0	1	.222
Cal Ripken Jr., ss	4	1	1	1	0	0	.500
Eddie Murray, dh	4	1	2	0	0	0	.364
B.J. Surhoff, lf	4	1	2	3	0	1	.333
Mike Devereaux, pr	0	0	0	0	0	0	—
Chris Hoiles, c	2	0	1	0	1	0	.250
Manny Alexander, pr	0	0	0	0	0	0	—
Mark Parent, c	1	0	0	0	0	0	.250
TOTALS	34	4	8	4	3	8	.293

Indians	AB	R	H	RBI	BB	K	Avg
Kenny Lofton, cf	3	2	0	0	2	0	.231
Kevin Seitzer, dh	4	1	2	3	1	0	.385
Jim Thome, 3b	2	0	0	0	1	1	.300
Casey Candaele, ph	0	1	0	0	1	0	—
Jeff Kent, 3b	1	0	0	0	0	0	.200
Albert Belle, lf	4	1	2	4	1	1	.273
Julio Franco, 1b	4	0	0	0	0	2	.091
Manny Ramirez, rf	4	1	1	1	0	1	.333
Sandy Alomar Jr., c	4	0	0	0	0	2	.091
Omar Vizquel, ss	4	3	3	0	0	1	.444
Jose Vizcaino, 2b	4	0	2	1	0	0	.429
TOTALS	34	9	10	9	6	8	.275

	1	2	3	4	5	6	7	8	9	R	H	E
Orioles	0	1	0	3	0	0	0	0		4	8	2
Indians	1	2	0	1	0	0	4	1	x		9	10	0

E—Bonilla, Zeile. DP—Orioles 1 (Alomar to Ripken Jr. to Palmeiro), Indians 1 (Vizquel to Vizcaino to Franco). LOB—Orioles 7, Indians 7. Scoring Position—Orioles 1-for-6, Indians 4-for-14. 2B—Vizcaino 2 (2). HR—Surhoff 2 (2), Belle (2), Ramirez (2). GDP—Zeile, Ramirez. SB—Murray (1), Lofton 3 (5), Belle (1), Vizquel (3).

Orioles	IP	H	R	ER	BB	K	ERA
Mike Mussina	6.0	7	4	3	2	4	4.50
Jesse Orosco (L, 0-1)	0.0	0	3	3	3	0	108.00
Armando Benitez	1.0	1	1	1	0	1	4.50
Arthur Rhodes	0.1	1	1	1	1	0	9.00
Terry Mathews	0.2	1	0	0	0	1	0.00

Indians	IP	H	R	ER	BB	K	ERA
Jack McDowell	5.2	6	4	4	1	5	6.35
Alan Embree	0.1	0	0	0	1	0	13.50
Paul Shuey	0.2	1	0	0	2	0	9.00
Paul Assenmacher (W, 1-0)	0.1	0	0	0	0	0	0.00
Eric Plunk	1.0	0	0	0	0	2	9.00
Jose Mesa	1.0	1	0	0	0	1	0.00

Orosco pitched to four batters in the 7th.

HBP—Anderson by McDowell. Time—3:44. Attendance—44,250. Umpires—HP, Merrill. 1B, Young. 2B, Clark. 3B, Johnson.

Game 4
Saturday, October 5

Orioles	AB	R	H	RBI	BB	K	Avg
Brady Anderson, cf	5	0	1	0	1	1	.294
Todd Zeile, 3b	6	0	2	0	0	1	.263
Roberto Alomar, 2b	6	1	3	2	0	1	.294
Rafael Palmeiro, 1b	6	1	1	1	0	4	.176
Bobby Bonilla, rf	6	1	1	1	0	4	.200
Cal Ripken Jr., ss	6	0	2	0	0	2	.444
Eddie Murray, dh	4	0	2	0	2	2	.400
Pete Incaviglia, lf	5	0	1	0	0	4	.200
Mike Devereaux, lf	1	0	0	0	0	0	.000
Chris Hoiles, c	3	0	0	0	0	3	.143
B.J. Surhoff, ph	1	0	1	0	0	0	.385
Manny Alexander, pr	0	1	0	0	0	0	—
Mark Parent, c	1	0	0	0	0	1	.200
TOTALS	50	4	14	4	3	23	.289

Indians	AB	R	H	RBI	BB	K	Avg
Kenny Lofton, cf	5	0	0	0	0	1	.167
Omar Vizquel, ss	5	0	2	1	1	3	.429
Kevin Seitzer, dh	4	0	0	0	1	2	.294
Casey Candaele, pr-dh	0	0	0	0	0	0	—
Albert Belle, lf	4	0	0	0	1	1	.200
Julio Franco, 1b	4	1	1	0	1	2	.133
Manny Ramirez, rf	4	1	2	0	1	1	.375
Jeff Kent, 3b	3	0	0	0	0	0	.125
Nigel Wilson, ph	1	0	0	0	0	0	.000
Jim Thome, 3b	0	0	0	0	0	0	.300
Sandy Alomar Jr., c	5	0	1	2	0	0	.125
Jose Vizcaino, 2b	5	1	1	0	0	0	.333
TOTALS	40	3	7	3	5	10	.246

	1	2	3	4	5	6	7	8	9	10	11	12	R	H	E
Orioles	0	2	0	0	0	0	0	1	0	0	1		4	14	1
Indians	0	0	0	2	1	0	0	0	0	0	0	0	3	7	1

E—Palmeiro, Vizcaino. LOB—Orioles 13, Indians 8. Scoring Position—Orioles 1-for-11, Indians 2-for-11. 2B—Zeile (1), Ripken Jr. (3), Ramirez 2 (2). HR—Alomar (1), Palmeiro (1), Bonilla (2). S—Lofton, Kent. SB—Vizquel (4), Seitzer (1). CS—Anderson (1), Vizquel (2), Alomar Jr. (1).

Orioles	IP	H	R	ER	BB	K	ERA
David Wells	7.0	7	3	3	3	3	4.61
Terry Mathews	1.1	0	0	0	1	1	0.00
Jesse Orosco	0.2	0	0	0	0	1	36.00
Armando Benitez (W, 2-0)	2.0	0	0	0	1	4	2.25
Randy Myers (S, 2)	1.0	0	0	0	0	1	0.00

Indians	IP	H	R	ER	BB	K	ERA
Charles Nagy	6.0	6	2	2	2	12	7.15
Alan Embree (H, 1)	0.1	0	0	0	0	1	9.00
Paul Shuey	0.0	1	0	0	0	0	9.00
Paul Assenmacher (H, 1)	0.2	0	0	0	0	2	0.00
Eric Plunk (H, 1)	1.0	0	0	0	0	2	6.75
Jose Mesa (BS, 1; L, 0-1)	3.2	7	2	2	0	6	3.86
Chad Ogea	0.1	0	0	0	1	0	0.00

Shuey pitched to one batter in the 7th.

Time—4:41. Attendance—44,280. Umpires—HP, Young. 1B, Clark. 2B, Johnson. 3B, Evans.

1996 AL Division Series—Composite Statistics

Batting

Orioles	G	AB	R	H	RBI	2B	3B	HR	BB	SO	SB	CS	Avg	OBP	Slg
Manny Alexander	3	0	2	0	0	0	0	0	0	0	0	0	—	—	—
Roberto Alomar	4	17	2	5	4	0	0	1	2	3	0	0	.294	.350	.471
Brady Anderson	4	17	3	5	4	0	0	2	2	3	0	1	.294	.381	.647
Bobby Bonilla	4	15	4	3	5	0	0	2	4	6	0	0	.200	.368	.600
Mike Devereaux	4	1	0	0	0	0	0	0	0	0	0	0	.000	.000	.000
Chris Hoiles	4	7	1	1	0	0	0	0	3	3	0	0	.143	.455	.143
Pete Incaviglia	2	5	1	1	0	0	0	0	0	4	0	0	.200	.200	.200
Eddie Murray	4	15	1	6	1	1	0	0	3	4	1	0	.400	.500	.467
Rafael Palmeiro	4	17	4	3	2	1	0	1	1	6	0	0	.176	.263	.412
Mark Parent	4	5	0	1	0	0	0	0	0	2	0	0	.200	.200	.200
Cal Ripken Jr.	4	18	2	8	2	3	0	0	1	3	0	0	.444	.474	.611
B.J. Surhoff	4	13	3	5	5	0	0	3	0	1	0	0	.385	.385	1.077
Todd Zeile	4	19	2	5	0	1	0	0	2	5	0	0	.263	.333	.316
Totals	4	149	25	43	23	6	0	9	17	40	1	1	.289	.372	.510

Batting

Indians	G	AB	R	H	RBI	2B	3B	HR	BB	SO	SB	CS	Avg	OBP	Slg
Sandy Alomar Jr.	4	16	0	2	3	0	0	0	0	2	0	1	.125	.125	.125
Albert Belle	4	15	2	3	6	0	0	2	3	2	1	0	.200	.333	.600
Casey Candaele	2	0	1	0	0	0	0	0	1	0	0	0	—	1.000	—
Julio Franco	4	15	1	2	1	0	0	0	1	6	0	0	.133	.176	.133
Brian Giles	1	1	0	0	0	0	0	0	0	1	0	0	.000	.000	.000
Jeff Kent	4	8	2	1	0	1	0	0	0	0	0	0	.125	.125	.250
Kenny Lofton	4	18	3	3	1	0	0	0	2	3	5	0	.167	.250	.167
Manny Ramirez	4	16	4	6	2	2	0	2	1	4	0	0	.375	.412	.875
Kevin Seitzer	4	17	1	5	4	1	0	0	2	4	1	0	.294	.368	.353
Jim Thome	4	10	1	3	0	0	0	0	1	5	0	0	.300	.417	.300
Jose Vizcaino	3	12	1	4	1	2	0	0	1	1	0	0	.333	.385	.500
Omar Vizquel	4	14	4	6	2	1	0	0	3	4	4	2	.429	.500	.500
Nigel Wilson	1	1	0	0	0	0	0	0	0	0	0	0	.000	.000	.000
Totals	4	143	20	35	20	7	0	4	15	32	11	3	.245	.317	.378

Pitching

Orioles	G	GS	CG	IP	H	R	ER	BB	SO	W-L	Sv-Op	Hld	ERA
Armando Benitez	3	0	0	4.0	1	1	1	2	6	2-0	0-1	0	2.25
Scott Erickson	1	1	0	6.2	6	3	3	2	6	0-0	0-0	0	4.05
Terry Mathews	3	0	0	2.2	3	0	0	1	2	0-0	0-0	0	0.00
Mike Mussina	1	1	0	6.0	7	4	3	2	6	0-0	0-0	0	4.50
Randy Myers	3	0	0	3.0	0	0	0	0	3	0-0	2-2	0	0.00
Jesse Orosco	4	0	0	1.0	2	4	4	3	2	0-1	0-0	1	36.00
Arthur Rhodes	2	0	0	1.0	1	1	1	1	1	0-0	0-0	0	9.00
David Wells	2	2	0	13.2	15	7	7	4	6	1-0	0-0	0	4.61
Totals	4	4	0	38.0	35	20	19	15	32	3-1	2-3	1	4.50

Pitching

Indians	G	GS	CG	IP	H	R	ER	BB	SO	W-L	Sv-Op	Hld	ERA
Paul Assenmacher	3	0	0	1.2	0	0	0	1	2	1-0	0-0	1	0.00
Alan Embree	3	0	0	1.0	0	1	1	0	1	0-0	0-0	1	9.00
Orel Hershiser	1	1	0	5.0	7	4	3	3	3	0-0	0-0	0	5.40
Jack McDowell	1	1	0	5.2	6	4	4	1	5	0-0	0-0	0	6.35
Jose Mesa	2	0	0	4.2	8	2	2	0	7	0-1	0-1	0	3.86
Charles Nagy	2	2	0	11.1	15	9	9	5	13	0-1	0-0	0	7.15
Chad Ogea	1	0	0	0.1	0	0	0	1	0	0-0	0-0	0	0.00
Eric Plunk	3	0	0	4.0	1	3	3	2	6	0-1	0-0	1	6.75
Paul Shuey	3	0	0	2.0	5	2	2	2	0	0-0	0-0	0	9.00
Julian Tavarez	2	0	0	1.1	1	0	0	2	1	0-0	0-0	0	0.00
Totals	4	4	0	37.0	43	25	24	17	40	1-3	0-1	3	5.84

Fielding

Orioles	Pos	G	PO	Ast	E	DP	PB	FPct
Roberto Alomar	2b	4	10	6	0	2	—	1.000
Brady Anderson	cf	4	7	0	0	0	—	1.000
Armando Benitez	p	3	0	2	0	0	—	1.000
Bobby Bonilla	rf	4	9	0	1	0	—	.900
Mike Devereaux	rf	2	1	0	0	0	—	1.000
	lf	1	1	0	0	0	—	1.000
Scott Erickson	p	1	1	3	0	1	—	1.000
Chris Hoiles	c	4	14	3	0	0	0	1.000
Pete Incaviglia	lf	2	0	0	0	0	—	—
Terry Mathews	p	3	0	1	0	0	—	1.000
Mike Mussina	p	1	0	0	0	0	—	—
Randy Myers	p	3	0	0	0	0	—	—
Jesse Orosco	p	4	0	0	0	0	—	—
Rafael Palmeiro	1b	4	35	1	1	2	—	.973
Mark Parent	c	4	19	0	0	0	0	1.000
Arthur Rhodes	p	2	0	0	0	0	—	—
Cal Ripken Jr.	ss	4	7	15	0	1	—	1.000
B.J. Surhoff	lf	3	6	0	0	0	—	1.000
David Wells	p	2	0	3	0	0	—	1.000
Todd Zeile	3b	4	4	9	2	0	—	.867
Totals		4	114	43	4	6	0	.975

Fielding

Indians	Pos	G	PO	Ast	E	DP	PB	FPct
Sandy Alomar Jr.	c	4	40	4	1	0	0	.978
Paul Assenmacher	p	3	0	1	0	0	—	1.000
Albert Belle	lf	4	11	1	0	0	—	1.000
Alan Embree	p	3	0	0	0	0	—	—
Julio Franco	1b	3	18	1	0	1	—	1.000
Orel Hershiser	p	1	1	1	0	1	—	1.000
Jeff Kent	3b	2	1	1	0	0	—	1.000
	2b	1	2	2	0	0	—	1.000
	1b	1	0	0	0	0	—	—
Kenny Lofton	cf	4	10	0	0	0	—	1.000
Jack McDowell	p	1	1	2	0	0	—	1.000
Jose Mesa	p	2	0	0	0	0	—	—
Charles Nagy	p	2	0	4	0	0	—	1.000
Chad Ogea	p	1	0	0	0	0	—	—
Tony Pena	c	1	1	0	0	0	0	1.000
Eric Plunk	p	3	0	0	0	0	—	—
Manny Ramirez	rf	4	8	2	0	0	—	1.000
Kevin Seitzer	1b	1	7	1	1	1	—	.889
Paul Shuey	p	3	0	0	0	0	—	—
Julian Tavarez	p	2	0	0	0	0	—	—
Jim Thome	3b	4	1	1	0	0	—	1.000
Jose Vizcaino	2b	3	4	3	1	1	—	.875
Omar Vizquel	ss	4	6	10	0	2	—	1.000
Totals		4	111	34	3	6	0	.980

1996 New York Yankees (AL) 3, Texas Rangers (AL) 1

Juan Gonzalez almost did it all by himself, but the Yankees' bullpen was near-perfect, and the Yankees beat the Rangers in four games. Gonzalez hit a three-run homer in the opener and John Burkett went the distance for a 6-2 Rangers victory. Gonzalez hit two more homers in Game 2, but the Yankees won 5-4 in 12 innings when Dean Palmer threw away Charlie Hayes' sacrifice bunt. New York won Game 3, 3-2, on Mariano Duncan's RBI single in the top of the ninth. Cecil Fielder drove in the go-ahead run in Game 4 as the Yankees won 6-4 to move on to the ALCS. Bernie Williams went 7-for-15 with three home runs in the series, while Gonzalez went 7-for-16 with five home runs and nine RBI. The Yankees' bullpen allowed only one earned run over 19.2 innings, and the Rangers didn't score a single run after the sixth inning.

Game 1

Tuesday, October 1

Rangers	AB	R	H	RBI	BB	K	Avg
Darryl Hamilton, cf	4	0	0	0	0	0	.000
Ivan Rodriguez, c	4	1	1	0	0	1	.250
Rusty Greer, lf	3	1	1	0	1	1	.333
Juan Gonzalez, rf	4	1	1	3	0	1	.250
Will Clark, 1b	4	1	1	0	0	0	.250
Mickey Tettleton, dh	3	1	0	0	1	3	.000
Dean Palmer, 3b	4	1	2	2	0	1	.500
Mark McLemore, 2b	4	0	1	1	0	1	.250
Kevin Elster, ss	4	0	1	0	0	2	.250
TOTALS	34	6	8	6	2	10	.235

Yankees	AB	R	H	RBI	BB	K	Avg
Tim Raines, lf	5	1	1	0	0	1	.200
Wade Boggs, 3b	5	0	1	0	0	1	.200
Paul O'Neill, rf	4	0	0	0	0	1	.000
Bernie Williams, cf	4	0	1	1	0	0	.250
Tino Martinez, 1b	4	1	3	0	0	0	.750
Darryl Strawberry, dh	4	0	0	0	0	2	.000
Mariano Duncan, 2b	4	0	2	1	0	1	.500
Joe Girardi, c	3	0	1	0	1	0	.333
Derek Jeter, ss	4	0	1	0	0	1	.250
TOTALS	37	2	10	2	1	7	.270

	1	2	3	4	5	6	7	8	9		R	H	E
Rangers	0	0	0	5	0	1	0	0	0		6	8	0
Yankees	1	0	0	1	0	0	0	0	0		2	10	0

DP—Yankees 1 (Girardi to Duncan). LOB—Rangers 3, Yankees 9. Scoring Position—Rangers 2-for-4, Yankees 1-for-12. 2B—Elster (1), Boggs (1), Martinez 2 (2). HR—Gonzalez (1), Palmer (1). CS—McLemore (1).

Rangers	IP	H	R	ER	BB	K	ERA
John Burkett (W, 1-0)	9.0	10	2	2	1	7	2.00

Yankees	IP	H	R	ER	BB	K	ERA
David Cone (L, 0-1)	6.0	8	6	6	2	8	9.00
Graeme Lloyd	1.0	0	0	0	0	0	0.00
Dave Weathers	2.0	0	0	0	0	2	0.00

Time—2:50. Attendance—57,205. Umpires—HP, Evans. 1B, Kaiser. 2B, Merrill. 3B, Young.

Game 2

Wednesday, October 2

Rangers	AB	R	H	RBI	BB	K	Avg
Darryl Hamilton, cf	6	0	2	0	0	0	.200
Ivan Rodriguez, c	4	0	0	0	1	2	.125
Rusty Greer, lf	5	1	0	0	1	1	.125
Juan Gonzalez, rf	5	2	3	4	1	0	.444
Will Clark, 1b	4	0	1	0	2	0	.250
Dean Palmer, 3b	6	0	1	0	0	1	.300
Mickey Tettleton, dh	3	0	0	0	2	2	.000
Mark McLemore, 2b	4	0	0	0	0	2	.125
Kevin Elster, ss	4	1	1	0	0	0	.250
TOTALS	41	4	8	4	8	8	.213

Yankees	AB	R	H	RBI	BB	K	Avg
Tim Raines, lf	4	0	1	0	1	0	.222
Wade Boggs, 3b	3	0	0	0	1	0	.125
Charlie Hayes, ph-3b	1	0	0	1	0	0	.000
Paul O'Neill, rf	5	0	1	0	0	1	.111
Bernie Williams, cf	3	1	1	0	2	0	.286
Tino Martinez, 1b	4	1	0	0	0	1	.375
Cecil Fielder, dh	3	1	2	2	1	0	.667
Andy Fox, pr-dh	0	0	0	0	0	0	—
Darryl Strawberry, ph-dh	1	0	0	0	0	0	.000
Mariano Duncan, 2b	5	0	0	0	0	1	.222
Jim Leyritz, c	2	0	0	1	0	0	.000
Joe Girardi, pr-c	1	1	0	0	1	0	.250
Derek Jeter, ss	5	1	3	0	0	0	.444
TOTALS	37	5	8	4	6	2	.243

Game 3

Friday, October 4

Yankees	AB	R	H	RBI	BB	K	Avg
Derek Jeter, ss	4	1	2	0	0	1	.462
Tim Raines, lf	3	1	1	0	1	0	.250
Bernie Williams, cf	3	1	2	2	0	0	.400
Cecil Fielder, dh	4	0	0	0	0	1	.286
Tino Martinez, 1b	3	0	0	0	1	0	.273
Mariano Duncan, 2b	3	0	2	1	0	0	.333
Luis Sojo, 2b	0	0	0	0	0	0	—
Paul O'Neill, rf	3	0	0	0	0	1	.083
Ruben Rivera, ph-rf	1	0	0	0	0	1	.000
Charlie Hayes, 3b	3	0	0	0	0	0	.167
Joe Girardi, c	2	0	0	0	1	0	.167
TOTALS	29	3	7	3	3	4	.273

Rangers	AB	R	H	RBI	BB	K	Avg
Darryl Hamilton, cf	5	0	1	0	0	1	.200
Ivan Rodriguez, c	4	0	2	1	0	0	.250
Rusty Greer, lf	4	0	1	0	0	0	.167
Juan Gonzalez, rf	4	1	2	1	0	0	.462
Will Clark, 1b	3	0	0	0	1	2	.182
Dean Palmer, 3b	4	0	0	0	0	2	.214
Mickey Tettleton, dh	3	0	0	0	1	1	.000
Damon Buford, pr	0	0	0	0	0	0	—
Mark McLemore, 2b	3	0	0	0	0	1	.091
Kevin Elster, ss	1	1	0	0	2	0	.222
Warren Newson, ph	1	0	0	0	0	0	.000
TOTALS	32	2	6	2	4	7	.206

	1	2	3	4	5	6	7	8	9	R	H	E
Yankees	1	0	0	0	0	0	0	0	2	3	7	1
Rangers	0	0	0	1	1	0	0	0	0	2	6	1

E—Elster, Jeter. DP—Rangers 2 (Oliver to Elster to Clark; Elster to McLemore to Clark). LOB—Yankees 4, Rangers 8. Scoring Position—Yankees 1-for-6, Rangers 1-for-7. 2B—Rodriguez (1). HR—Williams (1), Gonzalez (4). S—McLemore. SF—Williams. GDP—O'Neill 2. SB—Elster (1). CS—Williams (1), Hayes (1).

[Game 2 box score — continued]

	1	2	3	4	5	6	7	8	9	10	11	12	R	H	E
Rangers	0	1	3	0	0	0	0	0	0	0	0	0	4	8	1
Yankees	0	1	0	1	0	0	1	1	0	0	0	1	5	8	0

E—Palmer. DP—Rangers 1 (Hamilton to Clark), Yankees 1 (Pettitte to Jeter to Martinez). LOB—Rangers 11, Yankees 9. Scoring Position—Rangers 1-for-9, Yankees 2-for-9. 2B—Elster (2), Jeter (1). HR—Gonzalez 2 (3), Fielder (1). S—Rodriguez, McLemore, Raines, Hayes. SF—Hayes. GDP—Greer.

Rangers	IP	H	R	ER	BB	K	ERA
Ken Hill	6.0	5	3	3	3	1	4.50
Dennis Cook (H, 1)	1.0	0	0	0	0	0	0.00
Jeff Russell (BS, 1)	2.1	2	1	1	0	0	3.86
Mike Stanton (L, 0-1)	1.2	1	1	0	3	1	4.50
Mike Henneman	0.0	0	0	0	0	0	—

Yankees	IP	H	R	ER	BB	K	ERA
Andy Pettitte	6.1	4	4	4	6	3	5.68
Mariano Rivera	2.2	0	0	0	1	0	0.00
John Wetteland	2.0	2	0	0	1	2	0.00
Graeme Lloyd	0.0	1	0	0	0	0	0.00
Jeff Nelson	0.2	1	0	0	0	0	0.00
Kenny Rogers	0.0	0	0	0	1	0	—
Brian Boehringer (W, 1-0)	0.1	0	0	0	0	0	—

Hill pitched to two batters in the 7th. Stanton pitched to two batters in the 12th. Lloyd pitched to one batter in the 12th. Rogers pitched to one batter in the 12th. Henneman pitched to one batter in the 12th.

WP—Pettitte. HBP—Leyritz by Hill. Time—4:25. Attendance—57,156. Umpires—HP, Kaiser. 1B, Merrill. 2B, Young. 3B, Clark.

Game 4

Saturday, October 5

Yankees	AB	R	H	RBI	BB	K	Avg
Tim Raines, lf	4	1	1	0	1	0	.250
Wade Boggs, 3b	4	0	0	0	0	1	.083
Bernie Williams, cf	5	3	3	2	0	1	.467
Tino Martinez, 1b	4	1	1	0	1	0	.267
Cecil Fielder, dh	4	1	2	2	0	1	.364
Andy Fox, pr-dh	0	0	0	0	0	0	—
Jim Leyritz, ph-dh	1	0	0	0	0	1	.000
Paul O'Neill, rf	3	0	0	0	0	1	.133
Charlie Hayes, ph	1	0	1	0	0	0	.200
Ruben Rivera, rf	0	0	0	0	0	0	.000
Mariano Duncan, 2b	4	0	1	0	0	2	.313
Luis Sojo, 2b	0	0	0	0	0	0	—
Joe Girardi, c	3	0	1	0	1	1	.222
Derek Jeter, ss	4	0	1	0	0	0	.412
TOTALS	37	6	12	6	3	7	.274

Rangers	AB	R	H	RBI	BB	K	Avg
Darryl Hamilton, cf	4	0	0	0	0	0	.158
Ivan Rodriguez, c	4	0	3	1	1	0	.375
Rusty Greer, lf	4	0	0	0	1	1	.125
Juan Gonzalez, rf	3	1	1	1	2	1	.438
Will Clark, 1b	5	0	0	0	0	0	.125
Dean Palmer, 3b	5	2	1	0	0	1	.211
Mickey Tettleton, dh	3	0	1	1	1	1	.083
Mark McLemore, 2b	4	1	1	1	0	0	.133
Kevin Elster, ss	3	0	2	0	0	0	.333
Warren Newson, ph	0	0	0	0	1	0	.000
Damon Buford, pr	0	0	0	0	0	0	—
Rene Gonzales, ss	0	0	0	0	0	0	—
TOTALS	35	4	9	4	6	5	.218

	1	2	3	4	5	6	7	8	9	R	H	E
Yankees	0	0	0	3	1	0	1	0	1	6	12	1
Rangers	0	2	2	0	0	0	0	0	0	4	9	0

E—Jeter. DP—Yankees 1 (Jeter to Duncan to Martinez), Rangers 1 (Elster to McLemore to Clark). LOB—Yankees 8, Rangers 11. Scoring Position—Yankees 6-for-11, Rangers 3-for-14. 2B—Palmer (1). HR—Williams 2 (3), Gonzalez (5). S—Boggs, Hamilton. GDP—Raines, Clark. SB—Williams (1).

Yankees	IP	H	R	ER	BB	K	ERA
Kenny Rogers	2.0	5	2	2	1	1	9.00
Brian Boehringer	1.0	3	2	1	2	0	6.75
Dave Weathers (W, 1-0)	3.0	1	0	0	0	3	0.00
Mariano Rivera (H, 1)	2.0	0	0	0	0	1	0.00
John Wetteland (S, 2)	1.0	0	0	0	2	1	0.00

Rangers	IP	H	R	ER	BB	K	ERA
Bobby Witt	3.1	4	3	3	2	3	8.10
Danny Patterson	0.1	1	0	0	0	0	0.00
Dennis Cook	0.1	0	0	0	1	0	0.00
Roger Pavlik (L, 0-1)	2.2	4	2	2	0	1	6.75
Ed Vosberg	0.0	1	0	0	0	0	—
Jeff Russell	0.2	1	0	0	0	1	3.00
Mike Stanton	1.1	1	1	1	0	1	2.70
Mike Henneman	0.1	0	0	0	0	1	0.00

Boehringer pitched to two batters in the 4th. Vosberg pitched to one batter in the 7th.

WP—Witt. Time—3:57. Attendance—50,066. Umpires—HP, Welke. 1B, Shulock. 2B, Hendry. 3B, Coble.

Yankees	IP	H	R	ER	BB	K	ERA
Jimmy Key	5.0	5	2	2	1	3	3.60
Jeff Nelson (W, 1-0)	3.0	1	0	0	2	3	0.00
John Wetteland (S, 1)	1.0	0	0	0	1	1	0.00

Rangers	IP	H	R	ER	BB	K	ERA
Darren Oliver (L, 0-1)	8.0	6	3	3	2	3	3.38
Mike Henneman (BS, 1)	0.2	1	0	0	1	0	0.00
Mike Stanton	0.1	0	0	0	0	1	0.00

Oliver pitched to two batters in the 9th.

HBP—Duncan by Oliver. Time—3:09. Attendance—50,860. Umpires—HP, Tschida. 1B, Welke. 2B, Shulock. 3B, Hendry.

1996 AL Division Series—Composite Statistics

Batting

Yankees	G	AB	R	H	RBI	2B	3B	HR	BB	SO	SB	CS	Avg	OBP	Slg
Wade Boggs	3	12	0	1	0	1	0	0	0	2	0	0	.083	.083	.167
Mariano Duncan	4	16	0	5	3	0	0	0	0	4	0	0	.313	.353	.313
Cecil Fielder	3	11	2	4	4	0	0	1	1	2	0	0	.364	.417	.636
Andy Fox	2	0	0	0	0	0	0	0	0	0	0	0	—	—	—
Joe Girardi	4	9	1	2	0	0	0	0	4	1	0	0	.222	.462	.222
Charlie Hayes	3	5	0	1	1	0	0	0	0	0	0	1	.200	.167	.200
Derek Jeter	4	17	2	7	1	1	0	0	0	2	0	0	.412	.412	.471
Jim Leyritz	2	3	0	0	1	0	0	0	0	1	0	0	.000	.250	.000
Tino Martinez	4	15	3	4	0	2	0	0	3	1	0	0	.267	.389	.400
Paul O'Neill	4	15	0	2	0	0	0	0	0	2	0	0	.133	.133	.133
Tim Raines	4	16	3	4	0	0	0	0	3	1	0	0	.250	.368	.250
Ruben Rivera	2	1	0	0	0	0	0	0	0	1	0	0	.000	.000	.000
Darryl Strawberry	2	5	0	0	0	0	0	0	0	0	0	0	.000	.000	.000
Bernie Williams	4	15	5	7	5	0	0	3	2	1	1	1	.467	.500	1.067
Totals	4	140	16	37	15	4	0	4	13	20	1	2	.264	.331	.379

Batting

Rangers	G	AB	R	H	RBI	2B	3B	HR	BB	SO	SB	CS	Avg	OBP	Slg
Damon Buford	2	0	0	0	0	0	0	0	0	0	0	0	—	—	—
Will Clark	4	16	1	2	0	0	0	0	3	2	0	0	.125	.263	.125
Kevin Elster	4	12	2	4	0	2	0	0	3	2	1	0	.333	.467	.500
Juan Gonzalez	4	16	5	7	9	0	0	5	3	2	0	0	.438	.526	1.375
Rusty Greer	4	16	2	2	0	0	0	0	3	3	0	0	.125	.263	.125
Darryl Hamilton	4	19	0	3	0	0	0	0	0	2	0	0	.158	.158	.158
Mark McLemore	4	15	1	2	2	0	0	0	4	0	1		.133	.133	.133
Warren Newson	2	1	0	0	0	0	0	0	1	0	0	0	.000	.500	.000
Dean Palmer	4	19	3	4	2	1	0	1	0	5	0	0	.211	.211	.421
Ivan Rodriguez	4	16	1	6	2	1	0	0	2	3	0	0	.375	.444	.438
Mickey Tettleton	4	12	1	1	1	0	0	0	5	7	0	0	.083	.353	.083
Totals	4	142	16	31	16	4	0	6	20	30	1	1	.218	.315	.373

Pitching

Yankees	G	GS	CG	IP	H	R	ER	BB	SO	W-L	Sv-Op	Hld	ERA
Brian Boehringer	2	0	0	1.1	3	2	1	2	0	1-0	0-0	0	6.75
David Cone	1	1	0	6.0	8	6	6	2	8	0-1	0-0	0	9.00
Jimmy Key	1	1	0	5.0	5	2	2	1	3	0-0	0-0	0	3.60
Graeme Lloyd	2	0	0	1.0	1	0	0	0	0	0-0	0-0	0	0.00
Jeff Nelson	2	0	0	3.2	2	0	0	2	5	1-0	0-0	0	0.00
Andy Pettitte	1	1	0	6.1	4	4	4	6	3	0-0	0-0	0	5.68
Mariano Rivera	2	0	0	4.2	0	0	0	1	1	0-0	0-0	1	0.00
Kenny Rogers	2	1	0	2.0	5	2	2	2	1	0-0	0-0	0	9.00
Dave Weathers	2	0	0	5.0	1	0	0	0	5	1-0	0-0	0	0.00
John Wetteland	3	0	0	4.0	2	0	0	4	4	0-0	2-2	0	0.00
Totals	4	4	0	39.0	31	16	15	20	30	3-1	2-2	1	3.46

Pitching

Rangers	G	GS	CG	IP	H	R	ER	BB	SO	W-L	Sv-Op	Hld	ERA
John Burkett	1	1	1	9.0	10	2	2	1	7	1-0	0-0	0	2.00
Dennis Cook	2	0	0	1.1	0	0	0	1	0	0-0	0-0	1	0.00
Mike Henneman	3	0	0	1.0	1	0	0	1	1	0-0	0-1	0	0.00
Ken Hill	1	1	0	6.0	5	3	3	3	1	0-0	0-0	0	4.50
Darren Oliver	1	1	0	8.0	6	3	3	2	3	0-1	0-0	0	3.38
Danny Patterson	1	0	0	0.1	1	0	0	0	0	0-0	0-0	0	0.00
Roger Pavlik	1	0	0	2.2	4	2	2	1	0	1-0	0-0	0	6.75
Jeff Russell	2	0	0	3.0	3	1	1	0	1	0-0	0-1	0	3.00
Mike Stanton	3	0	0	3.1	2	2	1	3	3	0-1	0-0	0	2.70
Ed Vosberg	1	0	0	0.0	1	0	0	0	0	0-0	0-0	0	—
Bobby Witt	1	1	0	3.1	4	3	3	2	3	0-0	0-0	0	8.10
Totals	4	4	1	38.0	37	16	15	13	20	1-3	0-2	1	3.55

Fielding

Yankees	Pos	G	PO	Ast	E	DP	PB	FPct
Brian Boehringer	p	2	0	0	0	0	—	—
Wade Boggs	3b	3	2	1	0	0	—	1.000
David Cone	p	1	1	0	0	0	—	1.000
Mariano Duncan	2b	4	9	13	0	2	—	1.000
Joe Girardi	c	4	28	1	0	1	0	1.000
Charlie Hayes	3b	2	1	3	0	0	—	1.000
Derek Jeter	ss	4	8	10	2	2	—	.900
Jimmy Key	p	1	0	0	0	0	—	—
Jim Leyritz	c	1	4	0	0	0	0	1.000
Graeme Lloyd	p	2	1	0	0	0	—	1.000
Tino Martinez	1b	4	33	3	0	2	—	1.000
Jeff Nelson	p	2	0	1	0	0	—	1.000
Paul O'Neill	rf	4	13	0	0	0	—	1.000
Andy Pettitte	p	1	0	2	0	1	—	1.000
Tim Raines	lf	4	5	0	0	0	—	1.000
Mariano Rivera	p	2	0	0	0	0	—	—
Ruben Rivera	rf	2	0	0	0	0	—	—
Kenny Rogers	p	2	0	0	0	0	—	—
Luis Sojo	2b	2	1	1	0	0	—	1.000
Dave Weathers	p	2	0	1	0	0	—	1.000
John Wetteland	p	3	1	2	0	0	—	1.000
Bernie Williams	cf	4	10	0	0	0	—	1.000
Totals		4	117	38	2	8	0	.987

Fielding

Rangers	Pos	G	PO	Ast	E	DP	PB	FPct
John Burkett	p	1	1	0	0	0	—	1.000
Will Clark	1b	4	35	4	0	4	—	1.000
Dennis Cook	p	2	0	0	0	0	—	—
Kevin Elster	ss	4	6	7	1	3	—	.929
Rene Gonzales	ss	1	0	0	0	0	—	—
Juan Gonzalez	rf	4	8	0	0	0	—	1.000
Rusty Greer	lf	4	12	0	0	0	—	1.000
Darryl Hamilton	cf	4	16	1	0	1	—	1.000
Mike Henneman	p	3	0	0	0	0	—	—
Ken Hill	p	1	1	2	0	0	—	1.000
Mark McLemore	2b	4	10	16	0	2	—	1.000
Darren Oliver	p	1	0	3	0	1	—	1.000
Dean Palmer	3b	4	3	10	1	0	—	.929
Danny Patterson	p	1	0	0	0	0	—	—
Roger Pavlik	p	1	1	0	0	0	—	—
Ivan Rodriguez	c	4	21	3	0	0	0	1.000
Jeff Russell	p	2	0	0	0	0	—	—
Mike Stanton	p	3	0	1	0	0	—	1.000
Ed Vosberg	p	1	0	0	0	0	—	—
Bobby Witt	p	1	0	0	0	0	—	—
Totals		4	114	47	2	11	0	.988

1996 St. Louis Cardinals (NL) 3, San Diego Padres (NL) 0

The St. Louis Cardinals made short work of the San Diego Padres, sweeping them three straight. Gary Gaetti crushed a three-run homer in the first inning of the opener, and Todd Stottlemyre made it stand up for a 3-1 victory. In Game 2, Tom Pagnozzi drove in the go-ahead run in the bottom of the eighth inning on a soft liner that Padres reliever Trevor Hoffman failed to field cleanly. Hoffman was hit much harder in Game 3. He entered in the top of the ninth with the game tied at five apiece, but Brian Jordan lit into a slider for a game-winning two-run homer. The inning before, Jordan had preserved the tie with a diving catch of a sinking liner with a runner on second and two out.

Game 1
Tuesday, October 1

Padres	AB	R	H	RBI	BB	K	Avg
Rickey Henderson, lf	4	1	2	1	1	0	.500
Tony Gwynn, rf	5	0	2	0	0	0	.400
Steve Finley, cf	3	0	1	0	0	1	.333
Ken Caminiti, 3b	3	0	0	0	1	3	.000
Wally Joyner, 1b	3	0	1	0	0	0	.333
Greg Vaughn, ph	1	0	0	0	0	0	.000
Archi Cianfrocco, 1b	0	0	0	0	0	0	—
Chris Gomez, ss	4	0	0	0	0	2	.000
Brian Johnson, c	4	0	0	0	0	1	.000
Jody Reed, 2b	4	0	1	0	0	0	.250
Joey Hamilton, p	2	0	0	0	0	2	.000
Scott Livingstone, ph	1	0	0	0	0	0	.000
Willie Blair, p	0	0	0	0	0	0	—
Chris Gwynn, ph	1	0	1	0	0	0	1.000
TOTALS	35	1	8	1	2	9	.229

Cardinals	AB	R	H	RBI	BB	K	Avg
Royce Clayton, ss	3	0	1	0	1	1	.333
Willie McGee, cf	4	0	0	0	0	1	.000
Ron Gant, lf	2	1	1	0	1	0	.500
Brian Jordan, rf	4	1	1	0	0	1	.250
Gary Gaetti, 3b	3	1	1	3	0	1	.333
John Mabry, 1b	3	0	0	0	0	0	.000
Tom Pagnozzi, c	3	0	0	0	0	2	.000
Luis Alicea, 2b	3	0	2	0	0	0	.667
Todd Stottlemyre, p	2	0	0	0	0	2	.000
Rick Honeycutt, p	1	0	0	0	0	1	.000
Dennis Eckersley, p	0	0	0	0	0	0	—
TOTALS	28	3	6	3	2	9	.214

	1	2	3	4	5	6	7	8	9	R	H	E
Padres	0	0	0	0	0	1	0	0	0	1	8	1
Cardinals	3	0	0	0	0	0	0	0	x	3	6	0

E—Caminiti. DP—Padres 2 (Reed to Gomez to Joyner; Johnson to Gomez). LOB—Padres 10, Cardinals 4. Scoring Position—Padres 0-for-6, Cardinals 1-for-7. 2B—TGwynn (1), Alicea 2 (2). HR—Henderson (1), Gaetti (1). GDP—McGee. SB—TGwynn (1), Finley (1), Gant 2 (2). CS—Clayton (1), Alicea (1).

Padres	IP	H	R	ER	BB	K	ERA
Joey Hamilton (L, 0-1)	6.0	5	3	3	0	6	4.50
Willie Blair	2.0	1	0	0	2	3	0.00

Cardinals	IP	H	R	ER	BB	K	ERA
Todd Stottlemyre (W, 1-0)	6.2	5	1	1	2	7	1.35
Rick Honeycutt (H, 1)	0.2	1	0	0	0	1	0.00
Dennis Eckersley (S, 1)	1.2	2	0	0	0	1	0.00

HBP—Finley by Stottlemyre, Gant by Hamilton. Time—2:39. Attendance—54,193. Umpires—HP, Quick. 1B, Davis. 2B, DeMuth. 3B, Pulli.

Game 2
Thursday, October 3

Padres	AB	R	H	RBI	BB	K	Avg
Rickey Henderson, lf	3	1	1	0	1	2	.429
Tony Gwynn, rf	3	0	1	1	0	0	.375
Steve Finley, cf	4	0	0	1	0	2	.143
Ken Caminiti, 3b	3	1	1	1	1	1	.167
Wally Joyner, 1b	4	0	0	0	0	2	.143
Trevor Hoffman, p	0	0	0	0	0	0	—
John Flaherty, c	4	0	0	0	0	1	.000
Chris Gomez, ss	4	0	1	0	0	1	.125
Jody Reed, 2b	3	0	0	0	0	1	.143
Greg Vaughn, ph	1	0	0	0	0	0	.000
Scott Sanders, p	1	0	0	0	0	0	.000
Dario Veras, p	0	0	0	0	0	0	—
Chris Gwynn, ph	1	1	1	0	0	0	1.000
Tim Worrell, p	0	0	0	0	0	0	—
Scott Livingstone, ph	1	1	1	0	0	0	.500
Doug Bochtler, p	0	0	0	0	0	0	—
Archi Cianfrocco, 1b	0	0	0	0	0	0	—
TOTALS	32	4	6	3	2	10	.230

Cardinals	AB	R	H	RBI	BB	K	Avg
Ozzie Smith, ss	2	1	1	0	2	0	.500
Willie McGee, cf	3	1	1	1	1	1	.143
Ron Gant, lf	4	0	1	3	0	0	.333
Brian Jordan, rf	3	1	0	0	1	2	.143
Gary Gaetti, 3b	4	0	0	0	0	0	.143
John Mabry, 1b	3	0	0	0	1	1	.000
Tom Pagnozzi, c	4	0	1	1	0	1	.143
Luis Alicea, 2b	3	1	0	0	1	1	.333
Dennis Eckersley, p	0	0	0	0	0	0	—
Andy Benes, p	2	1	1	0	0	1	.500
Rick Honeycutt, p	0	0	0	0	0	0	.000
Mike Gallego, 2b	0	0	0	0	0	0	—
TOTALS	28	5	5	5	6	7	.196

	1	2	3	4	5	6	7	8	9	R	H	E
Padres	0	0	0	0	1	2	0	1	0	4	6	0
Cardinals	0	0	1	0	3	0	0	1	x	5	5	1

E—McGee. LOB—Padres 4, Cardinals 6. Scoring Position—Padres 1-for-5, Cardinals 2-for-8. 2B—Gant (1). HR—Caminiti (1). S—TGwynn, Benes.

Padres	IP	H	R	ER	BB	K	ERA
Scott Sanders	4.1	3	4	4	4	4	8.31
Dario Veras	0.2	1	0	0	0	1	0.00
Tim Worrell	2.0	1	0	0	0	2	0.00
Doug Bochtler (L, 0-1)	0.1	0	1	1	2	0	27.00
Trevor Hoffman	0.2	0	0	0	0	0	0.00

Cardinals	IP	H	R	ER	BB	K	ERA
Andy Benes	7.0	6	4	4	1	9	5.14
Rick Honeycutt (BS, 1; W, 1-0)	1.0	0	0	0	1	0	0.00
Dennis Eckersley (S, 2)	1.0	0	0	0	0	1	0.00

Benes pitched to two batters in the 8th.

WP—Bochtler. Time—2:55. Attendance—56,752. Umpires—HP, Davis. 1B, DeMuth. 2B, Pulli. 3B, Wendelstedt.

Game 3
Saturday, October 5

Cardinals	AB	R	H	RBI	BB	K	Avg
Royce Clayton, ss	3	1	1	0	2	0	.333
Willie McGee, cf	3	0	0	0	0	1	.100
Mark Petkovsek, p	0	0	0	0	0	0	—
Mark Sweeney, ph	1	0	1	0	0	0	1.000
Rick Honeycutt, p	0	0	0	0	0	0	.000
T.J. Mathews, p	0	0	0	0	0	0	—
Ozzie Smith, ph	1	0	0	0	0	0	.333
Dennis Eckersley, p	0	0	0	0	0	0	—
Ron Gant, lf	4	2	2	1	1	0	.400
Brian Jordan, rf	5	2	3	3	0	0	.333
Gary Gaetti, 3b	4	0	0	0	0	2	.091
Miguel Mejia, pr	0	0	0	0	0	0	—
Mike Gallego, 3b	1	0	0	0	0	1	.000
John Mabry, 1b	4	1	3	1	0	0	.300
Tom Pagnozzi, c	4	0	2	1	1	0	.273
Luis Alicea, 2b	5	0	0	0	0	3	.182
Donovan Osborne, p	1	0	0	0	0	0	.000
Ray Lankford, ph-cf	2	1	1	0	1	0	.500
TOTALS	38	7	13	6	5	7	.256

Padres	AB	R	H	RBI	BB	K	Avg
Rickey Henderson, lf	5	0	1	0	0	1	.333
Tony Gwynn, rf	5	0	1	0	0	2	.308
Steve Finley, cf	5	0	0	0	0	1	.083
Ken Caminiti, 3b	4	2	2	2	0	1	.300
Archi Cianfrocco, 1b	3	1	1	0	0	1	.333
Tim Worrell, p	0	0	0	0	0	0	—
Fernando Valenzuela, p	0	0	0	0	0	0	—
Dario Veras, p	0	0	0	0	0	0	—
Greg Vaughn, ph	1	0	0	0	0	1	.000
John Flaherty, c	0	0	0	0	0	0	.000
Brian Johnson, c	4	2	3	0	0	0	.375
Luis Lopez, pr	0	0	0	0	0	0	—
Trevor Hoffman, p	0	0	0	0	0	0	—
Chris Gomez, ss	4	0	1	1	0	1	.167
Jody Reed, 2b	4	0	2	2	0	0	.273
Andy Ashby, p	1	0	0	0	0	1	.000
Wally Joyner, 1b	2	0	0	0	0	0	.111
TOTALS	38	5	11	5	0	9	.224

	1	2	3	4	5	6	7	8	9	R	H	E
Cardinals	1	0	0	0	0	3	1	0	2	7	13	1
Padres	0	2	1	1	0	0	0	1	0	5	11	2

E—Caminiti 2, Alicea. DP—Padres 2 (Cianfrocco to Johnson; Gomez to Reed to Joyner). LOB—Cardinals 10, Padres 7. Scoring Position—Cardinals 4-for-12, Padres 2-for-11. 2B—Johnson (1), Reed (1). 3B—Mabry (1). HR—Gant (1), Jordan (1), Caminiti 2 (3). S—Mabry, Ashby. GDP—Gant. SB—Jordan (1). CS—Alicea (2).

Cardinals	IP	H	R	ER	BB	K	ERA
Donovan Osborne, p	4.0	7	4	4	0	5	9.00
Mark Petkovsek	2.0	0	0	0	0	0	0.00
Rick Honeycutt (BS, 2)	1.0	2	1	1	0	1	3.38
T.J. Mathews (W, 1-0)	1.0	1	0	0	0	2	0.00
Dennis Eckersley (S, 3)	1.0	1	0	0	0	0	0.00

Padres	IP	H	R	ER	BB	K	ERA
Andy Ashby	5.1	7	4	4	1	5	6.75
Tim Worrell (BS, 1)	1.2	3	1	1	1	0	2.45
Fernando Valenzuela	0.2	0	0	0	0	2	0.00
Dario Veras	0.1	0	0	0	0	0	0.00
Trevor Hoffman (L, 0-1)	1.0	3	2	2	1	2	10.80

Worrell pitched to one batter in the 8th. Honeycutt pitched to one batter in the 8th.

WP—Ashby. Time—3:32. Attendance—53,899. Umpires—HP, Hallion. 1B, Tata. 2B, Froemming. 3B, Hohn.

1996 NL Division Series—Composite Statistics

Batting

Cardinals	G	AB	R	H	RBI	2B	3B	HR	BB	SO	SB	CS	Avg	OBP	Slg
Luis Alicea	3	11	1	2	0	2	0	0	1	4	0	2	.182	.250	.364
Andy Benes	1	2	1	1	0	0	0	0	0	1	0	0	.500	.500	.500
Royce Clayton	2	6	1	2	0	0	0	0	3	1	0	1	.333	.556	.333
Gary Gaetti	3	11	1	1	0	0	0	1	0	3	0	0	.091	.091	.364
Mike Gallego	2	1	0	0	0	0	0	0	0	1	0	0	.000	.000	.000
Ron Gant	3	10	3	4	4	1	0	1	2	0	2	0	.400	.538	.800
Rick Honeycutt	3	1	0	0	0	0	0	0	0	1	0	0	.000	.000	.000
Brian Jordan	3	12	4	4	3	0	0	1	1	3	1	0	.333	.385	.583
Ray Lankford	1	2	1	1	0	0	0	0	1	0	0	0	.500	.667	.500
John Mabry	3	10	1	3	1	0	1	0	1	1	0	0	.300	.364	.500
Willie McGee	3	10	1	1	1	0	0	0	1	3	0	0	.100	.182	.100
Miguel Mejia	1	0	0	0	0	0	0	0	0	0	0	0	—	—	—
Donovan Osborne	1	1	0	0	0	0	0	0	0	0	0	0	.000	.000	.000
Tom Pagnozzi	3	11	0	3	2	0	0	1	3	0	0	0	.273	.333	.273
Ozzie Smith	2	3	1	1	0	0	0	0	2	0	0	0	.333	.600	.333
Todd Stottlemyre	1	2	0	0	0	0	0	0	0	2	0	0	.000	.000	.000
Mark Sweeney	1	1	0	1	0	0	0	0	0	0	0	0	1.000	1.000	1.000
Totals	**3**	**94**	**15**	**24**	**14**	**3**	**1**	**3**	**13**	**23**	**3**	**3**	**.255**	**.352**	**.404**

Padres	G	AB	R	H	RBI	2B	3B	HR	BB	SO	SB	CS	Avg	OBP	Slg
Andy Ashby	1	1	0	0	0	0	0	0	0	1	0	0	.000	.000	.000
Ken Caminiti	3	10	3	3	3	0	0	3	2	5	0	0	.300	.417	1.200
Archi Cianfrocco	3	3	1	1	0	0	0	0	0	1	0	0	.333	.333	.333
Steve Finley	3	12	0	1	1	0	0	0	0	4	1	0	.083	.154	.083
John Flaherty	2	4	0	0	0	0	0	0	0	1	0	0	.000	.000	.000
Chris Gomez	3	12	0	2	1	0	0	0	0	4	0	0	.167	.167	.167
Chris Gwynn	2	2	1	2	0	0	0	0	0	0	0	0	1.000	1.000	1.000
Tony Gwynn	3	13	0	4	1	1	0	0	0	2	1	0	.308	.308	.385
Joey Hamilton	1	2	0	0	0	0	0	0	0	0	0	0	.000	.000	.000
Rickey Henderson	3	12	2	4	1	0	0	1	2	3	0	0	.333	.429	.583
Brian Johnson	2	8	2	3	0	1	0	0	0	1	0	0	.375	.375	.500
Wally Joyner	3	9	0	1	0	0	0	0	0	2	0	0	.111	.111	.111
Scott Livingstone	2	2	1	1	0	0	0	0	0	0	0	0	.500	.500	.500
Luis Lopez	1	0	0	0	0	0	0	0	0	0	0	0	—	—	—
Jody Reed	3	11	0	3	2	1	0	0	1	0	0	0	.273	.273	.364
Scott Sanders	1	1	0	0	0	0	0	0	0	0	0	0	.000	.000	.000
Greg Vaughn	3	3	0	0	0	0	0	0	1	0	0	0	.000	.000	.000
Totals	**3**	**105**	**10**	**25**	**9**	**3**	**0**	**4**	**4**	**28**	**2**	**0**	**.238**	**.273**	**.381**

Pitching

Cardinals	G	GS	CG	IP	H	R	ER	BB	SO	W-L	Sv-Op	Hld	ERA
Andy Benes	1	1	0	7.0	6	4	4	1	9	0-0	0-0	0	5.14
Dennis Eckersley	3	0	0	3.2	3	0	0	0	2	0-0	3-3	0	0.00
Rick Honeycutt	3	0	0	2.2	3	1	1	1	2	1-0	0-2	1	3.38
T.J. Mathews	1	0	0	1.0	1	0	0	0	2	1-0	0-0	0	0.00
Donovan Osborne	1	1	0	4.0	7	4	4	0	5	0-0	0-0	0	9.00
Mark Petkovsek	1	0	0	2.0	0	0	0	0	1	0-0	0-0	0	0.00
Todd Stottlemyre	1	1	0	6.2	5	1	1	2	7	1-0	0-0	0	1.35
Totals	**3**	**3**	**0**	**27.0**	**25**	**10**	**10**	**4**	**28**	**3-0**	**3-5**	**1**	**3.33**

Padres	G	GS	CG	IP	H	R	ER	BB	SO	W-L	Sv-Op	Hld	ERA
Andy Ashby	1	1	0	5.1	7	4	4	1	5	0-0	0-0	0	6.75
Willie Blair	1	0	0	2.0	1	0	0	2	3	0-0	0-0	0	0.00
Doug Bochtler	1	0	0	0.1	0	1	1	2	0	0-1	0-0	0	27.00
Joey Hamilton	1	1	0	6.0	5	3	3	0	6	0-1	0-0	0	4.50
Trevor Hoffman	2	0	0	1.2	3	2	2	1	2	0-1	0-0	0	10.80
Scott Sanders	1	1	0	4.1	3	4	4	4	4	0-0	0-0	0	8.31
Fernando Valenzuela	1	0	0	0.2	0	0	0	2	0	0-0	0-0	0	0.00
Dario Veras	2	0	0	1.0	1	0	0	0	1	0-0	0-0	0	0.00
Tim Worrell	2	0	0	3.2	4	1	1	1	2	0-0	0-1	0	2.45
Totals	**3**	**3**	**0**	**25.0**	**24**	**15**	**15**	**13**	**23**	**0-3**	**0-1**	**0**	**5.40**

Fielding

Cardinals	Pos	G	PO	Ast	E	DP	PB	FPct
Luis Alicea	2b	3	2	5	1	0	—	.875
Andy Benes	p	1	1	0	0	0	—	1.000
Royce Clayton	ss	2	4	5	0	0	—	1.000
Dennis Eckersley	p	3	0	1	0	0	—	1.000
Gary Gaetti	3b	3	1	3	0	0	—	1.000
Mike Gallego	2b	1	0	0	0	0	—	—
	3b	1	0	0	0	0	—	—
Ron Gant	lf	3	5	0	0	0	—	1.000
Rick Honeycutt	p	3	0	1	0	0	—	1.000
Brian Jordan	rf	3	5	0	0	0	—	1.000
Ray Lankford	cf	1	4	0	0	0	—	1.000
John Mabry	1b	3	20	1	0	0	—	1.000
T.J. Mathews	p	1	0	0	0	0	—	—
Willie McGee	cf	3	9	0	1	0	—	.900
Donovan Osborne	p	1	0	1	0	0	—	1.000
Tom Pagnozzi	c	3	28	0	0	0	0	1.000
Mark Petkovsek	p	1	0	0	0	0	—	—
Ozzie Smith	ss	1	2	1	0	0	—	1.000
Todd Stottlemyre	p	1	0	0	0	0	—	—
Totals		**3**	**81**	**18**	**2**	**0**	**0**	**.980**

Padres	Pos	G	PO	Ast	E	DP	PB	FPct
Andy Ashby	p	1	0	0	0	0	—	—
Willie Blair	p	1	0	0	0	0	—	—
Doug Bochtler	p	1	0	0	0	0	—	—
Ken Caminiti	3b	3	0	5	3	0	—	.625
Archi Cianfrocco	1b	3	8	2	0	1	—	1.000
Steve Finley	cf	3	10	0	0	0	—	1.000
John Flaherty	c	2	9	0	0	0	0	1.000
Chris Gomez	ss	3	8	5	0	3	—	1.000
Tony Gwynn	rf	3	2	0	0	0	—	1.000
Joey Hamilton	p	1	1	0	0	0	—	1.000
Rickey Henderson	lf	3	4	0	0	0	—	1.000
Trevor Hoffman	p	2	0	1	0	0	—	1.000
Brian Johnson	c	2	15	3	0	2	0	1.000
Wally Joyner	1b	3	12	2	0	2	—	1.000
Jody Reed	2b	3	6	6	0	2	—	1.000
Scott Sanders	p	1	0	1	0	0	—	1.000
Fernando Valenzuela	p	1	0	1	0	0	—	1.000
Dario Veras	p	2	0	1	0	0	—	1.000
Tim Worrell	p	2	0	1	0	0	—	1.000
Totals		**3**	**75**	**28**	**3**	**10**	**0**	**.972**

1996 Atlanta Braves (NL) 3, Los Angeles Dodgers (NL) 0

The Atlanta Braves allowed only three earned runs en route to a three-game sweep of the Los Angeles Dodgers. John Smoltz and Ramon Martinez each were stellar in the opener. The game went into extra innings tied 1-1, until Javy Lopez hit an opposite-field homer off Antonio Osuna in the top of the 10th. The Dodgers went ahead 2-1 against Greg Maddux in Game 2 with two unearned runs, but Fred McGriff and Jermaine Dye hit solo homers in the seventh to give Atlanta another one-run victory. In the finale, the Braves knocked out Hideo Nomo with a four-run fourth inning and went on to clinch a spot in the NLCS, winning 5-2.

Game 1
Wednesday, October 2

Braves	AB	R	H	RBI	BB	K	Avg
Marquis Grissom, cf	4	1	1	0	0	0	.250
Mark Lemke, 2b	4	0	0	0	0	0	.000
Chipper Jones, 3b	2	0	0	0	2	2	.000
Fred McGriff, 1b	3	0	1	1	0	0	.333
Ryan Klesko, lf	1	0	0	0	2	1	.000
Terry Pendleton, ph	1	0	0	0	0	1	.000
Andruw Jones, lf	0	0	0	0	0	0	—
Javy Lopez, c	4	1	1	1	0	0	.250
Jermaine Dye, rf	4	0	0	0	0	3	.000
Jeff Blauser, ss	3	0	1	0	0	1	.333
Mark Wohlers, p	0	0	0	0	0	0	—
John Smoltz, p	2	0	0	0	0	0	.000
Luis Polonia, ph	1	0	0	0	0	1	.000
Rafael Belliard, ss	0	0	0	0	0	0	—
TOTALS	29	2	4	2	4	9	.138

Dodgers	AB	R	H	RBI	BB	K	Avg
Wayne Kirby, cf	4	0	1	0	1	0	.250
Todd Hollandsworth, lf	4	0	1	1	0	1	.250
Mike Piazza, c	4	0	1	0	0	2	.250
Eric Karros, 1b	3	0	0	0	1	0	.000
Raul Mondesi, rf	4	0	0	0	0	1	.000
Tim Wallach, 3b	4	0	0	0	0	1	.000
Delino DeShields, 2b	4	0	0	0	0	1	.000
Greg Gagne, ss	4	1	2	0	0	1	.500
Ramon Martinez, p	3	0	0	0	0	2	.000
Scott Radinsky, p	0	0	0	0	0	0	—
Antonio Osuna, p	0	0	0	0	0	0	—
Dave Clark, ph	1	0	0	0	0	1	.000
TOTALS	35	1	5	1	2	9	.143

	1	2	3	4	5	6	7	8	9	10		R	H	E
Braves	0	0	0	1	0	0	0	0	0	1		2	4	1
Dodgers	0	0	0	0	1	0	0	0	0			1	5	0

E—Lopez. DP—Dodgers 2 (Piazza to DeShields; Piazza to DeShields). LOB—Braves 4, Dodgers 6. Scoring Position—Braves 0-for-6, Dodgers 1-for-6. 2B—Hollandsworth (1), Gagne (1). HR—Lopez (1). S—Smoltz. SF—McGriff. SB—Grissom (1), Klesko (1). CS—CJones (1), McGriff (1), Blauser (1), Kirby (1).

Braves	IP	H	R	ER	BB	K	ERA
John Smoltz (W, 1-0)	9.0	4	1	1	2	7	1.00
Mark Wohlers (S, 1)	1.0	1	0	0	0	2	0.00

Dodgers	IP	H	R	ER	BB	K	ERA
Ramon Martinez	8.0	3	1	1	3	6	1.13
Scott Radinsky	0.1	0	0	0	1	0	0.00
Antonio Osuna (L, 0-1)	1.2	1	1	1	0	3	5.40

HBP—Blauser by Osuna. Time—3:08. Attendance—47,428. Umpires—HP, Rippley. 1B, Gregg. 2B, Hallion. 3B, Tata.

Game 2
Thursday, October 3

Braves	AB	R	H	RBI	BB	K	Avg
Marquis Grissom, cf	4	0	0	0	0	1	.125
Mark Lemke, 2b	4	0	1	0	0	0	.125
Fred McGriff, 1b	4	1	1	1	0	1	.286
Ryan Klesko, lf	3	1	1	1	1	1	.250
Andruw Jones, pr-lf	0	0	0	0	0	0	—
Jermaine Dye, rf	3	1	1	1	0	1	.143
Eddie Perez, c	3	0	0	0	0	0	.333
Jeff Blauser, ss	3	0	0	0	0	0	.167
Rafael Belliard, ss	0	0	0	0	0	0	—
Greg Maddux, p	2	0	0	0	0	1	.000
Luis Polonia, ph	1	0	0	0	0	0	.000
Greg McMichael, p	0	0	0	0	0	0	—
Mark Wohlers, p	0	0	0	0	0	0	—
TOTALS	31	3	5	3	1	7	.151

Dodgers	AB	R	H	RBI	BB	K	Avg
Todd Hollandsworth, lf	4	1	1	0	0	2	.250
Wayne Kirby, cf	4	0	0	0	0	1	.125
Mike Piazza, c	4	1	1	1	0	0	.250
Eric Karros, 1b	3	0	0	0	0	2	.000
Raul Mondesi, rf	3	0	1	1	0	2	.143
Tim Wallach, 3b	3	0	0	0	0	0	.000
Greg Gagne, ss	3	0	0	0	0	0	.286
Juan Castro, 2b	2	0	0	0	0	0	.000
Dave Hansen, ph	1	0	0	0	0	0	.000
Delino DeShields, 2b	0	0	0	0	0	0	.000
Ismael Valdes, p	2	0	0	0	0	0	.000
Pedro Astacio, p	0	0	0	0	0	0	—
Billy Ashley, ph	1	0	0	0	0	1	.000
Todd Worrell, p	0	0	0	0	0	0	—
TOTALS	30	2	3	2	0	10	.131

	1	2	3	4	5	6	7	8	9		R	H	E
Braves	0	1	0	0	0	0	2	0	0		3	5	2
Dodgers	1	0	0	1	0	0	0	0	0		2	3	0

E—Grissom, Klesko. LOB—Braves 2, Dodgers 1. Scoring Position—Braves 0-for-0, Dodgers 1-for-5. 2B—Mondesi (1). HR—McGriff (1), Klesko (1), Dye (1).

Braves	IP	H	R	ER	BB	K	ERA
Greg Maddux (W, 1-0)	7.0	3	2	0	0	7	0.00
Greg McMichael (H, 1)	1.0	0	0	0	0	2	0.00
Mark Wohlers (S, 2)	1.0	0	0	0	0	1	0.00

Dodgers	IP	H	R	ER	BB	K	ERA
Ismael Valdes (L, 0-1)	6.1	5	3	3	0	5	4.26
Pedro Astacio	1.2	0	0	0	0	1	0.00
Todd Worrell	1.0	0	0	0	1	1	0.00

Time—2:08. Attendance—51,916. Umpires—HP, Gregg. 1B, Hallion. 2B, Tata. 3B, Froemming.

Game 3
Saturday, October 5

Dodgers	AB	R	H	RBI	BB	K	Avg
Chad Curtis, cf	2	0	0	0	1	1	.000
Wayne Kirby, ph-cf	0	1	0	0	1	0	.125
Todd Hollandsworth, lf	4	0	2	0	0	0	.333
Mike Piazza, c	2	0	1	1	0	0	.300
Eric Karros, 1b	3	0	0	0	0	1	.000
Raul Mondesi, rf	4	0	1	0	0	1	.182
Tim Wallach, 3b	4	0	0	0	0	1	.000
Antonio Osuna, p	0	0	0	0	0	0	—
Darren Dreifort, p	0	0	0	0	0	0	—
Greg Gagne, ss	4	1	1	0	0	2	.273
Juan Castro, 2b	3	0	1	1	1	1	.200
Hideo Nomo, p	1	0	0	0	0	1	.000
Mark Guthrie, p	0	0	0	0	0	0	—
Dave Clark, ph	1	0	0	0	0	1	.000
Tom Candiotti, p	0	0	0	0	0	0	—
Billy Ashley, ph	1	0	0	0	0	1	.000
Scott Radinsky, p	0	0	0	0	0	0	—
Dave Hansen, 3b	1	0	0	0	0	0	.000
TOTALS	30	2	6	2	5	10	.163

Braves	AB	R	H	RBI	BB	K	Avg
Marquis Grissom, cf	4	1	0	0	1	1	.083
Mark Lemke, 2b	4	1	1	2	0	1	.167
Chipper Jones, 3b	3	2	2	1	1	1	.222
Fred McGriff, 1b	2	0	1	1	2	0	.333
Ryan Klesko, lf	4	0	0	0	0	2	.125
Mark Wohlers, p	0	0	0	0	0	0	—
Javy Lopez, c	3	0	1	0	1	0	.286
Jermaine Dye, rf	4	0	1	0	0	2	.182
Jeff Blauser, ss	3	0	0	0	1	1	.111
Rafael Belliard, ss	0	0	0	0	0	0	—
Tom Glavine, p	2	1	1	0	0	0	.500
Greg McMichael, p	0	0	0	0	0	0	—
Mike Bielecki, p	0	0	0	0	0	0	—
Andruw Jones, lf	0	0	0	0	1	0	—
TOTALS	29	5	7	5	7	8	.190

	1	2	3	4	5	6	7	8	9		R	H	E
Dodgers	0	0	0	0	0	0	1	1	0		2	6	1
Braves	1	0	0	4	0	0	0	0	x		5	7	0

E—Wallach. DP—Dodgers 2 (Wallach to Castro to Karros; Dreifort to Hansen), Braves 1 (Blauser to Lemke to McGriff). LOB—Dodgers 7, Braves 8. Scoring Position—Dodgers 1-for-6, Braves 2-for-8. 2B—Hollandsworth 2 (3), Mondesi (2), Castro (1), Lemke (1), McGriff (1), Glavine (1). HR—CJones (1). S—Glavine. SF—Piazza. GDP—Karros, Lemke. SB—CJones (1), Lopez (1), Dye (1).

Dodgers	IP	H	R	ER	BB	K	ERA
Hideo Nomo (L, 0-1)	3.2	5	5	5	5	3	12.27
Mark Guthrie	0.1	0	0	0	1	1	0.00
Tom Candiotti	2.0	0	0	0	0	1	0.00
Scott Radinsky	1.0	0	0	0	0	2	0.00
Antonio Osuna	0.1	2	0	0	1	1	4.50
Darren Dreifort	0.2	0	0	0	0	0	0.00

Braves	IP	H	R	ER	BB	K	ERA
Tom Glavine (W, 1-0)	6.2	5	1	1	3	7	1.35
Greg McMichael	0.1	1	1	1	1	1	6.75
Mike Bielecki (H, 1)	0.2	0	0	0	1	1	0.00
Mark Wohlers (S, 3)	1.1	0	0	0	0	0	0.00

McMichael pitched to two batters in the 8th.

Time—3:19. Attendance—52,529. Umpires—HP, DeMuth. 1B, Pulli. 2B, Wendelstedt. 3B, Bonin.

1996 NL Division Series—Composite Statistics

Batting

Braves	G	AB	R	H	RBI	2B	3B	HR	BB	SO	SB	CS	Avg	OBP	Slg
Jeff Blauser	3	9	0	1	0	0	0	0	1	3	0	1	.111	.273	.111
Jermaine Dye	3	11	1	2	1	0	0	1	0	6	1	0	.182	.182	.455
Tom Glavine	1	2	1	1	0	1	0	0	0	0	0	0	.500	.500	1.000
Marquis Grissom	3	12	2	1	0	0	0	0	1	2	1	0	.083	.154	.083
Andruw Jones	3	0	0	0	0	0	0	0	1	0	0	0	—	1.000	—
Chipper Jones	3	9	2	2	2	0	0	1	3	4	1	1	.222	.417	.556
Ryan Klesko	3	8	1	1	1	0	0	1	3	4	1	0	.125	.364	.500
Mark Lemke	3	12	1	2	2	1	0	0	1	0	0	0	.167	.167	.250
Javy Lopez	2	7	1	2	1	0	1	1	0	1	0	0	.286	.375	.714
Greg Maddux	1	2	0	0	0	0	0	0	0	1	0	0	.000	.000	.000
Fred McGriff	3	9	1	3	3	1	0	1	2	1	0	1	.333	.417	.778
Terry Pendleton	1	1	0	0	0	0	0	0	0	1	0	0	.000	.000	.000
Eddie Perez	1	3	0	1	0	0	0	0	0	0	0	0	.333	.333	.333
Luis Polonia	2	2	0	0	0	0	0	0	0	1	0	0	.000	.000	.000
John Smoltz	1	2	0	0	0	0	0	0	0	0	0	0	.000	.000	.000
Totals	**3**	**89**	**10**	**16**	**10**	**3**	**0**	**5**	**12**	**24**	**5**	**3**	**.180**	**.282**	**.382**

Dodgers	G	AB	R	H	RBI	2B	3B	HR	BB	SO	SB	CS	Avg	OBP	Slg
Billy Ashley	2	2	0	0	0	0	0	0	0	2	0	0	.000	.000	.000
Juan Castro	2	5	0	1	1	1	0	0	1	1	0	0	.200	.333	.400
Dave Clark	2	2	0	0	0	0	0	0	0	0	0	0	.000	.000	.000
Chad Curtis	1	2	0	0	0	0	0	0	0	1	1	0	.000	.333	.000
Delino DeShields	2	4	0	0	0	0	0	0	0	1	0	0	.000	.000	.000
Greg Gagne	3	11	2	3	0	1	0	0	0	5	0	0	.273	.273	.364
Dave Hansen	2	2	0	0	0	0	0	0	0	0	0	0	.000	.000	.000
Todd Hollandsworth	3	12	1	4	1	3	0	0	0	3	0	0	.333	.333	.583
Eric Karros	3	9	0	0	0	0	0	0	2	3	0	0	.000	.182	.000
Wayne Kirby	3	8	1	1	0	0	0	0	2	1	0	1	.125	.300	.125
Ramon Martinez	1	3	0	0	0	0	0	0	0	2	0	0	.000	.000	.000
Raul Mondesi	3	11	0	2	1	2	0	0	4	0	0	0	.182	.182	.364
Hideo Nomo	1	1	0	0	0	0	0	0	0	1	0	0	.000	.000	.000
Mike Piazza	3	10	1	3	2	0	0	1	2	0	0	0	.300	.333	.300
Ismael Valdes	1	2	0	0	0	0	0	0	0	0	0	0	.000	.000	.000
Tim Wallach	3	11	0	0	0	0	0	0	1	0	0	0	.000	.000	.000
Totals	**3**	**95**	**5**	**14**	**5**	**7**	**0**	**0**	**7**	**29**	**0**	**1**	**.147**	**.204**	**.221**

Pitching

Braves	G	GS	CG	IP	H	R	ER	BB	SO	W-L	Sv-Op	Hld	ERA
Mike Bielecki	1	0	0	0.2	0	0	0	1	1	0-0	0-0	1	0.00
Tom Glavine	1	1	0	6.2	5	1	1	3	7	1-0	0-0	0	1.35
Greg Maddux	1	1	0	7.0	3	2	0	0	7	1-0	0-0	0	0.00
Greg McMichael	2	0	0	1.1	1	1	1	1	3	0-0	0-0	1	6.75
John Smoltz	1	1	0	9.0	4	1	1	2	7	1-0	0-0	0	1.00
Mark Wohlers	3	0	0	3.1	1	0	0	0	4	0-0	3-3	0	0.00
Totals	**3**	**3**	**0**	**28.0**	**14**	**5**	**3**	**7**	**29**	**3-0**	**3-3**	**2**	**0.96**

Dodgers	G	GS	CG	IP	H	R	ER	BB	SO	W-L	Sv-Op	Hld	ERA
Pedro Astacio	1	0	0	1.2	0	0	0	0	1	0-0	0-0	0	0.00
Tom Candiotti	1	0	0	2.0	0	0	0	0	1	0-0	0-0	0	0.00
Darren Dreifort	1	0	0	0.2	0	0	0	0	0	0-0	0-0	0	0.00
Mark Guthrie	1	0	0	0.1	0	0	0	1	1	0-0	0-0	0	0.00
Ramon Martinez	1	1	0	8.0	3	1	1	3	6	0-0	0-0	0	1.13
Hideo Nomo	1	1	0	3.2	5	5	5	3	3	0-1	0-0	0	12.27
Antonio Osuna	2	0	0	2.0	3	1	1	1	4	0-1	0-0	0	4.50
Scott Radinsky	2	0	0	1.1	0	0	0	1	2	0-0	0-0	0	0.00
Ismael Valdes	1	1	0	6.1	5	3	3	0	5	0-1	0-0	0	4.26
Todd Worrell	1	0	0	1.0	0	0	0	1	1	0-0	0-0	0	0.00
Totals	**3**	**3**	**0**	**27.0**	**16**	**10**	**10**	**12**	**24**	**0-3**	**0-0**	**0**	**3.33**

Fielding

Braves	Pos	G	PO	Ast	E	DP	PB	FPct
Rafael Belliard	ss	3	0	0	0	0	—	—
Mike Bielecki	p	1	0	0	0	0	—	—
Jeff Blauser	ss	3	0	7	0	1	—	1.000
Jermaine Dye	rf	3	11	1	0	0	—	1.000
Tom Glavine	p	1	0	1	0	0	—	1.000
Marquis Grissom	cf	3	4	0	1	0	—	.800
Andruw Jones	lf	3	2	0	0	0	—	1.000
Chipper Jones	3b	3	1	3	0	0	—	1.000
Ryan Klesko	lf	3	2	0	1	0	—	.667
Mark Lemke	2b	3	4	8	0	1	—	1.000
Javy Lopez	c	2	21	1	1	0	0	.957
Greg Maddux	p	1	2	2	0	0	—	1.000
Fred McGriff	1b	3	25	3	0	1	—	1.000
Greg McMichael	p	2	0	0	0	0	—	—
Eddie Perez	c	1	10	0	0	0	0	1.000
John Smoltz	p	1	2	1	0	0	—	1.000
Mark Wohlers	p	3	0	0	0	0	—	—
Totals		**3**	**84**	**27**	**3**	**3**	**0**	**.974**

Dodgers	Pos	G	PO	Ast	E	DP	PB	FPct
Pedro Astacio	p	1	0	1	0	0	—	1.000
Tom Candiotti	p	1	0	0	0	0	—	—
Juan Castro	2b	2	4	3	0	1	—	1.000
Chad Curtis	cf	1	2	0	0	0	—	1.000
Delino DeShields	2b	2	3	2	0	2	—	1.000
Darren Dreifort	p	1	1	1	0	1	—	1.000
Greg Gagne	ss	3	3	9	0	0	—	1.000
Mark Guthrie	p	1	0	0	0	0	—	—
Dave Hansen	3b	1	1	0	0	1	—	1.000
Todd Hollandsworth	lf	3	4	0	0	0	—	1.000
Eric Karros	1b	3	28	2	0	1	—	1.000
Wayne Kirby	cf	3	4	0	0	0	—	1.000
Ramon Martinez	p	1	0	0	0	0	—	—
Raul Mondesi	rf	3	2	0	0	0	—	1.000
Hideo Nomo	p	1	1	0	0	0	—	1.000
Antonio Osuna	p	2	0	0	0	0	—	—
Mike Piazza	c	3	25	4	0	2	0	1.000
Scott Radinsky	p	2	0	0	0	0	—	—
Ismael Valdes	p	1	1	2	0	0	—	1.000
Tim Wallach	3b	3	2	8	1	1	—	.909
Todd Worrell	p	1	0	0	0	0	—	—
Totals		**3**	**81**	**32**	**1**	**9**	**0**	**.991**

1997 Cleveland Indians (AL) 3, New York Yankees (AL) 2

The Cleveland Indians overturned the defending champion New York Yankees in a wild five-game Division Series. In the opener, Cleveland jumped out to a 5-0 lead in the top of the first inning. New York came back to take the lead with three consecutive home runs in the bottom of the sixth, and won 8-6. Game 2 produced an odd symmetry when the Yankees rocked Cleveland rookie Jaret Wright for three runs in the first inning before the Indians came back to take a 7-5 decision. Paul O'Neill belted a grand slam and David Wells tossed a five-hitter in Game 3, for a 6-1 New York win. The Yanks turned over a 2-1 lead to closer Mariano Rivera in the bottom of the eighth inning of Game 4, but Cleveland catcher Sandy Alomar tied it with a solo homer. In the bottom of the ninth, Omar Vizquel singled off the glove of pitcher Ramiro Mendoza to score Marquis Grissom with the winning run for Cleveland. The Indians took an early 4-0 lead in Game 5, and held on to win 4-3 as their bullpen provided 3.2 innings of shutout relief.

Game 1
Tuesday, September 30

Indians	AB	R	H	RBI	BB	K	Avg
Bip Roberts, 2b	3	1	2	1	2	0	.667
Omar Vizquel, ss	3	0	1	0	1	1	.333
Manny Ramirez, rf	5	1	2	1	0	1	.400
Jim Thome, 1b	5	0	2	0	0	0	.400
David Justice, dh	4	1	1	0	1	0	.250
Matt Williams, 3b	4	1	0	0	0	2	.000
Sandy Alomar Jr., c	4	1	2	3	0	0	.500
Brian Giles, lf	4	0	0	0	0	0	.000
Marquis Grissom, cf	4	1	1	0	0	1	.250
TOTALS	36	6	11	5	4	5	.306

Yankees	AB	R	H	RBI	BB	K	Avg
Tim Raines, dh	4	1	1	3	0	0	.250
Derek Jeter, ss	5	1	2	1	0	1	.400
Paul O'Neill, rf	3	1	1	1	1	0	.333
Bernie Williams, cf	2	1	0	0	1	0	.000
Tino Martinez, 1b	4	1	2	1	0	1	.500
Chad Curtis, lf	2	0	1	0	2	0	.500
Wade Boggs, 3b	4	1	1	1	0	0	.250
Charlie Hayes, 3b	0	0	0	0	0	0	—
Joe Girardi, c	4	1	1	0	0	1	.250
Rey Sanchez, 2b	3	1	2	1	1	0	.667
TOTALS	31	8	11	8	5	3	.355

	1	2	3	4	5	6	7	8	9	R	H	E
Indians	5	0	0	1	0	0	0	0	0	6	11	0
Yankees	0	1	0	1	1	5	0	0	x	8	11	0

DP—Indians 3 (MWilliams to Roberts to Thome; Roberts to Vizquel to Thome; Roberts to Vizquel to Thome), Yankees 1 (Boggs to Sanchez to Martinez). LOB—Indians 9, Yankees 6. Scoring Position—Indians 3-for-9, Yankees 2-for-7. 2B—Justice (1), Sanchez (1). 3B—Grissom (1). HR—Alomar Jr. (1), Raines (1), Jeter (1), O'Neill (1), Martinez (1). S—Vizquel. SF—Raines. GDP—Ramirez, Raines, Boggs, Girardi. SB—Roberts 2 (2).

Indians	IP	H	R	ER	BB	K	ERA
Orel Hershiser	4.1	6	3	3	2	1	6.23
Alvin Morman	0.0	0	0	0	1	0	—
Eric Plunk (L, 0-1)	1.1	4	4	4	0	1	27.00
Paul Assenmacher	0.2	1	1	1	1	0	13.50
Mike Jackson	1.2	0	0	0	1	1	0.00

Yankees	IP	H	R	ER	BB	K	ERA
David Cone	3.1	7	6	6	2	2	16.20
Ramiro Mendoza (W, 1-0)	3.1	1	0	0	0	2	0.00
Mike Stanton	0.0	1	0	0	1	0	—
Jeff Nelson (H, 1)	1.0	1	0	0	1	0	0.00
Mariano Rivera (S, 1)	1.1	1	0	0	0	1	0.00

Morman pitched to one batter in the 5th. Stanton pitched to two batters in the 7th.

WP—Cone. HBP—MWilliams by Cone, BWilliams by Assenmacher. Time—3:28. Attendance—57,398. Umpires—HP, Tschida. 1B, Morrison. 2B, Reed. 3B, Scott.

Game 2
Thursday, October 2

Indians	AB	R	H	RBI	BB	K	Avg
Bip Roberts, lf	5	0	2	0	0	0	.500
Omar Vizquel, ss	5	2	3	0	0	0	.500
Manny Ramirez, rf	4	0	0	0	0	2	.222
Matt Williams, 3b	2	2	1	2	2	1	.167
David Justice, dh	4	1	1	1	0	0	.250
Sandy Alomar Jr., c	4	1	1	0	0	0	.375
Jim Thome, 1b	4	1	1	1	0	2	.333
Tony Fernandez, 2b	4	0	2	2	0	0	.500
Marquis Grissom, cf	4	0	0	0	0	0	.125
TOTALS	36	7	11	7	2	6	.324

Yankees	AB	R	H	RBI	BB	K	Avg
Tim Raines, dh	5	0	1	0	0	0	.222
Derek Jeter, ss	4	2	2	1	1	2	.444
Paul O'Neill, rf	4	1	1	0	1	0	.286
Bernie Williams, cf	3	2	1	0	2	1	.200
Tino Martinez, 1b	4	0	1	2	1	0	.375
Charlie Hayes, 3b	3	0	1	1	0	1	.333
Chad Curtis, lf	3	0	0	0	1	1	.200
Joe Girardi, c	3	0	0	0	1	1	.143
Mike Stanley, ph	0	0	0	0	1	0	—
Andy Fox, pr-2b	0	0	0	0	0	0	—
Rey Sanchez, 2b	3	0	0	0	0	0	.333
Wade Boggs, ph	1	0	0	0	0	0	.200
Jorge Posada, c	0	0	0	0	0	0	—
TOTALS	33	5	7	5	6	7	.281

	1	2	3	4	5	6	7	8	9	R	H	E
Indians	0	0	0	5	2	0	0	0	0	7	11	1
Yankees	3	0	0	0	0	0	0	1	1	5	7	2

E—Hayes, Boehringer, Wright. DP—Indians 1 (Fernandez to Thome), Yankees 1 (Jeter to Martinez). LOB—Indians 4, Yankees 9. Scoring Position—Indians 4-for-8, Yankees 1-for-6. 2B—Fernandez (1), BWilliams (1), Martinez (1). HR—MWilliams (1), Jeter (2). SF—Hayes. GDP—Ramirez, Girardi. SB—Vizquel (1). CS—Roberts (1), Grissom (1).

Indians	IP	H	R	ER	BB	K	ERA
Jaret Wright (W, 1-0)	6.0	3	3	3	4	5	4.50
Mike Jackson	0.2	0	0	0	0	0	0.00
Paul Assenmacher (H, 1)	0.2	0	1	1	1	0	13.50
Jose Mesa	1.2	2	1	1	1	1	5.40

Yankees	IP	H	R	ER	BB	K	ERA
Andy Pettitte (L, 0-1)	5.0	9	7	7	1	3	12.60
Brian Boehringer	1.2	1	0	0	1	2	0.00
Graeme Lloyd	1.1	0	0	0	0	0	0.00
Jeff Nelson	1.0	1	0	0	0	0	0.00

HBP—Stanley by Mesa. Time—3:32. Attendance—57,360. Umpires—HP, Morrison. 1B, Reed. 2B, Scott. 3B, Garcia.

Game 3
Saturday, October 4

Yankees	AB	R	H	RBI	BB	K	Avg
Tim Raines, lf	2	2	0	0	2	0	.182
Chad Curtis, lf	1	0	0	0	0	0	.167
Derek Jeter, ss	3	2	0	0	2	0	.333
Paul O'Neill, rf	4	1	2	5	0	0	.364
Bernie Williams, cf	4	0	0	0	0	0	.111
Tino Martinez, 1b	3	0	1	1	1	0	.364
Cecil Fielder, dh	4	0	0	0	0	1	.000
Charlie Hayes, 3b	4	0	0	0	0	0	.143
Joe Girardi, c	3	1	1	0	1	1	.200
Rey Sanchez, 2b	3	0	0	0	0	0	.222
TOTALS	31	6	4	6	6	2	.233

Indians	AB	R	H	RBI	BB	K	Avg
Bip Roberts, lf	4	0	0	0	0	0	.333
Kevin Seitzer, 1b	4	0	0	0	0	0	.000
Manny Ramirez, rf	4	0	0	0	0	0	.154
Matt Williams, 3b	4	1	1	0	0	0	.200
David Justice, dh	4	0	2	0	0	0	.333
Sandy Alomar Jr., c	4	0	0	0	0	1	.250
Tony Fernandez, 2b	3	0	0	1	0	0	.286
Marquis Grissom, cf	3	0	1	0	0	0	.182
Omar Vizquel, ss	3	0	1	0	0	0	.455
TOTALS	33	1	5	1	0	1	.261

	1	2	3	4	5	6	7	8	9	R	H	E
Yankees	1	0	1	4	0	0	0	0	0	6	4	1
Indians	0	1	0	0	0	0	0	0	0	1	5	1

E—Hayes, Nagy. LOB—Yankees 5, Indians 5. Scoring Position—Yankees 3-for-8, Indians 0-for-5. 2B—Justice (2). HR—O'Neill (2). S—Sanchez. SB—Jeter (1).

Yankees	IP	H	R	ER	BB	K	ERA
David Wells (W, 1-0)	9.0	5	1	1	0	1	1.00

Indians	IP	H	R	ER	BB	K	ERA
Charles Nagy (L, 0-1)	3.2	2	5	4	6	1	9.82
Chad Ogea	5.1	2	1	1	0	1	1.69

Time—2:59. Attendance—45,274. Umpires—HP, Kaiser. 1B, Kosc. 2B, Phillips. 3B, Roe.

Game 4

Sunday, October 5

Yankees	AB	R	H	RBI	BB	K	Avg
Tim Raines, lf	4	0	1	0	0	1	.200
Chad Curtis, pr-lf	0	0	0	0	0	0	.167
Derek Jeter, ss	4	1	2	0	0	0	.375
Paul O'Neill, rf	4	1	2	1	0	0	.400
Bernie Williams, cf	4	0	0	0	0	1	.077
Tino Martinez, 1b	3	0	0	0	0	1	.286
Cecil Fielder, dh	4	0	1	1	0	2	.125
Charlie Hayes, 3b	4	0	2	0	0	0	.273
Joe Girardi, c	3	0	0	0	0	0	.154
Rey Sanchez, 2b	4	0	1	0	0	2	.231
TOTALS	34	2	9	2	0	7	.242

Indians	AB	R	H	RBI	BB	K	Avg
Bip Roberts, 2b-lf	4	0	0	0	0	1	.250
Omar Vizquel, ss	4	0	3	1	1	0	.533
Manny Ramirez, rf	4	0	0	0	0	0	.118
Jim Thome, 1b	4	0	0	0	0	3	.231
David Justice, dh	3	1	1	1	1	2	.333
Matt Williams, 3b	4	0	1	0	0	0	.214
Sandy Alomar Jr., c	4	1	2	1	0	0	.313
Brian Giles, lf	2	0	1	0	0	1	.167
Tony Fernandez, ph-2b	2	0	0	0	0	0	.222
Marquis Grissom, cf	3	1	1	0	1	0	.214
TOTALS	34	3	9	3	3	7	.267

	1	2	3	4	5	6	7	8	9	R	H	E
Yankees	2	0	0	0	0	0	0	0	0	2	9	1
Indians	0	1	0	0	0	0	0	1	1	3	9	0

E—Hayes. LOB—Yankees 7, Indians 10. Scoring Position—Yankees 4-for-8, Indians 1-for-8. 2B—Jeter (1), O'Neill (1), MWilliams (1). HR—Justice (1), Alomar Jr. (2). S—Girardi, Roberts. SB—Vizquel (2).

Yankees	IP	H	R	ER	BB	K	ERA
Dwight Gooden	5.2	5	1	1	3	5	1.59
Graeme Lloyd	0.0	0	0	0	0	0	0.00
Jeff Nelson (H, 2)	1.0	1	0	0	0	0	0.00
Mike Stanton (H, 1)	0.2	0	0	0	0	2	0.00
Mariano Rivera (BS, 1)	0.2	1	1	1	0	0	4.50
Ramiro Mendoza (L, 1-1)	0.1	2	1	1	0	0	2.45

Indians	IP	H	R	ER	BB	K	ERA
Orel Hershiser	7.0	8	2	2	0	3	3.97
Paul Assenmacher	0.2	1	0	0	0	2	9.00
Mike Jackson (W, 1-0)	1.1	0	0	0	0	2	0.00

Lloyd pitched to one batter in the 6th.

HBP—Martinez by Hershiser. Time—3:22. Attendance—45,231. Umpires—HP, Kosc. 1B, Phillips. 2B, Roe. 3B, McClelland.

Game 5

Monday, October 6

Yankees	AB	R	H	RBI	BB	K	Avg
Tim Raines, lf	4	1	1	0	1	0	.211
Derek Jeter, ss	5	0	1	0	0	2	.333
Paul O'Neill, rf	4	1	2	0	1	0	.421
Scott Pose, pr	0	0	0	0	0	0	—
Bernie Williams, cf	4	0	1	1	1	1	.118
Tino Martinez, 1b	4	0	0	0	0	1	.222
Mike Stanley, dh	4	1	3	0	0	1	.750
Charlie Hayes, 3b-2b	4	0	2	0	0	1	.333
Andy Fox, pr-2b	0	0	0	0	0	0	—
Joe Girardi, c	2	0	0	0	0	0	.133
Wade Boggs, ph-3b	2	0	2	1	0	0	.429
Rey Sanchez, 2b	2	0	0	0	0	0	.200
Jorge Posada, ph-c	2	0	0	0	0	1	.000
TOTALS	37	3	12	2	3	7	.270

Indians	AB	R	H	RBI	BB	K	Avg
Bip Roberts, lf	3	0	2	0	0	1	.316
Brian Giles, lf	1	0	0	0	0	0	.143
Omar Vizquel, ss	3	1	1	0	0	0	.500
Manny Ramirez, rf	4	1	1	2	0	0	.143
Matt Williams, 3b	3	0	1	1	1	0	.235
David Justice, dh	4	0	0	0	0	1	.263
Sandy Alomar Jr., c	3	1	1	0	0	0	.316
Jim Thome, 1b	2	0	0	0	0	0	.200
Tony Fernandez, 2b	2	0	0	1	0	0	.182
Marquis Grissom, cf	3	1	1	0	0	1	.235
TOTALS	28	4	7	4	1	3	.264

	1	2	3	4	5	6	7	8	9	R	H	E
Yankees	0	0	0	0	2	1	0	0	0	3	12	0
Indians	0	0	3	1	0	0	0	0	x	4	7	2

E—Alomar Jr., Ramirez. DP—Indians 2 (Wright to Fernandez to Vizquel to Thome; Vizquel to Thome). LOB—Yankees 10, Indians 4. Scoring Position—Yankees 2-for-12, Indians 2-for-6. 2B—O'Neill (2), Stanley (1), Ramirez (1), Alomar Jr. (1). S—Vizquel, Thome. SF—Fernandez. GDP—BWilliams, Girardi. SB—Raines 2 (2), Vizquel 2 (4).

Yankees	IP	H	R	ER	BB	K	ERA
Andy Pettitte (L, 0-2)	6.2	6	4	4	0	2	8.49
Jeff Nelson	1.0	1	0	0	1	0	0.00
Mike Stanton	0.1	0	0	0	0	1	0.00

Indians	IP	H	R	ER	BB	K	ERA
Jaret Wright (W, 2-0)	5.1	8	3	2	3	5	3.97
Mike Jackson (H, 1)	0.2	1	0	0	0	1	0.00
Paul Assenmacher (H, 2)	1.1	0	0	0	0	0	5.40
Jose Mesa (S, 1)	1.2	3	0	0	0	1	2.70

Jackson pitched to one batter in the 7th.

Time—3:29. Attendance—45,203. Umpires—HP, Phillips. 1B, Roe. 2B, McClelland. 3B, Ford.

1997 AL Division Series—Composite Statistics

Batting

Indians	G	AB	R	H	RBI	2B	3B	HR	BB	SO	SB	CS	Avg	OBP	Slg
Sandy Alomar Jr.	5	19	4	6	5	1	0	2	0	2	0	0	.316	.316	.684
Tony Fernandez	4	11	0	2	4	1	0	0	0	0	0	0	.182	.167	.273
Brian Giles	3	7	0	1	0	0	0	0	1	0	0	0	.143	.143	.143
Marquis Grissom	5	17	3	4	0	0	1	0	1	2	0	1	.235	.278	.353
David Justice	5	19	3	5	2	2	0	1	2	3	0	0	.263	.333	.526
Manny Ramirez	5	21	2	3	3	1	0	0	0	3	0	0	.143	.143	.190
Bip Roberts	5	19	1	6	1	0	0	0	2	2	2	1	.316	.381	.316
Kevin Seitzer	1	4	0	0	0	0	0	0	0	0	0	0	.000	.000	.000
Jim Thome	4	15	1	3	1	0	0	0	5	0	0	0	.200	.200	.200
Omar Vizquel	5	18	3	9	1	0	0	0	2	1	4	0	.500	.550	.500
Matt Williams	5	17	4	4	3	1	0	1	3	3	0	0	.235	.381	.471
Totals	5	167	21	43	20	6	1	4	10	22	6	2	.257	.302	.377

Yankees	G	AB	R	H	RBI	2B	3B	HR	BB	SO	SB	CS	Avg	OBP	Slg
Wade Boggs	3	7	1	3	2	0	0	0	0	0	0	0	.429	.429	.429
Chad Curtis	4	6	0	1	0	0	0	0	3	1	0	0	.167	.444	.167
Cecil Fielder	2	8	0	1	1	0	0	0	0	3	0	0	.125	.125	.125
Joe Girardi	5	15	2	2	0	0	0	0	1	3	0	0	.133	.188	.133
Charlie Hayes	5	15	0	5	1	0	0	0	0	2	0	0	.333	.313	.333
Derek Jeter	5	21	6	7	2	1	0	2	3	5	1	0	.333	.417	.667
Tino Martinez	5	18	1	4	4	1	0	1	2	4	0	0	.222	.333	.444
Paul O'Neill	5	19	5	8	7	2	0	2	3	0	0	0	.421	.500	.842
Jorge Posada	2	2	0	0	0	0	0	0	0	1	0	0	.000	.000	.000
Scott Pose	1	0	0	0	0	0	0	0	0	0	0	0	—	—	—
Tim Raines	5	19	4	4	3	0	0	1	3	1	2	0	.211	.304	.368
Rey Sanchez	5	15	1	3	1	1	0	0	1	2	0	0	.200	.250	.267
Mike Stanley	2	4	1	3	1	0	0	0	0	1	0	0	.750	.800	1.000
Bernie Williams	5	17	3	2	1	1	0	0	4	3	0	0	.118	.318	.176
Totals	5	166	24	43	23	7	0	6	20	26	3	0	.259	.346	.410

Pitching

Indians	G	GS	CG	IP	H	R	ER	BB	SO	W-L	Sv-Op	Hld	ERA
Paul Assenmacher	4	0	0	3.1	2	2	2	2	2	0-0	0-0	2	5.40
Orel Hershiser	2	2	0	11.1	14	5	5	2	4	1-0	0-0	0	3.97
Mike Jackson	4	0	0	4.1	3	0	0	1	5	1-0	0-0	1	0.00
Jose Mesa	2	0	0	3.1	5	1	1	1	2	0-0	1-1	0	2.70
Alvin Morman	1	0	0	0.0	0	0	0	0	0	0-0	0-0	0	—
Charles Nagy	1	1	0	3.2	2	5	4	6	1	0-1	0-0	0	9.82
Chad Ogea	1	0	0	5.1	2	1	1	0	1	1-0	0-0	0	1.69
Eric Plunk	1	0	0	1.1	4	4	4	0	1	0-1	0-0	0	27.00
Jaret Wright	2	2	0	11.1	11	6	5	7	10	2-0	0-0	0	3.97
Totals	5	5	0	44.0	43	24	22	20	26	3-2	1-1	3	4.50

Yankees	G	GS	CG	IP	H	R	ER	BB	SO	W-L	Sv-Op	Hld	ERA
Brian Boehringer	1	0	0	1.2	1	0	0	1	2	0-0	0-0	0	0.00
David Cone	1	1	0	3.1	7	6	6	2	2	0-0	0-0	0	16.20
Dwight Gooden	1	1	0	5.2	5	1	1	3	5	0-0	0-0	0	1.59
Graeme Lloyd	2	0	0	1.1	0	0	0	0	1	0-0	0-0	0	0.00
Ramiro Mendoza	2	0	0	3.2	3	1	1	0	2	1-1	0-0	0	2.45
Jeff Nelson	4	0	0	4.0	0	0	0	0	2	0-0	0-0	2	0.00
Andy Pettitte	2	2	0	11.2	15	11	11	1	5	0-2	0-0	0	8.49
Mariano Rivera	2	0	0	2.0	2	1	1	0	1	0-0	1-2	0	4.50
Mike Stanton	3	0	0	1.0	1	0	0	1	3	0-0	0-0	1	0.00
David Wells	1	1	1	9.0	5	1	1	0	1	1-0	0-0	0	1.00
Totals	5	5	1	43.1	43	21	21	10	22	2-3	1-2	3	4.36

Fielding

Indians	Pos	G	PO	Ast	E	DP	PB	FPct
Sandy Alomar Jr.	c	5	28	1	1	0	0	.967
Paul Assenmacher	p	4	0	0	0	0	—	—
Tony Fernandez	2b	4	8	9	0	2	—	1.000
Brian Giles	lf	3	4	1	0	0	—	1.000
Marquis Grissom	cf	5	14	0	0	0	—	1.000
Orel Hershiser	p	2	1	4	0	0	—	1.000
Mike Jackson	p	4	0	1	0	0	—	1.000
Jose Mesa	p	2	0	1	0	0	—	1.000
Alvin Morman	p	1	0	0	0	0	—	—
Charles Nagy	p	1	0	1	1	0	—	.500
Chad Ogea	p	1	0	1	0	0	—	1.000
Eric Plunk	p	1	0	0	0	0	—	—
Manny Ramirez	rf	5	3	0	1	0	—	.750
Bip Roberts	lf	4	3	0	0	0	—	1.000
	2b	2	2	8	0	3	—	1.000
Kevin Seitzer	1b	1	9	0	0	0	—	1.000
Jim Thome	1b	4	44	3	0	6	—	1.000
Omar Vizquel	ss	5	12	14	0	4	—	1.000
Matt Williams	3b	5	2	10	0	1	—	1.000
Jaret Wright	p	2	2	3	1	1	—	.833
Totals		5	132	57	4	17	0	.979

Yankees	Pos	G	PO	Ast	E	DP	PB	FPct
Brian Boehringer	p	1	0	0	1	0	—	.000
Wade Boggs	3b	2	0	1	0	1	—	1.000
David Cone	p	1	1	1	0	0	—	1.000
Chad Curtis	lf	4	4	0	0	0	—	1.000
Andy Fox	2b	2	0	0	0	0	—	—
Joe Girardi	c	5	21	2	0	0	0	1.000
Dwight Gooden	p	1	0	0	0	0	—	—
Charlie Hayes	3b	5	2	7	3	0	—	.750
	2b	1	1	2	0	0	—	1.000
Derek Jeter	ss	5	12	15	0	1	—	1.000
Graeme Lloyd	p	2	0	0	0	0	—	—
Tino Martinez	1b	5	48	6	0	2	—	1.000
Ramiro Mendoza	p	2	0	1	0	0	—	1.000
Jeff Nelson	p	4	0	0	0	0	—	—
Paul O'Neill	rf	5	9	0	0	0	—	1.000
Andy Pettitte	p	2	1	5	0	0	—	1.000
Jorge Posada	c	2	1	1	0	0	0	1.000
Tim Raines	lf	3	7	0	0	0	—	1.000
Mariano Rivera	p	2	1	0	0	0	—	1.000
Rey Sanchez	2b	5	15	14	0	1	—	1.000
Mike Stanton	p	3	0	0	0	0	—	—
David Wells	p	1	0	0	0	0	—	—
Bernie Williams	cf	5	7	0	0	0	—	1.000
Totals		5	130	55	4	5	0	.979

1997 Baltimore Orioles (AL) 3, Seattle Mariners (AL) 1

The Baltimore Orioles shut down the Seattle Mariners' powerful offense, and beat Randy Johnson twice to win the AL Division Series in four games. With Game 1 tied 1-1 in the fifth, Baltimore rallied for four runs to take a 5-1 lead and knock Johnson out of the game. The Mariners' beleaguered bullpen fared just as poorly in the O's 9-3 opening-game win. Seattle starter Jamie Moyer held a 2-1 lead with two out and two on base in the fifth inning of Game 2, when a sore elbow forced him to leave the game. Roberto Alomar greeted reliever Paul Spoljaric with a drive off center fielder Ken Griffey Jr.'s glove, plating both runners to put Baltimore ahead. The O's went on to pad their lead against Seattle's bullpen, winning 9-3. Seattle southpaw Jeff Fassero tossed eight three-hit innings in Game 3, winning 4-2 to keep Seattle's hopes alive. Baltimore's Mike Mussina once again outpitched Johnson in Game 4 for a 3-1 victory, wrapping things up for the Orioles.

Game 1

Wednesday, October 1

Orioles	AB	R	H	RBI	BB	K	Avg
Brady Anderson, cf	5	1	2	1	0	0	.400
Jeff Reboulet, 2b	2	0	0	0	0	1	.000
Roberto Alomar, ph-2b	1	1	0	0	1	0	.000
Eric Davis, rf	3	0	1	2	0	2	.333
B.J. Surhoff, ph-lf	2	0	1	2	0	0	.500
Geronimo Berroa, dh	5	1	1	1	0	0	.200
Cal Ripken Jr., 3b	5	0	3	0	0	0	.600
Chris Hoiles, c	2	1	1	1	1	0	.500
Lenny Webster, c	2	0	1	0	0	0	.500
Jerome Walton, 1b	2	0	0	0	0	0	.000
Rafael Palmeiro, 1b	2	1	1	0	0	0	.500
Jeffrey Hammonds, lf-rf	2	2	0	0	2	1	.000
Mike Bordick, ss	3	2	2	2	1	1	.667
TOTALS	36	9	13	9	5	5	.361

Mariners	AB	R	H	RBI	BB	K	Avg
Joey Cora, 2b	4	0	1	0	0	0	.250
Roberto Kelly, lf	4	0	1	0	0	1	.250
Ken Griffey Jr., cf	4	0	0	0	0	1	.000
Edgar Martinez, dh	4	1	1	1	0	0	.250
Alex Rodriguez, ss	4	1	2	1	0	2	.500
Jay Buhner, rf	3	1	1	1	1	2	.333
Paul Sorrento, 1b	4	0	1	0	0	2	.250
Dan Wilson, c	3	0	0	0	0	1	.000
Mike Blowers, 3b	2	0	0	0	0	2	.000
Brent Gates, ph-3b	1	0	0	0	0	0	.000
TOTALS	33	3	7	3	1	11	.212

	1	2	3	4	5	6	7	8	9	R	H	E
Orioles	0	0	1	0	4	4	0	0	0	9	13	0
Mariners	0	0	0	1	0	0	1	0	1	3	7	1

E—Sorrento. DP—Orioles 1 (Bordick to Palmeiro), Mariners 2 (Rodriguez to Sorrento; Blowers to Cora to Sorrento). LOB—Orioles 6, Mariners 4. Scoring Position—Orioles 5-for-10, Mariners 0-for-3. 2B—Bordick (1), Kelly (1), Sorrento (1), Palmeiro (1), Surhoff (1). HR—Berroa (1), Hoiles (1), Martinez (1), Rodriguez (1), Buhner (1). S—Reboulet. GDP—Hoiles, Walton, Kelly. SB—Anderson (1), Hammonds (1). CS—Davis (1).

Orioles	IP	H	R	ER	BB	K	ERA
Mike Mussina (W, 1-0)	7.0	5	2	2	0	9	2.57
Jesse Orosco	1.0	1	0	0	0	0	0.00
Armando Benitez	1.0	1	1	1	1	2	9.00

Mariners	IP	H	R	ER	BB	K	ERA
Randy Johnson (L, 0-1)	5.0	7	5	5	4	3	9.00
Mike Timlin	0.2	3	4	4	1	1	54.00
Paul Spoljaric	0.1	1	0	0	0	0	0.00
Bob Wells	1.1	1	0	0	0	1	0.00
Norm Charlton	1.2	1	0	0	0	0	0.00

Time—3:14. Attendance—59,579. Umpires—HP, McClelland. 1B, Ford. 2B, Kaiser. 3B, Kosc.

Game 2

Thursday, October 2

Orioles	AB	R	H	RBI	BB	K	Avg
Brady Anderson, cf	4	2	2	3	1	0	.444
Roberto Alomar, 2b	5	0	1	2	0	1	.167
B.J. Surhoff, lf	5	0	2	0	0	2	.429
Eric Davis, rf	2	0	0	0	0	1	.200
Geronimo Berroa, rf	2	0	2	0	0	0	.429
Jeffrey Hammonds, pr-rf	1	1	0	0	0	0	.000
Rafael Palmeiro, 1b	5	0	1	0	0	2	.286
Cal Ripken Jr., 3b	4	1	2	0	1	0	.556
Harold Baines, dh	4	2	2	1	1	0	.500
Lenny Webster, c	3	1	0	1	1	0	.200

Mike Bordick, ss	3	2	2	2	1	0	.667
TOTALS	38	9	14	9	5	6	.382

Mariners	AB	R	H	RBI	BB	K	Avg
Joey Cora, 2b	5	1	2	0	0	1	.333
Roberto Kelly, lf	4	1	1	0	0	1	.250
Ken Griffey Jr., cf	3	0	1	1	1	0	.143
Edgar Martinez, dh	4	0	0	1	0	0	.125
Alex Rodriguez, ss	4	0	1	0	0	1	.375
Jay Buhner, rf	4	0	1	0	0	1	.286
Paul Sorrento, 1b	2	1	1	0	1	0	.333
Rich Amaral, ph-1b	1	0	0	0	0	1	.000
Dan Wilson, c	4	0	0	0	0	4	.000
Andy Sheets, 3b	2	0	1	0	0	1	.500
Rob Ducey, ph	1	0	1	1	0	0	1.000
Mike Blowers, 3b	1	0	0	0	0	1	.000
TOTALS	35	3	9	3	2	11	.239

	1	2	3	4	5	6	7	8	9	R	H	E
Orioles	0	1	0	0	2	0	2	4	0	9	14	0
Mariners	2	0	0	0	0	0	1	0	0	3	9	0

DP—Mariners 1 (Rodriguez to Cora to Sorrento). LOB—Orioles 7, Mariners 7. Scoring Position—Orioles 3-for-9, Mariners 1-for-8. 2B—Anderson (1), Alomar (1), Palmeiro (2), Ripken Jr. 2 (2), Kelly (2). HR—Anderson (1), Baines (1). GDP—Webster. SB—Griffey Jr. 2 (2).

Orioles	IP	H	R	ER	BB	K	ERA
Scott Erickson (W, 1-0)	6.2	7	3	3	2	6	4.05
Armando Benitez (H, 1)	1.0	2	0	0	0	1	4.50
Jesse Orosco	0.1	0	0	0	0	1	0.00
Randy Myers	1.0	0	0	0	0	3	0.00

Mariners	IP	H	R	ER	BB	K	ERA
Jamie Moyer (L, 0-1)	4.2	5	3	3	1	2	5.79
Paul Spoljaric	1.1	3	0	0	0	0	0.00
Bobby Ayala	1.1	4	6	6	3	2	40.50
Norm Charlton	0.2	1	0	0	0	1	0.00
Heathcliff Slocumb	1.0	1	0	0	1	0	0.00

PB—Webster. Time—3:25. Attendance—59,309. Umpires—HP, Ford. 1B, Kaiser. 2B, Kosc. 3B, Phillips.

Game 3

Saturday, October 4

Mariners	AB	R	H	RBI	BB	K	Avg
Rich Amaral, 1b	3	2	2	0	0	0	.500
Andy Sheets, 3b	1	0	0	0	0	1	.333
Roberto Kelly, lf	4	0	2	1	0	0	.333
Ken Griffey Jr., cf	4	0	1	0	1	0	.182
Edgar Martinez, dh	4	0	1	0	0	1	.167
Alex Rodriguez, ss	4	0	1	0	0	1	.417
Jay Buhner, rf	4	1	1	1	0	2	.273
Mike Blowers, 3b	2	0	1	0	0	0	.200
Paul Sorrento, ph-1b	2	1	1	1	0	1	.375
Dan Wilson, c	4	0	0	0	0	3	.000
Joey Cora, 2b	4	0	0	0	0	0	.231
TOTALS	36	4	11	4	0	10	.255

Orioles	AB	R	H	RBI	BB	K	Avg
Brady Anderson, cf	4	0	2	0	0	0	.462
Roberto Alomar, 2b	3	0	1	0	0	0	.222
Geronimo Berroa, dh	2	1	0	0	2	1	.333
Rafael Palmeiro, 1b	4	1	1	0	0	0	.273
Cal Ripken Jr., 3b	3	0	0	1	0	2	.417
B.J. Surhoff, lf	4	0	0	0	0	0	.273
Jeffrey Hammonds, rf	4	0	1	2	0	0	.143
Chris Hoiles, c	3	0	0	0	0	0	.200
Harold Baines, ph	1	0	0	0	0	0	.400
Mike Bordick, ss	2	0	0	0	1	0	.500
TOTALS	30	2	5	2	4	3	.333

Game 4

Sunday, October 5

Mariners	AB	R	H	RBI	BB	K	Avg
Joey Cora, 2b	4	0	0	0	0	3	.176
Alex Rodriguez, ss	4	0	0	0	0	1	.313
Ken Griffey Jr., cf	4	0	0	0	0	1	.133
Edgar Martinez, dh	4	1	1	1	0	2	.188
Paul Sorrento, 1b	2	0	0	0	1	0	.300
Roberto Kelly, ph	1	0	0	0	0	1	.308
Jay Buhner, rf	2	0	0	0	2	1	.231
Rob Ducey, lf	3	0	1	0	0	0	.500
Brent Gates, 3b	3	0	0	0	0	0	.000
Dan Wilson, c	2	0	0	0	0	1	.000
Rick Wilkins, ph-c	0	0	0	0	1	0	—
TOTALS	29	1	2	1	4	10	.207

Orioles	AB	R	H	RBI	BB	K	Avg
Brady Anderson, cf	4	0	0	0	0	4	.353
Jeff Reboulet, 2b	3	1	1	1	0	1	.200
Roberto Alomar, 2b	1	0	0	0	0	0	.300
Geronimo Berroa, dh	4	2	2	1	0	1	.385
Eric Davis, rf	4	0	1	0	0	2	.222
Cal Ripken Jr., 3b	4	0	2	1	0	0	.438
Chris Hoiles, c	2	0	0	1	1	1	.143
Lenny Webster, c	1	0	0	0	0	1	.167
Jerome Walton, 1b	2	0	0	0	0	0	.000
Rafael Palmeiro, 1b	1	0	0	0	0	0	.250
Jeffrey Hammonds, lf	3	0	0	0	0	1	.100
Mike Bordick, ss	2	0	0	0	1	1	.400
TOTALS	31	3	7	3	2	13	.286

	1	2	3	4	5	6	7	8	9	R	H	E
Mariners	0	1	0	0	0	0	0	0	0	1	2	0
Orioles	2	0	0	0	1	0	0	0	x	3	7	0

LOB—Mariners 5, Orioles 6. Scoring Position—Mariners 0-for-3, Orioles 1-for-5. 2B—Berroa (1). HR—Martinez (2), Reboulet (1), Berroa (2).

Mariners	IP	H	R	ER	BB	K	ERA
Randy Johnson (L, 0-2)	8.0	7	3	3	2	13	5.54

Orioles	IP	H	R	ER	BB	K	ERA
Mike Mussina (W, 2-0)	7.0	2	1	1	3	7	1.93
Armando Benitez (H, 2)	1.0	0	0	0	0	1	3.00
Randy Myers (S, 1)	1.0	0	0	0	0	2	0.00

Time—2:42. Attendance—48,766. Umpires—HP, Scott. 1B, Garcia. 2B, Cousins. 3B, Tschida.

The following belongs to Game 3 (bottom of center column) — scoreline and notes:

	1	2	3	4	5	6	7	8	9	R	H	E
Mariners	0	0	1	0	1	0	0	0	2	4	11	0
Orioles	0	0	0	0	0	0	0	0	2	2	5	0

LOB—Mariners 5, Orioles 6. Scoring Position—Mariners 1-for-7, Orioles 1-for-9. 2B—Kelly (3), Rodriguez (1), Alomar (2), Hammonds (1). HR—Buhner (2), Sorrento (1). S—Alomar. CS—Bordick (1).

Mariners	IP	H	R	ER	BB	K	ERA
Jeff Fassero (W, 1-0)	8.0	3	1	1	4	3	1.13
Heathcliff Slocumb	1.0	2	1	1	0	0	4.50

Orioles	IP	H	R	ER	BB	K	ERA
Jimmy Key (L, 0-1)	4.2	8	2	2	0	4	3.86
Alan Mills	1.0	1	0	0	0	1	0.00
Arthur Rhodes	2.1	0	0	0	0	4	0.00
Terry Mathews	1.0	2	2	2	0	1	18.00

Fassero pitched to one batter in the 9th.

WP—Key. Time—3:26. Attendance—49,137. Umpires—HP, Reed. 1B, Scott. 2B, Garcia. 3B, Cousins.

1997 AL Division Series—Composite Statistics

Batting

Orioles	G	AB	R	H	RBI	2B	3B	HR	BB	SO	SB	CS	Avg	OBP	Slg
Roberto Alomar	4	10	1	3	2	2	0	0	1	1	0	0	.300	.364	.500
Brady Anderson	4	17	3	6	4	1	0	1	1	4	1	0	.353	.389	.588
Harold Baines	2	5	2	2	1	0	0	1	1	0	0	0	.400	.500	1.000
Geronimo Berroa	4	13	4	5	2	1	0	2	2	2	0	0	.385	.467	.923
Mike Bordick	4	10	4	4	4	1	0	0	4	2	0	1	.400	.571	.500
Eric Davis	3	9	0	2	2	0	0	0	0	5	0	1	.222	.222	.222
Jeffrey Hammonds	4	10	3	1	2	1	0	0	2	2	1	0	.100	.250	.200
Chris Hoiles	3	7	1	1	1	0	0	1	2	1	0	0	.143	.333	.571
Rafael Palmeiro	4	12	2	3	0	2	0	0	0	2	0	0	.250	.250	.417
Jeff Reboulet	2	5	1	1	1	0	0	1	0	2	0	0	.200	.200	.800
Cal Ripken Jr.	4	16	1	7	1	2	0	2	2	0	0	0	.438	.500	.563
B.J. Surhoff	3	11	0	3	2	1	0	0	0	2	0	0	.273	.273	.364
Jerome Walton	2	4	0	0	0	0	0	0	0	2	0	0	.000	.000	.000
Lenny Webster	3	6	1	1	1	0	0	0	1	0	0	0	.167	.286	.167
Totals	**4**	**135**	**23**	**39**	**23**	**11**	**0**	**6**	**16**	**27**	**2**	**2**	**.289**	**.364**	**.504**

Batting

Mariners	G	AB	R	H	RBI	2B	3B	HR	BB	SO	SB	CS	Avg	OBP	Slg
Rich Amaral	2	4	2	2	0	0	0	0	0	1	0	0	.500	.500	.500
Mike Blowers	3	5	0	1	0	0	0	0	0	3	0	0	.200	.200	.200
Jay Buhner	4	13	2	3	2	0	0	2	3	6	0	0	.231	.375	.692
Joey Cora	4	17	1	3	0	0	0	0	0	4	0	0	.176	.176	.176
Rob Ducey	2	4	0	2	1	0	0	0	0	0	0	0	.500	.500	.500
Brent Gates	2	4	0	0	0	0	0	0	0	0	0	0	.000	.000	.000
Ken Griffey Jr.	4	15	0	2	2	0	0	0	1	3	2	0	.133	.188	.133
Roberto Kelly	4	13	1	4	1	3	0	0	0	3	0	0	.308	.308	.538
Edgar Martinez	4	16	2	3	3	0	0	2	0	3	0	0	.188	.188	.563
Alex Rodriguez	4	16	1	5	1	1	0	1	0	5	0	0	.313	.313	.563
Andy Sheets	2	3	0	1	0	0	0	0	0	2	0	0	.333	.333	.333
Paul Sorrento	4	10	2	3	1	1	0	1	2	3	0	0	.300	.417	.700
Rick Wilkins	1	0	0	0	0	0	0	0	1	0	0	0	—	1.000	—
Dan Wilson	4	13	0	0	0	0	0	0	0	9	0	0	.000	.000	.000
Totals	**4**	**133**	**11**	**29**	**11**	**5**	**0**	**6**	**7**	**42**	**2**	**0**	**.218**	**.257**	**.391**

Pitching

Orioles	G	GS	CG	IP	H	R	ER	BB	SO	W-L	Sv-Op	Hld	ERA
Armando Benitez	3	0	0	3.0	3	1	1	2	4	0-0	0-0	2	3.00
Scott Erickson	1	1	0	6.2	7	3	3	2	6	1-0	0-0	0	4.05
Jimmy Key	1	1	0	4.2	8	2	2	0	4	0-1	0-0	0	3.86
Terry Mathews	1	0	0	1.0	2	2	2	0	1	0-0	0-0	0	18.00
Alan Mills	1	0	0	1.0	1	0	0	0	1	0-0	0-0	0	0.00
Mike Mussina	2	2	0	14.0	7	3	3	3	16	2-0	0-0	0	1.93
Randy Myers	2	0	0	2.0	0	0	0	0	5	0-0	1-1	0	0.00
Jesse Orosco	2	0	0	1.1	1	0	0	0	1	0-0	0-0	0	0.00
Arthur Rhodes	1	0	0	2.1	0	0	0	0	4	0-0	0-0	0	0.00
Totals	**4**	**4**	**0**	**36.0**	**29**	**11**	**11**	**7**	**42**	**3-1**	**1-1**	**2**	**2.75**

Pitching

Mariners	G	GS	CG	IP	H	R	ER	BB	SO	W-L	Sv-Op	Hld	ERA
Bobby Ayala	1	0	0	1.1	4	6	6	3	2	0-0	0-0	0	40.50
Norm Charlton	2	0	0	2.1	2	0	0	0	1	0-0	0-0	0	0.00
Jeff Fassero	1	1	0	8.0	3	1	1	4	3	1-0	0-0	0	1.13
Randy Johnson	2	2	1	13.0	14	8	8	6	16	0-2	0-0	0	5.54
Jamie Moyer	1	1	0	4.2	5	3	3	1	2	0-1	0-0	0	5.79
Heathcliff Slocumb	2	0	0	2.0	3	1	1	1	0	0-0	0-0	0	4.50
Paul Spoljaric	2	0	0	1.2	4	0	0	1	1	0-0	0-0	0	0.00
Mike Timlin	1	0	0	0.2	3	4	4	1	1	0-0	0-0	0	54.00
Bob Wells	1	0	0	1.1	1	0	0	0	1	0-0	0-0	0	0.00
Totals	**4**	**4**	**1**	**35.0**	**39**	**23**	**23**	**16**	**27**	**1-3**	**0-0**	**0**	**5.91**

Fielding

Orioles	Pos	G	PO	Ast	E	DP	PB	FPct
Roberto Alomar	2b	4	3	6	0	0	—	1.000
Brady Anderson	cf	4	6	0	0	0	—	1.000
Armando Benitez	p	3	0	0	0	0	—	—
Geronimo Berroa	rf	1	0	0	0	0	—	—
Mike Bordick	ss	4	4	15	0	1	—	1.000
Eric Davis	rf	3	1	0	0	0	—	1.000
Scott Erickson	p	1	1	0	0	0	—	1.000
Jeffrey Hammonds	rf	3	5	1	0	0	—	1.000
	lf	2	3	0	0	0	—	1.000
Chris Hoiles	c	3	23	0	0	0	0	1.000
Jimmy Key	p	1	0	1	0	0	—	1.000
Terry Mathews	p	1	0	0	0	0	—	—
Alan Mills	p	1	0	1	0	0	—	1.000
Mike Mussina	p	2	3	3	0	0	—	1.000
Randy Myers	p	2	0	0	0	0	—	—
Jesse Orosco	p	2	0	0	0	0	—	—
Rafael Palmeiro	1b	4	27	2	0	1	—	1.000
Jeff Reboulet	2b	2	2	3	0	0	—	1.000
Arthur Rhodes	p	1	0	0	0	0	—	—
Cal Ripken Jr.	3b	4	4	4	0	0	—	1.000
B.J. Surhoff	lf	3	1	1	0	0	—	1.000
Jerome Walton	1b	2	5	1	0	0	—	1.000
Lenny Webster	c	3	20	0	0	0	1	1.000
Totals		**4**	**108**	**38**	**0**	**2**	**1**	**1.000**

Fielding

Mariners	Pos	G	PO	Ast	E	DP	PB	FPct
Rich Amaral	1b	2	7	2	0	0	—	1.000
Bobby Ayala	p	1	0	0	0	0	—	—
Mike Blowers	3b	3	1	2	0	1	—	1.000
Jay Buhner	rf	4	5	1	0	0	—	1.000
Norm Charlton	p	2	1	0	0	0	—	1.000
Joey Cora	2b	4	7	11	0	2	—	1.000
Rob Ducey	lf	1	0	0	0	0	—	—
Jeff Fassero	p	1	1	4	0	0	—	1.000
Brent Gates	3b	2	1	2	0	0	—	1.000
Ken Griffey Jr.	cf	4	12	1	0	0	—	1.000
Randy Johnson	p	2	0	3	0	0	—	1.000
Roberto Kelly	lf	3	4	0	0	0	—	1.000
Jamie Moyer	p	1	2	1	0	0	—	1.000
Alex Rodriguez	ss	4	5	10	0	2	—	1.000
Andy Sheets	3b	2	0	0	0	0	—	—
Heathcliff Slocumb	p	2	1	0	0	0	—	1.000
Paul Sorrento	1b	4	27	4	1	3	—	.969
Paul Spoljaric	p	2	0	0	0	0	—	—
Mike Timlin	p	1	0	0	0	0	—	—
Bob Wells	p	1	0	0	0	0	—	—
Rick Wilkins	c	1	2	0	0	0	0	1.000
Dan Wilson	c	4	29	1	0	0	0	1.000
Totals		**4**	**105**	**42**	**1**	**8**	**0**	**.993**

1997 Atlanta Braves (NL) 3, Houston Astros (NL) 0

The Atlanta Braves knocked the Houston Astros out of the playoffs with ease, outscoring them 19-5 while taking three straight games. Ryan Klesko's second-inning homer was the difference in Game 1 as Greg Maddux bested Darryl Kile for a 2-1 Braves victory. With Game 2 tied 3-3 with two out in the Braves' half of the fifth, Houston starter Mike Hampton suddenly lost his command, and walked four straight batters to force in the go-ahead run. The Astros' bullpen let the game get out of hand, and the Braves ran away with a 13-3 victory. John Smoltz wrapped things up with a three-hitter in Game 3 to send the Braves to the NLCS. Houston's Jeff Bagwell and Craig Biggio combined for only two singles in 24 at-bats.

Game 1
Tuesday, September 30

Astros	AB	R	H	RBI	BB	K	Avg
Craig Biggio, 2b	4	0	0	0	0	0	.000
Derek Bell, rf	4	0	0	0	0	1	.000
Jeff Bagwell, 1b	4	0	0	0	0	2	.000
Luis Gonzalez, lf	4	0	2	0	0	0	.500
Bill Spiers, 3b	4	0	0	0	0	0	.000
Richard Hidalgo, cf	3	0	0	0	0	1	.000
Sean Berry, ph	1	0	0	0	0	0	.000
Tony Eusebio, c	3	1	2	0	0	1	.667
Ricky Gutierrez, ss	2	0	0	1	1	1	.000
Darryl Kile, p	2	0	2	1	0	0	1.000
Bob Abreu, ph	1	0	1	0	0	0	1.000
Russ Springer, p	0	0	0	0	0	0	—
Tom Martin, p	0	0	0	0	0	0	—
TOTALS	32	1	7	1	1	6	.219

Braves	AB	R	H	RBI	BB	K	Avg
Kenny Lofton, cf	4	1	1	0	0	0	.250
Keith Lockhart, 2b	3	0	0	0	0	0	.000
Tony Graffanino, 2b	0	0	0	0	0	0	—
Chipper Jones, 3b	2	0	0	1	0	1	.000
Fred McGriff, 1b	3	0	0	0	0	0	.000
Ryan Klesko, lf	3	1	1	1	0	2	.333
Andruw Jones, rf	0	0	0	0	0	0	—
Michael Tucker, rf	3	0	0	0	0	0	.000
Danny Bautista, lf	0	0	0	0	0	0	—
Eddie Perez, c	3	0	0	0	0	1	.000
Jeff Blauser, ss	2	0	0	0	1	1	.000
Greg Maddux, p	2	0	0	0	1	1	.000
TOTALS	25	2	2	2	2	6	.080

	1	2	3	4	5	6	7	8	9		R	H	E
Astros	0	0	0	1	0	0	0	0	0		1	7	1
Braves	1	1	0	0	0	0	0	x			2	2	0

E—Biggio. DP—Braves 1 (Lockhart to Blauser to McGriff). LOB—Astros 5, Braves 2. Scoring Position—Astros 1-for-5, Braves 0-for-1. 2B—Lofton (1). HR—Klesko (1). SF—CJones. GDP—Spiers. SB—Eusebio (1), Abreu (1). CS—Lofton (1).

Astros	IP	H	R	ER	BB	K	ERA
Darryl Kile (L, 0-1)	7.0	2	2	2	2	4	2.57
Russ Springer	0.2	0	0	0	0	2	0.00
Tom Martin	0.1	0	0	0	0	0	0.00

Braves	IP	H	R	ER	BB	K	ERA
Greg Maddux (W, 1-0)	9.0	7	1	1	1	6	1.00

Time—2:15. Attendance—46,467. Umpires—HP, Bonin. 1B, Rapuano. 2B, Reliford. 3B, Rippley.

Game 2
Wednesday, October 1

Astros	AB	R	H	RBI	BB	K	Avg
Craig Biggio, 2b	4	0	1	0	1	0	.125
Derek Bell, rf	5	0	0	0	0	1	.000
Jeff Bagwell, 1b	4	0	0	0	1	3	.000
Luis Gonzalez, lf	4	0	1	0	0	1	.375
Richard Hidalgo, cf	2	1	0	0	1	1	.000
Mike Magnante, p	0	0	0	0	0	0	—
Ramon Garcia, p	0	0	0	0	0	0	—
Jose Lima, p	0	0	0	0	0	0	—
Thomas Howard, ph	0	0	0	0	1	0	—
Tony Pena, c	0	0	0	0	0	0	—
Bill Spiers, 3b	3	1	0	0	1	0	.000
Ricky Gutierrez, ss	4	0	1	0	0	0	.167
Brad Ausmus, c	3	1	2	2	0	0	.667
Bob Abreu, ph	1	0	0	0	0	1	.500
Billy Wagner, p	0	0	0	0	0	0	—
Mike Hampton, p	2	0	1	1	0	0	.500
Chuck Carr, cf	1	0	0	0	1	1	.000
TOTALS	33	3	6	3	6	7	.153

Braves	AB	R	H	RBI	BB	K	Avg
Kenny Lofton, cf	4	1	0	0	1	2	.125
Jeff Blauser, ss	5	2	2	3	0	1	.286
Chipper Jones, 3b	2	2	1	0	3	1	.250
Fred McGriff, 1b	4	3	2	1	1	1	.286
Javy Lopez, c	3	2	1	1	2	0	.333
Andruw Jones, rf	4	1	0	1	1	0	.000
Ryan Klesko, lf	2	0	0	0	0	0	.200
Greg Colbrunn, ph	1	0	1	2	0	0	1.000
Danny Bautista, lf	2	0	1	2	0	1	.500
Tony Graffanino, 2b	2	0	0	0	2	0	.000
Tom Glavine, p	3	2	2	0	0	0	.667
Mike Cather, p	1	0	0	0	0	1	.000
Mark Wohlers, p	0	0	0	0	0	0	—
TOTALS	33	13	10	10	10	7	.255

	1	2	3	4	5	6	7	8	9		R	H	E
Astros	0	0	0	3	0	0	0	0	0		3	6	2
Braves	0	0	3	0	3	5	0	2	x		13	10	1

E—Gonzalez, Bagwell, Klesko. DP—Astros 1 (Biggio to Gutierrez to Bagwell). LOB—Astros 9, Braves 6. Scoring Position—Astros 2-for-8, Braves 5-for-9. 2B—Ausmus (1), Lopez (1). HR—Blauser (1). GDP—Lofton. SB—CJones (1).

Astros	IP	H	R	ER	BB	K	ERA
Mike Hampton (L, 0-1)	4.2	2	6	6	8	2	11.57
Mike Magnante	1.0	4	3	1	0	2	9.00
Ramon Garcia	0.1	1	2	0	1	0	0.00
Jose Lima	1.0	0	0	0	1	1	0.00
Billy Wagner	1.0	3	2	2	0	2	18.00

Braves	IP	H	R	ER	BB	K	ERA
Tom Glavine (W, 1-0)	6.0	5	3	3	5	4	4.50
Mike Cather	2.0	0	0	0	1	2	0.00
Mark Wohlers	1.0	1	0	0	0	1	0.00

Time—3:06. Attendance—49,200. Umpires—HP, Rapuano. 1B, Reliford. 2B, Rippley. 3B, Wendelstedt.

Game 3
Friday, October 3

Braves	AB	R	H	RBI	BB	K	Avg
Kenny Lofton, cf	5	0	1	0	0	0	.154
Keith Lockhart, 2b	3	0	0	0	0	1	.000
Tony Graffanino, 2b	1	0	0	0	0	1	.000
Chipper Jones, 3b	4	1	3	1	0	0	.500
Fred McGriff, 1b	2	1	0	2	2	1	.222
Ryan Klesko, lf	3	1	1	0	0	0	.250
Danny Bautista, lf	1	0	0	0	0	0	.333
Javy Lopez, c	4	1	1	0	0	1	.286
Michael Tucker, rf	3	0	1	1	0	1	.167
Andruw Jones, rf	1	0	0	0	0	1	.000
Jeff Blauser, ss	3	0	1	1	1	0	.300
John Smoltz, p	4	0	0	0	0	1	.000
TOTALS	34	4	8	3	3	7	.207

Astros	AB	R	H	RBI	BB	K	Avg
Craig Biggio, 2b	4	0	0	0	0	0	.083
Derek Bell, rf	4	0	0	0	0	1	.000
Jeff Bagwell, 1b	4	0	1	0	0	0	.083
Luis Gonzalez, lf	4	0	1	0	0	1	.333
Bill Spiers, 3b	4	0	0	0	0	2	.000
Chuck Carr, cf	3	1	1	1	0	2	.250
Ricky Gutierrez, ss	2	0	0	0	1	0	.125
Brad Ausmus, c	2	0	0	0	0	1	.400
Bob Abreu, ph	1	0	0	0	0	1	.333
Tony Pena, c	0	0	0	0	0	0	—
Shane Reynolds, p	1	0	0	0	0	0	.000
Russ Johnson, ph	1	0	0	0	0	1	.000
Russ Springer, p	0	0	0	0	0	0	—
Tom Martin, p	0	0	0	0	0	0	—
Ramon Garcia, p	0	0	0	0	0	0	—
Thomas Howard, ph	1	0	0	0	0	1	.000
Mike Magnante, p	0	0	0	0	0	0	—
TOTALS	31	1	3	1	1	11	.133

	1	2	3	4	5	6	7	8	9		R	H	E
Braves	1	1	0	0	0	0	1	1	0		4	8	2
Astros	0	0	0	0	0	0	1	0	0		1	3	1

E—Bagwell, CJones, Lockhart. DP—Braves 1 (Blauser to Lockhart to McGriff), Astros 1 (Gutierrez to Biggio to Bagwell). LOB—Braves 6, Astros 4. Scoring Position—Braves 2-for-12, Astros 0-for-1. 2B—Klesko (2). HR—CJones (1), Carr (1). GDP—Klesko, Ausmus.

Braves	IP	H	R	ER	BB	K	ERA
John Smoltz (W, 1-0)	9.0	3	1	1	1	11	1.00

Astros	IP	H	R	ER	BB	K	ERA
Shane Reynolds (L, 0-1)	6.0	5	2	2	1	5	3.00
Russ Springer	1.0	2	1	1	1	1	5.40
Tom Martin	0.1	1	1	0	1	0	0.00
Ramon Garcia	0.2	0	0	0	0	1	0.00
Mike Magnante	1.0	0	0	0	0	0	4.50

PB—Ausmus. Time—2:36. Attendance—53,688. Umpires—HP, Hallion. 1B, DeMuth. 2B, Tata. 3B, Gorman.

1997 NL Division Series—Composite Statistics

Batting

Braves	G	AB	R	H	RBI	2B	3B	HR	BB	SO	SB	CS	Avg	OBP	Slg
Danny Bautista	3	3	0	1	2	0	0	0	0	1	0	0	.333	.333	.333
Jeff Blauser	3	10	2	3	4	0	0	1	2	2	0	0	.300	.417	.600
Mike Cather	1	1	0	0	0	0	0	0	0	1	0	0	.000	.000	.000
Greg Colbrunn	1	1	0	1	2	0	0	0	0	0	0	0	1.000	1.000	1.000
Tom Glavine	1	3	2	2	0	0	0	0	0	0	0	0	.667	.667	.667
Tony Graffanino	3	3	0	0	0	0	0	0	2	1	0	0	.000	.400	.000
Andruw Jones	3	5	1	0	1	0	0	0	1	0	0	0	.000	.167	.000
Chipper Jones	3	8	3	4	2	0	0	1	3	2	1	0	.500	.583	.875
Ryan Klesko	3	8	2	2	1	1	0	1	0	2	0	0	.250	.250	.750
Keith Lockhart	2	6	0	0	0	0	0	0	0	1	0	0	.000	.000	.000
Kenny Lofton	3	13	2	2	0	1	0	0	1	2	0	1	.154	.214	.231
Javy Lopez	2	7	3	2	1	2	0	0	2	1	0	0	.286	.444	.571
Greg Maddux	1	2	0	0	0	0	0	0	1	1	0	0	.000	.333	.000
Fred McGriff	3	9	4	2	1	0	0	0	3	2	0	0	.222	.417	.222
Eddie Perez	1	3	0	0	0	0	0	0	0	1	0	0	.000	.000	.000
John Smoltz	1	4	0	0	0	0	0	0	0	1	0	0	.000	.000	.000
Michael Tucker	2	6	0	1	1	0	0	0	0	1	0	0	.167	.167	.167
Totals	**3**	**92**	**19**	**20**	**15**	**4**	**0**	**3**	**15**	**20**	**1**	**1**	**.217**	**.324**	**.359**

Batting

Astros	G	AB	R	H	RBI	2B	3B	HR	BB	SO	SB	CS	Avg	OBP	Slg
Bob Abreu	3	3	0	1	0	0	0	0	0	2	1	0	.333	.333	.333
Brad Ausmus	2	5	1	2	2	1	0	0	0	1	0	0	.400	.400	.600
Jeff Bagwell	3	12	0	1	0	0	0	0	1	5	0	0	.083	.154	.083
Derek Bell	3	13	0	0	0	0	0	0	0	3	0	0	.000	.000	.000
Sean Berry	1	1	0	0	0	0	0	0	0	0	0	0	.000	.000	.000
Craig Biggio	3	12	0	1	0	0	0	0	1	0	0	0	.083	.154	.083
Chuck Carr	2	4	1	1	0	0	0	0	1	3	0	0	.250	.400	1.000
Tony Eusebio	1	3	1	2	0	0	0	0	0	1	0	0	.667	.667	.667
Luis Gonzalez	3	12	0	4	0	0	0	0	0	1	0	0	.333	.333	.333
Ricky Gutierrez	3	8	0	1	0	0	0	0	2	1	0	0	.125	.300	.125
Mike Hampton	1	2	0	1	1	0	0	0	0	0	0	0	.500	.500	.500
Richard Hidalgo	2	5	1	0	0	0	0	0	1	2	0	0	.000	.167	.000
Thomas Howard	2	1	0	0	0	0	0	0	1	1	0	0	.000	.500	.000
Russ Johnson	1	1	0	0	0	0	0	0	0	0	0	0	.000	.000	.000
Darryl Kile	1	2	0	2	1	0	0	0	0	0	0	0	1.000	1.000	1.000
Shane Reynolds	1	1	0	0	0	0	0	0	0	1	0	0	.000	.000	.000
Bill Spiers	3	11	1	0	0	0	0	0	1	2	0	0	.000	.083	.000
Totals	**3**	**96**	**5**	**16**	**5**	**1**	**0**	**1**	**8**	**24**	**2**	**0**	**.167**	**.231**	**.208**

Pitching

Braves	G	GS	CG	IP	H	R	ER	BB	SO	W-L	Sv-Op	Hld	ERA
Mike Cather	1	0	0	2.0	0	0	0	1	2	0-0	0-0	0	0.00
Tom Glavine	1	1	0	6.0	5	3	3	5	4	1-0	0-0	0	4.50
Greg Maddux	1	1	1	9.0	7	1	1	1	6	1-0	0-0	0	1.00
John Smoltz	1	1	1	9.0	3	1	1	1	11	1-0	0-0	0	1.00
Mark Wohlers	1	0	0	1.0	1	0	0	0	1	0-0	0-0	0	0.00
Totals	**3**	**3**	**2**	**27.0**	**16**	**5**	**5**	**8**	**24**	**3-0**	**0-0**	**0**	**1.67**

Pitching

Astros	G	GS	CG	IP	H	R	ER	BB	SO	W-L	Sv-Op	Hld	ERA
Ramon Garcia	2	0	0	1.0	1	2	0	1	1	0-0	0-0	0	0.00
Mike Hampton	1	1	0	4.2	2	6	6	8	2	0-1	0-0	0	11.57
Darryl Kile	1	1	0	7.0	2	2	2	4	4	0-1	0-0	0	2.57
Jose Lima	1	0	0	1.0	0	0	0	1	1	0-0	0-0	0	0.00
Mike Magnante	2	0	0	2.0	4	3	1	0	2	0-0	0-0	0	4.50
Tom Martin	2	0	0	0.2	1	1	0	1	0	0-0	0-0	0	0.00
Shane Reynolds	1	1	0	6.0	5	2	2	1	5	0-1	0-0	0	3.00
Russ Springer	2	0	0	1.2	2	1	1	1	3	0-0	0-0	0	5.40
Billy Wagner	1	0	0	1.0	3	2	2	0	2	0-0	0-0	0	18.00
Totals	**3**	**3**	**0**	**25.0**	**20**	**19**	**14**	**15**	**20**	**0-3**	**0-0**	**0**	**5.04**

Fielding

Braves	Pos	G	PO	Ast	E	DP	PB	FPct
Danny Bautista	lf	3	0	0	0	0	—	—
Jeff Blauser	ss	3	2	10	0	2	—	1.000
Mike Cather	p	1	0	0	0	0	—	—
Tom Glavine	p	1	1	1	0	0	—	1.000
Tony Graffanino	2b	3	1	6	0	0	—	1.000
Andruw Jones	rf	3	10	0	0	0	—	1.000
Chipper Jones	3b	3	2	3	1	0	—	.833
Ryan Klesko	lf	3	3	0	1	0	—	.750
Keith Lockhart	2b	2	1	8	1	2	—	.900
Kenny Lofton	cf	3	6	1	0	0	—	1.000
Javy Lopez	c	2	18	0	0	0	0	1.000
Greg Maddux	p	1	1	1	0	0	—	1.000
Fred McGriff	1b	3	27	2	0	2	—	1.000
Eddie Perez	c	1	6	0	0	0	0	1.000
John Smoltz	p	1	0	0	0	0	—	—
Michael Tucker	rf	2	3	0	0	0	—	1.000
Mark Wohlers	p	1	0	0	0	0	—	—
Totals		**3**	**81**	**32**	**3**	**6**	**0**	**.974**

Fielding

Astros	Pos	G	PO	Ast	E	DP	PB	FPct
Brad Ausmus	c	2	13	0	0	0	1	1.000
Jeff Bagwell	1b	3	17	6	2	2	—	.920
Derek Bell	rf	3	3	0	0	0	—	1.000
Craig Biggio	2b	3	4	8	1	2	—	.923
Chuck Carr	cf	2	2	0	0	0	—	1.000
Tony Eusebio	c	1	6	1	0	0	0	1.000
Ramon Garcia	p	2	0	0	0	0	—	—
Luis Gonzalez	lf	3	13	1	1	0	—	.933
Ricky Gutierrez	ss	3	5	5	0	2	—	1.000
Mike Hampton	p	1	3	0	0	0	—	1.000
Richard Hidalgo	cf	2	5	0	0	0	—	1.000
Darryl Kile	p	1	0	0	0	0	—	—
Jose Lima	p	1	0	0	0	0	—	—
Mike Magnante	p	2	0	1	0	0	—	1.000
Tom Martin	p	2	0	1	0	0	—	1.000
Tony Pena	c	2	2	0	0	0	0	1.000
Shane Reynolds	p	1	1	1	0	0	—	1.000
Bill Spiers	3b	3	1	3	0	0	—	1.000
Russ Springer	p	2	0	0	0	0	—	—
Billy Wagner	p	1	0	0	0	0	—	—
Totals		**3**	**75**	**27**	**4**	**6**	**1**	**.962**

1997 Florida Marlins (NL) 3, San Francisco Giants (NL) 0

The Marlins won the first two games of the NL Division Series in their final at-bat, and swept past the San Francisco Giants in three games to advance to the NLCS. Starters Kirk Rueter and Kevin Brown were masterful in Game 1. With the score tied 1-1 and two out and the bases loaded in the bottom of the ninth, Florida's Edgar Renteria poked a single between first and second to win the game. Game 2 was a back-and-forth affair. The Giants tallied a single run in the top of the ninth to tie the game. In the bottom of the inning, Gary Sheffield led off with a single before stealing second. Moises Alou lined a single to center, and Sheffield tried to score. Center fielder Dante Powell's throw might have beaten him, but it hit the pitching rubber, and Sheffield came home to give the Marlins a 7-6 win. Devon White socked a grand slam in Game 3 to send the Marlins to a 6-2 victory and a trip to the NLCS.

Game 1

Tuesday, September 30

Giants	AB	R	H	RBI	BB	K	Avg
Darryl Hamilton, cf	4	0	0	0	0	1	.000
Bill Mueller, 3b	4	1	1	1	0	0	.250
Barry Bonds, lf	4	0	1	0	0	0	.250
J.T. Snow, 1b	3	0	0	0	0	1	.000
Jeff Kent, 2b	3	0	0	0	0	0	.000
Stan Javier, rf	3	0	1	0	0	1	.333
Jose Vizcaino, ss	3	0	0	0	0	3	.000
Brian Johnson, c	3	0	0	0	0	0	.000
Kirk Rueter, p	2	0	1	0	0	0	.500
Glenallen Hill, ph	1	0	0	0	0	1	.000
Julian Tavarez, p	0	0	0	0	0	0	—
Roberto Hernandez, p	0	0	0	0	0	0	—
TOTALS	30	1	4	1	0	8	.133

Marlins	AB	R	H	RBI	BB	K	Avg
Devon White, cf	5	0	0	0	0	1	.000
Edgar Renteria, ss	5	0	2	1	0	1	.400
Gary Sheffield, rf	2	0	1	0	2	0	.500
Bobby Bonilla, 3b	3	0	1	0	1	0	.333
Moises Alou, lf	4	0	0	0	0	0	.000
Jeff Conine, 1b	4	0	1	0	0	0	.250
Charles Johnson, c	3	2	1	1	0	1	.333
Craig Counsell, 2b	2	0	1	0	1	0	.500
Kevin Brown, p	2	0	0	0	0	2	.000
Kurt Abbott, ph	1	0	0	0	0	0	.000
Dennis Cook, p	0	0	0	0	0	0	—
Jim Eisenreich, ph	0	0	0	0	1	0	—
TOTALS	31	2	7	2	5	5	.226

	1	2	3	4	5	6	7	8	9		R	H	E
Giants	0	0	0	0	0	0	1	0	0		1	4	0
Marlins	0	0	0	0	0	0	1	0	1		2	7	0

DP—Giants 1 (Mueller to Kent to Snow). LOB—Giants 2, Marlins 10. Scoring Position—Giants 0-for-3, Marlins 1-for-7. 2B—Bonds (1), Sheffield (1). HR—Mueller (1), CJohnson (1). S—Counsell. GDP—Alou. CS—Javier (1).

Giants	IP	H	R	ER	BB	K	ERA
Kirk Rueter	7.0	4	1	1	3	5	1.29
Julian Tavarez (L, 0-1)	1.0	2	1	1	1	0	9.00
Roberto Hernandez	0.2	1	0	0	1	0	0.00

Marlins	IP	H	R	ER	BB	K	ERA
Kevin Brown	7.0	4	1	1	0	5	1.29
Dennis Cook (W, 1-0)	2.0	0	0	0	0	3	0.00

Tavarez pitched to two batters in the 9th.

HBP—CJohnson by Tavarez. Time—2:48. Attendance—42,167. Umpires—HP, Hirschbeck. 1B, Darling. 2B, Hallion. 3B, DeMuth.

Game 2

Wednesday, October 1

Giants	AB	R	H	RBI	BB	K	Avg
Stan Javier, cf-rf	5	2	4	1	0	0	.625
Jose Vizcaino, ss	4	1	1	0	0	2	.143
Barry Bonds, lf	4	0	2	2	0	1	.375
Jeff Kent, 1b-2b	3	0	0	0	2	1	.000
Mark Lewis, 2b	5	0	3	1	0	0	.600
Roberto Hernandez, p	0	0	0	0	0	0	—
Glenallen Hill, rf	3	0	0	0	1	1	.000
Rich Rodriguez, p	0	0	0	0	0	0	—
Dante Powell, cf	0	0	0	0	0	0	—
Bill Mueller, 3b	4	0	0	0	0	0	.125
Brian Johnson, c	3	2	1	1	1	1	.167
Shawn Estes, p	1	0	0	0	0	1	.000
Doug Henry, p	0	0	0	0	0	0	—
Marvin Benard, ph	1	0	0	0	0	0	.000
Julian Tavarez, p	0	0	0	0	0	0	—
Darryl Hamilton, cf	1	1	0	0	0	0	.000
J.T. Snow, 1b	0	0	0	0	0	0	.000
TOTALS	34	6	11	5	4	7	.226

Marlins	AB	R	H	RBI	BB	K	Avg
Kurt Abbott, 2b	4	0	1	0	0	0	.200
Craig Counsell, 2b	1	0	0	0	0	0	.333
Edgar Renteria, ss	3	1	0	0	2	1	.250
Gary Sheffield, rf	4	3	3	1	1	0	.667
Bobby Bonilla, 3b	4	1	3	3	1	0	.571
Moises Alou, lf	5	0	1	1	0	2	.111
Jeff Conine, 1b	3	1	1	0	1	0	.286
Charles Johnson, c	3	1	0	0	1	1	.167
Devon White, cf	2	0	0	0	2	1	.000
Al Leiter, p	1	0	0	0	0	0	.000
Alex Arias, ph	1	0	1	1	0	0	1.000
Livan Hernandez, p	1	0	0	0	0	0	.000
John Cangelosi, ph	1	0	0	0	0	0	.000
Robb Nen, p	0	0	0	0	0	0	—
TOTALS	33	7	10	6	8	5	.274

	1	2	3	4	5	6	7	8	9		R	H	E
Giants	1	1	1	1	0	0	1	0	1		6	11	0
Marlins	2	0	1	2	0	1	0	0	1		7	10	2

E—Conine, Counsell. DP—Giants 1 (Vizcaino to Lewis to Kent), Marlins 1 (Abbott to Renteria to Conine). LOB—Giants 8, Marlins 10. Scoring Position—Giants 3-for-11, Marlins 3-for-8. 2B—Javier (1), Vizcaino (1), Bonds (2), Conine (1). HR—BJohnson (1), Sheffield (1), Bonilla (1). S—Vizcaino, Estes. SF—Bonds. GDP—Mueller, Abbott. SB—Javier (1), Bonds (1), Sheffield (1). CS—Lewis (1).

Giants	IP	H	R	ER	BB	K	ERA
Shawn Estes	3.0	5	5	5	4	3	15.00
Doug Henry	2.0	1	0	0	3	2	0.00
Julian Tavarez	2.0	2	1	1	0	0	6.00
Rich Rodriguez	1.0	0	0	0	0	0	0.00
Roberto Hernandez (L, 0-1)	0.0	2	1	1	1	0	13.50

Marlins	IP	H	R	ER	BB	K	ERA
Al Leiter	4.0	7	4	4	3	3	9.00
Livan Hernandez	4.0	3	1	1	0	3	2.25
Robb Nen (BS, 1; W, 1-0)	1.0	1	1	0	1	1	0.00

Estes pitched to four batters in the 4th. RHernandez pitched to four batters in the 9th.

WP—Leiter. Time—3:12. Attendance—41,283. Umpires—HP, Darling. 1B, Hallion. 2B, DeMuth. 3B, Tata.

Game 3

Friday, October 3

Marlins	AB	R	H	RBI	BB	K	Avg
Kurt Abbott, 2b	3	0	1	0	0	0	.250
Craig Counsell, 2b	2	0	1	0	0	0	.400
Edgar Renteria, ss	5	0	0	0	0	2	.154
Gary Sheffield, rf	3	0	1	0	2	0	.556
John Wehner, pr-rf	0	0	0	0	0	0	—
Bobby Bonilla, 3b	5	0	0	0	0	1	.333
Moises Alou, lf	5	1	2	0	0	1	.214
Jeff Conine, 1b	4	2	2	0	0	0	.364
Charles Johnson, c	2	2	1	2	0	0	.250
Devon White, cf	4	1	2	4	0	1	.182
Alex Fernandez, p	2	0	0	0	1	1	.000
Jim Eisenreich, ph	0	0	0	0	1	0	—
Dennis Cook, p	0	0	0	0	0	0	—
Robb Nen, p	0	0	0	0	0	0	—
TOTALS	35	6	10	6	6	6	.280

Giants	AB	R	H	RBI	BB	K	Avg
Stan Javier, cf	4	0	0	0	0	1	.417
Bill Mueller, 3b	4	0	2	0	0	0	.250
Barry Bonds, lf	4	0	0	0	0	1	.250
Jeff Kent, 2b	4	2	3	2	0	0	.300
J.T. Snow, 1b	3	0	1	0	1	0	.167
Glenallen Hill, rf	3	0	0	0	0	0	.000
Jose Vizcaino, ss	4	0	1	0	0	0	.182
Brian Johnson, c	4	0	0	0	0	3	.100
Wilson Alvarez, p	2	0	0	0	0	0	.000
Julian Tavarez, p	0	0	0	0	0	0	—
Marvin Benard, ph	1	0	0	0	0	1	.000
Roberto Hernandez, p	0	0	0	0	0	0	—
Rich Rodriguez, p	0	0	0	0	0	0	—
Rod Beck, p	0	0	0	0	0	0	—
Damon Berryhill, ph	1	0	0	0	0	0	.000
TOTALS	34	2	7	2	2	6	.212

	1	2	3	4	5	6	7	8	9		R	H	E
Marlins	0	0	0	0	4	0	2	0			6	10	2
Giants	0	0	0	1	0	1	0	0	0		2	7	0

E—Renteria 2. DP—Marlins 2 (Renteria to Abbott to Conine; CJohnson to Renteria), Giants 2 (Kent to Vizcaino to Snow; Vizcaino to Snow). LOB—Marlins 8, Giants 7. Scoring Position—Marlins 2-for-7, Giants 0-for-7. 2B—Alou (1), CJohnson (1), Counsell (1). HR—White (1), Kent 2 (2). GDP—Renteria, Bonilla, Hill. CS—Mueller (1).

Marlins	IP	H	R	ER	BB	K	ERA
Alex Fernandez (W, 1-0)	7.0	7	2	2	0	5	2.57
Dennis Cook	1.0	0	0	0	1	0	0.00
Robb Nen	1.0	0	0	0	1	1	0.00

Giants	IP	H	R	ER	BB	K	ERA
Wilson Alvarez (L, 0-1)	6.0	6	4	4	4	4	6.00
Julian Tavarez	1.0	0	0	0	1	0	4.50
Roberto Hernandez	0.2	2	2	2	1	1	20.25
Rich Rodriguez	0.0	1	0	0	0	0	0.00
Rod Beck	1.1	1	0	0	0	1	0.00

Rodriguez pitched to one batter in the 8th. Cook pitched to one batter in the 9th.

WP—Nen. Time—3:22. Attendance—57,188. Umpires—HP, Reliford. 1B, Rippley. 2B, Wendelstedt. 3B, Hernandez.

1997 NL Division Series—Composite Statistics

Batting

Marlins	G	AB	R	H	RBI	2B	3B	HR	BB	SO	SB	CS	Avg	OBP	Slg
Kurt Abbott	3	8	0	2	0	0	0	0	0	0	0	0	.250	.250	.250
Moises Alou	3	14	1	3	1	1	0	0	0	3	0	0	.214	.214	.286
Alex Arias	1	1	0	1	1	0	0	0	0	0	0	0	1.000	1.000	1.000
Bobby Bonilla	3	12	1	4	3	0	0	1	2	1	0	0	.333	.429	.583
Kevin Brown	1	2	0	0	0	0	0	0	0	2	0	0	.000	.000	.000
John Cangelosi	1	1	0	0	0	0	0	0	0	0	0	0	.000	.000	.000
Jeff Conine	3	11	3	4	1	0	1	0	0	1	0	0	.364	.417	.455
Craig Counsell	3	5	0	2	1	1	0	0	1	0	0	0	.400	.500	.600
Jim Eisenreich	2	0	0	0	0	0	0	0	2	0	0	0	—	1.000	—
Alex Fernandez	1	2	0	0	0	0	0	0	1	1	0	0	.000	.333	.000
Livan Hernandez	1	1	0	0	0	0	0	0	0	0	0	0	.000	.000	.000
Charles Johnson	3	8	5	2	2	1	0	1	3	2	0	0	.250	.500	.750
Al Leiter	1	1	0	0	0	0	0	0	0	0	0	0	.000	.000	.000
Edgar Renteria	3	13	1	2	1	0	0	0	2	4	0	0	.154	.267	.154
Gary Sheffield	3	9	3	5	1	1	0	1	5	0	1	0	.556	.714	1.000
Devon White	3	11	1	2	4	0	0	1	2	3	0	0	.182	.308	.455
Totals	**3**	**99**	**15**	**27**	**14**	**5**	**0**	**4**	**19**	**16**	**1**	**0**	**.273**	**.395**	**.444**

Giants	G	AB	R	H	RBI	2B	3B	HR	BB	SO	SB	CS	Avg	OBP	Slg
Wilson Alvarez	1	2	0	0	0	0	0	0	0	0	0	0	.000	.000	.000
Marvin Benard	2	2	0	0	0	0	0	0	0	1	0	0	.000	.000	.000
Damon Berryhill	1	1	0	0	0	0	0	0	0	0	0	0	.000	.000	.000
Barry Bonds	3	12	0	3	2	2	0	0	0	3	1	0	.250	.231	.417
Shawn Estes	1	1	0	0	0	0	0	0	0	1	0	0	.000	.000	.000
Darryl Hamilton	2	5	1	0	0	0	0	0	0	1	0	0	.000	.000	.000
Glenallen Hill	3	7	0	0	0	0	0	0	0	2	0	0	.000	.222	.000
Stan Javier	3	12	2	5	1	1	0	0	1	1	1	1	.417	.417	.500
Brian Johnson	3	10	2	1	1	0	0	1	1	4	0	0	.100	.182	.400
Jeff Kent	3	10	2	3	2	0	0	2	2	1	0	0	.300	.417	.900
Mark Lewis	1	5	0	3	1	0	0	0	0	0	0	1	.600	.600	.600
Bill Mueller	3	12	1	3	1	0	0	1	0	0	0	1	.250	.250	.500
Kirk Rueter	1	2	0	1	0	0	0	0	0	0	0	0	.500	.500	.500
J.T. Snow	3	6	0	1	0	0	0	0	1	1	0	0	.167	.286	.167
Jose Vizcaino	3	11	1	2	0	1	0	0	0	5	0	0	.182	.182	.273
Totals	**3**	**98**	**9**	**22**	**8**	**4**	**0**	**4**	**6**	**21**	**2**	**3**	**.224**	**.267**	**.388**

Pitching

Marlins	G	GS	CG	IP	H	R	ER	BB	SO	W-L	Sv-Op	Hld	ERA
Kevin Brown	1	1	0	7.0	4	1	1	0	5	0-0	0-0	0	1.29
Dennis Cook	2	0	0	3.0	0	0	0	1	3	1-0	0-0	0	0.00
Alex Fernandez	1	1	0	7.0	7	2	2	0	5	1-0	0-0	0	2.57
Livan Hernandez	1	0	0	4.0	3	1	1	0	3	0-0	0-0	0	2.25
Al Leiter	1	1	0	4.0	7	4	4	3	3	0-0	0-0	0	9.00
Robb Nen	2	0	0	2.0	1	1	0	2	2	1-0	0-1	0	0.00
Totals	**3**	**3**	**0**	**27.0**	**22**	**9**	**8**	**6**	**21**	**3-0**	**0-1**	**0**	**2.67**

Giants	G	GS	CG	IP	H	R	ER	BB	SO	W-L	Sv-Op	Hld	ERA
Wilson Alvarez	1	1	0	6.0	6	4	4	4	4	0-1	0-0	0	6.00
Rod Beck	1	0	0	1.1	1	0	0	0	1	0-0	0-0	0	0.00
Shawn Estes	1	1	0	3.0	5	5	5	4	3	0-0	0-0	0	15.00
Doug Henry	1	0	0	2.0	0	0	0	0	3	0-0	0-0	0	0.00
Roberto Hernandez	3	0	0	1.1	5	3	3	3	1	0-1	0-0	0	20.25
Rich Rodriguez	2	0	0	1.0	1	0	0	0	0	0-0	0-0	0	0.00
Kirk Rueter	1	1	0	7.0	4	1	1	3	5	0-0	0-0	0	1.29
Julian Tavarez	3	0	0	4.0	4	2	2	2	0	0-1	0-0	0	4.50
Totals	**3**	**3**	**0**	**25.2**	**27**	**15**	**15**	**19**	**16**	**0-3**	**0-0**	**0**	**5.26**

Fielding

Marlins	Pos	G	PO	Ast	E	DP	PB	FPct
Kurt Abbott	2b	2	3	6	0	2	—	1.000
Moises Alou	lf	3	5	0	0	0	—	1.000
Bobby Bonilla	3b	3	3	5	0	0	—	1.000
Kevin Brown	p	1	2	1	0	0	—	1.000
Jeff Conine	1b	3	24	3	1	2	—	.964
Dennis Cook	p	2	0	0	0	0	—	—
Craig Counsell	2b	3	5	2	1	0	—	.875
Alex Fernandez	p	1	0	1	0	0	—	1.000
Livan Hernandez	p	1	0	0	0	0	—	—
Charles Johnson	c	3	21	3	0	1	0	1.000
Al Leiter	p	1	0	1	0	0	—	1.000
Robb Nen	p	2	0	0	0	0	—	—
Edgar Renteria	ss	3	9	11	2	3	—	.909
Gary Sheffield	rf	3	6	0	0	0	—	1.000
John Wehner	rf	1	0	0	0	0	—	—
Devon White	cf	3	3	0	0	0	—	1.000
Totals		**3**	**81**	**33**	**4**	**8**	**0**	**.966**

Giants	Pos	G	PO	Ast	E	DP	PB	FPct
Wilson Alvarez	p	1	0	0	0	0	—	—
Rod Beck	p	1	0	0	0	0	—	—
Barry Bonds	lf	3	6	0	0	0	—	1.000
Shawn Estes	p	1	0	1	0	0	—	1.000
Darryl Hamilton	cf	2	3	0	0	0	—	1.000
Doug Henry	p	1	0	0	0	0	—	—
Roberto Hernandez	p	3	0	0	0	0	—	—
Glenallen Hill	rf	2	2	0	0	0	—	1.000
Stan Javier	rf	2	6	0	0	0	—	1.000
	cf	2	5	0	0	0	—	1.000
Brian Johnson	c	3	18	0	0	0	0	1.000
Jeff Kent	2b	3	5	6	0	2	—	1.000
	1b	1	14	1	0	1	—	1.000
Mark Lewis	2b	1	1	3	0	1	—	1.000
Bill Mueller	3b	3	2	9	0	1	—	1.000
Dante Powell	cf	1	0	0	0	0	—	—
Rich Rodriguez	p	2	0	0	0	0	—	—
Kirk Rueter	p	1	0	1	0	0	—	1.000
J.T. Snow	1b	3	12	0	0	3	—	1.000
Julian Tavarez	p	3	0	0	0	0	—	—
Jose Vizcaino	ss	3	3	10	0	3	—	1.000
Totals		**3**	**77**	**31**	**0**	**11**	**0**	**1.000**

HANK AARON (HOF 1982-W)—Henry Louis Aaron—Nickname: Hammerin' Hank—Bats: Right; Throws: Right

Ht: 6'0"; Wt: 180 lbs; Born: 2/5/1934 in Mobile, Alabama; Debut: 4/13/1954

LCS		Batting																							Fielding						
Year Tm	Age	G	AB	H	2B	3B	HR	TB	R	RBI	GW	TBB	IBB	SO	HBP	SH	SF	SB	CS	SB%	GDP	Avg	OBP	SLG	Pos	G	PO	A	E	DP	FPct
1969 Atl	35	3	14	5	2	0	3	16	3	7	0	0	0	1	0	0	0	0	0	—	1	.357	.357	1.143	OF	3	5	1	1	0	.857

World Series		Batting																							Fielding						
Year Tm	Age	G	AB	H	2B	3B	HR	TB	R	RBI	GW	TBB	IBB	SO	HBP	SH	SF	SB	CS	SB%	GDP	Avg	OBP	SLG	Pos	G	PO	A	E	DP	FPct
1957 Mil-*M*	23	7	28	11	0	1	3	22	5	7	0	1	0	6	0	0	0	0	0	—	0	.393	.414	.786	OF	7	11	0	0	0	1.000
1958 Mil	24	7	27	9	2	0	0	11	3	2	0	4	0	6	0	0	0	0	0	—	1	.333	.419	.407	OF	7	15	0	0	0	1.000
WS Totals		14	55	20	2	1	3	33	8	9	0	5	0	12	0	0	0	0	0	—	1	.364	.417	.600	OF	14	26	0	0	0	1.000
Postseason Totals		17	69	25	4	1	6	49	11	16	0	5	0	13	0	0	0	0	0	—	2	.362	.405	.710	OF	17	31	1	1	0	.970

TOMMIE AARON—Tommie Lee Aaron—Bats: Right; Throws: Right

Ht: 6'3"; Wt: 190 lbs; Born: 8/5/1939 in Mobile, Alabama; Debut: 4/10/1962; Died: 8/16/1984

LCS		Batting																							Fielding						
Year Tm	Age	G	AB	H	2B	3B	HR	TB	R	RBI	GW	TBB	IBB	SO	HBP	SH	SF	SB	CS	SB%	GDP	Avg	OBP	SLG	Pos	G	PO	A	E	DP	FPct
1969 Atl	30	1	1	0	0	0	0	0	0	0	0	0	0	0	0	0	0	0	0	—	0	.000	.000	.000	—						

DON AASE—Donald William Aase—Throws: Right; Bats: Right

Ht: 6'3"; Wt: 190 lbs; Born: 9/8/1954 in Orange, California; Debut: 7/26/1977

LCS		Pitching																										
Year Tm	Age	G	GS	CG	GF	IP	BFP	H	R	ER	HR	SH	SF	HB	TBB	IBB	SO	WP	Bk	W	L	Pct	ShO	Sv-Op	Hld	OAvg	OOBP	ERA
1979 Cal	25	2	0	0	2	5.0	20	4	1	1	0	0	1	0	2	1	6	0	0	1	0	1.000	0	0- 1	0	.235	.300	1.80

LCS		Batting																							Fielding						
Year Tm	Age	G	AB	H	2B	3B	HR	TB	R	RBI	GW	TBB	IBB	SO	HBP	SH	SF	SB	CS	SB%	GDP	Avg	OBP	SLG	Pos	G	PO	A	E	DP	FPct
1979 Cal	25	2	0	0	0	0	0	0	0	0	0	0	0	0	0	0	0	0	0	—	0	—	—	—	P	2	0	1	0	0	1.000

ED ABBATICCHIO—Edward James Abbaticchio—Nickname: Batty—Bats: Right; Throws: Right

Ht: 5'11"; Wt: 170 lbs; Born: 4/15/1877 in Latrobe, Pennsylvania; Debut: 9/4/1897; Died: 1/6/1957

World Series		Batting																							Fielding						
Year Tm	Age	G	AB	H	2B	3B	HR	TB	R	RBI	GW	TBB	IBB	SO	HBP	SH	SF	SB	CS	SB%	GDP	Avg	OBP	SLG	Pos	G	PO	A	E	DP	FPct
1909 Pit	32	1	1	0	0	0	0	0	0	0	0	0	0	1	0	0	0	0	0	—	0	.000	.000	.000	—						

GLENN ABBOTT—William Glenn Abbott—Throws: Right; Bats: Right

Ht: 6'6"; Wt: 200 lbs; Born: 2/16/1951 in Little Rock, Arkansas; Debut: 7/29/1973

LCS		Pitching																										
Year Tm	Age	G	GS	CG	GF	IP	BFP	H	R	ER	HR	SH	SF	HB	TBB	IBB	SO	WP	Bk	W	L	Pct	ShO	Sv-Op	Hld	OAvg	OOBP	ERA
1975 Oak	24	1	0	0	1	1.0	3	0	0	0	0	0	0	0	0	0	0	0	0	0	0	—	0	0- 0	0	.000	.000	0.00

LCS		Batting																							Fielding						
Year Tm	Age	G	AB	H	2B	3B	HR	TB	R	RBI	GW	TBB	IBB	SO	HBP	SH	SF	SB	CS	SB%	GDP	Avg	OBP	SLG	Pos	G	PO	A	E	DP	FPct
1975 Oak	24	1	0	0	0	0	0	0	0	0	0	0	0	0	0	0	0	0	0	—	0	—	—	—	P	1	0	0	0	0	—

KURT ABBOTT—Kurt Thomas Abbott—Bats: Right; Throws: Right

Ht: 6'0"; Wt: 170 lbs; Born: 6/2/1969 in Zanesville, Ohio; Debut: 9/7/1993

Division Series		Batting																							Fielding						
Year Tm	Age	G	AB	H	2B	3B	HR	TB	R	RBI	GW	TBB	IBB	SO	HBP	SH	SF	SB	CS	SB%	GDP	Avg	OBP	SLG	Pos	G	PO	A	E	DP	FPct
1997 Fla	28	3	8	2	0	0	0	2	0	0	0	0	0	0	0	0	0	0	0	—	1	.250	.250	.250	2B	2	3	6	0	2	1.000

LCS		Batting																							Fielding						
Year Tm	Age	G	AB	H	2B	3B	HR	TB	R	RBI	GW	TBB	IBB	SO	HBP	SH	SF	SB	CS	SB%	GDP	Avg	OBP	SLG	Pos	G	PO	A	E	DP	FPct
1997 Fla	28	2	8	3	1	0	0	4	0	0	0	0	0	2	0	0	0	0	0	—	0	.375	.375	.500	2B	2	4	1	0	0	1.000

World Series		Batting																							Fielding						
Year Tm	Age	G	AB	H	2B	3B	HR	TB	R	RBI	GW	TBB	IBB	SO	HBP	SH	SF	SB	CS	SB%	GDP	Avg	OBP	SLG	Pos	G	PO	A	E	DP	FPct
1997 Fla	28	3	3	0	0	0	0	0	0	0	0	0	0	1	0	0	0	0	0	—	0	.000	.000	.000	—						
Postseason Totals		8	19	5	1	0	0	6	0	0	0	0	0	3	0	0	0	0	0	—	1	.263	.263	.316	2B	4	7	7	0	2	1.000

BOB ABREU—Bob Kelly Abreu—Bats: Left; Throws: Right

Ht: 6'0"; Wt: 160 lbs; Born: 3/11/1974 in Aragua, Venezuela; Debut: 9/1/1996

Division Series		Batting																							Fielding						
Year Tm	Age	G	AB	H	2B	3B	HR	TB	R	RBI	GW	TBB	IBB	SO	HBP	SH	SF	SB	CS	SB%	GDP	Avg	OBP	SLG	Pos	G	PO	A	E	DP	FPct
1997 Hou	23	3	3	1	0	0	0	1	0	0	0	0	0	2	0	0	0	1	0	1.00	0	.333	.333	.333	—						

BILL ABSTEIN—William Henry Abstein—Nickname: Big Bill—Bats: Right; Throws: Right

Ht: 6'0"; Wt: 185 lbs; Born: 2/2/1883 in St. Louis, Missouri; Debut: 9/25/1906; Died: 4/8/1940

World Series		Batting																							Fielding						
Year Tm	Age	G	AB	H	2B	3B	HR	TB	R	RBI	GW	TBB	IBB	SO	HBP	SH	SF	SB	CS	SB%	GDP	Avg	OBP	SLG	Pos	G	PO	A	E	DP	FPct
1909 Pit	26	7	26	6	2	0	0	8	3	2	0	3	0	9	0	0	0	1	0	1.00	0	.231	.310	.308	1B	7	71	4	5	3	.938

JIM ACKER—James Justin Acker—Throws: Right; Bats: Right

Ht: 6'2"; Wt: 210 lbs; Born: 9/24/1958 in Freer, Texas; Debut: 4/7/1983

LCS		Pitching																										
Year Tm	Age	G	GS	CG	GF	IP	BFP	H	R	ER	HR	SH	SF	HB	TBB	IBB	SO	WP	Bk	W	L	Pct	ShO	Sv-Op	Hld	OAvg	OOBP	ERA
1985 Tor	27	2	0	0	2	6.0	21	2	0	0	0	0	0	0	0	0	5	0	0	0	0	—	0	0- 0	0	.095	.095	0.00
1989 Tor	31	5	0	0	1	6.1	25	4	2	1	0	1	1	1	1	0	4	0	0	0	0	—	0	0- 0	1	.190	.250	1.42
1991 Tor	33	1	0	0	0	0.2	3	1	0	0	0	0	0	0	0	0	1	0	0	0	0	—	0	0- 0	0	.333	.333	0.00
LCS Totals		8	0	0	3	13.0	98	7	2	1	0	1	1	1	1	0	10	0	0	0	0	—	0	0-0	1	.156	.188	0.69

LCS		Batting																							Fielding						
Year Tm	Age	G	AB	H	2B	3B	HR	TB	R	RBI	GW	TBB	IBB	SO	HBP	SH	SF	SB	CS	SB%	GDP	Avg	OBP	SLG	Pos	G	PO	A	E	DP	FPct
1985 Tor	27	2	0	0	0	0	0	0	0	0	0	0	0	0	0	0	0	0	0	—	0	—	—	—	P	2	0	1	0	0	1.000
1989 Tor	31	5	0	0	0	0	0	0	0	0	0	0	0	0	0	0	0	0	0	—	0	—	—	—	P	5	1	1	0	0	1.000
1991 Tor	33	1	0	0	0	0	0	0	0	0	0	0	0	0	0	0	0	0	0	—	0	—	—	—	P	1	0	0	0	0	—
LCS Totals		8	0	0	0	0	0	0	0	0	0	0	0	0	0	0	0	0	0	—	0	—	—	—	P	8	1	2	0	0	1.000

JERRY ADAIR—Kenneth Jerry Adair—Bats: Right; Throws: Right

Ht: 6'0"; Wt: 175 lbs; Born: 12/17/1936 in Sand Springs, Oklahoma; Debut: 9/2/1958; Died: 5/31/1987

World Series		Batting																							Fielding						
Year Tm	Age	G	AB	H	2B	3B	HR	TB	R	RBI	GW	TBB	IBB	SO	HBP	SH	SF	SB	CS	SB%	GDP	Avg	OBP	SLG	Pos	G	PO	A	E	DP	FPct
1967 Bos	30	5	16	2	0	0	0	2	0	1	0	0	0	3	0	0	1	1	0	1.00	0	.125	.118	.125	2B	4	7	12	0	1	1.000

BABE ADAMS—Charles Benjamin Adams—Throws: Right; Bats: Left

Ht: 5'11"; Wt: 185 lbs; Born: 5/18/1882 in Tipton, Indiana; Debut: 4/18/1906; Died: 7/27/1968

World Series		Pitching																										
Year Tm	Age	G	GS	CG	GF	IP	BFP	H	R	ER	HR	SH	SF	HB	TBB	IBB	SO	WP	Bk	W	L	Pct	ShO	Sv-Op	Hld	OAvg	OOBP	ERA
1909 Pit	27	3	3	3	0	27.0	106	18	5	4	2	1	0	1	6	0	11	0	0	3	0	1.000	1	0- 0	0	.184	.238	1.33
1925 Pit	43	1	0	0	1	1.0	5	2	0	0	0	0	0	0	0	0	0	0	0	0	0	—	0	0- 0	0	.400	.400	0.00
WS Totals		4	3	3	1	28.0	222	20	5	4	2	1	0	1	6	0	11	0	0	3	0	1.000	1	0-0	0	.194	.245	1.29

World Series		Batting																							Fielding						
Year Tm	Age	G	AB	H	2B	3B	HR	TB	R	RBI	GW	TBB	IBB	SO	HBP	SH	SF	SB	CS	SB%	GDP	Avg	OBP	SLG	Pos	G	PO	A	E	DP	FPct
1909 Pit	27	3	9	0	0	0	0	0	0	0	0	1	0	1	0	2	0	0	0	—	0	.000	.100	.000	P	3	0	5	0	0	1.000
1925 Pit	43	1	0	0	0	0	0	0	0	0	0	0	0	0	0	0	0	0	0	—	0	—	—	—	P	1	0	0	0	0	—
WS Totals		4	9	0	0	0	0	0	0	0	0	1	0	1	0	2	0	0	0	—	0	.000	.100	.000	P	4	0	5	0	0	1.000

SPARKY ADAMS
—Earl John Adams—Bats: Right; Throws: Right — Ht: 5'5"; Wt: 151 lbs; Born: 8/26/1894 in Zerbe, Pennsylvania; Debut: 9/18/1922; Died: 2/24/1989

World Series		Batting																							Fielding						
Year Tm	Age	G	AB	H	2B	3B	HR	TB	R	RBI	GW	TBB	IBB	SO	HBP	SH	SF	SB	CS	SB%	GDP	Avg	OBP	SLG	Pos	G	PO	A	E	DP	FPct
1930 StL	36	6	21	3	0	0	0	3	0	1	0	0	0	4	0	0	1	0	0	—	0	.143	.136	.143	3B	6	4	7	0	1	1.000
1931 StL	37	2	4	1	0	0	0	1	0	0	0	0	0	1	0	0	0	0	0	—	0	.250	.250	.250	3B	1	0	1	0	0	1.000
WS Totals		8	25	4	0	0	0	4	0	1	0	0	0	5	0	0	1	0	0	—	0	.160	.154	.160	3B	7	4	8	0	1	1.000

SPENCER ADAMS
—Spencer Dewey Adams—Bats: Left; Throws: Right — Ht: 5'9"; Wt: 158 lbs; Born: 6/21/1898 in Layton, Utah; Debut: 5/8/1923; Died: 11/24/1970

World Series		Batting																							Fielding						
Year Tm	Age	G	AB	H	2B	3B	HR	TB	R	RBI	GW	TBB	IBB	SO	HBP	SH	SF	SB	CS	SB%	GDP	Avg	OBP	SLG	Pos	G	PO	A	E	DP	FPct
1925 Was	27	2	1	0	0	0	0	0	0	0	0	0	0	0	0	0	0	0	0	—	0	.000	.000	.000	2B	1	0	0	0	0	—
1926 NYA	28	2	0	0	0	0	0	0	0	0	0	0	0	0	0	0	0	0	0	—	0	—	—	—	—						
WS Totals		4	1	0	0	0	0	0	0	0	0	0	0	0	0	0	0	0	0	—	0	.000	.000	.000	2B	1	0	0	0	0	—

JOE ADCOCK
—Joseph Wilbur Adcock—Nickname: Goofy—Bats: Right; Throws: Right — Ht: 6'4"; Wt: 210 lbs; Born: 10/30/1927 in Coushatta, Louisiana; Debut: 4/23/1950

World Series		Batting																							Fielding						
Year Tm	Age	G	AB	H	2B	3B	HR	TB	R	RBI	GW	TBB	IBB	SO	HBP	SH	SF	SB	CS	SB%	GDP	Avg	OBP	SLG	Pos	G	PO	A	E	DP	FPct
1957 Mil	29	5	15	3	0	0	0	3	1	2	1	0	0	2	0	0	0	0	0	—	2	.200	.200	.200	1B	5	38	2	1	2	.976
1958 Mil	30	4	13	4	0	0	0	4	1	0	0	1	0	3	0	0	0	0	0	—	0	.308	.357	.308	1B	3	23	2	0	0	1.000
WS Totals		9	28	7	0	0	0	7	2	2	1	1	0	5	0	0	0	0	0	—	2	.250	.276	.250	1B	8	61	4	1	2	.985

TOMMIE AGEE
—Tommie Lee Agee—Bats: Right; Throws: Right — Ht: 5'11"; Wt: 195 lbs; Born: 8/9/1942 in Magnolia, Alabama; Debut: 9/14/1962

LCS		Batting																							Fielding						
Year Tm	Age	G	AB	H	2B	3B	HR	TB	R	RBI	GW	TBB	IBB	SO	HBP	SH	SF	SB	CS	SB%	GDP	Avg	OBP	SLG	Pos	G	PO	A	E	DP	FPct
1969 NYN	27	3	14	5	1	0	2	12	4	4	0	2	1	5	0	0	0	2	0	1.00	0	.357	.438	.857	OF	3	9	0	0	0	1.000
World Series		Batting																							Fielding						
Year Tm	Age	G	AB	H	2B	3B	HR	TB	R	RBI	GW	TBB	IBB	SO	HBP	SH	SF	SB	CS	SB%	GDP	Avg	OBP	SLG	Pos	G	PO	A	E	DP	FPct
1969 NYN	27	5	18	3	0	0	1	6	1	1	1	2	0	5	0	0	0	1	0	1.00	1	.167	.250	.333	OF	5	19	0	0	0	1.000
Postseason Totals		8	32	8	1	0	3	18	5	5	1	4	1	10	0	0	0	3	0	1.00	1	.250	.333	.563	OF	8	28	0	0	0	1.000

SAM AGNEW
—Samuel Lester Agnew—Nickname: Slam—Bats: Right; Throws: Right — Ht: 5'11"; Wt: 185 lbs; Born: 4/12/1887 in Farmington, Missouri; Debut: 4/10/1913; Died: 7/19/1951

World Series		Batting																							Fielding						
Year Tm	Age	G	AB	H	2B	3B	HR	TB	R	RBI	GW	TBB	IBB	SO	HBP	SH	SF	SB	CS	SB%	GDP	Avg	OBP	SLG	Pos	G	PO	A	E	DP	FPct
1918 Bos	31	4	9	0	0	0	0	0	0	0	0	0	0	0	0	0	0	0	0	—	1	.000	.000	.000	C	4	12	6	0	0	1.000

JUAN AGOSTO
—Juan Roberto Agosto—Throws: Left; Bats: Left — Ht: 6'2"; Wt: 190 lbs; Born: 2/23/1958 in Rio Piedras, Puerto Rico; Debut: 9/7/1981

LCS		Pitching																										
Year Tm	Age	G	GS	CG	GF	IP	BFP	H	R	ER	HR	SH	SF	HB	TBB	IBB	SO	WP	Bk	W	L	Pct	ShO	Sv-Op	Hld	OAvg	OOBP	ERA
1983 ChA	25	1	0	0	0	0.1	1	0	0	0	0	0	1	0	0	0	0	0	0	0	0	—	0	0- 0	0	—	.000	0.00

LCS		Batting																							Fielding						
Year Tm	Age	G	AB	H	2B	3B	HR	TB	R	RBI	GW	TBB	IBB	SO	HBP	SH	SF	SB	CS	SB%	GDP	Avg	OBP	SLG	Pos	G	PO	A	E	DP	FPct
1983 ChA	25	1	0	0	0	0	0	0	0	0	0	0	0	0	0	0	0	0	0	—	0	—	—	—	P	1	0	0	0	0	—

LUIS AGUAYO
—Bats: Right; Throws: Right — Ht: 5'9"; Wt: 173 lbs; Born: 3/13/1959 in Vega Baja, Puerto Rico; Debut: 4/19/1980

Division Series		Batting																							Fielding						
Year Tm	Age	G	AB	H	2B	3B	HR	TB	R	RBI	GW	TBB	IBB	SO	HBP	SH	SF	SB	CS	SB%	GDP	Avg	OBP	SLG	Pos	G	PO	A	E	DP	FPct
1981 Phi	22	2	0	0	0	0	0	0	1	0	0	0	0	0	0	0	0	0	0	—	0	—	—	—	—						

RICK AGUILERA
—Richard Warren Aguilera—Throws: Right; Bats: Right — Ht: 6'4"; Wt: 195 lbs; Born: 12/31/1961 in San Gabriel, California; Debut: 6/12/1985

Division Series		Pitching																										
Year Tm	Age	G	GS	CG	GF	IP	BFP	H	R	ER	HR	SH	SF	HB	TBB	IBB	SO	WP	Bk	W	L	Pct	ShO	Sv-Op	Hld	OAvg	OOBP	ERA
1995 Bos	33	1	0	0	0	0.2	5	3	1	1	1	0	0	0	0	0	1	0	0	0	0	—	0	0- 1	0	.600	.600	13.50
LCS		Pitching																										
Year Tm	Age	G	GS	CG	GF	IP	BFP	H	R	ER	HR	SH	SF	HB	TBB	IBB	SO	WP	Bk	W	L	Pct	ShO	Sv-Op	Hld	OAvg	OOBP	ERA
1986 NYN	24	2	0	0	0	5.0	19	2	1	0	0	1	0	0	2	0	2	0	0	0	0	—	0	0- 0	0	.125	.222	0.00
1988 NYN	26	3	0	0	1	7.0	26	3	1	1	0	0	0	0	2	0	4	0	0	0	0	—	0	0- 0	0	.125	.192	1.29
1991 Min	29	3	0	0	3	3.1	11	1	0	0	0	0	0	0	0	0	3	0	0	0	0	—	0	3- 3	0	.091	.091	0.00
LCS Totals		8	0	0	4	15.1	112	6	2	1	0	1	0	0	4	0	9	0	0	0	0	—	0	3-3	0	.118	.182	0.59
World Series		Pitching																										
Year Tm	Age	G	GS	CG	GF	IP	BFP	H	R	ER	HR	SH	SF	HB	TBB	IBB	SO	WP	Bk	W	L	Pct	ShO	Sv-Op	Hld	OAvg	OOBP	ERA
1986 NYN	24	2	0	0	1	3.0	19	8	4	4	1	0	0	1	1	0	4	0	0	1	0	1.000	0	0- 0	0	.471	.526	12.00
1991 Min	29	4	0	0	4	5.0	20	6	1	1	0	0	0	0	1	0	3	0	0	1	1	.500	0	2- 2	0	.316	.350	1.80
WS Totals		6	0	0	5	8.0	78	14	5	5	1	0	0	1	2	0	7	0	0	2	1	.667	0	2-2	0	.389	.436	5.63
Postseason Totals		15	0	0	9	24.0	200	23	8	7	2	1	0	1	6	0	17	0	0	2	1	.667	0	5-6	0	.250	.303	2.63

Division Series		Batting																							Fielding						
Year Tm	Age	G	AB	H	2B	3B	HR	TB	R	RBI	GW	TBB	IBB	SO	HBP	SH	SF	SB	CS	SB%	GDP	Avg	OBP	SLG	Pos	G	PO	A	E	DP	FPct
1995 Bos	33	1	0	0	0	0	0	0	0	0	0	0	0	0	0	0	0	0	0	—	0	—	—	—	P	1	0	0	0	0	—
LCS		Batting																							Fielding						
Year Tm	Age	G	AB	H	2B	3B	HR	TB	R	RBI	GW	TBB	IBB	SO	HBP	SH	SF	SB	CS	SB%	GDP	Avg	OBP	SLG	Pos	G	PO	A	E	DP	FPct
1986 NYN	24	2	0	0	0	0	0	0	0	0	0	0	0	0	0	0	0	0	0	—	0	—	—	—	P	2	1	1	0	0	1.000
1988 NYN	26	3	1	0	0	0	0	0	0	0	0	0	0	1	0	0	0	0	0	—	0	.000	.000	.000	P	3	0	1	0	0	1.000
1991 Min	29	3	0	0	0	0	0	0	0	0	0	0	0	0	0	0	0	0	0	—	0	—	—	—	P	3	0	0	0	0	—
LCS Totals		8	1	0	0	0	0	0	0	0	0	0	0	1	0	0	0	0	0	—	0	.000	.000	.000	P	8	1	2	0	0	1.000
World Series		Batting																							Fielding						
Year Tm	Age	G	AB	H	2B	3B	HR	TB	R	RBI	GW	TBB	IBB	SO	HBP	SH	SF	SB	CS	SB%	GDP	Avg	OBP	SLG	Pos	G	PO	A	E	DP	FPct
1986 NYN	24	2	0	0	0	0	0	0	0	0	0	0	0	0	0	0	0	0	0	—	0	—	—	—	P	2	0	0	0	0	—
1991 Min	29	4	1	0	0	0	0	0	0	0	0	0	0	0	0	0	0	0	0	—	0	.000	.000	.000	P	4	0	0	0	0	—
WS Totals		6	1	0	0	0	0	0	0	0	0	0	0	0	0	0	0	0	0	—	0	.000	.000	.000	P	6	0	0	0	0	—
Postseason Totals		15	2	0	0	0	0	0	0	0	0	0	0	1	0	0	0	0	0	—	0	.000	.000	.000	P	15	1	2	0	0	1.000

WILLIE AIKENS
—Willie Mays Aikens—Bats: Left; Throws: Right — Ht: 6'3"; Wt: 220 lbs; Born: 10/14/1954 in Seneca, South Carolina; Debut: 5/17/1977

Division Series		Batting																							Fielding						
Year Tm	Age	G	AB	H	2B	3B	HR	TB	R	RBI	GW	TBB	IBB	SO	HBP	SH	SF	SB	CS	SB%	GDP	Avg	OBP	SLG	Pos	G	PO	A	E	DP	FPct
1981 KC	26	3	9	3	0	0	0	3	0	0	0	3	0	2	0	0	0	0	0	—	0	.333	.500	.333	1B	3	28	1	0	1	1.000
LCS		Batting																							Fielding						
Year Tm	Age	G	AB	H	2B	3B	HR	TB	R	RBI	GW	TBB	IBB	SO	HBP	SH	SF	SB	CS	SB%	GDP	Avg	OBP	SLG	Pos	G	PO	A	E	DP	FPct
1980 KC	25	3	11	4	0	0	0	4	0	2	1	0	0	1	0	0	0	0	0	—	0	.364	.364	.364	1B	3	22	1	0	2	1.000
World Series		Batting																							Fielding						
Year Tm	Age	G	AB	H	2B	3B	HR	TB	R	RBI	GW	TBB	IBB	SO	HBP	SH	SF	SB	CS	SB%	GDP	Avg	OBP	SLG	Pos	G	PO	A	E	DP	FPct
1980 KC	25	6	20	8	0	1	4	22	5	8	1	6	0	8	0	0	0	0	0	—	0	.400	.538	1.100	1B	6	55	2	2	6	.966
Postseason Totals		12	40	15	0	1	4	29	5	10	2	9	0	11	0	0	0	0	0	—	0	.375	.490	.725	1B	12	105	4	2	9	.982

MIKE ALDRETE—Michael Peter Aldrete—Bats: Left; Throws: Left

Ht: 5'11"; Wt: 180 lbs; Born: 1/29/1961 in Carmel, California; Debut: 5/28/1986

LCS		Batting																							Fielding						
Year Tm	Age	G	AB	H	2B	3B	HR	TB	R	RBI	GW	TBB	IBB	SO	HBP	SH	SF	SB	CS	SB%	GDP	Avg	OBP	SLG	Pos	G	PO	A	E	DP	FPct
1987 SF	26	5	10	1	0	0	0	1	0	1	0	0	0	2	0	0	1	0	0	—	1	.100	.091	.100	OF	3	5	0	0	0	1.000
1996 NYA	35	1	0	0	0	0	0	0	0	0	0	0	0	0	0	0	0	0	0	—	0	—	—	—	—						
LCS Totals		6	10	1	0	0	0	1	0	1	0	0	0	2	0	0	1	0	0	—	1	.100	.091	.100	OF	3	5	0	0	0	1.000
World Series		Batting																							Fielding						
Year Tm	Age	G	AB	H	2B	3B	HR	TB	R	RBI	GW	TBB	IBB	SO	HBP	SH	SF	SB	CS	SB%	GDP	Avg	OBP	SLG	Pos	G	PO	A	E	DP	FPct
1996 NYA	35	2	1	0	0	0	0	0	0	0	0	0	0	0	0	0	0	0	0	—	0	.000	.000	.000	OF	1	0	0	0	0	—
Postseason Totals		8	11	1	0	0	0	1	0	1	0	0	0	2	0	0	1	0	0	—	1	.091	.083	.091	OF	4	5	0	0	0	1.000

VIC ALDRIDGE—Victor Eddington Aldridge—Nickname: Hoosier Schoolmaster—Throws: Right; Bats: Right

Ht: 5'9"; Wt: 175 lbs; Born: 10/25/1893 in Indian Springs, Indiana; Debut: 4/15/1917; Died: 4/17/1973

World Series		Pitching																										
Year Tm	Age	G	GS	CG	GF	IP	BFP	H	R	ER	HR	SH	SF	HB	TBB	IBB	SO	WP	Bk	W	L	Pct	ShO	Sv-Op	Hld	OAvg	OOBP	ERA
1925 Pit	31	3	3	2	0	18.1	81	18	9	9	2	5	1	1	9	0	9	2	1	2	0	1.000	0	0- 0	0	.277	.368	4.42
1927 Pit	33	1	1	0	0	7.1	36	10	6	6	0	0	3	0	4	0	4	1	0	0	1	.000	0	0- 0	0	.345	.389	7.36
WS Totals		4	4	2	0	25.2	234	28	15	15	2	5	4	1	13	0	13	3	1	2	1	.667	0	0-0	0	.298	.375	5.26

World Series		Batting																							Fielding						
Year Tm	Age	G	AB	H	2B	3B	HR	TB	R	RBI	GW	TBB	IBB	SO	HBP	SH	SF	SB	CS	SB%	GDP	Avg	OBP	SLG	Pos	G	PO	A	E	DP	FPct
1925 Pit	31	3	7	0	0	0	0	0	0	0	0	0	0	0	0	0	0	0	0	—	1	.000	.000	.000	P	3	0	4	0	0	1.000
1927 Pit	33	1	2	0	0	0	0	0	0	0	0	0	0	0	0	0	0	0	0	—	0	.000	.000	.000	P	1	0	2	0	0	1.000
WS Totals		4	9	0	0	0	0	0	0	0	0	0	0	0	0	0	0	0	0	—	1	.000	.000	.000	P	4	0	6	0	0	1.000

DOYLE ALEXANDER—Doyle Lafayette Alexander—Throws: Right; Bats: Right

Ht: 6'3"; Wt: 190 lbs; Born: 9/4/1950 in Cordova, Alabama; Debut: 6/26/1971

LCS		Pitching																										
Year Tm	Age	G	GS	CG	GF	IP	BFP	H	R	ER	HR	SH	SF	HB	TBB	IBB	SO	WP	Bk	W	L	Pct	ShO	Sv-Op	Hld	OAvg	OOBP	ERA
1973 Bal	23	1	1	0	0	3.2	16	5	3	2	0	1	0	1	0	0	1	0	0	0	1	.000	0	0- 0	0	.357	.400	4.91
1985 Tor	35	2	2	0	0	10.1	49	14	10	10	4	1	1	0	3	0	9	1	0	0	1	.000	0	0- 0	0	.318	.354	8.71
1987 Det	37	2	2	0	0	9.0	42	14	10	10	2	1	0	1	1	0	5	0	0	0	2	.000	0	0- 0	0	.359	.390	10.00
LCS Totals		5	5	0	0	23.0	214	33	23	22	6	3	1	2	4	0	15	1	0	0	4	.000	0	0-0	0	.340	.375	8.61
World Series		Pitching																										
Year Tm	Age	G	GS	CG	GF	IP	BFP	H	R	ER	HR	SH	SF	HB	TBB	IBB	SO	WP	Bk	W	L	Pct	ShO	Sv-Op	Hld	OAvg	OOBP	ERA
1976 NYA	26	1	1	0	0	6.0	25	9	5	5	1	0	1	0	2	0	1	0	0	0	1	.000	0	0- 0	0	.409	.440	7.50
Postseason Totals		6	6	0	0	29.0	264	42	28	27	7	3	2	2	6	0	16	1	0	0	5	.000	0	0-0	0	.353	.388	8.38

LCS		Batting																							Fielding						
Year Tm	Age	G	AB	H	2B	3B	HR	TB	R	RBI	GW	TBB	IBB	SO	HBP	SH	SF	SB	CS	SB%	GDP	Avg	OBP	SLG	Pos	G	PO	A	E	DP	FPct
1973 Bal	23	1	0	0	0	0	0	0	0	0	0	0	0	0	0	0	0	0	0	—	0	—	—	—	P	1	0	2	0	1	1.000
1985 Tor	35	2	0	0	0	0	0	0	0	0	0	0	0	0	0	0	0	0	0	—	0	—	—	—	P	2	1	0	0	0	1.000
1987 Det	37	2	0	0	0	0	0	0	0	0	0	0	0	0	0	0	0	0	0	—	0	—	—	—	P	2	1	1	0	0	1.000
LCS Totals		5	0	0	0	0	0	0	0	0	0	0	0	0	0	0	0	0	0	—	0	—	—	—	P	5	2	3	0	1	1.000
World Series		Batting																							Fielding						
Year Tm	Age	G	AB	H	2B	3B	HR	TB	R	RBI	GW	TBB	IBB	SO	HBP	SH	SF	SB	CS	SB%	GDP	Avg	OBP	SLG	Pos	G	PO	A	E	DP	FPct
1976 NYA	26	1	0	0	0	0	0	0	0	0	0	0	0	0	0	0	0	0	0	—	0	—	—	—	P	1	0	1	0	1	1.000
Postseason Totals		6	0	0	0	0	0	0	0	0	0	0	0	0	0	0	0	0	0	—	0	—	—	—	P	6	2	4	0	2	1.000

MANNY ALEXANDER—Manuel Dejesus Alexander—Bats: Right; Throws: Right

Ht: 5'10"; Wt: 150 lbs; Born: 3/20/1971 in San Pedro de Macoris, Dominican Republic; Debut: 9/18/1992

Division Series		Batting																							Fielding						
Year Tm	Age	G	AB	H	2B	3B	HR	TB	R	RBI	GW	TBB	IBB	SO	HBP	SH	SF	SB	CS	SB%	GDP	Avg	OBP	SLG	Pos	G	PO	A	E	DP	FPct
1996 Bal	25	3	0	0	0	0	0	0	2	0	0	0	0	0	0	0	0	0	0	—	0	—	—	—	—						

MATT ALEXANDER—Matthew Alexander—Bats: Both; Throws: Right

Ht: 5'11"; Wt: 168 lbs; Born: 1/30/1947 in Shreveport, Louisiana; Debut: 8/23/1973

LCS		Batting																							Fielding						
Year Tm	Age	G	AB	H	2B	3B	HR	TB	R	RBI	GW	TBB	IBB	SO	HBP	SH	SF	SB	CS	SB%	GDP	Avg	OBP	SLG	Pos	G	PO	A	E	DP	FPct
1979 Pit	32	1	0	0	0	0	0	0	1	0	0	0	0	0	0	0	0	0	0	—	0	—	—	—	—						
World Series		Batting																							Fielding						
Year Tm	Age	G	AB	H	2B	3B	HR	TB	R	RBI	GW	TBB	IBB	SO	HBP	SH	SF	SB	CS	SB%	GDP	Avg	OBP	SLG	Pos	G	PO	A	E	DP	FPct
1979 Pit	32	1	0	0	0	0	0	0	0	0	0	0	0	0	0	0	0	0	1	.00	0	—	—	—	OF	1	0	0	0	0	—
Postseason Totals		2	0	0	0	0	0	0	1	0	0	0	0	0	0	0	0	0	1	.00	0	—	—	—	OF	1	0	0	0	0	—

PETE ALEXANDER (HOF 1938-W)—Grover Cleveland Alexander—Throws: Right; Bats: Right

Ht: 6'1"; Wt: 185 lbs; Born: 1/26/1887 in Elba, Nebraska; Debut: 4/15/1911; Died: 11/4/1950

World Series		Pitching																										
Year Tm	Age	G	GS	CG	GF	IP	BFP	H	R	ER	HR	SH	SF	HB	TBB	IBB	SO	WP	Bk	W	L	Pct	ShO	Sv-Op	Hld	OAvg	OOBP	ERA
1915 Phi	28	2	2	2	0	17.2	69	14	3	3	0	4	1	0	4	1	10	0	0	1	1	.500	0	0- 0	0	.233	.277	1.53
1926 StL	39	3	2	2	1	20.1	76	12	4	3	0	0	0	0	4	0	17	0	0	2	0	1.000	0	1- 1	0	.167	.211	1.33
1928 StL	41	2	1	0	1	5.0	30	10	11	11	3	1	1	0	4	0	2	0	0	0	1	.000	0	0- 0	0	.417	.483	19.80
WS Totals		7	5	4	2	43.0	350	36	18	17	3	5	2	0	12	1	29	0	0	3	2	.600	0	1-1	0	.231	.282	3.56

World Series		Batting																							Fielding						
Year Tm	Age	G	AB	H	2B	3B	HR	TB	R	RBI	GW	TBB	IBB	SO	HBP	SH	SF	SB	CS	SB%	GDP	Avg	OBP	SLG	Pos	G	PO	A	E	DP	FPct
1915 Phi	28	2	5	1	0	0	0	1	0	0	0	0	0	1	0	1	0	0	0	—	0	.200	.200	.200	P	2	2	5	0	0	1.000
1926 StL	39	3	7	0	0	0	0	0	1	0	0	0	0	2	0	2	0	0	0	—	0	.000	.000	.000	P	3	0	6	1	1	.857
1928 StL	41	2	1	0	0	0	0	0	0	1	0	0	0	0	0	0	0	0	0	—	0	.000	.000	.000	P	2	0	4	0	0	1.000
WS Totals		7	13	1	0	0	0	1	1	1	0	0	0	3	0	3	0	0	0	—	0	.077	.077	.077	P	7	2	15	1	1	.944

ANTONIO ALFONSECA—Throws: Right; Bats: Right

Ht: 6'5"; Wt: 235 lbs; Born: 4/16/1972 in La Romana, Dominican Republic; Debut: 6/17/1997

World Series		Pitching																										
Year Tm	Age	G	GS	CG	GF	IP	BFP	H	R	ER	HR	SH	SF	HB	TBB	IBB	SO	WP	Bk	W	L	Pct	ShO	Sv-Op	Hld	OAvg	OOBP	ERA
1997 Fla	25	3	0	0	1	6.1	25	6	0	0	0	0	0	0	1	0	5	0	0	0	0	—	0	0- 0	0	.250	.280	0.00

World Series		Batting																							Fielding						
Year Tm	Age	G	AB	H	2B	3B	HR	TB	R	RBI	GW	TBB	IBB	SO	HBP	SH	SF	SB	CS	SB%	GDP	Avg	OBP	SLG	Pos	G	PO	A	E	DP	FPct
1997 Fla	25	3	0	0	0	0	0	0	0	0	0	0	0	0	0	0	0	0	0	—	0	—	—	—	P	3	1	1	0	0	1.000

LUIS ALICEA—Luis Rene Alicea—Bats: Both; Throws: Right

Ht: 5'9"; Wt: 165 lbs; Born: 7/29/1965 in Santurce, Puerto Rico; Debut: 4/23/1988

Division Series		Batting																							Fielding						
Year Tm	Age	G	AB	H	2B	3B	HR	TB	R	RBI	GW	TBB	IBB	SO	HBP	SH	SF	SB	CS	SB%	GDP	Avg	OBP	SLG	Pos	G	PO	A	E	DP	FPct
1995 Bos	30	3	10	6	1	0	1	10	1	1	0	2	0	2	0	0	0	1	0	1.00	0	.600	.667	1.000	2B	3	6	11	1	0	.944
1996 StL	31	3	11	2	2	0	0	4	1	0	0	1	0	4	0	0	0	0	2	.00	0	.182	.250	.364	2B	3	2	5	1	0	.875
DS Totals		6	21	8	3	0	1	14	2	1	0	3	0	6	0	0	0	1	2	.33	0	.381	.458	.667	2B	6	8	16	2	0	.923
LCS		Batting																							Fielding						
Year Tm	Age	G	AB	H	2B	3B	HR	TB	R	RBI	GW	TBB	IBB	SO	HBP	SH	SF	SB	CS	SB%	GDP	Avg	OBP	SLG	Pos	G	PO	A	E	DP	FPct
1996 StL	31	5	8	0	0	0	0	0	0	0	0	2	0	1	0	0	0	0	0	—	1	.000	.200	.000	2B	4	5	7	1	1	.923
Postseason Totals		11	29	8	3	0	1	14	2	1	0	5	0	7	0	0	0	1	2	.33	1	.276	.382	.483	2B	10	13	23	3	1	.923

DICK ALLEN—Richard Anthony Allen—Bats: Right; Throws: Right

Ht: 5'11"; Wt: 187 lbs; Born: 3/8/1942 in Wampum, Pennsylvania; Debut: 9/3/1963

LCS		Batting																							Fielding						
Year Tm	Age	G	AB	H	2B	3B	HR	TB	R	RBI	GW	TBB	IBB	SO	HBP	SH	SF	SB	CS	SB%	GDP	Avg	OBP	SLG	Pos	G	PO	A	E	DP	FPct
1976 Phi	34	3	9	2	0	0	0	2	1	0	0	3	0	2	0	0	0	0	0	—	0	.222	.417	.222	1B	3	28	0	1	1	.966

JOHNNY ALLEN—John Thomas Allen—Throws: Right; Bats: Right

Ht: 6'0"; Wt: 180 lbs; Born: 9/30/1905 in Lenoir, North Carolina; Debut: 4/19/1932; Died: 5/29/1959

World Series		Pitching																										
Year Tm	Age	G	GS	CG	GF	IP	BFP	H	R	ER	HR	SH	SF	HB	TBB	IBB	SO	WP	Bk	W	L	Pct	ShO	Sv-Op	Hld	OAvg	OOBP	ERA
1932 NYA	27	1	1	0	0	0.2	8	5	4	3	1	0	0	0	0	0	0	0	0	0	0	—	0	0- 0	0	.625	.625	40.50
1941 Bro	36	3	0	0	2	3.2	16	1	0	0	0	0	0	2	3	0	0	0	0	0	0	—	0	0- 0	0	.091	.375	0.00
WS Totals		4	1	0	2	4.1	48	6	4	3	1	0	0	2	3	0	0	0	0	0	0	—	0	0-0	0	.316	.458	6.23

World Series		Batting																							Fielding						
Year Tm	Age	G	AB	H	2B	3B	HR	TB	R	RBI	GW	TBB	IBB	SO	HBP	SH	SF	SB	CS	SB%	GDP	Avg	OBP	SLG	Pos	G	PO	A	E	DP	FPct
1932 NYA	27	1	0	0	0	0	0	0	0	0	0	0	0	0	0	0	0	0	0	—	0	—	—	—	P	1	0	0	0	0	—
1941 Bro	36	3	0	0	0	0	0	0	0	0	0	0	0	0	0	0	0	0	0	—	0	—	—	—	P	3	0	0	0	0	—
WS Totals		4	0	0	0	0	0	0	0	0	0	0	0	0	0	0	0	0	0	—	0	—	—	—	P	4	0	0	0	0	—

GENE ALLEY—Leonard Eugene Alley—Bats: Right; Throws: Right

Ht: 5'10"; Wt: 160 lbs; Born: 7/10/1940 in Richmond, Virginia; Debut: 9/4/1963

LCS		Batting																							Fielding						
Year Tm	Age	G	AB	H	2B	3B	HR	TB	R	RBI	GW	TBB	IBB	SO	HBP	SH	SF	SB	CS	SB%	GDP	Avg	OBP	SLG	Pos	G	PO	A	E	DP	FPct
1970 Pit	30	2	7	0	0	0	0	0	0	0	0	1	0	2	0	0	0	0	0	—	0	.000	.125	.000	SS	2	6	7	0	3	1.000
1971 Pit	31	1	2	1	0	0	0	1	1	0	0	0	0	0	0	0	0	0	0	—	0	.500	.500	.500	SS	1	1	1	0	1	1.000
1972 Pit	32	5	16	0	0	0	0	0	1	0	0	0	0	3	1	1	0	0	0	—	0	.000	.059	.000	SS	5	10	4	2	0	.875
LCS Totals		8	25	1	0	0	0	1	2	0	0	1	0	5	1	1	0	0	0	—	0	.040	.111	.040	SS	8	17	12	2	4	.935
World Series		Batting																							Fielding						
Year Tm	Age	G	AB	H	2B	3B	HR	TB	R	RBI	GW	TBB	IBB	SO	HBP	SH	SF	SB	CS	SB%	GDP	Avg	OBP	SLG	Pos	G	PO	A	E	DP	FPct
1971 Pit	31	2	2	0	0	0	0	0	0	0	0	1	0	0	0	0	0	0	0	—	0	.000	.333	.000	SS	2	1	4	0	0	1.000
Postseason Totals		10	27	1	0	0	0	1	2	0	0	2	0	5	1	1	0	0	0	—	0	.037	.133	.037	SS	10	18	16	2	4	.944

BOB ALLISON—William Robert Allison—Bats: Right; Throws: Right

Ht: 6'3"; Wt: 205 lbs; Born: 7/11/1934 in Raytown, Missouri; Debut: 9/16/1958; Died: 4/9/1995

LCS		Batting																							Fielding						
Year Tm	Age	G	AB	H	2B	3B	HR	TB	R	RBI	GW	TBB	IBB	SO	HBP	SH	SF	SB	CS	SB%	GDP	Avg	OBP	SLG	Pos	G	PO	A	E	DP	FPct
1969 Min	35	2	8	0	0	0	0	0	0	1	0	0	0	0	0	0	1	0	0	—	0	.000	.000	.000	OF	2	6	0	0	0	1.000
1970 Min	36	3	2	0	0	0	0	0	0	0	0	1	0	1	0	0	0	0	0	—	0	.000	.333	.000	—						
LCS Totals		5	10	0	0	0	0	0	0	1	0	1	0	1	0	0	1	0	0	—	0	.000	.083	.000	OF	2	6	0	0	0	1.000
World Series		Batting																							Fielding						
Year Tm	Age	G	AB	H	2B	3B	HR	TB	R	RBI	GW	TBB	IBB	SO	HBP	SH	SF	SB	CS	SB%	GDP	Avg	OBP	SLG	Pos	G	PO	A	E	DP	FPct
1965 Min	31	5	16	2	1	0	1	6	3	2	1	2	0	9	0	0	0	1	0	1.00	0	.125	.222	.375	OF	5	11	0	0	0	1.000
Postseason Totals		10	26	2	1	0	1	6	3	3	1	3	0	10	0	0	1	1	0	1.00	0	.077	.167	.231	OF	7	17	0	0	0	1.000

ROBERTO ALOMAR—Nickname: Robby—Bats: Both; Throws: Right

Ht: 6'0"; Wt: 184 lbs; Born: 2/5/1968 in Ponce, Puerto Rico; Debut: 4/22/1988

Division Series		Batting																							Fielding						
Year Tm	Age	G	AB	H	2B	3B	HR	TB	R	RBI	GW	TBB	IBB	SO	HBP	SH	SF	SB	CS	SB%	GDP	Avg	OBP	SLG	Pos	G	PO	A	E	DP	FPct
1996 Bal	28	4	17	5	0	0	1	8	2	4	1	2	0	3	0	0	1	0	0	—	0	.294	.350	.471	2B	4	10	6	0	2	1.000
1997 Bal	29	4	10	3	2	0	0	5	1	2	1	1	1	1	0	1	0	0	0	—	0	.300	.364	.500	2B	4	3	6	0	0	1.000
DS Totals		8	27	8	2	0	1	13	3	6	2	3	1	4	0	1	1	0	0	—	0	.296	.355	.481	2B	8	13	12	0	2	1.000
LCS		Batting																							Fielding						
Year Tm	Age	G	AB	H	2B	3B	HR	TB	R	RBI	GW	TBB	IBB	SO	HBP	SH	SF	SB	CS	SB%	GDP	Avg	OBP	SLG	Pos	G	PO	A	E	DP	FPct
1991 Tor	23	5	19	9	0	0	0	9	3	4	0	2	0	3	0	2	0	2	0	1.00	0	.474	.524	.474	2B	5	14	9	0	2	1.000
1992 Tor	24	6	26	11	1	0	2	18	4	4	0	2	0	1	0	0	0	5	0	1.00	2	.423	.464	.692	2B	6	16	15	0	4	1.000
1993 Tor	25	6	24	7	1	0	0	8	3	4	0	4	0	3	0	0	0	4	0	1.00	1	.292	.393	.333	2B	6	14	19	0	5	1.000
1996 Bal	28	5	23	5	2	0	0	7	2	1	0	0	0	4	0	0	1	0	0	—	0	.217	.208	.304	2B	5	15	26	2	7	.953
1997 Bal	29	6	22	4	0	0	1	7	2	2	0	7	2	3	0	0	0	0	0	—	2	.182	.379	.318	2B	6	10	17	2	2	.931
LCS Totals		28	114	36	4	0	3	49	14	15	0	15	2	14	0	2	1	11	0	1.00	5	.316	.392	.430	2B	28	69	86	4	20	.975
World Series		Batting																							Fielding						
Year Tm	Age	G	AB	H	2B	3B	HR	TB	R	RBI	GW	TBB	IBB	SO	HBP	SH	SF	SB	CS	SB%	GDP	Avg	OBP	SLG	Pos	G	PO	A	E	DP	FPct
1992 Tor	24	6	24	5	1	0	0	6	3	0	0	3	0	3	0	0	0	3	0	1.00	1	.208	.296	.250	2B	6	5	12	0	0	1.000
1993 Tor	25	6	25	12	2	1	0	16	5	6	0	2	0	3	0	0	0	4	2	.67	1	.480	.519	.640	2B	6	9	21	2	2	.938
WS Totals		12	49	17	3	1	0	22	8	6	0	5	0	6	0	0	0	7	2	.78	2	.347	.407	.449	2B	12	14	33	2	2	.959
Postseason Totals		48	190	61	9	1	4	84	25	27	2	23	3	24	0	3	2	18	2	.90	7	.321	.391	.442	2B	48	96	131	6	24	.974

SANDY ALOMAR—Santos Alomar—Nickname: Iron Pony—Bats: Both; Throws: Right

Ht: 5'9"; Wt: 140 lbs; Born: 10/19/1943 in Salinas, Puerto Rico; Debut: 9/15/1964

LCS		Batting																							Fielding						
Year Tm	Age	G	AB	H	2B	3B	HR	TB	R	RBI	GW	TBB	IBB	SO	HBP	SH	SF	SB	CS	SB%	GDP	Avg	OBP	SLG	Pos	G	PO	A	E	DP	FPct
1976 NYA	32	2	1	0	0	0	0	0	0	0	0	0	0	0	0	0	0	0	1	.00	0	.000	.000	.000	—						

SANDY ALOMAR JR.—Santos Alomar Jr.—Bats: Right; Throws: Right

Ht: 6'5"; Wt: 200 lbs; Born: 6/18/1966 in Salinas, Puerto Rico; Debut: 9/30/1988

Division Series		Batting																							Fielding						
Year Tm	Age	G	AB	H	2B	3B	HR	TB	R	RBI	GW	TBB	IBB	SO	HBP	SH	SF	SB	CS	SB%	GDP	Avg	OBP	SLG	Pos	G	PO	A	E	DP	FPct
1995 Cle	29	3	11	2	1	0	0	3	1	1	0	0	0	1	0	1	0	0	0	—	0	.182	.182	.273	C	3	22	1	0	0	1.000
1996 Cle	30	4	16	2	0	0	0	2	0	3	0	0	0	2	0	0	0	0	1	.00	0	.125	.125	.125	C	4	40	4	1	0	.978
1997 Cle	31	5	19	6	1	0	2	13	4	5	0	0	0	2	0	0	0	0	0	—	0	.316	.316	.684	C	5	28	1	1	0	.967
DS Totals		12	46	10	2	0	2	18	5	9	0	0	0	5	0	1	0	0	1	.00	0	.217	.217	.391	C	12	90	6	2	0	.980
LCS		Batting																							Fielding						
Year Tm	Age	G	AB	H	2B	3B	HR	TB	R	RBI	GW	TBB	IBB	SO	HBP	SH	SF	SB	CS	SB%	GDP	Avg	OBP	SLG	Pos	G	PO	A	E	DP	FPct
1995 Cle	29	5	15	4	1	1	0	7	0	1	0	1	0	1	0	0	0	0	0	—	0	.267	.313	.467	C	5	30	3	1	0	.971
1997 Cle	31	6	24	3	0	0	1	6	3	4	1	1	0	3	0	0	0	0	0	—	1	.125	.160	.250	C	6	49	1	0	1	1.000
LCS Totals		11	39	7	1	1	1	13	3	5	1	2	0	4	0	0	0	0	0	—	1	.179	.220	.333	C	11	79	4	1	1	.988
World Series		Batting																							Fielding						
Year Tm	Age	G	AB	H	2B	3B	HR	TB	R	RBI	GW	TBB	IBB	SO	HBP	SH	SF	SB	CS	SB%	GDP	Avg	OBP	SLG	Pos	G	PO	A	E	DP	FPct
1995 Cle	29	5	15	3	2	0	0	5	0	1	0	0	0	2	0	0	0	0	0	—	0	.200	.200	.333	C	5	28	0	0	0	1.000
1997 Cle	31	7	30	11	1	0	2	18	5	10	0	2	1	3	0	0	0	0	0	—	2	.367	.406	.600	C	7	49	3	0	0	1.000
WS Totals		12	45	14	3	0	2	23	5	11	0	2	1	5	0	0	0	0	0	—	2	.311	.340	.511	C	12	77	3	0	0	1.000
Postseason Totals		35	130	31	6	1	5	54	13	25	1	4	1	14	0	1	0	0	1	.00	3	.238	.261	.415	C	35	246	13	3	1	.989

FELIPE ALOU—Felipe Rojas Alou—Bats: Right; Throws: Right

Ht: 6'0"; Wt: 195 lbs; Born: 5/12/1935 in Haina, Dominican Republic; Debut: 6/8/1958

LCS		Batting																							Fielding						
Year Tm	Age	G	AB	H	2B	3B	HR	TB	R	RBI	GW	TBB	IBB	SO	HBP	SH	SF	SB	CS	SB%	GDP	Avg	OBP	SLG	Pos	G	PO	A	E	DP	FPct
1969 Atl	34	1	1	0	0	0	0	0	0	0	0	0	0	0	0	0	0	0	0	—	0	.000	.000	.000	—						
World Series		Batting																							Fielding						
Year Tm	Age	G	AB	H	2B	3B	HR	TB	R	RBI	GW	TBB	IBB	SO	HBP	SH	SF	SB	CS	SB%	GDP	Avg	OBP	SLG	Pos	G	PO	A	E	DP	FPct
1962 SF	27	7	26	7	1	1	0	10	2	1	0	1	0	4	0	1	0	0	0	—	1	.269	.296	.385	OF	7	9	0	1	0	.900
Postseason Totals		8	27	7	1	1	0	10	2	1	0	1	0	4	0	1	0	0	0	—	1	.259	.286	.370	OF	7	9	0	1	0	.900

JESUS ALOU—Jesus Maria Rojas Alou—Nickname: Jay—Bats: Right; Throws: Right

Ht: 6'2"; Wt: 190 lbs; Born: 3/24/1942 in Haina, Dominican Republic; Debut: 9/10/1963

LCS		Batting																							Fielding						
Year Tm	Age	G	AB	H	2B	3B	HR	TB	R	RBI	GW	TBB	IBB	SO	HBP	SH	SF	SB	CS	SB%	GDP	Avg	OBP	SLG	Pos	G	PO	A	E	DP	FPct
1973 Oak	31	4	6	2	0	0	0	2	0	1	0	0	0	1	0	0	0	0	0	—	0	.333	.333	.333	—						
1974 Oak	32	1	1	1	0	0	0	1	0	0	0	0	0	0	0	0	0	0	0	—	0	1.000	1.000	1.000	—						
LCS Totals		5	7	3	0	0	0	3	0	1	0	0	0	1	0	0	0	0	0	—	0	.429	.429	.429	—	0	0	0	0	0	—
World Series		Batting																							Fielding						
Year Tm	Age	G	AB	H	2B	3B	HR	TB	R	RBI	GW	TBB	IBB	SO	HBP	SH	SF	SB	CS	SB%	GDP	Avg	OBP	SLG	Pos	G	PO	A	E	DP	FPct
1973 Oak	31	7	19	3	1	0	0	4	0	3	0	0	0	0	0	0	1	0	0	—	0	.158	.150	.211	OF	6	5	0	0	0	1.000
1974 Oak	32	1	1	0	0	0	0	0	0	0	0	0	0	1	0	0	0	0	0	—	0	.000	.000	.000	—						
WS Totals		8	20	3	1	0	0	4	0	3	0	0	0	1	0	0	1	0	0	—	0	.150	.143	.200	OF	6	5	0	0	0	1.000
Postseason Totals		13	27	6	1	0	0	7	0	4	0	0	0	2	0	0	1	0	0	—	0	.222	.214	.259	OF	6	5	0	0	0	1.000

MATTY ALOU—Mateo Rojas Alou—Bats: Left; Throws: Left

Ht: 5'9"; Wt: 160 lbs; Born: 12/22/1938 in Haina, Dominican Republic; Debut: 9/26/1960

Year Tm	Age	G	AB	H	2B	3B	HR	TB	R	RBI	GW	TBB	IBB	SO	HBP	SH	SF	SB	CS	SB%	GDP	Avg	OBP	SLG	Pos	G	PO	A	E	DP	FPct
LCS		Batting																							Fielding						
1970 Pit	31	3	12	3	1	0	0	4	1	0	0	2	1	1	0	0	0	0	1	.00	0	.250	.357	.333	OF	3	6	0	0	0	1.000
1972 Oak	33	5	21	8	4	0	0	12	2	2	0	0	0	2	1	1	0	1	1	.50	1	.381	.409	.571	OF	5	8	0	0	0	1.000
LCS Totals		8	33	11	5	0	0	16	3	2	0	2	1	3	1	1	0	1	2	.33	1	.333	.389	.485	OF	8	14	0	0	0	1.000
World Series		Batting																							Fielding						
1962 SF	23	6	12	4	1	0	0	5	2	1	1	0	0	1	0	0	0	0	0	—	0	.333	.333	.417	OF	4	2	0	0	0	1.000
1972 Oak	33	7	24	1	0	0	0	1	0	0	0	3	1	0	0	1	0	1	0	1.00	0	.042	.148	.042	OF	7	11	1	1	1	.923
WS Totals		13	36	5	1	0	0	6	2	1	1	3	1	1	0	1	0	1	0	1.00	0	.139	.205	.167	OF	11	13	1	1	1	.933
Postseason Totals		21	69	16	6	0	0	22	5	3	1	5	2	4	1	2	0	2	2	.50	1	.232	.293	.319	OF	19	27	1	1	1	.966

MOISES ALOU—Moises Rojas Alou—Bats: Right; Throws: Right

Ht: 6'3"; Wt: 175 lbs; Born: 7/3/1966 in Atlanta, Georgia; Debut: 7/26/1990

Year Tm	Age	G	AB	H	2B	3B	HR	TB	R	RBI	GW	TBB	IBB	SO	HBP	SH	SF	SB	CS	SB%	GDP	Avg	OBP	SLG	Pos	G	PO	A	E	DP	FPct
Division Series		Batting																							Fielding						
1997 Fla	31	3	14	3	1	0	0	4	1	1	1	0	0	3	0	0	0	0	0	—	1	.214	.214	.286	OF	3	5	0	0	0	1.000
LCS		Batting																							Fielding						
1997 Fla	31	5	15	1	1	0	0	2	0	5	1	1	1	3	0	0	0	0	0	—	1	.067	.125	.133	OF	4	3	0	0	0	1.000
World Series		Batting																							Fielding						
1997 Fla	31	7	28	9	2	0	3	20	6	9	2	3	0	6	0	0	0	1	0	1.00	0	.321	.387	.714	OF	7	11	0	0	0	1.000
Postseason Totals		15	57	13	4	0	3	26	7	15	4	4	1	12	0	0	0	1	0	1.00	2	.228	.279	.456	OF	14	19	0	0	0	1.000

NICK ALTROCK—Nicholas Altrock—Throws: Left; Bats: Both

Ht: 5'10"; Wt: 197 lbs; Born: 9/15/1876 in Cincinnati, Ohio; Debut: 7/14/1898; Died: 1/20/1965

Year Tm	Age	G	GS	CG	GF	IP	BFP	H	R	ER	HR	SH	SF	HB	TBB	IBB	SO	WP	Bk	W	L	Pct	ShO	Sv-Op	Hld	OAvg	OOBP	ERA
World Series		Pitching																										
1906 ChA	30	2	2	2	0	18.0	65	11	2	2	0	7	0	0	2	0	5	1	0	1	1	.500	0	0- 0	0	.196	.224	1.00

Year Tm	Age	G	AB	H	2B	3B	HR	TB	R	RBI	GW	TBB	IBB	SO	HBP	SH	SF	SB	CS	SB%	GDP	Avg	OBP	SLG	Pos	G	PO	A	E	DP	FPct
World Series		Batting																							Fielding						
1906 ChA	30	2	4	1	0	0	0	1	0	0	0	1	0	1	0	0	0	0	0	—	0	.250	.400	.250	P	2	6	11	0	1	1.000

WILSON ALVAREZ—Wilson Eduardo Alvarez—Throws: Left; Bats: Left

Ht: 6'1"; Wt: 175 lbs; Born: 3/24/1970 in Maracaibo, Venezuela; Debut: 7/24/1989

Year Tm	Age	G	GS	CG	GF	IP	BFP	H	R	ER	HR	SH	SF	HB	TBB	IBB	SO	WP	Bk	W	L	Pct	ShO	Sv-Op	Hld	OAvg	OOBP	ERA
Division Series		Pitching																										
1997 SF	27	1	1	0	0	6.0	27	6	4	4	1	0	0	0	4	0	4	0	0	0	1	.000	0	0- 0	0	.261	.370	6.00
LCS		Pitching																										
1993 ChA	23	1	1	1	0	9.0	33	7	1	1	0	0	0	0	2	0	6	0	0	1	0	1.000	0	0- 0	0	.226	.273	1.00
Postseason Totals		2	2	1	0	15.0	120	13	5	5	1	0	0	0	6	0	10	0	0	1	1	.500	0	0-0	0	.241	.317	3.00

Year Tm	Age	G	AB	H	2B	3B	HR	TB	R	RBI	GW	TBB	IBB	SO	HBP	SH	SF	SB	CS	SB%	GDP	Avg	OBP	SLG	Pos	G	PO	A	E	DP	FPct
Division Series		Batting																							Fielding						
1997 SF	27	1	2	0	0	0	0	0	0	0	0	0	0	0	0	0	0	0	0	—	0	.000	.000	.000	P	1	0	0	0	0	—
LCS		Batting																							Fielding						
1993 ChA	23	1	0	0	0	0	0	0	0	0	0	0	0	0	0	0	0	0	0	—	0	—	—	—	P	1	0	2	0	1	1.000
Postseason Totals		2	2	0	0	0	0	0	0	0	0	0	0	0	0	0	0	0	0	—	0	.000	.000	.000	P	2	0	2	0	1	1.000

BRANT ALYEA—Garrabrant Ryerson Alyea—Bats: Right; Throws: Right

Ht: 6'3"; Wt: 215 lbs; Born: 12/8/1940 in Passaic, New Jersey; Debut: 9/11/1965

Year Tm	Age	G	AB	H	2B	3B	HR	TB	R	RBI	GW	TBB	IBB	SO	HBP	SH	SF	SB	CS	SB%	GDP	Avg	OBP	SLG	Pos	G	PO	A	E	DP	FPct
LCS		Batting																							Fielding						
1970 Min	29	3	7	0	0	0	0	0	1	0	0	2	0	3	0	0	0	0	0	—	0	.000	.222	.000	OF	2	0	0	0	0	—

RICH AMARAL—Richard Louis Amaral—Bats: Right; Throws: Right

Ht: 6'0"; Wt: 175 lbs; Born: 4/1/1962 in Visalia, California; Debut: 5/27/1991

Year Tm	Age	G	AB	H	2B	3B	HR	TB	R	RBI	GW	TBB	IBB	SO	HBP	SH	SF	SB	CS	SB%	GDP	Avg	OBP	SLG	Pos	G	PO	A	E	DP	FPct
Division Series		Batting																							Fielding						
1997 Sea	35	2	4	2	0	0	0	2	2	0	0	0	0	1	0	0	0	0	0	—	0	.500	.500	.500	1B	2	7	2	0	0	1.000
LCS		Batting																							Fielding						
1995 Sea	33	2	2	0	0	0	0	0	0	0	0	0	0	1	0	0	0	0	0	—	0	.000	.000	.000	—						
Postseason Totals		4	6	2	0	0	0	2	2	0	0	0	0	2	0	0	0	0	0	—	0	.333	.333	.333	1B	2	7	2	0	0	1.000

RUBEN AMARO—Bats: Both; Throws: Right

Ht: 5'10"; Wt: 170 lbs; Born: 2/12/1965 in Philadelphia, Pennsylvania; Debut: 6/8/1991

Year Tm	Age	G	AB	H	2B	3B	HR	TB	R	RBI	GW	TBB	IBB	SO	HBP	SH	SF	SB	CS	SB%	GDP	Avg	OBP	SLG	Pos	G	PO	A	E	DP	FPct
LCS		Batting																							Fielding						
1995 Cle	30	3	1	0	0	0	0	0	1	0	0	0	0	0	0	0	0	0	0	—	0	.000	.000	.000	—						
World Series		Batting																							Fielding						
1995 Cle	30	2	2	0	0	0	0	0	0	0	0	0	0	1	0	0	0	0	0	—	0	.000	.000	.000	OF	1	0	0	0	0	—
Postseason Totals		5	3	0	0	0	0	0	1	0	0	0	0	1	0	0	0	0	0	—	0	.000	.000	.000	OF	1	0	0	0	0	—

RED AMES—Leon Kessling Ames—Throws: Right; Bats: Both

Ht: 5'10"; Wt: 185 lbs; Born: 8/2/1882 in Warren, Ohio; Debut: 9/14/1903; Died: 10/8/1936

Year Tm	Age	G	GS	CG	GF	IP	BFP	H	R	ER	HR	SH	SF	HB	TBB	IBB	SO	WP	Bk	W	L	Pct	ShO	Sv-Op	Hld	OAvg	OOBP	ERA
World Series		Pitching																										
1905 NYG	23	1	0	0	1	1.0	5	1	0	0	0	0	0	0	1	0	1	0	0	0	0	—	0	0- 0	0	.250	.400	0.00
1911 NYG	29	2	1	0	0	8.0	33	6	5	2	0	1	0	0	1	0	6	0	0	0	1	.000	0	0- 0	0	.194	.219	2.25
1912 NYG	30	1	0	0	1	2.0	10	3	1	1	0	1	0	0	1	0	0	0	0	0	0	—	0	0- 0	0	.375	.444	4.50
WS Totals		4	1	0	2	11.0	96	10	6	3	0	2	0	0	3	0	7	0	0	0	1	.000	0	0-0	0	.233	.283	2.45

Year Tm	Age	G	AB	H	2B	3B	HR	TB	R	RBI	GW	TBB	IBB	SO	HBP	SH	SF	SB	CS	SB%	GDP	Avg	OBP	SLG	Pos	G	PO	A	E	DP	FPct
World Series		Batting																							Fielding						
1905 NYG	23	1	0	0	0	0	0	0	0	0	0	0	0	0	0	0	0	0	0	—	0	—	—	—	P	1	0	1	0	0	1.000
1911 NYG	29	2	2	1	0	0	0	1	0	0	0	0	0	1	0	0	0	0	0	—	0	.500	.500	.500	P	2	0	1	1	0	.500
1912 NYG	30	1	0	0	0	0	0	0	0	0	0	0	0	0	0	0	0	0	0	—	0	—	—	—	P	1	0	1	0	0	1.000
WS Totals		4	2	1	0	0	0	1	0	0	0	0	0	1	0	0	0	0	0	—	0	.500	.500	.500	P	4	0	3	1	0	.750

SANDY AMOROS—Edmundo Amoros—Bats: Left; Throws: Left

Ht: 5'7"; Wt: 170 lbs; Born: 1/30/1930 in Havana, Cuba; Debut: 8/22/1952; Died: 6/27/1992

Year Tm	Age	G	AB	H	2B	3B	HR	TB	R	RBI	GW	TBB	IBB	SO	HBP	SH	SF	SB	CS	SB%	GDP	Avg	OBP	SLG	Pos	G	PO	A	E	DP	FPct
World Series		Batting																							Fielding						
1952 Bro	22	1	0	0	0	0	0	0	0	0	0	0	0	0	0	0	0	0	0	—	0	—	—	—	—						
1955 Bro	25	5	12	4	0	0	1	7	3	3	1	4	1	4	1	0	0	0	0	—	0	.333	.529	.583	OF	5	10	1	0	1	1.000
1956 Bro	26	6	19	1	0	0	0	1	1	1	0	2	0	4	0	0	0	0	0	—	0	.053	.143	.053	OF	6	10	0	0	0	1.000
WS Totals		12	31	5	0	0	1	8	4	4	1	6	1	8	1	0	0	0	0	—	0	.161	.316	.258	OF	11	20	1	0	1	1.000

LARRY ANDERSEN—Larry Eugene Andersen—Throws: Right; Bats: Right

Ht: 6'3"; Wt: 200 lbs; Born: 5/6/1953 in Portland, Oregon; Debut: 9/5/1975

LCS — Pitching

Year Tm	Age	G	GS	CG	GF	IP	BFP	H	R	ER	HR	SH	SF	HB	TBB	IBB	SO	WP	Bk	W	L	Pct	ShO	Sv-Op	Hld	OAvg	OOBP	ERA
1986 Hou	33	2	0	0	0	5.0	19	1	0	0	0	0	0	0	2	1	3	0	0	0	0	—	0	0- 0	0	.059	.158	0.00
1990 Bos	37	3	0	0	1	3.0	15	3	2	2	0	0	1	0	3	0	3	0	0	0	1	.000	0	0- 1	0	.273	.400	6.00
1993 Phi	40	3	0	0	2	2.1	12	4	4	4	0	0	0	0	1	1	3	0	0	0	0	—	0	1- 1	0	.364	.417	15.43
LCS Totals		8	0	0	3	10.1	92	8	6	6	0	0	1	0	6	2	9	0	0	0	1	.000	0	1-2	0	.205	.304	5.23

World Series — Pitching

Year Tm	Age	G	GS	CG	GF	IP	BFP	H	R	ER	HR	SH	SF	HB	TBB	IBB	SO	WP	Bk	W	L	Pct	ShO	Sv-Op	Hld	OAvg	OOBP	ERA
1983 Phi	30	2	0	0	1	4.0	15	4	1	1	0	0	0	0	0	0	1	0	0	0	0	—	0	0- 0	0	.267	.267	2.25
1993 Phi	40	4	0	0	1	3.2	20	5	5	5	0	0	0	1	3	1	3	0	0	0	0	—	0	0- 0	1	.313	.450	12.27
WS Totals		6	0	0	2	7.2	70	9	6	6	0	0	0	1	3	1	4	0	0	0	0	—	0	0-0	1	.290	.371	7.04
Postseason Totals		14	0	0	5	18.0	162	17	12	12	0	0	1	1	9	3	13	0	0	0	1	.000	0	1-2	1	.243	.333	6.00

LCS — Batting / Fielding

Year Tm	Age	G	AB	H	2B	3B	HR	TB	R	RBI	GW	TBB	IBB	SO	HBP	SH	SF	SB	CS	SB%	GDP	Avg	OBP	SLG	Pos	G	PO	A	E	DP	FPct
1986 Hou	33	2	0	0	0	0	0	0	0	0	0	0	0	0	0	0	0	0	0	—	0	—	—	—	P	2	1	1	0	0	1.000
1990 Bos	37	3	0	0	0	0	0	0	0	0	0	0	0	0	0	0	0	0	0	—	0	—	—	—	P	3	1	0	0	0	1.000
1993 Phi	40	3	0	0	0	0	0	0	0	0	0	0	0	0	0	0	0	0	0	—	0	—	—	—	P	3	0	1	0	0	1.000
LCS Totals		8	0	0	0	0	0	0	0	0	0	0	0	0	0	0	0	0	0	—	0	—	—	—	P	8	2	2	0	0	1.000

World Series — Batting / Fielding

Year Tm	Age	G	AB	H	2B	3B	HR	TB	R	RBI	GW	TBB	IBB	SO	HBP	SH	SF	SB	CS	SB%	GDP	Avg	OBP	SLG	Pos	G	PO	A	E	DP	FPct
1983 Phi	30	2	0	0	0	0	0	0	0	0	0	0	0	0	0	0	0	0	0	—	0	—	—	—	P	2	1	1	0	1	1.000
1993 Phi	40	4	0	0	0	0	0	0	0	0	0	0	0	0	0	0	0	0	0	—	0	—	—	—	P	4	0	0	0	0	—
WS Totals		6	0	0	0	0	0	0	0	0	0	0	0	0	0	0	0	0	0	—	0	—	—	—	P	6	1	1	0	1	1.000
Postseason Totals		14	0	0	0	0	0	0	0	0	0	0	0	0	0	0	0	0	0	—	0	—	—	—	P	14	3	3	0	1	1.000

BRADY ANDERSON—Brady Kevin Anderson—Bats: Left; Throws: Left

Ht: 6'1"; Wt: 170 lbs; Born: 1/18/1964 in Silver Spring, Maryland; Debut: 4/4/1988

Division Series — Batting / Fielding

Year Tm	Age	G	AB	H	2B	3B	HR	TB	R	RBI	GW	TBB	IBB	SO	HBP	SH	SF	SB	CS	SB%	GDP	Avg	OBP	SLG	Pos	G	PO	A	E	DP	FPct
1996 Bal	32	4	17	5	0	0	2	11	3	4	0	2	0	3	1	0	1	0	1	.00	0	.294	.381	.647	OF	4	7	0	0	0	1.000
1997 Bal	33	4	17	6	1	0	1	10	3	4	1	1	0	4	0	0	0	1	0	1.00	0	.353	.389	.588	OF	4	6	0	0	0	1.000
DS Totals		8	34	11	1	0	3	21	6	8	1	3	0	7	1	0	1	1	1	.50	0	.324	.385	.618	OF	8	13	0	0	0	1.000

LCS — Batting / Fielding

Year Tm	Age	G	AB	H	2B	3B	HR	TB	R	RBI	GW	TBB	IBB	SO	HBP	SH	SF	SB	CS	SB%	GDP	Avg	OBP	SLG	Pos	G	PO	A	E	DP	FPct
1996 Bal	32	5	21	4	1	0	1	8	5	1	0	3	0	5	0	0	0	0	0	—	0	.190	.292	.381	OF	5	8	0	0	0	1.000
1997 Bal	33	6	25	9	2	0	2	17	5	3	1	4	0	4	0	0	0	2	0	1.00	0	.360	.448	.680	OF	6	13	0	1	0	.929
LCS Totals		11	46	13	3	0	3	25	10	4	1	7	0	9	0	0	0	2	0	1.00	0	.283	.377	.543	OF	11	21	0	1	0	.955
Postseason Totals		19	80	24	4	0	6	46	16	12	2	10	0	16	1	0	1	3	1	.75	0	.300	.380	.575	OF	19	34	0	1	0	.971

BRIAN ANDERSON—Brian James Anderson—Throws: Left; Bats: Both

Ht: 6'1"; Wt: 195 lbs; Born: 4/26/1972 in Geneva, Ohio; Debut: 9/10/1993

LCS — Pitching

Year Tm	Age	G	GS	CG	GF	IP	BFP	H	R	ER	HR	SH	SF	HB	TBB	IBB	SO	WP	Bk	W	L	Pct	ShO	Sv-Op	Hld	OAvg	OOBP	ERA
1997 Cle	25	3	0	0	1	6.1	24	1	1	1	0	0	0	0	3	1	7	0	0	1	0	1.000	0	0- 0	0	.048	.167	1.42

World Series — Pitching

Year Tm	Age	G	GS	CG	GF	IP	BFP	H	R	ER	HR	SH	SF	HB	TBB	IBB	SO	WP	Bk	W	L	Pct	ShO	Sv-Op	Hld	OAvg	OOBP	ERA
1997 Cle	25	3	0	0	1	3.2	13	2	1	1	0	0	0	0	0	0	2	0	0	0	0	—	0	1- 1	2	.154	.154	2.45
Postseason Totals		6	0	0	2	10.0	74	3	2	2	0	0	0	0	3	1	9	0	0	1	0	1.000	0	1-1	2	.088	.162	1.80

LCS — Batting / Fielding

Year Tm	Age	G	AB	H	2B	3B	HR	TB	R	RBI	GW	TBB	IBB	SO	HBP	SH	SF	SB	CS	SB%	GDP	Avg	OBP	SLG	Pos	G	PO	A	E	DP	FPct
1997 Cle	25	3	0	0	0	0	0	0	0	0	0	0	0	0	0	0	0	0	0	—	0	—	—	—	P	3	1	2	0	0	1.000

World Series — Batting / Fielding

Year Tm	Age	G	AB	H	2B	3B	HR	TB	R	RBI	GW	TBB	IBB	SO	HBP	SH	SF	SB	CS	SB%	GDP	Avg	OBP	SLG	Pos	G	PO	A	E	DP	FPct
1997 Cle	25	3	0	0	0	0	0	0	0	0	0	0	0	0	0	0	0	0	0	—	0	—	—	—	P	3	0	1	0	0	1.000
Postseason Totals		6	0	0	0	0	0	0	0	0	0	0	0	0	0	0	0	0	0	—	0	—	—	—	P	6	1	3	0	0	1.000

DAVE ANDERSON—David Carter Anderson—Bats: Right; Throws: Right

Ht: 6'2"; Wt: 185 lbs; Born: 8/1/1960 in Louisville, Kentucky; Debut: 5/8/1983

LCS — Batting / Fielding

Year Tm	Age	G	AB	H	2B	3B	HR	TB	R	RBI	GW	TBB	IBB	SO	HBP	SH	SF	SB	CS	SB%	GDP	Avg	OBP	SLG	Pos	G	PO	A	E	DP	FPct
1985 LA	25	4	5	0	0	0	0	0	1	0	0	3	0	1	0	0	0	0	0	—	0	.000	.375	.000	SS	3	3	4	0	1	1.000
																									3B	1	0	0	0	0	—

World Series — Batting / Fielding

Year Tm	Age	G	AB	H	2B	3B	HR	TB	R	RBI	GW	TBB	IBB	SO	HBP	SH	SF	SB	CS	SB%	GDP	Avg	OBP	SLG	Pos	G	PO	A	E	DP	FPct
1988 LA	28	1	1	0	0	0	0	0	0	0	0	0	0	1	0	0	0	0	0	—	0	.000	.000	.000	—						
Postseason Totals		5	6	0	0	0	0	0	1	0	0	3	0	2	0	0	0	0	0	—	0	.000	.333	.000	SS	3	3	4	0	1	1.000

FRED ANDERSON—John Frederick Anderson—Nickname: Spitball—Throws: Right; Bats: Right

Ht: 6'2"; Wt: 180 lbs; Born: 12/11/1885 in Calahan, North Carolina; Debut: 9/25/1909; Died: 11/8/1957

World Series — Pitching

Year Tm	Age	G	GS	CG	GF	IP	BFP	H	R	ER	HR	SH	SF	HB	TBB	IBB	SO	WP	Bk	W	L	Pct	ShO	Sv-Op	Hld	OAvg	OOBP	ERA
1917 NYG	31	1	0	0	0	2.0	11	5	4	4	0	0	0	0	0	0	3	0	0	0	1	.000	0	0- 0	0	.455	.455	18.00

World Series — Batting / Fielding

Year Tm	Age	G	AB	H	2B	3B	HR	TB	R	RBI	GW	TBB	IBB	SO	HBP	SH	SF	SB	CS	SB%	GDP	Avg	OBP	SLG	Pos	G	PO	A	E	DP	FPct
1917 NYG	31	1	0	0	0	0	0	0	0	0	0	0	0	0	0	0	0	0	0	—	0	—	—	—	P	1	0	1	0	0	1.000

JIM ANDERSON—James Lea Anderson—Bats: Right; Throws: Right

Ht: 6'0"; Wt: 170 lbs; Born: 2/23/1957 in Los Angeles, California; Debut: 7/2/1978

LCS — Batting / Fielding

Year Tm	Age	G	AB	H	2B	3B	HR	TB	R	RBI	GW	TBB	IBB	SO	HBP	SH	SF	SB	CS	SB%	GDP	Avg	OBP	SLG	Pos	G	PO	A	E	DP	FPct
1979 Cal	22	4	11	1	0	0	0	1	0	0	0	0	0	1	0	0	0	0	0	—	2	.091	.091	.091	SS	4	3	11	0	2	1.000

IVY ANDREWS—Ivy Paul Andrews—Nickname: Poison—Throws: Right; Bats: Right

Ht: 6'1"; Wt: 200 lbs; Born: 5/6/1907 in Dora, Alabama; Debut: 8/15/1931; Died: 11/24/1970

World Series — Pitching

Year Tm	Age	G	GS	CG	GF	IP	BFP	H	R	ER	HR	SH	SF	HB	TBB	IBB	SO	WP	Bk	W	L	Pct	ShO	Sv-Op	Hld	OAvg	OOBP	ERA
1937 NYA	30	1	0	0	0	5.2	26	6	2	2	0	0	0	0	4	1	1	0	0	0	0	—	0	0- 0	0	.273	.385	3.18

World Series — Batting / Fielding

Year Tm	Age	G	AB	H	2B	3B	HR	TB	R	RBI	GW	TBB	IBB	SO	HBP	SH	SF	SB	CS	SB%	GDP	Avg	OBP	SLG	Pos	G	PO	A	E	DP	FPct
1937 NYA	30	1	2	0	0	0	0	0	0	0	0	0	0	1	0	0	0	0	0	—	0	.000	.000	.000	P	1	0	1	0	0	1.000

MIKE ANDREWS—Michael Jay Andrews—Bats: Right; Throws: Right

Ht: 6'3"; Wt: 195 lbs; Born: 7/9/1943 in Los Angeles, California; Debut: 9/18/1966

LCS — Batting / Fielding

Year Tm	Age	G	AB	H	2B	3B	HR	TB	R	RBI	GW	TBB	IBB	SO	HBP	SH	SF	SB	CS	SB%	GDP	Avg	OBP	SLG	Pos	G	PO	A	E	DP	FPct
1973 Oak	30	2	1	0	0	0	0	0	0	0	0	0	0	0	0	1	0	0	0	—	0	.000	.000	.000	1B	1	1	0	0	0	1.000

World Series — Batting / Fielding

Year Tm	Age	G	AB	H	2B	3B	HR	TB	R	RBI	GW	TBB	IBB	SO	HBP	SH	SF	SB	CS	SB%	GDP	Avg	OBP	SLG	Pos	G	PO	A	E	DP	FPct
1967 Bos	24	5	13	4	0	0	0	4	2	1	0	0	0	1	0	2	0	0	0	—	0	.308	.308	.308	2B	3	2	6	0	0	1.000
1973 Oak	30	2	3	0	0	0	0	0	0	0	0	1	0	1	0	0	0	0	0	—	0	.000	.250	.000	2B	1	1	0	2	0	.333
WS Totals		7	16	4	0	0	0	4	2	1	0	1	0	2	0	2	0	0	0	—	0	.250	.294	.250	2B	4	3	6	2	0	.818
Postseason Totals		9	17	4	0	0	0	4	2	1	0	1	0	2	0	3	0	0	0	—	0	.235	.278	.235	2B	4	3	6	2	0	.818

JOAQUIN ANDUJAR—Throws: Right; Bats: Both

Ht: 6'0"; Wt: 170 lbs; Born: 12/21/1952 in San Pedro de Macoris, Dominican Republic; Debut: 4/8/1976

LCS		Pitching																										
Year Tm	Age	G	GS	CG	GF	IP	BFP	H	R	ER	HR	SH	SF	HB	TBB	IBB	SO	WP	Bk	W	L	Pct	ShO	Sv-Op	Hld	OAvg	OOBP	ERA
1980 Hou	27	1	0	0	1	1.0	4	0	0	0	0	0	0	0	1	0	0	0	0	0	0	—	0	1- 1	0	.000	.250	0.00
1982 StL	29	1	1	0	0	6.2	25	6	2	2	0	0	0	0	2	0	4	2	1	1	0	1.000	0	0- 0	0	.261	.320	2.70
1985 StL	32	2	2	0	0	10.1	50	14	10	8	2	0	1	0	4	2	9	0	0	0	1	.000	0	0- 0	0	.311	.360	6.97
LCS Totals		4	3	0	1	18.0	158	20	12	10	2	0	1	0	7	2	13	2	1	1	1	.500	0	1-1	0	.282	.342	5.00
World Series		Pitching																										
Year Tm	Age	G	GS	CG	GF	IP	BFP	H	R	ER	HR	SH	SF	HB	TBB	IBB	SO	WP	Bk	W	L	Pct	ShO	Sv-Op	Hld	OAvg	OOBP	ERA
1982 StL	29	2	2	0	0	13.1	49	10	3	2	1	0	1	0	1	0	4	0	0	2	0	1.000	0	0- 0	0	.213	.224	1.35
1985 StL	32	2	1	0	0	4.0	24	10	4	4	1	1	0	0	4	1	3	0	0	0	1	.000	0	0- 0	0	.526	.609	9.00
WS Totals		4	3	0	0	17.1	146	20	7	6	2	1	1	0	5	1	7	0	0	2	1	.667	0	0-0	0	.303	.347	3.12
Postseason Totals		8	6	0	1	35.1	304	40	19	16	4	1	2	0	12	3	20	2	1	3	2	.600	0	1-1	0	.292	.344	4.08

LCS		Batting																							Fielding						
Year Tm	Age	G	AB	H	2B	3B	HR	TB	R	RBI	GW	TBB	IBB	SO	HBP	SH	SF	SB	CS	SB%	GDP	Avg	OBP	SLG	Pos	G	PO	A	E	DP	FPct
1980 Hou	27	1	0	0	0	0	0	0	0	0	0	0	0	0	0	0	0	0	0	—	0	—	—	—	P	1	0	0	0	0	—
1982 StL	29	1	1	0	0	0	0	0	0	0	0	0	0	1	0	2	0	0	0	—	0	.000	.000	.000	P	1	0	1	0	0	1.000
1985 StL	32	2	4	1	1	0	0	2	1	0	0	0	0	1	0	0	0	0	0	—	1	.250	.250	.500	P	2	0	0	2	0	.000
LCS Totals		4	5	1	1	0	0	2	1	0	0	0	0	2	0	2	0	0	0	—	1	.200	.200	.400	P	4	0	1	2	0	.333
World Series		Batting																							Fielding						
Year Tm	Age	G	AB	H	2B	3B	HR	TB	R	RBI	GW	TBB	IBB	SO	HBP	SH	SF	SB	CS	SB%	GDP	Avg	OBP	SLG	Pos	G	PO	A	E	DP	FPct
1982 StL	29	2	0	0	0	0	0	0	0	0	0	0	0	0	0	0	0	0	0	—	0	—	—	—	P	2	1	2	1	0	.750
1985 StL	32	2	1	0	0	0	0	0	0	0	0	0	0	1	0	0	0	0	0	—	0	.000	.000	.000	P	2	0	1	0	0	1.000
WS Totals		4	1	0	0	0	0	0	0	0	0	0	0	1	0	0	0	0	0	—	0	.000	.000	.000	P	4	1	3	1	0	.800
Postseason Totals		8	6	1	1	0	0	2	1	0	0	0	0	3	0	2	0	0	0	—	1	.167	.167	.333	P	8	1	4	3	0	.625

ERIC ANTHONY—Eric Todd Anthony—Bats: Left; Throws: Left

Ht: 6'2"; Wt: 195 lbs; Born: 11/8/1967 in San Diego, California; Debut: 7/29/1989

LCS		Batting																							Fielding						
Year Tm	Age	G	AB	H	2B	3B	HR	TB	R	RBI	GW	TBB	IBB	SO	HBP	SH	SF	SB	CS	SB%	GDP	Avg	OBP	SLG	Pos	G	PO	A	E	DP	FPct
1995 Cin	27	2	1	0	0	0	0	0	0	0	0	1	0	1	0	0	0	0	0	—	0	.000	.500	.000	—						

JOHNNY ANTONELLI—John August Antonelli—Throws: Left; Bats: Left

Ht: 6'1"; Wt: 185 lbs; Born: 4/12/1930 in Rochester, New York; Debut: 7/4/1948

World Series		Pitching																										
Year Tm	Age	G	GS	CG	GF	IP	BFP	H	R	ER	HR	SH	SF	HB	TBB	IBB	SO	WP	Bk	W	L	Pct	ShO	Sv-Op	Hld	OAvg	OOBP	ERA
1954 NYG	24	2	1	1	1	10.2	47	8	1	1	1	1	0	0	7	0	12	0	0	1	0	1.000	0	1- 1	0	.205	.326	0.84

World Series		Batting																							Fielding						
Year Tm	Age	G	AB	H	2B	3B	HR	TB	R	RBI	GW	TBB	IBB	SO	HBP	SH	SF	SB	CS	SB%	GDP	Avg	OBP	SLG	Pos	G	PO	A	E	DP	FPct
1954 NYG	24	2	3	0	0	0	0	0	0	1	1	0	0	0	0	0	0	0	0	—	0	.000	.000	.000	P	2	0	1	0	0	1.000

LUIS APARICIO (HOF 1984-W)—Luis Ernesto Aparicio—Nickname: Little Louie—Bats: Right; Throws: Right

Ht: 5'9"; Wt: 160 lbs; Born: 4/29/1934 in Maracaibo, Venezuela; Debut: 4/17/1956

World Series		Batting																							Fielding						
Year Tm	Age	G	AB	H	2B	3B	HR	TB	R	RBI	GW	TBB	IBB	SO	HBP	SH	SF	SB	CS	SB%	GDP	Avg	OBP	SLG	Pos	G	PO	A	E	DP	FPct
1959 ChA	25	6	26	8	1	0	0	9	1	0	0	2	0	3	0	1	0	1	1	.50	0	.308	.357	.346	SS	6	10	16	2	2	.929
1966 Bal	32	4	16	4	1	0	0	5	0	2	0	0	0	0	0	0	0	0	2	.00	0	.250	.250	.313	SS	4	9	8	0	2	1.000
WS Totals		10	42	12	2	0	0	14	1	2	0	2	0	3	0	1	0	1	3	.25	0	.286	.318	.333	SS	10	19	24	2	4	.956

JIMMY ARCHER—James Patrick Archer—Bats: Right; Throws: Right

Ht: 5'10"; Wt: 168 lbs; Born: 5/13/1883 in Dublin, Ireland; Debut: 9/6/1904; Died: 3/29/1958

World Series		Batting																							Fielding						
Year Tm	Age	G	AB	H	2B	3B	HR	TB	R	RBI	GW	TBB	IBB	SO	HBP	SH	SF	SB	CS	SB%	GDP	Avg	OBP	SLG	Pos	G	PO	A	E	DP	FPct
1907 Det	24	1	3	0	0	0	0	0	0	0	0	0	0	1	0	0	0	0	0	—	0	.000	.000	.000	C	1	4	1	0	0	1.000
1910 ChN	27	3	11	2	1	0	0	3	1	0	0	0	0	4	0	0	0	0	0	—	0	.182	.182	.273	1B	1	9	0	0	1	1.000
																									C	2	18	4	0	1	1.000
WS Totals		4	14	2	1	0	0	3	1	0	0	0	0	5	0	0	0	0	0	—	0	.143	.143	.214	C	3	22	5	0	1	1.000

ALEX ARIAS—Alejandro Arias—Bats: Right; Throws: Right

Ht: 6'3"; Wt: 185 lbs; Born: 11/20/1967 in New York, New York; Debut: 5/12/1992

Division Series		Batting																							Fielding						
Year Tm	Age	G	AB	H	2B	3B	HR	TB	R	RBI	GW	TBB	IBB	SO	HBP	SH	SF	SB	CS	SB%	GDP	Avg	OBP	SLG	Pos	G	PO	A	E	DP	FPct
1997 Fla	29	1	1	1	0	0	0	1	0	1	0	0	0	0	0	0	0	0	0	—	0	1.000	1.000	1.000	—						
LCS		Batting																							Fielding						
Year Tm	Age	G	AB	H	2B	3B	HR	TB	R	RBI	GW	TBB	IBB	SO	HBP	SH	SF	SB	CS	SB%	GDP	Avg	OBP	SLG	Pos	G	PO	A	E	DP	FPct
1997 Fla	29	3	1	1	0	0	0	1	0	0	0	0	0	0	0	0	0	0	0	—	0	1.000	1.000	1.000	3B	2	0	0	0	0	—
World Series		Batting																							Fielding						
Year Tm	Age	G	AB	H	2B	3B	HR	TB	R	RBI	GW	TBB	IBB	SO	HBP	SH	SF	SB	CS	SB%	GDP	Avg	OBP	SLG	Pos	G	PO	A	E	DP	FPct
1997 Fla	29	2	1	0	0	0	0	0	1	0	0	0	0	0	0	0	0	0	0	—	0	.000	.000	.000	3B	1	0	0	0	0	—
Postseason Totals		6	3	2	0	0	0	2	1	1	0	0	0	0	0	0	0	0	0	—	0	.667	.667	.667	3B	3	0	0	0	0	—

TONY ARMAS—Antonio Rafael Armas—Bats: Right; Throws: Right

Ht: 5'11"; Wt: 182 lbs; Born: 7/2/1953 in Anzoategui, Venezuela; Debut: 9/6/1976

Division Series		Batting																							Fielding						
Year Tm	Age	G	AB	H	2B	3B	HR	TB	R	RBI	GW	TBB	IBB	SO	HBP	SH	SF	SB	CS	SB%	GDP	Avg	OBP	SLG	Pos	G	PO	A	E	DP	FPct
1981 Oak	28	3	11	6	2	0	0	8	1	3	2	1	0	1	0	0	0	0	0	—	0	.545	.583	.727	OF	3	6	0	1	0	.857
LCS		Batting																							Fielding						
Year Tm	Age	G	AB	H	2B	3B	HR	TB	R	RBI	GW	TBB	IBB	SO	HBP	SH	SF	SB	CS	SB%	GDP	Avg	OBP	SLG	Pos	G	PO	A	E	DP	FPct
1981 Oak	28	3	12	2	0	0	0	2	0	0	0	0	0	5	0	0	0	0	0	—	1	.167	.167	.167	OF	3	5	2	0	0	1.000
1986 Bos	33	5	16	2	1	0	0	3	1	0	0	0	0	2	0	0	0	0	0	—	0	.125	.125	.188	OF	5	12	0	0	0	1.000
LCS Totals		8	28	4	1	0	0	5	1	0	0	0	0	7	0	0	0	0	0	—	1	.143	.143	.179	OF	8	17	2	0	0	1.000
World Series		Batting																							Fielding						
Year Tm	Age	G	AB	H	2B	3B	HR	TB	R	RBI	GW	TBB	IBB	SO	HBP	SH	SF	SB	CS	SB%	GDP	Avg	OBP	SLG	Pos	G	PO	A	E	DP	FPct
1986 Bos	33	1	1	0	0	0	0	0	0	0	0	0	0	1	0	0	0	0	0	—	0	.000	.000	.000	—						
Postseason Totals		12	40	10	3	0	0	13	2	3	2	1	0	9	0	0	0	0	0	—	1	.250	.268	.325	OF	11	23	2	1	0	.962

ED ARMBRISTER—Edison Rosanda Armbrister—Bats: Right; Throws: Right

Ht: 5'11"; Wt: 160 lbs; Born: 7/4/1948 in Nassau, Bahamas; Debut: 8/31/1973

LCS		Batting																							Fielding						
Year Tm	Age	G	AB	H	2B	3B	HR	TB	R	RBI	GW	TBB	IBB	SO	HBP	SH	SF	SB	CS	SB%	GDP	Avg	OBP	SLG	Pos	G	PO	A	E	DP	FPct
1973 Cin	25	3	6	1	0	0	0	1	0	0	0	0	0	5	0	0	0	0	0	—	0	.167	.167	.167	OF	1	3	0	0	0	1.000
1975 Cin	27	2	0	0	0	0	0	0	0	1	1	0	0	0	0	0	1	0	0	—	0	—	.000	—	—						
1976 Cin	28	1	0	0	0	0	0	0	0	0	0	0	0	0	0	1	0	0	0	—	0	—	—	—	—						
LCS Totals		6	6	1	0	0	0	1	0	1	1	0	0	5	0	1	1	0	0	—	0	.167	.143	.167	OF	1	3	0	0	0	1.000
World Series		Batting																							Fielding						
Year Tm	Age	G	AB	H	2B	3B	HR	TB	R	RBI	GW	TBB	IBB	SO	HBP	SH	SF	SB	CS	SB%	GDP	Avg	OBP	SLG	Pos	G	PO	A	E	DP	FPct
1975 Cin	27	4	1	0	0	0	0	0	1	0	0	2	0	0	0	1	0	0	0	—	0	.000	.667	.000	—						
Postseason Totals		10	7	1	0	0	0	1	1	1	1	2	0	5	0	2	1	0	0	—	0	.143	.300	.143	OF	1	3	0	0	0	1.000

JACK ARMSTRONG—Jack William Armstrong—Throws: Right; Bats: Right

Ht: 6'5"; Wt: 220 lbs; Born: 3/7/1965 in Englewood, New Jersey; Debut: 6/21/1988

World Series		Pitching																										
Year Tm	Age	G	GS	CG	GF	IP	BFP	H	R	ER	HR	SH	SF	HB	TBB	IBB	SO	WP	Bk	W	L	Pct	ShO	Sv-Op	Hld	OAvg	OOBP	ERA
1990 Cin	25	1	0	0	0	3.0	10	1	0	0	0	0	0	0	0	0	3	0	0	0	0	—	0	0- 0	0	.100	.100	0.00

World Series — Batting / Fielding

Year Tm	Age	G	AB	H	2B	3B	HR	TB	R	RBI	GW	TBB	IBB	SO	HBP	SH	SF	SB	CS	SB%	GDP	Avg	OBP	SLG	Pos	G	PO	A	E	DP	FPct
1990 Cin	25	1	0	0	0	0	0	0	0	0	0	0	0	0	0	0	0	0	0	—	0	—	—	—	P	1	0	0	0	0	—

MORRIE ARNOVICH—Morris Arnovich—Nickname: Snooker—Bats: Right; Throws: Right

Ht: 5'10"; Wt: 168 lbs; Born: 11/16/1910 in Superior, Wisconsin; Debut: 9/14/1936; Died: 7/20/1959

World Series — Batting / Fielding

Year Tm	Age	G	AB	H	2B	3B	HR	TB	R	RBI	GW	TBB	IBB	SO	HBP	SH	SF	SB	CS	SB%	GDP	Avg	OBP	SLG	Pos	G	PO	A	E	DP	FPct
1940 Cin	29	1	1	0	0	0	0	0	0	0	0	0	0	0	0	1	0	0	0	—	0	.000	.000	.000	OF	1	2	0	0	0	1.000

LUIS ARROYO—Luis Enrique Arroyo—Nickname: Yo-Yo—Throws: Left; Bats: Left

Ht: 5'8"; Wt: 178 lbs; Born: 2/18/1927 in Penuelas, Puerto Rico; Debut: 4/20/1955

World Series — Pitching

Year Tm	Age	G	GS	CG	GF	IP	BFP	H	R	ER	HR	SH	SF	HB	TBB	IBB	SO	WP	Bk	W	L	Pct	ShO	Sv-Op	Hld	OAvg	OOBP	ERA
1960 NYA	33	1	0	0	0	0.2	4	2	1	1	0	0	0	0	0	0	1	0	0	0	0	—	0	0- 0	0	.500	.500	13.50
1961 NYA	34	2	0	0	2	4.0	18	4	2	1	0	0	0	0	2	1	3	0	0	1	0	1.000	0	0- 0	0	.250	.333	2.25
WS Totals		3	0	0	2	4.2	44	6	3	2	0	0	0	0	2	1	4	0	0	1	0	1.000	0	0-0	0	.300	.364	3.86

World Series — Batting / Fielding

Year Tm	Age	G	AB	H	2B	3B	HR	TB	R	RBI	GW	TBB	IBB	SO	HBP	SH	SF	SB	CS	SB%	GDP	Avg	OBP	SLG	Pos	G	PO	A	E	DP	FPct
1960 NYA	33	1	1	0	0	0	0	0	0	0	0	0	0	0	0	0	0	0	0	—	0	.000	.000	.000	P	1	0	0	0	0	—
1961 NYA	34	2	0	0	0	0	0	0	0	0	0	0	0	0	0	0	0	0	0	—	0	—	—	—	P	2	1	1	1	0	.667
WS Totals		3	1	0	0	0	0	0	0	0	0	0	0	0	0	0	0	0	0	—	0	.000	.000	.000	P	3	1	1	1	0	.667

RICHIE ASHBURN (HOF 1995-V)—Don Richard Ashburn—Nicknames: Whitey, Put Put—Bats: L; Throws: R

Ht: 5'10"; Wt: 170 lbs; Born: 3/19/1927 in Tilden, Neb.; Deb.: 4/20/1948; Died: 9/9/1997

World Series — Batting / Fielding

Year Tm	Age	G	AB	H	2B	3B	HR	TB	R	RBI	GW	TBB	IBB	SO	HBP	SH	SF	SB	CS	SB%	GDP	Avg	OBP	SLG	Pos	G	PO	A	E	DP	FPct
1950 Phi	23	4	17	3	1	0	0	4	0	1	0	0	0	4	0	0	0	0	0	—	0	.176	.176	.235	OF	4	9	0	0	0	1.000

ALAN ASHBY—Alan Dean Ashby—Bats: Both; Throws: Right

Ht: 6'2"; Wt: 185 lbs; Born: 7/8/1951 in Long Beach, California; Debut: 7/3/1973

Division Series — Batting / Fielding

Year Tm	Age	G	AB	H	2B	3B	HR	TB	R	RBI	GW	TBB	IBB	SO	HBP	SH	SF	SB	CS	SB%	GDP	Avg	OBP	SLG	Pos	G	PO	A	E	DP	FPct
1981 Hou	30	3	9	1	0	0	1	4	1	2	1	2	1	0	0	0	0	0	0	—	0	.111	.273	.444	C	3	24	2	0	0	1.000

LCS — Batting / Fielding

Year Tm	Age	G	AB	H	2B	3B	HR	TB	R	RBI	GW	TBB	IBB	SO	HBP	SH	SF	SB	CS	SB%	GDP	Avg	OBP	SLG	Pos	G	PO	A	E	DP	FPct
1980 Hou	29	2	8	1	0	0	0	1	0	1	0	0	0	0	0	0	0	0	0	—	0	.125	.125	.125	C	2	11	2	0	0	1.000
1986 Hou	35	6	23	3	1	0	1	7	2	2	1	2	0	1	0	0	0	0	0	—	1	.130	.200	.304	C	6	59	1	0	0	1.000
LCS Totals		8	31	4	1	0	1	8	2	3	1	2	0	1	0	0	0	0	0	—	1	.129	.182	.258	C	8	70	3	0	0	1.000
Postseason Totals		11	40	5	1	0	2	12	3	5	2	4	1	1	0	0	0	0	0	—	1	.125	.205	.300	C	11	94	5	0	0	1.000

ANDY ASHBY—Andrew Jason Ashby—Throws: Right; Bats: Right

Ht: 6'5"; Wt: 180 lbs; Born: 7/11/1967 in Kansas City, Missouri; Debut: 6/10/1991

Division Series — Pitching

Year Tm	Age	G	GS	CG	GF	IP	BFP	H	R	ER	HR	SH	SF	HB	TBB	IBB	SO	WP	Bk	W	L	Pct	ShO	Sv-Op	Hld	OAvg	OOBP	ERA
1996 SD	29	1	1	0	0	5.1	24	7	4	4	1	0	0	0	1	0	5	1	0	0	0	—	0	0- 0	0	.304	.333	6.75

Division Series — Batting / Fielding

Year Tm	Age	G	AB	H	2B	3B	HR	TB	R	RBI	GW	TBB	IBB	SO	HBP	SH	SF	SB	CS	SB%	GDP	Avg	OBP	SLG	Pos	G	PO	A	E	DP	FPct
1996 SD	29	1	1	0	0	0	0	0	0	0	0	0	0	1	0	1	0	0	0	—	0	.000	.000	.000	P	1	0	0	0	0	—

BILLY ASHLEY—Billy Manual Ashley—Bats: Right; Throws: Right

Ht: 6'7"; Wt: 220 lbs; Born: 7/11/1970 in Trenton, Michigan; Debut: 9/1/1992

Division Series — Batting / Fielding

Year Tm	Age	G	AB	H	2B	3B	HR	TB	R	RBI	GW	TBB	IBB	SO	HBP	SH	SF	SB	CS	SB%	GDP	Avg	OBP	SLG	Pos	G	PO	A	E	DP	FPct
1995 LA	25	1	0	0	0	0	0	0	0	0	0	1	0	0	0	0	0	0	0	—	0	—	1.000	—	—						
1996 LA	26	2	2	0	0	0	0	0	0	0	0	0	0	2	0	0	0	0	0	—	0	.000	.000	.000	—						
DS Totals		3	2	0	0	0	0	0	0	0	0	1	0	2	0	0	0	0	0	—	0	.000	.333	.000	—	0	0	0	0	0	—

BOB ASPROMONTE—Robert Thomas Aspromonte—Bats: Right; Throws: Right

Ht: 6'2"; Wt: 170 lbs; Born: 6/19/1938 in Brooklyn, New York; Debut: 9/19/1956

LCS — Batting / Fielding

Year Tm	Age	G	AB	H	2B	3B	HR	TB	R	RBI	GW	TBB	IBB	SO	HBP	SH	SF	SB	CS	SB%	GDP	Avg	OBP	SLG	Pos	G	PO	A	E	DP	FPct
1969 Atl	31	3	3	0	0	0	0	0	0	0	0	0	0	0	0	0	0	0	0	—	0	.000	.000	.000	—						

PAUL ASSENMACHER—Paul Andre Assenmacher—Throws: Left; Bats: Left

Ht: 6'3"; Wt: 195 lbs; Born: 12/10/1960 in Detroit, Michigan; Debut: 4/12/1986

Division Series — Pitching

Year Tm	Age	G	GS	CG	GF	IP	BFP	H	R	ER	HR	SH	SF	HB	TBB	IBB	SO	WP	Bk	W	L	Pct	ShO	Sv-Op	Hld	OAvg	OOBP	ERA
1995 Cle	34	3	0	0	1	1.2	5	0	0	0	0	0	0	0	0	0	3	0	0	0	0	—	0	0- 0	1	.000	.000	0.00
1996 Cle	35	3	0	0	0	1.2	6	0	0	0	0	0	1	0	1	1	2	0	0	1	0	1.000	0	0- 0	1	.000	.167	0.00
1997 Cle	36	4	0	0	0	3.1	14	2	2	2	1	0	0	1	2	0	2	0	0	0	0	—	0	0- 0	2	.182	.357	5.40
DS Totals		10	0	0	1	6.2	50	2	2	2	1	0	1	1	3	1	7	0	0	1	0	1.000	0	0-0	4	.100	.240	2.70

LCS — Pitching

Year Tm	Age	G	GS	CG	GF	IP	BFP	H	R	ER	HR	SH	SF	HB	TBB	IBB	SO	WP	Bk	W	L	Pct	ShO	Sv-Op	Hld	OAvg	OOBP	ERA
1989 ChN	28	2	0	0	0	0.2	5	3	1	1	0	0	0	0	0	0	0	0	0	0	0	—	0	0- 0	1	.600	.600	13.50
1995 Cle	34	3	0	0	0	1.1	5	0	0	0	0	0	0	0	1	0	2	0	0	0	0	—	0	0- 0	1	.000	.200	0.00
1997 Cle	36	5	0	0	0	2.0	12	5	2	2	1	0	0	0	1	0	3	0	0	1	0	1.000	0	0- 0	2	.455	.500	9.00
LCS Totals		10	0	0	0	4.0	44	8	3	3	1	0	0	0	2	0	5	0	0	1	0	1.000	0	0-0	4	.400	.455	6.75

World Series — Pitching

Year Tm	Age	G	GS	CG	GF	IP	BFP	H	R	ER	HR	SH	SF	HB	TBB	IBB	SO	WP	Bk	W	L	Pct	ShO	Sv-Op	Hld	OAvg	OOBP	ERA
1995 Cle	34	4	0	0	1	1.1	9	1	2	1	0	0	0	0	3	1	3	0	0	0	0	—	0	0- 1	0	.167	.444	6.75
1997 Cle	36	5	0	0	1	4.0	17	5	0	0	0	0	0	0	0	0	6	0	0	0	0	—	0	0- 0	2	.294	.294	0.00
WS Totals		9	0	0	2	5.1	52	6	2	1	0	0	0	0	3	1	9	0	0	0	0	—	0	0-1	2	.261	.346	1.69
Postseason Totals		29	0	0	3	16.0	146	16	7	6	2	0	1	1	8	2	21	0	0	2	0	1.000	0	0-1	10	.254	.342	3.38

Division Series — Batting / Fielding

Year Tm	Age	G	AB	H	2B	3B	HR	TB	R	RBI	GW	TBB	IBB	SO	HBP	SH	SF	SB	CS	SB%	GDP	Avg	OBP	SLG	Pos	G	PO	A	E	DP	FPct
1995 Cle	34	3	0	0	0	0	0	0	0	0	0	0	0	0	0	0	0	0	0	—	0	—	—	—	P	3	0	0	0	0	—
1996 Cle	35	3	0	0	0	0	0	0	0	0	0	0	0	0	0	0	0	0	0	—	0	—	—	—	P	3	0	1	0	0	1.000
1997 Cle	36	4	0	0	0	0	0	0	0	0	0	0	0	0	0	0	0	0	0	—	0	—	—	—	P	4	0	0	0	0	—
DS Totals		10	0	0	0	0	0	0	0	0	0	0	0	0	0	0	0	0	0	—	0	—	—	—	P	10	0	1	0	0	1.000

LCS — Batting / Fielding

Year Tm	Age	G	AB	H	2B	3B	HR	TB	R	RBI	GW	TBB	IBB	SO	HBP	SH	SF	SB	CS	SB%	GDP	Avg	OBP	SLG	Pos	G	PO	A	E	DP	FPct
1989 ChN	28	2	0	0	0	0	0	0	0	0	0	0	0	0	0	0	0	0	0	—	0	—	—	—	P	2	0	0	0	0	—
1995 Cle	34	3	0	0	0	0	0	0	0	0	0	0	0	0	0	0	0	0	0	—	0	—	—	—	P	3	0	0	0	0	—
1997 Cle	36	5	0	0	0	0	0	0	0	0	0	0	0	0	0	0	0	0	0	—	0	—	—	—	P	5	0	0	0	0	—
LCS Totals		10	0	0	0	0	0	0	0	0	0	0	0	0	0	0	0	0	0	—	0	—	—	—	P	10	0	0	0	0	—

World Series — Batting / Fielding

Year Tm	Age	G	AB	H	2B	3B	HR	TB	R	RBI	GW	TBB	IBB	SO	HBP	SH	SF	SB	CS	SB%	GDP	Avg	OBP	SLG	Pos	G	PO	A	E	DP	FPct
1995 Cle	34	4	0	0	0	0	0	0	0	0	0	0	0	0	0	0	0	0	0	—	0	—	—	—	P	4	0	0	0	0	—
1997 Cle	36	5	0	0	0	0	0	0	0	0	0	0	0	0	0	0	0	0	0	—	0	—	—	—	P	5	0	0	0	0	—
WS Totals		9	0	0	0	0	0	0	0	0	0	0	0	0	0	0	0	0	0	—	0	—	—	—	P	9	0	0	0	0	—
Postseason Totals		29	0	0	0	0	0	0	0	0	0	0	0	0	0	0	0	0	0	—	0	—	—	—	P	29	0	1	0	0	1.000

PEDRO ASTACIO—Pedro Julio Astacio—Throws: Right; Bats: Right

Ht: 6'2"; Wt: 174 lbs; Born: 11/28/1968 in Hato Mayor, Dominican Republic; Debut: 7/3/1992

Division Series — Pitching

Year Tm	Age	G	GS	CG	GF	IP	BFP	H	R	ER	HR	SH	SF	HB	TBB	IBB	SO	WP	Bk	W	L	Pct	ShO	Sv-Op	Hld	OAvg	OOBP	ERA
1995 LA	26	3	0	0	1	3.1	11	1	0	0	0	0	0	0	0	0	5	0	0	0	0	—	0	0- 0	0	.091	.091	0.00
1996 LA	27	1	0	0	0	1.2	5	0	0	0	0	0	0	0	0	0	1	0	0	0	0	—	0	0- 0	0	.000	.000	0.00
DS Totals		4	0	0	1	5.0	32	1	0	0	0	0	0	0	0	0	6	0	0	0	0	—	0	0-0	0	.063	.063	0.00

Division Series — Batting / Fielding

Year Tm	Age	G	AB	H	2B	3B	HR	TB	R	RBI	GW	TBB	IBB	SO	HBP	SH	SF	SB	CS	SB%	GDP	Avg	OBP	SLG	Pos	G	PO	A	E	DP	FPct
1995 LA	26	3	0	0	0	0	0	0	0	0	0	0	0	0	0	0	0	0	0	—	0	—	—	—	P	3	0	2	0	0	1.000
1996 LA	27	1	0	0	0	0	0	0	0	0	0	0	0	0	0	0	0	0	0	—	0	—	—	—	P	1	0	1	0	0	1.000
DS Totals		4	0	0	0	0	0	0	0	0	0	0	0	0	0	0	0	0	0	—	0	—	—	—	P	4	0	3	0	0	1.000

KEITH ATHERTON—Keith Rowe Atherton—Throws: Right; Bats: Right

Ht: 6'4"; Wt: 200 lbs; Born: 2/19/1959 in Newport News, Virginia; Debut: 7/14/1983

LCS — Pitching

Year Tm	Age	G	GS	CG	GF	IP	BFP	H	R	ER	HR	SH	SF	HB	TBB	IBB	SO	WP	Bk	W	L	Pct	ShO	Sv-Op	Hld	OAvg	OOBP	ERA
1987 Min	28	1	0	0	0	0.1	2	1	0	0	0	1	0	0	0	0	0	0	0	0	0	—	0	0- 0	1	1.000	1.000	0.00

World Series — Pitching

Year Tm	Age	G	GS	CG	GF	IP	BFP	H	R	ER	HR	SH	SF	HB	TBB	IBB	SO	WP	Bk	W	L	Pct	ShO	Sv-Op	Hld	OAvg	OOBP	ERA
1987 Min	28	2	0	0	1	1.1	5	0	1	1	0	0	0	0	1	0	0	0	1	0	0	—	0	0- 0	0	.000	.200	6.75
Postseason Totals		3	0	0	1	1.2	14	1	1	1	0	1	0	0	1	0	0	0	1	0	0	—	0	0-0	1	.200	.333	5.40

LCS — Batting / Fielding

Year Tm	Age	G	AB	H	2B	3B	HR	TB	R	RBI	GW	TBB	IBB	SO	HBP	SH	SF	SB	CS	SB%	GDP	Avg	OBP	SLG	Pos	G	PO	A	E	DP	FPct
1987 Min	28	1	0	0	0	0	0	0	0	0	0	0	0	0	0	0	0	0	0	—	0	—	—	—	P	1	0	0	0	0	—

World Series — Batting / Fielding

Year Tm	Age	G	AB	H	2B	3B	HR	TB	R	RBI	GW	TBB	IBB	SO	HBP	SH	SF	SB	CS	SB%	GDP	Avg	OBP	SLG	Pos	G	PO	A	E	DP	FPct
1987 Min	28	2	0	0	0	0	0	0	0	0	0	0	0	0	0	0	0	0	0	—	0	—	—	—	P	2	0	0	0	0	—
Postseason Totals		3	0	0	0	0	0	0	0	0	0	0	0	0	0	0	0	0	0	—	0	—	—	—	P	3	0	0	0	0	—

RICK AUERBACH—Frederick Steven Auerbach—Bats: Right; Throws: Right

Ht: 6'0"; Wt: 165 lbs; Born: 2/15/1950 in Woodland Hills, California; Debut: 4/13/1971

LCS — Batting / Fielding

Year Tm	Age	G	AB	H	2B	3B	HR	TB	R	RBI	GW	TBB	IBB	SO	HBP	SH	SF	SB	CS	SB%	GDP	Avg	OBP	SLG	Pos	G	PO	A	E	DP	FPct
1974 LA	24	1	1	1	1	0	0	2	0	0	0	0	0	0	0	0	0	0	0	—	0	1.000	1.000	2.000	—						
1979 Cin	29	2	2	0	0	0	0	0	0	0	0	0	0	1	0	0	0	0	0	—	0	.000	.000	.000	—						
LCS Totals		3	3	1	1	0	0	2	0	0	0	0	0	1	0	0	0	0	0	—	0	.333	.333	.667	—	0	0	0	0	0	—

World Series — Batting / Fielding

Year Tm	Age	G	AB	H	2B	3B	HR	TB	R	RBI	GW	TBB	IBB	SO	HBP	SH	SF	SB	CS	SB%	GDP	Avg	OBP	SLG	Pos	G	PO	A	E	DP	FPct
1974 LA	24	1	0	0	0	0	0	0	0	0	0	0	0	0	0	0	0	0	0	—	0	—	—	—	—						
Postseason Totals		4	3	1	1	0	0	2	0	0	0	0	0	1	0	0	0	0	0	—	0	.333	.333	.667	—	0	0	0	0	0	—

ELDON AUKER—Elden LeRoy Auker—Nicknames: Submarine, Big Six—Throws: Right; Bats: Right

Ht: 6'2"; Wt: 194 lbs; Born: 9/21/1910 in Norcatur, Kansas; Debut: 8/10/1933

World Series — Pitching

Year Tm	Age	G	GS	CG	GF	IP	BFP	H	R	ER	HR	SH	SF	HB	TBB	IBB	SO	WP	Bk	W	L	Pct	ShO	Sv-Op	Hld	OAvg	OOBP	ERA
1934 Det	24	2	2	1	0	11.1	51	16	8	7	0	0	0	0	5	0	2	0	0	1	1	.500	0	0- 0	0	.348	.412	5.56
1935 Det	25	1	1	0	0	6.0	24	6	3	2	1	1	0	0	2	0	1	0	0	0	0	—	0	0- 0	0	.286	.348	3.00
WS Totals		3	3	1	0	17.1	150	22	11	9	1	1	0	0	7	0	3	0	0	1	1	.500	0	0-0	0	.328	.392	4.67

World Series — Batting / Fielding

Year Tm	Age	G	AB	H	2B	3B	HR	TB	R	RBI	GW	TBB	IBB	SO	HBP	SH	SF	SB	CS	SB%	GDP	Avg	OBP	SLG	Pos	G	PO	A	E	DP	FPct
1934 Det	24	2	4	0	0	0	0	0	0	0	0	0	0	2	0	1	0	0	0	—	0	.000	.000	.000	P	2	0	2	0	1	1.000
1935 Det	25	1	2	0	0	0	0	0	0	0	0	0	0	1	0	0	0	0	0	—	0	.000	.000	.000	P	1	0	2	0	0	1.000
WS Totals		3	6	0	0	0	0	0	0	0	0	0	0	3	0	1	0	0	0	—	0	.000	.000	.000	P	3	0	4	0	1	1.000

BRAD AUSMUS—Bradley David Ausmus—Bats: Right; Throws: Right

Ht: 5'11"; Wt: 185 lbs; Born: 4/14/1969 in New Haven, Connecticut; Debut: 7/28/1993

Division Series — Batting / Fielding

Year Tm	Age	G	AB	H	2B	3B	HR	TB	R	RBI	GW	TBB	IBB	SO	HBP	SH	SF	SB	CS	SB%	GDP	Avg	OBP	SLG	Pos	G	PO	A	E	DP	FPct
1997 Hou	28	2	5	2	1	0	0	3	1	2	0	0	0	1	0	0	0	0	0	—	1	.400	.400	.600	C	2	13	0	0	0	1.000

EARL AVERILL (HOF 1975-V)—Howard Earl Averill—Nickname: Rock—Bats: Left; Throws: Right

Ht: 5'9"; Wt: 172 lbs; Born: 5/21/1902 in Snohomish, Washington; Debut: 4/16/1929; Died: 8/16/1983

World Series — Batting / Fielding

Year Tm	Age	G	AB	H	2B	3B	HR	TB	R	RBI	GW	TBB	IBB	SO	HBP	SH	SF	SB	CS	SB%	GDP	Avg	OBP	SLG	Pos	G	PO	A	E	DP	FPct
1940 Det	38	3	3	0	0	0	0	0	0	0	0	0	0	0	0	0	0	0	0	—	0	.000	.000	.000	—						

STEVE AVERY—Steven Thomas Avery—Throws: Left; Bats: Left

Ht: 6'4"; Wt: 180 lbs; Born: 4/14/1970 in Trenton, Michigan; Debut: 6/13/1990

Division Series — Pitching

Year Tm	Age	G	GS	CG	GF	IP	BFP	H	R	ER	HR	SH	SF	HB	TBB	IBB	SO	WP	Bk	W	L	Pct	ShO	Sv-Op	Hld	OAvg	OOBP	ERA
1995 Atl	25	1	0	0	0	0.2	3	1	1	1	0	0	0	0	0	0	1	0	0	0	0	—	0	0- 0	0	.333	.333	13.50

LCS — Pitching

Year Tm	Age	G	GS	CG	GF	IP	BFP	H	R	ER	HR	SH	SF	HB	TBB	IBB	SO	WP	Bk	W	L	Pct	ShO	Sv-Op	Hld	OAvg	OOBP	ERA
1991 Atl	21	2	2	0	0	16.1	58	9	0	0	0	0	0	0	4	0	17	0	0	2	0	1.000	0	0- 0	0	.167	.224	0.00
1992 Atl	22	3	2	0	0	8.0	38	13	8	8	0	0	0	0	2	0	3	1	0	1	1	.500	0	0- 0	0	.361	.395	9.00
1993 Atl	23	2	2	0	0	13.0	54	9	5	4	1	1	1	0	6	3	10	2	0	0	0	—	0	0- 0	0	.196	.283	2.77
1995 Atl	25	2	1	0	0	6.0	22	2	0	0	0	0	0	0	4	0	6	0	0	1	0	1.000	0	0- 0	0	.111	.273	0.00
1996 Atl	26	2	0	0	2	2.0	7	2	0	0	0	0	0	0	1	0	1	0	0	0	0	—	0	0- 0	0	.333	.429	0.00
LCS Totals		11	7	0	2	45.1	358	35	13	12	1	1	1	0	17	3	37	3	0	4	1	.800	0	0-0	0	.219	.292	2.38

World Series — Pitching

Year Tm	Age	G	GS	CG	GF	IP	BFP	H	R	ER	HR	SH	SF	HB	TBB	IBB	SO	WP	Bk	W	L	Pct	ShO	Sv-Op	Hld	OAvg	OOBP	ERA
1991 Atl	21	2	2	0	0	13.0	51	10	6	5	1	0	2	0	1	0	8	0	0	0	0	—	0	0- 0	0	.208	.216	3.46
1992 Atl	22	2	2	0	0	12.0	48	11	5	5	3	0	1	0	3	0	11	0	0	0	1	.000	0	0- 0	0	.250	.292	3.75
1995 Atl	25	1	1	0	0	6.0	25	3	1	1	1	0	0	0	5	1	3	0	1	1	0	1.000	0	0- 0	0	.150	.320	1.50
1996 Atl	26	1	0	0	0	0.2	6	1	2	1	0	0	0	0	3	1	0	0	0	0	1	.000	0	0- 0	0	.333	.667	13.50
WS Totals		6	5	0	0	31.2	260	25	14	12	5	0	3	0	12	2	22	0	1	1	2	.333	0	0-0	0	.217	.285	3.41
Postseason Totals		18	12	0	2	77.2	624	61	28	25	6	1	4	0	29	5	60	3	1	5	3	.625	0	0-0	0	.219	.289	2.90

Division Series — Batting / Fielding

Year Tm	Age	G	AB	H	2B	3B	HR	TB	R	RBI	GW	TBB	IBB	SO	HBP	SH	SF	SB	CS	SB%	GDP	Avg	OBP	SLG	Pos	G	PO	A	E	DP	FPct
1995 Atl	25	1	0	0	0	0	0	0	0	0	0	0	0	0	0	0	0	0	0	—	0	—	—	—	P	1	0	0	0	0	—

LCS — Batting / Fielding

Year Tm	Age	G	AB	H	2B	3B	HR	TB	R	RBI	GW	TBB	IBB	SO	HBP	SH	SF	SB	CS	SB%	GDP	Avg	OBP	SLG	Pos	G	PO	A	E	DP	FPct
1991 Atl	21	2	7	1	0	0	0	1	0	0	0	0	0	4	0	0	0	0	0	—	0	.143	.143	.143	P	2	1	2	0	0	1.000
1992 Atl	22	3	2	0	0	0	0	0	0	1	0	0	0	1	0	0	1	0	0	—	0	.000	.000	.000	P	3	0	0	0	0	—
1993 Atl	23	2	4	2	1	0	0	3	1	0	0	0	0	1	0	0	0	0	0	—	0	.500	.500	.750	P	2	0	2	0	0	1.000
1995 Atl	25	2	2	1	0	0	0	1	0	0	0	0	0	0	0	0	0	0	0	—	0	.500	.500	.500	P	2	0	2	0	0	1.000
1996 Atl	26	2	0	0	0	0	0	0	0	0	0	0	0	0	0	0	0	0	0	—	0	—	—	—	P	2	0	0	0	0	—
LCS Totals		11	15	4	1	0	0	5	1	1	0	0	0	6	0	0	1	0	0	—	0	.267	.250	.333	P	11	1	6	0	0	1.000

World Series — Batting / Fielding

Year Tm	Age	G	AB	H	2B	3B	HR	TB	R	RBI	GW	TBB	IBB	SO	HBP	SH	SF	SB	CS	SB%	GDP	Avg	OBP	SLG	Pos	G	PO	A	E	DP	FPct
1991 Atl	21	2	3	0	0	0	0	0	0	0	0	0	0	2	0	0	0	0	0	—	0	.000	.000	.000	P	2	1	0	0	0	1.000
1992 Atl	22	2	1	0	0	0	0	0	0	0	0	0	0	1	0	0	0	0	0	—	0	.000	.000	.000	P	2	0	2	0	0	1.000
1995 Atl	25	1	0	0	0	0	0	0	0	0	0	0	0	0	0	0	0	0	0	—	0	—	—	—	P	1	0	0	0	0	—
1996 Atl	26	1	0	0	0	0	0	0	0	0	0	0	0	0	0	0	0	0	0	—	0	—	—	—	P	1	0	0	0	0	—
WS Totals		6	4	0	0	0	0	0	0	0	0	0	0	3	0	0	0	0	0	—	0	.000	.000	.000	P	6	1	2	0	0	1.000
Postseason Totals		18	19	4	1	0	0	5	1	1	0	0	0	9	0	0	1	0	0	—	0	.211	.200	.263	P	18	2	8	0	0	1.000

BOBBY AVILA—Roberto Francisco Avila—Nickname: Beto—Bats: Right; Throws: Right

Ht: 5'10"; Wt: 175 lbs; Born: 4/2/1924 in Veracruz, Mexico; Debut: 4/30/1949

World Series — Batting / Fielding

Year Tm	Age	G	AB	H	2B	3B	HR	TB	R	RBI	GW	TBB	IBB	SO	HBP	SH	SF	SB	CS	SB%	GDP	Avg	OBP	SLG	Pos	G	PO	A	E	DP	FPct
1954 Cle	30	4	15	2	0	0	0	2	1	0	0	2	0	1	0	1	0	0	0	—	0	.133	.235	.133	2B	4	12	7	0	1	1.000

RAMON AVILES—Ramon Antonio Aviles—Bats: Right; Throws: Right

Ht: 5'9"; Wt: 155 lbs; Born: 1/22/1952 in Manati, Puerto Rico; Debut: 7/10/1977

Division Series — Batting / Fielding

Year Tm	Age	G	AB	H	2B	3B	HR	TB	R	RBI	GW	TBB	IBB	SO	HBP	SH	SF	SB	CS	SB%	GDP	Avg	OBP	SLG	Pos	G	PO	A	E	DP	FPct
1981 Phi	29	1	0	0	0	0	0	0	0	0	0	1	0	0	0	0	0	0	0	—	0	—	1.000	—	—						

LCS — Batting / Fielding

Year Tm	Age	G	AB	H	2B	3B	HR	TB	R	RBI	GW	TBB	IBB	SO	HBP	SH	SF	SB	CS	SB%	GDP	Avg	OBP	SLG	Pos	G	PO	A	E	DP	FPct
1980 Phi	28	1	0	0	0	0	0	0	1	0	0	0	0	0	0	0	0	0	0	—	0	—	—	—	—						
Postseason Totals		2	0	0	0	0	0	0	1	0	0	1	0	0	0	0	0	0	0	—	0	—	1.000	—	—	0	0	0	0	0	—

BENNIE AYALA—Benigno Ayala—Bats: Right; Throws: Right

Ht: 6'1"; Wt: 185 lbs; Born: 2/7/1951 in Yauco, Puerto Rico; Debut: 8/27/1974

LCS — Batting / Fielding

Year Tm	Age	G	AB	H	2B	3B	HR	TB	R	RBI	GW	TBB	IBB	SO	HBP	SH	SF	SB	CS	SB%	GDP	Avg	OBP	SLG	Pos	G	PO	A	E	DP	FPct
1983 Bal	32	1	0	0	0	0	0	0	0	1	0	0	0	0	0	0	1	0	0	—	0	—	.000	—	—						

World Series — Batting / Fielding

Year Tm	Age	G	AB	H	2B	3B	HR	TB	R	RBI	GW	TBB	IBB	SO	HBP	SH	SF	SB	CS	SB%	GDP	Avg	OBP	SLG	Pos	G	PO	A	E	DP	FPct
1979 Bal	28	4	6	2	0	0	1	5	1	2	0	1	0	0	0	0	0	0	0	—	0	.333	.429	.833	OF	3	4	0	0	0	1.000
1983 Bal	32	1	1	1	0	0	0	1	1	1	0	0	0	0	0	0	0	0	0	—	0	1.000	1.000	1.000	—						
WS Totals		5	7	3	0	0	1	6	2	3	0	1	0	0	0	0	0	0	0	—	0	.429	.500	.857	OF	3	4	0	0	0	1.000
Postseason Totals		6	7	3	0	0	1	6	2	4	0	1	0	0	0	0	1	0	0	—	0	.429	.444	.857	OF	3	4	0	0	0	1.000

BOBBY AYALA—Robert Joseph Ayala—Throws: Right; Bats: Right

Ht: 6'2"; Wt: 190 lbs; Born: 7/8/1969 in Ventura, California; Debut: 9/5/1992

Division Series — Pitching

Year Tm	Age	G	GS	CG	GF	IP	BFP	H	R	ER	HR	SH	SF	HB	TBB	IBB	SO	WP	Bk	W	L	Pct	ShO	Sv-Op	Hld	OAvg	OOBP	ERA
1995 Sea	26	2	0	0	0	0.2	9	6	4	4	1	0	1	0	1	0	0	0	0	0	0	—	0	0-0	0	.857	.778	54.00
1997 Sea	28	1	0	0	0	1.1	11	4	6	6	1	0	0	0	3	1	2	0	0	0	0	—	0	0-0	0	.500	.636	40.50
DS Totals		3	0	0	0	2.0	40	10	10	10	2	0	1	0	4	1	2	0	0	0	0	—	0	0-0	0	.667	.700	45.00

LCS — Pitching

Year Tm	Age	G	GS	CG	GF	IP	BFP	H	R	ER	HR	SH	SF	HB	TBB	IBB	SO	WP	Bk	W	L	Pct	ShO	Sv-Op	Hld	OAvg	OOBP	ERA
1995 Sea	26	2	0	0	0	3.2	16	3	1	1	1	0	0	0	3	0	3	0	0	0	0	—	0	0-0	0	.231	.375	2.45
Postseason Totals		5	0	0	0	5.2	72	13	11	11	3	0	1	0	7	1	5	0	0	0	0	—	0	0-0	0	.464	.556	17.47

Division Series — Batting / Fielding

Year Tm	Age	G	AB	H	2B	3B	HR	TB	R	RBI	GW	TBB	IBB	SO	HBP	SH	SF	SB	CS	SB%	GDP	Avg	OBP	SLG	Pos	G	PO	A	E	DP	FPct
1995 Sea	26	2	0	0	0	0	0	0	0	0	0	0	0	0	0	0	0	0	0	—	0	—	—	—	P	2	0	0	0	0	—
1997 Sea	28	1	0	0	0	0	0	0	0	0	0	0	0	0	0	0	0	0	0	—	0	—	—	—	P	1	0	0	0	0	—
DS Totals		3	0	0	0	0	0	0	0	0	0	0	0	0	0	0	0	0	0	—	0	—	—	—	P	3	0	0	0	0	—

LCS — Batting / Fielding

Year Tm	Age	G	AB	H	2B	3B	HR	TB	R	RBI	GW	TBB	IBB	SO	HBP	SH	SF	SB	CS	SB%	GDP	Avg	OBP	SLG	Pos	G	PO	A	E	DP	FPct
1995 Sea	26	2	0	0	0	0	0	0	0	0	0	0	0	0	0	0	0	0	0	—	0	—	—	—	P	2	0	1	0	1	1.000
Postseason Totals		5	0	0	0	0	0	0	0	0	0	0	0	0	0	0	0	0	0	—	0	—	—	—	P	5	0	1	0	1	1.000

WALLY BACKMAN—Walter Wayne Backman—Bats: Both; Throws: Right

Ht: 5'9"; Wt: 160 lbs; Born: 9/22/1959 in Hillsboro, Oregon; Debut: 9/2/1980

LCS — Batting / Fielding

Year Tm	Age	G	AB	H	2B	3B	HR	TB	R	RBI	GW	TBB	IBB	SO	HBP	SH	SF	SB	CS	SB%	GDP	Avg	OBP	SLG	Pos	G	PO	A	E	DP	FPct
1986 NYN	27	6	21	5	0	0	0	5	5	2	0	2	1	4	0	0	0	1	0	1.00	0	.238	.304	.238	2B	6	9	17	0	4	1.000
1988 NYN	29	7	22	6	1	0	0	7	2	2	0	2	0	5	0	2	0	1	0	1.00	0	.273	.333	.318	2B	7	7	19	2	1	.929
1990 Pit	31	3	7	1	1	0	0	2	1	0	0	1	0	3	0	0	0	1	0	1.00	0	.143	.250	.286	3B	2	1	3	0	0	1.000
LCS Totals		16	50	12	2	0	0	14	8	4	0	5	1	12	0	2	0	3	0	1.00	0	.240	.309	.280	2B	13	16	36	2	5	.963

World Series — Batting / Fielding

Year Tm	Age	G	AB	H	2B	3B	HR	TB	R	RBI	GW	TBB	IBB	SO	HBP	SH	SF	SB	CS	SB%	GDP	Avg	OBP	SLG	Pos	G	PO	A	E	DP	FPct
1986 NYN	27	6	18	6	0	0	0	6	4	1	0	3	0	2	0	1	0	1	1	.50	0	.333	.429	.333	2B	6	9	13	0	3	1.000
Postseason Totals		22	68	18	2	0	0	20	12	5	0	8	1	14	0	3	0	4	1	.80	0	.265	.342	.294	2B	19	25	49	2	8	.974

CARLOS BAERGA—Carlos Ortiz Baerga—Bats: Both; Throws: Right

Ht: 5'11"; Wt: 165 lbs; Born: 11/4/1968 in Santurce, Puerto Rico; Debut: 4/14/1990

Division Series — Batting / Fielding

Year Tm	Age	G	AB	H	2B	3B	HR	TB	R	RBI	GW	TBB	IBB	SO	HBP	SH	SF	SB	CS	SB%	GDP	Avg	OBP	SLG	Pos	G	PO	A	E	DP	FPct
1995 Cle	26	3	14	4	1	0	0	5	2	1	0	0	0	1	1	0	0	0	0	—	0	.286	.333	.357	2B	3	8	5	1	1	.929

LCS — Batting / Fielding

Year Tm	Age	G	AB	H	2B	3B	HR	TB	R	RBI	GW	TBB	IBB	SO	HBP	SH	SF	SB	CS	SB%	GDP	Avg	OBP	SLG	Pos	G	PO	A	E	DP	FPct
1995 Cle	26	6	25	10	0	0	1	13	3	4	2	2	0	3	0	0	0	0	0	—	0	.400	.444	.520	2B	6	12	22	0	2	1.000

World Series — Batting / Fielding

Year Tm	Age	G	AB	H	2B	3B	HR	TB	R	RBI	GW	TBB	IBB	SO	HBP	SH	SF	SB	CS	SB%	GDP	Avg	OBP	SLG	Pos	G	PO	A	E	DP	FPct
1995 Cle	26	6	26	5	2	0	0	7	1	4	0	1	0	1	0	0	0	0	0	—	1	.192	.222	.269	2B	6	15	24	1	7	.975
Postseason Totals		15	65	19	3	0	1	25	6	9	2	3	0	5	1	0	0	0	0	—	1	.292	.333	.385	2B	15	35	51	2	10	.977

JIM BAGBY—James Charles Jacob Bagby—Nickname: Sarge—Throws: Right; Bats: Both

Ht: 6'0"; Wt: 170 lbs; Born: 10/5/1889 in Barnett, Georgia; Debut: 4/22/1912; Died: 7/28/1954

World Series — Pitching

Year Tm	Age	G	GS	CG	GF	IP	BFP	H	R	ER	HR	SH	SF	HB	TBB	IBB	SO	WP	Bk	W	L	Pct	ShO	Sv-Op	Hld	OAvg	OOBP	ERA
1920 Cle	30	2	2	1	0	15.0	60	20	4	3	0	1	0	0	1	1	3	1	0	1	1	.500	0	0-0	0	.345	.356	1.80

World Series — Batting / Fielding

Year Tm	Age	G	AB	H	2B	3B	HR	TB	R	RBI	GW	TBB	IBB	SO	HBP	SH	SF	SB	CS	SB%	GDP	Avg	OBP	SLG	Pos	G	PO	A	E	DP	FPct
1920 Cle	30	2	6	2	0	0	1	5	1	3	0	0	0	0	0	0	0	0	0	—	0	.333	.333	.833	P	2	2	3	1	0	.833

JIM BAGBY JR.—James Charles Jacob Bagby Jr.—Throws: Right; Bats: Right

Ht: 6'2"; Wt: 170 lbs; Born: 9/8/1916 in Cleveland, Ohio; Debut: 4/18/1938; Died: 9/2/1988

World Series — Pitching

Year Tm	Age	G	GS	CG	GF	IP	BFP	H	R	ER	HR	SH	SF	HB	TBB	IBB	SO	WP	Bk	W	L	Pct	ShO	Sv-Op	Hld	OAvg	OOBP	ERA
1946 Bos	30	1	0	0	0	3.0	14	6	1	1	0	1	0	0	1	1	1	0	0	0	0	—	0	0-0	0	.500	.538	3.00

World Series — Batting / Fielding

Year Tm	Age	G	AB	H	2B	3B	HR	TB	R	RBI	GW	TBB	IBB	SO	HBP	SH	SF	SB	CS	SB%	GDP	Avg	OBP	SLG	Pos	G	PO	A	E	DP	FPct
1946 Bos	30	1	1	0	0	0	0	0	0	0	0	0	0	0	0	0	0	0	0	—	0	.000	.000	.000	P	1	0	1	0	0	1.000

JEFF BAGWELL—Jeffrey Robert Bagwell—Bats: Right; Throws: Right

Ht: 6'0"; Wt: 195 lbs; Born: 5/27/1968 in Boston, Massachusetts; Debut: 4/8/1991

Division Series — Batting / Fielding

Year Tm	Age	G	AB	H	2B	3B	HR	TB	R	RBI	GW	TBB	IBB	SO	HBP	SH	SF	SB	CS	SB%	GDP	Avg	OBP	SLG	Pos	G	PO	A	E	DP	FPct
1997 Hou	29	3	12	1	0	0	0	1	0	0	0	1	0	5	0	0	0	0	0	—	0	.083	.154	.083	1B	3	17	6	2	2	.920

STAN BAHNSEN—Stanley Raymond Bahnsen—Throws: Right; Bats: Right

Ht: 6'2"; Wt: 185 lbs; Born: 12/15/1944 in Council Bluffs, Iowa; Debut: 9/9/1966

Division Series — Pitching

Year Tm	Age	G	GS	CG	GF	IP	BFP	H	R	ER	HR	SH	SF	HB	TBB	IBB	SO	WP	Bk	W	L	Pct	ShO	Sv-Op	Hld	OAvg	OOBP	ERA
1981 Mon	36	1	0	0	0	1.1	5	1	0	0	0	0	0	0	1	0	1	0	0	0	0	—	0	0-0	0	.250	.400	0.00

Division Series		Batting																							Fielding						
Year Tm	Age	G	AB	H	2B	3B	HR	TB	R	RBI	GW	TBB	IBB	SO	HBP	SH	SF	SB	CS	SB%	GDP	Avg	OBP	SLG	Pos	G	PO	A	E	DP	FPct
1981 Mon	36	1	0	0	0	0	0	0	0	0	0	0	0	0	0	0	0	0	0	—	0	—	—	—	P	1	0	1	0	0	1.000

ED BAILEY—Lonas Edgar Bailey—Nickname: Gar—Bats: Left; Throws: Right

Ht: 6'2"; Wt: 205 lbs; Born: 4/15/1931 in Strawberry Plains, Tennessee; Debut: 9/26/1953

World Series		Batting																							Fielding						
Year Tm	Age	G	AB	H	2B	3B	HR	TB	R	RBI	GW	TBB	IBB	SO	HBP	SH	SF	SB	CS	SB%	GDP	Avg	OBP	SLG	Pos	G	PO	A	E	DP	FPct
1962 SF	31	6	14	1	0	0	1	4	1	2	0	0	0	3	0	0	0	0	0	—	0	.071	.071	.286	C	3	15	0	0	0	1.000

BOB BAILOR—Robert Michael Bailor—Bats: Right; Throws: Right

Ht: 5'11"; Wt: 170 lbs; Born: 7/10/1951 in Connellsville, Pennsylvania; Debut: 9/6/1975

LCS		Batting																							Fielding						
Year Tm	Age	G	AB	H	2B	3B	HR	TB	R	RBI	GW	TBB	IBB	SO	HBP	SH	SF	SB	CS	SB%	GDP	Avg	OBP	SLG	Pos	G	PO	A	E	DP	FPct
1985 LA	34	2	1	0	0	0	0	0	0	0	0	0	0	0	0	0	0	0	0	—	0	.000	.000	.000	3B	2	0	1	0	0	1.000

HAROLD BAINES—Harold Douglas Baines—Bats: Left; Throws: Left

Ht: 6'2"; Wt: 175 lbs; Born: 3/15/1959 in Easton, Maryland; Debut: 4/10/1980

Division Series		Batting																							Fielding						
Year Tm	Age	G	AB	H	2B	3B	HR	TB	R	RBI	GW	TBB	IBB	SO	HBP	SH	SF	SB	CS	SB%	GDP	Avg	OBP	SLG	Pos	G	PO	A	E	DP	FPct
1997 Bal	38	2	5	2	0	0	1	5	2	1	0	1	1	0	0	0	0	0	0	—	0	.400	.500	1.000	—						
LCS		Batting																							Fielding						
Year Tm	Age	G	AB	H	2B	3B	HR	TB	R	RBI	GW	TBB	IBB	SO	HBP	SH	SF	SB	CS	SB%	GDP	Avg	OBP	SLG	Pos	G	PO	A	E	DP	FPct
1983 ChA	24	4	16	2	0	0	0	2	0	0	0	1	0	3	0	0	0	0	0	—	2	.125	.176	.125	OF	4	5	1	0	0	1.000
1990 Oak	31	4	14	5	1	0	0	6	2	3	1	2	2	1	0	1	0	1	0	1.00	1	.357	.438	.429	—						
1992 Oak	33	6	25	11	2	0	1	16	6	4	1	0	0	3	0	1	0	0	0	—	1	.440	.440	.640	—						
1997 Bal	38	6	17	6	0	0	1	9	1	2	0	2	0	1	0	0	0	0	1	.00	1	.353	.421	.529	—						
LCS Totals		20	72	24	3	0	2	33	9	9	2	5	2	8	0	2	0	1	1	.50	5	.333	.377	.458	OF	4	5	1	0	0	1.000
World Series		Batting																							Fielding						
Year Tm	Age	G	AB	H	2B	3B	HR	TB	R	RBI	GW	TBB	IBB	SO	HBP	SH	SF	SB	CS	SB%	GDP	Avg	OBP	SLG	Pos	G	PO	A	E	DP	FPct
1990 Oak	31	3	7	1	0	0	1	4	1	2	0	1	1	2	0	0	0	0	0	—	0	.143	.250	.571	—						
Postseason Totals		25	84	27	3	0	4	42	12	12	2	7	4	10	0	2	0	1	1	.50	5	.321	.374	.500	OF	4	5	1	0	0	1.000

DOUG BAIR—Charles Douglas Bair—Throws: Right; Bats: Right

Ht: 6'0"; Wt: 170 lbs; Born: 8/22/1949 in Defiance, Ohio; Debut: 9/13/1976

LCS		Pitching																										
Year Tm	Age	G	GS	CG	GF	IP	BFP	H	R	ER	HR	SH	SF	HB	TBB	IBB	SO	WP	Bk	W	L	Pct	ShO	Sv-Op	Hld	OAvg	OOBP	ERA
1979 Cin	30	1	0	0	1	1.0	6	2	1	1	0	1	0	0	1	1	0	0	0	0	1	.000	0	0- 0	0	.500	.600	9.00
1982 StL	33	1	0	0	0	1.0	8	2	0	0	0	1	0	0	3	2	0	0	0	0	0	—	0	0- 0	0	.500	.714	0.00
LCS Totals		2	0	0	1	2.0	28	4	1	1	0	2	0	0	4	3	0	0	0	0	1	.000	0	0-0	0	.500	.667	4.50
World Series		Pitching																										
Year Tm	Age	G	GS	CG	GF	IP	BFP	H	R	ER	HR	SH	SF	HB	TBB	IBB	SO	WP	Bk	W	L	Pct	ShO	Sv-Op	Hld	OAvg	OOBP	ERA
1982 StL	33	3	0	0	0	2.0	10	2	2	2	0	0	0	0	2	0	3	0	0	0	1	.000	0	0- 1	0	.250	.400	9.00
1984 Det	35	1	0	0	0	0.2	1	0	0	0	0	0	0	0	0	0	1	0	0	0	0	—	0	0- 0	0	.000	.000	0.00
WS Totals		4	0	0	0	2.2	22	2	2	2	0	0	0	0	2	0	4	0	0	0	1	.000	0	0-1	0	.222	.364	6.75
Postseason Totals		6	0	0	1	4.2	50	6	3	3	0	2	0	0	6	3	4	0	0	0	2	.000	0	0-1	0	.353	.522	5.79

LCS		Batting																							Fielding						
Year Tm	Age	G	AB	H	2B	3B	HR	TB	R	RBI	GW	TBB	IBB	SO	HBP	SH	SF	SB	CS	SB%	GDP	Avg	OBP	SLG	Pos	G	PO	A	E	DP	FPct
1979 Cin	30	1	0	0	0	0	0	0	0	0	0	0	0	0	0	0	0	0	0	—	0	—	—	—	P	1	0	1	0	0	1.000
1982 StL	33	1	0	0	0	0	0	0	0	0	0	0	0	0	0	0	0	0	0	—	0	—	—	—	P	1	0	1	0	0	1.000
LCS Totals		2	0	0	0	0	0	0	0	0	0	0	0	0	0	0	0	0	0	—	0	—	—	—	P	2	0	2	0	0	1.000
World Series		Batting																							Fielding						
Year Tm	Age	G	AB	H	2B	3B	HR	TB	R	RBI	GW	TBB	IBB	SO	HBP	SH	SF	SB	CS	SB%	GDP	Avg	OBP	SLG	Pos	G	PO	A	E	DP	FPct
1982 StL	33	3	0	0	0	0	0	0	0	0	0	0	0	0	0	0	0	0	0	—	0	—	—	—	P	3	0	0	0	0	—
1984 Det	35	1	0	0	0	0	0	0	0	0	0	0	0	0	0	0	0	0	0	—	0	—	—	—	P	1	0	0	0	0	—
WS Totals		4	0	0	0	0	0	0	0	0	0	0	0	0	0	0	0	0	0	—	0	—	—	—	P	4	0	0	0	0	—
Postseason Totals		6	0	0	0	0	0	0	0	0	0	0	0	0	0	0	0	0	0	—	0	—	—	—	P	6	0	2	0	0	1.000

BILL BAKER—William Presley Baker—Bats: Right; Throws: Right

Ht: 6'0"; Wt: 200 lbs; Born: 2/22/1911 in Paw Creek, North Carolina; Debut: 5/4/1940

World Series		Batting																							Fielding						
Year Tm	Age	G	AB	H	2B	3B	HR	TB	R	RBI	GW	TBB	IBB	SO	HBP	SH	SF	SB	CS	SB%	GDP	Avg	OBP	SLG	Pos	G	PO	A	E	DP	FPct
1940 Cin	29	3	4	1	0	0	0	1	1	0	0	0	0	1	0	0	0	0	0	—	0	.250	.250	.250	C	3	7	0	1	1	.875

DOUG BAKER—Douglas Lee Baker—Bats: Both; Throws: Right

Ht: 5'9"; Wt: 165 lbs; Born: 4/3/1961 in Fullerton, California; Debut: 7/2/1984

LCS		Batting																							Fielding						
Year Tm	Age	G	AB	H	2B	3B	HR	TB	R	RBI	GW	TBB	IBB	SO	HBP	SH	SF	SB	CS	SB%	GDP	Avg	OBP	SLG	Pos	G	PO	A	E	DP	FPct
1984 Det	23	1	0	0	0	0	0	0	0	0	0	0	0	0	0	0	0	0	0	—	0	—	—	—	SS	1	0	0	0	0	—

DUSTY BAKER—Johnnie B. Baker—Bats: Right; Throws: Right

Ht: 6'2"; Wt: 183 lbs; Born: 6/15/1949 in Riverside, California; Debut: 9/7/1968

Division Series		Batting																							Fielding						
Year Tm	Age	G	AB	H	2B	3B	HR	TB	R	RBI	GW	TBB	IBB	SO	HBP	SH	SF	SB	CS	SB%	GDP	Avg	OBP	SLG	Pos	G	PO	A	E	DP	FPct
1981 LA	32	5	18	3	1	0	0	4	2	1	1	2	0	0	0	0	0	0	0	—	1	.167	.250	.222	OF	5	12	0	0	0	1.000
LCS		Batting																							Fielding						
Year Tm	Age	G	AB	H	2B	3B	HR	TB	R	RBI	GW	TBB	IBB	SO	HBP	SH	SF	SB	CS	SB%	GDP	Avg	OBP	SLG	Pos	G	PO	A	E	DP	FPct
1977 LA	28	4	14	5	1	0	2	12	4	8	2	2	0	3	0	0	0	0	0	—	0	.357	.438	.857	OF	4	3	0	0	0	1.000
1978 LA	29	4	15	7	2	0	0	9	1	1	0	3	0	0	0	0	0	0	0	—	1	.467	.556	.600	OF	4	5	0	0	0	1.000
1981 LA	32	5	19	6	1	0	0	7	3	3	0	1	0	0	1	0	0	0	0	—	0	.316	.381	.368	OF	5	10	0	1	0	.909
1983 LA	34	4	14	5	1	0	1	9	4	1	0	2	0	0	0	0	0	0	0	—	0	.357	.438	.643	OF	4	9	0	0	1	1.000
LCS Totals		17	62	23	5	0	3	37	12	13	2	8	0	3	1	0	0	0	0	—	1	.371	.451	.597	OF	17	27	0	1	1	.964
World Series		Batting																							Fielding						
Year Tm	Age	G	AB	H	2B	3B	HR	TB	R	RBI	GW	TBB	IBB	SO	HBP	SH	SF	SB	CS	SB%	GDP	Avg	OBP	SLG	Pos	G	PO	A	E	DP	FPct
1977 LA	28	6	24	7	0	0	1	10	4	5	0	0	0	2	1	0	0	0	0	—	0	.292	.320	.417	OF	6	12	0	1	0	.923
1978 LA	29	6	21	5	0	0	1	8	2	1	1	1	0	3	0	0	0	0	0	—	1	.238	.273	.381	OF	6	12	0	0	0	1.000
1981 LA	32	6	24	4	0	0	0	4	3	1	0	1	0	6	0	0	1	0	0	—	0	.167	.192	.167	OF	6	13	0	0	0	1.000
WS Totals		18	69	16	0	0	2	22	9	7	1	2	0	11	1	0	1	0	0	—	1	.232	.260	.319	OF	18	37	0	1	0	.974
Postseason Totals		40	149	42	6	0	5	63	23	21	4	12	0	14	2	0	1	0	0	—	3	.282	.341	.423	OF	40	76	0	2	1	.974

FLOYD BAKER—Floyd Wilson Baker—Bats: Left; Throws: Right

Ht: 5'9"; Wt: 160 lbs; Born: 10/10/1916 in Luray, Virginia; Debut: 5/4/1943

World Series		Batting																							Fielding						
Year Tm	Age	G	AB	H	2B	3B	HR	TB	R	RBI	GW	TBB	IBB	SO	HBP	SH	SF	SB	CS	SB%	GDP	Avg	OBP	SLG	Pos	G	PO	A	E	DP	FPct
1944 StL	27	2	2	0	0	0	0	0	0	0	0	0	0	2	0	0	0	0	0	—	0	.000	.000	.000	2B	2	1	0	0	0	1.000

FRANK BAKER—Frank Watts Baker—Bats: Left; Throws: Right

Ht: 6'2"; Wt: 178 lbs; Born: 10/29/1946 in Meridian, Mississippi; Debut: 8/9/1970

LCS		Batting																							Fielding						
Year Tm	Age	G	AB	H	2B	3B	HR	TB	R	RBI	GW	TBB	IBB	SO	HBP	SH	SF	SB	CS	SB%	GDP	Avg	OBP	SLG	Pos	G	PO	A	E	DP	FPct
1973 Bal	26	2	0	0	0	0	0	0	0	0	0	0	0	0	0	0	0	0	0	—	0	—	—	—	SS	2	0	0	0	0	—
1974 Bal	27	2	0	0	0	0	0	0	0	0	0	0	0	0	0	0	0	0	0	—	0	—	—	—	SS	2	1	1	1	0	.667
LCS Totals		4	0	0	0	0	0	0	0	0	0	0	0	0	0	0	0	0	0	—	0	—	—	—	SS	4	1	1	1	0	.667

GENE BAKER—Eugene Walter Baker—Bats: Right; Throws: Right

Ht: 6'1"; Wt: 170 lbs; Born: 6/15/1925 in Davenport, Iowa; Debut: 9/20/1953

World Series		Batting																							Fielding						
Year Tm	Age	G	AB	H	2B	3B	HR	TB	R	RBI	GW	TBB	IBB	SO	HBP	SH	SF	SB	CS	SB%	GDP	Avg	OBP	SLG	Pos	G	PO	A	E	DP	FPct
1960 Pit	35	3	3	0	0	0	0	0	0	0	0	0	0	1	0	0	0	0	0	—	0	.000	.000	.000	—						

HOME RUN BAKER (HOF 1955-V)—John Franklin Baker—Bats: Left; Throws: Right

Ht: 5'11"; Wt: 173 lbs; Born: 3/13/1886 in Trappe, Maryland; Debut: 9/21/1908; Died: 6/28/1963

World Series		Batting																							Fielding						
Year Tm	Age	G	AB	H	2B	3B	HR	TB	R	RBI	GW	TBB	IBB	SO	HBP	SH	SF	SB	CS	SB%	GDP	Avg	OBP	SLG	Pos	G	PO	A	E	DP	FPct
1910 Phi	24	5	22	9	3	0	0	12	6	4	1	2	0	1	0	0	0	0	3	.00	0	.409	.458	.545	3B	5	8	11	3	2	.864
1911 Phi	25	6	24	9	2	0	2	17	7	5	1	1	1	5	0	0	0	0	1	.00	0	.375	.400	.708	3B	6	10	11	2	1	.913
1913 Phi	27	5	20	9	0	0	1	12	2	7	2	0	0	2	0	0	1	1	1	.50	0	.450	.429	.600	3B	5	6	5	1	0	.917
1914 Phi	28	4	16	4	2	0	0	6	0	2	0	1	1	3	0	0	0	0	0	—	1	.250	.294	.375	3B	4	10	15	0	2	1.000
1921 NYA	35	4	8	2	0	0	0	2	0	0	0	1	0	0	0	0	0	0	0	—	0	.250	.333	.250	3B	2	2	3	0	0	1.000
1922 NYA	36	1	1	0	0	0	0	0	0	0	0	0	0	0	0	0	0	0	0	—	0	.000	.000	.000	—						
WS Totals		25	91	33	7	0	3	49	15	18	4	5	2	11	0	0	1	1	5	.17	1	.363	.392	.538	3B	22	36	45	6	5	.931

STEVE BALBONI—Stephen Charles Balboni—Nicknames: Bones, Bye-Bye—Bats: Right; Throws: Right

Ht: 6'3"; Wt: 225 lbs; Born: 1/16/1957 in Brockton, Massachusetts; Debut: 4/22/1981

LCS		Batting																							Fielding						
Year Tm	Age	G	AB	H	2B	3B	HR	TB	R	RBI	GW	TBB	IBB	SO	HBP	SH	SF	SB	CS	SB%	GDP	Avg	OBP	SLG	Pos	G	PO	A	E	DP	FPct
1984 KC	27	3	11	1	0	0	0	1	0	0	0	1	0	4	0	0	0	0	0	—	0	.091	.167	.091	1B	3	20	3	1	2	.958
1985 KC	28	7	25	3	0	0	0	3	1	1	1	2	0	8	0	0	0	0	0	—	0	.120	.185	.120	1B	7	72	7	2	6	.975
LCS Totals		10	36	4	0	0	0	4	1	1	1	3	0	12	0	0	0	0	0	—	0	.111	.179	.111	1B	10	92	10	3	8	.971
World Series		Batting																							Fielding						
Year Tm	Age	G	AB	H	2B	3B	HR	TB	R	RBI	GW	TBB	IBB	SO	HBP	SH	SF	SB	CS	SB%	GDP	Avg	OBP	SLG	Pos	G	PO	A	E	DP	FPct
1985 KC	28	7	25	8	0	0	0	8	2	3	0	5	1	4	0	0	0	0	0	—	0	.320	.433	.320	1B	7	70	3	0	1	1.000
Postseason Totals		17	61	12	0	0	0	12	3	4	1	8	1	16	0	0	0	0	0	—	0	.197	.290	.197	1B	17	162	13	3	9	.983

HARRY BALDWIN—Howard Edward Baldwin—Throws: Right; Bats: Right

Ht: 5'11"; Wt: 160 lbs; Born: 6/3/1900 in Baltimore, Maryland; Debut: 5/4/1924; Died: 1/23/1958

World Series		Pitching																										
Year Tm	Age	G	GS	CG	GF	IP	BFP	H	R	ER	HR	SH	SF	HB	TBB	IBB	SO	WP	Bk	W	L	Pct	ShO	Sv-Op	Hld	OAvg	OOBP	ERA
1924 NYG	24	1	0	0	0	2.0	7	1	0	0	0	0	0	0	0	0	1	0	0	0	0	—	0	0- 0	0	.143	.143	0.00

World Series		Batting																							Fielding						
Year Tm	Age	G	AB	H	2B	3B	HR	TB	R	RBI	GW	TBB	IBB	SO	HBP	SH	SF	SB	CS	SB%	GDP	Avg	OBP	SLG	Pos	G	PO	A	E	DP	FPct
1924 NYG	24	1	0	0	0	0	0	0	0	0	0	0	0	0	0	0	0	0	0	—	0	—	—	—	P	1	0	0	0	0	—

NEAL BALL—Cornelius Ball—Bats: Right; Throws: Right

Ht: 5'7"; Wt: 145 lbs; Born: 4/22/1881 in Grand Haven, Michigan; Debut: 9/12/1907; Died: 10/15/1957

World Series		Batting																							Fielding						
Year Tm	Age	G	AB	H	2B	3B	HR	TB	R	RBI	GW	TBB	IBB	SO	HBP	SH	SF	SB	CS	SB%	GDP	Avg	OBP	SLG	Pos	G	PO	A	E	DP	FPct
1912 Bos	31	1	1	0	0	0	0	0	0	0	0	0	0	1	0	0	0	0	0	—	0	.000	.000	.000	—						

WIN BALLOU—Noble Winfield Ballou—Throws: Left; Bats: Right

Ht: 5'10"; Wt: 170 lbs; Born: 11/30/1897 in Mount Morgan, Kentucky; Debut: 8/24/1925; Died: 1/30/1963

World Series		Pitching																										
Year Tm	Age	G	GS	CG	GF	IP	BFP	H	R	ER	HR	SH	SF	HB	TBB	IBB	SO	WP	Bk	W	L	Pct	ShO	Sv-Op	Hld	OAvg	OOBP	ERA
1925 Was	27	2	0	0	1	1.2	4	0	0	0	0	0	0	0	1	0	1	0	0	0	0	—	0	0- 0	0	.000	.250	0.00

World Series		Batting																							Fielding						
Year Tm	Age	G	AB	H	2B	3B	HR	TB	R	RBI	GW	TBB	IBB	SO	HBP	SH	SF	SB	CS	SB%	GDP	Avg	OBP	SLG	Pos	G	PO	A	E	DP	FPct
1925 Was	27	2	0	0	0	0	0	0	0	0	0	0	0	0	0	0	0	0	0	—	0	—	—	—	P	2	0	0	0	0	—

DAVE BANCROFT (HOF 1971-V)—David James Bancroft—Nickname: Beauty—Bats: Both; Throws: Right

Ht: 5'9"; Wt: 160 lbs; Born: 4/20/1891 in Sioux City, Iowa; Debut: 4/14/1915; Died: 10/9/1972

World Series		Batting																							Fielding						
Year Tm	Age	G	AB	H	2B	3B	HR	TB	R	RBI	GW	TBB	IBB	SO	HBP	SH	SF	SB	CS	SB%	GDP	Avg	OBP	SLG	Pos	G	PO	A	E	DP	FPct
1915 Phi	24	5	17	5	0	0	0	5	2	1	0	2	0	2	0	1	0	0	2	.00	0	.294	.368	.294	SS	5	13	10	1	2	.958
1921 NYG	30	8	33	5	1	0	0	6	3	3	0	1	0	5	0	0	1	0	1	.00	0	.152	.171	.182	SS	8	16	17	1	1	.971
1922 NYG	31	5	19	4	0	0	0	4	4	2	0	2	0	1	0	0	0	0	0	—	1	.211	.286	.211	SS	5	9	16	1	2	.962
1923 NYG	32	6	24	2	0	0	0	2	1	1	0	1	0	2	0	0	0	1	0	1.00	0	.083	.120	.083	SS	6	11	23	0	6	1.000
WS Totals		24	93	16	1	0	0	17	10	7	0	6	0	10	0	1	1	1	3	.25	1	.172	.220	.183	SS	24	49	66	3	11	.975

SAL BANDO—Salvatore Leonard Bando—Bats: Right; Throws: Right

Ht: 6'0"; Wt: 195 lbs; Born: 2/13/1944 in Cleveland, Ohio; Debut: 9/3/1966

Division Series		Batting																							Fielding						
Year Tm	Age	G	AB	H	2B	3B	HR	TB	R	RBI	GW	TBB	IBB	SO	HBP	SH	SF	SB	CS	SB%	GDP	Avg	OBP	SLG	Pos	G	PO	A	E	DP	FPct
1981 Mil	37	5	17	5	3	0	0	8	1	1	0	2	0	3	0	0	0	0	1	.00	0	.294	.368	.471	3B	5	3	5	0	0	1.000
LCS		Batting																							Fielding						
Year Tm	Age	G	AB	H	2B	3B	HR	TB	R	RBI	GW	TBB	IBB	SO	HBP	SH	SF	SB	CS	SB%	GDP	Avg	OBP	SLG	Pos	G	PO	A	E	DP	FPct
1971 Oak	27	3	11	4	2	0	1	9	3	1	0	1	0	0	0	0	0	0	0	—	1	.364	.417	.818	3B	3	6	2	0	2	1.000
1972 Oak	28	5	20	4	0	0	0	4	0	0	0	0	0	3	0	2	0	0	0	—	0	.200	.200	.200	3B	5	6	14	0	1	1.000
1973 Oak	29	5	18	3	0	0	2	9	2	3	0	3	0	6	1	0	0	0	0	—	0	.167	.318	.500	3B	5	7	11	0	0	1.000
1974 Oak	30	4	13	3	0	0	2	9	4	2	2	4	0	0	0	0	0	0	0	—	0	.231	.412	.692	3B	4	3	8	0	2	1.000
1975 Oak	31	3	12	6	2	0	0	8	1	2	0	0	0	3	0	0	0	0	0	—	0	.500	.500	.667	3B	3	3	11	1	0	.933
LCS Totals		20	74	20	4	0	5	39	10	8	2	8	0	12	1	2	0	0	0	—	1	.270	.349	.527	3B	20	25	46	1	5	.986
World Series		Batting																							Fielding						
Year Tm	Age	G	AB	H	2B	3B	HR	TB	R	RBI	GW	TBB	IBB	SO	HBP	SH	SF	SB	CS	SB%	GDP	Avg	OBP	SLG	Pos	G	PO	A	E	DP	FPct
1972 Oak	28	7	26	7	1	0	0	8	2	1	0	2	1	5	0	0	0	0	0	—	1	.269	.321	.308	3B	7	3	13	1	0	.941
1973 Oak	29	7	26	6	1	1	0	9	5	1	0	4	1	7	0	1	0	0	0	—	0	.231	.333	.346	3B	7	6	14	1	2	.952
1974 Oak	30	5	16	1	0	0	0	1	3	2	0	2	0	5	1	0	1	0	0	—	0	.063	.200	.063	3B	5	2	10	0	0	1.000
WS Totals		19	68	14	2	1	0	18	10	4	0	8	2	17	1	1	1	0	0	—	1	.206	.295	.265	3B	19	11	37	2	2	.960
Postseason Totals		44	159	39	9	1	5	65	21	13	2	18	2	32	2	3	1	0	1	.00	2	.245	.328	.409	3B	44	39	88	3	7	.977

DAN BANKHEAD—Daniel Robert Bankhead—Throws: Right; Bats: Right

Ht: 6'1"; Wt: 184 lbs; Born: 5/3/1920 in Empire, Alabama; Debut: 8/26/1947; Died: 5/2/1976

World Series		Batting																							Fielding						
Year Tm	Age	G	AB	H	2B	3B	HR	TB	R	RBI	GW	TBB	IBB	SO	HBP	SH	SF	SB	CS	SB%	GDP	Avg	OBP	SLG	Pos	G	PO	A	E	DP	FPct
1947 Bro	27	1	0	0	0	0	0	0	1	0	0	0	0	0	0	0	0	0	0	—	0	—	—	—	—						

FLOYD BANNISTER—Floyd Franklin Bannister—Throws: Left; Bats: Left

Ht: 6'1"; Wt: 190 lbs; Born: 6/10/1955 in Pierre, South Dakota; Debut: 4/19/1977

LCS		Pitching																										
Year Tm	Age	G	GS	CG	GF	IP	BFP	H	R	ER	HR	SH	SF	HB	TBB	IBB	SO	WP	Bk	W	L	Pct	ShO	Sv-Op	Hld	OAvg	OOBP	ERA
1983 ChA	28	1	1	0	0	6.0	25	5	4	3	1	0	0	0	1	0	5	0	0	0	1	.000	0	0- 0	0	.208	.240	4.50

LCS		Batting																							Fielding						
Year Tm	Age	G	AB	H	2B	3B	HR	TB	R	RBI	GW	TBB	IBB	SO	HBP	SH	SF	SB	CS	SB%	GDP	Avg	OBP	SLG	Pos	G	PO	A	E	DP	FPct
1983 ChA	28	1	0	0	0	0	0	0	0	0	0	0	0	0	0	0	0	0	0	—	0	—	—	—	P	1	0	0	0	0	—

JACK BANTA—Jackie Kay Banta—Throws: Right; Bats: Left

Ht: 6'2"; Wt: 175 lbs; Born: 6/24/1925 in Hutchinson, Kansas; Debut: 9/18/1947

World Series		Pitching																										
Year Tm	Age	G	GS	CG	GF	IP	BFP	H	R	ER	HR	SH	SF	HB	TBB	IBB	SO	WP	Bk	W	L	Pct	ShO	Sv-Op	Hld	OAvg	OOBP	ERA
1949 Bro	24	3	0	0	2	5.2	22	5	2	2	1	1	0	0	1	0	4	0	0	0	0	—	0	0- 0	0	.250	.286	3.18

World Series		Batting																							Fielding						
Year Tm	Age	G	AB	H	2B	3B	HR	TB	R	RBI	GW	TBB	IBB	SO	HBP	SH	SF	SB	CS	SB%	GDP	Avg	OBP	SLG	Pos	G	PO	A	E	DP	FPct
1949 Bro	24	3	1	0	0	0	0	0	0	0	0	0	0	0	0	0	0	0	0	—	0	.000	.000	.000	P	3	0	1	0	0	1.000

TURNER BARBER—Tyrus Turner Barber—Bats: Left; Throws: Right

Ht: 5'11"; Wt: 170 lbs; Born: 7/9/1893 in Lavinia, Tennessee; Debut: 8/19/1915; Died: 10/20/1968

World Series		Batting																							Fielding						
Year Tm	Age	G	AB	H	2B	3B	HR	TB	R	RBI	GW	TBB	IBB	SO	HBP	SH	SF	SB	CS	SB%	GDP	Avg	OBP	SLG	Pos	G	PO	A	E	DP	FPct
1918 ChN	25	3	2	0	0	0	0	0	0	0	0	0	0	0	0	0	0	0	0	—	1	.000	.000	.000	—						

JIM BARBIERI—James Patrick Barbieri—Bats: Left; Throws: Right

Ht: 5'7"; Wt: 155 lbs; Born: 9/15/1941 in Schenectady, New York; Debut: 7/5/1966

World Series		Batting																							Fielding						
Year Tm	Age	G	AB	H	2B	3B	HR	TB	R	RBI	GW	TBB	IBB	SO	HBP	SH	SF	SB	CS	SB%	GDP	Avg	OBP	SLG	Pos	G	PO	A	E	DP	FPct
1966 LA	25	1	1	0	0	0	0	0	0	0	0	0	0	1	0	0	0	0	0	—	0	.000	.000	.000	—						

JESSE BARFIELD—Jesse Lee Barfield—Bats: Right; Throws: Right

Ht: 6'1"; Wt: 200 lbs; Born: 10/29/1959 in Joliet, Illinois; Debut: 9/3/1981

LCS		Batting																							Fielding						
Year Tm	Age	G	AB	H	2B	3B	HR	TB	R	RBI	GW	TBB	IBB	SO	HBP	SH	SF	SB	CS	SB%	GDP	Avg	OBP	SLG	Pos	G	PO	A	E	DP	FPct
1985 Tor	25	7	25	7	1	0	1	11	3	4	0	3	0	7	0	0	0	1	1	.50	0	.280	.357	.440	OF	7	21	0	1	0	.955

MIKE BARLOW—Michael Roswell Barlow—Throws: Right; Bats: Left

Ht: 6'6"; Wt: 210 lbs; Born: 4/30/1948 in Stamford, New York; Debut: 6/18/1975

LCS		Pitching																										
Year Tm	Age	G	GS	CG	GF	IP	BFP	H	R	ER	HR	SH	SF	HB	TBB	IBB	SO	WP	Bk	W	L	Pct	ShO	Sv-Op	Hld	OAvg	OOBP	ERA
1979 Cal	31	1	0	0	1	1.0	3	0	0	0	0	0	0	0	0	0	0	0	0	0	0	—	0	0- 0	0	.000	.000	0.00

LCS		Batting																							Fielding						
Year Tm	Age	G	AB	H	2B	3B	HR	TB	R	RBI	GW	TBB	IBB	SO	HBP	SH	SF	SB	CS	SB%	GDP	Avg	OBP	SLG	Pos	G	PO	A	E	DP	FPct
1979 Cal	31	1	0	0	0	0	0	0	0	0	0	0	0	0	0	0	0	0	0	—	0	—	—	—	P	1	0	0	0	0	—

JESSE BARNES—Jesse Lawrence Barnes—Nickname: Nubby—Throws: Right; Bats: Left

Ht: 6'0"; Wt: 170 lbs; Born: 8/26/1892 in Perkins, Oklahoma; Debut: 7/30/1915; Died: 9/9/1961

World Series		Pitching																										
Year Tm	Age	G	GS	CG	GF	IP	BFP	H	R	ER	HR	SH	SF	HB	TBB	IBB	SO	WP	Bk	W	L	Pct	ShO	Sv-Op	Hld	OAvg	OOBP	ERA
1921 NYG	29	3	0	0	3	16.1	63	10	3	3	1	0	0	1	6	0	18	1	0	2	0	1.000	0	0- 0	0	.179	.270	1.65
1922 NYG	30	1	1	1	0	10.0	41	8	3	2	1	0	0	0	2	0	6	0	0	0	0	—	0	0- 0	0	.205	.244	1.80
1923 NYG	31	2	0	0	1	4.2	18	4	0	0	0	0	0	0	0	0	4	0	0	0	0	—	0	0- 0	0	.222	.222	0.00
WS Totals		6	1	1	4	31.0	244	22	6	5	2	0	0	1	8	0	28	1	0	2	0	1.000	0	0-0	0	.195	.254	1.45

World Series		Batting																							Fielding						
Year Tm	Age	G	AB	H	2B	3B	HR	TB	R	RBI	GW	TBB	IBB	SO	HBP	SH	SF	SB	CS	SB%	GDP	Avg	OBP	SLG	Pos	G	PO	A	E	DP	FPct
1921 NYG	29	3	9	4	0	0	0	4	3	0	0	0	0	0	0	0	0	0	0	—	1	.444	.444	.444	P	3	1	1	0	0	1.000
1922 NYG	30	1	4	0	0	0	0	0	0	0	0	0	0	1	0	0	0	0	0	—	1	.000	.000	.000	P	1	0	4	0	0	1.000
1923 NYG	31	2	1	0	0	0	0	0	0	0	0	0	0	1	0	0	0	0	0	—	0	.000	.000	.000	P	2	1	2	0	0	1.000
WS Totals		6	14	4	0	0	0	4	3	0	0	0	0	2	0	0	0	0	0	—	2	.286	.286	.286	P	6	2	7	0	0	1.000

VIRGIL BARNES—Virgil Jennings Barnes—Nickname: Zeke—Throws: Right; Bats: Right

Ht: 6'0"; Wt: 165 lbs; Born: 3/5/1897 in Ontario, Kansas; Debut: 9/25/1919; Died: 7/24/1958

World Series		Pitching																										
Year Tm	Age	G	GS	CG	GF	IP	BFP	H	R	ER	HR	SH	SF	HB	TBB	IBB	SO	WP	Bk	W	L	Pct	ShO	Sv-Op	Hld	OAvg	OOBP	ERA
1924 NYG	27	2	2	0	0	12.2	52	15	8	8	2	1	0	0	1	0	9	1	0	0	1	.000	0	0- 0	0	.300	.314	5.68

World Series		Batting																							Fielding						
Year Tm	Age	G	AB	H	2B	3B	HR	TB	R	RBI	GW	TBB	IBB	SO	HBP	SH	SF	SB	CS	SB%	GDP	Avg	OBP	SLG	Pos	G	PO	A	E	DP	FPct
1924 NYG	27	2	4	0	0	0	0	0	0	0	0	1	0	2	0	0	0	0	0	—	0	.000	.200	.000	P	2	2	3	0	0	1.000

REX BARNEY—Rex Edward Barney—Throws: Right; Bats: Right

Ht: 6'3"; Wt: 185 lbs; Born: 12/19/1924 in Omaha, Nebraska; Debut: 8/18/1943; Died: 8/12/1997

World Series		Pitching																										
Year Tm	Age	G	GS	CG	GF	IP	BFP	H	R	ER	HR	SH	SF	HB	TBB	IBB	SO	WP	Bk	W	L	Pct	ShO	Sv-Op	Hld	OAvg	OOBP	ERA
1947 Bro	22	3	1	0	1	6.2	32	4	2	2	1	0	0	0	10	0	3	2	0	0	1	.000	0	0- 0	0	.182	.438	2.70
1949 Bro	24	1	1	0	0	2.2	17	3	5	5	0	1	0	0	6	0	2	0	0	0	1	.000	0	0- 0	0	.300	.563	16.88
WS Totals		4	2	0	1	9.1	98	7	7	7	1	1	0	0	16	0	5	2	0	0	2	.000	0	0-0	0	.219	.479	6.75

World Series		Batting																							Fielding						
Year Tm	Age	G	AB	H	2B	3B	HR	TB	R	RBI	GW	TBB	IBB	SO	HBP	SH	SF	SB	CS	SB%	GDP	Avg	OBP	SLG	Pos	G	PO	A	E	DP	FPct
1947 Bro	22	3	1	0	0	0	0	0	0	0	0	0	0	0	0	0	0	0	0	—	0	.000	.000	.000	P	3	0	1	0	0	1.000
1949 Bro	24	1	0	0	0	0	0	0	0	0	0	0	0	0	0	0	0	0	0	—	0	—	—	—	P	1	1	1	1	0	.667
WS Totals		4	1	0	0	0	0	0	0	0	0	0	0	0	0	0	0	0	0	—	0	.000	.000	.000	P	4	1	2	1	0	.750

CLYDE BARNHART—Clyde Lee Barnhart—Nickname: Pooch—Bats: Right; Throws: Right

Ht: 5'10"; Wt: 155 lbs; Born: 12/29/1895 in Buck Valley, Pennsylvania; Debut: 9/22/1920; Died: 1/21/1980

World Series		Batting																							Fielding						
Year Tm	Age	G	AB	H	2B	3B	HR	TB	R	RBI	GW	TBB	IBB	SO	HBP	SH	SF	SB	CS	SB%	GDP	Avg	OBP	SLG	Pos	G	PO	A	E	DP	FPct
1925 Pit	29	7	28	7	1	0	0	8	1	5	0	3	0	5	0	0	0	1	0	1.00	1	.250	.323	.286	OF	7	12	1	0	0	1.000
1927 Pit	31	4	16	5	1	0	0	6	0	4	0	0	0	0	0	0	1	0	0	—	1	.313	.294	.375	OF	4	6	0	0	0	1.000
WS Totals		11	44	12	2	0	0	14	1	9	0	3	0	5	0	0	1	1	0	1.00	2	.273	.313	.318	OF	11	18	1	0	0	1.000

SALOME BAROJAS—Throws: Right; Bats: Right

Ht: 5'9"; Wt: 160 lbs; Born: 6/16/1957 in Cordoba, Mexico; Debut: 4/11/1982

LCS		Pitching																										
Year Tm	Age	G	GS	CG	GF	IP	BFP	H	R	ER	HR	SH	SF	HB	TBB	IBB	SO	WP	Bk	W	L	Pct	ShO	Sv-Op	Hld	OAvg	OOBP	ERA
1983 ChA	26	2	0	0	0	1.0	7	4	2	2	0	0	0	0	0	0	0	0	0	0	0	—	0	0- 0	0	.571	.571	18.00

LCS		Batting																							Fielding						
Year Tm	Age	G	AB	H	2B	3B	HR	TB	R	RBI	GW	TBB	IBB	SO	HBP	SH	SF	SB	CS	SB%	GDP	Avg	OBP	SLG	Pos	G	PO	A	E	DP	FPct
1983 ChA	26	2	0	0	0	0	0	0	0	0	0	0	0	0	0	0	0	0	0	—	0	—	—	—	P	2	0	1	0	0	1.000

JIM BARR—James Leland Barr—Throws: Right; Bats: Right

Ht: 6'3"; Wt: 205 lbs; Born: 2/10/1948 in Lynwood, California; Debut: 7/31/1971

LCS		Pitching																										
Year Tm	Age	G	GS	CG	GF	IP	BFP	H	R	ER	HR	SH	SF	HB	TBB	IBB	SO	WP	Bk	W	L	Pct	ShO	Sv-Op	Hld	OAvg	OOBP	ERA
1971 SF	23	1	0	0	0	1.0	6	3	1	1	1	0	0	0	0	0	2	0	0	0	0	—	0	0- 0	0	.500	.500	9.00

LCS		Batting																							Fielding						
Year Tm	Age	G	AB	H	2B	3B	HR	TB	R	RBI	GW	TBB	IBB	SO	HBP	SH	SF	SB	CS	SB%	GDP	Avg	OBP	SLG	Pos	G	PO	A	E	DP	FPct
1971 SF	23	1	1	0	0	0	0	0	0	0	0	0	0	0	0	0	0	0	0	—	0	.000	.000	.000	P	1	0	0	0	0	—

MARTY BARRETT—Martin Glenn Barrett—Bats: Right; Throws: Right

Ht: 5'10"; Wt: 175 lbs; Born: 6/23/1958 in Arcadia, California; Debut: 9/6/1982

		Batting																							Fielding						
LCS																															
Year Tm	Age	G	AB	H	2B	3B	HR	TB	R	RBI	GW	TBB	IBB	SO	HBP	SH	SF	SB	CS	SB%	GDP	Avg	OBP	SLG	Pos	G	PO	A	E	DP	FPct
1986 Bos	28	7	30	11	2	0	0	13	4	5	1	2	0	2	0	1	0	0	0	—	1	.367	.406	.433	2B	7	19	21	0	4	1.000
1988 Bos	30	4	15	1	0	0	0	1	2	0	0	1	0	0	0	1	0	0	0	—	1	.067	.125	.067	2B	4	6	9	0	1	1.000
1990 Bos	32	3	0	0	0	0	0	0	0	0	0	0	0	0	0	0	0	0	0	—	0	—	—	—	2B	3	2	0	0	0	1.000
LCS Totals		14	45	12	2	0	0	14	6	5	1	3	0	2	0	2	0	0	0	—	2	.267	.313	.311	2B	14	27	30	0	5	1.000
World Series																															
Year Tm	Age	G	AB	H	2B	3B	HR	TB	R	RBI	GW	TBB	IBB	SO	HBP	SH	SF	SB	CS	SB%	GDP	Avg	OBP	SLG	Pos	G	PO	A	E	DP	FPct
1986 Bos	28	7	30	13	2	0	0	15	1	4	0	5	1	2	0	0	0	0	0	—	0	.433	.514	.500	2B	7	14	25	0	5	1.000
Postseason Totals		21	75	25	4	0	0	29	7	9	1	8	1	4	0	2	0	0	0	—	2	.333	.398	.387	2B	21	41	55	0	10	1.000

RED BARRETT—Charles Henry Barrett—Throws: Right; Bats: Right

Ht: 5'11"; Wt: 183 lbs; Born: 2/14/1915 in Santa Barbara, California; Debut: 9/15/1937; Died: 7/28/1990

World Series		Pitching																									
Year Tm	Age	G	GS	CG	GF	IP	BFP	H	R	ER	HR	SH	SF	HB	TBB	IBB	SO	WP	Bk	W	L	Pct	ShO	Sv-Op	Hld	OAvg	OOBP	ERA
1948 Bos	33	2	0	0	1	3.2	13	1	0	0	0	0	0	0	0	0	1	0	0	0	0	—	0	0-0	0	.077	.077	0.00

World Series		Batting																							Fielding						
Year Tm	Age	G	AB	H	2B	3B	HR	TB	R	RBI	GW	TBB	IBB	SO	HBP	SH	SF	SB	CS	SB%	GDP	Avg	OBP	SLG	Pos	G	PO	A	E	DP	FPct
1948 Bos	33	2	0	0	0	0	0	0	0	0	0	0	0	0	0	0	0	0	0	—	0	—	—	—	P	2	0	0	0	0	—

JACK BARRY—John Joseph Barry—Bats: Right; Throws: Right

Ht: 5'9"; Wt: 158 lbs; Born: 4/26/1887 in Meriden, Connecticut; Debut: 7/13/1908; Died: 4/23/1961

World Series		Batting																							Fielding						
Year Tm	Age	G	AB	H	2B	3B	HR	TB	R	RBI	GW	TBB	IBB	SO	HBP	SH	SF	SB	CS	SB%	GDP	Avg	OBP	SLG	Pos	G	PO	A	E	DP	FPct
1910 Phi	23	5	17	4	2	0	0	6	3	3	0	1	0	3	1	2	0	0	0	—	1	.235	.316	.353	SS	5	9	12	0	1	1.000
1911 Phi	24	6	19	7	4	0	0	11	2	2	0	0	0	2	0	2	1	2	1	.67	0	.368	.350	.579	SS	6	8	12	3	0	.870
1913 Phi	26	5	20	6	3	0	0	9	3	1	1	0	0	0	0	0	0	0	0	—	0	.300	.300	.450	SS	5	8	15	1	5	.958
1914 Phi	27	4	14	1	0	0	0	1	1	0	0	1	0	3	0	0	0	1	0	1.00	0	.071	.133	.071	SS	4	5	20	1	2	.962
1915 Bos	28	5	17	3	0	0	0	3	1	1	0	1	0	2	0	0	0	0	0	—	0	.176	.222	.176	2B	5	10	8	1	1	.947
WS Totals		25	87	21	9	0	0	30	10	7	1	3	0	10	1	4	1	3	1	.75	1	.241	.272	.345	SS	20	30	59	5	8	.947

DICK BARTELL—Richard William Bartell—Nicknames: Rowdy Richard, Shortwave—Bats: Right; Throws: Right

Ht: 5'9"; Wt: 160 lbs; Born: 11/22/1907 in Chicago, Ill.; Debut: 10/2/1927; Died: 8/4/1995

World Series		Batting																							Fielding						
Year Tm	Age	G	AB	H	2B	3B	HR	TB	R	RBI	GW	TBB	IBB	SO	HBP	SH	SF	SB	CS	SB%	GDP	Avg	OBP	SLG	Pos	G	PO	A	E	DP	FPct
1936 NYG	28	6	21	8	3	0	1	14	5	3	0	4	0	4	0	2	0	0	0	—	0	.381	.480	.667	SS	6	8	13	1	4	.955
1937 NYG	29	5	21	5	1	0	0	6	3	1	0	0	0	3	0	0	0	0	0	—	0	.238	.238	.286	SS	5	13	11	3	3	.889
1940 Det	32	7	26	7	2	0	0	9	2	3	0	3	0	3	0	0	0	1	0	1.00	0	.269	.345	.346	SS	7	12	11	1	2	.958
WS Totals		18	68	20	6	0	1	29	10	7	0	7	0	10	0	2	0	1	0	1.00	0	.294	.360	.426	SS	18	33	35	5	9	.932

KEVIN BASS—Kevin Charles Bass—Bats: Both; Throws: Right

Ht: 6'0"; Wt: 183 lbs; Born: 5/12/1959 in Redwood City, California; Debut: 4/9/1982

LCS		Batting																							Fielding						
Year Tm	Age	G	AB	H	2B	3B	HR	TB	R	RBI	GW	TBB	IBB	SO	HBP	SH	SF	SB	CS	SB%	GDP	Avg	OBP	SLG	Pos	G	PO	A	E	DP	FPct
1986 Hou	27	6	24	7	2	0	0	9	0	0	0	4	0	4	0	0	0	2	3	.40	0	.292	.393	.375	OF	6	16	0	1	0	.941

BILLY BATES—William Derrick Bates—Bats: Left; Throws: Right

Ht: 5'7"; Wt: 155 lbs; Born: 12/7/1963 in Houston, Texas; Debut: 8/17/1989

		Batting																							Fielding						
LCS																															
Year Tm	Age	G	AB	H	2B	3B	HR	TB	R	RBI	GW	TBB	IBB	SO	HBP	SH	SF	SB	CS	SB%	GDP	Avg	OBP	SLG	Pos	G	PO	A	E	DP	FPct
1990 Cin	26	2	0	0	0	0	0	0	1	0	0	0	0	0	0	0	0	0	1	.00	0	—	—	—	—						
World Series																															
Year Tm	Age	G	AB	H	2B	3B	HR	TB	R	RBI	GW	TBB	IBB	SO	HBP	SH	SF	SB	CS	SB%	GDP	Avg	OBP	SLG	Pos	G	PO	A	E	DP	FPct
1990 Cin	26	1	1	1	0	0	0	1	1	0	0	0	0	0	0	0	0	0	0	—	0	1.000	1.000	1.000	—						
Postseason Totals		3	1	1	0	0	0	1	2	0	0	0	0	0	0	0	0	0	1	.00	0	1.000	1.000	1.000	—	0	0	0	0	0	—

JASON BATES—Jason Charles Bates—Bats: Both; Throws: Right

Ht: 5'11"; Wt: 170 lbs; Born: 1/5/1971 in Downey, California; Debut: 4/26/1995

Division Series		Batting																							Fielding						
Year Tm	Age	G	AB	H	2B	3B	HR	TB	R	RBI	GW	TBB	IBB	SO	HBP	SH	SF	SB	CS	SB%	GDP	Avg	OBP	SLG	Pos	G	PO	A	E	DP	FPct
1995 Col	24	4	4	1	0	0	0	1	0	0	0	0	0	0	0	1	0	0	0	—	0	.250	.250	.250	3B	1	0	1	0	0	1.000
																									2B	1	1	2	0	0	1.000

BILL BATHE—William David Bathe—Bats: Right; Throws: Right

Ht: 6'2"; Wt: 200 lbs; Born: 10/14/1960 in Downey, California; Debut: 4/12/1986

		Batting																							Fielding						
LCS																															
Year Tm	Age	G	AB	H	2B	3B	HR	TB	R	RBI	GW	TBB	IBB	SO	HBP	SH	SF	SB	CS	SB%	GDP	Avg	OBP	SLG	Pos	G	PO	A	E	DP	FPct
1989 SF	28	2	1	0	0	0	0	0	0	0	0	0	0	1	0	0	0	0	0	—	0	.000	.000	.000	—						
World Series																															
Year Tm	Age	G	AB	H	2B	3B	HR	TB	R	RBI	GW	TBB	IBB	SO	HBP	SH	SF	SB	CS	SB%	GDP	Avg	OBP	SLG	Pos	G	PO	A	E	DP	FPct
1989 SF	28	2	2	1	0	0	1	4	1	3	0	0	0	0	0	0	0	0	0	—	0	.500	.500	2.000	—						
Postseason Totals		4	3	1	0	0	1	4	1	3	0	0	0	1	0	0	0	0	0	—	0	.333	.333	1.333	—	0	0	0	0	0	—

KIM BATISTE—Kimothy Emil Batiste—Bats: Right; Throws: Right

Ht: 6'0"; Wt: 175 lbs; Born: 3/15/1968 in New Orleans, Louisiana; Debut: 9/8/1991

		Batting																							Fielding						
LCS																															
Year Tm	Age	G	AB	H	2B	3B	HR	TB	R	RBI	GW	TBB	IBB	SO	HBP	SH	SF	SB	CS	SB%	GDP	Avg	OBP	SLG	Pos	G	PO	A	E	DP	FPct
1993 Phi	25	4	1	1	0	0	0	1	0	1	1	0	0	0	0	0	0	0	0	—	0	1.000	1.000	1.000	3B	4	2	0	2	0	.500
World Series																															
Year Tm	Age	G	AB	H	2B	3B	HR	TB	R	RBI	GW	TBB	IBB	SO	HBP	SH	SF	SB	CS	SB%	GDP	Avg	OBP	SLG	Pos	G	PO	A	E	DP	FPct
1993 Phi	25	3	0	0	0	0	0	0	0	0	0	0	0	0	0	0	0	0	0	—	0	—	—	—	3B	3	0	1	0	0	1.000
Postseason Totals		7	1	1	0	0	0	1	0	1	1	0	0	0	0	0	0	0	0	—	0	1.000	1.000	1.000	3B	7	2	1	2	0	.600

EARL BATTEY—Earl Jesse Battey—Bats: Right; Throws: Right

Ht: 6'1"; Wt: 205 lbs; Born: 1/5/1935 in Los Angeles, California; Debut: 9/10/1955

World Series		Batting																							Fielding						
Year Tm	Age	G	AB	H	2B	3B	HR	TB	R	RBI	GW	TBB	IBB	SO	HBP	SH	SF	SB	CS	SB%	GDP	Avg	OBP	SLG	Pos	G	PO	A	E	DP	FPct
1965 Min	30	7	25	3	0	1	0	5	1	2	0	0	0	5	0	0	0	0	0	—	2	.120	.120	.200	C	7	31	6	0	2	1.000

HANK BAUER—Henry Albert Bauer—Bats: Right; Throws: Right

Ht: 6'0"; Wt: 192 lbs; Born: 7/31/1922 in East St. Louis, Illinois; Debut: 9/6/1948

World Series		Batting																							Fielding						
Year Tm	Age	G	AB	H	2B	3B	HR	TB	R	RBI	GW	TBB	IBB	SO	HBP	SH	SF	SB	CS	SB%	GDP	Avg	OBP	SLG	Pos	G	PO	A	E	DP	FPct
1949 NYA	27	3	6	1	0	0	0	1	0	0	0	0	0	0	0	0	0	0	0	—	0	.167	.167	.167	OF	3	3	0	0	0	1.000
1950 NYA	28	4	15	2	0	0	0	2	0	1	0	0	0	0	0	0	0	0	0	—	0	.133	.133	.133	OF	4	8	0	0	0	1.000
1951 NYA	29	6	18	3	0	1	0	5	0	3	1	1	0	1	0	0	0	0	0	—	0	.167	.211	.278	OF	6	7	0	0	0	1.000
1952 NYA	30	7	18	1	0	0	0	1	2	1	0	4	0	3	0	1	0	0	1	.00	1	.056	.227	.056	OF	7	10	0	0	0	1.000
1953 NYA	31	6	23	6	0	1	0	8	6	1	0	2	0	4	1	1	0	0	0	—	0	.261	.346	.348	OF	6	14	0	0	0	1.000
1955 NYA	33	6	14	6	0	0	0	6	1	1	0	0	0	1	0	0	0	0	1	.00	0	.429	.429	.429	OF	5	7	0	0	0	1.000
1956 NYA	34	7	32	9	0	0	1	12	3	3	0	0	0	5	0	0	0	1	0	1.00	0	.281	.281	.375	OF	7	14	1	1	0	.938
1957 NYA	35	7	31	8	2	1	2	18	3	6	2	1	0	6	0	0	0	0	0	—	0	.258	.281	.581	OF	7	10	0	0	0	1.000
1958 NYA	36	7	31	10	0	0	4	22	6	8	1	0	0	5	0	0	0	0	1	.00	1	.323	.323	.710	OF	7	7	0	0	0	1.000
WS Totals		53	188	46	2	3	7	75	21	24	4	8	0	25	1	2	0	1	3	.25	2	.245	.279	.399	OF	52	80	1	1	0	.988

DANNY BAUTISTA
Daniel Bautista—Bats: Right; Throws: Right   Ht: 5'11"; Wt: 170 lbs; Born: 5/24/1972 in Santo Domingo, Dominican Republic; Debut: 9/15/1993

Division Series
Year Tm	Age	G	AB	H	2B	3B	HR	TB	R	RBI	GW	TBB	IBB	SO	HBP	SH	SF	SB	CS	SB%	GDP	Avg	OBP	SLG	Pos	G	PO	A	E	DP	FPct
1997 Atl	25	3	3	1	0	0	0	1	0	2	0	0	0	1	0	0	0	0	0	—	0	.333	.333	.333	OF	3	0	0	0	0	

LCS
Year Tm	Age	G	AB	H	2B	3B	HR	TB	R	RBI	GW	TBB	IBB	SO	HBP	SH	SF	SB	CS	SB%	GDP	Avg	OBP	SLG	Pos	G	PO	A	E	DP	FPct
1997 Atl	25	2	4	1	0	0	0	1	0	0	0	0	0	0	0	0	0	0	0	—	0	.250	.250	.250	OF	2	4	0	0	0	1.000
Postseason Totals		5	7	2	0	0	0	2	0	2	0	0	0	1	0	0	0	0	0	—	0	.286	.286	.286	OF	5	4	0	0	0	1.000

DON BAYLOR
Don Edward Baylor—Nickname: Groove—Bats: Right; Throws: Right   Ht: 6'1"; Wt: 190 lbs; Born: 6/28/1949 in Austin, Texas; Debut: 9/18/1970

LCS
Year Tm	Age	G	AB	H	2B	3B	HR	TB	R	RBI	GW	TBB	IBB	SO	HBP	SH	SF	SB	CS	SB%	GDP	Avg	OBP	SLG	Pos	G	PO	A	E	DP	FPct
1973 Bal	24	4	11	3	0	0	0	3	3	1	0	3	0	5	0	0	0	0	0	—	1	.273	.429	.273	OF	3	7	0	0	0	1.000
1974 Bal	25	4	15	4	0	0	0	4	0	0	0	0	0	2	0	0	0	0	1	.00	0	.267	.267	.267	OF	4	9	0	0	0	1.000
1979 Cal-M	30	4	16	3	0	0	1	6	2	2	0	1	1	2	0	0	0	0	0	—	0	.188	.235	.375	OF	1	4	0	0	0	1.000
1982 Cal	33	5	17	5	1	1	1	11	2	10	1	2	0	0	0	0	1	0	0	—	1	.294	.350	.647	—						
1986 Bos	37	7	26	9	3	0	1	15	6	2	0	4	0	5	2	0	0	0	0	—	0	.346	.469	.577	—						
1987 Min	38	2	5	2	0	0	0	2	0	1	1	0	0	1	0	0	0	0	0	—	0	.400	.500	.400	—						
1988 Oak	39	2	8	0	0	0	0	0	0	1	0	1	0	2	1	0	0	0	0	—	1	.000	.125	.000	—						
LCS Totals		28	96	26	4	1	3	41	13	17	2	11	1	16	3	0	2	0	1	.00	3	.271	.357	.427	OF	8	20	0	0	0	1.000

World Series
Year Tm	Age	G	AB	H	2B	3B	HR	TB	R	RBI	GW	TBB	IBB	SO	HBP	SH	SF	SB	CS	SB%	GDP	Avg	OBP	SLG	Pos	G	PO	A	E	DP	FPct
1986 Bos	37	4	11	2	1	0	0	3	1	1	0	1	0	3	1	0	0	0	0	—	0	.182	.308	.273	—						
1987 Min	38	5	13	5	0	0	1	8	3	3	0	1	1	1	1	0	0	0	0	—	0	.385	.467	.615	—						
1988 Oak	39	1	1	0	0	0	0	0	0	0	0	0	0	1	0	0	0	0	0	—	0	.000	.000	.000	—						
WS Totals		10	25	7	1	0	1	11	4	4	0	2	1	5	2	0	0	0	0	—	0	.280	.379	.440	—		0	0	0	0	
Postseason Totals		38	121	33	5	1	4	52	17	21	2	13	2	21	5	0	2	0	1	.00	4	.273	.362	.430	OF	8	20	0	0	0	1.000

DAVE BEARD
Charles David Beard—Throws: Right; Bats: Left   Ht: 6'5"; Wt: 190 lbs; Born: 10/2/1959 in Atlanta, Georgia; Debut: 7/16/1980

Division Series
Year Tm	Age	G	GS	CG	GF	IP	BFP	H	R	ER	HR	SH	SF	HB	TBB	IBB	SO	WP	Bk	W	L	Pct	ShO	Sv-Op	Hld	OAvg	OOBP	ERA
1981 Oak	21	1	0	0	1	1.1	4	0	0	0	0	0	0	0	0	0	2	0	0	0	0	—	0	1-1	0	.000	.000	0.00

LCS
Year Tm	Age	G	GS	CG	GF	IP	BFP	H	R	ER	HR	SH	SF	HB	TBB	IBB	SO	WP	Bk	W	L	Pct	ShO	Sv-Op	Hld	OAvg	OOBP	ERA
1981 Oak	21	1	0	0	0	0.2	7	5	3	3	1	0	0	0	0	0	0	0	0	0	0	—	0	0-0	0	.714	.714	40.50
Postseason Totals		2	0	0	1	2.0	22	5	3	3	1	0	0	0	0	0	2	0	0	0	0	—	0	1-1	0	.455	.455	13.50

Division Series
Year Tm	Age	G	AB	H	2B	3B	HR	TB	R	RBI	GW	TBB	IBB	SO	HBP	SH	SF	SB	CS	SB%	GDP	Avg	OBP	SLG	Pos	G	PO	A	E	DP	FPct
1981 Oak	21	1	0	0	0	0	0	0	0	0	0	0	0	0	0	0	0	0	0	—	0	—	—	—	P	1	0	0	0	0	—

LCS
Year Tm	Age	G	AB	H	2B	3B	HR	TB	R	RBI	GW	TBB	IBB	SO	HBP	SH	SF	SB	CS	SB%	GDP	Avg	OBP	SLG	Pos	G	PO	A	E	DP	FPct
1981 Oak	21	1	0	0	0	0	0	0	0	0	0	0	0	0	0	0	0	0	0	—	0	—	—	—	P	1	0	1	0	0	1.000
Postseason Totals		2	0	0	0	0	0	0	0	0	0	0	0	0	0	0	0	0	0	—	0	—	—	—	P	2	0	1	0	0	1.000

GENE BEARDEN
Henry Eugene Bearden—Throws: Left; Bats: Left   Ht: 6'3"; Wt: 198 lbs; Born: 9/5/1920 in Lexa, Arkansas; Debut: 5/10/1947

World Series
Year Tm	Age	G	GS	CG	GF	IP	BFP	H	R	ER	HR	SH	SF	HB	TBB	IBB	SO	WP	Bk	W	L	Pct	ShO	Sv-Op	Hld	OAvg	OOBP	ERA
1948 Cle	28	2	1	1	1	10.2	36	6	0	0	0	1	0	0	1	0	4	0	0	1	0	1.000	1	1-1	0	.176	.200	0.00

World Series
Year Tm	Age	G	AB	H	2B	3B	HR	TB	R	RBI	GW	TBB	IBB	SO	HBP	SH	SF	SB	CS	SB%	GDP	Avg	OBP	SLG	Pos	G	PO	A	E	DP	FPct
1948 Cle	28	2	4	2	1	0	0	3	1	0	0	0	0	1	0	0	0	0	0	—	0	.500	.500	.750	P	2	0	7	0	1	1.000

JIM BEATTIE
James Louis Beattie—Throws: Right; Bats: Right   Ht: 6'5"; Wt: 210 lbs; Born: 7/4/1954 in Hampton, Virginia; Debut: 4/25/1978

LCS
Year Tm	Age	G	GS	CG	GF	IP	BFP	H	R	ER	HR	SH	SF	HB	TBB	IBB	SO	WP	Bk	W	L	Pct	ShO	Sv-Op	Hld	OAvg	OOBP	ERA
1978 NYA	24	1	1	0	0	5.1	23	2	1	1	0	0	0	0	5	0	3	0	0	1	0	1.000	0	0-0	0	.111	.304	1.69

World Series
Year Tm	Age	G	GS	CG	GF	IP	BFP	H	R	ER	HR	SH	SF	HB	TBB	IBB	SO	WP	Bk	W	L	Pct	ShO	Sv-Op	Hld	OAvg	OOBP	ERA
1978 NYA	24	1	1	1	0	9.0	38	9	2	2	0	0	0	0	4	0	8	0	0	1	0	1.000	0	0-0	0	.265	.342	2.00
Postseason Totals		2	2	1	0	14.1	122	11	3	3	0	0	0	0	9	0	11	0	0	2	0	1.000	0	0-0	0	.212	.328	1.88

LCS
Year Tm	Age	G	AB	H	2B	3B	HR	TB	R	RBI	GW	TBB	IBB	SO	HBP	SH	SF	SB	CS	SB%	GDP	Avg	OBP	SLG	Pos	G	PO	A	E	DP	FPct
1978 NYA	24	1	0	0	0	0	0	0	0	0	0	0	0	0	0	0	0	0	0	—	0	—	—	—	P	1	2	0	0	0	1.000

World Series
Year Tm	Age	G	AB	H	2B	3B	HR	TB	R	RBI	GW	TBB	IBB	SO	HBP	SH	SF	SB	CS	SB%	GDP	Avg	OBP	SLG	Pos	G	PO	A	E	DP	FPct
1978 NYA	24	1	0	0	0	0	0	0	0	0	0	0	0	0	0	0	0	0	0	—	0	—	—	—	P	1	0	1	0	0	1.000
Postseason Totals		2	0	0	0	0	0	0	0	0	0	0	0	0	0	0	0	0	0	—	0	—	—	—	P	2	2	1	0	0	1.000

JIM BEAUCHAMP
James Edward Beauchamp—Bats: Right; Throws: Right   Ht: 6'2"; Wt: 190 lbs; Born: 8/21/1939 in Vinita, Oklahoma; Debut: 9/22/1963

World Series
Year Tm	Age	G	AB	H	2B	3B	HR	TB	R	RBI	GW	TBB	IBB	SO	HBP	SH	SF	SB	CS	SB%	GDP	Avg	OBP	SLG	Pos	G	PO	A	E	DP	FPct
1973 NYN	34	4	4	0	0	0	0	0	0	0	0	0	0	1	0	0	0	0	0	—	0	.000	.000	.000	—						

GINGER BEAUMONT
Clarence Howeth Beaumont—Bats: Left; Throws: Right   Ht: 5'8"; Wt: 190 lbs; Born: 7/23/1876 in Rochester, Wisconsin; Debut: 4/21/1899; Died: 4/10/1956

World Series
Year Tm	Age	G	AB	H	2B	3B	HR	TB	R	RBI	GW	TBB	IBB	SO	HBP	SH	SF	SB	CS	SB%	GDP	Avg	OBP	SLG	Pos	G	PO	A	E	DP	FPct
1903 Pit	27	8	34	9	0	1	0	11	6	1	0	2	0	4	0	0	0	2	0	1.00	0	.265	.306	.324	OF	8	21	0	0	0	1.000
1910 ChN	34	3	2	0	0	0	0	0	1	0	0	1	0	1	0	0	0	0	0	—	0	.000	.333	.000	—						
WS Totals		11	36	9	0	1	0	11	7	1	0	3	0	5	0	0	0	2	0	1.00	0	.250	.308	.306	OF	8	21	0	0	0	1.000

JOHNNY BEAZLEY
John Andrew Beazley—Nickname: Nig—Throws: Right; Bats: Right   Ht: 6'1"; Wt: 190 lbs; Born: 5/25/1918 in Nashville, Tennessee; Debut: 9/28/1941; Died: 4/21/1990

World Series
Year Tm	Age	G	GS	CG	GF	IP	BFP	H	R	ER	HR	SH	SF	HB	TBB	IBB	SO	WP	Bk	W	L	Pct	ShO	Sv-Op	Hld	OAvg	OOBP	ERA
1942 StL	24	2	2	2	0	18.0	73	17	5	5	2	0	0	0	3	0	6	0	0	2	0	1.000	0	0-0	0	.243	.274	2.50
1946 StL	28	1	0	0	1	1.0	4	1	0	0	0	1	0	0	0	0	1	0	0	0	0	—	0	0-0	0	.333	.333	0.00
WS Totals		3	2	2	1	19.0	154	18	5	5	2	1	0	0	3	0	7	1	0	2	0	1.000	0	0-0	0	.247	.276	2.37

World Series
Year Tm	Age	G	AB	H	2B	3B	HR	TB	R	RBI	GW	TBB	IBB	SO	HBP	SH	SF	SB	CS	SB%	GDP	Avg	OBP	SLG	Pos	G	PO	A	E	DP	FPct
1942 StL	24	2	7	1	0	0	0	1	0	0	0	0	0	5	0	0	0	0	0	—	0	.143	.143	.143	P	2	2	0	1	0	.667
1946 StL	28	1	0	0	0	0	0	0	0	0	0	0	0	0	0	0	0	0	0	—	0	—	—	—	P	1	0	1	0	0	1.000
WS Totals		3	7	1	0	0	0	1	0	0	0	0	0	5	0	0	0	0	0	—	0	.143	.143	.143	P	3	2	1	1	0	.750

ROD BECK
Rodney Roy Beck—Throws: Right; Bats: Right   Ht: 6'1"; Wt: 215 lbs; Born: 8/3/1968 in Burbank, California; Debut: 5/6/1991

Division Series
Year Tm	Age	G	GS	CG	GF	IP	BFP	H	R	ER	HR	SH	SF	HB	TBB	IBB	SO	WP	Bk	W	L	Pct	ShO	Sv-Op	Hld	OAvg	OOBP	ERA
1997 SF	29	1	0	0	1	1.1	4	1	0	0	0	0	0	0	0	0	1	0	0	0	0	—	0	0-0	0	.250	.250	0.00

Division Series		Batting																							Fielding						
Year Tm	Age	G	AB	H	2B	3B	HR	TB	R	RBI	GW	TBB	IBB	SO	HBP	SH	SF	SB	CS	SB%	GDP	Avg	OBP	SLG	Pos	G	PO	A	E	DP	FPct
1997 SF	29	1	0	0	0	0	0	0	0	0	0	0	0	0	0	0	0	0	0	—	0	—	—	—	P	1	0	0	0	0	—

BEALS BECKER—David Beals Becker—Bats: Left; Throws: Left

Ht: 5'9"; Wt: 170 lbs; Born: 7/5/1886 in El Dorado, Kansas; Debut: 4/19/1908; Died: 8/16/1943

World Series		Batting																							Fielding						
Year Tm	Age	G	AB	H	2B	3B	HR	TB	R	RBI	GW	TBB	IBB	SO	HBP	SH	SF	SB	CS	SB%	GDP	Avg	OBP	SLG	Pos	G	PO	A	E	DP	FPct
1911 NYG	25	3	3	0	0	0	0	0	0	0	0	0	0	0	0	0	0	0	1	.00	0	.000	.000	.000	—						
1912 NYG	26	2	4	0	0	0	0	0	1	0	0	2	0	0	0	0	0	0	1	.00	0	.000	.333	.000	OF	1	0	0	0	0	—
1915 Phi	29	2	0	0	0	0	0	0	0	0	0	0	0	0	0	0	0	0	0	—	0	—	—	—	OF	2	0	0	0	0	—
WS Totals		7	7	0	0	0	0	0	1	0	0	2	0	0	0	0	0	0	2	.00	0	.000	.222	.000	OF	3	0	0	0	0	—

HEINZ BECKER—Heinz Reinhard Becker—Nicknames: Dutch, Bunions—Bats: Both; Throws: Right

Ht: 6'2"; Wt: 200 lbs; Born: 8/26/1915 in Berlin, Germany; Debut: 4/21/1943; Died: 11/11/1991

World Series		Batting																							Fielding						
Year Tm	Age	G	AB	H	2B	3B	HR	TB	R	RBI	GW	TBB	IBB	SO	HBP	SH	SF	SB	CS	SB%	GDP	Avg	OBP	SLG	Pos	G	PO	A	E	DP	FPct
1945 ChN	30	3	2	1	0	0	0	1	0	0	0	1	1	1	0	0	0	0	0	—	0	.500	.667	.500	—						

JOE BECKWITH—Thomas Joseph Beckwith—Throws: Right; Bats: Left

Ht: 6'3"; Wt: 200 lbs; Born: 1/28/1955 in Auburn, Alabama; Debut: 7/21/1979

LCS		Pitching																										
Year Tm	Age	G	GS	CG	GF	IP	BFP	H	R	ER	HR	SH	SF	HB	TBB	IBB	SO	WP	Bk	W	L	Pct	ShO	Sv-Op	Hld	OAvg	OOBP	ERA
1983 LA	28	2	0	0	0	2.1	11	1	0	0	0	1	0	0	2	2	3	0	0	0	0	—	0	0- 0	0	.125	.300	0.00
World Series		Pitching																										
Year Tm	Age	G	GS	CG	GF	IP	BFP	H	R	ER	HR	SH	SF	HB	TBB	IBB	SO	WP	Bk	W	L	Pct	ShO	Sv-Op	Hld	OAvg	OOBP	ERA
1985 KC	30	1	0	0	0	2.0	7	1	0	0	0	0	0	0	0	0	3	0	0	0	0	—	0	0- 0	0	.143	.143	0.00
Postseason Totals		3	0	0	0	4.1	36	2	0	0	0	1	0	0	2	2	6	0	0	0	0	—	0	0-0	0	.133	.235	0.00

LCS		Batting																							Fielding						
Year Tm	Age	G	AB	H	2B	3B	HR	TB	R	RBI	GW	TBB	IBB	SO	HBP	SH	SF	SB	CS	SB%	GDP	Avg	OBP	SLG	Pos	G	PO	A	E	DP	FPct
1983 LA	28	2	0	0	0	0	0	0	0	0	0	0	0	0	0	0	0	0	0	—	0	—	—	—	P	2	0	0	0	0	—
World Series		Batting																							Fielding						
Year Tm	Age	G	AB	H	2B	3B	HR	TB	R	RBI	GW	TBB	IBB	SO	HBP	SH	SF	SB	CS	SB%	GDP	Avg	OBP	SLG	Pos	G	PO	A	E	DP	FPct
1985 KC	30	1	0	0	0	0	0	0	0	0	0	0	0	0	0	0	0	0	0	—	0	—	—	—	P	1	0	0	0	0	—
Postseason Totals		3	0	0	0	0	0	0	0	0	0	0	0	0	0	0	0	0	0	—	0	—	—	—	P	3	0	0	0	0	—

HUGH BEDIENT—Hugh Carpenter Bedient—Throws: Right; Bats: Right

Ht: 6'0"; Wt: 185 lbs; Born: 10/23/1889 in Gerry, New York; Debut: 4/26/1912; Died: 7/21/1965

World Series		Pitching																										
Year Tm	Age	G	GS	CG	GF	IP	BFP	H	R	ER	HR	SH	SF	HB	TBB	IBB	SO	WP	Bk	W	L	Pct	ShO	Sv-Op	Hld	OAvg	OOBP	ERA
1912 Bos	22	4	2	1	2	18.0	69	10	2	2	0	1	0	2	7	0	7	0	0	1	0	1.000	0	0- 0	0	.169	.279	1.00

World Series		Batting																							Fielding						
Year Tm	Age	G	AB	H	2B	3B	HR	TB	R	RBI	GW	TBB	IBB	SO	HBP	SH	SF	SB	CS	SB%	GDP	Avg	OBP	SLG	Pos	G	PO	A	E	DP	FPct
1912 Bos	22	4	6	0	0	0	0	0	0	0	0	0	0	0	0	0	0	0	0	—	0	.000	.000	.000	P	4	0	1	0	0	1.000

STEVE BEDROSIAN—Stephen Wayne Bedrosian—Nickname: Bedrock—Throws: Right; Bats: Right

Ht: 6'3"; Wt: 200 lbs; Born: 12/6/1957 in Methuen, Massachusetts; Debut: 8/14/1981

LCS		Pitching																										
Year Tm	Age	G	GS	CG	GF	IP	BFP	H	R	ER	HR	SH	SF	HB	TBB	IBB	SO	WP	Bk	W	L	Pct	ShO	Sv-Op	Hld	OAvg	OOBP	ERA
1982 Atl	24	2	0	0	0	1.0	7	3	2	2	0	0	1	0	1	0	2	1	0	0	0	—	0	0- 0	0	.600	.571	18.00
1989 SF	31	4	0	0	4	3.1	16	4	1	1	0	0	0	0	2	0	2	0	0	0	0	—	0	3- 3	0	.286	.375	2.70
1991 Min	33	2	0	0	1	1.1	9	3	2	0	0	0	1	0	2	0	2	0	0	0	0	—	0	0- 0	0	.500	.556	0.00
LCS Totals		8	0	0	5	5.2	64	10	5	3	0	0	2	0	5	0	6	1	0	0	0	—	0	3-3	0	.400	.469	4.76
World Series		Pitching																										
Year Tm	Age	G	GS	CG	GF	IP	BFP	H	R	ER	HR	SH	SF	HB	TBB	IBB	SO	WP	Bk	W	L	Pct	ShO	Sv-Op	Hld	OAvg	OOBP	ERA
1989 SF	31	2	0	0	2	2.2	10	0	0	0	0	0	0	0	2	0	2	0	0	0	0	—	0	0- 0	0	.000	.200	0.00
1991 Min	33	3	0	0	1	3.1	13	3	2	2	0	0	1	0	0	0	2	1	0	0	0	—	0	0- 0	0	.250	.231	5.40
WS Totals		5	0	0	3	6.0	46	3	2	2	0	0	1	0	2	0	4	1	0	0	0	—	0	0-0	0	.150	.217	3.00
Postseason Totals		13	0	0	8	11.2	110	13	7	5	0	0	3	0	7	0	10	2	0	0	0	—	0	3-3	0	.289	.364	3.86

LCS		Batting																							Fielding						
Year Tm	Age	G	AB	H	2B	3B	HR	TB	R	RBI	GW	TBB	IBB	SO	HBP	SH	SF	SB	CS	SB%	GDP	Avg	OBP	SLG	Pos	G	PO	A	E	DP	FPct
1982 Atl	24	2	0	0	0	0	0	0	0	0	0	0	0	0	0	0	0	0	0	—	0	—	—	—	P	2	0	0	0	0	—
1989 SF	31	4	0	0	0	0	0	0	0	0	0	0	0	0	0	0	0	0	0	—	0	—	—	—	P	4	0	0	0	0	—
1991 Min	33	2	0	0	0	0	0	0	0	0	0	0	0	0	0	0	0	0	0	—	0	—	—	—	P	2	0	0	0	0	—
LCS Totals		8	0	0	0	0	0	0	0	0	0	0	0	0	0	0	0	0	0	—	0	—	—	—	P	8	0	0	0	0	—
World Series		Batting																							Fielding						
Year Tm	Age	G	AB	H	2B	3B	HR	TB	R	RBI	GW	TBB	IBB	SO	HBP	SH	SF	SB	CS	SB%	GDP	Avg	OBP	SLG	Pos	G	PO	A	E	DP	FPct
1989 SF	31	2	0	0	0	0	0	0	0	0	0	0	0	0	0	0	0	0	0	—	0	—	—	—	P	2	0	0	0	0	—
1991 Min	33	3	0	0	0	0	0	0	0	0	0	0	0	0	0	0	0	0	0	—	0	—	—	—	P	3	0	1	0	0	1.000
WS Totals		5	0	0	0	0	0	0	0	0	0	0	0	0	0	0	0	0	0	—	0	—	—	—	P	5	0	1	0	0	1.000
Postseason Totals		13	0	0	0	0	0	0	0	0	0	0	0	0	0	0	0	0	0	—	0	—	—	—	P	13	0	1	0	0	1.000

JOE BEGGS—Joseph Stanley Beggs—Nickname: Fireman—Throws: Right; Bats: Right

Ht: 6'1"; Wt: 182 lbs; Born: 11/4/1910 in Rankin, Pennsylvania; Debut: 4/19/1938; Died: 7/19/1983

World Series		Pitching																										
Year Tm	Age	G	GS	CG	GF	IP	BFP	H	R	ER	HR	SH	SF	HB	TBB	IBB	SO	WP	Bk	W	L	Pct	ShO	Sv-Op	Hld	OAvg	OOBP	ERA
1940 Cin	29	1	0	0	1	1.0	5	3	2	2	0	0	0	0	0	0	1	0	0	0	0	—	0	0- 0	0	.600	.600	18.00

World Series		Batting																							Fielding						
Year Tm	Age	G	AB	H	2B	3B	HR	TB	R	RBI	GW	TBB	IBB	SO	HBP	SH	SF	SB	CS	SB%	GDP	Avg	OBP	SLG	Pos	G	PO	A	E	DP	FPct
1940 Cin	29	1	0	0	0	0	0	0	0	0	0	0	0	0	0	0	0	0	0	—	0	—	—	—	P	1	0	0	0	0	—

HANK BEHRMAN—Henry Bernard Behrman—Throws: Right; Bats: Right

Ht: 5'11"; Wt: 174 lbs; Born: 6/27/1921 in Brooklyn, New York; Debut: 4/17/1946; Died: 1/20/1987

World Series		Pitching																										
Year Tm	Age	G	GS	CG	GF	IP	BFP	H	R	ER	HR	SH	SF	HB	TBB	IBB	SO	WP	Bk	W	L	Pct	ShO	Sv-Op	Hld	OAvg	OOBP	ERA
1947 Bro	26	5	0	0	0	6.1	35	9	5	5	0	2	0	0	5	1	3	1	0	0	0	—	0	0- 0	0	.321	.424	7.11

World Series		Batting																							Fielding						
Year Tm	Age	G	AB	H	2B	3B	HR	TB	R	RBI	GW	TBB	IBB	SO	HBP	SH	SF	SB	CS	SB%	GDP	Avg	OBP	SLG	Pos	G	PO	A	E	DP	FPct
1947 Bro	26	5	0	0	0	0	0	0	0	0	0	0	0	0	0	0	0	0	0	—	0	—	—	—	P	5	1	3	0	0	1.000

MARK BELANGER—Mark Henry Belanger—Nickname: Blade—Bats: Right; Throws: Right

Ht: 6'1"; Wt: 170 lbs; Born: 6/8/1944 in Pittsfield, Massachusetts; Debut: 8/7/1965

LCS — Batting / Fielding

Year Tm	Age	G	AB	H	2B	3B	HR	TB	R	RBI	GW	TBB	IBB	SO	HBP	SH	SF	SB	CS	SB%	GDP	Avg	OBP	SLG	Pos	G	PO	A	E	DP	FPct
1969 Bal	25	3	15	4	0	1	1	9	4	1	0	0	0	0	0	0	0	0	0	—	0	.267	.267	.600	SS	3	4	9	0	1	1.000
1970 Bal	26	3	12	4	0	0	0	4	5	1	0	1	0	0	0	0	0	0	0	—	0	.333	.385	.333	SS	3	7	13	0	3	1.000
1971 Bal	27	3	8	2	0	0	0	2	1	1	0	3	1	2	0	0	0	0	0	—	0	.250	.455	.250	SS	3	6	11	0	3	1.000
1973 Bal	29	5	16	2	0	0	0	2	0	1	0	1	0	1	0	0	0	0	0	—	0	.125	.176	.125	SS	5	8	17	0	1	1.000
1974 Bal	30	4	9	0	0	0	0	0	0	0	0	1	0	3	0	2	0	0	0	—	0	.000	.100	.000	SS	4	7	12	1	2	.950
1979 Bal	35	3	5	1	0	0	0	1	0	1	0	0	0	2	0	0	0	0	0	—	0	.200	.200	.200	SS	3	0	6	0	0	1.000
LCS Totals		21	65	13	0	1	1	18	10	5	0	6	1	8	0	2	0	0	0	—	0	.200	.268	.277	SS	21	32	68	1	10	.990

World Series — Batting / Fielding

Year Tm	Age	G	AB	H	2B	3B	HR	TB	R	RBI	GW	TBB	IBB	SO	HBP	SH	SF	SB	CS	SB%	GDP	Avg	OBP	SLG	Pos	G	PO	A	E	DP	FPct
1969 Bal	25	5	15	3	0	0	0	3	2	1	0	2	0	1	0	0	0	0	0	—	0	.200	.294	.200	SS	5	7	14	0	3	1.000
1970 Bal	26	5	19	2	0	0	0	2	0	1	0	1	1	2	0	0	0	0	0	—	0	.105	.150	.105	SS	5	11	14	1	1	.962
1971 Bal	27	7	21	5	0	1	0	7	4	0	0	5	0	2	0	0	0	1	0	1.00	1	.238	.385	.333	SS	7	10	21	3	1	.912
1979 Bal	35	5	6	0	0	0	0	0	1	0	0	1	0	1	0	0	0	0	0	—	0	.000	.143	.000	SS	5	3	7	1	2	.909
WS Totals		22	61	10	0	1	0	12	7	2	0	9	1	6	0	0	0	1	0	1.00	1	.164	.271	.197	SS	22	31	56	5	7	.946
Postseason Totals		43	126	23	0	2	1	30	17	7	0	15	2	14	0	2	0	1	0	1.00	1	.183	.270	.238	SS	43	63	124	6	17	.969

WAYNE BELARDI—Carroll Wayne Belardi—Bats: Left; Throws: Left

Ht: 6'1"; Wt: 185 lbs; Born: 9/5/1930 in St. Helena, California; Debut: 4/18/1950; Died: 10/21/1993

World Series — Batting / Fielding

Year Tm	Age	G	AB	H	2B	3B	HR	TB	R	RBI	GW	TBB	IBB	SO	HBP	SH	SF	SB	CS	SB%	GDP	Avg	OBP	SLG	Pos	G	PO	A	E	DP	FPct
1953 Bro	23	2	2	0	0	0	0	0	0	0	0	0	0	1	0	0	0	0	0	—	0	.000	.000	.000	—						

TIM BELCHER—Timothy Wayne Belcher—Throws: Right; Bats: Right

Ht: 6'3"; Wt: 210 lbs; Born: 10/19/1961 in Mount Gilead, Ohio; Debut: 9/6/1987

Division Series — Pitching

Year Tm	Age	G	GS	CG	GF	IP	BFP	H	R	ER	HR	SH	SF	HB	TBB	IBB	SO	WP	Bk	W	L	Pct	ShO	Sv-Op	Hld	OAvg	OOBP	ERA
1995 Sea	33	2	0	0	1	4.1	20	4	3	3	1	1	0	0	5	1	0	0	0	0	1	.000	0	0-1	1	.286	.474	6.23

LCS — Pitching

Year Tm	Age	G	GS	CG	GF	IP	BFP	H	R	ER	HR	SH	SF	HB	TBB	IBB	SO	WP	Bk	W	L	Pct	ShO	Sv-Op	Hld	OAvg	OOBP	ERA
1988 LA	26	2	2	0	0	15.1	59	12	7	7	2	0	0	0	4	0	16	0	0	2	0	1.000	0	0-0	0	.218	.271	4.11
1993 ChA	31	1	0	0	0	3.2	16	3	1	1	0	0	0	0	3	1	1	1	0	1	0	1.000	0	0-0	0	.231	.375	2.45
1995 Sea	33	1	1	0	0	5.2	27	9	4	4	1	0	0	0	2	0	1	0	0	0	1	.000	0	0-0	0	.360	.407	6.35
LCS Totals		4	3	0	0	24.2	204	24	12	12	3	0	0	0	9	1	18	1	0	3	1	.750	0	0-0	0	.258	.324	4.38

World Series — Pitching

Year Tm	Age	G	GS	CG	GF	IP	BFP	H	R	ER	HR	SH	SF	HB	TBB	IBB	SO	WP	Bk	W	L	Pct	ShO	Sv-Op	Hld	OAvg	OOBP	ERA
1988 LA	26	2	2	0	0	8.2	43	10	7	6	1	0	0	1	6	0	10	0	0	1	0	1.000	0	0-0	0	.278	.395	6.23
Postseason Totals		8	5	0	1	37.2	330	38	22	21	5	1	0	1	20	2	28	1	0	4	2	.667	0	0-1	1	.266	.360	5.02

Division Series — Batting / Fielding

Year Tm	Age	G	AB	H	2B	3B	HR	TB	R	RBI	GW	TBB	IBB	SO	HBP	SH	SF	SB	CS	SB%	GDP	Avg	OBP	SLG	Pos	G	PO	A	E	DP	FPct
1995 Sea	33	2	0	0	0	0	0	0	0	0	0	0	0	0	0	0	0	0	0	—	0	—	—	—	P	2	0	1	0	0	1.000

LCS — Batting / Fielding

Year Tm	Age	G	AB	H	2B	3B	HR	TB	R	RBI	GW	TBB	IBB	SO	HBP	SH	SF	SB	CS	SB%	GDP	Avg	OBP	SLG	Pos	G	PO	A	E	DP	FPct
1988 LA	26	2	8	1	0	0	0	1	1	0	0	0	0	3	0	0	0	0	0	—	0	.125	.125	.125	P	2	1	0	0	0	1.000
1993 ChA	31	1	0	0	0	0	0	0	0	0	0	0	0	0	0	0	0	0	0	—	0	—	—	—	P	1	1	1	0	0	1.000
1995 Sea	33	1	0	0	0	0	0	0	0	0	0	0	0	0	0	0	0	0	0	—	0	—	—	—	P	1	1	0	0	0	1.000
LCS Totals		4	8	1	0	0	0	1	1	0	0	0	0	3	0	0	0	0	0	—	0	.125	.125	.125	P	4	3	1	0	0	1.000

World Series — Batting / Fielding

Year Tm	Age	G	AB	H	2B	3B	HR	TB	R	RBI	GW	TBB	IBB	SO	HBP	SH	SF	SB	CS	SB%	GDP	Avg	OBP	SLG	Pos	G	PO	A	E	DP	FPct
1988 LA	26	2	0	0	0	0	0	0	0	0	0	0	0	0	0	0	0	0	0	—	0	—	—	—	P	2	0	0	0	0	—
Postseason Totals		8	8	1	0	0	0	1	1	0	0	0	0	3	0	0	0	0	0	—	0	.125	.125	.125	P	8	3	2	0	0	1.000

STAN BELINDA—Stanley Peter Belinda—Throws: Right; Bats: Right

Ht: 6'3"; Wt: 185 lbs; Born: 8/6/1966 in Huntingdon, Pennsylvania; Debut: 9/8/1989

Division Series — Pitching

Year Tm	Age	G	GS	CG	GF	IP	BFP	H	R	ER	HR	SH	SF	HB	TBB	IBB	SO	WP	Bk	W	L	Pct	ShO	Sv-Op	Hld	OAvg	OOBP	ERA
1995 Bos	29	1	0	0	0	0.1	1	0	0	0	0	0	0	0	0	0	0	0	0	0	0	—	0	0-0	0	.000	.000	0.00

LCS — Pitching

Year Tm	Age	G	GS	CG	GF	IP	BFP	H	R	ER	HR	SH	SF	HB	TBB	IBB	SO	WP	Bk	W	L	Pct	ShO	Sv-Op	Hld	OAvg	OOBP	ERA
1990 Pit	24	3	0	0	1	3.2	14	3	1	1	0	0	0	0	0	0	4	0	0	0	0	—	0	0-0	1	.214	.214	2.45
1991 Pit	25	3	0	0	3	5.0	18	0	0	0	0	1	0	0	3	0	4	0	0	1	0	1.000	0	0-0	0	.000	.176	0.00
1992 Pit	26	2	0	0	2	1.2	8	2	0	0	0	0	1	0	1	0	2	0	0	0	0	—	0	0-1	0	.333	.375	0.00
LCS Totals		8	0	0	6	10.1	80	5	1	1	0	1	1	0	4	0	10	0	0	1	0	1.000	0	0-1	1	.147	.231	0.87
Postseason Totals		9	0	0	6	10.2	82	5	1	1	0	1	1	0	4	0	10	0	0	1	0	1.000	0	0-1	1	.143	.225	0.84

Division Series — Batting / Fielding

Year Tm	Age	G	AB	H	2B	3B	HR	TB	R	RBI	GW	TBB	IBB	SO	HBP	SH	SF	SB	CS	SB%	GDP	Avg	OBP	SLG	Pos	G	PO	A	E	DP	FPct
1995 Bos	29	1	0	0	0	0	0	0	0	0	0	0	0	0	0	0	0	0	0	—	0	—	—	—	P	1	0	0	0	0	—

LCS — Batting / Fielding

Year Tm	Age	G	AB	H	2B	3B	HR	TB	R	RBI	GW	TBB	IBB	SO	HBP	SH	SF	SB	CS	SB%	GDP	Avg	OBP	SLG	Pos	G	PO	A	E	DP	FPct
1990 Pit	24	3	0	0	0	0	0	0	0	0	0	0	0	0	0	0	0	0	0	—	0	—	—	—	P	3	0	0	0	0	—
1991 Pit	25	3	0	0	0	0	0	0	0	0	0	0	0	0	0	0	0	0	0	—	0	—	—	—	P	3	0	2	0	0	1.000
1992 Pit	26	2	0	0	0	0	0	0	0	0	0	0	0	0	0	0	0	0	0	—	0	—	—	—	P	2	0	0	0	0	—
LCS Totals		8	0	0	0	0	0	0	0	0	0	0	0	0	0	0	0	0	0	—	0	—	—	—	P	8	0	2	0	0	1.000
Postseason Totals		9	0	0	0	0	0	0	0	0	0	0	0	0	0	0	0	0	0	—	0	—	—	—	P	9	0	2	0	0	1.000

DEREK BELL—Derek Nathaniel Bell—Bats: Right; Throws: Right

Ht: 6'2"; Wt: 200 lbs; Born: 12/11/1968 in Tampa, Florida; Debut: 6/28/1991

Division Series — Batting / Fielding

Year Tm	Age	G	AB	H	2B	3B	HR	TB	R	RBI	GW	TBB	IBB	SO	HBP	SH	SF	SB	CS	SB%	GDP	Avg	OBP	SLG	Pos	G	PO	A	E	DP	FPct
1997 Hou	28	3	13	0	0	0	0	0	0	0	0	0	0	3	0	0	0	0	0	—	0	.000	.000	.000	OF	3	3	0	0	0	1.000

LCS — Batting / Fielding

Year Tm	Age	G	AB	H	2B	3B	HR	TB	R	RBI	GW	TBB	IBB	SO	HBP	SH	SF	SB	CS	SB%	GDP	Avg	OBP	SLG	Pos	G	PO	A	E	DP	FPct
1992 Tor	23	2	0	0	0	0	0	0	1	0	0	1	0	0	0	0	0	0	0	—	0	—	1.000	—	OF	2	1	0	0	0	1.000

World Series — Batting / Fielding

Year Tm	Age	G	AB	H	2B	3B	HR	TB	R	RBI	GW	TBB	IBB	SO	HBP	SH	SF	SB	CS	SB%	GDP	Avg	OBP	SLG	Pos	G	PO	A	E	DP	FPct
1992 Tor	23	2	1	0	0	0	0	0	1	0	0	1	0	0	0	0	0	0	0	—	0	.000	.500	.000	—						
Postseason Totals		7	14	0	0	0	0	0	2	0	0	2	0	3	0	0	0	0	0	—	0	.000	.125	.000	OF	5	4	0	0	0	1.000

GARY BELL—Throws: Right; Bats: Right

Ht: 6'1"; Wt: 196 lbs; Born: 11/17/1936 in San Antonio, Texas; Debut: 6/1/1958

World Series — Pitching

Year Tm	Age	G	GS	CG	GF	IP	BFP	H	R	ER	HR	SH	SF	HB	TBB	IBB	SO	WP	Bk	W	L	Pct	ShO	Sv-Op	Hld	OAvg	OOBP	ERA
1967 Bos	30	3	1	0	1	5.1	23	8	3	3	1	0	0	0	1	0	1	0	0	0	1	.000	0	1-1	0	.364	.391	5.06

World Series — Batting / Fielding

Year Tm	Age	G	AB	H	2B	3B	HR	TB	R	RBI	GW	TBB	IBB	SO	HBP	SH	SF	SB	CS	SB%	GDP	Avg	OBP	SLG	Pos	G	PO	A	E	DP	FPct
1967 Bos	30	3	0	0	0	0	0	0	0	0	0	0	0	0	0	0	0	0	0	—	0	—	—	—	P	3	0	2	0	1	1.000

GEORGE BELL—Jorge Antonio Bell—Bats: Right; Throws: Right

Ht: 6'1"; Wt: 190 lbs; Born: 10/21/1959 in San Pedro de Macoris, Dominican Republic; Debut: 4/9/1981

LCS — Batting / Fielding

Year Tm	Age	G	AB	H	2B	3B	HR	TB	R	RBI	GW	TBB	IBB	SO	HBP	SH	SF	SB	CS	SB%	GDP	Avg	OBP	SLG	Pos	G	PO	A	E	DP	FPct
1985 Tor	25	7	28	9	3	0	0	12	4	1	0	0	0	4	1	0	1	0	1	.00	0	.321	.333	.429	OF	7	13	0	0	0	1.000
1989 Tor	29	5	20	4	0	0	1	7	2	2	0	0	0	3	0	0	1	0	0	—	1	.200	.190	.350	OF	2	3	1	0	0	1.000
LCS Totals		12	48	13	3	0	1	19	6	3	0	0	0	7	1	0	2	0	1	.00	1	.271	.275	.396	OF	9	16	1	0	0	1.000

GUS BELL—David Russell Bell—Bats: Left; Throws: Right

Ht: 6'1"; Wt: 190 lbs; Born: 11/15/1928 in Louisville, Kentucky; Debut: 5/30/1950; Died: 5/7/1995

World Series	Batting																								Fielding						
Year Tm	Age	G	AB	H	2B	3B	HR	TB	R	RBI	GW	TBB	IBB	SO	HBP	SH	SF	SB	CS	SB%	GDP	Avg	OBP	SLG	Pos	G	PO	A	E	DP	FPct
1961 Cin	32	3	3	0	0	0	0	0	0	0	0	0	0	0	0	0	0	0	0	—	0	.000	.000	.000	—						

HI BELL—Herman S. Bell—Throws: Right; Bats: Right

Ht: 6'0"; Wt: 185 lbs; Born: 7/16/1897 in Mt. Sherman, Kentucky; Debut: 4/16/1924; Died: 6/7/1949

World Series	Pitching																											
Year Tm	Age	G	GS	CG	GF	IP	BFP	H	R	ER	HR	SH	SF	HB	TBB	IBB	SO	WP	Bk	W	L	Pct	ShO	Sv-Op	Hld	OAvg	OOBP	ERA
1926 StL	29	1	0	0	0	2.0	10	4	2	2	1	0	1	0	1	0	1	0	1	0	0	—	0	0-0	0	.500	.500	9.00
1930 StL	33	1	0	0	1	1.0	3	0	0	0	0	0	0	0	0	0	0	0	0	0	0	—	0	0-0	0	.000	.000	0.00
1933 NYG	36	1	0	0	1	1.0	3	0	0	0	0	0	0	0	0	0	0	0	0	0	0	—	0	0-0	0	.000	.000	0.00
WS Totals		3	0	0	2	4.0	32	4	2	2	1	0	1	0	1	0	1	0	1	0	0	—	0	0-0	0	.286	.313	4.50

World Series	Batting																								Fielding						
Year Tm	Age	G	AB	H	2B	3B	HR	TB	R	RBI	GW	TBB	IBB	SO	HBP	SH	SF	SB	CS	SB%	GDP	Avg	OBP	SLG	Pos	G	PO	A	E	DP	FPct
1926 StL	29	1	0	0	0	0	0	0	0	0	0	0	0	0	0	0	0	0	0	—	0	—	—	—	P	1	0	0	0	0	—
1930 StL	33	1	0	0	0	0	0	0	0	0	0	0	0	0	0	0	0	0	0	—	0	—	—	—	P	1	0	1	0	0	1.000
1933 NYG	36	1	0	0	0	0	0	0	0	0	0	0	0	0	0	0	0	0	0	—	0	—	—	—	P	1	0	0	0	0	—
WS Totals		3	0	0	0	0	0	0	0	0	0	0	0	0	0	0	0	0	0	—	0	—	—	—	P	3	0	1	0	0	1.000

JAY BELL—Jay Stuart Bell—Bats: Right; Throws: Right

Ht: 6'1"; Wt: 180 lbs; Born: 12/11/1965 in Pensacola, Florida; Debut: 9/29/1986

LCS	Batting																								Fielding						
Year Tm	Age	G	AB	H	2B	3B	HR	TB	R	RBI	GW	TBB	IBB	SO	HBP	SH	SF	SB	CS	SB%	GDP	Avg	OBP	SLG	Pos	G	PO	A	E	DP	FPct
1990 Pit	24	6	20	5	1	0	1	9	3	1	0	4	0	3	1	0	0	0	0	—	0	.250	.400	.450	SS	6	4	22	1	2	.963
1991 Pit	25	7	29	12	2	0	1	17	2	1	0	0	0	10	0	1	0	0	1	.00	0	.414	.414	.586	SS	7	13	19	1	2	.970
1992 Pit	26	7	29	5	2	0	1	10	3	4	1	3	0	4	1	0	0	0	0	—	1	.172	.273	.345	SS	7	6	8	1	0	.933
LCS Totals		20	78	22	5	0	3	36	8	6	1	7	0	17	2	1	0	0	1	.00	1	.282	.356	.462	SS	20	23	49	3	4	.960

LES BELL—Lester Rowland Bell—Bats: Right; Throws: Right

Ht: 5'11"; Wt: 165 lbs; Born: 12/14/1901 in Harrisburg, Pennsylvania; Debut: 9/18/1923; Died: 12/26/1985

World Series	Batting																								Fielding						
Year Tm	Age	G	AB	H	2B	3B	HR	TB	R	RBI	GW	TBB	IBB	SO	HBP	SH	SF	SB	CS	SB%	GDP	Avg	OBP	SLG	Pos	G	PO	A	E	DP	FPct
1926 StL	24	7	27	7	1	0	1	11	4	6	0	2	0	5	0	0	1	0	2	.00	1	.259	.300	.407	3B	7	7	16	2	0	.920

ALBERT BELLE—Albert Jojuan Belle—Bats: Right; Throws: Right

Ht: 6'1"; Wt: 190 lbs; Born: 8/25/1966 in Shreveport, Louisiana; Debut: 7/15/1989

Division Series	Batting																								Fielding						
Year Tm	Age	G	AB	H	2B	3B	HR	TB	R	RBI	GW	TBB	IBB	SO	HBP	SH	SF	SB	CS	SB%	GDP	Avg	OBP	SLG	Pos	G	PO	A	E	DP	FPct
1995 Cle	29	3	11	3	1	0	1	7	3	3	0	4	2	3	0	0	0	0	0	—	0	.273	.467	.636	OF	3	7	0	1	0	.875
1996 Cle	30	4	15	3	0	0	2	9	2	6	1	3	1	2	0	0	0	1	0	1.00	0	.200	.333	.600	OF	4	11	1	0	0	1.000
DS Totals		7	26	6	1	0	3	16	5	9	1	7	3	5	0	0	0	1	0	1.00	0	.231	.394	.615	OF	7	18	1	1	0	.950
LCS	Batting																								Fielding						
Year Tm	Age	G	AB	H	2B	3B	HR	TB	R	RBI	GW	TBB	IBB	SO	HBP	SH	SF	SB	CS	SB%	GDP	Avg	OBP	SLG	Pos	G	PO	A	E	DP	FPct
1995 Cle	29	5	18	4	1	0	1	8	1	1	0	3	0	5	1	0	0	0	0	—	0	.222	.364	.444	OF	5	4	0	2	0	.667
World Series	Batting																								Fielding						
Year Tm	Age	G	AB	H	2B	3B	HR	TB	R	RBI	GW	TBB	IBB	SO	HBP	SH	SF	SB	CS	SB%	GDP	Avg	OBP	SLG	Pos	G	PO	A	E	DP	FPct
1995 Cle	29	6	17	4	0	0	2	10	4	4	0	7	2	5	0	0	0	0	1	.00	0	.235	.458	.588	OF	6	10	0	1	0	.909
Postseason Totals		18	61	14	2	0	6	34	10	14	1	17	5	15	1	0	0	1	1	.50	0	.230	.405	.557	OF	18	32	1	4	0	.892

RAFAEL BELLIARD—Rafael Leonidas Belliard—Bats: Right; Throws: Right

Ht: 5'6"; Wt: 160 lbs; Born: 10/24/1961 in Puerto Nuevo Mao, Dominican Republic; Debut: 9/6/1982

Division Series	Batting																								Fielding						
Year Tm	Age	G	AB	H	2B	3B	HR	TB	R	RBI	GW	TBB	IBB	SO	HBP	SH	SF	SB	CS	SB%	GDP	Avg	OBP	SLG	Pos	G	PO	A	E	DP	FPct
1995 Atl	33	4	5	0	0	0	0	0	1	0	0	0	0	1	0	0	0	0	0	—	0	.000	.000	.000	SS	4	2	5	0	1	1.000
1996 Atl	34	3	0	0	0	0	0	0	0	0	0	0	0	0	0	0	0	0	0	—	0	—	—	—	SS	3	0	0	0	0	—
DS Totals		7	5	0	0	0	0	0	1	0	0	0	0	1	0	0	0	0	0	—	0	.000	.000	.000	SS	7	2	5	0	1	1.000
LCS	Batting																								Fielding						
Year Tm	Age	G	AB	H	2B	3B	HR	TB	R	RBI	GW	TBB	IBB	SO	HBP	SH	SF	SB	CS	SB%	GDP	Avg	OBP	SLG	Pos	G	PO	A	E	DP	FPct
1991 Atl	29	7	19	4	0	0	0	4	0	1	0	3	2	3	0	2	0	0	0	—	0	.211	.318	.211	SS	7	9	15	1	4	.960
1992 Atl	30	4	2	0	0	0	0	0	1	0	0	1	0	0	0	0	0	0	0	—	0	.000	.333	.000	SS	3	1	3	0	0	1.000
																									2B	1	1	0	0	0	1.000
1993 Atl	31	2	1	0	0	0	0	0	1	0	0	0	0	1	0	1	0	0	0	—	0	.000	.000	.000	2B	1	0	0	0	0	—
																									SS	1	0	0	0	0	—
1995 Atl	33	4	11	3	0	0	0	3	1	0	0	0	0	3	0	0	0	0	0	—	0	.273	.273	.273	SS	4	6	7	1	3	.929
1996 Atl	34	4	6	4	0	0	0	4	0	2	0	0	0	0	0	0	0	0	0	—	0	.667	.667	.667	2B	1	0	1	0	0	1.000
																									SS	3	2	4	0	0	1.000
LCS Totals		21	39	11	0	0	0	11	3	3	0	4	2	7	0	3	0	0	0	—	0	.282	.349	.282	SS	18	18	29	2	7	.959
World Series	Batting																								Fielding						
Year Tm	Age	G	AB	H	2B	3B	HR	TB	R	RBI	GW	TBB	IBB	SO	HBP	SH	SF	SB	CS	SB%	GDP	Avg	OBP	SLG	Pos	G	PO	A	E	DP	FPct
1991 Atl	29	7	16	6	1	0	0	7	0	4	0	1	0	2	0	2	1	0	0	—	1	.375	.389	.438	SS	7	8	21	0	4	1.000
1992 Atl	30	4	0	0	0	0	0	0	0	0	0	0	0	0	0	1	0	0	0	—	0	—	—	—	SS	3	1	2	0	1	1.000
																									2B	1	1	0	0	0	1.000
1995 Atl	33	6	16	0	0	0	0	0	0	1	0	0	0	4	0	2	0	0	0	—	2	.000	.000	.000	SS	6	3	11	2	0	.875
1996 Atl	34	4	0	0	0	0	0	0	0	0	0	0	0	0	0	0	0	0	0	—	0	—	—	—	SS	3	0	3	0	0	1.000
WS Totals		21	32	6	1	0	0	7	0	5	0	1	0	6	0	5	1	0	0	—	3	.188	.206	.219	SS	19	12	37	2	5	.961
Postseason Totals		49	76	17	1	0	0	18	4	8	0	5	2	14	0	8	1	0	0	—	3	.224	.268	.237	SS	44	32	71	4	13	.963

MARVIN BENARD—Marvin Larry Benard—Bats: Left; Throws: Left

Ht: 5'9"; Wt: 180 lbs; Born: 1/20/1970 in Bluefields, Nicaragua; Debut: 9/5/1995

Division Series	Batting																								Fielding						
Year Tm	Age	G	AB	H	2B	3B	HR	TB	R	RBI	GW	TBB	IBB	SO	HBP	SH	SF	SB	CS	SB%	GDP	Avg	OBP	SLG	Pos	G	PO	A	E	DP	FPct
1997 SF	27	2	2	0	0	0	0	0	0	0	0	0	0	1	0	0	0	0	0	—	0	.000	.000	.000	—						

JOHNNY BENCH (HOF 1989-W)—Johnny Lee Bench—Bats: Right; Throws: Right

Ht: 6'1"; Wt: 197 lbs; Born: 12/7/1947 in Oklahoma City, Oklahoma; Debut: 8/28/1967

LCS	Batting																								Fielding						
Year Tm	Age	G	AB	H	2B	3B	HR	TB	R	RBI	GW	TBB	IBB	SO	HBP	SH	SF	SB	CS	SB%	GDP	Avg	OBP	SLG	Pos	G	PO	A	E	DP	FPct
1970 Cin-*M*	22	3	9	2	0	0	1	5	2	1	0	3	2	1	0	0	0	0	0	—	1	.222	.417	.556	C	3	20	2	0	0	1.000
1972 Cin-*M*	24	5	18	6	1	1	1	12	3	2	0	1	0	3	0	0	1	2	0	1.00	0	.333	.350	.667	C	5	29	3	1	1	.970
1973 Cin	25	5	19	5	2	0	1	10	1	1	1	2	1	3	0	0	0	0	0	—	0	.263	.333	.526	C	5	31	3	0	1	1.000
1975 Cin	27	3	13	1	0	0	0	1	1	0	0	1	0	6	0	0	0	1	0	1.00	0	.077	.143	.077	C	3	18	4	0	0	1.000
1976 Cin	28	3	12	4	1	0	1	8	3	1	0	1	0	2	0	0	0	1	0	1.00	1	.333	.385	.667	C	3	11	4	0	1	1.000
1979 Cin	31	3	12	3	0	1	1	8	1	1	0	2	0	2	0	0	0	0	1	.00	0	.250	.357	.667	C	3	17	2	0	0	1.000
LCS Totals		22	83	21	4	2	5	44	11	6	1	10	3	17	0	0	1	4	1	.80	2	.253	.330	.530	C	22	126	18	1	3	.993
World Series	Batting																								Fielding						
Year Tm	Age	G	AB	H	2B	3B	HR	TB	R	RBI	GW	TBB	IBB	SO	HBP	SH	SF	SB	CS	SB%	GDP	Avg	OBP	SLG	Pos	G	PO	A	E	DP	FPct
1970 Cin-*M*	22	5	19	4	0	0	1	7	3	3	0	1	0	2	0	0	0	0	0	—	0	.211	.250	.368	C	5	36	3	0	1	1.000
1972 Cin-*M*	24	7	23	6	1	0	1	10	4	1	0	5	3	5	0	0	0	2	0	1.00	0	.261	.393	.435	C	7	41	7	1	2	.980
1975 Cin	27	7	29	6	2	0	1	11	5	4	0	2	0	4	0	0	0	0	0	—	0	.207	.258	.379	C	7	44	5	0	3	1.000
1976 Cin	28	4	15	8	1	1	2	17	4	6	1	0	0	1	0	0	0	0	1	.00	2	.533	.533	1.133	C	4	18	2	0	0	1.000
WS Totals		23	86	24	4	1	5	45	16	14	1	8	3	12	0	0	0	2	1	.67	2	.279	.340	.523	C	23	139	17	1	6	.994
Postseason Totals		45	169	45	8	3	10	89	27	20	2	18	6	29	0	0	1	6	2	.75	4	.266	.335	.527	C	45	265	35	2	9	.993

CHIEF BENDER (HOF 1953-V)—Charles Albert Bender—Throws: Right; Bats: Right

Ht: 6'2"; Wt: 185 lbs; Born: 5/5/1884 in Crow Wing County, Minnesota; Debut: 4/20/1903; Died: 5/22/1954

World Series — Pitching

Year	Tm	Age	G	GS	CG	GF	IP	BFP	H	R	ER	HR	SH	SF	HB	TBB	IBB	SO	WP	Bk	W	L	Pct	ShO	Sv-Op	Hld	OAvg	OOBP	ERA
1905	Phi	21	2	2	2	0	17.0	64	9	2	2	0	2	0	0	6	0	13	0	0	1	1	.500	1	0-0	0	.161	.242	1.06
1910	Phi	26	2	2	2	0	18.2	67	12	5	4	0	1	0	0	4	0	14	0	0	1	1	.500	0	0-0	0	.194	.242	1.93
1911	Phi	27	3	3	3	0	26.0	104	16	6	3	0	1	1	1	8	0	20	1	0	2	1	.667	0	0-0	0	.172	.243	1.04
1913	Phi	29	2	2	2	0	18.0	73	19	9	8	1	1	0	1	1	0	9	0	0	2	0	1.000	0	0-0	0	.271	.292	4.00
1914	Phi	30	1	1	0	0	5.1	23	8	6	6	0	0	0	0	2	0	3	0	0	0	1	.000	0	0-0	0	.381	.435	10.13
WS Totals			10	10	9	0	85.0	662	64	28	23	1	5	1	2	21	0	59	1	0	6	4	.600	1	0-0	0	.212	.267	2.44

World Series — Batting / Fielding

Year	Tm	Age	G	AB	H	2B	3B	HR	TB	R	RBI	GW	TBB	IBB	SO	HBP	SH	SF	SB	CS	SB%	GDP	Avg	OBP	SLG	Pos	G	PO	A	E	DP	FPct
1905	Phi	21	2	5	0	0	0	0	0	0	0	0	0	0	1	0	1	0	0	0	—	0	.000	.000	.000	P	2	0	4	0	0	1.000
1910	Phi	26	2	6	2	0	0	0	2	1	1	0	1	0	1	0	0	0	0	0	—	0	.333	.429	.333	P	2	1	2	0	1	1.000
1911	Phi	27	3	11	1	0	0	0	1	0	0	0	0	0	1	0	0	0	0	0	—	0	.091	.091	.091	P	3	1	6	0	0	1.000
1913	Phi	29	2	8	0	0	0	0	0	0	1	0	0	0	1	0	0	0	0	0	—	0	.000	.000	.000	P	2	0	5	0	0	1.000
1914	Phi	30	1	2	0	0	0	0	0	0	0	0	0	0	0	0	0	0	0	0	—	0	.000	.000	.000	P	1	1	3	0	2	1.000
WS Totals			10	32	3	0	0	0	3	1	2	0	1	0	4	0	1	0	0	0	—	0	.094	.121	.094	P	10	3	20	0	3	1.000

BRUCE BENEDICT—Bruce Edwin Benedict—Bats: Right; Throws: Right

Ht: 6'1"; Wt: 175 lbs; Born: 8/18/1955 in Birmingham, Alabama; Debut: 8/18/1978

LCS — Batting / Fielding

Year	Tm	Age	G	AB	H	2B	3B	HR	TB	R	RBI	GW	TBB	IBB	SO	HBP	SH	SF	SB	CS	SB%	GDP	Avg	OBP	SLG	Pos	G	PO	A	E	DP	FPct
1982	Atl	27	3	8	2	1	0	0	3	1	0	0	2	0	1	0	0	0	0	0	—	0	.250	.400	.375	C	3	16	2	0	0	1.000

ALAN BENES—Alan Paul Benes—Throws: Right; Bats: Right

Ht: 6'5"; Wt: 215 lbs; Born: 1/21/1972 in Evansville, Indiana; Debut: 9/19/1995

LCS — Pitching

Year	Tm	Age	G	GS	CG	GF	IP	BFP	H	R	ER	HR	SH	SF	HB	TBB	IBB	SO	WP	Bk	W	L	Pct	ShO	Sv-Op	Hld	OAvg	OOBP	ERA
1996	StL	24	2	1	0	0	6.1	25	3	2	2	0	1	1	1	2	1	5	0	0	0	1	.000	0	0-0	0	.150	.250	2.84

LCS — Batting / Fielding

Year	Tm	Age	G	AB	H	2B	3B	HR	TB	R	RBI	GW	TBB	IBB	SO	HBP	SH	SF	SB	CS	SB%	GDP	Avg	OBP	SLG	Pos	G	PO	A	E	DP	FPct
1996	StL	24	2	1	0	0	0	0	0	0	0	0	0	0	1	0	0	0	0	0	—	0	.000	.000	.000	P	2	0	1	0	0	1.000

ANDY BENES—Andrew Charles Benes—Nicknames: Big Train, Rain Man—Throws: Right; Bats: Right

Ht: 6'6"; Wt: 235 lbs; Born: 8/20/1967 in Evansville, Indiana; Debut: 8/11/1989

Division Series — Pitching

Year	Tm	Age	G	GS	CG	GF	IP	BFP	H	R	ER	HR	SH	SF	HB	TBB	IBB	SO	WP	Bk	W	L	Pct	ShO	Sv-Op	Hld	OAvg	OOBP	ERA
1995	Sea	28	2	2	0	0	11.2	52	10	7	7	3	0	0	0	9	1	8	0	0	0	0	—	0	0-0	0	.233	.365	5.40
1996	StL	29	1	1	0	0	7.0	28	6	4	4	1	0	0	0	1	0	9	0	0	0	0	—	0	0-0	0	.222	.250	5.14
DS Totals			3	3	0	0	18.2	160	16	11	11	4	0	0	0	10	1	17	0	0	0	0	—	0	0-0	0	.229	.325	5.30

LCS — Pitching

Year	Tm	Age	G	GS	CG	GF	IP	BFP	H	R	ER	HR	SH	SF	HB	TBB	IBB	SO	WP	Bk	W	L	Pct	ShO	Sv-Op	Hld	OAvg	OOBP	ERA
1995	Sea	28	1	1	0	0	2.1	15	6	6	6	2	0	1	0	2	0	3	0	0	0	1	.000	0	0-0	0	.500	.533	23.14
1996	StL	29	3	2	0	0	15.1	67	19	9	9	3	1	0	0	3	0	9	0	0	0	0	—	0	0-0	0	.302	.333	5.28
LCS Totals			4	3	0	0	17.2	164	25	15	15	5	1	1	0	5	0	12	0	0	0	1	.000	0	0-0	0	.333	.370	7.64
Postseason Totals			7	6	0	0	36.1	324	41	26	26	9	1	1	0	15	1	29	0	0	0	1	.000	0	0-0	0	.283	.348	6.44

Division Series — Batting / Fielding

Year	Tm	Age	G	AB	H	2B	3B	HR	TB	R	RBI	GW	TBB	IBB	SO	HBP	SH	SF	SB	CS	SB%	GDP	Avg	OBP	SLG	Pos	G	PO	A	E	DP	FPct
1995	Sea	28	2	0	0	0	0	0	0	0	0	0	0	0	0	0	0	0	0	0	—	0	—	—	—	P	2	1	0	0	0	1.000
1996	StL	29	1	2	1	0	0	0	1	1	0	0	0	0	1	0	1	0	0	0	—	0	.500	.500	.500	P	1	1	0	0	0	1.000
DS Totals			3	2	1	0	0	0	1	1	0	0	0	0	1	0	1	0	0	0	—	0	.500	.500	.500	P	3	2	0	0	0	1.000

LCS — Batting / Fielding

Year	Tm	Age	G	AB	H	2B	3B	HR	TB	R	RBI	GW	TBB	IBB	SO	HBP	SH	SF	SB	CS	SB%	GDP	Avg	OBP	SLG	Pos	G	PO	A	E	DP	FPct
1995	Sea	28	1	0	0	0	0	0	0	0	0	0	0	0	0	0	0	0	0	0	—	0	—	—	—	P	1	0	0	0	0	—
1996	StL	29	3	4	1	1	0	0	2	0	0	0	1	0	2	0	0	0	0	0	—	0	.250	.400	.500	P	3	1	4	0	0	1.000
LCS Totals			4	4	1	1	0	0	2	0	0	0	1	0	2	0	0	0	0	0	—	0	.250	.400	.500	P	4	1	4	0	0	1.000
Postseason Totals			7	6	2	1	0	0	3	1	0	0	1	0	3	0	1	0	0	0	—	0	.333	.429	.500	P	7	3	4	0	0	1.000

BENNY BENGOUGH—Bernard Oliver Bengough—Bats: Right; Throws: Right

Ht: 5'7"; Wt: 168 lbs; Born: 7/27/1898 in Niagara Falls, New York; Debut: 5/18/1923; Died: 12/22/1968

World Series — Batting / Fielding

Year	Tm	Age	G	AB	H	2B	3B	HR	TB	R	RBI	GW	TBB	IBB	SO	HBP	SH	SF	SB	CS	SB%	GDP	Avg	OBP	SLG	Pos	G	PO	A	E	DP	FPct
1927	NYA	29	2	4	0	0	0	0	0	1	0	0	1	0	0	0	0	0	0	0	—	0	.000	.200	.000	C	2	4	0	0	0	1.000
1928	NYA	30	4	13	3	0	0	0	3	1	1	0	1	0	1	0	0	0	0	0	—	1	.231	.286	.231	C	4	33	2	0	0	1.000
WS Totals			6	17	3	0	0	0	3	2	1	0	2	0	1	0	0	0	0	0	—	1	.176	.263	.176	C	6	37	2	0	0	1.000

JUAN BENIQUEZ—Juan Jose Beniquez—Bats: Right; Throws: Right

Ht: 5'11"; Wt: 150 lbs; Born: 5/13/1950 in San Sebastian, Puerto Rico; Debut: 9/4/1971

LCS — Batting / Fielding

Year	Tm	Age	G	AB	H	2B	3B	HR	TB	R	RBI	GW	TBB	IBB	SO	HBP	SH	SF	SB	CS	SB%	GDP	Avg	OBP	SLG	Pos	G	PO	A	E	DP	FPct
1975	Bos	25	3	12	3	0	0	0	3	2	1	0	0	0	1	0	1	0	2	0	1.00	1	.250	.250	.250	—						
1982	Cal	32	2	0	0	0	0	0	0	0	0	0	0	0	0	0	0	0	0	0	—	0	—	—	—	OF	2	1	0	0	0	1.000
LCS Totals			5	12	3	0	0	0	3	2	1	0	0	0	1	0	1	0	2	0	1.00	1	.250	.250	.250	OF	2	1	0	0	0	1.000

World Series — Batting / Fielding

Year	Tm	Age	G	AB	H	2B	3B	HR	TB	R	RBI	GW	TBB	IBB	SO	HBP	SH	SF	SB	CS	SB%	GDP	Avg	OBP	SLG	Pos	G	PO	A	E	DP	FPct
1975	Bos	25	3	8	1	0	0	0	1	0	1	0	1	0	1	0	0	0	0	0	—	0	.125	.222	.125	OF	2	5	1	0	1	1.000
Postseason Totals			8	20	4	0	0	0	4	2	2	0	1	0	2	0	1	0	2	0	1.00	1	.200	.238	.200	OF	4	6	1	0	1	1.000

ARMANDO BENITEZ—Armando German Benitez—Throws: Right; Bats: Right

Ht: 6'4"; Wt: 220 lbs; Born: 11/3/1972 in Ramon Santana, Dominican Republic; Debut: 7/28/1994

Division Series — Pitching

Year	Tm	Age	G	GS	CG	GF	IP	BFP	H	R	ER	HR	SH	SF	HB	TBB	IBB	SO	WP	Bk	W	L	Pct	ShO	Sv-Op	Hld	OAvg	OOBP	ERA
1996	Bal	23	3	0	0	0	4.0	15	1	1	1	1	0	1	0	2	0	6	0	0	2	0	1.000	0	0-1	0	.083	.200	2.25
1997	Bal	24	3	0	0	1	3.0	14	3	1	1	1	0	0	0	2	0	4	0	0	0	0	—	0	0-0	2	.250	.357	3.00
DS Totals			6	0	0	1	7.0	58	4	2	2	2	0	1	0	4	0	10	0	0	2	0	1.000	0	0-1	2	.167	.276	2.57

LCS — Pitching

Year	Tm	Age	G	GS	CG	GF	IP	BFP	H	R	ER	HR	SH	SF	HB	TBB	IBB	SO	WP	Bk	W	L	Pct	ShO	Sv-Op	Hld	OAvg	OOBP	ERA
1996	Bal	23	3	0	0	1	2.1	13	3	2	2	2	0	0	0	3	1	2	0	0	0	0	—	0	1-2	0	.300	.462	7.71
1997	Bal	24	4	0	0	2	3.0	16	3	4	4	2	0	0	0	4	0	6	0	0	0	2	.000	0	0-1	0	.250	.438	12.00
LCS Totals			7	0	0	3	5.1	58	6	6	6	4	0	0	0	7	1	8	0	0	0	2	.000	0	1-3	0	.273	.448	10.13
Postseason Totals			13	0	0	4	12.1	116	10	8	8	6	0	1	0	11	1	18	0	0	2	2	.500	0	1-4	2	.217	.362	5.84

Division Series — Batting / Fielding

Year	Tm	Age	G	AB	H	2B	3B	HR	TB	R	RBI	GW	TBB	IBB	SO	HBP	SH	SF	SB	CS	SB%	GDP	Avg	OBP	SLG	Pos	G	PO	A	E	DP	FPct
1996	Bal	23	3	0	0	0	0	0	0	0	0	0	0	0	0	0	0	0	0	0	—	0	—	—	—	P	3	0	2	0	0	1.000
1997	Bal	24	3	0	0	0	0	0	0	0	0	0	0	0	0	0	0	0	0	0	—	0	—	—	—	P	3	0	0	0	0	—
DS Totals			6	0	0	0	0	0	0	0	0	0	0	0	0	0	0	0	0	0	—	0	—	—	—	P	6	0	2	0	0	1.000

LCS — Batting / Fielding

Year	Tm	Age	G	AB	H	2B	3B	HR	TB	R	RBI	GW	TBB	IBB	SO	HBP	SH	SF	SB	CS	SB%	GDP	Avg	OBP	SLG	Pos	G	PO	A	E	DP	FPct
1996	Bal	23	3	0	0	0	0	0	0	0	0	0	0	0	0	0	0	0	0	0	—	0	—	—	—	P	3	0	0	0	0	—
1997	Bal	24	4	0	0	0	0	0	0	0	0	0	0	0	0	0	0	0	0	0	—	0	—	—	—	P	4	0	1	0	0	1.000
LCS Totals			7	0	0	0	0	0	0	0	0	0	0	0	0	0	0	0	0	0	—	0	—	—	—	P	7	0	1	0	0	1.000
Postseason Totals			13	0	0	0	0	0	0	0	0	0	0	0	0	0	0	0	0	0	—	0	—	—	—	P	13	0	3	0	0	1.000

JACK BENTLEY—Jack Needles Bentley—Throws: Left; Bats: Left

Ht: 5'11"; Wt: 200 lbs; Born: 3/8/1895 in Sandy Spring, Maryland; Debut: 9/6/1913; Died: 10/24/1969

World Series — Pitching

Year Tm	Age	G	GS	CG	GF	IP	BFP	H	R	ER	HR	SH	SF	HB	TBB	IBB	SO	WP	Bk	W	L	Pct	ShO	Sv-Op	Hld	OAvg	OOBP	ERA
1923 NYG	28	2	1	0	1	6.2	34	10	8	7	2	0	1	1	4	0	1	0	0	0	1	.000	0	0- 0	0	.357	.441	9.45
1924 NYG	29	3	2	1	1	17.0	75	18	7	7	3	3	0	0	8	1	10	0	0	1	2	.333	0	0- 0	0	.281	.361	3.71
WS Totals		5	3	1	2	23.2	218	28	15	14	5	3	1	1	12	1	11	0	0	1	3	.250	0	0-0	0	.304	.387	5.32

World Series — Batting / Fielding

Year Tm	Age	G	AB	H	2B	3B	HR	TB	R	RBI	GW	TBB	IBB	SO	HBP	SH	SF	SB	CS	SB%	GDP	Avg	OBP	SLG	Pos	G	PO	A	E	DP	FPct
1923 NYG	28	5	5	3	1	0	0	4	0	0	0	0	0	0	0	0	0	0	0	—	0	.600	.600	.800	P	2	0	2	0	0	1.000
1924 NYG	29	5	7	2	0	0	1	5	1	2	1	1	0	1	0	0	0	0	0	—	0	.286	.375	.714	P	3	1	3	0	0	1.000
WS Totals		10	12	5	1	0	1	9	1	2	1	1	0	1	0	0	0	0	0	—	0	.417	.462	.750	P	5	1	5	0	0	1.000

AL BENTON—John Alton Benton—Throws: Right; Bats: Right

Ht: 6'4"; Wt: 215 lbs; Born: 3/18/1911 in Noble, Oklahoma; Debut: 4/18/1934; Died: 4/14/1968

World Series — Pitching

Year Tm	Age	G	GS	CG	GF	IP	BFP	H	R	ER	HR	SH	SF	HB	TBB	IBB	SO	WP	Bk	W	L	Pct	ShO	Sv-Op	Hld	OAvg	OOBP	ERA
1945 Det	34	3	0	0	1	4.2	20	6	1	1	0	2	0	0	0	0	5	0	0	0	0	—	0	0- 0	0	.333	.333	1.93

World Series — Batting / Fielding

Year Tm	Age	G	AB	H	2B	3B	HR	TB	R	RBI	GW	TBB	IBB	SO	HBP	SH	SF	SB	CS	SB%	GDP	Avg	OBP	SLG	Pos	G	PO	A	E	DP	FPct
1945 Det	34	3	0	0	0	0	0	0	0	0	0	0	0	0	0	0	0	0	0	—	0	—	—	—	P	3	0	3	0	0	1.000

RUBE BENTON—John Clebon Benton—Throws: Left; Bats: Right

Ht: 6'1"; Wt: 190 lbs; Born: 6/27/1887 in Clinton, North Carolina; Debut: 6/28/1910; Died: 12/12/1937

World Series — Pitching

Year Tm	Age	G	GS	CG	GF	IP	BFP	H	R	ER	HR	SH	SF	HB	TBB	IBB	SO	WP	Bk	W	L	Pct	ShO	Sv-Op	Hld	OAvg	OOBP	ERA
1917 NYG	30	2	2	1	0	14.0	53	9	3	0	0	0	0	0	1	0	8	0	0	1	1	.500	1	0- 0	0	.173	.189	0.00

World Series — Batting / Fielding

Year Tm	Age	G	AB	H	2B	3B	HR	TB	R	RBI	GW	TBB	IBB	SO	HBP	SH	SF	SB	CS	SB%	GDP	Avg	OBP	SLG	Pos	G	PO	A	E	DP	FPct
1917 NYG	30	2	4	0	0	0	0	0	0	0	0	0	0	3	0	0	0	0	0	—	0	.000	.000	.000	P	2	1	3	0	0	1.000

TODD BENZINGER—Todd Eric Benzinger—Bats: Both; Throws: Right

Ht: 6'1"; Wt: 185 lbs; Born: 2/11/1963 in Dayton, Kentucky; Debut: 6/21/1987

LCS — Batting / Fielding

Year Tm	Age	G	AB	H	2B	3B	HR	TB	R	RBI	GW	TBB	IBB	SO	HBP	SH	SF	SB	CS	SB%	GDP	Avg	OBP	SLG	Pos	G	PO	A	E	DP	FPct
1988 Bos	25	4	11	1	0	0	0	1	0	0	0	1	0	3	0	0	0	0	0	—	2	.091	.167	.091	1B	3	21	1	0	2	1.000
1990 Cin	27	5	9	3	0	0	0	3	0	0	0	2	2	0	0	0	0	0	0	—	0	.333	.455	.333	1B	2	17	0	0	0	1.000
LCS Totals		9	20	4	0	0	0	4	0	0	0	3	2	3	0	0	0	0	0	—	2	.200	.304	.200	1B	5	38	1	0	2	1.000

World Series — Batting / Fielding

Year Tm	Age	G	AB	H	2B	3B	HR	TB	R	RBI	GW	TBB	IBB	SO	HBP	SH	SF	SB	CS	SB%	GDP	Avg	OBP	SLG	Pos	G	PO	A	E	DP	FPct
1990 Cin	27	4	11	2	0	0	0	2	1	0	0	0	0	0	0	0	0	0	0	—	1	.182	.182	.182	1B	3	24	0	0	1	1.000
Postseason Totals		13	31	6	0	0	0	6	1	0	0	3	2	3	0	0	0	0	0	—	3	.194	.265	.194	1B	8	62	1	0	3	1.000

JASON BERE—Jason Phillip Bere—Throws: Right; Bats: Right

Ht: 6'3"; Wt: 185 lbs; Born: 5/26/1971 in Cambridge, Massachusetts; Debut: 5/27/1993

LCS — Pitching

Year Tm	Age	G	GS	CG	GF	IP	BFP	H	R	ER	HR	SH	SF	HB	TBB	IBB	SO	WP	Bk	W	L	Pct	ShO	Sv-Op	Hld	OAvg	OOBP	ERA
1993 ChA	22	1	1	0	0	2.1	15	5	3	3	0	0	0	1	2	0	3	0	0	0	0	—	0	0- 0	0	.417	.533	11.57

LCS — Batting / Fielding

Year Tm	Age	G	AB	H	2B	3B	HR	TB	R	RBI	GW	TBB	IBB	SO	HBP	SH	SF	SB	CS	SB%	GDP	Avg	OBP	SLG	Pos	G	PO	A	E	DP	FPct
1993 ChA	22	1	0	0	0	0	0	0	0	0	0	0	0	0	0	0	0	0	0	—	0	—	—	—	P	1	0	0	0	0	—

JUAN BERENGUER—Juan Bautista Berenguer—Throws: Right; Bats: Right

Ht: 5'11"; Wt: 186 lbs; Born: 11/30/1954 in Aguadulce, Panama; Debut: 8/17/1978

LCS — Pitching

Year Tm	Age	G	GS	CG	GF	IP	BFP	H	R	ER	HR	SH	SF	HB	TBB	IBB	SO	WP	Bk	W	L	Pct	ShO	Sv-Op	Hld	OAvg	OOBP	ERA
1987 Min	32	4	0	0	1	6.0	20	1	1	1	1	0	0	0	3	0	6	1	0	0	0	—	0	1- 1	3	.059	.200	1.50

World Series — Pitching

Year Tm	Age	G	GS	CG	GF	IP	BFP	H	R	ER	HR	SH	SF	HB	TBB	IBB	SO	WP	Bk	W	L	Pct	ShO	Sv-Op	Hld	OAvg	OOBP	ERA
1987 Min	32	3	0	0	0	4.1	22	10	5	5	0	1	0	0	0	0	1	0	0	0	1	.000	0	0- 1	1	.476	.476	10.38
Postseason Totals		7	0	0	1	10.1	84	11	6	6	1	1	0	0	3	0	7	1	0	0	1	.000	0	1-2	4	.289	.341	5.23

LCS — Batting / Fielding

Year Tm	Age	G	AB	H	2B	3B	HR	TB	R	RBI	GW	TBB	IBB	SO	HBP	SH	SF	SB	CS	SB%	GDP	Avg	OBP	SLG	Pos	G	PO	A	E	DP	FPct
1987 Min	32	4	0	0	0	0	0	0	0	0	0	0	0	0	0	0	0	0	0	—	0	—	—	—	P	4	0	0	0	0	—

World Series — Batting / Fielding

Year Tm	Age	G	AB	H	2B	3B	HR	TB	R	RBI	GW	TBB	IBB	SO	HBP	SH	SF	SB	CS	SB%	GDP	Avg	OBP	SLG	Pos	G	PO	A	E	DP	FPct
1987 Min	32	3	0	0	0	0	0	0	0	0	0	0	0	0	0	0	0	0	0	—	0	—	—	—	P	3	0	0	0	0	—
Postseason Totals		7	0	0	0	0	0	0	0	0	0	0	0	0	0	0	0	0	0	—	0	—	—	—	P	7	0	0	0	0	—

AUGIE BERGAMO—August Samuel Bergamo—Bats: Left; Throws: Left

Ht: 5'9"; Wt: 165 lbs; Born: 2/14/1917 in Detroit, Michigan; Debut: 4/25/1944; Died: 8/19/1974

World Series — Batting / Fielding

Year Tm	Age	G	AB	H	2B	3B	HR	TB	R	RBI	GW	TBB	IBB	SO	HBP	SH	SF	SB	CS	SB%	GDP	Avg	OBP	SLG	Pos	G	PO	A	E	DP	FPct
1944 StL	27	3	6	0	0	0	0	0	0	1	0	2	0	3	0	0	0	0	0	—	0	.000	.250	.000	OF	2	1	0	0	0	1.000

WALLY BERGER—Walter Antone Berger—Bats: Right; Throws: Right

Ht: 6'2"; Wt: 198 lbs; Born: 10/10/1905 in Chicago, Illinois; Debut: 4/15/1930; Died: 11/30/1988

World Series — Batting / Fielding

Year Tm	Age	G	AB	H	2B	3B	HR	TB	R	RBI	GW	TBB	IBB	SO	HBP	SH	SF	SB	CS	SB%	GDP	Avg	OBP	SLG	Pos	G	PO	A	E	DP	FPct
1937 NYG	31	3	3	0	0	0	0	0	0	0	0	0	0	1	0	0	0	0	0	—	0	.000	.000	.000	—						
1939 Cin	33	4	15	0	0	0	0	0	0	1	0	0	0	4	0	0	0	0	0	—	0	.000	.000	.000	OF	4	8	0	0	0	1.000
WS Totals		7	18	0	0	0	0	0	0	1	0	0	0	5	0	0	0	0	0	—	0	.000	.000	.000	OF	4	8	0	0	0	1.000

DAVE BERGMAN—David Bruce Bergman—Bats: Left; Throws: Left

Ht: 6'1"; Wt: 185 lbs; Born: 6/6/1953 in Evanston, Illinois; Debut: 8/26/1975

LCS — Batting / Fielding

Year Tm	Age	G	AB	H	2B	3B	HR	TB	R	RBI	GW	TBB	IBB	SO	HBP	SH	SF	SB	CS	SB%	GDP	Avg	OBP	SLG	Pos	G	PO	A	E	DP	FPct
1980 Hou	27	4	3	1	0	1	0	3	0	2	0	0	0	0	0	0	0	0	0	—	0	.333	.333	1.000	1B	3	8	2	1	0	.909
1984 Det	31	2	1	1	0	0	0	1	1	0	0	0	0	0	0	0	0	1	0	1.00	0	1.000	1.000	1.000	1B	2	5	0	0	0	1.000
1987 Det	34	4	4	1	0	0	0	1	0	2	0	0	0	1	0	0	1	0	0	—	0	.250	.200	.250	1B	1	6	0	0	0	1.000
LCS Totals		10	8	3	0	1	0	5	1	4	0	0	0	1	0	0	1	1	0	1.00	0	.375	.333	.625	1B	6	19	2	1	0	.955

World Series — Batting / Fielding

Year Tm	Age	G	AB	H	2B	3B	HR	TB	R	RBI	GW	TBB	IBB	SO	HBP	SH	SF	SB	CS	SB%	GDP	Avg	OBP	SLG	Pos	G	PO	A	E	DP	FPct
1984 Det	31	5	5	0	0	0	0	0	0	0	0	0	0	1	0	0	0	0	0	—	0	.000	.000	.000	1B	5	22	4	0	0	1.000
Postseason Totals		15	13	3	0	1	0	5	1	4	0	0	0	2	0	0	1	1	0	1.00	0	.231	.214	.385	1B	11	41	6	1	0	.979

DWIGHT BERNARD—Dwight Vern Bernard—Throws: Right; Bats: Right

Ht: 6'2"; Wt: 170 lbs; Born: 5/31/1952 in Mt. Vernon, Illinois; Debut: 6/29/1978

Division Series — Pitching

Year Tm	Age	G	GS	CG	GF	IP	BFP	H	R	ER	HR	SH	SF	HB	TBB	IBB	SO	WP	Bk	W	L	Pct	ShO	Sv-Op	Hld	OAvg	OOBP	ERA
1981 Mil	29	2	0	0	0	2.1	7	0	0	0	0	0	0	0	0	0	0	0	0	0	0	—	0	0- 0	0	.000	.000	0.00

LCS — Pitching

Year Tm	Age	G	GS	CG	GF	IP	BFP	H	R	ER	HR	SH	SF	HB	TBB	IBB	SO	WP	Bk	W	L	Pct	ShO	Sv-Op	Hld	OAvg	OOBP	ERA
1982 Mil	30	1	0	0	1	1.0	3	0	0	0	0	0	0	0	0	0	0	0	0	0	0	—	0	0- 0	0	.000	.000	0.00

World Series — Pitching

Year Tm	Age	G	GS	CG	GF	IP	BFP	H	R	ER	HR	SH	SF	HB	TBB	IBB	SO	WP	Bk	W	L	Pct	ShO	Sv-Op	Hld	OAvg	OOBP	ERA
1982 Mil	30	1	0	0	1	1.0	4	0	0	0	0	0	0	0	0	0	1	0	0	0	0	—	0	0- 0	0	.000	.000	0.00
Postseason Totals		4	0	0	2	4.1	28	0	0	0	0	0	0	0	0	0	1	0	0	0	0	—	0	0-0	0	.000	.000	0.00

Division Series — Batting / Fielding

Year Tm	Age	G	AB	H	2B	3B	HR	TB	R	RBI	GW	TBB	IBB	SO	HBP	SH	SF	SB	CS	SB%	GDP	Avg	OBP	SLG	Pos	G	PO	A	E	DP	FPct
1981 Mil	29	2	0	0	0	0	0	0	0	0	0	0	0	0	0	0	0	0	0	—	0	—	—	—	P	2	0	0	0	0	—

LCS — Batting / Fielding

Year Tm	Age	G	AB	H	2B	3B	HR	TB	R	RBI	GW	TBB	IBB	SO	HBP	SH	SF	SB	CS	SB%	GDP	Avg	OBP	SLG	Pos	G	PO	A	E	DP	FPct
1982 Mil	30	1	0	0	0	0	0	0	0	0	0	0	0	0	0	0	0	0	0	—	0	—	—	—	P	1	0	0	0	0	—

World Series — Batting / Fielding

Year Tm	Age	G	AB	H	2B	3B	HR	TB	R	RBI	GW	TBB	IBB	SO	HBP	SH	SF	SB	CS	SB%	GDP	Avg	OBP	SLG	Pos	G	PO	A	E	DP	FPct
1982 Mil	30	1	0	0	0	0	0	0	0	0	0	0	0	0	0	0	0	0	0	—	0	—	—	—	P	1	0	0	0	0	—
Postseason Totals		4	0	0	0	0	0	0	0	0	0	0	0	0	0	0	0	0	0	—	0	—	—	—	P	4	0	0	0	0	—

YOGI BERRA (HOF 1972-W)—Lawrence Peter Berra—Bats: Left; Throws: Right

Ht: 5'7"; Wt: 185 lbs; Born: 5/12/1925 in St. Louis, Missouri; Debut: 9/22/1946

World Series — Batting / Fielding

Year Tm	Age	G	AB	H	2B	3B	HR	TB	R	RBI	GW	TBB	IBB	SO	HBP	SH	SF	SB	CS	SB%	GDP	Avg	OBP	SLG	Pos	G	PO	A	E	DP	FPct
1947 NYA	22	6	19	3	0	0	1	6	2	2	0	1	1	2	0	0	0	0	0	—	0	.158	.200	.316	C	4	19	2	2	0	.913
																									OF	2	3	0	0	0	1.000
1949 NYA	24	4	16	1	0	0	0	1	2	1	0	1	0	3	0	0	0	0	0	—	0	.063	.118	.063	C	4	37	3	0	1	1.000
1950 NYA	25	4	15	3	0	0	1	6	2	2	1	2	0	1	0	0	0	0	0	—	0	.200	.294	.400	C	4	30	1	0	1	1.000
1951 NYA-*M*	26	6	23	6	1	0	0	7	4	0	0	2	0	1	0	0	0	0	0	—	0	.261	.320	.304	C	6	27	3	1	0	.968
1952 NYA	27	7	28	6	1	0	2	13	2	3	0	2	0	4	0	0	0	0	0	—	1	.214	.267	.464	C	7	59	7	1	1	.985
1953 NYA	28	6	21	9	1	0	1	13	3	4	0	3	0	3	2	0	0	0	1	.00	0	.429	.538	.619	C	6	37	3	0	0	1.000
1955 NYA-*M*	30	7	24	10	1	0	1	14	5	2	1	3	0	1	1	0	0	0	1	.00	0	.417	.500	.583	C	7	40	4	0	1	1.000
1956 NYA	31	7	25	9	2	0	3	20	5	10	1	4	2	1	0	0	0	0	0	—	0	.360	.448	.800	C	7	50	3	0	0	1.000
1957 NYA	32	7	25	8	1	0	1	12	5	2	0	4	1	0	0	0	0	0	0	—	0	.320	.414	.480	C	7	45	2	1	0	.979
1958 NYA	33	7	27	6	3	0	0	9	3	2	0	1	0	0	0	0	1	0	0	—	2	.222	.241	.333	C	7	60	6	0	1	1.000
1960 NYA	35	7	22	7	0	0	1	10	6	8	0	2	0	0	0	0	0	0	0	—	1	.318	.375	.455	C	3	13	1	0	0	1.000
																									OF	4	5	0	0	0	1.000
1961 NYA	36	4	11	3	0	0	1	6	2	3	0	5	2	1	0	0	0	0	0	—	0	.273	.500	.545	OF	4	11	0	1	0	.917
1962 NYA	37	2	2	0	0	0	0	0	0	0	0	2	0	0	0	0	0	0	0	—	1	.000	.500	.000	C	1	6	1	0	0	1.000
1963 NYA	38	1	1	0	0	0	0	0	0	0	0	0	0	0	0	0	0	0	0	—	0	.000	.000	.000	—						
WS Totals		75	259	71	10	0	12	117	41	39	3	32	6	17	3	0	1	0	2	.00	5	.274	.359	.452	C	63	423	36	5	5	.989

GERONIMO BERROA—Geronimo Emiliano Berroa—Bats: Right; Throws: Right

Ht: 6'0"; Wt: 165 lbs; Born: 3/18/1965 in Santo Domingo, Dominican Republic; Debut: 4/5/1989

Division Series — Batting / Fielding

Year Tm	Age	G	AB	H	2B	3B	HR	TB	R	RBI	GW	TBB	IBB	SO	HBP	SH	SF	SB	CS	SB%	GDP	Avg	OBP	SLG	Pos	G	PO	A	E	DP	FPct
1997 Bal	32	4	13	5	1	0	2	12	4	2	0	2	0	2	0	0	0	0	0	—	0	.385	.467	.923	OF	1	0	0	0	0	—

LCS — Batting / Fielding

Year Tm	Age	G	AB	H	2B	3B	HR	TB	R	RBI	GW	TBB	IBB	SO	HBP	SH	SF	SB	CS	SB%	GDP	Avg	OBP	SLG	Pos	G	PO	A	E	DP	FPct
1997 Bal	32	6	21	6	2	0	0	8	1	3	1	0	0	3	0	0	0	0	0	—	2	.286	.286	.381	OF	4	9	0	0	0	1.000
Postseason Totals		10	34	11	3	0	2	20	5	5	1	2	0	5	0	0	0	0	0	—	2	.324	.361	.588	OF	5	9	0	0	0	1.000

SEAN BERRY—Sean Robert Berry—Bats: Right; Throws: Right

Ht: 5'11"; Wt: 200 lbs; Born: 3/22/1966 in Santa Monica, California; Debut: 9/17/1990

Division Series — Batting / Fielding

Year Tm	Age	G	AB	H	2B	3B	HR	TB	R	RBI	GW	TBB	IBB	SO	HBP	SH	SF	SB	CS	SB%	GDP	Avg	OBP	SLG	Pos	G	PO	A	E	DP	FPct
1997 Hou	31	1	1	0	0	0	0	0	0	0	0	0	0	0	0	0	0	0	0	—	0	.000	.000	.000	—						

DAMON BERRYHILL—Damon Scott Berryhill—Bats: Both; Throws: Right

Ht: 6'0"; Wt: 205 lbs; Born: 12/3/1963 in South Laguna, California; Debut: 9/5/1987

Division Series — Batting / Fielding

Year Tm	Age	G	AB	H	2B	3B	HR	TB	R	RBI	GW	TBB	IBB	SO	HBP	SH	SF	SB	CS	SB%	GDP	Avg	OBP	SLG	Pos	G	PO	A	E	DP	FPct
1997 SF	33	1	1	0	0	0	0	0	0	0	0	0	0	0	0	0	0	0	0	—	0	.000	.000	.000	—						

LCS — Batting / Fielding

Year Tm	Age	G	AB	H	2B	3B	HR	TB	R	RBI	GW	TBB	IBB	SO	HBP	SH	SF	SB	CS	SB%	GDP	Avg	OBP	SLG	Pos	G	PO	A	E	DP	FPct
1992 Atl	28	7	24	4	1	0	0	5	1	1	1	3	0	2	0	0	0	0	0	—	0	.167	.259	.208	C	7	43	5	0	0	1.000
1993 Atl	29	6	19	4	0	0	1	7	2	3	0	1	0	5	0	0	0	0	0	—	1	.211	.250	.368	C	6	42	0	0	0	1.000
LCS Totals		13	43	8	1	0	1	12	3	4	1	4	0	7	0	0	0	0	0	—	1	.186	.255	.279	C	13	85	5	0	0	1.000

World Series — Batting / Fielding

Year Tm	Age	G	AB	H	2B	3B	HR	TB	R	RBI	GW	TBB	IBB	SO	HBP	SH	SF	SB	CS	SB%	GDP	Avg	OBP	SLG	Pos	G	PO	A	E	DP	FPct
1992 Atl	28	6	22	2	0	0	1	5	1	3	1	1	0	11	0	1	0	0	0	—	0	.091	.130	.227	C	6	33	2	0	0	1.000
Postseason Totals		20	66	10	1	0	2	17	4	7	2	5	0	18	0	1	0	0	0	—	1	.152	.211	.258	C	19	118	7	0	0	1.000

DON BESSENT—Fred Donald Bessent—Nickname: The Weasel—Throws: Right; Bats: Right

Ht: 6'0"; Wt: 175 lbs; Born: 3/13/1931 in Jacksonville, Florida; Debut: 7/17/1955; Died: 7/7/1990

World Series — Pitching

Year Tm	Age	G	GS	CG	GF	IP	BFP	H	R	ER	HR	SH	SF	HB	TBB	IBB	SO	WP	Bk	W	L	Pct	ShO	Sv-Op	Hld	OAvg	OOBP	ERA
1955 Bro	24	3	0	0	0	3.1	12	3	0	0	0	0	0	0	1	0	1	0	0	0	0	—	0	0- 0	0	.273	.333	0.00
1956 Bro	25	2	0	0	1	10.0	41	8	2	2	0	2	1	0	3	1	5	1	0	1	0	1.000	0	0- 0	0	.229	.282	1.80
WS Totals		5	0	0	1	13.1	106	11	2	2	0	2	1	0	4	1	6	1	0	1	0	1.000	0	0-0	0	.239	.294	1.35

World Series — Batting / Fielding

Year Tm	Age	G	AB	H	2B	3B	HR	TB	R	RBI	GW	TBB	IBB	SO	HBP	SH	SF	SB	CS	SB%	GDP	Avg	OBP	SLG	Pos	G	PO	A	E	DP	FPct
1955 Bro	24	3	1	0	0	0	0	0	0	0	0	0	0	1	0	0	0	0	0	—	0	.000	.000	.000	P	3	0	1	0	0	1.000
1956 Bro	25	2	2	1	0	0	0	1	0	1	0	1	0	1	0	1	0	0	0	—	0	.500	.667	.500	P	2	0	0	0	0	—
WS Totals		5	3	1	0	0	0	1	0	1	0	1	0	2	0	1	0	0	0	—	0	.333	.500	.333	P	5	0	1	0	0	1.000

KURT BEVACQUA—Kurt Anthony Bevacqua—Nickname: Dirty—Bats: Right; Throws: Right

Ht: 6'0"; Wt: 180 lbs; Born: 1/23/1947 in Miami Beach, Florida; Debut: 6/22/1971

LCS — Batting / Fielding

Year Tm	Age	G	AB	H	2B	3B	HR	TB	R	RBI	GW	TBB	IBB	SO	HBP	SH	SF	SB	CS	SB%	GDP	Avg	OBP	SLG	Pos	G	PO	A	E	DP	FPct
1984 SD	37	2	2	0	0	0	0	0	0	0	0	0	0	0	0	0	0	0	0	—	1	.000	.000	.000	—						

World Series — Batting / Fielding

Year Tm	Age	G	AB	H	2B	3B	HR	TB	R	RBI	GW	TBB	IBB	SO	HBP	SH	SF	SB	CS	SB%	GDP	Avg	OBP	SLG	Pos	G	PO	A	E	DP	FPct
1984 SD	37	5	17	7	2	0	2	15	4	4	1	1	0	2	0	0	0	0	1	.00	0	.412	.444	.882	—						
Postseason Totals		7	19	7	2	0	2	15	4	4	1	1	0	2	0	0	0	0	1	.00	1	.368	.400	.789	—	0	0	0	0	0	—

BILL BEVENS—Floyd Clifford Bevens—Throws: Right; Bats: Right

Ht: 6'3"; Wt: 210 lbs; Born: 10/21/1916 in Hubbard, Oregon; Debut: 5/12/1944; Died: 10/26/1991

World Series — Pitching

Year Tm	Age	G	GS	CG	GF	IP	BFP	H	R	ER	HR	SH	SF	HB	TBB	IBB	SO	WP	Bk	W	L	Pct	ShO	Sv-Op	Hld	OAvg	OOBP	ERA
1947 NYA	30	2	1	1	0	11.1	48	3	3	3	0	1	0	0	11	1	7	1	0	0	1	.000	0	0- 0	0	.083	.298	2.38

World Series — Batting / Fielding

Year Tm	Age	G	AB	H	2B	3B	HR	TB	R	RBI	GW	TBB	IBB	SO	HBP	SH	SF	SB	CS	SB%	GDP	Avg	OBP	SLG	Pos	G	PO	A	E	DP	FPct
1947 NYA	30	2	4	0	0	0	0	0	0	0	0	0	0	2	0	1	0	0	0	—	0	.000	.000	.000	P	2	0	1	0	0	1.000

BUDDY BIANCALANA—Roland Americo Biancalana—Bats: Both; Throws: Right

Ht: 5'11"; Wt: 160 lbs; Born: 2/2/1960 in Greenbrae, California; Debut: 9/12/1982

LCS		Batting																							Fielding						
Year Tm	Age	G	AB	H	2B	3B	HR	TB	R	RBI	GW	TBB	IBB	SO	HBP	SH	SF	SB	CS	SB%	GDP	Avg	OBP	SLG	Pos	G	PO	A	E	DP	FPct
1984 KC	24	2	1	0	0	0	0	0	0	0	0	0	0	1	0	0	0	0	0	—	0	.000	.000	.000	SS	2	1	2	0	0	1.000
1985 KC	25	7	18	4	1	0	0	5	2	1	0	1	0	6	0	1	0	0	0	—	0	.222	.263	.278	SS	7	9	20	0	4	1.000
LCS Totals		9	19	4	1	0	0	5	2	1	0	1	0	7	0	1	0	0	0	—	0	.211	.250	.263	SS	9	10	22	0	4	1.000
World Series		Batting																							Fielding						
Year Tm	Age	G	AB	H	2B	3B	HR	TB	R	RBI	GW	TBB	IBB	SO	HBP	SH	SF	SB	CS	SB%	GDP	Avg	OBP	SLG	Pos	G	PO	A	E	DP	FPct
1985 KC	25	7	18	5	0	0	0	5	2	2	1	5	0	4	0	0	0	0	0	—	1	.278	.435	.278	SS	7	6	20	0	1	1.000
Postseason Totals		16	37	9	1	0	0	10	4	3	1	6	0	11	0	1	0	0	0	—	1	.243	.349	.270	SS	16	16	42	0	5	1.000

JIM BIBBY—James Blair Bibby—Throws: Right; Bats: Right

Ht: 6'5"; Wt: 235 lbs; Born: 10/29/1944 in Franklinton, North Carolina; Debut: 9/4/1972

LCS		Pitching																									
Year Tm	Age	G	GS	CG	GF	IP	BFP	H	R	ER	HR	SH	SF	HB	TBB	IBB	SO	WP	Bk	W	L	Pct	ShO	Sv-Op	Hld	OAvg	OOBP	ERA
1979 Pit	34	1	1	0	0	7.0	28	4	1	1	0	1	1	0	4	0	5	0	0	0	0	—	0	0- 0	0	.182	.296	1.29
World Series		Pitching																										
Year Tm	Age	G	GS	CG	GF	IP	BFP	H	R	ER	HR	SH	SF	HB	TBB	IBB	SO	WP	Bk	W	L	Pct	ShO	Sv-Op	Hld	OAvg	OOBP	ERA
1979 Pit	34	2	2	0	0	10.1	41	10	4	3	1	0	0	0	2	0	10	0	0	0	0	—	0	0- 0	0	.256	.293	2.61
Postseason Totals		3	3	0	0	17.1	138	14	5	4	1	1	1	0	6	0	15	0	0	0	0	—	0	0-0	0	.230	.294	2.08

LCS		Batting																							Fielding						
Year Tm	Age	G	AB	H	2B	3B	HR	TB	R	RBI	GW	TBB	IBB	SO	HBP	SH	SF	SB	CS	SB%	GDP	Avg	OBP	SLG	Pos	G	PO	A	E	DP	FPct
1979 Pit	34	1	0	0	0	0	0	0	0	0	0	1	0	0	0	2	0	0	0	—	0	—	1.000	—	P	1	0	1	0	0	1.000
World Series		Batting																							Fielding						
Year Tm	Age	G	AB	H	2B	3B	HR	TB	R	RBI	GW	TBB	IBB	SO	HBP	SH	SF	SB	CS	SB%	GDP	Avg	OBP	SLG	Pos	G	PO	A	E	DP	FPct
1979 Pit	34	2	4	0	0	0	0	0	0	0	0	0	0	1	0	0	0	0	0	—	0	.000	.000	.000	P	2	1	0	0	0	1.000
Postseason Totals		3	4	0	0	0	0	0	0	0	0	1	0	1	0	2	0	0	0	—	0	.000	.200	.000	P	3	1	1	0	0	1.000

DANTE BICHETTE—Alphonse Dante Bichette—Bats: Right; Throws: Right

Ht: 6'3"; Wt: 215 lbs; Born: 11/18/1963 in West Palm Beach, Florida; Debut: 9/5/1988

Division Series		Batting																							Fielding						
Year Tm	Age	G	AB	H	2B	3B	HR	TB	R	RBI	GW	TBB	IBB	SO	HBP	SH	SF	SB	CS	SB%	GDP	Avg	OBP	SLG	Pos	G	PO	A	E	DP	FPct
1995 Col	31	4	17	10	3	0	1	16	6	3	0	1	0	3	0	0	0	0	0	—	0	.588	.611	.941	OF	4	9	0	0	0	1.000

VERN BICKFORD—Vernon Edgell Bickford—Throws: Right; Bats: Right

Ht: 6'0"; Wt: 180 lbs; Born: 8/17/1920 in Hellier, Kentucky; Debut: 4/24/1948; Died: 5/6/1960

World Series		Pitching																										
Year Tm	Age	G	GS	CG	GF	IP	BFP	H	R	ER	HR	SH	SF	HB	TBB	IBB	SO	WP	Bk	W	L	Pct	ShO	Sv-Op	Hld	OAvg	OOBP	ERA
1948 Bos	28	1	1	0	0	3.1	18	4	2	1	0	0	0	0	5	0	1	0	0	0	1	.000	0	0- 0	0	.308	.500	2.70

World Series		Batting																							Fielding						
Year Tm	Age	G	AB	H	2B	3B	HR	TB	R	RBI	GW	TBB	IBB	SO	HBP	SH	SF	SB	CS	SB%	GDP	Avg	OBP	SLG	Pos	G	PO	A	E	DP	FPct
1948 Bos	28	1	0	0	0	0	0	0	0	0	0	0	0	0	0	1	0	0	0	—	0	—	—	—	P	1	0	0	0	0	—

MIKE BIELECKI—Michael Joseph Bielecki—Throws: Right; Bats: Right

Ht: 6'3"; Wt: 195 lbs; Born: 7/31/1959 in Baltimore, Maryland; Debut: 9/14/1984

Division Series		Pitching																										
Year Tm	Age	G	GS	CG	GF	IP	BFP	H	R	ER	HR	SH	SF	HB	TBB	IBB	SO	WP	Bk	W	L	Pct	ShO	Sv-Op	Hld	OAvg	OOBP	ERA
1996 Atl	37	1	0	0	0	0.2	3	0	0	0	0	0	1	0	1	0	1	0	0	0	0	—	0	0- 0	1	.000	.333	0.00
LCS		Pitching																										
Year Tm	Age	G	GS	CG	GF	IP	BFP	H	R	ER	HR	SH	SF	HB	TBB	IBB	SO	WP	Bk	W	L	Pct	ShO	Sv-Op	Hld	OAvg	OOBP	ERA
1989 ChN	30	2	2	0	0	12.1	49	7	5	5	1	1	1	0	6	0	11	0	0	0	1	.000	0	0- 0	0	.171	.271	3.65
1996 Atl	37	3	0	0	0	3.0	10	0	0	0	0	0	0	0	1	0	5	0	0	0	0	—	0	0- 0	0	.000	.100	0.00
LCS Totals		5	2	0	0	15.1	118	7	5	5	1	1	1	0	7	0	16	0	0	0	1	.000	0	0-0	0	.140	.241	2.93
World Series		Pitching																										
Year Tm	Age	G	GS	CG	GF	IP	BFP	H	R	ER	HR	SH	SF	HB	TBB	IBB	SO	WP	Bk	W	L	Pct	ShO	Sv-Op	Hld	OAvg	OOBP	ERA
1996 Atl	37	2	0	0	1	3.0	12	0	0	0	0	0	0	0	3	0	6	0	0	0	0	—	0	0- 0	1	.000	.250	0.00
Postseason Totals		8	2	0	1	19.0	148	7	5	5	1	1	2	0	11	0	23	0	0	0	1	.000	0	0-0	2	.117	.247	2.37

Division Series		Batting																							Fielding						
Year Tm	Age	G	AB	H	2B	3B	HR	TB	R	RBI	GW	TBB	IBB	SO	HBP	SH	SF	SB	CS	SB%	GDP	Avg	OBP	SLG	Pos	G	PO	A	E	DP	FPct
1996 Atl	37	1	0	0	0	0	0	0	0	0	0	0	0	0	0	0	0	0	0	—	0	—	—	—	P	1	0	0	0	0	—
LCS		Batting																							Fielding						
Year Tm	Age	G	AB	H	2B	3B	HR	TB	R	RBI	GW	TBB	IBB	SO	HBP	SH	SF	SB	CS	SB%	GDP	Avg	OBP	SLG	Pos	G	PO	A	E	DP	FPct
1989 ChN	30	2	5	1	0	0	0	1	0	2	0	0	0	2	0	0	0	0	0	—	1	.200	.200	.200	P	2	1	2	0	0	1.000
1996 Atl	37	3	0	0	0	0	0	0	0	0	0	0	0	0	0	0	0	0	0	—	0	—	—	—	P	3	0	0	0	0	—
LCS Totals		5	5	1	0	0	0	1	0	2	0	0	0	2	0	0	0	0	0	—	1	.200	.200	.200	P	5	1	2	0	0	1.000
World Series		Batting																							Fielding						
Year Tm	Age	G	AB	H	2B	3B	HR	TB	R	RBI	GW	TBB	IBB	SO	HBP	SH	SF	SB	CS	SB%	GDP	Avg	OBP	SLG	Pos	G	PO	A	E	DP	FPct
1996 Atl	37	2	1	0	0	0	0	0	0	0	0	0	0	1	0	0	0	0	0	—	0	.000	.000	.000	P	2	1	0	0	0	1.000
Postseason Totals		8	6	1	0	0	0	1	0	2	0	0	0	3	0	0	0	0	0	—	1	.167	.167	.167	P	8	2	2	0	0	1.000

CARSON BIGBEE—Carson Lee Bigbee—Nickname: Skeeter—Bats: Left; Throws: Right

Ht: 5'9"; Wt: 157 lbs; Born: 3/31/1895 in Waterloo, Oregon; Debut: 8/25/1916; Died: 10/17/1964

World Series		Batting																							Fielding						
Year Tm	Age	G	AB	H	2B	3B	HR	TB	R	RBI	GW	TBB	IBB	SO	HBP	SH	SF	SB	CS	SB%	GDP	Avg	OBP	SLG	Pos	G	PO	A	E	DP	FPct
1925 Pit	30	4	3	1	1	0	0	2	1	1	0	0	0	0	0	0	0	1	0	1.00	0	.333	.333	.667	OF	1	0	0	0	0	—

CRAIG BIGGIO—Craig Alan Biggio—Bats: Right; Throws: Right

Ht: 5'11"; Wt: 185 lbs; Born: 12/14/1965 in Smithtown, New York; Debut: 6/26/1988

Division Series		Batting																							Fielding						
Year Tm	Age	G	AB	H	2B	3B	HR	TB	R	RBI	GW	TBB	IBB	SO	HBP	SH	SF	SB	CS	SB%	GDP	Avg	OBP	SLG	Pos	G	PO	A	E	DP	FPct
1997 Hou	31	3	12	1	0	0	0	1	0	0	0	1	0	0	0	0	0	0	0	—	0	.083	.154	.083	2B	3	4	8	1	2	.923

JACK BILLINGHAM—John Eugene Billingham—Throws: Right; Bats: Right

Ht: 6'4"; Wt: 195 lbs; Born: 2/21/1943 in Orlando, Florida; Debut: 4/11/1968

LCS		Pitching																										
Year Tm	Age	G	GS	CG	GF	IP	BFP	H	R	ER	HR	SH	SF	HB	TBB	IBB	SO	WP	Bk	W	L	Pct	ShO	Sv-Op	Hld	OAvg	OOBP	ERA
1972 Cin	29	1	1	0	0	4.2	21	5	2	2	0	0	0	1	2	0	4	0	0	0	0	—	0	0- 0	0	.278	.381	3.86
1973 Cin	30	2	2	0	0	12.0	50	9	6	6	0	2	0	0	4	0	9	0	0	0	1	.000	0	0- 0	0	.205	.271	4.50
LCS Totals		3	3	0	0	16.2	142	14	8	8	0	2	0	1	6	0	13	0	0	0	1	.000	0	0-0	0	.226	.304	4.32
World Series		Pitching																										
Year Tm	Age	G	GS	CG	GF	IP	BFP	H	R	ER	HR	SH	SF	HB	TBB	IBB	SO	WP	Bk	W	L	Pct	ShO	Sv-Op	Hld	OAvg	OOBP	ERA
1972 Cin	29	3	2	0	1	13.2	50	6	1	0	0	1	0	0	4	1	11	0	0	1	0	1.000	0	1- 1	0	.133	.204	0.00
1975 Cin	32	3	1	0	0	9.0	40	8	2	1	0	1	0	1	5	0	7	0	0	0	0	—	0	0- 0	0	.242	.359	1.00
1976 Cin	33	1	0	0	1	2.2	8	0	0	0	0	0	0	0	0	0	1	0	0	1	0	1.000	0	0- 1	0	.000	.000	0.00
WS Totals		7	3	0	2	25.1	196	14	3	1	0	2	0	1	9	1	19	0	0	2	0	1.000	0	1-2	0	.163	.250	0.36
Postseason Totals		10	6	0	2	42.0	338	28	11	9	0	4	0	2	15	1	32	0	0	2	1	.667	0	1-2	0	.189	.273	1.93

LCS		Batting																							Fielding						
Year Tm	Age	G	AB	H	2B	3B	HR	TB	R	RBI	GW	TBB	IBB	SO	HBP	SH	SF	SB	CS	SB%	GDP	Avg	OBP	SLG	Pos	G	PO	A	E	DP	FPct
1972 Cin	29	1	2	0	0	0	0	0	0	0	0	0	0	1	0	0	0	0	0	—	0	.000	.000	.000	P	1	1	0	0	0	1.000
1973 Cin	30	2	3	0	0	0	0	0	0	0	0	0	0	1	0	1	0	0	0	—	0	.000	.000	.000	P	2	0	2	0	0	1.000
LCS Totals		3	5	0	0	0	0	0	0	0	0	0	0	2	0	1	0	0	0	—	0	.000	.000	.000	P	3	1	2	0	0	1.000

World Series												Batting																Fielding			
Year Tm	Age	G	AB	H	2B	3B	HR	TB	R	RBI	GW	TBB	IBB	SO	HBP	SH	SF	SB	CS	SB%	GDP	Avg	OBP	SLG	Pos	G	PO	A	E	DP	FPct
1972 Cin	29	3	5	0	0	0	0	0	0	0	0	0	0	4	0	0	0	0	0	—	0	.000	.000	.000	P	3	1	1	0	0	1.000
1975 Cin	32	3	2	0	0	0	0	0	0	0	0	0	0	0	0	0	0	0	0	—	0	.000	.000	.000	P	3	0	2	0	1	1.000
1976 Cin	33	1	0	0	0	0	0	0	0	0	0	0	0	0	0	0	0	0	0	—	0	—	—	—	P	1	1	0	0	0	1.000
WS Totals		7	7	0	0	0	0	0	0	0	0	0	0	4	0	0	0	0	0	—	0	.000	.000	.000	P	7	2	3	0	1	1.000
Postseason Totals		10	12	0	0	0	0	0	0	0	0	0	0	6	0	1	0	0	0	—	0	.000	.000	.000	P	10	3	5	0	1	1.000

DOUG BIRD—James Douglas Bird—Throws: Right; Bats: Right

Ht: 6'4"; Wt: 180 lbs; Born: 3/5/1950 in Corona, California; Debut: 4/29/1973

LCS															Pitching													
Year Tm	Age	G	GS	CG	GF	IP	BFP	H	R	ER	HR	SH	SF	HB	TBB	IBB	SO	WP	Bk	W	L	Pct	ShO	Sv-Op	Hld	OAvg	OOBP	ERA
1976 KC	26	1	0	0	0	4.2	16	4	1	1	0	0	0	0	0	0	1	0	0	1	0	1.000	0	0- 0	0	.250	.250	1.93
1977 KC	27	3	0	0	2	2.0	9	4	0	0	0	0	1	0	0	0	1	0	0	0	0	—	0	0- 0	1	.500	.444	0.00
1978 KC	28	2	0	0	1	1.0	6	2	1	1	1	0	0	0	0	0	1	0	0	0	1	.000	0	0- 1	0	.333	.333	9.00
LCS Totals		6	0	0	3	7.2	62	10	2	2	1	0	1	0	0	0	3	0	0	1	1	.500	0	0-1	1	.333	.323	2.35

LCS												Batting																Fielding			
Year Tm	Age	G	AB	H	2B	3B	HR	TB	R	RBI	GW	TBB	IBB	SO	HBP	SH	SF	SB	CS	SB%	GDP	Avg	OBP	SLG	Pos	G	PO	A	E	DP	FPct
1976 KC	26	1	0	0	0	0	0	0	0	0	0	0	0	0	0	0	0	0	0	—	0	—	—	—	P	1	0	1	1	0	.500
1977 KC	27	3	0	0	0	0	0	0	0	0	0	0	0	0	0	0	0	0	0	—	0	—	—	—	P	3	0	0	0	0	—
1978 KC	28	2	0	0	0	0	0	0	0	0	0	0	0	0	0	0	0	0	0	—	0	—	—	—	P	2	0	1	0	0	1.000
LCS Totals		6	0	0	0	0	0	0	0	0	0	0	0	0	0	0	0	0	0	—	0	—	—	—	P	6	0	2	1	0	.667

MAX BISHOP—Max Frederick Bishop—Nicknames: Tilly, Camera Eye—Bats: Left; Throws: Right

Ht: 5'8"; Wt: 165 lbs; Born: 9/5/1899 in Waynesboro, Pennsylvania; Debut: 4/15/1924; Died: 2/24/1962

World Series												Batting																Fielding			
Year Tm	Age	G	AB	H	2B	3B	HR	TB	R	RBI	GW	TBB	IBB	SO	HBP	SH	SF	SB	CS	SB%	GDP	Avg	OBP	SLG	Pos	G	PO	A	E	DP	FPct
1929 Phi	30	5	21	4	0	0	0	4	2	1	0	2	0	3	0	0	0	0	0	—	0	.190	.261	.190	2B	5	9	13	0	2	1.000
1930 Phi	31	6	18	4	0	0	0	4	5	0	0	7	0	3	1	0	0	0	0	—	0	.222	.462	.222	2B	6	8	9	0	0	1.000
1931 Phi	32	7	27	4	0	0	0	4	4	0	0	3	0	5	0	0	0	0	0	—	0	.148	.233	.148	2B	7	12	18	0	4	1.000
WS Totals		18	66	12	0	0	0	12	11	1	0	12	0	11	1	0	0	0	0	—	0	.182	.316	.182	2B	18	29	40	0	6	1.000

BUD BLACK—Harry Ralston Black—Throws: Left; Bats: Left

Ht: 6'2"; Wt: 180 lbs; Born: 6/30/1957 in San Mateo, California; Debut: 9/5/1981

LCS															Pitching													
Year Tm	Age	G	GS	CG	GF	IP	BFP	H	R	ER	HR	SH	SF	HB	TBB	IBB	SO	WP	Bk	W	L	Pct	ShO	Sv-Op	Hld	OAvg	OOBP	ERA
1984 KC	27	1	1	0	0	5.0	23	7	4	4	2	0	1	0	1	0	3	0	0	0	1	.000	0	0- 0	0	.333	.348	7.20
1985 KC	28	3	1	0	0	10.2	47	11	3	2	0	0	0	1	4	0	8	2	0	0	0	—	0	0- 0	1	.262	.340	1.69
LCS Totals		4	2	0	0	15.2	140	18	7	6	2	0	1	1	5	0	11	2	0	0	1	.000	0	0-0	1	.286	.343	3.45
World Series															**Pitching**													
Year Tm	Age	G	GS	CG	GF	IP	BFP	H	R	ER	HR	SH	SF	HB	TBB	IBB	SO	WP	Bk	W	L	Pct	ShO	Sv-Op	Hld	OAvg	OOBP	ERA
1985 KC	28	2	1	0	1	5.1	23	4	3	3	2	1	0	0	5	2	4	0	0	0	1	.000	0	0- 0	0	.235	.409	5.06
Postseason Totals		6	3	0	1	21.0	186	22	10	9	4	1	1	1	10	2	15	2	0	0	2	.000	0	0-0	1	.275	.359	3.86

LCS												Batting																Fielding			
Year Tm	Age	G	AB	H	2B	3B	HR	TB	R	RBI	GW	TBB	IBB	SO	HBP	SH	SF	SB	CS	SB%	GDP	Avg	OBP	SLG	Pos	G	PO	A	E	DP	FPct
1984 KC	27	1	0	0	0	0	0	0	0	0	0	0	0	0	0	0	0	0	0	—	0	—	—	—	P	1	1	1	0	0	1.000
1985 KC	28	3	0	0	0	0	0	0	0	0	0	0	0	0	0	0	0	0	0	—	0	—	—	—	P	3	2	3	0	1	1.000
LCS Totals		4	0	0	0	0	0	0	0	0	0	0	0	0	0	0	0	0	0	—	0	—	—	—	P	4	3	4	0	1	1.000
World Series												**Batting**																**Fielding**			
Year Tm	Age	G	AB	H	2B	3B	HR	TB	R	RBI	GW	TBB	IBB	SO	HBP	SH	SF	SB	CS	SB%	GDP	Avg	OBP	SLG	Pos	G	PO	A	E	DP	FPct
1985 KC	28	2	1	0	0	0	0	0	0	0	0	0	0	1	0	0	0	0	0	—	0	.000	.000	.000	P	2	1	2	1	1	.750
Postseason Totals		6	1	0	0	0	0	0	0	0	0	0	0	1	0	0	0	0	0	—	0	.000	.000	.000	P	6	4	6	1	2	.909

JOE BLACK—Joseph Black—Throws: Right; Bats: Right

Ht: 6'2"; Wt: 220 lbs; Born: 2/8/1924 in Plainfield, New Jersey; Debut: 5/1/1952

World Series															Pitching													
Year Tm	Age	G	GS	CG	GF	IP	BFP	H	R	ER	HR	SH	SF	HB	TBB	IBB	SO	WP	Bk	W	L	Pct	ShO	Sv-Op	Hld	OAvg	OOBP	ERA
1952 Bro-*RY*	28	3	3	1	0	21.1	84	15	6	6	4	0	0	0	8	1	9	0	0	1	2	.333	0	0- 0	0	.197	.274	2.53
1953 Bro	29	1	0	0	1	1.0	4	1	1	1	1	0	0	0	0	0	2	0	0	0	0	—	0	0- 0	0	.250	.250	9.00
WS Totals		4	3	1	1	22.1	176	16	7	7	5	0	0	0	8	1	11	0	0	1	2	.333	0	0-0	0	.200	.273	2.82

World Series												Batting																Fielding			
Year Tm	Age	G	AB	H	2B	3B	HR	TB	R	RBI	GW	TBB	IBB	SO	HBP	SH	SF	SB	CS	SB%	GDP	Avg	OBP	SLG	Pos	G	PO	A	E	DP	FPct
1952 Bro	28	3	6	0	0	0	0	0	0	0	0	1	0	6	0	0	0	0	0	—	0	.000	.143	.000	P	3	1	2	0	0	1.000
1953 Bro	29	1	0	0	0	0	0	0	0	0	0	0	0	0	0	0	0	0	0	—	0	—	—	—	P	1	0	0	0	0	—
WS Totals		4	6	0	0	0	0	0	0	0	0	1	0	6	0	0	0	0	0	—	0	.000	.143	.000	P	4	1	2	0	0	1.000

EWELL BLACKWELL—Nickname: The Whip—Throws: Right; Bats: Right

Ht: 6'6"; Wt: 195 lbs; Born: 10/23/1922 in Fresno, California; Debut: 4/21/1942; Died: 10/29/1996

World Series															Pitching													
Year Tm	Age	G	GS	CG	GF	IP	BFP	H	R	ER	HR	SH	SF	HB	TBB	IBB	SO	WP	Bk	W	L	Pct	ShO	Sv-Op	Hld	OAvg	OOBP	ERA
1952 NYA	29	1	1	0	0	5.0	22	4	4	4	1	2	0	0	3	0	4	0	0	0	0	—	0	0- 0	0	.235	.350	7.20

World Series												Batting																Fielding			
Year Tm	Age	G	AB	H	2B	3B	HR	TB	R	RBI	GW	TBB	IBB	SO	HBP	SH	SF	SB	CS	SB%	GDP	Avg	OBP	SLG	Pos	G	PO	A	E	DP	FPct
1952 NYA	29	1	1	0	0	0	0	0	0	0	0	0	0	0	0	0	0	0	0	—	0	.000	.000	.000	P	1	0	1	0	0	1.000

RAY BLADES—Francis Raymond Blades—Bats: Right; Throws: Right

Ht: 5'7"; Wt: 163 lbs; Born: 8/6/1896 in Mt. Vernon, Illinois; Debut: 8/19/1922; Died: 5/18/1979

World Series												Batting																Fielding			
Year Tm	Age	G	AB	H	2B	3B	HR	TB	R	RBI	GW	TBB	IBB	SO	HBP	SH	SF	SB	CS	SB%	GDP	Avg	OBP	SLG	Pos	G	PO	A	E	DP	FPct
1928 StL	32	1	1	0	0	0	0	0	0	0	0	0	0	1	0	0	0	0	0	—	0	.000	.000	.000	—						
1930 StL	34	5	9	1	0	0	0	1	2	0	0	2	0	2	0	0	0	0	0	—	0	.111	.273	.111	OF	3	10	0	0	0	1.000
1931 StL	35	2	2	0	0	0	0	0	0	0	0	0	0	2	0	0	0	0	0	—	0	.000	.000	.000	—						
WS Totals		8	12	1	0	0	0	1	2	0	0	2	0	5	0	0	0	0	0	—	0	.083	.214	.083	OF	3	10	0	0	0	1.000

FOOTSIE BLAIR—Clarence Vick Blair—Bats: Left; Throws: Right

Ht: 6'1"; Wt: 180 lbs; Born: 7/13/1900 in Interprise, Oklahoma; Debut: 4/28/1929; Died: 7/1/1982

World Series												Batting																Fielding			
Year Tm	Age	G	AB	H	2B	3B	HR	TB	R	RBI	GW	TBB	IBB	SO	HBP	SH	SF	SB	CS	SB%	GDP	Avg	OBP	SLG	Pos	G	PO	A	E	DP	FPct
1929 ChN	29	1	1	0	0	0	0	0	0	0	0	0	0	0	0	0	0	0	0	—	0	.000	.000	.000	—						

PAUL BLAIR—Paul L.D. Blair—Nickname: Motormouth—Bats: Right; Throws: Right

Ht: 6'0"; Wt: 168 lbs; Born: 2/1/1944 in Cushing, Oklahoma; Debut: 9/9/1964

LCS												Batting																Fielding			
Year Tm	Age	G	AB	H	2B	3B	HR	TB	R	RBI	GW	TBB	IBB	SO	HBP	SH	SF	SB	CS	SB%	GDP	Avg	OBP	SLG	Pos	G	PO	A	E	DP	FPct
1969 Bal	25	3	15	6	2	0	1	11	1	6	1	2	0	2	0	0	0	0	1	.00	1	.400	.471	.733	OF	3	8	0	0	0	1.000
1970 Bal	26	3	13	1	0	0	0	1	0	0	0	1	0	4	0	1	0	0	0	—	0	.077	.143	.077	OF	3	4	0	0	0	1.000
1971 Bal	27	3	9	3	1	0	0	4	1	2	1	0	0	3	0	0	0	0	0	—	0	.333	.333	.444	OF	3	5	0	0	0	1.000
1973 Bal	29	5	18	3	0	0	0	3	2	0	0	1	0	5	1	0	0	0	1	.00	0	.167	.250	.167	OF	5	8	0	0	0	1.000
1974 Bal	30	4	14	4	0	0	1	7	3	2	0	2	0	2	0	0	0	0	2	.00	0	.286	.375	.500	OF	4	7	0	0	0	1.000
1977 NYA	33	3	5	2	0	0	0	2	1	0	0	0	0	0	0	0	0	0	0	—	0	.400	.400	.400	OF	3	2	0	0	0	1.000
1978 NYA	34	4	6	0	0	0	0	0	1	0	0	0	0	1	0	0	0	0	0	—	0	.000	.000	.000	2B	1	1	0	0	0	1.000
																									OF	3	7	0	0	0	1.000
LCS Totals		25	80	19	3	0	2	28	9	10	2	6	0	17	1	1	0	0	4	.00	1	.238	.299	.350	OF	24	41	0	0	0	1.000

World Series — Batting / Fielding

Year Tm	Age	G	AB	H	2B	3B	HR	TB	R	RBI	GW	TBB	IBB	SO	HBP	SH	SF	SB	CS	SB%	GDP	Avg	OBP	SLG	Pos	G	PO	A	E	DP	FPct
1966 Bal	22	4	6	1	0	0	1	4	2	1	1	1	1	0	0	0	0	0	0	—	0	.167	.286	.667	OF	4	9	0	0	0	1.000
1969 Bal	25	5	20	2	0	0	0	2	1	0	0	2	0	5	0	0	0	1	1	.50	0	.100	.182	.100	OF	5	7	0	0	0	1.000
1970 Bal	26	5	19	9	1	0	0	10	5	3	1	2	0	4	0	1	0	0	1	.00	1	.474	.524	.526	OF	5	18	0	1	0	.947
1971 Bal	27	4	9	3	1	0	0	4	2	0	0	0	0	1	0	0	0	0	0	—	0	.333	.333	.444	OF	4	6	2	1	0	.889
1977 NYA	33	4	4	1	0	0	0	1	0	1	1	0	0	0	0	0	0	0	0	—	0	.250	.250	.250	OF	3	1	0	0	0	1.000
1978 NYA	34	6	8	3	1	0	0	4	2	0	0	1	0	4	0	0	0	0	0	—	0	.375	.444	.500	OF	6	5	0	0	0	1.000
WS Totals		28	66	19	3	0	1	25	12	5	3	6	1	14	0	1	0	1	2	.33	1	.288	.347	.379	OF	27	46	2	2	0	.960
Postseason Totals		53	146	38	6	0	3	53	21	15	5	12	1	31	1	2	0	1	6	.14	2	.260	.321	.363	OF	51	87	2	2	0	.978

WILLIE BLAIR—William Allen Blair—Throws: Right; Bats: Right

Ht: 6'1"; Wt: 185 lbs; Born: 12/18/1965 in Paintsville, Kentucky; Debut: 4/11/1990

Division Series — Pitching

Year Tm	Age	G	GS	CG	GF	IP	BFP	H	R	ER	HR	SH	SF	HB	TBB	IBB	SO	WP	Bk	W	L	Pct	ShO	Sv-Op	Hld	OAvg	OOBP	ERA
1996 SD	30	1	0	0	1	2.0	8	1	0	0	0	0	0	0	2	0	3	0	0	0	0	—	0	0- 0	0	.167	.375	0.00

Division Series — Batting / Fielding

Year Tm	Age	G	AB	H	2B	3B	HR	TB	R	RBI	GW	TBB	IBB	SO	HBP	SH	SF	SB	CS	SB%	GDP	Avg	OBP	SLG	Pos	G	PO	A	E	DP	FPct
1996 SD	30	1	0	0	0	0	0	0	0	0	0	0	0	0	0	0	0	0	0	—	0	—	—	—	P	1	0	0	0	0	—

SHERIFF BLAKE—John Frederick Blake—Throws: Right; Bats: Both

Ht: 6'0"; Wt: 180 lbs; Born: 9/17/1899 in Ansted, West Virginia; Debut: 6/29/1920; Died: 10/31/1982

World Series — Pitching

Year Tm	Age	G	GS	CG	GF	IP	BFP	H	R	ER	HR	SH	SF	HB	TBB	IBB	SO	WP	Bk	W	L	Pct	ShO	Sv-Op	Hld	OAvg	OOBP	ERA
1929 ChN	30	2	0	0	0	1.1	8	4	2	2	0	1	0	0	0	0	1	0	0	0	1	.000	0	0- 1	0	.571	.571	13.50

World Series — Batting / Fielding

Year Tm	Age	G	AB	H	2B	3B	HR	TB	R	RBI	GW	TBB	IBB	SO	HBP	SH	SF	SB	CS	SB%	GDP	Avg	OBP	SLG	Pos	G	PO	A	E	DP	FPct
1929 ChN	30	2	1	1	0	0	0	1	0	0	0	0	0	0	0	0	0	0	0	—	0	1.000	1.000	1.000	P	2	0	0	0	0	—

JOHNNY BLANCHARD—John Edwin Blanchard—Bats: Left; Throws: Right

Ht: 6'1"; Wt: 193 lbs; Born: 2/26/1933 in Minneapolis, Minnesota; Debut: 9/25/1955

World Series — Batting / Fielding

Year Tm	Age	G	AB	H	2B	3B	HR	TB	R	RBI	GW	TBB	IBB	SO	HBP	SH	SF	SB	CS	SB%	GDP	Avg	OBP	SLG	Pos	G	PO	A	E	DP	FPct
1960 NYA	27	5	11	5	2	0	0	7	2	2	0	0	0	0	0	0	0	0	0	—	0	.455	.455	.636	C	2	5	2	0	1	1.000
1961 NYA	28	4	10	4	1	0	2	11	4	3	1	2	0	0	0	0	0	0	0	—	0	.400	.500	1.100	OF	2	2	1	0	0	1.000
1962 NYA	29	1	1	0	0	0	0	0	0	0	0	0	0	1	0	0	0	0	0	—	0	.000	.000	.000	—						
1963 NYA	30	1	3	0	0	0	0	0	0	0	0	0	0	0	0	0	0	0	0	—	0	.000	.000	.000	OF	1	1	0	0	0	1.000
1964 NYA	31	4	4	1	1	0	0	2	0	0	0	0	0	1	0	0	0	0	0	—	0	.250	.250	.500	—						
WS Totals		15	29	10	4	0	2	20	6	5	1	2	0	2	0	0	0	0	0	—	0	.345	.387	.690	OF	3	3	1	0	0	1.000

LANCE BLANKENSHIP—Lance Robert Blankenship—Bats: Right; Throws: Right

Ht: 6'0"; Wt: 190 lbs; Born: 12/6/1963 in Portland, Oregon; Debut: 9/4/1988

LCS — Batting / Fielding

Year Tm	Age	G	AB	H	2B	3B	HR	TB	R	RBI	GW	TBB	IBB	SO	HBP	SH	SF	SB	CS	SB%	GDP	Avg	OBP	SLG	Pos	G	PO	A	E	DP	FPct
1989 Oak	25	1	0	0	0	0	0	0	0	0	0	0	0	0	0	0	0	0	0	—	0	—	—	—	2B	1	0	1	0	0	1.000
1990 Oak	26	3	0	0	0	0	0	0	1	0	0	0	0	0	0	0	0	1	0	1.00	0	—	—	—	—						
1992 Oak	28	5	13	3	0	0	0	3	2	0	0	3	0	4	0	0	0	1	0	1.00	0	.231	.375	.231	2B	5	11	13	2	3	.923
LCS Totals		9	13	3	0	0	0	3	3	0	0	3	0	4	0	0	0	2	0	1.00	0	.231	.375	.231	2B	6	11	14	2	3	.926

World Series — Batting / Fielding

Year Tm	Age	G	AB	H	2B	3B	HR	TB	R	RBI	GW	TBB	IBB	SO	HBP	SH	SF	SB	CS	SB%	GDP	Avg	OBP	SLG	Pos	G	PO	A	E	DP	FPct
1989 Oak	25	1	2	1	0	0	0	1	1	0	0	0	0	0	0	0	0	0	0	—	0	.500	.500	.500	2B	1	1	0	0	0	1.000
1990 Oak	26	1	1	0	0	0	0	0	0	0	0	0	0	1	0	0	0	0	0	—	0	.000	.000	.000	—						
WS Totals		2	3	1	0	0	0	1	1	0	0	0	0	1	0	0	0	0	0	—	0	.333	.333	.333	2B	1	1	0	0	0	1.000
Postseason Totals		11	16	4	0	0	0	4	4	0	0	3	0	5	0	0	0	2	0	1.00	0	.250	.368	.250	2B	7	12	14	2	3	.929

DON BLASINGAME—Don Lee Blasingame—Nickname: The Blazer—Bats: Left; Throws: Right

Ht: 5'10"; Wt: 160 lbs; Born: 3/16/1932 in Corinth, Mississippi; Debut: 9/20/1955

World Series — Batting / Fielding

Year Tm	Age	G	AB	H	2B	3B	HR	TB	R	RBI	GW	TBB	IBB	SO	HBP	SH	SF	SB	CS	SB%	GDP	Avg	OBP	SLG	Pos	G	PO	A	E	DP	FPct
1961 Cin	29	3	7	1	0	0	0	1	1	0	0	0	0	3	0	0	0	0	0	—	0	.143	.143	.143	2B	3	5	4	0	0	1.000

STEVE BLASS—Stephen Robert Blass—Throws: Right; Bats: Right

Ht: 6'0"; Wt: 165 lbs; Born: 4/18/1942 in Canaan, Connecticut; Debut: 5/10/1964

LCS — Pitching

Year Tm	Age	G	GS	CG	GF	IP	BFP	H	R	ER	HR	SH	SF	HB	TBB	IBB	SO	WP	Bk	W	L	Pct	ShO	Sv-Op	Hld	OAvg	OOBP	ERA
1971 Pit	29	2	2	0	0	7.0	38	14	10	9	4	2	0	0	2	0	11	0	0	0	1	.000	0	0- 0	0	.412	.444	11.57
1972 Pit	30	2	2	0	0	15.2	65	12	3	3	2	2	0	0	6	0	5	0	0	1	0	1.000	0	0- 0	0	.211	.286	1.72
LCS Totals		4	4	0	0	22.2	206	26	13	12	6	4	0	0	8	0	16	0	0	1	1	.500	0	0-0	0	.286	.343	4.76

World Series — Pitching

Year Tm	Age	G	GS	CG	GF	IP	BFP	H	R	ER	HR	SH	SF	HB	TBB	IBB	SO	WP	Bk	W	L	Pct	ShO	Sv-Op	Hld	OAvg	OOBP	ERA
1971 Pit	29	2	2	2	0	18.0	64	7	2	2	1	1	0	0	4	0	13	0	0	2	0	1.000	0	0- 0	0	.119	.175	1.00
Postseason Totals		6	6	2	0	40.2	334	33	15	14	7	5	0	0	12	0	29	0	0	3	1	.750	0	0-0	0	.220	.278	3.10

LCS — Batting / Fielding

Year Tm	Age	G	AB	H	2B	3B	HR	TB	R	RBI	GW	TBB	IBB	SO	HBP	SH	SF	SB	CS	SB%	GDP	Avg	OBP	SLG	Pos	G	PO	A	E	DP	FPct
1971 Pit	29	2	1	0	0	0	0	0	0	0	0	0	0	1	0	1	0	0	0	—	0	.000	.000	.000	P	2	1	1	0	0	1.000
1972 Pit	30	2	6	0	0	0	0	0	0	0	0	0	0	3	0	0	0	0	0	—	1	.000	.000	.000	P	2	1	3	0	0	1.000
LCS Totals		4	7	0	0	0	0	0	0	0	0	0	0	4	0	1	0	0	0	—	1	.000	.000	.000	P	4	2	4	0	0	1.000

World Series — Batting / Fielding

Year Tm	Age	G	AB	H	2B	3B	HR	TB	R	RBI	GW	TBB	IBB	SO	HBP	SH	SF	SB	CS	SB%	GDP	Avg	OBP	SLG	Pos	G	PO	A	E	DP	FPct
1971 Pit	29	2	7	0	0	0	0	0	0	0	0	0	0	1	0	0	0	0	0	—	0	.000	.000	.000	P	2	2	4	0	0	1.000
Postseason Totals		6	14	0	0	0	0	0	0	0	0	0	0	5	0	1	0	0	0	—	1	.000	.000	.000	P	6	4	8	0	0	1.000

JEFF BLAUSER—Jeffrey Michael Blauser—Bats: Right; Throws: Right

Ht: 6'0"; Wt: 170 lbs; Born: 11/8/1965 in Los Gatos, California; Debut: 7/5/1987

Division Series — Batting / Fielding

Year Tm	Age	G	AB	H	2B	3B	HR	TB	R	RBI	GW	TBB	IBB	SO	HBP	SH	SF	SB	CS	SB%	GDP	Avg	OBP	SLG	Pos	G	PO	A	E	DP	FPct
1995 Atl	29	3	6	0	0	0	0	0	0	0	0	1	1	3	1	0	0	0	0	—	0	.000	.250	.000	SS	3	5	11	1	3	.941
1996 Atl	30	3	9	1	0	0	0	1	0	0	0	1	0	3	1	0	0	0	1	.00	0	.111	.273	.111	SS	3	0	7	0	1	1.000
1997 Atl	31	3	10	3	0	0	1	6	2	4	0	2	0	2	0	0	0	0	0	—	0	.300	.417	.600	SS	3	2	10	0	2	1.000
DS Totals		9	25	4	0	0	1	7	2	4	0	4	1	8	2	0	0	0	1	.00	0	.160	.323	.280	SS	9	7	28	1	6	.972

LCS — Batting / Fielding

Year Tm	Age	G	AB	H	2B	3B	HR	TB	R	RBI	GW	TBB	IBB	SO	HBP	SH	SF	SB	CS	SB%	GDP	Avg	OBP	SLG	Pos	G	PO	A	E	DP	FPct
1991 Atl	25	2	2	0	0	0	0	0	0	0	0	0	0	0	0	0	0	0	0	—	0	.000	.000	.000	SS	2	0	1	1	0	.500
1992 Atl	26	7	24	5	0	1	1	10	3	4	0	3	0	2	0	1	0	0	0	—	1	.208	.296	.417	SS	7	7	15	2	1	.917
1993 Atl	27	6	25	7	1	0	2	14	5	4	0	4	0	7	0	0	0	0	0	—	0	.280	.379	.560	SS	6	6	14	0	0	1.000
1995 Atl	29	1	4	0	0	0	0	0	0	0	0	1	0	2	0	0	0	0	0	—	0	.000	.200	.000	SS	1	4	6	0	3	1.000
1996 Atl	30	7	17	3	0	1	0	5	5	2	0	4	2	6	2	0	0	0	0	—	0	.176	.391	.294	SS	7	5	9	1	2	.933
1997 Atl	31	6	20	6	0	0	1	9	5	1	0	3	0	6	1	0	0	0	0	—	1	.300	.417	.450	SS	6	6	19	1	4	.962
LCS Totals		29	92	21	1	2	4	38	18	11	0	15	2	23	3	1	0	0	0	—	2	.228	.355	.413	SS	29	28	64	5	10	.948

World Series — Batting / Fielding

Year Tm	Age	G	AB	H	2B	3B	HR	TB	R	RBI	GW	TBB	IBB	SO	HBP	SH	SF	SB	CS	SB%	GDP	Avg	OBP	SLG	Pos	G	PO	A	E	DP	FPct
1991 Atl	25	5	6	1	0	0	0	1	0	0	0	1	1	1	0	0	0	0	0	—	0	.167	.286	.167	SS	5	3	3	0	1	1.000
1992 Atl	26	6	24	6	0	0	0	6	2	0	0	1	0	9	0	0	0	2	1	.67	0	.250	.280	.250	SS	6	7	22	0	5	1.000
1996 Atl	30	6	18	3	1	0	0	4	2	1	0	1	0	4	0	0	0	0	0	—	1	.167	.211	.222	SS	6	9	15	1	3	.960
WS Totals		17	48	10	1	0	0	11	4	1	0	3	1	14	0	0	0	2	1	.67	1	.208	.255	.229	SS	17	19	40	1	9	.983
Postseason Totals		55	165	35	2	2	5	56	24	16	0	22	4	45	5	1	0	2	2	.50	3	.212	.323	.339	SS	55	54	132	7	25	.964

CURT BLEFARY—Curtis Leroy Blefary—Bats: Left; Throws: Right

Ht: 6'2"; Wt: 195 lbs; Born: 7/5/1943 in Brooklyn, New York; Debut: 4/14/1965

LCS		Batting																							Fielding						
Year Tm	Age	G	AB	H	2B	3B	HR	TB	R	RBI	GW	TBB	IBB	SO	HBP	SH	SF	SB	CS	SB%	GDP	Avg	OBP	SLG	Pos	G	PO	A	E	DP	FPct
1971 Oak	28	1	1	0	0	0	0	0	0	0	0	0	0	1	0	0	0	0	0	—	0	.000	.000	.000	—						
World Series		Batting																							Fielding						
Year Tm	Age	G	AB	H	2B	3B	HR	TB	R	RBI	GW	TBB	IBB	SO	HBP	SH	SF	SB	CS	SB%	GDP	Avg	OBP	SLG	Pos	G	PO	A	E	DP	FPct
1966 Bal	23	4	13	1	0	0	0	1	0	0	0	2	1	3	0	0	0	0	0	—	0	.077	.200	.077	OF	4	7	0	0	0	1.000
Postseason Totals		5	14	1	0	0	0	1	0	0	0	2	1	4	0	0	0	0	0	—	0	.071	.188	.071	OF	4	7	0	0	0	1.000

CY BLOCK—Seymour Block—Bats: Right; Throws: Right

Ht: 6'0"; Wt: 180 lbs; Born: 5/4/1919 in Brooklyn, New York; Debut: 9/7/1942

World Series		Batting																							Fielding						
Year Tm	Age	G	AB	H	2B	3B	HR	TB	R	RBI	GW	TBB	IBB	SO	HBP	SH	SF	SB	CS	SB%	GDP	Avg	OBP	SLG	Pos	G	PO	A	E	DP	FPct
1945 ChN	26	1	0	0	0	0	0	0	0	0	0	0	0	0	0	0	0	0	0	—	0	—	—	—	—						

JIMMY BLOODWORTH—James Henry Bloodworth—Bats: Right; Throws: Right

Ht: 5'11"; Wt: 180 lbs; Born: 7/26/1917 in Tallahassee, Florida; Debut: 9/14/1937

World Series		Batting																							Fielding						
Year Tm	Age	G	AB	H	2B	3B	HR	TB	R	RBI	GW	TBB	IBB	SO	HBP	SH	SF	SB	CS	SB%	GDP	Avg	OBP	SLG	Pos	G	PO	A	E	DP	FPct
1950 Phi	33	1	0	0	0	0	0	0	0	0	0	0	0	0	0	0	0	0	0	—	0	—	—	—	2B	1	0	0	0	0	—

MIKE BLOWERS—Michael Roy Blowers—Bats: Right; Throws: Right

Ht: 6'2"; Wt: 190 lbs; Born: 4/24/1965 in Wurzburg, West Germany; Debut: 9/1/1989

Division Series		Batting																							Fielding						
Year Tm	Age	G	AB	H	2B	3B	HR	TB	R	RBI	GW	TBB	IBB	SO	HBP	SH	SF	SB	CS	SB%	GDP	Avg	OBP	SLG	Pos	G	PO	A	E	DP	FPct
1995 Sea	30	5	18	3	0	0	0	3	0	1	0	3	0	7	1	1	0	0	0	—	0	.167	.318	.167	3B	5	2	5	0	0	1.000
																									1B	1	0	1	0	0	1.000
1997 Sea	32	3	5	1	0	0	0	1	0	0	0	0	0	3	0	0	0	0	0	—	0	.200	.200	.200	3B	3	1	2	0	1	1.000
DS Totals		8	23	4	0	0	0	4	0	1	0	3	0	10	1	1	0	0	0	—	0	.174	.296	.174	3B	8	3	7	0	1	1.000
LCS		Batting																							Fielding						
Year Tm	Age	G	AB	H	2B	3B	HR	TB	R	RBI	GW	TBB	IBB	SO	HBP	SH	SF	SB	CS	SB%	GDP	Avg	OBP	SLG	Pos	G	PO	A	E	DP	FPct
1995 Sea	30	6	18	4	0	0	1	7	1	2	0	0	0	4	0	0	0	0	0	—	0	.222	.222	.389	3B	6	5	9	0	0	1.000
Postseason Totals		14	41	8	0	0	1	11	1	3	0	3	0	14	1	1	0	0	0	—	0	.195	.267	.268	3B	14	8	16	0	1	1.000

VIDA BLUE—Vida Rochelle Blue—Throws: Left; Bats: Both

Ht: 6'0"; Wt: 189 lbs; Born: 7/28/1949 in Mansfield, Louisiana; Debut: 7/20/1969

LCS		Pitching																										
Year Tm	Age	G	GS	CG	GF	IP	BFP	H	R	ER	HR	SH	SF	HB	TBB	IBB	SO	WP	Bk	W	L	Pct	ShO	Sv-Op	Hld	OAvg	OOBP	ERA
1971 Oak-*MC*	22	1	1	0	0	7.0	29	7	5	5	0	0	0	0	2	0	8	0	0	0	1	.000	0	0- 0	0	.259	.310	6.43
1972 Oak	23	4	0	0	1	5.1	22	4	0	0	0	1	0	0	1	1	5	0	0	0	0	—	0	1- 1	0	.200	.238	0.00
1973 Oak	24	2	2	0	0	7.0	33	8	8	8	1	0	0	0	5	0	3	1	0	0	1	.000	0	0- 0	0	.286	.394	10.29
1974 Oak	25	1	1	1	0	9.0	30	2	0	0	0	0	0	0	0	0	7	0	0	1	0	1.000	1	0- 0	0	.067	.067	0.00
1975 Oak	26	1	1	0	0	3.0	14	6	3	3	1	0	0	0	0	0	2	0	0	0	0	—	0	0- 0	0	.429	.429	9.00
LCS Totals		9	5	1	1	31.1	256	27	16	16	2	1	0	0	8	1	25	1	0	1	2	.333	1	1-1	0	.227	.276	4.60
World Series		Pitching																										
Year Tm	Age	G	GS	CG	GF	IP	BFP	H	R	ER	HR	SH	SF	HB	TBB	IBB	SO	WP	Bk	W	L	Pct	ShO	Sv-Op	Hld	OAvg	OOBP	ERA
1972 Oak	23	4	1	0	1	8.2	38	8	4	4	1	1	1	0	5	1	5	1	0	0	1	.000	0	1- 2	0	.258	.351	4.15
1973 Oak	24	2	2	0	0	11.0	48	10	6	6	2	0	0	0	3	0	8	1	0	0	1	.000	0	0- 0	0	.222	.271	4.91
1974 Oak	25	2	2	0	0	13.2	56	10	5	5	1	2	1	0	7	0	9	0	0	0	1	.000	0	0- 0	0	.217	.315	3.29
WS Totals		8	5	0	1	33.1	284	28	15	15	4	3	2	0	15	1	22	2	0	0	3	.000	0	1-2	0	.230	.309	4.05
Postseason Totals		17	10	1	2	64.2	540	55	31	31	6	4	2	0	23	2	47	3	0	1	5	.167	1	2-3	0	.228	.293	4.31

LCS		Batting																							Fielding						
Year Tm	Age	G	AB	H	2B	3B	HR	TB	R	RBI	GW	TBB	IBB	SO	HBP	SH	SF	SB	CS	SB%	GDP	Avg	OBP	SLG	Pos	G	PO	A	E	DP	FPct
1971 Oak	22	1	3	0	0	0	0	0	0	0	0	0	0	3	0	0	0	0	0	—	0	.000	.000	.000	P	1	0	1	0	0	1.000
1972 Oak	23	4	1	0	0	0	0	0	0	0	0	0	0	0	0	0	0	0	0	—	0	.000	.000	.000	P	4	0	1	0	0	1.000
1973 Oak	24	2	0	0	0	0	0	0	0	0	0	0	0	0	0	0	0	0	0	—	0	—	—	—	P	2	1	0	0	0	1.000
1974 Oak	25	1	0	0	0	0	0	0	0	0	0	0	0	0	0	0	0	0	0	—	0	—	—	—	P	1	0	1	0	0	1.000
1975 Oak	26	1	0	0	0	0	0	0	0	0	0	0	0	0	0	0	0	0	0	—	0	—	—	—	P	1	0	0	0	0	—
LCS Totals		9	4	0	0	0	0	0	0	0	0	0	0	3	0	0	0	0	0	—	0	.000	.000	.000	P	9	1	3	0	0	1.000
World Series		Batting																							Fielding						
Year Tm	Age	G	AB	H	2B	3B	HR	TB	R	RBI	GW	TBB	IBB	SO	HBP	SH	SF	SB	CS	SB%	GDP	Avg	OBP	SLG	Pos	G	PO	A	E	DP	FPct
1972 Oak	23	4	1	0	0	0	0	0	0	0	0	2	0	1	0	0	0	0	0	—	0	.000	.667	.000	P	4	0	1	0	0	1.000
1973 Oak	24	2	4	0	0	0	0	0	0	0	0	0	0	4	0	0	0	0	0	—	0	.000	.000	.000	P	2	2	1	0	0	1.000
1974 Oak	25	2	4	0	0	0	0	0	0	0	0	0	0	4	0	0	0	0	0	—	0	.000	.000	.000	P	2	0	3	0	0	1.000
WS Totals		8	9	0	0	0	0	0	0	0	0	2	0	9	0	0	0	0	0	—	0	.000	.182	.000	P	8	2	5	0	0	1.000
Postseason Totals		17	13	0	0	0	0	0	0	0	0	2	0	12	0	0	0	0	0	—	0	.000	.133	.000	P	17	3	8	0	0	1.000

OSSIE BLUEGE—Oswald Louis Bluege—Bats: Right; Throws: Right

Ht: 5'11"; Wt: 162 lbs; Born: 10/24/1900 in Chicago, Illinois; Debut: 4/24/1922; Died: 10/14/1985

World Series		Batting																							Fielding						
Year Tm	Age	G	AB	H	2B	3B	HR	TB	R	RBI	GW	TBB	IBB	SO	HBP	SH	SF	SB	CS	SB%	GDP	Avg	OBP	SLG	Pos	G	PO	A	E	DP	FPct
1924 Was	23	7	26	5	0	0	0	5	2	2	0	3	0	4	0	2	0	1	0	1.00	1	.192	.276	.192	3B	4	4	11	0	3	1.000
																									SS	5	3	13	3	3	.842
1925 Was	24	5	18	5	1	0	0	6	2	2	0	0	0	4	1	0	0	0	1	.00	0	.278	.316	.333	3B	5	1	13	0	1	1.000
1933 Was	32	5	16	2	1	0	0	3	1	0	0	1	0	6	0	2	0	0	0	—	0	.125	.176	.188	3B	5	3	14	0	0	1.000
WS Totals		17	60	12	2	0	0	14	5	4	0	4	0	14	1	4	0	1	1	.50	1	.200	.262	.233	3B	14	8	38	0	4	1.000

BERT BLYLEVEN—Rik Aalbert Blyleven—Throws: Right; Bats: Right

Ht: 6'3"; Wt: 200 lbs; Born: 4/6/1951 in Zeist, Netherlands; Debut: 6/5/1970

LCS		Pitching																										
Year Tm	Age	G	GS	CG	GF	IP	BFP	H	R	ER	HR	SH	SF	HB	TBB	IBB	SO	WP	Bk	W	L	Pct	ShO	Sv-Op	Hld	OAvg	OOBP	ERA
1970 Min	19	1	0	0	0	2.0	9	2	1	0	0	0	1	0	0	0	2	0	0	0	0	—	0	0- 0	0	.250	.222	0.00
1979 Pit	28	1	1	1	0	9.0	35	8	1	1	1	0	0	0	0	0	9	0	0	1	0	1.000	0	0- 0	0	.229	.229	1.00
1987 Min	36	2	2	0	0	13.1	56	12	6	6	3	1	0	2	3	0	9	0	0	2	0	1.000	0	0- 0	0	.240	.309	4.05
LCS Totals		4	3	1	0	24.1	200	22	8	7	4	1	1	2	3	0	20	0	0	3	0	1.000	0	0-0	0	.237	.273	2.59
World Series		Pitching																										
Year Tm	Age	G	GS	CG	GF	IP	BFP	H	R	ER	HR	SH	SF	HB	TBB	IBB	SO	WP	Bk	W	L	Pct	ShO	Sv-Op	Hld	OAvg	OOBP	ERA
1979 Pit	28	2	1	0	1	10.0	40	8	2	2	1	0	0	0	3	0	4	0	0	1	0	1.000	0	0- 0	0	.216	.275	1.80
1987 Min	36	2	2	0	0	13.0	53	13	5	4	0	1	0	0	2	1	12	0	0	1	1	.500	0	0- 0	0	.260	.288	2.77
WS Totals		4	3	0	1	23.0	186	21	7	6	1	1	0	0	5	1	16	0	0	2	1	.667	0	0-0	0	.241	.283	2.35
Postseason Totals		8	6	1	1	47.1	386	43	15	13	5	2	1	2	8	1	36	0	0	5	1	.833	0	0-0	0	.239	.277	2.47

LCS		Batting																							Fielding						
Year Tm	Age	G	AB	H	2B	3B	HR	TB	R	RBI	GW	TBB	IBB	SO	HBP	SH	SF	SB	CS	SB%	GDP	Avg	OBP	SLG	Pos	G	PO	A	E	DP	FPct
1970 Min	19	1	0	0	0	0	0	0	0	0	0	0	0	0	0	0	0	0	0	—	0	—	—	—	P	1	1	0	0	0	1.000
1979 Pit	28	1	3	1	0	0	0	1	1	0	0	0	0	1	0	1	0	0	0	—	0	.333	.333	.333	P	1	1	1	0	0	1.000
1987 Min	36	2	0	0	0	0	0	0	0	0	0	0	0	0	0	0	0	0	0	—	0	—	—	—	P	2	0	1	0	0	1.000
LCS Totals		4	3	1	0	0	0	1	1	0	0	0	0	1	0	1	0	0	0	—	0	.333	.333	.333	P	4	2	2	0	0	1.000
World Series		Batting																							Fielding						
Year Tm	Age	G	AB	H	2B	3B	HR	TB	R	RBI	GW	TBB	IBB	SO	HBP	SH	SF	SB	CS	SB%	GDP	Avg	OBP	SLG	Pos	G	PO	A	E	DP	FPct
1979 Pit	28	2	3	0	0	0	0	0	0	0	0	0	0	0	0	1	0	0	0	—	1	.000	.000	.000	P	2	0	1	0	1	1.000
1987 Min	36	2	1	0	0	0	0	0	0	0	0	0	0	1	0	1	0	0	0	—	0	.000	.000	.000	P	2	0	1	0	0	1.000
WS Totals		4	4	0	0	0	0	0	0	0	0	0	0	1	0	2	0	0	0	—	1	.000	.000	.000	P	4	0	2	0	1	1.000
Postseason Totals		8	7	1	0	0	0	1	1	0	0	0	0	2	0	3	0	0	0	—	1	.143	.143	.143	P	8	2	4	0	1	1.000

DOUG BOCHTLER—Douglas Eugene Bochtler—Throws: Right; Bats: Right

Ht: 6'3"; Wt: 200 lbs; Born: 7/5/1970 in West Palm Beach, Florida; Debut: 5/5/1995

Division Series	Age	G	GS	CG	GF	IP	BFP	H	R	ER	HR	SH	SF	HB	TBB	IBB	SO	WP	Bk	W	L	Pct	ShO	Sv-Op	Hld	OAvg	OOBP	ERA
1996 SD	26	1	0	0	0	0.1	3	0	1	1	0	0	0	0	2	1	0	1	0	0	1	.000	0	0-0	0	.000	.667	27.00

Division Series	Age	G	AB	H	2B	3B	HR	TB	R	RBI	GW	TBB	IBB	SO	HBP	SH	SF	SB	CS	SB%	GDP	Avg	OBP	SLG	Pos	G	PO	A	E	DP	FPct
1996 SD	26	1	0	0	0	0	0	0	0	0	0	0	0	0	0	0	0	0	0	—	0	—	—	—	P	1	0	0	0	0	—

BRUCE BOCHY—Bruce Douglas Bochy—Bats: Right; Throws: Right

Ht: 6'3"; Wt: 205 lbs; Born: 4/16/1955 in Landes de Bussac, France; Debut: 7/19/1978

Year Tm	Age	G	AB	H	2B	3B	HR	TB	R	RBI	GW	TBB	IBB	SO	HBP	SH	SF	SB	CS	SB%	GDP	Avg	OBP	SLG	Pos	G	PO	A	E	DP	FPct
LCS																															
1980 Hou	25	1	1	0	0	0	0	0	0	0	0	0	0	0	0	0	0	0	0	—	0	.000	.000	.000	C	1	5	1	0	1	1.000
World Series																															
1984 SD	29	1	1	1	0	0	0	1	0	0	0	0	0	0	0	0	0	0	0	—	0	1.000	1.000	1.000	—						
Postseason Totals		2	2	1	0	0	0	1	0	0	0	0	0	0	0	0	0	0	0	—	0	.500	.500	.500	C	1	5	1	0	1	1.000

MIKE BODDICKER—Michael James Boddicker—Throws: Right; Bats: Right

Ht: 5'11"; Wt: 172 lbs; Born: 8/23/1957 in Cedar Rapids, Iowa; Debut: 10/4/1980

Year Tm	Age	G	GS	CG	GF	IP	BFP	H	R	ER	HR	SH	SF	HB	TBB	IBB	SO	WP	Bk	W	L	Pct	ShO	Sv-Op	Hld	OAvg	OOBP	ERA
LCS																												
1983 Bal	26	1	1	1	0	9.0	36	5	0	0	0	0	0	2	3	0	14	0	0	1	0	1.000	1	0-0	0	.161	.278	0.00
1988 Bos	31	1	1	0	0	2.2	15	8	6	6	3	0	0	0	1	0	2	0	0	0	1	.000	0	0-0	0	.571	.600	20.25
1990 Bos	33	1	1	1	0	8.0	35	6	4	2	0	1	1	2	3	1	7	0	0	0	1	.000	0	0-0	0	.214	.324	2.25
LCS Totals		3	3	2	0	19.2	172	19	10	8	3	1	1	4	7	1	23	0	0	1	2	.333	1	0-0	0	.260	.353	3.66
World Series																												
1983 Bal	26	1	1	1	0	9.0	30	3	1	0	0	0	1	0	0	0	6	0	0	1	0	1.000	0	0-0	0	.103	.100	0.00
Postseason Totals		4	4	3	0	28.2	232	22	11	8	3	1	2	4	7	1	29	0	0	2	2	.500	1	0-0	0	.216	.287	2.51

Year Tm	Age	G	AB	H	2B	3B	HR	TB	R	RBI	GW	TBB	IBB	SO	HBP	SH	SF	SB	CS	SB%	GDP	Avg	OBP	SLG	Pos	G	PO	A	E	DP	FPct
LCS																															
1983 Bal	26	1	0	0	0	0	0	0	0	0	0	0	0	0	0	0	0	0	0	—	0	—	—	—	P	1	0	1	0	0	1.000
1988 Bos	31	1	0	0	0	0	0	0	0	0	0	0	0	0	0	0	0	0	0	—	0	—	—	—	P	1	0	0	0	0	—
1990 Bos	33	1	0	0	0	0	0	0	0	0	0	0	0	0	0	0	0	0	0	—	0	—	—	—	P	1	0	2	1	0	.667
LCS Totals		3	0	0	0	0	0	0	0	0	0	0	0	0	0	0	0	0	0	—	0	—	—	—	P	3	0	3	1	0	.750
World Series																															
1983 Bal	26	1	3	0	0	0	0	0	0	1	0	0	0	1	0	0	1	0	0	—	0	.000	.000	.000	P	1	1	2	0	0	1.000
Postseason Totals		4	3	0	0	0	0	0	0	1	0	0	0	1	0	0	1	0	0	—	0	.000	.000	.000	P	4	1	5	1	0	.857

BRIAN BOEHRINGER—Brian Edward Boehringer—Throws: Right; Bats: Both

Ht: 6'2"; Wt: 190 lbs; Born: 1/8/1970 in St. Louis, Missouri; Debut: 4/30/1995

Year Tm	Age	G	GS	CG	GF	IP	BFP	H	R	ER	HR	SH	SF	HB	TBB	IBB	SO	WP	Bk	W	L	Pct	ShO	Sv-Op	Hld	OAvg	OOBP	ERA
Division Series																												
1996 NYA	26	2	0	0	1	1.1	10	3	2	1	1	0	0	0	2	0	0	0	0	1	0	1.000	0	0-0	0	.375	.500	6.75
1997 NYA	27	1	0	0	0	1.2	8	1	0	0	0	0	0	0	1	0	2	0	0	0	0	—	0	0-0	0	.143	.250	0.00
DS Totals		3	0	0	1	3.0	36	4	2	1	1	0	0	0	3	0	2	0	0	1	0	1.000	0	0-0	0	.267	.389	3.00
World Series																												
1996 NYA	26	2	0	0	0	5.0	21	5	5	3	2	0	1	0	0	0	5	0	0	0	0	—	0	0-0	0	.250	.238	5.40
Postseason Totals		5	0	0	1	8.0	78	9	7	4	3	0	1	0	3	0	7	0	0	1	0	1.000	0	0-0	0	.257	.308	4.50

Year Tm	Age	G	AB	H	2B	3B	HR	TB	R	RBI	GW	TBB	IBB	SO	HBP	SH	SF	SB	CS	SB%	GDP	Avg	OBP	SLG	Pos	G	PO	A	E	DP	FPct
Division Series																															
1996 NYA	26	2	0	0	0	0	0	0	0	0	0	0	0	0	0	0	0	0	0	—	0	—	—	—	P	2	0	0	0	0	—
1997 NYA	27	1	0	0	0	0	0	0	0	0	0	0	0	0	0	0	0	0	0	—	0	—	—	—	P	1	0	0	1	0	.000
DS Totals		3	0	0	0	0	0	0	0	0	0	0	0	0	0	0	0	0	0	—	0	—	—	—	P	3	0	0	1	0	.000
World Series																															
1996 NYA	26	2	0	0	0	0	0	0	0	0	0	0	0	0	0	0	0	0	0	—	0	—	—	—	P	2	0	0	0	0	—
Postseason Totals		5	0	0	0	0	0	0	0	0	0	0	0	0	0	0	0	0	0	—	0	—	—	—	P	5	0	0	1	0	.000

WADE BOGGS—Wade Anthony Boggs—Bats: Left; Throws: Right

Ht: 6'2"; Wt: 190 lbs; Born: 6/15/1958 in Omaha, Nebraska; Debut: 4/10/1982

Year Tm	Age	G	AB	H	2B	3B	HR	TB	R	RBI	GW	TBB	IBB	SO	HBP	SH	SF	SB	CS	SB%	GDP	Avg	OBP	SLG	Pos	G	PO	A	E	DP	FPct
Division Series																															
1995 NYA	37	4	19	5	2	0	1	10	4	3	0	3	0	5	0	0	0	0	0	—	1	.263	.364	.526	3B	4	4	8	0	2	1.000
1996 NYA	38	3	12	1	1	0	0	2	0	0	0	0	0	2	0	1	0	0	0	—	0	.083	.083	.167	3B	3	2	1	0	0	1.000
1997 NYA	39	3	7	3	0	0	0	3	1	2	0	0	0	0	0	0	0	0	0	—	1	.429	.429	.429	3B	2	0	1	0	1	1.000
DS Totals		10	38	9	3	0	1	15	5	5	0	3	0	7	0	1	0	0	0	—	2	.237	.293	.395	3B	9	6	10	0	3	1.000
LCS																															
1986 Bos	28	7	30	7	1	1	0	10	3	2	0	4	0	1	0	1	0	0	0	—	2	.233	.324	.333	3B	7	7	13	2	1	.909
1988 Bos	30	4	13	5	0	0	0	5	2	3	0	3	0	4	0	0	2	0	0	—	1	.385	.444	.385	3B	4	6	6	0	1	1.000
1990 Bos	32	4	16	7	1	0	1	11	1	1	0	0	0	3	0	0	0	0	0	—	1	.438	.438	.688	3B	4	6	10	0	2	1.000
1996 NYA	38	3	15	2	0	0	0	2	1	0	0	1	0	3	0	0	0	0	0	—	0	.133	.188	.133	3B	3	2	11	0	0	1.000
LCS Totals		18	74	21	2	1	1	28	7	6	0	8	0	11	0	1	2	0	0	—	3	.284	.345	.378	3B	18	21	40	2	4	.968
World Series																															
1986 Bos	28	7	31	9	3	0	0	12	3	3	1	4	1	2	0	0	0	0	0	—	0	.290	.371	.387	3B	7	4	15	0	2	1.000
1996 NYA	38	4	11	3	1	0	0	4	0	2	1	1	1	0	0	0	0	0	0	—	1	.273	.333	.364	3B	4	0	0	0	0	—
WS Totals		11	42	12	4	0	0	16	3	5	2	5	2	2	0	0	0	0	0	—	1	.286	.362	.381	3B	11	4	15	0	2	1.000
Postseason Totals		39	154	42	9	1	2	59	15	16	2	16	1	20	0	2	2	0	0	—	6	.273	.337	.383	3B	38	31	65	2	9	.980

JOE BOLEY—John Peter Boley—Bats: Right; Throws: Right

Ht: 5'11"; Wt: 170 lbs; Born: 7/19/1896 in Mahanoy City, Pennsylvania; Debut: 4/12/1927; Died: 12/30/1962

World Series	Age	G	AB	H	2B	3B	HR	TB	R	RBI	GW	TBB	IBB	SO	HBP	SH	SF	SB	CS	SB%	GDP	Avg	OBP	SLG	Pos	G	PO	A	E	DP	FPct
1929 Phi	33	5	17	4	0	0	0	4	1	1	0	0	0	3	0	3	0	0	0	—	1	.235	.235	.235	SS	5	4	12	0	1	1.000
1930 Phi	34	6	21	2	0	0	0	2	1	1	0	0	0	1	0	1	0	0	0	—	0	.095	.095	.095	SS	6	9	13	1	0	.957
1931 Phi	35	1	1	0	0	0	0	0	0	0	0	0	0	1	0	0	0	0	0	—	0	.000	.000	.000	—						
WS Totals		12	39	6	0	0	0	6	2	2	0	0	0	5	0	4	0	0	0	—	1	.154	.154	.154	SS	11	13	25	1	1	.974

BOBBY BOLIN—Bobby Donald Bolin—Nickname: Bee Bee—Throws: Right; Bats: Right

Ht: 6'4"; Wt: 185 lbs; Born: 1/29/1939 in Hickory Grove, South Carolina; Debut: 4/18/1961

World Series	Age	G	GS	CG	GF	IP	BFP	H	R	ER	HR	SH	SF	HB	TBB	IBB	SO	WP	Bk	W	L	Pct	ShO	Sv-Op	Hld	OAvg	OOBP	ERA
1962 SF	23	2	0	0	1	2.2	14	4	2	2	0	0	0	0	2	0	2	0	0	0	0	—	0	0-0	0	.333	.429	6.75

World Series	Age	G	AB	H	2B	3B	HR	TB	R	RBI	GW	TBB	IBB	SO	HBP	SH	SF	SB	CS	SB%	GDP	Avg	OBP	SLG	Pos	G	PO	A	E	DP	FPct
1962 SF	23	2	0	0	0	0	0	0	0	0	0	0	0	0	0	0	0	0	0	—	0	—	—	—	P	2	0	0	0	0	—

DON BOLLWEG—Donald Raymond Bollweg—Bats: Left; Throws: Left

Ht: 6'1"; Wt: 190 lbs; Born: 2/12/1921 in Wheaton, Illinois; Debut: 9/28/1950; Died: 5/26/1996

World Series		Batting																							Fielding						
Year Tm	Age	G	AB	H	2B	3B	HR	TB	R	RBI	GW	TBB	IBB	SO	HBP	SH	SF	SB	CS	SB%	GDP	Avg	OBP	SLG	Pos	G	PO	A	E	DP	FPct
1953 NYA	32	3	2	0	0	0	0	0	0	0	0	0	0	2	0	0	0	0	0	—	0	.000	.000	.000	1B	1	0	0	0	0	—

CLIFF BOLTON—William Clifton Bolton—Bats: Left; Throws: Right

Ht: 5'9"; Wt: 160 lbs; Born: 4/10/1907 in High Point, North Carolina; Debut: 4/20/1931; Died: 4/21/1979

World Series		Batting																							Fielding						
Year Tm	Age	G	AB	H	2B	3B	HR	TB	R	RBI	GW	TBB	IBB	SO	HBP	SH	SF	SB	CS	SB%	GDP	Avg	OBP	SLG	Pos	G	PO	A	E	DP	FPct
1933 Was	26	2	2	0	0	0	0	0	0	0	0	0	0	0	0	0	0	0	0	—	1	.000	.000	.000	—						

TOM BOLTON—Thomas Edward Bolton—Throws: Left; Bats: Left

Ht: 6'2"; Wt: 172 lbs; Born: 5/6/1962 in Nashville, Tennessee; Debut: 5/17/1987

LCS		Pitching																										
Year Tm	Age	G	GS	CG	GF	IP	BFP	H	R	ER	HR	SH	SF	HB	TBB	IBB	SO	WP	Bk	W	L	Pct	ShO	Sv-Op	Hld	OAvg	OOBP	ERA
1990 Bos	28	2	0	0	0	3.0	12	2	0	0	0	1	0	0	2	0	3	0	0	0	0	—	0	0- 0	0	.222	.364	0.00

LCS		Batting																							Fielding						
Year Tm	Age	G	AB	H	2B	3B	HR	TB	R	RBI	GW	TBB	IBB	SO	HBP	SH	SF	SB	CS	SB%	GDP	Avg	OBP	SLG	Pos	G	PO	A	E	DP	FPct
1990 Bos	28	2	0	0	0	0	0	0	0	0	0	0	0	0	0	0	0	0	0	—	0	—	—	—	P	2	0	0	0	0	—

BARRY BONDS—Barry Lamar Bonds—Bats: Left; Throws: Left

Ht: 6'1"; Wt: 185 lbs; Born: 7/24/1964 in Riverside, California; Debut: 5/30/1986

Division Series		Batting																							Fielding						
Year Tm	Age	G	AB	H	2B	3B	HR	TB	R	RBI	GW	TBB	IBB	SO	HBP	SH	SF	SB	CS	SB%	GDP	Avg	OBP	SLG	Pos	G	PO	A	E	DP	FPct
1997 SF	33	3	12	3	2	0	0	5	0	2	0	0	0	3	0	0	1	1	0	1.00	0	.250	.231	.417	OF	3	6	0	0	0	1.000
LCS		**Batting**																							**Fielding**						
Year Tm	Age	G	AB	H	2B	3B	HR	TB	R	RBI	GW	TBB	IBB	SO	HBP	SH	SF	SB	CS	SB%	GDP	Avg	OBP	SLG	Pos	G	PO	A	E	DP	FPct
1990 Pit-*M*	26	6	18	3	0	0	0	3	4	1	1	6	0	5	0	0	0	2	0	1.00	0	.167	.375	.167	OF	6	13	0	0	0	1.000
1991 Pit	27	7	27	4	1	0	0	5	1	0	0	2	0	4	0	0	0	3	0	1.00	1	.148	.207	.185	OF	7	14	1	1	0	.938
1992 Pit-*M*	28	7	23	6	1	0	1	10	5	2	1	6	1	4	1	0	0	1	0	1.00	0	.261	.433	.435	OF	7	17	0	0	0	1.000
LCS Totals		20	68	13	2	0	1	18	10	3	2	14	1	13	1	0	0	6	0	1.00	1	.191	.337	.265	OF	20	44	1	1	0	.978
Postseason Totals		23	80	16	4	0	1	23	10	5	2	14	1	16	1	0	1	7	0	1.00	1	.200	.323	.288	OF	23	50	1	1	0	.981

BOBBY BONDS—Bobby Lee Bonds—Bats: Right; Throws: Right

Ht: 6'1"; Wt: 190 lbs; Born: 3/15/1946 in Riverside, California; Debut: 6/25/1968

LCS		Batting																							Fielding						
Year Tm	Age	G	AB	H	2B	3B	HR	TB	R	RBI	GW	TBB	IBB	SO	HBP	SH	SF	SB	CS	SB%	GDP	Avg	OBP	SLG	Pos	G	PO	A	E	DP	FPct
1971 SF	25	3	8	2	0	0	0	2	0	0	0	2	0	4	0	0	0	0	0	—	0	.250	.400	.250	OF	3	3	0	1	0	.750

NINO BONGIOVANNI—Anthony Thomas Bongiovanni—Bats: Left; Throws: Left

Ht: 5'10"; Wt: 175 lbs; Born: 12/21/1911 in New Orleans, Louisiana; Debut: 4/23/1938

World Series		Batting																							Fielding						
Year Tm	Age	G	AB	H	2B	3B	HR	TB	R	RBI	GW	TBB	IBB	SO	HBP	SH	SF	SB	CS	SB%	GDP	Avg	OBP	SLG	Pos	G	PO	A	E	DP	FPct
1939 Cin	27	1	1	0	0	0	0	0	0	0	0	0	0	0	0	0	0	0	0	—	0	.000	.000	.000	—						

TINY BONHAM—Ernest Edward Bonham—Throws: Right; Bats: Right

Ht: 6'2"; Wt: 215 lbs; Born: 8/16/1913 in Ione, California; Debut: 8/5/1940; Died: 9/15/1949

World Series		Pitching																										
Year Tm	Age	G	GS	CG	GF	IP	BFP	H	R	ER	HR	SH	SF	HB	TBB	IBB	SO	WP	Bk	W	L	Pct	ShO	Sv-Op	Hld	OAvg	OOBP	ERA
1941 NYA	28	1	1	1	0	9.0	33	4	1	1	0	0	0	0	2	0	2	0	0	1	0	1.000	0	0- 0	0	.129	.182	1.00
1942 NYA	29	2	1	1	1	11.0	46	9	5	5	0	4	0	0	3	2	3	0	0	0	1	.000	0	0- 0	0	.231	.286	4.09
1943 NYA	30	1	1	0	0	8.0	33	6	4	4	2	1	0	0	3	0	9	0	0	0	1	.000	0	0- 0	0	.207	.281	4.50
WS Totals		4	3	2	1	28.0	224	19	10	10	2	5	0	0	8	2	14	0	0	1	2	.333	0	0-0	0	.192	.252	3.21

World Series		Batting																							Fielding						
Year Tm	Age	G	AB	H	2B	3B	HR	TB	R	RBI	GW	TBB	IBB	SO	HBP	SH	SF	SB	CS	SB%	GDP	Avg	OBP	SLG	Pos	G	PO	A	E	DP	FPct
1941 NYA	28	1	4	0	0	0	0	0	0	0	0	0	0	4	0	0	0	0	0	—	0	.000	.000	.000	P	1	0	1	0	0	1.000
1942 NYA	29	2	2	0	0	0	0	0	0	0	0	1	0	0	0	0	0	0	0	—	0	.000	.333	.000	P	2	0	1	0	0	1.000
1943 NYA	30	1	2	0	0	0	0	0	0	0	0	0	0	0	0	0	0	0	0	—	0	.000	.000	.000	P	1	0	0	0	0	—
WS Totals		4	8	0	0	0	0	0	0	0	0	1	0	4	0	0	0	0	0	—	0	.000	.111	.000	P	4	0	2	0	0	1.000

BOBBY BONILLA—Roberto Martin Antonio Bonilla—Nickname: Bobby Bo—Bats: Both; Throws: Right

Ht: 6'3"; Wt: 210 lbs; Born: 2/23/1963 in Bronx, New York; Debut: 4/9/1986

Division Series		Batting																							Fielding						
Year Tm	Age	G	AB	H	2B	3B	HR	TB	R	RBI	GW	TBB	IBB	SO	HBP	SH	SF	SB	CS	SB%	GDP	Avg	OBP	SLG	Pos	G	PO	A	E	DP	FPct
1996 Bal	33	4	15	3	0	0	2	9	4	5	0	4	0	6	0	0	0	0	0	—	0	.200	.368	.600	OF	4	9	0	1	0	.900
1997 Fla	34	3	12	4	0	0	1	7	1	3	0	2	1	1	0	0	0	0	0	—	1	.333	.429	.583	3B	3	3	5	0	0	1.000
DS Totals		7	27	7	0	0	3	16	5	8	0	6	1	7	0	0	0	0	0	—	1	.259	.394	.593	OF	4	9	0	1	0	.900
LCS		**Batting**																							**Fielding**						
Year Tm	Age	G	AB	H	2B	3B	HR	TB	R	RBI	GW	TBB	IBB	SO	HBP	SH	SF	SB	CS	SB%	GDP	Avg	OBP	SLG	Pos	G	PO	A	E	DP	FPct
1990 Pit	27	6	21	4	1	0	0	5	0	1	0	3	0	1	0	0	0	0	1	.00	0	.190	.292	.238	3B	3	1	5	0	1	1.000
																									OF	5	3	0	1	0	.750
1991 Pit	28	7	23	7	2	0	0	9	2	1	0	6	2	2	0	0	0	0	1	.00	2	.304	.448	.391	OF	7	12	1	0	0	1.000
1996 Bal	33	5	20	1	0	0	1	4	1	2	0	1	0	4	0	0	0	0	0	—	0	.050	.095	.200	OF	5	11	0	0	0	1.000
1997 Fla	34	6	23	6	1	0	0	7	3	4	1	1	0	6	0	0	0	0	0	—	0	.261	.292	.304	3B	6	5	13	0	1	1.000
LCS Totals		24	87	18	4	0	1	25	6	8	1	11	2	13	0	0	0	0	2	.00	2	.207	.296	.287	OF	17	26	1	1	0	.964
World Series		**Batting**																							**Fielding**						
Year Tm	Age	G	AB	H	2B	3B	HR	TB	R	RBI	GW	TBB	IBB	SO	HBP	SH	SF	SB	CS	SB%	GDP	Avg	OBP	SLG	Pos	G	PO	A	E	DP	FPct
1997 Fla	34	7	29	6	1	0	1	10	5	3	0	3	0	5	0	0	0	0	0	—	3	.207	.281	.345	3B	7	3	20	2	2	.920
Postseason Totals		38	143	31	5	0	5	51	16	19	1	20	3	25	0	0	0	0	2	.00	6	.217	.313	.357	OF	21	35	1	2	0	.947

GREG BOOKER—Gregory Scott Booker—Throws: Right; Bats: Right

Ht: 6'6"; Wt: 230 lbs; Born: 6/22/1960 in Lynchburg, Virginia; Debut: 9/11/1983

LCS		Pitching																										
Year Tm	Age	G	GS	CG	GF	IP	BFP	H	R	ER	HR	SH	SF	HB	TBB	IBB	SO	WP	Bk	W	L	Pct	ShO	Sv-Op	Hld	OAvg	OOBP	ERA
1984 SD	24	1	0	0	1	2.0	9	2	0	0	0	0	0	0	1	0	2	0	0	0	0	—	0	0- 0	0	.250	.333	0.00
World Series		**Pitching**																										
Year Tm	Age	G	GS	CG	GF	IP	BFP	H	R	ER	HR	SH	SF	HB	TBB	IBB	SO	WP	Bk	W	L	Pct	ShO	Sv-Op	Hld	OAvg	OOBP	ERA
1984 SD	24	1	0	0	0	1.0	7	0	1	1	0	0	0	0	4	0	0	0	0	0	0	—	0	0- 0	0	.000	.571	9.00
Postseason Totals		2	0	0	1	3.0	32	2	1	1	0	0	0	0	5	0	2	0	0	0	0	—	0	0-0	0	.182	.438	3.00

LCS		Batting																							Fielding						
Year Tm	Age	G	AB	H	2B	3B	HR	TB	R	RBI	GW	TBB	IBB	SO	HBP	SH	SF	SB	CS	SB%	GDP	Avg	OBP	SLG	Pos	G	PO	A	E	DP	FPct
1984 SD	24	1	0	0	0	0	0	0	0	0	0	0	0	0	0	0	0	0	0	—	0	—	—	—	P	1	0	0	0	0	—
World Series		**Batting**																							**Fielding**						
Year Tm	Age	G	AB	H	2B	3B	HR	TB	R	RBI	GW	TBB	IBB	SO	HBP	SH	SF	SB	CS	SB%	GDP	Avg	OBP	SLG	Pos	G	PO	A	E	DP	FPct
1984 SD	24	1	0	0	0	0	0	0	0	0	0	0	0	0	0	0	0	0	0	—	0	—	—	—	P	1	0	1	0	0	1.000
Postseason Totals		2	0	0	0	0	0	0	0	0	0	0	0	0	0	0	0	0	0	—	0	—	—	—	P	2	0	1	0	0	1.000

BOB BOONE—Robert Raymond Boone—Bats: Right; Throws: Right

Ht: 6'2"; Wt: 195 lbs; Born: 11/19/1947 in San Diego, California; Debut: 9/10/1972

Division Series		Batting																							Fielding						
Year Tm	Age	G	AB	H	2B	3B	HR	TB	R	RBI	GW	TBB	IBB	SO	HBP	SH	SF	SB	CS	SB%	GDP	Avg	OBP	SLG	Pos	G	PO	A	E	DP	FPct
1981 Phi	33	3	5	0	0	0	0	0	0	0	0	0	0	0	0	0	0	0	1	.00	0	.000	.000	.000	C	3	10	2	0	0	1.000

LCS		Batting																							Fielding						
Year Tm	Age	G	AB	H	2B	3B	HR	TB	R	RBI	GW	TBB	IBB	SO	HBP	SH	SF	SB	CS	SB%	GDP	Avg	OBP	SLG	Pos	G	PO	A	E	DP	FPct
1976 Phi	28	3	7	2	0	0	0	2	0	1	0	1	0	0	0	1	0	0	0	—	0	.286	.375	.286	C	3	8	2	0	0	1.000
1977 Phi	29	4	10	4	0	0	0	4	1	0	0	0	0	0	0	0	0	0	0	—	0	.400	.400	.400	C	4	18	2	0	1	1.000
1978 Phi	30	3	11	2	0	0	0	2	0	0	0	0	0	1	0	0	0	0	0	—	1	.182	.182	.182	C	3	16	2	1	0	.947
1980 Phi	32	5	18	4	0	0	0	4	1	2	0	1	0	2	0	1	0	0	0	—	0	.222	.263	.222	C	5	22	3	0	1	1.000
1982 Cal	34	5	16	4	0	0	1	7	3	4	0	0	0	2	0	2	1	0	0	—	0	.250	.235	.438	C	5	30	3	0	0	1.000
1986 Cal	38	7	22	10	0	0	1	13	4	2	0	1	0	3	1	1	0	0	0	—	0	.455	.500	.591	C	7	33	2	0	0	1.000
LCS Totals		27	84	26	0	0	2	32	9	9	0	3	0	8	1	5	1	0	0	—	1	.310	.337	.381	C	27	127	14	1	2	.993
World Series		Batting																							Fielding						
Year Tm	Age	G	AB	H	2B	3B	HR	TB	R	RBI	GW	TBB	IBB	SO	HBP	SH	SF	SB	CS	SB%	GDP	Avg	OBP	SLG	Pos	G	PO	A	E	DP	FPct
1980 Phi	32	6	17	7	2	0	0	9	3	4	0	4	0	0	0	0	1	0	0	—	0	.412	.500	.529	C	6	49	3	0	0	1.000
Postseason Totals		36	106	33	2	0	2	41	12	13	0	7	0	8	1	5	2	0	1	.00	1	.311	.353	.387	C	36	186	19	1	2	.995

BRET BOONE—Bret Robert Boone—Bats: Right; Throws: Right

Ht: 5'10"; Wt: 175 lbs; Born: 4/6/1969 in El Cajon, California; Debut: 8/19/1992

Division Series		Batting																							Fielding						
Year Tm	Age	G	AB	H	2B	3B	HR	TB	R	RBI	GW	TBB	IBB	SO	HBP	SH	SF	SB	CS	SB%	GDP	Avg	OBP	SLG	Pos	G	PO	A	E	DP	FPct
1995 Cin	26	3	10	3	1	0	1	7	4	1	0	1	0	3	0	0	0	1	0	1.00	0	.300	.364	.700	2B	3	7	5	0	0	1.000
LCS		Batting																							Fielding						
Year Tm	Age	G	AB	H	2B	3B	HR	TB	R	RBI	GW	TBB	IBB	SO	HBP	SH	SF	SB	CS	SB%	GDP	Avg	OBP	SLG	Pos	G	PO	A	E	DP	FPct
1995 Cin	26	4	14	3	0	0	0	3	1	0	0	1	0	2	0	0	0	0	0	—	2	.214	.267	.214	2B	4	9	13	0	3	1.000
Postseason Totals		7	24	6	1	0	1	10	5	1	0	2	0	5	0	0	0	1	0	1.00	2	.250	.308	.417	2B	7	16	18	0	3	1.000

RAY BOONE—Raymond Otis Boone—Nickname: Ike—Bats: Right; Throws: Right

Ht: 6'0"; Wt: 172 lbs; Born: 7/27/1923 in San Diego, California; Debut: 9/3/1948

World Series		Batting																							Fielding						
Year Tm	Age	G	AB	H	2B	3B	HR	TB	R	RBI	GW	TBB	IBB	SO	HBP	SH	SF	SB	CS	SB%	GDP	Avg	OBP	SLG	Pos	G	PO	A	E	DP	FPct
1948 Cle	25	1	1	0	0	0	0	0	0	0	0	0	0	1	0	0	0	0	0	—	0	.000	.000	.000	—						

PEDRO BORBON—Nickname: Dracula—Throws: Right; Bats: Right

Ht: 6'2"; Wt: 185 lbs; Born: 12/2/1946 in Valverde de Mao, Dominican Republic; Debut: 4/9/1969

LCS		Pitching																										
Year Tm	Age	G	GS	CG	GF	IP	BFP	H	R	ER	HR	SH	SF	HB	TBB	IBB	SO	WP	Bk	W	L	Pct	ShO	Sv-Op	Hld	OAvg	OOBP	ERA
1972 Cin	25	3	0	0	1	4.1	15	2	1	1	0	1	0	1	0	0	1	0	0	0	0	—	0	0- 0	1	.154	.214	2.08
1973 Cin	26	4	0	0	4	4.2	17	3	0	0	0	0	0	0	0	0	3	0	0	1	0	1.000	0	1- 1	0	.176	.176	0.00
1975 Cin	28	1	0	0	1	1.0	3	0	0	0	0	0	0	0	0	0	1	0	0	0	0	—	0	1- 1	0	.000	.000	0.00
1976 Cin	29	2	0	0	1	4.1	17	4	0	0	0	0	0	0	1	0	0	0	0	0	0	—	0	1- 1	0	.250	.294	0.00
LCS Totals		10	0	0	7	14.1	104	9	1	1	0	1	0	1	1	0	5	0	0	1	0	1.000	0	3-3	1	.184	.216	0.63
World Series		Pitching																										
Year Tm	Age	G	GS	CG	GF	IP	BFP	H	R	ER	HR	SH	SF	HB	TBB	IBB	SO	WP	Bk	W	L	Pct	ShO	Sv-Op	Hld	OAvg	OOBP	ERA
1972 Cin	25	6	0	0	0	7.0	28	7	3	3	0	2	0	0	2	1	4	0	0	0	1	.000	0	0- 0	2	.292	.346	3.86
1975 Cin	28	3	0	0	0	3.0	15	3	3	2	0	0	0	0	2	0	1	0	0	0	0	—	0	0- 0	0	.231	.333	6.00
1976 Cin	29	1	0	0	1	1.2	5	0	0	0	0	0	0	0	0	0	0	0	0	0	0	—	0	0- 0	0	.000	.000	0.00
WS Totals		10	0	0	1	11.2	96	10	6	5	0	2	0	0	4	1	5	0	0	0	1	.000	0	0-0	2	.238	.304	3.86
Postseason Totals		20	0	0	8	26.0	200	19	7	6	0	3	0	1	5	1	10	0	0	1	1	.500	0	3-3	3	.209	.258	2.08

LCS		Batting																							Fielding						
Year Tm	Age	G	AB	H	2B	3B	HR	TB	R	RBI	GW	TBB	IBB	SO	HBP	SH	SF	SB	CS	SB%	GDP	Avg	OBP	SLG	Pos	G	PO	A	E	DP	FPct
1972 Cin	25	3	0	0	0	0	0	0	0	0	0	0	0	0	0	0	0	0	0	—	0	—	—	—	P	3	1	0	0	0	1.000
1973 Cin	26	4	0	0	0	0	0	0	0	0	0	0	0	0	0	0	0	0	0	—	0	—	—	—	P	4	0	2	0	0	1.000
1975 Cin	28	1	0	0	0	0	0	0	0	0	0	0	0	0	0	0	0	0	0	—	0	—	—	—	P	1	0	0	0	0	—
1976 Cin	29	2	2	0	0	0	0	0	1	0	0	0	0	2	0	0	0	0	0	—	0	.000	.000	.000	P	2	0	0	0	0	—
LCS Totals		10	2	0	0	0	0	0	1	0	0	0	0	2	0	0	0	0	0	—	0	.000	.000	.000	P	10	1	2	0	0	1.000
World Series		Batting																							Fielding						
Year Tm	Age	G	AB	H	2B	3B	HR	TB	R	RBI	GW	TBB	IBB	SO	HBP	SH	SF	SB	CS	SB%	GDP	Avg	OBP	SLG	Pos	G	PO	A	E	DP	FPct
1972 Cin	25	6	0	0	0	0	0	0	0	0	0	0	0	0	0	0	0	0	0	—	0	—	—	—	P	6	0	3	0	0	1.000
1975 Cin	28	3	1	0	0	0	0	0	0	0	0	0	0	0	0	0	0	0	0	—	0	.000	.000	.000	P	3	0	0	0	0	—
1976 Cin	29	1	0	0	0	0	0	0	0	0	0	0	0	0	0	0	0	0	0	—	0	—	—	—	P	1	0	1	0	0	1.000
WS Totals		10	1	0	0	0	0	0	0	0	0	0	0	0	0	0	0	0	0	—	0	.000	.000	.000	P	10	0	4	0	0	1.000
Postseason Totals		20	3	0	0	0	0	0	1	0	0	0	0	2	0	0	0	0	0	—	0	.000	.000	.000	P	20	1	6	0	0	1.000

PEDRO BORBON—Pedro Felix Borbon—Throws: Left; Bats: Left

Ht: 6'1"; Wt: 205 lbs; Born: 11/15/1967 in Mao, Dominican Republic; Debut: 10/2/1992

Division Series		Pitching																										
Year Tm	Age	G	GS	CG	GF	IP	BFP	H	R	ER	HR	SH	SF	HB	TBB	IBB	SO	WP	Bk	W	L	Pct	ShO	Sv-Op	Hld	OAvg	OOBP	ERA
1995 Atl	27	1	0	0	0	1.0	4	1	0	0	0	0	0	0	0	0	3	0	0	0	0	—	0	0- 0	0	.250	.250	0.00
World Series		Pitching																										
Year Tm	Age	G	GS	CG	GF	IP	BFP	H	R	ER	HR	SH	SF	HB	TBB	IBB	SO	WP	Bk	W	L	Pct	ShO	Sv-Op	Hld	OAvg	OOBP	ERA
1995 Atl	27	1	0	0	1	1.0	3	0	0	0	0	0	0	0	0	0	2	0	0	0	0	—	0	1- 1	0	.000	.000	0.00
Postseason Totals		2	0	0	1	2.0	14	1	0	0	0	0	0	0	0	0	5	0	0	0	0	—	0	1-1	0	.143	.143	0.00

Division Series		Batting																							Fielding						
Year Tm	Age	G	AB	H	2B	3B	HR	TB	R	RBI	GW	TBB	IBB	SO	HBP	SH	SF	SB	CS	SB%	GDP	Avg	OBP	SLG	Pos	G	PO	A	E	DP	FPct
1995 Atl	27	1	0	0	0	0	0	0	0	0	0	0	0	0	0	0	0	0	0	—	0	—	—	—	P	1	0	0	0	0	—
World Series		Batting																							Fielding						
Year Tm	Age	G	AB	H	2B	3B	HR	TB	R	RBI	GW	TBB	IBB	SO	HBP	SH	SF	SB	CS	SB%	GDP	Avg	OBP	SLG	Pos	G	PO	A	E	DP	FPct
1995 Atl	27	1	0	0	0	0	0	0	0	0	0	0	0	0	0	0	0	0	0	—	0	—	—	—	P	1	0	0	0	0	—
Postseason Totals		2	0	0	0	0	0	0	0	0	0	0	0	0	0	0	0	0	0	—	0	—	—	—	P	2	0	0	0	0	—

FRENCHY BORDAGARAY—Stanley George Bordagaray—Bats: Right; Throws: Right

Ht: 5'7"; Wt: 175 lbs; Born: 1/3/1910 in Coalinga, California; Debut: 4/17/1934

World Series		Batting																							Fielding						
Year Tm	Age	G	AB	H	2B	3B	HR	TB	R	RBI	GW	TBB	IBB	SO	HBP	SH	SF	SB	CS	SB%	GDP	Avg	OBP	SLG	Pos	G	PO	A	E	DP	FPct
1939 Cin	29	2	0	0	0	0	0	0	0	0	0	0	0	0	0	0	0	0	0	—	0	—	—	—	—						
1941 NYA	31	1	0	0	0	0	0	0	0	0	0	0	0	0	0	0	0	0	0	—	0	—	—	—	—						
WS Totals		3	0	0	0	0	0	0	0	0	0	0	0	0	0	0	0	0	0	—	0	—	—	—	—	0	0	0	0	0	—

PAT BORDERS—Patrick Lance Borders—Bats: Right; Throws: Right

Ht: 6'2"; Wt: 190 lbs; Born: 5/14/1963 in Columbus, Ohio; Debut: 4/6/1988

LCS		Batting																							Fielding						
Year Tm	Age	G	AB	H	2B	3B	HR	TB	R	RBI	GW	TBB	IBB	SO	HBP	SH	SF	SB	CS	SB%	GDP	Avg	OBP	SLG	Pos	G	PO	A	E	DP	FPct
1989 Tor	26	1	1	1	0	0	0	1	0	1	0	0	0	0	0	0	0	0	0	—	0	1.000	1.000	1.000	C	1	1	0	0	0	1.000
1991 Tor	28	5	19	5	1	0	0	6	0	2	0	0	0	0	0	1	0	0	0	—	2	.263	.263	.316	C	5	38	3	2	0	.953
1992 Tor	29	6	22	7	0	0	1	10	3	3	1	1	0	1	0	0	2	0	0	—	0	.318	.320	.455	C	6	38	3	1	1	.976
1993 Tor	30	6	24	6	1	0	0	7	1	3	1	0	0	6	0	0	0	1	0	1.00	0	.250	.250	.292	C	6	41	4	0	1	1.000
LCS Totals		18	66	19	2	0	1	24	4	9	2	1	0	7	0	1	2	1	0	1.00	2	.288	.290	.364	C	18	118	10	3	2	.977
World Series		Batting																							Fielding						
Year Tm	Age	G	AB	H	2B	3B	HR	TB	R	RBI	GW	TBB	IBB	SO	HBP	SH	SF	SB	CS	SB%	GDP	Avg	OBP	SLG	Pos	G	PO	A	E	DP	FPct
1992 Tor	29	6	20	9	3	0	1	15	2	3	1	2	1	1	0	0	0	0	0	—	0	.450	.500	.750	C	6	48	5	1	2	.981
1993 Tor	30	6	23	7	0	0	0	7	2	1	0	2	0	1	0	0	0	0	0	—	1	.304	.360	.304	C	6	50	2	1	0	.981
WS Totals		12	43	16	3	0	1	22	4	4	1	4	1	2	0	0	0	0	0	—	1	.372	.426	.512	C	12	98	7	2	2	.981
Postseason Totals		30	109	35	5	0	2	46	8	13	3	5	1	9	0	1	2	1	0	1.00	3	.321	.345	.422	C	30	216	17	5	4	.979

MIKE BORDICK—Michael Todd Bordick—Bats: Right; Throws: Right

Ht: 5'11"; Wt: 170 lbs; Born: 7/21/1965 in Marquette, Michigan; Debut: 4/11/1990

Division Series		Batting																							Fielding						
Year Tm	Age	G	AB	H	2B	3B	HR	TB	R	RBI	GW	TBB	IBB	SO	HBP	SH	SF	SB	CS	SB%	GDP	Avg	OBP	SLG	Pos	G	PO	A	E	DP	FPct
1997 Bal	32	4	10	4	1	0	0	5	4	4	0	4	0	2	0	0	0	0	1	.00	0	.400	.571	.500	SS	4	4	15	0	1	1.000

LCS		Batting																							Fielding						
Year Tm	Age	G	AB	H	2B	3B	HR	TB	R	RBI	GW	TBB	IBB	SO	HBP	SH	SF	SB	CS	SB%	GDP	Avg	OBP	SLG	Pos	G	PO	A	E	DP	FPct
1992 Oak	27	6	19	1	0	0	0	1	1	0	0	1	0	2	0	0	0	1	0	1.00	1	.053	.100	.053	SS	4	10	10	0	3	1.000
																									2B	2	5	4	0	2	1.000
1997 Bal	32	6	19	3	1	0	0	4	0	2	0	0	0	6	0	1	0	0	0	—	1	.158	.158	.211	SS	6	5	14	0	1	1.000
LCS Totals		12	38	4	1	0	0	5	1	2	0	1	0	8	0	1	0	1	0	1.00	2	.105	.128	.132	SS	10	15	24	0	4	1.000
World Series		Batting																							Fielding						
Year Tm	Age	G	AB	H	2B	3B	HR	TB	R	RBI	GW	TBB	IBB	SO	HBP	SH	SF	SB	CS	SB%	GDP	Avg	OBP	SLG	Pos	G	PO	A	E	DP	FPct
1990 Oak	25	3	0	0	0	0	0	0	0	0	0	0	0	0	0	0	0	0	0	—	0	—	—	—	SS	3	0	2	0	0	1.000
Postseason Totals		19	48	8	2	0	0	10	5	6	0	5	0	10	0	1	0	1	1	.50	2	.167	.245	.208	SS	17	19	41	0	5	1.000

RED BOROM—Edward Jones Borom—Bats: Left; Throws: Right

Ht: 5'11"; Wt: 180 lbs; Born: 10/30/1915 in Spartanburg, South Carolina; Debut: 4/23/1944

World Series		Batting																							Fielding						
Year Tm	Age	G	AB	H	2B	3B	HR	TB	R	RBI	GW	TBB	IBB	SO	HBP	SH	SF	SB	CS	SB%	GDP	Avg	OBP	SLG	Pos	G	PO	A	E	DP	FPct
1945 Det	29	2	1	0	0	0	0	0	0	0	0	0	0	0	0	0	0	0	0	—	0	.000	.000	.000	—						

HANK BOROWY—Henry Ludwig Borowy—Throws: Right; Bats: Right

Ht: 6'0"; Wt: 175 lbs; Born: 5/12/1916 in Bloomfield, New Jersey; Debut: 4/18/1942

World Series		Pitching																										
Year Tm	Age	G	GS	CG	GF	IP	BFP	H	R	ER	HR	SH	SF	HB	TBB	IBB	SO	WP	Bk	W	L	Pct	ShO	Sv-Op	Hld	OAvg	OOBP	ERA
1942 NYA	26	1	1	0	0	3.0	18	6	6	6	0	0	0	0	3	0	1	0	0	0	0	—	0	0- 0	0	.400	.500	18.00
1943 NYA	27	1	1	0	0	8.0	31	6	2	2	0	0	0	0	3	2	4	0	0	1	0	1.000	0	0- 0	0	.214	.290	2.25
1945 ChN	29	4	3	1	1	18.0	78	21	8	8	0	0	0	1	6	0	8	0	0	2	2	.500	1	0- 0	0	.296	.359	4.00
WS Totals		6	5	1	1	29.0	254	33	16	16	0	0	0	1	12	2	13	0	0	3	2	.600	1	0-0	0	.289	.362	4.97

World Series		Batting																							Fielding						
Year Tm	Age	G	AB	H	2B	3B	HR	TB	R	RBI	GW	TBB	IBB	SO	HBP	SH	SF	SB	CS	SB%	GDP	Avg	OBP	SLG	Pos	G	PO	A	E	DP	FPct
1942 NYA	26	1	1	0	0	0	0	0	0	0	0	0	0	1	0	0	0	0	0	—	0	.000	.000	.000	P	1	0	1	0	0	1.000
1943 NYA	27	1	2	1	1	0	0	2	1	0	0	0	0	1	0	0	0	0	0	—	0	.500	.500	1.000	P	1	2	0	0	0	1.000
1945 ChN	29	4	6	1	1	0	0	2	1	0	0	0	0	3	0	1	0	0	0	—	0	.167	.167	.333	P	4	1	2	0	0	1.000
WS Totals		6	9	2	2	0	0	4	2	0	0	0	0	5	0	1	0	0	0	—	0	.222	.222	.444	P	6	3	3	0	0	1.000

RICK BOSETTI—Richard Alan Bosetti—Bats: Right; Throws: Right

Ht: 5'11"; Wt: 185 lbs; Born: 8/5/1953 in Redding, California; Debut: 9/9/1976

Division Series		Batting																							Fielding						
Year Tm	Age	G	AB	H	2B	3B	HR	TB	R	RBI	GW	TBB	IBB	SO	HBP	SH	SF	SB	CS	SB%	GDP	Avg	OBP	SLG	Pos	G	PO	A	E	DP	FPct
1981 Oak	28	1	0	0	0	0	0	0	0	0	0	0	0	0	0	0	0	0	0	—	0	—	—	—	OF	1	0	0	0	0	—
LCS		Batting																							Fielding						
Year Tm	Age	G	AB	H	2B	3B	HR	TB	R	RBI	GW	TBB	IBB	SO	HBP	SH	SF	SB	CS	SB%	GDP	Avg	OBP	SLG	Pos	G	PO	A	E	DP	FPct
1981 Oak	28	2	4	1	1	0	0	2	1	0	0	0	0	1	0	0	0	0	0	—	0	.250	.250	.500	OF	1	2	0	0	0	1.000
Postseason Totals		3	4	1	1	0	0	2	1	0	0	0	0	1	0	0	0	0	0	—	0	.250	.250	.500	OF	2	2	0	0	0	1.000

CHRIS BOSIO—Christopher Louis Bosio—Throws: Right; Bats: Right

Ht: 6'3"; Wt: 220 lbs; Born: 4/3/1963 in Carmichael, California; Debut: 8/3/1986

Division Series		Pitching																										
Year Tm	Age	G	GS	CG	GF	IP	BFP	H	R	ER	HR	SH	SF	HB	TBB	IBB	SO	WP	Bk	W	L	Pct	ShO	Sv-Op	Hld	OAvg	OOBP	ERA
1995 Sea	32	2	2	0	0	7.2	36	10	9	9	2	0	1	0	4	0	2	0	0	0	0	—	0	0- 0	0	.323	.389	10.57
LCS		Pitching																										
Year Tm	Age	G	GS	CG	GF	IP	BFP	H	R	ER	HR	SH	SF	HB	TBB	IBB	SO	WP	Bk	W	L	Pct	ShO	Sv-Op	Hld	OAvg	OOBP	ERA
1995 Sea	32	1	1	0	0	5.1	24	7	3	2	1	0	0	0	2	0	3	0	0	0	1	.000	0	0- 0	0	.318	.375	3.38
Postseason Totals		3	3	0	0	13.0	120	17	12	11	3	0	1	0	6	0	5	0	0	0	1	.000	0	0-0	0	.321	.383	7.62

Division Series		Batting																							Fielding						
Year Tm	Age	G	AB	H	2B	3B	HR	TB	R	RBI	GW	TBB	IBB	SO	HBP	SH	SF	SB	CS	SB%	GDP	Avg	OBP	SLG	Pos	G	PO	A	E	DP	FPct
1995 Sea	32	2	0	0	0	0	0	0	0	0	0	0	0	0	0	0	0	0	0	—	0	—	—	—	P	2	1	0	0	0	1.000
LCS		Batting																							Fielding						
Year Tm	Age	G	AB	H	2B	3B	HR	TB	R	RBI	GW	TBB	IBB	SO	HBP	SH	SF	SB	CS	SB%	GDP	Avg	OBP	SLG	Pos	G	PO	A	E	DP	FPct
1995 Sea	32	1	0	0	0	0	0	0	0	0	0	0	0	0	0	0	0	0	0	—	0	—	—	—	P	1	0	2	0	0	1.000
Postseason Totals		3	0	0	0	0	0	0	0	0	0	0	0	0	0	0	0	0	0	—	0	—	—	—	P	3	1	2	0	0	1.000

THAD BOSLEY—Thaddis Bosley—Bats: Left; Throws: Left

Ht: 6'3"; Wt: 175 lbs; Born: 9/17/1956 in Oceanside, California; Debut: 6/29/1977

Division Series		Batting																							Fielding						
Year Tm	Age	G	AB	H	2B	3B	HR	TB	R	RBI	GW	TBB	IBB	SO	HBP	SH	SF	SB	CS	SB%	GDP	Avg	OBP	SLG	Pos	G	PO	A	E	DP	FPct
1981 Mil	25	1	0	0	0	0	0	0	0	0	0	0	0	0	0	0	0	0	0	—	0	—	—	—	—						
LCS		Batting																							Fielding						
Year Tm	Age	G	AB	H	2B	3B	HR	TB	R	RBI	GW	TBB	IBB	SO	HBP	SH	SF	SB	CS	SB%	GDP	Avg	OBP	SLG	Pos	G	PO	A	E	DP	FPct
1984 ChN	28	2	2	0	0	0	0	0	0	0	0	0	0	2	0	0	0	0	0	—	0	.000	.000	.000	—						
Postseason Totals		3	2	0	0	0	0	0	0	0	0	0	0	2	0	0	0	0	0	—	0	.000	.000	.000	—	0	0	0	0	0	—

DICK BOSMAN—Richard Allen Bosman—Throws: Right; Bats: Right

Ht: 6'2"; Wt: 195 lbs; Born: 2/17/1944 in Kenosha, Wisconsin; Debut: 6/1/1966

LCS		Pitching																										
Year Tm	Age	G	GS	CG	GF	IP	BFP	H	R	ER	HR	SH	SF	HB	TBB	IBB	SO	WP	Bk	W	L	Pct	ShO	Sv-Op	Hld	OAvg	OOBP	ERA
1975 Oak	31	1	0	0	0	0.1	1	0	0	0	0	0	0	0	0	0	0	0	0	0	0	—	0	0- 0	0	.000	.000	0.00

LCS		Batting																							Fielding						
Year Tm	Age	G	AB	H	2B	3B	HR	TB	R	RBI	GW	TBB	IBB	SO	HBP	SH	SF	SB	CS	SB%	GDP	Avg	OBP	SLG	Pos	G	PO	A	E	DP	FPct
1975 Oak	31	1	0	0	0	0	0	0	0	0	0	0	0	0	0	0	0	0	0	—	0	—	—	—	P	1	0	0	0	0	—

DAVE BOSWELL—David Wilson Boswell—Throws: Right; Bats: Right

Ht: 6'3"; Wt: 185 lbs; Born: 1/20/1945 in Baltimore, Maryland; Debut: 9/18/1964

LCS		Pitching																										
Year Tm	Age	G	GS	CG	GF	IP	BFP	H	R	ER	HR	SH	SF	HB	TBB	IBB	SO	WP	Bk	W	L	Pct	ShO	Sv-Op	Hld	OAvg	OOBP	ERA
1969 Min	24	1	1	0	0	10.2	43	7	1	1	0	1	0	0	7	1	4	1	0	0	1	.000	0	0- 0	0	.200	.333	0.84
World Series		Pitching																										
Year Tm	Age	G	GS	CG	GF	IP	BFP	H	R	ER	HR	SH	SF	HB	TBB	IBB	SO	WP	Bk	W	L	Pct	ShO	Sv-Op	Hld	OAvg	OOBP	ERA
1965 Min	20	1	0	0	0	2.2	13	3	1	1	0	0	0	0	2	0	3	0	0	0	0	—	0	0- 0	0	.273	.385	3.38
Postseason Totals		2	1	0	0	13.1	112	10	2	2	0	1	0	0	9	1	7	1	0	0	1	.000	0	0-0	0	.217	.345	1.35

LCS		Batting																							Fielding						
Year Tm	Age	G	AB	H	2B	3B	HR	TB	R	RBI	GW	TBB	IBB	SO	HBP	SH	SF	SB	CS	SB%	GDP	Avg	OBP	SLG	Pos	G	PO	A	E	DP	FPct
1969 Min	24	1	4	0	0	0	0	0	0	0	0	0	0	4	0	0	0	0	0	—	0	.000	.000	.000	P	1	1	4	0	1	1.000
World Series		Batting																							Fielding						
Year Tm	Age	G	AB	H	2B	3B	HR	TB	R	RBI	GW	TBB	IBB	SO	HBP	SH	SF	SB	CS	SB%	GDP	Avg	OBP	SLG	Pos	G	PO	A	E	DP	FPct
1965 Min	20	1	0	0	0	0	0	0	0	0	0	0	0	0	0	0	0	0	0	—	0	—	—	—	P	1	0	0	0	0	—
Postseason Totals		2	4	0	0	0	0	0	0	0	0	0	0	4	0	0	0	0	0	—	0	.000	.000	.000	P	2	1	4	0	1	1.000

KEN BOSWELL—Kenneth George Boswell—Bats: Left; Throws: Right

Ht: 6'0"; Wt: 170 lbs; Born: 2/23/1946 in Austin, Texas; Debut: 9/18/1967

LCS		Batting																							Fielding						
Year Tm	Age	G	AB	H	2B	3B	HR	TB	R	RBI	GW	TBB	IBB	SO	HBP	SH	SF	SB	CS	SB%	GDP	Avg	OBP	SLG	Pos	G	PO	A	E	DP	FPct
1969 NYN	23	3	12	4	0	0	2	10	4	5	0	1	0	2	0	0	0	0	0	—	0	.333	.385	.833	2B	3	3	2	1	1	.833
1973 NYN	27	1	1	0	0	0	0	0	0	0	0	0	0	0	0	0	0	0	0	—	0	.000	.000	.000	—						
LCS Totals		4	13	4	0	0	2	10	4	5	0	1	0	2	0	0	0	0	0	—	0	.308	.357	.769	2B	3	3	2	1	1	.833
World Series		Batting																							Fielding						
Year Tm	Age	G	AB	H	2B	3B	HR	TB	R	RBI	GW	TBB	IBB	SO	HBP	SH	SF	SB	CS	SB%	GDP	Avg	OBP	SLG	Pos	G	PO	A	E	DP	FPct
1969 NYN	23	1	3	1	0	0	0	1	1	0	0	0	0	0	0	0	0	0	0	—	0	.333	.333	.333	2B	1	0	1	0	0	1.000
1973 NYN	27	3	3	3	0	0	0	3	1	0	0	0	0	0	0	0	0	0	0	—	0	1.000	1.000	1.000	—						
WS Totals		4	6	4	0	0	0	4	2	0	0	0	0	0	0	0	0	0	0	—	0	.667	.667	.667	2B	1	0	1	0	0	1.000
Postseason Totals		8	19	8	0	0	2	14	6	5	0	1	0	2	0	0	0	0	0	—	0	.421	.450	.737	2B	4	3	3	1	1	.857

JIM BOTTOMLEY (HOF 1974-V)—James Leroy Bottomley—Nickname: Sunny Jim—Bats: Left; Throws: Left

Ht: 6'0"; Wt: 180 lbs; Born: 4/23/1900 in Oglesby, Ill.; Debut: 8/18/1922; Died: 12/11/1959

World Series		Batting																							Fielding						
Year Tm	Age	G	AB	H	2B	3B	HR	TB	R	RBI	GW	TBB	IBB	SO	HBP	SH	SF	SB	CS	SB%	GDP	Avg	OBP	SLG	Pos	G	PO	A	E	DP	FPct
1926 StL	26	7	29	10	3	0	0	13	4	5	1	1	0	2	0	1	0	0	1	.00	0	.345	.367	.448	1B	7	79	1	0	5	1.000
1928 StL-*M*	28	4	14	3	0	1	1	8	1	3	0	2	0	6	0	0	0	0	0	—	0	.214	.313	.571	1B	4	36	2	0	3	1.000
1930 StL	30	6	22	1	1	0	0	2	1	0	0	2	0	9	0	0	0	0	0	—	0	.045	.125	.091	1B	6	57	2	0	3	1.000
1931 StL	31	7	25	4	1	0	0	5	2	2	0	2	0	5	0	0	0	0	0	—	0	.160	.222	.200	1B	7	61	2	1	7	.984
WS Totals		24	90	18	5	1	1	28	8	10	1	7	0	22	0	1	0	0	1	.00	0	.200	.258	.311	1B	24	233	7	1	18	.996

LOU BOUDREAU (HOF 1970-W)—Louis Boudreau—Bats: Right; Throws: Right

Ht: 5'11"; Wt: 185 lbs; Born: 7/17/1917 in Harvey, Illinois; Debut: 9/9/1938

World Series		Batting																							Fielding						
Year Tm	Age	G	AB	H	2B	3B	HR	TB	R	RBI	GW	TBB	IBB	SO	HBP	SH	SF	SB	CS	SB%	GDP	Avg	OBP	SLG	Pos	G	PO	A	E	DP	FPct
1948 Cle-*M*	31	6	22	6	4	0	0	10	1	3	1	1	0	1	1	0	0	0	0	—	2	.273	.333	.455	SS	6	11	14	0	5	1.000

PAT BOURQUE—Patrick Daniel Bourque—Bats: Left; Throws: Left

Ht: 6'0"; Wt: 210 lbs; Born: 3/23/1947 in Worcester, Massachusetts; Debut: 9/6/1971

LCS		Batting																							Fielding						
Year Tm	Age	G	AB	H	2B	3B	HR	TB	R	RBI	GW	TBB	IBB	SO	HBP	SH	SF	SB	CS	SB%	GDP	Avg	OBP	SLG	Pos	G	PO	A	E	DP	FPct
1973 Oak	26	2	1	0	0	0	0	0	0	0	0	2	1	1	0	0	0	0	0	—	0	.000	.667	.000	—						
World Series		**Batting**																							**Fielding**						
Year Tm	Age	G	AB	H	2B	3B	HR	TB	R	RBI	GW	TBB	IBB	SO	HBP	SH	SF	SB	CS	SB%	GDP	Avg	OBP	SLG	Pos	G	PO	A	E	DP	FPct
1973 Oak	26	2	2	1	0	0	0	1	0	0	0	0	0	0	0	0	0	0	0	—	0	.500	.500	.500	1B	2	3	1	0	0	1.000
Postseason Totals		4	3	1	0	0	0	1	0	0	0	2	1	1	0	0	0	0	0	—	0	.333	.600	.333	1B	2	3	1	0	0	1.000

JIM BOUTON—James Alan Bouton—Throws: Right; Bats: Right

Ht: 6'0"; Wt: 170 lbs; Born: 3/8/1939 in Newark, New Jersey; Debut: 4/22/1962

World Series		Pitching																									
Year Tm	Age	G	GS	CG	GF	IP	BFP	H	R	ER	HR	SH	SF	HB	TBB	IBB	SO	WP	Bk	W	L	Pct	ShO	Sv-Op	Hld	OAvg	OOBP	ERA
1963 NYA	24	1	1	0	0	7.0	28	4	1	1	0	0	0	0	5	0	4	2	0	0	1	.000	0	0-0	0	.174	.321	1.29
1964 NYA	25	2	2	1	0	17.1	72	15	4	3	0	2	0	0	5	1	7	0	0	2	0	1.000	0	0-0	0	.231	.286	1.56
WS Totals		3	3	1	0	24.1	200	19	5	4	0	2	0	0	10	1	11	2	0	2	1	.667	0	0-0	0	.216	.296	1.48

World Series		Batting																							Fielding						
Year Tm	Age	G	AB	H	2B	3B	HR	TB	R	RBI	GW	TBB	IBB	SO	HBP	SH	SF	SB	CS	SB%	GDP	Avg	OBP	SLG	Pos	G	PO	A	E	DP	FPct
1963 NYA	24	1	2	0	0	0	0	0	0	0	0	0	0	2	0	0	0	0	0	—	0	.000	.000	.000	P	1	1	2	0	0	1.000
1964 NYA	25	2	7	1	0	0	0	1	0	1	0	0	0	2	0	0	0	0	0	—	0	.143	.143	.143	P	2	4	0	0	0	1.000
WS Totals		3	9	1	0	0	0	1	0	1	0	0	0	4	0	0	0	0	0	—	0	.111	.111	.111	P	3	5	2	0	0	1.000

LARRY BOWA—Lawrence Robert Bowa—Bats: Both; Throws: Right

Ht: 5'10"; Wt: 155 lbs; Born: 12/6/1945 in Sacramento, California; Debut: 4/7/1970

Division Series		Batting																							Fielding						
Year Tm	Age	G	AB	H	2B	3B	HR	TB	R	RBI	GW	TBB	IBB	SO	HBP	SH	SF	SB	CS	SB%	GDP	Avg	OBP	SLG	Pos	G	PO	A	E	DP	FPct
1981 Phi	35	5	17	3	1	0	0	4	0	1	0	0	0	0	0	1	0	0	1	.00	0	.176	.176	.235	SS	5	13	8	1	1	.955
LCS		**Batting**																							**Fielding**						
Year Tm	Age	G	AB	H	2B	3B	HR	TB	R	RBI	GW	TBB	IBB	SO	HBP	SH	SF	SB	CS	SB%	GDP	Avg	OBP	SLG	Pos	G	PO	A	E	DP	FPct
1976 Phi	30	3	8	1	1	0	0	2	1	1	0	3	0	0	0	0	0	0	0	—	0	.125	.364	.250	SS	3	2	11	0	1	1.000
1977 Phi	31	4	17	2	0	0	0	2	2	1	0	1	0	0	0	0	0	0	0	—	1	.118	.167	.118	SS	4	0	17	0	2	1.000
1978 Phi	32	4	18	6	0	0	0	6	2	0	0	1	0	2	0	0	0	0	0	—	0	.333	.368	.333	SS	4	5	16	0	4	1.000
1980 Phi	34	5	19	6	0	0	0	6	2	0	0	3	3	3	0	1	0	1	0	1.00	0	.316	.409	.316	SS	5	4	11	1	4	.938
1984 ChN	38	5	15	3	1	0	0	4	1	1	0	1	0	0	0	0	0	0	0	—	1	.200	.250	.267	SS	5	8	14	0	6	1.000
LCS Totals		21	77	18	2	0	0	20	8	3	0	9	3	5	0	1	0	1	0	1.00	2	.234	.314	.260	SS	21	19	69	1	17	.989
World Series		**Batting**																							**Fielding**						
Year Tm	Age	G	AB	H	2B	3B	HR	TB	R	RBI	GW	TBB	IBB	SO	HBP	SH	SF	SB	CS	SB%	GDP	Avg	OBP	SLG	Pos	G	PO	A	E	DP	FPct
1980 Phi	34	6	24	9	1	0	0	10	3	2	0	0	0	0	0	0	0	3	0	1.00	0	.375	.375	.417	SS	6	5	18	0	7	1.000
Postseason Totals		32	118	30	4	0	0	34	11	6	0	9	3	5	0	2	0	4	1	.80	2	.254	.307	.288	SS	32	37	95	2	25	.985

ERNIE BOWMAN—Ernest Ferrell Bowman—Nickname: Squeaky—Bats: Right; Throws: Right

Ht: 5'10"; Wt: 160 lbs; Born: 7/28/1935 in Johnson City, Tennessee; Debut: 4/12/1961

World Series		Batting																							Fielding						
Year Tm	Age	G	AB	H	2B	3B	HR	TB	R	RBI	GW	TBB	IBB	SO	HBP	SH	SF	SB	CS	SB%	GDP	Avg	OBP	SLG	Pos	G	PO	A	E	DP	FPct
1962 SF	27	2	1	0	0	0	0	0	1	0	0	0	0	0	0	0	0	0	0	—	0	.000	.000	.000	SS	2	0	5	0	0	1.000

OIL CAN BOYD—Dennis Ray Boyd—Throws: Right; Bats: Right

Ht: 6'1"; Wt: 155 lbs; Born: 10/6/1959 in Meridian, Mississippi; Debut: 9/13/1982

LCS		Pitching																									
Year Tm	Age	G	GS	CG	GF	IP	BFP	H	R	ER	HR	SH	SF	HB	TBB	IBB	SO	WP	Bk	W	L	Pct	ShO	Sv-Op	Hld	OAvg	OOBP	ERA
1986 Bos	26	2	2	0	0	13.2	59	17	7	7	3	0	0	1	3	0	8	0	0	1	1	.500	0	0-0	0	.309	.356	4.61
World Series		**Pitching**																									
Year Tm	Age	G	GS	CG	GF	IP	BFP	H	R	ER	HR	SH	SF	HB	TBB	IBB	SO	WP	Bk	W	L	Pct	ShO	Sv-Op	Hld	OAvg	OOBP	ERA
1986 Bos	26	1	1	0	0	7.0	31	9	6	6	1	0	0	0	1	0	3	0	0	0	1	.000	0	0-0	0	.300	.323	7.71
Postseason Totals		3	3	0	0	20.2	180	26	13	13	4	0	0	1	4	0	11	0	0	1	2	.333	0	0-0	0	.306	.344	5.66

LCS		Batting																							Fielding						
Year Tm	Age	G	AB	H	2B	3B	HR	TB	R	RBI	GW	TBB	IBB	SO	HBP	SH	SF	SB	CS	SB%	GDP	Avg	OBP	SLG	Pos	G	PO	A	E	DP	FPct
1986 Bos	26	2	0	0	0	0	0	0	0	0	0	0	0	0	0	0	0	0	0	—	0	—	—	—	P	2	2	2	0	0	1.000
World Series		**Batting**																							**Fielding**						
Year Tm	Age	G	AB	H	2B	3B	HR	TB	R	RBI	GW	TBB	IBB	SO	HBP	SH	SF	SB	CS	SB%	GDP	Avg	OBP	SLG	Pos	G	PO	A	E	DP	FPct
1986 Bos	26	1	0	0	0	0	0	0	0	0	0	0	0	0	0	0	0	0	0	—	0	—	—	—	P	1	1	0	0	0	1.000
Postseason Totals		3	0	0	0	0	0	0	0	0	0	0	0	0	0	0	0	0	0	—	0	—	—	—	P	3	3	2	0	0	1.000

CLETE BOYER—Cletis Leroy Boyer—Nickname: Spike—Bats: Right; Throws: Right

Ht: 6'0"; Wt: 165 lbs; Born: 2/9/1937 in Cassville, Missouri; Debut: 6/5/1955

LCS		Batting																							Fielding						
Year Tm	Age	G	AB	H	2B	3B	HR	TB	R	RBI	GW	TBB	IBB	SO	HBP	SH	SF	SB	CS	SB%	GDP	Avg	OBP	SLG	Pos	G	PO	A	E	DP	FPct
1969 Atl	32	3	9	1	0	0	0	1	0	3	0	2	1	3	0	0	1	0	0	—	0	.111	.250	.111	3B	3	4	8	1	1	.923
World Series		**Batting**																							**Fielding**						
Year Tm	Age	G	AB	H	2B	3B	HR	TB	R	RBI	GW	TBB	IBB	SO	HBP	SH	SF	SB	CS	SB%	GDP	Avg	OBP	SLG	Pos	G	PO	A	E	DP	FPct
1960 NYA	23	4	12	3	2	1	0	7	1	1	0	0	0	1	0	0	0	0	0	—	1	.250	.250	.583	3B	4	0	8	0	2	1.000
																									SS	1	0	0	0	0	—
1961 NYA	24	5	15	4	2	0	0	6	0	3	0	4	1	0	0	0	0	0	0	—	1	.267	.421	.400	3B	5	6	12	1	0	.947
1962 NYA	25	7	22	7	1	0	1	11	2	4	1	1	1	3	0	0	1	0	0	—	0	.318	.333	.500	3B	7	9	16	2	2	.926
1963 NYA	26	4	13	1	0	0	0	1	0	0	0	1	1	6	0	0	0	0	0	—	0	.077	.143	.077	3B	4	2	8	0	0	1.000
1964 NYA	27	7	24	5	1	0	1	9	2	3	0	1	1	5	0	0	1	1	0	1.00	0	.208	.231	.375	3B	7	6	22	2	0	.933
WS Totals		27	86	20	6	1	2	34	5	11	1	7	4	15	0	0	2	1	0	1.00	2	.233	.284	.395	3B	27	23	66	5	4	.947
Postseason Totals		30	95	21	6	1	2	35	5	14	1	9	5	18	0	0	3	1	0	1.00	2	.221	.280	.368	3B	30	27	74	6	5	.944

KEN BOYER—Kenton Lloyd Boyer—Bats: Right; Throws: Right

Ht: 6'1"; Wt: 190 lbs; Born: 5/20/1931 in Liberty, Missouri; Debut: 4/12/1955; Died: 9/7/1982

World Series		Batting																							Fielding						
Year Tm	Age	G	AB	H	2B	3B	HR	TB	R	RBI	GW	TBB	IBB	SO	HBP	SH	SF	SB	CS	SB%	GDP	Avg	OBP	SLG	Pos	G	PO	A	E	DP	FPct
1964 StL-*M*	33	7	27	6	1	0	2	13	5	6	1	1	0	5	0	0	1	0	0	—	1	.222	.241	.481	3B	7	9	16	1	0	.962

BOBBY BRAGAN—Robert Randall Bragan—Nickname: Nig—Bats: Right; Throws: Right

Ht: 5'10"; Wt: 175 lbs; Born: 10/30/1917 in Birmingham, Alabama; Debut: 4/16/1940

World Series		Batting																							Fielding						
Year Tm	Age	G	AB	H	2B	3B	HR	TB	R	RBI	GW	TBB	IBB	SO	HBP	SH	SF	SB	CS	SB%	GDP	Avg	OBP	SLG	Pos	G	PO	A	E	DP	FPct
1947 Bro	29	1	1	1	1	0	0	2	0	1	1	0	0	0	0	0	0	0	0	—	0	1.000	1.000	2.000	—						

GLENN BRAGGS—Glenn Erick Braggs—Bats: Right; Throws: Right

Ht: 6'3"; Wt: 210 lbs; Born: 10/17/1962 in San Bernardino, California; Debut: 7/18/1986

LCS		Batting																							Fielding						
Year Tm	Age	G	AB	H	2B	3B	HR	TB	R	RBI	GW	TBB	IBB	SO	HBP	SH	SF	SB	CS	SB%	GDP	Avg	OBP	SLG	Pos	G	PO	A	E	DP	FPct
1990 Cin	27	2	5	1	0	0	0	1	0	0	0	0	0	1	0	0	0	0	0	—	0	.200	.200	.200	OF	2	2	0	0	0	1.000
World Series		Batting																							Fielding						
Year Tm	Age	G	AB	H	2B	3B	HR	TB	R	RBI	GW	TBB	IBB	SO	HBP	SH	SF	SB	CS	SB%	GDP	Avg	OBP	SLG	Pos	G	PO	A	E	DP	FPct
1990 Cin	27	2	4	0	0	0	0	0	0	2	0	1	0	0	0	0	0	0	0	—	0	.000	.200	.000	OF	1	0	0	0	0	—
Postseason Totals		4	9	1	0	0	0	1	0	2	0	1	0	1	0	0	0	0	0	—	0	.111	.200	.111	OF	3	2	0	0	0	1.000

RALPH BRANCA—Ralph Theodore Joseph Branca—Nickname: Hawk—Throws: Right; Bats: Right

Ht: 6'3"; Wt: 220 lbs; Born: 1/6/1926 in Mt. Vernon, New York; Debut: 6/12/1944

World Series		Pitching																										
Year Tm	Age	G	GS	CG	GF	IP	BFP	H	R	ER	HR	SH	SF	HB	TBB	IBB	SO	WP	Bk	W	L	Pct	ShO	Sv-Op	Hld	OAvg	OOBP	ERA
1947 Bro	21	3	1	0	0	8.1	43	12	8	8	1	0	0	1	5	0	8	0	0	1	1	.500	0	0- 0	0	.324	.419	8.64
1949 Bro	23	1	1	0	0	8.2	34	4	4	4	0	0	0	0	4	0	6	0	0	0	1	.000	0	0- 0	0	.133	.235	4.15
WS Totals		4	2	0	0	17.0	154	16	12	12	1	0	0	1	9	0	14	0	0	1	2	.333	0	0-0	0	.239	.338	6.35

World Series		Batting																							Fielding						
Year Tm	Age	G	AB	H	2B	3B	HR	TB	R	RBI	GW	TBB	IBB	SO	HBP	SH	SF	SB	CS	SB%	GDP	Avg	OBP	SLG	Pos	G	PO	A	E	DP	FPct
1947 Bro	21	3	4	0	0	0	0	0	0	0	0	0	0	1	0	0	0	0	0	—	0	.000	.000	.000	P	3	0	1	0	0	1.000
1949 Bro	23	1	3	0	0	0	0	0	0	0	0	0	0	3	0	0	0	0	0	—	0	.000	.000	.000	P	1	1	0	0	0	1.000
WS Totals		4	7	0	0	0	0	0	0	0	0	0	0	4	0	0	0	0	0	—	0	.000	.000	.000	P	4	1	1	0	0	1.000

KITTY BRANSFIELD—William Edward Bransfield—Bats: Right; Throws: Right

Ht: 5'11"; Wt: 207 lbs; Born: 1/7/1875 in Worcester, Massachusetts; Debut: 8/22/1898; Died: 5/1/1947

World Series		Batting																							Fielding						
Year Tm	Age	G	AB	H	2B	3B	HR	TB	R	RBI	GW	TBB	IBB	SO	HBP	SH	SF	SB	CS	SB%	GDP	Avg	OBP	SLG	Pos	G	PO	A	E	DP	FPct
1903 Pit	28	8	29	6	0	2	0	10	3	1	0	1	0	6	0	1	0	1	0	1.00	0	.207	.233	.345	1B	8	81	6	3	5	.967

JEFF BRANSON—Jeffery Glenn Branson—Bats: Left; Throws: Right

Ht: 6'0"; Wt: 180 lbs; Born: 1/26/1967 in Waynesboro, Massachusetts; Debut: 4/12/1992

Division Series		Batting																							Fielding						
Year Tm	Age	G	AB	H	2B	3B	HR	TB	R	RBI	GW	TBB	IBB	SO	HBP	SH	SF	SB	CS	SB%	GDP	Avg	OBP	SLG	Pos	G	PO	A	E	DP	FPct
1995 Cin	28	3	7	2	1	0	0	3	0	2	0	2	1	0	0	0	0	0	0	—	1	.286	.444	.429	3B	3	1	8	0	0	1.000
LCS		Batting																							Fielding						
Year Tm	Age	G	AB	H	2B	3B	HR	TB	R	RBI	GW	TBB	IBB	SO	HBP	SH	SF	SB	CS	SB%	GDP	Avg	OBP	SLG	Pos	G	PO	A	E	DP	FPct
1995 Cin	28	4	9	1	1	0	0	2	2	0	0	0	0	2	0	1	0	1	0	1.00	0	.111	.111	.222	3B	4	1	3	0	1	1.000
1997 Cle	30	1	2	0	0	0	0	0	0	0	0	0	0	2	0	0	0	0	0	—	0	.000	.000	.000	—						
LCS Totals		5	11	1	1	0	0	2	2	0	0	0	0	4	0	1	0	1	0	1.00	0	.091	.091	.182	3B	4	1	3	0	1	1.000
World Series		Batting																							Fielding						
Year Tm	Age	G	AB	H	2B	3B	HR	TB	R	RBI	GW	TBB	IBB	SO	HBP	SH	SF	SB	CS	SB%	GDP	Avg	OBP	SLG	Pos	G	PO	A	E	DP	FPct
1997 Cle	30	1	1	0	0	0	0	0	0	0	0	0	0	1	0	0	0	0	0	—	0	.000	.000	.000	—						
Postseason Totals		9	19	3	2	0	0	5	2	2	0	2	1	5	0	1	0	1	0	1.00	1	.158	.238	.263	3B	7	2	11	0	1	1.000

JEFF BRANTLEY—Jeffrey Hoke Brantley—Throws: Right; Bats: Right

Ht: 5'11"; Wt: 180 lbs; Born: 9/5/1963 in Florence, Alabama; Debut: 8/5/1988

Division Series		Pitching																										
Year Tm	Age	G	GS	CG	GF	IP	BFP	H	R	ER	HR	SH	SF	HB	TBB	IBB	SO	WP	Bk	W	L	Pct	ShO	Sv-Op	Hld	OAvg	OOBP	ERA
1995 Cin	32	3	0	0	3	3.0	14	5	2	2	1	0	0	0	0	0	2	0	0	0	0	—	0	1- 1	0	.357	.357	6.00
LCS		Pitching																										
Year Tm	Age	G	GS	CG	GF	IP	BFP	H	R	ER	HR	SH	SF	HB	TBB	IBB	SO	WP	Bk	W	L	Pct	ShO	Sv-Op	Hld	OAvg	OOBP	ERA
1989 SF	26	3	0	0	0	5.0	17	1	0	0	0	0	0	0	2	0	3	1	0	0	0	—	0	0- 0	0	.067	.176	0.00
1995 Cin	32	2	0	0	0	2.2	10	0	0	0	0	0	0	0	2	1	1	0	0	0	0	—	0	0- 0	0	.000	.200	0.00
LCS Totals		5	0	0	0	7.2	54	1	0	0	0	0	0	0	4	1	4	1	0	0	0	—	0	0-0	0	.043	.185	0.00
World Series		Pitching																										
Year Tm	Age	G	GS	CG	GF	IP	BFP	H	R	ER	HR	SH	SF	HB	TBB	IBB	SO	WP	Bk	W	L	Pct	ShO	Sv-Op	Hld	OAvg	OOBP	ERA
1989 SF	26	3	0	0	0	4.1	21	5	2	2	1	0	0	0	3	0	1	0	1	0	0	—	0	0- 0	0	.278	.381	4.15
Postseason Totals		11	0	0	3	15.0	124	11	4	4	2	0	0	0	7	1	7	1	1	0	0	—	0	1-1	0	.200	.290	2.40

Division Series		Batting																							Fielding						
Year Tm	Age	G	AB	H	2B	3B	HR	TB	R	RBI	GW	TBB	IBB	SO	HBP	SH	SF	SB	CS	SB%	GDP	Avg	OBP	SLG	Pos	G	PO	A	E	DP	FPct
1995 Cin	32	3	0	0	0	0	0	0	0	0	0	0	0	0	0	0	0	0	0	—	0	—	—	—	P	3	0	0	0	0	—
LCS		Batting																							Fielding						
Year Tm	Age	G	AB	H	2B	3B	HR	TB	R	RBI	GW	TBB	IBB	SO	HBP	SH	SF	SB	CS	SB%	GDP	Avg	OBP	SLG	Pos	G	PO	A	E	DP	FPct
1989 SF	26	3	0	0	0	0	0	0	0	0	0	1	0	0	0	0	0	0	0	—	0	—	1.000	—	P	3	0	0	0	0	—
1995 Cin	32	2	0	0	0	0	0	0	0	0	0	0	0	0	0	0	0	0	0	—	0	—	—	—	P	2	2	0	0	0	1.000
LCS Totals		5	0	0	0	0	0	0	0	0	0	1	0	0	0	0	0	0	0	—	0	—	1.000	—	P	5	2	0	0	0	1.000
World Series		Batting																							Fielding						
Year Tm	Age	G	AB	H	2B	3B	HR	TB	R	RBI	GW	TBB	IBB	SO	HBP	SH	SF	SB	CS	SB%	GDP	Avg	OBP	SLG	Pos	G	PO	A	E	DP	FPct
1989 SF	26	3	0	0	0	0	0	0	0	0	0	0	0	0	0	0	0	0	0	—	0	—	—	—	P	3	1	0	0	0	1.000
Postseason Totals		11	0	0	0	0	0	0	0	0	0	1	0	0	0	0	0	0	0	—	0	—	1.000	—	P	11	3	0	0	0	1.000

STEVE BRAUN—Stephen Russell Braun—Bats: Left; Throws: Right

Ht: 5'10"; Wt: 180 lbs; Born: 5/8/1948 in Trenton, New Jersey; Debut: 4/6/1971

LCS		Batting																							Fielding						
Year Tm	Age	G	AB	H	2B	3B	HR	TB	R	RBI	GW	TBB	IBB	SO	HBP	SH	SF	SB	CS	SB%	GDP	Avg	OBP	SLG	Pos	G	PO	A	E	DP	FPct
1978 KC	30	2	5	0	0	0	0	0	0	0	0	1	0	1	0	0	0	0	0	—	0	.000	.167	.000	OF	1	5	0	0	0	1.000
1982 StL	34	1	1	0	0	0	0	0	0	0	0	0	0	0	0	0	0	0	0	—	0	.000	.000	.000	—						
1985 StL	37	2	2	0	0	0	0	0	0	0	0	0	0	0	0	0	0	0	0	—	0	.000	.000	.000	—						
LCS Totals		5	8	0	0	0	0	0	0	0	0	1	0	1	0	0	0	0	0	—	0	.000	.111	.000	OF	1	5	0	0	0	1.000
World Series		Batting																							Fielding						
Year Tm	Age	G	AB	H	2B	3B	HR	TB	R	RBI	GW	TBB	IBB	SO	HBP	SH	SF	SB	CS	SB%	GDP	Avg	OBP	SLG	Pos	G	PO	A	E	DP	FPct
1982 StL	34	2	2	1	0	0	0	1	0	2	1	1	0	0	0	0	0	0	0	—	0	.500	.667	.500	—						
1985 StL	37	1	1	0	0	0	0	0	0	0	0	0	0	0	0	0	0	0	0	—	0	.000	.000	.000	—						
WS Totals		3	3	1	0	0	0	1	0	2	1	1	0	0	0	0	0	0	0	—	0	.333	.500	.333	—	0	0	0	0	0	—
Postseason Totals		8	11	1	0	0	0	1	0	2	1	2	0	1	0	0	0	0	0	—	0	.091	.231	.091	OF	1	5	0	0	0	1.000

ANGEL BRAVO—Angel Alfonso Bravo—Bats: Left; Throws: Left

Ht: 5'8"; Wt: 150 lbs; Born: 8/4/1942 in Maracaibo, Venezuela; Debut: 6/6/1969

LCS		Batting																							Fielding						
Year Tm	Age	G	AB	H	2B	3B	HR	TB	R	RBI	GW	TBB	IBB	SO	HBP	SH	SF	SB	CS	SB%	GDP	Avg	OBP	SLG	Pos	G	PO	A	E	DP	FPct
1970 Cin	28	1	1	0	0	0	0	0	0	0	0	0	0	0	0	0	0	0	0	—	0	.000	.000	.000	—						
World Series		Batting																							Fielding						
Year Tm	Age	G	AB	H	2B	3B	HR	TB	R	RBI	GW	TBB	IBB	SO	HBP	SH	SF	SB	CS	SB%	GDP	Avg	OBP	SLG	Pos	G	PO	A	E	DP	FPct
1970 Cin	28	4	2	0	0	0	0	0	0	0	0	1	0	1	0	1	0	0	0	—	0	.000	.333	.000	—						
Postseason Totals		5	3	0	0	0	0	0	0	0	0	1	0	1	0	1	0	0	0	—	0	.000	.250	.000	—	0	0	0	0	0	—

AL BRAZLE—Alpha Eugene Brazle—Nickname: Cotton—Throws: Left; Bats: Left

Ht: 6'2"; Wt: 185 lbs; Born: 10/19/1913 in Loyal, Oklahoma; Debut: 7/25/1943; Died: 10/24/1973

World Series		Pitching																										
Year Tm	Age	G	GS	CG	GF	IP	BFP	H	R	ER	HR	SH	SF	HB	TBB	IBB	SO	WP	Bk	W	L	Pct	ShO	Sv-Op	Hld	OAvg	OOBP	ERA
1943 StL	29	1	1	0	0	7.1	31	5	6	3	0	1	0	0	2	1	4	0	0	0	1	.000	0	0- 0	0	.179	.233	3.68
1946 StL	32	1	0	0	0	6.2	33	7	4	4	1	1	0	0	6	4	4	0	0	0	1	.000	0	0- 0	0	.269	.406	5.40
WS Totals		2	1	0	0	14.0	128	12	10	7	1	2	0	0	8	5	8	0	0	0	2	.000	0	0-0	0	.222	.323	4.50

World Series		Batting																							Fielding						
Year Tm	Age	G	AB	H	2B	3B	HR	TB	R	RBI	GW	TBB	IBB	SO	HBP	SH	SF	SB	CS	SB%	GDP	Avg	OBP	SLG	Pos	G	PO	A	E	DP	FPct
1943 StL	29	1	3	0	0	0	0	0	0	0	0	0	0	1	0	0	0	0	0	—	0	.000	.000	.000	P	1	1	2	0	0	1.000
1946 StL	32	1	2	0	0	0	0	0	0	0	0	0	0	0	0	0	0	0	0	—	0	.000	.000	.000	P	1	0	1	0	0	1.000
WS Totals		2	5	0	0	0	0	0	0	0	0	0	0	1	0	0	0	0	0	—	0	.000	.000	.000	P	2	1	3	0	0	1.000

SID BREAM—Sidney Eugene Bream—Bats: Left; Throws: Left

Ht: 6'4"; Wt: 215 lbs; Born: 8/3/1960 in Carlisle, Pennsylvania; Debut: 9/1/1983

LCS		Batting																							Fielding						
Year Tm	Age	G	AB	H	2B	3B	HR	TB	R	RBI	GW	TBB	IBB	SO	HBP	SH	SF	SB	CS	SB%	GDP	Avg	OBP	SLG	Pos	G	PO	A	E	DP	FPct
1990 Pit	30	4	8	4	1	0	1	8	1	3	0	2	0	3	0	0	0	0	0	—	0	.500	.600	1.000	1B	4	26	3	0	3	1.000
1991 Atl	31	4	10	3	0	0	1	6	1	3	0	0	0	1	0	0	0	0	0	—	0	.300	.300	.600	1B	4	19	3	0	2	1.000
1992 Atl	32	7	22	6	3	0	1	12	5	2	0	3	0	0	0	0	0	0	0	—	0	.273	.360	.545	1B	7	53	3	0	3	1.000
1993 Atl	33	1	1	1	0	0	0	1	1	0	0	0	0	0	0	0	0	0	0	—	0	1.000	1.000	1.000	1B	1	1	0	0	0	1.000
LCS Totals		16	41	14	4	0	3	27	8	8	0	5	0	4	0	0	0	0	0	—	0	.341	.413	.659	1B	16	99	9	0	8	1.000
World Series		Batting																							Fielding						
Year Tm	Age	G	AB	H	2B	3B	HR	TB	R	RBI	GW	TBB	IBB	SO	HBP	SH	SF	SB	CS	SB%	GDP	Avg	OBP	SLG	Pos	G	PO	A	E	DP	FPct
1991 Atl	31	7	24	3	2	0	0	5	0	0	0	3	0	4	0	0	0	0	0	—	1	.125	.222	.208	1B	7	69	7	0	6	1.000
1992 Atl	32	5	15	3	0	0	0	3	1	0	0	4	0	0	0	0	0	0	0	—	0	.200	.368	.200	1B	5	41	1	1	4	.977
WS Totals		12	39	6	2	0	0	8	1	0	0	7	0	4	0	0	0	0	0	—	1	.154	.283	.205	1B	12	110	8	1	10	.992
Postseason Totals		28	80	20	6	0	3	35	9	8	0	12	0	8	0	0	0	0	0	—	1	.250	.348	.438	1B	28	209	17	1	18	.996

HARRY BRECHEEN—Harry David Brecheen—Nickname: Harry the Cat—Throws: Left; Bats: Left

Ht: 5'10"; Wt: 160 lbs; Born: 10/14/1914 in Broken Bow, Oklahoma; Debut: 4/22/1940

World Series		Pitching																										
Year Tm	Age	G	GS	CG	GF	IP	BFP	H	R	ER	HR	SH	SF	HB	TBB	IBB	SO	WP	Bk	W	L	Pct	ShO	Sv-Op	Hld	OAvg	OOBP	ERA
1943 StL	28	3	0	0	3	3.2	17	5	1	1	0	1	0	0	3	2	3	0	0	0	1	.000	0	0-0	0	.385	.500	2.45
1944 StL	29	1	1	1	0	9.0	38	9	1	1	0	0	0	0	4	0	4	0	0	1	0	1.000	0	0-0	0	.265	.342	1.00
1946 StL	31	3	2	2	1	20.0	74	14	1	1	0	0	0	0	5	1	11	0	0	3	0	1.000	1	0-1	0	.203	.257	0.45
WS Totals		7	3	3	4	32.2	258	28	3	3	0	1	0	0	12	3	18	0	0	4	1	.800	1	0-1	0	.241	.313	0.83

World Series		Batting																							Fielding						
Year Tm	Age	G	AB	H	2B	3B	HR	TB	R	RBI	GW	TBB	IBB	SO	HBP	SH	SF	SB	CS	SB%	GDP	Avg	OBP	SLG	Pos	G	PO	A	E	DP	FPct
1943 StL	28	3	0	0	0	0	0	0	0	0	0	0	0	0	0	0	0	0	0	—	0	—	—	—	P	3	0	2	0	0	1.000
1944 StL	29	1	4	0	0	0	0	0	0	0	0	0	0	1	0	0	0	0	0	—	0	.000	.000	.000	P	1	1	3	0	0	1.000
1946 StL	31	3	8	1	0	0	0	1	2	1	1	0	0	1	0	0	0	0	0	—	0	.125	.125	.125	P	3	0	2	0	1	1.000
WS Totals		7	12	1	0	0	0	1	2	1	1	0	0	2	0	0	0	0	0	—	0	.083	.083	.083	P	7	1	7	0	1	1.000

BOB BRENLY—Robert Earl Brenly—Bats: Right; Throws: Right

Ht: 6'2"; Wt: 210 lbs; Born: 2/25/1954 in Coshocton, Ohio; Debut: 8/14/1981

LCS		Batting																							Fielding						
Year Tm	Age	G	AB	H	2B	3B	HR	TB	R	RBI	GW	TBB	IBB	SO	HBP	SH	SF	SB	CS	SB%	GDP	Avg	OBP	SLG	Pos	G	PO	A	E	DP	FPct
1987 SF	33	6	17	4	1	0	1	8	3	2	0	3	0	7	0	0	0	0	0	—	0	.235	.350	.471	C	6	28	2	0	0	1.000

DON BRENNAN—James Donald Brennan—Throws: Right; Bats: Right

Ht: 6'0"; Wt: 210 lbs; Born: 12/2/1903 in Augusta, Maine; Debut: 4/16/1933; Died: 4/26/1953

World Series		Pitching																										
Year Tm	Age	G	GS	CG	GF	IP	BFP	H	R	ER	HR	SH	SF	HB	TBB	IBB	SO	WP	Bk	W	L	Pct	ShO	Sv-Op	Hld	OAvg	OOBP	ERA
1937 NYG	33	2	0	0	2	3.0	11	1	0	0	0	1	0	0	1	0	1	0	0	0	0	—	0	0-0	0	.111	.200	0.00

World Series		Batting																							Fielding						
Year Tm	Age	G	AB	H	2B	3B	HR	TB	R	RBI	GW	TBB	IBB	SO	HBP	SH	SF	SB	CS	SB%	GDP	Avg	OBP	SLG	Pos	G	PO	A	E	DP	FPct
1937 NYG	33	2	0	0	0	0	0	0	0	0	0	0	0	0	0	0	0	0	0	—	0	—	—	—	P	2	0	0	0	0	—

ROGER BRESNAHAN (HOF 1945-V)—Roger Philip Bresnahan—Nickname: The Duke of Tralee—B: R; T: R

Ht: 5'9"; Wt: 200 lbs; Born: 6/11/1879 in Toledo, Ohio; Deb.: 8/27/1897; Died: 12/4/1944

World Series		Batting																							Fielding						
Year Tm	Age	G	AB	H	2B	3B	HR	TB	R	RBI	GW	TBB	IBB	SO	HBP	SH	SF	SB	CS	SB%	GDP	Avg	OBP	SLG	Pos	G	PO	A	E	DP	FPct
1905 NYG	26	5	16	5	2	0	0	7	3	1	0	4	1	0	2	0	0	1	0	1.00	0	.313	.500	.438	C	5	27	8	1	1	.972

EDDIE BRESSOUD—Edward Francis Bressoud—Bats: Right; Throws: Right

Ht: 6'1"; Wt: 175 lbs; Born: 5/2/1932 in Los Angeles, California; Debut: 6/14/1956

World Series		Batting																							Fielding						
Year Tm	Age	G	AB	H	2B	3B	HR	TB	R	RBI	GW	TBB	IBB	SO	HBP	SH	SF	SB	CS	SB%	GDP	Avg	OBP	SLG	Pos	G	PO	A	E	DP	FPct
1967 StL	35	2	0	0	0	0	0	0	0	0	0	0	0	0	0	0	0	0	0	—	0	—	—	—	SS	2	0	0	0	0	—

GEORGE BRETT—George Howard Brett—Bats: Left; Throws: Right

Ht: 6'0"; Wt: 185 lbs; Born: 5/15/1953 in Glen Dale, West Virginia; Debut: 8/2/1973

Division Series		Batting																							Fielding						
Year Tm	Age	G	AB	H	2B	3B	HR	TB	R	RBI	GW	TBB	IBB	SO	HBP	SH	SF	SB	CS	SB%	GDP	Avg	OBP	SLG	Pos	G	PO	A	E	DP	FPct
1981 KC	28	3	12	2	0	0	0	2	0	0	0	0	0	0	0	0	0	0	0	—	0	.167	.167	.167	3B	3	1	6	1	0	.875
LCS		Batting																							Fielding						
Year Tm	Age	G	AB	H	2B	3B	HR	TB	R	RBI	GW	TBB	IBB	SO	HBP	SH	SF	SB	CS	SB%	GDP	Avg	OBP	SLG	Pos	G	PO	A	E	DP	FPct
1976 KC	23	5	18	8	1	1	1	14	4	5	0	2	0	1	0	0	1	0	1	.00	1	.444	.476	.778	3B	5	3	7	3	1	.769
1977 KC	24	5	20	6	0	2	0	10	2	2	0	1	0	0	0	0	0	0	1	.00	0	.300	.333	.500	3B	5	5	12	2	2	.895
1978 KC	25	4	18	7	1	1	3	19	7	3	0	0	0	1	0	0	0	0	0	—	0	.389	.389	1.056	3B	4	3	8	1	1	.917
1980 KC-*M*	27	3	11	3	1	0	2	10	3	4	1	1	0	0	0	0	0	0	0	—	1	.273	.333	.909	3B	3	2	7	0	0	1.000
1984 KC	31	3	13	3	0	0	0	3	0	0	0	0	0	2	0	0	0	0	0	—	0	.231	.231	.231	3B	3	2	7	0	1	1.000
1985 KC	32	7	23	8	2	0	3	19	6	5	2	7	3	5	0	0	0	0	1	.00	0	.348	.500	.826	3B	7	7	8	2	1	.882
LCS Totals		27	103	35	5	4	9	75	22	19	3	11	3	9	0	0	1	0	3	.00	2	.340	.400	.728	3B	27	22	49	8	6	.899
World Series		Batting																							Fielding						
Year Tm	Age	G	AB	H	2B	3B	HR	TB	R	RBI	GW	TBB	IBB	SO	HBP	SH	SF	SB	CS	SB%	GDP	Avg	OBP	SLG	Pos	G	PO	A	E	DP	FPct
1980 KC-*M*	27	6	24	9	2	1	1	16	3	3	1	2	1	4	0	0	0	1	0	1.00	1	.375	.423	.667	3B	6	4	17	1	1	.955
1985 KC	32	7	27	10	1	0	0	11	5	1	0	4	2	7	0	0	0	1	0	1.00	1	.370	.452	.407	3B	7	10	19	1	1	.967
WS Totals		13	51	19	3	1	1	27	8	4	1	6	3	11	0	0	0	2	0	1.00	2	.373	.439	.529	3B	13	14	36	2	2	.962
Postseason Totals		43	166	56	8	5	10	104	30	23	4	17	6	20	0	0	1	2	3	.40	4	.337	.397	.627	3B	43	37	91	11	8	.921

KEN BRETT—Kenneth Alven Brett—Throws: Left; Bats: Left

Ht: 6'0"; Wt: 190 lbs; Born: 9/18/1948 in Brooklyn, New York; Debut: 9/27/1967

LCS		Pitching																										
Year Tm	Age	G	GS	CG	GF	IP	BFP	H	R	ER	HR	SH	SF	HB	TBB	IBB	SO	WP	Bk	W	L	Pct	ShO	Sv-Op	Hld	OAvg	OOBP	ERA
1974 Pit	26	1	0	0	0	2.1	11	3	2	2	1	0	0	0	2	0	1	0	0	0	0	—	0	0-0	0	.333	.455	7.71
1975 Pit	27	2	0	0	0	2.1	7	1	0	0	0	0	0	0	0	0	1	0	1	0	0	—	0	0-0	0	.143	.143	0.00
LCS Totals		3	0	0	0	4.2	36	4	2	2	1	0	0	0	2	0	2	0	1	0	0	—	0	0-0	0	.250	.333	3.86
World Series		Pitching																										
Year Tm	Age	G	GS	CG	GF	IP	BFP	H	R	ER	HR	SH	SF	HB	TBB	IBB	SO	WP	Bk	W	L	Pct	ShO	Sv-Op	Hld	OAvg	OOBP	ERA
1967 Bos	19	2	0	0	2	1.1	5	0	0	0	0	0	0	0	1	0	1	0	0	0	0	—	0	0-0	0	.000	.200	0.00
Postseason Totals		5	0	0	2	6.0	46	4	2	2	1	0	0	0	3	0	3	0	1	0	0	—	0	0-0	0	.200	.304	3.00

LCS		Batting																							Fielding						
Year Tm	Age	G	AB	H	2B	3B	HR	TB	R	RBI	GW	TBB	IBB	SO	HBP	SH	SF	SB	CS	SB%	GDP	Avg	OBP	SLG	Pos	G	PO	A	E	DP	FPct
1974 Pit	26	1	1	0	0	0	0	0	0	0	0	0	0	1	0	0	0	0	0	—	0	.000	.000	.000	P	1	0	1	0	0	1.000
1975 Pit	27	2	0	0	0	0	0	0	0	0	0	0	0	0	0	0	0	0	0	—	0	—	—	—	P	2	0	0	0	0	—
LCS Totals		3	1	0	0	0	0	0	0	0	0	0	0	1	0	0	0	0	0	—	0	.000	.000	.000	P	3	0	1	0	0	1.000
World Series		Batting																							Fielding						
Year Tm	Age	G	AB	H	2B	3B	HR	TB	R	RBI	GW	TBB	IBB	SO	HBP	SH	SF	SB	CS	SB%	GDP	Avg	OBP	SLG	Pos	G	PO	A	E	DP	FPct
1967 Bos	19	2	0	0	0	0	0	0	0	0	0	0	0	0	0	0	0	0	0	—	0	—	—	—	P	2	0	0	0	0	—
Postseason Totals		5	1	0	0	0	0	0	0	0	0	0	0	1	0	0	0	0	0	—	0	.000	.000	.000	P	5	0	1	0	0	1.000

MARV BREUER—Marvin Howard Breuer—Nickname: Baby Face—Throws: Right; Bats: Right

Ht: 6'2"; Wt: 185 lbs; Born: 4/29/1914 in Rolla, Missouri; Debut: 5/4/1939; Died: 1/17/1991

World Series		Pitching																										
Year Tm	Age	G	GS	CG	GF	IP	BFP	H	R	ER	HR	SH	SF	HB	TBB	IBB	SO	WP	Bk	W	L	Pct	ShO	Sv-Op	Hld	OAvg	OOBP	ERA
1941 NYA	27	1	0	0	0	3.0	12	3	0	0	0	0	0	0	1	0	2	0	0	0	0	—	0	0-0	0	.273	.333	0.00
1942 NYA	28	1	0	0	0	0.0	3	2	1	0	0	0	0	0	0	0	0	0	0	0	0	—	0	0-0	0	.667	.667	—
WS Totals		2	0	0	0	3.0	30	5	1	0	0	0	0	0	1	0	2	0	0	0	0	—	0	0-0	0	.357	.400	0.00

World Series		Batting																							Fielding						
Year Tm	Age	G	AB	H	2B	3B	HR	TB	R	RBI	GW	TBB	IBB	SO	HBP	SH	SF	SB	CS	SB%	GDP	Avg	OBP	SLG	Pos	G	PO	A	E	DP	FPct
1941 NYA	27	1	1	0	0	0	0	0	0	0	0	0	0	0	0	0	0	0	0	—	0	.000	.000	.000	P	1	0	1	0	0	1.000
1942 NYA	28	1	0	0	0	0	0	0	0	0	0	0	0	0	0	0	0	0	0	—	0	—	—	—	P	1	0	0	1	0	.000
WS Totals		2	1	0	0	0	0	0	0	0	0	0	0	0	0	0	0	0	0	—	0	.000	.000	.000	P	2	0	1	1	0	.500

JIM BREWER—James Thomas Brewer—Throws: Left; Bats: Left

Ht: 6'1"; Wt: 186 lbs; Born: 11/14/1937 in Merced, California; Debut: 7/17/1960; Died: 11/16/1987

World Series		Pitching																										
Year Tm	Age	G	GS	CG	GF	IP	BFP	H	R	ER	HR	SH	SF	HB	TBB	IBB	SO	WP	Bk	W	L	Pct	ShO	Sv-Op	Hld	OAvg	OOBP	ERA
1965 LA	27	1	0	0	0	2.0	9	3	1	1	0	0	0	0	0	0	1	1	0	0	0	—	0	0-0	0	.333	.333	4.50
1966 LA	28	1	0	0	1	1.0	3	0	0	0	0	0	0	0	0	0	1	0	0	0	0	—	0	0-0	0	.000	.000	0.00
1974 LA	36	1	0	0	0	0.1	1	0	0	0	0	0	0	0	0	0	1	0	0	0	0	—	0	0-0	0	.000	.000	0.00
WS Totals		3	0	0	1	3.1	26	3	1	1	0	0	0	0	0	0	3	1	0	0	0	—	0	0-0	0	.231	.231	2.70

World Series		Batting																							Fielding						
Year Tm	Age	G	AB	H	2B	3B	HR	TB	R	RBI	GW	TBB	IBB	SO	HBP	SH	SF	SB	CS	SB%	GDP	Avg	OBP	SLG	Pos	G	PO	A	E	DP	FPct
1965 LA	27	1	0	0	0	0	0	0	0	0	0	0	0	0	0	0	0	0	0	—	0	—	—	—	P	1	0	0	0	0	—
1966 LA	28	1	0	0	0	0	0	0	0	0	0	0	0	0	0	0	0	0	0	—	0	—	—	—	P	1	0	0	0	0	—
1974 LA	36	1	0	0	0	0	0	0	0	0	0	0	0	0	0	0	0	0	0	—	0	—	—	—	P	1	0	0	0	0	—
WS Totals		3	0	0	0	0	0	0	0	0	0	0	0	0	0	0	0	0	0	—	0	—	—	—	P	3	0	0	0	0	—

GEORGE BRICKELL—George Frederick Brickell—Bats: Left; Throws: Right

Ht: 5'7"; Wt: 160 lbs; Born: 11/9/1906 in Saffordville, Kansas; Debut: 8/19/1926; Died: 4/8/1961

World Series		Batting																							Fielding						
Year Tm	Age	G	AB	H	2B	3B	HR	TB	R	RBI	GW	TBB	IBB	SO	HBP	SH	SF	SB	CS	SB%	GDP	Avg	OBP	SLG	Pos	G	PO	A	E	DP	FPct
1927 Pit	20	2	2	0	0	0	0	0	1	0	0	0	0	0	0	0	0	0	0	—	0	.000	.000	.000	—						

MARSHALL BRIDGES—Nickname: Sherriff—Throws: Left; Bats: Both

Ht: 6'1"; Wt: 165 lbs; Born: 6/2/1931 in Jackson, Mississippi; Debut: 6/17/1959; Died: 9/3/1990

World Series		Pitching																										
Year Tm	Age	G	GS	CG	GF	IP	BFP	H	R	ER	HR	SH	SF	HB	TBB	IBB	SO	WP	Bk	W	L	Pct	ShO	Sv-Op	Hld	OAvg	OOBP	ERA
1962 NYA	31	2	0	0	2	3.2	17	4	3	2	1	1	0	0	2	1	3	0	0	0	0	—	0	0-0	0	.286	.375	4.91

World Series		Batting																							Fielding						
Year Tm	Age	G	AB	H	2B	3B	HR	TB	R	RBI	GW	TBB	IBB	SO	HBP	SH	SF	SB	CS	SB%	GDP	Avg	OBP	SLG	Pos	G	PO	A	E	DP	FPct
1962 NYA	31	2	0	0	0	0	0	0	0	0	0	0	0	0	0	0	0	0	0	—	0	—	—	—	P	2	0	1	0	0	1.000

TOMMY BRIDGES—Thomas Jefferson Davis Bridges—Throws: Right; Bats: Right

Ht: 5'10"; Wt: 155 lbs; Born: 12/28/1906 in Gordonsville, Tennessee; Debut: 8/13/1930; Died: 4/19/1968

World Series		Pitching																										
Year Tm	Age	G	GS	CG	GF	IP	BFP	H	R	ER	HR	SH	SF	HB	TBB	IBB	SO	WP	Bk	W	L	Pct	ShO	Sv-Op	Hld	OAvg	OOBP	ERA
1934 Det	27	3	2	1	0	17.1	75	21	9	7	1	0	0	1	1	0	12	1	0	1	1	.500	0	0-0	0	.288	.307	3.63
1935 Det	28	2	2	2	0	18.0	74	18	6	5	1	0	0	0	4	0	9	0	0	2	0	1.000	0	0-0	0	.257	.297	2.50
1940 Det	33	1	1	1	0	9.0	38	10	4	3	0	0	0	0	1	0	5	0	0	1	0	1.000	0	0-0	0	.270	.289	3.00
1945 Det	38	1	0	0	0	1.2	10	3	3	3	0	0	0	0	3	0	1	0	0	0	0	—	0	0-0	0	.429	.600	16.20
WS Totals		7	5	4	0	46.0	394	52	22	18	2	0	0	1	9	0	27	1	0	4	1	.800	0	0-0	0	.278	.315	3.52

World Series		Batting																							Fielding						
Year Tm	Age	G	AB	H	2B	3B	HR	TB	R	RBI	GW	TBB	IBB	SO	HBP	SH	SF	SB	CS	SB%	GDP	Avg	OBP	SLG	Pos	G	PO	A	E	DP	FPct
1934 Det	27	3	7	1	0	0	0	1	0	0	0	1	0	4	0	0	0	0	0	—	0	.143	.250	.143	P	3	0	2	0	0	1.000
1935 Det	28	2	8	1	0	0	0	1	1	1	0	0	0	3	0	0	0	0	0	—	0	.125	.125	.125	P	2	1	5	0	1	1.000
1940 Det	33	1	3	0	0	0	0	0	0	0	0	0	0	1	0	0	0	0	0	—	0	.000	.000	.000	P	1	0	1	0	0	1.000
1945 Det	38	1	0	0	0	0	0	0	0	0	0	0	0	0	0	0	0	0	0	—	0	—	—	—	P	1	0	0	0	0	—
WS Totals		7	18	2	0	0	0	2	1	1	0	1	0	8	0	0	0	0	0	—	0	.111	.158	.111	P	7	1	8	0	1	1.000

HARRY BRIGHT—Harry James Bright—Bats: Right; Throws: Right

Ht: 6'0"; Wt: 190 lbs; Born: 9/22/1929 in Kansas City, Missouri; Debut: 8/7/1958

World Series		Batting																							Fielding						
Year Tm	Age	G	AB	H	2B	3B	HR	TB	R	RBI	GW	TBB	IBB	SO	HBP	SH	SF	SB	CS	SB%	GDP	Avg	OBP	SLG	Pos	G	PO	A	E	DP	FPct
1963 NYA	34	2	2	0	0	0	0	0	0	0	0	0	0	2	0	0	0	0	0	—	0	.000	.000	.000	—						

NELSON BRILES—Nelson Kelley Briles—Throws: Right; Bats: Right

Ht: 5'11"; Wt: 195 lbs; Born: 8/5/1943 in Dorris, California; Debut: 4/19/1965

LCS		Pitching																										
Year Tm	Age	G	GS	CG	GF	IP	BFP	H	R	ER	HR	SH	SF	HB	TBB	IBB	SO	WP	Bk	W	L	Pct	ShO	Sv-Op	Hld	OAvg	OOBP	ERA
1972 Pit	29	1	1	0	0	6.0	23	6	2	2	0	0	0	0	1	0	3	0	0	0	0	—	0	0-0	0	.273	.304	3.00
World Series		Pitching																										
Year Tm	Age	G	GS	CG	GF	IP	BFP	H	R	ER	HR	SH	SF	HB	TBB	IBB	SO	WP	Bk	W	L	Pct	ShO	Sv-Op	Hld	OAvg	OOBP	ERA
1967 StL	24	2	1	1	0	11.0	41	7	2	2	1	1	0	2	1	1	4	0	0	1	0	1.000	0	0-0	0	.189	.250	1.64
1968 StL	25	2	2	0	0	11.1	50	13	7	7	3	0	1	0	4	1	7	0	0	0	1	.000	0	0-0	0	.289	.340	5.56
1971 Pit	28	1	1	1	0	9.0	29	2	0	0	0	0	0	0	2	0	2	0	0	1	0	1.000	1	0-0	0	.074	.138	0.00
WS Totals		5	4	2	0	31.1	240	22	9	9	4	1	1	2	7	2	13	0	0	2	1	.667	1	0-0	0	.202	.261	2.59
Postseason Totals		6	5	2	0	37.1	286	28	11	11	4	1	1	2	8	2	16	0	0	2	1	.667	1	0-0	0	.214	.268	2.65

LCS		Batting																							Fielding						
Year Tm	Age	G	AB	H	2B	3B	HR	TB	R	RBI	GW	TBB	IBB	SO	HBP	SH	SF	SB	CS	SB%	GDP	Avg	OBP	SLG	Pos	G	PO	A	E	DP	FPct
1972 Pit	29	1	2	0	0	0	0	0	0	0	0	0	0	1	0	0	0	0	0	—	0	.000	.000	.000	P	1	1	1	0	0	1.000
World Series		Batting																							Fielding						
Year Tm	Age	G	AB	H	2B	3B	HR	TB	R	RBI	GW	TBB	IBB	SO	HBP	SH	SF	SB	CS	SB%	GDP	Avg	OBP	SLG	Pos	G	PO	A	E	DP	FPct
1967 StL	24	2	3	0	0	0	0	0	0	0	0	0	0	0	0	0	0	0	0	—	0	.000	.000	.000	P	2	0	4	0	0	1.000
1968 StL	25	2	4	0	0	0	0	0	0	0	0	0	0	4	1	0	0	0	0	—	0	.000	.200	.000	P	2	0	2	0	0	1.000
1971 Pit	28	1	2	1	0	0	0	1	0	1	0	0	0	1	0	2	0	0	0	—	0	.500	.500	.500	P	1	0	1	0	0	1.000
WS Totals		5	9	1	0	0	0	1	0	1	0	0	0	5	1	2	0	0	0	—	0	.111	.200	.111	P	5	0	7	0	0	1.000
Postseason Totals		6	11	1	0	0	0	1	0	1	0	0	0	6	1	2	0	0	0	—	0	.091	.167	.091	P	6	1	8	0	0	1.000

ED BRINKMAN—Edwin Albert Brinkman—Bats: Right; Throws: Right

Ht: 6'0"; Wt: 170 lbs; Born: 12/8/1941 in Cincinnati, Ohio; Debut: 9/6/1961

LCS		Batting																							Fielding						
Year Tm	Age	G	AB	H	2B	3B	HR	TB	R	RBI	GW	TBB	IBB	SO	HBP	SH	SF	SB	CS	SB%	GDP	Avg	OBP	SLG	Pos	G	PO	A	E	DP	FPct
1972 Det	30	1	4	1	1	0	0	2	0	0	0	0	0	0	0	0	0	0	0	—	0	.250	.250	.500	SS	1	1	5	0	0	1.000

JIM BRITTON—James Allan Britton—Throws: Right; Bats: Right

Ht: 6'5"; Wt: 225 lbs; Born: 3/25/1944 in North Tonawanda, New York; Debut: 9/20/1967

LCS		Pitching																										
Year Tm	Age	G	GS	CG	GF	IP	BFP	H	R	ER	HR	SH	SF	HB	TBB	IBB	SO	WP	Bk	W	L	Pct	ShO	Sv-Op	Hld	OAvg	OOBP	ERA
1969 Atl	25	1	0	0	0	0.1	2	0	0	0	0	0	0	0	1	0	0	0	0	0	0	—	0	0-0	0	.000	.500	0.00

LCS		Batting																							Fielding						
Year Tm	Age	G	AB	H	2B	3B	HR	TB	R	RBI	GW	TBB	IBB	SO	HBP	SH	SF	SB	CS	SB%	GDP	Avg	OBP	SLG	Pos	G	PO	A	E	DP	FPct
1969 Atl	25	1	0	0	0	0	0	0	0	0	0	0	0	0	0	0	0	0	0	—	0	—	—	—	P	1	0	0	0	0	—

GREG BROCK—Gregory Allen Brock—Bats: Left; Throws: Right

Ht: 6'3"; Wt: 200 lbs; Born: 6/14/1957 in McMinnville, Oregon; Debut: 9/1/1982

LCS		Batting																							Fielding						
Year Tm	Age	G	AB	H	2B	3B	HR	TB	R	RBI	GW	TBB	IBB	SO	HBP	SH	SF	SB	CS	SB%	GDP	Avg	OBP	SLG	Pos	G	PO	A	E	DP	FPct
1983 LA	26	3	9	0	0	0	0	0	1	0	0	0	0	3	0	0	0	0	0	—	0	.000	.000	.000	1B	3	13	0	0	2	1.000
1985 LA	28	5	12	1	0	0	1	4	2	2	0	2	0	2	0	0	0	0	0	—	0	.083	.214	.333	1B	4	35	4	0	0	1.000
LCS Totals		8	21	1	0	0	1	4	3	2	0	2	0	5	0	0	0	0	0	—	0	.048	.130	.190	1B	7	48	4	0	2	1.000

LOU BROCK (HOF 1985-W)—Louis Clark Brock—Bats: Left; Throws: Left

Ht: 5'11"; Wt: 170 lbs; Born: 6/18/1939 in El Dorado, Arkansas; Debut: 9/10/1961

World Series — Batting / Fielding

Year Tm	Age	G	AB	H	2B	3B	HR	TB	R	RBI	GW	TBB	IBB	SO	HBP	SH	SF	SB	CS	SB%	GDP	Avg	OBP	SLG	Pos	G	PO	A	E	DP	FPct
1964 StL	25	7	30	9	2	0	1	14	2	5	0	0	0	3	0	0	0	0	0	—	0	.300	.300	.467	OF	7	8	1	1	0	.900
1967 StL	28	7	29	12	2	1	1	19	8	3	0	2	0	3	0	0	0	7	0	1.00	0	.414	.452	.655	OF	7	13	0	0	0	1.000
1968 StL	29	7	28	13	3	1	2	24	6	5	1	3	0	4	0	0	0	7	3	.70	0	.464	.516	.857	OF	7	14	0	1	0	.933
WS Totals		21	87	34	7	2	4	57	16	13	1	5	0	10	0	0	0	14	3	.82	0	.391	.424	.655	OF	21	35	1	2	0	.947

TOM BROOKENS—Thomas Dale Brookens—Bats: Right; Throws: Right

Ht: 5'10"; Wt: 165 lbs; Born: 8/10/1953 in Chambersburg, Pennsylvania; Debut: 7/10/1979

LCS — Batting / Fielding

Year Tm	Age	G	AB	H	2B	3B	HR	TB	R	RBI	GW	TBB	IBB	SO	HBP	SH	SF	SB	CS	SB%	GDP	Avg	OBP	SLG	Pos	G	PO	A	E	DP	FPct
1984 Det	31	2	2	0	0	0	0	0	0	0	0	0	0	1	0	0	0	0	0	—	0	.000	.000	.000	2B	1	0	0	0	0	—
																									3B	1	0	2	1	0	.667
1987 Det	34	5	13	0	0	0	0	0	0	0	0	0	0	3	0	1	0	0	0	—	0	.000	.000	.000	3B	5	3	15	0	0	1.000
LCS Totals		7	15	0	0	0	0	0	0	0	0	0	0	4	0	1	0	0	0	—	0	.000	.000	.000	3B	6	3	17	1	0	.952

World Series — Batting / Fielding

Year Tm	Age	G	AB	H	2B	3B	HR	TB	R	RBI	GW	TBB	IBB	SO	HBP	SH	SF	SB	CS	SB%	GDP	Avg	OBP	SLG	Pos	G	PO	A	E	DP	FPct
1984 Det	31	3	3	0	0	0	0	0	0	0	0	0	0	1	0	0	0	0	0	—	0	.000	.000	.000	3B	3	0	3	0	0	1.000
Postseason Totals		10	18	0	0	0	0	0	0	0	0	0	0	5	0	1	0	0	0	—	0	.000	.000	.000	3B	9	3	20	1	0	.958

JIM BROSNAN—James Patrick Brosnan—Nickname: Professor—Throws: Right; Bats: Right

Ht: 6'4"; Wt: 197 lbs; Born: 10/24/1929 in Cincinnati, Ohio; Debut: 4/15/1954

World Series — Pitching

Year Tm	Age	G	GS	CG	GF	IP	BFP	H	R	ER	HR	SH	SF	HB	TBB	IBB	SO	WP	Bk	W	L	Pct	ShO	Sv-Op	Hld	OAvg	OOBP	ERA
1961 Cin	31	3	0	0	1	6.0	29	9	5	5	0	1	0	0	4	3	5	2	0	0	0	—	0	0-0	0	.375	.464	7.50

World Series — Batting / Fielding

Year Tm	Age	G	AB	H	2B	3B	HR	TB	R	RBI	GW	TBB	IBB	SO	HBP	SH	SF	SB	CS	SB%	GDP	Avg	OBP	SLG	Pos	G	PO	A	E	DP	FPct
1961 Cin	31	3	0	0	0	0	0	0	0	0	0	0	0	0	0	0	0	0	0	—	0	—	—	—	P	3	0	0	0	0	—

MARK BROUHARD—Mark Steven Brouhard—Bats: Right; Throws: Right

Ht: 6'1"; Wt: 210 lbs; Born: 5/22/1956 in Burbank, California; Debut: 4/12/1980

LCS — Batting / Fielding

Year Tm	Age	G	AB	H	2B	3B	HR	TB	R	RBI	GW	TBB	IBB	SO	HBP	SH	SF	SB	CS	SB%	GDP	Avg	OBP	SLG	Pos	G	PO	A	E	DP	FPct
1982 Mil	26	1	4	3	1	0	1	7	4	3	1	0	0	0	0	0	0	0	0	—	0	.750	.750	1.750	OF	1	1	0	0	0	1.000

BOBBY BROWN—Robert William Brown—Nickname: Doc—Bats: Left; Throws: Right

Ht: 6'1"; Wt: 180 lbs; Born: 10/25/1924 in Seattle, Washington; Debut: 9/22/1946

World Series — Batting / Fielding

Year Tm	Age	G	AB	H	2B	3B	HR	TB	R	RBI	GW	TBB	IBB	SO	HBP	SH	SF	SB	CS	SB%	GDP	Avg	OBP	SLG	Pos	G	PO	A	E	DP	FPct
1947 NYA	22	4	3	3	2	0	0	5	2	3	0	1	0	0	0	0	0	0	0	—	0	1.000	1.000	1.667	—						
1949 NYA	24	4	12	6	1	2	0	11	4	5	0	2	0	2	0	0	0	0	0	—	0	.500	.571	.917	3B	3	0	6	0	0	1.000
1950 NYA	25	4	12	4	1	1	0	7	2	1	0	0	0	0	0	0	0	0	0	—	0	.333	.333	.583	3B	3	0	1	1	0	.500
1951 NYA	26	5	14	5	1	0	0	6	1	0	0	2	0	1	0	0	0	0	0	—	0	.357	.438	.429	3B	4	1	8	0	0	1.000
WS Totals		17	41	18	5	3	0	29	9	9	0	5	0	3	0	0	0	0	0	—	0	.439	.500	.707	3B	10	1	15	1	0	.941

BOBBY BROWN—Rogers Lee Brown—Bats: Both; Throws: Right

Ht: 6'2"; Wt: 190 lbs; Born: 5/25/1954 in Norfolk, Virginia; Debut: 4/5/1979

Division Series — Batting / Fielding

Year Tm	Age	G	AB	H	2B	3B	HR	TB	R	RBI	GW	TBB	IBB	SO	HBP	SH	SF	SB	CS	SB%	GDP	Avg	OBP	SLG	Pos	G	PO	A	E	DP	FPct
1981 NYA	27	1	0	0	0	0	0	0	0	0	0	0	0	0	0	0	0	0	0	—	0	—	—	—	—						

LCS — Batting / Fielding

Year Tm	Age	G	AB	H	2B	3B	HR	TB	R	RBI	GW	TBB	IBB	SO	HBP	SH	SF	SB	CS	SB%	GDP	Avg	OBP	SLG	Pos	G	PO	A	E	DP	FPct
1980 NYA	26	3	10	0	0	0	0	0	1	0	0	1	0	2	0	0	0	0	0	—	0	.000	.091	.000	OF	3	7	0	0	0	1.000
1981 NYA	27	3	1	1	0	0	0	1	2	0	0	0	0	0	0	0	0	0	0	—	0	1.000	1.000	1.000	OF	2	0	0	0	0	—
1984 SD	30	3	4	0	0	0	0	0	1	0	0	1	0	2	0	0	0	1	0	1.00	0	.000	.200	.000	OF	1	3	0	0	0	1.000
LCS Totals		9	15	1	0	0	0	1	4	0	0	2	0	4	0	0	0	1	0	1.00	0	.067	.176	.067	OF	6	10	0	0	0	1.000

World Series — Batting / Fielding

Year Tm	Age	G	AB	H	2B	3B	HR	TB	R	RBI	GW	TBB	IBB	SO	HBP	SH	SF	SB	CS	SB%	GDP	Avg	OBP	SLG	Pos	G	PO	A	E	DP	FPct
1981 NYA	27	4	1	0	0	0	0	0	1	0	0	0	0	1	0	0	0	0	0	—	0	.000	.000	.000	OF	2	1	0	0	0	1.000
1984 SD	30	5	15	1	0	0	0	1	1	2	0	0	0	4	0	0	1	0	0	—	0	.067	.063	.067	OF	5	13	0	0	0	1.000
WS Totals		9	16	1	0	0	0	1	2	2	0	0	0	5	0	0	1	0	0	—	0	.063	.059	.063	OF	7	14	0	0	0	1.000
Postseason Totals		19	31	2	0	0	0	2	6	2	0	2	0	9	0	0	1	1	0	1.00	0	.065	.118	.065	OF	13	24	0	0	0	1.000

GATES BROWN—William James Brown—Bats: Left; Throws: Right

Ht: 5'11"; Wt: 220 lbs; Born: 5/2/1939 in Crestline, Ohio; Debut: 6/19/1963

LCS — Batting / Fielding

Year Tm	Age	G	AB	H	2B	3B	HR	TB	R	RBI	GW	TBB	IBB	SO	HBP	SH	SF	SB	CS	SB%	GDP	Avg	OBP	SLG	Pos	G	PO	A	E	DP	FPct
1972 Det	33	3	2	0	0	0	0	0	1	0	0	1	0	0	0	0	0	0	0	—	0	.000	.333	.000	—						

World Series — Batting / Fielding

Year Tm	Age	G	AB	H	2B	3B	HR	TB	R	RBI	GW	TBB	IBB	SO	HBP	SH	SF	SB	CS	SB%	GDP	Avg	OBP	SLG	Pos	G	PO	A	E	DP	FPct
1968 Det	29	1	1	0	0	0	0	0	0	0	0	0	0	0	0	0	0	0	0	—	0	.000	.000	.000	—						
Postseason Totals		4	3	0	0	0	0	0	1	0	0	1	0	0	0	0	0	0	0	—	0	.000	.250	.000	—	0	0	0	0	0	—

IKE BROWN—Isaac Brown—Bats: Right; Throws: Right

Ht: 6'0"; Wt: 190 lbs; Born: 4/13/1942 in Memphis, Tennessee; Debut: 6/17/1969

LCS — Batting / Fielding

Year Tm	Age	G	AB	H	2B	3B	HR	TB	R	RBI	GW	TBB	IBB	SO	HBP	SH	SF	SB	CS	SB%	GDP	Avg	OBP	SLG	Pos	G	PO	A	E	DP	FPct
1972 Det	30	1	2	1	0	0	0	1	0	2	1	0	0	1	0	0	0	0	0	—	0	.500	.500	.500	1B	1	2	0	0	0	1.000

JARVIS BROWN—Jarvis Ardel Brown—Bats: Right; Throws: Right

Ht: 5'7"; Wt: 165 lbs; Born: 3/26/1967 in Waukegan, Illinois; Debut: 7/2/1991

LCS — Batting / Fielding

Year Tm	Age	G	AB	H	2B	3B	HR	TB	R	RBI	GW	TBB	IBB	SO	HBP	SH	SF	SB	CS	SB%	GDP	Avg	OBP	SLG	Pos	G	PO	A	E	DP	FPct
1991 Min	24	1	0	0	0	0	0	0	1	0	0	0	0	0	0	0	0	0	0	—	0	—	—	—	—						

World Series — Batting / Fielding

Year Tm	Age	G	AB	H	2B	3B	HR	TB	R	RBI	GW	TBB	IBB	SO	HBP	SH	SF	SB	CS	SB%	GDP	Avg	OBP	SLG	Pos	G	PO	A	E	DP	FPct
1991 Min	24	3	2	0	0	0	0	0	0	0	0	0	0	0	0	0	0	0	0	—	0	.000	.000	.000	OF	2	0	0	0	0	—
Postseason Totals		4	2	0	0	0	0	0	1	0	0	0	0	0	0	0	0	0	0	—	0	.000	.000	.000	OF	2	0	0	0	0	—

JIMMY BROWN—James Robertson Brown—Bats: Both; Throws: Right

Ht: 5'8"; Wt: 165 lbs; Born: 4/25/1910 in Jamesville, North Carolina; Debut: 4/23/1937; Died: 12/29/1977

World Series — Batting / Fielding

Year Tm	Age	G	AB	H	2B	3B	HR	TB	R	RBI	GW	TBB	IBB	SO	HBP	SH	SF	SB	CS	SB%	GDP	Avg	OBP	SLG	Pos	G	PO	A	E	DP	FPct
1942 StL	32	5	20	6	0	0	0	6	2	1	1	3	0	0	0	0	0	0	0	—	0	.300	.391	.300	2B	5	6	16	3	3	.880

KEVIN BROWN—James Kevin Brown—Throws: Right; Bats: Right

Ht: 6'4"; Wt: 195 lbs; Born: 3/14/1965 in Milledgeville, Georgia; Debut: 9/30/1986

Division Series — Pitching

Year Tm	Age	G	GS	CG	GF	IP	BFP	H	R	ER	HR	SH	SF	HB	TBB	IBB	SO	WP	Bk	W	L	Pct	ShO	Sv-Op	Hld	OAvg	OOBP	ERA
1997 Fla	32	1	1	0	0	7.0	24	4	1	1	1	0	0	0	0	0	5	0	0	0	0	—	0	0-0	0	.167	.167	1.29

LCS — Pitching

Year Tm	Age	G	GS	CG	GF	IP	BFP	H	R	ER	HR	SH	SF	HB	TBB	IBB	SO	WP	Bk	W	L	Pct	ShO	Sv-Op	Hld	OAvg	OOBP	ERA
1997 Fla	32	2	2	1	0	15.0	66	16	7	7	2	2	0	1	5	0	11	0	0	2	0	1.000	0	0-0	0	.276	.344	4.20

World Series — Pitching

Year Tm	Age	G	GS	CG	GF	IP	BFP	H	R	ER	HR	SH	SF	HB	TBB	IBB	SO	WP	Bk	W	L	Pct	ShO	Sv-Op	Hld	OAvg	OOBP	ERA
1997 Fla	32	2	2	0	0	11.0	48	15	10	10	1	1	2	0	5	0	6	0	0	0	2	.000	0	0-0	0	.375	.426	8.18
Postseason Totals		5	5	1	0	33.0	276	35	18	18	4	3	2	1	10	0	22	0	0	2	2	.500	0	0-0	0	.287	.341	4.91

Division Series

Year Tm	Age	G	AB	H	2B	3B	HR	TB	R	RBI	GW	TBB	IBB	SO	HBP	SH	SF	SB	CS	SB%	GDP	Avg	OBP	SLG	Pos	G	PO	A	E	DP	FPct
1997 Fla	32	1	2	0	0	0	0	0	0	0	0	0	0	2	0	0	0	0	0	—	0	.000	.000	.000	P	1	2	1	0	0	1.000

LCS

Year Tm	Age	G	AB	H	2B	3B	HR	TB	R	RBI	GW	TBB	IBB	SO	HBP	SH	SF	SB	CS	SB%	GDP	Avg	OBP	SLG	Pos	G	PO	A	E	DP	FPct
1997 Fla	32	2	6	0	0	0	0	0	0	0	0	0	0	3	0	2	0	0	0	—	0	.000	.000	.000	P	2	3	2	0	0	1.000

World Series

Year Tm	Age	G	AB	H	2B	3B	HR	TB	R	RBI	GW	TBB	IBB	SO	HBP	SH	SF	SB	CS	SB%	GDP	Avg	OBP	SLG	Pos	G	PO	A	E	DP	FPct
1997 Fla	32	2	3	0	0	0	0	0	0	0	0	0	0	1	0	0	0	0	0	—	0	.000	.000	.000	P	2	0	3	0	0	1.000
Postseason Totals		5	11	0	0	0	0	0	0	0	0	0	0	6	0	2	0	0	0	—	0	.000	.000	.000	P	5	5	6	0	0	1.000

LARRY BROWN—Larry Leslie Brown—Bats: Right; Throws: Right
Ht: 5'10"; Wt: 160 lbs; Born: 3/1/1940 in Shinnston, West Virginia; Debut: 7/6/1963

LCS

Year Tm	Age	G	AB	H	2B	3B	HR	TB	R	RBI	GW	TBB	IBB	SO	HBP	SH	SF	SB	CS	SB%	GDP	Avg	OBP	SLG	Pos	G	PO	A	E	DP	FPct
1973 Bal	33	1	0	0	0	0	0	0	0	0	0	0	0	0	0	0	0	0	0	—	0	—	—	—	3B	1	0	0	0	0	—

MACE BROWN—Mace Stanley Brown—Throws: Right; Bats: Right
Ht: 6'1"; Wt: 190 lbs; Born: 5/21/1909 in North English, Iowa; Debut: 5/21/1935

World Series

Year Tm	Age	G	GS	CG	GF	IP	BFP	H	R	ER	HR	SH	SF	HB	TBB	IBB	SO	WP	Bk	W	L	Pct	ShO	Sv-Op	Hld	OAvg	OOBP	ERA
1946 Bos	37	1	0	0	0	1.0	7	4	3	3	0	0	0	0	1	0	0	0	0	0	0	—	0	0-0	0	.667	.714	27.00

World Series

Year Tm	Age	G	AB	H	2B	3B	HR	TB	R	RBI	GW	TBB	IBB	SO	HBP	SH	SF	SB	CS	SB%	GDP	Avg	OBP	SLG	Pos	G	PO	A	E	DP	FPct
1946 Bos	37	1	0	0	0	0	0	0	0	0	0	0	0	0	0	0	0	0	0	—	0	—	—	—	P	1	0	0	0	0	—

OLLIE BROWN—Ollie Lee Brown—Nickname: Downtown—Bats: Right; Throws: Right
Ht: 6'2"; Wt: 178 lbs; Born: 2/11/1944 in Tuscaloosa, Alabama; Debut: 9/10/1965

LCS

Year Tm	Age	G	AB	H	2B	3B	HR	TB	R	RBI	GW	TBB	IBB	SO	HBP	SH	SF	SB	CS	SB%	GDP	Avg	OBP	SLG	Pos	G	PO	A	E	DP	FPct
1976 Phi	32	1	2	0	0	0	0	0	0	0	0	1	0	1	0	0	0	0	0	—	0	.000	.333	.000	OF	1	2	0	0	0	1.000
1977 Phi	33	2	2	0	0	0	0	0	0	0	0	0	0	1	0	0	0	0	0	—	0	.000	.000	.000	—						
LCS Totals		3	4	0	0	0	0	0	0	0	0	1	0	2	0	0	0	0	0	—	0	.000	.200	.000	OF	1	2	0	0	0	1.000

THREE FINGER BROWN (HOF 1949-V)—Mordecai Peter Centennial Brown—Throws: R; Bats: B
Ht: 5'10"; Wt: 175 lbs; Born: 10/19/1876 in Nyesville, Ind.; Debut: 4/19/1903; Died: 2/14/1948

World Series

Year Tm	Age	G	GS	CG	GF	IP	BFP	H	R	ER	HR	SH	SF	HB	TBB	IBB	SO	WP	Bk	W	L	Pct	ShO	Sv-Op	Hld	OAvg	OOBP	ERA
1906 ChN	29	3	3	2	0	19.2	76	14	9	8	0	2	0	0	4	0	12	1	0	1	2	.333	1	0-0	0	.200	.243	3.66
1907 ChN	30	1	1	1	0	9.0	34	7	0	0	0	0	0	0	1	0	4	0	0	1	0	1.000	1	0-0	0	.212	.235	0.00
1908 ChN	31	2	1	1	1	11.0	40	6	1	0	0	2	0	1	1	0	5	1	0	2	0	1.000	1	0-1	0	.167	.211	0.00
1910 ChN	33	3	2	1	1	18.0	86	23	16	10	0	2	0	0	7	0	14	1	0	1	2	.333	0	0-0	0	.299	.357	5.00
WS Totals		9	7	5	2	57.2	472	50	26	18	0	6	0	1	13	0	35	3	0	5	4	.556	3	0-1	0	.231	.278	2.81

World Series

Year Tm	Age	G	AB	H	2B	3B	HR	TB	R	RBI	GW	TBB	IBB	SO	HBP	SH	SF	SB	CS	SB%	GDP	Avg	OBP	SLG	Pos	G	PO	A	E	DP	FPct
1906 ChN	29	3	6	2	0	0	0	2	0	0	0	0	0	4	0	1	0	0	0	—	0	.333	.333	.333	P	3	1	11	1	0	.923
1907 ChN	30	1	3	0	0	0	0	0	0	0	0	0	0	1	0	0	0	0	0	—	0	.000	.250	.000	P	1	1	1	0	0	1.000
1908 ChN	31	2	4	0	0	0	0	0	0	0	0	0	0	2	0	1	0	0	0	—	0	.000	.000	.000	P	2	0	6	0	1	1.000
1910 ChN	33	3	7	0	0	0	0	0	0	0	0	0	0	1	0	0	0	0	0	—	0	.000	.000	.000	P	3	0	10	1	0	.909
WS Totals		9	20	2	0	0	0	2	0	0	0	0	0	7	0	2	0	0	0	—	0	.100	.143	.100	P	9	2	28	2	1	.938

TOMMY BROWN—Thomas Michael Brown—Nickname: Buckshot—Bats: Right; Throws: Right
Ht: 6'1"; Wt: 170 lbs; Born: 12/6/1927 in Brooklyn, New York; Debut: 8/3/1944

World Series

Year Tm	Age	G	AB	H	2B	3B	HR	TB	R	RBI	GW	TBB	IBB	SO	HBP	SH	SF	SB	CS	SB%	GDP	Avg	OBP	SLG	Pos	G	PO	A	E	DP	FPct
1949 Bro	21	2	2	0	0	0	0	0	0	0	0	0	0	1	0	0	0	0	0	—	0	.000	.000	.000	—						

GEORGE BROWNE—George Edward Browne—Bats: Left; Throws: Right
Ht: 5'10"; Wt: 160 lbs; Born: 1/12/1876 in Richmond, Virginia; Debut: 9/27/1901; Died: 12/9/1920

World Series

Year Tm	Age	G	AB	H	2B	3B	HR	TB	R	RBI	GW	TBB	IBB	SO	HBP	SH	SF	SB	CS	SB%	GDP	Avg	OBP	SLG	Pos	G	PO	A	E	DP	FPct
1905 NYG	29	5	22	4	0	0	0	4	2	1	0	0	0	2	0	0	0	2	0	1.00	0	.182	.182	.182	OF	5	3	0	0	0	1.000

JERRY BROWNE—Jerome Austin Browne—Bats: Both; Throws: Right
Ht: 5'10"; Wt: 140 lbs; Born: 2/13/1966 in Christiansted, Virgin Islands; Debut: 9/6/1986

LCS

Year Tm	Age	G	AB	H	2B	3B	HR	TB	R	RBI	GW	TBB	IBB	SO	HBP	SH	SF	SB	CS	SB%	GDP	Avg	OBP	SLG	Pos	G	PO	A	E	DP	FPct
1992 Oak	26	4	10	4	0	0	0	4	3	2	0	2	0	0	0	1	0	0	0	—	0	.400	.500	.400	3B	2	3	0	0	0	1.000
																									OF	1	3	0	0	0	1.000

TOM BROWNING—Thomas Leo Browning—Throws: Left; Bats: Left
Ht: 6'1"; Wt: 190 lbs; Born: 4/28/1960 in Casper, Wyoming; Debut: 9/9/1984

LCS

Year Tm	Age	G	GS	CG	GF	IP	BFP	H	R	ER	HR	SH	SF	HB	TBB	IBB	SO	WP	Bk	W	L	Pct	ShO	Sv-Op	Hld	OAvg	OOBP	ERA
1990 Cin	30	2	2	0	0	11.0	46	9	4	4	1	0	1	1	0	0	5	0	0	1	1	.500	0	0-0	0	.237	.348	3.27

World Series

Year Tm	Age	G	GS	CG	GF	IP	BFP	H	R	ER	HR	SH	SF	HB	TBB	IBB	SO	WP	Bk	W	L	Pct	ShO	Sv-Op	Hld	OAvg	OOBP	ERA
1990 Cin	30	1	1	0	0	6.0	26	6	3	3	2	0	0	0	2	0	2	0	0	1	0	1.000	0	0-0	0	.250	.308	4.50
Postseason Totals		3	3	0	0	17.0	144	15	7	7	3	0	1	1	8	0	7	0	0	2	1	.667	0	0-0	0	.242	.333	3.71

LCS

Year Tm	Age	G	AB	H	2B	3B	HR	TB	R	RBI	GW	TBB	IBB	SO	HBP	SH	SF	SB	CS	SB%	GDP	Avg	OBP	SLG	Pos	G	PO	A	E	DP	FPct
1990 Cin	30	2	3	0	0	0	0	0	0	0	0	0	0	0	0	1	0	0	0	—	0	.000	.000	.000	P	2	1	1	0	0	1.000

World Series

Year Tm	Age	G	AB	H	2B	3B	HR	TB	R	RBI	GW	TBB	IBB	SO	HBP	SH	SF	SB	CS	SB%	GDP	Avg	OBP	SLG	Pos	G	PO	A	E	DP	FPct
1990 Cin	30	1	0	0	0	0	0	0	0	0	0	0	0	0	0	0	0	0	0	—	0	—	—	—	P	1	0	0	0	0	—
Postseason Totals		3	3	0	0	0	0	0	0	0	0	0	0	0	0	1	0	0	0	—	0	.000	.000	.000	P	3	1	1	0	0	1.000

GLENN BRUMMER—Glenn Edward Brummer—Bats: Right; Throws: Right
Ht: 6'0"; Wt: 200 lbs; Born: 11/23/1954 in Olney, Illinois; Debut: 5/25/1981

World Series

Year Tm	Age	G	AB	H	2B	3B	HR	TB	R	RBI	GW	TBB	IBB	SO	HBP	SH	SF	SB	CS	SB%	GDP	Avg	OBP	SLG	Pos	G	PO	A	E	DP	FPct
1982 StL	27	1	0	0	0	0	0	0	0	0	0	0	0	0	0	0	0	0	0	—	0	—	—	—	C	1	0	0	0	0	—

TOM BRUNANSKY—Thomas Andrew Brunansky—Nickname: Bruno—Bats: Right; Throws: Right
Ht: 6'4"; Wt: 205 lbs; Born: 8/20/1960 in Covina, California; Debut: 4/9/1981

LCS

Year Tm	Age	G	AB	H	2B	3B	HR	TB	R	RBI	GW	TBB	IBB	SO	HBP	SH	SF	SB	CS	SB%	GDP	Avg	OBP	SLG	Pos	G	PO	A	E	DP	FPct
1987 Min	27	5	17	7	4	0	2	17	5	9	1	4	0	3	0	0	0	0	0	—	0	.412	.524	1.000	OF	5	10	0	0	0	1.000
1990 Bos	30	4	12	1	0	0	0	1	0	1	0	1	0	3	0	0	1	0	0	—	0	.083	.143	.083	OF	4	13	0	0	0	1.000
LCS Totals		9	29	8	4	0	2	18	5	10	1	5	0	6	0	0	1	0	0	—	0	.276	.371	.621	OF	9	23	0	0	0	1.000

World Series

Year Tm	Age	G	AB	H	2B	3B	HR	TB	R	RBI	GW	TBB	IBB	SO	HBP	SH	SF	SB	CS	SB%	GDP	Avg	OBP	SLG	Pos	G	PO	A	E	DP	FPct
1987 Min	27	7	25	5	0	0	0	5	5	2	0	4	1	4	0	0	1	1	0	1.00	0	.200	.310	.200	OF	7	14	0	0	0	1.000
Postseason Totals		16	54	13	4	0	2	23	10	12	1	9	1	10	0	0	1	1	0	1.00	0	.241	.344	.426	OF	16	37	0	0	0	1.000

JERRY BROWNE—Jerome Austin Browne—Bats: Both; Throws: Right
Ht: 5'10"; Wt: 140 lbs; Born: 2/13/1966 in Christiansted, Virgin Islands; Debut: 9/6/1986

LCS

Year Tm	Age	G	AB	H	2B	3B	HR	TB	R	RBI	GW	TBB	IBB	SO	HBP	SH	SF	SB	CS	SB%	GDP	Avg	OBP	SLG	Pos	G	PO	A	E	DP	FPct
1992 Oak	26	4	10	4	0	0	0	4	3	2	0	2	0	0	0	1	0	0	0	—	0	.400	.500	.400	3B	2	3	0	0	0	1.000
																									OF	1	3	0	0	0	1.000

WARREN BRUSSTAR—Warren Scott Brusstar—Throws: Right; Bats: Right

Ht: 6'3"; Wt: 200 lbs; Born: 2/2/1952 in Oakland, California; Debut: 5/6/1977

Division Series		Pitching																										
Year Tm	Age	G	GS	CG	GF	IP	BFP	H	R	ER	HR	SH	SF	HB	TBB	IBB	SO	WP	Bk	W	L	Pct	ShO	Sv-Op	Hld	OAvg	OOBP	ERA
1981 Phi	29	2	0	0	0	3.2	17	5	2	2	0	0	1	0	1	1	3	0	0	0	0	—	0	0- 0	0	.333	.353	4.91
LCS		Pitching																										
Year Tm	Age	G	GS	CG	GF	IP	BFP	H	R	ER	HR	SH	SF	HB	TBB	IBB	SO	WP	Bk	W	L	Pct	ShO	Sv-Op	Hld	OAvg	OOBP	ERA
1977 Phi	25	2	0	0	1	2.2	10	2	1	1	0	0	0	0	1	1	2	0	0	0	0	—	0	0- 0	0	.222	.300	3.38
1978 Phi	26	3	0	0	0	2.2	10	2	0	0	0	0	0	0	1	1	0	0	0	0	0	—	0	0- 0	0	.222	.300	0.00
1980 Phi	28	2	0	0	0	2.2	9	1	1	1	0	1	0	0	1	0	0	0	0	1	0	1.000	0	0- 1	0	.143	.250	3.38
1984 ChN	32	3	0	0	2	4.1	16	6	0	0	0	0	0	0	0	0	1	0	0	0	0	—	0	0- 0	0	.375	.375	0.00
LCS Totals		10	0	0	3	12.1	90	11	2	2	0	1	0	0	3	2	3	0	0	1	0	1.000	0	0-1	0	.268	.318	1.46
World Series		Pitching																										
Year Tm	Age	G	GS	CG	GF	IP	BFP	H	R	ER	HR	SH	SF	HB	TBB	IBB	SO	WP	Bk	W	L	Pct	ShO	Sv-Op	Hld	OAvg	OOBP	ERA
1980 Phi	28	1	0	0	1	2.1	8	0	0	0	0	0	0	0	1	0	0	0	0	0	0	—	0	0- 0	0	.000	.125	0.00
Postseason Totals		13	0	0	4	18.1	140	16	4	4	0	1	1	0	5	3	6	0	0	1	0	1.000	0	0-1	0	.254	.304	1.96

Division Series		Batting																							Fielding						
Year Tm	Age	G	AB	H	2B	3B	HR	TB	R	RBI	GW	TBB	IBB	SO	HBP	SH	SF	SB	CS	SB%	GDP	Avg	OBP	SLG	Pos	G	PO	A	E	DP	FPct
1981 Phi	29	2	0	0	0	0	0	0	0	0	0	0	0	0	0	0	0	0	0	—	0	—	—	—	P	2	0	0	0	0	—
LCS		Batting																							Fielding						
Year Tm	Age	G	AB	H	2B	3B	HR	TB	R	RBI	GW	TBB	IBB	SO	HBP	SH	SF	SB	CS	SB%	GDP	Avg	OBP	SLG	Pos	G	PO	A	E	DP	FPct
1977 Phi	25	2	0	0	0	0	0	0	0	0	0	0	0	0	0	0	0	0	0	—	0	—	—	—	P	2	0	0	0	0	—
1978 Phi	26	3	0	0	0	0	0	0	0	0	0	0	0	0	0	0	0	0	0	—	0	—	—	—	P	3	0	0	0	0	—
1980 Phi	28	2	1	0	0	0	0	0	0	0	0	0	0	1	0	0	0	0	0	—	0	.000	.000	.000	P	2	0	0	0	0	—
1984 ChN	32	3	1	0	0	0	0	0	0	0	0	0	0	0	0	0	0	0	0	—	0	.000	.000	.000	P	3	0	1	0	0	1.000
LCS Totals		10	2	0	0	0	0	0	0	0	0	0	0	1	0	0	0	0	0	—	0	.000	.000	.000	P	10	0	1	0	0	1.000
World Series		Batting																							Fielding						
Year Tm	Age	G	AB	H	2B	3B	HR	TB	R	RBI	GW	TBB	IBB	SO	HBP	SH	SF	SB	CS	SB%	GDP	Avg	OBP	SLG	Pos	G	PO	A	E	DP	FPct
1980 Phi	28	1	0	0	0	0	0	0	0	0	0	0	0	0	0	0	0	0	0	—	0	—	—	—	P	1	0	0	0	0	—
Postseason Totals		13	2	0	0	0	0	0	0	0	0	0	0	1	0	0	0	0	0	—	0	.000	.000	.000	P	13	0	1	0	0	1.000

BILL BRUTON—William Haron Bruton—Bats: Left; Throws: Right

Ht: 6'0"; Wt: 169 lbs; Born: 12/22/1925 in Panola, Alabama; Debut: 4/13/1953; Died: 12/5/1995

World Series		Batting																							Fielding						
Year Tm	Age	G	AB	H	2B	3B	HR	TB	R	RBI	GW	TBB	IBB	SO	HBP	SH	SF	SB	CS	SB%	GDP	Avg	OBP	SLG	Pos	G	PO	A	E	DP	FPct
1958 Mil	32	7	17	7	0	0	1	10	2	2	1	5	0	5	0	0	0	0	0	—	1	.412	.545	.588	OF	7	12	0	1	0	.923

CLAY BRYANT—Claiborne Henry Bryant—Throws: Right; Bats: Right

Ht: 6'2"; Wt: 195 lbs; Born: 11/26/1911 in Madison Heights, Virginia; Debut: 4/19/1935

World Series		Pitching																										
Year Tm	Age	G	GS	CG	GF	IP	BFP	H	R	ER	HR	SH	SF	HB	TBB	IBB	SO	WP	Bk	W	L	Pct	ShO	Sv-Op	Hld	OAvg	OOBP	ERA
1938 ChN	26	1	1	0	0	5.1	26	6	4	4	1	0	0	0	5	0	3	0	0	0	1	.000	0	0- 0	0	.286	.423	6.75

World Series		Batting																							Fielding						
Year Tm	Age	G	AB	H	2B	3B	HR	TB	R	RBI	GW	TBB	IBB	SO	HBP	SH	SF	SB	CS	SB%	GDP	Avg	OBP	SLG	Pos	G	PO	A	E	DP	FPct
1938 ChN	26	1	2	0	0	0	0	0	0	0	0	0	0	1	0	0	0	0	0	—	0	.000	.000	.000	P	1	0	0	0	0	—

RON BRYANT—Ronald Raymond Bryant—Throws: Left; Bats: Both

Ht: 6'0"; Wt: 190 lbs; Born: 11/12/1947 in Redlands, California; Debut: 9/29/1967

LCS		Pitching																										
Year Tm	Age	G	GS	CG	GF	IP	BFP	H	R	ER	HR	SH	SF	HB	TBB	IBB	SO	WP	Bk	W	L	Pct	ShO	Sv-Op	Hld	OAvg	OOBP	ERA
1971 SF	23	1	0	0	0	2.0	9	1	1	1	1	0	0	1	1	0	2	0	0	0	0	—	0	0- 0	0	.143	.333	4.50

LCS		Batting																							Fielding						
Year Tm	Age	G	AB	H	2B	3B	HR	TB	R	RBI	GW	TBB	IBB	SO	HBP	SH	SF	SB	CS	SB%	GDP	Avg	OBP	SLG	Pos	G	PO	A	E	DP	FPct
1971 SF	23	1	0	0	0	0	0	0	0	0	0	0	0	0	0	0	0	0	0	—	0	—	—	—	P	1	0	0	0	0	—

JERRY BUCHEK—Gerald Peter Buchek—Bats: Right; Throws: Right

Ht: 5'11"; Wt: 185 lbs; Born: 5/9/1942 in St. Louis, Missouri; Debut: 6/30/1961

World Series		Batting																							Fielding						
Year Tm	Age	G	AB	H	2B	3B	HR	TB	R	RBI	GW	TBB	IBB	SO	HBP	SH	SF	SB	CS	SB%	GDP	Avg	OBP	SLG	Pos	G	PO	A	E	DP	FPct
1964 StL	22	4	1	1	0	0	0	1	1	0	0	0	0	0	0	0	0	0	0	—	0	1.000	1.000	1.000	2B	4	0	1	0	0	1.000

BILL BUCKNER—William Joseph Buckner—Bats: Left; Throws: Left

Ht: 6'0"; Wt: 185 lbs; Born: 12/14/1949 in Vallejo, California; Debut: 9/21/1969

LCS		Batting																							Fielding						
Year Tm	Age	G	AB	H	2B	3B	HR	TB	R	RBI	GW	TBB	IBB	SO	HBP	SH	SF	SB	CS	SB%	GDP	Avg	OBP	SLG	Pos	G	PO	A	E	DP	FPct
1974 LA	24	4	18	3	1	0	0	4	0	0	0	0	0	2	0	0	0	0	0	—	0	.167	.167	.222	OF	4	6	0	0	0	1.000
1986 Bos	36	7	28	6	1	0	0	7	3	3	0	0	0	2	0	0	1	0	0	—	1	.214	.207	.250	1B	7	49	5	0	4	1.000
LCS Totals		11	46	9	2	0	0	11	3	3	0	0	0	4	0	0	1	0	0	—	1	.196	.191	.239	1B	7	49	5	0	4	1.000
World Series		Batting																							Fielding						
Year Tm	Age	G	AB	H	2B	3B	HR	TB	R	RBI	GW	TBB	IBB	SO	HBP	SH	SF	SB	CS	SB%	GDP	Avg	OBP	SLG	Pos	G	PO	A	E	DP	FPct
1974 LA	24	5	20	5	1	0	1	9	1	1	0	0	0	1	0	1	0	0	1	.00	0	.250	.250	.450	OF	5	10	0	0	0	1.000
1986 Bos	36	7	32	6	0	0	0	6	2	1	0	0	0	3	1	0	0	0	0	—	1	.188	.212	.188	1B	7	53	7	1	5	.984
WS Totals		12	52	11	1	0	1	15	3	2	0	0	0	4	1	1	0	0	1	.00	1	.212	.226	.288	1B	7	53	7	1	5	.984
Postseason Totals		23	98	20	3	0	1	26	6	5	0	0	0	8	1	1	1	0	1	.00	2	.204	.210	.265	1B	14	102	12	1	9	.991

STEVE BUECHELE—Steven Bernard Buechele—Bats: Right; Throws: Right

Ht: 6'2"; Wt: 190 lbs; Born: 9/26/1961 in Lancaster, California; Debut: 7/19/1985

LCS		Batting																							Fielding						
Year Tm	Age	G	AB	H	2B	3B	HR	TB	R	RBI	GW	TBB	IBB	SO	HBP	SH	SF	SB	CS	SB%	GDP	Avg	OBP	SLG	Pos	G	PO	A	E	DP	FPct
1991 Pit	30	7	23	7	2	0	0	9	2	0	0	4	0	6	0	1	0	0	0	—	0	.304	.407	.391	3B	7	8	14	0	1	1.000

DAMON BUFORD—Damon Jackson Buford—Bats: Right; Throws: Right

Ht: 5'11"; Wt: 170 lbs; Born: 6/12/1970 in Baltimore, Maryland; Debut: 5/4/1993

Division Series		Batting																							Fielding						
Year Tm	Age	G	AB	H	2B	3B	HR	TB	R	RBI	GW	TBB	IBB	SO	HBP	SH	SF	SB	CS	SB%	GDP	Avg	OBP	SLG	Pos	G	PO	A	E	DP	FPct
1996 Tex	26	2	0	0	0	0	0	0	0	0	0	0	0	0	0	0	0	0	0	—	0	—	—	—	—						

DON BUFORD—Donald Alvin Buford—Bats: Both; Throws: Right

Ht: 5'7"; Wt: 160 lbs; Born: 2/2/1937 in Linden, Texas; Debut: 9/14/1963

LCS		Batting																							Fielding						
Year Tm	Age	G	AB	H	2B	3B	HR	TB	R	RBI	GW	TBB	IBB	SO	HBP	SH	SF	SB	CS	SB%	GDP	Avg	OBP	SLG	Pos	G	PO	A	E	DP	FPct
1969 Bal	32	3	14	4	1	0	0	5	3	1	0	3	0	0	0	0	0	0	1	.00	0	.286	.412	.357	OF	3	7	0	0	0	1.000
1970 Bal	33	2	7	3	1	0	1	7	2	3	0	2	0	0	0	0	1	0	0	—	0	.429	.500	1.000	OF	2	1	0	0	0	1.000
1971 Bal	34	2	7	3	0	1	0	5	1	0	0	2	0	1	0	0	0	0	0	—	0	.429	.556	.714	OF	2	1	0	0	0	1.000
LCS Totals		7	28	10	2	1	1	17	6	4	0	7	0	1	0	0	1	0	1	.00	0	.357	.472	.607	OF	7	9	0	0	0	1.000
World Series		Batting																							Fielding						
Year Tm	Age	G	AB	H	2B	3B	HR	TB	R	RBI	GW	TBB	IBB	SO	HBP	SH	SF	SB	CS	SB%	GDP	Avg	OBP	SLG	Pos	G	PO	A	E	DP	FPct
1969 Bal	32	5	20	2	1	0	1	6	1	2	1	2	0	4	0	0	0	0	0	—	0	.100	.182	.300	OF	5	8	0	0	0	1.000
1970 Bal	33	4	15	4	0	0	1	7	3	1	0	3	0	2	0	0	0	0	0	—	0	.267	.389	.467	OF	4	6	0	0	0	1.000
1971 Bal	34	6	23	6	1	0	2	13	3	4	0	3	0	3	0	0	0	0	1	.00	0	.261	.346	.565	OF	6	13	1	0	0	1.000
WS Totals		15	58	12	2	0	4	26	7	7	1	8	0	9	0	0	0	0	1	.00	0	.207	.303	.448	OF	15	27	1	0	0	1.000
Postseason Totals		22	86	22	4	1	5	43	13	11	1	15	0	10	0	0	1	0	2	.00	0	.256	.363	.500	OF	22	36	1	0	0	1.000

BOB BUHL—Robert Ray Buhl—Throws: Right; Bats: Right

Ht: 6'2"; Wt: 180 lbs; Born: 8/12/1928 in Saginaw, Michigan; Debut: 4/17/1953

World Series		Pitching																										
Year Tm	Age	G	GS	CG	GF	IP	BFP	H	R	ER	HR	SH	SF	HB	TBB	IBB	SO	WP	Bk	W	L	Pct	ShO	Sv-Op	Hld	OAvg	OOBP	ERA
1957 Mil	29	2	2	0	0	3.1	21	6	5	4	2	0	1	0	6	0	4	1	0	0	1	.000	0	0-0	0	.429	.571	10.80

World Series		Batting																							Fielding						
Year Tm	Age	G	AB	H	2B	3B	HR	TB	R	RBI	GW	TBB	IBB	SO	HBP	SH	SF	SB	CS	SB%	GDP	Avg	OBP	SLG	Pos	G	PO	A	E	DP	FPct
1957 Mil	29	2	1	0	0	0	0	0	0	0	0	0	0	1	0	0	0	0	0	—	0	.000	.000	.000	P	2	0	2	1	0	.667

JAY BUHNER—Jay Campbell Buhner—Nickname: Bone—Bats: Right; Throws: Right

Ht: 6'3"; Wt: 205 lbs; Born: 8/13/1964 in Louisville, Kentucky; Debut: 9/11/1987

Division Series		Batting																							Fielding						
Year Tm	Age	G	AB	H	2B	3B	HR	TB	R	RBI	GW	TBB	IBB	SO	HBP	SH	SF	SB	CS	SB%	GDP	Avg	OBP	SLG	Pos	G	PO	A	E	DP	FPct
1995 Sea	31	5	24	11	1	0	1	15	2	3	0	2	0	4	0	0	0	0	1	.00	1	.458	.500	.625	OF	5	11	1	0	0	1.000
1997 Sea	33	4	13	3	0	0	2	9	2	2	0	3	0	6	0	0	0	0	0	—	0	.231	.375	.692	OF	4	5	1	0	0	1.000
DS Totals		9	37	14	1	0	3	24	4	5	0	5	0	10	0	0	0	0	1	.00	1	.378	.452	.649	OF	9	16	2	0	0	1.000
LCS		Batting																							Fielding						
Year Tm	Age	G	AB	H	2B	3B	HR	TB	R	RBI	GW	TBB	IBB	SO	HBP	SH	SF	SB	CS	SB%	GDP	Avg	OBP	SLG	Pos	G	PO	A	E	DP	FPct
1995 Sea	31	6	23	7	2	0	3	18	5	5	1	2	0	8	0	0	0	0	0	—	0	.304	.360	.783	OF	6	15	0	1	0	.938
Postseason Totals		15	60	21	3	0	6	42	9	10	1	7	0	18	0	0	0	0	1	.00	1	.350	.418	.700	OF	15	31	2	1	0	.971

AL BUMBRY—Alonza Benjamin Bumbry—Bats: Left; Throws: Right

Ht: 5'8"; Wt: 170 lbs; Born: 4/21/1947 in Fredericksburg, Virginia; Debut: 9/5/1972

LCS		Batting																							Fielding						
Year Tm	Age	G	AB	H	2B	3B	HR	TB	R	RBI	GW	TBB	IBB	SO	HBP	SH	SF	SB	CS	SB%	GDP	Avg	OBP	SLG	Pos	G	PO	A	E	DP	FPct
1973 Bal-*RY*	26	2	7	0	0	0	0	0	1	0	0	2	0	2	0	0	0	1	0	1.00	0	.000	.222	.000	OF	2	4	1	1	0	.833
1974 Bal	27	2	1	0	0	0	0	0	0	0	0	0	0	1	0	0	0	0	0	—	0	.000	.000	.000	—						
1979 Bal	32	4	16	4	0	1	0	6	5	0	0	4	1	3	0	0	0	2	0	1.00	0	.250	.400	.375	OF	4	10	0	1	0	.909
1983 Bal	36	3	8	1	1	0	0	2	0	1	0	0	0	2	0	0	0	0	0	—	0	.125	.125	.250	OF	2	3	0	0	0	1.000
LCS Totals		11	32	5	1	1	0	8	6	1	0	6	1	8	0	0	0	3	0	1.00	0	.156	.289	.250	OF	8	17	1	2	0	.900
World Series		Batting																							Fielding						
Year Tm	Age	G	AB	H	2B	3B	HR	TB	R	RBI	GW	TBB	IBB	SO	HBP	SH	SF	SB	CS	SB%	GDP	Avg	OBP	SLG	Pos	G	PO	A	E	DP	FPct
1979 Bal	32	7	21	3	0	0	0	3	3	1	0	2	0	1	1	1	0	0	0	—	1	.143	.250	.143	OF	7	14	1	1	0	.938
1983 Bal	36	4	11	1	1	0	0	2	0	1	0	0	0	1	0	0	1	0	0	—	0	.091	.083	.182	OF	4	12	0	0	0	1.000
WS Totals		11	32	4	1	0	0	5	3	2	0	2	0	2	1	1	1	0	0	—	1	.125	.194	.156	OF	11	26	1	1	0	.964
Postseason Totals		22	64	9	2	1	0	13	9	3	0	8	1	10	1	1	1	3	0	1.00	1	.141	.243	.203	OF	19	43	2	3	0	.938

WALLY BUNKER—Wallace Edward Bunker—Throws: Right; Bats: Right

Ht: 6'2"; Wt: 197 lbs; Born: 1/25/1945 in Seattle, Washington; Debut: 9/29/1963

World Series		Pitching																										
Year Tm	Age	G	GS	CG	GF	IP	BFP	H	R	ER	HR	SH	SF	HB	TBB	IBB	SO	WP	Bk	W	L	Pct	ShO	Sv-Op	Hld	OAvg	OOBP	ERA
1966 Bal	21	1	1	1	0	9.0	33	6	0	0	0	1	0	0	1	0	6	0	0	1	0	1.000	1	0-0	0	.194	.219	0.00

World Series		Batting																							Fielding						
Year Tm	Age	G	AB	H	2B	3B	HR	TB	R	RBI	GW	TBB	IBB	SO	HBP	SH	SF	SB	CS	SB%	GDP	Avg	OBP	SLG	Pos	G	PO	A	E	DP	FPct
1966 Bal	21	1	2	0	0	0	0	0	0	0	0	0	0	1	0	0	0	0	0	—	0	.000	.000	.000	P	1	0	3	0	0	1.000

DAVE BURBA—David Allen Burba—Throws: Right; Bats: Right

Ht: 6'4"; Wt: 220 lbs; Born: 7/7/1966 in Dayton, Ohio; Debut: 9/8/1990

Division Series		Pitching																										
Year Tm	Age	G	GS	CG	GF	IP	BFP	H	R	ER	HR	SH	SF	HB	TBB	IBB	SO	WP	Bk	W	L	Pct	ShO	Sv-Op	Hld	OAvg	OOBP	ERA
1995 Cin	29	1	0	0	0	1.0	6	2	0	0	0	0	0	0	1	0	0	0	0	1	0	1.000	0	0-0	0	.400	.500	0.00
LCS		Pitching																										
Year Tm	Age	G	GS	CG	GF	IP	BFP	H	R	ER	HR	SH	SF	HB	TBB	IBB	SO	WP	Bk	W	L	Pct	ShO	Sv-Op	Hld	OAvg	OOBP	ERA
1995 Cin	29	2	0	0	1	3.2	17	3	0	0	0	0	0	0	4	1	0	1	0	0	0	—	0	0-0	0	.231	.412	0.00
Postseason Totals		3	0	0	1	4.2	46	5	0	0	0	0	0	0	5	1	0	1	0	1	0	1.000	0	0-0	0	.278	.435	0.00

Division Series		Batting																							Fielding						
Year Tm	Age	G	AB	H	2B	3B	HR	TB	R	RBI	GW	TBB	IBB	SO	HBP	SH	SF	SB	CS	SB%	GDP	Avg	OBP	SLG	Pos	G	PO	A	E	DP	FPct
1995 Cin	29	1	0	0	0	0	0	0	0	0	0	0	0	0	0	0	0	0	0	—	0	—	—	—	P	1	0	0	0	0	—
LCS		Batting																							Fielding						
Year Tm	Age	G	AB	H	2B	3B	HR	TB	R	RBI	GW	TBB	IBB	SO	HBP	SH	SF	SB	CS	SB%	GDP	Avg	OBP	SLG	Pos	G	PO	A	E	DP	FPct
1995 Cin	29	2	0	0	0	0	0	0	0	0	0	0	0	0	0	0	0	0	0	—	0	—	—	—	P	2	0	0	0	0	—
Postseason Totals		3	0	0	0	0	0	0	0	0	0	0	0	0	0	0	0	0	0	—	0	—	—	—	P	3	0	0	0	0	—

LEW BURDETTE—Selva Lewis Burdette—Throws: Right; Bats: Right

Ht: 6'2"; Wt: 180 lbs; Born: 11/22/1926 in Nitro, West Virginia; Debut: 9/26/1950

World Series		Pitching																										
Year Tm	Age	G	GS	CG	GF	IP	BFP	H	R	ER	HR	SH	SF	HB	TBB	IBB	SO	WP	Bk	W	L	Pct	ShO	Sv-Op	Hld	OAvg	OOBP	ERA
1957 Mil	30	3	3	3	0	27.0	104	21	2	2	1	1	0	0	4	1	13	0	0	3	0	1.000	2	0-0	0	.212	.243	0.67
1958 Mil	31	3	3	1	0	22.1	93	22	17	14	5	2	1	0	4	3	12	0	0	1	2	.333	0	0-0	0	.256	.286	5.64
WS Totals		6	6	4	0	49.1	394	43	19	16	6	3	1	0	8	4	25	0	0	4	2	.667	2	0-0	0	.232	.263	2.92

World Series		Batting																							Fielding						
Year Tm	Age	G	AB	H	2B	3B	HR	TB	R	RBI	GW	TBB	IBB	SO	HBP	SH	SF	SB	CS	SB%	GDP	Avg	OBP	SLG	Pos	G	PO	A	E	DP	FPct
1957 Mil	30	3	8	0	0	0	0	0	0	0	0	1	0	2	0	2	0	0	0	—	0	.000	.111	.000	P	3	0	9	0	1	1.000
1958 Mil	31	3	9	1	0	0	1	4	1	3	0	0	0	3	0	0	0	0	0	—	0	.111	.111	.444	P	3	2	2	0	0	1.000
WS Totals		6	17	1	0	0	1	4	1	3	0	1	0	5	0	2	0	0	0	—	0	.059	.111	.235	P	6	2	11	0	1	1.000

SMOKY BURGESS—Forrest Harrill Burgess—Bats: Left; Throws: Right

Ht: 5'8"; Wt: 185 lbs; Born: 2/6/1927 in Caroleen, North Carolina; Debut: 4/19/1949; Died: 9/15/1991

World Series		Batting																							Fielding						
Year Tm	Age	G	AB	H	2B	3B	HR	TB	R	RBI	GW	TBB	IBB	SO	HBP	SH	SF	SB	CS	SB%	GDP	Avg	OBP	SLG	Pos	G	PO	A	E	DP	FPct
1960 Pit	33	5	18	6	1	0	0	7	2	0	0	2	0	1	0	0	0	0	0	—	0	.333	.400	.389	C	5	27	2	0	0	1.000

GLENN BURKE—Glenn Lawrence Burke—Bats: Right; Throws: Right

Ht: 6'0"; Wt: 195 lbs; Born: 11/16/1952 in Oakland, California; Debut: 4/9/1976; Died: 5/30/1995

LCS		Batting																							Fielding						
Year Tm	Age	G	AB	H	2B	3B	HR	TB	R	RBI	GW	TBB	IBB	SO	HBP	SH	SF	SB	CS	SB%	GDP	Avg	OBP	SLG	Pos	G	PO	A	E	DP	FPct
1977 LA	24	4	7	0	0	0	0	0	0	0	0	0	0	3	0	0	0	0	0	—	0	.000	.000	.000	OF	4	3	0	0	0	1.000
World Series		Batting																							Fielding						
Year Tm	Age	G	AB	H	2B	3B	HR	TB	R	RBI	GW	TBB	IBB	SO	HBP	SH	SF	SB	CS	SB%	GDP	Avg	OBP	SLG	Pos	G	PO	A	E	DP	FPct
1977 LA	24	3	5	1	0	0	0	1	0	0	0	0	0	1	0	0	0	0	0	—	0	.200	.200	.200	OF	3	9	0	0	0	1.000
Postseason Totals		7	12	1	0	0	0	1	0	0	0	0	0	4	0	0	0	0	0	—	0	.083	.083	.083	OF	7	12	0	0	0	1.000

JOHN BURKETT—John David Burkett—Throws: Right; Bats: Right

Ht: 6'2"; Wt: 175 lbs; Born: 11/28/1964 in New Brighton, Pennsylvania; Debut: 9/15/1987

Division Series		Pitching																										
Year Tm	Age	G	GS	CG	GF	IP	BFP	H	R	ER	HR	SH	SF	HB	TBB	IBB	SO	WP	Bk	W	L	Pct	ShO	Sv-Op	Hld	OAvg	OOBP	ERA
1996 Tex	31	1	1	1	0	9.0	38	10	2	2	0	0	0	0	1	0	7	0	0	1	0	1.000	0	0-0	0	.270	.289	2.00

Division Series		Batting																							Fielding						
Year Tm	Age	G	AB	H	2B	3B	HR	TB	R	RBI	GW	TBB	IBB	SO	HBP	SH	SF	SB	CS	SB%	GDP	Avg	OBP	SLG	Pos	G	PO	A	E	DP	FPct
1996 Tex	31	1	0	0	0	0	0	0	0	0	0	0	0	0	0	0	0	0	0	—	0	—	—	—	P	1	1	0	0	0	1.000

ELLIS BURKS—Ellis Rena Burks—Bats: Right; Throws: Right

Ht: 6'2"; Wt: 175 lbs; Born: 9/11/1964 in Vicksburg, Mississippi; Debut: 4/30/1987

Division Series		Batting																							Fielding						
Year Tm	Age	G	AB	H	2B	3B	HR	TB	R	RBI	GW	TBB	IBB	SO	HBP	SH	SF	SB	CS	SB%	GDP	Avg	OBP	SLG	Pos	G	PO	A	E	DP	FPct
1995 Col	31	2	6	2	1	0	0	3	1	2	0	0	0	1	0	0	1	0	0	—	0	.333	.286	.500	OF	2	4	0	1	0	.800

LCS — Batting / Fielding

Year Tm	Age	G	AB	H	2B	3B	HR	TB	R	RBI	GW	TBB	IBB	SO	HBP	SH	SF	SB	CS	SB%	GDP	Avg	OBP	SLG	Pos	G	PO	A	E	DP	FPct
1988 Bos	24	4	17	4	1	0	0	5	2	1	0	0	0	3	0	0	0	0	0	—	0	.235	.235	.294	OF	4	10	0	0	0	1.000
1990 Bos	26	4	15	4	2	0	0	6	1	0	0	1	0	1	0	0	0	1	0	1.00	0	.267	.313	.400	OF	4	9	1	0	0	1.000
1993 ChA	29	6	23	7	1	0	1	11	4	3	0	3	0	5	1	0	0	0	1	.00	1	.304	.407	.478	OF	6	15	0	0	0	1.000
LCS Totals		14	55	15	4	0	1	22	7	4	0	4	0	9	1	0	0	1	1	.50	1	.273	.333	.400	OF	14	34	1	0	0	1.000
Postseason Totals		16	61	17	5	0	1	25	8	6	0	4	0	10	1	0	1	1	1	.50	1	.279	.328	.410	OF	16	38	1	1	0	.975

RICK BURLESON—Richard Paul Burleson—Nickname: Rooster—Bats: Right; Throws: Right

Ht: 5'10"; Wt: 165 lbs; Born: 4/29/1951 in Lynwood, California; Debut: 5/4/1974

LCS — Batting / Fielding

Year Tm	Age	G	AB	H	2B	3B	HR	TB	R	RBI	GW	TBB	IBB	SO	HBP	SH	SF	SB	CS	SB%	GDP	Avg	OBP	SLG	Pos	G	PO	A	E	DP	FPct
1975 Bos	24	3	9	4	2	0	0	6	2	1	0	1	0	0	0	1	0	0	0	—	0	.444	.500	.667	SS	3	3	12	1	1	.938
1986 Cal	35	4	11	3	0	0	0	3	0	0	0	0	0	0	0	1	0	0	0	—	0	.273	.273	.273	2B	2	3	5	0	0	1.000
LCS Totals		7	20	7	2	0	0	9	2	1	0	1	0	0	0	2	0	0	0	—	0	.350	.381	.450	SS	3	3	12	1	1	.938

World Series — Batting / Fielding

Year Tm	Age	G	AB	H	2B	3B	HR	TB	R	RBI	GW	TBB	IBB	SO	HBP	SH	SF	SB	CS	SB%	GDP	Avg	OBP	SLG	Pos	G	PO	A	E	DP	FPct
1975 Bos	24	7	24	7	1	0	0	8	1	2	1	4	1	2	0	0	0	0	1	.00	2	.292	.393	.333	SS	7	8	20	1	3	.966
Postseason Totals		14	44	14	3	0	0	17	3	3	1	5	1	2	0	2	0	0	1	.00	2	.318	.388	.386	SS	10	11	32	2	4	.956

BRITT BURNS—Robert Britt Burns—Throws: Left; Bats: Left

Ht: 6'5"; Wt: 215 lbs; Born: 6/8/1959 in Houston, Texas; Debut: 8/5/1978

LCS — Pitching

Year Tm	Age	G	GS	CG	GF	IP	BFP	H	R	ER	HR	SH	SF	HB	TBB	IBB	SO	WP	Bk	W	L	Pct	ShO	Sv-Op	Hld	OAvg	OOBP	ERA
1983 ChA	24	1	1	0	0	9.1	38	6	1	1	1	1	0	1	5	0	8	0	0	0	1	.000	0	0- 0	0	.194	.324	0.96

LCS — Batting / Fielding

Year Tm	Age	G	AB	H	2B	3B	HR	TB	R	RBI	GW	TBB	IBB	SO	HBP	SH	SF	SB	CS	SB%	GDP	Avg	OBP	SLG	Pos	G	PO	A	E	DP	FPct
1983 ChA	24	1	0	0	0	0	0	0	0	0	0	0	0	0	0	0	0	0	0	—	0	—	—	—	P	1	0	1	0	0	1.000

ED BURNS—Edward James Burns—Bats: Right; Throws: Right

Ht: 5'6"; Wt: 165 lbs; Born: 10/31/1888 in San Francisco, California; Debut: 6/25/1912; Died: 6/1/1942

World Series — Batting / Fielding

Year Tm	Age	G	AB	H	2B	3B	HR	TB	R	RBI	GW	TBB	IBB	SO	HBP	SH	SF	SB	CS	SB%	GDP	Avg	OBP	SLG	Pos	G	PO	A	E	DP	FPct
1915 Phi	26	5	16	3	0	0	0	3	1	0	0	1	0	2	0	0	0	0	0	—	0	.188	.235	.188	C	5	28	8	1	2	.973

GEORGE BURNS—George Joseph Burns—Bats: Right; Throws: Right

Ht: 5'7"; Wt: 160 lbs; Born: 11/24/1889 in Utica, New York; Debut: 10/3/1911; Died: 8/15/1966

World Series — Batting / Fielding

Year Tm	Age	G	AB	H	2B	3B	HR	TB	R	RBI	GW	TBB	IBB	SO	HBP	SH	SF	SB	CS	SB%	GDP	Avg	OBP	SLG	Pos	G	PO	A	E	DP	FPct
1913 NYG	23	5	19	3	2	0	0	5	2	2	0	1	0	5	0	0	0	1	0	1.00	1	.158	.200	.263	OF	5	14	0	1	0	.933
1917 NYG	27	6	22	5	0	0	0	5	3	2	0	3	0	6	0	0	0	1	0	1.00	2	.227	.320	.227	OF	6	11	0	0	0	1.000
1921 NYG	31	8	33	11	4	1	0	17	2	2	1	3	0	5	0	1	0	1	1	.50	0	.333	.389	.515	OF	8	9	0	0	0	1.000
WS Totals		19	74	19	6	1	0	27	7	6	1	7	0	16	0	1	0	3	1	.75	3	.257	.321	.365	OF	19	34	0	1	0	.971

GEORGE BURNS—George Henry Burns—Nickname: Tioga George—Bats: Right; Throws: Right

Ht: 6'1"; Wt: 180 lbs; Born: 1/31/1893 in Niles, Ohio; Debut: 4/14/1914; Died: 1/7/1978

World Series — Batting / Fielding

Year Tm	Age	G	AB	H	2B	3B	HR	TB	R	RBI	GW	TBB	IBB	SO	HBP	SH	SF	SB	CS	SB%	GDP	Avg	OBP	SLG	Pos	G	PO	A	E	DP	FPct
1920 Cle	27	5	10	3	1	0	0	4	1	2	1	3	0	3	0	0	0	0	0	—	0	.300	.462	.400	1B	4	38	1	1	4	.975
1929 Phi	36	1	2	0	0	0	0	0	0	0	0	0	0	1	0	0	0	0	0	—	0	.000	.000	.000	—						
WS Totals		6	12	3	1	0	0	4	1	2	1	3	0	4	0	0	0	0	0	—	0	.250	.400	.333	1B	4	38	1	1	4	.975

TODD BURNS—Todd Edward Burns—Throws: Right; Bats: Right

Ht: 6'2"; Wt: 186 lbs; Born: 7/6/1963 in Maywood, California; Debut: 5/31/1988

World Series — Pitching

Year Tm	Age	G	GS	CG	GF	IP	BFP	H	R	ER	HR	SH	SF	HB	TBB	IBB	SO	WP	Bk	W	L	Pct	ShO	Sv-Op	Hld	OAvg	OOBP	ERA
1988 Oak	25	1	0	0	1	0.1	1	0	0	0	0	0	0	0	0	0	0	0	0	0	0	—	0	0- 0	0	.000	.000	0.00
1989 Oak	26	2	0	0	1	1.2	7	1	0	0	0	0	0	0	1	0	0	0	0	0	0	—	0	0- 0	1	.167	.286	0.00
1990 Oak	27	2	0	0	0	1.2	12	5	3	3	0	0	0	0	2	0	0	1	0	0	0	—	0	0- 0	0	.500	.583	16.20
WS Totals		5	0	0	2	3.2	40	6	3	3	0	0	0	0	3	0	0	1	0	0	0	—	0	0-0	1	.353	.450	7.36

World Series — Batting / Fielding

Year Tm	Age	G	AB	H	2B	3B	HR	TB	R	RBI	GW	TBB	IBB	SO	HBP	SH	SF	SB	CS	SB%	GDP	Avg	OBP	SLG	Pos	G	PO	A	E	DP	FPct
1988 Oak	25	1	0	0	0	0	0	0	0	0	0	0	0	0	0	0	0	0	0	—	0	—	—	—	P	1	0	0	0	0	—
1989 Oak	26	2	0	0	0	0	0	0	0	0	0	0	0	0	0	0	0	0	0	—	0	—	—	—	P	2	0	0	0	0	—
1990 Oak	27	2	0	0	0	0	0	0	0	0	0	0	0	0	0	0	0	0	0	—	0	—	—	—	P	2	0	0	0	0	—
WS Totals		5	0	0	0	0	0	0	0	0	0	0	0	0	0	0	0	0	0	—	0	—	—	—	P	5	0	0	0	0	—

RAY BURRIS—Bertram Ray Burris—Throws: Right; Bats: Right

Ht: 6'5"; Wt: 200 lbs; Born: 8/22/1950 in Idabel, Oklahoma; Debut: 4/8/1973

Division Series — Pitching

Year Tm	Age	G	GS	CG	GF	IP	BFP	H	R	ER	HR	SH	SF	HB	TBB	IBB	SO	WP	Bk	W	L	Pct	ShO	Sv-Op	Hld	OAvg	OOBP	ERA
1981 Mon	31	1	1	0	0	5.1	26	7	4	3	0	1	0	0	4	1	4	0	0	0	1	.000	0	0- 0	0	.333	.440	5.06

LCS — Pitching

Year Tm	Age	G	GS	CG	GF	IP	BFP	H	R	ER	HR	SH	SF	HB	TBB	IBB	SO	WP	Bk	W	L	Pct	ShO	Sv-Op	Hld	OAvg	OOBP	ERA
1981 Mon	31	2	2	1	0	17.0	63	10	1	1	0	0	0	0	3	0	4	1	0	1	0	1.000	1	0- 0	0	.167	.206	0.53
Postseason Totals		3	3	1	0	22.1	178	17	5	4	0	1	0	0	7	1	8	1	0	1	1	.500	1	0-0	0	.210	.273	1.61

Division Series — Batting / Fielding

Year Tm	Age	G	AB	H	2B	3B	HR	TB	R	RBI	GW	TBB	IBB	SO	HBP	SH	SF	SB	CS	SB%	GDP	Avg	OBP	SLG	Pos	G	PO	A	E	DP	FPct
1981 Mon	31	1	2	0	0	0	0	0	0	0	0	0	0	2	0	0	0	0	0	—	0	.000	.000	.000	P	1	0	0	0	0	—

LCS — Batting / Fielding

Year Tm	Age	G	AB	H	2B	3B	HR	TB	R	RBI	GW	TBB	IBB	SO	HBP	SH	SF	SB	CS	SB%	GDP	Avg	OBP	SLG	Pos	G	PO	A	E	DP	FPct
1981 Mon	31	2	6	0	0	0	0	0	0	0	0	0	0	4	0	0	0	0	0	—	0	.000	.000	.000	P	2	0	1	0	0	1.000
Postseason Totals		3	8	0	0	0	0	0	0	0	0	0	0	6	0	0	0	0	0	—	0	.000	.000	.000	P	3	0	1	0	0	1.000

JEFF BURROUGHS—Jeffrey Alan Burroughs—Bats: Right; Throws: Right

Ht: 6'1"; Wt: 200 lbs; Born: 3/7/1951 in Long Beach, California; Debut: 7/20/1970

LCS — Batting / Fielding

Year Tm	Age	G	AB	H	2B	3B	HR	TB	R	RBI	GW	TBB	IBB	SO	HBP	SH	SF	SB	CS	SB%	GDP	Avg	OBP	SLG	Pos	G	PO	A	E	DP	FPct
1985 Tor	34	1	1	0	0	0	0	0	0	0	0	0	0	0	0	0	0	0	0	—	0	.000	.000	.000	—						

JIM BURTON—Jim Scott Burton—Throws: Left; Bats: Right

Ht: 6'3"; Wt: 195 lbs; Born: 10/27/1949 in Royal Oak, Michigan; Debut: 6/10/1975

World Series — Pitching

Year Tm	Age	G	GS	CG	GF	IP	BFP	H	R	ER	HR	SH	SF	HB	TBB	IBB	SO	WP	Bk	W	L	Pct	ShO	Sv-Op	Hld	OAvg	OOBP	ERA
1975 Bos	25	2	0	0	0	1.0	7	1	1	1	0	1	1	0	3	0	0	0	0	0	1	.000	0	0- 0	0	.500	.667	9.00

World Series — Batting / Fielding

Year Tm	Age	G	AB	H	2B	3B	HR	TB	R	RBI	GW	TBB	IBB	SO	HBP	SH	SF	SB	CS	SB%	GDP	Avg	OBP	SLG	Pos	G	PO	A	E	DP	FPct
1975 Bos	25	2	0	0	0	0	0	0	0	0	0	0	0	0	0	0	0	0	0	—	0	—	—	—	P	2	0	0	0	0	—

DONIE BUSH—Owen Joseph Bush—Bats: Both; Throws: Right

Ht: 5'6"; Wt: 140 lbs; Born: 10/8/1887 in Indianapolis, Indiana; Debut: 9/18/1908; Died: 3/28/1972

World Series — Batting / Fielding

Year Tm	Age	G	AB	H	2B	3B	HR	TB	R	RBI	GW	TBB	IBB	SO	HBP	SH	SF	SB	CS	SB%	GDP	Avg	OBP	SLG	Pos	G	PO	A	E	DP	FPct
1909 Det	21	7	23	6	1	0	0	7	5	3	0	5	0	3	2	2	0	1	2	.33	0	.261	.433	.304	SS	7	9	18	5	3	.844

GUY BUSH—Guy Terrell Bush—Nickname: The Mississippi Mudcat—Throws: Right; Bats: Right

Ht: 6'0"; Wt: 175 lbs; Born: 8/23/1901 in Aberdeen, Mississippi; Debut: 9/17/1923; Died: 7/2/1985

World Series		Pitching																									
Year Tm	Age	G	GS	CG	GF	IP	BFP	H	R	ER	HR	SH	SF	HB	TBB	IBB	SO	WP	Bk	W	L	Pct	ShO	Sv-Op	Hld	OAvg	OOBP	ERA
1929 ChN	28	2	1	1	1	11.0	49	12	3	1	0	1	1	0	2	0	4	1	0	1	0	1.000	0	0- 0	0	.267	.292	0.82
1932 ChN	31	2	2	0	0	5.2	31	5	9	9	1	1	0	1	6	0	2	0	0	0	1	.000	0	0- 0	0	.217	.400	14.29
WS Totals		4	3	1	1	16.2	160	17	12	10	1	2	1	1	8	0	6	1	0	1	1	.500	0	0-0	0	.250	.333	5.40

World Series		Batting																							Fielding						
Year Tm	Age	G	AB	H	2B	3B	HR	TB	R	RBI	GW	TBB	IBB	SO	HBP	SH	SF	SB	CS	SB%	GDP	Avg	OBP	SLG	Pos	G	PO	A	E	DP	FPct
1929 ChN	28	2	3	0	0	0	0	0	1	0	0	1	0	3	0	0	0	0	0	—	0	.000	.250	.000	P	2	0	3	0	0	1.000
1932 ChN	31	2	1	0	0	0	0	0	0	0	0	1	0	0	0	0	0	0	0	—	0	.000	.500	.000	P	2	0	2	0	0	1.000
WS Totals		4	4	0	0	0	0	0	1	0	0	2	0	3	0	0	0	0	0	—	0	.000	.333	.000	P	4	0	5	0	0	1.000

JOE BUSH—Leslie Ambrose Bush—Nickname: Bullett Joe—Throws: Right; Bats: Right

Ht: 5'9"; Wt: 173 lbs; Born: 11/27/1892 in Brainerd, Minnesota; Debut: 9/30/1912; Died: 11/1/1974

World Series		Pitching																									
Year Tm	Age	G	GS	CG	GF	IP	BFP	H	R	ER	HR	SH	SF	HB	TBB	IBB	SO	WP	Bk	W	L	Pct	ShO	Sv-Op	Hld	OAvg	OOBP	ERA
1913 Phi	20	1	1	1	0	9.0	34	5	2	1	0	0	0	1	4	0	3	0	0	1	0	1.000	0	0- 0	0	.172	.294	1.00
1914 Phi	21	1	1	1	0	11.0	46	9	5	4	1	1	1	0	4	1	4	0	0	0	1	.000	0	0- 0	0	.225	.289	3.27
1918 Bos	25	2	1	1	1	9.0	33	7	3	3	0	1	0	0	3	0	0	0	0	0	1	.000	0	1- 1	0	.241	.313	3.00
1922 NYA	29	2	2	1	0	15.0	66	21	8	8	0	1	0	0	5	1	6	0	0	0	2	.000	0	0- 0	0	.350	.400	4.80
1923 NYA	30	3	1	1	2	16.2	58	7	2	2	1	0	0	0	4	0	5	0	0	1	1	.500	0	0- 0	0	.130	.190	1.08
WS Totals		9	6	5	3	60.2	474	49	20	18	2	3	1	1	20	2	18	0	0	2	5	.286	0	1-1	0	.231	.299	2.67

World Series		Batting																							Fielding						
Year Tm	Age	G	AB	H	2B	3B	HR	TB	R	RBI	GW	TBB	IBB	SO	HBP	SH	SF	SB	CS	SB%	GDP	Avg	OBP	SLG	Pos	G	PO	A	E	DP	FPct
1913 Phi	20	1	4	1	0	0	0	1	0	0	0	0	0	1	0	0	0	0	0	—	0	.250	.250	.250	P	1	0	1	0	1	1.000
1914 Phi	21	1	5	0	0	0	0	0	0	0	0	0	0	2	0	0	0	0	0	—	0	.000	.000	.000	P	1	0	5	1	0	.833
1918 Bos	25	2	2	0	0	0	0	0	0	0	0	1	0	0	0	0	0	0	0	—	0	.000	.333	.000	P	2	0	3	0	0	1.000
1922 NYA	29	2	6	1	0	0	0	1	0	1	0	0	0	0	0	0	0	0	0	—	0	.167	.167	.167	P	2	1	3	0	2	1.000
1923 NYA	30	4	7	3	1	0	0	4	2	1	0	1	0	1	0	0	0	0	0	—	0	.429	.500	.571	P	3	2	3	0	0	1.000
WS Totals		10	24	5	1	0	0	6	2	2	0	2	0	4	0	0	0	0	0	—	0	.208	.269	.250	P	9	3	15	1	3	.947

RANDY BUSH—Robert Randall Bush—Bats: Left; Throws: Left

Ht: 6'1"; Wt: 186 lbs; Born: 10/5/1958 in Dover, Delaware; Debut: 5/1/1982

LCS		Batting																							Fielding						
Year Tm	Age	G	AB	H	2B	3B	HR	TB	R	RBI	GW	TBB	IBB	SO	HBP	SH	SF	SB	CS	SB%	GDP	Avg	OBP	SLG	Pos	G	PO	A	E	DP	FPct
1987 Min	28	4	12	3	0	1	0	5	4	2	0	3	0	2	0	0	1	3	0	1.00	0	.250	.375	.417	—						
World Series		**Batting**																							**Fielding**						
Year Tm	Age	G	AB	H	2B	3B	HR	TB	R	RBI	GW	TBB	IBB	SO	HBP	SH	SF	SB	CS	SB%	GDP	Avg	OBP	SLG	Pos	G	PO	A	E	DP	FPct
1987 Min	28	4	6	1	1	0	0	2	1	2	0	0	0	1	0	0	0	0	0	—	0	.167	.167	.333	—						
1991 Min	32	3	4	1	0	0	0	1	0	0	0	0	0	1	0	0	0	0	0	—	0	.250	.250	.250	OF	2	0	0	0	0	—
WS Totals		7	10	2	1	0	0	3	1	2	0	0	0	2	0	0	0	0	0	—	0	.200	.200	.300	OF	2	0	0	0	0	—
Postseason Totals		11	22	5	1	1	0	8	5	4	0	3	0	4	0	0	1	3	0	1.00	0	.227	.308	.364	OF	2	0	0	0	0	—

SAL BUTERA—Salvatore Philip Butera—Bats: Right; Throws: Right

Ht: 6'0"; Wt: 190 lbs; Born: 9/25/1952 in Richmond Hill, New York; Debut: 4/10/1980

LCS		Batting																							Fielding						
Year Tm	Age	G	AB	H	2B	3B	HR	TB	R	RBI	GW	TBB	IBB	SO	HBP	SH	SF	SB	CS	SB%	GDP	Avg	OBP	SLG	Pos	G	PO	A	E	DP	FPct
1987 Min	35	1	3	2	0	0	0	2	0	0	0	0	0	0	0	0	0	0	0	—	0	.667	.667	.667	C	1	6	0	0	0	1.000
World Series		**Batting**																							**Fielding**						
Year Tm	Age	G	AB	H	2B	3B	HR	TB	R	RBI	GW	TBB	IBB	SO	HBP	SH	SF	SB	CS	SB%	GDP	Avg	OBP	SLG	Pos	G	PO	A	E	DP	FPct
1987 Min	35	1	0	0	0	0	0	0	0	0	0	0	0	0	0	0	0	0	0	—	0	—	—	—	C	1	0	0	0	0	—
Postseason Totals		2	3	2	0	0	0	2	0	0	0	0	0	0	0	0	0	0	0	—	0	.667	.667	.667	C	2	6	0	0	0	1.000

BRETT BUTLER—Brett Morgan Butler—Bats: Left; Throws: Left

Ht: 5'10"; Wt: 160 lbs; Born: 6/15/1957 in Los Angeles, California; Debut: 8/20/1981

Division Series		Batting																							Fielding						
Year Tm	Age	G	AB	H	2B	3B	HR	TB	R	RBI	GW	TBB	IBB	SO	HBP	SH	SF	SB	CS	SB%	GDP	Avg	OBP	SLG	Pos	G	PO	A	E	DP	FPct
1995 LA	38	3	15	4	0	0	0	4	1	1	0	0	0	3	0	0	0	0	0	—	0	.267	.267	.267	OF	3	7	0	0	0	1.000
LCS		**Batting**																							**Fielding**						
Year Tm	Age	G	AB	H	2B	3B	HR	TB	R	RBI	GW	TBB	IBB	SO	HBP	SH	SF	SB	CS	SB%	GDP	Avg	OBP	SLG	Pos	G	PO	A	E	DP	FPct
1982 Atl	25	2	1	0	0	0	0	0	0	0	0	0	0	0	0	0	0	0	0	—	0	.000	.000	.000	OF	1	0	0	0	0	—
1989 SF	32	5	19	4	0	0	0	4	6	0	0	3	1	3	0	0	0	0	1	.00	0	.211	.318	.211	OF	5	9	0	0	0	1.000
LCS Totals		7	20	4	0	0	0	4	6	0	0	3	1	3	0	0	0	0	1	.00	0	.200	.304	.200	OF	6	9	0	0	0	1.000
World Series		**Batting**																							**Fielding**						
Year Tm	Age	G	AB	H	2B	3B	HR	TB	R	RBI	GW	TBB	IBB	SO	HBP	SH	SF	SB	CS	SB%	GDP	Avg	OBP	SLG	Pos	G	PO	A	E	DP	FPct
1989 SF	32	4	14	4	1	0	0	5	1	1	0	2	0	1	0	0	0	2	1	.67	0	.286	.375	.357	OF	4	9	0	0	0	1.000
Postseason Totals		14	49	12	1	0	0	13	8	2	0	5	1	7	0	0	0	2	2	.50	0	.245	.315	.265	OF	13	25	0	0	0	1.000

ROB BUTLER—Robert Frank John Butler—Bats: Left; Throws: Left

Ht: 5'11"; Wt: 185 lbs; Born: 4/10/1970 in Toronto, Ontario; Debut: 6/12/1993

World Series		Batting																							Fielding						
Year Tm	Age	G	AB	H	2B	3B	HR	TB	R	RBI	GW	TBB	IBB	SO	HBP	SH	SF	SB	CS	SB%	GDP	Avg	OBP	SLG	Pos	G	PO	A	E	DP	FPct
1993 Tor	23	2	2	1	0	0	0	1	1	0	0	0	0	0	0	0	0	0	0	—	0	.500	.500	.500	—						

BUD BYERLY—Eldred William Byerly—Throws: Right; Bats: Right

Ht: 6'2"; Wt: 185 lbs; Born: 10/26/1920 in Webster Groves, Missouri; Debut: 9/26/1943

World Series		Pitching																									
Year Tm	Age	G	GS	CG	GF	IP	BFP	H	R	ER	HR	SH	SF	HB	TBB	IBB	SO	WP	Bk	W	L	Pct	ShO	Sv-Op	Hld	OAvg	OOBP	ERA
1944 StL	23	1	0	0	1	1.1	4	0	0	0	0	0	0	0	0	0	1	0	0	0	0	—	0	0- 0	0	.000	.000	0.00

World Series		Batting																							Fielding						
Year Tm	Age	G	AB	H	2B	3B	HR	TB	R	RBI	GW	TBB	IBB	SO	HBP	SH	SF	SB	CS	SB%	GDP	Avg	OBP	SLG	Pos	G	PO	A	E	DP	FPct
1944 StL	23	1	0	0	0	0	0	0	0	0	0	0	0	0	0	0	0	0	0	—	0	—	—	—	P	1	0	0	0	0	—

SAMMY BYRD—Samuel Dewey Byrd—Nickname: Babe Ruth's Legs—Bats: Right; Throws: Right

Ht: 5'10"; Wt: 175 lbs; Born: 10/15/1907 in Bremen, Georgia; Debut: 5/11/1929; Died: 5/11/1981

World Series		Batting																							Fielding						
Year Tm	Age	G	AB	H	2B	3B	HR	TB	R	RBI	GW	TBB	IBB	SO	HBP	SH	SF	SB	CS	SB%	GDP	Avg	OBP	SLG	Pos	G	PO	A	E	DP	FPct
1932 NYA	24	1	0	0	0	0	0	0	0	0	0	0	0	0	0	0	0	0	0	—	0	—	—	—	OF	1	0	0	0	0	—

BOBBY BYRNE—Robert Matthew Byrne—Bats: Right; Throws: Right

Ht: 5'7"; Wt: 145 lbs; Born: 12/31/1884 in St. Louis, Missouri; Debut: 4/11/1907; Died: 12/31/1964

World Series		Batting																							Fielding						
Year Tm	Age	G	AB	H	2B	3B	HR	TB	R	RBI	GW	TBB	IBB	SO	HBP	SH	SF	SB	CS	SB%	GDP	Avg	OBP	SLG	Pos	G	PO	A	E	DP	FPct
1909 Pit	24	7	24	6	1	0	0	7	5	0	0	1	0	4	2	0	0	1	1	.50	0	.250	.333	.292	3B	6	11	16	0	3	1.000
1915 Phi	30	1	1	0	0	0	0	0	0	0	0	0	0	0	0	0	0	0	0	—	0	.000	.000	.000	—						
WS Totals		8	25	6	1	0	0	7	5	0	0	1	0	4	2	0	0	1	1	.50	0	.240	.321	.280	3B	6	11	16	0	3	1.000

TOMMY BYRNE—Thomas Joseph Byrne—Throws: Left; Bats: Left

Ht: 6'1"; Wt: 182 lbs; Born: 12/31/1919 in Baltimore, Maryland; Debut: 4/27/1943

World Series		Pitching																									
Year Tm	Age	G	GS	CG	GF	IP	BFP	H	R	ER	HR	SH	SF	HB	TBB	IBB	SO	WP	Bk	W	L	Pct	ShO	Sv-Op	Hld	OAvg	OOBP	ERA
1949 NYA	29	1	1	0	0	3.1	14	2	1	1	1	0	0	1	2	0	1	0	0	0	0	—	0	0- 0	0	.182	.357	2.70
1955 NYA	35	2	2	1	0	14.1	56	8	4	3	0	2	0	0	8	1	8	0	0	1	1	.500	0	0- 0	0	.174	.296	1.88
1956 NYA	36	1	0	0	0	0.1	2	1	1	0	1	0	0	0	0	0	1	0	0	0	0	—	0	0- 0	0	.500	.500	0.00
1957 NYA	37	2	0	0	1	3.1	13	1	2	2	1	0	0	1	2	0	1	0	0	0	0	—	0	0- 0	0	.100	.308	5.40
WS Totals		6	3	1	1	21.1	170	12	8	6	3	2	0	2	12	1	11	0	0	1	1	.500	0	0-0	0	.174	.313	2.53

World Series — Batting / Fielding

Year Tm	Age	G	AB	H	2B	3B	HR	TB	R	RBI	GW	TBB	IBB	SO	HBP	SH	SF	SB	CS	SB%	GDP	Avg	OBP	SLG	Pos	G	PO	A	E	DP	FPct
1949 NYA	29	1	1	1	0	0	0	1	0	0	0	0	0	0	0	0	0	0	0	—	0	1.000	1.000	1.000	P	1	0	0	0	0	—
1955 NYA	35	3	6	1	0	0	0	1	0	2	0	0	0	2	0	0	0	0	0	—	1	.167	.167	.167	P	2	0	2	0	0	1.000
1956 NYA	36	2	1	0	0	0	0	0	0	0	0	0	0	0	0	0	0	0	0	—	0	.000	.000	.000	P	1	0	0	0	0	—
1957 NYA	37	2	2	1	0	0	0	1	0	0	0	0	0	1	0	0	0	0	0	—	0	.500	.500	.500	P	2	0	0	0	0	—
WS Totals		8	10	3	0	0	0	3	0	2	0	0	0	3	0	0	0	0	0	—	1	.300	.300	.300	P	6	0	2	0	0	1.000

MILT BYRNES—Milton John Byrnes—Nickname: Skippy—Bats: Left; Throws: Left

Ht: 5'10"; Wt: 170 lbs; Born: 11/15/1916 in St. Louis, Missouri; Debut: 4/21/1943; Died: 2/1/1979

World Series — Batting / Fielding

Year Tm	Age	G	AB	H	2B	3B	HR	TB	R	RBI	GW	TBB	IBB	SO	HBP	SH	SF	SB	CS	SB%	GDP	Avg	OBP	SLG	Pos	G	PO	A	E	DP	FPct
1944 StL	27	3	2	0	0	0	0	0	0	0	0	1	0	2	0	0	0	0	0	—	0	.000	.333	.000	—						

MARTY BYSTROM—Martin Eugene Bystrom—Throws: Right; Bats: Right

Ht: 6'5"; Wt: 200 lbs; Born: 7/26/1958 in Coral Gables, Florida; Debut: 9/7/1980

LCS — Pitching

Year Tm	Age	G	GS	CG	GF	IP	BFP	H	R	ER	HR	SH	SF	HB	TBB	IBB	SO	WP	Bk	W	L	Pct	ShO	Sv-Op	Hld	OAvg	OOBP	ERA
1980 Phi	22	1	1	0	0	5.1	25	7	2	1	0	0	0	0	2	0	1	0	0	0	0	—	0	0- 0	0	.304	.360	1.69

World Series — Pitching

Year Tm	Age	G	GS	CG	GF	IP	BFP	H	R	ER	HR	SH	SF	HB	TBB	IBB	SO	WP	Bk	W	L	Pct	ShO	Sv-Op	Hld	OAvg	OOBP	ERA
1980 Phi	22	1	1	0	0	5.0	26	10	3	3	1	1	0	0	1	0	4	0	0	0	0	—	0	0- 0	0	.417	.440	5.40
1983 Phi	25	1	0	0	0	1.0	4	0	0	0	0	0	1	0	0	0	1	1	0	0	0	—	0	0- 0	0	.000	.000	0.00
WS Totals		2	1	0	0	6.0	60	10	3	3	1	1	1	0	1	0	5	1	0	0	0	—	0	0-0	0	.370	.379	4.50
Postseason Totals		3	2	0	0	11.1	110	17	5	4	1	1	1	0	3	0	6	1	0	0	0	—	0	0-0	0	.340	.370	3.18

LCS — Batting / Fielding

Year Tm	Age	G	AB	H	2B	3B	HR	TB	R	RBI	GW	TBB	IBB	SO	HBP	SH	SF	SB	CS	SB%	GDP	Avg	OBP	SLG	Pos	G	PO	A	E	DP	FPct
1980 Phi	22	1	2	0	0	0	0	0	0	0	0	0	0	1	0	0	0	0	0	—	0	.000	.000	.000	P	1	0	0	0	0	—

World Series — Batting / Fielding

Year Tm	Age	G	AB	H	2B	3B	HR	TB	R	RBI	GW	TBB	IBB	SO	HBP	SH	SF	SB	CS	SB%	GDP	Avg	OBP	SLG	Pos	G	PO	A	E	DP	FPct
1980 Phi	22	1	0	0	0	0	0	0	0	0	0	0	0	0	0	0	0	0	0	—	0	—	—	—	P	1	1	1	0	0	1.000
1983 Phi	25	1	0	0	0	0	0	0	0	0	0	0	0	0	0	0	0	0	0	—	0	—	—	—	P	1	0	0	0	0	—
WS Totals		2	0	0	0	0	0	0	0	0	0	0	0	0	0	0	0	0	0	—	0	—	—	—	P	2	1	1	0	0	1.000
Postseason Totals		3	2	0	0	0	0	0	0	0	0	0	0	1	0	0	0	0	0	—	0	.000	.000	.000	P	3	1	1	0	0	1.000

PUTSY CABALLERO—Ralph Joseph Caballero—Bats: Right; Throws: Right

Ht: 5'10"; Wt: 170 lbs; Born: 11/5/1927 in New Orleans, Louisiana; Debut: 9/14/1944

World Series — Batting / Fielding

Year Tm	Age	G	AB	H	2B	3B	HR	TB	R	RBI	GW	TBB	IBB	SO	HBP	SH	SF	SB	CS	SB%	GDP	Avg	OBP	SLG	Pos	G	PO	A	E	DP	FPct
1950 Phi	22	3	1	0	0	0	0	0	0	0	0	0	0	1	0	0	0	0	0	—	0	.000	.000	.000	—						

ENOS CABELL—Enos Milton Cabell—Bats: Right; Throws: Right

Ht: 6'4"; Wt: 170 lbs; Born: 10/8/1949 in Fort Riley, Kansas; Debut: 9/17/1972

LCS — Batting / Fielding

Year Tm	Age	G	AB	H	2B	3B	HR	TB	R	RBI	GW	TBB	IBB	SO	HBP	SH	SF	SB	CS	SB%	GDP	Avg	OBP	SLG	Pos	G	PO	A	E	DP	FPct
1974 Bal	24	3	4	1	0	0	0	1	0	0	0	0	0	2	0	0	0	0	0	—	0	.250	.250	.250	OF	1	2	0	0	0	1.000
1980 Hou	30	5	21	5	1	0	0	6	1	0	0	1	0	3	0	3	0	0	1	.00	0	.238	.273	.286	3B	5	1	9	0	1	1.000
1985 LA	35	5	13	1	0	0	0	1	1	0	0	0	0	3	0	0	0	0	0	—	1	.077	.077	.077	1B	3	20	2	0	2	1.000
LCS Totals		13	38	7	1	0	0	8	2	0	0	1	0	8	0	3	0	0	1	.00	1	.184	.205	.211	3B	5	1	9	0	1	1.000

FRANCISCO CABRERA—Bats: Right; Throws: Right

Ht: 6'4"; Wt: 195 lbs; Born: 10/10/1966 in Santo Domingo, Dominican Republic; Debut: 7/24/1989

LCS — Batting / Fielding

Year Tm	Age	G	AB	H	2B	3B	HR	TB	R	RBI	GW	TBB	IBB	SO	HBP	SH	SF	SB	CS	SB%	GDP	Avg	OBP	SLG	Pos	G	PO	A	E	DP	FPct
1992 Atl	25	2	2	1	0	0	0	1	0	2	1	0	0	0	0	0	0	0	0	—	0	.500	.500	.500	—						
1993 Atl	26	3	3	2	0	0	0	2	0	1	0	0	0	1	0	0	0	0	0	—	0	.667	.667	.667	C	1	1	0	0	0	1.000
LCS Totals		5	5	3	0	0	0	3	0	3	1	0	0	1	0	0	0	0	0	—	0	.600	.600	.600	C	1	1	0	0	0	1.000

World Series — Batting / Fielding

Year Tm	Age	G	AB	H	2B	3B	HR	TB	R	RBI	GW	TBB	IBB	SO	HBP	SH	SF	SB	CS	SB%	GDP	Avg	OBP	SLG	Pos	G	PO	A	E	DP	FPct
1991 Atl	24	3	1	0	0	0	0	0	0	0	0	0	0	0	0	0	0	0	0	—	0	.000	.000	.000	C	1	0	0	0	0	—
1992 Atl	25	1	1	0	0	0	0	0	0	0	0	0	0	0	0	0	0	0	0	—	0	.000	.000	.000	—						
WS Totals		4	2	0	0	0	0	0	0	0	0	0	0	0	0	0	0	0	0	—	0	.000	.000	.000	C	1	0	0	0	0	—
Postseason Totals		9	7	3	0	0	0	3	0	3	1	0	0	1	0	0	0	0	0	—	0	.429	.429	.429	C	2	1	0	0	0	1.000

GREG CADARET—Gregory James Cadaret—Throws: Left; Bats: Left

Ht: 6'3"; Wt: 200 lbs; Born: 2/27/1962 in Detroit, Michigan; Debut: 7/5/1987

LCS — Pitching

Year Tm	Age	G	GS	CG	GF	IP	BFP	H	R	ER	HR	SH	SF	HB	TBB	IBB	SO	WP	Bk	W	L	Pct	ShO	Sv-Op	Hld	OAvg	OOBP	ERA
1988 Oak	26	1	0	0	0	0.1	2	1	1	1	1	0	0	0	0	0	0	0	0	0	0	—	0	0- 1	0	.500	.500	27.00

World Series — Pitching

Year Tm	Age	G	GS	CG	GF	IP	BFP	H	R	ER	HR	SH	SF	HB	TBB	IBB	SO	WP	Bk	W	L	Pct	ShO	Sv-Op	Hld	OAvg	OOBP	ERA
1988 Oak	26	3	0	0	0	2.0	8	2	0	0	0	0	0	0	0	0	3	0	0	0	0	—	0	0- 0	0	.250	.250	0.00
Postseason Totals		4	0	0	0	2.1	20	3	1	1	1	0	0	0	0	0	3	0	0	0	0	—	0	0-1	0	.300	.300	3.86

LCS — Batting / Fielding

Year Tm	Age	G	AB	H	2B	3B	HR	TB	R	RBI	GW	TBB	IBB	SO	HBP	SH	SF	SB	CS	SB%	GDP	Avg	OBP	SLG	Pos	G	PO	A	E	DP	FPct
1988 Oak	26	1	0	0	0	0	0	0	0	0	0	0	0	0	0	0	0	0	0	—	0	—	—	—	P	1	0	0	0	0	—

World Series — Batting / Fielding

Year Tm	Age	G	AB	H	2B	3B	HR	TB	R	RBI	GW	TBB	IBB	SO	HBP	SH	SF	SB	CS	SB%	GDP	Avg	OBP	SLG	Pos	G	PO	A	E	DP	FPct
1988 Oak	26	3	0	0	0	0	0	0	0	0	0	0	0	0	0	0	0	0	0	—	0	—	—	—	P	3	0	0	0	0	—
Postseason Totals		4	0	0	0	0	0	0	0	0	0	0	0	0	0	0	0	0	0	—	0	—	—	—	P	4	0	0	0	0	—

LEON CADORE—Leon Joseph Cadore—Nickname: Caddy—Throws: Right; Bats: Right

Ht: 6'1"; Wt: 190 lbs; Born: 11/20/1890 in Chicago, Illinois; Debut: 4/28/1915; Died: 3/16/1958

World Series — Pitching

Year Tm	Age	G	GS	CG	GF	IP	BFP	H	R	ER	HR	SH	SF	HB	TBB	IBB	SO	WP	Bk	W	L	Pct	ShO	Sv-Op	Hld	OAvg	OOBP	ERA
1920 Bro	29	2	1	0	1	2.0	11	4	2	2	0	0	1	0	1	0	1	0	0	0	1	.000	0	0- 0	0	.444	.455	9.00

World Series — Batting / Fielding

Year Tm	Age	G	AB	H	2B	3B	HR	TB	R	RBI	GW	TBB	IBB	SO	HBP	SH	SF	SB	CS	SB%	GDP	Avg	OBP	SLG	Pos	G	PO	A	E	DP	FPct
1920 Bro	29	2	0	0	0	0	0	0	0	0	0	0	0	0	0	0	0	0	0	—	0	—	—	—	P	2	1	1	0	0	1.000

HICK CADY—Forrest Leroy Cady—Bats: Right; Throws: Right

Ht: 6'2"; Wt: 179 lbs; Born: 1/26/1886 in Bishop Hill, Illinois; Debut: 4/26/1912; Died: 3/3/1946

World Series — Batting / Fielding

Year Tm	Age	G	AB	H	2B	3B	HR	TB	R	RBI	GW	TBB	IBB	SO	HBP	SH	SF	SB	CS	SB%	GDP	Avg	OBP	SLG	Pos	G	PO	A	E	DP	FPct
1912 Bos	26	7	22	3	0	0	0	3	1	1	0	0	0	3	0	1	0	0	0	—	0	.136	.136	.136	C	7	35	8	1	0	.977
1915 Bos	29	4	6	2	0	0	0	2	0	0	0	1	0	2	0	1	0	0	0	—	0	.333	.429	.333	C	4	14	4	0	0	1.000
1916 Bos	30	2	4	1	0	0	0	1	1	0	0	3	0	0	0	0	0	0	0	—	0	.250	.571	.250	C	2	11	1	0	1	1.000
WS Totals		13	32	6	0	0	0	6	2	1	0	4	0	5	0	2	0	0	0	—	0	.188	.278	.188	C	13	60	13	1	1	.986

MIKE CALDWELL—Ralph Michael Caldwell—Nickname: Lefty—Throws: Left; Bats: Right

Ht: 6'0"; Wt: 185 lbs; Born: 1/22/1949 in Tarboro, North Carolina; Debut: 9/4/1971

Division Series — Pitching

Year Tm	Age	G	GS	CG	GF	IP	BFP	H	R	ER	HR	SH	SF	HB	TBB	IBB	SO	WP	Bk	W	L	Pct	ShO	Sv-Op	Hld	OAvg	OOBP	ERA
1981 Mil	32	2	1	0	0	8.1	33	9	4	4	2	0	0	0	0	0	4	0	0	0	1	.000	0	0- 0	0	.273	.273	4.32

LCS — Pitching

Year Tm	Age	G	GS	CG	GF	IP	BFP	H	R	ER	HR	SH	SF	HB	TBB	IBB	SO	WP	Bk	W	L	Pct	ShO	Sv-Op	Hld	OAvg	OOBP	ERA
1982 Mil	33	1	1	0	0	3.0	18	7	6	5	0	0	1	0	1	0	2	1	0	0	1	.000	0	0- 0	0	.438	.444	15.00

World Series (Pitching)																												
Year Tm	Age	G	GS	CG	GF	IP	BFP	H	R	ER	HR	SH	SF	HB	TBB	IBB	SO	WP	Bk	W	L	Pct	ShO	Sv-Op	Hld	OAvg	OOBP	ERA
1982 Mil	33	3	2	1	1	17.2	74	19	4	4	0	0	0	0	3	0	6	0	0	2	0	1.000	1	0- 0	0	.268	.297	2.04
Postseason Totals		6	4	1	1	29.0	250	35	14	13	2	0	1	0	4	0	12	1	0	2	2	.500	1	0-0	0	.292	.312	4.03

Year Tm	Age	G	AB	H	2B	3B	HR	TB	R	RBI	GW	TBB	IBB	SO	HBP	SH	SF	SB	CS	SB%	GDP	Avg	OBP	SLG	Pos	G	PO	A	E	DP	FPct
Division Series																															
1981 Mil	32	2	0	0	0	0	0	0	0	0	0	0	0	0	0	0	0	0	0	—	0	—	—	—	P	2	0	3	0	0	1.000
LCS																															
1982 Mil	33	1	0	0	0	0	0	0	0	0	0	0	0	0	0	0	0	0	0	—	0	—	—	—	P	1	0	2	1	0	.667
World Series																															
1982 Mil	33	3	0	0	0	0	0	0	0	0	0	0	0	0	0	0	0	0	0	—	0	—	—	—	P	3	4	2	0	0	1.000
Postseason Totals		6	0	0	0	0	0	0	0	0	0	0	0	0	0	0	0	0	0	—	0	—	—	—	P	6	4	7	1	0	.917

RAY CALDWELL—Raymond Benjamin Caldwell—Nicknames: Rube, Slim—Throws: Right; Bats: Left

Ht: 6'2"; Wt: 190 lbs; Born: 4/26/1888 in Croydon, Pennsylvania; Debut: 9/9/1910; Died: 8/17/1967

World Series (Pitching)																												
Year Tm	Age	G	GS	CG	GF	IP	BFP	H	R	ER	HR	SH	SF	HB	TBB	IBB	SO	WP	Bk	W	L	Pct	ShO	Sv-Op	Hld	OAvg	OOBP	ERA
1920 Cle	32	1	1	0	0	0.1	5	2	2	1	0	1	0	0	1	0	0	0	0	0	1	.000	0	0- 0	0	.667	.750	27.00

World Series (Batting / Fielding)																															
Year Tm	Age	G	AB	H	2B	3B	HR	TB	R	RBI	GW	TBB	IBB	SO	HBP	SH	SF	SB	CS	SB%	GDP	Avg	OBP	SLG	Pos	G	PO	A	E	DP	FPct
1920 Cle	32	1	0	0	0	0	0	0	0	0	0	0	0	0	0	0	0	0	0	—	0	—	—	—	P	1	0	0	0	0	—

JEFF CALHOUN—Jeffrey Wilton Calhoun—Throws: Left; Bats: Left

Ht: 6'2"; Wt: 190 lbs; Born: 4/11/1958 in LaGrange, Georgia; Debut: 9/2/1984

LCS (Pitching)																												
Year Tm	Age	G	GS	CG	GF	IP	BFP	H	R	ER	HR	SH	SF	HB	TBB	IBB	SO	WP	Bk	W	L	Pct	ShO	Sv-Op	Hld	OAvg	OOBP	ERA
1986 Hou	28	1	0	0	1	1.0	4	1	1	1	0	1	0	0	1	0	0	2	0	0	0	—	0	0- 0	0	.500	.667	9.00

LCS (Batting / Fielding)																															
Year Tm	Age	G	AB	H	2B	3B	HR	TB	R	RBI	GW	TBB	IBB	SO	HBP	SH	SF	SB	CS	SB%	GDP	Avg	OBP	SLG	Pos	G	PO	A	E	DP	FPct
1986 Hou	28	1	0	0	0	0	0	0	0	0	0	0	0	0	0	0	0	0	0	—	0	—	—	—	P	1	0	0	0	0	—

DOLPH CAMILLI—Adolph Louis Camilli—Bats: Left; Throws: Left

Ht: 5'10"; Wt: 185 lbs; Born: 4/23/1907 in San Francisco, California; Debut: 9/9/1933; Died: 10/21/1997

World Series (Batting / Fielding)																															
Year Tm	Age	G	AB	H	2B	3B	HR	TB	R	RBI	GW	TBB	IBB	SO	HBP	SH	SF	SB	CS	SB%	GDP	Avg	OBP	SLG	Pos	G	PO	A	E	DP	FPct
1941 Bro-*M*	34	5	18	3	1	0	0	4	1	1	1	1	0	6	0	0	0	0	0	—	1	.167	.211	.222	1B	5	45	4	0	4	1.000

KEN CAMINITI—Kenneth Gene Caminiti—Bats: Both; Throws: Right

Ht: 6'0"; Wt: 200 lbs; Born: 4/21/1963 in Hanford, California; Debut: 7/16/1987

Division Series (Batting / Fielding)																															
Year Tm	Age	G	AB	H	2B	3B	HR	TB	R	RBI	GW	TBB	IBB	SO	HBP	SH	SF	SB	CS	SB%	GDP	Avg	OBP	SLG	Pos	G	PO	A	E	DP	FPct
1996 SD-*M*	33	3	10	3	0	0	3	12	3	3	0	2	1	5	0	0	0	0	0	—	0	.300	.417	1.200	3B	3	0	5	3	0	.625

HOWIE CAMNITZ—Samuel Howard Camnitz—Throws: Right; Bats: Right

Ht: 5'9"; Wt: 169 lbs; Born: 8/22/1881 in Covington, Kentucky; Debut: 4/22/1904; Died: 3/2/1960

World Series (Pitching)																												
Year Tm	Age	G	GS	CG	GF	IP	BFP	H	R	ER	HR	SH	SF	HB	TBB	IBB	SO	WP	Bk	W	L	Pct	ShO	Sv-Op	Hld	OAvg	OOBP	ERA
1909 Pit	28	2	1	0	0	3.1	20	8	6	5	0	1	0	0	2	0	2	0	0	0	1	.000	0	0- 0	0	.471	.526	13.50

World Series (Batting / Fielding)																															
Year Tm	Age	G	AB	H	2B	3B	HR	TB	R	RBI	GW	TBB	IBB	SO	HBP	SH	SF	SB	CS	SB%	GDP	Avg	OBP	SLG	Pos	G	PO	A	E	DP	FPct
1909 Pit	28	2	1	0	0	0	0	0	0	0	0	0	0	0	0	0	0	0	0	—	0	.000	.000	.000	P	2	0	2	0	0	1.000

RICK CAMP—Rick Lamar Camp—Throws: Right; Bats: Right

Ht: 6'1"; Wt: 185 lbs; Born: 6/10/1953 in Trion, Georgia; Debut: 9/15/1976

LCS (Pitching)																												
Year Tm	Age	G	GS	CG	GF	IP	BFP	H	R	ER	HR	SH	SF	HB	TBB	IBB	SO	WP	Bk	W	L	Pct	ShO	Sv-Op	Hld	OAvg	OOBP	ERA
1982 Atl	29	1	1	0	0	1.0	8	4	4	4	0	0	0	0	1	0	0	0	0	0	1	.000	0	0- 0	0	.571	.625	36.00

LCS (Batting / Fielding)																															
Year Tm	Age	G	AB	H	2B	3B	HR	TB	R	RBI	GW	TBB	IBB	SO	HBP	SH	SF	SB	CS	SB%	GDP	Avg	OBP	SLG	Pos	G	PO	A	E	DP	FPct
1982 Atl	29	1	0	0	0	0	0	0	0	0	0	0	0	0	0	0	0	0	0	—	0	—	—	—	P	1	0	0	0	0	—

ROY CAMPANELLA (HOF 1969-W)—Nickname: Campy—Bats: Right; Throws: Right

Ht: 5'9"; Wt: 190 lbs; Born: 11/19/1921 in Philadelphia, Pennsylvania; Debut: 4/20/1948; Died: 6/26/1993

World Series (Batting / Fielding)																															
Year Tm	Age	G	AB	H	2B	3B	HR	TB	R	RBI	GW	TBB	IBB	SO	HBP	SH	SF	SB	CS	SB%	GDP	Avg	OBP	SLG	Pos	G	PO	A	E	DP	FPct
1949 Bro	27	5	15	4	1	0	1	8	2	2	0	3	1	1	0	0	0	0	0	—	0	.267	.389	.533	C	5	32	2	0	1	1.000
1952 Bro	30	7	28	6	0	0	0	6	0	1	0	1	0	6	0	0	0	0	1	.00	1	.214	.241	.214	C	7	39	5	0	0	1.000
1953 Bro-*M*	31	6	22	6	0	0	1	9	6	2	1	2	1	3	1	0	0	0	0	—	0	.273	.360	.409	C	6	47	9	0	1	1.000
1955 Bro-*M*	33	7	27	7	3	0	2	16	4	4	0	3	0	3	0	1	0	0	0	—	0	.259	.333	.593	C	7	42	3	1	1	.978
1956 Bro	34	7	22	4	1	0	0	5	2	3	0	3	1	7	0	0	2	0	1	.00	0	.182	.259	.227	C	7	49	3	0	1	1.000
WS Totals		32	114	27	5	0	4	44	14	12	1	12	3	20	1	1	2	0	2	.00	1	.237	.310	.386	C	32	209	22	1	4	.996

BERT CAMPANERIS—Dagoberto Campaneris—Nickname: Campy—Bats: Right; Throws: Right

Ht: 5'10"; Wt: 160 lbs; Born: 3/9/1942 in Pueblo Nuevo, Cuba; Debut: 7/23/1964

Year Tm	Age	G	AB	H	2B	3B	HR	TB	R	RBI	GW	TBB	IBB	SO	HBP	SH	SF	SB	CS	SB%	GDP	Avg	OBP	SLG	Pos	G	PO	A	E	DP	FPct
LCS																															
1971 Oak	29	3	12	2	1	0	0	3	0	0	0	0	0	1	0	0	0	0	1	.00	0	.167	.167	.250	SS	3	3	6	0	1	1.000
1972 Oak	30	2	7	3	0	0	0	3	3	0	0	1	0	0	1	0	0	2	0	1.00	0	.429	.556	.429	SS	2	3	7	0	1	1.000
1973 Oak	31	5	21	7	1	0	2	14	3	3	1	2	0	2	0	0	0	3	0	1.00	0	.333	.391	.667	SS	5	6	14	2	1	.909
1974 Oak	32	4	17	3	0	0	0	3	0	3	0	0	0	3	0	0	1	1	1	.50	1	.176	.167	.176	SS	4	3	17	0	1	1.000
1975 Oak	33	3	11	0	0	0	0	0	1	0	0	1	0	1	0	0	0	0	0	—	0	.000	.083	.000	SS	3	2	10	0	3	1.000
1979 Cal	37	1	0	0	0	0	0	0	0	0	0	0	0	0	0	0	0	0	0	—	0	—	—	—	SS	1	0	0	0	0	—
LCS Totals		18	68	15	2	0	2	23	7	6	1	4	0	7	1	0	1	6	2	.75	1	.221	.270	.338	SS	18	17	54	2	7	.973
World Series																															
1972 Oak	30	7	28	5	0	0	0	5	1	0	0	1	0	4	0	2	0	0	1	.00	0	.179	.207	.179	SS	7	17	15	1	2	.970
1973 Oak	31	7	31	9	0	1	1	14	6	3	2	1	0	7	2	0	0	3	0	1.00	0	.290	.353	.452	SS	7	10	28	1	3	.974
1974 Oak	32	5	17	6	2	0	0	8	1	2	0	0	0	2	1	2	0	1	1	.50	0	.353	.389	.471	SS	5	6	16	2	5	.917
WS Totals		19	76	20	2	1	1	27	8	5	2	2	0	13	3	4	0	4	2	.67	0	.263	.309	.355	SS	19	33	59	4	10	.958
Postseason Totals		37	144	35	4	1	3	50	15	11	3	6	0	20	4	4	1	10	4	.71	1	.243	.290	.347	SS	37	50	113	6	17	.964

BILL CAMPBELL—William Richard Campbell—Throws: Right; Bats: Left

Ht: 6'3"; Wt: 185 lbs; Born: 8/9/1948 in Highland Park, Michigan; Debut: 7/14/1973

Year Tm	Age	G	GS	CG	GF	IP	BFP	H	R	ER	HR	SH	SF	HB	TBB	IBB	SO	WP	Bk	W	L	Pct	ShO	Sv-Op	Hld	OAvg	OOBP	ERA
LCS																												
1985 StL	37	3	0	0	1	2.1	10	3	0	0	0	0	0	0	0	0	2	0	0	0	0	—	0	0- 0	0	.300	.300	0.00
World Series																												
1985 StL	37	3	0	0	0	4.0	17	4	1	1	0	0	0	0	2	0	5	0	0	0	0	—	0	0-0	0	.267	.353	2.25
Postseason Totals		6	0	0	1	6.1	54	7	1	1	0	0	0	0	2	0	7	0	0	0	0	—	0	0-0	0	.280	.333	1.42

LCS (Batting / Fielding)																															
Year Tm	Age	G	AB	H	2B	3B	HR	TB	R	RBI	GW	TBB	IBB	SO	HBP	SH	SF	SB	CS	SB%	GDP	Avg	OBP	SLG	Pos	G	PO	A	E	DP	FPct
1985 StL	37	3	0	0	0	0	0	0	0	0	0	0	0	0	0	0	0	0	0	—	0	—	—	—	P	3	0	0	0	0	—

World Series		Batting																							Fielding						
Year Tm	Age	G	AB	H	2B	3B	HR	TB	R	RBI	GW	TBB	IBB	SO	HBP	SH	SF	SB	CS	SB%	GDP	Avg	OBP	SLG	Pos	G	PO	A	E	DP	FPct
1985 StL	37	3	0	0	0	0	0	0	0	0	0	0	0	0	0	0	0	0	0	—	0	—	—	—	P	3	1	0	0	0	1.000
Postseason Totals		6	0	0	0	0	0	0	0	0	0	0	0	0	0	0	0	0	0	—	0	—	—	—	P	6	1	0	0	0	1.000

BRUCE CAMPBELL—Bruce Douglas Campbell—Bats: Left; Throws: Right

Ht: 6'1"; Wt: 185 lbs; Born: 10/20/1909 in Chicago, Illinois; Debut: 9/12/1930; Died: 6/17/1995

World Series		Batting																							Fielding						
Year Tm	Age	G	AB	H	2B	3B	HR	TB	R	RBI	GW	TBB	IBB	SO	HBP	SH	SF	SB	CS	SB%	GDP	Avg	OBP	SLG	Pos	G	PO	A	E	DP	FPct
1940 Det	30	7	25	9	1	0	1	13	4	5	0	4	0	4	0	1	0	0	2	.00	1	.360	.448	.520	OF	7	17	0	0	0	1.000

PAUL CAMPBELL—Paul McLaughlin Campbell—Bats: Left; Throws: Left

Ht: 5'10"; Wt: 185 lbs; Born: 9/1/1917 in Paw Creek, North Carolina; Debut: 4/15/1941

World Series		Batting																							Fielding						
Year Tm	Age	G	AB	H	2B	3B	HR	TB	R	RBI	GW	TBB	IBB	SO	HBP	SH	SF	SB	CS	SB%	GDP	Avg	OBP	SLG	Pos	G	PO	A	E	DP	FPct
1946 Bos	29	1	0	0	0	0	0	0	0	0	0	0	0	0	0	0	0	0	0	—	0	—	—	—	—						

WILLIE CANATE—Emisael William Canate—Bats: Right; Throws: Right

Ht: 6'0"; Wt: 170 lbs; Born: 12/11/1971 in Maracaibo, Venezuela; Debut: 4/16/1993

World Series		Batting																							Fielding						
Year Tm	Age	G	AB	H	2B	3B	HR	TB	R	RBI	GW	TBB	IBB	SO	HBP	SH	SF	SB	CS	SB%	GDP	Avg	OBP	SLG	Pos	G	PO	A	E	DP	FPct
1993 Tor	21	1	0	0	0	0	0	0	0	0	0	0	0	0	0	0	0	0	0	—	0	—	—	—	—						

CASEY CANDAELE—Casey Todd Candaele—Bats: Both; Throws: Right

Ht: 5'9"; Wt: 160 lbs; Born: 1/12/1961 in Lompoc, California; Debut: 6/5/1986

Division Series		Batting																							Fielding						
Year Tm	Age	G	AB	H	2B	3B	HR	TB	R	RBI	GW	TBB	IBB	SO	HBP	SH	SF	SB	CS	SB%	GDP	Avg	OBP	SLG	Pos	G	PO	A	E	DP	FPct
1996 Cle	35	2	0	0	0	0	0	0	1	0	0	1	0	0	0	0	0	0	0	—	0	—	1.000	—	—						

JOHN CANDELARIA—John Robert Candelaria—Nickname: Candy Man—Throws: Left; Bats: Left

Ht: 6'7"; Wt: 205 lbs; Born: 11/6/1953 in New York, New York; Debut: 6/8/1975

LCS		Pitching																										
Year Tm	Age	G	GS	CG	GF	IP	BFP	H	R	ER	HR	SH	SF	HB	TBB	IBB	SO	WP	Bk	W	L	Pct	ShO	Sv-Op	Hld	OAvg	OOBP	ERA
1975 Pit	21	1	1	0	0	7.2	29	3	3	3	2	0	0	0	2	0	14	0	0	0	0	—	0	0- 0	0	.111	.172	3.52
1979 Pit	25	1	1	0	0	7.0	26	5	2	2	1	0	0	0	1	0	4	0	0	0	0	—	0	0- 0	0	.200	.231	2.57
1986 Cal	32	2	2	0	0	10.2	50	11	8	1	1	0	0	0	6	1	7	0	0	1	1	.500	0	0- 0	0	.250	.340	0.84
LCS Totals		4	4	0	0	25.1	210	19	13	6	4	0	0	0	9	1	25	0	0	1	1	.500	0	0-0	0	.198	.267	2.13
World Series		**Pitching**																										
Year Tm	Age	G	GS	CG	GF	IP	BFP	H	R	ER	HR	SH	SF	HB	TBB	IBB	SO	WP	Bk	W	L	Pct	ShO	Sv-Op	Hld	OAvg	OOBP	ERA
1979 Pit	25	2	2	0	0	9.0	41	14	6	5	1	0	0	0	2	0	4	0	0	1	1	.500	0	0- 0	0	.359	.390	5.00
Postseason Totals		6	6	0	0	34.1	292	33	19	11	5	0	0	0	11	1	29	0	0	2	2	.500	0	0-0	0	.244	.301	2.88

LCS		Batting																							Fielding						
Year Tm	Age	G	AB	H	2B	3B	HR	TB	R	RBI	GW	TBB	IBB	SO	HBP	SH	SF	SB	CS	SB%	GDP	Avg	OBP	SLG	Pos	G	PO	A	E	DP	FPct
1975 Pit	21	1	3	0	0	0	0	0	0	0	0	0	0	3	0	0	0	0	0	—	0	.000	.000	.000	P	1	0	0	0	0	—
1979 Pit	25	1	3	0	0	0	0	0	0	0	0	0	0	2	0	0	0	0	0	—	0	.000	.000	.000	P	1	0	0	0	0	—
1986 Cal	32	2	0	0	0	0	0	0	0	0	0	0	0	0	0	0	0	0	0	—	0	—	—	—	P	2	0	1	0	0	1.000
LCS Totals		4	6	0	0	0	0	0	0	0	0	0	0	5	0	0	0	0	0	—	0	.000	.000	.000	P	4	0	1	0	0	1.000
World Series		**Batting**																							**Fielding**						
Year Tm	Age	G	AB	H	2B	3B	HR	TB	R	RBI	GW	TBB	IBB	SO	HBP	SH	SF	SB	CS	SB%	GDP	Avg	OBP	SLG	Pos	G	PO	A	E	DP	FPct
1979 Pit	25	2	3	1	0	0	0	1	0	0	0	0	0	2	0	0	0	0	0	—	0	.333	.333	.333	P	2	0	1	0	0	1.000
Postseason Totals		6	9	1	0	0	0	1	0	0	0	0	0	7	0	0	0	0	0	—	0	.111	.111	.111	P	6	0	2	0	0	1.000

TOM CANDIOTTI—Thomas Caesar Candiotti—Throws: Right; Bats: Right

Ht: 6'3"; Wt: 205 lbs; Born: 8/31/1957 in Walnut Creek, California; Debut: 8/8/1983

Division Series		Pitching																										
Year Tm	Age	G	GS	CG	GF	IP	BFP	H	R	ER	HR	SH	SF	HB	TBB	IBB	SO	WP	Bk	W	L	Pct	ShO	Sv-Op	Hld	OAvg	OOBP	ERA
1996 LA	39	1	0	0	0	2.0	6	0	0	0	0	0	0	0	0	0	1	0	0	0	0	—	0	0- 0	0	.000	.000	0.00
LCS		**Pitching**																										
Year Tm	Age	G	GS	CG	GF	IP	BFP	H	R	ER	HR	SH	SF	HB	TBB	IBB	SO	WP	Bk	W	L	Pct	ShO	Sv-Op	Hld	OAvg	OOBP	ERA
1991 Tor	34	2	2	0	0	7.2	42	17	9	7	1	1	0	0	2	0	5	1	0	0	1	.000	0	0- 0	0	.436	.463	8.22
Postseason Totals		3	2	0	0	9.2	96	17	9	7	1	1	0	0	2	0	6	1	0	0	1	.000	0	0-0	0	.378	.404	6.52

Division Series		Batting																							Fielding						
Year Tm	Age	G	AB	H	2B	3B	HR	TB	R	RBI	GW	TBB	IBB	SO	HBP	SH	SF	SB	CS	SB%	GDP	Avg	OBP	SLG	Pos	G	PO	A	E	DP	FPct
1996 LA	39	1	0	0	0	0	0	0	0	0	0	0	0	0	0	0	0	0	0	—	0	—	—	—	P	1	0	0	0	0	—
LCS		**Batting**																							**Fielding**						
Year Tm	Age	G	AB	H	2B	3B	HR	TB	R	RBI	GW	TBB	IBB	SO	HBP	SH	SF	SB	CS	SB%	GDP	Avg	OBP	SLG	Pos	G	PO	A	E	DP	FPct
1991 Tor	34	2	0	0	0	0	0	0	0	0	0	0	0	0	0	0	0	0	0	—	0	—	—	—	P	2	0	2	0	1	1.000
Postseason Totals		3	0	0	0	0	0	0	0	0	0	0	0	0	0	0	0	0	0	—	0	—	—	—	P	3	0	2	0	1	1.000

JOHN CANGELOSI—John Anthony Cangelosi—Bats: Both; Throws: Left

Ht: 5'8"; Wt: 150 lbs; Born: 3/10/1963 in Brooklyn, New York; Debut: 6/30/1985

Division Series		Batting																							Fielding						
Year Tm	Age	G	AB	H	2B	3B	HR	TB	R	RBI	GW	TBB	IBB	SO	HBP	SH	SF	SB	CS	SB%	GDP	Avg	OBP	SLG	Pos	G	PO	A	E	DP	FPct
1997 Fla	34	1	1	0	0	0	0	0	0	0	0	0	0	0	0	0	0	0	0	—	0	.000	.000	.000	—						
LCS		**Batting**																							**Fielding**						
Year Tm	Age	G	AB	H	2B	3B	HR	TB	R	RBI	GW	TBB	IBB	SO	HBP	SH	SF	SB	CS	SB%	GDP	Avg	OBP	SLG	Pos	G	PO	A	E	DP	FPct
1997 Fla	34	3	5	1	0	0	0	1	0	0	0	1	0	0	0	0	0	0	0	—	0	.200	.333	.200	OF	1	2	0	0	0	1.000
World Series		**Batting**																							**Fielding**						
Year Tm	Age	G	AB	H	2B	3B	HR	TB	R	RBI	GW	TBB	IBB	SO	HBP	SH	SF	SB	CS	SB%	GDP	Avg	OBP	SLG	Pos	G	PO	A	E	DP	FPct
1997 Fla	34	3	3	1	0	0	0	1	0	0	0	0	0	2	0	0	0	0	0	—	0	.333	.333	.333	—						
Postseason Totals		7	9	2	0	0	0	2	0	0	0	1	0	2	0	0	0	0	0	—	0	.222	.300	.222	OF	1	2	0	0	0	1.000

JOSE CANSECO—Bats: Right; Throws: Right

Ht: 6'3"; Wt: 195 lbs; Born: 7/2/1964 in Havana, Cuba; Debut: 9/2/1985

Division Series		Batting																							Fielding						
Year Tm	Age	G	AB	H	2B	3B	HR	TB	R	RBI	GW	TBB	IBB	SO	HBP	SH	SF	SB	CS	SB%	GDP	Avg	OBP	SLG	Pos	G	PO	A	E	DP	FPct
1995 Bos	31	3	13	0	0	0	0	0	0	0	0	2	0	2	0	0	0	0	0	—	0	.000	.133	.000	OF	1	4	0	0	0	1.000
LCS		**Batting**																							**Fielding**						
Year Tm	Age	G	AB	H	2B	3B	HR	TB	R	RBI	GW	TBB	IBB	SO	HBP	SH	SF	SB	CS	SB%	GDP	Avg	OBP	SLG	Pos	G	PO	A	E	DP	FPct
1988 Oak-*M*	24	4	16	5	1	0	3	15	4	4	1	1	0	2	0	0	0	1	1	.50	1	.313	.353	.938	OF	4	6	0	0	0	1.000
1989 Oak	25	5	17	5	0	0	1	8	1	3	1	3	0	7	0	0	0	0	2	.00	0	.294	.400	.471	OF	5	6	1	1	0	.875
1990 Oak	26	4	11	2	0	0	0	2	3	1	0	5	0	5	0	0	1	2	0	1.00	0	.182	.412	.182	OF	4	14	0	0	0	1.000
LCS Totals		13	44	12	1	0	4	25	8	8	2	9	0	14	0	0	1	3	3	.50	1	.273	.389	.568	OF	13	26	1	1	0	.964
World Series		**Batting**																							**Fielding**						
Year Tm	Age	G	AB	H	2B	3B	HR	TB	R	RBI	GW	TBB	IBB	SO	HBP	SH	SF	SB	CS	SB%	GDP	Avg	OBP	SLG	Pos	G	PO	A	E	DP	FPct
1988 Oak-*M*	24	5	19	1	0	0	1	4	1	5	0	2	0	5	1	0	0	1	0	1.00	0	.053	.182	.211	OF	5	7	0	0	0	1.000
1989 Oak	25	4	14	5	0	0	1	8	5	3	0	4	1	3	0	0	0	1	0	1.00	0	.357	.500	.571	OF	4	6	0	0	0	1.000
1990 Oak	26	4	12	1	0	0	1	4	1	2	0	2	0	3	0	0	0	0	0	—	1	.083	.214	.333	OF	3	4	0	0	0	1.000
WS Totals		13	45	7	0	0	3	16	7	10	0	8	1	11	1	0	0	2	0	1.00	1	.156	.296	.356	OF	12	17	0	0	0	1.000
Postseason Totals		29	102	19	1	0	7	41	15	18	2	19	1	27	1	0	1	5	3	.63	2	.186	.317	.402	OF	26	47	1	1	0	.980

BERNIE CARBO—Bernard Carbo—Bats: Left; Throws: Right

Ht: 5'11"; Wt: 173 lbs; Born: 8/5/1947 in Detroit, Michigan; Debut: 9/2/1969

LCS		Batting																							Fielding						
Year Tm	Age	G	AB	H	2B	3B	HR	TB	R	RBI	GW	TBB	IBB	SO	HBP	SH	SF	SB	CS	SB%	GDP	Avg	OBP	SLG	Pos	G	PO	A	E	DP	FPct
1970 Cin	23	2	6	0	0	0	0	0	0	0	0	1	1	2	0	0	0	0	0	—	0	.000	.143	.000	OF	2	0	0	0	0	

World Series		Batting																							Fielding						
Year Tm	Age	G	AB	H	2B	3B	HR	TB	R	RBI	GW	TBB	IBB	SO	HBP	SH	SF	SB	CS	SB%	GDP	Avg	OBP	SLG	Pos	G	PO	A	E	DP	FPct
1970 Cin	23	4	8	0	0	0	0	0	0	0	0	2	0	3	0	0	0	0	1	.00	1	.000	.200	.000	OF	2	4	0	0	0	1.000
1975 Bos	28	4	7	3	1	0	2	10	3	4	0	1	0	1	0	0	0	0	0	—	0	.429	.500	1.429	OF	2	1	1	0	0	1.000
WS Totals		8	15	3	1	0	2	10	3	4	0	3	0	4	0	0	0	0	1	.00	1	.200	.333	.667	OF	4	5	1	0	0	1.000
Postseason Totals		10	21	3	1	0	2	10	3	4	0	4	1	6	0	0	0	0	1	.00	1	.143	.280	.476	OF	6	5	1	0	0	1.000

JOSE CARDENAL—Jose Rosario Domec Cardenal—Bats: Right; Throws: Right

Ht: 5'10"; Wt: 150 lbs; Born: 10/7/1943 in Matanzas, Cuba; Debut: 4/14/1963

LCS		Batting																							Fielding						
Year Tm	Age	G	AB	H	2B	3B	HR	TB	R	RBI	GW	TBB	IBB	SO	HBP	SH	SF	SB	CS	SB%	GDP	Avg	OBP	SLG	Pos	G	PO	A	E	DP	FPct
1978 Phi	34	2	6	1	0	0	0	1	0	0	0	1	0	1	0	0	0	0	0	—	0	.167	.286	.167	1B	2	21	0	0	1	1.000
World Series		Batting																							Fielding						
Year Tm	Age	G	AB	H	2B	3B	HR	TB	R	RBI	GW	TBB	IBB	SO	HBP	SH	SF	SB	CS	SB%	GDP	Avg	OBP	SLG	Pos	G	PO	A	E	DP	FPct
1980 KC	36	4	10	2	0	0	0	2	0	0	0	0	0	3	0	0	0	0	0	—	1	.200	.200	.200	OF	4	7	0	0	0	1.000
Postseason Totals		6	16	3	0	0	0	3	0	0	0	1	0	4	0	0	0	0	0	—	1	.188	.235	.188	OF	4	7	0	0	0	1.000

LEO CARDENAS—Leonardo Lazaro Cardenas—Nicknames: Chico, Mr. Automatic—Bats: Right; Throws: Right

Ht: 5'11"; Wt: 150 lbs; Born: 12/17/1938 in Matanzas, Cuba; Debut: 7/25/1960

LCS		Batting																							Fielding						
Year Tm	Age	G	AB	H	2B	3B	HR	TB	R	RBI	GW	TBB	IBB	SO	HBP	SH	SF	SB	CS	SB%	GDP	Avg	OBP	SLG	Pos	G	PO	A	E	DP	FPct
1969 Min	30	3	13	2	0	1	0	4	0	0	0	0	0	7	0	0	0	0	0	—	0	.154	.154	.308	SS	3	13	12	1	3	.962
1970 Min	31	3	11	2	0	0	0	2	1	1	0	1	0	1	0	1	0	0	0	—	1	.182	.250	.182	SS	3	6	12	2	3	.900
LCS Totals		6	24	4	0	1	0	6	1	1	0	1	0	8	0	1	0	0	0	—	1	.167	.200	.250	SS	6	19	24	3	6	.935
World Series		Batting																							Fielding						
Year Tm	Age	G	AB	H	2B	3B	HR	TB	R	RBI	GW	TBB	IBB	SO	HBP	SH	SF	SB	CS	SB%	GDP	Avg	OBP	SLG	Pos	G	PO	A	E	DP	FPct
1961 Cin	22	3	3	1	1	0	0	2	0	0	0	0	0	1	0	0	0	0	0	—	0	.333	.333	.667	—						
Postseason Totals		9	27	5	1	1	0	8	1	1	0	1	0	9	0	1	0	0	0	—	1	.185	.214	.296	SS	6	19	24	3	6	.935

DON CARDWELL—Donald Eugene Cardwell—Throws: Right; Bats: Right

Ht: 6'4"; Wt: 210 lbs; Born: 12/7/1935 in Winston-Salem, North Carolina; Debut: 4/21/1957

World Series		Pitching																										
Year Tm	Age	G	GS	CG	GF	IP	BFP	H	R	ER	HR	SH	SF	HB	TBB	IBB	SO	WP	Bk	W	L	Pct	ShO	Sv-Op	Hld	OAvg	OOBP	ERA
1969 NYN	33	1	0	0	0	1.0	3	0	0	0	0	0	0	0	0	0	0	0	0	0	0	—	0	0-0	0	.000	.000	0.00

World Series		Batting																							Fielding						
Year Tm	Age	G	AB	H	2B	3B	HR	TB	R	RBI	GW	TBB	IBB	SO	HBP	SH	SF	SB	CS	SB%	GDP	Avg	OBP	SLG	Pos	G	PO	A	E	DP	FPct
1969 NYN	33	1	0	0	0	0	0	0	0	0	0	0	0	0	0	0	0	0	0	—	0	—	—	—	P	1	0	0	0	0	—

ROD CAREW (HOF 1991-W)—Rodney Cline Carew—Bats: Left; Throws: Right

Ht: 6'0"; Wt: 170 lbs; Born: 10/1/1945 in Gatun, Canal Zone; Debut: 4/11/1967

LCS		Batting																							Fielding						
Year Tm	Age	G	AB	H	2B	3B	HR	TB	R	RBI	GW	TBB	IBB	SO	HBP	SH	SF	SB	CS	SB%	GDP	Avg	OBP	SLG	Pos	G	PO	A	E	DP	FPct
1969 Min	24	3	14	1	0	0	0	1	0	0	0	1	0	4	0	0	0	0	0	—	0	.071	.133	.071	2B	3	6	3	1	1	.900
1970 Min	24	2	2	0	0	0	0	0	0	0	0	0	0	1	0	0	0	0	0	—	0	.000	.000	.000	—						
1979 Cal	33	4	17	7	3	0	0	10	4	1	0	0	0	0	0	0	0	1	1	.50	0	.412	.412	.588	1B	4	34	1	0	6	1.000
1982 Cal	37	5	17	3	1	0	0	4	2	0	0	4	0	4	0	0	0	1	1	.50	0	.176	.333	.235	1B	5	42	3	0	2	1.000
LCS Totals		14	50	11	4	0	0	15	6	1	0	5	0	9	0	0	0	2	2	.50	0	.220	.291	.300	1B	9	76	4	0	8	1.000

ANDY CAREY—Andrew Arthur Carey—Bats: Right; Throws: Right

Ht: 6'1"; Wt: 190 lbs; Born: 10/18/1931 in Oakland, California; Debut: 5/2/1952

World Series		Batting																							Fielding						
Year Tm	Age	G	AB	H	2B	3B	HR	TB	R	RBI	GW	TBB	IBB	SO	HBP	SH	SF	SB	CS	SB%	GDP	Avg	OBP	SLG	Pos	G	PO	A	E	DP	FPct
1955 NYA	23	2	2	1	0	1	0	3	0	1	0	0	0	0	0	0	0	0	0	—	0	.500	.500	1.500	—						
1956 NYA	24	7	19	3	0	0	0	3	2	0	0	1	0	6	0	0	0	0	0	—	0	.158	.200	.158	3B	7	7	10	2	0	.895
1957 NYA	25	2	7	2	1	0	0	3	0	1	0	1	0	0	0	0	0	0	0	—	0	.286	.375	.429	3B	2	3	6	0	0	1.000
1958 NYA	26	5	12	1	0	0	0	1	1	0	0	0	0	3	0	0	0	0	0	—	0	.083	.083	.083	3B	5	2	6	0	0	1.000
WS Totals		16	40	7	1	1	0	10	3	2	0	2	0	9	0	0	0	0	0	—	0	.175	.214	.250	3B	14	12	22	2	0	.944

MAX CAREY (HOF 1961-V)—Max George Carey—Nickname: Scoops—Bats: Both; Throws: Right

Ht: 5'11"; Wt: 170 lbs; Born: 1/11/1890 in Terre Haute, Indiana; Debut: 10/3/1910; Died: 5/30/1976

World Series		Batting																							Fielding						
Year Tm	Age	G	AB	H	2B	3B	HR	TB	R	RBI	GW	TBB	IBB	SO	HBP	SH	SF	SB	CS	SB%	GDP	Avg	OBP	SLG	Pos	G	PO	A	E	DP	FPct
1925 Pit	35	7	24	11	4	0	0	15	6	2	0	2	0	3	3	2	0	3	1	.75	0	.458	.552	.625	OF	7	14	0	1	0	.933

TEX CARLETON—James Otto Carleton—Throws: Right; Bats: Both

Ht: 6'1"; Wt: 180 lbs; Born: 8/19/1906 in Comanche, Texas; Debut: 4/17/1932; Died: 1/11/1977

World Series		Pitching																										
Year Tm	Age	G	GS	CG	GF	IP	BFP	H	R	ER	HR	SH	SF	HB	TBB	IBB	SO	WP	Bk	W	L	Pct	ShO	Sv-Op	Hld	OAvg	OOBP	ERA
1934 StL	28	2	1	0	1	3.2	18	5	3	3	0	0	0	0	2	0	2	0	0	0	0	—	0	0-0	0	.313	.389	7.36
1935 ChN	29	1	1	0	0	7.0	34	6	2	1	0	0	0	0	7	1	4	0	1	0	1	.000	0	0-0	0	.222	.382	1.29
1938 ChN	32	1	0	0	0	0.0	3	1	2	2	0	0	0	0	2	1	0	2	0	0	0	—	0	0-0	0	1.000	1.000	—
WS Totals		4	2	0	1	10.2	110	12	7	6	0	0	0	0	11	2	6	2	1	0	1	.000	0	0-0	0	.273	.418	5.06

World Series		Batting																							Fielding						
Year Tm	Age	G	AB	H	2B	3B	HR	TB	R	RBI	GW	TBB	IBB	SO	HBP	SH	SF	SB	CS	SB%	GDP	Avg	OBP	SLG	Pos	G	PO	A	E	DP	FPct
1934 StL	28	2	1	0	0	0	0	0	0	0	0	0	0	0	0	0	0	0	0	—	0	.000	.000	.000	P	2	0	0	0	0	—
1935 ChN	29	1	1	0	0	0	0	0	0	0	0	1	0	1	0	0	0	0	0	—	0	.000	.500	.000	P	1	0	1	0	0	1.000
1938 ChN	32	1	0	0	0	0	0	0	0	0	0	0	0	0	0	0	0	0	0	—	0	—	—	—	P	1	0	0	0	0	—
WS Totals		4	2	0	0	0	0	0	0	0	0	1	0	1	0	0	0	0	0	—	0	.000	.333	.000	P	4	0	1	0	0	1.000

HAL CARLSON—Harold Gust Carlson—Throws: Right; Bats: Right

Ht: 6'0"; Wt: 180 lbs; Born: 5/17/1892 in Rockford, Illinois; Debut: 4/13/1917; Died: 5/28/1930

World Series		Pitching																										
Year Tm	Age	G	GS	CG	GF	IP	BFP	H	R	ER	HR	SH	SF	HB	TBB	IBB	SO	WP	Bk	W	L	Pct	ShO	Sv-Op	Hld	OAvg	OOBP	ERA
1929 ChN	37	2	0	0	1	4.0	18	7	3	3	1	2	0	0	1	0	3	0	0	0	0	—	0	0-0	0	.467	.500	6.75

World Series		Batting																							Fielding						
Year Tm	Age	G	AB	H	2B	3B	HR	TB	R	RBI	GW	TBB	IBB	SO	HBP	SH	SF	SB	CS	SB%	GDP	Avg	OBP	SLG	Pos	G	PO	A	E	DP	FPct
1929 ChN	37	2	0	0	0	0	0	0	0	0	0	0	0	0	0	0	0	0	0	—	0	—	—	—	P	2	0	2	0	0	1.000

STEVE CARLTON (HOF 1994-W)—Steven Norman Carlton—Nickname: Lefty—Throws: Left; Bats: Left

Ht: 6'4"; Wt: 210 lbs; Born: 12/22/1944 in Miami, Florida; Debut: 4/12/1965

Division Series		Pitching																										
Year Tm	Age	G	GS	CG	GF	IP	BFP	H	R	ER	HR	SH	SF	HB	TBB	IBB	SO	WP	Bk	W	L	Pct	ShO	Sv-Op	Hld	OAvg	OOBP	ERA
1981 Phi	36	2	2	0	0	14.0	60	14	6	6	0	2	0	0	8	2	13	1	0	0	2	.000	0	0-0	0	.280	.379	3.86
LCS		Pitching																										
Year Tm	Age	G	GS	CG	GF	IP	BFP	H	R	ER	HR	SH	SF	HB	TBB	IBB	SO	WP	Bk	W	L	Pct	ShO	Sv-Op	Hld	OAvg	OOBP	ERA
1976 Phi	31	1	1	0	0	7.0	34	8	5	4	1	0	1	0	5	0	6	0	0	0	1	.000	0	0-0	0	.286	.382	5.14
1977 Phi-*C*	32	2	2	0	0	11.2	54	13	9	9	2	0	0	0	8	0	6	1	1	0	1	.000	0	0-0	0	.283	.389	6.94
1978 Phi	33	1	1	1	0	9.0	36	8	4	4	1	0	0	0	2	0	8	0	0	1	0	1.000	0	0-0	0	.235	.278	4.00
1980 Phi-*C*	35	2	2	0	0	12.1	54	11	3	3	0	1	1	0	8	1	6	0	0	1	0	1.000	0	0-0	0	.250	.358	2.19
1983 Phi	38	2	2	0	0	13.2	57	13	1	1	1	2	0	1	5	0	13	1	0	2	0	1.000	0	0-0	0	.265	.345	0.66
LCS Totals		8	8	1	0	53.2	470	53	22	21	5	3	2	1	28	1	39	2	1	4	2	.667	0	0-0	0	.264	.353	3.52
World Series		Pitching																										
Year Tm	Age	G	GS	CG	GF	IP	BFP	H	R	ER	HR	SH	SF	HB	TBB	IBB	SO	WP	Bk	W	L	Pct	ShO	Sv-Op	Hld	OAvg	OOBP	ERA
1967 StL	22	1	1	0	0	6.0	24	3	1	0	0	1	0	0	2	0	5	1	0	0	1	.000	0	0-0	0	.143	.217	0.00
1968 StL	23	2	0	0	0	4.0	19	7	3	3	1	0	0	0	1	0	3	0	0	0	0	—	0	0-0	0	.389	.421	6.75
1980 Phi-*C*	35	2	2	0	0	15.0	64	14	5	4	0	1	1	0	9	0	17	1	0	2	0	1.000	0	0-0	0	.264	.365	2.40
1983 Phi	38	1	1	0	0	6.2	27	5	3	2	1	0	0	0	3	0	7	1	0	0	1	.000	0	0-0	0	.208	.296	2.70
WS Totals		6	4	0	0	31.2	268	29	12	9	2	2	1	0	15	0	32	3	0	2	2	.500	0	0-0	0	.250	.333	2.56
Postseason Totals		16	14	1	0	99.1	858	96	40	36	7	7	3	1	51	3	84	6	1	6	6	.500	0	0-0	0	.262	.351	3.26

(Gary Carter — top table, continued)

Division Series								Batting																Fielding					
Year Tm	Age	G	AB	H	2B	3B	HR	TB	R	RBI	GW	TBB	IBB	SO	HBP	SH	SF	SB	CS	SB%	GDP	Avg	OBP	SLG	Pos	G	PO	A	E	DP	FPct
1981 Phi	36	2	4	1	0	0	0	1	0	0	0	0	0	0	0	0	0	0	0	—	0	.250	.250	.250	P	2	0	4	0	0	1.000

LCS								Batting																Fielding					
Year Tm	Age	G	AB	H	2B	3B	HR	TB	R	RBI	GW	TBB	IBB	SO	HBP	SH	SF	SB	CS	SB%	GDP	Avg	OBP	SLG	Pos	G	PO	A	E	DP	FPct
1976 Phi	31	1	2	0	0	0	0	0	0	0	0	0	0	0	0	0	0	0	0	—	0	.000	.000	.000	P	1	0	0	0	0	—
1977 Phi	32	2	4	2	0	0	0	2	0	1	0	0	0	2	1	0	0	0	0	—	0	.500	.600	.500	P	2	0	0	0	0	—
1978 Phi	33	1	4	2	0	0	1	5	2	4	0	0	0	0	0	0	0	0	0	—	0	.500	.500	1.250	P	1	0	0	0	0	—
1980 Phi	35	2	4	0	0	0	0	0	0	0	0	0	0	1	0	0	0	0	0	—	0	.000	.000	.000	P	2	1	1	0	0	1.000
1983 Phi	38	2	5	1	0	0	0	1	0	0	0	0	0	3	0	1	0	0	0	—	0	.200	.200	.200	P	2	1	5	0	0	1.000
LCS Totals		8	19	5	0	0	1	8	2	5	0	0	0	6	1	1	0	0	0	—	0	.263	.300	.421	P	8	2	6	0	0	1.000

World Series								Batting																Fielding					
Year Tm	Age	G	AB	H	2B	3B	HR	TB	R	RBI	GW	TBB	IBB	SO	HBP	SH	SF	SB	CS	SB%	GDP	Avg	OBP	SLG	Pos	G	PO	A	E	DP	FPct
1967 StL	22	1	1	0	0	0	0	0	0	0	0	0	0	0	0	0	0	0	0	—	0	.000	.000	.000	P	1	0	0	0	0	—
1968 StL	23	2	0	0	0	0	0	0	0	0	0	0	0	0	0	0	0	0	0	—	0	—	—	—	P	2	1	0	0	0	1.000
1980 Phi	35	2	0	0	0	0	0	0	0	0	0	0	0	0	0	0	0	0	0	—	0	—	—	—	P	2	3	0	0	0	1.000
1983 Phi	38	1	3	0	0	0	0	0	0	0	0	0	0	1	0	0	0	0	0	—	0	.000	.000	.000	P	1	0	0	0	0	—
WS Totals		6	4	0	0	0	0	0	0	0	0	0	0	1	0	0	0	0	0	—	0	.000	.000	.000	P	6	1	0	0	0	1.000
Postseason Totals		16	27	6	0	0	1	9	2	5	0	0	0	7	1	1	0	0	0	—	0	.222	.250	.333	P	16	2	13	0	0	1.000

CHUCK CARR
Charles Lee Glenn Carr—Nickname: Chuckie—Bats: Both; Throws: Right Ht: 5'10"; Wt: 155 lbs; Born: 8/10/1968 in San Bernardino, California; Debut: 4/28/1990

Division Series								Batting																Fielding					
Year Tm	Age	G	AB	H	2B	3B	HR	TB	R	RBI	GW	TBB	IBB	SO	HBP	SH	SF	SB	CS	SB%	GDP	Avg	OBP	SLG	Pos	G	PO	A	E	DP	FPct
1997 Hou	29	2	4	1	0	0	1	4	1	1	0	1	0	3	0	0	0	0	0	—	0	.250	.400	1.000	OF	2	2	0	0	0	1.000

HECTOR CARRASCO
Hector Pacheco Carrasco—Throws: Right; Bats: Right Ht: 6'2"; Wt: 175 lbs; Born: 10/22/1969 in San Pedro de Macoris, Dominican Republic; Debut: 4/4/1994

LCS									Pitching																		
Year Tm	Age	G	GS	CG	GF	IP	BFP	H	R	ER	HR	SH	SF	HB	TBB	IBB	SO	WP	Bk	W	L	Pct	ShO	Sv-Op	Hld	OAvg	OOBP	ERA
1995 Cin	25	1	0	0	1	1.1	5	1	0	0	0	0	0	0	0	0	3	0	0	0	0	—	0	0-0	0	.200	.200	0.00

LCS								Batting																Fielding					
Year Tm	Age	G	AB	H	2B	3B	HR	TB	R	RBI	GW	TBB	IBB	SO	HBP	SH	SF	SB	CS	SB%	GDP	Avg	OBP	SLG	Pos	G	PO	A	E	DP	FPct
1995 Cin	25	1	0	0	0	0	0	0	0	0	0	0	0	0	0	0	0	0	0	—	0	—	—	—	P	1	0	0	0	0	—

BILL CARRIGAN
William Francis Carrigan—Nickname: Rough—Bats: Right; Throws: Right Ht: 5'9"; Wt: 175 lbs; Born: 10/22/1883 in Lewiston, Maine; Debut: 7/7/1906; Died: 7/8/1969

World Series								Batting																Fielding					
Year Tm	Age	G	AB	H	2B	3B	HR	TB	R	RBI	GW	TBB	IBB	SO	HBP	SH	SF	SB	CS	SB%	GDP	Avg	OBP	SLG	Pos	G	PO	A	E	DP	FPct
1912 Bos	28	2	7	0	0	0	0	0	0	0	0	0	0	0	0	0	0	0	0	—	0	.000	.000	.000	C	2	10	4	0	0	1.000
1915 Bos	31	1	2	0	0	0	0	0	0	0	0	1	0	1	0	0	0	0	0	—	0	.000	.333	.000	C	1	8	0	0	0	1.000
1916 Bos	32	1	3	2	0	0	0	2	0	1	0	0	0	1	0	1	0	0	0	1.00	0	.667	.667	.667	C	1	3	1	0	0	1.000
WS Totals		4	12	2	0	0	0	2	0	1	0	1	0	2	0	1	0	0	1	.00	0	.167	.231	.167	C	4	21	5	0	0	1.000

DON CARRITHERS
Donald George Carrithers—Throws: Right; Bats: Right Ht: 6'2"; Wt: 180 lbs; Born: 9/15/1949 in Lynwood, California; Debut: 8/1/1970

LCS									Pitching																		
Year Tm	Age	G	GS	CG	GF	IP	BFP	H	R	ER	HR	SH	SF	HB	TBB	IBB	SO	WP	Bk	W	L	Pct	ShO	Sv-Op	Hld	OAvg	OOBP	ERA
1971 SF	22	1	0	0	0	0.0	3	3	3	3	0	0	0	0	0	0	0	0	0	0	0	—	0	0-0	0	1.000	1.000	ERA

LCS								Batting																Fielding					
Year Tm	Age	G	AB	H	2B	3B	HR	TB	R	RBI	GW	TBB	IBB	SO	HBP	SH	SF	SB	CS	SB%	GDP	Avg	OBP	SLG	Pos	G	PO	A	E	DP	FPct
1971 SF	22	1	0	0	0	0	0	0	0	0	0	0	0	0	0	0	0	0	0	—	0	—	—	—	P	1	0	0	0	0	—

CLAY CARROLL
Clay Palmer Carroll—Nickname: Hawk—Throws: Right; Bats: Right Ht: 6'1"; Wt: 178 lbs; Born: 5/2/1941 in Clanton, Alabama; Debut: 9/2/1964

LCS									Pitching																		
Year Tm	Age	G	GS	CG	GF	IP	BFP	H	R	ER	HR	SH	SF	HB	TBB	IBB	SO	WP	Bk	W	L	Pct	ShO	Sv-Op	Hld	OAvg	OOBP	ERA
1970 Cin	29	2	0	0	1	1.1	6	2	0	0	0	0	0	0	0	0	2	0	0	0	0	—	0	1-1	1	.333	.333	0.00
1972 Cin	31	2	0	0	1	2.2	12	2	1	1	0	0	0	0	3	2	0	0	0	1	1	.500	0	0-1	0	.222	.417	3.38
1973 Cin	32	3	0	0	0	7.0	25	5	1	1	0	1	0	0	1	0	1	0	0	1	0	1.000	0	0-0	0	.217	.250	1.29
1975 Cin	34	1	0	0	0	1.0	4	0	0	0	0	0	0	0	1	0	1	0	0	0	0	—	0	0-0	0	.000	.250	0.00
LCS Totals		8	0	0	2	12.0	94	9	2	2	0	1	0	0	5	2	5	0	0	2	1	.667	0	1-2	1	.220	.304	1.50

World Series									Pitching																		
Year Tm	Age	G	GS	CG	GF	IP	BFP	H	R	ER	HR	SH	SF	HB	TBB	IBB	SO	WP	Bk	W	L	Pct	ShO	Sv-Op	Hld	OAvg	OOBP	ERA
1970 Cin	29	4	0	0	3	9.0	34	5	0	0	0	0	0	0	2	1	11	0	0	1	0	1.000	0	0-0	0	.156	.206	0.00
1972 Cin	31	5	0	0	3	5.2	27	6	1	1	0	3	0	0	4	1	3	0	0	0	1	.000	0	1-2	0	.300	.417	1.59
1975 Cin	34	5	0	0	0	5.2	21	4	2	2	1	0	0	0	2	0	3	0	0	1	0	1.000	0	0-0	1	.211	.286	3.18
WS Totals		14	0	0	6	20.1	164	15	3	3	1	3	0	0	8	2	17	0	0	2	1	.667	0	1-2	1	.211	.291	1.33
Postseason Totals		22	0	0	8	32.1	258	24	5	5	1	4	0	0	13	4	22	0	0	4	2	.667	0	2-4	2	.214	.296	1.39

LCS								Batting																Fielding					
Year Tm	Age	G	AB	H	2B	3B	HR	TB	R	RBI	GW	TBB	IBB	SO	HBP	SH	SF	SB	CS	SB%	GDP	Avg	OBP	SLG	Pos	G	PO	A	E	DP	FPct
1970 Cin	29	2	0	0	0	0	0	0	0	0	0	0	0	0	0	0	0	0	0	—	0	—	—	—	P	2	0	0	0	0	—
1972 Cin	31	2	0	0	0	0	0	0	0	0	0	0	0	0	0	0	0	0	0	—	0	—	—	—	P	2	0	1	0	0	1.000
1973 Cin	32	3	0	0	0	0	0	0	0	0	0	0	0	0	0	0	0	0	0	—	0	—	—	—	P	3	0	1	0	0	1.000
1975 Cin	34	1	0	0	0	0	0	0	0	0	0	0	0	0	0	0	0	0	0	—	0	—	—	—	P	1	0	1	0	0	1.000
LCS Totals		8	0	0	0	0	0	0	0	0	0	0	0	0	0	0	0	0	0	—	0	—	—	—	P	8	0	3	0	0	1.000

World Series								Batting																Fielding					
Year Tm	Age	G	AB	H	2B	3B	HR	TB	R	RBI	GW	TBB	IBB	SO	HBP	SH	SF	SB	CS	SB%	GDP	Avg	OBP	SLG	Pos	G	PO	A	E	DP	FPct
1970 Cin	29	4	1	0	0	0	0	0	0	0	0	0	0	1	0	0	0	0	0	—	0	.000	.000	.000	P	4	0	0	0	0	—
1972 Cin	31	5	0	0	0	0	0	0	0	0	0	0	0	0	0	0	0	0	0	—	0	—	—	—	P	5	1	3	0	0	1.000
1975 Cin	34	5	0	0	0	0	0	0	0	0	0	0	0	0	0	0	0	0	0	—	0	—	—	—	P	5	2	0	0	0	1.000
WS Totals		14	1	0	0	0	0	0	0	0	0	0	0	1	0	0	0	0	0	—	0	.000	.000	.000	P	14	3	3	0	0	1.000
Postseason Totals		22	1	0	0	0	0	0	0	0	0	0	0	1	0	0	0	0	0	—	0	.000	.000	.000	P	22	3	6	0	0	1.000

TOM CARROLL
Thomas Edward Carroll—Bats: Right; Throws: Right Ht: 6'3"; Wt: 186 lbs; Born: 9/17/1936 in Jamaica, New York; Debut: 5/7/1955

World Series								Batting																Fielding					
Year Tm	Age	G	AB	H	2B	3B	HR	TB	R	RBI	GW	TBB	IBB	SO	HBP	SH	SF	SB	CS	SB%	GDP	Avg	OBP	SLG	Pos	G	PO	A	E	DP	FPct
1955 NYA	19	2	0	0	0	0	0	0	0	0	0	0	0	0	0	0	0	0	0	—	0	—	—	—							

GARY CARTER
Gary Edmund Carter—Nickname: The Kid—Bats: Right; Throws: Right Ht: 6'2"; Wt: 205 lbs; Born: 4/8/1954 in Culver City, California; Debut: 9/16/1974

Division Series								Batting																Fielding					
Year Tm	Age	G	AB	H	2B	3B	HR	TB	R	RBI	GW	TBB	IBB	SO	HBP	SH	SF	SB	CS	SB%	GDP	Avg	OBP	SLG	Pos	G	PO	A	E	DP	FPct
1981 Mon	27	5	19	8	3	0	2	17	3	6	0	1	1	1	0	0	1	0	0	—	0	.421	.429	.895	C	5	19	4	0	0	1.000

LCS								Batting																Fielding					
Year Tm	Age	G	AB	H	2B	3B	HR	TB	R	RBI	GW	TBB	IBB	SO	HBP	SH	SF	SB	CS	SB%	GDP	Avg	OBP	SLG	Pos	G	PO	A	E	DP	FPct
1981 Mon	27	5	16	7	1	0	0	8	3	0	0	4	0	2	0	0	0	0	0	—	0	.438	.550	.500	C	5	27	3	0	0	1.000
1986 NYN	32	6	27	4	1	0	0	5	1	2	2	2	0	5	0	0	0	0	0	—	1	.148	.207	.185	C	6	43	4	0	0	1.000
1988 NYN	34	7	27	6	1	1	0	9	0	4	1	1	0	3	0	0	0	0	0	—	0	.222	.250	.333	C	7	58	1	0	0	1.000
LCS Totals		18	70	17	3	1	0	22	4	6	3	7	0	10	0	0	0	0	0	—	1	.243	.312	.314	C	18	128	8	0	0	1.000

World Series								Batting																Fielding					
Year Tm	Age	G	AB	H	2B	3B	HR	TB	R	RBI	GW	TBB	IBB	SO	HBP	SH	SF	SB	CS	SB%	GDP	Avg	OBP	SLG	Pos	G	PO	A	E	DP	FPct
1986 NYN	32	7	29	8	2	0	2	16	4	9	1	0	0	4	0	0	0	0	0	—	1	.276	.267	.552	C	7	57	0	0	0	1.000
Postseason Totals		30	118	33	8	1	4	55	11	21	4	8	1	15	0	0	1	0	0	—	2	.280	.320	.466	C	30	204	13	0	0	1.000

JOE CARTER—Joseph Chris Carter—Bats: Right; Throws: Right

Ht: 6'3"; Wt: 215 lbs; Born: 3/7/1960 in Oklahoma City, Oklahoma; Debut: 7/30/1983

LCS — Batting / Fielding

Year Tm	Age	G	AB	H	2B	3B	HR	TB	R	RBI	GW	TBB	IBB	SO	HBP	SH	SF	SB	CS	SB%	GDP	Avg	OBP	SLG	Pos	G	PO	A	E	DP	FPct
1991 Tor	31	5	19	5	2	0	1	10	3	4	1	1	1	5	0	0	1	0	1	.00	0	.263	.286	.526	OF	3	4	1	0	0	1.000
1992 Tor	32	6	26	5	0	0	1	8	2	3	1	2	0	4	0	0	0	2	0	1.00	1	.192	.250	.308	1B	2	2	0	0	0	1.000
																									OF	6	14	1	1	1	.938
1993 Tor	33	6	27	7	0	0	0	7	2	2	0	1	0	5	0	0	0	0	0	—	0	.259	.286	.259	OF	6	12	1	0	0	1.000
LCS Totals		17	72	17	2	0	2	25	7	9	2	4	1	14	0	0	1	2	1	.67	1	.236	.273	.347	OF	15	30	3	1	1	.971

World Series — Batting / Fielding

Year Tm	Age	G	AB	H	2B	3B	HR	TB	R	RBI	GW	TBB	IBB	SO	HBP	SH	SF	SB	CS	SB%	GDP	Avg	OBP	SLG	Pos	G	PO	A	E	DP	FPct
1992 Tor	32	6	22	6	2	0	2	14	2	3	0	3	1	2	0	0	1	0	0	—	0	.273	.346	.636	1B	2	20	1	0	0	1.000
																									OF	4	7	0	0	0	1.000
1993 Tor	33	6	25	7	1	0	2	14	6	8	1	0	0	4	0	0	3	0	0	—	0	.280	.250	.560	OF	6	13	0	2	0	.867
WS Totals		12	47	13	3	0	4	28	8	11	1	3	1	6	0	0	4	0	0	—	0	.277	.296	.596	OF	10	20	0	2	0	.909
Postseason Totals		29	119	30	5	0	6	53	15	20	3	7	2	20	0	0	5	2	1	.67	1	.252	.282	.445	OF	25	50	3	3	1	.946

RICO CARTY—Ricardo Adolfo Jacobo Carty—Bats: Right; Throws: Right

Ht: 6'3"; Wt: 200 lbs; Born: 9/1/1939 in San Pedro de Macoris, Dominican Republic; Debut: 9/15/1963

LCS — Batting / Fielding

Year Tm	Age	G	AB	H	2B	3B	HR	TB	R	RBI	GW	TBB	IBB	SO	HBP	SH	SF	SB	CS	SB%	GDP	Avg	OBP	SLG	Pos	G	PO	A	E	DP	FPct
1969 Atl	30	3	10	3	2	0	0	5	4	0	0	3	1	1	0	0	0	0	0	—	1	.300	.462	.500	OF	3	2	0	0	0	1.000

HUGH CASEY—Hugh Thomas Casey—Throws: Right; Bats: Right

Ht: 6'1"; Wt: 207 lbs; Born: 10/14/1913 in Atlanta, Georgia; Debut: 4/29/1935; Died: 7/3/1951

World Series — Pitching

Year Tm	Age	G	GS	CG	GF	IP	BFP	H	R	ER	HR	SH	SF	HB	TBB	IBB	SO	WP	Bk	W	L	Pct	ShO	Sv-Op	Hld	OAvg	OOBP	ERA
1941 Bro	27	3	0	0	1	5.1	28	9	6	2	0	0	0	0	2	0	1	0	0	0	2	.000	0	0- 0	0	.346	.393	3.38
1947 Bro	33	6	0	0	6	10.1	35	5	1	1	0	0	0	1	1	0	3	0	0	2	0	1.000	0	1- 2	0	.152	.200	0.87
WS Totals		9	0	0	7	15.2	126	14	7	3	0	0	0	1	3	0	4	0	0	2	2	.500	0	1-2	0	.237	.286	1.72

World Series — Batting / Fielding

Year Tm	Age	G	AB	H	2B	3B	HR	TB	R	RBI	GW	TBB	IBB	SO	HBP	SH	SF	SB	CS	SB%	GDP	Avg	OBP	SLG	Pos	G	PO	A	E	DP	FPct
1941 Bro	27	3	2	1	0	0	0	1	0	0	0	0	0	1	0	0	0	0	0	—	0	.500	.500	.500	P	3	0	3	0	0	1.000
1947 Bro	33	6	1	0	0	0	0	0	0	0	0	0	0	1	0	0	0	0	0	—	0	.000	.000	.000	P	6	2	3	0	1	1.000
WS Totals		9	3	1	0	0	0	1	0	0	0	0	0	2	0	0	0	0	0	—	0	.333	.333	.333	P	9	2	6	0	1	1.000

DAVE CASH—David Cash—Bats: Right; Throws: Right

Ht: 5'11"; Wt: 170 lbs; Born: 6/11/1948 in Utica, New York; Debut: 9/13/1969

LCS — Batting / Fielding

Year Tm	Age	G	AB	H	2B	3B	HR	TB	R	RBI	GW	TBB	IBB	SO	HBP	SH	SF	SB	CS	SB%	GDP	Avg	OBP	SLG	Pos	G	PO	A	E	DP	FPct
1970 Pit	22	2	8	1	1	0	0	2	1	0	0	1	0	1	0	0	0	0	0	—	0	.125	.222	.250	2B	2	6	8	0	3	1.000
1971 Pit	23	4	19	8	2	0	0	10	5	1	0	0	0	1	0	0	0	1	1	.50	0	.421	.421	.526	2B	4	12	11	1	3	.958
1972 Pit	24	5	19	4	0	0	0	4	0	3	0	0	0	0	0	0	0	0	0	—	0	.211	.211	.211	2B	5	5	10	1	1	.938
1976 Phi	28	3	13	4	1	0	0	5	1	1	0	0	0	0	0	0	1	0	0	—	1	.308	.286	.385	2B	3	8	8	0	2	1.000
LCS Totals		14	59	17	4	0	0	21	7	5	0	1	0	2	0	0	1	1	1	.50	1	.288	.295	.356	2B	14	31	37	2	9	.971

World Series — Batting / Fielding

Year Tm	Age	G	AB	H	2B	3B	HR	TB	R	RBI	GW	TBB	IBB	SO	HBP	SH	SF	SB	CS	SB%	GDP	Avg	OBP	SLG	Pos	G	PO	A	E	DP	FPct
1971 Pit	23	7	30	4	1	0	0	5	2	1	0	3	1	1	0	0	0	1	0	1.00	1	.133	.212	.167	2B	7	20	23	0	6	1.000
Postseason Totals		21	89	21	5	0	0	26	9	6	0	4	1	3	0	0	1	2	1	.67	2	.236	.266	.292	2B	21	51	60	2	15	.982

NORM CASH—Norman Dalton Cash—Bats: Left; Throws: Left

Ht: 6'0"; Wt: 185 lbs; Born: 11/10/1934 in Justiceburg, Texas; Debut: 6/18/1958; Died: 10/12/1986

LCS — Batting / Fielding

Year Tm	Age	G	AB	H	2B	3B	HR	TB	R	RBI	GW	TBB	IBB	SO	HBP	SH	SF	SB	CS	SB%	GDP	Avg	OBP	SLG	Pos	G	PO	A	E	DP	FPct
1972 Det	37	5	15	4	0	0	1	7	1	2	0	2	0	3	0	1	0	0	0	—	0	.267	.353	.467	1B	5	39	2	0	3	1.000

World Series — Batting / Fielding

Year Tm	Age	G	AB	H	2B	3B	HR	TB	R	RBI	GW	TBB	IBB	SO	HBP	SH	SF	SB	CS	SB%	GDP	Avg	OBP	SLG	Pos	G	PO	A	E	DP	FPct
1959 ChA	24	4	4	0	0	0	0	0	0	0	0	0	0	2	0	0	0	0	0	—	0	.000	.000	.000	—						
1968 Det	33	7	26	10	0	0	1	13	5	5	0	3	0	5	0	0	1	0	0	—	0	.385	.433	.500	1B	7	58	7	2	3	.970
WS Totals		11	30	10	0	0	1	13	5	5	0	3	0	7	0	0	1	0	0	—	0	.333	.382	.433	1B	7	58	7	2	3	.970
Postseason Totals		16	45	14	0	0	2	20	6	7	0	5	0	10	0	1	1	0	0	—	0	.311	.373	.444	1B	12	97	9	2	6	.981

GEORGE CASTER—George Jasper Caster—Nickname: Ug—Throws: Right; Bats: Right

Ht: 6'1"; Wt: 180 lbs; Born: 8/4/1907 in Colton, California; Debut: 9/10/1934; Died: 12/18/1955

World Series — Pitching

Year Tm	Age	G	GS	CG	GF	IP	BFP	H	R	ER	HR	SH	SF	HB	TBB	IBB	SO	WP	Bk	W	L	Pct	ShO	Sv-Op	Hld	OAvg	OOBP	ERA
1945 Det	38	1	0	0	0	0.2	2	0	0	0	0	0	0	0	0	0	1	0	0	0	0	—	0	0- 0	0	.000	.000	0.00

World Series — Batting / Fielding

Year Tm	Age	G	AB	H	2B	3B	HR	TB	R	RBI	GW	TBB	IBB	SO	HBP	SH	SF	SB	CS	SB%	GDP	Avg	OBP	SLG	Pos	G	PO	A	E	DP	FPct
1945 Det	38	1	0	0	0	0	0	0	0	0	0	0	0	0	0	0	0	0	0	—	0	—	—	—	P	1	0	0	0	0	—

VINNY CASTILLA—Vinicio Castilla—Bats: Right; Throws: Right

Ht: 6'1"; Wt: 175 lbs; Born: 7/4/1967 in Oaxaca, Mexico; Debut: 9/1/1991

Division Series — Batting / Fielding

Year Tm	Age	G	AB	H	2B	3B	HR	TB	R	RBI	GW	TBB	IBB	SO	HBP	SH	SF	SB	CS	SB%	GDP	Avg	OBP	SLG	Pos	G	PO	A	E	DP	FPct
1995 Col	28	4	15	7	1	0	3	17	3	6	0	0	0	1	1	0	0	0	0	—	1	.467	.500	1.133	3B	4	3	13	1	1	.941

BOBBY CASTILLO—Robert Ernie Castillo—Nickname: Robert—Throws: Right; Bats: Right

Ht: 5'10"; Wt: 170 lbs; Born: 4/18/1955 in Los Angeles, California; Debut: 9/10/1977

LCS — Pitching

Year Tm	Age	G	GS	CG	GF	IP	BFP	H	R	ER	HR	SH	SF	HB	TBB	IBB	SO	WP	Bk	W	L	Pct	ShO	Sv-Op	Hld	OAvg	OOBP	ERA
1981 LA	26	1	0	0	1	1.0	3	0	0	0	0	0	0	0	0	0	1	0	0	0	0	—	0	0- 0	0	.000	.000	0.00
1985 LA	30	1	0	0	0	5.1	21	4	2	2	0	0	1	0	2	0	4	0	0	0	0	—	0	0- 0	0	.222	.286	3.38
LCS Totals		2	0	0	1	6.1	48	4	2	2	0	0	1	0	2	0	5	0	0	0	0	—	0	0-0	0	.190	.250	2.84

World Series — Pitching

Year Tm	Age	G	GS	CG	GF	IP	BFP	H	R	ER	HR	SH	SF	HB	TBB	IBB	SO	WP	Bk	W	L	Pct	ShO	Sv-Op	Hld	OAvg	OOBP	ERA
1981 LA	26	1	0	0	0	1.0	8	0	0	1	0	1	0	0	5	0	0	0	0	0	0	—	0	0- 0	0	.000	.714	9.00
Postseason Totals		3	0	0	1	7.1	64	4	2	3	0	1	1	0	7	0	5	0	0	0	0	—	0	0-0	0	.174	.355	3.68

LCS — Batting / Fielding

Year Tm	Age	G	AB	H	2B	3B	HR	TB	R	RBI	GW	TBB	IBB	SO	HBP	SH	SF	SB	CS	SB%	GDP	Avg	OBP	SLG	Pos	G	PO	A	E	DP	FPct
1981 LA	26	1	0	0	0	0	0	0	0	0	0	0	0	0	0	0	0	0	0	—	0	—	—	—	P	1	0	1	0	0	1.000
1985 LA	30	1	2	0	0	0	0	0	0	0	0	0	0	1	0	0	0	0	0	—	0	.000	.000	.000	P	1	1	3	0	1	1.000
LCS Totals		2	2	0	0	0	0	0	0	0	0	0	0	1	0	0	0	0	0	—	0	.000	.000	.000	P	2	1	4	0	1	1.000

World Series — Batting / Fielding

Year Tm	Age	G	AB	H	2B	3B	HR	TB	R	RBI	GW	TBB	IBB	SO	HBP	SH	SF	SB	CS	SB%	GDP	Avg	OBP	SLG	Pos	G	PO	A	E	DP	FPct
1981 LA	26	1	0	0	0	0	0	0	0	0	0	0	0	0	0	0	0	0	0	—	0	—	—	—	P	1	0	2	0	0	1.000
Postseason Totals		3	2	0	0	0	0	0	0	0	0	0	0	1	0	0	0	0	0	—	0	.000	.000	.000	P	3	1	6	0	1	1.000

MARTY CASTILLO—Martin Horace Castillo—Bats: Right; Throws: Right

Ht: 6'1"; Wt: 190 lbs; Born: 1/16/1957 in Long Beach, California; Debut: 8/19/1981

LCS — Batting / Fielding

Year Tm	Age	G	AB	H	2B	3B	HR	TB	R	RBI	GW	TBB	IBB	SO	HBP	SH	SF	SB	CS	SB%	GDP	Avg	OBP	SLG	Pos	G	PO	A	E	DP	FPct
1984 Det	27	3	8	2	0	0	0	2	0	2	1	0	0	3	0	0	0	1	0	1.00	0	.250	.250	.250	3B	3	3	4	0	0	1.000

World Series — Batting / Fielding

Year Tm	Age	G	AB	H	2B	3B	HR	TB	R	RBI	GW	TBB	IBB	SO	HBP	SH	SF	SB	CS	SB%	GDP	Avg	OBP	SLG	Pos	G	PO	A	E	DP	FPct
1984 Det	27	3	9	3	0	0	1	6	2	2	1	2	0	1	0	0	0	0	0	—	0	.333	.455	.667	3B	3	3	3	0	0	1.000
Postseason Totals		6	17	5	0	0	1	8	2	4	2	2	0	4	0	0	0	1	0	1.00	0	.294	.368	.471	3B	6	6	7	0	0	1.000

TONY CASTILLO—Antonio Jose Castillo—Throws: Left; Bats: Left

Ht: 5'10"; Wt: 177 lbs; Born: 3/1/1963 in Quibor, Venezuela; Debut: 8/14/1988

		Pitching																										
LCS																												
Year Tm	Age	G	GS	CG	GF	IP	BFP	H	R	ER	HR	SH	SF	HB	TBB	IBB	SO	WP	Bk	W	L	Pct	ShO	Sv-Op	Hld	OAvg	OOBP	ERA
1993 Tor	30	2	0	0	1	2.0	6	0	0	0	0	0	0	0	1	0	1	0	0	0	0	—	0	0- 0	0	.000	.167	0.00
World Series																												
Year Tm	Age	G	GS	CG	GF	IP	BFP	H	R	ER	HR	SH	SF	HB	TBB	IBB	SO	WP	Bk	W	L	Pct	ShO	Sv-Op	Hld	OAvg	OOBP	ERA
1993 Tor	30	2	0	0	0	3.1	20	6	3	3	1	0	0	1	3	0	1	0	0	1	0	1.000	0	0- 0	0	.375	.500	8.10
Postseason Totals		4	0	0	1	5.1	52	6	3	3	1	0	0	1	4	0	2	0	0	1	0	1.000	0	0-0	0	.286	.423	5.06

		Batting																							Fielding						
LCS																															
Year Tm	Age	G	AB	H	2B	3B	HR	TB	R	RBI	GW	TBB	IBB	SO	HBP	SH	SF	SB	CS	SB%	GDP	Avg	OBP	SLG	Pos	G	PO	A	E	DP	FPct
1993 Tor	30	2	0	0	0	0	0	0	0	0	0	0	0	0	0	0	0	0	0	—	0	—	—	—	P	2	0	1	0	0	1.000
World Series																															
Year Tm	Age	G	AB	H	2B	3B	HR	TB	R	RBI	GW	TBB	IBB	SO	HBP	SH	SF	SB	CS	SB%	GDP	Avg	OBP	SLG	Pos	G	PO	A	E	DP	FPct
1993 Tor	30	2	1	0	0	0	0	0	0	0	0	0	0	1	0	0	0	0	0	—	0	.000	.000	.000	P	2	0	0	0	0	—
Postseason Totals		4	1	0	0	0	0	0	0	0	0	0	0	1	0	0	0	0	0	—	0	.000	.000	.000	P	4	0	1	0	0	1.000

SLICK CASTLEMAN—Clydell Castleman—Throws: Right; Bats: Right

Ht: 6'0"; Wt: 185 lbs; Born: 9/8/1913 in Donelson, Tennessee; Debut: 5/9/1934; Died: 3/2/1998

		Pitching																										
World Series																												
Year Tm	Age	G	GS	CG	GF	IP	BFP	H	R	ER	HR	SH	SF	HB	TBB	IBB	SO	WP	Bk	W	L	Pct	ShO	Sv-Op	Hld	OAvg	OOBP	ERA
1936 NYG	23	1	0	0	0	4.1	18	3	1	1	0	0	0	0	2	0	5	0	0	0	0	—	0	0- 0	0	.188	.278	2.08

		Batting																							Fielding						
World Series																															
Year Tm	Age	G	AB	H	2B	3B	HR	TB	R	RBI	GW	TBB	IBB	SO	HBP	SH	SF	SB	CS	SB%	GDP	Avg	OBP	SLG	Pos	G	PO	A	E	DP	FPct
1936 NYG	23	1	2	1	0	0	0	1	0	0	0	0	0	0	0	0	0	0	0	—	0	.500	.500	.500	P	1	0	0	0	0	—

JUAN CASTRO—Juan Gabriel Castro—Bats: Right; Throws: Right

Ht: 5'10"; Wt: 163 lbs; Born: 6/20/1972 in Los Mochis, Mexico; Debut: 9/2/1995

		Batting																							Fielding						
Division Series																															
Year Tm	Age	G	AB	H	2B	3B	HR	TB	R	RBI	GW	TBB	IBB	SO	HBP	SH	SF	SB	CS	SB%	GDP	Avg	OBP	SLG	Pos	G	PO	A	E	DP	FPct
1996 LA	24	2	5	1	1	0	0	2	0	1	0	1	0	1	0	0	0	0	0	—	0	.200	.333	.400	2B	2	4	3	0	1	1.000

MIKE CATHER—Michael Peter Cather—Throws: Right; Bats: Right

Ht: 6'2"; Wt: 195 lbs; Born: 12/17/1970 in San Diego, California; Debut: 7/13/1997

		Pitching																										
Division Series																												
Year Tm	Age	G	GS	CG	GF	IP	BFP	H	R	ER	HR	SH	SF	HB	TBB	IBB	SO	WP	Bk	W	L	Pct	ShO	Sv-Op	Hld	OAvg	OOBP	ERA
1997 Atl	26	1	0	0	0	2.0	7	0	0	0	0	0	0	0	1	0	2	0	0	0	0	—	0	0- 0	0	.000	.143	0.00
LCS																												
Year Tm	Age	G	GS	CG	GF	IP	BFP	H	R	ER	HR	SH	SF	HB	TBB	IBB	SO	WP	Bk	W	L	Pct	ShO	Sv-Op	Hld	OAvg	OOBP	ERA
1997 Atl	26	4	0	0	1	2.2	11	3	0	0	0	1	0	0	0	0	3	0	0	0	0	—	0	0- 0	0	.300	.300	0.00
Postseason Totals		5	0	0	1	4.2	36	3	0	0	0	1	0	0	1	0	5	0	0	0	0	—	0	0-0	0	.188	.235	0.00

		Batting																							Fielding						
Division Series																															
Year Tm	Age	G	AB	H	2B	3B	HR	TB	R	RBI	GW	TBB	IBB	SO	HBP	SH	SF	SB	CS	SB%	GDP	Avg	OBP	SLG	Pos	G	PO	A	E	DP	FPct
1997 Atl	26	1	1	0	0	0	0	0	0	0	0	0	0	1	0	0	0	0	0	—	0	.000	.000	.000	P	1	0	0	0	0	—
LCS																															
Year Tm	Age	G	AB	H	2B	3B	HR	TB	R	RBI	GW	TBB	IBB	SO	HBP	SH	SF	SB	CS	SB%	GDP	Avg	OBP	SLG	Pos	G	PO	A	E	DP	FPct
1997 Atl	26	4	0	0	0	0	0	0	0	0	0	0	0	0	0	0	0	0	0	—	0	—	—	—	P	4	0	0	0	0	—
Postseason Totals		5	1	0	0	0	0	0	0	0	0	0	0	1	0	0	0	0	0	—	0	.000	.000	.000	P	5	0	0	0	0	—

TED CATHER—Theodore Physick Cather—Bats: Right; Throws: Right

Ht: 5'10"; Wt: 178 lbs; Born: 5/20/1889 in Chester, Pennsylvania; Debut: 9/23/1912; Died: 4/9/1945

		Batting																							Fielding						
World Series																															
Year Tm	Age	G	AB	H	2B	3B	HR	TB	R	RBI	GW	TBB	IBB	SO	HBP	SH	SF	SB	CS	SB%	GDP	Avg	OBP	SLG	Pos	G	PO	A	E	DP	FPct
1914 Bos	25	1	5	0	0	0	0	0	0	0	0	0	0	1	0	0	0	0	0	—	0	.000	.000	.000	OF	1	2	0	0	0	1.000

PHIL CAVARRETTA—Philip Joseph Cavarretta—Nickname: Philabuck—Bats: Left; Throws: Left

Ht: 5'11"; Wt: 175 lbs; Born: 7/19/1916 in Chicago, Illinois; Debut: 9/16/1934

		Batting																							Fielding						
World Series																															
Year Tm	Age	G	AB	H	2B	3B	HR	TB	R	RBI	GW	TBB	IBB	SO	HBP	SH	SF	SB	CS	SB%	GDP	Avg	OBP	SLG	Pos	G	PO	A	E	DP	FPct
1935 ChN	19	6	24	3	0	0	0	3	1	0	0	0	0	5	0	1	0	0	1	.00	0	.125	.125	.125	1B	6	59	4	1	4	.984
1938 ChN	22	4	13	6	1	0	0	7	1	0	0	0	0	1	0	0	0	0	0	—	0	.462	.462	.538	OF	3	4	1	0	0	1.000
1945 ChN-*M*	29	7	26	11	2	0	1	16	7	5	0	4	0	3	0	1	0	0	0	—	0	.423	.500	.615	1B	7	71	3	0	5	1.000
WS Totals		17	63	20	3	0	1	26	9	5	0	4	0	9	0	2	0	0	1	.00	0	.317	.358	.413	1B	13	130	7	1	9	.993

CESAR CEDENO—Bats: Right; Throws: Right

Ht: 6'2"; Wt: 175 lbs; Born: 2/25/1951 in Santo Domingo, Dominican Republic; Debut: 6/20/1970

		Batting																							Fielding						
Division Series																															
Year Tm	Age	G	AB	H	2B	3B	HR	TB	R	RBI	GW	TBB	IBB	SO	HBP	SH	SF	SB	CS	SB%	GDP	Avg	OBP	SLG	Pos	G	PO	A	E	DP	FPct
1981 Hou	30	4	13	3	1	0	0	4	0	0	0	2	1	2	0	0	0	2	2	.50	1	.231	.333	.308	1B	4	36	1	1	1	.974
LCS																															
Year Tm	Age	G	AB	H	2B	3B	HR	TB	R	RBI	GW	TBB	IBB	SO	HBP	SH	SF	SB	CS	SB%	GDP	Avg	OBP	SLG	Pos	G	PO	A	E	DP	FPct
1980 Hou	29	3	11	2	0	0	0	2	1	1	0	1	0	0	0	0	0	0	0	—	3	.182	.250	.182	OF	3	5	0	0	0	1.000
1985 StL	34	5	12	2	1	0	0	3	2	0	0	2	1	3	0	0	0	0	0	—	0	.167	.286	.250	OF	4	5	0	0	0	1.000
LCS Totals		8	23	4	1	0	0	5	3	1	0	3	1	3	0	0	0	0	0	—	3	.174	.269	.217	OF	7	10	0	0	0	1.000
World Series																															
Year Tm	Age	G	AB	H	2B	3B	HR	TB	R	RBI	GW	TBB	IBB	SO	HBP	SH	SF	SB	CS	SB%	GDP	Avg	OBP	SLG	Pos	G	PO	A	E	DP	FPct
1985 StL	34	5	15	2	1	0	0	3	1	1	1	2	1	2	0	0	0	0	0	—	0	.133	.235	.200	OF	5	9	0	0	0	1.000
Postseason Totals		17	51	9	3	0	0	12	4	2	1	7	3	7	0	0	0	2	2	.50	4	.176	.276	.235	OF	12	19	0	0	0	1.000

ORLANDO CEPEDA—Orlando Manuel Cepeda—Nicknames: Cha Cha, Baby Bull—Bats: Right; Throws: Right

Ht: 6'2"; Wt: 210 lbs; Born: 9/17/1937 in Ponce, Puerto Rico; Debut: 4/15/1958

		Batting																							Fielding						
LCS																															
Year Tm	Age	G	AB	H	2B	3B	HR	TB	R	RBI	GW	TBB	IBB	SO	HBP	SH	SF	SB	CS	SB%	GDP	Avg	OBP	SLG	Pos	G	PO	A	E	DP	FPct
1969 Atl	32	3	11	5	2	0	1	10	2	3	0	1	1	2	1	0	0	1	0	1.00	0	.455	.538	.909	1B	3	29	1	2	2	.938
World Series																															
Year Tm	Age	G	AB	H	2B	3B	HR	TB	R	RBI	GW	TBB	IBB	SO	HBP	SH	SF	SB	CS	SB%	GDP	Avg	OBP	SLG	Pos	G	PO	A	E	DP	FPct
1962 SF	25	5	19	3	1	0	0	4	1	2	0	0	0	4	0	0	0	0	1	.00	1	.158	.158	.211	1B	5	39	4	0	6	1.000
1967 StL-*M*	30	7	29	3	2	0	0	5	1	1	0	0	0	4	0	0	0	0	0	—	1	.103	.103	.172	1B	7	52	4	0	3	1.000
1968 StL	31	7	28	7	0	0	2	13	2	6	0	2	0	3	0	0	0	0	1	.00	0	.250	.300	.464	1B	7	47	4	0	7	1.000
WS Totals		19	76	13	3	0	2	22	4	9	0	2	0	11	0	0	0	0	2	.00	2	.171	.192	.289	1B	19	138	12	0	16	1.000
Postseason Totals		22	87	18	5	0	3	32	6	12	0	3	1	13	1	0	0	1	2	.33	2	.207	.242	.368	1B	22	167	13	2	18	.989

RICK CERONE—Richard Aldo Cerone—Bats: Right; Throws: Right

Ht: 5'11"; Wt: 192 lbs; Born: 5/19/1954 in Newark, New Jersey; Debut: 8/17/1975

		Batting																							Fielding						
Division Series																															
Year Tm	Age	G	AB	H	2B	3B	HR	TB	R	RBI	GW	TBB	IBB	SO	HBP	SH	SF	SB	CS	SB%	GDP	Avg	OBP	SLG	Pos	G	PO	A	E	DP	FPct
1981 NYA	27	5	18	6	2	0	1	11	1	5	1	0	0	2	0	0	0	0	0	—	0	.333	.333	.611	C	5	42	1	0	0	1.000
LCS																															
Year Tm	Age	G	AB	H	2B	3B	HR	TB	R	RBI	GW	TBB	IBB	SO	HBP	SH	SF	SB	CS	SB%	GDP	Avg	OBP	SLG	Pos	G	PO	A	E	DP	FPct
1980 NYA	26	3	12	4	0	0	1	7	1	2	0	0	0	1	0	0	0	0	0	—	0	.333	.333	.583	C	3	14	4	0	0	1.000
1981 NYA	27	3	10	1	0	0	0	1	1	0	0	0	0	0	1	1	0	0	0	—	0	.100	.182	.100	C	3	23	2	0	1	1.000
LCS Totals		6	22	5	0	0	1	8	2	2	0	0	0	1	1	1	0	0	0	—	0	.227	.261	.364	C	6	37	6	0	1	1.000
World Series																															
Year Tm	Age	G	AB	H	2B	3B	HR	TB	R	RBI	GW	TBB	IBB	SO	HBP	SH	SF	SB	CS	SB%	GDP	Avg	OBP	SLG	Pos	G	PO	A	E	DP	FPct
1981 NYA	27	6	21	4	1	0	1	8	2	3	0	4	1	2	0	0	0	0	0	—	1	.190	.320	.381	C	6	42	4	0	0	1.000
Postseason Totals		17	61	15	3	0	3	27	5	10	1	4	1	5	1	1	0	0	0	—	1	.246	.303	.443	C	17	121	11	0	1	1.000

JOHN CERUTTI—John Joseph Cerutti—Throws: Left; Bats: Left

Ht: 6'2"; Wt: 195 lbs; Born: 4/28/1960 in Albany, New York; Debut: 9/1/1985

LCS		Pitching																										
Year Tm	Age	G	GS	CG	GF	IP	BFP	H	R	ER	HR	SH	SF	HB	TBB	IBB	SO	WP	Bk	W	L	Pct	ShO	Sv-Op	Hld	OAvg	OOBP	ERA
1989 Tor	29	2	0	0	1	2.2	9	0	0	0	0	0	0	0	3	0	1	0	0	0	0	—	0	0- 0	0	.000	.333	0.00

LCS		Batting																							Fielding						
Year Tm	Age	G	AB	H	2B	3B	HR	TB	R	RBI	GW	TBB	IBB	SO	HBP	SH	SF	SB	CS	SB%	GDP	Avg	OBP	SLG	Pos	G	PO	A	E	DP	FPct
1989 Tor	29	2	0	0	0	0	0	0	0	0	0	0	0	0	0	0	0	0	0	—	0	—	—	—	P	2	0	2	0	0	1.000

BOB CERV—Robert Henry Cerv—Bats: Right; Throws: Right

Ht: 6'0"; Wt: 200 lbs; Born: 5/5/1926 in Weston, Nebraska; Debut: 8/1/1951

World Series		Batting																							Fielding						
Year Tm	Age	G	AB	H	2B	3B	HR	TB	R	RBI	GW	TBB	IBB	SO	HBP	SH	SF	SB	CS	SB%	GDP	Avg	OBP	SLG	Pos	G	PO	A	E	DP	FPct
1955 NYA	29	5	16	2	0	0	1	5	1	1	0	0	0	4	0	0	0	0	0	—	1	.125	.125	.313	OF	4	10	0	0	0	1.000
1956 NYA	30	1	1	1	0	0	0	1	0	0	0	0	0	0	0	0	0	0	0	—	0	1.000	1.000	1.000	—						
1960 NYA	34	4	14	5	0	0	0	5	1	0	0	0	0	3	0	0	0	0	0	—	0	.357	.357	.357	OF	3	8	0	1	0	.889
WS Totals		10	31	8	0	0	1	11	2	1	0	0	0	7	0	0	0	0	0	—	1	.258	.258	.355	OF	7	18	0	1	0	.947

RON CEY—Ronald Charles Cey—Nickname: The Penguin—Bats: Right; Throws: Right

Ht: 5'10"; Wt: 185 lbs; Born: 2/15/1948 in Tacoma, Washington; Debut: 9/3/1971

LCS		Batting																							Fielding						
Year Tm	Age	G	AB	H	2B	3B	HR	TB	R	RBI	GW	TBB	IBB	SO	HBP	SH	SF	SB	CS	SB%	GDP	Avg	OBP	SLG	Pos	G	PO	A	E	DP	FPct
1974 LA	26	4	16	5	3	0	1	11	2	1	0	3	3	2	0	0	0	0	0	—	0	.313	.421	.688	3B	4	2	5	2	1	.778
1977 LA	29	4	13	4	1	0	1	8	4	4	0	2	0	4	0	1	0	1	0	1.00	1	.308	.400	.615	3B	4	7	15	1	0	.957
1978 LA	30	4	16	5	1	0	1	9	4	3	0	2	0	4	0	0	0	0	0	—	0	.313	.389	.563	3B	4	2	15	0	1	1.000
1981 LA	33	5	18	5	1	0	0	6	1	3	1	3	0	2	0	0	0	0	0	—	0	.278	.381	.333	3B	5	5	16	1	1	.955
1984 ChN	36	5	19	3	1	0	1	7	3	3	0	3	0	3	0	0	0	0	0	—	0	.158	.273	.368	3B	5	1	6	0	0	1.000
LCS Totals		22	82	22	7	0	4	41	14	14	1	13	3	15	0	1	0	1	0	1.00	1	.268	.368	.500	3B	22	17	57	4	3	.949

World Series		Batting																							Fielding						
Year Tm	Age	G	AB	H	2B	3B	HR	TB	R	RBI	GW	TBB	IBB	SO	HBP	SH	SF	SB	CS	SB%	GDP	Avg	OBP	SLG	Pos	G	PO	A	E	DP	FPct
1974 LA	26	5	17	3	0	0	0	3	1	0	0	3	0	3	0	0	0	0	0	—	1	.176	.300	.176	3B	5	5	9	1	0	.933
1977 LA	29	6	21	4	1	0	1	8	2	3	1	3	0	5	0	0	1	0	0	—	0	.190	.280	.381	3B	6	5	7	0	0	1.000
1978 LA	30	6	21	6	0	0	1	9	2	4	1	3	0	3	0	0	0	0	0	—	0	.286	.375	.429	3B	6	2	12	0	1	1.000
1981 LA	33	6	20	7	0	0	1	10	3	6	1	3	0	3	1	0	0	0	0	—	0	.350	.458	.500	3B	6	4	11	0	1	1.000
WS Totals		23	79	20	1	0	3	30	8	13	3	12	0	14	1	0	1	0	0	—	1	.253	.355	.380	3B	23	16	39	1	2	.982
Postseason Totals		45	161	42	8	0	7	71	22	27	4	25	3	29	1	1	1	1	0	1.00	2	.261	.362	.441	3B	45	33	96	5	5	.963

ELIO CHACON—Bats: Right; Throws: Right

Ht: 5'9"; Wt: 160 lbs; Born: 10/26/1936 in Caracas, Venezuela; Debut: 4/20/1960; Died: 4/24/1992

World Series		Batting																							Fielding						
Year Tm	Age	G	AB	H	2B	3B	HR	TB	R	RBI	GW	TBB	IBB	SO	HBP	SH	SF	SB	CS	SB%	GDP	Avg	OBP	SLG	Pos	G	PO	A	E	DP	FPct
1961 Cin	24	4	12	3	0	0	0	3	2	0	0	1	0	2	0	0	0	0	0	—	0	.250	.308	.250	2B	3	12	9	0	4	1.000

DAVE CHALK—David Lee Chalk—Bats: Right; Throws: Right

Ht: 5'10"; Wt: 175 lbs; Born: 8/30/1950 in Del Rio, Texas; Debut: 9/4/1973

World Series		Batting																							Fielding						
Year Tm	Age	G	AB	H	2B	3B	HR	TB	R	RBI	GW	TBB	IBB	SO	HBP	SH	SF	SB	CS	SB%	GDP	Avg	OBP	SLG	Pos	G	PO	A	E	DP	FPct
1980 KC	30	1	0	0	0	0	0	0	1	0	0	1	0	0	0	0	0	1	0	1.00	0	—	1.000	—	3B	1	0	1	0	0	1.000

GEORGE CHALMERS—George W. Chalmers—Nickname: Dut—Throws: Right; Bats: Right

Ht: 6'1"; Wt: 189 lbs; Born: 6/7/1888 in Edinburgh, Scotland; Debut: 9/21/1910; Died: 8/5/1960

World Series		Pitching																										
Year Tm	Age	G	GS	CG	GF	IP	BFP	H	R	ER	HR	SH	SF	HB	TBB	IBB	SO	WP	Bk	W	L	Pct	ShO	Sv-Op	Hld	OAvg	OOBP	ERA
1915 Phi	27	1	1	1	0	8.0	33	8	2	2	0	2	0	0	3	0	6	0	0	0	1	.000	0	0- 0	0	.286	.355	2.25

World Series		Batting																							Fielding						
Year Tm	Age	G	AB	H	2B	3B	HR	TB	R	RBI	GW	TBB	IBB	SO	HBP	SH	SF	SB	CS	SB%	GDP	Avg	OBP	SLG	Pos	G	PO	A	E	DP	FPct
1915 Phi	27	1	3	1	0	0	0	1	0	0	0	0	0	1	0	0	0	0	0	—	0	.333	.333	.333	P	1	0	4	0	1	1.000

WES CHAMBERLAIN—Wesley Polk Chamberlain—Bats: Right; Throws: Right

Ht: 6'2"; Wt: 210 lbs; Born: 4/13/1966 in Chicago, Illinois; Debut: 8/31/1990

LCS		Batting																							Fielding						
Year Tm	Age	G	AB	H	2B	3B	HR	TB	R	RBI	GW	TBB	IBB	SO	HBP	SH	SF	SB	CS	SB%	GDP	Avg	OBP	SLG	Pos	G	PO	A	E	DP	FPct
1993 Phi	27	4	11	4	3	0	0	7	1	1	0	1	1	3	0	0	1	0	0	—	0	.364	.385	.636	OF	3	2	2	0	0	1.000

World Series		Batting																							Fielding						
Year Tm	Age	G	AB	H	2B	3B	HR	TB	R	RBI	GW	TBB	IBB	SO	HBP	SH	SF	SB	CS	SB%	GDP	Avg	OBP	SLG	Pos	G	PO	A	E	DP	FPct
1993 Phi	27	2	2	0	0	0	0	0	0	0	0	0	0	1	0	0	0	0	0	—	1	.000	.000	.000	—						
Postseason Totals		6	13	4	3	0	0	7	1	1	0	1	1	4	0	0	1	0	0	—	1	.308	.333	.538	OF	3	2	2	0	0	1.000

CHRIS CHAMBLISS—Carroll Christopher Chambliss—Bats: Left; Throws: Right

Ht: 6'1"; Wt: 195 lbs; Born: 12/26/1948 in Dayton, Ohio; Debut: 5/28/1971

LCS		Batting																							Fielding						
Year Tm	Age	G	AB	H	2B	3B	HR	TB	R	RBI	GW	TBB	IBB	SO	HBP	SH	SF	SB	CS	SB%	GDP	Avg	OBP	SLG	Pos	G	PO	A	E	DP	FPct
1976 NYA	27	5	21	11	1	1	2	20	5	8	2	0	0	1	0	0	1	2	0	1.00	1	.524	.500	.952	1B	5	50	3	1	3	.981
1977 NYA	28	5	17	1	0	0	0	1	0	0	0	3	2	4	0	0	0	0	0	—	0	.059	.200	.059	1B	5	35	7	0	2	1.000
1978 NYA	29	4	15	6	0	0	0	6	1	2	0	0	0	4	0	0	0	0	0	—	0	.400	.400	.400	1B	4	28	1	0	1	1.000
1982 Atl	33	3	10	0	0	0	0	0	0	0	0	1	1	0	0	0	0	0	0	—	1	.000	.091	.000	1B	3	31	5	0	0	1.000
LCS Totals		17	63	18	1	1	2	27	6	10	2	4	3	9	0	0	1	2	0	1.00	2	.286	.324	.429	1B	17	144	16	1	6	.994

World Series		Batting																							Fielding						
Year Tm	Age	G	AB	H	2B	3B	HR	TB	R	RBI	GW	TBB	IBB	SO	HBP	SH	SF	SB	CS	SB%	GDP	Avg	OBP	SLG	Pos	G	PO	A	E	DP	FPct
1976 NYA	27	4	16	5	1	0	0	6	1	1	0	0	0	2	1	0	0	0	0	—	0	.313	.353	.375	1B	4	26	3	1	6	.967
1977 NYA	28	6	24	7	2	0	1	12	4	4	0	0	0	2	0	0	0	0	0	—	1	.292	.292	.500	1B	6	55	5	0	2	1.000
1978 NYA	29	3	11	2	0	0	0	2	1	0	0	1	0	1	0	0	0	0	0	—	0	.182	.250	.182	1B	3	17	1	0	4	1.000
WS Totals		13	51	14	3	0	1	20	6	5	0	1	0	5	1	0	0	0	0	—	1	.275	.302	.392	1B	13	98	9	1	12	.991
Postseason Totals		30	114	32	4	1	3	47	12	15	2	5	3	14	1	0	1	2	0	1.00	3	.281	.314	.412	1B	30	242	25	2	18	.993

DEAN CHANCE—Wilmer Dean Chance—Throws: Right; Bats: Right

Ht: 6'3"; Wt: 200 lbs; Born: 6/1/1941 in Wooster, Ohio; Debut: 9/11/1961

LCS		Pitching																										
Year Tm	Age	G	GS	CG	GF	IP	BFP	H	R	ER	HR	SH	SF	HB	TBB	IBB	SO	WP	Bk	W	L	Pct	ShO	Sv-Op	Hld	OAvg	OOBP	ERA
1969 Min	28	1	0	0	0	2.0	10	4	3	3	1	0	0	0	0	0	2	0	0	0	0	—	0	0- 0	0	.400	.400	13.50

LCS		Batting																							Fielding						
Year Tm	Age	G	AB	H	2B	3B	HR	TB	R	RBI	GW	TBB	IBB	SO	HBP	SH	SF	SB	CS	SB%	GDP	Avg	OBP	SLG	Pos	G	PO	A	E	DP	FPct
1969 Min	28	1	0	0	0	0	0	0	0	0	0	0	0	0	0	0	0	0	0	—	0	—	—	—	P	1	0	0	0	0	—

FRANK CHANCE (HOF 1946-V)—Frank Leroy Chance—Nicknames: Husk, The Peerless Leader—B: R; T: R

Ht: 6'0"; Wt: 190 lbs; Born: 9/9/1877 in Fresno, Calif.; Deb.: 4/29/1898; Died: 9/15/1924

World Series		Batting																							Fielding						
Year Tm	Age	G	AB	H	2B	3B	HR	TB	R	RBI	GW	TBB	IBB	SO	HBP	SH	SF	SB	CS	SB%	GDP	Avg	OBP	SLG	Pos	G	PO	A	E	DP	FPct
1906 ChN	29	6	21	5	1	0	0	6	3	0	0	2	0	1	2	0	0	2	1	.67	0	.238	.360	.286	1B	6	60	2	0	1	1.000
1907 ChN	30	4	14	3	1	0	0	4	3	0	0	3	0	2	1	0	0	3	1	.75	0	.214	.389	.286	1B	4	44	1	0	3	1.000
1908 ChN	31	5	19	8	0	0	0	8	4	2	1	3	0	1	0	0	0	5	0	1.00	0	.421	.500	.421	1B	5	66	0	1	3	.985
1910 ChN	33	5	17	6	1	1	0	9	1	4	0	0	0	2	0	0	0	0	0	—	0	.353	.353	.529	1B	5	52	3	0	2	1.000
WS Totals		20	71	22	3	1	0	27	11	6	1	8	0	6	3	0	0	10	2	.83	0	.310	.402	.380	1B	20	222	6	1	9	.996

SPUD CHANDLER—Spurgeon Ferdinand Chandler—Throws: Right; Bats: Right

Ht: 6'0"; Wt: 181 lbs; Born: 9/12/1907 in Commerce, Georgia; Debut: 5/6/1937; Died: 1/9/1990

World Series — Pitching

Year Tm	Age	G	GS	CG	GF	IP	BFP	H	R	ER	HR	SH	SF	HB	TBB	IBB	SO	WP	Bk	W	L	Pct	ShO	Sv-Op	Hld	OAvg	OOBP	ERA
1941 NYA	34	1	1	0	0	5.0	20	4	3	2	0	0	0	0	2	0	2	0	0	0	1	.000	0	0- 0	0	.222	.300	3.60
1942 NYA	35	2	1	0	1	8.1	30	5	1	1	0	1	0	0	1	0	3	0	0	0	1	.000	0	1- 1	0	.179	.207	1.08
1943 NYA-*M*	36	2	2	2	0	18.0	72	17	2	1	0	3	0	0	3	0	10	0	0	2	0	1.000	1	0- 0	0	.258	.290	0.50
1947 NYA	40	1	0	0	0	2.0	11	2	2	2	0	1	0	0	3	0	1	0	0	0	0	—	0	0- 0	0	.286	.500	9.00
WS Totals		6	4	2	1	33.1	266	28	8	6	0	5	0	0	9	0	16	0	0	2	2	.500	1	1-1	0	.235	.289	1.62

World Series — Batting / Fielding

Year Tm	Age	G	AB	H	2B	3B	HR	TB	R	RBI	GW	TBB	IBB	SO	HBP	SH	SF	SB	CS	SB%	GDP	Avg	OBP	SLG	Pos	G	PO	A	E	DP	FPct
1941 NYA	34	1	2	1	0	0	0	1	0	1	0	0	0	0	0	0	0	0	0	—	0	.500	.500	.500	P	1	0	0	0	0	—
1942 NYA	35	2	2	0	0	0	0	0	0	0	0	0	0	1	0	0	0	0	0	—	0	.000	.000	.000	P	2	2	2	0	0	1.000
1943 NYA	36	2	6	1	0	0	0	1	0	0	0	0	0	2	0	1	0	0	0	—	0	.167	.167	.167	P	2	0	4	0	0	1.000
1947 NYA	40	1	0	0	0	0	0	0	0	0	0	0	0	0	0	0	0	0	0	—	0	—	—	—	P	1	0	0	0	0	—
WS Totals		6	10	2	0	0	0	2	0	1	0	0	0	3	0	1	0	0	0	—	0	.200	.200	.200	P	6	2	6	0	0	1.000

DARREL CHANEY—Darrel Lee Chaney—Bats: Both; Throws: Right

Ht: 6'2"; Wt: 188 lbs; Born: 3/9/1948 in Hammond, Indiana; Debut: 4/11/1969

LCS — Batting / Fielding

Year Tm	Age	G	AB	H	2B	3B	HR	TB	R	RBI	GW	TBB	IBB	SO	HBP	SH	SF	SB	CS	SB%	GDP	Avg	OBP	SLG	Pos	G	PO	A	E	DP	FPct
1972 Cin	24	5	16	3	0	0	0	3	3	1	0	1	1	1	0	0	0	1	0	1.00	0	.188	.235	.188	SS	5	8	16	3	2	.889
1973 Cin	25	5	9	0	0	0	0	0	0	0	0	3	1	4	0	0	0	0	0	—	0	.000	.250	.000	SS	5	2	11	0	3	1.000
LCS Totals		10	25	3	0	0	0	3	3	1	0	4	2	5	0	0	0	1	0	1.00	0	.120	.241	.120	SS	10	10	27	3	5	.925

World Series — Batting / Fielding

Year Tm	Age	G	AB	H	2B	3B	HR	TB	R	RBI	GW	TBB	IBB	SO	HBP	SH	SF	SB	CS	SB%	GDP	Avg	OBP	SLG	Pos	G	PO	A	E	DP	FPct
1970 Cin	22	3	1	0	0	0	0	0	0	0	0	0	0	1	0	0	0	0	0	—	0	.000	.000	.000	SS	3	1	2	0	0	1.000
1972 Cin	24	4	7	0	0	0	0	0	0	0	0	2	2	2	1	0	0	0	0	—	0	.000	.300	.000	SS	3	5	11	0	2	1.000
1975 Cin	27	2	2	0	0	0	0	0	0	0	0	0	0	1	0	0	0	0	0	—	0	.000	.000	.000	—						
WS Totals		9	10	0	0	0	0	0	0	0	0	2	2	4	1	0	0	0	0	—	0	.000	.231	.000	SS	6	6	13	0	2	1.000
Postseason Totals		19	35	3	0	0	0	3	3	1	0	6	4	9	1	0	0	1	0	1.00	0	.086	.238	.086	SS	16	16	40	3	7	.949

BEN CHAPMAN—William Benjamin Chapman—Bats: Right; Throws: Right

Ht: 6'0"; Wt: 190 lbs; Born: 12/25/1908 in Nashville, Tennessee; Debut: 4/15/1930; Died: 7/9/1993

World Series — Batting / Fielding

Year Tm	Age	G	AB	H	2B	3B	HR	TB	R	RBI	GW	TBB	IBB	SO	HBP	SH	SF	SB	CS	SB%	GDP	Avg	OBP	SLG	Pos	G	PO	A	E	DP	FPct
1932 NYA	23	4	17	5	2	0	0	7	1	6	1	2	0	4	0	0	0	0	1	.00	0	.294	.368	.412	OF	4	8	1	0	0	1.000

ED CHARLES—Edwin Douglas Charles—Nicknames: Ez, The Poet—Bats: Right; Throws: Right

Ht: 5'10"; Wt: 170 lbs; Born: 4/29/1933 in Daytona Beach, Florida; Debut: 4/11/1962

World Series — Batting / Fielding

Year Tm	Age	G	AB	H	2B	3B	HR	TB	R	RBI	GW	TBB	IBB	SO	HBP	SH	SF	SB	CS	SB%	GDP	Avg	OBP	SLG	Pos	G	PO	A	E	DP	FPct
1969 NYN	36	4	15	2	1	0	0	3	1	0	0	0	0	2	0	0	0	0	0	—	0	.133	.133	.200	3B	4	3	9	0	0	1.000

NORM CHARLTON—Norman Wood Charlton—Nickname: The Sheriff—Throws: Left; Bats: Both

Ht: 6'3"; Wt: 195 lbs; Born: 1/6/1963 in Fort Polk, Louisiana; Debut: 8/19/1988

Division Series — Pitching

Year Tm	Age	G	GS	CG	GF	IP	BFP	H	R	ER	HR	SH	SF	HB	TBB	IBB	SO	WP	Bk	W	L	Pct	ShO	Sv-Op	Hld	OAvg	OOBP	ERA
1995 Sea	32	4	0	0	1	7.1	30	4	2	2	1	0	0	0	3	0	9	1	0	1	0	1.000	0	1- 3	0	.148	.233	2.45
1997 Sea	34	2	0	0	1	2.1	8	2	0	0	0	0	0	0	0	0	1	0	0	0	0	—	0	0- 0	0	.250	.250	0.00
DS Totals		6	0	0	2	9.2	76	6	2	2	1	0	0	0	3	0	10	1	0	1	0	1.000	0	1-3	0	.171	.237	1.86

LCS — Pitching

Year Tm	Age	G	GS	CG	GF	IP	BFP	H	R	ER	HR	SH	SF	HB	TBB	IBB	SO	WP	Bk	W	L	Pct	ShO	Sv-Op	Hld	OAvg	OOBP	ERA
1990 Cin	27	4	0	0	0	5.0	20	4	2	1	0	0	0	0	3	0	3	0	0	1	1	.500	0	0- 0	1	.235	.350	1.80
1995 Sea	32	3	0	0	3	6.0	21	1	0	0	0	0	0	1	1	0	5	0	0	1	0	1.000	0	1- 1	0	.053	.143	0.00
LCS Totals		7	0	0	3	11.0	82	5	2	1	0	0	0	1	4	0	8	0	0	2	1	.667	0	1-1	1	.139	.244	0.82

World Series — Pitching

Year Tm	Age	G	GS	CG	GF	IP	BFP	H	R	ER	HR	SH	SF	HB	TBB	IBB	SO	WP	Bk	W	L	Pct	ShO	Sv-Op	Hld	OAvg	OOBP	ERA
1990 Cin	27	1	0	0	0	1.0	4	1	0	0	0	1	0	0	0	0	0	0	0	0	0	—	0	0- 0	0	.333	.333	0.00
Postseason Totals		14	0	0	5	21.2	166	12	4	3	1	1	0	1	7	0	18	1	0	3	1	.750	0	2-4	1	.162	.244	1.25

Division Series — Batting / Fielding

Year Tm	Age	G	AB	H	2B	3B	HR	TB	R	RBI	GW	TBB	IBB	SO	HBP	SH	SF	SB	CS	SB%	GDP	Avg	OBP	SLG	Pos	G	PO	A	E	DP	FPct
1995 Sea	32	4	0	0	0	0	0	0	0	0	0	0	0	0	0	0	0	0	0	—	0	—	—	—	P	4	0	0	0	0	—
1997 Sea	34	2	0	0	0	0	0	0	0	0	0	0	0	0	0	0	0	0	0	—	0	—	—	—	P	2	1	0	0	0	1.000
DS Totals		6	0	0	0	0	0	0	0	0	0	0	0	0	0	0	0	0	0	—	0	—	—	—	P	6	1	0	0	0	1.000

LCS — Batting / Fielding

Year Tm	Age	G	AB	H	2B	3B	HR	TB	R	RBI	GW	TBB	IBB	SO	HBP	SH	SF	SB	CS	SB%	GDP	Avg	OBP	SLG	Pos	G	PO	A	E	DP	FPct
1990 Cin	27	4	0	0	0	0	0	0	0	0	0	0	0	0	0	0	0	0	0	—	0	—	—	—	P	4	1	0	0	1	1.000
1995 Sea	32	3	0	0	0	0	0	0	0	0	0	0	0	0	0	0	0	0	0	—	0	—	—	—	P	3	0	0	0	0	—
LCS Totals		7	0	0	0	0	0	0	0	0	0	0	0	0	0	0	0	0	0	—	0	—	—	—	P	7	1	0	0	1	1.000

World Series — Batting / Fielding

Year Tm	Age	G	AB	H	2B	3B	HR	TB	R	RBI	GW	TBB	IBB	SO	HBP	SH	SF	SB	CS	SB%	GDP	Avg	OBP	SLG	Pos	G	PO	A	E	DP	FPct
1990 Cin	27	1	0	0	0	0	0	0	0	0	0	0	0	0	0	0	0	0	0	—	0	—	—	—	P	1	0	0	0	0	—
Postseason Totals		14	0	0	0	0	0	0	0	0	0	0	0	0	0	0	0	0	0	—	0	—	—	—	P	14	2	0	0	1	1.000

MIKE CHARTAK—Michael George Chartak—Nickname: Shotgun—Bats: Left; Throws: Left

Ht: 6'2"; Wt: 180 lbs; Born: 4/28/1916 in Brooklyn, New York; Debut: 9/13/1940; Died: 7/25/1967

World Series — Batting / Fielding

Year Tm	Age	G	AB	H	2B	3B	HR	TB	R	RBI	GW	TBB	IBB	SO	HBP	SH	SF	SB	CS	SB%	GDP	Avg	OBP	SLG	Pos	G	PO	A	E	DP	FPct
1944 StL	28	2	2	0	0	0	0	0	0	0	0	0	0	2	0	0	0	0	0	—	0	.000	.000	.000	—						

LARRY CHENEY—Laurence Russell Cheney—Throws: Right; Bats: Right

Ht: 6'1"; Wt: 185 lbs; Born: 5/2/1886 in Belleville, Kansas; Debut: 9/9/1911; Died: 1/6/1969

World Series — Pitching

Year Tm	Age	G	GS	CG	GF	IP	BFP	H	R	ER	HR	SH	SF	HB	TBB	IBB	SO	WP	Bk	W	L	Pct	ShO	Sv-Op	Hld	OAvg	OOBP	ERA
1916 Bro	30	1	0	0	0	3.0	14	4	2	1	0	0	0	0	1	0	5	0	0	0	0	—	0	0- 0	0	.308	.357	3.00

World Series — Batting / Fielding

Year Tm	Age	G	AB	H	2B	3B	HR	TB	R	RBI	GW	TBB	IBB	SO	HBP	SH	SF	SB	CS	SB%	GDP	Avg	OBP	SLG	Pos	G	PO	A	E	DP	FPct
1916 Bro	30	1	0	0	0	0	0	0	0	0	0	0	0	0	0	0	0	0	0	—	0	—	—	—	P	1	0	0	1	0	.000

TOM CHENEY—Thomas Edgar Cheney—Throws: Right; Bats: Right

Ht: 5'11"; Wt: 170 lbs; Born: 10/14/1934 in Morgan, Georgia; Debut: 4/21/1957

World Series — Pitching

Year Tm	Age	G	GS	CG	GF	IP	BFP	H	R	ER	HR	SH	SF	HB	TBB	IBB	SO	WP	Bk	W	L	Pct	ShO	Sv-Op	Hld	OAvg	OOBP	ERA
1960 Pit	25	3	0	0	1	4.0	17	4	2	2	0	0	1	0	1	0	6	1	0	0	0	—	0	0- 0	0	.267	.294	4.50

World Series — Batting / Fielding

Year Tm	Age	G	AB	H	2B	3B	HR	TB	R	RBI	GW	TBB	IBB	SO	HBP	SH	SF	SB	CS	SB%	GDP	Avg	OBP	SLG	Pos	G	PO	A	E	DP	FPct
1960 Pit	25	3	0	0	0	0	0	0	0	0	0	0	0	0	0	0	0	0	0	—	0	—	—	—	P	3	0	1	0	0	1.000

LOU CHIOZZA—Louis Peo Chiozza—Bats: Left; Throws: Right

Ht: 6'0"; Wt: 172 lbs; Born: 5/17/1910 in Tallulah, Alabama; Debut: 4/17/1934; Died: 2/28/1971

World Series — Batting / Fielding

Year Tm	Age	G	AB	H	2B	3B	HR	TB	R	RBI	GW	TBB	IBB	SO	HBP	SH	SF	SB	CS	SB%	GDP	Avg	OBP	SLG	Pos	G	PO	A	E	DP	FPct
1937 NYG	27	2	7	2	0	0	0	2	0	0	0	1	0	1	0	0	0	0	0	—	0	.286	.375	.286	OF	2	6	0	1	0	.857

BOB CHIPMAN—Robert Howard Chipman—Nickname: Mr. Chips—Throws: Left; Bats: Left

Ht: 6'2"; Wt: 190 lbs; Born: 10/11/1918 in Brooklyn, New York; Debut: 9/28/1941; Died: 11/8/1973

World Series — Pitching

Year	Tm	Age	G	GS	CG	GF	IP	BFP	H	R	ER	HR	SH	SF	HB	TBB	IBB	SO	WP	Bk	W	L	Pct	ShO	Sv-Op	Hld	OAvg	OOBP	ERA
1945	ChN	26	1	0	0	0	0.1	2	0	0	0	0	0	0	0	1	0	0	0	0	0	0	—	0	0- 0	0	.000	.500	0.00

World Series — Batting / Fielding

Year Tm	Age	G	AB	H	2B	3B	HR	TB	R	RBI	GW	TBB	IBB	SO	HBP	SH	SF	SB	CS	SB%	GDP	Avg	OBP	SLG	Pos	G	PO	A	E	DP	FPct
1945 ChN	26	1	0	0	0	0	0	0	0	0	0	0	0	0	0	0	0	0	0	—	0	—	—	—	P	1	0	0	0	0	—

LARRY CHRISTENSON—Larry Richard Christenson—Throws: Right; Bats: Right

Ht: 6'4"; Wt: 215 lbs; Born: 11/10/1953 in Everett, Washington; Debut: 4/13/1973

Division Series / LCS / World Series — Pitching

Year	Tm	Age	G	GS	CG	GF	IP	BFP	H	R	ER	HR	SH	SF	HB	TBB	IBB	SO	WP	Bk	W	L	Pct	ShO	Sv-Op	Hld	OAvg	OOBP	ERA
Division Series																													
1981	Phi	27	1	1	0	0	6.0	23	4	1	1	0	0	0	0	1	0	8	0	0	1	0	1.000	0	0- 0	0	.182	.217	1.50
LCS																													
1977	Phi	23	1	1	0	0	3.1	16	7	3	3	0	0	0	0	0	0	2	0	0	0	0	—	0	0- 0	0	.438	.438	8.10
1978	Phi	24	1	1	0	0	4.1	22	7	7	6	2	0	0	0	1	0	3	0	0	0	1	.000	0	0- 0	0	.333	.364	12.46
1980	Phi	26	2	1	0	0	6.2	28	5	3	3	0	1	0	0	5	3	2	1	0	0	0	—	0	0- 0	0	.227	.370	4.05
LCS Totals			4	3	0	0	14.1	132	19	13	12	2	1	0	0	6	3	7	1	0	0	1	.000	0	0-0	0	.322	.385	7.53
World Series																													
1980	Phi	26	1	1	0	0	0.1	6	5	4	4	1	0	0	0	0	0	0	0	0	0	1	.000	0	0- 0	0	.833	.833	108.00
Postseason Totals			6	5	0	0	20.2	190	28	18	17	3	1	0	0	7	3	15	1	0	1	2	.333	0	0-0	0	.322	.372	7.40

Division Series / LCS / World Series — Batting / Fielding

Year Tm	Age	G	AB	H	2B	3B	HR	TB	R	RBI	GW	TBB	IBB	SO	HBP	SH	SF	SB	CS	SB%	GDP	Avg	OBP	SLG	Pos	G	PO	A	E	DP	FPct
Division Series																															
1981 Phi	27	1	2	0	0	0	0	0	0	0	0	0	0	1	0	0	0	0	0	—	0	.000	.000	.000	P	1	0	0	0	0	—
LCS																															
1977 Phi	23	1	0	0	0	0	0	0	0	1	0	1	0	0	0	0	0	0	0	—	0	—	1.000	—	P	1	0	0	0	0	—
1978 Phi	24	1	1	0	0	0	0	0	0	0	0	0	0	1	0	0	0	0	0	—	0	.000	.000	.000	P	1	0	0	0	0	—
1980 Phi	26	2	2	0	0	0	0	0	0	0	0	0	0	1	0	0	0	0	0	—	0	.000	.000	.000	P	2	0	1	1	0	.500
LCS Totals		4	3	0	0	0	0	0	0	1	0	1	0	2	0	0	0	0	0	—	0	.000	.250	.000	P	4	0	1	1	0	.500
World Series																															
1980 Phi	26	1	0	0	0	0	0	0	0	0	0	0	0	0	0	0	0	0	0	—	0	—	—	—	P	1	0	0	1	0	.000
Postseason Totals		6	5	0	0	0	0	0	0	1	0	1	0	3	0	0	0	0	0	—	0	.000	.167	.000	P	6	0	1	2	0	.333

MARK CHRISTMAN—Marquette Joseph Christman—Bats: Right; Throws: Right

Ht: 5'11"; Wt: 175 lbs; Born: 10/21/1913 in Maplewood, Missouri; Debut: 4/20/1938; Died: 10/9/1976

World Series — Batting / Fielding

Year Tm	Age	G	AB	H	2B	3B	HR	TB	R	RBI	GW	TBB	IBB	SO	HBP	SH	SF	SB	CS	SB%	GDP	Avg	OBP	SLG	Pos	G	PO	A	E	DP	FPct
1944 StL	30	6	22	2	0	0	0	2	0	1	0	0	0	6	0	0	0	0	0	—	0	.091	.091	.091	3B	6	3	9	1	0	.923

JOE CHRISTOPHER—Joseph O'Neal Christopher—Bats: Right; Throws: Right

Ht: 5'10"; Wt: 175 lbs; Born: 12/13/1935 in Frederiksted, Virgin Islands; Debut: 5/26/1959

World Series — Batting / Fielding

Year Tm	Age	G	AB	H	2B	3B	HR	TB	R	RBI	GW	TBB	IBB	SO	HBP	SH	SF	SB	CS	SB%	GDP	Avg	OBP	SLG	Pos	G	PO	A	E	DP	FPct
1960 Pit	24	3	0	0	0	0	0	0	2	0	0	0	0	0	1	0	0	0	0	—	0	—	1.000	—	—						

RUSS CHRISTOPHER—Russell Ormand Christopher—Nickname: Daddy—Throws: Right; Bats: Right

Ht: 6'3"; Wt: 170 lbs; Born: 9/12/1917 in Richmond, California; Debut: 4/14/1942; Died: 12/5/1954

World Series — Pitching

Year	Tm	Age	G	GS	CG	GF	IP	BFP	H	R	ER	HR	SH	SF	HB	TBB	IBB	SO	WP	Bk	W	L	Pct	ShO	Sv-Op	Hld	OAvg	OOBP	ERA
1948	Cle	31	1	0	0	0	0.0	2	2	1	1	0	0	0	0	0	0	0	0	0	0	0	—	0	0- 0	0	1.000	1.000	—

World Series — Batting / Fielding

Year Tm	Age	G	AB	H	2B	3B	HR	TB	R	RBI	GW	TBB	IBB	SO	HBP	SH	SF	SB	CS	SB%	GDP	Avg	OBP	SLG	Pos	G	PO	A	E	DP	FPct
1948 Cle	31	1	0	0	0	0	0	0	0	0	0	0	0	0	0	0	0	0	0	—	0	—	—	—	P	1	0	0	0	0	—

CHUCK CHURN—Clarence Nottingham Churn—Throws: Right; Bats: Right

Ht: 6'3"; Wt: 205 lbs; Born: 2/1/1930 in Bridgetown, Virginia; Debut: 4/18/1957

World Series — Pitching

Year	Tm	Age	G	GS	CG	GF	IP	BFP	H	R	ER	HR	SH	SF	HB	TBB	IBB	SO	WP	Bk	W	L	Pct	ShO	Sv-Op	Hld	OAvg	OOBP	ERA
1959	LA	29	1	0	0	0	0.2	9	5	6	2	1	0	0	0	0	0	0	0	0	0	0	—	0	0- 0	0	.556	.556	27.00

World Series — Batting / Fielding

Year Tm	Age	G	AB	H	2B	3B	HR	TB	R	RBI	GW	TBB	IBB	SO	HBP	SH	SF	SB	CS	SB%	GDP	Avg	OBP	SLG	Pos	G	PO	A	E	DP	FPct
1959 LA	29	1	0	0	0	0	0	0	0	0	0	0	0	0	0	0	0	0	0	—	0	—	—	—	P	1	0	1	0	0	1.000

ARCHI CIANFROCCO—Angelo Dominic Cianfrocco—Bats: Right; Throws: Right

Ht: 6'5"; Wt: 200 lbs; Born: 10/6/1966 in Rome, New York; Debut: 4/8/1992

Division Series — Batting / Fielding

Year Tm	Age	G	AB	H	2B	3B	HR	TB	R	RBI	GW	TBB	IBB	SO	HBP	SH	SF	SB	CS	SB%	GDP	Avg	OBP	SLG	Pos	G	PO	A	E	DP	FPct
1996 SD	29	3	3	1	0	0	0	1	1	0	0	0	0	1	0	0	0	0	0	—	0	.333	.333	.333	1B	3	8	2	0	1	1.000

EDDIE CICOTTE—Edward Victor Cicotte—Nickname: Knuckles—Throws: Right; Bats: Both

Ht: 5'9"; Wt: 175 lbs; Born: 6/19/1884 in Springwells, Michigan; Debut: 9/3/1905; Died: 5/5/1969

World Series — Pitching

Year	Tm	Age	G	GS	CG	GF	IP	BFP	H	R	ER	HR	SH	SF	HB	TBB	IBB	SO	WP	Bk	W	L	Pct	ShO	Sv-Op	Hld	OAvg	OOBP	ERA
1917	ChA	33	3	2	2	0	23.0	95	23	5	4	0	2	0	0	2	1	13	0	0	1	1	.500	0	0- 0	0	.253	.269	1.57
1919	ChA	35	3	3	2	0	21.2	87	19	9	7	0	1	1	1	5	0	7	0	0	1	2	.333	0	0- 0	0	.241	.291	2.91
WS Totals			6	5	4	0	44.2	364	42	14	11	0	3	1	1	7	1	20	0	0	2	3	.400	0	0-0	0	.247	.279	2.22

World Series — Batting / Fielding

Year Tm	Age	G	AB	H	2B	3B	HR	TB	R	RBI	GW	TBB	IBB	SO	HBP	SH	SF	SB	CS	SB%	GDP	Avg	OBP	SLG	Pos	G	PO	A	E	DP	FPct
1917 ChA	33	3	7	1	0	0	0	1	0	0	0	1	0	2	0	0	0	0	0	—	0	.143	.250	.143	P	3	0	7	1	0	.875
1919 ChA	35	3	8	0	0	0	0	0	0	0	0	0	0	3	0	0	0	0	0	—	0	.000	.000	.000	P	3	0	6	2	1	.750
WS Totals		6	15	1	0	0	0	1	0	0	0	1	0	5	0	0	0	0	0	—	0	.067	.125	.067	P	6	0	13	3	1	.813

GINO CIMOLI—Gino Nicholas Cimoli—Bats: Right; Throws: Right

Ht: 6'1"; Wt: 180 lbs; Born: 12/18/1929 in San Francisco, California; Debut: 4/19/1956

World Series — Batting / Fielding

Year Tm	Age	G	AB	H	2B	3B	HR	TB	R	RBI	GW	TBB	IBB	SO	HBP	SH	SF	SB	CS	SB%	GDP	Avg	OBP	SLG	Pos	G	PO	A	E	DP	FPct
1956 Bro	26	1	0	0	0	0	0	0	0	0	0	0	0	0	0	0	0	0	0	—	0	—	—	—	OF	1	1	0	0	0	1.000
1960 Pit	30	7	20	5	0	0	0	5	4	1	0	2	0	4	0	0	0	0	0	—	0	.250	.318	.250	OF	6	5	0	0	0	1.000
WS Totals		8	20	5	0	0	0	5	4	1	0	2	0	4	0	0	0	0	0	—	0	.250	.318	.250	OF	7	6	0	0	0	1.000

JIM CLANCY—James Clancy—Throws: Right; Bats: Right

Ht: 6'4"; Wt: 220 lbs; Born: 12/18/1955 in Chicago, Illinois; Debut: 7/26/1977

LCS / World Series — Pitching

Year	Tm	Age	G	GS	CG	GF	IP	BFP	H	R	ER	HR	SH	SF	HB	TBB	IBB	SO	WP	Bk	W	L	Pct	ShO	Sv-Op	Hld	OAvg	OOBP	ERA
LCS																													
1985	Tor	29	1	0	0	1	1.0	6	2	1	1	0	1	0	0	1	1	0	0	0	0	1	.000	0	0- 0	0	.500	.600	9.00
1991	Atl	35	1	0	0	0	0.1	1	0	0	0	0	0	0	0	0	0	0	0	0	0	0	—	0	0- 0	0	.000	.000	0.00
LCS Totals			2	0	0	1	1.1	14	2	1	1	0	1	0	0	1	1	0	0	0	0	1	.000	0	0-0	0	.400	.500	6.75
World Series																													
1991	Atl	35	3	0	0	1	4.1	20	3	2	2	1	0	0	0	4	2	2	0	0	1	0	1.000	0	0- 0	1	.188	.350	4.15
Postseason Totals			5	0	0	2	5.2	54	5	3	3	1	1	0	0	5	3	2	0	0	1	1	.500	0	0-0	1	.238	.385	4.76

LCS		Batting																							Fielding						
Year Tm	Age	G	AB	H	2B	3B	HR	TB	R	RBI	GW	TBB	IBB	SO	HBP	SH	SF	SB	CS	SB%	GDP	Avg	OBP	SLG	Pos	G	PO	A	E	DP	FPct
1985 Tor	29	1	0	0	0	0	0	0	0	0	0	0	0	0	0	0	0	0	0	—	0	—	—	—	P	1	0	1	0	0	1.000
1991 Atl	35	1	0	0	0	0	0	0	0	0	0	0	0	0	0	0	0	0	0	—	0	—	—	—	P	1	0	0	0	0	—
LCS Totals		2	0	0	0	0	0	0	0	0	0	0	0	0	0	0	0	0	0	—	0	—	—	—	P	2	0	1	0	0	1.000
World Series		**Batting**																							**Fielding**						
Year Tm	Age	G	AB	H	2B	3B	HR	TB	R	RBI	GW	TBB	IBB	SO	HBP	SH	SF	SB	CS	SB%	GDP	Avg	OBP	SLG	Pos	G	PO	A	E	DP	FPct
1991 Atl	35	3	1	0	0	0	0	0	0	0	0	0	0	1	0	0	0	0	0	—	0	.000	.000	.000	P	3	0	0	0	0	—
Postseason Totals		5	1	0	0	0	0	0	0	0	0	0	0	1	0	0	0	0	0	—	0	.000	.000	.000	P	5	0	1	0	0	1.000

ALLIE CLARK—Alfred Aloysius Clark—Bats: Right; Throws: Right

Ht: 6'0"; Wt: 185 lbs; Born: 6/16/1923 in South Amboy, New Jersey; Debut: 8/5/1947

World Series		Batting																							Fielding						
Year Tm	Age	G	AB	H	2B	3B	HR	TB	R	RBI	GW	TBB	IBB	SO	HBP	SH	SF	SB	CS	SB%	GDP	Avg	OBP	SLG	Pos	G	PO	A	E	DP	FPct
1947 NYA	24	3	2	1	0	0	0	1	1	1	0	1	0	0	0	0	0	0	0	—	0	.500	.667	.500	OF	1	2	0	0	0	1.000
1948 Cle	25	1	3	0	0	0	0	0	0	0	0	0	0	1	0	1	0	0	0	—	0	.000	.000	.000	OF	1	2	0	0	0	1.000
WS Totals		4	5	1	0	0	0	1	1	1	0	1	0	1	0	1	0	0	0	—	0	.200	.333	.200	OF	2	4	0	0	0	1.000

BOBBY CLARK—Robert Cale Clark—Bats: Right; Throws: Right

Ht: 6'0"; Wt: 190 lbs; Born: 6/13/1955 in Sacramento, California; Debut: 8/21/1979

LCS		Batting																							Fielding						
Year Tm	Age	G	AB	H	2B	3B	HR	TB	R	RBI	GW	TBB	IBB	SO	HBP	SH	SF	SB	CS	SB%	GDP	Avg	OBP	SLG	Pos	G	PO	A	E	DP	FPct
1979 Cal	24	1	3	0	0	0	0	0	0	0	0	0	0	2	0	0	0	0	0	—	0	.000	.000	.000	OF	1	4	0	0	0	1.000
1982 Cal	27	2	0	0	0	0	0	0	0	0	0	0	0	0	0	0	0	0	0	—	0	—	—	—	OF	2	1	0	0	0	1.000
LCS Totals		3	3	0	0	0	0	0	0	0	0	0	0	2	0	0	0	0	0	—	0	.000	.000	.000	OF	3	5	0	0	0	1.000

DAVE CLARK—David Earl Clark—Bats: Left; Throws: Right

Ht: 6'2"; Wt: 200 lbs; Born: 9/3/1962 in Tupelo, Mississippi; Debut: 9/3/1986

Division Series		Batting																							Fielding						
Year Tm	Age	G	AB	H	2B	3B	HR	TB	R	RBI	GW	TBB	IBB	SO	HBP	SH	SF	SB	CS	SB%	GDP	Avg	OBP	SLG	Pos	G	PO	A	E	DP	FPct
1996 LA	34	2	2	0	0	0	0	0	0	0	0	0	0	2	0	0	0	0	0	—	0	.000	.000	.000	—						

JACK CLARK—Jack Anthony Clark—Bats: Right; Throws: Right

Ht: 6'2"; Wt: 175 lbs; Born: 11/10/1955 in New Brighton, Pennsylvania; Debut: 9/12/1975

LCS		Batting																							Fielding						
Year Tm	Age	G	AB	H	2B	3B	HR	TB	R	RBI	GW	TBB	IBB	SO	HBP	SH	SF	SB	CS	SB%	GDP	Avg	OBP	SLG	Pos	G	PO	A	E	DP	FPct
1985 StL	29	6	21	8	0	0	1	11	4	4	1	5	3	5	0	0	0	0	0	—	0	.381	.500	.524	1B	6	55	0	0	3	1.000
1987 StL	31	1	1	0	0	0	0	0	0	0	0	0	0	1	0	0	0	0	0	—	0	.000	.000	.000	—						
LCS Totals		7	22	8	0	0	1	11	4	4	1	5	3	6	0	0	0	0	0	—	0	.364	.481	.500	1B	6	55	0	0	3	1.000
World Series		**Batting**																							**Fielding**						
Year Tm	Age	G	AB	H	2B	3B	HR	TB	R	RBI	GW	TBB	IBB	SO	HBP	SH	SF	SB	CS	SB%	GDP	Avg	OBP	SLG	Pos	G	PO	A	E	DP	FPct
1985 StL	29	7	25	6	2	0	0	8	1	4	0	3	0	9	0	0	0	0	0	—	0	.240	.321	.320	1B	7	49	4	0	6	1.000
Postseason Totals		14	47	14	2	0	1	19	5	8	1	8	3	15	0	0	0	0	0	—	0	.298	.400	.404	1B	13	104	4	0	9	1.000

WILL CLARK—William Nuschler Clark—Nickname: The Thrill—Bats: Left; Throws: Left

Ht: 6'2"; Wt: 190 lbs; Born: 3/13/1964 in New Orleans, Louisiana; Debut: 4/8/1986

Division Series		Batting																							Fielding						
Year Tm	Age	G	AB	H	2B	3B	HR	TB	R	RBI	GW	TBB	IBB	SO	HBP	SH	SF	SB	CS	SB%	GDP	Avg	OBP	SLG	Pos	G	PO	A	E	DP	FPct
1996 Tex	32	4	16	2	0	0	0	2	1	0	0	3	1	2	0	0	0	0	0	—	1	.125	.263	.125	1B	4	35	4	0	4	1.000
LCS		**Batting**																							**Fielding**						
Year Tm	Age	G	AB	H	2B	3B	HR	TB	R	RBI	GW	TBB	IBB	SO	HBP	SH	SF	SB	CS	SB%	GDP	Avg	OBP	SLG	Pos	G	PO	A	E	DP	FPct
1987 SF	23	7	25	9	2	0	1	14	3	3	1	3	1	6	0	0	0	1	0	1.00	1	.360	.429	.560	1B	7	62	8	1	10	.986
1989 SF	25	5	20	13	3	1	2	24	8	8	2	2	0	2	0	0	0	0	0	—	0	.650	.682	1.200	1B	5	43	5	0	6	1.000
LCS Totals		12	45	22	5	1	3	38	11	11	3	5	1	8	0	0	0	1	0	1.00	1	.489	.540	.844	1B	12	105	13	1	16	.992
World Series		**Batting**																							**Fielding**						
Year Tm	Age	G	AB	H	2B	3B	HR	TB	R	RBI	GW	TBB	IBB	SO	HBP	SH	SF	SB	CS	SB%	GDP	Avg	OBP	SLG	Pos	G	PO	A	E	DP	FPct
1989 SF	25	4	16	4	1	0	0	5	2	0	0	1	0	3	0	0	0	0	0	—	0	.250	.294	.313	1B	4	40	2	0	2	1.000
Postseason Totals		20	77	28	6	1	3	45	14	11	3	9	2	13	0	0	0	1	0	1.00	2	.364	.430	.584	1B	20	180	19	1	22	.995

FRED CLARKE (HOF 1945-V)—Fred Clifford Clarke—Nickname: Cap—Bats: Left; Throws: Right

Ht: 5'10"; Wt: 165 lbs; Born: 10/3/1872 in Winterset, Iowa; Debut: 6/30/1894; Died: 8/14/1960

World Series		Batting																							Fielding						
Year Tm	Age	G	AB	H	2B	3B	HR	TB	R	RBI	GW	TBB	IBB	SO	HBP	SH	SF	SB	CS	SB%	GDP	Avg	OBP	SLG	Pos	G	PO	A	E	DP	FPct
1903 Pit	30	8	34	9	2	1	0	13	3	2	0	1	0	5	0	0	0	1	0	1.00	0	.265	.286	.382	OF	8	18	0	1	0	.947
1909 Pit	36	7	19	4	0	0	2	10	7	7	1	5	0	3	1	4	1	3	0	1.00	0	.211	.385	.526	OF	7	19	0	1	0	.950
WS Totals		15	53	13	2	1	2	23	10	9	1	6	0	8	1	4	1	4	0	1.00	0	.245	.328	.434	OF	15	37	0	2	0	.949

ELLIS CLARY—Nickname: Cat—Bats: Right; Throws: Right

Ht: 5'8"; Wt: 160 lbs; Born: 9/11/1916 in Valdosta, Georgia; Debut: 6/7/1942

World Series		Batting																							Fielding						
Year Tm	Age	G	AB	H	2B	3B	HR	TB	R	RBI	GW	TBB	IBB	SO	HBP	SH	SF	SB	CS	SB%	GDP	Avg	OBP	SLG	Pos	G	PO	A	E	DP	FPct
1944 StL	28	1	1	0	0	0	0	0	0	0	0	0	0	0	0	0	0	0	0	—	0	.000	.000	.000	—						

KEN CLAY—Kenneth Earl Clay—Throws: Right; Bats: Right

Ht: 6'3"; Wt: 185 lbs; Born: 4/6/1954 in Lynchburg, Virginia; Debut: 6/7/1977

LCS		Pitching																										
Year Tm	Age	G	GS	CG	GF	IP	BFP	H	R	ER	HR	SH	SF	HB	TBB	IBB	SO	WP	Bk	W	L	Pct	ShO	Sv-Op	Hld	OAvg	OOBP	ERA
1978 NYA	24	1	0	0	1	3.2	14	0	0	0	0	0	1	0	3	0	2	0	0	0	0	—	0	1- 1	0	.000	.214	0.00
World Series		**Pitching**																										
Year Tm	Age	G	GS	CG	GF	IP	BFP	H	R	ER	HR	SH	SF	HB	TBB	IBB	SO	WP	Bk	W	L	Pct	ShO	Sv-Op	Hld	OAvg	OOBP	ERA
1977 NYA	23	2	0	0	0	3.2	14	2	1	1	0	0	1	0	1	0	0	0	0	0	0	—	0	0- 0	0	.167	.214	2.45
1978 NYA	24	1	0	0	0	2.1	14	4	4	3	1	0	0	0	2	0	2	1	0	0	0	—	0	0- 0	0	.333	.429	11.57
WS Totals		3	0	0	0	6.0	56	6	5	4	1	0	1	0	3	0	2	1	0	0	0	—	0	0-0	0	.250	.321	6.00
Postseason Totals		4	0	0	1	9.2	84	6	5	4	1	0	2	0	6	0	4	1	0	0	0	—	0	1-1	0	.176	.286	3.72

LCS		Batting																							Fielding						
Year Tm	Age	G	AB	H	2B	3B	HR	TB	R	RBI	GW	TBB	IBB	SO	HBP	SH	SF	SB	CS	SB%	GDP	Avg	OBP	SLG	Pos	G	PO	A	E	DP	FPct
1978 NYA	24	1	0	0	0	0	0	0	0	0	0	0	0	0	0	0	0	0	0	—	0	—	—	—	P	1	0	0	0	0	—
World Series		**Batting**																							**Fielding**						
Year Tm	Age	G	AB	H	2B	3B	HR	TB	R	RBI	GW	TBB	IBB	SO	HBP	SH	SF	SB	CS	SB%	GDP	Avg	OBP	SLG	Pos	G	PO	A	E	DP	FPct
1977 NYA	23	2	0	0	0	0	0	0	0	0	0	0	0	0	0	0	0	0	0	—	0	—	—	—	P	2	1	1	0	0	1.000
1978 NYA	24	1	0	0	0	0	0	0	0	0	0	0	0	0	0	0	0	0	0	—	0	—	—	—	P	1	0	0	0	0	—
WS Totals		3	0	0	0	0	0	0	0	0	0	0	0	0	0	0	0	0	0	—	0	—	—	—	P	3	1	1	0	0	1.000
Postseason Totals		4	0	0	0	0	0	0	0	0	0	0	0	0	0	0	0	0	0	—	0	—	—	—	P	4	1	1	0	0	1.000

ROYCE CLAYTON—Royce Spencer Clayton—Bats: Right; Throws: Right

Ht: 6'0"; Wt: 175 lbs; Born: 1/2/1970 in Burbank, California; Debut: 9/20/1991

Division Series		Batting																							Fielding						
Year Tm	Age	G	AB	H	2B	3B	HR	TB	R	RBI	GW	TBB	IBB	SO	HBP	SH	SF	SB	CS	SB%	GDP	Avg	OBP	SLG	Pos	G	PO	A	E	DP	FPct
1996 StL	26	2	6	2	0	0	0	2	1	0	0	3	0	1	0	0	0	0	1	.00	0	.333	.556	.333	SS	2	4	5	0	0	1.000
LCS		**Batting**																							**Fielding**						
Year Tm	Age	G	AB	H	2B	3B	HR	TB	R	RBI	GW	TBB	IBB	SO	HBP	SH	SF	SB	CS	SB%	GDP	Avg	OBP	SLG	Pos	G	PO	A	E	DP	FPct
1996 StL	26	5	20	7	0	0	0	7	4	1	0	1	0	4	0	0	0	1	1	.50	0	.350	.381	.350	SS	5	5	16	2	2	.913
Postseason Totals		7	26	9	0	0	0	9	5	1	0	4	0	5	0	0	0	1	2	.33	0	.346	.433	.346	SS	7	9	21	2	2	.938

MARK CLEAR—Mark Alan Clear—Throws: Right; Bats: Right

Ht: 6'4"; Wt: 200 lbs; Born: 5/27/1956 in Los Angeles, California; Debut: 4/4/1979

LCS — Pitching

Year Tm	Age	G	GS	CG	GF	IP	BFP	H	R	ER	HR	SH	SF	HB	TBB	IBB	SO	WP	Bk	W	L	Pct	ShO	Sv-Op	Hld	OAvg	OOBP	ERA
1979 Cal	23	1	0	0	0	5.2	23	4	3	3	1	0	0	0	2	0	3	1	0	0	0	—	0	0-0	0	.190	.261	4.76

LCS — Batting / Fielding

Year Tm	Age	G	AB	H	2B	3B	HR	TB	R	RBI	GW	TBB	IBB	SO	HBP	SH	SF	SB	CS	SB%	GDP	Avg	OBP	SLG	Pos	G	PO	A	E	DP	FPct
1979 Cal	23	1	0	0	0	0	0	0	0	0	0	0	0	0	0	0	0	0	0	—	0	—	—	—	P	1	0	0	0	0	—

ROGER CLEMENS—William Roger Clemens—Nickname: Rocket—Throws: Right; Bats: Right

Ht: 6'4"; Wt: 205 lbs; Born: 8/4/1962 in Dayton, Ohio; Debut: 5/15/1984

Pitching

Year Tm	Age	G	GS	CG	GF	IP	BFP	H	R	ER	HR	SH	SF	HB	TBB	IBB	SO	WP	Bk	W	L	Pct	ShO	Sv-Op	Hld	OAvg	OOBP	ERA
Division Series																												
1995 Bos	33	1	1	0	0	7.0	27	5	3	3	0	0	0	0	1	0	5	0	0	0	0	—	0	0-0	0	.192	.222	3.86
LCS																												
1986 Bos-*MC*	24	3	3	0	0	22.2	99	22	12	11	1	0	0	2	7	0	17	0	0	1	1	.500	0	0-0	0	.244	.313	4.37
1988 Bos	26	1	1	0	0	7.0	26	6	3	3	1	0	0	0	0	0	8	1	1	0	0	—	0	0-0	0	.231	.231	3.86
1990 Bos	28	2	2	0	0	7.2	32	7	3	3	0	0	0	0	5	0	4	1	0	0	1	.000	0	0-0	0	.259	.375	3.52
LCS Totals		6	6	0	0	37.1	314	35	18	17	2	0	0	2	12	0	29	2	1	1	2	.333	0	0-0	0	.245	.312	4.10
World Series																												
1986 Bos-*MC*	24	2	2	0	0	11.1	47	9	5	4	0	1	0	0	6	0	11	0	0	0	0	—	0	0-0	0	.225	.326	3.18
Postseason Totals		9	9	0	0	55.2	462	49	26	24	2	1	0	2	19	0	45	2	1	1	2	.333	0	0-0	0	.234	.304	3.88

Batting / Fielding

Year Tm	Age	G	AB	H	2B	3B	HR	TB	R	RBI	GW	TBB	IBB	SO	HBP	SH	SF	SB	CS	SB%	GDP	Avg	OBP	SLG	Pos	G	PO	A	E	DP	FPct
Division Series																															
1995 Bos	33	1	0	0	0	0	0	0	0	0	0	0	0	0	0	0	0	0	0	—	0	—	—	—	P	1	0	0	0	0	—
LCS																															
1986 Bos	24	3	0	0	0	0	0	0	0	0	0	0	0	0	0	0	0	0	0	—	0	—	—	—	P	3	1	2	0	1	1.000
1988 Bos	26	1	0	0	0	0	0	0	0	0	0	0	0	0	0	0	0	0	0	—	0	—	—	—	P	1	0	0	1	0	.000
1990 Bos	28	2	0	0	0	0	0	0	0	0	0	0	0	0	0	0	0	0	0	—	0	—	—	—	P	2	0	1	0	0	1.000
LCS Totals		6	0	0	0	0	0	0	0	0	0	0	0	0	0	0	0	0	0	—	0	—	—	—	P	6	1	3	1	1	.800
World Series																															
1986 Bos	24	2	4	0	0	0	0	0	1	0	0	0	0	1	0	1	0	0	0	—	0	.000	.000	.000	P	2	1	2	0	0	1.000
Postseason Totals		9	4	0	0	0	0	0	1	0	0	0	0	1	0	1	0	0	0	—	0	.000	.000	.000	P	9	2	5	1	1	.875

ROBERTO CLEMENTE (HOF 1973-W)—Nicknames: Bob, Arriba—Bats: Right; Throws: Right

Ht: 5'11"; Wt: 175 lbs; Born: 8/18/1934 in Carolina, Puerto Rico; Debut: 4/17/1955; Died: 12/31/1972

Year Tm	Age	G	AB	H	2B	3B	HR	TB	R	RBI	GW	TBB	IBB	SO	HBP	SH	SF	SB	CS	SB%	GDP	Avg	OBP	SLG	Pos	G	PO	A	E	DP	FPct
LCS																															
1970 Pit	36	3	14	3	0	0	0	3	1	1	0	0	0	4	0	0	0	0	0	—	0	.214	.214	.214	OF	3	7	0	0	0	1.000
1971 Pit	37	4	18	6	0	0	0	6	2	4	1	1	0	6	0	0	0	0	0	—	0	.333	.368	.333	OF	4	12	0	0	0	1.000
1972 Pit	38	5	17	4	1	0	1	8	1	2	0	3	1	5	0	0	0	0	0	—	0	.235	.350	.471	OF	5	9	0	0	0	1.000
LCS Totals		12	49	13	1	0	1	17	4	7	1	4	1	15	0	0	0	0	0	—	0	.265	.321	.347	OF	12	28	0	0	0	1.000
World Series																															
1960 Pit	26	7	29	9	0	0	0	9	1	3	0	0	0	4	0	0	0	0	0	—	1	.310	.310	.310	OF	7	19	0	0	0	1.000
1971 Pit	37	7	29	12	2	1	2	22	3	4	2	2	1	2	0	0	0	0	0	—	0	.414	.452	.759	OF	7	15	0	0	0	1.000
WS Totals		14	58	21	2	1	2	31	4	7	2	2	1	6	0	0	0	0	0	—	1	.362	.383	.534	OF	14	34	0	0	0	1.000
Postseason Totals		26	107	34	3	1	3	48	8	14	3	6	2	21	0	0	0	0	0	—	1	.318	.354	.449	OF	26	62	0	0	0	1.000

DONN CLENDENON—Donn Alvin Clendenon—Bats: Right; Throws: Right

Ht: 6'4"; Wt: 209 lbs; Born: 7/15/1935 in Neosho, Missouri; Debut: 9/22/1961

Year Tm	Age	G	AB	H	2B	3B	HR	TB	R	RBI	GW	TBB	IBB	SO	HBP	SH	SF	SB	CS	SB%	GDP	Avg	OBP	SLG	Pos	G	PO	A	E	DP	FPct
World Series																															
1969 NYN	34	4	14	5	1	0	3	15	4	4	0	2	0	6	0	0	0	0	0	—	0	.357	.438	1.071	1B	4	30	4	0	0	1.000

REGGIE CLEVELAND—Reginald Leslie Cleveland—Throws: Right; Bats: Right

Ht: 6'1"; Wt: 195 lbs; Born: 5/23/1948 in Swift Current, Saskatchewan; Debut: 10/1/1969

Pitching

Year Tm	Age	G	GS	CG	GF	IP	BFP	H	R	ER	HR	SH	SF	HB	TBB	IBB	SO	WP	Bk	W	L	Pct	ShO	Sv-Op	Hld	OAvg	OOBP	ERA
LCS																												
1975 Bos	27	1	1	0	0	5.0	21	7	3	3	1	0	0	0	1	0	2	0	0	0	0	—	0	0-0	0	.350	.381	5.40
World Series																												
1975 Bos	27	3	1	0	1	6.2	29	7	5	5	2	0	0	0	3	0	5	0	0	0	1	.000	0	0-0	0	.269	.345	6.75
Postseason Totals		4	2	0	1	11.2	100	14	8	8	3	0	0	0	4	0	7	0	0	0	1	.000	0	0-0	0	.304	.360	6.17

Batting / Fielding

Year Tm	Age	G	AB	H	2B	3B	HR	TB	R	RBI	GW	TBB	IBB	SO	HBP	SH	SF	SB	CS	SB%	GDP	Avg	OBP	SLG	Pos	G	PO	A	E	DP	FPct
LCS																															
1975 Bos	27	1	0	0	0	0	0	0	0	0	0	0	0	0	0	0	0	0	0	—	0	—	—	—	P	1	0	1	0	0	1.000
World Series																															
1975 Bos	27	3	2	0	0	0	0	0	0	0	0	0	0	2	0	0	0	0	0	—	0	.000	.000	.000	P	3	0	0	0	0	—
Postseason Totals		4	2	0	0	0	0	0	0	0	0	0	0	2	0	0	0	0	0	—	0	.000	.000	.000	P	4	0	1	0	0	1.000

FLEA CLIFTON—Herman Earl Clifton—Bats: Right; Throws: Right

Ht: 5'10"; Wt: 160 lbs; Born: 12/12/1909 in Cincinnati, Ohio; Debut: 4/29/1934; Died: 12/22/1997

Year Tm	Age	G	AB	H	2B	3B	HR	TB	R	RBI	GW	TBB	IBB	SO	HBP	SH	SF	SB	CS	SB%	GDP	Avg	OBP	SLG	Pos	G	PO	A	E	DP	FPct
World Series																															
1935 Det	25	4	16	0	0	0	0	0	1	0	0	2	0	4	0	0	0	0	0	—	0	.000	.111	.000	3B	4	2	9	1	0	.917

TY CLINE—Tyrone Alexander Cline—Bats: Left; Throws: Left

Ht: 6'0"; Wt: 170 lbs; Born: 6/15/1939 in Hampton, South Carolina; Debut: 9/14/1960

Year Tm	Age	G	AB	H	2B	3B	HR	TB	R	RBI	GW	TBB	IBB	SO	HBP	SH	SF	SB	CS	SB%	GDP	Avg	OBP	SLG	Pos	G	PO	A	E	DP	FPct
LCS																															
1970 Cin	31	2	1	1	0	1	0	3	2	0	0	1	0	0	0	0	0	0	0	—	0	1.000	1.000	3.000	OF	1	0	0	0	0	—
World Series																															
1970 Cin	31	3	3	1	0	0	0	1	0	0	0	0	0	0	0	0	0	0	0	—	0	.333	.333	.333	—						
Postseason Totals		5	4	2	0	1	0	4	2	0	0	1	0	0	0	0	0	0	0	—	0	.500	.600	1.000	OF	1	0	0	0	0	—

GENE CLINES—Eugene Anthony Clines—Nickname: Road Runner—Bats: Right; Throws: Right

Ht: 5'9"; Wt: 170 lbs; Born: 10/6/1946 in San Pablo, California; Debut: 6/28/1970

Year Tm	Age	G	AB	H	2B	3B	HR	TB	R	RBI	GW	TBB	IBB	SO	HBP	SH	SF	SB	CS	SB%	GDP	Avg	OBP	SLG	Pos	G	PO	A	E	DP	FPct
LCS																															
1971 Pit	24	1	3	1	0	0	1	4	1	1	0	0	0	1	0	0	0	0	0	—	0	.333	.333	1.333	OF	1	1	0	0	0	1.000
1972 Pit	25	3	2	0	0	0	0	0	1	0	0	0	0	1	0	0	0	0	0	—	0	.000	.000	.000	—						
1974 Pit	27	2	1	0	0	0	0	0	1	0	0	0	0	0	0	0	0	0	0	—	0	.000	.000	.000	OF	2	0	0	0	0	—
LCS Totals		6	6	1	0	0	1	4	3	1	0	0	0	2	0	0	0	0	0	—	0	.167	.167	.667	OF	3	1	0	0	0	1.000
World Series																															
1971 Pit	24	3	11	1	0	1	0	3	2	0	0	1	0	1	0	0	0	1	0	1.00	0	.091	.167	.273	OF	3	6	0	0	0	1.000
Postseason Totals		9	17	2	0	1	1	7	5	1	0	1	0	3	0	0	0	1	0	1.00	0	.118	.167	.412	OF	6	7	0	0	0	1.000

TONY CLONINGER
—Tony Lee Cloninger—Throws: Right; Bats: Right — Ht: 6'0"; Wt: 210 lbs; Born: 8/13/1940 in Lincoln, North Carolina; Debut: 6/15/1961

LCS

Year	Tm	Age	G	GS	CG	GF	IP	BFP	H	R	ER	HR	SH	SF	HB	TBB	IBB	SO	WP	Bk	W	L	Pct	ShO	Sv-Op	Hld	OAvg	OOBP	ERA
1970	Cin	30	1	1	0	0	5.0	24	7	2	2	0	0	0	0	4	0	1	0	1	0	0	—	0	0-0	0	.350	.458	3.60

World Series

Year	Tm	Age	G	GS	CG	GF	IP	BFP	H	R	ER	HR	SH	SF	HB	TBB	IBB	SO	WP	Bk	W	L	Pct	ShO	Sv-Op	Hld	OAvg	OOBP	ERA
1970	Cin	30	2	1	0	0	7.1	35	10	6	6	3	0	0	0	5	1	4	0	0	0	1	.000	0	0-0	0	.333	.429	7.36
Postseason Totals			3	2	0	0	12.1	118	17	8	8	3	0	0	0	9	1	5	1	0	0	1	.000	0	0-0	0	.340	.441	5.84

LCS

Year	Tm	Age	G	AB	H	2B	3B	HR	TB	R	RBI	GW	TBB	IBB	SO	HBP	SH	SF	SB	CS	SB%	GDP	Avg	OBP	SLG	Pos	G	PO	A	E	DP	FPct
1970	Cin	30	1	1	0	0	0	0	0	0	0	0	0	0	0	0	0	0	0	0	—	0	.000	.000	.000	P	1	0	1	0	0	—

World Series

Year	Tm	Age	G	AB	H	2B	3B	HR	TB	R	RBI	GW	TBB	IBB	SO	HBP	SH	SF	SB	CS	SB%	GDP	Avg	OBP	SLG	Pos	G	PO	A	E	DP	FPct
1970	Cin	30	2	2	0	0	0	0	0	0	0	0	0	0	1	0	0	0	0	0	—	0	.000	.000	.000	P	2	0	1	0	0	1.000
Postseason Totals			3	3	0	0	0	0	0	0	0	0	0	0	1	0	0	0	0	0	—	0	.000	.000	.000	P	3	0	3	0	0	1.000

BRAD CLONTZ
—John Bradley Clontz—Throws: Right; Bats: Right — Ht: 6'1"; Wt: 180 lbs; Born: 4/25/1971 in Stuart, Virginia; Debut: 4/26/1995

Division Series

Year	Tm	Age	G	GS	CG	GF	IP	BFP	H	R	ER	HR	SH	SF	HB	TBB	IBB	SO	WP	Bk	W	L	Pct	ShO	Sv-Op	Hld	OAvg	OOBP	ERA
1995	Atl	24	1	0	0	0	1.1	4	0	0	0	0	0	0	0	0	0	0	0	0	0	0	—	0	0-0	0	.000	.000	0.00

LCS

Year	Tm	Age	G	GS	CG	GF	IP	BFP	H	R	ER	HR	SH	SF	HB	TBB	IBB	SO	WP	Bk	W	L	Pct	ShO	Sv-Op	Hld	OAvg	OOBP	ERA
1995	Atl	24	1	0	0	0	0.1	2	1	0	0	0	0	0	0	0	0	0	0	0	0	0	—	0	0-0	1	.500	.500	0.00
1996	Atl	25	1	0	0	1	0.2	2	0	0	0	0	0	0	0	0	0	0	0	0	0	0	—	0	0-0	0	.000	.000	0.00
LCS Totals			2	0	0	1	1.0	8	1	0	0	0	0	0	0	0	0	0	0	0	0	0	—	0	0-0	1	.250	.250	0.00

World Series

Year	Tm	Age	G	GS	CG	GF	IP	BFP	H	R	ER	HR	SH	SF	HB	TBB	IBB	SO	WP	Bk	W	L	Pct	ShO	Sv-Op	Hld	OAvg	OOBP	ERA
1995	Atl	24	2	0	0	1	3.1	11	2	1	1	1	0	0	0	0	0	2	0	0	0	0	—	0	0-0	0	.182	.182	2.70
1996	Atl	25	3	0	0	2	1.2	8	1	0	0	0	0	0	0	1	1	2	0	0	0	0	—	0	0-0	0	.143	.250	0.00
WS Totals			5	0	0	3	5.0	38	3	1	1	1	0	0	0	1	1	4	0	0	0	0	—	0	0-0	0	.167	.211	1.80
Postseason Totals			8	0	0	4	7.1	54	4	1	1	1	0	0	0	1	1	4	0	0	0	0	—	0	0-0	1	.154	.185	1.23

Division Series

Year	Tm	Age	G	AB	H	2B	3B	HR	TB	R	RBI	GW	TBB	IBB	SO	HBP	SH	SF	SB	CS	SB%	GDP	Avg	OBP	SLG	Pos	G	PO	A	E	DP	FPct
1995	Atl	24	1	0	0	0	0	0	0	0	0	0	0	0	0	0	0	0	0	0	—	0	—	—	—	P	1	0	1	0	0	1.000

LCS

Year	Tm	Age	G	AB	H	2B	3B	HR	TB	R	RBI	GW	TBB	IBB	SO	HBP	SH	SF	SB	CS	SB%	GDP	Avg	OBP	SLG	Pos	G	PO	A	E	DP	FPct
1995	Atl	24	1	0	0	0	0	0	0	0	0	0	0	0	0	0	0	0	0	0	—	0	—	—	—	P	1	0	0	0	0	—
1996	Atl	25	1	0	0	0	0	0	0	0	0	0	0	0	0	0	0	0	0	0	—	0	—	—	—	P	1	0	0	0	0	—
LCS Totals			2	0	0	0	0	0	0	0	0	0	0	0	0	0	0	0	0	0	—	0	—	—	—	P	2	0	0	0	0	—

World Series

Year	Tm	Age	G	AB	H	2B	3B	HR	TB	R	RBI	GW	TBB	IBB	SO	HBP	SH	SF	SB	CS	SB%	GDP	Avg	OBP	SLG	Pos	G	PO	A	E	DP	FPct
1995	Atl	24	2	0	0	0	0	0	0	0	0	0	0	0	0	0	0	0	0	0	—	0	—	—	—	P	2	0	0	0	0	—
1996	Atl	25	3	0	0	0	0	0	0	0	0	0	0	0	0	0	0	0	0	0	—	0	—	—	—	P	3	0	0	0	0	—
WS Totals			5	0	0	0	0	0	0	0	0	0	0	0	0	0	0	0	0	0	—	0	—	—	—	P	5	0	0	0	0	—
Postseason Totals			8	0	0	0	0	0	0	0	0	0	0	0	0	0	0	0	0	0	—	0	—	—	—	P	8	0	1	0	0	1.000

ANDY COAKLEY
—Andrew James Coakley—Throws: Right; Bats: Left — Ht: 6'0"; Wt: 165 lbs; Born: 11/20/1882 in Providence, Rhode Island; Debut: 9/17/1902; Died: 9/27/1963

World Series

Year	Tm	Age	G	GS	CG	GF	IP	BFP	H	R	ER	HR	SH	SF	HB	TBB	IBB	SO	WP	Bk	W	L	Pct	ShO	Sv-Op	Hld	OAvg	OOBP	ERA
1905	Phi	22	1	1	1	0	9.0	40	8	9	2	0	0	0	1	5	1	2	0	0	0	1	.000	0	0-0	0	.235	.350	2.00

World Series

Year	Tm	Age	G	AB	H	2B	3B	HR	TB	R	RBI	GW	TBB	IBB	SO	HBP	SH	SF	SB	CS	SB%	GDP	Avg	OBP	SLG	Pos	G	PO	A	E	DP	FPct
1905	Phi	22	1	2	0	0	0	0	0	0	0	0	0	1	1	0	0	0	0	—	0	.000	.333	.000	P	1	0	2	0	1	1.000

JIM COATES
—James Alton Coates—Throws: Right; Bats: Right — Ht: 6'4"; Wt: 192 lbs; Born: 8/4/1932 in Farnham, Virginia; Debut: 9/21/1956

World Series

Year	Tm	Age	G	GS	CG	GF	IP	BFP	H	R	ER	HR	SH	SF	HB	TBB	IBB	SO	WP	Bk	W	L	Pct	ShO	Sv-Op	Hld	OAvg	OOBP	ERA
1960	NYA	28	3	0	0	1	6.1	26	6	4	4	2	1	0	1	1	0	3	0	0	0	0	—	0	0-1	0	.261	.320	5.68
1961	NYA	29	1	0	0	1	4.0	15	1	0	0	0	0	0	0	1	0	2	0	0	0	0	—	0	1-1	0	.077	.200	0.00
1962	NYA	30	2	0	0	0	2.2	10	1	2	2	0	0	0	0	1	0	3	0	0	1	0	1.000	0	0-0	0	.111	.200	6.75
WS Totals			6	0	0	2	13.0	102	8	6	6	2	1	0	2	3	0	8	0	0	1	0	1.000	0	1-2	0	.178	.260	4.15

World Series

Year	Tm	Age	G	AB	H	2B	3B	HR	TB	R	RBI	GW	TBB	IBB	SO	HBP	SH	SF	SB	CS	SB%	GDP	Avg	OBP	SLG	Pos	G	PO	A	E	DP	FPct
1960	NYA	28	3	1	0	0	0	0	0	0	0	0	0	0	0	0	0	0	0	0	—	0	.000	.000	.000	P	3	1	1	0	0	1.000
1961	NYA	29	1	1	0	0	0	0	0	0	0	1	0	0	0	0	0	0	0	0	—	0	.000	.000	.000	P	1	0	0	0	0	—
1962	NYA	30	2	0	0	0	0	0	0	0	0	0	0	0	2	0	0	0	0	0	—	0	—	—	—	P	2	0	0	0	0	—
WS Totals			6	2	0	0	0	0	0	0	0	0	0	0	2	0	0	0	0	0	—	0	.000	.000	.000	P	6	1	1	0	0	1.000

TY COBB
(HOF 1936-W)—Tyrus Raymond Cobb—Nickname: The Georgia Peach—Bats: Left; Throws: Right — Ht: 6'1"; Wt: 175 lbs; Born: 12/18/1886 in Narrows, Georgia; Debut: 8/30/1905; Died: 7/17/1961

World Series

Year	Tm	Age	G	AB	H	2B	3B	HR	TB	R	RBI	GW	TBB	IBB	SO	HBP	SH	SF	SB	CS	SB%	GDP	Avg	OBP	SLG	Pos	G	PO	A	E	DP	FPct
1907	Det	20	5	20	4	0	1	0	6	1	0	0	0	0	3	1	0	0	0	1	1.00	1	.200	.238	.300	OF	5	10	0	0	0	1.000
1908	Det	21	5	19	7	1	0	0	8	3	4	1	0	0	1	0	1	0	2	1	.67	0	.368	.400	.421	OF	5	3	0	1	0	.750
1909	Det	22	7	26	6	3	0	0	9	3	5	0	2	0	2	1	0	0	2	1	.67	0	.231	.310	.346	OF	7	8	0	1	0	.889
WS Totals			17	65	17	4	1	0	23	7	9	0	3	0	7	2	1	0	4	3	.57	1	.262	.314	.354	OF	17	21	0	2	0	.913

MICKEY COCHRANE
(HOF 1947-W)—Gordon Stanley Cochrane—Nickname: Black Mike—B: L; T: R — Ht: 5'10"; Wt: 180 lbs; Born: 4/6/1903 in Bridgewater, Mass.; Deb.: 4/14/1925; Died: 6/28/1962

World Series

Year	Tm	Age	G	AB	H	2B	3B	HR	TB	R	RBI	GW	TBB	IBB	SO	HBP	SH	SF	SB	CS	SB%	GDP	Avg	OBP	SLG	Pos	G	PO	A	E	DP	FPct
1929	Phi	26	5	15	6	1	0	0	7	5	0	0	7	0	0	0	0	0	0	0	—	1	.400	.591	.467	C	5	59	2	0	0	1.000
1930	Phi	27	6	18	4	1	0	2	11	5	4	2	5	0	2	0	0	1	0	1	.00	0	.222	.375	.611	C	6	40	1	1	0	.976
1931	Phi	28	7	25	4	0	0	0	4	2	1	0	5	0	2	0	0	0	0	0	—	1	.160	.300	.160	C	7	44	1	1	0	.978
1934	Det-M	31	7	28	6	1	0	0	7	2	1	0	4	0	1	0	0	0	0	0	—	1	.214	.313	.250	C	7	40	4	1	0	1.000
1935	Det	32	6	24	7	1	0	0	8	3	1	1	4	0	3	0	1	0	0	0	—	0	.292	.393	.333	C	6	32	4	1	1	.973
WS Totals			31	110	27	4	0	2	37	17	7	3	25	0	8	0	1	1	0	1	.00	3	.245	.382	.336	C	31	207	16	3	2	.987

DICK COFFMAN
—Samuel Richard Coffman—Throws: Right; Bats: Right — Ht: 6'2"; Wt: 195 lbs; Born: 12/18/1906 in Veto, Alabama; Debut: 4/28/1927; Died: 3/24/1972

World Series

Year	Tm	Age	G	GS	CG	GF	IP	BFP	H	R	ER	HR	SH	SF	HB	TBB	IBB	SO	WP	Bk	W	L	Pct	ShO	Sv-Op	Hld	OAvg	OOBP	ERA
1936	NYG	29	2	0	0	0	1.2	11	5	6	6	1	0	0	0	1	1	1	0	0	0	0	—	0	0-0	0	.500	.545	32.40
1937	NYG	30	2	0	0	1	4.1	19	2	2	2	0	0	0	0	5	0	1	0	0	0	0	—	0	0-0	0	.143	.368	4.15
WS Totals			4	0	0	1	6.0	60	7	8	8	1	0	0	0	6	1	2	0	0	0	0	—	0	0-0	0	.292	.433	12.00

World Series

Year	Tm	Age	G	AB	H	2B	3B	HR	TB	R	RBI	GW	TBB	IBB	SO	HBP	SH	SF	SB	CS	SB%	GDP	Avg	OBP	SLG	Pos	G	PO	A	E	DP	FPct
1936	NYG	29	2	0	0	0	0	0	0	0	0	0	0	0	0	0	0	0	0	0	—	0	—	—	—	P	2	0	1	0	0	1.000
1937	NYG	30	2	1	0	0	0	0	0	0	0	0	0	0	1	0	0	0	0	0	—	0	.000	.000	.000	P	2	0	1	0	0	1.000
WS Totals			4	1	0	0	0	0	0	0	0	0	0	0	1	0	0	0	0	0	—	0	.000	.000	.000	P	4	0	2	0	0	1.000

RICH COGGINS—Richard Allen Coggins—Bats: Left; Throws: Left

Ht: 5'8"; Wt: 170 lbs; Born: 12/7/1950 in Indianapolis, Indiana; Debut: 8/29/1972

LCS

Year Tm	Age	G	AB	H	2B	3B	HR	TB	R	RBI	GW	TBB	IBB	SO	HBP	SH	SF	SB	CS	SB%	GDP	Avg	OBP	SLG	Pos	G	PO	A	E	DP	FPct
1973 Bal	22	2	9	4	1	0	0	5	1	0	0	0	0	0	0	0	0	0	0	—	0	.444	.444	.556	OF	2	4	0	0	0	1.000
1974 Bal	23	3	11	0	0	0	0	0	0	0	0	0	0	3	0	0	0	0	0	—	0	.000	.000	.000	OF	3	6	0	0	0	1.000
LCS Totals		5	20	4	1	0	0	5	1	0	0	0	0	3	0	0	0	0	0	—	0	.200	.200	.250	OF	5	10	0	0	0	1.000

GREG COLBRUNN—Gregory Joseph Colbrunn—Bats: Right; Throws: Right

Ht: 6'0"; Wt: 190 lbs; Born: 7/26/1969 in Fontana, California; Debut: 7/9/1992

Division Series

Year Tm	Age	G	AB	H	2B	3B	HR	TB	R	RBI	GW	TBB	IBB	SO	HBP	SH	SF	SB	CS	SB%	GDP	Avg	OBP	SLG	Pos	G	PO	A	E	DP	FPct
1997 Atl	28	1	1	1	0	0	0	1	0	2	0	0	0	0	0	0	0	0	0	—	0	1.000	1.000	1.000	—						

LCS

Year Tm	Age	G	AB	H	2B	3B	HR	TB	R	RBI	GW	TBB	IBB	SO	HBP	SH	SF	SB	CS	SB%	GDP	Avg	OBP	SLG	Pos	G	PO	A	E	DP	FPct
1997 Atl	28	3	3	2	0	0	0	2	0	0	0	0	0	0	0	0	0	0	0	—	0	.667	.667	.667	—						
Postseason Totals		4	4	3	0	0	0	3	0	2	0	0	0	0	0	0	0	0	0	—	0	.750	.750	.750	—	0	0	0	0	0	—

ALEX COLE—Alexander Cole—Bats: Left; Throws: Left

Ht: 6'2"; Wt: 170 lbs; Born: 8/17/1965 in Fayetteville, North Carolina; Debut: 7/27/1990

LCS

Year Tm	Age	G	AB	H	2B	3B	HR	TB	R	RBI	GW	TBB	IBB	SO	HBP	SH	SF	SB	CS	SB%	GDP	Avg	OBP	SLG	Pos	G	PO	A	E	DP	FPct
1992 Pit	27	4	10	2	0	0	0	2	2	1	0	3	0	2	0	0	0	0	0	—	0	.200	.385	.200	OF	4	7	1	0	1	1.000

KING COLE—Leonard Leslie Cole—Throws: Right; Bats: Right

Ht: 6'1"; Wt: 170 lbs; Born: 4/15/1886 in Toledo, Iowa; Debut: 10/6/1909; Died: 1/6/1916

World Series — Pitching

Year Tm	Age	G	GS	CG	GF	IP	BFP	H	R	ER	HR	SH	SF	HB	TBB	IBB	SO	WP	Bk	W	L	Pct	ShO	Sv-Op	Hld	OAvg	OOBP	ERA
1910 ChN	24	1	1	0	0	8.0	35	10	3	3	0	2	0	1	3	0	5	0	0	0	0	—	0	0-0	0	.345	.424	3.38

World Series — Batting

Year Tm	Age	G	AB	H	2B	3B	HR	TB	R	RBI	GW	TBB	IBB	SO	HBP	SH	SF	SB	CS	SB%	GDP	Avg	OBP	SLG	Pos	G	PO	A	E	DP	FPct
1910 ChN	24	1	2	0	0	0	0	0	0	0	0	0	0	2	0	0	0	0	0	—	0	.000	.000	.000	P	1	1	3	0	1	1.000

GORDY COLEMAN—Gordon Calvin Coleman—Bats: Left; Throws: Right

Ht: 6'3"; Wt: 208 lbs; Born: 7/5/1934 in Rockville, Maryland; Debut: 9/19/1959; Died: 3/12/1994

World Series

Year Tm	Age	G	AB	H	2B	3B	HR	TB	R	RBI	GW	TBB	IBB	SO	HBP	SH	SF	SB	CS	SB%	GDP	Avg	OBP	SLG	Pos	G	PO	A	E	DP	FPct
1961 Cin	27	5	20	5	0	0	1	8	2	2	0	0	0	1	0	0	0	0	0	—	0	.250	.250	.400	1B	5	30	4	1	6	.971

JERRY COLEMAN—Gerald Francis Coleman—Bats: Right; Throws: Right

Ht: 6'0"; Wt: 165 lbs; Born: 9/14/1924 in San Jose, California; Debut: 4/20/1949

World Series

Year Tm	Age	G	AB	H	2B	3B	HR	TB	R	RBI	GW	TBB	IBB	SO	HBP	SH	SF	SB	CS	SB%	GDP	Avg	OBP	SLG	Pos	G	PO	A	E	DP	FPct
1949 NYA	25	5	20	5	3	0	0	8	0	4	0	0	0	4	0	0	0	0	0	—	0	.250	.250	.400	2B	5	10	9	1	3	.950
1950 NYA	26	4	14	4	1	0	0	5	2	3	2	2	0	0	0	0	0	0	0	—	0	.286	.375	.357	2B	4	11	12	0	3	1.000
1951 NYA	27	5	8	2	0	0	0	2	2	0	0	1	0	2	0	0	0	0	0	—	0	.250	.333	.250	2B	5	7	6	0	3	1.000
1955 NYA	31	3	3	0	0	0	0	0	0	0	0	0	0	1	0	0	0	0	0	—	0	.000	.000	.000	SS	3	2	3	0	3	1.000
1956 NYA	32	2	2	0	0	0	0	0	0	0	0	0	0	0	0	1	0	0	0	—	0	.000	.000	.000	2B	2	2	2	0	0	1.000
1957 NYA	33	7	22	8	2	0	0	10	2	2	0	3	0	1	0	1	0	0	0	—	0	.364	.440	.455	2B	7	16	17	0	3	1.000
WS Totals		26	69	19	6	0	0	25	6	9	2	6	0	8	0	2	0	0	0	—	0	.275	.333	.362	2B	23	46	46	1	12	.989

JOE COLEMAN—Joseph Howard Coleman—Throws: Right; Bats: Right

Ht: 6'3"; Wt: 175 lbs; Born: 2/3/1947 in Boston, Massachusetts; Debut: 9/28/1965

LCS — Pitching

Year Tm	Age	G	GS	CG	GF	IP	BFP	H	R	ER	HR	SH	SF	HB	TBB	IBB	SO	WP	Bk	W	L	Pct	ShO	Sv-Op	Hld	OAvg	OOBP	ERA
1972 Det	25	1	1	1	0	9.0	37	7	0	0	0	0	0	0	3	0	14	0	0	1	0	1.000	1	0-0	0	.206	.270	0.00

LCS — Batting

Year Tm	Age	G	AB	H	2B	3B	HR	TB	R	RBI	GW	TBB	IBB	SO	HBP	SH	SF	SB	CS	SB%	GDP	Avg	OBP	SLG	Pos	G	PO	A	E	DP	FPct
1972 Det	25	1	2	1	0	0	0	1	0	0	0	1	0	0	0	0	0	0	0	—	0	.500	.667	.500	P	1	0	1	0	0	1.000

RIP COLEMAN—Walter Gary Coleman—Throws: Left; Bats: Left

Ht: 6'2"; Wt: 185 lbs; Born: 7/31/1931 in Troy, New York; Debut: 8/15/1955

World Series — Pitching

Year Tm	Age	G	GS	CG	GF	IP	BFP	H	R	ER	HR	SH	SF	HB	TBB	IBB	SO	WP	Bk	W	L	Pct	ShO	Sv-Op	Hld	OAvg	OOBP	ERA
1955 NYA	24	1	0	0	0	1.0	8	5	1	1	0	0	0	0	0	0	1	0	0	0	0	—	0	0-0	0	.625	.625	9.00

World Series — Batting

Year Tm	Age	G	AB	H	2B	3B	HR	TB	R	RBI	GW	TBB	IBB	SO	HBP	SH	SF	SB	CS	SB%	GDP	Avg	OBP	SLG	Pos	G	PO	A	E	DP	FPct
1955 NYA	24	1	0	0	0	0	0	0	0	0	0	0	0	0	0	0	0	0	0	—	0	—	—	—	P	1	0	0	0	0	—

VINCE COLEMAN—Vincent Maurice Coleman—Bats: Both; Throws: Right

Ht: 6'0"; Wt: 170 lbs; Born: 9/22/1961 in Jacksonville, Florida; Debut: 4/18/1985

Division Series

Year Tm	Age	G	AB	H	2B	3B	HR	TB	R	RBI	GW	TBB	IBB	SO	HBP	SH	SF	SB	CS	SB%	GDP	Avg	OBP	SLG	Pos	G	PO	A	E	DP	FPct
1995 Sea	34	5	23	5	0	1	1	10	6	1	0	2	0	4	0	0	0	1	0	1.00	0	.217	.280	.435	OF	5	14	0	0	0	1.000

LCS

Year Tm	Age	G	AB	H	2B	3B	HR	TB	R	RBI	GW	TBB	IBB	SO	HBP	SH	SF	SB	CS	SB%	GDP	Avg	OBP	SLG	Pos	G	PO	A	E	DP	FPct
1985 StL-*RY*	24	3	14	4	0	0	0	4	2	1	0	0	0	2	0	0	0	1	2	.33	1	.286	.286	.286	OF	3	8	0	0	0	1.000
1987 StL	26	7	26	7	1	0	0	8	3	4	1	4	0	6	0	0	0	1	2	.33	1	.269	.367	.308	OF	7	8	1	0	0	1.000
1995 Sea	34	6	20	2	0	0	0	2	0	0	0	2	0	6	0	0	0	4	0	1.00	0	.100	.182	.100	OF	5	12	0	0	0	1.000
LCS Totals		16	60	13	1	0	0	14	5	5	1	6	0	14	0	0	0	6	4	.60	2	.217	.288	.233	OF	15	28	1	0	0	1.000

World Series

Year Tm	Age	G	AB	H	2B	3B	HR	TB	R	RBI	GW	TBB	IBB	SO	HBP	SH	SF	SB	CS	SB%	GDP	Avg	OBP	SLG	Pos	G	PO	A	E	DP	FPct
1987 StL	26	7	28	4	2	0	0	6	5	2	1	2	0	10	0	0	0	6	0	1.00	0	.143	.200	.214	OF	7	10	2	0	0	1.000
Postseason Totals		28	111	22	3	1	1	30	16	8	2	10	0	28	0	0	0	13	4	.76	2	.198	.264	.270	OF	27	52	3	0	0	1.000

DAVE COLLINS—David S. Collins—Bats: Both; Throws: Left

Ht: 5'11"; Wt: 175 lbs; Born: 10/20/1952 in Rapid City, South Dakota; Debut: 6/7/1975

LCS

Year Tm	Age	G	AB	H	2B	3B	HR	TB	R	RBI	GW	TBB	IBB	SO	HBP	SH	SF	SB	CS	SB%	GDP	Avg	OBP	SLG	Pos	G	PO	A	E	DP	FPct
1979 Cin	26	3	14	5	1	0	0	6	0	1	0	0	0	2	0	0	0	2	0	1.00	0	.357	.357	.429	OF	3	5	0	0	0	1.000

EDDIE COLLINS (HOF 1939-W)—Edward Trowbridge Collins—Nickname: Cocky—Bats: Left; Throws: Right

Ht: 5'9"; Wt: 175 lbs; Born: 5/2/1887 in Millerton, N.Y; Debut: 9/17/1906; Died: 3/25/1951

World Series

Year Tm	Age	G	AB	H	2B	3B	HR	TB	R	RBI	GW	TBB	IBB	SO	HBP	SH	SF	SB	CS	SB%	GDP	Avg	OBP	SLG	Pos	G	PO	A	E	DP	FPct
1910 Phi	23	5	21	9	4	0	0	13	5	3	0	2	0	0	0	1	0	4	2	.67	0	.429	.478	.619	2B	5	17	18	1	4	.972
1911 Phi	24	6	21	6	1	0	0	7	4	1	0	2	0	3	0	2	0	2	0	1.00	0	.286	.348	.333	2B	6	13	22	4	1	.897
1913 Phi	26	5	19	8	0	2	0	12	5	3	0	1	0	2	0	2	0	3	0	1.00	0	.421	.450	.632	2B	5	17	18	1	5	.972
1914 Phi-*M*	27	4	14	3	0	0	0	3	0	1	0	2	0	1	0	0	1	1	0	1.00	0	.214	.294	.214	2B	4	9	12	0	1	1.000
1917 ChA	30	6	22	9	1	0	0	10	4	2	1	2	0	3	0	0	0	3	1	.75	0	.409	.458	.455	2B	6	11	23	0	3	1.000
1919 ChA	32	8	31	7	1	0	0	8	2	1	0	1	0	2	1	1	1	1	1	.50	0	.226	.265	.258	2B	8	21	30	2	6	.962
WS Totals		34	128	42	7	2	0	53	20	11	1	10	0	11	1	6	2	14	4	.78	0	.328	.376	.414	2B	34	88	123	8	20	.963

JIMMY COLLINS (HOF 1945-V)—James Joseph Collins—Bats: Right; Throws: Right

Ht: 5'9"; Wt: 178 lbs; Born: 1/16/1870 in Buffalo, New York; Debut: 4/19/1895; Died: 3/6/1943

World Series		Batting																							Fielding						
Year Tm	Age	G	AB	H	2B	3B	HR	TB	R	RBI	GW	TBB	IBB	SO	HBP	SH	SF	SB	CS	SB%	GDP	Avg	OBP	SLG	Pos	G	PO	A	E	DP	FPct
1903 Bos	33	8	36	9	1	2	0	14	5	1	1	1	0	1	0	0	0	3	0	1.00	1	.250	.270	.389	3B	8	9	18	1	1	.964

JOE COLLINS—Joseph Edward Collins—Bats: Left; Throws: Left

Ht: 6'0"; Wt: 185 lbs; Born: 12/3/1922 in Scranton, Pennsylvania; Debut: 9/25/1948; Died: 8/30/1989

World Series		Batting																							Fielding						
Year Tm	Age	G	AB	H	2B	3B	HR	TB	R	RBI	GW	TBB	IBB	SO	HBP	SH	SF	SB	CS	SB%	GDP	Avg	OBP	SLG	Pos	G	PO	A	E	DP	FPct
1950 NYA	27	1	0	0	0	0	0	0	0	0	0	0	0	0	0	0	0	0	0	—	0	—	—	—	1B	1	1	1	0	0	1.000
1951 NYA	28	6	18	4	0	0	1	7	2	3	0	2	0	1	0	0	0	0	0	—	1	.222	.300	.389	1B	6	40	2	0	6	1.000
																									OF	1	0	0	0	0	—
1952 NYA	29	6	12	0	0	0	0	0	1	0	0	1	0	3	0	0	0	0	0	—	0	.000	.077	.000	1B	6	27	1	0	2	1.000
1953 NYA	30	6	24	4	1	0	1	8	4	2	1	3	0	8	0	0	0	0	0	—	0	.167	.259	.333	1B	6	50	4	0	3	1.000
1955 NYA	32	5	12	2	0	0	2	8	6	3	1	6	0	4	0	0	0	1	0	1.00	0	.167	.444	.667	1B	5	27	3	0	3	1.000
																									OF	1	0	0	0	0	—
1956 NYA	33	6	21	5	2	0	0	7	2	2	0	2	0	3	0	0	0	0	0	—	2	.238	.304	.333	1B	5	30	3	2	4	.943
1957 NYA	34	6	5	0	0	0	0	0	0	0	0	0	0	3	0	0	0	0	0	—	0	.000	.000	.000	1B	5	12	2	0	1	1.000
WS Totals		36	92	15	3	0	4	30	15	10	2	14	0	22	0	0	0	1	0	1.00	3	.163	.274	.326	1B	34	187	16	2	19	.990

PAT COLLINS—Tharon Patrick Collins—Bats: Right; Throws: Right

Ht: 5'11"; Wt: 178 lbs; Born: 9/13/1896 in Sweet Springs, Missouri; Debut: 9/5/1919; Died: 5/20/1960

World Series		Batting																							Fielding						
Year Tm	Age	G	AB	H	2B	3B	HR	TB	R	RBI	GW	TBB	IBB	SO	HBP	SH	SF	SB	CS	SB%	GDP	Avg	OBP	SLG	Pos	G	PO	A	E	DP	FPct
1926 NYA	30	3	2	0	0	0	0	0	0	0	0	0	0	1	0	0	0	0	0	—	0	.000	.000	.000	C	3	1	0	0	0	1.000
1927 NYA	31	2	5	3	1	0	0	4	0	0	0	3	0	0	0	0	0	0	0	—	0	.600	.750	.800	C	2	5	1	0	0	1.000
1928 NYA	32	1	1	1	1	0	0	2	0	0	0	0	0	0	0	0	0	0	0	—	0	1.000	1.000	2.000	C	1	2	0	0	0	1.000
WS Totals		6	8	4	2	0	0	6	0	0	0	3	0	1	0	0	0	0	0	—	0	.500	.636	.750	C	6	8	1	0	0	1.000

RAY COLLINS—Raymond Williston Collins—Throws: Left; Bats: Left

Ht: 6'1"; Wt: 185 lbs; Born: 2/11/1887 in Colchester, Vermont; Debut: 7/19/1909; Died: 1/9/1970

World Series		Pitching																										
Year Tm	Age	G	GS	CG	GF	IP	BFP	H	R	ER	HR	SH	SF	HB	TBB	IBB	SO	WP	Bk	W	L	Pct	ShO	Sv-Op	Hld	OAvg	OOBP	ERA
1912 Bos	25	2	1	0	1	14.1	53	14	5	3	0	0	1	0	0	0	6	0	0	0	0	—	0	0-0	0	.269	.264	1.88

World Series		Batting																							Fielding						
Year Tm	Age	G	AB	H	2B	3B	HR	TB	R	RBI	GW	TBB	IBB	SO	HBP	SH	SF	SB	CS	SB%	GDP	Avg	OBP	SLG	Pos	G	PO	A	E	DP	FPct
1912 Bos	25	2	5	0	0	0	0	0	0	0	0	0	0	2	0	0	0	0	0	—	1	.000	.000	.000	P	2	0	3	0	0	1.000

RIP COLLINS—Harry Warren Collins—Throws: Right; Bats: Both

Ht: 6'1"; Wt: 205 lbs; Born: 2/26/1896 in Weatherford, Texas; Debut: 4/19/1920; Died: 5/27/1968

World Series		Pitching																										
Year Tm	Age	G	GS	CG	GF	IP	BFP	H	R	ER	HR	SH	SF	HB	TBB	IBB	SO	WP	Bk	W	L	Pct	ShO	Sv-Op	Hld	OAvg	OOBP	ERA
1921 NYA	25	1	0	0	0	0.2	7	5	4	4	0	0	1	0	1	0	0	0	0	0	0	—	0	0-0	0	1.000	.857	54.00

World Series		Batting																							Fielding						
Year Tm	Age	G	AB	H	2B	3B	HR	TB	R	RBI	GW	TBB	IBB	SO	HBP	SH	SF	SB	CS	SB%	GDP	Avg	OBP	SLG	Pos	G	PO	A	E	DP	FPct
1921 NYA	25	1	0	0	0	0	0	0	0	0	0	0	0	0	0	0	0	0	0	—	0	—	—	—	P	1	0	0	0	0	—

RIPPER COLLINS—James Anthony Collins—Bats: Both; Throws: Left

Ht: 5'9"; Wt: 165 lbs; Born: 3/30/1904 in Altoona, Pennsylvania; Debut: 4/18/1931; Died: 4/15/1970

World Series		Batting																							Fielding						
Year Tm	Age	G	AB	H	2B	3B	HR	TB	R	RBI	GW	TBB	IBB	SO	HBP	SH	SF	SB	CS	SB%	GDP	Avg	OBP	SLG	Pos	G	PO	A	E	DP	FPct
1931 StL	27	2	2	0	0	0	0	0	0	0	0	0	0	1	0	0	0	0	0	—	0	.000	.000	.000	—						
1934 StL	30	7	30	11	1	0	0	12	4	3	0	1	0	2	0	0	0	0	1	.00	0	.367	.387	.400	1B	7	56	7	1	1	.984
1938 ChN	34	4	15	2	0	0	0	2	1	0	0	0	0	3	0	0	0	0	0	—	0	.133	.133	.133	1B	4	38	1	0	3	1.000
WS Totals		13	47	13	1	0	0	14	5	3	0	1	0	6	0	0	0	0	1	.00	0	.277	.292	.298	1B	11	94	8	1	4	.990

SHANO COLLINS—John Francis Collins—Bats: Right; Throws: Right

Ht: 6'0"; Wt: 185 lbs; Born: 12/4/1885 in Charlestown, Massachusetts; Debut: 4/21/1910; Died: 9/10/1955

World Series		Batting																							Fielding						
Year Tm	Age	G	AB	H	2B	3B	HR	TB	R	RBI	GW	TBB	IBB	SO	HBP	SH	SF	SB	CS	SB%	GDP	Avg	OBP	SLG	Pos	G	PO	A	E	DP	FPct
1917 ChA	31	6	21	6	1	0	0	7	2	0	0	0	0	2	0	0	0	0	1	.00	0	.286	.286	.333	OF	6	4	1	3	0	.625
1919 ChA	33	4	16	4	1	0	0	5	2	0	0	0	0	0	0	0	0	0	0	—	0	.250	.250	.313	OF	4	5	0	0	0	1.000
WS Totals		10	37	10	2	0	0	12	4	0	0	0	0	2	0	0	0	0	1	.00	0	.270	.270	.324	OF	10	9	1	3	0	.769

EARLE COMBS (HOF 1970-V)—Earle Bryan Combs—Nickname: The Kentucky Colonel—Bats: L; Throws: R

Ht: 6'0"; Wt: 185 lbs; Born: 5/14/1899 in Pebworth, Ky.; Deb.: 4/16/1924; Died: 7/21/1976

World Series		Batting																							Fielding						
Year Tm	Age	G	AB	H	2B	3B	HR	TB	R	RBI	GW	TBB	IBB	SO	HBP	SH	SF	SB	CS	SB%	GDP	Avg	OBP	SLG	Pos	G	PO	A	E	DP	FPct
1926 NYA	27	7	28	10	2	0	0	12	3	2	0	5	0	2	0	0	0	0	0	—	0	.357	.455	.429	OF	7	17	0	0	0	1.000
1927 NYA	28	4	16	5	0	0	0	5	6	2	0	1	0	2	1	0	0	0	0	—	0	.313	.389	.313	OF	4	16	0	0	0	1.000
1928 NYA	29	1	0	0	0	0	0	0	0	1	0	0	0	0	0	0	1	0	0	—	0	—	.000	—	—						
1932 NYA	33	4	16	6	1	0	1	10	8	4	1	4	0	3	0	0	0	0	0	—	1	.375	.500	.625	OF	4	10	0	0	0	1.000
WS Totals		16	60	21	3	0	1	27	17	9	1	10	0	7	1	0	1	0	0	—	1	.350	.444	.450	OF	15	43	0	0	0	1.000

WAYNE COMER—Harry Wayne Comer—Bats: Right; Throws: Right

Ht: 5'10"; Wt: 175 lbs; Born: 2/3/1944 in Shenandoah, Virginia; Debut: 9/17/1967

World Series		Batting																							Fielding						
Year Tm	Age	G	AB	H	2B	3B	HR	TB	R	RBI	GW	TBB	IBB	SO	HBP	SH	SF	SB	CS	SB%	GDP	Avg	OBP	SLG	Pos	G	PO	A	E	DP	FPct
1968 Det	24	1	1	1	0	0	0	1	0	0	0	0	0	0	0	0	0	0	0	—	0	1.000	1.000	1.000	—						

CLINT CONATSER—Clinton Astor Conatser—Nickname: Connie—Bats: Right; Throws: Right

Ht: 5'11"; Wt: 182 lbs; Born: 7/24/1921 in Los Angeles, California; Debut: 4/21/1948

World Series		Batting																							Fielding						
Year Tm	Age	G	AB	H	2B	3B	HR	TB	R	RBI	GW	TBB	IBB	SO	HBP	SH	SF	SB	CS	SB%	GDP	Avg	OBP	SLG	Pos	G	PO	A	E	DP	FPct
1948 Bos	27	2	4	0	0	0	0	0	0	1	0	0	0	0	0	0	0	0	0	—	1	.000	.000	.000	OF	2	1	0	0	0	1.000

DAVE CONCEPCION—David Ismael Concepcion—Nickname: Elmer—Bats: Right; Throws: Right

Ht: 6'2"; Wt: 155 lbs; Born: 6/17/1948 in Aragua, Venezuela; Debut: 4/6/1970

LCS		Batting																							Fielding						
Year Tm	Age	G	AB	H	2B	3B	HR	TB	R	RBI	GW	TBB	IBB	SO	HBP	SH	SF	SB	CS	SB%	GDP	Avg	OBP	SLG	Pos	G	PO	A	E	DP	FPct
1970 Cin	22	3	0	0	0	0	0	0	0	0	0	0	0	0	0	0	0	0	0	—	0	—	—	—	SS	3	1	1	0	0	1.000
1972 Cin	24	3	2	0	0	0	0	0	0	0	0	0	0	0	0	0	0	0	0	—	0	.000	.000	.000	SS	1	0	0	0	0	—
1975 Cin	27	3	11	5	0	0	1	8	2	1	0	1	0	2	0	0	0	2	0	1.00	0	.455	.500	.727	SS	3	6	8	1	2	.933
1976 Cin	28	3	10	2	1	0	0	3	4	0	0	2	0	1	0	0	0	0	0	—	0	.200	.333	.300	SS	3	2	12	0	1	1.000
1979 Cin	31	3	14	6	1	0	0	7	1	0	0	0	0	3	0	0	0	0	1	.00	1	.429	.429	.500	SS	3	4	14	0	2	1.000
LCS Totals		15	37	13	2	0	1	18	7	1	0	3	0	6	0	0	0	2	1	.67	1	.351	.400	.486	SS	13	13	35	1	5	.980
World Series		**Batting**																							**Fielding**						
Year Tm	Age	G	AB	H	2B	3B	HR	TB	R	RBI	GW	TBB	IBB	SO	HBP	SH	SF	SB	CS	SB%	GDP	Avg	OBP	SLG	Pos	G	PO	A	E	DP	FPct
1970 Cin	22	3	9	3	0	1	0	5	0	3	0	0	0	0	0	0	1	0	0	—	0	.333	.300	.556	SS	3	2	2	0	0	1.000
1972 Cin	24	6	13	4	0	1	0	6	2	2	1	2	1	2	0	1	1	1	1	.50	0	.308	.375	.462	SS	5	4	11	1	1	.938
1975 Cin	27	7	28	5	1	0	1	9	3	4	0	0	0	1	1	0	1	3	0	1.00	0	.179	.200	.321	SS	7	12	23	1	4	.972
1976 Cin	28	4	14	5	1	1	0	8	1	3	0	1	0	3	0	0	0	1	1	.50	1	.357	.400	.571	SS	4	6	11	1	3	.944
WS Totals		20	64	17	2	3	1	28	6	12	1	3	1	6	1	1	3	5	2	.71	1	.266	.296	.438	SS	19	24	47	3	8	.959
Postseason Totals		35	101	30	4	3	2	46	13	13	1	6	1	12	1	1	3	7	3	.70	2	.297	.333	.455	SS	32	37	82	4	13	.967

ONIX CONCEPCION—Onix Cardona Concepcion—Bats: Right; Throws: Right

Ht: 5'6"; Wt: 160 lbs; Born: 10/5/1957 in Dorado, Puerto Rico; Debut: 8/30/1980

LCS — Batting / Fielding

Year Tm	Age	G	AB	H	2B	3B	HR	TB	R	RBI	GW	TBB	IBB	SO	HBP	SH	SF	SB	CS	SB%	GDP	Avg	OBP	SLG	Pos	G	PO	A	E	DP	FPct
1984 KC	26	3	7	0	0	0	0	0	0	0	0	0	0	0	0	0	0	0	0	—	0	.000	.000	.000	SS	3	0	6	1	1	.857
1985 KC	27	4	1	0	0	0	0	0	0	0	0	0	0	0	0	0	0	0	1	.00	0	.000	.000	.000	SS	3	2	4	0	2	1.000
LCS Totals		7	8	0	0	0	0	0	0	0	0	0	0	0	0	0	0	0	1	.00	0	.000	.000	.000	SS	6	2	10	1	3	.923

World Series — Batting / Fielding

Year Tm	Age	G	AB	H	2B	3B	HR	TB	R	RBI	GW	TBB	IBB	SO	HBP	SH	SF	SB	CS	SB%	GDP	Avg	OBP	SLG	Pos	G	PO	A	E	DP	FPct
1980 KC	22	3	0	0	0	0	0	0	0	0	0	0	0	0	0	0	0	0	0	—	0	—	—	—	—						
1985 KC	27	3	0	0	0	0	0	0	1	0	0	0	0	0	0	0	0	0	0	—	0	—	—	—	SS	2	0	2	0	0	1.000
WS Totals		6	0	0	0	0	0	0	1	0	0	0	0	0	0	0	0	0	0	—	0	—	—	—	SS	2	0	2	0	0	1.000
Postseason Totals		13	8	0	0	0	0	0	1	0	0	0	0	0	0	0	0	0	1	.00	0	.000	.000	.000	SS	8	2	12	1	3	.933

DAVID CONE—David Brian Cone—Throws: Right; Bats: Left

Ht: 6'1"; Wt: 180 lbs; Born: 1/2/1963 in Kansas City, Missouri; Debut: 6/8/1986

Division Series — Pitching

Year Tm	Age	G	GS	CG	GF	IP	BFP	H	R	ER	HR	SH	SF	HB	TBB	IBB	SO	WP	Bk	W	L	Pct	ShO	Sv-Op	Hld	OAvg	OOBP	ERA
1995 NYA	32	2	2	0	0	15.2	71	15	8	8	4	0	0	0	9	0	14	2	0	1	0	1.000	0	0- 0	0	.242	.338	4.60
1996 NYA	33	1	1	0	0	6.0	27	8	6	6	2	0	0	0	2	0	8	0	0	0	1	.000	0	0- 0	0	.320	.370	9.00
1997 NYA	34	1	1	0	0	3.1	20	7	6	6	1	1	0	1	2	0	2	1	0	0	0	—	0	0- 0	0	.438	.526	16.20
DS Totals		4	4	0	0	25.0	236	30	20	20	7	1	0	1	13	0	24	3	0	1	1	.500	0	0-0	0	.291	.376	7.20

LCS — Pitching

Year Tm	Age	G	GS	CG	GF	IP	BFP	H	R	ER	HR	SH	SF	HB	TBB	IBB	SO	WP	Bk	W	L	Pct	ShO	Sv-Op	Hld	OAvg	OOBP	ERA
1988 NYN	25	3	2	1	1	12.0	52	10	6	6	0	0	0	1	5	1	9	1	1	1	1	.500	0	0- 0	0	.217	.308	4.50
1992 Tor	29	2	2	0	0	12.0	51	11	7	4	1	0	0	0	5	0	9	0	0	1	1	.500	0	0- 0	0	.239	.314	3.00
1996 NYA	33	1	1	0	0	6.0	28	5	2	2	1	0	0	0	5	0	5	1	0	0	0	—	0	0- 0	0	.217	.357	3.00
LCS Totals		6	5	1	1	30.0	262	26	15	12	2	0	0	1	15	1	23	2	1	2	2	.500	0	0-0	0	.226	.321	3.60

World Series — Pitching

Year Tm	Age	G	GS	CG	GF	IP	BFP	H	R	ER	HR	SH	SF	HB	TBB	IBB	SO	WP	Bk	W	L	Pct	ShO	Sv-Op	Hld	OAvg	OOBP	ERA
1992 Tor	29	2	2	0	0	10.1	47	9	5	4	0	0	1	0	8	0	8	1	0	0	0	—	0	0- 0	0	.237	.362	3.48
1996 NYA	33	1	1	0	0	6.0	24	4	1	1	0	0	0	0	4	0	3	0	0	1	0	1.000	0	0- 0	0	.200	.333	1.50
WS Totals		3	3	0	0	16.1	142	13	6	5	0	0	1	0	12	0	11	1	0	1	0	1.000	0	0-0	0	.224	.352	2.76
Postseason Totals		13	12	1	1	71.1	640	69	41	37	9	1	1	2	40	1	58	6	1	4	3	.571	0	0-0	0	.250	.348	4.67

Division Series — Batting / Fielding

Year Tm	Age	G	AB	H	2B	3B	HR	TB	R	RBI	GW	TBB	IBB	SO	HBP	SH	SF	SB	CS	SB%	GDP	Avg	OBP	SLG	Pos	G	PO	A	E	DP	FPct
1995 NYA	32	2	0	0	0	0	0	0	0	0	0	0	0	0	0	0	0	0	0	—	0	—	—	—	P	2	1	0	0	0	1.000
1996 NYA	33	1	0	0	0	0	0	0	0	0	0	0	0	0	0	0	0	0	0	—	0	—	—	—	P	1	1	0	0	0	1.000
1997 NYA	34	1	0	0	0	0	0	0	0	0	0	0	0	0	0	0	0	0	0	—	0	—	—	—	P	1	1	1	0	0	1.000
DS Totals		4	0	0	0	0	0	0	0	0	0	0	0	0	0	0	0	0	0	—	0	—	—	—	P	4	3	1	0	0	1.000

LCS — Batting / Fielding

Year Tm	Age	G	AB	H	2B	3B	HR	TB	R	RBI	GW	TBB	IBB	SO	HBP	SH	SF	SB	CS	SB%	GDP	Avg	OBP	SLG	Pos	G	PO	A	E	DP	FPct
1988 NYN	25	3	4	0	0	0	0	0	0	0	0	0	0	0	0	1	0	0	0	—	1	.000	.000	.000	P	3	1	0	0	0	1.000
1992 Tor	29	2	0	0	0	0	0	0	0	0	0	0	0	0	0	0	0	0	0	—	0	—	—	—	P	2	0	1	1	0	.500
1996 NYA	33	1	0	0	0	0	0	0	0	0	0	0	0	0	0	0	0	0	0	—	0	—	—	—	P	1	0	1	0	0	1.000
LCS Totals		6	4	0	0	0	0	0	0	0	0	0	0	0	0	1	0	0	0	—	1	.000	.000	.000	P	6	1	2	1	0	.750

World Series — Batting / Fielding

Year Tm	Age	G	AB	H	2B	3B	HR	TB	R	RBI	GW	TBB	IBB	SO	HBP	SH	SF	SB	CS	SB%	GDP	Avg	OBP	SLG	Pos	G	PO	A	E	DP	FPct
1992 Tor	29	2	4	2	0	0	0	2	0	1	0	1	0	0	0	0	0	0	0	—	1	.500	.600	.500	P	2	0	0	0	0	—
1996 NYA	33	1	2	0	0	0	0	0	0	0	0	0	0	1	0	0	0	0	0	—	0	.000	.000	.000	P	1	2	1	0	0	1.000
WS Totals		3	6	2	0	0	0	2	0	1	0	1	0	1	0	0	0	0	0	—	1	.333	.429	.333	P	3	2	1	0	0	1.000
Postseason Totals		13	10	2	0	0	0	2	0	1	0	1	0	1	0	1	0	0	0	—	2	.200	.273	.200	P	13	6	4	1	0	.909

BILLY CONIGLIARO—William Michael Conigliaro—Bats: Right; Throws: Right

Ht: 6'0"; Wt: 180 lbs; Born: 8/15/1947 in Revere, Massachusetts; Debut: 4/11/1969

LCS — Batting / Fielding

Year Tm	Age	G	AB	H	2B	3B	HR	TB	R	RBI	GW	TBB	IBB	SO	HBP	SH	SF	SB	CS	SB%	GDP	Avg	OBP	SLG	Pos	G	PO	A	E	DP	FPct
1973 Oak	26	1	4	0	0	0	0	0	0	0	0	0	0	2	0	0	0	0	0	—	0	.000	.000	.000	OF	1	5	0	0	0	1.000

World Series — Batting / Fielding

Year Tm	Age	G	AB	H	2B	3B	HR	TB	R	RBI	GW	TBB	IBB	SO	HBP	SH	SF	SB	CS	SB%	GDP	Avg	OBP	SLG	Pos	G	PO	A	E	DP	FPct
1973 Oak	26	3	3	0	0	0	0	0	0	0	0	0	0	1	0	0	0	0	0	—	0	.000	.000	.000	—						
Postseason Totals		4	7	0	0	0	0	0	0	0	0	0	0	3	0	0	0	0	0	—	0	.000	.000	.000	OF	1	5	0	0	0	1.000

JEFF CONINE—Jeffrey Guy Conine—Bats: Right; Throws: Right

Ht: 6'1"; Wt: 205 lbs; Born: 6/27/1966 in Tacoma, Washington; Debut: 9/16/1990

Division Series — Batting / Fielding

Year Tm	Age	G	AB	H	2B	3B	HR	TB	R	RBI	GW	TBB	IBB	SO	HBP	SH	SF	SB	CS	SB%	GDP	Avg	OBP	SLG	Pos	G	PO	A	E	DP	FPct
1997 Fla	31	3	11	4	1	0	0	5	3	0	0	1	0	0	0	0	0	0	0	—	0	.364	.417	.455	1B	3	24	3	1	2	.964

LCS — Batting / Fielding

Year Tm	Age	G	AB	H	2B	3B	HR	TB	R	RBI	GW	TBB	IBB	SO	HBP	SH	SF	SB	CS	SB%	GDP	Avg	OBP	SLG	Pos	G	PO	A	E	DP	FPct
1997 Fla	31	6	18	2	0	0	0	2	1	1	1	1	0	4	0	1	0	0	0	—	1	.111	.158	.111	1B	6	34	5	0	2	1.000

World Series — Batting / Fielding

Year Tm	Age	G	AB	H	2B	3B	HR	TB	R	RBI	GW	TBB	IBB	SO	HBP	SH	SF	SB	CS	SB%	GDP	Avg	OBP	SLG	Pos	G	PO	A	E	DP	FPct
1997 Fla	31	6	13	3	0	0	0	3	1	2	0	0	0	0	0	0	0	0	0	—	1	.231	.231	.231	1B	6	30	2	0	5	1.000
Postseason Totals		15	42	9	1	0	0	10	5	3	1	2	0	4	0	1	0	0	0	—	2	.214	.250	.238	1B	15	88	10	1	9	.990

GENE CONLEY—Donald Eugene Conley—Throws: Right; Bats: Right

Ht: 6'8"; Wt: 225 lbs; Born: 11/10/1930 in Muskogee, Oklahoma; Debut: 4/17/1952

World Series — Pitching

Year Tm	Age	G	GS	CG	GF	IP	BFP	H	R	ER	HR	SH	SF	HB	TBB	IBB	SO	WP	Bk	W	L	Pct	ShO	Sv-Op	Hld	OAvg	OOBP	ERA
1957 Mil	26	1	0	0	0	1.2	8	2	2	2	1	0	0	0	1	0	0	0	0	0	0	—	0	0- 0	0	.286	.375	10.80

World Series — Batting / Fielding

Year Tm	Age	G	AB	H	2B	3B	HR	TB	R	RBI	GW	TBB	IBB	SO	HBP	SH	SF	SB	CS	SB%	GDP	Avg	OBP	SLG	Pos	G	PO	A	E	DP	FPct
1957 Mil	26	1	0	0	0	0	0	0	0	0	0	0	0	0	0	0	0	0	0	—	0	—	—	—	P	1	1	0	0	0	1.000

JOE CONNOLLY—Joseph Aloysius Connolly—Bats: Left; Throws: Right

Ht: 5'7"; Wt: 165 lbs; Born: 2/12/1888 in North Smithfield, Rhode Island; Debut: 4/10/1913; Died: 9/1/1943

World Series — Batting / Fielding

Year Tm	Age	G	AB	H	2B	3B	HR	TB	R	RBI	GW	TBB	IBB	SO	HBP	SH	SF	SB	CS	SB%	GDP	Avg	OBP	SLG	Pos	G	PO	A	E	DP	FPct
1914 Bos	26	3	9	1	0	0	0	1	1	1	0	1	0	1	0	0	1	0	0	—	0	.111	.182	.111	OF	3	1	2	1	0	.750

DENNIS COOK—Dennis Bryan Cook—Throws: Left; Bats: Left

Ht: 6'3"; Wt: 185 lbs; Born: 10/4/1962 in LaMarque, Texas; Debut: 9/12/1988

Division Series — Pitching

Year Tm	Age	G	GS	CG	GF	IP	BFP	H	R	ER	HR	SH	SF	HB	TBB	IBB	SO	WP	Bk	W	L	Pct	ShO	Sv-Op	Hld	OAvg	OOBP	ERA
1996 Tex	33	2	0	0	0	1.1	5	0	0	0	0	1	1	0	1	0	0	0	0	0	0	—	0	0- 0	1	.000	.250	0.00
1997 Fla	34	2	0	0	1	3.0	10	0	0	0	0	0	0	0	1	0	3	0	0	1	0	1.000	0	0- 0	0	.000	.100	0.00
DS Totals		4	0	0	1	4.1	30	0	0	0	0	1	1	0	2	0	3	0	0	1	0	1.000	0	0-0	1	.000	.143	0.00

LCS — Pitching

Year Tm	Age	G	GS	CG	GF	IP	BFP	H	R	ER	HR	SH	SF	HB	TBB	IBB	SO	WP	Bk	W	L	Pct	ShO	Sv-Op	Hld	OAvg	OOBP	ERA
1997 Fla	34	2	0	0	0	2.1	8	0	0	0	0	0	0	1	0	0	2	0	0	0	0	—	0	0- 0	2	.000	.125	0.00

World Series — Pitching

Year Tm	Age	G	GS	CG	GF	IP	BFP	H	R	ER	HR	SH	SF	HB	TBB	IBB	SO	WP	Bk	W	L	Pct	ShO	Sv-Op	Hld	OAvg	OOBP	ERA
1997 Fla	34	3	0	0	0	3.2	13	1	0	0	0	1	0	0	1	0	5	0	0	1	0	1.000	0	0- 0	1	.091	.167	0.00
Postseason Totals		9	0	0	1	10.1	72	1	0	0	0	2	1	1	3	0	10	0	0	2	0	1.000	0	0-0	4	.034	.147	0.00

JACK COOMBS—DOUG CORBETT

Jack Coombs (top table)

Division Series								Batting																		Fielding				
Year	Tm	Age	G	AB	H	2B	3B	HR	TB	R	RBI	GW	TBB	IBB	SO	HBP	SH	SF	SB	CS	SB%	GDP	Avg	OBP	SLG	Pos	G	PO	A	E	DP	FPct
1996	Tex	33	2	0	0	0	0	0	0	0	0	0	0	0	0	0	0	0	0	0	—	0	—	—	—	P	2	0	0	0	0	—
1997	Fla	34	2	0	0	0	0	0	0	0	0	0	0	0	0	0	0	0	0	0	—	0	—	—	—	P	2	0	0	0	0	—
DS Totals			4	0	0	0	0	0	0	0	0	0	0	0	0	0	0	0	0	0	—	0	—	—	—	P	4	0	0	0	0	—

LCS								Batting																		Fielding					
Year	Tm	Age	G	AB	H	2B	3B	HR	TB	R	RBI	GW	TBB	IBB	SO	HBP	SH	SF	SB	CS	SB%	GDP	Avg	OBP	SLG	Pos	G	PO	A	E	DP	FPct
1997	Fla	34	2	0	0	0	0	0	0	0	0	0	0	0	0	0	0	0	0	0	—	0	—	—	—	P	2	0	1	0	0	1.000

World Series								Batting																		Fielding					
Year	Tm	Age	G	AB	H	2B	3B	HR	TB	R	RBI	GW	TBB	IBB	SO	HBP	SH	SF	SB	CS	SB%	GDP	Avg	OBP	SLG	Pos	G	PO	A	E	DP	FPct
1997	Fla	34	3	0	0	0	0	0	0	0	0	0	0	0	0	0	0	0	0	0	—	0	—	—	—	P	3	0	0	0	0	—
Postseason Totals			9	0	0	0	0	0	0	0	0	0	0	0	0	0	0	0	0	0	—	0	—	—	—	P	9	0	1	0	0	1.000

JACK COOMBS —John Wesley Coombs—Nickname: Colby Jack—Throws: Right; Bats: Both
Ht: 6'0"; Wt: 185 lbs; Born: 11/18/1882 in Le Grand, Iowa; Debut: 7/5/1906; Died: 4/15/1957

World Series							Pitching																					
Year	Tm	Age	G	GS	CG	GF	IP	BFP	H	R	ER	HR	SH	SF	HB	TBB	IBB	SO	WP	Bk	W	L	Pct	ShO	Sv-Op	Hld	OAvg	OOBP	ERA
1910	Phi	27	3	3	3	0	27.0	116	23	10	10	0	4	2	0	14	0	17	1	0	3	0	1.000	0	0-0	0	.240	.330	3.33
1911	Phi	28	2	2	1	0	20.0	73	11	5	3	0	2	1	1	6	0	16	0	0	1	0	1.000	0	0-0	0	.175	.254	1.35
1916	Bro	33	1	1	0	0	6.1	24	7	3	3	1	0	0	0	1	0	1	0	0	1	0	1.000	0	0-0	0	.304	.333	4.26
WS Totals			6	6	4	0	53.1	426	41	18	16	1	6	3	1	21	0	34	1	0	5	0	1.000	0	0-0	0	.225	.304	2.70

World Series								Batting																		Fielding					
Year	Tm	Age	G	AB	H	2B	3B	HR	TB	R	RBI	GW	TBB	IBB	SO	HBP	SH	SF	SB	CS	SB%	GDP	Avg	OBP	SLG	Pos	G	PO	A	E	DP	FPct
1910	Phi	27	3	13	5	1	0	0	6	0	3	0	0	0	3	0	0	0	0	0	—	1	.385	.385	.462	P	3	1	3	2	0	.667
1911	Phi	28	2	8	2	0	0	0	2	1	0	0	0	0	3	0	0	0	0	0	—	0	.250	.250	.250	P	2	1	2	0	0	1.000
1916	Bro	33	1	3	1	0	0	0	1	0	1	0	0	0	0	0	0	0	0	0	—	0	.333	.333	.333	P	1	0	2	0	0	1.000
WS Totals			6	24	8	1	0	0	9	1	4	0	0	0	3	0	0	0	0	0	—	1	.333	.333	.375	P	6	2	7	2	0	.818

CECIL COOPER —Cecil Celester Cooper—Bats: Left; Throws: Left
Ht: 6'2"; Wt: 165 lbs; Born: 12/20/1949 in Brenham, Texas; Debut: 9/8/1971

Division Series								Batting																		Fielding					
Year	Tm	Age	G	AB	H	2B	3B	HR	TB	R	RBI	GW	TBB	IBB	SO	HBP	SH	SF	SB	CS	SB%	GDP	Avg	OBP	SLG	Pos	G	PO	A	E	DP	FPct
1981	Mil	31	5	18	4	0	0	0	4	1	3	1	1	0	3	0	1	0	1	0	0	1	.222	.250	.222	1B	5	47	4	1	6	.981

LCS								Batting																		Fielding					
Year	Tm	Age	G	AB	H	2B	3B	HR	TB	R	RBI	GW	TBB	IBB	SO	HBP	SH	SF	SB	CS	SB%	GDP	Avg	OBP	SLG	Pos	G	PO	A	E	DP	FPct
1975	Bos	25	3	10	4	2	0	0	6	0	1	0	0	0	2	0	1	0	0	0	—	0	.400	.400	.600	1B	3	24	1	1	3	.962
1982	Mil	32	5	20	3	2	0	0	5	1	4	2	0	0	6	0	1	0	0	0	—	0	.150	.150	.250	1B	5	37	3	2	5	.952
LCS Totals			8	30	7	4	0	0	11	1	5	2	0	0	8	0	2	0	0	0	—	0	.233	.233	.367	1B	8	61	4	3	8	.956

World Series								Batting																		Fielding					
Year	Tm	Age	G	AB	H	2B	3B	HR	TB	R	RBI	GW	TBB	IBB	SO	HBP	SH	SF	SB	CS	SB%	GDP	Avg	OBP	SLG	Pos	G	PO	A	E	DP	FPct
1975	Bos	25	5	19	1	1	0	0	2	1	0	0	0	0	3	0	0	0	0	0	—	1	.053	.050	.105	1B	4	40	1	0	1	1.000
1982	Mil	32	7	28	8	1	0	1	12	3	6	1	0	0	1	0	0	0	0	0	—	1	.286	.300	.429	1B	7	71	10	1	3	.988
WS Totals			12	47	9	2	0	1	14	3	7	1	0	0	4	0	0	0	0	0	—	2	.191	.200	.298	1B	11	111	11	1	4	.992
Postseason Totals			25	95	20	6	0	1	29	5	15	4	2	0	15	0	3	0	1	0	0	3	.211	.220	.305	1B	24	219	19	5	18	.979

CLAUDE COOPER —Claude William Cooper—Bats: Left; Throws: Left
Ht: 5'9"; Wt: 158 lbs; Born: 4/1/1892 in Troup, Texas; Debut: 4/14/1913; Died: 1/21/1974

World Series								Batting																		Fielding					
Year	Tm	Age	G	AB	H	2B	3B	HR	TB	R	RBI	GW	TBB	IBB	SO	HBP	SH	SF	SB	CS	SB%	GDP	Avg	OBP	SLG	Pos	G	PO	A	E	DP	FPct
1913	NYG	21	2	0	0	0	0	0	0	0	0	0	0	0	0	0	0	0	1	1	.50	0	—	—	—	—						

MORT COOPER —Morton Cecil Cooper—Throws: Right; Bats: Right
Ht: 6'2"; Wt: 210 lbs; Born: 3/2/1913 in Atherton, Missouri; Debut: 9/14/1938; Died: 11/17/1958

World Series							Pitching																					
Year	Tm	Age	G	GS	CG	GF	IP	BFP	H	R	ER	HR	SH	SF	HB	TBB	IBB	SO	WP	Bk	W	L	Pct	ShO	Sv-Op	Hld	OAvg	OOBP	ERA
1942	StL-M	29	2	2	0	0	13.0	59	17	10	8	1	0	0	0	4	0	9	0	0	0	1	.000	0	0-0	0	.309	.356	5.54
1943	StL	30	2	2	1	0	16.0	62	11	5	5	1	2	0	0	3	0	10	1	0	1	1	.500	0	0-0	0	.196	.237	2.81
1944	StL	31	2	2	1	0	16.0	62	9	2	2	1	0	0	0	5	0	16	0	0	1	1	.500	1	0-0	0	.158	.226	1.13
WS Totals			6	6	2	0	45.0	366	37	17	15	3	2	0	0	12	0	35	1	0	2	3	.400	1	0-0	0	.220	.272	3.00

World Series								Batting																		Fielding					
Year	Tm	Age	G	AB	H	2B	3B	HR	TB	R	RBI	GW	TBB	IBB	SO	HBP	SH	SF	SB	CS	SB%	GDP	Avg	OBP	SLG	Pos	G	PO	A	E	DP	FPct
1942	StL	29	2	5	1	0	0	0	1	1	2	0	0	0	1	0	0	0	0	0	—	0	.200	.200	.200	P	2	0	1	0	0	1.000
1943	StL	30	2	5	0	0	0	0	0	0	0	0	0	0	3	0	1	0	0	0	—	0	.000	.000	.000	P	2	0	1	0	0	1.000
1944	StL	31	2	4	0	0	0	0	0	0	0	0	0	0	2	0	1	0	0	0	—	1	.000	.000	.000	P	2	0	6	0	0	1.000
WS Totals			6	14	1	0	0	0	1	1	2	0	0	0	6	0	2	0	0	0	—	1	.071	.071	.071	P	6	0	8	0	0	1.000

WALKER COOPER —William Walker Cooper—Nickname: Walk—Bats: Right; Throws: Right
Ht: 6'3"; Wt: 210 lbs; Born: 1/8/1915 in Atherton, Missouri; Debut: 9/25/1940; Died: 4/11/1991

World Series								Batting																		Fielding					
Year	Tm	Age	G	AB	H	2B	3B	HR	TB	R	RBI	GW	TBB	IBB	SO	HBP	SH	SF	SB	CS	SB%	GDP	Avg	OBP	SLG	Pos	G	PO	A	E	DP	FPct
1942	StL	27	5	21	6	1	0	0	7	3	4	0	0	0	1	0	0	0	0	0	—	0	.286	.286	.333	C	5	24	2	1	0	.963
1943	StL	28	5	17	5	0	0	0	5	1	0	0	0	0	1	0	1	0	0	1	1.00	1	.294	.294	.294	C	5	28	3	2	0	.939
1944	StL	29	6	22	7	2	1	0	11	1	2	0	3	2	2	0	1	0	0	0	—	1	.318	.400	.500	C	6	55	0	0	0	1.000
WS Totals			16	60	18	3	1	0	23	5	6	1	3	2	4	0	2	0	0	1	1.00	2	.300	.333	.383	C	16	107	5	3	0	.974

ROCKY COPPINGER —John Thomas Coppinger—Throws: Right; Bats: Right
Ht: 6'5"; Wt: 250 lbs; Born: 3/19/1974 in El Paso, Texas; Debut: 6/11/1996

LCS							Pitching																					
Year	Tm	Age	G	GS	CG	GF	IP	BFP	H	R	ER	HR	SH	SF	HB	TBB	IBB	SO	WP	Bk	W	L	Pct	ShO	Sv-Op	Hld	OAvg	OOBP	ERA
1996	Bal	22	1	1	0	0	5.1	23	6	5	5	3	0	0	0	1	0	3	0	0	0	1	.000	0	0-0	0	.273	.304	8.44

LCS								Batting																		Fielding					
Year	Tm	Age	G	AB	H	2B	3B	HR	TB	R	RBI	GW	TBB	IBB	SO	HBP	SH	SF	SB	CS	SB%	GDP	Avg	OBP	SLG	Pos	G	PO	A	E	DP	FPct
1996	Bal	22	1	0	0	0	0	0	0	0	0	0	0	0	0	0	0	0	0	0	—	0	—	—	—	P	1	1	1	0	0	1.000

JOEY CORA —Jose Manuel Cora—Bats: Both; Throws: Right
Ht: 5'7"; Wt: 150 lbs; Born: 5/14/1965 in Caguas, Puerto Rico; Debut: 4/6/1987

Division Series								Batting																		Fielding					
Year	Tm	Age	G	AB	H	2B	3B	HR	TB	R	RBI	GW	TBB	IBB	SO	HBP	SH	SF	SB	CS	SB%	GDP	Avg	OBP	SLG	Pos	G	PO	A	E	DP	FPct
1995	Sea	30	5	19	6	1	0	1	10	7	1	0	3	0	3	0	0	0	1	0	1.00	0	.316	.409	.526	2B	5	10	12	1	2	.957
1997	Sea	32	4	17	3	0	0	0	3	1	0	0	0	0	4	0	0	0	0	0	—	0	.176	.176	.176	2B	4	7	11	0	2	1.000
DS Totals			9	36	9	1	0	1	13	8	1	0	3	0	7	0	0	0	1	0	1.00	0	.250	.308	.361	2B	9	17	23	1	4	.976

LCS								Batting																		Fielding					
Year	Tm	Age	G	AB	H	2B	3B	HR	TB	R	RBI	GW	TBB	IBB	SO	HBP	SH	SF	SB	CS	SB%	GDP	Avg	OBP	SLG	Pos	G	PO	A	E	DP	FPct
1993	ChA	28	6	22	3	0	0	0	3	1	1	0	3	0	6	1	2	0	0	0	—	1	.136	.269	.136	2B	6	18	20	3	2	.927
1995	Sea	30	6	23	4	1	0	0	5	3	0	1	1	0	0	2	0	0	2	0	1.00	0	.174	.269	.217	2B	6	15	12	1	3	.964
LCS Totals			12	45	7	1	0	0	8	4	1	0	4	0	6	3	2	0	2	0	1.00	1	.156	.269	.178	2B	12	33	32	4	5	.942
Postseason Totals			21	81	16	2	0	1	21	12	2	0	7	0	10	3	5	0	3	0	1.00	1	.198	.286	.259	2B	21	50	55	5	9	.955

DOUG CORBETT —Douglas Mitchell Corbett—Throws: Right; Bats: Right
Ht: 6'1"; Wt: 185 lbs; Born: 11/4/1952 in Sarasota, Florida; Debut: 4/10/1980

LCS							Pitching																					
Year	Tm	Age	G	GS	CG	GF	IP	BFP	H	R	ER	HR	SH	SF	HB	TBB	IBB	SO	WP	Bk	W	L	Pct	ShO	Sv-Op	Hld	OAvg	OOBP	ERA
1986	Cal	33	3	0	0	2	6.2	31	9	4	4	1	0	1	0	2	0	2	0	0	1	0	1.000	0	0-0	0	.321	.387	5.40

LCS								Batting																		Fielding					
Year	Tm	Age	G	AB	H	2B	3B	HR	TB	R	RBI	GW	TBB	IBB	SO	HBP	SH	SF	SB	CS	SB%	GDP	Avg	OBP	SLG	Pos	G	PO	A	E	DP	FPct
1986	Cal	33	3	0	0	0	0	0	0	0	0	0	0	0	0	0	0	0	0	0	—	0	—	—	—	P	3	0	1	0	0	1.000

RHEAL CORMIER—Rheal Paul Cormier—Throws: Left; Bats: Left

Ht: 5'10"; Wt: 185 lbs; Born: 4/23/1967 in Moncton, New Brunswick; Debut: 8/15/1991

Division Series — Pitching

Year Tm	Age	G	GS	CG	GF	IP	BFP	H	R	ER	HR	SH	SF	HB	TBB	IBB	SO	WP	Bk	W	L	Pct	ShO	Sv-Op	Hld	OAvg	OOBP	ERA
1995 Bos	28	2	0	0	0	0.2	6	2	1	1	0	0	0	1	1	0	2	0	0	0	0	—	0	0- 0	0	.500	.667	13.50

Division Series — Batting / Fielding

Year Tm	Age	G	AB	H	2B	3B	HR	TB	R	RBI	GW	TBB	IBB	SO	HBP	SH	SF	SB	CS	SB%	GDP	Avg	OBP	SLG	Pos	G	PO	A	E	DP	FPct
1995 Bos	28	2	0	0	0	0	0	0	0	0	0	0	0	0	0	0	0	0	0	—	0	—	—	—	P	2	0	0	0	0	—

PAT CORRALES—Patrick Corrales—Bats: Right; Throws: Right

Ht: 6'0"; Wt: 180 lbs; Born: 3/20/1941 in Los Angeles, California; Debut: 8/2/1964

World Series — Batting / Fielding

Year Tm	Age	G	AB	H	2B	3B	HR	TB	R	RBI	GW	TBB	IBB	SO	HBP	SH	SF	SB	CS	SB%	GDP	Avg	OBP	SLG	Pos	G	PO	A	E	DP	FPct
1970 Cin	29	1	1	0	0	0	0	0	0	0	0	0	0	0	0	0	0	0	0	—	0	.000	.000	.000	—						

JIM CORSI—James Bernard Corsi—Throws: Right; Bats: Right

Ht: 6'1"; Wt: 210 lbs; Born: 9/9/1961 in Newton, Massachusetts; Debut: 6/28/1988

LCS — Pitching

Year Tm	Age	G	GS	CG	GF	IP	BFP	H	R	ER	HR	SH	SF	HB	TBB	IBB	SO	WP	Bk	W	L	Pct	ShO	Sv-Op	Hld	OAvg	OOBP	ERA
1992 Oak	31	3	0	0	0	2.0	10	2	0	0	0	0	0	0	3	0	0	0	0	0	0	—	0	0- 0	0	.286	.500	0.00

LCS — Batting / Fielding

Year Tm	Age	G	AB	H	2B	3B	HR	TB	R	RBI	GW	TBB	IBB	SO	HBP	SH	SF	SB	CS	SB%	GDP	Avg	OBP	SLG	Pos	G	PO	A	E	DP	FPct
1992 Oak	31	3	0	0	0	0	0	0	0	0	0	0	0	0	0	0	0	0	0	—	0	—	—	—	P	3	0	0	0	0	—

AL CORWIN—Elmer Nathan Corwin—Throws: Right; Bats: Right

Ht: 6'1"; Wt: 170 lbs; Born: 12/3/1926 in Newburgh, New York; Debut: 7/25/1951

World Series — Pitching

Year Tm	Age	G	GS	CG	GF	IP	BFP	H	R	ER	HR	SH	SF	HB	TBB	IBB	SO	WP	Bk	W	L	Pct	ShO	Sv-Op	Hld	OAvg	OOBP	ERA
1951 NYG	24	1	0	0	0	1.2	6	1	0	0	0	0	0	0	0	0	1	1	0	0	0	—	0	0- 0	0	.167	.167	0.00

World Series — Batting / Fielding

Year Tm	Age	G	AB	H	2B	3B	HR	TB	R	RBI	GW	TBB	IBB	SO	HBP	SH	SF	SB	CS	SB%	GDP	Avg	OBP	SLG	Pos	G	PO	A	E	DP	FPct
1951 NYG	24	1	0	0	0	0	0	0	0	0	0	0	0	0	0	0	0	0	0	—	0	—	—	—	P	1	1	0	0	0	1.000

PETE COSCARART—Peter Joseph Coscarart—Bats: Right; Throws: Right

Ht: 5'11"; Wt: 175 lbs; Born: 6/16/1913 in Escondido, California; Debut: 4/26/1938

World Series — Batting / Fielding

Year Tm	Age	G	AB	H	2B	3B	HR	TB	R	RBI	GW	TBB	IBB	SO	HBP	SH	SF	SB	CS	SB%	GDP	Avg	OBP	SLG	Pos	G	PO	A	E	DP	FPct
1941 Bro	28	3	7	0	0	0	0	0	1	0	0	1	0	2	0	0	0	0	0	—	0	.000	.125	.000	2B	3	7	8	0	1	1.000

HENRY COTTO—Bats: Right; Throws: Right

Ht: 6'2"; Wt: 178 lbs; Born: 1/5/1961 in New York, New York; Debut: 4/5/1984

LCS — Batting / Fielding

Year Tm	Age	G	AB	H	2B	3B	HR	TB	R	RBI	GW	TBB	IBB	SO	HBP	SH	SF	SB	CS	SB%	GDP	Avg	OBP	SLG	Pos	G	PO	A	E	DP	FPct
1984 ChN	23	3	1	1	0	0	0	1	1	0	0	0	0	0	1	0	0	0	0	—	0	1.000	1.000	1.000	OF	3	2	0	0	0	1.000

BILL COUGHLIN—William Paul Coughlin—Bats: Right; Throws: Right

Ht: 5'9"; Wt: 140 lbs; Born: 7/12/1878 in Scranton, Pennsylvania; Debut: 8/9/1899; Died: 5/7/1943

World Series — Batting / Fielding

Year Tm	Age	G	AB	H	2B	3B	HR	TB	R	RBI	GW	TBB	IBB	SO	HBP	SH	SF	SB	CS	SB%	GDP	Avg	OBP	SLG	Pos	G	PO	A	E	DP	FPct
1907 Det	29	5	20	5	0	0	0	5	0	0	0	1	0	4	0	0	0	1	0	1.00	0	.250	.286	.250	3B	5	9	7	2	0	.889
1908 Det	30	3	8	1	0	0	0	1	0	1	0	0	0	1	1	0	1	0	0	—	0	.125	.200	.125	3B	3	3	6	1	1	.900
WS Totals		8	28	6	0	0	0	6	0	1	0	1	0	5	1	0	1	1	0	1.00	0	.214	.258	.214	3B	8	12	13	3	1	.893

CRAIG COUNSELL—Craig John Counsell—Bats: Left; Throws: Right

Ht: 6'0"; Wt: 177 lbs; Born: 8/21/1970 in South Bend, Indiana; Debut: 9/17/1995

Division Series — Batting / Fielding

Year Tm	Age	G	AB	H	2B	3B	HR	TB	R	RBI	GW	TBB	IBB	SO	HBP	SH	SF	SB	CS	SB%	GDP	Avg	OBP	SLG	Pos	G	PO	A	E	DP	FPct
1997 Fla	27	3	5	2	1	0	0	3	0	1	0	1	0	0	0	1	0	0	0	—	0	.400	.500	.600	2B	3	5	2	1	0	.875

LCS — Batting / Fielding

Year Tm	Age	G	AB	H	2B	3B	HR	TB	R	RBI	GW	TBB	IBB	SO	HBP	SH	SF	SB	CS	SB%	GDP	Avg	OBP	SLG	Pos	G	PO	A	E	DP	FPct
1997 Fla	27	5	14	6	0	0	0	6	0	2	0	3	3	3	0	0	0	0	0	—	0	.429	.529	.429	2B	4	7	9	1	1	.941

World Series — Batting / Fielding

Year Tm	Age	G	AB	H	2B	3B	HR	TB	R	RBI	GW	TBB	IBB	SO	HBP	SH	SF	SB	CS	SB%	GDP	Avg	OBP	SLG	Pos	G	PO	A	E	DP	FPct
1997 Fla	27	7	22	4	1	0	0	5	4	2	0	6	0	5	0	0	1	1	0	1.00	0	.182	.345	.227	2B	7	18	15	1	7	.971
Postseason Totals		15	41	12	2	0	0	14	4	5	0	10	3	8	0	1	1	1	0	1.00	0	.293	.423	.341	2B	14	30	26	3	8	.949

STAN COVELESKI (HOF 1969-V)—Stanley Anthony Coveleski—Throws: Right; Bats: Right

Ht: 5'11"; Wt: 166 lbs; Born: 7/13/1889 in Shamokin, Pennsylvania; Debut: 9/10/1912; Died: 3/20/1984

World Series — Pitching

Year Tm	Age	G	GS	CG	GF	IP	BFP	H	R	ER	HR	SH	SF	HB	TBB	IBB	SO	WP	Bk	W	L	Pct	ShO	Sv-Op	Hld	OAvg	OOBP	ERA
1920 Cle	31	3	3	3	0	27.0	97	15	2	2	0	1	0	0	2	0	8	0	0	3	0	1.000	1	0- 0	0	.160	.177	0.67
1925 Was	36	2	2	1	0	14.1	65	16	7	6	2	1	1	0	5	0	3	0	0	0	2	.000	0	0- 0	0	.276	.328	3.77
WS Totals		5	5	4	0	41.1	324	31	9	8	2	2	1	0	7	0	11	0	0	3	2	.600	1	0-0	0	.204	.238	1.74

World Series — Batting / Fielding

Year Tm	Age	G	AB	H	2B	3B	HR	TB	R	RBI	GW	TBB	IBB	SO	HBP	SH	SF	SB	CS	SB%	GDP	Avg	OBP	SLG	Pos	G	PO	A	E	DP	FPct
1920 Cle	31	3	10	1	0	0	0	1	2	0	0	0	0	4	0	0	0	0	0	—	0	.100	.100	.100	P	3	2	5	1	0	.875
1925 Was	36	2	3	0	0	0	0	0	0	0	0	1	0	2	0	1	0	0	0	—	0	.000	.250	.000	P	2	0	4	0	1	1.000
WS Totals		5	13	1	0	0	0	1	2	0	0	1	0	6	0	1	0	0	0	—	0	.077	.143	.077	P	5	2	9	1	1	.917

WES COVINGTON—John Wesley Covington—Bats: Left; Throws: Right

Ht: 6'1"; Wt: 205 lbs; Born: 3/27/1932 in Laurinburg, North Carolina; Debut: 4/19/1956

World Series — Batting / Fielding

Year Tm	Age	G	AB	H	2B	3B	HR	TB	R	RBI	GW	TBB	IBB	SO	HBP	SH	SF	SB	CS	SB%	GDP	Avg	OBP	SLG	Pos	G	PO	A	E	DP	FPct
1957 Mil	25	7	24	5	1	0	0	6	1	1	1	2	0	6	0	2	0	1	0	1.00	1	.208	.269	.250	OF	7	13	1	0	1	1.000
1958 Mil	26	7	26	7	0	0	0	7	2	4	1	2	0	4	0	0	1	0	0	—	0	.269	.310	.269	OF	7	10	1	0	0	1.000
1966 LA	34	1	1	0	0	0	0	0	0	0	0	0	0	1	0	0	0	0	0	—	0	.000	.000	.000	—						
WS Totals		15	51	12	1	0	0	13	3	5	2	4	0	11	0	2	1	1	0	1.00	1	.235	.286	.255	OF	14	23	2	0	1	1.000

AL COWENS—Alfred Edward Cowens—Bats: Right; Throws: Right

Ht: 6'1"; Wt: 197 lbs; Born: 10/25/1951 in Los Angeles, California; Debut: 4/6/1974

LCS — Batting / Fielding

Year Tm	Age	G	AB	H	2B	3B	HR	TB	R	RBI	GW	TBB	IBB	SO	HBP	SH	SF	SB	CS	SB%	GDP	Avg	OBP	SLG	Pos	G	PO	A	E	DP	FPct
1976 KC	24	5	21	4	0	1	0	6	3	0	0	1	0	1	0	0	0	2	0	1.00	1	.190	.227	.286	OF	5	15	0	0	0	1.000
1977 KC	25	5	19	5	0	0	1	8	2	5	0	1	0	3	0	0	0	0	1	.00	1	.263	.300	.421	OF	5	14	0	0	0	1.000
1978 KC	26	4	15	2	0	0	0	2	2	1	0	0	0	2	0	0	0	0	0	—	0	.133	.133	.133	OF	4	5	0	0	0	1.000
LCS Totals		14	55	11	0	1	1	16	7	6	0	2	0	6	0	0	0	2	1	.67	2	.200	.228	.291	OF	14	34	0	0	0	1.000

BILLY COX—William Richard Cox—Bats: Right; Throws: Right

Ht: 5'10"; Wt: 150 lbs; Born: 8/29/1919 in Newport, Pennsylvania; Debut: 9/20/1941; Died: 3/30/1978

World Series — Batting / Fielding

Year Tm	Age	G	AB	H	2B	3B	HR	TB	R	RBI	GW	TBB	IBB	SO	HBP	SH	SF	SB	CS	SB%	GDP	Avg	OBP	SLG	Pos	G	PO	A	E	DP	FPct
1949 Bro	30	2	3	1	0	0	0	1	0	0	0	0	0	1	0	0	0	0	0	—	0	.333	.333	.333	3B	1	1	0	0	0	1.000
1952 Bro	33	7	27	8	2	0	0	10	4	0	0	3	2	4	0	1	0	0	1	.00	0	.296	.367	.370	3B	7	9	14	1	1	.958
1953 Bro	34	6	23	7	3	0	1	13	3	6	0	1	1	4	0	1	0	0	0	—	0	.304	.333	.565	3B	6	1	10	1	1	.917
WS Totals		15	53	16	5	0	1	24	7	6	0	4	3	9	0	2	0	0	1	.00	0	.302	.351	.453	3B	14	11	24	2	2	.946

DANNY COX—Danny Bradford Cox—Throws: Right; Bats: Right

Ht: 6'4"; Wt: 235 lbs; Born: 9/21/1959 in Northampton, England; Debut: 8/6/1983

LCS	Pitching																											
Year Tm	Age	G	GS	CG	GF	IP	BFP	H	R	ER	HR	SH	SF	HB	TBB	IBB	SO	WP	Bk	W	L	Pct	ShO	Sv-Op	Hld	OAvg	OOBP	ERA
1985 StL	26	1	1	0	0	6.0	26	4	2	2	0	0	0	0	5	1	4	0	0	1	0	1.000	0	0- 0	0	.190	.346	3.00
1987 StL	28	2	2	2	0	17.0	67	17	4	4	3	0	0	0	3	0	11	0	0	1	1	.500	1	0- 0	0	.266	.299	2.12
1992 Pit	33	2	0	0	1	1.1	6	1	0	0	0	0	0	0	1	0	1	0	0	0	0	—	0	0- 0	0	.200	.333	0.00
1993 Tor	34	2	0	0	0	5.0	19	3	0	0	0	2	1	0	2	2	5	0	0	0	0	—	0	0- 0	0	.214	.294	0.00
LCS Totals		7	3	2	1	29.1	236	25	6	6	3	2	1	0	11	3	21	0	0	2	1	.667	1	0-0	0	.240	.310	1.84
World Series	**Pitching**																											
Year Tm	Age	G	GS	CG	GF	IP	BFP	H	R	ER	HR	SH	SF	HB	TBB	IBB	SO	WP	Bk	W	L	Pct	ShO	Sv-Op	Hld	OAvg	OOBP	ERA
1985 StL	26	2	2	0	0	14.0	55	14	2	2	0	2	0	0	4	0	13	0	0	0	0	—	0	0- 0	0	.286	.340	1.29
1987 StL	28	3	2	0	0	11.2	54	13	10	10	1	1	0	0	8	1	9	1	0	1	2	.333	0	0- 0	0	.289	.396	7.71
1993 Tor	34	3	0	0	1	3.1	20	6	3	3	0	0	0	0	5	0	6	0	0	0	0	—	0	0- 1	0	.400	.550	8.10
WS Totals		8	4	0	1	29.0	258	33	15	15	1	3	0	0	17	1	28	1	0	1	2	.333	0	0-1	0	.303	.397	4.66
Postseason Totals		15	7	2	2	58.1	494	58	21	21	4	5	1	0	28	4	49	1	0	3	3	.500	1	0-1	0	.272	.355	3.24

LCS	Batting																								Fielding						
Year Tm	Age	G	AB	H	2B	3B	HR	TB	R	RBI	GW	TBB	IBB	SO	HBP	SH	SF	SB	CS	SB%	GDP	Avg	OBP	SLG	Pos	G	PO	A	E	DP	FPct
1985 StL	26	1	2	0	0	0	0	0	0	0	0	1	0	1	0	0	0	0	0	—	0	.000	.333	.000	P	1	0	0	0	0	—
1987 StL	28	2	6	2	0	0	0	2	0	1	0	0	0	2	0	1	0	0	0	—	0	.333	.333	.333	P	2	4	5	0	2	1.000
1992 Pit	33	2	0	0	0	0	0	0	0	0	0	0	0	0	0	0	0	0	0	—	0	—	—	—	P	2	0	0	0	0	—
1993 Tor	34	2	0	0	0	0	0	0	0	0	0	0	0	0	0	0	0	0	0	—	0	—	—	—	P	2	0	1	0	0	1.000
LCS Totals		7	8	2	0	0	0	2	0	1	0	1	0	3	0	1	0	0	0	—	0	.250	.333	.250	P	7	4	6	0	2	1.000
World Series	**Batting**																								**Fielding**						
Year Tm	Age	G	AB	H	2B	3B	HR	TB	R	RBI	GW	TBB	IBB	SO	HBP	SH	SF	SB	CS	SB%	GDP	Avg	OBP	SLG	Pos	G	PO	A	E	DP	FPct
1985 StL	26	2	4	0	0	0	0	0	0	0	0	0	0	2	0	0	0	0	0	—	0	.000	.000	.000	P	2	1	2	0	1	1.000
1987 StL	28	3	2	0	0	0	0	0	0	0	0	0	0	1	0	1	0	0	0	—	0	.000	.000	.000	P	3	1	1	0	0	1.000
1993 Tor	34	3	1	0	0	0	0	0	0	0	0	0	0	0	0	0	0	0	0	—	0	.000	.000	.000	P	3	1	0	0	1	1.000
WS Totals		8	7	0	0	0	0	0	0	0	0	0	0	3	0	1	0	0	0	—	0	.000	.000	.000	P	8	3	3	0	2	1.000
Postseason Totals		15	15	2	0	0	0	2	0	1	0	1	0	6	0	2	0	0	0	—	0	.133	.188	.133	P	15	7	9	0	4	1.000

HARRY CRAFT—Harry Francis Craft—Nickname: Wildfire—Bats: Right; Throws: Right

Ht: 6'1"; Wt: 185 lbs; Born: 4/19/1915 in Ellisville, Mississippi; Debut: 9/19/1937; Died: 8/3/1995

World Series	Batting																								Fielding						
Year Tm	Age	G	AB	H	2B	3B	HR	TB	R	RBI	GW	TBB	IBB	SO	HBP	SH	SF	SB	CS	SB%	GDP	Avg	OBP	SLG	Pos	G	PO	A	E	DP	FPct
1939 Cin	24	4	11	1	0	0	0	1	0	0	0	0	0	6	0	0	0	0	0	—	1	.091	.091	.091	OF	4	7	1	0	0	1.000
1940 Cin	25	1	1	0	0	0	0	0	0	0	0	0	0	0	0	0	0	0	0	—	0	.000	.000	.000	—						
WS Totals		5	12	1	0	0	0	1	0	0	0	0	0	6	0	0	0	0	0	—	1	.083	.083	.083	OF	4	7	1	0	0	1.000

ROGER CRAIG—Roger Lee Craig—Throws: Right; Bats: Right

Ht: 6'4"; Wt: 185 lbs; Born: 2/17/1930 in Durham, North Carolina; Debut: 7/17/1955

World Series	Pitching																											
Year Tm	Age	G	GS	CG	GF	IP	BFP	H	R	ER	HR	SH	SF	HB	TBB	IBB	SO	WP	Bk	W	L	Pct	ShO	Sv-Op	Hld	OAvg	OOBP	ERA
1955 Bro	25	1	1	0	0	6.0	28	4	2	2	1	0	0	0	5	0	4	0	0	1	0	1.000	0	0- 0	0	.174	.321	3.00
1956 Bro	26	2	1	0	0	6.0	29	10	8	8	3	0	0	0	3	1	4	1	0	0	1	.000	0	0- 0	0	.385	.448	12.00
1959 LA	29	2	2	0	0	9.1	46	15	9	9	2	1	1	0	5	1	8	0	0	0	1	.000	0	0- 0	0	.385	.444	8.68
1964 StL	34	2	0	0	1	5.0	19	2	0	0	0	0	0	0	3	0	9	0	0	1	0	1.000	0	0- 0	0	.125	.263	0.00
WS Totals		7	4	0	1	26.1	244	31	19	19	6	1	1	0	16	2	25	1	0	2	2	.500	0	0-0	0	.298	.388	6.49

World Series	Batting																								Fielding						
Year Tm	Age	G	AB	H	2B	3B	HR	TB	R	RBI	GW	TBB	IBB	SO	HBP	SH	SF	SB	CS	SB%	GDP	Avg	OBP	SLG	Pos	G	PO	A	E	DP	FPct
1955 Bro	25	1	0	0	0	0	0	0	0	0	0	1	0	0	0	1	0	0	0	—	0	—	1.000	—	P	1	0	1	0	0	1.000
1956 Bro	26	2	2	1	0	0	0	1	0	0	0	0	0	0	0	0	0	0	0	—	0	.500	.500	.500	P	2	1	1	0	1	1.000
1959 LA	29	2	3	0	0	0	0	0	0	0	0	0	0	2	0	1	0	0	0	—	0	.000	.000	.000	P	2	0	2	0	0	1.000
1964 StL	34	2	1	0	0	0	0	0	0	0	0	0	0	0	0	0	0	0	0	—	0	.000	.000	.000	P	2	0	2	0	0	1.000
WS Totals		7	6	1	0	0	0	1	0	0	0	1	0	2	0	2	0	0	0	—	0	.167	.286	.167	P	7	1	6	0	1	1.000

DOC CRAMER—Roger Maxwell Cramer—Nickname: Flit—Bats: Left; Throws: Right

Ht: 6'2"; Wt: 185 lbs; Born: 7/22/1905 in Beach Haven, New Jersey; Debut: 9/18/1929; Died: 9/9/1990

World Series	Batting																								Fielding						
Year Tm	Age	G	AB	H	2B	3B	HR	TB	R	RBI	GW	TBB	IBB	SO	HBP	SH	SF	SB	CS	SB%	GDP	Avg	OBP	SLG	Pos	G	PO	A	E	DP	FPct
1931 Phi	26	2	2	1	0	0	0	1	0	2	0	0	0	0	0	0	0	0	0	—	0	.500	.500	.500	—						
1945 Det	40	7	29	11	0	0	0	11	7	4	1	1	0	0	1	0	0	1	0	1.00	1	.379	.419	.379	OF	7	21	0	0	0	1.000
WS Totals		9	31	12	0	0	0	12	7	6	1	1	0	0	1	0	0	1	0	1.00	1	.387	.424	.387	OF	7	21	0	0	0	1.000

DEL CRANDALL—Delmar Wesley Crandall—Bats: Right; Throws: Right

Ht: 6'1"; Wt: 180 lbs; Born: 3/5/1930 in Ontario, California; Debut: 6/17/1949

World Series	Batting																								Fielding						
Year Tm	Age	G	AB	H	2B	3B	HR	TB	R	RBI	GW	TBB	IBB	SO	HBP	SH	SF	SB	CS	SB%	GDP	Avg	OBP	SLG	Pos	G	PO	A	E	DP	FPct
1957 Mil	27	6	19	4	0	0	1	7	1	1	0	1	0	1	0	0	0	0	1	.00	0	.211	.250	.368	C	6	21	4	0	2	1.000
1958 Mil	28	7	25	6	0	0	1	9	4	3	0	3	0	10	0	0	1	0	0	—	0	.240	.310	.360	C	7	43	5	0	2	1.000
WS Totals		13	44	10	0	0	2	16	5	4	0	4	0	11	0	0	1	0	1	.00	0	.227	.286	.364	C	13	64	9	0	4	1.000

DOC CRANDALL—James Otis Crandall—Throws: Right; Bats: Right

Ht: 5'10"; Wt: 180 lbs; Born: 10/8/1887 in Wadena, Indiana; Debut: 4/24/1908; Died: 8/17/1951

World Series	Pitching																											
Year Tm	Age	G	GS	CG	GF	IP	BFP	H	R	ER	HR	SH	SF	HB	TBB	IBB	SO	WP	Bk	W	L	Pct	ShO	Sv-Op	Hld	OAvg	OOBP	ERA
1911 NYG	23	2	0	0	2	4.0	14	2	0	0	0	0	0	0	0	0	2	1	0	1	0	1.000	0	0- 0	0	.143	.143	0.00
1912 NYG	24	1	0	0	1	2.0	7	1	0	0	0	1	0	0	0	0	2	0	0	0	0	—	0	0- 0	0	.167	.167	0.00
1913 NYG	25	2	0	0	1	4.2	17	4	2	2	1	0	0	0	0	0	2	0	0	0	0	—	0	0- 0	0	.235	.235	3.86
WS Totals		5	0	0	4	10.2	76	7	2	2	1	1	0	0	0	0	6	1	0	1	0	1.000	0	0-0	0	.189	.189	1.69

World Series	Batting																								Fielding						
Year Tm	Age	G	AB	H	2B	3B	HR	TB	R	RBI	GW	TBB	IBB	SO	HBP	SH	SF	SB	CS	SB%	GDP	Avg	OBP	SLG	Pos	G	PO	A	E	DP	FPct
1911 NYG	23	3	2	1	1	0	0	2	1	1	0	2	0	0	0	0	0	0	0	—	0	.500	.750	1.000	P	2	0	2	0	0	1.000
1912 NYG	24	1	1	0	0	0	0	0	0	0	0	0	0	1	0	0	0	0	0	—	0	.000	.000	.000	P	1	0	1	0	0	1.000
1913 NYG	25	4	4	0	0	0	0	0	0	0	0	0	0	0	0	0	0	0	0	—	0	.000	.000	.000	P	2	0	2	0	0	1.000
WS Totals		8	7	1	1	0	0	2	1	1	0	2	0	1	0	0	0	0	0	—	0	.143	.333	.286	P	5	0	5	0	0	1.000

GAVY CRAVATH—Clifford Carlton Cravath—Nickname: Cactus—Bats: Right; Throws: Right

Ht: 5'10"; Wt: 186 lbs; Born: 3/23/1881 in Escondido, California; Debut: 4/18/1908; Died: 5/23/1963

World Series	Batting																								Fielding						
Year Tm	Age	G	AB	H	2B	3B	HR	TB	R	RBI	GW	TBB	IBB	SO	HBP	SH	SF	SB	CS	SB%	GDP	Avg	OBP	SLG	Pos	G	PO	A	E	DP	FPct
1915 Phi	34	5	16	2	1	1	0	5	2	1	1	2	0	6	0	1	0	0	0	—	1	.125	.222	.313	OF	5	5	0	0	0	1.000

PAT CRAWFORD—Clifford Rankin Crawford—Bats: Left; Throws: Right

Ht: 5'11"; Wt: 170 lbs; Born: 1/28/1902 in Society Hill, South Carolina; Debut: 4/18/1929; Died: 1/25/1994

World Series	Batting																								Fielding						
Year Tm	Age	G	AB	H	2B	3B	HR	TB	R	RBI	GW	TBB	IBB	SO	HBP	SH	SF	SB	CS	SB%	GDP	Avg	OBP	SLG	Pos	G	PO	A	E	DP	FPct
1934 StL	32	2	2	0	0	0	0	0	0	0	0	0	0	0	0	0	0	0	0	—	0	.000	.000	.000	—						

SAM CRAWFORD (HOF 1957-V)—Samuel Earl Crawford—Nickname: Wahoo Sam—Bats: Left; Throws: Left

Ht: 6'0"; Wt: 190 lbs; Born: 4/18/1880 in Wahoo, Neb.; Deb.: 9/10/1899; Died: 6/15/1968

World Series	Batting																								Fielding						
Year Tm	Age	G	AB	H	2B	3B	HR	TB	R	RBI	GW	TBB	IBB	SO	HBP	SH	SF	SB	CS	SB%	GDP	Avg	OBP	SLG	Pos	G	PO	A	E	DP	FPct
1907 Det	27	5	21	5	1	0	0	6	1	3	0	0	0	3	0	0	0	0	0	—	0	.238	.238	.286	OF	5	6	2	0	1	1.000
1908 Det	28	5	20	4	1	0	0	5	2	1	0	1	0	2	0	1	0	0	0	—	1	.200	.238	.250	OF	5	16	0	0	0	1.000
1909 Det	29	7	28	7	3	0	1	13	4	4	0	1	0	1	0	0	0	1	0	1.00	1	.250	.276	.464	1B	1	0	1	0	0	1.000
																									OF	7	17	0	2	0	.895
WS Totals		17	69	16	5	0	1	24	7	8	0	2	0	6	0	1	0	1	0	1.00	2	.232	.254	.348	OF	17	39	2	2	1	.953

STEVE CRAWFORD—Steven Ray Crawford—Throws: Right; Bats: Right

Ht: 6'5"; Wt: 225 lbs; Born: 4/29/1958 in Pryor, Oklahoma; Debut: 9/2/1980

LCS		Pitching																										
Year Tm	Age	G	GS	CG	GF	IP	BFP	H	R	ER	HR	SH	SF	HB	TBB	IBB	SO	WP	Bk	W	L	Pct	ShO	Sv-Op	Hld	OAvg	OOBP	ERA
1986 Bos	28	1	0	0	0	1.2	8	1	0	0	0	0	0	0	2	1	1	0	0	1	0	1.000	0	0- 0	0	.167	.375	0.00
World Series		Pitching																										
Year Tm	Age	G	GS	CG	GF	IP	BFP	H	R	ER	HR	SH	SF	HB	TBB	IBB	SO	WP	Bk	W	L	Pct	ShO	Sv-Op	Hld	OAvg	OOBP	ERA
1986 Bos	28	3	0	0	1	4.1	18	5	3	3	2	0	0	1	0	0	4	0	0	1	0	1.000	0	0- 0	0	.294	.333	6.23
Postseason Totals		4	0	0	1	6.0	52	6	3	3	2	0	0	1	2	1	5	0	0	2	0	1.000	0	0-0	0	.261	.346	4.50

LCS		Batting																							Fielding						
Year Tm	Age	G	AB	H	2B	3B	HR	TB	R	RBI	GW	TBB	IBB	SO	HBP	SH	SF	SB	CS	SB%	GDP	Avg	OBP	SLG	Pos	G	PO	A	E	DP	FPct
1986 Bos	28	1	0	0	0	0	0	0	0	0	0	0	0	0	0	0	0	0	0	—	0	—	—	—	P	1	1	0	0	0	1.000
World Series		Batting																							Fielding						
Year Tm	Age	G	AB	H	2B	3B	HR	TB	R	RBI	GW	TBB	IBB	SO	HBP	SH	SF	SB	CS	SB%	GDP	Avg	OBP	SLG	Pos	G	PO	A	E	DP	FPct
1986 Bos	28	3	1	0	0	0	0	0	0	0	0	0	0	0	0	0	0	0	0	—	0	.000	.000	.000	P	3	0	0	0	0	—
Postseason Totals		4	1	0	0	0	0	0	0	0	0	0	0	0	0	0	0	0	0	—	0	.000	.000	.000	P	4	1	0	0	0	1.000

WILLIE CRAWFORD—Willie Murphy Crawford—Bats: Left; Throws: Left

Ht: 6'1"; Wt: 197 lbs; Born: 9/7/1946 in Los Angeles, California; Debut: 9/16/1964

LCS		Batting																							Fielding						
Year Tm	Age	G	AB	H	2B	3B	HR	TB	R	RBI	GW	TBB	IBB	SO	HBP	SH	SF	SB	CS	SB%	GDP	Avg	OBP	SLG	Pos	G	PO	A	E	DP	FPct
1974 LA	28	2	4	1	0	0	0	1	1	1	1	1	0	1	0	0	0	0	0	—	0	.250	.400	.250	OF	2	0	0	0	0	—
World Series		Batting																							Fielding						
Year Tm	Age	G	AB	H	2B	3B	HR	TB	R	RBI	GW	TBB	IBB	SO	HBP	SH	SF	SB	CS	SB%	GDP	Avg	OBP	SLG	Pos	G	PO	A	E	DP	FPct
1965 LA	19	2	2	1	0	0	0	1	0	0	0	0	0	1	0	0	0	0	0	—	0	.500	.500	.500	—						
1974 LA	28	3	6	2	0	0	1	5	1	1	0	0	0	0	0	0	0	0	0	—	0	.333	.333	.833	OF	2	1	0	0	0	1.000
WS Totals		5	8	3	0	0	1	6	1	1	0	0	0	1	0	0	0	0	0	—	0	.375	.375	.750	OF	2	1	0	0	0	1.000
Postseason Totals		7	12	4	0	0	1	7	2	2	1	1	0	2	0	0	0	0	0	—	0	.333	.385	.583	OF	4	1	0	0	0	1.000

CREEPY CRESPI—Frank Angelo Joseph Crespi—Bats: Right; Throws: Right

Ht: 5'8"; Wt: 175 lbs; Born: 2/16/1918 in St. Louis, Missouri; Debut: 9/14/1938; Died: 3/1/1990

World Series		Batting																							Fielding						
Year Tm	Age	G	AB	H	2B	3B	HR	TB	R	RBI	GW	TBB	IBB	SO	HBP	SH	SF	SB	CS	SB%	GDP	Avg	OBP	SLG	Pos	G	PO	A	E	DP	FPct
1942 StL	24	1	0	0	0	0	0	0	1	0	0	0	0	0	0	0	0	0	0	—	0	—	—	—	—						

LOU CRIGER—Louis Criger—Bats: Right; Throws: Right

Ht: 5'10"; Wt: 165 lbs; Born: 2/3/1872 in Elkhart, Indiana; Debut: 9/21/1896; Died: 5/14/1934

World Series		Batting																							Fielding						
Year Tm	Age	G	AB	H	2B	3B	HR	TB	R	RBI	GW	TBB	IBB	SO	HBP	SH	SF	SB	CS	SB%	GDP	Avg	OBP	SLG	Pos	G	PO	A	E	DP	FPct
1903 Bos	31	8	26	6	0	0	0	6	1	4	0	2	0	3	0	1	0	0	0	—	1	.231	.286	.231	C	8	54	5	3	0	.952

HUGHIE CRITZ—Hugh Melville Critz—Bats: Right; Throws: Right

Ht: 5'8"; Wt: 147 lbs; Born: 9/17/1900 in Starkville, Mississippi; Debut: 5/31/1924; Died: 1/10/1980

World Series		Batting																							Fielding						
Year Tm	Age	G	AB	H	2B	3B	HR	TB	R	RBI	GW	TBB	IBB	SO	HBP	SH	SF	SB	CS	SB%	GDP	Avg	OBP	SLG	Pos	G	PO	A	E	DP	FPct
1933 NYG	33	5	22	3	0	0	0	3	2	0	0	1	0	0	0	0	0	0	0	—	0	.136	.174	.136	2B	5	16	18	1	2	.971

WARREN CROMARTIE—Warren Livingston Cromartie—Bats: Left; Throws: Left

Ht: 6'0"; Wt: 180 lbs; Born: 9/29/1953 in Miami Beach, Florida; Debut: 9/6/1974

Division Series		Batting																							Fielding						
Year Tm	Age	G	AB	H	2B	3B	HR	TB	R	RBI	GW	TBB	IBB	SO	HBP	SH	SF	SB	CS	SB%	GDP	Avg	OBP	SLG	Pos	G	PO	A	E	DP	FPct
1981 Mon	28	5	22	5	2	0	0	7	1	1	0	0	0	9	0	0	0	0	1	.00	0	.227	.227	.318	1B	5	38	2	1	4	.976
LCS		Batting																							Fielding						
Year Tm	Age	G	AB	H	2B	3B	HR	TB	R	RBI	GW	TBB	IBB	SO	HBP	SH	SF	SB	CS	SB%	GDP	Avg	OBP	SLG	Pos	G	PO	A	E	DP	FPct
1981 Mon	28	5	18	3	1	0	0	4	0	2	1	0	0	2	0	0	0	0	0	—	1	.167	.167	.222	1B	5	48	2	0	6	1.000
Postseason Totals		10	40	8	3	0	0	11	1	3	1	0	0	11	0	0	0	0	1	.00	1	.200	.200	.275	1B	10	86	4	1	10	.989

JOE CRONIN (HOF 1956-W)—Joseph Edward Cronin—Bats: Right; Throws: Right

Ht: 5'11"; Wt: 180 lbs; Born: 10/12/1906 in San Francisco, California; Debut: 4/29/1926; Died: 9/7/1984

World Series		Batting																							Fielding						
Year Tm	Age	G	AB	H	2B	3B	HR	TB	R	RBI	GW	TBB	IBB	SO	HBP	SH	SF	SB	CS	SB%	GDP	Avg	OBP	SLG	Pos	G	PO	A	E	DP	FPct
1933 Was	26	5	22	7	0	0	0	7	1	2	1	0	0	2	0	0	0	0	0	—	1	.318	.318	.318	SS	5	7	15	1	3	.957

ED CROSBY—Edward Carlton Crosby—Bats: Left; Throws: Right

Ht: 6'2"; Wt: 175 lbs; Born: 5/26/1949 in Long Beach, California; Debut: 7/12/1970

LCS		Batting																							Fielding						
Year Tm	Age	G	AB	H	2B	3B	HR	TB	R	RBI	GW	TBB	IBB	SO	HBP	SH	SF	SB	CS	SB%	GDP	Avg	OBP	SLG	Pos	G	PO	A	E	DP	FPct
1973 Cin	24	3	2	1	0	0	0	1	0	0	0	0	0	1	0	0	0	0	0	—	0	.500	.500	.500	SS	2	1	2	0	0	1.000

FRANKIE CROSETTI—Frank Peter Joseph Crosetti—Nickname: Crow—Bats: Right; Throws: Right

Ht: 5'10"; Wt: 165 lbs; Born: 10/4/1910 in San Francisco, California; Debut: 4/12/1932

World Series		Batting																							Fielding						
Year Tm	Age	G	AB	H	2B	3B	HR	TB	R	RBI	GW	TBB	IBB	SO	HBP	SH	SF	SB	CS	SB%	GDP	Avg	OBP	SLG	Pos	G	PO	A	E	DP	FPct
1932 NYA	21	4	15	2	1	0	0	3	2	0	0	2	1	3	0	1	0	0	0	—	1	.133	.235	.200	SS	4	9	13	4	0	.846
1936 NYA	25	6	26	7	2	0	0	9	5	3	1	3	0	5	0	0	0	0	0	—	0	.269	.345	.346	SS	6	13	14	2	2	.931
1937 NYA	26	5	21	1	0	0	0	1	2	0	0	3	0	2	0	0	0	0	0	—	1	.048	.167	.048	SS	5	6	18	0	1	1.000
1938 NYA	27	4	16	4	2	1	1	11	1	6	1	2	0	4	1	0	0	0	1	.00	0	.250	.368	.688	SS	4	16	11	1	4	.964
1939 NYA	28	4	16	1	0	0	0	1	2	1	1	2	0	2	0	0	0	0	0	—	0	.063	.167	.063	SS	4	6	13	0	3	1.000
1942 NYA	31	1	3	0	0	0	0	0	0	0	0	0	0	1	0	0	0	0	0	—	0	.000	.000	.000	3B	1	1	1	0	0	1.000
1943 NYA	32	5	18	5	0	0	0	5	4	1	1	2	1	3	0	1	0	1	0	1.00	0	.278	.350	.278	SS	5	9	16	3	3	.893
WS Totals		29	115	20	5	1	1	30	16	11	4	14	2	20	1	2	0	1	1	.50	2	.174	.269	.261	SS	28	59	85	10	13	.935

LAVE CROSS—Lafayette Napoleon Cross—Bats: Right; Throws: Right

Ht: 5'8"; Wt: 155 lbs; Born: 5/12/1866 in Milwaukee, Wisconsin; Debut: 4/23/1887; Died: 9/6/1927

World Series		Batting																							Fielding						
Year Tm	Age	G	AB	H	2B	3B	HR	TB	R	RBI	GW	TBB	IBB	SO	HBP	SH	SF	SB	CS	SB%	GDP	Avg	OBP	SLG	Pos	G	PO	A	E	DP	FPct
1905 Phi	39	5	19	2	0	0	0	2	0	0	0	1	0	1	0	0	0	0	0	—	0	.105	.150	.105	3B	5	5	6	1	0	.917

MONTE CROSS—Montford Montgomery Cross—Bats: Right; Throws: Right

Ht: 5'9"; Wt: 148 lbs; Born: 8/31/1869 in Philadelphia, Pennsylvania; Debut: 9/27/1892; Died: 6/21/1934

World Series		Batting																							Fielding						
Year Tm	Age	G	AB	H	2B	3B	HR	TB	R	RBI	GW	TBB	IBB	SO	HBP	SH	SF	SB	CS	SB%	GDP	Avg	OBP	SLG	Pos	G	PO	A	E	DP	FPct
1905 Phi	36	5	17	3	0	0	0	3	0	0	0	0	0	7	0	0	0	0	1	.00	0	.176	.176	.176	SS	5	13	12	2	0	.926

FRANK CROUCHER—Frank Donald Croucher—Nickname: Dingle—Bats: Right; Throws: Right

Ht: 5'11"; Wt: 165 lbs; Born: 7/23/1914 in San Antonio, Texas; Debut: 4/18/1939; Died: 5/21/1980

World Series		Batting																							Fielding						
Year Tm	Age	G	AB	H	2B	3B	HR	TB	R	RBI	GW	TBB	IBB	SO	HBP	SH	SF	SB	CS	SB%	GDP	Avg	OBP	SLG	Pos	G	PO	A	E	DP	FPct
1940 Det	26	1	0	0	0	0	0	0	0	0	0	0	0	0	0	0	0	0	0	—	0	—	—	—	SS	1	0	0	0	0	—

GENERAL CROWDER—Alvin Floyd Crowder—Throws: Right; Bats: Left

Ht: 5'10"; Wt: 170 lbs; Born: 1/11/1899 in Winston-Salem, North Carolina; Debut: 7/24/1926; Died: 4/3/1972

World Series		Pitching																										
Year Tm	Age	G	GS	CG	GF	IP	BFP	H	R	ER	HR	SH	SF	HB	TBB	IBB	SO	WP	Bk	W	L	Pct	ShO	Sv-Op	Hld	OAvg	OOBP	ERA
1933 Was	34	2	2	0	0	11.0	53	16	9	9	0	3	0	0	5	1	7	1	0	0	1	.000	0	0- 0	0	.356	.420	7.36
1934 Det	35	2	1	0	1	6.0	29	6	4	1	1	0	0	0	1	0	2	0	0	0	1	.000	0	0- 0	0	.214	.241	1.50
1935 Det	36	1	1	1	0	9.0	34	5	1	1	1	0	0	0	3	0	5	0	0	1	0	1.000	0	0- 0	0	.161	.235	1.00
WS Totals		5	4	1	1	26.0	232	27	14	11	2	3	0	0	9	1	14	1	0	1	2	.333	0	0-0	0	.260	.319	3.81

World Series		Batting																							Fielding						
Year Tm	Age	G	AB	H	2B	3B	HR	TB	R	RBI	GW	TBB	IBB	SO	HBP	SH	SF	SB	CS	SB%	GDP	Avg	OBP	SLG	Pos	G	PO	A	E	DP	FPct
1933 Was	34	2	4	1	0	0	0	1	0	0	0	0	0	0	0	0	0	0	0	—	0	.250	.250	.250	P	2	0	3	0	0	1.000
1934 Det	35	2	1	0	0	0	0	0	0	0	0	0	0	0	0	0	0	0	0	—	0	.000	.000	.000	P	2	0	0	0	0	—
1935 Det	36	1	3	1	0	0	0	1	1	0	0	1	0	0	0	0	0	0	0	—	0	.333	.500	.333	P	1	2	1	0	0	1.000
WS Totals		5	8	2	0	0	0	2	1	0	0	1	0	0	0	0	0	0	0	—	0	.250	.333	.250	P	5	2	4	0	0	1.000

TERRY CROWLEY—Terrence Michael Crowley—Bats: Left; Throws: Left

Ht: 6'0"; Wt: 180 lbs; Born: 2/16/1947 in Staten Island, New York; Debut: 9/4/1969

LCS		Batting																							Fielding						
Year Tm	Age	G	AB	H	2B	3B	HR	TB	R	RBI	GW	TBB	IBB	SO	HBP	SH	SF	SB	CS	SB%	GDP	Avg	OBP	SLG	Pos	G	PO	A	E	DP	FPct
1973 Bal	26	2	2	0	0	0	0	0	0	0	0	0	0	0	0	0	0	0	0	—	0	.000	.000	.000	OF	1	1	0	0	0	1.000
1975 Cin	28	1	0	0	0	0	0	0	0	0	0	0	0	0	0	0	0	0	0	—	0	—	—	—	—						
1979 Bal	32	2	2	1	0	0	0	1	0	1	0	0	0	0	0	0	0	0	0	—	0	.500	.500	.500	—						
LCS Totals		5	4	1	0	0	0	1	0	1	0	0	0	0	0	0	0	0	0	—	0	.250	.250	.250	OF	1	1	0	0	0	1.000
World Series		Batting																							Fielding						
Year Tm	Age	G	AB	H	2B	3B	HR	TB	R	RBI	GW	TBB	IBB	SO	HBP	SH	SF	SB	CS	SB%	GDP	Avg	OBP	SLG	Pos	G	PO	A	E	DP	FPct
1970 Bal	23	1	1	0	0	0	0	0	0	0	0	0	0	0	0	0	0	0	0	—	0	.000	.000	.000	—						
1975 Cin	28	2	2	1	0	0	0	1	0	0	0	0	0	1	0	0	0	0	0	—	0	.500	.500	.500	—						
1979 Bal	32	5	4	1	1	0	0	2	0	2	1	1	0	0	0	0	0	0	0	—	0	.250	.400	.500	—						
WS Totals		8	7	2	1	0	0	3	0	2	1	1	0	1	0	0	0	0	0	—	0	.286	.375	.429	—	0	0	0	0	0	—
Postseason Totals		13	11	3	1	0	0	4	0	3	1	1	0	1	0	0	0	0	0	—	0	.273	.333	.364	OF	1	1	0	0	0	1.000

HEITY CRUZ—Hector Louis Cruz—Bats: Right; Throws: Right

Ht: 5'11"; Wt: 170 lbs; Born: 4/2/1953 in Arroyo, Puerto Rico; Debut: 8/11/1973

LCS		Batting																							Fielding						
Year Tm	Age	G	AB	H	2B	3B	HR	TB	R	RBI	GW	TBB	IBB	SO	HBP	SH	SF	SB	CS	SB%	GDP	Avg	OBP	SLG	Pos	G	PO	A	E	DP	FPct
1979 Cin	26	2	5	1	1	0	0	2	1	0	0	0	0	1	0	0	0	0	0	—	0	.200	.200	.400	OF	1	2	0	0	0	1.000

JOSE CRUZ—Bats: Left; Throws: Left

Ht: 6'0"; Wt: 170 lbs; Born: 8/8/1947 in Arroyo, Puerto Rico; Debut: 9/19/1970

Division Series		Batting																							Fielding						
Year Tm	Age	G	AB	H	2B	3B	HR	TB	R	RBI	GW	TBB	IBB	SO	HBP	SH	SF	SB	CS	SB%	GDP	Avg	OBP	SLG	Pos	G	PO	A	E	DP	FPct
1981 Hou	34	5	20	6	1	0	0	7	0	0	0	1	0	3	0	0	0	1	0	1.00	0	.300	.333	.350	OF	5	16	0	1	0	.941
LCS		Batting																							Fielding						
Year Tm	Age	G	AB	H	2B	3B	HR	TB	R	RBI	GW	TBB	IBB	SO	HBP	SH	SF	SB	CS	SB%	GDP	Avg	OBP	SLG	Pos	G	PO	A	E	DP	FPct
1980 Hou	33	5	15	6	1	1	0	9	3	4	1	8	4	1	0	0	0	0	0	—	1	.400	.609	.600	OF	5	19	0	0	0	1.000
1986 Hou	39	6	26	5	0	0	0	5	0	2	0	1	0	8	0	0	0	0	0	—	0	.192	.222	.192	OF	6	10	0	0	0	1.000
LCS Totals		11	41	11	1	1	0	14	3	6	1	9	4	9	0	0	0	0	0	—	1	.268	.400	.341	OF	11	29	0	0	0	1.000
Postseason Totals		16	61	17	2	1	0	21	3	6	1	10	4	12	0	0	0	1	0	1.00	1	.279	.380	.344	OF	16	45	0	1	0	.978

JULIO CRUZ—Julio Louis Cruz—Nickname: Juice—Bats: Both; Throws: Right

Ht: 5'9"; Wt: 165 lbs; Born: 12/2/1954 in Brooklyn, New York; Debut: 7/4/1977

LCS		Batting																							Fielding						
Year Tm	Age	G	AB	H	2B	3B	HR	TB	R	RBI	GW	TBB	IBB	SO	HBP	SH	SF	SB	CS	SB%	GDP	Avg	OBP	SLG	Pos	G	PO	A	E	DP	FPct
1983 ChA	28	4	12	4	0	0	0	4	0	0	0	3	0	4	0	0	0	2	0	1.00	0	.333	.467	.333	2B	4	10	14	0	3	1.000

TODD CRUZ—Todd Ruben Cruz—Bats: Right; Throws: Right

Ht: 6'0"; Wt: 175 lbs; Born: 11/23/1955 in Highland Park, Michigan; Debut: 9/4/1978

LCS		Batting																							Fielding						
Year Tm	Age	G	AB	H	2B	3B	HR	TB	R	RBI	GW	TBB	IBB	SO	HBP	SH	SF	SB	CS	SB%	GDP	Avg	OBP	SLG	Pos	G	PO	A	E	DP	FPct
1983 Bal	27	4	15	2	0	0	0	2	0	1	0	0	0	5	0	0	0	0	0	—	0	.133	.133	.133	3B	4	6	13	0	1	1.000
World Series		Batting																							Fielding						
Year Tm	Age	G	AB	H	2B	3B	HR	TB	R	RBI	GW	TBB	IBB	SO	HBP	SH	SF	SB	CS	SB%	GDP	Avg	OBP	SLG	Pos	G	PO	A	E	DP	FPct
1983 Bal	27	5	16	2	0	0	0	2	1	0	0	1	0	3	0	0	0	0	0	—	0	.125	.176	.125	3B	5	1	18	2	1	.905
Postseason Totals		9	31	4	0	0	0	4	1	1	0	1	0	8	0	0	0	0	0	—	0	.129	.156	.129	3B	9	7	31	2	2	.950

MIKE CUELLAR—Miguel Angel Cuellar—Nickname: Crazy Horse—Throws: Left; Bats: Left

Ht: 6'0"; Wt: 165 lbs; Born: 5/8/1937 in Las Villas, Cuba; Debut: 4/18/1959

LCS		Pitching																									
Year Tm	Age	G	GS	CG	GF	IP	BFP	H	R	ER	HR	SH	SF	HB	TBB	IBB	SO	WP	Bk	W	L	Pct	ShO	Sv-Op	Hld	OAvg	OOBP	ERA
1969 Bal-*C*	32	1	1	0	0	8.0	27	3	3	2	1	0	1	0	1	0	7	0	0	0	0	—	0	0- 0	0	.120	.148	2.25
1970 Bal	33	1	1	0	0	4.1	25	10	6	6	1	1	0	0	1	0	2	0	0	0	0	—	0	0- 0	0	.435	.458	12.46
1971 Bal	34	1	1	1	0	9.0	33	6	1	1	0	1	0	0	1	0	2	0	0	1	0	1.000	0	0- 0	0	.194	.219	1.00
1973 Bal	36	1	1	1	0	10.0	37	4	2	2	1	1	0	0	3	0	11	0	0	0	1	.000	0	0- 0	0	.121	.194	1.80
1974 Bal	37	2	2	0	0	12.2	60	9	4	4	0	0	0	0	13	1	6	1	0	1	1	.500	0	0- 0	0	.191	.367	2.84
LCS Totals		6	6	2	0	44.0	364	32	16	15	3	3	1	0	19	1	28	1	0	2	2	.500	0	0-0	0	.201	.285	3.07
World Series		Pitching																									
Year Tm	Age	G	GS	CG	GF	IP	BFP	H	R	ER	HR	SH	SF	HB	TBB	IBB	SO	WP	Bk	W	L	Pct	ShO	Sv-Op	Hld	OAvg	OOBP	ERA
1969 Bal-*C*	32	2	2	1	0	16.0	61	13	2	2	1	0	1	0	4	0	13	0	0	1	0	1.000	0	0- 0	0	.232	.279	1.13
1970 Bal	33	2	2	1	0	11.1	46	10	7	4	1	0	0	0	2	0	5	0	0	1	0	1.000	0	0- 0	0	.227	.261	3.18
1971 Bal	34	2	2	0	0	14.0	60	11	7	6	2	0	0	0	6	1	10	0	0	0	2	.000	0	0- 0	0	.204	.283	3.86
WS Totals		6	6	2	0	41.1	334	34	16	12	4	0	1	0	12	1	28	0	0	2	2	.500	0	0-0	0	.221	.275	2.61
Postseason Totals		12	12	4	0	85.1	698	66	32	27	7	3	2	0	31	2	56	1	0	4	4	.500	0	0-0	0	.211	.280	2.85

LCS		Batting																							Fielding						
Year Tm	Age	G	AB	H	2B	3B	HR	TB	R	RBI	GW	TBB	IBB	SO	HBP	SH	SF	SB	CS	SB%	GDP	Avg	OBP	SLG	Pos	G	PO	A	E	DP	FPct
1969 Bal	32	1	2	0	0	0	0	0	0	0	0	0	0	1	0	0	0	0	0	—	0	.000	.000	.000	P	1	0	0	0	0	—
1970 Bal	33	1	2	1	0	0	1	4	1	4	0	0	0	1	0	0	0	0	0	—	0	.500	.500	2.000	P	1	1	3	0	0	1.000
1971 Bal	34	1	3	1	0	0	0	1	0	0	0	0	0	2	0	0	0	0	0	—	0	.333	.333	.333	P	1	0	2	0	0	1.000
1973 Bal	36	1	0	0	0	0	0	0	0	0	0	0	0	0	0	0	0	0	0	—	0	—	—	—	P	1	0	2	0	0	1.000
1974 Bal	37	2	0	0	0	0	0	0	0	0	0	0	0	0	0	0	0	0	0	—	0	—	—	—	P	2	0	5	0	0	1.000
LCS Totals		6	7	2	0	0	1	5	1	4	0	0	0	4	0	0	0	0	0	—	0	.286	.286	.714	P	6	1	12	0	0	1.000
World Series		Batting																							Fielding						
Year Tm	Age	G	AB	H	2B	3B	HR	TB	R	RBI	GW	TBB	IBB	SO	HBP	SH	SF	SB	CS	SB%	GDP	Avg	OBP	SLG	Pos	G	PO	A	E	DP	FPct
1969 Bal	32	2	5	2	0	0	0	2	0	1	0	0	0	3	0	0	0	0	0	—	0	.400	.400	.400	P	2	0	1	0	0	1.000
1970 Bal	33	2	4	0	0	0	0	0	0	0	0	0	0	2	0	1	0	0	0	—	0	.000	.000	.000	P	2	0	1	0	1	1.000
1971 Bal	34	2	3	0	0	0	0	0	0	0	0	1	0	2	0	0	0	0	0	—	0	.000	.250	.000	P	2	0	3	1	0	.750
WS Totals		6	12	2	0	0	0	2	0	1	0	1	0	7	0	1	0	0	0	—	0	.167	.231	.167	P	6	0	5	1	1	.833
Postseason Totals		12	19	4	0	0	1	7	1	5	0	1	0	11	0	1	0	0	0	—	0	.211	.250	.368	P	12	1	17	1	1	.947

LEON CULBERSON—Delbert Leon Culberson—Nickname: Lee—Bats: Right; Throws: Right

Ht: 5'11"; Wt: 180 lbs; Born: 8/6/1919 in Hall's Station, Georgia; Debut: 5/16/1943; Died: 9/17/1989

World Series		Batting																							Fielding						
Year Tm	Age	G	AB	H	2B	3B	HR	TB	R	RBI	GW	TBB	IBB	SO	HBP	SH	SF	SB	CS	SB%	GDP	Avg	OBP	SLG	Pos	G	PO	A	E	DP	FPct
1946 Bos	27	5	9	2	0	0	1	5	1	1	0	1	1	2	0	0	0	1	0	1.00	0	.222	.300	.556	OF	3	7	0	0	0	1.000

TIM CULLEN—Timothy Leo Cullen—Bats: Right; Throws: Right

Ht: 6'1"; Wt: 185 lbs; Born: 2/16/1942 in San Francisco, California; Debut: 8/8/1966

LCS		Batting																							Fielding						
Year Tm	Age	G	AB	H	2B	3B	HR	TB	R	RBI	GW	TBB	IBB	SO	HBP	SH	SF	SB	CS	SB%	GDP	Avg	OBP	SLG	Pos	G	PO	A	E	DP	FPct
1972 Oak	30	2	1	0	0	0	0	0	0	0	0	0	0	0	0	0	0	0	0	—	0	.000	.000	.000	SS	2	0	2	0	1	1.000

ROY CULLENBINE—Roy Joseph Cullenbine—Bats: Both; Throws: Right

Ht: 6'1"; Wt: 190 lbs; Born: 10/18/1913 in Nashville, Tennessee; Debut: 4/19/1938; Died: 5/28/1991

World Series		Batting																							Fielding						
Year Tm	Age	G	AB	H	2B	3B	HR	TB	R	RBI	GW	TBB	IBB	SO	HBP	SH	SF	SB	CS	SB%	GDP	Avg	OBP	SLG	Pos	G	PO	A	E	DP	FPct
1942 NYA	28	5	19	5	1	0	0	6	3	2	0	1	0	2	0	1	0	1	0	1.00	0	.263	.300	.316	OF	5	6	0	0	0	1.000
1945 Det	31	7	22	5	2	0	0	7	5	4	0	8	1	2	0	1	0	1	0	1.00	0	.227	.433	.318	OF	7	8	0	0	0	1.000
WS Totals		12	41	10	3	0	0	13	8	6	0	9	1	4	0	2	0	2	0	1.00	0	.244	.380	.317	OF	12	14	0	0	0	1.000

JOHN CUMBERLAND—John Sheldon Cumberland—Throws: Left; Bats: Right

Ht: 6'0"; Wt: 185 lbs; Born: 5/10/1947 in Westbrook, Maine; Debut: 9/27/1968

LCS — Pitching

Year Tm	Age	G	GS	CG	GF	IP	BFP	H	R	ER	HR	SH	SF	HB	TBB	IBB	SO	WP	Bk	W	L	Pct	ShO	Sv-Op	Hld	OAvg	OOBP	ERA
1971 SF	24	1	1	0	0	3.0	15	7	3	3	1	0	0	0	0	0	4	0	0	0	1	.000	0	0-0	0	.467	.467	9.00

LCS — Batting / Fielding

Year Tm	Age	G	AB	H	2B	3B	HR	TB	R	RBI	GW	TBB	IBB	SO	HBP	SH	SF	SB	CS	SB%	GDP	Avg	OBP	SLG	Pos	G	PO	A	E	DP	FPct
1971 SF	24	1	0	0	0	0	0	0	0	0	0	0	0	0	0	1	0	0	0	—	0	—	—	—	P	1	0	0	0	0	—

JOHN CUMMINGS—John Russell Cummings—Throws: Left; Bats: Left

Ht: 6'3"; Wt: 200 lbs; Born: 5/10/1969 in Torrance, California; Debut: 4/10/1993

Division Series — Pitching

Year Tm	Age	G	GS	CG	GF	IP	BFP	H	R	ER	HR	SH	SF	HB	TBB	IBB	SO	WP	Bk	W	L	Pct	ShO	Sv-Op	Hld	OAvg	OOBP	ERA
1995 LA	26	2	0	0	0	1.1	9	3	3	3	0	0	0	0	2	1	3	0	0	0	0	—	0	0-0	0	.429	.556	20.25

Division Series — Batting / Fielding

Year Tm	Age	G	AB	H	2B	3B	HR	TB	R	RBI	GW	TBB	IBB	SO	HBP	SH	SF	SB	CS	SB%	GDP	Avg	OBP	SLG	Pos	G	PO	A	E	DP	FPct
1995 LA	26	2	0	0	0	0	0	0	0	0	0	0	0	0	0	0	0	0	0	—	0	—	—	—	P	2	0	0	0	0	—

BILL CUNNINGHAM—William Aloysius Cunningham—Bats: Right; Throws: Right

Ht: 5'8"; Wt: 155 lbs; Born: 7/30/1895 in San Francisco, California; Debut: 7/14/1921; Died: 9/26/1953

World Series — Batting / Fielding

Year Tm	Age	G	AB	H	2B	3B	HR	TB	R	RBI	GW	TBB	IBB	SO	HBP	SH	SF	SB	CS	SB%	GDP	Avg	OBP	SLG	Pos	G	PO	A	E	DP	FPct
1922 NYG	27	4	10	2	0	0	0	2	0	2	0	2	0	1	0	0	0	0	0	—	1	.200	.333	.200	OF	4	10	2	0	0	1.000
1923 NYG	28	4	7	1	0	0	0	1	0	1	0	0	0	1	0	0	0	0	0	—	1	.143	.143	.143	OF	3	2	0	1	0	.667
WS Totals		8	17	3	0	0	0	3	0	3	0	2	0	2	0	0	0	0	0	—	2	.176	.263	.176	OF	7	12	2	1	0	.933

CHAD CURTIS—Chad David Curtis—Bats: Right; Throws: Right

Ht: 5'10"; Wt: 180 lbs; Born: 11/6/1968 in Marion, Indiana; Debut: 4/8/1992

Division Series — Batting / Fielding

Year Tm	Age	G	AB	H	2B	3B	HR	TB	R	RBI	GW	TBB	IBB	SO	HBP	SH	SF	SB	CS	SB%	GDP	Avg	OBP	SLG	Pos	G	PO	A	E	DP	FPct
1996 LA	27	1	2	0	0	0	0	0	0	0	0	1	0	1	0	0	0	0	0	—	0	.000	.333	.000	OF	1	2	0	0	0	1.000
1997 NYA	28	4	6	1	0	0	0	1	0	0	0	3	0	1	0	0	0	0	0	—	0	.167	.444	.167	OF	4	4	0	0	0	1.000
DS Totals		5	8	1	0	0	0	1	0	0	0	4	0	2	0	0	0	0	0	—	0	.125	.417	.125	OF	5	6	0	0	0	1.000

GEORGE CUTSHAW—George William Cutshaw—Nicknames: Clancy, Cutty—Bats: Right; Throws: Right

Ht: 5'9"; Wt: 160 lbs; Born: 7/27/1887 in Wilmington, Illinois; Debut: 4/25/1912; Died: 8/22/1973

World Series — Batting / Fielding

Year Tm	Age	G	AB	H	2B	3B	HR	TB	R	RBI	GW	TBB	IBB	SO	HBP	SH	SF	SB	CS	SB%	GDP	Avg	OBP	SLG	Pos	G	PO	A	E	DP	FPct
1916 Bro	29	5	19	2	1	0	0	3	2	2	1	1	0	1	1	0	0	0	0	—	1	.105	.190	.158	2B	5	18	12	2	1	.938

KIKI CUYLER (HOF 1968-V)—Hazen Shirley Cuyler—Bats: Right; Throws: Right

Ht: 5'10"; Wt: 180 lbs; Born: 8/30/1898 in Harrisville, Michigan; Debut: 9/29/1921; Died: 2/11/1950

World Series — Batting / Fielding

Year Tm	Age	G	AB	H	2B	3B	HR	TB	R	RBI	GW	TBB	IBB	SO	HBP	SH	SF	SB	CS	SB%	GDP	Avg	OBP	SLG	Pos	G	PO	A	E	DP	FPct
1925 Pit	27	7	26	7	3	0	1	13	3	6	3	1	0	4	1	3	0	0	2	.00	0	.269	.321	.500	OF	7	12	0	1	0	.923
1929 ChN	31	5	20	6	1	0	0	7	4	4	1	1	0	7	0	0	0	0	1	.00	0	.300	.333	.350	OF	5	8	0	1	0	.889
1932 ChN	34	4	18	5	1	1	1	11	2	2	0	0	0	3	0	0	0	1	0	1.00	0	.278	.278	.611	OF	4	5	0	0	0	1.000
WS Totals		16	64	18	5	1	2	31	9	12	4	2	0	14	1	3	0	1	3	.25	0	.281	.313	.484	OF	16	25	0	2	0	.926

MIKE CVENGROS—Michael John Cvengros—Throws: Left; Bats: Left

Ht: 5'8"; Wt: 159 lbs; Born: 12/1/1901 in Pana, Illinois; Debut: 9/30/1922; Died: 8/2/1970

World Series — Pitching

Year Tm	Age	G	GS	CG	GF	IP	BFP	H	R	ER	HR	SH	SF	HB	TBB	IBB	SO	WP	Bk	W	L	Pct	ShO	Sv-Op	Hld	OAvg	OOBP	ERA
1927 Pit	25	2	0	0	1	2.1	11	3	1	1	1	0	0	1	0	0	2	0	0	0	0	—	0	0-0	0	.300	.364	3.86

World Series — Batting / Fielding

Year Tm	Age	G	AB	H	2B	3B	HR	TB	R	RBI	GW	TBB	IBB	SO	HBP	SH	SF	SB	CS	SB%	GDP	Avg	OBP	SLG	Pos	G	PO	A	E	DP	FPct
1927 Pit	25	2	0	0	0	0	0	0	0	0	0	0	0	0	0	0	0	0	0	—	0	—	—	—	P	2	0	0	0	0	—

BILL DAHLEN—William Frederick Dahlen—Nickname: Bad Bill—Bats: Right; Throws: Right

Ht: 5'9"; Wt: 180 lbs; Born: 1/5/1870 in Nelliston, New York; Debut: 4/22/1891; Died: 12/5/1950

World Series — Batting / Fielding

Year Tm	Age	G	AB	H	2B	3B	HR	TB	R	RBI	GW	TBB	IBB	SO	HBP	SH	SF	SB	CS	SB%	GDP	Avg	OBP	SLG	Pos	G	PO	A	E	DP	FPct
1905 NYG	35	5	15	0	0	0	0	0	1	1	0	3	0	2	0	0	0	2	1	.67	0	.000	.167	.000	SS	5	10	19	0	3	1.000

BABE DAHLGREN—Ellsworth Tenney Dahlgren—Bats: Right; Throws: Right

Ht: 6'0"; Wt: 190 lbs; Born: 6/15/1912 in San Francisco, California; Debut: 4/16/1935; Died: 9/4/1996

World Series — Batting / Fielding

Year Tm	Age	G	AB	H	2B	3B	HR	TB	R	RBI	GW	TBB	IBB	SO	HBP	SH	SF	SB	CS	SB%	GDP	Avg	OBP	SLG	Pos	G	PO	A	E	DP	FPct
1939 NYA	27	4	14	3	2	0	1	8	2	2	0	0	0	4	0	0	0	0	0	—	0	.214	.214	.571	1B	4	41	2	0	4	1.000

BUD DALEY—Leavitt Leo Daley—Throws: Left; Bats: Left

Ht: 6'1"; Wt: 185 lbs; Born: 10/7/1932 in Orange, California; Debut: 9/10/1955

World Series — Pitching

Year Tm	Age	G	GS	CG	GF	IP	BFP	H	R	ER	HR	SH	SF	HB	TBB	IBB	SO	WP	Bk	W	L	Pct	ShO	Sv-Op	Hld	OAvg	OOBP	ERA
1961 NYA	28	2	0	0	1	7.0	27	5	2	0	1	0	0	1	0	0	3	0	0	1	0	1.000	0	0-0	0	.192	.222	0.00
1962 NYA	29	1	0	0	1	1.0	5	1	0	0	0	0	0	0	1	0	0	0	0	0	0	—	0	0-0	0	.250	.400	0.00
WS Totals		3	0	0	2	8.0	64	6	2	0	1	0	0	1	1	0	3	0	0	1	0	1.000	0	0-0	0	.200	.250	0.00

World Series — Batting / Fielding

Year Tm	Age	G	AB	H	2B	3B	HR	TB	R	RBI	GW	TBB	IBB	SO	HBP	SH	SF	SB	CS	SB%	GDP	Avg	OBP	SLG	Pos	G	PO	A	E	DP	FPct
1961 NYA	28	2	1	0	0	0	0	0	0	1	0	0	0	0	0	1	1	0	0	—	0	.000	.000	.000	P	2	0	0	1	0	.000
1962 NYA	29	1	0	0	0	0	0	0	0	0	0	0	0	0	0	0	0	0	0	—	0	—	—	—	P	1	0	0	0	0	—
WS Totals		3	1	0	0	0	0	0	0	1	0	0	0	0	0	1	1	0	0	—	0	.000	.000	.000	P	3	0	0	1	0	.000

CLAY DALRYMPLE—Clayton Errol Dalrymple—Bats: Left; Throws: Right

Ht: 6'0"; Wt: 190 lbs; Born: 12/3/1936 in Chico, California; Debut: 4/24/1960

World Series — Batting / Fielding

Year Tm	Age	G	AB	H	2B	3B	HR	TB	R	RBI	GW	TBB	IBB	SO	HBP	SH	SF	SB	CS	SB%	GDP	Avg	OBP	SLG	Pos	G	PO	A	E	DP	FPct
1969 Bal	32	2	2	2	0	0	0	2	0	0	0	0	0	0	0	0	0	0	0	—	0	1.000	1.000	1.000	—						

DAVE DANFORTH—David Charles Danforth—Nickname: Dauntless Dave—Throws: Left; Bats: Left

Ht: 6'0"; Wt: 167 lbs; Born: 3/7/1890 in Granger, Texas; Debut: 8/1/1911; Died: 9/19/1970

World Series — Pitching

Year Tm	Age	G	GS	CG	GF	IP	BFP	H	R	ER	HR	SH	SF	HB	TBB	IBB	SO	WP	Bk	W	L	Pct	ShO	Sv-Op	Hld	OAvg	OOBP	ERA
1917 ChA	27	1	0	0	1	1.0	5	3	2	2	1	0	0	0	0	0	2	0	0	0	0	—	0	0-0	0	.600	.600	18.00

World Series — Batting / Fielding

Year Tm	Age	G	AB	H	2B	3B	HR	TB	R	RBI	GW	TBB	IBB	SO	HBP	SH	SF	SB	CS	SB%	GDP	Avg	OBP	SLG	Pos	G	PO	A	E	DP	FPct
1917 ChA	27	1	0	0	0	0	0	0	0	0	0	0	0	0	0	0	0	0	0	—	0	—	—	—	P	1	0	1	0	0	1.000

HARRY DANNING—Nickname: Harry the Horse—Bats: Right; Throws: Right

Ht: 6'1"; Wt: 190 lbs; Born: 9/6/1911 in Los Angeles, California; Debut: 7/30/1933

World Series — Batting / Fielding

Year Tm	Age	G	AB	H	2B	3B	HR	TB	R	RBI	GW	TBB	IBB	SO	HBP	SH	SF	SB	CS	SB%	GDP	Avg	OBP	SLG	Pos	G	PO	A	E	DP	FPct
1936 NYG	25	2	2	0	0	0	0	0	0	0	0	0	0	1	0	0	0	0	0	—	0	.000	.000	.000	C	1	3	0	1	0	.750
1937 NYG	26	3	12	3	1	0	0	4	0	2	0	0	0	2	0	0	0	0	0	—	0	.250	.250	.333	C	3	20	1	0	0	1.000
WS Totals		5	14	3	1	0	0	4	0	2	0	0	0	3	0	0	0	0	0	—	0	.214	.214	.286	C	4	23	1	1	0	.960

PAT DARCY—Patrick Leonard Darcy—Throws: Right; Bats: Left

Ht: 6'3"; Wt: 175 lbs; Born: 5/12/1950 in Troy, Ohio; Debut: 9/12/1974

World Series		Pitching																										
Year Tm	Age	G	GS	CG	GF	IP	BFP	H	R	ER	HR	SH	SF	HB	TBB	IBB	SO	WP	Bk	W	L	Pct	ShO	Sv-Op	Hld	OAvg	OOBP	ERA
1975 Cin	25	2	0	0	1	4.0	17	3	2	2	1	0	1	0	2	0	1	1	0	0	1	.000	0	0- 0	0	.214	.294	4.50

World Series		Batting																							Fielding						
Year Tm	Age	G	AB	H	2B	3B	HR	TB	R	RBI	GW	TBB	IBB	SO	HBP	SH	SF	SB	CS	SB%	GDP	Avg	OBP	SLG	Pos	G	PO	A	E	DP	FPct
1975 Cin	25	2	1	0	0	0	0	0	0	0	0	0	0	1	0	0	0	0	0	—	0	.000	.000	.000	P	2	0	1	0	0	1.000

AL DARK—Alvin Ralph Dark—Nicknames: Blackie, The Swamp Fox—Bats: Right; Throws: Right

Ht: 5'11"; Wt: 185 lbs; Born: 1/7/1922 in Comanche, Oklahoma; Debut: 7/14/1946

World Series		Batting																							Fielding						
Year Tm	Age	G	AB	H	2B	3B	HR	TB	R	RBI	GW	TBB	IBB	SO	HBP	SH	SF	SB	CS	SB%	GDP	Avg	OBP	SLG	Pos	G	PO	A	E	DP	FPct
1948 Bos-*RY*	26	6	24	4	1	0	0	5	2	0	0	0	0	2	0	1	0	0	0	—	1	.167	.167	.208	SS	6	7	12	3	1	.864
1951 NYG	29	6	24	10	3	0	1	16	5	4	0	2	0	3	0	0	0	0	0	—	1	.417	.462	.667	SS	6	10	16	0	4	1.000
1954 NYG	32	4	17	7	0	0	0	7	2	0	0	1	0	1	0	1	0	0	0	—	0	.412	.444	.412	SS	4	7	11	1	1	.947
WS Totals		16	65	21	4	0	1	28	9	4	0	3	0	6	0	2	0	0	0	—	2	.323	.353	.431	SS	16	24	39	4	6	.940

RON DARLING—Ronald Maurice Darling—Throws: Right; Bats: Right

Ht: 6'3"; Wt: 195 lbs; Born: 8/19/1960 in Honolulu, Hawaii; Debut: 9/6/1983

LCS		Pitching																										
Year Tm	Age	G	GS	CG	GF	IP	BFP	H	R	ER	HR	SH	SF	HB	TBB	IBB	SO	WP	Bk	W	L	Pct	ShO	Sv-Op	Hld	OAvg	OOBP	ERA
1986 NYN	26	1	1	0	0	5.0	23	6	4	4	1	0	0	1	2	0	5	1	0	0	0	—	0	0- 0	0	.300	.391	7.20
1988 NYN	28	2	2	0	0	7.0	37	11	9	6	0	0	1	0	4	0	7	0	0	0	1	.000	0	0- 0	0	.344	.405	7.71
1992 Oak	32	1	1	0	0	6.0	22	4	3	2	2	0	0	0	2	0	3	2	0	0	1	.000	0	0- 0	0	.200	.273	3.00
LCS Totals		4	4	0	0	18.0	164	21	16	12	3	0	1	1	8	0	15	3	0	0	2	.000	0	0-0	0	.292	.366	6.00
World Series		Pitching																										
Year Tm	Age	G	GS	CG	GF	IP	BFP	H	R	ER	HR	SH	SF	HB	TBB	IBB	SO	WP	Bk	W	L	Pct	ShO	Sv-Op	Hld	OAvg	OOBP	ERA
1986 NYN	26	3	3	0	0	17.2	75	13	4	3	2	2	0	1	10	1	12	2	0	1	1	.500	0	0- 0	0	.210	.329	1.53
Postseason Totals		7	7	0	0	35.2	314	34	20	15	5	2	1	2	18	1	27	5	0	1	3	.250	0	0-0	0	.254	.348	3.79

LCS		Batting																							Fielding						
Year Tm	Age	G	AB	H	2B	3B	HR	TB	R	RBI	GW	TBB	IBB	SO	HBP	SH	SF	SB	CS	SB%	GDP	Avg	OBP	SLG	Pos	G	PO	A	E	DP	FPct
1986 NYN	26	1	1	0	0	0	0	0	0	0	0	0	0	0	0	0	0	0	0	—	0	.000	.000	.000	P	1	1	2	0	0	1.000
1988 NYN	28	3	3	0	0	0	0	0	0	0	0	0	0	2	0	0	0	0	0	—	0	.000	.000	.000	P	2	1	3	0	0	1.000
1992 Oak	32	1	0	0	0	0	0	0	0	0	0	0	0	0	0	0	0	0	0	—	0	—	—	—	P	1	1	0	0	0	1.000
LCS Totals		5	4	0	0	0	0	0	0	0	0	0	0	2	0	0	0	0	0	—	0	.000	.000	.000	P	4	3	5	0	0	1.000
World Series		Batting																							Fielding						
Year Tm	Age	G	AB	H	2B	3B	HR	TB	R	RBI	GW	TBB	IBB	SO	HBP	SH	SF	SB	CS	SB%	GDP	Avg	OBP	SLG	Pos	G	PO	A	E	DP	FPct
1986 NYN	26	3	3	0	0	0	0	0	0	0	0	0	0	1	0	0	0	0	0	—	0	.000	.000	.000	P	3	0	4	0	0	1.000
Postseason Totals		8	7	0	0	0	0	0	0	0	0	0	0	3	0	0	0	0	0	—	0	.000	.000	.000	P	7	3	9	0	0	1.000

JAKE DAUBERT—Jacob Ellsworth Daubert—Nickname: Gentleman Jake—Bats: Left; Throws: Left

Ht: 5'10"; Wt: 160 lbs; Born: 4/17/1884 in Shamokin, Pennsylvania; Debut: 4/14/1910; Died: 10/9/1924

World Series		Batting																							Fielding						
Year Tm	Age	G	AB	H	2B	3B	HR	TB	R	RBI	GW	TBB	IBB	SO	HBP	SH	SF	SB	CS	SB%	GDP	Avg	OBP	SLG	Pos	G	PO	A	E	DP	FPct
1916 Bro	32	4	17	3	0	1	0	5	1	0	0	2	0	3	0	0	0	0	0	—	0	.176	.263	.294	1B	4	41	2	0	1	1.000
1919 Cin	35	8	29	7	0	1	0	9	4	1	0	1	0	2	1	5	0	1	1	.50	1	.241	.290	.310	1B	8	81	4	2	4	.977
WS Totals		12	46	10	0	2	0	14	5	1	0	3	0	5	1	5	0	1	1	.50	1	.217	.280	.304	1B	12	122	6	2	5	.985

RICH DAUER—Richard Fremont Dauer—Bats: Right; Throws: Right

Ht: 6'0"; Wt: 180 lbs; Born: 7/27/1952 in San Bernardino, California; Debut: 9/11/1976

LCS		Batting																							Fielding						
Year Tm	Age	G	AB	H	2B	3B	HR	TB	R	RBI	GW	TBB	IBB	SO	HBP	SH	SF	SB	CS	SB%	GDP	Avg	OBP	SLG	Pos	G	PO	A	E	DP	FPct
1979 Bal	27	4	11	2	0	0	0	2	0	0	0	0	0	1	0	1	0	0	0	—	0	.182	.182	.182	2B	4	11	12	0	2	1.000
1983 Bal	31	4	14	0	0	0	0	0	0	1	0	0	0	0	0	1	1	0	0	—	0	.000	.000	.000	2B	4	8	12	0	3	1.000
LCS Totals		8	25	2	0	0	0	2	0	1	0	0	0	1	0	2	1	0	0	—	0	.080	.077	.080	2B	8	19	24	0	5	1.000
World Series		Batting																							Fielding						
Year Tm	Age	G	AB	H	2B	3B	HR	TB	R	RBI	GW	TBB	IBB	SO	HBP	SH	SF	SB	CS	SB%	GDP	Avg	OBP	SLG	Pos	G	PO	A	E	DP	FPct
1979 Bal	27	6	17	5	1	0	1	9	2	1	0	0	0	1	0	0	0	0	0	—	1	.294	.294	.529	2B	6	10	10	0	1	1.000
1983 Bal	31	5	19	4	1	0	0	5	2	3	0	0	0	3	0	0	0	0	0	—	0	.211	.211	.263	2B	5	13	7	0	4	1.000
																									3B	1	1	1	0	0	1.000
WS Totals		11	36	9	2	0	1	14	4	4	0	0	0	4	0	0	0	0	0	—	1	.250	.250	.389	2B	11	23	17	0	5	1.000
Postseason Totals		19	61	11	2	0	1	16	4	5	0	0	0	5	0	2	1	0	0	—	1	.180	.177	.262	2B	19	42	41	0	10	1.000

DARREN DAULTON—Darren Arthur Daulton—Nickname: Dutch—Bats: Left; Throws: Right

Ht: 6'2"; Wt: 201 lbs; Born: 1/3/1962 in Arkansas City, Kansas; Debut: 9/25/1983

LCS		Batting																							Fielding						
Year Tm	Age	G	AB	H	2B	3B	HR	TB	R	RBI	GW	TBB	IBB	SO	HBP	SH	SF	SB	CS	SB%	GDP	Avg	OBP	SLG	Pos	G	PO	A	E	DP	FPct
1993 Phi	31	6	19	5	1	0	1	9	2	3	1	6	1	3	0	0	0	0	0	—	0	.263	.440	.474	C	6	54	3	0	0	1.000
1997 Fla	35	3	4	1	1	0	0	2	1	1	0	1	0	2	0	0	0	0	0	—	0	.250	.400	.500	1B	2	8	1	0	2	1.000
LCS Totals		9	23	6	2	0	1	11	3	4	1	7	1	5	0	0	0	0	0	—	0	.261	.433	.478	C	6	54	3	0	0	1.000
World Series		Batting																							Fielding						
Year Tm	Age	G	AB	H	2B	3B	HR	TB	R	RBI	GW	TBB	IBB	SO	HBP	SH	SF	SB	CS	SB%	GDP	Avg	OBP	SLG	Pos	G	PO	A	E	DP	FPct
1993 Phi	31	6	23	5	2	0	1	10	4	4	0	4	1	5	1	0	0	0	0	—	0	.217	.357	.435	C	6	31	4	0	1	1.000
1997 Fla	35	7	18	7	2	0	1	12	7	2	0	3	1	0	0	0	1	1	0	1.00	1	.389	.455	.667	1B	5	28	4	0	3	1.000
WS Totals		13	41	12	4	0	2	22	11	6	0	7	2	5	1	0	1	1	0	1.00	1	.293	.400	.537	C	6	31	4	0	1	1.000
Postseason Totals		22	64	18	6	0	3	33	14	10	1	14	3	10	1	0	1	1	0	1.00	1	.281	.413	.516	C	12	85	7	0	1	1.000

VIC DAVALILLO—Victor Jose Davalillo—Bats: Left; Throws: Left

Ht: 5'7"; Wt: 150 lbs; Born: 7/31/1936 in Cabimas, Venezuela; Debut: 4/9/1963

LCS		Batting																							Fielding						
Year Tm	Age	G	AB	H	2B	3B	HR	TB	R	RBI	GW	TBB	IBB	SO	HBP	SH	SF	SB	CS	SB%	GDP	Avg	OBP	SLG	Pos	G	PO	A	E	DP	FPct
1971 Pit	35	2	2	0	0	0	0	0	0	0	0	0	0	1	0	0	0	0	0	—	0	.000	.000	.000	—						
1972 Pit	36	1	0	0	0	0	0	0	0	0	0	1	1	0	0	0	0	0	0	—	0	—	1.000	—	—						
1973 Oak	37	4	8	5	1	1	0	8	2	1	0	1	1	0	0	0	0	0	0	—	1	.625	.667	1.000	1B	2	3	0	1	0	.750
																									OF	2	4	0	0	0	1.000
1977 LA	41	1	1	1	0	0	0	1	1	0	0	0	0	0	0	0	0	0	0	—	0	1.000	1.000	1.000	—						
LCS Totals		8	11	6	1	1	0	9	3	1	0	2	2	1	0	0	0	0	0	—	1	.545	.615	.818	1B	2	3	0	1	0	.750
World Series		Batting																							Fielding						
Year Tm	Age	G	AB	H	2B	3B	HR	TB	R	RBI	GW	TBB	IBB	SO	HBP	SH	SF	SB	CS	SB%	GDP	Avg	OBP	SLG	Pos	G	PO	A	E	DP	FPct
1971 Pit	35	3	3	1	0	0	0	1	1	0	0	0	0	0	0	0	0	0	0	—	0	.333	.333	.333	OF	2	2	0	0	0	1.000
1973 Oak	37	6	11	1	0	0	0	1	0	0	0	2	0	1	0	0	0	0	0	—	0	.091	.231	.091	1B	1	5	0	0	0	1.000
																									OF	4	12	0	0	0	1.000
1977 LA	41	3	3	1	0	0	0	1	0	1	0	0	0	0	0	0	0	0	0	—	0	.333	.333	.333	—						
1978 LA	42	2	3	1	0	0	0	1	0	0	0	0	0	0	0	1	0	0	0	—	0	.333	.333	.333	—						
WS Totals		14	20	4	0	0	0	4	1	1	0	2	0	1	0	1	0	0	0	—	0	.200	.273	.200	OF	6	14	0	0	0	1.000
Postseason Totals		22	31	10	1	1	0	13	4	2	0	4	2	2	0	1	0	0	0	—	1	.323	.400	.419	OF	8	18	0	0	0	1.000

JIM DAVENPORT—James Houston Davenport—Bats: Right; Throws: Right

Ht: 5'11"; Wt: 170 lbs; Born: 8/17/1933 in Siluria, Alabama; Debut: 4/15/1958

World Series		Batting																							Fielding						
Year Tm	Age	G	AB	H	2B	3B	HR	TB	R	RBI	GW	TBB	IBB	SO	HBP	SH	SF	SB	CS	SB%	GDP	Avg	OBP	SLG	Pos	G	PO	A	E	DP	FPct
1962 SF	29	7	22	3	1	0	0	4	1	1	0	4	0	7	0	0	0	0	0	—	0	.136	.269	.182	3B	7	6	12	3	4	.857

MARK DAVIDSON

John Mark Davidson—Bats: Right; Throws: Right — Ht: 6'2"; Wt: 180 lbs; Born: 2/15/1961 in Knoxville, Tennessee; Debut: 6/20/1986

LCS		Batting																							Fielding						
Year Tm	Age	G	AB	H	2B	3B	HR	TB	R	RBI	GW	TBB	IBB	SO	HBP	SH	SF	SB	CS	SB%	GDP	Avg	OBP	SLG	Pos	G	PO	A	E	DP	FPct
1987 Min	26	1	0	0	0	0	0	0	0	0	0	0	0	0	0	0	0	0	0	—	0	—	—	—	—						
World Series		Batting																							Fielding						
Year Tm	Age	G	AB	H	2B	3B	HR	TB	R	RBI	GW	TBB	IBB	SO	HBP	SH	SF	SB	CS	SB%	GDP	Avg	OBP	SLG	Pos	G	PO	A	E	DP	FPct
1987 Min	26	2	1	0	0	0	0	0	0	0	0	0	0	0	0	0	0	0	0	—	0	.000	.000	.000	OF	1	0	0	0	0	—
Postseason Totals		3	1	0	0	0	0	0	0	0	0	0	0	0	0	0	0	0	0	—	0	.000	.000	.000	OF	1	0	0	0	0	—

CHILI DAVIS

Charles Theodore Davis—Bats: Both; Throws: Right — Ht: 6'3"; Wt: 195 lbs; Born: 1/17/1960 in Kingston, Jamaica; Debut: 4/10/1981

LCS		Batting																							Fielding						
Year Tm	Age	G	AB	H	2B	3B	HR	TB	R	RBI	GW	TBB	IBB	SO	HBP	SH	SF	SB	CS	SB%	GDP	Avg	OBP	SLG	Pos	G	PO	A	E	DP	FPct
1987 SF	27	6	20	3	1	0	0	4	2	0	0	1	0	4	0	0	0	0	0	—	1	.150	.190	.200	OF	6	11	1	1	1	.923
1991 Min	31	5	17	5	2	0	0	7	3	2	1	5	1	8	0	0	0	1	0	1.00	0	.294	.455	.412	—						
LCS Totals		11	37	8	3	0	0	11	5	2	1	6	1	12	0	0	0	1	0	1.00	1	.216	.326	.297	OF	6	11	1	1	1	.923
World Series		Batting																							Fielding						
Year Tm	Age	G	AB	H	2B	3B	HR	TB	R	RBI	GW	TBB	IBB	SO	HBP	SH	SF	SB	CS	SB%	GDP	Avg	OBP	SLG	Pos	G	PO	A	E	DP	FPct
1991 Min	31	6	18	4	0	0	2	10	4	4	0	2	1	3	0	0	0	0	0	—	1	.222	.300	.556	OF	1	1	0	0	0	1.000
Postseason Totals		17	55	12	3	0	2	21	9	6	1	8	2	15	0	0	0	1	0	1.00	2	.218	.317	.382	OF	7	12	1	1	1	.929

CURT DAVIS

Curtis Benton Davis—Nickname: Coonskin—Throws: Right; Bats: Right — Ht: 6'2"; Wt: 185 lbs; Born: 9/7/1903 in Greenfield, Missouri; Debut: 4/21/1934; Died: 10/13/1965

World Series		Pitching																										
Year Tm	Age	G	GS	CG	GF	IP	BFP	H	R	ER	HR	SH	SF	HB	TBB	IBB	SO	WP	Bk	W	L	Pct	ShO	Sv-Op	Hld	OAvg	OOBP	ERA
1941 Bro	38	1	1	0	0	5.1	25	6	3	3	1	0	0	0	3	1	1	0	0	0	1	.000	0	0-0	0	.273	.360	5.06

World Series		Batting																							Fielding						
Year Tm	Age	G	AB	H	2B	3B	HR	TB	R	RBI	GW	TBB	IBB	SO	HBP	SH	SF	SB	CS	SB%	GDP	Avg	OBP	SLG	Pos	G	PO	A	E	DP	FPct
1941 Bro	38	1	2	0	0	0	0	0	0	0	0	0	0	0	0	0	0	0	0	—	0	.000	.000	.000	P	1	1	0	0	0	1.000

DICK DAVIS

Richard Earl Davis—Bats: Right; Throws: Right — Ht: 6'3"; Wt: 190 lbs; Born: 9/25/1953 in Long Beach, California; Debut: 7/12/1977

Division Series		Batting																							Fielding						
Year Tm	Age	G	AB	H	2B	3B	HR	TB	R	RBI	GW	TBB	IBB	SO	HBP	SH	SF	SB	CS	SB%	GDP	Avg	OBP	SLG	Pos	G	PO	A	E	DP	FPct
1981 Phi	28	1	2	0	0	0	0	0	0	0	0	0	0	1	0	0	0	0	0	—	0	.000	.000	.000	OF	1	2	0	0	0	1.000

ERIC DAVIS

Eric Keith Davis—Bats: Right; Throws: Right — Ht: 6'2"; Wt: 165 lbs; Born: 5/29/1962 in Los Angeles, California; Debut: 5/19/1984

Division Series		Batting																							Fielding						
Year Tm	Age	G	AB	H	2B	3B	HR	TB	R	RBI	GW	TBB	IBB	SO	HBP	SH	SF	SB	CS	SB%	GDP	Avg	OBP	SLG	Pos	G	PO	A	E	DP	FPct
1997 Bal	35	3	9	2	0	0	0	2	0	2	0	0	0	5	0	0	0	0	1	.00	0	.222	.222	.222	OF	3	1	0	0	0	1.000
LCS		Batting																							Fielding						
Year Tm	Age	G	AB	H	2B	3B	HR	TB	R	RBI	GW	TBB	IBB	SO	HBP	SH	SF	SB	CS	SB%	GDP	Avg	OBP	SLG	Pos	G	PO	A	E	DP	FPct
1990 Cin	28	6	23	4	1	0	0	5	2	1	0	1	0	9	0	0	0	0	1	.00	0	.174	.208	.217	OF	6	12	1	0	0	1.000
1997 Bal	35	6	13	2	0	0	1	5	1	1	0	1	1	3	0	0	0	0	0	—	0	.154	.214	.385	OF	3	3	0	0	0	1.000
LCS Totals		12	36	6	1	0	1	10	3	2	0	2	1	12	0	0	0	0	1	.00	0	.167	.211	.278	OF	9	15	1	0	0	1.000
World Series		Batting																							Fielding						
Year Tm	Age	G	AB	H	2B	3B	HR	TB	R	RBI	GW	TBB	IBB	SO	HBP	SH	SF	SB	CS	SB%	GDP	Avg	OBP	SLG	Pos	G	PO	A	E	DP	FPct
1990 Cin	28	4	14	4	0	0	1	7	3	5	1	0	0	0	0	0	0	0	0	—	0	.286	.286	.500	OF	4	4	0	0	0	1.000
Postseason Totals		19	59	12	1	0	2	19	6	9	1	2	1	17	0	0	0	0	2	.00	0	.203	.230	.322	OF	16	20	1	0	0	1.000

GEORGE DAVIS

(HOF 1998-V)—George Stacey Davis—Bats: Both; Throws: Right — Ht: 5'9"; Wt: 180 lbs; Born: 8/23/1870 in Cohoes, New York; Debut: 4/19/1890; Died: 10/17/1940

World Series		Batting																							Fielding						
Year Tm	Age	G	AB	H	2B	3B	HR	TB	R	RBI	GW	TBB	IBB	SO	HBP	SH	SF	SB	CS	SB%	GDP	Avg	OBP	SLG	Pos	G	PO	A	E	DP	FPct
1906 ChA	36	3	13	4	3	0	0	7	4	6	0	0	0	1	0	0	0	1	1	.50	0	.308	.308	.538	SS	3	7	15	2	1	.917

GLENN DAVIS

Glenn Earle Davis—Bats: Right; Throws: Right — Ht: 6'3"; Wt: 205 lbs; Born: 3/28/1961 in Jacksonville, Florida; Debut: 9/2/1984

LCS		Batting																							Fielding						
Year Tm	Age	G	AB	H	2B	3B	HR	TB	R	RBI	GW	TBB	IBB	SO	HBP	SH	SF	SB	CS	SB%	GDP	Avg	OBP	SLG	Pos	G	PO	A	E	DP	FPct
1986 Hou	25	6	26	7	1	0	1	11	3	3	1	1	0	3	1	0	0	0	0	—	0	.269	.321	.423	1B	6	62	3	1	3	.985

HARRY DAVIS

Harry H Davis—Nickname: Jasper—Bats: Right; Throws: Right — Ht: 5'10"; Wt: 180 lbs; Born: 7/19/1873 in Philadelphia, Pennsylvania; Debut: 9/21/1895; Died: 8/11/1947

World Series		Batting																							Fielding						
Year Tm	Age	G	AB	H	2B	3B	HR	TB	R	RBI	GW	TBB	IBB	SO	HBP	SH	SF	SB	CS	SB%	GDP	Avg	OBP	SLG	Pos	G	PO	A	E	DP	FPct
1905 Phi	32	5	20	4	1	0	0	5	0	0	0	0	0	1	0	0	0	0	0	—	0	.200	.200	.250	1B	5	52	1	0	2	1.000
1910 Phi	37	5	17	6	3	0	0	9	5	2	0	3	0	4	1	2	0	0	0	—	0	.353	.476	.529	1B	5	44	2	3	6	.939
1911 Phi	38	6	24	5	1	0	0	6	3	5	1	0	0	3	0	0	0	0	1	.00	0	.208	.208	.250	1B	6	54	3	0	1	1.000
WS Totals		16	61	15	5	0	0	20	8	7	1	3	0	8	1	2	0	0	1	.00	0	.246	.292	.328	1B	16	150	6	3	9	.981

JODY DAVIS

Jody Richard Davis—Bats: Right; Throws: Right — Ht: 6'4"; Wt: 192 lbs; Born: 11/12/1956 in Gainesville, Georgia; Debut: 4/21/1981

LCS		Batting																							Fielding						
Year Tm	Age	G	AB	H	2B	3B	HR	TB	R	RBI	GW	TBB	IBB	SO	HBP	SH	SF	SB	CS	SB%	GDP	Avg	OBP	SLG	Pos	G	PO	A	E	DP	FPct
1984 ChN	27	5	18	7	2	0	2	15	3	6	0	0	0	3	0	0	1	0	0	—	0	.389	.368	.833	C	5	24	1	0	0	1.000

KIDDO DAVIS

George Willis Davis—Bats: Right; Throws: Right — Ht: 5'11"; Wt: 178 lbs; Born: 2/12/1902 in Bridgeport, Connecticut; Debut: 6/15/1926; Died: 3/4/1983

World Series		Batting																							Fielding						
Year Tm	Age	G	AB	H	2B	3B	HR	TB	R	RBI	GW	TBB	IBB	SO	HBP	SH	SF	SB	CS	SB%	GDP	Avg	OBP	SLG	Pos	G	PO	A	E	DP	FPct
1933 NYG	31	5	19	7	1	0	0	8	1	0	0	0	0	3	0	1	0	0	0	—	0	.368	.368	.421	OF	5	6	0	0	0	1.000
1936 NYG	34	4	2	1	0	0	0	1	2	0	0	0	0	0	0	0	0	0	0	—	0	.500	.500	.500	—						
WS Totals		9	21	8	1	0	0	9	3	0	0	0	0	3	0	1	0	0	0	—	0	.381	.381	.429	OF	5	6	0	0	0	1.000

MIKE DAVIS

Michael Dwayne Davis—Bats: Left; Throws: Left — Ht: 6'2"; Wt: 175 lbs; Born: 6/11/1959 in San Diego, California; Debut: 4/10/1980

LCS		Batting																							Fielding						
Year Tm	Age	G	AB	H	2B	3B	HR	TB	R	RBI	GW	TBB	IBB	SO	HBP	SH	SF	SB	CS	SB%	GDP	Avg	OBP	SLG	Pos	G	PO	A	E	DP	FPct
1981 Oak	22	1	1	1	0	0	0	1	0	0	0	0	0	0	0	0	0	0	0	—	0	1.000	1.000	1.000	—						
1988 LA	29	4	2	0	0	0	0	0	0	0	0	1	0	0	0	0	0	0	0	—	0	.000	.333	.000	—						
LCS Totals		5	3	1	0	0	0	1	0	0	0	1	0	0	0	0	0	0	0	—	0	.333	.500	.333	—	0	0	0	0	0	—
World Series		Batting																							Fielding						
Year Tm	Age	G	AB	H	2B	3B	HR	TB	R	RBI	GW	TBB	IBB	SO	HBP	SH	SF	SB	CS	SB%	GDP	Avg	OBP	SLG	Pos	G	PO	A	E	DP	FPct
1988 LA	29	4	7	1	0	0	1	4	3	2	0	4	0	0	0	0	0	2	0	1.00	0	.143	.455	.571	OF	1	0	0	0	0	—
Postseason Totals		9	10	2	0	0	1	5	3	2	0	5	0	0	0	0	0	2	0	1.00	0	.200	.467	.500	OF	1	0	0	0	0	—

RON DAVIS

Ronald Everette Davis—Bats: Right; Throws: Right — Ht: 6'0"; Wt: 175 lbs; Born: 10/21/1941 in Roanoke Rapids, North Carolina; Debut: 8/1/1962; Died: 9/5/1992

World Series		Batting																							Fielding						
Year Tm	Age	G	AB	H	2B	3B	HR	TB	R	RBI	GW	TBB	IBB	SO	HBP	SH	SF	SB	CS	SB%	GDP	Avg	OBP	SLG	Pos	G	PO	A	E	DP	FPct
1968 StL	26	2	7	0	0	0	0	0	0	0	0	0	0	2	0	0	0	0	0	—	0	.000	.000	.000	OF	2	5	0	0	0	1.000

RON DAVIS—Ronald Gene Davis—Throws: Right; Bats: Right

Ht: 6'4"; Wt: 205 lbs; Born: 8/6/1955 in Houston, Texas; Debut: 7/29/1978

Division Series — Pitching

Year Tm	Age	G	GS	CG	GF	IP	BFP	H	R	ER	HR	SH	SF	HB	TBB	IBB	SO	WP	Bk	W	L	Pct	ShO	Sv-Op	Hld	OAvg	OOBP	ERA
1981 NYA	26	3	0	0	1	6.0	21	1	0	0	0	0	0	0	2	0	6	1	0	1	0	1.000	0	0-0	1	.053	.143	0.00

LCS — Pitching

Year Tm	Age	G	GS	CG	GF	IP	BFP	H	R	ER	HR	SH	SF	HB	TBB	IBB	SO	WP	Bk	W	L	Pct	ShO	Sv-Op	Hld	OAvg	OOBP	ERA
1980 NYA	25	1	0	0	0	4.0	15	3	1	1	1	0	0	1	1	0	3	0	0	0	0	—	0	0-0	0	.231	.333	2.25
1981 NYA	26	2	0	0	0	3.1	12	0	0	0	0	0	0	0	2	0	4	0	0	0	0	—	0	0-0	2	.000	.167	0.00
LCS Totals		3	0	0	0	7.1	54	3	1	1	1	0	0	1	3	0	7	0	0	0	0	—	0	0-0	2	.130	.259	1.23

World Series — Pitching

Year Tm	Age	G	GS	CG	GF	IP	BFP	H	R	ER	HR	SH	SF	HB	TBB	IBB	SO	WP	Bk	W	L	Pct	ShO	Sv-Op	Hld	OAvg	OOBP	ERA
1981 NYA	26	4	0	0	1	2.1	17	4	8	6	1	0	0	0	5	0	4	0	0	0	0	—	0	0-0	0	.333	.529	23.14
Postseason Totals		10	0	0	2	15.2	130	8	9	7	2	0	0	1	10	0	17	1	0	1	0	1.000	0	0-0	3	.148	.292	4.02

Division Series — Batting / Fielding

Year Tm	Age	G	AB	H	2B	3B	HR	TB	R	RBI	GW	TBB	IBB	SO	HBP	SH	SF	SB	CS	SB%	GDP	Avg	OBP	SLG	Pos	G	PO	A	E	DP	FPct
1981 NYA	26	3	0	0	0	0	0	0	0	0	0	0	0	0	0	0	0	0	0	—	0	—	—	—	P	3	1	0	0	0	1.000

LCS — Batting / Fielding

Year Tm	Age	G	AB	H	2B	3B	HR	TB	R	RBI	GW	TBB	IBB	SO	HBP	SH	SF	SB	CS	SB%	GDP	Avg	OBP	SLG	Pos	G	PO	A	E	DP	FPct
1980 NYA	25	1	0	0	0	0	0	0	0	0	0	0	0	0	0	0	0	0	0	—	0	—	—	—	P	1	0	2	0	0	1.000
1981 NYA	26	2	0	0	0	0	0	0	0	0	0	0	0	0	0	0	0	0	0	—	0	—	—	—	P	2	0	0	0	0	—
LCS Totals		3	0	0	0	0	0	0	0	0	0	0	0	0	0	0	0	0	0	—	0	—	—	—	P	3	0	2	0	0	1.000

World Series — Batting / Fielding

Year Tm	Age	G	AB	H	2B	3B	HR	TB	R	RBI	GW	TBB	IBB	SO	HBP	SH	SF	SB	CS	SB%	GDP	Avg	OBP	SLG	Pos	G	PO	A	E	DP	FPct
1981 NYA	26	4	0	0	0	0	0	0	0	0	0	0	0	0	0	0	0	0	0	—	0	—	—	—	P	4	0	0	0	0	—
Postseason Totals		10	0	0	0	0	0	0	0	0	0	0	0	0	0	0	0	0	0	—	0	—	—	—	P	10	1	2	0	0	1.000

RUSS DAVIS—Russell Stuart Davis—Bats: Right; Throws: Right

Ht: 6'0"; Wt: 170 lbs; Born: 9/13/1969 in Hueytown, Alabama; Debut: 7/6/1994

Division Series — Batting / Fielding

Year Tm	Age	G	AB	H	2B	3B	HR	TB	R	RBI	GW	TBB	IBB	SO	HBP	SH	SF	SB	CS	SB%	GDP	Avg	OBP	SLG	Pos	G	PO	A	E	DP	FPct
1995 NYA	26	2	5	1	0	0	0	1	0	0	0	0	0	2	0	0	0	0	0	—	0	.200	.200	.200	3B	2	0	1	0	0	1.000

SPUD DAVIS—Virgil Lawrence Davis—Bats: Right; Throws: Right

Ht: 6'1"; Wt: 197 lbs; Born: 12/20/1904 in Birmingham, Alabama; Debut: 4/30/1928; Died: 8/14/1984

World Series — Batting / Fielding

Year Tm	Age	G	AB	H	2B	3B	HR	TB	R	RBI	GW	TBB	IBB	SO	HBP	SH	SF	SB	CS	SB%	GDP	Avg	OBP	SLG	Pos	G	PO	A	E	DP	FPct
1934 StL	29	2	2	2	0	0	0	2	0	1	0	0	0	0	0	0	0	0	0	—	0	1.000	1.000	1.000	—						

STORM DAVIS—George Earl Davis—Throws: Right; Bats: Right

Ht: 6'4"; Wt: 207 lbs; Born: 12/26/1961 in Dallas, Texas; Debut: 4/29/1982

LCS — Pitching

Year Tm	Age	G	GS	CG	GF	IP	BFP	H	R	ER	HR	SH	SF	HB	TBB	IBB	SO	WP	Bk	W	L	Pct	ShO	Sv-Op	Hld	OAvg	OOBP	ERA
1983 Bal	21	1	1	0	0	6.0	24	5	0	0	0	0	0	0	2	0	2	0	0	0	0	—	0	0-0	0	.227	.292	0.00
1988 Oak	26	1	1	0	0	6.1	26	2	2	0	0	1	0	0	5	0	4	1	0	0	0	—	0	0-0	0	.100	.280	0.00
1989 Oak	27	1	1	0	0	6.1	25	5	6	5	0	0	1	0	2	1	3	0	0	0	1	.000	0	0-0	0	.227	.280	7.11
LCS Totals		3	3	0	0	18.2	150	12	8	5	0	1	1	0	9	1	9	1	0	0	1	.000	0	0-0	0	.188	.284	2.41

World Series — Pitching

Year Tm	Age	G	GS	CG	GF	IP	BFP	H	R	ER	HR	SH	SF	HB	TBB	IBB	SO	WP	Bk	W	L	Pct	ShO	Sv-Op	Hld	OAvg	OOBP	ERA
1983 Bal	21	1	1	0	0	5.0	21	6	3	3	0	0	0	0	1	0	3	1	0	1	0	1.000	0	0-0	0	.300	.333	5.40
1988 Oak	26	2	2	0	0	8.0	37	14	10	10	3	0	0	0	1	0	7	0	0	0	2	.000	0	0-0	0	.389	.405	11.25
WS Totals		3	3	0	0	13.0	116	20	13	13	3	0	0	0	2	0	10	1	0	1	2	.333	0	0-0	0	.357	.379	9.00
Postseason Totals		6	6	0	0	31.2	266	32	21	18	3	1	1	0	11	1	19	2	0	1	3	.250	0	0-0	0	.267	.326	5.12

LCS — Batting / Fielding

Year Tm	Age	G	AB	H	2B	3B	HR	TB	R	RBI	GW	TBB	IBB	SO	HBP	SH	SF	SB	CS	SB%	GDP	Avg	OBP	SLG	Pos	G	PO	A	E	DP	FPct
1983 Bal	21	1	0	0	0	0	0	0	0	0	0	0	0	0	0	0	0	0	0	—	0	—	—	—	P	1	0	0	0	0	—
1988 Oak	26	1	0	0	0	0	0	0	0	0	0	0	0	0	0	0	0	0	0	—	0	—	—	—	P	1	0	2	0	0	1.000
1989 Oak	27	1	0	0	0	0	0	0	0	0	0	0	0	0	0	0	0	0	0	—	0	—	—	—	P	1	0	0	0	0	—
LCS Totals		3	0	0	0	0	0	0	0	0	0	0	0	0	0	0	0	0	0	—	0	—	—	—	P	3	0	2	0	0	1.000

World Series — Batting / Fielding

Year Tm	Age	G	AB	H	2B	3B	HR	TB	R	RBI	GW	TBB	IBB	SO	HBP	SH	SF	SB	CS	SB%	GDP	Avg	OBP	SLG	Pos	G	PO	A	E	DP	FPct
1983 Bal	21	1	2	0	0	0	0	0	0	0	0	0	0	2	0	0	0	0	0	—	0	.000	.000	.000	P	1	0	1	0	0	1.000
1988 Oak	26	2	1	0	0	0	0	0	0	0	0	0	0	1	0	0	0	0	0	—	0	.000	.000	.000	P	2	2	1	0	0	1.000
WS Totals		3	3	0	0	0	0	0	0	0	0	0	0	3	0	0	0	0	0	—	0	.000	.000	.000	P	3	2	2	0	0	1.000
Postseason Totals		6	3	0	0	0	0	0	0	0	0	0	0	3	0	0	0	0	0	—	0	.000	.000	.000	P	6	2	4	0	0	1.000

TOMMY DAVIS—Herman Thomas Davis—Bats: Right; Throws: Right

Ht: 6'2"; Wt: 195 lbs; Born: 3/21/1939 in Brooklyn, New York; Debut: 9/22/1959

LCS — Batting / Fielding

Year Tm	Age	G	AB	H	2B	3B	HR	TB	R	RBI	GW	TBB	IBB	SO	HBP	SH	SF	SB	CS	SB%	GDP	Avg	OBP	SLG	Pos	G	PO	A	E	DP	FPct
1971 Oak	32	3	8	3	1	0	0	4	1	0	0	0	0	0	0	1	0	0	1	.00	0	.375	.375	.500	1B	2	8	0	0	1	1.000
1973 Bal	34	5	21	6	1	0	0	7	1	2	1	1	0	0	0	0	0	0	1	.00	1	.286	.318	.333	—						
1974 Bal	35	4	15	4	0	0	0	4	0	1	1	0	0	1	0	0	0	0	0	—	0	.267	.267	.267	—						
LCS Totals		12	44	13	2	0	0	15	2	3	2	1	0	1	0	1	0	0	2	.00	1	.295	.311	.341	1B	2	8	0	0	1	1.000

World Series — Batting / Fielding

Year Tm	Age	G	AB	H	2B	3B	HR	TB	R	RBI	GW	TBB	IBB	SO	HBP	SH	SF	SB	CS	SB%	GDP	Avg	OBP	SLG	Pos	G	PO	A	E	DP	FPct
1963 LA	24	4	15	6	0	2	0	10	0	2	1	0	0	2	0	0	0	1	0	1.00	0	.400	.400	.667	OF	4	6	0	0	0	1.000
1966 LA	27	4	8	2	0	0	0	2	0	0	0	1	0	1	0	0	0	0	0	—	1	.250	.333	.250	OF	3	3	0	0	0	1.000
WS Totals		8	23	8	0	2	0	12	0	2	1	1	0	3	0	0	0	1	0	1.00	1	.348	.375	.522	OF	7	9	0	0	0	1.000
Postseason Totals		20	67	21	2	2	0	27	2	5	3	2	0	4	0	1	0	1	2	.33	2	.313	.333	.403	OF	7	9	0	0	0	1.000

WILLIE DAVIS—William Henry Davis—Bats: Left; Throws: Left

Ht: 5'11"; Wt: 180 lbs; Born: 4/15/1940 in Mineral Springs, Arkansas; Debut: 9/8/1960

LCS — Batting / Fielding

Year Tm	Age	G	AB	H	2B	3B	HR	TB	R	RBI	GW	TBB	IBB	SO	HBP	SH	SF	SB	CS	SB%	GDP	Avg	OBP	SLG	Pos	G	PO	A	E	DP	FPct
1979 Cal	39	2	2	1	1	0	0	2	1	0	0	0	0	0	0	0	0	0	0	—	0	.500	.500	1.000	—						

World Series — Batting / Fielding

Year Tm	Age	G	AB	H	2B	3B	HR	TB	R	RBI	GW	TBB	IBB	SO	HBP	SH	SF	SB	CS	SB%	GDP	Avg	OBP	SLG	Pos	G	PO	A	E	DP	FPct
1963 LA	23	4	12	2	2	0	0	4	2	3	2	0	0	6	0	2	1	0	0	—	0	.167	.154	.333	OF	4	6	0	0	0	1.000
1965 LA	25	7	26	6	0	0	0	6	3	0	0	0	0	2	1	2	0	3	0	1.00	0	.231	.259	.231	OF	7	11	0	0	0	1.000
1966 LA	26	4	16	1	0	0	0	1	0	0	0	0	0	4	0	0	0	0	0	—	0	.063	.063	.063	OF	4	6	0	3	0	.667
WS Totals		15	54	9	2	0	0	11	5	3	2	0	0	12	1	4	1	3	0	1.00	0	.167	.179	.204	OF	15	23	0	3	0	.885
Postseason Totals		17	56	10	3	0	0	13	6	3	2	0	0	12	1	4	1	3	0	1.00	0	.179	.190	.232	OF	15	23	0	3	0	.885

ANDRE DAWSON—Andre Nolan Dawson—Nickname: Hawk—Bats: Right; Throws: Right

Ht: 6'3"; Wt: 180 lbs; Born: 7/10/1954 in Miami, Florida; Debut: 9/11/1976

Division Series — Batting / Fielding

Year Tm	Age	G	AB	H	2B	3B	HR	TB	R	RBI	GW	TBB	IBB	SO	HBP	SH	SF	SB	CS	SB%	GDP	Avg	OBP	SLG	Pos	G	PO	A	E	DP	FPct
1981 Mon	27	5	20	6	0	1	0	8	1	0	0	1	0	6	0	0	0	2	0	1.00	0	.300	.333	.400	OF	5	12	1	1	0	.929

LCS — Batting / Fielding

Year Tm	Age	G	AB	H	2B	3B	HR	TB	R	RBI	GW	TBB	IBB	SO	HBP	SH	SF	SB	CS	SB%	GDP	Avg	OBP	SLG	Pos	G	PO	A	E	DP	FPct
1981 Mon	27	5	20	3	0	0	0	3	2	0	0	0	0	4	0	0	0	0	0	—	2	.150	.150	.150	OF	5	12	0	0	0	1.000
1989 ChN	35	5	19	2	1	0	0	3	0	3	0	2	1	6	1	0	0	0	0	—	1	.105	.227	.158	OF	5	4	0	0	0	1.000
LCS Totals		10	39	5	1	0	0	6	2	3	0	2	1	10	1	0	0	0	0	—	3	.128	.190	.154	OF	10	16	0	0	0	1.000
Postseason Totals		15	59	11	1	1	0	14	3	3	0	3	1	16	1	0	0	2	0	1.00	3	.186	.238	.237	OF	15	28	1	1	0	.967

JOE DAWSON—Ralph Fenton Dawson—Throws: Right; Bats: Right

Ht: 5'11"; Wt: 182 lbs; Born: 3/9/1897 in Bow, Washington; Debut: 7/4/1924; Died: 1/4/1978

World Series — Pitching

Year Tm	Age	G	GS	CG	GF	IP	BFP	H	R	ER	HR	SH	SF	HB	TBB	IBB	SO	WP	Bk	W	L	Pct	ShO	Sv-Op	Hld	OAvg	OOBP	ERA
1927 Pit	30	1	0	0	1	1.0	3	0	0	0	0	0	0	0	0	0	0	0	0	0	0	—	0	0- 0	0	.000	.000	0.00

World Series — Batting / Fielding

Year Tm	Age	G	AB	H	2B	3B	HR	TB	R	RBI	GW	TBB	IBB	SO	HBP	SH	SF	SB	CS	SB%	GDP	Avg	OBP	SLG	Pos	G	PO	A	E	DP	FPct
1927 Pit	30	1	0	0	0	0	0	0	0	0	0	0	0	0	0	0	0	0	0	—	0	—	—	—	P	1	0	0	0	0	—

KEN DAYLEY—Kenneth Grant Dayley—Throws: Left; Bats: Left

Ht: 6'0"; Wt: 171 lbs; Born: 2/25/1959 in Jerome, Idaho; Debut: 5/13/1982

LCS — Pitching

Year Tm	Age	G	GS	CG	GF	IP	BFP	H	R	ER	HR	SH	SF	HB	TBB	IBB	SO	WP	Bk	W	L	Pct	ShO	Sv-Op	Hld	OAvg	OOBP	ERA
1985 StL	26	5	0	0	2	6.0	20	2	0	0	0	0	0	0	1	0	3	0	0	0	0	—	0	2- 2	0	.105	.150	0.00
1987 StL	28	3	0	0	3	4.0	14	1	0	0	0	0	0	1	2	0	4	0	0	0	0	—	0	2- 2	0	.091	.286	0.00
LCS Totals		8	0	0	5	10.0	68	3	0	0	0	0	0	1	3	0	7	0	0	0	0	—	0	4-4	0	.100	.206	0.00

World Series — Pitching

Year Tm	Age	G	GS	CG	GF	IP	BFP	H	R	ER	HR	SH	SF	HB	TBB	IBB	SO	WP	Bk	W	L	Pct	ShO	Sv-Op	Hld	OAvg	OOBP	ERA
1985 StL	26	4	0	0	2	6.0	22	1	0	0	0	0	0	0	3	0	5	0	0	1	0	1.000	0	0- 0	1	.053	.182	0.00
1987 StL	28	4	0	0	1	4.2	16	2	1	1	1	0	0	0	0	0	3	0	0	0	0	—	0	1- 1	1	.125	.125	1.93
WS Totals		8	0	0	3	10.2	76	3	1	1	1	0	0	0	3	0	8	0	0	1	0	1.000	0	1-1	2	.086	.158	0.84
Postseason Totals		16	0	0	8	20.2	144	6	1	1	1	0	0	1	6	0	15	0	0	1	0	1.000	0	5-5	2	.092	.181	0.44

LCS — Batting / Fielding

Year Tm	Age	G	AB	H	2B	3B	HR	TB	R	RBI	GW	TBB	IBB	SO	HBP	SH	SF	SB	CS	SB%	GDP	Avg	OBP	SLG	Pos	G	PO	A	E	DP	FPct
1985 StL	26	5	2	1	0	0	0	1	0	0	0	0	0	0	0	0	0	0	0	—	0	.500	.500	.500	P	5	0	1	0	0	1.000
1987 StL	28	3	0	0	0	0	0	0	0	0	0	0	0	0	0	0	0	0	0	—	0	—	—	—	P	3	0	0	0	0	—
LCS Totals		8	2	1	0	0	0	1	0	0	0	0	0	0	0	0	0	0	0	—	0	.500	.500	.500	P	8	0	1	0	0	1.000

World Series — Batting / Fielding

Year Tm	Age	G	AB	H	2B	3B	HR	TB	R	RBI	GW	TBB	IBB	SO	HBP	SH	SF	SB	CS	SB%	GDP	Avg	OBP	SLG	Pos	G	PO	A	E	DP	FPct
1985 StL	26	4	0	0	0	0	0	0	0	0	0	0	0	0	0	0	0	0	0	—	0	—	—	—	P	4	0	0	0	0	—
1987 StL	28	4	1	0	0	0	0	0	0	0	0	0	0	1	0	0	0	0	0	—	0	.000	.000	.000	P	4	0	0	0	0	—
WS Totals		8	1	0	0	0	0	0	0	0	0	0	0	1	0	0	0	0	0	—	0	.000	.000	.000	P	8	0	0	0	0	—
Postseason Totals		16	3	1	0	0	0	1	0	0	0	0	0	1	0	0	0	0	0	—	0	.333	.333	.333	P	16	0	1	0	0	1.000

CHARLIE DEAL—Charles Albert Deal—Bats: Right; Throws: Right

Ht: 6'0"; Wt: 160 lbs; Born: 10/30/1891 in Wilkinsburg, Pennsylvania; Debut: 7/19/1912; Died: 9/16/1979

World Series — Batting / Fielding

Year Tm	Age	G	AB	H	2B	3B	HR	TB	R	RBI	GW	TBB	IBB	SO	HBP	SH	SF	SB	CS	SB%	GDP	Avg	OBP	SLG	Pos	G	PO	A	E	DP	FPct
1914 Bos	22	4	16	2	2	0	0	4	1	0	0	0	0	0	0	0	0	2	0	1.00	2	.125	.125	.250	3B	4	6	11	0	1	1.000
1918 ChN	26	6	17	3	0	0	0	3	0	0	0	0	0	1	0	1	0	0	0	—	0	.176	.176	.176	3B	6	7	9	1	0	.941
WS Totals		10	33	5	2	0	0	7	1	0	0	0	0	1	0	1	0	2	0	1.00	2	.152	.152	.212	3B	10	13	20	1	1	.971

DIZZY DEAN (HOF 1953-W)—Jay Hanna Dean—Throws: Right; Bats: Right

Ht: 6'2"; Wt: 182 lbs; Born: 1/16/1910 in Lucas, Arkansas; Debut: 9/28/1930; Died: 7/17/1974

World Series — Pitching

Year Tm	Age	G	GS	CG	GF	IP	BFP	H	R	ER	HR	SH	SF	HB	TBB	IBB	SO	WP	Bk	W	L	Pct	ShO	Sv-Op	Hld	OAvg	OOBP	ERA
1934 StL-*M*	24	3	3	2	0	26.0	103	20	6	5	2	0	0	1	5	0	17	0	0	2	1	.667	1	0- 0	0	.206	.252	1.73
1938 ChN	28	2	1	0	1	8.1	33	8	6	6	2	0	0	0	1	0	2	0	0	0	1	.000	0	0- 0	0	.250	.273	6.48
WS Totals		5	4	2	1	34.1	272	28	12	11	4	0	0	1	6	0	19	0	0	2	2	.500	1	0-0	0	.217	.257	2.88

World Series — Batting / Fielding

Year Tm	Age	G	AB	H	2B	3B	HR	TB	R	RBI	GW	TBB	IBB	SO	HBP	SH	SF	SB	CS	SB%	GDP	Avg	OBP	SLG	Pos	G	PO	A	E	DP	FPct
1934 StL	24	4	12	3	2	0	0	5	3	1	0	0	0	3	0	0	0	0	0	—	0	.250	.250	.417	P	3	2	2	0	0	1.000
1938 ChN	28	2	3	2	0	0	0	2	0	0	0	0	0	0	0	0	0	0	1	.00	0	.667	.667	.667	P	2	0	2	0	0	1.000
WS Totals		6	15	5	2	0	0	7	3	1	0	0	0	3	0	0	0	0	1	.00	0	.333	.333	.467	P	5	2	4	0	0	1.000

PAUL DEAN—Paul Dee Dean—Nickname: Daffy—Throws: Right; Bats: Right

Ht: 6'0"; Wt: 175 lbs; Born: 8/14/1913 in Lucas, Arkansas; Debut: 4/18/1934; Died: 3/17/1981

World Series — Pitching

Year Tm	Age	G	GS	CG	GF	IP	BFP	H	R	ER	HR	SH	SF	HB	TBB	IBB	SO	WP	Bk	W	L	Pct	ShO	Sv-Op	Hld	OAvg	OOBP	ERA
1934 StL	21	2	2	2	0	18.0	77	15	4	2	0	1	0	1	7	1	11	0	0	2	0	1.000	0	0- 0	0	.221	.303	1.00

World Series — Batting / Fielding

Year Tm	Age	G	AB	H	2B	3B	HR	TB	R	RBI	GW	TBB	IBB	SO	HBP	SH	SF	SB	CS	SB%	GDP	Avg	OBP	SLG	Pos	G	PO	A	E	DP	FPct
1934 StL	21	2	6	1	0	0	0	1	0	2	1	0	0	1	0	1	0	0	0	—	0	.167	.167	.167	P	2	0	0	1	0	.000

WAYLAND DEAN—Wayland Ogden Dean—Throws: Right; Bats: Both

Ht: 6'1"; Wt: 178 lbs; Born: 6/20/1902 in Richwood, West Virginia; Debut: 4/17/1924; Died: 4/10/1930

World Series — Pitching

Year Tm	Age	G	GS	CG	GF	IP	BFP	H	R	ER	HR	SH	SF	HB	TBB	IBB	SO	WP	Bk	W	L	Pct	ShO	Sv-Op	Hld	OAvg	OOBP	ERA
1924 NYG	22	1	0	0	1	2.0	9	3	2	1	0	0	0	0	0	0	2	0	0	0	0	—	0	0- 0	0	.333	.333	4.50

World Series — Batting / Fielding

Year Tm	Age	G	AB	H	2B	3B	HR	TB	R	RBI	GW	TBB	IBB	SO	HBP	SH	SF	SB	CS	SB%	GDP	Avg	OBP	SLG	Pos	G	PO	A	E	DP	FPct
1924 NYG	22	1	0	0	0	0	0	0	0	0	0	0	0	0	0	0	0	0	0	—	0	—	—	—	P	1	0	0	0	0	—

DOUG DeCINCES—Douglas Vernon DeCinces—Bats: Right; Throws: Right

Ht: 6'2"; Wt: 190 lbs; Born: 8/29/1950 in Burbank, California; Debut: 9/9/1973

LCS — Batting / Fielding

Year Tm	Age	G	AB	H	2B	3B	HR	TB	R	RBI	GW	TBB	IBB	SO	HBP	SH	SF	SB	CS	SB%	GDP	Avg	OBP	SLG	Pos	G	PO	A	E	DP	FPct
1979 Bal	29	4	13	4	1	0	0	5	4	3	0	1	0	1	0	0	2	0	0	—	1	.308	.313	.385	3B	4	5	8	0	1	1.000
1982 Cal	32	5	19	6	2	0	0	8	5	0	0	1	0	5	0	0	0	0	1	.00	0	.316	.350	.421	3B	5	8	12	3	2	.870
1986 Cal	36	7	32	9	3	0	1	15	2	3	0	0	0	2	0	0	0	0	0	—	3	.281	.281	.469	3B	7	6	18	2	3	.923
LCS Totals		16	64	19	6	0	1	28	11	6	0	2	0	8	0	0	2	0	1	.00	4	.297	.309	.438	3B	16	19	38	5	6	.919

World Series — Batting / Fielding

Year Tm	Age	G	AB	H	2B	3B	HR	TB	R	RBI	GW	TBB	IBB	SO	HBP	SH	SF	SB	CS	SB%	GDP	Avg	OBP	SLG	Pos	G	PO	A	E	DP	FPct
1979 Bal	29	7	25	5	0	0	1	8	2	3	0	5	0	5	0	0	0	1	0	1.00	0	.200	.333	.320	3B	7	7	21	3	0	.903
Postseason Totals		23	89	24	6	0	2	36	13	9	0	7	0	13	0	0	2	1	1	.50	4	.270	.316	.404	3B	23	26	59	8	6	.914

IVAN DeJESUS—Bats: Right; Throws: Right

Ht: 5'11"; Wt: 175 lbs; Born: 1/9/1953 in Santurce, Puerto Rico; Debut: 9/13/1974

LCS — Batting / Fielding

Year Tm	Age	G	AB	H	2B	3B	HR	TB	R	RBI	GW	TBB	IBB	SO	HBP	SH	SF	SB	CS	SB%	GDP	Avg	OBP	SLG	Pos	G	PO	A	E	DP	FPct
1983 Phi	30	4	12	3	0	0	0	3	0	1	0	3	2	3	0	0	0	0	0	—	0	.250	.400	.250	SS	4	4	12	2	0	.889

World Series — Batting / Fielding

Year Tm	Age	G	AB	H	2B	3B	HR	TB	R	RBI	GW	TBB	IBB	SO	HBP	SH	SF	SB	CS	SB%	GDP	Avg	OBP	SLG	Pos	G	PO	A	E	DP	FPct
1983 Phi	30	5	16	2	0	0	0	2	0	0	0	1	0	2	0	0	0	0	0	—	1	.125	.176	.125	SS	5	5	14	1	2	.950
1985 StL	32	1	1	0	0	0	0	0	0	0	0	0	0	0	0	0	0	0	0	—	0	.000	.000	.000	—						
WS Totals		6	17	2	0	0	0	2	0	0	0	1	0	2	0	0	0	0	0	—	1	.118	.167	.118	SS	5	5	14	1	2	.950
Postseason Totals		10	29	5	0	0	0	5	0	1	0	4	2	5	0	0	0	0	0	—	1	.172	.273	.172	SS	9	9	26	3	2	.921

JIM DELAHANTY—James Christopher Delahanty—Bats: Right; Throws: Right

Ht: 5'10"; Wt: 170 lbs; Born: 6/20/1879 in Cleveland, Ohio; Debut: 4/19/1901; Died: 10/17/1953

World Series — Batting / Fielding

Year Tm	Age	G	AB	H	2B	3B	HR	TB	R	RBI	GW	TBB	IBB	SO	HBP	SH	SF	SB	CS	SB%	GDP	Avg	OBP	SLG	Pos	G	PO	A	E	DP	FPct
1909 Det	30	7	26	9	4	0	0	13	2	4	2	2	0	5	1	0	0	0	0	—	0	.346	.414	.500	2B	7	10	17	2	1	.931

BILL DeLANCEY—William Pinkney Delancey—Bats: Left; Throws: Right

Ht: 5'11"; Wt: 185 lbs; Born: 11/28/1911 in Greensboro, North Carolina; Debut: 9/11/1932; Died: 11/28/1946

World Series		Batting																							Fielding						
Year Tm	Age	G	AB	H	2B	3B	HR	TB	R	RBI	GW	TBB	IBB	SO	HBP	SH	SF	SB	CS	SB%	GDP	Avg	OBP	SLG	Pos	G	PO	A	E	DP	FPct
1934 StL	22	7	29	5	3	0	1	11	3	4	0	2	0	8	0	0	0	0	0	—	1	.172	.226	.379	C	7	50	6	2	1	.966

JOSE DeLEON—Throws: Right; Bats: Right

Ht: 6'3"; Wt: 210 lbs; Born: 12/20/1960 in Rancho Viejo, Dominican Republic; Debut: 7/23/1983

LCS		Pitching																								
Year Tm	Age	G	GS	CG	GF	IP	BFP	H	R	ER	HR	SH	SF	HB	TBB	IBB	SO	WP	Bk	W	L	Pct	ShO	Sv-Op	Hld	OAvg	OOBP	ERA
1993 ChA	32	2	0	0	0	4.2	21	7	1	1	0	0	0	0	1	0	6	0	0	0	0	—	0	0-0	0	.350	.381	1.93

LCS		Batting																							Fielding						
Year Tm	Age	G	AB	H	2B	3B	HR	TB	R	RBI	GW	TBB	IBB	SO	HBP	SH	SF	SB	CS	SB%	GDP	Avg	OBP	SLG	Pos	G	PO	A	E	DP	FPct
1993 ChA	32	2	0	0	0	0	0	0	0	0	0	0	0	0	0	0	0	0	0	—	0	—	—	—	P	2	0	0	0	0	—

WHEEZER DELL—William George Dell—Throws: Right; Bats: Right

Ht: 6'4"; Wt: 210 lbs; Born: 6/11/1887 in Tuscarora, Nevada; Debut: 4/22/1912; Died: 8/24/1966

World Series		Pitching																								
Year Tm	Age	G	GS	CG	GF	IP	BFP	H	R	ER	HR	SH	SF	HB	TBB	IBB	SO	WP	Bk	W	L	Pct	ShO	Sv-Op	Hld	OAvg	OOBP	ERA
1916 Bro	29	1	0	0	1	1.0	4	1	0	0	0	1	0	0	0	0	0	0	0	0	0	—	0	0-0	0	.333	.333	0.00

World Series		Batting																							Fielding						
Year Tm	Age	G	AB	H	2B	3B	HR	TB	R	RBI	GW	TBB	IBB	SO	HBP	SH	SF	SB	CS	SB%	GDP	Avg	OBP	SLG	Pos	G	PO	A	E	DP	FPct
1916 Bro	29	1	0	0	0	0	0	0	0	0	0	0	0	0	0	0	0	0	0	—	0	—	—	—	P	1	0	0	0	0	—

JOE DeMAESTRI—Joseph Paul DeMaestri—Nickname: Oats—Bats: Right; Throws: Right

Ht: 6'0"; Wt: 170 lbs; Born: 12/9/1928 in San Francisco, California; Debut: 4/19/1951

World Series		Batting																							Fielding						
Year Tm	Age	G	AB	H	2B	3B	HR	TB	R	RBI	GW	TBB	IBB	SO	HBP	SH	SF	SB	CS	SB%	GDP	Avg	OBP	SLG	Pos	G	PO	A	E	DP	FPct
1960 NYA	31	4	2	1	0	0	0	1	1	0	0	0	0	1	0	0	0	0	0	—	0	.500	.500	.500	SS	3	0	2	0	0	1.000

AL DEMAREE—Albert Wentworth Demaree—Throws: Right; Bats: Left

Ht: 6'0"; Wt: 170 lbs; Born: 9/8/1884 in Quincy, Illinois; Debut: 9/26/1912; Died: 4/30/1962

World Series		Pitching																								
Year Tm	Age	G	GS	CG	GF	IP	BFP	H	R	ER	HR	SH	SF	HB	TBB	IBB	SO	WP	Bk	W	L	Pct	ShO	Sv-Op	Hld	OAvg	OOBP	ERA
1913 NYG	29	1	1	0	0	4.0	21	7	4	2	0	1	0	0	1	0	0	0	0	0	1	.000	0	0-0	0	.368	.400	4.50

World Series		Batting																							Fielding						
Year Tm	Age	G	AB	H	2B	3B	HR	TB	R	RBI	GW	TBB	IBB	SO	HBP	SH	SF	SB	CS	SB%	GDP	Avg	OBP	SLG	Pos	G	PO	A	E	DP	FPct
1913 NYG	29	1	1	0	0	0	0	0	0	0	0	0	0	0	0	0	0	0	0	—	0	.000	.000	.000	P	1	0	2	0	0	1.000

FRANK DEMAREE—Joseph Franklin Demaree—Bats: Right; Throws: Right

Ht: 5'11"; Wt: 185 lbs; Born: 6/10/1910 in Winters, California; Debut: 7/22/1932; Died: 8/30/1958

World Series		Batting																							Fielding						
Year Tm	Age	G	AB	H	2B	3B	HR	TB	R	RBI	GW	TBB	IBB	SO	HBP	SH	SF	SB	CS	SB%	GDP	Avg	OBP	SLG	Pos	G	PO	A	E	DP	FPct
1932 ChN	22	2	7	2	0	0	1	5	1	4	0	1	0	0	0	0	0	0	0	—	0	.286	.375	.714	OF	2	4	0	1	0	.800
1935 ChN	25	6	24	6	1	0	2	13	2	2	0	1	0	4	0	0	0	0	0	—	1	.250	.280	.542	OF	6	7	2	0	0	1.000
1938 ChN	28	3	10	1	0	0	0	1	1	0	0	1	0	2	0	1	0	0	0	—	0	.100	.182	.100	OF	3	6	0	0	0	1.000
1943 StL	33	1	1	0	0	0	0	0	0	0	0	0	0	0	0	0	0	0	0	—	0	.000	.000	.000	—						
WS Totals		12	42	9	1	0	3	19	4	6	0	3	0	6	0	1	0	0	0	—	1	.214	.267	.452	OF	11	17	2	1	0	.950

JOHN DeMERIT—John Stephen DeMerit—Nickname: Thumper—Bats: Right; Throws: Right

Ht: 6'1"; Wt: 195 lbs; Born: 1/8/1936 in West Bend, Wisconsin; Debut: 6/18/1957

World Series		Batting																							Fielding						
Year Tm	Age	G	AB	H	2B	3B	HR	TB	R	RBI	GW	TBB	IBB	SO	HBP	SH	SF	SB	CS	SB%	GDP	Avg	OBP	SLG	Pos	G	PO	A	E	DP	FPct
1957 Mil	21	1	0	0	0	0	0	0	0	0	0	0	0	0	0	0	0	0	0	—	0	—	—	—	—						

LARRY DEMERY—Lawrence Calvin Demery—Throws: Right; Bats: Right

Ht: 6'0"; Wt: 170 lbs; Born: 6/4/1953 in Bakersfield, California; Debut: 6/2/1974

LCS		Pitching																								
Year Tm	Age	G	GS	CG	GF	IP	BFP	H	R	ER	HR	SH	SF	HB	TBB	IBB	SO	WP	Bk	W	L	Pct	ShO	Sv-Op	Hld	OAvg	OOBP	ERA
1974 Pit	21	2	0	0	0	1.0	8	3	4	4	0	0	0	0	2	0	0	1	0	0	0	—	0	0-0	0	.500	.625	36.00
1975 Pit	22	1	0	0	0	2.0	11	4	4	4	1	0	1	0	1	0	1	0	0	0	0	—	0	0-0	0	.444	.455	18.00
LCS Totals		3	0	0	0	3.0	38	7	8	8	1	0	1	0	3	0	1	1	0	0	0	—	0	0-0	0	.467	.526	24.00

LCS		Batting																							Fielding						
Year Tm	Age	G	AB	H	2B	3B	HR	TB	R	RBI	GW	TBB	IBB	SO	HBP	SH	SF	SB	CS	SB%	GDP	Avg	OBP	SLG	Pos	G	PO	A	E	DP	FPct
1974 Pit	21	2	0	0	0	0	0	0	0	0	0	0	0	0	0	0	0	0	0	—	0	—	—	—	P	2	0	1	0	0	1.000
1975 Pit	22	1	0	0	0	0	0	0	0	0	0	0	0	0	0	0	0	0	0	—	0	—	—	—	P	1	0	0	0	0	—
LCS Totals		3	0	0	0	0	0	0	0	0	0	0	0	0	0	0	0	0	0	—	0	—	—	—	P	3	0	1	0	0	1.000

DON DEMETER—Donald Lee Demeter—Bats: Right; Throws: Right

Ht: 6'4"; Wt: 190 lbs; Born: 6/25/1935 in Oklahoma City, Oklahoma; Debut: 9/18/1956

World Series		Batting																							Fielding						
Year Tm	Age	G	AB	H	2B	3B	HR	TB	R	RBI	GW	TBB	IBB	SO	HBP	SH	SF	SB	CS	SB%	GDP	Avg	OBP	SLG	Pos	G	PO	A	E	DP	FPct
1959 LA	24	6	12	3	0	0	0	3	2	0	0	1	0	3	0	0	0	0	1	.00	1	.250	.308	.250	OF	6	9	0	0	0	1.000

RICK DEMPSEY—John Rikard Dempsey—Bats: Right; Throws: Right

Ht: 6'0"; Wt: 190 lbs; Born: 9/13/1949 in Fayetteville, Tennessee; Debut: 9/23/1969

LCS		Batting																							Fielding						
Year Tm	Age	G	AB	H	2B	3B	HR	TB	R	RBI	GW	TBB	IBB	SO	HBP	SH	SF	SB	CS	SB%	GDP	Avg	OBP	SLG	Pos	G	PO	A	E	DP	FPct
1979 Bal	30	3	10	4	2	0	0	6	3	2	0	1	0	0	0	0	0	1	0	1.00	0	.400	.455	.600	C	3	10	1	0	0	1.000
1983 Bal	34	4	12	2	0	0	0	2	1	0	0	1	0	1	0	0	0	0	0	—	0	.167	.231	.167	C	4	29	5	1	2	.971
1988 LA	39	4	5	2	2	0	0	4	1	2	1	1	0	0	0	0	0	0	0	—	0	.400	.500	.800	C	3	7	0	0	0	1.000
LCS Totals		11	27	8	4	0	0	12	5	4	1	3	0	1	0	0	0	1	0	1.00	0	.296	.367	.444	C	10	46	6	1	2	.981

World Series		Batting																							Fielding						
Year Tm	Age	G	AB	H	2B	3B	HR	TB	R	RBI	GW	TBB	IBB	SO	HBP	SH	SF	SB	CS	SB%	GDP	Avg	OBP	SLG	Pos	G	PO	A	E	DP	FPct
1979 Bal	30	7	21	6	2	0	0	8	3	0	0	1	0	3	0	0	0	0	0	—	1	.286	.318	.381	C	7	38	2	0	0	1.000
1983 Bal	34	5	13	5	4	0	1	12	3	2	1	2	2	2	0	0	0	0	0	—	1	.385	.467	.923	C	5	27	4	0	0	1.000
1988 LA	39	2	5	1	0	0	0	2	0	1	0	1	0	2	0	0	0	0	0	—	1	.200	.333	.400	C	2	13	1	0	0	1.000
WS Totals		14	39	12	7	0	1	22	6	3	1	4	2	7	0	0	0	0	0	—	3	.308	.372	.564	C	14	78	7	0	0	1.000
Postseason Totals		25	66	20	11	0	1	34	11	7	2	7	2	8	0	0	0	1	0	1.00	3	.303	.370	.515	C	24	124	13	1	2	.993

JOHN DENNY—John Allen Denny—Throws: Right; Bats: Right

Ht: 6'3"; Wt: 185 lbs; Born: 11/8/1952 in Prescott, Arizona; Debut: 9/12/1974

LCS		Pitching																								
Year Tm	Age	G	GS	CG	GF	IP	BFP	H	R	ER	HR	SH	SF	HB	TBB	IBB	SO	WP	Bk	W	L	Pct	ShO	Sv-Op	Hld	OAvg	OOBP	ERA
1983 Phi-*C*	30	1	1	0	0	6.0	28	5	3	0	0	0	0	1	3	1	3	0	0	0	1	.000	0	0-0	0	.208	.321	0.00
World Series																												
Year Tm	Age	G	GS	CG	GF	IP	BFP	H	R	ER	HR	SH	SF	HB	TBB	IBB	SO	WP	Bk	W	L	Pct	ShO	Sv-Op	Hld	OAvg	OOBP	ERA
1983 Phi-*C*	30	2	2	0	0	13.0	54	12	5	5	1	0	0	0	3	2	9	0	0	1	1	.500	0	0-0	0	.235	.278	3.46
Postseason Totals		3	3	0	0	19.0	164	17	8	5	1	0	0	1	6	3	12	0	0	1	2	.333	0	0-0	0	.227	.293	2.37

LCS		Batting																							Fielding						
Year Tm	Age	G	AB	H	2B	3B	HR	TB	R	RBI	GW	TBB	IBB	SO	HBP	SH	SF	SB	CS	SB%	GDP	Avg	OBP	SLG	Pos	G	PO	A	E	DP	FPct
1983 Phi	30	1	1	0	0	0	0	0	0	0	0	0	0	0	0	1	0	0	0	—	0	.000	.000	.000	P	1	0	0	0	0	—
World Series																															
Year Tm	Age	G	AB	H	2B	3B	HR	TB	R	RBI	GW	TBB	IBB	SO	HBP	SH	SF	SB	CS	SB%	GDP	Avg	OBP	SLG	Pos	G	PO	A	E	DP	FPct
1983 Phi	30	2	5	1	0	0	0	1	1	1	0	0	0	1	0	0	0	0	0	—	0	.200	.200	.200	P	2	3	1	0	0	1.000
Postseason Totals		3	6	1	0	0	0	1	1	1	0	0	0	1	0	1	0	0	0	—	0	.167	.167	.167	P	3	3	1	0	0	1.000

BUCKY DENT—Russell Earl Dent—Bats: Right; Throws: Right

Ht: 5'9"; Wt: 170 lbs; Born: 11/25/1951 in Savannah, Georgia; Debut: 6/1/1973

LCS		Batting																							Fielding						
Year Tm	Age	G	AB	H	2B	3B	HR	TB	R	RBI	GW	TBB	IBB	SO	HBP	SH	SF	SB	CS	SB%	GDP	Avg	OBP	SLG	Pos	G	PO	A	E	DP	FPct
1977 NYA	25	5	14	3	1	0	0	4	1	2	0	1	0	0	0	1	0	0	0	—	0	.214	.267	.286	SS	5	10	14	1	0	.960
1978 NYA	26	4	15	3	0	0	0	3	0	4	1	0	0	0	0	0	0	0	0	—	1	.200	.200	.200	SS	4	2	7	1	0	.900
1980 NYA	28	3	11	2	0	0	0	2	0	0	0	0	0	1	0	1	0	0	0	—	1	.182	.182	.182	SS	3	10	12	0	2	1.000
LCS Totals		12	40	8	1	0	0	9	1	6	1	1	0	1	0	2	0	0	0	—	2	.200	.220	.225	SS	12	22	33	2	2	.965
World Series		Batting																							Fielding						
Year Tm	Age	G	AB	H	2B	3B	HR	TB	R	RBI	GW	TBB	IBB	SO	HBP	SH	SF	SB	CS	SB%	GDP	Avg	OBP	SLG	Pos	G	PO	A	E	DP	FPct
1977 NYA	25	6	19	5	0	0	0	5	0	2	0	2	0	1	0	0	0	0	0	—	0	.263	.333	.263	SS	6	2	15	1	2	.944
1978 NYA	26	6	24	10	1	0	0	11	3	7	1	1	0	2	0	0	0	0	0	—	0	.417	.440	.458	SS	6	8	16	2	4	.923
WS Totals		12	43	15	1	0	0	16	3	9	1	3	0	3	0	0	0	0	0	—	0	.349	.391	.372	SS	12	10	31	3	6	.932
Postseason Totals		24	83	23	2	0	0	25	4	15	2	4	0	4	0	2	0	0	0	—	2	.277	.310	.301	SS	24	32	64	5	8	.950

SAM DENTE—Samuel Joseph Dente—Nickname: Blackie—Bats: Right; Throws: Right

Ht: 5'11"; Wt: 175 lbs; Born: 4/26/1922 in Harrison, New Jersey; Debut: 7/10/1947

World Series		Batting																							Fielding						
Year Tm	Age	G	AB	H	2B	3B	HR	TB	R	RBI	GW	TBB	IBB	SO	HBP	SH	SF	SB	CS	SB%	GDP	Avg	OBP	SLG	Pos	G	PO	A	E	DP	FPct
1954 Cle	32	3	3	0	0	0	0	0	1	0	0	1	0	0	0	1	0	0	0	—	0	.000	.250	.000	SS	3	1	1	0	1	1.000

BOB DERNIER—Robert Eugene Dernier—Bats: Right; Throws: Right

Ht: 6'0"; Wt: 160 lbs; Born: 1/5/1957 in Kansas City, Missouri; Debut: 9/7/1980

LCS		Batting																							Fielding						
Year Tm	Age	G	AB	H	2B	3B	HR	TB	R	RBI	GW	TBB	IBB	SO	HBP	SH	SF	SB	CS	SB%	GDP	Avg	OBP	SLG	Pos	G	PO	A	E	DP	FPct
1983 Phi	26	1	0	0	0	0	0	0	0	0	0	0	0	0	0	0	0	0	0	—	0	—	—	—	OF	1	0	0	0	0	—
1984 ChN	27	5	17	4	2	0	1	9	5	1	1	5	0	4	0	0	0	2	1	.67	0	.235	.409	.529	OF	5	12	1	0	0	1.000
LCS Totals		6	17	4	2	0	1	9	5	1	1	5	0	4	0	0	0	2	1	.67	0	.235	.409	.529	OF	6	12	1	0	0	1.000
World Series		Batting																							Fielding						
Year Tm	Age	G	AB	H	2B	3B	HR	TB	R	RBI	GW	TBB	IBB	SO	HBP	SH	SF	SB	CS	SB%	GDP	Avg	OBP	SLG	Pos	G	PO	A	E	DP	FPct
1983 Phi	26	1	0	0	0	0	0	0	1	0	0	0	0	0	0	0	0	0	0	—	0	—	—	—	—						
Postseason Totals		7	17	4	2	0	1	9	6	1	1	5	0	4	0	0	0	2	1	.67	0	.235	.409	.529	OF	6	12	1	0	0	1.000

PAUL DERRINGER—Samuel Paul Derringer—Nicknames: Duke, 'Oom Paul—Throws: Right; Bats: Right

Ht: 6'3"; Wt: 205 lbs; Born: 10/17/1906 in Springfield, Kentucky; Debut: 4/16/1931; Died: 11/17/1987

World Series		Pitching																									
Year Tm	Age	G	GS	CG	GF	IP	BFP	H	R	ER	HR	SH	SF	HB	TBB	IBB	SO	WP	Bk	W	L	Pct	ShO	Sv-Op	Hld	OAvg	OOBP	ERA
1931 StL	24	3	2	0	1	12.2	59	14	10	6	1	1	0	0	7	0	14	1	0	0	2	.000	0	0- 0	0	.275	.362	4.26
1939 Cin	32	2	2	1	0	15.1	58	9	4	4	2	0	0	0	3	1	9	0	0	0	1	.000	0	0- 0	0	.164	.207	2.35
1940 Cin	33	3	3	2	0	19.1	84	17	8	6	0	2	0	0	10	2	6	0	0	2	1	.667	0	0- 0	0	.236	.329	2.79
1945 ChN	38	3	0	0	0	5.1	29	5	4	4	0	2	0	0	7	2	1	0	0	0	0	—	0	0- 0	0	.250	.444	6.75
WS Totals		11	7	3	1	52.2	460	45	26	20	3	5	0	0	27	5	30	1	0	2	4	.333	0	0-0	0	.227	.320	3.42

World Series		Batting																							Fielding						
Year Tm	Age	G	AB	H	2B	3B	HR	TB	R	RBI	GW	TBB	IBB	SO	HBP	SH	SF	SB	CS	SB%	GDP	Avg	OBP	SLG	Pos	G	PO	A	E	DP	FPct
1931 StL	24	3	2	0	0	0	0	0	0	0	0	0	0	1	0	1	0	0	0	—	0	.000	.000	.000	P	3	0	2	0	0	1.000
1939 Cin	32	2	5	1	0	0	0	1	0	0	0	0	0	0	0	0	0	0	0	—	1	.200	.200	.200	P	2	2	0	0	0	1.000
1940 Cin	33	3	7	0	0	0	0	0	0	0	0	0	0	1	0	0	0	0	0	—	0	.000	.000	.000	P	3	0	5	0	1	1.000
1945 ChN	38	3	0	0	0	0	0	0	0	0	0	0	0	0	0	0	0	0	0	—	0	—	—	—	P	3	0	0	0	0	—
WS Totals		11	14	1	0	0	0	1	0	0	0	0	0	2	0	1	0	0	0	—	1	.071	.071	.071	P	11	2	7	0	1	1.000

DELINO DeSHIELDS—Delino Lamont DeShields—Bats: Left; Throws: Right

Ht: 6'1"; Wt: 170 lbs; Born: 1/15/1969 in Seaford, Delaware; Debut: 4/9/1990

Division Series		Batting																							Fielding						
Year Tm	Age	G	AB	H	2B	3B	HR	TB	R	RBI	GW	TBB	IBB	SO	HBP	SH	SF	SB	CS	SB%	GDP	Avg	OBP	SLG	Pos	G	PO	A	E	DP	FPct
1995 LA	26	3	12	3	0	0	0	3	1	0	0	1	0	3	0	0	0	0	0	—	0	.250	.308	.250	2B	3	8	7	0	2	1.000
1996 LA	27	2	4	0	0	0	0	0	0	0	0	0	0	1	0	0	0	0	0	—	0	.000	.000	.000	2B	2	3	2	0	2	1.000
DS Totals		5	16	3	0	0	0	3	1	0	0	1	0	4	0	0	0	0	0	—	0	.188	.235	.188	2B	5	11	9	0	4	1.000

MIKE DEVEREAUX—Michael Devereaux—Bats: Right; Throws: Right

Ht: 6'0"; Wt: 195 lbs; Born: 4/10/1963 in Casper, Wyoming; Debut: 9/2/1987

Division Series		Batting																							Fielding						
Year Tm	Age	G	AB	H	2B	3B	HR	TB	R	RBI	GW	TBB	IBB	SO	HBP	SH	SF	SB	CS	SB%	GDP	Avg	OBP	SLG	Pos	G	PO	A	E	DP	FPct
1995 Atl	32	4	5	1	0	0	0	1	1	0	0	0	0	0	0	0	0	0	0	—	0	.200	.200	.200	OF	3	2	0	0	0	1.000
1996 Bal	33	4	1	0	0	0	0	0	0	0	0	0	0	0	0	0	0	0	0	—	0	.000	.000	.000	OF	3	2	0	0	0	1.000
DS Totals		8	6	1	0	0	0	1	1	0	0	0	0	0	0	0	0	0	0	—	0	.167	.167	.167	OF	6	4	0	0	0	1.000
LCS		Batting																							Fielding						
Year Tm	Age	G	AB	H	2B	3B	HR	TB	R	RBI	GW	TBB	IBB	SO	HBP	SH	SF	SB	CS	SB%	GDP	Avg	OBP	SLG	Pos	G	PO	A	E	DP	FPct
1995 Atl	32	4	13	4	1	0	1	8	2	5	1	1	0	2	0	0	0	0	0	—	2	.308	.357	.615	OF	4	2	0	0	0	1.000
1996 Bal	33	3	2	0	0	0	0	0	0	0	0	0	0	1	0	0	0	0	0	—	0	.000	.000	.000	OF	3	1	0	0	0	1.000
LCS Totals		7	15	4	1	0	1	8	2	5	1	1	0	3	0	0	0	0	0	—	2	.267	.313	.533	OF	7	3	0	0	0	1.000
World Series		Batting																							Fielding						
Year Tm	Age	G	AB	H	2B	3B	HR	TB	R	RBI	GW	TBB	IBB	SO	HBP	SH	SF	SB	CS	SB%	GDP	Avg	OBP	SLG	Pos	G	PO	A	E	DP	FPct
1995 Atl	32	5	4	1	0	0	0	1	0	1	0	2	0	1	0	0	0	0	0	—	0	.250	.500	.250	OF	4	0	0	1	0	.000
Postseason Totals		20	25	6	1	0	1	10	3	6	1	3	0	4	0	0	0	0	0	—	2	.240	.321	.400	OF	17	7	0	1	0	.875

ART DEVLIN—Arthur McArthur Devlin—Bats: Right; Throws: Right

Ht: 6'0"; Wt: 175 lbs; Born: 10/16/1879 in Washington, DC; Debut: 4/14/1904; Died: 9/18/1948

World Series		Batting																							Fielding						
Year Tm	Age	G	AB	H	2B	3B	HR	TB	R	RBI	GW	TBB	IBB	SO	HBP	SH	SF	SB	CS	SB%	GDP	Avg	OBP	SLG	Pos	G	PO	A	E	DP	FPct
1905 NYG	25	5	16	4	1	0	0	5	0	1	0	1	0	3	0	1	0	3	0	1.00	1	.250	.294	.313	3B	5	7	15	1	0	.957

JOSH DEVORE—Joshua D. Devore—Bats: Left; Throws: Left

Ht: 5'6"; Wt: 160 lbs; Born: 11/13/1887 in Murray City, Ohio; Debut: 9/25/1908; Died: 10/6/1954

World Series		Batting																							Fielding						
Year Tm	Age	G	AB	H	2B	3B	HR	TB	R	RBI	GW	TBB	IBB	SO	HBP	SH	SF	SB	CS	SB%	GDP	Avg	OBP	SLG	Pos	G	PO	A	E	DP	FPct
1911 NYG	23	6	24	4	1	0	0	5	1	3	1	1	0	8	0	0	0	0	3	.00	0	.167	.200	.208	OF	6	15	0	1	0	.938
1912 NYG	24	7	24	6	0	0	0	6	4	0	0	7	0	5	0	0	0	4	2	.67	0	.250	.419	.250	OF	7	12	2	1	1	.933
1914 Bos	26	1	1	0	0	0	0	0	0	0	0	0	0	1	0	0	0	0	0	—	0	.000	.000	.000	—						
WS Totals		14	49	10	1	0	0	11	5	3	1	8	0	14	0	0	0	4	5	.44	0	.204	.316	.224	OF	13	27	2	2	1	.935

AL DeVORMER—Albert E. DeVormer—Bats: Right; Throws: Right

Ht: 6'0"; Wt: 175 lbs; Born: 8/19/1891 in Grand Rapids, Michigan; Debut: 8/4/1918; Died: 8/29/1966

World Series		Batting																							Fielding						
Year Tm	Age	G	AB	H	2B	3B	HR	TB	R	RBI	GW	TBB	IBB	SO	HBP	SH	SF	SB	CS	SB%	GDP	Avg	OBP	SLG	Pos	G	PO	A	E	DP	FPct
1921 NYA	30	2	1	0	0	0	0	0	0	0	0	0	0	0	0	0	0	0	0	—	0	.000	.000	.000	C	1	1	0	0	0	1.000

ALEX DIAZ—Alexis Diaz—Bats: Both; Throws: Right

Ht: 5'11"; Wt: 175 lbs; Born: 10/5/1968 in Brooklyn, New York; Debut: 7/25/1992

Division Series		Batting																							Fielding						
Year Tm	Age	G	AB	H	2B	3B	HR	TB	R	RBI	GW	TBB	IBB	SO	HBP	SH	SF	SB	CS	SB%	GDP	Avg	OBP	SLG	Pos	G	PO	A	E	DP	FPct
1995 Sea	26	2	3	1	0	0	0	1	0	0	0	1	0	1	0	0	0	0	0	—	0	.333	.500	.333	OF	1	1	1	0	0	1.000
LCS		Batting																							Fielding						
Year Tm	Age	G	AB	H	2B	3B	HR	TB	R	RBI	GW	TBB	IBB	SO	HBP	SH	SF	SB	CS	SB%	GDP	Avg	OBP	SLG	Pos	G	PO	A	E	DP	FPct
1995 Sea	26	4	7	3	1	0	0	4	0	0	0	1	0	1	0	0	0	0	0	—	0	.429	.500	.571	OF	3	1	0	0	0	1.000
Postseason Totals		6	10	4	1	0	0	5	0	0	0	2	0	2	0	0	0	0	0	—	0	.400	.500	.500	OF	4	2	1	0	0	1.000

BO DIAZ—Baudilio Jose Diaz—Bats: Right; Throws: Right

Ht: 5'11"; Wt: 185 lbs; Born: 3/23/1953 in Cua, Venezuela; Debut: 9/6/1977; Died: 11/23/1990

LCS		Batting																							Fielding						
Year Tm	Age	G	AB	H	2B	3B	HR	TB	R	RBI	GW	TBB	IBB	SO	HBP	SH	SF	SB	CS	SB%	GDP	Avg	OBP	SLG	Pos	G	PO	A	E	DP	FPct
1983 Phi	30	4	13	2	1	0	0	3	0	0	0	2	0	2	0	0	0	0	0	—	1	.154	.267	.231	C	4	32	2	0	0	1.000
World Series		Batting																							Fielding						
Year Tm	Age	G	AB	H	2B	3B	HR	TB	R	RBI	GW	TBB	IBB	SO	HBP	SH	SF	SB	CS	SB%	GDP	Avg	OBP	SLG	Pos	G	PO	A	E	DP	FPct
1983 Phi	30	5	15	5	1	0	0	6	1	0	0	1	0	2	0	0	0	0	0	—	0	.333	.375	.400	C	5	37	1	1	0	.974
Postseason Totals		9	28	7	2	0	0	9	1	0	0	3	0	4	0	0	0	0	0	—	1	.250	.323	.321	C	9	69	3	1	0	.986

CARLOS DIAZ—Carlos Antonio Diaz—Throws: Left; Bats: Right

Ht: 6'0"; Wt: 161 lbs; Born: 1/7/1958 in Kaneohe, Hawaii; Debut: 6/30/1982

LCS		Pitching																										
Year Tm	Age	G	GS	CG	GF	IP	BFP	H	R	ER	HR	SH	SF	HB	TBB	IBB	SO	WP	Bk	W	L	Pct	ShO	Sv-Op	Hld	OAvg	OOBP	ERA
1985 LA	27	2	0	0	1	3.0	15	5	1	1	0	0	0	0	1	1	2	0	0	0	0	—	0	0- 0	0	.357	.400	3.00

LCS		Batting																							Fielding						
Year Tm	Age	G	AB	H	2B	3B	HR	TB	R	RBI	GW	TBB	IBB	SO	HBP	SH	SF	SB	CS	SB%	GDP	Avg	OBP	SLG	Pos	G	PO	A	E	DP	FPct
1985 LA	27	2	0	0	0	0	0	0	0	0	0	0	0	0	0	0	0	0	0	—	0	—	—	—	P	2	1	0	0	0	1.000

ROB DIBBLE—Robert Keith Dibble—Throws: Right; Bats: Left

Ht: 6'4"; Wt: 230 lbs; Born: 1/24/1964 in Bridgeport, Connecticut; Debut: 6/29/1988

LCS		Pitching																										
Year Tm	Age	G	GS	CG	GF	IP	BFP	H	R	ER	HR	SH	SF	HB	TBB	IBB	SO	WP	Bk	W	L	Pct	ShO	Sv-Op	Hld	OAvg	OOBP	ERA
1990 Cin	26	4	0	0	2	5.0	16	0	0	0	0	0	0	0	1	0	10	0	0	0	0	—	0	1- 1	2	.000	.063	0.00
World Series		Pitching																										
Year Tm	Age	G	GS	CG	GF	IP	BFP	H	R	ER	HR	SH	SF	HB	TBB	IBB	SO	WP	Bk	W	L	Pct	ShO	Sv-Op	Hld	OAvg	OOBP	ERA
1990 Cin	26	3	0	0	1	4.2	17	3	0	0	0	0	0	0	1	0	4	1	0	1	0	1.000	0	0- 0	0	.188	.235	0.00
Postseason Totals		7	0	0	3	9.2	66	3	0	0	0	0	0	0	2	0	14	1	0	1	0	1.000	0	1-1	2	.097	.152	0.00

LCS		Batting																							Fielding						
Year Tm	Age	G	AB	H	2B	3B	HR	TB	R	RBI	GW	TBB	IBB	SO	HBP	SH	SF	SB	CS	SB%	GDP	Avg	OBP	SLG	Pos	G	PO	A	E	DP	FPct
1990 Cin	26	4	2	0	0	0	0	0	0	0	0	0	0	1	0	0	0	0	0	—	0	.000	.000	.000	P	4	0	0	0	0	—
World Series		Batting																							Fielding						
Year Tm	Age	G	AB	H	2B	3B	HR	TB	R	RBI	GW	TBB	IBB	SO	HBP	SH	SF	SB	CS	SB%	GDP	Avg	OBP	SLG	Pos	G	PO	A	E	DP	FPct
1990 Cin	26	3	0	0	0	0	0	0	0	0	0	0	0	0	0	0	0	0	0	—	0	—	—	—	P	3	0	0	0	0	—
Postseason Totals		7	2	0	0	0	0	0	0	0	0	0	0	1	0	0	0	0	0	—	0	.000	.000	.000	P	7	0	0	0	0	—

BILL DICKEY (HOF 1954-W)—William Malcolm Dickey—Bats: Left; Throws: Right

Ht: 6'1"; Wt: 185 lbs; Born: 6/6/1907 in Bastrop, Louisiana; Debut: 8/15/1928; Died: 11/12/1993

World Series		Batting																							Fielding						
Year Tm	Age	G	AB	H	2B	3B	HR	TB	R	RBI	GW	TBB	IBB	SO	HBP	SH	SF	SB	CS	SB%	GDP	Avg	OBP	SLG	Pos	G	PO	A	E	DP	FPct
1932 NYA	25	4	16	7	0	0	0	7	2	4	0	2	1	1	1	0	0	0	1	.00	1	.438	.526	.438	C	4	25	1	0	0	1.000
1936 NYA	29	6	25	3	0	0	1	6	5	5	0	3	0	4	0	0	0	0	0	—	0	.120	.214	.240	C	6	38	4	1	0	.977
1937 NYA	30	5	19	4	0	1	0	6	3	3	0	2	0	2	0	0	0	0	0	—	0	.211	.286	.316	C	5	26	1	0	0	1.000
1938 NYA	31	4	15	6	0	0	1	9	2	2	0	1	0	0	0	0	0	1	0	1.00	1	.400	.438	.600	C	4	30	5	0	0	1.000
1939 NYA	32	4	15	4	0	0	2	10	2	5	1	1	0	2	0	0	0	0	0	—	0	.267	.313	.667	C	4	27	2	0	1	1.000
1941 NYA	34	5	18	3	1	0	0	4	3	1	0	3	0	1	0	0	0	0	0	—	1	.167	.286	.222	C	5	24	2	0	1	1.000
1942 NYA	35	5	19	5	0	0	0	5	1	0	0	1	0	0	0	0	0	0	0	—	0	.263	.300	.263	C	5	25	1	1	1	.963
1943 NYA	36	5	18	5	0	0	1	8	1	4	1	2	1	2	0	0	0	0	0	—	1	.278	.350	.444	C	5	28	3	0	0	1.000
WS Totals		38	145	37	1	1	5	55	19	24	2	15	2	12	1	0	0	1	1	.50	4	.255	.329	.379	C	38	223	19	2	3	.992

MURRY DICKSON—Murry Monroe Dickson—Throws: Right; Bats: Right

Ht: 5'10"; Wt: 157 lbs; Born: 8/21/1916 in Tracy, Missouri; Debut: 9/30/1939; Died: 9/21/1989

World Series		Pitching																										
Year Tm	Age	G	GS	CG	GF	IP	BFP	H	R	ER	HR	SH	SF	HB	TBB	IBB	SO	WP	Bk	W	L	Pct	ShO	Sv-Op	Hld	OAvg	OOBP	ERA
1943 StL	27	1	0	0	1	0.2	3	0	0	0	0	0	0	0	1	0	0	0	0	0	0	—	0	0- 0	0	.000	.333	0.00
1946 StL	30	2	2	0	0	14.0	57	11	6	6	1	1	0	0	4	1	7	0	0	0	1	.000	0	0- 0	0	.212	.268	3.86
1958 NYA	42	2	0	0	1	4.0	16	4	2	2	0	0	1	0	0	0	1	0	0	0	0	—	0	0- 0	0	.267	.250	4.50
WS Totals		5	2	0	2	18.2	152	15	8	8	1	1	1	0	5	1	8	0	0	0	1	.000	0	0-0	0	.217	.267	3.86

World Series		Batting																							Fielding						
Year Tm	Age	G	AB	H	2B	3B	HR	TB	R	RBI	GW	TBB	IBB	SO	HBP	SH	SF	SB	CS	SB%	GDP	Avg	OBP	SLG	Pos	G	PO	A	E	DP	FPct
1943 StL	27	1	0	0	0	0	0	0	0	0	0	0	0	0	0	0	0	0	0	—	0	—	—	—	P	1	1	0	0	0	1.000
1946 StL	30	2	5	2	2	0	0	4	1	1	0	0	0	1	0	0	0	0	0	—	0	.400	.400	.800	P	2	0	3	0	0	1.000
1958 NYA	42	2	0	0	0	0	0	0	0	0	0	0	0	0	0	0	0	0	0	—	0	—	—	—	P	2	0	0	0	0	—
WS Totals		5	5	2	2	0	0	4	1	1	0	0	0	1	0	0	0	0	0	—	0	.400	.400	.800	P	5	1	3	0	0	1.000

BOB DIDIER—Robert Daniel Didier—Bats: Both; Throws: Right

Ht: 6'0"; Wt: 190 lbs; Born: 2/16/1949 in Hattiesburg, Mississippi; Debut: 4/7/1969

LCS		Batting																							Fielding						
Year Tm	Age	G	AB	H	2B	3B	HR	TB	R	RBI	GW	TBB	IBB	SO	HBP	SH	SF	SB	CS	SB%	GDP	Avg	OBP	SLG	Pos	G	PO	A	E	DP	FPct
1969 Atl	20	3	11	0	0	0	0	0	0	0	0	0	0	2	0	0	0	0	0	—	0	.000	.000	.000	C	3	24	1	0	1	1.000

DICK DIETZ—Richard Allen Dietz—Bats: Right; Throws: Right

Ht: 6'1"; Wt: 195 lbs; Born: 9/18/1941 in Crawfordsville, Indiana; Debut: 6/18/1966

LCS		Batting																							Fielding						
Year Tm	Age	G	AB	H	2B	3B	HR	TB	R	RBI	GW	TBB	IBB	SO	HBP	SH	SF	SB	CS	SB%	GDP	Avg	OBP	SLG	Pos	G	PO	A	E	DP	FPct
1971 SF	30	4	15	1	0	0	0	1	0	0	0	2	0	5	0	0	0	0	0	—	1	.067	.176	.067	C	4	34	2	0	1	1.000

DOM DiMAGGIO—Dominic Paul DiMaggio—Nickname: The Little Professor—Bats: Right; Throws: Right

Ht: 5'9"; Wt: 168 lbs; Born: 2/12/1917 in San Francisco, California; Debut: 4/16/1940

World Series		Batting																							Fielding						
Year Tm	Age	G	AB	H	2B	3B	HR	TB	R	RBI	GW	TBB	IBB	SO	HBP	SH	SF	SB	CS	SB%	GDP	Avg	OBP	SLG	Pos	G	PO	A	E	DP	FPct
1946 Bos	29	7	27	7	3	0	0	10	2	3	0	2	0	2	0	1	0	0	0	—	3	.259	.310	.370	OF	7	20	3	0	1	1.000

JOE DiMAGGIO (HOF 1955-W)—Joseph Paul DiMaggio—Nicknames: Joltin' Joe, The Yankee Clipper, Giuseppe—B: R; T: R

Ht: 6'2"; Wt: 193 lbs; Born: 11/25/1914 in Martinez, Calif.; Deb.: 5/3/1936

World Series		Batting																							Fielding						
Year Tm	Age	G	AB	H	2B	3B	HR	TB	R	RBI	GW	TBB	IBB	SO	HBP	SH	SF	SB	CS	SB%	GDP	Avg	OBP	SLG	Pos	G	PO	A	E	DP	FPct
1936 NYA	21	6	26	9	3	0	0	12	3	3	0	1	0	3	0	0	1	0	0	—	1	.346	.357	.462	OF	6	17	0	1	0	.944
1937 NYA	22	5	22	6	0	0	1	9	2	4	1	0	0	3	0	0	0	0	0	—	0	.273	.273	.409	OF	5	18	0	0	0	1.000
1938 NYA	23	4	15	4	0	0	1	7	4	2	0	1	0	1	0	0	0	0	0	—	0	.267	.313	.467	OF	4	10	0	0	0	1.000
1939 NYA-*M*	24	4	16	5	0	0	1	8	3	3	2	1	1	1	0	0	0	0	0	—	1	.313	.353	.500	OF	4	11	0	0	0	1.000
1941 NYA-*M*	26	5	19	5	0	0	0	5	1	1	1	2	0	2	0	0	0	0	0	—	1	.263	.333	.263	OF	5	18	0	0	0	1.000
1942 NYA	27	5	21	7	0	0	0	7	3	3	0	0	0	1	0	0	0	0	0	—	0	.333	.333	.333	OF	5	20	0	0	0	1.000
1947 NYA-*M*	32	7	26	6	0	0	2	12	4	5	0	6	1	2	0	0	0	0	0	—	3	.231	.375	.462	OF	7	23	0	0	0	1.000
1949 NYA	34	5	18	2	0	0	1	5	2	2	1	3	1	5	0	0	0	0	0	—	0	.111	.238	.278	OF	5	7	0	0	0	1.000
1950 NYA	35	4	13	4	1	0	1	8	2	2	1	3	1	1	1	0	0	0	0	—	0	.308	.471	.615	OF	4	8	0	0	0	1.000
1951 NYA	36	6	23	6	2	0	1	11	3	5	0	2	2	4	0	0	0	0	0	—	1	.261	.320	.478	OF	6	17	0	0	0	1.000
WS Totals		51	199	54	6	0	8	84	27	30	6	19	6	23	1	0	1	0	0	—	7	.271	.336	.422	OF	51	149	0	1	0	.993

BILL DINNEEN—William Henry Dinneen—Nickname: Big Bill—Throws: Right; Bats: Right

Ht: 6'1"; Wt: 190 lbs; Born: 4/5/1876 in Syracuse, New York; Debut: 4/22/1898; Died: 1/13/1955

World Series		Pitching																										
Year Tm	Age	G	GS	CG	GF	IP	BFP	H	R	ER	HR	SH	SF	HB	TBB	IBB	SO	WP	Bk	W	L	Pct	ShO	Sv-Op	Hld	OAvg	OOBP	ERA
1903 Bos	27	4	4	4	0	35.0	134	29	8	8	0	0	0	0	8	0	28	0	0	3	1	.750	2	0- 0	0	.230	.276	2.06

World Series Year Tm	Age	G	AB	H	2B	3B	HR	TB	R	RBI	GW	TBB	IBB	SO	HBP	SH	SF	SB	CS	SB%	GDP	Avg	OBP	SLG	Pos	G	PO	A	E	DP	FPct
1903 Bos	27	4	11	2	0	0	0	2	1	0	0	2	0	2	0	1	0	0	0	—	0	.182	.308	.182	P	4	2	9	0	0	1.000

ART DITMAR—Arthur John Ditmar—Throws: Right; Bats: Right

Ht: 6'2"; Wt: 185 lbs; Born: 4/3/1929 in Winthrop, Massachusetts; Debut: 4/19/1954

World Series Year Tm	Age	G	GS	CG	GF	IP	BFP	H	R	ER	HR	SH	SF	HB	TBB	IBB	SO	WP	Bk	W	L	Pct	ShO	Sv-Op	Hld	OAvg	OOBP	ERA
1957 NYA	28	2	0	0	0	6.0	22	2	0	0	0	1	0	1	0	0	2	0	0	0	0	—	0	0- 0	0	.100	.143	0.00
1958 NYA	29	1	0	0	0	3.2	12	2	0	0	0	1	0	0	0	0	2	0	0	0	0	—	0	0- 0	0	.182	.182	0.00
1960 NYA	31	2	2	0	0	1.2	13	6	6	4	0	0	0	0	1	0	0	0	0	0	2	.000	0	0- 0	0	.500	.538	21.60
WS Totals		5	2	0	0	11.1	94	10	6	4	0	2	0	1	1	0	4	0	0	0	2	.000	0	0-0	0	.233	.267	3.18

World Series Year Tm	Age	G	AB	H	2B	3B	HR	TB	R	RBI	GW	TBB	IBB	SO	HBP	SH	SF	SB	CS	SB%	GDP	Avg	OBP	SLG	Pos	G	PO	A	E	DP	FPct
1957 NYA	28	2	1	0	0	0	0	0	0	0	0	0	0	1	0	0	0	0	0	—	0	.000	.000	.000	P	2	0	0	0	0	—
1958 NYA	29	1	1	0	0	0	0	0	0	0	0	0	0	0	0	0	0	0	0	—	0	.000	.000	.000	P	1	1	0	1	0	.500
1960 NYA	31	2	0	0	0	0	0	0	0	0	0	0	0	0	0	0	0	0	0	—	0	—	—	—	P	2	0	0	0	0	—
WS Totals		5	2	0	0	0	0	0	0	0	0	0	0	1	0	0	0	0	0	—	0	.000	.000	.000	P	5	1	0	1	0	.500

JOE DOBSON—Joseph Gordon Dobson—Nickname: Burrhead—Throws: Right; Bats: Right

Ht: 6'2"; Wt: 197 lbs; Born: 1/20/1917 in Durant, Oklahoma; Debut: 4/26/1939; Died: 6/23/1994

World Series Year Tm	Age	G	GS	CG	GF	IP	BFP	H	R	ER	HR	SH	SF	HB	TBB	IBB	SO	WP	Bk	W	L	Pct	ShO	Sv-Op	Hld	OAvg	OOBP	ERA
1946 Bos	29	3	1	1	1	12.2	48	4	3	0	0	0	0	1	3	1	10	0	0	1	0	1.000	0	0- 0	0	.091	.167	0.00

World Series Year Tm	Age	G	AB	H	2B	3B	HR	TB	R	RBI	GW	TBB	IBB	SO	HBP	SH	SF	SB	CS	SB%	GDP	Avg	OBP	SLG	Pos	G	PO	A	E	DP	FPct
1946 Bos	29	3	3	0	0	0	0	0	0	0	0	0	0	2	0	1	0	0	0	—	0	.000	.000	.000	P	3	0	2	0	0	1.000

PAT DOBSON—Patrick Edward Dobson—Nickname: Snake—Throws: Right; Bats: Right

Ht: 6'3"; Wt: 190 lbs; Born: 2/12/1942 in DePew, New York; Debut: 5/31/1967

World Series Year Tm	Age	G	GS	CG	GF	IP	BFP	H	R	ER	HR	SH	SF	HB	TBB	IBB	SO	WP	Bk	W	L	Pct	ShO	Sv-Op	Hld	OAvg	OOBP	ERA
1968 Det	26	3	0	0	1	4.2	19	5	2	2	2	0	0	0	1	0	0	0	0	0	0	—	0	0- 0	0	.278	.316	3.86
1971 Bal	29	3	1	0	0	6.2	36	13	3	3	0	0	0	0	4	2	6	0	0	0	0	—	0	0- 0	0	.406	.472	4.05
WS Totals		6	1	0	1	11.1	110	18	5	5	2	0	0	0	5	2	6	0	0	0	0	—	0	0-0	0	.360	.418	3.97

World Series Year Tm	Age	G	AB	H	2B	3B	HR	TB	R	RBI	GW	TBB	IBB	SO	HBP	SH	SF	SB	CS	SB%	GDP	Avg	OBP	SLG	Pos	G	PO	A	E	DP	FPct
1968 Det	26	3	0	0	0	0	0	0	0	0	0	0	0	0	0	0	0	0	0	—	0	—	—	—	P	3	1	0	0	0	1.000
1971 Bal	29	3	2	0	0	0	0	0	0	0	0	0	0	2	0	0	0	0	0	—	0	.000	.000	.000	P	3	0	3	0	0	1.000
WS Totals		6	2	0	0	0	0	0	0	0	0	0	0	2	0	0	0	0	0	—	0	.000	.000	.000	P	6	1	3	0	0	1.000

LARRY DOBY (HOF 1998-V)—Lawrence Eugene Doby—Bats: Left; Throws: Right

Ht: 6'1"; Wt: 180 lbs; Born: 12/13/1923 in Camden, South Carolina; Debut: 7/5/1947

World Series Year Tm	Age	G	AB	H	2B	3B	HR	TB	R	RBI	GW	TBB	IBB	SO	HBP	SH	SF	SB	CS	SB%	GDP	Avg	OBP	SLG	Pos	G	PO	A	E	DP	FPct
1948 Cle	24	6	22	7	1	0	1	11	1	2	1	2	0	4	0	0	0	0	0	—	0	.318	.375	.500	OF	6	11	0	1	0	.917
1954 Cle	30	4	16	2	0	0	0	2	0	0	0	2	1	4	0	0	0	0	0	—	0	.125	.222	.125	OF	4	7	0	0	0	1.000
WS Totals		10	38	9	1	0	1	13	1	2	1	4	1	8	0	0	0	0	0	—	0	.237	.310	.342	OF	10	18	0	1	0	.947

BOBBY DOERR (HOF 1986-V)—Robert Pershing Doerr—Bats: Right; Throws: Right

Ht: 5'11"; Wt: 175 lbs; Born: 4/7/1918 in Los Angeles, California; Debut: 4/20/1937

World Series Year Tm	Age	G	AB	H	2B	3B	HR	TB	R	RBI	GW	TBB	IBB	SO	HBP	SH	SF	SB	CS	SB%	GDP	Avg	OBP	SLG	Pos	G	PO	A	E	DP	FPct
1946 Bos	28	6	22	9	1	0	1	13	1	3	0	2	0	2	0	0	0	0	0	—	0	.409	.458	.591	2B	6	17	32	0	3	1.000

FRANK DOLJACK—Frank Joseph Doljack—Nickname: Dolie—Bats: Right; Throws: Right

Ht: 5'11"; Wt: 175 lbs; Born: 10/5/1907 in Cleveland, Ohio; Debut: 9/4/1930; Died: 1/23/1948

World Series Year Tm	Age	G	AB	H	2B	3B	HR	TB	R	RBI	GW	TBB	IBB	SO	HBP	SH	SF	SB	CS	SB%	GDP	Avg	OBP	SLG	Pos	G	PO	A	E	DP	FPct
1934 Det	26	2	2	0	0	0	0	0	0	0	0	0	0	0	0	0	0	0	0	—	0	.000	.000	.000	OF	1	1	0	0	0	1.000

JIGGS DONAHUE—John Augustus Donahue—Bats: Left; Throws: Left

Ht: 6'1"; Wt: 178 lbs; Born: 7/13/1879 in Springfield, Ohio; Debut: 9/10/1900; Died: 7/19/1913

World Series Year Tm	Age	G	AB	H	2B	3B	HR	TB	R	RBI	GW	TBB	IBB	SO	HBP	SH	SF	SB	CS	SB%	GDP	Avg	OBP	SLG	Pos	G	PO	A	E	DP	FPct
1906 ChA	27	6	18	5	2	1	0	9	0	4	1	3	0	4	1	2	0	0	2	.00	1	.278	.409	.500	1B	6	80	8	1	2	.989

ATLEY DONALD—Richard Atley Donald—Nickname: Swampy—Throws: Right; Bats: Left

Ht: 6'1"; Wt: 186 lbs; Born: 8/19/1910 in Morton, Mississippi; Debut: 4/21/1938; Died: 10/19/1992

World Series Year Tm	Age	G	GS	CG	GF	IP	BFP	H	R	ER	HR	SH	SF	HB	TBB	IBB	SO	WP	Bk	W	L	Pct	ShO	Sv-Op	Hld	OAvg	OOBP	ERA
1941 NYA	31	1	1	0	0	4.0	21	6	4	4	1	0	0	0	3	0	2	0	0	0	0	—	0	0- 0	0	.333	.429	9.00
1942 NYA	32	1	0	0	0	3.0	14	3	2	2	0	0	0	0	2	0	1	0	0	0	1	.000	0	0- 0	0	.250	.357	6.00
WS Totals		2	1	0	0	7.0	70	9	6	6	1	0	0	0	5	0	3	0	0	0	1	.000	0	0-0	0	.300	.400	7.71

World Series Year Tm	Age	G	AB	H	2B	3B	HR	TB	R	RBI	GW	TBB	IBB	SO	HBP	SH	SF	SB	CS	SB%	GDP	Avg	OBP	SLG	Pos	G	PO	A	E	DP	FPct
1941 NYA	31	1	2	0	0	0	0	0	0	0	0	0	0	1	0	0	0	0	0	—	0	.000	.000	.000	P	1	0	1	0	0	1.000
1942 NYA	32	1	2	0	0	0	0	0	0	0	0	0	0	0	0	0	0	0	0	—	0	.000	.000	.000	P	1	0	0	0	0	—
WS Totals		2	4	0	0	0	0	0	0	0	0	0	0	1	0	0	0	0	0	—	0	.000	.000	.000	P	2	0	1	0	0	1.000

MIKE DONLIN—Michael Joseph Donlin—Nickname: Turkey Mike—Bats: Left; Throws: Left

Ht: 5'9"; Wt: 170 lbs; Born: 5/30/1878 in Peoria, Illinois; Debut: 7/19/1899; Died: 9/24/1933

World Series Year Tm	Age	G	AB	H	2B	3B	HR	TB	R	RBI	GW	TBB	IBB	SO	HBP	SH	SF	SB	CS	SB%	GDP	Avg	OBP	SLG	Pos	G	PO	A	E	DP	FPct
1905 NYG	27	5	19	5	1	0	0	6	4	1	1	2	1	1	0	1	0	2	1	.67	0	.263	.333	.316	OF	5	16	0	1	0	.941

BLIX DONNELLY—Sylvester Urban Donnelly—Throws: Right; Bats: Right

Ht: 5'10"; Wt: 166 lbs; Born: 1/21/1914 in Olivia, Minnesota; Debut: 5/6/1944; Died: 6/20/1976

World Series Year Tm	Age	G	GS	CG	GF	IP	BFP	H	R	ER	HR	SH	SF	HB	TBB	IBB	SO	WP	Bk	W	L	Pct	ShO	Sv-Op	Hld	OAvg	OOBP	ERA
1944 StL	30	2	0	0	2	6.0	21	2	0	0	0	0	0	0	1	1	9	0	0	1	0	1.000	0	0- 0	0	.100	.143	0.00

World Series Year Tm	Age	G	AB	H	2B	3B	HR	TB	R	RBI	GW	TBB	IBB	SO	HBP	SH	SF	SB	CS	SB%	GDP	Avg	OBP	SLG	Pos	G	PO	A	E	DP	FPct
1944 StL	30	2	1	0	0	0	0	0	0	0	0	0	0	1	0	0	0	0	0	—	0	.000	.000	.000	P	2	0	2	0	0	1.000

DICK DONOVAN—Richard Edward Donovan—Throws: Right; Bats: Left

Ht: 6'3"; Wt: 190 lbs; Born: 12/7/1927 in Boston, Massachusetts; Debut: 4/24/1950; Died: 1/6/1997

World Series Year Tm	Age	G	GS	CG	GF	IP	BFP	H	R	ER	HR	SH	SF	HB	TBB	IBB	SO	WP	Bk	W	L	Pct	ShO	Sv-Op	Hld	OAvg	OOBP	ERA
1959 ChA	31	3	1	0	1	8.1	31	4	5	5	1	0	0	0	3	0	5	0	0	0	1	.000	0	1- 1	0	.143	.226	5.40

World Series Year Tm	Age	G	AB	H	2B	3B	HR	TB	R	RBI	GW	TBB	IBB	SO	HBP	SH	SF	SB	CS	SB%	GDP	Avg	OBP	SLG	Pos	G	PO	A	E	DP	FPct
1959 ChA	31	3	3	1	0	0	0	1	0	0	0	0	0	1	0	0	0	0	0	—	0	.333	.333	.333	P	3	1	1	0	0	1.000

WILD BILL DONOVAN—William Edward Donovan—Throws: Right; Bats: Right

Ht: 5'11"; Wt: 190 lbs; Born: 10/13/1876 in Lawrence, Massachusetts; Debut: 4/22/1898; Died: 12/9/1923

World Series — Pitching

Year Tm	Age	G	GS	CG	GF	IP	BFP	H	R	ER	HR	SH	SF	HB	TBB	IBB	SO	WP	Bk	W	L	Pct	ShO	Sv-Op	Hld	OAvg	OOBP	ERA
1907 Det	30	2	2	2	0	21.0	86	17	9	4	0	6	0	3	5	0	16	0	0	0	1	.000	0	0- 0	0	.236	.313	1.71
1908 Det	31	2	2	2	0	17.0	67	17	8	8	1	3	0	0	4	0	10	1	0	0	2	.000	0	0- 0	0	.283	.328	4.24
1909 Det	32	2	2	1	0	12.0	52	7	4	4	0	3	1	1	8	0	7	0	0	1	1	.500	0	0- 0	0	.179	.327	3.00
WS Totals		6	6	5	0	50.0	410	41	21	16	1	12	1	4	17	0	33	1	0	1	4	.200	0	0-0	0	.240	.321	2.88

World Series — Batting / Fielding

Year Tm	Age	G	AB	H	2B	3B	HR	TB	R	RBI	GW	TBB	IBB	SO	HBP	SH	SF	SB	CS	SB%	GDP	Avg	OBP	SLG	Pos	G	PO	A	E	DP	FPct
1907 Det	30	2	8	0	0	0	0	0	0	0	0	0	0	3	0	0	0	0	0	—	0	.000	.000	.000	P	2	2	3	0	0	1.000
1908 Det	31	2	4	0	0	0	0	0	0	0	0	1	0	1	0	1	0	1	0	1.00	0	.000	.200	.000	P	2	1	2	1	0	.750
1909 Det	32	2	4	0	0	0	0	0	0	0	0	0	0	1	0	0	0	0	0	—	0	.000	.000	.000	P	2	0	5	1	0	.833
WS Totals		6	16	0	0	0	0	0	0	0	0	1	0	5	0	1	0	1	0	1.00	0	.000	.059	.000	P	6	3	10	2	0	.867

BILL DORAN—William Donald Doran—Bats: Both; Throws: Right

Ht: 5'11"; Wt: 175 lbs; Born: 5/28/1958 in Cincinnati, Ohio; Debut: 9/6/1982

LCS — Batting / Fielding

Year Tm	Age	G	AB	H	2B	3B	HR	TB	R	RBI	GW	TBB	IBB	SO	HBP	SH	SF	SB	CS	SB%	GDP	Avg	OBP	SLG	Pos	G	PO	A	E	DP	FPct
1986 Hou	28	6	27	6	0	0	1	9	3	3	0	2	0	2	0	0	0	2	0	1.00	0	.222	.276	.333	2B	6	10	17	0	2	1.000

RICH DOTSON—Richard Elliott Dotson—Throws: Right; Bats: Right

Ht: 6'1"; Wt: 190 lbs; Born: 1/10/1959 in Cincinnati, Ohio; Debut: 9/4/1979

LCS — Pitching

Year Tm	Age	G	GS	CG	GF	IP	BFP	H	R	ER	HR	SH	SF	HB	TBB	IBB	SO	WP	Bk	W	L	Pct	ShO	Sv-Op	Hld	OAvg	OOBP	ERA
1983 ChA	24	1	1	0	0	5.0	23	6	6	6	1	0	0	1	3	0	3	0	0	0	1	.000	0	0- 0	0	.316	.435	10.80

LCS — Batting / Fielding

Year Tm	Age	G	AB	H	2B	3B	HR	TB	R	RBI	GW	TBB	IBB	SO	HBP	SH	SF	SB	CS	SB%	GDP	Avg	OBP	SLG	Pos	G	PO	A	E	DP	FPct
1983 ChA	24	1	0	0	0	0	0	0	0	0	0	0	0	0	0	0	0	0	0	—	0	—	—	—	P	1	1	1	0	0	1.000

PATSY DOUGHERTY—Patrick Henry Dougherty—Bats: Left; Throws: Right

Ht: 6'2"; Wt: 190 lbs; Born: 10/27/1876 in Andover, New York; Debut: 4/19/1902; Died: 4/30/1940

World Series — Batting / Fielding

Year Tm	Age	G	AB	H	2B	3B	HR	TB	R	RBI	GW	TBB	IBB	SO	HBP	SH	SF	SB	CS	SB%	GDP	Avg	OBP	SLG	Pos	G	PO	A	E	DP	FPct
1903 Bos	26	8	34	8	0	2	2	18	3	5	1	2	0	6	1	0	0	0	0	—	0	.235	.297	.529	OF	8	12	3	1	1	.938
1906 ChA	29	6	20	2	0	0	0	2	1	1	0	3	0	3	0	0	0	2	0	1.00	0	.100	.217	.100	OF	6	4	0	1	0	.800
WS Totals		14	54	10	0	2	2	20	4	6	1	5	0	9	1	0	0	2	0	1.00	0	.185	.267	.370	OF	14	16	3	2	1	.905

PHIL DOUGLAS—Phillip Brooks Douglas—Nickname: Shufflin' Phil—Throws: Right; Bats: Right

Ht: 6'3"; Wt: 190 lbs; Born: 6/17/1890 in Cedartown, Georgia; Debut: 8/30/1912; Died: 8/2/1952

World Series — Pitching

Year Tm	Age	G	GS	CG	GF	IP	BFP	H	R	ER	HR	SH	SF	HB	TBB	IBB	SO	WP	Bk	W	L	Pct	ShO	Sv-Op	Hld	OAvg	OOBP	ERA
1918 ChN	28	1	0	0	1	1.0	5	1	1	0	0	1	0	0	0	0	0	0	0	0	1	.000	0	0- 0	0	.250	.250	0.00
1921 NYG	31	3	3	2	0	26.0	97	20	6	6	1	5	0	0	5	0	17	1	0	2	1	.667	0	0- 0	0	.230	.272	2.08
WS Totals		4	3	2	1	27.0	204	21	7	6	1	6	0	0	5	0	17	1	0	2	2	.500	0	0-0	0	.231	.271	2.00

World Series — Batting / Fielding

Year Tm	Age	G	AB	H	2B	3B	HR	TB	R	RBI	GW	TBB	IBB	SO	HBP	SH	SF	SB	CS	SB%	GDP	Avg	OBP	SLG	Pos	G	PO	A	E	DP	FPct
1918 ChN	28	1	0	0	0	0	0	0	0	0	0	0	0	0	0	0	0	0	0	—	0	—	—	—	P	1	0	0	1	0	.000
1921 NYG	31	3	7	0	0	0	0	0	0	0	0	0	0	2	0	1	0	0	0	—	0	.000	.000	.000	P	3	3	8	0	0	1.000
WS Totals		4	7	0	0	0	0	0	0	0	0	0	0	2	0	1	0	0	0	—	0	.000	.000	.000	P	4	3	8	1	0	.917

TAYLOR DOUTHIT—Taylor Lee Douthit—Nickname: Ball Hawk—Bats: Right; Throws: Right

Ht: 5'11"; Wt: 175 lbs; Born: 4/22/1901 in Little Rock, Arkansas; Debut: 9/14/1923; Died: 5/28/1986

World Series — Batting / Fielding

Year Tm	Age	G	AB	H	2B	3B	HR	TB	R	RBI	GW	TBB	IBB	SO	HBP	SH	SF	SB	CS	SB%	GDP	Avg	OBP	SLG	Pos	G	PO	A	E	DP	FPct
1926 StL	25	4	15	4	2	0	0	6	3	1	0	3	0	2	0	0	0	0	0	—	0	.267	.389	.400	OF	4	5	2	0	0	1.000
1928 StL	27	3	11	1	0	0	0	1	1	1	0	1	0	1	1	0	0	0	0	—	1	.091	.231	.091	OF	3	6	1	0	0	1.000
1930 StL	29	6	24	2	0	0	1	5	1	2	1	0	0	2	0	0	1	0	0	—	0	.083	.080	.208	OF	6	14	0	0	0	1.000
WS Totals		13	50	7	2	0	1	12	5	4	1	4	0	5	1	0	1	0	0	—	1	.140	.214	.240	OF	13	25	3	0	0	1.000

AL DOWNING—Alphonso Erwin Downing—Throws: Left; Bats: Right

Ht: 5'11"; Wt: 175 lbs; Born: 6/28/1941 in Trenton, New Jersey; Debut: 7/19/1961

LCS — Pitching

Year Tm	Age	G	GS	CG	GF	IP	BFP	H	R	ER	HR	SH	SF	HB	TBB	IBB	SO	WP	Bk	W	L	Pct	ShO	Sv-Op	Hld	OAvg	OOBP	ERA
1974 LA	33	1	0	0	0	4.0	15	1	0	0	0	0	0	0	1	0	0	0	0	0	0	—	0	0- 0	0	.077	.143	0.00

World Series — Pitching

Year Tm	Age	G	GS	CG	GF	IP	BFP	H	R	ER	HR	SH	SF	HB	TBB	IBB	SO	WP	Bk	W	L	Pct	ShO	Sv-Op	Hld	OAvg	OOBP	ERA
1963 NYA	22	1	1	0	0	5.0	21	7	3	3	1	0	0	0	1	0	6	0	0	0	1	.000	0	0- 0	0	.350	.381	5.40
1964 NYA	23	3	1	0	0	7.2	35	9	8	7	2	0	0	0	2	0	5	0	0	0	1	.000	0	0- 0	0	.273	.314	8.22
1974 LA	33	1	1	0	0	3.2	20	4	3	1	0	1	0	0	4	0	3	0	0	0	1	.000	0	0- 0	0	.267	.421	2.45
WS Totals		5	3	0	0	16.1	152	20	14	11	3	1	0	0	7	0	14	0	0	0	3	.000	0	0-0	0	.294	.360	6.06
Postseason Totals		6	3	0	0	20.1	182	21	14	11	3	1	0	0	8	0	14	0	0	0	3	.000	0	0-0	0	.259	.326	4.87

LCS — Batting / Fielding

Year Tm	Age	G	AB	H	2B	3B	HR	TB	R	RBI	GW	TBB	IBB	SO	HBP	SH	SF	SB	CS	SB%	GDP	Avg	OBP	SLG	Pos	G	PO	A	E	DP	FPct
1974 LA	33	1	1	0	0	0	0	0	0	0	0	0	0	0	0	0	0	0	0	—	0	.000	.000	.000	P	1	0	0	1	0	.000

World Series — Batting / Fielding

Year Tm	Age	G	AB	H	2B	3B	HR	TB	R	RBI	GW	TBB	IBB	SO	HBP	SH	SF	SB	CS	SB%	GDP	Avg	OBP	SLG	Pos	G	PO	A	E	DP	FPct
1963 NYA	22	1	1	0	0	0	0	0	0	0	0	0	0	1	0	0	0	0	0	—	0	.000	.000	.000	P	1	0	1	0	0	1.000
1964 NYA	23	3	2	0	0	0	0	0	0	0	0	0	0	2	0	0	0	0	0	—	0	.000	.000	.000	P	3	0	1	0	0	1.000
1974 LA	33	1	1	0	0	0	0	0	0	0	0	0	0	0	0	0	0	0	0	—	0	.000	.000	.000	P	1	0	3	0	0	1.000
WS Totals		5	4	0	0	0	0	0	0	0	0	0	0	3	0	0	0	0	0	—	0	.000	.000	.000	P	5	0	5	0	0	1.000
Postseason Totals		6	5	0	0	0	0	0	0	0	0	0	0	3	0	0	0	0	0	—	0	.000	.000	.000	P	6	0	5	1	0	.833

BRIAN DOWNING—Brian Jay Downing—Nickname: The Incredible Hulk—Bats: Right; Throws: Right

Ht: 5'10"; Wt: 170 lbs; Born: 10/9/1950 in Los Angeles, California; Debut: 5/31/1973

LCS — Batting / Fielding

Year Tm	Age	G	AB	H	2B	3B	HR	TB	R	RBI	GW	TBB	IBB	SO	HBP	SH	SF	SB	CS	SB%	GDP	Avg	OBP	SLG	Pos	G	PO	A	E	DP	FPct
1979 Cal	28	4	15	3	0	0	0	3	1	1	0	1	0	1	0	0	1	0	0	—	0	.200	.235	.200	C	4	27	0	0	1	1.000
1982 Cal	31	5	19	3	1	0	0	4	4	0	0	3	0	2	0	1	0	0	0	—	1	.158	.273	.211	OF	5	5	0	0	0	1.000
1986 Cal	35	7	27	6	0	0	1	9	2	7	0	4	1	5	1	0	1	0	1	.00	0	.222	.333	.333	OF	7	18	0	0	0	1.000
LCS Totals		16	61	12	1	0	1	16	7	8	0	8	1	8	1	1	2	0	1	.00	1	.197	.292	.262	OF	12	23	0	0	0	1.000

KELLY DOWNS—Kelly Robert Downs—Throws: Right; Bats: Right

Ht: 6'4"; Wt: 195 lbs; Born: 10/25/1960 in Ogden, Utah; Debut: 7/29/1986

LCS — Pitching

Year Tm	Age	G	GS	CG	GF	IP	BFP	H	R	ER	HR	SH	SF	HB	TBB	IBB	SO	WP	Bk	W	L	Pct	ShO	Sv-Op	Hld	OAvg	OOBP	ERA
1987 SF	26	1	0	0	0	1.1	5	1	0	0	0	0	0	0	0	0	0	0	0	0	0	—	0	0- 0	0	.200	.200	0.00
1989 SF	28	2	0	0	0	8.2	37	8	3	3	0	0	0	0	6	1	6	0	0	1	0	1.000	0	0- 0	0	.258	.378	3.12
1992 Oak	31	2	0	0	1	2.1	12	3	3	1	0	0	1	0	1	0	0	0	0	0	1	.000	0	0- 0	0	.300	.333	3.86
LCS Totals		5	0	0	1	12.1	108	12	6	4	0	0	1	0	7	1	6	0	0	1	1	.500	0	0-0	0	.261	.352	2.92

World Series — Pitching

Year Tm	Age	G	GS	CG	GF	IP	BFP	H	R	ER	HR	SH	SF	HB	TBB	IBB	SO	WP	Bk	W	L	Pct	ShO	Sv-Op	Hld	OAvg	OOBP	ERA
1989 SF	28	3	0	0	0	4.2	18	3	4	4	2	0	0	0	2	0	4	0	0	0	0	—	0	0- 0	0	.188	.278	7.71
Postseason Totals		8	0	0	1	17.0	144	15	10	8	2	0	1	0	9	1	10	0	0	1	1	.500	0	0-0	0	.242	.333	4.24

LCS — Batting / Fielding

Year Tm	Age	G	AB	H	2B	3B	HR	TB	R	RBI	GW	TBB	IBB	SO	HBP	SH	SF	SB	CS	SB%	GDP	Avg	OBP	SLG	Pos	G	PO	A	E	DP	FPct
1987 SF	26	1	0	0	0	0	0	0	0	0	0	0	0	0	0	0	0	0	0	—	0	—	—	—	P	1	0	0	0	0	—
1989 SF	28	2	3	0	0	0	0	0	0	0	0	0	0	1	0	1	0	0	0	—	0	.000	.000	.000	P	2	0	1	0	1	1.000
1992 Oak	31	2	0	0	0	0	0	0	0	0	0	0	0	0	0	0	0	0	0	—	0	—	—	—	P	2	0	0	0	0	—
LCS Totals		5	3	0	0	0	0	0	0	0	0	0	0	1	0	1	0	0	0	—	0	.000	.000	.000	P	5	0	1	0	1	1.000
World Series																															
Year Tm	Age	G	AB	H	2B	3B	HR	TB	R	RBI	GW	TBB	IBB	SO	HBP	SH	SF	SB	CS	SB%	GDP	Avg	OBP	SLG	Pos	G	PO	A	E	DP	FPct
1989 SF	28	3	0	0	0	0	0	0	0	0	0	0	0	0	0	0	0	0	0	—	0	—	—	—	P	3	0	0	0	0	—
Postseason Totals		8	3	0	0	0	0	0	0	0	0	0	0	1	0	1	0	0	0	—	0	.000	.000	.000	P	8	0	1	0	1	1.000

RED DOWNS—Jerome Willis Downs—Bats: Right; Throws: Right

Ht: 5'11"; Wt: 155 lbs; Born: 8/22/1883 in Neola, Iowa; Debut: 5/2/1907; Died: 10/19/1939

World Series — Batting / Fielding

Year Tm	Age	G	AB	H	2B	3B	HR	TB	R	RBI	GW	TBB	IBB	SO	HBP	SH	SF	SB	CS	SB%	GDP	Avg	OBP	SLG	Pos	G	PO	A	E	DP	FPct
1908 Det	25	2	6	1	1	0	0	2	1	1	0	1	0	2	0	0	0	0	0	—	0	.167	.286	.333	2B	2	2	8	1	1	.909

BRIAN DOYLE—Brian Reed Doyle—Bats: Left; Throws: Right

Ht: 5'10"; Wt: 160 lbs; Born: 1/26/1955 in Glasgow, Kentucky; Debut: 4/30/1978

LCS — Batting / Fielding

Year Tm	Age	G	AB	H	2B	3B	HR	TB	R	RBI	GW	TBB	IBB	SO	HBP	SH	SF	SB	CS	SB%	GDP	Avg	OBP	SLG	Pos	G	PO	A	E	DP	FPct
1978 NYA	23	3	7	2	0	0	0	2	0	1	0	1	0	1	0	0	0	0	0	—	0	.286	.375	.286	2B	3	3	6	0	0	1.000
World Series																															
Year Tm	Age	G	AB	H	2B	3B	HR	TB	R	RBI	GW	TBB	IBB	SO	HBP	SH	SF	SB	CS	SB%	GDP	Avg	OBP	SLG	Pos	G	PO	A	E	DP	FPct
1978 NYA	23	6	16	7	1	0	0	8	4	2	0	0	0	0	0	0	0	0	0	—	0	.438	.438	.500	2B	6	17	7	0	6	1.000
Postseason Totals		9	23	9	1	0	0	10	4	3	0	1	0	1	0	0	0	0	0	—	0	.391	.417	.435	2B	9	20	13	0	6	1.000

DENNY DOYLE—Robert Dennis Doyle—Bats: Left; Throws: Right

Ht: 5'9"; Wt: 175 lbs; Born: 1/17/1944 in Glasgow, Kentucky; Debut: 4/7/1970

LCS — Batting / Fielding

Year Tm	Age	G	AB	H	2B	3B	HR	TB	R	RBI	GW	TBB	IBB	SO	HBP	SH	SF	SB	CS	SB%	GDP	Avg	OBP	SLG	Pos	G	PO	A	E	DP	FPct
1975 Bos	31	3	11	3	0	0	0	3	3	2	0	0	0	1	0	1	1	0	0	—	0	.273	.250	.273	2B	3	6	8	1	2	.933
World Series																															
Year Tm	Age	G	AB	H	2B	3B	HR	TB	R	RBI	GW	TBB	IBB	SO	HBP	SH	SF	SB	CS	SB%	GDP	Avg	OBP	SLG	Pos	G	PO	A	E	DP	FPct
1975 Bos	31	7	30	8	1	1	0	11	3	0	0	2	0	1	0	1	0	0	0	—	0	.267	.313	.367	2B	7	12	23	3	2	.921
Postseason Totals		10	41	11	1	1	0	14	6	2	0	2	0	2	0	2	1	0	0	—	0	.268	.295	.341	2B	10	18	31	4	4	.925

LARRY DOYLE—Lawrence Joseph Doyle—Nickname: Laughing Larry—Bats: Left; Throws: Right

Ht: 5'10"; Wt: 165 lbs; Born: 7/31/1886 in Caseyville, Illinois; Debut: 7/22/1907; Died: 3/1/1974

World Series — Batting / Fielding

Year Tm	Age	G	AB	H	2B	3B	HR	TB	R	RBI	GW	TBB	IBB	SO	HBP	SH	SF	SB	CS	SB%	GDP	Avg	OBP	SLG	Pos	G	PO	A	E	DP	FPct
1911 NYG	25	6	23	7	3	1	0	12	3	1	0	2	0	1	0	0	0	2	0	1.00	0	.304	.360	.522	2B	6	13	15	1	2	.966
1912 NYG-*M*	26	8	33	8	1	0	1	12	5	2	0	3	1	2	0	0	0	2	0	1.00	0	.242	.306	.364	2B	8	15	26	5	1	.891
1913 NYG	27	5	20	3	0	0	0	3	1	2	0	0	0	1	1	0	0	0	0	—	0	.150	.190	.150	2B	5	13	19	3	1	.914
WS Totals		19	76	18	4	1	1	27	9	5	0	5	1	4	1	0	0	4	0	1.00	0	.237	.293	.355	2B	19	41	60	9	4	.918

PAUL DOYLE—Paul Sinnott Doyle—Throws: Left; Bats: Left

Ht: 5'11"; Wt: 172 lbs; Born: 10/2/1939 in Philadelphia, Pennsylvania; Debut: 5/28/1969

LCS — Pitching

Year Tm	Age	G	GS	CG	GF	IP	BFP	H	R	ER	HR	SH	SF	HB	TBB	IBB	SO	WP	Bk	W	L	Pct	ShO	Sv-Op	Hld	OAvg	OOBP	ERA
1969 Atl	29	1	0	0	0	1.0	7	2	2	0	0	0	0	0	1	1	3	0	0	0	0	—	0	0- 0	0	.333	.429	0.00

LCS — Batting / Fielding

Year Tm	Age	G	AB	H	2B	3B	HR	TB	R	RBI	GW	TBB	IBB	SO	HBP	SH	SF	SB	CS	SB%	GDP	Avg	OBP	SLG	Pos	G	PO	A	E	DP	FPct
1969 Atl	29	1	0	0	0	0	0	0	0	0	0	0	0	0	0	0	0	0	0	—	0	—	—	—	P	1	0	0	0	0	—

DOUG DRABEK—Douglas Dean Drabek—Throws: Right; Bats: Right

Ht: 6'1"; Wt: 185 lbs; Born: 7/25/1962 in Victoria, Texas; Debut: 5/30/1986

LCS — Pitching

Year Tm	Age	G	GS	CG	GF	IP	BFP	H	R	ER	HR	SH	SF	HB	TBB	IBB	SO	WP	Bk	W	L	Pct	ShO	Sv-Op	Hld	OAvg	OOBP	ERA
1990 Pit-*C*	28	2	2	1	0	16.1	63	12	4	3	0	1	1	1	3	1	13	1	0	1	1	.500	0	0- 0	0	.211	.258	1.65
1991 Pit	29	2	2	1	0	15.0	59	10	1	1	0	1	0	0	5	1	10	0	0	1	1	.500	0	0- 0	0	.189	.259	0.60
1992 Pit	30	3	3	0	0	17.0	76	18	11	7	1	2	0	0	6	1	10	0	0	0	3	.000	0	0- 0	0	.265	.324	3.71
LCS Totals		7	7	2	0	48.1	396	40	16	11	1	4	1	1	14	3	33	1	0	2	5	.286	0	0-0	0	.225	.284	2.05

LCS — Batting / Fielding

Year Tm	Age	G	AB	H	2B	3B	HR	TB	R	RBI	GW	TBB	IBB	SO	HBP	SH	SF	SB	CS	SB%	GDP	Avg	OBP	SLG	Pos	G	PO	A	E	DP	FPct
1990 Pit	28	2	6	1	0	0	0	1	0	0	0	0	0	2	0	0	0	0	0	—	0	.167	.167	.167	P	2	1	6	1	0	.875
1991 Pit	29	2	5	1	1	0	0	2	0	1	0	0	0	2	0	0	0	0	0	—	0	.200	.200	.400	P	2	3	0	0	0	1.000
1992 Pit	30	3	6	0	0	0	0	0	0	0	0	1	0	4	0	1	0	0	0	—	0	.000	.143	.000	P	3	0	0	0	0	—
LCS Totals		7	17	2	1	0	0	3	0	1	0	1	0	8	0	1	0	0	0	—	0	.118	.167	.176	P	7	4	6	1	0	.909

MOE DRABOWSKY—Myron Walter Drabowsky—Nickname: The Snakeman—Throws: Right; Bats: Right

Ht: 6'3"; Wt: 190 lbs; Born: 7/21/1935 in Ozanna, Poland; Debut: 8/7/1956

World Series — Pitching

Year Tm	Age	G	GS	CG	GF	IP	BFP	H	R	ER	HR	SH	SF	HB	TBB	IBB	SO	WP	Bk	W	L	Pct	ShO	Sv-Op	Hld	OAvg	OOBP	ERA
1966 Bal	31	1	0	0	1	6.2	23	1	0	0	0	0	0	0	2	0	11	0	0	1	0	1.000	0	0- 0	0	.048	.130	0.00
1970 Bal	35	2	0	0	1	3.1	12	2	1	1	1	1	0	0	1	0	1	0	0	0	0	—	0	0- 0	0	.200	.273	2.70
WS Totals		3	0	0	2	10.0	70	3	1	1	1	1	0	0	3	0	12	0	0	1	0	1.000	0	0-0	0	.097	.176	0.90

World Series — Batting / Fielding

Year Tm	Age	G	AB	H	2B	3B	HR	TB	R	RBI	GW	TBB	IBB	SO	HBP	SH	SF	SB	CS	SB%	GDP	Avg	OBP	SLG	Pos	G	PO	A	E	DP	FPct
1966 Bal	31	1	2	0	0	0	0	0	0	0	0	1	0	1	0	0	0	0	0	—	0	.000	.333	.000	P	1	0	0	0	0	—
1970 Bal	35	2	1	0	0	0	0	0	0	0	0	0	0	1	0	0	0	0	0	—	0	.000	.000	.000	P	2	1	0	0	0	1.000
WS Totals		3	3	0	0	0	0	0	0	0	0	1	0	2	0	0	0	0	0	—	0	.000	.250	.000	P	3	1	0	0	0	1.000

DICK DRAGO—Richard Anthony Drago—Throws: Right; Bats: Right

Ht: 6'1"; Wt: 190 lbs; Born: 6/25/1945 in Toledo, Ohio; Debut: 4/11/1969

LCS — Pitching

Year Tm	Age	G	GS	CG	GF	IP	BFP	H	R	ER	HR	SH	SF	HB	TBB	IBB	SO	WP	Bk	W	L	Pct	ShO	Sv-Op	Hld	OAvg	OOBP	ERA
1975 Bos	30	2	0	0	2	4.2	15	2	0	0	0	0	0	0	1	0	2	1	0	0	0	—	0	2- 2	0	.143	.200	0.00
World Series																												
Year Tm	Age	G	GS	CG	GF	IP	BFP	H	R	ER	HR	SH	SF	HB	TBB	IBB	SO	WP	Bk	W	L	Pct	ShO	Sv-Op	Hld	OAvg	OOBP	ERA
1975 Bos	30	2	0	0	1	4.0	16	3	1	1	0	0	0	1	1	1	1	0	0	0	1	.000	0	0- 1	0	.214	.313	2.25
Postseason Totals		4	0	0	3	8.2	62	5	1	1	0	0	0	1	2	1	3	1	0	0	1	.000	0	2-3	0	.179	.258	1.04

LCS — Batting / Fielding

Year Tm	Age	G	AB	H	2B	3B	HR	TB	R	RBI	GW	TBB	IBB	SO	HBP	SH	SF	SB	CS	SB%	GDP	Avg	OBP	SLG	Pos	G	PO	A	E	DP	FPct
1975 Bos	30	2	0	0	0	0	0	0	0	0	0	0	0	0	0	0	0	0	0	—	0	—	—	—	P	2	1	0	0	0	1.000
World Series																															
Year Tm	Age	G	AB	H	2B	3B	HR	TB	R	RBI	GW	TBB	IBB	SO	HBP	SH	SF	SB	CS	SB%	GDP	Avg	OBP	SLG	Pos	G	PO	A	E	DP	FPct
1975 Bos	30	2	0	0	0	0	0	0	0	0	0	0	0	0	0	0	0	0	0	—	0	—	—	—	P	2	0	0	0	0	—
Postseason Totals		4	0	0	0	0	0	0	0	0	0	0	0	0	0	0	0	0	0	—	0	—	—	—	P	4	1	0	0	0	1.000

DAVE DRAVECKY—David Francis Dravecky—Throws: Left; Bats: Right

Ht: 6'1"; Wt: 195 lbs; Born: 2/14/1956 in Youngstown, Ohio; Debut: 6/15/1982

LCS — Pitching

Year Tm	Age	G	GS	CG	GF	IP	BFP	H	R	ER	HR	SH	SF	HB	TBB	IBB	SO	WP	Bk	W	L	Pct	ShO	Sv-Op	Hld	OAvg	OOBP	ERA
1984 SD	28	3	0	0	0	6.0	19	2	0	0	0	0	0	0	0	0	5	0	0	0	0	—	0	0- 0	0	.105	.105	0.00
1987 SF	31	2	2	1	0	15.0	53	7	1	1	0	0	1	0	4	0	14	0	0	1	1	.500	1	0- 0	0	.146	.208	0.60
LCS Totals		5	2	1	0	21.0	144	9	1	1	0	0	1	0	4	0	19	0	0	1	1	.500	1	0-0	0	.134	.181	0.43

World Series		Pitching																								
Year Tm	Age	G	GS	CG	GF	IP	BFP	H	R	ER	HR	SH	SF	HB	TBB	IBB	SO	WP	Bk	W	L	Pct	ShO	Sv-Op	Hld	OAvg	OOBP	ERA
1984 SD	28	2	0	0	1	4.2	16	3	0	0	0	0	0	0	1	0	5	0	0	0	0	—	0	0-0	0	.200	.250	0.00
Postseason Totals		7	2	1	1	25.2	176	12	1	1	0	0	1	0	5	0	24	0	0	1	1	.500	1	0-0	0	.146	.193	0.35

LCS		Batting																						Fielding						
Year Tm	Age	G	AB	H	2B	3B	HR	TB	R	RBI	GW	TBB	IBB	SO	HBP	SH	SF	SB	CS	SB%	GDP	Avg	OBP	SLG	Pos	G	PO	A	E	DP	FPct
1984 SD	28	3	0	0	0	0	0	0	0	0	0	0	0	0	0	0	0	0	0	—	0	—	—	—	P	3	1	1	0	0	1.000
1987 SF	31	2	6	1	0	0	0	1	0	0	0	0	0	1	0	0	0	0	0	—	0	.167	.167	.167	P	2	0	2	0	0	1.000
LCS Totals		5	6	1	0	0	0	1	0	0	0	0	0	1	0	0	0	0	0	—	0	.167	.167	.167	P	5	1	3	0	0	1.000
World Series		**Batting**																							**Fielding**						
Year Tm	Age	G	AB	H	2B	3B	HR	TB	R	RBI	GW	TBB	IBB	SO	HBP	SH	SF	SB	CS	SB%	GDP	Avg	OBP	SLG	Pos	G	PO	A	E	DP	FPct
1984 SD	28	2	0	0	0	0	0	0	0	0	0	0	0	0	0	0	0	0	0	—	0	—	—	—	P	2	0	0	0	0	—
Postseason Totals		7	6	1	0	0	0	1	0	0	0	0	0	1	0	0	0	0	0	—	0	.167	.167	.167	P	7	1	3	0	0	1.000

DARREN DREIFORT—Darren James Dreifort—Throws: Right; Bats: Right

Ht: 6'2"; Wt: 200 lbs; Born: 5/18/1972 in Wichita, Kansas; Debut: 4/7/1994

Division Series		Pitching																								
Year Tm	Age	G	GS	CG	GF	IP	BFP	H	R	ER	HR	SH	SF	HB	TBB	IBB	SO	WP	Bk	W	L	Pct	ShO	Sv-Op	Hld	OAvg	OOBP	ERA
1996 LA	24	1	0	0	1	0.2	1	0	0	0	0	0	0	0	0	0	0	0	0	0	0	—	0	0-0	0	.000	.000	0.00

Division Series		Batting																						Fielding						
Year Tm	Age	G	AB	H	2B	3B	HR	TB	R	RBI	GW	TBB	IBB	SO	HBP	SH	SF	SB	CS	SB%	GDP	Avg	OBP	SLG	Pos	G	PO	A	E	DP	FPct
1996 LA	24	1	0	0	0	0	0	0	0	0	0	0	0	0	0	0	0	0	0	—	0	—	—	—	P	1	1	1	0	1	1.000

CLEM DREISEWERD—Clement John Dreisewerd—Nickname: Steamboat—Throws: Left; Bats: Left

Ht: 6'1"; Wt: 195 lbs; Born: 1/24/1916 in Old Monroe, Missouri; Debut: 8/29/1944

World Series		Pitching																								
Year Tm	Age	G	GS	CG	GF	IP	BFP	H	R	ER	HR	SH	SF	HB	TBB	IBB	SO	WP	Bk	W	L	Pct	ShO	Sv-Op	Hld	OAvg	OOBP	ERA
1946 Bos	30	1	0	0	1	0.1	1	0	0	0	0	0	0	0	0	0	0	0	0	0	0	—	0	0-0	0	.000	.000	0.00

World Series		Batting																						Fielding						
Year Tm	Age	G	AB	H	2B	3B	HR	TB	R	RBI	GW	TBB	IBB	SO	HBP	SH	SF	SB	CS	SB%	GDP	Avg	OBP	SLG	Pos	G	PO	A	E	DP	FPct
1946 Bos	30	1	0	0	0	0	0	0	0	0	0	0	0	0	0	0	0	0	0	—	0	—	—	—	P	1	0	0	0	0	—

KARL DREWS—Karl August Drews—Throws: Right; Bats: Right

Ht: 6'4"; Wt: 192 lbs; Born: 2/22/1920 in Staten Island, New York; Debut: 9/8/1946; Died: 8/15/1963

World Series		Pitching																								
Year Tm	Age	G	GS	CG	GF	IP	BFP	H	R	ER	HR	SH	SF	HB	TBB	IBB	SO	WP	Bk	W	L	Pct	ShO	Sv-Op	Hld	OAvg	OOBP	ERA
1947 NYA	27	2	0	0	0	3.0	13	2	1	1	0	0	0	1	1	0	0	1	0	0	0	—	0	0-0	0	.182	.308	3.00

World Series		Batting																						Fielding						
Year Tm	Age	G	AB	H	2B	3B	HR	TB	R	RBI	GW	TBB	IBB	SO	HBP	SH	SF	SB	CS	SB%	GDP	Avg	OBP	SLG	Pos	G	PO	A	E	DP	FPct
1947 NYA	27	2	2	0	0	0	0	0	0	0	0	0	0	2	0	0	0	0	0	—	0	.000	.000	.000	P	2	0	3	0	0	1.000

DAN DRIESSEN—Daniel Driessen—Bats: Left; Throws: Right

Ht: 5'11"; Wt: 187 lbs; Born: 7/29/1951 in Hilton Head Island, South Carolina; Debut: 6/9/1973

LCS		Batting																						Fielding						
Year Tm	Age	G	AB	H	2B	3B	HR	TB	R	RBI	GW	TBB	IBB	SO	HBP	SH	SF	SB	CS	SB%	GDP	Avg	OBP	SLG	Pos	G	PO	A	E	DP	FPct
1973 Cin	22	4	12	2	1	0	0	3	0	1	0	0	0	2	0	0	1	0	1	.00	0	.167	.154	.250	3B	4	3	4	1	1	.875
1976 Cin	25	1	1	0	0	0	0	0	0	0	0	0	0	0	0	0	0	0	0	—	0	.000	.000	.000	—						
1979 Cin	28	3	12	1	0	0	0	1	1	0	0	1	1	3	0	0	0	0	0	—	0	.083	.154	.083	1B	3	32	0	0	2	1.000
1987 StL	36	5	12	3	2	0	0	5	1	1	0	1	0	1	0	0	0	0	0	—	1	.250	.308	.417	1B	4	26	3	1	2	.967
LCS Totals		13	37	6	3	0	0	9	2	2	0	2	1	6	0	0	1	0	1	.00	1	.162	.200	.243	1B	7	58	3	1	4	.984
World Series		**Batting**																							**Fielding**						
Year Tm	Age	G	AB	H	2B	3B	HR	TB	R	RBI	GW	TBB	IBB	SO	HBP	SH	SF	SB	CS	SB%	GDP	Avg	OBP	SLG	Pos	G	PO	A	E	DP	FPct
1975 Cin	24	2	2	0	0	0	0	0	0	0	0	0	0	0	0	0	0	0	0	—	0	.000	.000	.000	—						
1976 Cin	25	4	14	5	2	0	1	10	4	1	0	2	1	0	0	0	0	1	0	1.00	0	.357	.438	.714	—						
1987 StL	36	4	13	3	2	0	0	5	3	1	0	1	1	1	0	0	0	0	0	—	0	.231	.286	.385	1B	4	27	1	0	0	1.000
WS Totals		10	29	8	4	0	1	15	7	2	0	3	2	1	0	0	0	1	0	1.00	0	.276	.344	.517	1B	4	27	1	0	0	1.000
Postseason Totals		23	66	14	7	0	1	24	9	4	0	5	3	7	0	0	1	1	1	.50	1	.212	.264	.364	1B	11	85	4	1	4	.989

KEITH DRUMRIGHT—Keith Alan Drumright—Bats: Left; Throws: Right

Ht: 5'10"; Wt: 170 lbs; Born: 10/21/1954 in Springfield, Missouri; Debut: 9/1/1978

Division Series		Batting																						Fielding						
Year Tm	Age	G	AB	H	2B	3B	HR	TB	R	RBI	GW	TBB	IBB	SO	HBP	SH	SF	SB	CS	SB%	GDP	Avg	OBP	SLG	Pos	G	PO	A	E	DP	FPct
1981 Oak	26	1	4	1	0	0	0	1	0	0	0	0	0	0	0	0	0	0	0	—	1	.250	.250	.250	—						
LCS		**Batting**																							**Fielding**						
Year Tm	Age	G	AB	H	2B	3B	HR	TB	R	RBI	GW	TBB	IBB	SO	HBP	SH	SF	SB	CS	SB%	GDP	Avg	OBP	SLG	Pos	G	PO	A	E	DP	FPct
1981 Oak	26	3	4	0	0	0	0	0	0	0	0	1	1	0	0	0	0	0	0	—	0	.000	.200	.000	—						
Postseason Totals		4	8	1	0	0	0	1	0	0	0	1	1	0	0	0	0	0	0	—	1	.125	.222	.125	—	0	0	0	0	0	—

DON DRYSDALE (HOF 1984-W)—Donald Scott Drysdale—Nickname: Big D—Throws: Right; Bats: Right

Ht: 6'5"; Wt: 190 lbs; Born: 7/23/1936 in Van Nuys, Calif.; Debut: 4/17/1956; Died: 7/3/1993

World Series		Pitching																								
Year Tm	Age	G	GS	CG	GF	IP	BFP	H	R	ER	HR	SH	SF	HB	TBB	IBB	SO	WP	Bk	W	L	Pct	ShO	Sv-Op	Hld	OAvg	OOBP	ERA
1956 Bro	20	1	0	0	1	2.0	9	2	2	2	1	0	0	0	1	0	1	0	0	0	0	—	0	0-0	0	.250	.333	9.00
1959 LA	23	1	1	0	0	7.0	32	11	1	1	0	0	0	0	4	1	5	0	0	1	0	1.000	0	0-0	0	.393	.469	1.29
1963 LA	27	1	1	1	0	9.0	32	3	0	0	0	1	0	1	1	1	9	0	0	1	0	1.000	1	0-0	0	.103	.161	0.00
1965 LA	29	2	2	1	0	11.2	50	12	9	5	4	1	0	0	3	0	15	0	0	1	1	.500	0	0-0	0	.261	.306	3.86
1966 LA	30	2	2	1	0	10.0	39	8	5	5	3	1	0	0	3	0	6	0	0	0	2	.000	0	0-0	0	.229	.289	4.50
WS Totals		7	6	3	1	39.2	324	36	17	13	8	3	0	1	12	2	36	0	0	3	3	.500	1	0-0	0	.247	.308	2.95

World Series		Batting																						Fielding						
Year Tm	Age	G	AB	H	2B	3B	HR	TB	R	RBI	GW	TBB	IBB	SO	HBP	SH	SF	SB	CS	SB%	GDP	Avg	OBP	SLG	Pos	G	PO	A	E	DP	FPct
1956 Bro	20	1	0	0	0	0	0	0	0	0	0	0	0	0	0	0	0	0	0	—	0	—	—	—	P	1	0	0	0	0	—
1959 LA	23	1	2	0	0	0	0	0	0	0	0	0	0	2	0	0	0	0	0	—	0	.000	.000	.000	P	1	1	1	0	0	1.000
1963 LA	27	1	1	0	0	0	0	0	0	0	0	2	0	0	0	0	0	0	0	—	0	.000	.667	.000	P	1	1	3	0	0	1.000
1965 LA	29	3	5	0	0	0	0	0	0	0	0	0	0	4	0	0	0	0	0	—	0	.000	.000	.000	P	2	0	2	0	0	1.000
1966 LA	30	2	2	0	0	0	0	0	0	0	0	0	0	1	0	0	0	0	0	—	0	.000	.000	.000	P	2	0	3	0	0	1.000
WS Totals		8	10	0	0	0	0	0	0	0	0	2	0	7	0	0	0	0	0	—	0	.000	.167	.000	P	7	2	9	0	0	1.000

JEAN DUBUC—Jean Joseph Octave Dubuc—Nickname: Chauncey—Throws: Right; Bats: Right

Ht: 5'10"; Wt: 185 lbs; Born: 9/15/1888 in St. Johnsbury, Vermont; Debut: 6/25/1908; Died: 8/28/1958

World Series		Batting																						Fielding						
Year Tm	Age	G	AB	H	2B	3B	HR	TB	R	RBI	GW	TBB	IBB	SO	HBP	SH	SF	SB	CS	SB%	GDP	Avg	OBP	SLG	Pos	G	PO	A	E	DP	FPct
1918 Bos	30	1	1	0	0	0	0	0	0	0	0	0	0	1	0	0	0	0	0	—	0	.000	.000	.000	—						

ROB DUCEY—Robert Thomas Ducey—Bats: Left; Throws: Right

Ht: 6'2"; Wt: 175 lbs; Born: 5/24/1965 in Toronto, Ontario; Debut: 5/1/1987

Division Series		Batting																						Fielding						
Year Tm	Age	G	AB	H	2B	3B	HR	TB	R	RBI	GW	TBB	IBB	SO	HBP	SH	SF	SB	CS	SB%	GDP	Avg	OBP	SLG	Pos	G	PO	A	E	DP	FPct
1997 Sea	32	2	4	2	0	0	0	2	0	1	0	0	0	0	0	0	0	0	0	—	0	.500	.500	.500	OF	1	0	0	0	0	—
LCS		**Batting**																							**Fielding**						
Year Tm	Age	G	AB	H	2B	3B	HR	TB	R	RBI	GW	TBB	IBB	SO	HBP	SH	SF	SB	CS	SB%	GDP	Avg	OBP	SLG	Pos	G	PO	A	E	DP	FPct
1991 Tor	26	1	1	0	0	0	0	0	0	0	0	0	0	0	0	0	0	0	0	—	0	.000	.000	.000	OF	1	0	0	0	0	—
Postseason Totals		3	5	2	0	0	0	2	0	1	0	0	0	0	0	0	0	0	0	—	0	.400	.400	.400	OF	2	0	0	0	0	—

FRANK DUFFY—Frank Thomas Duffy—Bats: Right; Throws: Right

Ht: 6'1"; Wt: 180 lbs; Born: 10/14/1946 in Oakland, California; Debut: 9/4/1970

LCS		Batting																							Fielding						
Year Tm	Age	G	AB	H	2B	3B	HR	TB	R	RBI	GW	TBB	IBB	SO	HBP	SH	SF	SB	CS	SB%	GDP	Avg	OBP	SLG	Pos	G	PO	A	E	DP	FPct
1971 SF	24	1	1	0	0	0	0	0	0	0	0	0	0	1	0	0	0	0	0	—	0	.000	.000	.000	—						

JOE DUGAN—Joseph Anthony Dugan—Nickname: Jumping Joe—Bats: Right; Throws: Right

Ht: 5'11"; Wt: 160 lbs; Born: 5/12/1897 in Mahanoy City, Pennsylvania; Debut: 7/5/1917; Died: 7/7/1982

World Series		Batting																							Fielding						
Year Tm	Age	G	AB	H	2B	3B	HR	TB	R	RBI	GW	TBB	IBB	SO	HBP	SH	SF	SB	CS	SB%	GDP	Avg	OBP	SLG	Pos	G	PO	A	E	DP	FPct
1922 NYA	25	5	20	5	1	0	0	6	4	0	0	0	0	1	1	0	0	0	0	—	0	.250	.286	.300	3B	5	5	8	0	0	1.000
1923 NYA	26	6	25	7	2	1	1	14	5	5	0	3	0	0	0	0	0	0	0	—	0	.280	.357	.560	3B	6	7	13	0	2	1.000
1926 NYA	29	7	24	8	1	0	0	9	2	2	0	1	0	1	0	0	0	0	1	.00	1	.333	.360	.375	3B	7	7	14	1	0	.955
1927 NYA	30	4	15	3	0	0	0	3	2	0	0	0	0	0	0	2	0	0	0	—	0	.200	.200	.200	3B	4	3	6	0	1	1.000
1928 NYA	31	3	7	1	0	0	0	1	0	2	0	0	0	0	0	0	1	0	0	—	0	.143	.125	.143	3B	3	3	0	0	0	1.000
WS Totals		25	91	24	4	1	1	33	13	9	0	4	0	2	1	2	1	0	1	.00	1	.264	.299	.363	3B	25	25	41	1	3	.985

OSCAR DUGEY—Oscar Joseph Dugey—Nickname: Jake—Bats: Right; Throws: Right

Ht: 5'8"; Wt: 160 lbs; Born: 10/25/1887 in Palestine, Texas; Debut: 9/13/1913; Died: 1/1/1966

World Series		Batting																							Fielding						
Year Tm	Age	G	AB	H	2B	3B	HR	TB	R	RBI	GW	TBB	IBB	SO	HBP	SH	SF	SB	CS	SB%	GDP	Avg	OBP	SLG	Pos	G	PO	A	E	DP	FPct
1915 Phi	27	2	0	0	0	0	0	0	0	0	0	0	0	0	0	0	0	1	0	1.00	0	—	—	—	—						

TOM DUKES—Thomas Earl Dukes—Throws: Right; Bats: Right

Ht: 6'2"; Wt: 185 lbs; Born: 8/31/1942 in Knoxville, Tennessee; Debut: 8/15/1967

World Series		Pitching																										
Year Tm	Age	G	GS	CG	GF	IP	BFP	H	R	ER	HR	SH	SF	HB	TBB	IBB	SO	WP	Bk	W	L	Pct	ShO	Sv-Op	Hld	OAvg	OOBP	ERA
1971 Bal	29	2	0	0	1	4.0	15	2	0	0	0	1	0	1	0	0	1	0	0	0	0	—	0	0-0	0	.154	.214	0.00

World Series		Batting																							Fielding						
Year Tm	Age	G	AB	H	2B	3B	HR	TB	R	RBI	GW	TBB	IBB	SO	HBP	SH	SF	SB	CS	SB%	GDP	Avg	OBP	SLG	Pos	G	PO	A	E	DP	FPct
1971 Bal	29	2	0	0	0	0	0	0	0	0	0	0	0	0	0	0	0	0	0	—	0	—	—	—	P	2	0	0	0	0	—

DAVE DUNCAN—David Edwin Duncan—Bats: Right; Throws: Right

Ht: 6'2"; Wt: 190 lbs; Born: 9/26/1945 in Dallas, Texas; Debut: 5/6/1964

LCS		Batting																							Fielding						
Year Tm	Age	G	AB	H	2B	3B	HR	TB	R	RBI	GW	TBB	IBB	SO	HBP	SH	SF	SB	CS	SB%	GDP	Avg	OBP	SLG	Pos	G	PO	A	E	DP	FPct
1971 Oak	26	2	6	3	1	0	0	4	0	2	0	0	0	0	0	0	0	0	1	.00	0	.500	.500	.667	C	2	15	0	0	0	1.000
1972 Oak	27	2	2	0	0	0	0	0	0	0	0	1	0	1	0	0	0	0	0	—	0	.000	.333	.000	C	2	5	1	0	0	1.000
LCS Totals		4	8	3	1	0	0	4	0	2	0	1	0	1	0	0	0	0	1	.00	0	.375	.444	.500	C	4	20	1	0	0	1.000
World Series		Batting																							Fielding						
Year Tm	Age	G	AB	H	2B	3B	HR	TB	R	RBI	GW	TBB	IBB	SO	HBP	SH	SF	SB	CS	SB%	GDP	Avg	OBP	SLG	Pos	G	PO	A	E	DP	FPct
1972 Oak	27	3	5	1	0	0	0	1	0	0	0	1	0	3	0	0	0	0	1	.00	0	.200	.333	.200	C	1	5	1	0	0	1.000
Postseason Totals		7	13	4	1	0	0	5	0	2	0	2	0	4	0	0	0	0	2	.00	0	.308	.400	.385	C	5	25	2	0	0	1.000

MARIANO DUNCAN—Bats: Both; Throws: Right

Ht: 6'0"; Wt: 160 lbs; Born: 3/13/1963 in San Pedro de Macoris, Dominican Republic; Debut: 4/9/1985

Division Series		Batting																							Fielding						
Year Tm	Age	G	AB	H	2B	3B	HR	TB	R	RBI	GW	TBB	IBB	SO	HBP	SH	SF	SB	CS	SB%	GDP	Avg	OBP	SLG	Pos	G	PO	A	E	DP	FPct
1995 Cin	32	2	3	2	0	0	0	2	1	1	0	0	0	0	0	0	0	1	0	1.00	1	.667	.667	.667	2B	1	0	1	0	0	1.000
1996 NYA	33	4	16	5	0	0	0	5	0	3	1	0	0	4	1	0	0	0	0	—	0	.313	.353	.313	2B	4	9	13	0	2	1.000
DS Totals		6	19	7	0	0	0	7	1	4	1	0	0	4	1	0	0	1	0	1.00	1	.368	.400	.368	2B	5	9	14	0	2	1.000
LCS		Batting																							Fielding						
Year Tm	Age	G	AB	H	2B	3B	HR	TB	R	RBI	GW	TBB	IBB	SO	HBP	SH	SF	SB	CS	SB%	GDP	Avg	OBP	SLG	Pos	G	PO	A	E	DP	FPct
1985 LA	22	5	18	4	2	1	0	8	2	1	0	1	0	3	0	0	0	1	0	1.00	0	.222	.263	.444	SS	5	7	16	1	2	.958
1990 Cin	27	6	20	6	0	0	1	9	1	4	1	0	0	8	0	0	0	0	0	—	0	.300	.300	.450	2B	6	6	11	1	0	.944
1993 Phi	30	3	15	4	0	2	0	8	3	0	0	0	0	5	0	0	0	0	0	—	0	.267	.267	.533	2B	3	5	6	1	0	.917
1995 Cin	32	3	3	0	0	0	0	0	0	0	0	1	0	1	0	0	0	0	0	—	1	.000	.250	.000	1B	1	9	0	0	1	1.000
1996 NYA	33	4	15	3	2	0	0	5	0	0	0	0	0	3	1	0	0	0	0	—	2	.200	.250	.333	2B	4	5	7	1	0	.923
LCS Totals		21	71	17	4	3	1	30	6	5	1	2	0	20	1	0	0	1	0	1.00	3	.239	.270	.423	2B	13	16	24	3	0	.930
World Series		Batting																							Fielding						
Year Tm	Age	G	AB	H	2B	3B	HR	TB	R	RBI	GW	TBB	IBB	SO	HBP	SH	SF	SB	CS	SB%	GDP	Avg	OBP	SLG	Pos	G	PO	A	E	DP	FPct
1990 Cin	27	4	14	2	0	0	0	2	1	1	0	2	0	2	0	0	0	1	0	1.00	0	.143	.250	.143	2B	4	9	9	0	2	1.000
1993 Phi	30	6	29	10	0	1	0	12	5	2	0	1	0	7	0	0	0	3	0	1.00	1	.345	.367	.414	2B	5	11	17	1	5	.966
1996 NYA	33	6	19	1	0	0	0	1	1	0	0	0	0	4	0	0	0	1	0	1.00	0	.053	.053	.053	2B	6	9	14	2	5	.920
WS Totals		16	62	13	0	1	0	15	7	3	0	3	0	13	0	0	0	5	0	1.00	1	.210	.246	.242	2B	15	29	40	3	12	.958
Postseason Totals		43	152	37	4	4	1	52	14	12	2	5	0	37	2	0	0	7	0	1.00	5	.243	.277	.342	2B	33	54	78	6	14	.957

PAT DUNCAN—Louis Baird Duncan—Bats: Right; Throws: Right

Ht: 5'9"; Wt: 170 lbs; Born: 10/6/1893 in Coalton, Ohio; Debut: 7/16/1915; Died: 7/17/1960

World Series		Batting																							Fielding						
Year Tm	Age	G	AB	H	2B	3B	HR	TB	R	RBI	GW	TBB	IBB	SO	HBP	SH	SF	SB	CS	SB%	GDP	Avg	OBP	SLG	Pos	G	PO	A	E	DP	FPct
1919 Cin	25	8	26	7	2	0	0	9	3	8	0	2	0	2	0	2	1	0	1	.00	0	.269	.310	.346	OF	8	9	0	0	0	1.000

SHAWON DUNSTON—Shawon Donnell Dunston—Bats: Right; Throws: Right

Ht: 6'1"; Wt: 175 lbs; Born: 3/21/1963 in Brooklyn, New York; Debut: 4/9/1985

LCS		Batting																							Fielding						
Year Tm	Age	G	AB	H	2B	3B	HR	TB	R	RBI	GW	TBB	IBB	SO	HBP	SH	SF	SB	CS	SB%	GDP	Avg	OBP	SLG	Pos	G	PO	A	E	DP	FPct
1989 ChN	26	5	19	6	0	0	0	6	2	0	0	1	0	1	0	0	0	1	0	1.00	1	.316	.350	.316	SS	5	10	14	1	1	.960

RYNE DUREN—Rinold George Duren—Nickname: The Flame—Throws: Right; Bats: Right

Ht: 6'2"; Wt: 190 lbs; Born: 2/22/1929 in Cazenovia, Wisconsin; Debut: 9/25/1954

World Series		Pitching																										
Year Tm	Age	G	GS	CG	GF	IP	BFP	H	R	ER	HR	SH	SF	HB	TBB	IBB	SO	WP	Bk	W	L	Pct	ShO	Sv-Op	Hld	OAvg	OOBP	ERA
1958 NYA	29	3	0	0	2	9.1	40	7	2	2	0	0	1	0	6	0	14	1	0	1	1	.500	0	1-2	0	.212	.325	1.93
1960 NYA	31	2	0	0	2	4.0	15	2	1	1	0	0	0	1	1	0	5	1	0	0	0	—	0	0-0	0	.154	.267	2.25
WS Totals		5	0	0	4	13.1	110	9	3	3	0	0	1	1	7	0	19	2	0	1	1	.500	0	1-2	0	.196	.309	2.03

World Series		Batting																							Fielding						
Year Tm	Age	G	AB	H	2B	3B	HR	TB	R	RBI	GW	TBB	IBB	SO	HBP	SH	SF	SB	CS	SB%	GDP	Avg	OBP	SLG	Pos	G	PO	A	E	DP	FPct
1958 NYA	29	3	3	0	0	0	0	0	0	0	0	0	0	2	0	0	0	0	0	—	0	.000	.000	.000	P	3	0	1	0	1	1.000
1960 NYA	31	2	0	0	0	0	0	0	0	0	0	0	0	0	0	0	0	0	0	—	0	—	—	—	P	2	0	2	0	0	1.000
WS Totals		5	3	0	0	0	0	0	0	0	0	0	0	2	0	0	0	0	0	—	0	.000	.000	.000	P	5	0	3	0	1	1.000

LEON DURHAM—Nickname: Bull—Bats: Left; Throws: Left

Ht: 6'1"; Wt: 185 lbs; Born: 7/31/1957 in Cincinnati, Ohio; Debut: 5/27/1980

LCS		Batting																							Fielding						
Year Tm	Age	G	AB	H	2B	3B	HR	TB	R	RBI	GW	TBB	IBB	SO	HBP	SH	SF	SB	CS	SB%	GDP	Avg	OBP	SLG	Pos	G	PO	A	E	DP	FPct
1984 ChN	27	5	20	3	0	0	2	9	2	4	0	1	1	4	0	0	0	0	0	—	1	.150	.190	.450	1B	5	45	3	1	6	.980

LEO DUROCHER (HOF 1994-V)—Leo Ernest Durocher—Nickname: The Lip—Bats: R; Throws: R

Ht: 5'10"; Wt: 160 lbs; Born: 7/27/1905 in West Springfield, Mass.; Debut: 10/2/1925; Died: 10/7/1991

World Series		Batting																							Fielding						
Year Tm	Age	G	AB	H	2B	3B	HR	TB	R	RBI	GW	TBB	IBB	SO	HBP	SH	SF	SB	CS	SB%	GDP	Avg	OBP	SLG	Pos	G	PO	A	E	DP	FPct
1928 NYA	23	4	2	0	0	0	0	0	0	0	0	0	0	1	0	0	0	0	0	—	0	.000	.000	.000	2B	4	1	1	0	1	1.000
1934 StL	29	7	27	7	1	1	0	10	4	0	0	0	0	0	0	0	0	0	0	—	0	.259	.259	.370	SS	7	13	17	0	1	1.000
WS Totals		11	29	7	1	1	0	10	4	0	0	0	0	1	0	0	0	0	0	—	0	.241	.241	.345	SS	7	13	17	0	1	1.000

CEDRIC DURST—Cedric Montgomery Durst—Bats: Left; Throws: Left

Ht: 5'11"; Wt: 160 lbs; Born: 8/23/1896 in Austin, Texas; Debut: 5/30/1922; Died: 2/16/1971

World Series		Batting																							Fielding						
Year Tm	Age	G	AB	H	2B	3B	HR	TB	R	RBI	GW	TBB	IBB	SO	HBP	SH	SF	SB	CS	SB%	GDP	Avg	OBP	SLG	Pos	G	PO	A	E	DP	FPct
1927 NYA	31	1	1	0	0	0	0	0	0	0	0	0	0	0	0	0	0	0	0	—	0	.000	.000	.000	—						
1928 NYA	32	4	8	3	0	0	1	6	3	2	1	0	0	1	0	0	0	0	0	—	0	.375	.375	.750	OF	4	3	0	0	0	1.000
WS Totals		5	9	3	0	0	1	6	3	2	1	0	0	1	0	0	0	0	0	—	0	.333	.333	.667	OF	4	3	0	0	0	1.000

ERV DUSAK—Ervin Frank Dusak—Nickname: Foursack—Bats: Right; Throws: Right

Ht: 6'2"; Wt: 185 lbs; Born: 7/29/1920 in Chicago, Illinois; Debut: 9/18/1941; Died: 11/6/1994

World Series		Batting																							Fielding						
Year Tm	Age	G	AB	H	2B	3B	HR	TB	R	RBI	GW	TBB	IBB	SO	HBP	SH	SF	SB	CS	SB%	GDP	Avg	OBP	SLG	Pos	G	PO	A	E	DP	FPct
1946 StL	26	4	4	1	1	0	0	2	0	0	0	2	0	2	0	0	0	0	0	—	0	.250	.500	.500	OF	4	1	1	0	0	1.000

JIM DWYER—James Edward Dwyer—Bats: Left; Throws: Left

Ht: 5'10"; Wt: 165 lbs; Born: 6/3/1950 in Evergreen Park, Illinois; Debut: 6/10/1973

LCS		Batting																							Fielding						
Year Tm	Age	G	AB	H	2B	3B	HR	TB	R	RBI	GW	TBB	IBB	SO	HBP	SH	SF	SB	CS	SB%	GDP	Avg	OBP	SLG	Pos	G	PO	A	E	DP	FPct
1983 Bal	33	2	4	1	1	0	0	2	1	0	0	1	0	0	0	0	0	0	0	—	0	.250	.400	.500	OF	1	4	0	0	0	1.000
World Series		Batting																							Fielding						
Year Tm	Age	G	AB	H	2B	3B	HR	TB	R	RBI	GW	TBB	IBB	SO	HBP	SH	SF	SB	CS	SB%	GDP	Avg	OBP	SLG	Pos	G	PO	A	E	DP	FPct
1983 Bal	33	2	8	3	1	0	1	7	3	1	0	0	0	0	0	0	0	0	0	—	0	.375	.375	.875	OF	2	2	0	0	0	1.000
Postseason Totals		4	12	4	2	0	1	9	4	1	0	1	0	0	0	0	0	0	0	—	0	.333	.385	.750	OF	3	6	0	0	0	1.000

JERRY DYBZINSKI—Jerome Mathew Dybzinski—Bats: Right; Throws: Right

Ht: 6'2"; Wt: 180 lbs; Born: 7/7/1955 in Cleveland, Ohio; Debut: 4/11/1980

LCS		Batting																							Fielding						
Year Tm	Age	G	AB	H	2B	3B	HR	TB	R	RBI	GW	TBB	IBB	SO	HBP	SH	SF	SB	CS	SB%	GDP	Avg	OBP	SLG	Pos	G	PO	A	E	DP	FPct
1983 ChA	28	2	4	1	0	0	0	1	0	0	0	0	0	0	0	0	0	0	0	—	0	.250	.250	.250	SS	2	3	8	0	2	1.000

JERMAINE DYE—Jermaine Terrell Dye—Bats: Right; Throws: Right

Ht: 6'4"; Wt: 210 lbs; Born: 1/28/1974 in Oakland, California; Debut: 5/17/1996

Division Series		Batting																							Fielding						
Year Tm	Age	G	AB	H	2B	3B	HR	TB	R	RBI	GW	TBB	IBB	SO	HBP	SH	SF	SB	CS	SB%	GDP	Avg	OBP	SLG	Pos	G	PO	A	E	DP	FPct
1996 Atl	22	3	11	2	0	0	1	5	1	1	1	0	0	6	0	0	0	1	0	1.00	0	.182	.182	.455	OF	3	11	1	0	0	1.000
LCS		Batting																							Fielding						
Year Tm	Age	G	AB	H	2B	3B	HR	TB	R	RBI	GW	TBB	IBB	SO	HBP	SH	SF	SB	CS	SB%	GDP	Avg	OBP	SLG	Pos	G	PO	A	E	DP	FPct
1996 Atl	22	7	28	6	1	0	0	7	2	4	1	1	0	7	0	0	2	0	1	.00	0	.214	.226	.250	OF	7	14	0	0	0	1.000
World Series		Batting																							Fielding						
Year Tm	Age	G	AB	H	2B	3B	HR	TB	R	RBI	GW	TBB	IBB	SO	HBP	SH	SF	SB	CS	SB%	GDP	Avg	OBP	SLG	Pos	G	PO	A	E	DP	FPct
1996 Atl	22	5	17	2	0	0	0	2	0	1	0	1	0	1	0	1	0	0	0	—	0	.118	.167	.118	OF	5	15	0	1	0	.938
Postseason Totals		15	56	10	1	0	1	14	3	6	2	2	0	14	0	1	2	1	1	.50	0	.179	.200	.250	OF	15	40	1	1	0	.976

DUFFY DYER—Don Robert Dyer—Bats: Right; Throws: Right

Ht: 6'0"; Wt: 187 lbs; Born: 8/15/1945 in Dayton, Ohio; Debut: 9/21/1968

LCS		Batting																							Fielding						
Year Tm	Age	G	AB	H	2B	3B	HR	TB	R	RBI	GW	TBB	IBB	SO	HBP	SH	SF	SB	CS	SB%	GDP	Avg	OBP	SLG	Pos	G	PO	A	E	DP	FPct
1975 Pit	30	1	0	0	0	0	0	0	0	1	0	1	0	0	0	0	0	0	0	—	0	—	1.000	—	—						
World Series		Batting																							Fielding						
Year Tm	Age	G	AB	H	2B	3B	HR	TB	R	RBI	GW	TBB	IBB	SO	HBP	SH	SF	SB	CS	SB%	GDP	Avg	OBP	SLG	Pos	G	PO	A	E	DP	FPct
1969 NYN	24	1	1	0	0	0	0	0	0	0	0	0	0	0	0	0	0	0	0	—	0	.000	.000	.000	—						
Postseason Totals		2	1	0	0	0	0	0	0	1	0	1	0	0	0	0	0	0	0	—	0	.000	.500	.000	—	0	0	0	0	0	—

JIMMY DYKES—James Joseph Dykes—Nickname: Roundman—Bats: Right; Throws: Right

Ht: 5'9"; Wt: 185 lbs; Born: 11/10/1896 in Philadelphia, Pennsylvania; Debut: 5/6/1918; Died: 6/15/1976

World Series		Batting																							Fielding						
Year Tm	Age	G	AB	H	2B	3B	HR	TB	R	RBI	GW	TBB	IBB	SO	HBP	SH	SF	SB	CS	SB%	GDP	Avg	OBP	SLG	Pos	G	PO	A	E	DP	FPct
1929 Phi	32	5	19	8	1	0	0	9	2	4	1	1	0	1	0	0	0	0	0	—	0	.421	.450	.474	3B	5	3	4	2	1	.778
1930 Phi	33	6	18	4	3	0	1	10	2	5	1	5	0	3	0	2	0	0	0	—	0	.222	.391	.556	3B	6	8	6	1	1	.933
1931 Phi	34	7	22	5	0	0	0	5	2	2	0	5	0	1	0	1	0	0	0	—	1	.227	.370	.227	3B	7	4	12	0	1	1.000
WS Totals		18	59	17	4	0	1	24	6	11	2	11	0	5	0	3	0	0	0	—	1	.288	.400	.407	3B	18	15	22	3	3	.925

LENNY DYKSTRA—Leonard Kyle Dykstra—Nickname: Nails—Bats: Left; Throws: Left

Ht: 5'10"; Wt: 160 lbs; Born: 2/10/1963 in Santa Ana, California; Debut: 5/3/1985

LCS		Batting																							Fielding						
Year Tm	Age	G	AB	H	2B	3B	HR	TB	R	RBI	GW	TBB	IBB	SO	HBP	SH	SF	SB	CS	SB%	GDP	Avg	OBP	SLG	Pos	G	PO	A	E	DP	FPct
1986 NYN	23	6	23	7	1	1	1	13	3	3	1	2	1	4	0	0	0	1	0	1.00	0	.304	.360	.565	OF	6	10	0	0	0	1.000
1988 NYN	25	7	14	6	3	0	1	12	6	3	0	4	0	0	2	0	0	0	0	—	0	.429	.600	.857	OF	7	9	0	0	0	1.000
1993 Phi	30	6	25	7	1	0	2	14	5	2	1	5	1	8	0	0	0	0	0	—	0	.280	.400	.560	OF	6	13	0	0	0	1.000
LCS Totals		19	62	20	5	1	4	39	14	8	2	11	2	12	2	0	0	1	0	1.00	0	.323	.440	.629	OF	19	32	0	0	0	1.000
World Series		Batting																							Fielding						
Year Tm	Age	G	AB	H	2B	3B	HR	TB	R	RBI	GW	TBB	IBB	SO	HBP	SH	SF	SB	CS	SB%	GDP	Avg	OBP	SLG	Pos	G	PO	A	E	DP	FPct
1986 NYN	23	7	27	8	0	0	2	14	4	3	1	2	0	7	0	2	0	0	0	—	0	.296	.345	.519	OF	7	15	0	0	0	1.000
1993 Phi	30	6	23	8	1	0	4	21	9	8	0	7	1	4	0	0	0	4	0	1.00	0	.348	.500	.913	OF	6	18	1	0	0	1.000
WS Totals		13	50	16	1	0	6	35	13	11	1	9	1	11	0	2	0	4	0	1.00	0	.320	.424	.700	OF	13	33	1	0	0	1.000
Postseason Totals		32	112	36	6	1	10	74	27	19	3	20	3	23	2	2	0	5	0	1.00	0	.321	.433	.661	OF	32	65	1	0	0	1.000

GEORGE EARNSHAW—George Livingston Earnshaw—Nickname: Moose—Throws: Right; Bats: Right

Ht: 6'4"; Wt: 210 lbs; Born: 2/15/1900 in New York, New York; Debut: 6/3/1928; Died: 12/1/1976

World Series		Pitching																										
Year Tm	Age	G	GS	CG	GF	IP	BFP	H	R	ER	HR	SH	SF	HB	TBB	IBB	SO	WP	Bk	W	L	Pct	ShO	Sv-Op	Hld	OAvg	OOBP	ERA
1929 Phi	29	2	2	1	0	13.2	62	14	6	4	0	0	0	0	6	0	17	0	0	0	1	.000	0	0- 0	0	.250	.323	2.63
1930 Phi	30	3	3	2	0	25.0	95	13	2	2	1	1	0	0	7	1	19	0	0	2	0	1.000	0	0- 0	0	.149	.213	0.72
1931 Phi	31	3	3	2	0	24.0	88	12	6	5	1	3	0	0	4	0	20	1	0	1	2	.333	1	0- 0	0	.148	.188	1.88
WS Totals		8	8	5	0	62.2	490	39	14	11	2	4	0	0	17	1	56	1	0	3	3	.500	1	0-0	0	.174	.232	1.58

World Series		Batting																							Fielding						
Year Tm	Age	G	AB	H	2B	3B	HR	TB	R	RBI	GW	TBB	IBB	SO	HBP	SH	SF	SB	CS	SB%	GDP	Avg	OBP	SLG	Pos	G	PO	A	E	DP	FPct
1929 Phi	29	2	5	0	0	0	0	0	1	0	0	0	0	4	0	1	0	0	0	—	0	.000	.000	.000	P	2	0	2	0	0	1.000
1930 Phi	30	3	9	0	0	0	0	0	0	0	0	0	0	5	0	0	0	0	0	—	0	.000	.000	.000	P	3	1	6	0	0	1.000
1931 Phi	31	3	8	0	0	0	0	0	0	0	0	0	0	2	0	0	0	0	0	—	2	.000	.000	.000	P	3	1	7	0	0	1.000
WS Totals		8	22	0	0	0	0	0	1	0	0	0	0	11	0	1	0	0	0	—	2	.000	.000	.000	P	8	2	15	0	0	1.000

MIKE EASLER—Michael Anthony Easler—Nickname: The Hit Man—Bats: Left; Throws: Right

Ht: 6'0"; Wt: 190 lbs; Born: 11/29/1950 in Cleveland, Ohio; Debut: 9/5/1973

LCS		Batting																							Fielding						
Year Tm	Age	G	AB	H	2B	3B	HR	TB	R	RBI	GW	TBB	IBB	SO	HBP	SH	SF	SB	CS	SB%	GDP	Avg	OBP	SLG	Pos	G	PO	A	E	DP	FPct
1979 Pit	28	1	1	0	0	0	0	0	0	0	0	0	0	0	0	0	0	0	0	—	0	.000	.000	.000	—						
World Series		Batting																							Fielding						
Year Tm	Age	G	AB	H	2B	3B	HR	TB	R	RBI	GW	TBB	IBB	SO	HBP	SH	SF	SB	CS	SB%	GDP	Avg	OBP	SLG	Pos	G	PO	A	E	DP	FPct
1979 Pit	28	2	1	0	0	0	0	0	0	0	0	1	0	0	0	0	0	0	0	—	0	.000	.500	.000	—						
Postseason Totals		3	2	0	0	0	0	0	0	0	0	1	0	0	0	0	0	0	0	—	0	.000	.333	.000	—	0	0	0	0	0	—

JAMIE EASTERLY—James Morris Easterly—Throws: Left; Bats: Left

Ht: 5'9"; Wt: 180 lbs; Born: 2/17/1953 in Houston, Texas; Debut: 4/6/1974

Division Series		Pitching																										
Year Tm	Age	G	GS	CG	GF	IP	BFP	H	R	ER	HR	SH	SF	HB	TBB	IBB	SO	WP	Bk	W	L	Pct	ShO	Sv-Op	Hld	OAvg	OOBP	ERA
1981 Mil	28	2	0	0	0	1.1	6	2	1	1	0	0	1	0	0	0	1	0	0	0	0	—	0	0- 0	1	.400	.333	6.75

Division Series — Batting / Fielding

Year Tm	Age	G	AB	H	2B	3B	HR	TB	R	RBI	GW	TBB	IBB	SO	HBP	SH	SF	SB	CS	SB%	GDP	Avg	OBP	SLG	Pos	G	PO	A	E	DP	FPct
1981 Mil	28	2	0	0	0	0	0	0	0	0	0	0	0	0	0	0	0	0	0	—	0	—	—	—	P	2	0	0	0	0	—

RAWLY EASTWICK—Rawlins Jackson Eastwick—Throws: Right; Bats: Right

Ht: 6'3"; Wt: 180 lbs; Born: 10/24/1950 in Camden, New Jersey; Debut: 9/12/1974

LCS — Pitching

Year	Tm	Age	G	GS	CG	GF	IP	BFP	H	R	ER	HR	SH	SF	HB	TBB	IBB	SO	WP	Bk	W	L	Pct	ShO	Sv-Op	Hld	OAvg	OOBP	ERA
1975	Cin	24	2	0	0	1	3.2	15	2	0	0	0	0	0	0	2	0	1	0	0	1	0	1.000	0	1- 2	0	.154	.267	0.00
1976	Cin	25	2	0	0	2	3.0	19	7	5	4	0	0	1	0	2	1	1	2	0	1	0	1.000	0	0- 1	0	.438	.474	12.00
1978	Phi	27	1	0	0	0	1.0	7	3	1	1	1	0	0	1	0	0	1	0	0	0	0	—	0	0- 0	0	.500	.571	9.00
LCS Totals			5	0	0	3	7.2	82	12	6	5	1	0	1	1	4	1	3	2	0	2	0	1.000	0	1-3	0	.343	.415	5.87

World Series — Pitching

Year	Tm	Age	G	GS	CG	GF	IP	BFP	H	R	ER	HR	SH	SF	HB	TBB	IBB	SO	WP	Bk	W	L	Pct	ShO	Sv-Op	Hld	OAvg	OOBP	ERA
1975	Cin	24	5	0	0	4	8.0	32	6	2	2	2	1	0	0	3	0	4	0	0	2	0	1.000	0	1- 3	0	.214	.290	2.25
Postseason Totals			10	0	0	7	15.2	146	18	8	7	3	1	1	1	7	1	7	2	0	4	0	1.000	0	2-6	0	.286	.361	4.02

LCS — Batting / Fielding

Year Tm	Age	G	AB	H	2B	3B	HR	TB	R	RBI	GW	TBB	IBB	SO	HBP	SH	SF	SB	CS	SB%	GDP	Avg	OBP	SLG	Pos	G	PO	A	E	DP	FPct
1975 Cin	24	2	0	0	0	0	0	0	0	0	0	0	0	0	0	0	0	0	0	—	0	—	—	—	P	2	1	0	0	0	1.000
1976 Cin	25	2	0	0	0	0	0	0	0	0	0	0	0	0	0	0	0	0	0	—	0	—	—	—	P	2	0	1	0	0	1.000
1978 Phi	27	1	0	0	0	0	0	0	0	0	0	0	0	0	0	0	0	0	0	—	0	—	—	—	P	1	0	0	0	0	—
LCS Totals		5	0	0	0	0	0	0	0	0	0	0	0	0	0	0	0	0	0	—	0	—	—	—	P	5	1	1	0	0	1.000

World Series — Batting / Fielding

Year Tm	Age	G	AB	H	2B	3B	HR	TB	R	RBI	GW	TBB	IBB	SO	HBP	SH	SF	SB	CS	SB%	GDP	Avg	OBP	SLG	Pos	G	PO	A	E	DP	FPct
1975 Cin	24	5	1	0	0	0	0	0	0	0	0	0	0	0	0	0	0	0	0	—	0	.000	.000	.000	P	5	0	0	0	0	—
Postseason Totals		10	1	0	0	0	0	0	0	0	0	0	0	0	0	0	0	0	0	—	0	.000	.000	.000	P	10	1	1	0	0	1.000

ZEB EATON—Zebulon Vance Eaton—Nickname: Red—Throws: Right; Bats: Right

Ht: 5'10"; Wt: 185 lbs; Born: 2/2/1920 in Cooleemee, North Carolina; Debut: 4/18/1944; Died: 12/17/1989

World Series — Batting / Fielding

Year Tm	Age	G	AB	H	2B	3B	HR	TB	R	RBI	GW	TBB	IBB	SO	HBP	SH	SF	SB	CS	SB%	GDP	Avg	OBP	SLG	Pos	G	PO	A	E	DP	FPct
1945 Det	25	1	1	0	0	0	0	0	0	0	0	0	0	1	0	0	0	0	0	—	0	.000	.000	.000	—						

DENNIS ECKERSLEY—Dennis Lee Eckersley—Nickname: The Eck—Throws: Right; Bats: Right

Ht: 6'2"; Wt: 190 lbs; Born: 10/3/1954 in Oakland, California; Debut: 4/12/1975

Division Series — Pitching

Year	Tm	Age	G	GS	CG	GF	IP	BFP	H	R	ER	HR	SH	SF	HB	TBB	IBB	SO	WP	Bk	W	L	Pct	ShO	Sv-Op	Hld	OAvg	OOBP	ERA
1996	StL	41	3	0	0	3	3.2	14	3	0	0	0	0	0	0	0	0	2	0	0	0	0	—	0	3- 3	0	.214	.214	0.00

LCS — Pitching

Year	Tm	Age	G	GS	CG	GF	IP	BFP	H	R	ER	HR	SH	SF	HB	TBB	IBB	SO	WP	Bk	W	L	Pct	ShO	Sv-Op	Hld	OAvg	OOBP	ERA
1984	ChN	29	1	1	0	0	5.1	22	9	5	5	0	0	0	0	0	0	0	0	0	0	1	.000	0	0- 0	0	.409	.409	8.44
1988	Oak	33	4	0	0	4	6.0	21	1	0	0	0	0	0	0	2	0	5	0	0	0	0	—	0	4- 4	0	.053	.143	0.00
1989	Oak	34	4	0	0	4	5.2	20	4	1	1	0	0	1	0	0	0	2	0	0	0	0	—	0	3- 3	0	.211	.200	1.59
1990	Oak	35	3	0	0	3	3.1	12	2	0	0	0	0	0	0	0	0	3	0	0	0	0	—	0	2- 2	0	.167	.167	0.00
1992	Oak-*MC*	37	3	0	0	2	3.0	17	8	2	2	1	0	0	0	0	0	2	0	0	0	0	—	0	1- 2	0	.471	.471	6.00
1996	StL	41	3	0	0	3	3.1	12	2	0	0	0	0	0	0	0	0	4	0	0	1	0	1.000	0	1- 1	0	.167	.167	0.00
LCS Totals			18	1	0	16	26.2	208	26	8	8	1	0	1	0	2	0	16	0	0	1	1	.500	0	11-12	0	.257	.269	2.70

World Series — Pitching

Year	Tm	Age	G	GS	CG	GF	IP	BFP	H	R	ER	HR	SH	SF	HB	TBB	IBB	SO	WP	Bk	W	L	Pct	ShO	Sv-Op	Hld	OAvg	OOBP	ERA
1988	Oak	33	2	0	0	2	1.2	7	2	2	2	1	0	0	0	1	0	2	0	0	0	1	.000	0	0- 1	0	.333	.429	10.80
1989	Oak	34	2	0	0	2	1.2	5	0	0	0	0	0	0	0	0	0	0	0	0	0	0	—	0	1- 1	0	.000	.000	0.00
1990	Oak	35	2	0	0	2	1.1	7	3	1	1	0	0	0	0	0	0	1	0	0	0	1	.000	0	0- 0	0	.429	.429	6.75
WS Totals			6	0	0	6	4.2	38	5	3	3	1	0	0	0	1	0	3	0	0	0	2	.000	0	1-2	0	.278	.316	5.79
Postseason Totals			27	1	0	25	35.0	274	34	11	11	2	0	1	0	3	0	21	0	0	1	3	.250	0	15-17	0	.256	.270	2.83

Division Series — Batting / Fielding

Year Tm	Age	G	AB	H	2B	3B	HR	TB	R	RBI	GW	TBB	IBB	SO	HBP	SH	SF	SB	CS	SB%	GDP	Avg	OBP	SLG	Pos	G	PO	A	E	DP	FPct
1996 StL	41	3	0	0	0	0	0	0	0	0	0	0	0	0	0	0	0	0	0	—	0	—	—	—	P	3	0	1	0	0	1.000

LCS — Batting / Fielding

Year Tm	Age	G	AB	H	2B	3B	HR	TB	R	RBI	GW	TBB	IBB	SO	HBP	SH	SF	SB	CS	SB%	GDP	Avg	OBP	SLG	Pos	G	PO	A	E	DP	FPct
1984 ChN	29	1	2	0	0	0	0	0	0	0	0	0	0	1	0	0	0	0	0	—	0	.000	.000	.000	P	1	0	0	0	0	—
1988 Oak	33	4	0	0	0	0	0	0	0	0	0	0	0	0	0	0	0	0	0	—	0	—	—	—	P	4	2	0	0	0	1.000
1989 Oak	34	4	0	0	0	0	0	0	0	0	0	0	0	0	0	0	0	0	0	—	0	—	—	—	P	4	0	1	0	0	1.000
1990 Oak	35	3	0	0	0	0	0	0	0	0	0	0	0	0	0	0	0	0	0	—	0	—	—	—	P	3	0	0	0	0	—
1992 Oak	37	3	0	0	0	0	0	0	0	0	0	0	0	0	0	0	0	0	0	—	0	—	—	—	P	3	0	0	0	0	—
1996 StL	41	3	0	0	0	0	0	0	0	0	0	0	0	0	0	0	0	0	0	—	0	—	—	—	P	3	0	1	0	0	1.000
LCS Totals		18	2	0	0	0	0	0	0	0	0	0	0	1	0	0	0	0	0	—	0	.000	.000	.000	P	18	2	2	0	0	1.000

World Series — Batting / Fielding

Year Tm	Age	G	AB	H	2B	3B	HR	TB	R	RBI	GW	TBB	IBB	SO	HBP	SH	SF	SB	CS	SB%	GDP	Avg	OBP	SLG	Pos	G	PO	A	E	DP	FPct
1988 Oak	33	2	0	0	0	0	0	0	0	0	0	0	0	0	0	0	0	0	0	—	0	—	—	—	P	2	0	0	0	0	—
1989 Oak	34	2	0	0	0	0	0	0	0	0	0	0	0	0	0	0	0	0	0	—	0	—	—	—	P	2	1	0	0	0	1.000
1990 Oak	35	2	0	0	0	0	0	0	0	0	0	0	0	0	0	0	0	0	0	—	0	—	—	—	P	2	0	0	0	0	—
WS Totals		6	0	0	0	0	0	0	0	0	0	0	0	0	0	0	0	0	0	—	0	—	—	—	P	6	1	0	0	0	1.000
Postseason Totals		27	2	0	0	0	0	0	0	0	0	0	0	1	0	0	0	0	0	—	0	.000	.000	.000	P	27	3	3	0	0	1.000

BRUCE EDWARDS—Charles Bruce Edwards—Nickname: Bull—Bats: Right; Throws: Right

Ht: 5'8"; Wt: 180 lbs; Born: 7/15/1923 in Quincy, Illinois; Debut: 6/23/1946; Died: 4/25/1975

World Series — Batting / Fielding

Year Tm	Age	G	AB	H	2B	3B	HR	TB	R	RBI	GW	TBB	IBB	SO	HBP	SH	SF	SB	CS	SB%	GDP	Avg	OBP	SLG	Pos	G	PO	A	E	DP	FPct
1947 Bro	24	7	27	6	1	0	0	7	3	2	1	2	0	7	0	0	0	0	0	—	1	.222	.276	.259	C	7	44	4	1	1	.980
1949 Bro	26	2	2	1	0	0	0	1	0	0	0	0	0	1	0	0	0	0	0	—	0	.500	.500	.500	—						
WS Totals		9	29	7	1	0	0	8	3	2	1	2	0	8	0	0	0	0	0	—	1	.241	.290	.276	C	7	44	4	1	1	.980

JOHNNY EDWARDS—John Alban Edwards—Bats: Left; Throws: Right

Ht: 6'4"; Wt: 220 lbs; Born: 6/10/1938 in Columbus, Ohio; Debut: 6/27/1961

World Series — Batting / Fielding

Year Tm	Age	G	AB	H	2B	3B	HR	TB	R	RBI	GW	TBB	IBB	SO	HBP	SH	SF	SB	CS	SB%	GDP	Avg	OBP	SLG	Pos	G	PO	A	E	DP	FPct
1961 Cin	23	3	11	4	2	0	0	6	1	2	0	0	0	0	0	0	0	0	0	—	0	.364	.364	.545	C	3	17	1	0	0	1.000
1968 StL	30	1	1	0	0	0	0	0	0	0	0	0	0	1	0	0	0	0	0	—	0	.000	.000	.000	—						
WS Totals		4	12	4	2	0	0	6	1	2	0	0	0	1	0	0	0	0	0	—	0	.333	.333	.500	C	3	17	1	0	0	1.000

MARSHALL EDWARDS—Marshall Lynn Edwards—Bats: Left; Throws: Left

Ht: 5'9"; Wt: 157 lbs; Born: 8/27/1952 in Fort Lewis, Washington; Debut: 4/11/1981

Division Series — Batting / Fielding

Year Tm	Age	G	AB	H	2B	3B	HR	TB	R	RBI	GW	TBB	IBB	SO	HBP	SH	SF	SB	CS	SB%	GDP	Avg	OBP	SLG	Pos	G	PO	A	E	DP	FPct
1981 Mil	29	2	1	0	0	0	0	0	0	0	0	0	0	1	0	0	0	0	0	—	0	.000	.000	.000	OF	2	0	0	0	0	—

LCS — Batting / Fielding

Year Tm	Age	G	AB	H	2B	3B	HR	TB	R	RBI	GW	TBB	IBB	SO	HBP	SH	SF	SB	CS	SB%	GDP	Avg	OBP	SLG	Pos	G	PO	A	E	DP	FPct
1982 Mil	30	3	1	0	0	0	0	0	2	0	0	0	0	0	0	0	0	1	0	1.00	0	.000	.000	.000	OF	1	2	0	0	0	1.000

World Series — Batting / Fielding

Year Tm	Age	G	AB	H	2B	3B	HR	TB	R	RBI	GW	TBB	IBB	SO	HBP	SH	SF	SB	CS	SB%	GDP	Avg	OBP	SLG	Pos	G	PO	A	E	DP	FPct
1982 Mil	30	1	0	0	0	0	0	0	0	0	0	0	0	0	0	0	0	0	0	—	0	—	—	—	OF	1	0	0	0	0	—
Postseason Totals		6	2	0	0	0	0	0	2	0	0	0	0	1	0	0	0	1	0	1.00	0	.000	.000	.000	OF	4	2	0	0	0	1.000

HOWARD EHMKE—Howard Jonathan Ehmke—Nickname: Bob—Throws: Right; Bats: Right

Ht: 6'3"; Wt: 190 lbs; Born: 4/24/1894 in Silver Creek, New York; Debut: 4/12/1915; Died: 3/17/1959

World Series — Pitching

Year	Tm	Age	G	GS	CG	GF	IP	BFP	H	R	ER	HR	SH	SF	HB	TBB	IBB	SO	WP	Bk	W	L	Pct	ShO	Sv-Op	Hld	OAvg	OOBP	ERA
1929	Phi	35	2	2	1	0	12.2	53	14	3	2	0	1	0	0	3	0	13	0	0	1	0	1.000	0	0- 0	0	.286	.327	1.42

World Series — Batting / Fielding

Year Tm	Age	G	AB	H	2B	3B	HR	TB	R	RBI	GW	TBB	IBB	SO	HBP	SH	SF	SB	CS	SB%	GDP	Avg	OBP	SLG	Pos	G	PO	A	E	DP	FPct
1929 Phi	35	2	5	1	0	0	0	1	0	0	0	0	0	0	0	0	0	0	0	—	0	.200	.200	.200	P	2	0	4	0	0	1.000

MARK EICHHORN—Mark Anthony Eichhorn—Throws: Right; Bats: Right

Ht: 6'4"; Wt: 200 lbs; Born: 11/21/1960 in San Jose, California; Debut: 8/30/1982

LCS — Pitching

Year Tm	Age	G	GS	CG	GF	IP	BFP	H	R	ER	HR	SH	SF	HB	TBB	IBB	SO	WP	Bk	W	L	Pct	ShO	Sv-Op	Hld	OAvg	OOBP	ERA
1992 Tor	31	1	0	0	1	1.0	3	0	0	0	0	0	0	0	0	0	0	0	0	0	0	—	0	0-0	0	.000	.000	0.00
1993 Tor	32	1	0	0	0	2.0	8	1	0	0	0	0	0	0	1	0	1	0	0	0	0	—	0	0-0	0	.143	.250	0.00
LCS Totals		2	0	0	1	3.0	22	1	0	0	0	0	0	0	1	0	1	0	0	0	0	—	0	0-0	0	.100	.182	0.00

World Series — Pitching

Year Tm	Age	G	GS	CG	GF	IP	BFP	H	R	ER	HR	SH	SF	HB	TBB	IBB	SO	WP	Bk	W	L	Pct	ShO	Sv-Op	Hld	OAvg	OOBP	ERA
1992 Tor	31	1	0	0	0	1.0	3	0	0	0	0	0	0	0	0	0	1	0	0	0	0	—	0	0-0	0	.000	.000	0.00
1993 Tor	32	1	0	0	0	0.1	3	1	0	0	0	0	0	0	1	0	0	0	0	0	0	—	0	0-0	0	.500	.667	0.00
WS Totals		2	0	0	0	1.1	12	1	0	0	0	0	0	0	1	0	1	0	0	0	0	—	0	0-0	0	.200	.333	0.00
Postseason Totals		4	0	0	1	4.1	34	2	0	0	0	0	0	0	2	0	2	0	0	0	0	—	0	0-0	0	.133	.235	0.00

LCS — Batting / Fielding

Year Tm	Age	G	AB	H	2B	3B	HR	TB	R	RBI	GW	TBB	IBB	SO	HBP	SH	SF	SB	CS	SB%	GDP	Avg	OBP	SLG	Pos	G	PO	A	E	DP	FPct
1992 Tor	31	1	0	0	0	0	0	0	0	0	0	0	0	0	0	0	0	0	0	—	0	—	—	—	P	1	0	0	0	0	—
1993 Tor	32	1	0	0	0	0	0	0	0	0	0	0	0	0	0	0	0	0	0	—	0	—	—	—	P	1	0	0	0	0	—
LCS Totals		2	0	0	0	0	0	0	0	0	0	0	0	0	0	0	0	0	0	—	0	—	—	—	P	2	0	0	0	0	—

World Series — Batting / Fielding

Year Tm	Age	G	AB	H	2B	3B	HR	TB	R	RBI	GW	TBB	IBB	SO	HBP	SH	SF	SB	CS	SB%	GDP	Avg	OBP	SLG	Pos	G	PO	A	E	DP	FPct
1992 Tor	31	1	0	0	0	0	0	0	0	0	0	0	0	0	0	0	0	0	0	—	0	—	—	—	P	1	0	0	0	0	—
1993 Tor	32	1	0	0	0	0	0	0	0	0	0	0	0	0	0	0	0	0	0	—	0	—	—	—	P	1	0	0	0	0	—
WS Totals		2	0	0	0	0	0	0	0	0	0	0	0	0	0	0	0	0	0	—	0	—	—	—	P	2	0	0	0	0	—
Postseason Totals		4	0	0	0	0	0	0	0	0	0	0	0	0	0	0	0	0	0	—	0	—	—	—	P	4	0	0	0	0	—

JIM EISENREICH—James Michael Eisenreich—Bats: Left; Throws: Left

Ht: 5'11"; Wt: 180 lbs; Born: 4/18/1959 in St. Cloud, Minnesota; Debut: 4/6/1982

Division Series — Batting / Fielding

Year Tm	Age	G	AB	H	2B	3B	HR	TB	R	RBI	GW	TBB	IBB	SO	HBP	SH	SF	SB	CS	SB%	GDP	Avg	OBP	SLG	Pos	G	PO	A	E	DP	FPct
1997 Fla	38	2	0	0	0	0	0	0	0	0	0	2	1	0	0	0	0	0	0	—	0	—	1.000	—	—						

LCS — Batting / Fielding

Year Tm	Age	G	AB	H	2B	3B	HR	TB	R	RBI	GW	TBB	IBB	SO	HBP	SH	SF	SB	CS	SB%	GDP	Avg	OBP	SLG	Pos	G	PO	A	E	DP	FPct
1993 Phi	34	6	15	2	1	0	0	3	0	1	0	0	0	2	0	0	0	0	0	—	0	.133	.133	.200	OF	5	6	0	0	0	1.000
1997 Fla	38	1	3	0	0	0	0	0	0	0	0	0	0	0	0	0	0	0	0	—	1	.000	.000	.000	OF	1	2	0	0	0	1.000
LCS Totals		7	18	2	1	0	0	3	0	1	0	0	0	2	0	0	0	0	0	—	1	.111	.111	.167	OF	6	8	0	0	0	1.000

World Series — Batting / Fielding

Year Tm	Age	G	AB	H	2B	3B	HR	TB	R	RBI	GW	TBB	IBB	SO	HBP	SH	SF	SB	CS	SB%	GDP	Avg	OBP	SLG	Pos	G	PO	A	E	DP	FPct
1993 Phi	34	6	26	6	0	0	1	9	3	7	0	2	0	4	0	0	0	0	0	—	1	.231	.286	.346	OF	6	18	0	0	0	1.000
1997 Fla	38	5	8	4	0	0	1	7	1	3	0	3	1	1	0	0	0	0	0	—	0	.500	.636	.875	1B	2	3	1	0	1	1.000
WS Totals		11	34	10	0	0	2	16	4	10	0	5	1	5	0	0	0	0	0	—	1	.294	.385	.471	OF	6	18	0	0	0	1.000
Postseason Totals		20	52	12	1	0	2	19	4	11	0	7	2	7	0	0	0	0	0	—	2	.231	.322	.365	OF	12	26	0	0	0	1.000

HOD ELLER—Horace Owen Eller—Throws: Right; Bats: Right

Ht: 5'11"; Wt: 185 lbs; Born: 7/5/1894 in Muncie, Indiana; Debut: 4/16/1917; Died: 7/18/1961

World Series — Pitching

Year Tm	Age	G	GS	CG	GF	IP	BFP	H	R	ER	HR	SH	SF	HB	TBB	IBB	SO	WP	Bk	W	L	Pct	ShO	Sv-Op	Hld	OAvg	OOBP	ERA
1919 Cin	25	2	2	2	0	18.0	71	13	5	4	1	0	0	1	2	0	15	0	0	2	0	1.000	1	0-0	0	.191	.225	2.00

World Series — Batting / Fielding

Year Tm	Age	G	AB	H	2B	3B	HR	TB	R	RBI	GW	TBB	IBB	SO	HBP	SH	SF	SB	CS	SB%	GDP	Avg	OBP	SLG	Pos	G	PO	A	E	DP	FPct
1919 Cin	25	2	7	2	1	0	0	3	2	0	0	0	0	2	1	0	0	0	0	—	0	.286	.375	.429	P	2	0	2	0	0	1.000

GLENN ELLIOTT—Herbert Glenn Elliott—Nickname: Lefty—Throws: Left; Bats: Both

Ht: 5'10"; Wt: 170 lbs; Born: 11/11/1919 in Sapulpa, Oklahoma; Debut: 4/17/1947; Died: 7/27/1969

World Series — Batting / Fielding

Year Tm	Age	G	AB	H	2B	3B	HR	TB	R	RBI	GW	TBB	IBB	SO	HBP	SH	SF	SB	CS	SB%	GDP	Avg	OBP	SLG	Pos	G	PO	A	E	DP	FPct
1948 Bos	28	6	21	7	0	0	2	13	4	5	0	2	0	2	0	0	0	0	0	—	2	.333	.391	.619	3B	6	11	13	3	1	.889

DOCK ELLIS—Dock Phillip Ellis—Throws: Right; Bats: Both

Ht: 6'3"; Wt: 205 lbs; Born: 3/11/1945 in Los Angeles, California; Debut: 6/18/1968

LCS — Pitching

Year Tm	Age	G	GS	CG	GF	IP	BFP	H	R	ER	HR	SH	SF	HB	TBB	IBB	SO	WP	Bk	W	L	Pct	ShO	Sv-Op	Hld	OAvg	OOBP	ERA
1970 Pit	25	1	1	0	0	9.2	41	9	3	3	0	0	0	0	4	2	1	0	0	0	1	.000	0	0-0	0	.243	.317	2.79
1971 Pit	26	1	1	0	0	5.0	26	6	2	2	0	1	0	1	4	0	1	0	0	1	0	1.000	0	0-0	0	.300	.440	3.60
1972 Pit	27	1	1	0	0	5.0	22	5	3	0	0	1	0	0	1	0	3	0	0	0	1	.000	0	0-0	0	.250	.286	0.00
1975 Pit	30	1	0	0	1	2.0	8	2	0	0	0	0	0	0	0	0	2	0	0	0	0	—	0	0-0	0	.250	.250	0.00
1976 NYA	31	1	1	0	0	8.0	29	6	3	3	0	0	1	1	2	0	5	0	0	1	0	1.000	0	0-0	0	.240	.310	3.38
LCS Totals		5	4	0	1	29.2	252	28	11	8	0	2	1	2	11	2	12	0	0	2	2	.500	0	0-0	0	.255	.331	2.43

World Series — Pitching

Year Tm	Age	G	GS	CG	GF	IP	BFP	H	R	ER	HR	SH	SF	HB	TBB	IBB	SO	WP	Bk	W	L	Pct	ShO	Sv-Op	Hld	OAvg	OOBP	ERA
1971 Pit	26	1	1	0	0	2.1	12	4	4	4	2	0	0	0	1	0	1	0	0	0	1	.000	0	0-0	0	.364	.417	15.43
1976 NYA	31	1	1	0	0	3.1	16	7	4	4	1	0	0	0	0	0	1	0	0	0	1	.000	0	0-0	0	.438	.438	10.80
WS Totals		2	2	0	0	5.2	56	11	8	8	3	0	0	0	1	0	2	0	0	0	2	.000	0	0-0	0	.407	.429	12.71
Postseason Totals		7	6	0	1	35.1	308	39	19	16	3	2	1	2	12	2	14	0	0	2	4	.333	0	0-0	0	.285	.349	4.08

LCS — Batting / Fielding

Year Tm	Age	G	AB	H	2B	3B	HR	TB	R	RBI	GW	TBB	IBB	SO	HBP	SH	SF	SB	CS	SB%	GDP	Avg	OBP	SLG	Pos	G	PO	A	E	DP	FPct
1970 Pit	25	1	2	0	0	0	0	0	0	0	0	0	0	1	0	2	0	0	0	—	0	.000	.000	.000	P	1	0	3	0	0	1.000
1971 Pit	26	1	3	0	0	0	0	0	0	0	0	0	0	2	0	0	0	0	0	—	0	.000	.000	.000	P	1	0	0	0	0	—
1972 Pit	27	2	1	0	0	0	0	0	0	0	0	0	0	0	0	0	0	0	0	—	0	.000	.000	.000	P	1	0	0	0	0	—
1975 Pit	30	1	0	0	0	0	0	0	0	0	0	0	0	0	0	0	0	0	0	—	0	—	—	—	P	1	0	0	0	0	—
1976 NYA	31	1	0	0	0	0	0	0	0	0	0	0	0	0	0	0	0	0	0	—	0	—	—	—	P	1	1	0	0	0	1.000
LCS Totals		6	6	0	0	0	0	0	0	0	0	0	0	3	0	2	0	0	0	—	0	.000	.000	.000	P	5	1	3	0	0	1.000

World Series — Batting / Fielding

Year Tm	Age	G	AB	H	2B	3B	HR	TB	R	RBI	GW	TBB	IBB	SO	HBP	SH	SF	SB	CS	SB%	GDP	Avg	OBP	SLG	Pos	G	PO	A	E	DP	FPct
1971 Pit	26	1	1	0	0	0	0	0	0	0	0	0	0	1	0	0	0	0	0	—	0	.000	.000	.000	P	1	1	0	0	0	1.000
1976 NYA	31	1	0	0	0	0	0	0	0	0	0	0	0	0	0	0	0	0	0	—	0	—	—	—	P	1	0	0	0	0	—
WS Totals		2	1	0	0	0	0	0	0	0	0	0	0	1	0	0	0	0	0	—	0	.000	.000	.000	P	2	1	0	0	0	1.000
Postseason Totals		8	7	0	0	0	0	0	0	0	0	0	0	4	0	2	0	0	0	—	0	.000	.000	.000	P	7	2	3	0	0	1.000

KEVIN ELSTER—Kevin Daniel Elster—Bats: Right; Throws: Right

Ht: 6'2"; Wt: 180 lbs; Born: 8/3/1964 in San Pedro, California; Debut: 9/2/1986

Division Series — Batting / Fielding

Year Tm	Age	G	AB	H	2B	3B	HR	TB	R	RBI	GW	TBB	IBB	SO	HBP	SH	SF	SB	CS	SB%	GDP	Avg	OBP	SLG	Pos	G	PO	A	E	DP	FPct
1996 Tex	32	4	12	4	2	0	0	6	2	0	0	3	0	2	0	0	0	1	0	1.00	0	.333	.467	.500	SS	4	6	7	1	3	.929

LCS — Batting / Fielding

Year Tm	Age	G	AB	H	2B	3B	HR	TB	R	RBI	GW	TBB	IBB	SO	HBP	SH	SF	SB	CS	SB%	GDP	Avg	OBP	SLG	Pos	G	PO	A	E	DP	FPct
1986 NYN	22	4	3	0	0	0	0	0	0	0	0	0	0	1	0	0	0	0	0	—	0	.000	.000	.000	SS	4	2	3	0	0	1.000
1988 NYN	24	5	8	2	1	0	0	3	1	1	0	3	1	0	0	0	0	0	0	—	0	.250	.455	.375	SS	5	7	7	2	2	.875
LCS Totals		9	11	2	1	0	0	3	1	1	0	3	1	1	0	0	0	0	0	—	0	.182	.357	.273	SS	9	9	10	2	2	.905

World Series — Batting / Fielding

Year Tm	Age	G	AB	H	2B	3B	HR	TB	R	RBI	GW	TBB	IBB	SO	HBP	SH	SF	SB	CS	SB%	GDP	Avg	OBP	SLG	Pos	G	PO	A	E	DP	FPct
1986 NYN	22	1	1	0	0	0	0	0	0	0	0	0	0	0	0	0	0	0	0	—	0	.000	.000	.000	SS	1	3	3	1	1	.857
Postseason Totals		14	24	6	3	0	0	9	3	1	0	6	1	3	0	0	0	1	0	1.00	0	.250	.400	.375	SS	14	18	20	4	6	.905

ALAN EMBREE—Alan Duane Embree—Throws: Left; Bats: Left

Ht: 6'3"; Wt: 185 lbs; Born: 1/23/1970 in Vancouver, Washington; Debut: 9/15/1992

Division Series — Pitching

Year Tm	Age	G	GS	CG	GF	IP	BFP	H	R	ER	HR	SH	SF	HB	TBB	IBB	SO	WP	Bk	W	L	Pct	ShO	Sv-Op	Hld	OAvg	OOBP	ERA
1996 Cle	26	3	0	0	0	1.0	4	0	1	1	0	0	1	1	0	0	1	0	0	0	0	—	0	0- 0	1	.000	.250	9.00

LCS — Pitching

Year Tm	Age	G	GS	CG	GF	IP	BFP	H	R	ER	HR	SH	SF	HB	TBB	IBB	SO	WP	Bk	W	L	Pct	ShO	Sv-Op	Hld	OAvg	OOBP	ERA
1995 Cle	25	1	0	0	1	0.1	1	0	0	0	0	0	0	0	0	0	1	0	0	0	0	—	0	0- 0	0	.000	.000	0.00
1997 Atl	27	1	0	0	1	1.0	3	0	0	0	0	0	0	0	1	0	1	0	0	0	0	—	0	0- 0	0	.000	.333	0.00
LCS Totals		2	0	0	2	1.1	8	0	0	0	0	0	0	0	1	0	2	0	0	0	0	—	0	0-0	0	.000	.250	0.00

World Series — Pitching

Year Tm	Age	G	GS	CG	GF	IP	BFP	H	R	ER	HR	SH	SF	HB	TBB	IBB	SO	WP	Bk	W	L	Pct	ShO	Sv-Op	Hld	OAvg	OOBP	ERA
1995 Cle	25	4	0	0	2	3.1	14	2	1	1	0	1	0	0	2	1	2	0	0	0	0	—	0	0- 0	0	.182	.308	2.70
Postseason Totals		9	0	0	4	5.2	44	2	2	2	0	1	1	1	3	1	5	0	0	0	0	—	0	0-0	1	.125	.286	3.18

Division Series — Batting / Fielding

Year Tm	Age	G	AB	H	2B	3B	HR	TB	R	RBI	GW	TBB	IBB	SO	HBP	SH	SF	SB	CS	SB%	GDP	Avg	OBP	SLG	Pos	G	PO	A	E	DP	FPct
1996 Cle	26	3	0	0	0	0	0	0	0	0	0	0	0	0	0	0	0	0	0	—	0	—	—	—	P	3	0	0	0	0	—

LCS — Batting / Fielding

Year Tm	Age	G	AB	H	2B	3B	HR	TB	R	RBI	GW	TBB	IBB	SO	HBP	SH	SF	SB	CS	SB%	GDP	Avg	OBP	SLG	Pos	G	PO	A	E	DP	FPct
1995 Cle	25	1	0	0	0	0	0	0	0	0	0	0	0	0	0	0	0	0	0	—	0	—	—	—	P	1	0	0	0	0	—
1997 Atl	27	1	0	0	0	0	0	0	0	0	0	0	0	0	0	0	0	0	0	—	0	—	—	—	P	1	0	0	0	0	—
LCS Totals		2	0	0	0	0	0	0	0	0	0	0	0	0	0	0	0	0	0	—	0	—	—	—	P	2	0	0	0	0	—

World Series — Batting / Fielding

Year Tm	Age	G	AB	H	2B	3B	HR	TB	R	RBI	GW	TBB	IBB	SO	HBP	SH	SF	SB	CS	SB%	GDP	Avg	OBP	SLG	Pos	G	PO	A	E	DP	FPct
1995 Cle	25	4	0	0	0	0	0	0	0	0	0	0	0	0	0	0	0	0	0	—	0	—	—	—	P	4	0	1	0	0	1.000
Postseason Totals		9	0	0	0	0	0	0	0	0	0	0	0	0	0	0	0	0	0	—	0	—	—	—	P	9	0	1	0	0	1.000

CLYDE ENGLE—Arthur Clyde Engle—Nickname: Hack—Bats: Right; Throws: Right

Ht: 5'10"; Wt: 190 lbs; Born: 3/19/1884 in Dayton, Ohio; Debut: 4/12/1909; Died: 12/26/1939

World Series — Batting / Fielding

Year Tm	Age	G	AB	H	2B	3B	HR	TB	R	RBI	GW	TBB	IBB	SO	HBP	SH	SF	SB	CS	SB%	GDP	Avg	OBP	SLG	Pos	G	PO	A	E	DP	FPct
1912 Bos	28	3	3	1	1	0	0	2	1	2	0	0	0	0	0	0	0	0	0	—	0	.333	.333	.667	—						

WOODY ENGLISH—Elwood George English—Bats: Right; Throws: Right

Ht: 5'10"; Wt: 155 lbs; Born: 3/2/1907 in Fredonia, Ohio; Debut: 4/26/1927; Died: 9/26/1997

World Series — Batting / Fielding

Year Tm	Age	G	AB	H	2B	3B	HR	TB	R	RBI	GW	TBB	IBB	SO	HBP	SH	SF	SB	CS	SB%	GDP	Avg	OBP	SLG	Pos	G	PO	A	E	DP	FPct
1929 ChN	22	5	21	4	2	0	0	6	1	0	0	1	0	6	0	0	0	0	1	.00	0	.190	.227	.286	SS	5	9	11	4	3	.833
1932 ChN	25	4	17	3	0	0	0	3	2	1	0	2	0	2	0	0	0	0	1	.00	0	.176	.263	.176	3B	4	3	4	1	0	.875
WS Totals		9	38	7	2	0	0	9	3	1	0	3	0	8	0	0	0	0	2	.00	0	.184	.244	.237	SS	5	9	11	4	3	.833

DEL ENNIS—Delmer Ennis—Bats: Right; Throws: Right

Ht: 6'0"; Wt: 195 lbs; Born: 6/8/1925 in Philadelphia, Pennsylvania; Debut: 4/28/1946; Died: 2/8/1996

World Series — Batting / Fielding

Year Tm	Age	G	AB	H	2B	3B	HR	TB	R	RBI	GW	TBB	IBB	SO	HBP	SH	SF	SB	CS	SB%	GDP	Avg	OBP	SLG	Pos	G	PO	A	E	DP	FPct
1950 Phi	25	4	14	2	1	0	0	3	1	0	0	0	0	1	1	0	0	0	0	—	1	.143	.200	.214	OF	4	9	0	0	0	1.000

MIKE EPSTEIN—Michael Peter Epstein—Nickname: Superjew—Bats: Left; Throws: Left

Ht: 6'3"; Wt: 230 lbs; Born: 4/4/1943 in Bronx, New York; Debut: 9/16/1966

LCS — Batting / Fielding

Year Tm	Age	G	AB	H	2B	3B	HR	TB	R	RBI	GW	TBB	IBB	SO	HBP	SH	SF	SB	CS	SB%	GDP	Avg	OBP	SLG	Pos	G	PO	A	E	DP	FPct
1971 Oak	28	2	5	1	0	0	0	1	0	0	0	0	0	3	0	0	0	0	0	—	0	.200	.200	.200	1B	1	4	0	0	2	1.000
1972 Oak	29	5	16	3	0	0	1	6	1	1	0	4	0	5	1	0	0	1	0	1.00	0	.188	.381	.375	1B	5	55	2	0	5	1.000
LCS Totals		7	21	4	0	0	1	7	1	1	0	4	0	8	1	0	0	1	0	1.00	0	.190	.346	.333	1B	6	59	2	0	7	1.000

World Series — Batting / Fielding

Year Tm	Age	G	AB	H	2B	3B	HR	TB	R	RBI	GW	TBB	IBB	SO	HBP	SH	SF	SB	CS	SB%	GDP	Avg	OBP	SLG	Pos	G	PO	A	E	DP	FPct
1972 Oak	29	6	16	0	0	0	0	0	1	0	0	5	1	3	0	0	0	0	0	—	0	.000	.238	.000	1B	6	35	2	2	1	.949
Postseason Totals		13	37	4	0	0	1	7	2	1	0	9	1	11	1	0	0	1	0	1.00	0	.108	.298	.189	1B	12	94	4	2	8	.980

PAUL ERICKSON—Paul Walford Erickson—Nickname: Li'l Abner—Throws: Right; Bats: Right

Ht: 6'2"; Wt: 200 lbs; Born: 12/14/1915 in Zion, Illinois; Debut: 6/29/1941

World Series — Pitching

Year Tm	Age	G	GS	CG	GF	IP	BFP	H	R	ER	HR	SH	SF	HB	TBB	IBB	SO	WP	Bk	W	L	Pct	ShO	Sv-Op	Hld	OAvg	OOBP	ERA
1945 ChN	29	4	0	0	3	7.0	32	8	3	3	0	0	0	1	3	0	5	0	0	0	0	—	0	0- 0	0	.286	.375	3.86

World Series — Batting / Fielding

Year Tm	Age	G	AB	H	2B	3B	HR	TB	R	RBI	GW	TBB	IBB	SO	HBP	SH	SF	SB	CS	SB%	GDP	Avg	OBP	SLG	Pos	G	PO	A	E	DP	FPct
1945 ChN	29	4	0	0	0	0	0	0	0	0	0	0	0	0	0	0	0	0	0	—	0	—	—	—	P	4	0	1	0	0	1.000

SCOTT ERICKSON—Scott Gavin Erickson—Throws: Right; Bats: Right

Ht: 6'4"; Wt: 220 lbs; Born: 2/2/1968 in Long Beach, California; Debut: 6/25/1990

Division Series — Pitching

Year Tm	Age	G	GS	CG	GF	IP	BFP	H	R	ER	HR	SH	SF	HB	TBB	IBB	SO	WP	Bk	W	L	Pct	ShO	Sv-Op	Hld	OAvg	OOBP	ERA
1996 Bal	28	1	1	0	0	6.2	27	6	3	3	1	0	0	0	2	0	6	0	0	0	0	—	0	0- 0	0	.240	.296	4.05
1997 Bal	29	1	1	0	0	6.2	28	7	3	3	0	0	0	0	2	0	6	0	0	1	0	1.000	0	0- 0	0	.269	.321	4.05
DS Totals		2	2	0	0	13.1	110	13	6	6	1	0	0	0	4	0	12	0	0	1	0	1.000	0	0-0	0	.255	.309	4.05

LCS — Pitching

Year Tm	Age	G	GS	CG	GF	IP	BFP	H	R	ER	HR	SH	SF	HB	TBB	IBB	SO	WP	Bk	W	L	Pct	ShO	Sv-Op	Hld	OAvg	OOBP	ERA
1991 Min	23	1	1	0	0	4.0	20	3	2	2	1	1	0	0	5	0	2	0	0	0	0	—	0	0- 0	0	.214	.421	4.50
1996 Bal	28	2	2	0	0	11.1	53	14	9	3	3	0	0	0	4	0	8	0	0	0	1	.000	0	0- 0	0	.286	.340	2.38
1997 Bal	29	2	2	0	0	12.2	51	15	7	6	2	0	0	0	1	0	6	0	0	1	0	1.000	0	0- 0	0	.300	.314	4.26
LCS Totals		5	5	0	0	28.0	248	32	18	11	6	1	0	0	10	0	16	0	0	1	1	.500	0	0-0	0	.283	.341	3.54

World Series — Pitching

Year Tm	Age	G	GS	CG	GF	IP	BFP	H	R	ER	HR	SH	SF	HB	TBB	IBB	SO	WP	Bk	W	L	Pct	ShO	Sv-Op	Hld	OAvg	OOBP	ERA
1991 Min	23	2	2	0	0	10.2	48	10	7	6	3	0	0	1	4	0	5	1	0	0	0	—	0	0- 0	0	.233	.313	5.06
Postseason Totals		9	9	0	0	52.0	454	55	31	23	10	1	0	1	18	0	33	1	0	2	1	.667	0	0-0	0	.266	.327	3.98

Division Series — Batting / Fielding

Year Tm	Age	G	AB	H	2B	3B	HR	TB	R	RBI	GW	TBB	IBB	SO	HBP	SH	SF	SB	CS	SB%	GDP	Avg	OBP	SLG	Pos	G	PO	A	E	DP	FPct
1996 Bal	28	1	0	0	0	0	0	0	0	0	0	0	0	0	0	0	0	0	0	—	0	—	—	—	P	1	1	3	0	1	1.000
1997 Bal	29	1	0	0	0	0	0	0	0	0	0	0	0	0	0	0	0	0	0	—	0	—	—	—	P	1	1	0	0	0	1.000
DS Totals		2	0	0	0	0	0	0	0	0	0	0	0	0	0	0	0	0	0	—	0	—	—	—	P	2	2	3	0	1	1.000

LCS — Batting / Fielding

Year Tm	Age	G	AB	H	2B	3B	HR	TB	R	RBI	GW	TBB	IBB	SO	HBP	SH	SF	SB	CS	SB%	GDP	Avg	OBP	SLG	Pos	G	PO	A	E	DP	FPct
1991 Min	23	1	0	0	0	0	0	0	0	0	0	0	0	0	0	0	0	0	0	—	0	—	—	—	P	1	1	1	0	0	1.000
1996 Bal	28	2	0	0	0	0	0	0	0	0	0	0	0	0	0	0	0	0	0	—	0	—	—	—	P	2	0	2	0	0	1.000
1997 Bal	29	2	0	0	0	0	0	0	0	0	0	0	0	0	0	0	0	0	0	—	0	—	—	—	P	2	0	5	0	1	1.000
LCS Totals		5	0	0	0	0	0	0	0	0	0	0	0	0	0	0	0	0	0	—	0	—	—	—	P	5	1	8	0	1	1.000

World Series — Batting / Fielding

Year Tm	Age	G	AB	H	2B	3B	HR	TB	R	RBI	GW	TBB	IBB	SO	HBP	SH	SF	SB	CS	SB%	GDP	Avg	OBP	SLG	Pos	G	PO	A	E	DP	FPct
1991 Min	23	2	1	0	0	0	0	0	0	0	0	0	0	1	0	0	0	0	0	—	0	.000	.000	.000	P	2	1	0	0	0	1.000
Postseason Totals		9	1	0	0	0	0	0	0	0	0	0	0	1	0	0	0	0	0	—	0	.000	.000	.000	P	9	4	11	0	2	1.000

CARL ERSKINE—Carl Daniel Erskine—Nickname: Oisk—Throws: Right; Bats: Right

Ht: 5'10"; Wt: 165 lbs; Born: 12/13/1926 in Anderson, Indiana; Debut: 7/25/1948

World Series		Pitching																										
Year Tm	Age	G	GS	CG	GF	IP	BFP	H	R	ER	HR	SH	SF	HB	TBB	IBB	SO	WP	Bk	W	L	Pct	ShO	Sv-Op	Hld	OAvg	OOBP	ERA
1949 Bro	22	2	0	0	0	1.2	9	3	3	3	0	0	0	0	1	0	0	0	0	0	0	—	0	0- 0	0	.375	.444	16.20
1952 Bro	25	3	2	1	1	18.0	72	12	10	9	1	0	0	0	10	0	10	1	0	1	1	.500	0	0- 0	0	.194	.306	4.50
1953 Bro	26	3	3	1	0	14.0	67	14	9	9	0	1	0	2	9	1	16	1	0	1	0	1.000	0	0- 0	0	.255	.379	5.79
1955 Bro	28	1	1	0	0	3.0	14	3	3	3	1	1	0	0	2	0	3	0	0	0	0	—	0	0- 0	0	.273	.385	9.00
1956 Bro	29	2	1	0	1	5.0	20	4	3	3	0	0	1	0	2	1	2	0	0	0	1	.000	0	0- 0	0	.235	.300	5.40
WS Totals		11	7	2	2	41.2	364	36	28	27	2	2	1	2	24	2	31	2	0	2	2	.500	0	0-0	0	.235	.344	5.83

World Series		Batting																							Fielding						
Year Tm	Age	G	AB	H	2B	3B	HR	TB	R	RBI	GW	TBB	IBB	SO	HBP	SH	SF	SB	CS	SB%	GDP	Avg	OBP	SLG	Pos	G	PO	A	E	DP	FPct
1949 Bro	22	2	0	0	0	0	0	0	0	0	0	0	0	0	0	0	0	0	0	—	0	—	—	—	P	2	0	0	0	0	—
1952 Bro	25	3	6	0	0	0	0	0	1	0	0	0	0	1	0	1	0	0	0	—	0	.000	.000	.000	P	3	0	2	0	0	1.000
1953 Bro	26	3	4	1	0	0	0	1	0	0	0	0	0	1	0	0	0	0	0	—	0	.250	.250	.250	P	3	1	2	1	0	.750
1955 Bro	28	1	1	0	0	0	0	0	0	0	0	0	0	0	0	0	0	0	0	—	0	.000	.000	.000	P	1	0	1	0	0	1.000
1956 Bro	29	2	1	0	0	0	0	0	0	0	0	0	0	1	0	0	0	0	0	—	0	.000	.000	.000	P	2	1	2	0	0	1.000
WS Totals		11	12	1	0	0	0	1	1	0	0	0	0	3	0	1	0	0	0	—	0	.083	.083	.083	P	11	2	7	1	0	.900

ALVARO ESPINOZA—Alvaro Alberto Espinoza—Bats: Right; Throws: Right

Ht: 6'0"; Wt: 170 lbs; Born: 2/19/1962 in Valencia, Venezuela; Debut: 9/14/1984

Division Series		Batting																							Fielding						
Year Tm	Age	G	AB	H	2B	3B	HR	TB	R	RBI	GW	TBB	IBB	SO	HBP	SH	SF	SB	CS	SB%	GDP	Avg	OBP	SLG	Pos	G	PO	A	E	DP	FPct
1995 Cle	33	1	1	0	0	0	0	0	0	0	0	0	0	0	0	0	0	0	0	—	0	.000	.000	.000	3B	1	0	0	0	0	—
LCS		Batting																							Fielding						
Year Tm	Age	G	AB	H	2B	3B	HR	TB	R	RBI	GW	TBB	IBB	SO	HBP	SH	SF	SB	CS	SB%	GDP	Avg	OBP	SLG	Pos	G	PO	A	E	DP	FPct
1995 Cle	33	4	8	1	0	0	0	1	1	0	0	0	0	3	0	0	0	0	0	—	0	.125	.125	.125	3B	4	0	3	1	0	.750
World Series		Batting																							Fielding						
Year Tm	Age	G	AB	H	2B	3B	HR	TB	R	RBI	GW	TBB	IBB	SO	HBP	SH	SF	SB	CS	SB%	GDP	Avg	OBP	SLG	Pos	G	PO	A	E	DP	FPct
1995 Cle	33	2	2	1	0	0	0	1	1	0	0	0	0	0	0	0	0	0	1	.00	0	.500	.500	.500	3B	1	1	1	0	0	1.000
Postseason Totals		7	11	2	0	0	0	2	2	0	0	0	0	3	0	0	0	0	1	.00	0	.182	.182	.182	3B	6	1	4	1	0	.833

SAMMY ESPOSITO—Samuel Esposito—Bats: Right; Throws: Right

Ht: 5'9"; Wt: 165 lbs; Born: 12/15/1931 in Chicago, Illinois; Debut: 9/28/1952

World Series		Batting																							Fielding						
Year Tm	Age	G	AB	H	2B	3B	HR	TB	R	RBI	GW	TBB	IBB	SO	HBP	SH	SF	SB	CS	SB%	GDP	Avg	OBP	SLG	Pos	G	PO	A	E	DP	FPct
1959 ChA	27	2	2	0	0	0	0	0	0	0	0	0	0	1	0	0	0	0	0	—	0	.000	.000	.000	3B	2	1	0	0	0	1.000

CECIL ESPY—Cecil Edward Espy—Bats: Both; Throws: Right

Ht: 6'3"; Wt: 195 lbs; Born: 1/20/1963 in San Diego, California; Debut: 9/2/1983

LCS		Batting																							Fielding						
Year Tm	Age	G	AB	H	2B	3B	HR	TB	R	RBI	GW	TBB	IBB	SO	HBP	SH	SF	SB	CS	SB%	GDP	Avg	OBP	SLG	Pos	G	PO	A	E	DP	FPct
1991 Pit	28	2	2	0	0	0	0	0	0	0	0	0	0	2	0	0	0	0	0	—	0	.000	.000	.000	—						
1992 Pit	29	4	3	2	0	0	0	2	0	0	0	0	0	1	0	0	0	0	0	—	0	.667	.667	.667	OF	2	0	0	0	0	—
LCS Totals		6	5	2	0	0	0	2	0	0	0	0	0	3	0	0	0	0	0	—	0	.400	.400	.400	OF	2	0	0	0	0	—

CHUCK ESSEGIAN—Charles Abraham Essegian—Bats: Right; Throws: Right

Ht: 5'11"; Wt: 200 lbs; Born: 8/9/1931 in Boston, Massachusetts; Debut: 4/15/1958

World Series		Batting																							Fielding						
Year Tm	Age	G	AB	H	2B	3B	HR	TB	R	RBI	GW	TBB	IBB	SO	HBP	SH	SF	SB	CS	SB%	GDP	Avg	OBP	SLG	Pos	G	PO	A	E	DP	FPct
1959 LA	28	4	3	2	0	0	2	8	2	2	0	1	0	1	0	0	0	0	0	—	0	.667	.750	2.667	—						

SHAWN ESTES—Aaron Shawn Estes—Throws: Left; Bats: Right

Ht: 6'2"; Wt: 185 lbs; Born: 2/18/1973 in San Bernardino, California; Debut: 9/16/1995

Division Series		Pitching																										
Year Tm	Age	G	GS	CG	GF	IP	BFP	H	R	ER	HR	SH	SF	HB	TBB	IBB	SO	WP	Bk	W	L	Pct	ShO	Sv-Op	Hld	OAvg	OOBP	ERA
1997 SF	24	1	1	0	0	3.0	18	5	5	5	1	0	0	0	4	0	3	0	0	0	0	—	0	0- 0	0	.357	.500	15.00

Division Series		Batting																							Fielding						
Year Tm	Age	G	AB	H	2B	3B	HR	TB	R	RBI	GW	TBB	IBB	SO	HBP	SH	SF	SB	CS	SB%	GDP	Avg	OBP	SLG	Pos	G	PO	A	E	DP	FPct
1997 SF	24	1	1	0	0	0	0	0	0	0	0	0	0	1	0	1	0	0	0	—	0	.000	.000	.000	P	1	0	1	0	0	1.000

ANDY ETCHEBARREN—Andrew Auguste Etchebarren—Bats: Right; Throws: Right

Ht: 6'1"; Wt: 190 lbs; Born: 6/20/1943 in Whittier, California; Debut: 9/26/1962

LCS		Batting																							Fielding						
Year Tm	Age	G	AB	H	2B	3B	HR	TB	R	RBI	GW	TBB	IBB	SO	HBP	SH	SF	SB	CS	SB%	GDP	Avg	OBP	SLG	Pos	G	PO	A	E	DP	FPct
1969 Bal	26	2	4	0	0	0	0	0	0	0	0	0	0	0	0	1	0	0	0	—	1	.000	.000	.000	C	2	11	0	0	0	1.000
1970 Bal	27	2	9	1	0	0	0	1	1	0	0	0	0	3	0	0	0	0	0	—	1	.111	.111	.111	C	2	19	0	0	0	1.000
1971 Bal	28	2	5	0	0	0	0	0	0	0	0	0	0	0	0	0	0	0	0	—	0	.000	.000	.000	C	2	11	0	0	1	1.000
1973 Bal	30	4	14	5	1	0	1	9	1	4	0	0	0	1	1	0	0	0	0	—	0	.357	.400	.643	C	4	30	2	0	0	1.000
1974 Bal	31	2	6	2	0	0	0	2	0	0	0	0	0	0	0	0	0	0	0	—	0	.333	.333	.333	C	2	7	1	0	0	1.000
LCS Totals		12	38	8	1	0	1	12	2	4	0	0	0	4	1	1	0	0	0	—	2	.211	.231	.316	C	12	78	3	0	1	1.000
World Series		Batting																							Fielding						
Year Tm	Age	G	AB	H	2B	3B	HR	TB	R	RBI	GW	TBB	IBB	SO	HBP	SH	SF	SB	CS	SB%	GDP	Avg	OBP	SLG	Pos	G	PO	A	E	DP	FPct
1966 Bal	23	4	12	1	0	0	0	1	2	0	0	2	0	4	0	0	0	0	0	—	1	.083	.214	.083	C	4	32	1	0	1	1.000
1969 Bal	26	2	6	0	0	0	0	0	0	0	0	0	0	1	0	0	0	0	0	—	0	.000	.000	.000	C	2	16	0	0	0	1.000
1970 Bal	27	2	7	1	0	0	0	1	1	0	0	2	1	3	0	0	0	0	0	—	0	.143	.333	.143	C	2	10	0	1	0	.909
1971 Bal	28	1	2	0	0	0	0	0	0	0	0	0	0	0	1	0	0	0	0	—	1	.000	.333	.000	C	1	6	0	0	0	1.000
WS Totals		9	27	2	0	0	0	2	3	0	0	4	1	8	1	0	0	0	0	—	2	.074	.219	.074	C	9	64	1	1	1	.985
Postseason Totals		21	65	10	1	0	1	14	5	4	0	4	1	12	2	1	0	0	0	—	4	.154	.225	.215	C	21	142	4	1	2	.993

NICK ETTEN—Nicholas Raymond Thomas Etten—Bats: Left; Throws: Left

Ht: 6'2"; Wt: 198 lbs; Born: 9/19/1913 in Spring Grove, Illinois; Debut: 9/8/1938; Died: 10/18/1990

World Series		Batting																							Fielding						
Year Tm	Age	G	AB	H	2B	3B	HR	TB	R	RBI	GW	TBB	IBB	SO	HBP	SH	SF	SB	CS	SB%	GDP	Avg	OBP	SLG	Pos	G	PO	A	E	DP	FPct
1943 NYA	30	5	19	2	0	0	0	2	0	2	0	1	0	2	0	0	0	0	0	—	0	.105	.150	.105	1B	5	46	2	1	3	.980

TONY EUSEBIO—Raul Antonio Eusebio—Bats: Right; Throws: Right

Ht: 6'2"; Wt: 180 lbs; Born: 4/27/1967 in San Jose De Los Llamos, Dominican Republic; Debut: 8/8/1991

Division Series		Batting																							Fielding						
Year Tm	Age	G	AB	H	2B	3B	HR	TB	R	RBI	GW	TBB	IBB	SO	HBP	SH	SF	SB	CS	SB%	GDP	Avg	OBP	SLG	Pos	G	PO	A	E	DP	FPct
1997 Hou	30	1	3	2	0	0	0	2	1	0	0	0	0	1	0	0	0	1	0	1.00	0	.667	.667	.667	C	1	6	1	0	0	1.000

DARRELL EVANS—Darrell Wayne Evans—Bats: Left; Throws: Right

Ht: 6'2"; Wt: 200 lbs; Born: 5/26/1947 in Pasadena, California; Debut: 4/20/1969

LCS		Batting																							Fielding						
Year Tm	Age	G	AB	H	2B	3B	HR	TB	R	RBI	GW	TBB	IBB	SO	HBP	SH	SF	SB	CS	SB%	GDP	Avg	OBP	SLG	Pos	G	PO	A	E	DP	FPct
1984 Det	37	3	10	3	1	0	0	4	1	1	0	1	0	0	0	1	0	1	0	1.00	0	.300	.364	.400	1B	3	22	3	0	0	1.000
																									3B	1	0	1	0	0	1.000
1987 Det	40	5	17	5	0	0	0	5	0	0	0	4	0	2	1	0	0	0	0	—	1	.294	.455	.294	1B	5	43	3	1	1	.979
																									3B	1	0	1	2	0	.333
LCS Totals		8	27	8	1	0	0	9	1	1	0	5	0	2	1	1	0	1	0	1.00	1	.296	.424	.333	1B	8	65	6	1	1	.986
World Series		Batting																							Fielding						
Year Tm	Age	G	AB	H	2B	3B	HR	TB	R	RBI	GW	TBB	IBB	SO	HBP	SH	SF	SB	CS	SB%	GDP	Avg	OBP	SLG	Pos	G	PO	A	E	DP	FPct
1984 Det	37	5	15	1	0	0	0	1	1	1	0	4	1	4	0	0	0	0	0	—	0	.067	.263	.067	1B	4	15	3	0	1	1.000
																									3B	2	3	2	0	0	1.000
Postseason Totals		13	42	9	1	0	0	10	2	2	0	9	1	6	1	1	0	1	0	1.00	1	.214	.365	.238	1B	12	80	9	1	2	.989

DWIGHT EVANS—Dwight Michael Evans—Nickname: Dewey—Bats: Right; Throws: Right

Ht: 6'2"; Wt: 180 lbs; Born: 11/3/1951 in Santa Monica, California; Debut: 9/16/1972

LCS		Batting																							Fielding						
Year Tm	Age	G	AB	H	2B	3B	HR	TB	R	RBI	GW	TBB	IBB	SO	HBP	SH	SF	SB	CS	SB%	GDP	Avg	OBP	SLG	Pos	G	PO	A	E	DP	FPct
1975 Bos	23	3	10	1	1	0	0	2	1	0	0	1	1	2	0	0	0	0	0	—	0	.100	.182	.200	OF	3	7	0	0	0	1.000
1986 Bos	34	7	28	6	1	0	1	10	2	4	1	3	0	3	0	0	0	0	0	—	0	.214	.290	.357	OF	7	11	0	0	0	1.000
1988 Bos	36	4	12	2	1	0	0	3	1	1	0	3	0	5	0	0	0	0	0	—	0	.167	.333	.250	OF	4	11	0	0	0	1.000
1990 Bos	38	4	13	3	1	0	0	4	0	0	0	1	0	3	0	0	0	0	0	—	0	.231	.286	.308	—						
LCS Totals		18	63	12	4	0	1	19	4	5	1	8	1	13	0	0	0	0	0	—	0	.190	.282	.302	OF	14	29	0	0	0	1.000
World Series		Batting																							Fielding						
Year Tm	Age	G	AB	H	2B	3B	HR	TB	R	RBI	GW	TBB	IBB	SO	HBP	SH	SF	SB	CS	SB%	GDP	Avg	OBP	SLG	Pos	G	PO	A	E	DP	FPct
1975 Bos	23	7	24	7	1	1	1	13	3	5	0	3	0	4	1	1	0	0	1	.00	0	.292	.393	.542	OF	7	25	0	0	1	1.000
1986 Bos	34	7	26	8	2	0	2	16	4	9	0	4	0	3	0	0	0	0	0	—	1	.308	.400	.615	OF	7	16	1	1	0	.944
WS Totals		14	50	15	3	1	3	29	7	14	0	7	0	7	1	1	0	0	1	.00	1	.300	.397	.580	OF	14	41	1	1	1	.977
Postseason Totals		32	113	27	7	1	4	48	11	19	1	15	1	20	1	1	0	0	1	.00	1	.239	.333	.425	OF	28	70	1	1	1	.986

JOE EVANS—Joseph Patton Evans—Nickname: Doc—Bats: Right; Throws: Right

Ht: 5'9"; Wt: 160 lbs; Born: 5/15/1895 in Meridan, Mississippi; Debut: 7/3/1915; Died: 8/9/1953

World Series		Batting																							Fielding						
Year Tm	Age	G	AB	H	2B	3B	HR	TB	R	RBI	GW	TBB	IBB	SO	HBP	SH	SF	SB	CS	SB%	GDP	Avg	OBP	SLG	Pos	G	PO	A	E	DP	FPct
1920 Cle	25	4	13	4	0	0	0	4	0	0	0	1	0	0	0	0	0	0	1	.00	0	.308	.357	.308	OF	4	7	0	0	0	1.000

JOHNNY EVERS (HOF 1946-V)—John Joseph Evers—Nicknames: Crab, Trojan—Bats: Left; Throws: Right

Ht: 5'9"; Wt: 125 lbs; Born: 7/21/1881 in Troy, New York; Debut: 9/1/1902; Died: 3/28/1947

World Series		Batting																							Fielding						
Year Tm	Age	G	AB	H	2B	3B	HR	TB	R	RBI	GW	TBB	IBB	SO	HBP	SH	SF	SB	CS	SB%	GDP	Avg	OBP	SLG	Pos	G	PO	A	E	DP	FPct
1906 ChN	25	6	20	3	1	0	0	4	2	1	1	1	0	3	0	0	0	2	1	.67	0	.150	.190	.200	2B	6	14	19	1	3	.971
1907 ChN	26	5	20	7	2	0	0	9	2	1	1	0	0	1	0	1	0	3	1	.75	0	.350	.350	.450	2B	5	11	12	2	2	.920
																									SS	1	0	0	1	0	.000
1908 ChN	27	5	20	7	1	0	0	8	5	2	0	1	0	2	0	1	0	2	2	.50	0	.350	.381	.400	2B	5	5	20	1	1	.962
1914 Bos-*M*	33	4	16	7	0	0	0	7	2	2	1	2	0	2	0	0	0	1	1	.50	0	.438	.500	.438	2B	4	8	16	1	2	.960
WS Totals		20	76	24	4	0	0	28	11	6	3	4	0	8	0	2	0	8	5	.62	0	.316	.350	.368	2B	20	38	67	5	8	.955

RED FABER (HOF 1964-V)—Urban Charles Faber—Throws: Right; Bats: Both

Ht: 6'2"; Wt: 180 lbs; Born: 9/6/1888 in Cascade, Iowa; Debut: 4/17/1914; Died: 9/25/1976

World Series		Pitching																									
Year Tm	Age	G	GS	CG	GF	IP	BFP	H	R	ER	HR	SH	SF	HB	TBB	IBB	SO	WP	Bk	W	L	Pct	ShO	Sv-Op	Hld	OAvg	OOBP	ERA
1917 ChA	29	4	3	2	1	27.0	101	21	7	7	1	1	0	2	3	0	9	1	0	3	1	.750	0	0- 0	0	.221	.260	2.33

World Series		Batting																							Fielding						
Year Tm	Age	G	AB	H	2B	3B	HR	TB	R	RBI	GW	TBB	IBB	SO	HBP	SH	SF	SB	CS	SB%	GDP	Avg	OBP	SLG	Pos	G	PO	A	E	DP	FPct
1917 ChA	29	4	7	1	0	0	0	1	0	0	0	2	0	3	0	1	0	0	0	—	0	.143	.333	.143	P	4	1	9	0	2	1.000

ROY FACE—Elroy Leon Face—Throws: Right; Bats: Both

Ht: 5'8"; Wt: 155 lbs; Born: 2/20/1928 in Stephentown, New York; Debut: 4/16/1953

World Series		Pitching																									
Year Tm	Age	G	GS	CG	GF	IP	BFP	H	R	ER	HR	SH	SF	HB	TBB	IBB	SO	WP	Bk	W	L	Pct	ShO	Sv-Op	Hld	OAvg	OOBP	ERA
1960 Pit	32	4	0	0	3	10.1	41	9	6	6	2	0	0	0	2	0	4	0	0	0	0	—	0	3- 4	0	.231	.268	5.23

World Series		Batting																							Fielding						
Year Tm	Age	G	AB	H	2B	3B	HR	TB	R	RBI	GW	TBB	IBB	SO	HBP	SH	SF	SB	CS	SB%	GDP	Avg	OBP	SLG	Pos	G	PO	A	E	DP	FPct
1960 Pit	32	4	3	0	0	0	0	0	0	0	0	0	0	2	0	0	0	0	0	—	0	.000	.000	.000	P	4	0	2	0	0	1.000

RON FAIRLY—Ronald Ray Fairly—Bats: Left; Throws: Left

Ht: 5'10"; Wt: 175 lbs; Born: 7/12/1938 in Macon, Georgia; Debut: 9/9/1958

World Series		Batting																							Fielding						
Year Tm	Age	G	AB	H	2B	3B	HR	TB	R	RBI	GW	TBB	IBB	SO	HBP	SH	SF	SB	CS	SB%	GDP	Avg	OBP	SLG	Pos	G	PO	A	E	DP	FPct
1959 LA	21	6	3	0	0	0	0	0	0	0	0	0	0	1	0	0	0	0	0	—	0	.000	.000	.000	OF	4	0	0	0	0	—
1963 LA	25	4	1	0	0	0	0	0	0	0	0	3	1	0	0	0	0	0	0	—	0	.000	.750	.000	OF	4	3	0	0	0	1.000
1965 LA	27	7	29	11	3	0	2	20	7	6	1	0	0	1	0	0	0	0	0	—	0	.379	.379	.690	OF	7	8	0	0	0	1.000
1966 LA	28	3	7	1	0	0	0	1	0	0	0	2	0	4	0	0	0	0	0	—	0	.143	.333	.143	1B	1	2	0	0	0	1.000
																									OF	2	3	0	1	0	.750
WS Totals		20	40	12	3	0	2	21	7	6	1	5	1	6	0	0	0	0	0	—	0	.300	.378	.525	OF	17	14	0	1	0	.933

GEORGE FALLON—George Decatur Fallon—Nickname: Flash—Bats: Right; Throws: Right

Ht: 5'9"; Wt: 155 lbs; Born: 7/8/1914 in Jersey City, New Jersey; Debut: 9/27/1937; Died: 10/25/1994

World Series		Batting																							Fielding						
Year Tm	Age	G	AB	H	2B	3B	HR	TB	R	RBI	GW	TBB	IBB	SO	HBP	SH	SF	SB	CS	SB%	GDP	Avg	OBP	SLG	Pos	G	PO	A	E	DP	FPct
1944 StL	30	2	2	0	0	0	0	0	0	0	0	0	0	1	0	0	0	0	0	—	0	.000	.000	.000	2B	2	0	0	0	0	—

STEVE FARR—Steven Michael Farr—Throws: Right; Bats: Right

Ht: 5'10"; Wt: 198 lbs; Born: 12/12/1956 in Cheverly, Maryland; Debut: 5/16/1984

LCS		Pitching																									
Year Tm	Age	G	GS	CG	GF	IP	BFP	H	R	ER	HR	SH	SF	HB	TBB	IBB	SO	WP	Bk	W	L	Pct	ShO	Sv-Op	Hld	OAvg	OOBP	ERA
1985 KC	28	2	0	0	1	6.1	22	4	1	1	0	0	1	0	1	0	3	0	0	1	0	1.000	0	0- 0	0	.200	.227	1.42

LCS		Batting																							Fielding						
Year Tm	Age	G	AB	H	2B	3B	HR	TB	R	RBI	GW	TBB	IBB	SO	HBP	SH	SF	SB	CS	SB%	GDP	Avg	OBP	SLG	Pos	G	PO	A	E	DP	FPct
1985 KC	28	2	0	0	0	0	0	0	0	0	0	0	0	0	0	0	0	0	0	—	0	—	—	—	P	2	0	1	0	1	1.000

DUKE FARRELL—Charles Andrew Farrell—Bats: Both; Throws: Right

Ht: 6'1"; Wt: 208 lbs; Born: 8/31/1866 in Oakdale, Massachusetts; Debut: 4/21/1888; Died: 2/15/1925

World Series		Batting																							Fielding						
Year Tm	Age	G	AB	H	2B	3B	HR	TB	R	RBI	GW	TBB	IBB	SO	HBP	SH	SF	SB	CS	SB%	GDP	Avg	OBP	SLG	Pos	G	PO	A	E	DP	FPct
1903 Bos	37	2	2	0	0	0	0	0	0	1	0	0	0	0	0	0	0	0	0	—	0	.000	.000	.000	—						

JEFF FASSERO—Jeffrey Joseph Fassero—Throws: Left; Bats: Left

Ht: 6'1"; Wt: 180 lbs; Born: 1/5/1963 in Springfield, Illinois; Debut: 5/4/1991

Division Series		Pitching																									
Year Tm	Age	G	GS	CG	GF	IP	BFP	H	R	ER	HR	SH	SF	HB	TBB	IBB	SO	WP	Bk	W	L	Pct	ShO	Sv-Op	Hld	OAvg	OOBP	ERA
1997 Sea	34	1	1	0	0	8.0	30	3	1	1	0	1	0	0	4	0	3	0	0	1	0	1.000	0	0- 0	0	.120	.241	1.13

Division Series		Batting																							Fielding						
Year Tm	Age	G	AB	H	2B	3B	HR	TB	R	RBI	GW	TBB	IBB	SO	HBP	SH	SF	SB	CS	SB%	GDP	Avg	OBP	SLG	Pos	G	PO	A	E	DP	FPct
1997 Sea	34	1	0	0	0	0	0	0	0	0	0	0	0	0	0	0	0	0	0	—	0	—	—	—	P	1	1	4	0	0	1.000

JUNIOR FELIX—Junior Francisco Felix—Bats: Both; Throws: Right

Ht: 6'0"; Wt: 170 lbs; Born: 10/3/1967 in Laguna Salada, Dominican Republic; Debut: 5/3/1989

LCS		Batting																							Fielding						
Year Tm	Age	G	AB	H	2B	3B	HR	TB	R	RBI	GW	TBB	IBB	SO	HBP	SH	SF	SB	CS	SB%	GDP	Avg	OBP	SLG	Pos	G	PO	A	E	DP	FPct
1989 Tor	21	3	11	3	1	0	0	4	0	3	0	0	0	2	0	0	0	0	0	—	0	.273	.273	.364	OF	3	8	0	0	0	1.000

BOB FELLER (HOF 1962-W)—Robert William Andrew Feller—Nickname: Rapid Robert—Throws: Right; Bats: Right

Ht: 6'0"; Wt: 185 lbs; Born: 11/3/1918 in Van Meter, Iowa; Debut: 7/19/1936

World Series		Pitching																									
Year Tm	Age	G	GS	CG	GF	IP	BFP	H	R	ER	HR	SH	SF	HB	TBB	IBB	SO	WP	Bk	W	L	Pct	ShO	Sv-Op	Hld	OAvg	OOBP	ERA
1948 Cle	29	2	2	1	0	14.1	59	10	8	8	3	3	0	0	5	1	7	0	0	0	2	.000	0	0- 0	0	.196	.268	5.02

World Series

Year Tm	Age	G	AB	H	2B	3B	HR	TB	R	RBI	GW	TBB	IBB	SO	HBP	SH	SF	SB	CS	SB%	GDP	Avg	OBP	SLG	Pos	G	PO	A	E	DP	FPct
1948 Cle	29	2	4	0	0	0	0	0	0	0	0	0	0	2	0	1	0	0	0	—	0	.000	.000	.000	P	2	2	4	0	0	1.000

HAPPY FELSCH—Oscar Emil Felsch—Bats: Right; Throws: Right

Ht: 5'11"; Wt: 175 lbs; Born: 8/22/1891 in Milwaukee, Wisconsin; Debut: 4/14/1915; Died: 8/17/1964

World Series

Year Tm	Age	G	AB	H	2B	3B	HR	TB	R	RBI	GW	TBB	IBB	SO	HBP	SH	SF	SB	CS	SB%	GDP	Avg	OBP	SLG	Pos	G	PO	A	E	DP	FPct
1917 ChA	26	6	22	6	1	0	1	10	4	3	0	1	0	5	0	0	0	0	2	.00	0	.273	.304	.455	OF	6	16	2	0	1	1.000
1919 ChA	28	8	26	5	1	0	0	6	2	3	0	1	0	4	0	4	0	0	1	.00	1	.192	.222	.231	OF	8	23	1	2	1	.923
WS Totals		14	48	11	2	0	1	16	6	6	0	2	0	9	0	4	0	0	3	.00	1	.229	.260	.333	OF	14	39	3	2	2	.955

ALEX FERGUSON—James Alexander Ferguson—Throws: Right; Bats: Right

Ht: 6'0"; Wt: 180 lbs; Born: 2/16/1897 in Montclair, New Jersey; Debut: 8/16/1918; Died: 4/26/1976

World Series — Pitching

Year Tm	Age	G	GS	CG	GF	IP	BFP	H	R	ER	HR	SH	SF	HB	TBB	IBB	SO	WP	Bk	W	L	Pct	ShO	Sv-Op	Hld	OAvg	OOBP	ERA
1925 Was	28	2	2	0	0	14.0	64	13	6	5	1	3	1	1	6	1	11	0	0	1	1	.500	0	0-0	0	.245	.328	3.21

World Series — Batting / Fielding

Year Tm	Age	G	AB	H	2B	3B	HR	TB	R	RBI	GW	TBB	IBB	SO	HBP	SH	SF	SB	CS	SB%	GDP	Avg	OBP	SLG	Pos	G	PO	A	E	DP	FPct
1925 Was	28	2	4	0	0	0	0	0	0	0	0	0	0	3	0	0	0	0	0	—	0	.000	.000	.000	P	2	0	1	0	0	1.000

JOE FERGUSON—Joseph Vance Ferguson—Bats: Right; Throws: Right

Ht: 6'2"; Wt: 200 lbs; Born: 9/19/1946 in San Francisco, California; Debut: 9/12/1970

Year Tm	Age	G	AB	H	2B	3B	HR	TB	R	RBI	GW	TBB	IBB	SO	HBP	SH	SF	SB	CS	SB%	GDP	Avg	OBP	SLG	Pos	G	PO	A	E	DP	FPct
LCS																															
1974 LA	28	4	13	3	0	0	0	3	3	2	0	5	0	1	0	1	0	0	0	—	0	.231	.444	.231	C	2	3	0	0	0	1.000
																									OF	3	6	0	0	0	1.000
1978 LA	32	2	2	0	0	0	0	0	0	0	0	0	0	1	0	0	0	0	0	—	1	.000	.000	.000	—						
LCS Totals		6	15	3	0	0	0	3	3	2	0	5	0	2	0	1	0	0	0	—	1	.200	.400	.200	OF	3	6	0	0	0	1.000
World Series																															
1974 LA	28	5	16	2	0	0	1	5	2	2	0	4	0	6	1	0	0	1	0	1.00	0	.125	.333	.313	C	2	10	0	2	0	.833
																									OF	4	5	1	0	1	1.000
1978 LA	32	2	4	2	2	0	0	4	1	0	0	0	0	1	0	0	0	0	0	—	0	.500	.500	1.000	C	2	11	0	1	0	.917
WS Totals		7	20	4	2	0	1	9	3	2	0	4	0	7	1	0	0	1	0	1.00	0	.200	.360	.450	C	4	21	0	3	0	.875
Postseason Totals		13	35	7	2	0	1	12	6	4	0	9	0	9	1	1	0	1	0	1.00	1	.200	.378	.343	OF	7	11	1	0	1	1.000

FELIX FERMIN—Felix Jose Fermin—Nickname: Gato—Bats: Right; Throws: Right

Ht: 5'11"; Wt: 160 lbs; Born: 10/9/1963 in Mao Valverde, Dominican Republic; Debut: 7/8/1987

Year Tm	Age	G	AB	H	2B	3B	HR	TB	R	RBI	GW	TBB	IBB	SO	HBP	SH	SF	SB	CS	SB%	GDP	Avg	OBP	SLG	Pos	G	PO	A	E	DP	FPct
Division Series																															
1995 Sea	31	3	1	0	0	0	0	0	0	0	0	0	0	1	0	0	0	0	0	—	0	.000	.000	.000	SS	2	1	1	0	0	1.000
																									2B	1	2	2	0	1	1.000
LCS																															
1995 Sea	31	2	0	0	0	0	0	0	0	0	0	0	0	0	0	0	0	0	0	—	0	—	—	—	2B	1	0	0	0	0	—
																									SS	1	0	0	0	0	—
Postseason Totals		5	1	0	0	0	0	0	0	0	0	0	0	1	0	0	0	0	0	—	0	.000	.000	.000	SS	3	1	1	0	0	1.000

ALEX FERNANDEZ—Alexander Fernandez—Throws: Right; Bats: Right

Ht: 6'1"; Wt: 205 lbs; Born: 8/13/1969 in Miami Beach, Florida; Debut: 8/2/1990

Pitching

Year Tm	Age	G	GS	CG	GF	IP	BFP	H	R	ER	HR	SH	SF	HB	TBB	IBB	SO	WP	Bk	W	L	Pct	ShO	Sv-Op	Hld	OAvg	OOBP	ERA
Division Series																												
1997 Fla	28	1	1	0	0	7.0	28	7	2	2	2	0	0	0	0	0	5	0	0	1	0	1.000	0	0-0	0	.250	.250	2.57
LCS																												
1993 ChA	24	2	2	0	0	15.0	66	15	6	3	0	1	0	1	6	3	10	0	0	0	2	.000	0	0-0	0	.259	.338	1.80
1997 Fla	28	1	1	0	0	2.2	15	6	5	5	2	0	0	0	1	0	3	0	0	0	1	.000	0	0-0	0	.429	.467	16.88
LCS Totals		3	3	0	0	17.2	162	21	11	8	2	1	0	1	7	3	13	0	0	0	3	.000	0	0-0	0	.292	.363	4.08
Postseason Totals		4	4	0	0	24.2	218	28	13	10	4	1	0	1	7	3	18	0	0	1	3	.250	0	0-0	0	.280	.333	3.65

Batting / Fielding

Year Tm	Age	G	AB	H	2B	3B	HR	TB	R	RBI	GW	TBB	IBB	SO	HBP	SH	SF	SB	CS	SB%	GDP	Avg	OBP	SLG	Pos	G	PO	A	E	DP	FPct
Division Series																															
1997 Fla	28	1	2	0	0	0	0	0	0	0	0	1	0	1	0	0	0	0	0	—	0	.000	.333	.000	P	1	0	1	0	0	1.000
LCS																															
1993 ChA	24	2	0	0	0	0	0	0	0	0	0	0	0	0	0	0	0	0	0	—	0	—	—	—	P	2	2	1	0	1	1.000
1997 Fla	28	1	1	0	0	0	0	0	0	0	0	0	0	1	0	0	0	0	0	—	0	.000	.000	.000	P	1	0	0	0	0	—
LCS Totals		3	1	0	0	0	0	0	0	0	0	0	0	1	0	0	0	0	0	—	0	.000	.000	.000	P	3	2	1	0	1	1.000
Postseason Totals		4	3	0	0	0	0	0	0	0	0	1	0	2	0	0	0	0	0	—	0	.000	.250	.000	P	4	2	2	0	1	1.000

SID FERNANDEZ—Charles Sidney Fernandez—Nickname: El Sid—Throws: Left; Bats: Left

Ht: 6'1"; Wt: 220 lbs; Born: 10/12/1962 in Honolulu, Hawaii; Debut: 9/20/1983

Pitching

Year Tm	Age	G	GS	CG	GF	IP	BFP	H	R	ER	HR	SH	SF	HB	TBB	IBB	SO	WP	Bk	W	L	Pct	ShO	Sv-Op	Hld	OAvg	OOBP	ERA
LCS																												
1986 NYN	23	1	1	0	0	6.0	22	3	3	3	2	0	0	0	1	0	5	0	0	0	1	.000	0	0-0	0	.143	.182	4.50
1988 NYN	25	1	1	0	0	4.0	21	7	6	6	1	0	0	0	1	0	5	0	0	0	1	.000	0	0-0	0	.350	.381	13.50
LCS Totals		2	2	0	0	10.0	86	10	9	9	3	0	0	0	2	0	10	0	0	0	2	.000	0	0-0	0	.244	.279	8.10
World Series																												
1986 NYN	23	3	0	0	1	6.2	27	6	1	1	0	0	0	0	1	0	10	0	0	0	0	—	0	0-0	0	.231	.259	1.35
Postseason Totals		5	2	0	1	16.2	140	16	10	10	3	0	0	0	3	0	20	0	0	0	2	.000	0	0-0	0	.239	.271	5.40

Batting / Fielding

Year Tm	Age	G	AB	H	2B	3B	HR	TB	R	RBI	GW	TBB	IBB	SO	HBP	SH	SF	SB	CS	SB%	GDP	Avg	OBP	SLG	Pos	G	PO	A	E	DP	FPct
LCS																															
1986 NYN	23	1	1	0	0	0	0	0	0	0	0	0	0	0	0	0	0	0	0	—	0	.000	.000	.000	P	1	0	0	0	0	—
1988 NYN	25	1	1	0	0	0	0	0	0	0	0	0	0	0	0	0	0	0	0	—	0	.000	.000	.000	P	1	0	0	0	0	—
LCS Totals		2	2	0	0	0	0	0	0	0	0	0	0	0	0	0	0	0	0	—	0	.000	.000	.000	P	2	0	0	0	0	—
World Series																															
1986 NYN	23	3	0	0	0	0	0	0	0	0	0	0	0	0	0	0	0	0	0	—	0	—	—	—	P	3	0	0	0	0	—
Postseason Totals		5	2	0	0	0	0	0	0	0	0	0	0	0	0	0	0	0	0	—	0	.000	.000	.000	P	5	0	0	0	0	—

TONY FERNANDEZ—Octavio Antonio Fernandez—Bats: Both; Throws: Right

Ht: 6'2"; Wt: 165 lbs; Born: 6/30/1962 in San Pedro de Macoris, Dominican Republic; Debut: 9/2/1983

Year Tm	Age	G	AB	H	2B	3B	HR	TB	R	RBI	GW	TBB	IBB	SO	HBP	SH	SF	SB	CS	SB%	GDP	Avg	OBP	SLG	Pos	G	PO	A	E	DP	FPct
Division Series																															
1995 NYA	33	5	21	5	2	0	0	7	0	0	0	2	1	2	0	1	0	0	0	—	1	.238	.304	.333	SS	5	9	15	0	2	1.000
1997 Cle	35	4	11	2	1	0	0	3	0	4	1	0	0	0	0	0	1	0	0	—	0	.182	.167	.273	2B	4	8	9	0	2	1.000
DS Totals		9	32	7	3	0	0	10	0	4	1	2	1	2	0	1	1	0	0	—	1	.219	.257	.313	SS	5	9	15	0	2	1.000
LCS																															
1985 Tor	23	7	24	8	2	0	0	10	2	2	0	1	0	2	0	0	1	0	0	—	0	.333	.346	.417	SS	7	11	15	2	2	.929
1989 Tor	27	5	20	7	3	0	0	10	6	1	0	1	0	2	0	0	0	5	0	1.00	0	.350	.381	.500	SS	5	9	15	0	3	1.000
1993 Tor	31	6	22	7	0	0	0	7	1	1	1	2	2	4	0	1	0	0	0	—	1	.318	.375	.318	SS	6	12	8	0	5	1.000
1997 Cle	35	5	14	5	1	0	1	9	1	2	1	1	0	2	1	0	0	0	0	—	0	.357	.438	.643	2B	5	9	10	1	2	.950
LCS Totals		23	80	27	6	0	1	36	10	6	2	5	2	10	1	1	1	5	0	1.00	2	.338	.379	.450	SS	18	32	38	2	10	.972

World Series		Batting																							Fielding						
Year Tm	Age	G	AB	H	2B	3B	HR	TB	R	RBI	GW	TBB	IBB	SO	HBP	SH	SF	SB	CS	SB%	GDP	Avg	OBP	SLG	Pos	G	PO	A	E	DP	FPct
1993 Tor	31	6	21	7	1	0	0	8	2	9	0	3	0	3	1	0	1	0	1	.00	0	.333	.423	.381	SS	6	11	8	0	4	1.000
1997 Cle	35	5	17	8	1	0	0	9	1	4	0	0	0	1	0	0	1	0	0	—	0	.471	.444	.529	2B	5	9	14	2	3	.920
WS Totals		11	38	15	2	0	0	17	3	13	0	3	0	4	1	0	2	0	1	.00	0	.395	.432	.447	SS	6	11	8	0	4	1.000
Postseason Totals		43	150	49	11	0	1	63	13	23	3	10	3	16	2	2	4	5	1	.83	3	.327	.367	.420	SS	29	52	61	2	16	.983

AL FERRARA—Alfred John Ferrara—Nickname: The Bull—Bats: Right; Throws: Right

Ht: 6'1"; Wt: 200 lbs; Born: 12/22/1939 in Brooklyn, New York; Debut: 7/30/1963

World Series		Batting																							Fielding						
Year Tm	Age	G	AB	H	2B	3B	HR	TB	R	RBI	GW	TBB	IBB	SO	HBP	SH	SF	SB	CS	SB%	GDP	Avg	OBP	SLG	Pos	G	PO	A	E	DP	FPct
1966 LA	26	1	1	1	0	0	0	1	0	0	0	0	0	0	0	0	0	0	0	—	0	1.000	1.000	1.000	—						

TOM FERRICK—Thomas Jerome Ferrick—Throws: Right; Bats: Right

Ht: 6'2"; Wt: 220 lbs; Born: 1/6/1915 in New York, New York; Debut: 4/19/1941; Died: 10/15/1996

World Series		Pitching																										
Year Tm	Age	G	GS	CG	GF	IP	BFP	H	R	ER	HR	SH	SF	HB	TBB	IBB	SO	WP	Bk	W	L	Pct	ShO	Sv-Op	Hld	OAvg	OOBP	ERA
1950 NYA	35	1	0	0	1	1.0	5	1	0	0	0	1	0	0	1	1	0	0	0	1	0	1.000	0	0- 0	0	.333	.500	0.00

World Series		Batting																							Fielding						
Year Tm	Age	G	AB	H	2B	3B	HR	TB	R	RBI	GW	TBB	IBB	SO	HBP	SH	SF	SB	CS	SB%	GDP	Avg	OBP	SLG	Pos	G	PO	A	E	DP	FPct
1950 NYA	35	1	0	0	0	0	0	0	0	0	0	0	0	0	0	0	0	0	0	—	0	—	—	—	P	1	0	0	0	0	—

HOBE FERRIS—Albert Sayles Ferris—Bats: Right; Throws: Right

Ht: 5'8"; Wt: 162 lbs; Born: 12/7/1877 in Providence, Rhode Island; Debut: 4/26/1901; Died: 3/18/1938

World Series		Batting																							Fielding						
Year Tm	Age	G	AB	H	2B	3B	HR	TB	R	RBI	GW	TBB	IBB	SO	HBP	SH	SF	SB	CS	SB%	GDP	Avg	OBP	SLG	Pos	G	PO	A	E	DP	FPct
1903 Bos	25	8	31	9	0	1	0	11	3	5	1	0	0	6	1	1	0	0	0	—	0	.290	.313	.355	2B	8	18	23	2	2	.953

BOO FERRISS—David Meadow Ferriss—Throws: Right; Bats: Left

Ht: 6'2"; Wt: 208 lbs; Born: 12/5/1921 in Shaw, Mississippi; Debut: 4/29/1945

World Series		Pitching																										
Year Tm	Age	G	GS	CG	GF	IP	BFP	H	R	ER	HR	SH	SF	HB	TBB	IBB	SO	WP	Bk	W	L	Pct	ShO	Sv-Op	Hld	OAvg	OOBP	ERA
1946 Bos	24	2	2	1	0	13.1	51	13	3	3	0	1	0	0	2	0	4	0	0	1	0	1.000	1	0- 0	0	.271	.300	2.03

World Series		Batting																							Fielding						
Year Tm	Age	G	AB	H	2B	3B	HR	TB	R	RBI	GW	TBB	IBB	SO	HBP	SH	SF	SB	CS	SB%	GDP	Avg	OBP	SLG	Pos	G	PO	A	E	DP	FPct
1946 Bos	24	2	6	0	0	0	0	0	0	0	0	0	0	1	0	0	0	0	0	—	0	.000	.000	.000	P	2	0	3	0	0	1.000

CHICK FEWSTER—Wilson Lloyd Fewster—Bats: Right; Throws: Right

Ht: 5'11"; Wt: 160 lbs; Born: 11/10/1895 in Baltimore, Maryland; Debut: 9/19/1917; Died: 4/16/1945

World Series		Batting																							Fielding						
Year Tm	Age	G	AB	H	2B	3B	HR	TB	R	RBI	GW	TBB	IBB	SO	HBP	SH	SF	SB	CS	SB%	GDP	Avg	OBP	SLG	Pos	G	PO	A	E	DP	FPct
1921 NYA	25	4	10	2	0	0	1	5	3	2	0	3	0	3	0	0	0	0	0	—	0	.200	.385	.500	OF	4	7	0	0	0	1.000

CECIL FIELDER—Cecil Grant Fielder—Nickname: Big Daddy—Bats: Right; Throws: Right

Ht: 6'3"; Wt: 230 lbs; Born: 9/21/1963 in Los Angeles, California; Debut: 7/20/1985

Division Series		Batting																							Fielding						
Year Tm	Age	G	AB	H	2B	3B	HR	TB	R	RBI	GW	TBB	IBB	SO	HBP	SH	SF	SB	CS	SB%	GDP	Avg	OBP	SLG	Pos	G	PO	A	E	DP	FPct
1996 NYA	33	3	11	4	0	0	1	7	2	4	1	1	0	2	0	0	0	0	0	—	0	.364	.417	.636	—						
1997 NYA	34	2	8	1	0	0	0	1	0	1	0	0	0	3	0	0	0	0	0	—	0	.125	.125	.125	—						
DS Totals		5	19	5	0	0	1	8	2	5	1	1	0	5	0	0	0	0	0	—	0	.263	.300	.421	—	0	0	0	0	0	—
LCS		Batting																							Fielding						
Year Tm	Age	G	AB	H	2B	3B	HR	TB	R	RBI	GW	TBB	IBB	SO	HBP	SH	SF	SB	CS	SB%	GDP	Avg	OBP	SLG	Pos	G	PO	A	E	DP	FPct
1985 Tor	22	3	3	1	1	0	0	2	0	0	0	0	0	1	0	0	0	0	0	—	0	.333	.333	.667	—						
1996 NYA	33	5	18	3	0	0	2	9	3	8	0	4	1	5	0	0	0	0	0	—	1	.167	.318	.500	—						
LCS Totals		8	21	4	1	0	2	11	3	8	0	4	1	6	0	0	0	0	0	—	1	.190	.320	.524	—	0	0	0	0	0	—
World Series		Batting																							Fielding						
Year Tm	Age	G	AB	H	2B	3B	HR	TB	R	RBI	GW	TBB	IBB	SO	HBP	SH	SF	SB	CS	SB%	GDP	Avg	OBP	SLG	Pos	G	PO	A	E	DP	FPct
1996 NYA	33	6	23	9	2	0	0	11	1	2	1	2	0	2	0	0	0	0	0	—	0	.391	.440	.478	1B	3	21	5	0	3	1.000
Postseason Totals		19	63	18	3	0	3	30	6	15	2	7	1	13	0	0	0	0	0	—	1	.286	.357	.476	1B	3	21	5	0	3	1.000

ED FIGUEROA—Eduardo Figueroa—Throws: Right; Bats: Right

Ht: 6'1"; Wt: 190 lbs; Born: 10/14/1948 in Ciales, Puerto Rico; Debut: 4/9/1974

LCS		Pitching																										
Year Tm	Age	G	GS	CG	GF	IP	BFP	H	R	ER	HR	SH	SF	HB	TBB	IBB	SO	WP	Bk	W	L	Pct	ShO	Sv-Op	Hld	OAvg	OOBP	ERA
1976 NYA	27	2	2	0	0	12.1	52	14	8	8	1	0	1	0	2	0	5	0	0	0	1	.000	0	0- 0	0	.286	.308	5.84
1977 NYA	28	1	1	0	0	3.1	17	5	4	4	0	0	1	0	2	0	3	0	0	0	0	—	0	0- 0	0	.357	.412	10.80
1978 NYA	29	1	1	0	0	1.0	9	5	5	3	0	0	1	0	0	0	0	0	0	0	1	.000	0	0- 0	0	.625	.556	27.00
LCS Totals		4	4	0	0	16.2	156	24	17	15	1	0	3	0	4	0	8	0	0	0	2	.000	0	0-0	0	.338	.359	8.10
World Series		Pitching																										
Year Tm	Age	G	GS	CG	GF	IP	BFP	H	R	ER	HR	SH	SF	HB	TBB	IBB	SO	WP	Bk	W	L	Pct	ShO	Sv-Op	Hld	OAvg	OOBP	ERA
1976 NYA	27	1	1	0	0	8.0	32	6	5	5	1	0	0	0	5	0	2	1	0	0	1	.000	0	0- 0	0	.222	.344	5.63
1978 NYA	29	2	2	0	0	6.2	32	9	6	6	3	0	0	0	5	0	2	0	0	0	1	.000	0	0- 0	0	.333	.438	8.10
WS Totals		3	3	0	0	14.2	128	15	11	11	4	0	0	0	10	0	4	1	0	0	2	.000	0	0-0	0	.278	.391	6.75
Postseason Totals		7	7	0	0	31.1	284	39	28	26	5	0	3	0	14	0	12	1	0	0	4	.000	0	0-0	0	.312	.373	7.47

LCS		Batting																							Fielding						
Year Tm	Age	G	AB	H	2B	3B	HR	TB	R	RBI	GW	TBB	IBB	SO	HBP	SH	SF	SB	CS	SB%	GDP	Avg	OBP	SLG	Pos	G	PO	A	E	DP	FPct
1976 NYA	27	2	0	0	0	0	0	0	0	0	0	0	0	0	0	0	0	0	0	—	0	—	—	—	P	2	0	2	0	0	1.000
1977 NYA	28	1	0	0	0	0	0	0	0	0	0	0	0	0	0	0	0	0	0	—	0	—	—	—	P	1	0	0	0	0	—
1978 NYA	29	1	0	0	0	0	0	0	0	0	0	0	0	0	0	0	0	0	0	—	0	—	—	—	P	1	0	0	0	0	—
LCS Totals		4	0	0	0	0	0	0	0	0	0	0	0	0	0	0	0	0	0	—	0	—	—	—	P	4	0	2	0	0	1.000
World Series		Batting																							Fielding						
Year Tm	Age	G	AB	H	2B	3B	HR	TB	R	RBI	GW	TBB	IBB	SO	HBP	SH	SF	SB	CS	SB%	GDP	Avg	OBP	SLG	Pos	G	PO	A	E	DP	FPct
1976 NYA	27	1	0	0	0	0	0	0	0	0	0	0	0	0	0	0	0	0	0	—	0	—	—	—	P	1	0	1	0	0	1.000
1978 NYA	29	2	0	0	0	0	0	0	0	0	0	0	0	0	0	0	0	0	0	—	0	—	—	—	P	2	0	0	0	0	—
WS Totals		3	0	0	0	0	0	0	0	0	0	0	0	0	0	0	0	0	0	—	0	—	—	—	P	3	0	1	0	0	1.000
Postseason Totals		7	0	0	0	0	0	0	0	0	0	0	0	0	0	0	0	0	0	—	0	—	—	—	P	7	0	3	0	0	1.000

JACK FIMPLE—John Joseph Fimple—Bats: Right; Throws: Right

Ht: 6'2"; Wt: 185 lbs; Born: 2/10/1959 in Darby, Pennsylvania; Debut: 7/30/1983

LCS		Batting																							Fielding						
Year Tm	Age	G	AB	H	2B	3B	HR	TB	R	RBI	GW	TBB	IBB	SO	HBP	SH	SF	SB	CS	SB%	GDP	Avg	OBP	SLG	Pos	G	PO	A	E	DP	FPct
1983 LA	24	3	7	1	0	0	0	1	0	1	0	0	0	3	0	0	0	0	0	—	0	.143	.143	.143	C	3	14	2	0	1	1.000

ROLLIE FINGERS (HOF 1992-W)—Roland Glen Fingers—Throws: Right; Bats: Right

Ht: 6'4"; Wt: 190 lbs; Born: 8/25/1946 in Steubenville, Ohio; Debut: 9/15/1968

Division Series		Pitching																										
Year Tm	Age	G	GS	CG	GF	IP	BFP	H	R	ER	HR	SH	SF	HB	TBB	IBB	SO	WP	Bk	W	L	Pct	ShO	Sv-Op	Hld	OAvg	OOBP	ERA
1981 Mil-*MC*	35	3	0	0	3	4.2	23	7	3	2	0	0	0	0	1	0	5	0	0	1	0	1.000	0	1- 2	0	.318	.348	3.86
LCS		Pitching																										
Year Tm	Age	G	GS	CG	GF	IP	BFP	H	R	ER	HR	SH	SF	HB	TBB	IBB	SO	WP	Bk	W	L	Pct	ShO	Sv-Op	Hld	OAvg	OOBP	ERA
1971 Oak	25	2	0	0	1	2.1	9	2	2	2	0	0	0	0	1	0	2	0	0	0	0	—	0	0- 0	0	.250	.333	7.71
1972 Oak	26	3	0	0	1	5.1	18	4	1	1	1	1	0	0	1	0	3	0	0	1	0	1.000	0	0- 0	0	.250	.294	1.69
1973 Oak	27	3	0	0	3	4.2	18	4	1	1	1	0	0	0	2	0	4	0	0	0	1	.000	0	1- 1	0	.250	.333	1.93
1974 Oak	28	2	0	0	2	3.0	13	3	1	1	0	0	0	0	1	0	3	0	0	0	0	—	0	1- 1	0	.250	.308	3.00
1975 Oak	29	1	0	0	1	4.0	16	5	3	3	1	2	0	0	1	1	3	0	0	0	1	.000	0	0- 0	0	.385	.429	6.75
LCS Totals		11	0	0	8	19.1	148	18	8	8	3	3	0	0	6	1	15	0	0	1	2	.333	0	2-2	0	.277	.338	3.72

World Series		Pitching																										
Year Tm	Age	G	GS	CG	GF	IP	BFP	H	R	ER	HR	SH	SF	HB	TBB	IBB	SO	WP	Bk	W	L	Pct	ShO	Sv-Op	Hld	OAvg	OOBP	ERA
1972 Oak	26	6	0	0	4	10.1	39	4	2	2	0	1	1	1	4	2	11	1	0	1	1	.500	0	2- 2	1	.125	.237	1.74
1973 Oak	27	6	0	0	3	13.2	60	13	5	1	0	3	0	1	4	1	8	0	0	0	1	.000	0	2- 2	1	.250	.316	0.66
1974 Oak	28	4	0	0	3	9.1	36	8	2	2	2	0	0	1	2	0	6	0	0	1	0	1.000	0	2- 3	0	.242	.306	1.93
WS Totals		16	0	0	10	33.1	270	25	9	5	2	4	1	3	10	3	25	1	0	2	2	.500	0	6-7	2	.214	.290	1.35
Postseason Totals		30	0	0	21	57.1	464	50	20	15	5	7	1	3	17	4	45	1	0	4	4	.500	0	9-11	2	.245	.311	2.35

Division Series		Batting																							Fielding						
Year Tm	Age	G	AB	H	2B	3B	HR	TB	R	RBI	GW	TBB	IBB	SO	HBP	SH	SF	SB	CS	SB%	GDP	Avg	OBP	SLG	Pos	G	PO	A	E	DP	FPct
1981 Mil	35	3	0	0	0	0	0	0	0	0	0	0	0	0	0	0	0	0	0	—	0	—	—	—	P	3	0	0	0	0	—
LCS		Batting																							Fielding						
Year Tm	Age	G	AB	H	2B	3B	HR	TB	R	RBI	GW	TBB	IBB	SO	HBP	SH	SF	SB	CS	SB%	GDP	Avg	OBP	SLG	Pos	G	PO	A	E	DP	FPct
1971 Oak	25	2	0	0	0	0	0	0	0	0	0	0	0	0	0	0	0	0	0	—	0	—	—	—	P	2	0	0	0	0	—
1972 Oak	26	3	1	0	0	0	0	0	0	0	0	0	0	0	0	0	0	0	0	—	0	.000	.000	.000	P	3	0	0	0	0	—
1973 Oak	27	3	0	0	0	0	0	0	0	0	0	0	0	0	0	0	0	0	0	—	0	—	—	—	P	3	0	0	0	0	—
1974 Oak	28	2	0	0	0	0	0	0	0	0	0	0	0	0	0	0	0	0	0	—	0	—	—	—	P	2	0	0	0	0	—
1975 Oak	29	1	0	0	0	0	0	0	0	0	0	0	0	0	0	0	0	0	0	—	0	—	—	—	P	1	1	0	0	0	1.000
LCS Totals		11	1	0	0	0	0	0	0	0	0	0	0	0	0	0	0	0	0	—	0	.000	.000	.000	P	11	1	0	0	0	1.000
World Series		Batting																							Fielding						
Year Tm	Age	G	AB	H	2B	3B	HR	TB	R	RBI	GW	TBB	IBB	SO	HBP	SH	SF	SB	CS	SB%	GDP	Avg	OBP	SLG	Pos	G	PO	A	E	DP	FPct
1972 Oak	26	6	1	0	0	0	0	0	0	0	0	0	0	0	0	1	0	0	0	—	0	.000	.000	.000	P	6	0	2	0	0	1.000
1973 Oak	27	6	3	1	0	0	0	1	0	0	0	0	0	1	0	0	0	0	0	—	0	.333	.333	.333	P	6	0	2	0	0	1.000
1974 Oak	28	4	2	0	0	0	0	0	0	0	0	0	0	1	0	0	0	0	0	—	0	.000	.000	.000	P	4	0	1	0	0	1.000
WS Totals		16	6	1	0	0	0	1	0	0	0	0	0	2	0	1	0	0	0	—	0	.167	.167	.167	P	16	0	5	0	0	1.000
Postseason Totals		30	7	1	0	0	0	1	0	0	0	0	0	2	0	1	0	0	0	—	0	.143	.143	.143	P	30	1	5	0	0	1.000

CHUCK FINLEY—Charles Edward Finley—Throws: Left; Bats: Left

Ht: 6'6"; Wt: 220 lbs; Born: 11/26/1962 in Monroe, Louisiana; Debut: 5/29/1986

LCS		Pitching																										
Year Tm	Age	G	GS	CG	GF	IP	BFP	H	R	ER	HR	SH	SF	HB	TBB	IBB	SO	WP	Bk	W	L	Pct	ShO	Sv-Op	Hld	OAvg	OOBP	ERA
1986 Cal	23	3	0	0	2	2.0	7	1	0	0	0	0	0	0	0	0	1	0	0	0	0	—	0	0- 0	0	.143	.143	0.00

LCS		Batting																							Fielding						
Year Tm	Age	G	AB	H	2B	3B	HR	TB	R	RBI	GW	TBB	IBB	SO	HBP	SH	SF	SB	CS	SB%	GDP	Avg	OBP	SLG	Pos	G	PO	A	E	DP	FPct
1986 Cal	23	3	0	0	0	0	0	0	0	0	0	0	0	0	0	0	0	0	0	—	0	—	—	—	P	3	0	0	0	0	—

STEVE FINLEY—Steven Allen Finley—Bats: Left; Throws: Left

Ht: 6'2"; Wt: 175 lbs; Born: 3/12/1965 in Paducah, Kentucky; Debut: 4/3/1989

Division Series		Batting																							Fielding						
Year Tm	Age	G	AB	H	2B	3B	HR	TB	R	RBI	GW	TBB	IBB	SO	HBP	SH	SF	SB	CS	SB%	GDP	Avg	OBP	SLG	Pos	G	PO	A	E	DP	FPct
1996 SD	31	3	12	1	0	0	0	1	0	1	0	0	0	4	1	0	0	1	0	1.00	0	.083	.154	.083	OF	3	10	0	0	0	1.000

RAY FISHER—Ray Lyle Fisher—Nickname: Chic—Throws: Right; Bats: Right

Ht: 5'11"; Wt: 180 lbs; Born: 10/4/1887 in Middlebury, Vermont; Debut: 7/2/1910; Died: 11/3/1982

World Series		Pitching																										
Year Tm	Age	G	GS	CG	GF	IP	BFP	H	R	ER	HR	SH	SF	HB	TBB	IBB	SO	WP	Bk	W	L	Pct	ShO	Sv-Op	Hld	OAvg	OOBP	ERA
1919 Cin	31	2	1	0	0	7.2	29	7	3	2	0	0	0	0	2	0	2	0	0	0	1	.000	0	0- 0	0	.259	.310	2.35

World Series		Batting																							Fielding						
Year Tm	Age	G	AB	H	2B	3B	HR	TB	R	RBI	GW	TBB	IBB	SO	HBP	SH	SF	SB	CS	SB%	GDP	Avg	OBP	SLG	Pos	G	PO	A	E	DP	FPct
1919 Cin	31	2	2	1	0	0	0	1	0	0	0	0	0	0	0	0	0	0	0	—	0	.500	.500	.500	P	2	0	6	1	0	.857

SHOWBOAT FISHER—George Aloys Fisher—Bats: Left; Throws: Right

Ht: 5'10"; Wt: 170 lbs; Born: 1/16/1899 in Wesley, Iowa; Debut: 4/24/1923; Died: 5/15/1994

World Series		Batting																							Fielding						
Year Tm	Age	G	AB	H	2B	3B	HR	TB	R	RBI	GW	TBB	IBB	SO	HBP	SH	SF	SB	CS	SB%	GDP	Avg	OBP	SLG	Pos	G	PO	A	E	DP	FPct
1930 StL	31	2	2	1	1	0	0	2	0	0	0	0	0	1	0	0	0	0	0	—	0	.500	.500	1.000	—						

CARLTON FISK—Carlton Ernest Fisk—Nickname: Pudge—Bats: Right; Throws: Right

Ht: 6'3"; Wt: 200 lbs; Born: 12/26/1947 in Bellows Falls, Vermont; Debut: 9/18/1969

LCS		Batting																							Fielding						
Year Tm	Age	G	AB	H	2B	3B	HR	TB	R	RBI	GW	TBB	IBB	SO	HBP	SH	SF	SB	CS	SB%	GDP	Avg	OBP	SLG	Pos	G	PO	A	E	DP	FPct
1975 Bos	27	3	12	5	1	0	0	6	4	2	1	0	0	2	0	0	0	1	0	1.00	0	.417	.417	.500	C	3	15	0	0	0	1.000
1983 ChA	35	4	17	3	1	0	0	4	0	0	0	1	0	3	0	0	0	0	0	—	0	.176	.222	.235	C	4	27	3	0	0	1.000
LCS Totals		7	29	8	2	0	0	10	4	2	1	1	0	5	0	0	0	1	0	1.00	0	.276	.300	.345	C	7	42	3	0	0	1.000
World Series		Batting																							Fielding						
Year Tm	Age	G	AB	H	2B	3B	HR	TB	R	RBI	GW	TBB	IBB	SO	HBP	SH	SF	SB	CS	SB%	GDP	Avg	OBP	SLG	Pos	G	PO	A	E	DP	FPct
1975 Bos	27	7	25	6	0	0	2	12	5	4	1	7	3	7	0	0	0	0	0	—	1	.240	.406	.480	C	7	37	3	2	1	.952
Postseason Totals		14	54	14	2	0	2	22	9	6	2	8	3	12	0	0	0	1	0	1.00	1	.259	.355	.407	C	14	79	6	2	1	.977

FREDDIE FITZSIMMONS—Frederick Landis Fitzsimmons—Throws: Right; Bats: Right

Ht: 5'11"; Wt: 185 lbs; Born: 7/26/1901 in Mishawaka, Ind.; Debut: 8/12/1925; Died: 11/18/1979

World Series		Pitching																										
Year Tm	Age	G	GS	CG	GF	IP	BFP	H	R	ER	HR	SH	SF	HB	TBB	IBB	SO	WP	Bk	W	L	Pct	ShO	Sv-Op	Hld	OAvg	OOBP	ERA
1933 NYG	32	1	1	0	0	7.0	29	9	4	4	0	0	0	0	0	0	2	0	0	0	1	.000	0	0- 0	0	.310	.310	5.14
1936 NYG	35	2	2	1	0	11.2	49	13	7	7	2	1	0	0	2	0	6	0	0	0	2	.000	0	0- 0	0	.283	.313	5.40
1941 Bro	40	1	1	0	0	7.0	27	4	0	0	0	0	0	0	3	1	1	0	0	0	0	—	0	0- 0	0	.167	.259	0.00
WS Totals		4	4	1	0	25.2	210	26	11	11	2	1	0	0	5	1	9	0	0	0	3	.000	0	0-0	0	.263	.298	3.86

World Series		Batting																							Fielding						
Year Tm	Age	G	AB	H	2B	3B	HR	TB	R	RBI	GW	TBB	IBB	SO	HBP	SH	SF	SB	CS	SB%	GDP	Avg	OBP	SLG	Pos	G	PO	A	E	DP	FPct
1933 NYG	32	1	2	1	0	0	0	1	0	0	0	0	0	0	0	0	0	0	0	—	0	.500	.500	.500	P	1	0	1	0	0	1.000
1936 NYG	35	2	4	2	0	0	0	2	0	0	0	0	0	1	0	0	0	0	0	—	0	.500	.500	.500	P	2	1	2	0	0	1.000
1941 Bro	40	1	2	0	0	0	0	0	0	0	0	0	0	0	0	0	0	0	0	—	0	.000	.000	.000	P	1	0	2	0	0	1.000
WS Totals		4	8	3	0	0	0	3	0	0	0	0	0	1	0	0	0	0	0	—	0	.375	.375	.375	P	4	1	5	0	0	1.000

MAX FLACK—Max John Flack—Bats: Left; Throws: Left

Ht: 5'7"; Wt: 148 lbs; Born: 2/5/1890 in Belleville, Illinois; Debut: 4/16/1914; Died: 7/31/1975

World Series		Batting																							Fielding						
Year Tm	Age	G	AB	H	2B	3B	HR	TB	R	RBI	GW	TBB	IBB	SO	HBP	SH	SF	SB	CS	SB%	GDP	Avg	OBP	SLG	Pos	G	PO	A	E	DP	FPct
1918 ChN	28	6	19	5	0	0	0	5	2	0	0	4	0	1	1	0	0	1	1	.50	0	.263	.417	.263	OF	6	14	2	1	0	.941

JOHN FLAHERTY—John Timothy Flaherty—Nickname: Flash—Bats: Right; Throws: Right

Ht: 6'1"; Wt: 195 lbs; Born: 10/21/1967 in Bronx, New York; Debut: 4/12/1992

Division Series		Batting																							Fielding						
Year Tm	Age	G	AB	H	2B	3B	HR	TB	R	RBI	GW	TBB	IBB	SO	HBP	SH	SF	SB	CS	SB%	GDP	Avg	OBP	SLG	Pos	G	PO	A	E	DP	FPct
1996 SD	28	2	4	0	0	0	0	0	0	0	0	0	0	1	0	0	0	0	0	—	0	.000	.000	.000	C	2	9	0	0	0	1.000

MIKE FLANAGAN—Michael Kendall Flanagan—Throws: Left; Bats: Left

Ht: 6'0"; Wt: 185 lbs; Born: 12/16/1951 in Manchester, New Hampshire; Debut: 9/5/1975

LCS		Pitching																										
Year Tm	Age	G	GS	CG	GF	IP	BFP	H	R	ER	HR	SH	SF	HB	TBB	IBB	SO	WP	Bk	W	L	Pct	ShO	Sv-Op	Hld	OAvg	OOBP	ERA
1979 Bal-*C*	27	1	1	0	0	7.0	29	6	6	4	1	0	1	0	1	0	2	0	0	1	0	1.000	0	0- 0	0	.222	.241	5.14
1983 Bal	31	1	1	0	0	5.0	20	5	1	1	0	0	0	1	0	0	1	0	0	1	0	1.000	0	0- 0	0	.263	.300	1.80
1989 Tor	37	1	1	0	0	4.1	19	7	5	5	3	1	0	0	1	0	3	0	0	0	1	.000	0	0- 0	0	.412	.444	10.38
LCS Totals		3	3	0	0	16.1	136	18	12	10	4	1	1	1	2	0	6	0	0	2	1	.667	0	0-0	0	.286	.313	5.51
World Series		Pitching																										
Year Tm	Age	G	GS	CG	GF	IP	BFP	H	R	ER	HR	SH	SF	HB	TBB	IBB	SO	WP	Bk	W	L	Pct	ShO	Sv-Op	Hld	OAvg	OOBP	ERA
1979 Bal-*C*	27	3	2	1	0	15.0	67	18	7	5	1	1	1	0	2	0	13	0	0	1	1	.500	0	0- 0	0	.286	.303	3.00
1983 Bal	31	1	1	0	0	4.0	18	6	2	2	2	0	0	0	1	0	1	0	0	0	0	—	0	0- 0	0	.353	.389	4.50
WS Totals		4	3	1	0	19.0	170	24	9	7	3	1	1	0	3	0	14	0	0	1	1	.500	0	0-0	0	.300	.321	3.32
Postseason Totals		7	6	1	0	35.1	306	42	21	17	7	2	2	1	5	0	20	0	0	3	2	.600	0	0-0	0	.294	.318	4.33

LCS		Batting																							Fielding						
Year Tm	Age	G	AB	H	2B	3B	HR	TB	R	RBI	GW	TBB	IBB	SO	HBP	SH	SF	SB	CS	SB%	GDP	Avg	OBP	SLG	Pos	G	PO	A	E	DP	FPct
1979 Bal	27	1	0	0	0	0	0	0	0	0	0	0	0	0	0	0	0	0	0	—	0	—	—	—	P	1	0	0	0	0	—
1983 Bal	31	1	0	0	0	0	0	0	0	0	0	0	0	0	0	0	0	0	0	—	0	—	—	—	P	1	0	0	0	0	—
1989 Tor	37	1	0	0	0	0	0	0	0	0	0	0	0	0	0	0	0	0	0	—	0	—	—	—	P	1	2	3	0	2	1.000
LCS Totals		3	0	0	0	0	0	0	0	0	0	0	0	0	0	0	0	0	0	—	0	—	—	—	P	3	2	3	0	2	1.000
World Series		**Batting**																							**Fielding**						
Year Tm	Age	G	AB	H	2B	3B	HR	TB	R	RBI	GW	TBB	IBB	SO	HBP	SH	SF	SB	CS	SB%	GDP	Avg	OBP	SLG	Pos	G	PO	A	E	DP	FPct
1979 Bal	27	3	5	0	0	0	0	0	0	0	0	1	0	2	0	0	0	0	0	—	0	.000	.167	.000	P	3	0	4	0	0	1.000
1983 Bal	31	1	1	0	0	0	0	0	0	0	0	0	0	1	0	0	0	0	0	—	0	.000	.000	.000	P	1	0	0	0	0	—
WS Totals		4	6	0	0	0	0	0	0	0	0	1	0	3	0	0	0	0	0	—	0	.000	.143	.000	P	4	0	4	0	0	1.000
Postseason Totals		7	6	0	0	0	0	0	0	0	0	1	0	3	0	0	0	0	0	—	0	.000	.143	.000	P	7	2	7	0	2	1.000

TIM FLANNERY—Timothy Earl Flannery—Bats: Left; Throws: Right

Ht: 5'11"; Wt: 175 lbs; Born: 9/29/1957 in Tulsa, Oklahoma; Debut: 9/3/1979

LCS		Batting																							Fielding						
Year Tm	Age	G	AB	H	2B	3B	HR	TB	R	RBI	GW	TBB	IBB	SO	HBP	SH	SF	SB	CS	SB%	GDP	Avg	OBP	SLG	Pos	G	PO	A	E	DP	FPct
1984 SD	27	3	2	1	0	0	0	1	2	0	0	0	0	0	1	0	0	0	0	—	0	.500	.667	.500	—						
World Series		**Batting**																							**Fielding**						
Year Tm	Age	G	AB	H	2B	3B	HR	TB	R	RBI	GW	TBB	IBB	SO	HBP	SH	SF	SB	CS	SB%	GDP	Avg	OBP	SLG	Pos	G	PO	A	E	DP	FPct
1984 SD	27	1	1	1	0	0	0	1	0	0	0	0	0	0	0	0	0	0	0	—	0	1.000	1.000	1.000	2B	1	1	0	0	0	1.000
Postseason Totals		4	3	2	0	0	0	2	2	0	0	0	0	0	1	0	0	0	0	—	0	.667	.750	.667	2B	1	1	0	0	0	1.000

ART FLETCHER—Arthur Fletcher—Bats: Right; Throws: Right

Ht: 5'10"; Wt: 170 lbs; Born: 1/5/1885 in Collinsville, Illinois; Debut: 4/15/1909; Died: 2/6/1950

World Series		Batting																							Fielding						
Year Tm	Age	G	AB	H	2B	3B	HR	TB	R	RBI	GW	TBB	IBB	SO	HBP	SH	SF	SB	CS	SB%	GDP	Avg	OBP	SLG	Pos	G	PO	A	E	DP	FPct
1911 NYG	26	6	23	3	1	0	0	4	1	1	0	0	0	4	0	0	0	0	0	—	0	.130	.130	.174	SS	6	11	18	4	1	.879
1912 NYG	27	8	28	5	1	0	0	6	1	3	0	1	0	4	0	0	0	1	0	1.00	0	.179	.207	.214	SS	8	16	24	4	3	.909
1913 NYG	28	5	18	5	0	0	0	5	1	3	0	1	0	1	1	0	0	1	1	.50	1	.278	.350	.278	SS	5	8	10	1	0	.947
1917 NYG	32	6	25	5	1	0	0	6	2	0	0	0	0	2	0	0	0	0	0	—	0	.200	.200	.240	SS	6	9	17	3	1	.897
WS Totals		25	94	18	3	0	0	21	5	7	0	2	0	11	1	0	0	2	1	.67	1	.191	.216	.223	SS	25	44	69	12	5	.904

SCOTT FLETCHER—Scott Brian Fletcher—Bats: Right; Throws: Right

Ht: 5'11"; Wt: 168 lbs; Born: 7/30/1958 in Fort Walton Beach, Florida; Debut: 4/25/1981

LCS		Batting																							Fielding						
Year Tm	Age	G	AB	H	2B	3B	HR	TB	R	RBI	GW	TBB	IBB	SO	HBP	SH	SF	SB	CS	SB%	GDP	Avg	OBP	SLG	Pos	G	PO	A	E	DP	FPct
1983 ChA	25	3	7	0	0	0	0	0	0	0	0	1	0	0	0	1	0	0	0	—	0	.000	.125	.000	SS	3	3	8	0	2	1.000

CURT FLOOD—Curtis Charles Flood—Bats: Right; Throws: Right

Ht: 5'9"; Wt: 165 lbs; Born: 1/18/1938 in Houston, Texas; Debut: 9/9/1956; Died: 1/20/1997

World Series		Batting																							Fielding						
Year Tm	Age	G	AB	H	2B	3B	HR	TB	R	RBI	GW	TBB	IBB	SO	HBP	SH	SF	SB	CS	SB%	GDP	Avg	OBP	SLG	Pos	G	PO	A	E	DP	FPct
1964 StL	26	7	30	6	0	1	0	8	5	3	0	3	0	1	0	0	0	0	0	—	1	.200	.273	.267	OF	7	13	0	0	0	1.000
1967 StL	29	7	28	5	1	0	0	6	2	3	2	3	0	3	0	0	0	0	0	—	0	.179	.258	.214	OF	7	15	0	0	0	1.000
1968 StL	30	7	28	8	1	0	0	9	4	2	0	2	0	2	0	0	0	3	1	.75	0	.286	.333	.321	OF	7	12	0	0	0	1.000
WS Totals		21	86	19	2	1	0	23	11	8	2	8	0	6	0	0	0	3	1	.75	1	.221	.287	.267	OF	21	40	0	0	0	1.000

JAKE FLOWERS—D'Arcy Raymond Flowers—Bats: Right; Throws: Right

Ht: 5'11"; Wt: 170 lbs; Born: 3/16/1902 in Cambridge, Maryland; Debut: 9/7/1923; Died: 12/27/1962

World Series		Batting																							Fielding						
Year Tm	Age	G	AB	H	2B	3B	HR	TB	R	RBI	GW	TBB	IBB	SO	HBP	SH	SF	SB	CS	SB%	GDP	Avg	OBP	SLG	Pos	G	PO	A	E	DP	FPct
1926 StL	24	3	3	0	0	0	0	0	0	0	0	0	0	1	0	0	0	0	0	—	0	.000	.000	.000	—						
1931 StL	29	5	11	1	1	0	0	2	1	0	0	1	0	0	0	0	0	0	0	—	0	.091	.167	.182	3B	4	3	4	1	0	.875
WS Totals		8	14	1	1	0	0	2	1	0	0	1	0	1	0	0	0	0	0	—	0	.071	.133	.143	3B	4	3	4	1	0	.875

CLIFF FLOYD—Cornelius Cliff Floyd—Bats: Left; Throws: Left

Ht: 6'4"; Wt: 220 lbs; Born: 12/5/1972 in Chicago, Illinois; Debut: 9/18/1993

World Series		Batting																							Fielding						
Year Tm	Age	G	AB	H	2B	3B	HR	TB	R	RBI	GW	TBB	IBB	SO	HBP	SH	SF	SB	CS	SB%	GDP	Avg	OBP	SLG	Pos	G	PO	A	E	DP	FPct
1997 Fla	24	4	2	0	0	0	0	0	1	0	0	1	1	1	0	0	0	0	0	—	0	.000	.333	.000	—						

DOUG FLYNN—Robert Douglas Flynn—Bats: Right; Throws: Right

Ht: 5'11"; Wt: 165 lbs; Born: 4/18/1951 in Lexington, Kentucky; Debut: 4/9/1975

LCS		Batting																							Fielding						
Year Tm	Age	G	AB	H	2B	3B	HR	TB	R	RBI	GW	TBB	IBB	SO	HBP	SH	SF	SB	CS	SB%	GDP	Avg	OBP	SLG	Pos	G	PO	A	E	DP	FPct
1976 Cin	25	1	0	0	0	0	0	0	0	0	0	0	0	0	0	0	0	0	0	—	0	—	—	—	2B	1	0	0	0	0	—

TIM FOLI—Timothy John Foli—Bats: Right; Throws: Right

Ht: 6'0"; Wt: 179 lbs; Born: 12/6/1950 in Culver City, California; Debut: 9/11/1970

LCS		Batting																							Fielding						
Year Tm	Age	G	AB	H	2B	3B	HR	TB	R	RBI	GW	TBB	IBB	SO	HBP	SH	SF	SB	CS	SB%	GDP	Avg	OBP	SLG	Pos	G	PO	A	E	DP	FPct
1979 Pit	28	3	12	4	1	0	0	5	1	3	0	0	0	0	0	1	2	0	0	—	0	.333	.286	.417	SS	3	3	9	0	1	1.000
1982 Cal	31	5	16	2	0	0	0	2	0	1	1	0	0	3	0	1	0	0	0	—	0	.125	.125	.125	SS	5	6	6	0	0	1.000
LCS Totals		8	28	6	1	0	0	7	1	4	1	0	0	3	0	2	2	0	0	—	0	.214	.200	.250	SS	8	9	15	0	1	1.000
World Series		**Batting**																							**Fielding**						
Year Tm	Age	G	AB	H	2B	3B	HR	TB	R	RBI	GW	TBB	IBB	SO	HBP	SH	SF	SB	CS	SB%	GDP	Avg	OBP	SLG	Pos	G	PO	A	E	DP	FPct
1979 Pit	28	7	30	10	1	1	0	13	6	3	0	2	0	0	0	1	0	0	0	—	0	.333	.375	.433	SS	7	8	32	3	7	.930
Postseason Totals		15	58	16	2	1	0	20	7	7	1	2	0	3	0	3	2	0	0	—	0	.276	.290	.345	SS	15	17	47	3	8	.955

CHAD FONVILLE—Chad Everette Fonville—Bats: Both; Throws: Right

Ht: 5'6"; Wt: 155 lbs; Born: 3/5/1971 in Jacksonville, North Carolina; Debut: 4/28/1995

Division Series		Batting																							Fielding						
Year Tm	Age	G	AB	H	2B	3B	HR	TB	R	RBI	GW	TBB	IBB	SO	HBP	SH	SF	SB	CS	SB%	GDP	Avg	OBP	SLG	Pos	G	PO	A	E	DP	FPct
1995 LA	24	3	12	6	0	0	0	6	1	0	0	0	0	1	0	1	0	0	0	—	1	.500	.500	.500	SS	3	1	7	1	2	.889

BARRY FOOTE—Barry Clifton Foote—Bats: Right; Throws: Right

Ht: 6'3"; Wt: 205 lbs; Born: 2/16/1952 in Smithfield, North Carolina; Debut: 9/14/1973

Division Series		Batting																							Fielding						
Year Tm	Age	G	AB	H	2B	3B	HR	TB	R	RBI	GW	TBB	IBB	SO	HBP	SH	SF	SB	CS	SB%	GDP	Avg	OBP	SLG	Pos	G	PO	A	E	DP	FPct
1981 NYA	29	1	0	0	0	0	0	0	0	0	0	0	0	0	0	0	0	0	0	—	0	—	—	—	—						
LCS		**Batting**																							**Fielding**						
Year Tm	Age	G	AB	H	2B	3B	HR	TB	R	RBI	GW	TBB	IBB	SO	HBP	SH	SF	SB	CS	SB%	GDP	Avg	OBP	SLG	Pos	G	PO	A	E	DP	FPct
1978 Phi	26	1	1	0	0	0	0	0	0	0	0	0	0	1	0	0	0	0	0	—	0	.000	.000	.000	—						
1981 NYA	29	2	1	1	0	0	0	1	0	0	0	0	0	0	0	0	0	0	0	—	0	1.000	1.000	1.000	C	1	0	0	0	0	—
LCS Totals		3	2	1	0	0	0	1	0	0	0	0	0	1	0	0	0	0	0	—	0	.500	.500	.500	C	1	0	0	0	0	—
World Series		**Batting**																							**Fielding**						
Year Tm	Age	G	AB	H	2B	3B	HR	TB	R	RBI	GW	TBB	IBB	SO	HBP	SH	SF	SB	CS	SB%	GDP	Avg	OBP	SLG	Pos	G	PO	A	E	DP	FPct
1981 NYA	29	1	1	0	0	0	0	0	0	0	0	0	0	1	0	0	0	0	0	—	0	.000	.000	.000	—						
Postseason Totals		5	3	1	0	0	0	1	0	0	0	0	0	2	0	0	0	0	0	—	0	.333	.333	.333	C	1	0	0	0	0	—

CURT FORD—Curtis Glenn Ford—Bats: Left; Throws: Right

Ht: 5'10"; Wt: 150 lbs; Born: 10/11/1960 in Jackson, Mississippi; Debut: 6/22/1985

LCS		Batting																							Fielding						
Year Tm	Age	G	AB	H	2B	3B	HR	TB	R	RBI	GW	TBB	IBB	SO	HBP	SH	SF	SB	CS	SB%	GDP	Avg	OBP	SLG	Pos	G	PO	A	E	DP	FPct
1987 StL	26	4	9	3	0	0	0	3	2	0	0	1	0	1	0	0	0	0	0	—	1	.333	.400	.333	OF	4	6	0	0	0	1.000

World Series		Batting																							Fielding						
Year Tm	Age	G	AB	H	2B	3B	HR	TB	R	RBI	GW	TBB	IBB	SO	HBP	SH	SF	SB	CS	SB%	GDP	Avg	OBP	SLG	Pos	G	PO	A	E	DP	FPct
1987 StL	26	5	13	4	0	0	0	4	1	2	1	1	0	1	0	0	0	0	1	.00	0	.308	.357	.308	OF	4	5	0	0	0	1.000
Postseason Totals		9	22	7	0	0	0	7	3	2	1	2	0	2	0	0	0	0	1	.00	1	.318	.375	.318	OF	8	11	0	0	0	1.000

DAN FORD—Darnell Glenn Ford—Nickname: Disco Dan—Bats: Right; Throws: Right

Ht: 6'1"; Wt: 185 lbs; Born: 5/19/1952 in Los Angeles, California; Debut: 4/12/1975

LCS		Batting																							Fielding						
Year Tm	Age	G	AB	H	2B	3B	HR	TB	R	RBI	GW	TBB	IBB	SO	HBP	SH	SF	SB	CS	SB%	GDP	Avg	OBP	SLG	Pos	G	PO	A	E	DP	FPct
1979 Cal	27	4	17	5	1	0	2	12	2	4	0	0	0	0	0	0	0	0	0	—	1	.294	.294	.706	OF	4	6	0	0	0	1.000
1983 Bal	31	2	5	1	1	0	0	2	0	0	0	0	0	1	0	0	0	0	0	—	1	.200	.200	.400	OF	1	1	0	0	0	1.000
LCS Totals		6	22	6	2	0	2	14	2	4	0	0	0	1	0	0	0	0	0	—	2	.273	.273	.636	OF	5	7	0	0	0	1.000

World Series		Batting																							Fielding						
Year Tm	Age	G	AB	H	2B	3B	HR	TB	R	RBI	GW	TBB	IBB	SO	HBP	SH	SF	SB	CS	SB%	GDP	Avg	OBP	SLG	Pos	G	PO	A	E	DP	FPct
1983 Bal	31	5	12	2	0	0	1	5	1	1	0	1	0	5	1	0	0	0	0	—	0	.167	.286	.417	OF	4	5	1	0	0	1.000
Postseason Totals		11	34	8	2	0	3	19	3	5	0	1	0	6	1	0	0	0	0	—	2	.235	.278	.559	OF	9	12	1	0	0	1.000

WHITEY FORD (HOF 1974-W)—Edward Charles Ford—Nicknames: The Chairman of the Board, Slick—Throws: Left; Bats: Left

Ht: 5'10"; Wt: 178 lbs; Born: 10/21/1928 in New York, N.Y.; Deb.: 7/1/1950

World Series		Pitching																										
Year Tm	Age	G	GS	CG	GF	IP	BFP	H	R	ER	HR	SH	SF	HB	TBB	IBB	SO	WP	Bk	W	L	Pct	ShO	Sv-Op	Hld	OAvg	OOBP	ERA
1950 NYA	21	1	1	0	0	8.2	35	7	2	0	0	0	0	1	1	0	7	0	0	1	0	1.000	0	0- 0	0	.212	.257	0.00
1953 NYA	24	2	2	0	0	8.0	34	9	4	4	0	0	0	0	2	1	7	1	0	0	1	.000	0	0- 0	0	.281	.324	4.50
1955 NYA	26	2	2	1	0	17.0	72	13	6	4	2	0	1	1	8	0	10	1	0	2	0	1.000	0	0- 0	0	.210	.306	2.12
1956 NYA	27	2	2	1	0	12.0	50	14	8	7	2	0	2	0	2	0	8	0	0	1	1	.500	0	0- 0	0	.304	.320	5.25
1957 NYA	28	2	2	1	0	16.0	62	11	2	2	0	1	0	0	5	0	7	0	0	1	1	.500	0	0- 0	0	.196	.262	1.13
1958 NYA	29	3	3	0	0	15.1	71	19	8	7	0	1	0	0	5	0	16	2	0	0	1	.000	0	0- 0	0	.292	.343	4.11
1960 NYA	31	2	2	2	0	18.0	65	11	0	0	0	0	0	0	2	0	8	0	0	2	0	1.000	2	0- 0	0	.175	.200	0.00
1961 NYA-*C*	32	2	2	1	0	14.0	49	6	0	0	0	0	0	1	1	0	7	0	0	2	0	1.000	1	0- 0	0	.128	.163	0.00
1962 NYA	33	3	3	1	0	19.2	83	24	9	9	1	0	0	0	4	0	12	0	0	1	1	.500	0	0- 0	0	.304	.337	4.12
1963 NYA	34	2	2	0	0	12.0	48	10	7	6	2	1	1	0	3	1	8	0	0	0	2	.000	0	0- 0	0	.233	.277	4.50
1964 NYA	35	1	1	0	0	5.1	25	8	5	5	1	0	1	0	1	0	4	0	0	0	1	.000	0	0- 0	0	.348	.360	8.44
WS Totals		22	22	7	0	146.0	1188	132	51	44	8	3	5	3	34	2	94	4	0	10	8	.556	3	0-0	0	.240	.286	2.71

World Series		Batting																							Fielding						
Year Tm	Age	G	AB	H	2B	3B	HR	TB	R	RBI	GW	TBB	IBB	SO	HBP	SH	SF	SB	CS	SB%	GDP	Avg	OBP	SLG	Pos	G	PO	A	E	DP	FPct
1950 NYA	21	1	3	0	0	0	0	0	0	0	0	0	0	2	0	0	0	0	0	—	0	.000	.000	.000	P	1	1	0	0	0	1.000
1953 NYA	24	2	3	1	0	0	0	1	0	0	0	0	0	0	0	0	0	0	0	—	0	.333	.333	.333	P	2	0	1	0	0	1.000
1955 NYA	26	2	6	0	0	0	0	0	1	0	0	1	0	1	0	0	0	0	0	—	0	.000	.143	.000	P	2	1	4	0	0	1.000
1956 NYA	27	2	4	0	0	0	0	0	0	0	0	0	0	3	0	0	0	0	0	—	1	.000	.000	.000	P	2	1	0	0	0	1.000
1957 NYA	28	2	5	0	0	0	0	0	0	0	0	0	0	1	0	0	0	0	0	—	0	.000	.000	.000	P	2	1	1	0	0	1.000
1958 NYA	29	3	4	0	0	0	0	0	1	0	0	2	0	2	0	0	0	0	0	—	0	.000	.333	.000	P	3	1	1	0	0	1.000
1960 NYA	31	2	8	2	0	0	0	2	1	2	1	0	0	2	0	1	0	0	0	—	0	.250	.250	.250	P	2	3	5	0	1	1.000
1961 NYA	32	2	5	0	0	0	0	0	1	0	0	1	0	0	0	0	0	0	0	—	0	.000	.167	.000	P	2	0	1	0	0	1.000
1962 NYA	33	3	7	0	0	0	0	0	0	0	0	1	0	3	0	0	0	0	0	—	0	.000	.125	.000	P	3	0	4	1	0	.800
1963 NYA	34	2	3	0	0	0	0	0	0	0	0	0	0	0	0	0	0	0	0	—	0	.000	.000	.000	P	2	3	2	0	0	1.000
1964 NYA	35	1	1	1	0	0	0	1	0	1	0	2	0	0	0	0	0	0	0	—	0	1.000	1.000	1.000	P	1	0	1	0	0	1.000
WS Totals		22	49	4	0	0	0	4	4	3	1	7	0	14	0	1	0	0	0	—	1	.082	.196	.082	P	22	11	20	1	1	.969

BOB FORSCH—Robert Herbert Forsch—Throws: Right; Bats: Right

Ht: 6'4"; Wt: 200 lbs; Born: 1/13/1950 in Sacramento, California; Debut: 7/7/1974

LCS		Pitching																										
Year Tm	Age	G	GS	CG	GF	IP	BFP	H	R	ER	HR	SH	SF	HB	TBB	IBB	SO	WP	Bk	W	L	Pct	ShO	Sv-Op	Hld	OAvg	OOBP	ERA
1982 StL	32	1	1	1	0	9.0	30	3	0	0	0	0	0	0	0	0	6	0	0	1	0	1.000	1	0- 0	0	.100	.100	0.00
1985 StL	35	1	1	0	0	3.1	15	3	2	2	1	0	0	0	2	0	0	0	0	0	0	—	0	0- 0	0	.250	.357	5.40
1987 StL	37	3	0	0	1	3.0	16	4	4	4	0	0	0	1	1	0	3	0	0	1	1	.500	0	0- 0	0	.286	.375	12.00
LCS Totals		5	2	1	1	15.1	122	10	6	6	1	0	0	1	3	0	9	0	0	2	1	.667	1	0-0	0	.179	.233	3.52

World Series		Pitching																										
Year Tm	Age	G	GS	CG	GF	IP	BFP	H	R	ER	HR	SH	SF	HB	TBB	IBB	SO	WP	Bk	W	L	Pct	ShO	Sv-Op	Hld	OAvg	OOBP	ERA
1982 StL	32	2	2	0	0	12.2	59	18	10	7	2	1	0	1	3	0	4	0	0	0	2	.000	0	0- 0	0	.333	.379	4.97
1985 StL	35	2	1	0	0	3.0	15	6	4	4	0	0	0	0	1	0	3	1	0	0	1	.000	0	0- 0	0	.429	.467	12.00
1987 StL	37	3	0	0	0	6.1	34	8	7	7	2	0	0	1	5	1	3	0	0	1	0	1.000	0	0- 0	0	.286	.412	9.95
WS Totals		7	3	0	0	22.0	216	32	21	18	4	1	0	2	9	1	10	1	0	1	3	.250	0	0-0	0	.333	.402	7.36
Postseason Totals		12	5	1	1	37.1	338	42	27	24	5	1	0	3	12	1	19	1	0	3	4	.429	1	0-0	0	.276	.341	5.79

LCS		Batting																							Fielding						
Year Tm	Age	G	AB	H	2B	3B	HR	TB	R	RBI	GW	TBB	IBB	SO	HBP	SH	SF	SB	CS	SB%	GDP	Avg	OBP	SLG	Pos	G	PO	A	E	DP	FPct
1982 StL	32	1	3	2	0	0	0	2	1	1	0	0	0	0	0	0	1	0	0	—	0	.667	.500	.667	P	1	0	2	0	0	1.000
1985 StL	35	1	0	0	0	0	0	0	0	0	0	0	0	0	0	1	0	0	0	—	0	—	—	—	P	1	0	1	0	0	1.000
1987 StL	37	3	0	0	0	0	0	0	0	0	0	0	0	0	0	0	0	0	0	—	0	—	—	—	P	3	0	1	0	0	1.000
LCS Totals		5	3	2	0	0	0	2	1	1	0	0	0	0	0	1	1	0	0	—	0	.667	.500	.667	P	5	0	4	0	0	1.000

World Series		Batting																							Fielding						
Year Tm	Age	G	AB	H	2B	3B	HR	TB	R	RBI	GW	TBB	IBB	SO	HBP	SH	SF	SB	CS	SB%	GDP	Avg	OBP	SLG	Pos	G	PO	A	E	DP	FPct
1982 StL	32	2	0	0	0	0	0	0	0	0	0	0	0	0	0	0	0	0	0	—	0	—	—	—	P	2	1	0	1	0	.500
1985 StL	35	2	0	0	0	0	0	0	0	0	0	0	0	0	0	0	0	0	0	—	0	—	—	—	P	2	0	0	0	0	—
1987 StL	37	3	2	0	0	0	0	0	0	0	0	0	0	0	0	0	0	0	0	—	0	.000	.000	.000	P	3	1	0	0	1	1.000
WS Totals		7	2	0	0	0	0	0	0	0	0	0	0	0	0	0	0	0	0	—	0	.000	.000	.000	P	7	2	0	1	1	.667
Postseason Totals		12	5	2	0	0	0	2	1	1	0	0	0	0	0	1	1	0	0	—	0	.400	.333	.400	P	12	2	4	1	1	.857

KEN FORSCH—Kenneth Roth Forsch—Throws: Right; Bats: Right

Ht: 6'4"; Wt: 195 lbs; Born: 9/8/1946 in Sacramento, California; Debut: 9/7/1970

LCS		Pitching																										
Year Tm	Age	G	GS	CG	GF	IP	BFP	H	R	ER	HR	SH	SF	HB	TBB	IBB	SO	WP	Bk	W	L	Pct	ShO	Sv-Op	Hld	OAvg	OOBP	ERA
1980 Hou	34	2	1	1	0	8.2	36	10	4	4	1	1	0	0	1	0	6	0	0	0	1	.000	0	0- 1	0	.294	.314	4.15

LCS		Batting																							Fielding						
Year Tm	Age	G	AB	H	2B	3B	HR	TB	R	RBI	GW	TBB	IBB	SO	HBP	SH	SF	SB	CS	SB%	GDP	Avg	OBP	SLG	Pos	G	PO	A	E	DP	FPct
1980 Hou	34	2	2	2	0	0	0	2	0	0	0	0	0	0	0	1	0	0	0	—	0	1.000	1.000	1.000	P	2	1	0	0	0	1.000

TERRY FORSTER—Terry Jay Forster—Nickname: Fat Tub of Goo—Throws: Left; Bats: Left

Ht: 6'3"; Wt: 200 lbs; Born: 1/14/1952 in Sioux Falls, South Dakota; Debut: 4/11/1971

Division Series		Pitching																										
Year Tm	Age	G	GS	CG	GF	IP	BFP	H	R	ER	HR	SH	SF	HB	TBB	IBB	SO	WP	Bk	W	L	Pct	ShO	Sv-Op	Hld	OAvg	OOBP	ERA
1981 LA	29	1	0	0	0	0.1	1	0	0	0	0	0	0	0	0	0	0	0	0	0	0	—	0	0- 0	0	.000	.000	0.00

LCS		Pitching																										
Year Tm	Age	G	GS	CG	GF	IP	BFP	H	R	ER	HR	SH	SF	HB	TBB	IBB	SO	WP	Bk	W	L	Pct	ShO	Sv-Op	Hld	OAvg	OOBP	ERA
1978 LA	26	1	0	0	1	1.0	4	1	0	0	0	0	0	0	0	0	2	0	0	1	0	1.000	0	0- 0	0	.250	.250	0.00
1981 LA	29	1	0	0	0	0.1	1	0	0	0	0	0	0	0	0	0	1	0	0	0	0	—	0	0- 0	0	.000	.000	0.00
LCS Totals		2	0	0	1	1.1	10	1	0	0	0	0	0	0	0	0	3	0	0	1	0	1.000	0	0-0	0	.200	.200	0.00

World Series		Pitching																										
Year Tm	Age	G	GS	CG	GF	IP	BFP	H	R	ER	HR	SH	SF	HB	TBB	IBB	SO	WP	Bk	W	L	Pct	ShO	Sv-Op	Hld	OAvg	OOBP	ERA
1978 LA	26	3	0	0	1	4.0	18	5	0	0	0	1	0	1	1	0	6	0	0	0	0	—	0	0- 1	1	.333	.412	0.00
1981 LA	29	2	0	0	0	2.0	9	1	0	0	0	2	0	0	3	1	0	0	0	0	0	—	0	0- 0	0	.250	.571	0.00
WS Totals		5	0	0	1	6.0	54	6	0	0	0	3	0	1	4	1	6	0	0	0	0	—	0	0-1	1	.316	.458	0.00
Postseason Totals		8	0	0	2	7.2	66	7	0	0	0	3	0	1	4	1	9	0	0	1	0	1.000	0	0-1	1	.280	.400	0.00

Division Series		Batting																							Fielding						
Year Tm	Age	G	AB	H	2B	3B	HR	TB	R	RBI	GW	TBB	IBB	SO	HBP	SH	SF	SB	CS	SB%	GDP	Avg	OBP	SLG	Pos	G	PO	A	E	DP	FPct
1981 LA	29	1	0	0	0	0	0	0	0	0	0	0	0	0	0	0	0	0	0	—	0	—	—	—	P	1	0	0	0	0	—

LCS / World Series (batting & fielding)

	Year	Tm	Age	G	AB	H	2B	3B	HR	TB	R	RBI	GW	TBB	IBB	SO	HBP	SH	SF	SB	CS	SB%	GDP	Avg	OBP	SLG	Pos	G	PO	A	E	DP	FPct
LCS	1978	LA	26	1	0	0	0	0	0	0	0	0	0	0	0	0	0	0	0	0	0	—	0	—	—	—	P	1	0	0	0	0	—
	1981	LA	29	1	0	0	0	0	0	0	0	0	0	0	0	0	0	0	0	0	0	—	0	—	—	—	P	1	0	0	0	0	—
	LCS Totals			2	0	0	0	0	0	0	0	0	0	0	0	0	0	0	0	0	0	—	0	—	—	—	P	2	0	0	0	0	—
World Series	1978	LA	26	3	0	0	0	0	0	0	0	0	0	0	0	0	0	0	0	0	0	—	0	—	—	—	P	3	0	1	0	0	1.000
	1981	LA	29	2	0	0	0	0	0	0	0	0	0	0	0	0	0	0	0	0	0	—	0	—	—	—	P	2	0	1	0	0	1.000
	WS Totals			5	0	0	0	0	0	0	0	0	0	0	0	0	0	0	0	0	0	—	0	—	—	—	P	5	0	2	0	0	1.000
	Postseason Totals			8	0	0	0	0	0	0	0	0	0	0	0	0	0	0	0	0	0	—	0	—	—	—	P	8	0	2	0	0	1.000

TONY FOSSAS
—Emilio Antonio Fossas—Throws: Left; Bats: Left. Ht: 6'0"; Wt: 195 lbs; Born: 9/23/1957 in Havana, Cuba; Debut: 5/15/1988

LCS — Pitching

	Year	Tm	Age	G	GS	CG	GF	IP	BFP	H	R	ER	HR	SH	SF	HB	TBB	IBB	SO	WP	Bk	W	L	Pct	ShO	Sv-Op	Hld	OAvg	OOBP	ERA
LCS	1996	StL	39	5	0	0	1	4.1	15	1	1	1	1	0	0	0	3	1	0	0	0	0	0	—	0	0-0	0	.083	.267	2.08

LCS — Batting & Fielding

	Year	Tm	Age	G	AB	H	2B	3B	HR	TB	R	RBI	GW	TBB	IBB	SO	HBP	SH	SF	SB	CS	SB%	GDP	Avg	OBP	SLG	Pos	G	PO	A	E	DP	FPct
LCS	1996	StL	39	5	0	0	0	0	0	0	0	0	0	0	0	0	0	0	0	0	0	—	0	—	—	—	P	5	0	0	0	0	—

RAY FOSSE
—Raymond Earl Fosse—Bats: Right; Throws: Right. Ht: 6'2"; Wt: 215 lbs; Born: 4/4/1947 in Marion, Illinois; Debut: 9/8/1967

	Year	Tm	Age	G	AB	H	2B	3B	HR	TB	R	RBI	GW	TBB	IBB	SO	HBP	SH	SF	SB	CS	SB%	GDP	Avg	OBP	SLG	Pos	G	PO	A	E	DP	FPct
LCS	1973	Oak	26	5	11	1	1	0	0	2	2	3	0	2	0	2	0	1	1	0	0	—	0	.091	.214	.182	C	5	25	4	0	2	1.000
	1974	Oak	27	4	12	4	1	0	1	8	1	3	0	1	0	2	0	1	0	0	0	—	0	.333	.385	.667	C	4	21	3	0	1	1.000
	1975	Oak	28	1	2	0	0	0	0	0	0	0	0	0	0	1	0	0	0	0	0	—	0	.000	.000	.000	C	1	3	0	0	0	1.000
	LCS Totals			10	25	5	2	0	1	10	3	6	0	3	0	5	0	2	1	0	0	—	0	.200	.276	.400	C	10	49	7	0	4	1.000
World Series	1973	Oak	26	7	19	3	1	0	0	4	0	0	1	1	0	4	0	0	0	0	0	—	0	.158	.200	.211	C	7	32	3	0	2	1.000
	1974	Oak	27	5	14	2	0	0	1	5	1	1	0	1	0	5	0	0	0	0	0	—	0	.143	.200	.357	C	5	27	1	0	0	1.000
	WS Totals			12	33	5	1	0	1	9	1	1	1	2	0	9	0	0	0	0	0	—	0	.152	.200	.273	C	12	59	4	0	2	1.000
	Postseason Totals			22	58	10	3	0	2	19	4	7	0	5	1	14	0	2	1	0	0	—	0	.172	.234	.328	C	22	108	11	0	6	1.000

GEORGE FOSTER
—George Arthur Foster—Bats: Right; Throws: Right. Ht: 6'1"; Wt: 180 lbs; Born: 12/1/1948 in Tuscaloosa, Alabama; Debut: 9/10/1969

	Year	Tm	Age	G	AB	H	2B	3B	HR	TB	R	RBI	GW	TBB	IBB	SO	HBP	SH	SF	SB	CS	SB%	GDP	Avg	OBP	SLG	Pos	G	PO	A	E	DP	FPct
LCS	1972	Cin	23	1	0	0	0	0	0	0	1	0	0	0	0	0	0	0	0	0	0	—	0	—	—	—	—						
	1975	Cin	26	3	11	4	0	0	0	4	0	0	1	0	2	0	0	0	0	1	0	1.00	1	.364	.417	.364	OF	3	7	0	0	0	1.000
	1976	Cin	27	3	12	2	0	0	2	8	2	4	1	0	0	4	0	0	1	0	0	—	0	.167	.154	.667	OF	3	7	0	0	0	1.000
	1979	Cin	30	3	10	2	0	0	1	5	1	2	0	4	0	3	0	0	0	0	0	—	0	.200	.429	.500	OF	3	6	2	0	0	1.000
	LCS Totals			10	33	8	0	0	3	17	7	6	1	5	0	9	0	0	1	1	0	1.00	1	.242	.333	.515	OF	9	20	2	0	0	1.000
World Series	1972	Cin	23	2	0	0	0	0	0	0	0	0	0	0	0	0	0	0	0	0	0	—	0	—	—	—	OF	1	0	0	0	0	—
	1975	Cin	26	7	29	8	1	0	0	9	1	2	0	1	0	1	0	0	0	1	1	.50	0	.276	.300	.310	OF	7	14	1	0	1	1.000
	1976	Cin	27	4	14	6	1	0	0	7	3	4	1	2	0	3	0	0	0	0	2	.00	0	.429	.500	.500	OF	4	14	0	0	0	1.000
	WS Totals			13	43	14	2	0	0	16	4	6	1	3	0	4	0	0	0	1	3	.25	0	.326	.370	.372	OF	12	28	1	0	1	1.000
	Postseason Totals			23	76	22	2	0	3	33	11	12	2	8	0	13	0	0	1	2	3	.40	1	.289	.353	.434	OF	21	48	3	0	1	1.000

RUBE FOSTER
—George Foster—Throws: Right; Bats: Right. Ht: 5'7"; Wt: 170 lbs; Born: 1/5/1888 in Lehigh, Oklahoma; Debut: 4/10/1913; Died: 3/1/1976

World Series — Pitching

	Year	Tm	Age	G	GS	CG	GF	IP	BFP	H	R	ER	HR	SH	SF	HB	TBB	IBB	SO	WP	Bk	W	L	Pct	ShO	Sv-Op	Hld	OAvg	OOBP	ERA
World Series	1915	Bos	27	2	2	2	0	18.0	66	12	5	4	1	0	0	2	2	0	13	0	0	2	0	1.000	0	0-0	0	.194	.242	2.00
	1916	Bos	28	1	0	0	1	3.0	11	3	0	0	0	0	0	0	0	0	1	0	0	0	0	—	0	0-0	0	.273	.273	0.00
	WS Totals			3	2	2	1	21.0	77	15	5	4	1	0	0	2	2	0	14	0	0	2	0	1.000	0	0-0	0	.205	.247	1.71

World Series — Batting & Fielding

	Year	Tm	Age	G	AB	H	2B	3B	HR	TB	R	RBI	GW	TBB	IBB	SO	HBP	SH	SF	SB	CS	SB%	GDP	Avg	OBP	SLG	Pos	G	PO	A	E	DP	FPct
World Series	1915	Bos	27	2	8	4	1	0	0	5	0	1	1	0	0	2	0	0	0	0	0	—	0	.500	.500	.625	P	2	4	3	0	1	1.000
	1916	Bos	28	1	1	0	0	0	0	0	0	0	0	0	0	1	0	0	0	0	0	—	0	.000	.000	.000	P	1	1	2	0	0	1.000
	WS Totals			3	9	4	1	0	0	5	0	1	1	0	0	3	0	0	0	0	0	—	0	.444	.444	.556	P	3	5	5	0	1	1.000

ANDY FOX
—Andrew Junipero Fox—Bats: Left; Throws: Right. Ht: 6'4"; Wt: 205 lbs; Born: 1/12/1971 in Sacramento, California; Debut: 4/7/1996

	Year	Tm	Age	G	AB	H	2B	3B	HR	TB	R	RBI	GW	TBB	IBB	SO	HBP	SH	SF	SB	CS	SB%	GDP	Avg	OBP	SLG	Pos	G	PO	A	E	DP	FPct
Division Series	1996	NYA	25	2	0	0	0	0	0	0	0	0	0	0	0	0	0	0	0	0	0	—	0	—	—	—	—						
	1997	NYA	26	2	0	0	0	0	0	0	0	0	0	0	0	0	0	0	0	0	0	—	0	—	—	—	2B	2	0	0	0	0	—
	DS Totals			4	0	0	0	0	0	0	0	0	0	0	0	0	0	0	0	0	0	—	0	—	—	—	2B	2	0	0	0	0	—
LCS	1996	NYA	25	2	0	0	0	0	0	0	0	0	0	0	0	0	0	0	0	0	0	—	0	—	—	—	—						
World Series	1996	NYA	25	4	0	0	0	0	0	0	1	0	0	0	0	0	0	0	0	0	0	—	0	—	—	—	2B	1	0	0	0	0	1.000
																											3B	1	0	0	0	0	—
	Postseason Totals			10	0	0	0	0	0	0	1	0	0	0	0	0	0	0	0	0	0	—	0	—	—	—	2B	3	1	0	0	0	1.000

ERIC FOX
—Eric Hollis Fox—Bats: Both; Throws: Left. Ht: 5'10"; Wt: 180 lbs; Born: 8/15/1963 in LeMoore, California; Debut: 7/7/1992

	Year	Tm	Age	G	AB	H	2B	3B	HR	TB	R	RBI	GW	TBB	IBB	SO	HBP	SH	SF	SB	CS	SB%	GDP	Avg	OBP	SLG	Pos	G	PO	A	E	DP	FPct
LCS	1992	Oak	29	4	1	0	0	0	0	0	0	0	0	1	0	0	0	0	0	2	0	1.00	0	.000	.500	.000	OF	1	1	0	0	0	1.000

NELLIE FOX
(HOF 1997-V)—Jacob Nelson Fox—Nickname: Little Nel—Bats: Left; Throws: Right. Ht: 5'10"; Wt: 160 lbs; Born: 12/25/1927 in St. Thomas, Pennsylvania; Debut: 6/8/1947; Died: 12/1/1975

	Year	Tm	Age	G	AB	H	2B	3B	HR	TB	R	RBI	GW	TBB	IBB	SO	HBP	SH	SF	SB	CS	SB%	GDP	Avg	OBP	SLG	Pos	G	PO	A	E	DP	FPct
World Series	1959	ChA-M	31	6	24	9	3	0	0	12	4	0	0	4	0	1	0	0	1	0	0	.00	0	.375	.464	.500	2B	6	14	23	0	2	1.000

PETE FOX
—Ervin Fox—Bats: Right; Throws: Right. Ht: 5'11"; Wt: 165 lbs; Born: 3/8/1909 in Evansville, Indiana; Debut: 4/12/1933; Died: 7/5/1966

	Year	Tm	Age	G	AB	H	2B	3B	HR	TB	R	RBI	GW	TBB	IBB	SO	HBP	SH	SF	SB	CS	SB%	GDP	Avg	OBP	SLG	Pos	G	PO	A	E	DP	FPct
World Series	1934	Det	25	7	28	8	6	0	0	14	1	2	1	1	1	4	0	0	0	0	0	—	0	.286	.310	.500	OF	7	16	0	0	0	1.000
	1935	Det	26	6	26	10	3	1	0	15	1	4	0	0	0	1	0	0	0	0	0	—	0	.385	.385	.577	OF	6	10	2	1	0	.923
	1940	Det	31	1	1	0	0	0	0	0	0	0	0	0	0	0	0	0	0	0	0	—	0	.000	.000	.000	—						
	WS Totals			14	55	18	9	1	0	29	2	6	1	1	1	5	0	0	0	0	0	—	0	.327	.339	.527	OF	13	26	2	1	0	.966

JIMMIE FOXX

(HOF 1951-W)—James Emory Foxx—Nicknames: Beast, Double X—Bats: Right; Throws: Right — Ht: 6'0"; Wt: 195 lbs; Born: 10/22/1907 in Sudlersville, Md.; Deb.: 5/1/1925; Died: 7/21/1967

World Series		Batting																							Fielding						
Year Tm	Age	G	AB	H	2B	3B	HR	TB	R	RBI	GW	TBB	IBB	SO	HBP	SH	SF	SB	CS	SB%	GDP	Avg	OBP	SLG	Pos	G	PO	A	E	DP	FPct
1929 Phi	21	5	20	7	1	0	2	14	5	5	2	1	1	1	0	0	0	0	0	—	2	.350	.381	.700	1B	5	38	1	0	2	1.000
1930 Phi	22	6	21	7	2	1	1	14	3	3	1	2	1	4	0	0	0	0	0	—	1	.333	.391	.667	1B	6	52	3	0	2	1.000
1931 Phi	23	7	23	8	0	0	1	11	3	3	1	6	0	5	0	0	0	0	0	—	0	.348	.483	.478	1B	7	69	2	1	4	.986
WS Totals		18	64	22	3	1	4	39	11	11	4	9	2	10	0	0	0	0	0	—	3	.344	.425	.609	1B	18	159	6	1	8	.994

JOE FOY

—Joseph Anthony Foy—Bats: Right; Throws: Right — Ht: 6'0"; Wt: 215 lbs; Born: 2/21/1943 in New York, New York; Debut: 4/13/1966; Died: 10/12/1989

World Series		Batting																							Fielding						
Year Tm	Age	G	AB	H	2B	3B	HR	TB	R	RBI	GW	TBB	IBB	SO	HBP	SH	SF	SB	CS	SB%	GDP	Avg	OBP	SLG	Pos	G	PO	A	E	DP	FPct
1967 Bos	24	6	15	2	1	0	0	3	2	1	1	1	0	5	0	1	0	0	0	—	0	.133	.188	.200	3B	3	7	10	1	0	.944

JULIO FRANCO

—Julio Cesar Franco—Bats: Right; Throws: Right — Ht: 6'0"; Wt: 160 lbs; Born: 8/23/1961 in Hato Mayor, Dominican Republic; Debut: 4/23/1982

Division Series		Batting																							Fielding						
Year Tm	Age	G	AB	H	2B	3B	HR	TB	R	RBI	GW	TBB	IBB	SO	HBP	SH	SF	SB	CS	SB%	GDP	Avg	OBP	SLG	Pos	G	PO	A	E	DP	FPct
1996 Cle	35	4	15	2	0	0	0	2	1	1	0	1	0	6	0	0	1	0	0	—	0	.133	.176	.133	1B	3	18	1	0	1	1.000

TERRY FRANCONA

—Terry Jon Francona—Bats: Left; Throws: Left — Ht: 6'1"; Wt: 190 lbs; Born: 4/22/1959 in Aberdeen, South Dakota; Debut: 8/19/1981

Division Series		Batting																							Fielding						
Year Tm	Age	G	AB	H	2B	3B	HR	TB	R	RBI	GW	TBB	IBB	SO	HBP	SH	SF	SB	CS	SB%	GDP	Avg	OBP	SLG	Pos	G	PO	A	E	DP	FPct
1981 Mon	22	5	12	4	0	0	0	4	0	0	0	2	1	2	0	0	0	2	0	1.00	0	.333	.429	.333	OF	5	8	0	0	0	1.000
LCS		Batting																							Fielding						
Year Tm	Age	G	AB	H	2B	3B	HR	TB	R	RBI	GW	TBB	IBB	SO	HBP	SH	SF	SB	CS	SB%	GDP	Avg	OBP	SLG	Pos	G	PO	A	E	DP	FPct
1981 Mon	22	2	1	0	0	0	0	0	0	0	0	0	0	1	0	0	0	0	0	—	0	.000	.000	.000	OF	1	0	0	0	0	—
Postseason Totals		7	13	4	0	0	0	4	0	0	0	2	1	3	0	0	0	2	0	1.00	0	.308	.400	.308	OF	6	8	0	0	0	1.000

HERMAN FRANKS

—Herman Louis Franks—Bats: Left; Throws: Right — Ht: 5'10"; Wt: 187 lbs; Born: 1/4/1914 in Price, Utah; Debut: 4/27/1939

World Series		Batting																							Fielding						
Year Tm	Age	G	AB	H	2B	3B	HR	TB	R	RBI	GW	TBB	IBB	SO	HBP	SH	SF	SB	CS	SB%	GDP	Avg	OBP	SLG	Pos	G	PO	A	E	DP	FPct
1941 Bro	27	1	1	0	0	0	0	0	0	0	0	0	0	0	0	0	0	0	0	—	1	.000	.000	.000	C	1	0	1	0	0	1.000

GEORGE FRAZIER

—George Allen Frazier—Throws: Right; Bats: Right — Ht: 6'5"; Wt: 205 lbs; Born: 10/13/1954 in Oklahoma City, Oklahoma; Debut: 5/25/1978

LCS		Pitching																									
Year Tm	Age	G	GS	CG	GF	IP	BFP	H	R	ER	HR	SH	SF	HB	TBB	IBB	SO	WP	Bk	W	L	Pct	ShO	Sv-Op	Hld	OAvg	OOBP	ERA
1981 NYA	26	1	0	0	1	5.2	22	5	0	0	0	0	0	0	1	1	5	1	0	1	0	1.000	0	0- 0	0	.238	.273	0.00
1984 ChN	29	1	0	0	0	1.2	7	2	2	2	1	0	0	0	0	0	1	0	0	0	0	—	0	0- 0	0	.286	.286	10.80
LCS Totals		2	0	0	1	7.1	58	7	2	2	1	0	0	0	1	1	6	1	0	1	0	1.000	0	0-0	0	.250	.276	2.45
World Series		Pitching																									
Year Tm	Age	G	GS	CG	GF	IP	BFP	H	R	ER	HR	SH	SF	HB	TBB	IBB	SO	WP	Bk	W	L	Pct	ShO	Sv-Op	Hld	OAvg	OOBP	ERA
1981 NYA	26	3	0	0	0	3.2	23	9	7	7	0	1	0	0	3	2	2	0	0	0	3	.000	0	0- 0	0	.474	.545	17.18
1987 Min	32	1	0	0	1	2.0	7	1	0	0	0	0	0	0	0	0	2	0	0	0	0	—	0	0- 0	0	.143	.143	0.00
WS Totals		4	0	0	1	5.2	60	10	7	7	0	1	0	0	3	2	4	0	0	0	3	.000	0	0-0	0	.385	.448	11.12
Postseason Totals		6	0	0	2	13.0	118	17	9	9	1	1	0	0	4	3	10	1	0	1	3	.250	0	0-0	0	.315	.362	6.23

LCS		Batting																							Fielding						
Year Tm	Age	G	AB	H	2B	3B	HR	TB	R	RBI	GW	TBB	IBB	SO	HBP	SH	SF	SB	CS	SB%	GDP	Avg	OBP	SLG	Pos	G	PO	A	E	DP	FPct
1981 NYA	26	1	0	0	0	0	0	0	0	0	0	0	0	0	0	0	0	0	0	—	0	—	—	—	P	1	0	2	0	1	1.000
1984 ChN	29	1	0	0	0	0	0	0	0	0	0	0	0	0	0	0	0	0	0	—	0	—	—	—	P	1	0	0	0	0	—
LCS Totals		2	0	0	0	0	0	0	0	0	0	0	0	0	0	0	0	0	0	—	0	—	—	—	P	2	0	2	0	1	1.000
World Series		Batting																							Fielding						
Year Tm	Age	G	AB	H	2B	3B	HR	TB	R	RBI	GW	TBB	IBB	SO	HBP	SH	SF	SB	CS	SB%	GDP	Avg	OBP	SLG	Pos	G	PO	A	E	DP	FPct
1981 NYA	26	3	2	0	0	0	0	0	0	0	0	0	0	1	0	0	0	0	0	—	0	.000	.000	.000	P	3	0	0	0	0	—
1987 Min	32	1	0	0	0	0	0	0	0	0	0	0	0	0	0	0	0	0	0	—	0	—	—	—	P	1	0	1	0	0	1.000
WS Totals		4	2	0	0	0	0	0	0	0	0	0	0	1	0	0	0	0	0	—	0	.000	.000	.000	P	4	0	1	0	0	1.000
Postseason Totals		6	2	0	0	0	0	0	0	0	0	0	0	1	0	0	0	0	0	—	0	.000	.000	.000	P	6	0	3	0	1	1.000

BILL FREEHAN

—William Ashley Freehan—Bats: Right; Throws: Right — Ht: 6'3"; Wt: 203 lbs; Born: 11/29/1941 in Detroit, Michigan; Debut: 9/26/1961

LCS		Batting																							Fielding						
Year Tm	Age	G	AB	H	2B	3B	HR	TB	R	RBI	GW	TBB	IBB	SO	HBP	SH	SF	SB	CS	SB%	GDP	Avg	OBP	SLG	Pos	G	PO	A	E	DP	FPct
1972 Det	30	3	12	3	1	0	1	7	2	3	0	0	0	1	0	1	0	0	0	—	0	.250	.250	.583	C	3	24	3	0	0	1.000
World Series		Batting																							Fielding						
Year Tm	Age	G	AB	H	2B	3B	HR	TB	R	RBI	GW	TBB	IBB	SO	HBP	SH	SF	SB	CS	SB%	GDP	Avg	OBP	SLG	Pos	G	PO	A	E	DP	FPct
1968 Det	26	7	24	2	1	0	0	3	0	2	0	4	1	8	0	0	0	0	0	—	0	.083	.214	.125	C	7	45	6	2	2	.962
Postseason Totals		10	36	5	2	0	1	10	2	5	0	4	1	9	0	1	0	0	0	—	0	.139	.225	.278	C	10	69	9	2	2	.975

BUCK FREEMAN

—John Frank Freeman—Bats: Left; Throws: Left — Ht: 5'9"; Wt: 169 lbs; Born: 10/30/1871 in Catasauqua, Pennsylvania; Debut: 6/27/1891; Died: 6/25/1949

World Series		Batting																							Fielding						
Year Tm	Age	G	AB	H	2B	3B	HR	TB	R	RBI	GW	TBB	IBB	SO	HBP	SH	SF	SB	CS	SB%	GDP	Avg	OBP	SLG	Pos	G	PO	A	E	DP	FPct
1903 Bos	31	8	32	9	0	3	0	15	6	4	0	2	0	2	0	0	0	0	1	.00	0	.281	.324	.469	OF	8	11	0	0	0	1.000

MARVIN FREEMAN

—Throws: Right; Bats: Right — Ht: 6'7"; Wt: 200 lbs; Born: 4/10/1963 in Chicago, Illinois; Debut: 9/16/1986

LCS		Pitching																									
Year Tm	Age	G	GS	CG	GF	IP	BFP	H	R	ER	HR	SH	SF	HB	TBB	IBB	SO	WP	Bk	W	L	Pct	ShO	Sv-Op	Hld	OAvg	OOBP	ERA
1992 Atl	29	3	0	0	0	3.2	21	8	6	6	1	1	0	0	2	0	1	0	0	0	0	—	0	0- 0	0	.444	.500	14.73

LCS		Batting																							Fielding						
Year Tm	Age	G	AB	H	2B	3B	HR	TB	R	RBI	GW	TBB	IBB	SO	HBP	SH	SF	SB	CS	SB%	GDP	Avg	OBP	SLG	Pos	G	PO	A	E	DP	FPct
1992 Atl	29	3	0	0	0	0	0	0	0	0	0	0	0	0	0	0	0	0	0	—	0	—	—	—	P	3	0	2	0	0	1.000

GENE FREESE

—Eugene Lewis Freese—Nickname: Augie—Bats: Right; Throws: Right — Ht: 5'11"; Wt: 175 lbs; Born: 1/8/1934 in Wheeling, West Virginia; Debut: 4/13/1955

World Series		Batting																							Fielding						
Year Tm	Age	G	AB	H	2B	3B	HR	TB	R	RBI	GW	TBB	IBB	SO	HBP	SH	SF	SB	CS	SB%	GDP	Avg	OBP	SLG	Pos	G	PO	A	E	DP	FPct
1961 Cin	27	5	16	1	1	0	0	2	0	0	0	3	2	4	0	0	0	0	0	—	0	.063	.211	.125	3B	5	6	4	0	1	1.000

LARRY FRENCH

—Lawrence Herbert French—Throws: Left; Bats: Both — Ht: 6'1"; Wt: 195 lbs; Born: 11/1/1907 in Visalia, California; Debut: 4/18/1929; Died: 2/9/1987

World Series		Pitching																									
Year Tm	Age	G	GS	CG	GF	IP	BFP	H	R	ER	HR	SH	SF	HB	TBB	IBB	SO	WP	Bk	W	L	Pct	ShO	Sv-Op	Hld	OAvg	OOBP	ERA
1935 ChN	27	2	1	1	1	10.2	50	15	5	4	0	1	0	0	2	2	8	0	0	0	2	.000	0	0- 0	0	.319	.347	3.38
1938 ChN	30	3	0	0	2	3.1	13	1	1	1	1	0	0	0	1	0	2	0	0	0	0	—	0	0- 0	0	.083	.154	2.70
1941 Bro	33	2	0	0	0	1.0	1	0	0	0	0	0	0	0	0	0	0	0	0	0	0	—	0	0- 0	0	.000	.000	0.00
WS Totals		7	1	1	3	15.0	128	16	6	5	1	1	0	0	3	2	10	0	0	0	2	.000	0	0-0	0	.267	.302	3.00

World Series		Batting																							Fielding						
Year Tm	Age	G	AB	H	2B	3B	HR	TB	R	RBI	GW	TBB	IBB	SO	HBP	SH	SF	SB	CS	SB%	GDP	Avg	OBP	SLG	Pos	G	PO	A	E	DP	FPct
1935 ChN	27	2	4	1	0	0	0	1	1	0	0	0	0	2	0	0	0	0	0	—	0	.250	.250	.250	P	2	1	2	0	0	1.000
1938 ChN	30	3	0	0	0	0	0	0	0	0	0	0	0	0	0	0	0	0	0	—	0	—	—	—	P	3	0	2	0	0	1.000
1941 Bro	33	2	0	0	0	0	0	0	0	0	0	0	0	0	0	0	0	0	0	—	0	—	—	—	P	2	0	0	0	0	—
WS Totals		7	4	1	0	0	0	1	1	0	0	0	0	2	0	0	0	0	0	—	0	.250	.250	.250	P	7	1	4	0	0	1.000

WALT FRENCH—Walter Edward French—Nicknames: Piggy, Fritz—Bats: Left; Throws: Right

Ht: 5'7"; Wt: 155 lbs; Born: 7/12/1899 in Moorestown, New Jersey; Debut: 9/15/1923; Died: 5/13/1984

World Series		Batting																							Fielding						
Year Tm	Age	G	AB	H	2B	3B	HR	TB	R	RBI	GW	TBB	IBB	SO	HBP	SH	SF	SB	CS	SB%	GDP	Avg	OBP	SLG	Pos	G	PO	A	E	DP	FPct
1929 Phi	30	1	1	0	0	0	0	0	0	0	0	0	0	1	0	0	0	0	0	—	0	.000	.000	.000	—						

LONNY FREY—Linus Reinhard Frey—Nickname: Junior—Bats: Left; Throws: Right

Ht: 5'10"; Wt: 160 lbs; Born: 8/23/1910 in St. Louis, Missouri; Debut: 8/29/1933

World Series		Batting																							Fielding						
Year Tm	Age	G	AB	H	2B	3B	HR	TB	R	RBI	GW	TBB	IBB	SO	HBP	SH	SF	SB	CS	SB%	GDP	Avg	OBP	SLG	Pos	G	PO	A	E	DP	FPct
1939 Cin	29	4	17	0	0	0	0	0	0	0	0	1	0	4	0	0	0	0	0	—	0	.000	.056	.000	2B	4	9	9	0	0	1.000
1940 Cin	30	3	2	0	0	0	0	0	0	0	0	0	0	0	0	0	0	0	0	—	0	.000	.000	.000	2B	1	0	1	0	0	1.000
1947 NYA	37	1	1	0	0	0	0	0	0	1	0	0	0	0	0	0	0	0	0	—	0	.000	.000	.000	—						
WS Totals		8	20	0	0	0	0	0	0	1	0	1	0	4	0	0	0	0	0	—	0	.000	.048	.000	2B	5	9	10	0	0	1.000

BOB FRIEND—Robert Bartmess Friend—Nickname: Warrior—Throws: Right; Bats: Right

Ht: 6'0"; Wt: 190 lbs; Born: 11/24/1930 in Lafayette, Indiana; Debut: 4/28/1951

World Series		Pitching																										
Year Tm	Age	G	GS	CG	GF	IP	BFP	H	R	ER	HR	SH	SF	HB	TBB	IBB	SO	WP	Bk	W	L	Pct	ShO	Sv-Op	Hld	OAvg	OOBP	ERA
1960 Pit	29	3	2	0	0	6.0	35	13	10	9	0	1	0	2	3	0	7	0	0	0	2	.000	0	0- 0	0	.448	.529	13.50

World Series		Batting																							Fielding						
Year Tm	Age	G	AB	H	2B	3B	HR	TB	R	RBI	GW	TBB	IBB	SO	HBP	SH	SF	SB	CS	SB%	GDP	Avg	OBP	SLG	Pos	G	PO	A	E	DP	FPct
1960 Pit	29	3	1	0	0	0	0	0	0	0	0	0	0	0	0	0	0	0	0	—	0	.000	.000	.000	P	3	1	3	0	0	1.000

FRANKIE FRISCH (HOF 1947-W)—Frank Francis Frisch—Nickname: The Fordham Flash—Bats: B; Throws: R

Ht: 5'11"; Wt: 165 lbs; Born: 9/9/1898 in Bronx, N.Y.; Deb.: 6/14/1919; Died: 3/12/1973

World Series		Batting																							Fielding						
Year Tm	Age	G	AB	H	2B	3B	HR	TB	R	RBI	GW	TBB	IBB	SO	HBP	SH	SF	SB	CS	SB%	GDP	Avg	OBP	SLG	Pos	G	PO	A	E	DP	FPct
1921 NYG	23	8	30	9	0	1	0	11	5	0	0	4	0	3	0	0	0	3	0	1.00	0	.300	.382	.367	3B	8	12	23	2	3	.946
1922 NYG	24	5	17	8	1	0	0	9	3	2	1	1	0	0	0	1	1	1	1	.50	1	.471	.474	.529	2B	5	10	19	1	3	.967
1923 NYG	25	6	25	10	0	1	0	12	2	1	0	0	0	0	0	0	0	0	1	.00	0	.400	.400	.480	2B	6	17	17	1	7	.971
1924 NYG	26	7	30	10	4	1	0	16	1	0	0	4	0	1	1	0	0	1	0	1.00	0	.333	.429	.533	2B	7	17	26	0	3	1.000
																									3B	1	0	0	0	0	—
1928 StL	30	4	13	3	0	0	0	3	1	1	0	2	0	2	0	1	1	2	0	1.00	0	.231	.313	.231	2B	4	8	13	0	2	1.000
1930 StL	32	6	24	5	2	0	0	7	0	0	0	0	0	0	0	0	0	1	0	1.00	0	.208	.208	.292	2B	6	13	14	3	3	.900
1931 StL-*M*	33	7	27	7	2	0	0	9	2	1	0	1	0	2	0	1	0	1	0	1.00	1	.259	.286	.333	2B	7	23	19	0	5	1.000
1934 StL	36	7	31	6	1	0	0	7	2	4	1	0	0	1	0	1	0	0	1	.00	1	.194	.194	.226	2B	7	17	26	2	1	.956
WS Totals		50	197	58	10	3	0	74	16	9	2	12	0	9	1	4	2	9	3	.75	3	.294	.335	.376	2B	42	105	134	7	24	.972

DAVE FROST—Carl David Frost—Throws: Right; Bats: Right

Ht: 6'6"; Wt: 235 lbs; Born: 11/17/1952 in Long Beach, California; Debut: 9/11/1977

LCS		Pitching																										
Year Tm	Age	G	GS	CG	GF	IP	BFP	H	R	ER	HR	SH	SF	HB	TBB	IBB	SO	WP	Bk	W	L	Pct	ShO	Sv-Op	Hld	OAvg	OOBP	ERA
1979 Cal	26	2	1	0	0	4.1	24	8	10	9	0	0	0	0	5	1	1	1	0	0	1	.000	0	0- 0	0	.421	.542	18.69

LCS		Batting																							Fielding						
Year Tm	Age	G	AB	H	2B	3B	HR	TB	R	RBI	GW	TBB	IBB	SO	HBP	SH	SF	SB	CS	SB%	GDP	Avg	OBP	SLG	Pos	G	PO	A	E	DP	FPct
1979 Cal	26	2	0	0	0	0	0	0	0	0	0	0	0	0	0	0	0	0	0	—	0	—	—	—	P	2	0	0	0	0	—

WOODIE FRYMAN—Woodrow Thompson Fryman—Throws: Left; Bats: Right

Ht: 6'3"; Wt: 197 lbs; Born: 4/15/1940 in Ewing, Kentucky; Debut: 4/15/1966

Division Series		Pitching																										
Year Tm	Age	G	GS	CG	GF	IP	BFP	H	R	ER	HR	SH	SF	HB	TBB	IBB	SO	WP	Bk	W	L	Pct	ShO	Sv-Op	Hld	OAvg	OOBP	ERA
1981 Mon	41	1	0	0	0	1.1	8	3	1	1	1	0	0	0	1	0	0	0	0	0	0	—	0	0- 0	0	.429	.500	6.75
LCS		**Pitching**																										
Year Tm	Age	G	GS	CG	GF	IP	BFP	H	R	ER	HR	SH	SF	HB	TBB	IBB	SO	WP	Bk	W	L	Pct	ShO	Sv-Op	Hld	OAvg	OOBP	ERA
1972 Det	32	2	2	0	0	12.1	52	11	6	5	0	3	0	2	2	0	8	0	1	0	2	.000	0	0- 0	0	.244	.306	3.65
1981 Mon	41	1	0	0	0	1.0	7	3	4	4	0	1	0	0	1	1	1	0	0	0	0	—	0	0- 0	0	.600	.667	36.00
LCS Totals		3	2	0	0	13.1	118	14	10	9	0	4	0	2	3	1	9	0	1	0	2	.000	0	0-0	0	.280	.345	6.08
Postseason Totals		4	2	0	0	14.2	134	17	11	10	1	4	0	2	4	1	9	0	1	0	2	.000	0	0-0	0	.298	.365	6.14

Division Series		Batting																							Fielding						
Year Tm	Age	G	AB	H	2B	3B	HR	TB	R	RBI	GW	TBB	IBB	SO	HBP	SH	SF	SB	CS	SB%	GDP	Avg	OBP	SLG	Pos	G	PO	A	E	DP	FPct
1981 Mon	41	1	0	0	0	0	0	0	0	0	0	0	0	0	0	0	0	0	0	—	0	—	—	—	P	1	0	1	0	0	1.000
LCS		**Batting**																							**Fielding**						
Year Tm	Age	G	AB	H	2B	3B	HR	TB	R	RBI	GW	TBB	IBB	SO	HBP	SH	SF	SB	CS	SB%	GDP	Avg	OBP	SLG	Pos	G	PO	A	E	DP	FPct
1972 Det	32	2	3	0	0	0	0	0	0	0	0	0	0	0	0	0	0	0	0	—	0	.000	.000	.000	P	2	0	3	0	1	1.000
1981 Mon	41	1	0	0	0	0	0	0	0	0	0	0	0	0	0	0	0	0	0	—	0	—	—	—	P	1	0	0	0	0	—
LCS Totals		3	3	0	0	0	0	0	0	0	0	0	0	0	0	0	0	0	0	—	0	.000	.000	.000	P	3	0	3	0	1	1.000
Postseason Totals		4	3	0	0	0	0	0	0	0	0	0	0	0	0	0	0	0	0	—	0	.000	.000	.000	P	4	0	4	0	1	1.000

TITO FUENTES—Rigoberto Fuentes—Nickname: Parakeet—Bats: Both; Throws: Right

Ht: 5'11"; Wt: 175 lbs; Born: 1/4/1944 in Havana, Cuba; Debut: 8/18/1965

LCS		Batting																							Fielding						
Year Tm	Age	G	AB	H	2B	3B	HR	TB	R	RBI	GW	TBB	IBB	SO	HBP	SH	SF	SB	CS	SB%	GDP	Avg	OBP	SLG	Pos	G	PO	A	E	DP	FPct
1971 SF	27	4	16	5	1	0	1	9	4	2	1	1	0	3	0	1	0	0	0	—	0	.313	.353	.563	2B	4	9	4	1	1	.929

CHICK FULLIS—Charles Philip Fullis—Bats: Right; Throws: Right

Ht: 5'9"; Wt: 170 lbs; Born: 2/27/1904 in Girardville, Pennsylvania; Debut: 4/13/1928; Died: 3/28/1946

World Series		Batting																							Fielding						
Year Tm	Age	G	AB	H	2B	3B	HR	TB	R	RBI	GW	TBB	IBB	SO	HBP	SH	SF	SB	CS	SB%	GDP	Avg	OBP	SLG	Pos	G	PO	A	E	DP	FPct
1934 StL	30	3	5	2	0	0	0	2	0	0	0	0	0	0	0	0	0	0	0	—	0	.400	.400	.400	OF	3	6	0	1	0	.857

CARL FURILLO—Carl Anthony Furillo—Nicknames: Skoonj, The Reading Rifle—Bats: R; Throws: R

Ht: 6'0"; Wt: 190 lbs; Born: 3/8/1922 in Stony Creek Mills, Pa.; Deb.: 4/16/1946; Died: 1/21/1989

World Series		Batting																							Fielding						
Year Tm	Age	G	AB	H	2B	3B	HR	TB	R	RBI	GW	TBB	IBB	SO	HBP	SH	SF	SB	CS	SB%	GDP	Avg	OBP	SLG	Pos	G	PO	A	E	DP	FPct
1947 Bro	25	6	17	6	2	0	0	8	2	3	0	3	0	0	0	1	0	0	0	—	0	.353	.450	.471	OF	6	14	1	1	0	.938
1949 Bro	27	3	8	1	0	0	0	1	0	0	0	1	0	0	0	0	0	0	0	—	0	.125	.222	.125	OF	2	2	0	0	0	1.000
1952 Bro	30	7	23	4	2	0	0	6	1	0	0	3	0	3	0	1	0	0	0	—	1	.174	.269	.261	OF	7	13	0	0	0	1.000
1953 Bro	31	6	24	8	2	0	1	13	4	4	0	1	0	3	0	0	0	0	0	—	3	.333	.360	.542	OF	6	10	0	2	0	.833
1955 Bro	33	7	26	8	1	0	1	12	4	3	0	3	1	5	1	0	1	0	0	—	1	.308	.387	.462	OF	7	8	0	0	0	1.000
1956 Bro	34	7	25	6	2	0	0	8	2	1	0	2	0	3	0	0	0	0	0	—	0	.240	.296	.320	OF	7	7	0	0	0	1.000
1959 LA	37	4	4	1	0	0	0	1	0	2	1	0	0	1	0	0	0	0	0	—	0	.250	.250	.250	OF	1	0	0	0	0	—
WS Totals		40	127	34	9	0	2	49	13	13	1	13	1	15	1	2	1	0	0	—	5	.268	.338	.386	OF	36	54	1	3	0	.948

FRANK GABLER—Frank Harold Gabler—Nickname: The Great Gabbo—Throws: Right; Bats: Right

Ht: 6'1"; Wt: 175 lbs; Born: 11/6/1911 in East Highland, California; Debut: 4/19/1935; Died: 11/1/1967

World Series		Pitching																										
Year Tm	Age	G	GS	CG	GF	IP	BFP	H	R	ER	HR	SH	SF	HB	TBB	IBB	SO	WP	Bk	W	L	Pct	ShO	Sv-Op	Hld	OAvg	OOBP	ERA
1936 NYG	24	2	0	0	1	5.0	26	7	4	4	0	0	1	0	4	0	0	0	0	0	0	—	0	0- 0	0	.333	.423	7.20

World Series		Batting																							Fielding						
Year Tm	Age	G	AB	H	2B	3B	HR	TB	R	RBI	GW	TBB	IBB	SO	HBP	SH	SF	SB	CS	SB%	GDP	Avg	OBP	SLG	Pos	G	PO	A	E	DP	FPct
1936 NYG	24	2	0	0	0	0	0	0	0	0	0	1	0	0	0	0	0	0	0	—	0	—	1.000	—	P	2	1	0	0	0	1.000

GARY GAETTI

—Gary Joseph Gaetti—Bats: Right; Throws: Right — Ht: 6'0"; Wt: 180 lbs; Born: 8/19/1958 in Centralia, Illinois; Debut: 9/20/1981

Division Series — Batting / Fielding

Year Tm	Age	G	AB	H	2B	3B	HR	TB	R	RBI	GW	TBB	IBB	SO	HBP	SH	SF	SB	CS	SB%	GDP	Avg	OBP	SLG	Pos	G	PO	A	E	DP	FPct
1996 StL	38	3	11	1	0	0	1	4	1	3	1	0	0	3	0	0	0	0	0	—	0	.091	.091	.364	3B	3	1	3	0	0	1.000

LCS — Batting / Fielding

Year Tm	Age	G	AB	H	2B	3B	HR	TB	R	RBI	GW	TBB	IBB	SO	HBP	SH	SF	SB	CS	SB%	GDP	Avg	OBP	SLG	Pos	G	PO	A	E	DP	FPct
1987 Min	29	5	20	6	1	0	2	13	5	5	0	1	0	3	1	0	1	0	0	—	0	.300	.348	.650	3B	5	8	7	0	1	1.000
1996 StL	38	7	24	7	0	0	1	10	1	4	0	1	0	5	0	0	0	0	0	—	1	.292	.320	.417	3B	7	4	12	0	1	1.000
LCS Totals		12	44	13	1	0	3	23	6	9	0	2	0	8	1	0	1	0	0	—	1	.295	.333	.523	3B	12	12	19	0	2	1.000

World Series — Batting / Fielding

Year Tm	Age	G	AB	H	2B	3B	HR	TB	R	RBI	GW	TBB	IBB	SO	HBP	SH	SF	SB	CS	SB%	GDP	Avg	OBP	SLG	Pos	G	PO	A	E	DP	FPct
1987 Min	29	7	27	7	2	1	1	14	4	4	1	2	0	5	1	0	0	2	0	1.00	0	.259	.333	.519	3B	7	6	15	0	2	1.000
Postseason Totals		22	82	21	3	1	5	41	11	16	2	4	0	16	2	0	1	2	0	1.00	1	.256	.303	.500	3B	22	19	37	0	4	1.000

PHIL GAGLIANO

—Philip Joseph Gagliano—Bats: Right; Throws: Right — Ht: 6'1"; Wt: 180 lbs; Born: 12/27/1941 in Memphis, Tennessee; Debut: 4/16/1963

LCS — Batting / Fielding

Year Tm	Age	G	AB	H	2B	3B	HR	TB	R	RBI	GW	TBB	IBB	SO	HBP	SH	SF	SB	CS	SB%	GDP	Avg	OBP	SLG	Pos	G	PO	A	E	DP	FPct
1973 Cin	31	3	3	0	0	0	0	0	0	0	0	0	0	1	0	0	0	0	0	—	0	.000	.000	.000	—						

World Series — Batting / Fielding

Year Tm	Age	G	AB	H	2B	3B	HR	TB	R	RBI	GW	TBB	IBB	SO	HBP	SH	SF	SB	CS	SB%	GDP	Avg	OBP	SLG	Pos	G	PO	A	E	DP	FPct
1967 StL	25	1	1	0	0	0	0	0	0	0	0	0	0	0	0	0	0	0	0	—	0	.000	.000	.000	—						
1968 StL	26	3	3	0	0	0	0	0	0	0	0	0	0	0	0	0	0	0	0	—	0	.000	.000	.000	—						
WS Totals		4	4	0	0	0	0	0	0	0	0	0	0	0	0	0	0	0	0	—	0	.000	.000	.000	—	0	0	0	0	0	—
Postseason Totals		7	7	0	0	0	0	0	0	0	0	0	0	1	0	0	0	0	0	—	0	.000	.000	.000	—	0	0	0	0	0	—

GREG GAGNE

—Gregory Christopher Gagne—Bats: Right; Throws: Right — Ht: 5'11"; Wt: 185 lbs; Born: 11/12/1961 in Fall River, Massachusetts; Debut: 6/5/1983

Division Series — Batting / Fielding

Year Tm	Age	G	AB	H	2B	3B	HR	TB	R	RBI	GW	TBB	IBB	SO	HBP	SH	SF	SB	CS	SB%	GDP	Avg	OBP	SLG	Pos	G	PO	A	E	DP	FPct
1996 LA	34	3	11	3	1	0	0	4	2	0	0	0	0	5	0	0	0	0	0	—	0	.273	.273	.364	SS	3	3	9	0	0	1.000

LCS — Batting / Fielding

Year Tm	Age	G	AB	H	2B	3B	HR	TB	R	RBI	GW	TBB	IBB	SO	HBP	SH	SF	SB	CS	SB%	GDP	Avg	OBP	SLG	Pos	G	PO	A	E	DP	FPct
1987 Min	25	5	18	5	3	0	2	14	5	3	1	3	0	4	1	0	0	0	0	—	0	.278	.409	.778	SS	5	9	13	2	2	.917
1991 Min	29	5	17	4	0	0	0	4	1	1	0	1	0	5	1	0	0	0	2	.00	1	.235	.316	.235	SS	5	9	9	2	1	.900
LCS Totals		10	35	9	3	0	2	18	6	4	1	4	0	9	2	0	0	0	2	.00	1	.257	.366	.514	SS	10	18	22	4	3	.909

World Series — Batting / Fielding

Year Tm	Age	G	AB	H	2B	3B	HR	TB	R	RBI	GW	TBB	IBB	SO	HBP	SH	SF	SB	CS	SB%	GDP	Avg	OBP	SLG	Pos	G	PO	A	E	DP	FPct
1987 Min	25	7	30	6	1	0	1	10	5	3	1	1	0	6	0	0	0	0	0	—	0	.200	.226	.333	SS	7	6	20	2	2	.929
1991 Min	29	7	24	4	1	0	1	8	1	3	0	0	0	7	0	0	0	0	0	—	0	.167	.167	.333	SS	7	13	24	0	5	1.000
WS Totals		14	54	10	2	0	2	18	6	6	1	1	0	13	0	0	0	0	0	—	0	.185	.200	.333	SS	14	19	44	2	7	.969
Postseason Totals		27	100	22	6	0	4	40	14	10	2	5	0	27	2	0	0	0	2	.00	1	.220	.271	.400	SS	27	40	75	6	10	.950

DEL GAINER

—Dellos Clinton Gainer—Nickname: Sheriff—Bats: Right; Throws: Right — Ht: 6'0"; Wt: 180 lbs; Born: 11/10/1886 in Montrose, West Virginia; Debut: 10/2/1909; Died: 1/29/1947

World Series — Batting / Fielding

Year Tm	Age	G	AB	H	2B	3B	HR	TB	R	RBI	GW	TBB	IBB	SO	HBP	SH	SF	SB	CS	SB%	GDP	Avg	OBP	SLG	Pos	G	PO	A	E	DP	FPct
1915 Bos	28	1	3	1	0	0	0	1	1	0	0	0	0	0	0	0	0	0	0	—	1	.333	.333	.333	1B	1	9	0	0	0	1.000
1916 Bos	29	1	1	1	0	0	0	1	0	1	1	0	0	0	0	0	0	0	0	—	0	1.000	1.000	1.000	—						
WS Totals		2	4	2	0	0	0	2	1	1	1	0	0	0	0	0	0	0	0	—	1	.500	.500	.500	1B	1	9	0	0	0	1.000

AUGIE GALAN

—August John Galan—Nickname: Goo Goo—Bats: Both; Throws: Right — Ht: 6'0"; Wt: 175 lbs; Born: 5/25/1912 in Berkeley, California; Debut: 4/29/1934; Died: 12/28/1993

World Series — Batting / Fielding

Year Tm	Age	G	AB	H	2B	3B	HR	TB	R	RBI	GW	TBB	IBB	SO	HBP	SH	SF	SB	CS	SB%	GDP	Avg	OBP	SLG	Pos	G	PO	A	E	DP	FPct
1935 ChN	23	6	25	4	1	0	0	5	2	2	0	2	0	2	0	0	0	0	0	—	0	.160	.222	.200	OF	6	13	1	1	0	.933
1938 ChN	26	2	2	0	0	0	0	0	0	0	0	0	0	1	0	0	0	0	0	—	0	.000	.000	.000	—						
1941 Bro	29	2	2	0	0	0	0	0	0	0	0	0	0	1	0	0	0	0	0	—	0	.000	.000	.000	—						
WS Totals		10	29	4	1	0	0	5	2	2	0	2	0	4	0	0	0	0	0	—	0	.138	.194	.172	OF	6	13	1	1	0	.933

ANDRES GALARRAGA

—Andres Jose Galarraga—Nickname: Big Cat—Bats: Right; Throws: Right — Ht: 6'3"; Wt: 235 lbs; Born: 6/18/1961 in Caracas, Venezuela; Debut: 8/23/1985

Division Series — Batting / Fielding

Year Tm	Age	G	AB	H	2B	3B	HR	TB	R	RBI	GW	TBB	IBB	SO	HBP	SH	SF	SB	CS	SB%	GDP	Avg	OBP	SLG	Pos	G	PO	A	E	DP	FPct
1995 Col	34	4	18	5	1	0	0	6	1	2	1	0	0	6	0	0	0	0	0	—	0	.278	.278	.333	1B	4	41	2	0	4	1.000

RICH GALE

—Richard Blackwell Gale—Throws: Right; Bats: Right — Ht: 6'7"; Wt: 225 lbs; Born: 1/19/1954 in Littleton, New Hampshire; Debut: 4/30/1978

World Series — Pitching

Year Tm	Age	G	GS	CG	GF	IP	BFP	H	R	ER	HR	SH	SF	HB	TBB	IBB	SO	WP	Bk	W	L	Pct	ShO	Sv-Op	Hld	OAvg	OOBP	ERA
1980 KC	26	2	2	0	0	6.1	35	11	4	3	1	0	0	0	4	0	4	0	0	0	1	.000	0	0- 0	0	.355	.429	4.26

World Series — Batting / Fielding

Year Tm	Age	G	AB	H	2B	3B	HR	TB	R	RBI	GW	TBB	IBB	SO	HBP	SH	SF	SB	CS	SB%	GDP	Avg	OBP	SLG	Pos	G	PO	A	E	DP	FPct
1980 KC	26	2	0	0	0	0	0	0	0	0	0	0	0	0	0	0	0	0	0	—	0	—	—	—	P	2	0	1	0	0	1.000

DENNY GALEHOUSE

—Dennis Ward Galehouse—Throws: Right; Bats: Right — Ht: 6'1"; Wt: 195 lbs; Born: 12/7/1911 in Marshallville, Ohio; Debut: 4/30/1934

World Series — Pitching

Year Tm	Age	G	GS	CG	GF	IP	BFP	H	R	ER	HR	SH	SF	HB	TBB	IBB	SO	WP	Bk	W	L	Pct	ShO	Sv-Op	Hld	OAvg	OOBP	ERA
1944 StL	32	2	2	2	0	18.0	71	13	3	3	2	2	0	0	5	1	15	0	0	1	1	.500	0	0- 0	0	.203	.261	1.50

World Series — Batting / Fielding

Year Tm	Age	G	AB	H	2B	3B	HR	TB	R	RBI	GW	TBB	IBB	SO	HBP	SH	SF	SB	CS	SB%	GDP	Avg	OBP	SLG	Pos	G	PO	A	E	DP	FPct
1944 StL	32	2	5	1	0	0	0	1	0	0	0	1	0	1	0	0	0	0	0	—	0	.200	.333	.200	P	2	0	5	0	0	1.000

AL GALLAGHER

—Alan Mitchell Edward Geor Gallagher—Nicknames: Dirty Al, Pig Pen—Bats: Right; Throws: Right — Ht: 6'0"; Wt: 180 lbs; Born: 10/19/1945 in San Francisco, Calif.; Debut: 4/7/1970

LCS — Batting / Fielding

Year Tm	Age	G	AB	H	2B	3B	HR	TB	R	RBI	GW	TBB	IBB	SO	HBP	SH	SF	SB	CS	SB%	GDP	Avg	OBP	SLG	Pos	G	PO	A	E	DP	FPct
1971 SF	25	4	10	1	0	0	0	1	0	0	0	0	0	2	1	0	0	0	0	—	0	.100	.182	.100	3B	4	0	4	0	0	1.000

MIKE GALLEGO

—Michael Anthony Gallego—Bats: Right; Throws: Right — Ht: 5'8"; Wt: 160 lbs; Born: 10/31/1960 in Whittier, California; Debut: 4/11/1985

Division Series — Batting / Fielding

Year Tm	Age	G	AB	H	2B	3B	HR	TB	R	RBI	GW	TBB	IBB	SO	HBP	SH	SF	SB	CS	SB%	GDP	Avg	OBP	SLG	Pos	G	PO	A	E	DP	FPct
1996 StL	35	2	1	0	0	0	0	0	0	0	0	0	0	1	0	0	0	0	0	—	0	.000	.000	.000	2B	1	0	0	0	0	—
																									3B	1	0	0	0	0	—

LCS — Batting / Fielding

Year Tm	Age	G	AB	H	2B	3B	HR	TB	R	RBI	GW	TBB	IBB	SO	HBP	SH	SF	SB	CS	SB%	GDP	Avg	OBP	SLG	Pos	G	PO	A	E	DP	FPct
1988 Oak	27	4	12	1	0	0	0	1	1	0	0	0	0	3	0	0	0	0	0	—	0	.083	.083	.083	2B	4	7	6	0	4	1.000
1989 Oak	28	4	11	3	1	0	0	4	3	1	0	0	0	2	0	2	0	0	0	—	0	.273	.273	.364	SS	2	3	5	0	1	1.000
																									2B	2	3	9	0	1	1.000
1990 Oak	29	4	10	4	1	0	0	5	1	2	0	1	0	1	1	0	0	0	1	.00	0	.400	.500	.500	2B	2	5	4	0	2	1.000
																									SS	3	3	5	0	0	1.000
1996 StL	35	7	14	2	0	0	0	2	1	0	0	1	0	3	0	0	0	0	0	—	1	.143	.200	.143	3B	2	0	0	0	0	—
																									2B	5	8	12	1	2	.952
LCS Totals		19	47	10	2	0	0	12	6	3	0	2	0	9	1	2	0	0	1	.00	1	.213	.260	.255	2B	13	23	31	1	9	.982

World Series								Batting																	Fielding						
Year Tm	Age	G	AB	H	2B	3B	HR	TB	R	RBI	GW	TBB	IBB	SO	HBP	SH	SF	SB	CS	SB%	GDP	Avg	OBP	SLG	Pos	G	PO	A	E	DP	FPct
1988 Oak	27	1	0	0	0	0	0	0	0	0	0	0	0	0	0	0	0	0	0	—	0	—	—	—	2B	1	0	0	0	0	—
1989 Oak	28	2	1	0	0	0	0	0	0	0	0	0	0	0	0	0	0	0	0	—	0	.000	.000	.000	2B	1	0	0	0	0	—
																									3B	1	0	0	0	0	—
1990 Oak	29	4	11	1	0	0	0	1	0	1	0	1	0	3	0	0	0	1	0	1.00	0	.091	.167	.091	SS	4	7	10	1	3	.944
WS Totals		7	12	1	0	0	0	1	0	1	0	1	0	3	0	0	0	1	0	1.00	0	.083	.154	.083	SS	4	7	10	1	3	.944
Postseason Totals		28	60	11	2	0	0	13	6	4	0	3	0	13	1	2	0	1	1	.50	1	.183	.234	.217	2B	16	23	31	1	9	.982

LEE GAMBLE—Lee Jesse Gamble—Bats: Left; Throws: Right

Ht: 6'1"; Wt: 170 lbs; Born: 6/28/1910 in Renovo, Pennsylvania; Debut: 9/15/1935; Died: 10/5/1994

World Series								Batting																	Fielding						
Year Tm	Age	G	AB	H	2B	3B	HR	TB	R	RBI	GW	TBB	IBB	SO	HBP	SH	SF	SB	CS	SB%	GDP	Avg	OBP	SLG	Pos	G	PO	A	E	DP	FPct
1939 Cin	29	1	1	0	0	0	0	0	0	0	0	0	0	1	0	0	0	0	0	—	0	.000	.000	.000	—						

OSCAR GAMBLE—Oscar Charles Gamble—Bats: Left; Throws: Right

Ht: 5'11"; Wt: 160 lbs; Born: 12/20/1949 in Ramer, Alabama; Debut: 8/27/1969

Division Series								Batting																	Fielding						
Year Tm	Age	G	AB	H	2B	3B	HR	TB	R	RBI	GW	TBB	IBB	SO	HBP	SH	SF	SB	CS	SB%	GDP	Avg	OBP	SLG	Pos	G	PO	A	E	DP	FPct
1981 NYA	31	4	9	5	1	0	2	12	2	3	1	1	0	2	0	0	0	0	0	—	0	.556	.600	1.333	—						
LCS								**Batting**																	**Fielding**						
Year Tm	Age	G	AB	H	2B	3B	HR	TB	R	RBI	GW	TBB	IBB	SO	HBP	SH	SF	SB	CS	SB%	GDP	Avg	OBP	SLG	Pos	G	PO	A	E	DP	FPct
1976 NYA	26	3	8	2	1	0	0	3	1	1	0	1	0	1	0	1	0	0	0	—	0	.250	.333	.375	OF	3	4	0	2	0	.667
1980 NYA	30	2	5	1	0	0	0	1	1	0	0	1	0	1	0	0	0	0	0	—	0	.200	.333	.200	OF	1	1	0	0	0	1.000
1981 NYA	31	3	6	1	0	0	0	1	2	1	0	5	0	3	0	0	1	0	0	—	0	.167	.500	.167	OF	1	4	0	0	0	1.000
LCS Totals		8	19	4	1	0	0	5	4	2	0	7	0	5	0	1	1	0	0	—	0	.211	.407	.263	OF	5	9	0	2	0	.818
World Series								**Batting**																	**Fielding**						
Year Tm	Age	G	AB	H	2B	3B	HR	TB	R	RBI	GW	TBB	IBB	SO	HBP	SH	SF	SB	CS	SB%	GDP	Avg	OBP	SLG	Pos	G	PO	A	E	DP	FPct
1976 NYA	26	3	8	1	0	0	0	1	0	1	0	0	0	0	0	0	0	0	0	—	0	.125	.125	.125	OF	2	3	0	0	0	1.000
1981 NYA	31	3	6	2	0	0	0	2	1	1	0	1	0	0	0	0	0	0	0	—	0	.333	.429	.333	OF	2	4	0	0	0	1.000
WS Totals		6	14	3	0	0	0	3	1	2	0	1	0	0	0	0	0	0	0	—	0	.214	.267	.214	OF	4	7	0	0	0	1.000
Postseason Totals		18	42	12	2	0	2	20	7	7	1	9	0	7	0	1	1	0	0	—	0	.286	.404	.476	OF	9	16	0	2	0	.889

CHICK GANDIL—Arnold Gandil—Bats: Right; Throws: Right

Ht: 6'1"; Wt: 190 lbs; Born: 1/19/1887 in St. Paul, Minnesota; Debut: 4/14/1910; Died: 12/13/1970

World Series								Batting																	Fielding						
Year Tm	Age	G	AB	H	2B	3B	HR	TB	R	RBI	GW	TBB	IBB	SO	HBP	SH	SF	SB	CS	SB%	GDP	Avg	OBP	SLG	Pos	G	PO	A	E	DP	FPct
1917 ChA	30	6	23	6	1	0	0	7	1	5	0	0	0	2	0	0	0	1	0	1.00	0	.261	.261	.304	1B	6	67	4	1	6	.986
1919 ChA	32	8	30	7	0	1	0	9	1	5	2	1	0	3	0	0	0	1	1	.50	0	.233	.258	.300	1B	8	79	2	1	6	.988
WS Totals		14	53	13	1	1	0	16	2	10	2	1	0	5	0	0	0	2	1	.67	0	.245	.259	.302	1B	14	146	6	2	12	.987

RON GANT—Ronald Edwin Gant—Bats: Right; Throws: Right

Ht: 6'0"; Wt: 172 lbs; Born: 3/2/1965 in Victoria, Texas; Debut: 9/6/1987

Division Series								Batting																	Fielding						
Year Tm	Age	G	AB	H	2B	3B	HR	TB	R	RBI	GW	TBB	IBB	SO	HBP	SH	SF	SB	CS	SB%	GDP	Avg	OBP	SLG	Pos	G	PO	A	E	DP	FPct
1995 Cin	30	3	13	3	0	0	1	6	3	2	1	0	0	3	0	0	0	0	0	—	0	.231	.231	.462	OF	3	8	1	0	0	1.000
1996 StL	31	3	10	4	1	0	1	8	3	4	0	2	0	0	1	0	0	2	0	1.00	1	.400	.538	.800	OF	3	5	0	0	0	1.000
DS Totals		6	23	7	1	0	2	14	6	6	1	2	0	3	1	0	0	2	0	1.00	1	.304	.385	.609	OF	6	13	1	0	0	1.000
LCS								**Batting**																	**Fielding**						
Year Tm	Age	G	AB	H	2B	3B	HR	TB	R	RBI	GW	TBB	IBB	SO	HBP	SH	SF	SB	CS	SB%	GDP	Avg	OBP	SLG	Pos	G	PO	A	E	DP	FPct
1991 Atl	26	7	27	7	1	0	1	11	4	3	1	2	0	4	1	0	1	7	0	1.00	0	.259	.323	.407	OF	7	15	2	0	0	1.000
1992 Atl	27	7	22	4	0	0	2	10	5	6	0	4	0	4	0	1	1	1	0	1.00	2	.182	.296	.455	OF	7	16	0	0	0	1.000
1993 Atl	28	6	27	5	3	0	0	8	4	3	0	2	0	9	0	0	0	0	1	.00	1	.185	.241	.296	OF	6	10	1	1	0	.917
1995 Cin	30	4	16	3	0	0	0	3	1	1	0	0	0	3	1	0	0	0	0	—	1	.188	.235	.188	OF	4	9	0	0	0	1.000
1996 StL	31	7	25	6	1	0	2	13	3	4	1	2	0	6	0	0	0	0	0	—	0	.240	.296	.520	OF	7	12	0	0	0	1.000
LCS Totals		31	117	25	5	0	5	45	17	17	2	10	0	26	2	1	2	8	1	.89	4	.214	.282	.385	OF	31	62	3	1	0	.985
World Series								**Batting**																	**Fielding**						
Year Tm	Age	G	AB	H	2B	3B	HR	TB	R	RBI	GW	TBB	IBB	SO	HBP	SH	SF	SB	CS	SB%	GDP	Avg	OBP	SLG	Pos	G	PO	A	E	DP	FPct
1991 Atl	26	7	30	8	0	1	0	10	3	4	0	2	0	3	0	0	0	1	0	1.00	0	.267	.313	.333	OF	7	19	0	0	0	1.000
1992 Atl	27	4	8	1	1	0	0	2	2	0	0	1	0	2	0	0	0	2	0	1.00	0	.125	.222	.250	OF	3	3	1	0	0	1.000
WS Totals		11	38	9	1	1	0	12	5	4	0	3	0	5	0	0	0	3	0	1.00	0	.237	.293	.316	OF	10	22	1	0	0	1.000
Postseason Totals		48	178	41	7	1	7	71	28	27	3	15	0	34	3	1	2	13	1	.93	5	.230	.298	.399	OF	47	97	5	1	0	.990

JIM GANTNER—James Elmer Gantner—Nickname: Gumby—Bats: Left; Throws: Right

Ht: 6'0"; Wt: 180 lbs; Born: 1/5/1953 in Fond du Lac, Wisconsin; Debut: 9/3/1976

Division Series								Batting																	Fielding						
Year Tm	Age	G	AB	H	2B	3B	HR	TB	R	RBI	GW	TBB	IBB	SO	HBP	SH	SF	SB	CS	SB%	GDP	Avg	OBP	SLG	Pos	G	PO	A	E	DP	FPct
1981 Mil	28	4	14	2	1	0	0	3	1	0	0	0	0	2	0	0	0	0	0	—	0	.143	.143	.214	2B	4	3	14	2	2	.895
LCS								**Batting**																	**Fielding**						
Year Tm	Age	G	AB	H	2B	3B	HR	TB	R	RBI	GW	TBB	IBB	SO	HBP	SH	SF	SB	CS	SB%	GDP	Avg	OBP	SLG	Pos	G	PO	A	E	DP	FPct
1982 Mil	29	5	16	3	0	0	0	3	1	2	0	1	0	1	0	0	0	0	0	—	0	.188	.235	.188	2B	5	12	8	0	4	1.000
World Series								**Batting**																	**Fielding**						
Year Tm	Age	G	AB	H	2B	3B	HR	TB	R	RBI	GW	TBB	IBB	SO	HBP	SH	SF	SB	CS	SB%	GDP	Avg	OBP	SLG	Pos	G	PO	A	E	DP	FPct
1982 Mil	29	7	24	8	4	1	0	14	5	4	0	1	0	1	0	1	0	0	0	—	1	.333	.360	.583	2B	7	9	33	5	2	.894
Postseason Totals		16	54	13	5	1	0	20	7	6	0	2	0	4	0	1	0	0	0	—	1	.241	.268	.370	2B	16	24	55	7	8	.919

JOE GARAGIOLA—Joseph Henry Garagiola—Bats: Left; Throws: Right

Ht: 6'0"; Wt: 190 lbs; Born: 2/12/1926 in St. Louis, Missouri; Debut: 5/26/1946

World Series								Batting																	Fielding						
Year Tm	Age	G	AB	H	2B	3B	HR	TB	R	RBI	GW	TBB	IBB	SO	HBP	SH	SF	SB	CS	SB%	GDP	Avg	OBP	SLG	Pos	G	PO	A	E	DP	FPct
1946 StL	20	5	19	6	2	0	0	8	2	4	0	0	0	3	0	0	0	0	0	—	0	.316	.316	.421	C	5	22	2	0	1	1.000

GENE GARBER—Henry Eugene Garber—Throws: Right; Bats: Right

Ht: 5'10"; Wt: 175 lbs; Born: 11/13/1947 in Lancaster, Pennsylvania; Debut: 6/17/1969

LCS													Pitching															
Year Tm	Age	G	GS	CG	GF	IP	BFP	H	R	ER	HR	SH	SF	HB	TBB	IBB	SO	WP	Bk	W	L	Pct	ShO	Sv-Op	Hld	OAvg	OOBP	ERA
1976 Phi	28	2	0	0	0	0.2	6	2	2	1	0	0	0	0	1	1	0	0	0	0	1	.000	0	0- 1	0	.400	.500	13.50
1977 Phi	29	3	0	0	2	5.1	20	4	3	2	0	0	0	0	0	0	3	0	0	1	1	.500	0	0- 0	0	.200	.200	3.38
1982 Atl	34	2	0	0	2	3.1	15	4	3	3	1	1	0	0	1	0	3	0	0	0	1	.000	0	0- 1	0	.308	.357	8.10
LCS Totals		7	0	0	4	9.1	82	10	8	6	1	1	0	0	2	1	6	0	0	1	3	.250	0	0-2	0	.263	.300	5.79

LCS								Batting																	Fielding						
Year Tm	Age	G	AB	H	2B	3B	HR	TB	R	RBI	GW	TBB	IBB	SO	HBP	SH	SF	SB	CS	SB%	GDP	Avg	OBP	SLG	Pos	G	PO	A	E	DP	FPct
1976 Phi	28	2	0	0	0	0	0	0	0	0	0	0	0	0	0	0	0	0	0	—	0	—	—	—	P	2	0	0	0	0	—
1977 Phi	29	3	0	0	0	0	0	0	0	0	0	0	0	0	0	1	0	0	0	—	0	—	—	—	P	3	0	2	1	0	.667
1982 Atl	34	2	1	0	0	0	0	0	0	0	0	0	0	0	0	0	0	0	0	—	0	.000	.000	.000	P	2	0	1	0	0	1.000
LCS Totals		7	1	0	0	0	0	0	0	0	0	0	0	0	0	1	0	0	0	—	0	.000	.000	.000	P	7	0	3	1	0	.750

BARBARO GARBEY—Bats: Right; Throws: Right

Ht: 5'10"; Wt: 170 lbs; Born: 12/4/1956 in Santiago de Cuba, Cuba; Debut: 4/3/1984

LCS								Batting																	Fielding						
Year Tm	Age	G	AB	H	2B	3B	HR	TB	R	RBI	GW	TBB	IBB	SO	HBP	SH	SF	SB	CS	SB%	GDP	Avg	OBP	SLG	Pos	G	PO	A	E	DP	FPct
1984 Det	27	3	9	3	0	0	0	3	1	0	0	0	0	1	0	0	0	0	0	—	1	.333	.333	.333	—						
World Series								**Batting**																	**Fielding**						
Year Tm	Age	G	AB	H	2B	3B	HR	TB	R	RBI	GW	TBB	IBB	SO	HBP	SH	SF	SB	CS	SB%	GDP	Avg	OBP	SLG	Pos	G	PO	A	E	DP	FPct
1984 Det	27	4	12	0	0	0	0	0	0	0	0	0	0	2	0	0	0	0	0	—	0	.000	.000	.000	—						
Postseason Totals		7	21	3	0	0	0	3	1	0	0	0	0	3	0	0	0	0	0	—	1	.143	.143	.143	—	0	0	0	0	0	—

CARLOS GARCIA—Carlos Jesus Garcia—Bats: Right; Throws: Right

Ht: 6'1"; Wt: 185 lbs; Born: 10/15/1967 in Tachira, Venezuela; Debut: 9/20/1990

LCS — Batting / Fielding

Year Tm	Age	G	AB	H	2B	3B	HR	TB	R	RBI	GW	TBB	IBB	SO	HBP	SH	SF	SB	CS	SB%	GDP	Avg	OBP	SLG	Pos	G	PO	A	E	DP	FPct
1992 Pit	24	1	1	0	0	0	0	0	0	0	0	0	0	0	0	0	0	0	0	—	0	.000	.000	.000	2B	1	0	0	0	0	—

DAMASO GARCIA—Damaso Domingo Garcia—Bats: Right; Throws: Right

Ht: 6'1"; Wt: 165 lbs; Born: 2/7/1957 in Moca, Dominican Republic; Debut: 6/24/1978

LCS — Batting / Fielding

Year Tm	Age	G	AB	H	2B	3B	HR	TB	R	RBI	GW	TBB	IBB	SO	HBP	SH	SF	SB	CS	SB%	GDP	Avg	OBP	SLG	Pos	G	PO	A	E	DP	FPct
1985 Tor	28	7	30	7	4	0	0	11	4	1	0	3	0	3	0	0	0	0	0	—	0	.233	.303	.367	2B	7	10	12	0	3	1.000

KIKO GARCIA—Alfonso Rafael Garcia—Bats: Right; Throws: Right

Ht: 5'11"; Wt: 180 lbs; Born: 10/14/1953 in Martinez, California; Debut: 9/11/1976

Division Series — Batting / Fielding

Year Tm	Age	G	AB	H	2B	3B	HR	TB	R	RBI	GW	TBB	IBB	SO	HBP	SH	SF	SB	CS	SB%	GDP	Avg	OBP	SLG	Pos	G	PO	A	E	DP	FPct
1981 Hou	27	2	4	0	0	0	0	0	0	0	0	0	0	1	0	0	0	0	0	—	0	.000	.000	.000	SS	1	2	4	0	1	1.000

LCS — Batting / Fielding

Year Tm	Age	G	AB	H	2B	3B	HR	TB	R	RBI	GW	TBB	IBB	SO	HBP	SH	SF	SB	CS	SB%	GDP	Avg	OBP	SLG	Pos	G	PO	A	E	DP	FPct
1979 Bal	25	3	11	3	0	0	0	3	1	2	0	2	0	4	0	0	0	0	0	—	0	.273	.385	.273	SS	3	7	17	2	3	.923

World Series — Batting / Fielding

Year Tm	Age	G	AB	H	2B	3B	HR	TB	R	RBI	GW	TBB	IBB	SO	HBP	SH	SF	SB	CS	SB%	GDP	Avg	OBP	SLG	Pos	G	PO	A	E	DP	FPct
1979 Bal	25	6	20	8	2	1	0	12	4	6	1	1	0	3	0	0	0	0	1	.00	0	.400	.429	.600	SS	6	10	17	1	2	.964
Postseason Totals		11	35	11	2	1	0	15	5	8	1	3	0	8	0	0	0	0	1	.00	0	.314	.368	.429	SS	10	19	38	3	6	.950

MIKE GARCIA—Edward Miguel Garcia—Nickname: The Big Bear—Throws: Right; Bats: Right

Ht: 6'1"; Wt: 195 lbs; Born: 11/17/1923 in San Gabriel, California; Debut: 10/3/1948; Died: 1/13/1986

World Series — Pitching

Year Tm	Age	G	GS	CG	GF	IP	BFP	H	R	ER	HR	SH	SF	HB	TBB	IBB	SO	WP	Bk	W	L	Pct	ShO	Sv-Op	Hld	OAvg	OOBP	ERA
1954 Cle	30	2	1	0	1	5.0	26	6	4	3	0	3	0	0	4	1	4	1	0	0	1	.000	0	0- 0	0	.316	.435	5.40

World Series — Batting / Fielding

Year Tm	Age	G	AB	H	2B	3B	HR	TB	R	RBI	GW	TBB	IBB	SO	HBP	SH	SF	SB	CS	SB%	GDP	Avg	OBP	SLG	Pos	G	PO	A	E	DP	FPct
1954 Cle	30	2	0	0	0	0	0	0	0	0	0	0	0	0	0	0	0	0	0	—	0	—	—	—	P	2	0	2	1	0	.667

RAMON GARCIA—Ramon Antonio Garcia—Throws: Right; Bats: Right

Ht: 6'2"; Wt: 200 lbs; Born: 2/9/1969 in Guanare, Venezuela; Debut: 5/31/1991

Division Series — Pitching

Year Tm	Age	G	GS	CG	GF	IP	BFP	H	R	ER	HR	SH	SF	HB	TBB	IBB	SO	WP	Bk	W	L	Pct	ShO	Sv-Op	Hld	OAvg	OOBP	ERA
1997 Hou	28	2	0	0	0	1.0	5	1	2	0	0	0	0	0	1	0	1	0	0	0	0	—	0	0- 0	0	.250	.400	0.00

Division Series — Batting / Fielding

Year Tm	Age	G	AB	H	2B	3B	HR	TB	R	RBI	GW	TBB	IBB	SO	HBP	SH	SF	SB	CS	SB%	GDP	Avg	OBP	SLG	Pos	G	PO	A	E	DP	FPct
1997 Hou	28	2	0	0	0	0	0	0	0	0	0	0	0	0	0	0	0	0	0	—	0	—	—	—	P	2	0	0	0	0	—

BILLY GARDNER—William Frederick Gardner—Nickname: Shotgun—Bats: Right; Throws: Right

Ht: 6'0"; Wt: 170 lbs; Born: 7/19/1927 in Waterford, Connecticut; Debut: 4/22/1954

World Series — Batting / Fielding

Year Tm	Age	G	AB	H	2B	3B	HR	TB	R	RBI	GW	TBB	IBB	SO	HBP	SH	SF	SB	CS	SB%	GDP	Avg	OBP	SLG	Pos	G	PO	A	E	DP	FPct
1961 NYA	34	1	1	0	0	0	0	0	0	0	0	0	0	0	0	0	0	0	0	—	0	.000	.000	.000	—						

LARRY GARDNER—William Lawrence Gardner—Bats: Left; Throws: Right

Ht: 5'8"; Wt: 165 lbs; Born: 5/13/1886 in Enosburg Falls, Vermont; Debut: 6/25/1908; Died: 3/11/1976

World Series — Batting / Fielding

Year Tm	Age	G	AB	H	2B	3B	HR	TB	R	RBI	GW	TBB	IBB	SO	HBP	SH	SF	SB	CS	SB%	GDP	Avg	OBP	SLG	Pos	G	PO	A	E	DP	FPct
1912 Bos	26	8	28	5	2	1	1	12	4	5	1	2	0	5	1	2	1	0	0	—	0	.179	.250	.429	3B	8	9	13	4	0	.846
1915 Bos	29	5	17	4	0	1	0	6	2	0	0	1	0	0	0	1	0	0	0	—	1	.235	.278	.353	3B	5	5	14	0	0	1.000
1916 Bos	30	5	17	3	0	0	2	9	2	6	1	0	0	2	0	1	1	0	0	—	0	.176	.167	.529	3B	5	7	19	2	1	.929
1920 Cle	34	7	24	5	1	0	0	6	1	2	0	1	0	1	0	0	1	0	0	—	0	.208	.231	.250	3B	7	8	14	2	3	.917
WS Totals		25	86	17	3	2	3	33	9	13	2	4	0	8	1	4	3	0	0	—	1	.198	.234	.384	3B	25	29	60	8	4	.918

WES GARDNER—Wesley Brian Gardner—Throws: Right; Bats: Right

Ht: 6'4"; Wt: 197 lbs; Born: 4/29/1961 in Benton, Arkansas; Debut: 7/29/1984

LCS — Pitching

Year Tm	Age	G	GS	CG	GF	IP	BFP	H	R	ER	HR	SH	SF	HB	TBB	IBB	SO	WP	Bk	W	L	Pct	ShO	Sv-Op	Hld	OAvg	OOBP	ERA
1988 Bos	27	1	0	0	0	4.2	22	6	3	3	0	0	0	0	2	2	8	0	0	0	0	—	0	0- 0	0	.300	.364	5.79

LCS — Batting / Fielding

Year Tm	Age	G	AB	H	2B	3B	HR	TB	R	RBI	GW	TBB	IBB	SO	HBP	SH	SF	SB	CS	SB%	GDP	Avg	OBP	SLG	Pos	G	PO	A	E	DP	FPct
1988 Bos	27	1	0	0	0	0	0	0	0	0	0	0	0	0	0	0	0	0	0	—	0	—	—	—	P	1	0	0	0	0	—

WAYNE GARLAND—Marcus Wayne Garland—Throws: Right; Bats: Right

Ht: 6'0"; Wt: 195 lbs; Born: 10/26/1950 in Nashville, Tennessee; Debut: 9/13/1973

LCS — Pitching

Year Tm	Age	G	GS	CG	GF	IP	BFP	H	R	ER	HR	SH	SF	HB	TBB	IBB	SO	WP	Bk	W	L	Pct	ShO	Sv-Op	Hld	OAvg	OOBP	ERA
1974 Bal	23	1	0	0	0	0.2	4	1	0	0	0	0	0	0	1	1	0	0	0	0	0	—	0	0- 0	0	.333	.500	0.00

LCS — Batting / Fielding

Year Tm	Age	G	AB	H	2B	3B	HR	TB	R	RBI	GW	TBB	IBB	SO	HBP	SH	SF	SB	CS	SB%	GDP	Avg	OBP	SLG	Pos	G	PO	A	E	DP	FPct
1974 Bal	23	1	0	0	0	0	0	0	0	0	0	0	0	0	0	0	0	0	0	—	0	—	—	—	P	1	0	0	0	0	—

MIKE GARMAN—Michael Douglas Garman—Throws: Right; Bats: Right

Ht: 6'3"; Wt: 195 lbs; Born: 9/16/1949 in Caldwell, Idaho; Debut: 9/22/1969

LCS — Pitching

Year Tm	Age	G	GS	CG	GF	IP	BFP	H	R	ER	HR	SH	SF	HB	TBB	IBB	SO	WP	Bk	W	L	Pct	ShO	Sv-Op	Hld	OAvg	OOBP	ERA
1977 LA	28	2	0	0	1	1.1	5	0	0	0	0	0	0	1	0	0	1	0	0	0	0	—	0	1- 1	0	.000	.200	0.00

World Series — Pitching

Year Tm	Age	G	GS	CG	GF	IP	BFP	H	R	ER	HR	SH	SF	HB	TBB	IBB	SO	WP	Bk	W	L	Pct	ShO	Sv-Op	Hld	OAvg	OOBP	ERA
1977 LA	28	2	0	0	1	4.0	14	2	0	0	0	0	0	0	1	0	3	0	0	0	0	—	0	0- 0	0	.154	.214	0.00
Postseason Totals		4	0	0	2	5.1	38	2	0	0	0	0	0	1	1	0	4	0	0	0	0	—	0	1-1	0	.118	.211	0.00

LCS — Batting / Fielding

Year Tm	Age	G	AB	H	2B	3B	HR	TB	R	RBI	GW	TBB	IBB	SO	HBP	SH	SF	SB	CS	SB%	GDP	Avg	OBP	SLG	Pos	G	PO	A	E	DP	FPct
1977 LA	28	2	0	0	0	0	0	0	0	0	0	0	0	0	0	0	0	0	0	—	0	—	—	—	P	2	0	0	0	0	—

World Series — Batting / Fielding

Year Tm	Age	G	AB	H	2B	3B	HR	TB	R	RBI	GW	TBB	IBB	SO	HBP	SH	SF	SB	CS	SB%	GDP	Avg	OBP	SLG	Pos	G	PO	A	E	DP	FPct
1977 LA	28	2	0	0	0	0	0	0	0	0	0	0	0	0	0	0	0	0	0	—	0	—	—	—	P	2	0	0	0	0	—
Postseason Totals		4	0	0	0	0	0	0	0	0	0	0	0	0	0	0	0	0	0	—	0	—	—	—	P	4	0	0	0	0	—

DEBS GARMS—Debs C. Garms—Nickname: Tex—Bats: Left; Throws: Right

Ht: 5'8"; Wt: 165 lbs; Born: 6/26/1908 in Bangs, Texas; Debut: 8/10/1932; Died: 12/16/1984

World Series — Batting / Fielding

Year Tm	Age	G	AB	H	2B	3B	HR	TB	R	RBI	GW	TBB	IBB	SO	HBP	SH	SF	SB	CS	SB%	GDP	Avg	OBP	SLG	Pos	G	PO	A	E	DP	FPct
1943 StL	35	2	5	0	0	0	0	0	0	0	0	0	0	2	0	1	0	0	0	—	0	.000	.000	.000	OF	1	1	0	0	0	1.000
1944 StL	36	2	2	0	0	0	0	0	0	0	0	0	0	0	0	0	0	0	0	—	0	.000	.000	.000	—						
WS Totals		4	7	0	0	0	0	0	0	0	0	0	0	2	0	1	0	0	0	—	0	.000	.000	.000	OF	1	1	0	0	0	1.000

PHIL GARNER—Philip Mason Garner—Nickname: Scrap Iron—Bats: Right; Throws: Right

Ht: 5'10"; Wt: 175 lbs; Born: 4/30/1949 in Jefferson City, Tennessee; Debut: 9/10/1973

Division Series — Batting / Fielding

Year Tm	Age	G	AB	H	2B	3B	HR	TB	R	RBI	GW	TBB	IBB	SO	HBP	SH	SF	SB	CS	SB%	GDP	Avg	OBP	SLG	Pos	G	PO	A	E	DP	FPct
1981 Hou	32	5	18	2	0	0	0	2	1	0	0	3	0	3	0	0	0	0	0	—	0	.111	.238	.111	2B	5	4	8	1	0	.923

LCS — Batting / Fielding

Year Tm	Age	G	AB	H	2B	3B	HR	TB	R	RBI	GW	TBB	IBB	SO	HBP	SH	SF	SB	CS	SB%	GDP	Avg	OBP	SLG	Pos	G	PO	A	E	DP	FPct
1975 Oak	26	3	5	0	0	0	0	0	0	0	0	0	0	1	0	0	0	0	0	—	0	.000	.000	.000	2B	3	7	4	1	2	.917
1979 Pit	30	3	12	5	0	1	1	10	4	1	0	1	1	0	0	0	0	0	0	—	0	.417	.462	.833	2B	3	8	9	0	2	1.000
																									SS	1	0	0	0	0	—
1986 Hou	37	3	9	2	1	0	0	3	1	2	0	1	0	2	0	0	0	0	0	—	0	.222	.300	.333	3B	3	1	8	0	0	1.000
LCS Totals		9	26	7	1	1	1	13	5	3	0	2	1	3	0	0	0	0	0	—	0	.269	.321	.500	2B	6	15	13	1	4	.966

World Series — Batting / Fielding

Year Tm	Age	G	AB	H	2B	3B	HR	TB	R	RBI	GW	TBB	IBB	SO	HBP	SH	SF	SB	CS	SB%	GDP	Avg	OBP	SLG	Pos	G	PO	A	E	DP	FPct
1979 Pit	30	7	24	12	4	0	0	16	4	5	0	3	2	1	1	0	0	0	0	—	0	.500	.571	.667	2B	7	21	22	2	9	.956
Postseason Totals		21	68	21	5	1	1	31	10	8	0	8	3	7	1	0	0	0	0	—	0	.309	.390	.456	2B	18	40	43	4	13	.954

SCOTT GARRELTS—Scott William Garrelts—Throws: Right; Bats: Right

Ht: 6'4"; Wt: 195 lbs; Born: 10/30/1961 in Champaign, Illinois; Debut: 10/2/1982

LCS — Pitching

Year Tm	Age	G	GS	CG	GF	IP	BFP	H	R	ER	HR	SH	SF	HB	TBB	IBB	SO	WP	Bk	W	L	Pct	ShO	Sv-Op	Hld	OAvg	OOBP	ERA
1987 SF	25	2	0	0	1	2.2	13	2	2	2	0	1	0	0	4	0	4	1	0	0	0	—	0	0-0	0	.250	.500	6.75
1989 SF	27	2	2	0	0	11.2	53	16	7	7	3	0	1	0	2	0	8	1	0	1	0	1.000	0	0-0	0	.320	.340	5.40
LCS Totals		4	2	0	1	14.1	132	18	9	9	3	1	1	0	6	0	12	2	0	1	0	1.000	0	0-0	0	.310	.369	5.65

World Series — Pitching

Year Tm	Age	G	GS	CG	GF	IP	BFP	H	R	ER	HR	SH	SF	HB	TBB	IBB	SO	WP	Bk	W	L	Pct	ShO	Sv-Op	Hld	OAvg	OOBP	ERA
1989 SF	27	2	2	0	0	7.1	37	13	9	8	4	0	0	0	1	0	8	0	0	0	2	.000	0	0-0	0	.361	.378	9.82
Postseason Totals		6	4	0	1	21.2	206	31	18	17	7	1	1	0	7	0	20	2	0	1	2	.333	0	0-0	0	.330	.373	7.06

LCS — Batting / Fielding

Year Tm	Age	G	AB	H	2B	3B	HR	TB	R	RBI	GW	TBB	IBB	SO	HBP	SH	SF	SB	CS	SB%	GDP	Avg	OBP	SLG	Pos	G	PO	A	E	DP	FPct
1987 SF	25	2	0	0	0	0	0	0	0	0	0	0	0	0	0	0	0	0	0	—	0	—	—	—	P	2	2	0	0	0	1.000
1989 SF	27	2	4	0	0	0	0	0	0	0	0	1	0	1	0	0	0	0	0	—	0	.000	.200	.000	P	2	0	1	0	0	1.000
LCS Totals		4	4	0	0	0	0	0	0	0	0	1	0	1	0	0	0	0	0	—	0	.000	.200	.000	P	4	2	1	0	0	1.000

World Series — Batting / Fielding

Year Tm	Age	G	AB	H	2B	3B	HR	TB	R	RBI	GW	TBB	IBB	SO	HBP	SH	SF	SB	CS	SB%	GDP	Avg	OBP	SLG	Pos	G	PO	A	E	DP	FPct
1989 SF	27	2	1	0	0	0	0	0	0	0	0	0	0	1	0	0	0	0	0	—	0	.000	.000	.000	P	2	0	2	0	0	1.000
Postseason Totals		6	5	0	0	0	0	0	0	0	0	1	0	2	0	0	0	0	0	—	0	.000	.167	.000	P	6	2	3	0	0	1.000

WAYNE GARRETT—Ronald Wayne Garrett—Bats: Left; Throws: Right

Ht: 5'11"; Wt: 175 lbs; Born: 12/3/1947 in Brooksville, Florida; Debut: 4/12/1969

LCS — Batting / Fielding

Year Tm	Age	G	AB	H	2B	3B	HR	TB	R	RBI	GW	TBB	IBB	SO	HBP	SH	SF	SB	CS	SB%	GDP	Avg	OBP	SLG	Pos	G	PO	A	E	DP	FPct
1969 NYN	21	3	13	5	2	0	1	10	3	3	1	2	0	2	0	0	0	1	0	1.00	0	.385	.467	.769	3B	3	1	6	0	0	1.000
1973 NYN	25	5	23	2	1	0	0	3	1	1	0	0	0	5	0	0	1	0	0	—	0	.087	.083	.130	3B	5	4	6	1	0	.909
LCS Totals		8	36	7	3	0	1	13	4	4	1	2	0	7	0	0	1	1	0	1.00	0	.194	.231	.361	3B	8	5	12	1	0	.944

World Series — Batting / Fielding

Year Tm	Age	G	AB	H	2B	3B	HR	TB	R	RBI	GW	TBB	IBB	SO	HBP	SH	SF	SB	CS	SB%	GDP	Avg	OBP	SLG	Pos	G	PO	A	E	DP	FPct
1969 NYN	21	2	1	0	0	0	0	0	0	0	0	2	0	1	0	1	0	0	0	—	0	.000	.667	.000	3B	2	1	0	1	0	.500
1973 NYN	25	7	30	5	0	0	2	11	4	2	0	5	1	11	1	0	0	0	0	—	1	.167	.306	.367	3B	7	4	19	3	1	.885
WS Totals		9	31	5	0	0	2	11	4	2	0	7	1	12	1	1	0	0	0	—	1	.161	.333	.355	3B	9	5	19	4	1	.857
Postseason Totals		17	67	12	3	0	3	24	8	6	1	9	1	19	1	1	1	1	0	1.00	1	.179	.282	.358	3B	17	10	31	5	1	.891

GIL GARRIDO—Gil Gonzalo Garrido—Bats: Right; Throws: Right

Ht: 5'9"; Wt: 150 lbs; Born: 6/26/1941 in Panama City, Panama; Debut: 4/24/1964

LCS — Batting / Fielding

Year Tm	Age	G	AB	H	2B	3B	HR	TB	R	RBI	GW	TBB	IBB	SO	HBP	SH	SF	SB	CS	SB%	GDP	Avg	OBP	SLG	Pos	G	PO	A	E	DP	FPct
1969 Atl	28	3	10	2	0	0	0	2	0	0	0	1	0	1	0	0	0	0	1	.00	0	.200	.273	.200	SS	3	4	8	0	3	1.000

STEVE GARVEY—Steven Patrick Garvey—Bats: Right; Throws: Right

Ht: 5'10"; Wt: 192 lbs; Born: 12/22/1948 in Tampa, Florida; Debut: 9/1/1969

Division Series — Batting / Fielding

Year Tm	Age	G	AB	H	2B	3B	HR	TB	R	RBI	GW	TBB	IBB	SO	HBP	SH	SF	SB	CS	SB%	GDP	Avg	OBP	SLG	Pos	G	PO	A	E	DP	FPct
1981 LA	32	5	19	7	0	1	2	15	4	4	0	0	0	2	0	0	0	0	0	—	0	.368	.368	.789	1B	5	49	5	0	2	1.000

LCS — Batting / Fielding

Year Tm	Age	G	AB	H	2B	3B	HR	TB	R	RBI	GW	TBB	IBB	SO	HBP	SH	SF	SB	CS	SB%	GDP	Avg	OBP	SLG	Pos	G	PO	A	E	DP	FPct
1974 LA-*M*	25	4	18	7	1	0	2	14	4	5	0	1	1	1	0	0	0	0	0	—	1	.389	.421	.778	1B	4	41	2	1	6	.977
1977 LA	28	4	13	4	0	0	0	4	2	0	0	2	2	1	0	1	0	1	0	1.00	0	.308	.400	.308	1B	4	40	1	0	3	1.000
1978 LA	29	4	18	7	1	1	4	22	6	7	1	0	0	1	0	0	0	0	1	.00	0	.389	.389	1.222	1B	4	44	4	0	4	1.000
1981 LA	32	5	21	6	0	0	1	9	2	2	1	0	0	4	0	0	0	0	0	—	1	.286	.286	.429	1B	5	49	2	0	4	1.000
1984 SD	35	5	20	8	1	0	1	12	1	7	1	1	0	2	0	0	0	0	0	—	1	.400	.429	.600	1B	5	35	3	0	4	1.000
LCS Totals		22	90	32	3	1	8	61	15	21	3	4	3	9	0	1	0	1	1	.50	3	.356	.383	.678	1B	22	209	12	1	21	.995

World Series — Batting / Fielding

Year Tm	Age	G	AB	H	2B	3B	HR	TB	R	RBI	GW	TBB	IBB	SO	HBP	SH	SF	SB	CS	SB%	GDP	Avg	OBP	SLG	Pos	G	PO	A	E	DP	FPct
1974 LA-*M*	25	5	21	8	0	0	0	8	2	1	0	0	0	3	0	0	0	0	0	—	0	.381	.381	.381	1B	5	34	3	0	4	1.000
1977 LA	28	6	24	9	1	1	1	15	5	3	0	1	0	4	0	0	0	0	1	.00	0	.375	.400	.625	1B	6	59	5	0	4	1.000
1978 LA	29	6	24	5	1	0	0	6	1	0	0	1	0	7	0	0	0	1	0	1.00	0	.208	.240	.250	1B	6	58	3	1	4	.984
1981 LA	32	6	24	10	1	0	0	11	3	0	0	2	1	5	0	0	0	0	0	—	0	.417	.462	.458	1B	6	45	3	0	6	1.000
1984 SD	35	5	20	4	2	0	0	6	2	2	0	0	0	2	0	1	0	0	0	—	1	.200	.200	.300	1B	5	34	3	0	4	1.000
WS Totals		28	113	36	5	1	1	46	13	6	0	4	1	21	0	1	0	1	1	.50	1	.319	.342	.407	1B	28	230	17	1	22	.996
Postseason Totals		55	222	75	8	3	11	122	32	31	3	8	4	32	0	2	0	2	2	.50	4	.338	.361	.550	1B	55	488	34	2	45	.996

ROD GASPAR—Rodney Earl Gaspar—Bats: Both; Throws: Left

Ht: 5'11"; Wt: 165 lbs; Born: 4/3/1946 in Long Beach, California; Debut: 4/8/1969

LCS — Batting / Fielding

Year Tm	Age	G	AB	H	2B	3B	HR	TB	R	RBI	GW	TBB	IBB	SO	HBP	SH	SF	SB	CS	SB%	GDP	Avg	OBP	SLG	Pos	G	PO	A	E	DP	FPct
1969 NYN	23	3	0	0	0	0	0	0	0	0	0	0	0	0	0	0	0	0	0	—	0	—	—	—	OF	3	2	0	0	0	1.000

World Series — Batting / Fielding

Year Tm	Age	G	AB	H	2B	3B	HR	TB	R	RBI	GW	TBB	IBB	SO	HBP	SH	SF	SB	CS	SB%	GDP	Avg	OBP	SLG	Pos	G	PO	A	E	DP	FPct
1969 NYN	23	3	2	0	0	0	0	0	1	0	0	0	0	0	0	0	0	0	0	—	0	.000	.000	.000	OF	1	2	0	0	0	1.000
Postseason Totals		6	2	0	0	0	0	0	1	0	0	0	0	0	0	0	0	0	0	—	0	.000	.000	.000	OF	4	4	0	0	0	1.000

BRENT GATES—Brent Robert Gates—Bats: Both; Throws: Right

Ht: 6'1"; Wt: 180 lbs; Born: 3/14/1970 in Grand Rapids, Michigan; Debut: 5/5/1993

Division Series — Batting / Fielding

Year Tm	Age	G	AB	H	2B	3B	HR	TB	R	RBI	GW	TBB	IBB	SO	HBP	SH	SF	SB	CS	SB%	GDP	Avg	OBP	SLG	Pos	G	PO	A	E	DP	FPct
1997 Sea	27	2	4	0	0	0	0	0	0	0	0	0	0	0	0	0	0	0	0	—	0	.000	.000	.000	3B	2	1	2	0	0	1.000

MIKE GAZELLA—Michael Gazella—Bats: Right; Throws: Right

Ht: 5'7"; Wt: 165 lbs; Born: 10/13/1896 in Olyphant, Pennsylvania; Debut: 7/2/1923; Died: 9/11/1978

World Series — Batting / Fielding

Year Tm	Age	G	AB	H	2B	3B	HR	TB	R	RBI	GW	TBB	IBB	SO	HBP	SH	SF	SB	CS	SB%	GDP	Avg	OBP	SLG	Pos	G	PO	A	E	DP	FPct
1926 NYA	29	1	0	0	0	0	0	0	0	0	0	0	0	0	1	0	0	0	0	—	0	—	1.000	—	3B	1	1	2	0	0	1.000

DINTY GEARIN—Dennis John Gearin—Throws: Left; Bats: Left

Ht: 5'4"; Wt: 148 lbs; Born: 10/15/1897 in Providence, Rhode Island; Debut: 8/6/1923; Died: 3/11/1959

World Series — Batting / Fielding

Year Tm	Age	G	AB	H	2B	3B	HR	TB	R	RBI	GW	TBB	IBB	SO	HBP	SH	SF	SB	CS	SB%	GDP	Avg	OBP	SLG	Pos	G	PO	A	E	DP	FPct
1923 NYG	25	1	0	0	0	0	0	0	0	0	0	0	0	0	0	0	0	0	0	—	0	—	—	—	—						

RICH GEDMAN—Richard Leo Gedman—Bats: Left; Throws: Right

Ht: 6'0"; Wt: 210 lbs; Born: 9/26/1959 in Worcester, Massachusetts; Debut: 9/7/1980

LCS		Batting																							Fielding						
Year Tm	Age	G	AB	H	2B	3B	HR	TB	R	RBI	GW	TBB	IBB	SO	HBP	SH	SF	SB	CS	SB%	GDP	Avg	OBP	SLG	Pos	G	PO	A	E	DP	FPct
1986 Bos	27	7	28	10	1	0	1	14	4	6	1	0	0	4	1	0	0	0	0	—	0	.357	.379	.500	C	7	45	4	0	0	1.000
1988 Bos	29	4	14	5	0	0	1	8	1	1	0	2	0	1	0	0	0	0	0	—	0	.357	.438	.571	C	4	34	5	0	1	1.000
LCS Totals		11	42	15	1	0	2	22	5	7	1	2	0	5	1	0	0	0	0	—	0	.357	.400	.524	C	11	79	9	0	1	1.000
World Series		Batting																							Fielding						
Year Tm	Age	G	AB	H	2B	3B	HR	TB	R	RBI	GW	TBB	IBB	SO	HBP	SH	SF	SB	CS	SB%	GDP	Avg	OBP	SLG	Pos	G	PO	A	E	DP	FPct
1986 Bos	27	7	30	6	1	0	1	10	1	1	0	0	0	10	0	0	0	0	0	—	1	.200	.200	.333	C	7	46	3	2	2	.961
Postseason Totals		18	72	21	2	0	3	32	6	8	1	2	0	15	1	0	0	0	0	—	1	.292	.320	.444	C	18	125	12	2	3	.986

LOU GEHRIG (HOF 1939-W)—Henry Louis Gehrig—Nicknames: The Iron Horse, Biscuit Pants—Bats: L; Throws: L

Ht: 6'0"; Wt: 200 lbs; Born: 6/19/1903 in New York, N.Y.; Deb.: 6/15/1923; Died: 6/2/1941

World Series		Batting																							Fielding						
Year Tm	Age	G	AB	H	2B	3B	HR	TB	R	RBI	GW	TBB	IBB	SO	HBP	SH	SF	SB	CS	SB%	GDP	Avg	OBP	SLG	Pos	G	PO	A	E	DP	FPct
1926 NYA	23	7	23	8	2	0	0	10	1	4	2	5	1	4	0	1	0	0	0	—	0	.348	.464	.435	1B	7	77	1	0	3	1.000
1927 NYA-*M*	24	4	13	4	2	2	0	10	2	4	1	3	0	3	0	0	2	0	0	—	0	.308	.389	.769	1B	4	41	3	0	3	1.000
1928 NYA	25	4	11	6	1	0	4	19	5	9	2	6	0	0	0	0	0	0	0	—	0	.545	.706	1.727	1B	4	33	0	0	3	1.000
1932 NYA	29	4	17	9	1	0	3	19	9	8	1	2	0	1	1	0	0	0	0	—	1	.529	.600	1.118	1B	4	37	2	1	1	.975
1936 NYA-*M*	33	6	24	7	1	0	2	14	5	7	2	3	0	2	1	0	0	0	1	.00	0	.292	.393	.583	1B	6	45	2	0	2	1.000
1937 NYA	34	5	17	5	1	1	1	11	4	3	0	5	1	4	0	0	0	0	0	—	0	.294	.455	.647	1B	5	51	1	0	2	1.000
1938 NYA	35	4	14	4	0	0	0	4	4	0	0	2	0	3	0	0	0	0	0	—	0	.286	.375	.286	1B	4	26	3	0	4	1.000
WS Totals		34	119	43	8	3	10	87	30	35	8	26	2	17	2	1	2	0	1	.00	1	.361	.477	.731	1B	34	310	12	1	18	.997

CHARLIE GEHRINGER (HOF 1949-W)—Charles Leonard Gehringer—Bats: Left; Throws: Left

Ht: 5'11"; Wt: 180 lbs; Born: 5/11/1903 in Fowlerville, Mich.; Debut: 9/22/1924; Died: 1/21/1993

World Series		Batting																							Fielding						
Year Tm	Age	G	AB	H	2B	3B	HR	TB	R	RBI	GW	TBB	IBB	SO	HBP	SH	SF	SB	CS	SB%	GDP	Avg	OBP	SLG	Pos	G	PO	A	E	DP	FPct
1934 Det	31	7	29	11	1	0	1	15	5	2	0	3	0	0	0	1	0	1	0	1.00	0	.379	.438	.517	2B	7	18	26	3	3	.936
1935 Det	32	6	24	9	3	0	0	12	4	4	0	2	0	1	0	1	0	1	0	1.00	0	.375	.423	.500	2B	6	14	25	0	6	1.000
1940 Det	37	7	28	6	0	0	0	6	3	1	0	2	0	0	0	0	0	0	0	—	3	.214	.267	.214	2B	7	18	18	0	3	1.000
WS Totals		20	81	26	4	0	1	33	12	7	0	7	0	1	0	2	0	2	0	1.00	3	.321	.375	.407	2B	20	50	69	3	12	.975

CHARLIE GELBERT—Charles Magnus Gelbert—Bats: Right; Throws: Right

Ht: 5'11"; Wt: 170 lbs; Born: 1/26/1906 in Scranton, Pennsylvania; Debut: 4/16/1929; Died: 1/13/1967

World Series		Batting																							Fielding						
Year Tm	Age	G	AB	H	2B	3B	HR	TB	R	RBI	GW	TBB	IBB	SO	HBP	SH	SF	SB	CS	SB%	GDP	Avg	OBP	SLG	Pos	G	PO	A	E	DP	FPct
1930 StL	24	6	17	6	0	1	0	8	2	2	0	3	1	3	0	0	0	0	0	—	0	.353	.450	.471	SS	6	5	23	0	3	1.000
1931 StL	25	7	23	6	1	0	0	7	0	3	0	0	0	4	0	1	0	0	0	—	1	.261	.261	.304	SS	7	13	29	0	6	1.000
WS Totals		13	40	12	1	1	0	15	2	5	0	3	1	7	0	1	0	0	0	—	1	.300	.349	.375	SS	13	18	52	0	9	1.000

GARY GENTRY—Gary Edward Gentry—Throws: Right; Bats: Right

Ht: 6'0"; Wt: 170 lbs; Born: 10/6/1946 in Phoenix, Arizona; Debut: 4/10/1969

LCS		Pitching																									
Year Tm	Age	G	GS	CG	GF	IP	BFP	H	R	ER	HR	SH	SF	HB	TBB	IBB	SO	WP	Bk	W	L	Pct	ShO	Sv-Op	Hld	OAvg	OOBP	ERA
1969 NYN	22	1	1	0	0	2.0	12	5	2	2	1	0	0	0	1	0	1	0	0	0	0	—	0	0- 0	0	.455	.500	9.00
World Series		Pitching																										
Year Tm	Age	G	GS	CG	GF	IP	BFP	H	R	ER	HR	SH	SF	HB	TBB	IBB	SO	WP	Bk	W	L	Pct	ShO	Sv-Op	Hld	OAvg	OOBP	ERA
1969 NYN	22	1	1	0	0	6.2	28	3	0	0	0	0	0	0	5	0	4	0	0	1	0	1.000	0	0- 0	0	.130	.286	0.00
Postseason Totals		2	2	0	0	8.2	80	8	2	2	1	0	0	0	6	0	5	0	0	1	0	1.000	0	0-0	0	.235	.350	2.08

LCS		Batting																							Fielding						
Year Tm	Age	G	AB	H	2B	3B	HR	TB	R	RBI	GW	TBB	IBB	SO	HBP	SH	SF	SB	CS	SB%	GDP	Avg	OBP	SLG	Pos	G	PO	A	E	DP	FPct
1969 NYN	22	1	0	0	0	0	0	0	0	0	0	0	0	0	0	0	0	0	0	—	0	—	—	—	P	1	0	0	0	0	—
World Series		Batting																							Fielding						
Year Tm	Age	G	AB	H	2B	3B	HR	TB	R	RBI	GW	TBB	IBB	SO	HBP	SH	SF	SB	CS	SB%	GDP	Avg	OBP	SLG	Pos	G	PO	A	E	DP	FPct
1969 NYN	22	1	3	1	1	0	0	2	0	2	0	0	0	2	0	0	0	0	0	—	0	.333	.333	.667	P	1	0	0	0	0	—
Postseason Totals		2	3	1	1	0	0	2	0	2	0	0	0	2	0	0	0	0	0	—	0	.333	.333	.667	P	2	0	0	0	0	—

DICK GERNERT—Richard Edward Gernert—Bats: Right; Throws: Right

Ht: 6'3"; Wt: 209 lbs; Born: 9/28/1928 in Reading, Pennsylvania; Debut: 4/16/1952

World Series		Batting																							Fielding						
Year Tm	Age	G	AB	H	2B	3B	HR	TB	R	RBI	GW	TBB	IBB	SO	HBP	SH	SF	SB	CS	SB%	GDP	Avg	OBP	SLG	Pos	G	PO	A	E	DP	FPct
1961 Cin	33	4	4	0	0	0	0	0	0	0	0	0	0	1	0	0	0	0	0	—	0	.000	.000	.000	—						

CESAR GERONIMO—Cesar Francisco Geronimo—Bats: Left; Throws: Left

Ht: 6'0"; Wt: 165 lbs; Born: 3/11/1948 in El Seibo, Dominican Republic; Debut: 4/16/1969

Division Series		Batting																							Fielding						
Year Tm	Age	G	AB	H	2B	3B	HR	TB	R	RBI	GW	TBB	IBB	SO	HBP	SH	SF	SB	CS	SB%	GDP	Avg	OBP	SLG	Pos	G	PO	A	E	DP	FPct
1981 KC	33	1	0	0	0	0	0	0	0	0	0	0	0	0	0	0	0	0	0	—	0	—	—	—	—						
LCS		Batting																							Fielding						
Year Tm	Age	G	AB	H	2B	3B	HR	TB	R	RBI	GW	TBB	IBB	SO	HBP	SH	SF	SB	CS	SB%	GDP	Avg	OBP	SLG	Pos	G	PO	A	E	DP	FPct
1972 Cin	24	5	20	2	0	0	1	5	2	1	0	0	0	2	0	0	0	0	0	—	0	.100	.100	.250	OF	5	9	1	0	1	1.000
1973 Cin	25	4	15	1	0	0	0	1	0	0	0	0	0	7	0	0	0	0	0	—	0	.067	.067	.067	OF	4	12	1	0	0	1.000
1975 Cin	27	3	10	0	0	0	0	0	0	1	0	1	0	7	0	0	1	0	0	—	0	.000	.083	.000	OF	3	13	0	0	0	1.000
1976 Cin	28	3	11	2	0	1	0	4	0	2	0	1	0	3	0	0	0	0	1	.00	0	.182	.250	.364	OF	3	10	0	0	0	1.000
1979 Cin	31	2	7	1	0	0	0	1	0	0	0	0	0	5	0	1	0	0	0	—	0	.143	.143	.143	OF	2	8	0	1	0	.889
LCS Totals		17	63	6	0	1	1	11	2	4	0	2	0	24	0	1	1	0	1	.00	0	.095	.121	.175	OF	17	52	2	1	1	.982
World Series		Batting																							Fielding						
Year Tm	Age	G	AB	H	2B	3B	HR	TB	R	RBI	GW	TBB	IBB	SO	HBP	SH	SF	SB	CS	SB%	GDP	Avg	OBP	SLG	Pos	G	PO	A	E	DP	FPct
1972 Cin	24	6	19	3	0	0	0	3	1	3	1	1	0	4	0	0	0	1	0	1.00	0	.158	.200	.158	OF	6	9	0	0	0	1.000
1975 Cin	27	7	25	7	0	1	2	15	3	3	0	3	3	5	0	1	0	0	0	—	1	.280	.357	.600	OF	7	23	1	0	1	1.000
1976 Cin	28	4	13	4	2	0	0	6	3	1	0	2	0	2	0	0	0	2	0	1.00	1	.308	.400	.462	OF	4	12	0	1	0	.923
WS Totals		17	57	14	2	1	2	24	7	7	1	6	3	11	0	1	0	3	0	1.00	2	.246	.317	.421	OF	17	44	1	1	1	.978
Postseason Totals		35	120	20	2	2	3	35	9	11	1	8	3	35	0	2	1	3	1	.75	2	.167	.217	.292	OF	34	96	3	2	2	.980

DOC GESSLER—Harry Homer Gessler—Nickname: Brownie—Bats: Left; Throws: Right

Ht: 5'10"; Wt: 180 lbs; Born: 12/23/1880 in Greensburg, Pennsylvania; Debut: 4/23/1903; Died: 12/25/1924

World Series		Batting																							Fielding						
Year Tm	Age	G	AB	H	2B	3B	HR	TB	R	RBI	GW	TBB	IBB	SO	HBP	SH	SF	SB	CS	SB%	GDP	Avg	OBP	SLG	Pos	G	PO	A	E	DP	FPct
1906 ChN	25	2	1	0	0	0	0	0	0	0	0	1	0	0	0	0	0	0	0	—	0	.000	.500	.000	—						

GUS GETZ—Gustave Getz—Nickname: Gee-Gee—Bats: Right; Throws: Right

Ht: 5'11"; Wt: 165 lbs; Born: 8/3/1889 in Pittsburgh, Pennsylvania; Debut: 8/15/1909; Died: 5/28/1969

World Series		Batting																							Fielding						
Year Tm	Age	G	AB	H	2B	3B	HR	TB	R	RBI	GW	TBB	IBB	SO	HBP	SH	SF	SB	CS	SB%	GDP	Avg	OBP	SLG	Pos	G	PO	A	E	DP	FPct
1916 Bro	27	1	1	0	0	0	0	0	0	0	0	0	0	0	0	0	0	0	0	—	0	.000	.000	.000	—						

JOE GIBBON—Joseph Charles Gibbon—Throws: Left; Bats: Right

Ht: 6'4"; Wt: 200 lbs; Born: 4/10/1935 in Hickory, Mississippi; Debut: 4/17/1960

LCS		Pitching																									
Year Tm	Age	G	GS	CG	GF	IP	BFP	H	R	ER	HR	SH	SF	HB	TBB	IBB	SO	WP	Bk	W	L	Pct	ShO	Sv-Op	Hld	OAvg	OOBP	ERA
1970 Pit	35	2	0	0	1	0.1	2	1	0	0	0	0	0	0	0	0	1	0	0	0	0	—	0	0- 0	0	.500	.500	0.00
World Series		Pitching																										
Year Tm	Age	G	GS	CG	GF	IP	BFP	H	R	ER	HR	SH	SF	HB	TBB	IBB	SO	WP	Bk	W	L	Pct	ShO	Sv-Op	Hld	OAvg	OOBP	ERA
1960 Pit	25	2	0	0	1	3.0	14	4	3	3	1	0	0	0	1	0	2	0	0	0	0	—	0	0- 0	0	.308	.357	9.00
Postseason Totals		4	0	0	2	3.1	32	5	3	3	1	0	0	0	1	0	3	0	0	0	0	—	0	0-0	0	.333	.375	8.10

LCS — Batting / Fielding

Year Tm	Age	G	AB	H	2B	3B	HR	TB	R	RBI	GW	TBB	IBB	SO	HBP	SH	SF	SB	CS	SB%	GDP	Avg	OBP	SLG	Pos	G	PO	A	E	DP	FPct
1970 Pit	35	2	0	0	0	0	0	0	0	0	0	0	0	0	0	0	0	0	0	—	0	—	—	—	P	2	0	0	0	0	—

World Series — Batting / Fielding

Year Tm	Age	G	AB	H	2B	3B	HR	TB	R	RBI	GW	TBB	IBB	SO	HBP	SH	SF	SB	CS	SB%	GDP	Avg	OBP	SLG	Pos	G	PO	A	E	DP	FPct
1960 Pit	25	2	0	0	0	0	0	0	0	0	0	0	0	0	0	0	0	0	0	—	0	—	—	—	P	2	1	0	0	0	1.000
Postseason Totals		4	0	0	0	0	0	0	0	0	0	0	0	0	0	0	0	0	0	—	0	—	—	—	P	4	1	0	0	0	1.000

BOB GIBSON (HOF 1981-W)—Pack Robert Gibson—Throws: Right; Bats: Right

Ht: 6'1"; Wt: 189 lbs; Born: 11/9/1935 in Omaha, Nebraska; Debut: 4/15/1959

World Series — Pitching

Year Tm	Age	G	GS	CG	GF	IP	BFP	H	R	ER	HR	SH	SF	HB	TBB	IBB	SO	WP	Bk	W	L	Pct	ShO	Sv-Op	Hld	OAvg	OOBP	ERA
1964 StL	28	3	3	2	0	27.0	113	23	11	9	4	0	1	2	8	2	31	1	0	2	1	.667	0	0- 0	0	.225	.292	3.00
1967 StL	31	3	3	3	0	27.0	98	14	3	3	1	2	0	0	5	0	26	1	0	3	0	1.000	1	0- 0	0	.154	.198	1.00
1968 StL-*MC*	32	3	3	3	0	27.0	101	18	5	5	1	0	0	0	4	1	35	0	0	2	1	.667	1	0- 0	0	.186	.218	1.67
WS Totals		9	9	8	0	81.0	624	55	19	17	6	2	1	2	17	3	92	2	0	7	2	.778	2	0-0	0	.190	.239	1.89

World Series — Batting / Fielding

Year Tm	Age	G	AB	H	2B	3B	HR	TB	R	RBI	GW	TBB	IBB	SO	HBP	SH	SF	SB	CS	SB%	GDP	Avg	OBP	SLG	Pos	G	PO	A	E	DP	FPct
1964 StL	28	3	9	2	0	0	0	2	1	0	0	0	0	3	0	1	0	0	0	—	0	.222	.222	.222	P	3	1	2	0	0	1.000
1967 StL	31	3	11	1	0	0	1	4	1	1	0	1	0	2	0	0	0	0	0	—	1	.091	.167	.364	P	3	2	3	0	0	1.000
1968 StL	32	3	8	1	0	0	1	4	2	2	0	1	0	2	0	1	0	0	0	—	0	.125	.222	.500	P	3	2	0	0	0	1.000
WS Totals		9	28	4	0	0	2	10	4	3	0	2	0	7	0	2	0	0	0	—	1	.143	.200	.357	P	9	5	5	0	0	1.000

GEORGE GIBSON—George C. Gibson—Nickname: Moon—Bats: Right; Throws: Right

Ht: 5'11"; Wt: 190 lbs; Born: 7/22/1880 in London, Ontario; Debut: 7/2/1905; Died: 1/25/1967

World Series — Batting / Fielding

Year Tm	Age	G	AB	H	2B	3B	HR	TB	R	RBI	GW	TBB	IBB	SO	HBP	SH	SF	SB	CS	SB%	GDP	Avg	OBP	SLG	Pos	G	PO	A	E	DP	FPct
1909 Pit	29	7	25	6	2	0	0	8	2	2	1	1	0	1	0	0	0	2	1	.67	1	.240	.269	.320	C	7	28	9	0	1	1.000

KIRK GIBSON—Kirk Harold Gibson—Bats: Left; Throws: Left

Ht: 6'3"; Wt: 215 lbs; Born: 5/28/1957 in Pontiac, Michigan; Debut: 9/8/1979

LCS — Batting / Fielding

Year Tm	Age	G	AB	H	2B	3B	HR	TB	R	RBI	GW	TBB	IBB	SO	HBP	SH	SF	SB	CS	SB%	GDP	Avg	OBP	SLG	Pos	G	PO	A	E	DP	FPct
1984 Det	27	3	12	5	1	0	1	9	2	2	0	2	0	1	0	0	0	1	0	1.00	0	.417	.500	.750	OF	3	7	0	0	0	1.000
1987 Det	30	5	21	6	1	0	1	10	4	4	0	3	0	8	0	0	0	3	0	1.00	0	.286	.375	.476	OF	5	10	1	0	0	1.000
1988 LA-*M*	31	7	26	4	0	0	2	10	2	6	2	3	2	6	0	0	1	2	0	1.00	0	.154	.233	.385	OF	7	17	1	1	0	.947
LCS Totals		15	59	15	2	0	4	29	8	12	2	8	2	15	0	0	1	6	0	1.00	0	.254	.338	.492	OF	15	34	2	1	0	.973

World Series — Batting / Fielding

Year Tm	Age	G	AB	H	2B	3B	HR	TB	R	RBI	GW	TBB	IBB	SO	HBP	SH	SF	SB	CS	SB%	GDP	Avg	OBP	SLG	Pos	G	PO	A	E	DP	FPct
1984 Det	27	5	18	6	0	0	2	12	4	7	0	4	0	4	1	0	0	3	1	.75	0	.333	.478	.667	OF	5	5	1	2	0	.750
1988 LA-*M*	31	1	1	1	0	0	1	4	1	2	1	0	0	0	0	0	0	0	0	—	0	1.000	1.000	4.000	—						
WS Totals		6	19	7	0	0	3	16	5	9	1	4	0	4	1	0	0	3	1	.75	0	.368	.500	.842	OF	5	5	1	2	0	.750
Postseason Totals		21	78	22	2	0	7	45	13	21	3	12	2	19	1	0	1	9	1	.90	0	.282	.380	.577	OF	20	39	3	3	0	.933

RUSS GIBSON—John Russell Gibson—Bats: Right; Throws: Right

Ht: 6'1"; Wt: 195 lbs; Born: 5/6/1939 in Fall River, Massachusetts; Debut: 4/14/1967

World Series — Batting / Fielding

Year Tm	Age	G	AB	H	2B	3B	HR	TB	R	RBI	GW	TBB	IBB	SO	HBP	SH	SF	SB	CS	SB%	GDP	Avg	OBP	SLG	Pos	G	PO	A	E	DP	FPct
1967 Bos	28	2	2	0	0	0	0	0	0	0	0	0	0	2	0	0	0	0	0	—	0	.000	.000	.000	C	2	9	0	0	0	1.000

BILLY GILBERT—William Oliver Gilbert—Bats: Right; Throws: Right

Ht: 5'4"; Wt: 153 lbs; Born: 6/21/1876 in Tullytown, Pennsylvania; Debut: 4/25/1901; Died: 8/8/1927

World Series — Batting / Fielding

Year Tm	Age	G	AB	H	2B	3B	HR	TB	R	RBI	GW	TBB	IBB	SO	HBP	SH	SF	SB	CS	SB%	GDP	Avg	OBP	SLG	Pos	G	PO	A	E	DP	FPct
1905 NYG	29	5	17	4	0	0	0	4	1	2	2	0	0	2	0	0	0	1	1	.50	0	.235	.235	.235	2B	5	9	15	0	0	1.000

LARRY GILBERT—Lawrence William Gilbert—Bats: Left; Throws: Left

Ht: 5'9"; Wt: 158 lbs; Born: 12/3/1891 in New Orleans, Louisiana; Debut: 4/14/1914; Died: 2/17/1965

World Series — Batting / Fielding

Year Tm	Age	G	AB	H	2B	3B	HR	TB	R	RBI	GW	TBB	IBB	SO	HBP	SH	SF	SB	CS	SB%	GDP	Avg	OBP	SLG	Pos	G	PO	A	E	DP	FPct
1914 Bos	22	1	0	0	0	0	0	0	0	0	0	1	1	0	0	0	0	0	0	—	0	—	1.000	—	—						

BRIAN GILES—Brian Stephen Giles—Bats: Left; Throws: Left

Ht: 5'11"; Wt: 195 lbs; Born: 1/21/1971 in El Cajon, California; Debut: 9/16/1995

Division Series — Batting / Fielding

Year Tm	Age	G	AB	H	2B	3B	HR	TB	R	RBI	GW	TBB	IBB	SO	HBP	SH	SF	SB	CS	SB%	GDP	Avg	OBP	SLG	Pos	G	PO	A	E	DP	FPct
1996 Cle	25	1	1	0	0	0	0	0	0	0	0	0	0	1	0	0	0	0	0	—	0	.000	.000	.000	—						
1997 Cle	26	3	7	1	0	0	0	1	0	0	0	0	0	1	0	0	0	0	0	—	0	.143	.143	.143	OF	3	4	1	0	0	1.000
DS Totals		4	8	1	0	0	0	1	0	0	0	0	0	2	0	0	0	0	0	—	0	.125	.125	.125	OF	3	4	1	0	0	1.000

LCS — Batting / Fielding

Year Tm	Age	G	AB	H	2B	3B	HR	TB	R	RBI	GW	TBB	IBB	SO	HBP	SH	SF	SB	CS	SB%	GDP	Avg	OBP	SLG	Pos	G	PO	A	E	DP	FPct
1997 Cle	26	6	16	3	3	0	0	6	1	0	0	2	0	6	0	0	0	0	0	—	0	.188	.278	.375	OF	6	9	0	0	0	1.000

World Series — Batting / Fielding

Year Tm	Age	G	AB	H	2B	3B	HR	TB	R	RBI	GW	TBB	IBB	SO	HBP	SH	SF	SB	CS	SB%	GDP	Avg	OBP	SLG	Pos	G	PO	A	E	DP	FPct
1997 Cle	26	5	4	2	1	0	0	3	1	2	0	4	0	1	0	0	0	0	1	.00	0	.500	.750	.750	OF	2	2	0	0	0	1.000
Postseason Totals		15	28	6	4	0	0	10	2	2	0	6	0	9	0	0	0	0	1	.00	0	.214	.353	.357	OF	11	15	1	0	0	1.000

PAUL GILLESPIE—Paul Allen Gillespie—Bats: Left; Throws: Right

Ht: 6'3"; Wt: 195 lbs; Born: 9/18/1920 in Cartersville, Georgia; Debut: 9/11/1942; Died: 8/11/1970

World Series — Batting / Fielding

Year Tm	Age	G	AB	H	2B	3B	HR	TB	R	RBI	GW	TBB	IBB	SO	HBP	SH	SF	SB	CS	SB%	GDP	Avg	OBP	SLG	Pos	G	PO	A	E	DP	FPct
1945 ChN	25	3	6	0	0	0	0	0	0	0	0	0	0	0	0	0	0	0	0	—	0	.000	.000	.000	C	1	3	0	0	0	1.000

JIM GILLIAM—James William Gilliam—Nickname: Junior—Bats: Both; Throws: Right

Ht: 5'10"; Wt: 175 lbs; Born: 10/17/1928 in Nashville, Tennessee; Debut: 4/14/1953; Died: 10/8/1978

World Series — Batting / Fielding

Year Tm	Age	G	AB	H	2B	3B	HR	TB	R	RBI	GW	TBB	IBB	SO	HBP	SH	SF	SB	CS	SB%	GDP	Avg	OBP	SLG	Pos	G	PO	A	E	DP	FPct
1953 Bro-*RY*	24	6	27	8	3	0	2	17	4	4	0	0	0	2	1	0	0	0	1	.00	0	.296	.321	.630	2B	6	15	16	1	3	.969
1955 Bro	26	7	24	7	1	0	0	8	2	3	1	8	0	1	0	0	0	1	1	.50	1	.292	.469	.333	2B	5	4	12	0	4	1.000
																									OF	4	4	1	0	0	1.000
1956 Bro	27	7	24	2	0	0	0	2	2	2	0	7	0	3	0	0	0	1	1	.50	1	.083	.290	.083	2B	6	17	17	0	4	1.000
																									OF	1	2	0	0	0	1.000
1959 LA	30	6	25	6	0	0	0	6	2	0	0	2	0	2	0	0	0	2	0	1.00	0	.240	.296	.240	3B	6	4	10	0	1	1.000
1963 LA	34	4	13	2	0	0	0	2	3	0	0	3	0	1	0	0	0	0	1	.00	2	.154	.313	.154	3B	4	2	2	0	0	1.000
1965 LA	36	7	28	6	1	0	0	7	2	2	1	1	0	0	1	0	0	0	0	—	0	.214	.267	.250	3B	7	4	6	2	0	.833
1966 LA	37	2	6	0	0	0	0	0	0	1	0	2	0	0	0	0	0	0	0	—	0	.000	.250	.000	3B	2	3	4	1	1	.875
WS Totals		39	147	31	5	0	2	42	15	12	2	23	0	9	2	0	0	4	4	.50	4	.211	.326	.286	3B	19	13	22	3	2	.921

AL GIONFRIDDO—Albert Francis Gionfriddo—Nickname: The Little Italian—Bats: Left; Throws: Left

Ht: 5'6"; Wt: 165 lbs; Born: 3/8/1922 in Dysart, Pennsylvania; Debut: 9/23/1944

World Series — Batting / Fielding

Year Tm	Age	G	AB	H	2B	3B	HR	TB	R	RBI	GW	TBB	IBB	SO	HBP	SH	SF	SB	CS	SB%	GDP	Avg	OBP	SLG	Pos	G	PO	A	E	DP	FPct
1947 Bro	25	4	3	0	0	0	0	0	2	0	0	1	0	0	0	0	0	1	0	1.00	0	.000	.250	.000	OF	1	1	0	0	0	1.000

JOE GIRARDI—Joseph Elliott Girardi—Bats: Right; Throws: Right

Ht: 5'11"; Wt: 195 lbs; Born: 10/14/1964 in Peoria, Illinois; Debut: 4/4/1989

Division Series		Batting																							Fielding						
Year Tm	Age	G	AB	H	2B	3B	HR	TB	R	RBI	GW	TBB	IBB	SO	HBP	SH	SF	SB	CS	SB%	GDP	Avg	OBP	SLG	Pos	G	PO	A	E	DP	FPct
1995 Col	30	4	16	2	0	0	0	2	0	0	0	0	0	2	0	0	0	0	0	—	2	.125	.125	.125	C	4	25	3	1	2	.966
1996 NYA	31	4	9	2	0	0	0	2	1	0	0	4	0	1	0	0	0	0	0	—	0	.222	.462	.222	C	4	28	1	0	1	1.000
1997 NYA	32	5	15	2	0	0	0	2	2	0	0	1	0	3	0	1	0	0	0	—	3	.133	.188	.133	C	5	21	2	0	0	1.000
DS Totals		13	40	6	0	0	0	6	3	0	0	5	0	6	0	1	0	0	0	—	5	.150	.244	.150	C	13	74	6	1	3	.988
LCS		Batting																							Fielding						
Year Tm	Age	G	AB	H	2B	3B	HR	TB	R	RBI	GW	TBB	IBB	SO	HBP	SH	SF	SB	CS	SB%	GDP	Avg	OBP	SLG	Pos	G	PO	A	E	DP	FPct
1989 ChN	24	4	10	1	0	0	0	1	1	0	0	1	0	2	0	1	0	0	0	—	1	.100	.182	.100	C	4	20	0	0	0	1.000
1996 NYA	31	4	12	3	0	1	0	5	1	0	0	1	0	3	0	0	0	0	0	—	1	.250	.308	.417	C	4	22	0	0	0	1.000
LCS Totals		8	22	4	0	1	0	6	2	0	0	2	0	5	0	1	0	0	0	—	2	.182	.250	.273	C	8	42	0	0	0	1.000
World Series		Batting																							Fielding						
Year Tm	Age	G	AB	H	2B	3B	HR	TB	R	RBI	GW	TBB	IBB	SO	HBP	SH	SF	SB	CS	SB%	GDP	Avg	OBP	SLG	Pos	G	PO	A	E	DP	FPct
1996 NYA	31	4	10	2	0	1	0	4	1	1	1	1	0	2	0	1	0	0	0	—	0	.200	.273	.400	C	4	23	4	0	0	1.000
Postseason Totals		25	72	12	0	2	0	16	6	1	1	8	0	13	0	3	0	0	0	—	7	.167	.250	.222	C	25	139	10	1	3	.993

DAVE GIUSTI—David John Giusti—Throws: Right; Bats: Right

Ht: 5'11"; Wt: 190 lbs; Born: 11/27/1939 in Seneca Falls, New York; Debut: 4/13/1962

LCS		Pitching																										
Year Tm	Age	G	GS	CG	GF	IP	BFP	H	R	ER	HR	SH	SF	HB	TBB	IBB	SO	WP	Bk	W	L	Pct	ShO	Sv-Op	Hld	OAvg	OOBP	ERA
1970 Pit	30	2	0	0	2	2.1	10	3	1	1	0	0	0	0	1	1	1	0	0	0	0	—	0	0- 0	0	.333	.400	3.86
1971 Pit	31	4	0	0	4	5.1	19	1	0	0	0	0	0	0	2	1	3	0	0	0	0	—	0	3- 3	0	.059	.158	0.00
1972 Pit	32	3	0	0	2	2.2	13	5	2	2	1	0	0	0	0	0	3	0	0	0	1	.000	0	1- 2	0	.385	.385	6.75
1974 Pit	34	3	0	0	1	3.1	28	13	8	8	0	1	0	0	5	4	1	0	0	0	1	.000	0	0- 0	0	.591	.667	21.60
1975 Pit	35	1	0	0	0	1.1	4	0	0	0	0	0	0	0	0	0	1	0	0	0	0	—	0	0- 0	0	.000	.000	0.00
LCS Totals		13	0	0	9	15.0	148	22	11	11	1	1	0	0	8	6	9	0	0	0	2	.000	0	4-5	0	.338	.411	6.60
World Series		Pitching																										
Year Tm	Age	G	GS	CG	GF	IP	BFP	H	R	ER	HR	SH	SF	HB	TBB	IBB	SO	WP	Bk	W	L	Pct	ShO	Sv-Op	Hld	OAvg	OOBP	ERA
1971 Pit	31	3	0	0	2	5.1	21	3	0	0	0	0	0	0	2	0	4	0	0	0	0	—	0	1- 2	0	.158	.238	0.00
Postseason Totals		16	0	0	11	20.1	190	25	11	11	1	1	0	0	10	6	13	0	0	0	2	.000	0	5-7	0	.298	.372	4.87

LCS		Batting																							Fielding						
Year Tm	Age	G	AB	H	2B	3B	HR	TB	R	RBI	GW	TBB	IBB	SO	HBP	SH	SF	SB	CS	SB%	GDP	Avg	OBP	SLG	Pos	G	PO	A	E	DP	FPct
1970 Pit	30	2	0	0	0	0	0	0	0	0	0	0	0	0	0	0	0	0	0	—	0	—	—	—	P	2	1	0	0	0	1.000
1971 Pit	31	4	1	0	0	0	0	0	0	0	0	0	0	0	0	0	0	0	0	—	0	.000	.000	.000	P	4	0	1	0	0	1.000
1972 Pit	32	3	1	0	0	0	0	0	0	0	0	0	0	0	0	0	0	0	0	—	0	.000	.000	.000	P	3	0	1	0	0	1.000
1974 Pit	34	3	0	0	0	0	0	0	0	0	0	0	0	0	0	0	0	0	0	—	0	—	—	—	P	3	1	2	0	0	1.000
1975 Pit	35	1	0	0	0	0	0	0	0	0	0	0	0	0	0	0	0	0	0	—	0	—	—	—	P	1	0	0	0	0	—
LCS Totals		13	2	0	0	0	0	0	0	0	0	0	0	0	0	0	0	0	0	—	0	.000	.000	.000	P	13	2	4	0	0	1.000
World Series		Batting																							Fielding						
Year Tm	Age	G	AB	H	2B	3B	HR	TB	R	RBI	GW	TBB	IBB	SO	HBP	SH	SF	SB	CS	SB%	GDP	Avg	OBP	SLG	Pos	G	PO	A	E	DP	FPct
1971 Pit	31	3	0	0	0	0	0	0	0	0	0	0	0	0	0	0	0	0	0	—	0	—	—	—	P	3	0	0	0	0	—
Postseason Totals		16	2	0	0	0	0	0	0	0	0	0	0	0	0	0	0	0	0	—	0	.000	.000	.000	P	16	2	4	0	0	1.000

DAN GLADDEN—Clinton Daniel Gladden—Bats: Right; Throws: Right

Ht: 5'11"; Wt: 180 lbs; Born: 7/7/1957 in San Jose, California; Debut: 9/5/1983

LCS		Batting																							Fielding						
Year Tm	Age	G	AB	H	2B	3B	HR	TB	R	RBI	GW	TBB	IBB	SO	HBP	SH	SF	SB	CS	SB%	GDP	Avg	OBP	SLG	Pos	G	PO	A	E	DP	FPct
1987 Min	30	5	20	7	2	0	0	9	5	5	0	2	1	1	2	0	0	0	1	.00	0	.350	.458	.450	OF	5	12	0	0	0	1.000
1991 Min	34	5	23	6	0	0	0	6	4	3	0	1	0	3	0	0	0	3	0	1.00	1	.261	.292	.261	OF	5	20	0	0	0	1.000
LCS Totals		10	43	13	2	0	0	15	9	8	0	3	1	4	2	0	0	3	1	.75	1	.302	.375	.349	OF	10	32	0	0	0	1.000
World Series		Batting																							Fielding						
Year Tm	Age	G	AB	H	2B	3B	HR	TB	R	RBI	GW	TBB	IBB	SO	HBP	SH	SF	SB	CS	SB%	GDP	Avg	OBP	SLG	Pos	G	PO	A	E	DP	FPct
1987 Min	30	7	31	9	2	1	1	16	3	7	0	3	0	4	0	0	0	2	0	1.00	0	.290	.353	.516	OF	7	12	0	0	0	1.000
1991 Min	34	7	30	7	2	2	0	13	5	0	0	3	0	4	0	0	0	2	1	.67	1	.233	.303	.433	OF	7	25	1	1	0	.963
WS Totals		14	61	16	4	3	1	29	8	7	0	6	0	8	0	0	0	4	1	.80	1	.262	.328	.475	OF	14	37	1	1	0	.974
Postseason Totals		24	104	29	6	3	1	44	17	15	0	9	1	12	2	0	0	7	2	.78	2	.279	.348	.423	OF	24	69	1	1	0	.986

TOM GLAVINE—Thomas Michael Glavine—Throws: Left; Bats: Left

Ht: 6'0"; Wt: 175 lbs; Born: 3/25/1966 in Concord, Massachusetts; Debut: 8/17/1987

Division Series		Pitching																										
Year Tm	Age	G	GS	CG	GF	IP	BFP	H	R	ER	HR	SH	SF	HB	TBB	IBB	SO	WP	Bk	W	L	Pct	ShO	Sv-Op	Hld	OAvg	OOBP	ERA
1995 Atl	29	1	1	0	0	7.0	28	5	3	2	1	0	0	0	1	0	3	0	0	0	0	—	0	0- 0	0	.185	.214	2.57
1996 Atl	30	1	1	0	0	6.2	26	5	1	1	0	0	0	0	3	0	7	0	0	1	0	1.000	0	0- 0	0	.217	.308	1.35
1997 Atl	31	1	1	0	0	6.0	28	5	3	3	0	0	0	0	5	0	4	0	0	1	0	1.000	0	0- 0	0	.217	.357	4.50
DS Totals		3	3	0	0	19.2	164	15	7	6	1	0	0	0	9	0	14	0	0	2	0	1.000	0	0-0	0	.205	.293	2.75
LCS		Pitching																										
Year Tm	Age	G	GS	CG	GF	IP	BFP	H	R	ER	HR	SH	SF	HB	TBB	IBB	SO	WP	Bk	W	L	Pct	ShO	Sv-Op	Hld	OAvg	OOBP	ERA
1991 Atl-*C*	25	2	2	0	0	14.0	59	12	5	5	1	0	0	0	6	2	11	0	0	0	2	.000	0	0- 0	0	.226	.305	3.21
1992 Atl	26	2	2	0	0	7.1	40	13	11	10	3	1	0	2	3	1	2	0	0	0	2	.000	0	0- 0	0	.382	.462	12.27
1993 Atl	27	1	1	0	0	7.0	27	6	2	2	1	0	0	0	0	0	5	0	0	1	0	1.000	0	0- 0	0	.222	.222	2.57
1995 Atl	29	1	1	0	0	7.0	27	7	1	1	0	0	0	1	2	1	5	0	0	0	0	—	0	0- 0	0	.292	.370	1.29
1996 Atl	30	2	2	0	0	13.0	47	10	3	3	2	0	0	1	0	0	9	0	0	1	1	.500	0	0- 0	0	.217	.234	2.08
1997 Atl	31	2	2	0	0	13.1	62	13	8	8	0	2	0	1	11	3	9	0	0	1	1	.500	0	0- 0	0	.271	.417	5.40
LCS Totals		10	10	0	0	61.2	524	61	30	29	7	3	0	5	22	7	41	0	0	3	6	.333	0	0-0	0	.263	.340	4.23
World Series		Pitching																										
Year Tm	Age	G	GS	CG	GF	IP	BFP	H	R	ER	HR	SH	SF	HB	TBB	IBB	SO	WP	Bk	W	L	Pct	ShO	Sv-Op	Hld	OAvg	OOBP	ERA
1991 Atl-*C*	25	2	2	1	0	13.1	54	8	6	4	2	1	0	0	7	0	8	0	1	1	1	.500	0	0- 0	0	.174	.283	2.70
1992 Atl	26	2	2	2	0	17.0	61	10	3	3	2	0	0	0	4	0	8	0	0	1	1	.500	0	0- 0	0	.175	.230	1.59
1995 Atl	29	2	2	0	0	14.0	52	4	2	2	1	0	0	0	6	0	11	1	0	2	0	1.000	0	0- 0	0	.087	.192	1.29
1996 Atl	30	1	1	0	0	7.0	28	4	2	1	0	2	0	0	3	0	8	0	0	0	1	.000	0	0- 0	0	.174	.269	1.29
WS Totals		7	7	3	0	51.1	390	26	13	10	5	3	0	0	20	0	35	1	1	4	3	.571	0	0-0	0	.151	.240	1.75
Postseason Totals		20	20	3	0	132.2	1078	102	50	45	13	6	0	5	51	7	90	1	1	9	9	.500	0	0-0	0	.214	.296	3.05

Division Series		Batting																							Fielding						
Year Tm	Age	G	AB	H	2B	3B	HR	TB	R	RBI	GW	TBB	IBB	SO	HBP	SH	SF	SB	CS	SB%	GDP	Avg	OBP	SLG	Pos	G	PO	A	E	DP	FPct
1995 Atl	29	1	3	1	0	0	0	1	0	0	0	0	0	1	0	0	0	0	0	—	0	.333	.333	.333	P	1	1	1	0	0	1.000
1996 Atl	30	1	2	1	1	0	0	2	1	0	0	0	0	0	0	1	0	0	0	—	0	.500	.500	1.000	P	1	0	1	0	0	1.000
1997 Atl	31	1	3	2	0	0	0	2	2	0	0	0	0	0	0	0	0	0	0	—	0	.667	.667	.667	P	1	1	1	0	0	1.000
DS Totals		3	8	4	1	0	0	5	3	0	0	0	0	1	0	1	0	0	0	—	0	.500	.500	.625	P	3	2	3	0	0	1.000
LCS		Batting																							Fielding						
Year Tm	Age	G	AB	H	2B	3B	HR	TB	R	RBI	GW	TBB	IBB	SO	HBP	SH	SF	SB	CS	SB%	GDP	Avg	OBP	SLG	Pos	G	PO	A	E	DP	FPct
1991 Atl	25	2	4	1	0	0	0	1	0	0	0	0	0	2	0	0	0	0	0	—	0	.250	.250	.250	P	2	1	3	0	0	1.000
1992 Atl	26	2	2	0	0	0	0	0	0	0	0	0	0	0	0	0	0	0	0	—	0	.000	.000	.000	P	2	1	2	0	0	1.000
1993 Atl	27	1	3	0	0	0	0	0	0	0	0	0	0	0	0	0	0	0	0	—	0	.000	.000	.000	P	1	0	3	0	0	1.000
1995 Atl	29	1	1	0	0	0	0	0	0	0	0	1	0	0	0	0	0	0	0	—	0	.000	.500	.000	P	1	0	1	0	1	1.000
1996 Atl	30	2	6	1	0	1	0	3	0	3	0	0	0	3	0	0	0	0	0	—	0	.167	.167	.500	P	2	0	3	0	1	1.000
1997 Atl	31	2	3	1	0	0	0	1	0	0	0	0	0	2	0	2	0	0	0	—	0	.333	.333	.333	P	2	0	5	0	0	1.000
LCS Totals		10	19	3	0	1	0	5	0	3	0	1	0	7	0	2	0	0	0	—	0	.158	.200	.263	P	10	2	17	0	2	1.000
World Series		Batting																							Fielding						
Year Tm	Age	G	AB	H	2B	3B	HR	TB	R	RBI	GW	TBB	IBB	SO	HBP	SH	SF	SB	CS	SB%	GDP	Avg	OBP	SLG	Pos	G	PO	A	E	DP	FPct
1991 Atl	25	2	2	0	0	0	0	0	0	0	0	0	0	0	0	0	0	0	0	—	0	.000	.000	.000	P	2	0	3	0	1	1.000
1992 Atl	26	2	2	0	0	0	0	0	0	0	0	1	0	0	0	0	0	0	0	—	0	.000	.333	.000	P	2	0	2	0	0	1.000
1995 Atl	29	2	4	0	0	0	0	0	0	0	0	1	0	2	0	0	0	0	0	—	0	.000	.200	.000	P	2	1	3	0	0	1.000
1996 Atl	30	1	1	0	0	0	0	0	1	0	0	1	0	0	0	0	0	0	0	—	0	.000	.500	.000	P	1	0	2	0	0	1.000
WS Totals		7	9	0	0	0	0	0	1	0	0	3	0	2	0	0	0	0	0	—	0	.000	.250	.000	P	7	1	10	0	1	1.000
Postseason Totals		20	36	7	1	1	0	10	4	3	0	4	0	10	0	3	0	0	0	—	0	.194	.275	.278	P	20	5	30	0	3	1.000

BILL GLYNN—William Vincent Glynn—Bats: Left; Throws: Left

Ht: 6'0"; Wt: 190 lbs; Born: 7/30/1925 in Sussex, New Jersey; Debut: 9/16/1949

World Series		Batting																							Fielding						
Year Tm	Age	G	AB	H	2B	3B	HR	TB	R	RBI	GW	TBB	IBB	SO	HBP	SH	SF	SB	CS	SB%	GDP	Avg	OBP	SLG	Pos	G	PO	A	E	DP	FPct
1954 Cle	29	2	2	1	1	0	0	2	1	0	0	0	0	1	0	0	0	0	0	—	0	.500	.500	1.000	1B	1	0	0	0	0	—

MIKE GOLIAT—Mike Mitchell Goliat—Bats: Right; Throws: Right

Ht: 6'0"; Wt: 180 lbs; Born: 11/5/1925 in Yatesboro, Pennsylvania; Debut: 8/3/1949

World Series		Batting																							Fielding						
Year Tm	Age	G	AB	H	2B	3B	HR	TB	R	RBI	GW	TBB	IBB	SO	HBP	SH	SF	SB	CS	SB%	GDP	Avg	OBP	SLG	Pos	G	PO	A	E	DP	FPct
1950 Phi	24	4	14	3	0	0	0	3	1	1	0	1	1	2	0	0	0	0	0	—	1	.214	.267	.214	2B	4	13	9	1	0	.957

DAVE GOLTZ—David Allan Goltz—Throws: Right; Bats: Right

Ht: 6'4"; Wt: 200 lbs; Born: 6/23/1949 in Pelican Rapids, Minnesota; Debut: 7/18/1972

LCS		Pitching																									
Year Tm	Age	G	GS	CG	GF	IP	BFP	H	R	ER	HR	SH	SF	HB	TBB	IBB	SO	WP	Bk	W	L	Pct	ShO	Sv-Op	Hld	OAvg	OOBP	ERA
1982 Cal	33	1	0	0	0	3.2	16	4	3	3	1	1	0	0	2	0	2	0	0	0	0	—	0	0-0	0	.308	.400	7.36
World Series		Pitching																										
Year Tm	Age	G	GS	CG	GF	IP	BFP	H	R	ER	HR	SH	SF	HB	TBB	IBB	SO	WP	Bk	W	L	Pct	ShO	Sv-Op	Hld	OAvg	OOBP	ERA
1981 LA	32	2	0	0	0	3.1	15	4	2	2	1	0	1	0	1	0	2	0	0	0	0	—	0	0-0	0	.308	.333	5.40
Postseason Totals		3	0	0	0	7.0	62	8	5	5	2	1	1	0	3	0	4	0	0	0	0	—	0	0-0	0	.308	.367	6.43

LCS		Batting																							Fielding						
Year Tm	Age	G	AB	H	2B	3B	HR	TB	R	RBI	GW	TBB	IBB	SO	HBP	SH	SF	SB	CS	SB%	GDP	Avg	OBP	SLG	Pos	G	PO	A	E	DP	FPct
1982 Cal	33	1	0	0	0	0	0	0	0	0	0	0	0	0	0	0	0	0	0	—	0	—	—	—	P	1	0	0	0	0	—
World Series		Batting																							Fielding						
Year Tm	Age	G	AB	H	2B	3B	HR	TB	R	RBI	GW	TBB	IBB	SO	HBP	SH	SF	SB	CS	SB%	GDP	Avg	OBP	SLG	Pos	G	PO	A	E	DP	FPct
1981 LA	32	2	0	0	0	0	0	0	0	0	0	0	0	0	0	0	0	0	0	—	0	—	—	—	P	2	0	0	0	0	—
Postseason Totals		3	0	0	0	0	0	0	0	0	0	0	0	0	0	0	0	0	0	—	0	—	—	—	P	3	0	0	0	0	—

CHRIS GOMEZ—Christopher Cory Gomez—Bats: Right; Throws: Right

Ht: 6'1"; Wt: 183 lbs; Born: 6/16/1971 in Los Angeles, California; Debut: 7/19/1993

Division Series		Batting																							Fielding						
Year Tm	Age	G	AB	H	2B	3B	HR	TB	R	RBI	GW	TBB	IBB	SO	HBP	SH	SF	SB	CS	SB%	GDP	Avg	OBP	SLG	Pos	G	PO	A	E	DP	FPct
1996 SD	25	3	12	2	0	0	0	2	0	1	0	0	0	4	0	0	0	0	0	—	0	.167	.167	.167	SS	3	8	5	0	3	1.000

LEFTY GOMEZ (HOF 1972-V)—Vernon Louis Gomez—Nickname: Goofy—Throws: Left; Bats: Left

Ht: 6'2"; Wt: 173 lbs; Born: 11/26/1908 in Rodeo, California; Debut: 4/29/1930; Died: 2/17/1989

World Series		Pitching																									
Year Tm	Age	G	GS	CG	GF	IP	BFP	H	R	ER	HR	SH	SF	HB	TBB	IBB	SO	WP	Bk	W	L	Pct	ShO	Sv-Op	Hld	OAvg	OOBP	ERA
1932 NYA	23	1	1	1	0	9.0	36	9	2	1	0	1	0	0	1	0	8	0	0	1	0	1.000	0	0-0	0	.265	.286	1.00
1936 NYA	27	2	2	1	0	15.1	72	14	8	7	1	2	0	0	11	0	9	1	0	2	0	1.000	0	0-0	0	.237	.357	4.11
1937 NYA	28	2	2	2	0	18.0	70	16	3	3	1	0	0	0	2	0	8	0	0	2	0	1.000	0	0-0	0	.235	.257	1.50
1938 NYA	29	1	1	0	0	7.0	29	9	3	3	0	1	0	0	1	0	5	0	0	1	0	1.000	0	0-0	0	.333	.357	3.86
1939 NYA	30	1	1	0	0	1.0	6	3	1	1	0	0	0	0	0	0	1	0	0	0	0	—	0	0-0	0	.500	.500	9.00
WS Totals		7	7	4	0	50.1	426	51	17	15	2	4	0	0	15	0	31	1	0	6	0	1.000	0	0-0	0	.263	.316	2.68

World Series		Batting																							Fielding						
Year Tm	Age	G	AB	H	2B	3B	HR	TB	R	RBI	GW	TBB	IBB	SO	HBP	SH	SF	SB	CS	SB%	GDP	Avg	OBP	SLG	Pos	G	PO	A	E	DP	FPct
1932 NYA	23	1	3	0	0	0	0	0	0	0	0	0	0	2	0	0	0	0	0	—	0	.000	.000	.000	P	1	0	3	0	0	1.000
1936 NYA	27	2	8	2	0	0	0	2	1	3	0	0	0	3	0	0	0	0	0	—	0	.250	.250	.250	P	2	0	3	0	0	1.000
1937 NYA	28	2	6	1	0	0	0	1	2	1	1	2	0	1	0	0	0	0	0	—	0	.167	.375	.167	P	2	1	3	0	0	1.000
1938 NYA	29	1	2	0	0	0	0	0	0	0	0	0	0	0	0	0	0	0	0	—	0	.000	.000	.000	P	1	0	1	0	0	1.000
1939 NYA	30	1	1	0	0	0	0	0	0	0	0	0	0	1	0	0	0	0	0	—	0	.000	.000	.000	P	1	0	0	0	0	—
WS Totals		7	20	3	0	0	0	3	3	4	1	2	0	7	0	0	0	0	0	—	0	.150	.227	.150	P	7	1	10	0	0	1.000

RUBEN GOMEZ—Nickname: El Divino Loco—Throws: Right; Bats: Right

Ht: 6'0"; Wt: 170 lbs; Born: 7/13/1927 in Arroyo, Puerto Rico; Debut: 4/17/1953

World Series		Pitching																									
Year Tm	Age	G	GS	CG	GF	IP	BFP	H	R	ER	HR	SH	SF	HB	TBB	IBB	SO	WP	Bk	W	L	Pct	ShO	Sv-Op	Hld	OAvg	OOBP	ERA
1954 NYG	27	1	1	0	0	7.1	29	4	2	2	1	1	0	0	3	0	2	0	0	1	0	1.000	0	0-0	0	.160	.250	2.45

World Series		Batting																							Fielding						
Year Tm	Age	G	AB	H	2B	3B	HR	TB	R	RBI	GW	TBB	IBB	SO	HBP	SH	SF	SB	CS	SB%	GDP	Avg	OBP	SLG	Pos	G	PO	A	E	DP	FPct
1954 NYG	27	1	4	0	0	0	0	0	0	0	0	0	0	2	0	0	0	0	0	—	0	.000	.000	.000	P	1	1	2	0	0	1.000

RENE GONZALES—Rene Adrian Gonzales—Bats: Right; Throws: Right

Ht: 6'3"; Wt: 180 lbs; Born: 9/3/1960 in Austin, Texas; Debut: 7/27/1984

Division Series		Batting																							Fielding						
Year Tm	Age	G	AB	H	2B	3B	HR	TB	R	RBI	GW	TBB	IBB	SO	HBP	SH	SF	SB	CS	SB%	GDP	Avg	OBP	SLG	Pos	G	PO	A	E	DP	FPct
1996 Tex	36	1	0	0	0	0	0	0	0	0	0	0	0	0	0	0	0	0	0	—	0	—	—	—	SS	1	0	0	0	0	—
LCS		Batting																							Fielding						
Year Tm	Age	G	AB	H	2B	3B	HR	TB	R	RBI	GW	TBB	IBB	SO	HBP	SH	SF	SB	CS	SB%	GDP	Avg	OBP	SLG	Pos	G	PO	A	E	DP	FPct
1991 Tor	31	2	0	0	0	0	0	0	0	0	0	0	0	0	0	0	0	0	0	—	0	—	—	—	1B	1	2	0	0	0	1.000
																									SS	1	0	0	0	0	—
Postseason Totals		3	0	0	0	0	0	0	0	0	0	0	0	0	0	0	0	0	0	—	0	—	—	—	SS	2	0	0	0	0	—

JOSE GONZALEZ—Jose Rafael Gonzalez—Bats: Right; Throws: Right

Ht: 6'2"; Wt: 190 lbs; Born: 11/23/1964 in Puerta Plata, Dominican Republic; Debut: 9/2/1985

LCS		Batting																							Fielding						
Year Tm	Age	G	AB	H	2B	3B	HR	TB	R	RBI	GW	TBB	IBB	SO	HBP	SH	SF	SB	CS	SB%	GDP	Avg	OBP	SLG	Pos	G	PO	A	E	DP	FPct
1988 LA	23	5	0	0	0	0	0	0	2	0	0	0	0	0	0	0	0	0	0	—	0	—	—	—	OF	4	3	0	0	0	1.000
World Series		Batting																							Fielding						
Year Tm	Age	G	AB	H	2B	3B	HR	TB	R	RBI	GW	TBB	IBB	SO	HBP	SH	SF	SB	CS	SB%	GDP	Avg	OBP	SLG	Pos	G	PO	A	E	DP	FPct
1988 LA	23	4	2	0	0	0	0	0	0	0	0	0	0	2	0	0	0	0	0	—	0	.000	.000	.000	OF	3	2	0	0	0	1.000
Postseason Totals		9	2	0	0	0	0	0	2	0	0	0	0	2	0	0	0	0	0	—	0	.000	.000	.000	OF	7	5	0	0	0	1.000

JUAN GONZALEZ—Juan Alberto Gonzalez—Nickname: Igor—Bats: Right; Throws: Right

Ht: 6'3"; Wt: 175 lbs; Born: 10/20/1969 in Arecibo, Puerto Rico; Debut: 9/1/1989

Division Series		Batting																							Fielding						
Year Tm	Age	G	AB	H	2B	3B	HR	TB	R	RBI	GW	TBB	IBB	SO	HBP	SH	SF	SB	CS	SB%	GDP	Avg	OBP	SLG	Pos	G	PO	A	E	DP	FPct
1996 Tex-*M*	26	4	16	7	0	0	5	22	5	9	1	3	1	2	0	0	0	0	0	—	0	.438	.526	1.375	OF	4	8	0	0	0	1.000

LUIS GONZALEZ—Luis Emilio Gonzalez—Bats: Left; Throws: Right

Ht: 6'2"; Wt: 180 lbs; Born: 9/3/1967 in Tampa, Florida; Debut: 9/4/1990

Division Series		Batting																							Fielding						
Year Tm	Age	G	AB	H	2B	3B	HR	TB	R	RBI	GW	TBB	IBB	SO	HBP	SH	SF	SB	CS	SB%	GDP	Avg	OBP	SLG	Pos	G	PO	A	E	DP	FPct
1997 Hou	30	3	12	4	0	0	0	4	0	0	0	0	0	1	0	0	0	0	0	—	0	.333	.333	.333	OF	3	13	1	1	0	.933

MIKE GONZALEZ—Miguel Angel Gonzalez—Bats: Right; Throws: Right

Ht: 6'1"; Wt: 200 lbs; Born: 9/24/1890 in Havana, Cuba; Debut: 9/28/1912; Died: 2/19/1977

World Series		Batting																							Fielding						
Year Tm	Age	G	AB	H	2B	3B	HR	TB	R	RBI	GW	TBB	IBB	SO	HBP	SH	SF	SB	CS	SB%	GDP	Avg	OBP	SLG	Pos	G	PO	A	E	DP	FPct
1929 ChN	39	2	1	0	0	0	0	0	0	0	0	0	0	1	0	0	0	0	0	—	0	.000	.000	.000	C	1	2	0	0	0	1.000

ORLANDO GONZALEZ—Orlando Eugene Gonzalez—Bats: Left; Throws: Left

Ht: 6'2"; Wt: 180 lbs; Born: 11/15/1951 in Havana, Cuba; Debut: 6/7/1976

LCS — Batting / Fielding

Year Tm	Age	G	AB	H	2B	3B	HR	TB	R	RBI	GW	TBB	IBB	SO	HBP	SH	SF	SB	CS	SB%	GDP	Avg	OBP	SLG	Pos	G	PO	A	E	DP	FPct
1978 Phi	26	1	1	0	0	0	0	0	0	0	0	0	0	1	0	0	0	0	0	—	0	.000	.000	.000	—						

PEDRO GONZALEZ—Bats: Right; Throws: Right

Ht: 6'0"; Wt: 176 lbs; Born: 12/12/1937 in San Pedro de Macoris, Dominican Republic; Debut: 4/11/1963

World Series — Batting / Fielding

Year Tm	Age	G	AB	H	2B	3B	HR	TB	R	RBI	GW	TBB	IBB	SO	HBP	SH	SF	SB	CS	SB%	GDP	Avg	OBP	SLG	Pos	G	PO	A	E	DP	FPct
1964 NYA	26	1	1	0	0	0	0	0	0	0	0	0	0	0	0	0	0	0	0	—	0	.000	.000	.000	3B	1	1	3	0	0	1.000

TONY GONZALEZ—Andres Antonio Gonzalez—Bats: Left; Throws: Right

Ht: 5'9"; Wt: 170 lbs; Born: 8/28/1936 in Central Cunagua, Cuba; Debut: 4/12/1960

LCS — Batting / Fielding

Year Tm	Age	G	AB	H	2B	3B	HR	TB	R	RBI	GW	TBB	IBB	SO	HBP	SH	SF	SB	CS	SB%	GDP	Avg	OBP	SLG	Pos	G	PO	A	E	DP	FPct
1969 Atl	33	3	14	5	1	0	1	9	4	2	0	1	0	4	0	0	0	0	0	—	0	.357	.400	.643	OF	3	3	0	1	0	.750

JOHNNY GOOCH—John Beverley Gooch—Bats: Both; Throws: Right

Ht: 5'11"; Wt: 175 lbs; Born: 11/9/1897 in Smyrna, Tennessee; Debut: 9/9/1921; Died: 3/15/1975

World Series — Batting / Fielding

Year Tm	Age	G	AB	H	2B	3B	HR	TB	R	RBI	GW	TBB	IBB	SO	HBP	SH	SF	SB	CS	SB%	GDP	Avg	OBP	SLG	Pos	G	PO	A	E	DP	FPct
1925 Pit	27	3	3	0	0	0	0	0	0	0	0	0	0	0	0	0	0	0	0	—	0	.000	.000	.000	C	3	9	3	0	0	1.000
1927 Pit	29	3	5	0	0	0	0	0	0	0	0	1	1	1	0	0	0	0	0	—	0	.000	.167	.000	C	3	19	1	0	0	1.000
WS Totals		6	8	0	0	0	0	0	0	0	0	1	1	1	0	0	0	0	0	—	0	.000	.111	.000	C	6	28	4	0	0	1.000

DWIGHT GOODEN—Dwight Eugene Gooden—Nicknames: Doc, Dr. K.—Throws: Right; Bats: Right

Ht: 6'2"; Wt: 190 lbs; Born: 11/16/1964 in Tampa, Florida; Debut: 4/7/1984

Division Series — Pitching

Year Tm	Age	G	GS	CG	GF	IP	BFP	H	R	ER	HR	SH	SF	HB	TBB	IBB	SO	WP	Bk	W	L	Pct	ShO	Sv-Op	Hld	OAvg	OOBP	ERA
1997 NYA	32	1	1	0	0	5.2	25	5	1	1	1	0	0	0	3	0	5	0	0	0	0	—	0	0-0	0	.227	.320	1.59

LCS — Pitching

Year Tm	Age	G	GS	CG	GF	IP	BFP	H	R	ER	HR	SH	SF	HB	TBB	IBB	SO	WP	Bk	W	L	Pct	ShO	Sv-Op	Hld	OAvg	OOBP	ERA
1986 NYN	21	2	2	0	0	17.0	68	16	2	2	1	1	0	0	5	0	9	0	0	0	1	.000	0	0-0	0	.258	.313	1.06
1988 NYN	23	3	2	0	0	18.1	74	10	6	6	1	0	1	1	8	2	20	2	1	0	0	—	0	0-0	0	.156	.257	2.95
LCS Totals		5	4	0	0	35.1	284	26	8	8	2	1	1	1	13	2	29	2	1	0	1	.000	0	0-0	0	.206	.284	2.04

World Series — Pitching

Year Tm	Age	G	GS	CG	GF	IP	BFP	H	R	ER	HR	SH	SF	HB	TBB	IBB	SO	WP	Bk	W	L	Pct	ShO	Sv-Op	Hld	OAvg	OOBP	ERA
1986 NYN	21	2	2	0	0	9.0	50	17	10	8	2	1	1	1	4	0	9	0	0	0	2	.000	0	0-0	0	.395	.449	8.00
Postseason Totals		8	7	0	0	50.0	434	48	19	17	5	2	2	2	20	2	43	2	1	0	3	.000	0	0-0	0	.251	.326	3.06

Division Series — Batting / Fielding

Year Tm	Age	G	AB	H	2B	3B	HR	TB	R	RBI	GW	TBB	IBB	SO	HBP	SH	SF	SB	CS	SB%	GDP	Avg	OBP	SLG	Pos	G	PO	A	E	DP	FPct
1997 NYA	32	1	0	0	0	0	0	0	0	0	0	0	0	0	0	0	0	0	0	—	0	—	—	—	P	1	0	0	0	0	—

LCS — Batting / Fielding

Year Tm	Age	G	AB	H	2B	3B	HR	TB	R	RBI	GW	TBB	IBB	SO	HBP	SH	SF	SB	CS	SB%	GDP	Avg	OBP	SLG	Pos	G	PO	A	E	DP	FPct
1986 NYN	21	2	5	0	0	0	0	0	0	0	0	0	0	2	0	0	0	0	0	—	0	.000	.000	.000	P	2	3	2	0	0	1.000
1988 NYN	23	3	5	1	0	0	0	1	0	0	0	0	0	2	0	0	0	0	0	—	1	.200	.200	.200	P	3	1	3	0	0	1.000
LCS Totals		5	10	1	0	0	0	1	0	0	0	0	0	4	0	0	0	0	0	—	1	.100	.100	.100	P	5	4	5	0	0	1.000

World Series — Batting / Fielding

Year Tm	Age	G	AB	H	2B	3B	HR	TB	R	RBI	GW	TBB	IBB	SO	HBP	SH	SF	SB	CS	SB%	GDP	Avg	OBP	SLG	Pos	G	PO	A	E	DP	FPct
1986 NYN	21	2	2	1	0	0	0	1	1	0	0	0	0	0	0	0	0	0	0	—	0	.500	.500	.500	P	2	1	2	0	0	1.000
Postseason Totals		8	12	2	0	0	0	2	1	0	0	0	0	4	0	0	0	0	0	—	1	.167	.167	.167	P	8	5	7	0	0	1.000

BILLY GOODMAN—William Dale Goodman—Bats: Left; Throws: Right

Ht: 5'11"; Wt: 165 lbs; Born: 3/22/1926 in Concord, North Carolina; Debut: 4/19/1947; Died: 10/1/1984

World Series — Batting / Fielding

Year Tm	Age	G	AB	H	2B	3B	HR	TB	R	RBI	GW	TBB	IBB	SO	HBP	SH	SF	SB	CS	SB%	GDP	Avg	OBP	SLG	Pos	G	PO	A	E	DP	FPct
1959 ChA	33	5	13	3	0	0	0	3	1	1	0	0	0	5	1	0	0	0	0	—	0	.231	.286	.231	3B	5	1	2	0	0	1.000

IVAL GOODMAN—Ival Richard Goodman—Nickname: Goodie—Bats: Left; Throws: Right

Ht: 5'11"; Wt: 170 lbs; Born: 7/23/1908 in Northview, Missouri; Debut: 4/16/1935; Died: 11/25/1984

World Series — Batting / Fielding

Year Tm	Age	G	AB	H	2B	3B	HR	TB	R	RBI	GW	TBB	IBB	SO	HBP	SH	SF	SB	CS	SB%	GDP	Avg	OBP	SLG	Pos	G	PO	A	E	DP	FPct
1939 Cin	31	4	15	5	1	0	0	6	3	1	0	1	0	2	0	0	0	1	0	1.00	0	.333	.375	.400	OF	4	11	2	1	0	.929
1940 Cin	32	7	29	8	2	0	0	10	5	5	2	0	0	3	0	1	0	0	0	—	0	.276	.276	.345	OF	7	11	0	0	0	1.000
WS Totals		11	44	13	3	0	0	16	8	6	2	1	0	5	0	1	0	1	0	1.00	0	.295	.311	.364	OF	11	22	2	1	0	.960

ED GOODSON—James Edward Goodson—Bats: Left; Throws: Right

Ht: 6'3"; Wt: 180 lbs; Born: 1/25/1948 in Pulaski, Virginia; Debut: 9/5/1970

LCS — Batting / Fielding

Year Tm	Age	G	AB	H	2B	3B	HR	TB	R	RBI	GW	TBB	IBB	SO	HBP	SH	SF	SB	CS	SB%	GDP	Avg	OBP	SLG	Pos	G	PO	A	E	DP	FPct
1977 LA	29	1	1	0	0	0	0	0	0	0	0	0	0	0	0	0	0	0	0	—	0	.000	.000	.000	—						

World Series — Batting / Fielding

Year Tm	Age	G	AB	H	2B	3B	HR	TB	R	RBI	GW	TBB	IBB	SO	HBP	SH	SF	SB	CS	SB%	GDP	Avg	OBP	SLG	Pos	G	PO	A	E	DP	FPct
1977 LA	29	1	1	0	0	0	0	0	0	0	0	0	0	1	0	0	0	0	0	—	0	.000	.000	.000	—						
Postseason Totals		2	2	0	0	0	0	0	0	0	0	0	0	1	0	0	0	0	0	—	0	.000	.000	.000	—	0	0	0	0	0	—

JOE GORDON—Joseph Lowell Gordon—Nickname: Flash—Bats: Right; Throws: Right

Ht: 5'10"; Wt: 180 lbs; Born: 2/18/1915 in Los Angeles, California; Debut: 4/18/1938; Died: 4/14/1978

World Series — Batting / Fielding

Year Tm	Age	G	AB	H	2B	3B	HR	TB	R	RBI	GW	TBB	IBB	SO	HBP	SH	SF	SB	CS	SB%	GDP	Avg	OBP	SLG	Pos	G	PO	A	E	DP	FPct
1938 NYA	23	4	15	6	2	0	1	11	3	6	0	1	1	3	0	0	0	1	0	1.00	0	.400	.438	.733	2B	4	12	11	2	3	.920
1939 NYA	24	4	14	2	0	0	0	2	1	1	0	0	0	2	0	0	0	0	0	—	0	.143	.143	.143	2B	4	6	13	0	4	1.000
1941 NYA	26	5	14	7	1	1	1	13	2	5	1	7	2	0	0	0	0	0	0	—	1	.500	.667	.929	2B	5	7	19	1	5	.963
1942 NYA-*M*	27	5	21	2	1	0	0	3	1	0	0	0	0	7	0	0	0	0	0	—	0	.095	.095	.143	2B	5	11	12	0	1	1.000
1943 NYA	28	5	17	4	1	0	1	8	2	2	0	3	0	3	0	0	0	0	0	—	0	.235	.350	.471	2B	5	20	23	0	3	1.000
1948 Cle	33	6	22	4	0	0	1	7	3	2	1	1	0	2	0	0	0	1	0	1.00	0	.182	.217	.318	2B	6	15	13	1	7	.966
WS Totals		29	103	25	5	1	4	44	12	16	2	12	3	17	0	0	0	2	0	1.00	1	.243	.322	.427	2B	29	71	91	4	23	.976

TOM GORMAN—Thomas Aloysius Gorman—Throws: Right; Bats: Right

Ht: 6'1"; Wt: 190 lbs; Born: 1/4/1925 in New York, New York; Debut: 7/16/1952; Died: 12/26/1992

World Series — Pitching

Year Tm	Age	G	GS	CG	GF	IP	BFP	H	R	ER	HR	SH	SF	HB	TBB	IBB	SO	WP	Bk	W	L	Pct	ShO	Sv-Op	Hld	OAvg	OOBP	ERA
1952 NYA	27	1	0	0	1	0.2	3	1	0	0	0	0	0	0	0	0	0	0	0	0	0	—	0	0-0	0	.333	.333	0.00
1953 NYA	28	1	0	0	0	3.0	13	4	1	1	0	0	0	0	0	0	1	0	0	0	0	—	0	0-0	0	.308	.308	3.00
WS Totals		2	0	0	1	3.2	32	5	1	1	0	0	0	0	0	0	1	0	0	0	0	—	0	0-0	0	.313	.313	2.45

World Series — Batting / Fielding

Year Tm	Age	G	AB	H	2B	3B	HR	TB	R	RBI	GW	TBB	IBB	SO	HBP	SH	SF	SB	CS	SB%	GDP	Avg	OBP	SLG	Pos	G	PO	A	E	DP	FPct
1952 NYA	27	1	0	0	0	0	0	0	0	0	0	0	0	0	0	0	0	0	0	—	0	—	—	—	P	1	0	0	0	0	—
1953 NYA	28	1	1	0	0	0	0	0	0	0	0	0	0	1	0	0	0	0	0	—	0	.000	.000	.000	P	1	1	0	0	0	1.000
WS Totals		2	1	0	0	0	0	0	0	0	0	0	0	1	0	0	0	0	0	—	0	.000	.000	.000	P	2	1	0	0	0	1.000

JOHNNY GORSICA—John Joseph Perry Gorsica—Throws: Right; Bats: Right

Ht: 6'2"; Wt: 180 lbs; Born: 3/29/1915 in Bayonne, New Jersey; Debut: 4/22/1940

World Series — Pitching

Year Tm	Age	G	GS	CG	GF	IP	BFP	H	R	ER	HR	SH	SF	HB	TBB	IBB	SO	WP	Bk	W	L	Pct	ShO	Sv-Op	Hld	OAvg	OOBP	ERA
1940 Det	25	2	0	0	1	11.1	44	6	1	1	0	1	0	0	4	1	4	0	0	0	0	—	0	0-0	0	.154	.233	0.79

World Series — Batting / Fielding

Year Tm	Age	G	AB	H	2B	3B	HR	TB	R	RBI	GW	TBB	IBB	SO	HBP	SH	SF	SB	CS	SB%	GDP	Avg	OBP	SLG	Pos	G	PO	A	E	DP	FPct
1940 Det	25	2	4	0	0	0	0	0	0	0	0	0	0	2	0	0	0	0	0	—	0	.000	.000	.000	P	2	0	6	0	1	1.000

GOOSE GOSLIN (HOF 1968-V)—Leon Allen Goslin—Bats: Left; Throws: Right

Ht: 5'11"; Wt: 185 lbs; Born: 10/16/1900 in Salem, New Jersey; Debut: 9/16/1921; Died: 5/15/1971

World Series — Batting / Fielding

Year Tm	Age	G	AB	H	2B	3B	HR	TB	R	RBI	GW	TBB	IBB	SO	HBP	SH	SF	SB	CS	SB%	GDP	Avg	OBP	SLG	Pos	G	PO	A	E	DP	FPct
1924 Was	23	7	32	11	2	0	3	22	4	7	1	0	0	7	0	0	0	0	2	.00	0	.344	.344	.688	OF	7	15	1	0	0	1.000
1925 Was	24	7	26	8	1	0	3	18	6	6	1	3	0	3	0	0	0	0	0	—	0	.308	.379	.692	OF	7	15	0	0	0	1.000
1933 Was	32	5	20	5	1	0	1	9	2	1	0	1	0	3	0	1	0	0	0	—	0	.250	.286	.450	OF	5	10	1	0	0	1.000
1934 Det	33	7	29	7	1	0	0	8	2	2	1	3	2	1	0	1	0	0	1	.00	0	.241	.313	.276	OF	7	20	1	2	0	.913
1935 Det	34	6	22	6	1	0	0	7	2	3	1	5	2	0	0	0	0	0	0	—	0	.273	.407	.318	OF	6	12	0	1	0	.923
WS Totals		32	129	37	6	0	7	64	16	19	4	12	4	14	0	2	0	0	3	.00	0	.287	.348	.496	OF	32	72	3	3	0	.962

GOOSE GOSSAGE—Richard Michael Gossage—Throws: Right; Bats: Right

Ht: 6'3"; Wt: 180 lbs; Born: 7/5/1951 in Colorado Springs, Colorado; Debut: 4/16/1972

Division Series — Pitching

Year Tm	Age	G	GS	CG	GF	IP	BFP	H	R	ER	HR	SH	SF	HB	TBB	IBB	SO	WP	Bk	W	L	Pct	ShO	Sv-Op	Hld	OAvg	OOBP	ERA
1981 NYA	30	3	0	0	3	6.2	25	3	0	0	0	0	0	0	2	0	8	0	0	0	0	—	0	3- 3	0	.130	.200	0.00

LCS — Pitching

Year Tm	Age	G	GS	CG	GF	IP	BFP	H	R	ER	HR	SH	SF	HB	TBB	IBB	SO	WP	Bk	W	L	Pct	ShO	Sv-Op	Hld	OAvg	OOBP	ERA
1978 NYA	27	2	0	0	2	4.0	15	3	2	2	0	0	0	0	0	0	3	0	0	1	0	1.000	0	1- 2	0	.200	.200	4.50
1980 NYA	29	1	0	0	0	0.1	3	3	2	2	1	0	0	0	0	0	0	0	0	0	1	.000	0	0- 1	0	1.000	1.000	54.00
1981 NYA	30	2	0	0	2	2.2	9	1	0	0	0	0	0	0	0	0	2	0	0	0	0	—	0	1- 1	0	.111	.111	0.00
1984 SD	33	3	0	0	2	4.0	19	5	2	2	0	0	0	1	1	1	5	0	0	0	0	—	0	1- 2	0	.294	.368	4.50
LCS Totals		8	0	0	6	11.0	92	12	6	6	1	0	0	1	1	1	10	0	0	1	1	.500	0	3-6	0	.273	.304	4.91

World Series — Pitching

Year Tm	Age	G	GS	CG	GF	IP	BFP	H	R	ER	HR	SH	SF	HB	TBB	IBB	SO	WP	Bk	W	L	Pct	ShO	Sv-Op	Hld	OAvg	OOBP	ERA
1978 NYA	27	3	0	0	3	6.0	19	1	0	0	0	0	0	0	1	0	4	0	0	1	0	1.000	0	0- 0	0	.056	.105	0.00
1981 NYA	30	3	0	0	3	5.0	20	2	0	0	0	0	1	1	2	0	5	0	0	0	0	—	0	2- 2	0	.125	.250	0.00
1984 SD	33	2	0	0	2	2.2	14	3	4	4	2	2	0	0	1	0	2	0	0	0	0	—	0	0- 0	0	.273	.333	13.50
WS Totals		8	0	0	8	13.2	106	6	4	4	2	2	1	1	4	0	11	0	0	1	0	1.000	0	2-2	0	.133	.216	2.63
Postseason Totals		19	0	0	17	31.1	248	21	10	10	3	2	1	2	7	1	29	0	0	2	1	.667	0	8-11	0	.188	.246	2.87

Division Series — Batting / Fielding

Year Tm	Age	G	AB	H	2B	3B	HR	TB	R	RBI	GW	TBB	IBB	SO	HBP	SH	SF	SB	CS	SB%	GDP	Avg	OBP	SLG	Pos	G	PO	A	E	DP	FPct
1981 NYA	30	3	0	0	0	0	0	0	0	0	0	0	0	0	0	0	0	0	0	—	0	—	—	—	P	3	0	0	0	0	—

LCS — Batting / Fielding

Year Tm	Age	G	AB	H	2B	3B	HR	TB	R	RBI	GW	TBB	IBB	SO	HBP	SH	SF	SB	CS	SB%	GDP	Avg	OBP	SLG	Pos	G	PO	A	E	DP	FPct
1978 NYA	27	2	0	0	0	0	0	0	0	0	0	0	0	0	0	0	0	0	0	—	0	—	—	—	P	2	0	1	0	0	1.000
1980 NYA	29	1	0	0	0	0	0	0	0	0	0	0	0	0	0	0	0	0	0	—	0	—	—	—	P	1	0	0	0	0	—
1981 NYA	30	2	0	0	0	0	0	0	0	0	0	0	0	0	0	0	0	0	0	—	0	—	—	—	P	2	0	0	0	0	—
1984 SD	33	3	0	0	0	0	0	0	0	0	0	0	0	0	0	0	0	0	0	—	0	—	—	—	P	3	0	0	0	0	—
LCS Totals		8	0	0	0	0	0	0	0	0	0	0	0	0	0	0	0	0	0	—	0	—	—	—	P	8	0	1	0	0	1.000

World Series — Batting / Fielding

Year Tm	Age	G	AB	H	2B	3B	HR	TB	R	RBI	GW	TBB	IBB	SO	HBP	SH	SF	SB	CS	SB%	GDP	Avg	OBP	SLG	Pos	G	PO	A	E	DP	FPct
1978 NYA	27	3	0	0	0	0	0	0	0	0	0	0	0	0	0	0	0	0	0	—	0	—	—	—	P	3	0	0	0	0	—
1981 NYA	30	3	1	0	0	0	0	0	0	0	0	0	0	1	0	0	0	0	0	—	0	.000	.000	.000	P	3	0	0	0	0	—
1984 SD	33	2	0	0	0	0	0	0	0	0	0	0	0	0	0	0	0	0	0	—	0	—	—	—	P	2	0	1	0	0	1.000
WS Totals		8	1	0	0	0	0	0	0	0	0	0	0	1	0	0	0	0	0	—	0	.000	.000	.000	P	8	0	1	0	0	1.000
Postseason Totals		19	1	0	0	0	0	0	0	0	0	0	0	1	0	0	0	0	0	—	0	.000	.000	.000	P	19	0	2	0	0	1.000

HANK GOWDY—Henry Morgan Gowdy—Bats: Right; Throws: Right

Ht: 6'2"; Wt: 182 lbs; Born: 8/24/1889 in Columbus, Ohio; Debut: 9/13/1910; Died: 8/1/1966

World Series — Batting / Fielding

Year Tm	Age	G	AB	H	2B	3B	HR	TB	R	RBI	GW	TBB	IBB	SO	HBP	SH	SF	SB	CS	SB%	GDP	Avg	OBP	SLG	Pos	G	PO	A	E	DP	FPct
1914 Bos	25	4	11	6	3	1	1	14	3	3	1	5	0	1	0	0	0	1	0	1.00	0	.545	.688	1.273	C	4	31	4	0	1	1.000
1923 NYG	34	3	4	0	0	0	0	0	0	0	0	1	0	0	0	0	0	0	0	—	0	.000	.200	.000	C	2	7	0	0	0	1.000
1924 NYG	35	7	27	7	0	0	0	7	4	2	1	2	0	2	0	0	0	0	0	—	1	.259	.310	.259	C	7	37	5	1	0	.977
WS Totals		14	42	13	3	1	1	21	7	5	2	8	0	3	0	0	0	1	0	1.00	1	.310	.420	.500	C	13	75	9	1	1	.988

JOHNNY GRABOWSKI—John Patrick Grabowski—Nickname: Nig—Bats: Right; Throws: Right

Ht: 5'10"; Wt: 185 lbs; Born: 1/7/1900 in Ware, Massachusetts; Debut: 7/11/1924; Died: 5/23/1946

World Series — Batting / Fielding

Year Tm	Age	G	AB	H	2B	3B	HR	TB	R	RBI	GW	TBB	IBB	SO	HBP	SH	SF	SB	CS	SB%	GDP	Avg	OBP	SLG	Pos	G	PO	A	E	DP	FPct
1927 NYA	27	1	2	0	0	0	0	0	0	0	0	0	0	0	0	0	0	0	0	—	0	.000	.000	.000	C	1	3	0	0	0	1.000

MARK GRACE—Mark Eugene Grace—Bats: Left; Throws: Left

Ht: 6'2"; Wt: 190 lbs; Born: 6/28/1964 in Winston-Salem, North Carolina; Debut: 5/2/1988

LCS — Batting / Fielding

Year Tm	Age	G	AB	H	2B	3B	HR	TB	R	RBI	GW	TBB	IBB	SO	HBP	SH	SF	SB	CS	SB%	GDP	Avg	OBP	SLG	Pos	G	PO	A	E	DP	FPct
1989 ChN	25	5	17	11	3	1	1	19	3	8	0	4	2	1	0	0	1	1	0	1.00	0	.647	.682	1.118	1B	5	44	3	0	1	1.000

TONY GRAFFANINO—Anthony Joseph Graffanino—Bats: Right; Throws: Right

Ht: 6'1"; Wt: 175 lbs; Born: 6/6/1972 in Amityville, New York; Debut: 4/19/1996

Division Series — Batting / Fielding

Year Tm	Age	G	AB	H	2B	3B	HR	TB	R	RBI	GW	TBB	IBB	SO	HBP	SH	SF	SB	CS	SB%	GDP	Avg	OBP	SLG	Pos	G	PO	A	E	DP	FPct
1997 Atl	25	3	3	0	0	0	0	0	0	0	0	2	0	1	0	0	0	0	0	—	0	.000	.400	.000	2B	3	1	6	0	0	1.000

LCS — Batting / Fielding

Year Tm	Age	G	AB	H	2B	3B	HR	TB	R	RBI	GW	TBB	IBB	SO	HBP	SH	SF	SB	CS	SB%	GDP	Avg	OBP	SLG	Pos	G	PO	A	E	DP	FPct
1997 Atl	25	3	8	2	1	0	0	3	1	0	0	0	0	3	0	0	0	0	0	—	1	.250	.250	.375	2B	3	4	2	0	0	1.000
Postseason Totals		6	11	2	1	0	0	3	1	0	0	2	0	4	0	0	0	0	0	—	1	.182	.308	.273	2B	6	5	8	0	0	1.000

JACK GRANEY—John Gladstone Graney—Bats: Left; Throws: Left

Ht: 5'9"; Wt: 180 lbs; Born: 6/10/1886 in St. Thomas, Ontario; Debut: 4/30/1908; Died: 4/20/1978

World Series — Batting / Fielding

Year Tm	Age	G	AB	H	2B	3B	HR	TB	R	RBI	GW	TBB	IBB	SO	HBP	SH	SF	SB	CS	SB%	GDP	Avg	OBP	SLG	Pos	G	PO	A	E	DP	FPct
1920 Cle	34	3	3	0	0	0	0	0	0	0	0	0	0	2	0	0	0	0	0	—	0	.000	.000	.000	OF	2	0	0	0	0	—

WAYNE GRANGER—Wayne Allan Granger—Throws: Right; Bats: Right

Ht: 6'2"; Wt: 165 lbs; Born: 3/15/1944 in Springfield, Massachusetts; Debut: 6/5/1968

LCS — Pitching

Year Tm	Age	G	GS	CG	GF	IP	BFP	H	R	ER	HR	SH	SF	HB	TBB	IBB	SO	WP	Bk	W	L	Pct	ShO	Sv-Op	Hld	OAvg	OOBP	ERA
1970 Cin	26	1	0	0	0	0.2	3	1	0	0	0	0	0	0	0	0	0	0	0	0	0	—	0	0- 0	1	.333	.333	0.00

World Series — Pitching

Year Tm	Age	G	GS	CG	GF	IP	BFP	H	R	ER	HR	SH	SF	HB	TBB	IBB	SO	WP	Bk	W	L	Pct	ShO	Sv-Op	Hld	OAvg	OOBP	ERA
1968 StL	24	1	0	0	0	2.0	7	0	0	0	0	0	0	2	1	0	1	0	0	0	0	—	0	0- 0	0	.000	.429	0.00
1970 Cin	26	2	0	0	0	1.1	12	7	5	5	1	0	0	0	1	1	1	0	0	0	0	—	0	0- 0	0	.636	.667	33.75
WS Totals		3	0	0	0	3.1	38	7	5	5	1	0	0	2	2	1	2	0	0	0	0	—	0	0-0	0	.467	.579	13.50
Postseason Totals		4	0	0	0	4.0	44	8	5	5	1	0	0	2	2	1	2	0	0	0	0	—	0	0-0	1	.444	.545	11.25

LCS — Batting / Fielding

Year Tm	Age	G	AB	H	2B	3B	HR	TB	R	RBI	GW	TBB	IBB	SO	HBP	SH	SF	SB	CS	SB%	GDP	Avg	OBP	SLG	Pos	G	PO	A	E	DP	FPct
1970 Cin	26	1	0	0	0	0	0	0	0	0	0	0	0	0	0	0	0	0	0	—	0	—	—	—	P	1	0	0	0	0	—

World Series — Batting / Fielding

Year Tm	Age	G	AB	H	2B	3B	HR	TB	R	RBI	GW	TBB	IBB	SO	HBP	SH	SF	SB	CS	SB%	GDP	Avg	OBP	SLG	Pos	G	PO	A	E	DP	FPct
1968 StL	24	1	0	0	0	0	0	0	0	0	0	0	0	0	0	0	0	0	0	—	0	—	—	—	P	1	0	1	0	1	1.000
1970 Cin	26	2	0	0	0	0	0	0	0	0	0	0	0	0	0	0	0	0	0	—	0	—	—	—	P	2	0	1	0	0	1.000
WS Totals		3	0	0	0	0	0	0	0	0	0	0	0	0	0	0	0	0	0	—	0	—	—	—	P	3	0	2	0	1	1.000
Postseason Totals		4	0	0	0	0	0	0	0	0	0	0	0	0	0	0	0	0	0	—	0	—	—	—	P	4	0	2	0	1	1.000

EDDIE GRANT—Edward Leslie Grant—Nickname: Harvard Eddie—Bats: Left; Throws: Right

Ht: 5'11"; Wt: 168 lbs; Born: 5/21/1883 in Franklin, Massachusetts; Debut: 8/4/1905; Died: 10/5/1918

World Series		Batting																							Fielding						
Year Tm	Age	G	AB	H	2B	3B	HR	TB	R	RBI	GW	TBB	IBB	SO	HBP	SH	SF	SB	CS	SB%	GDP	Avg	OBP	SLG	Pos	G	PO	A	E	DP	FPct
1913 NYG	30	2	1	0	0	0	0	0	1	0	0	0	0	0	0	0	0	0	0	—	0	.000	.000	.000	—						

MUDCAT GRANT—James Timothy Grant—Throws: Right; Bats: Right

Ht: 6'1"; Wt: 186 lbs; Born: 8/13/1935 in Lacoochee, Florida; Debut: 4/17/1958

LCS		Pitching																										
Year Tm	Age	G	GS	CG	GF	IP	BFP	H	R	ER	HR	SH	SF	HB	TBB	IBB	SO	WP	Bk	W	L	Pct	ShO	Sv-Op	Hld	OAvg	OOBP	ERA
1971 Oak	36	1	0	0	1	2.0	9	3	0	0	0	0	0	0	0	0	2	0	0	0	0	—	0	0-0	0	.333	.333	0.00
World Series		Pitching																										
Year Tm	Age	G	GS	CG	GF	IP	BFP	H	R	ER	HR	SH	SF	HB	TBB	IBB	SO	WP	Bk	W	L	Pct	ShO	Sv-Op	Hld	OAvg	OOBP	ERA
1965 Min	30	3	3	2	0	23.0	92	22	8	7	3	0	0	0	2	0	12	1	0	2	1	.667	0	0-0	0	.244	.261	2.74
Postseason Totals		4	3	2	1	25.0	202	25	8	7	3	0	0	0	2	0	14	1	0	2	1	.667	0	0-0	0	.253	.267	2.52

LCS		Batting																							Fielding						
Year Tm	Age	G	AB	H	2B	3B	HR	TB	R	RBI	GW	TBB	IBB	SO	HBP	SH	SF	SB	CS	SB%	GDP	Avg	OBP	SLG	Pos	G	PO	A	E	DP	FPct
1971 Oak	36	1	0	0	0	0	0	0	0	0	0	0	0	0	0	0	0	0	0	—	0	—	—	—	P	1	0	1	0	0	1.000
World Series		Batting																							Fielding						
Year Tm	Age	G	AB	H	2B	3B	HR	TB	R	RBI	GW	TBB	IBB	SO	HBP	SH	SF	SB	CS	SB%	GDP	Avg	OBP	SLG	Pos	G	PO	A	E	DP	FPct
1965 Min	30	3	8	2	1	0	1	6	3	3	0	0	0	1	0	1	0	0	0	—	0	.250	.250	.750	P	3	0	1	0	0	1.000
Postseason Totals		4	8	2	1	0	1	6	3	3	0	0	0	1	0	1	0	0	0	—	0	.250	.250	.750	P	4	0	2	0	0	1.000

GEORGE GRANTHAM—George Farley Grantham—Nickname: Boots—Bats: Left; Throws: Right

Ht: 5'10"; Wt: 170 lbs; Born: 5/20/1900 in Galena, Kansas; Debut: 9/20/1922; Died: 3/16/1954

World Series		Batting																							Fielding						
Year Tm	Age	G	AB	H	2B	3B	HR	TB	R	RBI	GW	TBB	IBB	SO	HBP	SH	SF	SB	CS	SB%	GDP	Avg	OBP	SLG	Pos	G	PO	A	E	DP	FPct
1925 Pit	25	5	15	2	0	0	0	2	0	0	0	0	0	3	0	0	0	1	0	1.00	0	.133	.133	.133	1B	4	41	6	0	3	1.000
1927 Pit	27	3	11	4	1	0	0	5	0	0	0	1	0	1	0	0	0	0	0	—	0	.364	.417	.455	2B	3	7	7	1	1	.933
WS Totals		8	26	6	1	0	0	7	0	0	0	1	0	4	0	0	0	1	0	1.00	0	.231	.259	.269	1B	4	41	6	0	3	1.000

MICKEY GRASSO—Newton Michael Grasso—Bats: Right; Throws: Right

Ht: 6'0"; Wt: 195 lbs; Born: 5/10/1920 in Newark, New Jersey; Debut: 9/18/1946; Died: 10/15/1975

World Series		Batting																							Fielding						
Year Tm	Age	G	AB	H	2B	3B	HR	TB	R	RBI	GW	TBB	IBB	SO	HBP	SH	SF	SB	CS	SB%	GDP	Avg	OBP	SLG	Pos	G	PO	A	E	DP	FPct
1954 Cle	34	1	0	0	0	0	0	0	0	0	0	0	0	0	0	0	0	0	0	—	0	—	—	—	C	1	1	0	0	0	1.000

JEFF GRAY—Jeffrey Edward Gray—Throws: Right; Bats: Right

Ht: 6'1"; Wt: 175 lbs; Born: 4/10/1963 in Richmond, Virginia; Debut: 6/21/1988

LCS		Pitching																										
Year Tm	Age	G	GS	CG	GF	IP	BFP	H	R	ER	HR	SH	SF	HB	TBB	IBB	SO	WP	Bk	W	L	Pct	ShO	Sv-Op	Hld	OAvg	OOBP	ERA
1990 Bos	27	2	0	0	0	3.1	16	4	2	1	0	2	0	0	1	0	2	0	0	0	0	—	0	0-0	0	.308	.357	2.70

LCS		Batting																							Fielding						
Year Tm	Age	G	AB	H	2B	3B	HR	TB	R	RBI	GW	TBB	IBB	SO	HBP	SH	SF	SB	CS	SB%	GDP	Avg	OBP	SLG	Pos	G	PO	A	E	DP	FPct
1990 Bos	27	2	0	0	0	0	0	0	0	0	0	0	0	0	0	0	0	0	0	—	0	—	—	—	P	2	0	0	1	0	.000

ELI GRBA—Throws: Right; Bats: Right

Ht: 6'2"; Wt: 205 lbs; Born: 8/9/1934 in Chicago, Illinois; Debut: 7/10/1959

World Series		Batting																							Fielding						
Year Tm	Age	G	AB	H	2B	3B	HR	TB	R	RBI	GW	TBB	IBB	SO	HBP	SH	SF	SB	CS	SB%	GDP	Avg	OBP	SLG	Pos	G	PO	A	E	DP	FPct
1960 NYA	26	1	0	0	0	0	0	0	0	0	0	0	0	0	0	0	0	0	0	—	0	—	—	—	—						

CRAIG GREBECK—Craig Allen Grebeck—Nickname: Little Hurt—Bats: Right; Throws: Right

Ht: 5'8"; Wt: 160 lbs; Born: 12/29/1964 in Cerritos, California; Debut: 4/13/1990

LCS		Batting																							Fielding						
Year Tm	Age	G	AB	H	2B	3B	HR	TB	R	RBI	GW	TBB	IBB	SO	HBP	SH	SF	SB	CS	SB%	GDP	Avg	OBP	SLG	Pos	G	PO	A	E	DP	FPct
1993 ChA	28	1	1	1	0	0	0	1	0	0	0	0	0	0	0	0	0	0	0	—	0	1.000	1.000	1.000	3B	1	0	0	0	0	—

DAVID GREEN—David Alejandro Green—Bats: Right; Throws: Right

Ht: 6'3"; Wt: 170 lbs; Born: 12/4/1960 in Managua, Nicaragua; Debut: 9/4/1981

LCS		Batting																							Fielding						
Year Tm	Age	G	AB	H	2B	3B	HR	TB	R	RBI	GW	TBB	IBB	SO	HBP	SH	SF	SB	CS	SB%	GDP	Avg	OBP	SLG	Pos	G	PO	A	E	DP	FPct
1982 StL	21	2	1	1	0	0	0	1	1	0	0	0	0	0	0	0	0	0	0	—	0	1.000	1.000	1.000	OF	2	0	0	0	0	—
World Series		Batting																							Fielding						
Year Tm	Age	G	AB	H	2B	3B	HR	TB	R	RBI	GW	TBB	IBB	SO	HBP	SH	SF	SB	CS	SB%	GDP	Avg	OBP	SLG	Pos	G	PO	A	E	DP	FPct
1982 StL	21	7	10	2	1	1	0	5	3	0	0	1	0	3	0	0	0	0	0	—	0	.200	.273	.500	OF	4	4	0	0	0	1.000
Postseason Totals		9	11	3	1	1	0	6	4	0	0	1	0	3	0	0	0	0	0	—	0	.273	.333	.545	OF	6	4	0	0	0	1.000

DICK GREEN—Richard Larry Green—Bats: Right; Throws: Right

Ht: 5'10"; Wt: 180 lbs; Born: 4/21/1941 in Sioux City, Iowa; Debut: 9/9/1963

LCS		Batting																							Fielding						
Year Tm	Age	G	AB	H	2B	3B	HR	TB	R	RBI	GW	TBB	IBB	SO	HBP	SH	SF	SB	CS	SB%	GDP	Avg	OBP	SLG	Pos	G	PO	A	E	DP	FPct
1971 Oak	30	3	7	2	0	0	0	2	0	0	0	1	0	1	0	1	0	0	0	—	1	.286	.375	.286	2B	3	8	4	0	3	1.000
1972 Oak	31	5	8	1	1	0	0	2	0	0	0	0	0	0	0	0	0	0	0	—	1	.125	.125	.250	2B	5	5	7	0	1	1.000
1973 Oak	32	5	13	1	1	0	0	2	0	1	0	0	0	4	0	1	0	0	0	—	0	.077	.077	.154	2B	5	12	11	1	4	.958
1974 Oak	33	4	9	2	0	0	0	2	0	0	0	2	0	1	0	1	0	0	0	—	0	.222	.364	.222	2B	4	10	8	2	3	.900
LCS Totals		17	37	6	2	0	0	8	0	1	0	3	0	6	0	3	0	0	0	—	2	.162	.225	.216	2B	17	35	30	3	11	.956
World Series		Batting																							Fielding						
Year Tm	Age	G	AB	H	2B	3B	HR	TB	R	RBI	GW	TBB	IBB	SO	HBP	SH	SF	SB	CS	SB%	GDP	Avg	OBP	SLG	Pos	G	PO	A	E	DP	FPct
1972 Oak	31	7	18	6	2	0	0	8	0	1	0	0	0	4	0	0	0	0	0	—	0	.333	.333	.444	2B	7	12	13	0	2	1.000
1973 Oak	32	7	16	1	0	0	0	1	0	0	0	1	0	6	0	0	0	0	1	.00	0	.063	.118	.063	2B	7	14	11	1	4	.962
1974 Oak	33	5	13	0	0	0	0	0	1	1	0	1	0	4	0	1	0	0	0	—	0	.000	.071	.000	2B	5	15	14	1	6	.967
WS Totals		19	47	7	2	0	0	9	1	2	0	2	0	14	0	1	0	0	1	.00	0	.149	.184	.191	2B	19	41	38	2	12	.975
Postseason Totals		36	84	13	4	0	0	17	1	3	0	5	0	20	0	4	0	0	1	.00	2	.155	.202	.202	2B	36	76	68	5	23	.966

FRED GREEN—Fred Allen Green—Throws: Left; Bats: Right

Ht: 6'4"; Wt: 190 lbs; Born: 9/14/1933 in Titusville, New Jersey; Debut: 4/15/1959; Died: 12/22/1996

World Series		Pitching																										
Year Tm	Age	G	GS	CG	GF	IP	BFP	H	R	ER	HR	SH	SF	HB	TBB	IBB	SO	WP	Bk	W	L	Pct	ShO	Sv-Op	Hld	OAvg	OOBP	ERA
1960 Pit	27	3	0	0	0	4.0	23	11	10	10	2	0	0	0	1	0	3	1	0	0	0	—	0	0-0	0	.500	.522	22.50

World Series		Batting																							Fielding						
Year Tm	Age	G	AB	H	2B	3B	HR	TB	R	RBI	GW	TBB	IBB	SO	HBP	SH	SF	SB	CS	SB%	GDP	Avg	OBP	SLG	Pos	G	PO	A	E	DP	FPct
1960 Pit	27	3	1	0	0	0	0	0	0	0	0	0	0	0	0	0	0	0	0	—	0	.000	.000	.000	P	3	0	0	0	0	—

HANK GREENBERG (HOF 1956-W)—Henry Benjamin Greenberg—Nickname: Hammerin' Hank—B: R; T: R

Ht: 6'3"; Wt: 210 lbs; Born: 1/1/1911 in New York, N.Y.; Deb.: 9/14/1930; Died: 9/4/1986

World Series		Batting																							Fielding						
Year Tm	Age	G	AB	H	2B	3B	HR	TB	R	RBI	GW	TBB	IBB	SO	HBP	SH	SF	SB	CS	SB%	GDP	Avg	OBP	SLG	Pos	G	PO	A	E	DP	FPct
1934 Det	23	7	28	9	2	1	1	16	4	7	1	4	0	9	0	0	0	1	0	1.00	0	.321	.406	.571	1B	7	60	4	1	5	.985
1935 Det-*M*	24	2	6	1	0	0	1	4	1	2	0	1	0	0	1	0	0	0	0	—	1	.167	.375	.667	1B	2	17	2	3	2	.864
1940 Det-*M*	29	7	28	10	2	1	1	17	5	6	1	2	0	5	0	0	0	0	0	—	2	.357	.400	.607	OF	7	12	0	0	0	1.000
1945 Det	34	7	23	7	3	0	2	16	7	7	3	6	0	5	1	1	0	0	0	—	1	.304	.467	.696	OF	7	8	1	0	0	1.000
WS Totals		23	85	27	7	2	5	53	17	22	5	13	0	19	2	1	0	1	0	1.00	4	.318	.420	.624	OF	14	20	1	0	0	1.000

TOMMY GREENE
Ira Thomas Greene—Throws: Right; Bats: Right — Ht: 6'5"; Wt: 225 lbs; Born: 4/6/1967 in Lumberton, North Carolina; Debut: 9/10/1989

LCS — Pitching

Year	Tm	Age	G	GS	CG	GF	IP	BFP	H	R	ER	HR	SH	SF	HB	TBB	IBB	SO	WP	Bk	W	L	Pct	ShO	Sv-Op	Hld	OAvg	OOBP	ERA
1993	Phi	26	2	2	0	0	9.1	45	12	10	10	3	2	0	0	7	0	7	0	0	1	1	.500	0	0-0	0	.333	.442	9.64

World Series — Pitching

Year	Tm	Age	G	GS	CG	GF	IP	BFP	H	R	ER	HR	SH	SF	HB	TBB	IBB	SO	WP	Bk	W	L	Pct	ShO	Sv-Op	Hld	OAvg	OOBP	ERA
1993	Phi	26	1	1	0	0	2.1	17	7	7	7	0	0	0	0	4	0	1	0	0	0	0	—	0	0-0	0	.538	.647	27.00
Postseason Totals			3	3	0	0	11.2	124	19	17	17	3	2	0	0	11	0	8	0	0	1	1	.500	0	0-0	0	.388	.500	13.11

LCS — Batting / Fielding

Year	Tm	Age	G	AB	H	2B	3B	HR	TB	R	RBI	GW	TBB	IBB	SO	HBP	SH	SF	SB	CS	SB%	GDP	Avg	OBP	SLG	Pos	G	PO	A	E	DP	FPct
1993	Phi	26	2	0	0	0	0	0	0	1	0	0	1	0	0	0	0	2	0	0	—	0	—	1.000	—	P	2	0	3	0	0	1.000

World Series — Batting / Fielding

Year	Tm	Age	G	AB	H	2B	3B	HR	TB	R	RBI	GW	TBB	IBB	SO	HBP	SH	SF	SB	CS	SB%	GDP	Avg	OBP	SLG	Pos	G	PO	A	E	DP	FPct
1993	Phi	26	1	1	1	0	0	0	1	1	0	0	0	0	0	0	0	0	0	0	—	0	1.000	1.000	1.000	P	1	0	0	0	0	—
Postseason Totals			3	1	1	0	0	0	1	2	0	0	1	0	0	0	0	2	0	0	—	0	1.000	1.000	1.000	P	3	0	3	0	0	1.000

MIKE GREENWELL
Michael Lewis Greenwell—Bats: Left; Throws: Right — Ht: 6'0"; Wt: 170 lbs; Born: 7/18/1963 in Louisville, Kentucky; Debut: 9/5/1985

Division Series — Batting / Fielding

Year	Tm	Age	G	AB	H	2B	3B	HR	TB	R	RBI	GW	TBB	IBB	SO	HBP	SH	SF	SB	CS	SB%	GDP	Avg	OBP	SLG	Pos	G	PO	A	E	DP	FPct
1995	Bos	32	3	15	3	0	0	0	3	0	0	0	0	0	1	0	0	0	0	0	—	0	.200	.200	.200	OF	3	8	0	0	0	1.000

LCS — Batting / Fielding

Year	Tm	Age	G	AB	H	2B	3B	HR	TB	R	RBI	GW	TBB	IBB	SO	HBP	SH	SF	SB	CS	SB%	GDP	Avg	OBP	SLG	Pos	G	PO	A	E	DP	FPct
1986	Bos	23	2	2	1	0	0	0	1	0	0	0	0	0	0	0	0	0	0	0	—	0	.500	.500	.500	—						
1988	Bos	25	4	14	3	1	0	1	7	2	3	0	3	0	0	0	0	0	0	0	—	0	.214	.353	.500	OF	4	4	0	0	0	1.000
1990	Bos	27	4	14	0	0	0	0	0	1	0	0	2	0	2	0	0	0	0	0	—	0	.000	.125	.000	OF	4	3	0	1	0	.750
LCS Totals			10	30	4	1	0	1	8	3	3	0	5	0	2	0	0	0	0	0	—	0	.133	.257	.267	OF	8	7	0	1	0	.875

World Series — Batting / Fielding

Year	Tm	Age	G	AB	H	2B	3B	HR	TB	R	RBI	GW	TBB	IBB	SO	HBP	SH	SF	SB	CS	SB%	GDP	Avg	OBP	SLG	Pos	G	PO	A	E	DP	FPct
1986	Bos	23	4	3	0	0	0	0	0	0	0	0	1	0	2	0	0	0	0	0	—	0	.000	.250	.000	—						
Postseason Totals			17	48	7	1	0	1	11	3	3	0	6	0	5	0	0	0	0	0	—	0	.146	.241	.229	OF	11	15	0	1	0	.938

RUSTY GREER
Thurman Clyde Greer—Bats: Left; Throws: Left — Ht: 6'0"; Wt: 190 lbs; Born: 1/21/1969 in Fort Rucker, Alabama; Debut: 5/16/1994

Division Series — Batting / Fielding

Year	Tm	Age	G	AB	H	2B	3B	HR	TB	R	RBI	GW	TBB	IBB	SO	HBP	SH	SF	SB	CS	SB%	GDP	Avg	OBP	SLG	Pos	G	PO	A	E	DP	FPct
1996	Tex	27	4	16	2	0	0	0	2	2	0	0	3	0	3	0	0	0	0	0	—	1	.125	.263	.125	OF	4	12	0	0	0	1.000

HAL GREGG
Harold Dana Gregg—Nickname: Skeets—Throws: Right; Bats: Right — Ht: 6'3"; Wt: 195 lbs; Born: 7/11/1921 in Anaheim, California; Debut: 8/18/1943; Died: 5/13/1991

World Series — Pitching

Year	Tm	Age	G	GS	CG	GF	IP	BFP	H	R	ER	HR	SH	SF	HB	TBB	IBB	SO	WP	Bk	W	L	Pct	ShO	Sv-Op	Hld	OAvg	OOBP	ERA
1947	Bro	26	3	1	0	0	12.2	53	9	5	5	0	1	0	0	8	0	10	0	0	0	1	.000	0	0-0	0	.205	.327	3.55

World Series — Batting / Fielding

Year	Tm	Age	G	AB	H	2B	3B	HR	TB	R	RBI	GW	TBB	IBB	SO	HBP	SH	SF	SB	CS	SB%	GDP	Avg	OBP	SLG	Pos	G	PO	A	E	DP	FPct
1947	Bro	26	3	3	0	0	0	0	0	0	0	0	1	0	1	0	0	0	0	0	—	0	.000	.250	.000	P	3	1	3	0	1	1.000

TOMMY GREGG
William Thomas Gregg—Bats: Left; Throws: Left — Ht: 6'1"; Wt: 190 lbs; Born: 7/29/1963 in Boone, North Carolina; Debut: 9/14/1987

LCS — Batting / Fielding

Year	Tm	Age	G	AB	H	2B	3B	HR	TB	R	RBI	GW	TBB	IBB	SO	HBP	SH	SF	SB	CS	SB%	GDP	Avg	OBP	SLG	Pos	G	PO	A	E	DP	FPct
1991	Atl	28	4	4	1	0	0	0	1	0	0	0	0	0	2	0	0	0	0	0	—	0	.250	.250	.250	—						
1997	Atl	34	4	4	0	0	0	0	0	0	0	0	0	0	1	0	0	0	0	0	—	0	.000	.000	.000	—						
LCS Totals			8	8	1	0	0	0	1	0	0	0	0	0	3	0	0	0	0	0	—	0	.125	.125	.125	—	0	0	0	0	0	

World Series — Batting / Fielding

Year	Tm	Age	G	AB	H	2B	3B	HR	TB	R	RBI	GW	TBB	IBB	SO	HBP	SH	SF	SB	CS	SB%	GDP	Avg	OBP	SLG	Pos	G	PO	A	E	DP	FPct
1991	Atl	28	4	3	0	0	0	0	0	0	0	0	0	0	2	0	0	0	0	0	—	0	.000	.000	.000	—						
Postseason Totals			12	11	1	0	0	0	1	0	0	0	0	0	5	0	0	0	0	0	—	0	.091	.091	.091	—	0	0	0	0	0	

BOBBY GRICH
Robert Anthony Grich—Bats: Right; Throws: Right — Ht: 6'2"; Wt: 180 lbs; Born: 1/15/1949 in Muskegon, Michigan; Debut: 6/29/1970

LCS — Batting / Fielding

Year	Tm	Age	G	AB	H	2B	3B	HR	TB	R	RBI	GW	TBB	IBB	SO	HBP	SH	SF	SB	CS	SB%	GDP	Avg	OBP	SLG	Pos	G	PO	A	E	DP	FPct
1973	Bal	24	5	20	2	0	0	1	5	1	1	1	2	0	5	0	0	0	0	0	—	0	.100	.182	.250	2B	5	17	9	0	1	1.000
1974	Bal	25	4	16	4	1	0	1	8	2	2	0	1	0	0	0	0	0	0	0	—	1	.250	.250	.500	2B	4	13	12	1	3	.962
1979	Cal	30	4	13	2	1	0	0	3	0	2	0	1	0	1	0	0	0	0	0	—	0	.154	.200	.231	2B	4	4	12	2	4	.889
1982	Cal	33	5	15	3	1	0	0	4	1	1	0	2	0	7	1	1	0	0	0	—	0	.200	.333	.267	2B	5	11	17	0	3	1.000
1986	Cal	37	6	24	5	0	0	1	8	1	3	1	0	0	8	2	0	0	0	0	—	0	.208	.269	.333	2B	3	3	7	2	0	.833
																										1B	3	26	2	1	5	.966
LCS Totals			24	88	16	3	0	3	28	5	9	2	5	0	22	3	1	1	0	0	—	1	.182	.247	.318	2B	21	48	57	5	11	.955

KEN GRIFFEY JR.
George Kenneth Griffey Jr.—Nicknames: Junior, The Kid—Bats: Left; Throws: Left — Ht: 6'3"; Wt: 195 lbs; Born: 11/21/1969 in Donora, Pennsylvania; Debut: 4/3/1989

Division Series — Batting / Fielding

Year	Tm	Age	G	AB	H	2B	3B	HR	TB	R	RBI	GW	TBB	IBB	SO	HBP	SH	SF	SB	CS	SB%	GDP	Avg	OBP	SLG	Pos	G	PO	A	E	DP	FPct
1995	Sea	25	5	23	9	0	0	5	24	9	7	0	2	1	4	1	0	1	1	0	1.00	0	.391	.444	1.043	OF	5	15	1	0	0	1.000
1997	Sea-M	27	4	15	2	0	0	0	2	0	2	0	1	0	3	0	0	0	2	0	1.00	0	.133	.188	.133	OF	4	12	1	0	0	1.000
DS Totals			9	38	11	0	0	5	26	9	9	0	3	1	7	1	0	1	3	0	1.00	0	.289	.349	.684	OF	9	27	2	0	0	1.000

LCS — Batting / Fielding

Year	Tm	Age	G	AB	H	2B	3B	HR	TB	R	RBI	GW	TBB	IBB	SO	HBP	SH	SF	SB	CS	SB%	GDP	Avg	OBP	SLG	Pos	G	PO	A	E	DP	FPct
1995	Sea	25	6	21	7	2	0	1	12	2	2	0	4	0	4	0	0	0	2	1	.67	0	.333	.440	.571	OF	6	13	0	1	0	.929
Postseason Totals			15	59	18	2	0	6	38	11	11	0	7	1	11	1	0	1	5	1	.83	0	.305	.382	.644	OF	15	40	2	1	0	.977

KEN GRIFFEY SR.
George Kenneth Griffey Sr.—Bats: Left; Throws: Left — Ht: 5'11"; Wt: 190 lbs; Born: 4/10/1950 in Donora, Pennsylvania; Debut: 8/25/1973

LCS — Batting / Fielding

Year	Tm	Age	G	AB	H	2B	3B	HR	TB	R	RBI	GW	TBB	IBB	SO	HBP	SH	SF	SB	CS	SB%	GDP	Avg	OBP	SLG	Pos	G	PO	A	E	DP	FPct
1973	Cin	23	3	7	1	1	0	0	2	0	0	0	0	0	1	1	0	0	0	0	—	0	.143	.250	.286	OF	2	1	0	0	0	1.000
1975	Cin	25	3	12	4	1	0	0	5	3	4	1	0	0	3	0	0	0	3	0	1.00	1	.333	.333	.417	OF	3	4	1	0	0	1.000
1976	Cin	26	3	13	5	0	1	0	7	2	2	1	2	0	1	0	0	0	2	0	1.00	0	.385	.467	.538	OF	3	11	0	0	0	1.000
LCS Totals			9	32	10	2	1	0	14	5	6	2	2	0	5	1	0	0	5	0	1.00	1	.313	.371	.438	OF	8	16	1	0	0	1.000

World Series — Batting / Fielding

Year	Tm	Age	G	AB	H	2B	3B	HR	TB	R	RBI	GW	TBB	IBB	SO	HBP	SH	SF	SB	CS	SB%	GDP	Avg	OBP	SLG	Pos	G	PO	A	E	DP	FPct
1975	Cin	25	7	26	7	3	1	0	12	4	4	1	4	0	2	0	0	0	2	0	1.00	0	.269	.367	.462	OF	7	10	1	0	0	1.000
1976	Cin	26	4	17	1	0	0	0	1	2	1	0	0	0	1	0	0	0	1	0	1.00	0	.059	.056	.059	OF	4	5	0	0	0	1.000
WS Totals			11	43	8	3	1	0	13	6	5	1	4	0	3	0	0	0	3	0	1.00	0	.186	.250	.302	OF	11	15	1	0	0	1.000
Postseason Totals			20	75	18	5	2	0	27	11	11	3	6	0	8	1	0	1	8	0	1.00	1	.240	.301	.360	OF	19	31	2	0	0	1.000

ALFREDO GRIFFIN
Alfredo Claudino Griffin—Bats: Both; Throws: Right — Ht: 5'11"; Wt: 160 lbs; Born: 10/6/1957 in Santo Domingo, Dominican Republic; Debut: 9/4/1976

LCS — Batting / Fielding

Year	Tm	Age	G	AB	H	2B	3B	HR	TB	R	RBI	GW	TBB	IBB	SO	HBP	SH	SF	SB	CS	SB%	GDP	Avg	OBP	SLG	Pos	G	PO	A	E	DP	FPct
1988	LA	30	7	25	4	1	0	0	5	1	3	0	0	0	5	0	1	0	0	1	.00	0	.160	.160	.200	SS	7	17	13	0	7	1.000
1992	Tor	34	2	2	0	0	0	0	0	0	0	0	0	0	0	0	0	0	0	0	—	0	.000	.000	.000	SS	1	0	3	0	0	1.000
LCS Totals			9	27	4	1	0	0	5	1	3	0	0	0	5	0	1	0	0	1	.00	0	.148	.148	.185	SS	8	17	16	0	7	1.000

World Series		Batting																							Fielding						
Year Tm	Age	G	AB	H	2B	3B	HR	TB	R	RBI	GW	TBB	IBB	SO	HBP	SH	SF	SB	CS	SB%	GDP	Avg	OBP	SLG	Pos	G	PO	A	E	DP	FPct
1988 LA	30	5	16	3	0	0	0	3	2	0	0	2	0	4	0	1	0	0	1	.00	0	.188	.278	.188	SS	5	7	12	1	1	.950
1992 Tor	34	2	0	0	0	0	0	0	0	0	0	0	0	0	0	0	0	0	0	—	0	—	—	—	SS	2	0	1	1	0	.500
1993 Tor	35	3	0	0	0	0	0	0	0	0	0	0	0	0	0	0	0	0	0	—	0	—	—	—	3B	2	0	0	0	0	—
WS Totals		10	16	3	0	0	0	3	2	0	0	2	0	4	0	1	0	0	1	.00	0	.188	.278	.188	SS	7	7	13	2	1	.909
Postseason Totals		19	43	7	1	0	0	8	3	3	0	2	0	9	0	2	0	0	2	.00	0	.163	.200	.186	SS	15	24	29	2	8	.964

DOUG GRIFFIN—Douglas Lee Griffin—Bats: Right; Throws: Right

Ht: 6'0"; Wt: 160 lbs; Born: 6/4/1947 in South Gate, California; Debut: 9/11/1970

World Series		Batting																							Fielding						
Year Tm	Age	G	AB	H	2B	3B	HR	TB	R	RBI	GW	TBB	IBB	SO	HBP	SH	SF	SB	CS	SB%	GDP	Avg	OBP	SLG	Pos	G	PO	A	E	DP	FPct
1975 Bos	28	1	1	0	0	0	0	0	0	0	0	0	0	0	0	0	0	0	0	—	0	.000	.000	.000	—						

TOMMY GRIFFITH—Thomas Herman Griffith—Bats: Left; Throws: Right

Ht: 5'10"; Wt: 175 lbs; Born: 10/26/1889 in Prospect, Ohio; Debut: 8/28/1913; Died: 4/13/1967

World Series		Batting																							Fielding						
Year Tm	Age	G	AB	H	2B	3B	HR	TB	R	RBI	GW	TBB	IBB	SO	HBP	SH	SF	SB	CS	SB%	GDP	Avg	OBP	SLG	Pos	G	PO	A	E	DP	FPct
1920 Bro	30	7	21	4	2	0	0	6	1	3	0	0	0	2	0	0	0	0	1	.00	0	.190	.190	.286	OF	7	10	0	0	0	1.000

BOB GRIM—Robert Anton Grim—Throws: Right; Bats: Right

Ht: 6'1"; Wt: 175 lbs; Born: 3/8/1930 in New York, New York; Debut: 4/18/1954; Died: 10/23/1996

World Series		Pitching																										
Year Tm	Age	G	GS	CG	GF	IP	BFP	H	R	ER	HR	SH	SF	HB	TBB	IBB	SO	WP	Bk	W	L	Pct	ShO	Sv-Op	Hld	OAvg	OOBP	ERA
1955 NYA	25	3	1	0	1	8.2	36	8	4	4	3	1	1	0	5	0	8	1	0	0	1	.000	0	1- 1	0	.276	.371	4.15
1957 NYA	27	2	0	0	2	2.1	10	3	2	2	1	1	0	0	0	0	2	0	0	0	1	.000	0	0- 1	0	.333	.333	7.71
WS Totals		5	1	0	3	11.0	92	11	6	6	4	2	1	0	5	0	10	1	0	0	2	.000	0	1-2	0	.289	.364	4.91

World Series		Batting																							Fielding						
Year Tm	Age	G	AB	H	2B	3B	HR	TB	R	RBI	GW	TBB	IBB	SO	HBP	SH	SF	SB	CS	SB%	GDP	Avg	OBP	SLG	Pos	G	PO	A	E	DP	FPct
1955 NYA	25	3	2	0	0	0	0	0	0	0	0	0	0	0	0	0	0	0	0	—	0	.000	.000	.000	P	3	1	1	0	0	1.000
1957 NYA	27	2	0	0	0	0	0	0	0	0	0	0	0	0	0	0	0	0	0	—	0	—	—	—	P	2	0	0	0	0	—
WS Totals		5	2	0	0	0	0	0	0	0	0	0	0	0	0	0	0	0	0	—	0	.000	.000	.000	P	5	1	1	0	0	1.000

BURLEIGH GRIMES (HOF 1964-V)—Burleigh Arland Grimes—Nickname: Ol' Stubblebeard—T: R; B: R

Ht: 5'10"; Wt: 175 lbs; Born: 8/18/1893 in Emerald, Wis.; Deb.: 9/10/1916; Died: 12/6/1985

World Series		Pitching																										
Year Tm	Age	G	GS	CG	GF	IP	BFP	H	R	ER	HR	SH	SF	HB	TBB	IBB	SO	WP	Bk	W	L	Pct	ShO	Sv-Op	Hld	OAvg	OOBP	ERA
1920 Bro	27	3	3	1	0	19.1	88	23	10	9	2	0	0	0	9	1	4	0	0	1	2	.333	1	0- 0	0	.291	.364	4.19
1930 StL	37	2	2	2	0	17.0	65	10	7	7	3	1	1	0	6	1	13	0	0	0	2	.000	0	0- 0	0	.175	.250	3.71
1931 StL	38	2	2	1	0	17.2	68	9	4	4	1	0	0	0	9	0	11	0	0	2	0	1.000	0	0- 0	0	.153	.265	2.04
1932 ChN	39	2	0	0	1	2.2	17	7	7	7	2	0	0	1	2	0	0	1	0	0	0	—	0	0- 0	0	.500	.588	23.63
WS Totals		9	7	4	1	56.2	476	49	28	27	8	1	1	1	26	2	28	1	0	3	4	.429	1	0-0	0	.234	.321	4.29

World Series		Batting																							Fielding						
Year Tm	Age	G	AB	H	2B	3B	HR	TB	R	RBI	GW	TBB	IBB	SO	HBP	SH	SF	SB	CS	SB%	GDP	Avg	OBP	SLG	Pos	G	PO	A	E	DP	FPct
1920 Bro	27	3	6	2	0	0	0	2	1	0	0	0	0	0	0	0	0	0	0	—	1	.333	.333	.333	P	3	1	7	1	0	.889
1930 StL	37	2	5	2	0	0	0	2	0	0	0	0	0	1	0	1	0	0	0	—	0	.400	.400	.400	P	2	0	3	0	0	1.000
1931 StL	38	2	7	2	0	0	0	2	0	2	0	0	0	2	0	0	0	0	0	—	0	.286	.286	.286	P	2	0	3	0	0	1.000
1932 ChN	39	2	1	0	0	0	0	0	0	0	0	0	0	1	0	0	0	0	0	—	0	.000	.000	.000	P	2	0	0	0	0	—
WS Totals		9	19	6	0	0	0	6	1	2	0	0	0	4	0	1	0	0	0	—	1	.316	.316	.316	P	9	1	13	1	0	.933

CHARLIE GRIMM—Charles John Grimm—Nickname: Jolly Cholly—Bats: Left; Throws: Left

Ht: 5'11"; Wt: 173 lbs; Born: 8/28/1898 in St. Louis, Missouri; Debut: 7/30/1916; Died: 11/15/1983

World Series		Batting																							Fielding						
Year Tm	Age	G	AB	H	2B	3B	HR	TB	R	RBI	GW	TBB	IBB	SO	HBP	SH	SF	SB	CS	SB%	GDP	Avg	OBP	SLG	Pos	G	PO	A	E	DP	FPct
1929 ChN	31	5	18	7	0	0	1	10	2	4	0	1	0	2	0	1	0	0	1	.00	0	.389	.421	.556	1B	5	40	1	0	4	1.000
1932 ChN	34	4	15	5	2	0	0	7	2	1	0	2	0	2	0	0	0	0	0	—	0	.333	.412	.467	1B	4	28	3	0	5	1.000
WS Totals		9	33	12	2	0	1	17	4	5	0	3	0	4	0	1	0	0	1	.00	0	.364	.417	.515	1B	9	68	4	0	9	1.000

ROSS GRIMSLEY—Ross Albert, II Grimsley—Throws: Left; Bats: Left

Ht: 6'3"; Wt: 195 lbs; Born: 1/7/1950 in Topeka, Kansas; Debut: 5/16/1971

LCS		Pitching																										
Year Tm	Age	G	GS	CG	GF	IP	BFP	H	R	ER	HR	SH	SF	HB	TBB	IBB	SO	WP	Bk	W	L	Pct	ShO	Sv-Op	Hld	OAvg	OOBP	ERA
1972 Cin	22	1	1	1	0	9.0	30	2	1	1	1	0	0	0	0	0	5	0	0	1	0	1.000	0	0- 0	0	.067	.067	1.00
1973 Cin	23	2	1	0	1	3.2	20	7	5	5	1	0	1	0	2	0	3	0	0	0	1	.000	0	0- 0	0	.412	.450	12.27
1974 Bal	24	2	0	0	2	5.1	18	1	1	1	0	0	1	0	2	1	2	0	0	0	0	—	0	0- 1	0	.067	.167	1.69
LCS Totals		5	2	1	3	18.0	136	10	7	7	2	0	2	0	4	1	10	0	0	1	1	.500	0	0-1	0	.161	.206	3.50
World Series		**Pitching**																										
Year Tm	Age	G	GS	CG	GF	IP	BFP	H	R	ER	HR	SH	SF	HB	TBB	IBB	SO	WP	Bk	W	L	Pct	ShO	Sv-Op	Hld	OAvg	OOBP	ERA
1972 Cin	22	4	1	0	0	7.0	30	7	2	2	1	0	0	0	3	1	2	0	0	2	1	.667	0	0- 0	0	.259	.333	2.57
Postseason Totals		9	3	1	3	25.0	196	17	9	9	3	0	2	0	7	2	12	0	0	3	2	.600	0	0-1	0	.191	.245	3.24

LCS		Batting																							Fielding						
Year Tm	Age	G	AB	H	2B	3B	HR	TB	R	RBI	GW	TBB	IBB	SO	HBP	SH	SF	SB	CS	SB%	GDP	Avg	OBP	SLG	Pos	G	PO	A	E	DP	FPct
1972 Cin	22	1	4	2	1	0	0	3	0	1	0	0	0	1	0	0	0	0	0	—	0	.500	.500	.750	P	1	0	0	0	0	—
1973 Cin	23	2	0	0	0	0	0	0	0	0	0	0	0	0	0	0	0	0	0	—	0	—	—	—	P	2	1	0	0	0	1.000
1974 Bal	24	2	0	0	0	0	0	0	0	0	0	0	0	0	0	0	0	0	0	—	0	—	—	—	P	2	0	1	0	0	1.000
LCS Totals		5	4	2	1	0	0	3	0	1	0	0	0	1	0	0	0	0	0	—	0	.500	.500	.750	P	5	1	1	0	0	1.000
World Series		**Batting**																							**Fielding**						
Year Tm	Age	G	AB	H	2B	3B	HR	TB	R	RBI	GW	TBB	IBB	SO	HBP	SH	SF	SB	CS	SB%	GDP	Avg	OBP	SLG	Pos	G	PO	A	E	DP	FPct
1972 Cin	22	4	2	0	0	0	0	0	0	0	0	0	0	2	0	1	0	0	0	—	0	.000	.000	.000	P	4	0	2	0	0	1.000
Postseason Totals		9	6	2	1	0	0	3	0	1	0	0	0	3	0	1	0	0	0	—	0	.333	.333	.500	P	9	1	3	0	0	1.000

LEE GRISSOM—Lee Theo Grissom—Throws: Left; Bats: Both

Ht: 6'3"; Wt: 200 lbs; Born: 10/23/1907 in Sherman, Texas; Debut: 9/2/1934

World Series		Pitching																										
Year Tm	Age	G	GS	CG	GF	IP	BFP	H	R	ER	HR	SH	SF	HB	TBB	IBB	SO	WP	Bk	W	L	Pct	ShO	Sv-Op	Hld	OAvg	OOBP	ERA
1939 Cin	31	1	0	0	0	1.1	5	0	0	0	0	0	0	0	1	0	0	0	0	0	0	—	0	0- 0	0	.000	.200	0.00

World Series		Batting																							Fielding						
Year Tm	Age	G	AB	H	2B	3B	HR	TB	R	RBI	GW	TBB	IBB	SO	HBP	SH	SF	SB	CS	SB%	GDP	Avg	OBP	SLG	Pos	G	PO	A	E	DP	FPct
1939 Cin	31	1	0	0	0	0	0	0	0	0	0	0	0	0	0	0	0	0	0	—	0	—	—	—	P	1	0	0	0	0	—

MARQUIS GRISSOM—Marquis Deon Grissom—Bats: Right; Throws: Right

Ht: 5'11"; Wt: 190 lbs; Born: 4/17/1967 in Atlanta, Georgia; Debut: 8/22/1989

Division Series		Batting																							Fielding						
Year Tm	Age	G	AB	H	2B	3B	HR	TB	R	RBI	GW	TBB	IBB	SO	HBP	SH	SF	SB	CS	SB%	GDP	Avg	OBP	SLG	Pos	G	PO	A	E	DP	FPct
1995 Atl	28	4	21	11	2	0	3	22	5	4	0	0	0	3	0	0	0	2	1	.67	0	.524	.524	1.048	OF	4	9	0	0	0	1.000
1996 Atl	29	3	12	1	0	0	0	1	2	0	0	1	0	2	0	0	0	1	0	1.00	0	.083	.154	.083	OF	3	4	0	1	0	.800
1997 Cle	30	5	17	4	0	1	0	6	3	0	0	1	0	2	0	0	0	0	1	.00	0	.235	.278	.353	OF	5	14	0	0	0	1.000
DS Totals		12	50	16	2	1	3	29	10	4	0	2	0	7	0	0	0	3	2	.60	0	.320	.346	.580	OF	12	27	0	1	0	.964
LCS		**Batting**																							**Fielding**						
Year Tm	Age	G	AB	H	2B	3B	HR	TB	R	RBI	GW	TBB	IBB	SO	HBP	SH	SF	SB	CS	SB%	GDP	Avg	OBP	SLG	Pos	G	PO	A	E	DP	FPct
1995 Atl	28	4	19	5	0	1	0	7	2	0	0	1	0	4	0	0	0	0	0	—	0	.263	.300	.368	OF	4	8	0	1	0	.889
1996 Atl	29	7	35	10	1	0	1	14	7	3	0	0	0	8	0	0	0	2	0	1.00	0	.286	.286	.400	OF	7	17	0	1	0	.944
1997 Cle	30	6	23	6	0	0	1	9	2	4	1	1	0	9	0	0	0	3	0	1.00	0	.261	.292	.391	OF	6	13	1	0	0	1.000
LCS Totals		17	77	21	1	1	2	30	11	7	1	2	0	21	0	0	0	5	0	1.00	0	.273	.291	.390	OF	17	38	1	2	0	.951

World Series		Batting																							Fielding						
Year Tm	Age	G	AB	H	2B	3B	HR	TB	R	RBI	GW	TBB	IBB	SO	HBP	SH	SF	SB	CS	SB%	GDP	Avg	OBP	SLG	Pos	G	PO	A	E	DP	FPct
1995 Atl	28	6	25	9	1	0	0	10	3	1	0	1	0	3	1	0	0	3	1	.75	1	.360	.407	.400	OF	6	13	0	0	0	1.000
1996 Atl	29	6	27	12	2	1	0	16	4	5	0	1	0	2	0	0	0	1	0	1.00	0	.444	.464	.593	OF	6	7	0	1	0	.875
1997 Cle	30	7	25	9	1	0	0	10	5	2	1	4	0	4	0	0	0	0	0	—	1	.360	.448	.400	OF	7	19	0	1	0	.950
WS Totals		19	77	30	4	1	0	36	12	8	1	6	0	9	1	0	0	4	1	.80	2	.390	.440	.468	OF	19	39	0	2	0	.951
Postseason Totals		48	204	67	7	3	5	95	33	19	2	10	0	37	1	0	0	12	3	.80	2	.328	.363	.466	OF	48	104	1	5	0	.955

MARV GRISSOM—Marvin Edward Grissom—Throws: Right; Bats: Right

Ht: 6'3"; Wt: 190 lbs; Born: 3/31/1918 in Los Molinas, California; Debut: 9/10/1946

World Series		Pitching																										
Year Tm	Age	G	GS	CG	GF	IP	BFP	H	R	ER	HR	SH	SF	HB	TBB	IBB	SO	WP	Bk	W	L	Pct	ShO	Sv-Op	Hld	OAvg	OOBP	ERA
1954 NYG	36	1	0	0	1	2.2	13	1	0	0	0	1	0	0	3	2	2	0	0	1	0	1.000	0	0-0	0	.111	.333	0.00

World Series		Batting																							Fielding						
Year Tm	Age	G	AB	H	2B	3B	HR	TB	R	RBI	GW	TBB	IBB	SO	HBP	SH	SF	SB	CS	SB%	GDP	Avg	OBP	SLG	Pos	G	PO	A	E	DP	FPct
1954 NYG	36	1	1	0	0	0	0	0	0	0	0	0	0	1	0	0	0	0	0	—	0	.000	.000	.000	P	1	0	0	0	0	—

DICK GROAT—Richard Morrow Groat—Bats: Right; Throws: Right

Ht: 5'11"; Wt: 180 lbs; Born: 11/4/1930 in Wilkinsburg, Pennsylvania; Debut: 6/19/1952

World Series		Batting																							Fielding						
Year Tm	Age	G	AB	H	2B	3B	HR	TB	R	RBI	GW	TBB	IBB	SO	HBP	SH	SF	SB	CS	SB%	GDP	Avg	OBP	SLG	Pos	G	PO	A	E	DP	FPct
1960 Pit-*M*	29	7	28	6	2	0	0	8	3	2	0	0	0	1	0	0	0	0	0	—	1	.214	.214	.286	SS	7	12	12	2	2	.923
1964 StL	33	7	26	5	1	1	0	8	3	1	0	4	0	3	0	0	0	0	0	—	0	.192	.300	.308	SS	7	11	16	2	6	.931
WS Totals		14	54	11	3	1	0	16	6	3	0	4	0	4	0	0	0	0	0	—	1	.204	.259	.296	SS	14	23	28	4	8	.927

HEINE GROH—Henry Knight Groh—Bats: Right; Throws: Right

Ht: 5'8"; Wt: 158 lbs; Born: 9/18/1889 in Rochester, New York; Debut: 4/12/1912; Died: 8/22/1968

World Series		Batting																							Fielding						
Year Tm	Age	G	AB	H	2B	3B	HR	TB	R	RBI	GW	TBB	IBB	SO	HBP	SH	SF	SB	CS	SB%	GDP	Avg	OBP	SLG	Pos	G	PO	A	E	DP	FPct
1919 Cin	30	8	29	5	2	0	0	7	6	2	0	6	0	4	0	0	1	0	1	.00	0	.172	.306	.241	3B	8	8	18	2	2	.929
1922 NYG	33	5	19	9	0	1	0	11	4	0	0	2	0	1	0	0	0	0	1	.00	0	.474	.524	.579	3B	5	6	16	0	0	1.000
1923 NYG	34	6	22	4	0	1	0	6	3	2	0	3	0	1	0	0	0	0	0	—	0	.182	.280	.273	3B	6	4	17	0	1	1.000
1924 NYG	35	1	1	1	0	0	0	1	0	0	0	0	0	0	0	0	0	0	0	—	0	1.000	1.000	1.000	—						
1927 Pit	38	1	1	0	0	0	0	0	0	0	0	0	0	0	0	0	0	0	0	—	0	.000	.000	.000	—						
WS Totals		21	72	19	2	2	0	25	13	4	0	11	0	6	0	0	1	0	2	.00	0	.264	.357	.347	3B	19	18	51	2	3	.972

STEVE GROMEK—Stephen Joseph Gromek—Throws: Right; Bats: Both

Ht: 6'2"; Wt: 180 lbs; Born: 1/15/1920 in Hamtramck, Michigan; Debut: 8/18/1941

World Series		Pitching																										
Year Tm	Age	G	GS	CG	GF	IP	BFP	H	R	ER	HR	SH	SF	HB	TBB	IBB	SO	WP	Bk	W	L	Pct	ShO	Sv-Op	Hld	OAvg	OOBP	ERA
1948 Cle	28	1	1	1	0	9.0	34	7	1	1	1	1	0	0	1	0	2	0	0	1	0	1.000	0	0-0	0	.219	.242	1.00

World Series		Batting																							Fielding						
Year Tm	Age	G	AB	H	2B	3B	HR	TB	R	RBI	GW	TBB	IBB	SO	HBP	SH	SF	SB	CS	SB%	GDP	Avg	OBP	SLG	Pos	G	PO	A	E	DP	FPct
1948 Cle	28	1	3	0	0	0	0	0	0	0	0	0	0	1	0	0	0	0	0	—	0	.000	.000	.000	P	1	1	1	0	0	1.000

GREG GROSS—Gregory Eugene Gross—Bats: Left; Throws: Left

Ht: 5'10"; Wt: 160 lbs; Born: 8/1/1952 in York, Pennsylvania; Debut: 9/5/1973

Division Series		Batting																							Fielding						
Year Tm	Age	G	AB	H	2B	3B	HR	TB	R	RBI	GW	TBB	IBB	SO	HBP	SH	SF	SB	CS	SB%	GDP	Avg	OBP	SLG	Pos	G	PO	A	E	DP	FPct
1981 Phi	29	4	4	0	0	0	0	0	0	0	0	0	0	0	0	0	0	0	0	—	1	.000	.000	.000	OF	2	0	0	0	0	—
LCS		**Batting**																							**Fielding**						
Year Tm	Age	G	AB	H	2B	3B	HR	TB	R	RBI	GW	TBB	IBB	SO	HBP	SH	SF	SB	CS	SB%	GDP	Avg	OBP	SLG	Pos	G	PO	A	E	DP	FPct
1980 Phi	28	4	4	3	0	0	0	3	2	1	0	0	0	0	0	1	0	0	0	—	0	.750	.750	.750	OF	1	1	0	0	0	1.000
1983 Phi	31	4	5	0	0	0	0	0	1	0	0	2	0	2	0	0	0	0	0	—	0	.000	.286	.000	OF	3	4	0	0	0	1.000
LCS Totals		8	9	3	0	0	0	3	3	1	0	2	0	2	0	1	0	0	0	—	0	.333	.455	.333	OF	4	5	0	0	0	1.000
World Series		**Batting**																							**Fielding**						
Year Tm	Age	G	AB	H	2B	3B	HR	TB	R	RBI	GW	TBB	IBB	SO	HBP	SH	SF	SB	CS	SB%	GDP	Avg	OBP	SLG	Pos	G	PO	A	E	DP	FPct
1980 Phi	28	4	2	0	0	0	0	0	0	0	0	0	0	0	0	1	0	0	0	—	1	.000	.000	.000	OF	4	1	0	0	0	1.000
1983 Phi	31	2	6	0	0	0	0	0	0	0	0	0	0	0	0	0	0	0	0	—	1	.000	.000	.000	OF	2	8	0	0	0	1.000
WS Totals		6	8	0	0	0	0	0	0	0	0	0	0	0	0	1	0	0	0	—	2	.000	.000	.000	OF	6	9	0	0	0	1.000
Postseason Totals		18	21	3	0	0	0	3	3	1	0	2	0	2	0	2	0	0	0	—	3	.143	.217	.143	OF	12	14	0	0	0	1.000

WAYNE GROSS—Wayne Dale Gross—Bats: Left; Throws: Right

Ht: 6'2"; Wt: 210 lbs; Born: 1/14/1952 in Riverside, California; Debut: 8/21/1976

Division Series		Batting																							Fielding						
Year Tm	Age	G	AB	H	2B	3B	HR	TB	R	RBI	GW	TBB	IBB	SO	HBP	SH	SF	SB	CS	SB%	GDP	Avg	OBP	SLG	Pos	G	PO	A	E	DP	FPct
1981 Oak	29	2	5	2	0	0	1	5	1	3	1	0	0	0	0	0	0	0	0	—	0	.400	.400	1.000	3B	1	1	4	0	2	1.000
LCS		**Batting**																							**Fielding**						
Year Tm	Age	G	AB	H	2B	3B	HR	TB	R	RBI	GW	TBB	IBB	SO	HBP	SH	SF	SB	CS	SB%	GDP	Avg	OBP	SLG	Pos	G	PO	A	E	DP	FPct
1981 Oak	29	3	5	0	0	0	0	0	0	0	0	0	0	0	0	0	0	0	0	—	0	.000	.000	.000	3B	3	2	0	0	0	1.000
Postseason Totals		5	10	2	0	0	1	5	1	3	1	0	0	0	0	0	0	0	0	—	0	.200	.200	.500	3B	4	3	4	0	2	1.000

JERRY GROTE—Gerald Wayne Grote—Bats: Right; Throws: Right

Ht: 5'10"; Wt: 185 lbs; Born: 10/6/1942 in San Antonio, Texas; Debut: 9/21/1963

LCS		Batting																							Fielding						
Year Tm	Age	G	AB	H	2B	3B	HR	TB	R	RBI	GW	TBB	IBB	SO	HBP	SH	SF	SB	CS	SB%	GDP	Avg	OBP	SLG	Pos	G	PO	A	E	DP	FPct
1969 NYN	26	3	12	2	1	0	0	3	3	1	0	1	0	4	0	0	0	0	0	—	0	.167	.231	.250	C	3	22	1	0	0	1.000
1973 NYN	30	5	19	4	0	0	0	4	2	2	0	1	0	3	0	0	0	0	0	—	1	.211	.250	.211	C	5	42	1	1	0	.977
1977 LA	34	2	0	0	0	0	0	0	0	0	0	1	0	0	0	0	0	0	0	—	0	—	1.000	—	C	1	0	0	0	0	—
1978 LA	35	1	0	0	0	0	0	0	0	0	0	0	0	0	0	0	0	0	0	—	0	—	—	—	C	1	2	0	0	0	1.000
LCS Totals		11	31	6	1	0	0	7	5	3	0	3	0	7	0	0	0	0	0	—	1	.194	.265	.226	C	10	66	2	1	0	.986
World Series		**Batting**																							**Fielding**						
Year Tm	Age	G	AB	H	2B	3B	HR	TB	R	RBI	GW	TBB	IBB	SO	HBP	SH	SF	SB	CS	SB%	GDP	Avg	OBP	SLG	Pos	G	PO	A	E	DP	FPct
1969 NYN	26	5	19	4	2	0	0	6	1	1	0	1	0	3	0	0	0	0	0	—	0	.211	.250	.316	C	5	29	2	0	0	1.000
1973 NYN	30	7	30	8	0	0	0	8	2	0	0	0	0	1	1	1	0	0	0	—	1	.267	.290	.267	C	7	67	5	0	1	1.000
1977 LA	34	1	1	0	0	0	0	0	0	0	0	0	0	0	0	0	0	0	0	—	0	.000	.000	.000	C	1	3	3	0	0	1.000
1978 LA	35	2	0	0	0	0	0	0	0	0	0	0	0	0	0	0	0	0	0	—	0	—	—	—	C	2	3	0	0	0	1.000
WS Totals		15	50	12	2	0	0	14	3	1	0	1	0	4	1	1	0	0	0	—	1	.240	.269	.280	C	15	102	10	0	1	1.000
Postseason Totals		26	81	18	3	0	0	21	8	4	0	4	0	11	1	1	0	0	0	—	2	.222	.267	.259	C	25	168	12	1	1	.994

LEFTY GROVE (HOF 1947-W)—Robert Moses Grove—Throws: Left; Bats: Left

Ht: 6'3"; Wt: 190 lbs; Born: 3/6/1900 in Lonaconing, Maryland; Debut: 4/14/1925; Died: 5/22/1975

World Series		Pitching																										
Year Tm	Age	G	GS	CG	GF	IP	BFP	H	R	ER	HR	SH	SF	HB	TBB	IBB	SO	WP	Bk	W	L	Pct	ShO	Sv-Op	Hld	OAvg	OOBP	ERA
1929 Phi	29	2	0	0	2	6.1	22	3	0	0	0	0	0	0	1	0	10	0	0	1	0	1.000	0	1-1	0	.143	.182	0.00
1930 Phi	30	3	2	2	1	19.0	76	15	5	3	0	1	2	0	3	0	10	0	0	2	1	.667	0	0-0	0	.214	.240	1.42
1931 Phi-*M*	31	3	3	2	0	26.0	107	28	7	7	0	1	0	0	2	0	16	0	0	2	1	.667	0	0-0	0	.269	.283	2.42
WS Totals		8	5	4	3	51.1	410	46	12	10	0	2	2	0	6	0	36	0	0	5	2	.714	0	1-1	0	.236	.256	1.75

World Series		Batting																							Fielding						
Year Tm	Age	G	AB	H	2B	3B	HR	TB	R	RBI	GW	TBB	IBB	SO	HBP	SH	SF	SB	CS	SB%	GDP	Avg	OBP	SLG	Pos	G	PO	A	E	DP	FPct
1929 Phi	29	2	2	0	0	0	0	0	0	0	0	0	0	1	0	0	0	0	0	—	0	.000	.000	.000	P	2	0	1	0	0	1.000
1930 Phi	30	3	6	0	0	0	0	0	0	0	0	0	0	3	0	0	0	0	0	—	0	.000	.000	.000	P	3	0	1	0	0	1.000
1931 Phi	31	3	10	0	0	0	0	0	0	0	0	0	0	7	0	0	0	0	0	—	0	.000	.000	.000	P	3	0	0	0	0	—
WS Totals		8	18	0	0	0	0	0	0	0	0	0	0	11	0	0	0	0	0	—	0	.000	.000	.000	P	8	0	2	0	0	1.000

JOHN GRUBB—John Raymond Grubb—Bats: Left; Throws: Right

Ht: 6'3"; Wt: 175 lbs; Born: 8/4/1948 in Richmond, Virginia; Debut: 9/10/1972

LCS — Batting / Fielding

Year Tm	Age	G	AB	H	2B	3B	HR	TB	R	RBI	GW	TBB	IBB	SO	HBP	SH	SF	SB	CS	SB%	GDP	Avg	OBP	SLG	Pos	G	PO	A	E	DP	FPct
1984 Det	36	1	4	1	1	0	0	2	0	2	1	0	0	0	0	1	0	0	0	—	0	.250	.250	.500	—						
1987 Det	39	4	7	4	0	0	0	4	0	0	0	0	0	1	0	0	0	0	0	—	0	.571	.571	.571	—						
LCS Totals		5	11	5	1	0	0	6	0	2	1	0	0	1	0	1	0	0	0	—	0	.455	.455	.545	—	0	0	0	0	0	—

World Series — Batting / Fielding

Year Tm	Age	G	AB	H	2B	3B	HR	TB	R	RBI	GW	TBB	IBB	SO	HBP	SH	SF	SB	CS	SB%	GDP	Avg	OBP	SLG	Pos	G	PO	A	E	DP	FPct
1984 Det	36	4	3	1	0	0	0	1	0	0	0	0	0	0	1	0	0	0	0	—	0	.333	.500	.333	—						
Postseason Totals		9	14	6	1	0	0	7	0	2	1	0	0	1	1	1	0	0	0	—	0	.429	.467	.500	—	0	0	0	0	0	—

KELLY GRUBER—Kelly Wayne Gruber—Bats: Right; Throws: Right

Ht: 6'0"; Wt: 180 lbs; Born: 2/26/1962 in Houston, Texas; Debut: 4/20/1984

LCS — Batting / Fielding

Year Tm	Age	G	AB	H	2B	3B	HR	TB	R	RBI	GW	TBB	IBB	SO	HBP	SH	SF	SB	CS	SB%	GDP	Avg	OBP	SLG	Pos	G	PO	A	E	DP	FPct
1989 Tor	27	5	17	5	1	0	0	6	2	1	0	3	1	2	0	0	1	1	0	1.00	1	.294	.381	.353	3B	5	4	8	0	1	1.000
1991 Tor	29	5	21	6	1	0	0	7	1	4	0	0	0	4	0	0	0	1	0	1.00	0	.286	.286	.333	3B	5	3	6	3	0	.750
1992 Tor	30	6	22	2	1	0	1	6	3	2	1	2	0	3	0	1	0	0	0	—	1	.091	.167	.273	3B	6	5	16	1	1	.955
LCS Totals		16	60	13	3	0	1	19	6	7	1	5	1	9	0	1	1	2	0	1.00	2	.217	.273	.317	3B	16	12	30	4	2	.913

World Series — Batting / Fielding

Year Tm	Age	G	AB	H	2B	3B	HR	TB	R	RBI	GW	TBB	IBB	SO	HBP	SH	SF	SB	CS	SB%	GDP	Avg	OBP	SLG	Pos	G	PO	A	E	DP	FPct
1992 Tor	30	6	19	2	0	0	1	5	2	1	0	2	0	5	0	1	0	1	0	1.00	1	.105	.190	.263	3B	6	5	5	1	0	.909
Postseason Totals		22	79	15	3	0	2	24	8	8	1	7	1	14	0	2	1	3	0	1.00	3	.190	.253	.304	3B	22	17	35	5	2	.912

JOE GRZENDA—Joseph Charles Grzenda—Throws: Left; Bats: Right

Ht: 6'2"; Wt: 180 lbs; Born: 6/8/1937 in Scranton, Pennsylvania; Debut: 4/26/1961

LCS — Pitching

Year Tm	Age	G	GS	CG	GF	IP	BFP	H	R	ER	HR	SH	SF	HB	TBB	IBB	SO	WP	Bk	W	L	Pct	ShO	Sv-Op	Hld	OAvg	OOBP	ERA
1969 Min	32	1	0	0	0	0.2	2	0	0	0	0	0	0	0	0	0	0	0	0	0	0	—	0	0-0	0	.000	.000	0.00

LCS — Batting / Fielding

Year Tm	Age	G	AB	H	2B	3B	HR	TB	R	RBI	GW	TBB	IBB	SO	HBP	SH	SF	SB	CS	SB%	GDP	Avg	OBP	SLG	Pos	G	PO	A	E	DP	FPct
1969 Min	32	1	0	0	0	0	0	0	0	0	0	0	0	0	0	0	0	0	0	—	0	—	—	—	P	1	0	0	0	0	—

MARK GUBICZA—Mark Steven Gubicza—Throws: Right; Bats: Right

Ht: 6'6"; Wt: 215 lbs; Born: 8/14/1962 in Philadelphia, Pennsylvania; Debut: 4/6/1984

LCS — Pitching

Year Tm	Age	G	GS	CG	GF	IP	BFP	H	R	ER	HR	SH	SF	HB	TBB	IBB	SO	WP	Bk	W	L	Pct	ShO	Sv-Op	Hld	OAvg	OOBP	ERA
1985 KC	23	2	1	0	0	8.1	32	4	3	3	0	0	0	0	4	0	4	1	0	1	0	1.000	0	0-0	0	.143	.250	3.24

LCS — Batting / Fielding

Year Tm	Age	G	AB	H	2B	3B	HR	TB	R	RBI	GW	TBB	IBB	SO	HBP	SH	SF	SB	CS	SB%	GDP	Avg	OBP	SLG	Pos	G	PO	A	E	DP	FPct
1985 KC	23	2	0	0	0	0	0	0	0	0	0	0	0	0	0	0	0	0	0	—	0	—	—	—	P	2	0	1	0	1	1.000

MARV GUDAT—Marvin John Gudat—Bats: Left; Throws: Left

Ht: 5'11"; Wt: 162 lbs; Born: 8/27/1905 in Goliad, Texas; Debut: 5/21/1929; Died: 3/1/1954

World Series — Batting / Fielding

Year Tm	Age	G	AB	H	2B	3B	HR	TB	R	RBI	GW	TBB	IBB	SO	HBP	SH	SF	SB	CS	SB%	GDP	Avg	OBP	SLG	Pos	G	PO	A	E	FPct
1932 ChN	27	2	2	0	0	0	0	0	0	0	0	0	0	1	0	0	0	0	0	—	0	.000	.000	.000	—					

PEDRO GUERRERO—Bats: Right; Throws: Right

Ht. 5'11"; Wt: 176 lbs; Born: 6/29/1956 in San Pedro de Macoris, Dominican Republic; Debut: 9/22/1978

Division Series — Batting / Fielding

Year Tm	Age	G	AB	H	2B	3B	HR	TB	R	RBI	GW	TBB	IBB	SO	HBP	SH	SF	SB	CS	SB%	GDP	Avg	OBP	SLG	Pos	G	PO	A	E	DP	FPct
1981 LA	25	5	17	3	1	0	1	7	1	1	1	2	1	4	0	0	0	1	0	1.00	0	.176	.263	.412	3B	5	3	14	1	1	.944

LCS — Batting / Fielding

Year Tm	Age	G	AB	H	2B	3B	HR	TB	R	RBI	GW	TBB	IBB	SO	HBP	SH	SF	SB	CS	SB%	GDP	Avg	OBP	SLG	Pos	G	PO	A	E	DP	FPct
1981 LA	25	5	19	2	0	0	1	5	1	2	0	1	0	4	0	0	0	0	0	—	4	.105	.150	.263	OF	5	9	2	0	1	1.000
1983 LA	27	4	12	3	1	1	0	6	1	2	1	3	0	3	1	0	0	0	0	—	0	.250	.438	.500	3B	4	1	9	0	0	1.000
1985 LA	29	6	20	5	1	0	0	6	2	4	1	5	5	2	0	0	1	2	0	1.00	1	.250	.385	.300	OF	6	11	0	0	0	1.000
LCS Totals		15	51	10	2	1	1	17	4	8	2	9	5	9	1	0	1	2	0	1.00	5	.196	.323	.333	OF	11	20	2	0	1	1.000

World Series — Batting / Fielding

Year Tm	Age	G	AB	H	2B	3B	HR	TB	R	RBI	GW	TBB	IBB	SO	HBP	SH	SF	SB	CS	SB%	GDP	Avg	OBP	SLG	Pos	G	PO	A	E	DP	FPct
1981 LA	25	6	21	7	1	1	2	16	2	7	0	2	1	6	1	0	0	0	0	—	0	.333	.417	.762	OF	6	17	1	0	0	1.000
Postseason Totals		26	89	20	4	2	4	40	7	16	3	13	7	19	2	0	1	3	0	1.00	5	.225	.333	.449	OF	17	37	3	0	1	1.000

RON GUIDRY—Ronald Ames Guidry—Nickname: Louisiana Lightning—Throws: Left; Bats: Left

Ht: 5'11"; Wt: 161 lbs; Born: 8/28/1950 in Lafayette, Louisiana; Debut: 7/27/1975

Division Series — Pitching

Year Tm	Age	G	GS	CG	GF	IP	BFP	H	R	ER	HR	SH	SF	HB	TBB	IBB	SO	WP	Bk	W	L	Pct	ShO	Sv-Op	Hld	OAvg	OOBP	ERA
1981 NYA	31	2	2	0	0	8.1	39	11	5	5	1	1	2	0	3	0	8	0	0	0	0	—	0	0-0	0	.333	.368	5.40

LCS — Pitching

Year Tm	Age	G	GS	CG	GF	IP	BFP	H	R	ER	HR	SH	SF	HB	TBB	IBB	SO	WP	Bk	W	L	Pct	ShO	Sv-Op	Hld	OAvg	OOBP	ERA
1977 NYA	27	2	2	1	0	11.1	45	9	5	5	0	0	1	0	3	0	8	0	0	1	0	1.000	0	0-0	0	.220	.267	3.97
1978 NYA-*C*	28	1	1	0	0	8.0	30	7	1	1	0	0	0	0	1	0	7	0	0	1	0	1.000	0	0-0	0	.241	.267	1.13
1980 NYA	30	1	1	0	0	3.0	17	5	4	4	0	0	0	0	4	1	2	0	0	0	1	.000	0	0-0	0	.385	.529	12.00
LCS Totals		4	4	1	0	22.1	184	21	10	10	0	0	1	0	8	1	17	0	0	2	1	.667	0	0-0	0	.253	.315	4.03

World Series — Pitching

Year Tm	Age	G	GS	CG	GF	IP	BFP	H	R	ER	HR	SH	SF	HB	TBB	IBB	SO	WP	Bk	W	L	Pct	ShO	Sv-Op	Hld	OAvg	OOBP	ERA
1977 NYA	27	1	1	1	0	9.0	33	4	2	2	1	0	0	0	3	0	7	0	0	1	0	1.000	0	0-0	0	.133	.212	2.00
1978 NYA-*C*	28	1	1	1	0	9.0	39	8	1	1	0	0	0	0	7	0	4	0	0	1	0	1.000	0	0-0	0	.250	.385	1.00
1981 NYA	31	2	2	0	0	14.0	53	8	3	3	3	0	0	0	4	0	15	0	0	1	1	.500	0	0-0	0	.163	.226	1.93
WS Totals		4	4	2	0	32.0	250	20	6	6	4	0	0	0	14	0	26	0	0	3	1	.750	0	0-0	0	.180	.272	1.69
Postseason Totals		10	10	3	0	62.2	512	52	21	21	5	1	3	0	25	1	51	0	0	5	2	.714	0	0-0	0	.229	.302	3.02

Division Series — Batting / Fielding

Year Tm	Age	G	AB	H	2B	3B	HR	TB	R	RBI	GW	TBB	IBB	SO	HBP	SH	SF	SB	CS	SB%	GDP	Avg	OBP	SLG	Pos	G	PO	A	E	DP	FPct
1981 NYA	31	2	0	0	0	0	0	0	0	0	0	0	0	0	0	0	0	0	0	—	0	—	—	—	P	2	0	0	0	0	—

LCS — Batting / Fielding

Year Tm	Age	G	AB	H	2B	3B	HR	TB	R	RBI	GW	TBB	IBB	SO	HBP	SH	SF	SB	CS	SB%	GDP	Avg	OBP	SLG	Pos	G	PO	A	E	DP	FPct
1976 NYA	26	1	0	0	0	0	0	0	0	0	0	0	0	0	0	0	0	0	0	—	0	—	—	—	—						
1977 NYA	27	2	0	0	0	0	0	0	0	0	0	0	0	0	0	0	0	0	0	—	0	—	—	—	P	2	2	0	0	0	1.000
1978 NYA	28	1	0	0	0	0	0	0	0	0	0	0	0	0	0	0	0	0	0	—	0	—	—	—	P	1	0	0	0	0	—
1980 NYA	30	1	0	0	0	0	0	0	0	0	0	0	0	0	0	0	0	0	0	—	0	—	—	—	P	1	0	1	0	0	1.000
LCS Totals		5	0	0	0	0	0	0	0	0	0	0	0	0	0	0	0	0	0	—	0	—	—	—	P	4	2	1	0	0	1.000

World Series — Batting / Fielding

Year Tm	Age	G	AB	H	2B	3B	HR	TB	R	RBI	GW	TBB	IBB	SO	HBP	SH	SF	SB	CS	SB%	GDP	Avg	OBP	SLG	Pos	G	PO	A	E	DP	FPct
1977 NYA	27	1	2	0	0	0	0	0	0	0	0	0	0	1	0	1	0	0	0	—	0	.000	.000	.000	P	1	0	0	0	0	—
1978 NYA	28	1	0	0	0	0	0	0	0	0	0	0	0	0	0	0	0	0	0	—	0	—	—	—	P	1	1	1	0	0	1.000
1981 NYA	31	2	5	0	0	0	0	0	0	0	0	0	0	3	0	1	0	0	0	—	0	.000	.000	.000	P	2	0	0	0	0	—
WS Totals		4	7	0	0	0	0	0	0	0	0	0	0	4	0	2	0	0	0	—	0	.000	.000	.000	P	4	1	1	0	0	1.000
Postseason Totals		11	7	0	0	0	0	0	0	0	0	0	0	4	0	2	0	0	0	—	0	.000	.000	.000	P	10	3	2	0	0	1.000

OZZIE GUILLEN—Oswaldo Jose Guillen—Bats: Left; Throws: Right

Ht: 5'11"; Wt: 150 lbs; Born: 1/20/1964 in Oculare del Tuy, Venezuela; Debut: 4/9/1985

LCS — Batting / Fielding

Year Tm	Age	G	AB	H	2B	3B	HR	TB	R	RBI	GW	TBB	IBB	SO	HBP	SH	SF	SB	CS	SB%	GDP	Avg	OBP	SLG	Pos	G	PO	A	E	DP	FPct
1993 ChA	29	6	22	6	1	0	0	7	4	2	0	0	0	2	0	1	0	1	0	1.00	1	.273	.273	.318	SS	6	12	14	0	4	1.000

DON GULLETT
Donald Edward Gullett—Throws: Left; Bats: Right — Ht: 6'0"; Wt: 190 lbs; Born: 1/6/1951 in Lynn, Kentucky; Debut: 4/10/1970

LCS — Pitching

Year	Tm	Age	G	GS	CG	GF	IP	BFP	H	R	ER	HR	SH	SF	HB	TBB	IBB	SO	WP	Bk	W	L	Pct	ShO	Sv-Op	Hld	OAvg	OOBP	ERA
1970	Cin	19	2	0	0	2	3.2	14	1	0	0	0	0	0	0	2	0	3	0	0	0	0	—	0	2-2	0	.083	.214	0.00
1972	Cin	21	2	2	0	0	9.0	39	12	8	8	1	0	0	0	0	0	5	1	0	0	1	.000	0	0-0	0	.308	.308	8.00
1973	Cin	22	3	1	0	0	9.0	33	4	2	2	1	0	0	0	3	0	6	0	0	0	0	.000	0	0-0	0	.133	.212	2.00
1975	Cin	24	1	1	1	0	9.0	37	8	3	3	0	0	0	1	2	0	5	1	0	1	0	1.000	0	0-0	0	.235	.297	3.00
1976	Cin	25	1	1	0	0	8.0	28	2	1	1	0	0	1	0	3	0	4	0	0	1	0	1.000	0	0-0	0	.083	.179	1.13
1977	NYA	26	1	1	0	0	2.0	11	4	4	4	1	0	0	0	2	0	0	0	0	0	1	.000	0	0-0	0	.444	.545	18.00
LCS Totals			10	6	1	2	40.2	324	31	18	18	3	0	1	1	12	0	23	2	0	2	3	.400	0	2-2	0	.209	.272	3.98

World Series — Pitching

Year	Tm	Age	G	GS	CG	GF	IP	BFP	H	R	ER	HR	SH	SF	HB	TBB	IBB	SO	WP	Bk	W	L	Pct	ShO	Sv-Op	Hld	OAvg	OOBP	ERA
1970	Cin	19	3	0	0	2	6.2	27	5	2	1	0	0	0	0	4	0	4	0	0	0	0	—	0	0-0	0	.217	.333	1.35
1972	Cin	21	1	1	0	0	7.0	27	5	1	1	1	0	0	0	2	1	4	0	0	0	0	—	0	0-0	0	.200	.259	1.29
1975	Cin	24	3	3	0	0	18.2	83	19	9	9	0	2	1	0	10	2	15	1	0	1	1	.500	0	0-0	0	.271	.358	4.34
1976	Cin	25	1	1	0	0	7.1	29	5	1	1	0	0	1	1	3	0	4	0	0	1	0	1.000	0	0-0	0	.208	.310	1.23
1977	NYA	26	2	2	0	0	12.2	58	13	10	9	1	0	1	1	7	0	10	0	0	0	1	.000	0	0-0	0	.265	.362	6.39
WS Totals			10	7	0	2	52.1	448	47	23	21	2	2	3	2	26	3	37	1	0	2	2	.500	0	0-0	0	.246	.338	3.61
Postseason Totals			20	13	1	4	93.0	772	78	41	39	5	2	4	3	38	3	60	3	0	4	5	.444	0	2-2	0	.230	.310	3.77

LCS — Batting / Fielding

Year	Tm	Age	G	AB	H	2B	3B	HR	TB	R	RBI	GW	TBB	IBB	SO	HBP	SH	SF	SB	CS	SB%	GDP	Avg	OBP	SLG	Pos	G	PO	A	E	DP	FPct
1970	Cin	19	2	1	0	0	0	0	0	0	0	0	0	0	0	0	0	0	0	0	—	0	.000	.000	.000	P	2	0	0	0	0	—
1972	Cin	21	2	2	1	0	0	0	1	0	0	0	0	0	0	0	1	0	0	0	—	0	.500	.500	.500	P	2	0	0	0	0	—
1973	Cin	22	3	1	0	0	0	0	0	0	0	0	0	0	0	0	1	0	0	0	—	0	.000	.000	.000	P	3	1	0	0	0	1.000
1975	Cin	24	1	4	2	0	0	1	5	1	3	0	0	0	0	0	0	0	0	0	—	0	.500	.500	1.250	P	1	4	1	0	0	1.000
1976	Cin	25	1	4	2	1	0	0	3	1	3	0	0	0	0	0	0	0	0	0	—	0	.500	.500	.750	P	1	0	0	0	0	—
1977	NYA	26	1	0	0	0	0	0	0	0	0	0	0	0	0	0	0	0	0	0	—	0	.000	.000	.000	P	1	0	0	0	0	—
LCS Totals			10	12	5	1	0	1	9	2	6	0	0	0	0	0	2	0	0	0	—	0	.417	.417	.750	P	10	5	1	0	0	1.000

World Series — Batting / Fielding

Year	Tm	Age	G	AB	H	2B	3B	HR	TB	R	RBI	GW	TBB	IBB	SO	HBP	SH	SF	SB	CS	SB%	GDP	Avg	OBP	SLG	Pos	G	PO	A	E	DP	FPct
1970	Cin	19	3	1	0	0	0	0	0	0	0	0	0	0	0	1	0	0	0	0	—	0	.000	.000	.000	P	3	0	0	0	0	—
1972	Cin	21	1	2	0	0	0	0	0	0	0	0	0	0	0	0	0	0	0	0	—	0	.000	.000	.000	P	1	0	1	0	0	1.000
1975	Cin	24	3	7	2	0	0	0	2	1	0	0	0	0	2	0	0	0	0	0	—	0	.286	.286	.286	P	3	0	0	0	0	—
1976	Cin	25	1	0	0	0	0	0	0	0	0	0	0	0	0	0	0	0	0	0	—	0	—	—	—	P	1	0	1	0	0	1.000
1977	NYA	26	2	2	0	0	0	0	0	0	0	0	0	0	2	0	0	0	0	0	—	0	.000	.000	.000	P	2	1	2	0	0	1.000
WS Totals			10	12	2	0	0	0	2	1	0	0	0	0	5	0	2	0	0	0	—	0	.167	.167	.167	P	10	1	4	0	0	1.000
Postseason Totals			20	24	7	1	0	1	11	3	6	0	0	0	5	0	4	0	0	0	—	0	.292	.292	.458	P	20	6	5	0	0	1.000

BILL GULLICKSON
William Lee Gullickson—Throws: Right; Bats: Right — Ht: 6'3"; Wt: 200 lbs; Born: 2/20/1959 in Marshall, Minnesota; Debut: 9/26/1979

Division Series — Pitching

Year	Tm	Age	G	GS	CG	GF	IP	BFP	H	R	ER	HR	SH	SF	HB	TBB	IBB	SO	WP	Bk	W	L	Pct	ShO	Sv-Op	Hld	OAvg	OOBP	ERA
1981	Mon	22	1	1	0	0	7.2	30	6	1	1	0	0	0	0	1	0	3	0	0	1	0	1.000	0	0-0	0	.207	.233	1.17

LCS — Pitching

Year	Tm	Age	G	GS	CG	GF	IP	BFP	H	R	ER	HR	SH	SF	HB	TBB	IBB	SO	WP	Bk	W	L	Pct	ShO	Sv-Op	Hld	OAvg	OOBP	ERA
1981	Mon	22	2	2	0	0	14.1	61	12	5	4	1	3	0	1	6	0	12	0	0	0	2	.000	0	0-0	0	.235	.328	2.51
Postseason Totals			3	3	0	0	22.0	182	18	6	5	1	3	0	1	7	0	15	0	0	1	2	.333	0	0-0	0	.225	.295	2.05

Division Series — Batting / Fielding

Year	Tm	Age	G	AB	H	2B	3B	HR	TB	R	RBI	GW	TBB	IBB	SO	HBP	SH	SF	SB	CS	SB%	GDP	Avg	OBP	SLG	Pos	G	PO	A	E	DP	FPct
1981	Mon	22	1	3	0	0	0	0	0	0	0	0	0	0	1	0	0	0	0	0	—	0	.000	.000	.000	P	1	0	1	0	0	1.000

LCS — Batting / Fielding

Year	Tm	Age	G	AB	H	2B	3B	HR	TB	R	RBI	GW	TBB	IBB	SO	HBP	SH	SF	SB	CS	SB%	GDP	Avg	OBP	SLG	Pos	G	PO	A	E	DP	FPct
1981	Mon	22	2	3	0	0	0	0	0	0	0	0	1	0	2	0	1	0	0	0	—	0	.000	.250	.000	P	2	0	2	0	0	1.000
Postseason Totals			3	6	0	0	0	0	0	0	0	0	1	0	3	0	1	0	0	0	—	0	.000	.143	.000	P	3	0	3	0	0	1.000

HARRY GUMBERT
Harry Edward Gumbert—Nickname: Gunboat—Throws: Right; Bats: Right — Ht: 6'2"; Wt: 185 lbs; Born: 11/5/1909 in Elizabeth, Pennsylvania; Debut: 9/12/1935; Died: 1/4/1995

World Series — Pitching

Year	Tm	Age	G	GS	CG	GF	IP	BFP	H	R	ER	HR	SH	SF	HB	TBB	IBB	SO	WP	Bk	W	L	Pct	ShO	Sv-Op	Hld	OAvg	OOBP	ERA
1936	NYG	26	2	0	0	2	2.0	17	7	8	8	1	0	0	0	4	0	2	0	0	0	0	—	0	0-0	0	.538	.647	36.00
1937	NYG	27	2	0	0	0	1.1	10	4	4	4	0	0	0	0	1	1	1	0	0	0	0	—	0	0-0	0	.444	.500	27.00
1942	StL	32	2	0	0	0	0.2	4	1	1	0	0	0	0	0	0	0	0	0	0	0	0	—	0	0-1	0	.250	.250	0.00
WS Totals			6	0	0	2	4.0	62	12	13	12	1	0	0	0	5	1	3	0	0	0	0	—	0	0-1	0	.462	.548	27.00

World Series — Batting / Fielding

Year	Tm	Age	G	AB	H	2B	3B	HR	TB	R	RBI	GW	TBB	IBB	SO	HBP	SH	SF	SB	CS	SB%	GDP	Avg	OBP	SLG	Pos	G	PO	A	E	DP	FPct
1936	NYG	26	2	0	0	0	0	0	0	0	0	0	0	0	0	0	0	0	0	0	—	0	—	—	—	P	2	0	0	0	0	—
1937	NYG	27	2	0	0	0	0	0	0	0	0	0	0	0	0	0	0	0	0	0	—	0	—	—	—	P	2	0	0	0	0	—
1942	StL	32	2	0	0	0	0	0	0	0	0	0	0	0	0	0	0	0	0	0	—	0	—	—	—	P	2	0	1	0	0	1.000
WS Totals			6	0	0	0	0	0	0	0	0	0	0	0	0	0	0	0	0	0	—	0	—	—	—	P	6	0	1	0	0	1.000

LARRY GURA
Lawrence Cyril Gura—Throws: Left; Bats: Both — Ht: 6'0"; Wt: 170 lbs; Born: 11/26/1947 in Joliet, Illinois; Debut: 4/30/1970

Division Series — Pitching

Year	Tm	Age	G	GS	CG	GF	IP	BFP	H	R	ER	HR	SH	SF	HB	TBB	IBB	SO	WP	Bk	W	L	Pct	ShO	Sv-Op	Hld	OAvg	OOBP	ERA
1981	KC	33	1	1	0	0	3.2	20	7	4	3	1	0	0	0	3	0	3	0	0	0	1	.000	0	0-0	0	.412	.500	7.36

LCS — Pitching

Year	Tm	Age	G	GS	CG	GF	IP	BFP	H	R	ER	HR	SH	SF	HB	TBB	IBB	SO	WP	Bk	W	L	Pct	ShO	Sv-Op	Hld	OAvg	OOBP	ERA
1976	KC	28	2	2	0	0	10.2	50	18	6	5	1	0	0	0	1	0	4	0	0	0	1	.000	0	0-0	0	.367	.380	4.22
1977	KC	29	2	1	0	0	2.0	14	7	5	4	0	0	0	0	1	0	2	0	0	0	1	.000	0	0-1	0	.538	.571	18.00
1978	KC	30	1	1	0	0	6.1	28	8	2	2	0	0	0	0	2	0	2	0	0	1	0	1.000	0	0-0	0	.308	.357	2.84
1980	KC	32	1	1	1	0	9.0	38	10	2	2	2	1	0	0	1	0	4	0	0	1	0	1.000	0	0-0	0	.278	.297	2.00
LCS Totals			6	5	1	0	28.0	260	43	15	13	3	1	0	0	5	0	12	0	0	2	2	.500	0	0-1	0	.347	.372	4.18

World Series — Pitching

Year	Tm	Age	G	GS	CG	GF	IP	BFP	H	R	ER	HR	SH	SF	HB	TBB	IBB	SO	WP	Bk	W	L	Pct	ShO	Sv-Op	Hld	OAvg	OOBP	ERA
1980	KC	32	2	2	0	0	12.1	46	8	4	3	1	0	1	0	3	0	4	0	0	0	0	—	0	0-0	0	.190	.239	2.19
Postseason Totals			9	8	1	0	44.0	392	58	23	19	5	1	1	0	11	0	19	0	0	2	3	.400	0	0-1	0	.317	.354	3.89

Division Series — Batting / Fielding

Year	Tm	Age	G	AB	H	2B	3B	HR	TB	R	RBI	GW	TBB	IBB	SO	HBP	SH	SF	SB	CS	SB%	GDP	Avg	OBP	SLG	Pos	G	PO	A	E	DP	FPct
1981	KC	33	1	0	0	0	0	0	0	0	0	0	0	0	0	0	0	0	0	0	—	0	—	—	—	P	1	0	0	0	0	—

LCS — Batting / Fielding

Year	Tm	Age	G	AB	H	2B	3B	HR	TB	R	RBI	GW	TBB	IBB	SO	HBP	SH	SF	SB	CS	SB%	GDP	Avg	OBP	SLG	Pos	G	PO	A	E	DP	FPct
1976	KC	28	2	0	0	0	0	0	0	0	0	0	0	0	0	0	0	0	0	0	—	0	—	—	—	P	2	0	0	0	0	—
1977	KC	29	2	0	0	0	0	0	0	0	0	0	0	0	0	0	0	0	0	0	—	0	—	—	—	P	2	0	0	0	0	—
1978	KC	30	1	0	0	0	0	0	0	0	0	0	0	0	0	0	0	0	0	0	—	0	—	—	—	P	1	1	4	0	0	1.000
1980	KC	32	1	0	0	0	0	0	0	0	0	0	0	0	0	0	0	0	0	0	—	0	—	—	—	P	1	0	1	0	0	1.000
LCS Totals			6	0	0	0	0	0	0	0	0	0	0	0	0	0	0	0	0	0	—	0	—	—	—	P	6	1	5	0	0	1.000

World Series — Batting / Fielding

Year	Tm	Age	G	AB	H	2B	3B	HR	TB	R	RBI	GW	TBB	IBB	SO	HBP	SH	SF	SB	CS	SB%	GDP	Avg	OBP	SLG	Pos	G	PO	A	E	DP	FPct
1980	KC	32	2	0	0	0	0	0	0	0	0	0	0	0	0	0	0	0	0	0	—	0	—	—	—	P	2	2	4	0	2	1.000
Postseason Totals			9	0	0	0	0	0	0	0	0	0	0	0	0	0	0	0	0	0	—	0	—	—	—	P	9	3	9	0	2	1.000

MARK GUTHRIE
Mark Andrew Guthrie—Throws: Right; Bats: Both — Ht: 6'4"; Wt: 192 lbs; Born: 9/22/1965 in Buffalo, New York; Debut: 7/25/1989

Division Series — Pitching

Year	Tm	Age	G	GS	CG	GF	IP	BFP	H	R	ER	HR	SH	SF	HB	TBB	IBB	SO	WP	Bk	W	L	Pct	ShO	Sv-Op	Hld	OAvg	OOBP	ERA
1995	LA	30	3	0	0	0	1.1	6	2	1	1	1	0	0	0	1	0	1	0	0	0	0	—	0	0-0	0	.400	.500	6.75
1996	LA	31	1	0	0	0	0.1	2	0	0	0	0	0	0	0	1	0	1	0	0	0	0	—	0	0-0	0	.000	.500	0.00
DS Totals			4	0	0	0	1.2	16	2	1	1	1	0	0	0	2	0	2	0	0	0	0	—	0	0-0	0	.333	.500	5.40

LCS — Pitching

Year Tm	Age	G	GS	CG	GF	IP	BFP	H	R	ER	HR	SH	SF	HB	TBB	IBB	SO	WP	Bk	W	L	Pct	ShO	Sv-Op	Hld	OAvg	OOBP	ERA
1991 Min	26	2	0	0	1	2.2	8	0	0	0	0	0	0	0	0	0	0	0	0	1	0	1.000	0	0- 0	0	.000	.000	0.00

World Series — Pitching

Year Tm	Age	G	GS	CG	GF	IP	BFP	H	R	ER	HR	SH	SF	HB	TBB	IBB	SO	WP	Bk	W	L	Pct	ShO	Sv-Op	Hld	OAvg	OOBP	ERA
1991 Min	26	4	0	0	0	4.0	18	3	1	1	0	0	0	0	4	1	3	1	0	0	1	.000	0	0- 0	2	.214	.389	2.25
Postseason Totals		10	0	0	1	8.1	68	5	2	2	1	0	0	0	6	1	5	1	0	1	1	.500	0	0-0	2	.179	.324	2.16

Division Series — Batting / Fielding

Year Tm	Age	G	AB	H	2B	3B	HR	TB	R	RBI	GW	TBB	IBB	SO	HBP	SH	SF	SB	CS	SB%	GDP	Avg	OBP	SLG	Pos	G	PO	A	E	DP	FPct
1995 LA	30	3	0	0	0	0	0	0	0	0	0	0	0	0	0	0	0	0	0	—	0	—	—	—	P	3	0	0	0	0	—
1996 LA	31	1	0	0	0	0	0	0	0	0	0	0	0	0	0	0	0	0	0	—	0	—	—	—	P	1	0	0	0	0	—
DS Totals		4	0	0	0	0	0	0	0	0	0	0	0	0	0	0	0	0	0	—	0	—	—	—	P	4	0	0	0	0	—

LCS — Batting / Fielding

Year Tm	Age	G	AB	H	2B	3B	HR	TB	R	RBI	GW	TBB	IBB	SO	HBP	SH	SF	SB	CS	SB%	GDP	Avg	OBP	SLG	Pos	G	PO	A	E	DP	FPct
1991 Min	26	2	0	0	0	0	0	0	0	0	0	0	0	0	0	0	0	0	0	—	0	—	—	—	P	2	0	1	0	0	1.000

World Series — Batting / Fielding

Year Tm	Age	G	AB	H	2B	3B	HR	TB	R	RBI	GW	TBB	IBB	SO	HBP	SH	SF	SB	CS	SB%	GDP	Avg	OBP	SLG	Pos	G	PO	A	E	DP	FPct
1991 Min	26	4	0	0	0	0	0	0	0	0	0	0	0	0	0	0	0	0	0	—	0	—	—	—	P	4	0	1	0	0	1.000
Postseason Totals		10	0	0	0	0	0	0	0	0	0	0	0	0	0	0	0	0	0	—	0	—	—	—	P	10	0	2	0	0	1.000

RICKY GUTIERREZ—Ricardo Gutierrez—Bats: Right; Throws: Right

Ht: 6'1"; Wt: 175 lbs; Born: 5/23/1970 in Miami, Florida; Debut: 4/13/1993

Division Series — Batting / Fielding

Year Tm	Age	G	AB	H	2B	3B	HR	TB	R	RBI	GW	TBB	IBB	SO	HBP	SH	SF	SB	CS	SB%	GDP	Avg	OBP	SLG	Pos	G	PO	A	E	DP	FPct
1997 Hou	27	3	8	1	0	0	0	1	0	0	0	2	0	1	0	0	0	0	0	—	0	.125	.300	.125	SS	3	5	5	0	2	1.000

DON GUTTERIDGE—Donald Joseph Gutteridge—Bats: Right; Throws: Right

Ht: 5'10"; Wt: 165 lbs; Born: 6/19/1912 in Pittsburg, Kansas; Debut: 9/7/1936

World Series — Batting / Fielding

Year Tm	Age	G	AB	H	2B	3B	HR	TB	R	RBI	GW	TBB	IBB	SO	HBP	SH	SF	SB	CS	SB%	GDP	Avg	OBP	SLG	Pos	G	PO	A	E	DP	FPct
1944 StL	32	6	21	3	1	0	0	4	1	0	0	3	0	5	0	0	0	0	0	—	0	.143	.250	.190	2B	6	15	11	3	3	.897
1946 Bos	34	3	5	2	0	0	0	2	1	1	1	0	0	0	0	0	0	0	0	—	0	.400	.400	.400	2B	2	0	2	0	0	1.000
WS Totals		9	26	5	1	0	0	6	2	1	1	3	0	5	0	0	0	0	0	—	0	.192	.276	.231	2B	8	15	13	3	3	.903

JUAN GUZMAN—Juan Andres Guzman—Throws: Right; Bats: Right

Ht: 6'0"; Wt: 190 lbs; Born: 10/28/1966 in Santo Domingo, Dominican Republic; Debut: 6/7/1991

LCS — Pitching

Year Tm	Age	G	GS	CG	GF	IP	BFP	H	R	ER	HR	SH	SF	HB	TBB	IBB	SO	WP	Bk	W	L	Pct	ShO	Sv-Op	Hld	OAvg	OOBP	ERA
1991 Tor	24	1	1	0	0	5.2	24	4	2	2	0	0	0	0	4	0	2	1	0	1	0	1.000	0	0- 0	0	.200	.333	3.18
1992 Tor	25	2	2	0	0	13.0	56	12	3	3	0	0	0	1	5	0	11	0	0	2	0	1.000	0	0- 0	0	.240	.321	2.08
1993 Tor	26	2	2	0	0	13.0	56	8	4	3	1	1	0	1	9	1	9	3	0	2	0	1.000	0	0- 0	0	.178	.327	2.08
LCS Totals		5	5	0	0	31.2	272	24	9	8	1	1	0	2	18	1	22	4	0	5	0	1.000	0	0-0	0	.209	.326	2.27

World Series — Pitching

Year Tm	Age	G	GS	CG	GF	IP	BFP	H	R	ER	HR	SH	SF	HB	TBB	IBB	SO	WP	Bk	W	L	Pct	ShO	Sv-Op	Hld	OAvg	OOBP	ERA
1992 Tor	25	1	1	0	0	8.0	32	8	2	1	0	0	0	0	1	1	7	0	0	0	0	—	0	0- 0	0	.258	.281	1.13
1993 Tor	26	2	2	0	0	12.0	53	10	6	5	0	1	0	0	8	2	12	1	0	0	1	.000	0	0- 0	0	.227	.346	3.75
WS Totals		3	3	0	0	20.0	170	18	8	6	0	1	0	0	9	3	19	1	0	0	1	.000	0	0-0	0	.240	.321	2.70
Postseason Totals		8	8	0	0	51.2	442	42	17	14	1	2	0	2	27	4	41	5	0	5	1	.833	0	0-0	0	.221	.324	2.44

LCS — Batting / Fielding

Year Tm	Age	G	AB	H	2B	3B	HR	TB	R	RBI	GW	TBB	IBB	SO	HBP	SH	SF	SB	CS	SB%	GDP	Avg	OBP	SLG	Pos	G	PO	A	E	DP	FPct
1991 Tor	24	1	0	0	0	0	0	0	0	0	0	0	0	0	0	0	0	0	0	—	0	—	—	—	P	1	0	0	0	0	—
1992 Tor	25	2	0	0	0	0	0	0	0	0	0	0	0	0	0	0	0	0	0	—	0	—	—	—	P	2	0	0	0	0	—
1993 Tor	26	2	0	0	0	0	0	0	0	0	0	0	0	0	0	0	0	0	0	—	0	—	—	—	P	2	0	4	0	0	1.000
LCS Totals		5	0	0	0	0	0	0	0	0	0	0	0	0	0	0	0	0	0	—	0	—	—	—	P	5	0	4	0	0	1.000

World Series — Batting / Fielding

Year Tm	Age	G	AB	H	2B	3B	HR	TB	R	RBI	GW	TBB	IBB	SO	HBP	SH	SF	SB	CS	SB%	GDP	Avg	OBP	SLG	Pos	G	PO	A	E	DP	FPct
1992 Tor	25	1	0	0	0	0	0	0	0	0	0	0	0	0	0	0	0	0	0	—	0	—	—	—	P	1	2	0	0	0	1.000
1993 Tor	26	2	2	0	0	0	0	0	0	0	0	0	0	1	0	0	0	0	0	—	1	.000	.000	.000	P	2	0	1	0	0	1.000
WS Totals		3	2	0	0	0	0	0	0	0	0	0	0	1	0	0	0	0	0	—	1	.000	.000	.000	P	3	2	1	0	0	1.000
Postseason Totals		8	2	0	0	0	0	0	0	0	0	0	0	1	0	0	0	0	0	—	1	.000	.000	.000	P	8	2	5	0	0	1.000

CHRIS GWYNN—Christopher Karlton Gwynn—Bats: Left; Throws: Left

Ht: 6'0"; Wt: 200 lbs; Born: 10/13/1964 in Los Angeles, California; Debut: 8/14/1987

Division Series — Batting / Fielding

Year Tm	Age	G	AB	H	2B	3B	HR	TB	R	RBI	GW	TBB	IBB	SO	HBP	SH	SF	SB	CS	SB%	GDP	Avg	OBP	SLG	Pos	G	PO	A	E	DP	FPct
1995 LA	30	1	1	0	0	0	0	0	0	0	0	0	0	1	0	0	0	0	0	—	0	.000	.000	.000	—						
1996 SD	31	2	2	2	0	0	0	2	1	0	0	0	0	0	0	0	0	0	0	—	0	1.000	1.000	1.000	—						
DS Totals		3	3	2	0	0	0	2	1	0	0	0	0	1	0	0	0	0	0	—	0	.667	.667	.667	—	0	0	0	0	0	—

TONY GWYNN—Anthony Keith Gwynn—Bats: Left; Throws: Left

Ht: 5'11"; Wt: 185 lbs; Born: 5/9/1960 in Los Angeles, California; Debut: 7/19/1982

Division Series — Batting / Fielding

Year Tm	Age	G	AB	H	2B	3B	HR	TB	R	RBI	GW	TBB	IBB	SO	HBP	SH	SF	SB	CS	SB%	GDP	Avg	OBP	SLG	Pos	G	PO	A	E	DP	FPct
1996 SD	36	3	13	4	1	0	0	5	0	1	0	0	0	2	0	1	0	1	0	1.00	0	.308	.308	.385	OF	3	2	0	0	0	1.000

LCS — Batting / Fielding

Year Tm	Age	G	AB	H	2B	3B	HR	TB	R	RBI	GW	TBB	IBB	SO	HBP	SH	SF	SB	CS	SB%	GDP	Avg	OBP	SLG	Pos	G	PO	A	E	DP	FPct
1984 SD	24	5	19	7	3	0	0	10	6	3	1	1	1	2	0	0	1	0	0	—	0	.368	.381	.526	OF	5	9	0	0	0	1.000

World Series — Batting / Fielding

Year Tm	Age	G	AB	H	2B	3B	HR	TB	R	RBI	GW	TBB	IBB	SO	HBP	SH	SF	SB	CS	SB%	GDP	Avg	OBP	SLG	Pos	G	PO	A	E	DP	FPct
1984 SD	24	5	19	5	0	0	0	5	1	0	0	3	0	2	0	0	0	1	2	.33	0	.263	.364	.263	OF	5	12	1	1	1	.929
Postseason Totals		13	51	16	4	0	0	20	7	4	1	4	1	6	0	1	1	2	2	.50	0	.314	.357	.392	OF	13	23	1	1	1	.960

MOOSE HAAS—Bryan Edmund Haas—Throws: Right; Bats: Right

Ht: 6'0"; Wt: 180 lbs; Born: 4/22/1956 in Baltimore, Maryland; Debut: 9/8/1976

Division Series — Pitching

Year Tm	Age	G	GS	CG	GF	IP	BFP	H	R	ER	HR	SH	SF	HB	TBB	IBB	SO	WP	Bk	W	L	Pct	ShO	Sv-Op	Hld	OAvg	OOBP	ERA
1981 Mil	25	2	2	0	0	6.2	32	13	7	7	3	0	0	0	1	0	1	0	0	0	2	.000	0	0- 0	0	.419	.438	9.45

LCS — Pitching

Year Tm	Age	G	GS	CG	GF	IP	BFP	H	R	ER	HR	SH	SF	HB	TBB	IBB	SO	WP	Bk	W	L	Pct	ShO	Sv-Op	Hld	OAvg	OOBP	ERA
1982 Mil	26	1	1	0	0	7.1	32	5	5	4	1	0	0	0	5	0	7	0	0	1	0	1.000	0	0- 0	0	.185	.313	4.91

World Series — Pitching

Year Tm	Age	G	GS	CG	GF	IP	BFP	H	R	ER	HR	SH	SF	HB	TBB	IBB	SO	WP	Bk	W	L	Pct	ShO	Sv-Op	Hld	OAvg	OOBP	ERA
1982 Mil	26	2	1	0	0	7.1	33	8	7	6	0	0	1	0	3	1	4	1	0	0	0	—	0	0- 0	0	.276	.333	7.36
Postseason Totals		5	4	0	0	21.1	194	26	19	17	4	0	1	0	9	1	12	1	0	1	2	.333	0	0-0	0	.299	.361	7.17

Division Series — Batting / Fielding

Year Tm	Age	G	AB	H	2B	3B	HR	TB	R	RBI	GW	TBB	IBB	SO	HBP	SH	SF	SB	CS	SB%	GDP	Avg	OBP	SLG	Pos	G	PO	A	E	DP	FPct
1981 Mil	25	2	0	0	0	0	0	0	0	0	0	0	0	0	0	0	0	0	0	—	0	—	—	—	P	2	2	0	0	0	1.000

LCS — Batting / Fielding

Year Tm	Age	G	AB	H	2B	3B	HR	TB	R	RBI	GW	TBB	IBB	SO	HBP	SH	SF	SB	CS	SB%	GDP	Avg	OBP	SLG	Pos	G	PO	A	E	DP	FPct
1982 Mil	26	1	0	0	0	0	0	0	0	0	0	0	0	0	0	0	0	0	0	—	0	—	—	—	P	1	0	0	0	0	—

World Series — Batting / Fielding

Year Tm	Age	G	AB	H	2B	3B	HR	TB	R	RBI	GW	TBB	IBB	SO	HBP	SH	SF	SB	CS	SB%	GDP	Avg	OBP	SLG	Pos	G	PO	A	E	DP	FPct
1982 Mil	26	2	0	0	0	0	0	0	0	0	0	0	0	0	0	0	0	0	0	—	0	—	—	—	P	2	1	2	0	0	1.000
Postseason Totals		5	0	0	0	0	0	0	0	0	0	0	0	0	0	0	0	0	0	—	0	—	—	—	P	5	3	2	0	0	1.000

MULE HAAS—George William Haas—Bats: Left; Throws: Right

Ht: 6'1"; Wt: 175 lbs; Born: 10/15/1903 in Montclair, New Jersey; Debut: 8/15/1925; Died: 6/30/1974

World Series		Batting																							Fielding						
Year Tm	Age	G	AB	H	2B	3B	HR	TB	R	RBI	GW	TBB	IBB	SO	HBP	SH	SF	SB	CS	SB%	GDP	Avg	OBP	SLG	Pos	G	PO	A	E	DP	FPct
1929 Phi	25	5	21	5	0	0	2	11	3	6	0	1	0	3	0	1	0	0	0	—	0	.238	.273	.524	OF	5	5	0	0	0	1.000
1930 Phi	26	6	18	2	0	1	0	4	1	1	0	1	0	3	0	0	1	0	1	.00	1	.111	.150	.222	OF	6	13	0	0	0	1.000
1931 Phi	27	7	23	3	1	0	0	4	1	2	0	3	0	5	0	2	0	0	0	—	0	.130	.231	.174	OF	7	15	0	0	0	1.000
WS Totals		18	62	10	1	1	2	19	5	9	0	5	0	11	0	3	1	0	1	.00	1	.161	.221	.306	OF	18	33	0	0	0	1.000

STAN HACK—Stanley Camfield Hack—Nickname: Smiling Stan—Bats: Left; Throws: Right

Ht: 6'0"; Wt: 170 lbs; Born: 12/6/1909 in Sacramento, California; Debut: 4/12/1932; Died: 12/15/1979

World Series		Batting																							Fielding						
Year Tm	Age	G	AB	H	2B	3B	HR	TB	R	RBI	GW	TBB	IBB	SO	HBP	SH	SF	SB	CS	SB%	GDP	Avg	OBP	SLG	Pos	G	PO	A	E	DP	FPct
1932 ChN	22	1	0	0	0	0	0	0	0	0	0	0	0	0	0	0	0	0	0	—	0	—	—	—	—						
1935 ChN	25	6	22	5	1	1	0	8	2	0	0	2	0	2	0	0	0	1	0	1.00	1	.227	.292	.364	3B	6	4	10	0	0	1.000
																									SS	1	1	0	0	0	1.000
1938 ChN	28	4	17	8	1	0	0	9	3	1	0	1	0	2	0	0	0	0	1	.00	2	.471	.500	.529	3B	4	4	4	0	0	1.000
1945 ChN	35	7	30	11	3	0	0	14	1	4	1	4	0	2	0	0	0	0	2	.00	0	.367	.441	.467	3B	7	12	13	3	0	.893
WS Totals		18	69	24	5	1	0	31	6	5	1	7	0	6	0	0	0	1	3	.25	3	.348	.408	.449	3B	17	20	27	3	0	.940

HARVEY HADDIX—Nickname: The Kitten—Throws: Left; Bats: Left

Ht: 5'9"; Wt: 170 lbs; Born: 9/18/1925 in Medway, Ohio; Debut: 8/20/1952; Died: 1/8/1994

World Series		Pitching																									
Year Tm	Age	G	GS	CG	GF	IP	BFP	H	R	ER	HR	SH	SF	HB	TBB	IBB	SO	WP	Bk	W	L	Pct	ShO	Sv-Op	Hld	OAvg	OOBP	ERA
1960 Pit	35	2	1	0	1	7.1	31	6	2	2	1	0	0	0	2	1	6	0	0	2	0	1.000	0	0- 1	0	.207	.258	2.45

World Series		Batting																							Fielding						
Year Tm	Age	G	AB	H	2B	3B	HR	TB	R	RBI	GW	TBB	IBB	SO	HBP	SH	SF	SB	CS	SB%	GDP	Avg	OBP	SLG	Pos	G	PO	A	E	DP	FPct
1960 Pit	35	2	3	1	0	0	0	1	0	0	0	0	0	1	0	0	0	0	0	—	1	.333	.333	.333	P	2	1	1	0	0	1.000

BUMP HADLEY—Irving Darius Hadley—Throws: Right; Bats: Right

Ht: 5'11"; Wt: 190 lbs; Born: 7/5/1904 in Lynn, Massachusetts; Debut: 4/20/1926; Died: 2/15/1963

World Series		Pitching																									
Year Tm	Age	G	GS	CG	GF	IP	BFP	H	R	ER	HR	SH	SF	HB	TBB	IBB	SO	WP	Bk	W	L	Pct	ShO	Sv-Op	Hld	OAvg	OOBP	ERA
1936 NYA	32	1	1	0	0	8.0	33	10	1	1	1	1	0	0	1	0	2	0	0	1	0	1.000	0	0- 0	0	.323	.344	1.13
1937 NYA	33	1	1	0	0	1.1	10	6	5	5	0	0	0	0	0	0	0	0	0	0	1	.000	0	0- 0	0	.600	.600	33.75
1939 NYA	35	1	0	0	1	8.0	35	7	2	2	0	1	0	1	3	0	2	0	0	1	0	1.000	0	0- 0	0	.233	.324	2.25
WS Totals		3	2	0	1	17.1	156	23	8	8	1	2	0	1	4	0	4	0	0	2	1	.667	0	0-0	0	.324	.368	4.15

World Series		Batting																							Fielding						
Year Tm	Age	G	AB	H	2B	3B	HR	TB	R	RBI	GW	TBB	IBB	SO	HBP	SH	SF	SB	CS	SB%	GDP	Avg	OBP	SLG	Pos	G	PO	A	E	DP	FPct
1936 NYA	32	1	2	0	0	0	0	0	0	0	0	0	0	1	0	0	0	0	0	—	0	.000	.000	.000	P	1	0	3	0	0	1.000
1937 NYA	33	1	0	0	0	0	0	0	0	0	0	0	0	0	0	0	0	0	0	—	0	—	—	—	P	1	0	0	0	0	—
1939 NYA	35	1	3	0	0	0	0	0	0	0	0	0	0	0	0	0	0	0	0	—	0	.000	.000	.000	P	1	1	1	1	0	.667
WS Totals		3	5	0	0	0	0	0	0	0	0	0	0	1	0	0	0	0	0	—	0	.000	.000	.000	P	3	1	4	1	0	.833

CHICK HAFEY (HOF 1971-V)—Charles James Hafey—Bats: Right; Throws: Right

Ht: 6'0"; Wt: 185 lbs; Born: 2/12/1903 in Berkeley, California; Debut: 8/28/1924; Died: 7/2/1973

World Series		Batting																							Fielding						
Year Tm	Age	G	AB	H	2B	3B	HR	TB	R	RBI	GW	TBB	IBB	SO	HBP	SH	SF	SB	CS	SB%	GDP	Avg	OBP	SLG	Pos	G	PO	A	E	DP	FPct
1926 StL	23	7	27	5	2	0	0	7	2	0	0	0	0	7	0	2	0	0	1	.00	0	.185	.185	.259	OF	7	20	1	0	0	1.000
1928 StL	25	4	15	3	0	0	0	3	0	0	0	1	0	4	0	0	0	0	0	—	0	.200	.250	.200	OF	4	8	0	1	0	.889
1930 StL	27	6	22	6	5	0	0	11	2	2	0	1	0	3	0	0	0	0	0	—	0	.273	.304	.500	OF	6	9	0	0	0	1.000
1931 StL	28	6	24	4	0	0	0	4	1	0	0	0	0	5	0	0	0	1	0	1.00	0	.167	.167	.167	OF	6	8	0	1	0	.889
WS Totals		23	88	18	7	0	0	25	5	2	0	2	0	19	0	2	0	1	1	.50	0	.205	.222	.284	OF	23	45	1	2	0	.958

JOE HAGUE—Joe Clarence Hague—Bats: Left; Throws: Left

Ht: 6'0"; Wt: 195 lbs; Born: 4/25/1944 in Huntington, West Virginia; Debut: 9/19/1968; Died: 11/5/1994

LCS		Batting																							Fielding						
Year Tm	Age	G	AB	H	2B	3B	HR	TB	R	RBI	GW	TBB	IBB	SO	HBP	SH	SF	SB	CS	SB%	GDP	Avg	OBP	SLG	Pos	G	PO	A	E	DP	FPct
1972 Cin	28	3	1	0	0	0	0	0	0	0	0	2	0	1	0	0	0	0	0	—	0	.000	.667	.000	—						

World Series		Batting																							Fielding						
Year Tm	Age	G	AB	H	2B	3B	HR	TB	R	RBI	GW	TBB	IBB	SO	HBP	SH	SF	SB	CS	SB%	GDP	Avg	OBP	SLG	Pos	G	PO	A	E	DP	FPct
1972 Cin	28	3	3	0	0	0	0	0	0	0	0	0	0	0	0	0	0	0	0	—	0	.000	.000	.000	OF	1	0	0	0	0	—
Postseason Totals		6	4	0	0	0	0	0	0	0	0	2	0	1	0	0	0	0	0	—	0	.000	.333	.000	OF	1	0	0	0	0	—

DON HAHN—Donald Antone Hahn—Bats: Right; Throws: Right

Ht: 6'1"; Wt: 180 lbs; Born: 11/16/1948 in San Francisco, California; Debut: 4/8/1969

LCS		Batting																							Fielding						
Year Tm	Age	G	AB	H	2B	3B	HR	TB	R	RBI	GW	TBB	IBB	SO	HBP	SH	SF	SB	CS	SB%	GDP	Avg	OBP	SLG	Pos	G	PO	A	E	DP	FPct
1973 NYN	24	5	17	4	0	0	0	4	2	1	0	2	0	4	0	0	0	0	0	—	0	.235	.316	.235	OF	5	12	0	0	0	1.000

World Series		Batting																							Fielding						
Year Tm	Age	G	AB	H	2B	3B	HR	TB	R	RBI	GW	TBB	IBB	SO	HBP	SH	SF	SB	CS	SB%	GDP	Avg	OBP	SLG	Pos	G	PO	A	E	DP	FPct
1973 NYN	24	7	29	7	1	1	0	10	2	2	0	1	0	6	0	0	0	0	0	—	1	.241	.267	.345	OF	7	13	1	1	0	.933
Postseason Totals		12	46	11	1	1	0	14	4	3	0	3	0	10	0	0	0	0	0	—	1	.239	.286	.304	OF	12	25	1	1	0	.963

ED HAHN—William Edgar Hahn—Bats: Left; Throws: Right

Ht: Unknown; Wt: 160 lbs; Born: 8/27/1875 in Nevada, Ohio; Debut: 8/31/1905; Died: 11/29/1941

World Series		Batting																							Fielding						
Year Tm	Age	G	AB	H	2B	3B	HR	TB	R	RBI	GW	TBB	IBB	SO	HBP	SH	SF	SB	CS	SB%	GDP	Avg	OBP	SLG	Pos	G	PO	A	E	DP	FPct
1906 ChA	31	6	22	6	0	0	0	6	4	0	0	1	0	1	1	1	0	0	2	.00	0	.273	.333	.273	OF	6	3	0	0	0	1.000

HINKEY HAINES—Henry Luther Haines—Bats: Right; Throws: Right

Ht: 5'10"; Wt: 170 lbs; Born: 12/23/1898 in Red Lion, Pennsylvania; Debut: 4/20/1923; Died: 1/9/1979

World Series		Batting																							Fielding						
Year Tm	Age	G	AB	H	2B	3B	HR	TB	R	RBI	GW	TBB	IBB	SO	HBP	SH	SF	SB	CS	SB%	GDP	Avg	OBP	SLG	Pos	G	PO	A	E	DP	FPct
1923 NYA	24	2	1	0	0	0	0	0	1	0	0	0	0	0	0	0	0	0	0	—	0	.000	.000	.000	OF	2	0	0	0	0	—

JESSE HAINES (HOF 1970-V)—Jesse Joseph Haines—Nickname: Pop—Throws: Right; Bats: Right

Ht: 6'0"; Wt: 190 lbs; Born: 7/22/1893 in Clayton, Ohio; Debut: 7/20/1918; Died: 8/5/1978

World Series		Pitching																									
Year Tm	Age	G	GS	CG	GF	IP	BFP	H	R	ER	HR	SH	SF	HB	TBB	IBB	SO	WP	Bk	W	L	Pct	ShO	Sv-Op	Hld	OAvg	OOBP	ERA
1926 StL	33	3	2	1	1	16.2	69	13	2	2	1	2	0	0	9	1	5	0	0	2	0	1.000	1	0- 0	0	.224	.328	1.08
1928 StL	35	1	1	0	0	6.0	26	6	6	3	2	0	0	0	3	0	3	0	0	0	1	.000	0	0- 0	0	.261	.346	4.50
1930 StL	37	1	1	1	0	9.0	35	4	1	1	0	1	0	0	4	0	2	1	0	1	0	1.000	0	0- 0	0	.133	.235	1.00
1934 StL	41	1	0	0	0	0.2	3	1	0	0	0	0	0	0	0	0	2	0	0	0	0	—	0	0- 0	0	.333	.333	0.00
WS Totals		6	4	2	1	32.1	266	24	9	6	3	3	0	0	16	1	12	1	0	3	1	.750	1	0-0	0	.211	.308	1.67

World Series		Batting																							Fielding						
Year Tm	Age	G	AB	H	2B	3B	HR	TB	R	RBI	GW	TBB	IBB	SO	HBP	SH	SF	SB	CS	SB%	GDP	Avg	OBP	SLG	Pos	G	PO	A	E	DP	FPct
1926 StL	33	3	5	3	0	0	1	6	1	2	0	0	0	1	0	1	0	0	0	—	0	.600	.600	1.200	P	3	0	6	0	0	1.000
1928 StL	35	1	2	0	0	0	0	0	0	0	0	0	0	0	0	0	0	0	0	—	0	.000	.000	.000	P	1	0	1	0	0	1.000
1930 StL	37	1	2	1	0	0	0	1	0	1	0	0	0	0	0	1	0	0	0	—	0	.500	.500	.500	P	1	0	1	0	0	1.000
1934 StL	41	1	0	0	0	0	0	0	0	0	0	0	0	0	0	0	0	0	0	—	0	—	—	—	P	1	0	0	0	0	—
WS Totals		6	9	4	0	0	1	7	1	3	0	0	0	1	0	2	0	0	0	—	0	.444	.444	.778	P	6	0	8	0	0	1.000

JERRY HAIRSTON—Jerry Wayne Hairston—Bats: Both; Throws: Right

Ht: 5'10"; Wt: 170 lbs; Born: 2/16/1952 in Birmingham, Alabama; Debut: 7/26/1973

LCS		Batting																							Fielding						
Year Tm	Age	G	AB	H	2B	3B	HR	TB	R	RBI	GW	TBB	IBB	SO	HBP	SH	SF	SB	CS	SB%	GDP	Avg	OBP	SLG	Pos	G	PO	A	E	DP	FPct
1983 ChA	31	2	3	0	0	0	0	0	0	0	0	1	0	1	0	0	0	0	0	—	0	.000	.250	.000	OF	2	0	0	1	0	.000

DICK HALL—Richard Wallace Hall—Nickname: Turkey—Throws: Right; Bats: Right

Ht: 6'6"; Wt: 200 lbs; Born: 9/27/1930 in St. Louis, Missouri; Debut: 4/15/1952

LCS		Pitching																										
Year Tm	Age	G	GS	CG	GF	IP	BFP	H	R	ER	HR	SH	SF	HB	TBB	IBB	SO	WP	Bk	W	L	Pct	ShO	Sv-Op	Hld	OAvg	OOBP	ERA
1969 Bal	39	1	0	0	1	0.2	2	0	0	0	0	0	0	0	0	0	1	0	0	1	0	1.000	0	0- 0	0	.000	.000	0.00
1970 Bal	40	1	0	0	1	4.2	14	1	0	0	0	0	0	0	0	0	3	0	0	1	0	1.000	0	0- 0	0	.071	.071	0.00
LCS Totals		2	0	0	2	5.1	32	1	0	0	0	0	0	0	0	0	4	0	0	2	0	1.000	0	0-0	0	.063	.063	0.00
World Series		Pitching																										
Year Tm	Age	G	GS	CG	GF	IP	BFP	H	R	ER	HR	SH	SF	HB	TBB	IBB	SO	WP	Bk	W	L	Pct	ShO	Sv-Op	Hld	OAvg	OOBP	ERA
1969 Bal	39	1	0	0	0	0.0	2	1	1	0	0	0	0	0	1	1	0	0	0	0	1	.000	0	0- 0	0	1.000	1.000	—
1970 Bal	40	1	0	0	1	2.1	7	0	0	0	0	0	0	0	0	0	0	0	0	0	0	—	0	1- 1	0	.000	.000	0.00
1971 Bal	41	1	0	0	1	1.0	4	1	0	0	0	0	0	0	0	0	0	0	0	0	0	—	0	1- 1	0	.250	.250	0.00
WS Totals		3	0	0	2	3.1	26	2	1	0	0	0	0	0	1	1	0	0	0	0	1	.000	0	2-2	0	.167	.231	0.00
Postseason Totals		5	0	0	4	8.2	58	3	1	0	0	0	0	0	1	1	4	0	0	2	1	.667	0	2-2	0	.107	.138	0.00

LCS		Batting																							Fielding						
Year Tm	Age	G	AB	H	2B	3B	HR	TB	R	RBI	GW	TBB	IBB	SO	HBP	SH	SF	SB	CS	SB%	GDP	Avg	OBP	SLG	Pos	G	PO	A	E	DP	FPct
1969 Bal	39	1	0	0	0	0	0	0	0	0	0	0	0	0	0	0	0	0	0	—	0	—	—	—	P	1	0	0	0	0	—
1970 Bal	40	1	2	1	0	0	0	1	1	0	0	0	0	1	0	0	0	0	0	—	0	.500	.500	.500	P	1	0	0	0	0	—
LCS Totals		2	2	1	0	0	0	1	1	0	0	0	0	1	0	0	0	0	0	—	0	.500	.500	.500	P	2	0	0	0	0	—
World Series		Batting																							Fielding						
Year Tm	Age	G	AB	H	2B	3B	HR	TB	R	RBI	GW	TBB	IBB	SO	HBP	SH	SF	SB	CS	SB%	GDP	Avg	OBP	SLG	Pos	G	PO	A	E	DP	FPct
1969 Bal	39	1	0	0	0	0	0	0	0	0	0	0	0	0	0	0	0	0	0	—	0	—	—	—	P	1	0	0	0	0	—
1970 Bal	40	1	1	0	0	0	0	0	0	0	0	0	0	1	0	0	0	0	0	—	0	.000	.000	.000	P	1	0	0	0	0	—
1971 Bal	41	1	0	0	0	0	0	0	0	0	0	0	0	0	0	0	0	0	0	—	0	—	—	—	P	1	1	0	0	0	1.000
WS Totals		3	1	0	0	0	0	0	0	0	0	0	0	1	0	0	0	0	0	—	0	.000	.000	.000	P	3	1	0	0	0	1.000
Postseason Totals		5	3	1	0	0	0	1	1	0	0	0	0	2	0	0	0	0	0	—	0	.333	.333	.333	P	5	1	0	0	0	1.000

JIMMIE HALL—Jimmie Randolph Hall—Bats: Left; Throws: Right

Ht: 6'0"; Wt: 175 lbs; Born: 3/7/1938 in Mt. Holly, North Carolina; Debut: 4/9/1963

World Series		Batting																							Fielding						
Year Tm	Age	G	AB	H	2B	3B	HR	TB	R	RBI	GW	TBB	IBB	SO	HBP	SH	SF	SB	CS	SB%	GDP	Avg	OBP	SLG	Pos	G	PO	A	E	DP	FPct
1965 Min	27	2	7	1	0	0	0	1	0	0	0	1	0	5	0	0	0	0	0	—	0	.143	.250	.143	OF	2	2	0	0	0	1.000

SEA LION HALL—Charles Louis Hall—Throws: Right; Bats: Left

Ht: 6'1"; Wt: 187 lbs; Born: 7/27/1885 in Ventura, California; Debut: 7/12/1906; Died: 12/6/1943

World Series		Pitching																										
Year Tm	Age	G	GS	CG	GF	IP	BFP	H	R	ER	HR	SH	SF	HB	TBB	IBB	SO	WP	Bk	W	L	Pct	ShO	Sv-Op	Hld	OAvg	OOBP	ERA
1912 Bos	27	2	0	0	1	10.2	51	11	6	4	1	0	1	0	9	2	1	0	0	0	0	—	0	0- 1	0	.268	.392	3.38

World Series		Batting																							Fielding						
Year Tm	Age	G	AB	H	2B	3B	HR	TB	R	RBI	GW	TBB	IBB	SO	HBP	SH	SF	SB	CS	SB%	GDP	Avg	OBP	SLG	Pos	G	PO	A	E	DP	FPct
1912 Bos	27	2	4	3	1	0	0	4	0	0	0	1	0	0	0	0	0	0	0	—	0	.750	.800	1.000	P	2	0	5	1	0	.833

TOM HALL—Tom Edward Hall—Nickname: The Blade—Throws: Left; Bats: Left

Ht: 6'0"; Wt: 150 lbs; Born: 11/23/1947 in Thomasville, North Carolina; Debut: 6/9/1968

LCS		Pitching																										
Year Tm	Age	G	GS	CG	GF	IP	BFP	H	R	ER	HR	SH	SF	HB	TBB	IBB	SO	WP	Bk	W	L	Pct	ShO	Sv-Op	Hld	OAvg	OOBP	ERA
1969 Min	21	1	0	0	0	0.2	2	0	0	0	0	0	0	0	0	0	0	0	0	0	0	—	0	0- 0	0	.000	.000	0.00
1970 Min	22	2	1	0	0	5.1	26	6	4	4	1	0	0	0	4	0	6	0	0	0	1	.000	0	0- 0	0	.273	.385	6.75
1972 Cin	24	2	0	0	1	7.1	28	3	1	1	0	1	0	0	3	1	8	0	0	1	0	1.000	0	0- 0	0	.125	.222	1.23
1973 Cin	25	3	0	0	0	0.2	9	3	5	5	1	0	0	0	4	0	1	0	0	0	0	—	0	0- 0	0	.600	.778	67.50
1976 KC	28	1	0	0	0	0.1	2	1	0	0	0	0	0	0	0	0	0	0	0	0	0	—	0	0- 1	0	.500	.500	0.00
LCS Totals		9	1	0	1	14.1	134	13	10	10	2	1	0	0	11	1	15	0	0	1	1	.500	0	0-1	0	.236	.364	6.28
World Series		Pitching																										
Year Tm	Age	G	GS	CG	GF	IP	BFP	H	R	ER	HR	SH	SF	HB	TBB	IBB	SO	WP	Bk	W	L	Pct	ShO	Sv-Op	Hld	OAvg	OOBP	ERA
1972 Cin	24	4	0	0	3	8.1	33	6	0	0	0	0	0	0	2	0	7	0	0	0	0	—	0	1- 1	0	.194	.242	0.00
Postseason Totals		13	1	0	4	22.2	200	19	10	10	2	1	0	0	13	1	22	0	0	1	1	.500	0	1-2	0	.221	.323	3.97

LCS		Batting																							Fielding						
Year Tm	Age	G	AB	H	2B	3B	HR	TB	R	RBI	GW	TBB	IBB	SO	HBP	SH	SF	SB	CS	SB%	GDP	Avg	OBP	SLG	Pos	G	PO	A	E	DP	FPct
1969 Min	21	1	0	0	0	0	0	0	0	0	0	0	0	0	0	0	0	0	0	—	0	—	—	—	P	1	0	0	0	0	—
1970 Min	22	2	1	0	0	0	0	0	0	0	0	0	0	1	0	0	0	0	0	—	0	.000	.000	.000	P	2	0	0	0	0	—
1972 Cin	24	2	1	0	0	0	0	0	0	0	0	0	0	0	0	0	0	0	0	—	0	.000	.000	.000	P	2	1	0	0	0	1.000
1973 Cin	25	3	0	0	0	0	0	0	0	0	0	0	0	0	0	0	0	0	0	—	0	—	—	—	P	3	1	0	0	0	1.000
1976 KC	28	1	0	0	0	0	0	0	0	0	0	0	0	0	0	0	0	0	0	—	0	—	—	—	P	1	0	0	0	0	—
LCS Totals		9	2	0	0	0	0	0	0	0	0	0	0	1	0	0	0	0	0	—	0	.000	.000	.000	P	9	2	0	0	0	1.000
World Series		Batting																							Fielding						
Year Tm	Age	G	AB	H	2B	3B	HR	TB	R	RBI	GW	TBB	IBB	SO	HBP	SH	SF	SB	CS	SB%	GDP	Avg	OBP	SLG	Pos	G	PO	A	E	DP	FPct
1972 Cin	24	4	2	0	0	0	0	0	0	0	0	0	0	1	0	0	0	0	0	—	0	.000	.000	.000	P	4	0	2	0	0	1.000
Postseason Totals		13	4	0	0	0	0	0	0	0	0	0	0	2	0	0	0	0	0	—	0	.000	.000	.000	P	13	2	2	0	0	1.000

WILD BILL HALLAHAN—William Anthony Hallahan—Throws: Left; Bats: Right

Ht: 5'10"; Wt: 170 lbs; Born: 8/4/1902 in Binghamton, New York; Debut: 4/16/1925; Died: 7/8/1981

World Series		Pitching																										
Year Tm	Age	G	GS	CG	GF	IP	BFP	H	R	ER	HR	SH	SF	HB	TBB	IBB	SO	WP	Bk	W	L	Pct	ShO	Sv-Op	Hld	OAvg	OOBP	ERA
1926 StL	24	1	0	0	0	2.0	11	2	1	1	0	2	0	0	3	0	1	0	0	0	0	—	0	0- 0	0	.333	.556	4.50
1930 StL	28	2	2	1	0	11.0	50	9	2	2	0	0	0	1	8	0	8	0	0	1	1	.500	1	0- 0	0	.220	.360	1.64
1931 StL	29	3	2	2	1	18.1	74	12	1	1	0	1	0	0	8	1	12	1	0	2	0	1.000	1	1- 1	0	.185	.274	0.49
1934 StL	32	1	1	0	0	8.1	37	6	2	2	0	1	0	0	4	0	6	0	0	0	0	—	0	0- 0	0	.188	.278	2.16
WS Totals		7	5	3	1	39.2	344	29	6	6	0	4	0	1	23	1	27	1	0	3	1	.750	2	1-1	0	.201	.315	1.36

World Series		Batting																							Fielding						
Year Tm	Age	G	AB	H	2B	3B	HR	TB	R	RBI	GW	TBB	IBB	SO	HBP	SH	SF	SB	CS	SB%	GDP	Avg	OBP	SLG	Pos	G	PO	A	E	DP	FPct
1926 StL	24	1	0	0	0	0	0	0	0	0	0	0	0	0	0	0	0	0	0	—	0	—	—	—	P	1	1	0	0	0	1.000
1930 StL	28	2	2	0	0	0	0	0	0	0	0	1	0	1	0	0	0	0	0	—	0	.000	.333	.000	P	2	0	1	0	0	1.000
1931 StL	29	3	6	0	0	0	0	0	0	0	0	0	0	3	0	1	0	0	0	—	0	.000	.000	.000	P	3	0	0	0	0	—
1934 StL	32	1	3	0	0	0	0	0	0	0	0	0	0	1	0	0	0	0	0	—	0	.000	.000	.000	P	1	1	3	1	0	.800
WS Totals		7	11	0	0	0	0	0	0	0	0	1	0	5	0	1	0	0	0	—	0	.000	.083	.000	P	7	2	4	1	0	.857

TOM HALLER—Thomas Frank Haller—Bats: Left; Throws: Right

Ht: 6'4"; Wt: 195 lbs; Born: 6/23/1937 in Lockport, Illinois; Debut: 4/11/1961

LCS		Batting																							Fielding						
Year Tm	Age	G	AB	H	2B	3B	HR	TB	R	RBI	GW	TBB	IBB	SO	HBP	SH	SF	SB	CS	SB%	GDP	Avg	OBP	SLG	Pos	G	PO	A	E	DP	FPct
1972 Det	35	1	1	0	0	0	0	0	0	0	0	0	0	0	0	0	0	0	0	—	0	.000	.000	.000	—						
World Series		Batting																							Fielding						
Year Tm	Age	G	AB	H	2B	3B	HR	TB	R	RBI	GW	TBB	IBB	SO	HBP	SH	SF	SB	CS	SB%	GDP	Avg	OBP	SLG	Pos	G	PO	A	E	DP	FPct
1962 SF	25	4	14	4	1	0	1	8	1	3	0	0	0	2	0	0	0	0	1	.00	0	.286	.286	.571	C	4	29	2	0	1	1.000
Postseason Totals		5	15	4	1	0	1	8	1	3	0	0	0	2	0	0	0	0	1	.00	0	.267	.267	.533	C	4	29	2	0	1	1.000

DARRYL HAMILTON—Darryl Quinn Hamilton—Bats: Left; Throws: Right

Ht: 6'1"; Wt: 180 lbs; Born: 12/3/1964 in Baton Rouge, Louisiana; Debut: 6/3/1988

Division Series — Batting / Fielding

Year Tm	Age	G	AB	H	2B	3B	HR	TB	R	RBI	GW	TBB	IBB	SO	HBP	SH	SF	SB	CS	SB%	GDP	Avg	OBP	SLG	Pos	G	PO	A	E	DP	FPct
1996 Tex	31	4	19	3	0	0	0	3	0	0	0	0	0	2	0	1	0	0	0	—	0	.158	.158	.158	OF	4	16	1	0	1	1.000
1997 SF	32	2	5	0	0	0	0	0	1	0	0	0	0	1	0	0	0	0	0	—	0	.000	.000	.000	OF	2	3	0	0	0	1.000
DS Totals		6	24	3	0	0	0	3	1	0	0	0	0	3	0	1	0	0	0	—	0	.125	.125	.125	OF	6	19	1	0	1	1.000

DAVE HAMILTON—David Edward Hamilton—Throws: Left; Bats: Left

Ht: 6'0"; Wt: 180 lbs; Born: 12/13/1947 in Seattle, Washington; Debut: 5/29/1972

LCS — Pitching

Year Tm	Age	G	GS	CG	GF	IP	BFP	H	R	ER	HR	SH	SF	HB	TBB	IBB	SO	WP	Bk	W	L	Pct	ShO	Sv-Op	Hld	OAvg	OOBP	ERA
1972 Oak	24	1	0	0	1	0.0	2	1	0	0	0	0	0	0	1	0	0	0	0	0	0	—	0	0-1	0	1.000	1.000	—

World Series — Pitching

Year Tm	Age	G	GS	CG	GF	IP	BFP	H	R	ER	HR	SH	SF	HB	TBB	IBB	SO	WP	Bk	W	L	Pct	ShO	Sv-Op	Hld	OAvg	OOBP	ERA
1972 Oak	24	2	0	0	1	1.1	7	3	4	4	0	0	0	0	1	1	1	0	0	0	0	—	0	0-0	0	.500	.571	27.00
Postseason Totals		3	0	0	2	1.1	18	4	4	4	0	0	0	0	2	1	1	0	0	0	0	—	0	0-1	0	.571	.667	27.00

LCS — Batting / Fielding

Year Tm	Age	G	AB	H	2B	3B	HR	TB	R	RBI	GW	TBB	IBB	SO	HBP	SH	SF	SB	CS	SB%	GDP	Avg	OBP	SLG	Pos	G	PO	A	E	DP	FPct
1972 Oak	24	1	0	0	0	0	0	0	0	0	0	0	0	0	0	0	0	0	0	—	0	—	—	—	P	1	0	0	0	0	—

World Series — Batting / Fielding

Year Tm	Age	G	AB	H	2B	3B	HR	TB	R	RBI	GW	TBB	IBB	SO	HBP	SH	SF	SB	CS	SB%	GDP	Avg	OBP	SLG	Pos	G	PO	A	E	DP	FPct
1972 Oak	24	2	0	0	0	0	0	0	0	0	0	0	0	0	0	0	0	0	0	—	0	—	—	—	P	2	0	0	0	0	—
Postseason Totals		3	0	0	0	0	0	0	0	0	0	0	0	0	0	0	0	0	0	—	0	—	—	—	P	3	0	0	0	0	—

JEFF HAMILTON—Jeffrey Robert Hamilton—Bats: Right; Throws: Right

Ht: 6'3"; Wt: 190 lbs; Born: 3/19/1964 in Flint, Michigan; Debut: 6/28/1986

LCS — Batting / Fielding

Year Tm	Age	G	AB	H	2B	3B	HR	TB	R	RBI	GW	TBB	IBB	SO	HBP	SH	SF	SB	CS	SB%	GDP	Avg	OBP	SLG	Pos	G	PO	A	E	DP	FPct
1988 LA	24	7	23	5	0	0	0	5	2	1	0	3	0	4	1	0	0	0	0	—	0	.217	.333	.217	3B	7	9	10	2	0	.905

World Series — Batting / Fielding

Year Tm	Age	G	AB	H	2B	3B	HR	TB	R	RBI	GW	TBB	IBB	SO	HBP	SH	SF	SB	CS	SB%	GDP	Avg	OBP	SLG	Pos	G	PO	A	E	DP	FPct
1988 LA	24	5	19	2	0	0	0	2	1	0	0	1	0	4	0	0	0	0	0	—	1	.105	.150	.105	3B	5	2	6	1	1	.889
Postseason Totals		12	42	7	0	0	0	7	3	1	0	4	0	8	1	0	0	0	0	—	1	.167	.255	.167	3B	12	11	16	3	1	.900

JOEY HAMILTON—Johns Joseph Hamilton—Nickname: Big Daddy—Throws: Right; Bats: Right

Ht: 6'4"; Wt: 220 lbs; Born: 9/9/1970 in Statesboro, Georgia; Debut: 5/24/1994

Division Series — Pitching

Year Tm	Age	G	GS	CG	GF	IP	BFP	H	R	ER	HR	SH	SF	HB	TBB	IBB	SO	WP	Bk	W	L	Pct	ShO	Sv-Op	Hld	OAvg	OOBP	ERA
1996 SD	26	1	1	0	0	6.0	23	5	3	3	1	0	0	1	0	0	6	0	0	0	1	.000	0	0-0	0	.227	.261	4.50

Division Series — Batting / Fielding

Year Tm	Age	G	AB	H	2B	3B	HR	TB	R	RBI	GW	TBB	IBB	SO	HBP	SH	SF	SB	CS	SB%	GDP	Avg	OBP	SLG	Pos	G	PO	A	E	DP	FPct
1996 SD	26	1	2	0	0	0	0	0	0	0	0	0	0	2	0	0	0	0	0	—	0	.000	.000	.000	P	1	1	0	0	0	1.000

STEVE HAMILTON—Steven Absher Hamilton—Throws: Left; Bats: Left

Ht: 6'6"; Wt: 190 lbs; Born: 11/30/1935 in Columbia, Kentucky; Debut: 4/23/1961; Died: 12/2/1997

LCS — Pitching

Year Tm	Age	G	GS	CG	GF	IP	BFP	H	R	ER	HR	SH	SF	HB	TBB	IBB	SO	WP	Bk	W	L	Pct	ShO	Sv-Op	Hld	OAvg	OOBP	ERA
1971 SF	35	1	0	0	1	1.0	4	1	1	1	1	0	0	0	0	0	3	0	0	0	0	—	0	0-0	0	.250	.250	9.00

World Series — Pitching

Year Tm	Age	G	GS	CG	GF	IP	BFP	H	R	ER	HR	SH	SF	HB	TBB	IBB	SO	WP	Bk	W	L	Pct	ShO	Sv-Op	Hld	OAvg	OOBP	ERA
1963 NYA	27	1	0	0	1	1.0	3	0	0	0	0	0	0	0	0	0	1	0	0	0	0	—	0	0-0	0	.000	.000	0.00
1964 NYA	28	2	0	0	1	2.0	9	3	1	1	1	1	0	0	0	0	2	0	0	0	0	—	0	1-1	0	.375	.375	4.50
WS Totals		3	0	0	2	3.0	24	3	1	1	1	1	0	0	0	0	3	0	0	0	0	—	0	1-1	0	.273	.273	3.00
Postseason Totals		4	0	0	3	4.0	32	4	2	2	2	1	0	0	0	0	6	0	0	0	0	—	0	1-1	0	.267	.267	4.50

LCS — Batting / Fielding

Year Tm	Age	G	AB	H	2B	3B	HR	TB	R	RBI	GW	TBB	IBB	SO	HBP	SH	SF	SB	CS	SB%	GDP	Avg	OBP	SLG	Pos	G	PO	A	E	DP	FPct
1971 SF	35	1	0	0	0	0	0	0	0	0	0	0	0	0	0	0	0	0	0	—	0	—	—	—	P	1	0	0	0	0	—

World Series — Batting / Fielding

Year Tm	Age	G	AB	H	2B	3B	HR	TB	R	RBI	GW	TBB	IBB	SO	HBP	SH	SF	SB	CS	SB%	GDP	Avg	OBP	SLG	Pos	G	PO	A	E	DP	FPct
1963 NYA	27	1	0	0	0	0	0	0	0	0	0	0	0	0	0	0	0	0	0	—	0	—	—	—	P	1	0	0	0	0	—
1964 NYA	28	2	0	0	0	0	0	0	0	0	0	0	0	0	0	0	0	0	0	—	0	—	—	—	P	2	0	0	0	0	—
WS Totals		3	0	0	0	0	0	0	0	0	0	0	0	0	0	0	0	0	0	—	0	—	—	—	P	3	0	0	0	0	—
Postseason Totals		4	0	0	0	0	0	0	0	0	0	0	0	0	0	0	0	0	0	—	0	—	—	—	P	4	0	0	0	0	—

ATLEE HAMMAKER—Charlton Atlee Hammaker—Throws: Left; Bats: Both

Ht: 6'3"; Wt: 200 lbs; Born: 1/24/1958 in Carmel, California; Debut: 8/13/1981

LCS — Pitching

Year Tm	Age	G	GS	CG	GF	IP	BFP	H	R	ER	HR	SH	SF	HB	TBB	IBB	SO	WP	Bk	W	L	Pct	ShO	Sv-Op	Hld	OAvg	OOBP	ERA
1987 SF	29	2	2	0	0	8.0	35	12	7	7	2	0	0	0	0	0	7	0	0	0	1	.000	0	0-0	0	.343	.343	7.88
1989 SF	31	1	0	0	1	1.0	4	1	0	0	0	0	0	0	0	0	0	0	0	0	0	—	0	0-0	0	.250	.250	0.00
LCS Totals		3	2	0	1	9.0	78	13	7	7	2	0	0	0	0	0	7	0	0	0	1	.000	0	0-0	0	.333	.333	7.00

World Series — Pitching

Year Tm	Age	G	GS	CG	GF	IP	BFP	H	R	ER	HR	SH	SF	HB	TBB	IBB	SO	WP	Bk	W	L	Pct	ShO	Sv-Op	Hld	OAvg	OOBP	ERA
1989 SF	31	2	0	0	0	2.1	16	8	4	4	0	0	0	1	0	0	2	0	0	0	0	—	0	0-0	0	.533	.563	15.43
Postseason Totals		5	2	0	1	11.1	110	21	11	11	2	0	0	1	0	0	9	0	0	0	1	.000	0	0-0	0	.389	.400	8.74

LCS — Batting / Fielding

Year Tm	Age	G	AB	H	2B	3B	HR	TB	R	RBI	GW	TBB	IBB	SO	HBP	SH	SF	SB	CS	SB%	GDP	Avg	OBP	SLG	Pos	G	PO	A	E	DP	FPct
1987 SF	29	2	3	0	0	0	0	0	0	0	0	0	0	2	0	0	0	0	0	—	0	.000	.000	.000	P	2	0	1	0	0	1.000
1989 SF	31	1	0	0	0	0	0	0	0	0	0	0	0	0	0	0	0	0	0	—	0	—	—	—	P	1	0	0	0	0	—
LCS Totals		3	3	0	0	0	0	0	0	0	0	0	0	2	0	0	0	0	0	—	0	.000	.000	.000	P	3	0	1	0	0	1.000

World Series — Batting / Fielding

Year Tm	Age	G	AB	H	2B	3B	HR	TB	R	RBI	GW	TBB	IBB	SO	HBP	SH	SF	SB	CS	SB%	GDP	Avg	OBP	SLG	Pos	G	PO	A	E	DP	FPct
1989 SF	31	2	0	0	0	0	0	0	0	0	0	0	0	0	0	0	0	0	0	—	0	—	—	—	P	2	0	1	0	0	1.000
Postseason Totals		5	3	0	0	0	0	0	0	0	0	0	0	2	0	0	0	0	0	—	0	.000	.000	.000	P	5	0	2	0	0	1.000

JEFFREY HAMMONDS—Jeffrey Bryan Hammonds—Bats: Right; Throws: Right

Ht: 6'0"; Wt: 195 lbs; Born: 3/5/1971 in Plainfield, New Jersey; Debut: 6/25/1993

Division Series — Batting / Fielding

Year Tm	Age	G	AB	H	2B	3B	HR	TB	R	RBI	GW	TBB	IBB	SO	HBP	SH	SF	SB	CS	SB%	GDP	Avg	OBP	SLG	Pos	G	PO	A	E	DP	FPct
1997 Bal	26	4	10	1	1	0	0	2	3	2	0	2	0	2	0	0	0	1	0	1.00	0	.100	.250	.200	OF	4	8	1	0	0	1.000

LCS — Batting / Fielding

Year Tm	Age	G	AB	H	2B	3B	HR	TB	R	RBI	GW	TBB	IBB	SO	HBP	SH	SF	SB	CS	SB%	GDP	Avg	OBP	SLG	Pos	G	PO	A	E	DP	FPct
1997 Bal	26	5	3	0	0	0	0	0	0	0	0	1	0	2	0	0	0	1	0	1.00	0	.000	.250	.000	OF	4	2	0	0	0	1.000
Postseason Totals		9	13	1	1	0	0	2	3	2	0	3	0	4	0	0	0	2	0	1.00	0	.077	.250	.154	OF	8	10	1	0	0	1.000

GRANNY HAMNER—Granville Wilbur Hamner—Bats: Right; Throws: Right

Ht: 5'10"; Wt: 163 lbs; Born: 4/26/1927 in Richmond, Virginia; Debut: 9/14/1944; Died: 9/12/1993

World Series — Batting / Fielding

Year Tm	Age	G	AB	H	2B	3B	HR	TB	R	RBI	GW	TBB	IBB	SO	HBP	SH	SF	SB	CS	SB%	GDP	Avg	OBP	SLG	Pos	G	PO	A	E	DP	FPct
1950 Phi	23	4	14	6	2	1	0	10	1	0	0	1	0	2	0	0	0	1	0	1.00	0	.429	.467	.714	SS	4	6	7	1	1	.929

MIKE HAMPTON—Michael William Hampton—Throws: Left; Bats: Right

Ht: 5'10"; Wt: 180 lbs; Born: 9/9/1972 in Brooksville, Florida; Debut: 4/17/1993

Division Series — Pitching

Year Tm	Age	G	GS	CG	GF	IP	BFP	H	R	ER	HR	SH	SF	HB	TBB	IBB	SO	WP	Bk	W	L	Pct	ShO	Sv-Op	Hld	OAvg	OOBP	ERA
1997 Hou	25	1	1	0	0	4.2	24	2	6	6	1	0	0	0	8	0	2	0	0	0	1	.000	0	0-0	0	.125	.417	11.57

Division Series		Batting																							Fielding						
Year Tm	Age	G	AB	H	2B	3B	HR	TB	R	RBI	GW	TBB	IBB	SO	HBP	SH	SF	SB	CS	SB%	GDP	Avg	OBP	SLG	Pos	G	PO	A	E	DP	FPct
1997 Hou	25	1	2	1	0	0	0	1	0	1	0	0	0	0	0	0	0	0	0	—	0	.500	.500	.500	P	1	3	0	0	0	1.000

HARRY HANEBRINK—Harry Aloysius Hanebrink—Bats: Left; Throws: Right

Ht: 6'0"; Wt: 165 lbs; Born: 11/12/1927 in St. Louis, Missouri; Debut: 5/3/1953; Died: 9/9/1996

World Series		Batting																							Fielding						
Year Tm	Age	G	AB	H	2B	3B	HR	TB	R	RBI	GW	TBB	IBB	SO	HBP	SH	SF	SB	CS	SB%	GDP	Avg	OBP	SLG	Pos	G	PO	A	E	DP	FPct
1958 Mil	30	2	2	0	0	0	0	0	0	0	0	0	0	0	0	0	0	0	0	—	0	.000	.000	.000	—						

LARRY HANEY—Wallace Larry Haney—Bats: Right; Throws: Right

Ht: 6'2"; Wt: 195 lbs; Born: 11/19/1942 in Charlottesville, Virginia; Debut: 7/27/1966

World Series		Batting																							Fielding						
Year Tm	Age	G	AB	H	2B	3B	HR	TB	R	RBI	GW	TBB	IBB	SO	HBP	SH	SF	SB	CS	SB%	GDP	Avg	OBP	SLG	Pos	G	PO	A	E	DP	FPct
1974 Oak	31	2	0	0	0	0	0	0	0	0	0	0	0	0	0	0	0	0	0	—	0	—	—	—	C	2	6	0	0	0	1.000

DAVE HANSEN—David Andrew Hansen—Bats: Left; Throws: Right

Ht: 6'0"; Wt: 180 lbs; Born: 11/24/1968 in Long Beach, California; Debut: 9/16/1990

Division Series		Batting																							Fielding						
Year Tm	Age	G	AB	H	2B	3B	HR	TB	R	RBI	GW	TBB	IBB	SO	HBP	SH	SF	SB	CS	SB%	GDP	Avg	OBP	SLG	Pos	G	PO	A	E	DP	FPct
1995 LA	26	3	3	2	0	0	0	2	0	0	0	0	0	0	0	0	0	0	0	—	0	.667	.667	.667	—						
1996 LA	27	2	2	0	0	0	0	0	0	0	0	0	0	0	0	0	0	0	0	—	0	.000	.000	.000	3B	1	1	0	0	1	1.000
DS Totals		5	5	2	0	0	0	2	0	0	0	0	0	0	0	0	0	0	0	—	0	.400	.400	.400	3B	1	1	0	0	1	1.000

ERIK HANSON—Erik Brian Hanson—Throws: Right; Bats: Right

Ht: 6'6"; Wt: 210 lbs; Born: 5/18/1965 in Kinnelon, New Jersey; Debut: 9/5/1988

Division Series		Pitching																										
Year Tm	Age	G	GS	CG	GF	IP	BFP	H	R	ER	HR	SH	SF	HB	TBB	IBB	SO	WP	Bk	W	L	Pct	ShO	Sv-Op	Hld	OAvg	OOBP	ERA
1995 Bos	30	1	1	1	0	8.0	34	4	4	4	1	1	0	1	4	1	5	0	0	0	1	.000	0	0- 0	0	.143	.273	4.50

Division Series		Batting																							Fielding						
Year Tm	Age	G	AB	H	2B	3B	HR	TB	R	RBI	GW	TBB	IBB	SO	HBP	SH	SF	SB	CS	SB%	GDP	Avg	OBP	SLG	Pos	G	PO	A	E	DP	FPct
1995 Bos	30	1	0	0	0	0	0	0	0	0	0	0	0	0	0	0	0	0	0	—	0	—	—	—	P	1	1	3	0	0	1.000

LARRY HARLOW—Larry Duane Harlow—Bats: Left; Throws: Left

Ht: 6'2"; Wt: 185 lbs; Born: 11/13/1951 in Colorado Springs, Colorado; Debut: 9/20/1975

LCS		Batting																							Fielding						
Year Tm	Age	G	AB	H	2B	3B	HR	TB	R	RBI	GW	TBB	IBB	SO	HBP	SH	SF	SB	CS	SB%	GDP	Avg	OBP	SLG	Pos	G	PO	A	E	DP	FPct
1979 Cal	27	3	8	1	1	0	0	2	0	1	1	1	0	2	0	0	0	0	0	—	0	.125	.222	.250	OF	2	6	0	0	0	1.000

TERRY HARMON—Terry Walter Harmon—Bats: Right; Throws: Right

Ht: 6'2"; Wt: 180 lbs; Born: 4/12/1944 in Toledo, Ohio; Debut: 7/23/1967

LCS		Batting																							Fielding						
Year Tm	Age	G	AB	H	2B	3B	HR	TB	R	RBI	GW	TBB	IBB	SO	HBP	SH	SF	SB	CS	SB%	GDP	Avg	OBP	SLG	Pos	G	PO	A	E	DP	FPct
1976 Phi	32	1	0	0	0	0	0	0	1	0	0	0	0	0	0	0	0	0	0	—	0	—	—	—	—						

BRIAN HARPER—Brian David Harper—Bats: Right; Throws: Right

Ht: 6'2"; Wt: 195 lbs; Born: 10/16/1959 in Los Angeles, California; Debut: 9/29/1979

LCS		Batting																							Fielding						
Year Tm	Age	G	AB	H	2B	3B	HR	TB	R	RBI	GW	TBB	IBB	SO	HBP	SH	SF	SB	CS	SB%	GDP	Avg	OBP	SLG	Pos	G	PO	A	E	DP	FPct
1985 StL	25	1	1	0	0	0	0	0	0	0	0	0	0	0	0	0	0	0	0	—	0	.000	.000	.000	—						
1991 Min	31	5	18	5	2	0	0	7	1	1	0	0	0	2	0	0	0	0	0	—	0	.278	.278	.389	C	5	23	1	1	0	.960
LCS Totals		6	19	5	2	0	0	7	1	1	0	0	0	2	0	0	0	0	0	—	0	.263	.263	.368	C	5	23	1	1	0	.960
World Series		**Batting**																							**Fielding**						
Year Tm	Age	G	AB	H	2B	3B	HR	TB	R	RBI	GW	TBB	IBB	SO	HBP	SH	SF	SB	CS	SB%	GDP	Avg	OBP	SLG	Pos	G	PO	A	E	DP	FPct
1985 StL	25	4	4	1	0	0	0	1	0	1	0	0	0	1	0	0	0	0	0	—	0	.250	.250	.250	—						
1991 Min	31	7	21	8	2	0	0	10	2	1	0	2	0	2	0	0	0	0	0	—	0	.381	.435	.476	C	7	33	5	1	1	.974
WS Totals		11	25	9	2	0	0	11	2	2	0	2	0	3	0	0	0	0	0	—	0	.360	.407	.440	C	7	33	5	1	1	.974
Postseason Totals		17	44	14	4	0	0	18	3	3	0	2	0	5	0	0	0	0	0	—	0	.318	.348	.409	C	12	56	6	2	1	.969

GEORGE HARPER—George Washington Harper—Bats: Left; Throws: Right

Ht: 5'8"; Wt: 167 lbs; Born: 6/24/1892 in Arlington, Kentucky; Debut: 4/15/1916; Died: 8/18/1978

World Series		Batting																							Fielding						
Year Tm	Age	G	AB	H	2B	3B	HR	TB	R	RBI	GW	TBB	IBB	SO	HBP	SH	SF	SB	CS	SB%	GDP	Avg	OBP	SLG	Pos	G	PO	A	E	DP	FPct
1928 StL	36	3	9	1	0	0	0	1	1	0	0	2	0	2	0	0	0	0	0	—	1	.111	.273	.111	OF	3	5	0	0	0	1.000

HARRY HARPER—Harry Clayton Harper—Throws: Left; Bats: Left

Ht: 6'2"; Wt: 165 lbs; Born: 4/24/1895 in Hackensack, New Jersey; Debut: 6/27/1913; Died: 4/23/1963

World Series		Pitching																										
Year Tm	Age	G	GS	CG	GF	IP	BFP	H	R	ER	HR	SH	SF	HB	TBB	IBB	SO	WP	Bk	W	L	Pct	ShO	Sv-Op	Hld	OAvg	OOBP	ERA
1921 NYA	26	1	1	0	0	1.1	9	3	3	3	2	0	0	0	2	0	1	0	0	0	0	—	0	0- 0	0	.429	.556	20.25

World Series		Batting																							Fielding						
Year Tm	Age	G	AB	H	2B	3B	HR	TB	R	RBI	GW	TBB	IBB	SO	HBP	SH	SF	SB	CS	SB%	GDP	Avg	OBP	SLG	Pos	G	PO	A	E	DP	FPct
1921 NYA	26	1	0	0	0	0	0	0	0	0	0	0	0	0	0	0	0	0	0	—	0	—	—	—	P	1	0	0	0	0	—

TERRY HARPER—Terry Joe Harper—Bats: Right; Throws: Right

Ht: 6'4"; Wt: 195 lbs; Born: 8/19/1955 in Douglasville, Georgia; Debut: 9/12/1980

LCS		Batting																							Fielding						
Year Tm	Age	G	AB	H	2B	3B	HR	TB	R	RBI	GW	TBB	IBB	SO	HBP	SH	SF	SB	CS	SB%	GDP	Avg	OBP	SLG	Pos	G	PO	A	E	DP	FPct
1982 Atl	27	1	1	0	0	0	0	0	1	0	0	0	0	0	0	0	0	0	0	—	0	.000	.000	.000	OF	1	0	0	0	0	—

TOMMY HARPER—Bats: Right; Throws: Right

Ht: 5'9"; Wt: 165 lbs; Born: 10/14/1940 in Oak Grove, Louisiana; Debut: 4/9/1962

LCS		Batting																							Fielding						
Year Tm	Age	G	AB	H	2B	3B	HR	TB	R	RBI	GW	TBB	IBB	SO	HBP	SH	SF	SB	CS	SB%	GDP	Avg	OBP	SLG	Pos	G	PO	A	E	DP	FPct
1975 Oak	34	1	0	0	0	0	0	0	0	0	0	1	0	0	0	0	0	0	0	—	0	—	1.000	—	—						

BUD HARRELSON—Derrel McKinley Harrelson—Bats: Both; Throws: Right

Ht: 5'11"; Wt: 160 lbs; Born: 6/6/1944 in Niles, California; Debut: 9/2/1965

LCS		Batting																							Fielding						
Year Tm	Age	G	AB	H	2B	3B	HR	TB	R	RBI	GW	TBB	IBB	SO	HBP	SH	SF	SB	CS	SB%	GDP	Avg	OBP	SLG	Pos	G	PO	A	E	DP	FPct
1969 NYN	25	3	11	2	1	1	0	5	2	3	0	1	1	2	0	1	0	0	0	—	0	.182	.250	.455	SS	3	6	6	1	2	.923
1973 NYN	29	5	18	3	0	0	0	3	1	2	0	1	0	1	0	0	0	0	0	—	0	.167	.211	.167	SS	5	11	14	0	4	1.000
LCS Totals		8	29	5	1	1	0	8	3	5	0	2	1	3	0	1	0	0	0	—	0	.172	.226	.276	SS	8	17	20	1	6	.974
World Series		**Batting**																							**Fielding**						
Year Tm	Age	G	AB	H	2B	3B	HR	TB	R	RBI	GW	TBB	IBB	SO	HBP	SH	SF	SB	CS	SB%	GDP	Avg	OBP	SLG	Pos	G	PO	A	E	DP	FPct
1969 NYN	25	5	17	3	0	0	0	3	1	0	0	3	0	4	0	0	0	0	0	—	0	.176	.300	.176	SS	5	13	17	0	0	1.000
1973 NYN	29	7	24	6	1	0	0	7	2	1	0	5	3	3	0	0	0	0	0	—	0	.250	.379	.292	SS	7	11	24	0	1	1.000
WS Totals		12	41	9	1	0	0	10	3	1	0	8	3	7	0	0	0	0	0	—	0	.220	.347	.244	SS	12	24	41	0	1	1.000
Postseason Totals		20	70	14	2	1	0	18	6	6	0	10	4	10	0	1	0	0	0	—	0	.200	.300	.257	SS	20	41	61	1	7	.990

KEN HARRELSON—Kenneth Smith Harrelson—Nickname: Hawk—Bats: Right; Throws: Right

Ht: 6'2"; Wt: 190 lbs; Born: 9/4/1941 in Woodruff, South Carolina; Debut: 6/9/1963

World Series		Batting																							Fielding						
Year Tm	Age	G	AB	H	2B	3B	HR	TB	R	RBI	GW	TBB	IBB	SO	HBP	SH	SF	SB	CS	SB%	GDP	Avg	OBP	SLG	Pos	G	PO	A	E	DP	FPct
1967 Bos	26	4	13	1	0	0	0	1	0	1	1	1	0	3	0	0	0	0	0	—	1	.077	.143	.077	OF	4	5	0	0	0	1.000

BUCKY HARRIS (HOF 1975-V)—Stanley Raymond Harris—Bats: Right; Throws: Right

Ht: 5'9"; Wt: 156 lbs; Born: 11/8/1896 in Port Jervis, New York; Debut: 8/28/1919; Died: 11/8/1977

World Series — Batting / Fielding

Year Tm	Age	G	AB	H	2B	3B	HR	TB	R	RBI	GW	TBB	IBB	SO	HBP	SH	SF	SB	CS	SB%	GDP	Avg	OBP	SLG	Pos	G	PO	A	E	DP	FPct
1924 Was	27	7	33	11	2	0	2	19	5	7	1	1	0	4	0	0	0	0	1	.00	0	.333	.353	.576	2B	7	27	27	2	8	.964
1925 Was	28	7	23	2	0	0	0	2	2	0	0	1	0	3	1	4	0	0	1	.00	1	.087	.160	.087	2B	7	23	18	0	5	1.000
WS Totals		14	56	13	2	0	2	21	7	7	1	2	0	7	1	4	0	0	2	.00	1	.232	.271	.375	2B	14	50	45	2	13	.979

DAVE HARRIS—David Stanley Harris—Nickname: Sheriff—Bats: Right; Throws: Right

Ht: 5'11"; Wt: 170 lbs; Born: 7/14/1900 in Summerfield, North Carolina; Debut: 4/14/1925; Died: 9/18/1973

World Series — Batting / Fielding

Year Tm	Age	G	AB	H	2B	3B	HR	TB	R	RBI	GW	TBB	IBB	SO	HBP	SH	SF	SB	CS	SB%	GDP	Avg	OBP	SLG	Pos	G	PO	A	E	DP	FPct
1933 Was	33	3	2	0	0	0	0	0	0	0	0	2	0	0	0	0	0	0	0	—	0	.000	.500	.000	OF	1	0	0	0	0	—

GREG HARRIS—Greg Allen Harris—Throws: Right; Bats: Both

Ht: 6'0"; Wt: 165 lbs; Born: 11/2/1955 in Lynwood, California; Debut: 5/20/1981

LCS — Pitching

Year Tm	Age	G	GS	CG	GF	IP	BFP	H	R	ER	HR	SH	SF	HB	TBB	IBB	SO	WP	Bk	W	L	Pct	ShO	Sv-Op	Hld	OAvg	OOBP	ERA
1984 SD	28	1	0	0	0	2.0	18	9	8	7	2	0	0	0	3	0	2	0	0	0	0	—	0	0-0	0	.600	.667	31.50
1990 Bos	34	1	0	0	0	0.1	4	3	1	1	0	0	0	0	0	0	0	0	0	0	1	.000	0	0-0	0	.750	.750	27.00
LCS Totals		2	0	0	0	2.1	44	12	9	8	2	0	0	0	3	0	2	0	0	0	1	.000	0	0-0	0	.632	.682	30.86

World Series — Pitching

Year Tm	Age	G	GS	CG	GF	IP	BFP	H	R	ER	HR	SH	SF	HB	TBB	IBB	SO	WP	Bk	W	L	Pct	ShO	Sv-Op	Hld	OAvg	OOBP	ERA
1984 SD	28	1	0	0	1	5.1	23	3	0	0	0	0	0	1	3	0	5	0	0	0	0	—	0	0-0	0	.158	.304	0.00
Postseason Totals		3	0	0	1	7.2	90	15	9	8	2	0	0	1	6	0	7	0	0	0	1	.000	0	0-0	0	.395	.489	9.39

LCS — Batting / Fielding

Year Tm	Age	G	AB	H	2B	3B	HR	TB	R	RBI	GW	TBB	IBB	SO	HBP	SH	SF	SB	CS	SB%	GDP	Avg	OBP	SLG	Pos	G	PO	A	E	DP	FPct
1984 SD	28	1	0	0	0	0	0	0	0	0	0	0	0	0	0	0	0	0	0	—	0	—	—	—	P	1	0	0	0	0	—
1990 Bos	34	1	0	0	0	0	0	0	0	0	0	0	0	0	0	0	0	0	0	—	0	—	—	—	P	1	0	0	0	0	—
LCS Totals		2	0	0	0	0	0	0	0	0	0	0	0	0	0	0	0	0	0	—	0	—	—	—	P	2	0	0	0	0	—

World Series — Batting / Fielding

Year Tm	Age	G	AB	H	2B	3B	HR	TB	R	RBI	GW	TBB	IBB	SO	HBP	SH	SF	SB	CS	SB%	GDP	Avg	OBP	SLG	Pos	G	PO	A	E	DP	FPct
1984 SD	28	1	0	0	0	0	0	0	0	0	0	0	0	0	0	0	0	0	0	—	0	—	—	—	P	1	0	0	0	0	—
Postseason Totals		3	0	0	0	0	0	0	0	0	0	0	0	0	0	0	0	0	0	—	0	—	—	—	P	3	0	0	0	0	—

JOE HARRIS—Joseph Harris—Nickname: Moon—Bats: Right; Throws: Right

Ht: 5'9"; Wt: 170 lbs; Born: 5/30/1891 in Coulters, Pennsylvania; Debut: 6/9/1914; Died: 12/10/1959

World Series — Batting / Fielding

Year Tm	Age	G	AB	H	2B	3B	HR	TB	R	RBI	GW	TBB	IBB	SO	HBP	SH	SF	SB	CS	SB%	GDP	Avg	OBP	SLG	Pos	G	PO	A	E	DP	FPct
1925 Was	34	7	25	11	2	0	3	22	5	6	2	3	0	4	0	0	0	0	2	.00	1	.440	.500	.880	OF	7	11	1	0	0	1.000
1927 Pit	36	4	15	3	0	0	0	3	0	1	0	0	0	0	0	0	0	0	0	—	1	.200	.200	.200	1B	4	35	1	0	2	1.000
WS Totals		11	40	14	2	0	3	25	5	7	2	3	0	4	0	0	0	0	2	.00	2	.350	.395	.625	OF	7	11	1	0	0	1.000

LENNY HARRIS—Leonard Anthony Harris—Bats: Left; Throws: Right

Ht: 5'10"; Wt: 195 lbs; Born: 10/28/1964 in Miami, Florida; Debut: 9/7/1988

LCS — Batting / Fielding

Year Tm	Age	G	AB	H	2B	3B	HR	TB	R	RBI	GW	TBB	IBB	SO	HBP	SH	SF	SB	CS	SB%	GDP	Avg	OBP	SLG	Pos	G	PO	A	E	DP	FPct
1995 Cin	30	3	2	2	0	0	0	2	0	1	0	0	0	0	0	0	0	1	0	1.00	0	1.000	1.000	1.000	—						

MICKEY HARRIS—Maurice Charles Harris—Throws: Left; Bats: Left

Ht: 6'0"; Wt: 195 lbs; Born: 1/30/1917 in New York, New York; Debut: 4/23/1940; Died: 4/15/1971

World Series — Pitching

Year Tm	Age	G	GS	CG	GF	IP	BFP	H	R	ER	HR	SH	SF	HB	TBB	IBB	SO	WP	Bk	W	L	Pct	ShO	Sv-Op	Hld	OAvg	OOBP	ERA
1946 Bos	29	2	2	0	0	9.2	45	11	6	5	0	1	0	0	4	1	5	0	0	0	2	.000	0	0-0	0	.275	.341	4.66

World Series — Batting / Fielding

Year Tm	Age	G	AB	H	2B	3B	HR	TB	R	RBI	GW	TBB	IBB	SO	HBP	SH	SF	SB	CS	SB%	GDP	Avg	OBP	SLG	Pos	G	PO	A	E	DP	FPct
1946 Bos	29	2	3	1	0	0	0	1	0	0	0	0	0	1	0	0	0	0	0	—	0	.333	.333	.333	P	2	1	0	0	0	1.000

JIM RAY HART—James Ray Hart—Bats: Right; Throws: Right

Ht: 5'11"; Wt: 185 lbs; Born: 10/30/1941 in Hookerton, North Carolina; Debut: 7/7/1963

LCS — Batting / Fielding

Year Tm	Age	G	AB	H	2B	3B	HR	TB	R	RBI	GW	TBB	IBB	SO	HBP	SH	SF	SB	CS	SB%	GDP	Avg	OBP	SLG	Pos	G	PO	A	E	DP	FPct
1971 SF	29	3	5	0	0	0	0	0	0	0	0	0	0	2	0	0	0	0	0	—	1	.000	.000	.000	3B	1	0	2	0	0	1.000

GABBY HARTNETT (HOF 1955-W)—Charles Leo Hartnett—Bats: Right; Throws: Right

Ht: 6'1"; Wt: 195 lbs; Born: 12/20/1900 in Woonsocket, Rhode Island; Debut: 4/12/1922; Died: 12/20/1972

World Series — Batting / Fielding

Year Tm	Age	G	AB	H	2B	3B	HR	TB	R	RBI	GW	TBB	IBB	SO	HBP	SH	SF	SB	CS	SB%	GDP	Avg	OBP	SLG	Pos	G	PO	A	E	DP	FPct
1929 ChN	28	3	3	0	0	0	0	0	0	0	0	0	0	3	0	0	0	0	0	—	0	.000	.000	.000	—						
1932 ChN	31	4	16	5	2	0	1	10	2	1	0	1	0	3	0	0	0	0	0	—	0	.313	.353	.625	C	4	32	5	1	2	.974
1935 ChN-*M*	34	6	24	7	0	0	1	10	1	2	0	0	0	3	0	1	0	0	0	—	2	.292	.292	.417	C	6	33	6	0	0	1.000
1938 ChN	37	3	11	1	0	1	0	3	0	0	0	0	0	2	0	0	0	0	0	—	0	.091	.091	.273	C	3	14	3	0	0	1.000
WS Totals		16	54	13	2	1	2	23	3	3	0	1	0	11	0	1	0	0	0	—	2	.241	.255	.426	C	13	79	14	1	2	.989

TOPSY HARTSEL—Tully Frederick Hartsel—Bats: Left; Throws: Left

Ht: 5'5"; Wt: 155 lbs; Born: 6/26/1874 in Polk, Ohio; Debut: 9/14/1898; Died: 10/14/1944

World Series — Batting / Fielding

Year Tm	Age	G	AB	H	2B	3B	HR	TB	R	RBI	GW	TBB	IBB	SO	HBP	SH	SF	SB	CS	SB%	GDP	Avg	OBP	SLG	Pos	G	PO	A	E	DP	FPct
1905 Phi	31	5	17	5	1	0	0	6	1	0	0	2	0	1	0	1	0	2	0	1.00	0	.294	.368	.353	OF	5	9	1	1	0	.909
1910 Phi	36	1	5	1	0	0	0	1	2	0	0	0	0	1	0	0	0	2	0	1.00	0	.200	.200	.200	OF	1	2	0	0	0	1.000
WS Totals		6	22	6	1	0	0	7	3	0	0	2	0	2	0	1	0	4	0	1.00	0	.273	.333	.318	OF	6	11	1	1	0	.923

CLINT HARTUNG—Clinton Clarence Hartung—Nicknames: Floppy, The Hondo Hurricane—Throws: Right; Bats: Right

Ht: 6'5"; Wt: 210 lbs; Born: 8/10/1922 in Hondo, Texas; Debut: 4/15/1947

World Series — Batting / Fielding

Year Tm	Age	G	AB	H	2B	3B	HR	TB	R	RBI	GW	TBB	IBB	SO	HBP	SH	SF	SB	CS	SB%	GDP	Avg	OBP	SLG	Pos	G	PO	A	E	DP	FPct
1951 NYG	29	2	4	0	0	0	0	0	0	0	0	0	0	0	0	0	0	0	0	—	1	.000	.000	.000	OF	2	1	1	1	0	.667

BILL HASELMAN—William Joseph Haselman—Bats: Right; Throws: Right

Ht: 6'3"; Wt: 205 lbs; Born: 5/25/1966 in Long Branch, New Jersey; Debut: 9/3/1990

Division Series — Batting / Fielding

Year Tm	Age	G	AB	H	2B	3B	HR	TB	R	RBI	GW	TBB	IBB	SO	HBP	SH	SF	SB	CS	SB%	GDP	Avg	OBP	SLG	Pos	G	PO	A	E	DP	FPct
1995 Bos	29	1	2	0	0	0	0	0	0	0	0	0	0	0	0	0	0	0	0	—	0	.000	.000	.000	C	1	6	0	0	0	1.000

BUDDY HASSETT—John Aloysius Hassett—Bats: Left; Throws: Left

Ht: 5'11"; Wt: 180 lbs; Born: 9/5/1911 in New York, New York; Debut: 4/14/1936; Died: 8/23/1997

World Series — Batting / Fielding

Year Tm	Age	G	AB	H	2B	3B	HR	TB	R	RBI	GW	TBB	IBB	SO	HBP	SH	SF	SB	CS	SB%	GDP	Avg	OBP	SLG	Pos	G	PO	A	E	DP	FPct
1942 NYA	31	3	9	3	1	0	0	4	1	2	1	0	0	1	0	0	0	0	0	—	0	.333	.333	.444	1B	3	15	1	1	0	.941

RON HASSEY—Ronald William Hassey—Bats: Left; Throws: Right

Ht: 6'2"; Wt: 200 lbs; Born: 2/27/1953 in Tucson, Arizona; Debut: 4/23/1978

LCS — Batting / Fielding

Year Tm	Age	G	AB	H	2B	3B	HR	TB	R	RBI	GW	TBB	IBB	SO	HBP	SH	SF	SB	CS	SB%	GDP	Avg	OBP	SLG	Pos	G	PO	A	E	DP	FPct
1988 Oak	35	4	8	4	1	0	1	8	2	3	1	1	1	1	0	0	0	0	0	—	0	.500	.556	1.000	C	4	13	0	0	0	1.000
1989 Oak	36	2	6	1	0	0	0	1	0	1	0	1	0	2	0	0	1	0	0	—	1	.167	.250	.167	C	2	10	0	0	0	1.000
1990 Oak	37	2	3	1	0	0	0	1	0	0	0	2	0	0	1	0	0	0	0	—	1	.333	.667	.333	C	1	6	0	0	0	1.000
LCS Totals		8	17	6	1	0	1	10	2	4	1	4	1	3	1	0	1	0	0	—	2	.353	.478	.588	C	7	29	0	0	0	1.000

World Series		Batting																							Fielding						
Year Tm	Age	G	AB	H	2B	3B	HR	TB	R	RBI	GW	TBB	IBB	SO	HBP	SH	SF	SB	CS	SB%	GDP	Avg	OBP	SLG	Pos	G	PO	A	E	DP	FPct
1988 Oak	35	5	8	2	0	0	0	2	0	1	0	3	0	3	0	0	0	0	0	—	0	.250	.455	.250	C	4	28	1	0	0	1.000
1990 Oak	37	3	6	2	0	0	0	2	0	1	0	0	0	0	0	0	0	0	0	—	0	.333	.286	.333	C	1	2	0	1	0	.667
WS Totals		8	14	4	0	0	0	4	0	2	0	3	0	3	0	0	1	0	0	—	0	.286	.389	.286	C	5	30	1	1	0	.969
Postseason Totals		16	31	10	1	0	1	14	2	6	1	7	1	6	1	0	2	0	0	—	2	.323	.439	.452	C	12	59	1	1	0	.984

ANDY HASSLER—Andrew Earl Hassler—Throws: Left; Bats: Left

Ht: 6'5"; Wt: 220 lbs; Born: 10/18/1951 in Texas City, Texas; Debut: 5/30/1971

LCS		Pitching																										
Year Tm	Age	G	GS	CG	GF	IP	BFP	H	R	ER	HR	SH	SF	HB	TBB	IBB	SO	WP	Bk	W	L	Pct	ShO	Sv-Op	Hld	OAvg	OOBP	ERA
1976 KC	24	2	1	0	0	7.1	34	8	6	5	1	2	0	0	6	0	4	0	0	0	1	.000	0	0- 0	0	.308	.438	6.14
1977 KC	25	1	1	0	0	5.2	22	5	3	3	1	0	0	0	0	0	3	0	1	0	1	.000	0	0- 0	0	.227	.227	4.76
1982 Cal	30	2	0	0	2	2.2	8	0	0	0	0	0	0	0	0	0	2	0	0	0	0	—	0	0- 0	0	.000	.000	0.00
LCS Totals		5	2	0	2	15.2	128	13	9	8	2	2	0	0	6	0	9	0	1	0	2	.000	0	0-0	0	.232	.306	4.60

LCS		Batting																							Fielding						
Year Tm	Age	G	AB	H	2B	3B	HR	TB	R	RBI	GW	TBB	IBB	SO	HBP	SH	SF	SB	CS	SB%	GDP	Avg	OBP	SLG	Pos	G	PO	A	E	DP	FPct
1976 KC	24	2	0	0	0	0	0	0	0	0	0	0	0	0	0	0	0	0	0	—	0	—	—	—	P	2	0	0	0	0	—
1977 KC	25	1	0	0	0	0	0	0	0	0	0	0	0	0	0	0	0	0	0	—	0	—	—	—	P	1	1	0	0	0	1.000
1982 Cal	30	2	0	0	0	0	0	0	0	0	0	0	0	0	0	0	0	0	0	—	0	—	—	—	P	2	0	1	0	0	1.000
LCS Totals		5	0	0	0	0	0	0	0	0	0	0	0	0	0	0	0	0	0	—	0	—	—	—	P	5	1	1	0	0	1.000

BILLY HATCHER—William Augustus Hatcher—Bats: Right; Throws: Right

Ht: 5'9"; Wt: 175 lbs; Born: 10/4/1960 in Williams, Arizona; Debut: 9/10/1984

LCS		Batting																							Fielding						
Year Tm	Age	G	AB	H	2B	3B	HR	TB	R	RBI	GW	TBB	IBB	SO	HBP	SH	SF	SB	CS	SB%	GDP	Avg	OBP	SLG	Pos	G	PO	A	E	DP	FPct
1986 Hou	25	6	25	7	0	0	1	10	4	2	0	3	0	2	0	2	0	3	0	1.00	0	.280	.357	.400	OF	6	12	0	1	0	.923
1990 Cin	29	4	15	5	1	0	1	9	2	2	0	0	0	2	0	1	0	0	0	—	0	.333	.333	.600	OF	4	5	1	0	0	1.000
LCS Totals		10	40	12	1	0	2	19	6	4	0	3	0	4	0	3	0	3	0	1.00	0	.300	.349	.475	OF	10	17	1	1	0	.947
World Series		Batting																							Fielding						
Year Tm	Age	G	AB	H	2B	3B	HR	TB	R	RBI	GW	TBB	IBB	SO	HBP	SH	SF	SB	CS	SB%	GDP	Avg	OBP	SLG	Pos	G	PO	A	E	DP	FPct
1990 Cin	29	4	12	9	4	1	0	15	6	2	0	2	1	0	1	0	0	0	1	.00	1	.750	.800	1.250	OF	4	11	0	0	0	1.000
Postseason Totals		14	52	21	5	1	2	34	12	6	0	5	1	4	1	3	0	3	1	.75	1	.404	.466	.654	OF	14	28	1	1	0	.967

MICKEY HATCHER—Michael Vaughn Hatcher—Bats: Right; Throws: Right

Ht: 6'2"; Wt: 200 lbs; Born: 3/15/1955 in Cleveland, Ohio; Debut: 8/3/1979

LCS		Batting																							Fielding						
Year Tm	Age	G	AB	H	2B	3B	HR	TB	R	RBI	GW	TBB	IBB	SO	HBP	SH	SF	SB	CS	SB%	GDP	Avg	OBP	SLG	Pos	G	PO	A	E	DP	FPct
1988 LA	33	6	21	5	2	0	0	7	4	3	0	3	0	0	0	0	0	0	0	—	0	.238	.333	.333	1B	6	33	1	2	6	.944
																									OF	1	1	0	0	0	1.000
World Series		Batting																							Fielding						
Year Tm	Age	G	AB	H	2B	3B	HR	TB	R	RBI	GW	TBB	IBB	SO	HBP	SH	SF	SB	CS	SB%	GDP	Avg	OBP	SLG	Pos	G	PO	A	E	DP	FPct
1988 LA	33	5	19	7	1	0	2	14	5	5	1	1	0	3	0	0	0	0	0	—	0	.368	.400	.737	OF	5	8	0	0	0	1.000
Postseason Totals		11	40	12	3	0	2	21	9	8	1	4	0	3	0	0	0	0	0	—	0	.300	.364	.525	1B	6	33	1	2	6	.944

JOE HATTEN—Joseph Hilarian Hatten—Throws: Left; Bats: Right

Ht: 6'0"; Wt: 176 lbs; Born: 11/17/1916 in Bancroft, Iowa; Debut: 4/21/1946; Died: 12/16/1988

World Series		Pitching																										
Year Tm	Age	G	GS	CG	GF	IP	BFP	H	R	ER	HR	SH	SF	HB	TBB	IBB	SO	WP	Bk	W	L	Pct	ShO	Sv-Op	Hld	OAvg	OOBP	ERA
1947 Bro	30	4	1	0	0	9.0	45	12	7	7	1	0	0	0	7	0	5	0	0	0	0	—	0	0- 0	1	.316	.422	7.00
1949 Bro	32	2	0	0	0	1.2	10	4	3	3	0	0	0	0	2	1	0	0	0	0	0	—	0	0- 0	0	.500	.600	16.20
WS Totals		6	1	0	0	10.2	110	16	10	10	1	0	0	0	9	1	5	0	0	0	0	—	0	0-0	1	.348	.455	8.44

World Series		Batting																							Fielding						
Year Tm	Age	G	AB	H	2B	3B	HR	TB	R	RBI	GW	TBB	IBB	SO	HBP	SH	SF	SB	CS	SB%	GDP	Avg	OBP	SLG	Pos	G	PO	A	E	DP	FPct
1947 Bro	30	4	3	1	0	0	0	1	1	0	0	0	0	0	0	0	0	0	0	—	0	.333	.333	.333	P	4	0	0	0	0	—
1949 Bro	32	2	0	0	0	0	0	0	0	0	0	0	0	0	0	0	0	0	0	—	0	—	—	—	P	2	0	0	0	0	—
WS Totals		6	3	1	0	0	0	1	1	0	0	0	0	0	0	0	0	0	0	—	0	.333	.333	.333	P	6	0	0	0	0	—

ANDY HAWKINS—Melton Andrew Hawkins—Throws: Right; Bats: Right

Ht: 6'4"; Wt: 200 lbs; Born: 1/21/1960 in Waco, Texas; Debut: 7/17/1982

LCS		Pitching																										
Year Tm	Age	G	GS	CG	GF	IP	BFP	H	R	ER	HR	SH	SF	HB	TBB	IBB	SO	WP	Bk	W	L	Pct	ShO	Sv-Op	Hld	OAvg	OOBP	ERA
1984 SD	24	3	0	0	0	3.2	10	0	0	0	0	0	0	0	2	0	1	0	0	0	0	—	0	0- 0	0	.000	.200	0.00
World Series		Pitching																										
Year Tm	Age	G	GS	CG	GF	IP	BFP	H	R	ER	HR	SH	SF	HB	TBB	IBB	SO	WP	Bk	W	L	Pct	ShO	Sv-Op	Hld	OAvg	OOBP	ERA
1984 SD	24	3	0	0	0	12.0	44	4	1	1	0	0	0	1	6	1	4	1	0	1	1	.500	0	0- 0	0	.108	.250	0.75
Postseason Totals		6	0	0	0	15.2	108	4	1	1	0	0	0	1	8	1	5	1	0	1	1	.500	0	0-0	0	.089	.241	0.57

LCS		Batting																							Fielding						
Year Tm	Age	G	AB	H	2B	3B	HR	TB	R	RBI	GW	TBB	IBB	SO	HBP	SH	SF	SB	CS	SB%	GDP	Avg	OBP	SLG	Pos	G	PO	A	E	DP	FPct
1984 SD	24	3	0	0	0	0	0	0	0	0	0	0	0	0	0	0	0	0	0	—	0	—	—	—	P	3	0	1	0	1	1.000
World Series		Batting																							Fielding						
Year Tm	Age	G	AB	H	2B	3B	HR	TB	R	RBI	GW	TBB	IBB	SO	HBP	SH	SF	SB	CS	SB%	GDP	Avg	OBP	SLG	Pos	G	PO	A	E	DP	FPct
1984 SD	24	3	0	0	0	0	0	0	0	0	0	0	0	0	0	0	0	0	0	—	0	—	—	—	P	3	0	1	0	0	1.000
Postseason Totals		6	0	0	0	0	0	0	0	0	0	0	0	0	0	0	0	0	0	—	0	—	—	—	P	6	0	2	0	1	1.000

CHARLIE HAYES—Charles Dewayne Hayes—Bats: Right; Throws: Right

Ht: 6'0"; Wt: 190 lbs; Born: 5/29/1965 in Hattiesburg, Mississippi; Debut: 9/11/1988

Division Series		Batting																							Fielding						
Year Tm	Age	G	AB	H	2B	3B	HR	TB	R	RBI	GW	TBB	IBB	SO	HBP	SH	SF	SB	CS	SB%	GDP	Avg	OBP	SLG	Pos	G	PO	A	E	DP	FPct
1996 NYA	31	3	5	1	0	0	0	1	0	1	0	0	0	0	0	1	1	0	1	.00	0	.200	.167	.200	3B	2	1	3	0	0	1.000
1997 NYA	32	5	15	5	0	0	0	5	0	1	0	0	0	2	0	0	1	0	0	—	0	.333	.313	.333	3B	5	2	7	3	0	.750
																									2B	1	1	2	0	0	1.000
DS Totals		8	20	6	0	0	0	6	0	2	0	0	0	2	0	1	2	0	1	.00	0	.300	.273	.300	3B	7	3	10	3	0	.813
LCS		Batting																							Fielding						
Year Tm	Age	G	AB	H	2B	3B	HR	TB	R	RBI	GW	TBB	IBB	SO	HBP	SH	SF	SB	CS	SB%	GDP	Avg	OBP	SLG	Pos	G	PO	A	E	DP	FPct
1996 NYA	31	4	7	1	0	0	0	1	0	0	0	2	0	2	0	0	0	0	0	—	0	.143	.333	.143	3B	2	0	3	0	0	1.000
World Series		Batting																							Fielding						
Year Tm	Age	G	AB	H	2B	3B	HR	TB	R	RBI	GW	TBB	IBB	SO	HBP	SH	SF	SB	CS	SB%	GDP	Avg	OBP	SLG	Pos	G	PO	A	E	DP	FPct
1996 NYA	31	5	16	3	0	0	0	3	2	1	0	1	0	5	0	0	0	0	0	—	0	.188	.235	.188	3B	4	2	6	0	0	1.000
																									1B	1	1	0	0	1	1.000
Postseason Totals		17	43	10	0	0	0	10	2	3	0	3	0	9	0	1	2	0	1	.00	0	.233	.271	.233	3B	13	5	19	3	0	.889

VON HAYES—Von Francis Hayes—Bats: Left; Throws: Right

Ht: 6'5"; Wt: 185 lbs; Born: 8/31/1958 in Stockton, California; Debut: 4/14/1981

LCS		Batting																							Fielding						
Year Tm	Age	G	AB	H	2B	3B	HR	TB	R	RBI	GW	TBB	IBB	SO	HBP	SH	SF	SB	CS	SB%	GDP	Avg	OBP	SLG	Pos	G	PO	A	E	DP	FPct
1983 Phi	25	2	2	0	0	0	0	0	0	0	0	0	0	0	0	0	0	0	0	—	0	.000	.000	.000	OF	1	0	0	0	0	—
World Series		Batting																							Fielding						
Year Tm	Age	G	AB	H	2B	3B	HR	TB	R	RBI	GW	TBB	IBB	SO	HBP	SH	SF	SB	CS	SB%	GDP	Avg	OBP	SLG	Pos	G	PO	A	E	DP	FPct
1983 Phi	25	4	3	0	0	0	0	0	0	0	0	0	0	1	0	0	0	0	0	—	0	.000	.000	.000	OF	2	1	0	0	0	1.000
Postseason Totals		6	5	0	0	0	0	0	0	0	0	0	0	1	0	0	0	0	0	—	0	.000	.000	.000	OF	3	1	0	0	0	1.000

RAY HAYWORTH—Raymond Hall Hayworth—Bats: Right; Throws: Right

Ht: 6'0"; Wt: 180 lbs; Born: 1/29/1904 in High Point, North Carolina; Debut: 6/27/1926

World Series		Batting																							Fielding						
Year Tm	Age	G	AB	H	2B	3B	HR	TB	R	RBI	GW	TBB	IBB	SO	HBP	SH	SF	SB	CS	SB%	GDP	Avg	OBP	SLG	Pos	G	PO	A	E	DP	FPct
1934 Det	30	1	0	0	0	0	0	0	0	0	0	0	0	0	0	0	0	0	0	—	0	—	—	—	C	1	1	0	0	0	1.000

RED HAYWORTH—Myron Claude Hayworth—Bats: Right; Throws: Right

Ht: 6'1"; Wt: 200 lbs; Born: 5/14/1915 in High Point, North Carolina; Debut: 4/21/1944

World Series — Batting / Fielding

Year Tm	Age	G	AB	H	2B	3B	HR	TB	R	RBI	GW	TBB	IBB	SO	HBP	SH	SF	SB	CS	SB%	GDP	Avg	OBP	SLG	Pos	G	PO	A	E	DP	FPct
1944 StL	29	6	17	2	1	0	0	3	1	1	0	3	2	1	0	0	0	0	0	—	1	.118	.250	.176	C	6	45	2	1	0	.979

BOB HAZLE—Robert Sidney Hazle—Nickname: Hurricane—Bats: Left; Throws: Right

Ht: 6'0"; Wt: 190 lbs; Born: 12/9/1930 in Laurens, South Carolina; Debut: 9/8/1955; Died: 4/25/1992

World Series — Batting / Fielding

Year Tm	Age	G	AB	H	2B	3B	HR	TB	R	RBI	GW	TBB	IBB	SO	HBP	SH	SF	SB	CS	SB%	GDP	Avg	OBP	SLG	Pos	G	PO	A	E	DP	FPct
1957 Mil	26	4	13	2	0	0	0	2	2	0	0	1	0	2	0	0	0	0	0	—	0	.154	.214	.154	OF	4	6	0	0	0	1.000

JIM HEARN—James Tolbert Hearn—Throws: Right; Bats: Right

Ht: 6'3"; Wt: 205 lbs; Born: 4/11/1921 in Atlanta, Georgia; Debut: 4/17/1947; Died: 6/10/1998

World Series — Pitching

Year Tm	Age	G	GS	CG	GF	IP	BFP	H	R	ER	HR	SH	SF	HB	TBB	IBB	SO	WP	Bk	W	L	Pct	ShO	Sv-Op	Hld	OAvg	OOBP	ERA
1951 NYG	30	2	1	0	0	8.2	38	5	1	1	0	0	0	1	8	0	1	0	0	1	0	1.000	0	0- 0	0	.172	.368	1.04

World Series — Batting / Fielding

Year Tm	Age	G	AB	H	2B	3B	HR	TB	R	RBI	GW	TBB	IBB	SO	HBP	SH	SF	SB	CS	SB%	GDP	Avg	OBP	SLG	Pos	G	PO	A	E	DP	FPct
1951 NYG	30	2	3	0	0	0	0	0	0	0	0	0	0	1	0	0	0	0	0	—	0	.000	.000	.000	P	2	0	2	0	1	1.000

JEFF HEARRON—Jeffrey Vernon Hearron—Bats: Right; Throws: Right

Ht: 6'1"; Wt: 195 lbs; Born: 11/19/1961 in Long Beach, California; Debut: 8/25/1985

LCS — Batting / Fielding

Year Tm	Age	G	AB	H	2B	3B	HR	TB	R	RBI	GW	TBB	IBB	SO	HBP	SH	SF	SB	CS	SB%	GDP	Avg	OBP	SLG	Pos	G	PO	A	E	DP	FPct
1985 Tor	23	2	0	0	0	0	0	0	0	0	0	0	0	0	0	0	0	0	0	—	0	—	—	—	C	2	2	0	0	0	1.000

MIKE HEATH—Michael Thomas Heath—Bats: Right; Throws: Right

Ht: 5'11"; Wt: 180 lbs; Born: 2/5/1955 in Tampa, Florida; Debut: 6/3/1978

Division Series — Batting / Fielding

Year Tm	Age	G	AB	H	2B	3B	HR	TB	R	RBI	GW	TBB	IBB	SO	HBP	SH	SF	SB	CS	SB%	GDP	Avg	OBP	SLG	Pos	G	PO	A	E	DP	FPct
1981 Oak	26	2	8	0	0	0	0	0	0	0	0	0	0	1	0	0	0	0	0	—	0	.000	.000	.000	C	2	9	1	0	0	1.000

LCS — Batting / Fielding

Year Tm	Age	G	AB	H	2B	3B	HR	TB	R	RBI	GW	TBB	IBB	SO	HBP	SH	SF	SB	CS	SB%	GDP	Avg	OBP	SLG	Pos	G	PO	A	E	DP	FPct
1981 Oak	26	3	6	2	0	0	0	2	1	0	0	0	0	1	0	0	0	0	0	—	0	.333	.333	.333	C	2	3	0	0	0	1.000
																									OF	1	0	1	0	0	1.000
1987 Det	32	3	7	2	0	0	1	5	1	2	0	0	0	0	0	1	0	0	0	—	0	.286	.286	.714	C	3	14	0	0	0	1.000
LCS Totals		6	13	4	0	0	1	7	2	2	0	0	0	1	0	1	0	0	0	—	0	.308	.308	.538	C	5	17	0	0	0	1.000

World Series — Batting / Fielding

Year Tm	Age	G	AB	H	2B	3B	HR	TB	R	RBI	GW	TBB	IBB	SO	HBP	SH	SF	SB	CS	SB%	GDP	Avg	OBP	SLG	Pos	G	PO	A	E	DP	FPct
1978 NYA	23	1	0	0	0	0	0	0	0	0	0	0	0	0	0	0	0	0	0	—	0	—	—	—	C	1	0	0	0	0	—
Postseason Totals		9	21	4	0	0	1	7	2	2	0	0	0	2	0	1	0	0	0	—	0	.190	.190	.333	C	8	26	1	0	0	1.000

CLIFF HEATHCOTE—Clifton Earl Heathcote—Nickname: Rubberhead—Bats: Left; Throws: Left

Ht: 5'10"; Wt: 160 lbs; Born: 1/24/1898 in Glen Rock, Pennsylvania; Debut: 6/4/1918; Died: 1/19/1939

World Series — Batting / Fielding

Year Tm	Age	G	AB	H	2B	3B	HR	TB	R	RBI	GW	TBB	IBB	SO	HBP	SH	SF	SB	CS	SB%	GDP	Avg	OBP	SLG	Pos	G	PO	A	E	DP	FPct
1929 ChN	31	2	1	0	0	0	0	0	0	0	0	0	0	0	0	0	0	0	0	—	0	.000	.000	.000	—						

RICHIE HEBNER—Richard Joseph Hebner—Bats: Left; Throws: Right

Ht: 6'1"; Wt: 195 lbs; Born: 11/26/1947 in Boston, Massachusetts; Debut: 9/23/1968

LCS — Batting / Fielding

Year Tm	Age	G	AB	H	2B	3B	HR	TB	R	RBI	GW	TBB	IBB	SO	HBP	SH	SF	SB	CS	SB%	GDP	Avg	OBP	SLG	Pos	G	PO	A	E	DP	FPct
1970 Pit	22	2	6	4	2	0	0	6	0	0	0	2	0	1	0	0	0	0	0	—	0	.667	.750	1.000	3B	2	0	4	0	0	1.000
1971 Pit	23	4	17	5	1	0	2	12	3	4	1	0	0	4	1	0	0	0	0	—	0	.294	.333	.706	3B	4	4	3	1	0	.875
1972 Pit	24	5	16	3	1	0	0	4	2	1	0	1	1	3	1	0	0	0	0	—	0	.188	.278	.250	3B	5	5	11	0	1	1.000
1974 Pit	26	4	13	3	0	0	1	6	1	4	0	1	0	4	1	0	0	0	0	—	1	.231	.333	.462	3B	4	5	7	0	1	1.000
1975 Pit	27	3	12	4	1	0	0	5	2	2	0	1	0	1	0	0	0	0	0	—	0	.333	.385	.417	3B	3	0	2	0	0	1.000
1977 Phi	29	4	14	5	2	0	0	7	2	0	0	0	0	1	0	0	0	0	0	—	0	.357	.357	.500	1B	3	32	0	0	2	1.000
1978 Phi	30	3	9	1	0	0	0	1	0	1	0	0	0	0	0	1	0	0	0	—	0	.111	.111	.111	1B	2	21	0	0	3	1.000
1984 ChN	36	2	1	0	0	0	0	0	0	0	0	0	0	0	1	0	0	0	0	—	0	.000	.500	.000	—						
LCS Totals		27	88	25	7	0	3	41	10	12	1	5	1	14	4	1	0	0	0	—	1	.284	.351	.466	3B	18	14	27	1	2	.976

World Series — Batting / Fielding

Year Tm	Age	G	AB	H	2B	3B	HR	TB	R	RBI	GW	TBB	IBB	SO	HBP	SH	SF	SB	CS	SB%	GDP	Avg	OBP	SLG	Pos	G	PO	A	E	DP	FPct
1971 Pit	23	3	12	2	0	0	1	5	2	3	0	3	0	3	0	0	0	0	0	—	0	.167	.333	.417	3B	3	1	3	1	1	.800
Postseason Totals		30	100	27	7	0	4	46	12	15	1	8	1	17	4	1	0	0	0	—	1	.270	.348	.460	3B	21	15	30	2	3	.957

DANNY HEEP—Daniel William Heep—Bats: Left; Throws: Left

Ht: 5'11"; Wt: 185 lbs; Born: 7/3/1957 in San Antonio, Texas; Debut: 8/31/1979

LCS — Batting / Fielding

Year Tm	Age	G	AB	H	2B	3B	HR	TB	R	RBI	GW	TBB	IBB	SO	HBP	SH	SF	SB	CS	SB%	GDP	Avg	OBP	SLG	Pos	G	PO	A	E	DP	FPct
1980 Hou	23	1	1	0	0	0	0	0	0	0	0	0	0	0	0	0	0	0	0	—	0	.000	.000	.000	—						
1986 NYN	29	5	4	1	0	0	0	1	0	1	0	0	0	2	0	0	1	0	0	—	0	.250	.200	.250	OF	1	0	0	0	0	—
1988 LA	31	3	1	0	0	0	0	0	0	0	0	1	0	1	0	0	0	0	0	—	0	.000	.500	.000	—						
1990 Bos	33	2	2	0	0	0	0	0	0	0	0	0	0	0	0	0	0	0	0	—	0	.000	.000	.000	—						
LCS Totals		11	8	1	0	0	0	1	0	1	0	1	0	3	0	0	1	0	0	—	0	.125	.200	.125	OF	1	0	0	0	0	—

World Series — Batting / Fielding

Year Tm	Age	G	AB	H	2B	3B	HR	TB	R	RBI	GW	TBB	IBB	SO	HBP	SH	SF	SB	CS	SB%	GDP	Avg	OBP	SLG	Pos	G	PO	A	E	DP	FPct
1986 NYN	29	5	11	1	0	0	0	1	0	2	0	1	0	1	0	0	0	0	0	—	2	.091	.167	.091	OF	1	1	0	0	0	1.000
1988 LA	31	3	8	2	1	0	0	3	0	0	0	0	0	2	0	0	0	0	1	.00	0	.250	.250	.375	OF	1	0	0	0	0	—
WS Totals		8	19	3	1	0	0	4	0	2	0	1	0	3	0	0	0	0	1	.00	2	.158	.200	.211	OF	2	1	0	0	0	1.000
Postseason Totals		19	27	4	1	0	0	5	0	3	0	2	0	6	0	0	1	0	1	.00	2	.148	.200	.185	OF	3	1	0	0	0	1.000

JIM HEGAN—James Edward Hegan—Bats: Right; Throws: Right

Ht: 6'2"; Wt: 195 lbs; Born: 8/3/1920 in Lynn, Massachusetts; Debut: 9/9/1941; Died: 6/17/1984

World Series — Batting / Fielding

Year Tm	Age	G	AB	H	2B	3B	HR	TB	R	RBI	GW	TBB	IBB	SO	HBP	SH	SF	SB	CS	SB%	GDP	Avg	OBP	SLG	Pos	G	PO	A	E	DP	FPct
1948 Cle	28	6	19	4	0	0	1	7	2	5	0	1	1	4	0	1	0	1	0	1.00	0	.211	.250	.368	C	6	25	5	0	1	1.000
1954 Cle	34	4	13	2	1	0	0	3	1	0	0	1	0	1	0	0	0	0	0	—	0	.154	.214	.231	C	4	27	2	0	0	1.000
WS Totals		10	32	6	1	0	1	10	3	5	0	2	1	5	0	1	0	1	0	1.00	0	.188	.235	.313	C	10	52	7	0	1	1.000

MIKE HEGAN—James Michael Hegan—Bats: Left; Throws: Left

Ht: 6'1"; Wt: 188 lbs; Born: 7/21/1942 in Cleveland, Ohio; Debut: 9/13/1964

LCS — Batting / Fielding

Year Tm	Age	G	AB	H	2B	3B	HR	TB	R	RBI	GW	TBB	IBB	SO	HBP	SH	SF	SB	CS	SB%	GDP	Avg	OBP	SLG	Pos	G	PO	A	E	DP	FPct
1971 Oak	29	1	1	0	0	0	0	0	0	0	0	0	0	1	0	0	0	0	0	—	0	.000	.000	.000	—						
1972 Oak	30	3	1	0	0	0	0	0	1	0	0	0	0	0	0	0	0	0	0	—	0	.000	.000	.000	1B	1	1	0	0	0	1.000
LCS Totals		4	2	0	0	0	0	0	1	0	0	0	0	1	0	0	0	0	0	—	0	.000	.000	.000	1B	1	1	0	0	0	1.000

World Series — Batting / Fielding

Year Tm	Age	G	AB	H	2B	3B	HR	TB	R	RBI	GW	TBB	IBB	SO	HBP	SH	SF	SB	CS	SB%	GDP	Avg	OBP	SLG	Pos	G	PO	A	E	DP	FPct
1964 NYA	22	3	1	0	0	0	0	0	1	0	0	1	0	1	0	0	0	0	0	—	0	.000	.500	.000	—						
1972 Oak	30	6	5	1	0	0	0	1	0	0	0	0	0	2	0	0	0	0	0	—	0	.200	.200	.200	1B	5	11	1	0	1	1.000
WS Totals		9	6	1	0	0	0	1	1	0	0	1	0	3	0	0	0	0	0	—	0	.167	.286	.167	1B	5	11	1	0	1	1.000
Postseason Totals		13	8	1	0	0	0	1	2	0	0	1	0	4	0	0	0	0	0	—	0	.125	.222	.125	1B	6	12	1	0	1	1.000

KEN HEINTZELMAN—Kenneth Alphonse Heintzelman—Throws: Left; Bats: Right

Ht: 5'11"; Wt: 185 lbs; Born: 10/14/1915 in Peruque, Missouri; Debut: 10/3/1937

World Series															Pitching													
Year Tm	Age	G	GS	CG	GF	IP	BFP	H	R	ER	HR	SH	SF	HB	TBB	IBB	SO	WP	Bk	W	L	Pct	ShO	Sv-Op	Hld	OAvg	OOBP	ERA
1950 Phi	34	1	1	0	0	7.2	31	4	2	1	0	0	0	0	6	0	3	0	0	0	0	—	0	0-0	0	.160	.323	1.17

World Series													Batting														Fielding				
Year Tm	Age	G	AB	H	2B	3B	HR	TB	R	RBI	GW	TBB	IBB	SO	HBP	SH	SF	SB	CS	SB%	GDP	Avg	OBP	SLG	Pos	G	PO	A	E	DP	FPct
1950 Phi	34	1	2	0	0	0	0	0	0	0	0	0	0	0	0	1	0	0	0	—	0	.000	.000	.000	P	1	0	2	0	0	1.000

TOMMY HELMS—Tommy Vann Helms—Bats: Right; Throws: Right

Ht: 5'10"; Wt: 165 lbs; Born: 5/5/1941 in Charlotte, North Carolina; Debut: 9/23/1964

LCS													Batting														Fielding				
Year Tm	Age	G	AB	H	2B	3B	HR	TB	R	RBI	GW	TBB	IBB	SO	HBP	SH	SF	SB	CS	SB%	GDP	Avg	OBP	SLG	Pos	G	PO	A	E	DP	FPct
1970 Cin	29	3	11	3	0	0	0	3	0	0	0	0	0	1	0	0	0	0	0	—	0	.273	.273	.273	2B	3	11	12	0	1	1.000
World Series													Batting														Fielding				
Year Tm	Age	G	AB	H	2B	3B	HR	TB	R	RBI	GW	TBB	IBB	SO	HBP	SH	SF	SB	CS	SB%	GDP	Avg	OBP	SLG	Pos	G	PO	A	E	DP	FPct
1970 Cin	29	5	18	4	0	0	0	4	1	0	0	1	0	1	0	0	0	0	0	—	0	.222	.263	.222	2B	5	10	13	0	2	1.000
Postseason Totals		8	29	7	0	0	0	7	1	0	0	1	0	2	0	0	0	0	0	—	0	.241	.267	.241	2B	8	21	25	0	3	1.000

ROLLIE HEMSLEY—Ralston Burdett Hemsley—Bats: Right; Throws: Right

Ht: 5'10"; Wt: 170 lbs; Born: 6/24/1907 in Syracuse, Ohio; Debut: 4/13/1928; Died: 7/31/1972

World Series													Batting														Fielding				
Year Tm	Age	G	AB	H	2B	3B	HR	TB	R	RBI	GW	TBB	IBB	SO	HBP	SH	SF	SB	CS	SB%	GDP	Avg	OBP	SLG	Pos	G	PO	A	E	DP	FPct
1932 ChN	25	3	3	0	0	0	0	0	0	0	0	0	0	3	0	0	0	0	0	—	0	.000	.000	.000	C	1	0	0	0	0	—

DAVE HENDERSON—David Lee Henderson—Bats: Right; Throws: Right

Ht: 6'2"; Wt: 210 lbs; Born: 7/21/1958 in Merced, California; Debut: 4/9/1981

LCS													Batting														Fielding				
Year Tm	Age	G	AB	H	2B	3B	HR	TB	R	RBI	GW	TBB	IBB	SO	HBP	SH	SF	SB	CS	SB%	GDP	Avg	OBP	SLG	Pos	G	PO	A	E	DP	FPct
1986 Bos	28	5	9	1	0	0	1	4	3	4	1	2	1	2	0	0	1	0	0	—	0	.111	.250	.444	OF	5	11	0	0	0	1.000
1988 Oak	30	4	16	6	1	0	1	10	2	4	1	1	0	7	0	0	0	0	0	—	0	.375	.412	.625	OF	4	11	0	2	0	.846
1989 Oak	31	5	19	5	3	0	1	11	4	1	0	2	0	5	0	0	0	0	0	—	0	.263	.333	.579	OF	5	22	0	0	0	1.000
1990 Oak	32	2	6	1	0	0	0	1	0	1	0	0	0	2	1	0	1	1	0	1.00	1	.167	.250	.167	OF	2	7	0	0	0	1.000
LCS Totals		16	50	13	4	0	3	26	9	10	2	5	1	16	1	0	2	1	0	1.00	1	.260	.328	.520	OF	16	51	0	2	0	.962
World Series													Batting														Fielding				
Year Tm	Age	G	AB	H	2B	3B	HR	TB	R	RBI	GW	TBB	IBB	SO	HBP	SH	SF	SB	CS	SB%	GDP	Avg	OBP	SLG	Pos	G	PO	A	E	DP	FPct
1986 Bos	28	7	25	10	1	1	2	19	6	5	0	2	0	6	1	0	1	0	0	—	0	.400	.448	.760	OF	7	22	0	0	0	1.000
1988 Oak	30	5	20	6	2	0	0	8	1	1	0	2	0	7	0	0	0	0	0	—	0	.300	.364	.400	OF	5	13	0	0	0	1.000
1989 Oak	31	4	13	4	2	0	2	12	6	4	2	4	0	3	1	0	0	0	0	—	1	.308	.500	.923	OF	4	13	0	0	0	1.000
1990 Oak	32	4	13	3	1	0	0	4	2	0	0	1	0	3	0	0	0	0	0	—	0	.231	.286	.308	OF	3	7	0	0	0	1.000
WS Totals		20	71	23	6	1	4	43	15	10	2	9	0	19	2	0	1	0	0	—	1	.324	.410	.606	OF	19	55	0	0	0	1.000
Postseason Totals		36	121	36	10	1	7	69	24	20	4	14	1	35	3	0	3	1	0	1.00	2	.298	.376	.570	OF	35	106	0	2	0	.981

KEN HENDERSON—Kenneth Joseph Henderson—Bats: Both; Throws: Right

Ht: 6'2"; Wt: 180 lbs; Born: 6/15/1946 in Carroll, Iowa; Debut: 4/23/1965

LCS													Batting														Fielding				
Year Tm	Age	G	AB	H	2B	3B	HR	TB	R	RBI	GW	TBB	IBB	SO	HBP	SH	SF	SB	CS	SB%	GDP	Avg	OBP	SLG	Pos	G	PO	A	E	DP	FPct
1971 SF	25	4	16	5	1	0	0	6	3	2	0	2	0	1	0	0	0	1	0	1.00	0	.313	.389	.375	OF	4	4	0	0	0	1.000

RICKEY HENDERSON—Rickey Henley Henderson—Bats: Right; Throws: Left

Ht: 5'10"; Wt: 180 lbs; Born: 12/25/1958 in Chicago, Illinois; Debut: 6/24/1979

Division Series													Batting														Fielding				
Year Tm	Age	G	AB	H	2B	3B	HR	TB	R	RBI	GW	TBB	IBB	SO	HBP	SH	SF	SB	CS	SB%	GDP	Avg	OBP	SLG	Pos	G	PO	A	E	DP	FPct
1981 Oak	22	3	11	2	0	0	0	2	3	0	0	2	0	0	0	0	0	2	0	1.00	0	.182	.308	.182	OF	3	8	0	0	0	1.000
1996 SD	37	3	12	4	0	0	1	7	2	1	0	2	0	3	0	0	0	0	0	—	0	.333	.429	.583	OF	3	4	0	0	0	1.000
DS Totals		6	23	6	0	0	1	9	5	1	0	4	0	3	0	0	0	2	0	1.00	0	.261	.370	.391	OF	6	12	0	0	0	1.000
LCS													Batting														Fielding				
Year Tm	Age	G	AB	H	2B	3B	HR	TB	R	RBI	GW	TBB	IBB	SO	HBP	SH	SF	SB	CS	SB%	GDP	Avg	OBP	SLG	Pos	G	PO	A	E	DP	FPct
1981 Oak	22	3	11	4	2	1	0	8	0	1	0	1	0	2	0	0	0	2	0	1.00	1	.364	.417	.727	OF	3	6	0	1	0	.857
1989 Oak	30	5	15	6	1	1	2	15	8	5	1	7	0	0	1	0	0	8	1	.89	0	.400	.609	1.000	OF	5	13	0	1	0	.929
1990 Oak-*M*	31	4	17	5	0	0	0	5	1	3	0	1	0	2	0	0	1	2	1	.67	0	.294	.316	.294	OF	4	10	0	0	0	1.000
1992 Oak	33	6	23	6	0	0	0	6	5	1	0	4	0	4	0	0	0	2	0	1.00	0	.261	.370	.261	OF	6	15	0	3	0	.833
1993 Tor	34	6	25	3	2	0	0	5	4	0	0	4	0	5	0	0	0	2	1	.67	0	.120	.241	.200	OF	6	9	0	1	0	.900
LCS Totals		24	91	24	5	2	2	39	18	10	1	17	0	13	1	0	1	16	3	.84	1	.264	.382	.429	OF	24	53	0	6	0	.898
World Series													Batting														Fielding				
Year Tm	Age	G	AB	H	2B	3B	HR	TB	R	RBI	GW	TBB	IBB	SO	HBP	SH	SF	SB	CS	SB%	GDP	Avg	OBP	SLG	Pos	G	PO	A	E	DP	FPct
1989 Oak	30	4	19	9	1	2	1	17	4	3	0	2	0	2	0	0	0	3	1	.75	0	.474	.524	.895	OF	4	9	0	0	0	1.000
1990 Oak-*M*	31	4	15	5	2	0	1	10	2	1	0	3	0	4	0	0	0	3	0	1.00	0	.333	.444	.667	OF	4	12	1	0	0	1.000
1993 Tor	34	6	22	5	2	0	0	7	6	2	0	5	0	2	1	0	0	1	1	.50	0	.227	.393	.318	OF	6	8	0	0	0	1.000
WS Totals		14	56	19	5	2	2	34	12	6	0	10	0	8	1	0	0	7	2	.78	0	.339	.448	.607	OF	14	29	1	0	0	1.000
Postseason Totals		44	170	49	10	4	5	82	35	17	1	31	0	24	2	0	1	25	5	.83	1	.288	.402	.482	OF	44	94	1	6	0	.941

GEORGE HENDRICK—George Andrew Hendrick—Bats: Right; Throws: Right

Ht: 6'3"; Wt: 195 lbs; Born: 10/18/1949 in Los Angeles, California; Debut: 6/4/1971

LCS													Batting														Fielding				
Year Tm	Age	G	AB	H	2B	3B	HR	TB	R	RBI	GW	TBB	IBB	SO	HBP	SH	SF	SB	CS	SB%	GDP	Avg	OBP	SLG	Pos	G	PO	A	E	DP	FPct
1972 Oak	22	5	7	1	0	0	0	1	2	0	0	0	0	1	0	0	0	0	0	—	0	.143	.143	.143	OF	1	1	0	0	0	1.000
1982 StL	32	3	13	4	0	0	0	4	2	2	1	1	0	2	0	0	0	0	0	—	0	.308	.357	.308	OF	3	5	0	0	0	1.000
1986 Cal	36	3	12	1	0	0	0	1	0	0	0	0	0	2	0	0	0	0	0	—	1	.083	.083	.083	1B	1	14	2	0	0	1.000
																									OF	2	2	0	0	0	1.000
LCS Totals		11	32	6	0	0	0	6	4	2	1	1	0	5	0	0	0	0	0	—	1	.188	.212	.188	OF	6	8	0	0	0	1.000
World Series													Batting														Fielding				
Year Tm	Age	G	AB	H	2B	3B	HR	TB	R	RBI	GW	TBB	IBB	SO	HBP	SH	SF	SB	CS	SB%	GDP	Avg	OBP	SLG	Pos	G	PO	A	E	DP	FPct
1972 Oak	22	5	15	2	0	0	0	2	3	0	0	1	0	2	0	1	0	0	0	—	1	.133	.188	.133	OF	5	12	0	0	0	1.000
1982 StL	32	7	28	9	0	0	0	9	5	5	1	2	0	2	0	0	0	0	1	.00	0	.321	.367	.321	OF	7	10	1	0	0	1.000
WS Totals		12	43	11	0	0	0	11	8	5	1	3	0	4	0	1	0	0	1	.00	1	.256	.304	.256	OF	12	22	1	0	0	1.000
Postseason Totals		23	75	17	0	0	0	17	12	7	2	4	0	9	0	1	0	0	1	.00	2	.227	.266	.227	OF	18	30	1	0	0	1.000

HARVEY HENDRICK—Nickname: Gink—Bats: Left; Throws: Right

Ht: 6'2"; Wt: 190 lbs; Born: 11/9/1897 in Mason, Tennessee; Debut: 4/20/1923; Died: 10/29/1941

World Series													Batting														Fielding				
Year Tm	Age	G	AB	H	2B	3B	HR	TB	R	RBI	GW	TBB	IBB	SO	HBP	SH	SF	SB	CS	SB%	GDP	Avg	OBP	SLG	Pos	G	PO	A	E	DP	FPct
1923 NYA	25	1	1	0	0	0	0	0	0	0	0	0	0	0	0	0	0	0	0	—	0	.000	.000	.000	—						

ELLIE HENDRICKS—Elrod Jerome Hendricks—Bats: Left; Throws: Right

Ht: 6'1"; Wt: 175 lbs; Born: 12/22/1940 in Charlotte Amalie, Virgin Islands; Debut: 4/13/1968

LCS													Batting														Fielding				
Year Tm	Age	G	AB	H	2B	3B	HR	TB	R	RBI	GW	TBB	IBB	SO	HBP	SH	SF	SB	CS	SB%	GDP	Avg	OBP	SLG	Pos	G	PO	A	E	DP	FPct
1969 Bal	28	3	8	2	2	0	0	4	2	3	1	1	0	2	0	0	0	0	0	—	0	.250	.333	.500	C	3	18	0	0	0	1.000
1970 Bal	29	1	5	2	0	0	0	2	2	0	0	0	0	1	0	0	0	0	0	—	1	.400	.400	.400	C	1	5	0	0	0	1.000
1971 Bal	30	2	4	2	0	0	1	5	1	2	0	1	1	1	0	0	1	0	0	—	0	.500	.500	1.250	C	2	6	0	0	0	1.000
1974 Bal	33	3	6	1	0	0	0	1	1	0	0	1	0	3	0	0	0	0	0	—	0	.167	.286	.167	C	3	11	1	0	0	1.000
1976 NYA	35	1	1	1	0	0	0	1	0	0	0	0	0	0	0	0	0	0	0	—	0	1.000	1.000	1.000	—						
LCS Totals		10	24	8	2	0	1	13	6	5	1	3	1	7	0	0	1	0	0	—	1	.333	.393	.542	C	9	40	1	0	0	1.000

World Series		Batting																							Fielding						
Year Tm	Age	G	AB	H	2B	3B	HR	TB	R	RBI	GW	TBB	IBB	SO	HBP	SH	SF	SB	CS	SB%	GDP	Avg	OBP	SLG	Pos	G	PO	A	E	DP	FPct
1969 Bal	28	3	10	1	0	0	0	1	1	0	0	1	0	0	0	0	0	0	0	—	0	.100	.182	.100	C	3	21	1	0	1	1.000
1970 Bal	29	3	11	4	1	0	1	8	1	4	1	1	0	2	0	0	0	0	0	—	0	.364	.417	.727	C	3	17	2	1	0	.950
1971 Bal	30	6	19	5	1	0	0	6	3	1	0	3	0	3	1	0	0	0	0	—	0	.263	.391	.316	C	6	40	4	1	0	.978
1976 NYA	35	2	2	0	0	0	0	0	0	0	0	0	0	0	0	0	0	0	0	—	0	.000	.000	.000	—						
WS Totals		14	42	10	2	0	1	15	5	5	1	5	0	5	1	0	0	0	0	—	0	.238	.333	.357	C	12	78	7	2	1	.977
Postseason Totals		24	66	18	4	0	2	28	11	10	2	8	1	12	1	0	1	0	0	—	1	.273	.355	.424	C	21	118	8	2	1	.984

CLAUDE HENDRIX—Claude Raymond Hendrix—Throws: Right; Bats: Right

Ht: 6'0"; Wt: 195 lbs; Born: 4/13/1889 in Olathe, Kansas; Debut: 6/7/1911; Died: 3/22/1944

World Series		Pitching																									
Year Tm	Age	G	GS	CG	GF	IP	BFP	H	R	ER	HR	SH	SF	HB	TBB	IBB	SO	WP	Bk	W	L	Pct	ShO	Sv-Op	Hld	OAvg	OOBP	ERA
1918 ChN	29	1	0	0	1	1.0	3	0	0	0	0	0	0	0	0	0	0	0	0	0	0	—	0	0-0	0	.000	.000	0.00

World Series		Batting																							Fielding						
Year Tm	Age	G	AB	H	2B	3B	HR	TB	R	RBI	GW	TBB	IBB	SO	HBP	SH	SF	SB	CS	SB%	GDP	Avg	OBP	SLG	Pos	G	PO	A	E	DP	FPct
1918 ChN	29	2	1	1	0	0	0	1	0	0	0	0	0	0	0	0	0	0	0	—	0	1.000	1.000	1.000	P	1	0	0	0	0	—

TOM HENKE—Thomas Anthony Henke—Nickname: The Terminator—Throws: Right; Bats: Right

Ht: 6'5"; Wt: 215 lbs; Born: 12/21/1957 in Kansas City, Missouri; Debut: 9/10/1982

LCS		Pitching																									
Year Tm	Age	G	GS	CG	GF	IP	BFP	H	R	ER	HR	SH	SF	HB	TBB	IBB	SO	WP	Bk	W	L	Pct	ShO	Sv-Op	Hld	OAvg	OOBP	ERA
1985 Tor	27	3	0	0	3	6.1	26	5	3	3	1	0	0	0	4	0	4	0	0	2	0	1.000	0	0-0	0	.227	.346	4.26
1989 Tor	31	3	0	0	2	2.2	8	0	0	0	0	0	0	0	0	0	3	0	0	0	0	—	0	0-0	0	.000	.000	0.00
1991 Tor	33	2	0	0	0	2.2	9	0	0	0	0	0	0	0	1	0	5	0	0	0	0	—	0	0-0	1	.000	.111	0.00
1992 Tor	34	4	0	0	4	4.2	19	3	0	0	0	0	0	0	2	0	2	0	0	0	0	—	0	3-3	0	.176	.263	0.00
LCS Totals		12	0	0	9	16.1	124	8	3	3	1	0	0	0	7	0	14	0	0	2	0	1.000	0	3-3	1	.145	.242	1.65
World Series		**Pitching**																									
Year Tm	Age	G	GS	CG	GF	IP	BFP	H	R	ER	HR	SH	SF	HB	TBB	IBB	SO	WP	Bk	W	L	Pct	ShO	Sv-Op	Hld	OAvg	OOBP	ERA
1992 Tor	34	3	0	0	2	3.1	15	2	1	1	0	1	0	1	2	0	1	0	0	0	0	—	0	2-3	0	.182	.357	2.70
Postseason Totals		15	0	0	11	19.2	154	10	4	4	1	1	0	1	9	0	15	0	0	2	0	1.000	0	5-6	1	.152	.263	1.83

LCS		Batting																							Fielding						
Year Tm	Age	G	AB	H	2B	3B	HR	TB	R	RBI	GW	TBB	IBB	SO	HBP	SH	SF	SB	CS	SB%	GDP	Avg	OBP	SLG	Pos	G	PO	A	E	DP	FPct
1985 Tor	27	3	0	0	0	0	0	0	0	0	0	0	0	0	0	0	0	0	0	—	0	—	—	—	P	3	1	0	0	0	1.000
1989 Tor	31	3	0	0	0	0	0	0	0	0	0	0	0	0	0	0	0	0	0	—	0	—	—	—	P	3	0	1	0	0	1.000
1991 Tor	33	2	0	0	0	0	0	0	0	0	0	0	0	0	0	0	0	0	0	—	0	—	—	—	P	2	0	2	0	0	1.000
1992 Tor	34	4	0	0	0	0	0	0	0	0	0	0	0	0	0	0	0	0	0	—	0	—	—	—	P	4	0	0	0	0	—
LCS Totals		12	0	0	0	0	0	0	0	0	0	0	0	0	0	0	0	0	0	—	0	—	—	—	P	12	1	3	0	0	1.000
World Series		**Batting**																							**Fielding**						
Year Tm	Age	G	AB	H	2B	3B	HR	TB	R	RBI	GW	TBB	IBB	SO	HBP	SH	SF	SB	CS	SB%	GDP	Avg	OBP	SLG	Pos	G	PO	A	E	DP	FPct
1992 Tor	34	3	0	0	0	0	0	0	0	0	0	0	0	0	0	0	0	0	0	—	0	—	—	—	P	3	0	2	0	0	1.000
Postseason Totals		15	0	0	0	0	0	0	0	0	0	0	0	0	0	0	0	0	0	—	0	—	—	—	P	15	1	5	0	0	1.000

MIKE HENNEMAN—Michael Alan Henneman—Throws: Right; Bats: Right

Ht: 6'4"; Wt: 205 lbs; Born: 12/11/1961 in St. Charles, Missouri; Debut: 5/11/1987

Division Series		Pitching																									
Year Tm	Age	G	GS	CG	GF	IP	BFP	H	R	ER	HR	SH	SF	HB	TBB	IBB	SO	WP	Bk	W	L	Pct	ShO	Sv-Op	Hld	OAvg	OOBP	ERA
1996 Tex	34	3	0	0	2	1.0	6	1	0	0	0	1	1	0	1	1	1	0	0	0	0	—	0	0-1	0	.333	.400	0.00
LCS		**Pitching**																									
Year Tm	Age	G	GS	CG	GF	IP	BFP	H	R	ER	HR	SH	SF	HB	TBB	IBB	SO	WP	Bk	W	L	Pct	ShO	Sv-Op	Hld	OAvg	OOBP	ERA
1987 Det	25	3	0	0	1	5.0	27	6	6	6	1	0	0	0	6	3	3	0	0	1	0	1.000	0	0-1	0	.286	.444	10.80
Postseason Totals		6	0	0	3	6.0	66	7	6	6	1	1	1	0	7	4	4	0	0	1	0	1.000	0	0-2	0	.292	.438	9.00

Division Series		Batting																							Fielding						
Year Tm	Age	G	AB	H	2B	3B	HR	TB	R	RBI	GW	TBB	IBB	SO	HBP	SH	SF	SB	CS	SB%	GDP	Avg	OBP	SLG	Pos	G	PO	A	E	DP	FPct
1996 Tex	34	3	0	0	0	0	0	0	0	0	0	0	0	0	0	0	0	0	0	—	0	—	—	—	P	3	0	0	0	0	—
LCS		**Batting**																							**Fielding**						
Year Tm	Age	G	AB	H	2B	3B	HR	TB	R	RBI	GW	TBB	IBB	SO	HBP	SH	SF	SB	CS	SB%	GDP	Avg	OBP	SLG	Pos	G	PO	A	E	DP	FPct
1987 Det	25	3	0	0	0	0	0	0	0	0	0	0	0	0	0	0	0	0	0	—	0	—	—	—	P	3	0	2	0	0	1.000
Postseason Totals		6	0	0	0	0	0	0	0	0	0	0	0	0	0	0	0	0	0	—	0	—	—	—	P	6	0	2	0	0	1.000

TOMMY HENRICH—Thomas David Henrich—Nicknames: The Clutch, Old Reliable—Bats: Left; Throws: Left

Ht: 6'0"; Wt: 180 lbs; Born: 2/20/1913 in Massillon, Ohio; Debut: 5/11/1937

World Series		Batting																							Fielding						
Year Tm	Age	G	AB	H	2B	3B	HR	TB	R	RBI	GW	TBB	IBB	SO	HBP	SH	SF	SB	CS	SB%	GDP	Avg	OBP	SLG	Pos	G	PO	A	E	DP	FPct
1938 NYA	25	4	16	4	1	0	1	8	3	1	0	0	0	1	0	0	0	0	1	.00	0	.250	.250	.500	OF	4	6	0	1	0	.857
1941 NYA	28	5	18	3	1	0	1	7	4	1	0	3	0	3	1	0	0	0	0	—	0	.167	.318	.389	OF	5	6	0	0	0	1.000
1947 NYA	34	7	31	10	2	0	1	15	2	5	1	2	0	3	0	1	0	0	0	—	3	.323	.364	.484	OF	7	11	0	0	0	1.000
1949 NYA	36	5	19	5	0	0	1	8	4	1	1	3	0	0	0	0	0	0	0	—	0	.263	.364	.421	1B	5	48	1	0	4	1.000
WS Totals		21	84	22	4	0	4	38	13	8	2	8	0	7	1	1	0	0	1	.00	3	.262	.333	.452	OF	16	23	0	1	0	.958

OLAF HENRIKSEN—Nickname: Swede—Bats: Left; Throws: Left

Ht: 5'7"; Wt: 158 lbs; Born: 4/26/1888 in Kirkerup, Denmark; Debut: 8/11/1911; Died: 10/17/1962

World Series		Batting																							Fielding						
Year Tm	Age	G	AB	H	2B	3B	HR	TB	R	RBI	GW	TBB	IBB	SO	HBP	SH	SF	SB	CS	SB%	GDP	Avg	OBP	SLG	Pos	G	PO	A	E	DP	FPct
1912 Bos	24	2	1	1	1	0	0	2	0	1	0	0	0	0	0	0	0	0	0	—	0	1.000	1.000	2.000	—						
1915 Bos	27	2	2	0	0	0	0	0	0	0	0	0	0	0	0	0	0	0	0	—	0	.000	.000	.000	—						
1916 Bos	28	1	0	0	0	0	0	0	1	0	0	1	0	0	0	0	0	0	0	—	0	—	1.000	—	—						
WS Totals		5	3	1	1	0	0	2	1	1	0	1	0	0	0	0	0	0	0	—	0	.333	.500	.667	—	0	0	0	0	0	—

BILL HENRY—William Rodman Henry—Nickname: Gabby—Throws: Left; Bats: Left

Ht: 6'2"; Wt: 180 lbs; Born: 10/15/1927 in Alice, Texas; Debut: 4/17/1952

World Series		Pitching																									
Year Tm	Age	G	GS	CG	GF	IP	BFP	H	R	ER	HR	SH	SF	HB	TBB	IBB	SO	WP	Bk	W	L	Pct	ShO	Sv-Op	Hld	OAvg	OOBP	ERA
1961 Cin	33	2	0	0	1	2.1	13	4	5	5	1	1	0	0	2	1	3	0	0	0	0	—	0	0-0	0	.400	.500	19.29

World Series		Batting																							Fielding						
Year Tm	Age	G	AB	H	2B	3B	HR	TB	R	RBI	GW	TBB	IBB	SO	HBP	SH	SF	SB	CS	SB%	GDP	Avg	OBP	SLG	Pos	G	PO	A	E	DP	FPct
1961 Cin	33	2	0	0	0	0	0	0	0	0	0	0	0	0	0	0	0	0	0	—	0	—	—	—	P	2	0	1	0	0	1.000

DOUG HENRY—Richard Douglas Henry—Throws: Right; Bats: Right

Ht: 6'4"; Wt: 185 lbs; Born: 12/10/1963 in Sacramento, California; Debut: 7/15/1991

Division Series		Pitching																									
Year Tm	Age	G	GS	CG	GF	IP	BFP	H	R	ER	HR	SH	SF	HB	TBB	IBB	SO	WP	Bk	W	L	Pct	ShO	Sv-Op	Hld	OAvg	OOBP	ERA
1997 SF	33	1	0	0	0	2.0	9	1	0	0	0	0	0	0	3	1	2	0	0	0	0	—	0	0-0	0	.167	.444	0.00

Division Series		Batting																							Fielding						
Year Tm	Age	G	AB	H	2B	3B	HR	TB	R	RBI	GW	TBB	IBB	SO	HBP	SH	SF	SB	CS	SB%	GDP	Avg	OBP	SLG	Pos	G	PO	A	E	DP	FPct
1997 SF	33	1	0	0	0	0	0	0	0	0	0	0	0	0	0	0	0	0	0	—	0	—	—	—	P	1	0	0	0	0	—

ROY HENSHAW—Roy Kniklebine Henshaw—Throws: Left; Bats: Right

Ht: 5'8"; Wt: 155 lbs; Born: 7/29/1911 in Chicago, Illinois; Debut: 4/15/1933; Died: 6/8/1993

World Series		Pitching																									
Year Tm	Age	G	GS	CG	GF	IP	BFP	H	R	ER	HR	SH	SF	HB	TBB	IBB	SO	WP	Bk	W	L	Pct	ShO	Sv-Op	Hld	OAvg	OOBP	ERA
1935 ChN	24	1	0	0	0	3.2	17	2	3	3	0	0	0	1	5	0	2	1	0	0	0	—	0	0-0	0	.182	.471	7.36

World Series		Batting																							Fielding						
Year Tm	Age	G	AB	H	2B	3B	HR	TB	R	RBI	GW	TBB	IBB	SO	HBP	SH	SF	SB	CS	SB%	GDP	Avg	OBP	SLG	Pos	G	PO	A	E	DP	FPct
1935 ChN	24	1	1	0	0	0	0	0	0	0	0	0	0	0	0	0	0	0	0	—	0	.000	.000	.000	P	1	0	1	0	0	1.000

PAT HENTGEN—Patrick George Hentgen—Throws: Right; Bats: Right
Ht: 6'2"; Wt: 210 lbs; Born: 11/13/1968 in Detroit, Michigan; Debut: 9/3/1991

LCS

Year	Tm	Age	G	GS	CG	GF	IP	BFP	H	R	ER	HR	SH	SF	HB	TBB	IBB	SO	WP	Bk	W	L	Pct	ShO	Sv-Op	Hld	OAvg	OOBP	ERA
1993	Tor	24	1	1	0	0	3.0	19	9	6	6	0	0	0	0	2	0	3	0	0	0	1	.000	0	0-0	0	.529	.579	18.00

World Series

Year	Tm	Age	G	GS	CG	GF	IP	BFP	H	R	ER	HR	SH	SF	HB	TBB	IBB	SO	WP	Bk	W	L	Pct	ShO	Sv-Op	Hld	OAvg	OOBP	ERA
1993	Tor	24	1	1	0	0	6.0	25	5	1	1	0	0	0	0	3	0	6	0	0	1	0	1.000	0	0-0	0	.227	.320	1.50
Postseason Totals			2	2	0	0	9.0	88	14	7	7	0	0	0	0	5	0	9	0	0	1	1	.500	0	0-0	0	.359	.432	7.00

LCS

Year	Tm	Age	G	AB	H	2B	3B	HR	TB	R	RBI	GW	TBB	IBB	SO	HBP	SH	SF	SB	CS	SB%	GDP	Avg	OBP	SLG	Pos	G	PO	A	E	DP	FPct
1993	Tor	24	1	0	0	0	0	0	0	0	0	0	0	0	0	0	0	0	0	0	—	0	—	—	—	P	1	1	0	0	0	1.000

World Series

Year	Tm	Age	G	AB	H	2B	3B	HR	TB	R	RBI	GW	TBB	IBB	SO	HBP	SH	SF	SB	CS	SB%	GDP	Avg	OBP	SLG	Pos	G	PO	A	E	DP	FPct
1993	Tor	24	1	3	0	0	0	0	0	0	0	0	0	0	1	0	0	0	0	0	—	0	.000	.000	.000	P	1	0	0	0	0	—
Postseason Totals			2	3	0	0	0	0	0	0	0	0	0	0	1	0	0	0	0	0	—	0	.000	.000	.000	P	2	1	0	0	0	1.000

FELIX HEREDIA—Throws: Left; Bats: Left
Ht: 6'0"; Wt: 165 lbs; Born: 6/18/1976 in Barahona, Dominican Republic; Debut: 8/9/1996

LCS

Year	Tm	Age	G	GS	CG	GF	IP	BFP	H	R	ER	HR	SH	SF	HB	TBB	IBB	SO	WP	Bk	W	L	Pct	ShO	Sv-Op	Hld	OAvg	OOBP	ERA
1997	Fla	21	2	0	0	0	3.1	15	3	2	2	0	0	1	0	2	0	4	0	0	0	0	—	0	0-0	0	.250	.333	5.40

World Series

Year	Tm	Age	G	GS	CG	GF	IP	BFP	H	R	ER	HR	SH	SF	HB	TBB	IBB	SO	WP	Bk	W	L	Pct	ShO	Sv-Op	Hld	OAvg	OOBP	ERA
1997	Fla	21	4	0	0	0	5.1	19	2	0	0	0	0	0	0	1	0	5	0	0	0	0	—	0	0-0	0	.111	.158	0.00
Postseason Totals			6	0	0	0	8.2	68	5	2	2	0	0	1	0	3	0	9	0	0	0	0	—	0	0-0	0	.167	.235	2.08

LCS

Year	Tm	Age	G	AB	H	2B	3B	HR	TB	R	RBI	GW	TBB	IBB	SO	HBP	SH	SF	SB	CS	SB%	GDP	Avg	OBP	SLG	Pos	G	PO	A	E	DP	FPct
1997	Fla	21	2	0	0	0	0	0	0	0	0	0	0	0	0	0	0	0	0	0	—	0	—	—	—	P	2	0	0	0	0	—

World Series

Year	Tm	Age	G	AB	H	2B	3B	HR	TB	R	RBI	GW	TBB	IBB	SO	HBP	SH	SF	SB	CS	SB%	GDP	Avg	OBP	SLG	Pos	G	PO	A	E	DP	FPct
1997	Fla	21	4	0	0	0	0	0	0	0	0	0	0	0	0	0	0	0	0	0	—	0	—	—	—	P	4	1	0	0	0	1.000
Postseason Totals			6	0	0	0	0	0	0	0	0	0	0	0	0	0	0	0	0	0	—	0	—	—	—	P	6	1	0	0	0	1.000

BILLY HERMAN (HOF 1975-V)—William Jennings Bryan Herman—Bats: Right; Throws: Right
Ht: 5'11"; Wt: 180 lbs; Born: 7/7/1909 in New Albany, Indiana; Debut: 8/29/1931; Died: 9/5/1992

World Series

Year	Tm	Age	G	AB	H	2B	3B	HR	TB	R	RBI	GW	TBB	IBB	SO	HBP	SH	SF	SB	CS	SB%	GDP	Avg	OBP	SLG	Pos	G	PO	A	E	DP	FPct
1932	ChN	23	4	18	4	1	0	0	5	5	1	0	1	0	3	0	0	0	0	0	—	0	.222	.263	.278	2B	4	5	12	1	6	.944
1935	ChN	26	6	24	8	2	1	1	15	3	6	0	0	0	2	0	1	0	0	0	—	1	.333	.333	.625	2B	6	15	19	1	4	.971
1938	ChN	29	4	16	3	0	0	0	3	1	0	0	1	0	4	0	0	0	0	0	—	0	.188	.235	.188	2B	4	5	15	2	2	.909
1941	Bro	32	4	8	1	0	0	0	1	0	0	0	2	0	0	0	0	0	0	0	—	0	.125	.300	.125	2B	4	4	13	0	2	1.000
WS Totals			18	66	16	3	1	1	24	9	7	0	4	0	9	0	1	0	0	0	—	1	.242	.286	.364	2B	18	29	59	4	14	.957

GENE HERMANSKI—Eugene Victor Hermanski—Bats: Left; Throws: Right
Ht: 5'11"; Wt: 185 lbs; Born: 5/11/1920 in Pittsfield, Massachusetts; Debut: 8/15/1943

World Series

Year	Tm	Age	G	AB	H	2B	3B	HR	TB	R	RBI	GW	TBB	IBB	SO	HBP	SH	SF	SB	CS	SB%	GDP	Avg	OBP	SLG	Pos	G	PO	A	E	DP	FPct
1947	Bro	27	7	19	3	0	1	0	5	4	1	0	3	0	3	1	0	0	0	0	—	0	.158	.304	.263	OF	7	15	0	0	0	1.000
1949	Bro	29	4	13	4	0	1	0	6	1	2	0	3	0	3	0	0	0	0	0	—	0	.308	.438	.462	OF	4	6	0	0	0	1.000
WS Totals			11	32	7	0	2	0	11	5	3	0	6	0	6	1	0	0	0	0	—	0	.219	.359	.344	OF	11	21	0	0	0	1.000

JACKIE HERNANDEZ—Jacinto Hernandez—Bats: Right; Throws: Right
Ht: 5'11"; Wt: 165 lbs; Born: 9/11/1940 in Central Tinguaro, Cuba; Debut: 9/14/1965

LCS

Year	Tm	Age	G	AB	H	2B	3B	HR	TB	R	RBI	GW	TBB	IBB	SO	HBP	SH	SF	SB	CS	SB%	GDP	Avg	OBP	SLG	Pos	G	PO	A	E	DP	FPct
1971	Pit	31	4	13	3	0	0	0	3	2	1	0	0	0	4	0	0	0	0	0	—	0	.231	.231	.231	SS	4	7	9	1	2	.941

World Series

Year	Tm	Age	G	AB	H	2B	3B	HR	TB	R	RBI	GW	TBB	IBB	SO	HBP	SH	SF	SB	CS	SB%	GDP	Avg	OBP	SLG	Pos	G	PO	A	E	DP	FPct
1971	Pit	31	7	18	4	0	0	0	4	2	1	0	2	0	5	1	1	0	1	0	1.00	0	.222	.333	.222	SS	7	9	16	0	3	1.000
Postseason Totals			11	31	7	0	0	0	7	4	2	0	2	0	9	1	1	0	1	0	1.00	0	.226	.294	.226	SS	11	16	25	1	5	.976

KEITH HERNANDEZ—Nickname: Mex—Bats: Left; Throws: Left
Ht: 6'0"; Wt: 180 lbs; Born: 10/20/1953 in San Francisco, California; Debut: 8/30/1974

LCS

Year	Tm	Age	G	AB	H	2B	3B	HR	TB	R	RBI	GW	TBB	IBB	SO	HBP	SH	SF	SB	CS	SB%	GDP	Avg	OBP	SLG	Pos	G	PO	A	E	DP	FPct
1982	StL	28	3	12	4	0	0	0	4	3	1	0	2	2	3	0	0	0	0	0	—	0	.333	.429	.333	1B	3	35	1	0	3	1.000
1986	NYN	32	6	26	7	1	1	0	10	3	3	0	3	3	6	0	0	0	0	0	—	0	.269	.345	.385	1B	6	66	11	0	5	1.000
1988	NYN	34	7	26	7	0	0	1	10	2	5	0	6	1	7	0	0	0	1	0	1.00	2	.269	.406	.385	1B	7	57	4	1	2	.984
LCS Totals			16	64	18	1	1	1	24	8	9	0	11	6	16	0	0	0	1	0	1.00	2	.281	.387	.375	1B	16	158	16	1	10	.994

World Series

Year	Tm	Age	G	AB	H	2B	3B	HR	TB	R	RBI	GW	TBB	IBB	SO	HBP	SH	SF	SB	CS	SB%	GDP	Avg	OBP	SLG	Pos	G	PO	A	E	DP	FPct
1982	StL	28	7	27	7	2	0	1	12	4	8	0	4	1	2	0	0	0	0	0	—	1	.259	.355	.444	1B	7	62	7	2	8	.972
1986	NYN	32	7	26	6	0	0	0	6	1	4	0	5	1	1	0	0	1	0	0	—	1	.231	.344	.231	1B	7	48	4	1	4	.981
WS Totals			14	53	13	2	0	1	18	5	12	0	9	2	3	0	0	1	0	0	—	1	.245	.349	.340	1B	14	110	11	3	12	.976
Postseason Totals			30	117	31	3	1	2	42	13	21	0	20	8	19	0	0	1	1	0	1.00	3	.265	.370	.359	1B	30	268	27	4	22	.987

LIVAN HERNANDEZ—Eisler Livan Hernandez—Throws: Right; Bats: Right
Ht: 6'2"; Wt: 220 lbs; Born: 2/20/1975 in Villa Clara, Cuba; Debut: 9/24/1996

Division Series

Year	Tm	Age	G	GS	CG	GF	IP	BFP	H	R	ER	HR	SH	SF	HB	TBB	IBB	SO	WP	Bk	W	L	Pct	ShO	Sv-Op	Hld	OAvg	OOBP	ERA
1997	Fla	22	1	0	0	0	4.0	15	3	1	1	0	0	0	0	0	0	3	0	0	0	0	—	0	0-0	0	.200	.200	2.25

LCS

Year	Tm	Age	G	GS	CG	GF	IP	BFP	H	R	ER	HR	SH	SF	HB	TBB	IBB	SO	WP	Bk	W	L	Pct	ShO	Sv-Op	Hld	OAvg	OOBP	ERA
1997	Fla	22	2	1	0	1	10.2	38	5	1	1	1	0	1	0	2	0	16	0	0	2	0	1.000	0	0-0	0	.143	.184	0.84

World Series

Year	Tm	Age	G	GS	CG	GF	IP	BFP	H	R	ER	HR	SH	SF	HB	TBB	IBB	SO	WP	Bk	W	L	Pct	ShO	Sv-Op	Hld	OAvg	OOBP	ERA
1997	Fla	22	2	2	0	0	13.2	65	15	9	8	3	2	0	0	10	0	7	1	0	2	0	1.000	0	0-0	0	.283	.397	5.27
Postseason Totals			5	3	1	0	28.1	236	23	11	10	4	2	1	0	12	0	26	1	0	4	0	1.000	0	0-0	0	.223	.302	3.18

Division Series

Year	Tm	Age	G	AB	H	2B	3B	HR	TB	R	RBI	GW	TBB	IBB	SO	HBP	SH	SF	SB	CS	SB%	GDP	Avg	OBP	SLG	Pos	G	PO	A	E	DP	FPct
1997	Fla	22	1	1	0	0	0	0	0	0	0	0	0	0	0	0	0	0	0	0	—	0	.000	.000	.000	P	1	0	0	0	0	—

LCS

Year	Tm	Age	G	AB	H	2B	3B	HR	TB	R	RBI	GW	TBB	IBB	SO	HBP	SH	SF	SB	CS	SB%	GDP	Avg	OBP	SLG	Pos	G	PO	A	E	DP	FPct
1997	Fla	22	2	3	0	0	0	0	0	0	0	0	0	0	1	0	1	0	0	0	—	0	.000	.000	.000	P	2	1	0	0	0	1.000

World Series

Year	Tm	Age	G	AB	H	2B	3B	HR	TB	R	RBI	GW	TBB	IBB	SO	HBP	SH	SF	SB	CS	SB%	GDP	Avg	OBP	SLG	Pos	G	PO	A	E	DP	FPct
1997	Fla	22	2	2	0	0	0	0	0	0	0	0	0	0	1	0	0	0	0	0	—	0	.000	.000	.000	P	2	0	4	1	1	.800
Postseason Totals			5	6	0	0	0	0	0	0	0	0	0	0	2	0	1	0	0	0	—	0	.000	.000	.000	P	5	1	4	1	1	.833

RAMON HERNANDEZ—Throws: Left; Bats: Both
Ht: 5'11"; Wt: 165 lbs; Born: 8/31/1940 in Carolina, Puerto Rico; Debut: 4/11/1967

LCS

Year	Tm	Age	G	GS	CG	GF	IP	BFP	H	R	ER	HR	SH	SF	HB	TBB	IBB	SO	WP	Bk	W	L	Pct	ShO	Sv-Op	Hld	OAvg	OOBP	ERA
1972	Pit	32	3	0	0	1	3.1	11	1	1	1	1	0	0	0	0	0	3	0	0	0	0	—	0	1-1	1	.091	.091	2.70
1974	Pit	34	2	0	0	2	4.1	16	3	0	0	0	0	0	0	1	1	2	0	0	0	0	—	0	0-0	0	.200	.250	0.00
1975	Pit	35	1	0	0	0	0.2	3	3	2	2	0	0	0	1	0	0	0	0	0	0	1	.000	0	0-0	0	.750	.600	27.00
LCS Totals			6	0	0	3	8.1	64	7	3	3	1	0	0	1	1	1	5	0	0	0	1	.000	0	1-1	1	.233	.250	3.24

LCS — Batting / Fielding

Year Tm	Age	G	AB	H	2B	3B	HR	TB	R	RBI	GW	TBB	IBB	SO	HBP	SH	SF	SB	CS	SB%	GDP	Avg	OBP	SLG	Pos	G	PO	A	E	DP	FPct
1972 Pit	32	3	0	0	0	0	0	0	0	0	0	0	0	0	0	0	0	0	0	—	0	—	—	—	P	3	0	0	0	0	—
1974 Pit	34	2	1	0	0	0	0	0	0	0	0	0	0	1	0	0	0	0	0	—	0	.000	.000	.000	P	2	0	1	0	1	1.000
1975 Pit	35	1	0	0	0	0	0	0	0	0	0	0	0	0	0	0	0	0	0	—	0	—	—	—	P	1	0	0	0	0	—
LCS Totals		6	1	0	0	0	0	0	0	0	0	0	0	1	0	0	0	0	0	—	0	.000	.000	.000	P	6	0	1	0	1	1.000

ROBERTO HERNANDEZ—Roberto Manuel Hernandez—Throws: Right; Bats: Right

Ht: 6'4"; Wt: 220 lbs; Born: 11/11/1964 in Santurce, Puerto Rico; Debut: 9/2/1991

Division Series — Pitching

Year Tm	Age	G	GS	CG	GF	IP	BFP	H	R	ER	HR	SH	SF	HB	TBB	IBB	SO	WP	Bk	W	L	Pct	ShO	Sv-Op	Hld	OAvg	OOBP	ERA
1997 SF	32	3	0	0	2	1.1	12	5	3	3	0	1	0	0	3	1	1	0	0	0	1	.000	0	0- 0	0	.625	.727	20.25

LCS — Pitching

Year Tm	Age	G	GS	CG	GF	IP	BFP	H	R	ER	HR	SH	SF	HB	TBB	IBB	SO	WP	Bk	W	L	Pct	ShO	Sv-Op	Hld	OAvg	OOBP	ERA
1993 ChA	28	4	0	0	4	4.0	15	4	0	0	0	0	0	0	0	0	1	0	0	0	0	—	0	1- 1	0	.267	.267	0.00
Postseason Totals		7	0	0	6	5.1	54	9	3	3	0	1	0	0	3	1	2	0	0	0	1	.000	0	1-1	0	.391	.462	5.06

Division Series — Batting / Fielding

Year Tm	Age	G	AB	H	2B	3B	HR	TB	R	RBI	GW	TBB	IBB	SO	HBP	SH	SF	SB	CS	SB%	GDP	Avg	OBP	SLG	Pos	G	PO	A	E	DP	FPct
1997 SF	32	3	0	0	0	0	0	0	0	0	0	0	0	0	0	0	0	0	0	—	0	—	—	—	P	3	0	0	0	0	—

LCS — Batting / Fielding

Year Tm	Age	G	AB	H	2B	3B	HR	TB	R	RBI	GW	TBB	IBB	SO	HBP	SH	SF	SB	CS	SB%	GDP	Avg	OBP	SLG	Pos	G	PO	A	E	DP	FPct
1993 ChA	28	4	0	0	0	0	0	0	0	0	0	0	0	0	0	0	0	0	0	—	0	—	—	—	P	4	0	0	0	0	—
Postseason Totals		7	0	0	0	0	0	0	0	0	0	0	0	0	0	0	0	0	0	—	0	—	—	—	P	7	0	0	0	0	—

WILLIE HERNANDEZ—Guillermo Hernandez—Throws: Left; Bats: Left

Ht: 6'3"; Wt: 180 lbs; Born: 11/14/1954 in Aguada, Puerto Rico; Debut: 4/8/1977

LCS — Pitching

Year Tm	Age	G	GS	CG	GF	IP	BFP	H	R	ER	HR	SH	SF	HB	TBB	IBB	SO	WP	Bk	W	L	Pct	ShO	Sv-Op	Hld	OAvg	OOBP	ERA
1984 Det-*MC*	29	3	0	0	2	4.0	16	3	1	1	0	0	0	0	1	1	3	0	0	0	0	—	0	1- 2	0	.200	.250	2.25
1987 Det	32	1	0	0	0	0.1	2	2	0	0	0	0	0	0	0	0	0	0	0	0	0	—	0	0- 0	0	1.000	1.000	0.00
LCS Totals		4	0	0	2	4.1	36	5	1	1	0	0	0	0	1	1	3	0	0	0	0	—	0	1-2	0	.294	.333	2.08

World Series — Pitching

Year Tm	Age	G	GS	CG	GF	IP	BFP	H	R	ER	HR	SH	SF	HB	TBB	IBB	SO	WP	Bk	W	L	Pct	ShO	Sv-Op	Hld	OAvg	OOBP	ERA
1983 Phi	28	3	0	0	0	4.0	14	0	0	0	0	0	1	1	1	0	4	0	0	0	0	—	0	0- 0	0	.000	.143	0.00
1984 Det-*MC*	29	3	0	0	3	5.1	19	4	1	1	1	0	0	0	0	0	0	0	0	0	0	—	0	2- 2	0	.211	.211	1.69
WS Totals		6	0	0	3	9.1	66	4	1	1	1	0	1	1	1	0	4	0	0	0	0	—	0	2-2	0	.133	.182	0.96
Postseason Totals		10	0	0	5	13.2	102	9	2	2	1	0	1	1	2	1	7	0	0	0	0	—	0	3-4	0	.191	.235	1.32

LCS — Batting / Fielding

Year Tm	Age	G	AB	H	2B	3B	HR	TB	R	RBI	GW	TBB	IBB	SO	HBP	SH	SF	SB	CS	SB%	GDP	Avg	OBP	SLG	Pos	G	PO	A	E	DP	FPct
1984 Det	29	3	0	0	0	0	0	0	0	0	0	0	0	0	0	0	0	0	0	—	0	—	—	—	P	3	0	0	0	0	—
1987 Det	32	1	0	0	0	0	0	0	0	0	0	0	0	0	0	0	0	0	0	—	0	—	—	—	P	1	0	0	0	0	—
LCS Totals		4	0	0	0	0	0	0	0	0	0	0	0	0	0	0	0	0	0	—	0	—	—	—	P	4	0	0	0	0	—

World Series — Batting / Fielding

Year Tm	Age	G	AB	H	2B	3B	HR	TB	R	RBI	GW	TBB	IBB	SO	HBP	SH	SF	SB	CS	SB%	GDP	Avg	OBP	SLG	Pos	G	PO	A	E	DP	FPct
1983 Phi	28	3	0	0	0	0	0	0	0	0	0	0	0	0	0	0	0	0	0	—	0	—	—	—	P	3	1	0	0	0	1.000
1984 Det	29	3	0	0	0	0	0	0	0	0	0	0	0	0	0	0	0	0	0	—	0	—	—	—	P	3	0	1	0	0	1.000
WS Totals		6	0	0	0	0	0	0	0	0	0	0	0	0	0	0	0	0	0	—	0	—	—	—	P	6	1	1	0	0	1.000
Postseason Totals		10	0	0	0	0	0	0	0	0	0	0	0	0	0	0	0	0	0	—	0	—	—	—	P	10	1	1	0	0	1.000

XAVIER HERNANDEZ—Francis Xavier Hernandez—Throws: Right; Bats: Left

Ht: 6'2"; Wt: 185 lbs; Born: 8/16/1965 in Port Arthur, Texas; Debut: 6/4/1989

LCS — Pitching

Year Tm	Age	G	GS	CG	GF	IP	BFP	H	R	ER	HR	SH	SF	HB	TBB	IBB	SO	WP	Bk	W	L	Pct	ShO	Sv-Op	Hld	OAvg	OOBP	ERA
1995 Cin	30	1	0	0	0	0.2	5	3	2	2	1	0	0	0	0	0	0	0	0	0	0	—	0	0- 0	0	.600	.600	27.00

LCS — Batting / Fielding

Year Tm	Age	G	AB	H	2B	3B	HR	TB	R	RBI	GW	TBB	IBB	SO	HBP	SH	SF	SB	CS	SB%	GDP	Avg	OBP	SLG	Pos	G	PO	A	E	DP	FPct
1995 Cin	30	1	0	0	0	0	0	0	0	0	0	0	0	0	0	0	0	0	0	—	0	—	—	—	P	1	0	0	0	0	—

LARRY HERNDON—Larry Darnell Herndon—Nickname: Hondo—Bats: Right; Throws: Right

Ht: 6'3"; Wt: 190 lbs; Born: 11/3/1953 in Sunflower, Texas; Debut: 9/4/1974

LCS — Batting / Fielding

Year Tm	Age	G	AB	H	2B	3B	HR	TB	R	RBI	GW	TBB	IBB	SO	HBP	SH	SF	SB	CS	SB%	GDP	Avg	OBP	SLG	Pos	G	PO	A	E	DP	FPct
1984 Det	30	2	5	1	0	0	1	4	1	1	0	1	0	2	0	0	0	0	0	—	0	.200	.333	.800	OF	2	6	0	0	0	1.000
1987 Det	33	3	9	3	1	0	0	4	1	2	0	1	0	1	0	0	0	0	0	—	0	.333	.400	.444	OF	2	2	0	1	0	.667
LCS Totals		5	14	4	1	0	1	8	2	3	0	2	0	3	0	0	0	0	0	—	0	.286	.375	.571	OF	4	8	0	1	0	.889

World Series — Batting / Fielding

Year Tm	Age	G	AB	H	2B	3B	HR	TB	R	RBI	GW	TBB	IBB	SO	HBP	SH	SF	SB	CS	SB%	GDP	Avg	OBP	SLG	Pos	G	PO	A	E	DP	FPct
1984 Det	30	5	15	5	0	0	1	8	1	3	1	3	0	2	0	0	0	0	1	.00	0	.333	.444	.533	OF	5	6	0	0	0	1.000
Postseason Totals		10	29	9	1	0	2	16	3	6	1	5	0	5	0	0	0	0	1	.00	0	.310	.412	.552	OF	9	14	0	1	0	.933

TOM HERR—Thomas Mitchell Herr—Bats: Both; Throws: Right

Ht: 6'0"; Wt: 175 lbs; Born: 4/4/1956 in Lancaster, Pennsylvania; Debut: 8/13/1979

LCS — Batting / Fielding

Year Tm	Age	G	AB	H	2B	3B	HR	TB	R	RBI	GW	TBB	IBB	SO	HBP	SH	SF	SB	CS	SB%	GDP	Avg	OBP	SLG	Pos	G	PO	A	E	DP	FPct
1982 StL	26	3	13	3	1	0	0	4	1	0	0	1	0	2	0	1	0	0	0	—	0	.231	.286	.308	2B	3	6	10	0	3	1.000
1985 StL	29	6	21	7	4	0	1	14	2	6	0	5	1	2	0	0	1	1	0	1.00	0	.333	.444	.667	2B	6	13	12	0	3	1.000
1987 StL	31	7	27	6	0	0	0	6	0	3	0	0	0	1	0	1	1	1	0	1.00	3	.222	.214	.222	2B	7	12	11	1	3	.958
LCS Totals		16	61	16	5	0	1	24	3	9	0	6	1	5	0	2	2	2	0	1.00	3	.262	.319	.393	2B	16	31	33	1	9	.985

World Series — Batting / Fielding

Year Tm	Age	G	AB	H	2B	3B	HR	TB	R	RBI	GW	TBB	IBB	SO	HBP	SH	SF	SB	CS	SB%	GDP	Avg	OBP	SLG	Pos	G	PO	A	E	DP	FPct
1982 StL	26	7	25	4	2	0	0	6	2	5	0	3	0	3	0	1	1	0	0	—	0	.160	.241	.240	2B	7	11	19	1	6	.968
1985 StL	29	7	26	4	2	0	0	6	2	0	0	2	1	2	0	0	0	0	0	—	0	.154	.214	.231	2B	7	11	13	0	8	1.000
1987 StL	31	7	28	7	0	0	1	10	2	1	0	2	1	2	0	0	0	0	1	.00	1	.250	.300	.357	2B	7	24	17	0	1	1.000
WS Totals		21	79	15	4	0	1	22	6	6	0	7	2	7	0	1	1	0	1	.00	1	.190	.253	.278	2B	21	46	49	1	15	.990
Postseason Totals		37	140	31	9	0	2	46	9	15	0	13	3	12	0	3	3	2	1	.67	4	.221	.282	.329	2B	37	77	82	2	24	.988

WILLARD HERSHBERGER—Willard McKee Hershberger—Nickname: Bill—Bats: R; Throws: R

Ht: 5'10"; Wt: 167 lbs; Born: 5/28/1910 in Lemon Cove, Calif.; Deb.: 4/19/1938; Died: 8/3/1940

World Series — Batting / Fielding

Year Tm	Age	G	AB	H	2B	3B	HR	TB	R	RBI	GW	TBB	IBB	SO	HBP	SH	SF	SB	CS	SB%	GDP	Avg	OBP	SLG	Pos	G	PO	A	E	DP	FPct
1939 Cin	29	3	2	1	0	0	0	1	0	1	0	0	0	0	0	0	0	0	0	—	0	.500	.500	.500	C	2	1	0	0	0	1.000

OREL HERSHISER—Orel Leonard Quinton Hershiser—Nickname: Bulldog—Throws: Right; Bats: Right

Ht: 6'3"; Wt: 190 lbs; Born: 9/16/1958 in Buffalo, New York; Debut: 9/1/1983

Division Series — Pitching

Year Tm	Age	G	GS	CG	GF	IP	BFP	H	R	ER	HR	SH	SF	HB	TBB	IBB	SO	WP	Bk	W	L	Pct	ShO	Sv-Op	Hld	OAvg	OOBP	ERA
1995 Cle	37	1	1	0	0	7.1	28	3	0	0	0	0	0	0	2	0	7	1	0	1	0	1.000	0	0- 0	0	.115	.179	0.00
1996 Cle	38	1	1	0	0	5.0	25	7	4	3	1	0	0	1	3	0	3	0	0	0	0	—	0	0- 0	0	.333	.440	5.40
1997 Cle	39	2	2	0	0	11.1	49	14	5	5	1	1	1	1	2	0	4	0	0	0	0	—	0	0- 0	0	.318	.354	3.97
DS Totals		4	4	0	0	23.2	204	24	9	8	2	1	1	2	7	0	14	1	0	1	0	1.000	0	0-0	0	.264	.327	3.04

LCS — Pitching

Year Tm	Age	G	GS	CG	GF	IP	BFP	H	R	ER	HR	SH	SF	HB	TBB	IBB	SO	WP	Bk	W	L	Pct	ShO	Sv-Op	Hld	OAvg	OOBP	ERA
1985 LA	27	2	2	1	0	15.1	66	17	6	6	0	0	0	0	6	0	5	1	0	1	0	1.000	0	0- 0	0	.283	.348	3.52
1988 LA-*C*	30	4	3	1	1	24.2	98	18	5	3	0	1	0	2	7	1	15	2	0	1	0	1.000	1	1- 1	0	.205	.278	1.09
1995 Cle	37	2	2	0	0	14.0	57	9	3	2	1	1	0	1	3	1	15	1	0	2	0	1.000	0	0- 0	0	.173	.232	1.29
1997 Cle	39	1	1	0	0	7.0	22	4	0	0	0	0	0	0	1	0	7	0	0	0	0	—	0	0- 0	0	.190	.227	0.00
LCS Totals		9	8	2	1	61.0	486	48	14	11	1	2	0	3	17	2	42	4	0	4	0	1.000	1	1-1	0	.217	.282	1.62

World Series		Pitching																										
Year Tm	Age	G	GS	CG	GF	IP	BFP	H	R	ER	HR	SH	SF	HB	TBB	IBB	SO	WP	Bk	W	L	Pct	ShO	Sv-Op	Hld	OAvg	OOBP	ERA
1988 LA-*C*	30	2	2	2	0	18.0	66	7	2	2	0	1	1	0	6	0	17	1	0	2	0	1.000	1	0- 0	0	.121	.200	1.00
1995 Cle	37	2	2	0	0	14.0	52	8	5	4	2	1	0	0	4	1	13	0	0	1	1	.500	0	0- 0	0	.170	.235	2.57
1997 Cle	39	2	2	0	0	10.0	49	15	13	13	3	1	0	0	6	0	5	0	0	0	2	.000	0	0- 0	0	.357	.438	11.70
WS Totals		6	6	2	0	42.0	334	30	20	19	5	3	1	0	16	1	35	1	0	3	3	.500	1	0-0	0	.204	.280	4.07
Postseason Totals		19	18	4	1	126.2	1024	102	43	38	8	6	2	5	40	3	91	6	0	8	3	.727	2	1-1	0	.222	.291	2.70

Division Series		Batting																							Fielding						
Year Tm	Age	G	AB	H	2B	3B	HR	TB	R	RBI	GW	TBB	IBB	SO	HBP	SH	SF	SB	CS	SB%	GDP	Avg	OBP	SLG	Pos	G	PO	A	E	DP	FPct
1995 Cle	37	1	0	0	0	0	0	0	0	0	0	0	0	0	0	0	0	0	0	—	0	—	—	—	P	1	0	0	0	0	—
1996 Cle	38	1	0	0	0	0	0	0	0	0	0	0	0	0	0	0	0	0	0	—	0	—	—	—	P	1	1	1	0	1	1.000
1997 Cle	39	2	0	0	0	0	0	0	0	0	0	0	0	0	0	0	0	0	0	—	0	—	—	—	P	2	1	4	0	0	1.000
DS Totals		4	0	0	0	0	0	0	0	0	0	0	0	0	0	0	0	0	0	—	0	—	—	—	P	4	2	5	0	1	1.000
LCS		**Batting**																							**Fielding**						
Year Tm	Age	G	AB	H	2B	3B	HR	TB	R	RBI	GW	TBB	IBB	SO	HBP	SH	SF	SB	CS	SB%	GDP	Avg	OBP	SLG	Pos	G	PO	A	E	DP	FPct
1985 LA	27	2	7	2	0	0	0	2	1	1	0	0	0	2	0	0	0	0	0	—	0	.286	.286	.286	P	2	2	2	0	1	1.000
1988 LA	30	4	9	0	0	0	0	0	1	1	0	1	0	2	0	0	0	0	0	—	0	.000	.100	.000	P	4	3	3	0	0	1.000
1995 Cle	37	2	0	0	0	0	0	0	0	0	0	0	0	0	0	0	0	0	0	—	0	—	—	—	P	2	0	4	0	0	1.000
1997 Cle	39	1	0	0	0	0	0	0	0	0	0	0	0	0	0	0	0	0	0	—	0	—	—	—	P	1	0	0	0	0	—
LCS Totals		9	16	2	0	0	0	2	2	2	0	1	0	4	0	0	0	0	0	—	0	.125	.176	.125	P	9	5	9	0	1	1.000
World Series		**Batting**																							**Fielding**						
Year Tm	Age	G	AB	H	2B	3B	HR	TB	R	RBI	GW	TBB	IBB	SO	HBP	SH	SF	SB	CS	SB%	GDP	Avg	OBP	SLG	Pos	G	PO	A	E	DP	FPct
1988 LA	30	2	3	3	2	0	0	5	1	1	0	0	0	0	0	0	0	0	0	—	0	1.000	1.000	1.667	P	2	1	1	0	0	1.000
1995 Cle	37	2	2	0	0	0	0	0	0	0	0	0	0	0	0	0	0	0	0	—	0	.000	.000	.000	P	2	1	7	1	1	.889
1997 Cle	39	2	2	0	0	0	0	0	0	0	0	0	0	1	0	0	0	0	0	—	0	.000	.000	.000	P	2	1	1	0	0	1.000
WS Totals		6	7	3	2	0	0	5	1	1	0	0	0	1	0	0	0	0	0	—	0	.429	.429	.714	P	6	3	9	1	1	.923
Postseason Totals		19	23	5	2	0	0	7	3	3	0	1	0	5	0	0	0	0	0	—	0	.217	.250	.304	P	19	10	23	1	3	.971

BUCK HERZOG—Charles Lincoln Herzog—Bats: Right; Throws: Right

Ht: 5'11"; Wt: 160 lbs; Born: 7/9/1885 in Baltimore, Maryland; Debut: 4/17/1908; Died: 9/4/1953

World Series		Batting																							Fielding						
Year Tm	Age	G	AB	H	2B	3B	HR	TB	R	RBI	GW	TBB	IBB	SO	HBP	SH	SF	SB	CS	SB%	GDP	Avg	OBP	SLG	Pos	G	PO	A	E	DP	FPct
1911 NYG	26	6	21	4	2	0	0	6	3	0	0	2	0	3	0	0	0	2	1	.67	0	.190	.261	.286	3B	6	7	13	3	0	.870
1912 NYG	27	8	30	12	4	1	0	18	6	5	1	1	0	3	1	0	2	2	1	.67	0	.400	.412	.600	3B	8	11	15	0	1	1.000
1913 NYG	28	5	19	1	0	0	0	1	1	0	0	0	0	1	0	0	0	0	0	—	1	.053	.053	.053	3B	5	6	7	0	0	1.000
1917 NYG	32	6	24	6	0	1	0	8	1	2	0	0	0	4	0	1	0	0	0	—	0	.250	.250	.333	2B	6	11	11	2	3	.917
WS Totals		25	94	23	6	2	0	33	11	7	1	3	0	11	1	1	2	4	2	.67	1	.245	.270	.351	3B	19	24	35	3	1	.952

JOHNNY HEVING—John Aloysius Heving—Bats: Right; Throws: Right

Ht: 6'0"; Wt: 175 lbs; Born: 4/29/1896 in Covington, Kentucky; Debut: 9/24/1920; Died: 12/24/1968

World Series		Batting																							Fielding						
Year Tm	Age	G	AB	H	2B	3B	HR	TB	R	RBI	GW	TBB	IBB	SO	HBP	SH	SF	SB	CS	SB%	GDP	Avg	OBP	SLG	Pos	G	PO	A	E	DP	FPct
1931 Phi	35	1	1	0	0	0	0	0	0	0	0	0	0	0	0	0	0	0	0	—	0	.000	.000	.000	—						

RICHARD HIDALGO—Richard Jose Hidalgo—Bats: Right; Throws: Right

Ht: 6'3"; Wt: 190 lbs; Born: 7/2/1975 in Caracas, Venezuela; Debut: 9/1/1997

Division Series		Batting																							Fielding						
Year Tm	Age	G	AB	H	2B	3B	HR	TB	R	RBI	GW	TBB	IBB	SO	HBP	SH	SF	SB	CS	SB%	GDP	Avg	OBP	SLG	Pos	G	PO	A	E	DP	FPct
1997 Hou	22	2	5	0	0	0	0	0	1	0	0	1	0	2	0	0	0	0	0	—	0	.000	.167	.000	OF	2	5	0	0	0	1.000

KIRBY HIGBE—Walter Kirby Higbe—Nickname: Old Hig—Throws: Right; Bats: Right

Ht: 5'11"; Wt: 190 lbs; Born: 4/8/1915 in Columbia, South Carolina; Debut: 10/3/1937; Died: 5/6/1985

World Series		Pitching																										
Year Tm	Age	G	GS	CG	GF	IP	BFP	H	R	ER	HR	SH	SF	HB	TBB	IBB	SO	WP	Bk	W	L	Pct	ShO	Sv-Op	Hld	OAvg	OOBP	ERA
1941 Bro	26	1	1	0	0	3.2	19	6	3	3	0	0	0	0	2	0	1	0	0	0	0	—	0	0- 0	0	.353	.421	7.36

World Series		Batting																							Fielding						
Year Tm	Age	G	AB	H	2B	3B	HR	TB	R	RBI	GW	TBB	IBB	SO	HBP	SH	SF	SB	CS	SB%	GDP	Avg	OBP	SLG	Pos	G	PO	A	E	DP	FPct
1941 Bro	26	1	1	1	0	0	0	1	0	0	0	0	0	0	0	0	0	0	0	—	0	1.000	1.000	1.000	P	1	0	1	0	0	1.000

MIKE HIGGINS—Michael Franklin Higgins—Nickname: Pinky—Bats: Right; Throws: Right

Ht: 6'1"; Wt: 185 lbs; Born: 5/27/1909 in Red Oak, Texas; Debut: 6/25/1930; Died: 3/21/1969

World Series		Batting																							Fielding						
Year Tm	Age	G	AB	H	2B	3B	HR	TB	R	RBI	GW	TBB	IBB	SO	HBP	SH	SF	SB	CS	SB%	GDP	Avg	OBP	SLG	Pos	G	PO	A	E	DP	FPct
1940 Det	31	7	24	8	3	1	1	16	2	6	1	3	0	3	0	0	0	0	0	—	0	.333	.407	.667	3B	7	4	30	2	1	.944
1946 Bos	37	7	24	5	1	0	0	6	1	2	0	2	1	0	0	0	0	0	0	—	0	.208	.269	.250	3B	7	6	6	2	0	.857
WS Totals		14	48	13	4	1	1	22	3	8	1	5	1	3	0	0	0	0	0	—	0	.271	.340	.458	3B	14	10	36	4	1	.920

ANDY HIGH—Andrew Aird High—Nicknames: Handy Andy, Knee High—Bats: Left; Throws: Right

Ht: 5'6"; Wt: 155 lbs; Born: 11/21/1897 in Ava, Illinois; Debut: 4/12/1922; Died: 2/22/1981

World Series		Batting																							Fielding						
Year Tm	Age	G	AB	H	2B	3B	HR	TB	R	RBI	GW	TBB	IBB	SO	HBP	SH	SF	SB	CS	SB%	GDP	Avg	OBP	SLG	Pos	G	PO	A	E	DP	FPct
1928 StL	30	4	17	5	2	0	0	7	1	1	0	1	0	3	0	0	0	0	0	—	0	.294	.333	.412	3B	4	2	5	0	1	1.000
1930 StL	32	1	2	1	0	0	0	1	1	0	0	0	0	0	0	0	0	0	0	—	0	.500	.500	.500	3B	1	0	0	0	0	—
1931 StL	33	4	15	4	0	0	0	4	3	0	0	0	0	2	0	0	0	0	0	—	0	.267	.267	.267	3B	4	3	9	0	0	1.000
WS Totals		9	34	10	2	0	0	12	5	1	0	1	0	5	0	0	0	0	0	—	0	.294	.314	.353	3B	9	5	14	0	1	1.000

ORAL HILDEBRAND—Oral Clyde Hildebrand—Throws: Right; Bats: Right

Ht: 6'3"; Wt: 175 lbs; Born: 4/7/1907 in Indianapolis, Indiana; Debut: 9/8/1931; Died: 9/8/1977

World Series		Pitching																										
Year Tm	Age	G	GS	CG	GF	IP	BFP	H	R	ER	HR	SH	SF	HB	TBB	IBB	SO	WP	Bk	W	L	Pct	ShO	Sv-Op	Hld	OAvg	OOBP	ERA
1939 NYA	32	1	1	0	0	4.0	14	2	0	0	0	0	0	0	0	0	3	0	0	0	0	—	0	0- 0	0	.143	.143	0.00

World Series		Batting																							Fielding						
Year Tm	Age	G	AB	H	2B	3B	HR	TB	R	RBI	GW	TBB	IBB	SO	HBP	SH	SF	SB	CS	SB%	GDP	Avg	OBP	SLG	Pos	G	PO	A	E	DP	FPct
1939 NYA	32	1	1	0	0	0	0	0	0	0	0	0	0	1	0	0	0	0	0	—	0	.000	.000	.000	P	1	0	0	0	0	—

CARMEN HILL—Carmen Proctor Hill—Nicknames: Specs, Bunker—Throws: Right; Bats: Right

Ht: 6'1"; Wt: 180 lbs; Born: 10/1/1895 in Royalton, Minnesota; Debut: 8/24/1915; Died: 1/1/1990

World Series		Pitching																										
Year Tm	Age	G	GS	CG	GF	IP	BFP	H	R	ER	HR	SH	SF	HB	TBB	IBB	SO	WP	Bk	W	L	Pct	ShO	Sv-Op	Hld	OAvg	OOBP	ERA
1927 Pit	31	1	1	0	0	6.0	28	9	3	3	1	0	0	0	1	0	6	0	0	0	0	—	0	0- 0	0	.333	.357	4.50

World Series		Batting																							Fielding						
Year Tm	Age	G	AB	H	2B	3B	HR	TB	R	RBI	GW	TBB	IBB	SO	HBP	SH	SF	SB	CS	SB%	GDP	Avg	OBP	SLG	Pos	G	PO	A	E	DP	FPct
1927 Pit	31	1	1	0	0	0	0	0	0	0	0	1	0	0	0	0	0	0	0	—	0	.000	.500	.000	P	1	0	0	0	0	—

GLENALLEN HILL—Bats: Right; Throws: Right

Ht: 6'3"; Wt: 210 lbs; Born: 3/22/1965 in Santa Cruz, California; Debut: 9/1/1989

Division Series		Batting																							Fielding						
Year Tm	Age	G	AB	H	2B	3B	HR	TB	R	RBI	GW	TBB	IBB	SO	HBP	SH	SF	SB	CS	SB%	GDP	Avg	OBP	SLG	Pos	G	PO	A	E	DP	FPct
1997 SF	32	3	7	0	0	0	0	0	0	0	0	2	0	2	0	0	0	0	0	—	1	.000	.222	.000	OF	2	2	0	0	0	1.000

KEN HILL—Kenneth Wade Hill—Throws: Right; Bats: Right

Ht: 6'4"; Wt: 200 lbs; Born: 12/14/1965 in Lynn, Massachusetts; Debut: 9/3/1988

Division Series		Pitching																										
Year Tm	Age	G	GS	CG	GF	IP	BFP	H	R	ER	HR	SH	SF	HB	TBB	IBB	SO	WP	Bk	W	L	Pct	ShO	Sv-Op	Hld	OAvg	OOBP	ERA
1995 Cle	29	1	0	0	1	1.1	5	1	0	0	0	0	0	0	0	0	2	0	0	1	0	1.000	0	0- 0	0	.200	.200	0.00
1996 Tex	30	1	1	0	0	6.0	27	5	3	3	1	0	0	1	3	0	1	0	0	0	0	—	0	0- 0	0	.217	.333	4.50
DS Totals		2	1	0	1	7.1	64	6	3	3	1	0	0	1	3	0	3	0	0	1	0	1.000	0	0-0	0	.214	.313	3.68

LCS — Pitching																												
Year Tm	Age	G	GS	CG	GF	IP	BFP	H	R	ER	HR	SH	SF	HB	TBB	IBB	SO	WP	Bk	W	L	Pct	ShO	Sv-Op	Hld	OAvg	OOBP	ERA
1995 Cle	29	1	1	0	0	7.0	29	5	0	0	0	0	0	0	3	0	6	0	0	1	0	1.000	0	0-0	0	.192	.276	0.00
World Series — Pitching																												
Year Tm	Age	G	GS	CG	GF	IP	BFP	H	R	ER	HR	SH	SF	HB	TBB	IBB	SO	WP	Bk	W	L	Pct	ShO	Sv-Op	Hld	OAvg	OOBP	ERA
1995 Cle	29	2	1	0	0	6.1	30	7	3	3	1	0	0	0	4	0	1	0	0	0	1	.000	0	0-0	0	.269	.367	4.26
Postseason Totals		5	3	0	1	20.2	182	18	6	6	2	0	0	1	10	0	10	0	0	2	1	.667	0	0-0	0	.225	.319	2.61

Division Series — Batting / Fielding																															
Year Tm	Age	G	AB	H	2B	3B	HR	TB	R	RBI	GW	TBB	IBB	SO	HBP	SH	SF	SB	CS	SB%	GDP	Avg	OBP	SLG	Pos	G	PO	A	E	DP	FPct
1995 Cle	29	1	0	0	0	0	0	0	0	0	0	0	0	0	0	0	0	0	0	—	0	—	—	—	P	1	0	2	0	0	1.000
1996 Tex	30	1	0	0	0	0	0	0	0	0	0	0	0	0	0	0	0	0	0	—	0	—	—	—	P	1	1	2	0	0	1.000
DS Totals		2	0	0	0	0	0	0	0	0	0	0	0	0	0	0	0	0	0	—	0	—	—	—	P	2	1	4	0	0	1.000
LCS — Batting / Fielding																															
Year Tm	Age	G	AB	H	2B	3B	HR	TB	R	RBI	GW	TBB	IBB	SO	HBP	SH	SF	SB	CS	SB%	GDP	Avg	OBP	SLG	Pos	G	PO	A	E	DP	FPct
1995 Cle	29	1	0	0	0	0	0	0	0	0	0	0	0	0	0	0	0	0	0	—	0	—	—	—	P	1	1	1	0	0	1.000
World Series — Batting / Fielding																															
Year Tm	Age	G	AB	H	2B	3B	HR	TB	R	RBI	GW	TBB	IBB	SO	HBP	SH	SF	SB	CS	SB%	GDP	Avg	OBP	SLG	Pos	G	PO	A	E	DP	FPct
1995 Cle	29	2	0	0	0	0	0	0	0	0	0	0	0	0	0	0	0	0	0	—	0	—	—	—	P	2	1	2	0	0	1.000
Postseason Totals		5	0	0	0	0	0	0	0	0	0	0	0	0	0	0	0	0	0	—	0	—	—	—	P	5	3	7	0	0	1.000

CHUCK HILLER—Charles Joseph Hiller—Bats: Left; Throws: Right

Ht: 5'11"; Wt: 170 lbs; Born: 10/1/1934 in Johnsburg, Illinois; Debut: 4/11/1961

World Series — Batting / Fielding																															
Year Tm	Age	G	AB	H	2B	3B	HR	TB	R	RBI	GW	TBB	IBB	SO	HBP	SH	SF	SB	CS	SB%	GDP	Avg	OBP	SLG	Pos	G	PO	A	E	DP	FPct
1962 SF	28	7	26	7	3	0	1	13	4	5	1	3	0	4	0	0	0	0	0	—	0	.269	.345	.500	2B	7	16	22	1	7	.974

JOHN HILLER—John Frederick Hiller—Throws: Left; Bats: Right

Ht: 6'1"; Wt: 185 lbs; Born: 4/8/1943 in Toronto, Ontario; Debut: 9/6/1965

LCS — Pitching																												
Year Tm	Age	G	GS	CG	GF	IP	BFP	H	R	ER	HR	SH	SF	HB	TBB	IBB	SO	WP	Bk	W	L	Pct	ShO	Sv-Op	Hld	OAvg	OOBP	ERA
1972 Det	29	3	0	0	3	3.1	10	1	0	0	0	0	0	0	1	0	1	0	0	1	0	1.000	0	0-0	0	.111	.200	0.00
World Series — Pitching																												
Year Tm	Age	G	GS	CG	GF	IP	BFP	H	R	ER	HR	SH	SF	HB	TBB	IBB	SO	WP	Bk	W	L	Pct	ShO	Sv-Op	Hld	OAvg	OOBP	ERA
1968 Det	25	2	0	0	1	2.0	16	6	4	3	0	0	0	0	3	0	1	0	0	0	0	—	0	0-0	0	.462	.563	13.50
Postseason Totals		5	0	0	4	5.1	52	7	4	3	0	0	0	0	4	0	2	0	0	1	0	1.000	0	0-0	0	.318	.423	5.06

LCS — Batting / Fielding																															
Year Tm	Age	G	AB	H	2B	3B	HR	TB	R	RBI	GW	TBB	IBB	SO	HBP	SH	SF	SB	CS	SB%	GDP	Avg	OBP	SLG	Pos	G	PO	A	E	DP	FPct
1972 Det	29	3	0	0	0	0	0	0	0	0	0	0	0	0	0	0	0	0	0	—	0	—	—	—	P	3	0	0	0	0	—
World Series — Batting / Fielding																															
Year Tm	Age	G	AB	H	2B	3B	HR	TB	R	RBI	GW	TBB	IBB	SO	HBP	SH	SF	SB	CS	SB%	GDP	Avg	OBP	SLG	Pos	G	PO	A	E	DP	FPct
1968 Det	25	2	0	0	0	0	0	0	0	0	0	0	0	0	0	0	0	0	0	—	0	—	—	—	P	2	1	0	0	0	1.000
Postseason Totals		5	0	0	0	0	0	0	0	0	0	0	0	0	0	0	0	0	0	—	0	—	—	—	P	5	1	0	0	0	1.000

STERLING HITCHCOCK—Sterling Alex Hitchcock—Throws: Left; Bats: Left

Ht: 6'1"; Wt: 195 lbs; Born: 4/29/1971 in Fayetteville, North Carolina; Debut: 9/11/1992

Division Series — Pitching																												
Year Tm	Age	G	GS	CG	GF	IP	BFP	H	R	ER	HR	SH	SF	HB	TBB	IBB	SO	WP	Bk	W	L	Pct	ShO	Sv-Op	Hld	OAvg	OOBP	ERA
1995 NYA	24	2	0	0	0	1.2	9	2	2	1	1	1	0	0	2	1	1	0	0	0	0	—	0	0-0	0	.333	.500	5.40

Division Series — Batting / Fielding																															
Year Tm	Age	G	AB	H	2B	3B	HR	TB	R	RBI	GW	TBB	IBB	SO	HBP	SH	SF	SB	CS	SB%	GDP	Avg	OBP	SLG	Pos	G	PO	A	E	DP	FPct
1995 NYA	24	2	0	0	0	0	0	0	0	0	0	0	0	0	0	0	0	0	0	—	0	—	—	—	P	2	0	1	0	0	1.000

MYRIL HOAG—Myrill Oliver Hoag—Bats: Right; Throws: Right

Ht: 5'11"; Wt: 180 lbs; Born: 3/9/1908 in Davis, California; Debut: 4/15/1931; Died: 7/28/1971

World Series — Batting / Fielding																															
Year Tm	Age	G	AB	H	2B	3B	HR	TB	R	RBI	GW	TBB	IBB	SO	HBP	SH	SF	SB	CS	SB%	GDP	Avg	OBP	SLG	Pos	G	PO	A	E	DP	FPct
1932 NYA	24	1	0	0	0	0	0	0	1	0	0	0	0	0	0	0	0	0	0	—	0	—	—	—	—						
1937 NYA	29	5	20	6	1	0	1	10	4	2	0	0	0	1	0	1	0	0	0	—	1	.300	.300	.500	OF	5	11	0	0	0	1.000
1938 NYA	30	2	5	2	1	0	0	3	3	1	0	0	0	0	0	0	0	0	0	—	0	.400	.400	.600	OF	1	1	0	0	0	1.000
WS Totals		8	25	8	2	0	1	13	8	3	0	0	0	1	0	1	0	0	0	—	1	.320	.320	.520	OF	6	12	0	0	0	1.000

DON HOAK—Donald Albert Hoak—Nickname: Tiger—Bats: Right; Throws: Right

Ht: 6'1"; Wt: 170 lbs; Born: 2/5/1928 in Roulette, Pennsylvania; Debut: 4/18/1954; Died: 10/9/1969

World Series — Batting / Fielding																															
Year Tm	Age	G	AB	H	2B	3B	HR	TB	R	RBI	GW	TBB	IBB	SO	HBP	SH	SF	SB	CS	SB%	GDP	Avg	OBP	SLG	Pos	G	PO	A	E	DP	FPct
1955 Bro	27	3	3	1	0	0	0	1	0	0	0	2	0	0	0	0	0	0	0	—	0	.333	.600	.333	3B	1	1	1	0	0	1.000
1960 Pit	32	7	23	5	2	0	0	7	3	3	1	4	0	1	0	0	0	0	1	.00	1	.217	.333	.304	3B	7	8	10	1	2	.947
WS Totals		10	26	6	2	0	0	8	3	3	1	6	0	1	0	0	0	0	1	.00	1	.231	.375	.308	3B	8	9	11	1	2	.952

DOC HOBLITZELL—Richard Carleton Hoblitzell—Bats: Right; Throws: Right

Ht: 6'0"; Wt: 172 lbs; Born: 10/26/1888 in Waverly, West Virginia; Debut: 9/5/1908; Died: 11/14/1962

World Series — Batting / Fielding																															
Year Tm	Age	G	AB	H	2B	3B	HR	TB	R	RBI	GW	TBB	IBB	SO	HBP	SH	SF	SB	CS	SB%	GDP	Avg	OBP	SLG	Pos	G	PO	A	E	DP	FPct
1915 Bos	26	5	16	5	0	0	0	5	1	1	0	0	0	1	0	0	1	1	1	.50	1	.313	.294	.313	1B	5	35	5	1	2	.976
1916 Bos	27	5	17	4	1	1	0	7	3	2	0	6	0	0	0	0	0	0	0	—	0	.235	.435	.412	1B	5	69	4	0	4	1.000
WS Totals		10	33	9	1	1	0	12	4	3	0	6	0	1	0	0	1	1	1	.50	1	.273	.375	.364	1B	10	104	9	1	6	.991

GIL HODGES—Gilbert Raymond Hodges—Bats: Right; Throws: Right

Ht: 6'1"; Wt: 200 lbs; Born: 4/4/1924 in Princeton, Indiana; Debut: 10/3/1943; Died: 4/2/1972

World Series — Batting / Fielding																															
Year Tm	Age	G	AB	H	2B	3B	HR	TB	R	RBI	GW	TBB	IBB	SO	HBP	SH	SF	SB	CS	SB%	GDP	Avg	OBP	SLG	Pos	G	PO	A	E	DP	FPct
1947 Bro	23	1	1	0	0	0	0	0	0	0	0	0	0	1	0	0	0	0	0	—	0	.000	.000	.000	—						
1949 Bro	25	5	17	4	0	0	1	7	2	4	1	1	0	4	0	1	0	0	0	—	2	.235	.278	.412	1B	5	38	3	0	0	1.000
1952 Bro	28	7	21	0	0	0	0	0	1	1	0	5	1	6	0	0	0	0	0	—	2	.000	.192	.000	1B	7	60	6	1	4	.985
1953 Bro	29	6	22	8	0	0	1	11	3	1	0	3	0	3	0	0	0	1	0	1.00	0	.364	.440	.500	1B	6	47	4	1	2	.981
1955 Bro	31	7	24	7	0	0	1	10	2	5	2	3	0	2	0	1	1	0	1	.00	0	.292	.357	.417	1B	7	73	4	0	10	1.000
1956 Bro	32	7	23	7	2	0	1	12	5	8	2	4	0	4	0	0	0	0	0	—	0	.304	.407	.522	1B	7	54	5	0	8	1.000
1959 LA	35	6	23	9	0	1	1	14	2	2	1	1	0	2	0	0	0	0	0	—	0	.391	.417	.609	1B	6	53	3	0	6	1.000
WS Totals		39	131	35	2	1	5	54	15	21	6	17	1	22	0	2	1	1	1	.50	4	.267	.349	.412	1B	38	325	25	2	30	.994

RON HODGES—Ronald Wray Hodges—Bats: Left; Throws: Right

Ht: 6'1"; Wt: 185 lbs; Born: 6/22/1949 in Rocky Mount, Virginia; Debut: 6/13/1973

World Series — Batting / Fielding																															
Year Tm	Age	G	AB	H	2B	3B	HR	TB	R	RBI	GW	TBB	IBB	SO	HBP	SH	SF	SB	CS	SB%	GDP	Avg	OBP	SLG	Pos	G	PO	A	E	DP	FPct
1973 NYN	24	1	0	0	0	0	0	0	0	0	0	1	0	0	0	0	0	0	0	—	0	—	1.000	—	—						

JOE HOERNER—Joseph Walter Hoerner—Throws: Left; Bats: Right

Ht: 6'1"; Wt: 200 lbs; Born: 11/12/1936 in Dubuque, Iowa; Debut: 9/27/1963; Died: 10/4/1996

World Series — Pitching																												
Year Tm	Age	G	GS	CG	GF	IP	BFP	H	R	ER	HR	SH	SF	HB	TBB	IBB	SO	WP	Bk	W	L	Pct	ShO	Sv-Op	Hld	OAvg	OOBP	ERA
1967 StL	30	2	0	0	0	0.2	7	4	3	3	1	0	0	0	1	0	0	0	0	0	0	—	0	0-0	0	.667	.714	40.50
1968 StL	31	3	0	0	2	4.2	25	5	4	2	0	1	0	0	5	1	3	0	0	0	1	.000	0	1-2	0	.263	.417	3.86
WS Totals		5	0	0	2	5.1	64	9	7	5	1	1	0	0	6	1	3	0	0	0	1	.000	0	1-2	0	.360	.484	8.44

World Series — Batting / Fielding																															
Year Tm	Age	G	AB	H	2B	3B	HR	TB	R	RBI	GW	TBB	IBB	SO	HBP	SH	SF	SB	CS	SB%	GDP	Avg	OBP	SLG	Pos	G	PO	A	E	DP	FPct
1967 StL	30	2	0	0	0	0	0	0	0	0	0	0	0	0	0	0	0	0	0	—	0	—	—	—	P	2	0	0	0	0	—
1968 StL	31	3	2	1	0	0	0	1	0	0	0	0	0	1	0	0	0	0	0	—	0	.500	.500	.500	P	3	0	0	0	0	—
WS Totals		5	2	1	0	0	0	1	0	0	0	0	0	1	0	0	0	0	0	—	0	.500	.500	.500	P	5	0	0	0	0	—

DANNY HOFFMAN—Daniel John Hoffman—Bats: Left; Throws: Left

Ht: 5'9"; Wt: 175 lbs; Born: 3/2/1880 in Canton, Connecticut; Debut: 4/20/1903; Died: 3/14/1922

World Series		Batting																							Fielding						
Year Tm	Age	G	AB	H	2B	3B	HR	TB	R	RBI	GW	TBB	IBB	SO	HBP	SH	SF	SB	CS	SB%	GDP	Avg	OBP	SLG	Pos	G	PO	A	E	DP	FPct
1905 Phi	25	1	1	0	0	0	0	0	0	0	0	0	0	1	0	0	0	0	0	—	0	.000	.000	.000	—						

TREVOR HOFFMAN—Trevor William Hoffman—Throws: Right; Bats: Right

Ht: 6'1"; Wt: 200 lbs; Born: 10/13/1967 in Bellflower, California; Debut: 4/6/1993

Division Series		Pitching																										
Year Tm	Age	G	GS	CG	GF	IP	BFP	H	R	ER	HR	SH	SF	HB	TBB	IBB	SO	WP	Bk	W	L	Pct	ShO	Sv-Op	Hld	OAvg	OOBP	ERA
1996 SD	28	2	0	0	2	1.2	9	3	2	2	1	0	0	0	1	0	2	0	0	0	1	.000	0	0- 0	0	.375	.444	10.80

Division Series		Batting																							Fielding						
Year Tm	Age	G	AB	H	2B	3B	HR	TB	R	RBI	GW	TBB	IBB	SO	HBP	SH	SF	SB	CS	SB%	GDP	Avg	OBP	SLG	Pos	G	PO	A	E	DP	FPct
1996 SD	28	2	0	0	0	0	0	0	0	0	0	0	0	0	0	0	0	0	0	—	0	—	—	—	P	2	0	1	0	0	1.000

SOLLY HOFMAN—Arthur Frederick Hofman—Nickname: Circus Solly—Bats: Right; Throws: Right

Ht: 6'0"; Wt: 160 lbs; Born: 10/29/1882 in St. Louis, Missouri; Debut: 7/28/1903; Died: 3/10/1956

World Series		Batting																							Fielding						
Year Tm	Age	G	AB	H	2B	3B	HR	TB	R	RBI	GW	TBB	IBB	SO	HBP	SH	SF	SB	CS	SB%	GDP	Avg	OBP	SLG	Pos	G	PO	A	E	DP	FPct
1906 ChN	23	6	23	7	1	0	0	8	3	2	0	3	0	5	0	1	0	1	1	.50	0	.304	.385	.348	OF	6	10	1	0	0	1.000
1908 ChN	25	5	19	6	0	1	0	8	2	4	1	1	0	4	0	0	0	2	0	1.00	0	.316	.350	.421	OF	5	10	1	0	1	1.000
1910 ChN	27	5	15	4	0	0	0	4	2	2	0	4	0	3	0	1	1	0	0	—	0	.267	.400	.267	OF	5	7	0	1	0	.875
WS Totals		16	57	17	1	1	0	20	7	8	1	8	0	12	0	2	1	3	1	.75	0	.298	.379	.351	OF	16	27	2	1	1	.967

FRED HOFMANN—Nickname: Bootnose—Bats: Right; Throws: Right

Ht: 5'11"; Wt: 175 lbs; Born: 6/10/1894 in St. Louis, Missouri; Debut: 9/26/1919; Died: 11/19/1964

World Series		Batting																							Fielding						
Year Tm	Age	G	AB	H	2B	3B	HR	TB	R	RBI	GW	TBB	IBB	SO	HBP	SH	SF	SB	CS	SB%	GDP	Avg	OBP	SLG	Pos	G	PO	A	E	DP	FPct
1923 NYA	29	2	1	0	0	0	0	0	0	0	0	1	0	0	0	0	0	0	0	—	0	.000	.500	.000	—						

CHIEF HOGSETT—Elon Chester Hogsett—Throws: Left; Bats: Left

Ht: 6'0"; Wt: 190 lbs; Born: 11/2/1903 in Bromwell, Kansas; Debut: 9/18/1929

World Series		Pitching																										
Year Tm	Age	G	GS	CG	GF	IP	BFP	H	R	ER	HR	SH	SF	HB	TBB	IBB	SO	WP	Bk	W	L	Pct	ShO	Sv-Op	Hld	OAvg	OOBP	ERA
1934 Det	30	3	0	0	2	7.1	30	6	1	1	0	1	0	0	3	0	3	0	0	0	0	—	0	0- 0	0	.231	.310	1.23
1935 Det	31	1	0	0	0	1.0	5	0	0	0	0	1	0	1	1	0	0	0	0	0	0	—	0	0- 0	0	.000	.500	0.00
WS Totals		4	0	0	2	8.1	70	6	1	1	0	2	0	1	4	0	3	0	0	0	0	—	0	0-0	0	.214	.333	1.08

World Series		Batting																							Fielding						
Year Tm	Age	G	AB	H	2B	3B	HR	TB	R	RBI	GW	TBB	IBB	SO	HBP	SH	SF	SB	CS	SB%	GDP	Avg	OBP	SLG	Pos	G	PO	A	E	DP	FPct
1934 Det	30	3	3	0	0	0	0	0	0	0	0	0	0	1	0	0	0	0	0	—	0	.000	.000	.000	P	3	0	2	0	0	1.000
1935 Det	31	1	0	0	0	0	0	0	0	0	0	0	0	0	0	0	0	0	0	—	0	—	—	—	P	1	1	0	0	0	1.000
WS Totals		4	3	0	0	0	0	0	0	0	0	0	0	1	0	0	0	0	0	—	0	.000	.000	.000	P	4	1	2	0	0	1.000

BOBBY HOGUE—Robert Clinton Hogue—Throws: Right; Bats: Right

Ht: 5'10"; Wt: 195 lbs; Born: 4/5/1921 in Miami, Florida; Debut: 4/24/1948; Died: 12/22/1987

World Series		Pitching																										
Year Tm	Age	G	GS	CG	GF	IP	BFP	H	R	ER	HR	SH	SF	HB	TBB	IBB	SO	WP	Bk	W	L	Pct	ShO	Sv-Op	Hld	OAvg	OOBP	ERA
1951 NYA	30	2	0	0	0	2.2	9	1	0	0	0	0	0	0	0	0	0	0	0	0	0	—	0	0- 0	0	.111	.111	0.00

World Series		Batting																							Fielding						
Year Tm	Age	G	AB	H	2B	3B	HR	TB	R	RBI	GW	TBB	IBB	SO	HBP	SH	SF	SB	CS	SB%	GDP	Avg	OBP	SLG	Pos	G	PO	A	E	DP	FPct
1951 NYA	30	2	0	0	0	0	0	0	0	0	0	0	0	0	0	0	0	0	0	—	0	—	—	—	P	2	0	1	0	0	1.000

CHRIS HOILES—Christopher Allen Hoiles—Bats: Right; Throws: Right

Ht: 6'0"; Wt: 195 lbs; Born: 3/20/1965 in Bowling Green, Ohio; Debut: 4/25/1989

Division Series		Batting																							Fielding						
Year Tm	Age	G	AB	H	2B	3B	HR	TB	R	RBI	GW	TBB	IBB	SO	HBP	SH	SF	SB	CS	SB%	GDP	Avg	OBP	SLG	Pos	G	PO	A	E	DP	FPct
1996 Bal	31	4	7	1	0	0	0	1	1	0	0	3	1	3	1	0	0	0	0	—	0	.143	.455	.143	C	4	14	3	0	0	1.000
1997 Bal	32	3	7	1	0	0	1	4	1	1	0	2	0	1	0	0	0	0	0	—	1	.143	.333	.571	C	3	23	0	0	0	1.000
DS Totals		7	14	2	0	0	1	5	2	1	0	5	1	4	1	0	0	0	0	—	1	.143	.400	.357	C	7	37	3	0	0	1.000
LCS		Batting																							Fielding						
Year Tm	Age	G	AB	H	2B	3B	HR	TB	R	RBI	GW	TBB	IBB	SO	HBP	SH	SF	SB	CS	SB%	GDP	Avg	OBP	SLG	Pos	G	PO	A	E	DP	FPct
1996 Bal	31	4	12	2	0	0	1	5	1	2	0	1	0	3	0	0	0	0	0	—	0	.167	.231	.417	C	4	23	2	0	0	1.000
1997 Bal	32	4	14	2	0	0	0	2	1	0	0	2	0	5	0	0	0	0	0	—	2	.143	.250	.143	C	4	47	2	0	0	1.000
LCS Totals		8	26	4	0	0	1	7	2	2	0	3	0	8	0	0	0	0	0	—	2	.154	.241	.269	C	8	70	4	0	0	1.000
Postseason Totals		15	40	6	0	0	2	12	4	3	0	8	1	12	1	0	0	0	0	—	3	.150	.306	.300	C	15	107	7	0	0	1.000

WALTER HOLKE—Walter Henry Holke—Nickname: Union Man—Bats: Both; Throws: Left

Ht: 6'1"; Wt: 185 lbs; Born: 12/25/1892 in St. Louis, Missouri; Debut: 10/6/1914; Died: 10/12/1954

World Series		Batting																							Fielding						
Year Tm	Age	G	AB	H	2B	3B	HR	TB	R	RBI	GW	TBB	IBB	SO	HBP	SH	SF	SB	CS	SB%	GDP	Avg	OBP	SLG	Pos	G	PO	A	E	DP	FPct
1917 NYG	24	6	21	6	2	0	0	8	2	1	1	0	0	6	1	0	0	0	1	.00	0	.286	.318	.381	1B	6	67	0	1	1	.985

AL HOLLAND—Alfred Willis Holland—Throws: Left; Bats: Right

Ht: 5'11"; Wt: 207 lbs; Born: 8/16/1952 in Roanoke, Virginia; Debut: 9/5/1977

LCS		Pitching																										
Year Tm	Age	G	GS	CG	GF	IP	BFP	H	R	ER	HR	SH	SF	HB	TBB	IBB	SO	WP	Bk	W	L	Pct	ShO	Sv-Op	Hld	OAvg	OOBP	ERA
1983 Phi	31	2	0	0	2	3.0	11	1	0	0	0	0	0	0	0	0	3	0	0	0	0	—	0	1- 1	0	.091	.091	0.00
World Series		Pitching																										
Year Tm	Age	G	GS	CG	GF	IP	BFP	H	R	ER	HR	SH	SF	HB	TBB	IBB	SO	WP	Bk	W	L	Pct	ShO	Sv-Op	Hld	OAvg	OOBP	ERA
1983 Phi	31	2	0	0	2	3.2	13	1	0	0	0	0	0	0	0	0	5	0	0	0	0	—	0	1- 1	0	.077	.077	0.00
Postseason Totals		4	0	0	4	6.2	48	2	0	0	0	0	0	0	0	0	8	0	0	0	0	—	0	2-2	0	.083	.083	0.00

LCS		Batting																							Fielding						
Year Tm	Age	G	AB	H	2B	3B	HR	TB	R	RBI	GW	TBB	IBB	SO	HBP	SH	SF	SB	CS	SB%	GDP	Avg	OBP	SLG	Pos	G	PO	A	E	DP	FPct
1983 Phi	31	2	0	0	0	0	0	0	0	0	0	0	0	0	0	0	0	0	0	—	0	—	—	—	P	2	0	0	0	0	—
World Series		Batting																							Fielding						
Year Tm	Age	G	AB	H	2B	3B	HR	TB	R	RBI	GW	TBB	IBB	SO	HBP	SH	SF	SB	CS	SB%	GDP	Avg	OBP	SLG	Pos	G	PO	A	E	DP	FPct
1983 Phi	31	2	0	0	0	0	0	0	0	0	0	0	0	0	0	0	0	0	0	—	0	—	—	—	P	2	0	0	0	0	—
Postseason Totals		4	0	0	0	0	0	0	0	0	0	0	0	0	0	0	0	0	0	—	0	—	—	—	P	4	0	0	0	0	—

TODD HOLLANDSWORTH—Todd Mathew Hollandsworth—Bats: Left; Throws: Left

Ht: 6'2"; Wt: 193 lbs; Born: 4/20/1973 in Dayton, Ohio; Debut: 4/25/1995

Division Series		Batting																							Fielding						
Year Tm	Age	G	AB	H	2B	3B	HR	TB	R	RBI	GW	TBB	IBB	SO	HBP	SH	SF	SB	CS	SB%	GDP	Avg	OBP	SLG	Pos	G	PO	A	E	DP	FPct
1995 LA	22	2	2	0	0	0	0	0	0	0	0	0	0	0	0	0	0	0	0	—	0	.000	.000	.000	OF	2	0	0	0	0	—
1996 LA-*RY*	23	3	12	4	3	0	0	7	1	1	0	0	0	3	0	0	0	0	0	—	0	.333	.333	.583	OF	3	4	0	0	0	1.000
DS Totals		5	14	4	3	0	0	7	1	1	0	0	0	3	0	0	0	0	0	—	0	.286	.286	.500	OF	5	4	0	0	0	1.000

AL HOLLINGSWORTH—Albert Wayne Hollingsworth—Nickname: Boots—Throws: Left; Bats: Left

Ht: 6'0"; Wt: 174 lbs; Born: 2/25/1908 in St. Louis, Missouri; Debut: 4/16/1935; Died: 4/28/1996

World Series		Pitching																										
Year Tm	Age	G	GS	CG	GF	IP	BFP	H	R	ER	HR	SH	SF	HB	TBB	IBB	SO	WP	Bk	W	L	Pct	ShO	Sv-Op	Hld	OAvg	OOBP	ERA
1944 StL	36	1	0	0	0	4.0	18	5	1	1	0	0	0	0	2	1	1	0	0	0	0	—	0	0- 0	0	.313	.389	2.25

World Series		Batting																							Fielding						
Year Tm	Age	G	AB	H	2B	3B	HR	TB	R	RBI	GW	TBB	IBB	SO	HBP	SH	SF	SB	CS	SB%	GDP	Avg	OBP	SLG	Pos	G	PO	A	E	DP	FPct
1944 StL	36	1	1	0	0	0	0	0	0	0	0	0	0	0	0	0	0	0	0	—	0	.000	.000	.000	P	1	0	1	0	0	1.000

DAVE HOLLINS—David Michaels Hollins—Bats: Both; Throws: Right

Ht: 6'1"; Wt: 195 lbs; Born: 5/25/1966 in Buffalo, New York; Debut: 4/12/1990

LCS		Batting																							Fielding						
Year Tm	Age	G	AB	H	2B	3B	HR	TB	R	RBI	GW	TBB	IBB	SO	HBP	SH	SF	SB	CS	SB%	GDP	Avg	OBP	SLG	Pos	G	PO	A	E	DP	FPct
1993 Phi	27	6	20	4	1	0	2	11	2	4	0	5	0	4	0	0	0	1	0	1.00	1	.200	.360	.550	3B	6	5	4	0	0	1.000
World Series		Batting																							Fielding						
Year Tm	Age	G	AB	H	2B	3B	HR	TB	R	RBI	GW	TBB	IBB	SO	HBP	SH	SF	SB	CS	SB%	GDP	Avg	OBP	SLG	Pos	G	PO	A	E	DP	FPct
1993 Phi	27	6	23	6	1	0	0	7	5	2	0	6	0	5	0	0	0	0	0	—	1	.261	.414	.304	3B	6	9	9	0	0	1.000
Postseason Totals		12	43	10	2	0	2	18	7	6	0	11	0	9	0	0	0	1	0	1.00	2	.233	.389	.419	3B	12	14	13	0	0	1.000

CHARLIE HOLLOCHER—Charles Jacob Hollocher—Bats: Left; Throws: Right

Ht: 5'7"; Wt: 154 lbs; Born: 6/11/1896 in St. Louis, Missouri; Debut: 4/16/1918; Died: 8/14/1940

World Series		Batting																							Fielding						
Year Tm	Age	G	AB	H	2B	3B	HR	TB	R	RBI	GW	TBB	IBB	SO	HBP	SH	SF	SB	CS	SB%	GDP	Avg	OBP	SLG	Pos	G	PO	A	E	DP	FPct
1918 ChN	22	6	21	4	0	1	0	6	2	1	0	1	0	1	0	2	0	1	0	1.00	0	.190	.227	.286	SS	6	11	17	1	6	.966

WATTIE HOLM—Roscoe Albert Holm—Bats: Right; Throws: Right

Ht: 5'9"; Wt: 160 lbs; Born: 12/28/1901 in Peterson, Iowa; Debut: 4/15/1924; Died: 5/19/1950

World Series		Batting																							Fielding						
Year Tm	Age	G	AB	H	2B	3B	HR	TB	R	RBI	GW	TBB	IBB	SO	HBP	SH	SF	SB	CS	SB%	GDP	Avg	OBP	SLG	Pos	G	PO	A	E	DP	FPct
1926 StL	24	5	16	2	0	0	0	2	1	1	0	1	0	2	0	0	0	0	0	—	1	.125	.176	.125	OF	4	7	0	0	0	1.000
1928 StL	26	3	6	1	0	0	0	1	0	1	0	0	0	1	0	0	0	0	0	—	0	.167	.167	.167	OF	1	4	0	0	0	1.000
WS Totals		8	22	3	0	0	0	3	1	2	0	1	0	3	0	0	0	0	0	—	1	.136	.174	.136	OF	5	11	0	0	0	1.000

DARREN HOLMES—Darren Lee Holmes—Throws: Right; Bats: Right

Ht: 6'0"; Wt: 200 lbs; Born: 4/25/1966 in Asheville, North Carolina; Debut: 9/1/1990

Division Series		Pitching																										
Year Tm	Age	G	GS	CG	GF	IP	BFP	H	R	ER	HR	SH	SF	HB	TBB	IBB	SO	WP	Bk	W	L	Pct	ShO	Sv-Op	Hld	OAvg	OOBP	ERA
1995 Col	29	3	0	0	1	1.2	12	6	2	0	0	0	0	0	0	0	2	0	0	1	0	1.000	0	0- 1	0	.500	.500	0.00

Division Series		Batting																							Fielding						
Year Tm	Age	G	AB	H	2B	3B	HR	TB	R	RBI	GW	TBB	IBB	SO	HBP	SH	SF	SB	CS	SB%	GDP	Avg	OBP	SLG	Pos	G	PO	A	E	DP	FPct
1995 Col	29	3	0	0	0	0	0	0	0	0	0	0	0	0	0	0	0	0	0	—	0	—	—	—	P	3	0	0	0	0	—

TOMMY HOLMES—Thomas Francis Holmes—Nickname: Kelly—Bats: Left; Throws: Left

Ht: 5'10"; Wt: 180 lbs; Born: 3/29/1917 in Brooklyn, New York; Debut: 4/14/1942

World Series		Batting																							Fielding						
Year Tm	Age	G	AB	H	2B	3B	HR	TB	R	RBI	GW	TBB	IBB	SO	HBP	SH	SF	SB	CS	SB%	GDP	Avg	OBP	SLG	Pos	G	PO	A	E	DP	FPct
1948 Bos	31	6	26	5	0	0	0	5	3	1	1	0	0	0	0	0	0	0	0	—	0	.192	.192	.192	OF	6	10	2	0	1	1.000
1952 Bro	35	3	1	0	0	0	0	0	0	0	0	0	0	0	0	0	0	0	0	—	0	.000	.000	.000	OF	3	2	0	0	0	1.000
WS Totals		9	27	5	0	0	0	5	3	1	1	0	0	0	0	0	0	0	0	—	0	.185	.185	.185	OF	9	12	2	0	1	1.000

JIM HOLT—James William Holt—Bats: Left; Throws: Right

Ht: 6'0"; Wt: 180 lbs; Born: 5/27/1944 in Graham, North Carolina; Debut: 4/17/1968

LCS		Batting																							Fielding						
Year Tm	Age	G	AB	H	2B	3B	HR	TB	R	RBI	GW	TBB	IBB	SO	HBP	SH	SF	SB	CS	SB%	GDP	Avg	OBP	SLG	Pos	G	PO	A	E	DP	FPct
1970 Min	26	3	5	0	0	0	0	0	0	0	0	0	0	2	0	0	0	0	0	—	0	.000	.000	.000	OF	3	3	0	1	0	.750
1974 Oak	30	2	0	0	0	0	0	0	0	0	0	1	1	0	0	0	0	0	0	—	0	—	1.000	—	1B	1	1	0	0	0	1.000
1975 Oak	31	3	3	1	1	0	0	2	0	0	0	0	0	0	0	0	0	0	0	—	0	.333	.333	.667	1B	1	1	2	0	0	1.000
LCS Totals		8	8	1	1	0	0	2	0	0	0	1	1	2	0	0	0	0	0	—	0	.125	.222	.250	OF	3	3	0	1	0	.750
World Series		Batting																							Fielding						
Year Tm	Age	G	AB	H	2B	3B	HR	TB	R	RBI	GW	TBB	IBB	SO	HBP	SH	SF	SB	CS	SB%	GDP	Avg	OBP	SLG	Pos	G	PO	A	E	DP	FPct
1974 Oak	30	4	3	2	0	0	0	2	0	2	1	0	0	0	0	0	0	0	0	—	0	.667	.667	.667	1B	1	1	0	0	1	1.000
Postseason Totals		12	11	3	1	0	0	4	0	2	1	1	1	2	0	0	0	0	0	—	0	.273	.333	.364	1B	3	3	2	0	1	1.000

BRIAN HOLTON—Brian John Holton—Throws: Right; Bats: Right

Ht: 6'2"; Wt: 190 lbs; Born: 11/29/1959 in McKeesport, Pennsylvania; Debut: 9/9/1985

LCS		Pitching																										
Year Tm	Age	G	GS	CG	GF	IP	BFP	H	R	ER	HR	SH	SF	HB	TBB	IBB	SO	WP	Bk	W	L	Pct	ShO	Sv-Op	Hld	OAvg	OOBP	ERA
1988 LA	28	3	0	0	1	4.0	13	2	1	1	0	0	0	0	1	0	2	0	0	0	0	—	0	1- 1	0	.167	.231	2.25
World Series		Pitching																										
Year Tm	Age	G	GS	CG	GF	IP	BFP	H	R	ER	HR	SH	SF	HB	TBB	IBB	SO	WP	Bk	W	L	Pct	ShO	Sv-Op	Hld	OAvg	OOBP	ERA
1988 LA	28	1	0	0	0	2.0	7	0	0	0	0	0	0	0	1	0	0	0	0	0	0	—	0	0- 0	0	.000	.143	0.00
Postseason Totals		4	0	0	1	6.0	40	2	1	1	0	0	0	0	2	0	2	0	0	0	0	—	0	1-1	0	.111	.200	1.50

LCS		Batting																							Fielding						
Year Tm	Age	G	AB	H	2B	3B	HR	TB	R	RBI	GW	TBB	IBB	SO	HBP	SH	SF	SB	CS	SB%	GDP	Avg	OBP	SLG	Pos	G	PO	A	E	DP	FPct
1988 LA	28	3	1	1	0	0	0	1	1	0	0	0	0	0	0	0	0	0	0	—	0	1.000	1.000	1.000	P	3	0	1	0	0	1.000
World Series		Batting																							Fielding						
Year Tm	Age	G	AB	H	2B	3B	HR	TB	R	RBI	GW	TBB	IBB	SO	HBP	SH	SF	SB	CS	SB%	GDP	Avg	OBP	SLG	Pos	G	PO	A	E	DP	FPct
1988 LA	28	1	0	0	0	0	0	0	0	0	0	0	0	0	0	0	0	0	0	—	0	—	—	—	P	1	0	1	0	0	1.000
Postseason Totals		4	1	1	0	0	0	1	1	0	0	0	0	0	0	0	0	0	0	—	0	1.000	1.000	1.000	P	4	0	2	0	0	1.000

KEN HOLTZMAN—Kenneth Dale Holtzman—Throws: Left; Bats: Right

Ht: 6'2"; Wt: 175 lbs; Born: 11/3/1945 in St. Louis, Missouri; Debut: 9/4/1965

LCS		Pitching																										
Year Tm	Age	G	GS	CG	GF	IP	BFP	H	R	ER	HR	SH	SF	HB	TBB	IBB	SO	WP	Bk	W	L	Pct	ShO	Sv-Op	Hld	OAvg	OOBP	ERA
1972 Oak	26	1	1	0	0	4.0	17	4	2	2	0	0	0	0	2	0	2	0	0	0	1	.000	0	0- 0	0	.267	.353	4.50
1973 Oak	27	1	1	1	0	11.0	38	3	1	1	1	0	0	0	1	0	7	0	0	1	0	1.000	0	0- 0	0	.081	.105	0.82
1974 Oak	28	1	1	1	0	9.0	32	5	0	0	0	0	0	0	2	0	3	0	0	1	0	1.000	1	0- 0	0	.167	.219	0.00
1975 Oak	29	2	2	0	0	11.0	48	12	8	5	0	1	0	0	1	0	7	0	0	0	2	.000	0	0- 0	0	.261	.277	4.09
LCS Totals		5	5	2	0	35.0	270	24	11	8	1	1	0	0	6	0	19	0	0	2	3	.400	1	0-0	0	.188	.224	2.06
World Series		Pitching																										
Year Tm	Age	G	GS	CG	GF	IP	BFP	H	R	ER	HR	SH	SF	HB	TBB	IBB	SO	WP	Bk	W	L	Pct	ShO	Sv-Op	Hld	OAvg	OOBP	ERA
1972 Oak	26	3	2	0	0	12.2	51	11	3	3	0	1	0	0	3	1	4	0	0	1	0	1.000	0	0- 0	0	.234	.280	2.13
1973 Oak	27	3	3	0	0	10.2	48	13	5	5	1	1	0	0	5	0	6	0	0	2	1	.667	0	0- 0	0	.310	.383	4.22
1974 Oak	28	2	2	0	0	12.0	52	13	3	2	0	1	0	0	4	0	10	1	0	1	0	1.000	0	0- 0	0	.277	.333	1.50
WS Totals		8	7	0	0	35.1	302	37	11	10	1	3	0	0	12	1	20	1	0	4	1	.800	0	0-0	0	.272	.331	2.55
Postseason Totals		13	12	2	0	70.1	572	61	22	18	2	4	0	0	18	1	39	1	0	6	4	.600	1	0-0	0	.231	.280	2.30

LCS		Batting																							Fielding						
Year Tm	Age	G	AB	H	2B	3B	HR	TB	R	RBI	GW	TBB	IBB	SO	HBP	SH	SF	SB	CS	SB%	GDP	Avg	OBP	SLG	Pos	G	PO	A	E	DP	FPct
1972 Oak	26	1	1	0	0	0	0	0	0	0	0	0	0	1	0	0	0	0	0	—	0	.000	.000	.000	P	1	0	1	0	0	1.000
1973 Oak	27	1	0	0	0	0	0	0	0	0	0	0	0	0	0	0	0	0	0	—	0	—	—	—	P	1	1	2	0	1	1.000
1974 Oak	28	1	0	0	0	0	0	0	0	0	0	0	0	0	0	0	0	0	0	—	0	—	—	—	P	1	0	1	0	0	1.000
1975 Oak	29	2	0	0	0	0	0	0	0	0	0	0	0	0	0	0	0	0	0	—	0	—	—	—	P	2	1	1	0	0	1.000
LCS Totals		5	1	0	0	0	0	0	0	0	0	0	0	1	0	0	0	0	0	—	0	.000	.000	.000	P	5	2	5	0	1	1.000
World Series		Batting																							Fielding						
Year Tm	Age	G	AB	H	2B	3B	HR	TB	R	RBI	GW	TBB	IBB	SO	HBP	SH	SF	SB	CS	SB%	GDP	Avg	OBP	SLG	Pos	G	PO	A	E	DP	FPct
1972 Oak	26	3	5	0	0	0	0	0	0	0	0	0	0	0	0	0	0	0	0	—	0	.000	.000	.000	P	3	0	3	1	1	.750
1973 Oak	27	3	3	2	2	0	0	4	2	0	0	0	0	0	0	0	0	0	0	—	0	.667	.667	1.333	P	3	1	3	0	1	1.000
1974 Oak	28	2	4	2	1	0	1	6	2	1	0	1	0	1	0	0	0	0	0	—	0	.500	.600	1.500	P	2	0	3	0	0	1.000
WS Totals		8	12	4	3	0	1	10	4	1	0	1	0	1	0	0	0	0	0	—	0	.333	.385	.833	P	8	1	9	1	2	.909
Postseason Totals		13	13	4	3	0	1	10	4	1	0	1	0	2	0	0	0	0	0	—	0	.308	.357	.769	P	13	3	14	1	3	.944

RICK HONEYCUTT—Frederick Wayne Honeycutt—Throws: Left; Bats: Left

Ht: 6'1"; Wt: 185 lbs; Born: 6/29/1954 in Chattanooga, Tennessee; Debut: 8/24/1977

Division Series		Pitching																										
Year Tm	Age	G	GS	CG	GF	IP	BFP	H	R	ER	HR	SH	SF	HB	TBB	IBB	SO	WP	Bk	W	L	Pct	ShO	Sv-Op	Hld	OAvg	OOBP	ERA
1996 StL	42	3	0	0	0	2.2	12	3	1	1	1	1	0	0	1	1	2	0	0	1	0	1.000	0	0- 2	1	.300	.364	3.38

LCS Pitching

Year Tm	Age	G	GS	CG	GF	IP	BFP	H	R	ER	HR	SH	SF	HB	TBB	IBB	SO	WP	Bk	W	L	Pct	ShO	Sv-Op	Hld	OAvg	OOBP	ERA
1983 LA	29	2	0	0	0	1.2	9	4	4	4	1	0	0	0	0	0	2	0	0	0	0	—	0	0- 0	0	.444	.444	21.60
1985 LA	31	2	0	0	0	1.1	10	4	2	2	0	0	0	0	2	1	1	0	0	0	0	—	0	0- 0	0	.500	.600	13.50
1988 Oak	34	3	0	0	0	2.0	7	0	0	0	0	0	1	0	2	0	0	0	0	1	0	1.000	0	0- 1	2	.000	.286	0.00
1989 Oak	35	3	0	0	0	1.2	16	6	6	6	0	0	0	0	5	0	1	1	0	0	0	—	0	0- 0	1	.545	.688	32.40
1990 Oak	36	3	0	0	1	1.2	4	0	0	0	0	0	0	0	0	0	0	0	0	0	0	—	0	1- 1	2	.000	.000	0.00
1992 Oak	38	2	0	0	0	2.0	6	0	0	0	0	0	0	0	0	0	1	0	0	0	0	—	0	0- 0	0	.000	.000	0.00
1996 StL	42	5	0	0	1	4.0	22	5	4	4	2	0	0	0	3	0	3	0	0	0	0	—	0	0- 0	1	.263	.364	9.00
LCS Totals		20	0	0	2	14.1	148	19	16	16	3	0	1	0	12	1	8	1	0	1	0	1.000	0	1-2	6	.311	.419	10.05

World Series Pitching

Year Tm	Age	G	GS	CG	GF	IP	BFP	H	R	ER	HR	SH	SF	HB	TBB	IBB	SO	WP	Bk	W	L	Pct	ShO	Sv-Op	Hld	OAvg	OOBP	ERA
1988 Oak	34	3	0	0	2	3.1	10	0	0	0	0	0	0	0	0	0	5	0	0	1	0	1.000	0	0- 0	0	.000	.000	0.00
1989 Oak	35	3	0	0	0	2.2	11	4	2	2	0	0	0	0	0	0	2	0	0	0	0	—	0	0- 0	0	.364	.364	6.75
1990 Oak	36	1	0	0	0	1.2	8	2	0	0	0	0	0	0	1	1	0	0	0	0	0	—	0	0- 1	0	.286	.375	0.00
WS Totals		7	0	0	2	7.2	58	6	2	2	0	0	0	0	1	1	7	0	0	1	0	1.000	0	0-1	0	.214	.241	2.35
Postseason Totals		30	0	0	4	24.2	230	28	19	19	4	1	1	0	14	3	17	1	0	3	0	1.000	0	1-5	7	.283	.368	6.93

Division Series Batting / Fielding

Year Tm	Age	G	AB	H	2B	3B	HR	TB	R	RBI	GW	TBB	IBB	SO	HBP	SH	SF	SB	CS	SB%	GDP	Avg	OBP	SLG	Pos	G	PO	A	E	DP	FPct
1996 StL	42	3	1	0	0	0	0	0	0	0	0	0	0	1	0	0	0	0	0	—	0	.000	.000	.000	P	3	0	1	0	0	1.000

LCS Batting / Fielding

Year Tm	Age	G	AB	H	2B	3B	HR	TB	R	RBI	GW	TBB	IBB	SO	HBP	SH	SF	SB	CS	SB%	GDP	Avg	OBP	SLG	Pos	G	PO	A	E	DP	FPct
1983 LA	29	2	0	0	0	0	0	0	0	0	0	0	0	0	0	0	0	0	0	—	0	—	—	—	P	2	1	0	0	0	1.000
1985 LA	31	2	0	0	0	0	0	0	0	0	0	0	0	0	0	0	0	0	0	—	0	—	—	—	P	2	0	1	0	0	1.000
1988 Oak	34	3	0	0	0	0	0	0	0	0	0	0	0	0	0	0	0	0	0	—	0	—	—	—	P	3	0	0	0	0	—
1989 Oak	35	3	0	0	0	0	0	0	0	0	0	0	0	0	0	0	0	0	0	—	0	—	—	—	P	3	0	0	0	0	—
1990 Oak	36	3	0	0	0	0	0	0	0	0	0	0	0	0	0	0	0	0	0	—	0	—	—	—	P	3	0	1	0	0	1.000
1992 Oak	38	2	0	0	0	0	0	0	0	0	0	0	0	0	0	0	0	0	0	—	0	—	—	—	P	2	0	0	0	0	—
1996 StL	42	5	0	0	0	0	0	0	0	0	0	0	0	0	0	0	0	0	0	—	0	—	—	—	P	5	0	0	0	0	—
LCS Totals		20	0	0	0	0	0	0	0	0	0	0	0	0	0	0	0	0	0	—	0	—	—	—	P	20	1	2	0	0	1.000

World Series Batting / Fielding

Year Tm	Age	G	AB	H	2B	3B	HR	TB	R	RBI	GW	TBB	IBB	SO	HBP	SH	SF	SB	CS	SB%	GDP	Avg	OBP	SLG	Pos	G	PO	A	E	DP	FPct
1988 Oak	34	3	0	0	0	0	0	0	0	0	0	0	0	0	0	0	0	0	0	—	0	—	—	—	P	3	0	0	0	0	—
1989 Oak	35	3	0	0	0	0	0	0	0	0	0	0	0	0	0	0	0	0	0	—	0	—	—	—	P	3	0	0	0	0	—
1990 Oak	36	1	0	0	0	0	0	0	0	0	0	0	0	0	0	0	0	0	0	—	0	—	—	—	P	1	0	0	0	0	—
WS Totals		7	0	0	0	0	0	0	0	0	0	0	0	0	0	0	0	0	0	—	0	—	—	—	P	7	0	0	0	0	—
Postseason Totals		30	1	0	0	0	0	0	0	0	0	0	0	1	0	0	0	0	0	—	0	.000	.000	.000	P	30	1	3	0	0	1.000

DON HOOD—Donald Harris Hood—Throws: Left; Bats: Left

Ht: 6'2"; Wt: 180 lbs; Born: 10/16/1949 in Florence, South Carolina; Debut: 7/16/1973

LCS Batting / Fielding

Year Tm	Age	G	AB	H	2B	3B	HR	TB	R	RBI	GW	TBB	IBB	SO	HBP	SH	SF	SB	CS	SB%	GDP	Avg	OBP	SLG	Pos	G	PO	A	E	DP	FPct
1973 Bal	23	1	0	0	0	0	0	0	0	0	0	0	0	0	0	0	0	0	0	—	0	—	—	—	—						

HARRY HOOPER (HOF 1971-V)—Harry Bartholomew Hooper—Bats: Left; Throws: Right

Ht: 5'10"; Wt: 168 lbs; Born: 8/24/1887 in Bell Station, California; Debut: 4/16/1909; Died: 12/18/1974

World Series Batting / Fielding

Year Tm	Age	G	AB	H	2B	3B	HR	TB	R	RBI	GW	TBB	IBB	SO	HBP	SH	SF	SB	CS	SB%	GDP	Avg	OBP	SLG	Pos	G	PO	A	E	DP	FPct
1912 Bos	25	8	31	9	2	1	0	13	3	2	0	4	0	4	0	1	1	2	1	.67	0	.290	.361	.419	OF	8	16	2	0	1	1.000
1915 Bos	28	5	20	7	0	0	2	13	4	3	2	2	0	4	1	0	0	0	0	—	0	.350	.435	.650	OF	5	8	0	1	0	.889
1916 Bos	29	5	21	7	1	1	0	10	6	1	0	3	0	1	0	0	0	1	2	.33	0	.333	.417	.476	OF	5	8	2	0	1	1.000
1918 Bos	31	6	20	4	0	0	0	4	0	0	0	2	0	2	0	2	0	0	2	.00	0	.200	.273	.200	OF	6	11	0	0	0	1.000
WS Totals		24	92	27	3	2	2	40	13	6	2	11	0	11	1	3	1	3	5	.38	0	.293	.371	.435	OF	24	43	4	1	2	.979

BURT HOOTON—Burt Carlton Hooton—Nickname: Happy—Throws: Right; Bats: Right

Ht: 6'1"; Wt: 210 lbs; Born: 2/7/1950 in Greenville, Texas; Debut: 6/17/1971

Division Series Pitching

Year Tm	Age	G	GS	CG	GF	IP	BFP	H	R	ER	HR	SH	SF	HB	TBB	IBB	SO	WP	Bk	W	L	Pct	ShO	Sv-Op	Hld	OAvg	OOBP	ERA
1981 LA	31	1	1	0	0	7.0	25	3	1	1	1	0	0	0	3	0	2	0	0	1	0	1.000	0	0- 0	0	.136	.240	1.29

LCS Pitching

Year Tm	Age	G	GS	CG	GF	IP	BFP	H	R	ER	HR	SH	SF	HB	TBB	IBB	SO	WP	Bk	W	L	Pct	ShO	Sv-Op	Hld	OAvg	OOBP	ERA
1977 LA	27	1	1	0	0	1.2	11	2	3	3	0	0	0	0	4	0	1	0	0	0	0	—	0	0- 0	0	.286	.545	16.20
1978 LA	28	1	1	0	0	4.2	23	10	4	4	0	0	1	0	0	0	5	0	0	0	0	—	0	0- 0	0	.455	.435	7.71
1981 LA	31	2	2	0	0	14.2	59	11	1	0	0	1	0	0	6	1	7	0	0	2	0	1.000	0	0- 0	0	.212	.293	0.00
LCS Totals		4	4	0	0	21.0	186	23	8	7	0	1	1	0	10	1	13	0	0	2	0	1.000	0	0-0	0	.284	.359	3.00

World Series Pitching

Year Tm	Age	G	GS	CG	GF	IP	BFP	H	R	ER	HR	SH	SF	HB	TBB	IBB	SO	WP	Bk	W	L	Pct	ShO	Sv-Op	Hld	OAvg	OOBP	ERA
1977 LA	27	2	2	1	0	12.0	45	8	5	5	2	0	0	0	2	0	9	0	0	1	1	.500	0	0- 0	0	.186	.222	3.75
1978 LA	28	2	2	0	0	8.1	42	13	7	6	0	0	0	1	3	1	6	1	0	1	1	.500	0	0- 0	0	.342	.405	6.48
1981 LA	31	2	2	0	0	11.1	52	8	3	2	1	1	0	0	9	1	3	0	0	1	1	.500	0	0- 0	0	.190	.333	1.59
WS Totals		6	6	1	0	31.2	278	29	15	13	3	1	0	1	14	2	18	1	0	3	3	.500	0	0-0	0	.236	.319	3.69
Postseason Totals		11	11	1	0	59.2	514	55	24	21	4	2	1	1	27	3	33	1	0	6	3	.667	0	0-0	0	.243	.325	3.17

Division Series Batting / Fielding

Year Tm	Age	G	AB	H	2B	3B	HR	TB	R	RBI	GW	TBB	IBB	SO	HBP	SH	SF	SB	CS	SB%	GDP	Avg	OBP	SLG	Pos	G	PO	A	E	DP	FPct
1981 LA	31	1	3	0	0	0	0	0	0	0	0	0	0	0	0	0	0	0	0	—	0	.000	.000	.000	P	1	1	0	0	0	1.000

LCS Batting / Fielding

Year Tm	Age	G	AB	H	2B	3B	HR	TB	R	RBI	GW	TBB	IBB	SO	HBP	SH	SF	SB	CS	SB%	GDP	Avg	OBP	SLG	Pos	G	PO	A	E	DP	FPct
1977 LA	27	1	1	1	1	0	0	2	0	0	0	0	0	0	0	0	0	0	0	—	0	1.000	1.000	2.000	P	1	0	1	0	0	1.000
1978 LA	28	1	2	0	0	0	0	0	0	0	0	0	0	1	0	0	0	0	0	—	0	.000	.000	.000	P	1	1	0	0	0	1.000
1981 LA	31	2	5	0	0	0	0	0	0	0	0	0	0	2	0	1	0	0	0	—	0	.000	.000	.000	P	2	0	1	0	0	1.000
LCS Totals		4	8	1	1	0	0	2	0	0	0	0	0	3	0	1	0	0	0	—	0	.125	.125	.250	P	4	1	2	0	0	1.000

World Series Batting / Fielding

Year Tm	Age	G	AB	H	2B	3B	HR	TB	R	RBI	GW	TBB	IBB	SO	HBP	SH	SF	SB	CS	SB%	GDP	Avg	OBP	SLG	Pos	G	PO	A	E	DP	FPct
1977 LA	27	2	5	0	0	0	0	0	0	0	0	0	0	2	0	0	0	0	0	—	0	.000	.000	.000	P	2	0	0	0	0	—
1978 LA	28	2	0	0	0	0	0	0	0	0	0	0	0	0	0	0	0	0	0	—	0	—	—	—	P	2	1	0	0	0	1.000
1981 LA	31	2	4	0	0	0	0	0	1	0	0	1	0	3	0	0	0	0	0	—	0	.000	.200	.000	P	2	1	0	0	0	1.000
WS Totals		6	9	0	0	0	0	0	1	0	0	1	0	5	0	0	0	0	0	—	0	.000	.100	.000	P	6	2	0	0	0	1.000
Postseason Totals		11	20	1	1	0	0	2	1	0	0	1	0	8	0	1	0	0	0	—	0	.050	.095	.100	P	11	4	2	0	0	1.000

JOE HOOVER—Robert Joseph Hoover—Bats: Right; Throws: Right

Ht: 5'11"; Wt: 175 lbs; Born: 4/15/1915 in Brawley, California; Debut: 4/21/1943; Died: 9/2/1965

World Series Batting / Fielding

Year Tm	Age	G	AB	H	2B	3B	HR	TB	R	RBI	GW	TBB	IBB	SO	HBP	SH	SF	SB	CS	SB%	GDP	Avg	OBP	SLG	Pos	G	PO	A	E	DP	FPct
1945 Det	30	1	3	1	0	0	0	1	1	1	0	0	0	0	0	0	0	0	1	.00	0	.333	.333	.333	SS	1	1	1	0	1	1.000

DON HOPKINS—Donald Hopkins—Bats: Left; Throws: Right

Ht: 6'0"; Wt: 175 lbs; Born: 1/9/1952 in West Point, Mississippi; Debut: 4/8/1975

LCS Batting / Fielding

Year Tm	Age	G	AB	H	2B	3B	HR	TB	R	RBI	GW	TBB	IBB	SO	HBP	SH	SF	SB	CS	SB%	GDP	Avg	OBP	SLG	Pos	G	PO	A	E	DP	FPct
1975 Oak	23	1	0	0	0	0	0	0	0	0	0	0	0	0	0	0	0	0	0	—	0	—	—	—	—						

JOHNNY HOPP—John Leonard Hopp—Nickname: Hippity—Bats: Left; Throws: Left

Ht: 5'10"; Wt: 170 lbs; Born: 7/18/1916 in Hastings, Nebraska; Debut: 9/18/1939

World Series		Batting																							Fielding						
Year Tm	Age	G	AB	H	2B	3B	HR	TB	R	RBI	GW	TBB	IBB	SO	HBP	SH	SF	SB	CS	SB%	GDP	Avg	OBP	SLG	Pos	G	PO	A	E	DP	FPct
1942 StL	26	5	17	3	0	0	0	3	3	0	0	1	0	1	0	2	0	0	0	—	0	.176	.222	.176	1B	5	46	3	1	2	.980
1943 StL	27	1	4	0	0	0	0	0	0	0	0	0	0	1	0	0	0	0	0	—	0	.000	.000	.000	OF	1	1	0	0	0	1.000
1944 StL	28	6	27	5	0	0	0	5	2	0	0	0	0	8	0	0	0	0	0	—	0	.185	.185	.185	OF	6	14	0	0	0	1.000
1950 NYA	34	3	2	0	0	0	0	0	0	0	0	0	0	0	0	0	0	0	0	—	0	.000	.000	.000	1B	3	7	1	0	2	1.000
1951 NYA	35	1	0	0	0	0	0	0	0	0	0	1	0	0	0	0	0	0	0	—	0	—	1.000	—	—						
WS Totals		16	50	8	0	0	0	8	5	0	0	2	0	10	0	2	0	0	0	—	0	.160	.192	.160	1B	8	53	4	1	4	.983

JOE HORLEN—Joel Edward Horlen—Throws: Right; Bats: Right

Ht: 6'0"; Wt: 170 lbs; Born: 8/14/1937 in San Antonio, Texas; Debut: 9/4/1961

LCS		Pitching																									
Year Tm	Age	G	GS	CG	GF	IP	BFP	H	R	ER	HR	SH	SF	HB	TBB	IBB	SO	WP	Bk	W	L	Pct	ShO	Sv-Op	Hld	OAvg	OOBP	ERA
1972 Oak	35	1	0	0	0	0.0	2	0	1	1	0	0	0	0	1	0	0	1	0	0	1	.000	0	0-0	0	.000	.500	—
World Series		Pitching																										
Year Tm	Age	G	GS	CG	GF	IP	BFP	H	R	ER	HR	SH	SF	HB	TBB	IBB	SO	WP	Bk	W	L	Pct	ShO	Sv-Op	Hld	OAvg	OOBP	ERA
1972 Oak	35	1	0	0	1	1.1	8	2	1	1	0	0	0	0	2	1	1	1	0	0	0	—	0	0-0	0	.333	.500	6.75
Postseason Totals		2	0	0	1	1.1	20	2	2	2	0	0	0	0	3	1	1	2	0	0	1	.000	0	0-0	0	.286	.500	13.50

LCS		Batting																							Fielding						
Year Tm	Age	G	AB	H	2B	3B	HR	TB	R	RBI	GW	TBB	IBB	SO	HBP	SH	SF	SB	CS	SB%	GDP	Avg	OBP	SLG	Pos	G	PO	A	E	DP	FPct
1972 Oak	35	1	0	0	0	0	0	0	0	0	0	0	0	0	0	0	0	0	0	—	0	—	—	—	P	1	0	0	0	0	—
World Series		Batting																							Fielding						
Year Tm	Age	G	AB	H	2B	3B	HR	TB	R	RBI	GW	TBB	IBB	SO	HBP	SH	SF	SB	CS	SB%	GDP	Avg	OBP	SLG	Pos	G	PO	A	E	DP	FPct
1972 Oak	35	1	0	0	0	0	0	0	0	0	0	0	0	0	0	0	0	0	0	—	0	—	—	—	P	1	1	0	0	0	1.000
Postseason Totals		2	0	0	0	0	0	0	0	0	0	0	0	0	0	0	0	0	0	—	0	—	—	—	P	2	1	0	0	0	1.000

BOB HORNER—James Robert Horner—Bats: Right; Throws: Right

Ht: 6'1"; Wt: 195 lbs; Born: 8/6/1957 in Junction City, Kansas; Debut: 6/16/1978

LCS		Batting																							Fielding						
Year Tm	Age	G	AB	H	2B	3B	HR	TB	R	RBI	GW	TBB	IBB	SO	HBP	SH	SF	SB	CS	SB%	GDP	Avg	OBP	SLG	Pos	G	PO	A	E	DP	FPct
1982 Atl	25	3	11	1	0	0	0	1	0	0	0	0	0	2	0	0	0	0	0	—	0	.091	.091	.091	3B	3	2	5	0	0	1.000

ROGERS HORNSBY (HOF 1942-W)—Nickname: Rajah—Bats: Right; Throws: Right

Ht: 5'11"; Wt: 175 lbs; Born: 4/27/1896 in Winters, Texas; Debut: 9/10/1915; Died: 1/5/1963

World Series		Batting																							Fielding						
Year Tm	Age	G	AB	H	2B	3B	HR	TB	R	RBI	GW	TBB	IBB	SO	HBP	SH	SF	SB	CS	SB%	GDP	Avg	OBP	SLG	Pos	G	PO	A	E	DP	FPct
1926 StL	30	7	28	7	1	0	0	8	2	4	0	2	0	2	0	1	0	1	0	1.00	1	.250	.300	.286	2B	7	16	21	0	5	1.000
1929 ChN-*M*	33	5	21	5	1	1	0	8	4	1	0	1	0	8	0	0	0	0	0	—	0	.238	.273	.381	2B	5	8	11	1	4	.950
WS Totals		12	49	12	2	1	0	16	6	5	0	3	0	10	0	1	0	1	0	1.00	1	.245	.288	.327	2B	12	24	32	1	9	.982

RICKY HORTON—Ricky Neal Horton—Throws: Left; Bats: Left

Ht: 6'2"; Wt: 195 lbs; Born: 7/30/1959 in Poughkeepsie, New York; Debut: 4/7/1984

LCS		Pitching																										
Year Tm	Age	G	GS	CG	GF	IP	BFP	H	R	ER	HR	SH	SF	HB	TBB	IBB	SO	WP	Bk	W	L	Pct	ShO	Sv-Op	Hld	OAvg	OOBP	ERA
1985 StL	26	3	0	0	0	3.0	14	4	3	3	0	0	0	0	2	1	1	0	0	0	0	—	0	0-0	1	.333	.429	9.00
1987 StL	28	1	0	0	0	3.0	10	2	0	0	0	0	1	0	0	0	2	0	0	0	0	—	0	0-0	0	.222	.200	0.00
1988 LA	29	4	0	0	1	4.1	18	4	0	0	0	0	0	0	2	0	3	0	0	0	0	—	0	0-0	1	.250	.333	0.00
LCS Totals		8	0	0	1	10.1	84	10	3	3	0	0	1	0	4	1	6	0	0	0	0	—	0	0-0	2	.270	.333	2.61
World Series		Pitching																										
Year Tm	Age	G	GS	CG	GF	IP	BFP	H	R	ER	HR	SH	SF	HB	TBB	IBB	SO	WP	Bk	W	L	Pct	ShO	Sv-Op	Hld	OAvg	OOBP	ERA
1985 StL	26	3	0	0	0	4.0	21	4	3	3	0	0	0	0	5	2	5	0	1	0	0	—	0	0-0	0	.250	.429	6.75
1987 StL	28	2	0	0	1	3.0	13	5	2	2	0	0	0	0	0	0	1	0	0	0	0	—	0	0-0	0	.385	.385	6.00
WS Totals		5	0	0	1	7.0	68	9	5	5	0	0	0	0	5	2	6	0	1	0	0	—	0	0-0	0	.310	.412	6.43
Postseason Totals		13	0	0	2	17.1	152	19	8	8	0	0	1	0	9	3	12	0	1	0	0	—	0	0-0	2	.288	.368	4.15

LCS		Batting																							Fielding						
Year Tm	Age	G	AB	H	2B	3B	HR	TB	R	RBI	GW	TBB	IBB	SO	HBP	SH	SF	SB	CS	SB%	GDP	Avg	OBP	SLG	Pos	G	PO	A	E	DP	FPct
1985 StL	26	3	0	0	0	0	0	0	0	0	0	0	0	0	0	0	0	0	0	—	0	—	—	—	P	3	1	2	0	1	1.000
1987 StL	28	1	0	0	0	0	0	0	0	0	0	0	0	0	0	0	0	0	0	—	0	—	—	—	P	1	0	0	0	0	—
1988 LA	29	4	0	0	0	0	0	0	0	0	0	0	0	0	0	0	0	0	0	—	0	—	—	—	P	4	0	1	0	1	1.000
LCS Totals		8	0	0	0	0	0	0	0	0	0	0	0	0	0	0	0	0	0	—	0	—	—	—	P	8	1	3	0	2	1.000
World Series		Batting																							Fielding						
Year Tm	Age	G	AB	H	2B	3B	HR	TB	R	RBI	GW	TBB	IBB	SO	HBP	SH	SF	SB	CS	SB%	GDP	Avg	OBP	SLG	Pos	G	PO	A	E	DP	FPct
1985 StL	26	3	1	0	0	0	0	0	0	0	0	0	0	1	0	0	0	0	0	—	0	.000	.000	.000	P	3	2	0	0	0	1.000
1987 StL	28	2	0	0	0	0	0	0	0	0	0	0	0	0	0	0	0	0	0	—	0	—	—	—	P	2	0	1	0	0	1.000
WS Totals		5	1	0	0	0	0	0	0	0	0	0	0	1	0	0	0	0	0	—	0	.000	.000	.000	P	5	2	1	0	0	1.000
Postseason Totals		13	1	0	0	0	0	0	0	0	0	0	0	1	0	0	0	0	0	—	0	.000	.000	.000	P	13	3	4	0	2	1.000

WILLIE HORTON—William Watterson Horton—Bats: Right; Throws: Right

Ht: 5'11"; Wt: 209 lbs; Born: 10/18/1942 in Arno, Virginia; Debut: 9/10/1963

LCS		Batting																							Fielding						
Year Tm	Age	G	AB	H	2B	3B	HR	TB	R	RBI	GW	TBB	IBB	SO	HBP	SH	SF	SB	CS	SB%	GDP	Avg	OBP	SLG	Pos	G	PO	A	E	DP	FPct
1972 Det	29	5	10	1	0	0	0	1	0	0	0	1	0	3	0	0	0	0	0	—	0	.100	.182	.100	OF	3	7	0	0	0	1.000
World Series		Batting																							Fielding						
Year Tm	Age	G	AB	H	2B	3B	HR	TB	R	RBI	GW	TBB	IBB	SO	HBP	SH	SF	SB	CS	SB%	GDP	Avg	OBP	SLG	Pos	G	PO	A	E	DP	FPct
1968 Det	25	7	23	7	1	1	1	13	6	3	2	5	0	6	1	0	0	0	0	—	1	.304	.448	.565	OF	7	5	1	1	0	.857
Postseason Totals		12	33	8	1	1	1	14	6	3	2	6	0	9	1	0	0	0	0	—	1	.242	.375	.424	OF	10	12	1	1	0	.929

DWAYNE HOSEY—Dwayne Samuel Hosey—Bats: Both; Throws: Right

Ht: 5'10"; Wt: 175 lbs; Born: 3/11/1967 in Sharon, Pennsylvania; Debut: 9/1/1995

Division Series		Batting																							Fielding						
Year Tm	Age	G	AB	H	2B	3B	HR	TB	R	RBI	GW	TBB	IBB	SO	HBP	SH	SF	SB	CS	SB%	GDP	Avg	OBP	SLG	Pos	G	PO	A	E	DP	FPct
1995 Bos	28	3	12	0	0	0	0	0	1	0	0	2	0	3	0	0	0	1	0	1.00	0	.000	.143	.000	OF	3	7	0	0	0	1.000

CHUCK HOSTETLER—Charles Cloyd Hostetler—Bats: Left; Throws: Right

Ht: 6'0"; Wt: 175 lbs; Born: 9/22/1903 in McClellandtown, Pennsylvania; Debut: 4/18/1944; Died: 2/18/1971

World Series		Batting																							Fielding						
Year Tm	Age	G	AB	H	2B	3B	HR	TB	R	RBI	GW	TBB	IBB	SO	HBP	SH	SF	SB	CS	SB%	GDP	Avg	OBP	SLG	Pos	G	PO	A	E	DP	FPct
1945 Det	42	3	3	0	0	0	0	0	0	0	0	0	0	0	0	0	0	0	0	—	0	.000	.000	.000	—						

CHARLIE HOUGH—Charles Oliver Hough—Throws: Right; Bats: Right

Ht: 6'2"; Wt: 190 lbs; Born: 1/5/1948 in Honolulu, Hawaii; Debut: 8/12/1970

LCS		Pitching																										
Year Tm	Age	G	GS	CG	GF	IP	BFP	H	R	ER	HR	SH	SF	HB	TBB	IBB	SO	WP	Bk	W	L	Pct	ShO	Sv-Op	Hld	OAvg	OOBP	ERA
1974 LA	26	1	0	0	0	2.1	11	4	2	2	0	0	0	0	0	0	2	0	0	0	0	—	0	0-0	0	.364	.364	7.71
1977 LA	29	1	0	0	0	2.0	8	2	1	1	0	1	0	0	0	0	3	0	0	0	0	—	0	0-0	0	.286	.286	4.50
1978 LA	30	1	0	0	1	2.0	7	1	1	1	1	0	0	0	0	0	1	0	0	0	0	—	0	0-0	0	.143	.143	4.50
LCS Totals		3	0	0	1	6.1	52	7	4	4	1	1	0	0	0	0	6	0	0	0	0	—	0	0-0	0	.280	.280	5.68
World Series		Pitching																										
Year Tm	Age	G	GS	CG	GF	IP	BFP	H	R	ER	HR	SH	SF	HB	TBB	IBB	SO	WP	Bk	W	L	Pct	ShO	Sv-Op	Hld	OAvg	OOBP	ERA
1974 LA	26	1	0	0	0	2.0	7	0	0	0	0	0	0	0	1	0	4	1	0	0	0	—	0	0-0	0	.000	.143	0.00
1977 LA	29	2	0	0	2	5.0	18	3	1	1	1	0	0	0	0	0	5	0	0	0	0	—	0	0-0	0	.167	.167	1.80
1978 LA	30	2	0	0	2	5.1	29	10	5	5	0	0	0	0	2	0	5	2	0	0	0	—	0	0-0	0	.370	.414	8.44
WS Totals		5	0	0	4	12.1	108	13	6	6	1	0	0	0	3	0	14	3	0	0	0	—	0	0-0	0	.255	.296	4.38
Postseason Totals		8	0	0	5	18.2	160	20	10	10	2	1	0	0	3	0	20	3	0	0	0	—	0	0-0	0	.263	.291	4.82

LCS		Batting																							Fielding						
Year Tm	Age	G	AB	H	2B	3B	HR	TB	R	RBI	GW	TBB	IBB	SO	HBP	SH	SF	SB	CS	SB%	GDP	Avg	OBP	SLG	Pos	G	PO	A	E	DP	FPct
1974 LA	26	1	0	0	0	0	0	0	0	0	0	0	0	0	0	0	0	0	0	—	0	—	—	—	P	1	0	0	1	0	.000
1977 LA	29	1	0	0	0	0	0	0	0	0	0	0	0	0	0	0	0	0	0	—	0	—	—	—	P	1	0	1	0	0	1.000
1978 LA	30	1	0	0	0	0	0	0	0	0	0	0	0	0	0	0	0	0	0	—	0	—	—	—	P	1	1	1	0	0	1.000
LCS Totals		3	0	0	0	0	0	0	0	0	0	0	0	0	0	0	0	0	0	—	0	—	—	—	P	3	1	2	1	0	.750
World Series		Batting																							Fielding						
Year Tm	Age	G	AB	H	2B	3B	HR	TB	R	RBI	GW	TBB	IBB	SO	HBP	SH	SF	SB	CS	SB%	GDP	Avg	OBP	SLG	Pos	G	PO	A	E	DP	FPct
1974 LA	26	1	0	0	0	0	0	0	0	0	0	0	0	0	0	0	0	0	0	—	0	—	—	—	P	1	0	0	0	0	—
1977 LA	29	2	0	0	0	0	0	0	0	0	0	0	0	0	0	0	0	0	0	—	0	—	—	—	P	2	0	0	0	0	—
1978 LA	30	2	0	0	0	0	0	0	0	0	0	0	0	0	0	0	0	0	0	—	0	—	—	—	P	2	1	0	0	0	1.000
WS Totals		5	0	0	0	0	0	0	0	0	0	0	0	0	0	0	0	0	0	—	0	—	—	—	P	5	1	0	0	0	1.000
Postseason Totals		8	0	0	0	0	0	0	0	0	0	0	0	0	0	0	0	0	0	—	0	—	—	—	P	8	2	2	1	0	.800

RALPH HOUK—Ralph George Houk—Nickname: Major—Bats: Right; Throws: Right

Ht: 5'11"; Wt: 193 lbs; Born: 8/9/1919 in Lawrence, Kansas; Debut: 4/26/1947

World Series		Batting																							Fielding						
Year Tm	Age	G	AB	H	2B	3B	HR	TB	R	RBI	GW	TBB	IBB	SO	HBP	SH	SF	SB	CS	SB%	GDP	Avg	OBP	SLG	Pos	G	PO	A	E	DP	FPct
1947 NYA	28	1	1	1	0	0	0	1	0	0	0	0	0	0	0	0	0	0	0	—	0	1.000	1.000	1.000	—						
1952 NYA	33	1	1	0	0	0	0	0	0	0	0	0	0	0	0	0	0	0	0	—	0	.000	.000	.000	—						
WS Totals		2	2	1	0	0	0	1	0	0	0	0	0	0	0	0	0	0	0	—	0	.500	.500	.500	—	0	0	0	0	0	—

ART HOUTTEMAN—Arthur Joseph Houtteman—Throws: Right; Bats: Right

Ht: 6'2"; Wt: 188 lbs; Born: 8/7/1927 in Detroit, Michigan; Debut: 4/29/1945

World Series		Pitching																										
Year Tm	Age	G	GS	CG	GF	IP	BFP	H	R	ER	HR	SH	SF	HB	TBB	IBB	SO	WP	Bk	W	L	Pct	ShO	Sv-Op	Hld	OAvg	OOBP	ERA
1954 Cle	27	1	0	0	0	2.0	9	2	1	1	0	0	0	0	1	1	1	0	0	0	0	—	0	0-0	0	.250	.333	4.50

World Series		Batting																							Fielding						
Year Tm	Age	G	AB	H	2B	3B	HR	TB	R	RBI	GW	TBB	IBB	SO	HBP	SH	SF	SB	CS	SB%	GDP	Avg	OBP	SLG	Pos	G	PO	A	E	DP	FPct
1954 Cle	27	1	0	0	0	0	0	0	0	0	0	0	0	0	0	0	0	0	0	—	0	—	—	—	P	1	0	0	0	0	—

DEL HOWARD—George Elmer Howard—Bats: Left; Throws: Right

Ht: 6'0"; Wt: 180 lbs; Born: 12/24/1877 in Kenney, Illinois; Debut: 4/15/1905; Died: 12/24/1956

World Series		Batting																							Fielding						
Year Tm	Age	G	AB	H	2B	3B	HR	TB	R	RBI	GW	TBB	IBB	SO	HBP	SH	SF	SB	CS	SB%	GDP	Avg	OBP	SLG	Pos	G	PO	A	E	DP	FPct
1907 ChN	29	2	5	1	0	0	0	1	0	0	0	0	0	2	0	0	0	1	0	1.00	0	.200	.200	.200	1B	1	10	1	0	0	1.000
1908 ChN	30	1	1	0	0	0	0	0	0	0	0	0	0	0	0	0	0	0	0	—	0	.000	.000	.000	—						
WS Totals		3	6	1	0	0	0	1	0	0	0	0	0	2	0	0	0	1	0	1.00	0	.167	.167	.167	1B	1	10	1	0	0	1.000

ELSTON HOWARD—Elston Gene Howard—Bats: Right; Throws: Right

Ht: 6'2"; Wt: 196 lbs; Born: 2/23/1929 in St. Louis, Missouri; Debut: 4/14/1955; Died: 12/14/1980

World Series		Batting																							Fielding						
Year Tm	Age	G	AB	H	2B	3B	HR	TB	R	RBI	GW	TBB	IBB	SO	HBP	SH	SF	SB	CS	SB%	GDP	Avg	OBP	SLG	Pos	G	PO	A	E	DP	FPct
1955 NYA	26	7	26	5	0	0	1	8	3	3	0	1	0	8	0	1	0	0	0	—	0	.192	.222	.308	OF	7	11	1	0	0	1.000
1956 NYA	27	1	5	2	1	0	1	6	1	1	0	0	0	0	0	0	0	0	0	—	0	.400	.400	1.200	OF	1	2	0	0	0	1.000
1957 NYA	28	6	11	3	0	0	1	6	2	3	0	1	0	3	0	0	0	0	0	—	1	.273	.333	.545	1B	3	21	1	1	1	.957
1958 NYA	29	6	18	4	0	0	0	4	4	2	1	1	1	4	0	1	0	1	0	1.00	0	.222	.263	.222	OF	5	14	2	0	2	1.000
1960 NYA	31	5	13	6	1	1	1	12	4	4	0	1	0	4	1	0	0	0	0	—	0	.462	.533	.923	C	4	11	0	0	0	1.000
1961 NYA	32	5	20	5	3	0	1	11	5	1	1	2	1	3	0	0	0	0	0	—	2	.250	.318	.550	C	5	31	0	0	0	1.000
1962 NYA	33	6	21	3	1	0	0	4	1	1	0	1	0	4	1	0	0	0	0	—	2	.143	.217	.190	C	6	37	1	0	1	1.000
1963 NYA-*M*	34	4	15	5	0	0	0	5	0	1	0	0	0	3	0	0	0	0	0	—	0	.333	.333	.333	C	4	30	2	0	1	1.000
1964 NYA	35	7	24	7	1	0	0	8	5	2	0	4	2	6	1	0	0	0	0	—	1	.292	.414	.333	C	7	40	2	1	0	.977
1967 Bos	38	7	18	2	0	0	0	2	0	1	0	1	1	2	0	1	0	0	0	—	0	.111	.158	.111	C	7	23	1	0	0	1.000
WS Totals		54	171	42	7	1	5	66	25	19	2	12	5	37	3	3	0	1	0	1.00	6	.246	.306	.386	C	33	172	6	1	2	.994

FRANK HOWARD—Frank Oliver Howard—Nicknames: Hondo, The Capital Punisher—Bats: Right; Throws: Right

Ht: 6'7"; Wt: 255 lbs; Born: 8/8/1936 in Columbus, Ohio; Debut: 9/10/1958

World Series		Batting																							Fielding						
Year Tm	Age	G	AB	H	2B	3B	HR	TB	R	RBI	GW	TBB	IBB	SO	HBP	SH	SF	SB	CS	SB%	GDP	Avg	OBP	SLG	Pos	G	PO	A	E	DP	FPct
1963 LA	27	3	10	3	1	0	1	7	2	1	0	0	0	2	0	0	0	0	0	—	0	.300	.300	.700	OF	3	4	0	0	0	1.000

THOMAS HOWARD—Thomas Sylvester Howard—Bats: Both; Throws: Right

Ht: 6'2"; Wt: 200 lbs; Born: 12/11/1964 in Middletown, Ohio; Debut: 7/3/1990

Division Series		Batting																							Fielding						
Year Tm	Age	G	AB	H	2B	3B	HR	TB	R	RBI	GW	TBB	IBB	SO	HBP	SH	SF	SB	CS	SB%	GDP	Avg	OBP	SLG	Pos	G	PO	A	E	DP	FPct
1995 Cin	30	3	10	1	1	0	0	2	0	0	0	0	0	2	0	0	0	0	0	—	0	.100	.100	.200	OF	3	5	0	0	0	1.000
1997 Hou	32	2	1	0	0	0	0	0	0	0	0	1	0	1	0	0	0	0	0	—	0	.000	.500	.000	—						
DS Totals		5	11	1	1	0	0	2	0	0	0	1	0	3	0	0	0	0	0	—	0	.091	.167	.182	OF	3	5	0	0	0	1.000
LCS		Batting																							Fielding						
Year Tm	Age	G	AB	H	2B	3B	HR	TB	R	RBI	GW	TBB	IBB	SO	HBP	SH	SF	SB	CS	SB%	GDP	Avg	OBP	SLG	Pos	G	PO	A	E	DP	FPct
1995 Cin	30	4	8	2	1	0	0	3	0	1	0	2	0	0	0	0	1	0	1	.00	0	.250	.364	.375	OF	3	2	0	0	0	1.000
Postseason Totals		9	19	3	2	0	0	5	0	1	0	3	0	3	0	0	1	0	1	.00	0	.158	.261	.263	OF	6	7	0	0	0	1.000

ART HOWE—Arthur Henry Howe—Bats: Right; Throws: Right

Ht: 6'2"; Wt: 190 lbs; Born: 12/15/1946 in Pittsburgh, Pennsylvania; Debut: 7/10/1974

Division Series		Batting																							Fielding						
Year Tm	Age	G	AB	H	2B	3B	HR	TB	R	RBI	GW	TBB	IBB	SO	HBP	SH	SF	SB	CS	SB%	GDP	Avg	OBP	SLG	Pos	G	PO	A	E	DP	FPct
1981 Hou	34	5	17	4	0	0	1	7	1	1	0	2	1	1	0	0	0	0	0	—	0	.235	.316	.412	3B	5	5	8	0	0	1.000
LCS		Batting																							Fielding						
Year Tm	Age	G	AB	H	2B	3B	HR	TB	R	RBI	GW	TBB	IBB	SO	HBP	SH	SF	SB	CS	SB%	GDP	Avg	OBP	SLG	Pos	G	PO	A	E	DP	FPct
1974 Pit	27	1	1	0	0	0	0	0	0	0	0	0	0	0	0	0	0	0	0	—	0	.000	.000	.000							
1980 Hou	33	5	15	3	1	1	0	6	0	2	0	2	2	2	0	0	1	0	0	—	0	.200	.278	.400	1B	4	29	3	0	3	1.000
LCS Totals		6	16	3	1	1	0	6	0	2	0	2	2	2	0	0	1	0	0	—	0	.188	.263	.375	1B	4	29	3	0	3	1.000
Postseason Totals		11	33	7	1	1	1	13	1	3	0	4	3	3	0	0	1	0	0	—	0	.212	.289	.394	3B	5	5	8	0	0	1.000

STEVE HOWE—Steven Roy Howe—Throws: Left; Bats: Left

Ht: 6'1"; Wt: 180 lbs; Born: 3/10/1958 in Pontiac, Michigan; Debut: 4/11/1980

Division Series		Pitching																										
Year Tm	Age	G	GS	CG	GF	IP	BFP	H	R	ER	HR	SH	SF	HB	TBB	IBB	SO	WP	Bk	W	L	Pct	ShO	Sv-Op	Hld	OAvg	OOBP	ERA
1981 LA	23	2	0	0	0	2.0	7	1	0	0	0	1	0	0	0	0	2	0	0	0	0	—	0	0-0	1	.167	.167	0.00
1995 NYA	37	2	0	0	1	1.0	6	4	2	2	1	0	0	0	0	0	0	0	0	0	0	—	0	0-0	0	.667	.667	18.00
DS Totals		4	0	0	1	3.0	26	5	2	2	1	1	0	0	0	0	2	0	0	0	0	—	0	0-0	1	.417	.417	6.00
LCS		Pitching																										
Year Tm	Age	G	GS	CG	GF	IP	BFP	H	R	ER	HR	SH	SF	HB	TBB	IBB	SO	WP	Bk	W	L	Pct	ShO	Sv-Op	Hld	OAvg	OOBP	ERA
1981 LA	23	2	0	0	2	2.0	6	1	0	0	0	0	0	0	0	0	2	0	0	0	0	—	0	0-0	0	.167	.167	0.00
World Series		Pitching																										
Year Tm	Age	G	GS	CG	GF	IP	BFP	H	R	ER	HR	SH	SF	HB	TBB	IBB	SO	WP	Bk	W	L	Pct	ShO	Sv-Op	Hld	OAvg	OOBP	ERA
1981 LA	23	3	0	0	2	7.0	30	7	3	3	1	0	0	0	1	0	4	0	0	1	0	1.000	0	1-1	0	.241	.267	3.86
Postseason Totals		9	0	0	5	12.0	98	13	5	5	2	1	0	0	1	0	8	0	0	1	0	1.000	0	1-1	1	.277	.292	3.75

Division Series		Batting																							Fielding						
Year Tm	Age	G	AB	H	2B	3B	HR	TB	R	RBI	GW	TBB	IBB	SO	HBP	SH	SF	SB	CS	SB%	GDP	Avg	OBP	SLG	Pos	G	PO	A	E	DP	FPct
1981 LA	23	2	0	0	0	0	0	0	0	0	0	0	0	0	0	0	0	0	0	—	0	—	—	—	P	2	0	1	0	0	1.000
1995 NYA	37	2	0	0	0	0	0	0	0	0	0	0	0	0	0	0	0	0	0	—	0	—	—	—	P	2	0	0	0	0	—
DS Totals		4	0	0	0	0	0	0	0	0	0	0	0	0	0	0	0	0	0	—	0	—	—	—	P	4	0	1	0	0	1.000
LCS		Batting																							Fielding						
Year Tm	Age	G	AB	H	2B	3B	HR	TB	R	RBI	GW	TBB	IBB	SO	HBP	SH	SF	SB	CS	SB%	GDP	Avg	OBP	SLG	Pos	G	PO	A	E	DP	FPct
1981 LA	23	2	0	0	0	0	0	0	0	0	0	0	0	0	0	0	0	0	0	—	0	—	—	—	P	2	0	0	0	0	—

World Series — Batting / Fielding

Year Tm	Age	G	AB	H	2B	3B	HR	TB	R	RBI	GW	TBB	IBB	SO	HBP	SH	SF	SB	CS	SB%	GDP	Avg	OBP	SLG	Pos	G	PO	A	E	DP	FPct
1981 LA	23	3	2	0	0	0	0	0	0	0	0	0	0	2	0	1	0	0	0	—	0	.000	.000	.000	P	3	0	1	1	0	.500
Postseason Totals		9	2	0	0	0	0	0	0	0	0	0	0	2	0	1	0	0	0	—	0	.000	.000	.000	P	9	0	2	1	0	.667

JACK HOWELL—Jack Robert Howell—Bats: Left; Throws: Right

Ht: 6'0"; Wt: 180 lbs; Born: 8/18/1961 in Tucson, Arizona; Debut: 5/20/1985

LCS — Batting / Fielding

Year Tm	Age	G	AB	H	2B	3B	HR	TB	R	RBI	GW	TBB	IBB	SO	HBP	SH	SF	SB	CS	SB%	GDP	Avg	OBP	SLG	Pos	G	PO	A	E	DP	FPct
1986 Cal	25	2	1	0	0	0	0	0	0	0	0	1	0	1	0	0	0	0	0	—	0	.000	.500	.000	—						

JAY HOWELL—Jay Canfield Howell—Throws: Right; Bats: Right

Ht: 6'3"; Wt: 200 lbs; Born: 11/26/1955 in Miami, Florida; Debut: 8/10/1980

LCS — Pitching

Year Tm	Age	G	GS	CG	GF	IP	BFP	H	R	ER	HR	SH	SF	HB	TBB	IBB	SO	WP	Bk	W	L	Pct	ShO	Sv-Op	Hld	OAvg	OOBP	ERA
1988 LA	32	2	0	0	1	0.2	5	1	2	2	0	0	0	0	2	0	1	0	0	0	1	.000	0	0- 1	0	.333	.600	27.00

World Series — Pitching

Year Tm	Age	G	GS	CG	GF	IP	BFP	H	R	ER	HR	SH	SF	HB	TBB	IBB	SO	WP	Bk	W	L	Pct	ShO	Sv-Op	Hld	OAvg	OOBP	ERA
1988 LA	32	2	0	0	2	2.2	13	3	1	1	1	0	0	0	1	0	2	0	0	0	1	.000	0	1- 1	0	.250	.308	3.38
Postseason Totals		4	0	0	3	3.1	36	4	3	3	1	0	0	0	3	0	3	0	0	0	2	.000	0	1-2	0	.267	.389	8.10

LCS — Batting / Fielding

Year Tm	Age	G	AB	H	2B	3B	HR	TB	R	RBI	GW	TBB	IBB	SO	HBP	SH	SF	SB	CS	SB%	GDP	Avg	OBP	SLG	Pos	G	PO	A	E	DP	FPct
1988 LA	32	2	0	0	0	0	0	0	0	0	0	0	0	0	0	0	0	0	0	—	0	—	—	—	P	2	0	0	0	0	—

World Series — Batting / Fielding

Year Tm	Age	G	AB	H	2B	3B	HR	TB	R	RBI	GW	TBB	IBB	SO	HBP	SH	SF	SB	CS	SB%	GDP	Avg	OBP	SLG	Pos	G	PO	A	E	DP	FPct
1988 LA	32	2	0	0	0	0	0	0	0	0	0	0	0	0	0	0	0	0	0	—	0	—	—	—	P	2	0	0	0	0	—
Postseason Totals		4	0	0	0	0	0	0	0	0	0	0	0	0	0	0	0	0	0	—	0	—	—	—	P	4	0	0	0	0	—

KEN HOWELL—Kenneth Howell—Throws: Right; Bats: Right

Ht: 6'3"; Wt: 200 lbs; Born: 11/28/1960 in Detroit, Michigan; Debut: 6/25/1984

LCS — Pitching

Year Tm	Age	G	GS	CG	GF	IP	BFP	H	R	ER	HR	SH	SF	HB	TBB	IBB	SO	WP	Bk	W	L	Pct	ShO	Sv-Op	Hld	OAvg	OOBP	ERA
1985 LA	24	1	0	0	1	2.0	6	0	0	0	0	0	0	0	0	0	2	0	0	0	0	—	0	0- 0	0	.000	.000	0.00

LCS — Batting / Fielding

Year Tm	Age	G	AB	H	2B	3B	HR	TB	R	RBI	GW	TBB	IBB	SO	HBP	SH	SF	SB	CS	SB%	GDP	Avg	OBP	SLG	Pos	G	PO	A	E	DP	FPct
1985 LA	24	1	0	0	0	0	0	0	0	0	0	0	0	0	0	0	0	0	0	—	0	—	—	—	P	1	0	1	0	0	1.000

ROY HOWELL—Roy Lee Howell—Bats: Left; Throws: Right

Ht: 6'1"; Wt: 190 lbs; Born: 12/18/1953 in Lompoc, California; Debut: 9/9/1974

Division Series — Batting / Fielding

Year Tm	Age	G	AB	H	2B	3B	HR	TB	R	RBI	GW	TBB	IBB	SO	HBP	SH	SF	SB	CS	SB%	GDP	Avg	OBP	SLG	Pos	G	PO	A	E	DP	FPct
1981 Mil	27	4	5	2	0	0	0	2	0	0	0	2	0	2	0	0	0	0	1	.00	0	.400	.571	.400	—						

LCS — Batting / Fielding

Year Tm	Age	G	AB	H	2B	3B	HR	TB	R	RBI	GW	TBB	IBB	SO	HBP	SH	SF	SB	CS	SB%	GDP	Avg	OBP	SLG	Pos	G	PO	A	E	DP	FPct
1982 Mil	28	1	3	0	0	0	0	0	0	0	0	0	0	1	0	0	0	0	0	—	0	.000	.000	.000	—						

World Series — Batting / Fielding

Year Tm	Age	G	AB	H	2B	3B	HR	TB	R	RBI	GW	TBB	IBB	SO	HBP	SH	SF	SB	CS	SB%	GDP	Avg	OBP	SLG	Pos	G	PO	A	E	DP	FPct
1982 Mil	28	4	11	0	0	0	0	0	1	0	0	0	0	3	1	0	0	0	0	—	0	.000	.083	.000	—						
Postseason Totals		9	19	2	0	0	0	2	1	0	0	2	0	6	1	0	0	0	1	.00	0	.105	.227	.105	—	0	0	0	0	0	—

LAMARR HOYT—Dewey LaMarr Hoyt—Throws: Right; Bats: Right

Ht: 6'3"; Wt: 195 lbs; Born: 1/1/1955 in Columbia, South Carolina; Debut: 9/14/1979

LCS — Pitching

Year Tm	Age	G	GS	CG	GF	IP	BFP	H	R	ER	HR	SH	SF	HB	TBB	IBB	SO	WP	Bk	W	L	Pct	ShO	Sv-Op	Hld	OAvg	OOBP	ERA
1983 ChA-*C*	28	1	1	1	0	9.0	31	5	1	1	0	0	0	0	0	0	4	0	0	1	0	1.000	0	0- 0	0	.161	.161	1.00

LCS — Batting / Fielding

Year Tm	Age	G	AB	H	2B	3B	HR	TB	R	RBI	GW	TBB	IBB	SO	HBP	SH	SF	SB	CS	SB%	GDP	Avg	OBP	SLG	Pos	G	PO	A	E	DP	FPct
1983 ChA	28	1	0	0	0	0	0	0	0	0	0	0	0	0	0	0	0	0	0	—	0	—	—	—	P	1	2	1	0	0	1.000

WAITE HOYT (HOF 1969-V)—Waite Charles Hoyt—Nickname: Schoolboy—Throws: Right; Bats: Right

Ht: 6'0"; Wt: 180 lbs; Born: 9/9/1899 in Brooklyn, New York; Debut: 7/24/1918; Died: 8/25/1984

World Series — Pitching

Year Tm	Age	G	GS	CG	GF	IP	BFP	H	R	ER	HR	SH	SF	HB	TBB	IBB	SO	WP	Bk	W	L	Pct	ShO	Sv-Op	Hld	OAvg	OOBP	ERA
1921 NYA	22	3	3	3	0	27.0	106	18	2	0	0	2	0	0	11	0	18	0	0	2	1	.667	1	0- 0	0	.194	.279	0.00
1922 NYA	23	2	1	0	1	8.0	34	11	3	1	0	0	2	0	2	0	4	0	0	0	1	.000	0	0- 0	0	.367	.382	1.13
1923 NYA	24	1	1	0	0	2.1	11	4	4	4	0	0	0	0	1	0	0	0	0	0	0	—	0	0- 0	0	.400	.455	15.43
1926 NYA	27	2	2	1	0	15.0	67	19	8	2	0	1	3	0	1	0	10	0	0	1	1	.500	0	0- 0	0	.306	.303	1.20
1927 NYA	28	1	1	0	0	7.1	32	8	4	4	0	0	2	1	1	0	2	0	0	1	0	1.000	0	0- 0	0	.286	.313	4.91
1928 NYA	29	2	2	2	0	18.0	71	14	4	3	1	0	1	0	6	0	14	0	0	2	0	1.000	0	0- 0	0	.219	.282	1.50
1931 Phi	32	1	1	0	0	6.0	24	7	3	3	1	0	0	0	0	0	1	0	0	0	1	.000	0	0- 0	0	.292	.292	4.50
WS Totals		12	11	6	1	83.2	690	81	28	17	2	3	8	1	22	0	49	0	0	6	4	.600	1	0-0	0	.260	.304	1.83

World Series — Batting / Fielding

Year Tm	Age	G	AB	H	2B	3B	HR	TB	R	RBI	GW	TBB	IBB	SO	HBP	SH	SF	SB	CS	SB%	GDP	Avg	OBP	SLG	Pos	G	PO	A	E	DP	FPct
1921 NYA	22	3	9	2	0	0	0	2	0	1	1	0	0	1	0	0	0	0	0	—	0	.222	.222	.222	P	3	0	6	0	0	1.000
1922 NYA	23	2	2	1	0	0	0	1	0	0	0	0	0	0	0	0	0	0	0	—	0	.500	.500	.500	P	2	1	2	0	0	1.000
1923 NYA	24	1	1	0	0	0	0	0	0	0	0	0	0	1	0	0	0	0	0	—	0	.000	.000	.000	P	1	0	0	0	0	—
1926 NYA	27	2	6	0	0	0	0	0	0	0	0	0	0	1	0	1	0	0	0	—	0	.000	.000	.000	P	2	0	1	0	0	1.000
1927 NYA	28	1	3	0	0	0	0	0	0	0	0	0	0	0	0	0	0	0	0	—	1	.000	.000	.000	P	1	0	0	0	0	—
1928 NYA	29	2	7	1	0	0	0	1	0	0	0	0	0	0	0	1	0	0	0	—	0	.143	.143	.143	P	2	0	3	1	0	.750
1931 Phi	32	1	2	0	0	0	0	0	0	0	0	0	0	0	0	0	0	0	0	—	0	.000	.000	.000	P	1	0	0	0	0	—
WS Totals		12	30	4	0	0	0	4	0	1	1	0	0	3	0	2	0	0	0	—	1	.133	.133	.133	P	12	1	12	1	0	.929

AL HRABOSKY—Alan Thomas Hrabosky—Nickname: The Mad Hungarian—Throws: Left; Bats: Right

Ht: 5'11"; Wt: 185 lbs; Born: 7/21/1949 in Oakland, California; Debut: 6/16/1970

LCS — Pitching

Year Tm	Age	G	GS	CG	GF	IP	BFP	H	R	ER	HR	SH	SF	HB	TBB	IBB	SO	WP	Bk	W	L	Pct	ShO	Sv-Op	Hld	OAvg	OOBP	ERA
1978 KC	29	3	0	0	2	3.0	12	3	1	1	1	0	0	0	0	0	2	0	0	0	0	—	0	0- 0	0	.250	.250	3.00

LCS — Batting / Fielding

Year Tm	Age	G	AB	H	2B	3B	HR	TB	R	RBI	GW	TBB	IBB	SO	HBP	SH	SF	SB	CS	SB%	GDP	Avg	OBP	SLG	Pos	G	PO	A	E	DP	FPct
1978 KC	29	3	0	0	0	0	0	0	0	0	0	0	0	0	0	0	0	0	0	—	0	—	—	—	P	3	0	0	0	0	—

KENT HRBEK—Kent Allen Hrbek—Bats: Left; Throws: Right

Ht: 6'4"; Wt: 200 lbs; Born: 5/21/1960 in Minneapolis, Minnesota; Debut: 8/24/1981

LCS — Batting / Fielding

Year Tm	Age	G	AB	H	2B	3B	HR	TB	R	RBI	GW	TBB	IBB	SO	HBP	SH	SF	SB	CS	SB%	GDP	Avg	OBP	SLG	Pos	G	PO	A	E	DP	FPct
1987 Min	27	5	20	3	0	0	1	6	4	1	0	3	2	0	0	0	0	0	0	—	1	.150	.261	.300	1B	5	40	3	0	3	1.000
1991 Min	31	5	21	3	0	0	0	3	0	3	0	1	0	3	0	0	0	0	0	—	1	.143	.182	.143	1B	5	40	7	0	3	1.000
LCS Totals		10	41	6	0	0	1	9	4	4	0	4	2	3	0	0	0	0	0	—	2	.146	.222	.220	1B	10	80	10	0	6	1.000

World Series — Batting / Fielding

Year Tm	Age	G	AB	H	2B	3B	HR	TB	R	RBI	GW	TBB	IBB	SO	HBP	SH	SF	SB	CS	SB%	GDP	Avg	OBP	SLG	Pos	G	PO	A	E	DP	FPct
1987 Min	27	7	24	5	0	0	1	8	4	6	1	5	0	3	0	0	0	0	0	—	0	.208	.345	.333	1B	7	68	2	0	3	1.000
1991 Min	31	7	26	3	1	0	1	7	2	2	0	2	1	6	1	0	0	0	0	—	1	.115	.207	.269	1B	7	65	8	0	4	1.000
WS Totals		14	50	8	1	0	2	15	6	8	1	7	1	9	1	0	0	0	0	—	1	.160	.276	.300	1B	14	133	10	0	7	1.000
Postseason Totals		24	91	14	1	0	3	24	10	12	1	11	3	12	1	0	0	0	0	—	3	.154	.252	.264	1B	24	213	20	0	13	1.000

GLENN HUBBARD—Glenn Dee Hubbard—Bats: Right; Throws: Right

Ht: 5'9"; Wt: 150 lbs; Born: 9/25/1957 in Hahn, West Germany; Debut: 7/14/1978

LCS		Batting																							Fielding						
Year Tm	Age	G	AB	H	2B	3B	HR	TB	R	RBI	GW	TBB	IBB	SO	HBP	SH	SF	SB	CS	SB%	GDP	Avg	OBP	SLG	Pos	G	PO	A	E	DP	FPct
1982 Atl	25	3	9	2	0	0	0	2	1	1	0	0	0	3	0	1	0	0	0	—	0	.222	.222	.222	2B	3	4	13	0	0	1.000
World Series																															
Year Tm	Age	G	AB	H	2B	3B	HR	TB	R	RBI	GW	TBB	IBB	SO	HBP	SH	SF	SB	CS	SB%	GDP	Avg	OBP	SLG	Pos	G	PO	A	E	DP	FPct
1988 Oak	31	4	12	3	0	0	0	3	2	0	0	1	0	2	0	0	0	1	0	1.00	0	.250	.308	.250	2B	4	5	7	1	0	.923
Postseason Totals		7	21	5	0	0	0	5	3	1	0	1	0	5	0	1	0	1	0	1.00	0	.238	.273	.238	2B	7	9	20	1	0	.967

TRENT HUBBARD—Trenidad Aviel Hubbard—Bats: Right; Throws: Right

Ht: 5'8"; Wt: 180 lbs; Born: 5/11/1966 in Chicago, Illinois; Debut: 7/7/1994

Division Series		Batting																							Fielding						
Year Tm	Age	G	AB	H	2B	3B	HR	TB	R	RBI	GW	TBB	IBB	SO	HBP	SH	SF	SB	CS	SB%	GDP	Avg	OBP	SLG	Pos	G	PO	A	E	DP	FPct
1995 Col	29	3	2	0	0	0	0	0	0	0	0	0	0	0	0	0	0	0	0	—	0	.000	.000	.000	—						

CARL HUBBELL (HOF 1947-W)—Carl Owen Hubbell—Nicknames: King Carl, Meal Ticket—Throws: L; Bats: R

Ht: 6'0"; Wt: 170 lbs; Born: 6/22/1903 in Carthage, Mo.; Deb.: 7/26/1928; Died: 11/21/1988

World Series		Pitching																									
Year Tm	Age	G	GS	CG	GF	IP	BFP	H	R	ER	HR	SH	SF	HB	TBB	IBB	SO	WP	Bk	W	L	Pct	ShO	Sv-Op	Hld	OAvg	OOBP	ERA
1933 NYG-*M*	30	2	2	2	0	20.0	80	13	3	0	0	3	0	0	6	1	15	0	0	2	0	1.000	0	0-0	0	.183	.247	0.00
1936 NYG-*M*	33	2	2	1	0	16.0	65	15	5	4	2	1	0	1	2	0	10	1	0	1	1	.500	0	0-0	0	.246	.281	2.25
1937 NYG	34	2	2	1	0	14.1	59	12	10	6	1	0	0	0	4	1	7	0	0	1	1	.500	0	0-0	0	.218	.271	3.77
WS Totals		6	6	4	0	50.1	408	40	18	10	3	4	0	1	12	2	32	1	0	4	2	.667	0	0-0	0	.214	.265	1.79

World Series		Batting																							Fielding						
Year Tm	Age	G	AB	H	2B	3B	HR	TB	R	RBI	GW	TBB	IBB	SO	HBP	SH	SF	SB	CS	SB%	GDP	Avg	OBP	SLG	Pos	G	PO	A	E	DP	FPct
1933 NYG	30	2	7	2	0	0	0	2	0	0	0	0	0	0	0	1	0	0	0	—	0	.286	.286	.286	P	2	1	4	1	0	.833
1936 NYG	33	2	6	2	0	0	0	2	0	1	0	0	0	0	0	0	0	0	0	—	0	.333	.333	.333	P	2	2	2	1	0	.800
1937 NYG	34	2	6	0	0	0	0	0	1	1	1	0	0	0	0	0	0	0	0	—	0	.000	.000	.000	P	2	0	3	0	1	1.000
WS Totals		6	19	4	0	0	0	4	1	2	1	0	0	0	0	1	0	0	0	—	0	.211	.211	.211	P	6	3	9	2	1	.857

CHARLES HUDSON—Charles Lynn Hudson—Throws: Right; Bats: Both

Ht: 6'3"; Wt: 185 lbs; Born: 3/16/1959 in Ennis, Texas; Debut: 5/31/1983

LCS		Pitching																									
Year Tm	Age	G	GS	CG	GF	IP	BFP	H	R	ER	HR	SH	SF	HB	TBB	IBB	SO	WP	Bk	W	L	Pct	ShO	Sv-Op	Hld	OAvg	OOBP	ERA
1983 Phi	24	1	1	1	0	9.0	34	4	2	2	1	0	0	0	2	0	9	0	0	1	0	1.000	0	0-0	0	.125	.176	2.00
World Series																												
Year Tm	Age	G	GS	CG	GF	IP	BFP	H	R	ER	HR	SH	SF	HB	TBB	IBB	SO	WP	Bk	W	L	Pct	ShO	Sv-Op	Hld	OAvg	OOBP	ERA
1983 Phi	24	2	2	0	0	8.1	35	9	8	8	4	0	1	0	1	0	6	0	0	0	2	.000	0	0-0	0	.273	.286	8.64
Postseason Totals		3	3	1	0	17.1	138	13	10	10	5	0	1	0	3	0	15	0	0	1	2	.333	0	0-0	0	.200	.232	5.19

LCS		Batting																							Fielding						
Year Tm	Age	G	AB	H	2B	3B	HR	TB	R	RBI	GW	TBB	IBB	SO	HBP	SH	SF	SB	CS	SB%	GDP	Avg	OBP	SLG	Pos	G	PO	A	E	DP	FPct
1983 Phi	24	1	4	0	0	0	0	0	0	0	0	0	0	2	0	0	0	0	0	—	0	.000	.000	.000	P	1	0	0	0	0	—
World Series																															
Year Tm	Age	G	AB	H	2B	3B	HR	TB	R	RBI	GW	TBB	IBB	SO	HBP	SH	SF	SB	CS	SB%	GDP	Avg	OBP	SLG	Pos	G	PO	A	E	DP	FPct
1983 Phi	24	2	2	0	0	0	0	0	0	0	0	0	0	1	0	0	0	0	0	—	0	.000	.000	.000	P	2	0	0	0	0	—
Postseason Totals		3	6	0	0	0	0	0	0	0	0	0	0	3	0	0	0	0	0	—	0	.000	.000	.000	P	3	0	0	0	0	—

JOE HUDSON—Joseph Paul Hudson—Throws: Right; Bats: Right

Ht: 6'1"; Wt: 175 lbs; Born: 9/29/1970 in Philadelphia, Pennsylvania; Debut: 6/10/1995

Division Series		Pitching																									
Year Tm	Age	G	GS	CG	GF	IP	BFP	H	R	ER	HR	SH	SF	HB	TBB	IBB	SO	WP	Bk	W	L	Pct	ShO	Sv-Op	Hld	OAvg	OOBP	ERA
1995 Bos	25	1	0	0	1	1.0	6	2	0	0	0	0	0	0	1	0	0	1	0	0	0	—	0	0-0	0	.400	.500	0.00

Division Series		Batting																							Fielding						
Year Tm	Age	G	AB	H	2B	3B	HR	TB	R	RBI	GW	TBB	IBB	SO	HBP	SH	SF	SB	CS	SB%	GDP	Avg	OBP	SLG	Pos	G	PO	A	E	DP	FPct
1995 Bos	25	1	0	0	0	0	0	0	0	0	0	0	0	0	0	0	0	0	0	—	0	—	—	—	P	1	0	0	0	0	—

DICK HUGHES—Richard Henry Hughes—Throws: Right; Bats: Right

Ht: 6'3"; Wt: 195 lbs; Born: 2/13/1938 in Stephens, Arkansas; Debut: 9/11/1966

World Series		Pitching																									
Year Tm	Age	G	GS	CG	GF	IP	BFP	H	R	ER	HR	SH	SF	HB	TBB	IBB	SO	WP	Bk	W	L	Pct	ShO	Sv-Op	Hld	OAvg	OOBP	ERA
1967 StL	29	2	2	0	0	9.0	40	9	6	5	5	0	0	0	3	0	7	0	0	0	1	.000	0	0-0	0	.243	.300	5.00
1968 StL	30	1	0	0	0	0.1	3	2	0	0	0	0	0	0	0	0	0	0	0	0	0	—	0	0-0	0	.667	.667	0.00
WS Totals		3	2	0	0	9.1	86	11	6	5	5	0	0	0	3	0	7	0	0	0	1	.000	0	0-0	0	.275	.326	4.82

World Series		Batting																							Fielding						
Year Tm	Age	G	AB	H	2B	3B	HR	TB	R	RBI	GW	TBB	IBB	SO	HBP	SH	SF	SB	CS	SB%	GDP	Avg	OBP	SLG	Pos	G	PO	A	E	DP	FPct
1967 StL	29	2	3	0	0	0	0	0	0	0	0	0	0	3	0	0	0	0	0	—	0	.000	.000	.000	P	2	1	0	0	0	1.000
1968 StL	30	1	0	0	0	0	0	0	0	0	0	0	0	0	0	0	0	0	0	—	0	—	—	—	P	1	0	0	0	0	—
WS Totals		3	3	0	0	0	0	0	0	0	0	0	0	3	0	0	0	0	0	—	0	.000	.000	.000	P	3	1	0	0	0	1.000

JIM HUGHES—James Robert Hughes—Throws: Right; Bats: Right

Ht: 6'1"; Wt: 200 lbs; Born: 3/21/1923 in Chicago, Illinois; Debut: 9/13/1952

World Series		Pitching																									
Year Tm	Age	G	GS	CG	GF	IP	BFP	H	R	ER	HR	SH	SF	HB	TBB	IBB	SO	WP	Bk	W	L	Pct	ShO	Sv-Op	Hld	OAvg	OOBP	ERA
1953 Bro	30	1	0	0	0	4.0	15	3	1	1	1	0	0	0	1	0	3	0	0	0	0	—	0	0-0	0	.214	.267	2.25

World Series		Batting																							Fielding						
Year Tm	Age	G	AB	H	2B	3B	HR	TB	R	RBI	GW	TBB	IBB	SO	HBP	SH	SF	SB	CS	SB%	GDP	Avg	OBP	SLG	Pos	G	PO	A	E	DP	FPct
1953 Bro	30	1	1	0	0	0	0	0	0	0	0	0	0	1	0	0	0	0	0	—	0	.000	.000	.000	P	1	0	0	1	0	.000

LONG TOM HUGHES—Thomas James Hughes—Throws: Right; Bats: Right

Ht: 6'1"; Wt: 175 lbs; Born: 11/29/1878 in Chicago, Illinois; Debut: 9/7/1900; Died: 2/8/1956

World Series		Pitching																									
Year Tm	Age	G	GS	CG	GF	IP	BFP	H	R	ER	HR	SH	SF	HB	TBB	IBB	SO	WP	Bk	W	L	Pct	ShO	Sv-Op	Hld	OAvg	OOBP	ERA
1903 Bos	24	1	1	0	0	2.0	12	4	2	2	0	0	0	0	2	0	0	0	0	0	1	.000	0	0-0	0	.400	.500	9.00

World Series		Batting																							Fielding						
Year Tm	Age	G	AB	H	2B	3B	HR	TB	R	RBI	GW	TBB	IBB	SO	HBP	SH	SF	SB	CS	SB%	GDP	Avg	OBP	SLG	Pos	G	PO	A	E	DP	FPct
1903 Bos	24	1	0	0	0	0	0	0	0	0	0	0	0	0	0	0	0	0	0	—	0	—	—	—	P	1	0	0	0	0	—

ROY HUGHES—Roy John Hughes—Nicknames: Jeep, Sage—Bats: Right; Throws: Right

Ht: 5'10"; Wt: 167 lbs; Born: 1/11/1911 in Cincinnati, Ohio; Debut: 4/16/1935; Died: 3/5/1995

World Series		Batting																							Fielding						
Year Tm	Age	G	AB	H	2B	3B	HR	TB	R	RBI	GW	TBB	IBB	SO	HBP	SH	SF	SB	CS	SB%	GDP	Avg	OBP	SLG	Pos	G	PO	A	E	DP	FPct
1945 ChN	34	6	17	5	1	0	0	6	1	3	0	4	0	5	0	1	0	0	1	.00	0	.294	.429	.353	SS	6	13	18	0	2	1.000

TEX HUGHSON—Cecil Carlton Hughson—Throws: Right; Bats: Right

Ht: 6'3"; Wt: 198 lbs; Born: 2/9/1916 in Kyle, Texas; Debut: 4/16/1941; Died: 8/6/1993

World Series		Pitching																									
Year Tm	Age	G	GS	CG	GF	IP	BFP	H	R	ER	HR	SH	SF	HB	TBB	IBB	SO	WP	Bk	W	L	Pct	ShO	Sv-Op	Hld	OAvg	OOBP	ERA
1946 Bos	30	3	2	0	0	14.1	61	14	8	5	1	3	0	1	3	1	8	0	0	0	1	.000	0	0-0	0	.259	.310	3.14

World Series		Batting																							Fielding						
Year Tm	Age	G	AB	H	2B	3B	HR	TB	R	RBI	GW	TBB	IBB	SO	HBP	SH	SF	SB	CS	SB%	GDP	Avg	OBP	SLG	Pos	G	PO	A	E	DP	FPct
1946 Bos	30	3	3	1	0	0	0	1	0	0	0	1	0	0	0	0	0	0	0	—	0	.333	.500	.333	P	3	0	1	1	0	.500

MARK HUISMANN—Mark Lawrence Huismann—Throws: Right; Bats: Right

Ht: 6'3"; Wt: 195 lbs; Born: 5/11/1958 in Lincoln, Nebraska; Debut: 8/16/1983

LCS			Pitching																										
Year	Tm	Age	G	GS	CG	GF	IP	BFP	H	R	ER	HR	SH	SF	HB	TBB	IBB	SO	WP	Bk	W	L	Pct	ShO	Sv-Op	Hld	OAvg	OOBP	ERA
1984	KC	26	1	0	0	0	2.2	15	6	3	2	0	0	0	0	1	0	2	1	0	0	0	—	0	0- 0	0	.429	.467	6.75

LCS			Batting																						Fielding						
Year	Tm	Age	G	AB	H	2B	3B	HR	TB	R	RBI	GW	TBB	IBB	SO	HBP	SH	SF	SB	CS	SB%	GDP	Avg	OBP	SLG	Pos	G	PO	A	E	DP	FPct
1984	KC	26	1	0	0	0	0	0	0	0	0	0	0	0	0	0	0	0	0	0	—	0	—	—	—	P	1	0	0	0	0	—

TOM HUME—Thomas Hubert Hume—Throws: Right; Bats: Right

Ht: 6'1"; Wt: 185 lbs; Born: 3/29/1953 in Cincinnati, Ohio; Debut: 5/25/1977

LCS			Pitching																										
Year	Tm	Age	G	GS	CG	GF	IP	BFP	H	R	ER	HR	SH	SF	HB	TBB	IBB	SO	WP	Bk	W	L	Pct	ShO	Sv-Op	Hld	OAvg	OOBP	ERA
1979	Cin	26	3	0	0	1	4.0	19	6	3	3	1	0	0	0	0	0	2	0	0	0	1	.000	0	0- 0	0	.316	.316	6.75

LCS			Batting																						Fielding						
Year	Tm	Age	G	AB	H	2B	3B	HR	TB	R	RBI	GW	TBB	IBB	SO	HBP	SH	SF	SB	CS	SB%	GDP	Avg	OBP	SLG	Pos	G	PO	A	E	DP	FPct
1979	Cin	26	3	1	0	0	0	0	0	0	0	0	0	0	1	0	0	0	0	0	—	0	.000	.000	.000	P	3	0	2	0	0	1.000

BOB HUMPHREYS—Robert William Humphreys—Throws: Right; Bats: Right

Ht: 5'11"; Wt: 165 lbs; Born: 8/18/1935 in Covington, Virginia; Debut: 9/8/1962

World Series			Pitching																										
Year	Tm	Age	G	GS	CG	GF	IP	BFP	H	R	ER	HR	SH	SF	HB	TBB	IBB	SO	WP	Bk	W	L	Pct	ShO	Sv-Op	Hld	OAvg	OOBP	ERA
1964	StL	29	1	0	0	1	1.0	3	0	0	0	0	0	0	0	0	0	1	0	0	0	0	—	0	0- 0	0	.000	.000	0.00

World Series			Batting																						Fielding						
Year	Tm	Age	G	AB	H	2B	3B	HR	TB	R	RBI	GW	TBB	IBB	SO	HBP	SH	SF	SB	CS	SB%	GDP	Avg	OBP	SLG	Pos	G	PO	A	E	DP	FPct
1964	StL	29	1	0	0	0	0	0	0	0	0	0	0	0	0	0	0	0	0	0	—	0	—	—	—	P	1	0	0	0	0	—

KEN HUNT—Kenneth Raymond Hunt—Throws: Right; Bats: Right

Ht: 6'4"; Wt: 200 lbs; Born: 12/14/1938 in Ogden, Utah; Debut: 4/16/1961

World Series			Pitching																										
Year	Tm	Age	G	GS	CG	GF	IP	BFP	H	R	ER	HR	SH	SF	HB	TBB	IBB	SO	WP	Bk	W	L	Pct	ShO	Sv-Op	Hld	OAvg	OOBP	ERA
1961	Cin	22	1	0	0	1	1.0	4	0	0	0	0	0	0	0	1	0	1	0	0	0	0	—	0	0- 0	0	.000	.250	0.00

World Series			Batting																						Fielding						
Year	Tm	Age	G	AB	H	2B	3B	HR	TB	R	RBI	GW	TBB	IBB	SO	HBP	SH	SF	SB	CS	SB%	GDP	Avg	OBP	SLG	Pos	G	PO	A	E	DP	FPct
1961	Cin	22	1	0	0	0	0	0	0	0	0	0	0	0	0	0	0	0	0	0	—	0	—	—	—	P	1	0	1	0	0	1.000

BRIAN HUNTER—Brian Raynold Hunter—Bats: Right; Throws: Left

Ht: 6'0"; Wt: 195 lbs; Born: 3/4/1968 in Torrance, California; Debut: 5/31/1991

LCS			Batting																						Fielding						
Year	Tm	Age	G	AB	H	2B	3B	HR	TB	R	RBI	GW	TBB	IBB	SO	HBP	SH	SF	SB	CS	SB%	GDP	Avg	OBP	SLG	Pos	G	PO	A	E	DP	FPct
1991	Atl	23	5	18	6	2	0	1	11	2	4	1	0	0	2	0	0	0	0	1	.00	0	.333	.333	.611	1B	5	30	4	0	3	1.000
1992	Atl	24	3	5	1	0	0	0	1	1	0	0	0	0	1	0	0	0	0	0	—	0	.200	.200	.200	1B	2	7	0	0	0	1.000
LCS Totals			8	23	7	2	0	1	12	3	4	1	0	0	3	0	0	0	0	1	.00	0	.304	.304	.522	1B	7	37	4	0	3	1.000
World Series			**Batting**																						**Fielding**						
Year	Tm	Age	G	AB	H	2B	3B	HR	TB	R	RBI	GW	TBB	IBB	SO	HBP	SH	SF	SB	CS	SB%	GDP	Avg	OBP	SLG	Pos	G	PO	A	E	DP	FPct
1991	Atl	23	7	21	4	1	0	1	8	2	3	0	0	0	2	0	0	1	0	0	—	0	.190	.182	.381	1B	4	3	0	0	0	1.000
																										OF	4	3	1	1	1	.800
1992	Atl	24	4	5	1	0	0	0	1	0	2	0	0	0	1	0	0	1	0	1	.00	0	.200	.167	.200	1B	3	14	1	0	2	1.000
WS Totals			11	26	5	1	0	1	9	2	5	0	0	0	3	0	0	2	0	1	.00	0	.192	.179	.346	1B	7	17	1	0	2	1.000
Postseason Totals			19	49	12	3	0	2	21	5	9	1	0	0	6	0	0	2	0	2	.00	0	.245	.235	.429	1B	14	54	5	0	5	1.000

CATFISH HUNTER (HOF 1987-W)—James Augustus Hunter—Throws: Right; Bats: Right

Ht: 6'0"; Wt: 190 lbs; Born: 4/8/1946 in Hertford, North Carolina; Debut: 5/13/1965

LCS			Pitching																										
Year	Tm	Age	G	GS	CG	GF	IP	BFP	H	R	ER	HR	SH	SF	HB	TBB	IBB	SO	WP	Bk	W	L	Pct	ShO	Sv-Op	Hld	OAvg	OOBP	ERA
1971	Oak	25	1	1	1	0	8.0	32	7	5	5	4	0	0	0	2	0	6	0	0	0	1	.000	0	0- 0	0	.233	.281	5.63
1972	Oak	26	2	2	0	0	15.1	60	10	2	2	2	1	0	0	5	1	9	0	0	0	0	—	0	0- 0	0	.185	.254	1.17
1973	Oak	27	2	2	1	0	16.1	66	12	3	3	0	0	0	1	5	1	6	0	0	2	0	1.000	1	0- 0	0	.200	.273	1.65
1974	Oak-*C*	28	2	2	0	0	11.2	45	11	6	6	3	2	0	0	2	0	6	0	0	1	1	.500	0	0- 0	0	.268	.302	4.63
1976	NYA	30	2	2	1	0	12.0	45	10	6	6	0	0	0	0	1	0	5	0	0	1	1	.500	0	0- 0	0	.227	.244	4.50
1978	NYA	32	1	1	0	0	6.0	26	7	3	3	3	0	0	0	3	0	5	0	0	0	0	—	0	0- 0	0	.304	.385	4.50
LCS Totals			10	10	3	0	69.1	548	57	25	25	12	3	0	1	18	2	37	0	0	4	3	.571	1	0-0	0	.226	.280	3.25
World Series			**Pitching**																										
Year	Tm	Age	G	GS	CG	GF	IP	BFP	H	R	ER	HR	SH	SF	HB	TBB	IBB	SO	WP	Bk	W	L	Pct	ShO	Sv-Op	Hld	OAvg	OOBP	ERA
1972	Oak	26	3	2	0	0	16.0	67	12	5	5	2	1	1	0	6	2	11	1	0	2	0	1.000	0	0- 0	0	.203	.273	2.81
1973	Oak	27	2	2	0	0	13.1	56	11	3	3	1	0	0	0	4	1	6	1	0	1	0	1.000	0	0- 0	0	.212	.268	2.03
1974	Oak-*C*	28	2	1	0	1	7.2	30	5	1	1	1	0	0	0	2	0	5	0	0	1	0	1.000	0	1- 1	0	.179	.233	1.17
1976	NYA	30	1	1	1	0	8.2	40	10	4	3	0	0	1	0	4	1	5	0	0	0	1	.000	0	0- 0	0	.286	.350	3.12
1977	NYA	31	2	1	0	1	4.1	19	6	5	5	3	0	0	0	0	0	1	0	0	0	1	.000	0	0- 0	0	.316	.316	10.38
1978	NYA	32	2	2	0	0	13.0	50	13	6	6	2	1	0	0	1	0	5	0	0	1	1	.500	0	0- 0	0	.271	.286	4.15
WS Totals			12	9	1	2	63.0	524	57	24	23	9	2	2	0	17	4	33	2	0	5	3	.625	0	1-1	0	.237	.285	3.29
Postseason Totals			22	19	4	2	132.1	1072	114	49	48	21	5	2	1	35	6	70	2	0	9	6	.600	1	1-1	0	.231	.282	3.26

LCS			Batting																						Fielding						
Year	Tm	Age	G	AB	H	2B	3B	HR	TB	R	RBI	GW	TBB	IBB	SO	HBP	SH	SF	SB	CS	SB%	GDP	Avg	OBP	SLG	Pos	G	PO	A	E	DP	FPct
1971	Oak	25	1	3	0	0	0	0	0	0	0	0	0	0	1	0	0	0	0	0	—	0	.000	.000	.000	P	1	0	0	0	0	—
1972	Oak	26	2	6	1	0	0	0	1	0	0	0	0	0	2	0	0	0	0	0	—	0	.167	.167	.167	P	2	0	0	0	0	—
1973	Oak	27	2	0	0	0	0	0	0	0	0	0	0	0	0	0	0	0	0	0	—	0	—	—	—	P	2	1	0	0	0	1.000
1974	Oak	28	2	0	0	0	0	0	0	0	0	0	0	0	0	0	0	0	0	0	—	0	—	—	—	P	2	3	2	0	0	1.000
1976	NYA	30	2	0	0	0	0	0	0	0	0	0	0	0	0	0	0	0	0	0	—	0	—	—	—	P	2	0	3	0	0	1.000
1978	NYA	32	1	0	0	0	0	0	0	0	0	0	0	0	0	0	0	0	0	0	—	0	—	—	—	P	1	0	1	0	0	1.000
LCS Totals			10	9	1	0	0	0	1	0	0	0	0	0	3	0	0	0	0	0	—	0	.111	.111	.111	P	10	4	6	0	0	1.000
World Series			**Batting**																						**Fielding**						
Year	Tm	Age	G	AB	H	2B	3B	HR	TB	R	RBI	GW	TBB	IBB	SO	HBP	SH	SF	SB	CS	SB%	GDP	Avg	OBP	SLG	Pos	G	PO	A	E	DP	FPct
1972	Oak	26	3	5	1	0	0	0	1	0	1	1	2	0	1	0	0	0	0	0	—	0	.200	.429	.200	P	3	0	3	1	0	.750
1973	Oak	27	2	5	0	0	0	0	0	0	0	0	0	0	3	0	0	0	0	0	—	0	.000	.000	.000	P	2	1	2	1	0	.750
1974	Oak	28	2	2	0	0	0	0	0	0	0	0	0	0	2	0	1	0	0	0	—	0	.000	.000	.000	P	2	1	2	0	0	1.000
1976	NYA	30	1	0	0	0	0	0	0	0	0	0	0	0	0	0	0	0	0	0	—	0	—	—	—	P	1	0	1	0	0	1.000
1977	NYA	31	2	0	0	0	0	0	0	0	0	0	0	0	0	0	0	0	0	0	—	0	—	—	—	P	2	1	0	0	0	1.000
1978	NYA	32	2	0	0	0	0	0	0	0	0	0	0	0	0	0	0	0	0	0	—	0	—	—	—	P	2	2	0	0	0	1.000
WS Totals			12	12	1	0	0	0	1	0	1	1	2	0	6	0	1	0	0	0	—	0	.083	.214	.083	P	12	5	8	2	0	.867
Postseason Totals			22	21	2	0	0	0	2	0	1	1	2	0	9	0	1	0	0	0	—	0	.095	.174	.095	P	22	9	14	2	0	.920

CLINT HURDLE—Clinton Merrick Hurdle—Bats: Left; Throws: Right

Ht: 6'3"; Wt: 195 lbs; Born: 7/30/1957 in Big Rapids, Michigan; Debut: 9/18/1977

Division Series			Batting																						Fielding						
Year	Tm	Age	G	AB	H	2B	3B	HR	TB	R	RBI	GW	TBB	IBB	SO	HBP	SH	SF	SB	CS	SB%	GDP	Avg	OBP	SLG	Pos	G	PO	A	E	DP	FPct
1981	KC	24	3	11	3	0	0	0	3	0	0	0	1	0	1	0	0	0	0	1	.00	0	.273	.333	.273	OF	3	6	0	0	0	1.000
LCS			**Batting**																						**Fielding**						
Year	Tm	Age	G	AB	H	2B	3B	HR	TB	R	RBI	GW	TBB	IBB	SO	HBP	SH	SF	SB	CS	SB%	GDP	Avg	OBP	SLG	Pos	G	PO	A	E	DP	FPct
1978	KC	21	4	8	3	0	1	0	5	1	1	0	2	0	3	0	0	0	0	0	—	0	.375	.500	.625	OF	2	6	1	0	1	1.000
1980	KC	23	3	2	0	0	0	0	0	0	0	0	0	0	1	0	0	0	0	0	—	1	.000	.000	.000	OF	3	1	0	0	0	1.000
LCS Totals			7	10	3	0	1	0	5	1	1	0	2	0	4	0	0	0	0	0	—	1	.300	.417	.500	OF	5	7	1	0	1	1.000
World Series			**Batting**																						**Fielding**						
Year	Tm	Age	G	AB	H	2B	3B	HR	TB	R	RBI	GW	TBB	IBB	SO	HBP	SH	SF	SB	CS	SB%	GDP	Avg	OBP	SLG	Pos	G	PO	A	E	DP	FPct
1980	KC	23	4	12	5	1	0	0	6	1	0	0	2	0	1	0	0	0	1	0	1.00	0	.417	.500	.500	OF	4	8	0	0	0	1.000
Postseason Totals			14	33	11	1	1	0	14	2	1	0	5	0	6	0	0	0	1	1	.50	1	.333	.421	.424	OF	12	21	1	0	1	1.000

BRUCE HURST—Bruce Vee Hurst—Throws: Left; Bats: Left

Ht: 6'4"; Wt: 200 lbs; Born: 3/24/1958 in St. George, Utah; Debut: 4/12/1980

LCS Pitching																												
Year Tm	Age	G	GS	CG	GF	IP	BFP	H	R	ER	HR	SH	SF	HB	TBB	IBB	SO	WP	Bk	W	L	Pct	ShO	Sv-Op	Hld	OAvg	OOBP	ERA
1986 Bos	28	2	2	1	0	15.0	61	18	5	4	3	1	0	0	1	0	8	0	0	1	0	1.000	0	0-0	0	.305	.317	2.40
1988 Bos	30	2	2	1	0	13.0	53	10	4	4	2	0	0	0	5	1	12	0	0	0	2	.000	0	0-0	0	.208	.283	2.77
LCS Totals		4	4	2	0	28.0	228	28	9	8	5	1	0	0	6	1	20	0	0	1	2	.333	0	0-0	0	.262	.301	2.57
World Series Pitching																												
Year Tm	Age	G	GS	CG	GF	IP	BFP	H	R	ER	HR	SH	SF	HB	TBB	IBB	SO	WP	Bk	W	L	Pct	ShO	Sv-Op	Hld	OAvg	OOBP	ERA
1986 Bos	28	3	3	1	0	23.0	91	18	5	5	1	2	0	0	6	0	17	0	0	2	0	1.000	0	0-0	0	.217	.270	1.96
Postseason Totals		7	7	3	0	51.0	410	46	14	13	6	3	0	0	12	1	37	0	0	3	2	.600	0	0-0	0	.242	.287	2.29

LCS Batting / Fielding																															
Year Tm	Age	G	AB	H	2B	3B	HR	TB	R	RBI	GW	TBB	IBB	SO	HBP	SH	SF	SB	CS	SB%	GDP	Avg	OBP	SLG	Pos	G	PO	A	E	DP	FPct
1986 Bos	28	2	0	0	0	0	0	0	0	0	0	0	0	0	0	0	0	0	0	—	0	—	—	—	P	2	1	2	0	0	1.000
1988 Bos	30	2	0	0	0	0	0	0	0	0	0	0	0	0	0	0	0	0	0	—	0	—	—	—	P	2	0	3	0	0	1.000
LCS Totals		4	0	0	0	0	0	0	0	0	0	0	0	0	0	0	0	0	0	—	0	—	—	—	P	4	1	5	0	0	1.000
World Series Batting / Fielding																															
Year Tm	Age	G	AB	H	2B	3B	HR	TB	R	RBI	GW	TBB	IBB	SO	HBP	SH	SF	SB	CS	SB%	GDP	Avg	OBP	SLG	Pos	G	PO	A	E	DP	FPct
1986 Bos	28	3	3	0	0	0	0	0	0	0	0	0	0	3	0	2	0	0	0	—	0	.000	.000	.000	P	3	1	3	0	0	1.000
Postseason Totals		7	3	0	0	0	0	0	0	0	0	0	0	3	0	2	0	0	0	—	0	.000	.000	.000	P	7	2	8	0	0	1.000

JOHNNY HUTCHINGS—John Richard Joseph Hutchings—Throws: Right; Bats: Both

Ht: 6'2"; Wt: 250 lbs; Born: 4/14/1916 in Chicago, Illinois; Debut: 4/26/1940; Died: 4/27/1963

World Series Pitching																												
Year Tm	Age	G	GS	CG	GF	IP	BFP	H	R	ER	HR	SH	SF	HB	TBB	IBB	SO	WP	Bk	W	L	Pct	ShO	Sv-Op	Hld	OAvg	OOBP	ERA
1940 Cin	24	1	0	0	1	1.0	6	2	1	1	0	0	0	0	1	0	0	1	0	0	0	—	0	0-0	0	.400	.500	9.00

World Series Batting / Fielding																															
Year Tm	Age	G	AB	H	2B	3B	HR	TB	R	RBI	GW	TBB	IBB	SO	HBP	SH	SF	SB	CS	SB%	GDP	Avg	OBP	SLG	Pos	G	PO	A	E	DP	FPct
1940 Cin	24	1	0	0	0	0	0	0	0	0	0	0	0	0	0	0	0	0	0	—	0	—	—	—	P	1	0	1	0	0	1.000

FRED HUTCHINSON—Frederick Charles Hutchinson—Nickname: Hutch—Throws: Right; Bats: Left

Ht: 6'2"; Wt: 190 lbs; Born: 8/12/1919 in Seattle, Washington; Debut: 5/2/1939; Died: 11/12/1964

World Series Pitching																												
Year Tm	Age	G	GS	CG	GF	IP	BFP	H	R	ER	HR	SH	SF	HB	TBB	IBB	SO	WP	Bk	W	L	Pct	ShO	Sv-Op	Hld	OAvg	OOBP	ERA
1940 Det	21	1	0	0	1	1.0	5	1	1	1	1	0	0	0	1	0	1	0	0	0	0	—	0	0-0	0	.250	.400	9.00

World Series Batting / Fielding																															
Year Tm	Age	G	AB	H	2B	3B	HR	TB	R	RBI	GW	TBB	IBB	SO	HBP	SH	SF	SB	CS	SB%	GDP	Avg	OBP	SLG	Pos	G	PO	A	E	DP	FPct
1940 Det	21	1	0	0	0	0	0	0	0	0	0	0	0	0	0	0	0	0	0	—	0	—	—	—	P	1	0	0	0	0	—

TOM HUTTON—Thomas George Hutton—Bats: Left; Throws: Left

Ht: 5'11"; Wt: 180 lbs; Born: 4/20/1946 in Los Angeles, California; Debut: 9/16/1966

LCS Batting / Fielding																															
Year Tm	Age	G	AB	H	2B	3B	HR	TB	R	RBI	GW	TBB	IBB	SO	HBP	SH	SF	SB	CS	SB%	GDP	Avg	OBP	SLG	Pos	G	PO	A	E	DP	FPct
1976 Phi	30	1	1	0	0	0	0	0	0	0	0	0	0	0	0	0	0	0	0	—	0	.000	.000	.000	—						
1977 Phi	31	3	3	0	0	0	0	0	0	0	0	0	0	0	0	0	0	0	0	—	0	.000	.000	.000	1B	1	5	0	0	0	1.000
LCS Totals		4	4	0	0	0	0	0	0	0	0	0	0	0	0	0	0	0	0	—	0	.000	.000	.000	1B	1	5	0	0	0	1.000

HAM HYATT—Robert Hamilton Hyatt—Bats: Left; Throws: Right

Ht: 6'1"; Wt: 185 lbs; Born: 11/1/1884 in Buncombe County, North Carolina; Debut: 4/15/1909; Died: 9/11/1963

World Series Batting / Fielding																															
Year Tm	Age	G	AB	H	2B	3B	HR	TB	R	RBI	GW	TBB	IBB	SO	HBP	SH	SF	SB	CS	SB%	GDP	Avg	OBP	SLG	Pos	G	PO	A	E	DP	FPct
1909 Pit	24	2	4	0	0	0	0	0	1	1	1	1	0	0	0	0	1	0	0	—	0	.000	.167	.000	OF	1	0	0	0	0	—

PETE INCAVIGLIA—Peter Joseph Incaviglia—Nickname: Inky—Bats: Right; Throws: Right

Ht: 6'1"; Wt: 225 lbs; Born: 4/2/1964 in Pebble Beach, California; Debut: 4/8/1986

Division Series Batting / Fielding																															
Year Tm	Age	G	AB	H	2B	3B	HR	TB	R	RBI	GW	TBB	IBB	SO	HBP	SH	SF	SB	CS	SB%	GDP	Avg	OBP	SLG	Pos	G	PO	A	E	DP	FPct
1996 Bal	32	2	5	1	0	0	0	1	1	0	0	0	0	4	0	0	0	0	0	—	0	.200	.200	.200	OF	2	0	0	0	0	—
LCS Batting / Fielding																															
Year Tm	Age	G	AB	H	2B	3B	HR	TB	R	RBI	GW	TBB	IBB	SO	HBP	SH	SF	SB	CS	SB%	GDP	Avg	OBP	SLG	Pos	G	PO	A	E	DP	FPct
1993 Phi	29	3	12	2	0	0	1	5	2	1	0	0	0	3	0	0	0	0	0	—	0	.167	.167	.417	OF	3	8	0	0	0	1.000
1996 Bal	32	1	2	1	0	0	0	1	1	0	0	0	0	0	0	0	0	0	0	—	0	.500	.500	.500	—						
LCS Totals		4	14	3	0	0	1	6	3	1	0	0	0	3	0	0	0	0	0	—	0	.214	.214	.429	OF	3	8	0	0	0	1.000
World Series Batting / Fielding																															
Year Tm	Age	G	AB	H	2B	3B	HR	TB	R	RBI	GW	TBB	IBB	SO	HBP	SH	SF	SB	CS	SB%	GDP	Avg	OBP	SLG	Pos	G	PO	A	E	DP	FPct
1993 Phi	29	4	8	1	0	0	0	1	0	1	0	0	0	4	0	0	1	0	0	—	0	.125	.111	.125	OF	4	7	0	0	0	1.000
Postseason Totals		10	27	5	0	0	1	8	4	2	0	0	0	11	0	0	1	0	0	—	0	.185	.179	.296	OF	9	15	0	0	0	1.000

DANE IORG—Dane Charles Iorg—Bats: Left; Throws: Right

Ht: 6'0"; Wt: 180 lbs; Born: 5/11/1950 in Eureka, California; Debut: 4/9/1977

LCS Batting / Fielding																															
Year Tm	Age	G	AB	H	2B	3B	HR	TB	R	RBI	GW	TBB	IBB	SO	HBP	SH	SF	SB	CS	SB%	GDP	Avg	OBP	SLG	Pos	G	PO	A	E	DP	FPct
1984 KC	34	2	2	1	0	0	0	1	0	1	0	0	0	0	0	0	0	0	0	—	0	.500	.500	.500	—						
1985 KC	35	4	2	1	1	0	0	2	0	0	0	2	0	0	0	0	0	0	0	—	0	.500	.750	1.000	—						
LCS Totals		6	4	2	1	0	0	3	0	1	0	2	0	0	0	0	0	0	0	—	0	.500	.667	.750	—	0	0	0	0	0	—
World Series Batting / Fielding																															
Year Tm	Age	G	AB	H	2B	3B	HR	TB	R	RBI	GW	TBB	IBB	SO	HBP	SH	SF	SB	CS	SB%	GDP	Avg	OBP	SLG	Pos	G	PO	A	E	DP	FPct
1982 StL	32	5	17	9	4	1	0	15	4	1	0	0	0	0	0	0	0	0	0	—	0	.529	.529	.882	—						
1985 KC	35	2	2	1	0	0	0	1	0	2	1	0	0	0	0	0	0	0	0	—	0	.500	.500	.500	—						
WS Totals		7	19	10	4	1	0	16	4	3	1	0	0	0	0	0	0	0	0	—	0	.526	.526	.842	—	0	0	0	0	0	—
Postseason Totals		13	23	12	5	1	0	19	4	4	1	2	0	0	0	0	0	0	0	—	0	.522	.560	.826	—	0	0	0	0	0	—

GARTH IORG—Garth Ray Iorg—Bats: Right; Throws: Right

Ht: 5'11"; Wt: 170 lbs; Born: 10/12/1954 in Arcata, California; Debut: 4/9/1978

LCS Batting / Fielding																															
Year Tm	Age	G	AB	H	2B	3B	HR	TB	R	RBI	GW	TBB	IBB	SO	HBP	SH	SF	SB	CS	SB%	GDP	Avg	OBP	SLG	Pos	G	PO	A	E	DP	FPct
1985 Tor	30	6	15	2	0	0	0	2	1	0	0	1	0	3	0	0	0	0	0	—	0	.133	.188	.133	3B	6	5	10	0	0	1.000

MONTE IRVIN (HOF 1973-N)—Montford Merrill Irvin—Bats: Right; Throws: Right

Ht: 6'1"; Wt: 195 lbs; Born: 2/25/1919 in Columbus, Alabama; Debut: 7/8/1949

World Series Batting / Fielding																															
Year Tm	Age	G	AB	H	2B	3B	HR	TB	R	RBI	GW	TBB	IBB	SO	HBP	SH	SF	SB	CS	SB%	GDP	Avg	OBP	SLG	Pos	G	PO	A	E	DP	FPct
1951 NYG	32	6	24	11	0	1	0	13	3	2	0	2	0	1	0	0	0	2	1	.67	0	.458	.500	.542	OF	6	17	0	1	0	.944
1954 NYG	35	4	9	2	1	0	0	3	1	2	0	0	0	3	0	1	0	0	0	—	1	.222	.222	.333	OF	4	8	0	1	0	.889
WS Totals		10	33	13	1	1	0	16	4	4	0	2	0	4	0	1	0	2	1	.67	1	.394	.429	.485	OF	10	25	0	2	0	.926

FRANK ISBELL—William Frank Isbell—Nickname: Bald Eagle—Bats: Left; Throws: Right

Ht: 5'11"; Wt: 190 lbs; Born: 8/21/1875 in Delevan, New York; Debut: 5/1/1898; Died: 7/15/1941

World Series Batting / Fielding																															
Year Tm	Age	G	AB	H	2B	3B	HR	TB	R	RBI	GW	TBB	IBB	SO	HBP	SH	SF	SB	CS	SB%	GDP	Avg	OBP	SLG	Pos	G	PO	A	E	DP	FPct
1906 ChA	31	6	26	8	4	0	0	12	4	4	1	0	0	6	0	0	0	1	0	1.00	0	.308	.308	.462	2B	6	11	16	5	0	.844

BO JACKSON
—Vincent Edward Jackson—Bats: Right; Throws: Right — Ht: 6'1"; Wt: 220 lbs; Born: 11/30/1962 in Bessemer, Alabama; Debut: 9/2/1986

LCS

Year	Tm	Age	G	AB	H	2B	3B	HR	TB	R	RBI	GW	TBB	IBB	SO	HBP	SH	SF	SB	CS	SB%	GDP	Avg	OBP	SLG	Pos	G	PO	A	E	DP	FPct
1993	ChA	30	3	10	0	0	0	0	0	1	0	0	3	0	6	0	0	0	0	0	—	0	.000	.231	.000	—						

DANNY JACKSON
—Danny Lynn Jackson—Throws: Left; Bats: Right — Ht: 6'0"; Wt: 205 lbs; Born: 1/5/1962 in San Antonio, Texas; Debut: 9/11/1983

LCS — Pitching

Year	Tm	Age	G	GS	CG	GF	IP	BFP	H	R	ER	HR	SH	SF	HB	TBB	IBB	SO	WP	Bk	W	L	Pct	ShO	Sv-Op	Hld	OAvg	OOBP	ERA
1985	KC	23	2	1	1	1	10.0	40	10	0	0	0	0	0	0	1	0	7	0	0	1	0	1.000	1	0-0	0	.256	.275	0.00
1990	Cin	28	2	2	0	0	11.1	49	8	3	3	0	0	0	0	7	1	8	0	0	1	0	1.000	0	0-0	0	.190	.306	2.38
1992	Pit	30	1	1	0	0	1.2	11	4	4	4	0	0	1	0	2	0	0	0	0	0	1	.000	0	0-0	0	.500	.545	21.60
1993	Phi	31	1	1	0	0	7.2	34	9	1	1	0	1	0	1	2	0	6	0	0	1	0	1.000	0	0-0	0	.300	.364	1.17
1996	StL	34	1	0	0	0	3.0	18	7	3	3	0	0	0	0	3	0	3	0	0	0	0	—	0	0-0	0	.467	.556	9.00
LCS Totals			7	5	1	1	33.2	304	38	11	11	0	1	1	1	15	1	24	0	0	3	1	.750	1	0-0	0	.284	.358	2.94

World Series — Pitching

Year	Tm	Age	G	GS	CG	GF	IP	BFP	H	R	ER	HR	SH	SF	HB	TBB	IBB	SO	WP	Bk	W	L	Pct	ShO	Sv-Op	Hld	OAvg	OOBP	ERA
1985	KC	23	2	2	1	0	16.0	61	9	3	3	0	1	0	0	5	0	12	0	0	1	1	.500	1	0-0	0	.164	.233	1.69
1990	Cin	28	1	1	0	0	2.2	17	6	4	3	1	1	1	0	2	0	0	0	0	0	0	—	0	0-0	0	.462	.500	10.13
1993	Phi	31	1	1	0	0	5.0	22	6	4	4	1	0	1	0	1	0	1	0	0	0	1	.000	0	0-0	0	.300	.318	7.20
WS Totals			4	4	1	0	23.2	200	21	11	10	2	2	2	0	8	0	13	0	0	1	2	.333	1	0-0	0	.239	.296	3.80
Postseason Totals			11	9	2	1	57.1	504	59	22	21	2	3	3	1	23	1	37	0	0	4	3	.571	1	0-0	0	.266	.333	3.30

LCS — Batting / Fielding

Year	Tm	Age	G	AB	H	2B	3B	HR	TB	R	RBI	GW	TBB	IBB	SO	HBP	SH	SF	SB	CS	SB%	GDP	Avg	OBP	SLG	Pos	G	PO	A	E	DP	FPct
1985	KC	23	2	0	0	0	0	0	0	0	0	0	0	0	0	0	0	0	0	0	—	0	—	—	—	P	2	1	1	0	0	1.000
1990	Cin	28	2	3	0	0	0	0	0	0	0	0	0	0	2	0	1	0	0	0	—	0	.000	.000	.000	P	2	0	2	0	0	1.000
1992	Pit	30	1	0	0	0	0	0	0	0	0	0	0	0	0	0	0	0	0	0	—	0	—	—	—	P	1	0	0	0	0	—
1993	Phi	31	1	4	1	0	0	0	1	0	1	1	0	0	3	0	0	0	0	0	—	0	.250	.250	.250	P	1	0	0	0	0	—
1996	StL	34	1	1	0	0	0	0	0	0	0	0	0	0	1	0	0	0	0	0	—	0	.000	.000	.000	P	1	0	0	0	0	—
LCS Totals			7	8	1	0	0	0	1	0	1	1	0	0	6	0	1	0	0	0	—	0	.125	.125	.125	P	7	1	3	0	0	1.000

World Series — Batting / Fielding

Year	Tm	Age	G	AB	H	2B	3B	HR	TB	R	RBI	GW	TBB	IBB	SO	HBP	SH	SF	SB	CS	SB%	GDP	Avg	OBP	SLG	Pos	G	PO	A	E	DP	FPct
1985	KC	23	2	6	0	0	0	0	0	0	0	0	0	0	5	0	0	0	0	0	—	0	.000	.000	.000	P	2	0	4	1	0	.800
1990	Cin	28	1	1	0	0	0	0	0	0	0	0	0	0	1	0	0	0	0	0	—	0	.000	.000	.000	P	1	0	1	1	0	.500
1993	Phi	31	1	1	0	0	0	0	0	0	0	0	0	0	1	0	0	0	0	0	—	0	.000	.000	.000	P	1	0	0	0	0	—
WS Totals			4	8	0	0	0	0	0	0	0	0	0	0	7	0	0	0	0	0	—	0	.000	.000	.000	P	4	0	5	2	0	.714
Postseason Totals			11	16	1	0	0	0	1	0	1	1	0	0	13	0	1	0	0	0	—	0	.063	.063	.063	P	11	1	8	2	0	.818

GRANT JACKSON
—Grant Dwight Jackson—Nickname: Buck—Throws: Left; Bats: Both — Ht: 6'0"; Wt: 180 lbs; Born: 9/28/1942 in Fostoria, Ohio; Debut: 9/3/1965

LCS — Pitching

Year	Tm	Age	G	GS	CG	GF	IP	BFP	H	R	ER	HR	SH	SF	HB	TBB	IBB	SO	WP	Bk	W	L	Pct	ShO	Sv-Op	Hld	OAvg	OOBP	ERA
1973	Bal	31	2	0	0	2	3.0	10	0	0	0	0	0	0	0	1	0	0	0	0	1	0	1.000	0	0-0	0	.000	.100	0.00
1974	Bal	32	1	0	0	0	0.1	3	1	2	0	1	0	0	0	0	0	1	0	0	0	0	—	0	0-0	0	.333	.333	0.00
1976	NYA	34	2	0	0	1	3.1	15	4	3	3	1	0	0	0	1	0	3	0	0	0	0	—	0	0-1	0	.286	.333	8.10
1979	Pit	37	2	0	0	0	2.0	8	1	0	0	0	0	0	0	1	0	2	0	0	1	0	1.000	0	0-0	0	.143	.250	0.00
LCS Totals			7	0	0	4	8.2	72	6	5	3	2	0	0	0	3	0	6	0	0	2	0	1.000	0	0-1	1	.182	.250	3.12

World Series — Pitching

Year	Tm	Age	G	GS	CG	GF	IP	BFP	H	R	ER	HR	SH	SF	HB	TBB	IBB	SO	WP	Bk	W	L	Pct	ShO	Sv-Op	Hld	OAvg	OOBP	ERA
1971	Bal	29	1	0	0	0	0.2	3	0	0	0	0	0	0	0	1	0	0	0	0	0	0	—	0	0-0	0	.000	.333	0.00
1976	NYA	34	1	0	0	0	3.2	14	4	2	2	0	0	0	0	0	0	3	0	0	0	0	—	0	0-0	0	.286	.286	4.91
1979	Pit	37	4	0	0	1	4.2	16	1	0	0	0	0	0	0	2	0	2	0	0	1	0	1.000	0	0-0	1	.071	.188	0.00
WS Totals			6	0	0	1	9.0	66	5	2	2	0	0	0	0	3	0	5	0	0	1	0	1.000	0	0-0	1	.167	.242	2.00
Postseason Totals			13	0	0	5	17.2	138	11	7	5	2	0	0	0	6	0	11	0	0	3	0	1.000	0	0-1	2	.175	.246	2.55

LCS — Batting / Fielding

Year	Tm	Age	G	AB	H	2B	3B	HR	TB	R	RBI	GW	TBB	IBB	SO	HBP	SH	SF	SB	CS	SB%	GDP	Avg	OBP	SLG	Pos	G	PO	A	E	DP	FPct
1973	Bal	31	2	0	0	0	0	0	0	0	0	0	0	0	0	0	0	0	0	0	—	0	—	—	—	P	2	0	0	0	0	—
1974	Bal	32	1	0	0	0	0	0	0	0	0	0	0	0	0	0	0	0	0	0	—	0	—	—	—	P	1	0	0	0	0	—
1976	NYA	34	2	0	0	0	0	0	0	0	0	0	0	0	0	0	0	0	0	0	—	0	—	—	—	P	2	0	1	0	0	1.000
1979	Pit	37	2	1	0	0	0	0	0	0	0	0	0	0	0	0	0	0	0	0	—	0	.000	.000	.000	P	2	0	0	0	0	—
LCS Totals			7	1	0	0	0	0	0	0	0	0	0	0	0	0	0	0	0	0	—	0	.000	.000	.000	P	7	0	1	0	0	1.000

World Series — Batting / Fielding

Year	Tm	Age	G	AB	H	2B	3B	HR	TB	R	RBI	GW	TBB	IBB	SO	HBP	SH	SF	SB	CS	SB%	GDP	Avg	OBP	SLG	Pos	G	PO	A	E	DP	FPct
1971	Bal	29	1	0	0	0	0	0	0	0	0	0	0	0	0	0	0	0	0	0	—	0	—	—	—	P	1	0	0	0	0	—
1976	NYA	34	1	0	0	0	0	0	0	0	0	0	0	0	0	0	0	0	0	0	—	0	—	—	—	P	1	0	3	0	0	1.000
1979	Pit	37	4	1	0	0	0	0	0	0	0	0	0	0	0	0	0	0	0	0	—	0	.000	.000	.000	P	4	0	0	0	0	—
WS Totals			6	1	0	0	0	0	0	0	0	0	0	0	0	0	0	0	0	0	—	0	.000	.000	.000	P	6	0	3	0	0	1.000
Postseason Totals			13	2	0	0	0	0	0	0	0	0	0	0	0	0	0	0	0	0	—	0	.000	.000	.000	P	13	0	4	0	0	1.000

JOE JACKSON
—Joseph Jefferson Jackson—Nickname: Shoeless Joe—Bats: Left; Throws: Right — Ht: 6'1"; Wt: 200 lbs; Born: 7/16/1889 in Pickens County, South Carolina; Debut: 8/25/1908; Died: 12/5/1951

World Series — Batting / Fielding

Year	Tm	Age	G	AB	H	2B	3B	HR	TB	R	RBI	GW	TBB	IBB	SO	HBP	SH	SF	SB	CS	SB%	GDP	Avg	OBP	SLG	Pos	G	PO	A	E	DP	FPct
1917	ChA	28	6	23	7	0	0	0	7	4	2	0	1	0	0	0	0	0	1	0	1.00	0	.304	.333	.304	OF	6	9	1	0	0	1.000
1919	ChA	30	8	32	12	3	0	1	18	5	6	1	1	0	2	0	0	2	0	1	.00	0	.375	.394	.563	OF	8	16	1	0	1	1.000
WS Totals			14	55	19	3	0	1	25	9	8	1	2	0	2	0	0	2	1	1	.50	0	.345	.368	.455	OF	14	25	2	0	1	1.000

MIKE JACKSON
—Michael Ray Jackson—Throws: Right; Bats: Right — Ht: 6'1"; Wt: 185 lbs; Born: 12/22/1964 in Houston, Texas; Debut: 8/11/1986

Division Series — Pitching

Year	Tm	Age	G	GS	CG	GF	IP	BFP	H	R	ER	HR	SH	SF	HB	TBB	IBB	SO	WP	Bk	W	L	Pct	ShO	Sv-Op	Hld	OAvg	OOBP	ERA
1995	Cin	30	3	0	0	0	3.2	15	4	0	0	0	0	0	0	0	0	1	0	0	0	0	—	0	0-0	1	.267	.267	0.00
1997	Cle	32	4	0	0	2	4.1	15	3	0	0	0	0	0	0	1	0	5	0	0	1	0	1.000	0	0-0	1	.214	.267	0.00
DS Totals			7	0	0	2	8.0	60	7	0	0	0	0	0	0	1	0	6	0	0	1	0	1.000	0	0-0	2	.241	.267	0.00

LCS — Pitching

Year	Tm	Age	G	GS	CG	GF	IP	BFP	H	R	ER	HR	SH	SF	HB	TBB	IBB	SO	WP	Bk	W	L	Pct	ShO	Sv-Op	Hld	OAvg	OOBP	ERA
1995	Cin	30	3	0	0	1	2.1	16	5	6	6	1	1	0	0	4	2	1	0	1	0	1	.000	0	0-0	0	.455	.600	23.14
1997	Cle	32	5	0	0	1	4.1	14	1	0	0	0	0	0	0	1	0	7	0	0	0	0	—	0	0-0	3	.077	.143	0.00
LCS Totals			8	0	0	2	6.2	60	6	6	6	1	1	0	0	5	2	8	0	1	0	1	.000	0	0-0	3	.250	.379	8.10

World Series — Pitching

Year	Tm	Age	G	GS	CG	GF	IP	BFP	H	R	ER	HR	SH	SF	HB	TBB	IBB	SO	WP	Bk	W	L	Pct	ShO	Sv-Op	Hld	OAvg	OOBP	ERA
1997	Cle	32	4	0	0	0	4.2	22	5	1	1	0	0	0	0	3	1	4	0	0	0	0	—	0	0-1	2	.263	.364	1.93
Postseason Totals			19	0	0	4	19.1	164	18	7	7	1	1	0	0	9	3	18	0	1	1	1	.500	0	0-1	7	.250	.333	3.26

Division Series — Batting / Fielding

Year	Tm	Age	G	AB	H	2B	3B	HR	TB	R	RBI	GW	TBB	IBB	SO	HBP	SH	SF	SB	CS	SB%	GDP	Avg	OBP	SLG	Pos	G	PO	A	E	DP	FPct
1995	Cin	30	3	1	1	1	0	0	2	0	3	0	0	0	0	0	0	0	0	0	1.000	0	1.000	1.000	2.000	P	3	1	1	0	0	1.000
1997	Cle	32	4	0	0	0	0	0	0	0	0	0	0	0	0	0	0	0	0	0	—	0	—	—	—	P	4	1	0	0	0	1.000
DS Totals			7	1	1	1	0	0	2	0	3	0	0	0	0	0	0	0	0	0	1.000	0	1.000	1.000	2.000	P	7	2	1	0	0	1.000

LCS — Batting / Fielding

Year	Tm	Age	G	AB	H	2B	3B	HR	TB	R	RBI	GW	TBB	IBB	SO	HBP	SH	SF	SB	CS	SB%	GDP	Avg	OBP	SLG	Pos	G	PO	A	E	DP	FPct
1995	Cin	30	3	0	0	0	0	0	0	0	0	0	0	0	0	0	0	0	0	0	—	0	—	—	—	P	3	0	1	0	0	1.000
1997	Cle	32	5	0	0	0	0	0	0	0	0	0	0	0	0	0	0	0	0	0	—	0	—	—	—	P	5	0	0	0	0	—
LCS Totals			8	0	0	0	0	0	0	0	0	0	0	0	0	0	0	0	0	0	—	0	—	—	—	P	8	0	1	0	0	1.000

World Series — Batting / Fielding

Year	Tm	Age	G	AB	H	2B	3B	HR	TB	R	RBI	GW	TBB	IBB	SO	HBP	SH	SF	SB	CS	SB%	GDP	Avg	OBP	SLG	Pos	G	PO	A	E	DP	FPct
1997	Cle	32	4	0	0	0	0	0	0	0	0	0	0	0	0	1	0	0	0	0	—	0	.000	.000	.000	P	4	1	0	0	0	1.000
Postseason Totals			19	3	1	1	0	0	2	0	3	0	0	0	0	1	0	0	0	0	—	0	.333	.333	.667	P	19	2	4	0	0	1.000

RANDY JACKSON

—Ransom Joseph Jackson—Nickname: Handsom Ransom—Bats: Right; Throws: Right   Ht: 6'1"; Wt: 180 lbs; Born: 2/10/1926 in Little Rock, Arkansas; Debut: 5/2/1950

World Series		Batting																							Fielding						
Year Tm	Age	G	AB	H	2B	3B	HR	TB	R	RBI	GW	TBB	IBB	SO	HBP	SH	SF	SB	CS	SB%	GDP	Avg	OBP	SLG	Pos	G	PO	A	E	DP	FPct
1956 Bro	30	3	3	0	0	0	0	0	0	0	0	0	0	2	0	0	0	0	0	—	0	.000	.000	.000	—						

REGGIE JACKSON

(HOF 1993-W)—Reginald Martinez Jackson—Nickname: Mr. October—Bats: Left; Throws: Left   Ht: 6'0"; Wt: 195 lbs; Born: 5/18/1946 in Wyncote, Pennsylvania; Debut: 6/9/1967

Division Series		Batting																							Fielding						
Year Tm	Age	G	AB	H	2B	3B	HR	TB	R	RBI	GW	TBB	IBB	SO	HBP	SH	SF	SB	CS	SB%	GDP	Avg	OBP	SLG	Pos	G	PO	A	E	DP	FPct
1981 NYA	35	5	20	6	0	0	2	12	4	4	0	1	0	5	0	0	0	0	0	—	1	.300	.333	.600	OF	5	7	0	0	0	1.000
LCS		**Batting**																							**Fielding**						
Year Tm	Age	G	AB	H	2B	3B	HR	TB	R	RBI	GW	TBB	IBB	SO	HBP	SH	SF	SB	CS	SB%	GDP	Avg	OBP	SLG	Pos	G	PO	A	E	DP	FPct
1971 Oak	25	3	12	4	1	0	2	11	2	2	0	0	0	1	0	0	0	0	0	—	0	.333	.333	.917	OF	3	10	1	0	0	1.000
1972 Oak	26	5	18	5	1	0	0	6	1	2	0	1	0	6	0	0	0	2	0	1.00	0	.278	.316	.333	OF	5	14	0	1	0	.933
1973 Oak-*M*	27	5	21	3	0	0	0	3	0	0	0	0	0	6	0	0	0	0	1	.00	0	.143	.143	.143	OF	5	19	0	0	0	1.000
1974 Oak	28	4	12	2	1	0	0	3	0	1	0	5	0	2	0	0	0	0	0	—	0	.167	.412	.250	OF	1	0	0	0	0	—
1975 Oak	29	3	12	5	0	0	1	8	1	3	0	0	0	2	0	0	0	0	0	—	0	.417	.417	.667	OF	3	5	1	0	1	1.000
1977 NYA	31	5	16	2	0	0	0	2	1	1	0	2	0	2	0	0	0	1	0	1.00	0	.125	.222	.125	OF	4	10	1	0	0	1.000
1978 NYA	32	4	13	6	1	0	2	13	5	6	0	3	0	4	0	0	1	0	0	—	0	.462	.529	1.000	OF	1	4	0	0	0	1.000
1980 NYA	34	3	11	3	1	0	0	4	1	0	0	1	0	4	0	0	0	0	0	—	0	.273	.333	.364	OF	3	5	0	0	0	1.000
1981 NYA	35	2	4	0	0	0	0	0	1	1	0	1	0	0	0	0	0	1	0	1.00	0	.000	.200	.000	OF	2	1	0	0	0	1.000
1982 Cal	36	5	18	2	0	0	1	5	2	2	0	2	0	7	0	0	0	0	0	—	1	.111	.200	.278	OF	5	3	0	0	0	1.000
1986 Cal	40	6	26	5	2	0	0	7	2	2	0	2	0	7	0	0	0	0	0	—	0	.192	.250	.269	—						
LCS Totals		45	163	37	7	0	6	62	16	20	0	17	0	41	0	0	1	4	1	.80	1	.227	.298	.380	OF	32	71	3	1	1	.987
World Series		**Batting**																							**Fielding**						
Year Tm	Age	G	AB	H	2B	3B	HR	TB	R	RBI	GW	TBB	IBB	SO	HBP	SH	SF	SB	CS	SB%	GDP	Avg	OBP	SLG	Pos	G	PO	A	E	DP	FPct
1973 Oak-*M*	27	7	29	9	3	1	1	17	3	6	1	2	0	7	0	0	0	0	0	—	1	.310	.355	.586	OF	7	15	0	0	0	1.000
1974 Oak	28	5	14	4	1	0	1	8	3	1	1	5	0	3	0	0	0	1	0	1.00	0	.286	.474	.571	OF	5	8	1	1	0	.900
1977 NYA	31	6	20	9	1	0	5	25	10	8	1	3	0	4	1	0	0	0	0	—	0	.450	.542	1.250	OF	6	9	0	0	0	1.000
1978 NYA	32	6	23	9	1	0	2	16	2	8	0	3	1	7	2	0	0	0	0	—	0	.391	.500	.696	—						
1981 NYA	35	3	12	4	1	0	1	8	3	1	0	2	1	3	0	0	0	0	0	—	1	.333	.429	.667	OF	3	5	0	1	0	.833
WS Totals		27	98	35	7	1	10	74	21	24	3	15	2	24	3	0	0	1	0	1.00	2	.357	.457	.755	OF	21	37	1	2	0	.950
Postseason Totals		77	281	78	14	1	18	148	41	48	3	33	2	70	3	0	1	5	1	.83	4	.278	.358	.527	OF	58	115	4	3	1	.975

RON JACKSON

—Ronnie Damien Jackson—Bats: Right; Throws: Right   Ht: 6'0"; Wt: 200 lbs; Born: 5/9/1953 in Birmingham, Alabama; Debut: 9/12/1975

LCS		Batting																							Fielding						
Year Tm	Age	G	AB	H	2B	3B	HR	TB	R	RBI	GW	TBB	IBB	SO	HBP	SH	SF	SB	CS	SB%	GDP	Avg	OBP	SLG	Pos	G	PO	A	E	DP	FPct
1982 Cal	29	1	1	1	0	0	0	1	0	0	0	0	0	0	0	0	0	0	0	—	0	1.000	1.000	1.000	—						

SONNY JACKSON

—Roland Thomas Jackson—Bats: Left; Throws: Right   Ht: 5'9"; Wt: 150 lbs; Born: 7/9/1944 in Washington, DC; Debut: 9/27/1963

LCS		Batting																							Fielding						
Year Tm	Age	G	AB	H	2B	3B	HR	TB	R	RBI	GW	TBB	IBB	SO	HBP	SH	SF	SB	CS	SB%	GDP	Avg	OBP	SLG	Pos	G	PO	A	E	DP	FPct
1969 Atl	25	1	0	0	0	0	0	0	0	0	0	0	0	0	0	0	0	0	0	—	0	—	—	—	SS	1	0	0	0	0	—

TRAVIS JACKSON

(HOF 1982-V)—Travis Calvin Jackson—Nickname: Stonewall—Bats: R; Throws: R   Ht: 5'10"; Wt: 160 lbs; Born: 11/2/1903 in Waldo, Ark.; Deb.: 9/27/1922; Died: 7/27/1987

World Series		Batting																							Fielding						
Year Tm	Age	G	AB	H	2B	3B	HR	TB	R	RBI	GW	TBB	IBB	SO	HBP	SH	SF	SB	CS	SB%	GDP	Avg	OBP	SLG	Pos	G	PO	A	E	DP	FPct
1923 NYG	19	1	1	0	0	0	0	0	0	0	0	0	0	0	0	0	0	0	0	—	0	.000	.000	.000	—						
1924 NYG	20	7	27	2	0	0	0	2	3	1	0	1	0	4	0	1	1	1	0	1.00	2	.074	.103	.074	SS	7	8	20	3	3	.903
1933 NYG	29	5	18	4	1	0	0	5	3	2	0	1	0	3	0	2	0	0	0	—	1	.222	.263	.278	3B	5	3	16	1	2	.950
1936 NYG	32	6	21	4	0	0	0	4	1	1	0	1	0	3	0	0	0	0	0	—	0	.190	.227	.190	3B	6	2	8	3	1	.769
WS Totals		19	67	10	1	0	0	11	7	4	0	3	0	10	0	3	1	1	0	1.00	3	.149	.183	.164	3B	11	5	24	4	3	.879

SIG JAKUCKI

—Sigmund Jakucki—Nickname: Jack—Throws: Right; Bats: Right   Ht: 6'2"; Wt: 198 lbs; Born: 8/20/1909 in Camden, New Jersey; Debut: 8/30/1936; Died: 5/29/1979

World Series			Pitching																										
Year	Tm	Age	G	GS	CG	GF	IP	BFP	H	R	ER	HR	SH	SF	HB	TBB	IBB	SO	WP	Bk	W	L	Pct	ShO	Sv-Op	Hld	OAvg	OOBP	ERA
1944	StL	35	1	1	0	0	3.0	15	5	4	3	1	0	0	0	0	0	4	0	0	0	1	.000	0	0- 0	0	.333	.333	9.00

World Series		Batting																							Fielding						
Year Tm	Age	G	AB	H	2B	3B	HR	TB	R	RBI	GW	TBB	IBB	SO	HBP	SH	SF	SB	CS	SB%	GDP	Avg	OBP	SLG	Pos	G	PO	A	E	DP	FPct
1944 StL	35	1	0	0	0	0	0	0	0	0	0	0	0	0	0	0	0	0	0	—	0	—	—	—	P	1	0	1	0	0	1.000

BILL JAMES

—William Henry James—Nickname: Big Bill—Throws: Right; Bats: Both   Ht: 6'4"; Wt: 195 lbs; Born: 1/20/1887 in Detroit, Michigan; Debut: 6/12/1911; Died: 5/24/1942

World Series			Pitching																										
Year	Tm	Age	G	GS	CG	GF	IP	BFP	H	R	ER	HR	SH	SF	HB	TBB	IBB	SO	WP	Bk	W	L	Pct	ShO	Sv-Op	Hld	OAvg	OOBP	ERA
1919	ChA	32	1	0	0	0	4.2	23	8	4	3	0	0	0	1	3	0	2	0	0	0	0	—	0	0- 0	0	.421	.522	5.79

World Series		Batting																							Fielding						
Year Tm	Age	G	AB	H	2B	3B	HR	TB	R	RBI	GW	TBB	IBB	SO	HBP	SH	SF	SB	CS	SB%	GDP	Avg	OBP	SLG	Pos	G	PO	A	E	DP	FPct
1919 ChA	32	1	2	0	0	0	0	0	0	0	0	0	0	1	0	0	0	0	0	—	0	.000	.000	.000	P	1	0	0	0	0	—

BILL JAMES

—William Lawrence James—Nickname: Seattle Bill—Throws: Right; Bats: Right   Ht: 6'3"; Wt: 196 lbs; Born: 3/12/1892 in Iowa Hill, California; Debut: 4/17/1913; Died: 3/10/1971

World Series			Pitching																										
Year	Tm	Age	G	GS	CG	GF	IP	BFP	H	R	ER	HR	SH	SF	HB	TBB	IBB	SO	WP	Bk	W	L	Pct	ShO	Sv-Op	Hld	OAvg	OOBP	ERA
1914	Bos	22	2	1	1	1	11.0	37	2	0	0	0	0	0	0	6	1	9	0	0	2	0	1.000	1	0- 0	0	.065	.216	0.00

World Series		Batting																							Fielding						
Year Tm	Age	G	AB	H	2B	3B	HR	TB	R	RBI	GW	TBB	IBB	SO	HBP	SH	SF	SB	CS	SB%	GDP	Avg	OBP	SLG	Pos	G	PO	A	E	DP	FPct
1914 Bos	22	2	4	0	0	0	0	0	0	0	0	0	0	4	0	0	0	0	0	—	0	.000	.000	.000	P	2	0	4	0	0	1.000

CHARLIE JAMES

—Charles Wesley James—Nickname: Chopdown Charlie—Bats: Right; Throws: Right   Ht: 6'1"; Wt: 195 lbs; Born: 12/22/1937 in St. Louis, Missouri; Debut: 8/2/1960

World Series		Batting																							Fielding						
Year Tm	Age	G	AB	H	2B	3B	HR	TB	R	RBI	GW	TBB	IBB	SO	HBP	SH	SF	SB	CS	SB%	GDP	Avg	OBP	SLG	Pos	G	PO	A	E	DP	FPct
1964 StL	26	3	3	0	0	0	0	0	0	0	0	0	0	1	0	0	0	0	0	—	0	.000	.000	.000	—						

DION JAMES

—Bats: Left; Throws: Left   Ht: 6'1"; Wt: 170 lbs; Born: 11/9/1962 in Philadelphia, Pennsylvania; Debut: 9/16/1983

Division Series		Batting																							Fielding						
Year Tm	Age	G	AB	H	2B	3B	HR	TB	R	RBI	GW	TBB	IBB	SO	HBP	SH	SF	SB	CS	SB%	GDP	Avg	OBP	SLG	Pos	G	PO	A	E	DP	FPct
1995 NYA	32	4	12	1	0	0	0	1	0	0	0	1	1	1	0	0	0	0	0	—	0	.083	.154	.083	OF	4	6	0	0	0	1.000

CHARLIE JAMIESON

—Charles Devine Jamieson—Bats: Left; Throws: Left   Ht: 5'8"; Wt: 165 lbs; Born: 2/7/1893 in Paterson, New Jersey; Debut: 9/20/1915; Died: 10/27/1969

World Series		Batting																							Fielding						
Year Tm	Age	G	AB	H	2B	3B	HR	TB	R	RBI	GW	TBB	IBB	SO	HBP	SH	SF	SB	CS	SB%	GDP	Avg	OBP	SLG	Pos	G	PO	A	E	DP	FPct
1920 Cle	27	6	15	5	1	0	0	6	2	1	0	1	0	0	0	0	0	1	1	.50	0	.333	.375	.400	OF	5	8	1	0	1	1.000

LARRY JANSEN—Lawrence Joseph Jansen—Throws: Right; Bats: Right

Ht: 6'2"; Wt: 190 lbs; Born: 7/16/1920 in Verboort, Oregon; Debut: 4/17/1947

World Series — Pitching

Year Tm	Age	G	GS	CG	GF	IP	BFP	H	R	ER	HR	SH	SF	HB	TBB	IBB	SO	WP	Bk	W	L	Pct	ShO	Sv-Op	Hld	OAvg	OOBP	ERA
1951 NYG	31	3	2	0	1	10.0	41	8	7	7	2	0	0	0	4	1	6	0	0	0	2	.000	0	0-0	0	.216	.293	6.30

World Series — Batting / Fielding

Year Tm	Age	G	AB	H	2B	3B	HR	TB	R	RBI	GW	TBB	IBB	SO	HBP	SH	SF	SB	CS	SB%	GDP	Avg	OBP	SLG	Pos	G	PO	A	E	DP	FPct
1951 NYG	31	3	2	0	0	0	0	0	0	0	0	0	0	0	0	0	0	0	0	—	0	.000	.000	.000	P	3	1	2	0	0	1.000

HAL JANVRIN—Harold Chandler Janvrin—Nickname: Childe Harold—Bats: Right; Throws: Right

Ht: 5'11"; Wt: 168 lbs; Born: 8/27/1892 in Haverhill, Massachusetts; Debut: 7/9/1911; Died: 3/1/1962

World Series — Batting / Fielding

Year Tm	Age	G	AB	H	2B	3B	HR	TB	R	RBI	GW	TBB	IBB	SO	HBP	SH	SF	SB	CS	SB%	GDP	Avg	OBP	SLG	Pos	G	PO	A	E	DP	FPct
1915 Bos	23	1	1	0	0	0	0	0	0	0	0	0	0	0	0	0	0	0	0	—	0	.000	.000	.000	SS	1	1	0	0	0	1.000
1916 Bos	24	5	23	5	3	0	0	8	2	1	0	0	0	6	0	1	0	0	1	.00	0	.217	.217	.348	2B	5	8	15	2	4	.920
WS Totals		6	24	5	3	0	0	8	2	1	0	0	0	6	0	1	0	0	1	.00	0	.208	.208	.333	2B	5	8	15	2	4	.920

PAT JARVIS—Robert Patrick Jarvis—Throws: Right; Bats: Right

Ht: 5'10"; Wt: 180 lbs; Born: 3/18/1941 in Carlyle, Illinois; Debut: 8/4/1966

LCS — Pitching

Year Tm	Age	G	GS	CG	GF	IP	BFP	H	R	ER	HR	SH	SF	HB	TBB	IBB	SO	WP	Bk	W	L	Pct	ShO	Sv-Op	Hld	OAvg	OOBP	ERA
1969 Atl	28	1	1	0	0	4.1	21	10	6	6	3	0	0	0	0	0	6	0	0	0	1	.000	0	0-0	0	.476	.476	12.46

LCS — Batting / Fielding

Year Tm	Age	G	AB	H	2B	3B	HR	TB	R	RBI	GW	TBB	IBB	SO	HBP	SH	SF	SB	CS	SB%	GDP	Avg	OBP	SLG	Pos	G	PO	A	E	DP	FPct
1969 Atl	28	1	2	0	0	0	0	0	0	0	0	0	0	2	0	0	0	0	0	—	0	.000	.000	.000	P	1	1	2	0	1	1.000

LARRY JASTER—Larry Edward Jaster—Throws: Left; Bats: Left

Ht: 6'3"; Wt: 190 lbs; Born: 1/13/1944 in Midland, Michigan; Debut: 9/17/1965

World Series — Pitching

Year Tm	Age	G	GS	CG	GF	IP	BFP	H	R	ER	HR	SH	SF	HB	TBB	IBB	SO	WP	Bk	W	L	Pct	ShO	Sv-Op	Hld	OAvg	OOBP	ERA
1967 StL	23	1	0	0	0	0.1	3	2	0	0	0	0	1	0	0	0	0	0	0	0	0	—	0	0-0	0	1.000	.667	0.00
1968 StL	24	1	0	0	0	0.0	3	2	3	3	1	0	0	0	1	0	0	0	0	0	0	—	0	0-0	0	1.000	1.000	—
WS Totals		2	0	0	0	0.1	12	4	3	3	1	0	1	0	1	0	0	0	0	0	0	—	0	0-0	0	1.000	.833	81.00

World Series — Batting / Fielding

Year Tm	Age	G	AB	H	2B	3B	HR	TB	R	RBI	GW	TBB	IBB	SO	HBP	SH	SF	SB	CS	SB%	GDP	Avg	OBP	SLG	Pos	G	PO	A	E	DP	FPct
1967 StL	23	1	0	0	0	0	0	0	0	0	0	0	0	0	0	0	0	0	0	—	0	—	—	—	P	1	0	0	0	0	—
1968 StL	24	1	0	0	0	0	0	0	0	0	0	0	0	0	0	0	0	0	0	—	0	—	—	—	P	1	0	0	0	0	—
WS Totals		2	0	0	0	0	0	0	0	0	0	0	0	0	0	0	0	0	0	—	0	—	—	—	P	2	0	0	0	0	—

JULIAN JAVIER—Manuel Julian Javier—Nicknames: Hoolie, The Phantom—Bats: Right; Throws: Right

Ht: 6'1"; Wt: 175 lbs; Born: 8/9/1936 in San Francisco de Macoris, Dominican Republic; Debut: 5/28/1960

World Series — Batting / Fielding

Year Tm	Age	G	AB	H	2B	3B	HR	TB	R	RBI	GW	TBB	IBB	SO	HBP	SH	SF	SB	CS	SB%	GDP	Avg	OBP	SLG	Pos	G	PO	A	E	DP	FPct
1964 StL	28	1	0	0	0	0	0	0	1	0	0	0	0	0	0	0	0	0	0	—	0	—	—	—	2B	1	0	1	0	0	1.000
1967 StL	31	7	25	9	3	0	1	15	2	4	0	0	0	6	0	0	0	0	1	.00	0	.360	.360	.600	2B	7	12	20	1	4	.970
1968 StL	32	7	27	9	1	0	0	10	1	3	0	3	0	4	0	0	0	1	2	.33	0	.333	.400	.370	2B	7	15	13	0	4	1.000
1972 Cin	36	4	2	0	0	0	0	0	0	0	0	0	0	0	0	1	0	0	0	—	0	.000	.000	.000	—						
WS Totals		19	54	18	4	0	1	25	4	7	0	3	0	10	0	1	0	1	3	.25	0	.333	.368	.463	2B	15	27	34	1	8	.984

STAN JAVIER—Stanley Julian Antonio Javier—Bats: Both; Throws: Right

Ht: 6'0"; Wt: 185 lbs; Born: 1/9/1964 in San Francisco de Macoris, Dominican Republic; Debut: 4/15/1984

Division Series — Batting / Fielding

Year Tm	Age	G	AB	H	2B	3B	HR	TB	R	RBI	GW	TBB	IBB	SO	HBP	SH	SF	SB	CS	SB%	GDP	Avg	OBP	SLG	Pos	G	PO	A	E	DP	FPct
1997 SF	33	3	12	5	1	0	0	6	2	1	0	0	0	2	0	0	0	1	1	.50	0	.417	.417	.500	OF	3	11	0	0	0	1.000

LCS — Batting / Fielding

Year Tm	Age	G	AB	H	2B	3B	HR	TB	R	RBI	GW	TBB	IBB	SO	HBP	SH	SF	SB	CS	SB%	GDP	Avg	OBP	SLG	Pos	G	PO	A	E	DP	FPct
1988 Oak	24	2	4	2	0	0	0	2	0	1	0	1	1	0	0	0	0	0	0	—	0	.500	.600	.500	OF	2	5	0	0	0	1.000
1989 Oak	25	1	2	0	0	0	0	0	0	0	0	0	0	1	0	0	0	0	0	—	0	.000	.000	.000	OF	1	1	0	0	0	1.000
LCS Totals		3	6	2	0	0	0	2	0	1	0	1	1	1	0	0	0	0	0	—	0	.333	.429	.333	OF	3	6	0	0	0	1.000

World Series — Batting / Fielding

Year Tm	Age	G	AB	H	2B	3B	HR	TB	R	RBI	GW	TBB	IBB	SO	HBP	SH	SF	SB	CS	SB%	GDP	Avg	OBP	SLG	Pos	G	PO	A	E	DP	FPct
1988 Oak	24	3	4	2	0	0	0	2	0	2	0	0	0	1	0	0	1	0	0	—	0	.500	.400	.500	OF	2	1	0	0	0	1.000
1989 Oak	25	1	0	0	0	0	0	0	0	0	0	0	0	0	0	0	0	0	0	—	0	—	—	—	OF	1	0	0	0	0	—
WS Totals		4	4	2	0	0	0	2	0	2	0	0	0	1	0	0	1	0	0	—	0	.500	.400	.500	OF	3	1	0	0	0	1.000
Postseason Totals		10	22	9	1	0	0	10	2	4	0	1	1	4	0	0	1	1	1	.50	0	.409	.417	.455	OF	9	18	0	0	0	1.000

JOEY JAY—Joseph Richard Jay—Throws: Right; Bats: Both

Ht: 6'4"; Wt: 228 lbs; Born: 8/15/1935 in Middletown, Connecticut; Debut: 7/21/1953

World Series — Pitching

Year Tm	Age	G	GS	CG	GF	IP	BFP	H	R	ER	HR	SH	SF	HB	TBB	IBB	SO	WP	Bk	W	L	Pct	ShO	Sv-Op	Hld	OAvg	OOBP	ERA
1961 Cin	26	2	2	1	0	9.2	42	8	6	6	2	0	0	0	6	0	6	0	0	1	1	.500	0	0-0	0	.222	.333	5.59

World Series — Batting / Fielding

Year Tm	Age	G	AB	H	2B	3B	HR	TB	R	RBI	GW	TBB	IBB	SO	HBP	SH	SF	SB	CS	SB%	GDP	Avg	OBP	SLG	Pos	G	PO	A	E	DP	FPct
1961 Cin	26	2	4	0	0	0	0	0	0	0	0	0	0	2	0	0	0	0	0	—	0	.000	.000	.000	P	2	1	0	0	0	1.000

GREGG JEFFERIES—Gregory Scott Jefferies—Nickname: Puggsly—Bats: Both; Throws: Right

Ht: 5'11"; Wt: 175 lbs; Born: 8/1/1967 in Burlingame, California; Debut: 9/6/1987

LCS — Batting / Fielding

Year Tm	Age	G	AB	H	2B	3B	HR	TB	R	RBI	GW	TBB	IBB	SO	HBP	SH	SF	SB	CS	SB%	GDP	Avg	OBP	SLG	Pos	G	PO	A	E	DP	FPct
1988 NYN	21	7	27	9	2	0	0	11	2	1	0	4	0	0	1	0	0	0	0	—	1	.333	.438	.407	3B	7	5	8	1	0	.929

REGGIE JEFFERSON—Reginald Jirod Jefferson—Bats: Both; Throws: Left

Ht: 6'4"; Wt: 210 lbs; Born: 9/25/1968 in Tallahassee, Florida; Debut: 5/18/1991

Division Series — Batting / Fielding

Year Tm	Age	G	AB	H	2B	3B	HR	TB	R	RBI	GW	TBB	IBB	SO	HBP	SH	SF	SB	CS	SB%	GDP	Avg	OBP	SLG	Pos	G	PO	A	E	DP	FPct
1995 Bos	27	1	4	1	0	0	0	1	1	0	0	0	0	1	0	0	0	0	0	—	0	.250	.250	.250	—						

DOUG JENNINGS—James Douglas Jennings—Bats: Left; Throws: Left

Ht: 5'10"; Wt: 175 lbs; Born: 9/30/1964 in Atlanta, Georgia; Debut: 4/8/1988

LCS — Batting / Fielding

Year Tm	Age	G	AB	H	2B	3B	HR	TB	R	RBI	GW	TBB	IBB	SO	HBP	SH	SF	SB	CS	SB%	GDP	Avg	OBP	SLG	Pos	G	PO	A	E	DP	FPct
1990 Oak	26	1	1	0	0	0	0	0	0	0	0	0	0	0	0	0	0	0	0	—	0	.000	.000	.000	OF	1	0	0	0	0	—

World Series — Batting / Fielding

Year Tm	Age	G	AB	H	2B	3B	HR	TB	R	RBI	GW	TBB	IBB	SO	HBP	SH	SF	SB	CS	SB%	GDP	Avg	OBP	SLG	Pos	G	PO	A	E	DP	FPct
1990 Oak	26	1	1	1	0	0	0	1	0	0	0	0	0	0	0	0	0	0	0	—	0	1.000	1.000	1.000	—						
Postseason Totals		2	2	1	0	0	0	1	0	0	0	0	0	0	0	0	0	0	0	—	0	.500	.500	.500	OF	1	0	0	0	0	—

JACKIE JENSEN—Jack Eugene Jensen—Bats: Right; Throws: Right

Ht: 5'11"; Wt: 190 lbs; Born: 3/9/1927 in San Francisco, California; Debut: 4/18/1950; Died: 7/14/1982

World Series — Batting / Fielding

Year Tm	Age	G	AB	H	2B	3B	HR	TB	R	RBI	GW	TBB	IBB	SO	HBP	SH	SF	SB	CS	SB%	GDP	Avg	OBP	SLG	Pos	G	PO	A	E	DP	FPct
1950 NYA	23	1	0	0	0	0	0	0	0	0	0	0	0	0	0	0	0	0	0	—	0	—	—	—	—						

DEREK JETER—Derek Sanderson Jeter—Bats: Right; Throws: Right

Ht: 6'3"; Wt: 185 lbs; Born: 6/26/1974 in Pequannock, New Jersey; Debut: 5/29/1995

Division Series		Batting																							Fielding						
Year Tm	Age	G	AB	H	2B	3B	HR	TB	R	RBI	GW	TBB	IBB	SO	HBP	SH	SF	SB	CS	SB%	GDP	Avg	OBP	SLG	Pos	G	PO	A	E	DP	FPct
1996 NYA-*RY*	22	4	17	7	1	0	0	8	2	1	0	0	0	2	0	0	0	0	0	—	0	.412	.412	.471	SS	4	8	10	2	2	.900
1997 NYA	23	5	21	7	1	0	2	14	6	2	1	3	0	5	0	0	0	1	0	1.00	0	.333	.417	.667	SS	5	12	15	0	1	1.000
DS Totals		9	38	14	2	0	2	22	8	3	1	3	0	7	0	0	0	1	0	1.00	0	.368	.415	.579	SS	9	20	25	2	3	.957

LCS		Batting																							Fielding						
Year Tm	Age	G	AB	H	2B	3B	HR	TB	R	RBI	GW	TBB	IBB	SO	HBP	SH	SF	SB	CS	SB%	GDP	Avg	OBP	SLG	Pos	G	PO	A	E	DP	FPct
1996 NYA-*RY*	22	5	24	10	2	0	1	15	5	1	0	0	0	5	0	0	0	2	0	1.00	0	.417	.417	.625	SS	5	6	13	0	0	1.000

World Series		Batting																							Fielding						
Year Tm	Age	G	AB	H	2B	3B	HR	TB	R	RBI	GW	TBB	IBB	SO	HBP	SH	SF	SB	CS	SB%	GDP	Avg	OBP	SLG	Pos	G	PO	A	E	DP	FPct
1996 NYA-*RY*	22	6	20	5	0	0	0	5	5	1	0	4	0	6	1	1	0	1	0	1.00	1	.250	.400	.250	SS	6	14	22	2	5	.947
Postseason Totals		20	82	29	4	0	3	42	18	5	1	7	0	18	1	1	0	4	0	1.00	1	.354	.411	.512	SS	20	40	60	4	8	.962

JOHNNY JETER—John Jeter—Bats: Right; Throws: Right

Ht: 6'1"; Wt: 180 lbs; Born: 10/24/1944 in Shreveport, Louisiana; Debut: 6/14/1969

LCS		Batting																							Fielding						
Year Tm	Age	G	AB	H	2B	3B	HR	TB	R	RBI	GW	TBB	IBB	SO	HBP	SH	SF	SB	CS	SB%	GDP	Avg	OBP	SLG	Pos	G	PO	A	E	DP	FPct
1970 Pit	25	3	2	0	0	0	0	0	0	0	0	0	0	2	0	0	0	0	0	—	0	.000	.000	.000	OF	1	2	0	0	0	1.000

TOMMY JOHN—Thomas Edward John—Nickname: T.J.—Throws: Left; Bats: Right

Ht: 6'3"; Wt: 180 lbs; Born: 5/22/1943 in Terre Haute, Indiana; Debut: 9/6/1963

Division Series		Pitching																										
Year Tm	Age	G	GS	CG	GF	IP	BFP	H	R	ER	HR	SH	SF	HB	TBB	IBB	SO	WP	Bk	W	L	Pct	ShO	Sv-Op	Hld	OAvg	OOBP	ERA
1981 NYA	38	1	1	0	0	7.0	29	8	5	5	2	1	0	0	2	0	0	0	0	0	1	.000	0	0-0	0	.308	.357	6.43

LCS		Pitching																										
Year Tm	Age	G	GS	CG	GF	IP	BFP	H	R	ER	HR	SH	SF	HB	TBB	IBB	SO	WP	Bk	W	L	Pct	ShO	Sv-Op	Hld	OAvg	OOBP	ERA
1977 LA	34	2	2	1	0	13.2	60	11	5	1	1	0	0	2	5	0	11	0	0	1	0	1.000	0	0-0	0	.208	.000	0.66
1978 LA	35	1	1	1	0	9.0	30	4	0	0	0	0	0	0	2	0	4	0	0	1	0	1.000	1	0-0	0	.143	.200	0.00
1980 NYA	37	1	1	0	0	6.2	28	8	2	2	1	0	0	0	1	0	3	1	0	0	0	—	0	0-0	0	.296	.321	2.70
1981 NYA	38	1	1	0	0	6.0	24	6	1	1	0	0	0	0	1	0	3	0	0	1	0	1.000	0	0-0	0	.261	.292	1.50
1982 Cal	39	2	2	1	0	12.1	54	11	9	7	1	0	0	1	6	1	6	3	0	1	1	.500	0	0-0	0	.234	.333	5.11
LCS Totals		7	7	3	0	47.2	392	40	17	11	3	0	0	3	15	1	27	4	0	4	1	.800	1	0-0	0	.225	.296	2.08

World Series		Pitching																										
Year Tm	Age	G	GS	CG	GF	IP	BFP	H	R	ER	HR	SH	SF	HB	TBB	IBB	SO	WP	Bk	W	L	Pct	ShO	Sv-Op	Hld	OAvg	OOBP	ERA
1977 LA	34	1	1	0	0	6.0	30	9	5	4	0	1	0	1	3	0	7	0	0	0	1	.000	0	0-0	0	.360	.448	6.00
1978 LA	35	2	2	0	0	14.2	61	14	8	5	1	0	0	0	4	0	6	0	0	1	0	1.000	0	0-0	0	.246	.295	3.07
1981 NYA	38	3	2	0	1	13.0	51	11	1	1	0	1	1	0	0	0	8	0	0	1	0	1.000	0	0-0	0	.224	.220	0.69
WS Totals		6	5	0	1	33.2	284	34	14	10	1	2	1	1	7	0	21	0	0	2	1	.667	0	0-0	0	.260	.300	2.67
Postseason Totals		14	13	3	1	88.1	734	82	36	26	6	3	1	4	24	1	48	4	0	6	3	.667	1	0-0	0	.245	.302	2.65

Division Series		Batting																							Fielding						
Year Tm	Age	G	AB	H	2B	3B	HR	TB	R	RBI	GW	TBB	IBB	SO	HBP	SH	SF	SB	CS	SB%	GDP	Avg	OBP	SLG	Pos	G	PO	A	E	DP	FPct
1981 NYA	38	1	0	0	0	0	0	0	0	0	0	0	0	0	0	0	0	0	0	—	0	—	—	—	P	1	0	3	0	0	1.000

LCS		Batting																							Fielding						
Year Tm	Age	G	AB	H	2B	3B	HR	TB	R	RBI	GW	TBB	IBB	SO	HBP	SH	SF	SB	CS	SB%	GDP	Avg	OBP	SLG	Pos	G	PO	A	E	DP	FPct
1977 LA	34	2	5	1	0	0	0	1	0	0	0	0	0	2	0	0	0	0	0	—	0	.200	.200	.200	P	2	0	1	0	0	1.000
1978 LA	35	1	3	0	0	0	0	0	0	0	0	0	0	0	0	1	0	0	0	—	0	.000	.000	.000	P	1	0	0	0	0	—
1980 NYA	37	1	0	0	0	0	0	0	0	0	0	0	0	0	0	0	0	0	0	—	0	—	—	—	P	1	0	1	0	0	1.000
1981 NYA	38	1	0	0	0	0	0	0	0	0	0	0	0	0	0	0	0	0	0	—	0	—	—	—	P	1	0	1	0	0	1.000
1982 Cal	39	2	0	0	0	0	0	0	0	0	0	0	0	0	0	0	0	0	0	—	0	—	—	—	P	2	3	1	0	0	1.000
LCS Totals		7	8	1	0	0	0	1	0	0	0	0	0	2	0	1	0	0	0	—	0	.125	.125	.125	P	7	3	4	0	0	1.000

World Series		Batting																							Fielding						
Year Tm	Age	G	AB	H	2B	3B	HR	TB	R	RBI	GW	TBB	IBB	SO	HBP	SH	SF	SB	CS	SB%	GDP	Avg	OBP	SLG	Pos	G	PO	A	E	DP	FPct
1977 LA	34	1	2	0	0	0	0	0	0	0	0	0	0	2	0	0	0	0	0	—	0	.000	.000	.000	P	1	0	0	0	0	—
1978 LA	35	2	0	0	0	0	0	0	0	0	0	0	0	0	0	0	0	0	0	—	0	—	—	—	P	2	0	4	0	0	1.000
1981 NYA	38	3	2	0	0	0	0	0	0	0	0	0	0	0	0	1	0	0	0	—	0	.000	.000	.000	P	3	0	3	0	0	1.000
WS Totals		6	4	0	0	0	0	0	0	0	0	0	0	2	0	1	0	0	0	—	0	.000	.000	.000	P	6	0	7	0	0	1.000
Postseason Totals		14	12	1	0	0	0	1	0	0	0	0	0	4	0	2	0	0	0	—	0	.083	.083	.083	P	14	3	14	0	0	1.000

BILL JOHNSON—William Russell Johnson—Nickname: Bull—Bats: Right; Throws: Right

Ht: 5'10"; Wt: 180 lbs; Born: 8/30/1918 in Montclair, New Jersey; Debut: 4/22/1943

World Series		Batting																							Fielding						
Year Tm	Age	G	AB	H	2B	3B	HR	TB	R	RBI	GW	TBB	IBB	SO	HBP	SH	SF	SB	CS	SB%	GDP	Avg	OBP	SLG	Pos	G	PO	A	E	DP	FPct
1943 NYA	25	5	20	6	1	1	0	9	3	3	1	0	0	3	0	0	0	0	0	—	2	.300	.300	.450	3B	5	2	9	1	0	.917
1947 NYA	29	7	26	7	0	3	0	13	8	2	0	3	0	4	1	0	0	0	0	—	1	.269	.367	.500	3B	7	11	14	0	1	1.000
1949 NYA	31	2	7	1	0	0	0	1	0	0	0	0	0	2	0	0	0	1	0	1.00	0	.143	.143	.143	3B	2	2	5	0	0	1.000
1950 NYA	32	4	6	0	0	0	0	0	0	0	0	0	0	3	0	0	0	0	0	—	0	.000	.000	.000	3B	4	1	5	0	1	1.000
WS Totals		18	59	14	1	4	0	23	11	5	1	3	0	12	1	0	0	1	0	1.00	3	.237	.286	.390	3B	18	16	33	1	2	.980

BOB JOHNSON—Robert Dale Johnson—Throws: Right; Bats: Left

Ht: 6'4"; Wt: 220 lbs; Born: 4/25/1943 in Aurora, Indiana; Debut: 9/19/1969

LCS		Pitching																										
Year Tm	Age	G	GS	CG	GF	IP	BFP	H	R	ER	HR	SH	SF	HB	TBB	IBB	SO	WP	Bk	W	L	Pct	ShO	Sv-Op	Hld	OAvg	OOBP	ERA
1971 Pit	28	1	1	0	0	8.0	33	5	1	0	0	1	0	0	3	1	7	0	0	1	0	1.000	0	0-0	0	.172	.250	0.00
1972 Pit	29	2	0	0	0	6.0	22	4	2	2	0	0	0	0	2	1	7	1	0	0	0	—	0	0-0	0	.200	.273	3.00
LCS Totals		3	1	0	0	14.0	110	9	3	2	0	1	0	0	5	2	14	1	0	1	0	1.000	0	0-0	0	.184	.259	1.29

World Series		Pitching																										
Year Tm	Age	G	GS	CG	GF	IP	BFP	H	R	ER	HR	SH	SF	HB	TBB	IBB	SO	WP	Bk	W	L	Pct	ShO	Sv-Op	Hld	OAvg	OOBP	ERA
1971 Pit	28	2	1	0	0	5.0	23	5	5	5	0	0	0	1	3	0	3	0	0	0	1	.000	0	0-0	1	.263	.391	9.00
Postseason Totals		5	2	0	0	19.0	156	14	8	7	0	1	0	1	8	2	17	1	0	1	1	.500	0	0-0	1	.206	.299	3.32

LCS		Batting																							Fielding						
Year Tm	Age	G	AB	H	2B	3B	HR	TB	R	RBI	GW	TBB	IBB	SO	HBP	SH	SF	SB	CS	SB%	GDP	Avg	OBP	SLG	Pos	G	PO	A	E	DP	FPct
1971 Pit	28	1	2	0	0	0	0	0	0	0	0	0	0	1	0	0	0	0	0	—	0	.000	.000	.000	P	1	0	0	0	0	—
1972 Pit	29	2	1	0	0	0	0	0	0	0	0	0	0	1	0	0	0	0	0	—	0	.000	.000	.000	P	2	0	0	0	0	—
LCS Totals		3	3	0	0	0	0	0	0	0	0	0	0	2	0	0	0	0	0	—	0	.000	.000	.000	P	3	0	0	0	0	—

World Series		Batting																							Fielding						
Year Tm	Age	G	AB	H	2B	3B	HR	TB	R	RBI	GW	TBB	IBB	SO	HBP	SH	SF	SB	CS	SB%	GDP	Avg	OBP	SLG	Pos	G	PO	A	E	DP	FPct
1971 Pit	28	2	3	0	0	0	0	0	0	0	0	0	0	2	0	0	0	0	0	—	0	.000	.000	.000	P	2	2	0	0	0	1.000
Postseason Totals		5	6	0	0	0	0	0	0	0	0	0	0	4	0	0	0	0	0	—	0	.000	.000	.000	P	5	2	0	0	0	1.000

BRIAN JOHNSON—Brian David Johnson—Bats: Right; Throws: Right

Ht: 6'2"; Wt: 210 lbs; Born: 1/8/1968 in Oakland, California; Debut: 4/5/1994

Division Series		Batting																							Fielding						
Year Tm	Age	G	AB	H	2B	3B	HR	TB	R	RBI	GW	TBB	IBB	SO	HBP	SH	SF	SB	CS	SB%	GDP	Avg	OBP	SLG	Pos	G	PO	A	E	DP	FPct
1996 SD	28	2	8	3	1	0	0	4	2	0	0	0	0	1	0	0	0	0	0	—	0	.375	.375	.500	C	2	15	3	0	2	1.000
1997 SF	29	3	10	1	0	0	1	4	2	1	0	1	0	4	0	0	0	0	0	—	0	.100	.182	.400	C	3	18	0	0	0	1.000
DS Totals		5	18	4	1	0	1	8	4	1	0	1	0	5	0	0	0	0	0	—	0	.222	.263	.444	C	5	33	3	0	2	1.000

CHARLES JOHNSON—Charles Edward Johnson—Bats: Right; Throws: Right

Ht: 6'2"; Wt: 215 lbs; Born: 7/20/1971 in Fort Pierce, Florida; Debut: 5/6/1994

Division Series		Batting																							Fielding						
Year Tm	Age	G	AB	H	2B	3B	HR	TB	R	RBI	GW	TBB	IBB	SO	HBP	SH	SF	SB	CS	SB%	GDP	Avg	OBP	SLG	Pos	G	PO	A	E	DP	FPct
1997 Fla	26	3	8	2	1	0	1	6	5	2	0	3	0	2	1	0	0	0	0	—	0	.250	.500	.750	C	3	21	3	0	1	1.000

LCS		Batting																							Fielding						
Year Tm	Age	G	AB	H	2B	3B	HR	TB	R	RBI	GW	TBB	IBB	SO	HBP	SH	SF	SB	CS	SB%	GDP	Avg	OBP	SLG	Pos	G	PO	A	E	DP	FPct
1997 Fla	26	6	17	2	2	0	0	4	1	5	1	3	1	8	1	1	0	0	1	.00	0	.118	.286	.235	C	6	52	3	2	1	.965

World Series — Batting / Fielding

Year Tm	Age	G	AB	H	2B	3B	HR	TB	R	RBI	GW	TBB	IBB	SO	HBP	SH	SF	SB	CS	SB%	GDP	Avg	OBP	SLG	Pos	G	PO	A	E	DP	FPct
1997 Fla	26	7	28	10	0	0	1	13	4	3	0	1	0	6	0	0	0	0	0	—	0	.357	.379	.464	C	7	49	2	0	0	1.000
Postseason Totals		16	53	14	3	0	2	23	10	10	1	7	1	16	2	1	0	0	1	.00	0	.264	.371	.434	C	16	122	8	2	2	.985

CLIFF JOHNSON—Clifford Johnson—Bats: Right; Throws: Right

Ht: 6'4"; Wt: 215 lbs; Born: 7/22/1947 in San Antonio, Texas; Debut: 9/13/1972

Division Series — Batting / Fielding

Year Tm	Age	G	AB	H	2B	3B	HR	TB	R	RBI	GW	TBB	IBB	SO	HBP	SH	SF	SB	CS	SB%	GDP	Avg	OBP	SLG	Pos	G	PO	A	E	DP	FPct
1981 Oak	34	2	7	2	1	0	0	3	0	0	0	0	0	1	0	1	0	0	0	—	0	.286	.286	.429	—						

LCS — Batting / Fielding

Year Tm	Age	G	AB	H	2B	3B	HR	TB	R	RBI	GW	TBB	IBB	SO	HBP	SH	SF	SB	CS	SB%	GDP	Avg	OBP	SLG	Pos	G	PO	A	E	DP	FPct
1977 NYA	30	5	15	6	2	0	1	11	2	2	1	1	0	2	0	0	0	0	0	—	0	.400	.438	.733	—						
1978 NYA	31	1	1	0	0	0	0	0	0	0	0	0	0	0	0	0	0	0	0	—	0	.000	.000	.000	—						
1981 Oak	34	2	6	0	0	0	0	0	0	0	0	2	0	2	0	0	0	0	0	—	0	.000	.250	.000	—						
1985 Tor	38	7	19	7	2	0	0	9	1	2	0	1	0	4	0	0	0	0	0	—	0	.368	.400	.474	—						
LCS Totals		15	41	13	4	0	1	20	3	4	1	4	0	8	0	0	0	0	0	—	0	.317	.378	.488	—	0	0	0	0	0	—

World Series — Batting / Fielding

Year Tm	Age	G	AB	H	2B	3B	HR	TB	R	RBI	GW	TBB	IBB	SO	HBP	SH	SF	SB	CS	SB%	GDP	Avg	OBP	SLG	Pos	G	PO	A	E	DP	FPct
1977 NYA	30	1	1	0	0	0	0	0	0	0	0	0	0	0	0	0	0	0	0	—	0	.000	.000	.000	—						
1978 NYA	31	2	2	0	0	0	0	0	0	0	0	0	0	1	0	0	0	0	0	—	1	.000	.000	.000	—						
WS Totals		3	3	0	0	0	0	0	0	0	0	0	0	1	0	0	0	0	0	—	1	.000	.000	.000	—	0	0	0	0	0	—
Postseason Totals		20	51	15	5	0	1	23	3	4	1	4	0	10	0	1	0	0	0	—	1	.294	.345	.451	—	0	0	0	0	0	—

DARRELL JOHNSON—Darrell Dean Johnson—Bats: Right; Throws: Right

Ht: 6'1"; Wt: 180 lbs; Born: 8/25/1928 in Horace, Nebraska; Debut: 4/20/1952

World Series — Batting / Fielding

Year Tm	Age	G	AB	H	2B	3B	HR	TB	R	RBI	GW	TBB	IBB	SO	HBP	SH	SF	SB	CS	SB%	GDP	Avg	OBP	SLG	Pos	G	PO	A	E	DP	FPct
1961 Cin	33	2	4	2	0	0	0	2	0	0	0	0	0	0	0	0	0	0	0	—	0	.500	.500	.500	C	2	8	1	0	1	1.000

DAVE JOHNSON—David Allen Johnson—Bats: Right; Throws: Right

Ht: 6'1"; Wt: 170 lbs; Born: 1/30/1943 in Orlando, Florida; Debut: 4/13/1965

LCS — Batting / Fielding

Year Tm	Age	G	AB	H	2B	3B	HR	TB	R	RBI	GW	TBB	IBB	SO	HBP	SH	SF	SB	CS	SB%	GDP	Avg	OBP	SLG	Pos	G	PO	A	E	DP	FPct
1969 Bal	26	3	13	3	0	0	0	3	2	0	0	2	1	1	0	0	0	0	0	—	0	.231	.333	.231	2B	3	5	11	0	2	1.000
1970 Bal	27	3	11	4	0	0	2	10	4	4	0	1	0	1	1	0	0	0	0	—	1	.364	.462	.909	2B	3	9	4	0	3	1.000
1971 Bal	28	3	10	3	2	0	0	5	2	0	0	3	0	1	0	0	0	0	0	—	0	.300	.462	.500	2B	3	5	6	1	3	.917
1977 Phi	34	1	4	1	0	0	0	1	0	2	0	0	0	1	0	0	0	0	0	—	0	.250	.250	.250	1B	1	8	0	0	0	1.000
LCS Totals		10	38	11	2	0	2	19	8	6	0	6	1	4	1	0	0	0	0	—	1	.289	.400	.500	2B	9	19	21	1	8	.976

World Series — Batting / Fielding

Year Tm	Age	G	AB	H	2B	3B	HR	TB	R	RBI	GW	TBB	IBB	SO	HBP	SH	SF	SB	CS	SB%	GDP	Avg	OBP	SLG	Pos	G	PO	A	E	DP	FPct
1966 Bal	23	4	14	4	1	0	0	5	1	1	0	0	0	1	0	0	0	0	0	—	2	.286	.286	.357	2B	4	12	12	0	4	1.000
1969 Bal	26	5	16	1	0	0	0	1	1	0	0	2	0	1	0	0	0	0	1	.00	0	.063	.167	.063	2B	5	8	15	0	4	1.000
1970 Bal	27	5	16	5	2	0	0	7	2	2	0	5	1	2	0	0	0	0	1	.00	0	.313	.476	.438	2B	5	15	9	0	1	1.000
1971 Bal	28	7	27	4	0	0	0	4	1	3	0	0	0	1	1	0	0	0	0	—	1	.148	.179	.148	2B	7	18	11	0	2	1.000
WS Totals		21	73	14	3	0	0	17	5	6	0	7	1	5	1	0	0	0	2	.00	3	.192	.272	.233	2B	21	53	47	0	11	1.000
Postseason Totals		31	111	25	5	0	2	36	13	12	0	13	2	9	2	0	0	0	2	.00	4	.225	.317	.324	2B	30	72	68	1	19	.993

DERON JOHNSON—Deron Roger Johnson—Bats: Right; Throws: Right

Ht: 6'2"; Wt: 200 lbs; Born: 7/17/1938 in San Diego, California; Debut: 9/20/1960; Died: 4/23/1992

LCS — Batting / Fielding

Year Tm	Age	G	AB	H	2B	3B	HR	TB	R	RBI	GW	TBB	IBB	SO	HBP	SH	SF	SB	CS	SB%	GDP	Avg	OBP	SLG	Pos	G	PO	A	E	DP	FPct
1973 Oak	35	4	10	1	0	0	0	1	0	0	0	2	0	6	0	0	0	0	0	—	0	.100	.250	.100	—						

World Series — Batting / Fielding

Year Tm	Age	G	AB	H	2B	3B	HR	TB	R	RBI	GW	TBB	IBB	SO	HBP	SH	SF	SB	CS	SB%	GDP	Avg	OBP	SLG	Pos	G	PO	A	E	DP	FPct
1973 Oak	35	6	10	3	1	0	0	4	0	0	0	1	0	4	0	0	0	0	0	—	0	.300	.364	.400	1B	2	8	1	0	0	1.000
Postseason Totals		10	20	4	1	0	0	5	0	0	0	3	0	10	0	0	0	0	0	—	0	.200	.304	.250	1B	2	8	1	0	0	1.000

DON JOHNSON—Donald Spore Johnson—Nickname: Pep—Bats: Right; Throws: Right

Ht: 6'0"; Wt: 170 lbs; Born: 12/7/1911 in Chicago, Illinois; Debut: 9/26/1943

World Series — Batting / Fielding

Year Tm	Age	G	AB	H	2B	3B	HR	TB	R	RBI	GW	TBB	IBB	SO	HBP	SH	SF	SB	CS	SB%	GDP	Avg	OBP	SLG	Pos	G	PO	A	E	DP	FPct
1945 ChN	33	7	29	5	2	1	0	9	4	0	0	0	0	8	0	4	0	1	0	1.00	0	.172	.172	.310	2B	7	11	23	1	5	.971

EARL JOHNSON—Earl Douglas Johnson—Nickname: Lefty—Throws: Left; Bats: Left

Ht: 6'3"; Wt: 190 lbs; Born: 4/2/1919 in Redmond, Washington; Debut: 7/20/1940; Died: 12/3/1994

World Series — Pitching

Year Tm	Age	G	GS	CG	GF	IP	BFP	H	R	ER	HR	SH	SF	HB	TBB	IBB	SO	WP	Bk	W	L	Pct	ShO	Sv-Op	Hld	OAvg	OOBP	ERA
1946 Bos	27	3	0	0	3	3.1	14	1	1	1	0	1	0	0	2	1	1	0	0	1	0	1.000	0	0- 0	0	.091	.231	2.70

World Series — Batting / Fielding

Year Tm	Age	G	AB	H	2B	3B	HR	TB	R	RBI	GW	TBB	IBB	SO	HBP	SH	SF	SB	CS	SB%	GDP	Avg	OBP	SLG	Pos	G	PO	A	E	DP	FPct
1946 Bos	27	3	1	0	0	0	0	0	0	0	0	0	0	0	0	0	0	0	0	—	0	.000	.000	.000	P	3	0	2	0	0	1.000

ERNIE JOHNSON—Ernest Rudolph Johnson—Bats: Left; Throws: Right

Ht: 5'9"; Wt: 151 lbs; Born: 4/29/1888 in Chicago, Illinois; Debut: 8/5/1912; Died: 5/1/1952

World Series — Batting / Fielding

Year Tm	Age	G	AB	H	2B	3B	HR	TB	R	RBI	GW	TBB	IBB	SO	HBP	SH	SF	SB	CS	SB%	GDP	Avg	OBP	SLG	Pos	G	PO	A	E	DP	FPct
1923 NYA	35	2	0	0	0	0	0	0	1	0	0	0	0	0	0	0	0	0	0	—	0	—	—	—	SS	1	0	1	0	0	1.000

ERNIE JOHNSON—Ernest Thorwald Johnson—Throws: Right; Bats: Right

Ht: 6'3"; Wt: 190 lbs; Born: 6/16/1924 in Brattleboro, Vermont; Debut: 4/28/1950

World Series — Pitching

Year Tm	Age	G	GS	CG	GF	IP	BFP	H	R	ER	HR	SH	SF	HB	TBB	IBB	SO	WP	Bk	W	L	Pct	ShO	Sv-Op	Hld	OAvg	OOBP	ERA
1957 Mil	33	3	0	0	0	7.0	24	2	1	1	1	1	0	0	1	0	8	0	0	0	1	.000	0	0- 0	0	.091	.130	1.29

World Series — Batting / Fielding

Year Tm	Age	G	AB	H	2B	3B	HR	TB	R	RBI	GW	TBB	IBB	SO	HBP	SH	SF	SB	CS	SB%	GDP	Avg	OBP	SLG	Pos	G	PO	A	E	DP	FPct
1957 Mil	33	3	1	0	0	0	0	0	0	0	0	0	0	1	0	0	0	0	0	—	0	.000	.000	.000	P	3	1	4	0	0	1.000

HOWARD JOHNSON—Howard Michael Johnson—Nickname: HoJo—Bats: Both; Throws: Right

Ht: 5'11"; Wt: 178 lbs; Born: 11/29/1960 in Clearwater, Florida; Debut: 4/14/1982

LCS — Batting / Fielding

Year Tm	Age	G	AB	H	2B	3B	HR	TB	R	RBI	GW	TBB	IBB	SO	HBP	SH	SF	SB	CS	SB%	GDP	Avg	OBP	SLG	Pos	G	PO	A	E	DP	FPct
1986 NYN	25	2	2	0	0	0	0	0	0	0	0	0	0	0	0	0	0	0	0	—	0	.000	.000	.000	—						
1988 NYN	27	6	18	1	0	0	0	1	3	0	0	1	0	6	0	0	0	1	0	1.00	0	.056	.105	.056	SS	5	6	9	1	0	.938
																									3B	1	0	0	0	0	—
LCS Totals		8	20	1	0	0	0	1	3	0	0	1	0	6	0	0	0	1	0	1.00	0	.050	.095	.050	SS	5	6	9	1	0	.938

World Series — Batting / Fielding

Year Tm	Age	G	AB	H	2B	3B	HR	TB	R	RBI	GW	TBB	IBB	SO	HBP	SH	SF	SB	CS	SB%	GDP	Avg	OBP	SLG	Pos	G	PO	A	E	DP	FPct
1984 Det	23	1	1	0	0	0	0	0	0	0	0	0	0	0	0	0	0	0	0	—	0	.000	.000	.000	—						
1986 NYN	25	2	5	0	0	0	0	0	0	0	0	0	0	2	0	0	0	0	0	—	0	.000	.000	.000	3B	1	1	0	0	0	1.000
																									SS	1	0	0	0	0	—
WS Totals		3	6	0	0	0	0	0	0	0	0	0	0	2	0	0	0	0	0	—	0	.000	.000	.000	3B	1	1	0	0	0	1.000
Postseason Totals		11	26	1	0	0	0	1	3	0	0	1	0	8	0	0	0	1	0	1.00	0	.038	.074	.038	SS	6	6	9	1	0	.938

JERRY JOHNSON—Jerry Michael Johnson—Throws: Right; Bats: Right

Ht: 6'3"; Wt: 200 lbs; Born: 12/3/1943 in Miami, Florida; Debut: 7/17/1968

LCS		Pitching																									
Year Tm	Age	G	GS	CG	GF	IP	BFP	H	R	ER	HR	SH	SF	HB	TBB	IBB	SO	WP	Bk	W	L	Pct	ShO	Sv-Op	Hld	OAvg	OOBP	ERA
1971 SF	27	1	0	0	0	1.1	6	1	2	2	1	0	0	0	1	1	2	0	0	0	0	—	0	0-0	0	.200	.333	13.50

LCS		Batting																							Fielding						
Year Tm	Age	G	AB	H	2B	3B	HR	TB	R	RBI	GW	TBB	IBB	SO	HBP	SH	SF	SB	CS	SB%	GDP	Avg	OBP	SLG	Pos	G	PO	A	E	DP	FPct
1971 SF	27	1	0	0	0	0	0	0	0	0	0	0	0	0	0	0	0	0	0	—	0	—	—	—	P	1	0	0	0	0	—

KEN JOHNSON—Kenneth Wandersee Johnson—Nickname: Hook—Throws: Left; Bats: Left

Ht: 6'1"; Wt: 185 lbs; Born: 1/14/1923 in Topeka, Kansas; Debut: 9/18/1947

World Series		Batting																							Fielding						
Year Tm	Age	G	AB	H	2B	3B	HR	TB	R	RBI	GW	TBB	IBB	SO	HBP	SH	SF	SB	CS	SB%	GDP	Avg	OBP	SLG	Pos	G	PO	A	E	DP	FPct
1950 Phi	27	1	0	0	0	0	0	0	1	0	0	0	0	0	0	0	0	0	0	—	0	—	—	—	—						

KEN JOHNSON—Kenneth Travis Johnson—Throws: Right; Bats: Right

Ht: 6'4"; Wt: 210 lbs; Born: 6/16/1933 in West Palm Beach, Florida; Debut: 9/13/1958

World Series		Pitching																									
Year Tm	Age	G	GS	CG	GF	IP	BFP	H	R	ER	HR	SH	SF	HB	TBB	IBB	SO	WP	Bk	W	L	Pct	ShO	Sv-Op	Hld	OAvg	OOBP	ERA
1961 Cin	28	1	0	0	0	0.2	2	0	0	0	0	0	0	0	0	0	0	0	0	0	0	—	0	0-0	0	.000	.000	0.00

World Series		Batting																							Fielding						
Year Tm	Age	G	AB	H	2B	3B	HR	TB	R	RBI	GW	TBB	IBB	SO	HBP	SH	SF	SB	CS	SB%	GDP	Avg	OBP	SLG	Pos	G	PO	A	E	DP	FPct
1961 Cin	28	1	0	0	0	0	0	0	0	0	0	0	0	0	0	0	0	0	0	—	0	—	—	—	P	1	0	0	0	0	—

LANCE JOHNSON—Kenneth Lance Johnson—Bats: Left; Throws: Left

Ht: 5'10"; Wt: 160 lbs; Born: 7/6/1963 in Cincinnati, Ohio; Debut: 7/10/1987

LCS		Batting																							Fielding						
Year Tm	Age	G	AB	H	2B	3B	HR	TB	R	RBI	GW	TBB	IBB	SO	HBP	SH	SF	SB	CS	SB%	GDP	Avg	OBP	SLG	Pos	G	PO	A	E	DP	FPct
1987 StL	24	1	0	0	0	0	0	0	1	0	0	0	0	0	0	0	0	1	0	1.00	0	—	—	—	—						
1993 ChA	30	6	23	5	1	1	1	11	2	6	1	2	0	1	0	0	0	1	0	1.00	1	.217	.280	.478	OF	6	15	0	0	0	1.000
LCS Totals		7	23	5	1	1	1	11	3	6	1	2	0	1	0	0	0	2	0	1.00	1	.217	.280	.478	OF	6	15	0	0	0	1.000
World Series		**Batting**																							**Fielding**						
Year Tm	Age	G	AB	H	2B	3B	HR	TB	R	RBI	GW	TBB	IBB	SO	HBP	SH	SF	SB	CS	SB%	GDP	Avg	OBP	SLG	Pos	G	PO	A	E	DP	FPct
1987 StL	24	1	0	0	0	0	0	0	0	0	0	0	0	0	0	0	0	1	0	1.00	0	—	—	—	—						
Postseason Totals		8	23	5	1	1	1	11	3	6	1	2	0	1	0	0	0	3	0	1.00	1	.217	.280	.478	OF	6	15	0	0	0	1.000

LOU JOHNSON—Louis Brown Johnson—Nickname: Slick—Bats: Right; Throws: Right

Ht: 5'11"; Wt: 170 lbs; Born: 9/22/1934 in Lexington, Kentucky; Debut: 4/17/1960

World Series		Batting																							Fielding						
Year Tm	Age	G	AB	H	2B	3B	HR	TB	R	RBI	GW	TBB	IBB	SO	HBP	SH	SF	SB	CS	SB%	GDP	Avg	OBP	SLG	Pos	G	PO	A	E	DP	FPct
1965 LA	31	7	27	8	2	0	2	16	3	4	1	1	0	3	0	1	0	0	1	.00	0	.296	.321	.593	OF	7	13	1	1	0	.933
1966 LA	32	4	15	4	1	0	0	5	1	0	0	1	0	1	0	0	0	0	0	—	1	.267	.313	.333	OF	4	9	0	0	0	1.000
WS Totals		11	42	12	3	0	2	21	4	4	1	2	0	4	0	1	0	0	1	.00	1	.286	.318	.500	OF	11	22	1	1	0	.958

RANDY JOHNSON—Randall David Johnson—Nickname: Big Unit—Throws: Left; Bats: Right

Ht: 6'10"; Wt: 225 lbs; Born: 9/10/1963 in Walnut Creek, California; Debut: 9/15/1988

Division Series		Pitching																									
Year Tm	Age	G	GS	CG	GF	IP	BFP	H	R	ER	HR	SH	SF	HB	TBB	IBB	SO	WP	Bk	W	L	Pct	ShO	Sv-Op	Hld	OAvg	OOBP	ERA
1995 Sea-*C*	32	2	1	0	1	10.0	40	5	3	3	1	1	1	0	6	1	16	0	0	2	0	1.000	0	0-0	0	.156	.282	2.70
1997 Sea	34	2	2	1	0	13.0	56	14	8	8	3	1	0	0	6	0	16	0	0	0	2	.000	0	0-0	0	.286	.364	5.54
DS Totals		4	3	1	1	23.0	192	19	11	11	4	2	1	0	12	1	32	0	0	2	2	.500	0	0-0	0	.235	.330	4.30
LCS		**Pitching**																									
Year Tm	Age	G	GS	CG	GF	IP	BFP	H	R	ER	HR	SH	SF	HB	TBB	IBB	SO	WP	Bk	W	L	Pct	ShO	Sv-Op	Hld	OAvg	OOBP	ERA
1995 Sea-*C*	32	2	2	0	0	15.1	60	12	6	4	1	0	1	0	2	0	13	0	0	0	1	.000	0	0-0	0	.211	.233	2.35
Postseason Totals		6	5	1	1	38.1	312	31	17	15	5	2	2	0	14	1	45	0	0	2	3	.400	0	0-0	0	.225	.292	3.52

Division Series		Batting																							Fielding						
Year Tm	Age	G	AB	H	2B	3B	HR	TB	R	RBI	GW	TBB	IBB	SO	HBP	SH	SF	SB	CS	SB%	GDP	Avg	OBP	SLG	Pos	G	PO	A	E	DP	FPct
1995 Sea	32	2	0	0	0	0	0	0	0	0	0	0	0	0	0	0	0	0	0	—	0	—	—	—	P	2	0	0	0	0	—
1997 Sea	34	2	0	0	0	0	0	0	0	0	0	0	0	0	0	0	0	0	0	—	0	—	—	—	P	2	0	3	0	0	1.000
DS Totals		4	0	0	0	0	0	0	0	0	0	0	0	0	0	0	0	0	0	—	0	—	—	—	P	4	0	3	0	0	1.000
LCS		**Batting**																							**Fielding**						
Year Tm	Age	G	AB	H	2B	3B	HR	TB	R	RBI	GW	TBB	IBB	SO	HBP	SH	SF	SB	CS	SB%	GDP	Avg	OBP	SLG	Pos	G	PO	A	E	DP	FPct
1995 Sea	32	2	0	0	0	0	0	0	0	0	0	0	0	0	0	0	0	0	0	—	0	—	—	—	P	2	1	1	0	0	1.000
Postseason Totals		6	0	0	0	0	0	0	0	0	0	0	0	0	0	0	0	0	0	—	0	—	—	—	P	6	1	4	0	0	1.000

ROY JOHNSON—Roy Cleveland Johnson—Bats: Left; Throws: Right

Ht: 5'9"; Wt: 175 lbs; Born: 2/23/1903 in Pryor, Oklahoma; Debut: 4/18/1929; Died: 9/10/1973

World Series		Batting																							Fielding						
Year Tm	Age	G	AB	H	2B	3B	HR	TB	R	RBI	GW	TBB	IBB	SO	HBP	SH	SF	SB	CS	SB%	GDP	Avg	OBP	SLG	Pos	G	PO	A	E	DP	FPct
1936 NYA	33	2	1	0	0	0	0	0	0	0	0	0	0	1	0	0	0	0	0	—	0	.000	.000	.000	—						

RUSS JOHNSON—William Russell Johnson—Bats: Right; Throws: Right

Ht: 5'10"; Wt: 180 lbs; Born: 2/22/1973 in Baton Rouge, Louisiana; Debut: 4/8/1997

Division Series		Batting																							Fielding						
Year Tm	Age	G	AB	H	2B	3B	HR	TB	R	RBI	GW	TBB	IBB	SO	HBP	SH	SF	SB	CS	SB%	GDP	Avg	OBP	SLG	Pos	G	PO	A	E	DP	FPct
1997 Hou	24	1	1	0	0	0	0	0	0	0	0	0	0	1	0	0	0	0	0	—	0	.000	.000	.000	—						

SYL JOHNSON—Sylvester Johnson—Throws: Right; Bats: Right

Ht: 5'11"; Wt: 180 lbs; Born: 12/31/1900 in Portland, Oregon; Debut: 4/24/1922; Died: 2/20/1985

World Series		Pitching																									
Year Tm	Age	G	GS	CG	GF	IP	BFP	H	R	ER	HR	SH	SF	HB	TBB	IBB	SO	WP	Bk	W	L	Pct	ShO	Sv-Op	Hld	OAvg	OOBP	ERA
1928 StL	27	2	0	0	1	2.0	12	4	2	1	0	0	0	0	1	0	1	0	0	0	0	—	0	0-0	0	.364	.417	4.50
1930 StL	29	2	0	0	1	5.0	22	4	4	4	2	2	1	0	3	0	4	0	0	0	0	—	0	0-0	0	.250	.350	7.20
1931 StL	30	3	1	0	1	9.0	37	10	3	3	1	1	0	0	1	0	6	0	0	0	1	.000	0	0-0	0	.286	.306	3.00
WS Totals		7	1	0	3	16.0	142	18	9	8	3	3	1	0	5	0	11	0	0	0	1	.000	0	0-0	0	.290	.338	4.50

World Series		Batting																							Fielding						
Year Tm	Age	G	AB	H	2B	3B	HR	TB	R	RBI	GW	TBB	IBB	SO	HBP	SH	SF	SB	CS	SB%	GDP	Avg	OBP	SLG	Pos	G	PO	A	E	DP	FPct
1928 StL	27	2	0	0	0	0	0	0	0	0	0	0	0	0	0	0	0	0	0	—	0	—	—	—	P	2	0	0	0	0	—
1930 StL	29	2	0	0	0	0	0	0	0	0	0	0	0	0	0	0	0	0	0	—	0	—	—	—	P	2	0	0	0	0	—
1931 StL	30	3	2	0	0	0	0	0	0	0	0	0	0	2	0	0	0	0	0	—	0	.000	.000	.000	P	3	0	1	0	0	1.000
WS Totals		7	2	0	0	0	0	0	0	0	0	0	0	2	0	0	0	0	0	—	0	.000	.000	.000	P	7	0	1	0	0	1.000

WALLACE JOHNSON—Wallace Darnell Johnson—Bats: Both; Throws: Right

Ht: 6'0"; Wt: 173 lbs; Born: 12/25/1956 in Gary, Indiana; Debut: 9/8/1981

Division Series		Batting																							Fielding						
Year Tm	Age	G	AB	H	2B	3B	HR	TB	R	RBI	GW	TBB	IBB	SO	HBP	SH	SF	SB	CS	SB%	GDP	Avg	OBP	SLG	Pos	G	PO	A	E	DP	FPct
1981 Mon	24	2	2	1	0	0	0	1	0	1	0	0	0	0	0	0	0	0	0	—	0	.500	.500	.500	—						

WALTER JOHNSON (HOF 1936-W)—Walter Perry Johnson—Nickname: The Big Train—T: R; B: R

Ht: 6'1"; Wt: 200 lbs; Born: 11/6/1887 in Humboldt, Kan.; Deb.: 8/2/1907; Died: 12/10/1946

World Series		Pitching																									
Year Tm	Age	G	GS	CG	GF	IP	BFP	H	R	ER	HR	SH	SF	HB	TBB	IBB	SO	WP	Bk	W	L	Pct	ShO	Sv-Op	Hld	OAvg	OOBP	ERA
1924 Was-*M*	36	3	2	2	1	24.0	106	30	10	6	3	3	2	0	11	3	20	1	0	1	2	.333	0	0-0	0	.337	.408	2.25
1925 Was	37	3	3	3	0	26.0	106	26	10	6	1	1	0	2	4	0	15	0	0	2	1	.667	1	0-0	0	.263	.305	2.08
WS Totals		6	5	5	1	50.0	424	56	20	12	4	4	2	3	15	3	35	1	0	3	3	.500	1	0-0	0	.298	.356	2.16

World Series		Batting																							Fielding						
Year Tm	Age	G	AB	H	2B	3B	HR	TB	R	RBI	GW	TBB	IBB	SO	HBP	SH	SF	SB	CS	SB%	GDP	Avg	OBP	SLG	Pos	G	PO	A	E	DP	FPct
1924 Was	36	3	9	1	0	0	0	1	0	0	0	0	0	0	0	0	0	0	0	—	1	.111	.111	.111	P	3	1	4	1	2	.833
1925 Was	37	3	11	1	0	0	0	1	0	0	0	0	0	3	0	0	0	0	0	—	0	.091	.091	.091	P	3	0	4	0	0	1.000
WS Totals		6	20	2	0	0	0	2	0	0	0	0	0	3	0	0	0	0	0	—	1	.100	.100	.100	P	6	1	8	1	2	.900

DOC JOHNSTON—Wheeler Roger Johnston—Bats: Left; Throws: Left

Ht: 6'0"; Wt: 170 lbs; Born: 9/9/1887 in Cleveland, Tennessee; Debut: 10/3/1909; Died: 2/17/1961

World Series		Batting																							Fielding						
Year Tm	Age	G	AB	H	2B	3B	HR	TB	R	RBI	GW	TBB	IBB	SO	HBP	SH	SF	SB	CS	SB%	GDP	Avg	OBP	SLG	Pos	G	PO	A	E	DP	FPct
1920 Cle	33	5	11	3	0	0	0	3	1	0	0	2	0	1	0	1	0	1	2	.33	0	.273	.385	.273	1B	5	29	6	0	3	1.000

JIMMY JOHNSTON—James Harle Johnston—Bats: Right; Throws: Right

Ht: 5'10"; Wt: 160 lbs; Born: 12/10/1889 in Cleveland, Tennessee; Debut: 5/3/1911; Died: 2/14/1967

World Series		Batting																							Fielding						
Year Tm	Age	G	AB	H	2B	3B	HR	TB	R	RBI	GW	TBB	IBB	SO	HBP	SH	SF	SB	CS	SB%	GDP	Avg	OBP	SLG	Pos	G	PO	A	E	DP	FPct
1916 Bro	26	3	10	3	0	1	0	5	1	0	0	1	0	0	0	0	0	0	2	.00	0	.300	.364	.500	OF	2	1	0	1	0	.500
1920 Bro	30	4	14	3	0	0	0	3	2	0	0	0	0	2	0	2	0	1	0	1.00	0	.214	.214	.214	3B	4	2	8	0	2	1.000
WS Totals		7	24	6	0	1	0	8	3	0	0	1	0	2	0	2	0	1	2	.33	0	.250	.280	.333	3B	4	2	8	0	2	1.000

JAY JOHNSTONE—John William Johnstone—Bats: Left; Throws: Right

Ht: 6'1"; Wt: 175 lbs; Born: 11/20/1945 in Manchester, Connecticut; Debut: 7/30/1966

Division Series		Batting																							Fielding						
Year Tm	Age	G	AB	H	2B	3B	HR	TB	R	RBI	GW	TBB	IBB	SO	HBP	SH	SF	SB	CS	SB%	GDP	Avg	OBP	SLG	Pos	G	PO	A	E	DP	FPct
1981 LA	35	1	1	0	0	0	0	0	0	0	0	0	0	0	0	0	0	0	0	—	0	.000	.000	.000	—						
LCS		Batting																							Fielding						
Year Tm	Age	G	AB	H	2B	3B	HR	TB	R	RBI	GW	TBB	IBB	SO	HBP	SH	SF	SB	CS	SB%	GDP	Avg	OBP	SLG	Pos	G	PO	A	E	DP	FPct
1976 Phi	30	3	9	7	1	1	0	10	1	2	0	1	0	0	0	0	0	0	0	—	0	.778	.800	1.111	OF	2	3	0	0	0	1.000
1977 Phi	31	2	5	1	0	0	0	1	0	0	0	0	0	1	0	0	0	0	0	—	0	.200	.200	.200	OF	2	4	0	0	0	1.000
1981 LA	35	2	2	0	0	0	0	0	0	0	0	0	0	0	0	0	0	0	0	—	0	.000	.000	.000	—						
1985 LA	39	1	1	0	0	0	0	0	0	0	0	0	0	0	0	0	0	0	0	—	0	.000	.000	.000	—						
LCS Totals		8	17	8	1	1	0	11	1	2	0	1	0	1	0	0	0	0	0	—	0	.471	.500	.647	OF	4	7	0	0	0	1.000
World Series		Batting																							Fielding						
Year Tm	Age	G	AB	H	2B	3B	HR	TB	R	RBI	GW	TBB	IBB	SO	HBP	SH	SF	SB	CS	SB%	GDP	Avg	OBP	SLG	Pos	G	PO	A	E	DP	FPct
1978 NYA	32	2	0	0	0	0	0	0	0	0	0	0	0	0	0	0	0	0	0	—	0	—	—	—	OF	2	1	0	0	0	1.000
1981 LA	35	3	3	2	0	0	1	5	1	3	0	0	0	0	0	0	0	0	0	—	0	.667	.667	1.667	—						
WS Totals		5	3	2	0	0	1	5	1	3	0	0	0	0	0	0	0	0	0	—	0	.667	.667	1.667	OF	2	1	0	0	0	1.000
Postseason Totals		14	21	10	1	1	1	16	2	5	0	1	0	1	0	0	0	0	0	—	0	.476	.500	.762	OF	6	8	0	0	0	1.000

ANDRUW JONES—Andruw Rudolf Jones—Bats: Right; Throws: Right

Ht: 6'1"; Wt: 185 lbs; Born: 4/23/1977 in Wellemstad, Curacao; Debut: 8/15/1996

Division Series		Batting																							Fielding						
Year Tm	Age	G	AB	H	2B	3B	HR	TB	R	RBI	GW	TBB	IBB	SO	HBP	SH	SF	SB	CS	SB%	GDP	Avg	OBP	SLG	Pos	G	PO	A	E	DP	FPct
1996 Atl	19	3	0	0	0	0	0	0	0	0	0	1	0	0	0	0	0	0	0	—	0	—	1.000	—	OF	3	2	0	0	0	1.000
1997 Atl	20	3	5	0	0	0	0	0	1	1	1	1	0	1	0	0	0	0	0	—	0	.000	.167	.000	OF	3	10	0	0	0	1.000
DS Totals		6	5	0	0	0	0	0	1	1	1	2	0	1	0	0	0	0	0	—	0	.000	.286	.000	OF	6	12	0	0	0	1.000
LCS		Batting																							Fielding						
Year Tm	Age	G	AB	H	2B	3B	HR	TB	R	RBI	GW	TBB	IBB	SO	HBP	SH	SF	SB	CS	SB%	GDP	Avg	OBP	SLG	Pos	G	PO	A	E	DP	FPct
1996 Atl	19	5	9	2	0	0	1	5	3	3	0	3	0	2	0	0	0	0	0	—	0	.222	.417	.556	OF	5	5	0	0	0	1.000
1997 Atl	20	5	9	4	0	0	0	4	0	1	0	1	0	1	0	0	0	0	0	—	0	.444	.500	.444	OF	5	12	1	0	1	1.000
LCS Totals		10	18	6	0	0	1	9	3	4	0	4	0	3	0	0	0	0	0	—	0	.333	.455	.500	OF	10	17	1	0	1	1.000
World Series		Batting																							Fielding						
Year Tm	Age	G	AB	H	2B	3B	HR	TB	R	RBI	GW	TBB	IBB	SO	HBP	SH	SF	SB	CS	SB%	GDP	Avg	OBP	SLG	Pos	G	PO	A	E	DP	FPct
1996 Atl	19	6	20	8	1	0	2	15	4	6	1	3	0	6	1	0	0	1	2	.33	0	.400	.500	.750	OF	6	7	1	0	1	1.000
Postseason Totals		22	43	14	1	0	3	24	8	11	2	9	0	10	1	0	0	1	2	.33	0	.326	.453	.558	OF	22	36	2	0	2	1.000

CHIPPER JONES—Larry Wayne Jones—Bats: Both; Throws: Right

Ht: 6'3"; Wt: 185 lbs; Born: 4/24/1972 in Deland, Florida; Debut: 9/11/1993

Division Series		Batting																							Fielding						
Year Tm	Age	G	AB	H	2B	3B	HR	TB	R	RBI	GW	TBB	IBB	SO	HBP	SH	SF	SB	CS	SB%	GDP	Avg	OBP	SLG	Pos	G	PO	A	E	DP	FPct
1995 Atl	23	4	18	7	2	0	2	15	4	4	1	2	1	2	0	0	0	0	0	—	2	.389	.450	.833	3B	4	3	4	0	0	1.000
1996 Atl	24	3	9	2	0	0	1	5	2	2	0	3	0	4	0	0	0	1	1	.50	0	.222	.417	.556	3B	3	1	3	0	0	1.000
1997 Atl	25	3	8	4	0	0	1	7	3	2	2	3	0	2	0	0	1	1	0	1.00	0	.500	.583	.875	3B	3	2	3	1	0	.833
DS Totals		10	35	13	2	0	4	27	9	8	3	8	1	8	0	0	1	2	1	.67	2	.371	.477	.771	3B	10	6	10	1	0	.941
LCS		Batting																							Fielding						
Year Tm	Age	G	AB	H	2B	3B	HR	TB	R	RBI	GW	TBB	IBB	SO	HBP	SH	SF	SB	CS	SB%	GDP	Avg	OBP	SLG	Pos	G	PO	A	E	DP	FPct
1995 Atl	23	4	16	7	0	0	1	10	3	3	0	3	0	1	0	0	0	1	0	1.00	0	.438	.526	.625	3B	4	4	13	0	2	1.000
1996 Atl	24	7	25	11	2	0	0	13	6	4	1	3	0	1	0	0	1	1	0	1.00	0	.440	.483	.520	3B	7	5	7	1	2	.923
1997 Atl	25	6	24	7	1	0	2	14	5	4	0	2	0	3	0	1	0	0	0	—	0	.292	.346	.583	3B	6	1	8	0	0	1.000
LCS Totals		17	65	25	3	0	3	37	14	11	1	8	0	5	0	1	1	2	0	1.00	0	.385	.446	.569	3B	17	10	28	1	4	.974
World Series		Batting																							Fielding						
Year Tm	Age	G	AB	H	2B	3B	HR	TB	R	RBI	GW	TBB	IBB	SO	HBP	SH	SF	SB	CS	SB%	GDP	Avg	OBP	SLG	Pos	G	PO	A	E	DP	FPct
1995 Atl	23	6	21	6	3	0	0	9	3	1	0	4	2	3	0	0	1	0	0	—	0	.286	.385	.429	3B	6	6	12	1	1	.947
1996 Atl	24	6	21	6	3	0	0	9	3	3	0	4	0	2	0	0	1	1	0	1.00	1	.286	.385	.429	3B	6	4	6	0	1	1.000
																									SS	1	0	1	0	0	1.000
WS Totals		12	42	12	6	0	0	18	6	4	0	8	2	5	0	0	2	1	0	1.00	1	.286	.385	.429	3B	12	10	18	1	2	.966
Postseason Totals		39	142	50	11	0	7	82	29	23	4	24	3	18	0	1	4	5	1	.83	3	.352	.435	.577	3B	39	26	56	3	6	.965

CLEON JONES—Cleon Joseph Jones—Bats: Right; Throws: Left

Ht: 6'0"; Wt: 185 lbs; Born: 8/4/1942 in Plateau, Alabama; Debut: 9/14/1963

LCS		Batting																							Fielding						
Year Tm	Age	G	AB	H	2B	3B	HR	TB	R	RBI	GW	TBB	IBB	SO	HBP	SH	SF	SB	CS	SB%	GDP	Avg	OBP	SLG	Pos	G	PO	A	E	DP	FPct
1969 NYN	27	3	14	6	2	0	1	11	4	4	0	1	0	2	0	0	0	2	0	1.00	2	.429	.467	.786	OF	3	11	0	0	0	1.000
1973 NYN	31	5	20	6	2	0	0	8	3	3	1	2	0	4	0	0	0	0	0	—	1	.300	.364	.400	OF	5	9	0	1	0	.900
LCS Totals		8	34	12	4	0	1	19	7	7	1	3	0	6	0	0	0	2	0	1.00	3	.353	.405	.559	OF	8	20	0	1	0	.952
World Series		Batting																							Fielding						
Year Tm	Age	G	AB	H	2B	3B	HR	TB	R	RBI	GW	TBB	IBB	SO	HBP	SH	SF	SB	CS	SB%	GDP	Avg	OBP	SLG	Pos	G	PO	A	E	DP	FPct
1969 NYN	27	5	19	3	1	0	0	4	2	0	0	0	0	1	1	0	0	0	0	—	1	.158	.200	.211	OF	5	7	0	0	0	1.000
1973 NYN	31	7	28	8	2	0	1	13	5	1	0	4	1	2	1	0	0	0	0	—	0	.286	.394	.464	OF	7	11	1	1	0	.923
WS Totals		12	47	11	3	0	1	17	7	1	0	4	1	3	2	0	0	0	0	—	1	.234	.321	.362	OF	12	18	1	1	0	.950
Postseason Totals		20	81	23	7	0	2	36	14	8	1	7	1	9	2	0	0	2	0	1.00	4	.284	.356	.444	OF	20	38	1	2	0	.951

DALTON JONES—James Dalton Jones—Bats: Left; Throws: Right

Ht: 6'1"; Wt: 180 lbs; Born: 12/10/1943 in McComb, Mississippi; Debut: 4/17/1964

World Series		Batting																							Fielding						
Year Tm	Age	G	AB	H	2B	3B	HR	TB	R	RBI	GW	TBB	IBB	SO	HBP	SH	SF	SB	CS	SB%	GDP	Avg	OBP	SLG	Pos	G	PO	A	E	DP	FPct
1967 Bos	23	6	18	7	0	0	0	7	2	1	0	1	0	3	0	0	0	0	0	—	0	.389	.421	.389	3B	5	4	8	0	2	1.000

DAVY JONES—David Jefferson Jones—Nickname: Kangaroo—Bats: Left; Throws: Right

Ht: 5'10"; Wt: 165 lbs; Born: 6/30/1880 in Cambria, Wisconsin; Debut: 9/15/1901; Died: 3/31/1972

World Series		Batting																							Fielding						
Year Tm	Age	G	AB	H	2B	3B	HR	TB	R	RBI	GW	TBB	IBB	SO	HBP	SH	SF	SB	CS	SB%	GDP	Avg	OBP	SLG	Pos	G	PO	A	E	DP	FPct
1907 Det	27	5	17	6	0	0	0	6	1	0	0	4	0	0	0	1	0	3	1	.75	0	.353	.476	.353	OF	5	10	2	1	0	.923
1908 Det	28	3	2	0	0	0	0	0	1	0	0	1	0	1	0	0	0	0	0	—	0	.000	.333	.000	—						
1909 Det	29	7	30	7	0	0	1	10	6	1	0	2	0	1	0	0	0	1	2	.33	0	.233	.281	.333	OF	7	14	0	1	0	.933
WS Totals		15	49	13	0	0	1	16	8	1	0	7	0	2	0	1	0	4	3	.57	0	.265	.357	.327	OF	12	24	2	2	0	.929

FIELDER JONES—Fielder Allison Jones—Bats: Left; Throws: Right

Ht: 5'11"; Wt: 180 lbs; Born: 8/13/1871 in Shinglehouse, Pennsylvania; Debut: 4/18/1896; Died: 3/13/1934

World Series		Batting																							Fielding						
Year Tm	Age	G	AB	H	2B	3B	HR	TB	R	RBI	GW	TBB	IBB	SO	HBP	SH	SF	SB	CS	SB%	GDP	Avg	OBP	SLG	Pos	G	PO	A	E	DP	FPct
1906 ChA	35	6	21	3	0	0	0	3	4	0	0	3	0	3	0	2	0	0	1	.00	0	.143	.250	.143	OF	6	9	0	0	0	1.000

JEFF JONES—Jeffrey Allen Jones—Throws: Right; Bats: Right

Ht: 6'3"; Wt: 210 lbs; Born: 7/29/1956 in Detroit, Michigan; Debut: 4/10/1980

LCS		Pitching																										
Year Tm	Age	G	GS	CG	GF	IP	BFP	H	R	ER	HR	SH	SF	HB	TBB	IBB	SO	WP	Bk	W	L	Pct	ShO	Sv-Op	Hld	OAvg	OOBP	ERA
1981 Oak	25	1	0	0	0	2.0	10	2	1	1	0	0	0	1	1	0	0	0	0	0	0	—	0	0- 0	0	.250	.400	4.50

LCS		Batting																							Fielding						
Year Tm	Age	G	AB	H	2B	3B	HR	TB	R	RBI	GW	TBB	IBB	SO	HBP	SH	SF	SB	CS	SB%	GDP	Avg	OBP	SLG	Pos	G	PO	A	E	DP	FPct
1981 Oak	25	1	0	0	0	0	0	0	0	0	0	0	0	0	0	0	0	0	0	—	0	—	—	—	P	1	1	0	0	0	1.000

LYNN JONES—Lynn Morris Jones—Bats: Right; Throws: Right

Ht: 5'9"; Wt: 175 lbs; Born: 1/1/1953 in Meadville, Pennsylvania; Debut: 4/13/1979

LCS		Batting																							Fielding						
Year Tm	Age	G	AB	H	2B	3B	HR	TB	R	RBI	GW	TBB	IBB	SO	HBP	SH	SF	SB	CS	SB%	GDP	Avg	OBP	SLG	Pos	G	PO	A	E	DP	FPct
1984 KC	31	3	5	1	0	0	0	1	1	0	0	0	0	0	0	0	0	0	0	—	0	.200	.200	.200	OF	2	2	0	0	0	1.000
1985 KC	32	5	0	0	0	0	0	0	0	0	0	0	0	0	0	0	0	0	0	—	0	—	—	—	OF	5	2	0	0	0	1.000
LCS Totals		8	5	1	0	0	0	1	1	0	0	0	0	0	0	0	0	0	0	—	0	.200	.200	.200	OF	7	4	0	0	0	1.000
World Series		Batting																							Fielding						
Year Tm	Age	G	AB	H	2B	3B	HR	TB	R	RBI	GW	TBB	IBB	SO	HBP	SH	SF	SB	CS	SB%	GDP	Avg	OBP	SLG	Pos	G	PO	A	E	DP	FPct
1985 KC	32	6	3	2	1	1	0	5	0	0	0	0	0	0	0	0	0	0	0	—	0	.667	.667	1.667	OF	4	4	0	0	0	1.000
Postseason Totals		14	8	3	1	1	0	6	1	0	0	0	0	0	0	0	0	0	0	—	0	.375	.375	.750	OF	11	8	0	0	0	1.000

MIKE JONES—Michael Carl Jones—Throws: Left; Bats: Left

Ht: 6'6"; Wt: 215 lbs; Born: 7/30/1959 in Rochester, New York; Debut: 9/6/1980

Division Series		Pitching																										
Year Tm	Age	G	GS	CG	GF	IP	BFP	H	R	ER	HR	SH	SF	HB	TBB	IBB	SO	WP	Bk	W	L	Pct	ShO	Sv-Op	Hld	OAvg	OOBP	ERA
1981 KC	22	1	1	0	0	8.0	33	9	2	2	0	2	0	0	0	0	2	0	0	0	1	.000	0	0- 0	0	.290	.290	2.25
LCS		Pitching																										
Year Tm	Age	G	GS	CG	GF	IP	BFP	H	R	ER	HR	SH	SF	HB	TBB	IBB	SO	WP	Bk	W	L	Pct	ShO	Sv-Op	Hld	OAvg	OOBP	ERA
1984 KC	25	1	0	0	1	1.1	5	1	1	1	1	0	0	0	0	0	0	0	0	0	0	—	0	0- 0	0	.200	.200	6.75
Postseason Totals		2	1	0	1	9.1	76	10	3	3	1	2	0	0	0	0	2	0	0	0	1	.000	0	0-0	0	.278	.278	2.89

Division Series		Batting																							Fielding						
Year Tm	Age	G	AB	H	2B	3B	HR	TB	R	RBI	GW	TBB	IBB	SO	HBP	SH	SF	SB	CS	SB%	GDP	Avg	OBP	SLG	Pos	G	PO	A	E	DP	FPct
1981 KC	22	1	0	0	0	0	0	0	0	0	0	0	0	0	0	0	0	0	0	—	0	—	—	—	P	1	0	0	0	0	—
LCS		Batting																							Fielding						
Year Tm	Age	G	AB	H	2B	3B	HR	TB	R	RBI	GW	TBB	IBB	SO	HBP	SH	SF	SB	CS	SB%	GDP	Avg	OBP	SLG	Pos	G	PO	A	E	DP	FPct
1984 KC	25	1	0	0	0	0	0	0	0	0	0	0	0	0	0	0	0	0	0	—	0	—	—	—	P	1	0	0	0	0	—
Postseason Totals		2	0	0	0	0	0	0	0	0	0	0	0	0	0	0	0	0	0	—	0	—	—	—	P	2	0	0	0	0	—

NIPPY JONES—Vernal Leroy Jones—Bats: Right; Throws: Right

Ht: 6'1"; Wt: 185 lbs; Born: 6/29/1925 in Los Angeles, California; Debut: 6/8/1946; Died: 10/3/1995

World Series		Batting																							Fielding						
Year Tm	Age	G	AB	H	2B	3B	HR	TB	R	RBI	GW	TBB	IBB	SO	HBP	SH	SF	SB	CS	SB%	GDP	Avg	OBP	SLG	Pos	G	PO	A	E	DP	FPct
1946 StL	21	1	1	0	0	0	0	0	0	0	0	0	0	1	0	0	0	0	0	—	0	.000	.000	.000	—						
1957 Mil	32	3	2	0	0	0	0	0	0	0	0	0	0	0	1	0	0	0	0	—	0	.000	.333	.000	—						
WS Totals		4	3	0	0	0	0	0	0	0	0	0	0	1	1	0	0	0	0	—	0	.000	.250	.000	—	0	0	0	0	0	—

PUDDIN' HEAD JONES—Willie Edward Jones—Bats: Right; Throws: Right

Ht: 6'1"; Wt: 188 lbs; Born: 8/16/1925 in Dillon, South Carolina; Debut: 9/10/1947; Died: 10/18/1983

World Series		Batting																							Fielding						
Year Tm	Age	G	AB	H	2B	3B	HR	TB	R	RBI	GW	TBB	IBB	SO	HBP	SH	SF	SB	CS	SB%	GDP	Avg	OBP	SLG	Pos	G	PO	A	E	DP	FPct
1950 Phi	25	4	14	4	1	0	0	5	1	0	0	0	0	3	0	1	0	0	0	—	0	.286	.286	.357	3B	4	8	9	1	0	.944

RUPPERT JONES—Ruppert Sanderson Jones—Bats: Left; Throws: Left

Ht: 5'10"; Wt: 170 lbs; Born: 3/12/1955 in Dallas, Texas; Debut: 8/1/1976

LCS		Batting																							Fielding						
Year Tm	Age	G	AB	H	2B	3B	HR	TB	R	RBI	GW	TBB	IBB	SO	HBP	SH	SF	SB	CS	SB%	GDP	Avg	OBP	SLG	Pos	G	PO	A	E	DP	FPct
1984 Det	29	2	5	0	0	0	0	0	1	0	0	1	0	1	0	0	0	0	0	—	0	.000	.167	.000	OF	2	5	0	0	0	1.000
1986 Cal	31	6	17	3	1	0	0	4	4	2	1	5	1	2	0	0	1	0	0	—	0	.176	.348	.235	OF	5	6	0	0	0	1.000
LCS Totals		8	22	3	1	0	0	4	5	2	1	6	1	3	0	0	1	0	0	—	0	.136	.310	.182	OF	7	11	0	0	0	1.000
World Series		Batting																							Fielding						
Year Tm	Age	G	AB	H	2B	3B	HR	TB	R	RBI	GW	TBB	IBB	SO	HBP	SH	SF	SB	CS	SB%	GDP	Avg	OBP	SLG	Pos	G	PO	A	E	DP	FPct
1984 Det	29	2	3	0	0	0	0	0	0	0	0	0	0	1	0	0	0	0	0	—	0	.000	.000	.000	OF	2	3	0	0	0	1.000
Postseason Totals		10	25	3	1	0	0	4	5	2	1	6	1	4	0	0	1	0	0	—	0	.120	.281	.160	OF	9	14	0	0	0	1.000

SAD SAM JONES—Samuel Pond Jones—Throws: Right; Bats: Right

Ht: 6'0"; Wt: 170 lbs; Born: 7/26/1892 in Woodsfield, Ohio; Debut: 6/13/1914; Died: 7/6/1966

World Series		Pitching																										
Year Tm	Age	G	GS	CG	GF	IP	BFP	H	R	ER	HR	SH	SF	HB	TBB	IBB	SO	WP	Bk	W	L	Pct	ShO	Sv-Op	Hld	OAvg	OOBP	ERA
1918 Bos	26	1	1	1	0	9.0	36	7	3	3	0	1	0	0	5	0	5	0	0	0	1	.000	0	0- 0	0	.233	.343	3.00
1922 NYA	30	2	0	0	2	2.0	8	1	0	0	0	1	0	0	1	0	0	0	0	0	0	—	0	0- 0	0	.167	.286	0.00
1923 NYA	31	2	1	0	1	10.0	37	5	1	1	1	0	0	0	2	0	3	0	0	0	1	.000	0	1- 1	0	.143	.189	0.90
1926 NYA	34	1	0	0	1	1.0	7	2	1	1	1	0	0	0	2	0	1	0	0	0	0	—	0	0- 0	0	.400	.571	9.00
WS Totals		6	2	1	4	22.0	176	15	5	5	2	2	0	0	10	0	9	0	0	0	2	.000	0	1-1	0	.197	.291	2.05

World Series		Batting																							Fielding						
Year Tm	Age	G	AB	H	2B	3B	HR	TB	R	RBI	GW	TBB	IBB	SO	HBP	SH	SF	SB	CS	SB%	GDP	Avg	OBP	SLG	Pos	G	PO	A	E	DP	FPct
1918 Bos	26	1	1	0	0	0	0	0	0	0	0	1	0	0	0	0	0	0	0	—	0	.000	.500	.000	P	1	1	3	0	0	1.000
1922 NYA	30	2	0	0	0	0	0	0	0	0	0	0	0	0	0	0	0	0	0	—	0	—	—	—	P	2	0	1	0	0	1.000
1923 NYA	31	2	2	0	0	0	0	0	0	0	0	0	0	1	0	0	0	0	0	—	1	.000	.000	.000	P	2	0	3	0	1	1.000
1926 NYA	34	1	0	0	0	0	0	0	0	0	0	0	0	0	0	0	0	0	0	—	0	—	—	—	P	1	0	0	0	0	—
WS Totals		6	3	0	0	0	0	0	0	0	0	1	0	1	0	0	0	0	0	—	1	.000	.250	.000	P	6	1	7	0	1	1.000

SHELDON JONES—Sheldon Leslie Jones—Nickname: Available—Throws: Right; Bats: Right

Ht: 6'0"; Wt: 180 lbs; Born: 2/2/1922 in Tecumseh, Nebraska; Debut: 9/9/1946; Died: 4/18/1991

World Series		Pitching																										
Year Tm	Age	G	GS	CG	GF	IP	BFP	H	R	ER	HR	SH	SF	HB	TBB	IBB	SO	WP	Bk	W	L	Pct	ShO	Sv-Op	Hld	OAvg	OOBP	ERA
1951 NYG	29	2	0	0	1	4.1	19	5	3	1	1	0	0	0	1	0	2	0	0	0	0	—	0	1- 1	0	.278	.316	2.08

World Series		Batting																							Fielding						
Year Tm	Age	G	AB	H	2B	3B	HR	TB	R	RBI	GW	TBB	IBB	SO	HBP	SH	SF	SB	CS	SB%	GDP	Avg	OBP	SLG	Pos	G	PO	A	E	DP	FPct
1951 NYG	29	2	0	0	0	0	0	0	0	0	0	0	0	0	0	0	0	0	0	—	0	—	—	—	P	2	0	1	0	0	1.000

SHERMAN JONES—Sherman Jarvis Jones—Nickname: Roadblock—Throws: Right; Bats: Left

Ht: 6'4"; Wt: 205 lbs; Born: 2/10/1935 in Winton, North Carolina; Debut: 8/2/1960

World Series		Pitching																										
Year Tm	Age	G	GS	CG	GF	IP	BFP	H	R	ER	HR	SH	SF	HB	TBB	IBB	SO	WP	Bk	W	L	Pct	ShO	Sv-Op	Hld	OAvg	OOBP	ERA
1961 Cin	26	1	0	0	0	0.2	2	0	0	0	0	0	0	0	0	0	0	0	0	0	0	—	0	0- 0	0	.000	.000	0.00

World Series		Batting																							Fielding						
Year Tm	Age	G	AB	H	2B	3B	HR	TB	R	RBI	GW	TBB	IBB	SO	HBP	SH	SF	SB	CS	SB%	GDP	Avg	OBP	SLG	Pos	G	PO	A	E	DP	FPct
1961 Cin	26	1	0	0	0	0	0	0	0	0	0	0	0	0	0	0	0	0	0	—	0	—	—	—	P	1	0	0	0	0	—

TOM JONES—Thomas Jones—Bats: Right; Throws: Right

Ht: 6'1"; Wt: 195 lbs; Born: 1/22/1877 in Honesdale, Pennsylvania; Debut: 8/25/1902; Died: 6/21/1923

World Series	Batting																							Fielding						
Year Tm	Age	G	AB	H	2B	3B	HR	TB	R	RBI	GW	TBB	IBB	SO	HBP	SH	SF	SB	CS	SB%	GDP	Avg	OBP	SLG	Pos	G	PO	A	E	DP	FPct
1909 Det	32	7	24	6	1	0	0	7	3	2	0	2	0	0	0	1	0	1	0	1.00	0	.250	.308	.292	1B	7	73	1	1	1	.987

CLAUDE JONNARD—Claude Alfred Jonnard—Throws: Right; Bats: Right

Ht: 6'1"; Wt: 165 lbs; Born: 11/23/1897 in Nashville, Tennessee; Debut: 10/1/1921; Died: 8/27/1959

World Series	Pitching																											
Year Tm	Age	G	GS	CG	GF	IP	BFP	H	R	ER	HR	SH	SF	HB	TBB	IBB	SO	WP	Bk	W	L	Pct	ShO	Sv-Op	Hld	OAvg	OOBP	ERA
1923 NYG	25	2	0	0	1	2.0	8	1	0	0	0	0	0	0	1	0	1	0	0	0	0	—	0	0-0	0	.143	.250	0.00
1924 NYG	26	1	0	0	0	0.0	1	0	0	0	0	0	0	0	1	0	0	0	0	0	0	—	0	0-0	0	—	1.000	—
WS Totals		3	0	0	1	2.0	18	1	0	0	0	0	0	0	2	0	1	0	0	0	0	—	0	0-0	0	.143	.333	0.00

World Series	Batting																							Fielding						
Year Tm	Age	G	AB	H	2B	3B	HR	TB	R	RBI	GW	TBB	IBB	SO	HBP	SH	SF	SB	CS	SB%	GDP	Avg	OBP	SLG	Pos	G	PO	A	E	DP	FPct
1923 NYG	25	2	0	0	0	0	0	0	0	0	0	0	0	0	0	0	0	0	0	—	0	—	—	—	P	2	0	1	0	0	1.000
1924 NYG	26	1	0	0	0	0	0	0	0	0	0	0	0	0	0	0	0	0	0	—	0	—	—	—	P	1	0	0	0	0	—
WS Totals		3	0	0	0	0	0	0	0	0	0	0	0	0	0	0	0	0	0	—	0	—	—	—	P	3	0	1	0	0	1.000

EDDIE JOOST—Edwin David Joost—Bats: Right; Throws: Right

Ht: 6'0"; Wt: 175 lbs; Born: 6/5/1916 in San Francisco, California; Debut: 9/11/1936

World Series	Batting																							Fielding						
Year Tm	Age	G	AB	H	2B	3B	HR	TB	R	RBI	GW	TBB	IBB	SO	HBP	SH	SF	SB	CS	SB%	GDP	Avg	OBP	SLG	Pos	G	PO	A	E	DP	FPct
1940 Cin	24	7	25	5	0	0	0	5	0	2	0	1	0	2	0	0	0	0	1	.00	1	.200	.231	.200	2B	7	14	12	0	6	1.000

BRIAN JORDAN—Brian O'Neal Jordan—Bats: Right; Throws: Right

Ht: 6'1"; Wt: 205 lbs; Born: 3/29/1967 in Baltimore, Maryland; Debut: 4/8/1992

Division Series	Batting																							Fielding						
Year Tm	Age	G	AB	H	2B	3B	HR	TB	R	RBI	GW	TBB	IBB	SO	HBP	SH	SF	SB	CS	SB%	GDP	Avg	OBP	SLG	Pos	G	PO	A	E	DP	FPct
1996 StL	29	3	12	4	0	0	1	7	4	3	1	1	0	3	0	0	0	1	0	1.00	0	.333	.385	.583	OF	3	5	0	0	0	1.000
LCS	Batting																							Fielding						
Year Tm	Age	G	AB	H	2B	3B	HR	TB	R	RBI	GW	TBB	IBB	SO	HBP	SH	SF	SB	CS	SB%	GDP	Avg	OBP	SLG	Pos	G	PO	A	E	DP	FPct
1996 StL	29	7	25	6	1	1	1	12	3	2	1	1	1	3	0	0	0	0	0	—	1	.240	.269	.480	OF	7	13	0	0	1	1.000
Postseason Totals		10	37	10	1	1	2	19	7	5	2	2	1	6	0	0	0	1	0	1.00	1	.270	.308	.514	OF	10	18	0	0	1	1.000

RICKY JORDAN—Paul Scott Jordan—Bats: Right; Throws: Right

Ht: 6'5"; Wt: 210 lbs; Born: 5/26/1965 in Richmond, California; Debut: 7/17/1988

LCS	Batting																							Fielding						
Year Tm	Age	G	AB	H	2B	3B	HR	TB	R	RBI	GW	TBB	IBB	SO	HBP	SH	SF	SB	CS	SB%	GDP	Avg	OBP	SLG	Pos	G	PO	A	E	DP	FPct
1993 Phi	28	2	1	0	0	0	0	0	0	0	0	1	0	0	0	0	0	0	0	—	0	.000	.500	.000	—						
World Series	Batting																							Fielding						
Year Tm	Age	G	AB	H	2B	3B	HR	TB	R	RBI	GW	TBB	IBB	SO	HBP	SH	SF	SB	CS	SB%	GDP	Avg	OBP	SLG	Pos	G	PO	A	E	DP	FPct
1993 Phi	28	3	10	2	0	0	0	2	0	0	0	0	0	2	0	0	0	0	0	—	0	.200	.200	.200	—						
Postseason Totals		5	11	2	0	0	0	2	0	0	0	1	0	2	0	0	0	0	0	—	0	.182	.250	.182	—	0	0	0	0	0	—

MIKE JORGENSEN—Michael Jorgensen—Bats: Left; Throws: Left

Ht: 6'0"; Wt: 195 lbs; Born: 8/16/1948 in Passaic, New Jersey; Debut: 9/10/1968

LCS	Batting																							Fielding						
Year Tm	Age	G	AB	H	2B	3B	HR	TB	R	RBI	GW	TBB	IBB	SO	HBP	SH	SF	SB	CS	SB%	GDP	Avg	OBP	SLG	Pos	G	PO	A	E	DP	FPct
1985 StL	37	2	2	0	0	0	0	0	0	0	0	0	0	1	0	0	0	0	0	—	0	.000	.000	.000	—						
World Series	Batting																							Fielding						
Year Tm	Age	G	AB	H	2B	3B	HR	TB	R	RBI	GW	TBB	IBB	SO	HBP	SH	SF	SB	CS	SB%	GDP	Avg	OBP	SLG	Pos	G	PO	A	E	DP	FPct
1985 StL	37	2	3	0	0	0	0	0	0	0	0	0	0	0	0	0	0	0	0	—	0	.000	.000	.000	OF	1	1	0	0	0	1.000
Postseason Totals		4	5	0	0	0	0	0	0	0	0	0	0	1	0	0	0	0	0	—	0	.000	.000	.000	OF	1	1	0	0	0	1.000

SPIDER JORGENSEN—John Donald Jorgensen—Bats: Left; Throws: Right

Ht: 5'9"; Wt: 155 lbs; Born: 11/3/1919 in Folsom, California; Debut: 4/15/1947

World Series	Batting																							Fielding						
Year Tm	Age	G	AB	H	2B	3B	HR	TB	R	RBI	GW	TBB	IBB	SO	HBP	SH	SF	SB	CS	SB%	GDP	Avg	OBP	SLG	Pos	G	PO	A	E	DP	FPct
1947 Bro	27	7	20	4	2	0	0	6	1	3	0	2	0	4	0	0	0	0	0	—	0	.200	.273	.300	3B	7	8	11	2	1	.905
1949 Bro	29	4	11	2	2	0	0	4	1	0	0	2	0	2	0	0	0	0	0	—	0	.182	.308	.364	3B	3	1	6	0	0	1.000
WS Totals		11	31	6	4	0	0	10	2	3	0	4	0	6	0	0	0	0	0	—	0	.194	.286	.323	3B	10	9	17	2	1	.929

VON JOSHUA—Von Everett Joshua—Bats: Left; Throws: Left

Ht: 5'10"; Wt: 170 lbs; Born: 5/1/1948 in Oakland, California; Debut: 9/2/1969

LCS	Batting																							Fielding						
Year Tm	Age	G	AB	H	2B	3B	HR	TB	R	RBI	GW	TBB	IBB	SO	HBP	SH	SF	SB	CS	SB%	GDP	Avg	OBP	SLG	Pos	G	PO	A	E	DP	FPct
1974 LA	26	1	0	0	0	0	0	0	0	0	0	1	0	0	0	0	0	0	0	—	0	—	1.000	—	—						
World Series	Batting																							Fielding						
Year Tm	Age	G	AB	H	2B	3B	HR	TB	R	RBI	GW	TBB	IBB	SO	HBP	SH	SF	SB	CS	SB%	GDP	Avg	OBP	SLG	Pos	G	PO	A	E	DP	FPct
1974 LA	26	4	4	0	0	0	0	0	0	0	0	0	0	0	0	0	0	0	0	—	1	.000	.000	.000	—						
Postseason Totals		5	4	0	0	0	0	0	0	0	0	1	0	0	0	0	0	0	0	—	1	.000	.200	.000	—	0	0	0	0	0	—

WALLY JOYNER—Wallace Keith Joyner—Bats: Left; Throws: Left

Ht: 6'2"; Wt: 185 lbs; Born: 6/16/1962 in Atlanta, Georgia; Debut: 4/8/1986

Division Series	Batting																							Fielding						
Year Tm	Age	G	AB	H	2B	3B	HR	TB	R	RBI	GW	TBB	IBB	SO	HBP	SH	SF	SB	CS	SB%	GDP	Avg	OBP	SLG	Pos	G	PO	A	E	DP	FPct
1996 SD	34	3	9	1	0	0	0	1	0	0	0	0	0	2	0	0	0	0	0	—	0	.111	.111	.111	1B	3	12	2	0	2	1.000
LCS	Batting																							Fielding						
Year Tm	Age	G	AB	H	2B	3B	HR	TB	R	RBI	GW	TBB	IBB	SO	HBP	SH	SF	SB	CS	SB%	GDP	Avg	OBP	SLG	Pos	G	PO	A	E	DP	FPct
1986 Cal	24	3	11	5	2	0	1	10	3	2	0	2	0	0	0	0	0	0	0	—	1	.455	.538	.909	1B	3	24	1	0	2	1.000
Postseason Totals		6	20	6	2	0	1	11	3	2	0	2	0	2	0	0	0	0	0	—	1	.300	.364	.550	1B	6	36	3	0	4	1.000

JEFF JUDEN—Jeffrey Daniel Juden—Throws: Right; Bats: Right

Ht: 6'7"; Wt: 245 lbs; Born: 1/19/1971 in Salem, Massachusetts; Debut: 9/15/1991

LCS	Pitching																											
Year Tm	Age	G	GS	CG	GF	IP	BFP	H	R	ER	HR	SH	SF	HB	TBB	IBB	SO	WP	Bk	W	L	Pct	ShO	Sv-Op	Hld	OAvg	OOBP	ERA
1997 Cle	26	3	0	0	0	1.0	7	2	0	0	0	0	0	0	2	1	2	0	0	0	0	—	0	0-0	0	.400	.571	0.00
World Series	Pitching																											
Year Tm	Age	G	GS	CG	GF	IP	BFP	H	R	ER	HR	SH	SF	HB	TBB	IBB	SO	WP	Bk	W	L	Pct	ShO	Sv-Op	Hld	OAvg	OOBP	ERA
1997 Cle	26	2	0	0	0	2.0	10	2	1	1	0	0	0	0	2	0	0	1	0	0	0	—	0	0-0	0	.250	.400	4.50
Postseason Totals		5	0	0	0	3.0	34	4	1	1	0	0	0	0	4	1	2	1	0	0	0	—	0	0-0	0	.308	.471	3.00

LCS	Batting																							Fielding						
Year Tm	Age	G	AB	H	2B	3B	HR	TB	R	RBI	GW	TBB	IBB	SO	HBP	SH	SF	SB	CS	SB%	GDP	Avg	OBP	SLG	Pos	G	PO	A	E	DP	FPct
1997 Cle	26	3	0	0	0	0	0	0	0	0	0	0	0	0	0	0	0	0	0	—	0	—	—	—	P	3	0	0	0	0	—
World Series	Batting																							Fielding						
Year Tm	Age	G	AB	H	2B	3B	HR	TB	R	RBI	GW	TBB	IBB	SO	HBP	SH	SF	SB	CS	SB%	GDP	Avg	OBP	SLG	Pos	G	PO	A	E	DP	FPct
1997 Cle	26	2	0	0	0	0	0	0	0	0	0	0	0	0	0	0	0	0	0	—	0	—	—	—	P	2	0	0	0	0	—
Postseason Totals		5	0	0	0	0	0	0	0	0	0	0	0	0	0	0	0	0	0	—	0	—	—	—	P	5	0	0	0	0	—

JOE JUDGE—Joseph Ignatius Judge—Bats: Left; Throws: Left

Ht: 5'8"; Wt: 155 lbs; Born: 5/25/1894 in Brooklyn, New York; Debut: 9/20/1915; Died: 3/11/1963

World Series	Batting																							Fielding						
Year Tm	Age	G	AB	H	2B	3B	HR	TB	R	RBI	GW	TBB	IBB	SO	HBP	SH	SF	SB	CS	SB%	GDP	Avg	OBP	SLG	Pos	G	PO	A	E	DP	FPct
1924 Was	30	7	26	10	2	0	0	12	4	0	0	5	1	2	0	0	0	0	1	.00	0	.385	.484	.462	1B	7	62	4	1	8	.985
1925 Was	31	7	23	4	1	0	1	8	2	3	0	3	0	2	0	1	1	0	1	.00	0	.174	.259	.348	1B	7	60	2	0	8	1.000
WS Totals		14	49	14	3	0	1	20	6	3	0	8	1	4	0	1	1	0	2	.00	0	.286	.379	.408	1B	14	122	6	1	16	.992

WALLY JUDNICH—Walter Franklin Judnich—Bats: Left; Throws: Left

Ht: 6'1"; Wt: 205 lbs; Born: 1/24/1917 in San Francisco, California; Debut: 4/16/1940; Died: 7/12/1971

World Series		Batting																							Fielding						
Year Tm	Age	G	AB	H	2B	3B	HR	TB	R	RBI	GW	TBB	IBB	SO	HBP	SH	SF	SB	CS	SB%	GDP	Avg	OBP	SLG	Pos	G	PO	A	E	DP	FPct
1948 Cle	31	4	13	1	0	0	0	1	1	1	0	1	0	4	0	0	0	0	0	—	0	.077	.143	.077	OF	4	7	0	0	0	1.000

BILLY JURGES—William Frederick Jurges—Bats: Right; Throws: Right

Ht: 5'11"; Wt: 175 lbs; Born: 5/9/1908 in Bronx, New York; Debut: 5/4/1931; Died: 3/3/1997

World Series		Batting																							Fielding						
Year Tm	Age	G	AB	H	2B	3B	HR	TB	R	RBI	GW	TBB	IBB	SO	HBP	SH	SF	SB	CS	SB%	GDP	Avg	OBP	SLG	Pos	G	PO	A	E	DP	FPct
1932 ChN	24	3	11	4	1	0	0	5	1	1	0	0	0	1	0	1	0	2	0	1.00	0	.364	.364	.455	SS	3	11	8	2	5	.905
1935 ChN	27	6	16	4	0	0	0	4	3	1	0	4	0	4	1	0	0	0	0	—	0	.250	.429	.250	SS	6	16	15	1	4	.969
1938 ChN	30	4	13	3	1	0	0	4	0	0	0	1	0	3	0	0	0	0	0	—	0	.231	.286	.308	SS	4	11	7	1	2	.947
WS Totals		13	40	11	2	0	0	13	4	2	0	5	0	8	1	1	0	2	0	1.00	0	.275	.370	.325	SS	13	38	30	4	11	.944

AL JURISICH—Alvin Joseph Jurisich—Throws: Right; Bats: Right

Ht: 6'2"; Wt: 193 lbs; Born: 8/25/1921 in New Orleans, Louisiana; Debut: 4/26/1944; Died: 11/3/1981

World Series		Pitching																										
Year Tm	Age	G	GS	CG	GF	IP	BFP	H	R	ER	HR	SH	SF	HB	TBB	IBB	SO	WP	Bk	W	L	Pct	ShO	Sv-Op	Hld	OAvg	OOBP	ERA
1944 StL	23	1	0	0	0	0.2	5	2	2	2	0	0	0	0	1	0	0	0	0	0	0	—	0	0-0	0	.500	.600	27.00

World Series		Batting																							Fielding						
Year Tm	Age	G	AB	H	2B	3B	HR	TB	R	RBI	GW	TBB	IBB	SO	HBP	SH	SF	SB	CS	SB%	GDP	Avg	OBP	SLG	Pos	G	PO	A	E	DP	FPct
1944 StL	23	1	0	0	0	0	0	0	0	0	0	0	0	0	0	0	0	0	0	—	0	—	—	—	P	1	0	0	0	0	—

DAVID JUSTICE—David Christopher Justice—Bats: Left; Throws: Left

Ht: 6'3"; Wt: 195 lbs; Born: 4/14/1966 in Cincinnati, Ohio; Debut: 5/24/1989

Division Series		Batting																							Fielding						
Year Tm	Age	G	AB	H	2B	3B	HR	TB	R	RBI	GW	TBB	IBB	SO	HBP	SH	SF	SB	CS	SB%	GDP	Avg	OBP	SLG	Pos	G	PO	A	E	DP	FPct
1995 Atl	29	4	13	3	0	0	0	3	2	0	0	5	0	2	0	0	0	0	0	—	0	.231	.444	.231	OF	4	6	0	1	0	.857
1997 Cle	31	5	19	5	2	0	1	10	3	2	0	2	0	3	0	0	0	0	0	—	0	.263	.333	.526	—						
DS Totals		9	32	8	2	0	1	13	5	2	0	7	0	5	0	0	0	0	0	—	0	.250	.385	.406	OF	4	6	0	1	0	.857
LCS		**Batting**																							**Fielding**						
Year Tm	Age	G	AB	H	2B	3B	HR	TB	R	RBI	GW	TBB	IBB	SO	HBP	SH	SF	SB	CS	SB%	GDP	Avg	OBP	SLG	Pos	G	PO	A	E	DP	FPct
1991 Atl	25	7	25	5	1	0	1	9	4	2	0	3	1	7	0	0	0	0	1	.00	0	.200	.286	.360	OF	7	17	0	1	0	.944
1992 Atl	26	7	25	7	1	0	2	14	5	6	0	6	1	2	0	0	0	0	0	—	0	.280	.419	.560	OF	7	19	3	0	0	1.000
1993 Atl	27	6	21	3	1	0	0	4	2	4	1	3	0	3	0	0	2	0	0	—	0	.143	.231	.190	OF	6	14	0	1	0	.933
1995 Atl	29	3	11	3	0	0	0	3	1	1	0	2	1	1	0	0	0	0	0	—	0	.273	.385	.273	OF	3	4	0	0	0	1.000
1997 Cle	31	6	21	7	1	0	0	8	3	0	0	2	0	4	1	0	0	0	0	—	1	.333	.417	.381	—						
LCS Totals		29	103	25	4	0	3	38	15	13	1	16	3	17	1	0	2	0	1	.00	1	.243	.344	.369	OF	23	54	3	2	0	.966
World Series		**Batting**																							**Fielding**						
Year Tm	Age	G	AB	H	2B	3B	HR	TB	R	RBI	GW	TBB	IBB	SO	HBP	SH	SF	SB	CS	SB%	GDP	Avg	OBP	SLG	Pos	G	PO	A	E	DP	FPct
1991 Atl	25	7	27	7	0	0	2	13	5	6	1	5	1	5	0	0	0	2	0	1.00	0	.259	.375	.481	OF	7	21	1	1	0	.957
1992 Atl	26	6	19	3	0	0	1	6	4	3	0	6	2	5	0	0	0	1	0	1.00	0	.158	.360	.316	OF	6	15	0	1	0	.938
1995 Atl	29	6	20	5	1	0	1	9	3	5	1	5	0	1	0	0	0	0	0	—	0	.250	.400	.450	OF	6	16	0	0	0	1.000
1997 Cle	31	7	27	5	0	0	0	5	4	4	0	6	0	8	0	0	0	0	1	.00	1	.185	.333	.185	OF	4	9	0	0	0	1.000
WS Totals		26	93	20	1	0	4	33	16	18	2	22	3	19	0	0	0	3	1	.75	1	.215	.365	.355	OF	23	61	1	2	0	.969
Postseason Totals		64	228	53	7	0	8	84	36	33	3	45	6	41	1	0	2	3	2	.60	2	.232	.359	.368	OF	50	121	4	5	0	.962

JIM KAAT—James Lee Kaat—Nickname: Kitty—Throws: Left; Bats: Left

Ht: 6'4"; Wt: 205 lbs; Born: 11/7/1938 in Zeeland, Michigan; Debut: 8/2/1959

LCS		Pitching																										
Year Tm	Age	G	GS	CG	GF	IP	BFP	H	R	ER	HR	SH	SF	HB	TBB	IBB	SO	WP	Bk	W	L	Pct	ShO	Sv-Op	Hld	OAvg	OOBP	ERA
1970 Min	31	1	1	0	0	2.0	15	6	4	2	0	1	0	0	2	1	1	0	0	0	1	.000	0	0-0	0	.500	.571	9.00
1976 Phi	37	1	1	0	0	6.0	21	2	2	2	0	0	0	0	2	0	1	0	0	0	0	—	0	0-0	0	.105	.190	3.00
LCS Totals		2	2	0	0	8.0	72	8	6	4	0	1	0	0	4	1	2	0	0	0	1	.000	0	0-0	0	.258	.343	4.50
World Series		**Pitching**																										
Year Tm	Age	G	GS	CG	GF	IP	BFP	H	R	ER	HR	SH	SF	HB	TBB	IBB	SO	WP	Bk	W	L	Pct	ShO	Sv-Op	Hld	OAvg	OOBP	ERA
1965 Min	26	3	3	1	0	14.1	65	18	7	6	1	3	0	1	2	0	6	0	0	1	2	.333	0	0-0	0	.305	.339	3.77
1982 StL	43	4	0	0	0	2.1	12	4	1	1	0	0	0	0	2	1	2	1	0	0	0	—	0	0-1	0	.400	.500	3.86
WS Totals		7	3	1	0	16.2	154	22	8	7	1	3	0	1	4	1	8	1	0	1	2	.333	0	0-1	0	.319	.365	3.78
Postseason Totals		9	5	1	0	24.2	226	30	14	11	1	4	0	1	8	2	10	1	0	1	3	.250	0	0-1	0	.300	.358	4.01

LCS		Batting																							Fielding						
Year Tm	Age	G	AB	H	2B	3B	HR	TB	R	RBI	GW	TBB	IBB	SO	HBP	SH	SF	SB	CS	SB%	GDP	Avg	OBP	SLG	Pos	G	PO	A	E	DP	FPct
1970 Min	31	1	1	0	0	0	0	0	0	0	0	0	0	1	0	0	0	0	0	—	0	.000	.000	.000	P	1	0	0	0	0	—
1976 Phi	37	1	2	1	0	0	0	1	0	0	0	0	0	0	0	1	0	0	0	—	0	.500	.500	.500	P	1	0	1	0	0	1.000
LCS Totals		2	3	1	0	0	0	1	0	0	0	0	0	1	0	1	0	0	0	—	0	.333	.333	.333	P	2	0	1	0	0	1.000
World Series		**Batting**																							**Fielding**						
Year Tm	Age	G	AB	H	2B	3B	HR	TB	R	RBI	GW	TBB	IBB	SO	HBP	SH	SF	SB	CS	SB%	GDP	Avg	OBP	SLG	Pos	G	PO	A	E	DP	FPct
1965 Min	26	3	6	1	0	0	0	1	0	2	0	0	0	5	0	0	0	0	0	—	0	.167	.167	.167	P	3	5	2	0	0	1.000
1982 StL	43	4	0	0	0	0	0	0	0	0	0	0	0	0	0	0	0	0	0	—	0	—	—	—	P	4	0	0	0	0	—
WS Totals		7	6	1	0	0	0	1	0	2	0	0	0	5	0	0	0	0	0	—	0	.167	.167	.167	P	7	5	2	0	0	1.000
Postseason Totals		9	9	2	0	0	0	2	0	2	0	0	0	6	0	1	0	0	0	—	0	.222	.222	.222	P	9	5	3	0	0	1.000

AL KALINE (HOF 1980-W)—Albert William Kaline—Bats: Right; Throws: Right

Ht: 6'1"; Wt: 175 lbs; Born: 12/19/1934 in Baltimore, Maryland; Debut: 6/25/1953

LCS		Batting																							Fielding						
Year Tm	Age	G	AB	H	2B	3B	HR	TB	R	RBI	GW	TBB	IBB	SO	HBP	SH	SF	SB	CS	SB%	GDP	Avg	OBP	SLG	Pos	G	PO	A	E	DP	FPct
1972 Det	37	5	19	5	0	0	1	8	3	1	0	2	0	2	0	1	0	0	0	—	0	.263	.333	.421	OF	5	13	0	1	0	.929
World Series		**Batting**																							**Fielding**						
Year Tm	Age	G	AB	H	2B	3B	HR	TB	R	RBI	GW	TBB	IBB	SO	HBP	SH	SF	SB	CS	SB%	GDP	Avg	OBP	SLG	Pos	G	PO	A	E	DP	FPct
1968 Det	33	7	29	11	2	0	2	19	6	8	1	0	0	7	1	0	0	0	0	—	0	.379	.400	.655	OF	7	19	0	0	0	1.000
Postseason Totals		12	48	16	2	0	3	27	9	9	1	2	0	9	1	1	0	0	0	—	0	.333	.373	.563	OF	12	32	0	1	0	.970

SCOTT KAMIENIECKI—Scott Andrew Kamieniecki—Throws: Right; Bats: Right

Ht: 6'0"; Wt: 195 lbs; Born: 4/19/1964 in Mt. Clemens, Michigan; Debut: 6/18/1991

Division Series		Pitching																										
Year Tm	Age	G	GS	CG	GF	IP	BFP	H	R	ER	HR	SH	SF	HB	TBB	IBB	SO	WP	Bk	W	L	Pct	ShO	Sv-Op	Hld	OAvg	OOBP	ERA
1995 NYA	31	1	1	0	0	5.0	28	9	5	4	1	1	1	0	4	0	4	0	0	0	0	—	0	0-0	0	.409	.481	7.20
LCS		**Pitching**																										
Year Tm	Age	G	GS	CG	GF	IP	BFP	H	R	ER	HR	SH	SF	HB	TBB	IBB	SO	WP	Bk	W	L	Pct	ShO	Sv-Op	Hld	OAvg	OOBP	ERA
1997 Bal	33	2	1	0	0	8.0	31	4	0	0	0	0	0	1	2	0	5	0	0	1	0	1.000	0	0-0	0	.143	.226	0.00
Postseason Totals		3	2	0	0	13.0	118	13	5	4	1	1	1	1	6	0	9	0	0	1	0	1.000	0	0-0	0	.260	.345	2.77

Division Series		Batting																							Fielding						
Year Tm	Age	G	AB	H	2B	3B	HR	TB	R	RBI	GW	TBB	IBB	SO	HBP	SH	SF	SB	CS	SB%	GDP	Avg	OBP	SLG	Pos	G	PO	A	E	DP	FPct
1995 NYA	31	1	0	0	0	0	0	0	0	0	0	0	0	0	0	0	0	0	0	—	0	—	—	—	P	1	0	0	0	0	—
LCS		**Batting**																							**Fielding**						
Year Tm	Age	G	AB	H	2B	3B	HR	TB	R	RBI	GW	TBB	IBB	SO	HBP	SH	SF	SB	CS	SB%	GDP	Avg	OBP	SLG	Pos	G	PO	A	E	DP	FPct
1997 Bal	33	2	0	0	0	0	0	0	0	0	0	0	0	0	0	0	0	0	0	—	0	—	—	—	P	2	0	2	0	0	1.000
Postseason Totals		3	0	0	0	0	0	0	0	0	0	0	0	0	0	0	0	0	0	—	0	—	—	—	P	3	0	2	0	0	1.000

JOHN KANE—John Francis Kane—Bats: Right; Throws: Right

Ht: 5'6"; Wt: 138 lbs; Born: 9/24/1882 in Chicago, Illinois; Debut: 4/11/1907; Died: 1/28/1934

World Series		Batting																							Fielding						
Year Tm	Age	G	AB	H	2B	3B	HR	TB	R	RBI	GW	TBB	IBB	SO	HBP	SH	SF	SB	CS	SB%	GDP	Avg	OBP	SLG	Pos	G	PO	A	E	DP	FPct
1910 ChN	28	2	0	0	0	0	0	0	0	0	0	0	0	0	0	0	0	0	0	—	0	—	—	—	—						

RON KARKOVICE—Ronald Joseph Karkovice—Nickname: Officer Karkovice—Bats: Right; Throws: Right

Ht: 6'1"; Wt: 210 lbs; Born: 8/8/1963 in Union, New Jersey; Debut: 8/17/1986

LCS	Batting																								Fielding						
Year Tm	Age	G	AB	H	2B	3B	HR	TB	R	RBI	GW	TBB	IBB	SO	HBP	SH	SF	SB	CS	SB%	GDP	Avg	OBP	SLG	Pos	G	PO	A	E	DP	FPct
1993 ChA	30	6	15	0	0	0	0	0	0	0	0	1	0	7	0	2	0	0	0	—	0	.000	.063	.000	C	6	30	2	0	0	1.000

ERIC KARROS—Eric Peter Karros—Bats: Right; Throws: Right

Ht: 6'4"; Wt: 205 lbs; Born: 11/4/1967 in Hackensack, New Jersey; Debut: 9/1/1991

Division Series	Batting																								Fielding						
Year Tm	Age	G	AB	H	2B	3B	HR	TB	R	RBI	GW	TBB	IBB	SO	HBP	SH	SF	SB	CS	SB%	GDP	Avg	OBP	SLG	Pos	G	PO	A	E	DP	FPct
1995 LA	27	3	12	6	1	0	2	13	3	4	0	1	0	0	0	0	0	0	0	—	0	.500	.538	1.083	1B	3	14	0	0	2	1.000
1996 LA	28	3	9	0	0	0	0	0	0	0	0	2	0	3	0	0	0	0	0	—	1	.000	.182	.000	1B	3	28	2	0	1	1.000
DS Totals		6	21	6	1	0	2	13	3	4	0	3	0	3	0	0	0	0	0	—	1	.286	.375	.619	1B	6	42	2	0	3	1.000

EDDIE KASKO—Edward Michael Kasko—Bats: Right; Throws: Right

Ht: 6'0"; Wt: 180 lbs; Born: 6/27/1932 in Linden, New Jersey; Debut: 4/18/1957

World Series	Batting																								Fielding						
Year Tm	Age	G	AB	H	2B	3B	HR	TB	R	RBI	GW	TBB	IBB	SO	HBP	SH	SF	SB	CS	SB%	GDP	Avg	OBP	SLG	Pos	G	PO	A	E	DP	FPct
1961 Cin	29	5	22	7	0	0	0	7	1	1	0	0	0	2	0	0	0	0	0	—	0	.318	.318	.318	SS	5	13	13	1	5	.963

BENNY KAUFF—Benjamin Michael Kauff—Bats: Left; Throws: Left

Ht: 5'8"; Wt: 157 lbs; Born: 1/5/1890 in Pomeroy, Ohio; Debut: 4/20/1912; Died: 11/17/1961

World Series	Batting																								Fielding						
Year Tm	Age	G	AB	H	2B	3B	HR	TB	R	RBI	GW	TBB	IBB	SO	HBP	SH	SF	SB	CS	SB%	GDP	Avg	OBP	SLG	Pos	G	PO	A	E	DP	FPct
1917 NYG	27	6	25	4	1	0	2	11	2	5	1	0	0	2	0	0	0	1	1	.50	0	.160	.160	.440	OF	6	6	0	0	0	1.000

VIC KEEN—Howard Victor Keen—Throws: Right; Bats: Right

Ht: 5'9"; Wt: 165 lbs; Born: 3/16/1899 in Bel Air, Maryland; Debut: 8/13/1918; Died: 12/10/1976

World Series	Pitching																											
Year Tm	Age	G	GS	CG	GF	IP	BFP	H	R	ER	HR	SH	SF	HB	TBB	IBB	SO	WP	Bk	W	L	Pct	ShO	Sv-Op	Hld	OAvg	OOBP	ERA
1926 StL	27	1	0	0	1	1.0	3	0	0	0	0	0	0	0	0	0	0	0	0	0	0	—	0	0- 0	0	.000	.000	0.00

World Series	Batting																								Fielding						
Year Tm	Age	G	AB	H	2B	3B	HR	TB	R	RBI	GW	TBB	IBB	SO	HBP	SH	SF	SB	CS	SB%	GDP	Avg	OBP	SLG	Pos	G	PO	A	E	DP	FPct
1926 StL	27	1	0	0	0	0	0	0	0	0	0	0	0	0	0	0	0	0	0	—	0	—	—	—	P	1	0	1	0	0	1.000

CHARLIE KELLER—Charles Ernest Keller—Nickname: King Kong—Bats: Left; Throws: Right

Ht: 5'10"; Wt: 185 lbs; Born: 9/12/1916 in Middletown, Maryland; Debut: 4/22/1939; Died: 5/23/1990

World Series	Batting																								Fielding						
Year Tm	Age	G	AB	H	2B	3B	HR	TB	R	RBI	GW	TBB	IBB	SO	HBP	SH	SF	SB	CS	SB%	GDP	Avg	OBP	SLG	Pos	G	PO	A	E	DP	FPct
1939 NYA	23	4	16	7	1	1	3	19	8	6	0	1	0	2	0	0	0	0	0	—	0	.438	.471	1.188	OF	4	5	0	0	0	1.000
1941 NYA	25	5	18	7	2	0	0	9	5	5	1	3	0	1	0	0	0	0	0	—	1	.389	.476	.500	OF	5	12	0	0	2	1.000
1942 NYA	26	5	20	4	0	0	2	10	2	5	0	1	0	3	0	0	0	0	0	—	0	.200	.238	.500	OF	5	12	1	0	1	1.000
1943 NYA	27	5	18	4	0	1	0	6	3	2	0	2	0	5	0	0	0	1	0	1.00	1	.222	.300	.333	OF	5	10	1	0	1	1.000
WS Totals		19	72	22	3	2	5	44	18	18	1	7	0	11	0	0	0	1	0	1.00	2	.306	.367	.611	OF	19	39	2	0	1	1.000

FRANK KELLERT—Frank William Kellert—Bats: Right; Throws: Right

Ht: 6'2"; Wt: 185 lbs; Born: 7/6/1924 in Oklahoma City, Oklahoma; Debut: 4/18/1953; Died: 11/19/1976

World Series	Batting																								Fielding						
Year Tm	Age	G	AB	H	2B	3B	HR	TB	R	RBI	GW	TBB	IBB	SO	HBP	SH	SF	SB	CS	SB%	GDP	Avg	OBP	SLG	Pos	G	PO	A	E	DP	FPct
1955 Bro	31	3	3	1	0	0	0	1	0	0	0	0	0	0	0	0	0	0	0	—	1	.333	.333	.333	—						

GEORGE KELLY (HOF 1973-V)—George Lange Kelly—Nickname: High Pockets—Bats: R; Throws: R

Ht: 6'4"; Wt: 190 lbs; Born: 9/10/1895 in San Francisco, Calif.; Deb.: 8/18/1915; Died: 10/13/1984

World Series	Batting																								Fielding						
Year Tm	Age	G	AB	H	2B	3B	HR	TB	R	RBI	GW	TBB	IBB	SO	HBP	SH	SF	SB	CS	SB%	GDP	Avg	OBP	SLG	Pos	G	PO	A	E	DP	FPct
1921 NYG	26	8	30	7	1	0	0	8	3	5	1	3	0	10	0	0	0	0	1	.00	3	.233	.303	.267	1B	8	86	6	0	4	1.000
1922 NYG	27	5	18	5	0	0	0	5	0	2	1	0	0	3	0	2	0	0	1	.00	1	.278	.278	.278	1B	5	61	1	0	2	1.000
1923 NYG	28	6	22	4	0	0	0	4	1	1	0	1	0	2	0	0	0	0	0	—	3	.182	.217	.182	1B	6	63	3	1	5	.985
1924 NYG	29	7	31	9	1	0	1	13	7	4	0	1	0	8	0	0	1	0	0	—	2	.290	.303	.419	2B	1	1	1	0	0	1.000
																									1B	4	44	5	1	2	.980
																									OF	4	7	0	0	0	1.000
WS Totals		26	101	25	2	0	1	30	11	12	2	5	0	23	0	2	1	0	2	.00	9	.248	.280	.297	1B	23	254	15	2	13	.993

PAT KELLY—Harold Patrick Kelly—Bats: Left; Throws: Left

Ht: 6'1"; Wt: 185 lbs; Born: 7/30/1944 in Philadelphia, Pennsylvania; Debut: 9/6/1967

LCS	Batting																								Fielding						
Year Tm	Age	G	AB	H	2B	3B	HR	TB	R	RBI	GW	TBB	IBB	SO	HBP	SH	SF	SB	CS	SB%	GDP	Avg	OBP	SLG	Pos	G	PO	A	E	DP	FPct
1979 Bal	35	3	11	4	0	0	1	7	3	4	0	1	0	3	0	0	0	2	0	1.00	0	.364	.417	.636	OF	1	3	0	0	0	1.000
World Series	Batting																								Fielding						
Year Tm	Age	G	AB	H	2B	3B	HR	TB	R	RBI	GW	TBB	IBB	SO	HBP	SH	SF	SB	CS	SB%	GDP	Avg	OBP	SLG	Pos	G	PO	A	E	DP	FPct
1979 Bal	35	5	4	1	0	0	0	1	0	0	0	1	0	1	0	0	0	0	0	—	0	.250	.400	.250	—						
Postseason Totals		8	15	5	0	0	1	8	3	4	0	2	0	4	0	0	0	2	0	1.00	0	.333	.412	.533	OF	1	3	0	0	0	1.000

PAT KELLY—Patrick Franklin Kelly—Bats: Right; Throws: Right

Ht: 6'0"; Wt: 180 lbs; Born: 10/14/1967 in Philadelphia, Pennsylvania; Debut: 5/20/1991

Division Series	Batting																								Fielding						
Year Tm	Age	G	AB	H	2B	3B	HR	TB	R	RBI	GW	TBB	IBB	SO	HBP	SH	SF	SB	CS	SB%	GDP	Avg	OBP	SLG	Pos	G	PO	A	E	DP	FPct
1995 NYA	27	5	3	0	0	0	0	0	3	1	0	1	0	3	0	1	1	0	0	—	0	.000	.200	.000	2B	4	2	4	0	2	1.000

ROBERTO KELLY—Roberto Conrado Kelly—Nickname: Gray—Bats: Right; Throws: Right

Ht: 6'2"; Wt: 180 lbs; Born: 10/1/1964 in Panama City, Panama; Debut: 7/29/1987

Division Series	Batting																								Fielding						
Year Tm	Age	G	AB	H	2B	3B	HR	TB	R	RBI	GW	TBB	IBB	SO	HBP	SH	SF	SB	CS	SB%	GDP	Avg	OBP	SLG	Pos	G	PO	A	E	DP	FPct
1995 LA	30	3	11	4	0	0	0	4	0	0	0	1	0	0	0	0	0	0	0	—	0	.364	.417	.364	OF	3	8	0	1	0	.889
1997 Sea	32	4	13	4	3	0	0	7	1	1	1	0	0	3	0	0	0	0	0	—	1	.308	.308	.538	OF	3	4	0	0	0	1.000
DS Totals		7	24	8	3	0	0	11	1	1	1	1	0	3	0	0	0	0	0	—	1	.333	.360	.458	OF	6	12	0	1	0	.923

KEN KELTNER—Kenneth Frederick Keltner—Nickname: Butch—Bats: Right; Throws: Right

Ht: 6'0"; Wt: 190 lbs; Born: 10/31/1916 in Milwaukee, Wisconsin; Debut: 10/2/1937; Died: 12/12/1991

World Series	Batting																								Fielding						
Year Tm	Age	G	AB	H	2B	3B	HR	TB	R	RBI	GW	TBB	IBB	SO	HBP	SH	SF	SB	CS	SB%	GDP	Avg	OBP	SLG	Pos	G	PO	A	E	DP	FPct
1948 Cle	31	6	21	2	0	0	0	2	3	0	0	2	0	3	0	0	0	0	0	—	0	.095	.174	.095	3B	6	3	11	1	1	.933

BOB KENNEDY—Robert Daniel Kennedy—Bats: Right; Throws: Right

Ht: 6'2"; Wt: 193 lbs; Born: 8/18/1920 in Chicago, Illinois; Debut: 9/14/1939

World Series	Batting																								Fielding						
Year Tm	Age	G	AB	H	2B	3B	HR	TB	R	RBI	GW	TBB	IBB	SO	HBP	SH	SF	SB	CS	SB%	GDP	Avg	OBP	SLG	Pos	G	PO	A	E	DP	FPct
1948 Cle	28	3	2	1	0	0	0	1	0	1	0	0	0	1	0	0	0	0	0	—	0	.500	.500	.500	OF	3	2	0	0	0	1.000

BRICKYARD KENNEDY—William Park Kennedy—Throws: Right; Bats: Right

Ht: 5'11"; Wt: 160 lbs; Born: 10/7/1867 in Bellaire, Ohio; Debut: 4/26/1892; Died: 9/23/1915

World Series	Pitching																											
Year Tm	Age	G	GS	CG	GF	IP	BFP	H	R	ER	HR	SH	SF	HB	TBB	IBB	SO	WP	Bk	W	L	Pct	ShO	Sv-Op	Hld	OAvg	OOBP	ERA
1903 Pit	35	1	1	0	0	7.0	38	11	10	4	0	1	0	0	3	0	3	0	0	0	1	.000	0	0- 0	0	.324	.378	5.14

World Series		Batting																							Fielding						
Year Tm	Age	G	AB	H	2B	3B	HR	TB	R	RBI	GW	TBB	IBB	SO	HBP	SH	SF	SB	CS	SB%	GDP	Avg	OBP	SLG	Pos	G	PO	A	E	DP	FPct
1903 Pit	35	1	2	1	1	0	0	2	0	0	0	0	0	0	0	0	0	0	0	—	0	.500	.500	1.000	P	1	0	1	0	0	1.000

JOHN KENNEDY—John Edward Kennedy—Bats: Right; Throws: Right

Ht: 6'0"; Wt: 185 lbs; Born: 5/29/1941 in Chicago, Illinois; Debut: 9/5/1962

World Series		Batting																							Fielding						
Year Tm	Age	G	AB	H	2B	3B	HR	TB	R	RBI	GW	TBB	IBB	SO	HBP	SH	SF	SB	CS	SB%	GDP	Avg	OBP	SLG	Pos	G	PO	A	E	DP	FPct
1965 LA	24	4	1	0	0	0	0	0	0	0	0	0	0	0	0	0	0	0	0	—	0	.000	.000	.000	3B	4	0	2	1	0	.667
1966 LA	25	2	5	1	0	0	0	1	0	0	0	0	0	0	0	0	0	0	1	.00	0	.200	.200	.200	3B	2	0	3	0	0	1.000
WS Totals		6	6	1	0	0	0	1	0	0	0	0	0	0	0	0	0	0	1	.00	0	.167	.167	.167	3B	6	0	5	1	0	.833

MONTE KENNEDY—Monty Calvin Kennedy—Throws: Left; Bats: Right

Ht: 6'2"; Wt: 185 lbs; Born: 5/11/1922 in Amelia, Virginia; Debut: 4/18/1946; Died: 3/1/1997

World Series		Pitching																										
Year Tm	Age	G	GS	CG	GF	IP	BFP	H	R	ER	HR	SH	SF	HB	TBB	IBB	SO	WP	Bk	W	L	Pct	ShO	Sv-Op	Hld	OAvg	OOBP	ERA
1951 NYG	29	2	0	0	1	3.0	13	3	2	2	1	0	0	0	1	0	4	0	0	0	0	—	0	0- 0	0	.250	.308	6.00

World Series		Batting																							Fielding						
Year Tm	Age	G	AB	H	2B	3B	HR	TB	R	RBI	GW	TBB	IBB	SO	HBP	SH	SF	SB	CS	SB%	GDP	Avg	OBP	SLG	Pos	G	PO	A	E	DP	FPct
1951 NYG	29	2	0	0	0	0	0	0	0	0	0	0	0	0	0	0	0	0	0	—	0	—	—	—	P	2	0	1	0	0	1.000

TERRY KENNEDY—Terrance Edward Kennedy—Bats: Left; Throws: Right

Ht: 6'3"; Wt: 220 lbs; Born: 6/4/1956 in Euclid, Ohio; Debut: 9/4/1978

LCS		Batting																							Fielding						
Year Tm	Age	G	AB	H	2B	3B	HR	TB	R	RBI	GW	TBB	IBB	SO	HBP	SH	SF	SB	CS	SB%	GDP	Avg	OBP	SLG	Pos	G	PO	A	E	DP	FPct
1984 SD	28	5	18	4	0	0	0	4	2	1	0	1	0	3	0	0	1	0	0	—	1	.222	.250	.222	C	5	29	3	0	2	1.000
1989 SF	33	5	16	3	1	0	0	4	0	0	0	1	1	4	0	0	0	0	0	—	0	.188	.235	.250	C	5	26	1	0	2	1.000
LCS Totals		10	34	7	1	0	0	8	2	1	0	2	1	7	0	0	1	0	0	—	1	.206	.243	.235	C	10	55	4	0	4	1.000
World Series		Batting																							Fielding						
Year Tm	Age	G	AB	H	2B	3B	HR	TB	R	RBI	GW	TBB	IBB	SO	HBP	SH	SF	SB	CS	SB%	GDP	Avg	OBP	SLG	Pos	G	PO	A	E	DP	FPct
1984 SD	28	5	19	4	1	0	1	8	2	3	0	1	0	1	0	0	0	0	0	—	0	.211	.250	.421	C	5	30	2	0	1	1.000
1989 SF	33	4	12	2	0	0	0	2	1	2	0	1	0	3	0	0	0	0	0	—	0	.167	.231	.167	C	4	23	1	1	1	.960
WS Totals		9	31	6	1	0	1	10	3	5	0	2	0	4	0	0	0	0	0	—	0	.194	.242	.323	C	9	53	3	1	2	.982
Postseason Totals		19	65	13	2	0	1	18	5	6	0	4	1	11	0	0	1	0	0	—	1	.200	.243	.277	C	19	108	7	1	6	.991

JEFF KENT—Jeffrey Franklin Kent—Bats: Right; Throws: Right

Ht: 6'1"; Wt: 185 lbs; Born: 3/7/1968 in Bellflower, California; Debut: 4/12/1992

Division Series		Batting																							Fielding						
Year Tm	Age	G	AB	H	2B	3B	HR	TB	R	RBI	GW	TBB	IBB	SO	HBP	SH	SF	SB	CS	SB%	GDP	Avg	OBP	SLG	Pos	G	PO	A	E	DP	FPct
1996 Cle	28	4	8	1	1	0	0	2	2	0	0	0	0	0	0	1	0	0	0	—	0	.125	.125	.250	2B	1	2	2	0	0	1.000
																									1B	1	0	0	0	0	—
																									3B	2	1	1	0	0	1.000
1997 SF	29	3	10	3	0	0	2	9	2	2	0	2	0	1	0	0	0	0	0	—	0	.300	.417	.900	2B	3	5	6	0	2	1.000
																									1B	1	14	1	0	1	1.000
DS Totals		7	18	4	1	0	2	11	4	2	0	2	0	1	0	1	0	0	0	—	0	.222	.300	.611	2B	4	7	8	0	2	1.000

MATT KEOUGH—Matthew Lon Keough—Throws: Right; Bats: Right

Ht: 6'3"; Wt: 190 lbs; Born: 7/3/1955 in Pomona, California; Debut: 9/3/1977

LCS		Pitching																										
Year Tm	Age	G	GS	CG	GF	IP	BFP	H	R	ER	HR	SH	SF	HB	TBB	IBB	SO	WP	Bk	W	L	Pct	ShO	Sv-Op	Hld	OAvg	OOBP	ERA
1981 Oak	26	1	1	0	0	8.1	39	7	2	1	1	1	0	0	6	0	4	1	0	0	1	.000	0	0- 0	0	.219	.342	1.08

LCS		Batting																							Fielding						
Year Tm	Age	G	AB	H	2B	3B	HR	TB	R	RBI	GW	TBB	IBB	SO	HBP	SH	SF	SB	CS	SB%	GDP	Avg	OBP	SLG	Pos	G	PO	A	E	DP	FPct
1981 Oak	26	1	0	0	0	0	0	0	0	0	0	0	0	0	0	0	0	0	0	—	0	—	—	—	P	1	0	0	0	0	—

CHARLIE KERFELD—Charles Patrick Kerfeld—Throws: Right; Bats: Right

Ht: 6'6"; Wt: 225 lbs; Born: 9/28/1963 in Knob Noster, Missouri; Debut: 7/27/1985

LCS		Pitching																										
Year Tm	Age	G	GS	CG	GF	IP	BFP	H	R	ER	HR	SH	SF	HB	TBB	IBB	SO	WP	Bk	W	L	Pct	ShO	Sv-Op	Hld	OAvg	OOBP	ERA
1986 Hou	23	3	0	0	2	4.0	14	2	1	1	0	0	0	0	1	1	4	0	0	0	1	.000	0	0- 0	1	.154	.214	2.25

LCS		Batting																							Fielding						
Year Tm	Age	G	AB	H	2B	3B	HR	TB	R	RBI	GW	TBB	IBB	SO	HBP	SH	SF	SB	CS	SB%	GDP	Avg	OBP	SLG	Pos	G	PO	A	E	DP	FPct
1986 Hou	23	3	0	0	0	0	0	0	0	0	0	0	0	0	0	0	0	0	0	—	0	—	—	—	P	3	0	1	1	0	.500

DICKIE KERR—Richard Henry Kerr—Throws: Left; Bats: Left

Ht: 5'7"; Wt: 155 lbs; Born: 7/3/1893 in St. Louis, Missouri; Debut: 4/25/1919; Died: 5/4/1963

World Series		Pitching																										
Year Tm	Age	G	GS	CG	GF	IP	BFP	H	R	ER	HR	SH	SF	HB	TBB	IBB	SO	WP	Bk	W	L	Pct	ShO	Sv-Op	Hld	OAvg	OOBP	ERA
1919 ChA	26	2	2	2	0	19.0	72	14	4	3	0	1	0	1	3	0	6	0	0	2	0	1.000	1	0- 0	0	.209	.254	1.42

World Series		Batting																							Fielding						
Year Tm	Age	G	AB	H	2B	3B	HR	TB	R	RBI	GW	TBB	IBB	SO	HBP	SH	SF	SB	CS	SB%	GDP	Avg	OBP	SLG	Pos	G	PO	A	E	DP	FPct
1919 ChA	26	2	6	1	0	0	0	1	0	0	0	0	0	0	0	1	0	0	0	—	0	.167	.167	.167	P	2	1	4	0	0	1.000

JOHN KERR—John Francis Kerr—Bats: Right; Throws: Right

Ht: 5'8"; Wt: 158 lbs; Born: 11/26/1898 in San Francisco, California; Debut: 5/1/1923; Died: 10/19/1993

World Series		Batting																							Fielding						
Year Tm	Age	G	AB	H	2B	3B	HR	TB	R	RBI	GW	TBB	IBB	SO	HBP	SH	SF	SB	CS	SB%	GDP	Avg	OBP	SLG	Pos	G	PO	A	E	DP	FPct
1933 Was	34	1	0	0	0	0	0	0	0	0	0	0	0	0	0	0	0	0	0	—	0	—	—	—	—						

JIMMY KEY—James Edward Key—Throws: Left; Bats: Right

Ht: 6'1"; Wt: 185 lbs; Born: 4/22/1961 in Huntsville, Alabama; Debut: 4/6/1984

Division Series		Pitching																										
Year Tm	Age	G	GS	CG	GF	IP	BFP	H	R	ER	HR	SH	SF	HB	TBB	IBB	SO	WP	Bk	W	L	Pct	ShO	Sv-Op	Hld	OAvg	OOBP	ERA
1996 NYA	35	1	1	0	0	5.0	21	5	2	2	1	0	0	0	1	0	3	0	0	0	0	—	0	0- 0	0	.250	.286	3.60
1997 Bal	36	1	1	0	0	4.2	21	8	2	2	0	0	0	0	0	0	4	1	0	0	1	.000	0	0- 0	0	.381	.381	3.86
DS Totals		2	2	0	0	9.2	84	13	4	4	1	0	0	0	1	0	7	1	0	0	1	.000	0	0-0	0	.317	.333	3.72
LCS		Pitching																										
Year Tm	Age	G	GS	CG	GF	IP	BFP	H	R	ER	HR	SH	SF	HB	TBB	IBB	SO	WP	Bk	W	L	Pct	ShO	Sv-Op	Hld	OAvg	OOBP	ERA
1985 Tor	24	2	2	0	0	8.2	41	15	5	5	1	1	1	0	2	0	5	0	0	0	1	.000	0	0- 0	0	.405	.425	5.19
1989 Tor	28	1	1	0	0	6.0	26	7	3	3	1	0	1	0	2	0	2	0	0	1	0	1.000	0	0- 0	0	.304	.346	4.50
1991 Tor	30	1	1	0	0	6.0	23	5	2	2	0	0	0	0	1	0	1	0	0	0	0	—	0	0- 0	0	.227	.261	3.00
1992 Tor	31	1	0	0	0	3.0	12	2	0	0	0	1	0	0	2	1	1	0	0	0	0	—	0	0- 0	0	.222	.364	0.00
1996 NYA	35	1	1	0	0	8.0	27	3	2	2	1	0	0	0	1	0	5	0	0	1	0	1.000	0	0- 0	0	.115	.148	2.25
1997 Bal	36	2	1	0	0	7.0	31	5	2	2	1	0	0	3	3	0	7	0	0	0	0	—	0	0- 0	1	.200	.355	2.57
LCS Totals		8	6	0	0	38.2	320	37	14	14	4	2	2	3	11	1	21	0	0	2	1	.667	0	0-0	1	.261	.323	3.26
World Series		Pitching																										
Year Tm	Age	G	GS	CG	GF	IP	BFP	H	R	ER	HR	SH	SF	HB	TBB	IBB	SO	WP	Bk	W	L	Pct	ShO	Sv-Op	Hld	OAvg	OOBP	ERA
1992 Tor	31	2	1	0	0	9.0	33	6	2	1	0	1	0	0	0	0	6	0	0	2	0	1.000	0	0- 0	0	.188	.188	1.00
1996 NYA	35	2	2	0	0	11.1	51	15	5	5	0	1	1	1	5	0	1	0	0	1	1	.500	0	0- 0	0	.349	.420	3.97
WS Totals		4	3	0	0	20.1	168	21	7	6	0	2	1	1	5	0	7	0	0	3	1	.750	0	0-0	0	.280	.329	2.66
Postseason Totals		14	11	0	0	68.2	572	71	25	24	5	4	3	4	17	1	35	1	0	5	3	.625	0	0-0	1	.275	.326	3.15

Division Series		Batting																							Fielding						
Year Tm	Age	G	AB	H	2B	3B	HR	TB	R	RBI	GW	TBB	IBB	SO	HBP	SH	SF	SB	CS	SB%	GDP	Avg	OBP	SLG	Pos	G	PO	A	E	DP	FPct
1996 NYA	35	1	0	0	0	0	0	0	0	0	0	0	0	0	0	0	0	0	0	—	0	—	—	—	P	1	0	0	0	0	—
1997 Bal	36	1	0	0	0	0	0	0	0	0	0	0	0	0	0	0	0	0	0	—	0	—	—	—	P	1	0	1	0	0	1.000
DS Totals		2	0	0	0	0	0	0	0	0	0	0	0	0	0	0	0	0	0	—	0	—	—	—	P	2	0	1	0	0	1.000

LCS								Batting																	Fielding						
Year Tm	Age	G	AB	H	2B	3B	HR	TB	R	RBI	GW	TBB	IBB	SO	HBP	SH	SF	SB	CS	SB%	GDP	Avg	OBP	SLG	Pos	G	PO	A	E	DP	FPct
1985 Tor	24	2	0	0	0	0	0	0	0	0	0	0	0	0	0	0	0	0	0	—	0	—	—	—	P	2	0	3	0	0	1.000
1989 Tor	28	1	0	0	0	0	0	0	0	0	0	0	0	0	0	0	0	0	0	—	0	—	—	—	P	1	0	0	0	0	—
1991 Tor	30	1	0	0	0	0	0	0	0	0	0	0	0	0	0	0	0	0	0	—	0	—	—	—	P	1	0	3	0	1	1.000
1992 Tor	31	1	0	0	0	0	0	0	0	0	0	0	0	0	0	0	0	0	0	—	0	—	—	—	P	1	0	0	0	0	—
1996 NYA	35	1	0	0	0	0	0	0	0	0	0	0	0	0	0	0	0	0	0	—	0	—	—	—	P	1	1	0	0	0	1.000
1997 Bal	36	2	0	0	0	0	0	0	0	0	0	0	0	0	0	0	0	0	0	—	0	—	—	—	P	2	0	0	0	0	—
LCS Totals		8	0	0	0	0	0	0	0	0	0	0	0	0	0	0	0	0	0	—	0	—	—	—	P	8	1	6	0	1	1.000
World Series								Batting																	Fielding						
Year Tm	Age	G	AB	H	2B	3B	HR	TB	R	RBI	GW	TBB	IBB	SO	HBP	SH	SF	SB	CS	SB%	GDP	Avg	OBP	SLG	Pos	G	PO	A	E	DP	FPct
1992 Tor	31	2	1	0	0	0	0	0	0	0	0	0	0	0	0	0	0	0	0	—	0	.000	.000	.000	P	2	2	4	0	0	1.000
1996 NYA	35	2	0	0	0	0	0	0	0	0	0	0	0	0	0	0	0	0	0	—	0	—	—	—	P	2	0	3	0	1	1.000
WS Totals		4	1	0	0	0	0	0	0	0	0	0	0	0	0	0	0	0	0	—	0	.000	.000	.000	P	4	2	7	0	1	1.000
Postseason Totals		14	1	0	0	0	0	0	0	0	0	0	0	0	0	0	0	0	0	—	0	.000	.000	.000	P	14	3	14	0	2	1.000

DANA KIECKER—Dana Ervin Kiecker—Throws: Right; Bats: Right

Ht: 6'3"; Wt: 180 lbs; Born: 2/25/1961 in Sleepy Eye, Minnesota; Debut: 4/12/1990

LCS										Pitching																		
Year Tm	Age	G	GS	CG	GF	IP	BFP	H	R	ER	HR	SH	SF	HB	TBB	IBB	SO	WP	Bk	W	L	Pct	ShO	Sv-Op	Hld	OAvg	OOBP	ERA
1990 Bos	29	1	1	0	0	5.2	24	6	1	1	0	0	0	1	1	0	2	0	0	0	0	—	0	0-0	0	.273	.333	1.59

LCS								Batting																	Fielding						
Year Tm	Age	G	AB	H	2B	3B	HR	TB	R	RBI	GW	TBB	IBB	SO	HBP	SH	SF	SB	CS	SB%	GDP	Avg	OBP	SLG	Pos	G	PO	A	E	DP	FPct
1990 Bos	29	1	0	0	0	0	0	0	0	0	0	0	0	0	0	0	0	0	0	—	0	—	—	—	P	1	0	0	0	0	—

PETE KILDUFF—Peter John Kilduff—Bats: Right; Throws: Right

Ht: 5'7"; Wt: 155 lbs; Born: 4/4/1893 in Weir City, Kansas; Debut: 4/18/1917; Died: 2/14/1930

World Series								Batting																	Fielding						
Year Tm	Age	G	AB	H	2B	3B	HR	TB	R	RBI	GW	TBB	IBB	SO	HBP	SH	SF	SB	CS	SB%	GDP	Avg	OBP	SLG	Pos	G	PO	A	E	DP	FPct
1920 Bro	27	7	21	2	0	0	0	2	0	0	0	1	0	4	0	1	0	0	0	—	0	.095	.136	.095	2B	7	15	28	0	4	1.000

DARRYL KILE—Darryl Andrew Kile—Throws: Right; Bats: Right

Ht: 6'5"; Wt: 185 lbs; Born: 12/2/1968 in Garden Grove, California; Debut: 4/8/1991

Division Series										Pitching																		
Year Tm	Age	G	GS	CG	GF	IP	BFP	H	R	ER	HR	SH	SF	HB	TBB	IBB	SO	WP	Bk	W	L	Pct	ShO	Sv-Op	Hld	OAvg	OOBP	ERA
1997 Hou	28	1	1	0	0	7.0	25	2	2	2	1	0	1	0	2	0	4	0	0	0	1	.000	0	0-0	0	.091	.160	2.57

Division Series								Batting																	Fielding						
Year Tm	Age	G	AB	H	2B	3B	HR	TB	R	RBI	GW	TBB	IBB	SO	HBP	SH	SF	SB	CS	SB%	GDP	Avg	OBP	SLG	Pos	G	PO	A	E	DP	FPct
1997 Hou	28	1	2	2	0	0	0	2	0	1	0	0	0	0	0	0	0	0	0	—	0	1.000	1.000	1.000	P	1	0	0	0	0	—

PAUL KILGUS—Paul Nelson Kilgus—Throws: Left; Bats: Left

Ht: 6'1"; Wt: 175 lbs; Born: 2/2/1962 in Bowling Green, Kentucky; Debut: 6/7/1987

LCS										Pitching																		
Year Tm	Age	G	GS	CG	GF	IP	BFP	H	R	ER	HR	SH	SF	HB	TBB	IBB	SO	WP	Bk	W	L	Pct	ShO	Sv-Op	Hld	OAvg	OOBP	ERA
1989 ChN	27	1	0	0	0	3.0	13	4	0	0	0	0	0	0	1	0	1	0	0	0	0	—	0	0-0	0	.333	.385	0.00

LCS								Batting																	Fielding						
Year Tm	Age	G	AB	H	2B	3B	HR	TB	R	RBI	GW	TBB	IBB	SO	HBP	SH	SF	SB	CS	SB%	GDP	Avg	OBP	SLG	Pos	G	PO	A	E	DP	FPct
1989 ChN	27	1	0	0	0	0	0	0	0	0	0	0	0	0	0	0	0	0	0	—	0	—	—	—	P	1	0	0	0	0	—

HARMON KILLEBREW (HOF 1984-W)—Harmon Clayton Killebrew—Nickname: Killer—Bats: Right; Throws: Right

Ht: 6'0"; Wt: 195 lbs; Born: 6/29/1936 in Payette, Idaho; Debut: 6/23/1954

LCS								Batting																	Fielding						
Year Tm	Age	G	AB	H	2B	3B	HR	TB	R	RBI	GW	TBB	IBB	SO	HBP	SH	SF	SB	CS	SB%	GDP	Avg	OBP	SLG	Pos	G	PO	A	E	DP	FPct
1969 Min-*M*	33	3	8	1	1	0	0	2	2	0	0	6	1	2	0	0	0	0	0	—	1	.125	.500	.250	3B	3	6	3	0	0	1.000
1970 Min	34	3	11	3	0	0	2	9	2	4	0	2	0	4	0	0	0	0	0	—	0	.273	.385	.818	3B	2	0	4	1	0	.800
																									1B	1	7	0	0	1	1.000
LCS Totals		6	19	4	1	0	2	11	4	4	0	8	1	6	0	0	0	0	0	—	1	.211	.444	.579	3B	5	6	7	1	0	.929
World Series								Batting																	Fielding						
Year Tm	Age	G	AB	H	2B	3B	HR	TB	R	RBI	GW	TBB	IBB	SO	HBP	SH	SF	SB	CS	SB%	GDP	Avg	OBP	SLG	Pos	G	PO	A	E	DP	FPct
1965 Min	29	7	21	6	0	0	1	9	2	2	1	6	0	4	0	0	0	0	0	—	0	.286	.444	.429	3B	7	11	7	1	0	.947
Postseason Totals		13	40	10	1	0	3	20	6	6	0	14	1	10	0	0	0	0	0	—	1	.250	.444	.500	3B	12	17	14	2	0	.939

BILL KILLEFER—William Lavier Killefer—Bats: Right; Throws: Right

Ht: 5'10"; Wt: 200 lbs; Born: 10/10/1887 in Bloomingdale, Michigan; Debut: 9/13/1909; Died: 7/3/1960

World Series								Batting																	Fielding						
Year Tm	Age	G	AB	H	2B	3B	HR	TB	R	RBI	GW	TBB	IBB	SO	HBP	SH	SF	SB	CS	SB%	GDP	Avg	OBP	SLG	Pos	G	PO	A	E	DP	FPct
1915 Phi	27	1	1	0	0	0	0	0	0	0	0	0	0	0	0	0	0	0	0	—	0	.000	.000	.000	—						
1918 ChN	30	6	17	2	1	0	0	3	2	2	1	2	0	0	0	0	0	0	1	.00	1	.118	.211	.176	C	6	26	6	0	1	1.000
WS Totals		7	18	2	1	0	0	3	2	2	1	2	0	0	0	0	0	0	1	.00	1	.111	.200	.167	C	6	26	6	0	1	1.000

ED KILLIAN—Edwin Henry Killian—Throws: Left; Bats: Left

Ht: 5'11"; Wt: 170 lbs; Born: 11/12/1876 in Racine, Wisconsin; Debut: 8/25/1903; Died: 7/18/1928

World Series										Pitching																		
Year Tm	Age	G	GS	CG	GF	IP	BFP	H	R	ER	HR	SH	SF	HB	TBB	IBB	SO	WP	Bk	W	L	Pct	ShO	Sv-Op	Hld	OAvg	OOBP	ERA
1907 Det	30	1	0	0	1	4.0	16	3	1	1	0	0	0	0	1	0	1	0	0	0	0	—	0	0-0	0	.200	.250	2.25
1908 Det	31	1	1	0	0	2.1	15	5	4	3	0	0	0	0	3	0	1	0	0	0	0	—	0	0-0	0	.417	.533	11.57
WS Totals		2	1	0	1	6.1	62	8	5	4	0	0	0	0	4	0	2	0	0	0	0	—	0	0-0	0	.296	.387	5.68

World Series								Batting																	Fielding						
Year Tm	Age	G	AB	H	2B	3B	HR	TB	R	RBI	GW	TBB	IBB	SO	HBP	SH	SF	SB	CS	SB%	GDP	Avg	OBP	SLG	Pos	G	PO	A	E	DP	FPct
1907 Det	30	1	2	1	0	0	0	1	1	0	0	0	0	0	0	0	0	0	0	—	0	.500	.500	.500	P	1	0	0	0	0	—
1908 Det	31	1	0	0	0	0	0	0	0	0	0	0	0	0	0	0	0	0	0	—	0	—	—	—	P	1	0	1	0	0	1.000
WS Totals		2	2	1	0	0	0	1	1	0	0	0	0	0	0	0	0	0	0	—	0	.500	.500	.500	P	2	0	1	0	0	1.000

ERIC KING—Eric Steven King—Throws: Right; Bats: Right

Ht: 6'2"; Wt: 180 lbs; Born: 4/10/1964 in Oxnard, California; Debut: 5/15/1986

LCS										Pitching																		
Year Tm	Age	G	GS	CG	GF	IP	BFP	H	R	ER	HR	SH	SF	HB	TBB	IBB	SO	WP	Bk	W	L	Pct	ShO	Sv-Op	Hld	OAvg	OOBP	ERA
1987 Det	23	2	0	0	1	5.1	23	3	1	1	0	0	1	1	2	0	4	1	0	0	0	—	0	0-0	0	.158	.261	1.69

LCS								Batting																	Fielding						
Year Tm	Age	G	AB	H	2B	3B	HR	TB	R	RBI	GW	TBB	IBB	SO	HBP	SH	SF	SB	CS	SB%	GDP	Avg	OBP	SLG	Pos	G	PO	A	E	DP	FPct
1987 Det	23	2	0	0	0	0	0	0	0	0	0	0	0	0	0	0	0	0	0	—	0	—	—	—	P	2	1	1	0	0	1.000

HAL KING—Harold King—Bats: Left; Throws: Right

Ht: 6'1"; Wt: 200 lbs; Born: 2/1/1944 in Oviedo, Florida; Debut: 9/6/1967

LCS								Batting																	Fielding						
Year Tm	Age	G	AB	H	2B	3B	HR	TB	R	RBI	GW	TBB	IBB	SO	HBP	SH	SF	SB	CS	SB%	GDP	Avg	OBP	SLG	Pos	G	PO	A	E	DP	FPct
1973 Cin	29	3	2	1	0	0	0	1	0	0	0	1	0	1	0	0	0	0	0	—	0	.500	.667	.500	—						

JEFF KING—Jeffrey Wayne King—Bats: Right; Throws: Right

Ht: 6'1"; Wt: 175 lbs; Born: 12/26/1964 in Marion, Indiana; Debut: 6/2/1989

LCS								Batting																	Fielding						
Year Tm	Age	G	AB	H	2B	3B	HR	TB	R	RBI	GW	TBB	IBB	SO	HBP	SH	SF	SB	CS	SB%	GDP	Avg	OBP	SLG	Pos	G	PO	A	E	DP	FPct
1990 Pit	25	5	10	1	0	0	0	1	0	0	0	1	0	5	0	0	0	0	0	—	0	.100	.182	.100	3B	4	1	4	0	0	1.000
1992 Pit	27	7	29	7	4	0	0	11	4	2	0	0	0	1	0	0	0	0	1	.00	0	.241	.241	.379	3B	7	11	19	1	5	.968
LCS Totals		12	39	8	4	0	0	12	4	2	0	1	0	6	0	0	0	0	1	.00	0	.205	.225	.308	3B	11	12	23	1	5	.972

LEE KING—Edward Lee King—Bats: Right; Throws: Right

Ht: 5'8"; Wt: 160 lbs; Born: 12/26/1892 in Hundred, West Virginia; Debut: 9/20/1916; Died: 9/16/1967

World Series		Batting																							Fielding						
Year Tm	Age	G	AB	H	2B	3B	HR	TB	R	RBI	GW	TBB	IBB	SO	HBP	SH	SF	SB	CS	SB%	GDP	Avg	OBP	SLG	Pos	G	PO	A	E	DP	FPct
1922 NYG	29	2	1	1	0	0	0	1	0	1	0	0	0	0	0	0	0	0	0	—	0	1.000	1.000	1.000	OF	2	0	0	0	0	—

MIKE KINGERY—Michael Scott Kingery—Bats: Left; Throws: Left

Ht: 6'0"; Wt: 180 lbs; Born: 3/29/1961 in St. James, Minnesota; Debut: 7/7/1986

Division Series		Batting																							Fielding						
Year Tm	Age	G	AB	H	2B	3B	HR	TB	R	RBI	GW	TBB	IBB	SO	HBP	SH	SF	SB	CS	SB%	GDP	Avg	OBP	SLG	Pos	G	PO	A	E	DP	FPct
1995 Col	34	4	10	2	0	0	0	2	1	0	0	0	0	1	0	2	0	0	0	—	0	.200	.200	.200	OF	4	5	0	0	0	1.000

BRIAN KINGMAN—Brian Paul Kingman—Throws: Right; Bats: Right

Ht: 6'2"; Wt: 200 lbs; Born: 7/27/1954 in Los Angeles, California; Debut: 6/28/1979

LCS		Pitching																										
Year Tm	Age	G	GS	CG	GF	IP	BFP	H	R	ER	HR	SH	SF	HB	TBB	IBB	SO	WP	Bk	W	L	Pct	ShO	Sv-Op	Hld	OAvg	OOBP	ERA
1981 Oak	27	1	0	0	0	0.1	4	3	3	3	0	0	0	0	0	0	0	0	0	0	0	—	0	0- 0	0	.750	.750	81.00

LCS		Batting																							Fielding						
Year Tm	Age	G	AB	H	2B	3B	HR	TB	R	RBI	GW	TBB	IBB	SO	HBP	SH	SF	SB	CS	SB%	GDP	Avg	OBP	SLG	Pos	G	PO	A	E	DP	FPct
1981 Oak	27	1	0	0	0	0	0	0	0	0	0	0	0	0	0	0	0	0	0	—	0	—	—	—	P	1	0	0	0	0	—

DAVE KINGMAN—David Arthur Kingman—Nickname: Kong—Bats: Right; Throws: Right

Ht: 6'6"; Wt: 210 lbs; Born: 12/21/1948 in Pendleton, Oregon; Debut: 7/30/1971

LCS		Batting																							Fielding						
Year Tm	Age	G	AB	H	2B	3B	HR	TB	R	RBI	GW	TBB	IBB	SO	HBP	SH	SF	SB	CS	SB%	GDP	Avg	OBP	SLG	Pos	G	PO	A	E	DP	FPct
1971 SF	22	4	9	1	0	0	0	1	0	0	0	1	0	3	0	0	0	0	0	—	0	.111	.200	.111	OF	2	5	0	0	0	1.000

BOB KIPPER—Robert Wayne Kipper—Throws: Left; Bats: Right

Ht: 6'2"; Wt: 200 lbs; Born: 7/8/1964 in Aurora, Illinois; Debut: 4/12/1985

LCS		Pitching																										
Year Tm	Age	G	GS	CG	GF	IP	BFP	H	R	ER	HR	SH	SF	HB	TBB	IBB	SO	WP	Bk	W	L	Pct	ShO	Sv-Op	Hld	OAvg	OOBP	ERA
1991 Pit	27	1	0	0	0	2.0	7	2	1	1	1	0	0	0	0	0	1	0	0	0	0	—	0	0- 0	0	.286	.286	4.50

LCS		Batting																							Fielding						
Year Tm	Age	G	AB	H	2B	3B	HR	TB	R	RBI	GW	TBB	IBB	SO	HBP	SH	SF	SB	CS	SB%	GDP	Avg	OBP	SLG	Pos	G	PO	A	E	DP	FPct
1991 Pit	27	1	0	0	0	0	0	0	0	0	0	0	0	0	0	0	0	0	0	—	0	—	—	—	P	1	0	1	0	0	1.000

WAYNE KIRBY—Wayne Leonard Kirby—Bats: Left; Throws: Right

Ht: 5'11"; Wt: 185 lbs; Born: 1/22/1964 in Williamsburg, Virginia; Debut: 9/12/1991

Division Series		Batting																							Fielding						
Year Tm	Age	G	AB	H	2B	3B	HR	TB	R	RBI	GW	TBB	IBB	SO	HBP	SH	SF	SB	CS	SB%	GDP	Avg	OBP	SLG	Pos	G	PO	A	E	DP	FPct
1995 Cle	31	3	1	1	0	0	0	1	0	0	0	0	0	0	0	0	0	0	0	—	0	1.000	1.000	1.000	OF	2	0	0	0	0	—
1996 LA	32	3	8	1	0	0	0	1	1	0	0	2	0	1	0	0	0	0	1	.00	0	.125	.300	.125	OF	3	4	0	0	0	1.000
DS Totals		6	9	2	0	0	0	2	1	0	0	2	0	1	0	0	0	0	1	.00	0	.222	.364	.222	OF	5	4	0	0	0	1.000

LCS		Batting																							Fielding						
Year Tm	Age	G	AB	H	2B	3B	HR	TB	R	RBI	GW	TBB	IBB	SO	HBP	SH	SF	SB	CS	SB%	GDP	Avg	OBP	SLG	Pos	G	PO	A	E	DP	FPct
1995 Cle	31	5	5	1	0	0	0	1	2	0	0	0	0	0	0	1	0	1	0	1.00	1	.200	.200	.200	OF	4	3	0	0	0	1.000

World Series		Batting																							Fielding						
Year Tm	Age	G	AB	H	2B	3B	HR	TB	R	RBI	GW	TBB	IBB	SO	HBP	SH	SF	SB	CS	SB%	GDP	Avg	OBP	SLG	Pos	G	PO	A	E	DP	FPct
1995 Cle	31	3	1	0	0	0	0	0	0	0	0	0	0	1	0	0	0	0	0	—	0	.000	.000	.000	OF	1	1	0	0	0	1.000
Postseason Totals		14	15	3	0	0	0	3	3	0	0	2	0	2	0	1	0	1	1	.50	1	.200	.294	.200	OF	10	8	0	0	0	1.000

ED KIRKPATRICK—Edgar Leon Kirkpatrick—Nickname: Spanky—Bats: Left; Throws: Right

Ht: 5'11"; Wt: 195 lbs; Born: 10/8/1944 in Spokane, Washington; Debut: 9/13/1962

LCS		Batting																							Fielding						
Year Tm	Age	G	AB	H	2B	3B	HR	TB	R	RBI	GW	TBB	IBB	SO	HBP	SH	SF	SB	CS	SB%	GDP	Avg	OBP	SLG	Pos	G	PO	A	E	DP	FPct
1974 Pit	29	3	9	0	0	0	0	0	0	0	0	2	0	0	0	0	0	0	0	—	1	.000	.182	.000	1B	3	22	0	0	2	1.000
1975 Pit	30	2	2	0	0	0	0	0	0	0	0	0	0	0	0	0	0	0	0	—	0	.000	.000	.000	—						
LCS Totals		5	11	0	0	0	0	0	0	0	0	2	0	0	0	0	0	0	0	—	1	.000	.154	.000	1B	3	22	0	0	2	1.000

BRUCE KISON—Bruce Eugene Kison—Nickname: Sweetie—Throws: Right; Bats: Right

Ht: 6'4"; Wt: 178 lbs; Born: 2/18/1950 in Pasco, Washington; Debut: 7/4/1971

LCS		Pitching																										
Year Tm	Age	G	GS	CG	GF	IP	BFP	H	R	ER	HR	SH	SF	HB	TBB	IBB	SO	WP	Bk	W	L	Pct	ShO	Sv-Op	Hld	OAvg	OOBP	ERA
1971 Pit	21	1	0	0	0	4.2	17	2	0	0	0	0	0	0	2	0	3	1	0	1	0	1.000	0	0- 0	0	.133	.235	0.00
1972 Pit	22	2	0	0	0	2.1	8	1	0	0	0	0	0	0	0	0	3	0	0	1	0	1.000	0	0- 0	0	.125	.125	0.00
1974 Pit	24	1	1	0	0	6.2	28	2	0	0	0	0	0	0	6	0	5	0	0	1	0	1.000	0	0- 0	0	.091	.286	0.00
1975 Pit	25	1	0	0	1	2.0	7	2	1	1	0	0	0	0	1	0	1	0	0	0	0	—	0	0- 0	0	.333	.429	4.50
1982 Cal	32	2	2	1	0	14.0	53	8	4	3	2	0	1	0	3	0	12	0	0	1	0	1.000	0	0- 0	0	.163	.208	1.93
LCS Totals		7	3	1	1	29.2	226	15	5	4	2	0	1	0	12	0	24	1	0	4	0	1.000	0	0-0	0	.150	.239	1.21

World Series		Pitching																										
Year Tm	Age	G	GS	CG	GF	IP	BFP	H	R	ER	HR	SH	SF	HB	TBB	IBB	SO	WP	Bk	W	L	Pct	ShO	Sv-Op	Hld	OAvg	OOBP	ERA
1971 Pit	21	2	0	0	0	6.1	24	1	0	0	0	0	0	3	2	0	3	0	0	1	0	1.000	0	0- 0	0	.053	.250	0.00
1979 Pit	29	1	1	0	0	0.1	7	3	5	4	1	0	0	0	2	0	0	1	0	0	1	.000	0	0- 0	0	.600	.714	108.00
WS Totals		3	1	0	0	6.2	62	4	5	4	1	0	0	3	4	0	3	1	0	1	1	.500	0	0-0	0	.167	.355	5.40
Postseason Totals		10	4	1	1	36.1	288	19	10	8	3	0	1	3	16	0	27	2	0	5	1	.833	0	0-0	0	.153	.264	1.98

LCS		Batting																							Fielding						
Year Tm	Age	G	AB	H	2B	3B	HR	TB	R	RBI	GW	TBB	IBB	SO	HBP	SH	SF	SB	CS	SB%	GDP	Avg	OBP	SLG	Pos	G	PO	A	E	DP	FPct
1971 Pit	21	1	2	0	0	0	0	0	0	0	0	0	0	0	0	0	0	0	0	—	0	.000	.000	.000	P	1	0	1	0	0	1.000
1972 Pit	22	2	0	0	0	0	0	0	0	0	0	0	0	0	0	0	0	0	0	—	0	—	—	—	P	2	0	0	0	0	—
1974 Pit	24	1	3	0	0	0	0	0	0	0	0	0	0	2	0	0	0	0	0	—	0	.000	.000	.000	P	1	1	1	0	0	1.000
1975 Pit	25	1	0	0	0	0	0	0	0	0	0	0	0	0	0	0	0	0	0	—	0	—	—	—	P	1	0	0	0	0	—
1982 Cal	32	2	0	0	0	0	0	0	0	0	0	0	0	0	0	0	0	0	0	—	0	—	—	—	P	2	0	0	0	0	—
LCS Totals		7	5	0	0	0	0	0	0	0	0	0	0	2	0	0	0	0	0	—	0	.000	.000	.000	P	7	1	2	0	0	1.000

World Series		Batting																							Fielding						
Year Tm	Age	G	AB	H	2B	3B	HR	TB	R	RBI	GW	TBB	IBB	SO	HBP	SH	SF	SB	CS	SB%	GDP	Avg	OBP	SLG	Pos	G	PO	A	E	DP	FPct
1971 Pit	21	2	2	0	0	0	0	0	0	0	0	1	0	2	0	0	0	0	0	—	0	.000	.333	.000	P	2	0	1	0	0	1.000
1979 Pit	29	1	0	0	0	0	0	0	0	0	0	0	0	0	0	0	0	0	0	—	0	—	—	—	P	1	0	1	0	0	1.000
WS Totals		3	2	0	0	0	0	0	0	0	0	1	0	2	0	0	0	0	0	—	0	.000	.333	.000	P	3	0	2	0	0	1.000
Postseason Totals		10	7	0	0	0	0	0	0	0	0	1	0	4	0	0	0	0	0	—	0	.000	.125	.000	P	10	1	4	0	0	1.000

RON KITTLE—Ronald Dale Kittle—Bats: Right; Throws: Right

Ht: 6'4"; Wt: 200 lbs; Born: 1/5/1958 in Gary, Indiana; Debut: 9/2/1982

LCS		Batting																							Fielding						
Year Tm	Age	G	AB	H	2B	3B	HR	TB	R	RBI	GW	TBB	IBB	SO	HBP	SH	SF	SB	CS	SB%	GDP	Avg	OBP	SLG	Pos	G	PO	A	E	DP	FPct
1983 ChA-*RY*	25	3	7	2	1	0	0	3	1	0	0	1	0	2	1	0	0	0	0	—	1	.286	.444	.429	OF	3	3	0	0	0	1.000

CHUCK KLEIN (HOF 1980-V)—Charles Herbert Klein—Bats: Left; Throws: Right

Ht: 6'0"; Wt: 185 lbs; Born: 10/7/1904 in Indianapolis, Indiana; Debut: 7/30/1928; Died: 3/28/1958

World Series		Batting																							Fielding						
Year Tm	Age	G	AB	H	2B	3B	HR	TB	R	RBI	GW	TBB	IBB	SO	HBP	SH	SF	SB	CS	SB%	GDP	Avg	OBP	SLG	Pos	G	PO	A	E	DP	FPct
1935 ChN	30	5	12	4	0	0	1	7	2	2	1	0	0	2	0	0	0	0	0	—	0	.333	.333	.583	OF	3	4	0	0	0	1.000

LOU KLEIN—Louis Frank Klein—Bats: Right; Throws: Right

Ht: 5'11"; Wt: 167 lbs; Born: 10/22/1918 in New Orleans, Louisiana; Debut: 4/21/1943; Died: 6/20/1976

World Series — Batting / Fielding

Year Tm	Age	G	AB	H	2B	3B	HR	TB	R	RBI	GW	TBB	IBB	SO	HBP	SH	SF	SB	CS	SB%	GDP	Avg	OBP	SLG	Pos	G	PO	A	E	DP	FPct
1943 StL	24	5	22	3	0	0	0	3	0	0	0	1	0	2	0	0	0	0	0	—	0	.136	.174	.136	2B	5	10	13	2	4	.920

RYAN KLESKO—Ryan Anthony Klesko—Bats: Left; Throws: Left

Ht: 6'3"; Wt: 220 lbs; Born: 6/12/1971 in Westminster, California; Debut: 9/12/1992

Division Series — Batting / Fielding

Year Tm	Age	G	AB	H	2B	3B	HR	TB	R	RBI	GW	TBB	IBB	SO	HBP	SH	SF	SB	CS	SB%	GDP	Avg	OBP	SLG	Pos	G	PO	A	E	DP	FPct
1995 Atl	24	4	15	7	1	0	0	8	5	1	0	0	0	3	0	0	0	0	0	—	1	.467	.467	.533	OF	4	3	0	0	0	1.000
1996 Atl	25	3	8	1	0	0	1	4	1	1	0	3	0	4	0	0	0	1	0	1.00	0	.125	.364	.500	OF	3	2	0	1	0	.667
1997 Atl	26	3	8	2	1	0	1	6	2	1	0	0	0	2	0	0	0	0	0	—	1	.250	.250	.750	OF	3	3	0	1	0	.750
DS Totals		10	31	10	2	0	2	18	8	3	0	3	0	9	0	0	0	1	0	1.00	2	.323	.382	.581	OF	10	8	0	2	0	.800

LCS — Batting / Fielding

Year Tm	Age	G	AB	H	2B	3B	HR	TB	R	RBI	GW	TBB	IBB	SO	HBP	SH	SF	SB	CS	SB%	GDP	Avg	OBP	SLG	Pos	G	PO	A	E	DP	FPct
1995 Atl	24	4	7	0	0	0	0	0	0	0	0	3	2	4	0	0	0	0	1	.00	0	.000	.300	.000	OF	3	1	0	0	0	1.000
1996 Atl	25	6	16	4	0	0	1	7	1	3	0	2	0	6	0	0	0	0	0	—	1	.250	.333	.438	OF	6	13	0	0	0	1.000
1997 Atl	26	5	17	4	0	0	2	10	2	4	0	2	0	3	0	0	0	0	0	—	0	.235	.316	.588	OF	5	5	0	0	0	1.000
LCS Totals		15	40	8	0	0	3	17	3	7	0	7	2	13	0	0	0	0	1	.00	1	.200	.319	.425	OF	14	19	0	0	0	1.000

World Series — Batting / Fielding

Year Tm	Age	G	AB	H	2B	3B	HR	TB	R	RBI	GW	TBB	IBB	SO	HBP	SH	SF	SB	CS	SB%	GDP	Avg	OBP	SLG	Pos	G	PO	A	E	DP	FPct
1995 Atl	24	6	16	5	0	0	3	14	4	4	0	3	1	4	0	0	0	0	0	—	0	.313	.421	.875	OF	3	1	0	0	0	1.000
1996 Atl	25	5	10	1	0	0	0	1	2	1	0	2	1	4	0	0	0	0	0	—	0	.100	.250	.100	1B	1	0	0	1	0	.000
																									OF	2	1	0	0	0	1.000
WS Totals		11	26	6	0	0	3	15	6	5	0	5	2	8	0	0	0	0	0	—	0	.231	.355	.577	OF	5	2	0	0	0	1.000
Postseason Totals		36	97	24	2	0	8	50	17	15	0	15	4	30	0	0	0	1	1	.50	3	.247	.348	.515	OF	29	29	0	2	0	.935

ED KLIEMAN—Edward Frederick Klieman—Nicknames: Specs, Babe—Throws: Right; Bats: Right

Ht: 6'1"; Wt: 190 lbs; Born: 3/21/1918 in Norwood, Ohio; Debut: 9/24/1943; Died: 11/15/1979

World Series — Pitching

Year Tm	Age	G	GS	CG	GF	IP	BFP	H	R	ER	HR	SH	SF	HB	TBB	IBB	SO	WP	Bk	W	L	Pct	ShO	Sv-Op	Hld	OAvg	OOBP	ERA
1948 Cle	30	1	0	0	0	0.0	3	1	3	3	0	0	0	0	2	0	0	0	0	0	0	—	0	0-0	0	1.000	1.000	—

World Series — Batting / Fielding

Year Tm	Age	G	AB	H	2B	3B	HR	TB	R	RBI	GW	TBB	IBB	SO	HBP	SH	SF	SB	CS	SB%	GDP	Avg	OBP	SLG	Pos	G	PO	A	E	DP	FPct
1948 Cle	30	1	0	0	0	0	0	0	0	0	0	0	0	0	0	0	0	0	0	—	0	—	—	—	P	1	0	0	0	0	—

JOHNNY KLING—John Kling—Nickname: Noisy—Bats: Right; Throws: Right

Ht: 5'9"; Wt: 160 lbs; Born: 2/25/1875 in Kansas City, Missouri; Debut: 9/11/1900; Died: 1/31/1947

World Series — Batting / Fielding

Year Tm	Age	G	AB	H	2B	3B	HR	TB	R	RBI	GW	TBB	IBB	SO	HBP	SH	SF	SB	CS	SB%	GDP	Avg	OBP	SLG	Pos	G	PO	A	E	DP	FPct
1906 ChN	31	6	17	3	1	0	0	4	2	0	0	4	1	3	0	0	0	0	0	—	1	.176	.333	.235	C	6	45	9	1	3	.982
1907 ChN	32	5	19	4	0	0	0	4	2	1	0	1	0	4	0	1	0	0	0	—	0	.211	.250	.211	C	5	25	10	1	0	.972
1908 ChN	33	5	16	4	1	0	0	5	2	2	0	2	0	2	0	1	0	0	2	.00	0	.250	.333	.313	C	5	32	6	0	1	1.000
1910 ChN	35	5	13	1	0	0	0	1	0	1	0	1	0	2	0	0	0	0	0	—	1	.077	.143	.077	C	3	11	7	0	0	1.000
WS Totals		21	65	12	2	0	0	14	6	4	0	8	1	11	0	2	0	0	2	.00	3	.185	.274	.215	C	19	113	32	2	4	.986

BOB KLINGER—Robert Harold Klinger—Throws: Right; Bats: Right

Ht: 6'0"; Wt: 180 lbs; Born: 6/4/1908 in Allenton, Missouri; Debut: 4/19/1938; Died: 8/19/1977

World Series — Pitching

Year Tm	Age	G	GS	CG	GF	IP	BFP	H	R	ER	HR	SH	SF	HB	TBB	IBB	SO	WP	Bk	W	L	Pct	ShO	Sv-Op	Hld	OAvg	OOBP	ERA
1946 Bos	38	1	0	0	0	0.2	5	2	1	1	0	0	0	0	1	1	0	0	0	0	1	.000	0	0-0	0	.500	.600	13.50

World Series — Batting / Fielding

Year Tm	Age	G	AB	H	2B	3B	HR	TB	R	RBI	GW	TBB	IBB	SO	HBP	SH	SF	SB	CS	SB%	GDP	Avg	OBP	SLG	Pos	G	PO	A	E	DP	FPct
1946 Bos	38	1	0	0	0	0	0	0	0	0	0	0	0	0	0	0	0	0	0	—	0	—	—	—	P	1	1	0	0	0	1.000

JOE KLINK—Joseph Charles Klink—Throws: Left; Bats: Left

Ht: 5'11"; Wt: 170 lbs; Born: 2/3/1962 in Johnstown, Pennsylvania; Debut: 4/9/1987

World Series — Pitching

Year Tm	Age	G	GS	CG	GF	IP	BFP	H	R	ER	HR	SH	SF	HB	TBB	IBB	SO	WP	Bk	W	L	Pct	ShO	Sv-Op	Hld	OAvg	OOBP	ERA
1990 Oak	28	1	0	0	0	0.0	1	0	0	0	0	0	0	0	1	0	0	0	0	0	0	—	0	0-0	0	—	1.000	—

World Series — Batting / Fielding

Year Tm	Age	G	AB	H	2B	3B	HR	TB	R	RBI	GW	TBB	IBB	SO	HBP	SH	SF	SB	CS	SB%	GDP	Avg	OBP	SLG	Pos	G	PO	A	E	DP	FPct
1990 Oak	28	1	0	0	0	0	0	0	0	0	0	0	0	0	0	0	0	0	0	—	0	—	—	—	P	1	0	0	0	0	—

JOHNNY KLIPPSTEIN—John Calvin Klippstein—Throws: Right; Bats: Right

Ht: 6'1"; Wt: 173 lbs; Born: 10/17/1927 in Washington, DC; Debut: 5/3/1950

World Series — Pitching

Year Tm	Age	G	GS	CG	GF	IP	BFP	H	R	ER	HR	SH	SF	HB	TBB	IBB	SO	WP	Bk	W	L	Pct	ShO	Sv-Op	Hld	OAvg	OOBP	ERA
1959 LA	31	1	0	0	1	2.0	7	1	0	0	0	0	0	0	0	0	2	0	0	0	0	—	0	0-0	0	.143	.143	0.00
1965 Min	37	2	0	0	1	2.2	12	2	0	0	0	0	0	1	2	1	3	0	0	0	0	—	0	0-0	0	.222	.417	0.00
WS Totals		3	0	0	2	4.2	38	3	0	0	0	0	0	1	2	1	5	0	0	0	0	—	0	0-0	0	.188	.316	0.00

World Series — Batting / Fielding

Year Tm	Age	G	AB	H	2B	3B	HR	TB	R	RBI	GW	TBB	IBB	SO	HBP	SH	SF	SB	CS	SB%	GDP	Avg	OBP	SLG	Pos	G	PO	A	E	DP	FPct
1959 LA	31	1	0	0	0	0	0	0	0	0	0	0	0	0	0	0	0	0	0	—	0	—	—	—	P	1	0	1	0	0	1.000
1965 Min	37	2	0	0	0	0	0	0	0	0	0	0	0	0	0	0	0	0	0	—	0	—	—	—	P	2	0	0	0	0	—
WS Totals		3	0	0	0	0	0	0	0	0	0	0	0	0	0	0	0	0	0	—	0	—	—	—	P	3	0	1	0	0	1.000

TED KLUSZEWSKI—Theodore Bernard Kluszewski—Nickname: Big Klu—Bats: Left; Throws: Left

Ht: 6'2"; Wt: 225 lbs; Born: 9/10/1924 in Argo, Illinois; Debut: 4/18/1947; Died: 3/29/1988

World Series — Batting / Fielding

Year Tm	Age	G	AB	H	2B	3B	HR	TB	R	RBI	GW	TBB	IBB	SO	HBP	SH	SF	SB	CS	SB%	GDP	Avg	OBP	SLG	Pos	G	PO	A	E	DP	FPct
1959 ChA	35	6	23	9	1	0	3	19	5	10	1	2	2	0	0	0	0	0	0	—	1	.391	.440	.826	1B	6	58	3	0	2	1.000

MICKEY KLUTTS—Gene Ellis Klutts—Bats: Right; Throws: Right

Ht: 5'11"; Wt: 170 lbs; Born: 9/20/1954 in Montebello, California; Debut: 7/7/1976

Division Series — Batting / Fielding

Year Tm	Age	G	AB	H	2B	3B	HR	TB	R	RBI	GW	TBB	IBB	SO	HBP	SH	SF	SB	CS	SB%	GDP	Avg	OBP	SLG	Pos	G	PO	A	E	DP	FPct
1981 Oak	27	2	7	1	0	0	0	1	0	0	0	0	0	1	0	1	0	0	0	—	0	.143	.143	.143	3B	2	0	2	0	1	1.000

LCS — Batting / Fielding

Year Tm	Age	G	AB	H	2B	3B	HR	TB	R	RBI	GW	TBB	IBB	SO	HBP	SH	SF	SB	CS	SB%	GDP	Avg	OBP	SLG	Pos	G	PO	A	E	DP	FPct
1981 Oak	27	3	7	3	0	0	0	3	1	0	0	0	0	1	0	0	0	0	0	—	0	.429	.429	.429	3B	3	3	4	1	0	.875
Postseason Totals		5	14	4	0	0	0	4	1	0	0	0	0	2	0	1	0	0	0	—	0	.286	.286	.286	3B	5	3	6	1	1	.900

CHRIS KNAPP—Robert Christian Knapp—Throws: Right; Bats: Right

Ht: 6'5"; Wt: 195 lbs; Born: 9/16/1953 in Cherry Point, North Carolina; Debut: 9/4/1975

LCS — Pitching

Year Tm	Age	G	GS	CG	GF	IP	BFP	H	R	ER	HR	SH	SF	HB	TBB	IBB	SO	WP	Bk	W	L	Pct	ShO	Sv-Op	Hld	OAvg	OOBP	ERA
1979 Cal	26	1	1	0	0	2.1	13	5	2	2	0	0	1	0	1	0	0	0	0	0	1	.000	0	0-0	0	.455	.462	7.71

LCS — Batting / Fielding

Year Tm	Age	G	AB	H	2B	3B	HR	TB	R	RBI	GW	TBB	IBB	SO	HBP	SH	SF	SB	CS	SB%	GDP	Avg	OBP	SLG	Pos	G	PO	A	E	DP	FPct
1979 Cal	26	1	0	0	0	0	0	0	0	0	0	0	0	0	0	0	0	0	0	—	0	—	—	—	P	1	0	0	0	0	—

BOB KNEPPER—Robert Wesley Knepper—Throws: Left; Bats: Left

Ht: 6'3"; Wt: 195 lbs; Born: 5/25/1954 in Akron, Ohio; Debut: 9/10/1976

Division Series — Pitching

Year Tm	Age	G	GS	CG	GF	IP	BFP	H	R	ER	HR	SH	SF	HB	TBB	IBB	SO	WP	Bk	W	L	Pct	ShO	Sv-Op	Hld	OAvg	OOBP	ERA
1981 Hou	27	1	1	0	0	5.0	25	6	3	3	1	1	0	0	2	1	4	1	0	0	1	.000	0	0- 0	0	.273	.333	5.40

LCS — Pitching

Year Tm	Age	G	GS	CG	GF	IP	BFP	H	R	ER	HR	SH	SF	HB	TBB	IBB	SO	WP	Bk	W	L	Pct	ShO	Sv-Op	Hld	OAvg	OOBP	ERA
1986 Hou	32	2	2	0	0	15.1	60	13	7	6	1	0	0	0	1	0	9	0	0	0	0	—	0	0- 0	0	.220	.233	3.52
Postseason Totals		3	3	0	0	20.1	170	19	10	9	2	1	0	0	3	1	13	1	0	0	1	.000	0	0-0	0	.235	.262	3.98

Division Series — Batting / Fielding

Year Tm	Age	G	AB	H	2B	3B	HR	TB	R	RBI	GW	TBB	IBB	SO	HBP	SH	SF	SB	CS	SB%	GDP	Avg	OBP	SLG	Pos	G	PO	A	E	DP	FPct
1981 Hou	27	1	1	0	0	0	0	0	0	0	0	0	0	0	0	0	0	0	0	—	0	.000	.000	.000	P	1	0	1	0	0	1.000

LCS — Batting / Fielding

Year Tm	Age	G	AB	H	2B	3B	HR	TB	R	RBI	GW	TBB	IBB	SO	HBP	SH	SF	SB	CS	SB%	GDP	Avg	OBP	SLG	Pos	G	PO	A	E	DP	FPct
1986 Hou	32	2	5	0	0	0	0	0	0	0	0	1	0	2	0	0	0	0	0	—	0	.000	.167	.000	P	2	0	3	0	0	1.000
Postseason Totals		3	6	0	0	0	0	0	0	0	0	1	0	2	0	0	0	0	0	—	0	.000	.143	.000	P	3	0	4	0	0	1.000

RAY KNIGHT—Charles Ray Knight—Bats: Right; Throws: Right

Ht: 6'1"; Wt: 185 lbs; Born: 12/28/1952 in Albany, Georgia; Debut: 9/10/1974

LCS — Batting / Fielding

Year Tm	Age	G	AB	H	2B	3B	HR	TB	R	RBI	GW	TBB	IBB	SO	HBP	SH	SF	SB	CS	SB%	GDP	Avg	OBP	SLG	Pos	G	PO	A	E	DP	FPct
1979 Cin	26	3	14	4	1	0	0	5	0	0	0	0	0	2	0	0	0	1	0	1.00	1	.286	.286	.357	3B	3	0	5	0	0	1.000
1986 NYN	33	6	24	4	0	0	0	4	1	2	1	1	1	5	0	0	1	0	0	—	0	.167	.192	.167	3B	6	5	19	1	1	.960
LCS Totals		9	38	8	1	0	0	9	1	2	1	1	1	7	0	0	1	1	0	1.00	1	.211	.225	.237	3B	9	5	24	1	1	.967

World Series — Batting / Fielding

Year Tm	Age	G	AB	H	2B	3B	HR	TB	R	RBI	GW	TBB	IBB	SO	HBP	SH	SF	SB	CS	SB%	GDP	Avg	OBP	SLG	Pos	G	PO	A	E	DP	FPct
1986 NYN	33	6	23	9	1	0	1	13	4	5	1	2	0	2	0	0	0	0	0	—	2	.391	.440	.565	3B	6	5	6	1	0	.917
Postseason Totals		15	61	17	2	0	1	22	5	7	2	3	1	9	0	0	1	1	0	1.00	3	.279	.308	.361	3B	15	10	30	2	1	.952

CHUCK KNOBLAUCH—Edward Charles Knoblauch—Bats: Right; Throws: Right

Ht: 5'9"; Wt: 175 lbs; Born: 7/7/1968 in Houston, Texas; Debut: 4/9/1991

LCS — Batting / Fielding

Year Tm	Age	G	AB	H	2B	3B	HR	TB	R	RBI	GW	TBB	IBB	SO	HBP	SH	SF	SB	CS	SB%	GDP	Avg	OBP	SLG	Pos	G	PO	A	E	DP	FPct
1991 Min-*RY*	23	5	20	7	2	0	0	9	5	3	0	3	0	3	0	0	0	2	1	.67	0	.350	.435	.450	2B	5	8	14	0	3	1.000

World Series — Batting / Fielding

Year Tm	Age	G	AB	H	2B	3B	HR	TB	R	RBI	GW	TBB	IBB	SO	HBP	SH	SF	SB	CS	SB%	GDP	Avg	OBP	SLG	Pos	G	PO	A	E	DP	FPct
1991 Min-*RY*	23	7	26	8	1	0	0	9	3	2	1	4	0	2	0	1	1	4	0	1.00	0	.308	.387	.346	2B	7	15	14	1	1	.967
Postseason Totals		12	46	15	3	0	0	18	8	5	1	7	0	5	0	1	1	6	1	.86	0	.326	.407	.391	2B	12	23	28	1	4	.981

RANDY KNORR—Randy Duane Knorr—Bats: Right; Throws: Right

Ht: 6'2"; Wt: 205 lbs; Born: 11/12/1968 in San Gabriel, California; Debut: 9/5/1991

World Series — Batting / Fielding

Year Tm	Age	G	AB	H	2B	3B	HR	TB	R	RBI	GW	TBB	IBB	SO	HBP	SH	SF	SB	CS	SB%	GDP	Avg	OBP	SLG	Pos	G	PO	A	E	DP	FPct
1993 Tor	24	1	0	0	0	0	0	0	0	0	0	0	0	0	0	0	0	0	0	—	0	—	—	—	C	1	3	0	0	0	1.000

DAROLD KNOWLES—Darold Duane Knowles—Throws: Left; Bats: Left

Ht: 6'0"; Wt: 180 lbs; Born: 12/9/1941 in Brunswick, Missouri; Debut: 4/18/1965

LCS — Pitching

Year Tm	Age	G	GS	CG	GF	IP	BFP	H	R	ER	HR	SH	SF	HB	TBB	IBB	SO	WP	Bk	W	L	Pct	ShO	Sv-Op	Hld	OAvg	OOBP	ERA
1971 Oak	29	1	0	0	0	0.1	2	1	0	0	0	0	0	0	0	0	0	1	0	0	0	—	0	0- 0	0	.500	.500	0.00

World Series — Pitching

Year Tm	Age	G	GS	CG	GF	IP	BFP	H	R	ER	HR	SH	SF	HB	TBB	IBB	SO	WP	Bk	W	L	Pct	ShO	Sv-Op	Hld	OAvg	OOBP	ERA
1973 Oak	31	7	0	0	2	6.1	30	4	1	0	0	0	0	1	5	2	5	0	0	0	0	—	0	2- 2	1	.167	.333	0.00
Postseason Totals		8	0	0	2	6.2	64	5	1	0	0	0	0	1	5	2	5	1	0	0	0	—	0	2-2	1	.192	.344	0.00

LCS — Batting / Fielding

Year Tm	Age	G	AB	H	2B	3B	HR	TB	R	RBI	GW	TBB	IBB	SO	HBP	SH	SF	SB	CS	SB%	GDP	Avg	OBP	SLG	Pos	G	PO	A	E	DP	FPct
1971 Oak	29	1	0	0	0	0	0	0	0	0	0	0	0	0	0	0	0	0	0	—	0	—	—	—	P	1	0	0	0	0	—

World Series — Batting / Fielding

Year Tm	Age	G	AB	H	2B	3B	HR	TB	R	RBI	GW	TBB	IBB	SO	HBP	SH	SF	SB	CS	SB%	GDP	Avg	OBP	SLG	Pos	G	PO	A	E	DP	FPct
1973 Oak	31	7	0	0	0	0	0	0	0	0	0	0	0	0	0	0	0	0	0	—	0	—	—	—	P	7	0	1	1	1	.500
Postseason Totals		8	0	0	0	0	0	0	0	0	0	0	0	0	0	0	0	0	0	—	0	—	—	—	P	8	0	1	1	1	.500

JOHN KNOX—John Clinton Knox—Bats: Left; Throws: Right

Ht: 6'0"; Wt: 170 lbs; Born: 7/26/1948 in Newark, New Jersey; Debut: 8/1/1972

LCS — Batting / Fielding

Year Tm	Age	G	AB	H	2B	3B	HR	TB	R	RBI	GW	TBB	IBB	SO	HBP	SH	SF	SB	CS	SB%	GDP	Avg	OBP	SLG	Pos	G	PO	A	E	DP	FPct
1972 Det	24	1	0	0	0	0	0	0	0	0	0	0	0	0	0	0	0	0	0	—	0	—	—	—	—						

MARK KOENIG—Mark Anthony Koenig—Bats: Both; Throws: Right

Ht: 6'0"; Wt: 180 lbs; Born: 7/19/1904 in San Francisco, California; Debut: 9/8/1925; Died: 4/22/1993

World Series — Batting / Fielding

Year Tm	Age	G	AB	H	2B	3B	HR	TB	R	RBI	GW	TBB	IBB	SO	HBP	SH	SF	SB	CS	SB%	GDP	Avg	OBP	SLG	Pos	G	PO	A	E	DP	FPct
1926 NYA	22	7	32	4	1	0	0	5	2	2	0	0	0	6	0	1	0	0	0	—	3	.125	.125	.156	SS	7	12	24	4	3	.900
1927 NYA	23	4	18	9	2	0	0	11	5	2	0	0	0	2	0	0	0	0	0	—	0	.500	.500	.611	SS	4	6	8	0	1	1.000
1928 NYA	24	4	19	3	0	0	0	3	1	0	0	0	0	1	0	0	0	0	0	—	0	.158	.158	.158	SS	4	8	11	2	3	.905
1932 ChN	28	2	4	1	0	1	0	3	1	1	0	1	1	0	0	0	0	0	0	—	0	.250	.400	.750	SS	1	4	3	0	1	1.000
1936 NYG	32	3	3	1	0	0	0	1	0	0	0	0	0	1	0	0	0	0	0	—	0	.333	.333	.333	2B	1	1	0	0	0	1.000
WS Totals		20	76	18	3	1	0	23	9	5	0	1	1	10	0	1	0	0	0	—	3	.237	.247	.303	SS	16	30	46	6	8	.927

ED KONETCHY—Edward Joseph Konetchy—Nickname: Big Ed—Bats: Right; Throws: Right

Ht: 6'2"; Wt: 195 lbs; Born: 9/3/1885 in LaCrosse, Wisconsin; Debut: 6/29/1907; Died: 5/27/1947

World Series — Batting / Fielding

Year Tm	Age	G	AB	H	2B	3B	HR	TB	R	RBI	GW	TBB	IBB	SO	HBP	SH	SF	SB	CS	SB%	GDP	Avg	OBP	SLG	Pos	G	PO	A	E	DP	FPct
1920 Bro	35	7	23	4	0	1	0	6	0	2	0	3	0	2	0	0	0	0	0	—	1	.174	.269	.261	1B	7	70	7	1	4	.987

ALEX KONIKOWSKI—Alexander James Konikowski—Nickname: Whitey—Throws: Right; Bats: Right

Ht: 6'1"; Wt: 187 lbs; Born: 6/8/1928 in Throop, Pennsylvania; Debut: 6/16/1948; Died: 9/28/1997

World Series — Pitching

Year Tm	Age	G	GS	CG	GF	IP	BFP	H	R	ER	HR	SH	SF	HB	TBB	IBB	SO	WP	Bk	W	L	Pct	ShO	Sv-Op	Hld	OAvg	OOBP	ERA
1951 NYG	23	1	0	0	1	1.0	3	1	0	0	0	0	0	0	0	0	0	0	0	0	0	—	0	0- 0	0	.333	.333	0.00

World Series — Batting / Fielding

Year Tm	Age	G	AB	H	2B	3B	HR	TB	R	RBI	GW	TBB	IBB	SO	HBP	SH	SF	SB	CS	SB%	GDP	Avg	OBP	SLG	Pos	G	PO	A	E	DP	FPct
1951 NYG	23	1	0	0	0	0	0	0	0	0	0	0	0	0	0	0	0	0	0	—	0	—	—	—	P	1	0	0	0	0	—

JIM KONSTANTY—Casimir James Konstanty—Throws: Right; Bats: Right

Ht: 6'1"; Wt: 202 lbs; Born: 3/2/1917 in Strykersville, New York; Debut: 6/18/1944; Died: 6/11/1976

World Series — Pitching

Year Tm	Age	G	GS	CG	GF	IP	BFP	H	R	ER	HR	SH	SF	HB	TBB	IBB	SO	WP	Bk	W	L	Pct	ShO	Sv-Op	Hld	OAvg	OOBP	ERA
1950 Phi-*M*	33	3	1	0	0	15.0	60	9	4	4	1	1	0	1	4	1	3	0	0	0	1	.000	0	0- 1	0	.167	.237	2.40

World Series — Batting / Fielding

Year Tm	Age	G	AB	H	2B	3B	HR	TB	R	RBI	GW	TBB	IBB	SO	HBP	SH	SF	SB	CS	SB%	GDP	Avg	OBP	SLG	Pos	G	PO	A	E	DP	FPct
1950 Phi	33	3	4	1	0	0	0	1	0	0	0	0	0	1	0	0	0	0	0	—	0	.250	.250	.250	P	3	1	1	0	0	1.000

JERRY KOOSMAN—Jerome Martin Koosman—Throws: Left; Bats: Right

Ht: 6'2"; Wt: 205 lbs; Born: 12/23/1942 in Appleton, Minnesota; Debut: 4/14/1967

LCS	Pitching																											
Year Tm	Age	G	GS	CG	GF	IP	BFP	H	R	ER	HR	SH	SF	HB	TBB	IBB	SO	WP	Bk	W	L	Pct	ShO	Sv-Op	Hld	OAvg	OOBP	ERA
1969 NYN	26	1	1	0	0	4.2	24	7	6	6	1	0	0	0	4	0	5	0	0	0	0	—	0	0- 0	0	.350	.458	11.57
1973 NYN	30	1	1	1	0	9.0	35	8	2	2	1	0	0	0	0	0	9	0	0	1	0	1.000	0	0- 0	0	.229	.229	2.00
1983 ChA	40	1	0	0	0	0.1	4	1	3	2	0	0	0	0	2	1	0	0	0	0	0	—	0	0- 0	0	.500	.750	54.00
LCS Totals		3	2	1	0	14.0	126	16	11	10	2	0	0	0	6	1	14	0	0	1	0	1.000	0	0-0	0	.281	.349	6.43
World Series	Pitching																											
Year Tm	Age	G	GS	CG	GF	IP	BFP	H	R	ER	HR	SH	SF	HB	TBB	IBB	SO	WP	Bk	W	L	Pct	ShO	Sv-Op	Hld	OAvg	OOBP	ERA
1969 NYN	26	2	2	1	0	17.2	64	7	4	4	2	0	0	0	4	0	9	0	0	2	0	1.000	0	0- 0	0	.117	.172	2.04
1973 NYN	30	2	2	0	0	8.2	41	9	3	3	0	0	0	0	7	1	8	0	0	1	0	1.000	0	0- 0	0	.265	.390	3.12
WS Totals		4	4	1	0	26.1	210	16	7	7	2	0	0	0	11	1	17	0	0	3	0	1.000	0	0-0	0	.170	.257	2.39
Postseason Totals		7	6	2	0	40.1	336	32	18	17	4	0	0	0	17	2	31	0	0	4	0	1.000	0	0-0	0	.212	.292	3.79

LCS	Batting																								Fielding						
Year Tm	Age	G	AB	H	2B	3B	HR	TB	R	RBI	GW	TBB	IBB	SO	HBP	SH	SF	SB	CS	SB%	GDP	Avg	OBP	SLG	Pos	G	PO	A	E	DP	FPct
1969 NYN	26	1	2	0	0	0	0	0	1	0	0	1	0	2	0	0	0	0	0	—	0	.000	.333	.000	P	1	0	1	0	0	1.000
1973 NYN	30	1	4	2	0	0	0	2	1	1	0	0	0	0	0	0	0	0	0	—	0	.500	.500	.500	P	1	0	0	0	0	—
1983 ChA	40	1	0	0	0	0	0	0	0	0	0	0	0	0	0	0	0	0	0	—	0	—	—	—	P	1	0	0	0	0	—
LCS Totals		3	6	2	0	0	0	2	2	1	0	1	0	2	0	0	0	0	0	—	0	.333	.429	.333	P	3	0	1	0	0	1.000
World Series	Batting																								Fielding						
Year Tm	Age	G	AB	H	2B	3B	HR	TB	R	RBI	GW	TBB	IBB	SO	HBP	SH	SF	SB	CS	SB%	GDP	Avg	OBP	SLG	Pos	G	PO	A	E	DP	FPct
1969 NYN	26	2	7	1	1	0	0	2	0	0	0	0	0	4	0	0	0	0	0	—	0	.143	.143	.286	P	2	0	2	0	0	1.000
1973 NYN	30	2	4	0	0	0	0	0	0	0	0	0	0	3	0	0	0	0	0	—	0	.000	.000	.000	P	2	0	1	1	0	.500
WS Totals		4	11	1	1	0	0	2	0	0	0	0	0	7	0	0	0	0	0	—	0	.091	.091	.182	P	4	0	3	1	0	.750
Postseason Totals		7	17	3	1	0	0	4	2	1	0	1	0	9	0	0	0	0	0	—	0	.176	.222	.235	P	7	0	4	1	0	.800

LARRY KOPF—William Lorenz Kopf—Bats: Both; Throws: Right

Ht: 5'9"; Wt: 160 lbs; Born: 11/3/1890 in Bristol, Connecticut; Debut: 9/2/1913; Died: 10/15/1986

World Series	Batting																								Fielding						
Year Tm	Age	G	AB	H	2B	3B	HR	TB	R	RBI	GW	TBB	IBB	SO	HBP	SH	SF	SB	CS	SB%	GDP	Avg	OBP	SLG	Pos	G	PO	A	E	DP	FPct
1919 Cin	28	8	27	6	0	2	0	10	3	3	1	3	0	2	0	1	0	0	1	.00	1	.222	.300	.370	SS	8	11	28	1	4	.975

ANDY KOSCO—Andrew John Kosco—Bats: Right; Throws: Right

Ht: 6'3"; Wt: 205 lbs; Born: 10/5/1941 in Youngstown, Ohio; Debut: 8/13/1965

LCS	Batting																								Fielding						
Year Tm	Age	G	AB	H	2B	3B	HR	TB	R	RBI	GW	TBB	IBB	SO	HBP	SH	SF	SB	CS	SB%	GDP	Avg	OBP	SLG	Pos	G	PO	A	E	DP	FPct
1973 Cin	31	3	10	3	0	0	0	3	0	0	0	2	0	3	0	0	0	0	0	—	1	.300	.417	.300	OF	3	12	0	1	0	.923

DAVE KOSLO—George Bernard Koslo—Throws: Left; Bats: Left

Ht: 5'11"; Wt: 180 lbs; Born: 3/31/1920 in Menasha, Wisconsin; Debut: 9/12/1941; Died: 12/1/1975

World Series	Pitching																											
Year Tm	Age	G	GS	CG	GF	IP	BFP	H	R	ER	HR	SH	SF	HB	TBB	IBB	SO	WP	Bk	W	L	Pct	ShO	Sv-Op	Hld	OAvg	OOBP	ERA
1951 NYG	31	2	2	1	0	15.0	63	12	5	5	0	0	0	0	7	2	6	1	0	1	1	.500	0	0- 0	0	.214	.302	3.00

World Series	Batting																								Fielding						
Year Tm	Age	G	AB	H	2B	3B	HR	TB	R	RBI	GW	TBB	IBB	SO	HBP	SH	SF	SB	CS	SB%	GDP	Avg	OBP	SLG	Pos	G	PO	A	E	DP	FPct
1951 NYG	31	2	5	0	0	0	0	0	0	0	0	0	0	2	0	2	0	0	0	—	0	.000	.000	.000	P	2	2	1	0	0	1.000

SANDY KOUFAX (HOF 1972-W)—Sanford Koufax—Throws: Left; Bats: Right

Ht: 6'2"; Wt: 210 lbs; Born: 12/30/1935 in Brooklyn, New York; Debut: 6/24/1955

World Series	Pitching																											
Year Tm	Age	G	GS	CG	GF	IP	BFP	H	R	ER	HR	SH	SF	HB	TBB	IBB	SO	WP	Bk	W	L	Pct	ShO	Sv-Op	Hld	OAvg	OOBP	ERA
1959 LA	23	2	1	0	0	9.0	31	5	1	1	0	1	0	0	1	0	7	0	0	0	1	.000	0	0- 0	0	.172	.200	1.00
1963 LA-*MC*	27	2	2	2	0	18.0	69	12	3	3	2	0	0	0	3	0	23	0	0	2	0	1.000	0	0- 0	0	.182	.217	1.50
1965 LA-*C*	29	3	3	2	0	24.0	87	13	2	1	0	1	0	0	5	0	29	0	0	2	1	.667	2	0- 0	0	.160	.209	0.38
1966 LA-*C*	30	1	1	0	0	6.0	26	6	4	1	0	0	0	0	2	1	2	0	0	0	1	.000	0	0- 0	0	.250	.308	1.50
WS Totals		8	7	4	0	57.0	426	36	10	6	2	2	0	0	11	1	61	0	0	4	3	.571	2	0-0	0	.180	.223	0.95

World Series	Batting																								Fielding						
Year Tm	Age	G	AB	H	2B	3B	HR	TB	R	RBI	GW	TBB	IBB	SO	HBP	SH	SF	SB	CS	SB%	GDP	Avg	OBP	SLG	Pos	G	PO	A	E	DP	FPct
1959 LA	23	2	2	0	0	0	0	0	0	0	0	0	0	1	0	0	0	0	0	—	0	.000	.000	.000	P	2	0	0	0	0	—
1963 LA	27	2	6	0	0	0	0	0	0	0	0	0	0	2	0	0	0	0	0	—	0	.000	.000	.000	P	2	1	3	0	0	1.000
1965 LA	29	3	9	1	0	0	0	1	0	1	0	1	0	5	0	0	0	0	0	—	0	.111	.200	.111	P	3	1	4	0	0	1.000
1966 LA	30	1	2	0	0	0	0	0	0	0	0	0	0	0	0	0	0	0	0	—	0	.000	.000	.000	P	1	0	1	0	0	1.000
WS Totals		8	19	1	0	0	0	1	0	1	0	1	0	8	0	0	0	0	0	—	0	.053	.100	.053	P	8	2	8	0	0	1.000

FABIAN KOWALIK—Fabian Lorenz Kowalik—Throws: Right; Bats: Both

Ht: 5'11"; Wt: 185 lbs; Born: 4/22/1908 in Falls City, Texas; Debut: 9/4/1932; Died: 8/14/1954

World Series	Pitching																											
Year Tm	Age	G	GS	CG	GF	IP	BFP	H	R	ER	HR	SH	SF	HB	TBB	IBB	SO	WP	Bk	W	L	Pct	ShO	Sv-Op	Hld	OAvg	OOBP	ERA
1935 ChN	27	1	0	0	1	4.1	16	3	1	1	0	1	0	1	1	0	1	0	0	0	0	—	0	0- 0	0	.231	.333	2.08

World Series	Batting																								Fielding						
Year Tm	Age	G	AB	H	2B	3B	HR	TB	R	RBI	GW	TBB	IBB	SO	HBP	SH	SF	SB	CS	SB%	GDP	Avg	OBP	SLG	Pos	G	PO	A	E	DP	FPct
1935 ChN	27	1	2	1	0	0	0	1	1	0	0	0	0	0	0	0	0	0	0	—	0	.500	.500	.500	P	1	0	2	1	0	.667

JACK KRAMER—John Henry Kramer—Throws: Right; Bats: Right

Ht: 6'2"; Wt: 190 lbs; Born: 1/5/1918 in New Orleans, Louisiana; Debut: 4/25/1939; Died: 5/18/1995

World Series	Pitching																											
Year Tm	Age	G	GS	CG	GF	IP	BFP	H	R	ER	HR	SH	SF	HB	TBB	IBB	SO	WP	Bk	W	L	Pct	ShO	Sv-Op	Hld	OAvg	OOBP	ERA
1944 StL	26	2	1	1	1	11.0	46	9	2	0	0	1	0	0	4	1	12	0	0	1	0	1.000	0	0- 0	0	.220	.289	0.00

World Series	Batting																								Fielding						
Year Tm	Age	G	AB	H	2B	3B	HR	TB	R	RBI	GW	TBB	IBB	SO	HBP	SH	SF	SB	CS	SB%	GDP	Avg	OBP	SLG	Pos	G	PO	A	E	DP	FPct
1944 StL	26	2	4	0	0	0	0	0	0	0	0	0	0	2	0	0	0	0	0	—	0	.000	.000	.000	P	2	0	3	0	0	1.000

ED KRANEPOOL—Edward Emil Kranepool—Bats: Left; Throws: Left

Ht: 6'3"; Wt: 205 lbs; Born: 11/8/1944 in New York, New York; Debut: 9/22/1962

LCS	Batting																								Fielding						
Year Tm	Age	G	AB	H	2B	3B	HR	TB	R	RBI	GW	TBB	IBB	SO	HBP	SH	SF	SB	CS	SB%	GDP	Avg	OBP	SLG	Pos	G	PO	A	E	DP	FPct
1969 NYN	24	3	12	3	1	0	0	4	2	1	1	1	0	2	0	0	0	0	1	.00	0	.250	.308	.333	1B	3	20	3	0	2	1.000
1973 NYN	28	1	2	1	0	0	0	1	0	2	0	0	0	0	0	0	0	0	0	—	0	.500	.500	.500	OF	1	2	0	0	0	1.000
LCS Totals		4	14	4	1	0	0	5	2	3	1	1	0	2	0	0	0	0	1	.00	0	.286	.333	.357	1B	3	20	3	0	2	1.000
World Series	Batting																								Fielding						
Year Tm	Age	G	AB	H	2B	3B	HR	TB	R	RBI	GW	TBB	IBB	SO	HBP	SH	SF	SB	CS	SB%	GDP	Avg	OBP	SLG	Pos	G	PO	A	E	DP	FPct
1969 NYN	24	1	4	1	0	0	1	4	1	1	0	0	0	0	0	0	0	0	0	—	0	.250	.250	1.000	1B	1	7	0	0	0	1.000
1973 NYN	28	4	3	0	0	0	0	0	0	0	0	0	0	0	0	0	0	0	0	—	0	.000	.000	.000	—						
WS Totals		5	7	1	0	0	1	4	1	1	0	0	0	0	0	0	0	0	0	—	0	.143	.143	.571	1B	1	7	0	0	0	1.000
Postseason Totals		9	21	5	1	0	1	9	3	4	1	1	0	2	0	0	0	0	1	.00	0	.238	.273	.429	1B	4	27	3	0	2	1.000

MIKE KREEVICH—Michael Andreas Kreevich—Bats: Right; Throws: Right

Ht: 5'7"; Wt: 168 lbs; Born: 6/10/1908 in Mount Olive, Illinois; Debut: 9/7/1931; Died: 4/25/1994

World Series	Batting																								Fielding						
Year Tm	Age	G	AB	H	2B	3B	HR	TB	R	RBI	GW	TBB	IBB	SO	HBP	SH	SF	SB	CS	SB%	GDP	Avg	OBP	SLG	Pos	G	PO	A	E	DP	FPct
1944 StL	36	6	26	6	3	0	0	9	0	0	0	0	0	5	0	0	0	0	0	—	0	.231	.231	.346	OF	6	20	2	0	0	1.000

RAY KREMER—Remy Peter Kremer—Nickname: Wiz—Throws: Right; Bats: Right

Ht: 6'1"; Wt: 190 lbs; Born: 3/23/1893 in Oakland, California; Debut: 4/18/1924; Died: 2/8/1965

World Series		Pitching																										
Year Tm	Age	G	GS	CG	GF	IP	BFP	H	R	ER	HR	SH	SF	HB	TBB	IBB	SO	WP	Bk	W	L	Pct	ShO	Sv-Op	Hld	OAvg	OOBP	ERA
1925 Pit	32	3	2	2	0	21.0	83	17	7	7	3	2	1	0	4	0	9	0	0	2	1	.667	0	0- 0	0	.224	.259	3.00
1927 Pit	34	1	1	0	0	5.0	24	5	5	2	0	0	1	0	3	0	1	0	0	0	1	.000	0	0- 0	0	.250	.333	3.60
WS Totals		4	3	2	0	26.0	214	22	12	9	3	2	2	0	7	0	10	0	0	2	2	.500	0	0-0	0	.229	.276	3.12

World Series		Batting																							Fielding						
Year Tm	Age	G	AB	H	2B	3B	HR	TB	R	RBI	GW	TBB	IBB	SO	HBP	SH	SF	SB	CS	SB%	GDP	Avg	OBP	SLG	Pos	G	PO	A	E	DP	FPct
1925 Pit	32	3	7	1	0	0	0	1	0	1	0	0	0	5	0	0	0	0	0	—	0	.143	.143	.143	P	3	2	3	1	0	.833
1927 Pit	34	1	2	1	1	0	0	2	1	0	0	0	0	1	0	0	0	0	0	—	0	.500	.500	1.000	P	1	0	0	0	0	—
WS Totals		4	9	2	1	0	0	3	1	1	0	0	0	6	0	0	0	0	0	—	0	.222	.222	.333	P	4	2	3	1	0	.833

HOWIE KRIST—Howard Wilbur Krist—Nickname: Spud—Throws: Right; Bats: Left

Ht: 6'1"; Wt: 175 lbs; Born: 2/28/1916 in West Henrietta, New York; Debut: 9/12/1937; Died: 4/23/1989

World Series		Pitching																										
Year Tm	Age	G	GS	CG	GF	IP	BFP	H	R	ER	HR	SH	SF	HB	TBB	IBB	SO	WP	Bk	W	L	Pct	ShO	Sv-Op	Hld	OAvg	OOBP	ERA
1943 StL	27	1	0	0	0	0.0	1	1	0	0	0	0	0	0	0	0	0	0	0	0	0	—	0	0- 0	0	1.000	1.000	—

World Series		Batting																							Fielding						
Year Tm	Age	G	AB	H	2B	3B	HR	TB	R	RBI	GW	TBB	IBB	SO	HBP	SH	SF	SB	CS	SB%	GDP	Avg	OBP	SLG	Pos	G	PO	A	E	DP	FPct
1943 StL	27	1	0	0	0	0	0	0	0	0	0	0	0	0	0	0	0	0	0	—	0	—	—	—	P	1	0	0	0	0	—

ERNIE KRUEGER—Ernest George Krueger—Bats: Right; Throws: Right

Ht: 5'10"; Wt: 185 lbs; Born: 12/27/1890 in Chicago, Illinois; Debut: 8/4/1913; Died: 4/22/1976

World Series		Batting																							Fielding						
Year Tm	Age	G	AB	H	2B	3B	HR	TB	R	RBI	GW	TBB	IBB	SO	HBP	SH	SF	SB	CS	SB%	GDP	Avg	OBP	SLG	Pos	G	PO	A	E	DP	FPct
1920 Bro	29	4	6	1	0	0	0	1	0	0	0	0	0	0	0	0	0	0	0	—	0	.167	.167	.167	C	3	10	2	0	1	1.000

JOHN KRUK—John Martin Kruk—Bats: Left; Throws: Left

Ht: 5'10"; Wt: 170 lbs; Born: 2/9/1961 in Charleston, West Virginia; Debut: 4/7/1986

LCS		Batting																							Fielding						
Year Tm	Age	G	AB	H	2B	3B	HR	TB	R	RBI	GW	TBB	IBB	SO	HBP	SH	SF	SB	CS	SB%	GDP	Avg	OBP	SLG	Pos	G	PO	A	E	DP	FPct
1993 Phi	32	6	24	6	2	1	1	13	4	5	0	4	0	5	0	0	0	0	0	—	0	.250	.357	.542	1B	6	44	2	0	2	1.000
World Series		Batting																							Fielding						
Year Tm	Age	G	AB	H	2B	3B	HR	TB	R	RBI	GW	TBB	IBB	SO	HBP	SH	SF	SB	CS	SB%	GDP	Avg	OBP	SLG	Pos	G	PO	A	E	DP	FPct
1993 Phi	32	6	23	8	1	0	0	9	4	4	2	7	0	7	0	0	0	0	0	—	0	.348	.500	.391	1B	6	42	3	0	4	1.000
Postseason Totals		12	47	14	3	1	1	22	8	9	2	11	0	12	0	0	0	0	0	—	0	.298	.431	.468	1B	12	86	5	0	6	1.000

MIKE KRUKOW—Michael Edward Krukow—Throws: Right; Bats: Right

Ht: 6'5"; Wt: 205 lbs; Born: 1/21/1952 in Long Beach, California; Debut: 9/6/1976

LCS		Pitching																										
Year Tm	Age	G	GS	CG	GF	IP	BFP	H	R	ER	HR	SH	SF	HB	TBB	IBB	SO	WP	Bk	W	L	Pct	ShO	Sv-Op	Hld	OAvg	OOBP	ERA
1987 SF	35	1	1	1	0	9.0	34	9	2	2	0	0	0	0	1	0	3	0	0	1	0	1.000	0	0- 0	0	.273	.294	2.00

LCS		Batting																							Fielding						
Year Tm	Age	G	AB	H	2B	3B	HR	TB	R	RBI	GW	TBB	IBB	SO	HBP	SH	SF	SB	CS	SB%	GDP	Avg	OBP	SLG	Pos	G	PO	A	E	DP	FPct
1987 SF	35	1	2	0	0	0	0	0	0	0	0	1	0	0	0	0	0	0	0	—	0	.000	.333	.000	P	1	2	2	0	1	1.000

TONY KUBEK—Anthony Christopher Kubek—Bats: Left; Throws: Right

Ht: 6'3"; Wt: 190 lbs; Born: 10/12/1936 in Milwaukee, Wisconsin; Debut: 4/20/1957

World Series		Batting																							Fielding						
Year Tm	Age	G	AB	H	2B	3B	HR	TB	R	RBI	GW	TBB	IBB	SO	HBP	SH	SF	SB	CS	SB%	GDP	Avg	OBP	SLG	Pos	G	PO	A	E	DP	FPct
1957 NYA-*RY*	20	7	28	8	0	0	2	14	4	4	1	0	0	4	0	1	0	0	0	—	1	.286	.286	.500	3B	2	4	5	2	0	.818
																									OF	5	13	0	0	0	1.000
1958 NYA	21	7	21	1	0	0	0	1	0	1	0	1	1	7	0	0	1	0	0	—	0	.048	.087	.048	SS	7	8	15	2	2	.920
1960 NYA	23	7	30	10	1	0	0	11	6	3	1	2	1	2	1	0	0	0	1	.00	0	.333	.394	.367	SS	7	10	21	3	4	.912
																									OF	2	2	0	0	0	1.000
1961 NYA	24	5	22	5	0	0	0	5	3	1	0	1	0	4	0	0	0	0	0	—	0	.227	.261	.227	SS	5	5	11	0	1	1.000
1962 NYA	25	7	29	8	1	0	0	9	2	1	0	1	0	3	0	0	0	0	1	.00	1	.276	.300	.310	SS	7	12	17	1	3	.967
1963 NYA	26	4	16	3	0	0	0	3	1	0	0	0	0	3	0	0	0	0	1	.00	1	.188	.188	.188	SS	4	5	13	0	5	1.000
WS Totals		37	146	35	2	0	2	43	16	10	2	5	2	23	1	1	1	0	3	.00	3	.240	.268	.295	SS	30	40	77	6	15	.951

TED KUBIAK—Theodore Roger Kubiak—Bats: Both; Throws: Right

Ht: 6'0"; Wt: 175 lbs; Born: 5/12/1942 in New Brunswick, New Jersey; Debut: 4/14/1967

LCS		Batting																							Fielding						
Year Tm	Age	G	AB	H	2B	3B	HR	TB	R	RBI	GW	TBB	IBB	SO	HBP	SH	SF	SB	CS	SB%	GDP	Avg	OBP	SLG	Pos	G	PO	A	E	DP	FPct
1972 Oak	30	4	4	2	0	0	0	2	0	1	0	0	0	0	0	0	0	0	0	—	0	.500	.500	.500	2B	3	3	7	1	1	.909
																									SS	1	0	0	0	0	—
1973 Oak	31	3	2	0	0	0	0	0	0	0	0	0	0	1	0	0	0	0	0	—	1	.000	.000	.000	2B	3	0	1	0	0	1.000
LCS Totals		7	6	2	0	0	0	2	0	1	0	0	0	1	0	0	0	0	0	—	1	.333	.333	.333	2B	6	3	8	1	1	.917
World Series		Batting																							Fielding						
Year Tm	Age	G	AB	H	2B	3B	HR	TB	R	RBI	GW	TBB	IBB	SO	HBP	SH	SF	SB	CS	SB%	GDP	Avg	OBP	SLG	Pos	G	PO	A	E	DP	FPct
1972 Oak	30	4	3	1	0	0	0	1	0	0	0	0	0	0	0	0	0	0	0	—	0	.333	.333	.333	2B	4	4	3	0	0	1.000
1973 Oak	31	4	3	0	0	0	0	0	1	0	0	1	0	1	0	0	0	0	0	—	0	.000	.250	.000	2B	4	5	7	0	1	1.000
WS Totals		8	6	1	0	0	0	1	1	0	0	1	0	1	0	0	0	0	0	—	0	.167	.286	.167	2B	8	9	10	0	1	1.000
Postseason Totals		15	12	3	0	0	0	3	1	1	0	1	0	2	0	0	0	0	0	—	1	.250	.308	.250	2B	14	12	18	1	2	.968

JOHNNY KUCKS—John Charles Kucks—Throws: Right; Bats: Right

Ht: 6'3"; Wt: 170 lbs; Born: 7/27/1933 in Hoboken, New Jersey; Debut: 4/17/1955

World Series		Pitching																										
Year Tm	Age	G	GS	CG	GF	IP	BFP	H	R	ER	HR	SH	SF	HB	TBB	IBB	SO	WP	Bk	W	L	Pct	ShO	Sv-Op	Hld	OAvg	OOBP	ERA
1955 NYA	22	2	0	0	0	3.0	14	4	2	2	1	1	0	0	1	0	1	0	0	0	0	—	0	0- 0	0	.333	.385	6.00
1956 NYA	23	3	1	1	0	11.0	40	6	2	1	0	0	0	0	3	0	2	0	0	1	0	1.000	1	0- 0	0	.162	.225	0.82
1957 NYA	24	1	0	0	0	0.2	4	1	0	0	0	0	0	0	1	0	1	0	0	0	0	—	0	0- 0	0	.333	.500	0.00
1958 NYA	25	2	0	0	0	4.1	18	4	1	1	0	0	0	0	1	0	0	0	0	0	0	—	0	0- 0	0	.235	.278	2.08
WS Totals		8	1	1	0	19.0	152	15	5	4	1	1	0	0	6	0	4	0	0	1	0	1.000	1	0-0	0	.217	.280	1.89

World Series		Batting																							Fielding						
Year Tm	Age	G	AB	H	2B	3B	HR	TB	R	RBI	GW	TBB	IBB	SO	HBP	SH	SF	SB	CS	SB%	GDP	Avg	OBP	SLG	Pos	G	PO	A	E	DP	FPct
1955 NYA	22	2	0	0	0	0	0	0	0	0	0	0	0	0	0	0	0	0	0	—	0	—	—	—	P	2	0	1	0	0	1.000
1956 NYA	23	3	3	0	0	0	0	0	0	0	0	0	0	1	0	1	0	0	0	—	0	.000	.000	.000	P	3	1	2	0	1	1.000
1957 NYA	24	1	0	0	0	0	0	0	0	0	0	0	0	0	0	0	0	0	0	—	0	—	—	—	P	1	0	0	0	0	—
1958 NYA	25	2	1	1	0	0	0	1	0	0	0	0	0	0	0	0	0	0	0	—	0	1.000	1.000	1.000	P	2	0	0	0	0	—
WS Totals		8	4	1	0	0	0	1	0	0	0	0	0	1	0	1	0	0	0	—	0	.250	.250	.250	P	8	1	3	0	1	1.000

HARVEY KUENN—Harvey Edward Kuenn—Bats: Right; Throws: Right

Ht: 6'2"; Wt: 187 lbs; Born: 12/4/1930 in West Allis, Wisconsin; Debut: 9/6/1952; Died: 2/28/1988

World Series		Batting																							Fielding						
Year Tm	Age	G	AB	H	2B	3B	HR	TB	R	RBI	GW	TBB	IBB	SO	HBP	SH	SF	SB	CS	SB%	GDP	Avg	OBP	SLG	Pos	G	PO	A	E	DP	FPct
1962 SF	31	3	12	1	0	0	0	1	1	0	0	1	0	1	0	0	0	0	0	—	0	.083	.154	.083	OF	3	11	0	0	0	1.000

JOE KUHEL—Joseph Anthony Kuhel—Bats: Left; Throws: Left

Ht: 6'0"; Wt: 180 lbs; Born: 6/25/1906 in Cleveland, Ohio; Debut: 7/31/1930; Died: 2/26/1984

World Series		Batting																							Fielding						
Year Tm	Age	G	AB	H	2B	3B	HR	TB	R	RBI	GW	TBB	IBB	SO	HBP	SH	SF	SB	CS	SB%	GDP	Avg	OBP	SLG	Pos	G	PO	A	E	DP	FPct
1933 Was	27	5	20	3	0	0	0	3	1	1	0	1	0	4	0	0	0	0	1	.00	0	.150	.190	.150	1B	5	59	3	0	4	1.000

RUSTY KUNTZ—Russell Jay Kuntz—Bats: Right; Throws: Right

Ht: 6'3"; Wt: 190 lbs; Born: 2/4/1955 in Orange, California; Debut: 9/1/1979

LCS		Batting																							Fielding						
Year Tm	Age	G	AB	H	2B	3B	HR	TB	R	RBI	GW	TBB	IBB	SO	HBP	SH	SF	SB	CS	SB%	GDP	Avg	OBP	SLG	Pos	G	PO	A	E	DP	FPct
1984 Det	29	1	1	0	0	0	0	0	0	0	0	0	0	0	0	0	0	0	0	—	0	.000	.000	.000	OF	1	0	0	0	0	—
World Series		Batting																							Fielding						
Year Tm	Age	G	AB	H	2B	3B	HR	TB	R	RBI	GW	TBB	IBB	SO	HBP	SH	SF	SB	CS	SB%	GDP	Avg	OBP	SLG	Pos	G	PO	A	E	DP	FPct
1984 Det	29	2	1	0	0	0	0	0	0	1	1	0	0	1	0	0	1	0	0	—	0	.000	.000	.000	—						
Postseason Totals		3	2	0	0	0	0	0	0	1	1	0	0	1	0	0	1	0	0	—	0	.000	.000	.000	OF	1	0	0	0	0	—

WHITEY KUROWSKI—George John Kurowski—Bats: Right; Throws: Right

Ht: 5'11"; Wt: 193 lbs; Born: 4/19/1918 in Reading, Pennsylvania; Debut: 9/23/1941

World Series		Batting																							Fielding						
Year Tm	Age	G	AB	H	2B	3B	HR	TB	R	RBI	GW	TBB	IBB	SO	HBP	SH	SF	SB	CS	SB%	GDP	Avg	OBP	SLG	Pos	G	PO	A	E	DP	FPct
1942 StL	24	5	15	4	0	1	1	9	3	5	1	2	1	3	0	1	0	0	0	—	0	.267	.353	.600	3B	5	7	4	1	0	.917
1943 StL	25	5	18	4	1	0	0	5	2	1	0	0	0	3	0	1	0	0	0	—	1	.222	.222	.278	3B	5	8	8	2	0	.889
1944 StL	26	6	23	5	1	0	0	6	2	1	0	1	0	4	0	1	0	0	1	.00	0	.217	.250	.261	3B	6	4	15	0	1	1.000
1946 StL	28	7	27	8	3	0	0	11	5	2	0	0	0	3	1	0	0	0	0	—	1	.296	.321	.407	3B	7	12	10	1	2	.957
WS Totals		23	83	21	5	1	1	31	12	9	1	3	1	13	1	3	0	0	1	.00	2	.253	.287	.373	3B	23	31	37	4	3	.944

RANDY KUTCHER—Randy Scott Kutcher—Bats: Right; Throws: Right

Ht: 5'11"; Wt: 170 lbs; Born: 4/30/1960 in Anchorage, Alaska; Debut: 6/19/1986

LCS		Batting																							Fielding						
Year Tm	Age	G	AB	H	2B	3B	HR	TB	R	RBI	GW	TBB	IBB	SO	HBP	SH	SF	SB	CS	SB%	GDP	Avg	OBP	SLG	Pos	G	PO	A	E	DP	FPct
1990 Bos	30	2	0	0	0	0	0	0	0	0	0	0	0	0	0	0	0	0	0	—	0	—	—	—	—						

BOB KUZAVA—Robert Leroy Kuzava—Nickname: Sarge—Throws: Left; Bats: Both

Ht: 6'2"; Wt: 202 lbs; Born: 5/28/1923 in Wyandotte, Michigan; Debut: 9/21/1946

World Series		Pitching																										
Year Tm	Age	G	GS	CG	GF	IP	BFP	H	R	ER	HR	SH	SF	HB	TBB	IBB	SO	WP	Bk	W	L	Pct	ShO	Sv-Op	Hld	OAvg	OOBP	ERA
1951 NYA	28	1	0	0	1	1.0	3	0	0	0	0	0	0	0	0	0	0	0	0	0	0	—	0	1-1	0	.000	.000	0.00
1952 NYA	29	1	0	0	1	2.2	9	0	0	0	0	0	0	0	0	0	2	0	0	0	0	—	0	1-1	0	.000	.000	0.00
1953 NYA	30	1	0	0	0	0.2	4	2	1	1	1	0	0	0	0	0	1	0	0	0	0	—	0	0-0	0	.500	.500	13.50
WS Totals		3	0	0	2	4.1	32	2	1	1	1	0	0	0	0	0	3	0	0	0	0	—	0	2-2	0	.125	.125	2.08

World Series		Batting																							Fielding						
Year Tm	Age	G	AB	H	2B	3B	HR	TB	R	RBI	GW	TBB	IBB	SO	HBP	SH	SF	SB	CS	SB%	GDP	Avg	OBP	SLG	Pos	G	PO	A	E	DP	FPct
1951 NYA	28	1	0	0	0	0	0	0	0	0	0	0	0	0	0	0	0	0	0	—	0	—	—	—	P	1	0	0	0	0	—
1952 NYA	29	1	1	0	0	0	0	0	0	0	0	0	0	0	0	0	0	0	0	—	0	.000	.000	.000	P	1	0	0	0	0	—
1953 NYA	30	1	1	0	0	0	0	0	0	0	0	0	0	1	0	0	0	0	0	—	0	.000	.000	.000	P	1	0	0	0	0	—
WS Totals		3	2	0	0	0	0	0	0	0	0	0	0	1	0	0	0	0	0	—	0	.000	.000	.000	P	3	0	0	0	0	—

CHET LAABS—Chester Peter Laabs—Bats: Right; Throws: Right

Ht: 5'8"; Wt: 175 lbs; Born: 4/30/1912 in Milwaukee, Wisconsin; Debut: 5/5/1937; Died: 1/26/1983

World Series		Batting																							Fielding						
Year Tm	Age	G	AB	H	2B	3B	HR	TB	R	RBI	GW	TBB	IBB	SO	HBP	SH	SF	SB	CS	SB%	GDP	Avg	OBP	SLG	Pos	G	PO	A	E	DP	FPct
1944 StL	32	5	15	3	1	1	0	6	1	0	0	2	0	6	0	0	0	0	0	—	1	.200	.294	.400	OF	4	5	1	0	0	1.000

CLEM LABINE—Clement Walter Labine—Throws: Right; Bats: Right

Ht: 6'0"; Wt: 180 lbs; Born: 8/6/1926 in Lincoln, Rhode Island; Debut: 4/18/1950

World Series		Pitching																										
Year Tm	Age	G	GS	CG	GF	IP	BFP	H	R	ER	HR	SH	SF	HB	TBB	IBB	SO	WP	Bk	W	L	Pct	ShO	Sv-Op	Hld	OAvg	OOBP	ERA
1953 Bro	27	3	0	0	2	5.0	23	10	2	2	1	0	0	0	1	0	3	0	0	0	2	.000	0	1-1	0	.455	.478	3.60
1955 Bro	29	4	0	0	4	9.1	34	6	3	3	1	0	0	0	2	0	2	0	0	1	0	1.000	0	1-1	0	.188	.235	2.89
1956 Bro	30	2	1	1	1	12.0	47	8	1	0	0	0	0	0	3	2	7	0	0	1	0	1.000	1	0-0	0	.182	.234	0.00
1959 LA	33	1	0	0	0	1.0	3	0	0	0	0	0	0	0	0	0	1	0	0	0	0	—	0	0-0	0	.000	.000	0.00
1960 Pit	34	3	0	0	0	4.0	26	13	11	6	1	1	0	0	1	0	2	1	0	0	0	—	0	0-0	0	.542	.560	13.50
WS Totals		13	1	1	7	31.1	266	37	17	11	3	1	0	0	7	2	15	1	0	2	2	.500	1	2-2	0	.296	.333	3.16

World Series		Batting																							Fielding						
Year Tm	Age	G	AB	H	2B	3B	HR	TB	R	RBI	GW	TBB	IBB	SO	HBP	SH	SF	SB	CS	SB%	GDP	Avg	OBP	SLG	Pos	G	PO	A	E	DP	FPct
1953 Bro	27	3	2	0	0	0	0	0	0	0	0	0	0	1	0	0	0	0	0	—	0	.000	.000	.000	P	3	0	2	0	1	1.000
1955 Bro	29	4	4	0	0	0	0	0	0	0	0	0	0	3	0	0	0	0	0	—	0	.000	.000	.000	P	4	0	3	0	0	1.000
1956 Bro	30	2	4	1	1	0	0	2	0	0	0	0	0	2	0	0	0	0	0	—	0	.250	.250	.500	P	2	0	3	0	0	1.000
1959 LA	33	1	0	0	0	0	0	0	0	0	0	0	0	0	0	0	0	0	0	—	0	—	—	—	P	1	0	0	0	0	—
1960 Pit	34	3	0	0	0	0	0	0	0	0	0	0	0	0	0	0	0	0	0	—	0	—	—	—	P	3	0	2	0	0	1.000
WS Totals		13	10	1	1	0	0	2	0	0	0	0	0	6	0	0	0	0	0	—	0	.100	.100	.200	P	13	0	10	0	1	1.000

CANDY LaCHANCE—George Joseph LaChance—Bats: Both; Throws: Right

Ht: 6'1"; Wt: 183 lbs; Born: 2/15/1870 in Putnam, Connecticut; Debut: 8/15/1893; Died: 8/18/1932

World Series		Batting																							Fielding						
Year Tm	Age	G	AB	H	2B	3B	HR	TB	R	RBI	GW	TBB	IBB	SO	HBP	SH	SF	SB	CS	SB%	GDP	Avg	OBP	SLG	Pos	G	PO	A	E	DP	FPct
1903 Bos	33	8	27	6	2	1	0	10	5	4	1	3	0	2	0	3	0	0	0	—	1	.222	.300	.370	1B	8	77	3	3	2	.964

PETE LaCOCK—Ralph Pierre LaCock—Bats: Left; Throws: Left

Ht: 6'2"; Wt: 200 lbs; Born: 1/17/1952 in Burbank, California; Debut: 9/6/1972

LCS		Batting																							Fielding						
Year Tm	Age	G	AB	H	2B	3B	HR	TB	R	RBI	GW	TBB	IBB	SO	HBP	SH	SF	SB	CS	SB%	GDP	Avg	OBP	SLG	Pos	G	PO	A	E	DP	FPct
1977 KC	25	1	1	0	0	0	0	0	0	0	0	1	0	1	0	0	0	0	0	—	0	.000	.500	.000	1B	1	4	0	0	0	1.000
1978 KC	26	4	11	4	2	1	0	8	1	1	0	3	0	1	0	0	0	1	0	1.00	0	.364	.500	.727	1B	3	26	1	0	3	1.000
1980 KC	28	1	0	0	0	0	0	0	0	0	0	0	0	0	0	0	0	0	0	—	0	—	—	—	1B	1	0	0	0	0	—
LCS Totals		6	12	4	2	1	0	8	1	1	0	4	0	2	0	0	0	1	0	1.00	0	.333	.500	.667	1B	5	30	1	0	3	1.000
World Series		Batting																							Fielding						
Year Tm	Age	G	AB	H	2B	3B	HR	TB	R	RBI	GW	TBB	IBB	SO	HBP	SH	SF	SB	CS	SB%	GDP	Avg	OBP	SLG	Pos	G	PO	A	E	DP	FPct
1980 KC	28	1	0	0	0	0	0	0	0	0	0	0	0	0	0	0	0	0	0	—	0	—	—	—	1B	1	2	0	0	1	1.000
Postseason Totals		7	12	4	2	1	0	8	1	1	0	4	0	2	0	0	0	1	0	1.00	0	.333	.500	.667	1B	6	32	1	0	4	1.000

FRANK LaCORTE—Frank Joseph LaCorte—Throws: Right; Bats: Right

Ht: 6'1"; Wt: 180 lbs; Born: 10/13/1951 in San Jose, California; Debut: 9/8/1975

Division Series		Pitching																										
Year Tm	Age	G	GS	CG	GF	IP	BFP	H	R	ER	HR	SH	SF	HB	TBB	IBB	SO	WP	Bk	W	L	Pct	ShO	Sv-Op	Hld	OAvg	OOBP	ERA
1981 Hou	29	2	0	0	1	3.2	14	2	0	0	0	0	0	0	1	1	5	0	0	0	0	—	0	0-0	0	.154	.214	0.00
LCS		Pitching																										
Year Tm	Age	G	GS	CG	GF	IP	BFP	H	R	ER	HR	SH	SF	HB	TBB	IBB	SO	WP	Bk	W	L	Pct	ShO	Sv-Op	Hld	OAvg	OOBP	ERA
1980 Hou	28	2	0	0	1	3.0	18	7	2	1	0	1	0	0	2	1	2	0	0	1	1	.500	0	0-0	0	.467	.529	3.00
Postseason Totals		4	0	0	2	6.2	64	9	2	1	0	1	0	0	3	2	7	0	0	1	1	.500	0	0-0	0	.321	.387	1.35

Division Series		Batting																							Fielding						
Year Tm	Age	G	AB	H	2B	3B	HR	TB	R	RBI	GW	TBB	IBB	SO	HBP	SH	SF	SB	CS	SB%	GDP	Avg	OBP	SLG	Pos	G	PO	A	E	DP	FPct
1981 Hou	29	2	0	0	0	0	0	0	0	0	0	0	0	0	0	0	0	0	0	—	0	—	—	—	P	2	0	0	0	0	—
LCS		Batting																							Fielding						
Year Tm	Age	G	AB	H	2B	3B	HR	TB	R	RBI	GW	TBB	IBB	SO	HBP	SH	SF	SB	CS	SB%	GDP	Avg	OBP	SLG	Pos	G	PO	A	E	DP	FPct
1980 Hou	28	2	1	0	0	0	0	0	0	0	0	0	0	0	0	0	0	0	0	—	0	.000	.000	.000	P	2	0	0	0	0	—
Postseason Totals		4	1	0	0	0	0	0	0	0	0	0	0	0	0	0	0	0	0	—	0	.000	.000	.000	P	4	0	0	0	0	—

MIKE LaCOSS—Michael James LaCoss—Nickname: Goofy—Throws: Right; Bats: Right

Ht: 6'5"; Wt: 185 lbs; Born: 5/30/1956 in Glendale, California; Debut: 7/18/1978

LCS — Pitching

Year Tm	Age	G	GS	CG	GF	IP	BFP	H	R	ER	HR	SH	SF	HB	TBB	IBB	SO	WP	Bk	W	L	Pct	ShO	Sv-Op	Hld	OAvg	OOBP	ERA
1979 Cin	23	1	1	0	0	1.2	11	1	2	2	0	0	2	0	4	0	0	0	0	0	1	.000	0	0- 0	0	.200	.455	10.80
1987 SF	31	2	0	0	1	3.1	13	1	0	0	0	0	0	0	3	1	2	0	0	0	0	—	0	0- 0	0	.100	.308	0.00
1989 SF	33	1	1	0	0	3.0	17	7	3	3	0	2	0	0	0	0	2	1	0	0	0	—	0	0- 0	0	.467	.467	9.00
LCS Totals		4	2	0	1	8.0	82	9	5	5	0	2	2	0	7	1	4	1	0	0	1	.000	0	0-0	0	.300	.410	5.63

World Series — Pitching

Year Tm	Age	G	GS	CG	GF	IP	BFP	H	R	ER	HR	SH	SF	HB	TBB	IBB	SO	WP	Bk	W	L	Pct	ShO	Sv-Op	Hld	OAvg	OOBP	ERA
1989 SF	33	2	0	0	1	4.1	20	4	3	3	0	0	0	0	3	1	2	0	0	0	0	—	0	0- 0	0	.235	.350	6.23
Postseason Totals		6	2	0	2	12.1	122	13	8	8	0	2	2	0	10	2	6	1	0	0	1	.000	0	0-0	0	.277	.390	5.84

LCS — Batting / Fielding

Year Tm	Age	G	AB	H	2B	3B	HR	TB	R	RBI	GW	TBB	IBB	SO	HBP	SH	SF	SB	CS	SB%	GDP	Avg	OBP	SLG	Pos	G	PO	A	E	DP	FPct
1979 Cin	23	1	0	0	0	0	0	0	0	0	0	0	0	0	0	0	0	0	0	—	0	—	—	—	P	1	0	1	0	0	1.000
1987 SF	31	2	0	0	0	0	0	0	0	0	0	0	0	0	0	0	0	0	0	—	0	—	—	—	P	2	0	2	0	0	1.000
1989 SF	33	1	1	0	0	0	0	0	0	0	0	0	0	0	0	0	0	0	0	—	0	.000	.000	.000	P	1	0	0	1	0	.000
LCS Totals		4	1	0	0	0	0	0	0	0	0	0	0	0	0	0	0	0	0	—	0	.000	.000	.000	P	4	0	3	1	0	.750

World Series — Batting / Fielding

Year Tm	Age	G	AB	H	2B	3B	HR	TB	R	RBI	GW	TBB	IBB	SO	HBP	SH	SF	SB	CS	SB%	GDP	Avg	OBP	SLG	Pos	G	PO	A	E	DP	FPct
1989 SF	33	2	1	0	0	0	0	0	0	0	0	0	0	0	0	0	0	0	0	—	0	.000	.000	.000	P	2	1	0	0	0	1.000
Postseason Totals		6	2	0	0	0	0	0	0	0	0	0	0	0	0	0	0	0	0	—	0	.000	.000	.000	P	6	1	3	1	0	.800

LEE LACY—Leondaus Lacy—Bats: Right; Throws: Right

Ht: 6'1"; Wt: 175 lbs; Born: 4/10/1948 in Longview, Texas; Debut: 6/30/1972

LCS — Batting / Fielding

Year Tm	Age	G	AB	H	2B	3B	HR	TB	R	RBI	GW	TBB	IBB	SO	HBP	SH	SF	SB	CS	SB%	GDP	Avg	OBP	SLG	Pos	G	PO	A	E	DP	FPct
1974 LA	26	1	0	0	0	0	0	0	0	0	0	0	0	0	0	0	0	0	0	—	0	—	—	—	—						
1977 LA	29	1	1	1	0	0	0	1	1	0	0	0	0	0	0	0	0	0	0	—	0	1.000	1.000	1.000	—						
1978 LA	30	2	2	0	0	0	0	0	0	0	0	0	0	0	0	0	0	0	0	—	0	.000	.000	.000	—						
LCS Totals		4	3	1	0	0	0	1	1	0	0	0	0	0	0	0	0	0	0	—	0	.333	.333	.333	—	0	0	0	0	0	—

World Series — Batting / Fielding

Year Tm	Age	G	AB	H	2B	3B	HR	TB	R	RBI	GW	TBB	IBB	SO	HBP	SH	SF	SB	CS	SB%	GDP	Avg	OBP	SLG	Pos	G	PO	A	E	DP	FPct
1974 LA	26	1	1	0	0	0	0	0	0	0	0	0	0	1	0	0	0	0	0	—	0	.000	.000	.000	—						
1977 LA	29	4	7	3	0	0	0	3	1	2	0	1	0	1	0	0	0	0	0	—	0	.429	.500	.429	OF	2	2	0	0	0	1.000
1978 LA	30	4	14	2	0	0	0	2	0	1	0	1	0	3	0	0	0	0	0	—	2	.143	.200	.143	—						
1979 Pit	31	4	4	1	0	0	0	1	0	0	0	0	0	1	0	0	0	0	0	—	0	.250	.250	.250	—						
WS Totals		13	26	6	0	0	0	6	1	3	0	2	0	6	0	0	0	0	0	—	2	.231	.286	.231	OF	2	2	0	0	0	1.000
Postseason Totals		17	29	7	0	0	0	7	2	3	0	2	0	6	0	0	0	0	0	—	2	.241	.290	.241	OF	2	2	0	0	0	1.000

PETER LADD—Peter Linwood Ladd—Nickname: Bigfoot—Throws: Right; Bats: Right

Ht: 6'3"; Wt: 228 lbs; Born: 7/17/1956 in Portland, Maine; Debut: 8/17/1979

LCS — Pitching

Year Tm	Age	G	GS	CG	GF	IP	BFP	H	R	ER	HR	SH	SF	HB	TBB	IBB	SO	WP	Bk	W	L	Pct	ShO	Sv-Op	Hld	OAvg	OOBP	ERA
1982 Mil	26	3	0	0	2	3.1	10	0	0	0	0	1	0	0	0	0	5	0	0	0	0	—	0	2- 2	0	.000	.000	0.00

World Series — Pitching

Year Tm	Age	G	GS	CG	GF	IP	BFP	H	R	ER	HR	SH	SF	HB	TBB	IBB	SO	WP	Bk	W	L	Pct	ShO	Sv-Op	Hld	OAvg	OOBP	ERA
1982 Mil	26	1	0	0	1	0.2	4	1	0	0	0	0	0	0	2	0	0	0	0	0	0	—	0	0- 0	0	.500	.750	0.00
Postseason Totals		4	0	0	3	4.0	28	1	0	0	0	1	0	0	2	0	5	0	0	0	0	—	0	2-2	0	.091	.231	0.00

LCS — Batting / Fielding

Year Tm	Age	G	AB	H	2B	3B	HR	TB	R	RBI	GW	TBB	IBB	SO	HBP	SH	SF	SB	CS	SB%	GDP	Avg	OBP	SLG	Pos	G	PO	A	E	DP	FPct
1982 Mil	26	3	0	0	0	0	0	0	0	0	0	0	0	0	0	0	0	0	0	—	0	—	—	—	P	3	0	1	0	0	1.000

World Series — Batting / Fielding

Year Tm	Age	G	AB	H	2B	3B	HR	TB	R	RBI	GW	TBB	IBB	SO	HBP	SH	SF	SB	CS	SB%	GDP	Avg	OBP	SLG	Pos	G	PO	A	E	DP	FPct
1982 Mil	26	1	0	0	0	0	0	0	0	0	0	0	0	0	0	0	0	0	0	—	0	—	—	—	P	1	0	0	0	0	—
Postseason Totals		4	0	0	0	0	0	0	0	0	0	0	0	0	0	0	0	0	0	—	0	—	—	—	P	4	0	1	0	0	1.000

LERRIN LaGROW—Lerrin Harris LaGrow—Nickname: Lurch—Throws: Right; Bats: Right

Ht: 6'5"; Wt: 220 lbs; Born: 7/8/1948 in Phoenix, Arizona; Debut: 7/28/1970

LCS — Pitching

Year Tm	Age	G	GS	CG	GF	IP	BFP	H	R	ER	HR	SH	SF	HB	TBB	IBB	SO	WP	Bk	W	L	Pct	ShO	Sv-Op	Hld	OAvg	OOBP	ERA
1972 Det	24	1	0	0	0	1.0	4	0	0	0	0	0	0	1	0	0	1	0	0	0	0	—	0	0- 0	0	.000	.250	0.00

LCS — Batting / Fielding

Year Tm	Age	G	AB	H	2B	3B	HR	TB	R	RBI	GW	TBB	IBB	SO	HBP	SH	SF	SB	CS	SB%	GDP	Avg	OBP	SLG	Pos	G	PO	A	E	DP	FPct
1972 Det	24	1	0	0	0	0	0	0	0	0	0	0	0	0	0	0	0	0	0	—	0	—	—	—	P	1	0	0	0	0	—

JOE LAHOUD—Joseph Michael Lahoud—Nickname: Duck—Bats: Left; Throws: Left

Ht: 6'1"; Wt: 198 lbs; Born: 4/14/1947 in Danbury, Connecticut; Debut: 4/10/1968

LCS — Batting / Fielding

Year Tm	Age	G	AB	H	2B	3B	HR	TB	R	RBI	GW	TBB	IBB	SO	HBP	SH	SF	SB	CS	SB%	GDP	Avg	OBP	SLG	Pos	G	PO	A	E	DP	FPct
1977 KC	30	1	1	0	0	0	0	0	2	0	0	2	0	0	0	0	0	0	0	—	0	.000	.667	.000	—						

JEFF LAHTI—Jeffrey Allen Lahti—Throws: Right; Bats: Right

Ht: 6'0"; Wt: 180 lbs; Born: 10/8/1956 in Oregon City, Oregon; Debut: 6/27/1982

LCS — Pitching

Year Tm	Age	G	GS	CG	GF	IP	BFP	H	R	ER	HR	SH	SF	HB	TBB	IBB	SO	WP	Bk	W	L	Pct	ShO	Sv-Op	Hld	OAvg	OOBP	ERA
1985 StL	28	2	0	0	2	2.0	8	2	0	0	0	0	0	0	0	0	1	0	0	1	0	1.000	0	0- 0	0	.250	.250	0.00

World Series — Pitching

Year Tm	Age	G	GS	CG	GF	IP	BFP	H	R	ER	HR	SH	SF	HB	TBB	IBB	SO	WP	Bk	W	L	Pct	ShO	Sv-Op	Hld	OAvg	OOBP	ERA
1982 StL	25	2	0	0	2	1.2	10	4	2	2	0	0	0	0	1	1	1	0	0	0	0	—	0	0- 0	0	.444	.500	10.80
1985 StL	28	3	0	0	2	3.2	20	10	6	5	0	0	0	0	0	0	2	0	0	0	0	—	0	1- 1	0	.500	.500	12.27
WS Totals		5	0	0	4	5.1	60	14	8	7	0	0	0	0	1	1	3	0	0	0	0	—	0	1-1	0	.483	.500	11.81
Postseason Totals		7	0	0	6	7.1	76	16	8	7	0	0	0	0	1	1	4	0	0	1	0	1.000	0	1-1	0	.432	.447	8.59

LCS — Batting / Fielding

Year Tm	Age	G	AB	H	2B	3B	HR	TB	R	RBI	GW	TBB	IBB	SO	HBP	SH	SF	SB	CS	SB%	GDP	Avg	OBP	SLG	Pos	G	PO	A	E	DP	FPct
1985 StL	28	2	0	0	0	0	0	0	0	0	0	0	0	0	0	0	0	0	0	—	0	—	—	—	P	2	0	0	0	0	—

World Series — Batting / Fielding

Year Tm	Age	G	AB	H	2B	3B	HR	TB	R	RBI	GW	TBB	IBB	SO	HBP	SH	SF	SB	CS	SB%	GDP	Avg	OBP	SLG	Pos	G	PO	A	E	DP	FPct
1982 StL	25	2	0	0	0	0	0	0	0	0	0	0	0	0	0	0	0	0	0	—	0	—	—	—	P	2	0	1	0	0	1.000
1985 StL	28	3	0	0	0	0	0	0	0	0	0	0	0	0	0	0	0	0	0	—	0	—	—	—	P	3	0	0	0	0	—
WS Totals		5	0	0	0	0	0	0	0	0	0	0	0	0	0	0	0	0	0	—	0	—	—	—	P	5	0	1	0	0	1.000
Postseason Totals		7	0	0	0	0	0	0	0	0	0	0	0	0	0	0	0	0	0	—	0	—	—	—	P	7	0	1	0	0	1.000

STEVE LAKE—Steven Michael Lake—Bats: Right; Throws: Right

Ht: 6'1"; Wt: 180 lbs; Born: 3/14/1957 in Inglewood, California; Debut: 4/9/1983

LCS — Batting / Fielding

Year Tm	Age	G	AB	H	2B	3B	HR	TB	R	RBI	GW	TBB	IBB	SO	HBP	SH	SF	SB	CS	SB%	GDP	Avg	OBP	SLG	Pos	G	PO	A	E	DP	FPct
1984 ChN	27	1	1	1	1	0	0	2	0	0	0	0	0	0	0	0	0	0	0	—	0	1.000	1.000	2.000	C	1	0	0	0	0	—

World Series — Batting / Fielding

Year Tm	Age	G	AB	H	2B	3B	HR	TB	R	RBI	GW	TBB	IBB	SO	HBP	SH	SF	SB	CS	SB%	GDP	Avg	OBP	SLG	Pos	G	PO	A	E	DP	FPct
1987 StL	30	3	3	1	0	0	0	1	0	1	0	0	0	0	0	0	0	0	0	—	0	.333	.333	.333	C	3	8	1	0	0	1.000
Postseason Totals		4	4	2	1	0	0	3	0	1	0	0	0	0	0	0	0	0	0	—	0	.500	.500	.750	C	4	8	1	0	0	1.000

JACK LAMABE—John Alexander Lamabe—Nickname: Tomatoes—Throws: Right; Bats: Right

Ht: 6'1"; Wt: 198 lbs; Born: 10/3/1936 in Farmingdale, New York; Debut: 4/17/1962

World Series — Pitching

Year Tm	Age	G	GS	CG	GF	IP	BFP	H	R	ER	HR	SH	SF	HB	TBB	IBB	SO	WP	Bk	W	L	Pct	ShO	Sv-Op	Hld	OAvg	OOBP	ERA
1967 StL	30	3	0	0	2	2.2	12	5	2	2	0	0	0	0	0	0	4	0	0	0	1	.000	0	0-0	0	.417	.417	6.75

World Series — Batting / Fielding

Year Tm	Age	G	AB	H	2B	3B	HR	TB	R	RBI	GW	TBB	IBB	SO	HBP	SH	SF	SB	CS	SB%	GDP	Avg	OBP	SLG	Pos	G	PO	A	E	DP	FPct
1967 StL	30	3	0	0	0	0	0	0	0	0	0	0	0	0	0	0	0	0	0	—	0	—	—	—	P	3	0	1	0	1	1.000

BILL LAMAR—William Harmong Lamar—Nickname: Good Time Bill—Bats: Left; Throws: Right

Ht: 6'1"; Wt: 185 lbs; Born: 3/21/1897 in Rockville, Maryland; Debut: 9/19/1917; Died: 5/24/1970

World Series — Batting / Fielding

Year Tm	Age	G	AB	H	2B	3B	HR	TB	R	RBI	GW	TBB	IBB	SO	HBP	SH	SF	SB	CS	SB%	GDP	Avg	OBP	SLG	Pos	G	PO	A	E	DP	FPct
1920 Bro	23	3	3	0	0	0	0	0	0	0	0	0	0	0	0	0	0	0	0	—	0	.000	.000	.000	—						

DENNIS LAMP—Dennis Patrick Lamp—Throws: Right; Bats: Right

Ht: 6'4"; Wt: 200 lbs; Born: 9/23/1952 in Los Angeles, California; Debut: 8/21/1977

LCS — Pitching

Year Tm	Age	G	GS	CG	GF	IP	BFP	H	R	ER	HR	SH	SF	HB	TBB	IBB	SO	WP	Bk	W	L	Pct	ShO	Sv-Op	Hld	OAvg	OOBP	ERA
1983 ChA	31	3	0	0	3	2.0	9	0	1	0	0	0	2	0	2	0	1	0	0	0	0	—	0	0-0	0	.000	.222	0.00
1985 Tor	33	3	0	0	1	9.1	31	2	0	0	0	0	0	0	1	1	10	0	0	0	0	—	0	0-0	0	.067	.097	0.00
1990 Bos	38	1	0	0	0	0.1	5	2	4	4	0	0	1	0	2	1	0	0	0	0	0	—	0	0-0	0	1.000	.800	108.00
LCS Totals		7	0	0	4	11.2	90	4	5	4	0	0	3	0	5	2	11	0	0	0	0	—	0	0-0	0	.108	.200	3.09

LCS — Batting / Fielding

Year Tm	Age	G	AB	H	2B	3B	HR	TB	R	RBI	GW	TBB	IBB	SO	HBP	SH	SF	SB	CS	SB%	GDP	Avg	OBP	SLG	Pos	G	PO	A	E	DP	FPct
1983 ChA	31	3	0	0	0	0	0	0	0	0	0	0	0	0	0	0	0	0	0	—	0	—	—	—	P	3	0	0	0	0	—
1985 Tor	33	3	0	0	0	0	0	0	0	0	0	0	0	0	0	0	0	0	0	—	0	—	—	—	P	3	1	2	0	0	1.000
1990 Bos	38	1	0	0	0	0	0	0	0	0	0	0	0	0	0	0	0	0	0	—	0	—	—	—	P	1	0	0	0	0	—
LCS Totals		7	0	0	0	0	0	0	0	0	0	0	0	0	0	0	0	0	0	—	0	—	—	—	P	7	1	2	0	0	1.000

LES LANCASTER—Lester Wayne Lancaster—Throws: Right; Bats: Right

Ht: 6'2"; Wt: 200 lbs; Born: 4/21/1962 in Dallas, Texas; Debut: 4/7/1987

LCS — Pitching

Year Tm	Age	G	GS	CG	GF	IP	BFP	H	R	ER	HR	SH	SF	HB	TBB	IBB	SO	WP	Bk	W	L	Pct	ShO	Sv-Op	Hld	OAvg	OOBP	ERA
1989 ChN	27	3	0	0	3	6.0	25	6	4	4	3	0	0	0	1	0	3	0	0	1	1	.500	0	0-2	0	.250	.280	6.00

LCS — Batting / Fielding

Year Tm	Age	G	AB	H	2B	3B	HR	TB	R	RBI	GW	TBB	IBB	SO	HBP	SH	SF	SB	CS	SB%	GDP	Avg	OBP	SLG	Pos	G	PO	A	E	DP	FPct
1989 ChN	27	3	1	0	0	0	0	0	0	0	0	0	0	1	0	0	0	0	0	—	0	.000	.000	.000	P	3	0	1	0	0	1.000

RAFAEL LANDESTOY—Rafael Silvaldo Landestoy—Nickname: Santana—Bats: Both; Throws: Right

Ht: 5'10"; Wt: 165 lbs; Born: 5/28/1953 in Bani, Dominican Republic; Debut: 8/27/1977

LCS / World Series — Batting / Fielding

Year Tm	Age	G	AB	H	2B	3B	HR	TB	R	RBI	GW	TBB	IBB	SO	HBP	SH	SF	SB	CS	SB%	GDP	Avg	OBP	SLG	Pos	G	PO	A	E	DP	FPct
LCS																															
1980 Hou	27	5	9	2	0	0	0	2	3	2	0	1	0	0	0	0	0	1	0	1.00	0	.222	.300	.222	2B	3	3	4	0	0	1.000
																									SS	1	2	4	1	0	.857
1983 LA	30	2	2	0	0	0	0	0	0	0	0	0	0	1	0	0	0	0	0	—	0	.000	.000	.000	—						
LCS Totals		7	11	2	0	0	0	2	3	2	0	1	0	1	0	0	0	1	0	1.00	0	.182	.250	.182	2B	3	3	4	0	0	1.000
World Series																															
1977 LA	24	1	0	0	0	0	0	0	0	0	0	0	0	0	0	0	0	0	0	—	0	—	—	—	—						
Postseason Totals		8	11	2	0	0	0	2	3	2	0	1	0	1	0	0	0	1	0	1.00	0	.182	.250	.182	2B	3	3	4	0	0	1.000

JIM LANDIS—James Henry Landis—Bats: Right; Throws: Right

Ht: 6'1"; Wt: 180 lbs; Born: 3/9/1934 in Fresno, California; Debut: 4/16/1957

World Series — Batting / Fielding

Year Tm	Age	G	AB	H	2B	3B	HR	TB	R	RBI	GW	TBB	IBB	SO	HBP	SH	SF	SB	CS	SB%	GDP	Avg	OBP	SLG	Pos	G	PO	A	E	DP	FPct
1959 ChA	25	6	24	7	0	0	0	7	6	1	0	1	0	7	1	0	0	0	0	—	0	.292	.346	.292	OF	6	9	0	1	0	.900

KEN LANDREAUX—Kenneth Francis Landreaux—Bats: Left; Throws: Right

Ht: 5'10"; Wt: 165 lbs; Born: 12/22/1954 in Los Angeles, California; Debut: 9/11/1977

Division Series / LCS / World Series — Batting / Fielding

Year Tm	Age	G	AB	H	2B	3B	HR	TB	R	RBI	GW	TBB	IBB	SO	HBP	SH	SF	SB	CS	SB%	GDP	Avg	OBP	SLG	Pos	G	PO	A	E	DP	FPct
Division Series																															
1981 LA	26	5	20	4	1	0	0	5	1	1	0	0	0	1	0	2	0	0	0	—	0	.200	.200	.250	OF	5	16	0	0	0	1.000
LCS																															
1981 LA	26	5	10	1	1	0	0	2	0	0	0	3	0	2	0	0	0	0	0	—	0	.100	.308	.200	OF	5	4	0	0	0	1.000
1983 LA	28	4	14	2	0	0	0	2	0	1	0	1	1	3	0	0	0	0	0	—	0	.143	.200	.143	OF	4	12	0	0	0	1.000
1985 LA	30	5	18	7	3	0	0	10	4	2	1	1	0	1	0	0	0	0	0	—	0	.389	.421	.556	OF	5	7	0	0	0	1.000
LCS Totals		14	42	10	4	0	0	14	4	3	1	5	1	6	0	0	0	0	0	—	0	.238	.319	.333	OF	14	23	0	0	0	1.000
World Series																															
1981 LA	26	5	6	1	1	0	0	2	1	0	0	0	0	2	0	0	0	1	0	1.00	0	.167	.167	.333	OF	3	6	0	0	0	1.000
Postseason Totals		24	68	15	6	0	0	21	6	4	1	5	1	9	0	2	0	1	0	1.00	0	.221	.274	.309	OF	22	45	0	0	0	1.000

BILL LANDRUM—Thomas William Landrum—Throws: Right; Bats: Right

Ht: 6'2"; Wt: 185 lbs; Born: 8/17/1957 in Columbia, South Carolina; Debut: 8/31/1986

LCS — Pitching

Year Tm	Age	G	GS	CG	GF	IP	BFP	H	R	ER	HR	SH	SF	HB	TBB	IBB	SO	WP	Bk	W	L	Pct	ShO	Sv-Op	Hld	OAvg	OOBP	ERA
1990 Pit	33	2	0	0	1	2.0	6	0	0	0	0	0	0	0	0	0	1	0	0	0	0	—	0	0-0	0	.000	.000	0.00
1991 Pit	34	1	0	0	0	1.0	6	2	1	1	0	0	0	0	2	1	2	0	0	0	0	—	0	0-0	0	.500	.667	9.00
LCS Totals		3	0	0	1	3.0	24	2	1	1	0	0	0	0	2	1	3	0	0	0	0	—	0	0-0	0	.200	.333	3.00

LCS — Batting / Fielding

Year Tm	Age	G	AB	H	2B	3B	HR	TB	R	RBI	GW	TBB	IBB	SO	HBP	SH	SF	SB	CS	SB%	GDP	Avg	OBP	SLG	Pos	G	PO	A	E	DP	FPct
1990 Pit	33	2	0	0	0	0	0	0	0	0	0	0	0	0	0	0	0	0	0	—	0	—	—	—	P	2	0	0	0	0	—
1991 Pit	34	1	0	0	0	0	0	0	0	0	0	0	0	0	0	0	0	0	0	—	0	—	—	—	P	1	0	0	0	0	—
LCS Totals		3	0	0	0	0	0	0	0	0	0	0	0	0	0	0	0	0	0	—	0	—	—	—	P	3	0	0	0	0	—

TITO LANDRUM—Terry Lee Landrum—Bats: Right; Throws: Right

Ht: 5'11"; Wt: 175 lbs; Born: 10/25/1954 in Joplin, Missouri; Debut: 7/23/1980

LCS / World Series — Batting / Fielding

Year Tm	Age	G	AB	H	2B	3B	HR	TB	R	RBI	GW	TBB	IBB	SO	HBP	SH	SF	SB	CS	SB%	GDP	Avg	OBP	SLG	Pos	G	PO	A	E	DP	FPct
LCS																															
1983 Bal	28	4	10	2	0	0	1	5	2	1	1	0	0	2	0	0	0	0	0	—	0	.200	.200	.500	OF	3	5	0	0	0	1.000
1985 StL	30	5	14	6	0	0	0	6	2	4	1	1	0	1	0	0	0	1	0	1.00	0	.429	.467	.429	OF	4	6	0	0	0	1.000
LCS Totals		9	24	8	0	0	1	11	4	5	2	1	0	3	0	0	0	1	0	1.00	0	.333	.360	.458	OF	7	11	0	0	0	1.000
World Series																															
1983 Bal	28	3	0	0	0	0	0	0	0	0	0	0	0	0	0	0	0	1	0	1.00	0	—	—	—	OF	3	1	0	0	0	1.000
1985 StL	30	7	25	9	2	0	1	14	3	1	1	0	0	2	0	0	0	0	0	—	0	.360	.360	.560	OF	7	12	1	0	0	1.000
WS Totals		10	25	9	2	0	1	14	3	1	1	0	0	2	0	0	0	1	0	1.00	0	.360	.360	.560	OF	10	13	1	0	0	1.000
Postseason Totals		19	49	17	2	0	2	25	7	6	3	1	0	5	0	0	0	2	0	1.00	0	.347	.360	.510	OF	17	24	1	0	0	1.000

RICK LANGFORD—James Rick Langford—Throws: Right; Bats: Right

Ht: 6'0"; Wt: 180 lbs; Born: 3/20/1952 in Farmville, Virginia; Debut: 6/13/1976

Division Series — Pitching

Year Tm	Age	G	GS	CG	GF	IP	BFP	H	R	ER	HR	SH	SF	HB	TBB	IBB	SO	WP	Bk	W	L	Pct	ShO	Sv-Op	Hld	OAvg	OOBP	ERA
1981 Oak	29	1	1	0	0	7.1	30	10	1	1	0	0	0	0	0	0	3	0	0	1	0	1.000	0	0-0	0	.333	.333	1.23

Division Series — Batting / Fielding

Year Tm	Age	G	AB	H	2B	3B	HR	TB	R	RBI	GW	TBB	IBB	SO	HBP	SH	SF	SB	CS	SB%	GDP	Avg	OBP	SLG	Pos	G	PO	A	E	DP	FPct
1981 Oak	29	1	0	0	0	0	0	0	0	0	0	0	0	0	0	0	0	0	0	—	0	—	—	—	P	1	2	2	0	0	1.000

HAL LANIER—Harold Clifton Lanier—Bats: Right; Throws: Right

Ht: 6'2"; Wt: 180 lbs; Born: 7/4/1942 in Denton, North Carolina; Debut: 6/18/1964

LCS — Batting / Fielding

Year Tm	Age	G	AB	H	2B	3B	HR	TB	R	RBI	GW	TBB	IBB	SO	HBP	SH	SF	SB	CS	SB%	GDP	Avg	OBP	SLG	Pos	G	PO	A	E	DP	FPct
1971 SF	29	1	1	0	0	0	0	0	0	0	0	0	0	0	0	0	0	0	0	—	0	.000	.000	.000	3B	1	1	0	0	0	1.000

MAX LANIER—Hubert Max Lanier—Throws: Left; Bats: Right

Ht: 5'11"; Wt: 180 lbs; Born: 8/18/1915 in Denton, North Carolina; Debut: 4/20/1938

World Series — Pitching

Year Tm	Age	G	GS	CG	GF	IP	BFP	H	R	ER	HR	SH	SF	HB	TBB	IBB	SO	WP	Bk	W	L	Pct	ShO	Sv-Op	Hld	OAvg	OOBP	ERA
1942 StL	27	2	0	0	2	4.0	17	3	2	0	0	1	0	0	1	0	1	0	0	0	0	—	0	1-1	0	.200	.250	0.00
1943 StL	28	3	2	0	0	15.1	62	13	5	3	1	0	0	0	3	0	13	1	0	0	1	.000	0	0-0	0	.220	.258	1.76
1944 StL	29	2	2	0	0	12.1	53	8	3	3	0	1	0	0	8	1	11	1	0	1	0	1.000	0	0-0	0	.182	.308	2.19
WS Totals		7	4	0	2	31.2	264	24	10	6	1	2	0	0	12	1	25	2	0	1	1	.500	0	1-1	0	.203	.277	1.71

World Series — Batting / Fielding

Year Tm	Age	G	AB	H	2B	3B	HR	TB	R	RBI	GW	TBB	IBB	SO	HBP	SH	SF	SB	CS	SB%	GDP	Avg	OBP	SLG	Pos	G	PO	A	E	DP	FPct
1942 StL	27	2	1	1	0	0	0	1	0	1	0	0	0	0	0	0	0	0	0	—	0	1.000	1.000	1.000	P	2	0	1	2	0	.333
1943 StL	28	3	4	1	0	0	0	1	0	1	0	0	0	0	0	0	0	0	0	—	0	.250	.250	.250	P	3	0	3	1	0	.750
1944 StL	29	2	4	2	0	0	0	2	0	1	0	0	0	0	0	1	0	0	0	—	0	.500	.500	.500	P	2	1	1	0	0	1.000
WS Totals		7	9	4	0	0	0	4	0	3	0	0	0	0	0	1	0	0	0	—	0	.444	.444	.444	P	7	1	5	3	0	.667

RAY LANKFORD—Raymond Lewis Lankford—Bats: Left; Throws: Left

Ht: 5'11"; Wt: 180 lbs; Born: 6/5/1967 in Los Angeles, California; Debut: 8/21/1990

Division Series — Batting / Fielding

Year Tm	Age	G	AB	H	2B	3B	HR	TB	R	RBI	GW	TBB	IBB	SO	HBP	SH	SF	SB	CS	SB%	GDP	Avg	OBP	SLG	Pos	G	PO	A	E	DP	FPct
1996 StL	29	1	2	1	0	0	0	1	1	0	0	1	0	0	0	0	0	0	0	—	0	.500	.667	.500	OF	1	4	0	0	0	1.000

LCS — Batting / Fielding

Year Tm	Age	G	AB	H	2B	3B	HR	TB	R	RBI	GW	TBB	IBB	SO	HBP	SH	SF	SB	CS	SB%	GDP	Avg	OBP	SLG	Pos	G	PO	A	E	DP	FPct
1996 StL	29	5	13	0	0	0	0	0	1	1	1	1	0	4	0	0	1	0	0	—	0	.000	.067	.000	OF	3	7	0	0	0	1.000
Postseason Totals		6	15	1	0	0	0	1	2	1	1	2	0	4	0	0	1	0	0	—	0	.067	.167	.067	OF	4	11	0	0	0	1.000

CARNEY LANSFORD—Carney Ray Lansford—Bats: Right; Throws: Right

Ht: 6'2"; Wt: 195 lbs; Born: 2/7/1957 in San Jose, California; Debut: 4/8/1978

LCS — Batting / Fielding

Year Tm	Age	G	AB	H	2B	3B	HR	TB	R	RBI	GW	TBB	IBB	SO	HBP	SH	SF	SB	CS	SB%	GDP	Avg	OBP	SLG	Pos	G	PO	A	E	DP	FPct
1979 Cal	22	4	17	5	0	0	0	5	2	3	0	1	0	2	0	0	0	1	0	1.00	1	.294	.333	.294	3B	4	4	8	0	3	1.000
1988 Oak	31	4	17	5	1	0	1	9	4	2	0	0	0	2	0	0	0	0	1	.00	0	.294	.294	.529	3B	4	7	8	0	2	1.000
1989 Oak	32	3	11	5	0	0	0	5	2	4	1	2	0	1	0	0	0	2	0	1.00	0	.455	.538	.455	3B	3	1	2	0	0	1.000
1990 Oak	33	4	16	7	1	0	0	8	2	2	1	0	0	1	0	2	0	0	0	—	0	.438	.438	.500	3B	4	3	11	0	1	1.000
1992 Oak	35	5	18	3	0	0	0	3	0	1	0	1	0	1	0	0	0	0	0	—	1	.167	.211	.167	3B	5	2	9	1	1	.917
LCS Totals		20	79	25	2	0	1	30	10	12	2	4	0	7	0	2	0	3	1	.75	2	.316	.349	.380	3B	20	17	38	1	7	.982

World Series — Batting / Fielding

Year Tm	Age	G	AB	H	2B	3B	HR	TB	R	RBI	GW	TBB	IBB	SO	HBP	SH	SF	SB	CS	SB%	GDP	Avg	OBP	SLG	Pos	G	PO	A	E	DP	FPct
1988 Oak	31	5	18	3	0	0	0	3	2	1	0	2	0	2	0	0	0	0	0	—	0	.167	.250	.167	3B	5	8	7	0	1	1.000
1989 Oak	32	4	16	7	1	0	1	11	5	4	0	3	0	1	0	0	0	0	0	—	1	.438	.526	.688	3B	4	5	5	0	0	1.000
1990 Oak	33	4	15	4	0	0	0	4	0	1	0	1	0	0	0	1	0	1	0	1.00	0	.267	.313	.267	3B	4	1	14	0	0	1.000
WS Totals		13	49	14	1	0	1	18	7	6	0	6	0	3	0	1	0	1	0	1.00	1	.286	.364	.367	3B	13	14	26	0	1	1.000
Postseason Totals		33	128	39	3	0	2	48	17	18	2	10	0	10	0	3	0	4	1	.80	3	.305	.355	.375	3B	33	31	64	1	8	.990

DAVE LaPOINT—David Jeffrey LaPoint—Throws: Left; Bats: Left

Ht: 6'3"; Wt: 205 lbs; Born: 7/29/1959 in Glens Falls, New York; Debut: 9/10/1980

World Series — Pitching

Year Tm	Age	G	GS	CG	GF	IP	BFP	H	R	ER	HR	SH	SF	HB	TBB	IBB	SO	WP	Bk	W	L	Pct	ShO	Sv-Op	Hld	OAvg	OOBP	ERA
1982 StL	23	2	1	0	0	8.1	36	10	6	3	0	0	0	0	2	0	3	0	0	0	0	—	0	0-0	0	.294	.333	3.24

World Series — Batting / Fielding

Year Tm	Age	G	AB	H	2B	3B	HR	TB	R	RBI	GW	TBB	IBB	SO	HBP	SH	SF	SB	CS	SB%	GDP	Avg	OBP	SLG	Pos	G	PO	A	E	DP	FPct
1982 StL	23	2	0	0	0	0	0	0	0	0	0	0	0	0	0	0	0	0	0	—	0	—	—	—	P	2	0	2	1	0	.667

JACK LAPP—John Walker Lapp—Bats: Left; Throws: Right

Ht: 5'8"; Wt: 160 lbs; Born: 9/10/1884 in Frazer, Pennsylvania; Debut: 9/11/1908; Died: 2/6/1920

World Series — Batting / Fielding

Year Tm	Age	G	AB	H	2B	3B	HR	TB	R	RBI	GW	TBB	IBB	SO	HBP	SH	SF	SB	CS	SB%	GDP	Avg	OBP	SLG	Pos	G	PO	A	E	DP	FPct
1910 Phi	26	1	4	1	0	0	0	1	0	1	1	0	0	2	0	0	0	0	0	—	0	.250	.250	.250	C	1	4	2	0	0	1.000
1911 Phi	27	2	8	2	0	0	0	2	1	0	0	0	0	1	0	0	0	0	0	—	0	.250	.250	.250	C	2	18	8	0	1	1.000
1913 Phi	29	1	4	1	0	0	0	1	0	0	0	0	0	1	0	0	0	0	0	—	0	.250	.250	.250	C	1	7	1	0	0	1.000
1914 Phi	30	1	1	0	0	0	0	0	0	0	0	0	0	0	0	0	0	0	0	—	0	.000	.000	.000	C	1	2	1	0	1	1.000
WS Totals		5	17	4	0	0	0	4	1	1	1	0	0	4	0	0	0	0	0	—	0	.235	.235	.235	C	5	31	12	0	2	1.000

NORM LARKER—Norman Howard John Larker—Bats: Left; Throws: Left

Ht: 6'0"; Wt: 185 lbs; Born: 12/27/1930 in Beaver Meadows, Pennsylvania; Debut: 4/15/1958

World Series — Batting / Fielding

Year Tm	Age	G	AB	H	2B	3B	HR	TB	R	RBI	GW	TBB	IBB	SO	HBP	SH	SF	SB	CS	SB%	GDP	Avg	OBP	SLG	Pos	G	PO	A	E	DP	FPct
1959 LA	28	6	16	3	0	0	0	3	2	0	0	2	0	3	0	0	0	0	0	—	0	.188	.278	.188	OF	6	12	1	0	0	1.000

BARRY LARKIN—Barry Louis Larkin—Bats: Right; Throws: Right

Ht: 6'0"; Wt: 185 lbs; Born: 4/28/1964 in Cincinnati, Ohio; Debut: 8/13/1986

Division Series — Batting / Fielding

Year Tm	Age	G	AB	H	2B	3B	HR	TB	R	RBI	GW	TBB	IBB	SO	HBP	SH	SF	SB	CS	SB%	GDP	Avg	OBP	SLG	Pos	G	PO	A	E	DP	FPct
1995 Cin-*M*	31	3	13	5	0	0	0	5	2	1	1	1	0	2	0	0	0	4	0	1.00	0	.385	.429	.385	SS	3	3	8	0	1	1.000

LCS — Batting / Fielding

Year Tm	Age	G	AB	H	2B	3B	HR	TB	R	RBI	GW	TBB	IBB	SO	HBP	SH	SF	SB	CS	SB%	GDP	Avg	OBP	SLG	Pos	G	PO	A	E	DP	FPct
1990 Cin	26	6	23	6	2	0	0	8	5	1	0	3	0	1	0	0	0	3	0	1.00	1	.261	.346	.348	SS	6	21	15	1	2	.973
1995 Cin-*M*	31	4	18	7	2	1	0	11	1	0	0	1	0	1	0	0	0	1	1	.50	0	.389	.421	.611	SS	4	10	15	1	2	.962
LCS Totals		10	41	13	4	1	0	19	6	1	0	4	0	2	0	0	0	4	1	.80	1	.317	.378	.463	SS	10	31	30	2	4	.968

World Series — Batting / Fielding

Year Tm	Age	G	AB	H	2B	3B	HR	TB	R	RBI	GW	TBB	IBB	SO	HBP	SH	SF	SB	CS	SB%	GDP	Avg	OBP	SLG	Pos	G	PO	A	E	DP	FPct
1990 Cin	26	4	17	6	1	1	0	9	3	1	0	2	0	0	0	0	0	0	0	—	1	.353	.421	.529	SS	4	1	14	0	2	1.000
Postseason Totals		17	71	24	5	2	0	33	11	3	1	7	0	4	0	0	0	8	1	.89	2	.338	.397	.465	SS	17	35	52	2	7	.978

GENE LARKIN—Eugene Thomas Larkin—Bats: Both; Throws: Right

Ht: 6'3"; Wt: 195 lbs; Born: 10/24/1962 in Flushing, New York; Debut: 5/21/1987

LCS — Batting / Fielding

Year Tm	Age	G	AB	H	2B	3B	HR	TB	R	RBI	GW	TBB	IBB	SO	HBP	SH	SF	SB	CS	SB%	GDP	Avg	OBP	SLG	Pos	G	PO	A	E	DP	FPct
1987 Min	24	1	1	1	1	0	0	2	0	1	0	0	0	0	0	0	0	0	0	—	0	1.000	1.000	2.000	—						
1991 Min	28	3	3	0	0	0	0	0	0	0	0	0	0	1	0	0	0	0	0	—	0	.000	.000	.000	—						
LCS Totals		4	4	1	1	0	0	2	0	1	0	0	0	1	0	0	0	0	0	—	0	.250	.250	.500	—	0	0	0	0	0	—

World Series — Batting / Fielding

Year Tm	Age	G	AB	H	2B	3B	HR	TB	R	RBI	GW	TBB	IBB	SO	HBP	SH	SF	SB	CS	SB%	GDP	Avg	OBP	SLG	Pos	G	PO	A	E	DP	FPct
1987 Min	24	5	3	0	0	0	0	0	1	0	0	1	0	0	0	0	0	0	0	—	0	.000	.250	.000	1B	1	1	0	0	0	1.000
1991 Min	28	4	4	2	0	0	0	2	0	1	1	0	0	0	0	0	0	0	0	—	0	.500	.500	.500	—						
WS Totals		9	7	2	0	0	0	2	1	1	1	1	0	0	0	0	0	0	0	—	0	.286	.375	.286	1B	1	1	0	0	0	1.000
Postseason Totals		13	11	3	1	0	0	4	1	2	1	1	0	1	0	0	0	0	0	—	0	.273	.333	.364	1B	1	1	0	0	0	1.000

DAVE LaROCHE—David Eugene LaRoche—Throws: Left; Bats: Left

Ht: 6'2"; Wt: 200 lbs; Born: 5/14/1948 in Colorado Springs, Colorado; Debut: 5/11/1970

LCS		Pitching																										
Year Tm	Age	G	GS	CG	GF	IP	BFP	H	R	ER	HR	SH	SF	HB	TBB	IBB	SO	WP	Bk	W	L	Pct	ShO	Sv-Op	Hld	OAvg	OOBP	ERA
1979 Cal	31	1	0	0	0	1.1	6	2	1	1	0	0	0	0	1	0	1	0	0	0	0	—	0	0- 0	0	.400	.500	6.75
World Series		**Pitching**																										
Year Tm	Age	G	GS	CG	GF	IP	BFP	H	R	ER	HR	SH	SF	HB	TBB	IBB	SO	WP	Bk	W	L	Pct	ShO	Sv-Op	Hld	OAvg	OOBP	ERA
1981 NYA	33	1	0	0	1	1.0	3	0	0	0	0	0	0	0	0	0	2	0	0	0	0	—	0	0- 0	0	.000	.000	0.00
Postseason Totals		2	0	0	1	2.1	18	2	1	1	0	0	0	0	1	0	3	0	0	0	0	—	0	0-0	0	.250	.333	3.86

LCS		Batting																							Fielding						
Year Tm	Age	G	AB	H	2B	3B	HR	TB	R	RBI	GW	TBB	IBB	SO	HBP	SH	SF	SB	CS	SB%	GDP	Avg	OBP	SLG	Pos	G	PO	A	E	DP	FPct
1979 Cal	31	1	0	0	0	0	0	0	0	0	0	0	0	0	0	0	0	0	0	—	0	—	—	—	P	1	0	0	0	0	—
World Series		**Batting**																							**Fielding**						
Year Tm	Age	G	AB	H	2B	3B	HR	TB	R	RBI	GW	TBB	IBB	SO	HBP	SH	SF	SB	CS	SB%	GDP	Avg	OBP	SLG	Pos	G	PO	A	E	DP	FPct
1981 NYA	33	1	0	0	0	0	0	0	0	0	0	0	0	0	0	0	0	0	0	—	0	—	—	—	P	1	0	0	0	0	—
Postseason Totals		2	0	0	0	0	0	0	0	0	0	0	0	0	0	0	0	0	0	—	0	—	—	—	P	2	0	0	0	0	—

DON LARSEN—Don James Larsen—Nickname: Night Rider—Throws: Right; Bats: Right

Ht: 6'4"; Wt: 215 lbs; Born: 8/7/1929 in Michigan City, Indiana; Debut: 4/18/1953

World Series		Pitching																										
Year Tm	Age	G	GS	CG	GF	IP	BFP	H	R	ER	HR	SH	SF	HB	TBB	IBB	SO	WP	Bk	W	L	Pct	ShO	Sv-Op	Hld	OAvg	OOBP	ERA
1955 NYA	26	1	1	0	0	4.0	19	5	5	5	2	0	0	0	2	0	2	0	0	0	1	.000	0	0- 0	0	.294	.368	11.25
1956 NYA	27	2	2	1	0	10.2	37	1	4	0	0	0	1	0	4	0	7	0	0	1	0	1.000	1	0- 0	0	.031	.135	0.00
1957 NYA	28	2	1	0	1	9.2	44	8	5	4	1	1	0	1	5	0	6	0	0	1	1	.500	0	0- 0	0	.216	.326	3.72
1958 NYA	29	2	2	0	0	9.1	42	9	1	1	0	1	0	0	6	1	9	0	0	1	0	1.000	0	0- 0	0	.257	.366	0.96
1962 SF	33	3	0	0	0	2.1	11	1	1	1	0	0	1	1	2	0	0	0	0	1	0	1.000	0	0- 0	0	.143	.364	3.86
WS Totals		10	6	1	1	36.0	306	24	16	11	3	2	2	2	19	1	24	0	0	4	2	.667	1	0-0	0	.188	.298	2.75

World Series		Batting																							Fielding						
Year Tm	Age	G	AB	H	2B	3B	HR	TB	R	RBI	GW	TBB	IBB	SO	HBP	SH	SF	SB	CS	SB%	GDP	Avg	OBP	SLG	Pos	G	PO	A	E	DP	FPct
1955 NYA	26	1	2	0	0	0	0	0	0	0	0	0	0	0	0	0	0	0	0	—	0	.000	.000	.000	P	1	0	1	0	0	1.000
1956 NYA	27	2	3	1	0	0	0	1	1	1	0	0	0	1	0	1	0	0	0	—	0	.333	.333	.333	P	2	0	1	0	0	1.000
1957 NYA	28	2	2	0	0	0	0	0	1	0	0	2	0	1	0	0	0	0	0	—	0	.000	.500	.000	P	2	0	1	0	0	1.000
1958 NYA	29	2	2	0	0	0	0	0	0	0	0	1	0	0	0	0	0	0	0	—	0	.000	.333	.000	P	2	1	0	0	0	1.000
1962 SF	33	3	0	0	0	0	0	0	0	0	0	0	0	0	0	0	0	0	0	—	0	—	—	—	P	3	1	0	0	0	1.000
WS Totals		10	9	1	0	0	0	1	2	1	0	3	0	2	0	1	0	0	0	—	0	.111	.333	.111	P	10	2	3	0	0	1.000

FRED LASHER—Frederick Walter Lasher—Nickname: Whip—Throws: Right; Bats: Right

Ht: 6'3"; Wt: 190 lbs; Born: 8/19/1941 in Poughkeepsie, New York; Debut: 4/12/1963

World Series		Pitching																										
Year Tm	Age	G	GS	CG	GF	IP	BFP	H	R	ER	HR	SH	SF	HB	TBB	IBB	SO	WP	Bk	W	L	Pct	ShO	Sv-Op	Hld	OAvg	OOBP	ERA
1968 Det	27	1	0	0	0	2.0	7	1	0	0	0	0	0	0	0	0	1	0	0	0	0	—	0	0- 0	0	.143	.143	0.00

World Series		Batting																							Fielding						
Year Tm	Age	G	AB	H	2B	3B	HR	TB	R	RBI	GW	TBB	IBB	SO	HBP	SH	SF	SB	CS	SB%	GDP	Avg	OBP	SLG	Pos	G	PO	A	E	DP	FPct
1968 Det	27	1	0	0	0	0	0	0	0	0	0	0	0	0	0	0	0	0	0	—	0	—	—	—	P	1	0	1	0	0	1.000

TIM LAUDNER—Timothy Jon Laudner—Bats: Right; Throws: Right

Ht: 6'3"; Wt: 212 lbs; Born: 6/7/1958 in Mason City, Iowa; Debut: 8/28/1981

LCS		Batting																							Fielding						
Year Tm	Age	G	AB	H	2B	3B	HR	TB	R	RBI	GW	TBB	IBB	SO	HBP	SH	SF	SB	CS	SB%	GDP	Avg	OBP	SLG	Pos	G	PO	A	E	DP	FPct
1987 Min	29	5	14	1	1	0	0	2	1	2	1	2	0	5	0	0	0	0	0	—	0	.071	.188	.143	C	5	31	2	0	0	1.000
World Series		**Batting**																							**Fielding**						
Year Tm	Age	G	AB	H	2B	3B	HR	TB	R	RBI	GW	TBB	IBB	SO	HBP	SH	SF	SB	CS	SB%	GDP	Avg	OBP	SLG	Pos	G	PO	A	E	DP	FPct
1987 Min	29	7	22	7	1	0	1	11	4	4	0	5	0	4	0	0	0	0	0	—	1	.318	.444	.500	C	7	46	2	0	1	1.000
Postseason Totals		12	36	8	2	0	1	13	5	6	1	7	0	9	0	0	0	0	0	—	1	.222	.349	.361	C	12	77	4	0	1	1.000

COOKIE LAVAGETTO—Harry Arthur Lavagetto—Bats: Right; Throws: Right

Ht: 6'0"; Wt: 170 lbs; Born: 12/1/1912 in Oakland, California; Debut: 4/17/1934; Died: 8/10/1990

World Series		Batting																							Fielding						
Year Tm	Age	G	AB	H	2B	3B	HR	TB	R	RBI	GW	TBB	IBB	SO	HBP	SH	SF	SB	CS	SB%	GDP	Avg	OBP	SLG	Pos	G	PO	A	E	DP	FPct
1941 Bro	28	3	10	1	0	0	0	1	1	0	0	2	0	0	0	0	0	0	0	—	1	.100	.250	.100	3B	3	2	0	0	0	1.000
1947 Bro	34	5	7	1	1	0	0	2	0	3	1	0	0	2	0	0	0	0	0	—	0	.143	.143	.286	3B	3	0	1	0	0	1.000
WS Totals		8	17	2	1	0	0	3	1	3	1	2	0	2	0	0	0	0	0	—	1	.118	.211	.176	3B	6	2	1	0	0	1.000

MIKE LaVALLIERE—Michael Eugene LaValliere—Bats: Left; Throws: Right

Ht: 5'10"; Wt: 180 lbs; Born: 8/18/1960 in Charlotte, North Carolina; Debut: 9/9/1984

LCS		Batting																							Fielding						
Year Tm	Age	G	AB	H	2B	3B	HR	TB	R	RBI	GW	TBB	IBB	SO	HBP	SH	SF	SB	CS	SB%	GDP	Avg	OBP	SLG	Pos	G	PO	A	E	DP	FPct
1990 Pit	30	3	6	0	0	0	0	0	1	0	0	3	1	1	0	0	0	0	0	—	2	.000	.333	.000	C	3	17	2	0	0	1.000
1991 Pit	31	3	6	2	0	0	0	2	0	1	1	2	0	0	0	0	0	0	0	—	0	.333	.500	.333	C	3	14	3	0	0	1.000
1992 Pit	32	3	10	2	0	0	0	2	1	0	0	0	0	3	0	0	0	0	0	—	0	.200	.200	.200	C	3	14	0	0	0	1.000
1993 ChA	33	2	3	1	0	0	0	1	0	0	0	1	0	0	0	0	0	0	0	—	0	.333	.500	.333	C	2	8	0	0	0	1.000
LCS Totals		11	25	5	0	0	0	5	2	1	1	6	1	4	0	0	0	0	0	—	2	.200	.355	.200	C	11	53	5	0	0	1.000

GARY LAVELLE—Gary Robert Lavelle—Throws: Left; Bats: Both

Ht: 6'2"; Wt: 190 lbs; Born: 1/3/1949 in Scranton, Pennsylvania; Debut: 9/10/1974

LCS		Pitching																										
Year Tm	Age	G	GS	CG	GF	IP	BFP	H	R	ER	HR	SH	SF	HB	TBB	IBB	SO	WP	Bk	W	L	Pct	ShO	Sv-Op	Hld	OAvg	OOBP	ERA
1985 Tor	36	1	0	0	0	0.0	1	0	0	0	0	0	0	0	1	0	0	0	0	0	0	—	0	0- 0	0	—	1.000	—

LCS		Batting																							Fielding						
Year Tm	Age	G	AB	H	2B	3B	HR	TB	R	RBI	GW	TBB	IBB	SO	HBP	SH	SF	SB	CS	SB%	GDP	Avg	OBP	SLG	Pos	G	PO	A	E	DP	FPct
1985 Tor	36	1	0	0	0	0	0	0	0	0	0	0	0	0	0	0	0	0	0	—	0	—	—	—	P	1	0	0	0	0	—

RUDY LAW—Rudy Karl Law—Bats: Left; Throws: Left

Ht: 6'1"; Wt: 165 lbs; Born: 10/7/1956 in Waco, Texas; Debut: 9/12/1978

LCS		Batting																							Fielding						
Year Tm	Age	G	AB	H	2B	3B	HR	TB	R	RBI	GW	TBB	IBB	SO	HBP	SH	SF	SB	CS	SB%	GDP	Avg	OBP	SLG	Pos	G	PO	A	E	DP	FPct
1983 ChA	26	4	18	7	1	0	0	8	1	0	0	0	0	1	0	0	0	2	0	1.00	0	.389	.389	.444	OF	4	10	0	0	0	1.000

VANCE LAW—Vance Aaron Law—Bats: Right; Throws: Right

Ht: 6'2"; Wt: 185 lbs; Born: 10/1/1956 in Boise, Idaho; Debut: 6/1/1980

LCS		Batting																							Fielding						
Year Tm	Age	G	AB	H	2B	3B	HR	TB	R	RBI	GW	TBB	IBB	SO	HBP	SH	SF	SB	CS	SB%	GDP	Avg	OBP	SLG	Pos	G	PO	A	E	DP	FPct
1983 ChA	26	4	11	2	0	0	0	2	0	1	0	1	0	3	0	0	0	0	0	—	0	.182	.250	.182	3B	4	1	9	1	1	.909
1989 ChN	32	2	3	0	0	0	0	0	0	0	0	0	0	3	0	0	0	0	0	—	0	.000	.000	.000	3B	1	0	0	0	0	—
LCS Totals		6	14	2	0	0	0	2	0	1	0	1	0	6	0	0	0	0	0	—	0	.143	.200	.143	3B	5	1	9	1	1	.909

VERN LAW—Vernon Sanders Law—Nickname: Deacon—Throws: Right; Bats: Right

Ht: 6'2"; Wt: 195 lbs; Born: 3/12/1930 in Meridan, Idaho; Debut: 6/11/1950

World Series		Pitching																										
Year Tm	Age	G	GS	CG	GF	IP	BFP	H	R	ER	HR	SH	SF	HB	TBB	IBB	SO	WP	Bk	W	L	Pct	ShO	Sv-Op	Hld	OAvg	OOBP	ERA
1960 Pit-C	30	3	3	0	0	18.1	77	22	7	7	3	0	0	0	3	1	8	1	0	2	0	1.000	0	0- 0	0	.297	.325	3.44

World Series		Batting																							Fielding						
Year Tm	Age	G	AB	H	2B	3B	HR	TB	R	RBI	GW	TBB	IBB	SO	HBP	SH	SF	SB	CS	SB%	GDP	Avg	OBP	SLG	Pos	G	PO	A	E	DP	FPct
1960 Pit	30	3	6	2	1	0	0	3	1	1	0	0	0	1	1	1	0	0	0	—	1	.333	.429	.500	P	3	0	6	0	0	1.000

TOM LAWLESS—Thomas James Lawless—Bats: Right; Throws: Right

Ht: 5'11"; Wt: 170 lbs; Born: 12/19/1956 in Erie, Pennsylvania; Debut: 7/15/1982

LCS — Batting / Fielding

Year Tm	Age	G	AB	H	2B	3B	HR	TB	R	RBI	GW	TBB	IBB	SO	HBP	SH	SF	SB	CS	SB%	GDP	Avg	OBP	SLG	Pos	G	PO	A	E	DP	FPct
1987 StL	30	3	6	2	0	0	0	2	0	0	0	1	0	1	0	0	0	0	0	—	0	.333	.429	.333	3B	2	0	4	0	0	1.000
																									OF	1	1	0	0	0	1.000

World Series — Batting / Fielding

Year Tm	Age	G	AB	H	2B	3B	HR	TB	R	RBI	GW	TBB	IBB	SO	HBP	SH	SF	SB	CS	SB%	GDP	Avg	OBP	SLG	Pos	G	PO	A	E	DP	FPct
1985 StL	28	1	0	0	0	0	0	0	0	0	0	0	0	0	0	0	0	0	0	—	0	—	—	—	—						
1987 StL	30	3	10	1	0	0	1	4	1	3	1	0	0	4	0	0	0	0	0	—	0	.100	.100	.400	3B	3	3	6	1	1	.900
WS Totals		4	10	1	0	0	1	4	1	3	1	0	0	4	0	0	0	0	0	—	0	.100	.100	.400	3B	3	3	6	1	1	.900
Postseason Totals		7	16	3	0	0	1	6	1	3	1	1	0	5	0	0	0	0	0	—	0	.188	.235	.375	3B	5	3	10	1	1	.929

TONY LAZZERI (HOF 1991-V)—Anthony Michael Lazzeri—Nickname: Poosh 'Em Up Tony—B: R; T: R

Ht: 5'11"; Wt: 170 lbs; Born: 12/6/1903 in San Francisco, Calif.; Deb.: 4/13/1926; Died: 8/6/1946

World Series — Batting / Fielding

Year Tm	Age	G	AB	H	2B	3B	HR	TB	R	RBI	GW	TBB	IBB	SO	HBP	SH	SF	SB	CS	SB%	GDP	Avg	OBP	SLG	Pos	G	PO	A	E	DP	FPct
1926 NYA	22	7	26	5	1	0	0	6	2	3	1	1	0	6	0	0	2	0	1	.00	1	.192	.207	.231	2B	7	15	19	1	2	.971
1927 NYA	23	4	15	4	1	0	0	5	1	2	0	1	0	4	0	0	1	0	0	—	0	.267	.294	.333	2B	4	10	18	1	4	.966
1928 NYA	24	4	12	3	1	0	0	4	2	0	0	1	0	0	0	1	0	2	0	1.00	1	.250	.308	.333	2B	4	2	7	2	1	.818
1932 NYA	28	4	17	5	0	0	2	11	4	5	0	2	0	1	0	0	0	0	0	—	0	.294	.368	.647	2B	4	8	11	1	1	.950
1936 NYA	32	6	20	5	0	0	1	8	4	7	0	4	0	4	0	1	0	0	0	—	0	.250	.375	.400	2B	6	12	17	0	1	1.000
1937 NYA	33	5	15	6	0	1	1	11	3	2	1	3	3	3	1	0	0	0	0	—	0	.400	.526	.733	2B	5	10	15	0	1	1.000
1938 ChN	34	2	2	0	0	0	0	0	0	0	0	0	0	1	0	0	0	0	0	—	0	.000	.000	.000	—						
WS Totals		32	107	28	3	1	4	45	16	19	2	12	3	19	1	2	3	2	1	.67	2	.262	.333	.421	2B	30	57	87	5	10	.966

TERRY LEACH—Terry Hester Leach—Throws: Right; Bats: Right

Ht: 6'0"; Wt: 215 lbs; Born: 3/13/1954 in Selma, Alabama; Debut: 8/12/1981

LCS — Pitching

Year Tm	Age	G	GS	CG	GF	IP	BFP	H	R	ER	HR	SH	SF	HB	TBB	IBB	SO	WP	Bk	W	L	Pct	ShO	Sv-Op	Hld	OAvg	OOBP	ERA
1988 NYN	34	3	0	0	0	5.0	20	4	0	0	0	0	0	0	1	0	4	0	0	0	0	—	0	0-0	0	.211	.250	0.00

World Series — Pitching

Year Tm	Age	G	GS	CG	GF	IP	BFP	H	R	ER	HR	SH	SF	HB	TBB	IBB	SO	WP	Bk	W	L	Pct	ShO	Sv-Op	Hld	OAvg	OOBP	ERA
1991 Min	37	2	0	0	0	2.1	9	2	1	1	0	0	0	0	0	0	2	0	0	0	0	—	0	0-0	0	.222	.222	3.86
Postseason Totals		5	0	0	0	7.1	58	6	1	1	0	0	0	0	1	0	6	0	0	0	0	—	0	0-0	0	.214	.241	1.23

LCS — Batting / Fielding

Year Tm	Age	G	AB	H	2B	3B	HR	TB	R	RBI	GW	TBB	IBB	SO	HBP	SH	SF	SB	CS	SB%	GDP	Avg	OBP	SLG	Pos	G	PO	A	E	DP	FPct
1988 NYN	34	3	0	0	0	0	0	0	0	0	0	0	0	0	0	0	0	0	0	—	0	—	—	—	P	3	1	0	0	0	1.000

World Series — Batting / Fielding

Year Tm	Age	G	AB	H	2B	3B	HR	TB	R	RBI	GW	TBB	IBB	SO	HBP	SH	SF	SB	CS	SB%	GDP	Avg	OBP	SLG	Pos	G	PO	A	E	DP	FPct
1991 Min	37	2	0	0	0	0	0	0	0	0	0	0	0	0	0	0	0	0	0	—	0	—	—	—	P	2	0	0	0	0	—
Postseason Totals		5	0	0	0	0	0	0	0	0	0	0	0	0	0	0	0	0	0	—	0	—	—	—	P	5	1	0	0	0	1.000

TOMMY LEACH—Thomas William Leach—Nickname: The Wee—Bats: Right; Throws: Right

Ht: 5'6"; Wt: 150 lbs; Born: 11/4/1877 in French Creek, New York; Debut: 9/28/1898; Died: 9/29/1969

World Series — Batting / Fielding

Year Tm	Age	G	AB	H	2B	3B	HR	TB	R	RBI	GW	TBB	IBB	SO	HBP	SH	SF	SB	CS	SB%	GDP	Avg	OBP	SLG	Pos	G	PO	A	E	DP	FPct
1903 Pit	25	8	33	9	0	4	0	17	3	7	1	1	0	4	0	0	0	1	2	.33	1	.273	.294	.515	3B	8	5	16	4	0	.840
1909 Pit	31	7	25	9	4	0	0	13	8	2	0	2	0	1	1	1	1	1	1	.50	0	.360	.414	.520	3B	1	4	2	0	0	1.000
																									OF	6	16	1	0	0	1.000
WS Totals		15	58	18	4	4	0	30	11	9	1	3	0	5	1	1	1	2	3	.40	1	.310	.349	.517	3B	9	9	18	4	0	.871

TIM LEARY—Timothy James Leary—Throws: Right; Bats: Right

Ht: 6'3"; Wt: 205 lbs; Born: 3/21/1958 in Santa Monica, California; Debut: 4/12/1981

LCS — Pitching

Year Tm	Age	G	GS	CG	GF	IP	BFP	H	R	ER	HR	SH	SF	HB	TBB	IBB	SO	WP	Bk	W	L	Pct	ShO	Sv-Op	Hld	OAvg	OOBP	ERA
1988 LA	30	2	1	0	0	4.1	26	8	4	3	1	1	1	1	3	0	3	0	0	0	1	.000	0	0-0	1	.400	.480	6.23

World Series — Pitching

Year Tm	Age	G	GS	CG	GF	IP	BFP	H	R	ER	HR	SH	SF	HB	TBB	IBB	SO	WP	Bk	W	L	Pct	ShO	Sv-Op	Hld	OAvg	OOBP	ERA
1988 LA	30	2	0	0	0	6.2	27	6	1	1	0	0	0	0	2	1	4	0	1	0	0	—	0	0-0	0	.240	.296	1.35
Postseason Totals		4	1	0	0	11.0	106	14	5	4	1	1	1	1	5	1	7	0	1	0	1	.000	0	0-0	1	.311	.385	3.27

LCS — Batting / Fielding

Year Tm	Age	G	AB	H	2B	3B	HR	TB	R	RBI	GW	TBB	IBB	SO	HBP	SH	SF	SB	CS	SB%	GDP	Avg	OBP	SLG	Pos	G	PO	A	E	DP	FPct
1988 LA	30	2	1	0	0	0	0	0	0	0	0	0	0	0	0	0	0	0	0	—	0	.000	.000	.000	P	2	0	1	0	0	1.000

World Series — Batting / Fielding

Year Tm	Age	G	AB	H	2B	3B	HR	TB	R	RBI	GW	TBB	IBB	SO	HBP	SH	SF	SB	CS	SB%	GDP	Avg	OBP	SLG	Pos	G	PO	A	E	DP	FPct
1988 LA	30	2	0	0	0	0	0	0	0	0	0	0	0	0	0	0	0	0	0	—	0	—	—	—	P	2	1	3	0	1	1.000
Postseason Totals		4	1	0	0	0	0	0	0	0	0	0	0	0	0	0	0	0	0	—	0	.000	.000	.000	P	4	1	4	0	1	1.000

BILL LEE—William Crutcher Lee—Nickname: Big Bill—Throws: Right; Bats: Right

Ht: 6'3"; Wt: 195 lbs; Born: 10/21/1909 in Plaquemine, Louisiana; Debut: 4/29/1934; Died: 6/15/1977

World Series — Pitching

Year Tm	Age	G	GS	CG	GF	IP	BFP	H	R	ER	HR	SH	SF	HB	TBB	IBB	SO	WP	Bk	W	L	Pct	ShO	Sv-Op	Hld	OAvg	OOBP	ERA
1935 ChN	25	2	1	0	1	10.1	45	11	5	5	0	0	0	0	5	0	5	0	0	0	0	—	0	1-1	0	.275	.356	4.35
1938 ChN	28	2	2	0	0	11.0	48	15	6	3	0	1	0	1	1	0	8	0	0	0	2	.000	0	0-0	0	.333	.362	2.45
WS Totals		4	3	0	1	21.1	186	26	11	8	0	1	0	1	6	0	13	0	0	0	2	.000	0	1-1	0	.306	.359	3.38

World Series — Batting / Fielding

Year Tm	Age	G	AB	H	2B	3B	HR	TB	R	RBI	GW	TBB	IBB	SO	HBP	SH	SF	SB	CS	SB%	GDP	Avg	OBP	SLG	Pos	G	PO	A	E	DP	FPct
1935 ChN	25	2	1	0	0	0	0	0	0	1	0	0	0	0	0	3	0	0	0	—	0	.000	.000	.000	P	2	1	1	0	0	1.000
1938 ChN	28	2	3	0	0	0	0	0	0	0	0	0	0	1	0	0	0	0	0	—	0	.000	.000	.000	P	2	1	0	0	0	1.000
WS Totals		4	4	0	0	0	0	0	0	1	0	0	0	1	0	3	0	0	0	—	0	.000	.000	.000	P	4	2	1	0	0	1.000

BILL LEE—William Francis Lee—Nickname: Spaceman—Throws: Left; Bats: Left

Ht: 6'3"; Wt: 205 lbs; Born: 12/28/1946 in Burbank, California; Debut: 6/25/1969

Division Series — Pitching

Year Tm	Age	G	GS	CG	GF	IP	BFP	H	R	ER	HR	SH	SF	HB	TBB	IBB	SO	WP	Bk	W	L	Pct	ShO	Sv-Op	Hld	OAvg	OOBP	ERA
1981 Mon	34	1	0	0	0	0.2	4	2	0	0	0	0	0	0	0	0	1	0	0	0	0	—	0	0-0	0	.500	.500	0.00

LCS — Pitching

Year Tm	Age	G	GS	CG	GF	IP	BFP	H	R	ER	HR	SH	SF	HB	TBB	IBB	SO	WP	Bk	W	L	Pct	ShO	Sv-Op	Hld	OAvg	OOBP	ERA
1981 Mon	34	1	0	0	1	0.1	2	1	0	0	0	0	0	0	0	0	0	0	0	0	0	—	0	0-0	0	.500	.500	0.00

World Series — Pitching

Year Tm	Age	G	GS	CG	GF	IP	BFP	H	R	ER	HR	SH	SF	HB	TBB	IBB	SO	WP	Bk	W	L	Pct	ShO	Sv-Op	Hld	OAvg	OOBP	ERA
1975 Bos	28	2	2	0	0	14.1	55	12	5	5	1	0	0	0	3	0	7	0	0	0	0	—	0	0-0	0	.231	.273	3.14
Postseason Totals		4	2	0	1	15.1	122	15	5	5	1	0	0	0	3	0	8	0	0	0	0	—	0	0-0	0	.259	.295	2.93

Division Series — Batting / Fielding

Year Tm	Age	G	AB	H	2B	3B	HR	TB	R	RBI	GW	TBB	IBB	SO	HBP	SH	SF	SB	CS	SB%	GDP	Avg	OBP	SLG	Pos	G	PO	A	E	DP	FPct
1981 Mon	34	1	0	0	0	0	0	0	0	0	0	0	0	0	0	0	0	0	0	—	0	—	—	—	P	1	0	0	0	0	—

LCS — Batting / Fielding

Year Tm	Age	G	AB	H	2B	3B	HR	TB	R	RBI	GW	TBB	IBB	SO	HBP	SH	SF	SB	CS	SB%	GDP	Avg	OBP	SLG	Pos	G	PO	A	E	DP	FPct
1981 Mon	34	1	0	0	0	0	0	0	0	0	0	0	0	0	0	0	0	0	0	—	0	—	—	—	P	1	0	0	0	0	—

World Series — Batting / Fielding

Year Tm	Age	G	AB	H	2B	3B	HR	TB	R	RBI	GW	TBB	IBB	SO	HBP	SH	SF	SB	CS	SB%	GDP	Avg	OBP	SLG	Pos	G	PO	A	E	DP	FPct
1975 Bos	28	2	6	1	0	0	0	1	0	0	0	0	0	3	0	0	0	0	0	—	0	.167	.167	.167	P	2	0	1	0	0	1.000
Postseason Totals		4	6	1	0	0	0	1	0	0	0	0	0	3	0	0	0	0	0	—	0	.167	.167	.167	P	4	0	1	0	0	1.000

MANUEL LEE—Manuel Lora Lee—Bats: Both; Throws: Right

Ht: 5'10"; Wt: 145 lbs; Born: 6/17/1965 in San Pedro de Macoris, Dominican Republic; Debut: 4/10/1985

LCS		Batting																							Fielding						
Year Tm	Age	G	AB	H	2B	3B	HR	TB	R	RBI	GW	TBB	IBB	SO	HBP	SH	SF	SB	CS	SB%	GDP	Avg	OBP	SLG	Pos	G	PO	A	E	DP	FPct
1985 Tor	20	1	0	0	0	0	0	0	0	0	0	0	0	0	0	0	0	0	0	—	0	—	—	—	2B	1	0	0	0	0	—
1989 Tor	24	2	8	2	0	0	0	2	2	0	0	0	0	1	0	0	0	0	0	—	0	.250	.250	.250	2B	2	4	1	0	1	1.000
1991 Tor	26	5	16	2	0	0	0	2	3	0	0	1	0	5	0	0	0	0	0	—	0	.125	.176	.125	SS	5	8	16	1	3	.960
1992 Tor	27	6	18	5	1	1	0	8	2	3	0	1	0	2	0	0	1	0	0	—	0	.278	.300	.444	SS	6	12	15	3	5	.900
LCS Totals		14	42	9	1	1	0	12	7	3	0	2	0	8	0	0	1	0	0	—	0	.214	.244	.286	SS	11	20	31	4	8	.927
World Series		Batting																							Fielding						
Year Tm	Age	G	AB	H	2B	3B	HR	TB	R	RBI	GW	TBB	IBB	SO	HBP	SH	SF	SB	CS	SB%	GDP	Avg	OBP	SLG	Pos	G	PO	A	E	DP	FPct
1992 Tor	27	6	19	2	0	0	0	2	1	0	0	1	0	2	0	0	0	0	0	—	1	.105	.150	.105	SS	6	14	10	1	4	.960
Postseason Totals		20	61	11	1	1	0	14	8	3	0	3	0	10	0	0	1	0	0	—	1	.180	.215	.230	SS	17	34	41	5	12	.938

SAM LEEVER—Samuel Leever—Nickname: The Goshen Schoolmaster—Throws: Right; Bats: Right

Ht: 5'10"; Wt: 175 lbs; Born: 12/23/1871 in Goshen, Ohio; Debut: 5/26/1898; Died: 5/19/1953

World Series		Pitching																									
Year Tm	Age	G	GS	CG	GF	IP	BFP	H	R	ER	HR	SH	SF	HB	TBB	IBB	SO	WP	Bk	W	L	Pct	ShO	Sv-Op	Hld	OAvg	OOBP	ERA
1903 Pit	31	2	2	1	0	10.0	48	13	8	6	1	0	0	1	3	0	2	0	0	0	2	.000	0	0- 0	0	.295	.354	5.40

World Series		Batting																							Fielding						
Year Tm	Age	G	AB	H	2B	3B	HR	TB	R	RBI	GW	TBB	IBB	SO	HBP	SH	SF	SB	CS	SB%	GDP	Avg	OBP	SLG	Pos	G	PO	A	E	DP	FPct
1903 Pit	31	2	4	0	0	0	0	0	0	0	0	0	0	0	0	0	0	0	0	—	0	.000	.000	.000	P	2	0	2	0	0	1.000

JIM LEFEBVRE—James Kenneth Lefebvre—Nickname: Frenchy—Bats: Both; Throws: Right

Ht: 6'0"; Wt: 180 lbs; Born: 1/7/1942 in Inglewood, California; Debut: 4/12/1965

World Series		Batting																							Fielding						
Year Tm	Age	G	AB	H	2B	3B	HR	TB	R	RBI	GW	TBB	IBB	SO	HBP	SH	SF	SB	CS	SB%	GDP	Avg	OBP	SLG	Pos	G	PO	A	E	DP	FPct
1965 LA-*RY*	23	3	10	4	0	0	0	4	2	0	0	0	0	0	0	0	0	0	0	—	0	.400	.400	.400	2B	3	3	7	1	0	.909
1966 LA	24	4	12	2	0	0	1	5	1	1	0	3	0	4	0	0	0	0	0	—	0	.167	.333	.417	2B	4	11	11	0	3	1.000
WS Totals		7	22	6	0	0	1	9	3	1	0	3	0	4	0	0	0	0	0	—	0	.273	.360	.409	2B	7	14	18	1	3	.970

JOE LEFEBVRE—Joseph Henry Lefebvre—Bats: Left; Throws: Right

Ht: 5'10"; Wt: 170 lbs; Born: 2/22/1956 in Concord, New Hampshire; Debut: 5/22/1980

LCS		Batting																							Fielding						
Year Tm	Age	G	AB	H	2B	3B	HR	TB	R	RBI	GW	TBB	IBB	SO	HBP	SH	SF	SB	CS	SB%	GDP	Avg	OBP	SLG	Pos	G	PO	A	E	DP	FPct
1980 NYA	24	1	0	0	0	0	0	0	0	0	0	0	0	0	0	0	0	0	0	—	0	—	—	—	OF	1	0	0	0	0	—
1983 Phi	27	2	2	0	0	0	0	0	0	1	0	0	0	1	0	0	1	0	0	—	0	.000	.000	.000	OF	1	2	0	0	0	1.000
LCS Totals		3	2	0	0	0	0	0	0	1	0	0	0	1	0	0	1	0	0	—	0	.000	.000	.000	OF	2	2	0	0	0	1.000
World Series		Batting																							Fielding						
Year Tm	Age	G	AB	H	2B	3B	HR	TB	R	RBI	GW	TBB	IBB	SO	HBP	SH	SF	SB	CS	SB%	GDP	Avg	OBP	SLG	Pos	G	PO	A	E	DP	FPct
1983 Phi	27	3	5	1	1	0	0	2	0	2	0	0	0	1	0	0	1	0	0	—	0	.200	.167	.400	OF	2	3	0	0	0	1.000
Postseason Totals		6	7	1	1	0	0	2	0	3	0	0	0	2	0	0	2	0	0	—	0	.143	.111	.286	OF	4	5	0	0	0	1.000

CRAIG LEFFERTS—Craig Lindsay Lefferts—Throws: Left; Bats: Left

Ht: 6'1"; Wt: 180 lbs; Born: 9/29/1957 in Munich, West Germany; Debut: 4/7/1983

LCS		Pitching																									
Year Tm	Age	G	GS	CG	GF	IP	BFP	H	R	ER	HR	SH	SF	HB	TBB	IBB	SO	WP	Bk	W	L	Pct	ShO	Sv-Op	Hld	OAvg	OOBP	ERA
1984 SD	27	3	0	0	2	4.0	15	1	0	0	0	0	0	1	1	1	1	0	0	2	0	1.000	0	0- 0	0	.077	.200	0.00
1987 SF	30	3	0	0	0	2.0	9	3	0	0	0	1	1	0	1	0	0	0	0	0	0	—	0	0- 0	0	.500	.500	0.00
1989 SF	32	2	0	0	0	1.0	6	1	1	1	0	0	0	0	2	1	1	0	0	0	0	—	0	0- 0	1	.250	.500	9.00
LCS Totals		8	0	0	2	7.0	60	5	1	1	0	1	1	1	4	2	2	0	0	2	0	1.000	0	0-0	1	.217	.345	1.29
World Series		Pitching																									
Year Tm	Age	G	GS	CG	GF	IP	BFP	H	R	ER	HR	SH	SF	HB	TBB	IBB	SO	WP	Bk	W	L	Pct	ShO	Sv-Op	Hld	OAvg	OOBP	ERA
1984 SD	27	3	0	0	1	6.0	20	2	0	0	0	0	1	0	1	0	7	0	0	0	0	—	0	1- 1	0	.111	.150	0.00
1989 SF	32	3	0	0	1	2.2	13	2	1	1	0	0	0	0	2	1	1	0	0	0	0	—	0	0- 0	0	.182	.308	3.38
WS Totals		6	0	0	2	8.2	66	4	1	1	0	0	1	0	3	1	8	0	0	0	0	—	0	1-1	0	.138	.212	1.04
Postseason Totals		14	0	0	4	15.2	126	9	2	2	0	1	2	1	7	3	10	0	0	2	0	1.000	0	1-1	1	.173	.274	1.15

LCS		Batting																							Fielding						
Year Tm	Age	G	AB	H	2B	3B	HR	TB	R	RBI	GW	TBB	IBB	SO	HBP	SH	SF	SB	CS	SB%	GDP	Avg	OBP	SLG	Pos	G	PO	A	E	DP	FPct
1984 SD	27	3	0	0	0	0	0	0	0	0	0	0	0	0	0	0	0	0	0	—	0	—	—	—	P	3	0	0	0	0	—
1987 SF	30	3	0	0	0	0	0	0	0	0	0	0	0	0	0	0	0	0	0	—	0	—	—	—	P	3	0	2	0	1	1.000
1989 SF	32	2	0	0	0	0	0	0	0	0	0	0	0	0	0	0	0	0	0	—	0	—	—	—	P	2	0	0	0	0	—
LCS Totals		8	0	0	0	0	0	0	0	0	0	0	0	0	0	0	0	0	0	—	0	—	—	—	P	8	0	2	0	1	1.000
World Series		Batting																							Fielding						
Year Tm	Age	G	AB	H	2B	3B	HR	TB	R	RBI	GW	TBB	IBB	SO	HBP	SH	SF	SB	CS	SB%	GDP	Avg	OBP	SLG	Pos	G	PO	A	E	DP	FPct
1984 SD	27	3	0	0	0	0	0	0	0	0	0	0	0	0	0	0	0	0	0	—	0	—	—	—	P	3	0	0	0	0	—
1989 SF	32	3	0	0	0	0	0	0	0	0	0	0	0	0	0	0	0	0	0	—	0	—	—	—	P	3	0	1	1	0	.500
WS Totals		6	0	0	0	0	0	0	0	0	0	0	0	0	0	0	0	0	0	—	0	—	—	—	P	6	0	1	1	0	.500
Postseason Totals		14	0	0	0	0	0	0	0	0	0	0	0	0	0	0	0	0	0	—	0	—	—	—	P	14	0	3	1	1	.750

KEN LEHMAN—Kenneth Karl Lehman—Throws: Left; Bats: Left

Ht: 6'0"; Wt: 170 lbs; Born: 6/10/1928 in Seattle, Washington; Debut: 9/5/1952

World Series		Pitching																									
Year Tm	Age	G	GS	CG	GF	IP	BFP	H	R	ER	HR	SH	SF	HB	TBB	IBB	SO	WP	Bk	W	L	Pct	ShO	Sv-Op	Hld	OAvg	OOBP	ERA
1952 Bro	24	1	0	0	1	2.0	9	2	0	0	0	0	0	0	1	0	0	0	0	0	0	—	0	0- 0	0	.250	.333	0.00

World Series		Batting																							Fielding						
Year Tm	Age	G	AB	H	2B	3B	HR	TB	R	RBI	GW	TBB	IBB	SO	HBP	SH	SF	SB	CS	SB%	GDP	Avg	OBP	SLG	Pos	G	PO	A	E	DP	FPct
1952 Bro	24	1	0	0	0	0	0	0	0	0	0	0	0	0	0	0	0	0	0	—	0	—	—	—	P	1	0	1	0	0	1.000

HANK LEIBER—Henry Edward Leiber—Nickname: Goldilocks—Bats: Right; Throws: Right

Ht: 6'1"; Wt: 205 lbs; Born: 1/17/1911 in Phoenix, Arizona; Debut: 4/16/1933; Died: 11/8/1993

World Series		Batting																							Fielding						
Year Tm	Age	G	AB	H	2B	3B	HR	TB	R	RBI	GW	TBB	IBB	SO	HBP	SH	SF	SB	CS	SB%	GDP	Avg	OBP	SLG	Pos	G	PO	A	E	DP	FPct
1936 NYG	25	2	6	0	0	0	0	0	0	0	0	2	0	2	0	1	0	0	0	—	0	.000	.250	.000	OF	2	11	1	0	1	1.000
1937 NYG	26	3	11	4	0	0	0	4	2	2	0	1	0	1	0	0	0	0	0	—	0	.364	.417	.364	OF	3	7	0	0	0	1.000
WS Totals		5	17	4	0	0	0	4	2	2	0	3	0	3	0	1	0	0	0	—	0	.235	.350	.235	OF	5	18	1	0	1	1.000

NEMO LEIBOLD—Harry Loran Leibold—Bats: Left; Throws: Right

Ht: 5'7"; Wt: 157 lbs; Born: 2/17/1892 in Butler, Indiana; Debut: 4/12/1913; Died: 2/4/1977

World Series		Batting																							Fielding						
Year Tm	Age	G	AB	H	2B	3B	HR	TB	R	RBI	GW	TBB	IBB	SO	HBP	SH	SF	SB	CS	SB%	GDP	Avg	OBP	SLG	Pos	G	PO	A	E	DP	FPct
1917 ChA	25	2	5	2	0	0	0	2	1	2	1	1	0	1	0	0	0	0	1	.00	0	.400	.500	.400	OF	2	1	0	0	0	1.000
1919 ChA	27	5	18	1	0	0	0	1	0	0	0	2	0	3	0	0	0	1	0	1.00	0	.056	.150	.056	OF	5	5	2	0	0	1.000
1924 Was	32	3	6	1	1	0	0	2	1	0	0	1	0	0	0	0	0	0	0	—	0	.167	.286	.333	OF	1	2	0	0	0	1.000
1925 Was	33	3	2	1	1	0	0	2	1	0	0	1	0	0	0	0	0	0	0	—	0	.500	.667	1.000	—						
WS Totals		13	31	5	2	0	0	7	3	2	1	5	0	4	0	0	0	1	1	.50	0	.161	.278	.226	OF	8	8	2	0	0	1.000

CHARLIE LEIBRANDT—Charles Louis Leibrandt—Throws: Left; Bats: Right

Ht: 6'3"; Wt: 195 lbs; Born: 10/4/1956 in Chicago, Illinois; Debut: 9/17/1979

LCS		Pitching																									
Year Tm	Age	G	GS	CG	GF	IP	BFP	H	R	ER	HR	SH	SF	HB	TBB	IBB	SO	WP	Bk	W	L	Pct	ShO	Sv-Op	Hld	OAvg	OOBP	ERA
1979 Cin	22	1	0	0	0	0.1	1	0	0	0	0	0	0	0	0	0	0	0	1	0	0	—	0	0- 0	0	.000	.000	0.00
1984 KC	27	1	1	1	0	8.0	30	3	1	1	0	0	0	0	4	0	6	0	0	0	1	.000	0	0- 0	0	.115	.233	1.13
1985 KC	28	3	2	0	0	15.1	66	17	9	9	0	0	0	1	4	0	6	0	0	1	2	.333	0	0- 0	0	.279	.333	5.28
1991 Atl	34	1	1	0	0	6.2	30	8	2	1	0	0	0	0	3	0	6	0	0	0	0	—	0	0- 0	0	.296	.367	1.35
1992 Atl	35	2	0	0	0	4.2	20	4	1	1	0	0	0	0	3	0	3	0	0	0	0	—	0	0- 0	0	.235	.350	1.93
LCS Totals		8	4	1	0	35.0	294	32	13	12	0	0	0	1	14	0	21	0	1	1	3	.250	0	0-0	0	.242	.320	3.09

World Series		Pitching																										
Year Tm	Age	G	GS	CG	GF	IP	BFP	H	R	ER	HR	SH	SF	HB	TBB	IBB	SO	WP	Bk	W	L	Pct	ShO	Sv-Op	Hld	OAvg	OOBP	ERA
1985 KC	28	2	2	0	0	16.1	62	10	5	5	0	0	0	0	4	1	10	0	0	0	1	.000	0	0-0	0	.172	.226	2.76
1991 Atl	34	2	1	0	1	4.0	19	8	5	5	2	0	0	0	1	0	3	0	0	0	2	.000	0	0-0	0	.444	.474	11.25
1992 Atl	35	1	0	0	1	2.0	10	3	2	2	0	0	0	1	0	0	0	0	0	0	1	.000	0	0-0	0	.333	.400	9.00
WS Totals		5	3	0	2	22.1	182	21	12	12	2	0	0	1	5	1	13	0	0	0	4	.000	0	0-0	0	.247	.297	4.84
Postseason Totals		13	7	1	2	57.1	476	53	25	24	2	0	0	2	19	1	34	0	1	1	7	.125	0	0-0	0	.244	.311	3.77

LCS		Batting																							Fielding						
Year Tm	Age	G	AB	H	2B	3B	HR	TB	R	RBI	GW	TBB	IBB	SO	HBP	SH	SF	SB	CS	SB%	GDP	Avg	OBP	SLG	Pos	G	PO	A	E	DP	FPct
1979 Cin	22	1	0	0	0	0	0	0	0	0	0	0	0	0	0	0	0	0	0	—	0	—	—	—	P	1	0	0	0	0	—
1984 KC	27	1	0	0	0	0	0	0	0	0	0	0	0	0	0	0	0	0	0	—	0	—	—	—	P	1	1	2	0	0	1.000
1985 KC	28	3	0	0	0	0	0	0	0	0	0	0	0	0	0	0	0	0	0	—	0	—	—	—	P	3	3	8	0	0	1.000
1991 Atl	34	1	1	0	0	0	0	0	0	0	0	0	0	0	0	1	0	0	0	—	0	.000	.000	.000	P	1	0	1	0	0	1.000
1992 Atl	35	2	1	0	0	0	0	0	0	0	0	0	0	1	0	0	0	0	0	—	0	.000	.000	.000	P	2	0	1	0	0	1.000
LCS Totals		8	2	0	0	0	0	0	0	0	0	0	0	1	0	1	0	0	0	—	0	.000	.000	.000	P	8	4	12	0	0	1.000
World Series		**Batting**																							**Fielding**						
Year Tm	Age	G	AB	H	2B	3B	HR	TB	R	RBI	GW	TBB	IBB	SO	HBP	SH	SF	SB	CS	SB%	GDP	Avg	OBP	SLG	Pos	G	PO	A	E	DP	FPct
1985 KC	28	2	4	0	0	0	0	0	0	0	0	0	0	2	0	2	0	0	0	—	1	.000	.000	.000	P	2	1	2	0	0	1.000
1991 Atl	34	2	0	0	0	0	0	0	0	0	0	0	0	0	0	0	0	0	0	—	0	—	—	—	P	2	0	1	0	0	1.000
1992 Atl	35	1	0	0	0	0	0	0	0	0	0	0	0	0	0	0	0	0	0	—	0	—	—	—	P	1	1	0	0	0	1.000
WS Totals		5	4	0	0	0	0	0	0	0	0	0	0	2	0	2	0	0	0	—	1	.000	.000	.000	P	5	2	3	0	0	1.000
Postseason Totals		13	6	0	0	0	0	0	0	0	0	0	0	3	0	3	0	0	0	—	1	.000	.000	.000	P	13	6	15	0	0	1.000

LEFTY LEIFIELD—Albert Peter Leifield—Throws: Left; Bats: Left

Ht: 6'1"; Wt: 165 lbs; Born: 9/5/1883 in Trenton, Illinois; Debut: 9/3/1905; Died: 10/10/1970

World Series		Pitching																										
Year Tm	Age	G	GS	CG	GF	IP	BFP	H	R	ER	HR	SH	SF	HB	TBB	IBB	SO	WP	Bk	W	L	Pct	ShO	Sv-Op	Hld	OAvg	OOBP	ERA
1909 Pit	26	1	1	0	0	4.0	22	7	5	5	0	0	0	2	1	0	0	0	0	0	1	.000	0	0-0	0	.368	.455	11.25

World Series		Batting																							Fielding						
Year Tm	Age	G	AB	H	2B	3B	HR	TB	R	RBI	GW	TBB	IBB	SO	HBP	SH	SF	SB	CS	SB%	GDP	Avg	OBP	SLG	Pos	G	PO	A	E	DP	FPct
1909 Pit	26	1	1	0	0	0	0	0	0	0	0	0	0	1	0	0	0	0	0	—	0	.000	.000	.000	P	1	0	5	0	0	1.000

AL LEITER—Alois Terry Leiter—Throws: Left; Bats: Left

Ht: 6'2"; Wt: 200 lbs; Born: 10/23/1965 in Toms River, New Jersey; Debut: 9/15/1987

Division Series		Pitching																										
Year Tm	Age	G	GS	CG	GF	IP	BFP	H	R	ER	HR	SH	SF	HB	TBB	IBB	SO	WP	Bk	W	L	Pct	ShO	Sv-Op	Hld	OAvg	OOBP	ERA
1997 Fla	31	1	1	0	0	4.0	20	7	4	4	1	2	1	0	3	0	3	1	0	0	0	—	0	0-0	0	.500	.556	9.00
LCS		**Pitching**																										
Year Tm	Age	G	GS	CG	GF	IP	BFP	H	R	ER	HR	SH	SF	HB	TBB	IBB	SO	WP	Bk	W	L	Pct	ShO	Sv-Op	Hld	OAvg	OOBP	ERA
1993 Tor	27	2	0	0	0	2.2	13	4	1	1	0	0	0	0	2	1	2	0	0	0	0	—	0	0-0	1	.364	.462	3.38
1997 Fla	31	2	1	0	0	8.1	38	13	4	4	1	2	0	0	2	0	6	0	0	0	1	.000	0	0-0	0	.382	.417	4.32
LCS Totals		4	1	0	0	11.0	102	17	5	5	1	2	0	0	4	1	8	0	0	0	1	.000	0	0-0	1	.378	.429	4.09
World Series		**Pitching**																										
Year Tm	Age	G	GS	CG	GF	IP	BFP	H	R	ER	HR	SH	SF	HB	TBB	IBB	SO	WP	Bk	W	L	Pct	ShO	Sv-Op	Hld	OAvg	OOBP	ERA
1993 Tor	27	3	0	0	0	7.0	35	12	6	6	2	0	1	0	2	0	5	0	0	1	0	1.000	0	0-0	0	.375	.400	7.71
1997 Fla	31	2	2	0	0	10.2	52	10	9	6	1	1	0	0	10	1	10	0	0	0	0	—	0	0-0	0	.244	.392	5.06
WS Totals		5	2	0	0	17.2	174	22	15	12	3	1	1	0	12	1	15	0	0	1	0	1.000	0	0-0	0	.301	.395	6.11
Postseason Totals		10	4	0	0	32.2	316	46	24	21	5	5	2	0	19	2	26	1	0	1	1	.500	0	0-0	1	.348	.425	5.79

Division Series		Batting																							Fielding						
Year Tm	Age	G	AB	H	2B	3B	HR	TB	R	RBI	GW	TBB	IBB	SO	HBP	SH	SF	SB	CS	SB%	GDP	Avg	OBP	SLG	Pos	G	PO	A	E	DP	FPct
1997 Fla	31	1	1	0	0	0	0	0	0	0	0	0	0	0	0	0	0	0	0	—	0	.000	.000	.000	P	1	0	1	0	0	1.000
LCS		**Batting**																							**Fielding**						
Year Tm	Age	G	AB	H	2B	3B	HR	TB	R	RBI	GW	TBB	IBB	SO	HBP	SH	SF	SB	CS	SB%	GDP	Avg	OBP	SLG	Pos	G	PO	A	E	DP	FPct
1993 Tor	27	2	0	0	0	0	0	0	0	0	0	0	0	0	0	0	0	0	0	—	0	—	—	—	P	2	0	0	0	0	—
1997 Fla	31	2	1	0	0	0	0	0	0	0	0	0	0	1	0	0	0	0	0	—	0	.000	.000	.000	P	2	1	3	0	1	1.000
LCS Totals		4	1	0	0	0	0	0	0	0	0	0	0	1	0	0	0	0	0	—	0	.000	.000	.000	P	4	1	3	0	1	1.000
World Series		**Batting**																							**Fielding**						
Year Tm	Age	G	AB	H	2B	3B	HR	TB	R	RBI	GW	TBB	IBB	SO	HBP	SH	SF	SB	CS	SB%	GDP	Avg	OBP	SLG	Pos	G	PO	A	E	DP	FPct
1993 Tor	27	3	1	1	1	0	0	2	0	0	0	0	0	0	0	0	0	0	0	—	0	1.000	1.000	2.000	P	3	0	0	0	0	—
1997 Fla	31	2	0	0	0	0	0	0	0	0	0	2	0	0	0	0	0	0	0	—	0	—	1.000	—	P	2	1	0	1	0	.500
WS Totals		5	1	1	1	0	0	2	0	0	0	2	0	0	0	0	0	0	0	—	0	1.000	1.000	2.000	P	5	1	0	1	0	.500
Postseason Totals		10	3	1	1	0	0	2	0	0	0	2	0	1	0	0	0	0	0	—	0	.333	.600	.667	P	10	2	4	1	1	.857

SCOTT LEIUS—Scott Thomas Leius—Bats: Right; Throws: Right

Ht: 6'3"; Wt: 180 lbs; Born: 9/24/1965 in Yonkers, New York; Debut: 9/3/1990

LCS		Batting																							Fielding						
Year Tm	Age	G	AB	H	2B	3B	HR	TB	R	RBI	GW	TBB	IBB	SO	HBP	SH	SF	SB	CS	SB%	GDP	Avg	OBP	SLG	Pos	G	PO	A	E	DP	FPct
1991 Min	26	3	4	0	0	0	0	0	0	0	0	1	0	1	0	0	0	0	0	—	0	.000	.200	.000	3B	3	1	4	0	1	1.000
World Series		**Batting**																							**Fielding**						
Year Tm	Age	G	AB	H	2B	3B	HR	TB	R	RBI	GW	TBB	IBB	SO	HBP	SH	SF	SB	CS	SB%	GDP	Avg	OBP	SLG	Pos	G	PO	A	E	DP	FPct
1991 Min	26	7	14	5	0	0	1	8	2	2	1	1	0	2	0	0	0	0	1	.00	1	.357	.400	.571	3B	6	5	7	1	0	.923
																									SS	1	0	1	0	0	1.000
Postseason Totals		10	18	5	0	0	1	8	2	2	1	2	0	3	0	0	0	0	1	.00	1	.278	.350	.444	3B	9	6	11	1	1	.944

DON LeJOHN—Donald Everett LeJohn—Bats: Right; Throws: Right

Ht: 5'10"; Wt: 175 lbs; Born: 5/13/1934 in Daisytown, Pennsylvania; Debut: 6/30/1965

World Series		Batting																							Fielding						
Year Tm	Age	G	AB	H	2B	3B	HR	TB	R	RBI	GW	TBB	IBB	SO	HBP	SH	SF	SB	CS	SB%	GDP	Avg	OBP	SLG	Pos	G	PO	A	E	DP	FPct
1965 LA	31	1	1	0	0	0	0	0	0	0	0	0	0	1	0	0	0	0	0	—	0	.000	.000	.000	—						

MARK LEMKE—Mark Alan Lemke—Bats: Both; Throws: Right

Ht: 5'10"; Wt: 167 lbs; Born: 8/13/1965 in Utica, New York; Debut: 9/17/1988

Division Series		Batting																							Fielding						
Year Tm	Age	G	AB	H	2B	3B	HR	TB	R	RBI	GW	TBB	IBB	SO	HBP	SH	SF	SB	CS	SB%	GDP	Avg	OBP	SLG	Pos	G	PO	A	E	DP	FPct
1995 Atl	30	4	19	4	1	0	0	5	3	1	0	1	0	3	0	0	0	0	0	—	0	.211	.250	.263	2B	4	8	16	0	3	1.000
1996 Atl	31	3	12	2	1	0	0	3	1	2	0	0	0	1	0	0	0	0	0	—	1	.167	.167	.250	2B	3	4	8	0	1	1.000
DS Totals		7	31	6	2	0	0	8	4	3	0	1	0	4	0	0	0	0	0	—	1	.194	.219	.258	2B	7	12	24	0	4	1.000
LCS		**Batting**																							**Fielding**						
Year Tm	Age	G	AB	H	2B	3B	HR	TB	R	RBI	GW	TBB	IBB	SO	HBP	SH	SF	SB	CS	SB%	GDP	Avg	OBP	SLG	Pos	G	PO	A	E	DP	FPct
1991 Atl	26	7	20	4	1	0	0	5	1	1	1	4	1	0	0	0	0	0	0	—	0	.200	.333	.250	2B	7	12	10	1	2	.957
1992 Atl	27	7	21	7	1	0	0	8	2	2	1	5	1	3	0	0	0	0	0	—	0	.333	.462	.381	2B	7	11	16	0	3	1.000
																									3B	1	0	0	0	0	—
1993 Atl	28	6	24	5	2	0	0	7	2	4	0	1	0	6	0	0	0	0	0	—	0	.208	.240	.292	2B	6	6	19	2	1	.926
1995 Atl	30	4	18	3	0	0	0	3	2	1	1	1	0	0	0	0	0	0	0	—	1	.167	.211	.167	2B	4	13	16	0	5	1.000
1996 Atl	31	7	27	12	2	0	1	17	4	5	0	4	0	2	0	0	0	0	0	—	0	.444	.516	.630	2B	7	9	18	0	3	1.000
LCS Totals		31	110	31	6	0	1	40	11	13	3	15	2	11	0	0	0	0	0	—	1	.282	.368	.364	2B	31	51	79	3	14	.977
World Series		**Batting**																							**Fielding**						
Year Tm	Age	G	AB	H	2B	3B	HR	TB	R	RBI	GW	TBB	IBB	SO	HBP	SH	SF	SB	CS	SB%	GDP	Avg	OBP	SLG	Pos	G	PO	A	E	DP	FPct
1991 Atl	26	6	24	10	1	3	0	17	4	4	1	2	0	4	0	0	0	0	0	—	1	.417	.462	.708	2B	6	14	19	1	4	.971
1992 Atl	27	6	19	4	0	0	0	4	0	2	0	1	0	3	0	0	0	0	0	—	1	.211	.250	.211	2B	6	19	12	0	5	1.000
1995 Atl	30	6	22	6	0	0	0	6	1	0	0	3	0	2	0	1	0	0	1	.00	0	.273	.360	.273	2B	6	10	24	1	2	.971
1996 Atl	31	6	26	6	1	0	0	7	2	2	0	0	0	3	0	2	0	0	0	—	1	.231	.231	.269	2B	6	11	24	0	3	1.000
WS Totals		24	91	26	2	3	0	34	7	8	1	6	0	12	0	3	0	0	1	.00	3	.286	.330	.374	2B	24	54	79	2	14	.985
Postseason Totals		62	232	63	10	3	1	82	22	24	4	22	2	27	0	3	0	0	1	.00	5	.272	.335	.353	2B	62	117	182	5	32	.984

BOB LEMON (HOF 1976-W)—Robert Granville Lemon—Throws: Right; Bats: Left

Ht: 6'0"; Wt: 180 lbs; Born: 9/22/1920 in San Bernardino, California; Debut: 9/9/1941

World Series			Pitching																							
Year	Tm	Age	G	GS	CG	GF	IP	BFP	H	R	ER	HR	SH	SF	HB	TBB	IBB	SO	WP	Bk	W	L	Pct	ShO	Sv-Op	Hld	OAvg	OOBP	ERA
1948	Cle	28	2	2	1	0	16.1	67	16	4	3	0	2	0	0	7	0	6	0	1	2	0	1.000	0	0-0	0	.276	.354	1.65
1954	Cle	34	2	2	1	0	13.1	64	16	11	10	1	1	1	0	8	2	11	1	0	0	2	.000	0	0-0	0	.296	.381	6.75
WS Totals			4	4	2	0	29.2	262	32	15	13	1	3	1	0	15	2	17	1	1	2	2	.500	0	0-0	0	.286	.367	3.94

World Series			Batting																					Fielding						
Year	Tm	Age	G	AB	H	2B	3B	HR	TB	R	RBI	GW	TBB	IBB	SO	HBP	SH	SF	SB	CS	SB%	GDP	Avg	OBP	SLG	Pos	G	PO	A	E	DP	FPct
1948	Cle	28	2	7	0	0	0	0	0	0	0	0	0	0	0	0	0	0	0	0	—	0	.000	.000	.000	P	2	3	9	0	1	1.000
1954	Cle	34	3	6	0	0	0	0	0	0	0	0	1	0	1	0	0	0	0	0	—	0	.000	.143	.000	P	2	2	2	0	0	1.000
WS Totals			5	13	0	0	0	0	0	0	0	0	1	0	1	0	0	0	0	0	—	0	.000	.071	.000	P	4	5	11	0	1	1.000

CHET LEMON—Chester Earl Lemon—Bats: Right; Throws: Right

Ht: 6'0"; Wt: 190 lbs; Born: 2/12/1955 in Jackson, Mississippi; Debut: 9/9/1975

LCS			Batting																					Fielding						
Year	Tm	Age	G	AB	H	2B	3B	HR	TB	R	RBI	GW	TBB	IBB	SO	HBP	SH	SF	SB	CS	SB%	GDP	Avg	OBP	SLG	Pos	G	PO	A	E	DP	FPct
1984	Det	29	3	13	0	0	0	0	0	1	0	0	0	0	1	0	0	0	0	0	—	1	.000	.000	.000	OF	3	9	0	0	0	1.000
1987	Det	32	5	18	5	0	0	2	11	4	4	0	1	0	4	0	0	1	0	0	—	0	.278	.300	.611	OF	5	13	0	0	0	1.000
LCS Totals			8	31	5	0	0	2	11	5	4	0	1	0	5	0	0	1	0	0	—	1	.161	.182	.355	OF	8	22	0	0	0	1.000
World Series			Batting																					Fielding						
Year	Tm	Age	G	AB	H	2B	3B	HR	TB	R	RBI	GW	TBB	IBB	SO	HBP	SH	SF	SB	CS	SB%	GDP	Avg	OBP	SLG	Pos	G	PO	A	E	DP	FPct
1984	Det	29	5	17	5	0	0	0	5	1	1	0	2	0	2	0	0	0	2	1	.67	1	.294	.368	.294	OF	5	15	0	0	0	1.000
Postseason Totals			13	48	10	0	0	2	16	6	5	0	3	0	7	0	0	1	2	1	.67	2	.208	.250	.333	OF	13	37	0	0	0	1.000

DENNIS LEONARD—Dennis Patrick Leonard—Throws: Right; Bats: Right

Ht: 6'1"; Wt: 190 lbs; Born: 5/18/1951 in Brooklyn, New York; Debut: 9/4/1974

Division Series			Pitching																							
Year	Tm	Age	G	GS	CG	GF	IP	BFP	H	R	ER	HR	SH	SF	HB	TBB	IBB	SO	WP	Bk	W	L	Pct	ShO	Sv-Op	Hld	OAvg	OOBP	ERA
1981	KC	30	1	1	0	0	8.0	32	7	4	1	2	0	0	0	1	0	3	0	0	0	1	.000	0	0-0	0	.226	.250	1.13
LCS			Pitching																							
Year	Tm	Age	G	GS	CG	GF	IP	BFP	H	R	ER	HR	SH	SF	HB	TBB	IBB	SO	WP	Bk	W	L	Pct	ShO	Sv-Op	Hld	OAvg	OOBP	ERA
1976	KC	25	2	2	0	0	2.1	16	9	5	5	0	0	0	0	2	0	0	0	0	0	0	—	0	0-0	0	.643	.688	19.29
1977	KC	26	2	1	1	0	9.0	34	5	4	3	0	0	0	0	2	0	4	0	0	1	1	.500	0	0-0	0	.156	.206	3.00
1978	KC	27	2	2	1	0	12.0	51	13	5	5	2	0	0	0	2	0	11	1	0	0	2	.000	0	0-0	0	.265	.294	3.75
1980	KC	29	1	1	0	0	8.0	31	7	2	2	1	0	0	0	1	0	8	0	0	1	0	1.000	0	0-0	0	.233	.258	2.25
LCS Totals			7	6	2	0	31.1	264	34	16	15	3	0	0	0	7	0	23	1	0	2	3	.400	0	0-0	0	.272	.311	4.31
World Series			Pitching																							
Year	Tm	Age	G	GS	CG	GF	IP	BFP	H	R	ER	HR	SH	SF	HB	TBB	IBB	SO	WP	Bk	W	L	Pct	ShO	Sv-Op	Hld	OAvg	OOBP	ERA
1980	KC	29	2	2	0	0	10.2	47	15	9	8	1	0	1	1	2	0	5	1	0	1	1	.500	0	0-0	0	.349	.383	6.75
Postseason Totals			10	9	2	0	50.0	422	56	29	24	6	0	1	1	10	0	31	2	0	3	5	.375	0	0-0	0	.281	.318	4.32

Division Series			Batting																					Fielding						
Year	Tm	Age	G	AB	H	2B	3B	HR	TB	R	RBI	GW	TBB	IBB	SO	HBP	SH	SF	SB	CS	SB%	GDP	Avg	OBP	SLG	Pos	G	PO	A	E	DP	FPct
1981	KC	30	1	0	0	0	0	0	0	0	0	0	0	0	0	0	0	0	0	0	—	0	—	—	—	P	1	0	1	0	0	1.000
LCS			Batting																					Fielding						
Year	Tm	Age	G	AB	H	2B	3B	HR	TB	R	RBI	GW	TBB	IBB	SO	HBP	SH	SF	SB	CS	SB%	GDP	Avg	OBP	SLG	Pos	G	PO	A	E	DP	FPct
1976	KC	25	2	0	0	0	0	0	0	0	0	0	0	0	0	0	0	0	0	0	—	0	—	—	—	P	2	0	0	0	0	—
1977	KC	26	2	0	0	0	0	0	0	0	0	0	0	0	0	0	0	0	0	0	—	0	—	—	—	P	2	0	0	0	0	—
1978	KC	27	2	0	0	0	0	0	0	0	0	0	0	0	0	0	0	0	0	0	—	0	—	—	—	P	2	1	0	0	0	1.000
1980	KC	29	1	0	0	0	0	0	0	0	0	0	0	0	0	0	0	0	0	0	—	0	—	—	—	P	1	0	0	0	0	—
LCS Totals			7	0	0	0	0	0	0	0	0	0	0	0	0	0	0	0	0	0	—	0	—	—	—	P	7	1	0	0	0	1.000
World Series			Batting																					Fielding						
Year	Tm	Age	G	AB	H	2B	3B	HR	TB	R	RBI	GW	TBB	IBB	SO	HBP	SH	SF	SB	CS	SB%	GDP	Avg	OBP	SLG	Pos	G	PO	A	E	DP	FPct
1980	KC	29	2	0	0	0	0	0	0	0	0	0	0	0	0	0	0	0	0	0	—	0	—	—	—	P	2	0	0	1	0	.000
Postseason Totals			10	0	0	0	0	0	0	0	0	0	0	0	0	0	0	0	0	0	—	0	—	—	—	P	10	1	1	1	0	.667

DUTCH LEONARD—Hubert Benjamin Leonard—Throws: Left; Bats: Left

Ht: 5'10"; Wt: 185 lbs; Born: 4/16/1892 in Birmingham, Ohio; Debut: 4/12/1913; Died: 7/11/1952

World Series			Pitching																							
Year	Tm	Age	G	GS	CG	GF	IP	BFP	H	R	ER	HR	SH	SF	HB	TBB	IBB	SO	WP	Bk	W	L	Pct	ShO	Sv-Op	Hld	OAvg	OOBP	ERA
1915	Bos	23	1	1	1	0	9.0	31	3	1	1	0	3	0	0	0	0	6	0	0	1	0	1.000	0	0-0	0	.107	.107	1.00
1916	Bos	24	1	1	1	0	9.0	36	5	2	1	0	0	0	0	4	0	3	1	0	1	0	1.000	0	0-0	0	.156	.250	1.00
WS Totals			2	2	2	0	18.0	134	8	3	2	0	3	0	0	4	0	9	1	0	2	0	1.000	0	0-0	0	.133	.188	1.00

World Series			Batting																					Fielding						
Year	Tm	Age	G	AB	H	2B	3B	HR	TB	R	RBI	GW	TBB	IBB	SO	HBP	SH	SF	SB	CS	SB%	GDP	Avg	OBP	SLG	Pos	G	PO	A	E	DP	FPct
1915	Bos	23	1	3	0	0	0	0	0	0	0	0	0	0	2	0	0	0	0	0	—	0	.000	.000	.000	P	1	0	2	0	0	1.000
1916	Bos	24	1	3	0	0	0	0	0	0	0	0	1	0	3	0	0	0	0	0	—	0	.000	.250	.000	P	1	0	1	0	0	1.000
WS Totals			2	6	0	0	0	0	0	0	0	0	1	0	5	0	0	0	0	0	—	0	.000	.143	.000	P	2	0	3	0	0	1.000

JEFFREY LEONARD—Nicknames: Hac Man, Penitentiary Face—Bats: Right; Throws: Right

Ht: 6'2"; Wt: 200 lbs; Born: 9/22/1955 in Philadelphia, Pennsylvania; Debut: 9/2/1977

LCS			Batting																					Fielding						
Year	Tm	Age	G	AB	H	2B	3B	HR	TB	R	RBI	GW	TBB	IBB	SO	HBP	SH	SF	SB	CS	SB%	GDP	Avg	OBP	SLG	Pos	G	PO	A	E	DP	FPct
1980	Hou	25	3	3	0	0	0	0	0	0	0	0	0	0	2	0	0	0	0	0	—	0	.000	.000	.000	OF	1	2	1	0	1	1.000
1987	SF	32	7	24	10	0	0	4	22	5	5	1	3	0	4	1	0	0	0	0	—	0	.417	.500	.917	OF	7	14	1	0	0	1.000
LCS Totals			10	27	10	0	0	4	22	5	5	1	3	0	6	1	0	0	0	0	—	0	.370	.452	.815	OF	8	16	2	0	1	1.000

DAVE LEONHARD—David Paul Leonhard—Throws: Right; Bats: Right

Ht: 5'11"; Wt: 165 lbs; Born: 1/22/1941 in Arlington, Virginia; Debut: 9/21/1967

World Series			Pitching																							
Year	Tm	Age	G	GS	CG	GF	IP	BFP	H	R	ER	HR	SH	SF	HB	TBB	IBB	SO	WP	Bk	W	L	Pct	ShO	Sv-Op	Hld	OAvg	OOBP	ERA
1969	Bal	28	1	0	0	1	2.0	8	1	1	1	1	1	0	0	1	0	1	0	0	0	0	—	0	0-0	0	.167	.286	4.50
1971	Bal	30	1	0	0	0	1.0	4	0	0	0	0	0	0	0	1	0	0	0	0	0	0	—	0	0-0	0	.000	.250	0.00
WS Totals			2	0	0	1	3.0	24	1	1	1	1	1	0	0	2	0	1	0	0	0	0	—	0	0-0	0	.111	.273	3.00

World Series			Batting																					Fielding						
Year	Tm	Age	G	AB	H	2B	3B	HR	TB	R	RBI	GW	TBB	IBB	SO	HBP	SH	SF	SB	CS	SB%	GDP	Avg	OBP	SLG	Pos	G	PO	A	E	DP	FPct
1969	Bal	28	1	0	0	0	0	0	0	0	0	0	0	0	0	0	0	0	0	0	—	0	—	—	—	P	1	0	1	0	0	1.000
1971	Bal	30	1	0	0	0	0	0	0	0	0	0	0	0	0	0	0	0	0	0	—	0	—	—	—	P	1	0	0	0	0	—
WS Totals			2	0	0	0	0	0	0	0	0	0	0	0	0	0	0	0	0	0	—	0	—	—	—	P	2	0	1	0	0	1.000

RANDY LERCH—Randy Louis Lerch—Throws: Left; Bats: Left

Ht: 6'5"; Wt: 190 lbs; Born: 10/9/1954 in Sacramento, California; Debut: 9/14/1975

Division Series			Pitching																							
Year	Tm	Age	G	GS	CG	GF	IP	BFP	H	R	ER	HR	SH	SF	HB	TBB	IBB	SO	WP	Bk	W	L	Pct	ShO	Sv-Op	Hld	OAvg	OOBP	ERA
1981	Mil	26	1	1	0	0	6.0	23	3	1	1	0	0	0	0	4	0	3	0	0	0	0	—	0	0-0	0	.158	.304	1.50
LCS			Pitching																							
Year	Tm	Age	G	GS	CG	GF	IP	BFP	H	R	ER	HR	SH	SF	HB	TBB	IBB	SO	WP	Bk	W	L	Pct	ShO	Sv-Op	Hld	OAvg	OOBP	ERA
1978	Phi	23	1	1	0	0	5.1	22	7	3	3	2	1	0	0	0	0	0	0	0	0	0	—	0	0-0	0	.333	.333	5.06
Postseason Totals			2	2	0	0	11.1	90	10	4	4	2	1	0	0	4	0	3	0	0	0	0	—	0	0-0	0	.250	.318	3.18

Division Series			Batting																					Fielding						
Year	Tm	Age	G	AB	H	2B	3B	HR	TB	R	RBI	GW	TBB	IBB	SO	HBP	SH	SF	SB	CS	SB%	GDP	Avg	OBP	SLG	Pos	G	PO	A	E	DP	FPct
1981	Mil	26	1	0	0	0	0	0	0	0	0	0	0	0	0	0	0	0	0	0	—	0	—	—	—	P	1	0	1	0	1	1.000
LCS			Batting																					Fielding						
Year	Tm	Age	G	AB	H	2B	3B	HR	TB	R	RBI	GW	TBB	IBB	SO	HBP	SH	SF	SB	CS	SB%	GDP	Avg	OBP	SLG	Pos	G	PO	A	E	DP	FPct
1978	Phi	23	1	2	0	0	0	0	0	0	0	0	0	0	0	0	0	0	0	0	—	0	.000	.000	.000	P	1	0	1	0	0	1.000
Postseason Totals			2	2	0	0	0	0	0	0	0	0	0	0	0	0	0	0	0	0	—	0	.000	.000	.000	P	2	0	2	0	1	1.000

CURT LESKANIC—Curtis John Leskanic—Throws: Right; Bats: Right

Ht: 6'0"; Wt: 180 lbs; Born: 4/2/1968 in Homestead, Pennsylvania; Debut: 6/27/1993

Division Series — Pitching

Year Tm	Age	G	GS	CG	GF	IP	BFP	H	R	ER	HR	SH	SF	HB	TBB	IBB	SO	WP	Bk	W	L	Pct	ShO	Sv-Op	Hld	OAvg	OOBP	ERA
1995 Col	27	3	0	0	1	3.0	12	3	2	2	1	0	0	0	0	0	4	0	0	0	1	.000	0	0- 0	1	.250	.250	6.00

Division Series — Batting / Fielding

Year Tm	Age	G	AB	H	2B	3B	HR	TB	R	RBI	GW	TBB	IBB	SO	HBP	SH	SF	SB	CS	SB%	GDP	Avg	OBP	SLG	Pos	G	PO	A	E	DP	FPct
1995 Col	27	3	0	0	0	0	0	0	0	0	0	0	0	0	0	0	0	0	0	—	0	—	—	—	P	3	0	0	0	0	—

SAM LESLIE—Samuel Andrew Leslie—Nickname: Sambo—Bats: Left; Throws: Left

Ht: 6'0"; Wt: 192 lbs; Born: 7/26/1905 in Moss Point, Mississippi; Debut: 10/6/1929; Died: 1/21/1979

World Series — Batting / Fielding

Year Tm	Age	G	AB	H	2B	3B	HR	TB	R	RBI	GW	TBB	IBB	SO	HBP	SH	SF	SB	CS	SB%	GDP	Avg	OBP	SLG	Pos	G	PO	A	E	DP	FPct
1936 NYG	31	3	3	2	0	0	0	2	0	0	0	0	0	0	0	0	0	0	0	—	0	.667	.667	.667	—						
1937 NYG	32	2	1	0	0	0	0	0	0	0	0	1	0	0	0	0	0	0	0	—	0	.000	.500	.000	—						
WS Totals		5	4	2	0	0	0	2	0	0	0	1	0	0	0	0	0	0	0	—	0	.500	.600	.500	—	0	0	0	0	0	—

ALLAN LEWIS—Allan Sydney Lewis—Nickname: The Panamanian Express—Bats: Both; Throws: Right

Ht: 6'0"; Wt: 170 lbs; Born: 12/12/1941 in Colon, Panama; Debut: 4/11/1967

LCS — Batting / Fielding

Year Tm	Age	G	AB	H	2B	3B	HR	TB	R	RBI	GW	TBB	IBB	SO	HBP	SH	SF	SB	CS	SB%	GDP	Avg	OBP	SLG	Pos	G	PO	A	E	DP	FPct
1973 Oak	31	2	0	0	0	0	0	0	1	0	0	0	0	0	0	0	0	0	0	—	0	—	—	—	—						

World Series — Batting / Fielding

Year Tm	Age	G	AB	H	2B	3B	HR	TB	R	RBI	GW	TBB	IBB	SO	HBP	SH	SF	SB	CS	SB%	GDP	Avg	OBP	SLG	Pos	G	PO	A	E	DP	FPct
1972 Oak	30	6	0	0	0	0	0	0	2	0	0	0	0	0	0	0	0	0	2	.00	0	—	—	—	—						
1973 Oak	31	3	0	0	0	0	0	0	1	0	0	0	0	0	0	0	0	0	0	—	0	—	—	—	—						
WS Totals		9	0	0	0	0	0	0	3	0	0	0	0	0	0	0	0	0	2	.00	0	—	—	—	—	0	0	0	0	0	—
Postseason Totals		11	0	0	0	0	0	0	4	0	0	0	0	0	0	0	0	0	2	.00	0	—	—	—	—	0	0	0	0	0	—

DARREN LEWIS—Darren Joel Lewis—Bats: Right; Throws: Right

Ht: 6'0"; Wt: 175 lbs; Born: 8/28/1967 in Berkeley, California; Debut: 8/21/1990

Division Series — Batting / Fielding

Year Tm	Age	G	AB	H	2B	3B	HR	TB	R	RBI	GW	TBB	IBB	SO	HBP	SH	SF	SB	CS	SB%	GDP	Avg	OBP	SLG	Pos	G	PO	A	E	DP	FPct
1995 Cin	28	3	3	0	0	0	0	0	0	0	0	0	0	1	0	0	0	0	0	—	0	.000	.000	.000	OF	3	3	0	0	0	1.000

LCS — Batting / Fielding

Year Tm	Age	G	AB	H	2B	3B	HR	TB	R	RBI	GW	TBB	IBB	SO	HBP	SH	SF	SB	CS	SB%	GDP	Avg	OBP	SLG	Pos	G	PO	A	E	DP	FPct
1995 Cin	28	2	1	0	0	0	0	0	0	0	0	0	0	0	0	0	0	0	0	—	0	.000	.000	.000	OF	2	2	0	0	0	1.000
Postseason Totals		5	4	0	0	0	0	0	0	0	0	0	0	1	0	0	0	0	0	—	0	.000	.000	.000	OF	5	5	0	0	0	1.000

DUFFY LEWIS—George Edward Lewis—Bats: Right; Throws: Right

Ht: 5'10"; Wt: 165 lbs; Born: 4/18/1888 in San Francisco, California; Debut: 4/16/1910; Died: 6/17/1979

World Series — Batting / Fielding

Year Tm	Age	G	AB	H	2B	3B	HR	TB	R	RBI	GW	TBB	IBB	SO	HBP	SH	SF	SB	CS	SB%	GDP	Avg	OBP	SLG	Pos	G	PO	A	E	DP	FPct
1912 Bos	24	8	32	6	3	0	0	9	4	1	0	2	1	2	0	0	0	0	0	—	0	.188	.235	.281	OF	8	14	0	1	0	.933
1915 Bos	27	5	18	8	1	0	1	12	1	5	1	1	0	4	0	1	0	0	1	.00	0	.444	.474	.667	OF	5	10	1	0	0	1.000
1916 Bos	28	5	17	6	2	1	0	10	3	1	0	2	1	1	0	4	0	0	0	—	1	.353	.421	.588	OF	5	9	1	0	0	1.000
WS Totals		18	67	20	6	1	1	31	8	7	1	5	2	7	0	5	0	0	1	.00	1	.299	.347	.463	OF	18	33	2	1	0	.972

MARK LEWIS—Mark David Lewis—Bats: Right; Throws: Right

Ht: 6'1"; Wt: 190 lbs; Born: 11/30/1969 in Hamilton, Ohio; Debut: 4/26/1991

Division Series — Batting / Fielding

Year Tm	Age	G	AB	H	2B	3B	HR	TB	R	RBI	GW	TBB	IBB	SO	HBP	SH	SF	SB	CS	SB%	GDP	Avg	OBP	SLG	Pos	G	PO	A	E	DP	FPct
1995 Cin	25	2	2	1	0	0	1	4	2	5	0	1	1	0	0	0	0	0	0	—	0	.500	.667	2.000	3B	2	0	0	1	0	.000
1997 SF	27	1	5	3	0	0	0	3	0	1	0	0	0	0	0	0	0	0	1	.00	0	.600	.600	.600	2B	1	1	3	0	1	1.000
DS Totals		3	7	4	0	0	1	7	2	6	0	1	1	0	0	0	0	0	1	.00	0	.571	.625	1.000	3B	2	0	0	1	0	.000

LCS — Batting / Fielding

Year Tm	Age	G	AB	H	2B	3B	HR	TB	R	RBI	GW	TBB	IBB	SO	HBP	SH	SF	SB	CS	SB%	GDP	Avg	OBP	SLG	Pos	G	PO	A	E	DP	FPct
1995 Cin	25	2	4	1	0	0	0	1	0	0	0	1	0	1	0	0	0	0	0	—	0	.250	.400	.250	3B	2	2	3	0	0	1.000
Postseason Totals		5	11	5	0	0	1	8	2	6	0	2	1	1	0	0	0	0	1	.00	0	.455	.538	.727	3B	4	2	3	1	0	.833

JIM LEYRITZ—James Joseph Leyritz—Bats: Right; Throws: Right

Ht: 6'0"; Wt: 190 lbs; Born: 12/27/1963 in Lakewood, Ohio; Debut: 6/8/1990

Division Series — Batting / Fielding

Year Tm	Age	G	AB	H	2B	3B	HR	TB	R	RBI	GW	TBB	IBB	SO	HBP	SH	SF	SB	CS	SB%	GDP	Avg	OBP	SLG	Pos	G	PO	A	E	DP	FPct
1995 NYA	31	2	7	1	0	0	1	4	1	2	1	0	0	1	1	0	0	0	0	—	0	.143	.250	.571	C	2	13	0	0	0	1.000
1996 NYA	32	2	3	0	0	0	0	0	0	1	0	0	0	1	1	0	0	0	0	—	0	.000	.250	.000	C	1	4	0	0	0	1.000
DS Totals		4	10	1	0	0	1	4	1	3	1	0	0	2	2	0	0	0	0	—	0	.100	.250	.400	C	3	17	0	0	0	1.000

LCS — Batting / Fielding

Year Tm	Age	G	AB	H	2B	3B	HR	TB	R	RBI	GW	TBB	IBB	SO	HBP	SH	SF	SB	CS	SB%	GDP	Avg	OBP	SLG	Pos	G	PO	A	E	DP	FPct
1996 NYA	32	3	8	2	0	0	1	5	1	2	1	1	0	4	0	0	0	0	0	—	0	.250	.333	.625	C	2	11	2	0	0	1.000
																									OF	1	0	0	0	0	—

World Series — Batting / Fielding

Year Tm	Age	G	AB	H	2B	3B	HR	TB	R	RBI	GW	TBB	IBB	SO	HBP	SH	SF	SB	CS	SB%	GDP	Avg	OBP	SLG	Pos	G	PO	A	E	DP	FPct
1996 NYA	32	4	8	3	0	0	1	6	1	3	0	3	1	2	0	0	0	1	0	1.00	0	.375	.545	.750	C	3	15	0	0	0	1.000
Postseason Totals		11	26	6	0	0	3	15	3	8	2	4	1	8	2	0	0	1	0	1.00	0	.231	.375	.577	C	8	43	2	0	0	1.000

SIXTO LEZCANO—Sixto Joaquin Lezcano—Bats: Right; Throws: Right

Ht: 5'10"; Wt: 165 lbs; Born: 11/28/1953 in Arecibo, Puerto Rico; Debut: 9/10/1974

LCS — Batting / Fielding

Year Tm	Age	G	AB	H	2B	3B	HR	TB	R	RBI	GW	TBB	IBB	SO	HBP	SH	SF	SB	CS	SB%	GDP	Avg	OBP	SLG	Pos	G	PO	A	E	DP	FPct
1983 Phi	29	4	13	4	0	0	1	7	2	2	0	1	0	1	0	1	0	0	0	—	1	.308	.357	.538	OF	4	5	1	1	0	.857

World Series — Batting / Fielding

Year Tm	Age	G	AB	H	2B	3B	HR	TB	R	RBI	GW	TBB	IBB	SO	HBP	SH	SF	SB	CS	SB%	GDP	Avg	OBP	SLG	Pos	G	PO	A	E	DP	FPct
1983 Phi	29	4	8	1	0	0	0	1	0	0	0	0	0	2	0	0	0	0	0	—	0	.125	.125	.125	OF	3	2	0	0	0	1.000
Postseason Totals		8	21	5	0	0	1	8	2	2	0	1	0	3	0	1	0	0	0	—	1	.238	.273	.381	OF	7	7	1	1	0	.889

DON LIDDLE—Donald Eugene Liddle—Throws: Left; Bats: Left

Ht: 5'10"; Wt: 165 lbs; Born: 5/25/1925 in Mount Carmel, Illinois; Debut: 4/17/1953

World Series — Pitching

Year Tm	Age	G	GS	CG	GF	IP	BFP	H	R	ER	HR	SH	SF	HB	TBB	IBB	SO	WP	Bk	W	L	Pct	ShO	Sv-Op	Hld	OAvg	OOBP	ERA
1954 NYG	29	2	1	0	0	7.0	28	5	4	1	1	0	0	0	1	0	2	1	0	1	0	1.000	0	0- 0	0	.185	.214	1.29

World Series — Batting / Fielding

Year Tm	Age	G	AB	H	2B	3B	HR	TB	R	RBI	GW	TBB	IBB	SO	HBP	SH	SF	SB	CS	SB%	GDP	Avg	OBP	SLG	Pos	G	PO	A	E	DP	FPct
1954 NYG	29	2	3	0	0	0	0	0	0	0	0	0	0	2	0	0	0	0	0	—	0	.000	.000	.000	P	2	0	1	1	0	.500

KERRY LIGTENBERG—Kerry Dale Ligtenberg—Throws: Right; Bats: Right

Ht: 6'2"; Wt: 205 lbs; Born: 5/11/1971 in Rapid City, South Dakota; Debut: 8/12/1997

LCS — Pitching

Year Tm	Age	G	GS	CG	GF	IP	BFP	H	R	ER	HR	SH	SF	HB	TBB	IBB	SO	WP	Bk	W	L	Pct	ShO	Sv-Op	Hld	OAvg	OOBP	ERA
1997 Atl	26	2	0	0	1	3.0	10	1	0	0	0	1	0	0	0	0	4	0	0	0	0	—	0	0- 0	0	.111	.111	0.00

LCS — Batting / Fielding

Year Tm	Age	G	AB	H	2B	3B	HR	TB	R	RBI	GW	TBB	IBB	SO	HBP	SH	SF	SB	CS	SB%	GDP	Avg	OBP	SLG	Pos	G	PO	A	E	DP	FPct
1997 Atl	26	2	0	0	0	0	0	0	0	0	0	0	0	0	0	0	0	0	0	—	0	—	—	—	P	2	0	2	0	1	1.000

JOSE LIMA—Jose Desiderio Rodriguez Lima—Throws: Right; Bats: Right

Ht: 6'2"; Wt: 170 lbs; Born: 9/30/1972 in Santiago, Dominican Republic; Debut: 4/20/1994

Division Series		Pitching																										
Year Tm	Age	G	GS	CG	GF	IP	BFP	H	R	ER	HR	SH	SF	HB	TBB	IBB	SO	WP	Bk	W	L	Pct	ShO	Sv-Op	Hld	OAvg	OOBP	ERA
1997 Hou	25	1	0	0	0	1.0	3	0	0	0	0	0	0	0	1	0	1	0	0	0	0	—	0	0-0	0	.000	.333	0.00

Division Series		Batting																							Fielding						
Year Tm	Age	G	AB	H	2B	3B	HR	TB	R	RBI	GW	TBB	IBB	SO	HBP	SH	SF	SB	CS	SB%	GDP	Avg	OBP	SLG	Pos	G	PO	A	E	DP	FPct
1997 Hou	25	1	0	0	0	0	0	0	0	0	0	0	0	0	0	0	0	0	0	—	0	—	—	—	P	1	0	0	0	0	—

JOSE LIND—Nickname: Chico—Bats: Right; Throws: Right

Ht: 5'11"; Wt: 155 lbs; Born: 5/1/1964 in Toabaja, Puerto Rico; Debut: 8/28/1987

LCS		Batting																							Fielding						
Year Tm	Age	G	AB	H	2B	3B	HR	TB	R	RBI	GW	TBB	IBB	SO	HBP	SH	SF	SB	CS	SB%	GDP	Avg	OBP	SLG	Pos	G	PO	A	E	DP	FPct
1990 Pit	26	6	21	5	1	1	1	11	1	2	0	1	0	4	0	0	0	0	0	—	0	.238	.273	.524	2B	6	19	19	0	4	1.000
1991 Pit	27	7	25	4	0	0	0	4	0	3	1	0	0	6	0	0	1	0	0	—	0	.160	.154	.160	2B	7	12	24	1	1	.973
1992 Pit	28	7	27	6	2	1	1	13	5	5	0	1	1	4	0	0	0	0	0	—	0	.222	.250	.481	2B	7	16	23	2	3	.951
LCS Totals		20	73	15	3	2	2	28	6	10	1	2	1	14	0	0	1	0	0	—	0	.205	.224	.384	2B	20	47	66	3	8	.974

PAUL LINDBLAD—Paul Aaron Lindblad—Throws: Left; Bats: Left

Ht: 6'1"; Wt: 185 lbs; Born: 8/9/1941 in Chanute, Kansas; Debut: 9/15/1965

LCS		Pitching																										
Year Tm	Age	G	GS	CG	GF	IP	BFP	H	R	ER	HR	SH	SF	HB	TBB	IBB	SO	WP	Bk	W	L	Pct	ShO	Sv-Op	Hld	OAvg	OOBP	ERA
1975 Oak	34	2	0	0	1	4.2	20	5	3	0	0	2	1	0	1	1	0	1	0	0	0	—	0	0-0	0	.313	.333	0.00
World Series		Pitching																										
Year Tm	Age	G	GS	CG	GF	IP	BFP	H	R	ER	HR	SH	SF	HB	TBB	IBB	SO	WP	Bk	W	L	Pct	ShO	Sv-Op	Hld	OAvg	OOBP	ERA
1973 Oak	32	3	0	0	2	3.1	17	4	0	0	0	0	0	0	1	1	1	0	0	1	0	1.000	0	0-0	0	.250	.294	0.00
1978 NYA	37	1	0	0	0	2.1	11	4	3	3	0	0	0	0	0	0	1	0	0	0	0	—	0	0-0	0	.364	.364	11.57
WS Totals		4	0	0	2	5.2	56	8	3	3	0	0	0	0	1	1	2	0	0	1	0	1.000	0	0-0	0	.296	.321	4.76
Postseason Totals		6	0	0	3	10.1	96	13	6	3	0	2	1	0	2	2	2	1	0	1	0	1.000	0	0-0	0	.302	.326	2.61

LCS		Batting																							Fielding						
Year Tm	Age	G	AB	H	2B	3B	HR	TB	R	RBI	GW	TBB	IBB	SO	HBP	SH	SF	SB	CS	SB%	GDP	Avg	OBP	SLG	Pos	G	PO	A	E	DP	FPct
1975 Oak	34	2	0	0	0	0	0	0	0	0	0	0	0	0	0	0	0	0	0	—	0	—	—	—	P	2	1	4	0	0	1.000
World Series		Batting																							Fielding						
Year Tm	Age	G	AB	H	2B	3B	HR	TB	R	RBI	GW	TBB	IBB	SO	HBP	SH	SF	SB	CS	SB%	GDP	Avg	OBP	SLG	Pos	G	PO	A	E	DP	FPct
1973 Oak	32	3	1	0	0	0	0	0	0	0	0	0	0	0	0	0	0	0	0	—	0	.000	.000	.000	P	3	0	0	0	0	—
1978 NYA	37	1	0	0	0	0	0	0	0	0	0	0	0	0	0	0	0	0	0	—	0	—	—	—	P	1	0	0	0	0	—
WS Totals		4	1	0	0	0	0	0	0	0	0	0	0	0	0	0	0	0	0	—	0	.000	.000	.000	P	4	0	0	0	0	—
Postseason Totals		6	1	0	0	0	0	0	0	0	0	0	0	0	0	0	0	0	0	—	0	.000	.000	.000	P	6	1	4	0	0	1.000

JOHNNY LINDELL—John Harlan Lindell—Bats: Right; Throws: Right

Ht: 6'4"; Wt: 217 lbs; Born: 8/30/1916 in Greeley, Colorado; Debut: 4/18/1941; Died: 8/27/1985

World Series		Batting																							Fielding						
Year Tm	Age	G	AB	H	2B	3B	HR	TB	R	RBI	GW	TBB	IBB	SO	HBP	SH	SF	SB	CS	SB%	GDP	Avg	OBP	SLG	Pos	G	PO	A	E	DP	FPct
1943 NYA	27	4	9	1	0	0	0	1	1	0	0	1	1	4	0	0	0	0	0	—	0	.111	.200	.111	OF	4	8	0	0	0	1.000
1947 NYA	31	6	18	9	3	1	0	14	3	7	1	5	0	2	1	0	0	0	0	—	1	.500	.625	.778	OF	6	10	0	0	0	1.000
1949 NYA	33	2	7	1	0	0	0	1	0	0	0	0	0	2	0	0	0	0	0	—	0	.143	.143	.143	OF	2	2	1	1	0	.750
WS Totals		12	34	11	3	1	0	16	4	7	1	6	1	8	1	0	0	0	0	—	1	.324	.439	.471	OF	12	20	1	1	0	.955

JIM LINDEMAN—James William Lindeman—Bats: Right; Throws: Right

Ht: 6'1"; Wt: 200 lbs; Born: 1/10/1962 in Evanston, Illinois; Debut: 9/3/1986

LCS		Batting																							Fielding						
Year Tm	Age	G	AB	H	2B	3B	HR	TB	R	RBI	GW	TBB	IBB	SO	HBP	SH	SF	SB	CS	SB%	GDP	Avg	OBP	SLG	Pos	G	PO	A	E	DP	FPct
1987 StL	25	5	13	4	0	0	1	7	1	3	0	0	0	3	0	0	1	0	0	—	0	.308	.286	.538	1B	5	33	2	0	3	1.000
World Series		Batting																							Fielding						
Year Tm	Age	G	AB	H	2B	3B	HR	TB	R	RBI	GW	TBB	IBB	SO	HBP	SH	SF	SB	CS	SB%	GDP	Avg	OBP	SLG	Pos	G	PO	A	E	DP	FPct
1987 StL	25	6	15	5	1	0	0	6	3	2	0	0	0	3	1	0	0	0	0	—	0	.333	.375	.400	1B	6	28	2	3	2	.909
																									OF	1	0	0	0	0	—
Postseason Totals		11	28	9	1	0	1	13	4	5	0	0	0	6	1	0	1	0	0	—	0	.321	.333	.464	1B	11	61	4	3	5	.956

JIM LINDSEY—James Kendrick Lindsey—Throws: Right; Bats: Right

Ht: 6'1"; Wt: 175 lbs; Born: 1/24/1896 in Greensburg, Louisiana; Debut: 5/1/1922; Died: 10/25/1963

World Series		Pitching																										
Year Tm	Age	G	GS	CG	GF	IP	BFP	H	R	ER	HR	SH	SF	HB	TBB	IBB	SO	WP	Bk	W	L	Pct	ShO	Sv-Op	Hld	OAvg	OOBP	ERA
1930 StL	34	2	0	0	0	4.2	15	1	1	1	0	0	1	0	1	0	2	0	0	0	0	—	0	0-0	0	.077	.133	1.93
1931 StL	35	2	0	0	0	3.1	18	4	4	2	0	1	0	1	3	0	2	0	0	0	0	—	0	0-0	0	.308	.471	5.40
WS Totals		4	0	0	0	8.0	66	5	5	3	0	1	1	1	4	0	4	0	0	0	0	—	0	0-0	0	.192	.313	3.38

World Series		Batting																							Fielding						
Year Tm	Age	G	AB	H	2B	3B	HR	TB	R	RBI	GW	TBB	IBB	SO	HBP	SH	SF	SB	CS	SB%	GDP	Avg	OBP	SLG	Pos	G	PO	A	E	DP	FPct
1930 StL	34	2	1	1	0	0	0	1	0	0	0	0	0	0	0	0	0	0	0	—	0	1.000	1.000	1.000	P	2	0	1	0	0	1.000
1931 StL	35	2	0	0	0	0	0	0	0	0	0	0	0	0	0	0	0	0	0	—	0	—	—	—	P	2	0	0	0	0	—
WS Totals		4	1	1	0	0	0	1	0	0	0	0	0	0	0	0	0	0	0	—	0	1.000	1.000	1.000	P	4	0	1	0	0	1.000

FREDDY LINDSTROM (HOF 1976-V)—Frederick Charles Lindstrom—Nickname: Lindy—B: R; T: R

Ht: 5'11"; Wt: 170 lbs; Born: 11/21/1905 in Chicago, Ill.; Deb.: 4/15/1924; Died: 10/4/1981

World Series		Batting																							Fielding						
Year Tm	Age	G	AB	H	2B	3B	HR	TB	R	RBI	GW	TBB	IBB	SO	HBP	SH	SF	SB	CS	SB%	GDP	Avg	OBP	SLG	Pos	G	PO	A	E	DP	FPct
1924 NYG	18	7	30	10	2	0	0	12	1	4	0	3	0	6	0	1	0	0	2	.00	0	.333	.394	.400	3B	7	7	18	0	0	1.000
1935 ChN	29	4	15	3	1	0	0	4	0	0	0	1	0	1	0	1	0	0	1	.00	1	.200	.250	.267	3B	1	1	1	1	0	.667
																									OF	4	7	0	0	0	1.000
WS Totals		11	45	13	3	0	0	16	1	4	0	4	0	7	0	2	0	0	3	.00	1	.289	.347	.356	3B	8	8	19	1	0	.964

PHIL LINZ—Philip Francis Linz—Nickname: Super Sub—Bats: Right; Throws: Right

Ht: 6'1"; Wt: 180 lbs; Born: 6/4/1939 in Baltimore, Maryland; Debut: 4/13/1962

World Series		Batting																							Fielding						
Year Tm	Age	G	AB	H	2B	3B	HR	TB	R	RBI	GW	TBB	IBB	SO	HBP	SH	SF	SB	CS	SB%	GDP	Avg	OBP	SLG	Pos	G	PO	A	E	DP	FPct
1963 NYA	24	3	3	1	0	0	0	1	0	0	0	0	0	1	0	0	0	0	0	—	0	.333	.333	.333	—						
1964 NYA	25	7	31	7	1	0	2	14	5	2	0	2	0	5	0	0	0	0	1	.00	0	.226	.273	.452	SS	7	7	21	2	5	.933
WS Totals		10	34	8	1	0	2	15	5	2	0	2	0	6	0	0	0	0	1	.00	0	.235	.278	.441	SS	7	7	21	2	5	.933

NELSON LIRIANO—Nelson Arturo Liriano—Bats: Both; Throws: Right

Ht: 5'10"; Wt: 165 lbs; Born: 6/3/1964 in Puerto Plata, Dominican Republic; Debut: 8/25/1987

LCS		Batting																							Fielding						
Year Tm	Age	G	AB	H	2B	3B	HR	TB	R	RBI	GW	TBB	IBB	SO	HBP	SH	SF	SB	CS	SB%	GDP	Avg	OBP	SLG	Pos	G	PO	A	E	DP	FPct
1989 Tor	25	3	7	3	0	0	0	3	1	1	0	2	0	0	0	0	0	3	0	1.00	0	.429	.556	.429	2B	3	4	3	1	1	.875

MARK LITTELL—Mark Alan Littell—Throws: Right; Bats: Left

Ht: 6'3"; Wt: 210 lbs; Born: 1/17/1953 in Cape Girardeau, Missouri; Debut: 6/14/1973

LCS		Pitching																										
Year Tm	Age	G	GS	CG	GF	IP	BFP	H	R	ER	HR	SH	SF	HB	TBB	IBB	SO	WP	Bk	W	L	Pct	ShO	Sv-Op	Hld	OAvg	OOBP	ERA
1976 KC	23	3	0	0	3	4.2	19	4	1	1	1	0	0	0	1	0	3	0	0	0	1	.000	0	0-0	0	.222	.263	1.93
1977 KC	24	2	0	0	1	3.0	18	5	3	1	0	0	1	0	3	2	1	0	0	0	0	—	0	0-0	0	.357	.444	3.00
LCS Totals		5	0	0	4	7.2	74	9	4	2	1	0	1	0	4	2	4	0	0	0	1	.000	0	0-0	0	.281	.351	2.35

LCS		Batting																							Fielding						
Year Tm	Age	G	AB	H	2B	3B	HR	TB	R	RBI	GW	TBB	IBB	SO	HBP	SH	SF	SB	CS	SB%	GDP	Avg	OBP	SLG	Pos	G	PO	A	E	DP	FPct
1976 KC	23	3	0	0	0	0	0	0	0	0	0	0	0	0	0	0	0	0	0	—	0	—	—	—	P	3	0	1	0	0	1.000
1977 KC	24	2	0	0	0	0	0	0	0	0	0	0	0	0	0	0	0	0	0	—	0	—	—	—	P	2	0	0	0	0	—
LCS Totals		5	0	0	0	0	0	0	0	0	0	0	0	0	0	0	0	0	0	—	0	—	—	—	P	5	0	1	0	0	1.000

GREG LITTON—Jon Gregory Litton—Bats: Right; Throws: Right

Ht: 6'0"; Wt: 175 lbs; Born: 7/13/1964 in New Orleans, Louisiana; Debut: 5/2/1989

LCS		Batting																							Fielding						
Year Tm	Age	G	AB	H	2B	3B	HR	TB	R	RBI	GW	TBB	IBB	SO	HBP	SH	SF	SB	CS	SB%	GDP	Avg	OBP	SLG	Pos	G	PO	A	E	DP	FPct
1989 SF	25	1	1	1	0	0	0	1	0	0	0	0	0	0	0	0	0	0	0	—	0	1.000	1.000	1.000	3B	1	0	0	0	0	—
World Series		**Batting**																							**Fielding**						
Year Tm	Age	G	AB	H	2B	3B	HR	TB	R	RBI	GW	TBB	IBB	SO	HBP	SH	SF	SB	CS	SB%	GDP	Avg	OBP	SLG	Pos	G	PO	A	E	DP	FPct
1989 SF	25	2	6	3	1	0	1	7	1	3	0	0	0	0	0	0	0	0	0	—	0	.500	.500	1.167	2B	2	2	3	0	0	1.000
																									3B	1	0	0	0	0	—
Postseason Totals		3	7	4	1	0	1	8	1	3	0	0	0	0	0	0	0	0	0	—	0	.571	.571	1.143	2B	2	2	3	0	0	1.000

DANNY LITWHILER—Daniel Webster Litwhiler—Bats: Right; Throws: Right

Ht: 5'10"; Wt: 198 lbs; Born: 8/31/1916 in Ringtown, Pennsylvania; Debut: 4/25/1940

World Series		Batting																							Fielding						
Year Tm	Age	G	AB	H	2B	3B	HR	TB	R	RBI	GW	TBB	IBB	SO	HBP	SH	SF	SB	CS	SB%	GDP	Avg	OBP	SLG	Pos	G	PO	A	E	DP	FPct
1943 StL	27	5	15	4	1	0	0	5	0	2	0	2	0	4	0	0	0	0	0	—	0	.267	.353	.333	OF	4	11	0	0	0	1.000
1944 StL	28	5	20	4	1	0	1	8	2	1	0	2	0	7	0	0	0	0	0	—	0	.200	.273	.400	OF	5	5	0	0	0	1.000
WS Totals		10	35	8	2	0	1	13	2	3	0	4	0	11	0	0	0	0	0	—	0	.229	.308	.371	OF	9	16	0	0	0	1.000

MICKEY LIVINGSTON—Thompson Orville Livingston—Bats: Right; Throws: Right

Ht: 6'1"; Wt: 185 lbs; Born: 11/15/1914 in Newberry, South Carolina; Debut: 9/17/1938; Died: 4/3/1983

World Series		Batting																							Fielding						
Year Tm	Age	G	AB	H	2B	3B	HR	TB	R	RBI	GW	TBB	IBB	SO	HBP	SH	SF	SB	CS	SB%	GDP	Avg	OBP	SLG	Pos	G	PO	A	E	DP	FPct
1945 ChN	30	6	22	8	3	0	0	11	3	4	0	1	0	1	0	0	0	0	2	.00	0	.364	.391	.500	C	6	22	4	0	0	1.000

SCOTT LIVINGSTONE—Scott Louis Livingstone—Bats: Left; Throws: Right

Ht: 6'0"; Wt: 190 lbs; Born: 7/15/1965 in Dallas, Texas; Debut: 7/19/1991

Division Series		Batting																							Fielding						
Year Tm	Age	G	AB	H	2B	3B	HR	TB	R	RBI	GW	TBB	IBB	SO	HBP	SH	SF	SB	CS	SB%	GDP	Avg	OBP	SLG	Pos	G	PO	A	E	DP	FPct
1996 SD	31	2	2	1	0	0	0	1	1	0	0	0	0	0	0	0	0	0	0	—	0	.500	.500	.500	—						

GRAEME LLOYD—Graeme John Lloyd—Throws: Left; Bats: Left

Ht: 6'7"; Wt: 215 lbs; Born: 4/9/1967 in Geelong, Australia; Debut: 4/11/1993

Division Series		Pitching																									
Year Tm	Age	G	GS	CG	GF	IP	BFP	H	R	ER	HR	SH	SF	HB	TBB	IBB	SO	WP	Bk	W	L	Pct	ShO	Sv-Op	Hld	OAvg	OOBP	ERA
1996 NYA	29	2	0	0	0	1.0	4	1	0	0	0	0	0	0	0	0	0	0	0	0	0	—	0	0-0	0	.250	.250	0.00
1997 NYA	30	2	0	0	0	1.1	5	0	0	0	0	0	0	0	0	0	1	0	0	0	0	—	0	0-0	0	.000	.000	0.00
DS Totals		4	0	0	0	2.1	18	1	0	0	0	0	0	0	0	0	1	0	0	0	0	—	0	0-0	0	.111	.111	0.00
LCS		**Pitching**																										
Year Tm	Age	G	GS	CG	GF	IP	BFP	H	R	ER	HR	SH	SF	HB	TBB	IBB	SO	WP	Bk	W	L	Pct	ShO	Sv-Op	Hld	OAvg	OOBP	ERA
1996 NYA	29	2	0	0	0	1.2	4	0	0	0	0	0	1	0	0	0	1	0	0	0	0	—	0	0-0	1	.000	.000	0.00
World Series		**Pitching**																										
Year Tm	Age	G	GS	CG	GF	IP	BFP	H	R	ER	HR	SH	SF	HB	TBB	IBB	SO	WP	Bk	W	L	Pct	ShO	Sv-Op	Hld	OAvg	OOBP	ERA
1996 NYA	29	4	0	0	0	2.2	7	0	0	0	0	0	0	0	0	0	4	0	0	1	0	1.000	0	0-0	2	.000	.000	0.00
Postseason Totals		10	0	0	0	6.2	40	1	0	0	0	0	1	0	0	0	6	0	0	1	0	1.000	0	0-0	3	.053	.050	0.00

Division Series		Batting																							Fielding						
Year Tm	Age	G	AB	H	2B	3B	HR	TB	R	RBI	GW	TBB	IBB	SO	HBP	SH	SF	SB	CS	SB%	GDP	Avg	OBP	SLG	Pos	G	PO	A	E	DP	FPct
1996 NYA	29	2	0	0	0	0	0	0	0	0	0	0	0	0	0	0	0	0	0	—	0	—	—	—	P	2	1	0	0	0	1.000
1997 NYA	30	2	0	0	0	0	0	0	0	0	0	0	0	0	0	0	0	0	0	—	0	—	—	—	P	2	0	0	0	0	—
DS Totals		4	0	0	0	0	0	0	0	0	0	0	0	0	0	0	0	0	0	—	0	—	—	—	P	4	1	0	0	0	1.000
LCS		**Batting**																							**Fielding**						
Year Tm	Age	G	AB	H	2B	3B	HR	TB	R	RBI	GW	TBB	IBB	SO	HBP	SH	SF	SB	CS	SB%	GDP	Avg	OBP	SLG	Pos	G	PO	A	E	DP	FPct
1996 NYA	29	2	0	0	0	0	0	0	0	0	0	0	0	0	0	0	0	0	0	—	0	—	—	—	P	2	0	0	0	0	—
World Series		**Batting**																							**Fielding**						
Year Tm	Age	G	AB	H	2B	3B	HR	TB	R	RBI	GW	TBB	IBB	SO	HBP	SH	SF	SB	CS	SB%	GDP	Avg	OBP	SLG	Pos	G	PO	A	E	DP	FPct
1996 NYA	29	4	1	0	0	0	0	0	0	0	0	0	0	0	0	0	0	0	0	—	0	.000	.000	.000	P	4	0	0	0	0	—
Postseason Totals		10	1	0	0	0	0	0	0	0	0	0	0	0	0	0	0	0	0	—	0	.000	.000	.000	P	10	1	0	0	0	1.000

BOB LOCKER—Robert Awtry Locker—Throws: Right; Bats: Both

Ht: 6'3"; Wt: 200 lbs; Born: 3/15/1938 in George, Iowa; Debut: 4/14/1965

LCS		Pitching																									
Year Tm	Age	G	GS	CG	GF	IP	BFP	H	R	ER	HR	SH	SF	HB	TBB	IBB	SO	WP	Bk	W	L	Pct	ShO	Sv-Op	Hld	OAvg	OOBP	ERA
1971 Oak	33	1	0	0	0	0.2	3	0	0	0	0	0	0	0	2	0	0	0	0	0	0	—	0	0-0	0	.000	.667	0.00
1972 Oak	34	2	0	0	1	2.0	9	4	3	3	1	0	0	0	0	0	1	0	0	0	0	—	0	0-0	0	.444	.444	13.50
LCS Totals		3	0	0	1	2.2	24	4	3	3	1	0	0	0	2	0	1	0	0	0	0	—	0	0-0	0	.400	.500	10.13
World Series		**Pitching**																										
Year Tm	Age	G	GS	CG	GF	IP	BFP	H	R	ER	HR	SH	SF	HB	TBB	IBB	SO	WP	Bk	W	L	Pct	ShO	Sv-Op	Hld	OAvg	OOBP	ERA
1972 Oak	34	1	0	0	0	0.1	2	1	0	0	0	0	0	0	0	0	0	0	0	0	0	—	0	0-0	0	.500	.500	0.00
Postseason Totals		4	0	0	1	3.0	28	5	3	3	1	0	0	0	2	0	1	0	0	0	0	—	0	0-0	0	.417	.500	9.00

LCS		Batting																							Fielding						
Year Tm	Age	G	AB	H	2B	3B	HR	TB	R	RBI	GW	TBB	IBB	SO	HBP	SH	SF	SB	CS	SB%	GDP	Avg	OBP	SLG	Pos	G	PO	A	E	DP	FPct
1971 Oak	33	1	0	0	0	0	0	0	0	0	0	0	0	0	0	0	0	0	0	—	0	—	—	—	P	1	0	0	0	0	—
1972 Oak	34	2	0	0	0	0	0	0	0	0	0	0	0	0	0	0	0	0	0	—	0	—	—	—	P	2	0	0	0	0	—
LCS Totals		3	0	0	0	0	0	0	0	0	0	0	0	0	0	0	0	0	0	—	0	—	—	—	P	3	0	0	0	0	—
World Series		**Batting**																							**Fielding**						
Year Tm	Age	G	AB	H	2B	3B	HR	TB	R	RBI	GW	TBB	IBB	SO	HBP	SH	SF	SB	CS	SB%	GDP	Avg	OBP	SLG	Pos	G	PO	A	E	DP	FPct
1972 Oak	34	1	0	0	0	0	0	0	0	0	0	0	0	0	0	0	0	0	0	—	0	—	—	—	P	1	0	0	0	0	—
Postseason Totals		4	0	0	0	0	0	0	0	0	0	0	0	0	0	0	0	0	0	—	0	—	—	—	P	4	0	0	0	0	—

KEITH LOCKHART—Keith Virgil Lockhart—Bats: Left; Throws: Right

Ht: 5'10"; Wt: 170 lbs; Born: 11/10/1964 in Whittier, California; Debut: 4/5/1994

Division Series		Batting																							Fielding						
Year Tm	Age	G	AB	H	2B	3B	HR	TB	R	RBI	GW	TBB	IBB	SO	HBP	SH	SF	SB	CS	SB%	GDP	Avg	OBP	SLG	Pos	G	PO	A	E	DP	FPct
1997 Atl	32	2	6	0	0	0	0	0	0	0	0	0	0	1	0	0	0	0	0	—	0	.000	.000	.000	2B	2	1	8	1	2	.900
LCS		**Batting**																							**Fielding**						
Year Tm	Age	G	AB	H	2B	3B	HR	TB	R	RBI	GW	TBB	IBB	SO	HBP	SH	SF	SB	CS	SB%	GDP	Avg	OBP	SLG	Pos	G	PO	A	E	DP	FPct
1997 Atl	32	5	16	8	1	1	0	11	4	3	1	1	0	1	1	0	0	0	0	—	0	.500	.556	.688	2B	5	14	5	0	3	1.000
Postseason Totals		7	22	8	1	1	0	11	4	3	1	1	0	2	1	0	0	0	0	—	0	.364	.417	.500	2B	7	15	13	1	5	.966

WHITEY LOCKMAN—Carroll Walter Lockman—Bats: Left; Throws: Right

Ht: 6'1"; Wt: 175 lbs; Born: 7/25/1926 in Lowell, North Carolina; Debut: 7/5/1945

World Series		Batting																							Fielding						
Year Tm	Age	G	AB	H	2B	3B	HR	TB	R	RBI	GW	TBB	IBB	SO	HBP	SH	SF	SB	CS	SB%	GDP	Avg	OBP	SLG	Pos	G	PO	A	E	DP	FPct
1951 NYG	25	6	25	6	2	0	1	11	1	4	1	1	0	2	0	0	0	0	0	—	1	.240	.269	.440	1B	6	48	5	2	4	.964
1954 NYG	28	4	18	2	0	0	0	2	2	0	0	1	0	2	0	0	0	0	0	—	0	.111	.158	.111	1B	4	40	1	0	2	1.000
WS Totals		10	43	8	2	0	1	13	3	4	1	2	0	4	0	0	0	0	0	—	1	.186	.222	.302	1B	10	88	6	2	6	.979

BILLY LOES—William Loes—Throws: Right; Bats: Right

Ht: 6'1"; Wt: 165 lbs; Born: 12/13/1929 in Long Island City, New York; Debut: 5/18/1950

World Series		Pitching																									
Year Tm	Age	G	GS	CG	GF	IP	BFP	H	R	ER	HR	SH	SF	HB	TBB	IBB	SO	WP	Bk	W	L	Pct	ShO	Sv-Op	Hld	OAvg	OOBP	ERA
1952 Bro	22	2	1	0	0	10.1	46	11	5	5	3	0	0	0	5	0	5	0	1	0	1	.000	0	0-0	0	.268	.348	4.35
1953 Bro	23	1	1	0	0	8.0	34	8	3	3	1	0	0	0	2	0	8	0	0	1	0	1.000	0	0-0	0	.250	.294	3.38
1955 Bro	25	1	1	0	0	3.2	18	7	4	4	0	0	0	2	1	0	5	0	0	0	1	.000	0	0-0	0	.467	.556	9.82
WS Totals		4	3	0	0	22.0	196	26	12	12	4	0	0	2	8	0	18	0	1	1	2	.333	0	0-0	0	.295	.367	4.91

World Series		Batting																							Fielding						
Year Tm	Age	G	AB	H	2B	3B	HR	TB	R	RBI	GW	TBB	IBB	SO	HBP	SH	SF	SB	CS	SB%	GDP	Avg	OBP	SLG	Pos	G	PO	A	E	DP	FPct
1952 Bro	22	2	3	1	0	0	0	1	0	0	0	0	0	1	0	0	0	1	0	1.00	0	.333	.333	.333	P	2	0	2	0	0	1.000
1953 Bro	23	1	3	2	0	0	0	2	0	0	0	0	0	0	0	1	0	0	0	—	0	.667	.667	.667	P	1	0	0	0	0	—
1955 Bro	25	1	1	0	0	0	0	0	0	0	0	0	0	0	0	0	0	0	0	—	0	.000	.000	.000	P	1	0	0	0	0	—
WS Totals		4	7	3	0	0	0	3	0	0	0	0	0	1	0	1	0	1	0	1.00	0	.429	.429	.429	P	4	0	2	0	0	1.000

KENNY LOFTON—Kenneth Lofton—Bats: Left; Throws: Left

Ht: 6'0"; Wt: 180 lbs; Born: 5/31/1967 in East Chicago, Indiana; Debut: 9/14/1991

Division Series		Batting																							Fielding						
Year Tm	Age	G	AB	H	2B	3B	HR	TB	R	RBI	GW	TBB	IBB	SO	HBP	SH	SF	SB	CS	SB%	GDP	Avg	OBP	SLG	Pos	G	PO	A	E	DP	FPct
1995 Cle	28	3	13	2	0	0	0	2	1	0	0	1	0	3	1	0	0	0	0	—	0	.154	.267	.154	OF	3	9	0	2	0	.818
1996 Cle	29	4	18	3	0	0	0	3	3	1	0	2	0	3	0	1	0	5	0	1.00	0	.167	.250	.167	OF	4	10	0	0	0	1.000
1997 Atl	30	3	13	2	1	0	0	3	2	0	0	1	0	2	0	0	0	0	1	.00	1	.154	.214	.231	OF	3	6	1	0	0	1.000
DS Totals		10	44	7	1	0	0	8	6	1	0	4	0	8	1	1	0	5	1	.83	1	.159	.245	.182	OF	10	25	1	2	0	.929
LCS		Batting																							Fielding						
Year Tm	Age	G	AB	H	2B	3B	HR	TB	R	RBI	GW	TBB	IBB	SO	HBP	SH	SF	SB	CS	SB%	GDP	Avg	OBP	SLG	Pos	G	PO	A	E	DP	FPct
1995 Cle	28	6	24	11	0	2	0	15	4	3	1	4	0	6	0	0	1	5	0	1.00	0	.458	.517	.625	OF	6	15	0	0	0	1.000
1997 Atl	30	6	27	5	0	1	0	7	3	1	0	1	0	7	0	0	0	1	1	.50	1	.185	.214	.259	OF	6	9	1	2	0	.833
LCS Totals		12	51	16	0	3	0	22	7	4	1	5	0	13	0	0	1	6	1	.86	1	.314	.368	.431	OF	12	24	1	2	0	.926
World Series		Batting																							Fielding						
Year Tm	Age	G	AB	H	2B	3B	HR	TB	R	RBI	GW	TBB	IBB	SO	HBP	SH	SF	SB	CS	SB%	GDP	Avg	OBP	SLG	Pos	G	PO	A	E	DP	FPct
1995 Cle	28	6	25	5	1	0	0	6	6	0	0	3	2	1	0	0	0	6	1	.86	0	.200	.286	.240	OF	6	12	0	0	0	1.000
Postseason Totals		28	120	28	2	3	0	36	19	5	1	12	2	22	1	1	1	17	3	.85	2	.233	.306	.300	OF	28	61	2	4	0	.940

JOHNNY LOGAN—John Logan—Nickname: Yatcha—Bats: Right; Throws: Right

Ht: 5'11"; Wt: 175 lbs; Born: 3/23/1927 in Endicott, New York; Debut: 4/17/1951

World Series		Batting																							Fielding						
Year Tm	Age	G	AB	H	2B	3B	HR	TB	R	RBI	GW	TBB	IBB	SO	HBP	SH	SF	SB	CS	SB%	GDP	Avg	OBP	SLG	Pos	G	PO	A	E	DP	FPct
1957 Mil	30	7	27	5	1	0	1	9	5	2	0	3	0	6	1	0	0	0	0	—	0	.185	.290	.333	SS	7	13	24	0	7	1.000
1958 Mil	31	7	25	3	2	0	0	5	3	2	0	2	0	4	0	2	0	0	0	—	0	.120	.185	.200	SS	7	10	24	2	2	.944
WS Totals		14	52	8	3	0	1	14	8	4	0	5	0	10	1	2	0	0	0	—	0	.154	.241	.269	SS	14	23	48	2	9	.973

JACK LOHRKE—Jack Wayne Lohrke—Nickname: Lucky—Bats: Right; Throws: Right

Ht: 6'0"; Wt: 180 lbs; Born: 2/25/1924 in Los Angeles, California; Debut: 4/18/1947

World Series		Batting																							Fielding						
Year Tm	Age	G	AB	H	2B	3B	HR	TB	R	RBI	GW	TBB	IBB	SO	HBP	SH	SF	SB	CS	SB%	GDP	Avg	OBP	SLG	Pos	G	PO	A	E	DP	FPct
1951 NYG	27	2	2	0	0	0	0	0	0	0	0	0	0	1	0	0	0	0	0	—	0	.000	.000	.000	—						

MICKEY LOLICH—Michael Stephen Lolich—Throws: Left; Bats: Both

Ht: 6'1"; Wt: 170 lbs; Born: 9/12/1940 in Portland, Oregon; Debut: 5/12/1963

LCS		Pitching																										
Year Tm	Age	G	GS	CG	GF	IP	BFP	H	R	ER	HR	SH	SF	HB	TBB	IBB	SO	WP	Bk	W	L	Pct	ShO	Sv-Op	Hld	OAvg	OOBP	ERA
1972 Det	32	2	2	0	0	19.0	76	14	4	3	1	1	1	0	5	0	10	0	0	0	1	.000	0	0- 0	0	.203	.253	1.42
World Series		Pitching																										
Year Tm	Age	G	GS	CG	GF	IP	BFP	H	R	ER	HR	SH	SF	HB	TBB	IBB	SO	WP	Bk	W	L	Pct	ShO	Sv-Op	Hld	OAvg	OOBP	ERA
1968 Det	28	3	3	3	0	27.0	104	20	5	5	2	0	0	1	6	0	21	0	0	3	0	1.000	0	0- 0	0	.206	.260	1.67
Postseason Totals		5	5	3	0	46.0	360	34	9	8	3	1	1	1	11	0	31	0	0	3	1	.750	0	0-0	0	.205	.257	1.57

LCS		Batting																							Fielding						
Year Tm	Age	G	AB	H	2B	3B	HR	TB	R	RBI	GW	TBB	IBB	SO	HBP	SH	SF	SB	CS	SB%	GDP	Avg	OBP	SLG	Pos	G	PO	A	E	DP	FPct
1972 Det	32	2	7	0	0	0	0	0	0	0	0	0	0	2	0	0	0	0	0	—	0	.000	.000	.000	P	2	1	4	0	0	1.000
World Series		Batting																							Fielding						
Year Tm	Age	G	AB	H	2B	3B	HR	TB	R	RBI	GW	TBB	IBB	SO	HBP	SH	SF	SB	CS	SB%	GDP	Avg	OBP	SLG	Pos	G	PO	A	E	DP	FPct
1968 Det	28	3	12	3	0	0	1	6	2	2	0	1	0	5	0	0	0	0	0	—	0	.250	.308	.500	P	3	1	4	0	0	1.000
Postseason Totals		5	19	3	0	0	1	6	2	2	0	1	0	7	0	0	0	0	0	—	0	.158	.200	.316	P	5	2	8	0	0	1.000

SHERM LOLLAR—John Sherman Lollar—Bats: Right; Throws: Right

Ht: 6'1"; Wt: 185 lbs; Born: 8/23/1924 in Durham, Arkansas; Debut: 4/20/1946; Died: 9/24/1977

World Series		Batting																							Fielding						
Year Tm	Age	G	AB	H	2B	3B	HR	TB	R	RBI	GW	TBB	IBB	SO	HBP	SH	SF	SB	CS	SB%	GDP	Avg	OBP	SLG	Pos	G	PO	A	E	DP	FPct
1947 NYA	23	2	4	3	2	0	0	5	3	1	0	0	0	0	0	0	0	0	0	—	0	.750	.750	1.250	C	2	2	1	0	0	1.000
1959 ChA	35	6	22	5	0	0	1	8	3	5	0	1	0	3	0	0	1	0	0	—	2	.227	.250	.364	C	6	29	5	0	0	1.000
WS Totals		8	26	8	2	0	1	13	6	6	0	1	0	3	0	0	1	0	0	—	2	.308	.321	.500	C	8	31	6	0	0	1.000

TIM LOLLAR—William Timothy Lollar—Throws: Left; Bats: Left

Ht: 6'3"; Wt: 200 lbs; Born: 3/17/1956 in Poplar Bluff, Missouri; Debut: 6/28/1980

LCS		Pitching																										
Year Tm	Age	G	GS	CG	GF	IP	BFP	H	R	ER	HR	SH	SF	HB	TBB	IBB	SO	WP	Bk	W	L	Pct	ShO	Sv-Op	Hld	OAvg	OOBP	ERA
1984 SD	28	1	1	0	0	4.1	20	3	3	3	2	0	0	0	4	0	3	0	0	0	0	—	0	0- 0	0	.188	.350	6.23
World Series		Pitching																										
Year Tm	Age	G	GS	CG	GF	IP	BFP	H	R	ER	HR	SH	SF	HB	TBB	IBB	SO	WP	Bk	W	L	Pct	ShO	Sv-Op	Hld	OAvg	OOBP	ERA
1984 SD	28	1	1	0	0	1.2	13	4	4	4	1	0	0	0	4	0	0	1	0	0	1	.000	0	0- 0	0	.444	.615	21.60
Postseason Totals		2	2	0	0	6.0	66	7	7	7	3	0	0	0	8	0	3	1	0	0	1	.000	0	0-0	0	.280	.455	10.50

LCS		Batting																							Fielding						
Year Tm	Age	G	AB	H	2B	3B	HR	TB	R	RBI	GW	TBB	IBB	SO	HBP	SH	SF	SB	CS	SB%	GDP	Avg	OBP	SLG	Pos	G	PO	A	E	DP	FPct
1984 SD	28	1	1	0	0	0	0	0	0	0	0	0	0	1	0	0	0	0	0	—	0	.000	.000	.000	P	1	0	0	0	0	—
World Series		Batting																							Fielding						
Year Tm	Age	G	AB	H	2B	3B	HR	TB	R	RBI	GW	TBB	IBB	SO	HBP	SH	SF	SB	CS	SB%	GDP	Avg	OBP	SLG	Pos	G	PO	A	E	DP	FPct
1984 SD	28	1	0	0	0	0	0	0	0	0	0	0	0	0	0	0	0	0	0	—	0	—	—	—	P	1	0	0	0	0	—
Postseason Totals		2	1	0	0	0	0	0	0	0	0	0	0	1	0	0	0	0	0	—	0	.000	.000	.000	P	2	0	0	0	0	—

ERNIE LOMBARDI (HOF 1986-V)—Ernesto Natali Lombardi—Nicknames: Schnozz, Bocci—B: R; T: R

Ht: 6'3"; Wt: 230 lbs; Born: 4/6/1908 in Oakland, Calif.; Deb.: 4/15/1931; Died: 9/26/1977

World Series		Batting																							Fielding						
Year Tm	Age	G	AB	H	2B	3B	HR	TB	R	RBI	GW	TBB	IBB	SO	HBP	SH	SF	SB	CS	SB%	GDP	Avg	OBP	SLG	Pos	G	PO	A	E	DP	FPct
1939 Cin	31	4	14	3	0	0	0	3	0	2	0	0	0	1	1	0	0	0	0	—	1	.214	.267	.214	C	4	22	1	1	0	.958
1940 Cin	32	2	3	1	1	0	0	2	0	0	0	1	1	0	0	0	0	0	0	—	0	.333	.500	.667	C	1	4	0	0	0	1.000
WS Totals		6	17	4	1	0	0	5	0	2	0	1	1	1	1	0	0	0	0	—	1	.235	.316	.294	C	5	26	1	1	0	.964

VIC LOMBARDI—Victor Alvin Lombardi—Throws: Left; Bats: Left

Ht: 5'7"; Wt: 158 lbs; Born: 9/20/1922 in Reedley, California; Debut: 4/18/1945; Died: 12/3/1997

World Series		Pitching																										
Year Tm	Age	G	GS	CG	GF	IP	BFP	H	R	ER	HR	SH	SF	HB	TBB	IBB	SO	WP	Bk	W	L	Pct	ShO	Sv-Op	Hld	OAvg	OOBP	ERA
1947 Bro	25	2	2	0	0	6.2	34	14	9	9	1	0	0	0	1	1	5	1	0	0	1	.000	0	0- 0	0	.424	.441	12.15

World Series		Batting																							Fielding						
Year Tm	Age	G	AB	H	2B	3B	HR	TB	R	RBI	GW	TBB	IBB	SO	HBP	SH	SF	SB	CS	SB%	GDP	Avg	OBP	SLG	Pos	G	PO	A	E	DP	FPct
1947 Bro	25	3	3	0	0	0	0	0	0	0	0	0	0	0	0	0	0	0	0	—	0	.000	.000	.000	P	2	0	0	0	0	—

STEVE LOMBARDOZZI—Stephen Paul Lombardozzi—Bats: Right; Throws: Right

Ht: 6'0"; Wt: 175 lbs; Born: 4/26/1960 in Malden, Massachusetts; Debut: 7/12/1985

LCS		Batting																							Fielding						
Year Tm	Age	G	AB	H	2B	3B	HR	TB	R	RBI	GW	TBB	IBB	SO	HBP	SH	SF	SB	CS	SB%	GDP	Avg	OBP	SLG	Pos	G	PO	A	E	DP	FPct
1987 Min	27	5	15	4	0	0	0	4	2	1	0	2	0	2	0	1	0	0	0	—	0	.267	.353	.267	2B	5	8	9	1	3	.944
World Series		Batting																							Fielding						
Year Tm	Age	G	AB	H	2B	3B	HR	TB	R	RBI	GW	TBB	IBB	SO	HBP	SH	SF	SB	CS	SB%	GDP	Avg	OBP	SLG	Pos	G	PO	A	E	DP	FPct
1987 Min	27	6	17	7	1	0	1	11	3	4	1	2	0	2	0	0	0	0	0	—	0	.412	.474	.647	2B	6	9	24	0	3	1.000
Postseason Totals		11	32	11	1	0	1	15	5	5	1	4	0	4	0	1	0	0	0	—	0	.344	.417	.469	2B	11	17	33	1	6	.980

JIM LONBORG—James Reynold Lonborg—Nickname: Gentleman Jim—Throws: Right; Bats: Right

Ht: 6'5"; Wt: 200 lbs; Born: 4/16/1942 in Santa Maria, California; Debut: 4/23/1965

LCS — Pitching

Year Tm	Age	G	GS	CG	GF	IP	BFP	H	R	ER	HR	SH	SF	HB	TBB	IBB	SO	WP	Bk	W	L	Pct	ShO	Sv-Op	Hld	OAvg	OOBP	ERA
1976 Phi	34	1	1	0	0	5.1	20	2	3	1	0	0	0	0	2	0	2	0	0	0	1	.000	0	0-0	0	.111	.200	1.69
1977 Phi	35	1	1	0	0	4.0	18	5	5	5	1	1	0	0	1	1	1	0	0	0	1	.000	0	0-0	0	.313	.353	11.25
LCS Totals		2	2	0	0	9.1	76	7	8	6	1	1	0	0	3	1	3	0	0	0	2	.000	0	0-0	0	.206	.270	5.79

World Series — Pitching

Year Tm	Age	G	GS	CG	GF	IP	BFP	H	R	ER	HR	SH	SF	HB	TBB	IBB	SO	WP	Bk	W	L	Pct	ShO	Sv-Op	Hld	OAvg	OOBP	ERA
1967 Bos-*C*	25	3	3	2	0	24.0	89	14	8	7	3	0	1	0	2	0	11	1	0	2	1	.667	1	0-0	0	.163	.180	2.63
Postseason Totals		5	5	2	0	33.1	254	21	16	13	4	1	1	0	5	1	14	1	0	2	3	.400	1	0-0	0	.175	.206	3.51

LCS — Batting / Fielding

Year Tm	Age	G	AB	H	2B	3B	HR	TB	R	RBI	GW	TBB	IBB	SO	HBP	SH	SF	SB	CS	SB%	GDP	Avg	OBP	SLG	Pos	G	PO	A	E	DP	FPct
1976 Phi	34	1	1	0	0	0	0	0	0	0	0	0	0	0	0	1	0	0	0	—	1	.000	.000	.000	P	1	0	2	0	0	1.000
1977 Phi	35	1	1	0	0	0	0	0	0	0	0	0	0	1	0	0	0	0	0	—	0	.000	.000	.000	P	1	0	2	0	0	1.000
LCS Totals		2	2	0	0	0	0	0	0	0	0	0	0	1	0	1	0	0	0	—	1	.000	.000	.000	P	2	0	4	0	0	1.000

World Series — Batting / Fielding

Year Tm	Age	G	AB	H	2B	3B	HR	TB	R	RBI	GW	TBB	IBB	SO	HBP	SH	SF	SB	CS	SB%	GDP	Avg	OBP	SLG	Pos	G	PO	A	E	DP	FPct
1967 Bos	25	3	9	0	0	0	0	0	0	0	0	0	0	7	0	0	0	0	0	—	0	.000	.000	.000	P	3	1	2	0	0	1.000
Postseason Totals		5	11	0	0	0	0	0	0	0	0	0	0	8	0	1	0	0	0	—	1	.000	.000	.000	P	5	1	6	0	0	1.000

DALE LONG—Richard Dale Long—Bats: Left; Throws: Left

Ht: 6'4"; Wt: 205 lbs; Born: 2/6/1926 in Springfield, Missouri; Debut: 4/21/1951; Died: 1/27/1991

World Series — Batting / Fielding

Year Tm	Age	G	AB	H	2B	3B	HR	TB	R	RBI	GW	TBB	IBB	SO	HBP	SH	SF	SB	CS	SB%	GDP	Avg	OBP	SLG	Pos	G	PO	A	E	DP	FPct
1960 NYA	34	3	3	1	0	0	0	1	0	0	0	0	0	0	0	0	0	0	0	—	0	.333	.333	.333	—						
1962 NYA	36	2	5	1	0	0	0	1	0	1	0	0	0	1	0	0	0	0	0	—	0	.200	.200	.200	1B	2	9	3	0	1	1.000
WS Totals		5	8	2	0	0	0	2	0	1	0	0	0	1	0	0	0	0	0	—	0	.250	.250	.250	1B	2	9	3	0	1	1.000

TONY LONGMIRE—Anthony Eugene Longmire—Bats: Left; Throws: Right

Ht: 6'1"; Wt: 197 lbs; Born: 8/12/1968 in Vallejo, California; Debut: 9/3/1993

LCS — Batting / Fielding

Year Tm	Age	G	AB	H	2B	3B	HR	TB	R	RBI	GW	TBB	IBB	SO	HBP	SH	SF	SB	CS	SB%	GDP	Avg	OBP	SLG	Pos	G	PO	A	E	DP	FPct
1993 Phi	25	1	1	0	0	0	0	0	0	0	0	0	0	1	0	0	0	0	0	—	0	.000	.000	.000	—						

ED LOPAT—Edmund Walter Lopat—Nickname: Steady Eddie—Throws: Left; Bats: Left

Ht: 5'10"; Wt: 185 lbs; Born: 6/21/1918 in New York, New York; Debut: 4/30/1944; Died: 6/15/1992

World Series — Pitching

Year Tm	Age	G	GS	CG	GF	IP	BFP	H	R	ER	HR	SH	SF	HB	TBB	IBB	SO	WP	Bk	W	L	Pct	ShO	Sv-Op	Hld	OAvg	OOBP	ERA
1949 NYA	31	1	1	0	0	5.2	26	9	4	4	0	0	0	0	1	0	4	0	0	1	0	1.000	0	0-0	0	.360	.385	6.35
1950 NYA	32	1	1	0	0	8.0	32	9	2	2	0	3	0	0	0	0	5	0	0	0	0	—	0	0-0	0	.310	.310	2.25
1951 NYA	33	2	2	2	0	18.0	66	10	2	1	0	0	0	0	3	0	4	0	0	2	0	1.000	0	0-0	0	.159	.197	0.50
1952 NYA	34	2	2	0	0	11.1	53	14	6	6	0	2	0	0	4	3	3	0	0	0	1	.000	0	0-0	0	.298	.353	4.76
1953 NYA	35	1	1	1	0	9.0	39	9	2	2	0	0	0	0	4	1	3	0	0	1	0	1.000	0	0-0	0	.257	.333	2.00
WS Totals		7	7	3	0	52.0	432	51	16	15	0	5	0	0	12	4	19	0	0	4	1	.800	0	0-0	0	.256	.299	2.60

World Series — Batting / Fielding

Year Tm	Age	G	AB	H	2B	3B	HR	TB	R	RBI	GW	TBB	IBB	SO	HBP	SH	SF	SB	CS	SB%	GDP	Avg	OBP	SLG	Pos	G	PO	A	E	DP	FPct
1949 NYA	31	1	3	1	1	0	0	2	0	1	0	0	0	0	0	0	0	0	0	—	0	.333	.333	.667	P	1	0	1	0	0	1.000
1950 NYA	32	1	2	1	0	0	0	1	0	0	0	0	0	1	0	0	0	0	0	—	0	.500	.500	.500	P	1	1	4	0	0	1.000
1951 NYA	33	2	8	1	0	0	0	1	0	1	0	0	0	2	0	0	0	0	0	—	0	.125	.125	.125	P	2	2	4	0	1	1.000
1952 NYA	34	2	3	1	0	0	0	1	0	1	0	1	0	1	0	0	0	0	0	—	0	.333	.500	.333	P	2	0	1	0	0	1.000
1953 NYA	35	1	3	0	0	0	0	0	0	0	0	0	0	2	0	0	0	0	0	—	0	.000	.000	.000	P	1	0	2	0	0	1.000
WS Totals		7	19	4	1	0	0	5	0	3	0	1	0	6	0	0	0	0	0	—	0	.211	.250	.263	P	7	3	12	0	1	1.000

STAN LOPATA—Stanley Edward Lopata—Nickname: Stash—Bats: Right; Throws: Right

Ht: 6'2"; Wt: 210 lbs; Born: 9/12/1925 in Delray, Michigan; Debut: 9/19/1948

World Series — Batting / Fielding

Year Tm	Age	G	AB	H	2B	3B	HR	TB	R	RBI	GW	TBB	IBB	SO	HBP	SH	SF	SB	CS	SB%	GDP	Avg	OBP	SLG	Pos	G	PO	A	E	DP	FPct
1950 Phi	25	2	1	0	0	0	0	0	0	0	0	0	0	1	0	0	0	0	0	—	0	.000	.000	.000	C	1	1	0	0	0	1.000

DAVEY LOPES—David Earl Lopes—Bats: Right; Throws: Right

Ht: 5'9"; Wt: 170 lbs; Born: 5/3/1945 in East Providence, Rhode Island; Debut: 9/22/1972

Division Series — Batting / Fielding

Year Tm	Age	G	AB	H	2B	3B	HR	TB	R	RBI	GW	TBB	IBB	SO	HBP	SH	SF	SB	CS	SB%	GDP	Avg	OBP	SLG	Pos	G	PO	A	E	DP	FPct
1981 LA	36	5	20	4	1	0	0	5	1	0	0	3	1	7	0	0	0	1	0	1.00	0	.200	.304	.250	2B	5	7	12	0	1	1.000

LCS — Batting / Fielding

Year Tm	Age	G	AB	H	2B	3B	HR	TB	R	RBI	GW	TBB	IBB	SO	HBP	SH	SF	SB	CS	SB%	GDP	Avg	OBP	SLG	Pos	G	PO	A	E	DP	FPct
1974 LA	29	4	15	4	0	1	0	6	4	3	1	5	0	1	0	0	0	3	0	1.00	0	.267	.450	.400	2B	4	9	18	1	4	.964
1977 LA	32	4	17	4	0	0	0	4	2	3	0	2	0	0	0	0	0	0	1	.00	0	.235	.316	.235	2B	4	9	9	1	1	.947
1978 LA	33	4	18	7	1	1	2	16	3	5	1	0	0	1	0	0	0	1	0	1.00	0	.389	.389	.889	2B	4	10	10	2	3	.909
1981 LA	36	5	18	5	0	0	0	5	0	0	0	1	0	3	0	1	0	5	0	1.00	0	.278	.316	.278	2B	5	13	13	0	5	1.000
1984 ChN	39	2	1	0	0	0	0	0	0	0	0	0	0	0	0	0	0	0	0	—	0	.000	.000	.000	OF	1	0	0	0	0	—
1986 Hou	41	3	2	0	0	0	0	0	1	0	0	1	0	0	0	0	0	0	0	—	1	.000	.333	.000	—						
LCS Totals		22	71	20	1	2	2	31	10	11	2	9	0	5	0	1	0	9	1	.90	1	.282	.363	.437	2B	17	41	50	4	13	.958

World Series — Batting / Fielding

Year Tm	Age	G	AB	H	2B	3B	HR	TB	R	RBI	GW	TBB	IBB	SO	HBP	SH	SF	SB	CS	SB%	GDP	Avg	OBP	SLG	Pos	G	PO	A	E	DP	FPct
1974 LA	29	5	18	2	0	0	0	2	2	0	0	3	0	4	0	0	0	2	1	.67	0	.111	.238	.111	2B	5	19	9	0	3	1.000
1977 LA	32	6	24	4	0	1	1	9	3	2	0	4	0	3	0	0	0	2	1	.67	0	.167	.286	.375	2B	6	12	22	0	2	1.000
1978 LA	33	6	26	8	0	0	3	17	7	7	0	2	0	1	0	0	0	2	0	1.00	1	.308	.357	.654	2B	6	10	19	1	4	.967
1981 LA	36	6	22	5	1	0	0	6	6	2	0	4	0	3	0	1	0	4	0	1.00	0	.227	.346	.273	2B	6	25	14	6	4	.867
WS Totals		23	90	19	1	1	4	34	18	11	0	13	0	11	0	1	0	10	2	.83	1	.211	.311	.378	2B	23	66	64	7	13	.949
Postseason Totals		50	181	43	3	3	6	70	29	22	2	25	1	23	0	2	0	20	3	.87	2	.238	.330	.387	2B	45	114	126	11	27	.956

AURELIO LOPEZ—Aurelio Alejandro Lopez—Nickname: Senor Smoke—Throws: Right; Bats: Right

Ht: 6'0"; Wt: 185 lbs; Born: 9/21/1948 in Tecamachalco, Mexico; Debut: 9/1/1974; Died: 9/22/1992

LCS — Pitching

Year Tm	Age	G	GS	CG	GF	IP	BFP	H	R	ER	HR	SH	SF	HB	TBB	IBB	SO	WP	Bk	W	L	Pct	ShO	Sv-Op	Hld	OAvg	OOBP	ERA
1984 Det	36	1	0	0	1	3.0	13	4	0	0	0	0	0	0	1	0	2	0	0	1	0	1.000	0	0-0	0	.333	.385	0.00
1986 Hou	38	2	0	0	0	3.1	20	7	3	3	0	0	0	0	4	3	3	0	0	0	1	.000	0	0-0	0	.438	.550	8.10
LCS Totals		3	0	0	1	6.1	66	11	3	3	0	0	0	0	5	3	5	0	0	1	1	.500	0	0-0	0	.393	.485	4.26

World Series — Pitching

Year Tm	Age	G	GS	CG	GF	IP	BFP	H	R	ER	HR	SH	SF	HB	TBB	IBB	SO	WP	Bk	W	L	Pct	ShO	Sv-Op	Hld	OAvg	OOBP	ERA
1984 Det	36	2	0	0	0	3.0	11	1	0	0	0	0	0	0	1	0	4	0	0	1	0	1.000	0	0-0	0	.100	.182	0.00
Postseason Totals		5	0	0	1	9.1	88	12	3	3	0	0	0	0	6	3	9	0	0	2	1	.667	0	0-0	0	.316	.409	2.89

LCS — Batting / Fielding

Year Tm	Age	G	AB	H	2B	3B	HR	TB	R	RBI	GW	TBB	IBB	SO	HBP	SH	SF	SB	CS	SB%	GDP	Avg	OBP	SLG	Pos	G	PO	A	E	DP	FPct
1984 Det	36	1	0	0	0	0	0	0	0	0	0	0	0	0	0	0	0	0	0	—	0	—	—	—	P	1	0	0	0	0	—
1986 Hou	38	2	0	0	0	0	0	0	0	0	0	0	0	0	0	0	0	0	0	—	0	—	—	—	P	2	0	1	0	0	1.000
LCS Totals		3	0	0	0	0	0	0	0	0	0	0	0	0	0	0	0	0	0	—	0	—	—	—	P	3	0	1	0	0	1.000

World Series — Batting / Fielding

Year Tm	Age	G	AB	H	2B	3B	HR	TB	R	RBI	GW	TBB	IBB	SO	HBP	SH	SF	SB	CS	SB%	GDP	Avg	OBP	SLG	Pos	G	PO	A	E	DP	FPct
1984 Det	36	2	0	0	0	0	0	0	0	0	0	0	0	0	0	0	0	0	0	—	0	—	—	—	P	2	0	0	0	0	—
Postseason Totals		5	0	0	0	0	0	0	0	0	0	0	0	0	0	0	0	0	0	—	0	—	—	—	P	5	0	1	0	0	1.000

HECTOR LOPEZ—Hector Headley Lopez—Bats: Right; Throws: Right

Ht: 5'11"; Wt: 182 lbs; Born: 7/8/1929 in Colon, Panama; Debut: 5/12/1955

World Series		Batting																							Fielding						
Year Tm	Age	G	AB	H	2B	3B	HR	TB	R	RBI	GW	TBB	IBB	SO	HBP	SH	SF	SB	CS	SB%	GDP	Avg	OBP	SLG	Pos	G	PO	A	E	DP	FPct
1960 NYA	31	3	7	3	0	0	0	3	0	0	0	0	0	0	0	0	0	0	0	—	2	.429	.429	.429	OF	1	0	1	0	0	1.000
1961 NYA	32	4	9	3	0	1	1	8	3	7	0	2	0	3	0	1	0	0	0	—	0	.333	.455	.889	OF	3	8	0	0	0	1.000
1962 NYA	33	2	2	0	0	0	0	0	0	0	0	0	0	0	0	0	0	0	0	—	0	.000	.000	.000	—						
1963 NYA	34	3	8	2	2	0	0	4	1	0	0	0	0	1	0	0	0	0	0	—	0	.250	.250	.500	OF	2	2	0	0	0	1.000
1964 NYA	35	3	2	0	0	0	0	0	0	0	0	0	0	2	0	0	0	0	0	—	0	.000	.000	.000	OF	1	0	0	0	0	—
WS Totals		15	28	8	2	1	1	15	4	7	0	2	0	6	0	1	0	0	0	—	2	.286	.333	.536	OF	7	10	1	0	0	1.000

JAVY LOPEZ—Javier Torres Lopez—Bats: Right; Throws: Right

Ht: 6'2"; Wt: 185 lbs; Born: 11/5/1970 in Ponce, Puerto Rico; Debut: 9/18/1992

Division Series		Batting																							Fielding						
Year Tm	Age	G	AB	H	2B	3B	HR	TB	R	RBI	GW	TBB	IBB	SO	HBP	SH	SF	SB	CS	SB%	GDP	Avg	OBP	SLG	Pos	G	PO	A	E	DP	FPct
1995 Atl	24	3	9	4	0	0	0	4	0	3	0	0	0	3	0	0	1	0	1	.00	0	.444	.400	.444	C	3	22	3	0	1	1.000
1996 Atl	25	2	7	2	0	0	1	5	1	1	1	1	0	0	0	0	0	1	0	1.00	0	.286	.375	.714	C	2	21	1	1	0	.957
1997 Atl	26	2	7	2	2	0	0	4	3	1	0	2	0	1	0	0	0	0	0	—	0	.286	.444	.571	C	2	18	0	0	0	1.000
DS Totals		7	23	8	2	0	1	13	4	5	1	3	0	4	0	0	1	1	1	.50	0	.348	.407	.565	C	7	61	4	1	1	.985
LCS		**Batting**																							**Fielding**						
Year Tm	Age	G	AB	H	2B	3B	HR	TB	R	RBI	GW	TBB	IBB	SO	HBP	SH	SF	SB	CS	SB%	GDP	Avg	OBP	SLG	Pos	G	PO	A	E	DP	FPct
1992 Atl	21	1	1	0	0	0	0	0	0	0	0	0	0	0	0	0	0	0	0	—	0	.000	.000	.000	C	1	2	0	0	0	1.000
1995 Atl	24	3	14	5	1	0	1	9	2	3	0	0	0	1	0	0	0	0	0	—	0	.357	.357	.643	C	3	28	2	0	0	1.000
1996 Atl	25	7	24	13	5	0	2	24	8	6	1	3	1	1	1	0	0	1	0	1.00	0	.542	.607	1.000	C	7	48	3	0	0	1.000
1997 Atl	26	5	17	1	1	0	0	2	0	2	0	1	0	7	0	0	2	0	0	—	0	.059	.100	.118	C	5	40	3	0	2	1.000
LCS Totals		16	56	19	7	0	3	35	10	11	1	4	1	9	1	0	2	1	0	1.00	0	.339	.381	.625	C	16	118	8	0	2	1.000
World Series		**Batting**																							**Fielding**						
Year Tm	Age	G	AB	H	2B	3B	HR	TB	R	RBI	GW	TBB	IBB	SO	HBP	SH	SF	SB	CS	SB%	GDP	Avg	OBP	SLG	Pos	G	PO	A	E	DP	FPct
1995 Atl	24	6	17	3	2	0	1	8	1	3	1	1	0	1	1	0	0	0	0	—	1	.176	.263	.471	C	6	32	4	0	0	1.000
1996 Atl	25	6	21	4	0	0	0	4	3	1	0	3	0	4	0	0	1	0	0	—	2	.190	.280	.190	C	6	41	4	0	0	1.000
WS Totals		12	38	7	2	0	1	12	4	4	1	4	0	5	1	0	1	0	0	—	3	.184	.273	.316	C	12	73	8	0	0	1.000
Postseason Totals		35	117	34	11	0	5	60	18	20	3	11	1	18	2	0	4	2	1	.67	3	.291	.351	.513	C	35	252	20	1	3	.996

LUIS LOPEZ—Luis Manuel Lopez—Bats: Both; Throws: Right

Ht: 5'11"; Wt: 175 lbs; Born: 9/4/1970 in Cidra, Puerto Rico; Debut: 9/7/1993

Division Series		Batting																							Fielding						
Year Tm	Age	G	AB	H	2B	3B	HR	TB	R	RBI	GW	TBB	IBB	SO	HBP	SH	SF	SB	CS	SB%	GDP	Avg	OBP	SLG	Pos	G	PO	A	E	DP	FPct
1996 SD	26	1	0	0	0	0	0	0	0	0	0	0	0	0	0	0	0	0	0	—	0	—	—	—	—						

MARCELINO LOPEZ—Marcelino Pons Lopez—Throws: Left; Bats: Right

Ht: 6'3"; Wt: 195 lbs; Born: 9/23/1943 in Havana, Cuba; Debut: 4/14/1963

LCS		Pitching																										
Year Tm	Age	G	GS	CG	GF	IP	BFP	H	R	ER	HR	SH	SF	HB	TBB	IBB	SO	WP	Bk	W	L	Pct	ShO	Sv-Op	Hld	OAvg	OOBP	ERA
1969 Bal	26	1	0	0	0	0.1	4	1	0	0	0	0	0	0	2	1	0	1	0	0	0	—	0	0-0	0	.500	.750	0.00
World Series		**Pitching**																										
Year Tm	Age	G	GS	CG	GF	IP	BFP	H	R	ER	HR	SH	SF	HB	TBB	IBB	SO	WP	Bk	W	L	Pct	ShO	Sv-Op	Hld	OAvg	OOBP	ERA
1970 Bal	27	1	0	0	0	0.1	1	0	0	0	0	0	0	0	0	0	0	0	0	0	0	—	0	0-0	1	.000	.000	0.00
Postseason Totals		2	0	0	0	0.2	10	1	0	0	0	0	0	0	2	1	0	1	0	0	0	—	0	0-0	1	.333	.600	0.00

LCS		Batting																							Fielding						
Year Tm	Age	G	AB	H	2B	3B	HR	TB	R	RBI	GW	TBB	IBB	SO	HBP	SH	SF	SB	CS	SB%	GDP	Avg	OBP	SLG	Pos	G	PO	A	E	DP	FPct
1969 Bal	26	1	0	0	0	0	0	0	0	0	0	0	0	0	0	0	0	0	0	—	0	—	—	—	P	1	0	0	0	0	—
World Series		**Batting**																							**Fielding**						
Year Tm	Age	G	AB	H	2B	3B	HR	TB	R	RBI	GW	TBB	IBB	SO	HBP	SH	SF	SB	CS	SB%	GDP	Avg	OBP	SLG	Pos	G	PO	A	E	DP	FPct
1970 Bal	27	1	0	0	0	0	0	0	0	0	0	0	0	0	0	0	0	0	0	—	0	—	—	—	P	1	0	0	0	0	—
Postseason Totals		2	0	0	0	0	0	0	0	0	0	0	0	0	0	0	0	0	0	—	0	—	—	—	P	2	0	0	0	0	—

BRIS LORD—Bristol Robotham Lord—Nickname: The Human Eyeball—Bats: Right; Throws: Right

Ht: 5'9"; Wt: 185 lbs; Born: 9/21/1883 in Upland, Pennsylvania; Debut: 4/21/1905; Died: 11/13/1964

World Series		Batting																							Fielding						
Year Tm	Age	G	AB	H	2B	3B	HR	TB	R	RBI	GW	TBB	IBB	SO	HBP	SH	SF	SB	CS	SB%	GDP	Avg	OBP	SLG	Pos	G	PO	A	E	DP	FPct
1905 Phi	22	5	20	2	0	0	0	2	0	2	1	0	0	5	0	0	0	0	0	—	0	.100	.100	.100	OF	5	12	0	0	0	1.000
1910 Phi	27	5	22	4	2	0	0	6	3	1	0	1	0	3	0	1	0	0	1	.00	0	.182	.217	.273	OF	5	11	0	0	0	1.000
1911 Phi	28	6	27	5	2	0	0	7	2	1	0	0	0	5	0	0	0	0	0	—	0	.185	.185	.259	OF	6	14	1	0	0	1.000
WS Totals		16	69	11	4	0	0	15	5	4	1	1	0	13	0	1	0	0	1	.00	0	.159	.171	.217	OF	16	37	1	0	0	1.000

GROVER LOWDERMILK—Grover Cleveland Lowdermilk—Nickname: Slim—Throws: Right; Bats: Right

Ht: 6'4"; Wt: 190 lbs; Born: 1/15/1885 in Sandborn, Indiana; Debut: 7/3/1909; Died: 3/31/1968

World Series		Pitching																										
Year Tm	Age	G	GS	CG	GF	IP	BFP	H	R	ER	HR	SH	SF	HB	TBB	IBB	SO	WP	Bk	W	L	Pct	ShO	Sv-Op	Hld	OAvg	OOBP	ERA
1919 ChA	34	1	0	0	1	1.0	7	2	1	1	0	1	0	1	1	0	0	0	0	0	0	—	0	0-0	0	.500	.667	9.00

World Series		Batting																							Fielding						
Year Tm	Age	G	AB	H	2B	3B	HR	TB	R	RBI	GW	TBB	IBB	SO	HBP	SH	SF	SB	CS	SB%	GDP	Avg	OBP	SLG	Pos	G	PO	A	E	DP	FPct
1919 ChA	34	1	0	0	0	0	0	0	0	0	0	0	0	0	0	0	0	0	0	—	0	—	—	—	P	1	0	1	0	0	1.000

JOHN LOWENSTEIN—John Lee Lowenstein—Nickname: Captain Midnight—Bats: Left; Throws: Right

Ht: 6'0"; Wt: 175 lbs; Born: 1/27/1947 in Wolf Point, Montana; Debut: 9/2/1970

LCS		Batting																							Fielding						
Year Tm	Age	G	AB	H	2B	3B	HR	TB	R	RBI	GW	TBB	IBB	SO	HBP	SH	SF	SB	CS	SB%	GDP	Avg	OBP	SLG	Pos	G	PO	A	E	DP	FPct
1979 Bal	32	4	6	1	0	0	1	4	2	3	1	2	0	2	0	0	0	0	0	—	0	.167	.375	.667	OF	3	6	0	0	0	1.000
1983 Bal	36	3	6	1	1	0	0	2	0	2	0	1	0	2	0	0	0	0	0	—	0	.167	.286	.333	OF	2	4	0	0	0	1.000
LCS Totals		7	12	2	1	0	1	6	2	5	1	3	0	4	0	0	0	0	0	—	0	.167	.333	.500	OF	5	10	0	0	0	1.000
World Series		**Batting**																							**Fielding**						
Year Tm	Age	G	AB	H	2B	3B	HR	TB	R	RBI	GW	TBB	IBB	SO	HBP	SH	SF	SB	CS	SB%	GDP	Avg	OBP	SLG	Pos	G	PO	A	E	DP	FPct
1979 Bal	32	6	13	3	1	0	0	4	2	3	0	1	0	3	0	0	0	0	0	—	0	.231	.286	.308	OF	5	6	0	1	0	.857
1983 Bal	36	4	13	5	1	0	1	9	2	1	0	0	0	3	0	0	0	0	0	—	0	.385	.385	.692	OF	4	4	0	1	0	.800
WS Totals		10	26	8	2	0	1	13	4	4	0	1	0	6	0	0	0	0	0	—	0	.308	.333	.500	OF	9	10	0	2	0	.833
Postseason Totals		17	38	10	3	0	2	19	6	9	1	4	0	10	0	0	0	0	0	—	0	.263	.333	.500	OF	14	20	0	2	0	.909

TURK LOWN—Omar Joseph Lown—Throws: Right; Bats: Right

Ht: 6'0"; Wt: 180 lbs; Born: 5/30/1924 in Brooklyn, New York; Debut: 4/24/1951

World Series		Pitching																										
Year Tm	Age	G	GS	CG	GF	IP	BFP	H	R	ER	HR	SH	SF	HB	TBB	IBB	SO	WP	Bk	W	L	Pct	ShO	Sv-Op	Hld	OAvg	OOBP	ERA
1959 ChA	35	3	0	0	1	3.1	13	2	0	0	0	0	0	0	1	0	3	0	0	0	0	—	0	0-0	0	.167	.231	0.00

World Series		Batting																							Fielding						
Year Tm	Age	G	AB	H	2B	3B	HR	TB	R	RBI	GW	TBB	IBB	SO	HBP	SH	SF	SB	CS	SB%	GDP	Avg	OBP	SLG	Pos	G	PO	A	E	DP	FPct
1959 ChA	35	3	0	0	0	0	0	0	0	0	0	0	0	0	0	0	0	0	0	—	0	—	—	—	P	3	0	0	0	0	—

PEANUTS LOWREY—Harry Lee Lowrey—Bats: Right; Throws: Right

Ht: 5'8"; Wt: 170 lbs; Born: 8/27/1918 in Culver City, California; Debut: 4/14/1942; Died: 7/2/1986

World Series		Batting																							Fielding						
Year Tm	Age	G	AB	H	2B	3B	HR	TB	R	RBI	GW	TBB	IBB	SO	HBP	SH	SF	SB	CS	SB%	GDP	Avg	OBP	SLG	Pos	G	PO	A	E	DP	FPct
1945 ChN	27	7	29	9	1	0	0	10	4	0	0	1	0	2	0	1	0	0	0	—	1	.310	.333	.345	OF	7	23	1	0	0	1.000

GARY LUCAS—Gary Paul Lucas—Throws: Left; Bats: Left

Ht: 6'5"; Wt: 200 lbs; Born: 11/8/1954 in Riverside, California; Debut: 4/16/1980

LCS — Pitching

Year Tm	Age	G	GS	CG	GF	IP	BFP	H	R	ER	HR	SH	SF	HB	TBB	IBB	SO	WP	Bk	W	L	Pct	ShO	Sv-Op	Hld	OAvg	OOBP	ERA
1986 Cal	31	4	0	0	0	2.1	12	3	3	3	0	1	1	1	1	0	2	0	0	0	0	—	0	0-0	0	.375	.455	11.57

LCS — Batting / Fielding

Year Tm	Age	G	AB	H	2B	3B	HR	TB	R	RBI	GW	TBB	IBB	SO	HBP	SH	SF	SB	CS	SB%	GDP	Avg	OBP	SLG	Pos	G	PO	A	E	DP	FPct
1986 Cal	31	4	0	0	0	0	0	0	0	0	0	0	0	0	0	0	0	0	0	—	0	—	—	—	P	4	0	0	0	0	—

FRED LUDERUS—Frederick William Luderus—Bats: Left; Throws: Right

Ht: 5'11"; Wt: 185 lbs; Born: 9/12/1885 in Milwaukee, Wisconsin; Debut: 9/23/1909; Died: 1/5/1961

World Series — Batting / Fielding

Year Tm	Age	G	AB	H	2B	3B	HR	TB	R	RBI	GW	TBB	IBB	SO	HBP	SH	SF	SB	CS	SB%	GDP	Avg	OBP	SLG	Pos	G	PO	A	E	DP	FPct
1915 Phi	30	5	16	7	2	0	1	12	1	6	0	1	0	4	1	0	0	0	3	.00	0	.438	.500	.750	1B	5	39	4	1	2	.977

MIKE LUM—Michael Ken-Wai Lum—Bats: Left; Throws: Left

Ht: 6'0"; Wt: 180 lbs; Born: 10/27/1945 in Honolulu, Hawaii; Debut: 9/12/1967

LCS — Batting / Fielding

Year Tm	Age	G	AB	H	2B	3B	HR	TB	R	RBI	GW	TBB	IBB	SO	HBP	SH	SF	SB	CS	SB%	GDP	Avg	OBP	SLG	Pos	G	PO	A	E	DP	FPct
1969 Atl	23	2	2	2	1	0	0	3	0	0	0	0	0	0	0	0	0	0	0	—	0	1.000	1.000	1.500	OF	1	0	0	0	0	—
1976 Cin	30	1	1	0	0	0	0	0	0	0	0	0	0	0	0	0	0	0	0	—	0	.000	.000	.000	—						
LCS Totals		3	3	2	1	0	0	3	0	0	0	0	0	0	0	0	0	0	0	—	0	.667	.667	1.000	OF	1	0	0	0	0	—

JERRY LUMPE—Jerry Dean Lumpe—Bats: Left; Throws: Right

Ht: 6'2"; Wt: 185 lbs; Born: 6/2/1933 in Lincoln, Missouri; Debut: 4/17/1956

World Series — Batting / Fielding

Year Tm	Age	G	AB	H	2B	3B	HR	TB	R	RBI	GW	TBB	IBB	SO	HBP	SH	SF	SB	CS	SB%	GDP	Avg	OBP	SLG	Pos	G	PO	A	E	DP	FPct
1957 NYA	24	6	14	4	0	0	0	4	0	2	0	1	0	1	0	0	0	0	1	.00	0	.286	.333	.286	3B	3	3	6	0	0	1.000
1958 NYA	25	6	12	2	0	0	0	2	0	0	0	1	0	2	0	0	0	0	1	.00	0	.167	.231	.167	3B	3	2	4	0	0	1.000
																									SS	2	0	1	0	0	1.000
WS Totals		12	26	6	0	0	0	6	0	2	0	2	0	3	0	0	0	0	2	.00	0	.231	.286	.231	3B	6	5	10	0	0	1.000

HARRY LUNTE—Harry August Lunte—Bats: Right; Throws: Right

Ht: 5'11"; Wt: 165 lbs; Born: 9/15/1892 in St. Louis, Missouri; Debut: 5/19/1919; Died: 7/27/1965

World Series — Batting / Fielding

Year Tm	Age	G	AB	H	2B	3B	HR	TB	R	RBI	GW	TBB	IBB	SO	HBP	SH	SF	SB	CS	SB%	GDP	Avg	OBP	SLG	Pos	G	PO	A	E	DP	FPct
1920 Cle	28	1	0	0	0	0	0	0	0	0	0	0	0	0	0	0	0	0	0	—	0	—	—	—	2B	1	0	0	0	0	—

DOLF LUQUE—Adolfo Luque—Nickname: The Pride of Havana—Throws: Right; Bats: Right

Ht: 5'7"; Wt: 160 lbs; Born: 8/4/1890 in Havana, Cuba; Debut: 5/20/1914; Died: 7/3/1957

World Series — Pitching

Year Tm	Age	G	GS	CG	GF	IP	BFP	H	R	ER	HR	SH	SF	HB	TBB	IBB	SO	WP	Bk	W	L	Pct	ShO	Sv-Op	Hld	OAvg	OOBP	ERA
1919 Cin	29	2	0	0	2	5.0	16	1	0	0	0	0	0	0	0	0	6	0	0	0	0	—	0	0-0	0	.063	.063	0.00
1933 NYG	43	1	0	0	1	4.1	17	2	0	0	0	0	0	0	2	0	5	0	0	1	0	1.000	0	0-0	0	.133	.235	0.00
WS Totals		3	0	0	3	9.1	66	3	0	0	0	0	0	0	2	0	11	0	0	1	0	1.000	0	0-0	0	.097	.152	0.00

World Series — Batting / Fielding

Year Tm	Age	G	AB	H	2B	3B	HR	TB	R	RBI	GW	TBB	IBB	SO	HBP	SH	SF	SB	CS	SB%	GDP	Avg	OBP	SLG	Pos	G	PO	A	E	DP	FPct
1919 Cin	29	2	1	0	0	0	0	0	0	0	0	0	0	1	0	0	0	0	0	—	0	.000	.000	.000	P	2	1	0	0	0	1.000
1933 NYG	43	1	1	1	0	0	0	1	0	0	0	0	0	0	0	0	0	0	0	—	0	1.000	1.000	1.000	P	1	1	0	0	0	1.000
WS Totals		3	2	1	0	0	0	1	0	0	0	0	0	1	0	0	0	0	0	—	0	.500	.500	.500	P	3	2	0	0	0	1.000

GREG LUZINSKI—Gregory Michael Luzinski—Nickname: The Bull—Bats: Right; Throws: Right

Ht: 6'1"; Wt: 220 lbs; Born: 11/22/1950 in Chicago, Illinois; Debut: 9/9/1970

LCS — Batting / Fielding

Year Tm	Age	G	AB	H	2B	3B	HR	TB	R	RBI	GW	TBB	IBB	SO	HBP	SH	SF	SB	CS	SB%	GDP	Avg	OBP	SLG	Pos	G	PO	A	E	DP	FPct
1976 Phi	25	3	11	3	2	0	1	8	2	3	0	1	0	4	0	0	0	0	0	—	0	.273	.333	.727	OF	3	6	0	0	0	1.000
1977 Phi	26	4	14	4	1	0	1	8	2	2	0	3	0	3	1	0	0	1	0	1.00	0	.286	.444	.571	OF	4	4	1	0	0	1.000
1978 Phi	27	4	16	6	0	1	2	14	3	3	0	1	1	2	0	0	0	0	0	—	1	.375	.412	.875	OF	4	5	1	0	0	1.000
1980 Phi	29	5	17	5	2	0	1	10	3	4	2	0	0	6	0	0	0	0	0	—	0	.294	.294	.588	OF	4	5	0	1	0	.833
1983 ChA	32	4	15	2	1	0	0	3	0	0	0	1	0	5	1	0	0	0	0	—	0	.133	.235	.200	—						
LCS Totals		20	73	20	6	1	5	43	10	12	2	6	1	20	2	0	0	1	0	1.00	1	.274	.346	.589	OF	15	20	2	1	0	.957

World Series — Batting / Fielding

Year Tm	Age	G	AB	H	2B	3B	HR	TB	R	RBI	GW	TBB	IBB	SO	HBP	SH	SF	SB	CS	SB%	GDP	Avg	OBP	SLG	Pos	G	PO	A	E	DP	FPct
1980 Phi	29	3	9	0	0	0	0	0	0	0	0	1	0	5	1	0	0	0	0	—	0	.000	.182	.000	OF	1	1	0	0	0	1.000
Postseason Totals		23	82	20	6	1	5	43	10	12	2	7	1	25	3	0	0	1	0	1.00	1	.244	.326	.524	OF	16	21	2	1	0	.958

SPARKY LYLE—Albert Walter Lyle—Throws: Left; Bats: Left

Ht: 6'1"; Wt: 182 lbs; Born: 7/22/1944 in Du Bois, Pennsylvania; Debut: 7/4/1967

Division Series — Pitching

Year Tm	Age	G	GS	CG	GF	IP	BFP	H	R	ER	HR	SH	SF	HB	TBB	IBB	SO	WP	Bk	W	L	Pct	ShO	Sv-Op	Hld	OAvg	OOBP	ERA
1981 Phi	37	3	0	0	0	2.1	11	4	0	0	0	0	0	0	2	0	1	0	0	0	0	—	0	0-1	1	.444	.545	0.00

LCS — Pitching

Year Tm	Age	G	GS	CG	GF	IP	BFP	H	R	ER	HR	SH	SF	HB	TBB	IBB	SO	WP	Bk	W	L	Pct	ShO	Sv-Op	Hld	OAvg	OOBP	ERA
1976 NYA	32	1	0	0	1	1.0	4	0	0	0	0	0	0	0	1	0	0	0	0	0	0	—	0	1-1	0	.000	.250	0.00
1977 NYA-*C*	33	4	0	0	4	9.1	32	7	1	1	0	1	0	0	0	0	3	0	0	2	0	1.000	0	0-0	0	.226	.226	0.96
1978 NYA	34	1	0	0	1	1.1	7	3	2	2	0	1	0	0	0	0	0	0	0	0	0	—	0	0-0	0	.500	.500	13.50
LCS Totals		6	0	0	6	11.2	86	10	3	3	0	2	0	0	1	0	3	0	0	2	0	1.000	0	1-1	0	.250	.268	2.31

World Series — Pitching

Year Tm	Age	G	GS	CG	GF	IP	BFP	H	R	ER	HR	SH	SF	HB	TBB	IBB	SO	WP	Bk	W	L	Pct	ShO	Sv-Op	Hld	OAvg	OOBP	ERA
1976 NYA	32	2	0	0	2	2.2	10	1	0	0	0	0	0	0	0	0	3	1	0	0	0	—	0	0-0	0	.100	.100	0.00
1977 NYA-*C*	33	2	0	0	2	4.2	16	2	1	1	1	0	0	0	0	0	2	0	0	1	0	1.000	0	0-1	0	.125	.125	1.93
WS Totals		4	0	0	4	7.1	52	3	1	1	1	0	0	0	0	0	5	1	0	1	0	1.000	0	0-1	0	.115	.115	1.23
Postseason Totals		13	0	0	10	21.1	160	17	4	4	1	2	0	0	3	0	9	1	0	3	0	1.000	0	1-3	1	.227	.256	1.69

Division Series — Batting / Fielding

Year Tm	Age	G	AB	H	2B	3B	HR	TB	R	RBI	GW	TBB	IBB	SO	HBP	SH	SF	SB	CS	SB%	GDP	Avg	OBP	SLG	Pos	G	PO	A	E	DP	FPct
1981 Phi	37	3	0	0	0	0	0	0	0	0	0	0	0	0	0	0	0	0	0	—	0	—	—	—	P	3	0	0	0	0	—

LCS — Batting / Fielding

Year Tm	Age	G	AB	H	2B	3B	HR	TB	R	RBI	GW	TBB	IBB	SO	HBP	SH	SF	SB	CS	SB%	GDP	Avg	OBP	SLG	Pos	G	PO	A	E	DP	FPct
1976 NYA	32	1	0	0	0	0	0	0	0	0	0	0	0	0	0	0	0	0	0	—	0	—	—	—	P	1	0	0	0	0	—
1977 NYA	33	4	0	0	0	0	0	0	0	0	0	0	0	0	0	0	0	0	0	—	0	—	—	—	P	4	0	0	0	0	—
1978 NYA	34	1	0	0	0	0	0	0	0	0	0	0	0	0	0	0	0	0	0	—	0	—	—	—	P	1	1	1	0	0	1.000
LCS Totals		6	0	0	0	0	0	0	0	0	0	0	0	0	0	0	0	0	0	—	0	—	—	—	P	6	1	1	0	0	1.000

World Series — Batting / Fielding

Year Tm	Age	G	AB	H	2B	3B	HR	TB	R	RBI	GW	TBB	IBB	SO	HBP	SH	SF	SB	CS	SB%	GDP	Avg	OBP	SLG	Pos	G	PO	A	E	DP	FPct
1976 NYA	32	2	0	0	0	0	0	0	0	0	0	0	0	0	0	0	0	0	0	—	0	—	—	—	P	2	0	0	0	0	—
1977 NYA	33	2	2	0	0	0	0	0	0	0	0	0	0	2	0	0	0	0	0	—	0	.000	.000	.000	P	2	0	0	0	0	—
WS Totals		4	2	0	0	0	0	0	0	0	0	0	0	2	0	0	0	0	0	—	0	.000	.000	.000	P	4	0	0	0	0	—
Postseason Totals		13	2	0	0	0	0	0	0	0	0	0	0	2	0	0	0	0	0	—	0	.000	.000	.000	P	13	1	1	0	0	1.000

JERRY LYNCH—Gerald Thomas Lynch—Bats: Left; Throws: Right

Ht: 6'1"; Wt: 185 lbs; Born: 7/17/1930 in Bay City, Michigan; Debut: 4/15/1954

World Series — Batting / Fielding

Year Tm	Age	G	AB	H	2B	3B	HR	TB	R	RBI	GW	TBB	IBB	SO	HBP	SH	SF	SB	CS	SB%	GDP	Avg	OBP	SLG	Pos	G	PO	A	E	DP	FPct
1961 Cin	31	4	3	0	0	0	0	0	0	0	0	1	1	1	0	0	0	0	0	—	0	.000	.250	.000	—						

BYRD LYNN—Nickname: Birdie—Bats: Right; Throws: Right

Ht: 5'11"; Wt: 165 lbs; Born: 3/13/1889 in Unionville, Illinois; Debut: 4/16/1916; Died: 2/5/1940

World Series		Batting																							Fielding						
Year Tm	Age	G	AB	H	2B	3B	HR	TB	R	RBI	GW	TBB	IBB	SO	HBP	SH	SF	SB	CS	SB%	GDP	Avg	OBP	SLG	Pos	G	PO	A	E	DP	FPct
1917 ChA	28	1	1	0	0	0	0	0	0	0	0	0	0	1	0	0	0	0	0	—	0	.000	.000	.000	—						
1919 ChA	30	1	1	0	0	0	0	0	0	0	0	0	0	0	0	0	0	0	0	—	0	.000	.000	.000	C	1	1	0	0	0	1.000
WS Totals		2	2	0	0	0	0	0	0	0	0	0	0	1	0	0	0	0	0	—	0	.000	.000	.000	C	1	1	0	0	0	1.000

FRED LYNN—Frederic Michael Lynn—Bats: Left; Throws: Left

Ht: 6'1"; Wt: 185 lbs; Born: 2/3/1952 in Chicago, Illinois; Debut: 9/5/1974

LCS		Batting																							Fielding						
Year Tm	Age	G	AB	H	2B	3B	HR	TB	R	RBI	GW	TBB	IBB	SO	HBP	SH	SF	SB	CS	SB%	GDP	Avg	OBP	SLG	Pos	G	PO	A	E	DP	FPct
1975 Bos-*M RY*	23	3	11	4	1	0	0	5	1	3	0	0	0	0	0	1	0	0	0	—	1	.364	.364	.455	OF	3	12	1	1	1	.929
1982 Cal	30	5	18	11	2	0	1	16	4	5	0	2	0	3	0	0	0	0	0	—	1	.611	.650	.889	OF	5	16	0	1	0	.941
LCS Totals		8	29	15	3	0	1	21	5	8	0	2	0	3	0	1	0	0	0	—	2	.517	.548	.724	OF	8	28	1	2	1	.935
World Series		**Batting**																							**Fielding**						
Year Tm	Age	G	AB	H	2B	3B	HR	TB	R	RBI	GW	TBB	IBB	SO	HBP	SH	SF	SB	CS	SB%	GDP	Avg	OBP	SLG	Pos	G	PO	A	E	DP	FPct
1975 Bos-*M RY*	23	7	25	7	1	0	1	11	3	5	0	3	0	5	0	0	1	0	0	—	0	.280	.345	.440	OF	7	23	1	0	0	1.000
Postseason Totals		15	54	22	4	0	2	32	8	13	0	5	0	8	0	1	1	0	0	—	2	.407	.450	.593	OF	15	51	2	2	1	.964

DUKE MAAS—Duane Frederick Maas—Throws: Right; Bats: Right

Ht: 5'10"; Wt: 170 lbs; Born: 1/31/1929 in Utica, Michigan; Debut: 4/21/1955; Died: 12/7/1976

World Series		Pitching																										
Year Tm	Age	G	GS	CG	GF	IP	BFP	H	R	ER	HR	SH	SF	HB	TBB	IBB	SO	WP	Bk	W	L	Pct	ShO	Sv-Op	Hld	OAvg	OOBP	ERA
1958 NYA	29	1	0	0	0	0.1	4	2	3	3	1	0	0	0	1	0	0	0	0	0	0	—	0	0-0	0	.667	.750	81.00
1960 NYA	31	1	0	0	0	2.0	9	2	1	1	0	1	0	0	0	0	1	0	0	0	0	—	0	0-0	0	.250	.250	4.50
WS Totals		2	0	0	0	2.1	26	4	4	4	1	1	0	0	1	0	1	0	0	0	0	—	0	0-0	0	.364	.417	15.43

World Series		Batting																							Fielding						
Year Tm	Age	G	AB	H	2B	3B	HR	TB	R	RBI	GW	TBB	IBB	SO	HBP	SH	SF	SB	CS	SB%	GDP	Avg	OBP	SLG	Pos	G	PO	A	E	DP	FPct
1958 NYA	29	1	0	0	0	0	0	0	0	0	0	0	0	0	0	0	0	0	0	—	0	—	—	—	P	1	0	0	0	0	—
1960 NYA	31	1	0	0	0	0	0	0	0	0	0	0	0	0	0	0	0	0	0	—	0	—	—	—	P	1	0	0	0	0	—
WS Totals		2	0	0	0	0	0	0	0	0	0	0	0	0	0	0	0	0	0	—	0	—	—	—	P	2	0	0	0	0	—

JOHN MABRY—John Steven Mabry—Bats: Left; Throws: Right

Ht: 6'4"; Wt: 195 lbs; Born: 10/17/1970 in Wilmington, Delaware; Debut: 4/23/1994

Division Series		Batting																							Fielding						
Year Tm	Age	G	AB	H	2B	3B	HR	TB	R	RBI	GW	TBB	IBB	SO	HBP	SH	SF	SB	CS	SB%	GDP	Avg	OBP	SLG	Pos	G	PO	A	E	DP	FPct
1996 StL	25	3	10	3	0	1	0	5	1	1	0	1	1	1	0	1	0	0	0	—	0	.300	.364	.500	1B	3	20	1	0	0	1.000
LCS		**Batting**																							**Fielding**						
Year Tm	Age	G	AB	H	2B	3B	HR	TB	R	RBI	GW	TBB	IBB	SO	HBP	SH	SF	SB	CS	SB%	GDP	Avg	OBP	SLG	Pos	G	PO	A	E	DP	FPct
1996 StL	25	7	23	6	0	0	0	6	1	0	0	0	0	6	1	0	0	0	0	—	0	.261	.292	.261	1B	6	43	1	0	4	1.000
																									OF	2	2	0	0	0	1.000
Postseason Totals		10	33	9	0	1	0	11	2	1	0	1	1	7	1	1	0	0	0	—	0	.273	.314	.333	1B	9	63	2	0	4	1.000

BOB MacDONALD—Robert Joseph MacDonald—Throws: Left; Bats: Left

Ht: 6'3"; Wt: 208 lbs; Born: 4/27/1965 in East Orange, New Jersey; Debut: 8/14/1990

LCS		Pitching																										
Year Tm	Age	G	GS	CG	GF	IP	BFP	H	R	ER	HR	SH	SF	HB	TBB	IBB	SO	WP	Bk	W	L	Pct	ShO	Sv-Op	Hld	OAvg	OOBP	ERA
1991 Tor	26	1	0	0	1	1.0	5	1	1	1	0	0	1	0	1	0	0	0	0	0	0	—	0	0-0	0	.333	.400	9.00

LCS		Batting																							Fielding						
Year Tm	Age	G	AB	H	2B	3B	HR	TB	R	RBI	GW	TBB	IBB	SO	HBP	SH	SF	SB	CS	SB%	GDP	Avg	OBP	SLG	Pos	G	PO	A	E	DP	FPct
1991 Tor	26	1	0	0	0	0	0	0	0	0	0	0	0	0	0	0	0	0	0	—	0	—	—	—	P	1	0	0	0	0	—

MIKE MACFARLANE—Michael Andrew Macfarlane—Bats: Right; Throws: Right

Ht: 6'1"; Wt: 200 lbs; Born: 4/12/1964 in Stockton, California; Debut: 7/23/1987

Division Series		Batting																							Fielding						
Year Tm	Age	G	AB	H	2B	3B	HR	TB	R	RBI	GW	TBB	IBB	SO	HBP	SH	SF	SB	CS	SB%	GDP	Avg	OBP	SLG	Pos	G	PO	A	E	DP	FPct
1995 Bos	31	3	9	3	0	0	0	3	0	1	0	0	0	3	0	0	1	0	0	—	0	.333	.300	.333	C	3	18	0	2	0	.900

SHANE MACK—Shane Lee Mack—Bats: Right; Throws: Right

Ht: 6'0"; Wt: 185 lbs; Born: 12/7/1963 in Los Angeles, California; Debut: 5/25/1987

LCS		Batting																							Fielding						
Year Tm	Age	G	AB	H	2B	3B	HR	TB	R	RBI	GW	TBB	IBB	SO	HBP	SH	SF	SB	CS	SB%	GDP	Avg	OBP	SLG	Pos	G	PO	A	E	DP	FPct
1991 Min	27	5	18	6	1	1	0	9	4	3	0	2	1	4	0	0	1	2	1	.67	0	.333	.381	.500	OF	5	3	0	1	0	.750
World Series		**Batting**																							**Fielding**						
Year Tm	Age	G	AB	H	2B	3B	HR	TB	R	RBI	GW	TBB	IBB	SO	HBP	SH	SF	SB	CS	SB%	GDP	Avg	OBP	SLG	Pos	G	PO	A	E	DP	FPct
1991 Min	27	6	23	3	1	0	0	4	0	1	0	0	0	7	0	0	0	0	1	.00	1	.130	.130	.174	OF	6	11	0	0	0	1.000
Postseason Totals		11	41	9	2	1	0	13	4	4	0	2	1	11	0	0	1	2	2	.50	1	.220	.250	.317	OF	11	14	0	1	0	.933

ELLIOTT MADDOX—Bats: Right; Throws: Right

Ht: 5'11"; Wt: 180 lbs; Born: 12/21/1947 in East Orange, New Jersey; Debut: 4/7/1970

LCS		Batting																							Fielding						
Year Tm	Age	G	AB	H	2B	3B	HR	TB	R	RBI	GW	TBB	IBB	SO	HBP	SH	SF	SB	CS	SB%	GDP	Avg	OBP	SLG	Pos	G	PO	A	E	DP	FPct
1976 NYA	28	3	9	2	1	0	0	3	0	1	0	0	0	1	0	0	0	0	0	—	0	.222	.222	.333	OF	3	9	0	0	0	1.000
World Series		**Batting**																							**Fielding**						
Year Tm	Age	G	AB	H	2B	3B	HR	TB	R	RBI	GW	TBB	IBB	SO	HBP	SH	SF	SB	CS	SB%	GDP	Avg	OBP	SLG	Pos	G	PO	A	E	DP	FPct
1976 NYA	28	2	5	1	0	1	0	3	0	0	0	1	0	2	0	0	0	0	0	—	1	.200	.333	.600	OF	1	0	0	0	0	—
Postseason Totals		5	14	3	1	1	0	6	0	1	0	1	0	3	0	0	0	0	0	—	1	.214	.267	.429	OF	4	9	0	0	0	1.000

GARRY MADDOX—Garry Lee Maddox—Bats: Right; Throws: Right

Ht: 6'3"; Wt: 175 lbs; Born: 9/1/1949 in Cincinnati, Ohio; Debut: 4/25/1972

Division Series		Batting																							Fielding						
Year Tm	Age	G	AB	H	2B	3B	HR	TB	R	RBI	GW	TBB	IBB	SO	HBP	SH	SF	SB	CS	SB%	GDP	Avg	OBP	SLG	Pos	G	PO	A	E	DP	FPct
1981 Phi	32	2	3	1	1	0	0	2	0	0	0	0	0	0	0	0	0	0	0	—	0	.333	.333	.667	OF	2	3	0	0	0	1.000
LCS		**Batting**																							**Fielding**						
Year Tm	Age	G	AB	H	2B	3B	HR	TB	R	RBI	GW	TBB	IBB	SO	HBP	SH	SF	SB	CS	SB%	GDP	Avg	OBP	SLG	Pos	G	PO	A	E	DP	FPct
1976 Phi	27	3	13	3	1	0	0	4	2	1	0	1	0	0	0	0	0	0	1	.00	0	.231	.286	.308	OF	3	9	0	0	0	1.000
1977 Phi	28	2	7	3	0	0	0	3	1	2	0	0	0	1	1	0	0	0	0	—	0	.429	.500	.429	OF	2	6	0	0	0	1.000
1978 Phi	29	4	19	5	0	0	0	5	1	2	0	0	0	3	0	0	0	0	0	—	0	.263	.263	.263	OF	4	16	0	1	0	.941
1980 Phi	31	5	20	6	2	0	0	8	2	3	1	2	1	2	1	0	0	2	1	.67	2	.300	.391	.400	OF	5	23	0	0	0	1.000
1983 Phi	34	3	11	3	1	0	0	4	0	1	0	0	0	1	0	0	0	0	0	—	0	.273	.273	.364	OF	3	8	0	1	0	.889
LCS Totals		17	70	20	4	0	0	24	6	9	1	3	1	7	2	0	0	2	2	.50	2	.286	.333	.343	OF	17	62	0	2	0	.969
World Series		**Batting**																							**Fielding**						
Year Tm	Age	G	AB	H	2B	3B	HR	TB	R	RBI	GW	TBB	IBB	SO	HBP	SH	SF	SB	CS	SB%	GDP	Avg	OBP	SLG	Pos	G	PO	A	E	DP	FPct
1980 Phi	31	6	22	5	2	0	0	7	1	1	0	1	1	3	0	0	1	0	0	—	0	.227	.250	.318	OF	6	11	1	0	1	1.000
1983 Phi	34	4	12	3	1	0	1	7	1	1	1	0	0	2	0	0	0	0	0	—	1	.250	.250	.583	OF	3	7	0	0	0	1.000
WS Totals		10	34	8	3	0	1	14	2	2	1	1	1	5	0	0	1	0	0	—	1	.235	.250	.412	OF	9	18	1	0	1	1.000
Postseason Totals		29	107	29	8	0	1	40	8	11	2	4	2	12	2	0	1	2	2	.50	3	.271	.307	.374	OF	28	83	1	2	1	.977

NICK MADDOX—Nicholas Maddox—Throws: Right; Bats: Left

Ht: 6'0"; Wt: 175 lbs; Born: 11/9/1886 in Govans, Maryland; Debut: 9/13/1907; Died: 11/27/1954

World Series		Pitching																										
Year Tm	Age	G	GS	CG	GF	IP	BFP	H	R	ER	HR	SH	SF	HB	TBB	IBB	SO	WP	Bk	W	L	Pct	ShO	Sv-Op	Hld	OAvg	OOBP	ERA
1909 Pit	22	1	1	1	0	9.0	41	10	6	1	0	0	0	0	2	0	4	0	0	1	0	1.000	0	0-0	0	.256	.293	1.00

World Series — Batting / Fielding

Year Tm	Age	G	AB	H	2B	3B	HR	TB	R	RBI	GW	TBB	IBB	SO	HBP	SH	SF	SB	CS	SB%	GDP	Avg	OBP	SLG	Pos	G	PO	A	E	DP	FPct
1909 Pit	22	1	4	0	0	0	0	0	0	0	0	0	0	1	0	0	0	0	0	—	0	.000	.000	.000	P	1	0	1	0	0	1.000

GREG MADDUX—Gregory Alan Maddux—Throws: Right; Bats: Right

Ht: 6'0"; Wt: 170 lbs; Born: 4/14/1966 in San Angelo, Texas; Debut: 9/3/1986

Division Series — Pitching

Year Tm	Age	G	GS	CG	GF	IP	BFP	H	R	ER	HR	SH	SF	HB	TBB	IBB	SO	WP	Bk	W	L	Pct	ShO	Sv-Op	Hld	OAvg	OOBP	ERA
1995 Atl-*C*	29	2	2	0	0	14.0	58	19	7	7	3	2	1	1	2	1	7	0	0	1	0	1.000	0	0- 0	0	.365	.393	4.50
1996 Atl	30	1	1	0	0	7.0	24	3	2	0	0	0	0	0	0	0	7	0	0	1	0	1.000	0	0- 0	0	.125	.125	0.00
1997 Atl	31	1	1	1	0	9.0	33	7	1	1	0	0	0	0	1	0	6	0	0	1	0	1.000	0	0- 0	0	.219	.242	1.00
DS Totals		4	4	1	0	30.0	230	29	10	8	3	2	1	1	3	1	20	0	0	3	0	1.000	0	0-0	0	.269	.292	2.40

LCS — Pitching

Year Tm	Age	G	GS	CG	GF	IP	BFP	H	R	ER	HR	SH	SF	HB	TBB	IBB	SO	WP	Bk	W	L	Pct	ShO	Sv-Op	Hld	OAvg	OOBP	ERA
1989 ChN	23	2	2	0	0	7.1	40	13	12	11	2	1	0	1	4	2	5	1	0	0	1	.000	0	0- 0	0	.382	.462	13.50
1993 Atl-*C*	27	2	2	0	0	12.2	58	11	8	7	2	2	0	0	7	1	11	0	0	1	1	.500	0	0- 0	0	.224	.321	4.97
1995 Atl-*C*	29	1	1	0	0	8.0	34	7	1	1	0	0	0	1	2	0	4	1	0	1	0	1.000	0	0- 0	0	.226	.294	1.13
1996 Atl	30	2	2	0	0	14.1	61	15	9	4	1	1	1	0	2	1	10	1	0	1	1	.500	0	0- 0	0	.263	.283	2.51
1997 Atl	31	2	2	0	0	13.0	53	9	7	2	0	1	0	1	4	1	16	0	0	0	2	.000	0	0- 0	0	.191	.269	1.38
LCS Totals		9	9	0	0	55.1	492	55	37	25	5	5	1	3	19	5	46	3	0	3	5	.375	0	0-0	0	.252	.320	4.07

World Series — Pitching

Year Tm	Age	G	GS	CG	GF	IP	BFP	H	R	ER	HR	SH	SF	HB	TBB	IBB	SO	WP	Bk	W	L	Pct	ShO	Sv-Op	Hld	OAvg	OOBP	ERA
1995 Atl-*C*	29	2	2	1	0	16.0	60	9	6	4	1	0	0	0	3	1	8	0	0	1	1	.500	0	0- 0	0	.158	.200	2.25
1996 Atl	30	2	2	0	0	15.2	59	14	3	3	0	0	0	1	1	0	5	0	0	1	1	.500	0	0- 0	0	.246	.271	1.72
WS Totals		4	4	1	0	31.2	238	23	9	7	1	0	0	1	4	1	13	0	0	2	2	.500	0	0-0	0	.202	.235	1.99
Postseason Totals		17	17	2	0	117.0	960	107	56	40	9	7	2	5	26	7	79	3	0	8	7	.533	0	0-0	0	.243	.292	3.08

Division Series — Batting / Fielding

Year Tm	Age	G	AB	H	2B	3B	HR	TB	R	RBI	GW	TBB	IBB	SO	HBP	SH	SF	SB	CS	SB%	GDP	Avg	OBP	SLG	Pos	G	PO	A	E	DP	FPct
1995 Atl	29	2	6	1	0	0	0	1	1	0	0	0	0	1	0	0	0	0	0	—	0	.167	.167	.167	P	2	1	4	0	1	1.000
1996 Atl	30	1	2	0	0	0	0	0	0	0	0	0	0	1	0	0	0	0	0	—	0	.000	.000	.000	P	1	2	2	0	0	1.000
1997 Atl	31	1	2	0	0	0	0	0	0	0	0	1	0	1	0	0	0	0	0	—	0	.000	.333	.000	P	1	1	1	0	0	1.000
DS Totals		4	10	1	0	0	0	1	1	0	0	1	0	3	0	0	0	0	0	—	0	.100	.182	.100	P	4	4	7	0	1	1.000

LCS — Batting / Fielding

Year Tm	Age	G	AB	H	2B	3B	HR	TB	R	RBI	GW	TBB	IBB	SO	HBP	SH	SF	SB	CS	SB%	GDP	Avg	OBP	SLG	Pos	G	PO	A	E	DP	FPct
1989 ChN	23	3	3	0	0	0	0	0	1	0	0	0	0	0	0	0	0	0	0	—	0	.000	.000	.000	P	2	0	0	1	0	.000
1993 Atl	27	2	4	1	0	0	0	1	1	0	0	0	0	1	0	2	0	0	0	—	0	.250	.250	.250	P	2	3	5	1	0	.889
1995 Atl	29	1	3	0	0	0	0	0	0	0	0	0	0	1	0	0	0	0	0	—	0	.000	.000	.000	P	1	1	1	0	0	1.000
1996 Atl	30	2	4	0	0	0	0	0	0	0	0	0	0	2	0	1	0	0	0	—	0	.000	.000	.000	P	2	1	4	0	0	1.000
1997 Atl	31	2	3	0	0	0	0	0	0	0	0	0	0	2	0	1	0	0	0	—	0	.000	.000	.000	P	2	0	7	0	1	1.000
LCS Totals		10	17	1	0	0	0	1	2	0	0	0	0	6	0	4	0	0	0	—	0	.059	.059	.059	P	9	5	17	2	1	.917

World Series — Batting / Fielding

Year Tm	Age	G	AB	H	2B	3B	HR	TB	R	RBI	GW	TBB	IBB	SO	HBP	SH	SF	SB	CS	SB%	GDP	Avg	OBP	SLG	Pos	G	PO	A	E	DP	FPct
1995 Atl	29	2	3	0	0	0	0	0	0	0	0	0	0	1	0	0	0	0	0	—	0	.000	.000	.000	P	2	2	4	0	0	1.000
1996 Atl	30	2	0	0	0	0	0	0	0	0	0	0	0	0	0	0	0	0	0	—	0	—	—	—	P	2	2	7	0	0	1.000
WS Totals		4	3	0	0	0	0	0	0	0	0	0	0	1	0	0	0	0	0	—	0	.000	.000	.000	P	4	4	11	0	0	1.000
Postseason Totals		18	30	2	0	0	0	2	3	0	0	1	0	10	0	4	0	0	0	—	0	.067	.097	.067	P	17	13	35	2	2	.960

MIKE MADDUX—Michael Ausley Maddux—Throws: Right; Bats: Left

Ht: 6'2"; Wt: 180 lbs; Born: 8/27/1961 in Dayton, Ohio; Debut: 6/3/1986

Division Series — Pitching

Year Tm	Age	G	GS	CG	GF	IP	BFP	H	R	ER	HR	SH	SF	HB	TBB	IBB	SO	WP	Bk	W	L	Pct	ShO	Sv-Op	Hld	OAvg	OOBP	ERA
1995 Bos	34	2	0	0	0	3.0	14	2	0	0	0	1	0	1	1	1	1	0	0	0	0	—	0	0- 0	0	.182	.308	0.00

Division Series — Batting / Fielding

Year Tm	Age	G	AB	H	2B	3B	HR	TB	R	RBI	GW	TBB	IBB	SO	HBP	SH	SF	SB	CS	SB%	GDP	Avg	OBP	SLG	Pos	G	PO	A	E	DP	FPct
1995 Bos	34	2	0	0	0	0	0	0	0	0	0	0	0	0	0	0	0	0	0	—	0	—	—	—	P	2	1	2	0	0	1.000

BILL MADLOCK—Nickname: Mad Dog—Bats: Right; Throws: Right

Ht: 5'11"; Wt: 180 lbs; Born: 1/2/1951 in Memphis, Tennessee; Debut: 9/7/1973

LCS — Batting / Fielding

Year Tm	Age	G	AB	H	2B	3B	HR	TB	R	RBI	GW	TBB	IBB	SO	HBP	SH	SF	SB	CS	SB%	GDP	Avg	OBP	SLG	Pos	G	PO	A	E	DP	FPct
1979 Pit	28	3	12	3	0	0	1	6	1	2	0	2	1	0	0	0	0	2	0	1.00	1	.250	.357	.500	3B	3	1	7	0	1	1.000
1985 LA	34	6	24	8	1	0	3	18	5	7	0	0	0	2	0	0	0	1	0	1.00	1	.333	.333	.750	3B	6	6	9	0	0	1.000
1987 Det	36	1	5	0	0	0	0	0	0	0	0	0	0	3	0	0	0	0	0	—	0	.000	.000	.000	—						
LCS Totals		10	41	11	1	0	4	24	6	9	0	2	1	5	0	0	0	3	0	1.00	2	.268	.302	.585	3B	9	7	16	0	1	1.000

World Series — Batting / Fielding

Year Tm	Age	G	AB	H	2B	3B	HR	TB	R	RBI	GW	TBB	IBB	SO	HBP	SH	SF	SB	CS	SB%	GDP	Avg	OBP	SLG	Pos	G	PO	A	E	DP	FPct
1979 Pit	28	7	24	9	1	0	0	10	2	3	1	5	2	1	0	0	0	0	2	.00	1	.375	.483	.417	3B	7	3	10	1	4	.929
Postseason Totals		17	65	20	2	0	4	34	8	12	1	7	3	6	0	0	0	3	2	.60	3	.308	.375	.523	3B	16	10	26	1	5	.973

DAVE MAGADAN—David Joseph Magadan—Bats: Left; Throws: Right

Ht: 6'3"; Wt: 190 lbs; Born: 9/30/1962 in Tampa, Florida; Debut: 9/7/1986

LCS — Batting / Fielding

Year Tm	Age	G	AB	H	2B	3B	HR	TB	R	RBI	GW	TBB	IBB	SO	HBP	SH	SF	SB	CS	SB%	GDP	Avg	OBP	SLG	Pos	G	PO	A	E	DP	FPct
1988 NYN	26	3	3	0	0	0	0	0	0	0	0	0	0	2	0	0	0	0	0	—	0	.000	.000	.000	—						

SHERRY MAGEE—Sherwood Robert Magee—Bats: Right; Throws: Right

Ht: 5'11"; Wt: 179 lbs; Born: 8/6/1884 in Clarendon, Pennsylvania; Debut: 6/29/1904; Died: 3/13/1929

World Series — Batting / Fielding

Year Tm	Age	G	AB	H	2B	3B	HR	TB	R	RBI	GW	TBB	IBB	SO	HBP	SH	SF	SB	CS	SB%	GDP	Avg	OBP	SLG	Pos	G	PO	A	E	DP	FPct
1919 Cin	35	2	2	1	0	0	0	1	0	0	0	0	0	0	0	0	0	0	0	—	0	.500	.500	.500	—						

SAL MAGLIE—Salvatore Anthony Maglie—Nickname: The Barber—Throws: Right; Bats: Right

Ht: 6'2"; Wt: 180 lbs; Born: 4/26/1917 in Niagara Falls, New York; Debut: 8/9/1945; Died: 12/28/1992

World Series — Pitching

Year Tm	Age	G	GS	CG	GF	IP	BFP	H	R	ER	HR	SH	SF	HB	TBB	IBB	SO	WP	Bk	W	L	Pct	ShO	Sv-Op	Hld	OAvg	OOBP	ERA
1951 NYG	34	1	1	0	0	5.0	24	8	4	4	1	0	0	0	2	0	3	0	0	0	1	.000	0	0- 0	0	.364	.417	7.20
1954 NYG	37	1	1	0	0	7.0	31	7	2	2	0	0	0	1	2	0	2	0	0	0	0	—	0	0- 0	0	.250	.323	2.57
1956 Bro	39	2	2	2	0	17.0	68	14	5	5	3	1	0	0	6	0	15	0	0	1	1	.500	0	0- 0	0	.230	.299	2.65
WS Totals		4	4	2	0	29.0	246	29	11	11	4	1	0	1	10	0	20	0	0	1	2	.333	0	0-0	0	.261	.328	3.41

World Series — Batting / Fielding

Year Tm	Age	G	AB	H	2B	3B	HR	TB	R	RBI	GW	TBB	IBB	SO	HBP	SH	SF	SB	CS	SB%	GDP	Avg	OBP	SLG	Pos	G	PO	A	E	DP	FPct
1951 NYG	34	1	1	0	0	0	0	0	0	0	0	0	0	1	0	0	0	0	0	—	0	.000	.000	.000	P	1	0	0	0	0	—
1954 NYG	37	1	3	0	0	0	0	0	0	0	0	0	0	2	0	0	0	0	0	—	0	.000	.000	.000	P	1	0	2	0	0	1.000
1956 Bro	39	2	5	0	0	0	0	0	0	0	0	0	0	2	0	0	0	0	0	—	1	.000	.000	.000	P	2	0	1	0	0	1.000
WS Totals		4	9	0	0	0	0	0	0	0	0	0	0	5	0	0	0	0	0	—	1	.000	.000	.000	P	4	0	3	0	0	1.000

MIKE MAGNANTE—Michael Anthony Magnante—Throws: Left; Bats: Left

Ht: 6'1"; Wt: 180 lbs; Born: 6/17/1965 in Glendale, California; Debut: 4/22/1991

Division Series — Pitching

Year Tm	Age	G	GS	CG	GF	IP	BFP	H	R	ER	HR	SH	SF	HB	TBB	IBB	SO	WP	Bk	W	L	Pct	ShO	Sv-Op	Hld	OAvg	OOBP	ERA
1997 Hou	32	2	0	0	1	2.0	10	4	3	1	0	0	0	0	0	0	2	0	0	0	0	—	0	0- 0	0	.400	.400	4.50

Division Series — Batting / Fielding

Year Tm	Age	G	AB	H	2B	3B	HR	TB	R	RBI	GW	TBB	IBB	SO	HBP	SH	SF	SB	CS	SB%	GDP	Avg	OBP	SLG	Pos	G	PO	A	E	DP	FPct
1997 Hou	32	2	0	0	0	0	0	0	0	0	0	0	0	0	0	0	0	0	0	—	0	—	—	—	P	2	0	1	0	0	1.000

JOE MAGRANE—Joseph David Magrane—Throws: Left; Bats: Right

Ht: 6'6"; Wt: 225 lbs; Born: 7/2/1964 in Des Moines, Iowa; Debut: 4/25/1987

LCS			Pitching																										
Year	Tm	Age	G	GS	CG	GF	IP	BFP	H	R	ER	HR	SH	SF	HB	TBB	IBB	SO	WP	Bk	W	L	Pct	ShO	Sv-Op	Hld	OAvg	OOBP	ERA
1987	StL	23	1	1	0	0	4.0	18	4	4	4	1	0	0	0	2	0	3	1	0	0	0	—	0	0-0	0	.250	.333	9.00
World Series			Pitching																										
Year	Tm	Age	G	GS	CG	GF	IP	BFP	H	R	ER	HR	SH	SF	HB	TBB	IBB	SO	WP	Bk	W	L	Pct	ShO	Sv-Op	Hld	OAvg	OOBP	ERA
1987	StL	23	2	2	0	0	7.1	37	9	7	7	0	0	0	1	5	0	5	0	0	0	1	.000	0	0-0	0	.290	.405	8.59
Postseason Totals			3	3	0	0	11.1	110	13	11	11	1	0	0	1	7	0	8	1	0	0	1	.000	0	0-0	0	.277	.382	8.74

LCS			Batting																							Fielding						
Year	Tm	Age	G	AB	H	2B	3B	HR	TB	R	RBI	GW	TBB	IBB	SO	HBP	SH	SF	SB	CS	SB%	GDP	Avg	OBP	SLG	Pos	G	PO	A	E	DP	FPct
1987	StL	23	1	1	0	0	0	0	0	0	0	0	0	0	0	0	0	0	0	0	—	0	.000	.000	.000	P	1	0	1	0	0	1.000
World Series			Batting																							Fielding						
Year	Tm	Age	G	AB	H	2B	3B	HR	TB	R	RBI	GW	TBB	IBB	SO	HBP	SH	SF	SB	CS	SB%	GDP	Avg	OBP	SLG	Pos	G	PO	A	E	DP	FPct
1987	StL	23	2	0	0	0	0	0	0	0	0	0	0	0	0	0	0	0	0	0	—	0	—	—	—	P	2	1	1	0	0	1.000
Postseason Totals			3	1	0	0	0	0	0	0	0	0	0	0	0	0	0	0	0	0	—	0	.000	.000	.000	P	3	1	2	0	0	1.000

FREDDIE MAGUIRE—Frederick Edward Maguire—Bats: Right; Throws: Right

Ht: 5'11"; Wt: 155 lbs; Born: 5/10/1899 in Roxbury, Massachusetts; Debut: 9/22/1922; Died: 11/3/1961

World Series			Batting																							Fielding						
Year	Tm	Age	G	AB	H	2B	3B	HR	TB	R	RBI	GW	TBB	IBB	SO	HBP	SH	SF	SB	CS	SB%	GDP	Avg	OBP	SLG	Pos	G	PO	A	E	DP	FPct
1923	NYG	24	2	0	0	0	0	0	0	1	0	0	0	0	0	0	0	0	0	0	—	0	—	—	—	—						

ROY MAHAFFEY—Lee Roy Mahaffey—Nickname: Popeye—Throws: Right; Bats: Right

Ht: 6'0"; Wt: 180 lbs; Born: 2/9/1903 in Belton, South Carolina; Debut: 8/31/1926; Died: 7/23/1969

World Series			Pitching																										
Year	Tm	Age	G	GS	CG	GF	IP	BFP	H	R	ER	HR	SH	SF	HB	TBB	IBB	SO	WP	Bk	W	L	Pct	ShO	Sv-Op	Hld	OAvg	OOBP	ERA
1931	Phi	28	1	0	0	1	1.0	5	1	1	1	0	0	0	0	1	0	0	0	0	0	0	—	0	0-0	0	.250	.400	9.00

World Series			Batting																							Fielding						
Year	Tm	Age	G	AB	H	2B	3B	HR	TB	R	RBI	GW	TBB	IBB	SO	HBP	SH	SF	SB	CS	SB%	GDP	Avg	OBP	SLG	Pos	G	PO	A	E	DP	FPct
1931	Phi	28	1	0	0	0	0	0	0	0	0	0	0	0	0	0	0	0	0	0	—	0	—	—	—	P	1	0	1	0	0	1.000

RICK MAHLER—Richard Keith Mahler—Throws: Right; Bats: Right

Ht: 6'1"; Wt: 195 lbs; Born: 8/5/1953 in Austin, Texas; Debut: 4/20/1979

LCS			Pitching																										
Year	Tm	Age	G	GS	CG	GF	IP	BFP	H	R	ER	HR	SH	SF	HB	TBB	IBB	SO	WP	Bk	W	L	Pct	ShO	Sv-Op	Hld	OAvg	OOBP	ERA
1982	Atl	29	1	0	0	0	1.2	11	3	0	0	0	1	0	0	2	1	0	0	0	0	0	—	0	0-0	0	.375	.500	0.00
1990	Cin	37	1	0	0	0	1.2	7	2	0	0	0	0	0	0	0	0	0	0	0	0	0	—	0	0-0	0	.286	.286	0.00
LCS Totals			2	0	0	0	3.1	36	5	0	0	0	1	0	0	2	1	0	0	0	0	0	—	0	0-0	0	.333	.412	0.00

LCS			Batting																							Fielding						
Year	Tm	Age	G	AB	H	2B	3B	HR	TB	R	RBI	GW	TBB	IBB	SO	HBP	SH	SF	SB	CS	SB%	GDP	Avg	OBP	SLG	Pos	G	PO	A	E	DP	FPct
1982	Atl	29	1	0	0	0	0	0	0	0	0	0	0	0	0	0	0	0	0	0	—	0	—	—	—	P	1	0	1	0	0	1.000
1990	Cin	37	1	0	0	0	0	0	0	0	0	0	0	0	0	0	0	0	0	0	—	0	—	—	—	P	1	0	0	0	0	—
LCS Totals			2	0	0	0	0	0	0	0	0	0	0	0	0	0	0	0	0	0	—	0	—	—	—	P	2	0	1	0	0	1.000

BOB MAIER—Robert Phillip Maier—Bats: Right; Throws: Right

Ht: 5'8"; Wt: 180 lbs; Born: 9/5/1915 in Dunellen, New Jersey; Debut: 4/17/1945; Died: 8/4/1993

World Series			Batting																							Fielding						
Year	Tm	Age	G	AB	H	2B	3B	HR	TB	R	RBI	GW	TBB	IBB	SO	HBP	SH	SF	SB	CS	SB%	GDP	Avg	OBP	SLG	Pos	G	PO	A	E	DP	FPct
1945	Det	30	1	1	1	0	0	0	1	0	0	0	0	0	0	0	0	0	0	0	—	0	1.000	1.000	1.000	—						

DUSTER MAILS—John Walter Mails—Nickname: The Great—Throws: Left; Bats: Left

Ht: 6'0"; Wt: 195 lbs; Born: 10/1/1894 in San Quentin, California; Debut: 9/28/1915; Died: 7/5/1974

World Series			Pitching																										
Year	Tm	Age	G	GS	CG	GF	IP	BFP	H	R	ER	HR	SH	SF	HB	TBB	IBB	SO	WP	Bk	W	L	Pct	ShO	Sv-Op	Hld	OAvg	OOBP	ERA
1920	Cle	25	2	1	1	0	15.2	58	6	0	0	0	2	0	0	6	0	6	0	0	1	0	1.000	1	0-0	0	.120	.214	0.00

World Series			Batting																							Fielding						
Year	Tm	Age	G	AB	H	2B	3B	HR	TB	R	RBI	GW	TBB	IBB	SO	HBP	SH	SF	SB	CS	SB%	GDP	Avg	OBP	SLG	Pos	G	PO	A	E	DP	FPct
1920	Cle	25	2	5	0	0	0	0	0	0	0	0	0	0	1	0	0	0	0	0	—	1	.000	.000	.000	P	2	1	4	0	1	1.000

HANK MAJESKI—Henry Majeski—Nickname: Heeney—Bats: Right; Throws: Right

Ht: 5'9"; Wt: 174 lbs; Born: 12/13/1916 in Staten Island, New York; Debut: 5/17/1939; Died: 8/9/1991

World Series			Batting																							Fielding						
Year	Tm	Age	G	AB	H	2B	3B	HR	TB	R	RBI	GW	TBB	IBB	SO	HBP	SH	SF	SB	CS	SB%	GDP	Avg	OBP	SLG	Pos	G	PO	A	E	DP	FPct
1954	Cle	37	4	6	1	0	0	1	4	1	3	0	0	0	1	0	0	0	0	0	—	1	.167	.167	.667	3B	1	2	1	0	0	1.000

CANDY MALDONADO—Candido Maldonado—Bats: Right; Throws: Right

Ht: 6'0"; Wt: 185 lbs; Born: 9/5/1960 in Humacao, Puerto Rico; Debut: 9/7/1981

LCS			Batting																							Fielding						
Year	Tm	Age	G	AB	H	2B	3B	HR	TB	R	RBI	GW	TBB	IBB	SO	HBP	SH	SF	SB	CS	SB%	GDP	Avg	OBP	SLG	Pos	G	PO	A	E	DP	FPct
1983	LA	23	2	2	0	0	0	0	0	0	0	0	0	0	1	0	0	0	0	0	—	0	.000	.000	.000	—						
1985	LA	25	4	7	1	0	0	0	1	0	1	0	0	0	3	0	0	0	0	0	—	0	.143	.143	.143	OF	3	4	0	1	0	.800
1987	SF	27	5	19	4	1	0	0	5	2	2	0	0	0	3	0	0	0	0	0	—	0	.211	.211	.263	OF	5	7	0	0	0	1.000
1989	SF	29	3	3	0	0	0	0	0	1	1	0	2	0	0	0	0	0	0	0	—	0	.000	.400	.000	OF	3	2	0	0	0	1.000
1991	Tor	31	5	20	2	1	0	0	3	1	1	0	1	0	6	0	0	0	0	0	—	0	.100	.143	.150	OF	5	4	0	0	0	1.000
1992	Tor	32	6	22	6	0	0	2	12	3	6	1	3	0	4	0	0	0	0	1	.00	0	.273	.360	.545	OF	6	9	1	0	1	1.000
LCS Totals			25	73	13	2	0	2	21	7	11	1	6	0	17	0	0	0	0	1	.00	0	.178	.241	.288	OF	22	26	1	1	1	.964
World Series			Batting																							Fielding						
Year	Tm	Age	G	AB	H	2B	3B	HR	TB	R	RBI	GW	TBB	IBB	SO	HBP	SH	SF	SB	CS	SB%	GDP	Avg	OBP	SLG	Pos	G	PO	A	E	DP	FPct
1989	SF	29	4	11	1	0	1	0	3	1	0	0	0	0	4	0	0	0	0	0	—	0	.091	.091	.273	OF	3	5	0	0	0	1.000
1992	Tor	32	6	19	3	0	0	1	6	1	2	1	2	0	5	0	0	0	0	0	—	1	.158	.238	.316	OF	5	8	2	0	1	1.000
WS Totals			10	30	4	0	1	1	9	2	2	1	2	0	9	0	0	0	0	0	—	1	.133	.188	.300	OF	8	13	2	0	1	1.000
Postseason Totals			35	103	17	2	1	3	30	9	13	2	8	0	26	0	0	0	0	1	.00	1	.165	.225	.291	OF	30	39	3	1	2	.977

PAT MALONE—Perce Leigh Malone—Throws: Right; Bats: Left

Ht: 6'0"; Wt: 200 lbs; Born: 9/25/1902 in Altoona, Pennsylvania; Debut: 4/12/1928; Died: 5/13/1943

World Series			Pitching																										
Year	Tm	Age	G	GS	CG	GF	IP	BFP	H	R	ER	HR	SH	SF	HB	TBB	IBB	SO	WP	Bk	W	L	Pct	ShO	Sv-Op	Hld	OAvg	OOBP	ERA
1929	ChN	27	3	2	1	0	13.0	59	12	9	6	2	1	0	1	7	1	11	0	0	0	2	.000	0	0-0	0	.240	.345	4.15
1932	ChN	30	1	0	0	0	2.2	14	1	0	0	0	0	0	0	4	1	4	0	0	0	0	—	0	0-0	0	.100	.357	0.00
1936	NYA	34	2	0	0	2	5.0	17	2	1	1	0	1	0	0	1	0	2	0	0	0	1	.000	0	1-1	0	.133	.188	1.80
WS Totals			6	2	1	2	20.2	180	15	10	7	2	2	0	1	12	2	17	0	0	0	3	.000	0	1-1	0	.200	.318	3.05

World Series			Batting																							Fielding						
Year	Tm	Age	G	AB	H	2B	3B	HR	TB	R	RBI	GW	TBB	IBB	SO	HBP	SH	SF	SB	CS	SB%	GDP	Avg	OBP	SLG	Pos	G	PO	A	E	DP	FPct
1929	ChN	27	3	4	1	1	0	0	2	0	0	0	0	0	2	0	0	0	0	0	—	0	.250	.250	.500	P	3	0	1	0	0	1.000
1932	ChN	30	1	0	0	0	0	0	0	0	0	0	0	0	0	0	0	0	0	0	—	0	—	—	—	P	1	0	0	0	0	—
1936	NYA	34	2	1	1	0	0	0	1	0	0	0	0	0	0	0	0	0	0	0	—	0	1.000	1.000	1.000	P	2	0	2	0	0	1.000
WS Totals			6	5	2	1	0	0	3	0	0	0	0	0	2	0	0	0	0	0	—	0	.400	.400	.600	P	6	0	3	0	0	1.000

JIM MALONEY—James William Maloney—Throws: Right; Bats: Left

Ht: 6'2"; Wt: 190 lbs; Born: 6/2/1940 in Fresno, California; Debut: 7/27/1960

World Series			Pitching																										
Year	Tm	Age	G	GS	CG	GF	IP	BFP	H	R	ER	HR	SH	SF	HB	TBB	IBB	SO	WP	Bk	W	L	Pct	ShO	Sv-Op	Hld	OAvg	OOBP	ERA
1961	Cin	21	1	0	0	0	0.2	7	4	2	2	0	0	0	0	1	0	1	0	0	0	0	—	0	0-0	0	.667	.714	27.00

World Series		Batting																							Fielding						
Year Tm	Age	G	AB	H	2B	3B	HR	TB	R	RBI	GW	TBB	IBB	SO	HBP	SH	SF	SB	CS	SB%	GDP	Avg	OBP	SLG	Pos	G	PO	A	E	DP	FPct
1961 Cin	21	1	0	0	0	0	0	0	0	0	0	0	0	0	0	0	0	0	0	—	0	—	—	—	P	1	0	0	0	0	—

AL MAMAUX—Albert Leon Mamaux—Throws: Right; Bats: Right

Ht: 6'0"; Wt: 168 lbs; Born: 5/30/1894 in Pittsburgh, Pennsylvania; Debut: 9/23/1913; Died: 1/2/1963

World Series		Pitching																							
Year Tm	Age	G	GS	CG	GF	IP	BFP	H	R	ER	HR	SH	SF	HB	TBB	IBB	SO	WP	Bk	W	L	Pct	ShO	Sv-Op	Hld	OAvg	OOBP	ERA
1920 Bro	26	3	0	0	1	4.0	13	2	2	2	0	0	0	0	0	0	5	0	0	0	0	—	0	0- 0	0	.154	.154	4.50

World Series		Batting																							Fielding						
Year Tm	Age	G	AB	H	2B	3B	HR	TB	R	RBI	GW	TBB	IBB	SO	HBP	SH	SF	SB	CS	SB%	GDP	Avg	OBP	SLG	Pos	G	PO	A	E	DP	FPct
1920 Bro	26	3	1	0	0	0	0	0	0	0	0	0	0	1	0	0	0	0	0	—	0	.000	.000	.000	P	3	0	1	0	0	1.000

FRANK MANCUSO—Frank Octavius Mancuso—Bats: Right; Throws: Right

Ht: 6'0"; Wt: 195 lbs; Born: 5/23/1918 in Houston, Texas; Debut: 4/18/1944

World Series		Batting																							Fielding						
Year Tm	Age	G	AB	H	2B	3B	HR	TB	R	RBI	GW	TBB	IBB	SO	HBP	SH	SF	SB	CS	SB%	GDP	Avg	OBP	SLG	Pos	G	PO	A	E	DP	FPct
1944 StL	26	2	3	2	0	0	0	2	0	1	0	0	0	0	0	0	0	0	0	—	0	.667	.667	.667	C	1	3	0	0	0	1.000

GUS MANCUSO—August Rodney Mancuso—Nickname: Blackie—Bats: Right; Throws: Right

Ht: 5'10"; Wt: 185 lbs; Born: 12/5/1905 in Galveston, Texas; Debut: 4/30/1928; Died: 10/26/1984

World Series		Batting																							Fielding						
Year Tm	Age	G	AB	H	2B	3B	HR	TB	R	RBI	GW	TBB	IBB	SO	HBP	SH	SF	SB	CS	SB%	GDP	Avg	OBP	SLG	Pos	G	PO	A	E	DP	FPct
1930 StL	24	2	7	2	0	0	0	2	1	0	0	1	0	2	0	0	0	0	0	—	0	.286	.375	.286	C	2	13	1	0	0	1.000
1931 StL	25	2	1	0	0	0	0	0	0	0	0	0	0	0	0	0	0	0	0	—	0	.000	.000	.000	C	1	2	0	0	0	1.000
1933 NYG	27	5	17	2	1	0	0	3	2	2	0	3	1	0	0	1	0	0	0	—	1	.118	.250	.176	C	5	32	4	0	2	1.000
1936 NYG	30	6	19	5	2	0	0	7	3	1	1	3	1	3	0	1	0	0	0	—	1	.263	.364	.368	C	6	40	5	0	2	1.000
1937 NYG	31	3	8	0	0	0	0	0	0	0	0	0	0	1	0	0	0	0	0	—	1	.000	.000	.000	C	2	8	1	0	0	1.000
WS Totals		18	52	9	3	0	0	12	6	3	1	7	2	6	0	2	0	0	0	—	3	.173	.271	.231	C	16	95	11	0	4	1.000

ANGEL MANGUAL—Angel Luis Mangual—Bats: Right; Throws: Right

Ht: 5'10"; Wt: 178 lbs; Born: 3/19/1947 in Juana Diaz, Puerto Rico; Debut: 9/15/1969

LCS		Batting																							Fielding						
Year Tm	Age	G	AB	H	2B	3B	HR	TB	R	RBI	GW	TBB	IBB	SO	HBP	SH	SF	SB	CS	SB%	GDP	Avg	OBP	SLG	Pos	G	PO	A	E	DP	FPct
1971 Oak	24	3	12	2	1	1	0	5	1	2	0	0	0	1	0	0	0	0	0	—	1	.167	.167	.417	OF	3	6	0	0	0	1.000
1972 Oak	25	3	3	0	0	0	0	0	0	0	0	0	0	1	0	0	0	0	0	—	0	.000	.000	.000	—						
1973 Oak	26	3	9	1	0	0	0	1	1	0	0	0	0	3	0	0	0	0	0	—	0	.111	.111	.111	OF	3	2	0	0	0	1.000
1974 Oak	27	1	4	1	0	0	0	1	0	0	0	0	0	0	0	0	0	0	0	—	0	.250	.250	.250	—						
LCS Totals		10	28	4	1	1	0	7	2	2	0	0	0	5	0	0	0	0	0	—	1	.143	.143	.250	OF	6	8	0	0	0	1.000
World Series		**Batting**																							**Fielding**						
Year Tm	Age	G	AB	H	2B	3B	HR	TB	R	RBI	GW	TBB	IBB	SO	HBP	SH	SF	SB	CS	SB%	GDP	Avg	OBP	SLG	Pos	G	PO	A	E	DP	FPct
1972 Oak	25	4	10	3	0	0	0	3	1	1	1	0	0	0	0	1	0	0	0	—	0	.300	.300	.300	OF	3	6	0	1	0	.857
1973 Oak	26	5	6	0	0	0	0	0	0	0	0	0	0	3	0	0	0	0	0	—	0	.000	.000	.000	OF	1	1	0	0	0	1.000
1974 Oak	27	1	1	0	0	0	0	0	0	0	0	0	0	1	0	0	0	0	0	—	0	.000	.000	.000	—						
WS Totals		10	17	3	0	0	0	3	1	1	1	0	0	4	0	1	0	0	0	—	0	.176	.176	.176	OF	4	7	0	1	0	.875
Postseason Totals		20	45	7	1	1	0	10	3	3	1	0	0	9	0	1	0	0	0	—	1	.156	.156	.222	OF	10	15	0	1	0	.938

LES MANN—Leslie Mann—Nickname: Major—Bats: Right; Throws: Right

Ht: 5'9"; Wt: 172 lbs; Born: 11/18/1893 in Lincoln, Nebraska; Debut: 4/30/1913; Died: 1/14/1962

World Series		Batting																							Fielding						
Year Tm	Age	G	AB	H	2B	3B	HR	TB	R	RBI	GW	TBB	IBB	SO	HBP	SH	SF	SB	CS	SB%	GDP	Avg	OBP	SLG	Pos	G	PO	A	E	DP	FPct
1914 Bos	20	3	7	2	0	0	0	2	1	1	1	0	0	1	0	0	0	0	0	—	0	.286	.286	.286	OF	2	1	0	0	0	1.000
1918 ChN	24	6	22	5	2	0	0	7	0	2	1	0	0	0	1	1	0	0	1	.00	0	.227	.261	.318	OF	6	7	0	0	0	1.000
WS Totals		9	29	7	2	0	0	9	1	3	2	0	0	1	1	1	0	0	1	.00	0	.241	.267	.310	OF	8	8	0	0	0	1.000

FELIX MANTILLA—Nickname: The Cat—Bats: Right; Throws: Right

Ht: 6'0"; Wt: 160 lbs; Born: 7/29/1934 in Isabella, Puerto Rico; Debut: 6/21/1956

World Series		Batting																							Fielding						
Year Tm	Age	G	AB	H	2B	3B	HR	TB	R	RBI	GW	TBB	IBB	SO	HBP	SH	SF	SB	CS	SB%	GDP	Avg	OBP	SLG	Pos	G	PO	A	E	DP	FPct
1957 Mil	23	4	10	0	0	0	0	0	1	0	0	1	0	0	0	0	0	0	0	—	1	.000	.091	.000	2B	3	6	8	0	1	1.000
1958 Mil	24	4	0	0	0	0	0	0	1	0	0	0	0	0	0	0	0	0	0	—	0	—	—	—	SS	1	0	0	0	0	—
WS Totals		8	10	0	0	0	0	0	2	0	0	1	0	0	0	0	0	0	0	—	1	.000	.091	.000	2B	3	6	8	0	1	1.000

MICKEY MANTLE (HOF 1974-W)—Mickey Charles Mantle—Nickname: The Commerce Comet—B: B; T: R

Ht: 5'11"; Wt: 195 lbs; Born: 10/20/1931 in Spavinaw, Okla.; Deb.: 4/17/1951; Died: 8/13/1995

World Series		Batting																							Fielding						
Year Tm	Age	G	AB	H	2B	3B	HR	TB	R	RBI	GW	TBB	IBB	SO	HBP	SH	SF	SB	CS	SB%	GDP	Avg	OBP	SLG	Pos	G	PO	A	E	DP	FPct
1951 NYA	19	2	5	1	0	0	0	1	1	0	0	2	0	1	0	0	0	0	0	—	0	.200	.429	.200	OF	2	4	0	0	0	1.000
1952 NYA	20	7	29	10	1	1	2	19	5	3	1	3	0	4	0	0	0	0	0	—	0	.345	.406	.655	OF	7	16	0	0	0	1.000
1953 NYA	21	6	24	5	0	0	2	11	3	7	1	3	1	8	0	0	0	0	1	.00	0	.208	.296	.458	OF	6	14	0	0	0	1.000
1955 NYA	23	3	10	2	0	0	1	5	1	1	0	0	0	2	0	0	0	0	0	—	1	.200	.200	.500	OF	2	4	0	0	0	1.000
1956 NYA-*M*	24	7	24	6	1	0	3	16	6	4	1	6	1	5	0	0	0	1	0	1.00	1	.250	.400	.667	OF	7	18	1	0	0	1.000
1957 NYA-*M*	25	6	19	5	0	0	1	8	3	2	0	3	0	1	0	0	0	0	2	.00	0	.263	.364	.421	OF	5	8	0	1	0	.889
1958 NYA	26	7	24	6	0	1	2	14	4	3	0	7	1	4	0	0	0	0	0	—	0	.250	.419	.583	OF	7	16	0	0	0	1.000
1960 NYA	28	7	25	10	1	0	3	20	8	11	0	8	2	9	0	0	0	0	1	.00	0	.400	.545	.800	OF	7	14	0	0	0	1.000
1961 NYA	29	2	6	1	0	0	0	1	0	0	0	0	0	2	0	0	0	0	0	—	0	.167	.167	.167	OF	2	2	0	0	0	1.000
1962 NYA-*M*	30	7	25	3	1	0	0	4	2	0	0	4	0	5	0	0	0	2	0	1.00	0	.120	.241	.160	OF	7	11	0	0	0	1.000
1963 NYA	31	4	15	2	0	0	1	5	1	1	0	1	0	5	0	0	0	0	0	—	0	.133	.188	.333	OF	4	6	0	0	0	1.000
1964 NYA	32	7	24	8	2	0	3	19	8	8	1	6	1	8	0	0	0	0	0	—	0	.333	.467	.792	OF	7	12	0	2	0	.857
WS Totals		65	230	59	6	2	18	123	42	40	4	43	6	54	0	0	0	3	4	.43	2	.257	.374	.535	OF	63	125	1	3	0	.977

CHARLIE MANUEL—Charles Fuqua Manuel—Bats: Left; Throws: Right

Ht: 6'4"; Wt: 195 lbs; Born: 1/4/1944 in Northfork, West Virginia; Debut: 4/8/1969

LCS		Batting																							Fielding						
Year Tm	Age	G	AB	H	2B	3B	HR	TB	R	RBI	GW	TBB	IBB	SO	HBP	SH	SF	SB	CS	SB%	GDP	Avg	OBP	SLG	Pos	G	PO	A	E	DP	FPct
1969 Min	25	1	0	0	0	0	0	0	0	0	0	1	0	0	0	0	0	0	0	—	0	—	1.000	—	—						
1970 Min	26	1	1	0	0	0	0	0	0	0	0	0	0	1	0	0	0	0	0	—	0	.000	.000	.000	—						
LCS Totals		2	1	0	0	0	0	0	0	0	0	1	0	1	0	0	0	0	0	—	0	.000	.500	.000	—	0	0	0	0	0	—

JERRY MANUEL—Bats: Both; Throws: Right

Ht: 6'0"; Wt: 165 lbs; Born: 12/23/1953 in Hahira, Georgia; Debut: 9/18/1975

Division Series		Batting																							Fielding						
Year Tm	Age	G	AB	H	2B	3B	HR	TB	R	RBI	GW	TBB	IBB	SO	HBP	SH	SF	SB	CS	SB%	GDP	Avg	OBP	SLG	Pos	G	PO	A	E	DP	FPct
1981 Mon	27	5	14	1	0	0	0	1	0	0	0	2	0	5	0	0	0	0	0	—	1	.071	.188	.071	2B	5	14	17	3	5	.912
LCS		**Batting**																							**Fielding**						
Year Tm	Age	G	AB	H	2B	3B	HR	TB	R	RBI	GW	TBB	IBB	SO	HBP	SH	SF	SB	CS	SB%	GDP	Avg	OBP	SLG	Pos	G	PO	A	E	DP	FPct
1981 Mon	27	1	0	0	0	0	0	0	0	0	0	0	0	0	0	0	0	0	0	—	0	—	—	—	—						
Postseason Totals		6	14	1	0	0	0	1	0	0	0	2	0	5	0	0	0	0	0	—	1	.071	.188	.071	2B	5	14	17	3	5	.912

HEINIE MANUSH (HOF 1964-V)—Henry Emmett Manush—Bats: Left; Throws: Left

Ht: 6'1"; Wt: 200 lbs; Born: 7/20/1901 in Tuscumbia, Alabama; Debut: 4/20/1923; Died: 5/12/1971

World Series		Batting																							Fielding						
Year Tm	Age	G	AB	H	2B	3B	HR	TB	R	RBI	GW	TBB	IBB	SO	HBP	SH	SF	SB	CS	SB%	GDP	Avg	OBP	SLG	Pos	G	PO	A	E	DP	FPct
1933 Was	32	5	18	2	0	0	0	2	2	0	0	2	0	1	0	0	0	0	0	—	0	.111	.200	.111	OF	5	10	0	0	0	1.000

KIRT MANWARING—Kirt Dean Manwaring—Bats: Right; Throws: Right

Ht: 5'11"; Wt: 185 lbs; Born: 7/15/1965 in Elmira, New York; Debut: 9/15/1987

LCS		Batting																							Fielding						
Year Tm	Age	G	AB	H	2B	3B	HR	TB	R	RBI	GW	TBB	IBB	SO	HBP	SH	SF	SB	CS	SB%	GDP	Avg	OBP	SLG	Pos	G	PO	A	E	DP	FPct
1989 SF	24	3	2	0	0	0	0	0	0	0	0	0	0	0	0	0	0	0	0	—	0	.000	.000	.000	C	3	5	0	0	0	1.000
World Series		Batting																							Fielding						
Year Tm	Age	G	AB	H	2B	3B	HR	TB	R	RBI	GW	TBB	IBB	SO	HBP	SH	SF	SB	CS	SB%	GDP	Avg	OBP	SLG	Pos	G	PO	A	E	DP	FPct
1989 SF	24	1	1	1	1	0	0	2	1	0	0	0	0	0	0	0	0	0	0	—	0	1.000	1.000	2.000	C	1	0	0	0	0	—
Postseason Totals		4	3	1	1	0	0	2	1	0	0	0	0	0	0	0	0	0	0	—	0	.333	.333	.667	C	4	5	0	0	0	1.000

CLIFF MAPES—Clifford Franklin Mapes—Bats: Left; Throws: Right

Ht: 6'3"; Wt: 205 lbs; Born: 3/13/1922 in Sutherland, Nebraska; Debut: 4/20/1948; Died: 12/5/1996

World Series		Batting																							Fielding						
Year Tm	Age	G	AB	H	2B	3B	HR	TB	R	RBI	GW	TBB	IBB	SO	HBP	SH	SF	SB	CS	SB%	GDP	Avg	OBP	SLG	Pos	G	PO	A	E	DP	FPct
1949 NYA	27	4	10	1	1	0	0	2	3	2	1	2	0	4	0	1	0	0	0	—	0	.100	.250	.200	OF	4	8	0	1	0	.889
1950 NYA	28	1	4	0	0	0	0	0	0	0	0	0	0	1	0	0	0	0	0	—	0	.000	.000	.000	OF	1	3	0	0	0	1.000
WS Totals		5	14	1	1	0	0	2	3	2	1	2	0	5	0	1	0	0	0	—	0	.071	.188	.143	OF	5	11	0	1	0	.917

RABBIT MARANVILLE (HOF 1954-W)—Walter James Vincent Maranville—Bats: R; Throws: R

Ht: 5'5"; Wt: 155 lbs; Born: 11/11/1891 in Springfield, Mass.; Deb.: 9/10/1912; Died: 1/5/1954

World Series		Batting																							Fielding						
Year Tm	Age	G	AB	H	2B	3B	HR	TB	R	RBI	GW	TBB	IBB	SO	HBP	SH	SF	SB	CS	SB%	GDP	Avg	OBP	SLG	Pos	G	PO	A	E	DP	FPct
1914 Bos	22	4	13	4	0	0	0	4	1	3	0	1	0	1	1	1	0	2	1	.67	0	.308	.400	.308	SS	4	7	13	1	2	.952
1928 StL	36	4	13	4	1	0	0	5	2	0	0	1	0	1	0	0	0	1	0	1.00	0	.308	.357	.385	SS	4	11	3	1	2	.933
WS Totals		8	26	8	1	0	0	9	3	3	0	2	0	2	1	1	0	3	1	.75	0	.308	.379	.346	SS	8	18	16	2	4	.944

FIRPO MARBERRY—Frederick Marberry—Throws: Right; Bats: Right

Ht: 6'1"; Wt: 190 lbs; Born: 11/30/1898 in Streetman, Texas; Debut: 8/11/1923; Died: 6/30/1976

World Series		Pitching																										
Year Tm	Age	G	GS	CG	GF	IP	BFP	H	R	ER	HR	SH	SF	HB	TBB	IBB	SO	WP	Bk	W	L	Pct	ShO	Sv-Op	Hld	OAvg	OOBP	ERA
1924 Was	25	4	1	0	2	8.0	39	9	5	1	0	0	1	1	4	0	10	1	0	1	1	.500	0	1- 2	0	.273	.359	1.13
1925 Was	26	2	0	0	2	2.1	11	3	0	0	0	0	0	1	0	0	2	0	0	0	0	—	0	1- 1	0	.300	.364	0.00
1934 Det	35	2	0	0	0	1.2	11	5	4	4	0	1	0	0	1	0	0	0	0	0	0	—	0	0- 0	0	.556	.600	21.60
WS Totals		8	1	0	4	12.0	122	17	9	5	0	1	1	2	5	0	12	1	0	1	1	.500	0	2-3	0	.327	.400	3.75

World Series		Batting																							Fielding						
Year Tm	Age	G	AB	H	2B	3B	HR	TB	R	RBI	GW	TBB	IBB	SO	HBP	SH	SF	SB	CS	SB%	GDP	Avg	OBP	SLG	Pos	G	PO	A	E	DP	FPct
1924 Was	25	4	2	0	0	0	0	0	0	0	0	0	0	0	0	0	0	0	0	—	0	.000	.000	.000	P	4	1	1	0	1	1.000
1925 Was	26	2	0	0	0	0	0	0	0	0	0	0	0	0	0	1	0	0	0	—	0	—	—	—	P	2	0	0	0	0	—
1934 Det	35	2	0	0	0	0	0	0	0	0	0	0	0	0	0	0	0	0	0	—	0	—	—	—	P	2	0	1	0	0	1.000
WS Totals		8	2	0	0	0	0	0	0	0	0	0	0	0	0	1	0	0	0	—	0	.000	.000	.000	P	8	1	2	0	1	1.000

JUAN MARICHAL (HOF 1983-W)—Juan Antonio Marichal—Nicknames: Manito, The Dominican Dandy—T: R; B: R

Ht: 6'0"; Wt: 185 lbs; Born: 10/20/1937 in Laguna Verde, D.R.; Deb.: 7/19/1960

LCS		Pitching																										
Year Tm	Age	G	GS	CG	GF	IP	BFP	H	R	ER	HR	SH	SF	HB	TBB	IBB	SO	WP	Bk	W	L	Pct	ShO	Sv-Op	Hld	OAvg	OOBP	ERA
1971 SF	33	1	1	1	0	8.0	30	4	2	2	2	0	0	0	0	0	6	2	0	0	1	.000	0	0- 0	0	.133	.133	2.25
World Series		Pitching																										
Year Tm	Age	G	GS	CG	GF	IP	BFP	H	R	ER	HR	SH	SF	HB	TBB	IBB	SO	WP	Bk	W	L	Pct	ShO	Sv-Op	Hld	OAvg	OOBP	ERA
1962 SF	24	1	1	0	0	4.0	15	2	0	0	0	0	0	0	2	0	4	0	0	0	0	—	0	0- 0	0	.154	.267	0.00
Postseason Totals		2	2	1	0	12.0	90	6	2	2	2	0	0	0	2	0	10	2	0	0	1	.000	0	0-0	0	.140	.178	1.50

LCS		Batting																							Fielding						
Year Tm	Age	G	AB	H	2B	3B	HR	TB	R	RBI	GW	TBB	IBB	SO	HBP	SH	SF	SB	CS	SB%	GDP	Avg	OBP	SLG	Pos	G	PO	A	E	DP	FPct
1971 SF	33	1	3	0	0	0	0	0	0	0	0	0	0	1	0	0	0	0	0	—	0	.000	.000	.000	P	1	2	4	0	0	1.000
World Series		Batting																							Fielding						
Year Tm	Age	G	AB	H	2B	3B	HR	TB	R	RBI	GW	TBB	IBB	SO	HBP	SH	SF	SB	CS	SB%	GDP	Avg	OBP	SLG	Pos	G	PO	A	E	DP	FPct
1962 SF	24	1	2	0	0	0	0	0	0	0	0	0	0	1	0	0	0	0	0	—	0	.000	.000	.000	P	1	1	0	0	1	1.000
Postseason Totals		2	5	0	0	0	0	0	0	0	0	0	0	2	0	0	0	0	0	—	0	.000	.000	.000	P	2	3	4	0	1	1.000

MARTY MARION—Martin Whiteford Marion—Nicknames: Slats, The Octopus—Bats: Right; Throws: Right

Ht: 6'2"; Wt: 170 lbs; Born: 12/1/1917 in Richburg, South Carolina; Debut: 4/16/1940

World Series		Batting																							Fielding						
Year Tm	Age	G	AB	H	2B	3B	HR	TB	R	RBI	GW	TBB	IBB	SO	HBP	SH	SF	SB	CS	SB%	GDP	Avg	OBP	SLG	Pos	G	PO	A	E	DP	FPct
1942 StL	24	5	18	2	0	1	0	4	2	3	0	1	0	2	0	0	0	0	0	—	0	.111	.158	.222	SS	5	13	16	0	3	1.000
1943 StL	25	5	14	5	2	0	1	10	1	2	1	3	2	1	0	1	0	1	0	1.00	1	.357	.471	.714	SS	5	8	14	1	4	.957
1944 StL-*M*	26	6	22	5	3	0	0	8	1	2	0	2	2	3	0	1	0	0	0	—	0	.227	.292	.364	SS	6	7	22	0	2	1.000
1946 StL	28	7	24	6	2	0	0	8	1	4	0	1	1	1	0	3	0	0	0	—	1	.250	.280	.333	SS	7	12	22	2	3	.944
WS Totals		23	78	18	7	1	1	30	5	11	1	7	5	7	0	5	0	1	0	1.00	2	.231	.294	.385	SS	23	40	74	3	12	.974

ROGER MARIS—Roger Eugene Maris—Bats: Left; Throws: Right

Ht: 6'0"; Wt: 197 lbs; Born: 9/10/1934 in Hibbing, Minnesota; Debut: 4/16/1957; Died: 12/14/1985

World Series		Batting																							Fielding						
Year Tm	Age	G	AB	H	2B	3B	HR	TB	R	RBI	GW	TBB	IBB	SO	HBP	SH	SF	SB	CS	SB%	GDP	Avg	OBP	SLG	Pos	G	PO	A	E	DP	FPct
1960 NYA-*M*	26	7	30	8	1	0	2	15	6	2	0	2	0	4	0	0	0	0	0	—	0	.267	.313	.500	OF	7	12	0	1	0	.923
1961 NYA-*M*	27	5	19	2	1	0	1	6	4	2	1	4	1	6	0	0	0	0	0	—	0	.105	.261	.316	OF	5	11	1	0	0	1.000
1962 NYA	28	7	23	4	1	0	1	8	4	5	1	5	0	2	0	0	0	0	0	—	0	.174	.321	.348	OF	7	11	1	0	0	1.000
1963 NYA	29	2	5	0	0	0	0	0	0	0	0	0	0	1	0	0	0	0	0	—	0	.000	.000	.000	OF	2	3	0	0	0	1.000
1964 NYA	30	7	30	6	0	0	1	9	4	1	1	1	0	4	0	0	0	0	0	—	1	.200	.226	.300	OF	7	20	0	0	0	1.000
1967 StL	33	7	26	10	1	0	1	14	3	7	2	3	0	1	0	0	1	0	0	—	1	.385	.433	.538	OF	7	15	0	1	0	.938
1968 StL	34	6	19	3	1	0	0	4	5	1	0	3	0	3	0	0	0	0	0	—	1	.158	.273	.211	OF	5	8	0	0	0	1.000
WS Totals		41	152	33	5	0	6	56	26	18	5	18	1	21	0	0	1	0	0	—	3	.217	.298	.368	OF	40	80	2	2	0	.976

RUBE MARQUARD (HOF 1971-V)—Richard William Marquard—Throws: Left; Bats: Both

Ht: 6'3"; Wt: 180 lbs; Born: 10/9/1886 in Cleveland, Ohio; Debut: 9/25/1908; Died: 6/1/1980

World Series		Pitching																										
Year Tm	Age	G	GS	CG	GF	IP	BFP	H	R	ER	HR	SH	SF	HB	TBB	IBB	SO	WP	Bk	W	L	Pct	ShO	Sv-Op	Hld	OAvg	OOBP	ERA
1911 NYG	24	3	2	0	1	11.2	45	9	6	2	2	1	0	0	1	0	8	2	0	0	1	.000	0	0- 0	0	.209	.227	1.54
1912 NYG	25	2	2	2	0	18.0	69	14	3	1	0	1	0	0	2	0	9	0	0	2	0	1.000	0	0- 0	0	.212	.235	0.50
1913 NYG	26	2	1	0	1	9.0	39	10	7	7	1	1	0	0	3	0	3	0	0	0	1	.000	0	0- 0	0	.286	.342	7.00
1916 Bro	29	2	2	0	0	11.0	53	12	9	8	1	5	1	0	6	0	9	0	0	0	2	.000	0	0- 0	0	.293	.375	6.55
1920 Bro	33	2	1	0	0	9.0	36	7	3	2	0	1	0	0	3	1	6	0	0	0	1	.000	0	0- 0	0	.219	.286	2.00
WS Totals		11	8	2	2	58.2	484	52	28	20	4	9	1	0	15	1	35	2	0	2	5	.286	0	0-0	0	.240	.288	3.07

World Series		Batting																							Fielding						
Year Tm	Age	G	AB	H	2B	3B	HR	TB	R	RBI	GW	TBB	IBB	SO	HBP	SH	SF	SB	CS	SB%	GDP	Avg	OBP	SLG	Pos	G	PO	A	E	DP	FPct
1911 NYG	24	3	2	0	0	0	0	0	0	0	0	0	0	2	0	0	0	0	0	—	0	.000	.000	.000	P	3	0	2	0	0	1.000
1912 NYG	25	2	4	0	0	0	0	0	0	0	0	1	0	0	0	1	0	0	0	—	0	.000	.200	.000	P	2	0	4	1	0	.800
1913 NYG	26	2	1	0	0	0	0	0	0	0	0	0	0	0	0	1	0	0	0	—	0	.000	.000	.000	P	2	0	8	0	0	1.000
1916 Bro	29	2	3	0	0	0	0	0	0	0	0	0	0	1	0	0	0	0	0	—	0	.000	.000	.000	P	2	0	2	0	0	1.000
1920 Bro	33	2	1	0	0	0	0	0	0	0	0	0	0	0	0	0	0	0	0	—	0	.000	.000	.000	P	2	0	1	0	0	1.000
WS Totals		11	11	0	0	0	0	0	0	0	0	1	0	3	0	2	0	0	0	—	0	.000	.083	.000	P	11	0	17	1	0	.944

GONZALO MARQUEZ—Gonzalo Enrique Marquez—Bats: Left; Throws: Left

Ht: 5'11"; Wt: 180 lbs; Born: 3/31/1946 in Caupano, Venezuela; Debut: 8/11/1972; Died: 12/20/1984

LCS		Batting																							Fielding						
Year Tm	Age	G	AB	H	2B	3B	HR	TB	R	RBI	GW	TBB	IBB	SO	HBP	SH	SF	SB	CS	SB%	GDP	Avg	OBP	SLG	Pos	G	PO	A	E	DP	FPct
1972 Oak	26	3	3	2	0	0	0	2	1	1	0	0	0	0	0	0	0	0	0	—	0	.667	.667	.667	—						

Year Tm	Age	G	AB	H	2B	3B	HR	TB	R	RBI	GW	TBB	IBB	SO	HBP	SH	SF	SB	CS	SB%	GDP	Avg	OBP	SLG	Pos	G	PO	A	E	DP	FPct
World Series																															
1972 Oak	26	5	5	3	0	0	0	3	0	1	0	0	0	0	0	0	0	0	0	—	0	.600	.600	.600	—						
Postseason Totals		8	8	5	0	0	0	5	1	2	0	0	0	0	0	0	0	0	0	—	0	.625	.625	.625	—	0	0	0	0	0	—

MIKE MARSHALL—Michael Grant Marshall—Throws: Right; Bats: Right

Ht: 5'10"; Wt: 180 lbs; Born: 1/15/1943 in Adrian, Michigan; Debut: 5/31/1967

Year Tm	Age	G	GS	CG	GF	IP	BFP	H	R	ER	HR	SH	SF	HB	TBB	IBB	SO	WP	Bk	W	L	Pct	ShO	Sv-Op	Hld	OAvg	OOBP	ERA
LCS																												
1974 LA-*C*	31	2	0	0	2	3.0	9	0	0	0	0	0	0	0	0	0	1	0	0	0	0	—	0	0- 1	0	.000	.000	0.00
World Series																												
1974 LA-*C*	31	5	0	0	5	9.0	32	6	1	1	1	1	0	0	1	0	10	0	0	0	1	.000	0	1- 1	0	.200	.226	1.00
Postseason Totals		7	0	0	7	12.0	82	6	1	1	1	1	0	0	1	0	11	0	0	0	1	.000	0	1-2	0	.154	.175	0.75

Year Tm	Age	G	AB	H	2B	3B	HR	TB	R	RBI	GW	TBB	IBB	SO	HBP	SH	SF	SB	CS	SB%	GDP	Avg	OBP	SLG	Pos	G	PO	A	E	DP	FPct
LCS																															
1974 LA	31	2	0	0	0	0	0	0	0	0	0	0	0	0	0	0	0	0	0	—	0	—	—	—	P	2	0	0	0	0	—
World Series																															
1974 LA	31	5	0	0	0	0	0	0	0	0	0	1	0	0	0	0	0	0	0	—	0	—	1.000	—	P	5	0	4	0	0	1.000
Postseason Totals		7	0	0	0	0	0	0	0	0	0	1	0	0	0	0	0	0	0	—	0	—	1.000	—	P	7	0	4	0	0	1.000

MIKE MARSHALL—Michael Allen Marshall—Nickname: Moose—Bats: Right; Throws: Right

Ht: 6'5"; Wt: 215 lbs; Born: 1/12/1960 in Libertyville, Illinois; Debut: 9/7/1981

Year Tm	Age	G	AB	H	2B	3B	HR	TB	R	RBI	GW	TBB	IBB	SO	HBP	SH	SF	SB	CS	SB%	GDP	Avg	OBP	SLG	Pos	G	PO	A	E	DP	FPct
Division Series																															
1981 LA	21	1	1	0	0	0	0	0	0	0	0	0	0	1	0	0	0	0	0	—	0	.000	.000	.000	—						
LCS																															
1983 LA	23	4	15	2	1	0	1	6	1	2	0	1	0	6	0	0	0	0	1	.00	0	.133	.188	.400	1B	3	17	2	0	1	1.000
																									OF	2	4	0	0	0	1.000
1985 LA	25	6	23	5	2	0	1	10	1	3	0	1	0	3	0	0	0	0	0	—	0	.217	.250	.435	OF	6	8	0	0	0	1.000
1988 LA	28	7	30	7	1	1	0	10	3	5	1	2	0	9	0	0	0	0	0	—	1	.233	.281	.333	OF	7	14	0	0	0	1.000
1990 Bos	30	3	3	1	0	0	0	1	0	0	0	0	0	0	0	0	0	0	0	—	0	.333	.333	.333	—						
LCS Totals		20	71	15	4	1	2	27	5	10	1	4	0	18	0	0	0	0	1	.00	1	.211	.253	.380	OF	15	26	0	0	0	1.000
World Series																															
1988 LA	28	5	13	3	0	1	1	8	2	3	0	0	0	5	0	0	0	0	0	—	0	.231	.231	.615	OF	5	6	0	0	0	1.000
Postseason Totals		26	85	18	4	2	3	35	7	13	1	4	0	24	0	0	0	0	1	.00	1	.212	.247	.412	OF	20	32	0	0	0	1.000

BILLY MARTIN—Alfred Manuel Martin—Bats: Right; Throws: Right

Ht: 5'11"; Wt: 165 lbs; Born: 5/16/1928 in Berkeley, California; Debut: 4/18/1950; Died: 12/25/1989

Year Tm	Age	G	AB	H	2B	3B	HR	TB	R	RBI	GW	TBB	IBB	SO	HBP	SH	SF	SB	CS	SB%	GDP	Avg	OBP	SLG	Pos	G	PO	A	E	DP	FPct
World Series																															
1951 NYA	23	1	0	0	0	0	0	0	1	0	0	0	0	0	0	0	0	0	0	—	0	—	—	—	—						
1952 NYA	24	7	23	5	0	0	1	8	2	4	1	2	1	2	1	0	0	0	1	.00	0	.217	.308	.348	2B	7	15	16	1	5	.969
1953 NYA	25	6	24	12	1	2	2	23	5	8	1	1	0	2	0	0	0	1	2	.33	1	.500	.520	.958	2B	6	13	15	0	2	1.000
1955 NYA	27	7	25	8	1	1	0	11	2	4	1	1	0	5	0	0	0	0	2	.00	1	.320	.346	.440	2B	7	17	20	0	7	1.000
1956 NYA	28	7	27	8	0	0	2	14	5	3	1	1	0	6	0	0	0	0	0	—	2	.296	.321	.519	2B	7	12	18	0	4	1.000
																									3B	2	2	2	0	1	1.000
WS Totals		28	99	33	2	3	5	56	15	19	4	5	1	15	1	0	0	1	5	.17	4	.333	.371	.566	2B	27	57	69	1	18	.992

J.C. MARTIN—Joseph Clifton Martin—Bats: Left; Throws: Right

Ht: 6'2"; Wt: 188 lbs; Born: 12/13/1936 in Axton, Virginia; Debut: 9/10/1959

Year Tm	Age	G	AB	H	2B	3B	HR	TB	R	RBI	GW	TBB	IBB	SO	HBP	SH	SF	SB	CS	SB%	GDP	Avg	OBP	SLG	Pos	G	PO	A	E	DP	FPct
LCS																															
1969 NYN	32	2	2	1	0	0	0	1	0	2	0	0	0	0	0	0	0	0	0	—	0	.500	.500	.500	—						
World Series																															
1969 NYN	32	1	0	0	0	0	0	0	0	0	0	0	0	0	0	1	0	0	0	—	0	—	—	—	—						
Postseason Totals		3	2	1	0	0	0	1	0	2	0	0	0	0	0	1	0	0	0	—	0	.500	.500	.500	—	0	0	0	0	0	—

JERRY MARTIN—Jerry Lindsey Martin—Bats: Right; Throws: Right

Ht: 6'1"; Wt: 195 lbs; Born: 5/11/1949 in Columbia, South Carolina; Debut: 9/7/1974

Year Tm	Age	G	AB	H	2B	3B	HR	TB	R	RBI	GW	TBB	IBB	SO	HBP	SH	SF	SB	CS	SB%	GDP	Avg	OBP	SLG	Pos	G	PO	A	E	DP	FPct
LCS																															
1976 Phi	27	1	1	0	0	0	0	0	1	0	0	0	0	0	0	0	0	0	0	—	0	.000	.000	.000	OF	1	1	0	0	0	1.000
1977 Phi	28	3	4	0	0	0	0	0	0	0	0	0	0	2	0	0	0	0	0	—	0	.000	.000	.000	OF	1	1	0	0	0	1.000
1978 Phi	29	4	9	2	1	0	1	6	1	2	0	1	0	3	0	0	0	0	0	—	1	.222	.300	.667	OF	3	7	0	0	0	1.000
LCS Totals		8	14	2	1	0	1	6	2	2	0	1	0	5	0	0	0	0	0	—	1	.143	.200	.429	OF	5	9	0	0	0	1.000

PEPPER MARTIN—John Leonard Roosevelt Martin—Nickname: The Wild Horse of the Osage—B: R; T: R

Ht: 5'8"; Wt: 170 lbs; Born: 2/29/1904 in Temple, Okla.; Deb.: 4/16/1928; Died: 3/5/1965

Year Tm	Age	G	AB	H	2B	3B	HR	TB	R	RBI	GW	TBB	IBB	SO	HBP	SH	SF	SB	CS	SB%	GDP	Avg	OBP	SLG	Pos	G	PO	A	E	DP	FPct
World Series																															
1928 StL	24	1	0	0	0	0	0	0	1	0	0	0	0	0	0	0	0	0	0	—	0	—	—	—	—						
1931 StL	27	7	24	12	4	0	1	19	5	5	1	2	0	3	0	0	0	5	1	.83	0	.500	.538	.792	OF	7	11	0	0	0	1.000
1934 StL	30	7	31	11	3	1	0	16	8	4	0	3	0	3	0	0	0	2	1	.67	0	.355	.412	.516	3B	7	6	9	4	0	.789
WS Totals		15	55	23	7	1	1	35	14	9	1	5	0	6	0	0	0	7	2	.78	0	.418	.467	.636	3B	7	6	9	4	0	.789

RENIE MARTIN—Donald Renie Martin—Throws: Right; Bats: Right

Ht: 6'4"; Wt: 190 lbs; Born: 8/30/1955 in Dover, Delaware; Debut: 5/9/1979

Year Tm	Age	G	GS	CG	GF	IP	BFP	H	R	ER	HR	SH	SF	HB	TBB	IBB	SO	WP	Bk	W	L	Pct	ShO	Sv-Op	Hld	OAvg	OOBP	ERA
Division Series																												
1981 KC	26	2	0	0	2	5.1	19	1	0	0	0	0	0	0	2	0	2	0	0	0	0	—	0	0- 0	0	.059	.158	0.00
World Series																												
1980 KC	25	3	0	0	0	9.2	42	11	3	3	0	0	1	1	3	0	2	0	0	0	0	—	0	0- 0	0	.297	.357	2.79
Postseason Totals		5	0	0	2	15.0	122	12	3	3	0	0	1	1	5	0	4	0	0	0	0	—	0	0-0	0	.222	.295	1.80

Year Tm	Age	G	AB	H	2B	3B	HR	TB	R	RBI	GW	TBB	IBB	SO	HBP	SH	SF	SB	CS	SB%	GDP	Avg	OBP	SLG	Pos	G	PO	A	E	DP	FPct
Division Series																															
1981 KC	26	2	0	0	0	0	0	0	0	0	0	0	0	0	0	0	0	0	0	—	0	—	—	—	P	2	1	0	0	0	1.000
World Series																															
1980 KC	25	3	0	0	0	0	0	0	0	0	0	0	0	0	0	0	0	0	0	—	0	—	—	—	P	3	0	0	0	0	—
Postseason Totals		5	0	0	0	0	0	0	0	0	0	0	0	0	0	0	0	0	0	—	0	—	—	—	P	5	1	0	0	0	1.000

TOM MARTIN—Thomas Martin—Throws: Left; Bats: Left

Ht: 6'1"; Wt: 185 lbs; Born: 5/21/1970 in Panama City, Florida; Debut: 4/2/1997

Year Tm	Age	G	GS	CG	GF	IP	BFP	H	R	ER	HR	SH	SF	HB	TBB	IBB	SO	WP	Bk	W	L	Pct	ShO	Sv-Op	Hld	OAvg	OOBP	ERA
Division Series																												
1997 Hou	27	2	0	0	1	0.2	4	1	1	0	0	0	0	0	1	0	0	0	0	0	0	—	0	0- 0	0	.333	.500	0.00

Year Tm	Age	G	AB	H	2B	3B	HR	TB	R	RBI	GW	TBB	IBB	SO	HBP	SH	SF	SB	CS	SB%	GDP	Avg	OBP	SLG	Pos	G	PO	A	E	DP	FPct
Division Series																															
1997 Hou	27	2	0	0	0	0	0	0	0	0	0	0	0	0	0	0	0	0	0	—	0	—	—	—	P	2	0	1	0	0	1.000

JOE MARTINA—John Joseph Martina—Nickname: Oyster Joe—Throws: Right; Bats: Right

Ht: 6'0"; Wt: 183 lbs; Born: 7/8/1889 in New Orleans, Louisiana; Debut: 4/19/1924; Died: 3/22/1962

World Series		Pitching																										
Year Tm	Age	G	GS	CG	GF	IP	BFP	H	R	ER	HR	SH	SF	HB	TBB	IBB	SO	WP	Bk	W	L	Pct	ShO	Sv-Op	Hld	OAvg	OOBP	ERA
1924 Was	35	1	0	0	0	1.0	3	0	0	0	0	0	0	0	0	0	1	0	0	0	0	—	0	0-0	0	.000	.000	0.00

World Series		Batting																							Fielding						
Year Tm	Age	G	AB	H	2B	3B	HR	TB	R	RBI	GW	TBB	IBB	SO	HBP	SH	SF	SB	CS	SB%	GDP	Avg	OBP	SLG	Pos	G	PO	A	E	DP	FPct
1924 Was	35	1	0	0	0	0	0	0	0	0	0	0	0	0	0	0	0	0	0	—	0	—	—	—	P	1	0	0	0	0	—

BUCK MARTINEZ—John Albert Martinez—Bats: Right; Throws: Right

Ht: 5'10"; Wt: 190 lbs; Born: 11/7/1948 in Redding, California; Debut: 6/18/1969

LCS		Batting																							Fielding						
Year Tm	Age	G	AB	H	2B	3B	HR	TB	R	RBI	GW	TBB	IBB	SO	HBP	SH	SF	SB	CS	SB%	GDP	Avg	OBP	SLG	Pos	G	PO	A	E	DP	FPct
1976 KC	27	5	15	5	0	0	0	5	0	4	0	1	0	3	0	0	0	0	0	—	0	.333	.375	.333	C	5	15	4	0	1	1.000

CARMELO MARTINEZ—Nickname: Bitu—Bats: Right; Throws: Right

Ht: 6'2"; Wt: 190 lbs; Born: 7/28/1960 in Dorado, Puerto Rico; Debut: 8/22/1983

LCS		Batting																							Fielding						
Year Tm	Age	G	AB	H	2B	3B	HR	TB	R	RBI	GW	TBB	IBB	SO	HBP	SH	SF	SB	CS	SB%	GDP	Avg	OBP	SLG	Pos	G	PO	A	E	DP	FPct
1984 SD	24	5	17	3	0	0	0	3	1	0	0	2	0	4	0	0	0	0	0	—	1	.176	.263	.176	OF	5	6	0	0	0	1.000
1990 Pit	30	2	8	2	2	0	0	4	0	2	0	0	0	1	0	0	0	0	0	—	0	.250	.250	.500	1B	2	15	1	0	1	1.000
LCS Totals		7	25	5	2	0	0	7	1	2	0	2	0	5	0	0	0	0	0	—	1	.200	.259	.280	OF	5	6	0	0	0	1.000

World Series		Batting																							Fielding						
Year Tm	Age	G	AB	H	2B	3B	HR	TB	R	RBI	GW	TBB	IBB	SO	HBP	SH	SF	SB	CS	SB%	GDP	Avg	OBP	SLG	Pos	G	PO	A	E	DP	FPct
1984 SD	24	5	17	3	0	0	0	3	0	0	0	1	0	9	0	0	0	0	0	—	0	.176	.222	.176	OF	5	7	0	1	0	.875
Postseason Totals		12	42	8	2	0	0	10	1	2	0	3	0	14	0	0	0	0	0	—	1	.190	.244	.238	OF	10	13	0	1	0	.929

DENNIS MARTINEZ—Jose Dennis Martinez—Nickname: El Presidente—Throws: Right; Bats: Right

Ht: 6'1"; Wt: 160 lbs; Born: 5/14/1955 in Granada, Nicaragua; Debut: 9/14/1976

Division Series		Pitching																										
Year Tm	Age	G	GS	CG	GF	IP	BFP	H	R	ER	HR	SH	SF	HB	TBB	IBB	SO	WP	Bk	W	L	Pct	ShO	Sv-Op	Hld	OAvg	OOBP	ERA
1995 Cle	40	1	1	0	0	6.0	23	5	2	2	1	0	0	0	0	0	2	0	0	0	0	—	0	0-0	0	.217	.217	3.00

LCS		Pitching																										
Year Tm	Age	G	GS	CG	GF	IP	BFP	H	R	ER	HR	SH	SF	HB	TBB	IBB	SO	WP	Bk	W	L	Pct	ShO	Sv-Op	Hld	OAvg	OOBP	ERA
1979 Bal	24	1	1	0	0	8.1	32	8	3	3	1	0	0	0	0	0	4	0	0	0	0	—	0	0-0	0	.250	.250	3.24
1995 Cle	40	2	2	0	0	13.1	52	10	3	3	1	0	0	1	3	0	7	0	0	1	1	.500	0	0-0	0	.208	.269	2.03
LCS Totals		3	3	0	0	21.2	168	18	6	6	2	0	0	1	3	0	11	0	0	1	1	.500	0	0-0	0	.225	.262	2.49

World Series		Pitching																										
Year Tm	Age	G	GS	CG	GF	IP	BFP	H	R	ER	HR	SH	SF	HB	TBB	IBB	SO	WP	Bk	W	L	Pct	ShO	Sv-Op	Hld	OAvg	OOBP	ERA
1979 Bal	24	2	1	0	1	2.0	10	6	4	4	1	0	0	1	0	0	0	0	0	0	0	—	0	0-0	0	.667	.700	18.00
1995 Cle	40	2	2	0	0	10.1	49	12	4	4	1	0	1	1	8	1	5	0	0	0	1	.000	0	0-0	0	.308	.429	3.48
WS Totals		4	3	0	1	12.1	118	18	8	8	2	0	1	2	8	1	5	0	0	0	1	.000	0	0-0	0	.375	.475	5.84
Postseason Totals		8	7	0	1	40.0	332	41	16	16	5	0	1	3	11	1	18	0	0	1	2	.333	0	0-0	0	.272	.331	3.60

Division Series		Batting																							Fielding						
Year Tm	Age	G	AB	H	2B	3B	HR	TB	R	RBI	GW	TBB	IBB	SO	HBP	SH	SF	SB	CS	SB%	GDP	Avg	OBP	SLG	Pos	G	PO	A	E	DP	FPct
1995 Cle	40	1	0	0	0	0	0	0	0	0	0	0	0	0	0	0	0	0	0	—	0	—	—	—	P	1	0	1	0	0	1.000

LCS		Batting																							Fielding						
Year Tm	Age	G	AB	H	2B	3B	HR	TB	R	RBI	GW	TBB	IBB	SO	HBP	SH	SF	SB	CS	SB%	GDP	Avg	OBP	SLG	Pos	G	PO	A	E	DP	FPct
1979 Bal	24	1	0	0	0	0	0	0	0	0	0	0	0	0	0	0	0	0	0	—	0	—	—	—	P	1	2	0	0	0	1.000
1995 Cle	40	2	0	0	0	0	0	0	0	0	0	0	0	0	0	0	0	0	0	—	0	—	—	—	P	2	1	1	0	0	1.000
LCS Totals		3	0	0	0	0	0	0	0	0	0	0	0	0	0	0	0	0	0	—	0	—	—	—	P	3	3	1	0	0	1.000

World Series		Batting																							Fielding						
Year Tm	Age	G	AB	H	2B	3B	HR	TB	R	RBI	GW	TBB	IBB	SO	HBP	SH	SF	SB	CS	SB%	GDP	Avg	OBP	SLG	Pos	G	PO	A	E	DP	FPct
1979 Bal	24	2	0	0	0	0	0	0	0	0	0	0	0	0	0	0	0	0	0	—	0	—	—	—	P	2	0	1	0	1	1.000
1995 Cle	40	2	3	0	0	0	0	0	0	0	0	0	0	1	0	0	0	0	0	—	0	.000	.000	.000	P	2	0	3	1	0	.750
WS Totals		4	3	0	0	0	0	0	0	0	0	0	0	1	0	0	0	0	0	—	0	.000	.000	.000	P	4	0	4	1	1	.800
Postseason Totals		8	3	0	0	0	0	0	0	0	0	0	0	1	0	0	0	0	0	—	0	.000	.000	.000	P	8	3	6	1	1	.900

EDGAR MARTINEZ—Bats: Right; Throws: Right

Ht: 6'0"; Wt: 175 lbs; Born: 1/2/1963 in New York, New York; Debut: 9/12/1987

Division Series		Batting																							Fielding						
Year Tm	Age	G	AB	H	2B	3B	HR	TB	R	RBI	GW	TBB	IBB	SO	HBP	SH	SF	SB	CS	SB%	GDP	Avg	OBP	SLG	Pos	G	PO	A	E	DP	FPct
1995 Sea	32	5	21	12	3	0	2	21	6	10	2	6	2	2	0	0	0	0	0	—	0	.571	.667	1.000	—						
1997 Sea	34	4	16	3	0	0	2	9	2	3	0	0	0	3	0	0	0	0	0	—	0	.188	.188	.563	—						
DS Totals		9	37	15	3	0	4	30	8	13	2	6	2	5	0	0	0	0	0	—	0	.405	.488	.811	—	0	0	0	0	0	—

LCS		Batting																							Fielding						
Year Tm	Age	G	AB	H	2B	3B	HR	TB	R	RBI	GW	TBB	IBB	SO	HBP	SH	SF	SB	CS	SB%	GDP	Avg	OBP	SLG	Pos	G	PO	A	E	DP	FPct
1995 Sea	32	6	23	2	0	0	0	2	0	0	0	2	2	5	1	0	0	1	1	.50	1	.087	.192	.087	—						
Postseason Totals		15	60	17	3	0	4	32	8	13	2	8	4	10	1	0	0	1	1	.50	1	.283	.377	.533	—	0	0	0	0	0	—

RAMON MARTINEZ—Ramon Jaime Martinez—Throws: Right; Bats: Right

Ht: 6'4"; Wt: 165 lbs; Born: 3/22/1968 in Santo Domingo, Dominican Republic; Debut: 8/13/1988

Division Series		Pitching																										
Year Tm	Age	G	GS	CG	GF	IP	BFP	H	R	ER	HR	SH	SF	HB	TBB	IBB	SO	WP	Bk	W	L	Pct	ShO	Sv-Op	Hld	OAvg	OOBP	ERA
1995 LA	27	1	1	0	0	4.1	25	10	7	7	1	1	1	0	2	0	3	0	0	0	1	.000	0	0-0	0	.476	.500	14.54
1996 LA	28	1	1	0	0	8.0	29	3	1	1	0	1	1	0	3	0	6	0	0	0	0	—	0	0-0	0	.125	.214	1.13
DS Totals		2	2	0	0	12.1	108	13	8	8	1	2	2	0	5	0	9	0	0	0	1	.000	0	0-0	0	.289	.346	5.84

Division Series		Batting																							Fielding						
Year Tm	Age	G	AB	H	2B	3B	HR	TB	R	RBI	GW	TBB	IBB	SO	HBP	SH	SF	SB	CS	SB%	GDP	Avg	OBP	SLG	Pos	G	PO	A	E	DP	FPct
1995 LA	27	1	1	0	0	0	0	0	0	0	0	0	0	0	0	0	0	0	0	—	0	.000	.000	.000	P	1	0	1	0	0	1.000
1996 LA	28	1	3	0	0	0	0	0	0	0	0	0	0	2	0	0	0	0	0	—	0	.000	.000	.000	P	1	0	0	0	0	—
DS Totals		2	4	0	0	0	0	0	0	0	0	0	0	2	0	0	0	0	0	—	0	.000	.000	.000	P	2	0	1	0	0	1.000

TED MARTINEZ—Teodoro Noel Martinez—Bats: Right; Throws: Right

Ht: 6'0"; Wt: 165 lbs; Born: 12/10/1947 in Bahrahona, Dominican Republic; Debut: 7/18/1970

LCS		Batting																							Fielding						
Year Tm	Age	G	AB	H	2B	3B	HR	TB	R	RBI	GW	TBB	IBB	SO	HBP	SH	SF	SB	CS	SB%	GDP	Avg	OBP	SLG	Pos	G	PO	A	E	DP	FPct
1975 Oak	27	3	0	0	0	0	0	0	0	0	0	0	0	0	0	0	0	0	0	—	0	—	—	—	2B	3	1	1	0	0	1.000

World Series		Batting																							Fielding						
Year Tm	Age	G	AB	H	2B	3B	HR	TB	R	RBI	GW	TBB	IBB	SO	HBP	SH	SF	SB	CS	SB%	GDP	Avg	OBP	SLG	Pos	G	PO	A	E	DP	FPct
1973 NYN	25	2	0	0	0	0	0	0	0	0	0	0	0	0	0	0	0	0	0	—	0	—	—	—	—						
Postseason Totals		5	0	0	0	0	0	0	0	0	0	0	0	0	0	0	0	0	0	—	0	—	—	—	2B	3	1	1	0	0	1.000

TINO MARTINEZ—Constantino Martinez—Bats: Left; Throws: Right

Ht: 6'2"; Wt: 205 lbs; Born: 12/7/1967 in Tampa, Florida; Debut: 8/20/1990

Division Series		Batting																							Fielding						
Year Tm	Age	G	AB	H	2B	3B	HR	TB	R	RBI	GW	TBB	IBB	SO	HBP	SH	SF	SB	CS	SB%	GDP	Avg	OBP	SLG	Pos	G	PO	A	E	DP	FPct
1995 Sea	27	5	22	9	1	0	1	13	4	5	1	3	0	4	0	0	0	0	1	.00	0	.409	.480	.591	1B	5	39	5	0	4	1.000
1996 NYA	28	4	15	4	2	0	0	6	3	0	0	3	1	1	0	0	0	0	0	—	0	.267	.389	.400	1B	4	33	3	0	2	1.000
1997 NYA	29	5	18	4	1	0	1	8	1	4	1	2	1	4	1	0	0	0	0	—	0	.222	.333	.444	1B	5	48	6	0	2	1.000
DS Totals		14	55	17	4	0	2	27	8	9	2	8	2	9	1	0	0	0	1	.00	0	.309	.406	.491	1B	14	120	14	0	8	1.000

LCS		Batting																							Fielding						
Year Tm	Age	G	AB	H	2B	3B	HR	TB	R	RBI	GW	TBB	IBB	SO	HBP	SH	SF	SB	CS	SB%	GDP	Avg	OBP	SLG	Pos	G	PO	A	E	DP	FPct
1995 Sea	27	6	22	3	0	0	0	3	1	0	0	3	1	7	0	0	0	0	0	—	0	.136	.240	.136	1B	6	45	5	1	6	.980
1996 NYA	28	5	22	4	1	0	0	5	3	0	0	0	0	2	1	0	0	0	0	—	0	.182	.217	.227	1B	5	49	2	0	2	1.000
LCS Totals		11	44	7	1	0	0	8	4	0	0	3	1	9	1	0	0	0	0	—	0	.159	.229	.182	1B	11	94	7	1	8	.990

World Series		Batting																							Fielding						
Year Tm	Age	G	AB	H	2B	3B	HR	TB	R	RBI	GW	TBB	IBB	SO	HBP	SH	SF	SB	CS	SB%	GDP	Avg	OBP	SLG	Pos	G	PO	A	E	DP	FPct
1996 NYA	28	6	11	1	0	0	0	1	0	0	0	2	0	5	0	0	0	0	0	—	0	.091	.231	.091	1B	5	27	0	0	3	1.000
Postseason Totals		31	110	25	5	0	2	36	12	9	2	13	3	23	2	0	0	0	1	.00	0	.227	.320	.327	1B	30	241	21	1	19	.996

TIPPY MARTINEZ—Felix Anthony Martinez—Throws: Left; Bats: Left

Ht: 5'10"; Wt: 180 lbs; Born: 3/31/1950 in La Junta, Colorado; Debut: 8/9/1974

LCS		Pitching																										
Year Tm	Age	G	GS	CG	GF	IP	BFP	H	R	ER	HR	SH	SF	HB	TBB	IBB	SO	WP	Bk	W	L	Pct	ShO	Sv-Op	Hld	OAvg	OOBP	ERA
1983 Bal	33	2	0	0	2	6.0	25	5	0	0	0	0	0	0	3	0	5	1	0	1	0	1.000	0	0-0	0	.227	.320	0.00
World Series		**Pitching**																										
Year Tm	Age	G	GS	CG	GF	IP	BFP	H	R	ER	HR	SH	SF	HB	TBB	IBB	SO	WP	Bk	W	L	Pct	ShO	Sv-Op	Hld	OAvg	OOBP	ERA
1979 Bal	29	3	0	0	0	1.1	8	3	1	1	0	0	0	1	0	0	1	0	0	0	0	—	0	0-0	0	.429	.500	6.75
1983 Bal	33	3	0	0	3	3.0	11	3	1	1	0	0	0	0	0	0	0	0	0	0	0	—	0	2-2	0	.273	.273	3.00
WS Totals		6	0	0	3	4.1	38	6	2	2	0	0	0	1	0	0	1	0	0	0	0	—	0	2-2	0	.333	.368	4.15
Postseason Totals		8	0	0	5	10.1	88	11	2	2	0	0	0	1	3	0	6	1	0	1	0	1.000	0	2-2	0	.275	.341	1.74

LCS		Batting																							Fielding						
Year Tm	Age	G	AB	H	2B	3B	HR	TB	R	RBI	GW	TBB	IBB	SO	HBP	SH	SF	SB	CS	SB%	GDP	Avg	OBP	SLG	Pos	G	PO	A	E	DP	FPct
1983 Bal	33	2	0	0	0	0	0	0	0	0	0	0	0	0	0	0	0	0	0	—	0	—	—	—	P	2	0	2	0	0	1.000
World Series		**Batting**																							**Fielding**						
Year Tm	Age	G	AB	H	2B	3B	HR	TB	R	RBI	GW	TBB	IBB	SO	HBP	SH	SF	SB	CS	SB%	GDP	Avg	OBP	SLG	Pos	G	PO	A	E	DP	FPct
1979 Bal	29	3	0	0	0	0	0	0	0	0	0	0	0	0	0	0	0	0	0	—	0	—	—	—	P	3	0	0	0	0	—
1983 Bal	33	3	0	0	0	0	0	0	0	0	0	0	0	0	0	0	0	0	0	—	0	—	—	—	P	3	0	0	0	0	—
WS Totals		6	0	0	0	0	0	0	0	0	0	0	0	0	0	0	0	0	0	—	0	—	—	—	P	6	0	0	0	0	—
Postseason Totals		8	0	0	0	0	0	0	0	0	0	0	0	0	0	0	0	0	0	—	0	—	—	—	P	8	0	2	0	0	1.000

JOE MARTY—Joseph Anton Marty—Bats: Right; Throws: Right

Ht: 6'0"; Wt: 182 lbs; Born: 9/1/1913 in Sacramento, California; Debut: 4/22/1937; Died: 10/4/1984

World Series		Batting																							Fielding						
Year Tm	Age	G	AB	H	2B	3B	HR	TB	R	RBI	GW	TBB	IBB	SO	HBP	SH	SF	SB	CS	SB%	GDP	Avg	OBP	SLG	Pos	G	PO	A	E	DP	FPct
1938 ChN	25	3	12	6	1	0	1	10	1	5	0	0	0	2	0	0	0	0	1	.00	0	.500	.500	.833	OF	3	7	0	0	0	1.000

PHIL MASI—Philip Samuel Masi—Bats: Right; Throws: Right

Ht: 5'10"; Wt: 177 lbs; Born: 1/6/1916 in Chicago, Illinois; Debut: 4/23/1939; Died: 3/29/1990

World Series		Batting																							Fielding						
Year Tm	Age	G	AB	H	2B	3B	HR	TB	R	RBI	GW	TBB	IBB	SO	HBP	SH	SF	SB	CS	SB%	GDP	Avg	OBP	SLG	Pos	G	PO	A	E	DP	FPct
1948 Bos	32	5	8	1	1	0	0	2	1	1	0	0	0	0	0	0	0	0	0	—	0	.125	.125	.250	C	5	10	1	0	0	1.000

JIM MASON—James Percy Mason—Bats: Left; Throws: Right

Ht: 6'2"; Wt: 185 lbs; Born: 8/14/1950 in Mobile, Alabama; Debut: 9/26/1971

LCS		Batting																							Fielding						
Year Tm	Age	G	AB	H	2B	3B	HR	TB	R	RBI	GW	TBB	IBB	SO	HBP	SH	SF	SB	CS	SB%	GDP	Avg	OBP	SLG	Pos	G	PO	A	E	DP	FPct
1976 NYA	26	2	0	0	0	0	0	0	0	0	0	0	0	0	0	0	0	0	0	—	0	—	—	—	SS	2	1	2	0	0	1.000
World Series		**Batting**																							**Fielding**						
Year Tm	Age	G	AB	H	2B	3B	HR	TB	R	RBI	GW	TBB	IBB	SO	HBP	SH	SF	SB	CS	SB%	GDP	Avg	OBP	SLG	Pos	G	PO	A	E	DP	FPct
1976 NYA	26	3	1	1	0	0	1	4	1	1	0	0	0	0	0	0	0	0	0	—	0	1.000	1.000	4.000	SS	3	1	2	0	0	1.000
Postseason Totals		5	1	1	0	0	1	4	1	1	0	0	0	0	0	0	0	0	0	—	0	1.000	1.000	4.000	SS	5	2	4	0	0	1.000

ROGER MASON—Roger Leroy Mason—Throws: Right; Bats: Right

Ht: 6'6"; Wt: 215 lbs; Born: 9/18/1958 in Bellaire, Michigan; Debut: 9/4/1984

LCS		Pitching																										
Year Tm	Age	G	GS	CG	GF	IP	BFP	H	R	ER	HR	SH	SF	HB	TBB	IBB	SO	WP	Bk	W	L	Pct	ShO	Sv-Op	Hld	OAvg	OOBP	ERA
1991 Pit	33	3	0	0	1	4.1	16	3	0	0	0	1	0	0	1	0	2	0	0	0	0	—	0	1-1	0	.214	.267	0.00
1992 Pit	34	2	0	0	1	3.1	11	0	0	0	0	0	0	0	2	0	1	0	0	0	0	—	0	0-0	0	.000	.182	0.00
1993 Phi	35	2	0	0	0	3.0	11	1	0	0	0	0	0	0	0	0	2	0	0	0	0	—	0	0-0	0	.091	.091	0.00
LCS Totals		7	0	0	2	10.2	76	4	0	0	0	1	0	0	3	0	5	0	0	0	0	—	0	1-1	0	.118	.189	0.00
World Series		**Pitching**																										
Year Tm	Age	G	GS	CG	GF	IP	BFP	H	R	ER	HR	SH	SF	HB	TBB	IBB	SO	WP	Bk	W	L	Pct	ShO	Sv-Op	Hld	OAvg	OOBP	ERA
1993 Phi	35	4	0	0	1	7.2	28	4	1	1	0	0	0	0	1	0	7	0	0	0	0	—	0	0-0	1	.148	.179	1.17
Postseason Totals		11	0	0	3	18.1	132	8	1	1	0	1	0	0	4	0	12	0	0	0	0	—	0	1-1	1	.131	.185	0.49

LCS		Batting																							Fielding						
Year Tm	Age	G	AB	H	2B	3B	HR	TB	R	RBI	GW	TBB	IBB	SO	HBP	SH	SF	SB	CS	SB%	GDP	Avg	OBP	SLG	Pos	G	PO	A	E	DP	FPct
1991 Pit	33	3	1	0	0	0	0	0	0	0	0	0	0	1	0	0	0	0	0	—	0	.000	.000	.000	P	3	0	0	0	0	—
1992 Pit	34	2	0	0	0	0	0	0	0	0	0	0	0	0	0	0	0	0	0	—	0	—	—	—	P	2	2	0	0	0	1.000
1993 Phi	35	2	0	0	0	0	0	0	0	0	0	0	0	0	0	0	0	0	0	—	0	—	—	—	P	2	0	0	0	0	—
LCS Totals		7	1	0	0	0	0	0	0	0	0	0	0	1	0	0	0	0	0	—	0	.000	.000	.000	P	7	2	0	0	0	1.000
World Series		**Batting**																							**Fielding**						
Year Tm	Age	G	AB	H	2B	3B	HR	TB	R	RBI	GW	TBB	IBB	SO	HBP	SH	SF	SB	CS	SB%	GDP	Avg	OBP	SLG	Pos	G	PO	A	E	DP	FPct
1993 Phi	35	4	1	0	0	0	0	0	0	0	0	0	0	0	0	0	0	0	0	—	0	.000	.000	.000	P	4	0	0	0	0	—
Postseason Totals		11	2	0	0	0	0	0	0	0	0	0	0	1	0	0	0	0	0	—	0	.000	.000	.000	P	11	2	0	0	0	1.000

TOMMY MATCHICK—John Thomas Matchick—Bats: Left; Throws: Right

Ht: 6'1"; Wt: 173 lbs; Born: 9/7/1943 in Hazleton, Pennsylvania; Debut: 9/2/1967

World Series		Batting																							Fielding						
Year Tm	Age	G	AB	H	2B	3B	HR	TB	R	RBI	GW	TBB	IBB	SO	HBP	SH	SF	SB	CS	SB%	GDP	Avg	OBP	SLG	Pos	G	PO	A	E	DP	FPct
1968 Det	25	3	3	0	0	0	0	0	0	0	0	0	0	1	0	0	0	0	0	—	0	.000	.000	.000	—						

EDDIE MATHEWS (HOF 1978-W)—Edwin Lee Mathews—Bats: Left; Throws: Right

Ht: 6'1"; Wt: 190 lbs; Born: 10/13/1931 in Texarkana, Texas; Debut: 4/15/1952

World Series		Batting																							Fielding						
Year Tm	Age	G	AB	H	2B	3B	HR	TB	R	RBI	GW	TBB	IBB	SO	HBP	SH	SF	SB	CS	SB%	GDP	Avg	OBP	SLG	Pos	G	PO	A	E	DP	FPct
1957 Mil	25	7	22	5	3	0	1	11	4	4	2	8	0	5	0	1	0	0	0	—	1	.227	.433	.500	3B	7	9	18	1	2	.964
1958 Mil	26	7	25	4	2	0	0	6	3	3	0	6	2	11	0	0	0	1	0	1.00	0	.160	.323	.240	3B	7	5	12	1	1	.944
1968 Det	36	2	3	1	0	0	0	1	0	0	0	1	0	1	0	0	0	0	0	—	0	.333	.500	.333	3B	1	0	1	1	1	.500
WS Totals		16	50	10	5	0	1	18	7	7	2	15	2	17	0	1	0	1	0	1.00	1	.200	.385	.360	3B	15	14	31	3	3	.938

GREG MATHEWS—Gregory Inman Mathews—Throws: Left; Bats: Right

Ht: 6'2"; Wt: 180 lbs; Born: 5/17/1962 in Harbor City, California; Debut: 6/3/1986

LCS		Pitching																										
Year Tm	Age	G	GS	CG	GF	IP	BFP	H	R	ER	HR	SH	SF	HB	TBB	IBB	SO	WP	Bk	W	L	Pct	ShO	Sv-Op	Hld	OAvg	OOBP	ERA
1987 StL	25	2	2	0	0	10.1	41	6	5	4	2	1	0	0	3	0	10	0	0	1	0	1.000	0	0-0	0	.162	.225	3.48
World Series		**Pitching**																										
Year Tm	Age	G	GS	CG	GF	IP	BFP	H	R	ER	HR	SH	SF	HB	TBB	IBB	SO	WP	Bk	W	L	Pct	ShO	Sv-Op	Hld	OAvg	OOBP	ERA
1987 StL	25	1	1	0	0	3.2	16	2	1	1	1	0	0	1	2	0	3	1	0	0	0	—	0	0-0	0	.154	.313	2.45
Postseason Totals		3	3	0	0	14.0	114	8	6	5	3	1	0	1	5	0	13	1	0	1	0	1.000	0	0-0	0	.160	.250	3.21

LCS		Batting																							Fielding						
Year Tm	Age	G	AB	H	2B	3B	HR	TB	R	RBI	GW	TBB	IBB	SO	HBP	SH	SF	SB	CS	SB%	GDP	Avg	OBP	SLG	Pos	G	PO	A	E	DP	FPct
1987 StL	25	2	2	2	0	0	0	2	0	2	0	0	0	0	0	2	0	0	0	—	0	1.000	1.000	1.000	P	2	0	0	0	0	—
World Series		**Batting**																							**Fielding**						
Year Tm	Age	G	AB	H	2B	3B	HR	TB	R	RBI	GW	TBB	IBB	SO	HBP	SH	SF	SB	CS	SB%	GDP	Avg	OBP	SLG	Pos	G	PO	A	E	DP	FPct
1987 StL	25	1	1	0	0	0	0	0	0	0	0	0	0	0	0	0	0	0	0	—	0	.000	.000	.000	P	1	0	1	0	0	1.000
Postseason Totals		3	3	2	0	0	0	2	0	2	0	0	0	0	0	2	0	0	0	—	0	.667	.667	.667	P	3	0	1	0	0	1.000

T.J. MATHEWS—Timothy Jay Mathews—Throws: Right; Bats: Right

Ht: 6'2"; Wt: 200 lbs; Born: 1/19/1970 in Belleville, Illinois; Debut: 7/28/1995

Division Series — Pitching

Year Tm	Age	G	GS	CG	GF	IP	BFP	H	R	ER	HR	SH	SF	HB	TBB	IBB	SO	WP	Bk	W	L	Pct	ShO	Sv-Op	Hld	OAvg	OOBP	ERA
1996 StL	26	1	0	0	0	1.0	4	1	0	0	0	0	0	0	0	0	2	0	0	1	0	1.000	0	0- 0	0	.250	.250	0.00

LCS — Pitching

Year Tm	Age	G	GS	CG	GF	IP	BFP	H	R	ER	HR	SH	SF	HB	TBB	IBB	SO	WP	Bk	W	L	Pct	ShO	Sv-Op	Hld	OAvg	OOBP	ERA
1996 StL	26	2	0	0	1	0.2	5	2	0	0	0	0	0	0	1	1	2	0	0	0	0	—	0	0- 0	0	.500	.600	0.00
Postseason Totals		3	0	0	1	1.2	18	3	0	0	0	0	0	0	1	1	4	0	0	1	0	1.000	0	0-0	0	.375	.444	0.00

Division Series — Batting / Fielding

Year Tm	Age	G	AB	H	2B	3B	HR	TB	R	RBI	GW	TBB	IBB	SO	HBP	SH	SF	SB	CS	SB%	GDP	Avg	OBP	SLG	Pos	G	PO	A	E	DP	FPct
1996 StL	26	1	0	0	0	0	0	0	0	0	0	0	0	0	0	0	0	0	0	—	0	—	—	—	P	1	0	0	0	0	—

LCS — Batting / Fielding

Year Tm	Age	G	AB	H	2B	3B	HR	TB	R	RBI	GW	TBB	IBB	SO	HBP	SH	SF	SB	CS	SB%	GDP	Avg	OBP	SLG	Pos	G	PO	A	E	DP	FPct
1996 StL	26	2	0	0	0	0	0	0	0	0	0	0	0	0	0	0	0	0	0	—	0	—	—	—	P	2	0	0	0	0	—
Postseason Totals		3	0	0	0	0	0	0	0	0	0	0	0	0	0	0	0	0	0	—	0	—	—	—	P	3	0	0	0	0	—

TERRY MATHEWS—Terry Alan Mathews—Throws: Right; Bats: Left

Ht: 6'2"; Wt: 200 lbs; Born: 10/5/1964 in Alexandria, Louisiana; Debut: 6/21/1991

Division Series — Pitching

Year Tm	Age	G	GS	CG	GF	IP	BFP	H	R	ER	HR	SH	SF	HB	TBB	IBB	SO	WP	Bk	W	L	Pct	ShO	Sv-Op	Hld	OAvg	OOBP	ERA
1996 Bal	31	3	0	0	1	2.2	13	3	0	0	0	1	0	0	1	0	2	1	0	0	0	—	0	0- 0	0	.273	.333	0.00
1997 Bal	32	1	0	0	1	1.0	5	2	2	2	2	0	0	0	0	0	1	0	0	0	0	—	0	0- 0	0	.400	.400	18.00
DS Totals		4	0	0	2	3.2	36	5	2	2	2	1	0	0	1	0	3	1	0	0	0	—	0	0-0	0	.313	.353	4.91

LCS — Pitching

Year Tm	Age	G	GS	CG	GF	IP	BFP	H	R	ER	HR	SH	SF	HB	TBB	IBB	SO	WP	Bk	W	L	Pct	ShO	Sv-Op	Hld	OAvg	OOBP	ERA
1996 Bal	31	3	0	0	2	2.1	10	0	0	0	0	0	0	1	2	0	3	0	0	0	0	—	0	0- 0	0	.000	.300	0.00
Postseason Totals		7	0	0	4	6.0	56	5	2	2	2	1	0	1	3	0	6	1	0	0	0	—	0	0-0	0	.217	.333	3.00

Division Series — Batting / Fielding

Year Tm	Age	G	AB	H	2B	3B	HR	TB	R	RBI	GW	TBB	IBB	SO	HBP	SH	SF	SB	CS	SB%	GDP	Avg	OBP	SLG	Pos	G	PO	A	E	DP	FPct
1996 Bal	31	3	0	0	0	0	0	0	0	0	0	0	0	0	0	0	0	0	0	—	0	—	—	—	P	3	0	1	0	0	1.000
1997 Bal	32	1	0	0	0	0	0	0	0	0	0	0	0	0	0	0	0	0	0	—	0	—	—	—	P	1	0	0	0	0	—
DS Totals		4	0	0	0	0	0	0	0	0	0	0	0	0	0	0	0	0	0	—	0	—	—	—	P	4	0	1	0	0	1.000

LCS — Batting / Fielding

Year Tm	Age	G	AB	H	2B	3B	HR	TB	R	RBI	GW	TBB	IBB	SO	HBP	SH	SF	SB	CS	SB%	GDP	Avg	OBP	SLG	Pos	G	PO	A	E	DP	FPct
1996 Bal	31	3	0	0	0	0	0	0	0	0	0	0	0	0	0	0	0	0	0	—	0	—	—	—	P	3	0	1	0	0	1.000
Postseason Totals		7	0	0	0	0	0	0	0	0	0	0	0	0	0	0	0	0	0	—	0	—	—	—	P	7	0	2	0	0	1.000

CHRISTY MATHEWSON (HOF 1936-W)—Christopher Mathewson—Nickname: Big Six—T: R; B: R

Ht: 6'1"; Wt: 195 lbs; Born: 8/12/1878 in Factoryville, Pa.; Deb.: 7/17/1900; Died: 10/7/1925

World Series — Pitching

Year Tm	Age	G	GS	CG	GF	IP	BFP	H	R	ER	HR	SH	SF	HB	TBB	IBB	SO	WP	Bk	W	L	Pct	ShO	Sv-Op	Hld	OAvg	OOBP	ERA
1905 NYG	27	3	3	3	0	27.0	94	14	0	0	0	0	0	1	1	0	18	1	0	3	0	1.000	3	0- 0	0	.152	.170	0.00
1911 NYG	33	3	3	2	0	27.0	107	25	8	6	1	4	1	0	2	1	13	0	0	1	2	.333	0	0- 0	0	.250	.262	2.00
1912 NYG	34	3	3	3	0	28.2	115	23	11	4	0	1	1	0	5	1	10	0	0	0	2	.000	0	0- 0	0	.213	.246	1.26
1913 NYG	35	2	2	2	0	19.0	75	14	3	2	0	3	2	0	2	1	7	0	0	1	1	.500	1	0- 0	0	.206	.222	0.95
WS Totals		11	11	10	0	101.2	782	76	22	12	1	8	4	1	10	3	48	1	0	5	5	.500	4	0-0	0	.207	.227	1.06

World Series — Batting / Fielding

Year Tm	Age	G	AB	H	2B	3B	HR	TB	R	RBI	GW	TBB	IBB	SO	HBP	SH	SF	SB	CS	SB%	GDP	Avg	OBP	SLG	Pos	G	PO	A	E	DP	FPct
1905 NYG	27	3	8	2	0	0	0	2	1	0	0	1	0	1	0	2	0	0	0	—	0	.250	.333	.250	P	3	1	9	1	0	.909
1911 NYG	33	3	7	2	0	0	0	2	0	0	0	1	0	3	0	0	0	0	0	—	0	.286	.375	.286	P	3	2	9	1	0	.917
1912 NYG	34	3	12	2	0	0	0	2	0	0	0	0	0	4	0	0	0	0	0	—	0	.167	.167	.167	P	3	1	12	0	0	1.000
1913 NYG	35	2	5	3	0	0	0	3	1	1	1	1	0	0	0	0	0	0	0	—	0	.600	.667	.600	P	2	0	5	0	0	1.000
WS Totals		11	32	9	0	0	0	9	2	1	1	3	0	8	0	2	0	0	0	—	0	.281	.343	.281	P	11	4	35	2	0	.951

JON MATLACK—Jonathan Trumpbour Matlack—Throws: Left; Bats: Left

Ht: 6'3"; Wt: 205 lbs; Born: 1/19/1950 in West Chester, Pennsylvania; Debut: 7/11/1971

LCS — Pitching

Year Tm	Age	G	GS	CG	GF	IP	BFP	H	R	ER	HR	SH	SF	HB	TBB	IBB	SO	WP	Bk	W	L	Pct	ShO	Sv-Op	Hld	OAvg	OOBP	ERA
1973 NYN	23	1	1	1	0	9.0	31	2	0	0	0	1	0	0	3	0	9	0	0	1	0	1.000	1	0- 0	0	.074	.167	0.00

World Series — Pitching

Year Tm	Age	G	GS	CG	GF	IP	BFP	H	R	ER	HR	SH	SF	HB	TBB	IBB	SO	WP	Bk	W	L	Pct	ShO	Sv-Op	Hld	OAvg	OOBP	ERA
1973 NYN	23	3	3	0	0	16.2	67	10	7	4	2	0	0	1	5	0	11	0	0	1	2	.333	0	0- 0	0	.164	.239	2.16
Postseason Totals		4	4	1	0	25.2	196	12	7	4	2	1	0	1	8	0	20	0	0	2	2	.500	1	0-0	0	.136	.216	1.40

LCS — Batting / Fielding

Year Tm	Age	G	AB	H	2B	3B	HR	TB	R	RBI	GW	TBB	IBB	SO	HBP	SH	SF	SB	CS	SB%	GDP	Avg	OBP	SLG	Pos	G	PO	A	E	DP	FPct
1973 NYN	23	1	2	0	0	0	0	0	0	0	0	1	0	2	0	1	0	0	0	—	0	.000	.333	.000	P	1	0	1	0	1	1.000

World Series — Batting / Fielding

Year Tm	Age	G	AB	H	2B	3B	HR	TB	R	RBI	GW	TBB	IBB	SO	HBP	SH	SF	SB	CS	SB%	GDP	Avg	OBP	SLG	Pos	G	PO	A	E	DP	FPct
1973 NYN	23	3	4	1	0	0	0	1	0	0	0	2	0	1	0	1	0	0	0	—	2	.250	.500	.250	P	3	0	1	0	0	1.000
Postseason Totals		4	6	1	0	0	0	1	0	0	0	3	0	3	0	2	0	0	0	—	2	.167	.444	.167	P	4	0	2	0	1	1.000

GARY MATTHEWS—Gary Nathaniel Matthews—Nickname: Sarge—Bats: Right; Throws: Right

Ht: 6'2"; Wt: 185 lbs; Born: 7/5/1950 in San Fernando, California; Debut: 9/6/1972

Division Series — Batting / Fielding

Year Tm	Age	G	AB	H	2B	3B	HR	TB	R	RBI	GW	TBB	IBB	SO	HBP	SH	SF	SB	CS	SB%	GDP	Avg	OBP	SLG	Pos	G	PO	A	E	DP	FPct
1981 Phi	31	5	20	8	0	1	1	13	3	1	0	0	0	2	0	0	0	0	0	—	1	.400	.400	.650	OF	5	7	0	0	0	1.000

LCS — Batting / Fielding

Year Tm	Age	G	AB	H	2B	3B	HR	TB	R	RBI	GW	TBB	IBB	SO	HBP	SH	SF	SB	CS	SB%	GDP	Avg	OBP	SLG	Pos	G	PO	A	E	DP	FPct
1983 Phi	33	4	14	6	0	0	3	15	4	8	1	2	1	1	0	0	0	1	0	1.00	0	.429	.500	1.071	OF	4	6	0	0	0	1.000
1984 ChN	34	5	15	3	0	0	2	9	4	5	1	6	1	4	0	0	0	1	1	.50	1	.200	.429	.600	OF	5	11	0	0	0	1.000
LCS Totals		9	29	9	0	0	5	24	8	13	2	8	2	5	0	0	0	2	1	.67	1	.310	.459	.828	OF	9	17	0	0	0	1.000

World Series — Batting / Fielding

Year Tm	Age	G	AB	H	2B	3B	HR	TB	R	RBI	GW	TBB	IBB	SO	HBP	SH	SF	SB	CS	SB%	GDP	Avg	OBP	SLG	Pos	G	PO	A	E	DP	FPct
1983 Phi	33	5	16	4	0	0	1	7	1	1	0	2	0	2	0	0	0	0	0	—	1	.250	.333	.438	OF	5	15	0	0	0	1.000
Postseason Totals		19	65	21	0	1	7	44	12	15	2	10	2	9	0	0	0	2	1	.67	3	.323	.413	.677	OF	19	39	0	0	0	1.000

DON MATTINGLY—Donald Arthur Mattingly—Bats: Left; Throws: Left

Ht: 6'0"; Wt: 175 lbs; Born: 4/20/1961 in Evansville, Indiana; Debut: 9/8/1982

Division Series — Batting / Fielding

Year Tm	Age	G	AB	H	2B	3B	HR	TB	R	RBI	GW	TBB	IBB	SO	HBP	SH	SF	SB	CS	SB%	GDP	Avg	OBP	SLG	Pos	G	PO	A	E	DP	FPct
1995 NYA	34	5	24	10	4	0	1	17	3	6	0	1	0	5	0	0	0	0	0	—	1	.417	.440	.708	1B	5	36	4	1	3	.976

LEN MATUSZEK—Leonard James Matuszek—Bats: Left; Throws: Right

Ht: 6'2"; Wt: 190 lbs; Born: 9/27/1954 in Toledo, Ohio; Debut: 9/3/1981

LCS — Batting / Fielding

Year Tm	Age	G	AB	H	2B	3B	HR	TB	R	RBI	GW	TBB	IBB	SO	HBP	SH	SF	SB	CS	SB%	GDP	Avg	OBP	SLG	Pos	G	PO	A	E	DP	FPct
1985 LA	31	3	1	1	0	0	0	1	1	0	0	0	0	0	0	0	0	0	0	—	0	1.000	1.000	1.000	1B	1	0	0	0	0	—
																									OF	1	0	0	0	0	—

DAL MAXVILL—Charles Dallan Maxvill—Bats: Right; Throws: Right

Ht: 5'11"; Wt: 157 lbs; Born: 2/18/1939 in Granite City, Illinois; Debut: 6/10/1962

LCS — Batting / Fielding

Year Tm	Age	G	AB	H	2B	3B	HR	TB	R	RBI	GW	TBB	IBB	SO	HBP	SH	SF	SB	CS	SB%	GDP	Avg	OBP	SLG	Pos	G	PO	A	E	DP	FPct
1972 Oak	33	5	8	1	0	0	0	1	0	0	0	1	0	2	0	0	0	1	0	1.00	0	.125	.222	.125	SS	4	3	7	0	2	1.000
																									2B	1	0	1	0	0	1.000
1974 Oak	35	1	1	0	0	0	0	0	0	0	0	0	0	1	0	0	0	0	0	—	0	.000	.000	.000	2B	1	2	1	0	1	1.000
LCS Totals		6	9	1	0	0	0	1	0	0	0	1	0	3	0	0	0	1	0	1.00	0	.111	.200	.111	SS	4	3	7	0	2	1.000

World Series

Year Tm	Age	G	AB	H	2B	3B	HR	TB	R	RBI	GW	TBB	IBB	SO	HBP	SH	SF	SB	CS	SB%	GDP	Avg	OBP	SLG	Pos	G	PO	A	E	DP	FPct
1964 StL	25	7	20	4	1	0	0	5	0	1	0	1	0	4	0	1	0	0	0	—	0	.200	.238	.250	2B	7	13	15	0	5	1.000
1967 StL	28	7	19	3	0	1	0	5	1	1	0	4	0	1	0	0	0	0	0	—	0	.158	.304	.263	SS	7	13	17	0	3	1.000
1968 StL	29	7	22	0	0	0	0	0	1	0	0	3	0	5	0	0	0	0	0	—	0	.000	.120	.000	SS	7	15	15	0	6	1.000
1974 Oak	35	2	0	0	0	0	0	0	0	0	0	0	0	0	0	0	0	0	0	—	0	—	—	—	2B	2	0	0	0	0	—
WS Totals		23	61	7	1	1	0	10	2	2	0	8	0	10	0	1	0	0	0	—	0	.115	.217	.164	SS	14	28	32	0	9	1.000
Postseason Totals		29	70	8	1	1	0	11	2	2	0	9	0	13	0	1	0	1	0	1.00	0	.114	.215	.157	SS	18	31	39	0	11	1.000

CARLOS MAY—Bats: Left; Throws: Right

Ht: 5'11"; Wt: 200 lbs; Born: 5/17/1948 in Birmingham, Alabama; Debut: 9/6/1968

	Year Tm	Age	G	AB	H	2B	3B	HR	TB	R	RBI	GW	TBB	IBB	SO	HBP	SH	SF	SB	CS	SB%	GDP	Avg	OBP	SLG	Pos	G	PO	A	E	DP	FPct
LCS	1976 NYA	28	3	10	2	1	0	0	3	1	0	0	1	1	4	0	0	0	0	0	—	0	.200	.273	.300	—						
World Series	1976 NYA	28	4	9	0	0	0	0	0	0	0	0	0	0	1	0	0	0	0	0	—	0	.000	.000	.000	—						
	Postseason Totals		7	19	2	1	0	0	3	1	0	0	1	1	5	0	0	0	0	0	—	0	.105	.150	.158	—	0	0	0	0	0	—

DAVE MAY—David LaFrance May—Bats: Left; Throws: Right

Ht: 5'10"; Wt: 186 lbs; Born: 12/23/1943 in New Castle, Delaware; Debut: 7/28/1967

	Year Tm	Age	G	AB	H	2B	3B	HR	TB	R	RBI	GW	TBB	IBB	SO	HBP	SH	SF	SB	CS	SB%	GDP	Avg	OBP	SLG	Pos	G	PO	A	E	DP	FPct
LCS	1969 Bal	25	1	1	0	0	0	0	0	0	0	0	0	0	0	0	0	0	0	0	—	0	.000	.000	.000	—						
World Series	1969 Bal	25	2	1	0	0	0	0	0	0	0	0	1	0	1	0	0	0	0	0	—	0	.000	.500	.000	—						
	Postseason Totals		3	2	0	0	0	0	0	0	0	0	1	0	1	0	0	0	0	0	—	0	.000	.333	.000	—	0	0	0	0	0	—

JAKIE MAY—Frank Spruiell May—Throws: Left; Bats: Right

Ht: 5'8"; Wt: 178 lbs; Born: 11/25/1895 in Youngsville, North Carolina; Debut: 6/26/1917; Died: 6/3/1970

World Series — Pitching

Year Tm	Age	G	GS	CG	GF	IP	BFP	H	R	ER	HR	SH	SF	HB	TBB	IBB	SO	WP	Bk	W	L	Pct	ShO	Sv-Op	Hld	OAvg	OOBP	ERA
1932 ChN	36	2	0	0	0	4.2	28	9	7	6	0	0	0	2	3	1	4	0	0	0	1	.000	0	0-0	0	.391	.500	11.57

World Series — Batting / Fielding

Year Tm	Age	G	AB	H	2B	3B	HR	TB	R	RBI	GW	TBB	IBB	SO	HBP	SH	SF	SB	CS	SB%	GDP	Avg	OBP	SLG	Pos	G	PO	A	E	DP	FPct
1932 ChN	36	2	2	0	0	0	0	0	0	0	0	0	0	0	0	0	0	0	0	—	0	.000	.000	.000	P	2	1	0	0	0	1.000

LEE MAY—Lee Andrew May—Bats: Right; Throws: Right

Ht: 6'3"; Wt: 195 lbs; Born: 5/23/1943 in Birmingham, Alabama; Debut: 9/1/1965

	Year Tm	Age	G	AB	H	2B	3B	HR	TB	R	RBI	GW	TBB	IBB	SO	HBP	SH	SF	SB	CS	SB%	GDP	Avg	OBP	SLG	Pos	G	PO	A	E	DP	FPct
Division Series	1981 KC	38	1	0	0	0	0	0	0	0	0	0	0	0	0	0	0	0	0	0	—	0	—	—	—	1B	1	2	0	0	0	1.000
LCS	1970 Cin	27	3	12	2	1	0	0	3	0	2	0	0	0	2	0	0	0	0	0	—	1	.167	.167	.250	1B	3	31	1	0	1	1.000
	1979 Bal	36	2	7	1	0	0	0	1	0	1	0	1	0	3	0	0	0	0	0	—	1	.143	.250	.143	—						
	LCS Totals		5	19	3	1	0	0	4	0	3	0	1	0	5	0	0	0	0	0	—	2	.158	.200	.211	1B	3	31	1	0	1	1.000
World Series	1970 Cin	27	5	18	7	2	0	2	15	6	8	1	2	0	2	0	0	0	0	0	—	1	.389	.450	.833	1B	5	48	2	0	3	1.000
	1979 Bal	36	2	1	0	0	0	0	0	0	0	0	1	0	1	0	0	0	0	0	—	0	.000	.500	.000	—						
	WS Totals		7	19	7	2	0	2	15	6	8	1	3	0	3	0	0	0	0	0	—	0	.368	.455	.789	1B	5	48	2	0	3	1.000
	Postseason Totals		13	38	10	3	0	2	19	6	11	1	4	0	8	0	0	0	0	0	—	3	.263	.333	.500	1B	9	81	3	0	4	1.000

MILT MAY—Milton Scott May—Bats: Left; Throws: Right

Ht: 6'0"; Wt: 190 lbs; Born: 8/1/1950 in Gary, Indiana; Debut: 9/8/1970

	Year Tm	Age	G	AB	H	2B	3B	HR	TB	R	RBI	GW	TBB	IBB	SO	HBP	SH	SF	SB	CS	SB%	GDP	Avg	OBP	SLG	Pos	G	PO	A	E	DP	FPct
LCS	1971 Pit	21	1	1	0	0	0	0	0	0	0	0	0	0	0	0	0	0	0	0	—	0	.000	.000	.000	—						
	1972 Pit	22	1	2	1	0	0	0	1	0	1	0	0	0	0	0	0	0	0	0	—	0	.500	.500	.500	C	1	8	1	0	1	1.000
	LCS Totals		2	3	1	0	0	0	1	0	1	0	0	0	0	0	0	0	0	0	—	0	.333	.333	.333	C	1	8	1	0	1	1.000
World Series	1971 Pit	21	2	2	1	0	0	0	1	0	1	1	0	0	0	0	0	0	0	0	—	0	.500	.500	.500	—						
	Postseason Totals		4	5	2	0	0	0	2	0	2	1	0	0	0	0	0	0	0	0	—	0	.400	.400	.400	C	1	8	1	0	1	1.000

RUDY MAY—Rudolph May—Nickname: Dude—Throws: Left; Bats: Left

Ht: 6'2"; Wt: 205 lbs; Born: 7/18/1944 in Coffeyville, Kansas; Debut: 4/18/1965

Pitching

	Year Tm	Age	G	GS	CG	GF	IP	BFP	H	R	ER	HR	SH	SF	HB	TBB	IBB	SO	WP	Bk	W	L	Pct	ShO	Sv-Op	Hld	OAvg	OOBP	ERA
Division Series	1981 NYA	37	1	0	0	1	2.0	6	1	0	0	0	0	0	0	0	0	1	1	0	0	0	—	0	0-0	0	.167	.167	0.00
LCS	1980 NYA	36	1	1	1	0	8.0	32	6	3	3	0	0	0	0	3	0	4	0	0	0	1	.000	0	0-0	0	.207	.281	3.38
	1981 NYA	37	1	1	0	0	3.1	16	6	3	3	0	0	0	0	0	0	5	0	0	0	0	—	0	0-0	0	.375	.375	8.10
	LCS Totals		2	2	1	0	11.1	96	12	6	6	0	0	0	0	3	0	9	0	0	0	1	.000	0	0-0	0	.267	.313	4.76
World Series	1981 NYA	37	3	0	0	0	6.1	23	5	2	2	1	1	0	0	1	0	5	0	0	0	0	—	0	0-0	0	.238	.273	2.84
	Postseason Totals		6	2	1	1	19.2	154	18	8	8	1	1	0	0	4	0	15	1	0	0	1	.000	0	0-0	0	.250	.289	3.66

Batting / Fielding

	Year Tm	Age	G	AB	H	2B	3B	HR	TB	R	RBI	GW	TBB	IBB	SO	HBP	SH	SF	SB	CS	SB%	GDP	Avg	OBP	SLG	Pos	G	PO	A	E	DP	FPct
Division Series	1981 NYA	37	1	0	0	0	0	0	0	0	0	0	0	0	0	0	0	0	0	0	—	0	—	—	—	P	1	1	0	1	0	.500
LCS	1980 NYA	36	1	0	0	0	0	0	0	0	0	0	0	0	0	0	0	0	0	0	—	0	—	—	—	P	1	2	2	0	0	1.000
	1981 NYA	37	1	0	0	0	0	0	0	0	0	0	0	0	0	0	0	0	0	0	—	0	—	—	—	P	1	0	0	0	0	—
	LCS Totals		2	0	0	0	0	0	0	0	0	0	0	0	0	0	0	0	0	0	—	0	—	—	—	P	2	2	2	0	0	1.000
World Series	1981 NYA	37	3	1	0	0	0	0	0	0	0	0	0	0	0	0	0	0	0	0	—	0	.000	.000	.000	P	3	0	1	0	0	1.000
	Postseason Totals		6	1	0	0	0	0	0	0	0	0	0	0	0	0	0	0	0	0	—	0	.000	.000	.000	P	6	3	3	1	0	.857

JOHN MAYBERRY—John Claiborn Mayberry—Nickname: Big John—Bats: Left; Throws: Left

Ht: 6'3"; Wt: 215 lbs; Born: 2/18/1949 in Detroit, Michigan; Debut: 9/10/1968

LCS

Year Tm	Age	G	AB	H	2B	3B	HR	TB	R	RBI	GW	TBB	IBB	SO	HBP	SH	SF	SB	CS	SB%	GDP	Avg	OBP	SLG	Pos	G	PO	A	E	DP	FPct
1976 KC	27	5	18	4	0	0	1	7	4	3	0	1	0	0	0	0	0	0	0	—	0	.222	.263	.389	1B	5	48	1	0	4	1.000
1977 KC	28	4	12	2	1	0	1	6	1	3	0	1	0	2	0	0	0	0	0	—	0	.167	.231	.500	1B	4	29	1	2	0	.938
LCS Totals		9	30	6	1	0	2	13	5	6	0	2	0	2	0	0	0	0	0	—	0	.200	.250	.433	1B	9	77	2	2	4	.975

ERSKINE MAYER—Erskine John Mayer—Throws: Right; Bats: Right

Ht: 6'0"; Wt: 168 lbs; Born: 1/16/1889 in Atlanta, Georgia; Debut: 9/4/1912; Died: 3/10/1957

World Series — Pitching

Year Tm	Age	G	GS	CG	GF	IP	BFP	H	R	ER	HR	SH	SF	HB	TBB	IBB	SO	WP	Bk	W	L	Pct	ShO	Sv-Op	Hld	OAvg	OOBP	ERA
1915 Phi	26	2	2	1	0	11.1	49	16	4	3	1	0	0	0	2	0	7	0	0	0	1	.000	0	0-0	0	.340	.367	2.38
1919 ChA	30	1	0	0	1	1.0	5	0	1	0	0	0	0	0	1	0	0	0	0	0	0	—	0	0-0	0	.000	.250	0.00
WS Totals		3	2	1	1	12.1	108	16	5	3	1	1	0	0	3	0	7	0	0	0	1	.000	0	0-0	0	.320	.358	2.19

World Series		Batting																							Fielding						
Year Tm	Age	G	AB	H	2B	3B	HR	TB	R	RBI	GW	TBB	IBB	SO	HBP	SH	SF	SB	CS	SB%	GDP	Avg	OBP	SLG	Pos	G	PO	A	E	DP	FPct
1915 Phi	26	2	4	0	0	0	0	0	0	0	0	0	0	2	0	0	0	0	0	—	0	.000	.000	.000	P	2	2	3	0	0	1.000
1919 ChA	30	1	0	0	0	0	0	0	0	0	0	0	0	0	0	0	0	0	0	—	0	—	—	—	P	1	0	0	0	0	—
WS Totals		3	4	0	0	0	0	0	0	0	0	0	0	2	0	0	0	0	0	—	0	.000	.000	.000	P	3	2	3	0	0	1.000

EDDIE MAYO—Edward Joseph Mayo—Bats: Left; Throws: Right

Ht: 5'11"; Wt: 178 lbs; Born: 4/15/1910 in Holyoke, Massachusetts; Debut: 5/22/1936

World Series		Batting																							Fielding						
Year Tm	Age	G	AB	H	2B	3B	HR	TB	R	RBI	GW	TBB	IBB	SO	HBP	SH	SF	SB	CS	SB%	GDP	Avg	OBP	SLG	Pos	G	PO	A	E	DP	FPct
1936 NYG	26	1	1	0	0	0	0	0	0	0	0	0	0	0	0	0	0	0	0	—	0	.000	.000	.000	3B	1	0	1	0	0	1.000
1945 Det	35	7	28	7	1	0	0	8	4	2	0	3	0	2	0	0	0	0	0	—	0	.250	.323	.286	2B	7	18	13	2	4	.939
WS Totals		8	29	7	1	0	0	8	4	2	0	3	0	2	0	0	0	0	0	—	0	.241	.313	.276	2B	7	18	13	2	4	.939

JACKIE MAYO—John Lewis Mayo—Bats: Left; Throws: Right

Ht: 6'1"; Wt: 190 lbs; Born: 7/26/1925 in Litchfield, Illinois; Debut: 9/19/1948

World Series		Batting																							Fielding						
Year Tm	Age	G	AB	H	2B	3B	HR	TB	R	RBI	GW	TBB	IBB	SO	HBP	SH	SF	SB	CS	SB%	GDP	Avg	OBP	SLG	Pos	G	PO	A	E	DP	FPct
1950 Phi	25	3	0	0	0	0	0	0	0	0	0	1	0	0	0	0	0	0	0	—	0	—	1.000	—	OF	1	1	0	0	0	1.000

CARL MAYS—Carl William Mays—Nickname: Sub—Throws: Right; Bats: Left

Ht: 5'11"; Wt: 195 lbs; Born: 11/12/1891 in Liberty, Kentucky; Debut: 4/15/1915; Died: 4/4/1971

World Series		Pitching																										
Year Tm	Age	G	GS	CG	GF	IP	BFP	H	R	ER	HR	SH	SF	HB	TBB	IBB	SO	WP	Bk	W	L	Pct	ShO	Sv-Op	Hld	OAvg	OOBP	ERA
1916 Bos	24	2	1	0	1	5.1	28	8	4	3	0	3	0	1	3	1	2	0	0	0	1	.000	0	1- 1	0	.381	.480	5.06
1918 Bos	26	2	2	2	0	18.0	63	10	2	2	0	1	0	1	3	0	5	0	0	2	0	1.000	0	0- 0	0	.172	.226	1.00
1921 NYA	29	3	3	3	0	26.0	97	20	6	5	0	2	0	1	0	0	9	0	0	1	2	.333	1	0- 0	0	.213	.221	1.73
1922 NYA	30	1	1	0	0	8.0	33	9	4	4	0	1	0	0	2	0	1	0	0	0	1	.000	0	0- 0	0	.300	.344	4.50
WS Totals		8	7	5	1	57.1	442	47	16	14	0	7	0	3	8	1	17	0	0	3	4	.429	1	1-1	0	.232	.271	2.20

World Series		Batting																							Fielding						
Year Tm	Age	G	AB	H	2B	3B	HR	TB	R	RBI	GW	TBB	IBB	SO	HBP	SH	SF	SB	CS	SB%	GDP	Avg	OBP	SLG	Pos	G	PO	A	E	DP	FPct
1916 Bos	24	2	1	0	0	0	0	0	0	0	0	0	0	1	0	0	0	0	0	—	0	.000	.000	.000	P	2	0	4	0	0	1.000
1918 Bos	26	2	5	1	0	0	0	1	1	0	0	1	0	0	0	0	0	0	0	—	0	.200	.333	.200	P	2	0	8	0	0	1.000
1921 NYA	29	3	9	1	0	0	0	1	0	0	0	0	0	1	0	0	0	0	0	—	0	.111	.111	.111	P	3	0	9	0	0	1.000
1922 NYA	30	1	2	0	0	0	0	0	0	0	0	0	0	0	0	0	0	0	0	—	0	.000	.000	.000	P	1	0	4	0	0	1.000
WS Totals		8	17	2	0	0	0	2	1	0	0	1	0	2	0	0	0	0	0	—	0	.118	.167	.118	P	8	0	25	0	0	1.000

WILLIE MAYS (HOF 1979-W)—Willie Howard Mays—Nickname: Say Hey—Bats: Right; Throws: Right

Ht: 5'10"; Wt: 170 lbs; Born: 5/6/1931 in Westfield, Alabama; Debut: 5/25/1951

LCS		Batting																							Fielding						
Year Tm	Age	G	AB	H	2B	3B	HR	TB	R	RBI	GW	TBB	IBB	SO	HBP	SH	SF	SB	CS	SB%	GDP	Avg	OBP	SLG	Pos	G	PO	A	E	DP	FPct
1971 SF	40	4	15	4	2	0	1	9	2	3	0	3	0	3	0	0	0	1	0	1.00	0	.267	.389	.600	OF	4	5	0	0	0	1.000
1973 NYN	42	1	3	1	0	0	0	1	1	1	0	0	0	0	0	0	0	0	0	—	0	.333	.333	.333	OF	1	1	0	0	0	1.000
LCS Totals		5	18	5	2	0	1	10	3	4	0	3	0	3	0	0	0	1	0	1.00	0	.278	.381	.556	OF	5	6	0	0	0	1.000
World Series		**Batting**																							**Fielding**						
Year Tm	Age	G	AB	H	2B	3B	HR	TB	R	RBI	GW	TBB	IBB	SO	HBP	SH	SF	SB	CS	SB%	GDP	Avg	OBP	SLG	Pos	G	PO	A	E	DP	FPct
1951 NYG-*RY*	20	6	22	4	0	0	0	4	1	1	1	2	0	2	0	0	0	0	0	—	3	.182	.250	.182	OF	6	16	1	0	0	1.000
1954 NYG-*M*	23	4	14	4	1	0	0	5	4	3	1	4	0	1	0	0	0	1	0	1.00	0	.286	.444	.357	OF	4	10	0	0	0	1.000
1962 SF	31	7	28	7	2	0	0	9	3	1	0	1	0	5	0	0	0	1	0	1.00	1	.250	.276	.321	OF	7	19	0	0	0	1.000
1973 NYN	42	3	7	2	0	0	0	2	1	1	1	0	0	1	0	0	0	0	0	—	0	.286	.286	.286	OF	2	1	0	1	0	.500
WS Totals		20	71	17	3	0	0	20	9	6	3	7	0	9	0	0	0	2	0	1.00	4	.239	.308	.282	OF	19	46	1	1	0	.979
Postseason Totals		25	89	22	5	0	1	30	12	10	3	10	0	12	0	0	0	3	0	1.00	4	.247	.323	.337	OF	24	52	1	1	0	.981

BILL MAZEROSKI—William Stanley Mazeroski—Nickname: Maz—Bats: Right; Throws: Right

Ht: 5'11"; Wt: 183 lbs; Born: 9/5/1936 in Wheeling, West Virginia; Debut: 7/7/1956

LCS		Batting																							Fielding						
Year Tm	Age	G	AB	H	2B	3B	HR	TB	R	RBI	GW	TBB	IBB	SO	HBP	SH	SF	SB	CS	SB%	GDP	Avg	OBP	SLG	Pos	G	PO	A	E	DP	FPct
1970 Pit	34	1	2	0	0	0	0	0	0	0	0	2	0	0	0	0	0	0	0	—	0	.000	.500	.000	2B	1	1	4	0	0	1.000
1971 Pit	35	1	1	1	0	0	0	1	1	0	0	0	0	0	0	0	0	0	0	—	0	1.000	1.000	1.000	—						
1972 Pit	36	2	2	1	0	0	0	1	0	0	0	0	0	1	0	0	0	0	0	—	0	.500	.500	.500	—						
LCS Totals		4	5	2	0	0	0	2	1	0	0	2	0	1	0	0	0	0	0	—	0	.400	.571	.400	2B	1	1	4	0	0	1.000
World Series		**Batting**																							**Fielding**						
Year Tm	Age	G	AB	H	2B	3B	HR	TB	R	RBI	GW	TBB	IBB	SO	HBP	SH	SF	SB	CS	SB%	GDP	Avg	OBP	SLG	Pos	G	PO	A	E	DP	FPct
1960 Pit	24	7	25	8	2	0	2	16	4	5	1	0	0	3	0	1	0	0	0	—	2	.320	.320	.640	2B	7	17	23	0	6	1.000
1971 Pit	35	1	1	0	0	0	0	0	0	0	0	0	0	0	0	0	0	0	0	—	0	.000	.000	.000	—						
WS Totals		8	26	8	2	0	2	16	4	5	1	0	0	3	0	1	0	0	0	—	2	.308	.308	.615	2B	7	17	23	0	6	1.000
Postseason Totals		12	31	10	2	0	2	18	5	5	1	2	0	4	0	1	0	0	0	—	2	.323	.364	.581	2B	8	18	27	0	6	1.000

LEE MAZZILLI—Lee Louis Mazzilli—Bats: Both; Throws: Right

Ht: 6'1"; Wt: 180 lbs; Born: 3/25/1955 in New York, New York; Debut: 9/7/1976

LCS		Batting																							Fielding						
Year Tm	Age	G	AB	H	2B	3B	HR	TB	R	RBI	GW	TBB	IBB	SO	HBP	SH	SF	SB	CS	SB%	GDP	Avg	OBP	SLG	Pos	G	PO	A	E	DP	FPct
1986 NYN	31	5	5	1	0	0	0	1	0	0	0	0	0	3	0	0	0	0	0	—	0	.200	.200	.200	—						
1988 NYN	33	3	2	1	0	0	0	1	0	0	0	0	0	0	1	0	0	1	0	1.00	0	.500	.667	.500	—						
1989 Tor	34	3	8	0	0	0	0	0	0	0	0	0	0	2	0	0	0	0	0	—	0	.000	.000	.000	—						
LCS Totals		11	15	2	0	0	0	2	0	0	0	0	0	5	1	0	0	1	0	1.00	0	.133	.188	.133	—	0	0	0	0	0	—
World Series		**Batting**																							**Fielding**						
Year Tm	Age	G	AB	H	2B	3B	HR	TB	R	RBI	GW	TBB	IBB	SO	HBP	SH	SF	SB	CS	SB%	GDP	Avg	OBP	SLG	Pos	G	PO	A	E	DP	FPct
1986 NYN	31	4	5	2	0	0	0	2	2	0	0	0	0	0	0	0	0	0	0	—	0	.400	.400	.400	OF	1	1	0	0	0	1.000
Postseason Totals		15	20	4	0	0	0	4	2	0	0	0	0	5	1	0	0	1	0	1.00	0	.200	.238	.200	OF	1	1	0	0	0	1.000

JIM McANANY—James McAnany—Bats: Right; Throws: Right

Ht: 5'10"; Wt: 196 lbs; Born: 9/4/1936 in Los Angeles, California; Debut: 9/19/1958

World Series		Batting																							Fielding						
Year Tm	Age	G	AB	H	2B	3B	HR	TB	R	RBI	GW	TBB	IBB	SO	HBP	SH	SF	SB	CS	SB%	GDP	Avg	OBP	SLG	Pos	G	PO	A	E	DP	FPct
1959 ChA	23	3	5	0	0	0	0	0	0	0	0	1	0	0	0	0	0	0	0	—	0	.000	.167	.000	OF	3	5	0	0	0	1.000

DICK McAULIFFE—Richard John McAuliffe—Bats: Left; Throws: Right

Ht: 5'11"; Wt: 176 lbs; Born: 11/29/1939 in Hartford, Connecticut; Debut: 9/17/1960

LCS		Batting																							Fielding						
Year Tm	Age	G	AB	H	2B	3B	HR	TB	R	RBI	GW	TBB	IBB	SO	HBP	SH	SF	SB	CS	SB%	GDP	Avg	OBP	SLG	Pos	G	PO	A	E	DP	FPct
1972 Det	32	5	20	4	0	0	1	7	3	1	0	1	0	4	0	0	0	0	1	.00	0	.200	.238	.350	SS	4	10	7	3	2	.850
																									2B	1	2	0	1	1	.667
World Series		**Batting**																							**Fielding**						
Year Tm	Age	G	AB	H	2B	3B	HR	TB	R	RBI	GW	TBB	IBB	SO	HBP	SH	SF	SB	CS	SB%	GDP	Avg	OBP	SLG	Pos	G	PO	A	E	DP	FPct
1968 Det	28	7	27	6	0	0	1	9	5	3	0	4	1	6	0	0	0	0	0	—	0	.222	.323	.333	2B	7	12	16	0	2	1.000
Postseason Totals		12	47	10	0	0	2	16	8	4	0	5	1	10	0	0	0	0	1	.00	0	.213	.288	.340	2B	8	14	16	1	3	.968

BAKE McBRIDE—Arnold Ray McBride—Bats: Left; Throws: Right

Ht: 6'2"; Wt: 190 lbs; Born: 2/3/1949 in Fulton, Missouri; Debut: 7/26/1973

Division Series		Batting																							Fielding						
Year Tm	Age	G	AB	H	2B	3B	HR	TB	R	RBI	GW	TBB	IBB	SO	HBP	SH	SF	SB	CS	SB%	GDP	Avg	OBP	SLG	Pos	G	PO	A	E	DP	FPct
1981 Phi	32	4	15	3	1	0	0	4	1	0	0	0	0	5	0	0	0	0	0	—	0	.200	.200	.267	OF	4	7	0	0	0	1.000
LCS		**Batting**																							**Fielding**						
Year Tm	Age	G	AB	H	2B	3B	HR	TB	R	RBI	GW	TBB	IBB	SO	HBP	SH	SF	SB	CS	SB%	GDP	Avg	OBP	SLG	Pos	G	PO	A	E	DP	FPct
1977 Phi	28	4	18	4	0	0	1	7	2	2	0	1	0	2	0	0	0	0	0	—	0	.222	.263	.389	OF	4	6	2	0	1	1.000
1978 Phi	29	3	9	2	0	0	1	5	2	1	0	0	0	2	0	0	0	0	0	—	0	.222	.222	.556	OF	2	1	0	0	0	1.000
1980 Phi	31	5	21	5	0	0	0	5	0	0	0	1	0	5	0	0	0	2	0	1.00	0	.238	.273	.238	OF	5	11	3	1	2	.933
LCS Totals		12	48	11	0	0	2	17	4	3	0	2	0	9	0	0	0	2	0	1.00	0	.229	.260	.354	OF	11	18	5	1	3	.958

World Series	Batting																								Fielding						
Year Tm	Age	G	AB	H	2B	3B	HR	TB	R	RBI	GW	TBB	IBB	SO	HBP	SH	SF	SB	CS	SB%	GDP	Avg	OBP	SLG	Pos	G	PO	A	E	DP	FPct
1980 Phi	31	6	23	7	1	0	1	11	3	5	1	2	0	1	0	0	0	0	1	.00	0	.304	.360	.478	OF	6	13	1	0	0	1.000
Postseason Totals		22	86	21	2	0	3	32	8	8	1	4	0	15	0	0	0	2	1	.67	0	.244	.278	.372	OF	21	38	6	1	3	.978

TOM McBRIDE—Thomas Raymond McBride—Bats: Right; Throws: Right

Ht: 6'0"; Wt: 188 lbs; Born: 11/2/1914 in Bonham, Texas; Debut: 4/23/1943

World Series	Batting																								Fielding						
Year Tm	Age	G	AB	H	2B	3B	HR	TB	R	RBI	GW	TBB	IBB	SO	HBP	SH	SF	SB	CS	SB%	GDP	Avg	OBP	SLG	Pos	G	PO	A	E	DP	FPct
1946 Bos	31	5	12	2	0	0	0	2	0	1	0	0	0	1	0	0	0	0	0	—	0	.167	.167	.167	OF	2	4	0	1	0	.800

BILL McCABE—William Francis McCabe—Bats: Both; Throws: Right

Ht: 5'9"; Wt: 180 lbs; Born: 10/28/1892 in Chicago, Illinois; Debut: 4/16/1918; Died: 9/2/1966

World Series	Batting																								Fielding						
Year Tm	Age	G	AB	H	2B	3B	HR	TB	R	RBI	GW	TBB	IBB	SO	HBP	SH	SF	SB	CS	SB%	GDP	Avg	OBP	SLG	Pos	G	PO	A	E	DP	FPct
1918 ChN	25	3	1	0	0	0	0	0	1	0	0	0	0	0	0	0	0	0	0	—	0	.000	.000	.000	—						
1920 Bro	27	1	0	0	0	0	0	0	0	0	0	0	0	0	0	0	0	0	0	—	0	—	—	—	—						
WS Totals		4	1	0	0	0	0	0	1	0	0	0	0	0	0	0	0	0	0	—	0	.000	.000	.000	—	0	0	0	0	0	—

JOHNNY McCARTHY—John Joseph McCarthy—Bats: Left; Throws: Left

Ht: 6'1"; Wt: 185 lbs; Born: 1/7/1910 in Chicago, Illinois; Debut: 9/2/1934; Died: 9/13/1973

World Series	Batting																								Fielding						
Year Tm	Age	G	AB	H	2B	3B	HR	TB	R	RBI	GW	TBB	IBB	SO	HBP	SH	SF	SB	CS	SB%	GDP	Avg	OBP	SLG	Pos	G	PO	A	E	DP	FPct
1937 NYG	27	5	19	4	1	0	0	5	1	1	0	1	0	2	0	0	0	0	0	—	0	.211	.250	.263	1B	5	38	1	2	4	.951

LEW McCARTY—George Lewis McCarty—Bats: Right; Throws: Right

Ht: 5'11"; Wt: 192 lbs; Born: 11/17/1888 in Milton, Pennsylvania; Debut: 8/30/1913; Died: 6/9/1930

World Series	Batting																								Fielding						
Year Tm	Age	G	AB	H	2B	3B	HR	TB	R	RBI	GW	TBB	IBB	SO	HBP	SH	SF	SB	CS	SB%	GDP	Avg	OBP	SLG	Pos	G	PO	A	E	DP	FPct
1917 NYG	28	3	5	2	0	1	0	4	1	1	0	0	0	0	0	0	0	0	0	—	0	.400	.400	.800	C	2	7	1	1	0	.889

TIM McCARVER—James Timothy McCarver—Bats: Left; Throws: Right

Ht: 6'0"; Wt: 183 lbs; Born: 10/16/1941 in Memphis, Tennessee; Debut: 9/10/1959

LCS	Batting																								Fielding						
Year Tm	Age	G	AB	H	2B	3B	HR	TB	R	RBI	GW	TBB	IBB	SO	HBP	SH	SF	SB	CS	SB%	GDP	Avg	OBP	SLG	Pos	G	PO	A	E	DP	FPct
1976 Phi	34	2	4	0	0	0	0	0	0	0	0	0	0	1	0	0	0	0	0	—	0	.000	.000	.000	C	1	6	0	0	0	1.000
1977 Phi	35	3	6	1	0	0	0	1	1	0	0	1	0	3	0	0	0	0	0	—	0	.167	.286	.167	C	2	7	0	0	0	1.000
1978 Phi	36	2	4	0	0	0	0	0	2	1	0	2	0	0	0	0	0	0	0	—	0	.000	.333	.000	C	1	8	0	0	0	1.000
LCS Totals		7	14	1	0	0	0	1	3	1	0	3	0	4	0	0	0	0	0	—	0	.071	.235	.071	C	4	21	0	0	0	1.000

World Series	Batting																								Fielding						
Year Tm	Age	G	AB	H	2B	3B	HR	TB	R	RBI	GW	TBB	IBB	SO	HBP	SH	SF	SB	CS	SB%	GDP	Avg	OBP	SLG	Pos	G	PO	A	E	DP	FPct
1964 StL	22	7	23	11	1	1	1	17	4	5	1	5	1	1	0	0	1	1	0	1.00	0	.478	.552	.739	C	7	57	1	0	0	1.000
1967 StL	25	7	24	3	1	0	0	4	3	2	0	2	0	2	0	0	1	0	0	—	0	.125	.185	.167	C	7	55	3	0	1	1.000
1968 StL	26	7	27	9	0	2	1	16	3	4	1	3	0	2	0	0	0	0	1	.00	0	.333	.400	.593	C	7	61	1	0	0	1.000
WS Totals		21	74	23	2	3	2	37	10	11	2	10	1	5	0	0	2	1	1	.50	0	.311	.384	.500	C	21	173	5	0	1	1.000
Postseason Totals		28	88	24	2	3	2	38	13	12	2	13	1	9	0	0	2	1	1	.50	0	.273	.359	.432	C	25	194	5	0	1	1.000

KIRK McCASKILL—Kirk Edward McCaskill—Throws: Right; Bats: Right

Ht: 6'1"; Wt: 190 lbs; Born: 4/9/1961 in Kapuskasing, Ontario; Debut: 5/1/1985

LCS	Pitching																											
Year Tm	Age	G	GS	CG	GF	IP	BFP	H	R	ER	HR	SH	SF	HB	TBB	IBB	SO	WP	Bk	W	L	Pct	ShO	Sv-Op	Hld	OAvg	OOBP	ERA
1986 Cal	25	2	2	0	0	9.1	50	16	13	8	0	0	0	0	5	0	7	0	0	0	2	.000	0	0- 0	0	.356	.420	7.71
1993 ChA	32	3	0	0	1	3.2	15	3	0	0	0	0	0	0	1	0	3	0	0	0	0	—	0	0- 0	1	.214	.267	0.00
LCS Totals		5	2	0	1	13.0	130	19	13	8	0	0	0	0	6	0	10	0	0	0	2	.000	0	0-0	1	.322	.385	5.54

LCS	Batting																								Fielding						
Year Tm	Age	G	AB	H	2B	3B	HR	TB	R	RBI	GW	TBB	IBB	SO	HBP	SH	SF	SB	CS	SB%	GDP	Avg	OBP	SLG	Pos	G	PO	A	E	DP	FPct
1986 Cal	25	2	0	0	0	0	0	0	0	0	0	0	0	0	0	0	0	0	0	—	0	—	—	—	P	2	1	0	0	1	1.000
1993 ChA	32	3	0	0	0	0	0	0	0	0	0	0	0	0	0	0	0	0	0	—	0	—	—	—	P	3	0	2	0	0	1.000
LCS Totals		5	0	0	0	0	0	0	0	0	0	0	0	0	0	0	0	0	0	—	0	—	—	—	P	5	1	2	0	1	1.000

STEVE McCATTY—Steven Earl McCatty—Throws: Right; Bats: Right

Ht: 6'3"; Wt: 195 lbs; Born: 3/20/1954 in Detroit, Michigan; Debut: 9/17/1977

Division Series	Pitching																											
Year Tm	Age	G	GS	CG	GF	IP	BFP	H	R	ER	HR	SH	SF	HB	TBB	IBB	SO	WP	Bk	W	L	Pct	ShO	Sv-Op	Hld	OAvg	OOBP	ERA
1981 Oak	27	1	1	1	0	9.0	37	6	1	1	0	1	0	0	4	0	3	0	0	1	0	1.000	0	0- 0	0	.188	.278	1.00

LCS	Pitching																											
Year Tm	Age	G	GS	CG	GF	IP	BFP	H	R	ER	HR	SH	SF	HB	TBB	IBB	SO	WP	Bk	W	L	Pct	ShO	Sv-Op	Hld	OAvg	OOBP	ERA
1981 Oak	27	1	1	0	0	3.1	19	6	5	5	0	0	0	1	2	0	2	0	0	0	1	.000	0	0- 0	0	.375	.474	13.50
Postseason Totals		2	2	1	0	12.1	112	12	6	6	0	1	0	1	6	0	5	0	0	1	1	.500	0	0-0	0	.250	.345	4.38

Division Series	Batting																								Fielding						
Year Tm	Age	G	AB	H	2B	3B	HR	TB	R	RBI	GW	TBB	IBB	SO	HBP	SH	SF	SB	CS	SB%	GDP	Avg	OBP	SLG	Pos	G	PO	A	E	DP	FPct
1981 Oak	27	1	0	0	0	0	0	0	0	0	0	0	0	0	0	0	0	0	0	—	0	—	—	—	P	1	0	4	0	0	1.000

LCS	Batting																								Fielding						
Year Tm	Age	G	AB	H	2B	3B	HR	TB	R	RBI	GW	TBB	IBB	SO	HBP	SH	SF	SB	CS	SB%	GDP	Avg	OBP	SLG	Pos	G	PO	A	E	DP	FPct
1981 Oak	27	1	0	0	0	0	0	0	0	0	0	0	0	0	0	0	0	0	0	—	0	—	—	—	P	1	1	1	0	0	1.000
Postseason Totals		2	0	0	0	0	0	0	0	0	0	0	0	0	0	0	0	0	0	—	0	—	—	—	P	2	1	5	0	0	1.000

LLOYD McCLENDON—Lloyd Glenn McClendon—Bats: Right; Throws: Right

Ht: 5'10"; Wt: 190 lbs; Born: 1/11/1959 in Gary, Indiana; Debut: 4/6/1987

LCS	Batting																								Fielding						
Year Tm	Age	G	AB	H	2B	3B	HR	TB	R	RBI	GW	TBB	IBB	SO	HBP	SH	SF	SB	CS	SB%	GDP	Avg	OBP	SLG	Pos	G	PO	A	E	DP	FPct
1989 ChN	30	3	3	2	0	0	0	2	0	0	0	1	0	0	0	0	0	0	0	—	0	.667	.750	.667	C	2	3	0	0	0	1.000
																									OF	1	1	0	0	0	1.000
1991 Pit	32	3	2	0	0	0	0	0	0	0	0	1	0	0	0	0	0	0	0	—	0	.000	.333	.000	1B	1	0	0	0	0	—
1992 Pit	33	5	11	8	2	0	1	13	4	4	0	4	1	1	0	0	1	0	0	—	0	.727	.750	1.182	OF	5	10	0	0	0	1.000
LCS Totals		11	16	10	2	0	1	15	4	4	0	6	1	1	0	0	1	0	0	—	0	.625	.696	.938	OF	6	11	0	0	0	1.000

BOB McCLURE—Robert Craig McClure—Throws: Left; Bats: Right

Ht: 5'11"; Wt: 170 lbs; Born: 4/29/1952 in Oakland, California; Debut: 8/13/1975

Division Series	Pitching																											
Year Tm	Age	G	GS	CG	GF	IP	BFP	H	R	ER	HR	SH	SF	HB	TBB	IBB	SO	WP	Bk	W	L	Pct	ShO	Sv-Op	Hld	OAvg	OOBP	ERA
1981 Mil	29	3	0	0	0	3.1	13	4	0	0	0	0	0	0	0	0	2	0	0	0	0	—	0	0- 0	1	.308	.308	0.00

LCS	Pitching																											
Year Tm	Age	G	GS	CG	GF	IP	BFP	H	R	ER	HR	SH	SF	HB	TBB	IBB	SO	WP	Bk	W	L	Pct	ShO	Sv-Op	Hld	OAvg	OOBP	ERA
1982 Mil	30	1	0	0	0	1.2	6	2	0	0	0	0	0	0	0	0	0	0	0	1	0	1.000	0	0- 0	0	.333	.333	0.00

World Series	Pitching																											
Year Tm	Age	G	GS	CG	GF	IP	BFP	H	R	ER	HR	SH	SF	HB	TBB	IBB	SO	WP	Bk	W	L	Pct	ShO	Sv-Op	Hld	OAvg	OOBP	ERA
1982 Mil	30	5	0	0	3	4.1	20	5	2	2	0	0	0	0	3	0	5	0	0	0	2	.000	0	2- 3	0	.294	.400	4.15
Postseason Totals		9	0	0	3	9.1	78	11	2	2	0	0	0	0	3	0	7	0	0	1	2	.333	0	2-3	1	.306	.359	1.93

Division Series	Batting																								Fielding						
Year Tm	Age	G	AB	H	2B	3B	HR	TB	R	RBI	GW	TBB	IBB	SO	HBP	SH	SF	SB	CS	SB%	GDP	Avg	OBP	SLG	Pos	G	PO	A	E	DP	FPct
1981 Mil	29	3	0	0	0	0	0	0	0	0	0	0	0	0	0	0	0	0	0	—	0	—	—	—	P	3	1	1	0	1	1.000

LCS	Batting																								Fielding						
Year Tm	Age	G	AB	H	2B	3B	HR	TB	R	RBI	GW	TBB	IBB	SO	HBP	SH	SF	SB	CS	SB%	GDP	Avg	OBP	SLG	Pos	G	PO	A	E	DP	FPct
1982 Mil	30	1	0	0	0	0	0	0	0	0	0	0	0	0	0	0	0	0	0	—	0	—	—	—	P	1	0	0	0	0	—

World Series — Batting / Fielding

Year Tm	Age	G	AB	H	2B	3B	HR	TB	R	RBI	GW	TBB	IBB	SO	HBP	SH	SF	SB	CS	SB%	GDP	Avg	OBP	SLG	Pos	G	PO	A	E	DP	FPct
1982 Mil	30	5	0	0	0	0	0	0	0	0	0	0	0	0	0	0	0	0	0	—	0	—	—	—	P	5	0	0	0	0	—
Postseason Totals		9	0	0	0	0	0	0	0	0	0	0	0	0	0	0	0	0	0	—	0	—	—	—	P	9	1	1	0	1	1.000

ALEX McCOLL—Alexander Boyd McColl—Nickname: Red—Throws: Right; Bats: Both

Ht: 6'1"; Wt: 178 lbs; Born: 3/29/1894 in Eagleville, Ohio; Debut: 8/27/1933; Died: 2/6/1991

World Series — Pitching

Year Tm	Age	G	GS	CG	GF	IP	BFP	H	R	ER	HR	SH	SF	HB	TBB	IBB	SO	WP	Bk	W	L	Pct	ShO	Sv-Op	Hld	OAvg	OOBP	ERA
1933 Was	39	1	0	0	1	2.0	6	0	0	0	0	0	0	0	0	0	0	0	0	0	0	—	0	0- 0	0	.000	.000	0.00

World Series — Batting / Fielding

Year Tm	Age	G	AB	H	2B	3B	HR	TB	R	RBI	GW	TBB	IBB	SO	HBP	SH	SF	SB	CS	SB%	GDP	Avg	OBP	SLG	Pos	G	PO	A	E	DP	FPct
1933 Was	39	1	0	0	0	0	0	0	0	0	0	0	0	0	0	0	0	0	0	—	0	—	—	—	P	1	0	1	0	0	1.000

FRANK McCORMICK—Frank Andrew McCormick—Nickname: Buck—Bats: Right; Throws: Right

Ht: 6'4"; Wt: 205 lbs; Born: 6/9/1911 in New York, New York; Debut: 9/11/1934; Died: 11/21/1982

World Series — Batting / Fielding

Year Tm	Age	G	AB	H	2B	3B	HR	TB	R	RBI	GW	TBB	IBB	SO	HBP	SH	SF	SB	CS	SB%	GDP	Avg	OBP	SLG	Pos	G	PO	A	E	DP	FPct
1939 Cin	28	4	15	6	1	0	0	7	1	1	0	0	0	1	0	1	0	0	0	—	0	.400	.400	.467	1B	4	32	2	0	1	1.000
1940 Cin-*M*	29	7	28	6	1	0	0	7	2	0	0	1	0	1	0	0	0	0	0	—	0	.214	.241	.250	1B	7	59	4	1	8	.984
1948 Bos	37	3	5	1	0	0	0	1	0	0	0	0	0	2	0	0	0	0	0	—	1	.200	.200	.200	1B	1	5	1	0	1	1.000
WS Totals		14	48	13	2	0	0	15	3	1	0	1	0	4	0	1	0	0	0	—	1	.271	.286	.313	1B	12	96	7	1	10	.990

MIKE McCORMICK—Myron Winthrop McCormick—Bats: Right; Throws: Right

Ht: 6'0"; Wt: 195 lbs; Born: 5/6/1917 in Angel's Camp, California; Debut: 4/16/1940; Died: 4/14/1976

World Series — Batting / Fielding

Year Tm	Age	G	AB	H	2B	3B	HR	TB	R	RBI	GW	TBB	IBB	SO	HBP	SH	SF	SB	CS	SB%	GDP	Avg	OBP	SLG	Pos	G	PO	A	E	DP	FPct
1940 Cin	23	7	29	9	3	0	0	12	1	2	0	1	0	6	0	1	0	0	0	—	1	.310	.333	.414	OF	7	23	1	1	0	.960
1948 Bos	31	6	23	6	0	0	0	6	1	2	0	0	0	4	0	1	0	0	0	—	0	.261	.261	.261	OF	6	17	0	0	0	1.000
1949 Bro	32	1	0	0	0	0	0	0	0	0	0	0	0	0	0	0	0	0	0	—	0	—	—	—	OF	1	1	0	0	0	1.000
WS Totals		14	52	15	3	0	0	18	2	4	0	1	0	10	0	2	0	0	0	—	1	.288	.302	.346	OF	14	41	1	1	0	.977

MOOSE McCORMICK—Harry Elwood McCormick—Bats: Left; Throws: Left

Ht: 5'11"; Wt: 180 lbs; Born: 2/28/1881 in Philadelphia, Pennsylvania; Debut: 4/14/1904; Died: 7/9/1962

World Series — Batting / Fielding

Year Tm	Age	G	AB	H	2B	3B	HR	TB	R	RBI	GW	TBB	IBB	SO	HBP	SH	SF	SB	CS	SB%	GDP	Avg	OBP	SLG	Pos	G	PO	A	E	DP	FPct
1912 NYG	31	5	4	1	0	0	0	1	0	1	0	0	0	0	0	0	1	0	0	—	0	.250	.200	.250	—						
1913 NYG	32	2	2	1	0	0	0	1	1	0	0	0	0	0	0	0	0	0	0	—	0	.500	.500	.500	—						
WS Totals		7	6	2	0	0	0	2	1	1	0	0	0	0	0	0	1	0	0	—	0	.333	.286	.333	—	0	0	0	0	0	—

BARNEY McCOSKY—William Barney McCosky—Bats: Left; Throws: Right

Ht: 6'1"; Wt: 184 lbs; Born: 4/11/1917 in Coal Run, Pennsylvania; Debut: 4/18/1939; Died: 9/6/1996

World Series — Batting / Fielding

Year Tm	Age	G	AB	H	2B	3B	HR	TB	R	RBI	GW	TBB	IBB	SO	HBP	SH	SF	SB	CS	SB%	GDP	Avg	OBP	SLG	Pos	G	PO	A	E	DP	FPct
1940 Det	23	7	23	7	1	0	0	8	5	1	0	7	0	0	0	0	0	0	0	—	0	.304	.467	.348	OF	7	19	0	0	0	1.000

WILLIE McCOVEY (HOF 1986-W)—Willie Lee McCovey—Nickname: Stretch—Bats: Left; Throws: Left

Ht: 6'4"; Wt: 198 lbs; Born: 1/10/1938 in Mobile, Alabama; Debut: 7/30/1959

LCS — Batting / Fielding

Year Tm	Age	G	AB	H	2B	3B	HR	TB	R	RBI	GW	TBB	IBB	SO	HBP	SH	SF	SB	CS	SB%	GDP	Avg	OBP	SLG	Pos	G	PO	A	E	DP	FPct
1971 SF	33	4	14	6	0	0	2	12	2	6	0	4	2	2	0	0	0	0	0	—	1	.429	.556	.857	1B	4	34	3	1	0	.974

World Series — Batting / Fielding

Year Tm	Age	G	AB	H	2B	3B	HR	TB	R	RBI	GW	TBB	IBB	SO	HBP	SH	SF	SB	CS	SB%	GDP	Avg	OBP	SLG	Pos	G	PO	A	E	DP	FPct
1962 SF	24	4	15	3	0	1	1	8	2	1	0	1	0	3	0	0	0	0	0	—	0	.200	.250	.533	1B	2	18	4	1	2	.957
																									OF	2	5	0	1	0	.833
Postseason Totals		8	29	9	0	1	3	20	4	7	0	5	2	5	0	0	0	0	0	—	1	.310	.412	.690	1B	6	52	7	2	2	.967

CLYDE McCULLOUGH—Clyde Edward McCullough—Bats: Right; Throws: Right

Ht: 5'11"; Wt: 180 lbs; Born: 3/4/1917 in Nashville, Tennessee; Debut: 4/28/1940; Died: 9/18/1982

World Series — Batting / Fielding

Year Tm	Age	G	AB	H	2B	3B	HR	TB	R	RBI	GW	TBB	IBB	SO	HBP	SH	SF	SB	CS	SB%	GDP	Avg	OBP	SLG	Pos	G	PO	A	E	DP	FPct
1945 ChN	28	1	1	0	0	0	0	0	0	0	0	0	0	1	0	0	0	0	0	—	0	.000	.000	.000	—						

MICKEY McDERMOTT—Maurice Joseph McDermott—Nickname: Maury—Throws: Left; Bats: Left

Ht: 6'2"; Wt: 170 lbs; Born: 4/29/1928 in Poughkeepsie, New York; Debut: 4/24/1948

World Series — Pitching

Year Tm	Age	G	GS	CG	GF	IP	BFP	H	R	ER	HR	SH	SF	HB	TBB	IBB	SO	WP	Bk	W	L	Pct	ShO	Sv-Op	Hld	OAvg	OOBP	ERA
1956 NYA	28	1	0	0	1	3.0	15	2	2	1	0	1	0	0	3	0	3	0	0	0	0	—	0	0- 0	0	.182	.357	3.00

World Series — Batting / Fielding

Year Tm	Age	G	AB	H	2B	3B	HR	TB	R	RBI	GW	TBB	IBB	SO	HBP	SH	SF	SB	CS	SB%	GDP	Avg	OBP	SLG	Pos	G	PO	A	E	DP	FPct
1956 NYA	28	1	1	1	0	0	0	1	0	0	0	0	0	0	0	0	0	0	0	—	0	1.000	1.000	1.000	P	1	0	0	0	0	—

JIM McDONALD—Jimmie LeRoy McDonald—Nickname: Hot Rod—Throws: Right; Bats: Right

Ht: 5'10"; Wt: 185 lbs; Born: 5/17/1927 in Grant's Pass, Oregon; Debut: 7/27/1950

World Series — Pitching

Year Tm	Age	G	GS	CG	GF	IP	BFP	H	R	ER	HR	SH	SF	HB	TBB	IBB	SO	WP	Bk	W	L	Pct	ShO	Sv-Op	Hld	OAvg	OOBP	ERA
1953 NYA	26	1	1	0	0	7.2	35	12	6	5	1	0	0	1	0	0	3	0	0	1	0	1.000	0	0- 0	0	.353	.371	5.87

World Series — Batting / Fielding

Year Tm	Age	G	AB	H	2B	3B	HR	TB	R	RBI	GW	TBB	IBB	SO	HBP	SH	SF	SB	CS	SB%	GDP	Avg	OBP	SLG	Pos	G	PO	A	E	DP	FPct
1953 NYA	26	1	2	1	1	0	0	2	0	1	0	1	0	1	0	1	0	0	0	—	0	.500	.667	1.000	P	1	2	0	0	0	1.000

GIL McDOUGALD—Gilbert James McDougald—Bats: Right; Throws: Right

Ht: 6'0"; Wt: 175 lbs; Born: 5/19/1928 in San Francisco, California; Debut: 4/20/1951

World Series — Batting / Fielding

Year Tm	Age	G	AB	H	2B	3B	HR	TB	R	RBI	GW	TBB	IBB	SO	HBP	SH	SF	SB	CS	SB%	GDP	Avg	OBP	SLG	Pos	G	PO	A	E	DP	FPct
1951 NYA-*RY*	23	6	23	6	1	0	1	10	2	7	2	2	0	2	0	0	0	0	1	.00	0	.261	.320	.435	3B	5	2	8	1	1	.909
																									2B	4	8	6	0	3	1.000
1952 NYA	24	7	25	5	0	0	1	8	5	3	0	5	0	2	0	0	0	1	0	1.00	1	.200	.333	.320	3B	7	4	15	4	2	.826
1953 NYA	25	6	24	4	0	1	2	12	2	4	0	1	0	3	1	0	0	0	0	—	1	.167	.231	.500	3B	6	4	14	0	0	1.000
1955 NYA	27	7	27	7	0	0	1	10	2	1	0	2	0	6	0	0	0	0	0	—	0	.259	.310	.370	3B	7	6	13	1	1	.950
1956 NYA	28	7	21	3	0	0	0	3	0	1	0	3	0	6	0	1	1	0	0	—	0	.143	.240	.143	SS	7	15	16	0	4	1.000
1957 NYA	29	7	24	6	0	0	0	6	3	2	0	3	0	3	0	1	1	1	0	1.00	0	.250	.321	.250	SS	7	13	24	1	5	.974
1958 NYA	30	7	28	9	2	0	2	17	5	4	2	2	1	4	0	0	0	0	0	—	0	.321	.367	.607	2B	7	20	22	0	3	1.000
1960 NYA	32	6	18	5	1	0	0	6	4	2	0	2	0	3	0	0	0	0	0	—	0	.278	.350	.333	3B	6	5	7	1	0	.923
WS Totals		53	190	45	4	1	7	72	23	24	4	20	1	29	1	2	2	2	1	.67	2	.237	.310	.379	3B	31	21	57	7	4	.918

JACK McDOWELL—Jack Burns McDowell—Nickname: Black Jack—Throws: Right; Bats: Right

Ht: 6'5"; Wt: 180 lbs; Born: 1/16/1966 in Van Nuys, California; Debut: 9/15/1987

Division Series — Pitching

Year Tm	Age	G	GS	CG	GF	IP	BFP	H	R	ER	HR	SH	SF	HB	TBB	IBB	SO	WP	Bk	W	L	Pct	ShO	Sv-Op	Hld	OAvg	OOBP	ERA
1995 NYA	29	2	1	0	1	7.0	32	8	7	7	1	0	0	1	4	1	6	1	0	0	2	.000	0	0- 0	0	.296	.406	9.00
1996 Cle	30	1	1	0	0	5.2	25	6	4	4	1	0	0	1	1	0	5	0	0	0	0	—	0	0- 0	0	.261	.320	6.35
DS Totals		3	2	0	1	12.2	114	14	11	11	2	0	0	2	5	1	11	1	0	0	2	.000	0	0-0	0	.280	.368	7.82

LCS — Pitching

Year Tm	Age	G	GS	CG	GF	IP	BFP	H	R	ER	HR	SH	SF	HB	TBB	IBB	SO	WP	Bk	W	L	Pct	ShO	Sv-Op	Hld	OAvg	OOBP	ERA
1993 ChA-*C*	27	2	2	0	0	9.0	50	18	10	10	1	0	1	0	5	0	5	1	0	0	2	.000	0	0- 0	0	.409	.460	10.00
Postseason Totals		5	4	0	1	21.2	214	32	21	21	3	0	1	2	10	1	16	2	0	0	4	.000	0	0-0	0	.340	.411	8.72

Division Series — Batting / Fielding

Year Tm	Age	G	AB	H	2B	3B	HR	TB	R	RBI	GW	TBB	IBB	SO	HBP	SH	SF	SB	CS	SB%	GDP	Avg	OBP	SLG	Pos	G	PO	A	E	DP	FPct
1995 NYA	29	2	0	0	0	0	0	0	0	0	0	0	0	0	0	0	0	0	0	—	0	—	—	—	P	2	0	0	0	0	—
1996 Cle	30	1	0	0	0	0	0	0	0	0	0	0	0	0	0	0	0	0	0	—	0	—	—	—	P	1	1	2	0	0	1.000
DS Totals		3	0	0	0	0	0	0	0	0	0	0	0	0	0	0	0	0	0	—	0	—	—	—	P	3	1	2	0	0	1.000

LCS — Batting / Fielding

Year Tm	Age	G	AB	H	2B	3B	HR	TB	R	RBI	GW	TBB	IBB	SO	HBP	SH	SF	SB	CS	SB%	GDP	Avg	OBP	SLG	Pos	G	PO	A	E	DP	FPct
1993 ChA	27	2	0	0	0	0	0	0	0	0	0	0	0	0	0	0	0	0	0	—	0	—	—	—	P	2	0	1	1	0	.500
Postseason Totals		5	0	0	0	0	0	0	0	0	0	0	0	0	0	0	0	0	0	—	0	—	—	—	P	5	1	3	1	0	.800

ROGER McDOWELL—Roger Alan McDowell—Throws: Right; Bats: Right

Ht: 6'1"; Wt: 175 lbs; Born: 12/21/1960 in Cincinnati, Ohio; Debut: 4/11/1985

LCS — Pitching

Year Tm	Age	G	GS	CG	GF	IP	BFP	H	R	ER	HR	SH	SF	HB	TBB	IBB	SO	WP	Bk	W	L	Pct	ShO	Sv-Op	Hld	OAvg	OOBP	ERA
1986 NYN	25	2	0	0	0	7.0	21	1	0	0	0	0	0	0	0	0	3	0	0	0	0	—	0	0- 0	0	.048	.048	0.00
1988 NYN	27	4	0	0	3	6.0	26	6	3	3	1	0	0	0	2	1	5	0	0	0	1	.000	0	0- 0	0	.250	.308	4.50
LCS Totals		6	0	0	3	13.0	94	7	3	3	1	0	0	0	2	1	8	0	0	0	1	.000	0	0-0	0	.156	.191	2.08

World Series — Pitching

Year Tm	Age	G	GS	CG	GF	IP	BFP	H	R	ER	HR	SH	SF	HB	TBB	IBB	SO	WP	Bk	W	L	Pct	ShO	Sv-Op	Hld	OAvg	OOBP	ERA
1986 NYN	25	5	0	0	2	7.1	37	10	5	4	0	1	1	0	6	2	2	0	0	1	0	1.000	0	0- 0	0	.345	.444	4.91
Postseason Totals		11	0	0	5	20.1	168	17	8	7	1	1	1	0	8	3	10	0	0	1	1	.500	0	0-0	0	.230	.301	3.10

LCS — Batting / Fielding

Year Tm	Age	G	AB	H	2B	3B	HR	TB	R	RBI	GW	TBB	IBB	SO	HBP	SH	SF	SB	CS	SB%	GDP	Avg	OBP	SLG	Pos	G	PO	A	E	DP	FPct
1986 NYN	25	2	1	0	0	0	0	0	0	0	0	0	0	0	0	0	0	0	0	—	0	.000	.000	.000	P	2	3	1	0	0	1.000
1988 NYN	27	4	0	0	0	0	0	0	0	0	0	0	0	0	0	0	0	0	0	—	0	—	—	—	P	4	0	3	1	0	.750
LCS Totals		6	1	0	0	0	0	0	0	0	0	0	0	0	0	0	0	0	0	—	0	.000	.000	.000	P	6	3	4	1	0	.875

World Series — Batting / Fielding

Year Tm	Age	G	AB	H	2B	3B	HR	TB	R	RBI	GW	TBB	IBB	SO	HBP	SH	SF	SB	CS	SB%	GDP	Avg	OBP	SLG	Pos	G	PO	A	E	DP	FPct
1986 NYN	25	5	0	0	0	0	0	0	0	0	0	0	0	0	0	1	0	0	0	—	0	—	—	—	P	5	1	4	0	0	1.000
Postseason Totals		11	1	0	0	0	0	0	0	0	0	0	0	0	0	1	0	0	0	—	0	.000	.000	.000	P	11	4	8	1	0	.923

WILL McENANEY—William Henry McEnaney—Throws: Left; Bats: Left

Ht: 6'0"; Wt: 180 lbs; Born: 2/14/1952 in Springfield, Ohio; Debut: 7/3/1974

LCS — Pitching

Year Tm	Age	G	GS	CG	GF	IP	BFP	H	R	ER	HR	SH	SF	HB	TBB	IBB	SO	WP	Bk	W	L	Pct	ShO	Sv-Op	Hld	OAvg	OOBP	ERA
1975 Cin	23	1	0	0	0	1.1	5	1	1	1	0	0	0	0	0	0	1	0	0	0	0	—	0	0- 0	1	.200	.200	6.75

World Series — Pitching

Year Tm	Age	G	GS	CG	GF	IP	BFP	H	R	ER	HR	SH	SF	HB	TBB	IBB	SO	WP	Bk	W	L	Pct	ShO	Sv-Op	Hld	OAvg	OOBP	ERA
1975 Cin	23	5	0	0	2	6.2	23	3	2	2	0	0	1	0	2	1	5	0	0	0	0	—	0	1- 1	1	.150	.217	2.70
1976 Cin	24	2	0	0	2	4.2	18	2	0	0	0	0	0	0	1	0	2	0	0	0	0	—	0	2- 2	0	.118	.167	0.00
WS Totals		7	0	0	4	11.1	82	5	2	2	0	0	1	0	3	1	7	0	0	0	0	—	0	3-3	1	.135	.195	1.59
Postseason Totals		8	0	0	4	12.2	92	6	3	3	0	0	1	0	3	1	8	0	0	0	0	—	0	3-3	2	.143	.196	2.13

LCS — Batting / Fielding

Year Tm	Age	G	AB	H	2B	3B	HR	TB	R	RBI	GW	TBB	IBB	SO	HBP	SH	SF	SB	CS	SB%	GDP	Avg	OBP	SLG	Pos	G	PO	A	E	DP	FPct
1975 Cin	23	1	0	0	0	0	0	0	0	0	0	0	0	0	0	0	0	0	0	—	0	—	—	—	P	1	0	0	0	0	—

World Series — Batting / Fielding

Year Tm	Age	G	AB	H	2B	3B	HR	TB	R	RBI	GW	TBB	IBB	SO	HBP	SH	SF	SB	CS	SB%	GDP	Avg	OBP	SLG	Pos	G	PO	A	E	DP	FPct
1975 Cin	23	5	1	1	0	0	0	1	0	0	0	0	0	0	0	0	0	0	0	—	0	1.000	1.000	1.000	P	5	0	0	0	0	—
1976 Cin	24	2	0	0	0	0	0	0	0	0	0	0	0	0	0	0	0	0	0	—	0	—	—	—	P	2	1	0	0	0	1.000
WS Totals		7	1	1	0	0	0	1	0	0	0	0	0	0	0	0	0	0	0	—	0	1.000	1.000	1.000	P	7	1	0	0	0	1.000
Postseason Totals		8	1	1	0	0	0	1	0	0	0	0	0	0	0	0	0	0	0	—	0	1.000	1.000	1.000	P	8	1	0	0	0	1.000

ED McFARLAND—Edward William McFarland—Bats: Right; Throws: Right

Ht: 5'10"; Wt: 180 lbs; Born: 8/3/1874 in Cleveland, Ohio; Debut: 7/7/1893; Died: 11/28/1959

World Series — Batting / Fielding

Year Tm	Age	G	AB	H	2B	3B	HR	TB	R	RBI	GW	TBB	IBB	SO	HBP	SH	SF	SB	CS	SB%	GDP	Avg	OBP	SLG	Pos	G	PO	A	E	DP	FPct
1906 ChA	32	1	1	0	0	0	0	0	0	0	0	0	0	0	0	0	0	0	0	—	0	.000	.000	.000	—						

DAN McGANN—Dennis Lawrence McGann—Nickname: Cap—Bats: Both; Throws: Right

Ht: 6'0"; Wt: 190 lbs; Born: 7/15/1871 in Shelbyville, Kentucky; Debut: 8/8/1896; Died: 12/13/1910

World Series — Batting / Fielding

Year Tm	Age	G	AB	H	2B	3B	HR	TB	R	RBI	GW	TBB	IBB	SO	HBP	SH	SF	SB	CS	SB%	GDP	Avg	OBP	SLG	Pos	G	PO	A	E	DP	FPct
1905 NYG	34	5	17	4	2	0	0	6	1	4	1	2	0	7	0	1	0	0	1	.00	0	.235	.316	.353	1B	5	59	1	1	2	.984

WILLIE McGEE—Willie Dean McGee—Bats: Both; Throws: Right

Ht: 6'1"; Wt: 175 lbs; Born: 11/2/1958 in San Francisco, California; Debut: 5/10/1982

Division Series — Batting / Fielding

Year Tm	Age	G	AB	H	2B	3B	HR	TB	R	RBI	GW	TBB	IBB	SO	HBP	SH	SF	SB	CS	SB%	GDP	Avg	OBP	SLG	Pos	G	PO	A	E	DP	FPct
1995 Bos	36	2	4	1	0	0	0	1	0	1	0	0	0	2	0	0	0	0	0	—	0	.250	.250	.250	OF	2	0	0	0	0	—
1996 StL	37	3	10	1	0	0	0	1	1	1	0	1	0	3	0	0	0	0	0	—	1	.100	.182	.100	OF	3	9	0	1	0	.900
DS Totals		5	14	2	0	0	0	2	1	2	0	1	0	5	0	0	0	0	0	—	1	.143	.200	.143	OF	5	9	0	1	0	.900

LCS — Batting / Fielding

Year Tm	Age	G	AB	H	2B	3B	HR	TB	R	RBI	GW	TBB	IBB	SO	HBP	SH	SF	SB	CS	SB%	GDP	Avg	OBP	SLG	Pos	G	PO	A	E	DP	FPct
1982 StL	23	3	13	4	0	2	1	11	4	5	0	0	0	5	0	0	0	0	0	—	0	.308	.308	.846	OF	3	12	0	1	0	.923
1985 StL-*M*	26	6	26	7	1	0	0	8	6	3	0	3	0	6	0	0	0	2	3	.40	0	.269	.345	.308	OF	6	18	0	0	0	1.000
1987 StL	28	7	26	8	1	1	0	11	2	2	1	0	0	5	0	0	0	0	1	.00	0	.308	.308	.423	OF	7	17	0	0	0	1.000
1990 Oak	31	3	9	2	1	0	0	3	3	0	0	1	0	2	0	1	0	2	0	1.00	0	.222	.300	.333	OF	2	2	0	0	0	1.000
1996 StL	37	6	15	5	0	0	0	5	0	0	0	0	0	3	0	0	0	0	0	—	0	.333	.333	.333	OF	5	5	0	1	0	.833
LCS Totals		25	89	26	3	3	1	38	15	10	1	4	0	21	0	1	0	4	4	.50	0	.292	.323	.427	OF	23	54	0	2	0	.964

World Series — Batting / Fielding

Year Tm	Age	G	AB	H	2B	3B	HR	TB	R	RBI	GW	TBB	IBB	SO	HBP	SH	SF	SB	CS	SB%	GDP	Avg	OBP	SLG	Pos	G	PO	A	E	DP	FPct
1982 StL	23	6	25	6	0	0	2	12	6	5	1	1	1	3	0	0	0	2	0	1.00	1	.240	.269	.480	OF	6	24	0	0	0	1.000
1985 StL-*M*	26	7	27	7	2	0	1	12	2	2	0	1	1	3	0	0	0	1	2	.33	0	.259	.286	.444	OF	7	15	0	0	0	1.000
1987 StL	28	7	27	10	2	0	0	12	2	4	0	0	0	9	0	0	0	0	0	—	0	.370	.370	.444	OF	7	21	1	1	0	.957
1990 Oak	31	4	10	2	1	0	0	3	1	0	0	0	0	2	0	0	0	1	0	1.00	1	.200	.200	.300	OF	3	5	0	0	0	1.000
WS Totals		24	89	25	5	0	3	39	11	11	1	2	2	17	0	0	0	4	2	.67	2	.281	.297	.438	OF	23	65	1	1	0	.985
Postseason Totals		54	192	53	8	3	4	79	27	23	2	7	2	43	0	1	0	8	6	.57	3	.276	.302	.411	OF	51	128	1	4	0	.970

JOE McGINNITY (HOF 1946-V)—Joseph Jerome McGinnity—Nickname: Iron Man—Throws: R; Bats: R

Ht: 5'11"; Wt: 206 lbs; Born: 3/19/1871 in Rock Island, Ill.; Deb.: 4/18/1899; Died: 11/14/1929

World Series — Pitching

Year Tm	Age	G	GS	CG	GF	IP	BFP	H	R	ER	HR	SH	SF	HB	TBB	IBB	SO	WP	Bk	W	L	Pct	ShO	Sv-Op	Hld	OAvg	OOBP	ERA
1905 NYG	34	2	2	1	0	17.0	65	10	3	0	0	3	0	0	3	0	6	0	0	1	1	.500	1	0- 0	0	.169	.210	0.00

World Series — Batting / Fielding

Year Tm	Age	G	AB	H	2B	3B	HR	TB	R	RBI	GW	TBB	IBB	SO	HBP	SH	SF	SB	CS	SB%	GDP	Avg	OBP	SLG	Pos	G	PO	A	E	DP	FPct
1905 NYG	34	2	5	0	0	0	0	0	0	0	0	0	0	2	0	0	0	0	0	—	0	.000	.000	.000	P	2	0	6	0	0	1.000

JIM McGLOTHLIN—James Milton McGlothlin—Nickname: Red—Throws: Right; Bats: Right

Ht: 6'1"; Wt: 185 lbs; Born: 10/6/1943 in Los Angeles, California; Debut: 9/20/1965; Died: 12/23/1975

LCS — Pitching

Year Tm	Age	G	GS	CG	GF	IP	BFP	H	R	ER	HR	SH	SF	HB	TBB	IBB	SO	WP	Bk	W	L	Pct	ShO	Sv-Op	Hld	OAvg	OOBP	ERA
1972 Cin	28	1	0	0	1	1.0	3	0	0	0	0	0	0	0	0	0	0	0	0	0	0	—	0	0- 0	0	.000	.000	0.00

World Series — Pitching

Year Tm	Age	G	GS	CG	GF	IP	BFP	H	R	ER	HR	SH	SF	HB	TBB	IBB	SO	WP	Bk	W	L	Pct	ShO	Sv-Op	Hld	OAvg	OOBP	ERA
1970 Cin	26	1	1	0	0	4.1	20	6	4	4	1	0	0	0	2	0	2	0	0	0	0	—	0	0- 0	0	.333	.400	8.31
1972 Cin	28	1	1	0	0	3.0	14	2	4	4	1	0	0	1	2	0	3	0	0	0	0	—	0	0- 0	0	.182	.357	12.00
WS Totals		2	2	0	0	7.1	68	8	8	8	2	0	0	1	4	0	5	0	0	0	0	—	0	0-0	0	.276	.382	9.82
Postseason Totals		3	2	0	1	8.1	74	8	8	8	2	0	0	1	4	0	5	0	0	0	0	—	0	0-0	0	.250	.351	8.64

LCS		Batting																							Fielding					
Year Tm	Age	G	AB	H	2B	3B	HR	TB	R	RBI	GW	TBB	IBB	SO	HBP	SH	SF	SB	CS	SB%	GDP	Avg	OBP	SLG	Pos	G	PO	A	E	DP	FPct
1972 Cin	28	1	0	0	0	0	0	0	0	0	0	0	0	0	0	0	0	0	0	—	0	—	—	—	P	1	0	0	0	0	—
World Series		**Batting**																							**Fielding**						
Year Tm	Age	G	AB	H	2B	3B	HR	TB	R	RBI	GW	TBB	IBB	SO	HBP	SH	SF	SB	CS	SB%	GDP	Avg	OBP	SLG	Pos	G	PO	A	E	DP	FPct
1970 Cin	26	1	2	0	0	0	0	0	0	0	0	0	0	1	0	0	0	0	0	—	0	.000	.000	.000	P	1	0	0	0	0	—
1972 Cin	28	1	1	0	0	0	0	0	0	0	0	0	0	0	0	0	0	0	0	—	0	.000	.000	.000	P	1	0	1	0	0	1.000
WS Totals		2	3	0	0	0	0	0	0	0	0	0	0	1	0	0	0	0	0	—	0	.000	.000	.000	P	2	0	1	0	0	1.000
Postseason Totals		3	3	0	0	0	0	0	0	0	0	0	0	1	0	0	0	0	0	—	0	.000	.000	.000	P	3	0	1	0	0	1.000

TUG McGRAW—Frank Edwin McGraw—Throws: Left; Bats: Right

Ht: 6'0"; Wt: 170 lbs; Born: 8/30/1944 in Martinez, California; Debut: 4/18/1965

Division Series						Pitching																					
Year Tm	Age	G	GS	CG	GF	IP	BFP	H	R	ER	HR	SH	SF	HB	TBB	IBB	SO	WP	Bk	W	L	Pct	ShO	Sv-Op	Hld	OAvg	OOBP	ERA
1981 Phi	37	2	0	0	2	4.0	12	2	0	0	0	0	0	0	0	0	2	0	0	1	0	1.000	0	0-0	0	.167	.167	0.00
LCS						**Pitching**																						
Year Tm	Age	G	GS	CG	GF	IP	BFP	H	R	ER	HR	SH	SF	HB	TBB	IBB	SO	WP	Bk	W	L	Pct	ShO	Sv-Op	Hld	OAvg	OOBP	ERA
1969 NYN	25	1	0	0	1	3.0	11	1	0	0	0	0	0	0	1	0	1	0	0	0	0	—	0	1-1	0	.100	.182	0.00
1973 NYN	29	2	0	0	1	5.0	23	4	0	0	0	1	0	0	3	1	3	1	0	0	0	—	0	1-1	0	.211	.318	0.00
1976 Phi	32	2	0	0	1	2.1	12	4	3	3	0	0	0	0	1	0	5	2	0	0	0	—	0	0-0	0	.364	.417	11.57
1977 Phi	33	2	0	0	1	3.0	12	1	0	0	0	0	0	0	2	1	3	0	0	0	0	—	0	1-1	0	.100	.250	0.00
1978 Phi	34	3	0	0	3	5.2	25	3	2	1	1	0	0	0	5	0	5	0	0	0	1	.000	0	0-0	0	.150	.320	1.59
1980 Phi	36	5	0	0	3	8.0	34	8	4	4	0	0	1	0	4	3	5	0	0	0	1	.000	0	2-3	0	.276	.353	4.50
LCS Totals		15	0	0	10	27.0	234	21	9	8	1	1	1	0	16	5	22	3	0	0	2	.000	0	5-6	0	.212	.319	2.67
World Series						**Pitching**																						
Year Tm	Age	G	GS	CG	GF	IP	BFP	H	R	ER	HR	SH	SF	HB	TBB	IBB	SO	WP	Bk	W	L	Pct	ShO	Sv-Op	Hld	OAvg	OOBP	ERA
1973 NYN	29	5	0	0	3	13.2	58	8	5	4	0	1	1	1	9	2	14	0	0	1	0	1.000	0	1-2	0	.174	.316	2.63
1980 Phi	36	4	0	0	4	7.2	36	7	1	1	0	0	1	0	8	2	10	0	0	1	1	.500	0	2-2	0	.259	.417	1.17
WS Totals		9	0	0	7	21.1	188	15	6	5	0	1	2	1	17	4	24	0	0	2	1	.667	0	3-4	0	.205	.355	2.11
Postseason Totals		26	0	0	19	52.1	446	38	15	13	1	2	3	1	33	9	48	3	0	3	3	.500	0	8-10	0	.207	.326	2.24

Division Series		Batting																							Fielding						
Year Tm	Age	G	AB	H	2B	3B	HR	TB	R	RBI	GW	TBB	IBB	SO	HBP	SH	SF	SB	CS	SB%	GDP	Avg	OBP	SLG	Pos	G	PO	A	E	DP	FPct
1981 Phi	37	2	0	0	0	0	0	0	0	0	0	0	0	0	0	0	0	0	0	—	0	—	—	—	P	2	0	2	0	1	1.000
LCS		**Batting**																							**Fielding**						
Year Tm	Age	G	AB	H	2B	3B	HR	TB	R	RBI	GW	TBB	IBB	SO	HBP	SH	SF	SB	CS	SB%	GDP	Avg	OBP	SLG	Pos	G	PO	A	E	DP	FPct
1969 NYN	25	1	0	0	0	0	0	0	0	0	0	0	0	0	0	0	0	0	0	—	0	—	—	—	P	1	0	0	0	0	—
1973 NYN	29	2	1	0	0	0	0	0	0	0	0	0	0	1	0	0	0	0	0	—	0	.000	.000	.000	P	2	2	0	1	0	.667
1976 Phi	32	2	0	0	0	0	0	0	0	0	0	0	0	0	0	0	0	0	0	—	0	—	—	—	P	2	0	1	0	0	1.000
1977 Phi	33	2	0	0	0	0	0	0	0	0	0	0	0	0	0	0	0	0	0	—	0	—	—	—	P	2	0	0	0	0	—
1978 Phi	34	3	0	0	0	0	0	0	0	0	0	0	0	0	0	0	0	0	0	—	0	—	—	—	P	3	0	0	0	0	—
1980 Phi	36	5	1	0	0	0	0	0	0	0	0	0	0	0	0	0	0	0	0	—	0	.000	.000	.000	P	5	0	0	0	0	—
LCS Totals		15	2	0	0	0	0	0	0	0	0	0	0	1	0	0	0	0	0	—	0	.000	.000	.000	P	15	2	1	1	0	.750
World Series		**Batting**																							**Fielding**						
Year Tm	Age	G	AB	H	2B	3B	HR	TB	R	RBI	GW	TBB	IBB	SO	HBP	SH	SF	SB	CS	SB%	GDP	Avg	OBP	SLG	Pos	G	PO	A	E	DP	FPct
1973 NYN	29	5	3	1	0	0	0	1	1	0	0	0	0	1	0	1	0	0	0	—	0	.333	.333	.333	P	5	0	3	0	0	1.000
1980 Phi	36	4	0	0	0	0	0	0	0	0	0	0	0	0	0	0	0	0	0	—	0	—	—	—	P	4	0	1	0	0	1.000
WS Totals		9	3	1	0	0	0	1	1	0	0	0	0	1	0	1	0	0	0	—	0	.333	.333	.333	P	9	0	4	0	0	1.000
Postseason Totals		26	5	1	0	0	0	1	1	0	0	0	0	2	0	1	0	0	0	—	0	.200	.200	.200	P	26	2	7	1	1	.900

SCOTT McGREGOR—Scott Houston McGregor—Throws: Left; Bats: Both

Ht: 6'1"; Wt: 190 lbs; Born: 1/18/1954 in Inglewood, California; Debut: 9/19/1976

LCS						Pitching																						
Year Tm	Age	G	GS	CG	GF	IP	BFP	H	R	ER	HR	SH	SF	HB	TBB	IBB	SO	WP	Bk	W	L	Pct	ShO	Sv-Op	Hld	OAvg	OOBP	ERA
1979 Bal	25	1	1	1	0	9.0	32	6	0	0	0	0	0	0	1	0	4	0	0	1	0	1.000	1	0-0	0	.194	.219	0.00
1983 Bal	29	1	1	0	0	6.2	28	6	2	1	0	1	0	0	3	0	2	0	1	0	1	.000	0	0-0	0	.250	.333	1.35
LCS Totals		2	2	1	0	15.2	120	12	2	1	0	1	0	0	4	0	6	0	1	1	1	.500	1	0-0	0	.218	.271	0.57
World Series						**Pitching**																						
Year Tm	Age	G	GS	CG	GF	IP	BFP	H	R	ER	HR	SH	SF	HB	TBB	IBB	SO	WP	Bk	W	L	Pct	ShO	Sv-Op	Hld	OAvg	OOBP	ERA
1979 Bal	25	2	2	1	0	17.0	69	16	6	6	1	1	1	0	2	2	8	0	1	1	1	.500	0	0-0	0	.246	.265	3.18
1983 Bal	29	2	2	1	0	17.0	60	9	2	2	2	0	0	0	2	0	12	0	0	1	1	.500	1	0-0	0	.155	.183	1.06
WS Totals		4	4	2	0	34.0	258	25	8	8	3	1	1	0	4	2	20	0	1	2	2	.500	1	0-0	0	.203	.227	2.12
Postseason Totals		6	6	3	0	49.2	378	37	10	9	3	2	1	0	8	2	26	0	2	3	3	.500	2	0-0	0	.208	.241	1.63

LCS		Batting																							Fielding						
Year Tm	Age	G	AB	H	2B	3B	HR	TB	R	RBI	GW	TBB	IBB	SO	HBP	SH	SF	SB	CS	SB%	GDP	Avg	OBP	SLG	Pos	G	PO	A	E	DP	FPct
1979 Bal	25	1	0	0	0	0	0	0	0	0	0	0	0	0	0	0	0	0	0	—	0	—	—	—	P	1	0	0	0	0	—
1983 Bal	29	1	0	0	0	0	0	0	0	0	0	0	0	0	0	0	0	0	0	—	0	—	—	—	P	1	1	1	0	1	1.000
LCS Totals		2	0	0	0	0	0	0	0	0	0	0	0	0	0	0	0	0	0	—	0	—	—	—	P	2	1	1	0	1	1.000
World Series		**Batting**																							**Fielding**						
Year Tm	Age	G	AB	H	2B	3B	HR	TB	R	RBI	GW	TBB	IBB	SO	HBP	SH	SF	SB	CS	SB%	GDP	Avg	OBP	SLG	Pos	G	PO	A	E	DP	FPct
1979 Bal	25	2	4	0	0	0	0	0	1	0	0	2	0	1	0	0	0	0	0	—	0	.000	.333	.000	P	2	1	2	0	0	1.000
1983 Bal	29	2	5	0	0	0	0	0	0	0	0	0	0	0	0	0	0	0	0	—	0	.000	.000	.000	P	2	0	0	0	0	—
WS Totals		4	9	0	0	0	0	0	1	0	0	2	0	1	0	0	0	0	0	—	0	.000	.182	.000	P	4	1	2	0	1	1.000
Postseason Totals		6	9	0	0	0	0	0	1	0	0	2	0	1	0	0	0	0	0	—	0	.000	.182	.000	P	6	2	3	0	1	1.000

FRED McGRIFF—Frederick Stanley McGriff—Nickname: Crime Dog—Bats: Left; Throws: Left

Ht: 6'3"; Wt: 200 lbs; Born: 10/31/1963 in Tampa, Florida; Debut: 5/17/1986

Division Series		Batting																							Fielding						
Year Tm	Age	G	AB	H	2B	3B	HR	TB	R	RBI	GW	TBB	IBB	SO	HBP	SH	SF	SB	CS	SB%	GDP	Avg	OBP	SLG	Pos	G	PO	A	E	DP	FPct
1995 Atl	31	4	18	6	0	0	2	12	4	6	1	2	0	3	0	0	0	0	0	—	1	.333	.400	.667	1B	4	39	2	0	5	1.000
1996 Atl	32	3	9	3	1	0	1	7	1	3	1	2	0	1	0	0	1	0	1	.00	0	.333	.417	.778	1B	3	25	3	0	1	1.000
1997 Atl	33	3	9	2	0	0	0	2	4	1	0	3	0	2	0	0	0	0	0	—	0	.222	.417	.222	1B	3	27	2	0	2	1.000
DS Totals		10	36	11	1	0	3	21	9	10	2	7	0	6	0	0	1	0	1	.00	1	.306	.409	.583	1B	10	91	7	0	8	1.000
LCS		**Batting**																							**Fielding**						
Year Tm	Age	G	AB	H	2B	3B	HR	TB	R	RBI	GW	TBB	IBB	SO	HBP	SH	SF	SB	CS	SB%	GDP	Avg	OBP	SLG	Pos	G	PO	A	E	DP	FPct
1989 Tor	25	5	21	3	0	0	0	3	1	3	0	0	0	4	0	0	0	0	0	—	0	.143	.143	.143	1B	5	35	2	1	3	.974
1993 Atl	29	6	23	10	2	0	1	15	6	4	1	4	1	7	0	0	0	0	0	—	0	.435	.519	.652	1B	6	50	3	0	1	1.000
1995 Atl	31	4	16	7	4	0	0	11	5	0	0	3	2	0	0	0	0	0	0	—	0	.438	.526	.688	1B	4	42	4	0	8	1.000
1996 Atl	32	7	28	7	0	1	2	15	6	7	1	3	0	5	0	0	0	0	0	—	1	.250	.323	.536	1B	7	55	2	1	5	.983
1997 Atl	33	6	21	7	1	0	0	8	0	4	1	2	0	7	0	0	1	0	0	—	0	.333	.375	.381	1B	6	41	2	1	5	.977
LCS Totals		28	109	34	7	1	3	52	18	18	3	12	3	23	0	0	1	0	0	—	1	.312	.377	.477	1B	28	223	13	3	22	.987
World Series		**Batting**																							**Fielding**						
Year Tm	Age	G	AB	H	2B	3B	HR	TB	R	RBI	GW	TBB	IBB	SO	HBP	SH	SF	SB	CS	SB%	GDP	Avg	OBP	SLG	Pos	G	PO	A	E	DP	FPct
1995 Atl	31	6	23	6	2	0	2	14	5	3	0	3	0	7	0	0	0	1	0	1.00	1	.261	.346	.609	1B	6	68	2	1	2	.986
1996 Atl	32	6	20	6	0	0	2	12	4	6	1	5	1	4	0	0	1	0	0	—	0	.300	.423	.600	1B	6	62	5	0	6	1.000
WS Totals		12	43	12	2	0	4	26	9	9	1	8	1	11	0	0	1	1	0	1.00	2	.279	.385	.605	1B	12	130	7	1	8	.993
Postseason Totals		50	188	57	10	1	10	99	36	37	6	27	4	40	0	0	3	1	1	.50	4	.303	.385	.527	1B	50	444	27	4	38	.992

MARK McGWIRE—Mark David McGwire—Bats: Right; Throws: Right

Ht: 6'5"; Wt: 215 lbs; Born: 10/1/1963 in Pomona, California; Debut: 8/22/1986

LCS		Batting																							Fielding						
Year Tm	Age	G	AB	H	2B	3B	HR	TB	R	RBI	GW	TBB	IBB	SO	HBP	SH	SF	SB	CS	SB%	GDP	Avg	OBP	SLG	Pos	G	PO	A	E	DP	FPct
1988 Oak	25	4	15	5	0	0	1	8	4	3	0	1	1	5	0	0	0	0	0	—	0	.333	.375	.533	1B	4	24	2	0	4	1.000
1989 Oak	26	5	18	7	1	0	1	11	3	3	1	1	0	4	0	0	1	0	0	—	0	.389	.400	.611	1B	5	46	1	1	4	.979
1990 Oak	27	4	13	2	0	0	0	2	2	2	1	3	0	3	1	0	0	0	0	—	0	.154	.353	.154	1B	4	40	0	0	3	1.000
1992 Oak	29	6	20	3	0	0	1	6	1	3	0	5	2	4	1	1	0	0	0	—	1	.150	.346	.300	1B	6	46	2	1	4	.980
LCS Totals		19	66	17	1	0	3	27	10	11	2	10	3	16	2	1	1	0	0	—	1	.258	.367	.409	1B	19	156	5	2	15	.988

World Series — Batting / Fielding

Year Tm	Age	G	AB	H	2B	3B	HR	TB	R	RBI	GW	TBB	IBB	SO	HBP	SH	SF	SB	CS	SB%	GDP	Avg	OBP	SLG	Pos	G	PO	A	E	DP	FPct
1988 Oak	25	5	17	1	0	0	1	4	1	1	1	3	1	4	0	0	0	0	0	—	2	.059	.200	.235	1B	5	40	3	0	2	1.000
1989 Oak	26	4	17	5	1	0	0	6	0	1	0	1	0	3	0	0	0	0	0	—	0	.294	.333	.353	1B	4	28	2	0	1	1.000
1990 Oak	27	4	14	3	0	0	0	3	1	0	0	2	0	4	0	0	0	0	0	—	0	.214	.313	.214	1B	4	42	1	2	5	.956
WS Totals		13	48	9	1	0	1	13	2	2	1	6	1	11	0	0	0	0	0	—	2	.188	.278	.271	1B	13	110	6	2	8	.983
Postseason Totals		32	114	26	2	0	4	40	12	13	3	16	4	27	2	1	1	0	0	—	3	.228	.331	.351	1B	32	266	11	4	23	.986

JOHN McHALE—John Joseph McHale—Bats: Left; Throws: Right

Ht: 6'0"; Wt: 200 lbs; Born: 9/21/1921 in Detroit, Michigan; Debut: 5/28/1943

World Series — Batting / Fielding

Year Tm	Age	G	AB	H	2B	3B	HR	TB	R	RBI	GW	TBB	IBB	SO	HBP	SH	SF	SB	CS	SB%	GDP	Avg	OBP	SLG	Pos	G	PO	A	E	DP	FPct
1945 Det	24	3	3	0	0	0	0	0	0	0	0	0	0	1	0	0	0	0	0	—	0	.000	.000	.000	—						

STUFFY McINNIS—John Phalen McInnis—Nickname: Jack—Bats: Right; Throws: Right

Ht: 5'9"; Wt: 162 lbs; Born: 9/19/1890 in Gloucester, Massachusetts; Debut: 4/12/1909; Died: 2/16/1960

World Series — Batting / Fielding

Year Tm	Age	G	AB	H	2B	3B	HR	TB	R	RBI	GW	TBB	IBB	SO	HBP	SH	SF	SB	CS	SB%	GDP	Avg	OBP	SLG	Pos	G	PO	A	E	DP	FPct
1911 Phi	21	1	0	0	0	0	0	0	0	0	0	0	0	0	0	0	0	0	0	—	0	—	—	—	1B	1	1	0	0	0	1.000
1913 Phi	23	5	17	2	1	0	0	3	1	2	0	0	0	2	0	2	1	0	0	—	0	.118	.111	.176	1B	5	45	0	0	4	1.000
1914 Phi	24	4	14	2	1	0	0	3	2	0	0	3	0	3	0	0	0	0	0	—	0	.143	.294	.214	1B	4	50	1	0	4	1.000
1918 Bos	28	6	20	5	0	0	0	5	2	1	1	1	1	1	0	1	0	0	0	—	1	.250	.286	.250	1B	6	70	2	0	3	1.000
1925 Pit	35	4	14	4	0	0	0	4	0	1	0	0	0	2	0	0	0	0	0	—	0	.286	.286	.286	1B	3	30	3	0	0	1.000
WS Totals		20	65	13	2	0	0	15	5	4	1	4	1	8	0	3	1	0	0	—	1	.200	.243	.231	1B	19	196	6	0	11	1.000

HARRY McINTIRE—John Reid McIntire—Nickname: Rocks—Throws: Right; Bats: Right

Ht: 5'11"; Wt: 180 lbs; Born: 1/11/1879 in Dayton, Ohio; Debut: 4/14/1905; Died: 1/9/1949

World Series — Pitching

Year Tm	Age	G	GS	CG	GF	IP	BFP	H	R	ER	HR	SH	SF	HB	TBB	IBB	SO	WP	Bk	W	L	Pct	ShO	Sv-Op	Hld	OAvg	OOBP	ERA
1910 ChN	31	2	0	0	1	5.1	23	4	5	4	1	0	0	1	3	0	3	0	0	0	1	.000	0	0- 0	0	.211	.348	6.75

World Series — Batting / Fielding

Year Tm	Age	G	AB	H	2B	3B	HR	TB	R	RBI	GW	TBB	IBB	SO	HBP	SH	SF	SB	CS	SB%	GDP	Avg	OBP	SLG	Pos	G	PO	A	E	DP	FPct
1910 ChN	31	2	1	0	0	0	0	0	0	0	0	0	0	1	0	0	0	0	0	—	0	.000	.000	.000	P	2	0	1	1	0	.500

MATTY McINTYRE—Matthew W. McIntyre—Bats: Left; Throws: Left

Ht: 5'11"; Wt: 175 lbs; Born: 6/12/1880 in Stonington, Connecticut; Debut: 7/3/1901; Died: 4/2/1920

World Series — Batting / Fielding

Year Tm	Age	G	AB	H	2B	3B	HR	TB	R	RBI	GW	TBB	IBB	SO	HBP	SH	SF	SB	CS	SB%	GDP	Avg	OBP	SLG	Pos	G	PO	A	E	DP	FPct
1908 Det	28	5	18	4	1	0	0	5	2	0	0	3	0	2	1	0	0	1	0	1.00	0	.222	.364	.278	OF	5	10	0	1	0	.909
1909 Det	29	4	3	0	0	0	0	0	0	0	0	0	0	1	0	0	0	0	0	—	0	.000	.000	.000	OF	1	0	0	0	0	—
WS Totals		9	21	4	1	0	0	5	2	0	0	3	0	3	1	0	0	1	0	1.00	0	.190	.320	.238	OF	6	10	0	1	0	.909

ARCHIE McKAIN—Archie Richard McKain—Nickname: Happy—Throws: Left; Bats: Both

Ht: 5'10"; Wt: 175 lbs; Born: 5/12/1911 in Delphos, Kansas; Debut: 4/25/1937; Died: 5/21/1985

World Series — Pitching

Year Tm	Age	G	GS	CG	GF	IP	BFP	H	R	ER	HR	SH	SF	HB	TBB	IBB	SO	WP	Bk	W	L	Pct	ShO	Sv-Op	Hld	OAvg	OOBP	ERA
1940 Det	29	1	0	0	1	3.0	13	4	1	1	0	1	0	0	0	0	0	1	0	0	0	—	0	0- 0	0	.333	.333	3.00

World Series — Batting / Fielding

Year Tm	Age	G	AB	H	2B	3B	HR	TB	R	RBI	GW	TBB	IBB	SO	HBP	SH	SF	SB	CS	SB%	GDP	Avg	OBP	SLG	Pos	G	PO	A	E	DP	FPct
1940 Det	29	1	0	0	0	0	0	0	0	0	0	0	0	0	0	0	0	0	0	—	0	—	—	—	P	1	0	1	0	0	1.000

DAVE McKAY—David Lawrence McKay—Bats: Both; Throws: Right

Ht: 6'1"; Wt: 195 lbs; Born: 3/14/1950 in Vancouver, British Columbia; Debut: 8/22/1975

Division Series / LCS — Batting / Fielding

Year Tm	Age	G	AB	H	2B	3B	HR	TB	R	RBI	GW	TBB	IBB	SO	HBP	SH	SF	SB	CS	SB%	GDP	Avg	OBP	SLG	Pos	G	PO	A	E	DP	FPct
Division Series																															
1981 Oak	31	3	11	3	0	0	1	6	1	1	0	1	0	1	0	0	0	0	0	—	0	.273	.333	.545	2B	3	8	6	1	3	.933
LCS																															
1981 Oak	31	3	11	3	0	0	0	3	0	1	0	0	0	2	0	0	0	0	0	—	1	.273	.273	.273	2B	3	7	6	1	0	.929
Postseason Totals		6	22	6	0	0	1	9	1	2	0	1	0	3	0	0	0	0	0	—	1	.273	.304	.409	2B	6	15	12	2	3	.931

DENNY McLAIN—Dennis Dale McLain—Throws: Right; Bats: Right

Ht: 6'1"; Wt: 185 lbs; Born: 3/29/1944 in Chicago, Illinois; Debut: 9/21/1963

World Series — Pitching

Year Tm	Age	G	GS	CG	GF	IP	BFP	H	R	ER	HR	SH	SF	HB	TBB	IBB	SO	WP	Bk	W	L	Pct	ShO	Sv-Op	Hld	OAvg	OOBP	ERA
1968 Det-*MC*	24	3	3	1	0	16.2	73	18	8	6	1	1	0	0	4	0	13	0	0	1	2	.333	0	0- 0	0	.265	.306	3.24

World Series — Batting / Fielding

Year Tm	Age	G	AB	H	2B	3B	HR	TB	R	RBI	GW	TBB	IBB	SO	HBP	SH	SF	SB	CS	SB%	GDP	Avg	OBP	SLG	Pos	G	PO	A	E	DP	FPct
1968 Det	24	3	6	0	0	0	0	0	0	0	0	0	0	4	0	1	0	0	0	—	1	.000	.000	.000	P	3	0	3	1	0	.750

LARRY McLEAN—John Bannerman McLean—Bats: Right; Throws: Right

Ht: 6'5"; Wt: 228 lbs; Born: 7/18/1881 in Fredericton, New Brunswick; Debut: 4/26/1901; Died: 3/24/1921

World Series — Batting / Fielding

Year Tm	Age	G	AB	H	2B	3B	HR	TB	R	RBI	GW	TBB	IBB	SO	HBP	SH	SF	SB	CS	SB%	GDP	Avg	OBP	SLG	Pos	G	PO	A	E	DP	FPct
1913 NYG	32	5	12	6	0	0	0	6	0	2	0	0	0	0	0	0	0	0	0	—	0	.500	.500	.500	C	4	14	2	0	0	1.000

MARK McLEMORE—Mark Tremell McLemore—Bats: Both; Throws: Right

Ht: 5'11"; Wt: 175 lbs; Born: 10/4/1964 in San Diego, California; Debut: 9/13/1986

Division Series — Batting / Fielding

Year Tm	Age	G	AB	H	2B	3B	HR	TB	R	RBI	GW	TBB	IBB	SO	HBP	SH	SF	SB	CS	SB%	GDP	Avg	OBP	SLG	Pos	G	PO	A	E	DP	FPct
1996 Tex	31	4	15	2	0	0	0	2	1	2	0	0	0	4	0	2	0	0	1	.00	0	.133	.133	.133	2B	4	10	16	0	2	1.000

DON McMAHON—Donald John McMahon—Throws: Right; Bats: Right

Ht: 6'2"; Wt: 215 lbs; Born: 1/4/1930 in Brooklyn, New York; Debut: 6/30/1957; Died: 7/22/1987

LCS / World Series — Pitching

Year Tm	Age	G	GS	CG	GF	IP	BFP	H	R	ER	HR	SH	SF	HB	TBB	IBB	SO	WP	Bk	W	L	Pct	ShO	Sv-Op	Hld	OAvg	OOBP	ERA
LCS																												
1971 SF	41	2	0	0	1	3.0	9	0	0	0	0	0	0	0	0	0	3	0	0	0	0	—	0	0- 0	0	.000	.000	0.00
World Series																												
1957 Mil	27	3	0	0	3	5.0	18	3	0	0	0	1	0	0	3	0	5	0	0	0	0	—	0	0- 0	0	.214	.353	0.00
1958 Mil	28	3	0	0	3	3.1	16	3	2	2	1	0	0	0	3	0	5	0	0	0	0	—	0	0- 0	0	.231	.375	5.40
1968 Det	38	2	0	0	1	2.0	10	4	3	3	1	0	0	0	0	0	1	0	0	0	0	—	0	0- 0	0	.400	.400	13.50
WS Totals		8	0	0	7	10.1	88	10	5	5	2	1	0	0	6	0	11	0	0	0	0	—	0	0-0	0	.270	.372	4.35
Postseason Totals		10	0	0	8	13.1	106	10	5	5	2	1	0	0	6	0	14	0	0	0	0	—	0	0-0	0	.217	.308	3.38

LCS / World Series — Batting / Fielding

Year Tm	Age	G	AB	H	2B	3B	HR	TB	R	RBI	GW	TBB	IBB	SO	HBP	SH	SF	SB	CS	SB%	GDP	Avg	OBP	SLG	Pos	G	PO	A	E	DP	FPct
LCS																															
1971 SF	41	2	0	0	0	0	0	0	0	0	0	0	0	0	0	0	0	0	0	—	0	—	—	—	P	2	1	1	0	0	1.000
World Series																															
1957 Mil	27	3	0	0	0	0	0	0	0	0	0	0	0	0	0	0	0	0	0	—	0	—	—	—	P	3	0	2	0	0	1.000
1958 Mil	28	3	0	0	0	0	0	0	0	0	0	0	0	0	0	0	0	0	0	—	0	—	—	—	P	3	1	0	0	0	1.000
1968 Det	38	2	0	0	0	0	0	0	0	0	0	0	0	0	0	0	0	0	0	—	0	—	—	—	P	2	1	0	0	0	1.000
WS Totals		8	0	0	0	0	0	0	0	0	0	0	0	0	0	0	0	0	0	—	0	—	—	—	P	8	2	2	0	0	1.000
Postseason Totals		10	0	0	0	0	0	0	0	0	0	0	0	0	0	0	0	0	0	—	0	—	—	—	P	10	3	3	0	0	1.000

GREG McMICHAEL—Gregory Winston McMichael—Throws: Right; Bats: Right

Ht: 6'3"; Wt: 195 lbs; Born: 12/1/1966 in Knoxville, Tennessee; Debut: 4/12/1993

Year	Tm	Age	G	GS	CG	GF	IP	BFP	H	R	ER	HR	SH	SF	HB	TBB	IBB	SO	WP	Bk	W	L	Pct	ShO	Sv-Op	Hld	OAvg	OOBP	ERA
Division Series			Pitching																										
1995	Atl	28	2	0	0	0	1.1	7	1	1	1	0	0	0	0	2	0	1	0	0	0	0	—	0	0-0	1	.200	.429	6.75
1996	Atl	29	2	0	0	0	1.1	6	1	1	1	0	0	0	0	1	0	3	0	0	0	0	—	0	0-0	1	.200	.333	6.75
DS Totals			4	0	0	0	2.2	26	2	2	2	0	0	0	0	3	0	4	0	0	0	0	—	0	0-0	2	.200	.385	6.75
LCS			Pitching																										
1993	Atl	26	4	0	0	2	4.0	21	7	3	3	1	0	0	0	2	1	1	0	0	0	1	.000	0	0-0	0	.368	.429	6.75
1995	Atl	28	3	0	0	1	2.2	8	0	0	0	0	1	0	0	1	0	2	0	0	1	0	1.000	0	1-1	1	.000	.143	0.00
1996	Atl	29	3	0	0	1	2.0	11	4	2	2	1	0	0	0	1	0	3	0	0	0	1	.000	0	0-1	0	.400	.455	9.00
LCS Totals			10	0	0	4	8.2	80	11	5	5	2	1	0	0	4	1	6	0	0	1	2	.333	0	1-2	1	.314	.385	5.19
World Series			Pitching																										
1995	Atl	28	3	0	0	0	3.1	16	3	2	1	0	0	0	0	2	0	2	1	0	0	0	—	0	0-0	2	.214	.313	2.70
1996	Atl	29	2	0	0	0	1.0	8	5	3	3	1	0	0	0	0	0	1	0	0	0	0	—	0	0-0	0	.625	.625	27.00
WS Totals			5	0	0	0	4.1	48	8	5	4	1	0	0	0	2	0	3	1	0	0	0	—	0	0-0	2	.364	.417	8.31
Postseason Totals			19	0	0	4	15.2	154	21	12	11	3	1	0	0	9	1	13	1	0	1	2	.333	0	1-2	5	.313	.395	6.32

Year	Tm	Age	G	AB	H	2B	3B	HR	TB	R	RBI	GW	TBB	IBB	SO	HBP	SH	SF	SB	CS	SB%	GDP	Avg	OBP	SLG	Pos	G	PO	A	E	DP	FPct
Division Series			Batting																							Fielding						
1995	Atl	28	2	0	0	0	0	0	0	0	0	0	0	0	0	0	0	0	0	0	—	0	—	—	—	P	2	0	0	0	0	—
1996	Atl	29	2	0	0	0	0	0	0	0	0	0	0	0	0	0	0	0	0	0	—	0	—	—	—	P	2	0	0	0	0	—
DS Totals			4	0	0	0	0	0	0	0	0	0	0	0	0	0	0	0	0	0	—	0	—	—	—	P	4	0	0	0	0	—
LCS			Batting																							Fielding						
1993	Atl	26	4	0	0	0	0	0	0	0	0	0	0	0	0	0	0	0	0	0	—	0	—	—	—	P	4	0	1	0	0	1.000
1995	Atl	28	3	0	0	0	0	0	0	0	0	0	0	0	0	0	0	0	0	0	—	0	—	—	—	P	3	0	0	0	0	—
1996	Atl	29	3	0	0	0	0	0	0	0	0	0	0	0	0	0	0	0	0	0	—	0	—	—	—	P	3	1	0	0	0	1.000
LCS Totals			10	0	0	0	0	0	0	0	0	0	0	0	0	0	0	0	0	0	—	0	—	—	—	P	10	1	1	0	0	1.000
World Series			Batting																							Fielding						
1995	Atl	28	3	0	0	0	0	0	0	0	0	0	0	0	0	0	0	0	0	0	—	0	—	—	—	P	3	0	1	0	0	1.000
1996	Atl	29	2	0	0	0	0	0	0	0	0	0	0	0	0	0	0	0	0	0	—	0	—	—	—	P	2	0	0	0	0	—
WS Totals			5	0	0	0	0	0	0	0	0	0	0	0	0	0	0	0	0	0	—	0	—	—	—	P	5	0	1	0	0	1.000
Postseason Totals			19	0	0	0	0	0	0	0	0	0	0	0	0	0	0	0	0	0	—	0	—	—	—	P	19	1	2	0	0	1.000

NORM McMILLAN—Norman Alexis McMillan—Nickname: Bub—Bats: Right; Throws: Right

Ht: 6'0"; Wt: 175 lbs; Born: 10/5/1895 in Latta, South Carolina; Debut: 4/12/1922; Died: 9/28/1969

Year	Tm	Age	G	AB	H	2B	3B	HR	TB	R	RBI	GW	TBB	IBB	SO	HBP	SH	SF	SB	CS	SB%	GDP	Avg	OBP	SLG	Pos	G	PO	A	E	DP	FPct
World Series			Batting																							Fielding						
1922	NYA	26	1	2	0	0	0	0	0	0	0	0	0	0	0	0	0	0	0	0	—	0	.000	.000	.000	OF	1	1	0	0	0	1.000
1929	ChN	33	5	20	2	0	0	0	2	0	0	0	2	0	6	0	0	0	1	0	1.00	0	.100	.182	.100	3B	5	6	9	0	0	1.000
WS Totals			6	22	2	0	0	0	2	0	0	0	2	0	6	0	0	0	1	0	1.00	0	.091	.167	.091	3B	5	6	9	0	0	1.000

KEN McMULLEN—Kenneth Lee McMullen—Bats: Right; Throws: Right

Ht: 6'3"; Wt: 190 lbs; Born: 6/1/1942 in Oxnard, California; Debut: 9/17/1962

Year	Tm	Age	G	AB	H	2B	3B	HR	TB	R	RBI	GW	TBB	IBB	SO	HBP	SH	SF	SB	CS	SB%	GDP	Avg	OBP	SLG	Pos	G	PO	A	E	DP	FPct
LCS			Batting																							Fielding						
1974	LA	32	1	1	0	0	0	0	0	0	0	0	0	0	1	0	0	0	0	0	—	0	.000	.000	.000	—						

FRED McMULLIN—Frederick William McMullin—Bats: Right; Throws: Right

Ht: 5'11"; Wt: 170 lbs; Born: 10/13/1891 in Scammon, Kansas; Debut: 8/27/1914; Died: 11/21/1952

Year	Tm	Age	G	AB	H	2B	3B	HR	TB	R	RBI	GW	TBB	IBB	SO	HBP	SH	SF	SB	CS	SB%	GDP	Avg	OBP	SLG	Pos	G	PO	A	E	DP	FPct
World Series			Batting																							Fielding						
1917	ChA	25	6	24	3	1	0	0	4	1	2	1	1	0	6	0	2	0	0	1	.00	0	.125	.160	.167	3B	6	2	14	0	2	1.000
1919	ChA	27	2	2	1	0	0	0	1	0	0	0	0	0	0	0	0	0	0	0	—	0	.500	.500	.500	—						
WS Totals			8	26	4	1	0	0	5	1	2	1	1	0	6	0	2	0	0	1	.00	0	.154	.185	.192	3B	6	2	14	0	2	1.000

ERIC McNAIR—Donald Eric McNair—Nickname: Boob—Bats: Right; Throws: Right

Ht: 5'8"; Wt: 160 lbs; Born: 4/12/1909 in Meridian, Mississippi; Debut: 9/20/1929; Died: 3/11/1949

Year	Tm	Age	G	AB	H	2B	3B	HR	TB	R	RBI	GW	TBB	IBB	SO	HBP	SH	SF	SB	CS	SB%	GDP	Avg	OBP	SLG	Pos	G	PO	A	E	DP	FPct
World Series			Batting																							Fielding						
1930	Phi	21	1	1	0	0	0	0	0	0	0	0	0	0	0	0	0	0	0	0	—	0	.000	.000	.000	—						
1931	Phi	22	2	2	0	0	0	0	0	1	0	0	0	0	1	0	0	0	0	0	—	0	.000	.000	.000	2B	1	1	1	0	0	1.000
WS Totals			3	3	0	0	0	0	0	1	0	0	0	0	1	0	0	0	0	0	—	0	.000	.000	.000	2B	1	1	1	0	0	1.000

DAVE McNALLY—David Arthur McNally—Throws: Left; Bats: Right

Ht: 5'11"; Wt: 185 lbs; Born: 10/31/1942 in Billings, Montana; Debut: 9/26/1962

Year	Tm	Age	G	GS	CG	GF	IP	BFP	H	R	ER	HR	SH	SF	HB	TBB	IBB	SO	WP	Bk	W	L	Pct	ShO	Sv-Op	Hld	OAvg	OOBP	ERA
LCS			Pitching																										
1969	Bal	26	1	1	1	0	11.0	41	3	0	0	0	0	0	0	5	0	11	0	0	1	0	1.000	1	0-0	0	.083	.195	0.00
1970	Bal	27	1	1	1	0	9.0	36	6	3	3	2	0	0	0	5	0	5	0	0	1	0	1.000	0	0-0	0	.194	.306	3.00
1971	Bal	28	1	1	0	0	7.0	27	7	3	3	0	1	0	0	1	0	5	0	0	1	0	1.000	0	0-0	0	.280	.308	3.86
1973	Bal	30	1	1	0	0	7.2	32	7	5	5	4	0	0	0	2	0	7	1	0	0	1	.000	0	0-0	0	.233	.281	5.87
1974	Bal	31	1	1	0	0	5.2	23	6	2	1	1	1	0	0	2	0	2	1	0	0	1	.000	0	0-0	0	.300	.364	1.59
LCS Totals			5	5	2	0	40.1	318	29	13	12	7	2	0	0	15	0	30	2	0	3	2	.600	1	0-0	0	.204	.280	2.68
World Series			Pitching																										
1966	Bal	23	2	2	1	0	11.1	44	6	2	2	1	0	0	0	7	0	5	0	0	1	0	1.000	1	0-0	0	.162	.295	1.59
1969	Bal	26	2	2	1	0	16.0	65	11	5	5	3	0	0	1	5	1	13	1	0	0	1	.000	0	0-0	0	.186	.262	2.81
1970	Bal	27	1	1	1	0	9.0	37	9	3	3	0	0	1	0	2	0	5	0	0	1	0	1.000	0	0-0	0	.265	.297	3.00
1971	Bal	28	4	2	1	2	13.2	59	10	7	3	1	2	0	0	5	0	12	2	0	2	1	.667	0	0-0	0	.192	.263	1.98
WS Totals			9	7	4	2	50.0	410	36	17	13	5	2	1	1	19	1	35	3	0	4	2	.667	1	0-0	0	.198	.276	2.34
Postseason Totals			14	12	6	2	90.1	728	65	30	25	12	4	1	1	34	1	65	5	0	7	4	.636	2	0-0	0	.201	.278	2.49

Year	Tm	Age	G	AB	H	2B	3B	HR	TB	R	RBI	GW	TBB	IBB	SO	HBP	SH	SF	SB	CS	SB%	GDP	Avg	OBP	SLG	Pos	G	PO	A	E	DP	FPct
LCS			Batting																							Fielding						
1969	Bal	26	1	4	0	0	0	0	0	0	0	0	0	0	2	0	0	0	0	0	—	0	.000	.000	.000	P	1	0	0	0	0	—
1970	Bal	27	1	5	2	1	0	0	3	1	1	0	0	0	1	0	0	0	0	0	—	0	.400	.400	.600	P	1	0	0	0	0	—
1971	Bal	28	1	2	0	0	0	0	0	0	0	0	0	0	0	0	0	0	0	0	—	0	.000	.000	.000	P	1	0	2	0	1	1.000
1973	Bal	30	1	0	0	0	0	0	0	0	0	0	0	0	0	0	0	0	0	0	—	0	—	—	—	P	1	0	0	0	0	—
1974	Bal	31	1	0	0	0	0	0	0	0	0	0	0	0	0	0	0	0	0	0	—	0	—	—	—	P	1	0	0	0	0	—
LCS Totals			5	11	2	1	0	0	3	1	1	0	0	0	3	0	0	0	0	0	—	0	.182	.182	.273	P	5	0	2	0	1	1.000
World Series			Batting																							Fielding						
1966	Bal	23	2	3	0	0	0	0	0	0	0	0	0	0	1	0	1	0	0	0	—	0	.000	.000	.000	P	2	0	0	0	0	—
1969	Bal	26	2	5	1	0	0	1	4	1	2	0	0	0	2	0	0	0	0	0	—	0	.200	.200	.800	P	2	1	1	0	0	1.000
1970	Bal	27	1	4	1	0	0	1	4	1	4	0	0	0	2	0	0	0	0	0	—	0	.250	.250	1.000	P	1	0	1	0	0	1.000
1971	Bal	28	4	4	0	0	0	0	0	0	0	0	0	0	3	0	0	0	0	0	—	0	.000	.000	.000	P	4	0	2	0	0	1.000
WS Totals			9	16	2	0	0	2	8	2	6	0	0	0	8	0	1	0	0	0	—	0	.125	.125	.500	P	9	1	4	0	0	1.000
Postseason Totals			14	27	4	1	0	2	11	3	7	0	0	0	11	0	1	0	0	0	—	0	.148	.148	.407	P	14	1	6	0	1	1.000

MIKE McNALLY—Michael Joseph McNally—Nickname: Minooka Mike—Bats: Right; Throws: Right

Ht: 5'11"; Wt: 150 lbs; Born: 9/9/1892 in Minooka, Pennsylvania; Debut: 4/21/1915; Died: 5/29/1965

Year	Tm	Age	G	AB	H	2B	3B	HR	TB	R	RBI	GW	TBB	IBB	SO	HBP	SH	SF	SB	CS	SB%	GDP	Avg	OBP	SLG	Pos	G	PO	A	E	DP	FPct
World Series			Batting																							Fielding						
1916	Bos	24	1	0	0	0	0	0	0	1	0	0	0	0	0	0	0	0	0	0	—	0	—	—	—	—						
1921	NYA	29	7	20	4	1	0	0	5	3	1	0	1	0	3	1	0	0	2	2	.50	0	.200	.273	.250	3B	7	5	11	3	2	.842
1922	NYA	30	1	0	0	0	0	0	0	0	0	0	0	0	0	0	0	0	0	0	—	0	—	—	—	2B	1	1	1	0	0	1.000
WS Totals			9	20	4	1	0	0	5	4	1	0	1	0	3	1	0	0	2	2	.50	0	.200	.273	.250	3B	7	5	11	3	2	.842

EARL McNEELY—George Earl McNeely—Bats: Right; Throws: Right

Ht: 5'9"; Wt: 155 lbs; Born: 5/12/1898 in Sacramento, California; Debut: 8/9/1924; Died: 7/16/1971

World Series		Batting																							Fielding						
Year Tm	Age	G	AB	H	2B	3B	HR	TB	R	RBI	GW	TBB	IBB	SO	HBP	SH	SF	SB	CS	SB%	GDP	Avg	OBP	SLG	Pos	G	PO	A	E	DP	FPct
1924 Was	26	7	27	6	3	0	0	9	4	1	1	4	0	4	0	0	0	1	0	1.00	0	.222	.323	.333	OF	6	8	0	1	0	.889
1925 Was	27	4	0	0	0	0	0	0	2	0	0	0	0	0	0	0	0	1	0	1.00	0	—	—	—	OF	2	3	0	0	0	1.000
WS Totals		11	27	6	3	0	0	9	6	1	1	4	0	4	0	0	0	2	0	1.00	0	.222	.323	.333	OF	8	11	0	1	0	.917

HUGH McQUILLAN—Hugh A. McQuillan—Nickname: Handsome Hugh—Throws: Right; Bats: Right

Ht: 6'0"; Wt: 170 lbs; Born: 9/15/1897 in New York, New York; Debut: 7/26/1918; Died: 8/26/1947

World Series		Pitching																										
Year Tm	Age	G	GS	CG	GF	IP	BFP	H	R	ER	HR	SH	SF	HB	TBB	IBB	SO	WP	Bk	W	L	Pct	ShO	Sv-Op	Hld	OAvg	OOBP	ERA
1922 NYG	25	1	1	1	0	9.0	34	8	3	3	1	0	0	0	2	0	4	0	0	1	0	1.000	0	0-0	0	.250	.294	3.00
1923 NYG	26	2	1	0	0	9.0	41	11	5	5	2	2	0	0	4	0	3	0	0	0	1	.000	0	0-0	0	.314	.385	5.00
1924 NYG	27	3	1	0	1	7.0	27	2	2	2	0	0	1	0	6	0	2	0	0	1	0	1.000	0	1-1	0	.100	.296	2.57
WS Totals		6	3	1	1	25.0	204	21	10	10	3	2	1	0	12	0	9	0	0	2	1	.667	0	1-1	0	.241	.330	3.60

World Series		Batting																							Fielding						
Year Tm	Age	G	AB	H	2B	3B	HR	TB	R	RBI	GW	TBB	IBB	SO	HBP	SH	SF	SB	CS	SB%	GDP	Avg	OBP	SLG	Pos	G	PO	A	E	DP	FPct
1922 NYG	25	1	4	1	1	0	0	2	1	0	0	0	0	1	0	0	0	0	0	—	0	.250	.250	.500	P	1	0	0	0	0	—
1923 NYG	26	2	3	0	0	0	0	0	0	0	0	0	0	1	0	0	0	0	0	—	0	.000	.000	.000	P	2	0	1	0	0	1.000
1924 NYG	27	3	1	1	0	0	0	1	0	1	0	1	0	0	0	0	0	0	0	—	0	1.000	1.000	1.000	P	3	0	2	0	1	1.000
WS Totals		6	8	2	1	0	0	3	1	1	0	1	0	2	0	0	0	0	0	—	0	.250	.333	.375	P	6	0	3	0	1	1.000

GEORGE McQUINN—George Hartley McQuinn—Bats: Left; Throws: Left

Ht: 5'11"; Wt: 165 lbs; Born: 5/29/1910 in Arlington, Virginia; Debut: 4/14/1936; Died: 12/24/1978

World Series		Batting																							Fielding						
Year Tm	Age	G	AB	H	2B	3B	HR	TB	R	RBI	GW	TBB	IBB	SO	HBP	SH	SF	SB	CS	SB%	GDP	Avg	OBP	SLG	Pos	G	PO	A	E	DP	FPct
1944 StL	34	6	16	7	2	0	1	12	2	5	1	7	1	2	0	1	0	0	0	—	0	.438	.609	.750	1B	6	50	2	0	3	1.000
1947 NYA	37	7	23	3	0	0	0	3	3	1	0	5	0	8	0	1	0	0	0	—	0	.130	.286	.130	1B	7	48	4	1	3	.981
WS Totals		13	39	10	2	0	1	15	5	6	1	12	1	10	0	2	0	0	0	—	0	.256	.431	.385	1B	13	98	6	1	6	.990

HAL McRAE—Harold Abraham McRae—Bats: Right; Throws: Right

Ht: 5'11"; Wt: 180 lbs; Born: 7/10/1945 in Avon Park, Florida; Debut: 7/11/1968

Division Series		Batting																							Fielding						
Year Tm	Age	G	AB	H	2B	3B	HR	TB	R	RBI	GW	TBB	IBB	SO	HBP	SH	SF	SB	CS	SB%	GDP	Avg	OBP	SLG	Pos	G	PO	A	E	DP	FPct
1981 KC	36	3	11	1	1	0	0	2	0	0	0	1	0	1	0	0	0	0	0	—	0	.091	.167	.182	—						
LCS		**Batting**																							**Fielding**						
Year Tm	Age	G	AB	H	2B	3B	HR	TB	R	RBI	GW	TBB	IBB	SO	HBP	SH	SF	SB	CS	SB%	GDP	Avg	OBP	SLG	Pos	G	PO	A	E	DP	FPct
1970 Cin	25	2	4	0	0	0	0	0	0	0	0	0	0	2	0	0	0	0	0	—	0	.000	.000	.000	OF	1	2	0	0	0	1.000
1972 Cin	27	1	0	0	0	0	0	0	0	0	0	0	0	0	0	0	0	0	0	—	0	—	—	—	—						
1976 KC	31	5	17	2	1	1	0	5	2	1	0	1	0	4	1	0	1	0	1	.00	0	.118	.200	.294	OF	2	5	1	0	0	1.000
1977 KC	32	5	18	8	3	0	1	14	6	2	1	3	0	1	0	0	0	0	1	.00	0	.444	.524	.778	OF	2	2	1	0	0	1.000
1978 KC	33	4	14	3	0	0	0	3	0	2	0	2	0	2	0	1	1	1	1	.50	0	.214	.294	.214	—						
1980 KC	35	3	10	2	0	0	0	2	0	0	0	1	0	3	1	0	0	0	3	.00	0	.200	.333	.200	—						
1984 KC	39	2	2	2	1	0	0	3	0	1	0	0	0	0	0	0	0	0	0	—	0	1.000	1.000	1.500	—						
1985 KC	40	6	23	6	2	0	0	8	1	3	0	1	0	6	1	1	0	0	0	—	0	.261	.320	.348	—						
LCS Totals		28	88	23	7	1	1	35	9	9	1	8	0	18	3	2	2	1	6	.14	0	.261	.337	.398	OF	5	9	2	0	0	1.000
World Series		**Batting**																							**Fielding**						
Year Tm	Age	G	AB	H	2B	3B	HR	TB	R	RBI	GW	TBB	IBB	SO	HBP	SH	SF	SB	CS	SB%	GDP	Avg	OBP	SLG	Pos	G	PO	A	E	DP	FPct
1970 Cin	25	3	11	5	2	0	0	7	1	3	0	0	0	1	0	0	0	0	0	—	0	.455	.455	.636	OF	3	2	1	0	0	1.000
1972 Cin	27	5	9	4	1	0	0	5	1	2	0	0	0	1	0	0	1	0	0	—	0	.444	.400	.556	OF	2	4	0	0	0	1.000
1980 KC	35	6	24	9	3	0	0	12	3	1	0	2	0	2	0	0	0	0	0	—	0	.375	.423	.500	—						
1985 KC	40	3	1	0	0	0	0	0	0	0	0	1	1	0	1	0	0	0	0	—	0	.000	.667	.000	—						
WS Totals		17	45	18	6	0	0	24	5	6	0	3	1	4	1	0	1	0	0	—	0	.400	.440	.533	OF	5	6	1	0	0	1.000
Postseason Totals		48	144	42	14	1	1	61	14	15	1	12	1	23	4	2	3	1	6	.14	0	.292	.356	.424	OF	10	15	3	0	0	1.000

KEVIN McREYNOLDS—Walter Kevin McReynolds—Bats: Right; Throws: Right

Ht: 6'0"; Wt: 205 lbs; Born: 10/16/1959 in Little Rock, Arkansas; Debut: 6/2/1983

LCS		Batting																							Fielding						
Year Tm	Age	G	AB	H	2B	3B	HR	TB	R	RBI	GW	TBB	IBB	SO	HBP	SH	SF	SB	CS	SB%	GDP	Avg	OBP	SLG	Pos	G	PO	A	E	DP	FPct
1984 SD	24	4	10	3	0	0	1	6	2	4	0	3	0	1	0	0	1	0	0	—	0	.300	.429	.600	OF	4	10	0	0	0	1.000
1988 NYN	28	7	28	7	2	0	2	15	4	4	1	3	0	5	0	0	1	2	0	1.00	0	.250	.313	.536	OF	7	19	0	0	0	1.000
LCS Totals		11	38	10	2	0	3	21	6	8	1	6	0	6	0	0	2	2	0	1.00	0	.263	.348	.553	OF	11	29	0	0	0	1.000

LEE MEADOWS—Henry Lee Meadows—Nickname: Specs—Throws: Right; Bats: Left

Ht: 6'0"; Wt: 190 lbs; Born: 7/12/1894 in Oxford, North Carolina; Debut: 4/19/1915; Died: 1/29/1963

World Series		Pitching																										
Year Tm	Age	G	GS	CG	GF	IP	BFP	H	R	ER	HR	SH	SF	HB	TBB	IBB	SO	WP	Bk	W	L	Pct	ShO	Sv-Op	Hld	OAvg	OOBP	ERA
1925 Pit	31	1	1	0	0	8.0	29	6	3	3	1	0	0	1	0	0	4	0	0	0	1	.000	0	0-0	0	.214	.241	3.38
1927 Pit	33	1	1	0	0	6.1	29	7	7	7	0	1	0	0	1	0	6	0	0	0	1	.000	0	0-0	0	.259	.286	9.95
WS Totals		2	2	0	0	14.1	116	13	10	10	1	1	0	1	1	0	10	0	0	0	2	.000	0	0-0	0	.236	.263	6.28

World Series		Batting																							Fielding						
Year Tm	Age	G	AB	H	2B	3B	HR	TB	R	RBI	GW	TBB	IBB	SO	HBP	SH	SF	SB	CS	SB%	GDP	Avg	OBP	SLG	Pos	G	PO	A	E	DP	FPct
1925 Pit	31	1	1	0	0	0	0	0	0	0	0	1	0	1	0	0	0	0	0	—	0	.000	.500	.000	P	1	0	2	0	0	1.000
1927 Pit	33	1	2	0	0	0	0	0	0	0	0	0	0	0	0	0	0	0	0	—	0	.000	.000	.000	P	1	0	1	0	0	1.000
WS Totals		2	3	0	0	0	0	0	0	0	0	1	0	1	0	0	0	0	0	—	0	.000	.250	.000	P	2	0	3	0	0	1.000

DOC MEDICH—George Francis Medich—Throws: Right; Bats: Right

Ht: 6'5"; Wt: 225 lbs; Born: 12/9/1948 in Aliquippa, Pennsylvania; Debut: 9/5/1972

World Series		Pitching																										
Year Tm	Age	G	GS	CG	GF	IP	BFP	H	R	ER	HR	SH	SF	HB	TBB	IBB	SO	WP	Bk	W	L	Pct	ShO	Sv-Op	Hld	OAvg	OOBP	ERA
1982 Mil	33	1	0	0	0	2.0	13	5	6	4	0	0	0	0	1	0	0	2	0	0	0	—	0	0-0	0	.417	.462	18.00

World Series		Batting																							Fielding						
Year Tm	Age	G	AB	H	2B	3B	HR	TB	R	RBI	GW	TBB	IBB	SO	HBP	SH	SF	SB	CS	SB%	GDP	Avg	OBP	SLG	Pos	G	PO	A	E	DP	FPct
1982 Mil	33	1	0	0	0	0	0	0	0	0	0	0	0	0	0	0	0	0	0	—	0	—	—	—	P	1	0	0	0	0	—

JOE MEDWICK (HOF 1968-W)—Joseph Michael Medwick—Nicknames: Ducky, Muscles—Bats: R; Throws: R

Ht: 5'10"; Wt: 187 lbs; Born: 11/24/1911 in Carteret, N.J.; Deb.: 9/2/1932; Died: 3/21/1975

World Series		Batting																							Fielding						
Year Tm	Age	G	AB	H	2B	3B	HR	TB	R	RBI	GW	TBB	IBB	SO	HBP	SH	SF	SB	CS	SB%	GDP	Avg	OBP	SLG	Pos	G	PO	A	E	DP	FPct
1934 StL	22	7	29	11	0	1	1	16	4	5	0	1	0	7	0	0	0	0	0	—	1	.379	.400	.552	OF	7	9	0	0	0	1.000
1941 Bro	29	5	17	4	1	0	0	5	1	0	0	1	0	2	0	0	0	0	0	—	0	.235	.278	.294	OF	5	8	0	0	0	1.000
WS Totals		12	46	15	1	1	1	21	5	5	0	2	0	9	0	0	0	0	0	—	1	.326	.354	.457	OF	12	17	0	0	0	1.000

MIGUEL MEJIA—Bats: Right; Throws: Right

Ht: 6'1"; Wt: 155 lbs; Born: 3/25/1975 in San Pedro de Macoris, Dominican Republic; Debut: 4/4/1996

Division Series		Batting																							Fielding						
Year Tm	Age	G	AB	H	2B	3B	HR	TB	R	RBI	GW	TBB	IBB	SO	HBP	SH	SF	SB	CS	SB%	GDP	Avg	OBP	SLG	Pos	G	PO	A	E	DP	FPct
1996 StL	21	1	0	0	0	0	0	0	0	0	0	0	0	0	0	0	0	0	0	—	0	—	—	—	—						
LCS		**Batting**																							**Fielding**						
Year Tm	Age	G	AB	H	2B	3B	HR	TB	R	RBI	GW	TBB	IBB	SO	HBP	SH	SF	SB	CS	SB%	GDP	Avg	OBP	SLG	Pos	G	PO	A	E	DP	FPct
1996 StL	21	3	1	0	0	0	0	0	1	0	0	0	0	1	0	0	0	0	0	—	0	.000	.000	.000	OF	2	2	0	0	0	1.000
Postseason Totals		4	1	0	0	0	0	0	1	0	0	0	0	1	0	0	0	0	0	—	0	.000	.000	.000	OF	2	2	0	0	0	1.000

CLIFF MELTON
—Clifford George Melton—Nickname: Mountain Music—Throws: Left; Bats: Left
Ht: 6'5"; Wt: 203 lbs; Born: 1/3/1912 in Brevard, North Carolina; Debut: 4/25/1937; Died: 7/28/1986

World Series														Pitching													
Year Tm	Age	G	GS	CG	GF	IP	BFP	H	R	ER	HR	SH	SF	HB	TBB	IBB	SO	WP	Bk	W	L	Pct	ShO	Sv-Op	Hld	OAvg	OOBP	ERA
1937 NYG	25	3	2	0	0	11.0	50	12	6	6	2	0	0	0	6	1	7	1	0	0	2	.000	0	0-0	0	.273	.360	4.91

World Series									Batting														Fielding				
Year Tm	Age	G	AB	H	2B	3B	HR	TB	R	RBI	GW	TBB	IBB	SO	HBP	SH	SF	SB	CS	SB%	GDP	Avg	OBP	SLG	Pos	G	PO	A	E	DP	FPct
1937 NYG	25	3	2	0	0	0	0	0	0	0	0	1	0	1	0	0	0	0	0	—	0	.000	.333	.000	P	3	0	1	0	.000

BOB MELVIN
—Robert Paul Melvin—Bats: Right; Throws: Right
Ht: 6'4"; Wt: 205 lbs; Born: 10/28/1961 in Palo Alto, California; Debut: 5/25/1985

LCS									Batting														Fielding				
Year Tm	Age	G	AB	H	2B	3B	HR	TB	R	RBI	GW	TBB	IBB	SO	HBP	SH	SF	SB	CS	SB%	GDP	Avg	OBP	SLG	Pos	G	PO	A	E	DP	FPct
1987 SF	25	3	7	3	0	0	0	3	0	0	0	1	1	1	0	0	0	0	0	—	1	.429	.500	.429	C	2	14	1	0	0	1.000

MARIO MENDOZA
—Bats: Right; Throws: Right
Ht: 5'11"; Wt: 170 lbs; Born: 12/26/1950 in Chihuahua, Mexico; Debut: 4/26/1974

LCS									Batting														Fielding				
Year Tm	Age	G	AB	H	2B	3B	HR	TB	R	RBI	GW	TBB	IBB	SO	HBP	SH	SF	SB	CS	SB%	GDP	Avg	OBP	SLG	Pos	G	PO	A	E	DP	FPct
1974 Pit	23	3	5	1	0	0	0	1	0	1	0	1	0	0	0	0	0	0	0	—	0	.200	.333	.200	SS	3	4	7	0	0	1.000

RAMIRO MENDOZA
—Throws: Right; Bats: Right
Ht: 6'2"; Wt: 154 lbs; Born: 6/15/1972 in Los Santos, Panama; Debut: 5/25/1996

Division Series														Pitching													
Year Tm	Age	G	GS	CG	GF	IP	BFP	H	R	ER	HR	SH	SF	HB	TBB	IBB	SO	WP	Bk	W	L	Pct	ShO	Sv-Op	Hld	OAvg	OOBP	ERA
1997 NYA	25	2	0	0	1	3.2	13	3	1	1	0	1	0	0	0	0	2	0	0	1	1	.500	0	0-0	0	.250	.250	2.45

Division Series									Batting														Fielding				
Year Tm	Age	G	AB	H	2B	3B	HR	TB	R	RBI	GW	TBB	IBB	SO	HBP	SH	SF	SB	CS	SB%	GDP	Avg	OBP	SLG	Pos	G	PO	A	E	DP	FPct
1997 NYA	25	2	0	0	0	0	0	0	0	0	0	0	0	0	0	0	0	0	0	—	0	—	—	—	P	2	0	1	0	0	1.000

DENIS MENKE
—Denis John Menke—Bats: Right; Throws: Right
Ht: 6'0"; Wt: 185 lbs; Born: 7/21/1940 in Algona, Iowa; Debut: 4/14/1962

LCS									Batting														Fielding				
Year Tm	Age	G	AB	H	2B	3B	HR	TB	R	RBI	GW	TBB	IBB	SO	HBP	SH	SF	SB	CS	SB%	GDP	Avg	OBP	SLG	Pos	G	PO	A	E	DP	FPct
1972 Cin	32	5	16	4	1	0	0	5	1	0	0	4	0	3	0	0	0	0	0	—	1	.250	.400	.313	3B	5	3	11	0	0	1.000
1973 Cin	33	3	9	2	0	0	1	5	1	1	0	1	0	2	0	0	0	0	0	—	0	.222	.300	.556	SS	2	0	0	0	0	
																									3B	2	0	2	0	0	1.000
LCS Totals		8	25	6	1	0	1	10	2	1	0	5	0	5	0	0	0	0	0	—	1	.240	.367	.400	3B	7	3	13	0	0	1.000

World Series									Batting														Fielding				
Year Tm	Age	G	AB	H	2B	3B	HR	TB	R	RBI	GW	TBB	IBB	SO	HBP	SH	SF	SB	CS	SB%	GDP	Avg	OBP	SLG	Pos	G	PO	A	E	DP	FPct
1972 Cin	32	7	24	2	0	0	1	5	1	2	0	2	0	6	0	2	0	0	0	—	2	.083	.154	.208	3B	7	6	23	0	0	1.000
Postseason Totals		15	49	8	1	0	2	15	3	3	0	7	0	11	0	2	0	0	0	—	3	.163	.268	.306	3B	14	9	36	0	0	1.000

ORLANDO MERCED
—Orlando Luis Merced—Bats: Both; Throws: Right
Ht: 5'11"; Wt: 170 lbs; Born: 11/2/1966 in San Juan, Puerto Rico; Debut: 6/27/1990

LCS									Batting														Fielding				
Year Tm	Age	G	AB	H	2B	3B	HR	TB	R	RBI	GW	TBB	IBB	SO	HBP	SH	SF	SB	CS	SB%	GDP	Avg	OBP	SLG	Pos	G	PO	A	E	DP	FPct
1991 Pit	24	3	9	2	0	0	1	5	1	1	0	0	0	1	0	1	0	0	0	—	0	.222	.222	.556	1B	2	13	0	1	0	.929
1992 Pit	25	4	10	1	1	0	0	2	0	2	0	2	0	4	0	0	1	0	1	.00	0	.100	.231	.200	1B	4	27	2	1	3	.967
LCS Totals		7	19	3	1	0	1	7	1	3	0	2	0	5	0	1	1	0	1	.00	0	.158	.227	.368	1B	6	40	2	2	3	.955

KENT MERCKER
—Kent Franklin Mercker—Throws: Left; Bats: Left
Ht: 6'1"; Wt: 175 lbs; Born: 2/1/1968 in Indianapolis, Indiana; Debut: 9/22/1989

Division Series														Pitching													
Year Tm	Age	G	GS	CG	GF	IP	BFP	H	R	ER	HR	SH	SF	HB	TBB	IBB	SO	WP	Bk	W	L	Pct	ShO	Sv-Op	Hld	OAvg	OOBP	ERA
1995 Atl	27	1	0	0	1	0.1	1	0	0	0	0	0	0	0	0	0	0	0	0	0	0	—	0	0-0	0	.000	.000	0.00

LCS														Pitching													
Year Tm	Age	G	GS	CG	GF	IP	BFP	H	R	ER	HR	SH	SF	HB	TBB	IBB	SO	WP	Bk	W	L	Pct	ShO	Sv-Op	Hld	OAvg	OOBP	ERA
1991 Atl	23	1	0	0	0	0.2	4	0	1	1	0	0	0	0	2	0	0	0	0	0	1	.000	0	0-0	0	.000	.500	13.50
1992 Atl	24	2	0	0	1	3.0	11	1	0	0	0	0	0	0	1	0	1	0	0	0	0	—	0	0-0	0	.100	.182	0.00
1993 Atl	25	5	0	0	0	5.0	19	3	1	1	0	0	0	0	2	0	4	0	0	0	0	—	0	0-0	0	.176	.263	1.80
LCS Totals		8	0	0	1	8.2	68	4	2	2	0	0	0	0	5	0	5	0	0	0	1	.000	0	0-0	0	.138	.265	2.08

World Series														Pitching													
Year Tm	Age	G	GS	CG	GF	IP	BFP	H	R	ER	HR	SH	SF	HB	TBB	IBB	SO	WP	Bk	W	L	Pct	ShO	Sv-Op	Hld	OAvg	OOBP	ERA
1991 Atl	23	2	0	0	0	1.0	3	0	0	0	0	0	0	0	0	0	1	0	0	0	0	—	0	0-0	1	.000	.000	0.00
1995 Atl	27	1	0	0	0	2.0	9	1	1	1	0	0	0	0	2	0	2	0	0	0	0	—	0	0-0	0	.143	.333	4.50
WS Totals		3	0	0	0	3.0	24	1	1	1	0	0	0	0	2	0	3	0	0	0	0	—	0	0-0	1	.100	.250	3.00
Postseason Totals		12	0	0	2	12.0	94	5	3	3	0	0	0	0	7	0	8	0	0	0	1	.000	0	0-0	1	.125	.255	2.25

Division Series									Batting														Fielding				
Year Tm	Age	G	AB	H	2B	3B	HR	TB	R	RBI	GW	TBB	IBB	SO	HBP	SH	SF	SB	CS	SB%	GDP	Avg	OBP	SLG	Pos	G	PO	A	E	DP	FPct
1995 Atl	27	1	0	0	0	0	0	0	0	0	0	0	0	0	0	0	0	0	0	—	0	—	—	—	P	1	0	0	0	0	—

LCS									Batting														Fielding				
Year Tm	Age	G	AB	H	2B	3B	HR	TB	R	RBI	GW	TBB	IBB	SO	HBP	SH	SF	SB	CS	SB%	GDP	Avg	OBP	SLG	Pos	G	PO	A	E	DP	FPct
1991 Atl	23	1	0	0	0	0	0	0	0	0	0	0	0	0	0	0	0	0	0	—	0	—	—	—	P	1	0	0	0	0	—
1992 Atl	24	2	0	0	0	0	0	0	0	0	0	0	0	0	0	0	0	0	0	—	0	—	—	—	P	2	0	0	0	0	—
1993 Atl	25	5	0	0	0	0	0	0	0	0	0	0	0	0	0	0	0	0	0	—	0	—	—	—	P	5	0	0	0	0	—
LCS Totals		8	0	0	0	0	0	0	0	0	0	0	0	0	0	0	0	0	0	—	0	—	—	—	P	8	0	0	0	0	—

World Series									Batting														Fielding				
Year Tm	Age	G	AB	H	2B	3B	HR	TB	R	RBI	GW	TBB	IBB	SO	HBP	SH	SF	SB	CS	SB%	GDP	Avg	OBP	SLG	Pos	G	PO	A	E	DP	FPct
1991 Atl	23	2	0	0	0	0	0	0	0	0	0	0	0	0	0	0	0	0	0	—	0	—	—	—	P	2	0	0	0	0	—
1995 Atl	27	1	0	0	0	0	0	0	0	0	0	0	0	0	0	0	0	0	0	—	0	—	—	—	P	1	0	0	0	0	—
WS Totals		3	0	0	0	0	0	0	0	0	0	0	0	0	0	0	0	0	0	—	0	—	—	—	P	3	0	0	0	0	—
Postseason Totals		12	0	0	0	0	0	0	0	0	0	0	0	0	0	0	0	0	0	—	0	—	—	—	P	12	0	0	0	0	—

FRED MERKLE
—Frederick Charles Merkle—Bats: Right; Throws: Right
Ht: 6'1"; Wt: 190 lbs; Born: 12/20/1888 in Watertown, Wisconsin; Debut: 9/21/1907; Died: 3/2/1956

World Series									Batting														Fielding				
Year Tm	Age	G	AB	H	2B	3B	HR	TB	R	RBI	GW	TBB	IBB	SO	HBP	SH	SF	SB	CS	SB%	GDP	Avg	OBP	SLG	Pos	G	PO	A	E	DP	FPct
1911 NYG	22	6	20	3	1	0	0	4	1	1	1	2	0	6	1	0	1	0	1	.00	0	.150	.250	.200	1B	6	62	4	2	0	.971
1912 NYG	23	8	33	9	2	1	0	13	5	3	0	0	0	7	0	1	0	1	1	.50	0	.273	.273	.394	1B	8	83	0	2	2	.976
1913 NYG	24	4	13	3	0	0	1	6	3	3	0	1	0	2	0	0	0	0	0	—	1	.231	.286	.462	1B	4	37	1	2	0	.950
1916 Bro	27	3	4	1	0	0	0	1	0	0	0	2	0	0	0	0	0	0	0	—	0	.250	.500	.250	1B	1	9	1	1	0	.909
1918 ChN	29	6	18	5	0	0	0	5	1	2	0	4	0	3	0	0	0	1	1	.00	0	.278	.409	.278	1B	6	52	9	0	6	1.000
WS Totals		27	88	21	3	1	1	29	10	9	1	9	0	18	1	1	1	1	3	.25	1	.239	.313	.330	1B	25	243	15	7	8	.974

JIM MERRITT
—James Joseph Merritt—Throws: Left; Bats: Left
Ht: 6'3"; Wt: 175 lbs; Born: 12/9/1943 in Altadena, California; Debut: 8/2/1965

LCS														Pitching													
Year Tm	Age	G	GS	CG	GF	IP	BFP	H	R	ER	HR	SH	SF	HB	TBB	IBB	SO	WP	Bk	W	L	Pct	ShO	Sv-Op	Hld	OAvg	OOBP	ERA
1970 Cin	26	1	1	0	0	5.1	20	3	1	1	0	0	0	0	0	0	2	0	0	1	0	1.000	0	0-0	0	.150	.150	1.69

World Series														Pitching													
Year Tm	Age	G	GS	CG	GF	IP	BFP	H	R	ER	HR	SH	SF	HB	TBB	IBB	SO	WP	Bk	W	L	Pct	ShO	Sv-Op	Hld	OAvg	OOBP	ERA
1965 Min	21	2	0	0	0	3.1	11	2	1	1	0	1	0	0	1	0	1	0	0	0	0	—	0	0-0	0	.200	.200	2.70
1970 Cin	26	1	1	0	0	1.2	9	3	4	4	1	0	0	1	0	0	0	0	0	0	1	.000	0	0-0	0	.375	.444	21.60
WS Totals		3	1	0	0	5.0	40	5	5	5	1	1	0	1	1	0	1	0	0	0	1	.000	0	0-0	0	.278	.316	9.00
Postseason Totals		4	2	0	0	10.1	80	8	6	6	1	1	0	1	1	0	3	0	0	1	1	.500	0	0-0	0	.211	.231	5.23

LCS		Batting																							Fielding						
Year Tm	Age	G	AB	H	2B	3B	HR	TB	R	RBI	GW	TBB	IBB	SO	HBP	SH	SF	SB	CS	SB%	GDP	Avg	OBP	SLG	Pos	G	PO	A	E	DP	FPct
1970 Cin	26	1	2	0	0	0	0	0	0	0	0	0	0	2	0	0	0	0	0	—	0	.000	.000	.000	P	1	0	2	0	0	1.000
World Series		Batting																							Fielding						
Year Tm	Age	G	AB	H	2B	3B	HR	TB	R	RBI	GW	TBB	IBB	SO	HBP	SH	SF	SB	CS	SB%	GDP	Avg	OBP	SLG	Pos	G	PO	A	E	DP	FPct
1965 Min	21	2	0	0	0	0	0	0	0	0	0	0	0	0	0	0	0	0	0	—	0	—	—	—	P	2	0	2	0	0	1.000
1970 Cin	26	1	1	0	0	0	0	0	0	0	0	0	0	1	0	0	0	0	0	—	0	.000	.000	.000	P	1	0	0	0	0	—
WS Totals		3	1	0	0	0	0	0	0	0	0	0	0	1	0	0	0	0	0	—	0	.000	.000	.000	P	3	0	2	0	0	1.000
Postseason Totals		4	3	0	0	0	0	0	0	0	0	0	0	3	0	0	0	0	0	—	0	.000	.000	.000	P	4	0	4	0	0	1.000

SAM MERTES—Samuel Blair Mertes—Nickname: Sandow—Bats: Right; Throws: Right

Ht: 5'10"; Wt: 185 lbs; Born: 8/6/1872 in San Francisco, California; Debut: 6/30/1896; Died: 3/11/1945

World Series		Batting																							Fielding						
Year Tm	Age	G	AB	H	2B	3B	HR	TB	R	RBI	GW	TBB	IBB	SO	HBP	SH	SF	SB	CS	SB%	GDP	Avg	OBP	SLG	Pos	G	PO	A	E	DP	FPct
1905 NYG	33	5	17	3	1	0	0	4	2	2	0	2	0	5	0	0	0	0	2	.00	0	.176	.263	.235	OF	5	3	1	0	0	1.000

LENNIE MERULLO—Leonard Richard Merullo—Bats: Right; Throws: Right

Ht: 5'11"; Wt: 166 lbs; Born: 5/5/1917 in Boston, Massachusetts; Debut: 9/12/1941

World Series		Batting																							Fielding						
Year Tm	Age	G	AB	H	2B	3B	HR	TB	R	RBI	GW	TBB	IBB	SO	HBP	SH	SF	SB	CS	SB%	GDP	Avg	OBP	SLG	Pos	G	PO	A	E	DP	FPct
1945 ChN	28	3	2	0	0	0	0	0	0	0	0	0	0	1	0	0	0	0	0	—	0	.000	.000	.000	SS	3	4	2	0	2	1.000

JOSE MESA—Jose Ramon Nova Mesa—Throws: Right; Bats: Right

Ht: 6'3"; Wt: 170 lbs; Born: 5/22/1966 in Pueblo Viejo, Dominican Republic; Debut: 9/10/1987

Division Series		Pitching																										
Year Tm	Age	G	GS	CG	GF	IP	BFP	H	R	ER	HR	SH	SF	HB	TBB	IBB	SO	WP	Bk	W	L	Pct	ShO	Sv-Op	Hld	OAvg	OOBP	ERA
1995 Cle	29	2	0	0	1	2.0	7	0	0	0	0	0	0	0	2	0	0	0	0	0	0	—	0	0- 0	0	.000	.286	0.00
1996 Cle	30	2	0	0	1	4.2	21	8	2	2	1	0	0	0	0	0	7	0	0	0	1	.000	0	0- 1	0	.381	.381	3.86
1997 Cle	31	2	0	0	2	3.1	17	5	1	1	1	0	0	1	1	0	2	0	0	0	0	—	0	1- 1	0	.333	.412	2.70
DS Totals		6	0	0	4	10.0	90	13	3	3	2	0	0	1	3	0	9	0	0	0	1	.000	0	1-2	0	.317	.378	2.70
LCS		Pitching																										
Year Tm	Age	G	GS	CG	GF	IP	BFP	H	R	ER	HR	SH	SF	HB	TBB	IBB	SO	WP	Bk	W	L	Pct	ShO	Sv-Op	Hld	OAvg	OOBP	ERA
1995 Cle	29	4	0	0	3	4.0	15	3	1	1	1	0	0	0	1	0	1	0	0	0	0	—	0	1- 1	0	.214	.267	2.25
1997 Cle	31	4	0	0	3	5.1	24	5	2	2	0	0	0	0	3	1	5	0	0	1	0	1.000	0	2- 4	0	.238	.333	3.38
LCS Totals		8	0	0	6	9.1	78	8	3	3	1	0	0	0	4	1	6	0	0	1	0	1.000	0	3-5	0	.229	.308	2.89
World Series		Pitching																										
Year Tm	Age	G	GS	CG	GF	IP	BFP	H	R	ER	HR	SH	SF	HB	TBB	IBB	SO	WP	Bk	W	L	Pct	ShO	Sv-Op	Hld	OAvg	OOBP	ERA
1995 Cle	29	2	0	0	2	4.0	17	5	2	2	1	1	0	0	1	0	4	0	0	1	0	1.000	0	1- 1	0	.333	.375	4.50
1997 Cle	31	5	0	0	4	5.0	26	10	3	3	0	0	1	0	1	0	5	1	0	0	0	—	0	1- 2	0	.417	.423	5.40
WS Totals		7	0	0	6	9.0	86	15	5	5	1	1	1	0	2	0	9	1	0	1	0	1.000	0	2-3	0	.385	.405	5.00
Postseason Totals		21	0	0	16	28.1	254	36	11	11	4	1	1	1	9	1	24	1	0	2	1	.667	0	6-10	0	.313	.365	3.49

Division Series		Batting																							Fielding						
Year Tm	Age	G	AB	H	2B	3B	HR	TB	R	RBI	GW	TBB	IBB	SO	HBP	SH	SF	SB	CS	SB%	GDP	Avg	OBP	SLG	Pos	G	PO	A	E	DP	FPct
1995 Cle	29	2	0	0	0	0	0	0	0	0	0	0	0	0	0	0	0	0	0	—	0	—	—	—	P	2	0	0	0	0	—
1996 Cle	30	2	0	0	0	0	0	0	0	0	0	0	0	0	0	0	0	0	0	—	0	—	—	—	P	2	0	0	0	0	—
1997 Cle	31	2	0	0	0	0	0	0	0	0	0	0	0	0	0	0	0	0	0	—	0	—	—	—	P	2	0	1	0	0	1.000
DS Totals		6	0	0	0	0	0	0	0	0	0	0	0	0	0	0	0	0	0	—	0	—	—	—	P	6	0	1	0	0	1.000
LCS		Batting																							Fielding						
Year Tm	Age	G	AB	H	2B	3B	HR	TB	R	RBI	GW	TBB	IBB	SO	HBP	SH	SF	SB	CS	SB%	GDP	Avg	OBP	SLG	Pos	G	PO	A	E	DP	FPct
1995 Cle	29	4	0	0	0	0	0	0	0	0	0	0	0	0	0	0	0	0	0	—	0	—	—	—	P	4	1	2	0	1	1.000
1997 Cle	31	4	0	0	0	0	0	0	0	0	0	0	0	0	0	0	0	0	0	—	0	—	—	—	P	4	0	1	0	0	1.000
LCS Totals		8	0	0	0	0	0	0	0	0	0	0	0	0	0	0	0	0	0	—	0	—	—	—	P	8	1	3	0	1	1.000
World Series		Batting																							Fielding						
Year Tm	Age	G	AB	H	2B	3B	HR	TB	R	RBI	GW	TBB	IBB	SO	HBP	SH	SF	SB	CS	SB%	GDP	Avg	OBP	SLG	Pos	G	PO	A	E	DP	FPct
1995 Cle	29	2	0	0	0	0	0	0	0	0	0	0	0	0	0	0	0	0	0	—	0	—	—	—	P	2	0	0	0	0	—
1997 Cle	31	5	0	0	0	0	0	0	0	0	0	0	0	0	0	0	0	0	0	—	0	—	—	—	P	5	1	1	0	0	1.000
WS Totals		7	0	0	0	0	0	0	0	0	0	0	0	0	0	0	0	0	0	—	0	—	—	—	P	7	1	1	0	0	1.000
Postseason Totals		21	0	0	0	0	0	0	0	0	0	0	0	0	0	0	0	0	0	—	0	—	—	—	P	21	2	5	0	1	1.000

ANDY MESSERSMITH—John Alexander Messersmith—Throws: Right; Bats: Right

Ht: 6'1"; Wt: 200 lbs; Born: 8/6/1945 in Toms River, New Jersey; Debut: 7/4/1968

LCS		Pitching																										
Year Tm	Age	G	GS	CG	GF	IP	BFP	H	R	ER	HR	SH	SF	HB	TBB	IBB	SO	WP	Bk	W	L	Pct	ShO	Sv-Op	Hld	OAvg	OOBP	ERA
1974 LA	29	1	1	0	0	7.0	31	8	2	2	0	1	0	1	3	0	0	0	0	1	0	1.000	0	0- 0	0	.308	.400	2.57
World Series		Pitching																										
Year Tm	Age	G	GS	CG	GF	IP	BFP	H	R	ER	HR	SH	SF	HB	TBB	IBB	SO	WP	Bk	W	L	Pct	ShO	Sv-Op	Hld	OAvg	OOBP	ERA
1974 LA	29	2	2	0	0	14.0	58	11	8	7	2	5	0	1	7	1	12	1	0	0	2	.000	0	0- 0	0	.244	.358	4.50
Postseason Totals		3	3	0	0	21.0	178	19	10	9	2	6	0	2	10	1	12	1	0	1	2	.333	0	0-0	0	.268	.373	3.86

LCS		Batting																							Fielding						
Year Tm	Age	G	AB	H	2B	3B	HR	TB	R	RBI	GW	TBB	IBB	SO	HBP	SH	SF	SB	CS	SB%	GDP	Avg	OBP	SLG	Pos	G	PO	A	E	DP	FPct
1974 LA	29	1	3	0	0	0	0	0	0	0	0	0	0	1	0	0	0	0	0	—	0	.000	.000	.000	P	1	1	2	0	1	1.000
World Series		Batting																							Fielding						
Year Tm	Age	G	AB	H	2B	3B	HR	TB	R	RBI	GW	TBB	IBB	SO	HBP	SH	SF	SB	CS	SB%	GDP	Avg	OBP	SLG	Pos	G	PO	A	E	DP	FPct
1974 LA	29	2	4	2	0	0	0	2	0	0	0	0	0	2	0	1	0	0	0	—	0	.500	.500	.500	P	2	1	4	1	0	.833
Postseason Totals		3	7	2	0	0	0	2	0	0	0	0	0	3	0	1	0	0	0	—	0	.286	.286	.286	P	3	2	6	1	1	.889

BUD METHENY—Arthur Beauregard Metheny—Bats: Left; Throws: Left

Ht: 5'11"; Wt: 190 lbs; Born: 6/1/1915 in St. Louis, Missouri; Debut: 4/27/1943

World Series		Batting																							Fielding						
Year Tm	Age	G	AB	H	2B	3B	HR	TB	R	RBI	GW	TBB	IBB	SO	HBP	SH	SF	SB	CS	SB%	GDP	Avg	OBP	SLG	Pos	G	PO	A	E	DP	FPct
1943 NYA	28	2	8	1	0	0	0	1	0	0	0	0	0	2	0	0	0	0	0	—	0	.125	.125	.125	OF	2	3	0	0	0	1.000

CATFISH METKOVICH—George Michael Metkovich—Bats: Left; Throws: Left

Ht: 6'1"; Wt: 185 lbs; Born: 10/8/1920 in Angel's Camp, California; Debut: 7/16/1943; Died: 5/17/1995

World Series		Batting																							Fielding						
Year Tm	Age	G	AB	H	2B	3B	HR	TB	R	RBI	GW	TBB	IBB	SO	HBP	SH	SF	SB	CS	SB%	GDP	Avg	OBP	SLG	Pos	G	PO	A	E	DP	FPct
1946 Bos	25	2	2	1	1	0	0	2	1	0	0	0	0	0	0	0	0	0	0	—	0	.500	.500	1.000	—						

BOB MEUSEL—Robert William Meusel—Nickname: Long Bob—Bats: Right; Throws: Right

Ht: 6'3"; Wt: 190 lbs; Born: 7/19/1896 in San Jose, California; Debut: 4/14/1920; Died: 11/28/1977

World Series		Batting																							Fielding						
Year Tm	Age	G	AB	H	2B	3B	HR	TB	R	RBI	GW	TBB	IBB	SO	HBP	SH	SF	SB	CS	SB%	GDP	Avg	OBP	SLG	Pos	G	PO	A	E	DP	FPct
1921 NYA	25	8	30	6	2	0	0	8	3	3	1	2	0	5	0	0	0	1	2	.33	1	.200	.250	.267	OF	8	10	2	0	0	1.000
1922 NYA	26	5	20	6	1	0	0	7	2	2	0	1	0	3	0	0	0	1	0	1.00	0	.300	.333	.350	OF	5	7	1	0	0	1.000
1923 NYA	27	6	26	7	1	2	0	12	1	8	2	0	0	3	0	0	0	0	0	—	2	.269	.269	.462	OF	6	14	0	0	0	1.000
1926 NYA	30	7	21	5	1	1	0	8	3	0	0	6	0	1	0	2	1	0	0	—	0	.238	.393	.381	OF	7	13	0	1	0	.929
1927 NYA	31	4	17	2	0	0	0	2	1	1	1	1	0	7	0	0	0	1	0	1.00	0	.118	.167	.118	OF	4	8	0	1	0	.889
1928 NYA	32	4	15	3	1	0	1	7	5	3	0	2	0	5	0	0	0	2	0	1.00	0	.200	.294	.467	OF	4	7	0	0	0	1.000
WS Totals		34	129	29	6	3	1	44	15	17	4	12	0	24	0	2	1	5	2	.71	3	.225	.289	.341	OF	34	59	3	2	0	.969

IRISH MEUSEL—Emil Frederick Meusel—Bats: Right; Throws: Right

Ht: 5'11"; Wt: 178 lbs; Born: 6/9/1893 in Oakland, California; Debut: 10/1/1914; Died: 3/1/1963

World Series		Batting																							Fielding						
Year Tm	Age	G	AB	H	2B	3B	HR	TB	R	RBI	GW	TBB	IBB	SO	HBP	SH	SF	SB	CS	SB%	GDP	Avg	OBP	SLG	Pos	G	PO	A	E	DP	FPct
1921 NYG	28	8	29	10	2	1	1	17	4	7	1	2	0	3	0	0	0	1	2	.33	0	.345	.387	.586	OF	8	8	2	0	0	1.000
1922 NYG	29	5	20	5	0	0	1	8	3	7	1	0	0	1	0	0	0	0	0	—	0	.250	.250	.400	OF	5	3	0	0	0	1.000
1923 NYG	30	6	25	7	1	1	1	13	3	2	0	0	0	2	0	0	0	0	0	—	0	.280	.280	.520	OF	6	13	0	0	0	1.000
1924 NYG	31	4	13	2	0	0	0	2	0	1	0	2	0	0	0	0	1	0	0	—	1	.154	.250	.154	OF	4	5	0	1	0	.833
WS Totals		23	87	24	3	2	3	40	10	17	2	4	0	6	0	0	1	1	2	.33	1	.276	.304	.460	OF	23	29	2	1	0	.969

RUSS MEYER—Russell Charles Meyer—Nickname: The Mad Monk—Throws: Right; Bats: Both

Ht: 6'1"; Wt: 175 lbs; Born: 10/25/1923 in Peru, Illinois; Debut: 9/13/1946; Died: 11/16/1997

World Series			Pitching																										
Year	Tm	Age	G	GS	CG	GF	IP	BFP	H	R	ER	HR	SH	SF	HB	TBB	IBB	SO	WP	Bk	W	L	Pct	ShO	Sv-Op	Hld	OAvg	OOBP	ERA
1950	Phi	26	2	0	0	2	1.2	9	4	1	1	0	1	0	0	0	0	1	0	0	0	1	.000	0	0-0	0	.500	.500	5.40
1953	Bro	29	1	0	0	0	4.1	24	8	4	3	2	0	0	0	4	1	5	0	0	0	0	—	0	0-0	0	.400	.500	6.23
1955	Bro	31	1	0	0	0	5.2	22	4	0	0	0	0	0	0	2	0	4	0	0	0	0	—	0	0-0	0	.200	.273	0.00
WS Totals			4	0	0	2	11.2	110	16	5	4	2	1	0	0	6	1	10	0	0	0	1	.000	0	0-0	0	.333	.407	3.09

World Series			Batting																						Fielding					
Year	Tm	Age	G	AB	H	2B	3B	HR	TB	R	RBI	GW	TBB	IBB	SO	HBP	SH	SF	SB	CS	SB%	GDP	Avg	OBP	SLG	Pos	G	PO	A	E	DP	FPct
1950	Phi	26	2	0	0	0	0	0	0	0	0	0	0	0	0	0	0	0	0	0	—	0	—	—	—	P	2	0	1	0	0	1.000
1953	Bro	29	1	1	0	0	0	0	0	0	0	0	0	0	1	0	0	0	0	0	—	0	.000	.000	.000	P	1	0	1	0	0	1.000
1955	Bro	31	1	2	0	0	0	0	0	0	0	0	0	0	1	0	0	0	0	0	—	0	.000	.000	.000	P	1	0	1	0	0	1.000
WS Totals			4	3	0	0	0	0	0	0	0	0	0	0	2	0	0	0	0	0	—	0	.000	.000	.000	P	4	0	3	0	0	1.000

CHIEF MEYERS—John Tortes Meyers—Bats: Right; Throws: Right

Ht: 5'11"; Wt: 194 lbs; Born: 7/29/1880 in Riverside, California; Debut: 4/16/1909; Died: 7/25/1971

World Series			Batting																						Fielding					
Year	Tm	Age	G	AB	H	2B	3B	HR	TB	R	RBI	GW	TBB	IBB	SO	HBP	SH	SF	SB	CS	SB%	GDP	Avg	OBP	SLG	Pos	G	PO	A	E	DP	FPct
1911	NYG	31	6	20	6	2	0	0	8	2	2	0	0	0	3	0	0	1	0	1	.00	0	.300	.286	.400	C	6	37	12	0	1	1.000
1912	NYG	32	8	28	10	0	1	0	12	2	3	0	2	1	3	1	1	0	1	1	.50	0	.357	.419	.429	C	8	42	4	1	1	.979
1913	NYG	33	1	4	0	0	0	0	0	0	0	0	0	0	0	0	0	0	0	0	—	0	.000	.000	.000	C	1	4	1	0	0	1.000
1916	Bro	36	3	10	2	0	1	0	4	0	0	0	1	0	0	0	0	0	0	0	—	0	.200	.273	.400	C	3	21	8	0	0	1.000
WS Totals			18	62	18	2	2	0	24	4	5	0	3	1	6	1	1	1	1	2	.33	0	.290	.328	.387	C	18	104	25	1	2	.992

ED MIERKOWICZ—Edward Frank Mierkowicz—Nicknames: Butch, Mouse—Bats: Right; Throws: Right

Ht: 6'4"; Wt: 205 lbs; Born: 3/6/1924 in Wyandotte, Michigan; Debut: 8/31/1945

World Series			Batting																						Fielding					
Year	Tm	Age	G	AB	H	2B	3B	HR	TB	R	RBI	GW	TBB	IBB	SO	HBP	SH	SF	SB	CS	SB%	GDP	Avg	OBP	SLG	Pos	G	PO	A	E	DP	FPct
1945	Det	21	1	0	0	0	0	0	0	0	0	0	0	0	0	0	0	0	0	0	—	0	—	—	—	OF	1	0	0	0	0	—

PETE MIKKELSEN—Peter James Mikkelsen—Throws: Right; Bats: Right

Ht: 6'2"; Wt: 210 lbs; Born: 10/25/1939 in Staten Island, New York; Debut: 4/17/1964

World Series			Pitching																										
Year	Tm	Age	G	GS	CG	GF	IP	BFP	H	R	ER	HR	SH	SF	HB	TBB	IBB	SO	WP	Bk	W	L	Pct	ShO	Sv-Op	Hld	OAvg	OOBP	ERA
1964	NYA	24	4	0	0	3	4.2	20	4	4	3	1	0	0	0	2	0	4	0	0	0	1	.000	0	0-0	0	.222	.300	5.79

World Series			Batting																						Fielding					
Year	Tm	Age	G	AB	H	2B	3B	HR	TB	R	RBI	GW	TBB	IBB	SO	HBP	SH	SF	SB	CS	SB%	GDP	Avg	OBP	SLG	Pos	G	PO	A	E	DP	FPct
1964	NYA	24	4	0	0	0	0	0	0	0	0	0	0	0	0	0	0	0	0	0	—	0	—	—	—	P	4	1	1	0	0	1.000

EDDIE MIKSIS—Edward Thomas Miksis—Bats: Right; Throws: Right

Ht: 6'0"; Wt: 185 lbs; Born: 9/11/1926 in Burlington, New Jersey; Debut: 6/17/1944

World Series			Batting																						Fielding					
Year	Tm	Age	G	AB	H	2B	3B	HR	TB	R	RBI	GW	TBB	IBB	SO	HBP	SH	SF	SB	CS	SB%	GDP	Avg	OBP	SLG	Pos	G	PO	A	E	DP	FPct
1947	Bro	21	5	4	1	0	0	0	1	1	0	0	0	0	1	0	0	0	0	0	—	0	.250	.250	.250	2B	1	1	1	1	1	.667
																										OF	2	2	0	0	0	1.000
1949	Bro	23	3	7	2	1	0	0	3	0	0	0	0	0	1	0	0	0	0	0	—	0	.286	.286	.429	3B	2	3	3	1	1	.857
WS Totals			8	11	3	1	0	0	4	1	0	0	0	0	2	0	0	0	0	0	—	0	.273	.273	.364	3B	2	3	3	1	1	.857

LARRY MILBOURNE—Lawrence William Milbourne—Bats: Both; Throws: Right

Ht: 6'0"; Wt: 161 lbs; Born: 2/14/1951 in Port Norris, New Jersey; Debut: 4/6/1974

Division Series			Batting																						Fielding					
Year	Tm	Age	G	AB	H	2B	3B	HR	TB	R	RBI	GW	TBB	IBB	SO	HBP	SH	SF	SB	CS	SB%	GDP	Avg	OBP	SLG	Pos	G	PO	A	E	DP	FPct
1981	NYA	30	5	19	6	1	0	0	7	4	0	0	0	0	1	0	0	0	0	0	—	0	.316	.316	.368	SS	5	5	14	0	1	1.000
LCS			Batting																						Fielding					
Year	Tm	Age	G	AB	H	2B	3B	HR	TB	R	RBI	GW	TBB	IBB	SO	HBP	SH	SF	SB	CS	SB%	GDP	Avg	OBP	SLG	Pos	G	PO	A	E	DP	FPct
1981	NYA	30	3	13	6	0	0	0	6	4	1	0	0	0	0	0	1	0	0	0	—	0	.462	.462	.462	SS	3	2	7	0	2	1.000
World Series			Batting																						Fielding					
Year	Tm	Age	G	AB	H	2B	3B	HR	TB	R	RBI	GW	TBB	IBB	SO	HBP	SH	SF	SB	CS	SB%	GDP	Avg	OBP	SLG	Pos	G	PO	A	E	DP	FPct
1981	NYA	30	6	20	5	2	0	0	7	2	3	1	4	3	0	0	1	0	0	0	—	2	.250	.375	.350	SS	6	5	16	2	1	.913
Postseason Totals			14	52	17	3	0	0	20	10	4	1	4	3	1	0	2	0	0	0	—	2	.327	.375	.385	SS	14	12	37	2	4	.961

JOHNNY MILJUS—John Kenneth Miljus—Nickname: Big Sub—Throws: Right; Bats: Right

Ht: 6'1"; Wt: 178 lbs; Born: 6/30/1895 in Pittsburgh, Pennsylvania; Debut: 10/2/1915; Died: 2/11/1976

World Series			Pitching																										
Year	Tm	Age	G	GS	CG	GF	IP	BFP	H	R	ER	HR	SH	SF	HB	TBB	IBB	SO	WP	Bk	W	L	Pct	ShO	Sv-Op	Hld	OAvg	OOBP	ERA
1927	Pit	32	2	0	0	2	6.2	25	4	1	1	0	1	0	0	4	1	6	2	0	0	1	.000	0	0-0	0	.200	.333	1.35

World Series			Batting																						Fielding					
Year	Tm	Age	G	AB	H	2B	3B	HR	TB	R	RBI	GW	TBB	IBB	SO	HBP	SH	SF	SB	CS	SB%	GDP	Avg	OBP	SLG	Pos	G	PO	A	E	DP	FPct
1927	Pit	32	2	2	0	0	0	0	0	0	0	0	0	0	2	0	0	0	0	0	—	0	.000	.000	.000	P	2	1	2	0	0	1.000

FELIX MILLAN—Felix Bernardo Millan—Nickname: The Cat—Bats: Right; Throws: Right

Ht: 5'11"; Wt: 172 lbs; Born: 8/21/1943 in Yabucoa, Puerto Rico; Debut: 6/2/1966

LCS			Batting																						Fielding					
Year	Tm	Age	G	AB	H	2B	3B	HR	TB	R	RBI	GW	TBB	IBB	SO	HBP	SH	SF	SB	CS	SB%	GDP	Avg	OBP	SLG	Pos	G	PO	A	E	DP	FPct
1969	Atl	26	3	12	4	1	0	0	5	2	0	0	3	0	0	0	0	0	0	0	—	0	.333	.467	.417	2B	3	3	8	1	1	.917
1973	NYN	30	5	19	6	0	0	0	6	5	2	0	2	0	1	0	2	0	0	0	—	0	.316	.381	.316	2B	5	10	11	0	3	1.000
LCS Totals			8	31	10	1	0	0	11	7	2	0	5	0	1	0	2	0	0	0	—	0	.323	.417	.355	2B	8	13	19	1	4	.970
World Series			Batting																						Fielding					
Year	Tm	Age	G	AB	H	2B	3B	HR	TB	R	RBI	GW	TBB	IBB	SO	HBP	SH	SF	SB	CS	SB%	GDP	Avg	OBP	SLG	Pos	G	PO	A	E	DP	FPct
1973	NYN	30	7	32	6	1	1	0	9	3	1	0	1	1	1	0	1	0	0	0	—	0	.188	.212	.281	2B	7	17	13	3	3	.909
Postseason Totals			15	63	16	2	1	0	20	10	3	0	6	1	2	0	3	0	0	0	—	0	.254	.319	.317	2B	15	30	32	4	7	.939

BING MILLER—Edmund John Miller—Bats: Right; Throws: Right

Ht: 6'0"; Wt: 185 lbs; Born: 8/30/1894 in Vinton, Iowa; Debut: 4/16/1921; Died: 5/7/1966

World Series			Batting																						Fielding					
Year	Tm	Age	G	AB	H	2B	3B	HR	TB	R	RBI	GW	TBB	IBB	SO	HBP	SH	SF	SB	CS	SB%	GDP	Avg	OBP	SLG	Pos	G	PO	A	E	DP	FPct
1929	Phi	35	5	19	7	1	0	0	8	1	4	1	0	0	2	1	1	0	0	2	.00	0	.368	.400	.421	OF	5	13	0	1	0	.929
1930	Phi	36	6	21	3	2	0	0	5	0	3	0	0	0	4	0	1	1	0	0	—	0	.143	.136	.238	OF	6	13	0	0	0	1.000
1931	Phi	37	7	26	7	1	0	0	8	3	1	0	0	0	4	1	1	0	0	0	—	0	.269	.296	.308	OF	7	13	0	0	0	1.000
WS Totals			18	66	17	4	0	0	21	4	8	1	0	0	10	2	3	1	0	2	.00	0	.258	.275	.318	OF	18	39	0	1	0	.975

BOB MILLER—Robert John Miller—Throws: Right; Bats: Right

Ht: 6'3"; Wt: 190 lbs; Born: 6/16/1926 in Detroit, Michigan; Debut: 9/16/1949

World Series			Pitching																										
Year	Tm	Age	G	GS	CG	GF	IP	BFP	H	R	ER	HR	SH	SF	HB	TBB	IBB	SO	WP	Bk	W	L	Pct	ShO	Sv-Op	Hld	OAvg	OOBP	ERA
1950	Phi	24	1	1	0	0	0.1	4	2	2	1	0	0	0	0	0	0	0	1	0	0	1	.000	0	0-0	0	.500	.500	27.00

World Series			Batting																						Fielding					
Year	Tm	Age	G	AB	H	2B	3B	HR	TB	R	RBI	GW	TBB	IBB	SO	HBP	SH	SF	SB	CS	SB%	GDP	Avg	OBP	SLG	Pos	G	PO	A	E	DP	FPct
1950	Phi	24	1	0	0	0	0	0	0	0	0	0	0	0	0	0	0	0	0	0	—	0	—	—	—	P	1	0	0	0	0	—

BOB MILLER—Robert Lane Miller—Throws: Right; Bats: Right

Ht: 6'1"; Wt: 180 lbs; Born: 2/18/1939 in St. Louis, Missouri; Debut: 6/26/1957; Died: 8/6/1993

LCS — Pitching

Year Tm	Age	G	GS	CG	GF	IP	BFP	H	R	ER	HR	SH	SF	HB	TBB	IBB	SO	WP	Bk	W	L	Pct	ShO	Sv-Op	Hld	OAvg	OOBP	ERA
1969 Min	30	1	1	0	0	1.2	10	5	3	1	0	0	0	0	0	0	0	0	0	0	1	.000	0	0- 0	0	.500	.500	5.40
1971 Pit	32	1	0	0	0	3.0	14	3	2	2	1	0	0	0	3	0	3	0	0	0	0	—	0	0- 0	1	.273	.429	6.00
1972 Pit	33	1	0	0	1	1.0	3	0	0	0	0	0	0	0	0	0	1	0	0	0	0	—	0	0- 0	0	.000	.000	0.00
LCS Totals		3	1	0	1	5.2	54	8	5	3	1	0	0	0	3	0	4	0	0	0	1	.000	0	0-0	1	.333	.407	4.76

World Series — Pitching

Year Tm	Age	G	GS	CG	GF	IP	BFP	H	R	ER	HR	SH	SF	HB	TBB	IBB	SO	WP	Bk	W	L	Pct	ShO	Sv-Op	Hld	OAvg	OOBP	ERA
1965 LA	26	2	0	0	2	1.1	4	0	0	0	0	0	0	0	0	0	0	0	0	0	0	—	0	0- 0	0	.000	.000	0.00
1966 LA	27	1	0	0	0	3.0	13	2	0	0	0	0	0	0	2	1	1	0	0	0	0	—	0	0- 0	0	.182	.308	0.00
1971 Pit	32	3	0	0	2	4.2	22	7	2	2	0	0	1	0	1	0	2	0	0	0	1	.000	0	0- 0	0	.350	.364	3.86
WS Totals		6	0	0	4	9.0	78	9	2	2	0	0	1	0	3	1	3	0	0	0	1	.000	0	0-0	0	.257	.308	2.00
Postseason Totals		9	1	0	5	14.2	132	17	7	5	1	0	1	0	6	1	7	0	0	0	2	.000	0	0-0	1	.288	.348	3.07

LCS — Batting / Fielding

Year Tm	Age	G	AB	H	2B	3B	HR	TB	R	RBI	GW	TBB	IBB	SO	HBP	SH	SF	SB	CS	SB%	GDP	Avg	OBP	SLG	Pos	G	PO	A	E	DP	FPct
1969 Min	30	1	0	0	0	0	0	0	0	0	0	0	0	0	0	0	0	0	0	—	0	—	—	—	P	1	0	0	0	0	—
1971 Pit	32	1	1	0	0	0	0	0	0	0	0	0	0	0	0	0	0	0	0	—	0	.000	.000	.000	P	1	1	0	0	0	1.000
1972 Pit	33	1	0	0	0	0	0	0	0	0	0	0	0	0	0	0	0	0	0	—	0	—	—	—	P	1	0	0	0	0	—
LCS Totals		3	1	0	0	0	0	0	0	0	0	0	0	0	0	0	0	0	0	—	0	.000	.000	.000	P	3	1	0	0	0	1.000

World Series — Batting / Fielding

Year Tm	Age	G	AB	H	2B	3B	HR	TB	R	RBI	GW	TBB	IBB	SO	HBP	SH	SF	SB	CS	SB%	GDP	Avg	OBP	SLG	Pos	G	PO	A	E	DP	FPct
1965 LA	26	2	0	0	0	0	0	0	0	0	0	0	0	0	0	0	0	0	0	—	0	—	—	—	P	2	0	0	0	0	—
1966 LA	27	1	0	0	0	0	0	0	0	0	0	0	0	0	0	0	0	0	0	—	0	—	—	—	P	1	0	1	0	0	1.000
1971 Pit	32	3	0	0	0	0	0	0	0	0	0	0	0	0	0	0	0	0	0	—	0	—	—	—	P	3	1	1	0	0	1.000
WS Totals		6	0	0	0	0	0	0	0	0	0	0	0	0	0	0	0	0	0	—	0	—	—	—	P	6	1	2	0	0	1.000
Postseason Totals		9	1	0	0	0	0	0	0	0	0	0	0	0	0	0	0	0	0	—	0	.000	.000	.000	P	9	2	2	0	0	1.000

DOTS MILLER—John Barney Miller—Bats: Right; Throws: Right

Ht: 5'11"; Wt: 170 lbs; Born: 9/9/1886 in Kearny, New Jersey; Debut: 4/16/1909; Died: 9/5/1923

World Series — Batting / Fielding

Year Tm	Age	G	AB	H	2B	3B	HR	TB	R	RBI	GW	TBB	IBB	SO	HBP	SH	SF	SB	CS	SB%	GDP	Avg	OBP	SLG	Pos	G	PO	A	E	DP	FPct
1909 Pit	23	7	28	7	1	0	0	8	2	4	0	2	0	5	0	0	0	3	0	1.00	0	.250	.300	.286	2B	7	16	14	2	1	.938

ELMER MILLER—Bats: Right; Throws: Right

Ht: 6'0"; Wt: 175 lbs; Born: 7/28/1890 in Sandusky, Ohio; Debut: 4/26/1912; Died: 11/28/1944

World Series — Batting / Fielding

Year Tm	Age	G	AB	H	2B	3B	HR	TB	R	RBI	GW	TBB	IBB	SO	HBP	SH	SF	SB	CS	SB%	GDP	Avg	OBP	SLG	Pos	G	PO	A	E	DP	FPct
1921 NYA	31	8	31	5	1	0	0	6	3	2	0	2	0	5	0	0	1	0	0	—	0	.161	.206	.194	OF	8	10	1	0	0	1.000

HACK MILLER—Lawrence H. Miller—Bats: Right; Throws: Right

Ht: 5'9"; Wt: 195 lbs; Born: 1/1/1894 in New York, New York; Debut: 9/22/1916; Died: 9/17/1971

World Series — Batting / Fielding

Year Tm	Age	G	AB	H	2B	3B	HR	TB	R	RBI	GW	TBB	IBB	SO	HBP	SH	SF	SB	CS	SB%	GDP	Avg	OBP	SLG	Pos	G	PO	A	E	DP	FPct
1918 Bos	24	1	1	0	0	0	0	0	0	0	0	0	0	0	0	0	0	0	0	—	0	.000	.000	.000	—						

OTTO MILLER—Lowell Otto Miller—Nickname: Moonie—Bats: Right; Throws: Right

Ht: 6'0"; Wt: 196 lbs; Born: 6/1/1889 in Minden, Nebraska; Debut: 7/16/1910; Died: 3/29/1962

World Series — Batting / Fielding

Year Tm	Age	G	AB	H	2B	3B	HR	TB	R	RBI	GW	TBB	IBB	SO	HBP	SH	SF	SB	CS	SB%	GDP	Avg	OBP	SLG	Pos	G	PO	A	E	DP	FPct
1916 Bro	27	2	8	1	0	0	0	1	0	0	0	0	0	1	0	1	0	0	0	—	0	.125	.125	.125	C	2	8	3	0	1	1.000
1920 Bro	31	6	14	2	0	0	0	2	0	0	0	1	0	2	0	1	0	0	0	—	2	.143	.200	.143	C	6	17	6	0	0	1.000
WS Totals		8	22	3	0	0	0	3	0	0	0	1	0	3	0	2	0	0	0	—	2	.136	.174	.136	C	8	25	9	0	1	1.000

RALPH MILLER—Ralph Joseph Miller—Bats: Right; Throws: Right

Ht: 6'0"; Wt: 190 lbs; Born: 2/29/1896 in Fort Wayne, Indiana; Debut: 4/14/1920; Died: 3/18/1939

World Series — Batting / Fielding

Year Tm	Age	G	AB	H	2B	3B	HR	TB	R	RBI	GW	TBB	IBB	SO	HBP	SH	SF	SB	CS	SB%	GDP	Avg	OBP	SLG	Pos	G	PO	A	E	DP	FPct
1924 Was	28	4	11	2	0	0	0	2	0	2	0	1	0	0	0	0	1	0	0	—	1	.182	.231	.182	3B	4	6	4	2	0	.833

RICK MILLER—Richard Alan Miller—Bats: Left; Throws: Left

Ht: 6'0"; Wt: 175 lbs; Born: 4/19/1948 in Grand Rapids, Michigan; Debut: 9/4/1971

LCS — Batting / Fielding

Year Tm	Age	G	AB	H	2B	3B	HR	TB	R	RBI	GW	TBB	IBB	SO	HBP	SH	SF	SB	CS	SB%	GDP	Avg	OBP	SLG	Pos	G	PO	A	E	DP	FPct
1979 Cal	31	4	16	4	0	0	0	4	2	0	0	0	0	1	0	0	0	0	0	—	0	.250	.250	.250	OF	4	14	2	0	2	1.000

World Series — Batting / Fielding

Year Tm	Age	G	AB	H	2B	3B	HR	TB	R	RBI	GW	TBB	IBB	SO	HBP	SH	SF	SB	CS	SB%	GDP	Avg	OBP	SLG	Pos	G	PO	A	E	DP	FPct
1975 Bos	27	3	2	0	0	0	0	0	0	0	0	0	0	0	0	0	0	0	0	—	0	.000	.000	.000	OF	2	1	0	0	0	1.000
Postseason Totals		7	18	4	0	0	0	4	2	0	0	0	0	1	0	0	0	0	0	—	0	.222	.222	.222	OF	6	15	2	0	2	1.000

STU MILLER—Stuart Leonard Miller—Throws: Right; Bats: Right

Ht: 5'11"; Wt: 165 lbs; Born: 12/26/1927 in Northampton, Massachusetts; Debut: 8/12/1952

World Series — Pitching

Year Tm	Age	G	GS	CG	GF	IP	BFP	H	R	ER	HR	SH	SF	HB	TBB	IBB	SO	WP	Bk	W	L	Pct	ShO	Sv-Op	Hld	OAvg	OOBP	ERA
1962 SF	34	2	0	0	2	1.1	7	1	0	0	0	0	0	0	2	0	0	0	0	0	0	—	0	0- 0	0	.200	.429	0.00

World Series — Batting / Fielding

Year Tm	Age	G	AB	H	2B	3B	HR	TB	R	RBI	GW	TBB	IBB	SO	HBP	SH	SF	SB	CS	SB%	GDP	Avg	OBP	SLG	Pos	G	PO	A	E	DP	FPct
1962 SF	34	2	0	0	0	0	0	0	0	0	0	0	0	0	0	0	0	0	0	—	0	—	—	—	P	2	0	1	0	0	1.000

BOB MILLIKEN—Robert Fogle Milliken—Nickname: Bobo—Throws: Right; Bats: Right

Ht: 6'0"; Wt: 195 lbs; Born: 8/25/1926 in Majorsville, West Virginia; Debut: 4/22/1953

World Series — Pitching

Year Tm	Age	G	GS	CG	GF	IP	BFP	H	R	ER	HR	SH	SF	HB	TBB	IBB	SO	WP	Bk	W	L	Pct	ShO	Sv-Op	Hld	OAvg	OOBP	ERA
1953 Bro	27	1	0	0	0	2.0	9	2	0	0	0	0	0	0	1	0	0	0	0	0	0	—	0	0- 0	0	.250	.333	0.00

World Series — Batting / Fielding

Year Tm	Age	G	AB	H	2B	3B	HR	TB	R	RBI	GW	TBB	IBB	SO	HBP	SH	SF	SB	CS	SB%	GDP	Avg	OBP	SLG	Pos	G	PO	A	E	DP	FPct
1953 Bro	27	1	0	0	0	0	0	0	0	0	0	0	0	0	0	0	0	0	0	—	0	—	—	—	P	1	0	0	0	0	—

ALAN MILLS—Alan Bernard Mills—Throws: Right; Bats: Both

Ht: 6'1"; Wt: 190 lbs; Born: 10/18/1966 in Lakeland, Florida; Debut: 4/14/1990

Division Series — Pitching

Year Tm	Age	G	GS	CG	GF	IP	BFP	H	R	ER	HR	SH	SF	HB	TBB	IBB	SO	WP	Bk	W	L	Pct	ShO	Sv-Op	Hld	OAvg	OOBP	ERA
1997 Bal	30	1	0	0	0	1.0	3	1	0	0	0	0	0	0	0	0	1	0	0	0	0	—	0	0- 0	0	.333	.333	0.00

LCS — Pitching

Year Tm	Age	G	GS	CG	GF	IP	BFP	H	R	ER	HR	SH	SF	HB	TBB	IBB	SO	WP	Bk	W	L	Pct	ShO	Sv-Op	Hld	OAvg	OOBP	ERA
1996 Bal	29	3	0	0	0	2.1	11	3	1	1	0	0	0	0	1	0	3	0	0	0	0	—	0	0- 0	0	.300	.364	3.86
1997 Bal	30	3	0	0	1	3.1	13	1	1	1	0	0	0	0	2	0	3	0	0	0	1	.000	0	0- 0	0	.091	.231	2.70
LCS Totals		6	0	0	1	5.2	48	4	2	2	0	0	0	0	3	0	6	0	0	0	1	.000	0	0-0	0	.190	.292	3.18
Postseason Totals		7	0	0	1	6.2	54	5	2	2	0	0	0	0	3	0	7	0	0	0	1	.000	0	0-0	0	.208	.296	2.70

Division Series		Batting																							Fielding						
Year Tm	Age	G	AB	H	2B	3B	HR	TB	R	RBI	GW	TBB	IBB	SO	HBP	SH	SF	SB	CS	SB%	GDP	Avg	OBP	SLG	Pos	G	PO	A	E	DP	FPct
1997 Bal	30	1	0	0	0	0	0	0	0	0	0	0	0	0	0	0	0	0	0	—	0	—	—	—	P	1	0	1	0	0	1.000
LCS		**Batting**																							**Fielding**						
Year Tm	Age	G	AB	H	2B	3B	HR	TB	R	RBI	GW	TBB	IBB	SO	HBP	SH	SF	SB	CS	SB%	GDP	Avg	OBP	SLG	Pos	G	PO	A	E	DP	FPct
1996 Bal	29	3	0	0	0	0	0	0	0	0	0	0	0	0	0	0	0	0	0	—	0	—	—	—	P	3	0	0	0	0	—
1997 Bal	30	3	0	0	0	0	0	0	0	0	0	0	0	0	0	0	0	0	0	—	0	—	—	—	P	3	0	0	0	0	—
LCS Totals		6	0	0	0	0	0	0	0	0	0	0	0	0	0	0	0	0	0	—	0	—	—	—	P	6	0	0	0	0	—
Postseason Totals		7	0	0	0	0	0	0	0	0	0	0	0	0	0	0	0	0	0	—	0	—	—	—	P	7	0	1	0	0	1.000

BRAD MILLS—James Bradley Mills—Bats: Left; Throws: Right

Ht: 6'0"; Wt: 195 lbs; Born: 1/19/1957 in Exeter, California; Debut: 6/8/1980

Division Series		Batting																							Fielding						
Year Tm	Age	G	AB	H	2B	3B	HR	TB	R	RBI	GW	TBB	IBB	SO	HBP	SH	SF	SB	CS	SB%	GDP	Avg	OBP	SLG	Pos	G	PO	A	E	DP	FPct
1981 Mon	24	1	0	0	0	0	0	0	0	0	0	1	0	0	0	0	0	0	0	—	0	—	1.000	—	—						

EDDIE MILNER—Edward James Milner—Nickname: Greyhound—Bats: Left; Throws: Left

Ht: 5'11"; Wt: 173 lbs; Born: 5/21/1955 in Columbus, Ohio; Debut: 9/2/1980

LCS		Batting																							Fielding						
Year Tm	Age	G	AB	H	2B	3B	HR	TB	R	RBI	GW	TBB	IBB	SO	HBP	SH	SF	SB	CS	SB%	GDP	Avg	OBP	SLG	Pos	G	PO	A	E	DP	FPct
1987 SF	32	6	7	1	0	0	0	1	0	0	0	0	0	3	0	1	0	0	0	—	0	.143	.143	.143	OF	4	8	0	0	0	1.000

JOHN MILNER—John David Milner—Nickname: The Hammer—Bats: Left; Throws: Left

Ht: 6'0"; Wt: 185 lbs; Born: 12/28/1949 in Atlanta, Georgia; Debut: 9/15/1971

Division Series		Batting																							Fielding						
Year Tm	Age	G	AB	H	2B	3B	HR	TB	R	RBI	GW	TBB	IBB	SO	HBP	SH	SF	SB	CS	SB%	GDP	Avg	OBP	SLG	Pos	G	PO	A	E	DP	FPct
1981 Mon	31	2	2	1	0	0	0	1	0	1	0	0	0	0	0	0	0	0	0	—	0	.500	.500	.500	—						
LCS		**Batting**																							**Fielding**						
Year Tm	Age	G	AB	H	2B	3B	HR	TB	R	RBI	GW	TBB	IBB	SO	HBP	SH	SF	SB	CS	SB%	GDP	Avg	OBP	SLG	Pos	G	PO	A	E	DP	FPct
1973 NYN	23	5	17	3	0	0	0	3	2	1	0	5	0	3	0	0	0	0	0	—	1	.176	.364	.176	1B	5	37	5	0	4	1.000
1979 Pit	29	3	9	0	0	0	0	0	0	0	0	2	1	0	0	0	0	0	0	—	0	.000	.182	.000	OF	3	1	0	0	0	1.000
1981 Mon	31	1	1	0	0	0	0	0	0	0	0	0	0	1	0	0	0	0	0	—	0	.000	.000	.000	—						
LCS Totals		9	27	3	0	0	0	3	2	1	0	7	1	4	0	0	0	0	0	—	1	.111	.294	.111	1B	5	37	5	0	4	1.000
World Series		**Batting**																							**Fielding**						
Year Tm	Age	G	AB	H	2B	3B	HR	TB	R	RBI	GW	TBB	IBB	SO	HBP	SH	SF	SB	CS	SB%	GDP	Avg	OBP	SLG	Pos	G	PO	A	E	DP	FPct
1973 NYN	23	7	27	8	0	0	0	8	2	2	1	5	0	1	0	0	0	0	0	—	1	.296	.406	.296	1B	7	65	1	0	2	1.000
1979 Pit	29	3	9	3	1	0	0	4	2	1	0	2	1	0	0	0	0	0	0	—	0	.333	.455	.444	OF	3	5	0	0	0	1.000
WS Totals		10	36	11	1	0	0	12	4	3	1	7	1	1	0	0	0	0	0	—	1	.306	.419	.333	1B	7	65	1	0	2	1.000
Postseason Totals		21	65	15	1	0	0	16	6	5	1	14	2	5	0	0	0	0	0	—	2	.231	.367	.246	1B	12	102	6	0	6	1.000

DON MINCHER—Donald Ray Mincher—Bats: Left; Throws: Right

Ht: 6'3"; Wt: 205 lbs; Born: 6/24/1938 in Huntsville, Alabama; Debut: 4/18/1960

LCS		Batting																							Fielding						
Year Tm	Age	G	AB	H	2B	3B	HR	TB	R	RBI	GW	TBB	IBB	SO	HBP	SH	SF	SB	CS	SB%	GDP	Avg	OBP	SLG	Pos	G	PO	A	E	DP	FPct
1972 Oak	34	1	1	0	0	0	0	0	0	0	0	0	0	1	0	0	0	0	0	—	0	.000	.000	.000	—						
World Series		**Batting**																							**Fielding**						
Year Tm	Age	G	AB	H	2B	3B	HR	TB	R	RBI	GW	TBB	IBB	SO	HBP	SH	SF	SB	CS	SB%	GDP	Avg	OBP	SLG	Pos	G	PO	A	E	DP	FPct
1965 Min	27	7	23	3	0	0	1	6	3	1	0	2	0	7	0	0	0	0	0	—	1	.130	.200	.261	1B	7	51	4	0	0	1.000
1972 Oak	34	3	1	1	0	0	0	1	0	1	0	0	0	0	0	0	0	0	0	—	0	1.000	1.000	1.000	—						
WS Totals		10	24	4	0	0	1	7	3	2	0	2	0	7	0	0	0	0	0	—	1	.167	.231	.292	1B	7	51	4	0	0	1.000
Postseason Totals		11	25	4	0	0	1	7	3	2	0	2	0	8	0	0	0	0	0	—	1	.160	.222	.280	1B	7	51	4	0	0	1.000

STEVE MINGORI—Stephen Bernard Mingori—Throws: Left; Bats: Left

Ht: 5'10"; Wt: 165 lbs; Born: 2/29/1944 in Kansas City, Missouri; Debut: 8/5/1970

LCS		Pitching																										
Year Tm	Age	G	GS	CG	GF	IP	BFP	H	R	ER	HR	SH	SF	HB	TBB	IBB	SO	WP	Bk	W	L	Pct	ShO	Sv-Op	Hld	OAvg	OOBP	ERA
1976 KC	32	3	0	0	2	3.1	14	4	1	1	1	0	0	0	0	0	1	0	0	0	0	—	0	1- 1	0	.286	.286	2.70
1977 KC	33	3	0	0	1	1.1	4	0	0	0	0	0	0	0	0	0	1	1	0	0	0	—	0	0- 0	1	.000	.000	0.00
1978 KC	34	1	0	0	0	3.2	18	5	3	3	0	0	0	0	3	1	0	0	0	0	0	—	0	0- 0	0	.333	.444	7.36
LCS Totals		7	0	0	3	8.1	72	9	4	4	1	0	0	0	3	1	2	1	0	0	0	—	0	1-1	1	.273	.333	4.32

LCS		Batting																							Fielding						
Year Tm	Age	G	AB	H	2B	3B	HR	TB	R	RBI	GW	TBB	IBB	SO	HBP	SH	SF	SB	CS	SB%	GDP	Avg	OBP	SLG	Pos	G	PO	A	E	DP	FPct
1976 KC	32	3	0	0	0	0	0	0	0	0	0	0	0	0	0	0	0	0	0	—	0	—	—	—	P	3	0	0	0	0	—
1977 KC	33	3	0	0	0	0	0	0	0	0	0	0	0	0	0	0	0	0	0	—	0	—	—	—	P	3	0	0	0	0	—
1978 KC	34	1	0	0	0	0	0	0	0	0	0	0	0	0	0	0	0	0	0	—	0	—	—	—	P	1	0	0	0	0	—
LCS Totals		7	0	0	0	0	0	0	0	0	0	0	0	0	0	0	0	0	0	—	0	—	—	—	P	7	0	0	0	0	—

PAUL MINNER—Paul Edison Minner—Nickname: Lefty—Throws: Left; Bats: Left

Ht: 6'5"; Wt: 200 lbs; Born: 7/30/1923 in New Wilmington, Pennsylvania; Debut: 9/12/1946

World Series		Pitching																										
Year Tm	Age	G	GS	CG	GF	IP	BFP	H	R	ER	HR	SH	SF	HB	TBB	IBB	SO	WP	Bk	W	L	Pct	ShO	Sv-Op	Hld	OAvg	OOBP	ERA
1949 Bro	26	1	0	0	1	1.0	4	1	0	0	0	0	0	0	0	0	0	0	0	0	0	—	0	0- 0	0	.250	.250	0.00

World Series		Batting																							Fielding						
Year Tm	Age	G	AB	H	2B	3B	HR	TB	R	RBI	GW	TBB	IBB	SO	HBP	SH	SF	SB	CS	SB%	GDP	Avg	OBP	SLG	Pos	G	PO	A	E	DP	FPct
1949 Bro	26	1	0	0	0	0	0	0	0	0	0	0	0	0	0	0	0	0	0	—	0	—	—	—	P	1	0	1	0	0	1.000

CLARENCE MITCHELL—Clarence Elmer Mitchell—Throws: Left; Bats: Left

Ht: 5'11"; Wt: 190 lbs; Born: 2/22/1891 in Franklin, Nebraska; Debut: 6/2/1911; Died: 11/6/1963

World Series		Pitching																										
Year Tm	Age	G	GS	CG	GF	IP	BFP	H	R	ER	HR	SH	SF	HB	TBB	IBB	SO	WP	Bk	W	L	Pct	ShO	Sv-Op	Hld	OAvg	OOBP	ERA
1920 Bro	29	1	0	0	1	4.2	19	3	1	0	0	1	0	0	3	0	1	0	0	0	0	—	0	0- 0	0	.200	.333	0.00
1928 StL	37	1	0	0	1	5.2	21	2	1	1	0	1	1	1	2	0	3	0	0	0	0	—	0	0- 0	0	.125	.250	1.59
WS Totals		2	0	0	2	10.1	80	5	2	1	0	2	1	1	5	0	4	0	0	0	0	—	0	0-0	0	.161	.289	0.87

World Series		Batting																							Fielding						
Year Tm	Age	G	AB	H	2B	3B	HR	TB	R	RBI	GW	TBB	IBB	SO	HBP	SH	SF	SB	CS	SB%	GDP	Avg	OBP	SLG	Pos	G	PO	A	E	DP	FPct
1920 Bro	29	2	3	1	0	0	0	1	0	0	0	0	0	0	0	0	0	0	0	—	1	.333	.333	.333	P	1	1	0	0	0	1.000
1928 StL	37	1	2	0	0	0	0	0	0	0	0	0	0	0	0	0	0	0	0	—	0	.000	.000	.000	P	1	0	1	1	0	.500
WS Totals		3	5	1	0	0	0	1	0	0	0	0	0	0	0	0	0	0	0	—	1	.200	.200	.200	P	2	1	1	1	0	.667

DALE MITCHELL—Loren Dale Mitchell—Bats: Left; Throws: Left

Ht: 6'1"; Wt: 195 lbs; Born: 8/23/1921 in Colony, Oklahoma; Debut: 9/15/1946; Died: 1/5/1987

World Series		Batting																							Fielding						
Year Tm	Age	G	AB	H	2B	3B	HR	TB	R	RBI	GW	TBB	IBB	SO	HBP	SH	SF	SB	CS	SB%	GDP	Avg	OBP	SLG	Pos	G	PO	A	E	DP	FPct
1948 Cle	27	6	23	4	1	0	1	8	4	1	0	2	0	0	0	0	0	0	0	—	0	.174	.240	.348	OF	6	13	0	0	0	1.000
1954 Cle	33	3	2	0	0	0	0	0	0	0	0	1	0	0	0	0	0	0	0	—	0	.000	.333	.000	—						
1956 Bro	35	4	4	0	0	0	0	0	0	0	0	0	0	1	0	0	0	0	0	—	0	.000	.000	.000	—						
WS Totals		13	29	4	1	0	1	8	4	1	0	3	0	1	0	0	0	0	0	—	0	.138	.219	.276	OF	6	13	0	0	0	1.000

KEITH MITCHELL—Keith Alexander Mitchell—Bats: Right; Throws: Right

Ht: 5'10"; Wt: 180 lbs; Born: 8/6/1969 in San Diego, California; Debut: 7/23/1991

LCS		Batting																							Fielding						
Year Tm	Age	G	AB	H	2B	3B	HR	TB	R	RBI	GW	TBB	IBB	SO	HBP	SH	SF	SB	CS	SB%	GDP	Avg	OBP	SLG	Pos	G	PO	A	E	DP	FPct
1991 Atl	22	5	4	0	0	0	0	0	0	0	0	0	0	1	0	0	0	0	0	—	0	.000	.000	.000	OF	5	2	0	0	0	1.000
World Series		**Batting**																							**Fielding**						
Year Tm	Age	G	AB	H	2B	3B	HR	TB	R	RBI	GW	TBB	IBB	SO	HBP	SH	SF	SB	CS	SB%	GDP	Avg	OBP	SLG	Pos	G	PO	A	E	DP	FPct
1991 Atl	22	3	2	0	0	0	0	0	0	0	0	0	0	1	0	0	0	0	1	.00	0	.000	.000	.000	OF	3	0	0	0	0	—
Postseason Totals		8	6	0	0	0	0	0	0	0	0	0	0	2	0	0	0	0	1	.00	0	.000	.000	.000	OF	8	2	0	0	0	1.000

KEVIN MITCHELL—Kevin Darnell Mitchell—Bats: Right; Throws: Right

Ht: 5'10"; Wt: 186 lbs; Born: 1/13/1962 in San Diego, California; Debut: 9/4/1984

LCS — Batting / Fielding

Year Tm	Age	G	AB	H	2B	3B	HR	TB	R	RBI	GW	TBB	IBB	SO	HBP	SH	SF	SB	CS	SB%	GDP	Avg	OBP	SLG	Pos	G	PO	A	E	DP	FPct
1986 NYN	24	2	8	2	0	0	0	2	1	0	0	0	0	1	0	0	0	0	0	—	0	.250	.250	.250	OF	2	3	0	0	0	1.000
1987 SF	25	7	30	8	1	0	1	12	2	2	0	0	0	3	0	0	0	1	0	1.00	0	.267	.267	.400	3B	7	4	11	1	1	.938
1989 SF-*M*	27	5	17	6	0	0	2	12	5	7	0	3	2	3	0	0	1	0	0	—	1	.353	.429	.706	OF	5	15	1	1	1	.941
LCS Totals		14	55	16	1	0	3	26	8	9	0	3	2	7	0	0	1	1	0	1.00	1	.291	.322	.473	3B	7	4	11	1	1	.938

World Series — Batting / Fielding

Year Tm	Age	G	AB	H	2B	3B	HR	TB	R	RBI	GW	TBB	IBB	SO	HBP	SH	SF	SB	CS	SB%	GDP	Avg	OBP	SLG	Pos	G	PO	A	E	DP	FPct
1986 NYN	24	5	8	2	0	0	0	2	1	0	0	0	0	3	0	0	0	0	0	—	0	.250	.250	.250	OF	2	1	2	0	0	1.000
1989 SF-*M*	27	4	17	5	0	0	1	8	2	2	0	0	0	3	0	0	0	0	0	—	0	.294	.294	.471	OF	4	10	0	1	0	.909
WS Totals		9	25	7	0	0	1	10	3	2	0	0	0	6	0	0	0	0	0	—	0	.280	.280	.400	OF	6	11	2	1	0	.929
Postseason Totals		23	80	23	1	0	4	36	11	11	0	3	2	13	0	0	1	1	0	1.00	1	.288	.310	.450	OF	13	29	3	2	1	.941

GEORGE MITTERWALD—George Eugene Mitterwald—Bats: Right; Throws: Right

Ht: 6'2"; Wt: 195 lbs; Born: 6/7/1945 in Berkeley, California; Debut: 9/15/1966

LCS — Batting / Fielding

Year Tm	Age	G	AB	H	2B	3B	HR	TB	R	RBI	GW	TBB	IBB	SO	HBP	SH	SF	SB	CS	SB%	GDP	Avg	OBP	SLG	Pos	G	PO	A	E	DP	FPct
1969 Min	24	2	7	1	0	0	0	1	0	0	0	1	0	3	0	0	0	0	0	—	0	.143	.250	.143	C	2	10	4	0	0	1.000
1970 Min	25	2	8	4	1	0	0	5	2	2	0	0	0	2	0	0	0	0	0	—	0	.500	.500	.625	C	2	16	1	0	2	1.000
LCS Totals		4	15	5	1	0	0	6	2	2	0	1	0	5	0	0	0	0	0	—	0	.333	.375	.400	C	4	26	5	0	2	1.000

JOHNNY MIZE (HOF 1981-V)—John Robert Mize—Nickname: The Big Cat—Bats: Left; Throws: Right

Ht: 6'2"; Wt: 215 lbs; Born: 1/7/1913 in Demorest, Georgia; Debut: 4/16/1936; Died: 6/2/1993

World Series — Batting / Fielding

Year Tm	Age	G	AB	H	2B	3B	HR	TB	R	RBI	GW	TBB	IBB	SO	HBP	SH	SF	SB	CS	SB%	GDP	Avg	OBP	SLG	Pos	G	PO	A	E	DP	FPct
1949 NYA	36	2	2	2	0	0	0	2	0	2	1	0	0	0	0	0	0	0	0	—	0	1.000	1.000	1.000	—						
1950 NYA	37	4	15	2	0	0	0	2	0	0	0	0	0	1	0	0	0	0	0	—	0	.133	.133	.133	1B	4	27	3	0	2	1.000
1951 NYA	38	4	7	2	1	0	0	3	2	1	0	2	1	0	0	0	0	0	0	—	0	.286	.444	.429	1B	2	12	0	0	4	1.000
1952 NYA	39	5	15	6	1	0	3	16	3	6	1	3	0	1	0	0	0	0	0	—	0	.400	.500	1.067	1B	4	26	3	0	4	1.000
1953 NYA	40	3	3	0	0	0	0	0	0	0	0	0	0	1	0	0	0	0	0	—	0	.000	.000	.000	—						
WS Totals		18	42	12	2	0	3	23	5	9	2	5	1	3	0	0	0	0	0	—	0	.286	.362	.548	1B	10	65	6	0	10	1.000

VINEGAR BEND MIZELL—Wilmer David Mizell—Throws: Left; Bats: Right

Ht: 6'3"; Wt: 205 lbs; Born: 8/13/1930 in Leakesville, Mississippi; Debut: 4/22/1952

World Series — Pitching

Year Tm	Age	G	GS	CG	GF	IP	BFP	H	R	ER	HR	SH	SF	HB	TBB	IBB	SO	WP	Bk	W	L	Pct	ShO	Sv-Op	Hld	OAvg	OOBP	ERA
1960 Pit	30	2	1	0	0	2.1	13	4	4	4	0	0	0	0	2	0	1	0	0	0	1	.000	0	0-0	0	.364	.462	15.43

World Series — Batting / Fielding

Year Tm	Age	G	AB	H	2B	3B	HR	TB	R	RBI	GW	TBB	IBB	SO	HBP	SH	SF	SB	CS	SB%	GDP	Avg	OBP	SLG	Pos	G	PO	A	E	DP	FPct
1960 Pit	30	2	0	0	0	0	0	0	0	0	0	0	0	0	0	0	0	0	0	—	0	—	—	—	P	2	0	0	0	0	—

JOE MOELLER—Joseph Douglas Moeller—Nickname: Skeeter—Throws: Right; Bats: Right

Ht: 6'5"; Wt: 192 lbs; Born: 2/15/1943 in Blue Island, Illinois; Debut: 4/12/1962

World Series — Pitching

Year Tm	Age	G	GS	CG	GF	IP	BFP	H	R	ER	HR	SH	SF	HB	TBB	IBB	SO	WP	Bk	W	L	Pct	ShO	Sv-Op	Hld	OAvg	OOBP	ERA
1966 LA	23	1	0	0	0	2.0	8	1	1	1	0	0	0	0	1	0	0	0	0	0	0	—	0	0-0	0	.143	.250	4.50

World Series — Batting / Fielding

Year Tm	Age	G	AB	H	2B	3B	HR	TB	R	RBI	GW	TBB	IBB	SO	HBP	SH	SF	SB	CS	SB%	GDP	Avg	OBP	SLG	Pos	G	PO	A	E	DP	FPct
1966 LA	23	1	0	0	0	0	0	0	0	0	0	0	0	0	0	0	0	0	0	—	0	—	—	—	P	1	0	0	0	0	—

GEORGE MOGRIDGE—George Anthony Mogridge—Throws: Left; Bats: Left

Ht: 6'2"; Wt: 165 lbs; Born: 2/18/1889 in Rochester, New York; Debut: 8/17/1911; Died: 3/4/1962

World Series — Pitching

Year Tm	Age	G	GS	CG	GF	IP	BFP	H	R	ER	HR	SH	SF	HB	TBB	IBB	SO	WP	Bk	W	L	Pct	ShO	Sv-Op	Hld	OAvg	OOBP	ERA
1924 Was	35	2	1	0	0	12.0	52	7	5	3	0	0	0	0	6	0	5	0	0	1	0	1.000	0	0-0	0	.152	.250	2.25

World Series — Batting / Fielding

Year Tm	Age	G	AB	H	2B	3B	HR	TB	R	RBI	GW	TBB	IBB	SO	HBP	SH	SF	SB	CS	SB%	GDP	Avg	OBP	SLG	Pos	G	PO	A	E	DP	FPct
1924 Was	35	2	5	0	0	0	0	0	0	0	0	0	0	5	0	0	0	0	0	—	0	.000	.000	.000	P	2	0	0	0	0	—

PAUL MOLITOR—Paul Leo Molitor—Nickname: The Igniter—Bats: Right; Throws: Right

Ht: 6'0"; Wt: 185 lbs; Born: 8/22/1956 in St. Paul, Minnesota; Debut: 4/7/1978

Division Series — Batting / Fielding

Year Tm	Age	G	AB	H	2B	3B	HR	TB	R	RBI	GW	TBB	IBB	SO	HBP	SH	SF	SB	CS	SB%	GDP	Avg	OBP	SLG	Pos	G	PO	A	E	DP	FPct
1981 Mil	25	5	20	5	0	0	1	8	2	1	1	2	0	5	0	1	0	0	0	—	0	.250	.318	.400	OF	5	11	0	0	0	1.000

LCS — Batting / Fielding

Year Tm	Age	G	AB	H	2B	3B	HR	TB	R	RBI	GW	TBB	IBB	SO	HBP	SH	SF	SB	CS	SB%	GDP	Avg	OBP	SLG	Pos	G	PO	A	E	DP	FPct
1982 Mil	26	5	19	6	1	0	2	13	4	5	0	2	0	3	0	0	0	1	1	.50	1	.316	.381	.684	3B	5	4	11	1	2	.938
1993 Tor	37	6	23	9	2	1	1	16	7	5	0	3	1	3	1	0	0	0	0	—	0	.391	.481	.696	—						
LCS Totals		11	42	15	3	1	3	29	11	10	0	5	1	6	1	0	0	1	1	.50	1	.357	.438	.690	3B	5	4	11	1	2	.938

World Series — Batting / Fielding

Year Tm	Age	G	AB	H	2B	3B	HR	TB	R	RBI	GW	TBB	IBB	SO	HBP	SH	SF	SB	CS	SB%	GDP	Avg	OBP	SLG	Pos	G	PO	A	E	DP	FPct
1982 Mil	26	7	31	11	0	0	0	11	5	3	0	2	0	4	0	0	0	1	1	.50	1	.355	.394	.355	3B	7	4	9	0	1	1.000
1993 Tor	37	6	24	12	2	2	2	24	10	8	1	3	0	0	1	0	0	1	0	1.00	0	.500	.571	1.000	1B	1	7	1	0	2	1.000
																									3B	2	0	2	0	0	1.000
WS Totals		13	55	23	2	2	2	35	15	11	1	5	0	4	1	0	0	2	1	.67	1	.418	.475	.636	3B	9	4	11	0	1	1.000
Postseason Totals		29	117	43	5	3	6	72	28	22	2	12	1	15	2	1	0	3	2	.60	2	.368	.435	.615	3B	14	8	22	1	3	.968

RICK MONDAY—Robert James Monday—Bats: Left; Throws: Left

Ht: 6'3"; Wt: 193 lbs; Born: 11/20/1945 in Batesville, Arkansas; Debut: 9/3/1966

Division Series — Batting / Fielding

Year Tm	Age	G	AB	H	2B	3B	HR	TB	R	RBI	GW	TBB	IBB	SO	HBP	SH	SF	SB	CS	SB%	GDP	Avg	OBP	SLG	Pos	G	PO	A	E	DP	FPct
1981 LA	35	5	14	3	0	0	0	3	1	1	1	2	1	4	0	1	0	0	0	—	0	.214	.313	.214	OF	5	12	0	0	0	1.000

LCS — Batting / Fielding

Year Tm	Age	G	AB	H	2B	3B	HR	TB	R	RBI	GW	TBB	IBB	SO	HBP	SH	SF	SB	CS	SB%	GDP	Avg	OBP	SLG	Pos	G	PO	A	E	DP	FPct
1971 Oak	25	1	3	0	0	0	0	0	0	0	0	1	0	2	0	0	0	0	0	—	0	.000	.250	.000	OF	1	4	0	0	0	1.000
1977 LA	31	3	7	2	1	0	0	3	1	0	0	2	1	1	0	0	0	0	0	—	0	.286	.444	.429	OF	3	6	0	0	0	1.000
1978 LA	32	3	10	2	0	1	0	4	2	0	0	1	0	5	0	0	0	0	0	—	0	.200	.273	.400	OF	3	6	0	0	0	1.000
1981 LA	35	3	9	3	0	0	1	6	2	1	1	0	0	4	0	0	0	0	0	—	0	.333	.333	.667	OF	2	2	0	0	0	1.000
1983 LA	37	1	0	0	0	0	0	0	0	0	0	0	0	0	0	0	0	0	0	—	0	—	—	—	—						
LCS Totals		11	29	7	1	1	1	13	5	1	1	4	1	12	0	0	0	0	0	—	0	.241	.333	.448	OF	9	18	0	0	0	1.000

World Series — Batting / Fielding

Year Tm	Age	G	AB	H	2B	3B	HR	TB	R	RBI	GW	TBB	IBB	SO	HBP	SH	SF	SB	CS	SB%	GDP	Avg	OBP	SLG	Pos	G	PO	A	E	DP	FPct
1977 LA	31	4	12	2	0	0	0	2	0	0	0	0	0	3	0	0	0	0	1	.00	0	.167	.167	.167	OF	4	5	0	0	0	1.000
1978 LA	32	5	13	2	1	0	0	3	2	0	0	4	0	3	0	0	0	0	1	.00	0	.154	.353	.231	OF	4	5	0	0	0	1.000
1981 LA	35	5	13	3	1	0	0	4	1	0	0	3	2	6	0	0	0	0	0	—	0	.231	.375	.308	OF	4	9	0	0	0	1.000
WS Totals		14	38	7	2	0	0	9	3	0	0	7	2	12	0	0	0	0	2	.00	0	.184	.311	.237	OF	12	19	0	0	0	1.000
Postseason Totals		30	81	17	3	1	1	25	9	2	2	13	4	28	0	1	0	0	2	.00	0	.210	.319	.309	OF	26	49	0	0	0	1.000

RAUL MONDESI—Raul Ramon Mondesi—Bats: Right; Throws: Right

Ht: 5'11"; Wt: 150 lbs; Born: 3/12/1971 in San Cristobal, Dominican Republic; Debut: 7/19/1993

Division Series — Batting / Fielding

Year Tm	Age	G	AB	H	2B	3B	HR	TB	R	RBI	GW	TBB	IBB	SO	HBP	SH	SF	SB	CS	SB%	GDP	Avg	OBP	SLG	Pos	G	PO	A	E	DP	FPct
1995 LA	24	3	9	2	0	0	0	2	0	1	0	0	0	2	1	0	0	0	0	—	0	.222	.300	.222	OF	3	8	0	0	0	1.000
1996 LA	25	3	11	2	2	0	0	4	0	1	0	0	0	4	0	0	0	0	0	—	0	.182	.182	.364	OF	3	2	0	0	0	1.000
DS Totals		6	20	4	2	0	0	6	0	2	0	0	0	6	1	0	0	0	0	—	0	.200	.238	.300	OF	6	10	0	0	0	1.000

DON MONEY—Donald Wayne Money—Nickname: Brooks—Bats: Right; Throws: Right

Ht: 6'1"; Wt: 170 lbs; Born: 6/7/1947 in Washington, DC; Debut: 4/10/1968

Division Series — Batting / Fielding

Year Tm	Age	G	AB	H	2B	3B	HR	TB	R	RBI	GW	TBB	IBB	SO	HBP	SH	SF	SB	CS	SB%	GDP	Avg	OBP	SLG	Pos	G	PO	A	E	DP	FPct
1981 Mil	34	2	3	0	0	0	0	0	0	0	0	0	0	0	0	0	0	0	0	—	0	.000	.000	.000	2B	1	1	1	0	1	1.000

LCS — Batting / Fielding

Year Tm	Age	G	AB	H	2B	3B	HR	TB	R	RBI	GW	TBB	IBB	SO	HBP	SH	SF	SB	CS	SB%	GDP	Avg	OBP	SLG	Pos	G	PO	A	E	DP	FPct
1982 Mil	35	4	11	2	0	0	0	2	2	1	0	3	0	1	0	0	1	0	0	—	0	.182	.333	.182	—						

World Series — Batting / Fielding

Year Tm	Age	G	AB	H	2B	3B	HR	TB	R	RBI	GW	TBB	IBB	SO	HBP	SH	SF	SB	CS	SB%	GDP	Avg	OBP	SLG	Pos	G	PO	A	E	DP	FPct
1982 Mil	35	5	13	3	1	0	0	4	4	1	0	2	0	3	0	0	0	0	0	—	2	.231	.333	.308	—						
Postseason Totals		11	27	5	1	0	0	6	6	2	0	5	0	4	0	0	1	0	0	—	2	.185	.303	.222	2B	1	1	1	0	1	1.000

ZACK MONROE—Zachary Charles Monroe—Throws: Right; Bats: Right

Ht: 6'0"; Wt: 198 lbs; Born: 7/8/1931 in Peoria, Illinois; Debut: 6/27/1958

World Series — Pitching

Year Tm	Age	G	GS	CG	GF	IP	BFP	H	R	ER	HR	SH	SF	HB	TBB	IBB	SO	WP	Bk	W	L	Pct	ShO	Sv-Op	Hld	OAvg	OOBP	ERA
1958 NYA	27	1	0	0	1	1.0	7	3	3	3	0	0	1	0	1	0	1	0	0	0	0	—	0	0-0	0	.600	.571	27.00

World Series — Batting / Fielding

Year Tm	Age	G	AB	H	2B	3B	HR	TB	R	RBI	GW	TBB	IBB	SO	HBP	SH	SF	SB	CS	SB%	GDP	Avg	OBP	SLG	Pos	G	PO	A	E	DP	FPct
1958 NYA	27	1	0	0	0	0	0	0	0	0	0	0	0	0	0	0	0	0	0	—	0	—	—	—	P	1	0	0	0	0	—

JOHN MONTAGUE—John Evans Montague—Throws: Right; Bats: Right

Ht: 6'2"; Wt: 213 lbs; Born: 9/12/1947 in Newport News, Virginia; Debut: 9/9/1973

LCS — Pitching

Year Tm	Age	G	GS	CG	GF	IP	BFP	H	R	ER	HR	SH	SF	HB	TBB	IBB	SO	WP	Bk	W	L	Pct	ShO	Sv-Op	Hld	OAvg	OOBP	ERA
1979 Cal	32	2	0	0	1	4.0	17	4	4	4	2	1	0	0	2	1	2	0	0	0	1	.000	0	0-0	0	.286	.375	9.00

LCS — Batting / Fielding

Year Tm	Age	G	AB	H	2B	3B	HR	TB	R	RBI	GW	TBB	IBB	SO	HBP	SH	SF	SB	CS	SB%	GDP	Avg	OBP	SLG	Pos	G	PO	A	E	DP	FPct
1979 Cal	32	2	0	0	0	0	0	0	0	0	0	0	0	0	0	0	0	0	0	—	0	—	—	—	P	2	1	1	0	0	1.000

BOB MONTGOMERY—Robert Edward Montgomery—Bats: Right; Throws: Right

Ht: 6'1"; Wt: 195 lbs; Born: 4/16/1944 in Nashville, Tennessee; Debut: 9/6/1970

World Series — Batting / Fielding

Year Tm	Age	G	AB	H	2B	3B	HR	TB	R	RBI	GW	TBB	IBB	SO	HBP	SH	SF	SB	CS	SB%	GDP	Avg	OBP	SLG	Pos	G	PO	A	E	DP	FPct
1975 Bos	31	1	1	0	0	0	0	0	0	0	0	0	0	0	0	0	0	0	0	—	0	.000	.000	.000	—						

WALLY MOON—Wallace Wade Moon—Bats: Left; Throws: Right

Ht: 6'0"; Wt: 169 lbs; Born: 4/3/1930 in Bay, Arkansas; Debut: 4/13/1954

World Series — Batting / Fielding

Year Tm	Age	G	AB	H	2B	3B	HR	TB	R	RBI	GW	TBB	IBB	SO	HBP	SH	SF	SB	CS	SB%	GDP	Avg	OBP	SLG	Pos	G	PO	A	E	DP	FPct
1959 LA	29	6	23	6	0	0	1	9	3	2	0	2	0	2	0	0	0	1	0	1.00	0	.261	.320	.391	OF	6	10	1	0	0	1.000
1965 LA	35	2	2	0	0	0	0	0	0	0	0	0	0	0	0	0	0	0	0	—	0	.000	.000	.000	—						
WS Totals		8	25	6	0	0	1	9	3	2	0	2	0	2	0	0	0	1	0	1.00	0	.240	.296	.360	OF	6	10	1	0	0	1.000

JIM MOONEY—Jim Irving Mooney—Throws: Left; Bats: Right

Ht: 5'11"; Wt: 168 lbs; Born: 9/4/1906 in Mooresburg, Tennessee; Debut: 8/14/1931; Died: 4/27/1979

World Series — Pitching

Year Tm	Age	G	GS	CG	GF	IP	BFP	H	R	ER	HR	SH	SF	HB	TBB	IBB	SO	WP	Bk	W	L	Pct	ShO	Sv-Op	Hld	OAvg	OOBP	ERA
1934 StL	28	1	0	0	1	1.0	4	1	0	0	0	1	0	0	0	0	0	0	0	0	0	—	0	0-0	0	.333	.333	0.00

World Series — Batting / Fielding

Year Tm	Age	G	AB	H	2B	3B	HR	TB	R	RBI	GW	TBB	IBB	SO	HBP	SH	SF	SB	CS	SB%	GDP	Avg	OBP	SLG	Pos	G	PO	A	E	DP	FPct
1934 StL	28	1	0	0	0	0	0	0	0	0	0	0	0	0	0	0	0	0	0	—	0	—	—	—	P	1	0	1	0	0	1.000

CHARLIE MOORE—Charles William Moore—Bats: Right; Throws: Right

Ht: 5'11"; Wt: 180 lbs; Born: 6/21/1953 in Birmingham, Alabama; Debut: 9/8/1973

Division Series — Batting / Fielding

Year Tm	Age	G	AB	H	2B	3B	HR	TB	R	RBI	GW	TBB	IBB	SO	HBP	SH	SF	SB	CS	SB%	GDP	Avg	OBP	SLG	Pos	G	PO	A	E	DP	FPct
1981 Mil	28	4	9	2	0	0	0	2	0	1	0	1	0	2	0	0	0	0	0	—	0	.222	.300	.222	OF	2	7	0	0	0	1.000

LCS — Batting / Fielding

Year Tm	Age	G	AB	H	2B	3B	HR	TB	R	RBI	GW	TBB	IBB	SO	HBP	SH	SF	SB	CS	SB%	GDP	Avg	OBP	SLG	Pos	G	PO	A	E	DP	FPct
1982 Mil	29	5	13	6	0	0	0	6	3	0	0	1	1	2	1	2	0	0	0	—	0	.462	.533	.462	OF	5	7	1	0	0	1.000

World Series — Batting / Fielding

Year Tm	Age	G	AB	H	2B	3B	HR	TB	R	RBI	GW	TBB	IBB	SO	HBP	SH	SF	SB	CS	SB%	GDP	Avg	OBP	SLG	Pos	G	PO	A	E	DP	FPct
1982 Mil	29	7	26	9	3	0	0	12	3	2	0	1	0	0	0	0	0	0	0	—	0	.346	.370	.462	OF	7	13	0	0	0	1.000
Postseason Totals		16	48	17	3	0	0	20	6	3	0	3	1	4	1	2	0	0	0	—	0	.354	.404	.417	OF	14	27	1	0	0	1.000

DONNIE MOORE—Donnie Ray Moore—Throws: Right; Bats: Left

Ht: 6'0"; Wt: 185 lbs; Born: 2/13/1954 in Lubbock, Texas; Debut: 9/14/1975; Died: 7/18/1989

LCS — Pitching

Year Tm	Age	G	GS	CG	GF	IP	BFP	H	R	ER	HR	SH	SF	HB	TBB	IBB	SO	WP	Bk	W	L	Pct	ShO	Sv-Op	Hld	OAvg	OOBP	ERA
1982 Atl	28	2	0	0	0	2.2	11	2	0	0	0	1	0	1	0	0	1	0	0	0	0	—	0	0-0	0	.222	.300	0.00
1986 Cal	32	3	0	0	2	5.0	25	8	4	4	1	0	1	1	2	0	0	0	1	0	1	.000	0	1-2	0	.381	.440	7.20
LCS Totals		5	0	0	2	7.2	72	10	4	4	1	1	1	2	2	0	1	0	1	0	1	.000	0	1-2	0	.333	.400	4.70

LCS — Batting / Fielding

Year Tm	Age	G	AB	H	2B	3B	HR	TB	R	RBI	GW	TBB	IBB	SO	HBP	SH	SF	SB	CS	SB%	GDP	Avg	OBP	SLG	Pos	G	PO	A	E	DP	FPct
1982 Atl	28	2	0	0	0	0	0	0	0	0	0	0	0	0	0	0	0	0	0	—	0	—	—	—	P	2	1	0	0	0	1.000
1986 Cal	32	3	0	0	0	0	0	0	0	0	0	0	0	0	0	0	0	0	0	—	0	—	—	—	P	3	0	0	0	0	—
LCS Totals		5	0	0	0	0	0	0	0	0	0	0	0	0	0	0	0	0	0	—	0	—	—	—	P	5	1	0	0	0	1.000

EDDIE MOORE—Graham Edward Moore—Bats: Right; Throws: Right

Ht: 5'7"; Wt: 165 lbs; Born: 1/18/1899 in Barlow, Kentucky; Debut: 9/25/1923; Died: 2/10/1976

World Series — Batting / Fielding

Year Tm	Age	G	AB	H	2B	3B	HR	TB	R	RBI	GW	TBB	IBB	SO	HBP	SH	SF	SB	CS	SB%	GDP	Avg	OBP	SLG	Pos	G	PO	A	E	DP	FPct
1925 Pit	26	7	26	6	1	0	1	10	7	2	1	5	0	2	0	0	0	0	0	—	1	.231	.355	.385	2B	7	16	14	1	2	.968

GENE MOORE—Eugene Moore—Nickname: Rowdy—Bats: Left; Throws: Left

Ht: 5'11"; Wt: 175 lbs; Born: 8/26/1909 in Lancaster, Texas; Debut: 9/19/1931; Died: 3/12/1978

World Series — Batting / Fielding

Year Tm	Age	G	AB	H	2B	3B	HR	TB	R	RBI	GW	TBB	IBB	SO	HBP	SH	SF	SB	CS	SB%	GDP	Avg	OBP	SLG	Pos	G	PO	A	E	DP	FPct
1944 StL	35	6	22	4	0	0	0	4	4	0	0	3	0	6	0	0	0	0	0	—	0	.182	.280	.182	OF	6	8	0	0	0	1.000

JIMMY MOORE—James William Moore—Bats: Right; Throws: Right

Ht: 6'0"; Wt: 187 lbs; Born: 4/24/1903 in Paris, Tennessee; Debut: 8/31/1930; Died: 3/7/1986

World Series — Batting / Fielding

Year Tm	Age	G	AB	H	2B	3B	HR	TB	R	RBI	GW	TBB	IBB	SO	HBP	SH	SF	SB	CS	SB%	GDP	Avg	OBP	SLG	Pos	G	PO	A	E	DP	FPct
1930 Phi	27	3	3	1	0	0	0	1	0	0	0	1	0	1	0	0	0	0	0	—	0	.333	.500	.333	OF	1	0	0	0	0	—
1931 Phi	28	2	3	1	0	0	0	1	0	0	0	0	0	1	0	0	0	0	0	—	0	.333	.333	.333	OF	1	1	0	0	0	1.000
WS Totals		5	6	2	0	0	0	2	0	0	0	1	0	2	0	0	0	0	0	—	0	.333	.429	.333	OF	2	1	0	0	0	1.000

JO-JO MOORE—Joseph Gregg Moore—Nickname: The Gause Ghost—Bats: Left; Throws: Right
Ht: 5'11"; Wt: 155 lbs; Born: 12/25/1908 in Gause, Texas; Debut: 9/17/1930

World Series — Batting / Fielding

Year Tm	Age	G	AB	H	2B	3B	HR	TB	R	RBI	GW	TBB	IBB	SO	HBP	SH	SF	SB	CS	SB%	GDP	Avg	OBP	SLG	Pos	G	PO	A	E	DP	FPct
1933 NYG	24	5	22	5	1	0	0	6	1	1	0	1	0	3	0	0	0	0	0	—	0	.227	.261	.273	OF	5	13	1	0	1	1.000
1936 NYG	27	6	28	6	2	0	1	11	4	1	0	1	0	4	0	0	0	0	1	.00	0	.214	.241	.393	OF	6	11	0	0	0	1.000
1937 NYG	28	5	23	9	1	0	0	10	1	1	0	0	0	1	0	0	0	0	0	—	0	.391	.391	.435	OF	5	13	0	0	0	1.000
WS Totals		16	73	20	4	0	1	27	6	3	0	2	0	8	0	0	0	0	1	.00	0	.274	.293	.370	OF	16	37	1	0	1	1.000

JOHNNY MOORE—John Francis Moore—Bats: Left; Throws: Right
Ht: 5'10"; Wt: 175 lbs; Born: 3/23/1902 in Waterville, Connecticut; Debut: 9/15/1928; Died: 4/4/1991

World Series — Batting / Fielding

Year Tm	Age	G	AB	H	2B	3B	HR	TB	R	RBI	GW	TBB	IBB	SO	HBP	SH	SF	SB	CS	SB%	GDP	Avg	OBP	SLG	Pos	G	PO	A	E	DP	FPct
1932 ChN	30	2	7	0	0	0	0	0	1	0	0	2	0	1	0	0	0	0	0	—	0	.000	.222	.000	OF	2	4	0	0	0	1.000

KELVIN MOORE—Kelvin Orlando Moore—Bats: Right; Throws: Left
Ht: 6'1"; Wt: 195 lbs; Born: 9/26/1957 in Leroy, Alabama; Debut: 8/28/1981

Division Series — Batting / Fielding

Year Tm	Age	G	AB	H	2B	3B	HR	TB	R	RBI	GW	TBB	IBB	SO	HBP	SH	SF	SB	CS	SB%	GDP	Avg	OBP	SLG	Pos	G	PO	A	E	DP	FPct
1981 Oak	24	2	8	0	0	0	0	0	0	0	0	0	0	2	0	0	0	0	0	—	0	.000	.000	.000	1B	2	14	1	0	1	1.000

LCS — Batting / Fielding

Year Tm	Age	G	AB	H	2B	3B	HR	TB	R	RBI	GW	TBB	IBB	SO	HBP	SH	SF	SB	CS	SB%	GDP	Avg	OBP	SLG	Pos	G	PO	A	E	DP	FPct
1981 Oak	24	3	8	2	0	0	0	2	0	0	0	0	0	1	0	0	0	0	0	—	1	.250	.250	.250	1B	3	13	3	0	0	1.000
Postseason Totals		5	16	2	0	0	0	2	0	0	0	0	0	3	0	0	0	0	0	—	1	.125	.125	.125	1B	5	27	4	0	1	1.000

MIKE MOORE—Michael Wayne Moore—Throws: Right; Bats: Right
Ht: 6'4"; Wt: 205 lbs; Born: 11/26/1959 in Carnegie, Oklahoma; Debut: 4/11/1982

LCS — Pitching

Year Tm	Age	G	GS	CG	GF	IP	BFP	H	R	ER	HR	SH	SF	HB	TBB	IBB	SO	WP	Bk	W	L	Pct	ShO	Sv-Op	Hld	OAvg	OOBP	ERA
1989 Oak	29	1	1	0	0	7.0	26	3	1	0	0	0	0	0	2	0	3	0	0	1	0	1.000	0	0-0	0	.125	.192	0.00
1990 Oak	30	1	1	0	0	6.0	23	4	1	1	0	0	1	0	1	0	5	0	0	1	0	1.000	0	0-0	0	.190	.217	1.50
1992 Oak	32	2	2	0	0	9.2	45	11	9	8	3	0	1	0	5	1	7	0	0	0	2	.000	0	0-0	0	.282	.356	7.45
LCS Totals		4	4	0	0	22.2	188	18	11	9	3	0	2	0	8	1	15	0	0	2	2	.500	0	0-0	0	.214	.277	3.57

World Series — Pitching

Year Tm	Age	G	GS	CG	GF	IP	BFP	H	R	ER	HR	SH	SF	HB	TBB	IBB	SO	WP	Bk	W	L	Pct	ShO	Sv-Op	Hld	OAvg	OOBP	ERA
1989 Oak	29	2	2	0	0	13.0	50	9	3	3	1	0	1	0	3	0	10	2	0	2	0	1.000	0	0-0	0	.196	.240	2.08
1990 Oak	30	1	1	0	0	2.2	16	8	6	2	2	0	0	0	0	0	1	0	0	0	1	.000	0	0-0	0	.500	.500	6.75
WS Totals		3	3	0	0	15.2	132	17	9	5	3	0	1	0	3	0	11	2	0	2	1	.667	0	0-0	0	.274	.303	2.87
Postseason Totals		7	7	0	0	38.1	320	35	20	14	6	0	3	0	11	1	26	2	0	4	3	.571	0	0-0	0	.240	.288	3.29

LCS — Batting / Fielding

Year Tm	Age	G	AB	H	2B	3B	HR	TB	R	RBI	GW	TBB	IBB	SO	HBP	SH	SF	SB	CS	SB%	GDP	Avg	OBP	SLG	Pos	G	PO	A	E	DP	FPct
1989 Oak	29	1	0	0	0	0	0	0	0	0	0	0	0	0	0	0	0	0	0	—	0	—	—	—	P	1	0	1	0	0	1.000
1990 Oak	30	1	0	0	0	0	0	0	0	0	0	0	0	0	0	0	0	0	0	—	0	—	—	—	P	1	0	0	0	0	—
1992 Oak	32	2	0	0	0	0	0	0	0	0	0	0	0	0	0	0	0	0	0	—	0	—	—	—	P	2	1	1	0	0	1.000
LCS Totals		4	0	0	0	0	0	0	0	0	0	0	0	0	0	0	0	0	0	—	0	—	—	—	P	4	1	2	0	0	1.000

World Series — Batting / Fielding

Year Tm	Age	G	AB	H	2B	3B	HR	TB	R	RBI	GW	TBB	IBB	SO	HBP	SH	SF	SB	CS	SB%	GDP	Avg	OBP	SLG	Pos	G	PO	A	E	DP	FPct
1989 Oak	29	2	3	1	1	0	0	2	1	2	0	0	0	1	0	0	0	0	0	—	0	.333	.333	.667	P	2	0	3	0	0	1.000
1990 Oak	30	1	0	0	0	0	0	0	0	0	0	0	0	0	0	0	0	0	0	—	0	—	—	—	P	1	0	0	0	0	—
WS Totals		3	3	1	1	0	0	2	1	2	0	0	0	1	0	0	0	0	0	—	0	.333	.333	.667	P	3	0	3	0	0	1.000
Postseason Totals		7	3	1	1	0	0	2	1	2	0	0	0	1	0	0	0	0	0	—	0	.333	.333	.667	P	7	1	5	0	0	1.000

RAY MOORE—Raymond Leroy Moore—Nickname: Farmer—Throws: Right; Bats: Right
Ht: 6'0"; Wt: 195 lbs; Born: 6/1/1926 in Meadows, Maryland; Debut: 8/1/1952; Died: 3/2/1995

World Series — Pitching

Year Tm	Age	G	GS	CG	GF	IP	BFP	H	R	ER	HR	SH	SF	HB	TBB	IBB	SO	WP	Bk	W	L	Pct	ShO	Sv-Op	Hld	OAvg	OOBP	ERA
1959 ChA	33	1	0	0	1	1.0	4	1	1	1	1	0	0	0	0	0	1	0	0	0	0	—	0	0-0	0	.250	.250	9.00

World Series — Batting / Fielding

Year Tm	Age	G	AB	H	2B	3B	HR	TB	R	RBI	GW	TBB	IBB	SO	HBP	SH	SF	SB	CS	SB%	GDP	Avg	OBP	SLG	Pos	G	PO	A	E	DP	FPct
1959 ChA	33	1	0	0	0	0	0	0	0	0	0	0	0	0	0	0	0	0	0	—	0	—	—	—	P	1	0	0	0	0	—

TERRY MOORE—Terry Bluford Moore—Bats: Right; Throws: Right
Ht: 5'11"; Wt: 195 lbs; Born: 5/27/1912 in Vernon, Alabama; Debut: 4/16/1935; Died: 3/29/1995

World Series — Batting / Fielding

Year Tm	Age	G	AB	H	2B	3B	HR	TB	R	RBI	GW	TBB	IBB	SO	HBP	SH	SF	SB	CS	SB%	GDP	Avg	OBP	SLG	Pos	G	PO	A	E	DP	FPct
1942 StL	30	5	17	5	1	0	0	6	2	2	0	2	0	3	0	3	0	0	0	—	0	.294	.368	.353	OF	5	15	0	0	0	1.000
1946 StL	34	7	27	4	0	0	0	4	1	2	1	2	0	6	0	2	0	0	0	—	0	.148	.207	.148	OF	7	18	1	0	0	1.000
WS Totals		12	44	9	1	0	0	10	3	4	1	4	0	9	0	5	0	0	0	—	0	.205	.271	.227	OF	12	33	1	0	0	1.000

WHITEY MOORE—Lloyd Albert Moore—Throws: Right; Bats: Right
Ht: 6'1"; Wt: 195 lbs; Born: 6/10/1912 in Tuscarawas, Ohio; Debut: 9/27/1936; Died: 12/10/1987

World Series — Pitching

Year Tm	Age	G	GS	CG	GF	IP	BFP	H	R	ER	HR	SH	SF	HB	TBB	IBB	SO	WP	Bk	W	L	Pct	ShO	Sv-Op	Hld	OAvg	OOBP	ERA
1939 Cin	27	1	0	0	1	3.0	9	0	0	0	0	0	0	0	0	0	2	0	0	0	0	—	0	0-0	0	.000	.000	0.00
1940 Cin	28	3	0	0	0	8.1	38	8	3	3	1	0	0	0	6	0	7	0	0	0	0	—	0	0-0	0	.250	.368	3.24
WS Totals		4	0	0	1	11.1	94	8	3	3	1	0	0	0	6	0	9	0	0	0	0	—	0	0-0	0	.195	.298	2.38

World Series — Batting / Fielding

Year Tm	Age	G	AB	H	2B	3B	HR	TB	R	RBI	GW	TBB	IBB	SO	HBP	SH	SF	SB	CS	SB%	GDP	Avg	OBP	SLG	Pos	G	PO	A	E	DP	FPct
1939 Cin	27	1	1	0	0	0	0	0	0	0	0	0	0	0	0	0	0	0	0	—	0	.000	.000	.000	P	1	0	2	0	0	1.000
1940 Cin	28	3	2	0	0	0	0	0	0	0	0	0	0	1	0	0	0	0	0	—	0	.000	.000	.000	P	3	0	1	0	0	1.000
WS Totals		4	3	0	0	0	0	0	0	0	0	0	0	1	0	0	0	0	0	—	0	.000	.000	.000	P	4	0	3	0	0	1.000

WILCY MOORE—William Wilcy Moore—Nickname: Cy—Throws: Right; Bats: Right
Ht: 6'0"; Wt: 195 lbs; Born: 5/20/1897 in Bonita, Texas; Debut: 4/14/1927; Died: 3/29/1963

World Series — Pitching

Year Tm	Age	G	GS	CG	GF	IP	BFP	H	R	ER	HR	SH	SF	HB	TBB	IBB	SO	WP	Bk	W	L	Pct	ShO	Sv-Op	Hld	OAvg	OOBP	ERA
1927 NYA	30	2	1	1	1	10.2	45	11	3	1	0	1	1	0	2	1	2	0	0	1	0	1.000	0	1-1	0	.268	.295	0.84
1932 NYA	35	1	0	0	0	5.1	19	2	1	0	0	0	0	0	0	0	1	0	0	1	0	1.000	0	0-0	0	.105	.105	0.00
WS Totals		3	1	1	1	16.0	128	13	4	1	0	1	1	0	2	1	3	0	0	2	0	1.000	0	1-1	0	.217	.238	0.56

World Series — Batting / Fielding

Year Tm	Age	G	AB	H	2B	3B	HR	TB	R	RBI	GW	TBB	IBB	SO	HBP	SH	SF	SB	CS	SB%	GDP	Avg	OBP	SLG	Pos	G	PO	A	E	DP	FPct
1927 NYA	30	2	5	1	0	0	0	1	0	0	0	0	0	3	0	0	0	0	0	—	0	.200	.200	.200	P	2	0	5	1	0	.833
1932 NYA	35	1	3	1	0	0	0	1	0	0	0	0	0	2	0	0	0	0	0	—	0	.333	.333	.333	P	1	0	1	0	0	1.000
WS Totals		3	8	2	0	0	0	2	0	0	0	0	0	5	0	0	0	0	0	—	0	.250	.250	.250	P	3	0	6	1	0	.857

BOB MOOSE—Robert Ralph Moose—Throws: Right; Bats: Right
Ht: 6'0"; Wt: 200 lbs; Born: 10/9/1947 in Export, Pennsylvania; Debut: 9/19/1967; Died: 10/9/1976

LCS — Pitching

Year Tm	Age	G	GS	CG	GF	IP	BFP	H	R	ER	HR	SH	SF	HB	TBB	IBB	SO	WP	Bk	W	L	Pct	ShO	Sv-Op	Hld	OAvg	OOBP	ERA
1970 Pit	22	1	1	0	0	7.2	28	4	3	3	2	0	0	0	2	0	4	0	0	0	1	.000	0	0-0	0	.154	.214	3.52
1971 Pit	23	1	0	0	0	2.0	6	0	0	0	0	0	0	0	0	0	0	0	0	0	0	—	0	0-0	0	.000	.000	0.00
1972 Pit	24	2	1	0	1	0.2	7	5	4	4	0	0	0	0	0	0	0	1	0	0	1	.000	0	0-0	0	.714	.714	54.00
LCS Totals		4	2	0	1	10.1	82	9	7	7	2	0	0	0	2	0	4	1	0	0	2	.000	0	0-0	0	.231	.268	6.10

World Series — Pitching

Year Tm	Age	G	GS	CG	GF	IP	BFP	H	R	ER	HR	SH	SF	HB	TBB	IBB	SO	WP	Bk	W	L	Pct	ShO	Sv-Op	Hld	OAvg	OOBP	ERA
1971 Pit	23	3	1	0	0	9.2	42	12	7	7	2	1	0	0	2	0	7	1	0	0	0	—	0	0-0	0	.308	.341	6.52
Postseason Totals		7	3	0	1	20.0	166	21	14	14	4	1	0	0	4	0	11	2	0	0	2	.000	0	0-0	0	.269	.305	6.30

LCS — Batting / Fielding

Year Tm	Age	G	AB	H	2B	3B	HR	TB	R	RBI	GW	TBB	IBB	SO	HBP	SH	SF	SB	CS	SB%	GDP	Avg	OBP	SLG	Pos	G	PO	A	E	DP	FPct
1970 Pit	22	1	4	0	0	0	0	0	0	0	0	0	0	1	0	0	0	0	0	—	0	.000	.000	.000	P	1	0	3	0	0	1.000
1971 Pit	23	1	0	0	0	0	0	0	0	0	0	0	0	0	0	0	0	0	0	—	0	—	—	—	P	1	0	0	0	0	—
1972 Pit	24	2	0	0	0	0	0	0	0	0	0	0	0	0	0	0	0	0	0	—	0	—	—	—	P	2	0	0	0	0	—
LCS Totals		4	4	0	0	0	0	0	0	0	0	0	0	1	0	0	0	0	0	—	0	.000	.000	.000	P	4	0	3	0	0	1.000

World Series — Batting / Fielding

Year Tm	Age	G	AB	H	2B	3B	HR	TB	R	RBI	GW	TBB	IBB	SO	HBP	SH	SF	SB	CS	SB%	GDP	Avg	OBP	SLG	Pos	G	PO	A	E	DP	FPct
1971 Pit	23	3	2	0	0	0	0	0	0	0	0	0	0	1	0	1	0	0	0	—	0	.000	.000	.000	P	3	0	3	0	0	1.000
Postseason Totals		7	6	0	0	0	0	0	0	0	0	0	0	2	0	1	0	0	0	—	0	.000	.000	.000	P	7	0	6	0	0	1.000

JOSE MORALES—Jose Manuel Morales—Bats: Right; Throws: Right

Ht: 5'11"; Wt: 187 lbs; Born: 12/30/1944 in Frederiksted, Virgin Islands; Debut: 8/13/1973

LCS — Batting / Fielding

Year Tm	Age	G	AB	H	2B	3B	HR	TB	R	RBI	GW	TBB	IBB	SO	HBP	SH	SF	SB	CS	SB%	GDP	Avg	OBP	SLG	Pos	G	PO	A	E	DP	FPct
1983 LA	38	2	2	0	0	0	0	0	0	0	0	0	0	1	0	0	0	0	0	—	0	.000	.000	.000	—						

HERBIE MORAN—John Herbert Moran—Bats: Left; Throws: Right

Ht: 5'5"; Wt: 150 lbs; Born: 2/16/1884 in Costello, Pennsylvania; Debut: 4/16/1908; Died: 9/21/1954

World Series — Batting / Fielding

Year Tm	Age	G	AB	H	2B	3B	HR	TB	R	RBI	GW	TBB	IBB	SO	HBP	SH	SF	SB	CS	SB%	GDP	Avg	OBP	SLG	Pos	G	PO	A	E	DP	FPct
1914 Bos	30	3	13	1	1	0	0	2	2	0	0	1	0	1	0	1	0	1	0	1.00	0	.077	.143	.154	OF	3	2	0	1	0	.667

PAT MORAN—Patrick Joseph Moran—Bats: Right; Throws: Right

Ht: 5'10"; Wt: 180 lbs; Born: 2/7/1876 in Fitchburg, Massachusetts; Debut: 5/15/1901; Died: 3/7/1924

World Series — Batting / Fielding

Year Tm	Age	G	AB	H	2B	3B	HR	TB	R	RBI	GW	TBB	IBB	SO	HBP	SH	SF	SB	CS	SB%	GDP	Avg	OBP	SLG	Pos	G	PO	A	E	DP	FPct
1906 ChN	30	2	2	0	0	0	0	0	0	0	0	0	0	0	0	0	0	0	0	—	0	.000	.000	.000	—						
1907 ChN	31	1	0	0	0	0	0	0	0	0	0	0	0	0	0	0	0	0	0	—	0	—	—	—	—						
WS Totals		3	2	0	0	0	0	0	0	0	0	0	0	0	0	0	0	0	0	—	0	.000	.000	.000	—	0	0	0	0	0	—

MICKEY MORANDINI—Michael Robert Morandini—Bats: Left; Throws: Right

Ht: 5'11"; Wt: 170 lbs; Born: 4/22/1966 in Kittanning, Pennsylvania; Debut: 9/1/1990

LCS — Batting / Fielding

Year Tm	Age	G	AB	H	2B	3B	HR	TB	R	RBI	GW	TBB	IBB	SO	HBP	SH	SF	SB	CS	SB%	GDP	Avg	OBP	SLG	Pos	G	PO	A	E	DP	FPct
1993 Phi	27	4	16	4	0	1	0	6	1	2	0	0	0	3	0	0	0	1	0	1.00	0	.250	.250	.375	2B	4	8	9	1	2	.944

World Series — Batting / Fielding

Year Tm	Age	G	AB	H	2B	3B	HR	TB	R	RBI	GW	TBB	IBB	SO	HBP	SH	SF	SB	CS	SB%	GDP	Avg	OBP	SLG	Pos	G	PO	A	E	DP	FPct
1993 Phi	27	3	5	1	0	0	0	1	1	0	0	1	0	2	0	0	0	0	0	—	0	.200	.333	.200	2B	1	2	0	0	0	1.000
Postseason Totals		7	21	5	0	1	0	7	2	2	0	1	0	5	0	0	0	1	0	1.00	0	.238	.273	.333	2B	5	10	9	1	2	.950

MIKE MORDECAI—Michael Howard Mordecai—Bats: Both; Throws: Right

Ht: 5'11"; Wt: 175 lbs; Born: 12/13/1967 in Birmingham, Alabama; Debut: 5/8/1994

Division Series — Batting / Fielding

Year Tm	Age	G	AB	H	2B	3B	HR	TB	R	RBI	GW	TBB	IBB	SO	HBP	SH	SF	SB	CS	SB%	GDP	Avg	OBP	SLG	Pos	G	PO	A	E	DP	FPct
1995 Atl	27	2	3	2	1	0	0	3	1	2	1	0	0	0	0	0	0	0	0	—	0	.667	.667	1.000	SS	1	1	0	0	0	1.000

LCS — Batting / Fielding

Year Tm	Age	G	AB	H	2B	3B	HR	TB	R	RBI	GW	TBB	IBB	SO	HBP	SH	SF	SB	CS	SB%	GDP	Avg	OBP	SLG	Pos	G	PO	A	E	DP	FPct
1995 Atl	27	2	2	0	0	0	0	0	0	0	0	0	0	1	0	0	0	0	0	—	0	.000	.000	.000	SS	1	0	0	0	0	—
1996 Atl	28	4	4	1	0	0	0	1	1	0	0	0	0	1	0	0	0	0	0	—	0	.250	.250	.250	3B	1	0	0	0	0	—
																									2B	2	1	1	0	1	1.000
LCS Totals		6	6	1	0	0	0	1	1	0	0	0	0	2	0	0	0	0	0	—	0	.167	.167	.167	2B	2	1	1	0	1	1.000

World Series — Batting / Fielding

Year Tm	Age	G	AB	H	2B	3B	HR	TB	R	RBI	GW	TBB	IBB	SO	HBP	SH	SF	SB	CS	SB%	GDP	Avg	OBP	SLG	Pos	G	PO	A	E	DP	FPct
1995 Atl	27	3	3	1	0	0	0	1	0	0	0	0	0	1	0	1	0	0	0	—	0	.333	.333	.333	SS	2	0	6	0	0	1.000
1996 Atl	28	1	1	0	0	0	0	0	0	0	0	0	0	0	0	0	0	0	0	—	0	.000	.000	.000	—						
WS Totals		4	4	1	0	0	0	1	0	0	0	0	0	1	0	1	0	0	0	—	0	.250	.250	.250	SS	2	0	6	0	0	1.000
Postseason Totals		12	13	4	1	0	0	5	2	2	1	0	0	3	0	1	0	0	0	—	0	.308	.308	.385	SS	4	1	6	0	0	1.000

DAVE MOREHEAD—David Michael Morehead—Nickname: Moe—Throws: Right; Bats: Right

Ht: 6'1"; Wt: 185 lbs; Born: 9/5/1942 in San Diego, California; Debut: 4/13/1963

World Series — Pitching

Year Tm	Age	G	GS	CG	GF	IP	BFP	H	R	ER	HR	SH	SF	HB	TBB	IBB	SO	WP	Bk	W	L	Pct	ShO	Sv-Op	Hld	OAvg	OOBP	ERA
1967 Bos	25	2	0	0	0	3.1	14	0	0	0	0	0	0	0	4	0	3	0	0	0	0	—	0	0-0	0	.000	.286	0.00

World Series — Batting / Fielding

Year Tm	Age	G	AB	H	2B	3B	HR	TB	R	RBI	GW	TBB	IBB	SO	HBP	SH	SF	SB	CS	SB%	GDP	Avg	OBP	SLG	Pos	G	PO	A	E	DP	FPct
1967 Bos	25	2	0	0	0	0	0	0	0	0	0	0	0	0	0	0	0	0	0	—	0	—	—	—	P	2	0	0	0	0	—

KEITH MORELAND—Bobby Keith Moreland—Nickname: Zonk—Bats: Right; Throws: Right

Ht: 6'0"; Wt: 190 lbs; Born: 5/2/1954 in Dallas, Texas; Debut: 10/1/1978

Division Series — Batting / Fielding

Year Tm	Age	G	AB	H	2B	3B	HR	TB	R	RBI	GW	TBB	IBB	SO	HBP	SH	SF	SB	CS	SB%	GDP	Avg	OBP	SLG	Pos	G	PO	A	E	DP	FPct
1981 Phi	27	4	13	6	0	0	1	9	2	3	0	1	0	1	0	0	0	0	1	.00	0	.462	.500	.692	C	4	29	2	1	0	.969

LCS — Batting / Fielding

Year Tm	Age	G	AB	H	2B	3B	HR	TB	R	RBI	GW	TBB	IBB	SO	HBP	SH	SF	SB	CS	SB%	GDP	Avg	OBP	SLG	Pos	G	PO	A	E	DP	FPct
1980 Phi	26	2	1	0	0	0	0	0	0	1	0	0	0	0	0	0	0	0	0	—	0	.000	.000	.000	C	1	0	0	0	0	—
1984 ChN	30	5	18	6	2	0	0	8	3	2	0	1	0	1	0	0	1	0	0	—	0	.333	.350	.444	OF	5	9	0	0	0	1.000
LCS Totals		7	19	6	2	0	0	8	3	3	0	1	0	1	0	0	1	0	0	—	0	.316	.333	.421	OF	5	9	0	0	0	1.000

World Series — Batting / Fielding

Year Tm	Age	G	AB	H	2B	3B	HR	TB	R	RBI	GW	TBB	IBB	SO	HBP	SH	SF	SB	CS	SB%	GDP	Avg	OBP	SLG	Pos	G	PO	A	E	DP	FPct
1980 Phi	26	3	12	4	0	0	0	4	1	1	0	0	0	1	0	1	0	0	0	—	1	.333	.333	.333	—						
Postseason Totals		14	44	16	2	0	1	21	6	7	0	2	0	3	0	1	1	0	1	.00	1	.364	.383	.477	C	5	29	2	1	0	.969

OMAR MORENO—Omar Renan Moreno—Bats: Left; Throws: Left

Ht: 6'2"; Wt: 180 lbs; Born: 10/24/1952 in Puerto Armuelles, Panama; Debut: 9/6/1975

LCS — Batting / Fielding

Year Tm	Age	G	AB	H	2B	3B	HR	TB	R	RBI	GW	TBB	IBB	SO	HBP	SH	SF	SB	CS	SB%	GDP	Avg	OBP	SLG	Pos	G	PO	A	E	DP	FPct
1979 Pit	26	3	12	3	0	1	0	5	3	0	0	2	0	2	0	1	0	1	0	1.00	0	.250	.357	.417	OF	3	7	0	0	0	1.000

World Series — Batting / Fielding

Year Tm	Age	G	AB	H	2B	3B	HR	TB	R	RBI	GW	TBB	IBB	SO	HBP	SH	SF	SB	CS	SB%	GDP	Avg	OBP	SLG	Pos	G	PO	A	E	DP	FPct
1979 Pit	26	7	33	11	2	0	0	13	4	3	0	1	1	7	0	0	0	0	0	—	0	.333	.353	.394	OF	7	20	1	0	0	1.000
Postseason Totals		10	45	14	2	1	0	18	7	3	0	3	1	9	0	1	0	1	0	1.00	0	.311	.354	.400	OF	10	27	1	0	0	1.000

ROGER MORET—Rogelio Moret—Throws: Left; Bats: Both

Ht: 6'4"; Wt: 170 lbs; Born: 9/16/1949 in Guayama, Puerto Rico; Debut: 9/13/1970

LCS — Pitching

Year Tm	Age	G	GS	CG	GF	IP	BFP	H	R	ER	HR	SH	SF	HB	TBB	IBB	SO	WP	Bk	W	L	Pct	ShO	Sv-Op	Hld	OAvg	OOBP	ERA
1975 Bos	26	1	0	0	0	1.0	5	1	0	0	0	0	0	0	1	0	0	0	0	1	0	1.000	0	0-0	0	.250	.400	0.00

World Series — Pitching

Year Tm	Age	G	GS	CG	GF	IP	BFP	H	R	ER	HR	SH	SF	HB	TBB	IBB	SO	WP	Bk	W	L	Pct	ShO	Sv-Op	Hld	OAvg	OOBP	ERA
1975 Bos	26	3	0	0	1	1.2	10	2	0	0	0	0	0	0	3	1	1	0	0	0	0	—	0	0-1	0	.286	.500	0.00
Postseason Totals		4	0	0	1	2.2	30	3	0	0	0	0	0	0	4	1	1	0	0	1	0	1.000	0	0-1	0	.273	.467	0.00

LCS — Batting / Fielding

Year Tm	Age	G	AB	H	2B	3B	HR	TB	R	RBI	GW	TBB	IBB	SO	HBP	SH	SF	SB	CS	SB%	GDP	Avg	OBP	SLG	Pos	G	PO	A	E	DP	FPct
1975 Bos	26	1	0	0	0	0	0	0	0	0	0	0	0	0	0	0	0	0	0	—	0	—	—	—	P	1	0	0	0	0	—

World Series — Batting / Fielding

Year Tm	Age	G	AB	H	2B	3B	HR	TB	R	RBI	GW	TBB	IBB	SO	HBP	SH	SF	SB	CS	SB%	GDP	Avg	OBP	SLG	Pos	G	PO	A	E	DP	FPct
1975 Bos	26	3	0	0	0	0	0	0	0	0	0	0	0	0	0	0	0	0	0	—	0	—	—	—	P	3	0	1	0	0	1.000
Postseason Totals		4	0	0	0	0	0	0	0	0	0	0	0	0	0	0	0	0	0	—	0	—	—	—	P	4	0	1	0	0	1.000

BOBBY MORGAN—Robert Morris Morgan—Bats: Right; Throws: Right

Ht: 5'9"; Wt: 175 lbs; Born: 6/29/1926 in Oklahoma City, Oklahoma; Debut: 4/18/1950

World Series — Batting / Fielding

Year Tm	Age	G	AB	H	2B	3B	HR	TB	R	RBI	GW	TBB	IBB	SO	HBP	SH	SF	SB	CS	SB%	GDP	Avg	OBP	SLG	Pos	G	PO	A	E	DP	FPct
1952 Bro	26	2	1	0	0	0	0	0	0	0	0	0	0	0	0	0	0	0	0	—	0	.000	.000	.000	3B	1	0	1	0	0	1.000
1953 Bro	27	1	1	0	0	0	0	0	0	0	0	0	0	0	0	0	0	0	0	—	0	.000	.000	.000	—						
WS Totals		3	2	0	0	0	0	0	0	0	0	0	0	0	0	0	0	0	0	—	0	.000	.000	.000	3B	1	0	1	0	0	1.000

JOE MORGAN (HOF 1990-W)—Joe Leonard Morgan—Nickname: Little Joe—Bats: Left; Throws: Right

Ht: 5'7"; Wt: 160 lbs; Born: 9/19/1943 in Bonham, Texas; Debut: 9/21/1963

LCS — Batting / Fielding

Year Tm	Age	G	AB	H	2B	3B	HR	TB	R	RBI	GW	TBB	IBB	SO	HBP	SH	SF	SB	CS	SB%	GDP	Avg	OBP	SLG	Pos	G	PO	A	E	DP	FPct
1972 Cin	29	5	19	5	0	0	2	11	5	3	0	1	0	2	0	1	0	1	0	1.00	0	.263	.300	.579	2B	5	12	18	0	3	1.000
1973 Cin	30	5	20	2	1	0	0	3	1	1	0	2	0	2	0	1	0	0	0	—	1	.100	.182	.150	2B	5	12	25	0	4	1.000
1975 Cin-*M*	32	3	11	3	3	0	0	6	2	1	0	3	0	2	0	0	0	4	0	1.00	0	.273	.429	.545	2B	3	2	9	0	1	1.000
1976 Cin-*M*	33	3	7	0	0	0	0	0	2	0	0	6	2	1	0	0	0	2	0	1.00	0	.000	.462	.000	2B	3	9	5	0	2	1.000
1979 Cin	36	3	11	0	0	0	0	0	0	0	0	3	0	1	0	0	0	1	0	1.00	0	.000	.214	.000	2B	3	12	11	0	2	1.000
1980 Hou	37	4	13	2	1	1	0	5	1	0	0	6	1	1	0	0	0	0	0	—	0	.154	.421	.385	2B	4	9	8	0	3	1.000
1983 Phi	40	4	15	1	0	0	0	1	1	0	0	2	0	1	0	0	0	0	0	—	0	.067	.176	.067	2B	4	8	7	0	0	1.000
LCS Totals		27	96	13	5	1	2	26	12	5	0	23	3	10	0	2	0	8	0	1.00	1	.135	.303	.271	2B	27	64	83	0	15	1.000

World Series — Batting / Fielding

Year Tm	Age	G	AB	H	2B	3B	HR	TB	R	RBI	GW	TBB	IBB	SO	HBP	SH	SF	SB	CS	SB%	GDP	Avg	OBP	SLG	Pos	G	PO	A	E	DP	FPct
1972 Cin	29	7	24	3	2	0	0	5	4	1	0	6	0	3	0	0	0	2	1	.67	1	.125	.300	.208	2B	7	18	18	1	3	.973
1975 Cin-*M*	32	7	27	7	1	0	0	8	4	3	2	5	0	1	0	0	1	2	1	.67	0	.259	.364	.296	2B	7	16	27	0	4	1.000
1976 Cin-*M*	33	4	15	5	1	1	1	11	3	2	0	2	1	2	0	0	0	2	0	1.00	0	.333	.412	.733	2B	4	13	10	2	3	.920
1983 Phi	40	5	19	5	0	1	2	13	3	2	0	2	0	3	0	0	0	1	2	.33	0	.263	.333	.684	2B	5	8	10	0	3	1.000
WS Totals		23	85	20	4	2	3	37	14	8	2	15	1	9	0	0	1	7	4	.64	1	.235	.347	.435	2B	23	55	65	3	13	.976
Postseason Totals		50	181	33	9	3	5	63	26	13	2	38	4	19	0	2	1	15	4	.79	2	.182	.323	.348	2B	50	119	148	3	28	.989

TOM MORGAN—Tom Stephen Morgan—Nickname: Plowboy—Throws: Right; Bats: Right

Ht: 6'1"; Wt: 180 lbs; Born: 5/20/1930 in El Monte, California; Debut: 4/20/1951; Died: 1/13/1987

World Series — Pitching

Year Tm	Age	G	GS	CG	GF	IP	BFP	H	R	ER	HR	SH	SF	HB	TBB	IBB	SO	WP	Bk	W	L	Pct	ShO	Sv-Op	Hld	OAvg	OOBP	ERA
1951 NYA	21	1	0	0	1	2.0	10	2	0	0	0	0	0	0	1	0	3	0	0	0	0	—	0	0- 0	0	.222	.300	0.00
1955 NYA	25	2	0	0	0	3.2	17	3	2	2	0	0	1	0	3	1	1	0	0	0	0	—	0	0- 0	0	.231	.353	4.91
1956 NYA	26	2	0	0	0	4.0	21	6	4	4	0	0	0	0	4	2	3	0	0	0	1	.000	0	0- 0	0	.353	.476	9.00
WS Totals		5	0	0	1	9.2	96	11	6	6	0	0	1	0	8	3	7	0	0	0	1	.000	0	0-0	0	.282	.396	5.59

World Series — Batting / Fielding

Year Tm	Age	G	AB	H	2B	3B	HR	TB	R	RBI	GW	TBB	IBB	SO	HBP	SH	SF	SB	CS	SB%	GDP	Avg	OBP	SLG	Pos	G	PO	A	E	DP	FPct
1951 NYA	21	1	0	0	0	0	0	0	0	0	0	0	0	0	0	0	0	0	0	—	0	—	—	—	P	1	0	1	0	0	1.000
1955 NYA	25	2	0	0	0	0	0	0	0	0	0	0	0	0	0	0	0	0	0	—	0	—	—	—	P	2	0	0	0	0	—
1956 NYA	26	2	1	1	0	0	0	1	1	0	0	0	0	0	0	0	0	0	0	—	0	1.000	1.000	1.000	P	2	0	0	0	0	—
WS Totals		5	1	1	0	0	0	1	1	0	0	0	0	0	0	0	0	0	0	—	0	1.000	1.000	1.000	P	5	0	1	0	0	1.000

GEORGE MORIARTY—George Joseph Moriarty—Bats: Right; Throws: Right

Ht: 6'0"; Wt: 185 lbs; Born: 6/7/1884 in Chicago, Illinois; Debut: 9/27/1903; Died: 4/8/1964

World Series — Batting / Fielding

Year Tm	Age	G	AB	H	2B	3B	HR	TB	R	RBI	GW	TBB	IBB	SO	HBP	SH	SF	SB	CS	SB%	GDP	Avg	OBP	SLG	Pos	G	PO	A	E	DP	FPct
1909 Det	25	7	22	6	1	0	0	7	4	1	0	3	0	1	0	0	0	0	1	.00	0	.273	.360	.318	3B	7	7	15	0	1	1.000

ALVIN MORMAN—Throws: Left; Bats: Left

Ht: 6'3"; Wt: 210 lbs; Born: 1/6/1969 in Rockingham, North Carolina; Debut: 4/2/1996

Division Series — Pitching

Year Tm	Age	G	GS	CG	GF	IP	BFP	H	R	ER	HR	SH	SF	HB	TBB	IBB	SO	WP	Bk	W	L	Pct	ShO	Sv-Op	Hld	OAvg	OOBP	ERA
1997 Cle	28	1	0	0	0	0.0	1	0	0	0	0	0	0	0	1	0	0	0	0	0	0	—	0	0- 0	0	—	1.000	—

LCS — Pitching

Year Tm	Age	G	GS	CG	GF	IP	BFP	H	R	ER	HR	SH	SF	HB	TBB	IBB	SO	WP	Bk	W	L	Pct	ShO	Sv-Op	Hld	OAvg	OOBP	ERA
1997 Cle	28	2	0	0	0	1.1	4	0	0	0	0	0	0	0	0	0	1	0	0	0	0	—	0	0- 0	0	.000	.000	0.00

World Series — Pitching

Year Tm	Age	G	GS	CG	GF	IP	BFP	H	R	ER	HR	SH	SF	HB	TBB	IBB	SO	WP	Bk	W	L	Pct	ShO	Sv-Op	Hld	OAvg	OOBP	ERA
1997 Cle	28	2	0	0	0	0.1	4	0	2	0	0	0	0	0	2	0	1	0	0	0	0	—	0	0- 0	0	.000	.500	0.00
Postseason Totals		5	0	0	0	1.2	18	0	2	0	0	0	0	0	3	0	2	0	0	0	0	—	0	0-0	0	.000	.333	0.00

Division Series — Batting / Fielding

Year Tm	Age	G	AB	H	2B	3B	HR	TB	R	RBI	GW	TBB	IBB	SO	HBP	SH	SF	SB	CS	SB%	GDP	Avg	OBP	SLG	Pos	G	PO	A	E	DP	FPct
1997 Cle	28	1	0	0	0	0	0	0	0	0	0	0	0	0	0	0	0	0	0	—	0	—	—	—	P	1	0	0	0	0	—

LCS — Batting / Fielding

Year Tm	Age	G	AB	H	2B	3B	HR	TB	R	RBI	GW	TBB	IBB	SO	HBP	SH	SF	SB	CS	SB%	GDP	Avg	OBP	SLG	Pos	G	PO	A	E	DP	FPct
1997 Cle	28	2	0	0	0	0	0	0	0	0	0	0	0	0	0	0	0	0	0	—	0	—	—	—	P	2	0	0	0	0	—

World Series — Batting / Fielding

Year Tm	Age	G	AB	H	2B	3B	HR	TB	R	RBI	GW	TBB	IBB	SO	HBP	SH	SF	SB	CS	SB%	GDP	Avg	OBP	SLG	Pos	G	PO	A	E	DP	FPct
1997 Cle	28	2	0	0	0	0	0	0	0	0	0	0	0	0	0	0	0	0	0	—	0	—	—	—	P	2	0	0	0	0	—
Postseason Totals		5	0	0	0	0	0	0	0	0	0	0	0	0	0	0	0	0	0	—	0	—	—	—	P	5	0	0	0	0	—

HAL MORRIS—William Harold Morris—Bats: Left; Throws: Left

Ht: 6'3"; Wt: 200 lbs; Born: 4/9/1965 in Fort Rucker, Alabama; Debut: 7/29/1988

Division Series — Batting / Fielding

Year Tm	Age	G	AB	H	2B	3B	HR	TB	R	RBI	GW	TBB	IBB	SO	HBP	SH	SF	SB	CS	SB%	GDP	Avg	OBP	SLG	Pos	G	PO	A	E	DP	FPct
1995 Cin	30	3	10	5	1	0	0	6	5	2	1	3	2	1	0	0	0	1	0	1.00	0	.500	.615	.600	1B	3	22	2	0	1	1.000

LCS — Batting / Fielding

Year Tm	Age	G	AB	H	2B	3B	HR	TB	R	RBI	GW	TBB	IBB	SO	HBP	SH	SF	SB	CS	SB%	GDP	Avg	OBP	SLG	Pos	G	PO	A	E	DP	FPct
1990 Cin	25	5	12	5	1	0	0	6	3	1	0	1	1	0	1	1	0	0	0	—	0	.417	.500	.500	1B	4	20	2	0	2	1.000
1995 Cin	30	4	12	2	1	0	0	3	0	1	0	1	1	1	1	0	0	1	0	1.00	0	.167	.286	.250	1B	4	27	3	0	2	1.000
LCS Totals		9	24	7	2	0	0	9	3	2	0	2	2	1	2	1	0	1	0	1.00	0	.292	.393	.375	1B	8	47	5	0	4	1.000

World Series — Batting / Fielding

Year Tm	Age	G	AB	H	2B	3B	HR	TB	R	RBI	GW	TBB	IBB	SO	HBP	SH	SF	SB	CS	SB%	GDP	Avg	OBP	SLG	Pos	G	PO	A	E	DP	FPct
1990 Cin	25	4	14	1	0	0	0	1	0	2	2	1	0	1	0	0	1	0	0	—	1	.071	.125	.071	1B	2	18	1	0	1	1.000
Postseason Totals		16	48	13	3	0	0	16	8	6	3	6	4	3	2	1	1	2	0	1.00	1	.271	.368	.333	1B	13	87	8	0	6	1.000

JACK MORRIS—John Scott Morris—Throws: Right; Bats: Right

Ht: 6'3"; Wt: 195 lbs; Born: 5/16/1955 in St. Paul, Minnesota; Debut: 7/26/1977

LCS — Pitching

Year Tm	Age	G	GS	CG	GF	IP	BFP	H	R	ER	HR	SH	SF	HB	TBB	IBB	SO	WP	Bk	W	L	Pct	ShO	Sv-Op	Hld	OAvg	OOBP	ERA
1984 Det	29	1	1	0	0	7.0	27	5	1	1	0	0	0	0	1	0	4	0	0	1	0	1.000	0	0- 0	0	.192	.222	1.29
1987 Det	32	1	1	1	0	8.0	33	6	6	6	1	0	0	0	3	0	7	0	0	0	1	.000	0	0- 0	0	.200	.273	6.75
1991 Min	36	2	2	0	0	13.1	57	17	6	6	0	0	0	0	1	0	7	2	0	2	0	1.000	0	0- 0	0	.304	.316	4.05
1992 Tor	37	2	2	1	0	12.1	55	11	9	9	3	1	1	0	9	1	6	1	0	0	1	.000	0	0- 0	0	.250	.370	6.57
LCS Totals		6	6	2	0	40.2	344	39	22	22	4	1	1	0	14	1	24	3	0	3	2	.600	0	0-0	0	.250	.310	4.87

World Series — Pitching

Year Tm	Age	G	GS	CG	GF	IP	BFP	H	R	ER	HR	SH	SF	HB	TBB	IBB	SO	WP	Bk	W	L	Pct	ShO	Sv-Op	Hld	OAvg	OOBP	ERA
1984 Det	29	2	2	2	0	18.0	67	13	4	4	1	0	0	0	3	0	13	2	0	2	0	1.000	0	0- 0	0	.203	.239	2.00
1991 Min	36	3	3	1	0	23.0	92	18	3	3	1	2	0	0	9	1	15	1	0	2	0	1.000	1	0- 0	0	.222	.300	1.17
1992 Tor	37	2	2	0	0	10.2	50	13	10	10	3	0	0	0	6	1	12	1	0	0	2	.000	0	0- 0	0	.295	.380	8.44
WS Totals		7	7	3	0	51.2	418	44	17	17	5	2	0	0	18	2	40	4	0	4	2	.667	1	0-0	0	.233	.300	2.96
Postseason Totals		13	13	5	0	92.1	762	83	39	39	9	3	1	0	32	3	64	7	0	7	4	.636	1	0-0	0	.241	.304	3.80

LCS — Batting / Fielding

Year	Tm	Age	G	AB	H	2B	3B	HR	TB	R	RBI	GW	TBB	IBB	SO	HBP	SH	SF	SB	CS	SB%	GDP	Avg	OBP	SLG	Pos	G	PO	A	E	DP	FPct
1984	Det	29	1	0	0	0	0	0	0	0	0	0	0	0	0	0	0	0	0	0	—	0	—	—	—	P	1	1	1	0	0	1.000
1987	Det	32	2	0	0	0	0	0	0	1	0	0	0	0	0	0	0	0	0	0	—	0	—	—	—	P	1	0	0	0	0	—
1991	Min	36	2	0	0	0	0	0	0	0	0	0	0	0	0	0	0	0	0	0	—	0	—	—	—	P	2	3	2	0	0	1.000
1992	Tor	37	2	0	0	0	0	0	0	0	0	0	0	0	0	0	0	0	0	0	—	0	—	—	—	P	2	0	4	0	1	1.000
LCS Totals			7	0	0	0	0	0	0	1	0	0	0	0	0	0	0	0	0	0	—	0	—	—	—	P	6	4	7	0	1	1.000

World Series — Batting / Fielding

Year	Tm	Age	G	AB	H	2B	3B	HR	TB	R	RBI	GW	TBB	IBB	SO	HBP	SH	SF	SB	CS	SB%	GDP	Avg	OBP	SLG	Pos	G	PO	A	E	DP	FPct
1984	Det	29	2	0	0	0	0	0	0	0	0	0	0	0	0	0	0	0	0	0	—	0	—	—	—	P	2	5	1	0	0	1.000
1991	Min	36	3	2	0	0	0	0	0	0	0	0	0	0	1	0	0	0	0	0	—	0	.000	.000	.000	P	3	3	3	0	0	1.000
1992	Tor	37	2	2	0	0	0	0	0	0	0	0	0	0	2	0	0	0	0	0	—	0	.000	.000	.000	P	2	0	1	0	0	1.000
WS Totals			7	4	0	0	0	0	0	0	0	0	0	0	3	0	0	0	0	0	—	0	.000	.000	.000	P	7	8	5	0	0	1.000
Postseason Totals			14	4	0	0	0	0	0	1	0	0	0	0	3	0	0	0	0	0	—	0	.000	.000	.000	P	13	12	12	0	1	1.000

JOHN MORRIS
John Daniel Morris—Bats: Left; Throws: Left — Ht: 6'1"; Wt: 185 lbs; Born: 2/23/1961 in North Bellmore, New York; Debut: 8/5/1986

LCS — Batting / Fielding

Year	Tm	Age	G	AB	H	2B	3B	HR	TB	R	RBI	GW	TBB	IBB	SO	HBP	SH	SF	SB	CS	SB%	GDP	Avg	OBP	SLG	Pos	G	PO	A	E	DP	FPct
1987	StL	26	2	3	0	0	0	0	0	0	0	0	0	0	0	0	0	0	0	0	—	0	.000	.000	.000	OF	2	1	0	0	0	1.000

World Series — Batting / Fielding

Year	Tm	Age	G	AB	H	2B	3B	HR	TB	R	RBI	GW	TBB	IBB	SO	HBP	SH	SF	SB	CS	SB%	GDP	Avg	OBP	SLG	Pos	G	PO	A	E	DP	FPct
1987	StL	26	1	2	0	0	0	0	0	0	0	0	0	0	0	0	0	0	0	0	—	1	.000	.000	.000	OF	1	2	0	0	0	1.000
Postseason Totals			3	5	0	0	0	0	0	0	0	0	0	0	0	0	0	0	0	0	—	1	.000	.000	.000	OF	3	3	0	0	0	1.000

JIM MORRISON
James Forrest Morrison—Bats: Right; Throws: Right — Ht: 5'11"; Wt: 175 lbs; Born: 9/23/1952 in Pensacola, Florida; Debut: 9/18/1977

LCS — Batting / Fielding

Year	Tm	Age	G	AB	H	2B	3B	HR	TB	R	RBI	GW	TBB	IBB	SO	HBP	SH	SF	SB	CS	SB%	GDP	Avg	OBP	SLG	Pos	G	PO	A	E	DP	FPct
1978	Phi	26	1	1	0	0	0	0	0	0	0	0	0	0	1	0	0	0	0	0	—	0	.000	.000	—	—						
1987	Det	35	2	5	2	0	0	0	2	1	0	0	0	0	1	0	0	0	0	0	—	0	.400	.400	.400	3B	1	1	2	0	0	1.000
LCS Totals			3	6	2	0	0	0	2	1	0	0	0	0	2	0	0	0	0	0	—	0	.333	.333	.333	3B	1	1	2	0	0	1.000

JOHNNY MORRISON
John Dewey Morrison—Nickname: Jughandle Johnny—Throws: Right; Bats: Right — Ht: 5'11"; Wt: 188 lbs; Born: 10/22/1895 in Pellville, Kentucky; Debut: 9/28/1920; Died: 3/20/1966

World Series — Pitching

Year	Tm	Age	G	GS	CG	GF	IP	BFP	H	R	ER	HR	SH	SF	HB	TBB	IBB	SO	WP	Bk	W	L	Pct	ShO	Sv-Op	Hld	OAvg	OOBP	ERA
1925	Pit	29	3	0	0	1	9.1	40	11	3	3	0	1	0	0	1	0	7	0				—	0	0-0		.297	.316	2.89

World Series — Batting / Fielding

Year	Tm	Age	G	AB	H	2B	3B	HR	TB	R	RBI	GW	TBB	IBB	SO	HBP	SH	SF	SB	CS	SB%	GDP	Avg	OBP	SLG	Pos	G	PO	A	E	DP	FPct
1925	Pit	29	3	2	1	0	0	0	1	1	0	0	0	0	0	0	0	0	0	0	—	0	.500	.500	.500	P	3	0	3	0	0	1.000

LLOYD MOSEBY
Lloyd Anthony Moseby—Nickname: Shaker—Bats: Left; Throws: Right — Ht: 6'3"; Wt: 200 lbs; Born: 11/5/1959 in Portland, Arkansas; Debut: 5/24/1980

LCS — Batting / Fielding

Year	Tm	Age	G	AB	H	2B	3B	HR	TB	R	RBI	GW	TBB	IBB	SO	HBP	SH	SF	SB	CS	SB%	GDP	Avg	OBP	SLG	Pos	G	PO	A	E	DP	FPct
1985	Tor	25	7	31	7	1	0	0	8	5	4	0	2	0	3	0	0	0	1	1	.50	1	.226	.273	.258	OF	7	16	0	0	0	1.000
1989	Tor	29	5	16	5	0	0	1	8	4	2	0	5	0	2	0	0	0	1	0	1.00	0	.313	.476	.500	OF	5	15	0	0	0	1.000
LCS Totals			12	47	12	1	0	1	16	9	6	0	7	0	5	0	0	0	2	1	.67	1	.255	.352	.340	OF	12	31	0	0	0	1.000

WALLY MOSES
Wallace Moses—Nickname: Peepsight—Bats: Left; Throws: Left — Ht: 5'10"; Wt: 160 lbs; Born: 10/8/1910 in Uvalda, Georgia; Debut: 4/17/1935; Died: 10/10/1990

World Series — Batting / Fielding

Year	Tm	Age	G	AB	H	2B	3B	HR	TB	R	RBI	GW	TBB	IBB	SO	HBP	SH	SF	SB	CS	SB%	GDP	Avg	OBP	SLG	Pos	G	PO	A	E	DP	FPct
1946	Bos	35	4	12	5	0	0	0	5	1	0	0	1	0	2	0	0	0	0	0	—	0	.417	.462	.417	OF	4	5	0	0	0	1.000

DON MOSSI
Donald Louis Mossi—Nicknames: The Sphinx, Ears—Throws: Left; Bats: Left — Ht: 6'1"; Wt: 195 lbs; Born: 1/11/1929 in St. Helena, California; Debut: 4/17/1954

World Series — Pitching

Year	Tm	Age	G	GS	CG	GF	IP	BFP	H	R	ER	HR	SH	SF	HB	TBB	IBB	SO	WP	Bk	W	L	Pct	ShO	Sv-Op	Hld	OAvg	OOBP	ERA
1954	Cle	25	3	0	0	2	4.0	13	3	0	0	0	0	0	0	0	0	1	0	0	0	0	—	0	0-0	0	.231	.231	0.00

World Series — Batting / Fielding

Year	Tm	Age	G	AB	H	2B	3B	HR	TB	R	RBI	GW	TBB	IBB	SO	HBP	SH	SF	SB	CS	SB%	GDP	Avg	OBP	SLG	Pos	G	PO	A	E	DP	FPct
1954	Cle	25	3	0	0	0	0	0	0	0	0	0	0	0	0	0	0	0	0	0	—	0	—	—	—	P	3	0	2	0	0	1.000

MANNY MOTA
Manuel Rafael Mota—Bats: Right; Throws: Right — Ht: 5'10"; Wt: 160 lbs; Born: 2/18/1938 in Santo Domingo, Dominican Republic; Debut: 4/16/1962

LCS — Batting / Fielding

Year	Tm	Age	G	AB	H	2B	3B	HR	TB	R	RBI	GW	TBB	IBB	SO	HBP	SH	SF	SB	CS	SB%	GDP	Avg	OBP	SLG	Pos	G	PO	A	E	DP	FPct
1974	LA	36	3	3	1	0	0	0	1	0	1	0	0	0	0	0	0	0	0	0	—	1	.333	.333	.333	OF	1	1	0	0	0	1.000
1977	LA	39	1	1	1	1	0	0	2	1	0	0	0	0	0	0	0	0	0	0	—	0	1.000	1.000	2.000	—						
1978	LA	40	2	1	1	1	0	0	2	0	0	0	0	0	0	0	1	0	0	0	—	0	1.000	1.000	2.000	—						
LCS Totals			6	5	3	2	0	0	5	1	1	0	0	0	0	0	1	0	0	0	—	1	.600	.600	1.000	OF	1	1	0	0	0	1.000

World Series — Batting / Fielding

Year	Tm	Age	G	AB	H	2B	3B	HR	TB	R	RBI	GW	TBB	IBB	SO	HBP	SH	SF	SB	CS	SB%	GDP	Avg	OBP	SLG	Pos	G	PO	A	E	DP	FPct
1977	LA	39	3	3	0	0	0	0	0	0	0	0	0	0	1	0	0	0	0	0	—	0	.000	.000	.000	—						
1978	LA	40	1	0	0	0	0	0	0	0	0	0	1	0	0	0	0	0	0	0	—	0	—	1.000	—	0	0	0	0	0	—
WS Totals			4	3	0	0	0	0	0	0	0	0	1	0	1	0	0	0	0	0	—	0	.000	.250	.000	—						
Postseason Totals			10	8	3	2	0	0	5	1	1	0	1	0	1	0	1	0	0	0	—	1	.375	.444	.625	OF	1	1	0	0	0	1.000

DARRYL MOTLEY
Darryl DeWayne Motley—Bats: Right; Throws: Right — Ht: 5'9"; Wt: 196 lbs; Born: 1/21/1960 in Muskogee, Oklahoma; Debut: 8/10/1981

LCS — Batting / Fielding

Year	Tm	Age	G	AB	H	2B	3B	HR	TB	R	RBI	GW	TBB	IBB	SO	HBP	SH	SF	SB	CS	SB%	GDP	Avg	OBP	SLG	Pos	G	PO	A	E	DP	FPct
1984	KC	24	3	12	2	0	0	0	2	0	1	0	1	1	3	0	0	0	0	0	—	0	.167	.231	.167	OF	3	11	0	0	0	1.000
1985	KC	25	2	3	1	0	0	0	1	1	1	0	1	0	2	0	0	1	0	0	—	0	.333	.400	.333	OF	2	4	0	0	0	1.000
LCS Totals			5	15	3	0	0	0	3	1	2	0	2	1	5	0	0	1	0	0	—	0	.200	.278	.200	OF	5	15	0	0	0	1.000

World Series — Batting / Fielding

Year	Tm	Age	G	AB	H	2B	3B	HR	TB	R	RBI	GW	TBB	IBB	SO	HBP	SH	SF	SB	CS	SB%	GDP	Avg	OBP	SLG	Pos	G	PO	A	E	DP	FPct
1985	KC	25	5	11	4	0	0	1	7	1	3	1	0	0	1	0	0	0	0	1	.00	0	.364	.364	.636	OF	4	4	0	0	0	1.000
Postseason Totals			10	26	7	0	0	1	10	2	5	1	2	1	6	0	0	1	0	1	.00	0	.269	.310	.385	OF	9	19	0	0	0	1.000

CURT MOTTON
Curtell Howard Motton—Bats: Right; Throws: Right — Ht: 5'8"; Wt: 164 lbs; Born: 9/24/1940 in Darnell, Louisiana; Debut: 7/5/1967

LCS — Batting / Fielding

Year	Tm	Age	G	AB	H	2B	3B	HR	TB	R	RBI	GW	TBB	IBB	SO	HBP	SH	SF	SB	CS	SB%	GDP	Avg	OBP	SLG	Pos	G	PO	A	E	DP	FPct
1969	Bal	29	2	2	1	0	0	0	1	0	1	1	0	0	0	0	0	0	0	0	—	0	.500	.500	.500	—						
1971	Bal	31	1	1	1	1	0	0	2	0	1	0	0	0	0	0	0	0	0	0	—	0	1.000	1.000	2.000	—						
1974	Bal	34	1	1	0	0	0	0	0	0	0	0	0	0	0	0	0	0	0	0	—	0	.000	.000	.000	—						
LCS Totals			4	4	2	1	0	0	3	0	2	1	0	0	0	0	0	0	0	0	—	0	.500	.500	.750	—	0	0	0	0	0	

World Series — Batting / Fielding

Year	Tm	Age	G	AB	H	2B	3B	HR	TB	R	RBI	GW	TBB	IBB	SO	HBP	SH	SF	SB	CS	SB%	GDP	Avg	OBP	SLG	Pos	G	PO	A	E	DP	FPct
1969	Bal	29	1	1	0	0	0	0	0	0	0	0	0	0	0	0	0	0	0	0	—	0	.000	.000	.000	—						
Postseason Totals			5	5	2	1	0	0	3	0	2	1	0	0	0	0	0	0	0	0	—	0	.400	.400	.600	—	0	0	0	0	0	

MIKE MOWREY—Harry Harlan Mowrey—Bats: Right; Throws: Right

Ht: 5'10"; Wt: 180 lbs; Born: 4/20/1884 in Brown's Mill, Pennsylvania; Debut: 9/24/1905; Died: 3/20/1947

World Series — Batting / Fielding

Year Tm	Age	G	AB	H	2B	3B	HR	TB	R	RBI	GW	TBB	IBB	SO	HBP	SH	SF	SB	CS	SB%	GDP	Avg	OBP	SLG	Pos	G	PO	A	E	DP	FPct
1916 Bro	32	5	17	3	0	0	0	3	2	1	0	3	0	2	0	1	0	0	0	—	0	.176	.300	.176	3B	5	8	15	2	1	.920

JAMIE MOYER—Throws: Left; Bats: Left

Ht: 6'0"; Wt: 170 lbs; Born: 11/18/1962 in Sellersville, Pennsylvania; Debut: 6/16/1986

Division Series — Pitching

Year Tm	Age	G	GS	CG	GF	IP	BFP	H	R	ER	HR	SH	SF	HB	TBB	IBB	SO	WP	Bk	W	L	Pct	ShO	Sv-Op	Hld	OAvg	OOBP	ERA
1997 Sea	34	1	1	0	0	4.2	19	5	3	3	1	0	0	0	1	0	2	0	0	0	1	.000	0	0- 0	0	.278	.316	5.79

Division Series — Batting / Fielding

Year Tm	Age	G	AB	H	2B	3B	HR	TB	R	RBI	GW	TBB	IBB	SO	HBP	SH	SF	SB	CS	SB%	GDP	Avg	OBP	SLG	Pos	G	PO	A	E	DP	FPct
1997 Sea	34	1	0	0	0	0	0	0	0	0	0	0	0	0	0	0	0	0	0	—	0	—	—	—	P	1	2	1	0	0	1.000

BILL MUELLER—William Richard Mueller—Bats: Both; Throws: Right

Ht: 5'11"; Wt: 175 lbs; Born: 3/17/1971 in Maryland Heights, Missouri; Debut: 4/18/1996

Division Series — Batting / Fielding

Year Tm	Age	G	AB	H	2B	3B	HR	TB	R	RBI	GW	TBB	IBB	SO	HBP	SH	SF	SB	CS	SB%	GDP	Avg	OBP	SLG	Pos	G	PO	A	E	DP	FPct
1997 SF	26	3	12	3	0	0	1	6	1	1	0	0	0	0	0	0	0	0	1	.00	1	.250	.250	.500	3B	3	2	9	0	1	1.000

DON MUELLER—Donald Frederick Mueller—Nickname: Mandrake The Magician—Bats: Left; Throws: Right

Ht: 6'0"; Wt: 185 lbs; Born: 4/14/1927 in St. Louis, Missouri; Debut: 8/2/1948

World Series — Batting / Fielding

Year Tm	Age	G	AB	H	2B	3B	HR	TB	R	RBI	GW	TBB	IBB	SO	HBP	SH	SF	SB	CS	SB%	GDP	Avg	OBP	SLG	Pos	G	PO	A	E	DP	FPct
1954 NYG	27	4	18	7	0	0	0	7	4	1	0	0	0	1	0	1	0	0	0	—	0	.389	.389	.389	OF	4	3	0	2	0	.600

LES MUELLER—Leslie Clyde Mueller—Throws: Right; Bats: Right

Ht: 6'3"; Wt: 190 lbs; Born: 3/4/1919 in Belleville, Illinois; Debut: 8/15/1941

World Series — Pitching

Year Tm	Age	G	GS	CG	GF	IP	BFP	H	R	ER	HR	SH	SF	HB	TBB	IBB	SO	WP	Bk	W	L	Pct	ShO	Sv-Op	Hld	OAvg	OOBP	ERA
1945 Det	26	1	0	0	1	2.0	7	0	0	0	0	0	0	0	1	0	1	0	0	0	0	—	0	0- 0	0	.000	.143	0.00

World Series — Batting / Fielding

Year Tm	Age	G	AB	H	2B	3B	HR	TB	R	RBI	GW	TBB	IBB	SO	HBP	SH	SF	SB	CS	SB%	GDP	Avg	OBP	SLG	Pos	G	PO	A	E	DP	FPct
1945 Det	26	1	0	0	0	0	0	0	0	0	0	0	0	0	0	0	0	0	0	—	0	—	—	—	P	1	0	0	0	0	—

TERRY MULHOLLAND—Terence John Mulholland—Throws: Left; Bats: Right

Ht: 6'3"; Wt: 200 lbs; Born: 3/9/1963 in Uniontown, Pennsylvania; Debut: 6/8/1986

LCS / World Series — Pitching

Year Tm	Age	G	GS	CG	GF	IP	BFP	H	R	ER	HR	SH	SF	HB	TBB	IBB	SO	WP	Bk	W	L	Pct	ShO	Sv-Op	Hld	OAvg	OOBP	ERA
LCS																												
1993 Phi	30	1	1	0	0	5.0	24	9	5	4	0	0	0	0	1	0	2	0	0	0	1	.000	0	0- 0	0	.391	.417	7.20
World Series																												
1993 Phi	30	2	2	0	0	10.2	48	14	8	8	2	0	2	0	3	0	5	0	0	1	0	1.000	0	0- 0	0	.326	.354	6.75
Postseason Totals		3	3	0	0	15.2	144	23	13	12	2	0	2	0	4	0	7	0	0	1	1	.500	0	0-0	0	.348	.375	6.89

LCS / World Series — Batting / Fielding

Year Tm	Age	G	AB	H	2B	3B	HR	TB	R	RBI	GW	TBB	IBB	SO	HBP	SH	SF	SB	CS	SB%	GDP	Avg	OBP	SLG	Pos	G	PO	A	E	DP	FPct
LCS																															
1993 Phi	30	1	2	0	0	0	0	0	0	0	0	0	0	1	0	0	0	0	0	—	0	.000	.000	.000	P	1	0	2	0	0	1.000
World Series																															
1993 Phi	30	2	0	0	0	0	0	0	0	0	0	0	0	0	0	0	0	0	0	—	0	—	—	—	P	2	1	1	0	0	1.000
Postseason Totals		3	2	0	0	0	0	0	0	0	0	0	0	1	0	0	0	0	0	—	0	.000	.000	.000	P	3	1	3	0	0	1.000

GEORGE MULLIN—George Joseph Mullin—Nickname: Wabash George—Throws: Right; Bats: Right

Ht: 5'11"; Wt: 188 lbs; Born: 7/4/1880 in Toledo, Ohio; Debut: 5/4/1902; Died: 1/7/1944

World Series — Pitching

Year Tm	Age	G	GS	CG	GF	IP	BFP	H	R	ER	HR	SH	SF	HB	TBB	IBB	SO	WP	Bk	W	L	Pct	ShO	Sv-Op	Hld	OAvg	OOBP	ERA
1907 Det	27	2	2	2	0	17.0	71	16	5	4	0	2	0	1	6	0	8	0	0	0	2	.000	0	0- 0	0	.258	.333	2.12
1908 Det	28	1	1	1	0	9.0	33	7	3	0	0	0	0	0	1	0	8	0	0	1	0	1.000	0	0- 0	0	.219	.242	0.00
1909 Det	29	4	3	3	1	32.0	132	23	14	8	1	4	1	2	8	0	20	0	0	2	1	.667	1	0- 0	0	.197	.258	2.25
WS Totals		7	6	6	1	58.0	472	46	22	12	1	6	1	3	15	0	36	0	0	3	3	.500	1	0-0	0	.218	.278	1.86

World Series — Batting / Fielding

Year Tm	Age	G	AB	H	2B	3B	HR	TB	R	RBI	GW	TBB	IBB	SO	HBP	SH	SF	SB	CS	SB%	GDP	Avg	OBP	SLG	Pos	G	PO	A	E	DP	FPct
1907 Det	27	2	6	0	0	0	0	0	0	0	0	0	0	1	0	0	0	0	0	—	0	.000	.000	.000	P	2	1	5	0	0	1.000
1908 Det	28	1	3	1	0	0	0	1	1	1	0	1	0	0	0	0	0	0	0	—	0	.333	.500	.333	P	1	0	1	0	0	1.000
1909 Det	29	6	16	3	1	0	0	4	1	0	0	1	0	3	0	0	0	0	0	—	0	.188	.235	.250	P	4	0	12	0	0	1.000
WS Totals		9	25	4	1	0	0	5	2	1	0	2	0	4	0	0	0	0	0	—	0	.160	.222	.200	P	7	1	18	0	0	1.000

RANCE MULLINIKS—Steven Rance Mulliniks—Bats: Left; Throws: Right

Ht: 5'11"; Wt: 162 lbs; Born: 1/15/1956 in Tulare, California; Debut: 6/18/1977

LCS — Batting / Fielding

Year Tm	Age	G	AB	H	2B	3B	HR	TB	R	RBI	GW	TBB	IBB	SO	HBP	SH	SF	SB	CS	SB%	GDP	Avg	OBP	SLG	Pos	G	PO	A	E	DP	FPct
1985 Tor	29	5	11	4	1	0	1	8	1	3	0	2	0	2	0	0	0	0	0	—	1	.364	.462	.727	3B	5	1	4	0	0	1.000
1989 Tor	33	1	1	0	0	0	0	0	0	0	0	0	0	1	0	0	0	0	0	—	0	.000	.000	.000	—						
1991 Tor	35	5	8	1	0	0	0	1	1	0	0	3	0	0	0	0	0	0	0	—	1	.125	.364	.125	—						
LCS Totals		11	20	5	1	0	1	9	2	3	0	5	0	3	0	0	0	0	0	—	2	.250	.400	.450	3B	5	1	4	0	0	1.000

JERRY MUMPHREY—Jerry Wayne Mumphrey—Bats: Both; Throws: Right

Ht: 6'2"; Wt: 185 lbs; Born: 9/9/1952 in Tyler, Texas; Debut: 9/10/1974

Division Series / LCS / World Series — Batting / Fielding

Year Tm	Age	G	AB	H	2B	3B	HR	TB	R	RBI	GW	TBB	IBB	SO	HBP	SH	SF	SB	CS	SB%	GDP	Avg	OBP	SLG	Pos	G	PO	A	E	DP	FPct
Division Series																															
1981 NYA	29	5	21	2	0	0	0	2	2	0	0	0	0	1	0	0	0	1	1	.50	1	.095	.095	.095	OF	5	15	1	0	0	1.000
LCS																															
1981 NYA	29	3	12	6	1	0	0	7	2	0	0	3	0	2	0	0	0	0	1	.00	0	.500	.600	.583	OF	3	4	0	0	0	1.000
World Series																															
1981 NYA	29	5	15	3	0	0	0	3	2	0	0	3	1	2	0	0	0	1	0	1.00	0	.200	.333	.200	OF	5	6	0	0	0	1.000
Postseason Totals		13	48	11	1	0	0	12	6	0	0	6	1	5	0	0	0	2	2	.50	1	.229	.315	.250	OF	13	25	1	0	0	1.000

BOB MUNCRIEF—Robert Cleveland Muncrief—Throws: Right; Bats: Right

Ht: 6'2"; Wt: 190 lbs; Born: 1/28/1916 in Madill, Oklahoma; Debut: 9/30/1937; Died: 2/6/1996

World Series — Pitching

Year Tm	Age	G	GS	CG	GF	IP	BFP	H	R	ER	HR	SH	SF	HB	TBB	IBB	SO	WP	Bk	W	L	Pct	ShO	Sv-Op	Hld	OAvg	OOBP	ERA
1944 StL	28	2	0	0	1	6.2	28	5	1	1	0	3	0	0	4	2	4	0	0	0	1	.000	0	0- 0	0	.238	.360	1.35
1948 Cle	32	1	0	0	1	2.0	7	1	0	0	0	0	0	0	0	0	0	0	0	0	0	—	0	0- 0	0	.143	.143	0.00
WS Totals		3	0	0	2	8.2	70	6	1	1	0	3	0	0	4	2	4	0	0	0	1	.000	0	0-0	0	.214	.313	1.04

World Series — Batting / Fielding

Year Tm	Age	G	AB	H	2B	3B	HR	TB	R	RBI	GW	TBB	IBB	SO	HBP	SH	SF	SB	CS	SB%	GDP	Avg	OBP	SLG	Pos	G	PO	A	E	DP	FPct
1944 StL	28	2	1	0	0	0	0	0	0	0	0	0	0	1	0	0	0	0	0	—	0	.000	.000	.000	P	2	0	1	0	0	1.000
1948 Cle	32	1	0	0	0	0	0	0	0	0	0	0	0	0	0	0	0	0	0	—	0	—	—	—	P	1	1	0	0	0	1.000
WS Totals		3	1	0	0	0	0	0	0	0	0	0	0	1	0	0	0	0	0	—	0	.000	.000	.000	P	3	1	1	0	0	1.000

GEORGE MUNGER—George David Munger—Nickname: Red—Throws: Right; Bats: Right

Ht: 6'2"; Wt: 200 lbs; Born: 10/4/1918 in Houston, Texas; Debut: 5/1/1943; Died: 7/23/1996

World Series		Pitching																										
Year Tm	Age	G	GS	CG	GF	IP	BFP	H	R	ER	HR	SH	SF	HB	TBB	IBB	SO	WP	Bk	W	L	Pct	ShO	Sv-Op	Hld	OAvg	OOBP	ERA
1946 StL	27	1	1	1	0	9.0	38	9	3	1	1	0	0	0	3	0	2	0	0	1	0	1.000	0	0-0	0	.257	.316	1.00

World Series		Batting																						Fielding						
Year Tm	Age	G	AB	H	2B	3B	HR	TB	R	RBI	GW	TBB	IBB	SO	HBP	SH	SF	SB	CS	SB%	GDP	Avg	OBP	SLG	Pos	G	PO	A	E	DP	FPct
1946 StL	27	1	4	1	0	0	0	1	0	0	0	0	0	2	0	1	0	0	0	—	0	.250	.250	.250	P	1	1	0	0	0	1.000

MIKE MUNOZ—Michael Anthony Munoz—Throws: Left; Bats: Left

Ht: 6'2"; Wt: 190 lbs; Born: 7/12/1965 in Baldwin Park, California; Debut: 9/6/1989

Division Series		Pitching																										
Year Tm	Age	G	GS	CG	GF	IP	BFP	H	R	ER	HR	SH	SF	HB	TBB	IBB	SO	WP	Bk	W	L	Pct	ShO	Sv-Op	Hld	OAvg	OOBP	ERA
1995 Col	30	4	0	0	0	1.1	9	4	2	2	0	0	0	0	1	0	1	0	0	0	1	.000	0	0-1	0	.500	.556	13.50

Division Series		Batting																						Fielding						
Year Tm	Age	G	AB	H	2B	3B	HR	TB	R	RBI	GW	TBB	IBB	SO	HBP	SH	SF	SB	CS	SB%	GDP	Avg	OBP	SLG	Pos	G	PO	A	E	DP	FPct
1995 Col	30	4	0	0	0	0	0	0	0	0	0	0	0	0	0	0	0	0	0	—	0	—	—	—	P	4	0	0	0	0	—

THURMAN MUNSON—Thurman Lee Munson—Bats: Right; Throws: Right

Ht: 5'11"; Wt: 190 lbs; Born: 6/7/1947 in Akron, Ohio; Debut: 8/8/1969; Died: 8/2/1979

LCS		Batting																						Fielding						
Year Tm	Age	G	AB	H	2B	3B	HR	TB	R	RBI	GW	TBB	IBB	SO	HBP	SH	SF	SB	CS	SB%	GDP	Avg	OBP	SLG	Pos	G	PO	A	E	DP	FPct
1976 NYA-*M*	29	5	23	10	2	0	0	12	3	3	0	0	0	1	0	0	0	0	1	.00	1	.435	.435	.522	C	5	18	6	2	0	.923
1977 NYA	30	5	21	6	1	0	1	10	3	5	1	0	0	2	0	0	1	0	0	—	0	.286	.273	.476	C	5	24	4	0	0	1.000
1978 NYA	31	4	18	5	1	0	1	9	2	2	1	0	0	0	0	0	0	0	0	—	1	.278	.278	.500	C	4	22	4	0	0	1.000
LCS Totals		14	62	21	4	0	2	31	8	10	2	0	0	3	0	0	1	0	1	.00	2	.339	.333	.500	C	14	64	14	2	0	.975

World Series		Batting																						Fielding						
Year Tm	Age	G	AB	H	2B	3B	HR	TB	R	RBI	GW	TBB	IBB	SO	HBP	SH	SF	SB	CS	SB%	GDP	Avg	OBP	SLG	Pos	G	PO	A	E	DP	FPct
1976 NYA-*M*	29	4	17	9	0	0	0	9	2	2	0	0	0	1	0	0	0	0	0	—	0	.529	.529	.529	C	4	21	6	0	0	1.000
1977 NYA	30	6	25	8	2	0	1	13	4	3	0	2	1	8	0	0	0	0	0	—	1	.320	.370	.520	C	6	40	4	0	0	1.000
1978 NYA	31	6	25	8	3	0	0	11	5	7	1	3	0	7	0	0	0	1	0	1.00	1	.320	.393	.440	C	6	33	5	0	1	1.000
WS Totals		16	67	25	5	0	1	33	11	12	1	5	1	16	0	0	0	1	0	1.00	2	.373	.417	.493	C	16	94	15	0	1	1.000
Postseason Totals		30	129	46	9	0	3	64	19	22	3	5	1	19	0	0	1	1	1	.50	4	.357	.378	.496	C	30	158	29	2	1	.989

BOBBY MURCER—Bobby Ray Murcer—Bats: Left; Throws: Right

Ht: 5'11"; Wt: 160 lbs; Born: 5/20/1946 in Oklahoma City, Oklahoma; Debut: 9/8/1965

Division Series		Batting																						Fielding						
Year Tm	Age	G	AB	H	2B	3B	HR	TB	R	RBI	GW	TBB	IBB	SO	HBP	SH	SF	SB	CS	SB%	GDP	Avg	OBP	SLG	Pos	G	PO	A	E	DP	FPct
1981 NYA	35	2	1	0	0	0	0	0	0	0	0	1	0	0	0	0	0	0	0	—	0	.000	.500	.000	—						

LCS		Batting																						Fielding						
Year Tm	Age	G	AB	H	2B	3B	HR	TB	R	RBI	GW	TBB	IBB	SO	HBP	SH	SF	SB	CS	SB%	GDP	Avg	OBP	SLG	Pos	G	PO	A	E	DP	FPct
1980 NYA	34	1	4	0	0	0	0	0	0	0	0	0	0	2	0	0	0	0	0	—	0	.000	.000	.000	—						
1981 NYA	35	1	3	1	0	0	0	1	0	0	0	1	0	1	0	0	0	0	0	—	0	.333	.500	.333	—						
LCS Totals		2	7	1	0	0	0	1	0	0	0	1	0	3	0	0	0	0	0	—	0	.143	.250	.143	—	0	0	0	0	0	—

World Series		Batting																						Fielding						
Year Tm	Age	G	AB	H	2B	3B	HR	TB	R	RBI	GW	TBB	IBB	SO	HBP	SH	SF	SB	CS	SB%	GDP	Avg	OBP	SLG	Pos	G	PO	A	E	DP	FPct
1981 NYA	35	4	3	0	0	0	0	0	0	0	0	0	0	0	0	1	0	0	0	—	0	.000	.000	.000	—						
Postseason Totals		8	11	1	0	0	0	1	0	0	0	2	0	3	0	1	0	0	0	—	0	.091	.231	.091	—	0	0	0	0	0	—

DALE MURPHY—Dale Bryan Murphy—Bats: Right; Throws: Right

Ht: 6'4"; Wt: 210 lbs; Born: 3/12/1956 in Portland, Oregon; Debut: 9/13/1976

LCS		Batting																						Fielding						
Year Tm	Age	G	AB	H	2B	3B	HR	TB	R	RBI	GW	TBB	IBB	SO	HBP	SH	SF	SB	CS	SB%	GDP	Avg	OBP	SLG	Pos	G	PO	A	E	DP	FPct
1982 Atl-*M*	26	3	11	3	0	0	0	3	1	0	0	0	0	2	0	0	0	1	1	.50	0	.273	.273	.273	OF	3	7	0	0	0	1.000

DANNY MURPHY—Daniel Francis Murphy—Bats: Right; Throws: Right

Ht: 5'9"; Wt: 175 lbs; Born: 8/11/1876 in Philadelphia, Pennsylvania; Debut: 9/17/1900; Died: 11/22/1955

World Series		Batting																						Fielding						
Year Tm	Age	G	AB	H	2B	3B	HR	TB	R	RBI	GW	TBB	IBB	SO	HBP	SH	SF	SB	CS	SB%	GDP	Avg	OBP	SLG	Pos	G	PO	A	E	DP	FPct
1905 Phi	29	5	16	3	1	0	0	4	0	0	0	0	0	2	0	1	0	0	1	.00	1	.188	.188	.250	2B	5	3	12	4	0	.789
1910 Phi	34	5	20	7	3	0	1	13	6	9	1	1	0	0	0	1	0	1	0	1.00	0	.350	.381	.650	OF	5	6	2	0	2	1.000
1911 Phi	35	6	23	7	3	0	0	10	4	3	1	0	0	3	0	1	0	0	2	.00	0	.304	.304	.435	OF	6	8	0	1	0	.889
WS Totals		16	59	17	7	0	1	27	10	12	2	1	0	5	0	3	0	1	3	.25	1	.288	.300	.458	OF	11	14	2	1	2	.941

DWAYNE MURPHY—Dwayne Keith Murphy—Bats: Left; Throws: Right

Ht: 6'1"; Wt: 185 lbs; Born: 3/18/1955 in Merced, California; Debut: 4/8/1978

Division Series		Batting																						Fielding						
Year Tm	Age	G	AB	H	2B	3B	HR	TB	R	RBI	GW	TBB	IBB	SO	HBP	SH	SF	SB	CS	SB%	GDP	Avg	OBP	SLG	Pos	G	PO	A	E	DP	FPct
1981 Oak	26	3	11	6	1	0	1	10	4	2	0	1	0	1	0	0	0	0	1	.00	0	.545	.583	.909	OF	3	13	0	0	0	1.000

LCS		Batting																						Fielding						
Year Tm	Age	G	AB	H	2B	3B	HR	TB	R	RBI	GW	TBB	IBB	SO	HBP	SH	SF	SB	CS	SB%	GDP	Avg	OBP	SLG	Pos	G	PO	A	E	DP	FPct
1981 Oak	26	3	8	2	1	0	0	3	0	1	0	2	0	3	0	0	0	0	0	—	1	.250	.400	.375	OF	3	9	0	0	0	1.000
Postseason Totals		6	19	8	2	0	1	13	4	3	0	3	0	4	0	0	0	0	1	.00	1	.421	.500	.684	OF	6	22	0	0	0	1.000

EDDIE MURPHY—John Edward Murphy—Bats: Left; Throws: Right

Ht: 5'9"; Wt: 155 lbs; Born: 10/2/1891 in Hancock, New York; Debut: 8/26/1912; Died: 2/21/1969

World Series		Batting																						Fielding						
Year Tm	Age	G	AB	H	2B	3B	HR	TB	R	RBI	GW	TBB	IBB	SO	HBP	SH	SF	SB	CS	SB%	GDP	Avg	OBP	SLG	Pos	G	PO	A	E	DP	FPct
1913 Phi	21	5	22	5	0	0	0	5	2	0	0	2	0	0	0	0	0	0	1	.00	0	.227	.292	.227	OF	5	14	0	0	0	1.000
1914 Phi	22	4	16	3	2	0	0	5	2	0	0	2	0	2	0	0	0	0	1	.00	1	.188	.278	.313	OF	4	4	0	0	0	1.000
1919 ChA	27	3	2	0	0	0	0	0	0	0	0	0	0	1	1	0	0	0	0	—	0	.000	.333	.000	—						
WS Totals		12	40	8	2	0	0	10	4	0	0	4	0	3	1	0	0	0	2	.00	1	.200	.289	.250	OF	9	18	0	0	0	1.000

JOHNNY MURPHY—John Joseph Murphy—Nicknames: Fireman, Grandma, Fordham Johnny—T: R; B: R

Ht: 6'2"; Wt: 190 lbs; Born: 7/14/1908 in New York, N.Y.; Deb.: 5/19/1932; Died: 1/14/1970

World Series		Pitching																										
Year Tm	Age	G	GS	CG	GF	IP	BFP	H	R	ER	HR	SH	SF	HB	TBB	IBB	SO	WP	Bk	W	L	Pct	ShO	Sv-Op	Hld	OAvg	OOBP	ERA
1936 NYA	28	1	0	0	1	2.2	10	1	1	1	1	0	0	0	1	0	1	0	0	0	0	—	0	1-1	0	.111	.200	3.38
1937 NYA	29	1	0	0	1	0.1	1	0	0	0	0	0	0	0	0	0	0	0	0	0	0	—	0	1-1	0	.000	.000	0.00
1938 NYA	30	1	0	0	1	2.0	8	2	0	0	0	0	0	0	1	0	1	0	0	0	0	—	0	1-1	0	.286	.375	0.00
1939 NYA	31	1	0	0	1	3.1	15	5	1	1	0	1	0	0	0	0	2	0	0	1	0	1.000	0	0-0	0	.357	.357	2.70
1941 NYA	33	2	0	0	2	6.0	20	2	0	0	0	0	0	0	1	0	3	0	0	1	0	1.000	0	0-0	0	.105	.150	0.00
1943 NYA	35	2	0	0	2	2.0	8	1	0	0	0	1	0	0	1	0	1	0	0	0	0	—	0	1-1	0	.167	.286	0.00
WS Totals		8	0	0	8	16.1	124	11	2	2	1	2	0	0	4	0	8	0	0	2	0	1.000	0	4-4	0	.196	.250	1.10

World Series		Batting																						Fielding						
Year Tm	Age	G	AB	H	2B	3B	HR	TB	R	RBI	GW	TBB	IBB	SO	HBP	SH	SF	SB	CS	SB%	GDP	Avg	OBP	SLG	Pos	G	PO	A	E	DP	FPct
1936 NYA	28	1	2	1	0	0	0	1	1	1	0	0	0	1	0	0	0	0	0	—	0	.500	.500	.500	P	1	0	0	0	0	—
1937 NYA	29	1	0	0	0	0	0	0	0	0	0	0	0	0	0	0	0	0	0	—	0	—	—	—	P	1	0	0	0	0	—
1938 NYA	30	1	0	0	0	0	0	0	0	0	0	0	0	0	0	0	0	0	0	—	0	—	—	—	P	1	0	0	0	0	—
1939 NYA	31	1	2	0	0	0	0	0	0	0	0	0	0	1	0	0	0	0	0	—	0	.000	.000	.000	P	1	0	3	0	0	1.000
1941 NYA	33	2	2	0	0	0	0	0	0	0	0	0	0	1	0	0	0	0	0	—	0	.000	.000	.000	P	2	1	0	0	0	1.000
1943 NYA	35	2	0	0	0	0	0	0	0	0	0	0	0	0	0	0	0	0	0	—	0	—	—	—	P	2	0	1	0	0	1.000
WS Totals		8	6	1	0	0	0	1	1	1	0	0	0	3	0	0	0	0	0	—	0	.167	.167	.167	P	8	1	4	0	0	1.000

ROB MURPHY—Robert Albert Murphy—Throws: Left; Bats: Left

Ht: 6'2"; Wt: 200 lbs; Born: 5/26/1960 in Miami, Florida; Debut: 9/13/1985

LCS		Pitching																										
Year Tm	Age	G	GS	CG	GF	IP	BFP	H	R	ER	HR	SH	SF	HB	TBB	IBB	SO	WP	Bk	W	L	Pct	ShO	Sv-Op	Hld	OAvg	OOBP	ERA
1990 Bos	30	1	0	0	1	0.2	4	2	1	1	0	0	0	0	1	0	0	0	0	0	0	—	0	0- 0	0	.667	.750	13.50

LCS		Batting																							Fielding						
Year Tm	Age	G	AB	H	2B	3B	HR	TB	R	RBI	GW	TBB	IBB	SO	HBP	SH	SF	SB	CS	SB%	GDP	Avg	OBP	SLG	Pos	G	PO	A	E	DP	FPct
1990 Bos	30	1	0	0	0	0	0	0	0	0	0	0	0	0	0	0	0	0	0	—	0	—	—	—	P	1	0	0	0	0	—

EDDIE MURRAY—Eddie Clarence Murray—Bats: Both; Throws: Right

Ht: 6'2"; Wt: 190 lbs; Born: 2/24/1956 in Los Angeles, California; Debut: 4/7/1977

Division Series		Batting																							Fielding						
Year Tm	Age	G	AB	H	2B	3B	HR	TB	R	RBI	GW	TBB	IBB	SO	HBP	SH	SF	SB	CS	SB%	GDP	Avg	OBP	SLG	Pos	G	PO	A	E	DP	FPct
1995 Cle	39	3	13	5	0	1	1	10	3	3	0	2	0	1	0	0	0	0	0	—	0	.385	.467	.769	—						
1996 Bal	40	4	15	6	1	0	0	7	1	1	0	3	2	4	0	0	0	1	0	1.00	0	.400	.500	.467	—						
DS Totals		7	28	11	1	1	1	17	4	4	0	5	2	5	0	0	0	1	0	1.00	0	.393	.485	.607	—	0	0	0	0	0	—
LCS		Batting																							Fielding						
Year Tm	Age	G	AB	H	2B	3B	HR	TB	R	RBI	GW	TBB	IBB	SO	HBP	SH	SF	SB	CS	SB%	GDP	Avg	OBP	SLG	Pos	G	PO	A	E	DP	FPct
1979 Bal	23	4	12	5	0	0	1	8	3	5	0	5	2	2	0	0	0	0	1	.00	0	.417	.588	.667	1B	4	44	3	2	4	.959
1983 Bal	27	4	15	4	0	0	1	7	5	3	1	3	1	3	0	0	0	1	0	1.00	0	.267	.389	.467	1B	4	34	3	1	3	.974
1995 Cle	39	6	24	6	1	0	1	10	2	3	0	2	1	3	0	0	0	0	0	—	0	.250	.308	.417	—						
1996 Bal	40	5	15	4	0	0	1	7	1	2	0	2	0	2	0	0	0	0	0	—	0	.267	.353	.467	—						
LCS Totals		19	66	19	1	0	4	32	11	13	1	12	4	10	0	0	0	1	1	.50	0	.288	.397	.485	1B	8	78	6	3	7	.966
World Series		Batting																							Fielding						
Year Tm	Age	G	AB	H	2B	3B	HR	TB	R	RBI	GW	TBB	IBB	SO	HBP	SH	SF	SB	CS	SB%	GDP	Avg	OBP	SLG	Pos	G	PO	A	E	DP	FPct
1979 Bal	23	7	26	4	1	0	1	8	3	2	0	4	0	4	0	0	0	1	0	1.00	2	.154	.267	.308	1B	7	60	7	0	5	1.000
1983 Bal	27	5	20	5	0	0	2	11	2	3	1	1	0	4	0	0	0	0	0	—	0	.250	.286	.550	1B	5	45	1	1	5	.979
1995 Cle	39	6	19	2	0	0	1	5	1	3	1	5	0	4	0	0	0	0	0	—	0	.105	.292	.263	1B	3	27	0	0	3	1.000
WS Totals		18	65	11	1	0	4	24	6	8	2	10	0	12	0	0	0	1	0	1.00	2	.169	.280	.369	1B	15	132	8	1	13	.993
Postseason Totals		44	159	41	3	1	9	73	21	25	3	27	6	27	0	0	0	3	1	.75	2	.258	.366	.459	1B	23	210	14	4	20	.982

RED MURRAY—John Joseph Murray—Bats: Right; Throws: Right

Ht: 5'10"; Wt: 190 lbs; Born: 3/4/1884 in Arnot, Pennsylvania; Debut: 6/16/1906; Died: 12/4/1958

World Series		Batting																							Fielding						
Year Tm	Age	G	AB	H	2B	3B	HR	TB	R	RBI	GW	TBB	IBB	SO	HBP	SH	SF	SB	CS	SB%	GDP	Avg	OBP	SLG	Pos	G	PO	A	E	DP	FPct
1911 NYG	27	6	21	0	0	0	0	0	0	0	0	2	0	5	0	2	0	0	1	.00	0	.000	.087	.000	OF	6	4	1	3	0	.625
1912 NYG	28	8	31	10	4	1	0	16	5	4	0	2	0	2	0	1	0	0	1	.00	0	.323	.364	.516	OF	8	21	1	0	0	1.000
1913 NYG	29	5	16	4	0	0	0	4	2	1	0	2	0	2	1	0	0	2	1	.67	0	.250	.368	.250	OF	5	9	0	0	0	1.000
WS Totals		19	68	14	4	1	0	20	7	5	0	6	0	9	1	3	0	2	3	.40	0	.206	.280	.294	OF	19	34	2	3	0	.923

STAN MUSIAL (HOF 1969-W)—Stanley Frank Musial—Nickname: Stan the Man—Bats: Left; Throws: Left

Ht: 6'0"; Wt: 175 lbs; Born: 11/21/1920 in Donora, Pennsylvania; Debut: 9/17/1941

World Series		Batting																							Fielding						
Year Tm	Age	G	AB	H	2B	3B	HR	TB	R	RBI	GW	TBB	IBB	SO	HBP	SH	SF	SB	CS	SB%	GDP	Avg	OBP	SLG	Pos	G	PO	A	E	DP	FPct
1942 StL	21	5	18	4	1	0	0	5	2	2	1	4	2	0	0	0	0	0	1	.00	0	.222	.364	.278	OF	5	13	0	0	0	1.000
1943 StL-*M*	22	5	18	5	0	0	0	5	2	0	0	2	0	2	0	0	0	0	0	—	0	.278	.350	.278	OF	5	7	2	0	0	1.000
1944 StL	23	6	23	7	2	0	1	12	2	2	1	2	0	0	0	1	0	0	0	—	1	.304	.360	.522	OF	6	11	0	1	0	.917
1946 StL-*M*	25	7	27	6	4	1	0	12	3	4	0	4	0	2	0	0	0	1	1	.50	0	.222	.323	.444	1B	7	61	2	0	6	1.000
WS Totals		23	86	22	7	1	1	34	9	8	2	12	2	4	0	1	0	1	2	.33	1	.256	.347	.395	OF	16	31	2	1	0	.971

MIKE MUSSINA—Michael Cole Mussina—Nickname: Moose—Throws: Right; Bats: Right

Ht: 6'2"; Wt: 185 lbs; Born: 12/8/1968 in Williamsport, Pennsylvania; Debut: 8/4/1991

Division Series		Pitching																										
Year Tm	Age	G	GS	CG	GF	IP	BFP	H	R	ER	HR	SH	SF	HB	TBB	IBB	SO	WP	Bk	W	L	Pct	ShO	Sv-Op	Hld	OAvg	OOBP	ERA
1996 Bal	27	1	1	0	0	6.0	27	7	4	3	1	0	0	0	2	0	6	0	0	0	0	—	0	0- 0	0	.280	.333	4.50
1997 Bal	28	2	2	0	0	14.0	52	7	3	3	3	0	0	0	3	0	16	0	0	2	0	1.000	0	0- 0	0	.143	.192	1.93
DS Totals		3	3	0	0	20.0	158	14	7	6	4	0	0	0	5	0	22	0	0	2	0	1.000	0	0-0	0	.189	.241	2.70
LCS		Pitching																										
Year Tm	Age	G	GS	CG	GF	IP	BFP	H	R	ER	HR	SH	SF	HB	TBB	IBB	SO	WP	Bk	W	L	Pct	ShO	Sv-Op	Hld	OAvg	OOBP	ERA
1996 Bal	27	1	1	0	0	7.2	32	8	5	5	1	0	0	0	2	0	6	0	0	0	1	.000	0	0- 0	0	.267	.313	5.87
1997 Bal	28	2	2	0	0	15.0	53	4	1	1	0	0	0	0	4	0	25	0	0	0	0	—	0	0- 0	0	.082	.151	0.60
LCS Totals		3	3	0	0	22.2	170	12	6	6	1	0	0	0	6	0	31	0	0	0	1	.000	0	0-0	0	.152	.212	2.38
Postseason Totals		6	6	0	0	42.2	328	26	13	12	5	0	0	0	11	0	53	0	0	2	1	.667	0	0-0	0	.170	.226	2.53

Division Series		Batting																							Fielding						
Year Tm	Age	G	AB	H	2B	3B	HR	TB	R	RBI	GW	TBB	IBB	SO	HBP	SH	SF	SB	CS	SB%	GDP	Avg	OBP	SLG	Pos	G	PO	A	E	DP	FPct
1996 Bal	27	1	0	0	0	0	0	0	0	0	0	0	0	0	0	0	0	0	0	—	0	—	—	—	P	1	0	0	0	0	—
1997 Bal	28	2	0	0	0	0	0	0	0	0	0	0	0	0	0	0	0	0	0	—	0	—	—	—	P	2	3	3	0	0	1.000
DS Totals		3	0	0	0	0	0	0	0	0	0	0	0	0	0	0	0	0	0	—	0	—	—	—	P	3	3	3	0	0	1.000
LCS		Batting																							Fielding						
Year Tm	Age	G	AB	H	2B	3B	HR	TB	R	RBI	GW	TBB	IBB	SO	HBP	SH	SF	SB	CS	SB%	GDP	Avg	OBP	SLG	Pos	G	PO	A	E	DP	FPct
1996 Bal	27	1	0	0	0	0	0	0	0	0	0	0	0	0	0	0	0	0	0	—	0	—	—	—	P	1	0	0	0	0	—
1997 Bal	28	2	0	0	0	0	0	0	0	0	0	0	0	0	0	0	0	0	0	—	0	—	—	—	P	2	2	1	0	0	1.000
LCS Totals		3	0	0	0	0	0	0	0	0	0	0	0	0	0	0	0	0	0	—	0	—	—	—	P	3	2	1	0	0	1.000
Postseason Totals		6	0	0	0	0	0	0	0	0	0	0	0	0	0	0	0	0	0	—	0	—	—	—	P	6	5	4	0	0	1.000

BUDDY MYER—Charles Solomon Myer—Bats: Left; Throws: Right

Ht: 5'10"; Wt: 163 lbs; Born: 3/16/1904 in Ellisville, Mississippi; Debut: 9/26/1925; Died: 10/31/1974

World Series		Batting																							Fielding						
Year Tm	Age	G	AB	H	2B	3B	HR	TB	R	RBI	GW	TBB	IBB	SO	HBP	SH	SF	SB	CS	SB%	GDP	Avg	OBP	SLG	Pos	G	PO	A	E	DP	FPct
1925 Was	21	3	8	2	0	0	0	2	0	0	0	1	0	2	0	0	0	0	1	.00	0	.250	.333	.250	3B	3	1	1	0	0	1.000
1933 Was	29	5	20	6	1	0	0	7	2	2	0	2	0	3	0	0	0	0	0	—	0	.300	.364	.350	2B	5	15	12	3	3	.900
WS Totals		8	28	8	1	0	0	9	2	2	0	3	0	5	0	0	0	0	1	.00	0	.286	.355	.321	2B	5	15	12	3	3	.900

BILLY MYERS—William Harrison Myers—Bats: Right; Throws: Right

Ht: 5'8"; Wt: 168 lbs; Born: 8/14/1910 in Enola, Pennsylvania; Debut: 4/16/1935; Died: 4/10/1995

World Series		Batting																							Fielding						
Year Tm	Age	G	AB	H	2B	3B	HR	TB	R	RBI	GW	TBB	IBB	SO	HBP	SH	SF	SB	CS	SB%	GDP	Avg	OBP	SLG	Pos	G	PO	A	E	DP	FPct
1939 Cin	29	4	12	4	0	1	0	6	2	0	0	2	0	3	0	0	0	0	0	—	1	.333	.429	.500	SS	4	8	9	2	1	.895
1940 Cin	30	7	23	3	0	0	0	3	0	2	1	2	1	5	0	0	0	0	0	—	0	.130	.200	.130	SS	7	14	17	3	5	.912
WS Totals		11	35	7	0	1	0	9	2	2	1	4	1	8	0	0	0	0	0	—	1	.200	.282	.257	SS	11	22	26	5	6	.906

HI MYERS—Henry Harrison Myers—Bats: Right; Throws: Right

Ht: 5'9"; Wt: 175 lbs; Born: 4/27/1889 in East Liverpool, Ohio; Debut: 8/30/1909; Died: 5/1/1965

World Series		Batting																							Fielding						
Year Tm	Age	G	AB	H	2B	3B	HR	TB	R	RBI	GW	TBB	IBB	SO	HBP	SH	SF	SB	CS	SB%	GDP	Avg	OBP	SLG	Pos	G	PO	A	E	DP	FPct
1916 Bro	27	5	22	4	0	0	1	7	2	3	0	0	0	3	1	1	0	0	0	—	2	.182	.217	.318	OF	5	9	1	0	1	1.000
1920 Bro	31	7	26	6	0	0	0	6	0	1	0	0	0	1	0	0	0	0	2	.00	0	.231	.231	.231	OF	7	15	1	0	1	1.000
WS Totals		12	48	10	0	0	1	13	2	4	0	0	0	4	1	1	0	0	2	.00	2	.208	.224	.271	OF	12	24	2	0	2	1.000

RANDY MYERS—Randall Kirk Myers—Throws: Left; Bats: Left

Ht: 6'1"; Wt: 190 lbs; Born: 9/19/1962 in Vancouver, Washington; Debut: 10/6/1985

Division Series		Pitching																										
Year Tm	Age	G	GS	CG	GF	IP	BFP	H	R	ER	HR	SH	SF	HB	TBB	IBB	SO	WP	Bk	W	L	Pct	ShO	Sv-Op	Hld	OAvg	OOBP	ERA
1996 Bal	34	3	0	0	3	3.0	9	0	0	0	0	0	0	0	0	0	3	0	0	0	0	—	0	2- 2	0	.000	.000	0.00
1997 Bal	35	2	0	0	2	2.0	6	0	0	0	0	0	0	0	0	0	5	0	0	0	0	—	0	1- 1	0	.000	.000	0.00
DS Totals		5	0	0	5	5.0	30	0	0	0	0	0	0	0	0	0	8	0	0	0	0	—	0	3-3	0	.000	.000	0.00

LCS — Pitching

Year Tm	Age	G	GS	CG	GF	IP	BFP	H	R	ER	HR	SH	SF	HB	TBB	IBB	SO	WP	Bk	W	L	Pct	ShO	Sv-Op	Hld	OAvg	OOBP	ERA
1988 NYN	26	3	0	0	1	4.2	17	1	0	0	0	1	0	0	2	0	0	0	0	2	0	1.000	0	0-0	0	.071	.188	0.00
1990 Cin	28	4	0	0	3	5.2	21	2	0	0	0	0	0	0	3	0	7	0	0	0	0	—	0	3-3	1	.111	.238	0.00
1996 Bal	34	3	0	0	2	4.0	17	4	1	1	1	0	0	0	3	0	2	0	0	0	1	.000	0	0-0	1	.286	.412	2.25
1997 Bal	35	4	0	0	3	5.1	25	6	3	3	0	0	0	0	3	0	7	0	0	0	1	.000	0	1-1	0	.273	.360	5.06
LCS Totals		14	0	0	9	19.2	160	13	4	4	1	1	0	0	11	0	16	0	0	2	2	.500	0	4-4	2	.191	.304	1.83

World Series — Pitching

Year Tm	Age	G	GS	CG	GF	IP	BFP	H	R	ER	HR	SH	SF	HB	TBB	IBB	SO	WP	Bk	W	L	Pct	ShO	Sv-Op	Hld	OAvg	OOBP	ERA
1990 Cin	28	3	0	0	3	3.0	11	2	0	0	0	0	0	0	0	0	3	0	0	0	0	—	0	1-1	0	.182	.182	0.00
Postseason Totals		22	0	0	17	27.2	212	15	4	4	1	1	0	0	11	0	27	0	0	2	2	.500	0	8-8	2	.160	.248	1.30

Division Series — Batting / Fielding

Year Tm	Age	G	AB	H	2B	3B	HR	TB	R	RBI	GW	TBB	IBB	SO	HBP	SH	SF	SB	CS	SB%	GDP	Avg	OBP	SLG	Pos	G	PO	A	E	DP	FPct
1996 Bal	34	3	0	0	0	0	0	0	0	0	0	0	0	0	0	0	0	0	0	—	0	—	—	—	P	3	0	0	0	0	—
1997 Bal	35	2	0	0	0	0	0	0	0	0	0	0	0	0	0	0	0	0	0	—	0	—	—	—	P	2	0	0	0	0	—
DS Totals		5	0	0	0	0	0	0	0	0	0	0	0	0	0	0	0	0	0	—	0	—	—	—	P	5	0	0	0	0	—

LCS — Batting / Fielding

Year Tm	Age	G	AB	H	2B	3B	HR	TB	R	RBI	GW	TBB	IBB	SO	HBP	SH	SF	SB	CS	SB%	GDP	Avg	OBP	SLG	Pos	G	PO	A	E	DP	FPct
1988 NYN	26	3	0	0	0	0	0	0	0	0	0	0	0	0	0	0	0	0	0	—	0	—	—	—	P	3	0	1	0	0	1.000
1990 Cin	28	4	0	0	0	0	0	0	0	0	0	0	0	0	0	0	0	0	0	—	0	—	—	—	P	4	0	0	0	0	—
1996 Bal	34	3	0	0	0	0	0	0	0	0	0	0	0	0	0	0	0	0	0	—	0	—	—	—	P	3	0	0	0	0	—
1997 Bal	35	4	0	0	0	0	0	0	0	0	0	0	0	0	0	0	0	0	0	—	0	—	—	—	P	4	0	0	0	0	—
LCS Totals		14	0	0	0	0	0	0	0	0	0	0	0	0	0	0	0	0	0	—	0	—	—	—	P	14	0	1	0	0	1.000

World Series — Batting / Fielding

Year Tm	Age	G	AB	H	2B	3B	HR	TB	R	RBI	GW	TBB	IBB	SO	HBP	SH	SF	SB	CS	SB%	GDP	Avg	OBP	SLG	Pos	G	PO	A	E	DP	FPct
1990 Cin	28	3	0	0	0	0	0	0	0	0	0	0	0	0	0	0	0	0	0	—	0	—	—	—	P	3	0	0	0	0	—
Postseason Totals		22	0	0	0	0	0	0	0	0	0	0	0	0	0	0	0	0	0	—	0	—	—	—	P	22	0	1	0	0	1.000

TIM NAEHRING—Timothy James Naehring—Bats: Right; Throws: Right

Ht: 6'2"; Wt: 190 lbs; Born: 2/1/1967 in Cincinnati, Ohio; Debut: 7/15/1990

Division Series — Batting / Fielding

Year Tm	Age	G	AB	H	2B	3B	HR	TB	R	RBI	GW	TBB	IBB	SO	HBP	SH	SF	SB	CS	SB%	GDP	Avg	OBP	SLG	Pos	G	PO	A	E	DP	FPct
1995 Bos	28	3	13	4	0	0	1	7	2	1	0	0	0	1	0	1	0	0	0	—	0	.308	.308	.538	3B	3	5	5	0	0	1.000

CHARLES NAGY—Charles Harrison Nagy—Throws: Right; Bats: Left

Ht: 6'3"; Wt: 200 lbs; Born: 5/5/1967 in Bridgeport, Connecticut; Debut: 6/29/1990

Division Series — Pitching

Year Tm	Age	G	GS	CG	GF	IP	BFP	H	R	ER	HR	SH	SF	HB	TBB	IBB	SO	WP	Bk	W	L	Pct	ShO	Sv-Op	Hld	OAvg	OOBP	ERA
1995 Cle	28	1	1	0	0	7.0	32	4	1	1	0	0	1	0	5	0	6	0	0	1	0	1.000	0	0-0	0	.154	.281	1.29
1996 Cle	29	2	2	0	0	11.1	56	15	9	9	4	0	0	1	5	0	13	0	0	0	1	.000	0	0-0	0	.300	.375	7.15
1997 Cle	30	1	1	0	0	3.2	20	2	5	4	0	0	0	0	6	1	1	0	0	0	1	.000	0	0-0	0	.143	.400	9.82
DS Totals		4	4	0	0	22.0	216	21	15	14	4	0	1	1	16	1	20	0	0	1	2	.333	0	0-0	0	.233	.352	5.73

LCS — Pitching

Year Tm	Age	G	GS	CG	GF	IP	BFP	H	R	ER	HR	SH	SF	HB	TBB	IBB	SO	WP	Bk	W	L	Pct	ShO	Sv-Op	Hld	OAvg	OOBP	ERA
1995 Cle	28	1	1	0	0	8.0	30	5	2	1	1	0	0	1	0	0	6	0	0	0	0	—	0	0-0	0	.172	.200	1.13
1997 Cle	30	2	2	0	0	13.0	60	17	4	4	1	0	0	1	5	0	5	0	0	0	0	—	0	0-0	0	.315	.383	2.77
LCS Totals		3	3	0	0	21.0	180	22	6	5	2	0	0	2	5	0	11	0	0	0	0	—	0	0-0	0	.265	.322	2.14

World Series — Pitching

Year Tm	Age	G	GS	CG	GF	IP	BFP	H	R	ER	HR	SH	SF	HB	TBB	IBB	SO	WP	Bk	W	L	Pct	ShO	Sv-Op	Hld	OAvg	OOBP	ERA
1995 Cle	28	1	1	0	0	7.0	29	8	5	5	2	0	0	0	1	0	4	0	0	0	0	—	0	0-0	0	.286	.310	6.43
1997 Cle	30	2	1	0	1	7.0	33	8	6	5	3	0	0	0	5	1	5	0	0	0	1	.000	0	0-0	0	.286	.394	6.43
WS Totals		3	2	0	1	14.0	124	16	11	10	5	0	0	0	6	1	9	0	0	0	1	.000	0	0-0	0	.286	.355	6.43
Postseason Totals		10	9	0	1	57.0	520	59	32	29	11	0	1	3	27	2	40	0	0	1	3	.250	0	0-0	0	.258	.342	4.58

Division Series — Batting / Fielding

Year Tm	Age	G	AB	H	2B	3B	HR	TB	R	RBI	GW	TBB	IBB	SO	HBP	SH	SF	SB	CS	SB%	GDP	Avg	OBP	SLG	Pos	G	PO	A	E	DP	FPct
1995 Cle	28	1	0	0	0	0	0	0	0	0	0	0	0	0	0	0	0	0	0	—	0	—	—	—	P	1	2	1	0	0	1.000
1996 Cle	29	2	0	0	0	0	0	0	0	0	0	0	0	0	0	0	0	0	0	—	0	—	—	—	P	2	0	4	0	0	1.000
1997 Cle	30	1	0	0	0	0	0	0	0	0	0	0	0	0	0	0	0	0	0	—	0	—	—	—	P	1	0	1	1	0	.500
DS Totals		4	0	0	0	0	0	0	0	0	0	0	0	0	0	0	0	0	0	—	0	—	—	—	P	4	2	6	1	0	.889

LCS — Batting / Fielding

Year Tm	Age	G	AB	H	2B	3B	HR	TB	R	RBI	GW	TBB	IBB	SO	HBP	SH	SF	SB	CS	SB%	GDP	Avg	OBP	SLG	Pos	G	PO	A	E	DP	FPct
1995 Cle	28	1	0	0	0	0	0	0	0	0	0	0	0	0	0	0	0	0	0	—	0	—	—	—	P	1	0	1	0	0	1.000
1997 Cle	30	2	0	0	0	0	0	0	0	0	0	0	0	0	0	0	0	0	0	—	0	—	—	—	P	2	0	2	0	0	1.000
LCS Totals		3	0	0	0	0	0	0	0	0	0	0	0	0	0	0	0	0	0	—	0	—	—	—	P	3	0	3	0	0	1.000

World Series — Batting / Fielding

Year Tm	Age	G	AB	H	2B	3B	HR	TB	R	RBI	GW	TBB	IBB	SO	HBP	SH	SF	SB	CS	SB%	GDP	Avg	OBP	SLG	Pos	G	PO	A	E	DP	FPct
1995 Cle	28	1	0	0	0	0	0	0	0	0	0	0	0	0	0	0	0	0	0	—	0	—	—	—	P	1	1	1	0	0	1.000
1997 Cle	30	2	0	0	0	0	0	0	0	0	0	0	0	0	0	0	0	0	0	—	0	—	—	—	P	2	2	1	0	1	1.000
WS Totals		3	0	0	0	0	0	0	0	0	0	0	0	0	0	0	0	0	0	—	0	—	—	—	P	3	3	2	0	1	1.000
Postseason Totals		10	0	0	0	0	0	0	0	0	0	0	0	0	0	0	0	0	0	—	0	—	—	—	P	10	5	11	1	1	.941

HAL NARAGON—Harold Richard Naragon—Bats: Left; Throws: Right

Ht: 6'0"; Wt: 160 lbs; Born: 10/1/1928 in Zanesville, Ohio; Debut: 9/23/1951

World Series — Batting / Fielding

Year Tm	Age	G	AB	H	2B	3B	HR	TB	R	RBI	GW	TBB	IBB	SO	HBP	SH	SF	SB	CS	SB%	GDP	Avg	OBP	SLG	Pos	G	PO	A	E	DP	FPct
1954 Cle	25	1	0	0	0	0	0	0	0	0	0	0	0	0	0	0	0	0	0	—	0	—	—	—	C	1	1	0	0	0	1.000

RAY NARLESKI—Raymond Edmond Narleski—Throws: Right; Bats: Right

Ht: 6'1"; Wt: 175 lbs; Born: 11/25/1928 in Camden, New Jersey; Debut: 4/17/1954

World Series — Pitching

Year Tm	Age	G	GS	CG	GF	IP	BFP	H	R	ER	HR	SH	SF	HB	TBB	IBB	SO	WP	Bk	W	L	Pct	ShO	Sv-Op	Hld	OAvg	OOBP	ERA
1954 Cle	25	2	0	0	0	4.0	14	1	1	1	0	2	1	0	1	0	2	0	0	0	0	—	0	0-0	0	.100	.167	2.25

World Series — Batting / Fielding

Year Tm	Age	G	AB	H	2B	3B	HR	TB	R	RBI	GW	TBB	IBB	SO	HBP	SH	SF	SB	CS	SB%	GDP	Avg	OBP	SLG	Pos	G	PO	A	E	DP	FPct
1954 Cle	25	2	0	0	0	0	0	0	0	0	0	0	0	0	0	0	0	0	0	—	0	—	—	—	P	2	0	1	0	0	1.000

JERRY NARRON—Jerry Austin Narron—Bats: Left; Throws: Right

Ht: 6'3"; Wt: 205 lbs; Born: 1/15/1956 in Goldsboro, North Carolina; Debut: 4/13/1979

LCS — Batting / Fielding

Year Tm	Age	G	AB	H	2B	3B	HR	TB	R	RBI	GW	TBB	IBB	SO	HBP	SH	SF	SB	CS	SB%	GDP	Avg	OBP	SLG	Pos	G	PO	A	E	DP	FPct
1986 Cal	30	4	2	1	0	0	0	1	1	0	0	1	0	1	0	0	0	0	0	—	0	.500	.667	.500	C	3	1	0	0	0	1.000

SAM NARRON—Samuel Narron—Bats: Right; Throws: Right

Ht: 5'10"; Wt: 180 lbs; Born: 8/25/1913 in Middlesex, North Carolina; Debut: 9/15/1935; Died: 12/31/1996

World Series — Batting / Fielding

Year Tm	Age	G	AB	H	2B	3B	HR	TB	R	RBI	GW	TBB	IBB	SO	HBP	SH	SF	SB	CS	SB%	GDP	Avg	OBP	SLG	Pos	G	PO	A	E	DP	FPct
1943 StL	30	1	1	0	0	0	0	0	0	0	0	0	0	0	0	0	0	0	0	—	0	.000	.000	.000	—						

DENNY NEAGLE—Dennis Edward Neagle—Throws: Left; Bats: Left

Ht: 6'4"; Wt: 200 lbs; Born: 9/13/1968 in Gambrills, Maryland; Debut: 7/27/1991

LCS — Pitching

Year Tm	Age	G	GS	CG	GF	IP	BFP	H	R	ER	HR	SH	SF	HB	TBB	IBB	SO	WP	Bk	W	L	Pct	ShO	Sv-Op	Hld	OAvg	OOBP	ERA
1992 Pit	24	2	0	0	0	1.2	12	4	5	5	0	0	0	0	3	1	0	0	0	0	0	—	0	0-0	0	.444	.583	27.00
1996 Atl	28	2	1	0	0	7.2	28	2	2	2	0	0	0	0	3	0	8	0	0	0	0	—	0	0-0	0	.080	.179	2.35
1997 Atl	29	2	1	1	1	12.0	42	5	0	0	0	0	0	1	1	0	9	0	0	1	0	1.000	1	0-0	0	.125	.167	0.00
LCS Totals		6	2	1	1	21.1	164	11	7	7	0	0	0	1	7	1	17	0	0	1	0	1.000	1	0-0	0	.149	.232	2.95

World Series — Pitching

Year Tm	Age	G	GS	CG	GF	IP	BFP	H	R	ER	HR	SH	SF	HB	TBB	IBB	SO	WP	Bk	W	L	Pct	ShO	Sv-Op	Hld	OAvg	OOBP	ERA
1996 Atl	28	2	1	0	0	6.0	26	5	3	2	0	0	0	0	4	0	3	0	0	0	0	—	0	0- 0	0	.227	.346	3.00
Postseason Totals		8	3	1	1	27.1	216	16	10	9	0	0	0	1	11	1	20	0	0	1	0	1.000	1	0-0	0	.167	.259	2.96

LCS — Batting / Fielding

Year Tm	Age	G	AB	H	2B	3B	HR	TB	R	RBI	GW	TBB	IBB	SO	HBP	SH	SF	SB	CS	SB%	GDP	Avg	OBP	SLG	Pos	G	PO	A	E	DP	FPct
1992 Pit	24	2	0	0	0	0	0	0	0	0	0	0	0	0	0	0	0	0	0	—	0	—	—	—	P	2	0	0	0	0	—
1996 Atl	28	2	2	1	0	0	0	1	0	0	0	0	0	0	0	1	0	0	0	—	0	.500	.500	.500	P	2	0	1	0	0	1.000
1997 Atl	29	2	3	0	0	0	0	0	0	0	0	0	0	1	0	1	0	0	0	—	0	.000	.000	.000	P	2	1	0	0	0	1.000
LCS Totals		6	5	1	0	0	0	1	0	0	0	0	0	1	0	2	0	0	0	—	0	.200	.200	.200	P	6	1	1	0	0	1.000

World Series — Batting / Fielding

Year Tm	Age	G	AB	H	2B	3B	HR	TB	R	RBI	GW	TBB	IBB	SO	HBP	SH	SF	SB	CS	SB%	GDP	Avg	OBP	SLG	Pos	G	PO	A	E	DP	FPct
1996 Atl	28	2	1	0	0	0	0	0	0	0	0	0	0	1	0	1	0	0	0	—	0	.000	.000	.000	P	2	0	1	0	0	1.000
Postseason Totals		8	6	1	0	0	0	1	0	0	0	0	0	2	0	3	0	0	0	—	0	.167	.167	.167	P	8	1	2	0	0	1.000

CHARLIE NEAL—Charles Lenard Neal—Bats: Right; Throws: Right

Ht: 5'10"; Wt: 165 lbs; Born: 1/30/1931 in Longview, Texas; Debut: 4/17/1956; Died: 11/18/1996

World Series — Batting / Fielding

Year Tm	Age	G	AB	H	2B	3B	HR	TB	R	RBI	GW	TBB	IBB	SO	HBP	SH	SF	SB	CS	SB%	GDP	Avg	OBP	SLG	Pos	G	PO	A	E	DP	FPct
1956 Bro	25	1	4	0	0	0	0	0	0	0	0	0	0	1	0	0	0	0	0	—	0	.000	.000	.000	2B	1	2	2	1	1	.800
1959 LA	28	6	27	10	2	0	2	18	4	6	1	0	0	1	0	0	0	1	0	1.00	1	.370	.370	.667	2B	6	18	19	1	7	.974
WS Totals		7	31	10	2	0	2	18	4	6	1	0	0	2	0	0	0	1	0	1.00	1	.323	.323	.581	2B	7	20	21	2	8	.953

GREASY NEALE—Alfred Earle Neale—Bats: Left; Throws: Right

Ht: 6'0"; Wt: 170 lbs; Born: 11/5/1891 in Parkersburg, West Virginia; Debut: 4/12/1916; Died: 11/2/1973

World Series — Batting / Fielding

Year Tm	Age	G	AB	H	2B	3B	HR	TB	R	RBI	GW	TBB	IBB	SO	HBP	SH	SF	SB	CS	SB%	GDP	Avg	OBP	SLG	Pos	G	PO	A	E	DP	FPct
1919 Cin	27	8	28	10	1	1	0	13	3	4	0	2	0	5	0	0	0	1	4	.20	0	.357	.400	.464	OF	8	19	0	1	0	.950

TOM NEEDHAM—Thomas Joseph Needham—Nickname: Deerfoot—Bats: Right; Throws: Right

Ht: 5'10"; Wt: 180 lbs; Born: 5/17/1879 in Steubenville, Ohio; Debut: 5/12/1904; Died: 12/13/1926

World Series — Batting / Fielding

Year Tm	Age	G	AB	H	2B	3B	HR	TB	R	RBI	GW	TBB	IBB	SO	HBP	SH	SF	SB	CS	SB%	GDP	Avg	OBP	SLG	Pos	G	PO	A	E	DP	FPct
1910 ChN	31	1	1	0	0	0	0	0	0	0	0	0	0	0	0	0	0	0	0	—	0	.000	.000	.000	—						

ART NEHF—Arthur Neukom Nehf—Throws: Left; Bats: Left

Ht: 5'9"; Wt: 176 lbs; Born: 7/31/1892 in Terre Haute, Indiana; Debut: 8/13/1915; Died: 12/18/1960

World Series — Pitching

Year Tm	Age	G	GS	CG	GF	IP	BFP	H	R	ER	HR	SH	SF	HB	TBB	IBB	SO	WP	Bk	W	L	Pct	ShO	Sv-Op	Hld	OAvg	OOBP	ERA
1921 NYG	29	3	3	3	0	26.0	100	13	6	4	0	1	2	0	13	0	8	1	0	1	2	.333	1	0- 0	0	.155	.263	1.38
1922 NYG	30	2	2	1	0	16.0	61	11	5	4	0	4	2	1	3	1	6	1	0	1	0	1.000	0	0- 0	0	.216	.263	2.25
1923 NYG	31	2	2	1	0	16.1	62	10	5	5	1	0	0	0	6	0	7	0	0	1	1	.500	1	0- 0	0	.179	.258	2.76
1924 NYG	32	3	2	1	0	19.2	82	15	5	4	0	1	0	0	9	0	7	0	0	1	1	.500	0	0- 0	0	.208	.296	1.83
1929 ChN	37	2	0	0	1	1.0	5	1	2	2	1	0	0	0	1	0	0	0	0	0	0	—	0	0- 0	0	.250	.400	18.00
WS Totals		12	9	6	1	79.0	620	50	23	19	2	6	4	1	32	1	28	2	0	4	4	.500	2	0-0	0	.187	.273	2.16

World Series — Batting / Fielding

Year Tm	Age	G	AB	H	2B	3B	HR	TB	R	RBI	GW	TBB	IBB	SO	HBP	SH	SF	SB	CS	SB%	GDP	Avg	OBP	SLG	Pos	G	PO	A	E	DP	FPct
1921 NYG	29	3	9	0	0	0	0	0	0	0	0	1	0	3	0	0	0	0	0	—	0	.000	.100	.000	P	3	1	4	1	0	.833
1922 NYG	30	2	3	0	0	0	0	0	0	0	0	2	0	0	0	0	0	0	0	—	0	.000	.400	.000	P	2	0	3	1	0	.750
1923 NYG	31	2	6	1	0	0	0	1	0	0	0	0	0	4	0	0	0	0	0	—	0	.167	.167	.167	P	2	0	6	0	1	1.000
1924 NYG	32	3	7	3	0	0	0	3	1	0	0	0	0	0	0	0	0	0	0	—	0	.429	.429	.429	P	3	0	6	0	0	1.000
1929 ChN	37	2	0	0	0	0	0	0	0	0	0	0	0	0	0	0	0	0	0	—	0	—	—	—	P	2	0	0	0	0	—
WS Totals		12	25	4	0	0	0	4	1	0	0	3	0	7	0	0	0	0	0	—	0	.160	.250	.160	P	12	1	19	2	1	.909

GARY NEIBAUER—Gary Wayne Neibauer—Throws: Right; Bats: Right

Ht: 6'3"; Wt: 200 lbs; Born: 10/29/1944 in Billings, Montana; Debut: 4/12/1969

LCS — Pitching

Year Tm	Age	G	GS	CG	GF	IP	BFP	H	R	ER	HR	SH	SF	HB	TBB	IBB	SO	WP	Bk	W	L	Pct	ShO	Sv-Op	Hld	OAvg	OOBP	ERA
1969 Atl	24	1	0	0	1	1.0	4	0	0	0	0	0	0	0	0	0	1	0	0	0	0	—	0	0- 0	0	.000	.000	0.00

LCS — Batting / Fielding

Year Tm	Age	G	AB	H	2B	3B	HR	TB	R	RBI	GW	TBB	IBB	SO	HBP	SH	SF	SB	CS	SB%	GDP	Avg	OBP	SLG	Pos	G	PO	A	E	DP	FPct
1969 Atl	24	1	0	0	0	0	0	0	0	0	0	0	0	0	0	0	0	0	0	—	0	—	—	—	P	1	0	0	0	0	—

BERNIE NEIS—Bernard Edmund Neis—Bats: Both; Throws: Right

Ht: 5'7"; Wt: 160 lbs; Born: 9/26/1895 in Bloomington, Illinois; Debut: 4/14/1920; Died: 11/29/1972

World Series — Batting / Fielding

Year Tm	Age	G	AB	H	2B	3B	HR	TB	R	RBI	GW	TBB	IBB	SO	HBP	SH	SF	SB	CS	SB%	GDP	Avg	OBP	SLG	Pos	G	PO	A	E	DP	FPct
1920 Bro	25	4	5	0	0	0	0	0	0	0	0	1	0	0	0	0	0	0	0	—	0	.000	.167	.000	OF	2	3	0	0	0	1.000

DAVE NELSON—David Earl Nelson—Bats: Right; Throws: Right

Ht: 5'10"; Wt: 160 lbs; Born: 6/20/1944 in Fort Sill, Oklahoma; Debut: 4/11/1968

LCS — Batting / Fielding

Year Tm	Age	G	AB	H	2B	3B	HR	TB	R	RBI	GW	TBB	IBB	SO	HBP	SH	SF	SB	CS	SB%	GDP	Avg	OBP	SLG	Pos	G	PO	A	E	DP	FPct
1976 KC	32	2	2	0	0	0	0	0	0	0	0	0	0	1	0	0	0	0	0	—	0	.000	.000	.000	—						

GENE NELSON—Wayland Eugene Nelson—Throws: Right; Bats: Right

Ht: 6'0"; Wt: 172 lbs; Born: 12/3/1960 in Tampa, Florida; Debut: 5/4/1981

LCS — Pitching

Year Tm	Age	G	GS	CG	GF	IP	BFP	H	R	ER	HR	SH	SF	HB	TBB	IBB	SO	WP	Bk	W	L	Pct	ShO	Sv-Op	Hld	OAvg	OOBP	ERA
1988 Oak	27	2	0	0	0	4.2	18	5	0	0	0	0	0	0	1	0	0	0	0	2	0	1.000	0	0- 0	0	.294	.333	0.00
1989 Oak	28	1	0	0	0	1.1	4	1	0	0	0	0	0	0	0	0	2	0	0	0	0	—	0	0- 0	0	.250	.250	0.00
1990 Oak	29	1	0	0	0	1.2	8	3	0	0	0	0	0	0	0	0	0	0	0	0	0	—	0	0- 0	1	.375	.375	0.00
LCS Totals		4	0	0	0	7.2	60	9	0	0	0	0	0	0	1	0	2	0	0	2	0	1.000	0	0-0	1	.310	.333	0.00

World Series — Pitching

Year Tm	Age	G	GS	CG	GF	IP	BFP	H	R	ER	HR	SH	SF	HB	TBB	IBB	SO	WP	Bk	W	L	Pct	ShO	Sv-Op	Hld	OAvg	OOBP	ERA
1988 Oak	27	3	0	0	0	6.1	26	4	1	1	0	0	0	0	3	0	3	0	0	0	0	—	0	0- 0	0	.174	.269	1.42
1989 Oak	28	2	0	0	0	1.0	9	4	6	6	2	0	0	0	2	0	1	0	0	0	0	—	0	0- 0	0	.571	.667	54.00
1990 Oak	29	2	0	0	0	5.0	18	3	0	0	0	0	0	0	2	0	0	0	0	0	0	—	0	0- 0	0	.188	.278	0.00
WS Totals		7	0	0	0	12.1	106	11	7	7	2	0	0	0	7	0	4	0	0	0	0	—	0	0-0	0	.239	.340	5.11
Postseason Totals		11	0	0	0	20.0	166	20	7	7	2	0	0	0	8	0	6	0	0	2	0	1.000	0	0-0	1	.267	.337	3.15

LCS — Batting / Fielding

Year Tm	Age	G	AB	H	2B	3B	HR	TB	R	RBI	GW	TBB	IBB	SO	HBP	SH	SF	SB	CS	SB%	GDP	Avg	OBP	SLG	Pos	G	PO	A	E	DP	FPct
1988 Oak	27	2	0	0	0	0	0	0	0	0	0	0	0	0	0	0	0	0	0	—	0	—	—	—	P	2	0	0	0	0	—
1989 Oak	28	1	0	0	0	0	0	0	0	0	0	0	0	0	0	0	0	0	0	—	0	—	—	—	P	1	0	0	0	0	—
1990 Oak	29	1	0	0	0	0	0	0	0	0	0	0	0	0	0	0	0	0	0	—	0	—	—	—	P	1	0	0	0	0	—
LCS Totals		4	0	0	0	0	0	0	0	0	0	0	0	0	0	0	0	0	0	—	0	—	—	—	P	4	0	0	0	0	—

World Series — Batting / Fielding

Year Tm	Age	G	AB	H	2B	3B	HR	TB	R	RBI	GW	TBB	IBB	SO	HBP	SH	SF	SB	CS	SB%	GDP	Avg	OBP	SLG	Pos	G	PO	A	E	DP	FPct
1988 Oak	27	3	0	0	0	0	0	0	0	0	0	0	0	0	0	0	0	0	0	—	0	—	—	—	P	3	1	2	0	0	1.000
1989 Oak	28	2	0	0	0	0	0	0	0	0	0	0	0	0	0	0	0	0	0	—	0	—	—	—	P	2	0	0	0	0	—
1990 Oak	29	2	0	0	0	0	0	0	0	0	0	0	0	0	0	0	0	0	0	—	0	—	—	—	P	2	0	0	0	0	—
WS Totals		7	0	0	0	0	0	0	0	0	0	0	0	0	0	0	0	0	0	—	0	—	—	—	P	7	1	2	0	0	1.000
Postseason Totals		11	0	0	0	0	0	0	0	0	0	0	0	0	0	0	0	0	0	—	0	—	—	—	P	11	1	2	0	0	1.000

JEFF NELSON—Jeffrey Allan Nelson—Throws: Right; Bats: Right

Ht: 6'8"; Wt: 225 lbs; Born: 11/17/1966 in Baltimore, Maryland; Debut: 4/16/1992

Division Series — Pitching

Year	Tm	Age	G	GS	CG	GF	IP	BFP	H	R	ER	HR	SH	SF	HB	TBB	IBB	SO	WP	Bk	W	L	Pct	ShO	Sv-Op	Hld	OAvg	OOBP	ERA
1995	Sea	28	3	0	0	0	5.2	27	7	2	2	0	0	0	1	3	0	7	0	0	0	1	.000	0	0-0	0	.304	.407	3.18
1996	NYA	29	2	0	0	0	3.2	15	2	0	0	0	0	0	0	2	1	5	0	0	1	0	1.000	0	0-0	0	.154	.267	0.00
1997	NYA	30	4	0	0	1	4.0	17	4	0	0	0	0	0	0	2	0	0	0	0	0	0	—	0	0-0	2	.267	.353	0.00
DS Totals			9	0	0	1	13.1	118	13	2	2	0	0	0	1	7	1	12	0	0	1	1	.500	0	0-0	2	.255	.356	1.35

LCS — Pitching

Year	Tm	Age	G	GS	CG	GF	IP	BFP	H	R	ER	HR	SH	SF	HB	TBB	IBB	SO	WP	Bk	W	L	Pct	ShO	Sv-Op	Hld	OAvg	OOBP	ERA
1995	Sea	28	3	0	0	0	3.0	15	3	0	0	0	1	0	0	5	1	3	0	0	0	0	—	0	0-0	1	.333	.571	0.00
1996	NYA	29	2	0	0	0	2.1	13	5	3	3	1	0	0	0	0	0	2	0	0	0	1	.000	0	0-0	0	.385	.385	11.57
LCS Totals			5	0	0	0	5.1	56	8	3	3	1	1	0	0	5	1	5	0	0	0	1	.000	0	0-0	1	.364	.481	5.06

World Series — Pitching

Year	Tm	Age	G	GS	CG	GF	IP	BFP	H	R	ER	HR	SH	SF	HB	TBB	IBB	SO	WP	Bk	W	L	Pct	ShO	Sv-Op	Hld	OAvg	OOBP	ERA
1996	NYA	29	3	0	0	0	4.1	15	1	0	0	0	0	0	0	1	0	5	0	0	0	0	—	0	0-0	0	.071	.133	0.00
Postseason Totals			17	0	0	1	23.0	204	22	5	5	1	1	0	1	13	2	22	0	0	1	2	.333	0	0-0	3	.253	.356	1.96

Division Series — Batting / Fielding

Year	Tm	Age	G	AB	H	2B	3B	HR	TB	R	RBI	GW	TBB	IBB	SO	HBP	SH	SF	SB	CS	SB%	GDP	Avg	OBP	SLG	Pos	G	PO	A	E	DP	FPct
1995	Sea	28	3	0	0	0	0	0	0	0	0	0	0	0	0	0	0	0	0	0	—	0	—	—	—	P	3	0	1	0	0	1.000
1996	NYA	29	2	0	0	0	0	0	0	0	0	0	0	0	0	0	0	0	0	0	—	0	—	—	—	P	2	0	1	0	0	1.000
1997	NYA	30	4	0	0	0	0	0	0	0	0	0	0	0	0	0	0	0	0	0	—	0	—	—	—	P	4	0	0	0	0	—
DS Totals			9	0	0	0	0	0	0	0	0	0	0	0	0	0	0	0	0	0	—	0	—	—	—	P	9	0	2	0	0	1.000

LCS — Batting / Fielding

Year	Tm	Age	G	AB	H	2B	3B	HR	TB	R	RBI	GW	TBB	IBB	SO	HBP	SH	SF	SB	CS	SB%	GDP	Avg	OBP	SLG	Pos	G	PO	A	E	DP	FPct
1995	Sea	28	3	0	0	0	0	0	0	0	0	0	0	0	0	0	0	0	0	0	—	0	—	—	—	P	3	0	3	0	2	1.000
1996	NYA	29	2	0	0	0	0	0	0	0	0	0	0	0	0	0	0	0	0	0	—	0	—	—	—	P	2	0	0	0	0	—
LCS Totals			5	0	0	0	0	0	0	0	0	0	0	0	0	0	0	0	0	0	—	0	—	—	—	P	5	0	3	0	2	1.000

World Series — Batting / Fielding

Year	Tm	Age	G	AB	H	2B	3B	HR	TB	R	RBI	GW	TBB	IBB	SO	HBP	SH	SF	SB	CS	SB%	GDP	Avg	OBP	SLG	Pos	G	PO	A	E	DP	FPct
1996	NYA	29	3	0	0	0	0	0	0	0	0	0	0	0	0	0	0	0	0	0	—	0	—	—	—	P	3	2	0	0	0	1.000
Postseason Totals			17	0	0	0	0	0	0	0	0	0	0	0	0	0	0	0	0	0	—	0	—	—	—	P	17	2	5	0	2	1.000

MEL NELSON—Melvin Frederick Nelson—Nickname: Spider—Throws: Left; Bats: Right

Ht: 6'0"; Wt: 185 lbs; Born: 5/30/1936 in San Diego, California; Debut: 9/27/1960

World Series — Pitching

Year	Tm	Age	G	GS	CG	GF	IP	BFP	H	R	ER	HR	SH	SF	HB	TBB	IBB	SO	WP	Bk	W	L	Pct	ShO	Sv-Op	Hld	OAvg	OOBP	ERA
1968	StL	32	1	0	0	1	1.0	3	0	0	0	0	0	0	0	0	0	1	0	0	0	0	—	0	0-0	0	.000	.000	0.00

World Series — Batting / Fielding

Year	Tm	Age	G	AB	H	2B	3B	HR	TB	R	RBI	GW	TBB	IBB	SO	HBP	SH	SF	SB	CS	SB%	GDP	Avg	OBP	SLG	Pos	G	PO	A	E	DP	FPct
1968	StL	32	1	0	0	0	0	0	0	0	0	0	0	0	0	0	0	0	0	0	—	0	—	—	—	P	1	0	0	0	0	—

ROCKY NELSON—Glenn Richard Nelson—Bats: Left; Throws: Left

Ht: 5'10"; Wt: 175 lbs; Born: 11/18/1924 in Portsmouth, Ohio; Debut: 4/27/1949

World Series — Batting / Fielding

Year	Tm	Age	G	AB	H	2B	3B	HR	TB	R	RBI	GW	TBB	IBB	SO	HBP	SH	SF	SB	CS	SB%	GDP	Avg	OBP	SLG	Pos	G	PO	A	E	DP	FPct
1952	Bro	27	4	3	0	0	0	0	0	0	0	0	0	0	2	0	0	0	0	0	—	0	.000	.250	.000	—						
1960	Pit	35	4	9	3	0	0	1	6	2	2	0	1	0	1	0	0	0	0	0	—	0	.333	.400	.667	1B	3	13	3	0	0	1.000
WS Totals			8	12	3	0	0	1	6	2	2	0	2	0	3	0	0	0	0	0	—	0	.250	.357	.500	1B	3	13	3	0	0	1.000

ROGER NELSON—Roger Eugene Nelson—Throws: Right; Bats: Right

Ht: 6'3"; Wt: 200 lbs; Born: 6/7/1944 in Altadena, California; Debut: 9/9/1967

LCS — Pitching

Year	Tm	Age	G	GS	CG	GF	IP	BFP	H	R	ER	HR	SH	SF	HB	TBB	IBB	SO	WP	Bk	W	L	Pct	ShO	Sv-Op	Hld	OAvg	OOBP	ERA
1973	Cin	29	1	0	0	0	2.1	8	0	0	0	0	0	0	0	1	0	0	0	0	0	0	—	0	0-0	0	.000	.125	0.00

LCS — Batting / Fielding

Year	Tm	Age	G	AB	H	2B	3B	HR	TB	R	RBI	GW	TBB	IBB	SO	HBP	SH	SF	SB	CS	SB%	GDP	Avg	OBP	SLG	Pos	G	PO	A	E	DP	FPct
1973	Cin	29	1	1	0	0	0	0	0	0	0	0	0	0	1	0	0	0	0	0	—	0	.000	.000	.000	P	1	0	0	0	0	—

ROBB NEN—Robert Allen Nen—Throws: Right; Bats: Right

Ht: 6'4"; Wt: 190 lbs; Born: 11/28/1969 in San Pedro, California; Debut: 4/10/1993

Division Series — Pitching

Year	Tm	Age	G	GS	CG	GF	IP	BFP	H	R	ER	HR	SH	SF	HB	TBB	IBB	SO	WP	Bk	W	L	Pct	ShO	Sv-Op	Hld	OAvg	OOBP	ERA
1997	Fla	27	2	0	0	2	2.0	10	1	1	0	0	0	0	0	2	0	2	1	0	1	0	1.000	0	0-1	0	.125	.300	0.00

LCS — Pitching

Year	Tm	Age	G	GS	CG	GF	IP	BFP	H	R	ER	HR	SH	SF	HB	TBB	IBB	SO	WP	Bk	W	L	Pct	ShO	Sv-Op	Hld	OAvg	OOBP	ERA
1997	Fla	27	2	0	0	2	2.0	6	0	0	0	0	0	0	0	0	0	0	0	0	0	0	—	0	2-2	0	.000	.000	0.00

World Series — Pitching

Year	Tm	Age	G	GS	CG	GF	IP	BFP	H	R	ER	HR	SH	SF	HB	TBB	IBB	SO	WP	Bk	W	L	Pct	ShO	Sv-Op	Hld	OAvg	OOBP	ERA
1997	Fla	27	4	0	0	3	4.2	24	8	5	4	0	0	1	0	2	0	7	0	0	0	0	—	0	2-2	0	.381	.417	7.71
Postseason Totals			8	0	0	7	8.2	80	9	6	4	0	0	1	0	4	0	9	1	0	1	0	1.000	0	4-5	0	.257	.325	4.15

Division Series — Batting / Fielding

Year	Tm	Age	G	AB	H	2B	3B	HR	TB	R	RBI	GW	TBB	IBB	SO	HBP	SH	SF	SB	CS	SB%	GDP	Avg	OBP	SLG	Pos	G	PO	A	E	DP	FPct
1997	Fla	27	2	0	0	0	0	0	0	0	0	0	0	0	0	0	0	0	0	0	—	0	—	—	—	P	2	0	0	0	0	—

LCS — Batting / Fielding

Year	Tm	Age	G	AB	H	2B	3B	HR	TB	R	RBI	GW	TBB	IBB	SO	HBP	SH	SF	SB	CS	SB%	GDP	Avg	OBP	SLG	Pos	G	PO	A	E	DP	FPct
1997	Fla	27	2	0	0	0	0	0	0	0	0	0	0	0	0	0	0	0	0	0	—	0	—	—	—	P	2	0	1	0	0	1.000

World Series — Batting / Fielding

Year	Tm	Age	G	AB	H	2B	3B	HR	TB	R	RBI	GW	TBB	IBB	SO	HBP	SH	SF	SB	CS	SB%	GDP	Avg	OBP	SLG	Pos	G	PO	A	E	DP	FPct
1997	Fla	27	4	0	0	0	0	0	0	0	0	0	0	0	0	0	0	0	0	0	—	0	—	—	—	P	4	0	0	0	0	—
Postseason Totals			8	0	0	0	0	0	0	0	0	0	0	0	0	0	0	0	0	0	—	0	—	—	—	P	8	0	1	0	0	1.000

GRAIG NETTLES—Nickname: Puff—Bats: Left; Throws: Right

Ht: 6'0"; Wt: 180 lbs; Born: 8/20/1944 in San Diego, California; Debut: 9/6/1967

Division Series — Batting / Fielding

Year	Tm	Age	G	AB	H	2B	3B	HR	TB	R	RBI	GW	TBB	IBB	SO	HBP	SH	SF	SB	CS	SB%	GDP	Avg	OBP	SLG	Pos	G	PO	A	E	DP	FPct
1981	NYA	37	5	17	1	0	0	0	1	1	1	0	3	0	1	0	0	1	0	1	.00	1	.059	.190	.059	3B	5	8	7	0	0	1.000

LCS — Batting / Fielding

Year	Tm	Age	G	AB	H	2B	3B	HR	TB	R	RBI	GW	TBB	IBB	SO	HBP	SH	SF	SB	CS	SB%	GDP	Avg	OBP	SLG	Pos	G	PO	A	E	DP	FPct
1969	Min	25	1	1	1	0	0	0	1	0	0	0	0	0	0	0	0	0	0	0	—	0	1.000	1.000	1.000	—						
1976	NYA	32	5	17	4	1	0	2	11	2	4	1	3	0	3	0	0	0	0	0	—	0	.235	.350	.647	3B	5	5	14	0	0	1.000
1977	NYA	33	5	20	3	0	0	0	3	1	1	0	0	0	3	0	0	0	0	0	—	0	.150	.150	.150	3B	5	2	12	0	2	1.000
1978	NYA	34	4	15	5	0	1	1	10	3	2	0	0	0	1	0	0	0	0	0	—	0	.333	.333	.667	3B	4	6	8	0	2	1.000
1980	NYA	36	2	6	1	0	0	1	4	1	1	0	0	0	1	0	0	0	0	0	—	1	.167	.167	.667	3B	2	0	2	0	0	1.000
1981	NYA	37	3	12	6	2	0	1	11	2	9	1	1	0	0	1	0	0	0	0	—	0	.500	.571	.917	3B	3	4	4	1	2	.889
1984	SD	40	4	14	2	0	0	0	2	1	2	0	1	0	1	0	0	1	0	0	—	0	.143	.188	.143	3B	4	5	8	0	0	1.000
LCS Totals			24	85	22	3	1	5	42	10	19	2	5	0	9	1	0	1	0	0	—	1	.259	.304	.494	3B	23	22	48	1	6	.986

World Series — Batting / Fielding

Year	Tm	Age	G	AB	H	2B	3B	HR	TB	R	RBI	GW	TBB	IBB	SO	HBP	SH	SF	SB	CS	SB%	GDP	Avg	OBP	SLG	Pos	G	PO	A	E	DP	FPct
1976	NYA	32	4	12	3	0	0	0	3	0	2	0	3	0	1	0	0	1	0	1	.00	2	.250	.375	.250	3B	4	8	8	0	3	1.000
1977	NYA	33	6	21	4	1	0	0	5	1	2	0	2	0	3	0	0	0	0	0	—	0	.190	.261	.238	3B	6	2	20	1	0	.957
1978	NYA	34	6	25	4	0	0	0	4	2	1	0	0	0	6	0	0	0	0	0	—	1	.160	.160	.160	3B	6	8	18	0	4	1.000
1981	NYA	37	3	10	4	1	0	0	5	1	0	0	1	0	1	0	0	0	0	0	—	0	.400	.455	.500	3B	3	3	10	1	0	.929
1984	SD	40	5	12	3	0	0	0	3	2	2	0	5	0	0	0	0	2	0	0	—	0	.250	.421	.250	3B	5	7	12	0	1	1.000
WS Totals			24	80	18	2	0	0	20	6	7	0	11	0	11	0	0	3	0	1	.00	3	.225	.309	.250	3B	24	28	68	2	8	.980
Postseason Totals			53	182	41	5	1	5	63	17	27	2	19	0	21	1	0	5	0	2	.00	5	.225	.295	.346	3B	52	58	123	3	14	.984

DON NEWCOMBE—Donald Newcombe—Nickname: Newk—Throws: Right; Bats: Left

Ht: 6'4"; Wt: 220 lbs; Born: 6/14/1926 in Madison, New Jersey; Debut: 5/20/1949

World Series

Pitching																												
Year Tm	Age	G	GS	CG	GF	IP	BFP	H	R	ER	HR	SH	SF	HB	TBB	IBB	SO	WP	Bk	W	L	Pct	ShO	Sv-Op	Hld	OAvg	OOBP	ERA
1949 Bro-*RY*	23	2	2	1	0	11.2	47	10	4	4	1	0	0	0	3	0	11	0	0	0	2	.000	0	0- 0	0	.227	.277	3.09
1955 Bro	29	1	1	0	0	5.2	25	8	6	6	3	0	0	0	2	0	4	0	0	0	1	.000	0	0- 0	0	.348	.400	9.53
1956 Bro-*MC*	30	2	2	0	0	4.2	28	11	11	11	4	1	0	0	3	0	4	0	0	0	1	.000	0	0- 0	0	.458	.519	21.21
WS Totals		5	5	1	0	22.0	200	29	21	21	8	1	0	0	8	0	19	0	0	0	4	.000	0	0-0	0	.319	.374	8.59

World Series

Batting																									Fielding						
Year Tm	Age	G	AB	H	2B	3B	HR	TB	R	RBI	GW	TBB	IBB	SO	HBP	SH	SF	SB	CS	SB%	GDP	Avg	OBP	SLG	Pos	G	PO	A	E	DP	FPct
1949 Bro	23	2	4	0	0	0	0	0	0	0	0	0	0	3	0	0	0	0	0	—	0	.000	.000	.000	P	2	1	1	0	0	1.000
1955 Bro	29	1	3	0	0	0	0	0	0	0	0	0	0	0	0	0	0	0	0	—	0	.000	.000	.000	P	1	0	1	0	0	1.000
1956 Bro	30	2	1	0	0	0	0	0	0	0	0	0	0	0	0	0	0	0	0	—	0	.000	.000	.000	P	2	0	2	0	0	1.000
WS Totals		5	8	0	0	0	0	0	0	0	0	0	0	3	0	0	0	0	0	—	0	.000	.000	.000	P	5	1	4	0	0	1.000

HAL NEWHOUSER (HOF 1992-V)—Harold Newhouser—Nickname: Prince Hal—Throws: Left; Bats: Left

Ht: 6'2"; Wt: 180 lbs; Born: 5/20/1921 in Detroit, Michigan; Debut: 9/29/1939

World Series

Pitching																												
Year Tm	Age	G	GS	CG	GF	IP	BFP	H	R	ER	HR	SH	SF	HB	TBB	IBB	SO	WP	Bk	W	L	Pct	ShO	Sv-Op	Hld	OAvg	OOBP	ERA
1945 Det-*M*	24	3	3	2	0	20.2	89	25	14	14	0	2	0	0	4	1	22	1	0	2	1	.667	0	0- 0	0	.301	.333	6.10
1954 Cle	33	1	0	0	0	0.0	2	1	1	1	0	0	0	0	1	0	0	0	0	0	0	—	0	0- 0	0	1.000	1.000	—
WS Totals		4	3	2	0	20.2	182	26	15	15	0	2	0	0	5	1	22	1	0	2	1	.667	0	0-0	0	.310	.348	6.53

World Series

Batting																									Fielding						
Year Tm	Age	G	AB	H	2B	3B	HR	TB	R	RBI	GW	TBB	IBB	SO	HBP	SH	SF	SB	CS	SB%	GDP	Avg	OBP	SLG	Pos	G	PO	A	E	DP	FPct
1945 Det	24	3	8	0	0	0	0	0	0	1	0	1	0	1	0	0	0	0	0	—	2	.000	.111	.000	P	3	2	6	1	0	.889
1954 Cle	33	1	0	0	0	0	0	0	0	0	0	0	0	0	0	0	0	0	0	—	0	—	—	—	P	1	0	0	0	0	—
WS Totals		4	8	0	0	0	0	0	0	1	0	1	0	1	0	0	0	0	0	—	2	.000	.111	.000	P	4	2	6	1	0	.889

AL NEWMAN—Albert Dwayne Newman—Bats: Both; Throws: Right

Ht: 5'9"; Wt: 175 lbs; Born: 6/30/1960 in Kansas City, Missouri; Debut: 6/14/1985

LCS

Batting																									Fielding						
Year Tm	Age	G	AB	H	2B	3B	HR	TB	R	RBI	GW	TBB	IBB	SO	HBP	SH	SF	SB	CS	SB%	GDP	Avg	OBP	SLG	Pos	G	PO	A	E	DP	FPct
1987 Min	27	1	2	0	0	0	0	0	0	0	0	0	0	0	0	1	0	0	0	—	0	.000	.000	.000	2B	1	0	1	0	0	1.000
1991 Min	31	2	0	0	0	0	0	0	0	0	0	0	0	0	0	0	0	0	0	—	0	—	—	—	3B	1	0	0	0	0	—
																									SS	1	0	0	0	0	—
LCS Totals		3	2	0	0	0	0	0	0	0	0	0	0	0	0	1	0	0	0	—	0	.000	.000	.000	2B	1	0	1	0	0	1.000

World Series

Batting																									Fielding						
Year Tm	Age	G	AB	H	2B	3B	HR	TB	R	RBI	GW	TBB	IBB	SO	HBP	SH	SF	SB	CS	SB%	GDP	Avg	OBP	SLG	Pos	G	PO	A	E	DP	FPct
1987 Min	27	4	5	1	0	0	0	1	0	0	0	1	0	1	0	0	0	0	0	—	0	.200	.333	.200	2B	3	1	2	0	0	1.000
1991 Min	31	4	2	1	0	1	0	3	0	1	0	0	0	0	0	0	0	0	0	—	0	.500	.500	1.500	3B	2	0	0	0	0	—
																									2B	1	0	1	0	1	1.000
																									SS	1	0	1	0	0	1.000
WS Totals		8	7	2	0	1	0	4	0	1	0	1	0	1	0	0	0	0	0	—	0	.286	.375	.571	2B	4	1	3	0	1	1.000
Postseason Totals		11	9	2	0	1	0	4	0	1	0	1	0	1	0	1	0	0	0	—	0	.222	.300	.444	2B	5	1	4	0	1	1.000

JEFF NEWMAN—Jeffrey Lynn Newman—Bats: Right; Throws: Right

Ht: 6'2"; Wt: 215 lbs; Born: 9/11/1948 in Fort Worth, Texas; Debut: 6/30/1976

Division Series

Batting																									Fielding						
Year Tm	Age	G	AB	H	2B	3B	HR	TB	R	RBI	GW	TBB	IBB	SO	HBP	SH	SF	SB	CS	SB%	GDP	Avg	OBP	SLG	Pos	G	PO	A	E	DP	FPct
1981 Oak	33	1	3	0	0	0	0	0	0	0	0	0	0	1	0	1	0	0	0	—	0	.000	.000	.000	C	1	4	0	0	0	1.000

LCS

Batting																									Fielding						
Year Tm	Age	G	AB	H	2B	3B	HR	TB	R	RBI	GW	TBB	IBB	SO	HBP	SH	SF	SB	CS	SB%	GDP	Avg	OBP	SLG	Pos	G	PO	A	E	DP	FPct
1981 Oak	33	2	5	0	0	0	0	0	0	0	0	0	0	2	0	0	0	0	0	—	1	.000	.000	.000	C	2	9	1	0	0	1.000
Postseason Totals		3	8	0	0	0	0	0	0	0	0	0	0	3	0	1	0	0	0	—	1	.000	.000	.000	C	3	13	1	0	0	1.000

BOBO NEWSOM—Louis Norman Newsom—Nickname: Buck—Throws: Right; Bats: Right

Ht: 6'3"; Wt: 200 lbs; Born: 8/11/1907 in Hartsville, South Carolina; Debut: 9/11/1929; Died: 12/7/1962

World Series

Pitching																												
Year Tm	Age	G	GS	CG	GF	IP	BFP	H	R	ER	HR	SH	SF	HB	TBB	IBB	SO	WP	Bk	W	L	Pct	ShO	Sv-Op	Hld	OAvg	OOBP	ERA
1940 Det	33	3	3	3	0	26.0	97	18	4	4	0	1	0	0	4	1	17	0	0	2	1	.667	1	0- 0	0	.196	.229	1.38
1947 NYA	40	2	1	0	0	2.1	13	6	5	5	0	0	0	0	2	0	0	0	0	0	1	.000	0	0- 0	0	.545	.615	19.29
WS Totals		5	4	3	0	28.1	220	24	9	9	0	1	0	0	6	1	17	0	0	2	2	.500	1	0-0	0	.233	.275	2.86

World Series

Batting																									Fielding						
Year Tm	Age	G	AB	H	2B	3B	HR	TB	R	RBI	GW	TBB	IBB	SO	HBP	SH	SF	SB	CS	SB%	GDP	Avg	OBP	SLG	Pos	G	PO	A	E	DP	FPct
1940 Det	33	3	10	1	0	0	0	1	1	0	0	0	0	1	0	2	0	0	0	—	0	.100	.100	.100	P	3	2	0	0	0	1.000
1947 NYA	40	2	0	0	0	0	0	0	0	0	0	0	0	0	0	0	0	0	0	—	0	—	—	—	P	2	0	1	0	0	1.000
WS Totals		5	10	1	0	0	0	1	1	0	0	0	0	1	0	2	0	0	0	—	0	.100	.100	.100	P	5	2	1	0	0	1.000

WARREN NEWSON—Warren Dale Newson—Nickname: The Deacon—Bats: Left; Throws: Left

Ht: 5'7"; Wt: 190 lbs; Born: 7/3/1964 in Newnan, Georgia; Debut: 5/29/1991

Division Series

Batting																									Fielding						
Year Tm	Age	G	AB	H	2B	3B	HR	TB	R	RBI	GW	TBB	IBB	SO	HBP	SH	SF	SB	CS	SB%	GDP	Avg	OBP	SLG	Pos	G	PO	A	E	DP	FPct
1995 Sea	31	1	1	0	0	0	0	0	0	0	0	0	0	1	0	0	0	0	0	—	0	.000	.000	.000	—						
1996 Tex	32	2	1	0	0	0	0	0	0	0	0	1	0	0	0	0	0	0	0	—	0	.000	.500	.000	—						
DS Totals		3	2	0	0	0	0	0	0	0	0	1	0	1	0	0	0	0	0	—	0	.000	.333	.000	—	0	0	0	0	0	—

LCS

Batting																									Fielding						
Year Tm	Age	G	AB	H	2B	3B	HR	TB	R	RBI	GW	TBB	IBB	SO	HBP	SH	SF	SB	CS	SB%	GDP	Avg	OBP	SLG	Pos	G	PO	A	E	DP	FPct
1993 ChA	29	2	5	1	0	0	1	4	1	1	0	0	0	1	0	0	0	0	0	—	0	.200	.200	.800	—						
Postseason Totals		5	7	1	0	0	1	4	1	1	0	1	0	2	0	0	0	0	0	—	0	.143	.250	.571	—	0	0	0	0	0	—

GUS NIARHOS—Constantine Gregory Niarhos—Bats: Right; Throws: Right

Ht: 6'0"; Wt: 160 lbs; Born: 12/6/1920 in Birmingham, Alabama; Debut: 6/9/1946

World Series

Batting																									Fielding						
Year Tm	Age	G	AB	H	2B	3B	HR	TB	R	RBI	GW	TBB	IBB	SO	HBP	SH	SF	SB	CS	SB%	GDP	Avg	OBP	SLG	Pos	G	PO	A	E	DP	FPct
1949 NYA	28	1	0	0	0	0	0	0	0	0	0	0	0	0	0	0	0	0	0	—	0	—	—	—	C	1	0	0	0	0	—

BILL NICHOLSON—William Beck Nicholson—Nickname: Swish—Bats: Left; Throws: Right

Ht: 6'0"; Wt: 205 lbs; Born: 12/11/1914 in Chestertown, Maryland; Debut: 6/13/1936; Died: 3/8/1996

World Series

Batting																									Fielding						
Year Tm	Age	G	AB	H	2B	3B	HR	TB	R	RBI	GW	TBB	IBB	SO	HBP	SH	SF	SB	CS	SB%	GDP	Avg	OBP	SLG	Pos	G	PO	A	E	DP	FPct
1945 ChN	30	7	28	6	1	1	0	9	1	8	1	2	0	5	0	0	0	0	0	—	0	.214	.267	.321	OF	7	9	0	1	0	.900

STEVE NICOSIA—Steven Richard Nicosia—Bats: Right; Throws: Right

Ht: 5'10"; Wt: 185 lbs; Born: 8/6/1955 in Paterson, New Jersey; Debut: 7/8/1978

World Series

Batting																									Fielding						
Year Tm	Age	G	AB	H	2B	3B	HR	TB	R	RBI	GW	TBB	IBB	SO	HBP	SH	SF	SB	CS	SB%	GDP	Avg	OBP	SLG	Pos	G	PO	A	E	DP	FPct
1979 Pit	24	4	16	1	0	0	0	1	1	0	0	0	0	2	0	0	0	0	0	—	0	.063	.063	.063	C	4	23	2	0	0	1.000

TOM NIEDENFUER—Thomas Edward Niedenfuer—Throws: Right; Bats: Right

Ht: 6'5"; Wt: 225 lbs; Born: 8/13/1959 in St. Louis Park, Minnesota; Debut: 8/15/1981

Division Series

Pitching																												
Year Tm	Age	G	GS	CG	GF	IP	BFP	H	R	ER	HR	SH	SF	HB	TBB	IBB	SO	WP	Bk	W	L	Pct	ShO	Sv-Op	Hld	OAvg	OOBP	ERA
1981 LA	22	1	0	0	1	0.1	3	1	0	0	0	0	0	0	1	1	1	0	0	0	0	—	0	0- 0	0	.500	.667	0.00

LCS

Pitching																												
Year Tm	Age	G	GS	CG	GF	IP	BFP	H	R	ER	HR	SH	SF	HB	TBB	IBB	SO	WP	Bk	W	L	Pct	ShO	Sv-Op	Hld	OAvg	OOBP	ERA
1981 LA	22	1	0	0	0	0.1	3	2	0	0	0	0	0	0	0	0	0	0	0	0	0	—	0	0- 0	0	.667	.667	0.00
1983 LA	24	2	0	0	2	2.0	7	0	0	0	0	0	0	0	1	0	3	0	0	0	0	—	0	1- 1	0	.000	.143	0.00
1985 LA	26	3	0	0	3	5.2	23	5	4	4	2	0	0	0	2	1	5	0	0	0	2	.000	0	1- 2	0	.238	.304	6.35
LCS Totals		6	0	0	5	8.0	66	7	4	4	2	0	0	0	3	1	8	0	0	0	2	.000	0	2-3	0	.233	.303	4.50

World Series — Pitching

Year Tm	Age	G	GS	CG	GF	IP	BFP	H	R	ER	HR	SH	SF	HB	TBB	IBB	SO	WP	Bk	W	L	Pct	ShO	Sv-Op	Hld	OAvg	OOBP	ERA
1981 LA	22	2	0	0	0	5.0	20	3	2	0	0	0	0	0	1	1	0	0	0	0	0	—	0	0- 0	0	.158	.200	0.00
Postseason Totals		9	0	0	6	13.1	112	11	6	4	2	0	0	0	5	3	9	0	0	0	2	.000	0	2-3	0	.216	.286	2.70

Division Series — Batting / Fielding

Year Tm	Age	G	AB	H	2B	3B	HR	TB	R	RBI	GW	TBB	IBB	SO	HBP	SH	SF	SB	CS	SB%	GDP	Avg	OBP	SLG	Pos	G	PO	A	E	DP	FPct
1981 LA	22	1	0	0	0	0	0	0	0	0	0	0	0	0	0	0	0	0	0	—	0	—	—	—	P	1	0	0	0	0	—

LCS — Batting / Fielding

Year Tm	Age	G	AB	H	2B	3B	HR	TB	R	RBI	GW	TBB	IBB	SO	HBP	SH	SF	SB	CS	SB%	GDP	Avg	OBP	SLG	Pos	G	PO	A	E	DP	FPct
1981 LA	22	1	0	0	0	0	0	0	0	0	0	0	0	0	0	0	0	0	0	—	0	—	—	—	P	1	0	1	0	0	1.000
1983 LA	24	2	0	0	0	0	0	0	0	0	0	0	0	0	0	0	0	0	0	—	0	—	—	—	P	2	0	1	0	0	1.000
1985 LA	26	3	1	0	0	0	0	0	0	0	0	0	0	1	0	0	0	0	0	—	0	.000	.000	.000	P	3	2	0	0	0	1.000
LCS Totals		6	1	0	0	0	0	0	0	0	0	0	0	1	0	0	0	0	0	—	0	.000	.000	.000	P	6	2	2	0	0	1.000

World Series — Batting / Fielding

Year Tm	Age	G	AB	H	2B	3B	HR	TB	R	RBI	GW	TBB	IBB	SO	HBP	SH	SF	SB	CS	SB%	GDP	Avg	OBP	SLG	Pos	G	PO	A	E	DP	FPct
1981 LA	22	2	0	0	0	0	0	0	0	0	0	0	0	0	0	0	0	0	0	—	0	—	—	—	P	2	0	0	0	0	—
Postseason Totals		9	1	0	0	0	0	0	0	0	0	0	0	1	0	0	0	0	0	—	0	.000	.000	.000	P	9	2	2	0	0	1.000

BERT NIEHOFF—John Albert Niehoff—Bats: Right; Throws: Right

Ht: 5'10"; Wt: 170 lbs; Born: 5/13/1884 in Louisville, Colorado; Debut: 10/4/1913; Died: 12/8/1974

World Series — Batting / Fielding

Year Tm	Age	G	AB	H	2B	3B	HR	TB	R	RBI	GW	TBB	IBB	SO	HBP	SH	SF	SB	CS	SB%	GDP	Avg	OBP	SLG	Pos	G	PO	A	E	DP	FPct
1915 Phi	31	5	16	1	0	0	0	1	1	0	0	1	0	5	0	0	0	0	0	—	0	.063	.118	.063	2B	5	10	10	0	0	1.000

JOE NIEKRO—Joseph Franklin Niekro—Throws: Right; Bats: Right

Ht: 6'1"; Wt: 185 lbs; Born: 11/7/1944 in Martins Ferry, Ohio; Debut: 4/16/1967

Division Series — Pitching

Year Tm	Age	G	GS	CG	GF	IP	BFP	H	R	ER	HR	SH	SF	HB	TBB	IBB	SO	WP	Bk	W	L	Pct	ShO	Sv-Op	Hld	OAvg	OOBP	ERA
1981 Hou	36	1	1	0	0	8.0	34	7	0	0	0	1	0	0	3	0	4	0	0	0	0	—	0	0- 0	0	.233	.303	0.00

LCS — Pitching

Year Tm	Age	G	GS	CG	GF	IP	BFP	H	R	ER	HR	SH	SF	HB	TBB	IBB	SO	WP	Bk	W	L	Pct	ShO	Sv-Op	Hld	OAvg	OOBP	ERA
1980 Hou	35	1	1	0	0	10.0	39	6	0	0	0	0	0	1	1	1	2	0	0	0	0	—	0	0- 0	0	.162	.205	0.00

World Series — Pitching

Year Tm	Age	G	GS	CG	GF	IP	BFP	H	R	ER	HR	SH	SF	HB	TBB	IBB	SO	WP	Bk	W	L	Pct	ShO	Sv-Op	Hld	OAvg	OOBP	ERA
1987 Min	42	1	0	0	0	2.0	9	1	0	0	0	0	0	1	1	0	1	0	0	0	0	—	0	0- 0	0	.143	.333	0.00
Postseason Totals		3	2	0	0	20.0	164	14	0	0	0	1	0	2	5	1	7	0	0	0	0	—	0	0-0	0	.189	.259	0.00

Division Series — Batting / Fielding

Year Tm	Age	G	AB	H	2B	3B	HR	TB	R	RBI	GW	TBB	IBB	SO	HBP	SH	SF	SB	CS	SB%	GDP	Avg	OBP	SLG	Pos	G	PO	A	E	DP	FPct
1981 Hou	36	1	2	0	0	0	0	0	0	0	0	0	0	0	0	0	0	0	0	—	0	.000	.000	.000	P	1	0	1	0	0	1.000

LCS — Batting / Fielding

Year Tm	Age	G	AB	H	2B	3B	HR	TB	R	RBI	GW	TBB	IBB	SO	HBP	SH	SF	SB	CS	SB%	GDP	Avg	OBP	SLG	Pos	G	PO	A	E	DP	FPct
1972 Det	27	1	0	0	0	0	0	0	0	0	0	0	0	0	0	0	0	0	0	—	0	—	—	—	—						
1980 Hou	35	1	3	0	0	0	0	0	0	0	0	0	0	1	0	0	0	0	0	—	0	.000	.000	.000	P	1	1	0	0	0	1.000
LCS Totals		2	3	0	0	0	0	0	0	0	0	0	0	1	0	0	0	0	0	—	0	.000	.000	.000	P	1	1	0	0	0	1.000

World Series — Batting / Fielding

Year Tm	Age	G	AB	H	2B	3B	HR	TB	R	RBI	GW	TBB	IBB	SO	HBP	SH	SF	SB	CS	SB%	GDP	Avg	OBP	SLG	Pos	G	PO	A	E	DP	FPct
1987 Min	42	1	0	0	0	0	0	0	0	0	0	0	0	0	0	0	0	0	0	—	0	—	—	—	P	1	0	1	0	0	1.000
Postseason Totals		4	5	0	0	0	0	0	0	0	0	0	0	1	0	0	0	0	0	—	0	.000	.000	.000	P	3	1	2	0	0	1.000

PHIL NIEKRO (HOF 1997-W)—Philip Henry Niekro—Nickname: Knucksie—Throws: Right; Bats: Right

Ht: 6'1"; Wt: 180 lbs; Born: 4/1/1939 in Blaine, Ohio; Debut: 4/15/1964

LCS — Pitching

Year Tm	Age	G	GS	CG	GF	IP	BFP	H	R	ER	HR	SH	SF	HB	TBB	IBB	SO	WP	Bk	W	L	Pct	ShO	Sv-Op	Hld	OAvg	OOBP	ERA
1969 Atl	30	1	1	0	0	8.0	36	9	9	4	0	0	0	0	4	1	4	0	0	0	1	.000	0	0- 0	0	.281	.361	4.50
1982 Atl	43	1	1	0	0	6.0	27	6	2	2	0	1	0	0	4	0	5	1	0	0	0	—	0	0- 0	0	.273	.385	3.00
LCS Totals		2	2	0	0	14.0	126	15	11	6	0	1	0	0	8	1	9	1	0	0	1	.000	0	0-0	0	.278	.371	3.86

LCS — Batting / Fielding

Year Tm	Age	G	AB	H	2B	3B	HR	TB	R	RBI	GW	TBB	IBB	SO	HBP	SH	SF	SB	CS	SB%	GDP	Avg	OBP	SLG	Pos	G	PO	A	E	DP	FPct
1969 Atl	30	1	3	0	0	0	0	0	0	0	0	0	0	1	0	0	0	0	0	—	0	.000	.000	.000	P	1	0	3	0	0	1.000
1982 Atl	43	1	0	0	0	0	0	0	0	1	0	0	0	0	0	1	1	0	0	—	0	—	.000	—	P	1	1	1	0	0	1.000
LCS Totals		2	3	0	0	0	0	0	0	1	0	0	0	1	0	1	1	0	0	—	0	.000	.000	.000	P	2	1	4	0	0	1.000

BOB NIEMAN—Robert Charles Nieman—Nickname: Burly—Bats: Right; Throws: Right

Ht: 5'11"; Wt: 195 lbs; Born: 1/26/1927 in Cincinnati, Ohio; Debut: 9/14/1951; Died: 3/10/1985

World Series — Batting / Fielding

Year Tm	Age	G	AB	H	2B	3B	HR	TB	R	RBI	GW	TBB	IBB	SO	HBP	SH	SF	SB	CS	SB%	GDP	Avg	OBP	SLG	Pos	G	PO	A	E	DP	FPct
1962 SF	35	1	0	0	0	0	0	0	0	0	0	1	1	0	0	0	0	0	0	—	0	—	1.000	—	—						

TOM NIETO—Thomas Andrew Nieto—Bats: Right; Throws: Right

Ht: 6'1"; Wt: 193 lbs; Born: 10/27/1960 in Downey, California; Debut: 5/10/1984

LCS — Batting / Fielding

Year Tm	Age	G	AB	H	2B	3B	HR	TB	R	RBI	GW	TBB	IBB	SO	HBP	SH	SF	SB	CS	SB%	GDP	Avg	OBP	SLG	Pos	G	PO	A	E	DP	FPct
1985 StL	24	1	3	0	0	0	0	0	1	0	0	1	0	2	0	0	0	0	0	—	0	.000	.250	.000	C	1	7	0	0	0	1.000

World Series — Batting / Fielding

Year Tm	Age	G	AB	H	2B	3B	HR	TB	R	RBI	GW	TBB	IBB	SO	HBP	SH	SF	SB	CS	SB%	GDP	Avg	OBP	SLG	Pos	G	PO	A	E	DP	FPct
1985 StL	24	2	5	0	0	0	0	0	0	1	0	1	0	2	0	1	0	0	0	—	0	.000	.167	.000	C	2	23	1	0	0	1.000
Postseason Totals		3	8	0	0	0	0	0	1	1	0	2	0	4	0	1	0	0	0	—	0	.000	.200	.000	C	3	30	1	0	0	1.000

AL NIPPER—Albert Samuel Nipper—Throws: Right; Bats: Right

Ht: 6'0"; Wt: 188 lbs; Born: 4/2/1959 in San Diego, California; Debut: 9/6/1983

World Series — Pitching

Year Tm	Age	G	GS	CG	GF	IP	BFP	H	R	ER	HR	SH	SF	HB	TBB	IBB	SO	WP	Bk	W	L	Pct	ShO	Sv-Op	Hld	OAvg	OOBP	ERA
1986 Bos	27	2	1	0	0	6.1	29	10	5	5	2	0	0	0	2	1	2	0	0	0	1	.000	0	0- 0	0	.370	.414	7.11

World Series — Batting / Fielding

Year Tm	Age	G	AB	H	2B	3B	HR	TB	R	RBI	GW	TBB	IBB	SO	HBP	SH	SF	SB	CS	SB%	GDP	Avg	OBP	SLG	Pos	G	PO	A	E	DP	FPct
1986 Bos	27	2	0	0	0	0	0	0	0	0	0	0	0	0	0	0	0	0	0	—	0	—	—	—	P	2	1	2	0	0	1.000

DONELL NIXON—Robert Donell Nixon—Bats: Right; Throws: Right

Ht: 6'1"; Wt: 185 lbs; Born: 12/31/1961 in Evergreen, North Carolina; Debut: 4/7/1987

LCS — Batting / Fielding

Year Tm	Age	G	AB	H	2B	3B	HR	TB	R	RBI	GW	TBB	IBB	SO	HBP	SH	SF	SB	CS	SB%	GDP	Avg	OBP	SLG	Pos	G	PO	A	E	DP	FPct
1989 SF	27	3	3	0	0	0	0	0	0	0	0	0	0	1	0	0	0	1	0	1.00	0	.000	.000	.000	OF	2	2	0	0	0	1.000

World Series — Batting / Fielding

Year Tm	Age	G	AB	H	2B	3B	HR	TB	R	RBI	GW	TBB	IBB	SO	HBP	SH	SF	SB	CS	SB%	GDP	Avg	OBP	SLG	Pos	G	PO	A	E	DP	FPct
1989 SF	27	2	5	1	0	0	0	1	1	0	0	1	0	1	0	0	0	0	0	—	0	.200	.333	.200	OF	2	2	0	0	0	1.000
Postseason Totals		5	8	1	0	0	0	1	1	0	0	1	0	2	0	0	0	1	0	1.00	0	.125	.222	.125	OF	4	4	0	0	0	1.000

OTIS NIXON—Otis Junior Nixon—Bats: Both; Throws: Right

Ht: 6'2"; Wt: 180 lbs; Born: 1/9/1959 in Evergreen, North Carolina; Debut: 9/9/1983

LCS — Batting / Fielding

Year Tm	Age	G	AB	H	2B	3B	HR	TB	R	RBI	GW	TBB	IBB	SO	HBP	SH	SF	SB	CS	SB%	GDP	Avg	OBP	SLG	Pos	G	PO	A	E	DP	FPct
1992 Atl	33	7	28	8	2	0	0	10	5	2	0	4	1	4	0	0	0	3	0	1.00	0	.286	.375	.357	OF	7	16	0	0	0	1.000
1993 Atl	34	6	23	8	2	0	0	10	3	4	0	5	0	6	0	2	0	0	2	.00	0	.348	.464	.435	OF	6	13	0	0	0	1.000
LCS Totals		13	51	16	4	0	0	20	8	6	0	9	1	10	0	2	0	3	2	.60	0	.314	.417	.392	OF	13	29	0	0	0	1.000

World Series — Batting / Fielding

Year Tm	Age	G	AB	H	2B	3B	HR	TB	R	RBI	GW	TBB	IBB	SO	HBP	SH	SF	SB	CS	SB%	GDP	Avg	OBP	SLG	Pos	G	PO	A	E	DP	FPct
1992 Atl	33	6	27	8	1	0	0	9	3	1	0	1	0	3	0	0	0	5	1	.83	0	.296	.321	.333	OF	6	18	0	0	0	1.000
Postseason Totals		19	78	24	5	0	0	29	11	7	0	10	1	13	0	2	0	8	3	.73	0	.308	.386	.372	OF	19	47	0	0	0	1.000

RAY NOBLE—Rafael Miguel Noble—Nickname: Magee—Bats: Right; Throws: Right

Ht: 5'11"; Wt: 210 lbs; Born: 3/15/1919 in Central Hatillo, Cuba; Debut: 4/18/1951; Died: 5/9/1998

World Series — Batting / Fielding

Year Tm	Age	G	AB	H	2B	3B	HR	TB	R	RBI	GW	TBB	IBB	SO	HBP	SH	SF	SB	CS	SB%	GDP	Avg	OBP	SLG	Pos	G	PO	A	E	DP	FPct
1951 NYG	32	2	2	0	0	0	0	0	0	0	0	0	0	1	0	0	0	0	0	—	0	.000	.000	.000	C	2	0	1	0	0	1.000

MATT NOKES—Matthew Dodge Nokes—Bats: Left; Throws: Right

Ht: 6'1"; Wt: 185 lbs; Born: 10/31/1963 in San Diego, California; Debut: 9/3/1985

LCS — Batting / Fielding

Year Tm	Age	G	AB	H	2B	3B	HR	TB	R	RBI	GW	TBB	IBB	SO	HBP	SH	SF	SB	CS	SB%	GDP	Avg	OBP	SLG	Pos	G	PO	A	E	DP	FPct
1987 Det	23	5	14	2	0	0	1	5	2	2	0	1	0	4	0	0	0	0	0	—	0	.143	.200	.357	C	3	11	2	0	0	1.000

GARY NOLAN—Gary Lynn Nolan—Throws: Right; Bats: Right

Ht: 6'2"; Wt: 197 lbs; Born: 5/27/1948 in Herlong, California; Debut: 4/15/1967

LCS — Pitching

Year Tm	Age	G	GS	CG	GF	IP	BFP	H	R	ER	HR	SH	SF	HB	TBB	IBB	SO	WP	Bk	W	L	Pct	ShO	Sv-Op	Hld	OAvg	OOBP	ERA
1970 Cin	22	1	1	0	0	9.0	37	8	0	0	0	2	0	0	4	2	6	0	0	1	0	1.000	0	0- 0	0	.258	.343	0.00
1972 Cin	24	1	1	0	0	6.0	23	4	1	1	1	0	0	0	1	0	4	1	0	0	0	—	0	0- 0	0	.182	.217	1.50
1975 Cin	27	1	1	0	0	6.0	23	5	2	2	1	0	0	0	0	0	5	0	0	0	0	—	0	0- 0	0	.217	.217	3.00
1976 Cin	28	1	1	0	0	5.2	24	6	1	1	0	0	0	0	2	0	1	0	0	0	0	—	0	0- 0	0	.273	.333	1.59
LCS Totals		4	4	0	0	26.2	214	23	4	4	2	2	0	0	7	2	16	1	0	1	0	1.000	0	0-0	0	.235	.286	1.35

World Series — Pitching

Year Tm	Age	G	GS	CG	GF	IP	BFP	H	R	ER	HR	SH	SF	HB	TBB	IBB	SO	WP	Bk	W	L	Pct	ShO	Sv-Op	Hld	OAvg	OOBP	ERA
1970 Cin	22	2	2	0	0	9.1	39	9	8	8	4	1	0	0	3	0	9	0	0	0	1	.000	0	0- 0	0	.257	.316	7.71
1972 Cin	24	2	2	0	0	10.2	39	7	4	4	2	0	0	0	2	0	3	0	0	0	1	.000	0	0- 0	0	.189	.231	3.38
1975 Cin	27	2	2	0	0	6.0	24	6	4	4	2	0	0	0	1	0	2	0	0	0	0	—	0	0- 0	0	.261	.292	6.00
1976 Cin	28	1	1	0	0	6.2	30	8	2	2	0	0	0	0	1	0	1	0	0	1	0	1.000	0	0- 0	0	.276	.300	2.70
WS Totals		7	7	0	0	32.2	264	30	18	18	8	1	0	0	7	0	15	0	0	1	2	.333	0	0-0	0	.242	.282	4.96
Postseason Totals		11	11	0	0	59.1	478	53	22	22	10	3	0	0	14	2	31	1	0	2	2	.500	0	0-0	0	.239	.284	3.34

LCS — Batting / Fielding

Year Tm	Age	G	AB	H	2B	3B	HR	TB	R	RBI	GW	TBB	IBB	SO	HBP	SH	SF	SB	CS	SB%	GDP	Avg	OBP	SLG	Pos	G	PO	A	E	DP	FPct
1970 Cin	22	1	3	1	0	0	0	1	0	0	0	0	0	0	0	0	0	0	0	—	0	.333	.333	.333	P	1	0	3	0	0	1.000
1972 Cin	24	1	2	0	0	0	0	0	0	0	0	0	0	1	0	0	0	0	0	—	0	.000	.000	.000	P	1	0	0	0	0	—
1975 Cin	27	1	2	0	0	0	0	0	0	0	0	0	0	2	0	0	0	0	0	—	0	.000	.000	.000	P	1	0	0	0	0	—
1976 Cin	28	1	0	0	0	0	0	0	0	0	0	1	0	0	0	0	0	0	0	—	0	—	1.000	—	P	1	1	0	0	0	1.000
LCS Totals		4	7	1	0	0	0	1	0	0	0	1	0	3	0	0	0	0	0	—	0	.143	.250	.143	P	4	1	3	0	0	1.000

World Series — Batting / Fielding

Year Tm	Age	G	AB	H	2B	3B	HR	TB	R	RBI	GW	TBB	IBB	SO	HBP	SH	SF	SB	CS	SB%	GDP	Avg	OBP	SLG	Pos	G	PO	A	E	DP	FPct
1970 Cin	22	2	3	0	0	0	0	0	0	0	0	0	0	0	0	1	0	0	0	—	0	.000	.000	.000	P	2	0	1	0	0	1.000
1972 Cin	24	2	3	0	0	0	0	0	0	0	0	0	0	3	0	0	0	0	0	—	0	.000	.000	.000	P	2	0	2	0	0	1.000
1975 Cin	27	2	1	0	0	0	0	0	0	0	0	0	0	0	0	0	0	0	0	—	0	.000	.000	.000	P	2	1	0	0	0	1.000
1976 Cin	28	1	0	0	0	0	0	0	0	0	0	0	0	0	0	0	0	0	0	—	0	—	—	—	P	1	0	1	0	0	1.000
WS Totals		7	7	0	0	0	0	0	0	0	0	0	0	3	0	1	0	0	0	—	0	.000	.000	.000	P	7	1	4	0	0	1.000
Postseason Totals		11	14	1	0	0	0	1	0	0	0	1	0	6	0	1	0	0	0	—	0	.071	.133	.071	P	11	2	7	0	0	1.000

JOE NOLAN—Joseph William Nolan—Bats: Left; Throws: Right

Ht: 5'11"; Wt: 175 lbs; Born: 5/12/1951 in St. Louis, Missouri; Debut: 9/21/1972

LCS — Batting / Fielding

Year Tm	Age	G	AB	H	2B	3B	HR	TB	R	RBI	GW	TBB	IBB	SO	HBP	SH	SF	SB	CS	SB%	GDP	Avg	OBP	SLG	Pos	G	PO	A	E	DP	FPct
1983 Bal	32	1	0	0	0	0	0	0	0	1	0	0	0	0	0	0	1	0	0	—	0	—	.000	—	—						

World Series — Batting / Fielding

Year Tm	Age	G	AB	H	2B	3B	HR	TB	R	RBI	GW	TBB	IBB	SO	HBP	SH	SF	SB	CS	SB%	GDP	Avg	OBP	SLG	Pos	G	PO	A	E	DP	FPct
1983 Bal	32	2	2	0	0	0	0	0	0	0	0	1	1	0	0	0	0	0	0	—	0	.000	.333	.000	C	2	3	0	0	0	1.000
Postseason Totals		3	2	0	0	0	0	0	0	1	0	1	1	0	0	0	1	0	0	—	0	.000	.250	.000	C	2	3	0	0	0	1.000

DICKIE NOLES—Dickie Ray Noles—Throws: Right; Bats: Right

Ht: 6'2"; Wt: 160 lbs; Born: 11/19/1956 in Charlotte, North Carolina; Debut: 7/5/1979

Division Series — Pitching

Year Tm	Age	G	GS	CG	GF	IP	BFP	H	R	ER	HR	SH	SF	HB	TBB	IBB	SO	WP	Bk	W	L	Pct	ShO	Sv-Op	Hld	OAvg	OOBP	ERA
1981 Phi	24	1	1	0	0	4.0	18	4	2	2	1	0	0	0	2	0	5	0	0	0	0	—	0	0- 0	0	.250	.333	4.50

LCS — Pitching

Year Tm	Age	G	GS	CG	GF	IP	BFP	H	R	ER	HR	SH	SF	HB	TBB	IBB	SO	WP	Bk	W	L	Pct	ShO	Sv-Op	Hld	OAvg	OOBP	ERA
1980 Phi	23	2	0	0	0	2.2	11	1	0	0	0	2	0	0	3	0	0	0	0	0	0	—	0	0- 0	0	.167	.444	0.00

World Series — Pitching

Year Tm	Age	G	GS	CG	GF	IP	BFP	H	R	ER	HR	SH	SF	HB	TBB	IBB	SO	WP	Bk	W	L	Pct	ShO	Sv-Op	Hld	OAvg	OOBP	ERA
1980 Phi	23	1	0	0	0	4.2	21	5	1	1	1	0	0	0	2	0	6	0	0	0	0	—	0	0- 0	0	.263	.333	1.93
Postseason Totals		4	1	0	0	11.1	100	10	3	3	2	2	0	0	7	0	11	0	0	0	0	—	0	0-0	0	.244	.354	2.38

Division Series — Batting / Fielding

Year Tm	Age	G	AB	H	2B	3B	HR	TB	R	RBI	GW	TBB	IBB	SO	HBP	SH	SF	SB	CS	SB%	GDP	Avg	OBP	SLG	Pos	G	PO	A	E	DP	FPct
1981 Phi	24	1	0	0	0	0	0	0	0	0	0	1	0	0	0	1	0	0	0	—	0	—	1.000	—	P	1	0	1	0	0	1.000

LCS — Batting / Fielding

Year Tm	Age	G	AB	H	2B	3B	HR	TB	R	RBI	GW	TBB	IBB	SO	HBP	SH	SF	SB	CS	SB%	GDP	Avg	OBP	SLG	Pos	G	PO	A	E	DP	FPct
1980 Phi	23	2	0	0	0	0	0	0	0	0	0	0	0	0	0	0	0	0	0	—	0	—	—	—	P	2	1	2	0	1	1.000

World Series — Batting / Fielding

Year Tm	Age	G	AB	H	2B	3B	HR	TB	R	RBI	GW	TBB	IBB	SO	HBP	SH	SF	SB	CS	SB%	GDP	Avg	OBP	SLG	Pos	G	PO	A	E	DP	FPct
1980 Phi	23	1	0	0	0	0	0	0	0	0	0	0	0	0	0	0	0	0	0	—	0	—	—	—	P	1	1	0	0	0	1.000
Postseason Totals		4	0	0	0	0	0	0	0	0	0	1	0	0	0	1	0	0	0	—	0	—	1.000	—	P	4	2	3	0	1	1.000

HIDEO NOMO—Throws: Right; Bats: Right

Ht: 6'2"; Wt: 210 lbs; Born: 8/31/1968 in Kobe, Japan; Debut: 5/2/1995

Division Series — Pitching

Year Tm	Age	G	GS	CG	GF	IP	BFP	H	R	ER	HR	SH	SF	HB	TBB	IBB	SO	WP	Bk	W	L	Pct	ShO	Sv-Op	Hld	OAvg	OOBP	ERA
1995 LA-*RY*	27	1	1	0	0	5.0	24	7	5	5	2	0	0	0	2	1	6	1	0	0	1	.000	0	0- 0	0	.318	.375	9.00
1996 LA	28	1	1	0	0	3.2	21	5	5	5	1	1	0	0	5	0	3	0	0	0	1	.000	0	0- 0	0	.333	.500	12.27
DS Totals		2	2	0	0	8.2	90	12	10	10	3	1	0	0	7	1	9	1	0	0	2	.000	0	0-0	0	.324	.432	10.38

Division Series — Batting / Fielding

Year Tm	Age	G	AB	H	2B	3B	HR	TB	R	RBI	GW	TBB	IBB	SO	HBP	SH	SF	SB	CS	SB%	GDP	Avg	OBP	SLG	Pos	G	PO	A	E	DP	FPct
1995 LA	27	1	2	0	0	0	0	0	0	0	0	0	0	2	0	0	0	0	0	—	0	.000	.000	.000	P	1	0	0	0	0	—
1996 LA	28	1	1	0	0	0	0	0	0	0	0	0	0	1	0	0	0	0	0	—	0	.000	.000	.000	P	1	1	0	0	0	1.000
DS Totals		2	3	0	0	0	0	0	0	0	0	0	0	3	0	0	0	0	0	—	0	.000	.000	.000	P	2	1	0	0	0	1.000

IRV NOREN—Irving Arnold Noren—Bats: Left; Throws: Left

Ht: 6'0"; Wt: 190 lbs; Born: 11/29/1924 in Jamestown, New York; Debut: 4/18/1950

World Series — Batting / Fielding

Year Tm	Age	G	AB	H	2B	3B	HR	TB	R	RBI	GW	TBB	IBB	SO	HBP	SH	SF	SB	CS	SB%	GDP	Avg	OBP	SLG	Pos	G	PO	A	E	DP	FPct
1952 NYA	27	4	10	3	0	0	0	3	0	1	0	1	0	3	0	0	0	0	0	—	0	.300	.364	.300	OF	3	2	0	0	0	1.000
1953 NYA	28	2	1	0	0	0	0	0	0	0	0	1	0	0	0	0	0	0	0	—	0	.000	.500	.000	—						
1955 NYA	30	5	16	1	0	0	0	1	0	1	0	1	0	1	0	0	0	0	0	—	5	.063	.118	.063	OF	5	13	0	0	0	1.000
WS Totals		11	27	4	0	0	0	4	0	2	0	3	0	4	0	0	0	0	0	—	5	.148	.233	.148	OF	8	15	0	0	0	1.000

FRED NORMAN—Fredie Hubert Norman—Throws: Left; Bats: Both

Ht: 5'8"; Wt: 155 lbs; Born: 8/20/1942 in San Antonio, Texas; Debut: 9/21/1962

LCS — Pitching

Year Tm	Age	G	GS	CG	GF	IP	BFP	H	R	ER	HR	SH	SF	HB	TBB	IBB	SO	WP	Bk	W	L	Pct	ShO	Sv-Op	Hld	OAvg	OOBP	ERA
1973 Cin	31	1	1	0	0	5.0	18	1	1	1	0	0	0	0	3	0	3	0	0	0	0	—	0	0- 0	0	.067	.222	1.80
1975 Cin	33	1	1	0	0	6.0	25	4	1	1	0	0	0	0	5	0	4	1	0	1	0	1.000	0	0- 0	0	.200	.360	1.50
1979 Cin	37	1	0	0	0	2.0	11	4	4	4	2	1	0	0	1	0	1	0	0	0	0	—	0	0- 0	0	.444	.500	18.00
LCS Totals		3	2	0	0	13.0	108	9	6	6	2	1	0	0	9	0	8	1	0	1	0	1.000	0	0-0	0	.205	.340	4.15

World Series — Pitching

Year	Tm	Age	G	GS	CG	GF	IP	BFP	H	R	ER	HR	SH	SF	HB	TBB	IBB	SO	WP	Bk	W	L	Pct	ShO	Sv-Op	Hld	OAvg	OOBP	ERA
1975	Cin	33	2	1	0	0	4.0	22	8	4	4	0	0	0	0	3	1	2	1	0	0	1	.000	0	0- 0	0	.421	.500	9.00
1976	Cin	34	1	1	0	0	6.1	29	9	3	3	0	0	0	0	2	0	2	0	0	0	0	—	0	0- 0	0	.333	.379	4.26
WS Totals			3	2	0	0	10.1	102	17	7	7	0	0	0	0	5	1	4	1	0	0	1	.000	0	0-0	0	.370	.431	6.10
Postseason Totals			6	4	0	0	23.1	210	26	13	13	2	1	0	0	14	1	12	2	0	1	1	.500	0	0-0	0	.289	.385	5.01

LCS — Batting / Fielding

Year	Tm	Age	G	AB	H	2B	3B	HR	TB	R	RBI	GW	TBB	IBB	SO	HBP	SH	SF	SB	CS	SB%	GDP	Avg	OBP	SLG	Pos	G	PO	A	E	DP	FPct
1973	Cin	31	1	1	0	0	0	0	0	0	0	0	0	0	1	0	0	0	0	0	—	0	.000	.000	.000	P	1	1	0	0	0	1.000
1975	Cin	33	1	1	0	0	0	0	0	0	1	0	0	0	0	0	0	1	0	0	—	0	.000	.000	.000	P	1	0	1	0	0	1.000
1979	Cin	37	1	1	0	0	0	0	0	0	0	0	0	0	1	0	0	0	0	0	—	0	.000	.000	.000	P	1	0	0	0	0	—
LCS Totals			3	3	0	0	0	0	0	0	1	0	0	0	2	0	0	1	0	0	—	0	.000	.000	.000	P	3	1	1	0	0	1.000

World Series — Batting / Fielding

Year	Tm	Age	G	AB	H	2B	3B	HR	TB	R	RBI	GW	TBB	IBB	SO	HBP	SH	SF	SB	CS	SB%	GDP	Avg	OBP	SLG	Pos	G	PO	A	E	DP	FPct
1975	Cin	33	2	1	0	0	0	0	0	0	0	0	0	0	0	0	0	0	0	0	—	0	.000	.000	.000	P	2	0	0	0	0	—
1976	Cin	34	1	0	0	0	0	0	0	0	0	0	0	0	0	0	0	0	0	0	—	0	—	—	—	P	1	0	1	0	0	1.000
WS Totals			3	1	0	0	0	0	0	0	0	0	0	0	0	0	0	0	0	0	—	0	.000	.000	.000	P	3	0	1	0	0	1.000
Postseason Totals			6	4	0	0	0	0	0	0	1	0	0	0	2	0	0	1	0	0	—	0	.000	.000	.000	P	6	1	2	0	0	1.000

MIKE NORRIS—Michael Kelvin Norris—Throws: Right; Bats: Right

Ht: 6'2"; Wt: 175 lbs; Born: 3/19/1955 in San Francisco, California; Debut: 4/10/1975

Division Series — Pitching

Year	Tm	Age	G	GS	CG	GF	IP	BFP	H	R	ER	HR	SH	SF	HB	TBB	IBB	SO	WP	Bk	W	L	Pct	ShO	Sv-Op	Hld	OAvg	OOBP	ERA
1981	Oak	26	1	1	1	0	9.0	34	4	0	0	0	0	0	0	3	0	2	0	0	1	0	1.000	1	0- 0	0	.129	.206	0.00

LCS — Pitching

Year	Tm	Age	G	GS	CG	GF	IP	BFP	H	R	ER	HR	SH	SF	HB	TBB	IBB	SO	WP	Bk	W	L	Pct	ShO	Sv-Op	Hld	OAvg	OOBP	ERA
1981	Oak	26	1	1	0	0	7.1	30	6	3	3	0	1	0	0	2	0	4	0	0	0	1	.000	0	0- 0	0	.222	.276	3.68
Postseason Totals			2	2	1	0	16.1	128	10	3	3	0	1	0	0	5	0	6	0	0	1	1	.500	1	0-0	0	.172	.238	1.65

Division Series — Batting / Fielding

Year	Tm	Age	G	AB	H	2B	3B	HR	TB	R	RBI	GW	TBB	IBB	SO	HBP	SH	SF	SB	CS	SB%	GDP	Avg	OBP	SLG	Pos	G	PO	A	E	DP	FPct
1981	Oak	26	1	0	0	0	0	0	0	0	0	0	0	0	0	0	0	0	0	0	—	0	—	—	—	P	1	2	1	1	0	.750

LCS — Batting / Fielding

Year	Tm	Age	G	AB	H	2B	3B	HR	TB	R	RBI	GW	TBB	IBB	SO	HBP	SH	SF	SB	CS	SB%	GDP	Avg	OBP	SLG	Pos	G	PO	A	E	DP	FPct
1981	Oak	26	1	0	0	0	0	0	0	0	0	0	0	0	0	0	0	0	0	0	—	0	—	—	—	P	1	1	2	0	0	1.000
Postseason Totals			2	0	0	0	0	0	0	0	0	0	0	0	0	0	0	0	0	0	—	0	—	—	—	P	2	3	3	1	0	.857

BILL NORTH—William Alex North—Bats: Both; Throws: Right

Ht: 5'11"; Wt: 185 lbs; Born: 5/15/1948 in Seattle, Washington; Debut: 9/3/1971

LCS — Batting / Fielding

Year	Tm	Age	G	AB	H	2B	3B	HR	TB	R	RBI	GW	TBB	IBB	SO	HBP	SH	SF	SB	CS	SB%	GDP	Avg	OBP	SLG	Pos	G	PO	A	E	DP	FPct
1974	Oak	26	4	16	1	1	0	0	2	3	0	0	2	0	1	0	0	0	1	0	1.00	0	.063	.167	.125	OF	4	14	0	0	0	1.000
1975	Oak	27	3	10	0	0	0	0	0	0	1	0	2	0	0	0	0	0	0	0	—	0	.000	.167	.000	OF	3	6	1	1	0	.875
1978	LA	30	4	8	0	0	0	0	0	0	0	0	0	0	1	0	0	0	0	0	—	1	.000	.000	.000	OF	4	9	0	0	0	1.000
LCS Totals			11	34	1	1	0	0	2	3	1	0	4	0	2	0	0	0	1	0	1.00	1	.029	.132	.059	OF	11	29	1	1	0	.968

World Series — Batting / Fielding

Year	Tm	Age	G	AB	H	2B	3B	HR	TB	R	RBI	GW	TBB	IBB	SO	HBP	SH	SF	SB	CS	SB%	GDP	Avg	OBP	SLG	Pos	G	PO	A	E	DP	FPct
1974	Oak	26	5	17	1	0	0	0	1	3	0	0	2	0	5	0	1	0	1	1	.50	1	.059	.158	.059	OF	5	17	0	1	0	.944
1978	LA	30	4	8	1	1	0	0	2	2	2	0	1	0	0	0	0	0	1	0	1.00	0	.125	.222	.250	OF	4	7	0	0	0	1.000
WS Totals			9	25	2	1	0	0	3	5	2	0	3	0	5	0	1	0	2	1	.67	1	.080	.179	.120	OF	9	24	0	1	0	.960
Postseason Totals			20	59	3	2	0	0	5	8	3	0	7	0	7	0	1	0	3	1	.75	2	.051	.152	.085	OF	20	53	1	2	0	.964

JIM NORTHRUP—James Thomas Northrup—Bats: Left; Throws: Right

Ht: 6'3"; Wt: 190 lbs; Born: 11/24/1939 in Breckenridge, Michigan; Debut: 9/30/1964

LCS — Batting / Fielding

Year	Tm	Age	G	AB	H	2B	3B	HR	TB	R	RBI	GW	TBB	IBB	SO	HBP	SH	SF	SB	CS	SB%	GDP	Avg	OBP	SLG	Pos	G	PO	A	E	DP	FPct
1972	Det	32	5	14	5	0	0	0	5	0	1	1	2	0	3	0	0	0	0	1	.00	1	.357	.438	.357	OF	5	10	0	0	0	1.000

World Series — Batting / Fielding

Year	Tm	Age	G	AB	H	2B	3B	HR	TB	R	RBI	GW	TBB	IBB	SO	HBP	SH	SF	SB	CS	SB%	GDP	Avg	OBP	SLG	Pos	G	PO	A	E	DP	FPct
1968	Det	28	7	28	7	0	1	2	15	4	8	1	1	1	5	0	0	0	0	1	.00	3	.250	.276	.536	OF	7	20	0	2	0	.909
Postseason Totals			12	42	12	0	1	2	20	4	9	2	3	1	8	0	0	0	0	2	.00	4	.286	.333	.476	OF	12	30	0	2	0	.938

JOE NOSSEK—Joseph Rudolph Nossek—Bats: Right; Throws: Right

Ht: 6'0"; Wt: 178 lbs; Born: 11/8/1940 in Cleveland, Ohio; Debut: 4/18/1964

World Series — Batting / Fielding

Year	Tm	Age	G	AB	H	2B	3B	HR	TB	R	RBI	GW	TBB	IBB	SO	HBP	SH	SF	SB	CS	SB%	GDP	Avg	OBP	SLG	Pos	G	PO	A	E	DP	FPct
1965	Min	24	6	20	4	0	0	0	4	0	0	0	0	0	1	0	1	0	0	0	—	1	.200	.200	.200	OF	5	13	0	0	0	1.000

LES NUNAMAKER—Leslie Grant Nunamaker—Bats: Right; Throws: Right

Ht: 6'2"; Wt: 190 lbs; Born: 1/25/1889 in Malcolm, Nebraska; Debut: 4/28/1911; Died: 11/14/1938

World Series — Batting / Fielding

Year	Tm	Age	G	AB	H	2B	3B	HR	TB	R	RBI	GW	TBB	IBB	SO	HBP	SH	SF	SB	CS	SB%	GDP	Avg	OBP	SLG	Pos	G	PO	A	E	DP	FPct
1920	Cle	31	2	2	1	0	0	0	1	0	0	0	0	0	0	0	0	0	0	0	—	1	.500	.500	.500	C	1	0	0	0	0	—

JOHNNY OATES—Johnny Lane Oates—Nickname: Quaker—Bats: Left; Throws: Right

Ht: 5'11"; Wt: 188 lbs; Born: 1/21/1946 in Sylva, North Carolina; Debut: 9/17/1970

LCS — Batting / Fielding

Year	Tm	Age	G	AB	H	2B	3B	HR	TB	R	RBI	GW	TBB	IBB	SO	HBP	SH	SF	SB	CS	SB%	GDP	Avg	OBP	SLG	Pos	G	PO	A	E	DP	FPct
1976	Phi	30	1	1	0	0	0	0	0	0	0	0	0	0	0	0	0	0	0	0	—	0	.000	.000	.000	C	1	1	0	0	0	1.000

World Series — Batting / Fielding

Year	Tm	Age	G	AB	H	2B	3B	HR	TB	R	RBI	GW	TBB	IBB	SO	HBP	SH	SF	SB	CS	SB%	GDP	Avg	OBP	SLG	Pos	G	PO	A	E	DP	FPct
1977	LA	31	1	1	0	0	0	0	0	0	0	0	0	0	0	0	0	0	0	0	—	0	.000	.000	.000	C	1	1	0	0	0	1.000
1978	LA	32	1	1	1	0	0	0	1	0	0	0	1	0	0	0	0	0	0	0	—	0	1.000	1.000	1.000	C	1	3	1	0	0	1.000
WS Totals			2	2	1	0	0	0	1	0	0	0	1	0	0	0	0	0	0	0	—	0	.500	.667	.500	C	2	4	1	0	0	1.000
Postseason Totals			3	3	1	0	0	0	1	0	0	0	1	0	0	0	0	0	0	0	—	0	.333	.500	.333	C	3	5	1	0	0	1.000

KEN OBERKFELL—Kenneth Ray Oberkfell—Bats: Left; Throws: Right

Ht: 6'0"; Wt: 175 lbs; Born: 5/4/1956 in Highland, Illinois; Debut: 8/22/1977

LCS — Batting / Fielding

Year	Tm	Age	G	AB	H	2B	3B	HR	TB	R	RBI	GW	TBB	IBB	SO	HBP	SH	SF	SB	CS	SB%	GDP	Avg	OBP	SLG	Pos	G	PO	A	E	DP	FPct
1982	StL	26	3	15	3	0	0	0	3	1	2	1	0	0	0	0	0	0	0	0	—	0	.200	.200	.200	3B	3	2	4	1	2	.857
1989	SF	33	3	4	0	0	0	0	0	0	0	0	0	0	0	0	0	0	0	0	—	0	.000	.000	.000	3B	1	0	1	0	0	1.000
LCS Totals			6	19	3	0	0	0	3	1	2	1	0	0	0	0	0	0	0	0	—	0	.158	.158	.158	3B	4	2	5	1	2	.875

World Series — Batting / Fielding

Year	Tm	Age	G	AB	H	2B	3B	HR	TB	R	RBI	GW	TBB	IBB	SO	HBP	SH	SF	SB	CS	SB%	GDP	Avg	OBP	SLG	Pos	G	PO	A	E	DP	FPct
1982	StL	26	7	24	7	1	0	0	8	4	1	0	2	0	1	0	0	0	2	0	1.00	0	.292	.346	.333	3B	7	3	21	1	2	.960
1989	SF	33	4	6	2	0	0	0	2	1	0	0	3	0	0	0	0	0	0	0	—	0	.333	.556	.333	3B	4	0	5	1	1	.833
WS Totals			11	30	9	1	0	0	10	5	1	0	5	0	1	0	0	0	2	0	1.00	0	.300	.400	.333	3B	11	3	26	2	3	.935
Postseason Totals			17	49	12	1	0	0	13	6	3	1	5	0	1	0	0	0	2	0	1.00	0	.245	.315	.265	3B	15	5	31	3	5	.923

BUCK O'BRIEN—Thomas Joseph O'Brien—Throws: Right; Bats: Right

Ht: 5'10"; Wt: 188 lbs; Born: 5/9/1882 in Brockton, Massachusetts; Debut: 9/9/1911; Died: 7/25/1959

World Series — Pitching

Year	Tm	Age	G	GS	CG	GF	IP	BFP	H	R	ER	HR	SH	SF	HB	TBB	IBB	SO	WP	Bk	W	L	Pct	ShO	Sv-Op	Hld	OAvg	OOBP	ERA
1912	Bos	30	2	2	0	0	9.0	40	12	7	5	0	2	1	0	3	0	4	0	1	0	2	.000	0	0- 0	0	.353	.395	5.00

World Series — Batting / Fielding

Year	Tm	Age	G	AB	H	2B	3B	HR	TB	R	RBI	GW	TBB	IBB	SO	HBP	SH	SF	SB	CS	SB%	GDP	Avg	OBP	SLG	Pos	G	PO	A	E	DP	FPct
1912	Bos	30	2	2	0	0	0	0	0	0	0	0	0	0	2	0	0	0	0	0	—	0	.000	.000	.000	P	2	1	6	0	0	1.000

CHARLIE O'BRIEN—Charles Hugh O'Brien—Bats: Right; Throws: Right

Ht: 6'2"; Wt: 195 lbs; Born: 5/1/1960 in Tulsa, Oklahoma; Debut: 6/2/1985

Division Series		Batting																							Fielding						
Year Tm	Age	G	AB	H	2B	3B	HR	TB	R	RBI	GW	TBB	IBB	SO	HBP	SH	SF	SB	CS	SB%	GDP	Avg	OBP	SLG	Pos	G	PO	A	E	DP	FPct
1995 Atl	35	2	5	1	0	0	0	1	0	0	0	1	0	1	0	0	0	0	0	—	0	.200	.333	.200	C	2	8	1	0	0	1.000
LCS		**Batting**																							**Fielding**						
Year Tm	Age	G	AB	H	2B	3B	HR	TB	R	RBI	GW	TBB	IBB	SO	HBP	SH	SF	SB	CS	SB%	GDP	Avg	OBP	SLG	Pos	G	PO	A	E	DP	FPct
1995 Atl	35	2	5	2	0	0	1	5	1	3	1	0	0	1	0	0	0	0	0	—	0	.400	.400	1.000	C	1	3	1	0	0	1.000
World Series		**Batting**																							**Fielding**						
Year Tm	Age	G	AB	H	2B	3B	HR	TB	R	RBI	GW	TBB	IBB	SO	HBP	SH	SF	SB	CS	SB%	GDP	Avg	OBP	SLG	Pos	G	PO	A	E	DP	FPct
1995 Atl	35	2	3	0	0	0	0	0	0	0	0	0	0	1	0	1	0	0	0	—	0	.000	.000	.000	C	2	7	2	0	0	1.000
Postseason Totals		6	13	3	0	0	1	6	1	3	1	1	0	3	0	1	0	0	0	—	0	.231	.286	.462	C	5	18	4	0	0	1.000

JACK O'BRIEN—John Joseph O'Brien—Bats: Left; Throws: Right

Ht: 6'1"; Wt: 165 lbs; Born: 2/5/1873 in Watervliet, New York; Debut: 4/14/1899; Died: 6/10/1933

World Series		Batting																							Fielding						
Year Tm	Age	G	AB	H	2B	3B	HR	TB	R	RBI	GW	TBB	IBB	SO	HBP	SH	SF	SB	CS	SB%	GDP	Avg	OBP	SLG	Pos	G	PO	A	E	DP	FPct
1903 Bos	30	2	2	0	0	0	0	0	0	0	0	0	0	1	0	0	0	0	0	—	0	.000	.000	.000	—						

JIMMY O'CONNELL—James Joseph O'Connell—Bats: Left; Throws: Right

Ht: 5'10"; Wt: 175 lbs; Born: 2/11/1901 in Sacramento, California; Debut: 4/17/1923; Died: 11/11/1976

World Series		Batting																							Fielding						
Year Tm	Age	G	AB	H	2B	3B	HR	TB	R	RBI	GW	TBB	IBB	SO	HBP	SH	SF	SB	CS	SB%	GDP	Avg	OBP	SLG	Pos	G	PO	A	E	DP	FPct
1923 NYG	22	2	1	0	0	0	0	0	0	0	0	0	0	1	1	0	0	0	0	—	0	.000	.500	.000	—						

PADDY O'CONNOR—Patrick Francis O'Connor—Bats: Right; Throws: Right

Ht: 5'8"; Wt: 168 lbs; Born: 8/4/1879 in County Kerry, Ireland; Debut: 4/17/1908; Died: 8/17/1950

World Series		Batting																							Fielding						
Year Tm	Age	G	AB	H	2B	3B	HR	TB	R	RBI	GW	TBB	IBB	SO	HBP	SH	SF	SB	CS	SB%	GDP	Avg	OBP	SLG	Pos	G	PO	A	E	DP	FPct
1909 Pit	30	1	1	0	0	0	0	0	0	0	0	0	0	1	0	0	0	0	0	—	0	.000	.000	.000	—						

KEN O'DEA—James Kenneth O'Dea—Bats: Left; Throws: Right

Ht: 6'0"; Wt: 180 lbs; Born: 3/16/1913 in Lima, New York; Debut: 4/21/1935; Died: 12/17/1985

World Series		Batting																							Fielding						
Year Tm	Age	G	AB	H	2B	3B	HR	TB	R	RBI	GW	TBB	IBB	SO	HBP	SH	SF	SB	CS	SB%	GDP	Avg	OBP	SLG	Pos	G	PO	A	E	DP	FPct
1935 ChN	22	1	1	1	0	0	0	1	0	1	0	0	0	0	0	0	0	0	0	—	0	1.000	1.000	1.000	—						
1938 ChN	25	3	5	1	0	0	1	4	1	2	0	1	0	0	0	0	0	0	0	—	0	.200	.333	.800	C	1	5	0	0	0	1.000
1942 StL	29	1	1	1	0	0	0	1	0	1	0	0	0	0	0	0	0	0	0	—	0	1.000	1.000	1.000	—						
1943 StL	30	2	3	2	0	0	0	2	0	0	0	0	0	0	0	0	0	0	0	—	0	.667	.667	.667	C	1	2	0	0	0	1.000
1944 StL	31	3	3	1	0	0	0	1	0	2	1	0	0	0	0	0	0	0	0	—	0	.333	.333	.333	—						
WS Totals		10	13	6	0	0	1	9	1	6	1	1	0	0	0	0	0	0	0	—	0	.462	.500	.692	C	2	7	0	0	0	1.000

BILLY O'DELL—William Oliver O'Dell—Nickname: Digger—Throws: Left; Bats: Both

Ht: 5'11"; Wt: 170 lbs; Born: 2/10/1933 in Whitmire, South Carolina; Debut: 6/20/1954

World Series		Pitching																										
Year Tm	Age	G	GS	CG	GF	IP	BFP	H	R	ER	HR	SH	SF	HB	TBB	IBB	SO	WP	Bk	W	L	Pct	ShO	Sv-Op	Hld	OAvg	OOBP	ERA
1962 SF	29	3	1	0	2	12.1	51	12	6	6	1	0	0	1	3	0	9	0	0	0	1	.000	0	1- 1	0	.255	.314	4.38

World Series		Batting																							Fielding						
Year Tm	Age	G	AB	H	2B	3B	HR	TB	R	RBI	GW	TBB	IBB	SO	HBP	SH	SF	SB	CS	SB%	GDP	Avg	OBP	SLG	Pos	G	PO	A	E	DP	FPct
1962 SF	29	3	3	1	0	0	0	1	0	0	0	0	0	0	0	1	0	0	0	—	0	.333	.333	.333	P	3	0	0	0	0	—

BLUE MOON ODOM—Johnny Lee Odom—Throws: Right; Bats: Right

Ht: 6'0"; Wt: 178 lbs; Born: 5/29/1945 in Macon, Georgia; Debut: 9/5/1964

LCS		Pitching																										
Year Tm	Age	G	GS	CG	GF	IP	BFP	H	R	ER	HR	SH	SF	HB	TBB	IBB	SO	WP	Bk	W	L	Pct	ShO	Sv-Op	Hld	OAvg	OOBP	ERA
1972 Oak	27	2	2	1	0	14.0	48	5	1	0	0	0	0	0	2	0	5	1	0	2	0	1.000	1	0- 0	0	.109	.146	0.00
1973 Oak	28	1	0	0	0	5.0	23	6	2	1	0	0	0	0	2	0	4	0	0	0	0	—	0	0- 0	0	.286	.348	1.80
1974 Oak	29	1	0	0	0	3.1	11	1	0	0	0	0	0	0	0	0	1	0	0	0	0	—	0	0- 0	0	.091	.091	0.00
LCS Totals		4	2	1	0	22.1	164	12	3	1	0	0	0	0	4	0	10	1	0	2	0	1.000	1	0-0	0	.154	.195	0.40
World Series		**Pitching**																										
Year Tm	Age	G	GS	CG	GF	IP	BFP	H	R	ER	HR	SH	SF	HB	TBB	IBB	SO	WP	Bk	W	L	Pct	ShO	Sv-Op	Hld	OAvg	OOBP	ERA
1972 Oak	27	2	2	0	0	11.1	44	5	2	2	0	1	0	0	6	0	13	0	0	0	1	.000	0	0- 0	0	.135	.256	1.59
1973 Oak	28	2	0	0	0	4.2	19	5	2	2	0	0	0	0	2	0	2	1	0	0	0	—	0	0- 0	0	.294	.368	3.86
1974 Oak	29	2	0	0	1	1.1	5	0	0	0	0	0	0	0	1	0	2	0	0	1	0	1.000	0	0- 0	0	.000	.200	0.00
WS Totals		6	2	0	1	17.1	136	10	4	4	0	1	0	0	9	0	17	1	0	1	1	.500	0	0-0	0	.172	.284	2.08
Postseason Totals		10	4	1	1	39.2	300	22	7	5	0	1	0	0	13	0	27	2	0	3	1	.750	1	0-0	0	.162	.235	1.13

LCS		Batting																							Fielding						
Year Tm	Age	G	AB	H	2B	3B	HR	TB	R	RBI	GW	TBB	IBB	SO	HBP	SH	SF	SB	CS	SB%	GDP	Avg	OBP	SLG	Pos	G	PO	A	E	DP	FPct
1972 Oak	27	3	4	1	1	0	0	2	0	0	0	0	0	1	0	1	0	0	0	—	0	.250	.250	.500	P	2	2	2	0	0	1.000
1973 Oak	28	1	0	0	0	0	0	0	0	0	0	0	0	0	0	0	0	0	0	—	0	—	—	—	P	1	0	1	0	0	1.000
1974 Oak	29	3	0	0	0	0	0	0	0	0	0	0	0	0	0	0	0	0	0	—	0	—	—	—	P	1	0	0	0	0	—
LCS Totals		7	4	1	1	0	0	2	0	0	0	0	0	1	0	1	0	0	0	—	0	.250	.250	.500	P	4	2	3	0	0	1.000
World Series		**Batting**																							**Fielding**						
Year Tm	Age	G	AB	H	2B	3B	HR	TB	R	RBI	GW	TBB	IBB	SO	HBP	SH	SF	SB	CS	SB%	GDP	Avg	OBP	SLG	Pos	G	PO	A	E	DP	FPct
1972 Oak	27	4	4	0	0	0	0	0	0	0	0	0	0	3	0	0	0	0	0	—	0	.000	.000	.000	P	2	1	3	0	0	1.000
1973 Oak	28	3	1	0	0	0	0	0	0	0	0	0	0	1	0	0	0	0	0	—	0	.000	.000	.000	P	2	0	1	0	0	1.000
1974 Oak	29	2	0	0	0	0	0	0	0	0	0	0	0	0	0	0	0	0	0	—	0	—	—	—	P	2	0	0	0	0	—
WS Totals		9	5	0	0	0	0	0	0	0	0	0	0	4	0	0	0	0	0	—	0	.000	.000	.000	P	6	1	4	0	0	1.000
Postseason Totals		16	9	1	1	0	0	2	0	0	0	0	0	5	0	1	0	0	0	—	0	.111	.111	.222	P	10	3	7	0	0	1.000

LEFTY O'DOUL—Francis Joseph O'Doul—Bats: Left; Throws: Left

Ht: 6'0"; Wt: 180 lbs; Born: 3/4/1897 in San Francisco, California; Debut: 4/29/1919; Died: 12/7/1969

World Series		Batting																							Fielding						
Year Tm	Age	G	AB	H	2B	3B	HR	TB	R	RBI	GW	TBB	IBB	SO	HBP	SH	SF	SB	CS	SB%	GDP	Avg	OBP	SLG	Pos	G	PO	A	E	DP	FPct
1933 NYG	36	1	1	1	0	0	0	1	1	2	1	0	0	0	0	0	0	0	0	—	0	1.000	1.000	1.000	—						

RON OESTER—Ronald John Oester—Bats: Both; Throws: Right

Ht: 6'2"; Wt: 185 lbs; Born: 5/5/1956 in Cincinnati, Ohio; Debut: 9/10/1978

LCS		Batting																							Fielding						
Year Tm	Age	G	AB	H	2B	3B	HR	TB	R	RBI	GW	TBB	IBB	SO	HBP	SH	SF	SB	CS	SB%	GDP	Avg	OBP	SLG	Pos	G	PO	A	E	DP	FPct
1990 Cin	34	4	3	1	0	0	0	1	1	0	0	0	0	1	0	0	0	0	0	—	0	.333	.333	.333	2B	2	0	1	0	0	1.000
World Series		**Batting**																							**Fielding**						
Year Tm	Age	G	AB	H	2B	3B	HR	TB	R	RBI	GW	TBB	IBB	SO	HBP	SH	SF	SB	CS	SB%	GDP	Avg	OBP	SLG	Pos	G	PO	A	E	DP	FPct
1990 Cin	34	1	1	1	0	0	0	1	0	1	0	0	0	0	0	0	0	0	0	—	0	1.000	1.000	1.000	—						
Postseason Totals		5	4	2	0	0	0	2	1	1	0	0	0	1	0	0	0	0	0	—	0	.500	.500	.500	2B	2	0	1	0	0	1.000

BOB O'FARRELL—Robert Arthur O'Farrell—Bats: Right; Throws: Right

Ht: 5'9"; Wt: 180 lbs; Born: 10/19/1896 in Waukegan, Illinois; Debut: 9/5/1915; Died: 2/20/1988

World Series		Batting																							Fielding						
Year Tm	Age	G	AB	H	2B	3B	HR	TB	R	RBI	GW	TBB	IBB	SO	HBP	SH	SF	SB	CS	SB%	GDP	Avg	OBP	SLG	Pos	G	PO	A	E	DP	FPct
1918 ChN	21	3	3	0	0	0	0	0	0	0	0	0	0	0	0	0	0	0	0	—	1	.000	.000	.000	C	1	0	0	0	0	—
1926 StL-*M*	29	7	23	7	1	0	0	8	2	2	0	2	0	2	0	0	1	0	0	—	0	.304	.346	.348	C	7	35	8	0	0	1.000
WS Totals		10	26	7	1	0	0	8	2	2	0	2	0	2	0	0	1	0	0	—	1	.269	.310	.308	C	8	35	8	0	0	1.000

JOSE OFFERMAN—Jose Antonio Offerman—Bats: Both; Throws: Right

Ht: 6'0"; Wt: 160 lbs; Born: 11/8/1968 in San Pedro de Macoris, Dominican Republic; Debut: 8/19/1990

Division Series		Batting																							Fielding						
Year Tm	Age	G	AB	H	2B	3B	HR	TB	R	RBI	GW	TBB	IBB	SO	HBP	SH	SF	SB	CS	SB%	GDP	Avg	OBP	SLG	Pos	G	PO	A	E	DP	FPct
1995 LA	26	1	0	0	0	0	0	0	0	0	0	0	0	0	0	0	0	0	0	—	0	—	—	—	—						

CURLY OGDEN—Warren Harvey Ogden—Throws: Right; Bats: Right

Ht: 6'1"; Wt: 180 lbs; Born: 1/24/1901 in Ogden, Pennsylvania; Debut: 7/18/1922; Died: 8/6/1964

World Series		Pitching																										
Year Tm	Age	G	GS	CG	GF	IP	BFP	H	R	ER	HR	SH	SF	HB	TBB	IBB	SO	WP	Bk	W	L	Pct	ShO	Sv-Op	Hld	OAvg	OOBP	ERA
1924 Was	23	1	1	0	0	0.1	2	0	0	0	0	0	0	0	1	0	1	0	0	0	0	—	0	0-0	0	.000	.500	0.00

World Series		Batting																							Fielding						
Year Tm	Age	G	AB	H	2B	3B	HR	TB	R	RBI	GW	TBB	IBB	SO	HBP	SH	SF	SB	CS	SB%	GDP	Avg	OBP	SLG	Pos	G	PO	A	E	DP	FPct
1924 Was	23	1	0	0	0	0	0	0	0	0	0	0	0	0	0	0	0	0	0	—	0	—	—	—	P	1	0	0	0	0	—

CHAD OGEA—Chad Wayne Ogea—Throws: Right; Bats: Right

Ht: 6'2"; Wt: 200 lbs; Born: 11/9/1970 in Lake Charles, Louisiana; Debut: 5/3/1994

Division Series		Pitching																										
Year Tm	Age	G	GS	CG	GF	IP	BFP	H	R	ER	HR	SH	SF	HB	TBB	IBB	SO	WP	Bk	W	L	Pct	ShO	Sv-Op	Hld	OAvg	OOBP	ERA
1996 Cle	25	1	0	0	1	0.1	2	0	0	0	0	0	0	0	1	1	0	0	0	0	0	—	0	0-0	0	.000	.500	0.00
1997 Cle	26	1	0	0	1	5.1	18	2	1	1	1	1	0	0	0	0	1	0	0	0	0	—	0	0-0	0	.118	.118	1.69
DS Totals		2	0	0	2	5.2	40	2	1	1	1	1	0	0	1	1	1	0	0	0	0	—	0	0-0	0	.111	.158	1.59
LCS		Pitching																										
Year Tm	Age	G	GS	CG	GF	IP	BFP	H	R	ER	HR	SH	SF	HB	TBB	IBB	SO	WP	Bk	W	L	Pct	ShO	Sv-Op	Hld	OAvg	OOBP	ERA
1995 Cle	24	1	0	0	0	0.2	3	1	0	0	0	0	0	0	0	0	2	1	0	0	0	—	0	0-0	0	.333	.333	0.00
1997 Cle	26	2	2	0	0	14.0	56	12	5	5	2	1	0	0	5	0	7	0	0	0	2	.000	0	0-0	0	.240	.309	3.21
LCS Totals		3	2	0	0	14.2	118	13	5	5	2	1	0	0	5	0	9	1	0	0	2	.000	0	0-0	0	.245	.310	3.07
World Series		Pitching																										
Year Tm	Age	G	GS	CG	GF	IP	BFP	H	R	ER	HR	SH	SF	HB	TBB	IBB	SO	WP	Bk	W	L	Pct	ShO	Sv-Op	Hld	OAvg	OOBP	ERA
1997 Cle	26	2	2	0	0	11.2	49	11	2	2	0	0	1	1	3	0	5	0	0	2	0	1.000	0	0-0	0	.250	.306	1.54
Postseason Totals		7	4	0	2	32.0	256	26	8	8	3	2	1	1	9	1	15	1	0	2	2	.500	0	0-0	0	.226	.286	2.25

Division Series		Batting																							Fielding						
Year Tm	Age	G	AB	H	2B	3B	HR	TB	R	RBI	GW	TBB	IBB	SO	HBP	SH	SF	SB	CS	SB%	GDP	Avg	OBP	SLG	Pos	G	PO	A	E	DP	FPct
1996 Cle	25	1	0	0	0	0	0	0	0	0	0	0	0	0	0	0	0	0	0	—	0	—	—	—	P	1	0	0	0	0	—
1997 Cle	26	1	0	0	0	0	0	0	0	0	0	0	0	0	0	0	0	0	0	—	0	—	—	—	P	1	0	1	0	0	1.000
DS Totals		2	0	0	0	0	0	0	0	0	0	0	0	0	0	0	0	0	0	—	0	—	—	—	P	2	0	1	0	0	1.000
LCS		Batting																							Fielding						
Year Tm	Age	G	AB	H	2B	3B	HR	TB	R	RBI	GW	TBB	IBB	SO	HBP	SH	SF	SB	CS	SB%	GDP	Avg	OBP	SLG	Pos	G	PO	A	E	DP	FPct
1995 Cle	24	1	0	0	0	0	0	0	0	0	0	0	0	0	0	0	0	0	0	—	0	—	—	—	P	1	0	0	0	0	—
1997 Cle	26	2	0	0	0	0	0	0	0	0	0	0	0	0	0	0	0	0	0	—	0	—	—	—	P	2	0	1	0	0	1.000
LCS Totals		3	0	0	0	0	0	0	0	0	0	0	0	0	0	0	0	0	0	—	0	—	—	—	P	3	0	1	0	0	1.000
World Series		Batting																							Fielding						
Year Tm	Age	G	AB	H	2B	3B	HR	TB	R	RBI	GW	TBB	IBB	SO	HBP	SH	SF	SB	CS	SB%	GDP	Avg	OBP	SLG	Pos	G	PO	A	E	DP	FPct
1997 Cle	26	2	4	2	1	0	0	3	1	2	1	0	0	1	0	1	0	0	0	—	0	.500	.500	.750	P	2	0	2	0	0	1.000
Postseason Totals		7	4	2	1	0	0	3	1	2	1	0	0	1	0	1	0	0	0	—	0	.500	.500	.750	P	7	0	4	0	0	1.000

BEN OGLIVIE—Benjamin Ambrosio Oglivie—Bats: Left; Throws: Left

Ht: 6'2"; Wt: 160 lbs; Born: 2/11/1949 in Colon, Panama; Debut: 9/4/1971

Division Series		Batting																							Fielding						
Year Tm	Age	G	AB	H	2B	3B	HR	TB	R	RBI	GW	TBB	IBB	SO	HBP	SH	SF	SB	CS	SB%	GDP	Avg	OBP	SLG	Pos	G	PO	A	E	DP	FPct
1981 Mil	32	5	18	3	1	0	0	4	0	1	0	0	0	7	0	1	0	0	0	—	0	.167	.167	.222	OF	5	13	1	0	0	1.000
LCS		Batting																							Fielding						
Year Tm	Age	G	AB	H	2B	3B	HR	TB	R	RBI	GW	TBB	IBB	SO	HBP	SH	SF	SB	CS	SB%	GDP	Avg	OBP	SLG	Pos	G	PO	A	E	DP	FPct
1982 Mil	33	4	15	2	0	0	1	5	1	1	0	0	0	3	1	0	0	0	0	—	0	.133	.188	.333	OF	4	5	0	2	0	.714
World Series		Batting																							Fielding						
Year Tm	Age	G	AB	H	2B	3B	HR	TB	R	RBI	GW	TBB	IBB	SO	HBP	SH	SF	SB	CS	SB%	GDP	Avg	OBP	SLG	Pos	G	PO	A	E	DP	FPct
1982 Mil	33	7	27	6	0	1	1	11	4	1	0	2	1	4	0	0	0	0	1	.00	1	.222	.276	.407	OF	7	13	0	1	0	.929
Postseason Totals		16	60	11	1	1	2	20	5	3	0	2	1	14	1	1	0	0	1	.00	1	.183	.222	.333	OF	16	31	1	3	0	.914

BOBBY OJEDA—Robert Michael Ojeda—Nickname: Bobby O.—Throws: Left; Bats: Left

Ht: 6'1"; Wt: 185 lbs; Born: 12/17/1957 in Los Angeles, California; Debut: 7/13/1980

LCS		Pitching																										
Year Tm	Age	G	GS	CG	GF	IP	BFP	H	R	ER	HR	SH	SF	HB	TBB	IBB	SO	WP	Bk	W	L	Pct	ShO	Sv-Op	Hld	OAvg	OOBP	ERA
1986 NYN	28	2	2	1	0	14.0	57	15	4	4	0	0	0	0	4	0	6	0	0	1	0	1.000	0	0-0	0	.283	.333	2.57
World Series		Pitching																										
Year Tm	Age	G	GS	CG	GF	IP	BFP	H	R	ER	HR	SH	SF	HB	TBB	IBB	SO	WP	Bk	W	L	Pct	ShO	Sv-Op	Hld	OAvg	OOBP	ERA
1986 NYN	28	2	2	0	0	13.0	56	13	3	3	0	0	0	0	5	0	9	1	0	1	0	1.000	0	0-0	0	.255	.321	2.08
Postseason Totals		4	4	1	0	27.0	226	28	7	7	0	0	0	0	9	0	15	1	0	2	0	1.000	0	0-0	0	.269	.327	2.33

LCS		Batting																							Fielding						
Year Tm	Age	G	AB	H	2B	3B	HR	TB	R	RBI	GW	TBB	IBB	SO	HBP	SH	SF	SB	CS	SB%	GDP	Avg	OBP	SLG	Pos	G	PO	A	E	DP	FPct
1986 NYN	28	2	5	0	0	0	0	0	1	0	0	0	0	2	0	0	0	0	0	—	0	.000	.000	.000	P	2	2	4	0	0	1.000
World Series		Batting																							Fielding						
Year Tm	Age	G	AB	H	2B	3B	HR	TB	R	RBI	GW	TBB	IBB	SO	HBP	SH	SF	SB	CS	SB%	GDP	Avg	OBP	SLG	Pos	G	PO	A	E	DP	FPct
1986 NYN	28	2	2	0	0	0	0	0	0	0	0	0	0	1	0	0	0	0	0	—	0	.000	.000	.000	P	2	0	2	0	0	1.000
Postseason Totals		4	7	0	0	0	0	0	1	0	0	0	0	3	0	0	0	0	0	—	0	.000	.000	.000	P	4	2	6	0	0	1.000

RED OLDHAM—John Cyrus Oldham—Throws: Left; Bats: Both

Ht: 6'0"; Wt: 176 lbs; Born: 7/15/1893 in Zion, Maryland; Debut: 8/19/1914; Died: 1/28/1961

World Series		Pitching																										
Year Tm	Age	G	GS	CG	GF	IP	BFP	H	R	ER	HR	SH	SF	HB	TBB	IBB	SO	WP	Bk	W	L	Pct	ShO	Sv-Op	Hld	OAvg	OOBP	ERA
1925 Pit	32	1	0	0	1	1.0	3	0	0	0	0	0	0	0	0	0	2	0	0	0	0	—	0	1-1	0	.000	.000	0.00

World Series		Batting																							Fielding						
Year Tm	Age	G	AB	H	2B	3B	HR	TB	R	RBI	GW	TBB	IBB	SO	HBP	SH	SF	SB	CS	SB%	GDP	Avg	OBP	SLG	Pos	G	PO	A	E	DP	FPct
1925 Pit	32	1	0	0	0	0	0	0	0	0	0	0	0	0	0	0	0	0	0	—	0	—	—	—	P	1	0	0	0	0	—

BOB OLDIS—Robert Carl Oldis—Bats: Right; Throws: Right

Ht: 6'1"; Wt: 185 lbs; Born: 1/5/1928 in Preston, Iowa; Debut: 4/28/1953

World Series		Batting																							Fielding						
Year Tm	Age	G	AB	H	2B	3B	HR	TB	R	RBI	GW	TBB	IBB	SO	HBP	SH	SF	SB	CS	SB%	GDP	Avg	OBP	SLG	Pos	G	PO	A	E	DP	FPct
1960 Pit	32	2	0	0	0	0	0	0	0	0	0	0	0	0	0	0	0	0	0	—	0	—	—	—	C	2	0	0	0	0	—

RUBE OLDRING—Reuben Henry Oldring—Bats: Right; Throws: Right

Ht: 5'10"; Wt: 186 lbs; Born: 5/30/1884 in New York, New York; Debut: 10/2/1905; Died: 9/9/1961

World Series		Batting																							Fielding						
Year Tm	Age	G	AB	H	2B	3B	HR	TB	R	RBI	GW	TBB	IBB	SO	HBP	SH	SF	SB	CS	SB%	GDP	Avg	OBP	SLG	Pos	G	PO	A	E	DP	FPct
1911 Phi	27	6	25	5	2	0	1	10	2	3	0	0	0	4	0	2	0	0	0	—	0	.200	.200	.400	OF	6	8	0	1	0	.889
1913 Phi	29	5	22	6	0	1	0	8	5	0	0	0	0	1	0	0	0	1	0	1.00	0	.273	.273	.364	OF	5	10	0	0	0	1.000
1914 Phi	30	4	15	1	0	0	0	1	0	0	0	0	0	5	0	2	0	0	1	.00	0	.067	.067	.067	OF	4	6	0	0	0	1.000
WS Totals		15	62	12	2	1	1	19	7	3	0	0	0	10	0	4	0	1	1	.50	0	.194	.194	.306	OF	15	24	0	1	0	.960

CHARLEY O'LEARY—Charles Timothy O'Leary—Bats: Right; Throws: Right

Ht: 5'7"; Wt: 165 lbs; Born: 10/15/1882 in Chicago, Illinois; Debut: 4/14/1904; Died: 1/6/1941

World Series		Batting																							Fielding						
Year Tm	Age	G	AB	H	2B	3B	HR	TB	R	RBI	GW	TBB	IBB	SO	HBP	SH	SF	SB	CS	SB%	GDP	Avg	OBP	SLG	Pos	G	PO	A	E	DP	FPct
1907 Det	24	5	17	1	0	0	0	1	0	0	0	1	0	3	0	1	0	0	1	.00	0	.059	.111	.059	SS	5	12	15	2	0	.931
1908 Det	25	5	20	4	0	0	0	4	2	0	0	0	0	3	0	0	0	0	0	—	0	.200	.200	.200	SS	5	7	12	1	3	.950
1909 Det	26	1	3	0	0	0	0	0	0	0	0	0	0	0	0	0	0	0	0	—	0	.000	.000	.000	3B	1	1	1	0	0	1.000
WS Totals		11	40	5	0	0	0	5	2	0	0	1	0	6	0	1	0	0	1	.00	0	.125	.146	.125	SS	10	19	27	3	3	.939

JOHN OLERUD—John Garrett Olerud—Bats: Left; Throws: Left

Ht: 6'5"; Wt: 205 lbs; Born: 8/5/1968 in Seattle, Washington; Debut: 9/3/1989

LCS		Batting																							Fielding						
Year Tm	Age	G	AB	H	2B	3B	HR	TB	R	RBI	GW	TBB	IBB	SO	HBP	SH	SF	SB	CS	SB%	GDP	Avg	OBP	SLG	Pos	G	PO	A	E	DP	FPct
1991 Tor	23	5	19	3	0	0	0	3	1	3	0	3	0	1	0	0	0	0	0	—	0	.158	.273	.158	1B	5	40	3	0	5	1.000
1992 Tor	24	6	23	8	2	0	1	13	4	4	0	2	0	5	0	0	0	0	0	—	0	.348	.400	.565	1B	6	51	1	0	5	1.000
1993 Tor	25	6	23	8	1	0	0	9	5	3	1	4	0	1	1	0	0	0	0	—	1	.348	.464	.391	1B	6	48	9	1	5	.983
LCS Totals		17	65	19	3	0	1	25	10	10	1	9	0	7	1	0	0	0	0	—	1	.292	.387	.385	1B	17	139	13	1	15	.993

World Series		Batting																							Fielding						
Year Tm	Age	G	AB	H	2B	3B	HR	TB	R	RBI	GW	TBB	IBB	SO	HBP	SH	SF	SB	CS	SB%	GDP	Avg	OBP	SLG	Pos	G	PO	A	E	DP	FPct
1992 Tor	24	4	13	4	0	0	0	4	2	0	0	0	0	4	0	0	0	0	0	—	0	.308	.308	.308	1B	4	25	3	0	2	1.000
1993 Tor	25	5	17	4	1	0	1	8	5	2	1	4	1	1	0	0	1	0	0	—	0	.235	.364	.471	1B	5	36	0	0	3	1.000
WS Totals		9	30	8	1	0	1	12	7	2	1	4	1	5	0	0	1	0	0	—	0	.267	.343	.400	1B	9	61	3	0	5	1.000
Postseason Totals		26	95	27	4	0	2	37	17	12	2	13	1	12	1	0	1	0	0	—	1	.284	.373	.389	1B	26	200	16	1	20	.995

TONY OLIVA—Pedro Oliva—Bats: Left; Throws: Right

Ht: 6'1"; Wt: 175 lbs; Born: 7/20/1940 in Pinar del Rio, Cuba; Debut: 9/9/1962

LCS		Batting																							Fielding						
Year Tm	Age	G	AB	H	2B	3B	HR	TB	R	RBI	GW	TBB	IBB	SO	HBP	SH	SF	SB	CS	SB%	GDP	Avg	OBP	SLG	Pos	G	PO	A	E	DP	FPct
1969 Min	29	3	13	5	2	0	1	10	3	2	0	1	0	3	0	0	0	1	0	1.00	0	.385	.429	.769	OF	3	6	1	2	0	.778
1970 Min	30	3	12	6	2	0	1	11	2	1	0	0	0	1	0	0	0	0	0	—	0	.500	.500	.917	OF	3	10	1	0	1	1.000
LCS Totals		6	25	11	4	0	2	21	5	3	0	1	0	4	0	0	0	1	0	1.00	0	.440	.462	.840	OF	6	16	2	2	1	.900

World Series		Batting																							Fielding						
Year Tm	Age	G	AB	H	2B	3B	HR	TB	R	RBI	GW	TBB	IBB	SO	HBP	SH	SF	SB	CS	SB%	GDP	Avg	OBP	SLG	Pos	G	PO	A	E	DP	FPct
1965 Min	25	7	26	5	1	0	1	9	2	2	1	1	0	6	0	0	0	0	0	—	1	.192	.222	.346	OF	7	20	0	1	0	.952
Postseason Totals		13	51	16	5	0	3	30	7	5	1	2	0	10	0	0	0	1	0	1.00	1	.314	.340	.588	OF	13	36	2	3	1	.927

AL OLIVER—Albert Oliver—Nickname: Mr. Scoops—Bats: Left; Throws: Left

Ht: 6'0"; Wt: 195 lbs; Born: 10/14/1946 in Portsmouth, Ohio; Debut: 9/23/1968

LCS		Batting																							Fielding						
Year Tm	Age	G	AB	H	2B	3B	HR	TB	R	RBI	GW	TBB	IBB	SO	HBP	SH	SF	SB	CS	SB%	GDP	Avg	OBP	SLG	Pos	G	PO	A	E	DP	FPct
1970 Pit	23	2	8	2	0	0	0	2	0	1	0	1	1	0	0	0	0	0	0	—	0	.250	.333	.250	1B	2	23	0	0	1	1.000
1971 Pit	24	4	12	3	0	0	1	6	2	5	0	1	0	3	0	0	0	0	0	—	0	.250	.308	.500	OF	4	5	0	0	0	1.000
1972 Pit	25	5	20	5	2	1	1	12	3	3	0	0	0	4	0	1	0	0	0	—	0	.250	.250	.600	OF	5	17	1	0	0	1.000
1974 Pit	27	4	14	2	0	0	0	2	1	1	0	2	0	2	0	0	0	0	0	—	0	.143	.250	.143	OF	4	9	0	0	0	1.000
1975 Pit	28	3	11	2	0	0	1	5	1	2	0	2	0	0	0	0	0	0	0	—	0	.182	.308	.455	OF	3	5	0	0	0	1.000
1985 Tor	38	5	8	3	1	0	0	4	0	3	2	0	0	0	1	0	0	0	0	—	0	.375	.444	.500	—						
LCS Totals		23	73	17	3	1	3	31	7	15	2	6	1	9	1	1	0	0	0	—	0	.233	.300	.425	OF	16	36	1	0	0	1.000

World Series		Batting																							Fielding						
Year Tm	Age	G	AB	H	2B	3B	HR	TB	R	RBI	GW	TBB	IBB	SO	HBP	SH	SF	SB	CS	SB%	GDP	Avg	OBP	SLG	Pos	G	PO	A	E	DP	FPct
1971 Pit	24	5	19	4	2	0	0	6	1	2	0	2	1	5	0	0	0	0	0	—	0	.211	.286	.316	OF	4	11	0	1	0	.917
Postseason Totals		28	92	21	5	1	3	37	8	17	2	8	2	14	1	1	0	0	0	—	0	.228	.297	.402	OF	20	47	1	1	0	.980

DARREN OLIVER—Darren Christopher Oliver—Throws: Left; Bats: Right

Ht: 6'0"; Wt: 170 lbs; Born: 10/6/1970 in Kansas City, Missouri; Debut: 9/1/1993

Division Series		Pitching																										
Year Tm	Age	G	GS	CG	GF	IP	BFP	H	R	ER	HR	SH	SF	HB	TBB	IBB	SO	WP	Bk	W	L	Pct	ShO	Sv-Op	Hld	OAvg	OOBP	ERA
1996 Tex	25	1	1	0	0	8.0	29	6	3	3	1	0	0	1	2	0	3	0	0	0	1	.000	0	0- 0	0	.231	.310	3.38

Division Series		Batting																							Fielding						
Year Tm	Age	G	AB	H	2B	3B	HR	TB	R	RBI	GW	TBB	IBB	SO	HBP	SH	SF	SB	CS	SB%	GDP	Avg	OBP	SLG	Pos	G	PO	A	E	DP	FPct
1996 Tex	25	1	0	0	0	0	0	0	0	0	0	0	0	0	0	0	0	0	0	—	0	—	—	—	P	1	0	3	0	1	1.000

JOE OLIVER—Joseph Melton Oliver—Bats: Right; Throws: Right

Ht: 6'3"; Wt: 215 lbs; Born: 7/24/1965 in Memphis, Tennessee; Debut: 7/15/1989

LCS		Batting																							Fielding						
Year Tm	Age	G	AB	H	2B	3B	HR	TB	R	RBI	GW	TBB	IBB	SO	HBP	SH	SF	SB	CS	SB%	GDP	Avg	OBP	SLG	Pos	G	PO	A	E	DP	FPct
1990 Cin	25	5	14	2	0	0	0	2	1	0	0	0	0	2	0	0	0	0	0	—	1	.143	.143	.143	C	5	27	1	0	0	1.000

World Series		Batting																							Fielding						
Year Tm	Age	G	AB	H	2B	3B	HR	TB	R	RBI	GW	TBB	IBB	SO	HBP	SH	SF	SB	CS	SB%	GDP	Avg	OBP	SLG	Pos	G	PO	A	E	DP	FPct
1990 Cin	25	4	18	6	3	0	0	9	2	2	1	0	0	1	0	0	0	0	0	—	1	.333	.333	.500	C	4	27	1	3	0	.903
Postseason Totals		9	32	8	3	0	0	11	3	2	1	0	0	3	0	0	0	0	0	—	2	.250	.250	.344	C	9	54	2	3	0	.949

NATE OLIVER—Nathaniel Oliver—Nickname: Pee Wee—Bats: Right; Throws: Right

Ht: 5'10"; Wt: 160 lbs; Born: 12/13/1940 in St. Petersburg, Florida; Debut: 4/9/1963

World Series		Batting																							Fielding						
Year Tm	Age	G	AB	H	2B	3B	HR	TB	R	RBI	GW	TBB	IBB	SO	HBP	SH	SF	SB	CS	SB%	GDP	Avg	OBP	SLG	Pos	G	PO	A	E	DP	FPct
1966 LA	25	1	0	0	0	0	0	0	0	0	0	0	0	0	0	0	0	0	0	—	0	—	—	—	—						

LUIS OLMO—Luis Francisco Olmo—Bats: Right; Throws: Right

Ht: 5'11"; Wt: 185 lbs; Born: 8/11/1919 in Arecibo, Puerto Rico; Debut: 7/23/1943

World Series		Batting																							Fielding						
Year Tm	Age	G	AB	H	2B	3B	HR	TB	R	RBI	GW	TBB	IBB	SO	HBP	SH	SF	SB	CS	SB%	GDP	Avg	OBP	SLG	Pos	G	PO	A	E	DP	FPct
1949 Bro	30	4	11	3	0	0	1	6	2	2	0	0	0	2	0	0	0	0	0	—	0	.273	.273	.545	OF	4	6	1	0	0	1.000

GREG OLSON—Gregory William Olson—Bats: Right; Throws: Right

Ht: 6'0"; Wt: 200 lbs; Born: 9/6/1960 in Marshall, Minnesota; Debut: 6/27/1989

LCS		Batting																							Fielding						
Year Tm	Age	G	AB	H	2B	3B	HR	TB	R	RBI	GW	TBB	IBB	SO	HBP	SH	SF	SB	CS	SB%	GDP	Avg	OBP	SLG	Pos	G	PO	A	E	DP	FPct
1991 Atl	31	7	24	8	1	0	1	12	3	4	1	4	0	3	0	0	0	1	0	1.00	0	.333	.429	.500	C	7	62	1	0	2	1.000
1993 Atl	33	2	3	1	1	0	0	2	0	0	0	0	0	1	1	0	0	0	0	—	0	.333	.500	.667	C	2	10	0	0	0	1.000
LCS Totals		9	27	9	2	0	1	14	3	4	1	4	0	4	1	0	0	1	0	1.00	0	.333	.438	.519	C	9	72	1	0	2	1.000

World Series		Batting																							Fielding						
Year Tm	Age	G	AB	H	2B	3B	HR	TB	R	RBI	GW	TBB	IBB	SO	HBP	SH	SF	SB	CS	SB%	GDP	Avg	OBP	SLG	Pos	G	PO	A	E	DP	FPct
1991 Atl	31	7	27	6	2	0	0	8	3	1	0	5	0	4	0	0	0	1	0	1.00	0	.222	.344	.296	C	7	47	6	0	1	1.000
Postseason Totals		16	54	15	4	0	1	22	6	5	1	9	0	8	1	0	0	2	0	1.00	0	.278	.391	.407	C	16	119	7	0	3	1.000

IVY OLSON—Ivan Massie Olson—Bats: Right; Throws: Right

Ht: 5'10"; Wt: 175 lbs; Born: 10/14/1885 in Kansas City, Missouri; Debut: 4/12/1911; Died: 9/1/1965

World Series		Batting																							Fielding						
Year Tm	Age	G	AB	H	2B	3B	HR	TB	R	RBI	GW	TBB	IBB	SO	HBP	SH	SF	SB	CS	SB%	GDP	Avg	OBP	SLG	Pos	G	PO	A	E	DP	FPct
1916 Bro	30	5	16	4	0	1	0	6	1	2	0	2	0	2	0	2	0	0	0	—	1	.250	.333	.375	SS	5	9	12	4	0	.840
1920 Bro	34	7	25	8	1	0	0	9	2	0	0	3	0	1	0	0	0	0	1	.00	0	.320	.393	.360	SS	7	12	20	0	3	1.000
WS Totals		12	41	12	1	1	0	15	3	2	0	5	0	3	0	2	0	0	1	.00	1	.293	.370	.366	SS	12	21	32	4	3	.930

OLLIE O'MARA—Oliver Edward O'Mara—Bats: Right; Throws: Right

Ht: 5'9"; Wt: 155 lbs; Born: 3/8/1891 in St. Louis, Missouri; Debut: 9/8/1912; Died: 10/24/1989

World Series		Batting																							Fielding						
Year Tm	Age	G	AB	H	2B	3B	HR	TB	R	RBI	GW	TBB	IBB	SO	HBP	SH	SF	SB	CS	SB%	GDP	Avg	OBP	SLG	Pos	G	PO	A	E	DP	FPct
1916 Bro	25	1	1	0	0	0	0	0	0	0	0	0	0	1	0	0	0	0	0	—	0	.000	.000	.000	—						

BILL O'NEILL—William John O'Neill—Bats: Both; Throws: Right

Ht: 5'11"; Wt: 175 lbs; Born: 1/22/1880 in St. John, New Brunswick; Debut: 5/7/1904; Died: 7/20/1920

World Series		Batting																							Fielding						
Year Tm	Age	G	AB	H	2B	3B	HR	TB	R	RBI	GW	TBB	IBB	SO	HBP	SH	SF	SB	CS	SB%	GDP	Avg	OBP	SLG	Pos	G	PO	A	E	DP	FPct
1906 ChA	26	1	1	0	0	0	0	0	1	0	0	0	0	0	0	0	0	0	0	—	0	.000	.000	.000	OF	1	1	0	0	0	1.000

PAUL O'NEILL—Paul Andrew O'Neill—Bats: Left; Throws: Left

Ht: 6'4"; Wt: 200 lbs; Born: 2/25/1963 in Columbus, Ohio; Debut: 9/3/1985

Division Series

Year Tm	Age	G	AB	H	2B	3B	HR	TB	R	RBI	GW	TBB	IBB	SO	HBP	SH	SF	SB	CS	SB%	GDP	Avg	OBP	SLG	Pos	G	PO	A	E	DP	FPct
1995 NYA	32	5	18	6	0	0	3	15	5	6	0	5	0	5	0	0	1	0	0	—	0	.333	.458	.833	OF	5	13	0	0	0	1.000
1996 NYA	33	4	15	2	0	0	0	2	0	0	0	0	0	2	0	0	0	0	0	—	2	.133	.133	.133	OF	4	13	0	0	0	1.000
1997 NYA	34	5	19	8	2	0	2	16	5	7	0	3	0	0	0	0	0	0	0	—	0	.421	.500	.842	OF	5	9	0	0	0	1.000
DS Totals		14	52	16	2	0	5	33	10	13	0	8	0	7	0	0	1	0	0	—	2	.308	.393	.635	OF	14	35	0	0	0	1.000

LCS

Year Tm	Age	G	AB	H	2B	3B	HR	TB	R	RBI	GW	TBB	IBB	SO	HBP	SH	SF	SB	CS	SB%	GDP	Avg	OBP	SLG	Pos	G	PO	A	E	DP	FPct
1990 Cin	27	5	17	8	3	0	1	14	1	4	1	1	0	1	0	0	0	1	0	1.00	0	.471	.500	.824	OF	5	9	2	0	1	1.000
1996 NYA	33	4	11	3	0	0	1	6	1	2	0	3	0	2	0	0	0	0	0	—	1	.273	.429	.545	OF	4	9	1	0	1	1.000
LCS Totals		9	28	11	3	0	2	20	2	6	1	4	0	3	0	0	0	1	0	1.00	1	.393	.469	.714	OF	9	18	3	0	2	1.000

World Series

Year Tm	Age	G	AB	H	2B	3B	HR	TB	R	RBI	GW	TBB	IBB	SO	HBP	SH	SF	SB	CS	SB%	GDP	Avg	OBP	SLG	Pos	G	PO	A	E	DP	FPct
1990 Cin	27	4	12	1	0	0	0	1	2	1	0	5	0	2	0	1	0	1	0	1.00	0	.083	.353	.083	OF	4	11	0	0	0	1.000
1996 NYA	33	5	12	2	2	0	0	4	1	0	0	3	0	2	0	0	0	0	0	—	1	.167	.333	.333	OF	4	12	0	0	0	1.000
WS Totals		9	24	3	2	0	0	5	3	1	0	8	0	4	0	1	0	1	0	1.00	1	.125	.344	.208	OF	8	23	0	0	0	1.000
Postseason Totals		32	104	30	7	0	7	58	15	20	1	20	0	14	0	1	1	2	0	1.00	4	.288	.400	.558	OF	31	76	3	0	2	1.000

STEVE O'NEILL—Stephen Francis O'Neill—Bats: Right; Throws: Right

Ht: 5'10"; Wt: 165 lbs; Born: 7/6/1891 in Minooka, Pennsylvania; Debut: 9/18/1911; Died: 1/26/1962

World Series

Year Tm	Age	G	AB	H	2B	3B	HR	TB	R	RBI	GW	TBB	IBB	SO	HBP	SH	SF	SB	CS	SB%	GDP	Avg	OBP	SLG	Pos	G	PO	A	E	DP	FPct
1920 Cle	29	7	21	7	3	0	0	10	1	2	0	4	3	3	0	0	0	0	0	—	0	.333	.440	.476	C	7	23	6	1	2	.967

JOSE OQUENDO—Jose Manuel Oquendo—Bats: Both; Throws: Right

Ht: 5'10"; Wt: 160 lbs; Born: 7/4/1963 in Rio Piedras, Puerto Rico; Debut: 5/2/1983

LCS

Year Tm	Age	G	AB	H	2B	3B	HR	TB	R	RBI	GW	TBB	IBB	SO	HBP	SH	SF	SB	CS	SB%	GDP	Avg	OBP	SLG	Pos	G	PO	A	E	DP	FPct
1987 StL	24	5	12	2	0	0	1	5	3	4	1	3	1	2	0	0	1	0	0	—	0	.167	.313	.417	3B	1	0	0	0	0	—
																									OF	5	7	0	0	0	1.000

World Series

Year Tm	Age	G	AB	H	2B	3B	HR	TB	R	RBI	GW	TBB	IBB	SO	HBP	SH	SF	SB	CS	SB%	GDP	Avg	OBP	SLG	Pos	G	PO	A	E	DP	FPct
1987 StL	24	7	24	6	0	0	0	6	2	2	0	1	0	4	0	0	1	0	1	.00	0	.250	.269	.250	3B	4	1	10	0	0	1.000
																									OF	3	7	0	0	0	1.000
Postseason Totals		12	36	8	0	0	1	11	5	6	1	4	1	6	0	0	2	0	1	.00	0	.222	.286	.306	OF	8	14	0	0	0	1.000

JESSE OROSCO—Jesse Russell Orosco—Throws: Left; Bats: Right

Ht: 6'2"; Wt: 174 lbs; Born: 4/21/1957 in Santa Barbara, California; Debut: 4/5/1979

Division Series — Pitching

Year Tm	Age	G	GS	CG	GF	IP	BFP	H	R	ER	HR	SH	SF	HB	TBB	IBB	SO	WP	Bk	W	L	Pct	ShO	Sv-Op	Hld	OAvg	OOBP	ERA
1996 Bal	39	4	0	0	0	1.0	9	2	4	4	0	0	0	1	3	0	2	0	0	0	1	.000	0	0-0	1	.400	.667	36.00
1997 Bal	40	2	0	0	0	1.1	4	1	0	0	0	0	0	0	0	0	1	0	0	0	0	—	0	0-0	0	.250	.250	0.00
DS Totals		6	0	0	0	2.1	26	3	4	4	0	0	0	1	3	0	3	0	0	0	1	.000	0	0-0	1	.333	.538	15.43

LCS — Pitching

Year Tm	Age	G	GS	CG	GF	IP	BFP	H	R	ER	HR	SH	SF	HB	TBB	IBB	SO	WP	Bk	W	L	Pct	ShO	Sv-Op	Hld	OAvg	OOBP	ERA
1986 NYN	29	4	0	0	4	8.0	30	5	3	3	1	0	0	0	2	0	10	0	0	3	0	1.000	0	0-1	0	.179	.233	3.38
1988 LA	31	4	0	0	1	2.1	15	4	2	2	0	1	0	1	3	1	0	0	0	0	0	—	0	0-0	1	.400	.571	7.71
1996 Bal	39	4	0	0	0	2.0	9	2	1	1	0	0	0	0	1	1	2	0	0	0	0	—	0	0-0	2	.250	.333	4.50
1997 Bal	40	2	0	0	0	1.1	4	0	0	0	0	1	0	0	1	0	1	0	0	0	0	—	0	0-0	0	.000	.333	0.00
LCS Totals		14	0	0	5	13.2	116	11	6	6	1	2	0	1	7	2	13	0	0	3	0	1.000	0	0-1	3	.229	.339	3.95

World Series — Pitching

Year Tm	Age	G	GS	CG	GF	IP	BFP	H	R	ER	HR	SH	SF	HB	TBB	IBB	SO	WP	Bk	W	L	Pct	ShO	Sv-Op	Hld	OAvg	OOBP	ERA
1986 NYN	29	4	0	0	2	5.2	18	2	0	0	0	0	0	0	0	0	6	0	0	0	0	—	0	2-2	0	.111	.111	0.00
Postseason Totals		24	0	0	7	21.2	178	16	10	10	1	2	0	2	10	2	22	0	0	3	1	.750	0	2-3	4	.213	.322	4.15

Division Series — Batting

Year Tm	Age	G	AB	H	2B	3B	HR	TB	R	RBI	GW	TBB	IBB	SO	HBP	SH	SF	SB	CS	SB%	GDP	Avg	OBP	SLG	Pos	G	PO	A	E	DP	FPct
1996 Bal	39	4	0	0	0	0	0	0	0	0	0	0	0	0	0	0	0	0	0	—	0	—	—	—	P	4	0	0	0	0	—
1997 Bal	40	2	0	0	0	0	0	0	0	0	0	0	0	0	0	0	0	0	0	—	0	—	—	—	P	2	0	0	0	0	—
DS Totals		6	0	0	0	0	0	0	0	0	0	0	0	0	0	0	0	0	0	—	0	—	—	—	P	6	0	0	0	0	—

LCS — Batting

Year Tm	Age	G	AB	H	2B	3B	HR	TB	R	RBI	GW	TBB	IBB	SO	HBP	SH	SF	SB	CS	SB%	GDP	Avg	OBP	SLG	Pos	G	PO	A	E	DP	FPct
1986 NYN	29	4	0	0	0	0	0	0	0	0	0	0	0	0	0	1	0	0	0	—	0	—	—	—	P	4	1	1	0	0	1.000
1988 LA	31	4	0	0	0	0	0	0	0	0	0	0	0	0	0	0	0	0	0	—	0	—	—	—	P	4	1	0	0	0	1.000
1996 Bal	39	4	0	0	0	0	0	0	0	0	0	0	0	0	0	0	0	0	0	—	0	—	—	—	P	4	0	1	0	0	1.000
1997 Bal	40	2	0	0	0	0	0	0	0	0	0	0	0	0	0	0	0	0	0	—	0	—	—	—	P	2	0	2	0	0	1.000
LCS Totals		14	0	0	0	0	0	0	0	0	0	0	0	0	0	1	0	0	0	—	0	—	—	—	P	14	2	4	0	0	1.000

World Series — Batting

Year Tm	Age	G	AB	H	2B	3B	HR	TB	R	RBI	GW	TBB	IBB	SO	HBP	SH	SF	SB	CS	SB%	GDP	Avg	OBP	SLG	Pos	G	PO	A	E	DP	FPct
1986 NYN	29	4	1	1	0	0	0	1	0	1	0	0	0	0	0	0	0	0	0	—	0	1.000	1.000	1.000	P	4	0	0	0	0	—
Postseason Totals		24	1	1	0	0	0	1	0	1	0	0	0	0	0	1	0	0	0	—	0	1.000	1.000	1.000	P	24	2	4	0	0	1.000

ERNIE ORSATTI—Ernest Ralph Orsatti—Bats: Left; Throws: Left

Ht: 5'7"; Wt: 154 lbs; Born: 9/8/1902 in Los Angeles, California; Debut: 9/4/1927; Died: 9/4/1968

World Series

Year Tm	Age	G	AB	H	2B	3B	HR	TB	R	RBI	GW	TBB	IBB	SO	HBP	SH	SF	SB	CS	SB%	GDP	Avg	OBP	SLG	Pos	G	PO	A	E	DP	FPct
1928 StL	26	4	7	2	1	0	0	3	1	0	0	1	0	3	0	0	0	0	0	—	0	.286	.375	.429	OF	1	4	0	0	0	1.000
1930 StL	28	1	1	0	0	0	0	0	0	0	0	0	0	0	0	0	0	0	0	—	0	.000	.000	.000	—						
1931 StL	29	1	3	0	0	0	0	0	0	0	0	0	0	3	0	0	0	0	0	—	0	.000	.000	.000	OF	1	0	0	0	0	—
1934 StL	32	7	22	7	0	1	0	9	3	2	0	3	0	1	1	0	0	0	1	.00	0	.318	.423	.409	OF	6	16	1	2	0	.895
WS Totals		13	33	9	1	1	0	12	4	2	0	4	0	7	1	0	0	0	1	.00	0	.273	.368	.364	OF	8	20	1	2	0	.913

JOHN ORSINO—John Joseph Orsino—Nickname: Horse—Bats: Right; Throws: Right

Ht: 6'3"; Wt: 215 lbs; Born: 4/22/1938 in Teaneck, New Jersey; Debut: 7/14/1961

World Series

Year Tm	Age	G	AB	H	2B	3B	HR	TB	R	RBI	GW	TBB	IBB	SO	HBP	SH	SF	SB	CS	SB%	GDP	Avg	OBP	SLG	Pos	G	PO	A	E	DP	FPct
1962 SF	24	1	1	0	0	0	0	0	0	0	0	0	0	0	0	0	0	0	0	—	1	.000	.000	.000	C	1	0	0	0	0	—

JORGE ORTA—Bats: Left; Throws: Right

Ht: 5'10"; Wt: 170 lbs; Born: 11/26/1950 in Mazatlan, Mexico; Debut: 4/15/1972

LCS

Year Tm	Age	G	AB	H	2B	3B	HR	TB	R	RBI	GW	TBB	IBB	SO	HBP	SH	SF	SB	CS	SB%	GDP	Avg	OBP	SLG	Pos	G	PO	A	E	DP	FPct
1984 KC	33	3	10	1	0	1	0	3	1	1	0	0	0	2	0	0	0	0	0	—	0	.100	.100	.300	—						
1985 KC	34	2	5	0	0	0	0	0	0	0	0	0	0	1	0	0	0	0	0	—	0	.000	.000	.000	—						
LCS Totals		5	15	1	0	1	0	3	1	1	0	0	0	3	0	0	0	0	0	—	0	.067	.067	.200	—	0	0	0	0	0	—

World Series

Year Tm	Age	G	AB	H	2B	3B	HR	TB	R	RBI	GW	TBB	IBB	SO	HBP	SH	SF	SB	CS	SB%	GDP	Avg	OBP	SLG	Pos	G	PO	A	E	DP	FPct
1985 KC	34	3	3	1	0	0	0	1	0	0	0	0	0	0	0	0	0	0	0	—	1	.333	.333	.333	—						
Postseason Totals		8	18	2	0	1	0	4	1	1	0	0	0	3	0	0	0	0	0	—	1	.111	.111	.222	—	0	0	0	0	0	—

JUNIOR ORTIZ—Adalberto Colon Ortiz—Bats: Right; Throws: Right

Ht: 5'11"; Wt: 174 lbs; Born: 10/24/1959 in Humacao, Puerto Rico; Debut: 9/20/1982

LCS

Year Tm	Age	G	AB	H	2B	3B	HR	TB	R	RBI	GW	TBB	IBB	SO	HBP	SH	SF	SB	CS	SB%	GDP	Avg	OBP	SLG	Pos	G	PO	A	E	DP	FPct
1991 Min	31	3	3	0	0	0	0	0	0	0	0	0	0	0	0	0	0	0	0	—	1	.000	.000	.000	C	3	10	0	0	0	1.000

World Series		Batting																							Fielding						
Year Tm	Age	G	AB	H	2B	3B	HR	TB	R	RBI	GW	TBB	IBB	SO	HBP	SH	SF	SB	CS	SB%	GDP	Avg	OBP	SLG	Pos	G	PO	A	E	DP	FPct
1991 Min	31	3	5	1	0	0	0	1	0	1	0	0	0	1	0	0	0	0	0	—	0	.200	.200	.200	C	3	9	0	0	0	1.000
Postseason Totals		6	8	1	0	0	0	1	0	1	0	0	0	1	0	0	0	0	0	—	1	.125	.125	.125	C	6	19	0	0	0	1.000

DONOVAN OSBORNE—Donovan Alan Osborne—Throws: Left; Bats: Both

Ht: 6'2"; Wt: 195 lbs; Born: 6/21/1969 in Roseville, California; Debut: 4/9/1992

Division Series		Pitching																										
Year Tm	Age	G	GS	CG	GF	IP	BFP	H	R	ER	HR	SH	SF	HB	TBB	IBB	SO	WP	Bk	W	L	Pct	ShO	Sv-Op	Hld	OAvg	OOBP	ERA
1996 StL	27	1	1	0	0	4.0	20	7	4	4	1	1	0	0	0	0	5	0	0	0	0	—	0	0- 0	0	.368	.368	9.00
LCS		**Pitching**																										
Year Tm	Age	G	GS	CG	GF	IP	BFP	H	R	ER	HR	SH	SF	HB	TBB	IBB	SO	WP	Bk	W	L	Pct	ShO	Sv-Op	Hld	OAvg	OOBP	ERA
1996 StL	27	2	2	0	0	7.2	40	12	8	8	0	0	1	1	4	0	6	1	0	1	1	.500	0	0- 0	0	.353	.425	9.39
Postseason Totals		3	3	0	0	11.2	120	19	12	12	1	1	1	1	4	0	11	1	0	1	1	.500	0	0-0	0	.358	.407	9.26

Division Series		Batting																							Fielding						
Year Tm	Age	G	AB	H	2B	3B	HR	TB	R	RBI	GW	TBB	IBB	SO	HBP	SH	SF	SB	CS	SB%	GDP	Avg	OBP	SLG	Pos	G	PO	A	E	DP	FPct
1996 StL	27	1	1	0	0	0	0	0	0	0	0	0	0	0	0	0	0	0	0	—	0	.000	.000	.000	P	1	0	1	0	0	1.000
LCS		**Batting**																							**Fielding**						
Year Tm	Age	G	AB	H	2B	3B	HR	TB	R	RBI	GW	TBB	IBB	SO	HBP	SH	SF	SB	CS	SB%	GDP	Avg	OBP	SLG	Pos	G	PO	A	E	DP	FPct
1996 StL	27	2	3	0	0	0	0	0	0	0	0	0	0	3	0	0	0	0	0	—	0	.000	.000	.000	P	2	0	1	0	0	1.000
Postseason Totals		3	4	0	0	0	0	0	0	0	0	0	0	3	0	0	0	0	0	—	0	.000	.000	.000	P	3	0	2	0	0	1.000

DAN OSINSKI—Daniel Osinski—Throws: Right; Bats: Right

Ht: 6'1"; Wt: 190 lbs; Born: 11/17/1933 in Chicago, Illinois; Debut: 4/11/1962

World Series		Pitching																										
Year Tm	Age	G	GS	CG	GF	IP	BFP	H	R	ER	HR	SH	SF	HB	TBB	IBB	SO	WP	Bk	W	L	Pct	ShO	Sv-Op	Hld	OAvg	OOBP	ERA
1967 Bos	33	2	0	0	1	1.1	6	2	1	1	0	0	0	0	0	0	0	0	0	0	0	—	0	0- 0	0	.333	.333	6.75

World Series		Batting																							Fielding						
Year Tm	Age	G	AB	H	2B	3B	HR	TB	R	RBI	GW	TBB	IBB	SO	HBP	SH	SF	SB	CS	SB%	GDP	Avg	OBP	SLG	Pos	G	PO	A	E	DP	FPct
1967 Bos	33	2	0	0	0	0	0	0	0	0	0	0	0	0	0	0	0	0	0	—	0	—	—	—	P	2	0	0	0	0	—

CLAUDE OSTEEN—Claude Wilson Osteen—Throws: Left; Bats: Left

Ht: 5'11"; Wt: 160 lbs; Born: 8/9/1939 in Caney Springs, Tennessee; Debut: 7/6/1957

World Series		Pitching																										
Year Tm	Age	G	GS	CG	GF	IP	BFP	H	R	ER	HR	SH	SF	HB	TBB	IBB	SO	WP	Bk	W	L	Pct	ShO	Sv-Op	Hld	OAvg	OOBP	ERA
1965 LA	26	2	2	1	0	14.0	54	9	2	1	1	0	0	0	5	0	4	0	0	1	1	.500	1	0- 0	0	.184	.259	0.64
1966 LA	27	1	1	0	0	7.0	23	3	1	1	1	0	0	0	1	0	3	0	0	0	1	.000	0	0- 0	0	.136	.174	1.29
WS Totals		3	3	1	0	21.0	154	12	3	2	2	0	0	0	6	0	7	0	0	1	2	.333	1	0-0	0	.169	.234	0.86

World Series		Batting																							Fielding						
Year Tm	Age	G	AB	H	2B	3B	HR	TB	R	RBI	GW	TBB	IBB	SO	HBP	SH	SF	SB	CS	SB%	GDP	Avg	OBP	SLG	Pos	G	PO	A	E	DP	FPct
1965 LA	26	2	3	1	0	0	0	1	0	0	0	0	0	0	0	1	0	0	0	—	0	.333	.333	.333	P	2	2	3	0	1	1.000
1966 LA	27	1	2	0	0	0	0	0	0	0	0	0	0	1	0	0	0	0	0	—	0	.000	.000	.000	P	1	1	0	0	0	1.000
WS Totals		3	5	1	0	0	0	1	0	0	0	0	0	1	0	1	0	0	0	—	0	.200	.200	.200	P	3	3	3	0	1	1.000

JOE OSTROWSKI—Joseph Paul Ostrowski—Nickname: Professor—Throws: Left; Bats: Left

Ht: 6'0"; Wt: 180 lbs; Born: 11/15/1916 in West Wyoming, Pennsylvania; Debut: 7/18/1948

World Series		Pitching																										
Year Tm	Age	G	GS	CG	GF	IP	BFP	H	R	ER	HR	SH	SF	HB	TBB	IBB	SO	WP	Bk	W	L	Pct	ShO	Sv-Op	Hld	OAvg	OOBP	ERA
1951 NYA	34	1	0	0	1	2.0	6	1	0	0	0	0	0	0	0	0	1	0	0	0	0	—	0	0- 0	0	.167	.167	0.00

World Series		Batting																							Fielding						
Year Tm	Age	G	AB	H	2B	3B	HR	TB	R	RBI	GW	TBB	IBB	SO	HBP	SH	SF	SB	CS	SB%	GDP	Avg	OBP	SLG	Pos	G	PO	A	E	DP	FPct
1951 NYA	34	1	0	0	0	0	0	0	0	0	0	0	0	0	0	0	0	0	0	—	0	—	—	—	P	1	0	0	0	0	—

ANTONIO OSUNA—Antonio Melchor Osuna—Throws: Right; Bats: Right

Ht: 5'11"; Wt: 160 lbs; Born: 4/12/1973 in Sinaloa, Mexico; Debut: 4/25/1995

Division Series		Pitching																										
Year Tm	Age	G	GS	CG	GF	IP	BFP	H	R	ER	HR	SH	SF	HB	TBB	IBB	SO	WP	Bk	W	L	Pct	ShO	Sv-Op	Hld	OAvg	OOBP	ERA
1995 LA	22	3	0	0	2	3.1	14	3	1	1	0	0	0	0	1	1	3	0	0	0	1	.000	0	0- 0	0	.231	.286	2.70
1996 LA	23	2	0	0	1	2.0	9	3	1	1	1	0	0	1	1	0	4	0	0	0	1	.000	0	0- 0	0	.429	.556	4.50
DS Totals		5	0	0	3	5.1	46	6	2	2	1	0	0	1	2	1	7	0	0	0	2	.000	0	0-0	0	.300	.391	3.38

Division Series		Batting																							Fielding						
Year Tm	Age	G	AB	H	2B	3B	HR	TB	R	RBI	GW	TBB	IBB	SO	HBP	SH	SF	SB	CS	SB%	GDP	Avg	OBP	SLG	Pos	G	PO	A	E	DP	FPct
1995 LA	22	3	0	0	0	0	0	0	0	0	0	0	0	0	0	0	0	0	0	—	0	—	—	—	P	3	0	0	1	0	.000
1996 LA	23	2	0	0	0	0	0	0	0	0	0	0	0	0	0	0	0	0	0	—	0	—	—	—	P	2	0	0	0	0	—
DS Totals		5	0	0	0	0	0	0	0	0	0	0	0	0	0	0	0	0	0	—	0	—	—	—	P	5	0	0	1	0	.000

AMOS OTIS—Amos Joseph Otis—Bats: Right; Throws: Right

Ht: 5'11"; Wt: 165 lbs; Born: 4/26/1947 in Mobile, Alabama; Debut: 9/6/1967

Division Series		Batting																							Fielding						
Year Tm	Age	G	AB	H	2B	3B	HR	TB	R	RBI	GW	TBB	IBB	SO	HBP	SH	SF	SB	CS	SB%	GDP	Avg	OBP	SLG	Pos	G	PO	A	E	DP	FPct
1981 KC	34	3	12	0	0	0	0	0	0	1	0	0	0	4	0	0	0	0	0	—	2	.000	.000	.000	OF	3	12	0	0	0	1.000
LCS		**Batting**																							**Fielding**						
Year Tm	Age	G	AB	H	2B	3B	HR	TB	R	RBI	GW	TBB	IBB	SO	HBP	SH	SF	SB	CS	SB%	GDP	Avg	OBP	SLG	Pos	G	PO	A	E	DP	FPct
1976 KC	29	1	1	0	0	0	0	0	0	0	0	0	0	0	0	0	0	0	0	—	0	.000	.000	.000	OF	1	0	0	0	0	—
1977 KC	30	5	16	2	1	0	0	3	1	2	0	2	0	3	0	0	0	2	0	1.00	0	.125	.222	.188	OF	5	11	1	0	0	1.000
1978 KC	31	4	14	6	2	0	0	8	2	1	0	3	0	5	0	0	0	4	0	1.00	0	.429	.529	.571	OF	4	8	0	1	0	.889
1980 KC	33	3	12	4	1	0	0	5	2	0	0	0	0	3	0	0	0	2	1	.67	0	.333	.333	.417	OF	3	11	0	0	0	1.000
LCS Totals		13	43	12	4	0	0	16	5	3	0	5	0	11	0	0	0	8	1	.89	0	.279	.354	.372	OF	13	30	1	1	0	.969
World Series		**Batting**																							**Fielding**						
Year Tm	Age	G	AB	H	2B	3B	HR	TB	R	RBI	GW	TBB	IBB	SO	HBP	SH	SF	SB	CS	SB%	GDP	Avg	OBP	SLG	Pos	G	PO	A	E	DP	FPct
1980 KC	33	6	23	11	2	0	3	22	4	7	0	3	1	3	0	0	0	0	0	—	2	.478	.538	.957	OF	6	21	0	0	0	1.000
Postseason Totals		22	78	23	6	0	3	38	9	11	0	8	1	18	0	0	0	8	1	.89	4	.295	.360	.487	OF	22	63	1	1	0	.985

JIM O'TOOLE—James Jerome O'Toole—Nickname: Tootie—Throws: Left; Bats: Both

Ht: 6'0"; Wt: 190 lbs; Born: 1/10/1937 in Chicago, Illinois; Debut: 9/26/1958

World Series		Pitching																										
Year Tm	Age	G	GS	CG	GF	IP	BFP	H	R	ER	HR	SH	SF	HB	TBB	IBB	SO	WP	Bk	W	L	Pct	ShO	Sv-Op	Hld	OAvg	OOBP	ERA
1961 Cin	24	2	2	0	0	12.0	51	11	4	4	2	0	0	0	7	0	4	0	0	0	2	.000	0	0- 0	0	.250	.353	3.00

World Series		Batting																							Fielding						
Year Tm	Age	G	AB	H	2B	3B	HR	TB	R	RBI	GW	TBB	IBB	SO	HBP	SH	SF	SB	CS	SB%	GDP	Avg	OBP	SLG	Pos	G	PO	A	E	DP	FPct
1961 Cin	24	2	3	0	0	0	0	0	0	0	0	0	0	1	0	0	0	0	0	—	0	.000	.000	.000	P	2	1	0	0	0	1.000

ED OTT—Nathan Edward Ott—Bats: Left; Throws: Right

Ht: 5'10"; Wt: 190 lbs; Born: 7/11/1951 in Muncy, Pennsylvania; Debut: 6/10/1974

LCS		Batting																							Fielding						
Year Tm	Age	G	AB	H	2B	3B	HR	TB	R	RBI	GW	TBB	IBB	SO	HBP	SH	SF	SB	CS	SB%	GDP	Avg	OBP	SLG	Pos	G	PO	A	E	DP	FPct
1979 Pit	28	3	13	3	0	0	0	3	0	0	0	0	0	2	0	0	0	0	0	—	0	.231	.231	.231	C	3	25	3	0	0	1.000
World Series		**Batting**																							**Fielding**						
Year Tm	Age	G	AB	H	2B	3B	HR	TB	R	RBI	GW	TBB	IBB	SO	HBP	SH	SF	SB	CS	SB%	GDP	Avg	OBP	SLG	Pos	G	PO	A	E	DP	FPct
1979 Pit	28	3	12	4	1	0	0	5	2	3	0	0	0	2	0	0	1	0	0	—	0	.333	.308	.417	C	3	20	0	0	1	1.000
Postseason Totals		6	25	7	1	0	0	8	2	3	0	0	0	4	0	0	1	0	0	—	0	.280	.269	.320	C	6	45	3	0	1	1.000

MEL OTT (HOF 1951-W)—Melvin Thomas Ott—Nicknames: Master Melvin, Mr. McGraw's Boy—Bats: Left; Throws: Right

Ht: 5'9"; Wt: 170 lbs; Born: 3/2/1909 in Gretna, La.; Deb.: 4/27/1926; Died: 11/21/1958

World Series		Batting																							Fielding						
Year Tm	Age	G	AB	H	2B	3B	HR	TB	R	RBI	GW	TBB	IBB	SO	HBP	SH	SF	SB	CS	SB%	GDP	Avg	OBP	SLG	Pos	G	PO	A	E	DP	FPct
1933 NYG	24	5	18	7	0	0	2	13	3	4	2	4	1	4	0	0	0	0	1	.00	0	.389	.500	.722	OF	5	10	0	0	0	1.000
1936 NYG	27	6	23	7	2	0	1	12	4	3	0	3	0	1	0	0	0	0	0	—	1	.304	.385	.522	OF	6	12	0	1	0	.923
1937 NYG	28	5	20	4	0	0	1	7	1	3	0	1	0	4	0	0	0	0	0	—	0	.200	.238	.350	3B	5	5	9	1	1	.933
WS Totals		16	61	18	2	0	4	32	8	10	2	8	1	9	0	0	0	0	1	.00	1	.295	.377	.525	OF	11	22	0	1	0	.957

JIMMY OUTLAW—James Paulus Outlaw—Bats: Right; Throws: Right

Ht: 5'8"; Wt: 165 lbs; Born: 1/20/1913 in Orme, Tennessee; Debut: 4/20/1937

World Series		Batting																							Fielding						
Year Tm	Age	G	AB	H	2B	3B	HR	TB	R	RBI	GW	TBB	IBB	SO	HBP	SH	SF	SB	CS	SB%	GDP	Avg	OBP	SLG	Pos	G	PO	A	E	DP	FPct
1945 Det	32	7	28	5	0	0	0	5	1	3	0	2	1	1	0	1	0	1	0	1.00	0	.179	.233	.179	3B	7	5	15	0	0	1.000

ORVAL OVERALL—Nickname: Big Groundhog—Throws: Right; Bats: Both

Ht: 6'2"; Wt: 214 lbs; Born: 2/2/1881 in Farmersville, California; Debut: 4/16/1905; Died: 7/14/1947

World Series		Pitching																										
Year Tm	Age	G	GS	CG	GF	IP	BFP	H	R	ER	HR	SH	SF	HB	TBB	IBB	SO	WP	Bk	W	L	Pct	ShO	Sv-Op	Hld	OAvg	OOBP	ERA
1906 ChN	25	2	0	0	2	12.0	48	10	2	2	0	1	0	0	3	0	8	1	0	0	0	—	0	0- 0	0	.227	.277	1.50
1907 ChN	26	2	2	1	0	18.0	72	14	4	2	0	3	0	0	4	0	11	0	0	1	0	1.000	0	0- 0	0	.215	.261	1.00
1908 ChN	27	3	2	2	0	18.1	69	7	2	2	0	1	0	1	7	0	15	1	0	2	0	1.000	1	0- 0	1	.117	.221	0.98
1910 ChN	29	1	1	0	0	3.0	14	6	3	3	0	2	0	0	1	0	1	0	0	0	1	.000	0	0- 0	0	.545	.583	9.00
WS Totals		8	5	3	2	51.1	406	37	11	9	0	7	0	1	15	0	35	2	0	3	1	.750	1	0-0	1	.206	.270	1.58

World Series		Batting																							Fielding						
Year Tm	Age	G	AB	H	2B	3B	HR	TB	R	RBI	GW	TBB	IBB	SO	HBP	SH	SF	SB	CS	SB%	GDP	Avg	OBP	SLG	Pos	G	PO	A	E	DP	FPct
1906 ChN	25	2	4	1	1	0	0	2	1	0	0	1	0	1	0	0	0	0	0	—	0	.250	.400	.500	P	2	0	2	0	0	1.000
1907 ChN	26	2	5	1	0	0	0	1	0	2	1	0	0	1	0	2	0	0	0	—	0	.200	.200	.200	P	2	0	7	0	0	1.000
1908 ChN	27	3	6	2	0	0	0	2	0	0	0	0	0	1	0	1	0	0	0	—	0	.333	.333	.333	P	3	0	2	0	0	1.000
1910 ChN	29	1	1	0	0	0	0	0	0	0	0	0	0	0	0	0	0	0	0	—	0	.000	.000	.000	P	1	0	0	0	0	—
WS Totals		8	16	4	1	0	0	5	1	2	1	1	0	3	0	3	0	0	0	—	0	.250	.294	.313	P	8	0	11	0	0	1.000

STUBBY OVERMIRE—Frank W. Overmire—Throws: Left; Bats: Right

Ht: 5'7"; Wt: 170 lbs; Born: 5/16/1919 in Moline, Michigan; Debut: 4/25/1943; Died: 3/3/1977

World Series		Pitching																										
Year Tm	Age	G	GS	CG	GF	IP	BFP	H	R	ER	HR	SH	SF	HB	TBB	IBB	SO	WP	Bk	W	L	Pct	ShO	Sv-Op	Hld	OAvg	OOBP	ERA
1945 Det	26	1	1	0	0	6.0	24	4	2	2	0	1	0	0	2	0	2	0	0	0	1	.000	0	0- 0	0	.190	.261	3.00

World Series		Batting																							Fielding						
Year Tm	Age	G	AB	H	2B	3B	HR	TB	R	RBI	GW	TBB	IBB	SO	HBP	SH	SF	SB	CS	SB%	GDP	Avg	OBP	SLG	Pos	G	PO	A	E	DP	FPct
1945 Det	26	1	1	0	0	0	0	0	0	0	0	0	0	0	0	0	0	0	0	—	0	.000	.000	.000	P	1	0	1	0	0	1.000

BOB OWCHINKO—Robert Dennis Owchinko—Throws: Left; Bats: Left

Ht: 6'2"; Wt: 190 lbs; Born: 1/1/1955 in Detroit, Michigan; Debut: 9/25/1976

LCS		Pitching																										
Year Tm	Age	G	GS	CG	GF	IP	BFP	H	R	ER	HR	SH	SF	HB	TBB	IBB	SO	WP	Bk	W	L	Pct	ShO	Sv-Op	Hld	OAvg	OOBP	ERA
1981 Oak	26	1	0	0	1	1.2	8	3	1	1	1	0	1	0	0	0	0	0	0	0	0	—	0	0- 0	0	.429	.375	5.40

LCS		Batting																							Fielding						
Year Tm	Age	G	AB	H	2B	3B	HR	TB	R	RBI	GW	TBB	IBB	SO	HBP	SH	SF	SB	CS	SB%	GDP	Avg	OBP	SLG	Pos	G	PO	A	E	DP	FPct
1981 Oak	26	1	0	0	0	0	0	0	0	0	0	0	0	0	0	0	0	0	0	—	0	—	—	—	P	1	0	1	0	0	1.000

FRANK OWEN—Frank Malcolm Owen—Nickname: Yip—Throws: Right; Bats: Both

Ht: 5'11"; Wt: 160 lbs; Born: 12/23/1879 in Ypsilanti, Michigan; Debut: 4/29/1901; Died: 11/24/1942

World Series		Pitching																										
Year Tm	Age	G	GS	CG	GF	IP	BFP	H	R	ER	HR	SH	SF	HB	TBB	IBB	SO	WP	Bk	W	L	Pct	ShO	Sv-Op	Hld	OAvg	OOBP	ERA
1906 ChA	26	1	0	0	1	6.0	26	6	3	2	0	2	0	0	3	0	2	1	0	0	0	—	0	0- 0	0	.286	.375	3.00

World Series		Batting																							Fielding						
Year Tm	Age	G	AB	H	2B	3B	HR	TB	R	RBI	GW	TBB	IBB	SO	HBP	SH	SF	SB	CS	SB%	GDP	Avg	OBP	SLG	Pos	G	PO	A	E	DP	FPct
1906 ChA	26	1	2	0	0	0	0	0	0	0	0	0	0	1	0	0	0	0	0	—	0	.000	.000	.000	P	1	0	4	0	0	1.000

MARV OWEN—Marvin James Owen—Nickname: Freck—Bats: Right; Throws: Right

Ht: 6'1"; Wt: 175 lbs; Born: 3/22/1906 in Agnew, California; Debut: 4/16/1931; Died: 6/22/1991

World Series		Batting																							Fielding						
Year Tm	Age	G	AB	H	2B	3B	HR	TB	R	RBI	GW	TBB	IBB	SO	HBP	SH	SF	SB	CS	SB%	GDP	Avg	OBP	SLG	Pos	G	PO	A	E	DP	FPct
1934 Det	28	7	29	2	0	0	0	2	0	1	0	0	0	5	1	0	0	1	0	1.00	0	.069	.100	.069	3B	7	9	9	2	1	.900
1935 Det	29	6	20	1	0	0	0	1	2	1	0	2	1	3	1	1	0	0	0	—	0	.050	.174	.050	3B	2	2	0	0	0	1.000
																									1B	4	44	5	1	4	.980
WS Totals		13	49	3	0	0	0	3	2	2	0	2	1	8	2	1	0	1	0	1.00	0	.061	.132	.061	3B	9	11	9	2	1	.909

MICKEY OWEN—Arnold Malcolm Owen—Bats: Right; Throws: Right

Ht: 5'10"; Wt: 190 lbs; Born: 4/4/1916 in Nixa, Missouri; Debut: 5/2/1937

World Series		Batting																							Fielding						
Year Tm	Age	G	AB	H	2B	3B	HR	TB	R	RBI	GW	TBB	IBB	SO	HBP	SH	SF	SB	CS	SB%	GDP	Avg	OBP	SLG	Pos	G	PO	A	E	DP	FPct
1941 Bro	25	5	12	2	0	1	0	4	1	2	0	3	0	0	0	0	0	0	1	.00	0	.167	.333	.333	C	5	20	4	1	1	.960

SPIKE OWEN—Spike Dee Owen—Bats: Both; Throws: Right

Ht: 5'9"; Wt: 165 lbs; Born: 4/19/1961 in Cleburne, Texas; Debut: 6/25/1983

LCS		Batting																							Fielding						
Year Tm	Age	G	AB	H	2B	3B	HR	TB	R	RBI	GW	TBB	IBB	SO	HBP	SH	SF	SB	CS	SB%	GDP	Avg	OBP	SLG	Pos	G	PO	A	E	DP	FPct
1986 Bos	25	7	21	9	0	1	0	11	5	3	0	2	0	2	0	1	0	1	0	1.00	0	.429	.478	.524	SS	7	12	21	5	2	.868
1988 Bos	27	1	0	0	0	0	0	0	0	0	0	1	0	0	0	0	0	0	0	—	0	—	1.000	—	—						
LCS Totals		8	21	9	0	1	0	11	5	3	0	3	0	2	0	1	0	1	0	1.00	0	.429	.500	.524	SS	7	12	21	5	2	.868

World Series		Batting																							Fielding						
Year Tm	Age	G	AB	H	2B	3B	HR	TB	R	RBI	GW	TBB	IBB	SO	HBP	SH	SF	SB	CS	SB%	GDP	Avg	OBP	SLG	Pos	G	PO	A	E	DP	FPct
1986 Bos	25	7	20	6	0	0	0	6	2	2	1	5	2	6	0	1	1	0	0	—	1	.300	.423	.300	SS	7	9	13	0	3	1.000
Postseason Totals		15	41	15	0	1	0	17	7	5	1	8	2	8	0	2	1	1	0	1.00	1	.366	.460	.415	SS	14	21	34	5	5	.917

JAYHAWK OWENS—Claude Jayhawk Owens—Bats: Right; Throws: Right

Ht: 6'1"; Wt: 200 lbs; Born: 2/10/1969 in Sardinia, Ohio; Debut: 6/6/1993

Division Series		Batting																							Fielding						
Year Tm	Age	G	AB	H	2B	3B	HR	TB	R	RBI	GW	TBB	IBB	SO	HBP	SH	SF	SB	CS	SB%	GDP	Avg	OBP	SLG	Pos	G	PO	A	E	DP	FPct
1995 Col	26	1	1	0	0	0	0	0	0	0	0	0	0	1	0	0	0	0	0	—	0	.000	.000	.000	C	1	2	1	0	0	1.000

RAY OYLER—Raymond Francis Oyler—Bats: Right; Throws: Right

Ht: 5'11"; Wt: 165 lbs; Born: 8/4/1938 in Indianapolis, Indiana; Debut: 4/18/1965; Died: 1/26/1981

World Series		Batting																							Fielding						
Year Tm	Age	G	AB	H	2B	3B	HR	TB	R	RBI	GW	TBB	IBB	SO	HBP	SH	SF	SB	CS	SB%	GDP	Avg	OBP	SLG	Pos	G	PO	A	E	DP	FPct
1968 Det	30	4	0	0	0	0	0	0	0	0	0	0	0	0	0	1	0	0	0	—	0	—	—	—	SS	4	2	0	0	0	1.000

TOM PACIOREK—Thomas Marian Paciorek—Nickname: Wimpy—Bats: Right; Throws: Right

Ht: 6'4"; Wt: 215 lbs; Born: 11/2/1946 in Detroit, Michigan; Debut: 9/12/1970

LCS		Batting																							Fielding						
Year Tm	Age	G	AB	H	2B	3B	HR	TB	R	RBI	GW	TBB	IBB	SO	HBP	SH	SF	SB	CS	SB%	GDP	Avg	OBP	SLG	Pos	G	PO	A	E	DP	FPct
1974 LA	27	1	1	1	0	0	0	1	0	0	0	0	0	0	0	0	0	0	0	—	0	1.000	1.000	1.000	OF	1	0	0	0	0	—
1983 ChA	36	4	16	4	0	0	0	4	1	1	1	1	0	2	1	0	0	0	1	.00	0	.250	.333	.250	1B	3	29	3	0	3	1.000
																									OF	2	1	0	0	0	1.000
LCS Totals		5	17	5	0	0	0	5	1	1	1	1	0	2	1	0	0	0	1	.00	0	.294	.368	.294	1B	3	29	3	0	3	1.000

World Series		Batting																							Fielding						
Year Tm	Age	G	AB	H	2B	3B	HR	TB	R	RBI	GW	TBB	IBB	SO	HBP	SH	SF	SB	CS	SB%	GDP	Avg	OBP	SLG	Pos	G	PO	A	E	DP	FPct
1974 LA	27	3	2	1	1	0	0	2	1	0	0	0	0	0	0	0	0	0	0	—	0	.500	.500	1.000	—						
Postseason Totals		8	19	6	1	0	0	7	2	1	1	1	0	2	1	0	0	0	1	.00	0	.316	.381	.368	1B	3	29	3	0	3	1.000

ANDY PAFKO—Andrew Pafko—Nicknames: Handy Andy, Pruschka—Bats: Right; Throws: Right

Ht: 6'0"; Wt: 190 lbs; Born: 2/25/1921 in Boyceville, Wisconsin; Debut: 9/24/1943

World Series		Batting																							Fielding						
Year Tm	Age	G	AB	H	2B	3B	HR	TB	R	RBI	GW	TBB	IBB	SO	HBP	SH	SF	SB	CS	SB%	GDP	Avg	OBP	SLG	Pos	G	PO	A	E	DP	FPct
1945 ChN	24	7	28	6	2	1	0	10	5	2	0	2	1	5	0	1	0	1	0	1.00	1	.214	.267	.357	OF	7	22	2	1	0	.960
1952 Bro	31	7	21	4	0	0	0	4	0	2	0	0	0	4	0	0	0	0	1	.00	0	.190	.190	.190	OF	5	12	1	0	0	1.000
1957 Mil	36	6	14	3	0	0	0	3	1	0	0	0	0	1	1	0	0	0	0	—	0	.214	.267	.214	OF	5	9	0	0	0	1.000
1958 Mil	37	4	9	3	1	0	0	4	0	1	0	0	0	0	0	0	1	0	0	—	0	.333	.300	.444	OF	4	8	0	0	0	1.000
WS Totals		24	72	16	3	1	0	21	6	5	0	2	1	10	1	1	1	1	1	.50	1	.222	.250	.292	OF	21	51	3	1	0	.982

JOSE PAGAN—Jose Antonio Pagan—Bats: Right; Throws: Right

Ht: 5'9"; Wt: 160 lbs; Born: 5/5/1935 in Barceloneta, Puerto Rico; Debut: 8/4/1959

LCS		Batting																							Fielding						
Year Tm	Age	G	AB	H	2B	3B	HR	TB	R	RBI	GW	TBB	IBB	SO	HBP	SH	SF	SB	CS	SB%	GDP	Avg	OBP	SLG	Pos	G	PO	A	E	DP	FPct
1970 Pit	35	1	3	1	0	0	0	1	0	0	0	1	0	1	0	0	0	0	0	—	0	.333	.500	.333	3B	1	0	4	0	0	1.000
1971 Pit	36	1	1	0	0	0	0	0	0	0	0	0	0	0	0	0	0	0	0	—	0	.000	.000	.000	3B	1	1	2	0	0	1.000
LCS Totals		2	4	1	0	0	0	1	0	0	0	1	0	1	0	0	0	0	0	—	0	.250	.400	.250	3B	2	1	6	0	0	1.000
World Series		Batting																							Fielding						
Year Tm	Age	G	AB	H	2B	3B	HR	TB	R	RBI	GW	TBB	IBB	SO	HBP	SH	SF	SB	CS	SB%	GDP	Avg	OBP	SLG	Pos	G	PO	A	E	DP	FPct
1962 SF	27	7	19	7	0	0	1	10	2	2	0	0	0	1	1	1	0	0	0	—	0	.368	.400	.526	SS	7	8	14	1	2	.957
1971 Pit	36	4	15	4	2	0	0	6	0	2	0	0	0	1	0	0	0	0	0	—	0	.267	.267	.400	3B	4	2	8	0	1	1.000
WS Totals		11	34	11	2	0	1	16	2	4	0	0	0	2	1	1	0	0	0	—	0	.324	.343	.471	SS	7	8	14	1	2	.957
Postseason Totals		13	38	12	2	0	1	17	2	4	0	1	0	3	1	1	0	0	0	—	0	.316	.350	.447	SS	7	8	14	1	2	.957

JOE PAGE—Joseph Francis Page—Nicknames: Fireman, The Gay Reliever—Throws: Left; Bats: Left

Ht: 6'3"; Wt: 200 lbs; Born: 10/28/1917 in Cherry Valley, Pennsylvania; Debut: 4/19/1944; Died: 4/21/1980

World Series		Pitching																										
Year Tm	Age	G	GS	CG	GF	IP	BFP	H	R	ER	HR	SH	SF	HB	TBB	IBB	SO	WP	Bk	W	L	Pct	ShO	Sv-Op	Hld	OAvg	OOBP	ERA
1947 NYA	29	4	0	0	3	13.0	52	12	6	6	0	0	0	0	2	0	7	2	0	1	1	.500	0	1-1	0	.240	.269	4.15
1949 NYA	31	3	0	0	3	9.0	35	6	2	2	2	1	0	0	3	0	8	0	0	1	0	1.000	0	1- 1	0	.194	.265	2.00
WS Totals		7	0	0	6	22.0	174	18	8	8	2	1	0	0	5	0	15	2	0	2	1	.667	0	2-2	0	.222	.267	3.27

World Series		Batting																							Fielding						
Year Tm	Age	G	AB	H	2B	3B	HR	TB	R	RBI	GW	TBB	IBB	SO	HBP	SH	SF	SB	CS	SB%	GDP	Avg	OBP	SLG	Pos	G	PO	A	E	DP	FPct
1947 NYA	29	4	4	0	0	0	0	0	0	0	0	0	0	1	0	0	0	0	0	—	0	.000	.000	.000	P	4	1	2	0	0	1.000
1949 NYA	31	3	4	0	0	0	0	0	0	0	0	0	0	2	0	0	0	0	0	—	0	.000	.000	.000	P	3	0	2	0	1	1.000
WS Totals		7	8	0	0	0	0	0	0	0	0	0	0	3	0	0	0	0	0	—	0	.000	.000	.000	P	7	1	4	0	1	1.000

VANCE PAGE—Vance Linwood Page—Throws: Right; Bats: Right

Ht: 6'0"; Wt: 180 lbs; Born: 9/15/1905 in Elm City, North Carolina; Debut: 8/6/1938; Died: 7/14/1951

World Series		Pitching																										
Year Tm	Age	G	GS	CG	GF	IP	BFP	H	R	ER	HR	SH	SF	HB	TBB	IBB	SO	WP	Bk	W	L	Pct	ShO	Sv-Op	Hld	OAvg	OOBP	ERA
1938 ChN	33	1	0	0	0	1.1	6	2	2	2	0	0	0	0	0	0	0	0	0	0	0	—	0	0- 0	0	.333	.333	13.50

World Series		Batting																							Fielding						
Year Tm	Age	G	AB	H	2B	3B	HR	TB	R	RBI	GW	TBB	IBB	SO	HBP	SH	SF	SB	CS	SB%	GDP	Avg	OBP	SLG	Pos	G	PO	A	E	DP	FPct
1938 ChN	33	1	0	0	0	0	0	0	0	0	0	0	0	0	0	0	0	0	0	—	0	—	—	—	P	1	0	1	0	0	1.000

MIKE PAGLIARULO—Michael Timothy Pagliarulo—Bats: Left; Throws: Right

Ht: 6'1"; Wt: 205 lbs; Born: 3/15/1960 in Medford, Massachusetts; Debut: 7/7/1984

LCS		Batting																							Fielding						
Year Tm	Age	G	AB	H	2B	3B	HR	TB	R	RBI	GW	TBB	IBB	SO	HBP	SH	SF	SB	CS	SB%	GDP	Avg	OBP	SLG	Pos	G	PO	A	E	DP	FPct
1991 Min	31	5	15	5	1	0	1	9	4	3	2	0	0	2	0	1	0	0	0	—	0	.333	.333	.600	3B	5	4	10	0	1	1.000
World Series		Batting																							Fielding						
Year Tm	Age	G	AB	H	2B	3B	HR	TB	R	RBI	GW	TBB	IBB	SO	HBP	SH	SF	SB	CS	SB%	GDP	Avg	OBP	SLG	Pos	G	PO	A	E	DP	FPct
1991 Min	31	6	11	3	0	0	1	6	1	2	0	1	1	2	0	0	0	0	0	—	0	.273	.333	.545	3B	6	3	3	0	0	1.000
Postseason Totals		11	26	8	1	0	2	15	5	5	2	1	1	4	0	1	0	0	0	—	0	.308	.333	.577	3B	11	7	13	0	1	1.000

TOM PAGNOZZI—Thomas Alan Pagnozzi—Bats: Right; Throws: Right

Ht: 6'0"; Wt: 190 lbs; Born: 7/30/1962 in Tucson, Arizona; Debut: 4/12/1987

Division Series		Batting																							Fielding						
Year Tm	Age	G	AB	H	2B	3B	HR	TB	R	RBI	GW	TBB	IBB	SO	HBP	SH	SF	SB	CS	SB%	GDP	Avg	OBP	SLG	Pos	G	PO	A	E	DP	FPct
1996 StL	34	3	11	3	0	0	0	3	0	2	1	1	1	3	0	0	0	0	0	—	0	.273	.333	.273	C	3	28	0	0	0	1.000
LCS		Batting																							Fielding						
Year Tm	Age	G	AB	H	2B	3B	HR	TB	R	RBI	GW	TBB	IBB	SO	HBP	SH	SF	SB	CS	SB%	GDP	Avg	OBP	SLG	Pos	G	PO	A	E	DP	FPct
1987 StL	25	1	1	0	0	0	0	0	0	0	0	0	0	0	0	0	0	0	0	—	1	.000	.000	.000	—						
1996 StL	34	7	19	3	1	0	0	4	1	1	0	1	0	4	0	0	0	0	0	—	1	.158	.200	.211	C	7	49	1	0	0	1.000
LCS Totals		8	20	3	1	0	0	4	1	1	0	1	0	4	0	0	0	0	0	—	2	.150	.190	.200	C	7	49	1	0	0	1.000
World Series		Batting																							Fielding						
Year Tm	Age	G	AB	H	2B	3B	HR	TB	R	RBI	GW	TBB	IBB	SO	HBP	SH	SF	SB	CS	SB%	GDP	Avg	OBP	SLG	Pos	G	PO	A	E	DP	FPct
1987 StL	25	2	4	1	0	0	0	1	0	0	0	0	0	0	0	0	0	0	0	—	0	.250	.250	.250	—						
Postseason Totals		13	35	7	1	0	0	8	1	3	1	2	1	7	0	0	0	0	0	—	2	.200	.243	.229	C	10	77	1	0	0	1.000

SATCHEL PAIGE (HOF 1971-N)—Leroy Robert Paige—Throws: Right; Bats: Right

Ht: 6'3"; Wt: 180 lbs; Born: 7/7/1906 in Mobile, Alabama; Debut: 7/9/1948; Died: 6/8/1982

World Series		Pitching																										
Year Tm	Age	G	GS	CG	GF	IP	BFP	H	R	ER	HR	SH	SF	HB	TBB	IBB	SO	WP	Bk	W	L	Pct	ShO	Sv-Op	Hld	OAvg	OOBP	ERA
1948 Cle	42	1	0	0	0	0.2	2	0	0	0	0	0	0	0	0	0	0	0	1	0	0	—	0	0- 0	0	.000	.000	0.00

World Series		Batting																							Fielding						
Year Tm	Age	G	AB	H	2B	3B	HR	TB	R	RBI	GW	TBB	IBB	SO	HBP	SH	SF	SB	CS	SB%	GDP	Avg	OBP	SLG	Pos	G	PO	A	E	DP	FPct
1948 Cle	42	1	0	0	0	0	0	0	0	0	0	0	0	0	0	0	0	0	0	—	0	—	—	—	P	1	0	0	0	0	—

LANCE PAINTER—Lance Telford Painter—Throws: Left; Bats: Left

Ht: 6'1"; Wt: 195 lbs; Born: 7/21/1967 in Bedford, England; Debut: 5/19/1993

Division Series		Pitching																										
Year Tm	Age	G	GS	CG	GF	IP	BFP	H	R	ER	HR	SH	SF	HB	TBB	IBB	SO	WP	Bk	W	L	Pct	ShO	Sv-Op	Hld	OAvg	OOBP	ERA
1995 Col	28	1	1	0	0	5.0	23	5	3	3	2	0	1	0	2	0	4	0	0	0	0	—	0	0- 0	0	.250	.304	5.40

Division Series		Batting																							Fielding						
Year Tm	Age	G	AB	H	2B	3B	HR	TB	R	RBI	GW	TBB	IBB	SO	HBP	SH	SF	SB	CS	SB%	GDP	Avg	OBP	SLG	Pos	G	PO	A	E	DP	FPct
1995 Col	28	2	2	0	0	0	0	0	0	0	0	0	0	1	0	0	0	0	0	—	0	.000	.000	.000	P	1	0	0	0	0	—

ERV PALICA—Ervin Martin Palica—Throws: Right; Bats: Right

Ht: 6'1"; Wt: 180 lbs; Born: 2/9/1928 in Lomita, California; Debut: 4/21/1945; Died: 5/29/1982

World Series		Pitching																										
Year Tm	Age	G	GS	CG	GF	IP	BFP	H	R	ER	HR	SH	SF	HB	TBB	IBB	SO	WP	Bk	W	L	Pct	ShO	Sv-Op	Hld	OAvg	OOBP	ERA
1949 Bro	21	1	0	0	0	2.0	8	1	0	0	0	0	0	0	1	0	1	0	0	0	0	—	0	0- 0	0	.143	.250	0.00

World Series		Batting																							Fielding						
Year Tm	Age	G	AB	H	2B	3B	HR	TB	R	RBI	GW	TBB	IBB	SO	HBP	SH	SF	SB	CS	SB%	GDP	Avg	OBP	SLG	Pos	G	PO	A	E	DP	FPct
1949 Bro	21	1	0	0	0	0	0	0	0	0	0	0	0	0	0	0	0	0	0	—	0	—	—	—	P	1	0	1	0	0	1.000

RAFAEL PALMEIRO—Bats: Left; Throws: Left

Ht: 6'0"; Wt: 180 lbs; Born: 9/24/1964 in Havana, Cuba; Debut: 9/8/1986

Division Series		Batting																							Fielding						
Year Tm	Age	G	AB	H	2B	3B	HR	TB	R	RBI	GW	TBB	IBB	SO	HBP	SH	SF	SB	CS	SB%	GDP	Avg	OBP	SLG	Pos	G	PO	A	E	DP	FPct
1996 Bal	32	4	17	3	1	0	1	7	4	2	0	1	0	6	1	0	0	0	0	—	0	.176	.263	.412	1B	4	35	1	1	2	.973
1997 Bal	33	4	12	3	2	0	0	5	2	0	0	0	0	2	0	0	0	0	0	—	0	.250	.250	.417	1B	4	27	2	0	1	1.000
DS Totals		8	29	6	3	0	1	12	6	2	0	1	0	8	1	0	0	0	0	—	0	.207	.258	.414	1B	8	62	3	1	3	.985
LCS		Batting																							Fielding						
Year Tm	Age	G	AB	H	2B	3B	HR	TB	R	RBI	GW	TBB	IBB	SO	HBP	SH	SF	SB	CS	SB%	GDP	Avg	OBP	SLG	Pos	G	PO	A	E	DP	FPct
1996 Bal	32	5	17	4	0	0	2	10	4	4	1	4	0	4	0	0	1	0	0	—	0	.235	.364	.588	1B	5	44	3	0	6	1.000
1997 Bal	33	6	25	7	2	0	1	12	3	2	0	0	0	10	1	0	0	0	0	—	1	.280	.308	.480	1B	6	55	2	0	4	1.000
LCS Totals		11	42	11	2	0	3	22	7	6	1	4	0	14	1	0	1	0	0	—	1	.262	.333	.524	1B	11	99	5	0	10	1.000
Postseason Totals		19	71	17	5	0	4	34	13	8	1	5	0	22	2	0	1	0	0	—	1	.239	.304	.479	1B	19	161	8	1	13	.994

DEAN PALMER—Dean William Palmer—Bats: Right; Throws: Right

Ht: 6'1"; Wt: 175 lbs; Born: 12/27/1968 in Tallahassee, Florida; Debut: 9/1/1989

Division Series		Batting																							Fielding						
Year Tm	Age	G	AB	H	2B	3B	HR	TB	R	RBI	GW	TBB	IBB	SO	HBP	SH	SF	SB	CS	SB%	GDP	Avg	OBP	SLG	Pos	G	PO	A	E	DP	FPct
1996 Tex	27	4	19	4	1	0	1	8	3	2	0	0	0	5	0	0	0	0	0	—	0	.211	.211	.421	3B	4	3	10	1	0	.929

JIM PALMER (HOF 1990-W)—James Alvin Palmer—Nickname: Jockstrap Jim—Throws: Right; Bats: Right

Ht: 6'3"; Wt: 190 lbs; Born: 10/15/1945 in New York, New York; Debut: 4/17/1965

LCS		Pitching																										
Year Tm	Age	G	GS	CG	GF	IP	BFP	H	R	ER	HR	SH	SF	HB	TBB	IBB	SO	WP	Bk	W	L	Pct	ShO	Sv-Op	Hld	OAvg	OOBP	ERA
1969 Bal	23	1	1	1	0	9.0	38	10	2	2	0	0	0	0	2	0	4	1	0	1	0	1.000	0	0- 0	0	.278	.316	2.00
1970 Bal	24	1	1	1	0	9.0	36	7	1	1	0	0	0	0	3	0	12	0	0	1	0	1.000	0	0- 0	0	.212	.278	1.00
1971 Bal	25	1	1	1	0	9.0	36	7	3	3	3	0	0	0	3	0	8	1	0	1	0	1.000	0	0- 0	0	.212	.278	3.00
1973 Bal-*C*	27	3	2	1	1	14.2	62	11	3	3	0	0	0	0	8	1	15	0	0	1	0	1.000	1	0- 0	0	.204	.306	1.84
1974 Bal	28	1	1	1	0	9.0	32	4	1	1	1	1	0	1	1	0	4	0	0	0	1	.000	0	0- 0	0	.138	.194	1.00
1979 Bal	33	1	1	0	0	9.0	35	7	3	3	1	0	0	0	2	0	3	0	0	0	0	—	0	0- 0	0	.212	.257	3.00
LCS Totals		8	7	5	1	59.2	478	46	13	13	5	1	0	1	19	1	46	2	0	4	1	.800	1	0-0	0	.211	.277	1.96
World Series		Pitching																										
Year Tm	Age	G	GS	CG	GF	IP	BFP	H	R	ER	HR	SH	SF	HB	TBB	IBB	SO	WP	Bk	W	L	Pct	ShO	Sv-Op	Hld	OAvg	OOBP	ERA
1966 Bal	20	1	1	1	0	9.0	34	4	0	0	0	0	0	0	3	1	6	1	0	1	0	1.000	1	0- 0	0	.129	.206	0.00
1969 Bal	23	1	1	0	0	6.0	27	5	4	4	1	0	0	0	4	0	5	0	0	0	1	.000	0	0- 0	0	.217	.333	6.00
1970 Bal	24	2	2	0	0	15.2	68	11	8	8	2	1	0	0	9	0	9	1	0	1	0	1.000	0	0- 0	0	.193	.303	4.60
1971 Bal	25	2	2	0	0	17.0	75	15	5	5	2	1	0	0	9	0	15	0	0	1	0	1.000	0	0- 0	0	.231	.324	2.65
1979 Bal	33	2	2	0	0	15.0	66	18	6	6	0	0	3	1	5	1	8	1	0	0	1	.000	0	0- 0	0	.316	.364	3.60
1983 Bal	37	1	0	0	0	2.0	9	2	0	0	0	0	0	0	1	0	1	1	0	1	0	1.000	0	0- 0	0	.250	.333	0.00
WS Totals		9	8	1	0	64.2	558	55	23	23	5	2	3	1	31	2	44	4	0	4	2	.667	1	0-0	0	.228	.315	3.20
Postseason Totals		17	15	6	1	124.1	1036	101	36	36	10	3	3	2	50	3	90	6	0	8	3	.727	2	0-0	0	.220	.298	2.61

LCS		Batting																							Fielding						
Year Tm	Age	G	AB	H	2B	3B	HR	TB	R	RBI	GW	TBB	IBB	SO	HBP	SH	SF	SB	CS	SB%	GDP	Avg	OBP	SLG	Pos	G	PO	A	E	DP	FPct
1969 Bal	23	1	5	0	0	0	0	0	0	0	0	0	0	3	0	0	0	0	0	—	0	.000	.000	.000	P	1	0	1	0	0	1.000
1970 Bal	24	1	4	1	1	0	0	2	1	1	0	0	0	0	0	0	0	0	0	—	0	.250	.250	.500	P	1	1	1	0	0	1.000
1971 Bal	25	2	5	1	0	0	0	1	1	0	0	0	0	1	0	0	0	0	0	—	1	.200	.200	.200	P	1	1	0	0	0	1.000
1973 Bal	27	3	0	0	0	0	0	0	0	0	0	0	0	0	0	0	0	0	0	—	0	—	—	—	P	3	1	1	0	1	1.000
1974 Bal	28	2	0	0	0	0	0	0	0	0	0	0	0	0	0	0	0	0	0	—	0	—	—	—	P	1	0	2	0	0	1.000
1979 Bal	33	1	0	0	0	0	0	0	0	0	0	0	0	0	0	0	0	0	0	—	0	—	—	—	P	1	1	1	0	0	1.000
1983 Bal	37	1	0	0	0	0	0	0	0	0	0	0	0	0	0	0	0	0	0	—	0	—	—	—	—						
LCS Totals		11	14	2	1	0	0	3	2	1	0	0	0	4	0	0	0	0	0	—	1	.143	.143	.214	P	8	4	6	0	1	1.000
World Series		Batting																							Fielding						
Year Tm	Age	G	AB	H	2B	3B	HR	TB	R	RBI	GW	TBB	IBB	SO	HBP	SH	SF	SB	CS	SB%	GDP	Avg	OBP	SLG	Pos	G	PO	A	E	DP	FPct
1966 Bal	20	1	4	0	0	0	0	0	0	0	0	0	0	2	0	0	0	0	0	—	0	.000	.000	.000	P	1	0	2	0	0	1.000
1969 Bal	23	1	2	0	0	0	0	0	0	0	0	0	0	0	0	0	0	0	0	—	0	.000	.000	.000	P	1	1	0	1	0	.500
1970 Bal	24	2	7	1	0	0	0	1	1	0	0	0	0	3	0	0	0	0	0	—	0	.143	.143	.143	P	2	0	0	0	0	—
1971 Bal	25	2	4	0	0	0	0	0	0	2	0	2	0	2	0	1	0	0	0	—	0	.000	.333	.000	P	2	2	1	0	0	1.000
1979 Bal	33	2	4	0	0	0	0	0	0	0	0	0	0	3	0	0	0	0	0	—	0	.000	.000	.000	P	2	2	1	0	1	1.000
1983 Bal	37	1	0	0	0	0	0	0	0	0	0	0	0	0	0	0	0	0	0	—	0	—	—	—	P	1	0	0	0	0	—
WS Totals		9	21	1	0	0	0	1	1	2	0	2	0	10	0	1	0	0	0	—	0	.048	.130	.048	P	9	5	4	1	1	.900
Postseason Totals		20	35	3	1	0	0	4	3	3	0	2	0	14	0	1	0	0	0	—	1	.086	.135	.114	P	17	9	10	1	2	.950

JIM PANKOVITS—James Franklin Pankovits—Bats: Right; Throws: Right

Ht: 5'10"; Wt: 170 lbs; Born: 8/6/1955 in Pennington Gap, Virginia; Debut: 5/27/1984

LCS		Batting																							Fielding						
Year Tm	Age	G	AB	H	2B	3B	HR	TB	R	RBI	GW	TBB	IBB	SO	HBP	SH	SF	SB	CS	SB%	GDP	Avg	OBP	SLG	Pos	G	PO	A	E	DP	FPct
1986 Hou	31	2	2	0	0	0	0	0	0	0	0	0	0	1	0	0	0	0	0	—	0	.000	.000	.000	—						

MILT PAPPAS—Milton Stephen Pappas—Nickname: Gimpy—Throws: Right; Bats: Right

Ht: 6'3"; Wt: 190 lbs; Born: 5/11/1939 in Detroit, Michigan; Debut: 8/10/1957

LCS		Pitching																										
Year Tm	Age	G	GS	CG	GF	IP	BFP	H	R	ER	HR	SH	SF	HB	TBB	IBB	SO	WP	Bk	W	L	Pct	ShO	Sv-Op	Hld	OAvg	OOBP	ERA
1969 Atl	30	1	0	0	0	2.1	11	4	3	3	1	0	0	0	0	0	4	0	0	0	0	—	0	0- 0	0	.364	.364	11.57

LCS		Batting																							Fielding						
Year Tm	Age	G	AB	H	2B	3B	HR	TB	R	RBI	GW	TBB	IBB	SO	HBP	SH	SF	SB	CS	SB%	GDP	Avg	OBP	SLG	Pos	G	PO	A	E	DP	FPct
1969 Atl	30	1	1	0	0	0	0	0	0	0	0	0	0	1	0	0	0	0	0	—	0	.000	.000	.000	P	1	0	0	0	0	—

FREDDY PARENT—Frederick Alfred Parent—Bats: Right; Throws: Right

Ht: 5'7"; Wt: 154 lbs; Born: 11/25/1875 in Biddeford, Maine; Debut: 7/14/1899; Died: 11/2/1972

World Series		Batting																							Fielding						
Year Tm	Age	G	AB	H	2B	3B	HR	TB	R	RBI	GW	TBB	IBB	SO	HBP	SH	SF	SB	CS	SB%	GDP	Avg	OBP	SLG	Pos	G	PO	A	E	DP	FPct
1903 Bos	27	8	32	9	0	3	0	15	8	4	0	1	0	1	1	0	0	0	0	—	0	.281	.324	.469	SS	8	16	28	3	1	.936

MARK PARENT—Mark Alan Parent—Bats: Right; Throws: Right

Ht: 6'5"; Wt: 215 lbs; Born: 9/16/1961 in Ashland, Oregon; Debut: 9/20/1986

Division Series		Batting																							Fielding						
Year Tm	Age	G	AB	H	2B	3B	HR	TB	R	RBI	GW	TBB	IBB	SO	HBP	SH	SF	SB	CS	SB%	GDP	Avg	OBP	SLG	Pos	G	PO	A	E	DP	FPct
1996 Bal	35	4	5	1	0	0	0	1	0	0	0	0	0	2	0	0	0	0	0	—	0	.200	.200	.200	C	4	19	0	0	0	1.000
LCS		Batting																							Fielding						
Year Tm	Age	G	AB	H	2B	3B	HR	TB	R	RBI	GW	TBB	IBB	SO	HBP	SH	SF	SB	CS	SB%	GDP	Avg	OBP	SLG	Pos	G	PO	A	E	DP	FPct
1996 Bal	35	2	6	1	0	0	0	1	0	0	0	0	0	2	0	0	0	0	0	—	0	.167	.167	.167	C	2	14	0	0	0	1.000
Postseason Totals		6	11	2	0	0	0	2	0	0	0	0	0	4	0	0	0	0	0	—	0	.182	.182	.182	C	6	33	0	0	0	1.000

DAVE PARKER—David Gene Parker—Nickname: Cobra—Bats: Left; Throws: Right

Ht: 6'5"; Wt: 230 lbs; Born: 6/9/1951 in Calhoun, Mississippi; Debut: 7/12/1973

LCS		Batting																							Fielding						
Year Tm	Age	G	AB	H	2B	3B	HR	TB	R	RBI	GW	TBB	IBB	SO	HBP	SH	SF	SB	CS	SB%	GDP	Avg	OBP	SLG	Pos	G	PO	A	E	DP	FPct
1974 Pit	23	3	8	1	0	0	0	1	0	0	0	0	0	1	0	0	0	0	0	—	0	.125	.125	.125	OF	2	4	1	0	0	1.000
1975 Pit	24	3	10	0	0	0	0	0	2	0	0	1	0	3	1	0	0	0	0	—	1	.000	.167	.000	OF	3	13	1	0	1	1.000
1979 Pit	28	3	12	4	0	0	0	4	2	2	2	2	0	3	0	0	1	1	0	1.00	1	.333	.400	.333	OF	3	9	0	0	0	1.000
1988 Oak	37	3	12	3	1	0	0	4	1	0	0	0	0	4	0	0	0	0	0	—	0	.250	.250	.333	OF	1	1	0	1	0	.500
1989 Oak	38	4	16	3	0	0	2	9	2	3	0	0	0	0	0	0	0	0	0	—	0	.188	.188	.563	—						
LCS Totals		16	58	11	1	0	2	18	7	5	2	3	0	11	1	0	1	1	0	1.00	2	.190	.238	.310	OF	9	27	2	1	1	.967
World Series		Batting																							Fielding						
Year Tm	Age	G	AB	H	2B	3B	HR	TB	R	RBI	GW	TBB	IBB	SO	HBP	SH	SF	SB	CS	SB%	GDP	Avg	OBP	SLG	Pos	G	PO	A	E	DP	FPct
1979 Pit	28	7	29	10	3	0	0	13	2	4	1	2	1	7	1	0	1	0	1	.00	1	.345	.394	.448	OF	7	13	1	1	1	.933
1988 Oak	37	4	15	3	0	0	0	3	0	0	0	2	0	4	0	0	0	0	0	—	0	.200	.294	.200	OF	2	4	0	0	0	1.000
1989 Oak	38	3	9	2	1	0	1	6	2	2	1	0	0	2	0	0	0	0	0	—	0	.222	.222	.667	—						
WS Totals		14	53	15	4	0	1	22	4	6	2	4	1	13	1	0	1	0	1	.00	1	.283	.339	.415	OF	9	17	1	1	1	.947
Postseason Totals		30	111	26	5	0	3	40	11	11	4	7	1	24	2	0	2	1	1	.50	3	.234	.287	.360	OF	18	44	3	2	2	.959

HARRY PARKER

—Harry William Parker—Throws: Right; Bats: Right

Ht: 6'3"; Wt: 190 lbs; Born: 9/14/1947 in Highland, Illinois; Debut: 8/8/1970

LCS		Pitching																										
Year Tm	Age	G	GS	CG	GF	IP	BFP	H	R	ER	HR	SH	SF	HB	TBB	IBB	SO	WP	Bk	W	L	Pct	ShO	Sv-Op	Hld	OAvg	OOBP	ERA
1973 NYN	26	1	0	0	1	1.0	4	1	1	1	1	0	0	0	0	0	0	0	0	0	1	.000	0	0-0	0	.250	.250	9.00
World Series		**Pitching**																										
Year Tm	Age	G	GS	CG	GF	IP	BFP	H	R	ER	HR	SH	SF	HB	TBB	IBB	SO	WP	Bk	W	L	Pct	ShO	Sv-Op	Hld	OAvg	OOBP	ERA
1973 NYN	26	3	0	0	1	3.1	12	2	1	0	0	0	0	0	2	0	2	0	0	0	1	.000	0	0-0	0	.200	.333	0.00
Postseason Totals		4	0	0	2	4.1	32	3	2	1	1	0	0	0	2	0	2	0	0	0	2	.000	0	0-0	0	.214	.313	2.08

LCS		Batting																							Fielding						
Year Tm	Age	G	AB	H	2B	3B	HR	TB	R	RBI	GW	TBB	IBB	SO	HBP	SH	SF	SB	CS	SB%	GDP	Avg	OBP	SLG	Pos	G	PO	A	E	DP	FPct
1973 NYN	26	1	0	0	0	0	0	0	0	0	0	0	0	0	0	0	0	0	0	—	0	—	—	—	P	1	0	0	0	0	—
World Series		**Batting**																							**Fielding**						
Year Tm	Age	G	AB	H	2B	3B	HR	TB	R	RBI	GW	TBB	IBB	SO	HBP	SH	SF	SB	CS	SB%	GDP	Avg	OBP	SLG	Pos	G	PO	A	E	DP	FPct
1973 NYN	26	3	0	0	0	0	0	0	0	0	0	0	0	0	0	0	0	0	0	—	0	—	—	—	P	3	0	0	0	0	—
Postseason Totals		4	0	0	0	0	0	0	0	0	0	0	0	0	0	0	0	0	0	—	0	—	—	—	P	4	0	0	0	0	—

WES PARKER

—Maurice Wesley Parker—Bats: Both; Throws: Left

Ht: 6'1"; Wt: 180 lbs; Born: 11/13/1939 in Evanston, Illinois; Debut: 4/19/1964

World Series		Batting																							Fielding						
Year Tm	Age	G	AB	H	2B	3B	HR	TB	R	RBI	GW	TBB	IBB	SO	HBP	SH	SF	SB	CS	SB%	GDP	Avg	OBP	SLG	Pos	G	PO	A	E	DP	FPct
1965 LA	25	7	23	7	0	1	1	12	3	2	0	3	0	3	1	2	0	2	0	1.00	0	.304	.407	.522	1B	7	55	4	0	6	1.000
1966 LA	26	4	13	3	2	0	0	5	0	0	0	1	1	3	0	0	0	0	0	—	1	.231	.286	.385	1B	4	31	2	0	4	1.000
WS Totals		11	36	10	2	1	1	17	3	2	0	4	1	6	1	2	0	2	0	1.00	1	.278	.366	.472	1B	11	86	6	0	10	1.000

JEFF PARRETT

—Jeffrey Dale Parrett—Throws: Right; Bats: Right

Ht: 6'4"; Wt: 185 lbs; Born: 8/26/1961 in Indianapolis, Indiana; Debut: 4/11/1986

LCS		Pitching																										
Year Tm	Age	G	GS	CG	GF	IP	BFP	H	R	ER	HR	SH	SF	HB	TBB	IBB	SO	WP	Bk	W	L	Pct	ShO	Sv-Op	Hld	OAvg	OOBP	ERA
1992 Oak	31	3	0	0	1	2.1	12	6	3	3	0	1	1	0	0	0	1	0	0	0	0	—	0	0-0	0	.600	.545	11.57

LCS		Batting																							Fielding						
Year Tm	Age	G	AB	H	2B	3B	HR	TB	R	RBI	GW	TBB	IBB	SO	HBP	SH	SF	SB	CS	SB%	GDP	Avg	OBP	SLG	Pos	G	PO	A	E	DP	FPct
1992 Oak	31	3	0	0	0	0	0	0	0	0	0	0	0	0	0	0	0	0	0	—	0	—	—	—	P	3	0	1	0	0	1.000

LANCE PARRISH

—Lance Michael Parrish—Bats: Right; Throws: Right

Ht: 6'3"; Wt: 210 lbs; Born: 6/15/1956 in Clairton, Pennsylvania; Debut: 9/5/1977

LCS		Batting																							Fielding						
Year Tm	Age	G	AB	H	2B	3B	HR	TB	R	RBI	GW	TBB	IBB	SO	HBP	SH	SF	SB	CS	SB%	GDP	Avg	OBP	SLG	Pos	G	PO	A	E	DP	FPct
1984 Det	28	3	12	3	1	0	1	7	1	3	0	0	0	3	0	0	1	0	0	—	0	.250	.231	.583	C	3	21	2	0	0	1.000
World Series		**Batting**																							**Fielding**						
Year Tm	Age	G	AB	H	2B	3B	HR	TB	R	RBI	GW	TBB	IBB	SO	HBP	SH	SF	SB	CS	SB%	GDP	Avg	OBP	SLG	Pos	G	PO	A	E	DP	FPct
1984 Det	28	5	18	5	1	0	1	9	3	2	0	3	0	2	0	0	1	1	0	1.00	0	.278	.364	.500	C	5	30	3	1	1	.971
Postseason Totals		8	30	8	2	0	2	16	4	5	0	3	0	5	0	0	2	1	0	1.00	0	.267	.314	.533	C	8	51	5	1	1	.982

LARRY PARRISH

—Larry Alton Parrish—Bats: Right; Throws: Right

Ht: 6'3"; Wt: 190 lbs; Born: 11/10/1953 in Winter Haven, Florida; Debut: 9/6/1974

Division Series		Batting																							Fielding						
Year Tm	Age	G	AB	H	2B	3B	HR	TB	R	RBI	GW	TBB	IBB	SO	HBP	SH	SF	SB	CS	SB%	GDP	Avg	OBP	SLG	Pos	G	PO	A	E	DP	FPct
1981 Mon	27	5	20	3	1	0	0	4	3	1	0	1	0	3	0	0	0	0	0	—	0	.150	.190	.200	3B	5	8	6	0	1	1.000
LCS		**Batting**																							**Fielding**						
Year Tm	Age	G	AB	H	2B	3B	HR	TB	R	RBI	GW	TBB	IBB	SO	HBP	SH	SF	SB	CS	SB%	GDP	Avg	OBP	SLG	Pos	G	PO	A	E	DP	FPct
1981 Mon	27	5	19	5	2	0	0	7	2	2	0	1	0	1	0	0	0	0	0	—	0	.263	.300	.368	3B	5	3	13	1	3	.941
1988 Bos	34	4	6	0	0	0	0	0	0	0	0	0	0	2	0	0	0	0	0	—	0	.000	.000	.000	1B	2	7	0	0	0	1.000
LCS Totals		9	25	5	2	0	0	7	2	2	0	1	0	3	0	0	0	0	0	—	0	.200	.231	.280	3B	5	3	13	1	3	.941
Postseason Totals		14	45	8	3	0	0	11	5	3	0	2	0	6	0	0	0	0	0	—	0	.178	.213	.244	3B	10	11	19	1	4	.968

ROY PARTEE

—Roy Robert Partee—Bats: Right; Throws: Right

Ht: 5'10"; Wt: 180 lbs; Born: 9/7/1917 in Los Angeles, California; Debut: 4/23/1943

World Series		Batting																							Fielding						
Year Tm	Age	G	AB	H	2B	3B	HR	TB	R	RBI	GW	TBB	IBB	SO	HBP	SH	SF	SB	CS	SB%	GDP	Avg	OBP	SLG	Pos	G	PO	A	E	DP	FPct
1946 Bos	29	5	10	1	0	0	0	1	1	1	0	1	0	2	0	0	0	0	0	—	0	.100	.182	.100	C	5	14	1	0	1	1.000

BEN PASCHAL

—Benjamin Edwin Paschal—Bats: Right; Throws: Right

Ht: 5'11"; Wt: 185 lbs; Born: 10/13/1895 in Enterprise, Alabama; Debut: 8/16/1915; Died: 11/10/1974

World Series		Batting																							Fielding						
Year Tm	Age	G	AB	H	2B	3B	HR	TB	R	RBI	GW	TBB	IBB	SO	HBP	SH	SF	SB	CS	SB%	GDP	Avg	OBP	SLG	Pos	G	PO	A	E	DP	FPct
1926 NYA	30	5	4	1	0	0	0	1	0	1	0	1	0	2	0	0	0	0	0	—	0	.250	.400	.250	—						
1928 NYA	32	3	10	2	0	0	0	2	0	1	0	1	0	0	0	0	0	0	0	—	0	.200	.273	.200	OF	3	8	0	0	0	1.000
WS Totals		8	14	3	0	0	0	3	0	2	0	2	0	2	0	0	0	0	0	—	0	.214	.313	.214	OF	3	8	0	0	0	1.000

CAMILO PASCUAL

—Camilo Alberto Pascual—Nickname: Little Potato—Throws: Right; Bats: Right

Ht: 5'11"; Wt: 170 lbs; Born: 1/20/1934 in Havana, Cuba; Debut: 4/15/1954

World Series		Pitching																										
Year Tm	Age	G	GS	CG	GF	IP	BFP	H	R	ER	HR	SH	SF	HB	TBB	IBB	SO	WP	Bk	W	L	Pct	ShO	Sv-Op	Hld	OAvg	OOBP	ERA
1965 Min	31	1	1	0	0	5.0	24	8	3	3	0	1	0	0	1	0	0	0	0	0	1	.000	0	0-0	0	.364	.391	5.40

World Series		Batting																							Fielding						
Year Tm	Age	G	AB	H	2B	3B	HR	TB	R	RBI	GW	TBB	IBB	SO	HBP	SH	SF	SB	CS	SB%	GDP	Avg	OBP	SLG	Pos	G	PO	A	E	DP	FPct
1965 Min	31	1	1	0	0	0	0	0	0	0	0	0	0	0	0	0	0	0	0	—	0	.000	.000	.000	P	1	0	1	0	0	1.000

DODE PASKERT

—George Henry Paskert—Bats: Right; Throws: Right

Ht: 5'11"; Wt: 165 lbs; Born: 8/28/1881 in Cleveland, Ohio; Debut: 9/21/1907; Died: 2/12/1959

World Series		Batting																							Fielding						
Year Tm	Age	G	AB	H	2B	3B	HR	TB	R	RBI	GW	TBB	IBB	SO	HBP	SH	SF	SB	CS	SB%	GDP	Avg	OBP	SLG	Pos	G	PO	A	E	DP	FPct
1915 Phi	34	5	19	3	0	0	0	3	2	0	0	1	0	2	0	0	0	0	1	.00	0	.158	.200	.158	OF	5	17	0	0	0	1.000
1918 ChN	37	6	21	4	1	0	0	5	0	2	0	2	0	2	0	0	0	0	0	—	0	.190	.261	.238	OF	6	17	0	0	0	1.000
WS Totals		11	40	7	1	0	0	8	2	2	0	3	0	4	0	0	0	0	1	.00	0	.175	.233	.200	OF	11	34	0	0	0	1.000

DAN PASQUA

—Daniel Anthony Pasqua—Bats: Left; Throws: Left

Ht: 6'0"; Wt: 203 lbs; Born: 10/17/1961 in Yonkers, New York; Debut: 5/30/1985

LCS		Batting																							Fielding						
Year Tm	Age	G	AB	H	2B	3B	HR	TB	R	RBI	GW	TBB	IBB	SO	HBP	SH	SF	SB	CS	SB%	GDP	Avg	OBP	SLG	Pos	G	PO	A	E	DP	FPct
1993 ChA	31	2	6	0	0	0	0	0	1	0	0	1	0	2	1	0	0	0	0	—	0	.000	.250	.000	1B	2	13	2	1	2	.938

CLAUDE PASSEAU

—Claude William Passeau—Nickname: Deacon—Throws: Right; Bats: Right

Ht: 6'3"; Wt: 198 lbs; Born: 4/9/1909 in Waynesboro, Mississippi; Debut: 9/29/1935

World Series		Pitching																										
Year Tm	Age	G	GS	CG	GF	IP	BFP	H	R	ER	HR	SH	SF	HB	TBB	IBB	SO	WP	Bk	W	L	Pct	ShO	Sv-Op	Hld	OAvg	OOBP	ERA
1945 ChN	36	3	2	1	0	16.2	65	7	5	5	0	0	0	0	8	2	3	0	0	1	0	1.000	1	0-0	0	.123	.231	2.70

World Series		Batting																							Fielding						
Year Tm	Age	G	AB	H	2B	3B	HR	TB	R	RBI	GW	TBB	IBB	SO	HBP	SH	SF	SB	CS	SB%	GDP	Avg	OBP	SLG	Pos	G	PO	A	E	DP	FPct
1945 ChN	36	3	7	0	0	0	0	0	1	1	0	0	0	4	0	0	0	0	0	—	0	.000	.000	.000	P	3	1	3	0	0	1.000

FRANK PASTORE—Frank Enrico Pastore—Throws: Right; Bats: Right

Ht: 6'2"; Wt: 188 lbs; Born: 8/21/1957 in Alhambra, California; Debut: 4/4/1979

LCS — Pitching

Year Tm	Age	G	GS	CG	GF	IP	BFP	H	R	ER	HR	SH	SF	HB	TBB	IBB	SO	WP	Bk	W	L	Pct	ShO	Sv-Op	Hld	OAvg	OOBP	ERA
1979 Cin	22	1	1	0	0	7.0	28	7	2	2	0	2	0	0	3	1	1	0	0	0	0	—	0	0- 0	0	.304	.385	2.57

LCS — Batting / Fielding

Year Tm	Age	G	AB	H	2B	3B	HR	TB	R	RBI	GW	TBB	IBB	SO	HBP	SH	SF	SB	CS	SB%	GDP	Avg	OBP	SLG	Pos	G	PO	A	E	DP	FPct
1979 Cin	22	1	0	0	0	0	0	0	0	1	0	1	0	0	0	0	1	0	0	—	0	—	.500	—	P	1	0	0	0	0	—

FREDDIE PATEK—Frederick Joseph Patek—Nickname: The Flea—Bats: Right; Throws: Right

Ht: 5'5"; Wt: 148 lbs; Born: 10/9/1944 in Seguin, Texas; Debut: 6/3/1968

LCS — Batting / Fielding

Year Tm	Age	G	AB	H	2B	3B	HR	TB	R	RBI	GW	TBB	IBB	SO	HBP	SH	SF	SB	CS	SB%	GDP	Avg	OBP	SLG	Pos	G	PO	A	E	DP	FPct
1970 Pit	25	1	3	0	0	0	0	0	0	0	0	1	0	2	0	0	0	0	1	.00	1	.000	.250	.000	SS	1	1	2	0	0	1.000
1976 KC	31	5	18	7	2	0	0	9	2	4	1	0	0	1	0	0	0	0	3	.00	0	.389	.389	.500	SS	5	13	18	0	3	1.000
1977 KC	32	5	18	7	3	1	0	12	4	5	1	1	0	2	0	2	1	0	0	—	1	.389	.400	.667	SS	5	8	18	1	0	.963
1978 KC	33	4	13	1	0	0	1	4	2	2	0	1	0	4	0	0	0	0	1	.00	0	.077	.143	.308	SS	4	9	8	2	2	.895
LCS Totals		15	52	15	5	1	1	25	8	11	2	3	0	9	0	2	1	0	5	.00	2	.288	.321	.481	SS	15	31	46	3	5	.963

BOB PATTERSON—Robert Chandler Patterson—Throws: Left; Bats: Right

Ht: 6'2"; Wt: 185 lbs; Born: 5/16/1959 in Jacksonville, Florida; Debut: 9/2/1985

LCS — Pitching

Year Tm	Age	G	GS	CG	GF	IP	BFP	H	R	ER	HR	SH	SF	HB	TBB	IBB	SO	WP	Bk	W	L	Pct	ShO	Sv-Op	Hld	OAvg	OOBP	ERA
1990 Pit	31	2	0	0	1	1.0	5	1	0	0	0	0	0	0	2	1	0	0	0	0	0	—	0	1- 1	1	.333	.600	0.00
1991 Pit	32	1	0	0	0	2.0	7	1	0	0	0	0	0	0	0	0	3	0	0	0	0	—	0	0- 0	0	.143	.143	0.00
1992 Pit	33	2	0	0	0	1.2	9	3	1	1	0	0	0	0	1	0	1	0	0	0	0	—	0	0- 0	0	.375	.444	5.40
LCS Totals		5	0	0	1	4.2	42	5	1	1	0	0	0	0	3	1	4	0	0	0	0	—	0	1-1	1	.278	.381	1.93

LCS — Batting / Fielding

Year Tm	Age	G	AB	H	2B	3B	HR	TB	R	RBI	GW	TBB	IBB	SO	HBP	SH	SF	SB	CS	SB%	GDP	Avg	OBP	SLG	Pos	G	PO	A	E	DP	FPct
1990 Pit	31	2	0	0	0	0	0	0	0	0	0	0	0	0	0	0	0	0	0	—	0	—	—	—	P	2	0	1	0	0	1.000
1991 Pit	32	1	0	0	0	0	0	0	0	0	0	0	0	0	0	0	0	0	0	—	0	—	—	—	P	1	0	0	0	0	—
1992 Pit	33	2	0	0	0	0	0	0	0	0	0	0	0	0	0	0	0	0	0	—	0	—	—	—	P	2	0	0	0	0	—
LCS Totals		5	0	0	0	0	0	0	0	0	0	0	0	0	0	0	0	0	0	—	0	—	—	—	P	5	0	1	0	0	1.000

DANNY PATTERSON—Danny Shane Patterson—Throws: Right; Bats: Right

Ht: 6'0"; Wt: 185 lbs; Born: 2/17/1971 in San Gabriel, California; Debut: 7/26/1996

Division Series — Pitching

Year Tm	Age	G	GS	CG	GF	IP	BFP	H	R	ER	HR	SH	SF	HB	TBB	IBB	SO	WP	Bk	W	L	Pct	ShO	Sv-Op	Hld	OAvg	OOBP	ERA
1996 Tex	25	1	0	0	0	0.1	2	1	0	0	0	0	0	0	0	0	0	0	0	0	0	—	0	0- 0	0	.500	.500	0.00

Division Series — Batting / Fielding

Year Tm	Age	G	AB	H	2B	3B	HR	TB	R	RBI	GW	TBB	IBB	SO	HBP	SH	SF	SB	CS	SB%	GDP	Avg	OBP	SLG	Pos	G	PO	A	E	DP	FPct
1996 Tex	25	1	0	0	0	0	0	0	0	0	0	0	0	0	0	0	0	0	0	—	0	—	—	—	P	1	0	0	0	0	—

DARYL PATTERSON—Daryl Alan Patterson—Throws: Right; Bats: Left

Ht: 6'4"; Wt: 192 lbs; Born: 11/21/1943 in Coalinga, California; Debut: 4/10/1968

World Series — Pitching

Year Tm	Age	G	GS	CG	GF	IP	BFP	H	R	ER	HR	SH	SF	HB	TBB	IBB	SO	WP	Bk	W	L	Pct	ShO	Sv-Op	Hld	OAvg	OOBP	ERA
1968 Det	24	2	0	0	0	3.0	9	1	0	0	0	0	0	0	1	0	0	0	0	0	0	—	0	0- 0	0	.125	.222	0.00

World Series — Batting / Fielding

Year Tm	Age	G	AB	H	2B	3B	HR	TB	R	RBI	GW	TBB	IBB	SO	HBP	SH	SF	SB	CS	SB%	GDP	Avg	OBP	SLG	Pos	G	PO	A	E	DP	FPct
1968 Det	24	2	0	0	0	0	0	0	0	0	0	0	0	0	0	0	0	0	0	—	0	—	—	—	P	2	0	1	0	0	1.000

MARTY PATTIN—Martin William Pattin—Nicknames: Bulldog, Duck—Throws: Right; Bats: Right

Ht: 5'11"; Wt: 180 lbs; Born: 4/6/1943 in Charleston, Illinois; Debut: 5/14/1968

LCS — Pitching

Year Tm	Age	G	GS	CG	GF	IP	BFP	H	R	ER	HR	SH	SF	HB	TBB	IBB	SO	WP	Bk	W	L	Pct	ShO	Sv-Op	Hld	OAvg	OOBP	ERA
1976 KC	33	2	0	0	0	0.1	2	0	1	1	0	0	0	0	1	1	0	0	0	0	0	—	0	0- 0	0	.000	.500	27.00
1977 KC	34	1	0	0	0	6.0	24	6	2	1	0	1	0	0	0	0	0	0	0	0	0	—	0	0- 0	0	.261	.261	1.50
1978 KC	35	1	0	0	0	0.2	4	2	2	2	0	0	0	0	0	0	0	0	0	0	0	—	0	0- 0	1	.500	.500	27.00
LCS Totals		4	0	0	0	7.0	60	8	5	4	0	1	0	0	1	1	0	0	0	0	0	—	0	0-0	1	.286	.310	5.14

World Series — Pitching

Year Tm	Age	G	GS	CG	GF	IP	BFP	H	R	ER	HR	SH	SF	HB	TBB	IBB	SO	WP	Bk	W	L	Pct	ShO	Sv-Op	Hld	OAvg	OOBP	ERA
1980 KC	37	1	0	0	0	1.0	3	0	0	0	0	0	0	0	0	0	2	0	0	0	0	—	0	0- 0	0	.000	.000	0.00
Postseason Totals		5	0	0	0	8.0	66	8	5	4	0	1	0	0	1	1	2	0	0	0	0	—	0	0-0	1	.258	.281	4.50

LCS — Batting / Fielding

Year Tm	Age	G	AB	H	2B	3B	HR	TB	R	RBI	GW	TBB	IBB	SO	HBP	SH	SF	SB	CS	SB%	GDP	Avg	OBP	SLG	Pos	G	PO	A	E	DP	FPct
1976 KC	33	2	0	0	0	0	0	0	0	0	0	0	0	0	0	0	0	0	0	—	0	—	—	—	P	2	0	0	0	0	—
1977 KC	34	1	0	0	0	0	0	0	0	0	0	0	0	0	0	0	0	0	0	—	0	—	—	—	P	1	1	2	0	1	1.000
1978 KC	35	1	0	0	0	0	0	0	0	0	0	0	0	0	0	0	0	0	0	—	0	—	—	—	P	1	0	0	0	0	—
LCS Totals		4	0	0	0	0	0	0	0	0	0	0	0	0	0	0	0	0	0	—	0	—	—	—	P	4	1	2	0	1	1.000

World Series — Batting / Fielding

Year Tm	Age	G	AB	H	2B	3B	HR	TB	R	RBI	GW	TBB	IBB	SO	HBP	SH	SF	SB	CS	SB%	GDP	Avg	OBP	SLG	Pos	G	PO	A	E	DP	FPct
1980 KC	37	1	0	0	0	0	0	0	0	0	0	0	0	0	0	0	0	0	0	—	0	—	—	—	P	1	0	0	0	0	—
Postseason Totals		5	0	0	0	0	0	0	0	0	0	0	0	0	0	0	0	0	0	—	0	—	—	—	P	5	1	2	0	1	1.000

ROGER PAVLIK—Roger Allen Pavlik—Throws: Right; Bats: Right

Ht: 6'3"; Wt: 220 lbs; Born: 10/4/1967 in Houston, Texas; Debut: 5/2/1992

Division Series — Pitching

Year Tm	Age	G	GS	CG	GF	IP	BFP	H	R	ER	HR	SH	SF	HB	TBB	IBB	SO	WP	Bk	W	L	Pct	ShO	Sv-Op	Hld	OAvg	OOBP	ERA
1996 Tex	28	1	0	0	0	2.2	12	4	2	2	1	1	0	0	0	0	1	0	0	0	1	.000	0	0- 0	0	.364	.364	6.75

Division Series — Batting / Fielding

Year Tm	Age	G	AB	H	2B	3B	HR	TB	R	RBI	GW	TBB	IBB	SO	HBP	SH	SF	SB	CS	SB%	GDP	Avg	OBP	SLG	Pos	G	PO	A	E	DP	FPct
1996 Tex	28	1	0	0	0	0	0	0	0	0	0	0	0	0	0	0	0	0	0	—	0	—	—	—	P	1	1	0	0	0	1.000

FRED PAYNE—Frederick Thomas Payne—Bats: Right; Throws: Right

Ht: 5'10"; Wt: 162 lbs; Born: 9/2/1880 in Camden, New York; Debut: 4/21/1906; Died: 1/16/1954

World Series — Batting / Fielding

Year Tm	Age	G	AB	H	2B	3B	HR	TB	R	RBI	GW	TBB	IBB	SO	HBP	SH	SF	SB	CS	SB%	GDP	Avg	OBP	SLG	Pos	G	PO	A	E	DP	FPct
1907 Det	27	2	4	1	0	0	0	1	0	1	0	0	0	0	0	0	0	1	0	1.00	0	.250	.250	.250	C	1	6	1	1	0	.875

MONTE PEARSON—Montgomery Marcellus Pearson—Nickname: Hoot—Throws: Right; Bats: Right

Ht: 6'0"; Wt: 175 lbs; Born: 9/2/1909 in Oakland, California; Debut: 4/22/1932; Died: 1/27/1978

World Series — Pitching

Year Tm	Age	G	GS	CG	GF	IP	BFP	H	R	ER	HR	SH	SF	HB	TBB	IBB	SO	WP	Bk	W	L	Pct	ShO	Sv-Op	Hld	OAvg	OOBP	ERA
1936 NYA	27	1	1	1	0	9.0	35	7	2	2	0	0	0	0	2	0	7	0	0	1	0	1.000	0	0- 0	0	.212	.257	2.00
1937 NYA	28	1	1	0	0	8.2	33	5	1	1	0	0	0	0	2	0	4	0	0	1	0	1.000	0	0- 0	0	.161	.212	1.04
1938 NYA	29	1	1	1	0	9.0	36	5	2	1	1	0	0	0	2	0	9	0	0	1	0	1.000	0	0- 0	0	.147	.194	1.00
1939 NYA	30	1	1	1	0	9.0	29	2	0	0	0	0	0	0	1	0	8	0	0	1	0	1.000	1	0- 0	0	.071	.103	0.00
WS Totals		4	4	3	0	35.2	266	19	5	4	1	0	0	0	7	0	28	0	0	4	0	1.000	1	0-0	0	.151	.195	1.01

World Series — Batting / Fielding

Year Tm	Age	G	AB	H	2B	3B	HR	TB	R	RBI	GW	TBB	IBB	SO	HBP	SH	SF	SB	CS	SB%	GDP	Avg	OBP	SLG	Pos	G	PO	A	E	DP	FPct
1936 NYA	27	1	4	2	1	0	0	3	0	0	0	0	0	0	0	0	0	0	0	—	0	.500	.500	.750	P	1	1	2	0	0	1.000
1937 NYA	28	1	3	0	0	0	0	0	0	0	0	1	0	1	0	0	0	0	0	—	1	.000	.250	.000	P	1	0	0	0	0	—
1938 NYA	29	1	3	1	0	0	0	1	1	0	0	1	0	0	0	0	0	0	0	—	0	.333	.500	.333	P	1	2	0	0	0	1.000
1939 NYA	30	1	2	0	0	0	0	0	0	0	0	0	0	1	0	1	0	0	0	—	0	.000	.000	.000	P	1	0	5	0	0	1.000
WS Totals		4	12	3	1	0	0	4	1	0	0	2	0	2	0	1	0	0	0	—	1	.250	.357	.333	P	4	3	7	0	0	1.000

HAL PECK—Harold Arthur Peck—Bats: Left; Throws: Left

Ht: 5'11"; Wt: 175 lbs; Born: 4/20/1917 in Big Bend, Wisconsin; Debut: 5/13/1943; Died: 4/13/1995

World Series (Batting / Fielding)

Year Tm	Age	G	AB	H	2B	3B	HR	TB	R	RBI	GW	TBB	IBB	SO	HBP	SH	SF	SB	CS	SB%	GDP	Avg	OBP	SLG	Pos	G	PO	A	E	DP	FPct
1948 Cle	31	1	0	0	0	0	0	0	0	0	0	0	0	0	0	0	0	0	0	—	0	—	—	—	OF	1	0	0	0	0	—

ROGER PECKINPAUGH—Roger Thorpe Peckinpaugh—Bats: Right; Throws: Right

Ht: 5'10"; Wt: 165 lbs; Born: 2/5/1891 in Wooster, Ohio; Debut: 9/15/1910; Died: 11/17/1977

World Series (Batting / Fielding)

Year Tm	Age	G	AB	H	2B	3B	HR	TB	R	RBI	GW	TBB	IBB	SO	HBP	SH	SF	SB	CS	SB%	GDP	Avg	OBP	SLG	Pos	G	PO	A	E	DP	FPct
1921 NYA	30	8	28	5	1	0	0	6	2	0	0	4	0	3	0	1	0	0	1	.00	1	.179	.281	.214	SS	8	17	29	1	4	.979
1924 Was	33	4	12	5	2	0	0	7	1	2	1	1	0	0	0	0	0	1	0	1.00	0	.417	.462	.583	SS	4	7	14	0	3	1.000
1925 Was-*M*	34	7	24	6	1	0	1	10	1	3	0	1	0	2	0	1	0	1	1	.50	0	.250	.280	.417	SS	7	10	22	8	3	.800
WS Totals		19	64	16	4	0	1	23	4	5	1	6	0	5	0	2	0	2	2	.50	1	.250	.314	.359	SS	19	34	65	9	10	.917

BILL PECOTA—William Joseph Pecota—Nickname: I-29—Bats: Right; Throws: Right

Ht: 6'2"; Wt: 195 lbs; Born: 2/16/1960 in Redwood City, California; Debut: 9/19/1986

LCS (Batting / Fielding)

Year Tm	Age	G	AB	H	2B	3B	HR	TB	R	RBI	GW	TBB	IBB	SO	HBP	SH	SF	SB	CS	SB%	GDP	Avg	OBP	SLG	Pos	G	PO	A	E	DP	FPct
1993 Atl	33	4	3	1	0	0	0	1	1	0	0	1	0	1	0	0	0	0	0	—	0	.333	.500	.333	—						

HOMER PEEL—Homer Hefner Peel—Bats: Right; Throws: Right

Ht: 5'9"; Wt: 170 lbs; Born: 10/10/1902 in Fort Sullivan, Texas; Debut: 9/13/1927; Died: 4/8/1997

World Series (Batting / Fielding)

Year Tm	Age	G	AB	H	2B	3B	HR	TB	R	RBI	GW	TBB	IBB	SO	HBP	SH	SF	SB	CS	SB%	GDP	Avg	OBP	SLG	Pos	G	PO	A	E	DP	FPct
1933 NYG	30	2	2	1	0	0	0	1	0	0	0	0	0	0	0	0	0	0	0	—	0	.500	.500	.500	OF	1	0	0	0	0	—

ALEJANDRO PENA—Nickname: Slow—Throws: Right; Bats: Right

Ht: 6'1"; Wt: 200 lbs; Born: 6/25/1959 in Cambiaso Puerta Plata, Dominican Republic; Debut: 8/13/1981

Division Series (Pitching)

Year Tm	Age	G	GS	CG	GF	IP	BFP	H	R	ER	HR	SH	SF	HB	TBB	IBB	SO	WP	Bk	W	L	Pct	ShO	Sv-Op	Hld	OAvg	OOBP	ERA
1995 Atl	36	3	0	0	1	3.0	14	3	0	0	0	0	0	1	1	1	2	0	0	2	0	1.000	0	0- 1	0	.250	.357	0.00

LCS (Pitching)

Year Tm	Age	G	GS	CG	GF	IP	BFP	H	R	ER	HR	SH	SF	HB	TBB	IBB	SO	WP	Bk	W	L	Pct	ShO	Sv-Op	Hld	OAvg	OOBP	ERA
1981 LA	22	2	0	0	1	2.1	8	1	0	0	0	0	0	0	0	0	0	0	0	0	0	—	0	0- 0	0	.125	.125	0.00
1983 LA	24	1	0	0	0	2.2	12	4	2	2	1	0	1	0	1	0	3	1	0	0	0	—	0	0- 0	0	.400	.417	6.75
1988 LA	29	3	0	0	1	4.1	18	1	2	2	0	0	0	0	5	0	1	0	0	1	1	.500	0	1- 2	0	.077	.333	4.15
1991 Atl	32	4	0	0	4	4.1	15	1	0	0	0	2	0	0	0	0	4	2	0	0	0	—	0	3- 3	0	.077	.077	0.00
1995 Atl	36	3	0	0	0	3.0	12	2	0	0	0	0	0	0	1	1	4	0	0	0	0	—	0	0- 0	0	.182	.250	0.00
LCS Totals		13	0	0	6	16.2	130	9	4	4	1	2	1	0	7	1	12	3	0	1	1	.500	0	4-5	0	.164	.254	2.16

World Series (Pitching)

Year Tm	Age	G	GS	CG	GF	IP	BFP	H	R	ER	HR	SH	SF	HB	TBB	IBB	SO	WP	Bk	W	L	Pct	ShO	Sv-Op	Hld	OAvg	OOBP	ERA
1988 LA	29	2	0	0	1	5.0	18	2	0	0	0	0	0	0	1	0	7	0	0	1	0	1.000	0	0- 0	0	.118	.167	0.00
1991 Atl	32	3	0	0	1	5.1	24	6	2	2	1	1	0	0	3	3	7	1	0	0	1	.000	0	0- 1	0	.300	.391	3.38
1995 Atl	36	2	0	0	1	1.0	7	3	1	1	0	0	0	0	2	1	0	0	0	0	1	.000	0	0- 0	1	.600	.714	9.00
WS Totals		7	0	0	3	11.1	98	11	3	3	1	1	0	0	6	4	14	1	0	1	2	.333	0	0-1	1	.262	.354	2.38
Postseason Totals		23	0	0	10	31.0	256	23	7	7	2	3	1	1	14	6	28	4	0	4	3	.571	0	4-7	1	.211	.304	2.03

Division Series (Batting / Fielding)

Year Tm	Age	G	AB	H	2B	3B	HR	TB	R	RBI	GW	TBB	IBB	SO	HBP	SH	SF	SB	CS	SB%	GDP	Avg	OBP	SLG	Pos	G	PO	A	E	DP	FPct
1995 Atl	36	3	0	0	0	0	0	0	0	0	0	0	0	0	0	0	0	0	0	—	0	—	—	—	P	3	0	0	0	0	—

LCS (Batting / Fielding)

Year Tm	Age	G	AB	H	2B	3B	HR	TB	R	RBI	GW	TBB	IBB	SO	HBP	SH	SF	SB	CS	SB%	GDP	Avg	OBP	SLG	Pos	G	PO	A	E	DP	FPct
1981 LA	22	2	0	0	0	0	0	0	0	0	0	0	0	0	0	0	0	0	0	—	0	—	—	—	P	2	0	0	0	0	—
1983 LA	24	1	1	1	0	0	0	1	0	0	0	0	0	0	0	0	0	0	0	—	0	1.000	1.000	1.000	P	1	0	0	0	0	—
1988 LA	29	3	0	0	0	0	0	0	0	0	0	0	0	0	0	0	0	0	0	—	0	—	—	—	P	3	0	0	0	0	—
1991 Atl	32	4	0	0	0	0	0	0	0	0	0	0	0	0	0	0	0	0	0	—	0	—	—	—	P	4	1	2	0	0	1.000
1995 Atl	36	3	0	0	0	0	0	0	0	0	0	0	0	0	0	0	0	0	0	—	0	—	—	—	P	3	0	0	0	0	—
LCS Totals		13	1	1	0	0	0	1	0	0	0	0	0	0	0	0	0	0	0	—	0	1.000	1.000	1.000	P	13	1	2	0	0	1.000

World Series (Batting / Fielding)

Year Tm	Age	G	AB	H	2B	3B	HR	TB	R	RBI	GW	TBB	IBB	SO	HBP	SH	SF	SB	CS	SB%	GDP	Avg	OBP	SLG	Pos	G	PO	A	E	DP	FPct
1988 LA	29	2	0	0	0	0	0	0	0	0	0	0	0	0	0	0	0	0	0	—	0	—	—	—	P	2	0	0	0	0	—
1991 Atl	32	3	0	0	0	0	0	0	0	0	0	0	0	0	0	0	0	0	0	—	0	—	—	—	P	3	0	0	0	0	—
1995 Atl	36	2	0	0	0	0	0	0	0	0	0	0	0	0	0	0	0	0	0	—	0	—	—	—	P	2	0	0	0	0	—
WS Totals		7	0	0	0	0	0	0	0	0	0	0	0	0	0	0	0	0	0	—	0	—	—	—	P	7	0	0	0	0	—
Postseason Totals		23	1	1	0	0	0	1	0	0	0	0	0	0	0	0	0	0	0	—	0	1.000	1.000	1.000	P	23	1	2	0	0	1.000

TONY PENA—Antonio Francesco Pena—Nickname: El Gato—Bats: Right; Throws: Right

Ht: 6'0"; Wt: 175 lbs; Born: 6/4/1957 in Monte Cristi, Dominican Republic; Debut: 9/1/1980

Division Series (Batting / Fielding)

Year Tm	Age	G	AB	H	2B	3B	HR	TB	R	RBI	GW	TBB	IBB	SO	HBP	SH	SF	SB	CS	SB%	GDP	Avg	OBP	SLG	Pos	G	PO	A	E	DP	FPct
1995 Cle	38	2	2	1	0	0	1	4	1	1	1	0	0	0	0	0	0	0	0	—	0	.500	.500	2.000	C	2	5	0	0	0	1.000
1996 Cle	39	1	0	0	0	0	0	0	0	0	0	0	0	0	0	0	0	0	0	—	0	—	—	—	C	1	1	0	0	0	1.000
1997 Hou	40	2	0	0	0	0	0	0	0	0	0	0	0	0	0	0	0	0	0	—	0	—	—	—	C	2	2	0	0	0	1.000
DS Totals		5	2	1	0	0	1	4	1	1	1	0	0	0	0	0	0	0	0	—	0	.500	.500	2.000	C	5	8	0	0	0	1.000

LCS (Batting / Fielding)

Year Tm	Age	G	AB	H	2B	3B	HR	TB	R	RBI	GW	TBB	IBB	SO	HBP	SH	SF	SB	CS	SB%	GDP	Avg	OBP	SLG	Pos	G	PO	A	E	DP	FPct
1987 StL	30	7	21	8	0	1	0	10	5	0	0	3	0	4	0	0	0	1	1	.50	0	.381	.458	.476	C	7	55	5	0	0	1.000
1990 Bos	33	4	14	3	0	0	0	3	0	0	0	0	0	0	0	0	0	0	0	—	2	.214	.214	.214	C	4	22	4	1	1	.963
1995 Cle	38	4	6	2	1	0	0	3	1	0	0	1	0	0	0	0	0	0	0	—	0	.333	.429	.500	C	4	15	1	0	0	1.000
LCS Totals		15	41	13	1	1	0	16	6	0	0	4	0	4	0	0	0	1	1	.50	2	.317	.378	.390	C	15	92	10	1	1	.990

World Series (Batting / Fielding)

Year Tm	Age	G	AB	H	2B	3B	HR	TB	R	RBI	GW	TBB	IBB	SO	HBP	SH	SF	SB	CS	SB%	GDP	Avg	OBP	SLG	Pos	G	PO	A	E	DP	FPct
1987 StL	30	7	22	9	1	0	0	10	2	4	0	3	0	2	0	0	0	1	0	1.00	1	.409	.480	.455	C	6	32	1	1	0	.971
1995 Cle	38	2	6	1	0	0	0	1	0	0	0	0	0	0	0	0	0	0	0	—	0	.167	.167	.167	C	2	7	1	0	0	1.000
WS Totals		9	28	10	1	0	0	11	2	4	0	3	0	2	0	0	0	1	0	1.00	1	.357	.419	.393	C	8	39	2	1	0	.976
Postseason Totals		29	71	24	2	1	1	31	9	5	1	7	0	6	0	0	0	2	1	.67	3	.338	.397	.437	C	28	139	12	2	1	.987

TERRY PENDLETON—Terry Lee Pendleton—Bats: Both; Throws: Right

Ht: 5'9"; Wt: 178 lbs; Born: 7/16/1960 in Los Angeles, California; Debut: 7/18/1984

Division Series (Batting / Fielding)

Year Tm	Age	G	AB	H	2B	3B	HR	TB	R	RBI	GW	TBB	IBB	SO	HBP	SH	SF	SB	CS	SB%	GDP	Avg	OBP	SLG	Pos	G	PO	A	E	DP	FPct
1996 Atl	36	1	1	0	0	0	0	0	0	0	0	0	0	1	0	0	0	0	0	—	0	.000	.000	.000	—						

LCS (Batting / Fielding)

Year Tm	Age	G	AB	H	2B	3B	HR	TB	R	RBI	GW	TBB	IBB	SO	HBP	SH	SF	SB	CS	SB%	GDP	Avg	OBP	SLG	Pos	G	PO	A	E	DP	FPct
1985 StL	25	6	24	5	1	0	0	6	2	4	0	1	0	3	0	0	0	0	1	.00	1	.208	.240	.250	3B	6	6	18	1	2	.960
1987 StL	27	6	19	4	0	1	0	6	3	1	1	0	0	6	0	0	0	0	0	—	0	.211	.211	.316	3B	6	3	11	0	1	1.000
1991 Atl-*M*	31	7	30	5	1	1	0	8	1	1	0	1	0	3	0	0	0	0	0	—	2	.167	.194	.267	3B	7	5	11	0	1	1.000
1992 Atl	32	7	30	7	2	0	0	9	2	3	0	0	0	2	0	0	0	0	0	—	0	.233	.233	.300	3B	7	4	18	0	2	1.000
1993 Atl	33	6	26	9	1	0	1	13	4	5	0	0	0	2	0	0	0	0	0	—	0	.346	.346	.500	3B	6	7	5	0	1	1.000
1996 Atl	36	6	6	0	0	0	0	0	0	0	0	1	1	3	0	0	0	0	0	—	0	.000	.143	.000	3B	2	0	1	0	1	1.000
LCS Totals		38	135	30	5	2	1	42	12	14	1	3	1	19	0	0	0	0	1	.00	2	.222	.239	.311	3B	34	25	64	1	8	.989

World Series (Batting / Fielding)

Year Tm	Age	G	AB	H	2B	3B	HR	TB	R	RBI	GW	TBB	IBB	SO	HBP	SH	SF	SB	CS	SB%	GDP	Avg	OBP	SLG	Pos	G	PO	A	E	DP	FPct
1985 StL	25	7	23	6	1	1	0	9	3	3	1	3	1	2	0	0	0	0	0	—	0	.261	.346	.391	3B	7	6	14	1	3	.952
1987 StL	27	3	7	3	0	0	0	3	2	1	0	1	0	1	0	1	0	2	0	1.00	0	.429	.500	.429	—						
1991 Atl-*M*	31	7	30	11	3	0	2	20	6	3	0	3	1	1	0	0	0	0	0	—	1	.367	.424	.667	3B	7	3	20	2	2	.920
1992 Atl	32	6	25	6	2	0	0	8	2	2	0	1	0	5	0	0	1	0	0	—	0	.240	.259	.320	3B	6	4	19	0	1	1.000
1996 Atl	36	4	9	2	1	0	0	3	1	0	0	1	0	1	0	0	0	0	1	.00	1	.222	.300	.333	3B	1	0	2	0	0	1.000
WS Totals		27	94	28	7	1	2	43	14	9	1	9	2	10	0	1	1	2	1	.67	2	.298	.356	.457	3B	21	13	55	3	6	.958
Postseason Totals		66	230	58	12	3	3	85	26	23	2	12	3	30	0	1	1	2	2	.50	4	.252	.288	.370	3B	55	38	119	4	14	.975

HERB PENNOCK (HOF 1948-W)—Herbert Jeffries Pennock—Throws: Left; Bats: Both

Ht: 6'0"; Wt: 160 lbs; Born: 2/10/1894 in Kennett Square, Pennsylvania; Debut: 5/14/1912; Died: 1/30/1948

World Series		Pitching																										
Year Tm	Age	G	GS	CG	GF	IP	BFP	H	R	ER	HR	SH	SF	HB	TBB	IBB	SO	WP	Bk	W	L	Pct	ShO	Sv-Op	Hld	OAvg	OOBP	ERA
1914 Phi	20	1	0	0	1	3.0	12	2	0	0	0	0	0	0	2	0	3	0	0	0	0	—	0	0-0	0	.200	.333	0.00
1923 NYA	29	3	2	1	1	17.1	70	19	7	7	3	0	0	0	1	0	8	0	0	2	0	1.000	0	1-1	0	.275	.286	3.63
1926 NYA	32	3	2	2	1	22.0	82	13	3	3	0	2	0	0	4	0	8	0	0	2	0	1.000	0	0-0	0	.171	.213	1.23
1927 NYA	33	1	1	1	0	9.0	30	3	1	1	0	0	0	0	0	0	1	0	0	1	0	1.000	0	0-0	0	.100	.100	1.00
1932 NYA	38	2	0	0	2	4.0	16	2	1	1	0	0	0	0	1	0	4	0	0	0	0	—	0	2-2	0	.133	.188	2.25
WS Totals		10	5	4	5	55.1	420	39	12	12	3	2	0	0	8	0	24	0	0	5	0	1.000	0	3-3	0	.195	.226	1.95

World Series		Batting																							Fielding						
Year Tm	Age	G	AB	H	2B	3B	HR	TB	R	RBI	GW	TBB	IBB	SO	HBP	SH	SF	SB	CS	SB%	GDP	Avg	OBP	SLG	Pos	G	PO	A	E	DP	FPct
1914 Phi	20	1	1	0	0	0	0	0	0	0	0	0	0	0	0	0	0	0	0	—	0	.000	.000	.000	P	1	0	0	0	0	—
1923 NYA	29	3	6	0	0	0	0	0	0	0	0	0	0	2	1	0	0	0	0	—	1	.000	.143	.000	P	3	0	2	0	0	1.000
1926 NYA	32	3	7	1	1	0	0	2	1	0	0	0	0	0	0	1	0	0	0	—	0	.143	.143	.286	P	3	0	6	0	0	1.000
1927 NYA	33	1	4	0	0	0	0	0	1	1	0	0	0	1	0	0	0	0	0	—	0	.000	.000	.000	P	1	1	1	0	0	1.000
1932 NYA	38	2	1	0	0	0	0	0	0	0	0	0	0	0	0	0	0	0	0	—	0	.000	.000	.000	P	2	0	1	0	0	1.000
WS Totals		10	19	1	1	0	0	2	2	1	0	0	0	3	1	1	0	0	0	—	1	.053	.100	.105	P	10	1	10	0	0	1.000

JOE PEPITONE—Joseph Anthony Pepitone—Nickname: Pepi—Bats: Left; Throws: Left

Ht: 6'2"; Wt: 185 lbs; Born: 10/9/1940 in Brooklyn, New York; Debut: 4/10/1962

World Series		Batting																							Fielding						
Year Tm	Age	G	AB	H	2B	3B	HR	TB	R	RBI	GW	TBB	IBB	SO	HBP	SH	SF	SB	CS	SB%	GDP	Avg	OBP	SLG	Pos	G	PO	A	E	DP	FPct
1963 NYA	22	4	13	2	0	0	0	2	0	0	0	1	0	3	1	0	0	0	0	—	0	.154	.267	.154	1B	4	37	6	1	7	.977
1964 NYA	23	7	26	4	1	0	1	8	1	5	0	2	0	3	1	0	0	0	0	—	0	.154	.241	.308	1B	7	62	6	0	6	1.000
WS Totals		11	39	6	1	0	1	10	1	5	0	3	0	6	2	0	0	0	0	—	0	.154	.250	.256	1B	11	99	12	1	13	.991

EDDIE PEREZ—Eduardo Perez—Bats: Right; Throws: Right

Ht: 6'1"; Wt: 175 lbs; Born: 5/4/1968 in Cuidad Ojeda, Venezuela; Debut: 9/10/1995

Division Series		Batting																							Fielding						
Year Tm	Age	G	AB	H	2B	3B	HR	TB	R	RBI	GW	TBB	IBB	SO	HBP	SH	SF	SB	CS	SB%	GDP	Avg	OBP	SLG	Pos	G	PO	A	E	DP	FPct
1996 Atl	28	1	3	1	0	0	0	1	0	0	0	0	0	0	0	0	0	0	0	—	0	.333	.333	.333	C	1	10	0	0	0	1.000
1997 Atl	29	1	3	0	0	0	0	0	0	0	0	0	0	1	0	0	0	0	0	—	0	.000	.000	.000	C	1	6	0	0	0	1.000
DS Totals		2	6	1	0	0	0	1	0	0	0	0	0	1	0	0	0	0	0	—	0	.167	.167	.167	C	2	16	0	0	0	1.000
LCS		**Batting**																							**Fielding**						
Year Tm	Age	G	AB	H	2B	3B	HR	TB	R	RBI	GW	TBB	IBB	SO	HBP	SH	SF	SB	CS	SB%	GDP	Avg	OBP	SLG	Pos	G	PO	A	E	DP	FPct
1996 Atl	28	4	1	0	0	0	0	0	0	0	0	1	0	0	0	0	0	0	0	—	0	.000	.500	.000	C	3	5	0	0	0	1.000
																									1B	1	2	0	0	1	1.000
1997 Atl	29	2	3	0	0	0	0	0	0	0	0	0	0	0	0	0	0	0	0	—	0	.000	.000	.000	C	2	14	0	0	0	1.000
LCS Totals		6	4	0	0	0	0	0	0	0	0	1	0	0	0	0	0	0	0	—	0	.000	.200	.000	C	5	19	0	0	0	1.000
World Series		**Batting**																							**Fielding**						
Year Tm	Age	G	AB	H	2B	3B	HR	TB	R	RBI	GW	TBB	IBB	SO	HBP	SH	SF	SB	CS	SB%	GDP	Avg	OBP	SLG	Pos	G	PO	A	E	DP	FPct
1996 Atl	28	2	1	0	0	0	0	0	0	0	0	0	0	0	0	0	0	0	0	—	0	.000	.000	.000	C	2	2	0	0	0	1.000
Postseason Totals		10	11	1	0	0	0	1	0	0	0	1	0	1	0	0	0	0	0	—	0	.091	.167	.091	C	9	37	0	0	0	1.000

PASCUAL PEREZ—Pascual Gross Perez—Throws: Right; Bats: Right

Ht: 6'2"; Wt: 162 lbs; Born: 5/17/1957 in San Cristobal, Dominican Republic; Debut: 5/7/1980

LCS		Pitching																										
Year Tm	Age	G	GS	CG	GF	IP	BFP	H	R	ER	HR	SH	SF	HB	TBB	IBB	SO	WP	Bk	W	L	Pct	ShO	Sv-Op	Hld	OAvg	OOBP	ERA
1982 Atl	25	2	1	0	0	8.2	38	10	5	5	0	1	1	0	2	0	4	0	0	0	1	.000	0	0-0	0	.294	.324	5.19

LCS		Batting																							Fielding						
Year Tm	Age	G	AB	H	2B	3B	HR	TB	R	RBI	GW	TBB	IBB	SO	HBP	SH	SF	SB	CS	SB%	GDP	Avg	OBP	SLG	Pos	G	PO	A	E	DP	FPct
1982 Atl	25	2	3	0	0	0	0	0	0	0	0	0	0	1	0	0	0	0	0	—	0	.000	.000	.000	P	2	0	1	0	0	1.000

TONY PEREZ—Atanasio Perez—Nickname: Doggie—Bats: Right; Throws: Right

Ht: 6'2"; Wt: 175 lbs; Born: 5/14/1942 in Camaguey, Cuba; Debut: 7/26/1964

LCS		Batting																							Fielding						
Year Tm	Age	G	AB	H	2B	3B	HR	TB	R	RBI	GW	TBB	IBB	SO	HBP	SH	SF	SB	CS	SB%	GDP	Avg	OBP	SLG	Pos	G	PO	A	E	DP	FPct
1970 Cin	28	3	12	4	2	0	1	9	1	2	0	1	0	1	0	0	0	0	0	—	0	.333	.385	.750	3B	3	5	6	1	1	.917
																									1B	1	1	0	0	0	1.000
1972 Cin	30	5	20	4	1	0	0	5	0	2	0	0	0	7	0	0	0	0	0	—	0	.200	.200	.250	1B	5	45	3	0	2	1.000
1973 Cin	31	5	22	2	0	0	1	5	1	2	0	0	0	4	0	0	0	0	0	—	1	.091	.091	.227	1B	5	47	4	0	3	1.000
1975 Cin	33	3	12	5	0	0	1	8	3	4	1	1	0	2	0	0	0	0	0	—	0	.417	.462	.667	1B	3	27	5	0	2	1.000
1976 Cin	34	3	10	2	0	0	0	2	1	3	0	1	0	2	0	0	2	0	0	—	0	.200	.231	.200	1B	3	27	2	1	2	.967
1983 Phi	41	1	1	1	0	0	0	1	0	0	0	0	0	0	0	0	0	0	0	—	0	1.000	1.000	1.000	—						
LCS Totals		20	77	18	3	0	3	30	6	13	1	3	0	16	0	0	2	0	0	—	1	.234	.256	.390	1B	17	147	14	1	9	.994
World Series		**Batting**																							**Fielding**						
Year Tm	Age	G	AB	H	2B	3B	HR	TB	R	RBI	GW	TBB	IBB	SO	HBP	SH	SF	SB	CS	SB%	GDP	Avg	OBP	SLG	Pos	G	PO	A	E	DP	FPct
1970 Cin	28	5	18	1	0	0	0	1	2	0	0	3	0	4	0	0	0	0	0	—	1	.056	.190	.056	3B	5	3	14	1	0	.944
1972 Cin	30	7	23	10	2	0	0	12	3	2	0	4	1	4	0	0	1	0	1	.00	0	.435	.500	.522	1B	7	73	3	1	3	.987
1975 Cin	33	7	28	5	0	0	3	14	4	7	0	3	0	9	0	0	0	1	0	1.00	0	.179	.258	.500	1B	7	66	5	1	5	.986
1976 Cin	34	4	16	5	1	0	0	6	1	2	1	1	0	2	0	0	0	0	1	.00	0	.313	.353	.375	1B	4	32	4	0	4	1.000
1983 Phi	41	4	10	2	0	0	0	2	0	0	0	0	0	2	0	0	0	0	0	—	1	.200	.200	.200	1B	2	13	1	0	2	1.000
WS Totals		27	95	23	3	0	3	35	10	11	1	11	1	21	0	0	1	1	2	.33	2	.242	.318	.368	1B	20	184	13	2	14	.990
Postseason Totals		47	172	41	6	0	6	65	16	24	2	14	1	37	0	0	3	1	2	.33	3	.238	.291	.378	1B	37	331	27	3	23	.992

RON PERRANOSKI—Ronald Peter Perranoski—Throws: Left; Bats: Left

Ht: 6'0"; Wt: 180 lbs; Born: 4/1/1936 in Paterson, New Jersey; Debut: 4/14/1961

LCS		Pitching																										
Year Tm	Age	G	GS	CG	GF	IP	BFP	H	R	ER	HR	SH	SF	HB	TBB	IBB	SO	WP	Bk	W	L	Pct	ShO	Sv-Op	Hld	OAvg	OOBP	ERA
1969 Min	33	3	0	0	3	4.2	21	8	3	3	0	1	0	0	0	0	2	0	0	0	1	.000	0	0-0	0	.400	.400	5.79
1970 Min	34	2	0	0	1	2.1	12	5	5	5	0	0	0	0	1	0	3	0	0	0	0	—	0	0-0	0	.455	.500	19.29
LCS Totals		5	0	0	4	7.0	66	13	8	8	0	1	0	0	1	0	5	0	0	0	1	.000	0	0-0	0	.419	.438	10.29
World Series		**Pitching**																										
Year Tm	Age	G	GS	CG	GF	IP	BFP	H	R	ER	HR	SH	SF	HB	TBB	IBB	SO	WP	Bk	W	L	Pct	ShO	Sv-Op	Hld	OAvg	OOBP	ERA
1963 LA	27	1	0	0	1	0.2	3	1	0	0	0	0	0	0	0	0	1	0	0	0	0	—	0	1-1	0	.333	.333	0.00
1965 LA	29	2	0	0	1	3.2	18	3	3	3	0	0	0	0	4	1	1	1	1	0	0	—	0	0-0	0	.214	.389	7.36
1966 LA	30	2	0	0	1	3.1	15	4	2	2	0	1	0	0	1	0	2	0	0	0	0	—	0	0-0	0	.308	.357	5.40
WS Totals		5	0	0	3	7.2	72	8	5	5	0	1	0	0	5	1	4	1	1	0	0	—	0	1-1	0	.267	.371	5.87
Postseason Totals		10	0	0	7	14.2	138	21	13	13	0	2	0	0	6	1	9	1	1	0	1	.000	0	1-1	0	.344	.403	7.98

LCS		Batting																							Fielding						
Year Tm	Age	G	AB	H	2B	3B	HR	TB	R	RBI	GW	TBB	IBB	SO	HBP	SH	SF	SB	CS	SB%	GDP	Avg	OBP	SLG	Pos	G	PO	A	E	DP	FPct
1969 Min	33	3	1	0	0	0	0	0	0	0	0	0	0	0	0	0	0	0	0	—	0	.000	.000	.000	P	3	0	0	0	0	—
1970 Min	34	2	0	0	0	0	0	0	0	0	0	0	0	0	0	0	0	0	0	—	0	—	—	—	P	2	0	1	0	1	1.000
LCS Totals		5	1	0	0	0	0	0	0	0	0	0	0	0	0	0	0	0	0	—	0	.000	.000	.000	P	5	0	1	0	1	1.000
World Series		**Batting**																							**Fielding**						
Year Tm	Age	G	AB	H	2B	3B	HR	TB	R	RBI	GW	TBB	IBB	SO	HBP	SH	SF	SB	CS	SB%	GDP	Avg	OBP	SLG	Pos	G	PO	A	E	DP	FPct
1963 LA	27	1	0	0	0	0	0	0	0	0	0	0	0	0	0	0	0	0	0	—	0	—	—	—	P	1	0	0	0	0	—
1965 LA	29	2	0	0	0	0	0	0	0	0	0	0	0	0	0	0	0	0	0	—	0	—	—	—	P	2	0	1	0	1	1.000
1966 LA	30	2	0	0	0	0	0	0	0	0	0	0	0	0	0	0	0	0	0	—	0	—	—	—	P	2	0	2	1	0	.667
WS Totals		5	0	0	0	0	0	0	0	0	0	0	0	0	0	0	0	0	0	—	0	—	—	—	P	5	0	3	1	1	.750
Postseason Totals		10	1	0	0	0	0	0	0	0	0	0	0	0	0	0	0	0	0	—	0	.000	.000	.000	P	10	0	4	1	2	.800

POL PERRITT—William Dayton Perritt—Throws: Right; Bats: Right

Ht: 6'2"; Wt: 168 lbs; Born: 8/30/1892 in Arcadia, Louisiana; Debut: 9/7/1912; Died: 10/15/1947

World Series		Pitching																										
Year Tm	Age	G	GS	CG	GF	IP	BFP	H	R	ER	HR	SH	SF	HB	TBB	IBB	SO	WP	Bk	W	L	Pct	ShO	Sv-Op	Hld	OAvg	OOBP	ERA
1917 NYG	25	3	0	0	2	8.1	33	9	2	2	0	1	0	0	3	0	3	0	0	0	0	—	0	0-0	0	.310	.375	2.16

World Series		Batting																							Fielding						
Year Tm	Age	G	AB	H	2B	3B	HR	TB	R	RBI	GW	TBB	IBB	SO	HBP	SH	SF	SB	CS	SB%	GDP	Avg	OBP	SLG	Pos	G	PO	A	E	DP	FPct
1917 NYG	25	3	2	2	0	0	0	2	0	0	0	0	0	0	0	0	0	0	0	—	0	1.000	1.000	1.000	P	3	0	1	0	0	1.000

GAYLORD PERRY (HOF 1991-W)—Gaylord Jackson Perry—Throws: Right; Bats: Right

Ht: 6'4"; Wt: 205 lbs; Born: 9/15/1938 in Williamston, North Carolina; Debut: 4/14/1962

LCS		Pitching																										
Year Tm	Age	G	GS	CG	GF	IP	BFP	H	R	ER	HR	SH	SF	HB	TBB	IBB	SO	WP	Bk	W	L	Pct	ShO	Sv-Op	Hld	OAvg	OOBP	ERA
1971 SF	33	2	2	1	0	14.2	70	19	11	10	1	1	0	1	3	1	11	1	0	1	1	.500	0	0- 0	0	.292	.333	6.14

LCS		Batting																							Fielding						
Year Tm	Age	G	AB	H	2B	3B	HR	TB	R	RBI	GW	TBB	IBB	SO	HBP	SH	SF	SB	CS	SB%	GDP	Avg	OBP	SLG	Pos	G	PO	A	E	DP	FPct
1971 SF	33	2	4	1	0	0	0	1	0	0	0	0	0	0	0	2	0	0	0	—	0	.250	.250	.250	P	2	1	1	0	0	1.000

HERBERT PERRY—Herbert Edward Perry—Bats: Right; Throws: Right

Ht: 6'2"; Wt: 215 lbs; Born: 9/15/1969 in Live Oak, Florida; Debut: 5/3/1994

Division Series		Batting																							Fielding						
Year Tm	Age	G	AB	H	2B	3B	HR	TB	R	RBI	GW	TBB	IBB	SO	HBP	SH	SF	SB	CS	SB%	GDP	Avg	OBP	SLG	Pos	G	PO	A	E	DP	FPct
1995 Cle	26	1	1	0	0	0	0	0	0	0	0	0	0	0	0	0	0	0	0	—	0	.000	.000	.000	—						
LCS		**Batting**																							**Fielding**						
Year Tm	Age	G	AB	H	2B	3B	HR	TB	R	RBI	GW	TBB	IBB	SO	HBP	SH	SF	SB	CS	SB%	GDP	Avg	OBP	SLG	Pos	G	PO	A	E	DP	FPct
1995 Cle	26	3	8	0	0	0	0	0	0	0	0	1	0	3	0	0	0	0	1	.00	0	.000	.111	.000	1B	3	30	0	0	2	1.000
World Series		**Batting**																							**Fielding**						
Year Tm	Age	G	AB	H	2B	3B	HR	TB	R	RBI	GW	TBB	IBB	SO	HBP	SH	SF	SB	CS	SB%	GDP	Avg	OBP	SLG	Pos	G	PO	A	E	DP	FPct
1995 Cle	26	3	5	0	0	0	0	0	0	0	0	0	0	2	0	0	0	0	0	—	0	.000	.000	.000	1B	3	13	2	0	2	1.000
Postseason Totals		7	14	0	0	0	0	0	0	0	0	1	0	5	0	0	0	0	1	.00	0	.000	.067	.000	1B	6	43	2	0	4	1.000

JIM PERRY—James Evan Perry—Throws: Right; Bats: Both

Ht: 6'4"; Wt: 190 lbs; Born: 10/30/1935 in Williamston, North Carolina; Debut: 4/23/1959

LCS		Pitching																										
Year Tm	Age	G	GS	CG	GF	IP	BFP	H	R	ER	HR	SH	SF	HB	TBB	IBB	SO	WP	Bk	W	L	Pct	ShO	Sv-Op	Hld	OAvg	OOBP	ERA
1969 Min	33	1	1	0	0	8.0	32	6	3	3	3	0	0	0	3	0	3	0	0	0	0	—	0	0- 0	0	.207	.281	3.38
1970 Min-*C*	34	2	1	0	1	5.1	27	10	9	8	3	0	1	1	1	0	3	0	0	0	1	.000	0	0- 0	0	.417	.444	13.50
LCS Totals		3	2	0	1	13.1	118	16	12	11	6	0	1	1	4	0	6	0	0	0	1	.000	0	0-0	0	.302	.356	7.43
World Series		**Pitching**																										
Year Tm	Age	G	GS	CG	GF	IP	BFP	H	R	ER	HR	SH	SF	HB	TBB	IBB	SO	WP	Bk	W	L	Pct	ShO	Sv-Op	Hld	OAvg	OOBP	ERA
1965 Min	29	2	0	0	2	4.0	18	5	2	2	0	1	0	0	2	1	4	0	0	0	0	—	0	0- 0	0	.333	.412	4.50
Postseason Totals		5	2	0	3	17.1	154	21	14	13	6	1	1	1	6	1	10	0	0	0	1	.000	0	0-0	0	.309	.368	6.75

LCS		Batting																							Fielding						
Year Tm	Age	G	AB	H	2B	3B	HR	TB	R	RBI	GW	TBB	IBB	SO	HBP	SH	SF	SB	CS	SB%	GDP	Avg	OBP	SLG	Pos	G	PO	A	E	DP	FPct
1969 Min	33	1	3	0	0	0	0	0	0	0	0	0	0	1	0	0	0	0	0	—	0	.000	.000	.000	P	1	0	1	0	0	1.000
1970 Min	34	2	1	0	0	0	0	0	0	1	0	0	0	0	0	0	0	0	0	—	0	.000	.000	.000	P	2	1	0	0	0	1.000
LCS Totals		3	4	0	0	0	0	0	0	1	0	0	0	1	0	0	0	0	0	—	0	.000	.000	.000	P	3	1	1	0	0	1.000
World Series		**Batting**																							**Fielding**						
Year Tm	Age	G	AB	H	2B	3B	HR	TB	R	RBI	GW	TBB	IBB	SO	HBP	SH	SF	SB	CS	SB%	GDP	Avg	OBP	SLG	Pos	G	PO	A	E	DP	FPct
1965 Min	29	2	0	0	0	0	0	0	0	0	0	0	0	0	0	0	0	0	0	—	0	—	—	—	P	2	0	1	0	0	1.000
Postseason Totals		5	4	0	0	0	0	0	0	1	0	0	0	1	0	0	0	0	0	—	0	.000	.000	.000	P	5	1	2	0	0	1.000

JOHNNY PESKY—John Michael Pesky—Bats: Left; Throws: Right

Ht: 5'9"; Wt: 168 lbs; Born: 9/27/1919 in Portland, Oregon; Debut: 4/14/1942

World Series		Batting																							Fielding						
Year Tm	Age	G	AB	H	2B	3B	HR	TB	R	RBI	GW	TBB	IBB	SO	HBP	SH	SF	SB	CS	SB%	GDP	Avg	OBP	SLG	Pos	G	PO	A	E	DP	FPct
1946 Bos	27	7	30	7	0	0	0	7	2	0	0	1	0	3	0	0	0	1	1	.50	0	.233	.258	.233	SS	7	13	17	4	5	.882

MARK PETKOVSEK—Mark Joseph Petkovsek—Throws: Right; Bats: Right

Ht: 6'0"; Wt: 185 lbs; Born: 11/18/1965 in Beaumont, Texas; Debut: 6/8/1991

Division Series		Pitching																										
Year Tm	Age	G	GS	CG	GF	IP	BFP	H	R	ER	HR	SH	SF	HB	TBB	IBB	SO	WP	Bk	W	L	Pct	ShO	Sv-Op	Hld	OAvg	OOBP	ERA
1996 StL	30	1	0	0	0	2.0	6	0	0	0	0	0	0	0	0	0	1	0	0	0	0	—	0	0- 0	0	.000	.000	0.00
LCS		**Pitching**																										
Year Tm	Age	G	GS	CG	GF	IP	BFP	H	R	ER	HR	SH	SF	HB	TBB	IBB	SO	WP	Bk	W	L	Pct	ShO	Sv-Op	Hld	OAvg	OOBP	ERA
1996 StL	30	6	0	0	0	7.1	35	11	6	6	1	0	1	0	3	1	7	1	0	0	1	.000	0	0- 0	1	.355	.400	7.36
Postseason Totals		7	0	0	0	9.1	82	11	6	6	1	0	1	0	3	1	8	1	0	0	1	.000	0	0-0	1	.297	.341	5.79

Division Series		Batting																							Fielding						
Year Tm	Age	G	AB	H	2B	3B	HR	TB	R	RBI	GW	TBB	IBB	SO	HBP	SH	SF	SB	CS	SB%	GDP	Avg	OBP	SLG	Pos	G	PO	A	E	DP	FPct
1996 StL	30	1	0	0	0	0	0	0	0	0	0	0	0	0	0	0	0	0	0	—	0	—	—	—	P	1	0	0	0	0	—
LCS		**Batting**																							**Fielding**						
Year Tm	Age	G	AB	H	2B	3B	HR	TB	R	RBI	GW	TBB	IBB	SO	HBP	SH	SF	SB	CS	SB%	GDP	Avg	OBP	SLG	Pos	G	PO	A	E	DP	FPct
1996 StL	30	6	0	0	0	0	0	0	0	0	0	0	0	0	0	0	0	0	0	—	0	—	—	—	P	6	1	2	1	1	.750
Postseason Totals		7	0	0	0	0	0	0	0	0	0	0	0	0	0	0	0	0	0	—	0	—	—	—	P	7	1	2	1	1	.750

RICO PETROCELLI—Americo Peter Petrocelli—Bats: Right; Throws: Right

Ht: 6'0"; Wt: 175 lbs; Born: 6/27/1943 in Brooklyn, New York; Debut: 9/21/1963

LCS		Batting																							Fielding						
Year Tm	Age	G	AB	H	2B	3B	HR	TB	R	RBI	GW	TBB	IBB	SO	HBP	SH	SF	SB	CS	SB%	GDP	Avg	OBP	SLG	Pos	G	PO	A	E	DP	FPct
1975 Bos	32	3	12	2	0	0	1	5	1	2	1	0	0	3	0	0	0	0	0	—	1	.167	.167	.417	3B	3	4	3	0	1	1.000
World Series		**Batting**																							**Fielding**						
Year Tm	Age	G	AB	H	2B	3B	HR	TB	R	RBI	GW	TBB	IBB	SO	HBP	SH	SF	SB	CS	SB%	GDP	Avg	OBP	SLG	Pos	G	PO	A	E	DP	FPct
1967 Bos	24	7	20	4	1	0	2	11	3	3	0	3	2	8	0	0	1	0	1	.00	0	.200	.292	.550	SS	7	11	20	2	1	.939
1975 Bos	32	7	26	8	1	0	0	9	3	4	0	3	0	6	0	0	0	0	0	—	0	.308	.379	.346	3B	7	7	14	0	1	1.000
WS Totals		14	46	12	2	0	2	20	6	7	0	6	2	14	0	0	1	0	1	.00	0	.261	.340	.435	3B	7	7	14	0	1	1.000
Postseason Totals		17	58	14	2	0	3	25	7	9	1	6	2	17	0	0	1	0	1	.00	1	.241	.308	.431	3B	10	11	17	0	2	1.000

DAN PETRY—Daniel Joseph Petry—Throws: Right; Bats: Right

Ht: 6'4"; Wt: 185 lbs; Born: 11/13/1958 in Palo Alto, California; Debut: 7/8/1979

LCS		Pitching																										
Year Tm	Age	G	GS	CG	GF	IP	BFP	H	R	ER	HR	SH	SF	HB	TBB	IBB	SO	WP	Bk	W	L	Pct	ShO	Sv-Op	Hld	OAvg	OOBP	ERA
1984 Det	25	1	1	0	0	7.0	28	4	2	2	0	0	0	0	1	0	4	0	0	0	0	—	0	0- 0	0	.148	.179	2.57
1987 Det	28	1	0	0	0	3.1	13	1	1	0	0	0	0	0	0	0	1	1	0	0	0	—	0	0- 0	0	.077	.077	0.00
LCS Totals		2	1	0	0	10.1	82	5	3	2	0	0	0	0	1	0	5	1	0	0	0	—	0	0-0	0	.125	.146	1.74
World Series		**Pitching**																										
Year Tm	Age	G	GS	CG	GF	IP	BFP	H	R	ER	HR	SH	SF	HB	TBB	IBB	SO	WP	Bk	W	L	Pct	ShO	Sv-Op	Hld	OAvg	OOBP	ERA
1984 Det	25	2	2	0	0	8.0	43	14	8	8	1	1	2	0	5	0	4	0	1	0	1	.000	0	0- 0	0	.400	.452	9.00
Postseason Totals		4	3	0	0	18.1	168	19	11	10	1	1	2	0	6	0	9	1	1	0	1	.000	0	0-0	0	.253	.301	4.91

LCS		Batting																							Fielding						
Year Tm	Age	G	AB	H	2B	3B	HR	TB	R	RBI	GW	TBB	IBB	SO	HBP	SH	SF	SB	CS	SB%	GDP	Avg	OBP	SLG	Pos	G	PO	A	E	DP	FPct
1984 Det	25	1	0	0	0	0	0	0	0	0	0	0	0	0	0	0	0	0	0	—	0	—	—	—	P	1	0	0	0	0	—
1987 Det	28	1	0	0	0	0	0	0	0	0	0	0	0	0	0	0	0	0	0	—	0	—	—	—	P	1	0	1	0	0	1.000
LCS Totals		2	0	0	0	0	0	0	0	0	0	0	0	0	0	0	0	0	0	—	0	—	—	—	P	2	0	1	0	0	1.000
World Series		**Batting**																							**Fielding**						
Year Tm	Age	G	AB	H	2B	3B	HR	TB	R	RBI	GW	TBB	IBB	SO	HBP	SH	SF	SB	CS	SB%	GDP	Avg	OBP	SLG	Pos	G	PO	A	E	DP	FPct
1984 Det	25	2	0	0	0	0	0	0	0	0	0	0	0	0	0	0	0	0	0	—	0	—	—	—	P	2	1	1	0	0	1.000
Postseason Totals		4	0	0	0	0	0	0	0	0	0	0	0	0	0	0	0	0	0	—	0	—	—	—	P	4	1	2	0	0	1.000

GARY PETTIS—Gary George Pettis—Bats: Both; Throws: Right

Ht: 6'1"; Wt: 165 lbs; Born: 4/3/1958 in Oakland, California; Debut: 9/13/1982

LCS		Batting																							Fielding						
Year Tm	Age	G	AB	H	2B	3B	HR	TB	R	RBI	GW	TBB	IBB	SO	HBP	SH	SF	SB	CS	SB%	GDP	Avg	OBP	SLG	Pos	G	PO	A	E	DP	FPct
1986 Cal	28	7	26	9	1	0	1	13	4	4	0	3	0	5	0	2	0	0	2	.00	0	.346	.414	.500	OF	7	28	0	1	0	.966

ANDY PETTITTE—Andrew Eugene Pettitte—Throws: Left; Bats: Left

Ht: 6'5"; Wt: 235 lbs; Born: 6/15/1972 in Baton Rouge, Louisiana; Debut: 4/29/1995

Division Series		Pitching																										
Year Tm	Age	G	GS	CG	GF	IP	BFP	H	R	ER	HR	SH	SF	HB	TBB	IBB	SO	WP	Bk	W	L	Pct	ShO	Sv-Op	Hld	OAvg	OOBP	ERA
1995 NYA	23	1	1	0	0	7.0	30	9	4	4	1	0	1	0	3	0	0	0	0	0	0	—	0	0- 0	0	.346	.400	5.14
1996 NYA	24	1	1	0	0	6.1	28	4	4	4	2	1	0	0	6	0	3	1	0	0	0	—	0	0- 0	0	.190	.370	5.68
1997 NYA	25	2	2	0	0	11.2	49	15	11	11	1	2	1	0	1	0	5	0	0	0	2	.000	0	0- 0	0	.333	.340	8.49
DS Totals		4	4	0	0	25.0	214	28	19	19	4	3	2	0	10	0	8	1	0	0	2	.000	0	0-0	0	.304	.365	6.84
LCS		Pitching																										
Year Tm	Age	G	GS	CG	GF	IP	BFP	H	R	ER	HR	SH	SF	HB	TBB	IBB	SO	WP	Bk	W	L	Pct	ShO	Sv-Op	Hld	OAvg	OOBP	ERA
1996 NYA	24	2	2	0	0	15.0	60	10	6	6	4	0	1	0	5	0	7	0	1	1	0	1.000	0	0- 0	0	.185	.250	3.60
World Series		Pitching																										
Year Tm	Age	G	GS	CG	GF	IP	BFP	H	R	ER	HR	SH	SF	HB	TBB	IBB	SO	WP	Bk	W	L	Pct	ShO	Sv-Op	Hld	OAvg	OOBP	ERA
1996 NYA	24	2	2	0	0	10.2	45	11	7	7	1	1	0	0	4	0	5	0	0	1	1	.500	0	0- 0	0	.275	.341	5.91
Postseason Totals		8	8	0	0	50.2	424	49	32	32	9	4	3	0	19	0	20	1	1	2	3	.400	0	0-0	0	.263	.327	5.68

Division Series		Batting																							Fielding						
Year Tm	Age	G	AB	H	2B	3B	HR	TB	R	RBI	GW	TBB	IBB	SO	HBP	SH	SF	SB	CS	SB%	GDP	Avg	OBP	SLG	Pos	G	PO	A	E	DP	FPct
1995 NYA	23	1	0	0	0	0	0	0	0	0	0	0	0	0	0	0	0	0	0	—	0	—	—	—	P	1	0	3	0	0	1.000
1996 NYA	24	1	0	0	0	0	0	0	0	0	0	0	0	0	0	0	0	0	0	—	0	—	—	—	P	1	0	2	0	1	1.000
1997 NYA	25	2	0	0	0	0	0	0	0	0	0	0	0	0	0	0	0	0	0	—	0	—	—	—	P	2	1	5	0	0	1.000
DS Totals		4	0	0	0	0	0	0	0	0	0	0	0	0	0	0	0	0	0	—	0	—	—	—	P	4	1	10	0	1	1.000
LCS		Batting																							Fielding						
Year Tm	Age	G	AB	H	2B	3B	HR	TB	R	RBI	GW	TBB	IBB	SO	HBP	SH	SF	SB	CS	SB%	GDP	Avg	OBP	SLG	Pos	G	PO	A	E	DP	FPct
1996 NYA	24	2	0	0	0	0	0	0	0	0	0	0	0	0	0	0	0	0	0	—	0	—	—	—	P	2	2	0	0	0	1.000
World Series		Batting																							Fielding						
Year Tm	Age	G	AB	H	2B	3B	HR	TB	R	RBI	GW	TBB	IBB	SO	HBP	SH	SF	SB	CS	SB%	GDP	Avg	OBP	SLG	Pos	G	PO	A	E	DP	FPct
1996 NYA	24	2	4	0	0	0	0	0	0	0	0	0	0	1	0	0	0	0	0	—	0	.000	.000	.000	P	2	0	5	0	1	1.000
Postseason Totals		8	4	0	0	0	0	0	0	0	0	0	0	1	0	0	0	0	0	—	0	.000	.000	.000	P	8	3	15	0	2	1.000

JEFF PFEFFER—Edward Joseph Pfeffer—Throws: Right; Bats: Right

Ht: 6'3"; Wt: 210 lbs; Born: 3/4/1888 in Seymour, Illinois; Debut: 4/16/1911; Died: 8/15/1972

World Series		Pitching																										
Year Tm	Age	G	GS	CG	GF	IP	BFP	H	R	ER	HR	SH	SF	HB	TBB	IBB	SO	WP	Bk	W	L	Pct	ShO	Sv-Op	Hld	OAvg	OOBP	ERA
1916 Bro	28	3	1	0	2	10.2	42	7	5	2	0	1	1	0	4	0	5	2	0	0	1	.000	0	1- 1	0	.194	.268	1.69
1920 Bro	32	1	0	0	1	3.0	15	4	1	1	0	0	0	0	2	1	1	1	0	0	0	—	0	0- 0	0	.308	.400	3.00
WS Totals		4	1	0	3	13.2	114	11	6	3	0	1	1	0	6	1	6	3	0	0	1	.000	0	1-1	0	.224	.304	1.98

World Series		Batting																							Fielding						
Year Tm	Age	G	AB	H	2B	3B	HR	TB	R	RBI	GW	TBB	IBB	SO	HBP	SH	SF	SB	CS	SB%	GDP	Avg	OBP	SLG	Pos	G	PO	A	E	DP	FPct
1916 Bro	28	4	4	1	0	0	0	1	0	0	0	0	0	2	0	0	0	0	0	—	0	.250	.250	.250	P	3	0	2	0	0	1.000
1920 Bro	32	1	1	0	0	0	0	0	0	0	0	0	0	0	0	0	0	0	0	—	0	.000	.000	.000	P	1	0	0	0	0	—
WS Totals		5	5	1	0	0	0	1	0	0	0	0	0	2	0	0	0	0	0	—	0	.200	.200	.200	P	4	0	2	0	0	1.000

JACK PFIESTER—John Albert Pfiester—Nickname: Jack the Giant Killer—Throws: Left; Bats: Right

Ht: 5'11"; Wt: 180 lbs; Born: 5/24/1878 in Cincinnati, Ohio; Debut: 9/8/1903; Died: 9/3/1953

World Series		Pitching																										
Year Tm	Age	G	GS	CG	GF	IP	BFP	H	R	ER	HR	SH	SF	HB	TBB	IBB	SO	WP	Bk	W	L	Pct	ShO	Sv-Op	Hld	OAvg	OOBP	ERA
1906 ChN	28	2	1	1	0	10.1	43	7	7	7	0	2	0	2	3	0	11	0	0	0	2	.000	0	0- 0	0	.194	.293	6.10
1907 ChN	29	1	1	1	0	9.0	34	9	1	1	0	0	0	1	1	0	3	0	0	1	0	1.000	0	0- 0	0	.281	.324	1.00
1908 ChN	30	1	1	0	0	8.0	37	10	8	7	0	1	1	0	3	0	1	0	0	0	1	.000	0	0- 0	0	.313	.361	7.88
1910 ChN	32	1	0	0	1	6.2	31	9	5	0	0	0	0	0	1	0	1	0	0	0	0	—	0	0- 0	0	.300	.323	0.00
WS Totals		5	3	2	1	34.0	290	35	21	15	0	3	1	3	8	0	16	0	0	1	3	.250	0	0-0	0	.269	.324	3.97

World Series		Batting																							Fielding						
Year Tm	Age	G	AB	H	2B	3B	HR	TB	R	RBI	GW	TBB	IBB	SO	HBP	SH	SF	SB	CS	SB%	GDP	Avg	OBP	SLG	Pos	G	PO	A	E	DP	FPct
1906 ChN	28	2	2	0	0	0	0	0	0	0	0	0	0	1	0	0	0	0	0	—	0	.000	.000	.000	P	2	0	2	1	0	.667
1907 ChN	29	1	2	0	0	0	0	0	0	0	0	0	0	1	0	1	0	0	0	—	0	.000	.000	.000	P	1	0	0	0	0	—
1908 ChN	30	1	2	0	0	0	0	0	0	0	0	0	0	2	0	0	0	0	0	—	0	.000	.000	.000	P	1	0	0	0	0	—
1910 ChN	32	1	2	0	0	0	0	0	0	0	0	0	0	1	0	0	0	0	0	—	0	.000	.000	.000	P	1	0	1	0	0	1.000
WS Totals		5	8	0	0	0	0	0	0	0	0	0	0	5	0	1	0	0	0	—	0	.000	.000	.000	P	5	0	3	1	0	.750

ED PHELPS—Edward Jaykill Phelps—Nickname: Yaller—Bats: Right; Throws: Right

Ht: 5'11"; Wt: 185 lbs; Born: 3/3/1879 in Albany, New York; Debut: 9/3/1902; Died: 1/31/1942

World Series		Batting																							Fielding						
Year Tm	Age	G	AB	H	2B	3B	HR	TB	R	RBI	GW	TBB	IBB	SO	HBP	SH	SF	SB	CS	SB%	GDP	Avg	OBP	SLG	Pos	G	PO	A	E	DP	FPct
1903 Pit	24	8	26	6	2	0	0	8	1	1	1	1	0	6	0	1	0	0	0	—	0	.231	.259	.308	C	7	36	5	2	0	.953

KEN PHELPS—Kenneth Allen Phelps—Bats: Left; Throws: Left

Ht: 6'1"; Wt: 209 lbs; Born: 8/6/1954 in Seattle, Washington; Debut: 9/20/1980

LCS		Batting																							Fielding						
Year Tm	Age	G	AB	H	2B	3B	HR	TB	R	RBI	GW	TBB	IBB	SO	HBP	SH	SF	SB	CS	SB%	GDP	Avg	OBP	SLG	Pos	G	PO	A	E	DP	FPct
1989 Oak	35	1	1	1	1	0	0	2	0	0	0	0	0	0	0	0	0	0	0	—	0	1.000	1.000	2.000	—						
World Series		Batting																							Fielding						
Year Tm	Age	G	AB	H	2B	3B	HR	TB	R	RBI	GW	TBB	IBB	SO	HBP	SH	SF	SB	CS	SB%	GDP	Avg	OBP	SLG	Pos	G	PO	A	E	DP	FPct
1989 Oak	35	1	1	0	0	0	0	0	0	0	0	0	0	0	0	0	0	0	0	—	0	.000	.000	.000	—						
Postseason Totals		2	2	1	1	0	0	2	0	0	0	0	0	0	0	0	0	0	0	—	0	.500	.500	1.000	—	0	0	0	0	0	—

DAVE PHILLEY—David Earl Philley—Bats: Both; Throws: Right

Ht: 6'0"; Wt: 188 lbs; Born: 5/16/1920 in Paris, Texas; Debut: 9/6/1941

World Series		Batting																							Fielding						
Year Tm	Age	G	AB	H	2B	3B	HR	TB	R	RBI	GW	TBB	IBB	SO	HBP	SH	SF	SB	CS	SB%	GDP	Avg	OBP	SLG	Pos	G	PO	A	E	DP	FPct
1954 Cle	34	4	8	1	0	0	0	1	0	0	0	1	0	3	0	0	0	0	0	—	0	.125	.222	.125	OF	2	1	0	0	0	1.000

DEACON PHILLIPPE—Charles Louis Phillippe—Throws: Right; Bats: Right

Ht: 6'0"; Wt: 180 lbs; Born: 5/23/1872 in Rural Retreat, Virginia; Debut: 4/21/1899; Died: 3/30/1952

World Series		Pitching																										
Year Tm	Age	G	GS	CG	GF	IP	BFP	H	R	ER	HR	SH	SF	HB	TBB	IBB	SO	WP	Bk	W	L	Pct	ShO	Sv-Op	Hld	OAvg	OOBP	ERA
1903 Pit	31	5	5	5	0	44.0	178	38	19	14	0	3	0	1	3	0	22	1	0	3	2	.600	0	0- 0	0	.222	.240	2.86
1909 Pit	37	2	0	0	2	6.0	23	2	0	0	0	2	0	0	1	0	2	0	0	0	0	—	0	0- 0	0	.100	.143	0.00
WS Totals		7	5	5	2	50.0	402	40	19	14	0	5	0	1	4	0	24	1	0	3	2	.600	0	0-0	0	.209	.230	2.52

World Series		Batting																							Fielding						
Year Tm	Age	G	AB	H	2B	3B	HR	TB	R	RBI	GW	TBB	IBB	SO	HBP	SH	SF	SB	CS	SB%	GDP	Avg	OBP	SLG	Pos	G	PO	A	E	DP	FPct
1903 Pit	31	5	18	4	0	0	0	4	1	1	0	0	0	3	0	0	0	0	0	—	0	.222	.222	.222	P	5	2	9	1	0	.917
1909 Pit	37	2	1	0	0	0	0	0	0	0	0	0	0	1	0	0	0	0	0	—	0	.000	.000	.000	P	2	1	2	2	0	.600
WS Totals		7	19	4	0	0	0	4	1	1	0	0	0	4	0	0	0	0	0	—	0	.211	.211	.211	P	7	3	11	3	0	.824

BUBBA PHILLIPS—John Melvin Phillips—Bats: Right; Throws: Right

Ht: 5'9"; Wt: 180 lbs; Born: 2/24/1928 in West Point, Mississippi; Debut: 4/30/1955; Died: 6/22/1993

World Series		Batting																							Fielding						
Year Tm	Age	G	AB	H	2B	3B	HR	TB	R	RBI	GW	TBB	IBB	SO	HBP	SH	SF	SB	CS	SB%	GDP	Avg	OBP	SLG	Pos	G	PO	A	E	DP	FPct
1959 ChA	31	3	10	3	1	0	0	4	0	0	0	0	0	0	0	0	0	0	0	—	1	.300	.300	.400	3B	3	3	3	0	0	1.000
																									OF	1	3	0	0	0	1.000

JACK PHILLIPS—Jack Dorn Phillips—Nickname: Stretch—Bats: Right; Throws: Right

Ht: 6'4"; Wt: 193 lbs; Born: 9/6/1921 in Clarence, New York; Debut: 8/22/1947

World Series — Batting / Fielding

Year Tm	Age	G	AB	H	2B	3B	HR	TB	R	RBI	GW	TBB	IBB	SO	HBP	SH	SF	SB	CS	SB%	GDP	Avg	OBP	SLG	Pos	G	PO	A	E	DP	FPct
1947 NYA	26	2	2	0	0	0	0	0	0	0	0	0	0	0	0	0	0	0	0	—	0	.000	.000	.000	1B	1	4	0	0	1	1.000

MIKE PHILLIPS—Michael Dwaine Phillips—Bats: Left; Throws: Right

Ht: 6'0"; Wt: 170 lbs; Born: 8/19/1950 in Beaumont, Texas; Debut: 4/15/1973

Division Series — Batting / Fielding

Year Tm	Age	G	AB	H	2B	3B	HR	TB	R	RBI	GW	TBB	IBB	SO	HBP	SH	SF	SB	CS	SB%	GDP	Avg	OBP	SLG	Pos	G	PO	A	E	DP	FPct
1981 Mon	31	1	1	0	0	0	0	0	0	0	0	0	0	0	0	0	0	0	0	—	0	.000	.000	.000	2B	1	0	1	0	0	1.000

TONY PHILLIPS—Keith Anthony Phillips—Bats: Both; Throws: Right

Ht: 5'9"; Wt: 155 lbs; Born: 4/25/1959 in Atlanta, Georgia; Debut: 5/10/1982

LCS — Batting / Fielding

Year Tm	Age	G	AB	H	2B	3B	HR	TB	R	RBI	GW	TBB	IBB	SO	HBP	SH	SF	SB	CS	SB%	GDP	Avg	OBP	SLG	Pos	G	PO	A	E	DP	FPct
1988 Oak	29	2	7	2	1	0	0	3	0	0	0	1	0	3	0	0	0	0	0	—	0	.286	.375	.429	2B	1	4	0	0	1	1.000
																									OF	2	6	0	0	0	1.000
1989 Oak	30	5	18	3	1	0	0	4	1	1	0	2	0	4	0	0	0	2	0	1.00	0	.167	.250	.222	2B	3	2	11	0	2	1.000
																									3B	3	2	3	0	0	1.000
LCS Totals		7	25	5	2	0	0	7	1	1	0	3	0	7	0	0	0	2	0	1.00	0	.200	.286	.280	2B	4	6	11	0	3	1.000

World Series — Batting / Fielding

Year Tm	Age	G	AB	H	2B	3B	HR	TB	R	RBI	GW	TBB	IBB	SO	HBP	SH	SF	SB	CS	SB%	GDP	Avg	OBP	SLG	Pos	G	PO	A	E	DP	FPct
1988 Oak	29	2	4	1	0	0	0	1	1	0	0	1	0	2	0	0	0	0	0	—	0	.250	.400	.250	2B	1	3	5	0	1	1.000
																									OF	1	0	0	0	0	—
1989 Oak	30	4	17	4	1	0	1	8	2	3	1	0	0	3	0	0	0	0	0	—	0	.235	.235	.471	2B	4	7	13	0	1	1.000
																									3B	2	0	2	0	0	1.000
																									OF	1	1	0	0	0	1.000
WS Totals		6	21	5	1	0	1	9	3	3	1	1	0	5	0	0	0	0	0	—	0	.238	.273	.429	2B	5	10	18	0	2	1.000
Postseason Totals		13	46	10	3	0	1	16	4	4	1	4	0	12	0	0	0	2	0	1.00	0	.217	.280	.348	2B	9	16	29	0	5	1.000

TOM PHOEBUS—Thomas Harold Phoebus—Throws: Right; Bats: Right

Ht: 5'8"; Wt: 185 lbs; Born: 4/7/1942 in Baltimore, Maryland; Debut: 9/15/1966

World Series — Pitching

Year Tm	Age	G	GS	CG	GF	IP	BFP	H	R	ER	HR	SH	SF	HB	TBB	IBB	SO	WP	Bk	W	L	Pct	ShO	Sv-Op	Hld	OAvg	OOBP	ERA
1970 Bal	28	1	0	0	0	1.2	5	1	0	0	0	0	0	0	0	0	0	0	0	1	0	1.000	0	0-0	0	.200	.200	0.00

World Series — Batting / Fielding

Year Tm	Age	G	AB	H	2B	3B	HR	TB	R	RBI	GW	TBB	IBB	SO	HBP	SH	SF	SB	CS	SB%	GDP	Avg	OBP	SLG	Pos	G	PO	A	E	DP	FPct
1970 Bal	28	1	0	0	0	0	0	0	0	0	0	0	0	0	0	0	0	0	0	—	0	—	—	—	P	1	0	0	0	0	—

MIKE PIAZZA—Michael Joseph Piazza—Bats: Right; Throws: Right

Ht: 6'3"; Wt: 200 lbs; Born: 9/4/1968 in Norristown, Pennsylvania; Debut: 9/1/1992

Division Series — Batting / Fielding

Year Tm	Age	G	AB	H	2B	3B	HR	TB	R	RBI	GW	TBB	IBB	SO	HBP	SH	SF	SB	CS	SB%	GDP	Avg	OBP	SLG	Pos	G	PO	A	E	DP	FPct
1995 LA	27	3	14	3	1	0	1	7	1	1	0	0	0	2	0	0	0	0	0	—	0	.214	.214	.500	C	3	31	0	0	0	1.000
1996 LA	28	3	10	3	0	0	0	3	1	2	0	1	0	2	0	0	1	0	0	—	0	.300	.333	.300	C	3	25	4	0	2	1.000
DS Totals		6	24	6	1	0	1	10	2	3	0	1	0	4	0	0	1	0	0	—	0	.250	.269	.417	C	6	56	4	0	2	1.000

ROB PICCIOLO—Robert Michael Picciolo—Bats: Right; Throws: Right

Ht: 6'2"; Wt: 185 lbs; Born: 2/4/1953 in Santa Monica, California; Debut: 4/9/1977

Division Series — Batting / Fielding

Year Tm	Age	G	AB	H	2B	3B	HR	TB	R	RBI	GW	TBB	IBB	SO	HBP	SH	SF	SB	CS	SB%	GDP	Avg	OBP	SLG	Pos	G	PO	A	E	DP	FPct
1981 Oak	28	1	3	1	0	0	0	1	0	0	0	0	0	0	0	0	0	0	0	—	0	.333	.333	.333	SS	1	1	2	0	0	1.000

LCS — Batting / Fielding

Year Tm	Age	G	AB	H	2B	3B	HR	TB	R	RBI	GW	TBB	IBB	SO	HBP	SH	SF	SB	CS	SB%	GDP	Avg	OBP	SLG	Pos	G	PO	A	E	DP	FPct
1981 Oak	28	2	5	1	0	0	0	1	1	0	0	0	0	2	0	0	0	0	0	—	0	.200	.200	.200	SS	2	5	6	1	1	.917
Postseason Totals		3	8	2	0	0	0	2	1	0	0	0	0	2	0	0	0	0	0	—	0	.250	.250	.250	SS	3	6	8	1	1	.933

CHARLIE PICK—Charles Thomas Pick—Bats: Left; Throws: Right

Ht: 5'10"; Wt: 160 lbs; Born: 4/10/1888 in Brookneal, Virginia; Debut: 9/20/1914; Died: 6/26/1954

World Series — Batting / Fielding

Year Tm	Age	G	AB	H	2B	3B	HR	TB	R	RBI	GW	TBB	IBB	SO	HBP	SH	SF	SB	CS	SB%	GDP	Avg	OBP	SLG	Pos	G	PO	A	E	DP	FPct
1918 ChN	30	6	18	7	1	0	0	8	2	0	0	1	0	1	0	0	0	1	1	.50	0	.389	.421	.444	2B	6	12	11	0	3	1.000

BILLY PIERCE—Walter William Pierce—Throws: Left; Bats: Left

Ht: 5'10"; Wt: 160 lbs; Born: 4/2/1927 in Detroit, Michigan; Debut: 6/1/1945

World Series — Pitching

Year Tm	Age	G	GS	CG	GF	IP	BFP	H	R	ER	HR	SH	SF	HB	TBB	IBB	SO	WP	Bk	W	L	Pct	ShO	Sv-Op	Hld	OAvg	OOBP	ERA
1959 ChA	32	3	0	0	0	4.0	17	2	0	0	0	2	0	0	2	1	3	0	0	0	0	—	0	0-0	0	.154	.267	0.00
1962 SF	35	2	2	1	0	15.0	55	8	5	4	1	0	0	0	2	1	5	0	0	1	1	.500	0	0-0	0	.151	.182	2.40
WS Totals		5	2	1	0	19.0	144	10	5	4	1	2	0	0	4	2	8	0	0	1	1	.500	0	0-0	0	.152	.200	1.89

World Series — Batting / Fielding

Year Tm	Age	G	AB	H	2B	3B	HR	TB	R	RBI	GW	TBB	IBB	SO	HBP	SH	SF	SB	CS	SB%	GDP	Avg	OBP	SLG	Pos	G	PO	A	E	DP	FPct
1959 ChA	32	3	0	0	0	0	0	0	0	0	0	0	0	0	0	0	0	0	0	—	0	—	—	—	P	3	0	0	1	0	.000
1962 SF	35	2	5	0	0	0	0	0	0	0	0	0	0	1	0	0	0	0	0	—	0	.000	.000	.000	P	2	1	0	0	0	1.000
WS Totals		5	5	0	0	0	0	0	0	0	0	0	0	1	0	0	0	0	0	—	0	.000	.000	.000	P	5	1	0	1	0	.500

BILL PIERCY—William Benton Piercy—Nickname: Wild Bill—Throws: Right; Bats: Right

Ht: 6'1"; Wt: 170 lbs; Born: 5/2/1896 in El Monte, California; Debut: 10/3/1917; Died: 8/28/1951

World Series — Pitching

Year Tm	Age	G	GS	CG	GF	IP	BFP	H	R	ER	HR	SH	SF	HB	TBB	IBB	SO	WP	Bk	W	L	Pct	ShO	Sv-Op	Hld	OAvg	OOBP	ERA
1921 NYA	25	1	0	0	1	1.0	4	2	0	0	0	0	0	0	0	0	2	0	0	0	0	—	0	0-0	0	.500	.500	0.00

World Series — Batting / Fielding

Year Tm	Age	G	AB	H	2B	3B	HR	TB	R	RBI	GW	TBB	IBB	SO	HBP	SH	SF	SB	CS	SB%	GDP	Avg	OBP	SLG	Pos	G	PO	A	E	DP	FPct
1921 NYA	25	1	0	0	0	0	0	0	0	0	0	0	0	0	0	0	0	0	0	—	0	—	—	—	P	1	0	0	0	0	—

JOE PIGNATANO—Joseph Benjamin Pignatano—Bats: Right; Throws: Right

Ht: 5'10"; Wt: 180 lbs; Born: 8/4/1929 in Brooklyn, New York; Debut: 4/28/1957

World Series — Batting / Fielding

Year Tm	Age	G	AB	H	2B	3B	HR	TB	R	RBI	GW	TBB	IBB	SO	HBP	SH	SF	SB	CS	SB%	GDP	Avg	OBP	SLG	Pos	G	PO	A	E	DP	FPct
1959 LA	30	1	0	0	0	0	0	0	0	0	0	0	0	0	0	0	0	0	0	—	0	—	—	—	C	1	1	0	0	0	1.000

HORACIO PINA—Throws: Right; Bats: Right

Ht: 6'2"; Wt: 177 lbs; Born: 3/12/1945 in Coahuila, Mexico; Debut: 8/14/1968

LCS — Pitching

Year Tm	Age	G	GS	CG	GF	IP	BFP	H	R	ER	HR	SH	SF	HB	TBB	IBB	SO	WP	Bk	W	L	Pct	ShO	Sv-Op	Hld	OAvg	OOBP	ERA
1973 Oak	28	1	0	0	0	2.0	11	3	0	0	0	0	0	1	1	0	1	0	0	0	0	—	0	0-0	0	.333	.455	0.00

World Series — Pitching

Year Tm	Age	G	GS	CG	GF	IP	BFP	H	R	ER	HR	SH	SF	HB	TBB	IBB	SO	WP	Bk	W	L	Pct	ShO	Sv-Op	Hld	OAvg	OOBP	ERA
1973 Oak	28	2	0	0	0	3.0	16	6	2	0	0	0	0	1	2	1	0	0	0	0	0	—	0	0-1	0	.462	.563	0.00
Postseason Totals		3	0	0	0	5.0	54	9	2	0	0	0	0	2	3	1	1	0	0	0	0	—	0	0-1	0	.409	.519	0.00

LCS — Batting / Fielding

Year Tm	Age	G	AB	H	2B	3B	HR	TB	R	RBI	GW	TBB	IBB	SO	HBP	SH	SF	SB	CS	SB%	GDP	Avg	OBP	SLG	Pos	G	PO	A	E	DP	FPct
1973 Oak	28	1	0	0	0	0	0	0	0	0	0	0	0	0	0	0	0	0	0	—	0	—	—	—	P	1	0	0	0	0	—

World Series — Batting / Fielding

Year Tm	Age	G	AB	H	2B	3B	HR	TB	R	RBI	GW	TBB	IBB	SO	HBP	SH	SF	SB	CS	SB%	GDP	Avg	OBP	SLG	Pos	G	PO	A	E	DP	FPct
1973 Oak	28	2	0	0	0	0	0	0	0	0	0	0	0	0	0	0	0	0	0	—	0	—	—	—	P	2	0	0	0	0	—
Postseason Totals		3	0	0	0	0	0	0	0	0	0	0	0	0	0	0	0	0	0	—	0	—	—	—	P	3	0	0	0	0	—

LOU PINIELLA—Louis Victor Piniella—Nickname: Sweet Lou—Bats: Right; Throws: Right

Ht: 6'0"; Wt: 182 lbs; Born: 8/28/1943 in Tampa, Florida; Debut: 9/4/1964

Division Series — Batting / Fielding

Year Tm	Age	G	AB	H	2B	3B	HR	TB	R	RBI	GW	TBB	IBB	SO	HBP	SH	SF	SB	CS	SB%	GDP	Avg	OBP	SLG	Pos	G	PO	A	E	DP	FPct
1981 NYA	38	4	10	2	1	0	1	6	1	3	1	0	0	0	0	0	0	0	0	—	1	.200	.200	.600	—						

LCS — Batting / Fielding

Year Tm	Age	G	AB	H	2B	3B	HR	TB	R	RBI	GW	TBB	IBB	SO	HBP	SH	SF	SB	CS	SB%	GDP	Avg	OBP	SLG	Pos	G	PO	A	E	DP	FPct
1976 NYA	33	4	11	3	1	0	0	4	1	0	0	0	0	1	0	0	0	0	0	—	0	.273	.273	.364	—						
1977 NYA	34	5	21	7	3	0	0	10	1	2	0	0	0	1	0	0	0	0	0	—	0	.333	.333	.476	OF	4	9	1	0	0	1.000
1978 NYA	35	4	17	4	0	0	0	4	2	0	0	0	0	3	0	0	0	0	0	—	0	.235	.235	.235	OF	4	13	0	0	0	1.000
1980 NYA	37	2	5	1	0	0	1	4	1	1	0	2	0	1	0	0	0	0	0	—	0	.200	.429	.800	OF	2	5	0	0	0	1.000
1981 NYA	38	3	5	3	0	0	1	6	2	3	0	0	0	0	0	0	0	0	0	—	0	.600	.600	1.200	OF	1	0	0	0	0	—
LCS Totals		18	59	18	4	0	2	28	7	6	0	2	0	6	0	0	0	0	0	—	0	.305	.328	.475	OF	11	27	1	0	0	1.000

World Series — Batting / Fielding

Year Tm	Age	G	AB	H	2B	3B	HR	TB	R	RBI	GW	TBB	IBB	SO	HBP	SH	SF	SB	CS	SB%	GDP	Avg	OBP	SLG	Pos	G	PO	A	E	DP	FPct
1976 NYA	33	4	9	3	1	0	0	4	1	0	0	0	0	0	0	0	0	0	0	—	0	.333	.333	.444	OF	2	0	0	0	0	—
1977 NYA	34	6	22	6	0	0	0	6	1	3	1	0	0	3	1	0	1	0	0	—	1	.273	.292	.273	OF	6	16	1	1	0	.944
1978 NYA	35	6	25	7	0	0	0	7	3	4	1	0	0	0	0	0	0	1	0	1.00	1	.280	.280	.280	OF	6	14	1	0	1	1.000
1981 NYA	38	6	16	7	1	0	0	8	2	3	0	0	0	1	0	0	0	1	0	1.00	1	.438	.438	.500	OF	4	7	1	0	0	1.000
WS Totals		22	72	23	2	0	0	25	7	10	2	0	0	4	1	0	1	2	0	1.00	3	.319	.324	.347	OF	18	37	3	1	1	.976
Postseason Totals		44	141	43	7	0	3	59	15	19	3	2	0	10	1	0	1	2	0	1.00	4	.305	.317	.418	OF	29	64	4	1	1	.986

VADA PINSON—Vada Edward Pinson—Bats: Left; Throws: Left

Ht: 5'11"; Wt: 170 lbs; Born: 8/11/1938 in Memphis, Tennessee; Debut: 4/15/1958; Died: 10/21/1995

World Series — Batting / Fielding

Year Tm	Age	G	AB	H	2B	3B	HR	TB	R	RBI	GW	TBB	IBB	SO	HBP	SH	SF	SB	CS	SB%	GDP	Avg	OBP	SLG	Pos	G	PO	A	E	DP	FPct
1961 Cin	23	5	22	2	1	0	0	3	0	0	0	0	0	1	0	0	0	0	0	—	0	.091	.091	.136	OF	5	18	1	1	0	.950

GEORGE PIPGRAS—George William Pipgras—Nickname: Danish Viking—Throws: Right; Bats: Right

Ht: 6'1"; Wt: 185 lbs; Born: 12/20/1899 in Ida Grove, Iowa; Debut: 6/9/1923; Died: 10/19/1986

World Series — Pitching

Year Tm	Age	G	GS	CG	GF	IP	BFP	H	R	ER	HR	SH	SF	HB	TBB	IBB	SO	WP	Bk	W	L	Pct	ShO	Sv-Op	Hld	OAvg	OOBP	ERA
1927 NYA	27	1	1	1	0	9.0	34	7	2	2	0	0	2	0	1	0	2	0	0	1	0	1.000	0	0- 0	0	.226	.235	2.00
1928 NYA	28	1	1	1	0	9.0	36	4	3	2	0	0	0	0	4	0	8	0	0	1	0	1.000	0	0- 0	0	.125	.222	2.00
1932 NYA	32	1	1	0	0	8.0	35	9	5	4	2	0	0	0	3	0	1	0	0	1	0	1.000	0	0- 0	0	.281	.343	4.50
WS Totals		3	3	2	0	26.0	210	20	10	8	2	0	2	0	8	0	11	0	0	3	0	1.000	0	0-0	0	.211	.267	2.77

World Series — Batting / Fielding

Year Tm	Age	G	AB	H	2B	3B	HR	TB	R	RBI	GW	TBB	IBB	SO	HBP	SH	SF	SB	CS	SB%	GDP	Avg	OBP	SLG	Pos	G	PO	A	E	DP	FPct
1927 NYA	27	1	3	1	0	0	0	1	0	0	0	1	0	1	0	0	0	0	0	—	0	.333	.500	.333	P	1	1	2	0	0	1.000
1928 NYA	28	1	2	0	0	0	0	0	0	1	0	0	0	1	1	1	0	0	0	—	0	.000	.333	.000	P	1	0	1	0	0	1.000
1932 NYA	32	1	5	0	0	0	0	0	0	0	0	0	0	5	0	0	0	0	0	—	0	.000	.000	.000	P	1	0	0	0	0	—
WS Totals		3	10	1	0	0	0	1	0	1	0	1	0	7	1	1	0	0	0	—	0	.100	.250	.100	P	3	1	3	0	0	1.000

WALLY PIPP—Walter Clement Pipp—Bats: Left; Throws: Left

Ht: 6'1"; Wt: 180 lbs; Born: 2/17/1893 in Chicago, Illinois; Debut: 6/29/1913; Died: 1/11/1965

World Series — Batting / Fielding

Year Tm	Age	G	AB	H	2B	3B	HR	TB	R	RBI	GW	TBB	IBB	SO	HBP	SH	SF	SB	CS	SB%	GDP	Avg	OBP	SLG	Pos	G	PO	A	E	DP	FPct
1921 NYA	28	8	26	4	1	0	0	5	1	2	0	2	0	3	0	3	0	1	1	.50	0	.154	.214	.192	1B	8	91	1	0	5	1.000
1922 NYA	29	5	21	6	1	0	0	7	0	3	0	0	0	2	0	0	0	1	0	1.00	0	.286	.286	.333	1B	5	51	3	0	7	1.000
1923 NYA	30	6	20	5	0	0	0	5	2	2	0	4	0	1	0	0	1	0	0	—	0	.250	.360	.250	1B	6	63	3	0	6	1.000
WS Totals		19	67	15	2	0	0	17	3	7	0	6	0	6	0	3	1	2	1	.67	0	.224	.284	.254	1B	19	205	7	0	18	1.000

JOE PITTMAN—Joseph Wayne Pittman—Bats: Right; Throws: Right

Ht: 6'1"; Wt: 180 lbs; Born: 1/1/1954 in Houston, Texas; Debut: 4/25/1981

Division Series — Batting / Fielding

Year Tm	Age	G	AB	H	2B	3B	HR	TB	R	RBI	GW	TBB	IBB	SO	HBP	SH	SF	SB	CS	SB%	GDP	Avg	OBP	SLG	Pos	G	PO	A	E	DP	FPct
1981 Hou	27	2	2	0	0	0	0	0	0	0	0	0	0	0	0	0	0	0	0	—	0	.000	.000	.000	—						

JUAN PIZARRO—Juan Roman Pizarro—Throws: Left; Bats: Left

Ht: 5'11"; Wt: 170 lbs; Born: 2/7/1937 in Santurce, Puerto Rico; Debut: 5/4/1957

LCS — Pitching

Year Tm	Age	G	GS	CG	GF	IP	BFP	H	R	ER	HR	SH	SF	HB	TBB	IBB	SO	WP	Bk	W	L	Pct	ShO	Sv-Op	Hld	OAvg	OOBP	ERA
1974 Pit	37	1	0	0	1	0.2	2	0	0	0	0	0	0	0	1	1	0	0	0	0	0	—	0	0- 0	0	.000	.500	0.00

World Series — Pitching

Year Tm	Age	G	GS	CG	GF	IP	BFP	H	R	ER	HR	SH	SF	HB	TBB	IBB	SO	WP	Bk	W	L	Pct	ShO	Sv-Op	Hld	OAvg	OOBP	ERA
1957 Mil	20	1	0	0	0	1.2	10	3	2	2	0	0	0	0	2	0	1	0	0	0	0	—	0	0- 0	0	.375	.500	10.80
1958 Mil	21	1	0	0	0	1.2	8	2	1	1	0	0	0	0	1	0	3	1	0	0	0	—	0	0- 0	0	.286	.375	5.40
WS Totals		2	0	0	0	3.1	36	5	3	3	0	0	0	0	3	0	4	1	0	0	0	—	0	0-0	0	.333	.444	8.10
Postseason Totals		3	0	0	1	4.0	40	5	3	3	0	0	0	0	4	1	4	1	0	0	0	—	0	0-0	0	.313	.450	6.75

LCS — Batting / Fielding

Year Tm	Age	G	AB	H	2B	3B	HR	TB	R	RBI	GW	TBB	IBB	SO	HBP	SH	SF	SB	CS	SB%	GDP	Avg	OBP	SLG	Pos	G	PO	A	E	DP	FPct
1974 Pit	37	1	0	0	0	0	0	0	0	0	0	0	0	0	0	0	0	0	0	—	0	—	—	—	P	1	0	0	0	0	—

World Series — Batting / Fielding

Year Tm	Age	G	AB	H	2B	3B	HR	TB	R	RBI	GW	TBB	IBB	SO	HBP	SH	SF	SB	CS	SB%	GDP	Avg	OBP	SLG	Pos	G	PO	A	E	DP	FPct
1957 Mil	20	1	1	0	0	0	0	0	0	0	0	0	0	0	0	0	0	0	0	—	0	.000	.000	.000	P	1	0	0	0	0	—
1958 Mil	21	1	0	0	0	0	0	0	0	0	0	0	0	0	0	0	0	0	0	—	0	—	—	—	P	1	0	1	0	0	1.000
WS Totals		2	1	0	0	0	0	0	0	0	0	0	0	0	0	0	0	0	0	—	0	.000	.000	.000	P	2	0	1	0	0	1.000
Postseason Totals		3	1	0	0	0	0	0	0	0	0	0	0	0	0	0	0	0	0	—	0	.000	.000	.000	P	3	0	1	0	0	1.000

EDDIE PLANK (HOF 1946-V)—Edward Stewart Plank—Nickname: Gettysburg Eddie—Throws: L; Bats: L

Ht: 5'11"; Wt: 175 lbs; Born: 8/31/1875 in Gettysburg, Pa.; Deb.: 5/13/1901; Died: 2/24/1926

World Series — Pitching

Year Tm	Age	G	GS	CG	GF	IP	BFP	H	R	ER	HR	SH	SF	HB	TBB	IBB	SO	WP	Bk	W	L	Pct	ShO	Sv-Op	Hld	OAvg	OOBP	ERA
1905 Phi	30	2	2	2	0	17.0	71	14	4	3	0	3	0	1	4	1	11	1	0	0	2	.000	0	0- 0	0	.222	.279	1.59
1911 Phi	36	2	1	1	1	9.2	35	6	2	2	0	0	1	1	0	0	8	0	0	1	1	.500	0	0- 0	0	.182	.200	1.86
1913 Phi	38	2	2	2	0	19.0	70	9	4	2	0	1	0	1	3	0	7	0	0	1	1	.500	0	0- 0	0	.138	.188	0.95
1914 Phi	39	1	1	1	0	9.0	39	7	1	1	0	1	0	1	4	0	6	0	0	0	1	.000	0	0- 0	0	.212	.316	1.00
WS Totals		7	6	6	1	54.2	430	36	11	8	0	5	1	4	11	1	32	1	0	2	5	.286	0	0-0	0	.186	.243	1.32

World Series — Batting / Fielding

Year Tm	Age	G	AB	H	2B	3B	HR	TB	R	RBI	GW	TBB	IBB	SO	HBP	SH	SF	SB	CS	SB%	GDP	Avg	OBP	SLG	Pos	G	PO	A	E	DP	FPct
1905 Phi	30	2	6	1	0	0	0	1	0	0	0	0	0	2	0	0	0	0	0	—	1	.167	.167	.167	P	2	1	6	0	0	1.000
1911 Phi	36	2	3	0	0	0	0	0	0	0	0	0	0	2	0	0	0	0	0	—	0	.000	.000	.000	P	2	0	2	0	0	1.000
1913 Phi	38	2	7	1	0	0	0	1	0	0	0	0	0	0	0	0	0	0	0	—	0	.143	.143	.143	P	2	1	3	1	0	.800
1914 Phi	39	1	2	0	0	0	0	0	0	0	0	0	0	1	0	0	0	0	0	—	0	.000	.000	.000	P	1	0	1	0	0	1.000
WS Totals		7	18	2	0	0	0	2	0	0	0	0	0	5	0	0	0	0	0	—	1	.111	.111	.111	P	7	2	12	1	0	.933

BILL PLEIS—William Pleis—Throws: Left; Bats: Left

Ht: 5'10"; Wt: 170 lbs; Born: 8/5/1937 in St. Louis, Missouri; Debut: 4/16/1961

World Series — Pitching

Year Tm	Age	G	GS	CG	GF	IP	BFP	H	R	ER	HR	SH	SF	HB	TBB	IBB	SO	WP	Bk	W	L	Pct	ShO	Sv-Op	Hld	OAvg	OOBP	ERA
1965 Min	28	1	0	0	1	1.0	5	2	1	1	1	0	0	0	0	0	0	0	0	0	0	—	0	0- 0	0	.400	.400	9.00

World Series — Batting / Fielding

Year Tm	Age	G	AB	H	2B	3B	HR	TB	R	RBI	GW	TBB	IBB	SO	HBP	SH	SF	SB	CS	SB%	GDP	Avg	OBP	SLG	Pos	G	PO	A	E	DP	FPct
1965 Min	28	1	0	0	0	0	0	0	0	0	0	0	0	0	0	0	0	0	0	—	0	—	—	—	P	1	0	1	0	0	1.000

ERIC PLUNK—Eric Vaughn Plunk—Throws: Right; Bats: Right

Ht: 6'5"; Wt: 210 lbs; Born: 9/3/1963 in Wilmington, California; Debut: 5/12/1986

Division Series — Pitching

Year Tm	Age	G	GS	CG	GF	IP	BFP	H	R	ER	HR	SH	SF	HB	TBB	IBB	SO	WP	Bk	W	L	Pct	ShO	Sv-Op	Hld	OAvg	OOBP	ERA
1995 Cle	32	1	0	0	0	1.1	6	1	0	0	0	1	0	0	1	1	1	0	0	0	0	—	0	0- 0	0	.250	.400	0.00
1996 Cle	33	3	0	0	0	4.0	15	1	3	3	0	0	0	0	2	1	6	0	0	0	1	.000	0	0- 0	1	.077	.200	6.75
1997 Cle	34	1	0	0	0	1.1	8	4	4	4	2	0	0	0	0	0	1	0	0	0	1	.000	0	0- 0	0	.500	.500	27.00
DS Totals		5	0	0	0	6.2	58	6	7	7	2	1	0	0	3	2	8	0	0	0	2	.000	0	0-0	1	.240	.321	9.45

LCS — Pitching

Year Tm	Age	G	GS	CG	GF	IP	BFP	H	R	ER	HR	SH	SF	HB	TBB	IBB	SO	WP	Bk	W	L	Pct	ShO	Sv-Op	Hld	OAvg	OOBP	ERA
1988 Oak	25	1	0	0	0	0.1	2	1	0	0	0	0	0	0	0	0	1	0	0	0	0	—	0	0- 0	1	.500	.500	0.00
1995 Cle	32	3	0	0	2	2.0	9	1	2	2	1	0	0	0	3	1	2	0	0	0	0	—	0	0- 0	1	.167	.444	9.00
1997 Cle	34	1	0	0	1	0.2	3	1	0	0	0	0	0	0	0	0	0	0	0	1	0	1.000	0	0- 0	0	.333	.333	0.00
LCS Totals		5	0	0	3	3.0	28	3	2	2	1	0	0	0	3	1	3	0	0	1	0	1.000	0	0-0	2	.273	.429	6.00

World Series — Pitching

Year Tm	Age	G	GS	CG	GF	IP	BFP	H	R	ER	HR	SH	SF	HB	TBB	IBB	SO	WP	Bk	W	L	Pct	ShO	Sv-Op	Hld	OAvg	OOBP	ERA
1988 Oak	25	2	0	0	0	1.2	5	0	0	0	0	0	0	0	0	0	3	0	0	0	0	—	0	0- 0	0	.000	.000	0.00
1997 Cle	34	3	0	0	0	3.0	15	3	4	3	0	0	0	0	4	1	3	0	0	0	1	.000	0	0- 0	0	.273	.467	9.00
WS Totals		5	0	0	0	4.2	40	3	4	3	0	0	0	0	4	1	6	0	0	0	1	.000	0	0-0	0	.188	.350	5.79
Postseason Totals		15	0	0	3	14.1	126	12	13	12	3	1	0	0	10	4	17	0	0	1	3	.250	0	0-0	3	.231	.355	7.53

Division Series — Batting / Fielding

Year Tm	Age	G	AB	H	2B	3B	HR	TB	R	RBI	GW	TBB	IBB	SO	HBP	SH	SF	SB	CS	SB%	GDP	Avg	OBP	SLG	Pos	G	PO	A	E	DP	FPct
1995 Cle	32	1	0	0	0	0	0	0	0	0	0	0	0	0	0	0	0	0	0	—	0	—	—	—	P	1	0	1	0	0	1.000
1996 Cle	33	3	0	0	0	0	0	0	0	0	0	0	0	0	0	0	0	0	0	—	0	—	—	—	P	3	0	0	0	0	—
1997 Cle	34	1	0	0	0	0	0	0	0	0	0	0	0	0	0	0	0	0	0	—	0	—	—	—	P	1	0	0	0	0	—
DS Totals		5	0	0	0	0	0	0	0	0	0	0	0	0	0	0	0	0	0	—	0	—	—	—	P	5	0	1	0	0	1.000

LCS — Batting / Fielding

Year Tm	Age	G	AB	H	2B	3B	HR	TB	R	RBI	GW	TBB	IBB	SO	HBP	SH	SF	SB	CS	SB%	GDP	Avg	OBP	SLG	Pos	G	PO	A	E	DP	FPct
1988 Oak	25	1	0	0	0	0	0	0	0	0	0	0	0	0	0	0	0	0	0	—	0	—	—	—	P	1	0	0	0	0	—
1995 Cle	32	3	0	0	0	0	0	0	0	0	0	0	0	0	0	0	0	0	0	—	0	—	—	—	P	3	0	0	0	0	—
1997 Cle	34	1	0	0	0	0	0	0	0	0	0	0	0	0	0	0	0	0	0	—	0	—	—	—	P	1	0	0	0	0	—
LCS Totals		5	0	0	0	0	0	0	0	0	0	0	0	0	0	0	0	0	0	—	0	—	—	—	P	5	0	0	0	0	—

World Series — Batting / Fielding

Year Tm	Age	G	AB	H	2B	3B	HR	TB	R	RBI	GW	TBB	IBB	SO	HBP	SH	SF	SB	CS	SB%	GDP	Avg	OBP	SLG	Pos	G	PO	A	E	DP	FPct
1988 Oak	25	2	0	0	0	0	0	0	0	0	0	0	0	0	0	0	0	0	0	—	0	—	—	—	P	2	0	0	0	0	—
1997 Cle	34	3	0	0	0	0	0	0	0	0	0	0	0	0	0	0	0	0	0	—	0	—	—	—	P	3	0	0	0	0	—
WS Totals		5	0	0	0	0	0	0	0	0	0	0	0	0	0	0	0	0	0	—	0	—	—	—	P	5	0	0	0	0	—
Postseason Totals		15	0	0	0	0	0	0	0	0	0	0	0	0	0	0	0	0	0	—	0	—	—	—	P	15	0	1	0	0	1.000

BIFF POCOROBA—Biff Benedict Pocoroba—Bats: Both; Throws: Right

Ht: 5'10"; Wt: 175 lbs; Born: 7/25/1953 in Burbank, California; Debut: 4/25/1975

LCS — Batting / Fielding

Year Tm	Age	G	AB	H	2B	3B	HR	TB	R	RBI	GW	TBB	IBB	SO	HBP	SH	SF	SB	CS	SB%	GDP	Avg	OBP	SLG	Pos	G	PO	A	E	DP	FPct
1982 Atl	29	1	1	0	0	0	0	0	0	0	0	0	0	0	0	0	0	0	0	—	0	.000	.000	.000	—						

JOHNNY PODRES—John Joseph Podres—Nickname: The Point—Throws: Left; Bats: Left

Ht: 5'11"; Wt: 170 lbs; Born: 9/30/1932 in Witherbee, New York; Debut: 4/17/1953

World Series — Pitching

Year Tm	Age	G	GS	CG	GF	IP	BFP	H	R	ER	HR	SH	SF	HB	TBB	IBB	SO	WP	Bk	W	L	Pct	ShO	Sv-Op	Hld	OAvg	OOBP	ERA
1953 Bro	21	1	1	0	0	2.2	13	1	5	1	1	1	0	1	2	0	0	0	0	0	1	.000	0	0- 0	0	.111	.333	3.38
1955 Bro	23	2	2	2	0	18.0	70	15	3	2	1	0	0	0	4	0	10	0	0	2	0	1.000	1	0- 0	0	.227	.271	1.00
1959 LA	27	2	2	0	0	9.1	42	7	5	5	1	0	0	1	6	0	4	0	0	1	0	1.000	0	0- 0	0	.200	.333	4.82
1963 LA	31	1	1	0	0	8.1	32	6	1	1	0	0	0	0	1	0	4	0	0	1	0	1.000	0	0- 0	0	.194	.219	1.08
WS Totals		6	6	2	0	38.1	314	29	14	9	3	1	0	2	13	0	18	0	0	4	1	.800	1	0-0	0	.206	.282	2.11

World Series — Batting / Fielding

Year Tm	Age	G	AB	H	2B	3B	HR	TB	R	RBI	GW	TBB	IBB	SO	HBP	SH	SF	SB	CS	SB%	GDP	Avg	OBP	SLG	Pos	G	PO	A	E	DP	FPct
1953 Bro	21	1	1	1	0	0	0	1	0	0	0	0	0	0	0	0	0	0	0	—	0	1.000	1.000	1.000	P	1	0	1	0	0	1.000
1955 Bro	23	2	7	1	0	0	0	1	1	0	0	0	0	1	0	1	0	0	0	—	0	.143	.143	.143	P	2	0	2	0	0	1.000
1959 LA	27	3	4	2	1	0	0	3	1	1	0	0	0	0	0	0	0	0	0	—	0	.500	.500	.750	P	2	0	1	0	1	1.000
1963 LA	31	1	4	1	0	0	0	1	0	0	0	0	0	0	0	0	0	0	0	—	0	.250	.250	.250	P	1	0	2	1	0	.667
WS Totals		7	16	5	1	0	0	6	2	1	0	0	0	1	0	1	0	0	0	—	0	.313	.313	.375	P	6	0	6	1	1	.857

DICK POLE—Richard Henry Pole—Throws: Right; Bats: Right

Ht: 6'3"; Wt: 200 lbs; Born: 10/13/1950 in Trout Creek, Michigan; Debut: 8/3/1973

World Series — Pitching

Year Tm	Age	G	GS	CG	GF	IP	BFP	H	R	ER	HR	SH	SF	HB	TBB	IBB	SO	WP	Bk	W	L	Pct	ShO	Sv-Op	Hld	OAvg	OOBP	ERA
1975 Bos	24	1	0	0	0	0.0	2	0	1	1	0	0	0	0	2	0	0	0	0	0	0	—	0	0- 0	0	—	1.000	—

World Series — Batting / Fielding

Year Tm	Age	G	AB	H	2B	3B	HR	TB	R	RBI	GW	TBB	IBB	SO	HBP	SH	SF	SB	CS	SB%	GDP	Avg	OBP	SLG	Pos	G	PO	A	E	DP	FPct
1975 Bos	24	1	0	0	0	0	0	0	0	0	0	0	0	0	0	0	0	0	0	—	0	—	—	—	P	1	0	0	0	0	—

HOWIE POLLET—Howard Joseph Pollet—Throws: Left; Bats: Left

Ht: 6'1"; Wt: 175 lbs; Born: 6/26/1921 in New Orleans, Louisiana; Debut: 8/20/1941; Died: 8/8/1974

World Series — Pitching

Year Tm	Age	G	GS	CG	GF	IP	BFP	H	R	ER	HR	SH	SF	HB	TBB	IBB	SO	WP	Bk	W	L	Pct	ShO	Sv-Op	Hld	OAvg	OOBP	ERA
1942 StL	21	1	0	0	0	0.1	1	0	0	0	0	0	0	0	0	0	0	0	0	1	0	1.000	0	0- 0	0	.000	.000	0.00
1946 StL	25	2	2	1	0	10.1	47	12	5	4	1	0	0	1	4	0	3	0	0	0	1	.000	0	0- 0	0	.286	.362	3.48
WS Totals		3	2	1	0	10.2	96	12	5	4	1	0	0	1	4	0	3	0	0	1	1	.500	0	0-0	0	.279	.354	3.38

World Series — Batting / Fielding

Year Tm	Age	G	AB	H	2B	3B	HR	TB	R	RBI	GW	TBB	IBB	SO	HBP	SH	SF	SB	CS	SB%	GDP	Avg	OBP	SLG	Pos	G	PO	A	E	DP	FPct
1942 StL	21	1	0	0	0	0	0	0	0	0	0	0	0	0	0	0	0	0	0	—	0	—	—	—	P	1	0	0	0	0	—
1946 StL	25	2	4	0	0	0	0	0	0	0	0	0	0	1	0	0	0	0	0	—	0	.000	.000	.000	P	2	0	0	0	0	—
WS Totals		3	4	0	0	0	0	0	0	0	0	0	0	1	0	0	0	0	0	—	0	.000	.000	.000	P	3	0	0	0	0	—

LUIS POLONIA—Luis Andrew Polonia—Bats: Left; Throws: Left

Ht: 5'8"; Wt: 155 lbs; Born: 12/10/1964 in Santiago, Dominican Republic; Debut: 4/24/1987

Division Series — Batting / Fielding

Year Tm	Age	G	AB	H	2B	3B	HR	TB	R	RBI	GW	TBB	IBB	SO	HBP	SH	SF	SB	CS	SB%	GDP	Avg	OBP	SLG	Pos	G	PO	A	E	DP	FPct
1995 Atl	30	3	3	1	0	0	0	1	0	2	0	0	0	1	0	0	0	1	0	1.00	0	.333	.333	.333	—						
1996 Atl	31	2	2	0	0	0	0	0	0	0	0	0	0	1	0	0	0	0	0	—	0	.000	.000	.000	—						
DS Totals		5	5	1	0	0	0	1	0	2	0	0	0	2	0	0	0	1	0	1.00	0	.200	.200	.200	—	0	0	0	0	0	—

LCS — Batting / Fielding

Year Tm	Age	G	AB	H	2B	3B	HR	TB	R	RBI	GW	TBB	IBB	SO	HBP	SH	SF	SB	CS	SB%	GDP	Avg	OBP	SLG	Pos	G	PO	A	E	DP	FPct
1988 Oak	23	3	5	2	0	0	0	2	0	0	0	1	0	2	0	0	0	0	1	.00	0	.400	.500	.400	OF	1	2	0	0	0	1.000
1995 Atl	30	3	2	1	0	0	0	1	0	1	0	0	0	0	0	1	0	0	0	—	0	.500	.500	.500	OF	1	0	0	0	0	—
1996 Atl	31	3	3	0	0	0	0	0	0	0	0	0	0	0	0	0	0	0	0	—	0	.000	.000	.000	—						
LCS Totals		9	10	3	0	0	0	3	0	1	0	1	0	2	0	1	0	0	1	.00	0	.300	.364	.300	OF	2	2	0	0	0	1.000

World Series — Batting / Fielding

Year Tm	Age	G	AB	H	2B	3B	HR	TB	R	RBI	GW	TBB	IBB	SO	HBP	SH	SF	SB	CS	SB%	GDP	Avg	OBP	SLG	Pos	G	PO	A	E	DP	FPct
1988 Oak	23	3	9	1	0	0	0	1	1	0	0	0	0	2	0	0	0	0	0	—	0	.111	.111	.111	OF	2	2	0	0	0	1.000
1995 Atl	30	6	14	4	1	0	1	8	3	4	2	1	0	3	0	0	0	1	0	1.00	1	.286	.333	.571	OF	4	3	0	0	0	1.000
1996 Atl	31	6	5	0	0	0	0	0	0	0	0	1	0	3	0	0	0	0	1	.00	0	.000	.167	.000	—						
WS Totals		15	28	5	1	0	1	9	4	4	2	2	0	8	0	0	0	1	1	.50	1	.179	.233	.321	OF	6	5	0	0	0	1.000
Postseason Totals		29	43	9	1	0	1	13	4	7	2	3	0	12	0	1	0	2	2	.50	1	.209	.261	.302	OF	8	7	0	0	0	1.000

JIM POOLE—James Richard Poole—Throws: Left; Bats: Left

Ht: 6'2"; Wt: 190 lbs; Born: 4/28/1966 in Rochester, New York; Debut: 6/15/1990

Division Series — Pitching

Year	Tm	Age	G	GS	CG	GF	IP	BFP	H	R	ER	HR	SH	SF	HB	TBB	IBB	SO	WP	Bk	W	L	Pct	ShO	Sv-Op	Hld	OAvg	OOBP	ERA
1995	Cle	29	1	0	0	0	1.2	8	2	1	1	1	0	0	0	1	1	2	0	0	0	0	—	0	0-0	0	.286	.375	5.40

LCS — Pitching

Year	Tm	Age	G	GS	CG	GF	IP	BFP	H	R	ER	HR	SH	SF	HB	TBB	IBB	SO	WP	Bk	W	L	Pct	ShO	Sv-Op	Hld	OAvg	OOBP	ERA
1995	Cle	29	1	0	0	0	1.0	3	0	0	0	0	0	0	0	0	0	2	0	0	0	0	—	0	0-0	0	.000	.000	0.00

World Series — Pitching

Year	Tm	Age	G	GS	CG	GF	IP	BFP	H	R	ER	HR	SH	SF	HB	TBB	IBB	SO	WP	Bk	W	L	Pct	ShO	Sv-Op	Hld	OAvg	OOBP	ERA
1995	Cle	29	2	0	0	0	2.1	9	1	1	1	1	0	0	0	0	0	1	0	0	0	1	.000	0	0-0	0	.111	.111	3.86
Postseason Totals			4	0	0	0	5.0	40	3	2	2	2	0	0	0	1	1	5	0	0	0	1	.000	0	0-0	0	.158	.200	3.60

Division Series — Batting / Fielding

Year	Tm	Age	G	AB	H	2B	3B	HR	TB	R	RBI	GW	TBB	IBB	SO	HBP	SH	SF	SB	CS	SB%	GDP	Avg	OBP	SLG	Pos	G	PO	A	E	DP	FPct
1995	Cle	29	1	0	0	0	0	0	0	0	0	0	0	0	0	0	0	0	0	0	—	0	—	—	—	P	1	0	1	0	0	1.000

LCS — Batting / Fielding

Year	Tm	Age	G	AB	H	2B	3B	HR	TB	R	RBI	GW	TBB	IBB	SO	HBP	SH	SF	SB	CS	SB%	GDP	Avg	OBP	SLG	Pos	G	PO	A	E	DP	FPct
1995	Cle	29	1	0	0	0	0	0	0	0	0	0	0	0	0	0	0	0	0	0	—	0	—	—	—	P	1	0	0	0	0	—

World Series — Batting / Fielding

Year	Tm	Age	G	AB	H	2B	3B	HR	TB	R	RBI	GW	TBB	IBB	SO	HBP	SH	SF	SB	CS	SB%	GDP	Avg	OBP	SLG	Pos	G	PO	A	E	DP	FPct
1995	Cle	29	2	1	0	0	0	0	0	0	0	0	0	0	0	0	0	0	0	0	—	0	.000	.000	.000	P	2	0	0	0	0	—
Postseason Totals			4	1	0	0	0	0	0	0	0	0	0	0	0	0	0	0	0	0	—	0	.000	.000	.000	P	4	0	1	0	0	1.000

DAVE POPE—David Pope—Bats: Left; Throws: Right

Ht: 5'10"; Wt: 170 lbs; Born: 6/17/1921 in Talladega, Alabama; Debut: 7/1/1952

World Series — Batting / Fielding

Year	Tm	Age	G	AB	H	2B	3B	HR	TB	R	RBI	GW	TBB	IBB	SO	HBP	SH	SF	SB	CS	SB%	GDP	Avg	OBP	SLG	Pos	G	PO	A	E	DP	FPct
1954	Cle	33	3	3	0	0	0	0	0	0	0	0	1	1	1	0	0	0	0	0	—	0	.000	.250	.000	OF	2	0	0	0	0	—

PAUL POPOVICH—Paul Edward Popovich—Bats: Both; Throws: Right

Ht: 6'0"; Wt: 175 lbs; Born: 8/18/1940 in Flemington, West Virginia; Debut: 4/19/1964

LCS — Batting / Fielding

Year	Tm	Age	G	AB	H	2B	3B	HR	TB	R	RBI	GW	TBB	IBB	SO	HBP	SH	SF	SB	CS	SB%	GDP	Avg	OBP	SLG	Pos	G	PO	A	E	DP	FPct
1974	Pit	34	3	5	3	0	0	0	3	1	0	0	0	0	0	0	0	0	0	0	—	0	.600	.600	.600	SS	3	2	0	0	0	1.000

TOM POQUETTE—Thomas Arthur Poquette—Bats: Left; Throws: Right

Ht: 5'10"; Wt: 175 lbs; Born: 10/30/1951 in Eau Claire, Wisconsin; Debut: 9/1/1973

LCS — Batting / Fielding

Year	Tm	Age	G	AB	H	2B	3B	HR	TB	R	RBI	GW	TBB	IBB	SO	HBP	SH	SF	SB	CS	SB%	GDP	Avg	OBP	SLG	Pos	G	PO	A	E	DP	FPct
1976	KC	24	5	16	3	2	0	0	5	1	4	1	2	0	3	0	0	0	0	0	—	0	.188	.278	.313	OF	5	13	0	0	0	1.000
1977	KC	25	2	6	1	0	0	0	1	0	0	0	0	0	0	0	0	0	0	0	—	0	.167	.167	.167	OF	2	3	0	0	0	1.000
1978	KC	26	1	1	0	0	0	0	0	0	0	0	0	0	0	0	0	0	0	0	—	0	.000	.000	.000	—						
LCS Totals			8	23	4	2	0	0	6	1	4	1	2	0	3	0	0	0	0	0	—	0	.174	.240	.261	OF	7	16	0	0	0	1.000

DARRELL PORTER—Darrell Ray Porter—Bats: Left; Throws: Right

Ht: 6'0"; Wt: 193 lbs; Born: 1/17/1952 in Joplin, Missouri; Debut: 9/2/1971

LCS — Batting / Fielding

Year	Tm	Age	G	AB	H	2B	3B	HR	TB	R	RBI	GW	TBB	IBB	SO	HBP	SH	SF	SB	CS	SB%	GDP	Avg	OBP	SLG	Pos	G	PO	A	E	DP	FPct
1977	KC	25	5	15	5	0	0	0	5	3	0	0	3	0	0	0	0	0	0	0	—	0	.333	.444	.333	C	5	18	0	0	0	1.000
1978	KC	26	4	14	5	1	0	0	6	1	3	1	2	0	0	0	0	1	0	0	—	0	.357	.412	.429	C	4	21	1	0	1	1.000
1980	KC	28	3	10	1	0	0	0	1	2	0	0	1	0	0	0	0	0	0	0	—	0	.100	.182	.100	C	3	17	1	0	0	1.000
1982	StL	30	3	9	5	3	0	0	8	3	1	0	5	0	2	0	0	0	0	0	—	0	.556	.714	.889	C	3	15	3	0	1	1.000
1985	StL	33	5	15	4	1	0	0	5	1	0	0	5	1	4	0	0	0	0	0	—	0	.267	.450	.333	C	5	25	2	0	0	1.000
LCS Totals			20	63	20	5	0	0	25	10	4	1	16	1	6	0	0	1	0	0	—	0	.317	.450	.397	C	20	96	7	0	2	1.000

World Series — Batting / Fielding

Year	Tm	Age	G	AB	H	2B	3B	HR	TB	R	RBI	GW	TBB	IBB	SO	HBP	SH	SF	SB	CS	SB%	GDP	Avg	OBP	SLG	Pos	G	PO	A	E	DP	FPct
1980	KC	28	5	14	2	0	0	0	2	1	0	0	3	0	4	0	0	0	0	0	—	0	.143	.294	.143	C	4	13	2	0	0	1.000
1982	StL	30	7	28	8	2	0	1	13	1	5	0	1	0	4	0	0	0	0	0	—	0	.286	.310	.464	C	7	33	2	0	1	1.000
1985	StL	33	5	15	2	0	0	0	2	0	0	0	2	1	5	0	0	0	0	0	—	0	.133	.235	.133	C	5	36	4	0	1	1.000
WS Totals			17	57	12	2	0	1	17	2	5	0	6	1	13	0	0	0	0	0	—	0	.211	.286	.298	C	16	82	8	0	2	1.000
Postseason Totals			37	120	32	7	0	1	42	12	9	1	22	2	19	0	0	1	0	0	—	0	.267	.378	.350	C	36	178	15	0	4	1.000

MARK PORTUGAL—Mark Steven Portugal—Throws: Right; Bats: Right

Ht: 6'0"; Wt: 170 lbs; Born: 10/30/1962 in Los Angeles, California; Debut: 8/14/1985

LCS — Pitching

Year	Tm	Age	G	GS	CG	GF	IP	BFP	H	R	ER	HR	SH	SF	HB	TBB	IBB	SO	WP	Bk	W	L	Pct	ShO	Sv-Op	Hld	OAvg	OOBP	ERA
1995	Cin	32	1	0	0	1	1.0	7	3	4	4	1	0	0	0	1	1	0	1	0	0	1	.000	0	0-0	0	.500	.571	36.00

LCS — Batting / Fielding

Year	Tm	Age	G	AB	H	2B	3B	HR	TB	R	RBI	GW	TBB	IBB	SO	HBP	SH	SF	SB	CS	SB%	GDP	Avg	OBP	SLG	Pos	G	PO	A	E	DP	FPct
1995	Cin	32	1	0	0	0	0	0	0	0	0	0	0	0	0	0	0	0	0	0	—	0	—	—	—	P	1	0	0	0	0	—

JORGE POSADA—Jorge Rafael Posada—Bats: Both; Throws: Right

Ht: 6'2"; Wt: 205 lbs; Born: 8/17/1971 in Santurce, Puerto Rico; Debut: 9/4/1995

Division Series — Batting / Fielding

Year	Tm	Age	G	AB	H	2B	3B	HR	TB	R	RBI	GW	TBB	IBB	SO	HBP	SH	SF	SB	CS	SB%	GDP	Avg	OBP	SLG	Pos	G	PO	A	E	DP	FPct
1995	NYA	24	1	0	0	0	0	0	0	1	0	0	0	0	0	0	0	0	0	0	—	0	—	—	—	—						
1997	NYA	26	2	2	0	0	0	0	0	0	0	0	0	0	1	0	0	0	0	0	—	0	.000	.000	.000	C	2	1	1	0	0	1.000
DS Totals			3	2	0	0	0	0	0	1	0	0	0	0	1	0	0	0	0	0	—	0	.000	.000	.000	C	2	1	1	0	0	1.000

SCOTT POSE—Scott Vernon Pose—Bats: Left; Throws: Right

Ht: 5'11"; Wt: 165 lbs; Born: 2/11/1967 in Davenport, Iowa; Debut: 4/5/1993

Division Series — Batting / Fielding

Year	Tm	Age	G	AB	H	2B	3B	HR	TB	R	RBI	GW	TBB	IBB	SO	HBP	SH	SF	SB	CS	SB%	GDP	Avg	OBP	SLG	Pos	G	PO	A	E	DP	FPct
1997	NYA	30	1	0	0	0	0	0	0	0	0	0	0	0	0	0	0	0	0	0	—	0	—	—	—	—						

WALLY POST—Walter Charles Post—Bats: Right; Throws: Right

Ht: 6'1"; Wt: 190 lbs; Born: 7/9/1929 in St. Wendelin, Ohio; Debut: 9/18/1949; Died: 1/6/1982

World Series — Batting / Fielding

Year	Tm	Age	G	AB	H	2B	3B	HR	TB	R	RBI	GW	TBB	IBB	SO	HBP	SH	SF	SB	CS	SB%	GDP	Avg	OBP	SLG	Pos	G	PO	A	E	DP	FPct
1961	Cin	32	5	18	6	1	0	1	10	3	2	0	0	0	1	1	0	0	0	0	—	1	.333	.368	.556	OF	5	8	0	0	0	1.000

NELS POTTER—Nelson Thomas Potter—Throws: Right; Bats: Left

Ht: 5'11"; Wt: 180 lbs; Born: 8/23/1911 in Mt. Morris, Illinois; Debut: 4/25/1936; Died: 9/30/1990

World Series — Pitching

Year	Tm	Age	G	GS	CG	GF	IP	BFP	H	R	ER	HR	SH	SF	HB	TBB	IBB	SO	WP	Bk	W	L	Pct	ShO	Sv-Op	Hld	OAvg	OOBP	ERA
1944	StL	33	2	2	0	0	9.2	44	10	5	1	0	1	0	0	3	1	6	0	0	0	1	.000	0	0-0	0	.250	.302	0.93
1948	Bos	37	2	1	0	1	5.1	25	6	6	5	2	0	0	0	2	0	1	0	0	0	0	—	0	0-0	0	.261	.320	8.44
WS Totals			4	3	0	1	15.0	138	16	11	6	2	1	0	0	5	1	7	0	0	0	1	.000	0	0-0	0	.254	.309	3.60

World Series — Batting / Fielding

Year	Tm	Age	G	AB	H	2B	3B	HR	TB	R	RBI	GW	TBB	IBB	SO	HBP	SH	SF	SB	CS	SB%	GDP	Avg	OBP	SLG	Pos	G	PO	A	E	DP	FPct
1944	StL	33	2	4	0	0	0	0	0	0	0	0	0	0	1	0	0	0	0	0	—	0	.000	.000	.000	P	2	2	0	2	0	.500
1948	Bos	37	2	2	1	0	0	0	1	0	0	0	0	0	1	0	0	0	0	0	—	0	.500	.500	.500	P	2	1	0	0	0	1.000
WS Totals			4	6	1	0	0	0	1	0	0	0	0	0	2	0	0	0	0	0	—	0	.167	.167	.167	P	4	3	0	2	0	.600

BOOG POWELL—John Wesley Powell—Bats: Left; Throws: Right

Ht: 6'4"; Wt: 230 lbs; Born: 8/17/1941 in Lakeland, Florida; Debut: 9/26/1961

LCS		Batting																							Fielding						
Year Tm	Age	G	AB	H	2B	3B	HR	TB	R	RBI	GW	TBB	IBB	SO	HBP	SH	SF	SB	CS	SB%	GDP	Avg	OBP	SLG	Pos	G	PO	A	E	DP	FPct
1969 Bal	28	3	13	5	0	0	1	8	2	1	0	2	0	0	0	0	0	0	0	—	1	.385	.467	.615	1B	3	34	0	0	2	1.000
1970 Bal-*M*	29	3	14	6	2	0	1	11	2	6	2	0	0	3	0	0	0	0	0	—	1	.429	.429	.786	1B	3	24	1	0	3	1.000
1971 Bal	30	3	10	3	0	0	2	9	4	3	0	3	0	3	0	0	0	0	0	—	0	.300	.462	.900	1B	3	28	2	0	4	1.000
1973 Bal	32	1	4	0	0	0	0	0	1	0	0	0	0	1	0	0	0	0	0	—	0	.000	.000	.000	1B	1	7	0	0	0	1.000
1974 Bal	33	2	8	1	0	0	0	1	0	1	0	0	0	0	0	0	0	0	0	—	1	.125	.125	.125	1B	2	22	1	0	1	1.000
LCS Totals		12	49	15	2	0	4	29	9	11	2	5	0	7	0	0	0	0	0	—	3	.306	.370	.592	1B	12	115	4	0	10	1.000
World Series		Batting																							Fielding						
Year Tm	Age	G	AB	H	2B	3B	HR	TB	R	RBI	GW	TBB	IBB	SO	HBP	SH	SF	SB	CS	SB%	GDP	Avg	OBP	SLG	Pos	G	PO	A	E	DP	FPct
1966 Bal	25	4	14	5	1	0	0	6	1	1	0	0	0	1	0	1	0	0	0	—	1	.357	.357	.429	1B	4	27	1	0	3	1.000
1969 Bal	28	5	19	5	0	0	0	5	0	0	0	1	0	4	0	0	0	0	0	—	0	.263	.300	.263	1B	5	46	2	1	3	.980
1970 Bal-*M*	29	5	17	5	1	0	2	12	6	5	0	5	0	2	0	0	0	0	0	—	2	.294	.455	.706	1B	5	38	2	0	3	1.000
1971 Bal	30	7	27	3	0	0	0	3	1	1	0	1	0	3	0	0	1	0	0	—	0	.111	.138	.111	1B	7	52	4	1	1	.982
WS Totals		21	77	18	2	0	2	26	8	7	0	7	0	10	0	1	1	0	0	—	3	.234	.294	.338	1B	21	163	9	2	10	.989
Postseason Totals		33	126	33	4	0	6	55	17	18	2	12	0	17	0	1	1	0	0	—	6	.262	.324	.437	1B	33	278	13	2	20	.993

DANTE POWELL—LeJohn Dante Powell—Bats: Right; Throws: Right

Ht: 6'2"; Wt: 180 lbs; Born: 8/25/1973 in Long Beach, California; Debut: 4/15/1997

Division Series		Batting																							Fielding						
Year Tm	Age	G	AB	H	2B	3B	HR	TB	R	RBI	GW	TBB	IBB	SO	HBP	SH	SF	SB	CS	SB%	GDP	Avg	OBP	SLG	Pos	G	PO	A	E	DP	FPct
1997 SF	24	1	0	0	0	0	0	0	0	0	0	0	0	0	0	0	0	0	0	—	0	—	—	—	OF	1	0	0	0	0	—

JAKE POWELL—Alvin Jacob Powell—Bats: Right; Throws: Right

Ht: 5'11"; Wt: 180 lbs; Born: 7/15/1908 in Silver Spring, Maryland; Debut: 8/3/1930; Died: 11/4/1948

World Series		Batting																							Fielding						
Year Tm	Age	G	AB	H	2B	3B	HR	TB	R	RBI	GW	TBB	IBB	SO	HBP	SH	SF	SB	CS	SB%	GDP	Avg	OBP	SLG	Pos	G	PO	A	E	DP	FPct
1936 NYA	28	6	22	10	1	0	1	14	8	5	0	4	0	4	0	0	0	1	1	.50	1	.455	.538	.636	OF	6	12	0	0	0	1.000
1937 NYA	29	1	1	0	0	0	0	0	0	0	0	0	0	1	0	0	0	0	0	—	0	.000	.000	.000	—						
1938 NYA	30	1	0	0	0	0	0	0	0	0	0	0	0	0	0	0	0	0	0	—	0	—	—	—	OF	1	0	0	0	0	—
WS Totals		8	23	10	1	0	1	14	8	5	0	4	0	5	0	0	0	1	1	.50	1	.435	.519	.609	OF	7	12	0	0	0	1.000

JAY POWELL—James Willard Powell—Throws: Right; Bats: Right

Ht: 6'4"; Wt: 225 lbs; Born: 1/9/1972 in Meridian, Mississippi; Debut: 9/10/1995

LCS		Pitching																										
Year Tm	Age	G	GS	CG	GF	IP	BFP	H	R	ER	HR	SH	SF	HB	TBB	IBB	SO	WP	Bk	W	L	Pct	ShO	Sv-Op	Hld	OAvg	OOBP	ERA
1997 Fla	25	1	0	0	0	0.2	2	0	0	0	0	0	0	0	0	0	1	0	0	0	0	—	0	0- 0	1	.000	.000	0.00
World Series		Pitching																										
Year Tm	Age	G	GS	CG	GF	IP	BFP	H	R	ER	HR	SH	SF	HB	TBB	IBB	SO	WP	Bk	W	L	Pct	ShO	Sv-Op	Hld	OAvg	OOBP	ERA
1997 Fla	25	4	0	0	2	3.2	19	5	3	3	1	0	0	0	4	0	2	0	0	1	0	1.000	0	0- 0	0	.333	.474	7.36
Postseason Totals		5	0	0	2	4.1	42	5	3	3	1	0	0	0	4	0	3	0	0	1	0	1.000	0	0-0	1	.294	.429	6.23

LCS		Batting																							Fielding						
Year Tm	Age	G	AB	H	2B	3B	HR	TB	R	RBI	GW	TBB	IBB	SO	HBP	SH	SF	SB	CS	SB%	GDP	Avg	OBP	SLG	Pos	G	PO	A	E	DP	FPct
1997 Fla	25	1	0	0	0	0	0	0	0	0	0	0	0	0	0	0	0	0	0	—	0	—	—	—	P	1	0	0	0	0	—
World Series		Batting																							Fielding						
Year Tm	Age	G	AB	H	2B	3B	HR	TB	R	RBI	GW	TBB	IBB	SO	HBP	SH	SF	SB	CS	SB%	GDP	Avg	OBP	SLG	Pos	G	PO	A	E	DP	FPct
1997 Fla	25	4	0	0	0	0	0	0	0	0	0	0	0	0	0	0	0	0	0	—	0	—	—	—	P	4	0	2	0	0	1.000
Postseason Totals		5	0	0	0	0	0	0	0	0	0	0	0	0	0	0	0	0	0	—	0	—	—	—	P	5	0	2	0	0	1.000

TED POWER—Ted Henry Power—Throws: Right; Bats: Right

Ht: 6'4"; Wt: 215 lbs; Born: 1/31/1955 in Guthrie, Oklahoma; Debut: 9/9/1981

LCS		Pitching																										
Year Tm	Age	G	GS	CG	GF	IP	BFP	H	R	ER	HR	SH	SF	HB	TBB	IBB	SO	WP	Bk	W	L	Pct	ShO	Sv-Op	Hld	OAvg	OOBP	ERA
1990 Pit	35	3	1	0	2	5.0	21	6	2	2	0	0	1	0	2	1	3	0	0	0	0	—	0	1- 1	0	.333	.381	3.60

LCS		Batting																							Fielding						
Year Tm	Age	G	AB	H	2B	3B	HR	TB	R	RBI	GW	TBB	IBB	SO	HBP	SH	SF	SB	CS	SB%	GDP	Avg	OBP	SLG	Pos	G	PO	A	E	DP	FPct
1990 Pit	35	3	1	0	0	0	0	0	0	0	0	0	0	1	0	0	0	0	0	—	0	.000	.000	.000	P	3	0	1	0	0	1.000

MIKE POWERS—Michael Riley Powers—Nickname: Doc—Bats: Right; Throws: Right

Ht: Unknown; Wt: Unknown; Born: 9/22/1870 in Pittsfield, Massachusetts; Debut: 6/12/1898; Died: 4/26/1909

World Series		Batting																							Fielding						
Year Tm	Age	G	AB	H	2B	3B	HR	TB	R	RBI	GW	TBB	IBB	SO	HBP	SH	SF	SB	CS	SB%	GDP	Avg	OBP	SLG	Pos	G	PO	A	E	DP	FPct
1905 Phi	35	3	7	1	1	0	0	2	0	0	0	0	0	0	0	0	0	0	0	—	0	.143	.143	.286	C	3	13	5	0	0	1.000

TODD PRATT—Todd Alan Pratt—Bats: Right; Throws: Right

Ht: 6'3"; Wt: 195 lbs; Born: 2/9/1967 in Bellevue, Nebraska; Debut: 7/29/1992

LCS		Batting																							Fielding						
Year Tm	Age	G	AB	H	2B	3B	HR	TB	R	RBI	GW	TBB	IBB	SO	HBP	SH	SF	SB	CS	SB%	GDP	Avg	OBP	SLG	Pos	G	PO	A	E	DP	FPct
1993 Phi	26	1	1	0	0	0	0	0	0	0	0	0	0	1	0	0	0	0	0	—	0	.000	.000	.000	C	1	1	0	0	0	1.000

JIM PRICE—Jimmie William Price—Bats: Right; Throws: Right

Ht: 6'0"; Wt: 192 lbs; Born: 10/13/1941 in Harrisburg, Pennsylvania; Debut: 4/11/1967

World Series		Batting																							Fielding						
Year Tm	Age	G	AB	H	2B	3B	HR	TB	R	RBI	GW	TBB	IBB	SO	HBP	SH	SF	SB	CS	SB%	GDP	Avg	OBP	SLG	Pos	G	PO	A	E	DP	FPct
1968 Det	26	2	2	0	0	0	0	0	0	0	0	0	0	1	0	0	0	0	0	—	0	.000	.000	.000	—						

JOE PRICE—Joseph Walter Price—Throws: Left; Bats: Right

Ht: 6'4"; Wt: 220 lbs; Born: 11/29/1956 in Inglewood, California; Debut: 6/14/1980

LCS		Pitching																										
Year Tm	Age	G	GS	CG	GF	IP	BFP	H	R	ER	HR	SH	SF	HB	TBB	IBB	SO	WP	Bk	W	L	Pct	ShO	Sv-Op	Hld	OAvg	OOBP	ERA
1987 SF	30	2	0	0	1	5.2	21	3	0	0	0	0	0	0	1	0	7	0	0	1	0	1.000	0	0- 0	0	.150	.190	0.00

LCS		Batting																							Fielding						
Year Tm	Age	G	AB	H	2B	3B	HR	TB	R	RBI	GW	TBB	IBB	SO	HBP	SH	SF	SB	CS	SB%	GDP	Avg	OBP	SLG	Pos	G	PO	A	E	DP	FPct
1987 SF	30	2	1	0	0	0	0	0	0	0	0	0	0	1	0	0	0	0	0	—	0	.000	.000	.000	P	2	0	0	0	0	—

JERRY PRIDDY—Gerald Edward Priddy—Bats: Right; Throws: Right

Ht: 5'11"; Wt: 180 lbs; Born: 11/9/1919 in Los Angeles, California; Debut: 4/17/1941; Died: 3/3/1980

World Series		Batting																							Fielding						
Year Tm	Age	G	AB	H	2B	3B	HR	TB	R	RBI	GW	TBB	IBB	SO	HBP	SH	SF	SB	CS	SB%	GDP	Avg	OBP	SLG	Pos	G	PO	A	E	DP	FPct
1942 NYA	22	3	10	1	1	0	0	2	0	1	0	1	0	0	0	0	0	0	0	—	0	.100	.182	.200	3B	1	0	0	0	0	—
																									1B	3	22	4	1	1	.963

RAY PRIM—Raymond Lee Prim—Nickname: Pop—Throws: Left; Bats: Right

Ht: 6'0"; Wt: 178 lbs; Born: 12/30/1906 in Salitpa, Alabama; Debut: 9/24/1933; Died: 4/29/1995

World Series		Pitching																										
Year Tm	Age	G	GS	CG	GF	IP	BFP	H	R	ER	HR	SH	SF	HB	TBB	IBB	SO	WP	Bk	W	L	Pct	ShO	Sv-Op	Hld	OAvg	OOBP	ERA
1945 ChN	38	2	1	0	0	4.0	17	4	5	5	1	0	0	0	1	0	1	0	0	0	1	.000	0	0- 1	0	.250	.294	11.25

World Series		Batting																							Fielding						
Year Tm	Age	G	AB	H	2B	3B	HR	TB	R	RBI	GW	TBB	IBB	SO	HBP	SH	SF	SB	CS	SB%	GDP	Avg	OBP	SLG	Pos	G	PO	A	E	DP	FPct
1945 ChN	38	2	0	0	0	0	0	0	0	0	0	0	0	0	0	1	0	0	0	—	0	—	—	—	P	2	0	1	0	0	1.000

GREG PRYOR—Gregory Russell Pryor—Bats: Right; Throws: Right

Ht: 6'0"; Wt: 180 lbs; Born: 10/2/1949 in Marietta, Ohio; Debut: 6/4/1976

LCS		Batting																							Fielding						
Year Tm	Age	G	AB	H	2B	3B	HR	TB	R	RBI	GW	TBB	IBB	SO	HBP	SH	SF	SB	CS	SB%	GDP	Avg	OBP	SLG	Pos	G	PO	A	E	DP	FPct
1984 KC	34	1	0	0	0	0	0	0	0	0	0	0	0	0	0	0	0	0	0	—	0	—	—	—	3B	1	1	0	0	0	1.000
World Series		Batting																							Fielding						
Year Tm	Age	G	AB	H	2B	3B	HR	TB	R	RBI	GW	TBB	IBB	SO	HBP	SH	SF	SB	CS	SB%	GDP	Avg	OBP	SLG	Pos	G	PO	A	E	DP	FPct
1985 KC	35	1	0	0	0	0	0	0	0	0	0	0	0	0	0	0	0	0	0	—	0	—	—	—	3B	1	0	1	0	0	1.000
Postseason Totals		2	0	0	0	0	0	0	0	0	0	0	0	0	0	0	0	0	0	—	0	—	—	—	3B	2	1	1	0	0	1.000

GEORGE PUCCINELLI—George Lawrence Puccinelli—Nicknames: Pooch, Count—B: R; T: R

Ht: 6'0"; Wt: 190 lbs; Born: 6/22/1907 in San Francisco, Calif.; Deb.: 7/17/1930; Died: 4/16/1956

World Series		Batting																							Fielding						
Year Tm	Age	G	AB	H	2B	3B	HR	TB	R	RBI	GW	TBB	IBB	SO	HBP	SH	SF	SB	CS	SB%	GDP	Avg	OBP	SLG	Pos	G	PO	A	E	DP	FPct
1930 StL	23	1	1	0	0	0	0	0	0	0	0	0	0	0	0	0	0	0	0	—	0	.000	.000	.000	—						

KIRBY PUCKETT—Bats: Right; Throws: Right

Ht: 5'8"; Wt: 178 lbs; Born: 3/14/1961 in Chicago, Illinois; Debut: 5/8/1984

LCS		Batting																							Fielding						
Year Tm	Age	G	AB	H	2B	3B	HR	TB	R	RBI	GW	TBB	IBB	SO	HBP	SH	SF	SB	CS	SB%	GDP	Avg	OBP	SLG	Pos	G	PO	A	E	DP	FPct
1987 Min	26	5	24	5	1	0	1	9	3	3	0	0	0	5	0	0	0	1	0	1.00	0	.208	.208	.375	OF	5	7	0	0	0	1.000
1991 Min	30	5	21	9	1	0	2	16	4	6	1	1	0	4	0	0	1	0	0	—	0	.429	.435	.762	OF	5	13	1	0	0	1.000
LCS Totals		10	45	14	2	0	3	25	7	9	1	1	0	9	0	0	1	1	0	1.00	0	.311	.319	.556	OF	10	20	1	0	0	1.000
World Series		Batting																							Fielding						
Year Tm	Age	G	AB	H	2B	3B	HR	TB	R	RBI	GW	TBB	IBB	SO	HBP	SH	SF	SB	CS	SB%	GDP	Avg	OBP	SLG	Pos	G	PO	A	E	DP	FPct
1987 Min	26	7	28	10	1	1	0	13	5	3	0	2	0	1	1	0	0	1	1	.50	0	.357	.419	.464	OF	7	15	1	1	0	.941
1991 Min	30	7	24	6	0	1	2	14	4	4	1	5	4	7	0	1	1	1	0	1.00	1	.250	.367	.583	OF	7	16	1	0	0	1.000
WS Totals		14	52	16	1	2	2	27	9	7	1	7	4	8	1	1	1	2	1	.67	1	.308	.393	.519	OF	14	31	2	1	0	.971
Postseason Totals		24	97	30	3	2	5	52	16	16	2	8	4	17	1	1	2	3	1	.75	1	.309	.361	.536	OF	24	51	3	1	0	.982

TERRY PUHL—Terry Stephen Puhl—Bats: Left; Throws: Right

Ht: 6'2"; Wt: 195 lbs; Born: 7/8/1956 in Melville, Saskatchewan; Debut: 7/12/1977

Division Series		Batting																							Fielding						
Year Tm	Age	G	AB	H	2B	3B	HR	TB	R	RBI	GW	TBB	IBB	SO	HBP	SH	SF	SB	CS	SB%	GDP	Avg	OBP	SLG	Pos	G	PO	A	E	DP	FPct
1981 Hou	25	5	21	4	1	0	0	5	2	0	0	0	0	1	0	0	0	1	0	1.00	0	.190	.190	.238	OF	5	7	1	0	0	1.000
LCS		Batting																							Fielding						
Year Tm	Age	G	AB	H	2B	3B	HR	TB	R	RBI	GW	TBB	IBB	SO	HBP	SH	SF	SB	CS	SB%	GDP	Avg	OBP	SLG	Pos	G	PO	A	E	DP	FPct
1980 Hou	24	5	19	10	2	0	0	12	4	3	0	3	0	2	0	0	0	2	0	1.00	0	.526	.591	.632	OF	4	13	0	0	0	1.000
1986 Hou	30	3	3	2	0	0	0	2	0	0	0	0	0	0	0	0	0	1	0	1.00	0	.667	.667	.667	—						
LCS Totals		8	22	12	2	0	0	14	4	3	0	3	0	2	0	0	0	3	0	1.00	0	.545	.600	.636	OF	4	13	0	0	0	1.000
Postseason Totals		13	43	16	3	0	0	19	6	3	0	3	0	3	0	0	0	4	0	1.00	0	.372	.413	.442	OF	9	20	1	0	0	1.000

LUIS PUJOLS—Luis Bienvenido Pujols—Bats: Right; Throws: Right

Ht: 6'2"; Wt: 175 lbs; Born: 11/18/1955 in Santiago, Dominican Republic; Debut: 9/22/1977

Division Series		Batting																							Fielding						
Year Tm	Age	G	AB	H	2B	3B	HR	TB	R	RBI	GW	TBB	IBB	SO	HBP	SH	SF	SB	CS	SB%	GDP	Avg	OBP	SLG	Pos	G	PO	A	E	DP	FPct
1981 Hou	25	2	6	0	0	0	0	0	0	0	0	0	0	1	0	1	0	0	0	—	0	.000	.000	.000	C	2	12	0	0	0	1.000
LCS		Batting																							Fielding						
Year Tm	Age	G	AB	H	2B	3B	HR	TB	R	RBI	GW	TBB	IBB	SO	HBP	SH	SF	SB	CS	SB%	GDP	Avg	OBP	SLG	Pos	G	PO	A	E	DP	FPct
1980 Hou	24	4	10	1	0	1	0	3	1	0	0	3	0	0	0	0	0	0	0	—	0	.100	.308	.300	C	4	21	2	0	0	1.000
Postseason Totals		6	16	1	0	1	0	3	1	0	0	3	0	1	0	1	0	0	0	—	0	.063	.211	.188	C	6	33	2	0	0	1.000

BOB PURKEY—Robert Thomas Purkey—Throws: Right; Bats: Right

Ht: 6'2"; Wt: 175 lbs; Born: 7/14/1929 in Pittsburgh, Pennsylvania; Debut: 4/14/1954

World Series		Pitching																										
Year Tm	Age	G	GS	CG	GF	IP	BFP	H	R	ER	HR	SH	SF	HB	TBB	IBB	SO	WP	Bk	W	L	Pct	ShO	Sv-Op	Hld	OAvg	OOBP	ERA
1961 Cin	32	2	1	1	0	11.0	43	6	5	2	2	1	1	0	3	1	5	0	0	0	1	.000	0	0- 0	0	.158	.214	1.64

World Series		Batting																							Fielding						
Year Tm	Age	G	AB	H	2B	3B	HR	TB	R	RBI	GW	TBB	IBB	SO	HBP	SH	SF	SB	CS	SB%	GDP	Avg	OBP	SLG	Pos	G	PO	A	E	DP	FPct
1961 Cin	32	2	3	0	0	0	0	0	0	0	0	0	0	3	0	0	0	0	0	—	0	.000	.000	.000	P	2	4	3	1	0	.875

FRANK QUILICI—Francis Ralph Quilici—Nickname: Guido—Bats: Right; Throws: Right

Ht: 6'1"; Wt: 170 lbs; Born: 5/11/1939 in Chicago, Illinois; Debut: 7/18/1965

LCS		Batting																							Fielding						
Year Tm	Age	G	AB	H	2B	3B	HR	TB	R	RBI	GW	TBB	IBB	SO	HBP	SH	SF	SB	CS	SB%	GDP	Avg	OBP	SLG	Pos	G	PO	A	E	DP	FPct
1970 Min	31	3	2	0	0	0	0	0	0	0	0	0	0	1	0	0	0	0	0	—	0	.000	.000	.000	2B	2	1	1	0	1	1.000
World Series		Batting																							Fielding						
Year Tm	Age	G	AB	H	2B	3B	HR	TB	R	RBI	GW	TBB	IBB	SO	HBP	SH	SF	SB	CS	SB%	GDP	Avg	OBP	SLG	Pos	G	PO	A	E	DP	FPct
1965 Min	26	7	20	4	2	0	0	6	2	1	0	4	2	3	0	0	0	0	1	.00	0	.200	.333	.300	2B	7	15	18	2	0	.943
Postseason Totals		10	22	4	2	0	0	6	2	1	0	4	2	4	0	0	0	0	1	.00	0	.182	.308	.273	2B	9	16	19	2	1	.946

JACK QUINN—John Picus Quinn—Throws: Right; Bats: Right

Ht: 6'0"; Wt: 196 lbs; Born: 7/5/1883 in Janesville, Pennsylvania; Debut: 4/15/1909; Died: 4/17/1946

World Series		Pitching																										
Year Tm	Age	G	GS	CG	GF	IP	BFP	H	R	ER	HR	SH	SF	HB	TBB	IBB	SO	WP	Bk	W	L	Pct	ShO	Sv-Op	Hld	OAvg	OOBP	ERA
1921 NYA	38	1	0	0	0	3.2	19	7	4	4	0	0	0	0	2	0	2	0	0	0	1	.000	0	0- 0	0	.412	.474	9.82
1929 Phi	46	1	1	0	0	5.0	24	7	6	5	1	0	0	0	2	0	2	0	0	0	0	—	0	0- 0	0	.318	.375	9.00
1930 Phi	47	1	0	0	1	2.0	9	3	1	1	0	0	0	0	0	0	1	0	0	0	0	—	0	0- 0	0	.333	.333	4.50
WS Totals		3	1	0	1	10.2	104	17	11	10	1	0	0	0	4	0	5	0	0	0	1	.000	0	0-0	0	.354	.404	8.44

World Series		Batting																							Fielding						
Year Tm	Age	G	AB	H	2B	3B	HR	TB	R	RBI	GW	TBB	IBB	SO	HBP	SH	SF	SB	CS	SB%	GDP	Avg	OBP	SLG	Pos	G	PO	A	E	DP	FPct
1921 NYA	38	1	2	0	0	0	0	0	0	0	0	0	0	1	0	0	0	0	0	—	0	.000	.000	.000	P	1	0	1	0	1	1.000
1929 Phi	46	1	2	0	0	0	0	0	0	0	0	0	0	2	0	0	0	0	0	—	0	.000	.000	.000	P	1	0	0	0	0	—
1930 Phi	47	1	0	0	0	0	0	0	0	0	0	0	0	0	0	0	0	0	0	—	0	—	—	—	P	1	0	1	0	0	1.000
WS Totals		3	4	0	0	0	0	0	0	0	0	0	0	3	0	0	0	0	0	—	0	.000	.000	.000	P	3	0	2	0	1	1.000

LUIS QUINONES—Luis Raul Quinones—Bats: Both; Throws: Right

Ht: 5'11"; Wt: 165 lbs; Born: 4/28/1962 in Ponce, Puerto Rico; Debut: 5/27/1983

LCS		Batting																							Fielding						
Year Tm	Age	G	AB	H	2B	3B	HR	TB	R	RBI	GW	TBB	IBB	SO	HBP	SH	SF	SB	CS	SB%	GDP	Avg	OBP	SLG	Pos	G	PO	A	E	DP	FPct
1990 Cin	28	3	2	1	0	0	0	1	1	2	1	0	0	0	0	0	1	1	0	1.00	0	.500	.333	.500	—						

CARLOS QUINTANA—Carlos Narcis Quintana—Bats: Right; Throws: Right

Ht: 6'0"; Wt: 175 lbs; Born: 8/26/1965 in Estado Miranda, Venezuela; Debut: 9/16/1988

LCS		Batting																							Fielding						
Year Tm	Age	G	AB	H	2B	3B	HR	TB	R	RBI	GW	TBB	IBB	SO	HBP	SH	SF	SB	CS	SB%	GDP	Avg	OBP	SLG	Pos	G	PO	A	E	DP	FPct
1990 Bos	25	4	13	0	0	0	0	0	0	1	0	1	0	0	0	0	1	0	0	—	0	.000	.067	.000	1B	4	29	2	0	5	1.000

JAMIE QUIRK—James Patrick Quirk—Bats: Left; Throws: Right

Ht: 6'4"; Wt: 190 lbs; Born: 10/22/1954 in Whittier, California; Debut: 9/4/1975

LCS		Batting																							Fielding						
Year Tm	Age	G	AB	H	2B	3B	HR	TB	R	RBI	GW	TBB	IBB	SO	HBP	SH	SF	SB	CS	SB%	GDP	Avg	OBP	SLG	Pos	G	PO	A	E	DP	FPct
1976 KC	21	4	7	1	0	1	0	3	1	2	0	0	0	2	0	0	1	0	0	—	0	.143	.125	.429	—						
1985 KC	30	1	1	0	0	0	0	0	0	0	0	0	0	0	0	0	0	0	0	—	0	.000	.000	.000	—						
1990 Oak	35	1	1	1	0	0	0	1	0	0	0	0	0	0	0	0	0	0	0	—	0	1.000	1.000	1.000	—						
1992 Oak	37	1	1	0	0	0	0	0	0	0	0	0	0	0	0	0	0	0	0	—	0	.000	.000	.000	—						
LCS Totals		7	10	2	0	1	0	4	1	2	0	0	0	2	0	0	1	0	0	—	0	.200	.182	.400	—	0	0	0	0	0	—

World Series		Batting																							Fielding						
Year Tm	Age	G	AB	H	2B	3B	HR	TB	R	RBI	GW	TBB	IBB	SO	HBP	SH	SF	SB	CS	SB%	GDP	Avg	OBP	SLG	Pos	G	PO	A	E	DP	FPct
1990 Oak	35	1	3	0	0	0	0	0	0	0	0	0	0	2	0	0	0	0	0	—	0	.000	.000	.000	C	1	2	2	0	0	1.000
Postseason Totals		8	13	2	0	1	0	4	1	2	0	0	0	4	0	0	1	0	0	—	0	.154	.143	.308	C	1	2	2	0	0	1.000

DAN QUISENBERRY—Daniel Raymond Quisenberry—Nickname: Quiz—Throws: Right; Bats: Right

Ht: 6'2"; Wt: 170 lbs; Born: 2/7/1953 in Santa Monica, California; Debut: 7/8/1979

Division Series		Pitching																										
Year Tm	Age	G	GS	CG	GF	IP	BFP	H	R	ER	HR	SH	SF	HB	TBB	IBB	SO	WP	Bk	W	L	Pct	ShO	Sv-Op	Hld	OAvg	OOBP	ERA
1981 KC	28	1	0	0	1	1.0	4	1	0	0	0	1	0	0	0	0	0	0	0	0	0	—	0	0- 0	0	.333	.333	0.00
LCS		Pitching																										
Year Tm	Age	G	GS	CG	GF	IP	BFP	H	R	ER	HR	SH	SF	HB	TBB	IBB	SO	WP	Bk	W	L	Pct	ShO	Sv-Op	Hld	OAvg	OOBP	ERA
1980 KC	27	2	0	0	2	4.2	18	4	1	0	0	0	0	0	2	0	1	0	0	1	0	1.000	0	1- 2	0	.250	.333	0.00
1984 KC	31	1	0	0	1	3.0	13	2	2	1	0	2	0	0	1	0	1	0	0	0	1	.000	0	0- 0	0	.200	.273	3.00
1985 KC	32	4	0	0	4	4.2	21	7	4	2	0	0	1	0	0	0	3	0	0	0	1	.000	0	1- 1	0	.350	.333	3.86
LCS Totals		7	0	0	7	12.1	104	13	7	3	0	2	1	0	3	0	5	0	0	1	2	.333	0	2-3	0	.283	.320	2.19
World Series		Pitching																										
Year Tm	Age	G	GS	CG	GF	IP	BFP	H	R	ER	HR	SH	SF	HB	TBB	IBB	SO	WP	Bk	W	L	Pct	ShO	Sv-Op	Hld	OAvg	OOBP	ERA
1980 KC	27	6	0	0	6	10.1	43	10	6	6	0	2	1	0	3	2	0	0	0	1	2	.333	0	1- 3	0	.270	.317	5.23
1985 KC	32	4	0	0	3	4.1	19	5	1	1	0	1	0	0	3	2	3	1	0	1	0	1.000	0	0- 0	0	.333	.444	2.08
WS Totals		10	0	0	9	14.2	124	15	7	7	0	3	1	0	6	4	3	1	0	2	2	.500	0	1-3	0	.288	.356	4.30
Postseason Totals		18	0	0	17	28.0	236	29	14	10	0	6	2	0	9	4	8	1	0	3	4	.429	0	3-6	0	.287	.339	3.21

Division Series		Batting																							Fielding						
Year Tm	Age	G	AB	H	2B	3B	HR	TB	R	RBI	GW	TBB	IBB	SO	HBP	SH	SF	SB	CS	SB%	GDP	Avg	OBP	SLG	Pos	G	PO	A	E	DP	FPct
1981 KC	28	1	0	0	0	0	0	0	0	0	0	0	0	0	0	0	0	0	0	—	0	—	—	—	P	1	0	0	0	0	—
LCS		Batting																							Fielding						
Year Tm	Age	G	AB	H	2B	3B	HR	TB	R	RBI	GW	TBB	IBB	SO	HBP	SH	SF	SB	CS	SB%	GDP	Avg	OBP	SLG	Pos	G	PO	A	E	DP	FPct
1980 KC	27	2	0	0	0	0	0	0	0	0	0	0	0	0	0	0	0	0	0	—	0	—	—	—	P	2	1	0	0	0	1.000
1984 KC	31	1	0	0	0	0	0	0	0	0	0	0	0	0	0	0	0	0	0	—	0	—	—	—	P	1	1	1	0	0	1.000
1985 KC	32	4	0	0	0	0	0	0	0	0	0	0	0	0	0	0	0	0	0	—	0	—	—	—	P	4	1	1	0	0	1.000
LCS Totals		7	0	0	0	0	0	0	0	0	0	0	0	0	0	0	0	0	0	—	0	—	—	—	P	7	3	2	0	0	1.000
World Series		Batting																							Fielding						
Year Tm	Age	G	AB	H	2B	3B	HR	TB	R	RBI	GW	TBB	IBB	SO	HBP	SH	SF	SB	CS	SB%	GDP	Avg	OBP	SLG	Pos	G	PO	A	E	DP	FPct
1980 KC	27	6	0	0	0	0	0	0	0	0	0	0	0	0	0	0	0	0	0	—	0	—	—	—	P	6	1	1	0	0	1.000
1985 KC	32	4	0	0	0	0	0	0	0	0	0	0	0	0	0	0	0	0	0	—	0	—	—	—	P	4	1	1	0	0	1.000
WS Totals		10	0	0	0	0	0	0	0	0	0	0	0	0	0	0	0	0	0	—	0	—	—	—	P	10	2	2	0	0	1.000
Postseason Totals		18	0	0	0	0	0	0	0	0	0	0	0	0	0	0	0	0	0	—	0	—	—	—	P	18	5	4	0	0	1.000

MARV RACKLEY—Marvin Eugene Rackley—Bats: Left; Throws: Left

Ht: 5'10"; Wt: 170 lbs; Born: 7/25/1921 in Seneca, South Carolina; Debut: 4/15/1947

World Series		Batting																							Fielding						
Year Tm	Age	G	AB	H	2B	3B	HR	TB	R	RBI	GW	TBB	IBB	SO	HBP	SH	SF	SB	CS	SB%	GDP	Avg	OBP	SLG	Pos	G	PO	A	E	DP	FPct
1949 Bro	28	2	5	0	0	0	0	0	0	0	0	0	0	2	0	0	0	0	0	—	0	.000	.000	.000	OF	2	3	0	0	0	1.000

SCOTT RADINSKY—Scott David Radinsky—Nickname: Rads—Throws: Left; Bats: Left

Ht: 6'3"; Wt: 190 lbs; Born: 3/3/1968 in Glendale, California; Debut: 4/9/1990

Division Series		Pitching																										
Year Tm	Age	G	GS	CG	GF	IP	BFP	H	R	ER	HR	SH	SF	HB	TBB	IBB	SO	WP	Bk	W	L	Pct	ShO	Sv-Op	Hld	OAvg	OOBP	ERA
1996 LA	28	2	0	0	0	1.1	5	0	0	0	0	0	0	0	1	0	2	0	0	0	0	—	0	0- 0	0	.000	.200	0.00
LCS		Pitching																										
Year Tm	Age	G	GS	CG	GF	IP	BFP	H	R	ER	HR	SH	SF	HB	TBB	IBB	SO	WP	Bk	W	L	Pct	ShO	Sv-Op	Hld	OAvg	OOBP	ERA
1993 ChA	25	4	0	0	0	1.2	10	3	4	2	1	0	0	0	1	0	1	0	0	0	0	—	0	0- 0	1	.333	.400	10.80
Postseason Totals		6	0	0	0	3.0	30	3	4	2	1	0	0	0	2	0	3	0	0	0	0	—	0	0-0	1	.231	.333	6.00

Division Series		Batting																							Fielding						
Year Tm	Age	G	AB	H	2B	3B	HR	TB	R	RBI	GW	TBB	IBB	SO	HBP	SH	SF	SB	CS	SB%	GDP	Avg	OBP	SLG	Pos	G	PO	A	E	DP	FPct
1996 LA	28	2	0	0	0	0	0	0	0	0	0	0	0	0	0	0	0	0	0	—	0	—	—	—	P	2	0	0	0	0	—
LCS		Batting																							Fielding						
Year Tm	Age	G	AB	H	2B	3B	HR	TB	R	RBI	GW	TBB	IBB	SO	HBP	SH	SF	SB	CS	SB%	GDP	Avg	OBP	SLG	Pos	G	PO	A	E	DP	FPct
1993 ChA	25	4	0	0	0	0	0	0	0	0	0	0	0	0	0	0	0	0	0	—	0	—	—	—	P	4	0	0	1	0	.000
Postseason Totals		6	0	0	0	0	0	0	0	0	0	0	0	0	0	0	0	0	0	—	0	—	—	—	P	6	0	0	1	0	.000

TIM RAINES—Timothy Raines—Nickname: Rock—Bats: Both; Throws: Right

Ht: 5'8"; Wt: 160 lbs; Born: 9/16/1959 in Sanford, Florida; Debut: 9/11/1979

Division Series		Batting																							Fielding						
Year Tm	Age	G	AB	H	2B	3B	HR	TB	R	RBI	GW	TBB	IBB	SO	HBP	SH	SF	SB	CS	SB%	GDP	Avg	OBP	SLG	Pos	G	PO	A	E	DP	FPct
1996 NYA	37	4	16	4	0	0	0	4	3	0	0	3	0	1	0	1	0	0	0	—	1	.250	.368	.250	OF	4	5	0	0	0	1.000
1997 NYA	38	5	19	4	0	0	1	7	4	3	0	3	1	1	0	0	1	2	0	1.00	1	.211	.304	.368	OF	3	7	0	0	0	1.000
DS Totals		9	35	8	0	0	1	11	7	3	0	6	1	2	0	1	1	2	0	1.00	2	.229	.333	.314	OF	7	12	0	0	0	1.000
LCS		Batting																							Fielding						
Year Tm	Age	G	AB	H	2B	3B	HR	TB	R	RBI	GW	TBB	IBB	SO	HBP	SH	SF	SB	CS	SB%	GDP	Avg	OBP	SLG	Pos	G	PO	A	E	DP	FPct
1981 Mon	22	5	21	5	2	0	0	7	1	1	0	0	0	3	0	0	0	0	1	.00	0	.238	.238	.333	OF	5	9	0	0	0	1.000
1993 ChA	34	6	27	12	2	0	0	14	5	1	0	2	0	2	0	0	0	1	1	.50	0	.444	.483	.519	OF	6	12	2	0	0	1.000
1996 NYA	37	5	15	4	1	0	0	5	2	0	0	1	0	1	0	0	0	0	0	—	1	.267	.313	.333	OF	5	5	0	0	0	1.000
LCS Totals		16	63	21	5	0	0	26	8	2	0	3	0	6	0	0	0	1	2	.33	1	.333	.364	.413	OF	16	26	2	0	0	1.000
World Series		Batting																							Fielding						
Year Tm	Age	G	AB	H	2B	3B	HR	TB	R	RBI	GW	TBB	IBB	SO	HBP	SH	SF	SB	CS	SB%	GDP	Avg	OBP	SLG	Pos	G	PO	A	E	DP	FPct
1996 NYA	37	4	14	3	0	0	0	3	2	0	0	2	0	1	0	0	0	0	1	.00	0	.214	.313	.214	OF	4	5	0	1	0	.833
Postseason Totals		29	112	32	5	0	1	40	17	5	0	11	1	9	0	1	1	3	3	.50	3	.286	.347	.357	OF	27	43	2	1	0	.978

MANNY RAMIREZ—Manuel Aristedes Ramirez—Bats: Right; Throws: Right

Ht: 6'0"; Wt: 190 lbs; Born: 5/30/1972 in Santo Domingo, Dominican Republic; Debut: 9/2/1993

Division Series		Batting																							Fielding						
Year Tm	Age	G	AB	H	2B	3B	HR	TB	R	RBI	GW	TBB	IBB	SO	HBP	SH	SF	SB	CS	SB%	GDP	Avg	OBP	SLG	Pos	G	PO	A	E	DP	FPct
1995 Cle	23	3	12	0	0	0	0	0	1	0	0	1	0	2	1	0	0	0	0	—	0	.000	.143	.000	OF	3	3	0	0	0	1.000
1996 Cle	24	4	16	6	2	0	2	14	4	2	0	1	0	4	0	0	0	0	0	—	1	.375	.412	.875	OF	4	8	2	0	0	1.000
1997 Cle	25	5	21	3	1	0	0	4	2	3	1	0	0	3	0	0	0	0	0	—	2	.143	.143	.190	OF	5	3	0	1	0	.750
DS Totals		12	49	9	3	0	2	18	7	5	1	2	0	9	1	0	0	0	0	—	3	.184	.231	.367	OF	12	14	2	1	0	.941
LCS		Batting																							Fielding						
Year Tm	Age	G	AB	H	2B	3B	HR	TB	R	RBI	GW	TBB	IBB	SO	HBP	SH	SF	SB	CS	SB%	GDP	Avg	OBP	SLG	Pos	G	PO	A	E	DP	FPct
1995 Cle	23	6	21	6	0	0	2	12	2	2	0	2	0	5	0	0	0	0	0	—	1	.286	.348	.571	OF	6	9	0	0	0	1.000
1997 Cle	25	6	21	6	1	0	2	13	3	3	0	5	1	5	1	0	0	0	0	—	1	.286	.444	.619	OF	6	14	0	1	0	.933
LCS Totals		12	42	12	1	0	4	25	5	5	0	7	1	10	1	0	0	0	0	—	2	.286	.400	.595	OF	12	23	0	1	0	.958
World Series		Batting																							Fielding						
Year Tm	Age	G	AB	H	2B	3B	HR	TB	R	RBI	GW	TBB	IBB	SO	HBP	SH	SF	SB	CS	SB%	GDP	Avg	OBP	SLG	Pos	G	PO	A	E	DP	FPct
1995 Cle	23	6	18	4	0	0	1	7	2	2	0	4	1	5	0	0	0	1	0	1.00	1	.222	.364	.389	OF	6	8	0	0	0	1.000
1997 Cle	25	7	26	4	0	0	2	10	3	6	1	6	1	5	0	0	2	0	0	—	2	.154	.294	.385	OF	7	16	1	1	0	.944
WS Totals		13	44	8	0	0	3	17	5	8	1	10	2	10	0	0	2	1	0	1.00	3	.182	.321	.386	OF	13	24	1	1	0	.962
Postseason Totals		37	135	29	4	0	9	60	17	18	2	19	3	29	2	0	2	1	0	1.00	8	.215	.316	.444	OF	37	61	3	3	0	.955

MARIO RAMIREZ—Bats: Right; Throws: Right

Ht: 5'9"; Wt: 155 lbs; Born: 9/12/1957 in Yauco, Puerto Rico; Debut: 4/25/1980

LCS		Batting																							Fielding						
Year Tm	Age	G	AB	H	2B	3B	HR	TB	R	RBI	GW	TBB	IBB	SO	HBP	SH	SF	SB	CS	SB%	GDP	Avg	OBP	SLG	Pos	G	PO	A	E	DP	FPct
1984 SD	27	2	2	0	0	0	0	0	0	0	0	0	0	0	0	0	0	0	0	—	0	.000	.000	.000	—						

RAFAEL RAMIREZ—Rafael Emilio Ramirez—Bats: Right; Throws: Right

Ht: 6'0"; Wt: 170 lbs; Born: 2/18/1958 in San Pedro de Macoris, Dominican Republic; Debut: 8/4/1980

LCS		Batting																							Fielding						
Year Tm	Age	G	AB	H	2B	3B	HR	TB	R	RBI	GW	TBB	IBB	SO	HBP	SH	SF	SB	CS	SB%	GDP	Avg	OBP	SLG	Pos	G	PO	A	E	DP	FPct
1982 Atl	24	3	11	2	0	0	0	2	1	1	0	1	0	1	0	0	0	0	0	—	0	.182	.250	.182	SS	3	5	11	1	0	.941

DOMINGO RAMOS—Domingo Antonio Ramos—Bats: Right; Throws: Right

Ht: 5'10"; Wt: 154 lbs; Born: 3/29/1958 in Santiago, Dominican Republic; Debut: 9/8/1978

LCS		Batting																							Fielding						
Year Tm	Age	G	AB	H	2B	3B	HR	TB	R	RBI	GW	TBB	IBB	SO	HBP	SH	SF	SB	CS	SB%	GDP	Avg	OBP	SLG	Pos	G	PO	A	E	DP	FPct
1989 ChN	31	1	1	0	0	0	0	0	0	0	0	0	0	0	0	0	0	0	0	—	0	.000	.000	.000	—						

MIKE RAMSEY—Michael Jeffrey Ramsey—Bats: Both; Throws: Right

Ht: 6'1"; Wt: 170 lbs; Born: 3/29/1954 in Roanoke, Virginia; Debut: 9/4/1978

World Series		Batting																							Fielding						
Year Tm	Age	G	AB	H	2B	3B	HR	TB	R	RBI	GW	TBB	IBB	SO	HBP	SH	SF	SB	CS	SB%	GDP	Avg	OBP	SLG	Pos	G	PO	A	E	DP	FPct
1982 StL	28	3	1	0	0	0	0	0	1	0	0	0	0	1	0	0	0	0	0	—	0	.000	.000	.000	3B	2	0	0	0	0	—

WILLIE RANDOLPH—Willie Larry Randolph—Bats: Right; Throws: Right

Ht: 5'11"; Wt: 165 lbs; Born: 7/6/1954 in Holly Hill, South Carolina; Debut: 7/29/1975

Division Series		Batting																							Fielding						
Year Tm	Age	G	AB	H	2B	3B	HR	TB	R	RBI	GW	TBB	IBB	SO	HBP	SH	SF	SB	CS	SB%	GDP	Avg	OBP	SLG	Pos	G	PO	A	E	DP	FPct
1981 NYA	27	5	20	4	0	0	0	4	0	1	0	1	0	4	0	0	0	0	0	—	0	.200	.238	.200	2B	5	9	9	0	1	1.000
LCS		**Batting**																							**Fielding**						
Year Tm	Age	G	AB	H	2B	3B	HR	TB	R	RBI	GW	TBB	IBB	SO	HBP	SH	SF	SB	CS	SB%	GDP	Avg	OBP	SLG	Pos	G	PO	A	E	DP	FPct
1975 Pit	21	2	2	0	0	0	0	0	1	0	0	0	0	1	0	0	0	0	0	—	0	.000	.000	.000	2B	1	0	1	0	0	1.000
1976 NYA	22	5	17	2	0	0	0	2	0	1	0	3	0	1	0	0	0	1	0	1.00	2	.118	.250	.118	2B	5	8	14	0	2	1.000
1977 NYA	23	5	18	5	1	0	0	6	4	2	1	1	0	0	0	0	1	0	0	—	1	.278	.300	.333	2B	5	13	9	0	2	1.000
1980 NYA	26	3	13	5	2	0	0	7	0	1	0	1	0	3	0	0	0	0	0	—	0	.385	.429	.538	2B	3	1	9	0	2	1.000
1981 NYA	27	3	12	4	0	0	1	7	2	2	1	0	0	1	0	0	0	0	0	—	1	.333	.333	.583	2B	3	12	12	0	4	1.000
1990 Oak	36	4	8	3	0	0	0	3	1	3	1	1	0	0	0	0	0	0	0	—	1	.375	.444	.375	2B	4	5	9	0	1	1.000
LCS Totals		22	70	19	3	0	1	25	8	9	3	6	0	6	0	0	1	1	0	1.00	5	.271	.325	.357	2B	21	39	54	0	11	1.000
World Series		**Batting**																							**Fielding**						
Year Tm	Age	G	AB	H	2B	3B	HR	TB	R	RBI	GW	TBB	IBB	SO	HBP	SH	SF	SB	CS	SB%	GDP	Avg	OBP	SLG	Pos	G	PO	A	E	DP	FPct
1976 NYA	22	4	14	1	0	0	0	1	1	0	0	1	0	3	0	0	0	0	0	—	0	.071	.133	.071	2B	4	13	8	0	5	1.000
1977 NYA	23	6	25	4	2	0	1	9	5	1	0	2	0	2	0	0	0	0	0	—	0	.160	.222	.360	2B	6	13	14	0	1	1.000
1981 NYA	27	6	18	4	1	1	2	13	5	3	0	9	0	0	0	0	1	1	1	.50	0	.222	.464	.722	2B	6	13	11	0	2	1.000
1990 Oak	36	4	15	4	0	0	0	4	0	0	0	1	0	0	0	0	0	1	0	1.00	0	.267	.313	.267	2B	4	14	12	0	5	1.000
WS Totals		20	72	13	3	1	3	27	11	4	0	13	0	5	0	0	1	2	1	.67	0	.181	.302	.375	2B	20	53	45	0	13	1.000
Postseason Totals		47	162	36	6	1	4	56	19	14	3	20	0	15	0	0	2	3	1	.75	5	.222	.304	.346	2B	46	101	108	0	25	1.000

BILL RARIDEN—William Angel Rariden—Nickname: Bedford Bill—Bats: Right; Throws: Right

Ht: 5'10"; Wt: 168 lbs; Born: 2/4/1888 in Bedford, Indiana; Debut: 8/12/1909; Died: 8/28/1942

World Series		Batting																							Fielding						
Year Tm	Age	G	AB	H	2B	3B	HR	TB	R	RBI	GW	TBB	IBB	SO	HBP	SH	SF	SB	CS	SB%	GDP	Avg	OBP	SLG	Pos	G	PO	A	E	DP	FPct
1917 NYG	29	5	13	5	0	0	0	5	2	2	0	2	1	1	0	1	0	0	0	—	1	.385	.467	.385	C	5	25	11	0	1	1.000
1919 Cin	31	5	19	4	0	0	0	4	0	2	0	0	0	0	0	0	0	1	0	1.00	0	.211	.211	.211	C	5	25	3	1	0	.966
WS Totals		10	32	9	0	0	0	9	2	4	0	2	1	1	0	1	0	1	0	1.00	1	.281	.324	.281	C	10	50	14	1	1	.985

VIC RASCHI—Victor John Angelo Raschi—Nickname: The Springfield Rifle—Throws: Right; Bats: Right

Ht: 6'1"; Wt: 205 lbs; Born: 3/28/1919 in West Springfield, Massachusetts; Debut: 9/23/1946; Died: 10/14/1988

World Series		Pitching																										
Year Tm	Age	G	GS	CG	GF	IP	BFP	H	R	ER	HR	SH	SF	HB	TBB	IBB	SO	WP	Bk	W	L	Pct	ShO	Sv-Op	Hld	OAvg	OOBP	ERA
1947 NYA	28	2	0	0	0	1.1	6	2	1	1	0	0	0	0	0	0	1	0	0	0	0	—	0	0-0	0	.333	.333	6.75
1949 NYA	30	2	2	0	0	14.2	62	15	7	7	1	0	0	0	5	1	11	0	0	1	1	.500	0	0-0	0	.263	.323	4.30
1950 NYA	31	1	1	1	0	9.0	30	2	0	0	0	0	0	0	1	0	5	0	0	1	0	1.000	1	0-0	0	.069	.100	0.00
1951 NYA	32	2	2	0	0	10.1	50	12	7	1	1	0	0	1	8	0	4	0	0	1	1	.500	0	0-0	0	.293	.420	0.87
1952 NYA	33	3	2	1	0	17.0	71	12	3	3	2	0	0	0	8	0	18	0	0	2	0	1.000	0	0-0	1	.190	.282	1.59
1953 NYA	34	1	1	1	0	8.0	35	9	3	3	1	1	0	0	3	0	4	0	1	0	1	.000	0	0-0	0	.290	.353	3.38
WS Totals		11	8	3	0	60.1	508	52	21	15	5	1	0	1	25	1	43	0	1	5	3	.625	1	0-0	1	.229	.308	2.24

World Series		Batting																							Fielding						
Year Tm	Age	G	AB	H	2B	3B	HR	TB	R	RBI	GW	TBB	IBB	SO	HBP	SH	SF	SB	CS	SB%	GDP	Avg	OBP	SLG	Pos	G	PO	A	E	DP	FPct
1947 NYA	28	2	0	0	0	0	0	0	0	0	0	0	0	0	0	0	0	0	0	—	0	—	—	—	P	2	0	0	0	0	—
1949 NYA	30	2	5	1	0	0	0	1	0	1	0	1	0	1	0	0	0	0	0	—	0	.200	.333	.200	P	2	0	0	0	0	—
1950 NYA	31	1	3	1	0	0	0	1	0	0	0	0	0	0	0	1	0	0	0	—	0	.333	.333	.333	P	1	0	3	0	0	1.000
1951 NYA	32	2	2	0	0	0	0	0	0	0	0	2	0	1	0	0	0	0	0	—	0	.000	.500	.000	P	2	0	0	0	0	—
1952 NYA	33	3	6	1	0	0	0	1	0	1	1	1	0	2	0	0	0	0	0	—	1	.167	.286	.167	P	3	0	1	0	0	1.000
1953 NYA	34	1	2	0	0	0	0	0	0	0	0	0	0	1	0	1	0	0	0	—	0	.000	.000	.000	P	1	1	1	0	0	1.000
WS Totals		11	18	3	0	0	0	3	0	2	1	4	0	5	0	2	0	0	0	—	1	.167	.318	.167	P	11	1	5	0	0	1.000

MORRIE RATH—Morris Charles Rath—Bats: Left; Throws: Right

Ht: 5'8"; Wt: 160 lbs; Born: 12/25/1886 in Mobeetie, Texas; Debut: 9/28/1909; Died: 11/18/1945

World Series		Batting																							Fielding						
Year Tm	Age	G	AB	H	2B	3B	HR	TB	R	RBI	GW	TBB	IBB	SO	HBP	SH	SF	SB	CS	SB%	GDP	Avg	OBP	SLG	Pos	G	PO	A	E	DP	FPct
1919 Cin	32	8	31	7	1	0	0	8	5	2	1	4	0	1	1	1	0	2	0	1.00	0	.226	.333	.258	2B	8	21	16	2	4	.949

PAUL RATLIFF—Paul Hawthorne Ratliff—Bats: Left; Throws: Right

Ht: 6'2"; Wt: 190 lbs; Born: 1/23/1944 in San Diego, California; Debut: 4/14/1963

LCS		Batting																							Fielding						
Year Tm	Age	G	AB	H	2B	3B	HR	TB	R	RBI	GW	TBB	IBB	SO	HBP	SH	SF	SB	CS	SB%	GDP	Avg	OBP	SLG	Pos	G	PO	A	E	DP	FPct
1970 Min	26	1	4	1	0	0	0	1	0	0	0	0	0	1	0	0	0	0	0	—	0	.250	.250	.250	C	1	7	0	1	0	.875

DOUG RAU—Douglas James Rau—Throws: Left; Bats: Left

Ht: 6'2"; Wt: 175 lbs; Born: 12/15/1948 in Columbus, Texas; Debut: 9/2/1972

LCS		Pitching																										
Year Tm	Age	G	GS	CG	GF	IP	BFP	H	R	ER	HR	SH	SF	HB	TBB	IBB	SO	WP	Bk	W	L	Pct	ShO	Sv-Op	Hld	OAvg	OOBP	ERA
1974 LA	25	1	1	0	0	0.2	7	3	5	3	2	0	0	0	1	0	0	0	0	0	1	.000	0	0-0	0	.500	.571	40.50
1977 LA	28	1	0	0	0	1.0	3	0	0	0	0	0	0	0	0	0	1	0	0	0	0	—	0	0-0	0	.000	.000	0.00
1978 LA	29	1	1	0	0	5.0	21	5	2	2	1	0	0	0	2	0	1	0	0	0	0	—	0	0-0	0	.263	.333	3.60
LCS Totals		3	2	0	0	6.2	62	8	7	5	3	0	0	0	3	0	2	0	0	0	1	.000	0	0-0	0	.286	.355	6.75
World Series		**Pitching**																										
Year Tm	Age	G	GS	CG	GF	IP	BFP	H	R	ER	HR	SH	SF	HB	TBB	IBB	SO	WP	Bk	W	L	Pct	ShO	Sv-Op	Hld	OAvg	OOBP	ERA
1977 LA	28	2	1	0	0	2.1	10	4	3	3	0	0	0	0	0	0	1	0	0	0	1	.000	0	0-0	0	.400	.400	11.57
1978 LA	29	1	0	0	1	2.0	7	1	0	0	0	0	0	0	0	0	3	0	0	0	0	—	0	0-0	0	.143	.143	0.00
WS Totals		3	1	0	1	4.1	34	5	3	3	0	0	0	0	0	0	4	0	0	0	1	.000	0	0-0	0	.294	.294	6.23
Postseason Totals		6	3	0	1	11.0	96	13	10	8	3	0	0	0	3	0	6	0	0	0	2	.000	0	0-0	0	.289	.333	6.55

LCS		Batting																							Fielding						
Year Tm	Age	G	AB	H	2B	3B	HR	TB	R	RBI	GW	TBB	IBB	SO	HBP	SH	SF	SB	CS	SB%	GDP	Avg	OBP	SLG	Pos	G	PO	A	E	DP	FPct
1974 LA	25	1	0	0	0	0	0	0	0	0	0	0	0	0	0	0	0	0	0	—	0	—	—	—	P	1	0	0	0	0	—
1977 LA	28	1	0	0	0	0	0	0	0	0	0	0	0	0	0	0	0	0	0	—	0	—	—	—	P	1	0	0	0	0	—
1978 LA	29	1	1	0	0	0	0	0	0	0	0	0	0	0	0	0	0	0	0	—	0	.000	.000	.000	P	1	1	0	0	0	1.000
LCS Totals		3	1	0	0	0	0	0	0	0	0	0	0	0	0	0	0	0	0	—	0	.000	.000	.000	P	3	1	0	0	0	1.000
World Series		**Batting**																							**Fielding**						
Year Tm	Age	G	AB	H	2B	3B	HR	TB	R	RBI	GW	TBB	IBB	SO	HBP	SH	SF	SB	CS	SB%	GDP	Avg	OBP	SLG	Pos	G	PO	A	E	DP	FPct
1977 LA	28	2	0	0	0	0	0	0	0	0	0	0	0	0	0	0	0	0	0	—	0	—	—	—	P	2	0	0	0	0	—
1978 LA	29	1	0	0	0	0	0	0	0	0	0	0	0	0	0	0	0	0	0	—	0	—	—	—	P	1	0	1	0	0	1.000
WS Totals		3	0	0	0	0	0	0	0	0	0	0	0	0	0	0	0	0	0	—	0	—	—	—	P	3	0	1	0	0	1.000
Postseason Totals		6	1	0	0	0	0	0	0	0	0	0	0	0	0	0	0	0	0	—	0	.000	.000	.000	P	6	1	1	0	0	1.000

LANCE RAUTZHAN—Clarence George Rautzhan—Throws: Left; Bats: Right

Ht: 6'1"; Wt: 195 lbs; Born: 8/20/1952 in Pottsville, Pennsylvania; Debut: 7/23/1977

LCS — Pitching

Year Tm	Age	G	GS	CG	GF	IP	BFP	H	R	ER	HR	SH	SF	HB	TBB	IBB	SO	WP	Bk	W	L	Pct	ShO	Sv-Op	Hld	OAvg	OOBP	ERA
1977 LA	25	1	0	0	0	0.1	1	0	0	0	0	0	0	0	0	0	0	0	0	1	0	1.000	0	0-0	0	.000	.000	0.00
1978 LA	26	1	0	0	0	1.1	9	3	1	1	0	1	0	0	2	2	0	0	0	0	0	—	0	0-0	0	.500	.625	6.75
LCS Totals		2	0	0	0	1.2	20	3	1	1	0	1	0	0	2	2	0	0	0	1	0	1.000	0	0-0	0	.429	.556	5.40

World Series — Pitching

Year Tm	Age	G	GS	CG	GF	IP	BFP	H	R	ER	HR	SH	SF	HB	TBB	IBB	SO	WP	Bk	W	L	Pct	ShO	Sv-Op	Hld	OAvg	OOBP	ERA
1977 LA	25	1	0	0	0	0.1	3	0	0	0	0	0	0	0	2	0	0	0	0	0	0	—	0	0-0	0	.000	.667	0.00
1978 LA	26	2	0	0	0	2.0	9	4	3	3	0	0	0	0	0	0	0	0	0	0	0	—	0	0-0	0	.444	.444	13.50
WS Totals		3	0	0	0	2.1	24	4	3	3	0	0	0	0	2	0	0	0	0	0	0	—	0	0-0	0	.400	.500	11.57
Postseason Totals		5	0	0	0	4.0	44	7	4	4	0	1	0	0	4	2	0	0	0	1	0	1.000	0	0-0	0	.412	.524	9.00

LCS — Batting / Fielding

Year Tm	Age	G	AB	H	2B	3B	HR	TB	R	RBI	GW	TBB	IBB	SO	HBP	SH	SF	SB	CS	SB%	GDP	Avg	OBP	SLG	Pos	G	PO	A	E	DP	FPct
1977 LA	25	1	0	0	0	0	0	0	0	0	0	0	0	0	0	0	0	0	0	—	0	—	—	—	P	1	0	0	0	0	—
1978 LA	26	1	0	0	0	0	0	0	0	0	0	0	0	0	0	0	0	0	0	—	0	—	—	—	P	1	0	1	0	0	1.000
LCS Totals		2	0	0	0	0	0	0	0	0	0	0	0	0	0	0	0	0	0	—	0	—	—	—	P	2	0	1	0	0	1.000

World Series — Batting / Fielding

Year Tm	Age	G	AB	H	2B	3B	HR	TB	R	RBI	GW	TBB	IBB	SO	HBP	SH	SF	SB	CS	SB%	GDP	Avg	OBP	SLG	Pos	G	PO	A	E	DP	FPct
1977 LA	25	1	0	0	0	0	0	0	0	0	0	0	0	0	0	0	0	0	0	—	0	—	—	—	P	1	0	1	0	0	1.000
1978 LA	26	2	0	0	0	0	0	0	0	0	0	0	0	0	0	0	0	0	0	—	0	—	—	—	P	2	0	0	0	0	—
WS Totals		3	0	0	0	0	0	0	0	0	0	0	0	0	0	0	0	0	0	—	0	—	—	—	P	3	0	1	0	0	1.000
Postseason Totals		5	0	0	0	0	0	0	0	0	0	0	0	0	0	0	0	0	0	—	0	—	—	—	P	5	0	2	0	0	1.000

JOHNNY RAWLINGS—John William Rawlings—Nickname: Red—Bats: Right; Throws: Right

Ht: 5'8"; Wt: 158 lbs; Born: 8/17/1892 in Bloomfield, Iowa; Debut: 4/14/1914; Died: 10/16/1972

World Series — Batting / Fielding

Year Tm	Age	G	AB	H	2B	3B	HR	TB	R	RBI	GW	TBB	IBB	SO	HBP	SH	SF	SB	CS	SB%	GDP	Avg	OBP	SLG	Pos	G	PO	A	E	DP	FPct
1921 NYG	29	8	30	10	3	0	0	13	2	4	0	0	0	3	1	0	0	0	1	.00	0	.333	.355	.433	2B	8	20	27	0	5	1.000

RANDY READY—Randy Max Ready—Bats: Right; Throws: Right

Ht: 5'11"; Wt: 180 lbs; Born: 1/8/1960 in San Mateo, California; Debut: 9/4/1983

LCS — Batting / Fielding

Year Tm	Age	G	AB	H	2B	3B	HR	TB	R	RBI	GW	TBB	IBB	SO	HBP	SH	SF	SB	CS	SB%	GDP	Avg	OBP	SLG	Pos	G	PO	A	E	DP	FPct
1992 Oak	32	1	1	0	0	0	0	0	0	0	0	0	0	1	0	0	0	0	0	—	0	.000	.000	.000	—						

JEFF REARDON—Jeffrey James Reardon—Nickname: The Terminator—Throws: Right; Bats: Right

Ht: 6'0"; Wt: 190 lbs; Born: 10/1/1955 in Pittsfield, Massachusetts; Debut: 8/25/1979

Division Series — Pitching

Year Tm	Age	G	GS	CG	GF	IP	BFP	H	R	ER	HR	SH	SF	HB	TBB	IBB	SO	WP	Bk	W	L	Pct	ShO	Sv-Op	Hld	OAvg	OOBP	ERA
1981 Mon	26	3	0	0	3	4.1	15	1	1	1	1	0	0	0	1	1	2	0	0	0	1	.000	0	2-2	0	.071	.133	2.08

LCS — Pitching

Year Tm	Age	G	GS	CG	GF	IP	BFP	H	R	ER	HR	SH	SF	HB	TBB	IBB	SO	WP	Bk	W	L	Pct	ShO	Sv-Op	Hld	OAvg	OOBP	ERA
1981 Mon	26	1	0	0	1	1.0	6	3	3	3	2	0	0	0	0	0	0	0	0	0	0	—	0	0-0	0	.500	.500	27.00
1987 Min	32	4	0	0	4	5.1	26	7	3	3	1	0	2	0	3	0	5	1	0	1	1	.500	0	2-4	0	.333	.385	5.06
1990 Bos	35	1	0	0	1	2.0	10	3	2	2	0	0	0	1	1	0	0	0	0	0	0	—	0	0-0	0	.375	.500	9.00
1992 Atl	37	3	0	0	3	3.0	11	0	0	0	0	0	0	0	2	0	3	1	0	1	0	1.000	0	1-1	0	.000	.182	0.00
LCS Totals		9	0	0	9	11.1	106	13	8	8	3	0	2	1	6	0	8	2	0	2	1	.667	0	3-5	0	.295	.377	6.35

World Series — Pitching

Year Tm	Age	G	GS	CG	GF	IP	BFP	H	R	ER	HR	SH	SF	HB	TBB	IBB	SO	WP	Bk	W	L	Pct	ShO	Sv-Op	Hld	OAvg	OOBP	ERA
1987 Min	32	4	0	0	4	4.2	19	5	0	0	0	0	0	0	0	0	3	0	0	0	0	—	0	1-1	0	.263	.263	0.00
1992 Atl	37	2	0	0	2	1.1	7	2	2	2	1	0	0	0	1	0	1	0	0	0	1	.000	0	0-1	0	.333	.429	13.50
WS Totals		6	0	0	6	6.0	52	7	2	2	1	0	0	0	1	0	4	0	0	0	1	.000	0	1-2	0	.280	.308	3.00
Postseason Totals		18	0	0	18	21.2	188	21	11	11	5	0	2	1	8	1	14	2	0	2	3	.400	0	6-9	0	.253	.319	4.57

Division Series — Batting / Fielding

Year Tm	Age	G	AB	H	2B	3B	HR	TB	R	RBI	GW	TBB	IBB	SO	HBP	SH	SF	SB	CS	SB%	GDP	Avg	OBP	SLG	Pos	G	PO	A	E	DP	FPct
1981 Mon	26	3	1	0	0	0	0	0	0	0	0	0	0	1	0	0	0	0	0	—	0	.000	.000	.000	P	3	0	1	0	0	1.000

LCS — Batting / Fielding

Year Tm	Age	G	AB	H	2B	3B	HR	TB	R	RBI	GW	TBB	IBB	SO	HBP	SH	SF	SB	CS	SB%	GDP	Avg	OBP	SLG	Pos	G	PO	A	E	DP	FPct
1981 Mon	26	1	0	0	0	0	0	0	0	0	0	0	0	0	0	0	0	0	0	—	0	—	—	—	P	1	0	0	0	0	—
1987 Min	32	4	0	0	0	0	0	0	0	0	0	0	0	0	0	0	0	0	0	—	0	—	—	—	P	4	0	1	0	0	1.000
1990 Bos	35	1	0	0	0	0	0	0	0	0	0	0	0	0	0	0	0	0	0	—	0	—	—	—	P	1	0	0	0	0	—
1992 Atl	37	3	0	0	0	0	0	0	0	0	0	0	0	0	0	0	0	0	0	—	0	—	—	—	P	3	0	0	0	0	—
LCS Totals		9	0	0	0	0	0	0	0	0	0	0	0	0	0	0	0	0	0	—	0	—	—	—	P	9	0	1	0	0	1.000

World Series — Batting / Fielding

Year Tm	Age	G	AB	H	2B	3B	HR	TB	R	RBI	GW	TBB	IBB	SO	HBP	SH	SF	SB	CS	SB%	GDP	Avg	OBP	SLG	Pos	G	PO	A	E	DP	FPct
1987 Min	32	4	0	0	0	0	0	0	0	0	0	0	0	0	0	0	0	0	0	—	0	—	—	—	P	4	0	0	0	0	—
1992 Atl	37	2	0	0	0	0	0	0	0	0	0	0	0	0	0	0	0	0	0	—	0	—	—	—	P	2	0	0	0	0	—
WS Totals		6	0	0	0	0	0	0	0	0	0	0	0	0	0	0	0	0	0	—	0	—	—	—	P	6	0	0	0	0	—
Postseason Totals		18	1	0	0	0	0	0	0	0	0	0	0	1	0	0	0	0	0	—	0	.000	.000	.000	P	18	0	2	0	0	1.000

JEFF REBOULET—Jeffrey Allen Reboulet—Bats: Right; Throws: Right

Ht: 6'0"; Wt: 167 lbs; Born: 4/30/1964 in Dayton, Ohio; Debut: 5/12/1992

Division Series — Batting / Fielding

Year Tm	Age	G	AB	H	2B	3B	HR	TB	R	RBI	GW	TBB	IBB	SO	HBP	SH	SF	SB	CS	SB%	GDP	Avg	OBP	SLG	Pos	G	PO	A	E	DP	FPct
1997 Bal	33	2	5	1	0	0	1	4	1	1	1	0	0	2	0	1	0	0	0	—	0	.200	.200	.800	2B	2	2	3	0	0	1.000

LCS — Batting / Fielding

Year Tm	Age	G	AB	H	2B	3B	HR	TB	R	RBI	GW	TBB	IBB	SO	HBP	SH	SF	SB	CS	SB%	GDP	Avg	OBP	SLG	Pos	G	PO	A	E	DP	FPct
1997 Bal	33	1	2	0	0	0	0	0	1	0	0	0	0	1	0	0	0	0	0	—	0	.000	.000	.000	SS	1	0	0	0	0	—
Postseason Totals		3	7	1	0	0	1	4	2	1	1	0	0	3	0	1	0	0	0	—	0	.143	.143	.571	2B	2	2	3	0	0	1.000

GARY REDUS—Gary Eugene Redus—Bats: Right; Throws: Right

Ht: 6'1"; Wt: 180 lbs; Born: 11/1/1956 in Tanner, Alabama; Debut: 9/7/1982

LCS — Batting / Fielding

Year Tm	Age	G	AB	H	2B	3B	HR	TB	R	RBI	GW	TBB	IBB	SO	HBP	SH	SF	SB	CS	SB%	GDP	Avg	OBP	SLG	Pos	G	PO	A	E	DP	FPct
1990 Pit	33	5	8	2	0	0	0	2	1	0	0	1	0	3	0	0	0	1	1	.50	0	.250	.333	.250	1B	2	16	0	0	0	1.000
1991 Pit	34	5	19	3	0	0	0	3	1	0	0	1	0	4	0	0	0	2	0	1.00	1	.158	.200	.158	1B	5	51	0	2	2	.962
1992 Pit	35	5	16	7	4	1	0	13	4	3	0	2	0	3	0	0	0	0	0	—	0	.438	.500	.813	1B	5	31	4	0	1	1.000
LCS Totals		15	43	12	4	1	0	18	6	3	0	4	0	10	0	0	0	3	1	.75	1	.279	.340	.419	1B	12	98	4	2	3	.981

HOWIE REED—Howard Dean Reed—Nickname: Diz—Throws: Right; Bats: Right

Ht: 6'1"; Wt: 195 lbs; Born: 12/21/1936 in Dallas, Texas; Debut: 9/13/1958; Died: 12/7/1984

World Series — Pitching

Year Tm	Age	G	GS	CG	GF	IP	BFP	H	R	ER	HR	SH	SF	HB	TBB	IBB	SO	WP	Bk	W	L	Pct	ShO	Sv-Op	Hld	OAvg	OOBP	ERA
1965 LA	28	2	0	0	0	3.1	14	2	3	3	1	0	0	0	2	1	4	0	0	0	0	—	0	0-0	0	.167	.286	8.10

World Series — Batting / Fielding

Year Tm	Age	G	AB	H	2B	3B	HR	TB	R	RBI	GW	TBB	IBB	SO	HBP	SH	SF	SB	CS	SB%	GDP	Avg	OBP	SLG	Pos	G	PO	A	E	DP	FPct
1965 LA	28	2	0	0	0	0	0	0	0	0	0	0	0	0	0	0	0	0	0	—	0	—	—	—	P	2	1	0	0	0	1.000

JACK REED—John Burwell Reed—Bats: Right; Throws: Right

Ht: 6'0"; Wt: 185 lbs; Born: 2/2/1933 in Silver City, Mississippi; Debut: 4/23/1961

World Series — Batting / Fielding

Year Tm	Age	G	AB	H	2B	3B	HR	TB	R	RBI	GW	TBB	IBB	SO	HBP	SH	SF	SB	CS	SB%	GDP	Avg	OBP	SLG	Pos	G	PO	A	E	DP	FPct
1961 NYA	28	3	0	0	0	0	0	0	0	0	0	0	0	0	0	0	0	0	0	—	0	—	—	—	OF	3	0	0	0	0	—

JEFF REED—Jeffrey Scott Reed—Bats: Left; Throws: Right

Ht: 6'2"; Wt: 190 lbs; Born: 11/12/1962 in Joliet, Illinois; Debut: 4/5/1984

LCS		Batting																							Fielding						
Year Tm	Age	G	AB	H	2B	3B	HR	TB	R	RBI	GW	TBB	IBB	SO	HBP	SH	SF	SB	CS	SB%	GDP	Avg	OBP	SLG	Pos	G	PO	A	E	DP	FPct
1990 Cin	27	4	7	0	0	0	0	0	0	0	0	0	0	2	0	0	0	0	0	—	1	.000	.000	.000	C	4	24	1	0	0	1.000

JODY REED—Jody Eric Reed—Bats: Right; Throws: Right

Ht: 5'9"; Wt: 170 lbs; Born: 7/26/1962 in Tampa, Florida; Debut: 9/12/1987

Division Series		Batting																							Fielding						
Year Tm	Age	G	AB	H	2B	3B	HR	TB	R	RBI	GW	TBB	IBB	SO	HBP	SH	SF	SB	CS	SB%	GDP	Avg	OBP	SLG	Pos	G	PO	A	E	DP	FPct
1996 SD	34	3	11	3	1	0	0	4	0	2	0	0	0	1	0	0	0	0	0	—	0	.273	.273	.364	2B	3	6	6	0	2	1.000
LCS		Batting																							Fielding						
Year Tm	Age	G	AB	H	2B	3B	HR	TB	R	RBI	GW	TBB	IBB	SO	HBP	SH	SF	SB	CS	SB%	GDP	Avg	OBP	SLG	Pos	G	PO	A	E	DP	FPct
1988 Bos	26	4	11	3	1	0	0	4	0	0	0	2	0	1	1	1	0	0	0	—	1	.273	.429	.364	SS	4	3	10	0	2	1.000
1990 Bos	28	4	15	2	0	0	0	2	0	1	0	0	0	2	0	1	0	0	0	—	0	.133	.133	.133	2B	4	11	11	0	4	1.000
																									SS	3	0	0	0	0	—
LCS Totals		8	26	5	1	0	0	6	0	1	0	2	0	3	1	2	0	0	0	—	1	.192	.276	.231	SS	7	3	10	0	2	1.000
Postseason Totals		11	37	8	2	0	0	10	0	3	0	2	0	4	1	2	0	0	0	—	1	.216	.275	.270	2B	7	17	17	0	6	1.000

RON REED—Ronald Lee Reed—Throws: Right; Bats: Right

Ht: 6'6"; Wt: 215 lbs; Born: 11/2/1942 in LaPorte, Indiana; Debut: 9/26/1966

Division Series		Pitching																									
Year Tm	Age	G	GS	CG	GF	IP	BFP	H	R	ER	HR	SH	SF	HB	TBB	IBB	SO	WP	Bk	W	L	Pct	ShO	Sv-Op	Hld	OAvg	OOBP	ERA
1981 Phi	38	4	0	0	3	6.0	25	5	2	2	0	0	1	0	3	1	4	1	0	0	0	—	0	0- 1	0	.238	.320	3.00
LCS		Pitching																									
Year Tm	Age	G	GS	CG	GF	IP	BFP	H	R	ER	HR	SH	SF	HB	TBB	IBB	SO	WP	Bk	W	L	Pct	ShO	Sv-Op	Hld	OAvg	OOBP	ERA
1969 Atl	26	1	1	0	0	1.2	13	5	4	4	1	0	0	0	3	0	3	0	0	0	1	.000	0	0- 0	0	.500	.615	21.60
1976 Phi	33	2	0	0	1	4.2	21	6	4	4	2	0	2	0	2	1	2	0	0	0	0	—	0	0- 1	0	.353	.381	7.71
1977 Phi	34	3	0	0	0	5.0	19	3	1	1	0	1	0	0	2	1	5	0	0	0	0	—	0	0- 0	0	.188	.278	1.80
1978 Phi	35	2	0	0	0	4.0	17	6	1	1	0	1	0	0	0	0	2	0	0	0	0	—	0	0- 0	0	.375	.375	2.25
1980 Phi	37	3	0	0	0	2.0	11	3	4	4	0	1	0	0	1	1	1	0	0	0	1	.000	0	0- 0	0	.333	.400	18.00
1983 Phi	40	2	0	0	1	3.1	14	4	2	1	0	0	0	0	1	0	3	0	0	0	0	—	0	0- 0	0	.308	.357	2.70
LCS Totals		13	1	0	2	20.2	190	27	16	15	3	3	2	0	9	3	16	0	0	0	2	.000	0	0-1	0	.333	.391	6.53
World Series		Pitching																									
Year Tm	Age	G	GS	CG	GF	IP	BFP	H	R	ER	HR	SH	SF	HB	TBB	IBB	SO	WP	Bk	W	L	Pct	ShO	Sv-Op	Hld	OAvg	OOBP	ERA
1980 Phi	37	2	0	0	1	2.0	7	2	0	0	0	0	1	0	0	0	2	0	0	0	0	—	0	1- 1	0	.333	.286	0.00
1983 Phi	40	3	0	0	2	3.1	16	4	1	1	0	0	0	0	2	1	4	0	0	0	0	—	0	0- 0	0	.286	.375	2.70
WS Totals		5	0	0	3	5.1	46	6	1	1	0	0	1	0	2	1	6	0	0	0	0	—	0	1-1	0	.300	.348	1.69
Postseason Totals		22	1	0	8	32.0	286	38	19	18	3	3	4	0	14	5	26	1	0	0	2	.000	0	1-3	0	.311	.371	5.06

Division Series		Batting																							Fielding						
Year Tm	Age	G	AB	H	2B	3B	HR	TB	R	RBI	GW	TBB	IBB	SO	HBP	SH	SF	SB	CS	SB%	GDP	Avg	OBP	SLG	Pos	G	PO	A	E	DP	FPct
1981 Phi	38	4	0	0	0	0	0	0	0	0	0	0	0	0	0	0	0	0	0	—	0	—	—	—	P	4	0	0	0	0	—
LCS		Batting																							Fielding						
Year Tm	Age	G	AB	H	2B	3B	HR	TB	R	RBI	GW	TBB	IBB	SO	HBP	SH	SF	SB	CS	SB%	GDP	Avg	OBP	SLG	Pos	G	PO	A	E	DP	FPct
1969 Atl	26	1	0	0	0	0	0	0	0	0	0	0	0	0	0	0	0	0	0	—	0	—	—	—	P	1	0	1	0	0	1.000
1976 Phi	33	2	1	0	0	0	0	0	0	0	0	0	0	0	0	0	0	0	0	—	0	.000	.000	.000	P	2	0	0	0	0	—
1977 Phi	34	3	0	0	0	0	0	0	0	0	0	0	0	0	0	0	0	0	0	—	0	—	—	—	P	3	0	0	0	0	—
1978 Phi	35	2	0	0	0	0	0	0	0	0	0	0	0	0	0	0	0	0	0	—	0	—	—	—	P	2	0	0	0	0	—
1980 Phi	37	3	0	0	0	0	0	0	0	0	0	0	0	0	0	0	0	0	0	—	0	—	—	—	P	3	1	0	0	0	1.000
1983 Phi	40	2	0	0	0	0	0	0	0	0	0	0	0	0	0	0	0	0	0	—	0	—	—	—	P	2	0	1	0	0	1.000
LCS Totals		13	1	0	0	0	0	0	0	0	0	0	0	0	0	0	0	0	0	—	0	.000	.000	.000	P	13	1	2	0	0	1.000
World Series		Batting																							Fielding						
Year Tm	Age	G	AB	H	2B	3B	HR	TB	R	RBI	GW	TBB	IBB	SO	HBP	SH	SF	SB	CS	SB%	GDP	Avg	OBP	SLG	Pos	G	PO	A	E	DP	FPct
1980 Phi	37	2	0	0	0	0	0	0	0	0	0	0	0	0	0	0	0	0	0	—	0	—	—	—	P	2	0	0	0	0	—
1983 Phi	40	3	0	0	0	0	0	0	0	0	0	0	0	0	0	0	0	0	0	—	0	—	—	—	P	3	0	0	0	0	—
WS Totals		5	0	0	0	0	0	0	0	0	0	0	0	0	0	0	0	0	0	—	0	—	—	—	P	5	0	0	0	0	—
Postseason Totals		22	1	0	0	0	0	0	0	0	0	0	0	0	0	0	0	0	0	—	0	.000	.000	.000	P	22	1	2	0	0	1.000

STEVE REED—Steven Vincent Reed—Throws: Right; Bats: Right

Ht: 6'2"; Wt: 200 lbs; Born: 3/11/1966 in Los Angeles, California; Debut: 8/30/1992

Division Series		Pitching																									
Year Tm	Age	G	GS	CG	GF	IP	BFP	H	R	ER	HR	SH	SF	HB	TBB	IBB	SO	WP	Bk	W	L	Pct	ShO	Sv-Op	Hld	OAvg	OOBP	ERA
1995 Col	29	3	0	0	0	2.2	12	2	0	0	0	0	0	1	1	1	3	0	0	0	0	—	0	0- 1	1	.200	.333	0.00

Division Series		Batting																							Fielding						
Year Tm	Age	G	AB	H	2B	3B	HR	TB	R	RBI	GW	TBB	IBB	SO	HBP	SH	SF	SB	CS	SB%	GDP	Avg	OBP	SLG	Pos	G	PO	A	E	DP	FPct
1995 Col	29	3	0	0	0	0	0	0	0	0	0	0	0	0	0	0	0	0	0	—	0	—	—	—	P	3	0	1	0	0	1.000

PEE WEE REESE (HOF 1984-V)—Harold Henry Reese—Nickname: The Little Colonel—Bats: Right; Throws: Right

Ht: 5'10"; Wt: 160 lbs; Born: 7/23/1918 in Ekron, Kentucky; Debut: 4/23/1940

World Series		Batting																							Fielding						
Year Tm	Age	G	AB	H	2B	3B	HR	TB	R	RBI	GW	TBB	IBB	SO	HBP	SH	SF	SB	CS	SB%	GDP	Avg	OBP	SLG	Pos	G	PO	A	E	DP	FPct
1941 Bro	23	5	20	4	0	0	0	4	1	2	0	0	0	0	0	0	0	0	0	—	0	.200	.200	.200	SS	5	13	14	3	4	.900
1947 Bro	29	7	23	7	1	0	0	8	5	4	0	6	0	3	0	0	0	3	2	.60	0	.304	.448	.348	SS	7	8	16	1	5	.960
1949 Bro	31	5	19	6	1	0	1	10	2	2	0	1	0	0	1	0	0	1	0	1.00	1	.316	.381	.526	SS	5	5	9	1	0	.933
1952 Bro	34	7	29	10	0	0	1	13	4	4	1	2	0	2	0	1	0	1	1	.50	0	.345	.387	.448	SS	7	15	18	2	3	.943
1953 Bro	35	6	24	5	0	1	0	7	0	0	0	4	0	1	0	0	0	0	0	—	0	.208	.321	.292	SS	6	7	14	0	0	1.000
1955 Bro	37	7	27	8	1	0	0	9	5	2	0	3	0	5	0	1	0	0	0	—	1	.296	.367	.333	SS	7	15	22	1	6	.974
1956 Bro	38	7	27	6	0	1	0	8	3	2	0	2	0	6	0	1	0	0	0	—	0	.222	.276	.296	SS	7	14	21	1	7	.972
WS Totals		44	169	46	3	2	2	59	20	16	1	18	0	17	1	3	0	5	3	.63	2	.272	.346	.349	SS	44	77	114	9	25	.955

RICH REESE—Richard Benjamin Reese—Bats: Left; Throws: Left

Ht: 6'3"; Wt: 185 lbs; Born: 9/29/1941 in Leipsic, Ohio; Debut: 9/4/1964

LCS		Batting																							Fielding						
Year Tm	Age	G	AB	H	2B	3B	HR	TB	R	RBI	GW	TBB	IBB	SO	HBP	SH	SF	SB	CS	SB%	GDP	Avg	OBP	SLG	Pos	G	PO	A	E	DP	FPct
1969 Min	28	3	12	2	0	0	0	2	0	2	0	1	1	1	0	0	0	0	0	—	0	.167	.231	.167	1B	3	26	4	0	3	1.000
1970 Min	29	2	7	1	0	0	0	1	0	0	0	1	0	1	0	0	0	0	0	—	0	.143	.250	.143	1B	2	17	2	0	3	1.000
LCS Totals		5	19	3	0	0	0	3	0	2	0	2	1	2	0	0	0	0	0	—	0	.158	.238	.158	1B	5	43	6	0	6	1.000

RUDY REGALADO—Rudolph Valentino Regalado—Bats: Right; Throws: Right

Ht: 6'1"; Wt: 185 lbs; Born: 5/21/1930 in Los Angeles, California; Debut: 4/13/1954

World Series		Batting																							Fielding						
Year Tm	Age	G	AB	H	2B	3B	HR	TB	R	RBI	GW	TBB	IBB	SO	HBP	SH	SF	SB	CS	SB%	GDP	Avg	OBP	SLG	Pos	G	PO	A	E	DP	FPct
1954 Cle	24	4	3	1	0	0	0	1	0	1	0	0	0	0	0	0	0	0	0	—	0	.333	.333	.333	3B	1	0	0	0	0	—

PHIL REGAN—Philip Raymond Regan—Nickname: The Vulture—Throws: Right; Bats: Right

Ht: 6'3"; Wt: 200 lbs; Born: 4/6/1937 in Otsego, Michigan; Debut: 7/19/1960

World Series		Pitching																									
Year Tm	Age	G	GS	CG	GF	IP	BFP	H	R	ER	HR	SH	SF	HB	TBB	IBB	SO	WP	Bk	W	L	Pct	ShO	Sv-Op	Hld	OAvg	OOBP	ERA
1966 LA	29	2	0	0	1	1.2	6	0	0	0	0	0	0	0	1	0	2	1	0	0	0	—	0	0- 0	0	.000	.167	0.00

World Series		Batting																							Fielding						
Year Tm	Age	G	AB	H	2B	3B	HR	TB	R	RBI	GW	TBB	IBB	SO	HBP	SH	SF	SB	CS	SB%	GDP	Avg	OBP	SLG	Pos	G	PO	A	E	DP	FPct
1966 LA	29	2	0	0	0	0	0	0	0	0	0	0	0	0	0	0	0	0	0	—	0	—	—	—	P	2	0	1	0	0	1.000

ART REINHART—Arthur Conrad Reinhart—Throws: Left; Bats: Left

Ht: 6'1"; Wt: 170 lbs; Born: 5/29/1899 in Ackley, Iowa; Debut: 4/26/1919; Died: 11/11/1946

World Series		Pitching																									
Year Tm	Age	G	GS	CG	GF	IP	BFP	H	R	ER	HR	SH	SF	HB	TBB	IBB	SO	WP	Bk	W	L	Pct	ShO	Sv-Op	Hld	OAvg	OOBP	ERA
1926 StL	27	1	0	0	0	0.0	5	1	4	4	0	0	0	0	4	0	0	0	0	0	1	.000	0	0- 0	0	1.000	1.000	—

World Series — Batting / Fielding

Year Tm	Age	G	AB	H	2B	3B	HR	TB	R	RBI	GW	TBB	IBB	SO	HBP	SH	SF	SB	CS	SB%	GDP	Avg	OBP	SLG	Pos	G	PO	A	E	DP	FPct
1926 StL	27	1	0	0	0	0	0	0	0	0	0	0	0	0	0	0	0	0	0	—	0	—	—	—	P	1	0	0	0	0	—

PETE REISER—Harold Patrick Reiser—Nickname: Pistol Pete—Bats: Left; Throws: Right

Ht: 5'11"; Wt: 185 lbs; Born: 3/17/1919 in St. Louis, Missouri; Debut: 7/23/1940; Died: 10/25/1981

World Series — Batting / Fielding

Year Tm	Age	G	AB	H	2B	3B	HR	TB	R	RBI	GW	TBB	IBB	SO	HBP	SH	SF	SB	CS	SB%	GDP	Avg	OBP	SLG	Pos	G	PO	A	E	DP	FPct
1941 Bro	22	5	20	4	1	1	1	10	1	3	0	1	0	6	0	0	0	0	0	—	1	.200	.238	.500	OF	5	14	1	0	0	1.000
1947 Bro	28	5	8	2	0	0	0	2	1	0	0	3	2	1	0	0	0	0	1	.00	0	.250	.455	.250	OF	3	7	0	1	0	.875
WS Totals		10	28	6	1	1	1	12	2	3	0	4	2	7	0	0	0	0	1	.00	1	.214	.313	.429	OF	8	21	1	1	0	.957

RICK RENICK—Warren Richard Renick—Bats: Right; Throws: Right

Ht: 6'0"; Wt: 188 lbs; Born: 3/16/1944 in London, Ohio; Debut: 7/11/1968

LCS — Batting / Fielding

Year Tm	Age	G	AB	H	2B	3B	HR	TB	R	RBI	GW	TBB	IBB	SO	HBP	SH	SF	SB	CS	SB%	GDP	Avg	OBP	SLG	Pos	G	PO	A	E	DP	FPct
1969 Min	25	1	1	0	0	0	0	0	0	0	0	0	0	0	0	0	0	0	0	—	1	.000	.000	.000	—						
1970 Min	26	2	5	1	0	0	0	1	0	0	0	0	0	1	0	0	0	0	0	—	0	.200	.200	.200	3B	1	1	3	0	0	1.000
LCS Totals		3	6	1	0	0	0	1	0	0	0	0	0	1	0	0	0	0	0	—	1	.167	.167	.167	3B	1	1	3	0	0	1.000

HAL RENIFF—Harold Eugene Reniff—Nickname: Porky—Throws: Right; Bats: Right

Ht: 6'0"; Wt: 215 lbs; Born: 7/2/1938 in Warren, Ohio; Debut: 6/8/1961

World Series — Pitching

Year Tm	Age	G	GS	CG	GF	IP	BFP	H	R	ER	HR	SH	SF	HB	TBB	IBB	SO	WP	Bk	W	L	Pct	ShO	Sv-Op	Hld	OAvg	OOBP	ERA
1963 NYA	25	3	0	0	3	3.0	9	0	0	0	0	1	0	0	1	0	1	0	0	0	0	—	0	0- 0	0	.000	.125	0.00
1964 NYA	26	1	0	0	0	0.1	3	2	0	0	0	0	0	0	0	0	0	0	0	0	0	—	0	0- 0	0	.667	.667	0.00
WS Totals		4	0	0	3	3.1	24	2	0	0	0	1	0	0	1	0	1	0	0	0	0	—	0	0-0	0	.200	.273	0.00

World Series — Batting / Fielding

Year Tm	Age	G	AB	H	2B	3B	HR	TB	R	RBI	GW	TBB	IBB	SO	HBP	SH	SF	SB	CS	SB%	GDP	Avg	OBP	SLG	Pos	G	PO	A	E	DP	FPct
1963 NYA	25	3	0	0	0	0	0	0	0	0	0	0	0	0	0	0	0	0	0	—	0	—	—	—	P	3	1	0	0	0	1.000
1964 NYA	26	1	0	0	0	0	0	0	0	0	0	0	0	0	0	0	0	0	0	—	0	—	—	—	P	1	0	0	0	0	—
WS Totals		4	0	0	0	0	0	0	0	0	0	0	0	0	0	0	0	0	0	—	0	—	—	—	P	4	1	0	0	0	1.000

EDGAR RENTERIA—Edgar Enrique Renteria—Bats: Right; Throws: Right

Ht: 6'1"; Wt: 172 lbs; Born: 8/7/1975 in Barranquilla, Colombia; Debut: 5/10/1996

Division Series — Batting / Fielding

Year Tm	Age	G	AB	H	2B	3B	HR	TB	R	RBI	GW	TBB	IBB	SO	HBP	SH	SF	SB	CS	SB%	GDP	Avg	OBP	SLG	Pos	G	PO	A	E	DP	FPct
1997 Fla	22	3	13	2	0	0	0	2	1	1	1	2	0	4	0	0	0	0	0	—	1	.154	.267	.154	SS	3	9	11	2	3	.909

LCS — Batting / Fielding

Year Tm	Age	G	AB	H	2B	3B	HR	TB	R	RBI	GW	TBB	IBB	SO	HBP	SH	SF	SB	CS	SB%	GDP	Avg	OBP	SLG	Pos	G	PO	A	E	DP	FPct
1997 Fla	22	6	22	5	1	0	0	6	4	0	0	3	0	6	1	0	0	1	0	1.00	1	.227	.346	.273	SS	6	14	15	0	3	1.000

World Series — Batting / Fielding

Year Tm	Age	G	AB	H	2B	3B	HR	TB	R	RBI	GW	TBB	IBB	SO	HBP	SH	SF	SB	CS	SB%	GDP	Avg	OBP	SLG	Pos	G	PO	A	E	DP	FPct
1997 Fla	22	7	31	9	2	0	0	11	3	3	1	3	0	5	0	0	0	0	0	—	0	.290	.353	.355	SS	7	12	26	1	7	.974
Postseason Totals		16	66	16	3	0	0	19	8	4	2	8	0	15	1	0	0	1	0	1.00	2	.242	.333	.288	SS	16	35	52	3	13	.967

RIP REPULSKI—Eldon John Repulski—Bats: Right; Throws: Right

Ht: 6'0"; Wt: 195 lbs; Born: 10/4/1927 in Sauk Rapids, Minnesota; Debut: 4/14/1953; Died: 2/10/1993

World Series — Batting / Fielding

Year Tm	Age	G	AB	H	2B	3B	HR	TB	R	RBI	GW	TBB	IBB	SO	HBP	SH	SF	SB	CS	SB%	GDP	Avg	OBP	SLG	Pos	G	PO	A	E	DP	FPct
1959 LA	31	1	0	0	0	0	0	0	0	0	0	1	1	0	0	0	0	0	0	—	0	—	1.000	—	OF	1	0	0	0	0	—

MERV RETTENMUND—Mervin Weldon Rettenmund—Bats: Right; Throws: Right

Ht: 5'10"; Wt: 190 lbs; Born: 6/6/1943 in Flint, Michigan; Debut: 4/14/1968

LCS — Batting / Fielding

Year Tm	Age	G	AB	H	2B	3B	HR	TB	R	RBI	GW	TBB	IBB	SO	HBP	SH	SF	SB	CS	SB%	GDP	Avg	OBP	SLG	Pos	G	PO	A	E	DP	FPct
1969 Bal	26	1	0	0	0	0	0	0	0	0	0	0	0	0	0	0	0	0	0	—	0	—	—	—	—						
1970 Bal	27	1	3	1	0	0	0	1	1	1	0	2	0	1	0	0	0	1	0	1.00	0	.333	.600	.333	OF	1	3	1	0	0	1.000
1971 Bal	28	3	8	2	1	0	0	3	0	1	0	0	0	3	0	0	0	0	0	—	0	.250	.250	.375	OF	3	6	0	0	0	1.000
1973 Bal	30	3	11	1	0	0	0	1	1	0	0	3	0	2	0	0	0	0	2	.00	0	.091	.286	.091	OF	3	2	0	0	0	1.000
1975 Cin	32	2	1	0	0	0	0	0	1	0	0	1	0	0	0	0	0	0	0	—	0	.000	.500	.000	—						
1979 Cal	36	2	2	0	0	0	0	0	0	0	0	2	0	1	0	0	0	0	0	—	0	.000	.500	.000	—						
LCS Totals		12	25	4	1	0	0	5	3	2	0	8	0	7	0	0	0	1	2	.33	0	.160	.364	.200	OF	7	11	1	0	0	1.000

World Series — Batting / Fielding

Year Tm	Age	G	AB	H	2B	3B	HR	TB	R	RBI	GW	TBB	IBB	SO	HBP	SH	SF	SB	CS	SB%	GDP	Avg	OBP	SLG	Pos	G	PO	A	E	DP	FPct
1969 Bal	26	1	0	0	0	0	0	0	0	0	0	0	0	0	0	0	0	0	0	—	0	—	—	—	—						
1970 Bal	27	2	5	2	0	0	1	5	2	2	0	1	0	0	0	0	0	0	0	—	0	.400	.500	1.000	OF	1	3	0	0	0	1.000
1971 Bal	28	7	27	5	0	0	1	8	3	4	1	0	0	4	0	0	0	0	0	—	0	.185	.185	.296	OF	6	17	0	0	0	1.000
1975 Cin	32	3	3	0	0	0	0	0	0	0	0	0	0	1	0	0	0	0	0	—	1	.000	.000	.000	—						
WS Totals		13	35	7	0	0	2	13	5	6	1	1	0	5	0	0	0	0	0	—	1	.200	.222	.371	OF	7	20	0	0	0	1.000
Postseason Totals		25	60	11	1	0	2	18	8	8	1	9	0	12	0	0	0	1	2	.33	1	.183	.290	.300	OF	14	31	1	0	0	1.000

ED REULBACH—Edward Marvin Reulbach—Nickname: Big Ed—Throws: Right; Bats: Right

Ht: 6'1"; Wt: 190 lbs; Born: 12/1/1882 in Detroit, Michigan; Debut: 5/16/1905; Died: 7/17/1961

World Series — Pitching

Year Tm	Age	G	GS	CG	GF	IP	BFP	H	R	ER	HR	SH	SF	HB	TBB	IBB	SO	WP	Bk	W	L	Pct	ShO	Sv-Op	Hld	OAvg	OOBP	ERA
1906 ChN	23	2	2	1	0	11.0	47	6	4	3	0	1	0	1	8	0	4	1	0	1	0	1.000	0	0- 0	0	.162	.326	2.45
1907 ChN	24	2	1	1	1	12.0	45	6	1	1	0	0	0	0	3	0	4	0	0	1	0	1.000	0	0- 0	0	.143	.200	0.75
1908 ChN	25	2	1	0	1	7.2	31	9	4	4	0	0	0	0	1	0	5	0	0	0	0	—	0	0- 0	0	.300	.323	4.70
1910 ChN	27	1	1	0	0	2.0	10	3	3	3	0	1	0	0	2	0	0	0	0	0	0	—	0	0- 0	0	.429	.556	13.50
WS Totals		7	5	2	2	32.2	266	24	12	11	0	2	0	1	14	0	13	1	0	2	0	1.000	0	0-0	0	.207	.298	3.03

World Series — Batting / Fielding

Year Tm	Age	G	AB	H	2B	3B	HR	TB	R	RBI	GW	TBB	IBB	SO	HBP	SH	SF	SB	CS	SB%	GDP	Avg	OBP	SLG	Pos	G	PO	A	E	DP	FPct
1906 ChN	23	2	3	0	0	0	0	0	0	1	0	0	0	1	0	2	0	0	0	—	0	.000	.000	.000	P	2	0	4	0	0	1.000
1907 ChN	24	2	5	1	0	0	0	1	0	1	0	0	0	0	0	0	0	0	0	—	0	.200	.200	.200	P	2	1	3	0	0	1.000
1908 ChN	25	2	3	0	0	0	0	0	0	0	0	0	0	1	0	0	0	0	0	—	0	.000	.000	.000	P	2	0	5	0	0	1.000
1910 ChN	27	1	0	0	0	0	0	0	0	0	0	0	0	0	0	0	0	0	0	—	0	—	—	—	P	1	0	1	0	0	1.000
WS Totals		7	11	1	0	0	0	1	0	2	0	0	0	2	0	2	0	0	0	—	0	.091	.091	.091	P	7	1	13	0	0	1.000

RICK REUSCHEL—Rickey Eugene Reuschel—Nickname: Big Daddy—Throws: Right; Bats: Right

Ht: 6'3"; Wt: 215 lbs; Born: 5/16/1949 in Quincy, Illinois; Debut: 6/19/1972

Division Series — Pitching

Year Tm	Age	G	GS	CG	GF	IP	BFP	H	R	ER	HR	SH	SF	HB	TBB	IBB	SO	WP	Bk	W	L	Pct	ShO	Sv-Op	Hld	OAvg	OOBP	ERA
1981 NYA	32	1	1	0	0	6.0	22	4	2	2	0	1	0	0	1	0	3	0	0	0	1	.000	0	0- 0	0	.200	.238	3.00

LCS — Pitching

Year Tm	Age	G	GS	CG	GF	IP	BFP	H	R	ER	HR	SH	SF	HB	TBB	IBB	SO	WP	Bk	W	L	Pct	ShO	Sv-Op	Hld	OAvg	OOBP	ERA
1987 SF	38	2	2	0	0	10.0	45	15	8	7	0	3	2	0	2	0	2	1	0	0	1	.000	0	0- 0	0	.395	.405	6.30
1989 SF	40	2	2	0	0	8.2	39	12	6	5	0	1	0	1	2	1	5	0	0	1	1	.500	0	0- 0	0	.343	.395	5.19
LCS Totals		4	4	0	0	18.2	168	27	14	12	0	4	2	1	4	1	7	1	0	1	2	.333	0	0-0	0	.370	.400	5.79

World Series — Pitching

Year Tm	Age	G	GS	CG	GF	IP	BFP	H	R	ER	HR	SH	SF	HB	TBB	IBB	SO	WP	Bk	W	L	Pct	ShO	Sv-Op	Hld	OAvg	OOBP	ERA
1981 NYA	32	2	1	0	0	3.2	22	7	3	2	0	0	0	0	3	2	2	0	0	0	0	—	0	0- 0	0	.368	.455	4.91
1989 SF	40	1	1	0	0	4.0	20	5	5	5	1	0	0	0	4	0	2	0	0	0	1	.000	0	0- 0	0	.313	.450	11.25
WS Totals		3	2	0	0	7.2	84	12	8	7	1	0	0	0	7	2	4	0	0	0	1	.000	0	0-0	0	.343	.452	8.22
Postseason Totals		8	7	0	0	32.1	296	43	24	21	1	5	2	1	12	3	14	1	0	1	4	.200	0	0-0	0	.336	.392	5.85

Year Tm	Age	G	AB	H	2B	3B	HR	TB	R	RBI	GW	TBB	IBB	SO	HBP	SH	SF	SB	CS	SB%	GDP	Avg	OBP	SLG	Pos	G	PO	A	E	DP	FPct
Division Series																															
1981 NYA	32	1	0	0	0	0	0	0	0	0	0	0	0	0	0	0	0	0	0	—	0	—	—	—	P	1	1	2	0	0	1.000
LCS																															
1987 SF	38	2	2	0	0	0	0	0	0	0	0	0	0	1	0	1	0	0	0	—	0	.000	.000	.000	P	2	0	3	1	0	.750
1989 SF	40	2	2	0	0	0	0	0	0	0	0	0	0	0	0	0	0	0	0	—	0	.000	.000	.000	P	2	0	3	0	0	1.000
LCS Totals		4	4	0	0	0	0	0	0	0	0	0	0	1	0	1	0	0	0	—	0	.000	.000	.000	P	4	0	6	1	0	.857
World Series																															
1981 NYA	32	2	2	0	0	0	0	0	0	0	0	0	0	1	0	0	0	0	0	—	0	.000	.000	.000	P	2	0	0	0	0	—
1989 SF	40	1	0	0	0	0	0	0	0	0	0	0	0	0	0	0	0	0	0	—	0	—	—	—	P	1	0	0	0	0	—
WS Totals		3	2	0	0	0	0	0	0	0	0	0	0	1	0	0	0	0	0	—	0	.000	.000	.000	P	3	0	0	0	0	—
Postseason Totals		8	6	0	0	0	0	0	0	0	0	0	0	2	0	1	0	0	0	—	0	.000	.000	.000	P	8	1	8	1	0	.900

JERRY REUSS—Throws: Left; Bats: Left

Ht: 6'5"; Wt: 200 lbs; Born: 6/19/1949 in St. Louis, Missouri; Debut: 9/27/1969

Year Tm	Age	G	GS	CG	GF	IP	BFP	H	R	ER	HR	SH	SF	HB	TBB	IBB	SO	WP	Bk	W	L	Pct	ShO	Sv-Op	Hld	OAvg	OOBP	ERA
Division Series																												
1981 LA	32	2	2	1	0	18.0	69	10	0	0	0	0	0	0	5	1	7	0	0	1	0	1.000	1	0- 0	0	.156	.217	0.00
LCS																												
1974 Pit	25	2	2	0	0	9.2	44	7	4	4	1	0	0	0	8	0	3	0	0	0	2	.000	0	0- 0	0	.194	.341	3.72
1975 Pit	26	1	1	0	0	2.2	16	4	4	4	0	0	0	0	4	0	1	0	0	0	1	.000	0	0- 0	0	.333	.500	13.50
1981 LA	32	1	1	0	0	7.0	29	7	4	4	1	1	0	0	1	0	2	0	0	0	1	.000	0	0- 0	0	.259	.286	5.14
1983 LA	34	2	2	0	0	12.0	53	14	6	6	2	1	0	0	3	1	4	1	0	0	2	.000	0	0- 0	0	.286	.327	4.50
1985 LA	36	1	1	0	0	1.2	12	5	7	2	0	0	0	0	1	0	0	0	0	0	1	.000	0	0- 0	0	.455	.500	10.80
LCS Totals		7	7	0	0	33.0	308	37	25	20	4	2	0	0	17	1	10	1	0	0	7	.000	0	0-0	0	.274	.355	5.45
World Series																												
1981 LA	32	2	2	1	0	11.2	48	10	6	5	1	0	0	0	3	1	8	0	0	1	1	.500	0	0- 0	0	.222	.271	3.86
Postseason Totals		11	11	2	0	62.2	542	57	31	25	5	2	0	0	25	3	25	1	0	2	8	.200	1	0-0	0	.234	.305	3.59

Year Tm	Age	G	AB	H	2B	3B	HR	TB	R	RBI	GW	TBB	IBB	SO	HBP	SH	SF	SB	CS	SB%	GDP	Avg	OBP	SLG	Pos	G	PO	A	E	DP	FPct
Division Series																															
1981 LA	32	2	8	0	0	0	0	0	0	0	0	0	0	8	0	0	0	0	0	—	0	.000	.000	.000	P	2	1	1	0	0	1.000
LCS																															
1974 Pit	25	2	2	0	0	0	0	0	0	0	0	0	0	0	0	1	0	0	0	—	0	.000	.000	.000	P	2	0	0	0	0	—
1975 Pit	26	1	1	0	0	0	0	0	0	0	0	0	0	0	0	0	0	0	0	—	0	.000	.000	.000	P	1	0	1	0	0	1.000
1981 LA	32	1	2	0	0	0	0	0	0	0	0	0	0	0	0	0	0	0	0	—	1	.000	.000	.000	P	1	0	0	0	0	—
1983 LA	34	2	3	0	0	0	0	0	0	0	0	0	0	3	0	1	0	0	0	—	0	.000	.000	.000	P	2	0	1	0	0	1.000
1985 LA	36	1	0	0	0	0	0	0	0	0	0	0	0	0	0	0	0	0	0	—	0	—	—	—	P	1	0	0	1	0	.000
LCS Totals		7	8	0	0	0	0	0	0	0	0	0	0	3	0	2	0	0	0	—	1	.000	.000	.000	P	7	0	2	1	0	.667
World Series																															
1981 LA	32	2	3	0	0	0	0	0	0	0	0	1	0	2	0	0	0	0	0	—	0	.000	.250	.000	P	2	1	3	0	0	1.000
Postseason Totals		11	19	0	0	0	0	0	0	0	0	1	0	13	0	2	0	0	0	—	1	.000	.050	.000	P	11	2	6	1	0	.889

DAVE REVERING—David Allen Revering—Bats: Left; Throws: Right

Ht: 6'4"; Wt: 210 lbs; Born: 2/12/1953 in Roseville, California; Debut: 4/8/1978

Year Tm	Age	G	AB	H	2B	3B	HR	TB	R	RBI	GW	TBB	IBB	SO	HBP	SH	SF	SB	CS	SB%	GDP	Avg	OBP	SLG	Pos	G	PO	A	E	DP	FPct
Division Series																															
1981 NYA	28	2	0	0	0	0	0	0	0	0	0	0	0	0	0	0	0	0	0	—	0	—	—	—	1B	2	3	0	0	0	1.000
LCS																															
1981 NYA	28	2	2	1	0	0	0	1	0	0	0	0	0	0	0	0	0	0	0	—	0	.500	.500	.500	1B	2	6	1	0	1	1.000
Postseason Totals		4	2	1	0	0	0	1	0	0	0	0	0	0	0	0	0	0	0	—	0	.500	.500	.500	1B	4	9	1	0	1	1.000

ALLIE REYNOLDS—Allie Pierce Reynolds—Nickname: Superchief—Throws: Right; Bats: Right

Ht: 6'0"; Wt: 195 lbs; Born: 2/10/1915 in Bethany, Oklahoma; Debut: 9/17/1942; Died: 12/26/1994

Year Tm	Age	G	GS	CG	GF	IP	BFP	H	R	ER	HR	SH	SF	HB	TBB	IBB	SO	WP	Bk	W	L	Pct	ShO	Sv-Op	Hld	OAvg	OOBP	ERA
World Series																												
1947 NYA	32	2	2	1	0	11.1	49	15	7	6	1	0	0	0	3	0	6	0	0	1	0	1.000	0	0- 0	0	.326	.367	4.76
1949 NYA	34	2	1	1	1	12.1	43	2	0	0	0	1	0	0	4	0	14	0	0	1	0	1.000	1	1- 1	0	.053	.143	0.00
1950 NYA	35	2	1	1	1	10.1	40	7	1	1	0	2	0	0	4	1	7	0	0	1	0	1.000	0	1- 1	0	.206	.289	0.87
1951 NYA	36	2	2	1	0	15.0	66	16	7	7	1	2	0	0	11	0	8	0	0	1	1	.500	0	0- 0	0	.302	.422	4.20
1952 NYA	37	4	2	1	1	20.1	74	12	4	4	2	1	0	0	6	0	18	1	0	2	1	.667	1	1- 1	0	.179	.247	1.77
1953 NYA	38	3	1	0	2	8.0	37	9	6	6	4	0	0	1	4	0	9	0	0	1	0	1.000	0	1- 2	0	.281	.378	6.75
WS Totals		15	9	5	5	77.1	618	61	25	24	8	6	0	1	32	1	62	1	0	7	2	.778	2	4-5	0	.226	.310	2.79

Year Tm	Age	G	AB	H	2B	3B	HR	TB	R	RBI	GW	TBB	IBB	SO	HBP	SH	SF	SB	CS	SB%	GDP	Avg	OBP	SLG	Pos	G	PO	A	E	DP	FPct
World Series																															
1947 NYA	32	2	4	2	0	0	0	2	2	1	0	0	0	0	0	0	0	0	0	—	0	.500	.500	.500	P	2	1	0	0	0	1.000
1949 NYA	34	2	4	2	1	0	0	3	0	0	0	0	0	1	0	0	0	0	0	—	0	.500	.500	.750	P	2	0	1	0	1	1.000
1950 NYA	35	2	3	1	0	0	0	1	0	0	0	1	0	2	0	0	0	0	0	—	0	.333	.500	.333	P	2	1	2	0	0	1.000
1951 NYA	36	2	6	2	0	0	0	2	0	1	1	0	0	1	0	0	0	0	0	—	0	.333	.333	.333	P	2	0	5	0	2	1.000
1952 NYA	37	4	7	0	0	0	0	0	0	0	0	0	0	2	0	0	0	0	0	—	0	.000	.000	.000	P	4	2	1	2	0	.600
1953 NYA	38	3	2	1	0	0	0	1	0	0	0	1	0	1	0	0	0	0	0	—	0	.500	.667	.500	P	3	0	0	0	0	—
WS Totals		15	26	8	1	0	0	9	2	2	1	2	0	7	0	0	0	0	0	—	0	.308	.357	.346	P	15	4	9	2	3	.867

BOB REYNOLDS—Robert Allen Reynolds—Nickname: Bullet Bob—Throws: Right; Bats: Right

Ht: 6'0"; Wt: 205 lbs; Born: 1/21/1947 in Seattle, Washington; Debut: 9/19/1969

Year Tm	Age	G	GS	CG	GF	IP	BFP	H	R	ER	HR	SH	SF	HB	TBB	IBB	SO	WP	Bk	W	L	Pct	ShO	Sv-Op	Hld	OAvg	OOBP	ERA
LCS																												
1973 Bal	26	2	0	0	0	5.2	25	5	2	2	0	1	1	0	3	2	5	0	0	0	0	—	0	0- 0	0	.250	.333	3.18
1974 Bal	27	1	0	0	0	1.1	6	0	1	0	0	0	0	0	3	0	1	0	0	0	0	—	0	0- 0	0	.000	.500	0.00
LCS Totals		3	0	0	0	7.0	62	5	3	2	0	1	1	0	6	2	6	0	0	0	0	—	0	0-0	0	.217	.367	2.57

Year Tm	Age	G	AB	H	2B	3B	HR	TB	R	RBI	GW	TBB	IBB	SO	HBP	SH	SF	SB	CS	SB%	GDP	Avg	OBP	SLG	Pos	G	PO	A	E	DP	FPct
LCS																															
1973 Bal	26	2	0	0	0	0	0	0	0	0	0	0	0	0	0	0	0	0	0	—	0	—	—	—	P	2	1	0	0	0	1.000
1974 Bal	27	1	0	0	0	0	0	0	0	0	0	0	0	0	0	0	0	0	0	—	0	—	—	—	P	1	0	0	0	0	—
LCS Totals		3	0	0	0	0	0	0	0	0	0	0	0	0	0	0	0	0	0	—	0	—	—	—	P	3	1	0	0	0	1.000

CARL REYNOLDS—Carl Nettles Reynolds—Bats: Right; Throws: Right

Ht: 6'0"; Wt: 194 lbs; Born: 2/1/1903 in LaRue, Texas; Debut: 9/1/1927; Died: 5/29/1978

Year Tm	Age	G	AB	H	2B	3B	HR	TB	R	RBI	GW	TBB	IBB	SO	HBP	SH	SF	SB	CS	SB%	GDP	Avg	OBP	SLG	Pos	G	PO	A	E	DP	FPct
World Series																															
1938 ChN	35	4	12	0	0	0	0	0	0	0	0	1	0	3	0	0	0	0	0	—	2	.000	.077	.000	OF	3	7	0	0	0	1.000

CRAIG REYNOLDS—Gordon Craig Reynolds—Bats: Left; Throws: Right

Ht: 6'1"; Wt: 175 lbs; Born: 12/27/1952 in Houston, Texas; Debut: 8/1/1975

Year Tm	Age	G	AB	H	2B	3B	HR	TB	R	RBI	GW	TBB	IBB	SO	HBP	SH	SF	SB	CS	SB%	GDP	Avg	OBP	SLG	Pos	G	PO	A	E	DP	FPct
Division Series																															
1981 Hou	28	2	3	1	0	0	0	1	1	0	0	0	0	1	0	0	0	0	0	—	0	.333	.333	.333	SS	1	1	1	0	0	1.000
LCS																															
1975 Pit	22	2	1	0	0	0	0	0	0	0	0	0	0	0	0	0	0	0	0	—	0	.000	.000	.000	SS	1	0	0	1	0	.000
1980 Hou	27	4	13	2	1	0	0	3	2	0	0	3	1	1	0	1	0	0	0	—	0	.154	.313	.231	SS	4	8	12	1	1	.952
1986 Hou	33	4	12	4	0	0	0	4	1	0	0	1	0	3	0	0	0	0	0	—	1	.333	.385	.333	SS	4	7	8	2	1	.882
LCS Totals		10	26	6	1	0	0	7	3	0	0	4	1	4	0	1	0	0	0	—	1	.231	.333	.269	SS	9	15	20	4	2	.897
Postseason Totals		12	29	7	1	0	0	8	4	0	0	4	1	5	0	1	0	0	0	—	1	.241	.333	.276	SS	10	16	21	4	2	.902

R.J. REYNOLDS—Robert James Reynolds—Bats: Both; Throws: Right

Ht: 6'0"; Wt: 190 lbs; Born: 4/19/1959 in Sacramento, California; Debut: 9/1/1983

LCS — Batting / Fielding

Year Tm	Age	G	AB	H	2B	3B	HR	TB	R	RBI	GW	TBB	IBB	SO	HBP	SH	SF	SB	CS	SB%	GDP	Avg	OBP	SLG	Pos	G	PO	A	E	DP	FPct
1990 Pit	31	6	10	2	0	0	0	2	0	0	0	2	0	2	0	0	0	1	0	1.00	0	.200	.333	.200	OF	3	2	0	1	0	.667

SHANE REYNOLDS—Richard Shane Reynolds—Throws: Right; Bats: Right

Ht: 6'3"; Wt: 210 lbs; Born: 3/26/1968 in Bastrop, Louisiana; Debut: 7/20/1992

Division Series — Pitching

Year Tm	Age	G	GS	CG	GF	IP	BFP	H	R	ER	HR	SH	SF	HB	TBB	IBB	SO	WP	Bk	W	L	Pct	ShO	Sv-Op	Hld	OAvg	OOBP	ERA
1997 Hou	29	1	1	0	0	6.0	23	5	2	2	1	0	0	0	1	0	5	0	0	0	1	.000	0	0- 0	0	.227	.261	3.00

Division Series — Batting / Fielding

Year Tm	Age	G	AB	H	2B	3B	HR	TB	R	RBI	GW	TBB	IBB	SO	HBP	SH	SF	SB	CS	SB%	GDP	Avg	OBP	SLG	Pos	G	PO	A	E	DP	FPct
1997 Hou	29	1	1	0	0	0	0	0	0	0	0	0	0	1	0	0	0	0	0	—	0	.000	.000	.000	P	1	1	1	0	0	1.000

ARMANDO REYNOSO—Armando Martin Reynoso—Throws: Right; Bats: Right

Ht: 6'0"; Wt: 186 lbs; Born: 5/1/1966 in San Luis Potosi, Mexico; Debut: 8/11/1991

Division Series — Pitching

Year Tm	Age	G	GS	CG	GF	IP	BFP	H	R	ER	HR	SH	SF	HB	TBB	IBB	SO	WP	Bk	W	L	Pct	ShO	Sv-Op	Hld	OAvg	OOBP	ERA
1995 Col	29	1	0	0	0	1.0	5	2	0	0	0	0	0	0	0	0	0	0	0	0	0	—	0	0- 0	0	.400	.400	0.00

Division Series — Batting / Fielding

Year Tm	Age	G	AB	H	2B	3B	HR	TB	R	RBI	GW	TBB	IBB	SO	HBP	SH	SF	SB	CS	SB%	GDP	Avg	OBP	SLG	Pos	G	PO	A	E	DP	FPct
1995 Col	29	1	0	0	0	0	0	0	0	0	0	0	0	0	0	0	0	0	0	—	0	—	—	—	P	1	0	0	0	0	—

FLINT RHEM—Charles Flint Rhem—Nickname: Shad—Throws: Right; Bats: Right

Ht: 6'2"; Wt: 180 lbs; Born: 1/24/1901 in Rhems, South Carolina; Debut: 9/6/1924; Died: 7/30/1969

World Series — Pitching

Year Tm	Age	G	GS	CG	GF	IP	BFP	H	R	ER	HR	SH	SF	HB	TBB	IBB	SO	WP	Bk	W	L	Pct	ShO	Sv-Op	Hld	OAvg	OOBP	ERA
1926 StL	25	1	1	0	0	4.0	18	7	3	3	2	0	0	0	2	0	4	0	0	0	0	—	0	0- 0	0	.438	.500	6.75
1928 StL	27	1	0	0	1	2.0	6	0	0	0	0	0	0	0	0	0	1	0	0	0	0	—	0	0- 0	0	.000	.000	0.00
1930 StL	29	1	1	0	0	3.1	20	7	6	4	1	0	0	0	2	1	3	0	0	0	1	.000	0	0- 0	0	.389	.450	10.80
1931 StL	30	1	0	0	1	1.0	4	1	0	0	0	0	0	0	0	0	1	0	0	0	0	—	0	0- 0	0	.250	.250	0.00
WS Totals		4	2	0	2	10.1	96	15	9	7	3	0	0	0	4	1	9	0	0	0	1	.000	0	0-0	0	.341	.396	6.10

World Series — Batting / Fielding

Year Tm	Age	G	AB	H	2B	3B	HR	TB	R	RBI	GW	TBB	IBB	SO	HBP	SH	SF	SB	CS	SB%	GDP	Avg	OBP	SLG	Pos	G	PO	A	E	DP	FPct
1926 StL	25	1	1	0	0	0	0	0	0	0	0	0	0	1	0	0	0	0	0	—	0	.000	.000	.000	P	1	0	1	0	0	1.000
1928 StL	27	1	0	0	0	0	0	0	0	0	0	0	0	0	0	0	0	0	0	—	0	—	—	—	P	1	0	0	0	0	—
1930 StL	29	1	1	0	0	0	0	0	0	0	0	0	0	1	0	0	0	0	0	—	0	.000	.000	.000	P	1	0	0	1	0	.000
1931 StL	30	1	0	0	0	0	0	0	0	0	0	0	0	0	0	0	0	0	0	—	0	—	—	—	P	1	0	0	0	0	—
WS Totals		4	2	0	0	0	0	0	0	0	0	0	0	2	0	0	0	0	0	—	0	.000	.000	.000	P	4	0	1	1	0	.500

RICK RHODEN—Richard Alan Rhoden—Throws: Right; Bats: Right

Ht: 6'3"; Wt: 195 lbs; Born: 5/16/1953 in Boynton Beach, Florida; Debut: 7/5/1974

LCS — Pitching

Year Tm	Age	G	GS	CG	GF	IP	BFP	H	R	ER	HR	SH	SF	HB	TBB	IBB	SO	WP	Bk	W	L	Pct	ShO	Sv-Op	Hld	OAvg	OOBP	ERA
1977 LA	24	1	0	0	0	4.1	17	2	0	0	0	0	0	0	2	0	0	0	0	0	0	—	0	0- 0	0	.133	.235	0.00
1978 LA	25	1	0	0	0	4.0	15	2	1	1	1	0	0	0	1	1	3	0	0	0	0	—	0	0- 0	0	.143	.200	2.25
LCS Totals		2	0	0	0	8.1	64	4	1	1	1	0	0	0	3	1	3	0	0	0	0	—	0	0-0	0	.138	.219	1.08

World Series — Pitching

Year Tm	Age	G	GS	CG	GF	IP	BFP	H	R	ER	HR	SH	SF	HB	TBB	IBB	SO	WP	Bk	W	L	Pct	ShO	Sv-Op	Hld	OAvg	OOBP	ERA
1977 LA	24	2	0	0	1	7.0	26	4	2	2	1	1	0	0	1	1	5	0	0	0	1	.000	0	0- 0	0	.167	.200	2.57
Postseason Totals		4	0	0	1	15.1	116	8	3	3	2	1	0	0	4	2	8	0	0	0	1	.000	0	0-0	0	.151	.211	1.76

LCS — Batting / Fielding

Year Tm	Age	G	AB	H	2B	3B	HR	TB	R	RBI	GW	TBB	IBB	SO	HBP	SH	SF	SB	CS	SB%	GDP	Avg	OBP	SLG	Pos	G	PO	A	E	DP	FPct
1977 LA	24	1	1	0	0	0	0	0	0	0	0	0	0	0	0	0	0	0	0	—	0	.000	.000	.000	P	1	0	0	0	0	—
1978 LA	25	1	1	0	0	0	0	0	0	0	0	0	0	0	0	0	0	0	0	—	0	.000	.000	.000	P	1	0	2	0	0	1.000
LCS Totals		2	2	0	0	0	0	0	0	0	0	0	0	0	0	0	0	0	0	—	0	.000	.000	.000	P	2	0	2	0	0	1.000

World Series — Batting / Fielding

Year Tm	Age	G	AB	H	2B	3B	HR	TB	R	RBI	GW	TBB	IBB	SO	HBP	SH	SF	SB	CS	SB%	GDP	Avg	OBP	SLG	Pos	G	PO	A	E	DP	FPct
1977 LA	24	2	2	1	1	0	0	2	1	0	0	0	0	0	0	0	0	0	0	—	0	.500	.500	1.000	P	2	1	1	0	0	1.000
Postseason Totals		4	4	1	1	0	0	2	1	0	0	0	0	0	0	0	0	0	0	—	0	.250	.250	.500	P	4	1	3	0	0	1.000

ARTHUR RHODES—Arthur Lee Rhodes—Throws: Left; Bats: Left

Ht: 6'2"; Wt: 190 lbs; Born: 10/24/1969 in Waco, Texas; Debut: 8/21/1991

Division Series — Pitching

Year Tm	Age	G	GS	CG	GF	IP	BFP	H	R	ER	HR	SH	SF	HB	TBB	IBB	SO	WP	Bk	W	L	Pct	ShO	Sv-Op	Hld	OAvg	OOBP	ERA
1996 Bal	26	2	0	0	0	1.0	5	1	1	1	0	0	0	0	1	0	1	0	0	0	0	—	0	0- 0	0	.250	.400	9.00
1997 Bal	27	1	0	0	0	2.1	7	0	0	0	0	0	0	0	0	0	4	0	0	0	0	—	0	0- 0	0	.000	.000	0.00
DS Totals		3	0	0	0	3.1	24	1	1	1	0	0	0	0	1	0	5	0	0	0	0	—	0	0-0	0	.091	.167	2.70

LCS — Pitching

Year Tm	Age	G	GS	CG	GF	IP	BFP	H	R	ER	HR	SH	SF	HB	TBB	IBB	SO	WP	Bk	W	L	Pct	ShO	Sv-Op	Hld	OAvg	OOBP	ERA
1996 Bal	26	3	0	0	0	2.0	7	2	0	0	0	0	0	0	0	0	2	1	0	0	0	—	0	0- 0	0	.286	.286	0.00
1997 Bal	27	2	0	0	0	2.1	12	2	0	0	0	1	0	0	3	1	2	2	0	0	0	—	0	0- 0	0	.250	.455	0.00
LCS Totals		5	0	0	0	4.1	38	4	0	0	0	1	0	0	3	1	4	3	0	0	0	—	0	0-0	0	.267	.389	0.00
Postseason Totals		8	0	0	0	7.2	62	5	1	1	0	1	0	0	4	1	9	3	0	0	0	—	0	0-0	0	.192	.300	1.17

Division Series — Batting / Fielding

Year Tm	Age	G	AB	H	2B	3B	HR	TB	R	RBI	GW	TBB	IBB	SO	HBP	SH	SF	SB	CS	SB%	GDP	Avg	OBP	SLG	Pos	G	PO	A	E	DP	FPct
1996 Bal	26	2	0	0	0	0	0	0	0	0	0	0	0	0	0	0	0	0	0	—	0	—	—	—	P	2	0	0	0	0	—
1997 Bal	27	1	0	0	0	0	0	0	0	0	0	0	0	0	0	0	0	0	0	—	0	—	—	—	P	1	0	0	0	0	—
DS Totals		3	0	0	0	0	0	0	0	0	0	0	0	0	0	0	0	0	0	—	0	—	—	—	P	3	0	0	0	0	—

LCS — Batting / Fielding

Year Tm	Age	G	AB	H	2B	3B	HR	TB	R	RBI	GW	TBB	IBB	SO	HBP	SH	SF	SB	CS	SB%	GDP	Avg	OBP	SLG	Pos	G	PO	A	E	DP	FPct
1996 Bal	26	3	0	0	0	0	0	0	0	0	0	0	0	0	0	0	0	0	0	—	0	—	—	—	P	3	0	0	0	0	—
1997 Bal	27	2	0	0	0	0	0	0	0	0	0	0	0	0	0	0	0	0	0	—	0	—	—	—	P	2	0	0	0	0	—
LCS Totals		5	0	0	0	0	0	0	0	0	0	0	0	0	0	0	0	0	0	—	0	—	—	—	P	5	0	0	0	0	—
Postseason Totals		8	0	0	0	0	0	0	0	0	0	0	0	0	0	0	0	0	0	—	0	—	—	—	P	8	0	0	0	0	—

DUSTY RHODES—James Lamar Rhodes—Bats: Left; Throws: Right

Ht: 6'0"; Wt: 178 lbs; Born: 5/13/1927 in Mathews, Alabama; Debut: 7/15/1952

World Series — Batting / Fielding

Year Tm	Age	G	AB	H	2B	3B	HR	TB	R	RBI	GW	TBB	IBB	SO	HBP	SH	SF	SB	CS	SB%	GDP	Avg	OBP	SLG	Pos	G	PO	A	E	DP	FPct
1954 NYG	27	3	6	4	0	0	2	10	2	7	1	1	1	2	0	0	0	0	0	—	0	.667	.714	1.667	OF	2	4	0	0	0	1.000

HAL RHYNE—Harold J. Rhyne—Bats: Right; Throws: Right

Ht: 5'8"; Wt: 163 lbs; Born: 3/30/1899 in Paso Robles, California; Debut: 4/18/1926; Died: 1/7/1971

World Series — Batting / Fielding

Year Tm	Age	G	AB	H	2B	3B	HR	TB	R	RBI	GW	TBB	IBB	SO	HBP	SH	SF	SB	CS	SB%	GDP	Avg	OBP	SLG	Pos	G	PO	A	E	DP	FPct
1927 Pit	28	1	4	0	0	0	0	0	0	0	0	0	0	0	0	0	0	0	0	—	0	.000	.000	.000	2B	1	0	6	0	0	1.000

DEL RICE—Delbert W. Rice—Bats: Right; Throws: Right

Ht: 6'2"; Wt: 190 lbs; Born: 10/27/1922 in Portsmouth, Ohio; Debut: 5/2/1945; Died: 1/26/1983

World Series — Batting / Fielding

Year Tm	Age	G	AB	H	2B	3B	HR	TB	R	RBI	GW	TBB	IBB	SO	HBP	SH	SF	SB	CS	SB%	GDP	Avg	OBP	SLG	Pos	G	PO	A	E	DP	FPct
1946 StL	23	3	6	3	1	0	0	4	2	0	0	2	2	0	0	0	0	0	0	—	0	.500	.625	.667	C	3	9	1	0	0	1.000
1957 Mil	34	2	6	1	0	0	0	1	0	0	0	1	0	2	0	0	0	0	0	—	0	.167	.286	.167	C	2	15	2	0	2	1.000
WS Totals		5	12	4	1	0	0	5	2	0	0	3	2	2	0	0	0	0	0	—	0	.333	.467	.417	C	5	24	3	0	2	1.000

JIM RICE—James Edward Rice—Bats: Right; Throws: Right

Ht: 6'2"; Wt: 200 lbs; Born: 3/8/1953 in Anderson, South Carolina; Debut: 8/19/1974

Year Tm	Age	G	AB	H	2B	3B	HR	TB	R	RBI	GW	TBB	IBB	SO	HBP	SH	SF	SB	CS	SB%	GDP	Avg	OBP	SLG	Pos	G	PO	A	E	DP	FPct
LCS		Batting																							Fielding						
1986 Bos	33	7	31	5	1	0	2	12	8	6	0	1	0	8	0	0	0	0	0	—	2	.161	.188	.387	OF	7	13	1	0	0	1.000
1988 Bos	35	4	13	2	0	0	0	2	0	1	0	2	0	4	0	0	0	0	0	—	0	.154	.267	.154	—						
LCS Totals		11	44	7	1	0	2	14	8	7	0	3	0	12	0	0	0	0	0	—	2	.159	.213	.318	OF	7	13	1	0	0	1.000
World Series		Batting																							Fielding						
1986 Bos	33	7	27	9	1	1	0	12	6	0	0	6	0	9	0	0	0	0	0	—	0	.333	.455	.444	OF	7	16	2	0	1	1.000
Postseason Totals		18	71	16	2	1	2	26	14	7	0	9	0	21	0	0	0	0	0	—	2	.225	.313	.366	OF	14	29	3	0	1	1.000

SAM RICE (HOF 1963-V)—Edgar Charles Rice—Bats: Left; Throws: Right

Ht: 5'9"; Wt: 150 lbs; Born: 2/20/1890 in Morocco, Indiana; Debut: 8/7/1915; Died: 10/13/1974

Year Tm	Age	G	AB	H	2B	3B	HR	TB	R	RBI	GW	TBB	IBB	SO	HBP	SH	SF	SB	CS	SB%	GDP	Avg	OBP	SLG	Pos	G	PO	A	E	DP	FPct
World Series		Batting																							Fielding						
1924 Was	34	7	29	6	0	0	0	6	2	1	0	3	0	2	0	1	0	2	0	1.00	1	.207	.281	.207	OF	7	13	4	1	1	.944
1925 Was	35	7	33	12	0	0	0	12	5	3	0	0	0	1	0	0	0	0	0	—	0	.364	.364	.364	OF	7	15	0	0	0	1.000
1933 Was	43	1	1	1	0	0	0	1	0	0	0	0	0	0	0	0	0	0	0	—	0	1.000	1.000	1.000	—						
WS Totals		15	63	19	0	0	0	19	7	4	0	3	0	3	0	1	0	2	0	1.00	1	.302	.333	.302	OF	14	28	4	1	1	.970

PAUL RICHARDS—Paul Rapier Richards—Bats: Right; Throws: Right

Ht: 6'1"; Wt: 180 lbs; Born: 11/21/1908 in Waxahachie, Texas; Debut: 4/17/1932; Died: 5/4/1986

Year Tm	Age	G	AB	H	2B	3B	HR	TB	R	RBI	GW	TBB	IBB	SO	HBP	SH	SF	SB	CS	SB%	GDP	Avg	OBP	SLG	Pos	G	PO	A	E	DP	FPct
World Series		Batting																							Fielding						
1945 Det	36	7	19	4	2	0	0	6	0	6	0	4	2	3	0	0	0	0	0	—	0	.211	.348	.316	C	7	46	5	1	1	.981

BOBBY RICHARDSON—Robert Clinton Richardson—Bats: Right; Throws: Right

Ht: 5'9"; Wt: 170 lbs; Born: 8/19/1935 in Sumter, South Carolina; Debut: 8/5/1955

Year Tm	Age	G	AB	H	2B	3B	HR	TB	R	RBI	GW	TBB	IBB	SO	HBP	SH	SF	SB	CS	SB%	GDP	Avg	OBP	SLG	Pos	G	PO	A	E	DP	FPct
World Series		Batting																							Fielding						
1957 NYA	22	2	0	0	0	0	0	0	0	0	0	0	0	0	0	0	0	0	0	—	0	—	—	—	2B	1	0	0	0	0	—
1958 NYA	23	4	5	0	0	0	0	0	0	0	0	0	0	0	0	0	0	0	0	—	0	.000	.000	.000	3B	4	0	1	0	0	1.000
1960 NYA	25	7	30	11	2	2	1	20	8	12	0	1	0	1	0	0	0	0	0	—	0	.367	.387	.667	2B	7	21	28	2	7	.961
1961 NYA	26	5	23	9	1	0	0	10	2	0	0	0	0	0	0	0	0	1	1	.50	0	.391	.391	.435	2B	5	10	16	0	1	1.000
1962 NYA	27	7	27	4	0	0	0	4	3	0	0	3	0	1	0	0	0	0	0	—	1	.148	.233	.148	2B	7	19	19	1	4	.974
1963 NYA	28	4	14	3	1	0	0	4	0	0	0	1	0	3	0	1	0	0	0	—	0	.214	.267	.286	2B	4	7	14	0	5	1.000
1964 NYA	29	7	32	13	2	0	0	15	3	3	0	0	0	2	0	1	0	1	0	1.00	1	.406	.406	.469	2B	7	19	19	2	5	.950
WS Totals		36	131	40	6	2	1	53	16	15	0	5	0	7	0	2	0	2	1	.67	2	.305	.331	.405	2B	31	76	96	5	22	.972

GORDIE RICHARDSON—Gordon Clark Richardson—Throws: Left; Bats: Right

Ht: 6'0"; Wt: 185 lbs; Born: 7/19/1938 in Colquitt, Georgia; Debut: 7/26/1964

Year Tm	Age	G	GS	CG	GF	IP	BFP	H	R	ER	HR	SH	SF	HB	TBB	IBB	SO	WP	Bk	W	L	Pct	ShO	Sv-Op	Hld	OAvg	OOBP	ERA
World Series		Pitching																										
1964 StL	26	2	0	0	0	0.2	7	3	3	3	1	0	1	0	2	2	0	0	0	0	0	—	0	0- 0	0	.750	.714	40.50

Year Tm	Age	G	AB	H	2B	3B	HR	TB	R	RBI	GW	TBB	IBB	SO	HBP	SH	SF	SB	CS	SB%	GDP	Avg	OBP	SLG	Pos	G	PO	A	E	DP	FPct
World Series		Batting																							Fielding						
1964 StL	26	2	0	0	0	0	0	0	0	0	0	0	0	0	0	0	0	0	0	—	0	—	—	—	P	2	0	0	0	0	—

PETE RICHERT—Peter Gerard Richert—Throws: Left; Bats: Left

Ht: 5'11"; Wt: 165 lbs; Born: 10/29/1939 in Floral Park, New York; Debut: 4/12/1962

Year Tm	Age	G	GS	CG	GF	IP	BFP	H	R	ER	HR	SH	SF	HB	TBB	IBB	SO	WP	Bk	W	L	Pct	ShO	Sv-Op	Hld	OAvg	OOBP	ERA
LCS		Pitching																										
1969 Bal	29	1	0	0	0	1.0	5	0	0	0	0	0	0	0	2	1	2	0	0	0	0	—	0	0- 0	0	.000	.400	0.00
World Series		Pitching																										
1969 Bal	29	1	0	0	1	0.0	1	0	0	0	0	1	0	0	0	0	0	0	0	0	0	—	0	0- 0	0	—	—	—
1970 Bal	30	1	0	0	1	0.1	1	0	0	0	0	0	0	0	0	0	0	0	0	0	0	—	0	1- 1	0	.000	.000	0.00
1971 Bal	31	1	0	0	1	0.2	2	0	0	0	0	0	0	0	0	0	1	0	0	0	0	—	0	0- 0	0	.000	.000	0.00
WS Totals		3	0	0	3	1.0	8	0	0	0	0	1	0	0	0	0	1	0	0	0	0	—	0	1-1	0	.000	.000	0.00
Postseason Totals		4	0	0	3	2.0	18	0	0	0	0	1	0	0	2	1	3	0	0	0	0	—	0	1-1	0	.000	.250	0.00

Year Tm	Age	G	AB	H	2B	3B	HR	TB	R	RBI	GW	TBB	IBB	SO	HBP	SH	SF	SB	CS	SB%	GDP	Avg	OBP	SLG	Pos	G	PO	A	E	DP	FPct
LCS		Batting																							Fielding						
1969 Bal	29	1	0	0	0	0	0	0	0	0	0	0	0	0	0	0	0	0	0	—	0	—	—	—	P	1	0	0	0	0	—
World Series		Batting																							Fielding						
1969 Bal	29	1	0	0	0	0	0	0	0	0	0	0	0	0	0	0	0	0	0	—	0	—	—	—	P	1	0	0	1	0	.000
1970 Bal	30	1	0	0	0	0	0	0	0	0	0	0	0	0	0	0	0	0	0	—	0	—	—	—	P	1	0	0	0	0	—
1971 Bal	31	1	0	0	0	0	0	0	0	0	0	0	0	0	0	0	0	0	0	—	0	—	—	—	P	1	0	0	0	0	—
WS Totals		3	0	0	0	0	0	0	0	0	0	0	0	0	0	0	0	0	0	—	0	—	—	—	P	3	0	0	1	0	.000
Postseason Totals		4	0	0	0	0	0	0	0	0	0	0	0	0	0	0	0	0	0	—	0	—	—	—	P	4	0	0	1	0	.000

LEW RICHIE—Lewis A. Richie—Throws: Right; Bats: Right

Ht: 5'8"; Wt: 165 lbs; Born: 8/23/1883 in Ambler, Pennsylvania; Debut: 5/8/1906; Died: 8/15/1936

Year Tm	Age	G	GS	CG	GF	IP	BFP	H	R	ER	HR	SH	SF	HB	TBB	IBB	SO	WP	Bk	W	L	Pct	ShO	Sv-Op	Hld	OAvg	OOBP	ERA
World Series		Pitching																										
1910 ChN	27	1	0	0	1	1.0	4	1	0	0	0	0	0	0	0	0	0	0	0	0	0	—	0	0- 0	0	.250	.250	0.00

Year Tm	Age	G	AB	H	2B	3B	HR	TB	R	RBI	GW	TBB	IBB	SO	HBP	SH	SF	SB	CS	SB%	GDP	Avg	OBP	SLG	Pos	G	PO	A	E	DP	FPct
World Series		Batting																							Fielding						
1910 ChN	27	1	0	0	0	0	0	0	0	0	0	0	0	0	0	0	0	0	0	—	0	—	—	—	P	1	0	0	0	0	—

MARV RICKERT—Marvin August Rickert—Nickname: Twitch—Bats: Left; Throws: Right

Ht: 6'2"; Wt: 195 lbs; Born: 1/8/1921 in Longbranch, Washington; Debut: 9/10/1942; Died: 6/3/1978

Year Tm	Age	G	AB	H	2B	3B	HR	TB	R	RBI	GW	TBB	IBB	SO	HBP	SH	SF	SB	CS	SB%	GDP	Avg	OBP	SLG	Pos	G	PO	A	E	DP	FPct
World Series		Batting																							Fielding						
1948 Bos	27	5	19	4	0	0	1	7	2	2	0	0	0	4	0	0	0	0	0	—	1	.211	.211	.368	OF	5	20	0	0	0	1.000

DAVE RICKETTS—David William Ricketts—Bats: Both; Throws: Right

Ht: 6'0"; Wt: 190 lbs; Born: 7/12/1935 in Pottstown, Pennsylvania; Debut: 9/25/1963

Year Tm	Age	G	AB	H	2B	3B	HR	TB	R	RBI	GW	TBB	IBB	SO	HBP	SH	SF	SB	CS	SB%	GDP	Avg	OBP	SLG	Pos	G	PO	A	E	DP	FPct
World Series		Batting																							Fielding						
1967 StL	32	3	3	0	0	0	0	0	0	0	0	0	0	0	0	0	0	0	0	—	0	.000	.000	.000	—						
1968 StL	33	1	1	1	0	0	0	1	0	0	0	0	0	0	0	0	0	0	0	—	0	1.000	1.000	1.000	—						
WS Totals		4	4	1	0	0	0	1	0	0	0	0	0	0	0	0	0	0	0	—	0	.250	.250	.250	—	0	0	0	0	0	—

ELMER RIDDLE—Elmer Ray Riddle—Throws: Right; Bats: Right

Ht: 5'11"; Wt: 170 lbs; Born: 7/31/1914 in Columbus, Georgia; Debut: 10/1/1939; Died: 5/14/1984

Year Tm	Age	G	GS	CG	GF	IP	BFP	H	R	ER	HR	SH	SF	HB	TBB	IBB	SO	WP	Bk	W	L	Pct	ShO	Sv-Op	Hld	OAvg	OOBP	ERA
World Series		Pitching																										
1940 Cin	26	1	0	0	1	1.0	3	0	0	0	0	0	0	0	0	0	2	0	0	0	0	—	0	0- 0	0	.000	.000	0.00

Year Tm	Age	G	AB	H	2B	3B	HR	TB	R	RBI	GW	TBB	IBB	SO	HBP	SH	SF	SB	CS	SB%	GDP	Avg	OBP	SLG	Pos	G	PO	A	E	DP	FPct
World Series		Batting																							Fielding						
1940 Cin	26	1	0	0	0	0	0	0	0	0	0	0	0	0	0	0	0	0	0	—	0	—	—	—	P	1	0	0	0	0	—

LEW RIGGS—Lewis Sidney Riggs—Bats: Left; Throws: Right

Ht: 6'0"; Wt: 175 lbs; Born: 4/22/1910 in Mebane, North Carolina; Debut: 4/28/1934; Died: 8/12/1975

World Series — Batting / Fielding

Year Tm	Age	G	AB	H	2B	3B	HR	TB	R	RBI	GW	TBB	IBB	SO	HBP	SH	SF	SB	CS	SB%	GDP	Avg	OBP	SLG	Pos	G	PO	A	E	DP	FPct
1940 Cin	30	3	3	0	0	0	0	0	1	0	0	0	0	2	0	0	0	0	0	—	0	.000	.000	.000	—						
1941 Bro	31	3	8	2	0	0	0	2	0	1	0	1	0	1	0	0	0	0	0	—	0	.250	.333	.250	3B	2	1	4	0	1	1.000
WS Totals		6	11	2	0	0	0	2	1	1	0	1	0	3	0	0	0	0	0	—	0	.182	.250	.182	3B	2	1	4	0	1	1.000

DAVE RIGHETTI—David Allan Righetti—Nickname: Rags—Throws: Left; Bats: Left

Ht: 6'4"; Wt: 195 lbs; Born: 11/28/1958 in San Jose, California; Debut: 9/16/1979

Division Series — Pitching

Year Tm	Age	G	GS	CG	GF	IP	BFP	H	R	ER	HR	SH	SF	HB	TBB	IBB	SO	WP	Bk	W	L	Pct	ShO	Sv-Op	Hld	OAvg	OOBP	ERA
1981 NYA-*RY*	22	2	1	0	0	9.0	38	8	1	1	0	0	0	0	3	0	13	0	0	2	0	1.000	0	0- 0	0	.229	.289	1.00

LCS — Pitching

Year Tm	Age	G	GS	CG	GF	IP	BFP	H	R	ER	HR	SH	SF	HB	TBB	IBB	SO	WP	Bk	W	L	Pct	ShO	Sv-Op	Hld	OAvg	OOBP	ERA
1981 NYA-*RY*	22	1	1	0	0	6.0	22	4	0	0	0	0	0	0	2	0	4	0	0	1	0	1.000	0	0- 0	0	.200	.273	0.00

World Series — Pitching

Year Tm	Age	G	GS	CG	GF	IP	BFP	H	R	ER	HR	SH	SF	HB	TBB	IBB	SO	WP	Bk	W	L	Pct	ShO	Sv-Op	Hld	OAvg	OOBP	ERA
1981 NYA-*RY*	22	1	1	0	0	2.0	14	5	3	3	1	1	0	1	2	0	1	0	0	0	0	—	0	0- 0	0	.500	.615	13.50
Postseason Totals		4	3	0	0	17.0	148	17	4	4	1	1	0	1	7	0	18	0	0	3	0	1.000	0	0-0	0	.262	.342	2.12

Division Series — Batting / Fielding

Year Tm	Age	G	AB	H	2B	3B	HR	TB	R	RBI	GW	TBB	IBB	SO	HBP	SH	SF	SB	CS	SB%	GDP	Avg	OBP	SLG	Pos	G	PO	A	E	DP	FPct
1981 NYA	22	2	0	0	0	0	0	0	0	0	0	0	0	0	0	0	0	0	0	—	0	—	—	—	P	2	0	1	0	0	1.000

LCS — Batting / Fielding

Year Tm	Age	G	AB	H	2B	3B	HR	TB	R	RBI	GW	TBB	IBB	SO	HBP	SH	SF	SB	CS	SB%	GDP	Avg	OBP	SLG	Pos	G	PO	A	E	DP	FPct
1981 NYA	22	1	0	0	0	0	0	0	0	0	0	0	0	0	0	0	0	0	0	—	0	—	—	—	P	1	0	1	0	0	1.000

World Series — Batting / Fielding

Year Tm	Age	G	AB	H	2B	3B	HR	TB	R	RBI	GW	TBB	IBB	SO	HBP	SH	SF	SB	CS	SB%	GDP	Avg	OBP	SLG	Pos	G	PO	A	E	DP	FPct
1981 NYA	22	1	1	0	0	0	0	0	0	0	0	0	0	1	0	1	0	0	0	—	0	.000	.000	.000	P	1	0	0	0	0	—
Postseason Totals		4	1	0	0	0	0	0	0	0	0	0	0	1	0	1	0	0	0	—	0	.000	.000	.000	P	4	0	2	0	0	1.000

BILL RIGNEY—William Joseph Rigney—Nicknames: Specs, The Cricket—Bats: Right; Throws: Right

Ht: 6'1"; Wt: 178 lbs; Born: 1/29/1918 in Alameda, California; Debut: 4/16/1946

World Series — Batting / Fielding

Year Tm	Age	G	AB	H	2B	3B	HR	TB	R	RBI	GW	TBB	IBB	SO	HBP	SH	SF	SB	CS	SB%	GDP	Avg	OBP	SLG	Pos	G	PO	A	E	DP	FPct
1951 NYG	33	4	4	1	0	0	0	1	0	1	0	0	0	1	0	0	0	0	0	—	0	.250	.250	.250	—						

JOSE RIJO—Jose Antonio Rijo—Throws: Right; Bats: Right

Ht: 6'1"; Wt: 200 lbs; Born: 5/13/1965 in San Cristobal, Dominican Republic; Debut: 4/5/1984

LCS — Pitching

Year Tm	Age	G	GS	CG	GF	IP	BFP	H	R	ER	HR	SH	SF	HB	TBB	IBB	SO	WP	Bk	W	L	Pct	ShO	Sv-Op	Hld	OAvg	OOBP	ERA
1990 Cin	25	2	2	0	0	12.1	52	10	6	6	2	0	0	0	7	1	15	0	0	1	0	1.000	0	0- 0	0	.222	.327	4.38

World Series — Pitching

Year Tm	Age	G	GS	CG	GF	IP	BFP	H	R	ER	HR	SH	SF	HB	TBB	IBB	SO	WP	Bk	W	L	Pct	ShO	Sv-Op	Hld	OAvg	OOBP	ERA
1990 Cin	25	2	2	0	0	15.1	59	9	1	1	0	0	0	0	5	1	14	0	0	2	0	1.000	0	0- 0	0	.167	.237	0.59
Postseason Totals		4	4	0	0	27.2	222	19	7	7	2	0	0	0	12	2	29	0	0	3	0	1.000	0	0-0	0	.192	.279	2.28

LCS — Batting / Fielding

Year Tm	Age	G	AB	H	2B	3B	HR	TB	R	RBI	GW	TBB	IBB	SO	HBP	SH	SF	SB	CS	SB%	GDP	Avg	OBP	SLG	Pos	G	PO	A	E	DP	FPct
1990 Cin	25	2	5	0	0	0	0	0	0	0	0	0	0	1	0	0	0	0	0	—	1	.000	.000	.000	P	2	0	0	0	0	—

World Series — Batting / Fielding

Year Tm	Age	G	AB	H	2B	3B	HR	TB	R	RBI	GW	TBB	IBB	SO	HBP	SH	SF	SB	CS	SB%	GDP	Avg	OBP	SLG	Pos	G	PO	A	E	DP	FPct
1990 Cin	25	2	3	1	0	0	0	1	0	0	0	0	0	0	0	0	0	0	0	—	0	.333	.333	.333	P	2	0	2	0	0	1.000
Postseason Totals		4	8	1	0	0	0	1	0	0	0	0	0	1	0	0	0	0	0	—	1	.125	.125	.125	P	4	0	2	0	0	1.000

ERNEST RILES—Nickname: Ernie—Bats: Left; Throws: Right

Ht: 6'1"; Wt: 180 lbs; Born: 10/2/1960 in Cairo, Georgia; Debut: 5/14/1985

LCS — Batting / Fielding

Year Tm	Age	G	AB	H	2B	3B	HR	TB	R	RBI	GW	TBB	IBB	SO	HBP	SH	SF	SB	CS	SB%	GDP	Avg	OBP	SLG	Pos	G	PO	A	E	DP	FPct
1989 SF	28	1	1	0	0	0	0	0	0	0	0	0	0	0	0	0	0	0	0	—	0	.000	.000	.000	—						

World Series — Batting / Fielding

Year Tm	Age	G	AB	H	2B	3B	HR	TB	R	RBI	GW	TBB	IBB	SO	HBP	SH	SF	SB	CS	SB%	GDP	Avg	OBP	SLG	Pos	G	PO	A	E	DP	FPct
1989 SF	28	4	8	0	0	0	0	0	0	0	0	0	0	1	0	0	0	0	0	—	0	.000	.000	.000	—						
Postseason Totals		5	9	0	0	0	0	0	0	0	0	0	0	1	0	0	0	0	0	—	0	.000	.000	.000	—	0	0	0	0	0	—

JIMMY RING—James Joseph Ring—Throws: Right; Bats: Right

Ht: 6'1"; Wt: 170 lbs; Born: 2/15/1895 in Brooklyn, New York; Debut: 4/13/1917; Died: 7/6/1965

World Series — Pitching

Year Tm	Age	G	GS	CG	GF	IP	BFP	H	R	ER	HR	SH	SF	HB	TBB	IBB	SO	WP	Bk	W	L	Pct	ShO	Sv-Op	Hld	OAvg	OOBP	ERA
1919 Cin	24	2	1	1	1	14.0	57	7	1	1	0	1	0	2	6	0	4	0	0	1	1	.500	1	0- 1	0	.146	.268	0.64

World Series — Batting / Fielding

Year Tm	Age	G	AB	H	2B	3B	HR	TB	R	RBI	GW	TBB	IBB	SO	HBP	SH	SF	SB	CS	SB%	GDP	Avg	OBP	SLG	Pos	G	PO	A	E	DP	FPct
1919 Cin	24	2	5	0	0	0	0	0	0	0	0	0	0	2	0	0	0	0	0	—	1	.000	.000	.000	P	2	1	3	0	0	1.000

CAL RIPKEN JR.—Calvin Edwin Ripken Jr.—Nickname: Junior—Bats: Right; Throws: Right

Ht: 6'4"; Wt: 200 lbs; Born: 8/24/1960 in Havre de Grace, Maryland; Debut: 8/10/1981

Division Series — Batting / Fielding

Year Tm	Age	G	AB	H	2B	3B	HR	TB	R	RBI	GW	TBB	IBB	SO	HBP	SH	SF	SB	CS	SB%	GDP	Avg	OBP	SLG	Pos	G	PO	A	E	DP	FPct
1996 Bal	36	4	18	8	3	0	0	11	2	2	0	0	0	3	1	0	0	0	0	—	0	.444	.474	.611	SS	4	7	15	0	1	1.000
1997 Bal	37	4	16	7	2	0	0	9	1	1	0	2	0	2	0	0	0	0	0	—	0	.438	.500	.563	3B	4	4	4	0	0	1.000
DS Totals		8	34	15	5	0	0	20	3	3	0	2	0	5	1	0	0	0	0	—	0	.441	.486	.588	3B	4	4	4	0	0	1.000

LCS — Batting / Fielding

Year Tm	Age	G	AB	H	2B	3B	HR	TB	R	RBI	GW	TBB	IBB	SO	HBP	SH	SF	SB	CS	SB%	GDP	Avg	OBP	SLG	Pos	G	PO	A	E	DP	FPct
1983 Bal-*M*	23	4	15	6	2	0	0	8	5	1	0	2	0	3	1	0	0	0	0	—	1	.400	.500	.533	SS	4	7	11	0	3	1.000
1996 Bal	36	5	20	5	1	0	0	6	1	0	0	1	0	4	0	0	0	0	0	—	0	.250	.286	.300	SS	5	4	14	1	5	.947
1997 Bal	37	6	23	8	2	0	1	13	3	3	0	4	0	6	0	0	0	0	0	—	0	.348	.444	.565	3B	6	1	14	0	3	1.000
LCS Totals		15	58	19	5	0	1	27	9	4	0	7	0	13	1	0	0	0	0	—	1	.328	.409	.466	SS	9	11	25	1	8	.973

World Series — Batting / Fielding

Year Tm	Age	G	AB	H	2B	3B	HR	TB	R	RBI	GW	TBB	IBB	SO	HBP	SH	SF	SB	CS	SB%	GDP	Avg	OBP	SLG	Pos	G	PO	A	E	DP	FPct
1983 Bal-*M*	23	5	18	3	0	0	0	3	2	1	0	3	0	4	0	0	0	0	0	—	0	.167	.286	.167	SS	5	6	14	0	3	1.000
Postseason Totals		28	110	37	10	0	1	50	14	8	0	12	0	22	2	0	0	0	0	—	1	.336	.411	.455	SS	18	24	54	1	12	.987

JIMMY RIPPLE—James Albert Ripple—Bats: Left; Throws: Right

Ht: 5'10"; Wt: 170 lbs; Born: 10/14/1909 in Export, Pennsylvania; Debut: 4/20/1936; Died: 7/16/1959

World Series — Batting / Fielding

Year Tm	Age	G	AB	H	2B	3B	HR	TB	R	RBI	GW	TBB	IBB	SO	HBP	SH	SF	SB	CS	SB%	GDP	Avg	OBP	SLG	Pos	G	PO	A	E	DP	FPct
1936 NYG	26	5	12	4	0	0	1	7	2	3	0	3	0	3	0	2	0	0	1	.00	0	.333	.467	.583	OF	5	8	0	0	0	1.000
1937 NYG	27	5	17	5	0	0	0	5	2	0	0	3	0	1	0	0	0	0	1	.00	0	.294	.400	.294	OF	5	11	0	0	0	1.000
1940 Cin	30	7	21	7	2	0	1	12	3	6	1	4	2	2	0	0	0	0	0	—	0	.333	.440	.571	OF	7	14	0	0	0	1.000
WS Totals		17	50	16	2	0	2	24	7	9	1	10	2	6	0	2	0	0	2	.00	0	.320	.433	.480	OF	17	33	0	0	0	1.000

SWEDE RISBERG—Charles August Risberg—Bats: Right; Throws: Right

Ht: 6'0"; Wt: 175 lbs; Born: 10/13/1894 in San Francisco, California; Debut: 4/11/1917; Died: 10/13/1975

World Series — Batting / Fielding

Year Tm	Age	G	AB	H	2B	3B	HR	TB	R	RBI	GW	TBB	IBB	SO	HBP	SH	SF	SB	CS	SB%	GDP	Avg	OBP	SLG	Pos	G	PO	A	E	DP	FPct
1917 ChA	22	2	2	1	0	0	0	1	0	1	0	0	0	0	0	0	0	0	0	—	0	.500	.500	.500	—						
1919 ChA	24	8	25	2	0	1	0	4	3	0	0	5	0	3	0	0	0	1	0	1.00	1	.080	.233	.160	SS	8	23	30	4	6	.930
WS Totals		10	27	3	0	1	0	5	3	1	0	5	0	3	0	0	0	1	0	1.00	1	.111	.250	.185	SS	8	23	30	4	6	.930

BILL RISLEY—William Charles Risley—Throws: Right; Bats: Right

Ht: 6'2"; Wt: 215 lbs; Born: 5/29/1967 in Chicago, Illinois; Debut: 7/8/1992

Year	Tm	Age	G	GS	CG	GF	IP	BFP	H	R	ER	HR	SH	SF	HB	TBB	IBB	SO	WP	Bk	W	L	Pct	ShO	Sv-Op	Hld	OAvg	OOBP	ERA
Division Series			Pitching																										
1995	Sea	28	4	0	0	1	3.0	12	2	2	2	2	0	0	1	0	0	1	0	0	0	0	—	0	1-1	0	.182	.250	6.00
LCS			Pitching																										
1995	Sea	28	3	0	0	3	2.2	11	2	0	0	0	0	0	0	1	0	2	0	0	0	0	—	0	0-0	0	.200	.273	0.00
Postseason Totals			7	0	0	4	5.2	46	4	2	2	2	0	0	1	1	0	3	0	0	0	0	—	0	1-1	0	.190	.261	3.18

Year	Tm	Age	G	AB	H	2B	3B	HR	TB	R	RBI	GW	TBB	IBB	SO	HBP	SH	SF	SB	CS	SB%	GDP	Avg	OBP	SLG	Pos	G	PO	A	E	DP	FPct
Division Series			Batting																							Fielding						
1995	Sea	28	4	0	0	0	0	0	0	0	0	0	0	0	0	0	0	0	0	0	—	0	—	—	—	P	4	0	0	0	0	—
LCS			Batting																							Fielding						
1995	Sea	28	3	0	0	0	0	0	0	0	0	0	0	0	0	0	0	0	0	0	—	0	—	—	—	P	3	0	0	0	0	—
Postseason Totals			7	0	0	0	0	0	0	0	0	0	0	0	0	0	0	0	0	0	—	0	—	—	—	P	7	0	0	0	0	—

CLAUDE RITCHEY—Claude Cassius Ritchey—Nickname: Little All Right—Bats: Both; Throws: Right

Ht: 5'6"; Wt: 167 lbs; Born: 10/5/1873 in Emlenton, Pennsylvania; Debut: 4/22/1897; Died: 11/8/1951

Year	Tm	Age	G	AB	H	2B	3B	HR	TB	R	RBI	GW	TBB	IBB	SO	HBP	SH	SF	SB	CS	SB%	GDP	Avg	OBP	SLG	Pos	G	PO	A	E	DP	FPct
World Series			Batting																							Fielding						
1903	Pit	29	8	27	4	1	0	0	5	2	2	0	4	0	7	0	0	0	1	0	1.00	0	.148	.258	.185	2B	8	20	29	0	5	1.000

KEVIN RITZ—Kevin D. Ritz—Throws: Right; Bats: Right

Ht: 6'4"; Wt: 195 lbs; Born: 6/8/1965 in Eatontown, New Jersey; Debut: 7/15/1989

Year	Tm	Age	G	GS	CG	GF	IP	BFP	H	R	ER	HR	SH	SF	HB	TBB	IBB	SO	WP	Bk	W	L	Pct	ShO	Sv-Op	Hld	OAvg	OOBP	ERA
Division Series			Pitching																										
1995	Col	30	2	1	0	0	7.0	34	12	7	6	3	0	0	0	3	1	5	0	0	0	0	—	0	0-0	0	.387	.441	7.71

Year	Tm	Age	G	AB	H	2B	3B	HR	TB	R	RBI	GW	TBB	IBB	SO	HBP	SH	SF	SB	CS	SB%	GDP	Avg	OBP	SLG	Pos	G	PO	A	E	DP	FPct
Division Series			Batting																							Fielding						
1995	Col	30	2	2	0	0	0	0	0	0	0	0	0	0	0	0	0	0	0	0	—	0	.000	.000	.000	P	2	0	1	1	0	.500

BEN RIVERA—Bienvenido Santana Rivera—Throws: Right; Bats: Right

Ht: 6'6"; Wt: 210 lbs; Born: 1/11/1968 in San Pedro De Macoris, Dominican Republic; Debut: 4/9/1992

Year	Tm	Age	G	GS	CG	GF	IP	BFP	H	R	ER	HR	SH	SF	HB	TBB	IBB	SO	WP	Bk	W	L	Pct	ShO	Sv-Op	Hld	OAvg	OOBP	ERA
LCS			Pitching																										
1993	Phi	25	1	0	0	0	2.0	8	1	1	1	1	0	0	0	1	0	2	0	0	0	0	—	0	0-0	0	.143	.250	4.50
World Series			Pitching																										
1993	Phi	25	1	0	0	0	1.1	10	4	4	4	0	0	1	0	2	0	3	0	0	0	0	—	0	0-0	0	.571	.600	27.00
Postseason Totals			2	0	0	0	3.1	36	5	5	5	1	0	1	0	3	0	5	0	0	0	0	—	0	0-0	0	.357	.444	13.50

Year	Tm	Age	G	AB	H	2B	3B	HR	TB	R	RBI	GW	TBB	IBB	SO	HBP	SH	SF	SB	CS	SB%	GDP	Avg	OBP	SLG	Pos	G	PO	A	E	DP	FPct
LCS			Batting																							Fielding						
1993	Phi	25	1	0	0	0	0	0	0	0	0	0	0	0	0	0	0	0	0	0	—	0	—	—	—	P	1	0	0	0	0	—
World Series			Batting																							Fielding						
1993	Phi	25	1	0	0	0	0	0	0	0	0	0	0	0	0	0	0	0	0	0	—	0	—	—	—	P	1	0	0	0	0	—
Postseason Totals			2	0	0	0	0	0	0	0	0	0	0	0	0	0	0	0	0	0	—	0	—	—	—	P	2	0	0	0	0	—

JIM RIVERA—Manuel Joseph Rivera—Nickname: Jungle Jim—Bats: Left; Throws: Left

Ht: 6'0"; Wt: 196 lbs; Born: 7/22/1922 in New York, New York; Debut: 4/15/1952

Year	Tm	Age	G	AB	H	2B	3B	HR	TB	R	RBI	GW	TBB	IBB	SO	HBP	SH	SF	SB	CS	SB%	GDP	Avg	OBP	SLG	Pos	G	PO	A	E	DP	FPct
World Series			Batting																							Fielding						
1959	ChA	37	5	11	0	0	0	0	0	1	0	0	3	0	1	0	0	0	0	1	.00	0	.000	.214	.000	OF	5	10	0	0	0	1.000

LUIS RIVERA—Luis Antonio Rivera—Bats: Right; Throws: Right

Ht: 5'9"; Wt: 170 lbs; Born: 1/3/1964 in Cidra, Puerto Rico; Debut: 8/3/1986

Year	Tm	Age	G	AB	H	2B	3B	HR	TB	R	RBI	GW	TBB	IBB	SO	HBP	SH	SF	SB	CS	SB%	GDP	Avg	OBP	SLG	Pos	G	PO	A	E	DP	FPct
LCS			Batting																							Fielding						
1990	Bos	26	4	9	2	1	0	0	3	1	0	0	0	0	2	0	0	0	0	0	—	0	.222	.222	.333	SS	4	6	16	1	3	.957

MARIANO RIVERA—Throws: Right; Bats: Right

Ht: 6'2"; Wt: 168 lbs; Born: 11/29/1969 in Panama City, Panama; Debut: 5/23/1995

Year	Tm	Age	G	GS	CG	GF	IP	BFP	H	R	ER	HR	SH	SF	HB	TBB	IBB	SO	WP	Bk	W	L	Pct	ShO	Sv-Op	Hld	OAvg	OOBP	ERA
Division Series			Pitching																										
1995	NYA	25	3	0	0	2	5.1	20	3	0	0	0	1	0	0	1	1	8	0	0	1	0	1.000	0	0-0	0	.167	.211	0.00
1996	NYA	26	2	0	0	0	4.2	15	0	0	0	0	0	0	0	1	0	1	0	0	0	0	—	0	0-0	1	.000	.067	0.00
1997	NYA	27	2	0	0	1	2.0	8	2	1	1	1	0	0	0	0	0	1	0	0	0	0	—	0	1-2	0	.250	.250	4.50
DS Totals			7	0	0	3	12.0	86	5	1	1	1	1	0	0	2	1	10	0	0	1	0	1.000	0	1-2	1	.125	.167	0.75
LCS			Pitching																										
1996	NYA	26	2	0	0	1	4.0	19	6	0	0	0	0	0	0	1	0	5	0	0	1	0	1.000	0	0-0	1	.333	.368	0.00
World Series			Pitching																										
1996	NYA	26	4	0	0	1	5.2	23	4	1	1	0	1	0	0	3	0	4	0	0	0	0	—	0	0-0	2	.211	.318	1.59
Postseason Totals			13	0	0	5	21.2	170	15	2	2	1	2	0	0	6	1	19	0	0	2	0	1.000	0	1-2	4	.195	.253	0.83

Year	Tm	Age	G	AB	H	2B	3B	HR	TB	R	RBI	GW	TBB	IBB	SO	HBP	SH	SF	SB	CS	SB%	GDP	Avg	OBP	SLG	Pos	G	PO	A	E	DP	FPct
Division Series			Batting																							Fielding						
1995	NYA	25	3	0	0	0	0	0	0	0	0	0	0	0	0	0	0	0	0	0	—	0	—	—	—	P	3	0	0	0	0	—
1996	NYA	26	2	0	0	0	0	0	0	0	0	0	0	0	0	0	0	0	0	0	—	0	—	—	—	P	2	0	0	0	0	—
1997	NYA	27	2	0	0	0	0	0	0	0	0	0	0	0	0	0	0	0	0	0	—	0	—	—	—	P	2	1	0	0	0	1.000
DS Totals			7	0	0	0	0	0	0	0	0	0	0	0	0	0	0	0	0	0	—	0	—	—	—	P	7	1	0	0	0	1.000
LCS			Batting																							Fielding						
1996	NYA	26	2	0	0	0	0	0	0	0	0	0	0	0	0	0	0	0	0	0	—	0	—	—	—	P	2	0	0	0	0	—
World Series			Batting																							Fielding						
1996	NYA	26	4	1	0	0	0	0	0	0	0	0	0	0	0	0	0	0	0	0	—	0	.000	.000	.000	P	4	0	2	0	0	1.000
Postseason Totals			13	1	0	0	0	0	0	0	0	0	0	0	0	0	0	0	0	0	—	0	.000	.000	.000	P	13	1	2	0	0	1.000

RUBEN RIVERA—Ruben Moreno Rivera—Bats: Right; Throws: Right

Ht: 6'3"; Wt: 200 lbs; Born: 11/14/1973 in La Chorrera, Panama; Debut: 9/3/1995

Year	Tm	Age	G	AB	H	2B	3B	HR	TB	R	RBI	GW	TBB	IBB	SO	HBP	SH	SF	SB	CS	SB%	GDP	Avg	OBP	SLG	Pos	G	PO	A	E	DP	FPct
Division Series			Batting																							Fielding						
1996	NYA	22	2	1	0	0	0	0	0	0	0	0	0	0	1	0	0	0	0	0	—	0	.000	.000	.000	OF	2	0	0	0	0	—

MICKEY RIVERS—John Milton Rivers—Nicknames: Gozzlehead, Mick the Quick, Mickey Mouth—Bats: Left; Throws: Left

Ht: 5'10"; Wt: 165 lbs; Born: 10/31/1948 in Miami, Florida; Debut: 8/4/1970

Year	Tm	Age	G	AB	H	2B	3B	HR	TB	R	RBI	GW	TBB	IBB	SO	HBP	SH	SF	SB	CS	SB%	GDP	Avg	OBP	SLG	Pos	G	PO	A	E	DP	FPct
LCS			Batting																							Fielding						
1976	NYA	27	5	23	8	0	1	0	10	5	0	0	1	0	1	0	0	0	0	1	.00	0	.348	.375	.435	OF	5	11	0	0	0	1.000
1977	NYA	28	5	23	9	2	0	0	11	5	2	0	0	0	2	0	0	0	1	0	1.00	0	.391	.391	.478	OF	5	19	0	0	0	1.000
1978	NYA	29	4	11	5	0	0	0	5	0	0	0	2	0	0	0	0	0	0	0	—	0	.455	.538	.455	OF	4	8	1	0	1	1.000
LCS Totals			14	57	22	2	1	0	26	10	2	0	3	0	3	0	0	0	1	1	.50	0	.386	.417	.456	OF	14	38	1	0	1	1.000

World Series — Batting / Fielding

Year Tm	Age	G	AB	H	2B	3B	HR	TB	R	RBI	GW	TBB	IBB	SO	HBP	SH	SF	SB	CS	SB%	GDP	Avg	OBP	SLG	Pos	G	PO	A	E	DP	FPct
1976 NYA	27	4	18	3	0	0	0	3	1	0	0	1	0	2	0	0	0	1	1	.50	0	.167	.211	.167	OF	4	14	0	0	0	1.000
1977 NYA	28	6	27	6	2	0	0	8	1	1	1	0	0	2	0	0	0	1	0	1.00	0	.222	.222	.296	OF	6	24	1	0	0	1.000
1978 NYA	29	5	18	6	0	0	0	6	2	1	0	0	0	2	0	0	0	1	1	.50	0	.333	.333	.333	OF	4	7	0	0	0	1.000
WS Totals		15	63	15	2	0	0	17	4	2	1	1	0	6	0	0	0	3	2	.60	0	.238	.250	.270	OF	14	45	1	0	0	1.000
Postseason Totals		29	120	37	4	1	0	43	14	4	1	4	0	9	0	0	0	4	3	.57	0	.308	.331	.358	OF	28	83	2	0	1	1.000

EPPA RIXEY (HOF 1963-V)—Nickname: Eppa Jephtha—Throws: Left; Bats: Right

Ht: 6'5"; Wt: 210 lbs; Born: 5/3/1891 in Culpeper, Virginia; Debut: 6/21/1912; Died: 2/28/1963

World Series — Pitching

Year Tm	Age	G	GS	CG	GF	IP	BFP	H	R	ER	HR	SH	SF	HB	TBB	IBB	SO	WP	Bk	W	L	Pct	ShO	Sv-Op	Hld	OAvg	OOBP	ERA
1915 Phi	24	1	0	0	1	6.2	27	4	3	3	2	0	0	1	2	0	2	0	0	0	1	.000	0	0- 0	0	.167	.259	4.05

World Series — Batting / Fielding

Year Tm	Age	G	AB	H	2B	3B	HR	TB	R	RBI	GW	TBB	IBB	SO	HBP	SH	SF	SB	CS	SB%	GDP	Avg	OBP	SLG	Pos	G	PO	A	E	DP	FPct
1915 Phi	24	1	2	1	0	0	0	1	0	0	0	0	0	0	0	0	0	0	0	—	0	.500	.500	.500	P	1	0	1	0	0	1.000

PHIL RIZZUTO (HOF 1994-V)—Philip Francis Rizzuto—Nickname: Scooter—Bats: Right; Throws: Right

Ht: 5'6"; Wt: 150 lbs; Born: 9/25/1917 in Brooklyn, New York; Debut: 4/15/1941

World Series — Batting / Fielding

Year Tm	Age	G	AB	H	2B	3B	HR	TB	R	RBI	GW	TBB	IBB	SO	HBP	SH	SF	SB	CS	SB%	GDP	Avg	OBP	SLG	Pos	G	PO	A	E	DP	FPct
1941 NYA	24	5	18	2	0	0	0	2	0	0	0	3	1	1	0	0	0	1	0	1.00	0	.111	.238	.111	SS	5	12	18	1	6	.968
1942 NYA	25	5	21	8	0	0	1	11	2	1	0	2	0	1	0	0	0	2	0	1.00	0	.381	.435	.524	SS	5	15	15	1	1	.968
1947 NYA	30	7	26	8	1	0	0	9	3	2	1	4	0	0	0	0	0	2	1	.67	0	.308	.400	.346	SS	7	19	18	0	3	1.000
1949 NYA	32	5	18	3	0	0	0	3	2	1	0	3	0	1	0	2	0	1	0	1.00	0	.167	.286	.167	SS	5	5	15	0	3	1.000
1950 NYA-*M*	33	4	14	2	0	0	0	2	1	0	0	3	0	0	0	1	0	1	0	1.00	0	.143	.294	.143	SS	4	5	8	0	2	1.000
1951 NYA	34	6	25	8	0	0	1	11	5	3	0	2	0	3	1	0	0	0	1	.00	1	.320	.393	.440	SS	6	14	23	1	8	.974
1952 NYA	35	7	27	4	1	0	0	5	2	0	0	5	0	2	0	1	0	0	1	.00	0	.148	.281	.185	SS	7	13	17	1	4	.968
1953 NYA	36	6	19	6	1	0	0	7	4	0	0	3	0	2	0	1	0	1	0	1.00	0	.316	.409	.368	SS	6	11	19	1	3	.968
1955 NYA	38	7	15	4	0	0	0	4	2	1	0	5	0	1	0	0	0	2	0	1.00	1	.267	.450	.267	SS	7	13	14	0	1	1.000
WS Totals		52	183	45	3	0	2	54	21	8	1	30	1	11	1	5	0	10	3	.77	2	.246	.355	.295	SS	52	107	147	5	31	.981

BIP ROBERTS—Leon Joseph Roberts—Bats: Both; Throws: Right

Ht: 5'7"; Wt: 150 lbs; Born: 10/27/1963 in Berkeley, California; Debut: 4/7/1986

Division Series — Batting / Fielding

Year Tm	Age	G	AB	H	2B	3B	HR	TB	R	RBI	GW	TBB	IBB	SO	HBP	SH	SF	SB	CS	SB%	GDP	Avg	OBP	SLG	Pos	G	PO	A	E	DP	FPct
1997 Cle	33	5	19	6	0	0	0	6	1	1	0	2	0	2	0	1	0	2	1	.67	0	.316	.381	.316	2B	2	2	8	0	3	1.000
																									OF	4	3	0	0	0	1.000

LCS — Batting / Fielding

Year Tm	Age	G	AB	H	2B	3B	HR	TB	R	RBI	GW	TBB	IBB	SO	HBP	SH	SF	SB	CS	SB%	GDP	Avg	OBP	SLG	Pos	G	PO	A	E	DP	FPct
1997 Cle	33	5	20	3	1	0	0	4	0	0	0	0	0	8	0	0	0	1	0	1.00	0	.150	.150	.200	2B	4	8	7	0	5	1.000
																									OF	2	3	0	1	0	.750

World Series — Batting / Fielding

Year Tm	Age	G	AB	H	2B	3B	HR	TB	R	RBI	GW	TBB	IBB	SO	HBP	SH	SF	SB	CS	SB%	GDP	Avg	OBP	SLG	Pos	G	PO	A	E	DP	FPct
1997 Cle	33	6	22	6	4	0	0	10	3	4	0	3	0	5	0	1	0	0	1	.00	1	.273	.360	.455	2B	4	7	8	0	3	1.000
																									OF	2	1	0	0	0	1.000
Postseason Totals		16	61	15	5	0	0	20	4	5	0	5	0	15	0	2	0	3	2	.60	1	.246	.303	.328	2B	10	17	23	0	11	1.000

DAVE ROBERTS—David Arthur Roberts—Throws: Left; Bats: Left

Ht: 6'3"; Wt: 195 lbs; Born: 9/11/1944 in Gallipolis, Ohio; Debut: 7/6/1969

LCS — Pitching

Year Tm	Age	G	GS	CG	GF	IP	BFP	H	R	ER	HR	SH	SF	HB	TBB	IBB	SO	WP	Bk	W	L	Pct	ShO	Sv-Op	Hld	OAvg	OOBP	ERA
1979 Pit	35	1	0	0	0	0.0	1	0	0	0	0	0	0	0	1	0	0	0	0	0	0	—	0	0- 0	0	—	1.000	—

LCS — Batting / Fielding

Year Tm	Age	G	AB	H	2B	3B	HR	TB	R	RBI	GW	TBB	IBB	SO	HBP	SH	SF	SB	CS	SB%	GDP	Avg	OBP	SLG	Pos	G	PO	A	E	DP	FPct
1979 Pit	35	1	0	0	0	0	0	0	0	0	0	0	0	0	0	0	0	0	0	—	0	—	—	—	P	1	0	0	0	0	—

DAVE ROBERTS—David Wayne Roberts—Bats: Right; Throws: Right

Ht: 6'3"; Wt: 215 lbs; Born: 2/17/1951 in Lebanon, Oregon; Debut: 6/7/1972

Division Series — Batting / Fielding

Year Tm	Age	G	AB	H	2B	3B	HR	TB	R	RBI	GW	TBB	IBB	SO	HBP	SH	SF	SB	CS	SB%	GDP	Avg	OBP	SLG	Pos	G	PO	A	E	DP	FPct
1981 Hou	30	1	1	0	0	0	0	0	0	0	0	0	0	1	0	0	0	0	0	—	0	.000	.000	.000	—						

ROBIN ROBERTS (HOF 1976-W)—Robin Evan Roberts—Throws: Right; Bats: Both

Ht: 6'0"; Wt: 190 lbs; Born: 9/30/1926 in Springfield, Illinois; Debut: 6/18/1948

World Series — Pitching

Year Tm	Age	G	GS	CG	GF	IP	BFP	H	R	ER	HR	SH	SF	HB	TBB	IBB	SO	WP	Bk	W	L	Pct	ShO	Sv-Op	Hld	OAvg	OOBP	ERA
1950 Phi	24	2	1	1	1	11.0	47	11	2	2	1	0	0	0	3	0	5	0	0	0	1	.000	0	0- 0	0	.250	.298	1.64

World Series — Batting / Fielding

Year Tm	Age	G	AB	H	2B	3B	HR	TB	R	RBI	GW	TBB	IBB	SO	HBP	SH	SF	SB	CS	SB%	GDP	Avg	OBP	SLG	Pos	G	PO	A	E	DP	FPct
1950 Phi	24	2	2	0	0	0	0	0	0	0	0	0	0	1	0	1	0	0	0	—	0	.000	.000	.000	P	2	0	0	0	0	—

ANDRE ROBERTSON—Andre Levett Robertson—Bats: Right; Throws: Right

Ht: 5'10"; Wt: 155 lbs; Born: 10/2/1957 in Orange, Texas; Debut: 9/3/1981

LCS — Batting / Fielding

Year Tm	Age	G	AB	H	2B	3B	HR	TB	R	RBI	GW	TBB	IBB	SO	HBP	SH	SF	SB	CS	SB%	GDP	Avg	OBP	SLG	Pos	G	PO	A	E	DP	FPct
1981 NYA	23	1	1	0	0	0	0	0	0	0	0	0	0	0	0	0	0	0	0	—	0	.000	.000	.000	SS	1	2	1	0	1	1.000

World Series — Batting / Fielding

Year Tm	Age	G	AB	H	2B	3B	HR	TB	R	RBI	GW	TBB	IBB	SO	HBP	SH	SF	SB	CS	SB%	GDP	Avg	OBP	SLG	Pos	G	PO	A	E	DP	FPct
1981 NYA	23	1	0	0	0	0	0	0	0	0	0	0	0	0	0	0	0	0	0	—	0	—	—	—	—						
Postseason Totals		2	1	0	0	0	0	0	0	0	0	0	0	0	0	0	0	0	0	—	0	.000	.000	.000	SS	1	2	1	0	1	1.000

BOB ROBERTSON—Robert Eugene Robertson—Bats: Right; Throws: Right

Ht: 6'1"; Wt: 195 lbs; Born: 10/2/1946 in Frostburg, Maryland; Debut: 9/18/1967

LCS — Batting / Fielding

Year Tm	Age	G	AB	H	2B	3B	HR	TB	R	RBI	GW	TBB	IBB	SO	HBP	SH	SF	SB	CS	SB%	GDP	Avg	OBP	SLG	Pos	G	PO	A	E	DP	FPct
1970 Pit	23	2	5	1	1	0	0	2	0	0	0	0	0	0	0	0	0	0	0	—	0	.200	.200	.400	1B	1	11	1	0	1	1.000
1971 Pit	24	4	16	7	1	0	4	20	5	6	1	0	0	2	0	0	0	0	0	—	0	.438	.438	1.250	1B	4	24	2	0	3	1.000
1972 Pit	25	4	0	0	0	0	0	0	0	0	0	1	0	0	0	0	0	0	0	—	0	—	1.000	—	1B	4	3	0	0	0	1.000
1974 Pit	27	1	5	0	0	0	0	0	1	0	0	0	0	0	0	0	0	0	0	—	0	.000	.000	.000	1B	1	11	0	0	0	1.000
1975 Pit	28	3	2	1	0	0	0	1	0	1	0	1	0	0	0	0	0	0	0	—	0	.500	.667	.500	1B	1	1	0	0	0	1.000
LCS Totals		14	28	9	2	0	4	23	6	7	1	2	0	2	0	0	0	0	0	—	0	.321	.367	.821	1B	11	50	3	0	4	1.000

World Series — Batting / Fielding

Year Tm	Age	G	AB	H	2B	3B	HR	TB	R	RBI	GW	TBB	IBB	SO	HBP	SH	SF	SB	CS	SB%	GDP	Avg	OBP	SLG	Pos	G	PO	A	E	DP	FPct
1971 Pit	24	7	25	6	0	0	2	12	4	5	1	4	0	8	0	0	0	0	0	—	0	.240	.345	.480	1B	7	64	4	1	5	.986
Postseason Totals		21	53	15	2	0	6	35	10	12	2	6	0	10	0	0	0	0	0	—	0	.283	.356	.660	1B	18	114	7	1	9	.992

DAVE ROBERTSON—Davis Aydelotte Robertson—Bats: Left; Throws: Left

Ht: 6'0"; Wt: 186 lbs; Born: 9/25/1889 in Portsmouth, Virginia; Debut: 6/5/1912; Died: 11/5/1970

World Series — Batting / Fielding

Year Tm	Age	G	AB	H	2B	3B	HR	TB	R	RBI	GW	TBB	IBB	SO	HBP	SH	SF	SB	CS	SB%	GDP	Avg	OBP	SLG	Pos	G	PO	A	E	DP	FPct
1917 NYG	28	6	22	11	1	1	0	14	3	1	0	0	0	0	1	0	0	1	0	1.00	0	.500	.522	.636	OF	6	6	3	1	0	.900

GENE ROBERTSON—Eugene Edward Robertson—Bats: Left; Throws: Right

Ht: 5'7"; Wt: 152 lbs; Born: 12/25/1898 in St. Louis, Missouri; Debut: 7/4/1919; Died: 10/21/1981

World Series	Batting																								Fielding						
Year Tm	Age	G	AB	H	2B	3B	HR	TB	R	RBI	GW	TBB	IBB	SO	HBP	SH	SF	SB	CS	SB%	GDP	Avg	OBP	SLG	Pos	G	PO	A	E	DP	FPct
1928 NYA	29	3	7	1	0	0	0	1	1	1	0	1	0	0	0	0	0	0	0	—	0	.143	.250	.143	3B	3	2	1	1	0	.750

AARON ROBINSON—Aaron Andrew Robinson—Bats: Left; Throws: Right

Ht: 6'2"; Wt: 205 lbs; Born: 6/23/1915 in Lancaster, South Carolina; Debut: 5/6/1943; Died: 3/9/1966

World Series	Batting																								Fielding						
Year Tm	Age	G	AB	H	2B	3B	HR	TB	R	RBI	GW	TBB	IBB	SO	HBP	SH	SF	SB	CS	SB%	GDP	Avg	OBP	SLG	Pos	G	PO	A	E	DP	FPct
1947 NYA	32	3	10	2	0	0	0	2	2	1	0	2	0	1	0	0	0	0	0	—	0	.200	.333	.200	C	3	13	2	1	0	.938

BILL ROBINSON—William Henry Robinson—Bats: Right; Throws: Right

Ht: 6'2"; Wt: 189 lbs; Born: 6/26/1943 in McKeesport, Pennsylvania; Debut: 9/20/1966

LCS	Batting																								Fielding						
Year Tm	Age	G	AB	H	2B	3B	HR	TB	R	RBI	GW	TBB	IBB	SO	HBP	SH	SF	SB	CS	SB%	GDP	Avg	OBP	SLG	Pos	G	PO	A	E	DP	FPct
1975 Pit	32	2	2	0	0	0	0	0	0	0	0	0	0	1	0	0	0	0	0	—	0	.000	.000	.000	—						
1979 Pit	36	3	3	0	0	0	0	0	0	0	0	0	0	0	0	0	0	0	0	—	0	.000	.000	.000	OF	3	3	0	0	0	1.000
LCS Totals		5	5	0	0	0	0	0	0	0	0	0	0	1	0	0	0	0	0	—	0	.000	.000	.000	OF	3	3	0	0	0	1.000
World Series	Batting																								Fielding						
Year Tm	Age	G	AB	H	2B	3B	HR	TB	R	RBI	GW	TBB	IBB	SO	HBP	SH	SF	SB	CS	SB%	GDP	Avg	OBP	SLG	Pos	G	PO	A	E	DP	FPct
1979 Pit	36	7	19	5	1	0	0	6	2	2	0	0	0	4	1	1	1	0	0	—	0	.263	.286	.316	OF	6	11	1	0	0	1.000
Postseason Totals		12	24	5	1	0	0	6	2	2	0	0	0	5	1	1	1	0	0	—	0	.208	.231	.250	OF	9	14	1	0	0	1.000

BROOKS ROBINSON (HOF 1983-W)—Brooks Calbert Robinson—Nickname: The Human Vacuum Cleaner—B: R; T: R

Ht: 6'1"; Wt: 180 lbs; Born: 5/18/1937 in Little Rock, Ark.; Deb.: 9/17/1955

LCS	Batting																								Fielding						
Year Tm	Age	G	AB	H	2B	3B	HR	TB	R	RBI	GW	TBB	IBB	SO	HBP	SH	SF	SB	CS	SB%	GDP	Avg	OBP	SLG	Pos	G	PO	A	E	DP	FPct
1969 Bal	32	3	14	7	1	0	0	8	1	0	0	0	0	0	0	1	0	0	2	.00	0	.500	.500	.571	3B	3	6	10	0	0	1.000
1970 Bal	33	3	12	7	2	0	0	9	3	1	1	0	0	1	0	0	1	0	0	—	0	.583	.538	.750	3B	3	4	5	0	0	1.000
1971 Bal	34	3	11	4	1	0	1	8	2	3	2	0	0	1	0	0	0	0	0	—	0	.364	.364	.727	3B	3	4	7	0	0	1.000
1973 Bal	36	5	20	5	2	0	0	7	1	2	0	1	1	1	0	0	0	0	0	—	0	.250	.286	.350	3B	5	2	14	1	0	.941
1974 Bal	37	4	12	1	0	0	1	4	1	1	0	1	0	0	0	0	0	0	0	—	1	.083	.154	.333	3B	4	4	13	0	0	1.000
LCS Totals		18	69	24	6	0	2	36	8	7	3	2	1	3	0	1	1	0	2	.00	1	.348	.361	.522	3B	18	20	49	1	1	.986
World Series	Batting																								Fielding						
Year Tm	Age	G	AB	H	2B	3B	HR	TB	R	RBI	GW	TBB	IBB	SO	HBP	SH	SF	SB	CS	SB%	GDP	Avg	OBP	SLG	Pos	G	PO	A	E	DP	FPct
1966 Bal	29	4	14	3	0	0	1	6	2	1	0	1	0	0	0	0	0	0	0	—	0	.214	.267	.429	3B	4	4	6	0	1	1.000
1969 Bal	32	5	19	1	0	0	0	1	0	2	0	0	0	3	0	0	1	0	0	—	0	.053	.050	.053	3B	5	1	16	0	0	1.000
1970 Bal	33	5	21	9	2	0	2	17	5	6	2	0	0	2	0	0	0	0	0	—	0	.429	.429	.810	3B	5	9	14	1	2	.958
1971 Bal	34	7	22	7	0	0	0	7	2	5	2	3	0	1	0	0	2	0	0	—	1	.318	.370	.318	3B	7	6	17	2	1	.920
WS Totals		21	76	20	2	0	3	31	9	14	4	4	0	6	0	0	3	0	0	—	1	.263	.289	.408	3B	21	20	53	3	4	.961
Postseason Totals		39	145	44	8	0	5	67	17	21	7	6	1	9	0	1	4	0	2	.00	3	.303	.323	.462	3B	39	40	102	4	5	.973

DON ROBINSON—Don Allen Robinson—Throws: Right; Bats: Right

Ht: 6'4"; Wt: 225 lbs; Born: 6/8/1957 in Ashland, Kentucky; Debut: 4/10/1978

LCS	Pitching																											
Year Tm	Age	G	GS	CG	GF	IP	BFP	H	R	ER	HR	SH	SF	HB	TBB	IBB	SO	WP	Bk	W	L	Pct	ShO	Sv-Op	Hld	OAvg	OOBP	ERA
1979 Pit	22	2	0	0	2	2.0	7	0	0	0	0	0	0	0	1	0	3	0	0	1	0	1.000	0	1- 1	0	.000	.143	0.00
1987 SF	30	3	0	0	2	3.0	12	3	3	3	0	0	0	0	0	0	3	0	0	0	1	.000	0	0- 1	0	.250	.250	9.00
1989 SF	32	1	0	0	0	1.2	8	3	1	0	0	0	1	0	0	0	0	0	0	1	0	1.000	0	0- 0	0	.429	.375	0.00
LCS Totals		6	0	0	4	6.2	54	6	4	3	0	0	1	0	1	0	6	0	0	2	1	.667	0	1-2	0	.240	.259	4.05
World Series	Pitching																											
Year Tm	Age	G	GS	CG	GF	IP	BFP	H	R	ER	HR	SH	SF	HB	TBB	IBB	SO	WP	Bk	W	L	Pct	ShO	Sv-Op	Hld	OAvg	OOBP	ERA
1979 Pit	22	4	0	0	0	5.0	25	4	3	3	0	0	0	0	6	0	3	0	0	1	0	1.000	0	0- 0	1	.211	.400	5.40
1989 SF	32	1	1	0	0	1.2	10	4	4	4	1	0	0	0	1	1	0	0	0	0	1	.000	0	0- 0	0	.444	.500	21.60
WS Totals		5	1	0	0	6.2	70	8	7	7	1	0	0	0	7	1	3	0	0	1	1	.500	0	0-0	1	.286	.429	9.45
Postseason Totals		11	1	0	4	13.1	124	14	11	10	1	0	1	0	8	1	9	0	0	3	2	.600	0	1-2	1	.264	.355	6.75

LCS	Batting																								Fielding						
Year Tm	Age	G	AB	H	2B	3B	HR	TB	R	RBI	GW	TBB	IBB	SO	HBP	SH	SF	SB	CS	SB%	GDP	Avg	OBP	SLG	Pos	G	PO	A	E	DP	FPct
1979 Pit	22	2	0	0	0	0	0	0	0	0	0	0	0	0	0	0	0	0	0	—	0	—	—	—	P	2	0	0	0	0	—
1987 SF	30	3	0	0	0	0	0	0	0	0	0	0	0	0	0	0	0	0	0	—	0	—	—	—	P	3	0	0	0	0	—
1989 SF	32	1	0	0	0	0	0	0	0	0	0	0	0	0	0	0	0	0	0	—	0	—	—	—	P	1	0	0	0	0	—
LCS Totals		6	0	0	0	0	0	0	0	0	0	0	0	0	0	0	0	0	0	—	0	—	—	—	P	6	0	0	0	0	—
World Series	Batting																								Fielding						
Year Tm	Age	G	AB	H	2B	3B	HR	TB	R	RBI	GW	TBB	IBB	SO	HBP	SH	SF	SB	CS	SB%	GDP	Avg	OBP	SLG	Pos	G	PO	A	E	DP	FPct
1979 Pit	22	4	0	0	0	0	0	0	0	0	0	0	0	0	0	0	0	0	0	—	0	—	—	—	P	4	0	1	0	0	1.000
1989 SF	32	1	0	0	0	0	0	0	0	0	0	0	0	0	0	0	0	0	0	—	0	—	—	—	P	1	0	0	0	0	—
WS Totals		5	0	0	0	0	0	0	0	0	0	0	0	0	0	0	0	0	0	—	0	—	—	—	P	5	0	1	0	0	1.000
Postseason Totals		11	0	0	0	0	0	0	0	0	0	0	0	0	0	0	0	0	0	—	0	—	—	—	P	11	0	1	0	0	1.000

EDDIE ROBINSON—William Edward Robinson—Bats: Left; Throws: Right

Ht: 6'2"; Wt: 210 lbs; Born: 12/15/1920 in Paris, Texas; Debut: 9/9/1942

World Series	Batting																								Fielding						
Year Tm	Age	G	AB	H	2B	3B	HR	TB	R	RBI	GW	TBB	IBB	SO	HBP	SH	SF	SB	CS	SB%	GDP	Avg	OBP	SLG	Pos	G	PO	A	E	DP	FPct
1948 Cle	27	6	20	6	0	0	0	6	0	1	0	1	0	0	0	0	0	0	0	—	0	.300	.333	.300	1B	6	60	7	0	8	1.000
1955 NYA	34	4	3	2	0	0	0	2	0	1	0	2	0	1	1	0	0	0	0	—	0	.667	.833	.667	1B	1	6	0	0	2	1.000
WS Totals		10	23	8	0	0	0	8	0	2	0	3	0	1	1	0	0	0	0	—	0	.348	.444	.348	1B	7	66	7	0	10	1.000

FRANK ROBINSON (HOF 1982-W)—Nicknames: Robby, The Judge, Pencils—Bats: Right; Throws: Right

Ht: 6'1"; Wt: 183 lbs; Born: 8/31/1935 in Beaumont, Texas; Debut: 4/17/1956

LCS	Batting																								Fielding						
Year Tm	Age	G	AB	H	2B	3B	HR	TB	R	RBI	GW	TBB	IBB	SO	HBP	SH	SF	SB	CS	SB%	GDP	Avg	OBP	SLG	Pos	G	PO	A	E	DP	FPct
1969 Bal	34	3	12	4	2	0	1	9	1	2	0	3	0	3	0	0	0	0	0	—	0	.333	.467	.750	OF	3	3	0	1	0	.750
1970 Bal	35	3	10	2	0	0	1	5	3	2	0	5	1	2	0	0	0	0	0	—	0	.200	.467	.500	OF	3	3	0	0	0	1.000
1971 Bal	36	3	12	1	1	0	0	2	2	1	0	1	0	4	0	0	0	0	0	—	0	.083	.154	.167	OF	3	8	0	0	0	1.000
LCS Totals		9	34	7	3	0	2	16	6	5	0	9	1	9	0	0	0	0	0	—	0	.206	.372	.471	OF	9	14	0	1	0	.933
World Series	Batting																								Fielding						
Year Tm	Age	G	AB	H	2B	3B	HR	TB	R	RBI	GW	TBB	IBB	SO	HBP	SH	SF	SB	CS	SB%	GDP	Avg	OBP	SLG	Pos	G	PO	A	E	DP	FPct
1961 Cin-*M*	26	5	15	3	2	0	1	8	3	4	0	3	0	4	2	0	0	0	0	—	0	.200	.400	.533	OF	5	5	0	0	0	1.000
1966 Bal-*M*	31	4	14	4	0	1	2	12	4	3	2	2	0	3	0	0	0	0	0	—	0	.286	.375	.857	OF	4	6	0	0	0	1.000
1969 Bal	34	5	16	3	0	0	1	6	2	1	0	4	0	3	0	0	0	0	0	—	0	.188	.350	.375	OF	5	13	0	0	0	1.000
1970 Bal	35	5	22	6	0	0	2	12	5	4	0	0	0	5	0	0	0	0	0	—	0	.273	.273	.545	OF	5	7	0	0	0	1.000
1971 Bal	36	7	25	7	0	0	2	13	5	2	0	2	1	8	1	0	0	0	0	—	1	.280	.357	.520	OF	7	12	0	0	0	1.000
WS Totals		26	92	23	2	1	8	51	19	14	2	11	1	23	3	0	0	0	0	—	1	.250	.349	.554	OF	26	43	0	0	0	1.000
Postseason Totals		35	126	30	5	1	10	67	25	19	2	20	2	32	3	0	0	0	0	—	1	.238	.356	.532	OF	35	57	0	1	0	.983

JACKIE ROBINSON (HOF 1962-W)—Jack Roosevelt Robinson—Bats: Right; Throws: Right

Ht: 5'11"; Wt: 195 lbs; Born: 1/31/1919 in Cairo, Georgia; Debut: 4/15/1947; Died: 10/24/1972

World Series	Batting																								Fielding						
Year Tm	Age	G	AB	H	2B	3B	HR	TB	R	RBI	GW	TBB	IBB	SO	HBP	SH	SF	SB	CS	SB%	GDP	Avg	OBP	SLG	Pos	G	PO	A	E	DP	FPct
1947 Bro-*RY*	28	7	27	7	2	0	0	9	3	3	0	2	0	4	0	1	0	2	0	1.00	0	.259	.310	.333	1B	7	49	6	0	8	1.000
1949 Bro-*M*	30	5	16	3	1	0	0	4	2	2	0	4	0	2	0	1	0	0	0	—	0	.188	.350	.250	2B	5	12	9	1	1	.955
1952 Bro	33	7	23	4	0	0	1	7	4	2	0	7	2	5	0	0	0	2	0	1.00	0	.174	.367	.304	2B	7	10	19	0	4	1.000
1953 Bro	34	6	25	8	2	0	0	10	3	2	1	1	0	0	0	0	0	1	0	1.00	0	.320	.346	.400	OF	6	8	0	0	0	1.000
1955 Bro	36	6	22	4	1	1	0	7	5	1	0	2	0	1	0	0	0	1	0	1.00	2	.182	.250	.318	3B	6	4	18	2	3	.917
1956 Bro	37	7	24	6	1	0	1	10	5	2	1	5	0	2	0	0	0	0	0	—	2	.250	.379	.417	3B	7	5	11	0	1	1.000
WS Totals		38	137	32	7	1	2	47	22	12	2	21	2	14	0	2	0	6	0	1.00	5	.234	.335	.343	3B	13	9	29	2	4	.950

JEFF ROBINSON—Jeffrey Mark Robinson—Throws: Right; Bats: Right

Ht: 6'6"; Wt: 210 lbs; Born: 12/14/1961 in Ventura, California; Debut: 4/12/1987

LCS — Pitching

Year Tm	Age	G	GS	CG	GF	IP	BFP	H	R	ER	HR	SH	SF	HB	TBB	IBB	SO	WP	Bk	W	L	Pct	ShO	Sv-Op	Hld	OAvg	OOBP	ERA
1987 Det	25	1	0	0	1	0.1	2	1	0	0	0	0	0	0	0	0	0	0	0	0	0	—	0	0-0	0	.500	.500	0.00

LCS — Batting / Fielding

Year Tm	Age	G	AB	H	2B	3B	HR	TB	R	RBI	GW	TBB	IBB	SO	HBP	SH	SF	SB	CS	SB%	GDP	Avg	OBP	SLG	Pos	G	PO	A	E	DP	FPct
1987 Det	25	1	0	0	0	0	0	0	0	0	0	0	0	0	0	0	0	0	0	—	0	—	—	—	P	1	0	1	0	0	1.000

ALEX RODRIGUEZ—Alexander Emmanuel Rodriguez—Nickname: A-Rod—Bats: Right; Throws: Right

Ht: 6'2"; Wt: 190 lbs; Born: 7/27/1975 in New York, New York; Debut: 7/8/1994

Division Series — Batting / Fielding

Year Tm	Age	G	AB	H	2B	3B	HR	TB	R	RBI	GW	TBB	IBB	SO	HBP	SH	SF	SB	CS	SB%	GDP	Avg	OBP	SLG	Pos	G	PO	A	E	DP	FPct
1995 Sea	20	1	1	0	0	0	0	0	1	0	0	0	0	0	0	0	0	0	0	—	0	.000	.000	.000	SS	1	0	0	0	0	—
1997 Sea	22	4	16	5	1	0	1	9	1	1	0	0	0	5	0	0	0	0	0	—	0	.313	.313	.563	SS	4	5	10	0	2	1.000
DS Totals		5	17	5	1	0	1	9	2	1	0	0	0	5	0	0	0	0	0	—	0	.294	.294	.529	SS	5	5	10	0	2	1.000

LCS — Batting / Fielding

Year Tm	Age	G	AB	H	2B	3B	HR	TB	R	RBI	GW	TBB	IBB	SO	HBP	SH	SF	SB	CS	SB%	GDP	Avg	OBP	SLG	Pos	G	PO	A	E	DP	FPct
1995 Sea	20	1	1	0	0	0	0	0	0	0	0	0	0	1	0	0	0	0	0	—	0	.000	.000	.000	—						
Postseason Totals		6	18	5	1	0	1	9	2	1	0	0	0	6	0	0	0	0	0	—	0	.278	.278	.500	SS	5	5	10	0	2	1.000

AURELIO RODRIGUEZ—Nickname: Radio—Bats: Right; Throws: Right

Ht: 5'10"; Wt: 180 lbs; Born: 12/28/1947 in Cananea, Mexico; Debut: 9/1/1967

LCS — Batting / Fielding

Year Tm	Age	G	AB	H	2B	3B	HR	TB	R	RBI	GW	TBB	IBB	SO	HBP	SH	SF	SB	CS	SB%	GDP	Avg	OBP	SLG	Pos	G	PO	A	E	DP	FPct
1972 Det	24	5	16	0	0	0	0	0	0	0	0	2	2	2	0	0	0	0	0	—	0	.000	.111	.000	3B	5	2	13	1	2	.938
1980 NYA	32	2	6	2	1	0	0	3	0	0	0	0	0	0	0	0	0	0	0	—	0	.333	.333	.500	3B	2	2	2	0	0	1.000
1981 NYA	33	1	0	0	0	0	0	0	0	0	0	0	0	0	0	0	0	0	0	—	0	—	—	—	3B	1	0	0	0	0	—
1983 ChA	35	2	0	0	0	0	0	0	0	0	0	0	0	0	0	0	0	0	0	—	0	—	—	—	3B	2	0	0	1	0	.000
LCS Totals		10	22	2	1	0	0	3	0	0	0	2	2	2	0	0	0	0	0	—	0	.091	.167	.136	3B	10	4	15	2	2	.905

World Series — Batting / Fielding

Year Tm	Age	G	AB	H	2B	3B	HR	TB	R	RBI	GW	TBB	IBB	SO	HBP	SH	SF	SB	CS	SB%	GDP	Avg	OBP	SLG	Pos	G	PO	A	E	DP	FPct
1981 NYA	33	4	12	5	0	0	0	5	1	0	0	1	1	2	0	0	0	0	0	—	0	.417	.462	.417	3B	4	3	9	0	0	1.000
Postseason Totals		14	34	7	1	0	0	8	1	0	0	3	3	4	0	0	0	0	0	—	0	.206	.270	.235	3B	14	7	24	2	2	.939

IVAN RODRIGUEZ—Nickname: Pudge—Bats: Right; Throws: Right

Ht: 5'9"; Wt: 165 lbs; Born: 11/27/1971 in Manati, Puerto Rico; Debut: 6/20/1991

Division Series — Batting / Fielding

Year Tm	Age	G	AB	H	2B	3B	HR	TB	R	RBI	GW	TBB	IBB	SO	HBP	SH	SF	SB	CS	SB%	GDP	Avg	OBP	SLG	Pos	G	PO	A	E	DP	FPct
1996 Tex	24	4	16	6	1	0	0	7	1	2	0	2	0	3	0	1	0	0	0	—	0	.375	.444	.438	C	4	21	3	0	0	1.000

RICH RODRIGUEZ—Richard Anthony Rodriguez—Throws: Left; Bats: Left

Ht: 5'11"; Wt: 200 lbs; Born: 3/1/1963 in Downey, California; Debut: 6/30/1990

Division Series — Pitching

Year Tm	Age	G	GS	CG	GF	IP	BFP	H	R	ER	HR	SH	SF	HB	TBB	IBB	SO	WP	Bk	W	L	Pct	ShO	Sv-Op	Hld	OAvg	OOBP	ERA
1997 SF	34	2	0	0	0	1.0	4	1	0	0	0	0	0	0	0	0	0	0	0	0	0	—	0	0-0	0	.250	.250	0.00

Division Series — Batting / Fielding

Year Tm	Age	G	AB	H	2B	3B	HR	TB	R	RBI	GW	TBB	IBB	SO	HBP	SH	SF	SB	CS	SB%	GDP	Avg	OBP	SLG	Pos	G	PO	A	E	DP	FPct
1997 SF	34	2	0	0	0	0	0	0	0	0	0	0	0	0	0	0	0	0	0	—	0	—	—	—	P	2	0	0	0	0	—

ROSARIO RODRIGUEZ—Rosario Isabel Rodriguez—Throws: Left; Bats: Right

Ht: 6'0"; Wt: 185 lbs; Born: 7/8/1969 in Los Mochis, Mexico; Debut: 9/1/1989

LCS — Pitching

Year Tm	Age	G	GS	CG	GF	IP	BFP	H	R	ER	HR	SH	SF	HB	TBB	IBB	SO	WP	Bk	W	L	Pct	ShO	Sv-Op	Hld	OAvg	OOBP	ERA
1991 Pit	22	1	0	0	1	1.0	7	1	3	3	1	1	0	0	2	0	1	0	0	0	0	—	0	0-0	0	.250	.500	27.00

LCS — Batting / Fielding

Year Tm	Age	G	AB	H	2B	3B	HR	TB	R	RBI	GW	TBB	IBB	SO	HBP	SH	SF	SB	CS	SB%	GDP	Avg	OBP	SLG	Pos	G	PO	A	E	DP	FPct
1991 Pit	22	1	0	0	0	0	0	0	0	0	0	0	0	0	0	0	0	0	0	—	0	—	—	—	P	1	0	0	0	0	—

PREACHER ROE—Elwin Charles Roe—Nickname: Shad—Throws: Left; Bats: Right

Ht: 6'2"; Wt: 170 lbs; Born: 2/26/1915 in Ash Flat, Arkansas; Debut: 8/22/1938

World Series — Pitching

Year Tm	Age	G	GS	CG	GF	IP	BFP	H	R	ER	HR	SH	SF	HB	TBB	IBB	SO	WP	Bk	W	L	Pct	ShO	Sv-Op	Hld	OAvg	OOBP	ERA
1949 Bro	34	1	1	1	0	9.0	34	6	0	0	0	1	0	0	0	0	3	0	0	1	0	1.000	1	0-0	0	.182	.182	0.00
1952 Bro	37	3	1	1	1	11.1	50	9	4	4	2	2	0	1	6	1	7	0	0	1	0	1.000	0	0-0	0	.220	.333	3.18
1953 Bro	38	1	1	1	0	8.0	33	5	4	4	2	1	0	1	4	0	4	0	0	0	1	.000	0	0-0	0	.185	.313	4.50
WS Totals		5	3	3	1	28.1	234	20	8	8	4	4	0	2	10	1	14	0	0	2	1	.667	1	0-0	0	.198	.283	2.54

World Series — Batting / Fielding

Year Tm	Age	G	AB	H	2B	3B	HR	TB	R	RBI	GW	TBB	IBB	SO	HBP	SH	SF	SB	CS	SB%	GDP	Avg	OBP	SLG	Pos	G	PO	A	E	DP	FPct
1949 Bro	34	1	3	0	0	0	0	0	0	0	0	0	0	3	0	0	0	0	0	—	0	.000	.000	.000	P	1	1	1	1	0	.667
1952 Bro	37	3	2	0	0	0	0	0	0	0	0	0	0	0	0	2	0	0	0	—	0	.000	.000	.000	P	3	1	0	0	0	1.000
1953 Bro	38	1	3	0	0	0	0	0	0	0	0	0	0	2	0	0	0	0	0	—	0	.000	.000	.000	P	1	1	1	0	0	1.000
WS Totals		5	8	0	0	0	0	0	0	0	0	0	0	5	0	2	0	0	0	—	0	.000	.000	.000	P	5	3	2	1	0	.833

ED ROEBUCK—Edward Jack Roebuck—Throws: Right; Bats: Right

Ht: 6'2"; Wt: 185 lbs; Born: 7/3/1931 in East Millsboro, Pennsylvania; Debut: 4/18/1955

World Series — Pitching

Year Tm	Age	G	GS	CG	GF	IP	BFP	H	R	ER	HR	SH	SF	HB	TBB	IBB	SO	WP	Bk	W	L	Pct	ShO	Sv-Op	Hld	OAvg	OOBP	ERA
1955 Bro	24	1	0	0	1	2.0	8	1	0	0	0	0	0	0	0	0	0	0	0	0	0	—	0	0-0	0	.125	.125	0.00
1956 Bro	25	3	0	0	0	4.1	14	1	1	1	1	0	0	0	0	0	5	0	0	0	0	—	0	0-0	0	.071	.071	2.08
WS Totals		4	0	0	1	6.1	44	2	1	1	1	0	0	0	0	0	5	0	0	0	0	—	0	0-0	0	.091	.091	1.42

World Series — Batting / Fielding

Year Tm	Age	G	AB	H	2B	3B	HR	TB	R	RBI	GW	TBB	IBB	SO	HBP	SH	SF	SB	CS	SB%	GDP	Avg	OBP	SLG	Pos	G	PO	A	E	DP	FPct
1955 Bro	24	1	0	0	0	0	0	0	0	0	0	0	0	0	0	0	0	0	0	—	0	—	—	—	P	1	2	0	0	0	1.000
1956 Bro	25	3	0	0	0	0	0	0	0	0	0	0	0	0	0	0	0	0	0	—	0	—	—	—	P	3	0	0	0	0	—
WS Totals		4	0	0	0	0	0	0	0	0	0	0	0	0	0	0	0	0	0	—	0	—	—	—	P	4	2	0	0	0	1.000

GARY ROENICKE—Gary Steven Roenicke—Bats: Right; Throws: Right

Ht: 6'3"; Wt: 205 lbs; Born: 12/5/1954 in Covina, California; Debut: 6/8/1976

LCS — Batting / Fielding

Year Tm	Age	G	AB	H	2B	3B	HR	TB	R	RBI	GW	TBB	IBB	SO	HBP	SH	SF	SB	CS	SB%	GDP	Avg	OBP	SLG	Pos	G	PO	A	E	DP	FPct
1979 Bal	24	2	5	1	0	0	0	1	1	1	0	0	0	0	1	0	0	0	0	—	1	.200	.333	.200	OF	2	2	1	0	1	1.000
1983 Bal	28	3	4	3	1	0	1	7	4	4	0	5	0	0	1	0	0	0	0	—	1	.750	.900	1.750	OF	3	5	1	0	0	1.000
LCS Totals		5	9	4	1	0	1	8	5	5	0	5	0	0	2	0	0	0	0	—	2	.444	.688	.889	OF	5	7	2	0	1	1.000

World Series — Batting / Fielding

Year Tm	Age	G	AB	H	2B	3B	HR	TB	R	RBI	GW	TBB	IBB	SO	HBP	SH	SF	SB	CS	SB%	GDP	Avg	OBP	SLG	Pos	G	PO	A	E	DP	FPct
1979 Bal	24	6	16	2	1	0	0	3	1	0	0	0	0	6	0	0	0	0	0	—	0	.125	.125	.188	OF	6	14	1	0	0	1.000
1983 Bal	28	3	7	0	0	0	0	0	0	0	0	0	0	2	0	0	0	0	0	—	1	.000	.000	.000	OF	2	2	1	0	0	1.000
WS Totals		9	23	2	1	0	0	3	1	0	0	0	0	8	0	0	0	0	0	—	1	.087	.087	.130	OF	8	16	2	0	0	1.000
Postseason Totals		14	32	6	2	0	1	11	6	5	0	5	0	8	2	0	0	0	0	—	3	.188	.333	.344	OF	13	23	4	0	1	1.000

RON ROENICKE—Ronald Jon Roenicke—Bats: Both; Throws: Left

Ht: 6'0"; Wt: 180 lbs; Born: 8/19/1956 in Covina, California; Debut: 9/2/1981

World Series — Batting / Fielding

Year Tm	Age	G	AB	H	2B	3B	HR	TB	R	RBI	GW	TBB	IBB	SO	HBP	SH	SF	SB	CS	SB%	GDP	Avg	OBP	SLG	Pos	G	PO	A	E	DP	FPct
1984 SD	28	2	0	0	0	0	0	0	0	0	0	0	0	0	0	0	0	0	0	—	0	—	—	—	OF	1	0	0	0	0	—

WALLY ROETTGER—Walter Henry Roettger—Bats: Right; Throws: Right

Ht: 6'1"; Wt: 190 lbs; Born: 8/28/1902 in St. Louis, Missouri; Debut: 5/1/1927; Died: 9/14/1951

World Series — Batting / Fielding

Year Tm	Age	G	AB	H	2B	3B	HR	TB	R	RBI	GW	TBB	IBB	SO	HBP	SH	SF	SB	CS	SB%	GDP	Avg	OBP	SLG	Pos	G	PO	A	E	DP	FPct
1931 StL	29	3	14	4	1	0	0	5	1	0	0	0	0	3	0	0	0	0	0	—	0	.286	.286	.357	OF	3	4	0	0	0	1.000

BILLY ROGELL—William George Rogell—Bats: Both; Throws: Right

Ht: 5'10"; Wt: 163 lbs; Born: 11/24/1904 in Springfield, Illinois; Debut: 4/14/1925

World Series — Batting / Fielding

Year Tm	Age	G	AB	H	2B	3B	HR	TB	R	RBI	GW	TBB	IBB	SO	HBP	SH	SF	SB	CS	SB%	GDP	Avg	OBP	SLG	Pos	G	PO	A	E	DP	FPct
1934 Det	29	7	29	8	1	0	0	9	3	4	0	1	0	4	0	0	0	1	0	1.00	0	.276	.300	.310	SS	7	12	16	3	4	.903
1935 Det	30	6	24	7	2	0	0	9	1	1	0	2	0	5	0	0	0	0	1	.00	1	.292	.346	.375	SS	6	13	12	0	6	1.000
WS Totals		13	53	15	3	0	0	18	4	5	0	3	0	9	0	0	0	1	1	.50	1	.283	.321	.340	SS	13	25	28	3	10	.946

KENNY ROGERS—Kenneth Scott Rogers—Throws: Left; Bats: Left

Ht: 6'1"; Wt: 200 lbs; Born: 11/10/1964 in Savannah, Georgia; Debut: 4/6/1989

Division Series — Pitching

Year Tm	Age	G	GS	CG	GF	IP	BFP	H	R	ER	HR	SH	SF	HB	TBB	IBB	SO	WP	Bk	W	L	Pct	ShO	Sv-Op	Hld	OAvg	OOBP	ERA
1996 NYA	31	2	1	0	0	2.0	13	5	2	2	0	0	0	0	2	0	1	0	0	0	0	—	0	0- 0	0	.455	.538	9.00

LCS — Pitching

Year Tm	Age	G	GS	CG	GF	IP	BFP	H	R	ER	HR	SH	SF	HB	TBB	IBB	SO	WP	Bk	W	L	Pct	ShO	Sv-Op	Hld	OAvg	OOBP	ERA
1996 NYA	31	1	1	0	0	3.0	16	5	4	4	1	0	1	0	2	0	3	1	0	0	0	—	0	0- 0	0	.385	.438	12.00

World Series — Pitching

Year Tm	Age	G	GS	CG	GF	IP	BFP	H	R	ER	HR	SH	SF	HB	TBB	IBB	SO	WP	Bk	W	L	Pct	ShO	Sv-Op	Hld	OAvg	OOBP	ERA
1996 NYA	31	1	1	0	0	2.0	13	5	5	5	1	1	0	0	2	0	0	0	0	0	0	—	0	0- 0	0	.500	.583	22.50
Postseason Totals		4	3	0	0	7.0	84	15	11	11	2	1	1	0	6	0	4	1	0	0	0	—	0	0-0	0	.441	.512	14.14

Division Series — Batting / Fielding

Year Tm	Age	G	AB	H	2B	3B	HR	TB	R	RBI	GW	TBB	IBB	SO	HBP	SH	SF	SB	CS	SB%	GDP	Avg	OBP	SLG	Pos	G	PO	A	E	DP	FPct
1996 NYA	31	2	0	0	0	0	0	0	0	0	0	0	0	0	0	0	0	0	0	—	0	—	—	—	P	2	0	0	0	0	—

LCS — Batting / Fielding

Year Tm	Age	G	AB	H	2B	3B	HR	TB	R	RBI	GW	TBB	IBB	SO	HBP	SH	SF	SB	CS	SB%	GDP	Avg	OBP	SLG	Pos	G	PO	A	E	DP	FPct
1996 NYA	31	1	0	0	0	0	0	0	0	0	0	0	0	0	0	0	0	0	0	—	0	—	—	—	P	1	0	0	0	0	—

World Series — Batting / Fielding

Year Tm	Age	G	AB	H	2B	3B	HR	TB	R	RBI	GW	TBB	IBB	SO	HBP	SH	SF	SB	CS	SB%	GDP	Avg	OBP	SLG	Pos	G	PO	A	E	DP	FPct
1996 NYA	31	1	1	1	0	0	0	1	0	0	0	0	0	0	0	0	0	0	0	—	0	1.000	1.000	1.000	P	1	0	0	0	0	—
Postseason Totals		4	1	1	0	0	0	1	0	0	0	0	0	0	0	0	0	0	0	—	0	1.000	1.000	1.000	P	4	0	0	0	0	—

STEVE ROGERS—Stephen Douglas Rogers—Throws: Right; Bats: Right

Ht: 6'2"; Wt: 175 lbs; Born: 10/26/1949 in Jefferson City, Missouri; Debut: 7/18/1973

Division Series — Pitching

Year Tm	Age	G	GS	CG	GF	IP	BFP	H	R	ER	HR	SH	SF	HB	TBB	IBB	SO	WP	Bk	W	L	Pct	ShO	Sv-Op	Hld	OAvg	OOBP	ERA
1981 Mon	31	2	2	1	0	17.2	67	16	1	1	1	0	0	0	3	1	5	0	0	2	0	1.000	1	0- 0	0	.250	.284	0.51

LCS — Pitching

Year Tm	Age	G	GS	CG	GF	IP	BFP	H	R	ER	HR	SH	SF	HB	TBB	IBB	SO	WP	Bk	W	L	Pct	ShO	Sv-Op	Hld	OAvg	OOBP	ERA
1981 Mon	31	2	1	1	1	10.0	38	8	2	2	1	0	0	0	1	0	6	1	0	1	1	.500	0	0- 0	0	.216	.237	1.80
Postseason Totals		4	3	2	1	27.2	210	24	3	3	2	0	0	0	4	1	11	1	0	3	1	.750	1	0-0	0	.238	.267	0.98

Division Series — Batting / Fielding

Year Tm	Age	G	AB	H	2B	3B	HR	TB	R	RBI	GW	TBB	IBB	SO	HBP	SH	SF	SB	CS	SB%	GDP	Avg	OBP	SLG	Pos	G	PO	A	E	DP	FPct
1981 Mon	31	2	5	2	0	0	0	2	0	2	1	0	0	1	0	2	0	0	1	.00	0	.400	.400	.400	P	2	2	1	0	0	1.000

LCS — Batting / Fielding

Year Tm	Age	G	AB	H	2B	3B	HR	TB	R	RBI	GW	TBB	IBB	SO	HBP	SH	SF	SB	CS	SB%	GDP	Avg	OBP	SLG	Pos	G	PO	A	E	DP	FPct
1981 Mon	31	2	2	0	0	0	0	0	0	0	0	0	0	1	0	1	0	0	0	—	0	.000	.000	.000	P	2	0	1	0	0	1.000
Postseason Totals		4	7	2	0	0	0	2	0	2	1	0	0	2	0	3	0	0	1	.00	0	.286	.286	.286	P	4	2	2	0	0	1.000

TOM ROGERS—Thomas Andrew Rogers—Nickname: Shotgun—Throws: Right; Bats: Right

Ht: 6'0"; Wt: 180 lbs; Born: 2/12/1892 in Sparta, Tennessee; Debut: 4/14/1917; Died: 3/7/1936

World Series — Pitching

Year Tm	Age	G	GS	CG	GF	IP	BFP	H	R	ER	HR	SH	SF	HB	TBB	IBB	SO	WP	Bk	W	L	Pct	ShO	Sv-Op	Hld	OAvg	OOBP	ERA
1921 NYA	29	1	0	0	1	1.1	7	3	1	1	0	0	0	0	0	0	1	0	0	0	0	—	0	0- 0	0	.429	.429	6.75

World Series — Batting / Fielding

Year Tm	Age	G	AB	H	2B	3B	HR	TB	R	RBI	GW	TBB	IBB	SO	HBP	SH	SF	SB	CS	SB%	GDP	Avg	OBP	SLG	Pos	G	PO	A	E	DP	FPct
1921 NYA	29	1	0	0	0	0	0	0	0	0	0	0	0	0	0	0	0	0	0	—	0	—	—	—	P	1	0	1	0	0	1.000

GEORGE ROHE—George Anthony Rohe—Nickname: Whitey—Bats: Right; Throws: Right

Ht: 5'9"; Wt: 165 lbs; Born: 9/15/1875 in Cincinnati, Ohio; Debut: 5/7/1901; Died: 6/10/1957

World Series — Batting / Fielding

Year Tm	Age	G	AB	H	2B	3B	HR	TB	R	RBI	GW	TBB	IBB	SO	HBP	SH	SF	SB	CS	SB%	GDP	Avg	OBP	SLG	Pos	G	PO	A	E	DP	FPct
1906 ChA	31	6	21	7	1	2	0	12	2	4	1	3	0	1	1	0	0	2	0	1.00	0	.333	.440	.571	3B	6	4	17	3	0	.875

COOKIE ROJAS—Octavio Victor Rojas—Bats: Right; Throws: Right

Ht: 5'10"; Wt: 160 lbs; Born: 3/6/1939 in Havana, Cuba; Debut: 4/10/1962

LCS — Batting / Fielding

Year Tm	Age	G	AB	H	2B	3B	HR	TB	R	RBI	GW	TBB	IBB	SO	HBP	SH	SF	SB	CS	SB%	GDP	Avg	OBP	SLG	Pos	G	PO	A	E	DP	FPct
1976 KC	37	4	9	3	0	0	0	3	2	1	0	0	0	0	0	0	1	1	0	1.00	0	.333	.300	.333	2B	4	4	6	0	1	1.000
1977 KC	38	1	4	1	0	0	0	1	0	0	0	0	0	1	0	0	0	1	0	1.00	0	.250	.250	.250	—						
LCS Totals		5	13	4	0	0	0	4	2	1	0	0	0	1	0	0	1	2	0	1.00	0	.308	.286	.308	2B	4	4	6	0	1	1.000

RED ROLFE—Robert Abial Rolfe—Bats: Left; Throws: Right

Ht: 5'11"; Wt: 170 lbs; Born: 10/17/1908 in Penacook, New Hampshire; Debut: 6/29/1931; Died: 7/8/1969

World Series — Batting / Fielding

Year Tm	Age	G	AB	H	2B	3B	HR	TB	R	RBI	GW	TBB	IBB	SO	HBP	SH	SF	SB	CS	SB%	GDP	Avg	OBP	SLG	Pos	G	PO	A	E	DP	FPct
1936 NYA	27	6	25	10	0	0	0	10	5	4	0	3	0	1	0	1	0	0	1	.00	0	.400	.464	.400	3B	6	14	7	1	0	.955
1937 NYA	28	5	20	6	2	1	0	10	3	1	0	3	0	2	0	1	0	0	0	—	0	.300	.391	.500	3B	5	2	6	0	0	1.000
1938 NYA	29	4	18	3	0	0	0	3	0	1	1	0	0	3	0	0	0	1	0	1.00	0	.167	.167	.167	3B	4	0	4	2	0	.667
1939 NYA	30	4	16	2	0	0	0	2	2	0	0	0	0	0	0	1	0	0	0	—	0	.125	.125	.125	3B	4	4	8	1	2	.923
1941 NYA	32	5	20	6	0	0	0	6	2	0	0	2	0	1	0	0	0	0	1	.00	0	.300	.364	.300	3B	5	7	8	0	1	1.000
1942 NYA	33	4	17	6	2	0	0	8	5	0	0	1	0	2	0	0	0	0	0	—	1	.353	.389	.471	3B	4	3	5	0	0	1.000
WS Totals		28	116	33	4	1	0	39	17	6	1	9	0	9	0	3	0	1	2	.33	1	.284	.336	.336	3B	28	30	38	4	3	.944

RICH ROLLINS—Richard John Rollins—Nickname: Red—Bats: Right; Throws: Right

Ht: 5'10"; Wt: 185 lbs; Born: 4/16/1938 in Mount Pleasant, Pennsylvania; Debut: 6/16/1961

World Series — Batting / Fielding

Year Tm	Age	G	AB	H	2B	3B	HR	TB	R	RBI	GW	TBB	IBB	SO	HBP	SH	SF	SB	CS	SB%	GDP	Avg	OBP	SLG	Pos	G	PO	A	E	DP	FPct
1965 Min	27	3	2	0	0	0	0	0	0	0	0	1	0	0	0	0	0	0	0	—	0	.000	.333	.000	—						

JOHN ROMANO—John Anthony Romano—Nickname: Honey—Bats: Right; Throws: Right

Ht: 5'11"; Wt: 205 lbs; Born: 8/23/1934 in Hoboken, New Jersey; Debut: 9/12/1958

World Series — Batting / Fielding

Year Tm	Age	G	AB	H	2B	3B	HR	TB	R	RBI	GW	TBB	IBB	SO	HBP	SH	SF	SB	CS	SB%	GDP	Avg	OBP	SLG	Pos	G	PO	A	E	DP	FPct
1959 ChA	25	1	1	0	0	0	0	0	0	0	0	0	0	0	0	0	0	0	0	—	0	.000	.000	.000	—						

ED ROMERO—Edgardo Ralph Romero—Bats: Right; Throws: Right

Ht: 5'11"; Wt: 160 lbs; Born: 12/9/1957 in Santurce, Puerto Rico; Debut: 7/16/1977

Division Series — Batting / Fielding

Year Tm	Age	G	AB	H	2B	3B	HR	TB	R	RBI	GW	TBB	IBB	SO	HBP	SH	SF	SB	CS	SB%	GDP	Avg	OBP	SLG	Pos	G	PO	A	E	DP	FPct
1981 Mil	23	1	2	1	0	0	0	1	1	0	0	0	0	1	0	0	0	0	0	—	0	.500	.500	.500	2B	1	2	2	0	0	1.000

LCS		Batting																							Fielding						
Year Tm	Age	G	AB	H	2B	3B	HR	TB	R	RBI	GW	TBB	IBB	SO	HBP	SH	SF	SB	CS	SB%	GDP	Avg	OBP	SLG	Pos	G	PO	A	E	DP	FPct
1986 Bos	28	1	2	0	0	0	0	0	0	0	0	0	0	0	0	0	0	0	0	—	0	.000	.000	.000	SS	1	0	0	0	0	—
1988 Bos	30	1	0	0	0	0	0	0	0	0	0	0	0	0	0	0	0	0	0	—	0	—	—	—	—						
LCS Totals		2	2	0	0	0	0	0	0	0	0	0	0	0	0	0	0	0	0	—	0	.000	.000	.000	SS	1	0	0	0	0	—
World Series		Batting																							Fielding						
Year Tm	Age	G	AB	H	2B	3B	HR	TB	R	RBI	GW	TBB	IBB	SO	HBP	SH	SF	SB	CS	SB%	GDP	Avg	OBP	SLG	Pos	G	PO	A	E	DP	FPct
1986 Bos	28	3	1	0	0	0	0	0	0	0	0	0	0	0	0	0	0	0	0	—	0	.000	.000	.000	SS	3	0	1	0	0	1.000
Postseason Totals		6	5	1	0	0	0	1	1	0	0	0	0	1	0	0	0	0	0	—	0	.200	.200	.200	SS	4	0	1	0	0	1.000

KEVIN ROMINE—Kevin Andrew Romine—Bats: Right; Throws: Right

Ht: 5'11"; Wt: 185 lbs; Born: 5/23/1961 in Exeter, New Hampshire; Debut: 9/5/1985

LCS		Batting																							Fielding						
Year Tm	Age	G	AB	H	2B	3B	HR	TB	R	RBI	GW	TBB	IBB	SO	HBP	SH	SF	SB	CS	SB%	GDP	Avg	OBP	SLG	Pos	G	PO	A	E	DP	FPct
1988 Bos	27	2	0	0	0	0	0	0	1	0	0	0	0	0	0	0	0	0	0	—	0	—	—	—	—						

EDDIE ROMMEL—Edwin Americus Rommel—Throws: Right; Bats: Right

Ht: 6'2"; Wt: 197 lbs; Born: 9/13/1897 in Baltimore, Maryland; Debut: 4/19/1920; Died: 8/26/1970

World Series		Pitching																										
Year Tm	Age	G	GS	CG	GF	IP	BFP	H	R	ER	HR	SH	SF	HB	TBB	IBB	SO	WP	Bk	W	L	Pct	ShO	Sv-Op	Hld	OAvg	OOBP	ERA
1929 Phi	32	1	0	0	0	1.0	5	2	1	1	0	0	0	0	1	0	0	0	0	1	0	1.000	0	0- 0	0	.500	.600	9.00
1931 Phi	34	1	0	0	1	1.0	6	3	1	1	0	0	0	0	0	0	0	0	0	0	0	—	0	0- 0	0	.500	.500	9.00
WS Totals		2	0	0	1	2.0	22	5	2	2	0	0	0	0	1	0	0	0	0	1	0	1.000	0	0-0	0	.500	.545	9.00

World Series		Batting																							Fielding						
Year Tm	Age	G	AB	H	2B	3B	HR	TB	R	RBI	GW	TBB	IBB	SO	HBP	SH	SF	SB	CS	SB%	GDP	Avg	OBP	SLG	Pos	G	PO	A	E	DP	FPct
1929 Phi	32	1	0	0	0	0	0	0	0	0	0	0	0	0	0	0	0	0	0	—	0	—	—	—	P	1	0	0	0	0	—
1931 Phi	34	1	0	0	0	0	0	0	0	0	0	0	0	0	0	0	0	0	0	—	0	—	—	—	P	1	0	0	0	0	—
WS Totals		2	0	0	0	0	0	0	0	0	0	0	0	0	0	0	0	0	0	—	0	—	—	—	P	2	0	0	0	0	—

ENRIQUE ROMO—Throws: Right; Bats: Right

Ht: 5'11"; Wt: 185 lbs; Born: 7/15/1947 in Santa Rosalia, Mexico; Debut: 4/7/1977

LCS		Pitching																										
Year Tm	Age	G	GS	CG	GF	IP	BFP	H	R	ER	HR	SH	SF	HB	TBB	IBB	SO	WP	Bk	W	L	Pct	ShO	Sv-Op	Hld	OAvg	OOBP	ERA
1979 Pit	32	2	0	0	0	0.1	5	3	0	0	0	0	0	0	1	0	1	0	0	0	0	—	0	0- 0	0	.750	.800	0.00
World Series		Pitching																										
Year Tm	Age	G	GS	CG	GF	IP	BFP	H	R	ER	HR	SH	SF	HB	TBB	IBB	SO	WP	Bk	W	L	Pct	ShO	Sv-Op	Hld	OAvg	OOBP	ERA
1979 Pit	32	2	0	0	0	4.2	23	5	2	2	0	0	0	1	3	1	4	1	0	0	0	—	0	0- 0	0	.263	.391	3.86
Postseason Totals		4	0	0	0	5.0	56	8	2	2	0	0	0	1	4	1	5	1	0	0	0	—	0	0-0	0	.348	.464	3.60

LCS		Batting																							Fielding						
Year Tm	Age	G	AB	H	2B	3B	HR	TB	R	RBI	GW	TBB	IBB	SO	HBP	SH	SF	SB	CS	SB%	GDP	Avg	OBP	SLG	Pos	G	PO	A	E	DP	FPct
1979 Pit	32	2	0	0	0	0	0	0	0	0	0	0	0	0	0	0	0	0	0	—	0	—	—	—	P	2	0	0	0	0	—
World Series		Batting																							Fielding						
Year Tm	Age	G	AB	H	2B	3B	HR	TB	R	RBI	GW	TBB	IBB	SO	HBP	SH	SF	SB	CS	SB%	GDP	Avg	OBP	SLG	Pos	G	PO	A	E	DP	FPct
1979 Pit	32	2	1	0	0	0	0	0	0	0	0	0	0	0	0	0	0	0	0	—	0	.000	.000	.000	P	2	0	1	0	0	1.000
Postseason Totals		4	1	0	0	0	0	0	0	0	0	0	0	0	0	0	0	0	0	—	0	.000	.000	.000	P	4	0	1	0	0	1.000

JIM ROOKER—James Phillip Rooker—Throws: Left; Bats: Right

Ht: 6'0"; Wt: 195 lbs; Born: 9/23/1942 in Lakeview, Oregon; Debut: 6/30/1968

LCS		Pitching																										
Year Tm	Age	G	GS	CG	GF	IP	BFP	H	R	ER	HR	SH	SF	HB	TBB	IBB	SO	WP	Bk	W	L	Pct	ShO	Sv-Op	Hld	OAvg	OOBP	ERA
1974 Pit	32	1	1	0	0	7.0	32	6	2	2	1	0	0	0	5	2	4	0	0	0	0	—	0	0- 0	0	.222	.344	2.57
1975 Pit	33	1	1	0	0	4.0	19	7	4	4	1	0	1	0	0	0	5	0	0	0	1	.000	0	0- 0	0	.389	.368	9.00
LCS Totals		2	2	0	0	11.0	102	13	6	6	2	0	1	0	5	2	9	0	0	0	1	.000	0	0-0	0	.289	.353	4.91
World Series		Pitching																										
Year Tm	Age	G	GS	CG	GF	IP	BFP	H	R	ER	HR	SH	SF	HB	TBB	IBB	SO	WP	Bk	W	L	Pct	ShO	Sv-Op	Hld	OAvg	OOBP	ERA
1979 Pit	37	2	1	0	0	8.2	33	5	1	1	0	1	0	0	3	0	4	0	0	0	0	—	0	0- 0	0	.172	.250	1.04
Postseason Totals		4	3	0	0	19.2	168	18	7	7	2	1	1	0	8	2	13	0	0	0	1	.000	0	0-0	0	.243	.313	3.20

LCS		Batting																							Fielding						
Year Tm	Age	G	AB	H	2B	3B	HR	TB	R	RBI	GW	TBB	IBB	SO	HBP	SH	SF	SB	CS	SB%	GDP	Avg	OBP	SLG	Pos	G	PO	A	E	DP	FPct
1974 Pit	32	1	2	1	0	0	0	1	0	0	0	0	0	0	0	0	0	0	0	—	0	.500	.500	.500	P	1	0	3	1	0	.750
1975 Pit	33	1	1	0	0	0	0	0	0	0	0	0	0	1	0	0	0	0	0	—	0	.000	.000	.000	P	1	0	0	0	0	—
LCS Totals		2	3	1	0	0	0	1	0	0	0	0	0	1	0	0	0	0	0	—	0	.333	.333	.333	P	2	0	3	1	0	.750
World Series		Batting																							Fielding						
Year Tm	Age	G	AB	H	2B	3B	HR	TB	R	RBI	GW	TBB	IBB	SO	HBP	SH	SF	SB	CS	SB%	GDP	Avg	OBP	SLG	Pos	G	PO	A	E	DP	FPct
1979 Pit	37	2	2	0	0	0	0	0	0	0	0	0	0	1	0	0	0	0	0	—	0	.000	.000	.000	P	2	1	2	0	0	1.000
Postseason Totals		4	5	1	0	0	0	1	0	0	0	0	0	2	0	0	0	0	0	—	0	.200	.200	.200	P	4	1	5	1	0	.857

CHARLIE ROOT—Charles Henry Root—Nickname: Chinski—Throws: Right; Bats: Right

Ht: 5'10"; Wt: 190 lbs; Born: 3/17/1899 in Middletown, Ohio; Debut: 4/18/1923; Died: 11/5/1970

World Series		Pitching																										
Year Tm	Age	G	GS	CG	GF	IP	BFP	H	R	ER	HR	SH	SF	HB	TBB	IBB	SO	WP	Bk	W	L	Pct	ShO	Sv-Op	Hld	OAvg	OOBP	ERA
1929 ChN	30	2	2	0	0	13.1	53	12	7	7	2	1	0	0	2	0	8	0	0	0	1	.000	0	0- 0	0	.240	.269	4.73
1932 ChN	33	1	1	0	0	4.1	22	6	6	5	4	0	0	0	3	0	4	0	0	0	1	.000	0	0- 0	0	.316	.409	10.38
1935 ChN	36	2	1	0	1	2.0	12	5	4	4	1	1	0	0	1	1	2	0	0	0	1	.000	0	0- 0	0	.500	.545	18.00
1938 ChN	39	1	0	0	0	3.0	12	3	1	1	1	0	0	0	0	0	1	0	0	0	0	—	0	0- 0	0	.250	.250	3.00
WS Totals		6	4	0	1	22.2	198	26	18	17	8	2	0	0	6	1	15	0	0	0	3	.000	0	0-0	0	.286	.330	6.75

World Series		Batting																							Fielding						
Year Tm	Age	G	AB	H	2B	3B	HR	TB	R	RBI	GW	TBB	IBB	SO	HBP	SH	SF	SB	CS	SB%	GDP	Avg	OBP	SLG	Pos	G	PO	A	E	DP	FPct
1929 ChN	30	2	5	0	0	0	0	0	0	0	0	0	0	3	0	0	0	0	0	—	0	.000	.000	.000	P	2	0	0	0	0	—
1932 ChN	33	1	2	0	0	0	0	0	0	0	0	0	0	1	0	0	0	0	0	—	0	.000	.000	.000	P	1	0	0	0	0	—
1935 ChN	36	2	0	0	0	0	0	0	0	0	0	0	0	0	0	0	0	0	0	—	0	—	—	—	P	2	0	1	0	0	1.000
1938 ChN	39	1	0	0	0	0	0	0	0	0	0	0	0	0	0	0	0	0	0	—	0	—	—	—	P	1	0	0	0	0	—
WS Totals		6	7	0	0	0	0	0	0	0	0	0	0	4	0	0	0	0	0	—	0	.000	.000	.000	P	6	0	1	0	0	1.000

BUDDY ROSAR—Warren Vincent Rosar—Bats: Right; Throws: Right

Ht: 5'9"; Wt: 190 lbs; Born: 7/3/1914 in Buffalo, New York; Debut: 4/29/1939; Died: 3/13/1994

World Series		Batting																							Fielding						
Year Tm	Age	G	AB	H	2B	3B	HR	TB	R	RBI	GW	TBB	IBB	SO	HBP	SH	SF	SB	CS	SB%	GDP	Avg	OBP	SLG	Pos	G	PO	A	E	DP	FPct
1941 NYA	27	1	0	0	0	0	0	0	0	0	0	0	0	0	0	0	0	0	0	—	0	—	—	—	C	1	0	0	0	0	—
1942 NYA	28	1	1	1	0	0	0	1	0	0	0	0	0	0	0	0	0	0	0	—	0	1.000	1.000	1.000	—						
WS Totals		2	1	1	0	0	0	1	0	0	0	0	0	0	0	0	0	0	0	—	0	1.000	1.000	1.000	C	1	0	0	0	0	—

JIMMY ROSARIO—Angel Ramon Rosario—Bats: Both; Throws: Right

Ht: 5'10"; Wt: 155 lbs; Born: 5/5/1945 in Bayamon, Puerto Rico; Debut: 4/8/1971

LCS		Batting																							Fielding						
Year Tm	Age	G	AB	H	2B	3B	HR	TB	R	RBI	GW	TBB	IBB	SO	HBP	SH	SF	SB	CS	SB%	GDP	Avg	OBP	SLG	Pos	G	PO	A	E	DP	FPct
1971 SF	26	1	0	0	0	0	0	0	0	0	0	0	0	0	0	0	0	0	0	—	0	—	—	—	—						

PETE ROSE—Peter Edward Rose—Nickname: Charlie Hustle—Bats: Both; Throws: Right

Ht: 5'11"; Wt: 192 lbs; Born: 4/14/1941 in Cincinnati, Ohio; Debut: 4/8/1963

Division Series		Batting																							Fielding						
Year Tm	Age	G	AB	H	2B	3B	HR	TB	R	RBI	GW	TBB	IBB	SO	HBP	SH	SF	SB	CS	SB%	GDP	Avg	OBP	SLG	Pos	G	PO	A	E	DP	FPct
1981 Phi	40	5	20	6	1	0	0	7	1	2	0	2	0	0	0	0	0	0	0	—	1	.300	.364	.350	1B	5	29	7	0	0	1.000

LCS		Batting																							Fielding						
Year Tm	Age	G	AB	H	2B	3B	HR	TB	R	RBI	GW	TBB	IBB	SO	HBP	SH	SF	SB	CS	SB%	GDP	Avg	OBP	SLG	Pos	G	PO	A	E	DP	FPct
1970 Cin	29	3	13	3	0	0	0	3	1	1	1	0	0	0	0	0	0	0	0	—	0	.231	.231	.231	OF	3	3	0	0	0	1.000
1972 Cin	31	5	20	9	4	0	0	13	1	2	0	1	0	2	0	1	0	0	0	—	0	.450	.476	.650	OF	5	10	0	0	0	1.000
1973 Cin-*M*	32	5	21	8	1	0	2	15	3	2	1	2	1	2	0	0	0	0	0	—	0	.381	.435	.714	OF	5	10	1	0	0	1.000
1975 Cin	34	3	14	5	0	0	1	8	3	2	0	0	0	2	0	0	0	0	0	—	0	.357	.357	.571	3B	3	2	1	0	0	1.000
1976 Cin	35	3	14	6	2	1	0	10	3	2	0	1	1	0	0	0	0	0	0	—	0	.429	.467	.714	3B	3	2	5	1	1	.875
1980 Phi	39	5	20	8	0	0	0	8	3	2	0	5	2	3	0	0	0	0	2	.00	0	.400	.520	.400	1B	5	53	7	0	5	1.000
1983 Phi	42	4	16	6	0	0	0	6	3	0	0	1	0	1	0	0	0	1	1	.50	1	.375	.412	.375	1B	4	30	2	0	0	1.000
LCS Totals		28	118	45	7	1	3	63	17	11	2	10	4	10	0	1	0	1	3	.25	1	.381	.430	.534	OF	13	23	1	0	0	1.000
World Series		Batting																							Fielding						
Year Tm	Age	G	AB	H	2B	3B	HR	TB	R	RBI	GW	TBB	IBB	SO	HBP	SH	SF	SB	CS	SB%	GDP	Avg	OBP	SLG	Pos	G	PO	A	E	DP	FPct
1970 Cin	29	5	20	5	1	0	1	9	2	2	0	2	0	0	0	0	0	0	0	—	0	.250	.318	.450	OF	5	14	1	1	0	.938
1972 Cin	31	7	28	6	0	0	1	9	3	2	1	4	1	4	0	0	0	1	1	.50	0	.214	.313	.321	OF	7	14	1	0	0	1.000
1975 Cin	34	7	27	10	1	1	0	13	3	2	1	5	1	1	1	0	0	0	0	—	0	.370	.485	.481	3B	7	7	9	0	1	1.000
1976 Cin	35	4	16	3	1	0	0	4	1	1	1	2	0	2	0	0	1	0	0	—	1	.188	.263	.250	3B	4	6	3	0	0	1.000
1980 Phi	39	6	23	6	1	0	0	7	2	1	0	2	1	2	1	0	0	0	1	.00	0	.261	.346	.304	1B	6	49	6	0	8	1.000
1983 Phi	42	5	16	5	1	0	0	6	1	1	0	1	0	3	0	0	0	0	0	—	0	.313	.353	.375	1B	3	23	4	0	0	1.000
																									OF	1	3	0	0	0	1.000
WS Totals		34	130	35	5	1	2	48	12	9	3	16	3	12	2	0	1	1	2	.33	1	.269	.356	.369	OF	13	31	2	1	0	.971
Postseason Totals		67	268	86	13	2	5	118	30	22	5	28	7	22	2	1	1	2	5	.29	3	.321	.388	.440	OF	26	54	3	1	0	.983

JOHN ROSEBORO—John Junior Roseboro—Nickname: Gabby—Bats: Left; Throws: Right

Ht: 5'11"; Wt: 190 lbs; Born: 5/13/1933 in Ashland, Ohio; Debut: 6/14/1957

LCS		Batting																							Fielding						
Year Tm	Age	G	AB	H	2B	3B	HR	TB	R	RBI	GW	TBB	IBB	SO	HBP	SH	SF	SB	CS	SB%	GDP	Avg	OBP	SLG	Pos	G	PO	A	E	DP	FPct
1969 Min	36	2	5	1	0	0	0	1	0	0	0	0	0	0	0	0	0	0	0	—	0	.200	.200	.200	C	2	6	1	0	0	1.000
World Series		Batting																							Fielding						
Year Tm	Age	G	AB	H	2B	3B	HR	TB	R	RBI	GW	TBB	IBB	SO	HBP	SH	SF	SB	CS	SB%	GDP	Avg	OBP	SLG	Pos	G	PO	A	E	DP	FPct
1959 LA	26	6	21	2	0	0	0	2	0	1	0	0	0	2	0	2	0	0	0	—	0	.095	.095	.095	C	6	35	4	0	1	1.000
1963 LA	30	4	14	2	0	0	1	5	1	3	0	0	0	4	0	0	0	0	0	—	1	.143	.143	.357	C	4	43	0	0	0	1.000
1965 LA	32	7	21	6	1	0	0	7	1	3	1	5	2	3	0	0	0	1	2	.33	0	.286	.423	.333	C	7	57	4	0	0	1.000
1966 LA	33	4	14	1	0	0	0	1	0	0	0	0	0	3	0	0	0	0	0	—	0	.071	.071	.071	C	4	22	2	0	1	1.000
WS Totals		21	70	11	1	0	1	15	2	7	1	5	2	12	0	2	0	1	2	.33	1	.157	.213	.214	C	21	157	10	0	2	1.000
Postseason Totals		23	75	12	1	0	1	16	2	7	1	5	2	12	0	2	0	1	2	.33	1	.160	.213	.213	C	23	163	11	0	2	1.000

AL ROSEN—Albert Leonard Rosen—Nickname: Flip—Bats: Right; Throws: Right

Ht: 5'10"; Wt: 180 lbs; Born: 2/29/1924 in Spartanburg, South Carolina; Debut: 9/10/1947

World Series		Batting																							Fielding						
Year Tm	Age	G	AB	H	2B	3B	HR	TB	R	RBI	GW	TBB	IBB	SO	HBP	SH	SF	SB	CS	SB%	GDP	Avg	OBP	SLG	Pos	G	PO	A	E	DP	FPct
1948 Cle	24	1	1	0	0	0	0	0	0	0	0	0	0	0	0	0	0	0	0	—	0	.000	.000	.000	—						
1954 Cle	30	3	12	3	0	0	0	3	0	0	0	1	0	0	0	0	0	0	0	—	0	.250	.308	.250	3B	3	2	6	0	0	1.000
WS Totals		4	13	3	0	0	0	3	0	0	0	1	0	0	0	0	0	0	0	—	0	.231	.286	.231	3B	3	2	6	0	0	1.000

CLAUDE ROSSMAN—Claude R. Rossman—Bats: Left; Throws: Left

Ht: 6'0"; Wt: 188 lbs; Born: 6/17/1881 in Philmont, New York; Debut: 9/16/1904; Died: 1/16/1928

World Series		Batting																							Fielding						
Year Tm	Age	G	AB	H	2B	3B	HR	TB	R	RBI	GW	TBB	IBB	SO	HBP	SH	SF	SB	CS	SB%	GDP	Avg	OBP	SLG	Pos	G	PO	A	E	DP	FPct
1907 Det	26	5	20	8	0	1	0	10	1	2	0	1	0	0	0	0	0	1	0	1.00	0	.400	.429	.500	1B	5	47	4	1	1	.981
1908 Det	27	5	19	4	0	0	0	4	3	3	1	1	0	4	0	0	0	1	0	1.00	1	.211	.250	.211	1B	5	49	5	2	4	.964
WS Totals		10	39	12	0	1	0	14	4	5	1	2	0	4	0	0	0	2	0	1.00	1	.308	.341	.359	1B	10	96	9	3	5	.972

JACK ROTHROCK—John Houston Rothrock—Bats: Both; Throws: Right

Ht: 5'11"; Wt: 165 lbs; Born: 3/14/1905 in Long Beach, California; Debut: 7/28/1925; Died: 2/2/1980

World Series		Batting																							Fielding						
Year Tm	Age	G	AB	H	2B	3B	HR	TB	R	RBI	GW	TBB	IBB	SO	HBP	SH	SF	SB	CS	SB%	GDP	Avg	OBP	SLG	Pos	G	PO	A	E	DP	FPct
1934 StL	29	7	30	7	3	1	0	12	3	6	2	1	0	2	0	2	0	0	0	—	1	.233	.258	.400	OF	7	19	0	1	0	.950

EDD ROUSH (HOF 1986-V)—Edd J. Roush—Bats: Left; Throws: Left

Ht: 5'11"; Wt: 170 lbs; Born: 5/8/1893 in Oakland City, Indiana; Debut: 8/20/1913; Died: 3/21/1988

World Series		Batting																							Fielding						
Year Tm	Age	G	AB	H	2B	3B	HR	TB	R	RBI	GW	TBB	IBB	SO	HBP	SH	SF	SB	CS	SB%	GDP	Avg	OBP	SLG	Pos	G	PO	A	E	DP	FPct
1919 Cin	26	8	28	6	2	1	0	10	6	7	2	3	0	0	2	1	0	2	1	.67	1	.214	.333	.357	OF	8	31	3	2	2	.944

SCHOOLBOY ROWE—Lynwood Thomas Rowe—Throws: Right; Bats: Right

Ht: 6'4"; Wt: 210 lbs; Born: 1/11/1910 in Waco, Texas; Debut: 4/15/1933; Died: 1/8/1961

World Series		Pitching																										
Year Tm	Age	G	GS	CG	GF	IP	BFP	H	R	ER	HR	SH	SF	HB	TBB	IBB	SO	WP	Bk	W	L	Pct	ShO	Sv-Op	Hld	OAvg	OOBP	ERA
1934 Det	24	3	2	2	0	21.1	82	19	8	7	0	2	0	0	0	0	12	0	0	1	1	.500	0	0- 0	0	.238	.238	2.95
1935 Det	25	3	2	2	1	21.0	84	19	8	6	2	5	0	0	1	0	14	0	0	1	2	.333	0	0- 1	0	.244	.253	2.57
1940 Det	30	2	2	0	0	3.2	24	12	7	7	1	1	0	0	1	0	1	0	0	0	2	.000	0	0- 0	0	.545	.565	17.18
WS Totals		8	6	4	1	46.0	380	50	23	20	3	8	0	0	2	0	27	0	0	2	5	.286	0	0-1	0	.278	.286	3.91

World Series		Batting																							Fielding						
Year Tm	Age	G	AB	H	2B	3B	HR	TB	R	RBI	GW	TBB	IBB	SO	HBP	SH	SF	SB	CS	SB%	GDP	Avg	OBP	SLG	Pos	G	PO	A	E	DP	FPct
1934 Det	24	3	7	0	0	0	0	0	0	0	0	0	0	5	0	2	0	0	0	—	0	.000	.000	.000	P	3	1	1	0	0	1.000
1935 Det	25	3	8	2	1	0	0	3	0	0	0	0	0	1	0	0	0	0	0	—	0	.250	.250	.375	P	3	3	5	1	0	.889
1940 Det	30	2	1	0	0	0	0	0	0	0	0	0	0	1	0	0	0	0	0	—	0	.000	.000	.000	P	2	0	1	0	0	1.000
WS Totals		8	16	2	1	0	0	3	0	0	0	0	0	7	0	2	0	0	0	—	0	.125	.125	.188	P	8	4	7	1	0	.917

JERRY ROYSTER—Jeron Kennis Royster—Bats: Right; Throws: Right

Ht: 6'0"; Wt: 165 lbs; Born: 10/18/1952 in Sacramento, California; Debut: 8/14/1973

LCS		Batting																							Fielding						
Year Tm	Age	G	AB	H	2B	3B	HR	TB	R	RBI	GW	TBB	IBB	SO	HBP	SH	SF	SB	CS	SB%	GDP	Avg	OBP	SLG	Pos	G	PO	A	E	DP	FPct
1982 Atl	29	3	11	2	0	0	0	2	0	0	0	0	0	2	0	0	0	0	0	—	2	.182	.182	.182	3B	1	0	0	0	0	—
																									OF	3	4	0	0	0	1.000

NAP RUCKER—George Rucker—Throws: Left; Bats: Right

Ht: 5'11"; Wt: 190 lbs; Born: 9/30/1884 in Crabapple, Georgia; Debut: 4/15/1907; Died: 12/19/1970

World Series		Pitching																										
Year Tm	Age	G	GS	CG	GF	IP	BFP	H	R	ER	HR	SH	SF	HB	TBB	IBB	SO	WP	Bk	W	L	Pct	ShO	Sv-Op	Hld	OAvg	OOBP	ERA
1916 Bro	32	1	0	0	1	2.0	6	1	0	0	0	0	0	0	0	0	3	0	0	0	0	—	0	0- 0	0	.167	.167	0.00

World Series		Batting																							Fielding						
Year Tm	Age	G	AB	H	2B	3B	HR	TB	R	RBI	GW	TBB	IBB	SO	HBP	SH	SF	SB	CS	SB%	GDP	Avg	OBP	SLG	Pos	G	PO	A	E	DP	FPct
1916 Bro	32	1	0	0	0	0	0	0	0	0	0	0	0	0	0	0	0	0	0	—	0	—	—	—	P	1	0	0	0	0	—

JOE RUDI—Joseph Oden Rudi—Bats: Right; Throws: Right

Ht: 6'2"; Wt: 200 lbs; Born: 9/7/1946 in Modesto, California; Debut: 4/11/1967

LCS		Batting																							Fielding						
Year Tm	Age	G	AB	H	2B	3B	HR	TB	R	RBI	GW	TBB	IBB	SO	HBP	SH	SF	SB	CS	SB%	GDP	Avg	OBP	SLG	Pos	G	PO	A	E	DP	FPct
1971 Oak	25	2	7	1	1	0	0	2	0	0	0	1	0	0	0	0	0	0	0	—	0	.143	.250	.286	OF	2	3	0	0	0	1.000
1972 Oak	26	5	20	5	1	0	0	6	1	2	1	1	0	4	0	0	1	0	0	—	0	.250	.273	.300	OF	5	11	0	0	0	1.000
1973 Oak	27	5	18	4	0	0	1	7	1	3	2	3	1	1	0	1	0	0	0	—	0	.222	.333	.389	OF	5	11	0	0	0	1.000
1974 Oak	28	4	13	2	0	1	0	4	0	1	0	3	2	2	0	0	0	0	0	—	0	.154	.313	.308	OF	4	5	0	0	0	1.000
1975 Oak	29	3	12	3	2	0	0	5	1	0	0	0	0	1	0	0	0	0	0	—	1	.250	.250	.417	1B	2	21	2	0	0	1.000
																									OF	1	1	0	0	0	1.000
LCS Totals		19	70	15	4	1	1	24	3	6	3	8	3	8	0	1	1	0	0	—	1	.214	.291	.343	OF	17	31	0	0	0	1.000

World Series — Batting / Fielding

Year Tm	Age	G	AB	H	2B	3B	HR	TB	R	RBI	GW	TBB	IBB	SO	HBP	SH	SF	SB	CS	SB%	GDP	Avg	OBP	SLG	Pos	G	PO	A	E	DP	FPct
1972 Oak	26	7	25	6	0	0	1	9	1	1	0	2	1	5	1	0	0	0	0	—	0	.240	.321	.360	OF	7	20	0	0	0	1.000
1973 Oak	27	7	27	9	2	0	0	11	3	4	0	3	0	4	0	1	0	0	1	.00	0	.333	.400	.407	OF	7	20	2	0	1	1.000
1974 Oak	28	5	18	6	0	0	1	9	1	4	1	0	0	3	0	1	0	0	0	—	1	.333	.333	.500	1B	2	17	0	0	1	1.000
																									OF	5	11	0	0	0	1.000
WS Totals		19	70	21	2	0	2	29	5	9	1	5	1	12	1	2	0	0	1	.00	1	.300	.355	.414	OF	19	51	2	0	1	1.000
Postseason Totals		38	140	36	6	1	3	53	8	15	4	13	4	20	1	3	1	0	1	.00	2	.257	.323	.379	OF	36	82	2	0	1	1.000

DICK RUDOLPH—Richard Rudolph—Nickname: Baldy—Throws: Right; Bats: Right

Ht: 5'9"; Wt: 160 lbs; Born: 8/25/1887 in New York, New York; Debut: 9/30/1910; Died: 10/20/1949

World Series — Pitching

Year Tm	Age	G	GS	CG	GF	IP	BFP	H	R	ER	HR	SH	SF	HB	TBB	IBB	SO	WP	Bk	W	L	Pct	ShO	Sv-Op	Hld	OAvg	OOBP	ERA
1914 Bos	27	2	2	2	0	18.0	66	12	2	1	0	1	0	0	4	0	15	1	0	2	0	1.000	0	0- 0	0	.197	.246	0.50

World Series — Batting / Fielding

Year Tm	Age	G	AB	H	2B	3B	HR	TB	R	RBI	GW	TBB	IBB	SO	HBP	SH	SF	SB	CS	SB%	GDP	Avg	OBP	SLG	Pos	G	PO	A	E	DP	FPct
1914 Bos	27	2	6	2	0	0	0	2	1	0	0	1	0	1	0	0	0	0	0	—	0	.333	.429	.333	P	2	0	3	0	0	1.000

MUDDY RUEL—Herold Dominic Ruel—Bats: Right; Throws: Right

Ht: 5'9"; Wt: 150 lbs; Born: 2/20/1896 in St. Louis, Missouri; Debut: 5/29/1915; Died: 11/13/1963

World Series — Batting / Fielding

Year Tm	Age	G	AB	H	2B	3B	HR	TB	R	RBI	GW	TBB	IBB	SO	HBP	SH	SF	SB	CS	SB%	GDP	Avg	OBP	SLG	Pos	G	PO	A	E	DP	FPct
1924 Was	28	7	21	2	2	0	0	4	2	0	0	6	0	1	0	2	0	0	0	—	0	.095	.296	.190	C	7	51	4	0	1	1.000
1925 Was	29	7	19	6	1	0	0	7	0	1	0	3	0	2	0	0	0	0	0	—	0	.316	.409	.368	C	7	35	5	0	0	1.000
WS Totals		14	40	8	3	0	0	11	2	1	0	9	0	3	0	2	0	0	0	—	0	.200	.347	.275	C	14	86	9	0	1	1.000

KIRK RUETER—Kirk Wesley Rueter—Throws: Left; Bats: Left

Ht: 6'3"; Wt: 190 lbs; Born: 12/1/1970 in Nashville, Tennessee; Debut: 7/7/1993

Division Series — Pitching

Year Tm	Age	G	GS	CG	GF	IP	BFP	H	R	ER	HR	SH	SF	HB	TBB	IBB	SO	WP	Bk	W	L	Pct	ShO	Sv-Op	Hld	OAvg	OOBP	ERA
1997 SF	26	1	1	0	0	7.0	28	4	1	1	1	0	0	0	3	0	5	0	0	0	0	—	0	0- 0	0	.160	.250	1.29

Division Series — Batting / Fielding

Year Tm	Age	G	AB	H	2B	3B	HR	TB	R	RBI	GW	TBB	IBB	SO	HBP	SH	SF	SB	CS	SB%	GDP	Avg	OBP	SLG	Pos	G	PO	A	E	DP	FPct
1997 SF	26	1	2	1	0	0	0	1	0	0	0	0	0	0	0	0	0	0	0	—	0	.500	.500	.500	P	1	0	1	0	0	1.000

DUTCH RUETHER—Walter Henry Ruether—Throws: Left; Bats: Left

Ht: 6'1"; Wt: 180 lbs; Born: 9/13/1893 in Alameda, California; Debut: 4/13/1917; Died: 5/16/1970

World Series — Pitching

Year Tm	Age	G	GS	CG	GF	IP	BFP	H	R	ER	HR	SH	SF	HB	TBB	IBB	SO	WP	Bk	W	L	Pct	ShO	Sv-Op	Hld	OAvg	OOBP	ERA
1919 Cin	26	2	2	1	0	14.0	56	12	5	4	0	2	1	0	4	0	1	0	0	1	0	1.000	0	0- 0	0	.245	.296	2.57
1926 NYA	33	1	1	0	0	4.1	22	7	4	2	1	2	0	0	2	0	1	0	0	0	1	.000	0	0- 0	0	.389	.450	4.15
WS Totals		3	3	1	0	18.1	156	19	9	6	1	4	1	0	6	0	2	0	0	1	1	.500	0	0-0	0	.284	.338	2.95

World Series — Batting / Fielding

Year Tm	Age	G	AB	H	2B	3B	HR	TB	R	RBI	GW	TBB	IBB	SO	HBP	SH	SF	SB	CS	SB%	GDP	Avg	OBP	SLG	Pos	G	PO	A	E	DP	FPct
1919 Cin	26	3	6	4	1	2	0	9	2	4	0	1	0	0	0	0	0	0	0	—	0	.667	.714	1.500	P	2	0	2	0	0	1.000
1925 Was	32	1	1	0	0	0	0	0	0	0	0	0	0	1	0	0	0	0	0	—	0	.000	.000	.000	—						
1926 NYA	33	3	4	0	0	0	0	0	0	0	0	0	0	0	0	0	0	0	0	—	0	.000	.000	.000	P	1	0	2	0	0	1.000
WS Totals		7	11	4	1	2	0	9	2	4	0	1	0	1	0	0	0	0	0	—	0	.364	.417	.818	P	3	0	4	0	0	1.000

BRUCE RUFFIN—Bruce Wayne Ruffin—Throws: Left; Bats: Both

Ht: 6'2"; Wt: 205 lbs; Born: 10/4/1963 in Lubbock, Texas; Debut: 6/28/1986

Division Series — Pitching

Year Tm	Age	G	GS	CG	GF	IP	BFP	H	R	ER	HR	SH	SF	HB	TBB	IBB	SO	WP	Bk	W	L	Pct	ShO	Sv-Op	Hld	OAvg	OOBP	ERA
1995 Col	31	4	0	0	1	3.1	14	3	1	1	0	0	0	0	2	0	2	0	0	0	0	—	0	0- 0	1	.250	.357	2.70

Division Series — Batting / Fielding

Year Tm	Age	G	AB	H	2B	3B	HR	TB	R	RBI	GW	TBB	IBB	SO	HBP	SH	SF	SB	CS	SB%	GDP	Avg	OBP	SLG	Pos	G	PO	A	E	DP	FPct
1995 Col	31	4	0	0	0	0	0	0	0	0	0	0	0	0	0	0	0	0	0	—	0	—	—	—	P	4	0	0	0	0	—

RED RUFFING (HOF 1967-W)—Charles Herbert Ruffing—Throws: Right; Bats: Right

Ht: 6'1"; Wt: 205 lbs; Born: 5/3/1904 in Granville, Illinois; Debut: 5/31/1924; Died: 2/17/1986

World Series — Pitching

Year Tm	Age	G	GS	CG	GF	IP	BFP	H	R	ER	HR	SH	SF	HB	TBB	IBB	SO	WP	Bk	W	L	Pct	ShO	Sv-Op	Hld	OAvg	OOBP	ERA
1932 NYA	28	1	1	1	0	9.0	44	10	6	3	0	0	0	0	6	1	10	0	0	1	0	1.000	0	0- 0	0	.263	.364	3.00
1936 NYA	32	2	2	1	0	14.0	64	16	10	7	1	3	0	0	5	1	12	0	0	0	1	.000	0	0- 0	0	.286	.344	4.50
1937 NYA	33	1	1	1	0	9.0	37	7	1	1	0	0	0	0	3	0	8	0	0	1	0	1.000	0	0- 0	0	.206	.270	1.00
1938 NYA	34	2	2	2	0	18.0	70	17	4	3	1	0	0	0	2	0	11	0	0	2	0	1.000	0	0- 0	0	.250	.271	1.50
1939 NYA	35	1	1	1	0	9.0	29	4	1	1	0	0	0	0	1	0	4	0	0	1	0	1.000	0	0- 0	0	.143	.172	1.00
1941 NYA	37	1	1	1	0	9.0	35	6	2	1	0	0	0	0	3	0	5	0	0	1	0	1.000	0	0- 0	0	.188	.257	1.00
1942 NYA	38	2	2	1	0	17.2	73	14	8	8	2	2	0	0	7	0	11	0	0	1	1	.500	0	0- 0	0	.219	.296	4.08
WS Totals		10	10	8	0	85.2	704	74	32	24	4	5	0	0	27	2	61	0	0	7	2	.778	0	0-0	0	.231	.291	2.52

World Series — Batting / Fielding

Year Tm	Age	G	AB	H	2B	3B	HR	TB	R	RBI	GW	TBB	IBB	SO	HBP	SH	SF	SB	CS	SB%	GDP	Avg	OBP	SLG	Pos	G	PO	A	E	DP	FPct
1932 NYA	28	2	4	0	0	0	0	0	0	0	0	1	1	1	0	0	0	0	0	—	0	.000	.200	.000	P	1	1	3	0	0	1.000
1936 NYA	32	3	5	0	0	0	0	0	0	0	0	1	0	2	0	0	0	0	0	—	1	.000	.167	.000	P	2	1	3	0	0	1.000
1937 NYA	33	1	4	2	1	0	0	3	0	3	1	0	0	0	0	0	0	0	0	—	1	.500	.500	.750	P	1	0	2	0	0	1.000
1938 NYA	34	2	6	1	0	0	0	1	1	1	1	1	0	0	0	1	0	0	0	—	1	.167	.286	.167	P	2	2	4	0	0	1.000
1939 NYA	35	1	3	1	0	0	0	1	0	0	0	0	0	1	0	0	0	0	0	—	0	.333	.333	.333	P	1	0	3	0	1	1.000
1941 NYA	37	1	3	0	0	0	0	0	0	0	0	0	0	0	0	0	0	0	0	—	0	.000	.000	.000	P	1	0	0	0	0	—
1942 NYA	38	4	9	2	0	0	0	2	0	0	0	0	0	2	0	0	0	0	0	—	1	.222	.222	.222	P	2	0	1	0	0	1.000
WS Totals		14	34	6	1	0	0	7	1	4	2	3	1	6	0	1	0	0	0	—	4	.176	.243	.206	P	10	4	16	0	1	1.000

VERN RUHLE—Vernon Gerald Ruhle—Throws: Right; Bats: Right

Ht: 6'1"; Wt: 185 lbs; Born: 1/25/1951 in Coleman, Michigan; Debut: 9/9/1974

Division Series — Pitching

Year Tm	Age	G	GS	CG	GF	IP	BFP	H	R	ER	HR	SH	SF	HB	TBB	IBB	SO	WP	Bk	W	L	Pct	ShO	Sv-Op	Hld	OAvg	OOBP	ERA
1981 Hou	30	1	1	1	0	8.0	29	4	2	2	1	2	0	0	2	1	1	0	0	0	1	.000	0	0- 0	0	.160	.222	2.25

LCS — Pitching

Year Tm	Age	G	GS	CG	GF	IP	BFP	H	R	ER	HR	SH	SF	HB	TBB	IBB	SO	WP	Bk	W	L	Pct	ShO	Sv-Op	Hld	OAvg	OOBP	ERA
1980 Hou	29	1	1	0	0	7.0	29	8	3	3	0	0	0	0	1	0	3	0	0	0	0	—	0	0- 0	0	.286	.310	3.86
1986 Cal	35	1	0	0	0	0.2	4	2	2	1	0	0	0	0	0	0	0	1	0	0	0	—	0	0- 0	0	.500	.500	13.50
LCS Totals		2	1	0	0	7.2	66	10	5	4	0	0	0	0	1	0	3	1	0	0	0	—	0	0-0	0	.313	.333	4.70
Postseason Totals		3	2	1	0	15.2	124	14	7	6	1	2	0	0	3	1	4	1	0	0	1	.000	0	0-0	0	.246	.283	3.45

Division Series — Batting / Fielding

Year Tm	Age	G	AB	H	2B	3B	HR	TB	R	RBI	GW	TBB	IBB	SO	HBP	SH	SF	SB	CS	SB%	GDP	Avg	OBP	SLG	Pos	G	PO	A	E	DP	FPct
1981 Hou	30	1	1	0	0	0	0	0	0	0	0	0	0	1	0	1	0	0	0	—	0	.000	.000	.000	P	1	2	3	0	0	1.000

LCS — Batting / Fielding

Year Tm	Age	G	AB	H	2B	3B	HR	TB	R	RBI	GW	TBB	IBB	SO	HBP	SH	SF	SB	CS	SB%	GDP	Avg	OBP	SLG	Pos	G	PO	A	E	DP	FPct
1980 Hou	29	1	3	0	0	0	0	0	0	0	0	0	0	1	0	0	0	0	0	—	0	.000	.000	.000	P	1	1	1	0	1	1.000
1986 Cal	35	1	0	0	0	0	0	0	0	0	0	0	0	0	0	0	0	0	0	—	0	—	—	—	P	1	0	0	0	0	—
LCS Totals		2	3	0	0	0	0	0	0	0	0	0	0	1	0	0	0	0	0	—	0	.000	.000	.000	P	2	1	1	0	1	1.000
Postseason Totals		3	4	0	0	0	0	0	0	0	0	0	0	2	0	1	0	0	0	—	0	.000	.000	.000	P	3	3	4	0	1	1.000

BOB RUSH—Robert Ransom Rush—Throws: Right; Bats: Right

Ht: 6'4"; Wt: 205 lbs; Born: 12/21/1925 in Battle Creek, Michigan; Debut: 4/22/1948

World Series — Pitching

Year Tm	Age	G	GS	CG	GF	IP	BFP	H	R	ER	HR	SH	SF	HB	TBB	IBB	SO	WP	Bk	W	L	Pct	ShO	Sv-Op	Hld	OAvg	OOBP	ERA
1958 Mil	32	1	1	0	0	6.0	25	3	2	2	0	0	0	0	5	1	2	0	0	0	1	.000	0	0-0	0	.150	.320	3.00

World Series — Batting / Fielding

Year Tm	Age	G	AB	H	2B	3B	HR	TB	R	RBI	GW	TBB	IBB	SO	HBP	SH	SF	SB	CS	SB%	GDP	Avg	OBP	SLG	Pos	G	PO	A	E	DP	FPct
1958 Mil	32	1	2	0	0	0	0	0	0	0	0	0	0	2	0	0	0	0	0	—	0	.000	.000	.000	P	1	0	3	0	0	1.000

ALLAN RUSSELL—Allan E. Russell—Throws: Right; Bats: Both

Ht: 5'11"; Wt: 165 lbs; Born: 7/31/1893 in Baltimore, Maryland; Debut: 9/13/1915; Died: 10/20/1972

World Series — Pitching

Year Tm	Age	G	GS	CG	GF	IP	BFP	H	R	ER	HR	SH	SF	HB	TBB	IBB	SO	WP	Bk	W	L	Pct	ShO	Sv-Op	Hld	OAvg	OOBP	ERA
1924 Was	31	1	0	0	0	3.0	14	4	2	1	1	1	0	0	0	0	0	0	0	0	0	—	0	0-0	0	.308	.308	3.00

World Series — Batting / Fielding

Year Tm	Age	G	AB	H	2B	3B	HR	TB	R	RBI	GW	TBB	IBB	SO	HBP	SH	SF	SB	CS	SB%	GDP	Avg	OBP	SLG	Pos	G	PO	A	E	DP	FPct
1924 Was	31	1	0	0	0	0	0	0	0	0	0	0	0	0	0	0	0	0	0	—	0	—	—	—	P	1	0	1	0	0	1.000

BILL RUSSELL—William Ellis Russell—Bats: Right; Throws: Right

Ht: 6'0"; Wt: 175 lbs; Born: 10/21/1948 in Pittsburg, Kansas; Debut: 4/7/1969

Division Series — Batting / Fielding

Year Tm	Age	G	AB	H	2B	3B	HR	TB	R	RBI	GW	TBB	IBB	SO	HBP	SH	SF	SB	CS	SB%	GDP	Avg	OBP	SLG	Pos	G	PO	A	E	DP	FPct
1981 LA	32	5	16	4	1	0	0	5	1	2	0	3	0	1	0	0	0	0	0	—	0	.250	.368	.313	SS	5	10	15	2	1	.926

LCS — Batting / Fielding

Year Tm	Age	G	AB	H	2B	3B	HR	TB	R	RBI	GW	TBB	IBB	SO	HBP	SH	SF	SB	CS	SB%	GDP	Avg	OBP	SLG	Pos	G	PO	A	E	DP	FPct
1974 LA	25	4	18	7	0	0	0	7	1	3	0	1	1	0	0	0	0	0	0	—	0	.389	.421	.389	SS	4	13	15	0	6	1.000
1977 LA	28	4	18	5	1	0	0	6	3	2	1	0	0	0	0	0	0	0	0	—	1	.278	.278	.333	SS	4	11	12	2	3	.920
1978 LA	29	4	17	7	1	0	0	8	1	2	1	1	1	1	0	0	0	0	0	—	1	.412	.444	.471	SS	4	4	13	0	3	1.000
1981 LA	32	5	16	5	0	1	0	7	2	1	0	1	1	1	0	2	0	0	0	—	0	.313	.353	.438	SS	5	10	13	0	3	1.000
1983 LA	34	4	14	4	0	0	0	4	1	0	0	2	0	4	0	1	0	1	0	1.00	0	.286	.375	.286	SS	4	4	10	1	3	.933
LCS Totals		21	83	28	2	1	0	32	8	8	2	5	3	6	0	3	0	1	0	1.00	2	.337	.375	.386	SS	21	42	63	3	18	.972

World Series — Batting / Fielding

Year Tm	Age	G	AB	H	2B	3B	HR	TB	R	RBI	GW	TBB	IBB	SO	HBP	SH	SF	SB	CS	SB%	GDP	Avg	OBP	SLG	Pos	G	PO	A	E	DP	FPct
1974 LA	25	5	18	4	0	1	0	6	0	2	0	0	0	2	0	0	0	0	0	—	2	.222	.222	.333	SS	5	4	11	1	2	.938
1977 LA	28	6	26	4	0	1	0	6	3	2	1	1	0	3	0	0	0	0	0	—	0	.154	.185	.231	SS	6	9	21	0	4	1.000
1978 LA	29	6	26	11	2	0	0	13	1	2	0	2	0	2	0	0	0	1	2	.33	1	.423	.464	.500	SS	6	11	20	3	3	.912
1981 LA	32	6	25	6	0	0	0	6	1	2	0	0	0	1	0	1	0	1	1	.50	0	.240	.240	.240	SS	6	4	26	1	3	.968
WS Totals		23	95	25	2	2	0	31	5	8	1	3	0	8	0	1	0	2	3	.40	3	.263	.286	.326	SS	23	28	78	5	12	.955
Postseason Totals		49	194	57	5	3	0	68	14	18	3	11	3	15	0	4	0	3	3	.50	5	.294	.332	.351	SS	49	80	156	10	31	.959

JACK RUSSELL—Jack Erwin Russell—Throws: Right; Bats: Right

Ht: 6'1"; Wt: 178 lbs; Born: 10/24/1905 in Paris, Texas; Debut: 5/5/1926; Died: 11/3/1990

World Series — Pitching

Year Tm	Age	G	GS	CG	GF	IP	BFP	H	R	ER	HR	SH	SF	HB	TBB	IBB	SO	WP	Bk	W	L	Pct	ShO	Sv-Op	Hld	OAvg	OOBP	ERA
1933 Was	27	3	0	0	2	10.1	37	8	1	1	1	0	0	0	0	0	7	0	0	0	1	.000	0	0-0	0	.216	.216	0.87
1938 ChN	32	2	0	0	1	1.2	7	1	0	0	0	0	0	0	1	0	0	0	0	0	0	—	0	0-0	0	.167	.286	0.00
WS Totals		5	0	0	3	12.0	88	9	1	1	1	0	0	0	1	0	7	0	0	0	1	.000	0	0-0	0	.209	.227	0.75

World Series — Batting / Fielding

Year Tm	Age	G	AB	H	2B	3B	HR	TB	R	RBI	GW	TBB	IBB	SO	HBP	SH	SF	SB	CS	SB%	GDP	Avg	OBP	SLG	Pos	G	PO	A	E	DP	FPct
1933 Was	27	3	2	0	0	0	0	0	0	0	0	1	0	2	0	0	0	0	0	—	0	.000	.333	.000	P	3	1	5	0	0	1.000
1938 ChN	32	2	0	0	0	0	0	0	0	0	0	0	0	0	0	0	0	0	0	—	0	—	—	—	P	2	0	0	0	0	—
WS Totals		5	2	0	0	0	0	0	0	0	0	1	0	2	0	0	0	0	0	—	0	.000	.333	.000	P	5	1	5	0	0	1.000

JEFF RUSSELL—Jeffrey Lee Russell—Throws: Right; Bats: Right

Ht: 6'4"; Wt: 200 lbs; Born: 9/2/1961 in Cincinnati, Ohio; Debut: 8/13/1983

Division Series — Pitching

Year Tm	Age	G	GS	CG	GF	IP	BFP	H	R	ER	HR	SH	SF	HB	TBB	IBB	SO	WP	Bk	W	L	Pct	ShO	Sv-Op	Hld	OAvg	OOBP	ERA
1996 Tex	35	2	0	0	0	3.0	11	3	1	1	0	0	0	0	0	0	1	0	0	0	0	—	0	0-1	0	.273	.273	3.00

LCS — Pitching

Year Tm	Age	G	GS	CG	GF	IP	BFP	H	R	ER	HR	SH	SF	HB	TBB	IBB	SO	WP	Bk	W	L	Pct	ShO	Sv-Op	Hld	OAvg	OOBP	ERA
1992 Oak	31	3	0	0	0	2.0	13	2	2	2	0	0	0	0	4	0	0	1	0	1	0	1.000	0	0-1	0	.222	.462	9.00
Postseason Totals		5	0	0	0	5.0	48	5	3	3	0	0	0	0	4	0	1	1	0	1	0	1.000	0	0-2	0	.250	.375	5.40

Division Series — Batting / Fielding

Year Tm	Age	G	AB	H	2B	3B	HR	TB	R	RBI	GW	TBB	IBB	SO	HBP	SH	SF	SB	CS	SB%	GDP	Avg	OBP	SLG	Pos	G	PO	A	E	DP	FPct
1996 Tex	35	2	0	0	0	0	0	0	0	0	0	0	0	0	0	0	0	0	0	—	0	—	—	—	P	2	0	0	0	0	—

LCS — Batting / Fielding

Year Tm	Age	G	AB	H	2B	3B	HR	TB	R	RBI	GW	TBB	IBB	SO	HBP	SH	SF	SB	CS	SB%	GDP	Avg	OBP	SLG	Pos	G	PO	A	E	DP	FPct
1992 Oak	31	3	0	0	0	0	0	0	0	0	0	0	0	0	0	0	0	0	0	—	0	—	—	—	P	3	0	0	0	0	—
Postseason Totals		5	0	0	0	0	0	0	0	0	0	0	0	0	0	0	0	0	0	—	0	—	—	—	P	5	0	0	0	0	—

REB RUSSELL—Ewell Albert Russell—Throws: Left; Bats: Left

Ht: 5'11"; Wt: 185 lbs; Born: 4/12/1889 in Jackson, Mississippi; Debut: 4/18/1913; Died: 9/30/1973

World Series — Pitching

Year Tm	Age	G	GS	CG	GF	IP	BFP	H	R	ER	HR	SH	SF	HB	TBB	IBB	SO	WP	Bk	W	L	Pct	ShO	Sv-Op	Hld	OAvg	OOBP	ERA
1917 ChA	28	1	1	0	0	0.0	3	2	2	2	0	0	0	0	1	0	0	0	0	0	0	—	0	0-0	0	1.000	1.000	—

World Series — Batting / Fielding

Year Tm	Age	G	AB	H	2B	3B	HR	TB	R	RBI	GW	TBB	IBB	SO	HBP	SH	SF	SB	CS	SB%	GDP	Avg	OBP	SLG	Pos	G	PO	A	E	DP	FPct
1917 ChA	28	1	0	0	0	0	0	0	0	0	0	0	0	0	0	0	0	0	0	—	0	—	—	—	P	1	0	0	0	0	—

RIP RUSSELL—Glen David Russell—Bats: Right; Throws: Right

Ht: 6'1"; Wt: 180 lbs; Born: 1/26/1915 in Los Angeles, California; Debut: 5/5/1939; Died: 9/26/1976

World Series — Batting / Fielding

Year Tm	Age	G	AB	H	2B	3B	HR	TB	R	RBI	GW	TBB	IBB	SO	HBP	SH	SF	SB	CS	SB%	GDP	Avg	OBP	SLG	Pos	G	PO	A	E	DP	FPct
1946 Bos	31	2	2	2	0	0	0	2	1	0	0	0	0	0	0	0	0	0	0	—	0	1.000	1.000	1.000	3B	1	0	0	0	0	—

MARIUS RUSSO—Marius Ugo Russo—Nickname: Lefty—Throws: Left; Bats: Right

Ht: 6'1"; Wt: 190 lbs; Born: 7/19/1914 in Brooklyn, New York; Debut: 6/6/1939

World Series — Pitching

Year Tm	Age	G	GS	CG	GF	IP	BFP	H	R	ER	HR	SH	SF	HB	TBB	IBB	SO	WP	Bk	W	L	Pct	ShO	Sv-Op	Hld	OAvg	OOBP	ERA
1941 NYA	27	1	1	1	0	9.0	32	4	1	1	0	0	0	0	2	0	5	0	0	1	0	1.000	0	0-0	0	.133	.188	1.00
1943 NYA	29	1	1	1	0	9.0	37	7	1	0	0	0	0	0	1	1	2	0	0	1	0	1.000	0	0-0	0	.194	.216	0.00
WS Totals		2	2	2	0	18.0	138	11	2	1	0	0	0	0	3	1	7	0	0	2	0	1.000	0	0-0	0	.167	.203	0.50

World Series — Batting / Fielding

Year Tm	Age	G	AB	H	2B	3B	HR	TB	R	RBI	GW	TBB	IBB	SO	HBP	SH	SF	SB	CS	SB%	GDP	Avg	OBP	SLG	Pos	G	PO	A	E	DP	FPct
1941 NYA	27	1	4	0	0	0	0	0	0	0	0	0	0	1	0	0	0	0	0	—	0	.000	.000	.000	P	1	0	4	0	0	1.000
1943 NYA	29	1	3	2	2	0	0	4	1	0	0	1	0	1	0	0	0	0	0	—	0	.667	.750	1.333	P	1	0	2	0	0	1.000
WS Totals		2	7	2	2	0	0	4	1	0	0	1	0	2	0	0	0	0	0	—	0	.286	.375	.571	P	2	0	6	0	0	1.000

BABE RUTH

(HOF 1936-W)—George Herman Ruth—Nicknames: The Bambino, The Sultan of Swat—B: L; T: L

Ht: 6'2"; Wt: 215 lbs; Born: 2/6/1895 in Baltimore, Md.; Deb.: 7/11/1914; Died: 8/16/1948

World Series		Batting																							Fielding						
Year Tm	Age	G	AB	H	2B	3B	HR	TB	R	RBI	GW	TBB	IBB	SO	HBP	SH	SF	SB	CS	SB%	GDP	Avg	OBP	SLG	Pos	G	PO	A	E	DP	FPct
1915 Bos	20	1	1	0	0	0	0	0	0	0	0	0	0	0	0	0	0	0	0	—	0	.000	.000	.000	—						
1916 Bos	21	1	5	0	0	0	0	0	0	1	0	0	0	2	0	0	0	0	0	—	0	.000	.000	.000	P	1	2	4	0	0	1.000
1918 Bos	23	3	5	1	0	1	0	3	0	2	0	0	0	2	0	1	0	0	0	—	0	.200	.200	.600	P	2	0	5	0	1	1.000
																									OF	2	1	0	0	0	1.000
1921 NYA	26	6	16	5	0	0	1	8	3	4	1	5	0	8	0	0	0	2	1	.67	0	.313	.476	.500	OF	5	9	0	0	0	1.000
1922 NYA	27	5	17	2	1	0	0	3	1	1	0	2	0	3	1	1	0	0	1	.00	0	.118	.250	.176	OF	5	9	0	0	0	1.000
1923 NYA-*M*	28	6	19	7	1	1	3	19	8	3	1	8	0	6	0	0	0	0	1	.00	0	.368	.556	1.000	1B	1	2	0	0	0	1.000
																									OF	6	15	0	1	0	.938
1926 NYA	31	7	20	6	0	0	4	18	6	5	0	11	1	2	0	0	0	1	1	.50	0	.300	.548	.900	OF	7	8	2	0	0	1.000
1927 NYA	32	4	15	6	0	0	2	12	4	7	1	2	1	2	0	0	1	1	1	.50	1	.400	.444	.800	OF	4	10	0	0	0	1.000
1928 NYA	33	4	16	10	3	0	3	22	9	4	0	1	0	2	0	0	0	0	0	—	1	.625	.647	1.375	OF	4	6	1	0	0	1.000
1932 NYA	37	4	15	5	0	0	2	11	6	6	1	4	0	3	1	0	0	0	0	—	1	.333	.500	.733	OF	4	6	0	1	0	.857
WS Totals		41	129	42	5	2	15	96	37	33	4	33	2	30	2	2	1	4	5	.44	3	.326	.467	.744	OF	37	64	3	2	0	.971

World Series		Pitching																										
Year Tm	Age	G	GS	CG	GF	IP	BFP	H	R	ER	HR	SH	SF	HB	TBB	IBB	SO	WP	Bk	W	L	Pct	ShO	Sv-Op	Hld	OAvg	OOBP	ERA
1916 Bos	21	1	1	1	0	14.0	48	6	1	1	1	2	0	0	3	0	4	0	0	1	0	1.000	0	0- 0	0	.140	.196	0.64
1918 Bos	23	2	2	1	0	17.0	68	13	2	2	0	1	0	1	7	0	4	1	0	2	0	1.000	1	0- 0	0	.220	.313	1.06
WS Totals		3	3	2	0	31.0	232	19	3	3	1	3	0	1	10	0	8	1	0	3	0	1.000	1	0-0	0	.186	.265	0.87

JOHNNY RUTHERFORD

—John William Rutherford—Nickname: Doc—Throws: Right; Bats: Left

Ht: 5'10"; Wt: 170 lbs; Born: 5/5/1925 in Belleville, Ontario; Debut: 4/30/1952

World Series		Pitching																										
Year Tm	Age	G	GS	CG	GF	IP	BFP	H	R	ER	HR	SH	SF	HB	TBB	IBB	SO	WP	Bk	W	L	Pct	ShO	Sv-Op	Hld	OAvg	OOBP	ERA
1952 Bro	27	1	0	0	1	1.0	5	1	1	1	0	0	0	0	1	0	1	0	0	0	0	—	0	0- 0	0	.250	.400	9.00

World Series		Batting																							Fielding						
Year Tm	Age	G	AB	H	2B	3B	HR	TB	R	RBI	GW	TBB	IBB	SO	HBP	SH	SF	SB	CS	SB%	GDP	Avg	OBP	SLG	Pos	G	PO	A	E	DP	FPct
1952 Bro	27	1	0	0	0	0	0	0	0	0	0	0	0	0	0	0	0	0	0	—	0	—	—	—	P	1	0	0	0	0	—

DICK RUTHVEN

—Richard David Ruthven—Nickname: Rufus—Throws: Right; Bats: Right

Ht: 6'3"; Wt: 190 lbs; Born: 3/27/1951 in Sacramento, California; Debut: 4/17/1973

Division Series		Pitching																										
Year Tm	Age	G	GS	CG	GF	IP	BFP	H	R	ER	HR	SH	SF	HB	TBB	IBB	SO	WP	Bk	W	L	Pct	ShO	Sv-Op	Hld	OAvg	OOBP	ERA
1981 Phi	30	1	1	0	0	4.0	17	3	3	2	1	0	0	0	1	0	0	0	0	0	1	.000	0	0- 0	0	.188	.235	4.50
LCS		**Pitching**																										
Year Tm	Age	G	GS	CG	GF	IP	BFP	H	R	ER	HR	SH	SF	HB	TBB	IBB	SO	WP	Bk	W	L	Pct	ShO	Sv-Op	Hld	OAvg	OOBP	ERA
1978 Phi	27	1	1	0	0	4.2	20	6	3	3	1	0	0	0	0	0	3	0	0	0	1	.000	0	0- 0	0	.300	.300	5.79
1980 Phi	29	2	1	0	1	9.0	35	3	2	2	0	1	0	0	5	0	4	0	0	1	0	1.000	0	0- 0	0	.103	.235	2.00
LCS Totals		3	2	0	1	13.2	110	9	5	5	1	1	0	0	5	0	7	0	0	1	1	.500	0	0-0	0	.184	.259	3.29
World Series		**Pitching**																										
Year Tm	Age	G	GS	CG	GF	IP	BFP	H	R	ER	HR	SH	SF	HB	TBB	IBB	SO	WP	Bk	W	L	Pct	ShO	Sv-Op	Hld	OAvg	OOBP	ERA
1980 Phi	29	1	1	0	0	9.0	35	9	3	3	2	0	0	0	0	0	7	0	0	0	0	—	0	0- 0	0	.257	.257	3.00
Postseason Totals		5	4	0	1	26.2	214	21	11	10	4	1	0	0	6	0	14	0	0	1	2	.333	0	0-0	0	.210	.255	3.38

Division Series		Batting																							Fielding						
Year Tm	Age	G	AB	H	2B	3B	HR	TB	R	RBI	GW	TBB	IBB	SO	HBP	SH	SF	SB	CS	SB%	GDP	Avg	OBP	SLG	Pos	G	PO	A	E	DP	FPct
1981 Phi	30	1	1	0	0	0	0	0	0	0	0	0	0	0	0	0	0	0	0	—	0	.000	.000	.000	P	1	1	1	0	0	1.000
LCS		**Batting**																							**Fielding**						
Year Tm	Age	G	AB	H	2B	3B	HR	TB	R	RBI	GW	TBB	IBB	SO	HBP	SH	SF	SB	CS	SB%	GDP	Avg	OBP	SLG	Pos	G	PO	A	E	DP	FPct
1978 Phi	27	1	1	0	0	0	0	0	0	0	0	0	0	1	0	0	0	0	0	—	0	.000	.000	.000	P	1	0	0	0	0	—
1980 Phi	29	2	2	0	0	0	0	0	0	0	0	0	0	2	0	0	0	0	0	—	0	.000	.000	.000	P	2	2	0	0	0	1.000
LCS Totals		3	3	0	0	0	0	0	0	0	0	0	0	3	0	0	0	0	0	—	0	.000	.000	.000	P	3	2	0	0	0	1.000
World Series		**Batting**																							**Fielding**						
Year Tm	Age	G	AB	H	2B	3B	HR	TB	R	RBI	GW	TBB	IBB	SO	HBP	SH	SF	SB	CS	SB%	GDP	Avg	OBP	SLG	Pos	G	PO	A	E	DP	FPct
1980 Phi	29	1	0	0	0	0	0	0	0	0	0	0	0	0	0	0	0	0	0	—	0	—	—	—	P	1	0	0	0	0	—
Postseason Totals		5	4	0	0	0	0	0	0	0	0	0	0	3	0	0	0	0	0	—	0	.000	.000	.000	P	5	3	1	0	0	1.000

BLONDY RYAN

—John Collins Ryan—Bats: Right; Throws: Right

Ht: 6'1"; Wt: 178 lbs; Born: 1/4/1906 in Lynn, Massachusetts; Debut: 7/13/1930; Died: 11/28/1959

World Series		Batting																							Fielding						
Year Tm	Age	G	AB	H	2B	3B	HR	TB	R	RBI	GW	TBB	IBB	SO	HBP	SH	SF	SB	CS	SB%	GDP	Avg	OBP	SLG	Pos	G	PO	A	E	DP	FPct
1933 NYG	27	5	18	5	0	0	0	5	0	1	1	1	0	5	0	1	0	0	0	—	0	.278	.316	.278	SS	5	9	19	1	2	.966
1937 NYG	31	1	1	0	0	0	0	0	0	0	0	0	0	1	0	0	0	0	0	—	0	.000	.000	.000	—						
WS Totals		6	19	5	0	0	0	5	0	1	1	1	0	6	0	1	0	0	0	—	0	.263	.300	.263	SS	5	9	19	1	2	.966

CONNIE RYAN

—Cornelius Joseph Ryan—Bats: Right; Throws: Right

Ht: 5'11"; Wt: 175 lbs; Born: 2/27/1920 in New Orleans, Louisiana; Debut: 4/14/1942; Died: 1/3/1996

World Series		Batting																							Fielding						
Year Tm	Age	G	AB	H	2B	3B	HR	TB	R	RBI	GW	TBB	IBB	SO	HBP	SH	SF	SB	CS	SB%	GDP	Avg	OBP	SLG	Pos	G	PO	A	E	DP	FPct
1948 Bos	28	2	1	0	0	0	0	0	0	0	0	0	0	1	0	0	0	0	0	—	0	.000	.000	.000	—						

MIKE RYAN

—Michael James Ryan—Bats: Right; Throws: Right

Ht: 6'2"; Wt: 205 lbs; Born: 11/25/1941 in Haverhill, Massachusetts; Debut: 10/3/1964

World Series		Batting																							Fielding						
Year Tm	Age	G	AB	H	2B	3B	HR	TB	R	RBI	GW	TBB	IBB	SO	HBP	SH	SF	SB	CS	SB%	GDP	Avg	OBP	SLG	Pos	G	PO	A	E	DP	FPct
1967 Bos	25	1	2	0	0	0	0	0	0	0	0	0	0	1	0	0	0	0	0	—	0	.000	.000	.000	C	1	4	0	0	0	1.000

NOLAN RYAN

—Lynn Nolan Ryan—Nickname: The Ryan Express—Throws: Right; Bats: Right

Ht: 6'2"; Wt: 170 lbs; Born: 1/31/1947 in Refugio, Texas; Debut: 9/11/1966

Division Series		Pitching																										
Year Tm	Age	G	GS	CG	GF	IP	BFP	H	R	ER	HR	SH	SF	HB	TBB	IBB	SO	WP	Bk	W	L	Pct	ShO	Sv-Op	Hld	OAvg	OOBP	ERA
1981 Hou	34	2	2	1	0	15.0	56	6	4	3	1	0	0	0	3	0	14	0	0	1	1	.500	0	0- 0	0	.113	.161	1.80
LCS		**Pitching**																										
Year Tm	Age	G	GS	CG	GF	IP	BFP	H	R	ER	HR	SH	SF	HB	TBB	IBB	SO	WP	Bk	W	L	Pct	ShO	Sv-Op	Hld	OAvg	OOBP	ERA
1969 NYN	22	1	0	0	1	7.0	26	3	2	2	1	0	0	0	2	1	7	0	0	1	0	1.000	0	0- 0	0	.125	.192	2.57
1979 Cal	32	1	1	0	0	7.0	27	4	3	1	0	0	1	0	3	0	8	1	0	0	0	—	0	0- 0	0	.174	.259	1.29
1980 Hou	33	2	2	0	0	13.1	55	16	8	8	0	2	0	0	3	0	14	0	0	0	0	—	0	0- 0	0	.320	.358	5.40
1986 Hou	39	2	2	0	0	14.0	52	9	6	6	1	0	1	0	1	0	17	0	0	0	1	.000	0	0- 0	0	.180	.192	3.86
LCS Totals		6	5	0	1	41.1	320	32	19	17	2	2	2	0	9	1	46	1	0	1	1	.500	0	0-0	0	.218	.259	3.70
World Series		**Pitching**																										
Year Tm	Age	G	GS	CG	GF	IP	BFP	H	R	ER	HR	SH	SF	HB	TBB	IBB	SO	WP	Bk	W	L	Pct	ShO	Sv-Op	Hld	OAvg	OOBP	ERA
1969 NYN	22	1	0	0	1	2.1	10	1	0	0	0	0	0	0	2	0	3	0	0	0	0	—	0	1- 1	0	.125	.300	0.00
Postseason Totals		9	7	1	2	58.2	452	39	23	20	3	2	2	0	14	1	63	1	0	2	2	.500	0	1-1	0	.188	.237	3.07

Division Series		Batting																							Fielding						
Year Tm	Age	G	AB	H	2B	3B	HR	TB	R	RBI	GW	TBB	IBB	SO	HBP	SH	SF	SB	CS	SB%	GDP	Avg	OBP	SLG	Pos	G	PO	A	E	DP	FPct
1981 Hou	34	2	4	1	0	0	0	1	0	0	0	1	0	1	0	0	0	0	0	—	0	.250	.400	.250	P	2	1	4	0	1	1.000
LCS		**Batting**																							**Fielding**						
Year Tm	Age	G	AB	H	2B	3B	HR	TB	R	RBI	GW	TBB	IBB	SO	HBP	SH	SF	SB	CS	SB%	GDP	Avg	OBP	SLG	Pos	G	PO	A	E	DP	FPct
1969 NYN	22	1	4	2	0	0	0	2	1	0	0	0	0	1	0	0	0	0	0	—	0	.500	.500	.500	P	1	1	0	0	0	1.000
1979 Cal	32	1	0	0	0	0	0	0	0	0	0	0	0	0	0	0	0	0	0	—	0	—	—	—	P	1	0	0	0	0	—
1980 Hou	33	2	4	0	0	0	0	0	1	0	0	1	0	2	0	1	0	0	0	—	0	.000	.200	.000	P	2	1	3	0	0	1.000
1986 Hou	39	2	4	0	0	0	0	0	0	0	0	0	0	2	0	0	0	0	0	—	0	.000	.000	.000	P	2	0	2	0	0	1.000
LCS Totals		6	12	2	0	0	0	2	2	0	0	1	0	5	0	1	0	0	0	—	0	.167	.231	.167	P	6	2	5	0	0	1.000

World Series Year Tm	Age	G	AB	H	2B	3B	HR	TB	R	RBI	GW	TBB	IBB	SO	HBP	SH	SF	SB	CS	SB%	GDP	Avg	OBP	SLG	Pos	G	PO	A	E	DP	FPct
1969 NYN	22	1	0	0	0	0	0	0	0	0	0	0	0	0	0	0	0	0	0	—	0	—	—	—	P	1	0	0	0	0	—
Postseason Totals		9	16	3	0	0	0	3	2	0	0	2	0	6	0	1	0	0	0	—	0	.188	.278	.188	P	9	3	9	0	1	1.000

ROSY RYAN—Wilfred Patrick Dolan Ryan—Throws: Right; Bats: Left

Ht: 6'0"; Wt: 185 lbs; Born: 3/15/1898 in Worcester, Massachusetts; Debut: 9/7/1919; Died: 12/10/1980

World Series (Pitching) Year Tm	Age	G	GS	CG	GF	IP	BFP	H	R	ER	HR	SH	SF	HB	TBB	IBB	SO	WP	Bk	W	L	Pct	ShO	Sv-Op	Hld	OAvg	OOBP	ERA
1922 NYG	24	1	0	0	1	2.0	6	1	0	0	0	0	0	0	0	0	2	0	0	1	0	1.000	0	0-0	0	.167	.167	0.00
1923 NYG	25	3	0	0	2	9.1	39	11	4	1	0	0	1	0	3	0	3	1	0	1	0	1.000	0	0-1	0	.314	.359	0.96
1924 NYG	26	2	0	0	1	5.2	28	7	2	2	0	0	0	0	4	0	3	0	0	0	0	—	0	0-0	0	.292	.393	3.18
WS Totals		6	0	0	4	17.0	146	19	6	3	0	0	1	0	7	0	8	1	0	2	0	1.000	0	0-1	0	.292	.356	1.59

World Series (Batting/Fielding) Year Tm	Age	G	AB	H	2B	3B	HR	TB	R	RBI	GW	TBB	IBB	SO	HBP	SH	SF	SB	CS	SB%	GDP	Avg	OBP	SLG	Pos	G	PO	A	E	DP	FPct
1922 NYG	24	1	0	0	0	0	0	0	0	0	0	0	0	0	0	0	0	0	0	—	0	—	—	—	P	1	0	0	0	0	—
1923 NYG	25	3	2	0	0	0	0	0	0	0	0	0	0	1	0	0	0	0	0	—	0	.000	.000	.000	P	3	1	2	0	1	1.000
1924 NYG	26	2	2	1	0	0	1	4	1	1	0	0	0	0	0	1	0	0	0	—	0	.500	.500	2.000	P	2	0	1	0	0	1.000
WS Totals		6	4	1	0	0	1	4	1	1	0	0	0	1	0	1	0	0	0	—	0	.250	.250	1.000	P	6	1	3	0	1	1.000

MIKE RYBA—Dominic Joseph Ryba—Throws: Right; Bats: Right

Ht: 5'11"; Wt: 180 lbs; Born: 6/9/1903 in DeLancey, Pennsylvania; Debut: 9/22/1935; Died: 12/13/1971

World Series (Pitching) Year Tm	Age	G	GS	CG	GF	IP	BFP	H	R	ER	HR	SH	SF	HB	TBB	IBB	SO	WP	Bk	W	L	Pct	ShO	Sv-Op	Hld	OAvg	OOBP	ERA
1946 Bos	43	1	0	0	0	0.2	6	2	1	0	0	1	0	0	1	0	0	0	0	0	0	—	0	0-0	0	.500	.600	0.00

World Series (Batting/Fielding) Year Tm	Age	G	AB	H	2B	3B	HR	TB	R	RBI	GW	TBB	IBB	SO	HBP	SH	SF	SB	CS	SB%	GDP	Avg	OBP	SLG	Pos	G	PO	A	E	DP	FPct
1946 Bos	43	1	0	0	0	0	0	0	0	0	0	0	0	0	0	0	0	0	0	—	0	—	—	—	P	1	0	0	1	0	.000

BRET SABERHAGEN—Bret William Saberhagen—Throws: Right; Bats: Right

Ht: 6'1"; Wt: 160 lbs; Born: 4/11/1964 in Chicago Heights, Illinois; Debut: 4/4/1984

Division Series (Pitching) Year Tm	Age	G	GS	CG	GF	IP	BFP	H	R	ER	HR	SH	SF	HB	TBB	IBB	SO	WP	Bk	W	L	Pct	ShO	Sv-Op	Hld	OAvg	OOBP	ERA
1995 Col	31	1	1	0	0	4.0	20	7	6	5	1	0	0	0	1	0	3	0	0	0	1	.000	0	0-0	0	.368	.400	11.25
LCS																												
1984 KC	20	1	1	0	0	8.0	32	6	3	2	1	0	0	0	1	0	5	0	0	0	0	—	0	0-0	0	.194	.219	2.25
1985 KC-C	21	2	2	0	0	7.1	35	12	5	5	2	0	0	1	2	0	6	0	0	0	0	—	0	0-0	0	.375	.429	6.14
LCS Totals		3	3	0	0	15.1	134	18	8	7	3	0	0	1	3	0	11	0	0	0	0	—	0	0-0	0	.286	.328	4.11
World Series																												
1985 KC-C	21	2	2	2	0	18.0	65	11	1	1	0	0	0	0	1	0	10	0	0	2	0	1.000	1	0-0	0	.172	.185	0.50
Postseason Totals		6	6	2	0	37.1	304	36	15	13	4	0	0	1	5	0	24	0	0	2	1	.667	1	0-0	0	.247	.276	3.13

Division Series (Batting/Fielding) Year Tm	Age	G	AB	H	2B	3B	HR	TB	R	RBI	GW	TBB	IBB	SO	HBP	SH	SF	SB	CS	SB%	GDP	Avg	OBP	SLG	Pos	G	PO	A	E	DP	FPct
1995 Col	31	1	1	0	0	0	0	0	0	0	0	0	0	0	0	0	0	0	0	—	0	.000	.000	.000	P	1	0	1	0	0	1.000
LCS																															
1984 KC	20	1	0	0	0	0	0	0	0	0	0	0	0	0	0	0	0	0	0	—	0	—	—	—	P	1	1	1	1	0	.667
1985 KC	21	2	0	0	0	0	0	0	0	0	0	0	0	0	0	0	0	0	0	—	0	—	—	—	P	2	2	1	0	1	1.000
LCS Totals		3	0	0	0	0	0	0	0	0	0	0	0	0	0	0	0	0	0	—	0	—	—	—	P	3	3	2	1	1	.833
World Series																															
1985 KC	21	2	7	0	0	0	0	0	1	0	0	0	0	4	0	1	0	0	0	—	0	.000	.000	.000	P	2	0	0	0	0	—
Postseason Totals		6	8	0	0	0	0	0	1	0	0	0	0	4	0	1	0	0	0	—	0	.000	.000	.000	P	6	3	3	1	1	.857

CHRIS SABO—Christopher Andrew Sabo—Nickname: Spuds—Bats: Right; Throws: Right

Ht: 5'11"; Wt: 185 lbs; Born: 1/19/1962 in Detroit, Michigan; Debut: 4/4/1988

LCS (Batting/Fielding) Year Tm	Age	G	AB	H	2B	3B	HR	TB	R	RBI	GW	TBB	IBB	SO	HBP	SH	SF	SB	CS	SB%	GDP	Avg	OBP	SLG	Pos	G	PO	A	E	DP	FPct
1990 Cin	28	6	22	5	0	0	1	8	1	3	1	1	1	4	0	0	1	0	0	—	0	.227	.250	.364	3B	6	7	7	0	1	1.000
World Series																															
1990 Cin	28	4	16	9	1	0	2	16	2	5	0	2	0	2	0	0	0	0	1	.00	0	.563	.611	1.000	3B	4	3	14	0	0	1.000
Postseason Totals		10	38	14	1	0	3	24	3	8	1	3	1	6	0	0	1	0	1	.00	0	.368	.405	.632	3B	10	10	21	0	1	1.000

RAY SADECKI—Raymond Michael Sadecki—Throws: Left; Bats: Left

Ht: 5'11"; Wt: 180 lbs; Born: 12/26/1940 in Kansas City, Kansas; Debut: 5/19/1960

World Series (Pitching) Year Tm	Age	G	GS	CG	GF	IP	BFP	H	R	ER	HR	SH	SF	HB	TBB	IBB	SO	WP	Bk	W	L	Pct	ShO	Sv-Op	Hld	OAvg	OOBP	ERA
1964 StL	23	2	2	0	0	6.1	33	12	7	6	1	0	0	0	5	0	2	0	0	1	0	1.000	0	0-0	0	.429	.515	8.53
1973 NYN	32	4	0	0	1	4.2	20	5	1	1	0	0	0	0	1	0	6	0	0	0	0	—	0	1-1	0	.263	.300	1.93
WS Totals		6	2	0	1	11.0	106	17	8	7	1	0	0	0	6	0	8	0	0	1	0	1.000	0	1-1	0	.362	.434	5.73

World Series (Batting/Fielding) Year Tm	Age	G	AB	H	2B	3B	HR	TB	R	RBI	GW	TBB	IBB	SO	HBP	SH	SF	SB	CS	SB%	GDP	Avg	OBP	SLG	Pos	G	PO	A	E	DP	FPct
1964 StL	23	2	2	1	0	0	0	1	0	1	0	0	0	1	0	0	0	0	0	—	0	.500	.500	.500	P	2	0	1	0	0	1.000
1973 NYN	32	4	0	0	0	0	0	0	0	0	0	0	0	0	0	0	0	0	0	—	0	—	—	—	P	4	0	1	0	0	1.000
WS Totals		6	2	1	0	0	0	1	0	1	0	0	0	1	0	0	0	0	0	—	0	.500	.500	.500	P	6	0	2	0	0	1.000

JOHNNY SAIN—John Franklin Sain—Throws: Right; Bats: Right

Ht: 6'2"; Wt: 185 lbs; Born: 9/25/1917 in Havana, Arkansas; Debut: 4/24/1942

World Series (Pitching) Year Tm	Age	G	GS	CG	GF	IP	BFP	H	R	ER	HR	SH	SF	HB	TBB	IBB	SO	WP	Bk	W	L	Pct	ShO	Sv-Op	Hld	OAvg	OOBP	ERA
1948 Bos	31	2	2	2	0	17.0	61	9	2	2	1	2	0	0	0	0	9	0	0	1	1	.500	1	0-0	0	.153	.153	1.06
1951 NYA	34	1	0	0	0	2.0	12	4	2	2	0	0	0	0	2	0	2	0	0	0	0	—	0	0-0	1	.400	.500	9.00
1952 NYA	35	1	0	0	1	6.0	28	6	2	2	0	1	0	1	3	2	3	0	0	0	1	.000	0	0-1	0	.261	.370	3.00
1953 NYA	36	2	0	0	1	5.2	26	8	3	3	1	0	0	0	1	0	1	0	0	1	0	1.000	0	0-1	0	.320	.346	4.76
WS Totals		6	2	2	2	30.2	254	27	9	9	2	3	0	1	6	2	15	0	0	2	2	.500	1	0-2	1	.231	.274	2.64

World Series (Batting/Fielding) Year Tm	Age	G	AB	H	2B	3B	HR	TB	R	RBI	GW	TBB	IBB	SO	HBP	SH	SF	SB	CS	SB%	GDP	Avg	OBP	SLG	Pos	G	PO	A	E	DP	FPct
1948 Bos	31	2	5	1	0	0	0	1	0	0	0	0	0	0	0	1	0	0	0	—	0	.200	.200	.200	P	2	2	2	0	0	1.000
1951 NYA	34	1	1	0	0	0	0	0	0	0	0	0	0	0	0	0	0	0	0	—	0	.000	.000	.000	P	1	0	0	0	0	—
1952 NYA	35	2	3	0	0	0	0	0	0	0	0	0	0	0	0	0	0	0	0	—	0	.000	.000	.000	P	1	0	2	0	0	1.000
1953 NYA	36	2	2	1	1	0	0	2	1	2	0	0	0	1	0	0	0	0	0	—	0	.500	.500	1.000	P	2	0	0	0	0	—
WS Totals		7	11	2	1	0	0	3	1	2	0	0	0	1	0	1	0	0	0	—	0	.182	.182	.273	P	6	2	4	0	0	1.000

LENN SAKATA—Lenn Haruki Sakata—Bats: Right; Throws: Right

Ht: 5'9"; Wt: 160 lbs; Born: 6/8/1954 in Honolulu, Hawaii; Debut: 7/21/1977

World Series (Batting/Fielding) Year Tm	Age	G	AB	H	2B	3B	HR	TB	R	RBI	GW	TBB	IBB	SO	HBP	SH	SF	SB	CS	SB%	GDP	Avg	OBP	SLG	Pos	G	PO	A	E	DP	FPct
1983 Bal	29	1	1	0	0	0	0	0	0	0	0	0	0	0	0	0	0	0	0	—	0	.000	.000	.000	2B	1	2	2	0	1	1.000

LUIS SALAZAR—Luis Ernesto Salazar—Bats: Right; Throws: Right

Ht: 5'9"; Wt: 185 lbs; Born: 5/19/1956 in Barcelona, Venezuela; Debut: 8/15/1980

LCS — Batting / Fielding

Year Tm	Age	G	AB	H	2B	3B	HR	TB	R	RBI	GW	TBB	IBB	SO	HBP	SH	SF	SB	CS	SB%	GDP	Avg	OBP	SLG	Pos	G	PO	A	E	DP	FPct
1984 SD	28	3	5	1	0	1	0	3	0	0	0	0	0	1	0	0	0	0	1	.00	0	.200	.200	.600	3B	1	1	3	0	0	1.000
																									OF	2	0	0	0	0	—
1989 ChN	33	5	19	7	0	1	1	12	2	2	0	0	0	0	0	0	0	0	0	—	1	.368	.368	.632	3B	5	4	5	1	0	.900
LCS Totals		8	24	8	0	2	1	15	2	2	0	0	0	1	0	0	0	0	1	.00	1	.333	.333	.625	3B	6	5	8	1	0	.929

World Series — Batting / Fielding

Year Tm	Age	G	AB	H	2B	3B	HR	TB	R	RBI	GW	TBB	IBB	SO	HBP	SH	SF	SB	CS	SB%	GDP	Avg	OBP	SLG	Pos	G	PO	A	E	DP	FPct
1984 SD	28	4	3	1	0	0	0	1	0	0	0	0	0	0	0	0	0	0	1	.00	0	.333	.333	.333	3B	1	0	0	0	0	—
																									OF	2	1	0	0	0	1.000
Postseason Totals		12	27	9	0	2	1	16	2	2	0	0	0	1	0	0	0	0	2	.00	1	.333	.333	.593	3B	7	5	8	1	0	.929

BILL SALKELD—William Franklin Salkeld—Bats: Left; Throws: Right

Ht: 5'10"; Wt: 190 lbs; Born: 3/8/1917 in Pocatello, Idaho; Debut: 4/18/1945; Died: 4/22/1967

World Series — Batting / Fielding

Year Tm	Age	G	AB	H	2B	3B	HR	TB	R	RBI	GW	TBB	IBB	SO	HBP	SH	SF	SB	CS	SB%	GDP	Avg	OBP	SLG	Pos	G	PO	A	E	DP	FPct
1948 Bos	31	5	9	2	0	0	1	5	2	1	0	5	0	1	0	1	0	0	0	—	0	.222	.500	.556	C	4	19	1	0	0	1.000

SLIM SALLEE—Harry Franklin Sallee—Throws: Left; Bats: Left

Ht: 6'3"; Wt: 180 lbs; Born: 2/3/1885 in Higginsport, Ohio; Debut: 4/16/1908; Died: 3/22/1950

World Series — Pitching

Year Tm	Age	G	GS	CG	GF	IP	BFP	H	R	ER	HR	SH	SF	HB	TBB	IBB	SO	WP	Bk	W	L	Pct	ShO	Sv-Op	Hld	OAvg	OOBP	ERA
1917 NYG	32	2	2	1	0	15.1	69	20	10	9	1	2	0	0	4	0	4	0	0	0	2	.000	0	0- 0	0	.317	.358	5.28
1919 Cin	34	2	2	1	0	13.1	59	19	6	2	0	3	0	0	1	0	2	0	1	1	1	.500	0	0- 0	0	.345	.357	1.35
WS Totals		4	4	2	0	28.2	256	39	16	11	1	5	0	0	5	0	6	0	1	1	3	.250	0	0-0	0	.331	.358	3.45

World Series — Batting / Fielding

Year Tm	Age	G	AB	H	2B	3B	HR	TB	R	RBI	GW	TBB	IBB	SO	HBP	SH	SF	SB	CS	SB%	GDP	Avg	OBP	SLG	Pos	G	PO	A	E	DP	FPct
1917 NYG	32	2	6	1	0	0	0	1	0	1	0	0	0	2	0	1	0	0	0	—	0	.167	.167	.167	P	2	0	8	0	0	1.000
1919 Cin	34	2	4	0	0	0	0	0	0	0	0	0	0	0	0	0	0	0	0	—	0	.000	.000	.000	P	2	1	4	0	0	1.000
WS Totals		4	10	1	0	0	0	1	0	1	0	0	0	2	0	1	0	0	0	—	0	.100	.100	.100	P	4	1	12	0	0	1.000

CHICO SALMON—Ruthford Eduardo Salmon—Bats: Right; Throws: Right

Ht: 5'10"; Wt: 160 lbs; Born: 12/3/1940 in Colon, Panama; Debut: 6/28/1964

LCS — Batting / Fielding

Year Tm	Age	G	AB	H	2B	3B	HR	TB	R	RBI	GW	TBB	IBB	SO	HBP	SH	SF	SB	CS	SB%	GDP	Avg	OBP	SLG	Pos	G	PO	A	E	DP	FPct
1969 Bal	28	1	1	0	0	0	0	0	0	0	0	0	0	0	0	0	0	0	0	—	0	.000	.000	.000	—						

World Series — Batting / Fielding

Year Tm	Age	G	AB	H	2B	3B	HR	TB	R	RBI	GW	TBB	IBB	SO	HBP	SH	SF	SB	CS	SB%	GDP	Avg	OBP	SLG	Pos	G	PO	A	E	DP	FPct
1969 Bal	28	2	0	0	0	0	0	0	0	0	0	0	0	0	0	0	0	0	0	—	0	—	—	—	—						
1970 Bal	29	1	1	1	0	0	0	1	1	0	0	0	0	0	0	0	0	0	0	—	0	1.000	1.000	1.000	—						
WS Totals		3	1	1	0	0	0	1	1	0	0	0	0	0	0	0	0	0	0	—	0	1.000	1.000	1.000	—	0	0	0	0	0	—
Postseason Totals		4	2	1	0	0	0	1	1	0	0	0	0	0	0	0	0	0	0	—	0	.500	.500	.500	—	0	0	0	0	0	—

JOE SAMBITO—Joseph Charles Sambito—Throws: Left; Bats: Left

Ht: 6'1"; Wt: 185 lbs; Born: 6/28/1952 in Brooklyn, New York; Debut: 7/20/1976

Division Series — Pitching

Year Tm	Age	G	GS	CG	GF	IP	BFP	H	R	ER	HR	SH	SF	HB	TBB	IBB	SO	WP	Bk	W	L	Pct	ShO	Sv-Op	Hld	OAvg	OOBP	ERA
1981 Hou	29	2	0	0	1	1.2	12	5	3	3	0	0	1	0	2	1	2	0	0	1	0	1.000	0	0- 0	0	.556	.583	16.20

LCS — Pitching

Year Tm	Age	G	GS	CG	GF	IP	BFP	H	R	ER	HR	SH	SF	HB	TBB	IBB	SO	WP	Bk	W	L	Pct	ShO	Sv-Op	Hld	OAvg	OOBP	ERA
1980 Hou	28	3	0	0	1	3.2	16	4	2	2	0	0	1	0	2	2	6	0	0	0	1	.000	0	0- 0	1	.308	.375	4.91
1986 Bos	34	3	0	0	0	0.2	4	1	0	0	0	0	0	0	1	0	0	0	0	0	0	—	0	0- 1	0	.333	.500	0.00
LCS Totals		6	0	0	1	4.1	40	5	2	2	0	0	1	0	3	2	6	0	0	0	1	.000	0	0-1	1	.313	.400	4.15

World Series — Pitching

Year Tm	Age	G	GS	CG	GF	IP	BFP	H	R	ER	HR	SH	SF	HB	TBB	IBB	SO	WP	Bk	W	L	Pct	ShO	Sv-Op	Hld	OAvg	OOBP	ERA
1986 Bos	34	2	0	0	0	0.1	5	2	1	1	0	0	1	0	2	1	0	1	0	0	0	—	0	0- 0	0	1.000	.800	27.00
Postseason Totals		10	0	0	2	6.1	74	12	6	6	0	0	3	0	7	4	8	1	0	1	1	.500	0	0-1	1	.444	.514	8.53

Division Series — Batting / Fielding

Year Tm	Age	G	AB	H	2B	3B	HR	TB	R	RBI	GW	TBB	IBB	SO	HBP	SH	SF	SB	CS	SB%	GDP	Avg	OBP	SLG	Pos	G	PO	A	E	DP	FPct
1981 Hou	29	2	0	0	0	0	0	0	0	0	0	0	0	0	0	0	0	0	0	—	0	—	—	—	P	2	0	1	0	0	1.000

LCS — Batting / Fielding

Year Tm	Age	G	AB	H	2B	3B	HR	TB	R	RBI	GW	TBB	IBB	SO	HBP	SH	SF	SB	CS	SB%	GDP	Avg	OBP	SLG	Pos	G	PO	A	E	DP	FPct
1980 Hou	28	3	0	0	0	0	0	0	0	0	0	0	0	0	0	1	0	0	0	—	0	—	—	—	P	3	0	0	0	0	—
1986 Bos	34	3	0	0	0	0	0	0	0	0	0	0	0	0	0	0	0	0	0	—	0	—	—	—	P	3	0	0	0	0	—
LCS Totals		6	0	0	0	0	0	0	0	0	0	0	0	0	0	1	0	0	0	—	0	—	—	—	P	6	0	0	0	0	—

World Series — Batting / Fielding

Year Tm	Age	G	AB	H	2B	3B	HR	TB	R	RBI	GW	TBB	IBB	SO	HBP	SH	SF	SB	CS	SB%	GDP	Avg	OBP	SLG	Pos	G	PO	A	E	DP	FPct
1986 Bos	34	2	0	0	0	0	0	0	0	0	0	0	0	0	0	0	0	0	0	—	0	—	—	—	P	2	0	0	0	0	—
Postseason Totals		10	0	0	0	0	0	0	0	0	0	0	0	0	0	1	0	0	0	—	0	—	—	—	P	10	0	1	0	0	1.000

JUAN SAMUEL—Juan Milton Samuel—Bats: Right; Throws: Right

Ht: 5'11"; Wt: 170 lbs; Born: 12/9/1960 in San Pedro de Macoris, Dominican Republic; Debut: 8/24/1983

LCS — Batting / Fielding

Year Tm	Age	G	AB	H	2B	3B	HR	TB	R	RBI	GW	TBB	IBB	SO	HBP	SH	SF	SB	CS	SB%	GDP	Avg	OBP	SLG	Pos	G	PO	A	E	DP	FPct
1983 Phi	22	1	0	0	0	0	0	0	0	0	0	0	0	0	0	0	0	0	0	—	0	—	—	—	—						

World Series — Batting / Fielding

Year Tm	Age	G	AB	H	2B	3B	HR	TB	R	RBI	GW	TBB	IBB	SO	HBP	SH	SF	SB	CS	SB%	GDP	Avg	OBP	SLG	Pos	G	PO	A	E	DP	FPct
1983 Phi	22	3	1	0	0	0	0	0	0	0	0	0	0	0	0	0	0	0	0	—	0	.000	.000	.000	—						
Postseason Totals		4	1	0	0	0	0	0	0	0	0	0	0	0	0	0	0	0	0	—	0	.000	.000	.000	—	0	0	0	0	0	—

LUIS SANCHEZ—Luis Mercedes Escoba Sanchez—Throws: Right; Bats: Right

Ht: 6'2"; Wt: 170 lbs; Born: 8/24/1953 in Cariaco, Venezuela; Debut: 4/10/1981

LCS — Pitching

Year Tm	Age	G	GS	CG	GF	IP	BFP	H	R	ER	HR	SH	SF	HB	TBB	IBB	SO	WP	Bk	W	L	Pct	ShO	Sv-Op	Hld	OAvg	OOBP	ERA
1982 Cal	29	2	0	0	1	2.2	13	4	2	2	0	0	0	0	1	0	1	0	0	0	1	.000	0	0- 1	0	.333	.385	6.75

LCS — Batting / Fielding

Year Tm	Age	G	AB	H	2B	3B	HR	TB	R	RBI	GW	TBB	IBB	SO	HBP	SH	SF	SB	CS	SB%	GDP	Avg	OBP	SLG	Pos	G	PO	A	E	DP	FPct
1982 Cal	29	2	0	0	0	0	0	0	0	0	0	0	0	0	0	0	0	0	0	—	0	—	—	—	P	2	0	0	0	0	—

REY SANCHEZ—Rey Francisco Sanchez—Bats: Right; Throws: Right

Ht: 5'10"; Wt: 180 lbs; Born: 10/5/1967 in Rio Piedras, Puerto Rico; Debut: 9/8/1991

Division Series — Batting / Fielding

Year Tm	Age	G	AB	H	2B	3B	HR	TB	R	RBI	GW	TBB	IBB	SO	HBP	SH	SF	SB	CS	SB%	GDP	Avg	OBP	SLG	Pos	G	PO	A	E	DP	FPct
1997 NYA	29	5	15	3	1	0	0	4	1	1	0	1	0	2	0	1	0	0	0	—	0	.200	.250	.267	2B	5	15	14	0	1	1.000

RYNE SANDBERG—Ryne Dee Sandberg—Nickname: Ryno—Bats: Right; Throws: Right

Ht: 6'1"; Wt: 175 lbs; Born: 9/18/1959 in Spokane, Washington; Debut: 9/2/1981

LCS — Batting / Fielding

Year Tm	Age	G	AB	H	2B	3B	HR	TB	R	RBI	GW	TBB	IBB	SO	HBP	SH	SF	SB	CS	SB%	GDP	Avg	OBP	SLG	Pos	G	PO	A	E	DP	FPct
1984 ChN-*M*	25	5	19	7	2	0	0	9	3	2	0	3	0	2	0	0	0	3	1	.75	0	.368	.455	.474	2B	5	13	18	1	6	.969
1989 ChN	30	5	20	8	3	1	1	16	6	4	1	3	0	4	0	1	1	0	0	—	0	.400	.458	.800	2B	5	7	11	0	1	1.000
LCS Totals		10	39	15	5	1	1	25	9	6	1	6	0	6	0	1	1	3	1	.75	0	.385	.457	.641	2B	10	20	29	1	7	.980

DEION SANDERS—Deion Luwynn Sanders—Nicknames: Neon Deion, Prime Time—Bats: Left; Throws: Left

Ht: 6'1"; Wt: 195 lbs; Born: 8/9/1967 in Fort Myers, Florida; Debut: 6/1/1989

Year Tm	Age	G	AB	H	2B	3B	HR	TB	R	RBI	GW	TBB	IBB	SO	HBP	SH	SF	SB	CS	SB%	GDP	Avg	OBP	SLG	Pos	G	PO	A	E	DP	FPct
LCS — Batting / Fielding																															
1992 Atl	25	4	5	0	0	0	0	0	0	0	0	0	0	3	0	0	0	0	0	—	0	.000	.000	.000	OF	3	1	0	0	0	1.000
1993 Atl	26	5	3	0	0	0	0	0	0	0	0	0	0	1	0	0	0	0	0	—	0	.000	.000	.000	OF	1	0	0	0	0	—
LCS Totals		9	8	0	0	0	0	0	0	0	0	0	0	4	0	0	0	0	0	—	0	.000	.000	.000	OF	4	1	0	0	0	1.000
World Series — Batting / Fielding																															
Year Tm	Age	G	AB	H	2B	3B	HR	TB	R	RBI	GW	TBB	IBB	SO	HBP	SH	SF	SB	CS	SB%	GDP	Avg	OBP	SLG	Pos	G	PO	A	E	DP	FPct
1992 Atl	25	4	15	8	2	0	0	10	4	1	1	2	0	1	0	0	0	5	0	1.00	0	.533	.588	.667	OF	4	5	1	0	0	1.000
Postseason Totals		13	23	8	2	0	0	10	4	1	1	2	0	5	0	0	0	5	0	1.00	0	.348	.400	.435	OF	8	6	1	0	0	1.000

RAY SANDERS—Raymond Floyd Sanders—Bats: Left; Throws: Right

Ht: 6'2"; Wt: 185 lbs; Born: 12/4/1916 in Bonne Terre, Missouri; Debut: 4/14/1942; Died: 10/28/1983

Year Tm	Age	G	AB	H	2B	3B	HR	TB	R	RBI	GW	TBB	IBB	SO	HBP	SH	SF	SB	CS	SB%	GDP	Avg	OBP	SLG	Pos	G	PO	A	E	DP	FPct
World Series — Batting / Fielding																															
1942 StL	25	2	1	0	0	0	0	0	1	0	0	1	0	0	0	0	0	0	0	—	0	.000	.500	.000	—						
1943 StL	26	5	17	5	0	0	1	8	3	2	0	3	1	4	0	0	0	0	0	—	0	.294	.400	.471	1B	5	41	5	0	4	1.000
1944 StL	27	6	21	6	0	0	1	9	5	1	1	5	1	8	0	0	0	0	0	—	0	.286	.423	.429	1B	6	51	2	0	3	1.000
1948 Bos	31	1	1	0	0	0	0	0	0	0	0	0	0	0	0	0	0	0	0	—	0	.000	.000	.000	—						
WS Totals		14	40	11	0	0	2	17	9	3	1	9	2	12	0	0	0	0	0	—	0	.275	.408	.425	1B	11	92	7	0	7	1.000

REGGIE SANDERS—Reginald Laverne Sanders—Bats: Right; Throws: Right

Ht: 6'1"; Wt: 180 lbs; Born: 12/1/1967 in Florence, South Carolina; Debut: 8/22/1991

Year Tm	Age	G	AB	H	2B	3B	HR	TB	R	RBI	GW	TBB	IBB	SO	HBP	SH	SF	SB	CS	SB%	GDP	Avg	OBP	SLG	Pos	G	PO	A	E	DP	FPct
Division Series — Batting / Fielding																															
1995 Cin	27	3	13	2	1	0	1	6	3	2	0	1	0	9	0	0	0	2	0	1.00	0	.154	.214	.462	OF	3	7	0	1	0	.875
LCS — Batting / Fielding																															
Year Tm	Age	G	AB	H	2B	3B	HR	TB	R	RBI	GW	TBB	IBB	SO	HBP	SH	SF	SB	CS	SB%	GDP	Avg	OBP	SLG	Pos	G	PO	A	E	DP	FPct
1995 Cin	27	4	16	2	0	0	0	2	0	0	0	2	1	10	0	0	0	0	1	.00	2	.125	.222	.125	OF	4	7	0	1	0	.875
Postseason Totals		7	29	4	1	0	1	8	3	2	0	3	1	19	0	0	0	2	1	.67	2	.138	.219	.276	OF	7	14	0	2	0	.875

SCOTT SANDERS—Scott Gerald Sanders—Throws: Right; Bats: Right

Ht: 6'4"; Wt: 210 lbs; Born: 3/25/1969 in Hannibal, Missouri; Debut: 8/6/1993

Year Tm	Age	G	GS	CG	GF	IP	BFP	H	R	ER	HR	SH	SF	HB	TBB	IBB	SO	WP	Bk	W	L	Pct	ShO	Sv-Op	Hld	OAvg	OOBP	ERA
Division Series — Pitching																												
1996 SD	27	1	1	0	0	4.1	20	3	4	4	0	1	0	0	4	0	4	0	0	0	0	—	0	0- 0	0	.200	.368	8.31

Year Tm	Age	G	AB	H	2B	3B	HR	TB	R	RBI	GW	TBB	IBB	SO	HBP	SH	SF	SB	CS	SB%	GDP	Avg	OBP	SLG	Pos	G	PO	A	E	DP	FPct
Division Series — Batting / Fielding																															
1996 SD	27	1	1	0	0	0	0	0	0	0	0	0	0	0	0	0	0	0	0	—	0	.000	.000	.000	P	1	0	1	0	0	1.000

SCOTT SANDERSON—Scott Douglas Sanderson—Throws: Right; Bats: Right

Ht: 6'5"; Wt: 195 lbs; Born: 7/22/1956 in Dearborn, Michigan; Debut: 8/6/1978

Year Tm	Age	G	GS	CG	GF	IP	BFP	H	R	ER	HR	SH	SF	HB	TBB	IBB	SO	WP	Bk	W	L	Pct	ShO	Sv-Op	Hld	OAvg	OOBP	ERA
Division Series — Pitching																												
1981 Mon	25	1	1	0	0	2.2	14	4	4	2	1	1	0	0	2	0	2	0	0	0	0	—	0	0- 0	0	.364	.462	6.75
LCS — Pitching																												
Year Tm	Age	G	GS	CG	GF	IP	BFP	H	R	ER	HR	SH	SF	HB	TBB	IBB	SO	WP	Bk	W	L	Pct	ShO	Sv-Op	Hld	OAvg	OOBP	ERA
1984 ChN	28	1	1	0	0	4.2	21	6	3	3	0	1	1	0	1	0	2	0	0	0	0	—	0	0- 0	0	.333	.350	5.79
1989 ChN	33	1	0	0	0	2.0	8	2	0	0	0	0	0	0	0	0	1	0	0	0	0	—	0	0- 0	0	.250	.250	0.00
LCS Totals		2	1	0	0	6.2	58	8	3	3	0	1	1	0	1	0	3	0	0	0	0	—	0	0-0	0	.308	.321	4.05
World Series — Pitching																												
Year Tm	Age	G	GS	CG	GF	IP	BFP	H	R	ER	HR	SH	SF	HB	TBB	IBB	SO	WP	Bk	W	L	Pct	ShO	Sv-Op	Hld	OAvg	OOBP	ERA
1990 Oak	34	2	0	0	0	1.2	9	4	2	2	0	0	0	0	1	0	0	1	0	0	0	—	0	0- 0	0	.500	.556	10.80
Postseason Totals		5	2	0	0	11.0	104	16	9	7	1	2	1	0	4	0	5	1	0	0	0	—	0	0-0	0	.356	.400	5.73

Year Tm	Age	G	AB	H	2B	3B	HR	TB	R	RBI	GW	TBB	IBB	SO	HBP	SH	SF	SB	CS	SB%	GDP	Avg	OBP	SLG	Pos	G	PO	A	E	DP	FPct
Division Series — Batting / Fielding																															
1981 Mon	25	1	1	0	0	0	0	0	0	0	0	0	0	1	0	0	0	0	0	—	0	.000	.000	.000	P	1	0	1	0	0	1.000
LCS — Batting / Fielding																															
Year Tm	Age	G	AB	H	2B	3B	HR	TB	R	RBI	GW	TBB	IBB	SO	HBP	SH	SF	SB	CS	SB%	GDP	Avg	OBP	SLG	Pos	G	PO	A	E	DP	FPct
1984 ChN	28	1	2	0	0	0	0	0	0	0	0	0	0	1	0	0	0	0	0	—	0	.000	.000	.000	P	1	0	1	0	0	1.000
1989 ChN	33	1	0	0	0	0	0	0	0	0	0	0	0	0	0	0	0	0	0	—	0	—	—	—	P	1	0	0	0	0	—
LCS Totals		2	2	0	0	0	0	0	0	0	0	0	0	1	0	0	0	0	0	—	0	.000	.000	.000	P	2	0	1	0	0	1.000
World Series — Batting / Fielding																															
Year Tm	Age	G	AB	H	2B	3B	HR	TB	R	RBI	GW	TBB	IBB	SO	HBP	SH	SF	SB	CS	SB%	GDP	Avg	OBP	SLG	Pos	G	PO	A	E	DP	FPct
1990 Oak	34	2	0	0	0	0	0	0	0	0	0	0	0	0	0	0	0	0	0	—	0	—	—	—	P	2	0	0	0	0	—
Postseason Totals		5	3	0	0	0	0	0	0	0	0	0	0	2	0	0	0	0	0	—	0	.000	.000	.000	P	5	0	2	0	0	1.000

CHARLIE SANDS—Charles Duane Sands—Bats: Left; Throws: Right

Ht: 6'2"; Wt: 200 lbs; Born: 12/17/1947 in Newport News, Virginia; Debut: 6/21/1967

Year Tm	Age	G	AB	H	2B	3B	HR	TB	R	RBI	GW	TBB	IBB	SO	HBP	SH	SF	SB	CS	SB%	GDP	Avg	OBP	SLG	Pos	G	PO	A	E	DP	FPct
World Series — Batting / Fielding																															
1971 Pit	23	1	1	0	0	0	0	0	0	0	0	0	0	1	0	0	0	0	0	—	0	.000	.000	.000	—						

JACK SANFORD—John Stanley Sanford—Throws: Right; Bats: Right

Ht: 6'0"; Wt: 190 lbs; Born: 5/18/1929 in Wellesley Hills, Massachusetts; Debut: 9/16/1956

Year Tm	Age	G	GS	CG	GF	IP	BFP	H	R	ER	HR	SH	SF	HB	TBB	IBB	SO	WP	Bk	W	L	Pct	ShO	Sv-Op	Hld	OAvg	OOBP	ERA
World Series — Pitching																												
1962 SF	33	3	3	1	0	23.1	93	16	6	5	1	1	0	0	8	0	19	1	0	1	2	.333	1	0- 0	0	.190	.261	1.93

Year Tm	Age	G	AB	H	2B	3B	HR	TB	R	RBI	GW	TBB	IBB	SO	HBP	SH	SF	SB	CS	SB%	GDP	Avg	OBP	SLG	Pos	G	PO	A	E	DP	FPct
World Series — Batting / Fielding																															
1962 SF	33	3	7	3	0	0	0	3	0	0	0	0	0	2	0	1	0	0	0	—	0	.429	.429	.429	P	3	3	3	0	1	1.000

MANNY SANGUILLEN—Manuel de Jesus Sanguillen—Bats: Right; Throws: Right

Ht: 6'0"; Wt: 193 lbs; Born: 3/21/1944 in Colon, Panama; Debut: 7/23/1967

Year Tm	Age	G	AB	H	2B	3B	HR	TB	R	RBI	GW	TBB	IBB	SO	HBP	SH	SF	SB	CS	SB%	GDP	Avg	OBP	SLG	Pos	G	PO	A	E	DP	FPct
LCS — Batting / Fielding																															
1970 Pit	26	3	12	2	0	0	0	2	0	0	0	0	0	1	0	0	0	0	0	—	0	.167	.167	.167	C	3	13	1	1	0	.933
1971 Pit	27	4	15	4	0	0	0	4	1	1	0	1	0	1	0	0	0	1	0	1.00	0	.267	.313	.267	C	4	30	1	0	0	1.000
1972 Pit	28	5	16	5	1	0	1	9	4	2	1	0	0	0	0	0	0	0	0	—	0	.313	.313	.563	C	5	22	0	1	1	.957
1974 Pit	30	4	16	4	1	0	0	5	0	0	0	0	0	0	0	0	0	0	0	—	1	.250	.250	.313	C	4	19	2	2	1	.913
1975 Pit	31	3	12	2	0	0	0	2	0	0	0	0	0	0	0	0	0	0	0	—	1	.167	.167	.167	C	3	29	1	1	1	.968
LCS Totals		19	71	17	2	0	1	22	5	3	1	1	0	2	0	0	0	1	0	1.00	2	.239	.250	.310	C	19	113	5	5	3	.959
World Series — Batting / Fielding																															
Year Tm	Age	G	AB	H	2B	3B	HR	TB	R	RBI	GW	TBB	IBB	SO	HBP	SH	SF	SB	CS	SB%	GDP	Avg	OBP	SLG	Pos	G	PO	A	E	DP	FPct
1971 Pit	27	7	29	11	1	0	0	12	3	0	0	0	0	3	0	0	0	2	0	1.00	0	.379	.379	.414	C	7	37	0	0	1	1.000
1979 Pit	35	3	3	1	0	0	0	1	0	1	1	0	0	0	0	0	0	0	0	—	0	.333	.333	.333	—						
WS Totals		10	32	12	1	0	0	13	3	1	1	0	0	3	0	0	0	2	0	1.00	0	.375	.375	.406	C	7	37	0	0	1	1.000
Postseason Totals		29	103	29	3	0	1	35	8	4	2	1	0	5	0	0	0	3	0	1.00	2	.282	.288	.340	C	26	150	5	5	4	.969

RAFAEL SANTANA—Rafael Francisco Santana—Nickname: Renda Linda—Bats: Right; Throws: Right

Ht: 6'1"; Wt: 165 lbs; Born: 1/31/1958 in La Romana, Dominican Republic; Debut: 4/5/1983

Year Tm	Age	G	AB	H	2B	3B	HR	TB	R	RBI	GW	TBB	IBB	SO	HBP	SH	SF	SB	CS	SB%	GDP	Avg	OBP	SLG	Pos	G	PO	A	E	DP	FPct
LCS — Batting / Fielding																															
1986 NYN	28	6	17	3	0	0	0	3	0	0	0	0	0	3	0	0	0	0	0	—	1	.176	.176	.176	SS	6	13	18	0	4	1.000

World Series													Batting															Fielding			
Year Tm	Age	G	AB	H	2B	3B	HR	TB	R	RBI	GW	TBB	IBB	SO	HBP	SH	SF	SB	CS	SB%	GDP	Avg	OBP	SLG	Pos	G	PO	A	E	DP	FPct
1986 NYN	28	7	20	5	0	0	0	5	3	2	0	2	1	5	0	2	0	0	0	—	0	.250	.318	.250	SS	7	11	17	1	3	.966
Postseason Totals		13	37	8	0	0	0	8	3	2	0	2	1	8	0	2	0	0	0	—	1	.216	.256	.216	SS	13	24	35	1	7	.983

BENITO SANTIAGO—Bats: Right; Throws: Right

Ht: 6'1"; Wt: 180 lbs; Born: 3/9/1965 in Ponce, Puerto Rico; Debut: 9/14/1986

Division Series													Batting															Fielding			
Year Tm	Age	G	AB	H	2B	3B	HR	TB	R	RBI	GW	TBB	IBB	SO	HBP	SH	SF	SB	CS	SB%	GDP	Avg	OBP	SLG	Pos	G	PO	A	E	DP	FPct
1995 Cin	30	3	9	3	0	0	1	6	2	3	0	3	0	3	0	0	1	0	0	—	0	.333	.462	.667	C	3	20	0	0	0	1.000
LCS													Batting															Fielding			
Year Tm	Age	G	AB	H	2B	3B	HR	TB	R	RBI	GW	TBB	IBB	SO	HBP	SH	SF	SB	CS	SB%	GDP	Avg	OBP	SLG	Pos	G	PO	A	E	DP	FPct
1995 Cin	30	4	13	3	0	0	0	3	0	0	0	2	0	3	0	0	0	0	0	—	1	.231	.333	.231	C	4	23	1	0	1	1.000
Postseason Totals		7	22	6	0	0	1	9	2	3	0	5	0	6	0	0	1	0	0	—	1	.273	.393	.409	C	7	43	1	0	1	1.000

JOSE SANTIAGO—Jose Rafael Santiago—Throws: Right; Bats: Right

Ht: 6'2"; Wt: 185 lbs; Born: 8/15/1940 in Juana Diaz, Puerto Rico; Debut: 9/9/1963

World Series															Pitching													
Year Tm	Age	G	GS	CG	GF	IP	BFP	H	R	ER	HR	SH	SF	HB	TBB	IBB	SO	WP	Bk	W	L	Pct	ShO	Sv-Op	Hld	OAvg	OOBP	ERA
1967 Bos	27	3	2	0	0	9.2	45	16	6	6	0	0	0	0	3	0	6	0	0	0	2	.000	0	0- 0	0	.381	.422	5.59

World Series													Batting															Fielding			
Year Tm	Age	G	AB	H	2B	3B	HR	TB	R	RBI	GW	TBB	IBB	SO	HBP	SH	SF	SB	CS	SB%	GDP	Avg	OBP	SLG	Pos	G	PO	A	E	DP	FPct
1967 Bos	27	3	2	1	0	0	1	4	1	1	0	0	0	1	0	0	0	0	0	—	0	.500	.500	2.000	P	3	0	0	0	0	—

MANNY SARMIENTO—Manuel Eduardo Sarmiento—Throws: Right; Bats: Right

Ht: 6'0"; Wt: 170 lbs; Born: 2/2/1956 in Cagua, Venezuela; Debut: 7/30/1976

LCS															Pitching													
Year Tm	Age	G	GS	CG	GF	IP	BFP	H	R	ER	HR	SH	SF	HB	TBB	IBB	SO	WP	Bk	W	L	Pct	ShO	Sv-Op	Hld	OAvg	OOBP	ERA
1976 Cin	20	1	0	0	0	1.0	6	2	2	2	0	1	0	0	1	0	0	0	0	0	0	—	0	0- 0	0	.500	.600	18.00

LCS													Batting															Fielding			
Year Tm	Age	G	AB	H	2B	3B	HR	TB	R	RBI	GW	TBB	IBB	SO	HBP	SH	SF	SB	CS	SB%	GDP	Avg	OBP	SLG	Pos	G	PO	A	E	DP	FPct
1976 Cin	20	1	1	0	0	0	0	0	0	0	0	0	0	0	0	0	0	0	0	—	0	.000	.000	.000	P	1	0	0	0	0	—

MACKEY SASSER—Mack Daniel Sasser—Nickname: Mackey the Hacker—Bats: Left; Throws: Right

Ht: 6'1"; Wt: 190 lbs; Born: 8/3/1962 in Fort Gaines, Georgia; Debut: 7/17/1987

LCS													Batting															Fielding			
Year Tm	Age	G	AB	H	2B	3B	HR	TB	R	RBI	GW	TBB	IBB	SO	HBP	SH	SF	SB	CS	SB%	GDP	Avg	OBP	SLG	Pos	G	PO	A	E	DP	FPct
1988 NYN	26	4	5	1	0	0	0	1	0	0	0	0	0	1	0	0	0	0	0	—	0	.200	.200	.200	C	2	2	0	0	0	1.000

KEVIN SAUCIER—Kevin Andrew Saucier—Nickname: Hot Sauce—Throws: Left; Bats: Left

Ht: 6'1"; Wt: 190 lbs; Born: 8/9/1956 in Pensacola, Florida; Debut: 10/1/1978

LCS															Pitching													
Year Tm	Age	G	GS	CG	GF	IP	BFP	H	R	ER	HR	SH	SF	HB	TBB	IBB	SO	WP	Bk	W	L	Pct	ShO	Sv-Op	Hld	OAvg	OOBP	ERA
1980 Phi	24	2	0	0	1	0.2	5	1	0	0	0	0	0	0	2	1	0	0	0	0	0	—	0	0- 0	0	.333	.600	0.00
World Series															Pitching													
Year Tm	Age	G	GS	CG	GF	IP	BFP	H	R	ER	HR	SH	SF	HB	TBB	IBB	SO	WP	Bk	W	L	Pct	ShO	Sv-Op	Hld	OAvg	OOBP	ERA
1980 Phi	24	1	0	0	0	0.2	4	0	0	0	0	0	0	0	2	0	0	1	0	0	0	—	0	0- 0	0	.000	.500	0.00
Postseason Totals		3	0	0	1	1.1	18	1	0	0	0	0	0	0	4	1	0	1	0	0	0	—	0	0-0	0	.200	.556	0.00

LCS													Batting															Fielding			
Year Tm	Age	G	AB	H	2B	3B	HR	TB	R	RBI	GW	TBB	IBB	SO	HBP	SH	SF	SB	CS	SB%	GDP	Avg	OBP	SLG	Pos	G	PO	A	E	DP	FPct
1980 Phi	24	2	0	0	0	0	0	0	0	0	0	0	0	0	0	0	0	0	0	—	0	—	—	—	P	2	0	0	0	0	—
World Series													Batting															Fielding			
Year Tm	Age	G	AB	H	2B	3B	HR	TB	R	RBI	GW	TBB	IBB	SO	HBP	SH	SF	SB	CS	SB%	GDP	Avg	OBP	SLG	Pos	G	PO	A	E	DP	FPct
1980 Phi	24	1	0	0	0	0	0	0	0	0	0	0	0	0	0	0	0	0	0	—	0	—	—	—	P	1	0	0	0	0	—
Postseason Totals		3	0	0	0	0	0	0	0	0	0	0	0	0	0	0	0	0	0	—	0	—	—	—	P	3	0	0	0	0	—

EDDIE SAUER—Edward Sauer—Nickname: Horn—Bats: Right; Throws: Right

Ht: 6'1"; Wt: 188 lbs; Born: 1/3/1919 in Pittsburgh, Pennsylvania; Debut: 9/17/1943; Died: 7/1/1988

World Series													Batting															Fielding			
Year Tm	Age	G	AB	H	2B	3B	HR	TB	R	RBI	GW	TBB	IBB	SO	HBP	SH	SF	SB	CS	SB%	GDP	Avg	OBP	SLG	Pos	G	PO	A	E	DP	FPct
1945 ChN	26	2	2	0	0	0	0	0	0	0	0	0	0	2	0	0	0	0	0	—	0	.000	.000	.000	—						

TONY SAUNDERS—Anthony Scott Saunders—Throws: Left; Bats: Left

Ht: 6'2"; Wt: 205 lbs; Born: 4/29/1974 in Baltimore, Maryland; Debut: 4/5/1997

LCS															Pitching													
Year Tm	Age	G	GS	CG	GF	IP	BFP	H	R	ER	HR	SH	SF	HB	TBB	IBB	SO	WP	Bk	W	L	Pct	ShO	Sv-Op	Hld	OAvg	OOBP	ERA
1997 Fla	23	1	1	0	0	5.1	22	4	2	2	0	1	1	0	3	0	3	0	0	0	0	—	0	0- 0	0	.235	.333	3.38
World Series															Pitching													
Year Tm	Age	G	GS	CG	GF	IP	BFP	H	R	ER	HR	SH	SF	HB	TBB	IBB	SO	WP	Bk	W	L	Pct	ShO	Sv-Op	Hld	OAvg	OOBP	ERA
1997 Fla	23	1	1	0	0	2.0	16	7	6	6	1	0	0	0	3	0	2	0	0	0	1	.000	0	0- 0	0	.538	.625	27.00
Postseason Totals		2	2	0	0	7.1	76	11	8	8	1	1	1	0	6	0	5	0	0	0	1	.000	0	0-0	0	.367	.459	9.82

LCS													Batting															Fielding			
Year Tm	Age	G	AB	H	2B	3B	HR	TB	R	RBI	GW	TBB	IBB	SO	HBP	SH	SF	SB	CS	SB%	GDP	Avg	OBP	SLG	Pos	G	PO	A	E	DP	FPct
1997 Fla	23	1	2	0	0	0	0	0	0	0	0	0	0	2	0	0	0	0	0	—	0	.000	.000	.000	P	1	0	1	0	0	1.000
World Series													Batting															Fielding			
Year Tm	Age	G	AB	H	2B	3B	HR	TB	R	RBI	GW	TBB	IBB	SO	HBP	SH	SF	SB	CS	SB%	GDP	Avg	OBP	SLG	Pos	G	PO	A	E	DP	FPct
1997 Fla	23	1	0	0	0	0	0	0	0	0	0	0	0	0	0	0	0	0	0	—	0	—	—	—	P	1	0	1	1	0	.500
Postseason Totals		2	2	0	0	0	0	0	0	0	0	0	0	2	0	0	0	0	0	—	0	.000	.000	.000	P	2	0	2	1	0	.667

CARL SAWATSKI—Carl Ernest Sawatski—Nicknames: Swats, Swish—Bats: Left; Throws: Right

Ht: 5'10"; Wt: 210 lbs; Born: 11/4/1927 in Shickshinny, Pennsylvania; Debut: 9/29/1948; Died: 11/24/1991

World Series													Batting															Fielding			
Year Tm	Age	G	AB	H	2B	3B	HR	TB	R	RBI	GW	TBB	IBB	SO	HBP	SH	SF	SB	CS	SB%	GDP	Avg	OBP	SLG	Pos	G	PO	A	E	DP	FPct
1957 Mil	29	2	2	0	0	0	0	0	0	0	0	0	0	2	0	0	0	0	0	—	0	.000	.000	.000	—						

STEVE SAX—Stephen Louis Sax—Bats: Right; Throws: Right

Ht: 5'11"; Wt: 185 lbs; Born: 1/29/1960 in Sacramento, California; Debut: 8/18/1981

Division Series													Batting															Fielding			
Year Tm	Age	G	AB	H	2B	3B	HR	TB	R	RBI	GW	TBB	IBB	SO	HBP	SH	SF	SB	CS	SB%	GDP	Avg	OBP	SLG	Pos	G	PO	A	E	DP	FPct
1981 LA	21	1	0	0	0	0	0	0	0	0	0	0	0	0	0	0	0	0	0	—	0	—	—	—	2B	1	0	0	0	0	—
LCS													Batting															Fielding			
Year Tm	Age	G	AB	H	2B	3B	HR	TB	R	RBI	GW	TBB	IBB	SO	HBP	SH	SF	SB	CS	SB%	GDP	Avg	OBP	SLG	Pos	G	PO	A	E	DP	FPct
1981 LA	21	1	0	0	0	0	0	0	0	0	0	0	0	0	0	0	0	0	0	—	0	—	—	—	2B	1	0	1	0	0	1.000
1983 LA	23	4	16	4	0	0	0	4	0	0	0	1	0	0	0	0	0	1	2	.33	0	.250	.294	.250	2B	4	11	12	0	4	1.000
1985 LA	25	6	20	6	3	0	0	9	1	1	0	1	0	5	0	0	0	0	1	.00	0	.300	.333	.450	2B	6	11	21	0	1	1.000
1988 LA	28	7	30	8	0	0	0	8	7	3	0	3	0	3	1	0	0	5	0	1.00	0	.267	.353	.267	2B	7	12	22	0	6	1.000
LCS Totals		18	66	18	3	0	0	21	8	4	0	5	0	8	1	0	0	6	3	.67	0	.273	.333	.318	2B	18	34	56	0	11	1.000
World Series													Batting															Fielding			
Year Tm	Age	G	AB	H	2B	3B	HR	TB	R	RBI	GW	TBB	IBB	SO	HBP	SH	SF	SB	CS	SB%	GDP	Avg	OBP	SLG	Pos	G	PO	A	E	DP	FPct
1981 LA	21	2	1	0	0	0	0	0	0	0	0	0	0	0	0	0	0	0	0	—	0	.000	.000	.000	2B	1	0	0	0	0	—
1988 LA	28	5	20	6	0	0	0	6	3	0	0	1	0	1	1	0	0	1	1	.50	0	.300	.364	.300	2B	5	11	11	0	2	1.000
WS Totals		7	21	6	0	0	0	6	3	0	0	1	0	1	1	0	0	1	1	.50	0	.286	.348	.286	2B	6	11	11	0	2	1.000
Postseason Totals		26	87	24	3	0	0	27	11	4	0	6	0	9	2	0	0	7	4	.64	0	.276	.337	.310	2B	25	45	67	0	13	1.000

RAY SCARBOROUGH—Rae Wilson Scarborough—Throws: Right; Bats: Right

Ht: 6'0"; Wt: 185 lbs; Born: 7/23/1917 in Mt. Gilead, North Carolina; Debut: 6/26/1942; Died: 7/1/1982

World Series		Pitching																										
Year Tm	Age	G	GS	CG	GF	IP	BFP	H	R	ER	HR	SH	SF	HB	TBB	IBB	SO	WP	Bk	W	L	Pct	ShO	Sv-Op	Hld	OAvg	OOBP	ERA
1952 NYA	35	1	0	0	1	1.0	4	1	1	1	1	0	0	0	0	0	1	0	0	0	0	—	0	0-0	0	.250	.250	9.00

World Series		Batting																							Fielding						
Year Tm	Age	G	AB	H	2B	3B	HR	TB	R	RBI	GW	TBB	IBB	SO	HBP	SH	SF	SB	CS	SB%	GDP	Avg	OBP	SLG	Pos	G	PO	A	E	DP	FPct
1952 NYA	35	1	0	0	0	0	0	0	0	0	0	0	0	0	0	0	0	0	0	—	0	—	—	—	P	1	0	1	0	0	1.000

GERMANY SCHAEFER—Herman A. Schaefer—Bats: Right; Throws: Right

Ht: 5'9"; Wt: 175 lbs; Born: 2/4/1877 in Chicago, Illinois; Debut: 10/5/1901; Died: 5/16/1919

World Series		Batting																							Fielding						
Year Tm	Age	G	AB	H	2B	3B	HR	TB	R	RBI	GW	TBB	IBB	SO	HBP	SH	SF	SB	CS	SB%	GDP	Avg	OBP	SLG	Pos	G	PO	A	E	DP	FPct
1907 Det	30	5	21	3	0	0	0	3	1	0	0	0	0	3	0	1	0	0	2	.00	1	.143	.143	.143	2B	5	11	18	0	2	1.000
1908 Det	31	5	16	2	0	0	0	2	0	0	0	1	0	4	0	1	0	1	1	.50	0	.125	.176	.125	3B	2	1	3	1	0	.800
																									2B	3	9	8	0	3	1.000
WS Totals		10	37	5	0	0	0	5	1	0	0	1	0	7	0	2	0	1	3	.25	1	.135	.158	.135	2B	8	20	26	0	5	1.000

RAY SCHALK (HOF 1955-V)—Raymond William Schalk—Nickname: Cracker—Bats: Right; Throws: Right

Ht: 5'9"; Wt: 165 lbs; Born: 8/12/1892 in Harvey, Illinois; Debut: 8/11/1912; Died: 5/19/1970

World Series		Batting																							Fielding						
Year Tm	Age	G	AB	H	2B	3B	HR	TB	R	RBI	GW	TBB	IBB	SO	HBP	SH	SF	SB	CS	SB%	GDP	Avg	OBP	SLG	Pos	G	PO	A	E	DP	FPct
1917 ChA	25	6	19	5	0	0	0	5	1	0	0	2	0	1	0	0	0	1	1	.50	0	.263	.333	.263	C	6	32	6	2	1	.950
1919 ChA	27	8	23	7	0	0	0	7	1	2	0	4	0	2	1	0	0	1	1	.50	0	.304	.429	.304	C	8	29	15	1	1	.978
WS Totals		14	42	12	0	0	0	12	2	2	0	6	0	3	1	0	0	2	2	.50	0	.286	.388	.286	C	14	61	21	3	2	.965

ART SCHALLOCK—Arthur Lawrence Schallock—Throws: Left; Bats: Left

Ht: 5'9"; Wt: 160 lbs; Born: 4/25/1924 in Mill Valley, California; Debut: 7/16/1951

World Series		Pitching																										
Year Tm	Age	G	GS	CG	GF	IP	BFP	H	R	ER	HR	SH	SF	HB	TBB	IBB	SO	WP	Bk	W	L	Pct	ShO	Sv-Op	Hld	OAvg	OOBP	ERA
1953 NYA	29	1	0	0	1	2.0	9	2	1	1	0	1	0	0	1	0	1	0	0	0	0	—	0	0-0	0	.286	.375	4.50

World Series		Batting																							Fielding						
Year Tm	Age	G	AB	H	2B	3B	HR	TB	R	RBI	GW	TBB	IBB	SO	HBP	SH	SF	SB	CS	SB%	GDP	Avg	OBP	SLG	Pos	G	PO	A	E	DP	FPct
1953 NYA	29	1	0	0	0	0	0	0	0	0	0	0	0	0	0	0	0	0	0	—	0	—	—	—	P	1	0	1	0	0	1.000

WALLY SCHANG—Walter Henry Schang—Bats: Both; Throws: Right

Ht: 5'10"; Wt: 180 lbs; Born: 8/22/1889 in South Wales, New York; Debut: 5/1/1913; Died: 3/6/1965

World Series		Batting																							Fielding						
Year Tm	Age	G	AB	H	2B	3B	HR	TB	R	RBI	GW	TBB	IBB	SO	HBP	SH	SF	SB	CS	SB%	GDP	Avg	OBP	SLG	Pos	G	PO	A	E	DP	FPct
1913 Phi	24	4	14	5	0	1	1	10	2	7	1	2	0	4	0	0	0	0	0	—	0	.357	.438	.714	C	4	16	4	1	1	.952
1914 Phi	25	4	12	2	1	0	0	3	1	0	0	1	0	4	0	0	0	0	1	.00	0	.167	.231	.250	C	4	17	4	1	0	.955
1918 Bos	29	5	9	4	0	0	0	4	1	1	1	2	0	3	0	0	0	1	1	.50	0	.444	.545	.444	C	5	9	4	0	0	1.000
1921 NYA	32	8	21	6	1	1	0	9	1	1	0	5	0	4	0	1	0	0	0	—	0	.286	.423	.429	C	8	39	10	0	2	1.000
1922 NYA	33	5	16	3	1	0	0	4	0	0	0	0	0	3	0	3	0	0	0	—	0	.188	.188	.250	C	5	19	4	0	0	1.000
1923 NYA	34	6	22	7	1	0	0	8	3	0	0	1	0	2	0	2	0	0	0	—	1	.318	.348	.364	C	6	21	2	1	0	.958
WS Totals		32	94	27	4	2	1	38	8	9	2	11	0	20	0	6	0	1	2	.33	1	.287	.362	.404	C	32	121	28	3	3	.980

DAN SCHATZEDER—Daniel Ernest Schatzeder—Throws: Left; Bats: Left

Ht: 6'0"; Wt: 185 lbs; Born: 12/1/1954 in Elmhurst, Illinois; Debut: 9/4/1977

LCS		Pitching																										
Year Tm	Age	G	GS	CG	GF	IP	BFP	H	R	ER	HR	SH	SF	HB	TBB	IBB	SO	WP	Bk	W	L	Pct	ShO	Sv-Op	Hld	OAvg	OOBP	ERA
1987 Min	32	2	0	0	0	4.1	17	2	0	0	0	0	0	1	0	0	5	0	0	0	0	—	0	0-0	1	.125	.176	0.00
World Series		**Pitching**																										
Year Tm	Age	G	GS	CG	GF	IP	BFP	H	R	ER	HR	SH	SF	HB	TBB	IBB	SO	WP	Bk	W	L	Pct	ShO	Sv-Op	Hld	OAvg	OOBP	ERA
1987 Min	32	3	0	0	1	4.1	19	4	3	3	0	0	1	0	3	1	3	0	0	1	0	1.000	0	0-0	0	.267	.368	6.23
Postseason Totals		5	0	0	1	8.2	72	6	3	3	0	0	1	1	3	1	8	0	0	1	0	1.000	0	0-0	1	.194	.278	3.12

LCS		Batting																							Fielding						
Year Tm	Age	G	AB	H	2B	3B	HR	TB	R	RBI	GW	TBB	IBB	SO	HBP	SH	SF	SB	CS	SB%	GDP	Avg	OBP	SLG	Pos	G	PO	A	E	DP	FPct
1987 Min	32	2	0	0	0	0	0	0	0	0	0	0	0	0	0	0	0	0	0	—	0	—	—	—	P	2	1	1	0	0	1.000
World Series		**Batting**																							**Fielding**						
Year Tm	Age	G	AB	H	2B	3B	HR	TB	R	RBI	GW	TBB	IBB	SO	HBP	SH	SF	SB	CS	SB%	GDP	Avg	OBP	SLG	Pos	G	PO	A	E	DP	FPct
1987 Min	32	3	0	0	0	0	0	0	0	0	0	0	0	0	0	0	0	0	0	—	0	—	—	—	P	3	0	0	0	0	—
Postseason Totals		5	0	0	0	0	0	0	0	0	0	0	0	0	0	0	0	0	0	—	0	—	—	—	P	5	1	1	0	0	1.000

HANK SCHENZ—Henry Leonard Schenz—Bats: Right; Throws: Right

Ht: 5'9"; Wt: 175 lbs; Born: 4/11/1919 in New Richmond, Ohio; Debut: 9/18/1946; Died: 5/12/1988

World Series		Batting																							Fielding						
Year Tm	Age	G	AB	H	2B	3B	HR	TB	R	RBI	GW	TBB	IBB	SO	HBP	SH	SF	SB	CS	SB%	GDP	Avg	OBP	SLG	Pos	G	PO	A	E	DP	FPct
1951 NYG	32	1	0	0	0	0	0	0	0	0	0	0	0	0	0	0	0	0	0	—	0	—	—	—	—						

FRED SCHERMAN—Frederick John Scherman—Throws: Left; Bats: Left

Ht: 6'1"; Wt: 195 lbs; Born: 7/25/1944 in Dayton, Ohio; Debut: 4/26/1969

LCS		Pitching																										
Year Tm	Age	G	GS	CG	GF	IP	BFP	H	R	ER	HR	SH	SF	HB	TBB	IBB	SO	WP	Bk	W	L	Pct	ShO	Sv-Op	Hld	OAvg	OOBP	ERA
1972 Det	28	1	0	0	0	0.2	3	1	0	0	0	0	0	0	0	0	1	0	0	0	0	—	0	0-0	0	.333	.333	0.00

LCS		Batting																							Fielding						
Year Tm	Age	G	AB	H	2B	3B	HR	TB	R	RBI	GW	TBB	IBB	SO	HBP	SH	SF	SB	CS	SB%	GDP	Avg	OBP	SLG	Pos	G	PO	A	E	DP	FPct
1972 Det	28	1	0	0	0	0	0	0	0	0	0	0	0	0	0	0	0	0	0	—	0	—	—	—	P	1	0	0	0	0	—

BILL SCHERRER—William Joseph Scherrer—Throws: Left; Bats: Left

Ht: 6'4"; Wt: 170 lbs; Born: 1/20/1958 in Tonawanda, New York; Debut: 9/7/1982

World Series		Pitching																										
Year Tm	Age	G	GS	CG	GF	IP	BFP	H	R	ER	HR	SH	SF	HB	TBB	IBB	SO	WP	Bk	W	L	Pct	ShO	Sv-Op	Hld	OAvg	OOBP	ERA
1984 Det	26	3	0	0	0	3.0	13	5	1	1	0	0	1	0	0	0	0	0	0	0	0	—	0	0-0	0	.417	.385	3.00

World Series		Batting																							Fielding						
Year Tm	Age	G	AB	H	2B	3B	HR	TB	R	RBI	GW	TBB	IBB	SO	HBP	SH	SF	SB	CS	SB%	GDP	Avg	OBP	SLG	Pos	G	PO	A	E	DP	FPct
1984 Det	26	3	0	0	0	0	0	0	0	0	0	0	0	0	0	0	0	0	0	—	0	—	—	—	P	3	0	2	0	0	1.000

CURT SCHILLING—Curtis Montague Schilling—Throws: Right; Bats: Right

Ht: 6'5"; Wt: 205 lbs; Born: 11/14/1966 in Anchorage, Alaska; Debut: 9/7/1988

LCS		Pitching																										
Year Tm	Age	G	GS	CG	GF	IP	BFP	H	R	ER	HR	SH	SF	HB	TBB	IBB	SO	WP	Bk	W	L	Pct	ShO	Sv-Op	Hld	OAvg	OOBP	ERA
1993 Phi	26	2	2	0	0	16.0	63	11	4	3	0	0	1	0	5	0	19	0	0	0	0	—	0	0-0	0	.193	.254	1.69
World Series		**Pitching**																										
Year Tm	Age	G	GS	CG	GF	IP	BFP	H	R	ER	HR	SH	SF	HB	TBB	IBB	SO	WP	Bk	W	L	Pct	ShO	Sv-Op	Hld	OAvg	OOBP	ERA
1993 Phi	26	2	2	1	0	15.1	61	13	7	6	2	0	1	0	5	0	9	0	0	1	1	.500	1	0-0	0	.236	.295	3.52
Postseason Totals		4	4	1	0	31.1	248	24	11	9	2	0	2	0	10	0	28	0	0	1	1	.500	1	0-0	0	.214	.274	2.59

LCS		Batting																							Fielding						
Year Tm	Age	G	AB	H	2B	3B	HR	TB	R	RBI	GW	TBB	IBB	SO	HBP	SH	SF	SB	CS	SB%	GDP	Avg	OBP	SLG	Pos	G	PO	A	E	DP	FPct
1993 Phi	26	2	5	0	0	0	0	0	0	0	0	0	0	2	0	1	0	0	0	—	0	.000	.000	.000	P	2	0	0	0	0	—
World Series		**Batting**																							**Fielding**						
Year Tm	Age	G	AB	H	2B	3B	HR	TB	R	RBI	GW	TBB	IBB	SO	HBP	SH	SF	SB	CS	SB%	GDP	Avg	OBP	SLG	Pos	G	PO	A	E	DP	FPct
1993 Phi	26	2	2	1	0	0	0	1	0	0	0	0	0	1	0	1	0	0	0	—	0	.500	.500	.500	P	2	0	3	0	0	1.000
Postseason Totals		4	7	1	0	0	0	1	0	0	0	0	0	3	0	2	0	0	0	—	0	.143	.143	.143	P	4	0	3	0	0	1.000

CALVIN SCHIRALDI—Calvin Drew Schiraldi—Throws: Right; Bats: Right

Ht: 6'5"; Wt: 215 lbs; Born: 6/16/1962 in Houston, Texas; Debut: 9/1/1984

Year Tm	Age	G	GS	CG	GF	IP	BFP	H	R	ER	HR	SH	SF	HB	TBB	IBB	SO	WP	Bk	W	L	Pct	ShO	Sv-Op	Hld	OAvg	OOBP	ERA
LCS		Pitching																										
1986 Bos	24	4	0	0	4	6.0	28	5	2	1	0	1	1	1	3	1	9	0	0	0	1	.000	0	1-2	0	.227	.333	1.50
World Series		Pitching																										
Year Tm	Age	G	GS	CG	GF	IP	BFP	H	R	ER	HR	SH	SF	HB	TBB	IBB	SO	WP	Bk	W	L	Pct	ShO	Sv-Op	Hld	OAvg	OOBP	ERA
1986 Bos	24	3	0	0	1	4.0	24	7	7	6	1	3	1	0	3	1	2	1	0	0	2	.000	0	1-2	0	.412	.476	13.50
Postseason Totals		7	0	0	5	10.0	104	12	9	7	1	4	2	1	6	2	11	1	0	0	3	.000	0	2-4	0	.308	.396	6.30

Year Tm	Age	G	AB	H	2B	3B	HR	TB	R	RBI	GW	TBB	IBB	SO	HBP	SH	SF	SB	CS	SB%	GDP	Avg	OBP	SLG	Pos	G	PO	A	E	DP	FPct
LCS		Batting																							Fielding						
1986 Bos	24	4	0	0	0	0	0	0	0	0	0	0	0	0	0	0	0	0	0	—	0	—	—	—	P	4	0	0	0	0	—
World Series		Batting																							Fielding						
Year Tm	Age	G	AB	H	2B	3B	HR	TB	R	RBI	GW	TBB	IBB	SO	HBP	SH	SF	SB	CS	SB%	GDP	Avg	OBP	SLG	Pos	G	PO	A	E	DP	FPct
1986 Bos	24	3	1	0	0	0	0	0	0	0	0	0	0	1	0	0	0	0	0	—	0	.000	.000	.000	P	3	0	1	0	0	1.000
Postseason Totals		7	1	0	0	0	0	0	0	0	0	0	0	1	0	0	0	0	0	—	0	.000	.000	.000	P	7	0	1	0	0	1.000

RAY SCHMANDT—Raymond Henry Schmandt—Bats: Right; Throws: Right

Ht: 6'1"; Wt: 175 lbs; Born: 1/25/1896 in St. Louis, Missouri; Debut: 6/24/1915; Died: 2/2/1969

Year Tm	Age	G	AB	H	2B	3B	HR	TB	R	RBI	GW	TBB	IBB	SO	HBP	SH	SF	SB	CS	SB%	GDP	Avg	OBP	SLG	Pos	G	PO	A	E	DP	FPct
World Series		Batting																							Fielding						
1920 Bro	24	1	1	0	0	0	0	0	0	0	0	0	0	0	0	0	0	0	0	—	0	.000	.000	.000	—						

BOSS SCHMIDT—Charles Schmidt—Bats: Both; Throws: Right

Ht: 5'11"; Wt: 200 lbs; Born: 9/12/1880 in Coal Hill, Arkansas; Debut: 4/30/1906; Died: 11/14/1932

Year Tm	Age	G	AB	H	2B	3B	HR	TB	R	RBI	GW	TBB	IBB	SO	HBP	SH	SF	SB	CS	SB%	GDP	Avg	OBP	SLG	Pos	G	PO	A	E	DP	FPct
World Series		Batting																							Fielding						
1907 Det	27	4	12	2	0	0	0	2	0	0	0	2	0	1	0	0	0	0	0	—	0	.167	.286	.167	C	3	20	6	2	0	.929
1908 Det	28	4	14	1	0	0	0	1	0	1	0	0	0	2	0	0	0	0	0	—	0	.071	.071	.071	C	4	22	5	0	1	1.000
1909 Det	29	6	18	4	2	0	0	6	0	4	0	2	0	0	0	0	0	0	0	—	0	.222	.300	.333	C	6	31	10	4	2	.911
WS Totals		14	44	7	2	0	0	9	0	5	0	4	0	3	0	0	0	0	0	—	0	.159	.229	.205	C	13	73	21	6	3	.940

BUTCH SCHMIDT—Charles John Schmidt—Nickname: Butcher Boy—Bats: Left; Throws: Left

Ht: 6'1"; Wt: 200 lbs; Born: 7/19/1886 in Baltimore, Maryland; Debut: 5/11/1909; Died: 9/4/1952

Year Tm	Age	G	AB	H	2B	3B	HR	TB	R	RBI	GW	TBB	IBB	SO	HBP	SH	SF	SB	CS	SB%	GDP	Avg	OBP	SLG	Pos	G	PO	A	E	DP	FPct
World Series		Batting																							Fielding						
1914 Bos	28	4	17	5	0	0	0	5	2	2	0	0	0	2	0	0	0	1	1	.50	0	.294	.294	.294	1B	4	52	3	0	3	1.000

FREDDY SCHMIDT—Frederick Albert Schmidt—Throws: Right; Bats: Right

Ht: 6'1"; Wt: 185 lbs; Born: 2/9/1916 in Hartford, Connecticut; Debut: 4/25/1944

Year Tm	Age	G	GS	CG	GF	IP	BFP	H	R	ER	HR	SH	SF	HB	TBB	IBB	SO	WP	Bk	W	L	Pct	ShO	Sv-Op	Hld	OAvg	OOBP	ERA
World Series		Pitching																										
1944 StL	28	1	0	0	0	3.1	11	1	0	0	0	0	0	0	1	1	1	1	0	0	0	—	0	0-0	0	.100	.182	0.00

Year Tm	Age	G	AB	H	2B	3B	HR	TB	R	RBI	GW	TBB	IBB	SO	HBP	SH	SF	SB	CS	SB%	GDP	Avg	OBP	SLG	Pos	G	PO	A	E	DP	FPct
World Series		Batting																							Fielding						
1944 StL	28	1	1	0	0	0	0	0	0	0	0	0	0	1	0	0	0	0	0	—	0	.000	.000	.000	P	1	0	0	0	0	—

MIKE SCHMIDT (HOF 1995-W)—Michael Jack Schmidt—Nickname: Herbie—Bats: Right; Throws: Right

Ht: 6'2"; Wt: 195 lbs; Born: 9/27/1949 in Dayton, Ohio; Debut: 9/12/1972

Year Tm	Age	G	AB	H	2B	3B	HR	TB	R	RBI	GW	TBB	IBB	SO	HBP	SH	SF	SB	CS	SB%	GDP	Avg	OBP	SLG	Pos	G	PO	A	E	DP	FPct
Division Series		Batting																							Fielding						
1981 Phi-*M*	32	5	16	4	1	0	1	8	3	2	0	4	1	2	0	0	0	0	0	—	1	.250	.400	.500	3B	5	6	11	1	1	.944
LCS		Batting																							Fielding						
Year Tm	Age	G	AB	H	2B	3B	HR	TB	R	RBI	GW	TBB	IBB	SO	HBP	SH	SF	SB	CS	SB%	GDP	Avg	OBP	SLG	Pos	G	PO	A	E	DP	FPct
1976 Phi	27	3	13	4	2	0	0	6	1	2	0	0	0	1	0	0	1	0	0	—	0	.308	.286	.462	3B	3	4	9	1	2	.929
1977 Phi	28	4	16	1	0	0	0	1	2	1	1	2	0	3	0	0	0	0	0	—	0	.063	.167	.063	3B	4	4	15	0	0	1.000
1978 Phi	29	4	15	3	2	0	0	5	1	1	0	2	1	2	0	0	1	0	1	.00	0	.200	.278	.333	3B	4	3	18	2	0	.913
1980 Phi-*M*	31	5	24	5	1	0	0	6	1	1	0	1	0	6	0	0	0	1	0	1.00	0	.208	.240	.250	3B	5	3	17	1	2	.952
1983 Phi	34	4	15	7	2	0	1	12	5	2	1	2	0	3	0	0	0	0	0	—	0	.467	.529	.800	3B	4	5	7	1	0	.923
LCS Totals		20	83	20	7	0	1	30	10	7	2	7	1	15	0	0	2	1	1	.50	0	.241	.293	.361	3B	20	19	66	5	4	.944
World Series		Batting																							Fielding						
Year Tm	Age	G	AB	H	2B	3B	HR	TB	R	RBI	GW	TBB	IBB	SO	HBP	SH	SF	SB	CS	SB%	GDP	Avg	OBP	SLG	Pos	G	PO	A	E	DP	FPct
1980 Phi-*M*	31	6	21	8	1	0	2	15	6	7	2	4	0	3	0	0	1	0	0	—	0	.381	.462	.714	3B	6	9	8	0	1	1.000
1983 Phi	34	5	20	1	0	0	0	1	0	0	0	0	0	6	0	0	0	0	0	—	0	.050	.050	.050	3B	5	1	10	1	1	.917
WS Totals		11	41	9	1	0	2	16	6	7	2	4	0	9	0	0	1	0	0	—	0	.220	.283	.390	3B	11	10	18	1	2	.966
Postseason Totals		36	140	33	9	0	4	54	19	16	4	15	2	26	0	0	3	1	1	.50	1	.236	.304	.386	3B	36	35	95	7	7	.949

RED SCHOENDIENST (HOF 1989-V)—Albert Fred Schoendienst—Bats: Both; Throws: Right

Ht: 6'0"; Wt: 170 lbs; Born: 2/2/1923 in Germantown, Illinois; Debut: 4/17/1945

Year Tm	Age	G	AB	H	2B	3B	HR	TB	R	RBI	GW	TBB	IBB	SO	HBP	SH	SF	SB	CS	SB%	GDP	Avg	OBP	SLG	Pos	G	PO	A	E	DP	FPct
World Series		Batting																							Fielding						
1946 StL	23	7	30	7	1	0	0	8	3	1	0	0	0	2	0	1	0	1	1	.50	0	.233	.233	.267	2B	7	17	21	1	5	.974
1957 Mil	34	5	18	5	1	0	0	6	0	2	0	0	0	1	0	1	0	0	0	—	0	.278	.278	.333	2B	5	5	10	0	4	1.000
1958 Mil	35	7	30	9	3	1	0	14	5	0	0	2	0	1	0	1	0	0	0	—	1	.300	.344	.467	2B	7	19	19	1	3	.974
WS Totals		19	78	21	5	1	0	28	8	3	0	2	0	4	0	3	0	1	1	.50	1	.269	.288	.359	2B	19	41	50	2	12	.978

DICK SCHOFIELD—John Richard Schofield—Nickname: Ducky—Bats: Both; Throws: Right

Ht: 5'9"; Wt: 163 lbs; Born: 1/7/1935 in Springfield, Illinois; Debut: 7/3/1953

Year Tm	Age	G	AB	H	2B	3B	HR	TB	R	RBI	GW	TBB	IBB	SO	HBP	SH	SF	SB	CS	SB%	GDP	Avg	OBP	SLG	Pos	G	PO	A	E	DP	FPct
World Series		Batting																							Fielding						
1960 Pit	25	3	3	1	0	0	0	1	0	0	0	1	0	0	0	0	0	0	0	—	0	.333	.500	.333	SS	2	1	0	0	0	1.000
1968 StL	33	2	0	0	0	0	0	0	0	0	0	0	0	0	0	0	0	0	0	—	0	—	—	—	SS	1	0	0	0	0	—
WS Totals		5	3	1	0	0	0	1	0	0	0	1	0	0	0	0	0	0	0	—	0	.333	.500	.333	SS	3	1	0	0	0	1.000

DICK SCHOFIELD—Richard Craig Schofield—Nickname: Little Duck—Bats: Right; Throws: Right

Ht: 5'10"; Wt: 175 lbs; Born: 11/21/1962 in Springfield, Illinois; Debut: 9/8/1983

Year Tm	Age	G	AB	H	2B	3B	HR	TB	R	RBI	GW	TBB	IBB	SO	HBP	SH	SF	SB	CS	SB%	GDP	Avg	OBP	SLG	Pos	G	PO	A	E	DP	FPct
LCS		Batting																							Fielding						
1986 Cal	23	7	30	9	1	0	1	13	4	2	1	1	1	5	0	0	0	1	0	1.00	0	.300	.323	.433	SS	7	13	23	2	4	.947

PETE SCHOUREK—Peter Alan Schourek—Throws: Left; Bats: Left

Ht: 6'5"; Wt: 195 lbs; Born: 5/10/1969 in Austin, Texas; Debut: 4/9/1991

Year Tm	Age	G	GS	CG	GF	IP	BFP	H	R	ER	HR	SH	SF	HB	TBB	IBB	SO	WP	Bk	W	L	Pct	ShO	Sv-Op	Hld	OAvg	OOBP	ERA
Division Series		Pitching																										
1995 Cin	26	1	1	0	0	7.0	28	5	2	2	1	0	0	0	3	0	5	0	0	1	0	1.000	0	0-0	0	.200	.286	2.57
LCS		Pitching																										
Year Tm	Age	G	GS	CG	GF	IP	BFP	H	R	ER	HR	SH	SF	HB	TBB	IBB	SO	WP	Bk	W	L	Pct	ShO	Sv-Op	Hld	OAvg	OOBP	ERA
1995 Cin	26	2	2	0	0	14.1	59	14	2	2	0	0	0	0	3	0	13	1	0	0	1	.000	0	0-0	0	.250	.288	1.26
Postseason Totals		3	3	0	0	21.1	174	19	4	4	1	0	0	0	6	0	18	1	0	1	1	.500	0	0-0	0	.235	.287	1.69

Year Tm	Age	G	AB	H	2B	3B	HR	TB	R	RBI	GW	TBB	IBB	SO	HBP	SH	SF	SB	CS	SB%	GDP	Avg	OBP	SLG	Pos	G	PO	A	E	DP	FPct
Division Series		Batting																							Fielding						
1995 Cin	26	1	2	0	0	0	0	0	0	0	0	0	0	1	0	1	0	0	0	—	0	.000	.000	.000	P	1	0	2	0	1	1.000
LCS		Batting																							Fielding						
Year Tm	Age	G	AB	H	2B	3B	HR	TB	R	RBI	GW	TBB	IBB	SO	HBP	SH	SF	SB	CS	SB%	GDP	Avg	OBP	SLG	Pos	G	PO	A	E	DP	FPct
1995 Cin	26	2	5	0	0	0	0	0	0	0	0	0	0	4	0	0	0	0	0	—	0	.000	.000	.000	P	2	1	3	0	1	1.000
Postseason Totals		3	7	0	0	0	0	0	0	0	0	0	0	5	0	1	0	0	0	—	0	.000	.000	.000	P	3	1	5	0	2	1.000

OSSEE SCHRECKENGOST—Ossee Freeman Schreckengost—B: Right; T: Right

Ht: 5'10"; Wt: 180 lbs; Born: 4/11/1875 in New Bethlehem, Pennsylvania; Debut: 9/8/1897; Died: 7/9/1914

World Series		Batting																							Fielding						
Year Tm	Age	G	AB	H	2B	3B	HR	TB	R	RBI	GW	TBB	IBB	SO	HBP	SH	SF	SB	CS	SB%	GDP	Avg	OBP	SLG	Pos	G	PO	A	E	DP	FPct
1905 Phi	30	3	9	2	1	0	0	3	2	0	0	0	0	0	0	0	0	0	0	—	0	.222	.222	.333	C	3	17	4	0	1	1.000

FRED SCHULTE—Fred William Schulte—Nickname: Fritz—Bats: Right; Throws: Right

Ht: 6'1"; Wt: 183 lbs; Born: 1/13/1901 in Belleville, Illinois; Debut: 4/15/1927; Died: 5/20/1983

World Series		Batting																							Fielding						
Year Tm	Age	G	AB	H	2B	3B	HR	TB	R	RBI	GW	TBB	IBB	SO	HBP	SH	SF	SB	CS	SB%	GDP	Avg	OBP	SLG	Pos	G	PO	A	E	DP	FPct
1933 Was	32	5	21	7	1	0	1	11	1	4	0	1	0	1	0	0	0	0	1	.00	0	.333	.364	.524	OF	5	9	0	0	0	1.000

WILDFIRE SCHULTE—Frank M. Schulte—Bats: Left; Throws: Right

Ht: 5'11"; Wt: 170 lbs; Born: 9/17/1882 in Cohocton, New York; Debut: 9/21/1904; Died: 10/2/1949

World Series		Batting																							Fielding						
Year Tm	Age	G	AB	H	2B	3B	HR	TB	R	RBI	GW	TBB	IBB	SO	HBP	SH	SF	SB	CS	SB%	GDP	Avg	OBP	SLG	Pos	G	PO	A	E	DP	FPct
1906 ChN	24	6	26	7	3	0	0	10	1	3	0	1	0	3	0	0	0	0	3	.00	0	.269	.296	.385	OF	6	5	1	0	1	1.000
1907 ChN	25	5	20	5	0	0	0	5	3	2	0	1	0	2	0	0	0	0	0	—	0	.250	.286	.250	OF	5	4	2	1	0	.857
1908 ChN	26	5	18	7	0	1	0	9	4	2	0	2	0	1	0	2	0	2	2	.50	0	.389	.450	.500	OF	5	3	1	0	0	1.000
1910 ChN	28	5	17	6	3	0	0	9	3	2	0	2	0	3	0	2	0	0	5	.00	0	.353	.421	.529	OF	5	4	0	1	0	.800
WS Totals		21	81	25	6	1	0	33	11	9	0	6	0	9	0	4	0	2	10	.17	0	.309	.356	.407	OF	21	16	4	2	1	.909

BARNEY SCHULTZ—George Warren Schultz—Throws: Right; Bats: Right

Ht: 6'2"; Wt: 200 lbs; Born: 8/15/1926 in Beverly, New Jersey; Debut: 4/12/1955

World Series		Pitching																										
Year Tm	Age	G	GS	CG	GF	IP	BFP	H	R	ER	HR	SH	SF	HB	TBB	IBB	SO	WP	Bk	W	L	Pct	ShO	Sv-Op	Hld	OAvg	OOBP	ERA
1964 StL	38	4	0	0	2	4.0	24	9	8	8	2	1	0	0	3	1	1	0	0	0	1	.000	0	1- 1	0	.450	.522	18.00

World Series		Batting																							Fielding						
Year Tm	Age	G	AB	H	2B	3B	HR	TB	R	RBI	GW	TBB	IBB	SO	HBP	SH	SF	SB	CS	SB%	GDP	Avg	OBP	SLG	Pos	G	PO	A	E	DP	FPct
1964 StL	38	4	1	0	0	0	0	0	0	0	0	0	0	0	0	0	0	0	0	—	0	.000	.000	.000	P	4	0	0	0	0	—

HAL SCHUMACHER—Harold Henry Schumacher—Nickname: Prince Hal—Throws: Right; Bats: Right

Ht: 6'0"; Wt: 190 lbs; Born: 11/23/1910 in Hinckley, New York; Debut: 4/15/1931; Died: 4/21/1993

World Series		Pitching																										
Year Tm	Age	G	GS	CG	GF	IP	BFP	H	R	ER	HR	SH	SF	HB	TBB	IBB	SO	WP	Bk	W	L	Pct	ShO	Sv-Op	Hld	OAvg	OOBP	ERA
1933 NYG	22	2	2	1	0	14.2	60	13	4	4	2	0	0	0	5	0	3	2	0	1	0	1.000	0	0- 0	0	.236	.300	2.45
1936 NYG	25	2	2	1	0	12.0	55	13	9	7	1	0	0	0	10	0	11	2	0	1	1	.500	0	0- 0	0	.289	.418	5.25
1937 NYG	26	1	1	0	0	6.0	32	9	5	4	0	1	0	0	4	1	3	1	0	0	1	.000	0	0- 0	0	.333	.419	6.00
WS Totals		5	5	2	0	32.2	294	35	18	15	3	1	0	0	19	1	17	5	0	2	2	.500	0	0-0	0	.276	.370	4.13

World Series		Batting																							Fielding						
Year Tm	Age	G	AB	H	2B	3B	HR	TB	R	RBI	GW	TBB	IBB	SO	HBP	SH	SF	SB	CS	SB%	GDP	Avg	OBP	SLG	Pos	G	PO	A	E	DP	FPct
1933 NYG	22	2	7	2	0	0	0	2	0	3	0	0	0	3	0	0	0	0	0	—	1	.286	.286	.286	P	2	0	2	0	0	1.000
1936 NYG	25	2	4	0	0	0	0	0	0	0	0	1	0	3	0	0	0	0	0	—	0	.000	.200	.000	P	2	0	2	0	1	1.000
1937 NYG	26	1	1	0	0	0	0	0	0	0	0	0	0	1	0	0	0	0	0	—	0	.000	.000	.000	P	1	0	1	0	0	1.000
WS Totals		5	12	2	0	0	0	2	0	3	0	1	0	7	0	0	0	0	0	—	1	.167	.231	.167	P	5	0	5	0	1	1.000

FERDIE SCHUPP—Ferdinand Maurice Schupp—Throws: Left; Bats: Right

Ht: 5'10"; Wt: 150 lbs; Born: 1/16/1891 in Louisville, Kentucky; Debut: 4/19/1913; Died: 12/16/1971

World Series		Pitching																										
Year Tm	Age	G	GS	CG	GF	IP	BFP	H	R	ER	HR	SH	SF	HB	TBB	IBB	SO	WP	Bk	W	L	Pct	ShO	Sv-Op	Hld	OAvg	OOBP	ERA
1917 NYG	26	2	2	1	0	10.1	42	11	2	2	0	0	0	0	2	0	9	0	0	1	0	1.000	1	0- 0	0	.275	.310	1.74

World Series		Batting																							Fielding						
Year Tm	Age	G	AB	H	2B	3B	HR	TB	R	RBI	GW	TBB	IBB	SO	HBP	SH	SF	SB	CS	SB%	GDP	Avg	OBP	SLG	Pos	G	PO	A	E	DP	FPct
1917 NYG	26	2	4	1	0	0	0	1	0	1	0	0	0	1	0	0	0	0	0	—	0	.250	.250	.250	P	2	1	4	0	0	1.000

BILL SCHUSTER—William Charles Schuster—Nickname: Broadway Bill—Bats: Right; Throws: Right

Ht: 5'9"; Wt: 164 lbs; Born: 8/4/1912 in Buffalo, New York; Debut: 9/29/1937; Died: 6/28/1987

World Series		Batting																							Fielding						
Year Tm	Age	G	AB	H	2B	3B	HR	TB	R	RBI	GW	TBB	IBB	SO	HBP	SH	SF	SB	CS	SB%	GDP	Avg	OBP	SLG	Pos	G	PO	A	E	DP	FPct
1945 ChN	33	2	1	0	0	0	0	0	1	0	0	0	0	0	0	0	0	0	0	—	0	.000	.000	.000	SS	1	1	2	0	0	1.000

MIKE SCIOSCIA—Michael Lorri Scioscia—Bats: Left; Throws: Right

Ht: 6'2"; Wt: 200 lbs; Born: 11/27/1958 in Upper Darby, Pennsylvania; Debut: 4/20/1980

Division Series		Batting																							Fielding						
Year Tm	Age	G	AB	H	2B	3B	HR	TB	R	RBI	GW	TBB	IBB	SO	HBP	SH	SF	SB	CS	SB%	GDP	Avg	OBP	SLG	Pos	G	PO	A	E	DP	FPct
1981 LA	22	4	13	2	0	0	0	2	0	1	0	1	1	2	0	0	0	0	0	—	0	.154	.214	.154	C	4	21	4	0	0	1.000
LCS		Batting																							Fielding						
Year Tm	Age	G	AB	H	2B	3B	HR	TB	R	RBI	GW	TBB	IBB	SO	HBP	SH	SF	SB	CS	SB%	GDP	Avg	OBP	SLG	Pos	G	PO	A	E	DP	FPct
1981 LA	22	5	15	2	0	0	1	5	1	1	0	2	0	1	0	0	0	0	0	—	1	.133	.235	.333	C	5	27	1	0	0	1.000
1985 LA	26	6	16	4	0	0	0	4	2	1	0	4	1	0	0	0	0	0	0	—	0	.250	.400	.250	C	6	31	4	1	0	.972
1988 LA	29	7	22	8	1	0	1	12	3	2	0	1	1	2	0	0	0	0	0	—	1	.364	.391	.545	C	7	37	4	0	1	1.000
LCS Totals		18	53	14	1	0	2	21	6	4	0	7	2	3	0	0	0	0	0	—	2	.264	.350	.396	C	18	95	9	1	1	.990
World Series		Batting																							Fielding						
Year Tm	Age	G	AB	H	2B	3B	HR	TB	R	RBI	GW	TBB	IBB	SO	HBP	SH	SF	SB	CS	SB%	GDP	Avg	OBP	SLG	Pos	G	PO	A	E	DP	FPct
1981 LA	22	3	4	1	0	0	0	1	1	0	0	1	0	0	0	1	0	0	0	—	1	.250	.400	.250	C	3	7	1	0	0	1.000
1988 LA	29	4	14	3	0	0	0	3	0	1	0	0	0	2	0	0	0	0	1	.00	0	.214	.214	.214	C	4	28	0	1	0	.966
WS Totals		7	18	4	0	0	0	4	1	1	0	1	0	2	0	1	0	0	1	.00	1	.222	.263	.222	C	7	35	1	1	0	.973
Postseason Totals		29	84	20	1	0	2	27	7	6	0	9	3	7	0	1	0	0	1	.00	3	.238	.312	.321	C	29	151	14	2	1	.988

EVERETT SCOTT—Lewis Everett Scott—Nickname: Deacon—Bats: Right; Throws: Right

Ht: 5'8"; Wt: 148 lbs; Born: 11/19/1892 in Bluffton, Indiana; Debut: 4/14/1914; Died: 11/2/1960

World Series		Batting																							Fielding						
Year Tm	Age	G	AB	H	2B	3B	HR	TB	R	RBI	GW	TBB	IBB	SO	HBP	SH	SF	SB	CS	SB%	GDP	Avg	OBP	SLG	Pos	G	PO	A	E	DP	FPct
1915 Bos	22	5	18	1	0	0	0	1	0	0	0	0	0	3	0	2	0	0	0	—	0	.056	.056	.056	SS	5	8	12	0	1	1.000
1916 Bos	23	5	16	2	0	1	0	4	1	1	0	1	0	1	0	1	1	0	0	—	0	.125	.167	.250	SS	5	9	24	2	3	.943
1918 Bos	25	6	20	2	0	0	0	2	0	1	0	1	0	1	0	1	0	0	0	—	0	.100	.143	.100	SS	6	11	26	0	3	1.000
1922 NYA	29	5	14	2	0	0	0	2	0	1	0	1	0	0	0	0	1	0	0	—	0	.143	.188	.143	SS	5	14	15	0	6	1.000
1923 NYA	30	6	22	7	0	0	0	7	2	3	1	0	0	1	0	1	0	0	0	—	0	.318	.318	.318	SS	6	8	20	1	4	.966
WS Totals		27	90	14	0	1	0	16	3	6	1	3	0	6	0	5	2	0	0	—	0	.156	.179	.178	SS	27	50	97	3	17	.980

GEORGE SCOTT—George Charles Scott—Nickname: Boomer—Bats: Right; Throws: Right

Ht: 6'2"; Wt: 200 lbs; Born: 3/23/1944 in Greenville, Mississippi; Debut: 4/12/1966

World Series		Batting																							Fielding						
Year Tm	Age	G	AB	H	2B	3B	HR	TB	R	RBI	GW	TBB	IBB	SO	HBP	SH	SF	SB	CS	SB%	GDP	Avg	OBP	SLG	Pos	G	PO	A	E	DP	FPct
1967 Bos	23	7	26	6	1	1	0	9	3	0	0	3	0	6	0	0	0	0	0	—	1	.231	.310	.346	1B	7	70	3	0	3	1.000

JACK SCOTT—John William Scott—Throws: Right; Bats: Left

Ht: 6'2"; Wt: 199 lbs; Born: 4/18/1892 in Ridgeway, North Carolina; Debut: 9/6/1916; Died: 11/30/1959

World Series		Pitching																										
Year Tm	Age	G	GS	CG	GF	IP	BFP	H	R	ER	HR	SH	SF	HB	TBB	IBB	SO	WP	Bk	W	L	Pct	ShO	Sv-Op	Hld	OAvg	OOBP	ERA
1922 NYG	30	1	1	1	0	9.0	32	4	0	0	0	0	0	1	1	0	2	0	0	1	0	1.000	1	0- 0	0	.133	.188	0.00
1923 NYG	31	2	1	0	0	3.0	19	9	5	4	0	1	0	0	1	0	2	0	0	0	1	.000	0	0- 0	0	.529	.556	12.00
WS Totals		3	2	1	0	12.0	102	13	5	4	0	1	0	1	2	0	4	0	0	1	1	.500	1	0-0	0	.277	.320	3.00

World Series		Batting																							Fielding						
Year Tm	Age	G	AB	H	2B	3B	HR	TB	R	RBI	GW	TBB	IBB	SO	HBP	SH	SF	SB	CS	SB%	GDP	Avg	OBP	SLG	Pos	G	PO	A	E	DP	FPct
1922 NYG	30	1	4	1	0	0	0	1	0	0	0	0	0	1	0	0	0	0	0	—	0	.250	.250	.250	P	1	1	1	0	0	1.000
1923 NYG	31	2	1	0	0	0	0	0	0	0	0	0	0	0	0	0	0	0	0	—	0	.000	.000	.000	P	2	0	0	1	0	.000
WS Totals		3	5	1	0	0	0	1	0	0	0	0	0	1	0	0	0	0	0	—	0	.200	.200	.200	P	3	1	1	1	0	.667

MIKE SCOTT—Michael Warren Scott—Throws: Right; Bats: Right
Ht: 6'2"; Wt: 210 lbs; Born: 4/26/1955 in Santa Monica, California; Debut: 4/18/1979

LCS		Pitching																										
Year Tm	Age	G	GS	CG	GF	IP	BFP	H	R	ER	HR	SH	SF	HB	TBB	IBB	SO	WP	Bk	W	L	Pct	ShO	Sv-Op	Hld	OAvg	OOBP	ERA
1986 Hou-*C*	31	2	2	2	0	18.0	65	8	1	1	0	0	1	0	1	0	19	0	0	2	0	1.000	1	0-0	0	.127	.138	0.50

LCS		Batting																							Fielding						
Year Tm	Age	G	AB	H	2B	3B	HR	TB	R	RBI	GW	TBB	IBB	SO	HBP	SH	SF	SB	CS	SB%	GDP	Avg	OBP	SLG	Pos	G	PO	A	E	DP	FPct
1986 Hou	31	2	6	0	0	0	0	0	0	0	0	0	0	5	0	0	0	0	0	—	1	.000	.000	.000	P	2	2	4	1	0	.857

RODNEY SCOTT—Rodney Darrell Scott—Nickname: Cool Breeze—Bats: Both; Throws: Right
Ht: 6'0"; Wt: 160 lbs; Born: 10/16/1953 in Indianapolis, Indiana; Debut: 4/11/1975

LCS		Batting																							Fielding						
Year Tm	Age	G	AB	H	2B	3B	HR	TB	R	RBI	GW	TBB	IBB	SO	HBP	SH	SF	SB	CS	SB%	GDP	Avg	OBP	SLG	Pos	G	PO	A	E	DP	FPct
1981 Mon	27	5	18	3	0	0	0	3	0	0	0	1	0	3	0	1	0	1	0	1.00	0	.167	.211	.167	2B	5	12	14	1	7	.963

TONY SCOTT—Anthony Scott—Bats: Both; Throws: Right
Ht: 6'0"; Wt: 164 lbs; Born: 9/18/1951 in Cincinnati, Ohio; Debut: 9/1/1973

Division Series		Batting																							Fielding						
Year Tm	Age	G	AB	H	2B	3B	HR	TB	R	RBI	GW	TBB	IBB	SO	HBP	SH	SF	SB	CS	SB%	GDP	Avg	OBP	SLG	Pos	G	PO	A	E	DP	FPct
1981 Hou	30	5	20	3	0	0	0	3	0	2	0	1	0	6	0	0	0	0	1	.00	0	.150	.190	.150	OF	5	10	0	0	0	1.000

SCOTT SCUDDER—William Scott Scudder—Throws: Right; Bats: Right
Ht: 6'2"; Wt: 180 lbs; Born: 2/14/1968 in Paris, Texas; Debut: 6/6/1989

LCS		Pitching																										
Year Tm	Age	G	GS	CG	GF	IP	BFP	H	R	ER	HR	SH	SF	HB	TBB	IBB	SO	WP	Bk	W	L	Pct	ShO	Sv-Op	Hld	OAvg	OOBP	ERA
1990 Cin	22	1	0	0	1	1.0	4	1	0	0	0	0	0	0	0	0	1	0	0	0	0	—	0	0-0	0	.250	.250	0.00
World Series		Pitching																										
Year Tm	Age	G	GS	CG	GF	IP	BFP	H	R	ER	HR	SH	SF	HB	TBB	IBB	SO	WP	Bk	W	L	Pct	ShO	Sv-Op	Hld	OAvg	OOBP	ERA
1990 Cin	22	1	0	0	0	1.1	6	0	0	0	0	0	0	0	2	0	2	0	0	0	0	—	0	0-0	0	.000	.333	0.00
Postseason Totals		2	0	0	1	2.1	20	1	0	0	0	0	0	0	2	0	3	0	0	0	0	—	0	0-0	0	.125	.300	0.00

LCS		Batting																							Fielding						
Year Tm	Age	G	AB	H	2B	3B	HR	TB	R	RBI	GW	TBB	IBB	SO	HBP	SH	SF	SB	CS	SB%	GDP	Avg	OBP	SLG	Pos	G	PO	A	E	DP	FPct
1990 Cin	22	1	0	0	0	0	0	0	0	0	0	0	0	0	0	0	0	0	0	—	0	—	—	—	P	1	0	0	0	0	—
World Series		Batting																							Fielding						
Year Tm	Age	G	AB	H	2B	3B	HR	TB	R	RBI	GW	TBB	IBB	SO	HBP	SH	SF	SB	CS	SB%	GDP	Avg	OBP	SLG	Pos	G	PO	A	E	DP	FPct
1990 Cin	22	1	0	0	0	0	0	0	0	0	0	0	0	0	0	0	0	0	0	—	0	—	—	—	P	1	0	0	0	0	—
Postseason Totals		2	0	0	0	0	0	0	0	0	0	0	0	0	0	0	0	0	0	—	0	—	—	—	P	2	0	0	0	0	—

TOM SEAVER (HOF 1992-W)—George Thomas Seaver—Nickname: Tom Terrific—Throws: Right; Bats: Right
Ht: 6'1"; Wt: 195 lbs; Born: 11/17/1944 in Fresno, California; Debut: 4/13/1967

LCS		Pitching																										
Year Tm	Age	G	GS	CG	GF	IP	BFP	H	R	ER	HR	SH	SF	HB	TBB	IBB	SO	WP	Bk	W	L	Pct	ShO	Sv-Op	Hld	OAvg	OOBP	ERA
1969 NYN-*C*	24	1	1	0	0	7.0	33	8	5	5	2	0	1	1	3	2	2	0	0	1	0	1.000	0	0-0	0	.286	.364	6.43
1973 NYN-*C*	28	2	2	1	0	16.2	69	13	4	3	2	1	1	1	5	2	17	1	0	1	1	.500	0	0-0	0	.213	.279	1.62
1979 Cin	34	1	1	0	0	8.0	30	5	2	2	1	0	1	0	2	0	5	0	0	0	0	—	0	0-0	0	.185	.233	2.25
LCS Totals		4	4	1	0	31.2	264	26	11	10	5	1	3	2	10	4	24	1	0	2	1	.667	0	0-0	0	.224	.290	2.84
World Series		Pitching																										
Year Tm	Age	G	GS	CG	GF	IP	BFP	H	R	ER	HR	SH	SF	HB	TBB	IBB	SO	WP	Bk	W	L	Pct	ShO	Sv-Op	Hld	OAvg	OOBP	ERA
1969 NYN-*C*	24	2	2	1	0	15.0	61	12	5	5	1	0	1	0	3	0	9	0	0	1	1	.500	0	0-0	0	.211	.246	3.00
1973 NYN-*C*	28	2	2	0	0	15.0	62	13	4	4	0	1	0	0	3	0	18	1	0	0	1	.000	0	0-0	0	.224	.262	2.40
WS Totals		4	4	1	0	30.0	246	25	9	9	1	1	1	0	6	0	27	1	0	1	2	.333	0	0-0	0	.217	.254	2.70
Postseason Totals		8	8	2	0	61.2	510	51	20	19	6	2	4	2	16	4	51	2	0	3	3	.500	0	0-0	0	.221	.273	2.77

LCS		Batting																							Fielding						
Year Tm	Age	G	AB	H	2B	3B	HR	TB	R	RBI	GW	TBB	IBB	SO	HBP	SH	SF	SB	CS	SB%	GDP	Avg	OBP	SLG	Pos	G	PO	A	E	DP	FPct
1969 NYN	24	1	3	0	0	0	0	0	0	0	0	0	0	0	0	0	0	0	0	—	0	.000	.000	.000	P	1	1	0	0	0	1.000
1973 NYN	28	2	6	2	2	0	0	4	1	1	0	1	0	1	0	0	0	0	0	—	0	.333	.429	.667	P	2	0	4	0	0	1.000
1979 Cin	34	1	2	0	0	0	0	0	0	0	0	0	0	1	0	0	0	0	0	—	0	.000	.000	.000	P	1	0	0	0	0	—
LCS Totals		4	11	2	2	0	0	4	1	1	0	1	0	2	0	0	0	0	0	—	0	.182	.250	.364	P	4	1	5	0	0	1.000
World Series		Batting																							Fielding						
Year Tm	Age	G	AB	H	2B	3B	HR	TB	R	RBI	GW	TBB	IBB	SO	HBP	SH	SF	SB	CS	SB%	GDP	Avg	OBP	SLG	Pos	G	PO	A	E	DP	FPct
1969 NYN	24	2	4	0	0	0	0	0	0	0	0	0	0	2	0	0	0	0	0	—	1	.000	.000	.000	P	2	2	1	0	0	1.000
1973 NYN	28	2	5	0	0	0	0	0	0	0	0	0	0	2	0	0	0	0	0	—	0	.000	.000	.000	P	2	0	2	0	0	1.000
WS Totals		4	9	0	0	0	0	0	0	0	0	0	0	4	0	0	0	0	0	—	1	.000	.000	.000	P	4	2	3	0	0	1.000
Postseason Totals		8	20	2	2	0	0	4	1	1	0	1	0	6	0	0	0	0	0	—	1	.100	.143	.200	P	8	3	8	0	0	1.000

JIMMY SEBRING—James Dennison Sebring—Bats: Left; Throws: Right
Ht: 6'0"; Wt: 180 lbs; Born: 3/22/1882 in Liberty, Pennsylvania; Debut: 9/8/1902; Died: 12/22/1909

World Series		Batting																							Fielding						
Year Tm	Age	G	AB	H	2B	3B	HR	TB	R	RBI	GW	TBB	IBB	SO	HBP	SH	SF	SB	CS	SB%	GDP	Avg	OBP	SLG	Pos	G	PO	A	E	DP	FPct
1903 Pit	21	8	30	10	0	1	1	15	3	4	0	1	0	4	0	0	0	0	1	.00	0	.333	.355	.500	OF	8	13	1	0	0	1.000

FRANK SECORY—Frank Edward Secory—Bats: Right; Throws: Right
Ht: 6'1"; Wt: 200 lbs; Born: 8/24/1912 in Mason City, Iowa; Debut: 4/28/1940; Died: 4/7/1995

World Series		Batting																							Fielding						
Year Tm	Age	G	AB	H	2B	3B	HR	TB	R	RBI	GW	TBB	IBB	SO	HBP	SH	SF	SB	CS	SB%	GDP	Avg	OBP	SLG	Pos	G	PO	A	E	DP	FPct
1945 ChN	33	5	5	2	0	0	0	2	0	0	0	0	0	2	0	0	0	0	0	—	0	.400	.400	.400	—						

BOB SEEDS—Ira Robert Seeds—Nickname: Suitcase Bob—Bats: Right; Throws: Right
Ht: 6'0"; Wt: 180 lbs; Born: 2/24/1907 in Ringgold, Texas; Debut: 4/19/1930; Died: 10/28/1993

World Series		Batting																							Fielding						
Year Tm	Age	G	AB	H	2B	3B	HR	TB	R	RBI	GW	TBB	IBB	SO	HBP	SH	SF	SB	CS	SB%	GDP	Avg	OBP	SLG	Pos	G	PO	A	E	DP	FPct
1936 NYA	29	1	0	0	0	0	0	0	0	0	0	0	0	0	0	0	0	0	1	.00	0	—	—	—	—						

CHUCK SEELBACH—Charles Frederick Seelbach—Throws: Right; Bats: Right
Ht: 6'0"; Wt: 180 lbs; Born: 3/20/1948 in Lakewood, Ohio; Debut: 6/29/1971

LCS		Pitching																										
Year Tm	Age	G	GS	CG	GF	IP	BFP	H	R	ER	HR	SH	SF	HB	TBB	IBB	SO	WP	Bk	W	L	Pct	ShO	Sv-Op	Hld	OAvg	OOBP	ERA
1972 Det	24	2	0	0	1	1.0	7	4	2	2	0	0	0	0	0	0	0	0	0	0	0	—	0	0-1	0	.571	.571	18.00

LCS		Batting																							Fielding						
Year Tm	Age	G	AB	H	2B	3B	HR	TB	R	RBI	GW	TBB	IBB	SO	HBP	SH	SF	SB	CS	SB%	GDP	Avg	OBP	SLG	Pos	G	PO	A	E	DP	FPct
1972 Det	24	2	0	0	0	0	0	0	0	0	0	0	0	0	0	0	0	0	0	—	0	—	—	—	P	2	0	0	0	0	—

DIEGO SEGUI—Diego Pablo Segui—Throws: Right; Bats: Right
Ht: 6'0"; Wt: 190 lbs; Born: 8/17/1937 in Holguin, Cuba; Debut: 4/12/1962

LCS		Pitching																										
Year Tm	Age	G	GS	CG	GF	IP	BFP	H	R	ER	HR	SH	SF	HB	TBB	IBB	SO	WP	Bk	W	L	Pct	ShO	Sv-Op	Hld	OAvg	OOBP	ERA
1971 Oak	34	1	1	0	0	4.2	25	6	3	3	0	0	1	0	6	2	4	0	0	0	1	.000	0	0-0	0	.333	.480	5.79
World Series		Pitching																										
Year Tm	Age	G	GS	CG	GF	IP	BFP	H	R	ER	HR	SH	SF	HB	TBB	IBB	SO	WP	Bk	W	L	Pct	ShO	Sv-Op	Hld	OAvg	OOBP	ERA
1975 Bos	38	1	0	0	1	1.0	3	0	0	0	0	0	1	0	0	0	0	0	0	0	0	—	0	0-0	0	.000	.000	0.00
Postseason Totals		2	1	0	1	5.2	56	6	3	3	0	0	2	0	6	2	4	0	0	0	1	.000	0	0-0	0	.300	.429	4.76

LCS		Batting																							Fielding						
Year Tm	Age	G	AB	H	2B	3B	HR	TB	R	RBI	GW	TBB	IBB	SO	HBP	SH	SF	SB	CS	SB%	GDP	Avg	OBP	SLG	Pos	G	PO	A	E	DP	FPct
1971 Oak	34	1	2	0	0	0	0	0	0	0	0	0	0	0	0	0	0	0	0	—	0	.000	.000	.000	P	1	0	0	0	0	—

World Series		Batting																							Fielding						
Year Tm	Age	G	AB	H	2B	3B	HR	TB	R	RBI	GW	TBB	IBB	SO	HBP	SH	SF	SB	CS	SB%	GDP	Avg	OBP	SLG	Pos	G	PO	A	E	DP	FPct
1975 Bos	38	1	0	0	0	0	0	0	0	0	0	0	0	0	0	0	0	0	0	—	0	—	—	—	P	1	0	0	0	0	—
Postseason Totals		2	2	0	0	0	0	0	0	0	0	0	0	0	0	0	0	0	0	—	0	.000	.000	.000	P	2	0	0	0	0	—

KEVIN SEITZER—Kevin Lee Seitzer—Bats: Right; Throws: Right

Ht: 5'11"; Wt: 180 lbs; Born: 3/26/1962 in Springfield, Illinois; Debut: 9/3/1986

Division Series		Batting																							Fielding						
Year Tm	Age	G	AB	H	2B	3B	HR	TB	R	RBI	GW	TBB	IBB	SO	HBP	SH	SF	SB	CS	SB%	GDP	Avg	OBP	SLG	Pos	G	PO	A	E	DP	FPct
1996 Cle	34	4	17	5	1	0	0	6	1	4	0	2	0	4	0	0	0	1	0	1.00	1	.294	.368	.353	1B	1	7	1	1	1	.889
1997 Cle	35	1	4	0	0	0	0	0	0	0	0	0	0	0	0	0	0	0	0	—	0	.000	.000	.000	1B	1	9	0	0	0	1.000
DS Totals		5	21	5	1	0	0	6	1	4	0	2	0	4	0	0	0	1	0	1.00	1	.238	.304	.286	1B	2	16	1	1	1	.944

LCS		Batting																							Fielding						
Year Tm	Age	G	AB	H	2B	3B	HR	TB	R	RBI	GW	TBB	IBB	SO	HBP	SH	SF	SB	CS	SB%	GDP	Avg	OBP	SLG	Pos	G	PO	A	E	DP	FPct
1997 Cle	35	4	4	0	0	0	0	0	0	0	0	1	0	2	0	1	0	0	0	—	0	.000	.200	.000	1B	3	11	1	0	2	1.000

World Series		Batting																							Fielding						
Year Tm	Age	G	AB	H	2B	3B	HR	TB	R	RBI	GW	TBB	IBB	SO	HBP	SH	SF	SB	CS	SB%	GDP	Avg	OBP	SLG	Pos	G	PO	A	E	DP	FPct
1997 Cle	35	1	1	0	0	0	0	0	0	0	0	0	0	0	0	0	0	0	0	—	0	.000	.000	.000	—						
Postseason Totals		10	26	5	1	0	0	6	1	4	0	3	0	6	0	1	0	1	0	1.00	1	.192	.276	.231	1B	5	27	2	1	3	.967

GEORGE SELKIRK—George Alexander Selkirk—Nickname: Twinkletoes—Bats: Left; Throws: Right

Ht: 6'1"; Wt: 182 lbs; Born: 1/4/1908 in Huntsville, Ontario; Debut: 8/12/1934; Died: 1/19/1987

World Series		Batting																							Fielding						
Year Tm	Age	G	AB	H	2B	3B	HR	TB	R	RBI	GW	TBB	IBB	SO	HBP	SH	SF	SB	CS	SB%	GDP	Avg	OBP	SLG	Pos	G	PO	A	E	DP	FPct
1936 NYA	28	6	24	8	0	1	2	16	6	3	1	4	1	4	0	0	0	0	1	.00	0	.333	.429	.667	OF	6	9	0	1	0	.900
1937 NYA	29	5	19	5	1	0	0	6	5	6	0	2	0	0	0	0	0	0	0	—	0	.263	.333	.316	OF	5	7	0	0	0	1.000
1938 NYA	30	3	10	2	0	0	0	2	0	1	1	2	0	1	0	0	0	0	0	—	0	.200	.333	.200	OF	3	3	0	0	0	1.000
1939 NYA	31	4	12	2	1	0	0	3	0	0	0	3	0	2	0	0	0	0	0	—	0	.167	.333	.250	OF	4	10	0	0	0	1.000
1941 NYA	33	2	2	1	0	0	0	1	0	0	0	0	0	0	0	0	0	0	0	—	0	.500	.500	.500	—						
1942 NYA	34	1	1	0	0	0	0	0	0	0	0	0	0	0	0	0	0	0	0	—	0	.000	.000	.000	—						
WS Totals		21	68	18	2	1	2	28	11	10	2	11	1	7	0	0	0	0	1	.00	0	.265	.367	.412	OF	18	29	0	1	0	.967

ANDY SEMINICK—Andrew Wasil Seminick—Bats: Right; Throws: Right

Ht: 5'11"; Wt: 187 lbs; Born: 9/12/1920 in Pierce, West Virginia; Debut: 9/14/1943

World Series		Batting																							Fielding						
Year Tm	Age	G	AB	H	2B	3B	HR	TB	R	RBI	GW	TBB	IBB	SO	HBP	SH	SF	SB	CS	SB%	GDP	Avg	OBP	SLG	Pos	G	PO	A	E	DP	FPct
1950 Phi	30	4	11	2	0	0	0	2	0	0	0	1	0	3	0	2	0	0	0	—	0	.182	.250	.182	C	4	14	2	1	0	.941

HANK SEVEREID—Henry Levai Severeid—Bats: Right; Throws: Right

Ht: 6'0"; Wt: 175 lbs; Born: 6/1/1891 in Story City, Iowa; Debut: 5/15/1911; Died: 12/17/1968

World Series		Batting																							Fielding						
Year Tm	Age	G	AB	H	2B	3B	HR	TB	R	RBI	GW	TBB	IBB	SO	HBP	SH	SF	SB	CS	SB%	GDP	Avg	OBP	SLG	Pos	G	PO	A	E	DP	FPct
1925 Was	34	1	3	1	0	0	0	1	0	0	0	0	0	0	0	0	0	0	0	—	0	.333	.333	.333	C	1	6	0	1	0	.857
1926 NYA	35	7	22	6	1	0	0	7	1	1	0	1	0	2	0	1	0	0	0	—	0	.273	.304	.318	C	7	38	7	0	0	1.000
WS Totals		8	25	7	1	0	0	8	1	1	0	1	0	2	0	1	0	0	0	—	0	.280	.308	.320	C	8	44	7	1	0	.981

JOE SEWELL (HOF 1977-V)—Joseph Wheeler Sewell—Bats: Left; Throws: Right

Ht: 5'6"; Wt: 155 lbs; Born: 10/9/1898 in Titus, Alabama; Debut: 9/10/1920; Died: 3/6/1990

World Series		Batting																							Fielding						
Year Tm	Age	G	AB	H	2B	3B	HR	TB	R	RBI	GW	TBB	IBB	SO	HBP	SH	SF	SB	CS	SB%	GDP	Avg	OBP	SLG	Pos	G	PO	A	E	DP	FPct
1920 Cle	21	7	23	4	0	0	0	4	0	0	0	2	0	1	0	0	0	0	2	.00	1	.174	.240	.174	SS	7	12	28	5	3	.889
1932 NYA	33	4	15	5	1	0	0	6	4	3	0	4	0	0	1	0	0	0	0	—	0	.333	.500	.400	3B	4	4	6	1	1	.909
WS Totals		11	38	9	1	0	0	10	4	3	0	6	0	1	1	0	0	0	2	.00	1	.237	.356	.263	SS	7	12	28	5	3	.889

LUKE SEWELL—James Luther Sewell—Bats: Right; Throws: Right

Ht: 5'9"; Wt: 160 lbs; Born: 1/5/1901 in Titus, Alabama; Debut: 6/30/1921; Died: 5/14/1987

World Series		Batting																							Fielding						
Year Tm	Age	G	AB	H	2B	3B	HR	TB	R	RBI	GW	TBB	IBB	SO	HBP	SH	SF	SB	CS	SB%	GDP	Avg	OBP	SLG	Pos	G	PO	A	E	DP	FPct
1933 Was	32	5	17	3	0	0	0	3	1	1	0	2	1	0	0	0	0	1	0	1.00	0	.176	.263	.176	C	5	23	2	0	0	1.000

SOCKS SEYBOLD—Ralph Orlando Seybold—Bats: Right; Throws: Right

Ht: 5'11"; Wt: 175 lbs; Born: 11/23/1870 in Washingtonville, Ohio; Debut: 8/20/1899; Died: 12/22/1921

World Series		Batting																							Fielding						
Year Tm	Age	G	AB	H	2B	3B	HR	TB	R	RBI	GW	TBB	IBB	SO	HBP	SH	SF	SB	CS	SB%	GDP	Avg	OBP	SLG	Pos	G	PO	A	E	DP	FPct
1905 Phi	34	5	16	2	0	0	0	2	0	0	0	2	0	3	0	0	0	0	0	—	0	.125	.222	.125	OF	5	4	1	0	1	1.000

TILLIE SHAFER—Arthur Joseph Shafer—Bats: Both; Throws: Right

Ht: 5'10"; Wt: 165 lbs; Born: 3/22/1889 in Los Angeles, California; Debut: 4/24/1909; Died: 1/10/1962

World Series		Batting																							Fielding						
Year Tm	Age	G	AB	H	2B	3B	HR	TB	R	RBI	GW	TBB	IBB	SO	HBP	SH	SF	SB	CS	SB%	GDP	Avg	OBP	SLG	Pos	G	PO	A	E	DP	FPct
1912 NYG	23	3	0	0	0	0	0	0	0	0	0	0	0	0	0	0	0	0	0	—	0	—	—	—	SS	3	1	4	0	0	1.000
1913 NYG	24	5	19	3	1	1	0	6	2	1	0	2	0	3	0	0	0	0	1	.00	0	.158	.238	.316	3B	1	1	0	0	0	1.000
																									OF	5	7	0	0	0	1.000
WS Totals		8	19	3	1	1	0	6	2	1	0	2	0	3	0	0	0	0	1	.00	0	.158	.238	.316	OF	5	7	0	0	0	1.000

ART SHAMSKY—Arthur Louis Shamsky—Bats: Left; Throws: Left

Ht: 6'1"; Wt: 168 lbs; Born: 10/14/1941 in St. Louis, Missouri; Debut: 4/17/1965

LCS		Batting																							Fielding						
Year Tm	Age	G	AB	H	2B	3B	HR	TB	R	RBI	GW	TBB	IBB	SO	HBP	SH	SF	SB	CS	SB%	GDP	Avg	OBP	SLG	Pos	G	PO	A	E	DP	FPct
1969 NYN	27	3	13	7	0	0	0	7	3	1	0	0	0	3	0	0	0	0	0	—	0	.538	.538	.538	OF	3	3	0	0	0	1.000

World Series		Batting																							Fielding						
Year Tm	Age	G	AB	H	2B	3B	HR	TB	R	RBI	GW	TBB	IBB	SO	HBP	SH	SF	SB	CS	SB%	GDP	Avg	OBP	SLG	Pos	G	PO	A	E	DP	FPct
1969 NYN	27	3	6	0	0	0	0	0	0	0	0	0	0	0	0	0	0	0	0	—	0	.000	.000	.000	OF	1	1	0	0	0	1.000
Postseason Totals		6	19	7	0	0	0	7	3	1	0	0	0	3	0	0	0	0	0	—	0	.368	.368	.368	OF	4	4	0	0	0	1.000

MIKE SHANNON—Thomas Michael Shannon—Nickname: Moonman—Bats: Right; Throws: Right

Ht: 6'3"; Wt: 195 lbs; Born: 7/15/1939 in St. Louis, Missouri; Debut: 9/11/1962

World Series		Batting																							Fielding						
Year Tm	Age	G	AB	H	2B	3B	HR	TB	R	RBI	GW	TBB	IBB	SO	HBP	SH	SF	SB	CS	SB%	GDP	Avg	OBP	SLG	Pos	G	PO	A	E	DP	FPct
1964 StL	25	7	28	6	0	0	1	9	6	2	0	0	0	9	0	1	0	1	0	1.00	2	.214	.214	.321	OF	7	13	2	0	1	1.000
1967 StL	28	7	24	5	1	0	1	9	3	2	0	1	0	4	0	0	0	0	0	—	0	.208	.240	.375	3B	7	5	13	2	1	.900
1968 StL	29	7	29	8	1	0	1	12	3	4	1	1	0	5	0	0	0	0	0	—	2	.276	.300	.414	3B	7	5	10	1	1	.938
WS Totals		21	81	19	2	0	3	30	12	8	1	2	0	18	0	1	0	1	0	1.00	4	.235	.253	.370	3B	14	10	23	3	2	.917

BOBBY SHANTZ—Robert Clayton Shantz—Throws: Left; Bats: Right

Ht: 5'6"; Wt: 139 lbs; Born: 9/26/1925 in Pottstown, Pennsylvania; Debut: 5/1/1949

World Series		Pitching																										
Year Tm	Age	G	GS	CG	GF	IP	BFP	H	R	ER	HR	SH	SF	HB	TBB	IBB	SO	WP	Bk	W	L	Pct	ShO	Sv-Op	Hld	OAvg	OOBP	ERA
1957 NYA	32	3	1	0	0	6.2	30	8	5	3	1	0	0	0	2	0	7	0	0	0	1	.000	0	0- 0	0	.286	.333	4.05
1960 NYA	35	3	0	0	1	6.1	21	4	3	3	0	0	0	0	1	0	1	0	0	0	0	—	0	0- 0	0	.200	.238	4.26
WS Totals		6	1	0	1	13.0	102	12	8	6	1	0	0	0	3	0	8	0	0	0	1	.000	0	0-0	0	.250	.294	4.15

World Series		Batting																							Fielding						
Year Tm	Age	G	AB	H	2B	3B	HR	TB	R	RBI	GW	TBB	IBB	SO	HBP	SH	SF	SB	CS	SB%	GDP	Avg	OBP	SLG	Pos	G	PO	A	E	DP	FPct
1957 NYA	32	3	1	0	0	0	0	0	0	0	0	0	0	0	0	0	0	0	0	—	0	.000	.000	.000	P	3	0	1	0	0	1.000
1960 NYA	35	3	3	1	0	0	0	1	0	0	0	0	0	0	0	0	0	0	0	—	0	.333	.333	.333	P	3	3	2	0	1	1.000
WS Totals		6	4	1	0	0	0	1	0	0	0	0	0	0	0	0	0	0	0	—	0	.250	.250	.250	P	6	3	3	0	1	1.000

MIKE SHARPERSON—Michael Tyrone Sharperson—Bats: Right; Throws: Right

Ht: 6'3"; Wt: 190 lbs; Born: 10/4/1961 in Orangeburg, South Carolina; Debut: 4/6/1987; Died: 5/26/1996

LCS		Batting																							Fielding						
Year Tm	Age	G	AB	H	2B	3B	HR	TB	R	RBI	GW	TBB	IBB	SO	HBP	SH	SF	SB	CS	SB%	GDP	Avg	OBP	SLG	Pos	G	PO	A	E	DP	FPct
1988 LA	26	2	1	0	0	0	0	0	0	1	0	1	0	0	0	0	0	0	0	—	0	.000	.500	.000	SS	1	0	0	0	0	—
																									3B	1	1	0	0	0	1.000

BOB SHAW—Robert John Shaw—Throws: Right; Bats: Right

Ht: 6'2"; Wt: 195 lbs; Born: 6/29/1933 in Bronx, New York; Debut: 8/11/1957

World Series		Pitching																										
Year Tm	Age	G	GS	CG	GF	IP	BFP	H	R	ER	HR	SH	SF	HB	TBB	IBB	SO	WP	Bk	W	L	Pct	ShO	Sv-Op	Hld	OAvg	OOBP	ERA
1959 ChA	26	2	2	0	0	14.0	61	17	4	4	3	0	0	0	2	0	2	1	0	1	1	.500	0	0- 0	0	.288	.311	2.57

World Series		Batting																							Fielding						
Year Tm	Age	G	AB	H	2B	3B	HR	TB	R	RBI	GW	TBB	IBB	SO	HBP	SH	SF	SB	CS	SB%	GDP	Avg	OBP	SLG	Pos	G	PO	A	E	DP	FPct
1959 ChA	26	2	4	1	0	0	0	1	0	0	0	0	0	2	0	2	0	0	0	—	0	.250	.250	.250	P	2	0	4	0	0	1.000

BOB SHAWKEY—James Robert Shawkey—Nicknames: Sailor Bob, Bob the Gob—Throws: Right; Bats: Right

Ht: 5'11"; Wt: 168 lbs; Born: 12/4/1890 in Sigel, Pennsylvania; Debut: 7/16/1913; Died: 12/31/1980

World Series		Pitching																										
Year Tm	Age	G	GS	CG	GF	IP	BFP	H	R	ER	HR	SH	SF	HB	TBB	IBB	SO	WP	Bk	W	L	Pct	ShO	Sv-Op	Hld	OAvg	OOBP	ERA
1914 Phi	23	1	1	0	0	5.0	20	4	3	2	0	0	0	0	2	0	0	0	0	0	1	.000	0	0- 0	0	.222	.300	3.60
1921 NYA	30	2	1	0	0	9.0	44	13	9	7	0	1	0	0	6	0	5	0	0	0	1	.000	0	0- 0	0	.351	.442	7.00
1922 NYA	31	1	1	1	0	10.0	38	8	3	3	1	0	0	0	2	0	4	1	0	0	0	—	0	0- 0	0	.222	.263	2.70
1923 NYA	32	1	1	0	0	7.2	38	12	3	3	0	0	0	1	4	0	2	0	0	1	0	1.000	0	0- 0	0	.364	.447	3.52
1926 NYA	35	3	1	0	0	10.0	39	8	7	6	0	3	0	0	2	0	7	0	0	0	1	.000	0	0- 0	0	.235	.278	5.40
WS Totals		8	5	1	0	41.2	358	45	25	21	1	4	0	1	16	0	18	1	0	1	3	.250	0	0-0	0	.285	.354	4.54

World Series		Batting																							Fielding						
Year Tm	Age	G	AB	H	2B	3B	HR	TB	R	RBI	GW	TBB	IBB	SO	HBP	SH	SF	SB	CS	SB%	GDP	Avg	OBP	SLG	Pos	G	PO	A	E	DP	FPct
1914 Phi	23	1	2	1	1	0	0	2	0	1	0	0	0	1	0	0	0	0	0	—	0	.500	.500	1.000	P	1	0	3	0	0	1.000
1921 NYA	30	2	4	2	0	0	0	2	2	0	0	0	0	1	0	0	0	0	0	—	0	.500	.500	.500	P	2	0	0	0	0	—
1922 NYA	31	1	4	0	0	0	0	0	0	0	0	0	0	1	0	0	0	0	0	—	0	.000	.000	.000	P	1	0	2	0	0	1.000
1923 NYA	32	1	3	1	0	0	0	1	0	1	0	0	0	0	0	0	1	0	0	—	0	.333	.250	.333	P	1	1	2	0	1	1.000
1926 NYA	35	3	2	0	0	0	0	0	0	0	0	0	0	1	0	0	0	0	0	—	0	.000	.000	.000	P	3	0	1	0	0	1.000
WS Totals		8	15	4	1	0	0	5	2	2	0	0	0	4	0	0	1	0	0	—	0	.267	.250	.333	P	8	1	8	0	1	1.000

SPEC SHEA—Francis Joseph Shea—Nickname: The Naugatuck Nugget—Throws: Right; Bats: Right

Ht: 6'0"; Wt: 195 lbs; Born: 10/2/1920 in Naugatuck, Connecticut; Debut: 4/19/1947

World Series		Pitching																										
Year Tm	Age	G	GS	CG	GF	IP	BFP	H	R	ER	HR	SH	SF	HB	TBB	IBB	SO	WP	Bk	W	L	Pct	ShO	Sv-Op	Hld	OAvg	OOBP	ERA
1947 NYA	26	3	3	1	0	15.1	61	10	4	4	0	1	0	0	8	1	10	0	1	2	0	1.000	0	0- 0	0	.192	.300	2.35

World Series		Batting																							Fielding						
Year Tm	Age	G	AB	H	2B	3B	HR	TB	R	RBI	GW	TBB	IBB	SO	HBP	SH	SF	SB	CS	SB%	GDP	Avg	OBP	SLG	Pos	G	PO	A	E	DP	FPct
1947 NYA	26	3	5	2	1	0	0	3	0	1	1	0	0	2	0	0	0	0	0	—	0	.400	.400	.600	P	3	1	3	0	0	1.000

DANNY SHEAFFER—Danny Todd Sheaffer—Bats: Right; Throws: Right

Ht: 6'0"; Wt: 185 lbs; Born: 8/2/1961 in Jacksonville, Florida; Debut: 4/9/1987

LCS		Batting																							Fielding						
Year Tm	Age	G	AB	H	2B	3B	HR	TB	R	RBI	GW	TBB	IBB	SO	HBP	SH	SF	SB	CS	SB%	GDP	Avg	OBP	SLG	Pos	G	PO	A	E	DP	FPct
1996 StL	35	2	3	0	0	0	0	0	0	0	0	0	0	1	0	0	0	0	0	—	0	.000	.000	.000	C	2	3	0	0	0	1.000

DAVE SHEAN—David William Shean—Bats: Right; Throws: Right

Ht: 5'11"; Wt: 175 lbs; Born: 7/9/1883 in Arlington, Massachusetts; Debut: 9/10/1906; Died: 5/22/1963

World Series		Batting																							Fielding						
Year Tm	Age	G	AB	H	2B	3B	HR	TB	R	RBI	GW	TBB	IBB	SO	HBP	SH	SF	SB	CS	SB%	GDP	Avg	OBP	SLG	Pos	G	PO	A	E	DP	FPct
1918 Bos	35	6	19	4	1	0	0	5	2	0	0	4	0	3	0	1	0	1	0	1.00	0	.211	.348	.263	2B	6	15	16	0	3	1.000

JIMMY SHECKARD—Samuel James Tilden Sheckard—Bats: Left; Throws: Right

Ht: 5'9"; Wt: 175 lbs; Born: 11/23/1878 in Upper Chanceford, Pennsylvania; Debut: 9/14/1897; Died: 1/15/1947

World Series		Batting																							Fielding						
Year Tm	Age	G	AB	H	2B	3B	HR	TB	R	RBI	GW	TBB	IBB	SO	HBP	SH	SF	SB	CS	SB%	GDP	Avg	OBP	SLG	Pos	G	PO	A	E	DP	FPct
1906 ChN	27	6	21	0	0	0	0	0	0	1	0	2	0	4	0	3	0	1	0	1.00	0	.000	.087	.000	OF	6	10	1	0	1	1.000
1907 ChN	28	5	21	5	2	0	0	7	0	2	0	0	0	4	1	1	0	1	2	.33	0	.238	.273	.333	OF	5	10	0	0	0	1.000
1908 ChN	29	5	21	5	2	0	0	7	2	1	0	2	0	3	0	0	0	1	1	.50	2	.238	.304	.333	OF	5	7	0	0	0	1.000
1910 ChN	31	5	14	4	2	0	0	6	5	1	1	7	0	2	0	1	0	1	0	1.00	0	.286	.524	.429	OF	5	7	2	1	0	.900
WS Totals		21	77	14	6	0	0	20	7	5	1	11	0	13	1	5	0	4	3	.57	2	.182	.292	.260	OF	21	34	3	1	1	.974

JACK SHEEHAN—John Thomas Sheehan—Bats: Both; Throws: Right

Ht: 5'8"; Wt: 165 lbs; Born: 4/15/1893 in Chicago, Illinois; Debut: 9/11/1920; Died: 5/29/1987

World Series		Batting																							Fielding						
Year Tm	Age	G	AB	H	2B	3B	HR	TB	R	RBI	GW	TBB	IBB	SO	HBP	SH	SF	SB	CS	SB%	GDP	Avg	OBP	SLG	Pos	G	PO	A	E	DP	FPct
1920 Bro	27	3	11	2	0	0	0	2	0	0	0	0	0	1	0	1	0	0	0	—	0	.182	.182	.182	3B	3	3	5	2	0	.800

ANDY SHEETS—Andrew Mark Sheets—Bats: Right; Throws: Right

Ht: 6'2"; Wt: 180 lbs; Born: 11/19/1971 in Baton Rouge, Louisiana; Debut: 4/22/1996

Division Series		Batting																							Fielding						
Year Tm	Age	G	AB	H	2B	3B	HR	TB	R	RBI	GW	TBB	IBB	SO	HBP	SH	SF	SB	CS	SB%	GDP	Avg	OBP	SLG	Pos	G	PO	A	E	DP	FPct
1997 Sea	25	2	3	1	0	0	0	1	0	0	0	0	0	2	0	0	0	0	0	—	0	.333	.333	.333	3B	2	0	0	0	0	—

GARY SHEFFIELD—Gary Antonian Sheffield—Bats: Right; Throws: Right

Ht: 5'11"; Wt: 190 lbs; Born: 11/18/1968 in Tampa, Florida; Debut: 9/3/1988

Division Series		Batting																							Fielding						
Year Tm	Age	G	AB	H	2B	3B	HR	TB	R	RBI	GW	TBB	IBB	SO	HBP	SH	SF	SB	CS	SB%	GDP	Avg	OBP	SLG	Pos	G	PO	A	E	DP	FPct
1997 Fla	28	3	9	5	1	0	1	9	3	1	0	5	0	0	0	0	0	1	0	1.00	0	.556	.714	1.000	OF	3	6	0	0	0	1.000

LCS		Batting																							Fielding						
Year Tm	Age	G	AB	H	2B	3B	HR	TB	R	RBI	GW	TBB	IBB	SO	HBP	SH	SF	SB	CS	SB%	GDP	Avg	OBP	SLG	Pos	G	PO	A	E	DP	FPct
1997 Fla	28	6	17	4	0	0	1	7	6	1	0	7	0	3	0	0	0	0	0	—	0	.235	.458	.412	OF	6	5	2	0	0	1.000

World Series		Batting																							Fielding						
Year Tm	Age	G	AB	H	2B	3B	HR	TB	R	RBI	GW	TBB	IBB	SO	HBP	SH	SF	SB	CS	SB%	GDP	Avg	OBP	SLG	Pos	G	PO	A	E	DP	FPct
1997 Fla	28	7	24	7	1	0	1	11	4	5	0	8	0	5	1	0	0	0	0	—	2	.292	.485	.458	OF	7	16	0	1	0	.941
Postseason Totals		16	50	16	2	0	3	27	13	7	0	20	0	8	1	0	0	1	0	1.00	2	.320	.521	.540	OF	16	27	2	1	0	.967

JOHN SHELBY—John T. Shelby—Nickname: T-Bone—Bats: Both; Throws: Right

Ht: 6'1"; Wt: 175 lbs; Born: 2/23/1958 in Lexington, Kentucky; Debut: 9/15/1981

LCS		Batting																							Fielding						
Year Tm	Age	G	AB	H	2B	3B	HR	TB	R	RBI	GW	TBB	IBB	SO	HBP	SH	SF	SB	CS	SB%	GDP	Avg	OBP	SLG	Pos	G	PO	A	E	DP	FPct
1983 Bal	25	3	9	2	0	0	0	2	1	0	0	1	0	3	0	0	0	1	0	1.00	0	.222	.300	.222	OF	3	2	0	0	0	1.000
1988 LA	30	7	24	4	0	0	0	4	3	3	0	5	1	12	0	0	1	2	0	1.00	0	.167	.300	.167	OF	7	19	0	0	0	1.000
LCS Totals		10	33	6	0	0	0	6	4	3	0	6	1	15	0	0	1	3	0	1.00	0	.182	.300	.182	OF	10	21	0	0	0	1.000

World Series		Batting																							Fielding						
Year Tm	Age	G	AB	H	2B	3B	HR	TB	R	RBI	GW	TBB	IBB	SO	HBP	SH	SF	SB	CS	SB%	GDP	Avg	OBP	SLG	Pos	G	PO	A	E	DP	FPct
1983 Bal	25	5	9	4	0	0	0	4	1	1	1	0	0	4	0	0	1	0	0	—	0	.444	.400	.444	OF	5	10	0	0	0	1.000
1988 LA	30	5	18	4	1	0	0	5	0	1	0	2	0	7	0	0	0	1	0	1.00	0	.222	.300	.278	OF	5	14	0	0	0	1.000
WS Totals		10	27	8	1	0	0	9	1	2	1	2	0	11	0	0	1	1	0	1.00	0	.296	.333	.333	OF	10	24	0	0	0	1.000
Postseason Totals		20	60	14	1	0	0	15	5	5	1	8	1	26	0	0	2	4	0	1.00	0	.233	.314	.250	OF	20	45	0	0	0	1.000

ROLLIE SHELDON—Roland Frank Sheldon—Throws: Right; Bats: Right

Ht: 6'4"; Wt: 185 lbs; Born: 12/17/1936 in Putnam, Connecticut; Debut: 4/23/1961

World Series		Pitching																										
Year Tm	Age	G	GS	CG	GF	IP	BFP	H	R	ER	HR	SH	SF	HB	TBB	IBB	SO	WP	Bk	W	L	Pct	ShO	Sv-Op	Hld	OAvg	OOBP	ERA
1964 NYA	27	2	0	0	0	2.2	10	0	2	0	0	0	1	0	2	1	2	0	0	0	0	—	0	0-0	0	.000	.200	0.00

World Series		Batting																							Fielding						
Year Tm	Age	G	AB	H	2B	3B	HR	TB	R	RBI	GW	TBB	IBB	SO	HBP	SH	SF	SB	CS	SB%	GDP	Avg	OBP	SLG	Pos	G	PO	A	E	DP	FPct
1964 NYA	27	2	0	0	0	0	0	0	0	0	0	0	0	0	0	0	0	0	0	—	0	—	—	—	P	2	1	1	0	1	1.000

BILL SHERDEL—William Henry Sherdel—Nickname: Wee Willie—Throws: Left; Bats: Left

Ht: 5'10"; Wt: 160 lbs; Born: 8/15/1896 in McSherrystown, Pennsylvania; Debut: 4/22/1918; Died: 11/14/1968

World Series		Pitching																										
Year Tm	Age	G	GS	CG	GF	IP	BFP	H	R	ER	HR	SH	SF	HB	TBB	IBB	SO	WP	Bk	W	L	Pct	ShO	Sv-Op	Hld	OAvg	OOBP	ERA
1926 StL	30	2	2	1	0	17.0	73	15	5	4	0	3	2	1	8	1	3	1	0	0	2	.000	0	0-0	0	.254	.343	2.12
1928 StL	32	2	2	0	0	13.1	58	15	7	7	4	1	0	0	3	0	3	0	0	0	2	.000	0	0-0	0	.278	.316	4.73
WS Totals		4	4	1	0	30.1	262	30	12	11	4	4	2	1	11	1	6	1	0	0	4	.000	0	0-0	0	.265	.331	3.26

World Series		Batting																							Fielding						
Year Tm	Age	G	AB	H	2B	3B	HR	TB	R	RBI	GW	TBB	IBB	SO	HBP	SH	SF	SB	CS	SB%	GDP	Avg	OBP	SLG	Pos	G	PO	A	E	DP	FPct
1926 StL	30	2	5	0	0	0	0	0	0	0	0	0	0	2	0	0	0	0	0	—	0	.000	.000	.000	P	2	2	5	0	0	1.000
1928 StL	32	2	5	0	0	0	0	0	0	0	0	0	0	2	0	0	0	0	0	—	0	.000	.000	.000	P	2	0	4	0	0	1.000
WS Totals		4	10	0	0	0	0	0	0	0	0	0	0	4	0	0	0	0	0	—	0	.000	.000	.000	P	4	2	9	0	0	1.000

PAT SHERIDAN—Patrick Arthur Sheridan—Bats: Left; Throws: Right

Ht: 6'3"; Wt: 175 lbs; Born: 12/4/1957 in Ann Arbor, Michigan; Debut: 9/16/1981

LCS		Batting																							Fielding						
Year Tm	Age	G	AB	H	2B	3B	HR	TB	R	RBI	GW	TBB	IBB	SO	HBP	SH	SF	SB	CS	SB%	GDP	Avg	OBP	SLG	Pos	G	PO	A	E	DP	FPct
1984 KC	26	3	6	0	0	0	0	0	1	0	0	3	0	3	0	0	0	0	0	—	0	.000	.333	.000	OF	3	9	0	1	0	.900
1985 KC	27	7	20	3	0	0	2	9	4	3	0	2	1	3	0	0	0	0	0	—	0	.150	.227	.450	OF	7	13	0	0	0	1.000
1987 Det	29	5	10	3	1	0	1	7	2	2	1	0	0	2	2	0	0	1	0	1.00	0	.300	.417	.700	OF	4	7	1	0	0	1.000
1989 SF	31	5	13	2	0	1	0	4	1	0	0	0	0	4	0	0	0	0	1	.00	0	.154	.154	.308	OF	5	9	1	1	0	.909
LCS Totals		20	49	8	1	1	3	20	8	5	1	5	1	12	2	0	0	1	1	.50	0	.163	.268	.408	OF	19	38	2	2	0	.952

World Series		Batting																							Fielding						
Year Tm	Age	G	AB	H	2B	3B	HR	TB	R	RBI	GW	TBB	IBB	SO	HBP	SH	SF	SB	CS	SB%	GDP	Avg	OBP	SLG	Pos	G	PO	A	E	DP	FPct
1985 KC	27	5	18	4	2	0	0	6	0	1	0	0	0	7	0	0	0	0	0	—	0	.222	.222	.333	OF	4	6	0	0	0	1.000
1989 SF	31	1	2	0	0	0	0	0	0	0	0	0	0	0	0	0	0	0	0	—	0	.000	.000	.000	OF	1	0	0	0	0	—
WS Totals		6	20	4	2	0	0	6	0	1	0	0	0	7	0	0	0	0	0	—	0	.200	.200	.300	OF	5	6	0	0	0	1.000
Postseason Totals		26	69	12	3	1	3	26	8	6	1	5	1	19	2	0	0	1	1	.50	0	.174	.250	.377	OF	24	44	2	2	0	.958

LARRY SHERRY—Lawrence Sherry—Throws: Right; Bats: Right

Ht: 6'2"; Wt: 180 lbs; Born: 7/25/1935 in Los Angeles, California; Debut: 4/17/1958

World Series		Pitching																										
Year Tm	Age	G	GS	CG	GF	IP	BFP	H	R	ER	HR	SH	SF	HB	TBB	IBB	SO	WP	Bk	W	L	Pct	ShO	Sv-Op	Hld	OAvg	OOBP	ERA
1959 LA	24	4	0	0	4	12.2	47	8	1	1	0	0	0	1	2	0	5	0	0	2	0	1.000	0	2-2	0	.182	.234	0.71

World Series		Batting																							Fielding						
Year Tm	Age	G	AB	H	2B	3B	HR	TB	R	RBI	GW	TBB	IBB	SO	HBP	SH	SF	SB	CS	SB%	GDP	Avg	OBP	SLG	Pos	G	PO	A	E	DP	FPct
1959 LA	24	5	4	2	0	0	0	2	0	0	0	0	0	1	0	1	0	0	0	—	0	.500	.500	.500	P	4	1	3	0	0	1.000

MULE SHIRLEY—Ernest Raeford Shirley—Bats: Left; Throws: Left

Ht: 5'11"; Wt: 180 lbs; Born: 5/24/1901 in Snow Hill, North Carolina; Debut: 5/6/1924; Died: 8/4/1955

World Series		Batting																							Fielding						
Year Tm	Age	G	AB	H	2B	3B	HR	TB	R	RBI	GW	TBB	IBB	SO	HBP	SH	SF	SB	CS	SB%	GDP	Avg	OBP	SLG	Pos	G	PO	A	E	DP	FPct
1924 Was	23	3	2	1	0	0	0	1	1	1	0	0	0	0	0	0	0	0	0	—	0	.500	.500	.500	—						

TEX SHIRLEY—Alvis Newman Shirley—Throws: Right; Bats: Both

Ht: 6'1"; Wt: 175 lbs; Born: 4/25/1918 in Birthright, Texas; Debut: 9/6/1941

World Series		Pitching																										
Year Tm	Age	G	GS	CG	GF	IP	BFP	H	R	ER	HR	SH	SF	HB	TBB	IBB	SO	WP	Bk	W	L	Pct	ShO	Sv-Op	Hld	OAvg	OOBP	ERA
1944 StL	26	1	0	0	1	2.0	8	2	0	0	0	0	0	0	1	0	1	0	0	0	0	—	0	0-0	0	.286	.375	0.00

World Series		Batting																							Fielding						
Year Tm	Age	G	AB	H	2B	3B	HR	TB	R	RBI	GW	TBB	IBB	SO	HBP	SH	SF	SB	CS	SB%	GDP	Avg	OBP	SLG	Pos	G	PO	A	E	DP	FPct
1944 StL	26	2	0	0	0	0	0	0	0	0	0	0	0	0	0	0	0	0	0	—	0	—	—	—	P	1	0	1	0	0	1.000

URBAN SHOCKER—Urban James Shocker—Throws: Right; Bats: Right

Ht: 5'10"; Wt: 170 lbs; Born: 8/22/1890 in Cleveland, Ohio; Debut: 4/24/1916; Died: 9/9/1928

World Series		Pitching																										
Year Tm	Age	G	GS	CG	GF	IP	BFP	H	R	ER	HR	SH	SF	HB	TBB	IBB	SO	WP	Bk	W	L	Pct	ShO	Sv-Op	Hld	OAvg	OOBP	ERA
1926 NYA	36	2	1	0	0	7.2	36	13	7	7	2	1	0	0	0	0	3	0	0	0	1	.000	0	0-0	0	.371	.371	8.22

World Series		Batting																							Fielding						
Year Tm	Age	G	AB	H	2B	3B	HR	TB	R	RBI	GW	TBB	IBB	SO	HBP	SH	SF	SB	CS	SB%	GDP	Avg	OBP	SLG	Pos	G	PO	A	E	DP	FPct
1926 NYA	36	2	2	0	0	0	0	0	0	0	0	0	0	2	0	0	0	0	0	—	0	.000	.000	.000	P	2	0	2	0	0	1.000

TOM SHOPAY—Thomas Michael Shopay—Bats: Left; Throws: Right

Ht: 5'9"; Wt: 160 lbs; Born: 2/21/1945 in Bristol, Connecticut; Debut: 9/17/1967

World Series		Batting																							Fielding						
Year Tm	Age	G	AB	H	2B	3B	HR	TB	R	RBI	GW	TBB	IBB	SO	HBP	SH	SF	SB	CS	SB%	GDP	Avg	OBP	SLG	Pos	G	PO	A	E	DP	FPct
1971 Bal	26	5	4	0	0	0	0	0	0	0	0	0	0	0	0	1	0	0	0	—	0	.000	.000	.000	—						

ERNIE SHORE—Ernest Grady Shore—Throws: Right; Bats: Right

Ht: 6'4"; Wt: 220 lbs; Born: 3/24/1891 in East Bend, North Carolina; Debut: 6/20/1912; Died: 9/24/1980

World Series		Pitching																										
Year Tm	Age	G	GS	CG	GF	IP	BFP	H	R	ER	HR	SH	SF	HB	TBB	IBB	SO	WP	Bk	W	L	Pct	ShO	Sv-Op	Hld	OAvg	OOBP	ERA
1915 Bos	24	2	2	2	0	17.0	68	12	4	4	0	2	0	0	8	0	6	0	0	1	1	.500	0	0-0	0	.207	.303	2.12
1916 Bos	25	2	2	1	0	17.2	69	12	6	3	0	1	0	1	4	0	9	0	0	2	0	1.000	0	0-0	0	.190	.250	1.53
WS Totals		4	4	3	0	34.2	274	24	10	7	0	3	0	1	12	0	15	0	0	3	1	.750	0	0-0	0	.198	.276	1.82

World Series		Batting																							Fielding						
Year Tm	Age	G	AB	H	2B	3B	HR	TB	R	RBI	GW	TBB	IBB	SO	HBP	SH	SF	SB	CS	SB%	GDP	Avg	OBP	SLG	Pos	G	PO	A	E	DP	FPct
1915 Bos	24	2	5	1	0	0	0	1	0	0	0	0	0	3	0	1	0	0	0	—	0	.200	.200	.200	P	2	0	5	1	0	.833
1916 Bos	25	2	7	0	0	0	0	0	0	0	0	0	0	2	0	0	0	0	0	—	0	.000	.000	.000	P	2	2	7	0	1	1.000
WS Totals		4	12	1	0	0	0	1	0	0	0	0	0	5	0	1	0	0	0	—	0	.083	.083	.083	P	4	2	12	1	1	.933

BILL SHORES—William David Shores—Throws: Right; Bats: Right

Ht: 6'0"; Wt: 185 lbs; Born: 5/26/1904 in Abilene, Texas; Debut: 4/11/1928; Died: 2/19/1984

World Series		Pitching																										
Year Tm	Age	G	GS	CG	GF	IP	BFP	H	R	ER	HR	SH	SF	HB	TBB	IBB	SO	WP	Bk	W	L	Pct	ShO	Sv-Op	Hld	OAvg	OOBP	ERA
1930 Phi	26	1	0	0	0	1.1	7	3	2	2	0	0	0	0	0	0	0	0	0	0	0	—	0	0-0	0	.429	.429	13.50

World Series		Batting																							Fielding						
Year Tm	Age	G	AB	H	2B	3B	HR	TB	R	RBI	GW	TBB	IBB	SO	HBP	SH	SF	SB	CS	SB%	GDP	Avg	OBP	SLG	Pos	G	PO	A	E	DP	FPct
1930 Phi	26	1	0	0	0	0	0	0	0	0	0	1	0	0	0	0	0	0	0	—	0	—	1.000	—	P	1	0	0	0	0	—

CHICK SHORTEN—Charles Henry Shorten—Bats: Left; Throws: Left

Ht: 6'0"; Wt: 175 lbs; Born: 4/19/1892 in Scranton, Pennsylvania; Debut: 9/22/1915; Died: 10/23/1965

World Series		Batting																							Fielding						
Year Tm	Age	G	AB	H	2B	3B	HR	TB	R	RBI	GW	TBB	IBB	SO	HBP	SH	SF	SB	CS	SB%	GDP	Avg	OBP	SLG	Pos	G	PO	A	E	DP	FPct
1916 Bos	24	2	7	4	0	0	0	4	0	2	0	0	0	1	0	1	0	0	2	.00	0	.571	.571	.571	OF	2	3	0	0	0	1.000

ERIC SHOW—Eric Vaughn Show—Throws: Right; Bats: Right

Ht: 6'1"; Wt: 185 lbs; Born: 5/19/1956 in Riverside, California; Debut: 9/2/1981; Died: 3/16/1994

Year Tm	Age	G	GS	CG	GF	IP	BFP	H	R	ER	HR	SH	SF	HB	TBB	IBB	SO	WP	Bk	W	L	Pct	ShO	Sv-Op	Hld	OAvg	OOBP	ERA
LCS — Pitching																												
1984 SD	28	2	2	0	0	5.1	27	8	8	8	5	0	1	0	4	0	2	0	0	0	1	.000	0	0-0	0	.364	.444	13.50
World Series — Pitching																												
1984 SD	28	1	1	0	0	2.2	14	4	4	3	2	0	0	0	1	0	2	0	0	0	1	.000	0	0-0	0	.308	.357	10.13
Postseason Totals		3	3	0	0	8.0	82	12	12	11	7	0	1	0	5	0	4	0	0	0	2	.000	0	0-0	0	.343	.415	12.38

Year Tm	Age	G	AB	H	2B	3B	HR	TB	R	RBI	GW	TBB	IBB	SO	HBP	SH	SF	SB	CS	SB%	GDP	Avg	OBP	SLG	Pos	G	PO	A	E	DP	FPct
LCS — Batting / Fielding																															
1984 SD	28	2	1	0	0	0	0	0	0	0	0	0	0	1	0	0	0	0	0	—	0	.000	.000	.000	P	2	0	0	0	0	—
World Series — Batting / Fielding																															
1984 SD	28	1	0	0	0	0	0	0	0	0	0	0	0	0	0	0	0	0	0	—	0	—	—	—	P	1	0	0	0	0	—
Postseason Totals		3	1	0	0	0	0	0	0	0	0	0	0	1	0	0	0	0	0	—	0	.000	.000	.000	P	3	0	0	0	0	—

GEORGE SHUBA—George Thomas Shuba—Nickname: Shotgun—Bats: Left; Throws: Right

Ht: 5'11"; Wt: 180 lbs; Born: 12/13/1924 in Youngstown, Ohio; Debut: 7/2/1948

Year Tm	Age	G	AB	H	2B	3B	HR	TB	R	RBI	GW	TBB	IBB	SO	HBP	SH	SF	SB	CS	SB%	GDP	Avg	OBP	SLG	Pos	G	PO	A	E	DP	FPct
World Series — Batting / Fielding																															
1952 Bro	27	4	10	3	1	0	0	4	0	0	0	0	0	4	0	0	0	0	0	—	0	.300	.300	.400	OF	3	7	0	0	0	1.000
1953 Bro	28	2	1	1	0	0	1	4	1	2	0	0	0	0	0	0	0	0	0	—	0	1.000	1.000	4.000	—						
1955 Bro	30	1	1	0	0	0	0	0	0	0	0	0	0	0	0	0	0	0	0	—	0	.000	.000	.000	—						
WS Totals		7	12	4	1	0	1	8	1	2	0	0	0	4	0	0	0	0	0	—	0	.333	.333	.667	OF	3	7	0	0	0	1.000

PAUL SHUEY—Paul Kenneth Shuey—Throws: Right; Bats: Right

Ht: 6'3"; Wt: 215 lbs; Born: 9/16/1970 in Lima, Ohio; Debut: 5/8/1994

Year Tm	Age	G	GS	CG	GF	IP	BFP	H	R	ER	HR	SH	SF	HB	TBB	IBB	SO	WP	Bk	W	L	Pct	ShO	Sv-Op	Hld	OAvg	OOBP	ERA
Division Series — Pitching																												
1996 Cle	26	3	0	0	0	2.0	12	5	2	2	2	0	0	0	2	0	2	0	0	0	0	—	0	0-0	0	.500	.583	9.00

Year Tm	Age	G	AB	H	2B	3B	HR	TB	R	RBI	GW	TBB	IBB	SO	HBP	SH	SF	SB	CS	SB%	GDP	Avg	OBP	SLG	Pos	G	PO	A	E	DP	FPct
Division Series — Batting / Fielding																															
1996 Cle	26	3	0	0	0	0	0	0	0	0	0	0	0	0	0	0	0	0	0	—	0	—	—	—	P	3	0	0	0	0	—

NORM SIEBERN—Norman Leroy Siebern—Bats: Left; Throws: Right

Ht: 6'2"; Wt: 200 lbs; Born: 7/26/1933 in St. Louis, Missouri; Debut: 6/15/1956

Year Tm	Age	G	AB	H	2B	3B	HR	TB	R	RBI	GW	TBB	IBB	SO	HBP	SH	SF	SB	CS	SB%	GDP	Avg	OBP	SLG	Pos	G	PO	A	E	DP	FPct
World Series — Batting / Fielding																															
1956 NYA	23	1	1	0	0	0	0	0	0	0	0	0	0	0	0	0	0	0	0	—	0	.000	.000	.000	—						
1958 NYA	25	3	8	1	0	0	0	1	1	0	0	3	0	2	0	0	0	0	0	—	0	.125	.364	.125	OF	3	5	0	0	0	1.000
1967 Bos	34	3	3	1	0	0	0	1	0	1	0	0	0	0	0	0	0	0	0	—	0	.333	.333	.333	OF	1	0	0	0	0	—
WS Totals		7	12	2	0	0	0	2	1	1	0	3	0	2	0	0	0	0	0	—	0	.167	.333	.167	OF	4	5	0	0	0	1.000

RUBEN SIERRA—Ruben Angel Sierra—Bats: Both; Throws: Right

Ht: 6'1"; Wt: 175 lbs; Born: 10/6/1965 in Rio Piedras, Puerto Rico; Debut: 6/1/1986

Year Tm	Age	G	AB	H	2B	3B	HR	TB	R	RBI	GW	TBB	IBB	SO	HBP	SH	SF	SB	CS	SB%	GDP	Avg	OBP	SLG	Pos	G	PO	A	E	DP	FPct
Division Series — Batting / Fielding																															
1995 NYA	29	5	23	4	2	0	2	12	2	2	0	2	0	7	0	0	1	0	0	—	0	.174	.231	.522	—						
LCS — Batting / Fielding																															
1992 Oak	26	6	24	8	2	1	1	15	4	7	1	2	0	1	0	0	2	1	2	.33	1	.333	.357	.625	OF	6	12	0	0	0	1.000
Postseason Totals		11	47	12	4	1	3	27	6	12	1	4	0	8	0	0	3	1	2	.33	1	.255	.296	.574	OF	6	12	0	0	0	1.000

ED SIEVER—Edward Tilden Siever—Throws: Left; Bats: Left

Ht: 5'11"; Wt: 190 lbs; Born: 4/2/1877 in Goddard, Kansas; Debut: 4/26/1901; Died: 2/5/1920

Year Tm	Age	G	GS	CG	GF	IP	BFP	H	R	ER	HR	SH	SF	HB	TBB	IBB	SO	WP	Bk	W	L	Pct	ShO	Sv-Op	Hld	OAvg	OOBP	ERA
World Series — Pitching																												
1907 Det	30	1	1	0	0	4.0	19	7	4	2	0	1	0	0	0	0	1	0	0	0	1	.000	0	0-0	0	.389	.389	4.50

Year Tm	Age	G	AB	H	2B	3B	HR	TB	R	RBI	GW	TBB	IBB	SO	HBP	SH	SF	SB	CS	SB%	GDP	Avg	OBP	SLG	Pos	G	PO	A	E	DP	FPct
World Series — Batting / Fielding																															
1907 Det	30	1	1	0	0	0	0	0	0	0	0	0	0	0	0	0	0	0	0	—	0	.000	.000	.000	P	1	0	0	0	0	—

CHARLIE SILVERA—Charles Anthony Ryan Silvera—Nickname: Swede—Bats: Right; Throws: Right

Ht: 5'10"; Wt: 175 lbs; Born: 10/13/1924 in San Francisco, California; Debut: 9/29/1948

Year Tm	Age	G	AB	H	2B	3B	HR	TB	R	RBI	GW	TBB	IBB	SO	HBP	SH	SF	SB	CS	SB%	GDP	Avg	OBP	SLG	Pos	G	PO	A	E	DP	FPct
World Series — Batting / Fielding																															
1949 NYA	24	1	2	0	0	0	0	0	0	0	0	0	0	0	0	0	0	0	0	—	0	.000	.000	.000	C	1	6	0	0	0	1.000

KEN SILVESTRI—Kenneth Joseph Silvestri—Nickname: Hawk—Bats: Both; Throws: Right

Ht: 6'1"; Wt: 200 lbs; Born: 5/3/1916 in Chicago, Illinois; Debut: 4/18/1939; Died: 3/31/1992

Year Tm	Age	G	AB	H	2B	3B	HR	TB	R	RBI	GW	TBB	IBB	SO	HBP	SH	SF	SB	CS	SB%	GDP	Avg	OBP	SLG	Pos	G	PO	A	E	DP	FPct
World Series — Batting / Fielding																															
1950 Phi	34	1	0	0	0	0	0	0	0	0	0	0	0	0	0	0	0	0	0	—	0	—	—	—	C	1	1	0	0	0	1.000

AL SIMMONS (HOF 1953-W)—Aloysius Harry Simmons—Nickname: Bucketfoot Al—Bats: Right; Throws: Right

Ht: 5'11"; Wt: 190 lbs; Born: 5/22/1902 in Milwaukee, Wis.; Deb.: 4/15/1924; Died: 5/26/1956

Year Tm	Age	G	AB	H	2B	3B	HR	TB	R	RBI	GW	TBB	IBB	SO	HBP	SH	SF	SB	CS	SB%	GDP	Avg	OBP	SLG	Pos	G	PO	A	E	DP	FPct
World Series — Batting / Fielding																															
1929 Phi	27	5	20	6	1	0	2	13	6	5	0	1	0	4	0	0	1	0	0	—	0	.300	.318	.650	OF	5	4	0	0	0	1.000
1930 Phi	28	6	22	8	2	0	2	16	4	4	0	2	1	2	0	0	0	0	0	—	1	.364	.417	.727	OF	6	12	1	0	0	1.000
1931 Phi	29	7	27	9	2	0	2	17	4	8	1	3	0	3	0	0	0	0	0	—	1	.333	.400	.630	OF	7	20	0	0	0	1.000
1939 Cin	37	1	4	1	1	0	0	2	1	0	0	0	0	0	0	0	0	0	0	—	0	.250	.250	.500	OF	1	3	0	0	0	1.000
WS Totals		19	73	24	6	0	6	48	15	17	1	6	1	9	0	0	1	0	0	—	2	.329	.375	.658	OF	19	39	1	0	0	1.000

CURT SIMMONS—Curtis Thomas Simmons—Throws: Left; Bats: Left

Ht: 5'11"; Wt: 175 lbs; Born: 5/19/1929 in Egypt, Pennsylvania; Debut: 9/28/1947

Year Tm	Age	G	GS	CG	GF	IP	BFP	H	R	ER	HR	SH	SF	HB	TBB	IBB	SO	WP	Bk	W	L	Pct	ShO	Sv-Op	Hld	OAvg	OOBP	ERA
World Series — Pitching																												
1964 StL	35	2	2	0	0	14.1	56	11	4	4	2	0	0	0	3	1	8	0	0	0	1	.000	0	0-0	0	.208	.250	2.51

Year Tm	Age	G	AB	H	2B	3B	HR	TB	R	RBI	GW	TBB	IBB	SO	HBP	SH	SF	SB	CS	SB%	GDP	Avg	OBP	SLG	Pos	G	PO	A	E	DP	FPct
World Series — Batting / Fielding																															
1964 StL	35	2	4	2	0	0	0	2	0	1	0	0	0	1	0	1	0	0	0	—	0	.500	.500	.500	P	2	2	1	0	0	1.000

TED SIMMONS—Ted Lyle Simmons—Nickname: Simba—Bats: Both; Throws: Right

Ht: 5'11"; Wt: 193 lbs; Born: 8/9/1949 in Highland Park, Michigan; Debut: 9/21/1968

Year Tm	Age	G	AB	H	2B	3B	HR	TB	R	RBI	GW	TBB	IBB	SO	HBP	SH	SF	SB	CS	SB%	GDP	Avg	OBP	SLG	Pos	G	PO	A	E	DP	FPct
Division Series — Batting / Fielding																															
1981 Mil	32	5	18	4	1	0	1	8	1	4	0	2	0	2	0	0	0	0	0	—	0	.222	.300	.444	C	5	23	2	0	0	1.000
LCS — Batting / Fielding																															
1982 Mil	33	5	18	3	0	0	0	3	3	1	0	1	0	4	0	0	1	0	0	—	0	.167	.200	.167	C	5	36	3	0	0	1.000
World Series — Batting / Fielding																															
1982 Mil	33	7	23	4	0	0	2	10	2	3	0	5	2	3	0	0	0	0	0	—	1	.174	.321	.435	C	7	28	2	1	0	.968
Postseason Totals		17	59	11	1	0	3	21	6	8	0	8	2	9	0	0	1	0	0	—	1	.186	.279	.356	C	17	87	7	1	0	.989

HARRY SIMPSON—Harry Leon Simpson—Nicknames: Suitcase, Goody—Bats: Left; Throws: Right

Ht: 6'1"; Wt: 180 lbs; Born: 12/3/1925 in Atlanta, Georgia; Debut: 4/21/1951; Died: 4/3/1979

World Series		Batting																							Fielding						
Year Tm	Age	G	AB	H	2B	3B	HR	TB	R	RBI	GW	TBB	IBB	SO	HBP	SH	SF	SB	CS	SB%	GDP	Avg	OBP	SLG	Pos	G	PO	A	E	DP	FPct
1957 NYA	31	5	12	1	0	0	0	1	0	1	0	0	0	4	0	0	0	0	0	—	2	.083	.083	.083	1B	4	24	1	0	2	1.000

DUKE SIMS—Duane B. Sims—Bats: Left; Throws: Right

Ht: 6'2"; Wt: 197 lbs; Born: 6/5/1941 in Salt Lake City, Utah; Debut: 9/22/1964

LCS		Batting																							Fielding						
Year Tm	Age	G	AB	H	2B	3B	HR	TB	R	RBI	GW	TBB	IBB	SO	HBP	SH	SF	SB	CS	SB%	GDP	Avg	OBP	SLG	Pos	G	PO	A	E	DP	FPct
1972 Det	31	4	14	3	2	1	0	7	0	0	0	1	0	2	0	0	0	0	0	—	0	.214	.267	.500	C	2	13	1	0	0	1.000
																									OF	2	3	0	1	0	.750

KEN SINGLETON—Kenneth Wayne Singleton—Bats: Both; Throws: Right

Ht: 6'4"; Wt: 210 lbs; Born: 6/10/1947 in New York, New York; Debut: 6/24/1970

LCS		Batting																							Fielding						
Year Tm	Age	G	AB	H	2B	3B	HR	TB	R	RBI	GW	TBB	IBB	SO	HBP	SH	SF	SB	CS	SB%	GDP	Avg	OBP	SLG	Pos	G	PO	A	E	DP	FPct
1979 Bal	32	4	16	6	2	0	0	8	4	2	1	1	0	2	0	0	1	0	0	—	1	.375	.389	.500	OF	4	4	1	0	0	1.000
1983 Bal	36	4	12	3	2	0	0	5	0	1	0	2	1	2	0	0	0	0	0	—	2	.250	.357	.417	—						
LCS Totals		8	28	9	4	0	0	13	4	3	1	3	1	4	0	0	1	0	0	—	3	.321	.375	.464	OF	4	4	1	0	0	1.000
World Series		Batting																							Fielding						
Year Tm	Age	G	AB	H	2B	3B	HR	TB	R	RBI	GW	TBB	IBB	SO	HBP	SH	SF	SB	CS	SB%	GDP	Avg	OBP	SLG	Pos	G	PO	A	E	DP	FPct
1979 Bal	32	7	28	10	1	0	0	11	1	2	0	2	1	5	0	0	0	0	0	—	1	.357	.400	.393	OF	7	9	0	0	0	1.000
1983 Bal	36	2	1	0	0	0	0	0	0	1	0	1	0	1	0	0	0	0	0	—	0	.000	.500	.000	—						
WS Totals		9	29	10	1	0	0	11	1	3	0	3	1	6	0	0	0	0	0	—	1	.345	.406	.379	OF	7	9	0	0	0	1.000
Postseason Totals		17	57	19	5	0	0	24	5	6	1	6	2	10	0	0	1	0	0	—	4	.333	.391	.421	OF	11	13	1	0	0	1.000

DOUG SISK—Douglas Randall Sisk—Throws: Right; Bats: Right

Ht: 6'2"; Wt: 210 lbs; Born: 9/26/1957 in Renton, Washington; Debut: 9/6/1982

LCS		Pitching																										
Year Tm	Age	G	GS	CG	GF	IP	BFP	H	R	ER	HR	SH	SF	HB	TBB	IBB	SO	WP	Bk	W	L	Pct	ShO	Sv-Op	Hld	OAvg	OOBP	ERA
1986 NYN	29	1	0	0	1	1.0	5	1	0	0	0	0	0	0	1	0	0	0	0	0	0	—	0	0- 0	0	.250	.400	0.00
World Series		Pitching																										
Year Tm	Age	G	GS	CG	GF	IP	BFP	H	R	ER	HR	SH	SF	HB	TBB	IBB	SO	WP	Bk	W	L	Pct	ShO	Sv-Op	Hld	OAvg	OOBP	ERA
1986 NYN	29	1	0	0	1	0.2	3	0	0	0	0	0	0	0	1	1	1	0	0	0	0	—	0	0- 0	0	.000	.333	0.00
Postseason Totals		2	0	0	2	1.2	16	1	0	0	0	0	0	0	2	1	1	0	0	0	0	—	0	0-0	0	.167	.375	0.00

LCS		Batting																							Fielding						
Year Tm	Age	G	AB	H	2B	3B	HR	TB	R	RBI	GW	TBB	IBB	SO	HBP	SH	SF	SB	CS	SB%	GDP	Avg	OBP	SLG	Pos	G	PO	A	E	DP	FPct
1986 NYN	29	1	0	0	0	0	0	0	0	0	0	0	0	0	0	0	0	0	0	—	0	—	—	—	P	1	0	0	0	0	—
World Series		Batting																							Fielding						
Year Tm	Age	G	AB	H	2B	3B	HR	TB	R	RBI	GW	TBB	IBB	SO	HBP	SH	SF	SB	CS	SB%	GDP	Avg	OBP	SLG	Pos	G	PO	A	E	DP	FPct
1986 NYN	29	1	0	0	0	0	0	0	0	0	0	0	0	0	0	0	0	0	0	—	0	—	—	—	P	1	0	0	0	0	—
Postseason Totals		2	0	0	0	0	0	0	0	0	0	0	0	0	0	0	0	0	0	—	0	—	—	—	P	2	0	0	0	0	—

DICK SISLER—Richard Allan Sisler—Bats: Left; Throws: Right

Ht: 6'2"; Wt: 205 lbs; Born: 11/2/1920 in St. Louis, Missouri; Debut: 4/16/1946

World Series		Batting																							Fielding						
Year Tm	Age	G	AB	H	2B	3B	HR	TB	R	RBI	GW	TBB	IBB	SO	HBP	SH	SF	SB	CS	SB%	GDP	Avg	OBP	SLG	Pos	G	PO	A	E	DP	FPct
1946 StL	25	2	2	0	0	0	0	0	0	0	0	0	0	0	0	0	0	0	0	—	0	.000	.000	.000	—						
1950 Phi	29	4	17	1	0	0	0	1	0	1	0	0	0	5	0	0	0	0	0	—	1	.059	.059	.059	OF	4	10	1	0	0	1.000
WS Totals		6	19	1	0	0	0	1	0	1	0	0	0	5	0	0	0	0	0	—	1	.053	.053	.053	OF	4	10	1	0	0	1.000

SIBBY SISTI—Sebastian Daniel Sisti—Bats: Right; Throws: Right

Ht: 5'11"; Wt: 175 lbs; Born: 7/26/1920 in Buffalo, New York; Debut: 7/21/1939

World Series		Batting																							Fielding						
Year Tm	Age	G	AB	H	2B	3B	HR	TB	R	RBI	GW	TBB	IBB	SO	HBP	SH	SF	SB	CS	SB%	GDP	Avg	OBP	SLG	Pos	G	PO	A	E	DP	FPct
1948 Bos	28	2	1	0	0	0	0	0	0	0	0	0	0	0	0	0	0	0	0	—	0	.000	.000	.000	2B	1	0	0	0	0	—

TED SIZEMORE—Theodore Crawford Sizemore—Bats: Right; Throws: Right

Ht: 5'10"; Wt: 165 lbs; Born: 4/15/1945 in Gadsden, Alabama; Debut: 4/7/1969

LCS		Batting																							Fielding						
Year Tm	Age	G	AB	H	2B	3B	HR	TB	R	RBI	GW	TBB	IBB	SO	HBP	SH	SF	SB	CS	SB%	GDP	Avg	OBP	SLG	Pos	G	PO	A	E	DP	FPct
1977 Phi	32	4	13	3	0	0	0	3	1	0	0	2	0	0	0	1	0	0	0	—	1	.231	.333	.231	2B	4	10	8	2	2	.900
1978 Phi	33	4	13	5	0	1	0	7	3	1	1	1	1	0	0	1	0	0	0	—	1	.385	.429	.538	2B	4	7	8	0	4	1.000
LCS Totals		8	26	8	0	1	0	10	4	1	1	3	1	0	0	2	0	0	0	—	2	.308	.379	.385	2B	8	17	16	2	6	.943

DAVE SKAGGS—David Lindsey Skaggs—Bats: Right; Throws: Right

Ht: 6'2"; Wt: 200 lbs; Born: 6/12/1951 in Santa Monica, California; Debut: 4/17/1977

LCS		Batting																							Fielding						
Year Tm	Age	G	AB	H	2B	3B	HR	TB	R	RBI	GW	TBB	IBB	SO	HBP	SH	SF	SB	CS	SB%	GDP	Avg	OBP	SLG	Pos	G	PO	A	E	DP	FPct
1979 Bal	28	1	4	0	0	0	0	0	0	0	0	0	0	0	0	0	0	0	0	—	0	.000	.000	.000	C	1	3	1	0	0	1.000
World Series		Batting																							Fielding						
Year Tm	Age	G	AB	H	2B	3B	HR	TB	R	RBI	GW	TBB	IBB	SO	HBP	SH	SF	SB	CS	SB%	GDP	Avg	OBP	SLG	Pos	G	PO	A	E	DP	FPct
1979 Bal	28	1	3	1	0	0	0	1	1	0	0	0	0	0	0	0	0	0	0	—	1	.333	.333	.333	C	1	2	2	0	0	1.000
Postseason Totals		2	7	1	0	0	0	1	1	0	0	0	0	0	0	0	0	0	0	—	1	.143	.143	.143	C	2	5	3	0	0	1.000

BOB SKINNER—Robert Ralph Skinner—Bats: Left; Throws: Right

Ht: 6'4"; Wt: 190 lbs; Born: 10/3/1931 in La Jolla, California; Debut: 4/13/1954

World Series		Batting																							Fielding						
Year Tm	Age	G	AB	H	2B	3B	HR	TB	R	RBI	GW	TBB	IBB	SO	HBP	SH	SF	SB	CS	SB%	GDP	Avg	OBP	SLG	Pos	G	PO	A	E	DP	FPct
1960 Pit	28	2	5	1	0	0	0	1	2	1	1	1	0	0	1	1	0	1	0	1.00	0	.200	.429	.200	OF	2	4	1	0	1	1.000
1964 StL	32	4	3	2	1	0	0	3	0	1	0	1	1	0	0	0	0	0	0	—	0	.667	.750	1.000	—						
WS Totals		6	8	3	1	0	0	4	2	2	1	2	1	0	1	1	0	1	0	1.00	0	.375	.545	.500	OF	2	4	1	0	1	1.000

BILL SKOWRON—William Joseph Skowron—Nickname: Moose—Bats: Right; Throws: Right

Ht: 5'11"; Wt: 195 lbs; Born: 12/18/1930 in Chicago, Illinois; Debut: 4/13/1954

World Series		Batting																							Fielding						
Year Tm	Age	G	AB	H	2B	3B	HR	TB	R	RBI	GW	TBB	IBB	SO	HBP	SH	SF	SB	CS	SB%	GDP	Avg	OBP	SLG	Pos	G	PO	A	E	DP	FPct
1955 NYA	24	5	12	4	2	0	1	9	2	3	0	0	0	1	0	0	0	0	0	—	0	.333	.333	.750	1B	3	22	3	1	1	.962
1956 NYA	25	3	10	1	0	0	1	4	1	4	0	0	0	3	0	0	0	0	0	—	0	.100	.100	.400	1B	2	21	3	1	3	.960
1957 NYA	26	2	4	0	0	0	0	0	0	0	0	0	0	0	0	0	0	0	0	—	0	.000	.000	.000	1B	2	5	2	0	1	1.000
1958 NYA	27	7	27	7	0	0	2	13	3	7	0	1	0	4	0	0	0	0	0	—	0	.259	.286	.481	1B	7	54	4	0	4	1.000
1960 NYA	29	7	32	12	2	0	2	20	7	6	1	0	0	6	0	0	1	0	0	—	1	.375	.364	.625	1B	7	70	6	0	9	1.000
1961 NYA	30	5	17	6	0	0	1	9	3	5	0	3	0	4	0	0	0	0	0	—	1	.353	.450	.529	1B	5	46	5	0	1	1.000
1962 NYA	31	6	18	4	0	1	0	6	1	1	0	1	0	5	1	0	0	0	0	—	1	.222	.300	.333	1B	6	52	1	0	3	1.000
1963 LA	32	4	13	5	0	0	1	8	2	3	1	1	1	3	0	0	0	0	0	—	2	.385	.429	.615	1B	4	30	4	0	1	1.000
WS Totals		39	133	39	4	1	8	69	19	29	2	6	1	26	1	0	1	0	0	—	5	.293	.326	.519	1B	36	300	28	2	23	.994

JIMMY SLAGLE—James Franklin Slagle—Nicknames: Rabbit, Shorty—Bats: Left; Throws: Right

Ht: 5'7"; Wt: 144 lbs; Born: 7/11/1873 in Worthville, Pennsylvania; Debut: 4/17/1899; Died: 5/10/1956

World Series		Batting																							Fielding						
Year Tm	Age	G	AB	H	2B	3B	HR	TB	R	RBI	GW	TBB	IBB	SO	HBP	SH	SF	SB	CS	SB%	GDP	Avg	OBP	SLG	Pos	G	PO	A	E	DP	FPct
1907 ChN	34	5	22	6	0	0	0	6	3	4	1	2	0	3	0	0	0	6	2	.75	0	.273	.333	.273	OF	5	13	0	1	0	.929

JIM SLATON—James Michael Slaton—Throws: Right; Bats: Right

Ht: 6'0"; Wt: 185 lbs; Born: 6/19/1950 in Long Beach, California; Debut: 4/14/1971

Division Series — Pitching

Year Tm	Age	G	GS	CG	GF	IP	BFP	H	R	ER	HR	SH	SF	HB	TBB	IBB	SO	WP	Bk	W	L	Pct	ShO	Sv-Op	Hld	OAvg	OOBP	ERA
1981 Mil	31	4	0	0	1	6.0	22	6	2	2	1	0	0	0	0	0	2	0	0	0	0	—	0	0- 0	1	.273	.273	3.00

LCS — Pitching

Year Tm	Age	G	GS	CG	GF	IP	BFP	H	R	ER	HR	SH	SF	HB	TBB	IBB	SO	WP	Bk	W	L	Pct	ShO	Sv-Op	Hld	OAvg	OOBP	ERA
1982 Mil	32	2	0	0	1	4.2	18	3	2	1	1	0	0	0	1	0	3	0	0	0	0	—	0	1- 1	0	.176	.222	1.93

World Series — Pitching

Year Tm	Age	G	GS	CG	GF	IP	BFP	H	R	ER	HR	SH	SF	HB	TBB	IBB	SO	WP	Bk	W	L	Pct	ShO	Sv-Op	Hld	OAvg	OOBP	ERA
1982 Mil	32	2	0	0	0	2.2	11	1	0	0	0	0	0	0	2	0	1	0	0	1	0	1.000	0	0- 0	0	.111	.273	0.00
Postseason Totals		8	0	0	2	13.1	102	10	4	3	2	0	0	0	3	0	6	0	0	1	0	1.000	0	1-1	1	.208	.255	2.03

Division Series — Batting / Fielding

Year Tm	Age	G	AB	H	2B	3B	HR	TB	R	RBI	GW	TBB	IBB	SO	HBP	SH	SF	SB	CS	SB%	GDP	Avg	OBP	SLG	Pos	G	PO	A	E	DP	FPct
1981 Mil	31	4	0	0	0	0	0	0	0	0	0	0	0	0	0	0	0	0	0	—	0	—	—	—	P	4	0	0	0	0	—

LCS — Batting / Fielding

Year Tm	Age	G	AB	H	2B	3B	HR	TB	R	RBI	GW	TBB	IBB	SO	HBP	SH	SF	SB	CS	SB%	GDP	Avg	OBP	SLG	Pos	G	PO	A	E	DP	FPct
1982 Mil	32	2	0	0	0	0	0	0	0	0	0	0	0	0	0	0	0	0	0	—	0	—	—	—	P	2	1	0	0	0	1.000

World Series — Batting / Fielding

Year Tm	Age	G	AB	H	2B	3B	HR	TB	R	RBI	GW	TBB	IBB	SO	HBP	SH	SF	SB	CS	SB%	GDP	Avg	OBP	SLG	Pos	G	PO	A	E	DP	FPct
1982 Mil	32	2	0	0	0	0	0	0	0	0	0	0	0	0	0	0	0	0	0	—	0	—	—	—	P	2	0	0	0	0	—
Postseason Totals		8	0	0	0	0	0	0	0	0	0	0	0	0	0	0	0	0	0	—	0	—	—	—	P	8	1	0	0	0	1.000

DON SLAUGHT—Donald Martin Slaught—Nickname: Sluggo—Bats: Right; Throws: Right

Ht: 6'1"; Wt: 190 lbs; Born: 9/11/1958 in Long Beach, California; Debut: 7/6/1982

LCS — Batting / Fielding

Year Tm	Age	G	AB	H	2B	3B	HR	TB	R	RBI	GW	TBB	IBB	SO	HBP	SH	SF	SB	CS	SB%	GDP	Avg	OBP	SLG	Pos	G	PO	A	E	DP	FPct
1984 KC	26	3	11	4	0	0	0	4	0	0	0	0	0	0	0	0	0	0	0	—	0	.364	.364	.364	C	3	17	0	3	0	.850
1990 Pit	32	4	11	1	1	0	0	2	0	1	0	2	1	3	0	0	1	0	0	—	0	.091	.214	.182	C	4	22	1	1	0	.958
1991 Pit	33	6	17	4	0	0	0	4	0	1	0	1	1	4	0	1	0	0	0	—	0	.235	.278	.235	C	6	30	5	0	1	1.000
1992 Pit	34	5	12	4	1	0	1	8	5	5	0	6	1	3	0	0	0	0	0	—	1	.333	.556	.667	C	5	17	1	0	0	1.000
LCS Totals		18	51	13	2	0	1	18	5	7	0	9	3	10	0	1	1	0	0	—	1	.255	.361	.353	C	18	86	7	4	1	.959

ENOS SLAUGHTER (HOF 1985-V)—Enos Bradsher Slaughter—Nickname: Country—Bats: Left; Throws: Right

Ht: 5'9"; Wt: 180 lbs; Born: 4/27/1916 in Roxboro, North Carolina; Debut: 4/19/1938

World Series — Batting / Fielding

Year Tm	Age	G	AB	H	2B	3B	HR	TB	R	RBI	GW	TBB	IBB	SO	HBP	SH	SF	SB	CS	SB%	GDP	Avg	OBP	SLG	Pos	G	PO	A	E	DP	FPct
1942 StL	26	5	19	5	1	0	1	9	3	2	0	3	0	2	0	0	0	0	0	—	1	.263	.364	.474	OF	5	9	1	1	0	.909
1946 StL	30	7	25	8	1	1	1	14	5	2	1	4	2	3	1	0	0	1	0	1.00	0	.320	.433	.560	OF	7	20	1	0	1	1.000
1956 NYA	40	6	20	7	0	0	1	10	6	4	1	4	2	0	0	0	1	0	0	—	0	.350	.440	.500	OF	6	8	1	0	0	1.000
1957 NYA	41	5	12	3	1	0	0	4	2	0	0	3	0	2	0	0	0	0	1	.00	1	.250	.400	.333	OF	5	7	0	0	0	1.000
1958 NYA	42	4	3	0	0	0	0	0	1	0	0	1	0	1	0	0	0	0	0	—	0	.000	.250	.000	—						
WS Totals		27	79	23	3	1	3	37	17	8	2	15	4	8	1	0	1	1	1	.50	2	.291	.406	.468	OF	23	44	3	1	1	.979

HEATHCLIFF SLOCUMB—Throws: Right; Bats: Right

Ht: 6'3"; Wt: 210 lbs; Born: 6/7/1966 in Jamaica, New York; Debut: 4/11/1991

Division Series — Pitching

Year Tm	Age	G	GS	CG	GF	IP	BFP	H	R	ER	HR	SH	SF	HB	TBB	IBB	SO	WP	Bk	W	L	Pct	ShO	Sv-Op	Hld	OAvg	OOBP	ERA
1997 Sea	31	2	0	0	2	2.0	10	3	1	1	0	0	0	0	1	0	0	0	0	0	0	—	0	0- 0	0	.333	.400	4.50

Division Series — Batting / Fielding

Year Tm	Age	G	AB	H	2B	3B	HR	TB	R	RBI	GW	TBB	IBB	SO	HBP	SH	SF	SB	CS	SB%	GDP	Avg	OBP	SLG	Pos	G	PO	A	E	DP	FPct
1997 Sea	31	2	0	0	0	0	0	0	0	0	0	0	0	0	0	0	0	0	0	—	0	—	—	—	P	2	1	0	0	0	1.000

ROY SMALLEY—Roy Frederick Smalley—Bats: Both; Throws: Right

Ht: 6'1"; Wt: 185 lbs; Born: 10/25/1952 in Los Angeles, California; Debut: 4/30/1975

World Series — Batting / Fielding

Year Tm	Age	G	AB	H	2B	3B	HR	TB	R	RBI	GW	TBB	IBB	SO	HBP	SH	SF	SB	CS	SB%	GDP	Avg	OBP	SLG	Pos	G	PO	A	E	DP	FPct
1987 Min	34	4	2	1	1	0	0	2	0	0	0	2	0	0	0	0	0	0	0	—	0	.500	.750	1.000	—						

JOHN SMILEY—John Patrick Smiley—Throws: Left; Bats: Left

Ht: 6'4"; Wt: 180 lbs; Born: 3/17/1965 in Phoenixville, Pennsylvania; Debut: 9/1/1986

Division Series — Pitching

Year Tm	Age	G	GS	CG	GF	IP	BFP	H	R	ER	HR	SH	SF	HB	TBB	IBB	SO	WP	Bk	W	L	Pct	ShO	Sv-Op	Hld	OAvg	OOBP	ERA
1995 Cin	30	1	1	0	0	6.0	27	9	2	2	1	1	0	0	0	0	1	0	0	0	0	—	0	0- 0	0	.346	.346	3.00

LCS — Pitching

Year Tm	Age	G	GS	CG	GF	IP	BFP	H	R	ER	HR	SH	SF	HB	TBB	IBB	SO	WP	Bk	W	L	Pct	ShO	Sv-Op	Hld	OAvg	OOBP	ERA
1990 Pit	25	1	0	0	0	2.0	8	2	0	0	0	0	0	0	0	0	0	0	0	0	0	—	0	0- 0	0	.250	.250	0.00
1991 Pit	26	2	2	0	0	2.2	18	8	8	7	2	0	1	1	1	0	3	0	0	0	2	.000	0	0- 0	0	.533	.556	23.63
1995 Cin	30	1	1	0	0	5.0	20	5	2	2	0	0	0	0	0	0	1	0	0	0	0	—	0	0- 0	0	.250	.250	3.60
LCS Totals		4	3	0	0	9.2	92	15	10	9	2	0	1	1	1	0	4	0	0	0	2	.000	0	0-0	0	.349	.370	8.38
Postseason Totals		5	4	0	0	15.2	146	24	12	11	3	1	1	1	1	0	5	0	0	0	2	.000	0	0-0	0	.348	.361	6.32

Division Series — Batting / Fielding

Year Tm	Age	G	AB	H	2B	3B	HR	TB	R	RBI	GW	TBB	IBB	SO	HBP	SH	SF	SB	CS	SB%	GDP	Avg	OBP	SLG	Pos	G	PO	A	E	DP	FPct
1995 Cin	30	1	2	0	0	0	0	0	0	0	0	0	0	1	0	0	0	0	0	—	0	.000	.000	.000	P	1	0	1	0	0	1.000

LCS — Batting / Fielding

Year Tm	Age	G	AB	H	2B	3B	HR	TB	R	RBI	GW	TBB	IBB	SO	HBP	SH	SF	SB	CS	SB%	GDP	Avg	OBP	SLG	Pos	G	PO	A	E	DP	FPct
1990 Pit	25	1	0	0	0	0	0	0	0	0	0	0	0	0	0	0	0	0	0	—	0	—	—	—	P	1	0	0	0	0	—
1991 Pit	26	2	0	0	0	0	0	0	0	0	0	0	0	0	0	0	0	0	0	—	0	—	—	—	P	2	0	1	0	0	1.000
1995 Cin	30	1	1	0	0	0	0	0	0	0	0	0	0	0	0	0	0	0	0	—	0	.000	.000	.000	P	1	1	1	0	0	1.000
LCS Totals		4	1	0	0	0	0	0	0	0	0	0	0	0	0	0	0	0	0	—	0	.000	.000	.000	P	4	1	2	0	0	1.000
Postseason Totals		5	3	0	0	0	0	0	0	0	0	0	0	1	0	0	0	0	0	—	0	.000	.000	.000	P	5	1	3	0	0	1.000

AL SMITH—Alfred John Smith—Throws: Left; Bats: Left

Ht: 5'11"; Wt: 180 lbs; Born: 10/12/1907 in Belleville, Illinois; Debut: 5/5/1934; Died: 4/28/1977

World Series — Pitching

Year Tm	Age	G	GS	CG	GF	IP	BFP	H	R	ER	HR	SH	SF	HB	TBB	IBB	SO	WP	Bk	W	L	Pct	ShO	Sv-Op	Hld	OAvg	OOBP	ERA
1936 NYG	28	1	0	0	0	0.1	4	2	3	3	0	0	0	0	1	0	0	0	0	0	0	—	0	0- 0	0	.667	.750	81.00
1937 NYG	29	2	0	0	1	3.0	12	2	1	1	1	0	0	1	0	0	1	0	0	0	0	—	0	0- 0	0	.182	.250	3.00
WS Totals		3	0	0	1	3.1	32	4	4	4	1	0	0	1	1	0	1	0	0	0	0	—	0	0-0	0	.286	.375	10.80

World Series — Batting / Fielding

Year Tm	Age	G	AB	H	2B	3B	HR	TB	R	RBI	GW	TBB	IBB	SO	HBP	SH	SF	SB	CS	SB%	GDP	Avg	OBP	SLG	Pos	G	PO	A	E	DP	FPct
1936 NYG	28	1	0	0	0	0	0	0	0	0	0	0	0	0	0	0	0	0	0	—	0	—	—	—	P	1	0	0	0	0	—
1937 NYG	29	2	0	0	0	0	0	0	0	0	0	0	0	0	0	0	0	0	0	—	0	—	—	—	P	2	0	1	0	0	1.000
WS Totals		3	0	0	0	0	0	0	0	0	0	0	0	0	0	0	0	0	0	—	0	—	—	—	P	3	0	1	0	0	1.000

AL SMITH—Alphonse Eugene Smith—Nickname: Fuzzy—Bats: Right; Throws: Right

Ht: 6'0"; Wt: 189 lbs; Born: 2/7/1928 in Kirkwood, Missouri; Debut: 7/10/1953

World Series — Batting / Fielding

Year Tm	Age	G	AB	H	2B	3B	HR	TB	R	RBI	GW	TBB	IBB	SO	HBP	SH	SF	SB	CS	SB%	GDP	Avg	OBP	SLG	Pos	G	PO	A	E	DP	FPct
1954 Cle	26	4	14	3	0	0	1	6	2	2	0	2	0	2	1	0	0	0	0	—	1	.214	.353	.429	OF	4	4	0	0	0	1.000
1959 ChA	31	6	20	5	3	0	0	8	1	1	0	4	0	4	0	0	0	0	0	—	2	.250	.375	.400	OF	6	10	0	0	0	1.000
WS Totals		10	34	8	3	0	1	14	3	3	0	6	0	6	1	0	0	0	0	—	3	.235	.366	.412	OF	10	14	0	0	0	1.000

BILLY SMITH—Billy Edward Smith—Bats: Both; Throws: Right

Ht: 6'2"; Wt: 185 lbs; Born: 7/14/1953 in Hodge, Louisiana; Debut: 4/13/1975

LCS		Batting																							Fielding						
Year Tm	Age	G	AB	H	2B	3B	HR	TB	R	RBI	GW	TBB	IBB	SO	HBP	SH	SF	SB	CS	SB%	GDP	Avg	OBP	SLG	Pos	G	PO	A	E	DP	FPct
1979 Bal	26	1	4	0	0	0	0	0	0	0	0	0	0	1	0	0	0	0	0	—	0	.000	.000	.000	2B	1	1	2	0	2	1.000

World Series		Batting																							Fielding						
Year Tm	Age	G	AB	H	2B	3B	HR	TB	R	RBI	GW	TBB	IBB	SO	HBP	SH	SF	SB	CS	SB%	GDP	Avg	OBP	SLG	Pos	G	PO	A	E	DP	FPct
1979 Bal	26	4	7	2	0	0	0	2	1	0	0	2	2	0	0	0	0	0	0	—	2	.286	.444	.286	2B	4	4	3	0	1	1.000
Postseason Totals		5	11	2	0	0	0	2	1	0	0	2	2	1	0	0	0	0	0	—	2	.182	.308	.182	2B	5	5	5	0	3	1.000

BILLY SMITH—Billy Lavern Smith—Throws: Right; Bats: Right

Ht: 6'7"; Wt: 200 lbs; Born: 9/13/1954 in La Marque, Texas; Debut: 6/9/1981

Division Series		Pitching																										
Year Tm	Age	G	GS	CG	GF	IP	BFP	H	R	ER	HR	SH	SF	HB	TBB	IBB	SO	WP	Bk	W	L	Pct	ShO	Sv-Op	Hld	OAvg	OOBP	ERA
1981 Hou	27	1	0	0	1	0.1	1	0	0	0	0	0	0	0	0	0	0	0	0	0	0	—	0	0-0	0	.000	.000	0.00

Division Series		Batting																							Fielding						
Year Tm	Age	G	AB	H	2B	3B	HR	TB	R	RBI	GW	TBB	IBB	SO	HBP	SH	SF	SB	CS	SB%	GDP	Avg	OBP	SLG	Pos	G	PO	A	E	DP	FPct
1981 Hou	27	1	0	0	0	0	0	0	0	0	0	0	0	0	0	0	0	0	0	—	0	—	—	—	P	1	0	0	0	0	—

BOB SMITH—Robert Eldridge Smith—Throws: Right; Bats: Right

Ht: 5'10"; Wt: 175 lbs; Born: 4/22/1895 in Rogersville, Tennessee; Debut: 4/19/1923; Died: 7/19/1987

World Series		Pitching																										
Year Tm	Age	G	GS	CG	GF	IP	BFP	H	R	ER	HR	SH	SF	HB	TBB	IBB	SO	WP	Bk	W	L	Pct	ShO	Sv-Op	Hld	OAvg	OOBP	ERA
1932 ChN	37	1	0	0	1	1.0	5	2	1	1	0	0	0	0	0	0	1	0	0	0	0	—	0	0-0	0	.400	.400	9.00

World Series		Batting																							Fielding						
Year Tm	Age	G	AB	H	2B	3B	HR	TB	R	RBI	GW	TBB	IBB	SO	HBP	SH	SF	SB	CS	SB%	GDP	Avg	OBP	SLG	Pos	G	PO	A	E	DP	FPct
1932 ChN	37	1	0	0	0	0	0	0	0	0	0	0	0	0	0	0	0	0	0	—	0	—	—	—	P	1	0	0	0	0	—

CLAY SMITH—Clay Jamieson Smith—Throws: Right; Bats: Right

Ht: 6'2"; Wt: 190 lbs; Born: 9/11/1914 in Cambridge, Kansas; Debut: 9/13/1938

World Series		Pitching																										
Year Tm	Age	G	GS	CG	GF	IP	BFP	H	R	ER	HR	SH	SF	HB	TBB	IBB	SO	WP	Bk	W	L	Pct	ShO	Sv-Op	Hld	OAvg	OOBP	ERA
1940 Det	26	1	0	0	0	4.0	16	1	1	1	0	0	0	0	3	2	1	0	0	0	0	—	0	0-0	0	.077	.250	2.25

World Series		Batting																							Fielding						
Year Tm	Age	G	AB	H	2B	3B	HR	TB	R	RBI	GW	TBB	IBB	SO	HBP	SH	SF	SB	CS	SB%	GDP	Avg	OBP	SLG	Pos	G	PO	A	E	DP	FPct
1940 Det	26	1	1	0	0	0	0	0	0	0	0	0	0	1	0	0	0	0	0	—	0	.000	.000	.000	P	1	0	1	0	0	1.000

DAVE SMITH—David Stanley Smith—Throws: Right; Bats: Right

Ht: 6'1"; Wt: 195 lbs; Born: 1/21/1955 in Richmond, California; Debut: 4/11/1980

Division Series		Pitching																										
Year Tm	Age	G	GS	CG	GF	IP	BFP	H	R	ER	HR	SH	SF	HB	TBB	IBB	SO	WP	Bk	W	L	Pct	ShO	Sv-Op	Hld	OAvg	OOBP	ERA
1981 Hou	26	2	0	0	0	2.1	9	2	1	1	0	0	0	0	0	0	4	0	0	0	0	—	0	0-0	0	.222	.222	3.86
LCS		Pitching																										
Year Tm	Age	G	GS	CG	GF	IP	BFP	H	R	ER	HR	SH	SF	HB	TBB	IBB	SO	WP	Bk	W	L	Pct	ShO	Sv-Op	Hld	OAvg	OOBP	ERA
1980 Hou	25	3	0	0	1	2.1	13	4	1	1	0	1	0	0	2	2	4	0	0	1	0	1.000	0	0-1	0	.400	.500	3.86
1986 Hou	31	2	0	0	1	2.0	11	2	2	2	1	0	1	0	3	1	2	0	0	0	1	.000	0	0-2	0	.286	.455	9.00
LCS Totals		5	0	0	2	4.1	48	6	3	3	1	1	1	0	5	3	6	0	0	1	1	.500	0	0-3	0	.353	.478	6.23
Postseason Totals		7	0	0	2	6.2	66	8	4	4	1	1	1	0	5	3	10	0	0	1	1	.500	0	0-3	0	.308	.406	5.40

Division Series		Batting																							Fielding						
Year Tm	Age	G	AB	H	2B	3B	HR	TB	R	RBI	GW	TBB	IBB	SO	HBP	SH	SF	SB	CS	SB%	GDP	Avg	OBP	SLG	Pos	G	PO	A	E	DP	FPct
1981 Hou	26	2	0	0	0	0	0	0	0	0	0	0	0	0	0	0	0	0	0	—	0	—	—	—	P	2	0	0	0	0	—
LCS		Batting																							Fielding						
Year Tm	Age	G	AB	H	2B	3B	HR	TB	R	RBI	GW	TBB	IBB	SO	HBP	SH	SF	SB	CS	SB%	GDP	Avg	OBP	SLG	Pos	G	PO	A	E	DP	FPct
1980 Hou	25	3	0	0	0	0	0	0	0	0	0	0	0	0	0	0	0	0	0	—	0	—	—	—	P	3	0	0	0	0	—
1986 Hou	31	2	0	0	0	0	0	0	0	0	0	0	0	0	0	0	0	0	0	—	0	—	—	—	P	2	0	0	0	0	—
LCS Totals		5	0	0	0	0	0	0	0	0	0	0	0	0	0	0	0	0	0	—	0	—	—	—	P	5	0	0	0	0	—
Postseason Totals		7	0	0	0	0	0	0	0	0	0	0	0	0	0	0	0	0	0	—	0	—	—	—	P	7	0	0	0	0	—

DWIGHT SMITH—John Dwight Smith—Bats: Left; Throws: Right

Ht: 5'11"; Wt: 175 lbs; Born: 11/8/1963 in Tallahassee, Florida; Debut: 5/1/1989

Division Series		Batting																							Fielding						
Year Tm	Age	G	AB	H	2B	3B	HR	TB	R	RBI	GW	TBB	IBB	SO	HBP	SH	SF	SB	CS	SB%	GDP	Avg	OBP	SLG	Pos	G	PO	A	E	DP	FPct
1995 Atl	31	4	3	2	1	0	0	3	0	1	0	0	0	0	0	0	0	0	0	—	0	.667	.667	1.000	—						
LCS		Batting																							Fielding						
Year Tm	Age	G	AB	H	2B	3B	HR	TB	R	RBI	GW	TBB	IBB	SO	HBP	SH	SF	SB	CS	SB%	GDP	Avg	OBP	SLG	Pos	G	PO	A	E	DP	FPct
1989 ChN	25	4	15	3	1	0	0	4	2	0	0	2	0	2	0	0	0	1	0	1.00	0	.200	.294	.267	OF	4	9	0	0	0	1.000
1995 Atl	31	2	2	0	0	0	0	0	0	0	0	0	0	0	0	0	0	0	0	—	0	.000	.000	.000	—						
LCS Totals		6	17	3	1	0	0	4	2	0	0	2	0	2	0	0	0	1	0	1.00	0	.176	.263	.235	OF	4	9	0	0	0	1.000
World Series		Batting																							Fielding						
Year Tm	Age	G	AB	H	2B	3B	HR	TB	R	RBI	GW	TBB	IBB	SO	HBP	SH	SF	SB	CS	SB%	GDP	Avg	OBP	SLG	Pos	G	PO	A	E	DP	FPct
1995 Atl	31	3	2	1	0	0	0	1	0	0	0	1	1	0	0	0	0	0	0	—	0	.500	.667	.500	—						
Postseason Totals		13	22	6	2	0	0	8	2	1	0	3	1	2	0	0	0	1	0	1.00	0	.273	.360	.364	OF	4	9	0	0	0	1.000

EARL SMITH—Earl Sutton Smith—Nickname: Oil—Bats: Left; Throws: Right

Ht: 5'10"; Wt: 180 lbs; Born: 2/14/1897 in Hot Springs, Arkansas; Debut: 4/24/1919; Died: 6/8/1963

World Series		Batting																							Fielding						
Year Tm	Age	G	AB	H	2B	3B	HR	TB	R	RBI	GW	TBB	IBB	SO	HBP	SH	SF	SB	CS	SB%	GDP	Avg	OBP	SLG	Pos	G	PO	A	E	DP	FPct
1921 NYG	24	3	7	0	0	0	0	0	0	0	0	1	0	0	0	0	0	0	1	.00	0	.000	.125	.000	C	2	7	2	1	1	.900
1922 NYG	25	4	7	1	0	0	0	1	0	0	0	0	0	2	0	0	0	0	0	—	1	.143	.143	.143	C	1	2	1	0	0	1.000
1925 Pit	28	6	20	7	1	0	0	8	0	0	0	1	1	2	0	1	0	0	0	—	2	.350	.381	.400	C	6	29	7	1	1	.973
1927 Pit	30	3	8	0	0	0	0	0	0	0	0	0	0	0	0	0	0	0	0	—	0	.000	.000	.000	C	2	10	1	1	0	.917
1928 StL	31	1	4	3	0	0	0	3	0	0	0	0	0	0	0	0	0	0	1	.00	0	.750	.750	.750	C	1	3	1	0	0	1.000
WS Totals		17	46	11	1	0	0	12	0	0	0	2	1	4	0	1	0	0	2	.00	3	.239	.271	.261	C	12	51	12	3	2	.955

ELMER SMITH—Elmer John Smith—Bats: Left; Throws: Right

Ht: 5'10"; Wt: 165 lbs; Born: 9/21/1892 in Sandusky, Ohio; Debut: 9/20/1914; Died: 8/3/1984

World Series		Batting																							Fielding						
Year Tm	Age	G	AB	H	2B	3B	HR	TB	R	RBI	GW	TBB	IBB	SO	HBP	SH	SF	SB	CS	SB%	GDP	Avg	OBP	SLG	Pos	G	PO	A	E	DP	FPct
1920 Cle	28	5	13	4	0	1	1	9	1	5	2	1	0	1	0	0	0	0	0	—	0	.308	.357	.692	OF	5	7	1	0	0	1.000
1922 NYA	30	2	2	0	0	0	0	0	0	0	0	0	0	2	0	0	0	0	0	—	0	.000	.000	.000	—						
WS Totals		7	15	4	0	1	1	9	1	5	2	1	0	3	0	0	0	0	0	—	0	.267	.313	.600	OF	5	7	1	0	0	1.000

HAL SMITH—Harold Wayne Smith—Bats: Right; Throws: Right

Ht: 6'0"; Wt: 195 lbs; Born: 12/7/1930 in West Frankfort, Illinois; Debut: 4/11/1955

World Series		Batting																							Fielding						
Year Tm	Age	G	AB	H	2B	3B	HR	TB	R	RBI	GW	TBB	IBB	SO	HBP	SH	SF	SB	CS	SB%	GDP	Avg	OBP	SLG	Pos	G	PO	A	E	DP	FPct
1960 Pit	29	3	8	3	0	0	1	6	1	3	0	0	0	0	0	0	0	0	0	—	2	.375	.375	.750	C	3	14	1	0	0	1.000

HARRY SMITH—Harry Thomas Smith—Bats: Right; Throws: Right

Ht: Unknown; Wt: Unknown; Born: 10/31/1874 in Yorkshire, England; Debut: 7/11/1901; Died: 2/17/1933

World Series		Batting																							Fielding						
Year Tm	Age	G	AB	H	2B	3B	HR	TB	R	RBI	GW	TBB	IBB	SO	HBP	SH	SF	SB	CS	SB%	GDP	Avg	OBP	SLG	Pos	G	PO	A	E	DP	FPct
1903 Pit	28	1	3	0	0	0	0	0	0	0	0	0	0	0	0	0	0	0	0	—	0	.000	.000	.000	C	1	2	1	1	0	.750

JIMMY SMITH—James Lawrence Smith—Nicknames: Greenfield Jimmy, Bluejacket—Bats: Both; Throws: Right Ht: 5'9"; Wt: 152 lbs; Born: 5/15/1895 in Pittsburgh, Pennsylvania; Debut: 9/26/1914; Died: 1/1/1974

World Series — Batting / Fielding

Year Tm	Age	G	AB	H	2B	3B	HR	TB	R	RBI	GW	TBB	IBB	SO	HBP	SH	SF	SB	CS	SB%	GDP	Avg	OBP	SLG	Pos	G	PO	A	E	DP	FPct
1919 Cin	24	1	0	0	0	0	0	0	0	0	0	0	0	0	0	0	0	0	0	—	0	—	—	—	—						

LEE SMITH—Lee Arthur Smith—Throws: Right; Bats: Right Ht: 6'5"; Wt: 220 lbs; Born: 12/4/1957 in Jamestown, Louisiana; Debut: 9/1/1980

LCS — Pitching

Year Tm	Age	G	GS	CG	GF	IP	BFP	H	R	ER	HR	SH	SF	HB	TBB	IBB	SO	WP	Bk	W	L	Pct	ShO	Sv-Op	Hld	OAvg	OOBP	ERA
1984 ChN	26	2	0	0	2	2.0	10	3	2	2	1	0	0	0	0	0	3	0	0	0	1	.000	0	1- 1	0	.300	.300	9.00
1988 Bos	30	2	0	0	2	3.1	17	6	3	3	0	0	1	0	1	0	4	0	0	0	1	.000	0	0- 0	0	.400	.412	8.10
LCS Totals		4	0	0	4	5.1	54	9	5	5	1	0	1	0	1	0	7	0	0	0	2	.000	0	1-1	0	.360	.370	8.44

LCS — Batting / Fielding

Year Tm	Age	G	AB	H	2B	3B	HR	TB	R	RBI	GW	TBB	IBB	SO	HBP	SH	SF	SB	CS	SB%	GDP	Avg	OBP	SLG	Pos	G	PO	A	E	DP	FPct
1984 ChN	26	2	0	0	0	0	0	0	0	0	0	0	0	0	0	0	0	0	0	—	0	—	—	—	P	2	0	0	0	0	—
1988 Bos	30	2	0	0	0	0	0	0	0	0	0	0	0	0	0	0	0	0	0	—	0	—	—	—	P	2	0	0	0	0	—
LCS Totals		4	0	0	0	0	0	0	0	0	0	0	0	0	0	0	0	0	0	—	0	—	—	—	P	4	0	0	0	0	—

LONNIE SMITH—Nickname: Skates—Bats: Right; Throws: Right Ht: 5'9"; Wt: 170 lbs; Born: 12/22/1955 in Chicago, Illinois; Debut: 9/2/1978

Division Series — Batting / Fielding

Year Tm	Age	G	AB	H	2B	3B	HR	TB	R	RBI	GW	TBB	IBB	SO	HBP	SH	SF	SB	CS	SB%	GDP	Avg	OBP	SLG	Pos	G	PO	A	E	DP	FPct
1981 Phi	25	5	19	5	1	0	0	6	1	0	0	0	0	4	0	0	0	0	1	.00	0	.263	.263	.316	OF	5	5	0	0	0	1.000

LCS — Batting / Fielding

Year Tm	Age	G	AB	H	2B	3B	HR	TB	R	RBI	GW	TBB	IBB	SO	HBP	SH	SF	SB	CS	SB%	GDP	Avg	OBP	SLG	Pos	G	PO	A	E	DP	FPct
1980 Phi	24	3	5	3	0	0	0	3	2	0	0	0	0	0	0	0	0	1	0	1.00	0	.600	.600	.600	OF	2	2	1	0	1	1.000
1982 StL	26	3	11	3	0	0	0	3	1	1	0	0	0	1	1	1	1	0	0	—	0	.273	.308	.273	OF	3	2	0	0	0	1.000
1985 KC	29	7	28	7	2	0	0	9	2	1	0	3	0	6	0	0	0	1	1	.50	0	.250	.323	.321	OF	7	8	2	1	0	.909
1991 Atl	35	7	24	6	3	0	0	9	3	0	0	4	0	5	1	0	0	1	2	.33	0	.250	.379	.375	OF	7	10	2	0	1	1.000
1992 Atl	36	6	6	2	0	1	0	4	1	1	0	0	0	0	0	0	0	0	0	—	0	.333	.333	.667	—						
LCS Totals		26	74	21	5	1	0	28	9	3	0	7	0	12	2	1	1	3	3	.50	0	.284	.357	.378	OF	19	22	5	1	2	.964

World Series — Batting / Fielding

Year Tm	Age	G	AB	H	2B	3B	HR	TB	R	RBI	GW	TBB	IBB	SO	HBP	SH	SF	SB	CS	SB%	GDP	Avg	OBP	SLG	Pos	G	PO	A	E	DP	FPct
1980 Phi	24	6	19	5	1	0	0	6	2	1	0	1	0	1	0	0	0	0	1	.00	1	.263	.300	.316	OF	5	4	1	0	0	1.000
1982 StL	26	7	28	9	4	1	0	15	6	1	0	1	0	5	0	0	0	2	2	.50	0	.321	.345	.536	OF	6	11	0	0	0	1.000
1985 KC	29	7	27	9	3	0	0	12	4	4	1	3	0	8	0	0	0	2	2	.50	0	.333	.400	.444	OF	7	7	2	0	0	1.000
1991 Atl	35	7	26	6	0	0	3	15	5	3	0	3	0	4	1	1	0	1	0	1.00	1	.231	.333	.577	OF	3	2	0	0	0	1.000
1992 Atl	36	5	12	2	0	0	1	5	1	5	0	1	0	4	1	0	0	0	0	—	0	.167	.286	.417	—						
WS Totals		32	112	31	8	1	4	53	18	14	1	9	0	22	2	1	0	5	5	.50	2	.277	.341	.473	OF	21	24	3	0	0	1.000
Postseason Totals		63	205	57	14	2	4	87	28	17	1	16	0	38	4	2	1	8	9	.47	2	.278	.341	.424	OF	45	51	8	1	2	.983

OZZIE SMITH—Osborne Earl Smith—Nickname: The Wizard of Oz—Bats: Both; Throws: Right Ht: 5'11"; Wt: 150 lbs; Born: 12/26/1954 in Mobile, Alabama; Debut: 4/7/1978

Division Series — Batting / Fielding

Year Tm	Age	G	AB	H	2B	3B	HR	TB	R	RBI	GW	TBB	IBB	SO	HBP	SH	SF	SB	CS	SB%	GDP	Avg	OBP	SLG	Pos	G	PO	A	E	DP	FPct
1996 StL	41	2	3	1	0	0	0	1	1	0	0	2	0	0	0	0	0	0	0	—	0	.333	.600	.333	SS	1	2	1	0	0	1.000

LCS — Batting / Fielding

Year Tm	Age	G	AB	H	2B	3B	HR	TB	R	RBI	GW	TBB	IBB	SO	HBP	SH	SF	SB	CS	SB%	GDP	Avg	OBP	SLG	Pos	G	PO	A	E	DP	FPct
1982 StL	27	3	9	5	0	0	0	5	0	3	1	3	0	0	0	0	1	1	0	1.00	0	.556	.615	.556	SS	3	4	11	0	1	1.000
1985 StL	30	6	23	10	1	1	1	16	4	3	1	3	1	1	0	1	0	1	0	1.00	0	.435	.500	.696	SS	6	6	16	0	2	1.000
1987 StL	32	7	25	5	0	1	0	7	2	1	0	3	0	4	0	1	1	0	0	—	1	.200	.276	.280	SS	7	10	19	1	4	.967
1996 StL	41	3	9	0	0	0	0	0	0	0	0	0	0	1	0	0	0	0	0	—	0	.000	.000	.000	SS	2	7	2	0	1	1.000
LCS Totals		19	66	20	1	2	1	28	6	7	2	9	1	6	0	2	2	2	0	1.00	1	.303	.377	.424	SS	18	27	48	1	8	.987

World Series — Batting / Fielding

Year Tm	Age	G	AB	H	2B	3B	HR	TB	R	RBI	GW	TBB	IBB	SO	HBP	SH	SF	SB	CS	SB%	GDP	Avg	OBP	SLG	Pos	G	PO	A	E	DP	FPct
1982 StL	27	7	24	5	0	0	0	5	3	1	0	3	0	0	0	0	0	1	0	1.00	1	.208	.296	.208	SS	7	22	17	0	5	1.000
1985 StL	30	7	23	2	0	0	0	2	1	0	0	4	0	0	0	1	0	1	1	.50	1	.087	.222	.087	SS	7	10	16	1	5	.963
1987 StL	32	7	28	6	0	0	0	6	3	2	0	2	0	3	0	0	0	2	0	1.00	0	.214	.267	.214	SS	7	6	19	0	1	1.000
WS Totals		21	75	13	0	0	0	13	7	3	0	9	0	3	0	1	0	4	1	.80	2	.173	.262	.173	SS	21	38	52	1	11	.989
Postseason Totals		42	144	34	1	2	1	42	14	10	2	20	1	9	0	3	2	6	1	.86	3	.236	.325	.292	SS	40	67	101	2	19	.988

PETE SMITH—Peter John Smith—Throws: Right; Bats: Right Ht: 6'2"; Wt: 185 lbs; Born: 2/27/1966 in Abington, Massachusetts; Debut: 9/8/1987

LCS — Pitching

Year Tm	Age	G	GS	CG	GF	IP	BFP	H	R	ER	HR	SH	SF	HB	TBB	IBB	SO	WP	Bk	W	L	Pct	ShO	Sv-Op	Hld	OAvg	OOBP	ERA
1992 Atl	26	2	0	0	0	3.2	15	2	1	1	0	0	1	0	3	0	3	0	0	0	0	—	0	0- 0	0	.182	.333	2.45

World Series — Pitching

Year Tm	Age	G	GS	CG	GF	IP	BFP	H	R	ER	HR	SH	SF	HB	TBB	IBB	SO	WP	Bk	W	L	Pct	ShO	Sv-Op	Hld	OAvg	OOBP	ERA
1992 Atl	26	1	0	0	0	3.0	12	3	0	0	0	0	0	0	0	0	0	0	0	0	0	—	0	0- 0	0	.250	.250	0.00
Postseason Totals		3	0	0	0	6.2	54	5	1	1	0	0	1	0	3	0	3	0	0	0	0	—	0	0-0	0	.217	.296	1.35

LCS — Batting / Fielding

Year Tm	Age	G	AB	H	2B	3B	HR	TB	R	RBI	GW	TBB	IBB	SO	HBP	SH	SF	SB	CS	SB%	GDP	Avg	OBP	SLG	Pos	G	PO	A	E	DP	FPct
1992 Atl	26	2	1	0	0	0	0	0	0	0	0	0	0	0	0	0	0	0	0	—	0	.000	.000	.000	P	2	0	1	0	0	1.000

World Series — Batting / Fielding

Year Tm	Age	G	AB	H	2B	3B	HR	TB	R	RBI	GW	TBB	IBB	SO	HBP	SH	SF	SB	CS	SB%	GDP	Avg	OBP	SLG	Pos	G	PO	A	E	DP	FPct
1992 Atl	26	1	1	0	0	0	0	0	0	0	0	0	0	1	0	0	0	0	0	—	0	.000	.000	.000	P	1	0	0	0	0	—
Postseason Totals		3	2	0	0	0	0	0	0	0	0	0	0	1	0	0	0	0	0	—	0	.000	.000	.000	P	3	0	1	0	0	1.000

REGGIE SMITH—Carl Reginald Smith—Bats: Both; Throws: Right Ht: 6'0"; Wt: 180 lbs; Born: 4/2/1945 in Shreveport, Louisiana; Debut: 9/18/1966

Division Series — Batting / Fielding

Year Tm	Age	G	AB	H	2B	3B	HR	TB	R	RBI	GW	TBB	IBB	SO	HBP	SH	SF	SB	CS	SB%	GDP	Avg	OBP	SLG	Pos	G	PO	A	E	DP	FPct
1981 LA	36	2	1	0	0	0	0	0	0	1	0	0	0	1	0	0	1	0	0	—	0	.000	.000	.000	—						

LCS — Batting / Fielding

Year Tm	Age	G	AB	H	2B	3B	HR	TB	R	RBI	GW	TBB	IBB	SO	HBP	SH	SF	SB	CS	SB%	GDP	Avg	OBP	SLG	Pos	G	PO	A	E	DP	FPct
1977 LA	32	4	16	3	0	1	0	5	2	1	0	2	0	5	0	0	0	1	0	1.00	0	.188	.278	.313	OF	4	7	0	1	0	.875
1978 LA	33	4	16	3	1	0	0	4	2	1	0	0	0	2	1	0	0	0	0	—	0	.188	.235	.250	OF	4	5	0	1	0	.833
1981 LA	36	1	1	1	0	0	0	1	0	1	0	0	0	0	0	0	0	0	0	—	0	1.000	1.000	1.000	—						
LCS Totals		9	33	7	1	1	0	10	4	3	0	2	0	7	1	0	0	1	0	1.00	0	.212	.278	.303	OF	8	12	0	2	0	.857

World Series — Batting / Fielding

Year Tm	Age	G	AB	H	2B	3B	HR	TB	R	RBI	GW	TBB	IBB	SO	HBP	SH	SF	SB	CS	SB%	GDP	Avg	OBP	SLG	Pos	G	PO	A	E	DP	FPct
1967 Bos	22	7	24	6	1	0	2	13	3	3	0	2	0	2	0	0	0	0	1	.00	0	.250	.308	.542	OF	7	14	0	0	0	1.000
1977 LA	32	6	22	6	1	0	3	16	7	5	0	4	0	3	0	0	0	0	1	.00	2	.273	.385	.727	OF	6	14	1	0	0	1.000
1978 LA	33	6	25	5	0	0	1	8	3	5	0	2	0	6	0	0	0	0	1	.00	1	.200	.259	.320	OF	6	11	1	1	0	.923
1981 LA	36	2	2	1	0	0	0	1	0	0	0	0	0	1	0	0	0	0	0	—	0	.500	.500	.500	—						
WS Totals		21	73	18	2	0	6	38	13	13	0	8	0	12	0	0	0	0	3	.00	3	.247	.321	.521	OF	19	39	2	1	0	.976
Postseason Totals		32	107	25	3	1	6	48	17	17	0	10	0	20	1	0	1	1	3	.25	3	.234	.303	.449	OF	27	51	2	3	0	.946

SHERRY SMITH—Sherrod Malone Smith—Throws: Left; Bats: Right Ht: 6'1"; Wt: 170 lbs; Born: 2/18/1891 in Monticello, Georgia; Debut: 5/11/1911; Died: 9/12/1949

World Series — Pitching

Year Tm	Age	G	GS	CG	GF	IP	BFP	H	R	ER	HR	SH	SF	HB	TBB	IBB	SO	WP	Bk	W	L	Pct	ShO	Sv-Op	Hld	OAvg	OOBP	ERA
1916 Bro	25	1	1	1	0	13.1	51	7	2	2	0	3	0	0	6	1	2	0	0	0	1	.000	0	0- 0	0	.167	.271	1.35
1920 Bro	29	2	2	2	0	17.0	59	10	2	1	0	0	0	0	3	0	3	0	0	1	1	.500	0	0- 0	0	.179	.220	0.53
WS Totals		3	3	3	0	30.1	220	17	4	3	0	3	0	0	9	1	5	0	0	1	2	.333	0	0-0	0	.173	.243	0.89

World Series — Batting / Fielding

Year Tm	Age	G	AB	H	2B	3B	HR	TB	R	RBI	GW	TBB	IBB	SO	HBP	SH	SF	SB	CS	SB%	GDP	Avg	OBP	SLG	Pos	G	PO	A	E	DP	FPct
1916 Bro	25	1	5	1	1	0	0	2	0	0	0	0	0	0	0	0	0	0	0	—	0	.200	.200	.400	P	1	1	7	0	0	1.000
1920 Bro	29	2	6	0	0	0	0	0	0	0	0	0	0	2	0	0	0	0	0	—	0	.000	.000	.000	P	2	2	4	0	0	1.000
WS Totals		3	11	1	1	0	0	2	0	0	0	0	0	2	0	0	0	0	0	—	0	.091	.091	.182	P	3	3	11	0	0	1.000

ZANE SMITH—Zane William Smith—Throws: Left; Bats: Left

Ht: 6'2"; Wt: 185 lbs; Born: 12/28/1960 in Madison, Wisconsin; Debut: 9/10/1984

Division Series — Pitching

Year Tm	Age	G	GS	CG	GF	IP	BFP	H	R	ER	HR	SH	SF	HB	TBB	IBB	SO	WP	Bk	W	L	Pct	ShO	Sv-Op	Hld	OAvg	OOBP	ERA
1995 Bos	34	1	0	0	1	1.1	5	1	1	1	1	0	0	0	0	0	0	0	0	0	1	.000	0	0- 0	0	.200	.200	6.75

LCS — Pitching

Year Tm	Age	G	GS	CG	GF	IP	BFP	H	R	ER	HR	SH	SF	HB	TBB	IBB	SO	WP	Bk	W	L	Pct	ShO	Sv-Op	Hld	OAvg	OOBP	ERA
1990 Pit	29	2	1	0	0	9.0	42	14	6	6	2	1	0	0	1	1	8	0	0	0	2	.000	0	0- 0	0	.350	.366	6.00
1991 Pit	30	2	2	0	0	14.2	60	15	1	1	0	0	0	1	3	1	10	0	0	1	1	.500	0	0- 0	0	.268	.317	0.61
LCS Totals		4	3	0	0	23.2	204	29	7	7	2	1	0	1	4	2	18	0	0	1	3	.250	0	0-0	0	.302	.337	2.66
Postseason Totals		5	3	0	1	25.0	214	30	8	8	3	1	0	1	4	2	18	0	0	1	4	.200	0	0-0	0	.297	.330	2.88

Division Series — Batting / Fielding

Year Tm	Age	G	AB	H	2B	3B	HR	TB	R	RBI	GW	TBB	IBB	SO	HBP	SH	SF	SB	CS	SB%	GDP	Avg	OBP	SLG	Pos	G	PO	A	E	DP	FPct
1995 Bos	34	1	0	0	0	0	0	0	0	0	0	0	0	0	0	0	0	0	0	—	0	—	—	—	P	1	0	0	0	0	—

LCS — Batting / Fielding

Year Tm	Age	G	AB	H	2B	3B	HR	TB	R	RBI	GW	TBB	IBB	SO	HBP	SH	SF	SB	CS	SB%	GDP	Avg	OBP	SLG	Pos	G	PO	A	E	DP	FPct
1990 Pit	29	2	3	0	0	0	0	0	0	0	0	0	0	1	0	0	0	0	0	—	0	.000	.000	.000	P	2	0	1	0	0	1.000
1991 Pit	30	2	5	0	0	0	0	0	0	0	0	0	0	4	0	0	0	0	0	—	0	.000	.000	.000	P	2	0	3	0	0	1.000
LCS Totals		4	8	0	0	0	0	0	0	0	0	0	0	5	0	0	0	0	0	—	0	.000	.000	.000	P	4	0	4	0	0	1.000
Postseason Totals		5	8	0	0	0	0	0	0	0	0	0	0	5	0	0	0	0	0	—	0	.000	.000	.000	P	5	0	4	0	0	1.000

MIKE SMITHSON—Billy Mike Smithson—Throws: Right; Bats: Right

Ht: 6'8"; Wt: 215 lbs; Born: 1/21/1955 in Centerville, Tennessee; Debut: 8/27/1982

LCS — Pitching

Year Tm	Age	G	GS	CG	GF	IP	BFP	H	R	ER	HR	SH	SF	HB	TBB	IBB	SO	WP	Bk	W	L	Pct	ShO	Sv-Op	Hld	OAvg	OOBP	ERA
1988 Bos	33	1	0	0	0	2.1	9	3	0	0	0	0	0	0	0	0	1	0	0	0	0	—	0	0- 0	0	.333	.333	0.00

LCS — Batting / Fielding

Year Tm	Age	G	AB	H	2B	3B	HR	TB	R	RBI	GW	TBB	IBB	SO	HBP	SH	SF	SB	CS	SB%	GDP	Avg	OBP	SLG	Pos	G	PO	A	E	DP	FPct
1988 Bos	33	1	0	0	0	0	0	0	0	0	0	0	0	0	0	0	0	0	0	—	0	—	—	—	P	1	0	0	0	0	—

JOHN SMOLTZ—John Andrew Smoltz—Throws: Right; Bats: Right

Ht: 6'3"; Wt: 210 lbs; Born: 5/15/1967 in Detroit, Michigan; Debut: 7/23/1988

Division Series — Pitching

Year Tm	Age	G	GS	CG	GF	IP	BFP	H	R	ER	HR	SH	SF	HB	TBB	IBB	SO	WP	Bk	W	L	Pct	ShO	Sv-Op	Hld	OAvg	OOBP	ERA
1995 Atl	28	1	1	0	0	5.2	24	5	5	5	2	1	0	1	1	0	6	1	0	0	0	—	0	0- 0	0	.238	.304	7.94
1996 Atl-*C*	29	1	1	0	0	9.0	33	4	1	1	0	0	0	0	2	0	7	0	0	1	0	1.000	0	0- 0	0	.129	.182	1.00
1997 Atl	30	1	1	1	0	9.0	32	3	1	1	1	0	0	0	1	0	11	0	0	1	0	1.000	0	0- 0	0	.097	.125	1.00
DS Totals		3	3	1	0	23.2	178	12	7	7	3	1	0	1	4	0	24	1	0	2	0	1.000	0	0-0	0	.145	.193	2.66

LCS — Pitching

Year Tm	Age	G	GS	CG	GF	IP	BFP	H	R	ER	HR	SH	SF	HB	TBB	IBB	SO	WP	Bk	W	L	Pct	ShO	Sv-Op	Hld	OAvg	OOBP	ERA
1991 Atl	24	2	2	1	0	15.1	64	14	3	3	2	0	0	0	3	0	15	0	0	2	0	1.000	1	0- 0	0	.230	.266	1.76
1992 Atl	25	3	3	0	0	20.1	83	14	7	6	1	0	1	0	10	2	19	1	0	2	0	1.000	0	0- 0	0	.194	.289	2.66
1993 Atl	26	1	1	0	0	6.1	33	8	2	0	0	0	1	0	5	0	10	0	0	0	1	.000	0	0- 0	0	.296	.394	0.00
1995 Atl	28	1	1	0	0	7.0	28	7	2	2	0	0	0	0	2	0	2	0	0	0	0	—	0	0- 0	0	.269	.321	2.57
1996 Atl-*C*	29	2	2	0	0	15.0	59	12	2	2	0	0	0	0	3	0	12	2	0	2	0	1.000	0	0- 0	0	.214	.254	1.20
1997 Atl	30	1	1	0	0	6.0	27	5	5	5	1	0	0	0	5	2	9	0	0	0	1	.000	0	0- 0	0	.227	.370	7.50
LCS Totals		10	10	1	0	70.0	588	60	21	18	4	0	2	0	28	4	67	3	0	6	2	.750	1	0-0	0	.227	.299	2.31

World Series — Pitching

Year Tm	Age	G	GS	CG	GF	IP	BFP	H	R	ER	HR	SH	SF	HB	TBB	IBB	SO	WP	Bk	W	L	Pct	ShO	Sv-Op	Hld	OAvg	OOBP	ERA
1991 Atl	24	2	2	0	0	14.1	56	13	2	2	1	0	0	1	1	0	11	0	0	0	0	—	0	0- 0	0	.241	.268	1.26
1992 Atl	25	2	2	0	0	13.1	58	13	5	4	0	0	0	0	7	0	12	2	0	1	0	1.000	0	0- 0	0	.255	.345	2.70
1995 Atl	28	1	1	0	0	2.1	15	6	4	4	0	0	0	0	2	0	4	0	0	0	0	—	0	0- 0	0	.462	.533	15.43
1996 Atl-*C*	29	2	2	0	0	14.0	56	6	2	1	0	0	0	0	8	0	14	0	0	1	1	.500	0	0- 0	0	.125	.250	0.64
WS Totals		7	7	0	0	44.0	370	38	13	11	1	0	0	1	18	0	41	2	0	2	1	.667	0	0-0	0	.229	.308	2.25
Postseason Totals		20	20	2	0	137.2	1136	110	41	36	8	1	2	2	50	4	132	6	0	10	3	.769	1	0-0	0	.214	.286	2.35

Division Series — Batting / Fielding

Year Tm	Age	G	AB	H	2B	3B	HR	TB	R	RBI	GW	TBB	IBB	SO	HBP	SH	SF	SB	CS	SB%	GDP	Avg	OBP	SLG	Pos	G	PO	A	E	DP	FPct
1995 Atl	28	1	2	0	0	0	0	0	0	0	0	0	0	0	0	0	0	0	0	—	0	.000	.000	.000	P	1	1	1	0	0	1.000
1996 Atl	29	1	2	0	0	0	0	0	0	0	0	0	0	0	0	1	0	0	0	—	0	.000	.000	.000	P	1	2	1	0	0	1.000
1997 Atl	30	1	4	0	0	0	0	0	0	0	0	0	0	1	0	0	0	0	0	—	0	.000	.000	.000	P	1	0	0	0	0	—
DS Totals		3	8	0	0	0	0	0	0	0	0	0	0	1	0	1	0	0	0	—	0	.000	.000	.000	P	3	3	2	0	0	1.000

LCS — Batting / Fielding

Year Tm	Age	G	AB	H	2B	3B	HR	TB	R	RBI	GW	TBB	IBB	SO	HBP	SH	SF	SB	CS	SB%	GDP	Avg	OBP	SLG	Pos	G	PO	A	E	DP	FPct
1991 Atl	24	2	5	1	0	0	0	1	0	0	0	1	0	4	0	1	0	1	0	1.00	0	.200	.333	.200	P	2	3	0	0	0	1.000
1992 Atl	25	3	7	2	0	0	0	2	1	1	0	0	0	2	0	0	0	1	0	1.00	0	.286	.286	.286	P	3	0	1	0	0	1.000
1993 Atl	26	1	1	0	0	0	0	0	0	0	0	1	0	1	0	0	0	0	0	—	0	.000	.500	.000	P	1	0	0	0	0	—
1995 Atl	28	1	3	1	0	0	0	1	0	0	0	0	0	1	0	0	0	1	0	1.00	0	.333	.333	.333	P	1	0	1	1	0	.500
1996 Atl	29	2	7	2	0	0	0	2	1	1	0	0	0	3	0	0	0	0	0	—	1	.286	.286	.286	P	2	0	1	0	0	1.000
1997 Atl	30	1	2	0	0	0	0	0	0	0	0	0	0	1	0	0	0	0	0	—	0	.000	.000	.000	P	1	0	1	0	0	1.000
LCS Totals		10	25	6	0	0	0	6	2	2	0	2	0	12	0	1	0	3	0	1.00	1	.240	.296	.240	P	10	3	4	1	0	.875

World Series — Batting / Fielding

Year Tm	Age	G	AB	H	2B	3B	HR	TB	R	RBI	GW	TBB	IBB	SO	HBP	SH	SF	SB	CS	SB%	GDP	Avg	OBP	SLG	Pos	G	PO	A	E	DP	FPct
1991 Atl	24	2	2	0	0	0	0	0	0	0	0	0	0	1	0	0	0	0	0	—	0	.000	.000	.000	P	2	2	1	0	0	1.000
1992 Atl	25	3	3	0	0	0	0	0	0	0	0	0	0	2	0	0	0	0	0	—	1	.000	.000	.000	P	2	1	2	0	0	1.000
1995 Atl	28	1	0	0	0	0	0	0	0	0	0	0	0	0	0	0	0	0	0	—	0	—	—	—	P	1	0	0	0	0	—
1996 Atl	29	2	2	1	0	0	0	1	0	0	0	0	0	0	0	0	0	0	0	—	0	.500	.500	.500	P	2	0	1	0	0	1.000
WS Totals		8	7	1	0	0	0	1	0	0	0	0	0	3	0	0	0	0	0	—	1	.143	.143	.143	P	7	3	4	0	0	1.000
Postseason Totals		21	40	7	0	0	0	7	2	2	0	2	0	16	0	2	0	3	0	1.00	2	.175	.214	.175	P	20	9	10	1	0	.950

DUKE SNIDER (HOF 1980-W)—Edwin Donald Snider—Nickname: The Silver Fox—Bats: Left; Throws: Right

Ht: 6'0"; Wt: 179 lbs; Born: 9/19/1926 in Los Angeles, California; Debut: 4/17/1947

World Series — Batting / Fielding

Year Tm	Age	G	AB	H	2B	3B	HR	TB	R	RBI	GW	TBB	IBB	SO	HBP	SH	SF	SB	CS	SB%	GDP	Avg	OBP	SLG	Pos	G	PO	A	E	DP	FPct
1949 Bro	23	5	21	3	1	0	0	4	2	0	0	0	0	8	0	0	0	0	0	—	1	.143	.143	.190	OF	5	18	1	0	0	1.000
1952 Bro	26	7	29	10	2	0	4	24	5	8	2	1	0	5	1	0	0	1	0	1.00	1	.345	.387	.828	OF	7	23	0	0	0	1.000
1953 Bro	27	6	25	8	3	0	1	14	3	5	0	2	0	6	0	0	0	0	0	—	0	.320	.370	.560	OF	6	17	1	0	1	1.000
1955 Bro	29	7	25	8	1	0	4	21	5	7	0	2	1	6	0	1	0	0	0	—	0	.320	.370	.840	OF	7	13	0	0	0	1.000
1956 Bro	30	7	23	7	1	0	1	11	5	4	0	6	3	8	0	0	1	0	0	—	0	.304	.433	.478	OF	7	20	0	0	0	1.000
1959 LA	33	4	10	2	0	0	1	5	1	2	1	2	0	0	0	0	0	0	0	—	0	.200	.333	.500	OF	3	5	0	2	0	.714
WS Totals		36	133	38	8	0	11	79	21	26	3	13	4	33	1	1	1	1	0	1.00	2	.286	.351	.594	OF	35	96	2	2	1	.980

FRED SNODGRASS—Frederick Charles Snodgrass—Nickname: Snow—Bats: Right; Throws: Right

Ht: 5'11"; Wt: 175 lbs; Born: 10/19/1887 in Ventura, California; Debut: 6/4/1908; Died: 4/5/1974

World Series — Batting / Fielding

Year Tm	Age	G	AB	H	2B	3B	HR	TB	R	RBI	GW	TBB	IBB	SO	HBP	SH	SF	SB	CS	SB%	GDP	Avg	OBP	SLG	Pos	G	PO	A	E	DP	FPct
1911 NYG	23	6	19	2	0	0	0	2	1	1	0	2	0	7	2	1	1	0	2	.00	0	.105	.250	.105	OF	6	10	0	0	0	1.000
1912 NYG	24	8	33	7	2	0	0	9	2	2	1	2	0	5	1	0	0	1	2	.33	1	.212	.278	.273	OF	8	17	1	1	0	.947
1913 NYG	25	2	3	1	0	0	0	1	0	0	0	0	0	0	0	0	0	0	0	—	0	.333	.333	.333	1B	1	1	1	0	0	1.000
																									OF	1	2	0	0	0	1.000
WS Totals		16	55	10	2	0	0	12	3	3	1	4	0	12	3	1	1	1	4	.20	1	.182	.270	.218	OF	15	29	1	1	0	.968

J.T. SNOW—Jack Thomas Snow—Bats: Both; Throws: Left

Ht: 6'2"; Wt: 202 lbs; Born: 2/26/1968 in Long Beach, California; Debut: 9/20/1992

Division Series — Batting / Fielding

Year Tm	Age	G	AB	H	2B	3B	HR	TB	R	RBI	GW	TBB	IBB	SO	HBP	SH	SF	SB	CS	SB%	GDP	Avg	OBP	SLG	Pos	G	PO	A	E	DP	FPct
1997 SF	29	3	6	1	0	0	0	1	0	0	0	1	0	1	0	0	0	0	0	—	0	.167	.286	.167	1B	3	12	0	0	3	1.000

FRANK SNYDER—Frank Elton Snyder—Nickname: Pancho—Bats: Right; Throws: Right

Ht: 6'2"; Wt: 185 lbs; Born: 5/27/1893 in San Antonio, Texas; Debut: 8/25/1912; Died: 1/5/1962

World Series — Batting / Fielding

Year Tm	Age	G	AB	H	2B	3B	HR	TB	R	RBI	GW	TBB	IBB	SO	HBP	SH	SF	SB	CS	SB%	GDP	Avg	OBP	SLG	Pos	G	PO	A	E	DP	FPct
1921 NYG	28	7	22	8	1	0	1	12	4	3	1	0	0	2	0	2	0	0	1	.00	0	.364	.364	.545	C	6	43	5	0	0	1.000
1922 NYG	29	4	15	5	0	0	0	5	1	0	0	0	0	1	0	0	0	0	0	—	0	.333	.333	.333	C	4	23	3	1	1	.963
1923 NYG	30	5	17	2	0	0	1	5	1	2	0	0	0	2	0	0	0	0	0	—	1	.118	.118	.294	C	5	24	3	0	1	1.000
1924 NYG	31	1	1	0	0	0	0	0	0	0	0	0	0	0	0	0	0	0	0	—	0	.000	.000	.000	—						
WS Totals		17	55	15	1	0	2	22	6	5	1	0	0	5	0	2	0	0	1	.00	1	.273	.273	.400	C	15	90	11	1	2	.990

RUSS SNYDER—Russell Henry Snyder—Bats: Left; Throws: Right

Ht: 6'1"; Wt: 190 lbs; Born: 6/22/1934 in Oak, Nebraska; Debut: 4/18/1959

World Series — Batting / Fielding

Year Tm	Age	G	AB	H	2B	3B	HR	TB	R	RBI	GW	TBB	IBB	SO	HBP	SH	SF	SB	CS	SB%	GDP	Avg	OBP	SLG	Pos	G	PO	A	E	DP	FPct
1966 Bal	32	3	6	1	0	0	0	1	1	1	0	2	0	0	0	0	0	0	0	—	0	.167	.375	.167	OF	3	2	0	0	0	1.000

ERIC SODERHOLM—Eric Thane Soderholm—Bats: Right; Throws: Right

Ht: 5'11"; Wt: 187 lbs; Born: 9/24/1948 in Cortland, New York; Debut: 9/3/1971

LCS — Batting / Fielding

Year Tm	Age	G	AB	H	2B	3B	HR	TB	R	RBI	GW	TBB	IBB	SO	HBP	SH	SF	SB	CS	SB%	GDP	Avg	OBP	SLG	Pos	G	PO	A	E	DP	FPct
1980 NYA	32	2	6	1	0	0	0	1	0	0	0	0	0	0	0	0	0	0	0	—	0	.167	.167	.167	—						

LUIS SOJO—Luis Beltran Sojo—Bats: Right; Throws: Right

Ht: 5'11"; Wt: 165 lbs; Born: 1/3/1966 in Barquisimeto, Venezuela; Debut: 7/14/1990

Division Series — Batting / Fielding

Year Tm	Age	G	AB	H	2B	3B	HR	TB	R	RBI	GW	TBB	IBB	SO	HBP	SH	SF	SB	CS	SB%	GDP	Avg	OBP	SLG	Pos	G	PO	A	E	DP	FPct
1995 Sea	29	5	20	5	0	0	0	5	0	3	0	0	0	3	0	0	2	0	0	—	1	.250	.227	.250	SS	5	9	15	1	3	.960
1996 NYA	30	2	0	0	0	0	0	0	0	0	0	0	0	0	0	0	0	0	0	—	0	—	—	—	2B	2	1	1	0	0	1.000
DS Totals		7	20	5	0	0	0	5	0	3	0	0	0	3	0	0	2	0	0	—	1	.250	.227	.250	SS	5	9	15	1	3	.960

LCS — Batting / Fielding

Year Tm	Age	G	AB	H	2B	3B	HR	TB	R	RBI	GW	TBB	IBB	SO	HBP	SH	SF	SB	CS	SB%	GDP	Avg	OBP	SLG	Pos	G	PO	A	E	DP	FPct
1995 Sea	29	6	20	5	2	0	0	7	0	1	1	0	0	2	0	0	0	0	0	—	1	.250	.250	.350	SS	6	9	18	1	7	.964
1996 NYA	30	3	5	1	0	0	0	1	0	0	0	0	0	1	0	0	0	0	0	—	0	.200	.200	.200	2B	3	4	4	0	0	1.000
LCS Totals		9	25	6	2	0	0	8	0	1	1	0	0	3	0	0	0	0	0	—	1	.240	.240	.320	SS	6	9	18	1	7	.964

World Series — Batting / Fielding

Year Tm	Age	G	AB	H	2B	3B	HR	TB	R	RBI	GW	TBB	IBB	SO	HBP	SH	SF	SB	CS	SB%	GDP	Avg	OBP	SLG	Pos	G	PO	A	E	DP	FPct
1996 NYA	30	5	5	3	1	0	0	4	0	1	0	0	0	0	0	0	0	0	0	—	0	.600	.600	.800	2B	3	5	2	0	0	1.000
Postseason Totals		21	50	14	3	0	0	17	0	5	1	0	0	6	0	0	2	0	0	—	2	.280	.269	.340	SS	11	18	33	2	10	.962

EDDIE SOLOMON—Nickname: Buddy—Throws: Right; Bats: Right

Ht: 6'2"; Wt: 185 lbs; Born: 2/9/1951 in Perry, Georgia; Debut: 9/2/1973; Died: 1/12/1986

LCS — Pitching

Year Tm	Age	G	GS	CG	GF	IP	BFP	H	R	ER	HR	SH	SF	HB	TBB	IBB	SO	WP	Bk	W	L	Pct	ShO	Sv-Op	Hld	OAvg	OOBP	ERA
1974 LA	23	1	0	0	1	2.0	9	2	0	0	0	0	0	0	1	0	1	0	0	0	0	—	0	0- 0	0	.250	.333	0.00

LCS — Batting / Fielding

Year Tm	Age	G	AB	H	2B	3B	HR	TB	R	RBI	GW	TBB	IBB	SO	HBP	SH	SF	SB	CS	SB%	GDP	Avg	OBP	SLG	Pos	G	PO	A	E	DP	FPct
1974 LA	23	1	0	0	0	0	0	0	0	0	0	0	0	0	0	0	0	0	0	—	0	—	—	—	P	1	0	0	0	0	—

PAUL SORRENTO—Paul Anthony Sorrento—Bats: Left; Throws: Right

Ht: 6'2"; Wt: 195 lbs; Born: 11/17/1965 in Somerville, Massachusetts; Debut: 9/8/1989

Division Series — Batting / Fielding

Year Tm	Age	G	AB	H	2B	3B	HR	TB	R	RBI	GW	TBB	IBB	SO	HBP	SH	SF	SB	CS	SB%	GDP	Avg	OBP	SLG	Pos	G	PO	A	E	DP	FPct
1995 Cle	29	3	10	3	0	0	0	3	2	1	0	2	0	3	1	0	0	0	0	—	0	.300	.462	.300	1B	3	27	5	2	0	.941
1997 Sea	31	4	10	3	1	0	1	7	2	1	0	2	0	3	0	0	0	0	0	—	0	.300	.417	.700	1B	4	27	4	1	3	.969
DS Totals		7	20	6	1	0	1	10	4	2	0	4	0	6	1	0	0	0	0	—	0	.300	.440	.500	1B	7	54	9	3	3	.955

LCS — Batting / Fielding

Year Tm	Age	G	AB	H	2B	3B	HR	TB	R	RBI	GW	TBB	IBB	SO	HBP	SH	SF	SB	CS	SB%	GDP	Avg	OBP	SLG	Pos	G	PO	A	E	DP	FPct
1991 Min	25	1	1	0	0	0	0	0	0	0	0	0	0	1	0	0	0	0	0	—	0	.000	.000	.000	—						
1995 Cle	29	4	13	2	1	0	0	3	2	0	0	2	0	3	0	0	0	0	0	—	3	.154	.267	.231	1B	4	34	1	2	1	.946
LCS Totals		5	14	2	1	0	0	3	2	0	0	2	0	4	0	0	0	0	0	—	3	.143	.250	.214	1B	4	34	1	2	1	.946

World Series — Batting / Fielding

Year Tm	Age	G	AB	H	2B	3B	HR	TB	R	RBI	GW	TBB	IBB	SO	HBP	SH	SF	SB	CS	SB%	GDP	Avg	OBP	SLG	Pos	G	PO	A	E	DP	FPct
1991 Min	25	3	2	0	0	0	0	0	0	0	0	1	0	2	0	0	0	0	0	—	0	.000	.333	.000	1B	1	1	1	0	1	1.000
1995 Cle	29	6	11	2	1	0	0	3	0	0	0	0	0	4	0	0	0	0	0	—	0	.182	.182	.273	1B	3	19	2	1	2	.955
WS Totals		9	13	2	1	0	0	3	0	0	0	1	0	6	0	0	0	0	0	—	0	.154	.214	.231	1B	4	20	3	1	3	.958
Postseason Totals		21	47	10	3	0	1	16	6	2	0	7	0	16	1	0	0	0	0	—	3	.213	.327	.340	1B	15	108	13	6	7	.953

ELIAS SOSA—Throws: Right; Bats: Right

Ht: 6'2"; Wt: 186 lbs; Born: 6/10/1950 in La Vega, Dominican Republic; Debut: 9/8/1972

Division Series — Pitching

Year Tm	Age	G	GS	CG	GF	IP	BFP	H	R	ER	HR	SH	SF	HB	TBB	IBB	SO	WP	Bk	W	L	Pct	ShO	Sv-Op	Hld	OAvg	OOBP	ERA
1981 Mon	31	2	0	0	1	3.0	12	4	2	1	0	0	0	0	0	0	1	0	0	0	0	—	0	0- 0	0	.333	.333	3.00

LCS — Pitching

Year Tm	Age	G	GS	CG	GF	IP	BFP	H	R	ER	HR	SH	SF	HB	TBB	IBB	SO	WP	Bk	W	L	Pct	ShO	Sv-Op	Hld	OAvg	OOBP	ERA
1977 LA	27	2	0	0	1	2.2	14	5	4	3	0	1	0	0	0	0	0	0	1	0	1	.000	0	0- 0	0	.385	.385	10.13
1981 Mon	31	1	0	0	0	0.1	3	1	0	0	0	0	0	0	1	0	0	0	0	0	0	—	0	0- 0	0	.500	.667	0.00
LCS Totals		3	0	0	1	3.0	34	6	4	3	0	1	0	0	1	0	0	0	1	0	1	.000	0	0-0	0	.400	.438	9.00

World Series — Pitching

Year Tm	Age	G	GS	CG	GF	IP	BFP	H	R	ER	HR	SH	SF	HB	TBB	IBB	SO	WP	Bk	W	L	Pct	ShO	Sv-Op	Hld	OAvg	OOBP	ERA
1977 LA	27	2	0	0	0	2.1	11	3	3	3	1	0	1	0	1	0	1	0	0	0	0	—	0	0- 0	0	.333	.364	11.57
Postseason Totals		7	0	0	2	8.1	80	13	9	7	1	1	1	0	2	0	2	0	1	0	1	.000	0	0-0	0	.361	.385	7.56

Division Series — Batting / Fielding

Year Tm	Age	G	AB	H	2B	3B	HR	TB	R	RBI	GW	TBB	IBB	SO	HBP	SH	SF	SB	CS	SB%	GDP	Avg	OBP	SLG	Pos	G	PO	A	E	DP	FPct
1981 Mon	31	2	0	0	0	0	0	0	0	0	0	0	0	0	0	0	0	0	0	—	0	—	—	—	P	2	0	2	1	0	.667

LCS — Batting / Fielding

Year Tm	Age	G	AB	H	2B	3B	HR	TB	R	RBI	GW	TBB	IBB	SO	HBP	SH	SF	SB	CS	SB%	GDP	Avg	OBP	SLG	Pos	G	PO	A	E	DP	FPct
1977 LA	27	2	1	0	0	0	0	0	0	0	0	0	0	0	0	0	0	0	0	—	0	.000	.000	.000	P	2	0	1	0	0	1.000
1981 Mon	31	1	0	0	0	0	0	0	0	0	0	0	0	0	0	0	0	0	0	—	0	—	—	—	P	1	0	0	0	0	—
LCS Totals		3	1	0	0	0	0	0	0	0	0	0	0	0	0	0	0	0	0	—	0	.000	.000	.000	P	3	0	1	0	0	1.000

World Series — Batting / Fielding

Year Tm	Age	G	AB	H	2B	3B	HR	TB	R	RBI	GW	TBB	IBB	SO	HBP	SH	SF	SB	CS	SB%	GDP	Avg	OBP	SLG	Pos	G	PO	A	E	DP	FPct
1977 LA	27	2	0	0	0	0	0	0	0	0	0	0	0	0	0	0	0	0	0	—	0	—	—	—	P	2	0	0	0	0	—
Postseason Totals		7	1	0	0	0	0	0	0	0	0	0	0	0	0	0	0	0	0	—	0	.000	.000	.000	P	7	0	3	1	0	.750

MARIO SOTO—Mario Melvin Soto—Throws: Right; Bats: Right

Ht: 6'0"; Wt: 174 lbs; Born: 7/12/1956 in Bani, Dominican Republic; Debut: 7/21/1977

LCS — Pitching

Year Tm	Age	G	GS	CG	GF	IP	BFP	H	R	ER	HR	SH	SF	HB	TBB	IBB	SO	WP	Bk	W	L	Pct	ShO	Sv-Op	Hld	OAvg	OOBP	ERA
1979 Cin	23	1	0	0	0	2.0	6	0	0	0	0	0	0	0	0	0	1	0	0	0	0	—	0	0- 0	0	.000	.000	0.00

LCS		Batting																							Fielding						
Year Tm	Age	G	AB	H	2B	3B	HR	TB	R	RBI	GW	TBB	IBB	SO	HBP	SH	SF	SB	CS	SB%	GDP	Avg	OBP	SLG	Pos	G	PO	A	E	DP	FPct
1979 Cin	23	1	0	0	0	0	0	0	0	0	0	0	0	0	0	0	0	0	0	—	0	—	—	—	P	1	0	0	0	0	—

BILLY SOUTHWORTH—William Harrison Southworth—Bats: Left; Throws: Right

Ht: 5'9"; Wt: 170 lbs; Born: 3/9/1893 in Harvard, Nebraska; Debut: 8/4/1913; Died: 11/15/1969

World Series		Batting																							Fielding						
Year Tm	Age	G	AB	H	2B	3B	HR	TB	R	RBI	GW	TBB	IBB	SO	HBP	SH	SF	SB	CS	SB%	GDP	Avg	OBP	SLG	Pos	G	PO	A	E	DP	FPct
1924 NYG	31	5	1	0	0	0	0	0	1	0	0	0	0	0	0	0	0	0	0	—	0	.000	.000	.000	OF	2	1	1	0	0	1.000
1926 StL	33	7	29	10	1	1	1	16	6	4	1	0	0	0	0	1	0	0	0	—	0	.345	.345	.552	OF	7	8	3	0	1	1.000
WS Totals		12	30	10	1	1	1	16	7	4	1	0	0	0	0	1	0	0	0	—	0	.333	.333	.533	OF	9	9	4	0	1	1.000

WARREN SPAHN (HOF 1973-W)—Warren Edward Spahn—Throws: Left; Bats: Left

Ht: 6'0"; Wt: 172 lbs; Born: 4/23/1921 in Buffalo, New York; Debut: 4/19/1942

World Series		Pitching																										
Year Tm	Age	G	GS	CG	GF	IP	BFP	H	R	ER	HR	SH	SF	HB	TBB	IBB	SO	WP	Bk	W	L	Pct	ShO	Sv-Op	Hld	OAvg	OOBP	ERA
1948 Bos	27	3	1	0	2	12.0	48	10	4	4	0	1	0	0	3	1	12	0	0	1	1	.500	0	0-0	0	.227	.277	3.00
1957 Mil-*C*	36	2	2	1	0	15.1	63	18	8	8	1	0	0	0	2	0	2	0	0	1	1	.500	0	0-0	0	.295	.317	4.70
1958 Mil	37	3	3	2	0	28.2	113	19	7	7	4	0	1	0	8	0	18	1	0	2	1	.667	1	0-0	0	.183	.239	2.20
WS Totals		8	6	3	2	56.0	448	47	19	19	5	1	1	0	13	1	32	1	0	4	3	.571	1	0-0	0	.225	.269	3.05

World Series		Batting																							Fielding						
Year Tm	Age	G	AB	H	2B	3B	HR	TB	R	RBI	GW	TBB	IBB	SO	HBP	SH	SF	SB	CS	SB%	GDP	Avg	OBP	SLG	Pos	G	PO	A	E	DP	FPct
1948 Bos	27	3	4	0	0	0	0	0	0	1	0	0	0	1	0	0	0	0	0	—	0	.000	.000	.000	P	3	0	2	0	0	1.000
1957 Mil	36	2	4	0	0	0	0	0	0	0	0	1	0	2	0	0	0	0	0	—	0	.000	.200	.000	P	2	1	3	0	0	1.000
1958 Mil	37	3	12	4	0	0	0	4	0	3	0	0	0	6	0	0	0	0	0	—	0	.333	.333	.333	P	3	2	6	0	0	1.000
WS Totals		8	20	4	0	0	0	4	0	4	0	1	0	9	0	0	0	0	0	—	0	.200	.238	.200	P	8	3	11	0	0	1.000

JOE SPARMA—Joseph Blase Sparma—Throws: Right; Bats: Right

Ht: 6'1"; Wt: 190 lbs; Born: 2/4/1942 in Massillon, Ohio; Debut: 5/20/1964; Died: 5/14/1986

World Series		Pitching																										
Year Tm	Age	G	GS	CG	GF	IP	BFP	H	R	ER	HR	SH	SF	HB	TBB	IBB	SO	WP	Bk	W	L	Pct	ShO	Sv-Op	Hld	OAvg	OOBP	ERA
1968 Det	26	1	0	0	0	0.1	3	2	2	2	1	0	0	0	0	0	0	0	0	0	0	—	0	0-0	0	.667	.667	54.00

World Series		Batting																							Fielding						
Year Tm	Age	G	AB	H	2B	3B	HR	TB	R	RBI	GW	TBB	IBB	SO	HBP	SH	SF	SB	CS	SB%	GDP	Avg	OBP	SLG	Pos	G	PO	A	E	DP	FPct
1968 Det	26	1	0	0	0	0	0	0	0	0	0	0	0	0	0	0	0	0	0	—	0	—	—	—	P	1	0	0	0	0	—

TRIS SPEAKER (HOF 1937-W)—Tristram E. Speaker—Nickname: The Grey Eagle—Bats: Left; Throws: Left

Ht: 5'11"; Wt: 193 lbs; Born: 4/4/1888 in Hubbard, Texas; Debut: 9/14/1907; Died: 12/8/1958

World Series		Batting																							Fielding						
Year Tm	Age	G	AB	H	2B	3B	HR	TB	R	RBI	GW	TBB	IBB	SO	HBP	SH	SF	SB	CS	SB%	GDP	Avg	OBP	SLG	Pos	G	PO	A	E	DP	FPct
1912 Bos-*M*	24	8	30	9	1	2	0	14	4	2	0	4	0	2	0	0	0	1	1	.50	1	.300	.382	.467	OF	8	21	2	2	2	.920
1915 Bos	27	5	17	5	0	1	0	7	2	0	0	4	1	1	0	0	0	0	3	.00	0	.294	.429	.412	OF	5	10	0	0	0	1.000
1920 Cle	32	7	25	8	2	1	0	12	6	1	0	3	0	1	0	0	0	0	0	—	0	.320	.393	.480	OF	7	18	0	0	0	1.000
WS Totals		20	72	22	3	4	0	33	12	3	0	11	1	4	0	0	0	1	4	.20	1	.306	.398	.458	OF	20	49	2	2	2	.962

BYRON SPEECE—Byron Franklin Speece—Throws: Right; Bats: Right

Ht: 5'11"; Wt: 170 lbs; Born: 1/6/1897 in West Baden, Indiana; Debut: 4/21/1924; Died: 9/29/1974

World Series		Pitching																										
Year Tm	Age	G	GS	CG	GF	IP	BFP	H	R	ER	HR	SH	SF	HB	TBB	IBB	SO	WP	Bk	W	L	Pct	ShO	Sv-Op	Hld	OAvg	OOBP	ERA
1924 Was	27	1	0	0	1	1.0	5	3	1	1	0	0	0	0	0	0	0	0	0	0	0	—	0	0-0	0	.600	.600	9.00

World Series		Batting																							Fielding						
Year Tm	Age	G	AB	H	2B	3B	HR	TB	R	RBI	GW	TBB	IBB	SO	HBP	SH	SF	SB	CS	SB%	GDP	Avg	OBP	SLG	Pos	G	PO	A	E	DP	FPct
1924 Was	27	1	0	0	0	0	0	0	0	0	0	0	0	0	0	0	0	0	0	—	0	—	—	—	P	1	0	2	0	0	1.000

CHRIS SPEIER—Chris Edward Speier—Bats: Right; Throws: Right

Ht: 6'1"; Wt: 175 lbs; Born: 6/28/1950 in Alameda, California; Debut: 4/7/1971

Division Series		Batting																							Fielding						
Year Tm	Age	G	AB	H	2B	3B	HR	TB	R	RBI	GW	TBB	IBB	SO	HBP	SH	SF	SB	CS	SB%	GDP	Avg	OBP	SLG	Pos	G	PO	A	E	DP	FPct
1981 Mon	31	5	15	6	2	0	0	8	4	3	2	4	1	2	0	0	0	0	0	—	0	.400	.526	.533	SS	5	16	16	0	4	1.000
LCS		Batting																							Fielding						
Year Tm	Age	G	AB	H	2B	3B	HR	TB	R	RBI	GW	TBB	IBB	SO	HBP	SH	SF	SB	CS	SB%	GDP	Avg	OBP	SLG	Pos	G	PO	A	E	DP	FPct
1971 SF	21	4	14	5	1	0	1	9	4	1	0	1	0	1	0	0	0	0	0	—	0	.357	.400	.643	SS	4	3	14	1	0	.944
1981 Mon	31	5	16	3	0	0	0	3	0	0	0	2	1	0	0	0	0	0	0	—	1	.188	.278	.188	SS	5	15	16	2	6	.939
1987 SF	37	3	5	0	0	0	0	0	0	0	0	0	0	2	0	0	0	0	0	—	1	.000	.000	.000	2B	1	1	3	0	0	1.000
LCS Totals		12	35	8	1	0	1	12	4	1	0	3	1	3	0	0	0	0	0	—	2	.229	.289	.343	SS	9	18	30	3	6	.941
Postseason Totals		17	50	14	3	0	1	20	8	4	2	7	2	5	0	0	0	0	0	—	2	.280	.368	.400	SS	14	34	46	3	10	.964

GEORGE SPENCER—George Elwell Spencer—Throws: Right; Bats: Right

Ht: 6'1"; Wt: 215 lbs; Born: 7/7/1926 in Columbus, Ohio; Debut: 8/17/1950

World Series		Pitching																										
Year Tm	Age	G	GS	CG	GF	IP	BFP	H	R	ER	HR	SH	SF	HB	TBB	IBB	SO	WP	Bk	W	L	Pct	ShO	Sv-Op	Hld	OAvg	OOBP	ERA
1951 NYG	25	2	0	0	1	3.1	19	6	7	7	0	0	0	0	3	0	0	0	0	0	0	—	0	0-0	0	.375	.474	18.90

World Series		Batting																							Fielding						
Year Tm	Age	G	AB	H	2B	3B	HR	TB	R	RBI	GW	TBB	IBB	SO	HBP	SH	SF	SB	CS	SB%	GDP	Avg	OBP	SLG	Pos	G	PO	A	E	DP	FPct
1951 NYG	25	2	0	0	0	0	0	0	0	0	0	0	0	0	0	0	0	0	0	—	0	—	—	—	P	2	0	1	0	0	1.000

JIM SPENCER—James Lloyd Spencer—Bats: Left; Throws: Left

Ht: 6'2"; Wt: 195 lbs; Born: 7/30/1946 in Hanover, Pennsylvania; Debut: 9/7/1968

Division Series		Batting																							Fielding						
Year Tm	Age	G	AB	H	2B	3B	HR	TB	R	RBI	GW	TBB	IBB	SO	HBP	SH	SF	SB	CS	SB%	GDP	Avg	OBP	SLG	Pos	G	PO	A	E	DP	FPct
1981 Oak	35	1	4	1	1	0	0	2	0	0	0	0	0	0	0	0	0	0	0	—	0	.250	.250	.500	1B	1	6	2	0	1	1.000
LCS		Batting																							Fielding						
Year Tm	Age	G	AB	H	2B	3B	HR	TB	R	RBI	GW	TBB	IBB	SO	HBP	SH	SF	SB	CS	SB%	GDP	Avg	OBP	SLG	Pos	G	PO	A	E	DP	FPct
1980 NYA	34	1	1	0	0	0	0	0	0	0	0	0	0	0	0	0	0	0	0	—	0	.000	.000	.000	—						
1981 Oak	35	2	3	0	0	0	0	0	0	0	0	0	0	0	0	0	0	0	0	—	0	.000	.000	.000	1B	2	4	2	0	1	1.000
LCS Totals		3	4	0	0	0	0	0	0	0	0	0	0	0	0	0	0	0	0	—	0	.000	.000	.000	1B	2	4	2	0	1	1.000
World Series		Batting																							Fielding						
Year Tm	Age	G	AB	H	2B	3B	HR	TB	R	RBI	GW	TBB	IBB	SO	HBP	SH	SF	SB	CS	SB%	GDP	Avg	OBP	SLG	Pos	G	PO	A	E	DP	FPct
1978 NYA	32	4	12	2	0	0	0	2	3	0	0	2	0	4	0	0	0	0	0	—	0	.167	.286	.167	1B	3	23	2	0	4	1.000
Postseason Totals		8	20	3	1	0	0	4	3	0	0	2	0	4	0	0	0	0	0	—	0	.150	.227	.200	1B	6	33	6	0	6	1.000

ROY SPENCER—Roy Hampton Spencer—Bats: Right; Throws: Right

Ht: 5'10"; Wt: 168 lbs; Born: 2/22/1900 in Scranton, North Carolina; Debut: 4/19/1925; Died: 2/8/1973

World Series		Batting																							Fielding						
Year Tm	Age	G	AB	H	2B	3B	HR	TB	R	RBI	GW	TBB	IBB	SO	HBP	SH	SF	SB	CS	SB%	GDP	Avg	OBP	SLG	Pos	G	PO	A	E	DP	FPct
1927 Pit	27	1	1	0	0	0	0	0	0	0	0	0	0	0	0	0	0	0	0	—	0	.000	.000	.000	C	1	0	0	0	0	—

BILL SPIERS—William James Spiers—Bats: Left; Throws: Right

Ht: 6'2"; Wt: 190 lbs; Born: 6/5/1966 in Orangeburg, South Carolina; Debut: 4/7/1989

Division Series		Batting																							Fielding						
Year Tm	Age	G	AB	H	2B	3B	HR	TB	R	RBI	GW	TBB	IBB	SO	HBP	SH	SF	SB	CS	SB%	GDP	Avg	OBP	SLG	Pos	G	PO	A	E	DP	FPct
1997 Hou	31	3	11	0	0	0	0	0	1	0	0	1	0	2	0	0	0	0	0	—	1	.000	.083	.000	3B	3	1	3	0	0	1.000

ED SPIEZIO—Edward Wayne Spiezio—Bats: Right; Throws: Right

Ht: 5'11"; Wt: 180 lbs; Born: 10/31/1941 in Joliet, Illinois; Debut: 7/23/1964

World Series		Batting																							Fielding						
Year Tm	Age	G	AB	H	2B	3B	HR	TB	R	RBI	GW	TBB	IBB	SO	HBP	SH	SF	SB	CS	SB%	GDP	Avg	OBP	SLG	Pos	G	PO	A	E	DP	FPct
1967 StL	25	1	1	0	0	0	0	0	0	0	0	0	0	0	0	0	0	0	0	—	0	.000	.000	.000	—						
1968 StL	26	1	1	1	0	0	0	1	0	0	0	0	0	0	0	0	0	0	0	—	0	1.000	1.000	1.000	—						
WS Totals		2	2	1	0	0	0	1	0	0	0	0	0	0	0	0	0	0	0	—	0	.500	.500	.500	—	0	0	0	0	0	—

HARRY SPILMAN—William Harry Spilman—Bats: Left; Throws: Right

Ht: 6'1"; Wt: 180 lbs; Born: 7/18/1954 in Albany, Georgia; Debut: 9/11/1978

Division Series		Batting																							Fielding						
Year Tm	Age	G	AB	H	2B	3B	HR	TB	R	RBI	GW	TBB	IBB	SO	HBP	SH	SF	SB	CS	SB%	GDP	Avg	OBP	SLG	Pos	G	PO	A	E	DP	FPct
1981 Hou	27	1	1	0	0	0	0	0	0	0	0	0	0	0	0	0	0	0	0	—	0	.000	.000	.000	—						
LCS		**Batting**																							**Fielding**						
Year Tm	Age	G	AB	H	2B	3B	HR	TB	R	RBI	GW	TBB	IBB	SO	HBP	SH	SF	SB	CS	SB%	GDP	Avg	OBP	SLG	Pos	G	PO	A	E	DP	FPct
1979 Cin	25	2	2	0	0	0	0	0	0	0	0	0	0	0	0	0	0	0	0	—	0	.000	.000	.000	—						
1987 SF	33	3	2	1	0	0	1	4	1	1	0	0	0	0	0	0	0	0	0	—	0	.500	.500	2.000	—						
LCS Totals		5	4	1	0	0	1	4	1	1	0	0	0	0	0	0	0	0	0	—	0	.250	.250	1.000	—	0	0	0	0	0	—
Postseason Totals		6	5	1	0	0	1	4	1	1	0	0	0	0	0	0	0	0	0	—	0	.200	.200	.800	—	0	0	0	0	0	—

PAUL SPLITTORFF—Paul William Splittorff—Throws: Left; Bats: Left

Ht: 6'3"; Wt: 205 lbs; Born: 10/8/1946 in Evansville, Indiana; Debut: 9/23/1970

LCS		Pitching																										
Year Tm	Age	G	GS	CG	GF	IP	BFP	H	R	ER	HR	SH	SF	HB	TBB	IBB	SO	WP	Bk	W	L	Pct	ShO	Sv-Op	Hld	OAvg	OOBP	ERA
1976 KC	29	2	0	0	0	9.1	40	7	2	2	0	0	1	0	5	0	2	0	0	1	0	1.000	0	0- 0	0	.206	.300	1.93
1977 KC	30	2	2	0	0	15.0	62	14	4	4	1	0	0	0	3	0	4	0	0	1	0	1.000	0	0- 0	0	.237	.274	2.40
1978 KC	31	1	1	0	0	7.1	29	9	5	4	1	0	1	0	0	0	2	0	0	0	0	—	0	0- 0	0	.321	.310	4.91
1980 KC	33	1	1	0	0	5.1	22	5	1	1	0	0	0	0	2	0	3	0	1	0	0	—	0	0- 0	0	.250	.318	1.69
LCS Totals		6	4	0	0	37.0	306	35	12	11	2	0	2	0	10	0	11	0	1	2	0	1.000	0	0-0	0	.248	.294	2.68
World Series		**Pitching**																										
Year Tm	Age	G	GS	CG	GF	IP	BFP	H	R	ER	HR	SH	SF	HB	TBB	IBB	SO	WP	Bk	W	L	Pct	ShO	Sv-Op	Hld	OAvg	OOBP	ERA
1980 KC	33	1	0	0	0	1.2	8	4	1	1	0	0	0	0	0	0	0	0	0	0	0	—	0	0- 0	0	.500	.500	5.40
Postseason Totals		7	4	0	0	38.2	322	39	13	12	2	0	2	0	10	0	11	0	1	2	0	1.000	0	0-0	0	.262	.304	2.79

LCS		Batting																							Fielding						
Year Tm	Age	G	AB	H	2B	3B	HR	TB	R	RBI	GW	TBB	IBB	SO	HBP	SH	SF	SB	CS	SB%	GDP	Avg	OBP	SLG	Pos	G	PO	A	E	DP	FPct
1976 KC	29	2	0	0	0	0	0	0	0	0	0	0	0	0	0	0	0	0	0	—	0	—	—	—	P	2	0	1	0	0	1.000
1977 KC	30	2	0	0	0	0	0	0	0	0	0	0	0	0	0	0	0	0	0	—	0	—	—	—	P	2	0	3	0	0	1.000
1978 KC	31	1	0	0	0	0	0	0	0	0	0	0	0	0	0	0	0	0	0	—	0	—	—	—	P	1	0	0	0	0	—
1980 KC	33	1	0	0	0	0	0	0	0	0	0	0	0	0	0	0	0	0	0	—	0	—	—	—	P	1	0	1	0	1	1.000
LCS Totals		6	0	0	0	0	0	0	0	0	0	0	0	0	0	0	0	0	0	—	0	—	—	—	P	6	0	5	0	1	1.000
World Series		**Batting**																							**Fielding**						
Year Tm	Age	G	AB	H	2B	3B	HR	TB	R	RBI	GW	TBB	IBB	SO	HBP	SH	SF	SB	CS	SB%	GDP	Avg	OBP	SLG	Pos	G	PO	A	E	DP	FPct
1980 KC	33	1	0	0	0	0	0	0	0	0	0	0	0	0	0	0	0	0	0	—	0	—	—	—	P	1	0	1	0	1	1.000
Postseason Totals		7	0	0	0	0	0	0	0	0	0	0	0	0	0	0	0	0	0	—	0	—	—	—	P	7	0	6	0	2	1.000

PAUL SPOLJARIC—Paul Nikola Spoljaric—Throws: Left; Bats: Right

Ht: 6'3"; Wt: 205 lbs; Born: 9/24/1970 in Kelowna, British Columbia; Debut: 4/6/1994

Division Series		Pitching																										
Year Tm	Age	G	GS	CG	GF	IP	BFP	H	R	ER	HR	SH	SF	HB	TBB	IBB	SO	WP	Bk	W	L	Pct	ShO	Sv-Op	Hld	OAvg	OOBP	ERA
1997 Sea	27	2	0	0	0	1.2	8	4	0	0	0	0	0	0	0	0	1	0	0	0	0	—	0	0- 0	0	.500	.500	0.00

Division Series		Batting																							Fielding						
Year Tm	Age	G	AB	H	2B	3B	HR	TB	R	RBI	GW	TBB	IBB	SO	HBP	SH	SF	SB	CS	SB%	GDP	Avg	OBP	SLG	Pos	G	PO	A	E	DP	FPct
1997 Sea	27	2	0	0	0	0	0	0	0	0	0	0	0	0	0	0	0	0	0	—	0	—	—	—	P	2	0	0	0	0	—

KARL SPOONER—Karl Benjamin Spooner—Throws: Left; Bats: Right

Ht: 6'0"; Wt: 185 lbs; Born: 6/23/1931 in Oriskany Falls, New York; Debut: 9/22/1954; Died: 4/10/1984

World Series		Pitching																										
Year Tm	Age	G	GS	CG	GF	IP	BFP	H	R	ER	HR	SH	SF	HB	TBB	IBB	SO	WP	Bk	W	L	Pct	ShO	Sv-Op	Hld	OAvg	OOBP	ERA
1955 Bro	24	2	1	0	0	3.1	16	4	5	5	1	0	0	0	3	0	6	0	0	0	1	.000	0	0- 0	0	.308	.438	13.50

World Series		Batting																							Fielding						
Year Tm	Age	G	AB	H	2B	3B	HR	TB	R	RBI	GW	TBB	IBB	SO	HBP	SH	SF	SB	CS	SB%	GDP	Avg	OBP	SLG	Pos	G	PO	A	E	DP	FPct
1955 Bro	24	2	0	0	0	0	0	0	0	0	0	0	0	0	0	0	0	0	0	—	0	—	—	—	P	2	0	1	0	0	1.000

ED SPRAGUE—Edward Nelson Sprague—Bats: Right; Throws: Right

Ht: 6'2"; Wt: 215 lbs; Born: 7/25/1967 in Castro Valley, California; Debut: 5/7/1991

LCS		Batting																							Fielding						
Year Tm	Age	G	AB	H	2B	3B	HR	TB	R	RBI	GW	TBB	IBB	SO	HBP	SH	SF	SB	CS	SB%	GDP	Avg	OBP	SLG	Pos	G	PO	A	E	DP	FPct
1992 Tor	25	2	2	1	0	0	0	1	0	0	0	0	0	1	0	0	0	0	0	—	0	.500	.500	.500	—						
1993 Tor	26	6	21	6	0	1	0	8	0	4	0	2	1	4	0	0	1	0	0	—	2	.286	.333	.381	3B	6	5	9	0	1	1.000
LCS Totals		8	23	7	0	1	0	9	0	4	0	2	1	5	0	0	1	0	0	—	2	.304	.346	.391	3B	6	5	9	0	1	1.000
World Series		**Batting**																							**Fielding**						
Year Tm	Age	G	AB	H	2B	3B	HR	TB	R	RBI	GW	TBB	IBB	SO	HBP	SH	SF	SB	CS	SB%	GDP	Avg	OBP	SLG	Pos	G	PO	A	E	DP	FPct
1992 Tor	25	3	2	1	0	0	1	4	1	2	1	1	1	0	0	0	0	0	0	—	0	.500	.667	2.000	1B	1	0	0	0	0	—
1993 Tor	26	5	15	1	0	0	0	1	0	2	0	1	0	6	0	0	2	0	0	—	0	.067	.111	.067	3B	4	3	9	2	1	.857
																									1B	1	1	0	0	0	1.000
WS Totals		8	17	2	0	0	1	5	1	4	1	2	1	6	0	0	2	0	0	—	0	.118	.190	.294	3B	4	3	9	2	1	.857
Postseason Totals		16	40	9	0	1	1	14	1	8	1	4	2	11	0	0	3	0	0	—	2	.225	.277	.350	3B	10	8	18	2	2	.929

RUSS SPRINGER—Russell Paul Springer—Throws: Right; Bats: Right

Ht: 6'4"; Wt: 195 lbs; Born: 11/7/1968 in Alexandria, Louisiana; Debut: 4/17/1992

Division Series		Pitching																										
Year Tm	Age	G	GS	CG	GF	IP	BFP	H	R	ER	HR	SH	SF	HB	TBB	IBB	SO	WP	Bk	W	L	Pct	ShO	Sv-Op	Hld	OAvg	OOBP	ERA
1997 Hou	28	2	0	0	0	1.2	8	2	1	1	0	0	0	0	1	0	3	0	0	0	0	—	0	0- 0	0	.286	.375	5.40

Division Series		Batting																							Fielding						
Year Tm	Age	G	AB	H	2B	3B	HR	TB	R	RBI	GW	TBB	IBB	SO	HBP	SH	SF	SB	CS	SB%	GDP	Avg	OBP	SLG	Pos	G	PO	A	E	DP	FPct
1997 Hou	28	2	0	0	0	0	0	0	0	0	0	0	0	0	0	0	0	0	0	—	0	—	—	—	P	2	0	0	0	0	—

MIKE SQUIRES—Michael Lynn Squires—Nickname: Spanky—Bats: Left; Throws: Left

Ht: 5'11"; Wt: 185 lbs; Born: 3/5/1952 in Kalamazoo, Michigan; Debut: 9/1/1975

LCS		Batting																							Fielding						
Year Tm	Age	G	AB	H	2B	3B	HR	TB	R	RBI	GW	TBB	IBB	SO	HBP	SH	SF	SB	CS	SB%	GDP	Avg	OBP	SLG	Pos	G	PO	A	E	DP	FPct
1983 ChA	31	4	4	0	0	0	0	0	0	0	0	0	0	0	0	0	0	0	0	—	0	.000	.000	.000	1B	2	6	0	0	0	1.000

RANDY ST. CLAIRE—Randy Anthony St. Claire—Throws: Right; Bats: Right

Ht: 6'3"; Wt: 180 lbs; Born: 8/23/1960 in Glens Falls, New York; Debut: 9/11/1984

World Series		Pitching																										
Year Tm	Age	G	GS	CG	GF	IP	BFP	H	R	ER	HR	SH	SF	HB	TBB	IBB	SO	WP	Bk	W	L	Pct	ShO	Sv-Op	Hld	OAvg	OOBP	ERA
1991 Atl	31	1	0	0	1	1.0	4	1	1	1	0	0	0	0	0	0	0	0	0	0	0	—	0	0- 0	0	.250	.250	9.00

World Series		Batting																							Fielding						
Year Tm	Age	G	AB	H	2B	3B	HR	TB	R	RBI	GW	TBB	IBB	SO	HBP	SH	SF	SB	CS	SB%	GDP	Avg	OBP	SLG	Pos	G	PO	A	E	DP	FPct
1991 Atl	31	1	0	0	0	0	0	0	0	0	0	0	0	0	0	0	0	0	0	—	0	—	—	—	P	1	0	0	0	0	—

BILL STAFFORD—William Charles Stafford—Throws: Right; Bats: Right

Ht: 6'1"; Wt: 188 lbs; Born: 8/13/1939 in Catskill, New York; Debut: 4/17/1960

World Series — Pitching

Year Tm	Age	G	GS	CG	GF	IP	BFP	H	R	ER	HR	SH	SF	HB	TBB	IBB	SO	WP	Bk	W	L	Pct	ShO	Sv-Op	Hld	OAvg	OOBP	ERA
1960 NYA	21	2	0	0	0	6.0	22	5	1	1	0	0	0	0	1	0	2	0	0	0	0	—	0	0-0	0	.238	.273	1.50
1961 NYA	22	1	1	0	0	6.2	29	7	2	2	0	0	0	0	2	1	5	0	0	0	0	—	0	0-0	0	.259	.310	2.70
1962 NYA	23	1	1	1	0	9.0	34	4	2	2	1	0	0	0	2	0	5	0	0	1	0	1.000	0	0-0	0	.125	.176	2.00
WS Totals		4	2	1	0	21.2	170	16	5	5	1	0	0	0	5	1	12	0	0	1	0	1.000	0	0-0	0	.200	.247	2.08

World Series — Batting / Fielding

Year Tm	Age	G	AB	H	2B	3B	HR	TB	R	RBI	GW	TBB	IBB	SO	HBP	SH	SF	SB	CS	SB%	GDP	Avg	OBP	SLG	Pos	G	PO	A	E	DP	FPct
1960 NYA	21	2	1	0	0	0	0	0	0	0	0	0	0	1	0	0	0	0	0	—	0	.000	.000	.000	P	2	0	2	0	2	1.000
1961 NYA	22	1	2	0	0	0	0	0	0	0	0	0	0	0	0	0	0	0	0	—	0	.000	.000	.000	P	1	1	0	1	0	.500
1962 NYA	23	1	3	0	0	0	0	0	0	0	0	0	0	1	0	0	0	0	0	—	0	.000	.000	.000	P	1	0	1	0	0	1.000
WS Totals		4	6	0	0	0	0	0	0	0	0	0	0	2	0	0	0	0	0	—	0	.000	.000	.000	P	4	1	3	1	2	.800

CHICK STAHL—Charles Sylvester Stahl—Bats: Left; Throws: Left

Ht: 5'10"; Wt: 160 lbs; Born: 1/10/1873 in Avilla, Indiana; Debut: 4/19/1897; Died: 3/28/1907

World Series — Batting / Fielding

Year Tm	Age	G	AB	H	2B	3B	HR	TB	R	RBI	GW	TBB	IBB	SO	HBP	SH	SF	SB	CS	SB%	GDP	Avg	OBP	SLG	Pos	G	PO	A	E	DP	FPct
1903 Bos	30	8	33	10	1	3	0	17	6	3	1	1	0	2	0	0	0	2	1	.67	0	.303	.324	.515	OF	8	14	1	0	0	1.000

JAKE STAHL—Garland Stahl—Bats: Right; Throws: Right

Ht: 6'2"; Wt: 195 lbs; Born: 4/13/1879 in Elkhart, Illinois; Debut: 4/20/1903; Died: 9/18/1922

World Series — Batting / Fielding

Year Tm	Age	G	AB	H	2B	3B	HR	TB	R	RBI	GW	TBB	IBB	SO	HBP	SH	SF	SB	CS	SB%	GDP	Avg	OBP	SLG	Pos	G	PO	A	E	DP	FPct
1912 Bos	33	8	32	8	2	0	0	10	3	2	0	0	0	6	0	1	0	2	2	.50	0	.250	.250	.313	1B	8	76	3	1	4	.988

LARRY STAHL—Larry Floyd Stahl—Bats: Left; Throws: Left

Ht: 6'0"; Wt: 175 lbs; Born: 6/29/1941 in Belleville, Illinois; Debut: 9/11/1964

LCS — Batting / Fielding

Year Tm	Age	G	AB	H	2B	3B	HR	TB	R	RBI	GW	TBB	IBB	SO	HBP	SH	SF	SB	CS	SB%	GDP	Avg	OBP	SLG	Pos	G	PO	A	E	DP	FPct
1973 Cin	32	4	4	2	0	0	0	2	1	0	0	0	0	1	0	0	0	0	0	—	0	.500	.500	.500	—						

TUCK STAINBACK—George Tucker Stainback—Nickname: Goldilocks—Bats: Right; Throws: Right

Ht: 5'11"; Wt: 175 lbs; Born: 8/4/1911 in Los Angeles, California; Debut: 4/17/1934; Died: 11/29/1992

World Series — Batting / Fielding

Year Tm	Age	G	AB	H	2B	3B	HR	TB	R	RBI	GW	TBB	IBB	SO	HBP	SH	SF	SB	CS	SB%	GDP	Avg	OBP	SLG	Pos	G	PO	A	E	DP	FPct
1942 NYA	31	2	0	0	0	0	0	0	0	0	0	0	0	0	0	0	0	0	0	—	0	—	—	—	—						
1943 NYA	32	5	17	3	0	0	0	3	0	0	0	0	0	2	0	2	0	0	0	—	0	.176	.176	.176	OF	5	7	1	0	0	1.000
WS Totals		7	17	3	0	0	0	3	0	0	0	0	0	2	0	2	0	0	0	—	0	.176	.176	.176	OF	5	7	1	0	0	1.000

MATT STAIRS—Matthew Wade Stairs—Bats: Left; Throws: Right

Ht: 5'9"; Wt: 175 lbs; Born: 2/27/1969 in Fredericton, New Brunswick; Debut: 5/29/1992

Division Series — Batting / Fielding

Year Tm	Age	G	AB	H	2B	3B	HR	TB	R	RBI	GW	TBB	IBB	SO	HBP	SH	SF	SB	CS	SB%	GDP	Avg	OBP	SLG	Pos	G	PO	A	E	DP	FPct
1995 Bos	26	1	1	0	0	0	0	0	0	0	0	0	0	1	0	0	0	0	0	—	0	.000	.000	.000	—						

GERRY STALEY—Gerald Lee Staley—Throws: Right; Bats: Right

Ht: 6'0"; Wt: 195 lbs; Born: 8/21/1920 in Brush Prairie, Washington; Debut: 4/20/1947

World Series — Pitching

Year Tm	Age	G	GS	CG	GF	IP	BFP	H	R	ER	HR	SH	SF	HB	TBB	IBB	SO	WP	Bk	W	L	Pct	ShO	Sv-Op	Hld	OAvg	OOBP	ERA
1959 ChA	39	4	0	0	3	8.1	31	8	2	2	1	1	0	0	0	0	3	0	0	0	1	.000	0	1-1	0	.267	.267	2.16

World Series — Batting / Fielding

Year Tm	Age	G	AB	H	2B	3B	HR	TB	R	RBI	GW	TBB	IBB	SO	HBP	SH	SF	SB	CS	SB%	GDP	Avg	OBP	SLG	Pos	G	PO	A	E	DP	FPct
1959 ChA	39	4	1	0	0	0	0	0	0	0	0	1	0	1	0	0	0	0	0	—	0	.000	.500	.000	P	4	1	1	0	0	1.000

OSCAR STANAGE—Oscar Harland Stanage—Bats: Right; Throws: Right

Ht: 5'11"; Wt: 190 lbs; Born: 3/17/1883 in Tulare, California; Debut: 5/19/1906; Died: 11/11/1964

World Series — Batting / Fielding

Year Tm	Age	G	AB	H	2B	3B	HR	TB	R	RBI	GW	TBB	IBB	SO	HBP	SH	SF	SB	CS	SB%	GDP	Avg	OBP	SLG	Pos	G	PO	A	E	DP	FPct
1909 Det	26	2	5	1	0	0	0	1	0	2	1	0	0	2	0	1	0	0	0	—	1	.200	.200	.200	C	2	12	2	0	0	1.000

LEE STANGE—Albert Lee Stange—Throws: Right; Bats: Right

Ht: 5'10"; Wt: 170 lbs; Born: 10/27/1936 in Chicago, Illinois; Debut: 4/15/1961

World Series — Pitching

Year Tm	Age	G	GS	CG	GF	IP	BFP	H	R	ER	HR	SH	SF	HB	TBB	IBB	SO	WP	Bk	W	L	Pct	ShO	Sv-Op	Hld	OAvg	OOBP	ERA
1967 Bos	30	1	0	0	0	2.0	9	3	1	0	0	0	0	0	0	0	0	0	0	0	0	—	0	0-0	0	.333	.333	0.00

World Series — Batting / Fielding

Year Tm	Age	G	AB	H	2B	3B	HR	TB	R	RBI	GW	TBB	IBB	SO	HBP	SH	SF	SB	CS	SB%	GDP	Avg	OBP	SLG	Pos	G	PO	A	E	DP	FPct
1967 Bos	30	1	0	0	0	0	0	0	0	0	0	0	0	0	0	0	0	0	0	—	0	—	—	—	P	1	0	0	1	0	.000

DON STANHOUSE—Donald Joseph Stanhouse—Nicknames: Stan, The Man Unusual—Throws: Right; Bats: Right

Ht: 6'2"; Wt: 185 lbs; Born: 2/12/1951 in DuQuoin, Illinois; Debut: 4/19/1972

LCS / World Series — Pitching

Year Tm	Age	G	GS	CG	GF	IP	BFP	H	R	ER	HR	SH	SF	HB	TBB	IBB	SO	WP	Bk	W	L	Pct	ShO	Sv-Op	Hld	OAvg	OOBP	ERA
LCS																												
1979 Bal	28	3	0	0	3	3.0	18	5	3	2	0	0	1	0	3	1	0	0	0	1	1	.500	0	0-1	0	.357	.444	6.00
World Series																												
1979 Bal	28	3	0	0	2	2.0	14	6	3	3	0	1	0	0	3	2	0	0	0	0	1	.000	0	0-0	0	.600	.692	13.50
Postseason Totals		6	0	0	5	5.0	64	11	6	5	0	1	1	0	6	3	0	0	0	1	2	.333	0	0-1	0	.458	.548	9.00

LCS / World Series — Batting / Fielding

Year Tm	Age	G	AB	H	2B	3B	HR	TB	R	RBI	GW	TBB	IBB	SO	HBP	SH	SF	SB	CS	SB%	GDP	Avg	OBP	SLG	Pos	G	PO	A	E	DP	FPct
LCS																															
1979 Bal	28	3	0	0	0	0	0	0	0	0	0	0	0	0	0	0	0	0	0	—	0	—	—	—	P	3	0	0	0	0	—
World Series																															
1979 Bal	28	3	0	0	0	0	0	0	0	0	0	0	0	0	0	0	0	0	0	—	0	—	—	—	P	3	0	0	1	0	.000
Postseason Totals		6	0	0	0	0	0	0	0	0	0	0	0	0	0	0	0	0	0	—	0	—	—	—	P	6	0	0	1	0	.000

EDDIE STANKY—Edward Raymond Stanky—Nicknames: The Brat, Muggsy—Bats: Right; Throws: Right

Ht: 5'8"; Wt: 170 lbs; Born: 9/3/1916 in Philadelphia, Pennsylvania; Debut: 4/21/1943

World Series — Batting / Fielding

Year Tm	Age	G	AB	H	2B	3B	HR	TB	R	RBI	GW	TBB	IBB	SO	HBP	SH	SF	SB	CS	SB%	GDP	Avg	OBP	SLG	Pos	G	PO	A	E	DP	FPct
1947 Bro	31	7	25	6	1	0	0	7	4	2	0	3	0	2	0	1	0	0	1	.00	0	.240	.321	.280	2B	7	18	18	1	5	.973
1948 Bos	32	6	14	4	1	0	0	5	0	1	0	7	1	0	0	1	0	0	0	—	1	.286	.524	.357	2B	6	8	13	0	2	1.000
1951 NYG	35	6	22	3	0	0	0	3	3	1	0	3	0	2	1	0	0	0	1	.00	1	.136	.269	.136	2B	6	14	15	1	3	.967
WS Totals		19	61	13	2	0	0	15	7	4	0	13	1	4	1	2	0	0	2	.00	2	.213	.360	.246	2B	19	40	46	2	10	.977

BOB STANLEY—Robert William Stanley—Nickname: Bigfoot—Throws: Right; Bats: Right

Ht: 6'4"; Wt: 210 lbs; Born: 11/10/1954 in Portland, Maine; Debut: 4/16/1977

LCS / World Series — Pitching

Year Tm	Age	G	GS	CG	GF	IP	BFP	H	R	ER	HR	SH	SF	HB	TBB	IBB	SO	WP	Bk	W	L	Pct	ShO	Sv-Op	Hld	OAvg	OOBP	ERA
LCS																												
1986 Bos	31	3	0	0	2	5.2	27	7	4	3	0	2	1	0	3	1	1	0	0	0	0	—	0	0-0	0	.333	.400	4.76
1988 Bos	33	2	0	0	1	1.0	6	2	1	1	1	0	0	0	1	0	0	0	0	0	0	—	0	0-0	0	.400	.500	9.00
LCS Totals		5	0	0	3	6.2	66	9	5	4	1	2	1	0	4	1	1	0	0	0	0	—	0	0-0	0	.346	.419	5.40
World Series																												
1986 Bos	31	5	0	0	4	6.1	25	5	0	0	0	0	0	0	1	0	4	1	0	0	0	—	0	1-2	0	.208	.240	0.00
Postseason Totals		10	0	0	7	13.0	116	14	5	4	1	2	1	0	5	1	5	1	0	0	0	—	0	1-2	0	.280	.339	2.77

LCS		Batting																							Fielding						
Year Tm	Age	G	AB	H	2B	3B	HR	TB	R	RBI	GW	TBB	IBB	SO	HBP	SH	SF	SB	CS	SB%	GDP	Avg	OBP	SLG	Pos	G	PO	A	E	DP	FPct
1986 Bos	31	3	0	0	0	0	0	0	0	0	0	0	0	0	0	0	0	0	0	—	0	—	—	—	P	3	0	1	0	0	1.000
1988 Bos	33	2	0	0	0	0	0	0	0	0	0	0	0	0	0	0	0	0	0	—	0	—	—	—	P	2	0	0	0	0	—
LCS Totals		5	0	0	0	0	0	0	0	0	0	0	0	0	0	0	0	0	0	—	0	—	—	—	P	5	0	1	0	0	1.000

World Series		Batting																							Fielding						
Year Tm	Age	G	AB	H	2B	3B	HR	TB	R	RBI	GW	TBB	IBB	SO	HBP	SH	SF	SB	CS	SB%	GDP	Avg	OBP	SLG	Pos	G	PO	A	E	DP	FPct
1986 Bos	31	5	1	0	0	0	0	0	0	0	0	0	0	1	0	0	0	0	0	—	0	.000	.000	.000	P	5	1	2	0	0	1.000
Postseason Totals		10	1	0	0	0	0	0	0	0	0	0	0	1	0	0	0	0	0	—	0	.000	.000	.000	P	10	1	3	0	0	1.000

FRED STANLEY—Frederick Blair Stanley—Nickname: Chicken—Bats: Right; Throws: Right

Ht: 5'10"; Wt: 165 lbs; Born: 8/13/1947 in Farnhamville, Iowa; Debut: 9/11/1969

Division Series		Batting																							Fielding						
Year Tm	Age	G	AB	H	2B	3B	HR	TB	R	RBI	GW	TBB	IBB	SO	HBP	SH	SF	SB	CS	SB%	GDP	Avg	OBP	SLG	Pos	G	PO	A	E	DP	FPct
1981 Oak	34	3	6	0	0	0	0	0	0	0	0	1	0	1	0	0	0	0	0	—	0	.000	.143	.000	SS	3	7	4	0	0	1.000

LCS		Batting																							Fielding						
Year Tm	Age	G	AB	H	2B	3B	HR	TB	R	RBI	GW	TBB	IBB	SO	HBP	SH	SF	SB	CS	SB%	GDP	Avg	OBP	SLG	Pos	G	PO	A	E	DP	FPct
1976 NYA	29	5	15	5	2	0	0	7	1	0	0	2	0	0	0	0	0	0	0	—	0	.333	.412	.467	SS	5	7	15	1	2	.957
1977 NYA	30	2	0	0	0	0	0	0	0	0	0	0	0	0	0	0	0	0	0	—	0	—	—	—	SS	2	1	0	0	0	1.000
1978 NYA	31	2	5	1	0	0	0	1	0	0	0	0	0	2	0	0	0	0	0	—	0	.200	.200	.200	2B	2	3	3	0	0	1.000
1981 Oak	34	2	3	1	0	0	0	1	0	1	0	0	0	1	0	0	0	0	0	—	0	.333	.333	.333	SS	2	4	2	0	0	1.000
LCS Totals		11	23	7	2	0	0	9	1	1	0	2	0	3	0	0	0	0	0	—	0	.304	.360	.391	SS	9	12	17	1	2	.967

World Series		Batting																							Fielding						
Year Tm	Age	G	AB	H	2B	3B	HR	TB	R	RBI	GW	TBB	IBB	SO	HBP	SH	SF	SB	CS	SB%	GDP	Avg	OBP	SLG	Pos	G	PO	A	E	DP	FPct
1976 NYA	29	4	6	1	1	0	0	2	1	1	0	3	0	1	0	0	0	0	0	—	0	.167	.444	.333	SS	4	4	7	1	3	.917
1977 NYA	30	1	0	0	0	0	0	0	0	0	0	0	0	0	0	0	0	0	0	—	0	—	—	—	SS	1	1	0	0	0	1.000
1978 NYA	31	3	5	1	1	0	0	2	0	0	0	1	0	0	0	0	0	0	0	—	0	.200	.333	.400	2B	3	5	2	0	1	1.000
WS Totals		8	11	2	2	0	0	4	1	1	0	4	0	1	0	0	0	0	0	—	0	.182	.400	.364	SS	5	5	7	1	3	.923
Postseason Totals		22	40	9	4	0	0	13	2	2	0	7	0	5	0	0	0	0	0	—	0	.225	.340	.325	SS	17	24	28	2	5	.963

MICKEY STANLEY—Mitchell Jack Stanley—Bats: Right; Throws: Right

Ht: 6'1"; Wt: 185 lbs; Born: 7/20/1942 in Grand Rapids, Michigan; Debut: 9/13/1964

LCS		Batting																							Fielding						
Year Tm	Age	G	AB	H	2B	3B	HR	TB	R	RBI	GW	TBB	IBB	SO	HBP	SH	SF	SB	CS	SB%	GDP	Avg	OBP	SLG	Pos	G	PO	A	E	DP	FPct
1972 Det	30	4	6	2	0	0	0	2	0	0	0	0	0	0	0	0	0	0	0	—	0	.333	.333	.333	OF	3	7	0	0	0	1.000

World Series		Batting																							Fielding						
Year Tm	Age	G	AB	H	2B	3B	HR	TB	R	RBI	GW	TBB	IBB	SO	HBP	SH	SF	SB	CS	SB%	GDP	Avg	OBP	SLG	Pos	G	PO	A	E	DP	FPct
1968 Det	26	7	28	6	0	1	0	8	4	0	0	2	0	4	0	0	0	0	1	.00	2	.214	.267	.286	SS	7	14	16	2	3	.938
																									OF	4	2	0	0	0	1.000
Postseason Totals		11	34	8	0	1	0	10	4	0	0	2	0	4	0	0	0	0	1	.00	2	.235	.278	.294	SS	7	14	16	2	3	.938

MIKE STANLEY—Robert Michael Stanley—Bats: Right; Throws: Right

Ht: 6'1"; Wt: 185 lbs; Born: 6/25/1963 in Ft. Lauderdale, Florida; Debut: 6/24/1986

Division Series		Batting																							Fielding						
Year Tm	Age	G	AB	H	2B	3B	HR	TB	R	RBI	GW	TBB	IBB	SO	HBP	SH	SF	SB	CS	SB%	GDP	Avg	OBP	SLG	Pos	G	PO	A	E	DP	FPct
1995 NYA	32	4	16	5	0	0	1	8	2	3	0	2	0	1	0	0	0	0	0	—	0	.313	.389	.500	C	4	30	0	1	0	.968
1997 NYA	34	2	4	3	1	0	0	4	1	1	0	0	0	1	1	0	0	0	0	—	0	.750	.800	1.000	—						
DS Totals		6	20	8	1	0	1	12	3	4	0	2	0	2	1	0	0	0	0	—	0	.400	.478	.600	C	4	30	0	1	0	.968

MIKE STANTON—William Michael Stanton—Throws: Left; Bats: Left

Ht: 6'1"; Wt: 190 lbs; Born: 6/2/1967 in Houston, Texas; Debut: 8/24/1989

Division Series		Pitching																										
Year Tm	Age	G	GS	CG	GF	IP	BFP	H	R	ER	HR	SH	SF	HB	TBB	IBB	SO	WP	Bk	W	L	Pct	ShO	Sv-Op	Hld	OAvg	OOBP	ERA
1995 Bos	28	1	0	0	0	2.1	8	1	0	0	0	0	0	0	0	0	4	0	0	0	0	—	0	0-0	0	.125	.125	0.00
1996 Tex	29	3	0	0	1	3.1	13	2	2	1	1	0	0	0	3	0	3	0	0	0	1	.000	0	0-0	0	.200	.385	2.70
1997 NYA	30	3	0	0	1	1.0	5	1	0	0	0	0	0	0	1	0	3	0	0	0	0	—	0	0-0	1	.250	.400	0.00
DS Totals		7	0	0	2	6.2	52	4	2	1	1	0	0	0	4	0	10	0	0	0	1	.000	0	0-0	1	.182	.308	1.35

LCS		Pitching																										
Year Tm	Age	G	GS	CG	GF	IP	BFP	H	R	ER	HR	SH	SF	HB	TBB	IBB	SO	WP	Bk	W	L	Pct	ShO	Sv-Op	Hld	OAvg	OOBP	ERA
1991 Atl	24	3	0	0	1	3.2	17	4	1	1	0	1	1	0	3	1	3	1	0	0	0	—	0	0-0	1	.333	.438	2.45
1992 Atl	25	5	0	0	1	4.1	17	2	1	0	0	1	1	0	2	1	5	0	0	0	0	—	0	0-0	2	.154	.250	0.00
1993 Atl	26	1	0	0	0	1.0	5	1	0	0	0	0	0	0	1	0	0	0	0	0	0	—	0	0-0	0	.250	.400	0.00
LCS Totals		9	0	0	2	9.0	78	7	2	1	0	2	2	0	6	2	8	1	0	0	0	—	0	0-0	3	.241	.351	1.00

World Series		Pitching																										
Year Tm	Age	G	GS	CG	GF	IP	BFP	H	R	ER	HR	SH	SF	HB	TBB	IBB	SO	WP	Bk	W	L	Pct	ShO	Sv-Op	Hld	OAvg	OOBP	ERA
1991 Atl	24	5	0	0	2	7.1	27	5	0	0	0	0	0	0	2	2	7	0	0	1	0	1.000	0	0-0	0	.200	.259	0.00
1992 Atl	25	4	0	0	1	5.0	19	3	0	0	0	1	0	0	2	2	1	0	0	0	0	—	0	1-1	1	.188	.278	0.00
WS Totals		9	0	0	3	12.1	92	8	0	0	0	1	0	0	4	4	8	0	0	1	0	1.000	0	1-1	1	.195	.267	0.00
Postseason Totals		25	0	0	7	28.0	222	19	4	2	1	3	2	0	14	6	26	1	0	1	1	.500	0	1-1	5	.207	.306	0.64

Division Series		Batting																							Fielding						
Year Tm	Age	G	AB	H	2B	3B	HR	TB	R	RBI	GW	TBB	IBB	SO	HBP	SH	SF	SB	CS	SB%	GDP	Avg	OBP	SLG	Pos	G	PO	A	E	DP	FPct
1995 Bos	28	1	0	0	0	0	0	0	0	0	0	0	0	0	0	0	0	0	0	—	0	—	—	—	P	1	0	1	0	0	1.000
1996 Tex	29	3	0	0	0	0	0	0	0	0	0	0	0	0	0	0	0	0	0	—	0	—	—	—	P	3	0	1	0	0	1.000
1997 NYA	30	3	0	0	0	0	0	0	0	0	0	0	0	0	0	0	0	0	0	—	0	—	—	—	P	3	0	0	0	0	—
DS Totals		7	0	0	0	0	0	0	0	0	0	0	0	0	0	0	0	0	0	—	0	—	—	—	P	7	0	2	0	0	1.000

LCS		Batting																							Fielding						
Year Tm	Age	G	AB	H	2B	3B	HR	TB	R	RBI	GW	TBB	IBB	SO	HBP	SH	SF	SB	CS	SB%	GDP	Avg	OBP	SLG	Pos	G	PO	A	E	DP	FPct
1991 Atl	24	3	0	0	0	0	0	0	0	0	0	0	0	0	0	0	0	0	0	—	0	—	—	—	P	3	0	2	0	0	1.000
1992 Atl	25	5	1	1	1	0	0	2	1	1	0	0	0	0	0	0	0	0	0	—	0	1.000	1.000	2.000	P	5	0	1	0	0	1.000
1993 Atl	26	1	0	0	0	0	0	0	0	0	0	0	0	0	0	0	0	0	0	—	0	—	—	—	P	1	0	0	0	0	—
LCS Totals		9	1	1	1	0	0	2	1	1	0	0	0	0	0	0	0	0	0	—	0	1.000	1.000	2.000	P	9	0	3	0	0	1.000

World Series		Batting																							Fielding						
Year Tm	Age	G	AB	H	2B	3B	HR	TB	R	RBI	GW	TBB	IBB	SO	HBP	SH	SF	SB	CS	SB%	GDP	Avg	OBP	SLG	Pos	G	PO	A	E	DP	FPct
1991 Atl	24	5	0	0	0	0	0	0	0	0	0	0	0	0	0	0	0	0	0	—	0	—	—	—	P	5	0	0	0	0	—
1992 Atl	25	4	0	0	0	0	0	0	0	0	0	0	0	0	0	0	0	0	0	—	0	—	—	—	P	4	0	0	0	0	—
WS Totals		9	0	0	0	0	0	0	0	0	0	0	0	0	0	0	0	0	0	—	0	—	—	—	P	9	0	0	0	0	—
Postseason Totals		25	1	1	1	0	0	2	1	1	0	0	0	0	0	0	0	0	0	—	0	1.000	1.000	2.000	P	25	0	5	0	0	1.000

DAVE STAPLETON—David Leslie Stapleton—Bats: Right; Throws: Right

Ht: 6'1"; Wt: 178 lbs; Born: 1/16/1954 in Fairhope, Alabama; Debut: 5/30/1980

LCS		Batting																							Fielding						
Year Tm	Age	G	AB	H	2B	3B	HR	TB	R	RBI	GW	TBB	IBB	SO	HBP	SH	SF	SB	CS	SB%	GDP	Avg	OBP	SLG	Pos	G	PO	A	E	DP	FPct
1986 Bos	32	4	3	2	0	0	0	2	2	0	0	1	0	0	0	0	0	0	0	—	0	.667	.750	.667	1B	4	12	1	0	1	1.000

World Series		Batting																							Fielding						
Year Tm	Age	G	AB	H	2B	3B	HR	TB	R	RBI	GW	TBB	IBB	SO	HBP	SH	SF	SB	CS	SB%	GDP	Avg	OBP	SLG	Pos	G	PO	A	E	DP	FPct
1986 Bos	32	3	1	0	0	0	0	0	0	0	0	0	0	0	0	0	0	0	0	—	0	.000	.000	.000	1B	3	3	2	0	0	1.000
Postseason Totals		7	4	2	0	0	0	2	2	0	0	1	0	0	0	0	0	0	0	—	0	.500	.600	.500	1B	7	15	3	0	1	1.000

WILLIE STARGELL (HOF 1988-W)—Wilver Dornel Stargell—Nickname: Pops—Bats: Left; Throws: Left

Ht: 6'2"; Wt: 188 lbs; Born: 3/6/1940 in Earlsboro, Oklahoma; Debut: 9/16/1962

LCS		Batting																							Fielding						
Year Tm	Age	G	AB	H	2B	3B	HR	TB	R	RBI	GW	TBB	IBB	SO	HBP	SH	SF	SB	CS	SB%	GDP	Avg	OBP	SLG	Pos	G	PO	A	E	DP	FPct
1970 Pit	30	3	12	6	1	0	0	7	0	1	0	1	0	1	0	0	0	0	0	—	0	.500	.538	.583	OF	3	4	0	0	0	1.000
1971 Pit	31	4	14	0	0	0	0	0	1	0	0	2	2	6	1	0	0	0	0	—	0	.000	.176	.000	OF	4	6	0	0	0	1.000
1972 Pit	32	5	16	1	1	0	0	2	1	1	1	2	0	5	0	0	0	0	0	—	1	.063	.167	.125	1B	5	31	3	0	1	1.000
																									OF	1	0	0	0	0	—
1974 Pit	34	4	15	6	0	0	2	12	3	4	1	1	0	2	0	0	0	0	0	—	1	.400	.438	.800	OF	4	13	0	0	0	1.000
1975 Pit	35	3	11	2	1	0	0	3	1	0	0	1	0	3	0	0	0	0	0	—	0	.182	.250	.273	1B	3	15	0	0	2	1.000
1979 Pit-*M*	39	3	11	5	2	0	2	13	2	6	1	3	1	2	0	0	0	0	0	—	0	.455	.571	1.182	1B	3	32	2	0	2	1.000
LCS Totals		22	79	20	5	0	4	37	8	12	3	10	3	19	1	0	0	0	0	—	2	.253	.344	.468	OF	12	23	0	0	0	1.000

World Series		Batting																							Fielding						
Year Tm	Age	G	AB	H	2B	3B	HR	TB	R	RBI	GW	TBB	IBB	SO	HBP	SH	SF	SB	CS	SB%	GDP	Avg	OBP	SLG	Pos	G	PO	A	E	DP	FPct
1971 Pit	31	7	24	5	1	0	0	6	3	1	0	7	0	9	0	0	0	0	0	—	0	.208	.387	.250	OF	7	11	1	0	1	1.000
1979 Pit-*M*	39	7	30	12	4	0	3	25	7	7	1	0	0	6	0	0	2	0	0	—	1	.400	.375	.833	1B	7	59	2	2	9	.968
WS Totals		14	54	17	5	0	3	31	10	8	1	7	0	15	0	0	2	0	0	—	1	.315	.381	.574	1B	7	59	2	2	9	.968
Postseason Totals		36	133	37	10	0	7	68	18	20	4	17	3	34	1	0	2	0	0	—	3	.278	.359	.511	OF	19	34	1	0	1	1.000

RUSTY STAUB—Daniel Joseph Staub—Nickname: Le Grande Orange—Bats: Left; Throws: Right

Ht: 6'2"; Wt: 190 lbs; Born: 4/1/1944 in New Orleans, Louisiana; Debut: 4/9/1963

LCS		Batting																							Fielding						
Year Tm	Age	G	AB	H	2B	3B	HR	TB	R	RBI	GW	TBB	IBB	SO	HBP	SH	SF	SB	CS	SB%	GDP	Avg	OBP	SLG	Pos	G	PO	A	E	DP	FPct
1973 NYN	29	4	15	3	0	0	3	12	4	5	2	3	0	2	0	0	0	0	0	—	0	.200	.333	.800	OF	4	11	0	0	0	1.000

World Series		Batting																							Fielding						
Year Tm	Age	G	AB	H	2B	3B	HR	TB	R	RBI	GW	TBB	IBB	SO	HBP	SH	SF	SB	CS	SB%	GDP	Avg	OBP	SLG	Pos	G	PO	A	E	DP	FPct
1973 NYN	29	7	26	11	2	0	1	16	1	6	1	2	0	2	0	0	0	0	0	—	0	.423	.464	.615	OF	6	5	0	0	0	1.000
Postseason Totals		11	41	14	2	0	4	28	5	11	3	5	0	4	0	0	0	0	0	—	0	.341	.413	.683	OF	10	16	0	0	0	1.000

TERRY STEINBACH—Terry Lee Steinbach—Bats: Right; Throws: Right

Ht: 6'1"; Wt: 195 lbs; Born: 3/2/1962 in New Ulm, Minnesota; Debut: 9/12/1986

LCS		Batting																							Fielding						
Year Tm	Age	G	AB	H	2B	3B	HR	TB	R	RBI	GW	TBB	IBB	SO	HBP	SH	SF	SB	CS	SB%	GDP	Avg	OBP	SLG	Pos	G	PO	A	E	DP	FPct
1988 Oak	26	2	4	1	0	0	0	1	0	0	0	2	0	0	0	0	0	0	0	—	0	.250	.500	.250	C	2	12	0	0	0	1.000
1989 Oak	27	4	15	3	0	0	0	3	0	1	0	1	0	5	0	0	0	0	0	—	0	.200	.250	.200	C	3	17	0	0	0	1.000
1990 Oak	28	3	11	5	0	0	0	5	2	1	0	1	0	2	0	0	0	0	1	.00	1	.455	.500	.455	C	3	11	0	0	0	1.000
1992 Oak	30	6	24	7	0	0	1	10	1	5	0	2	0	7	0	0	0	0	0	—	1	.292	.346	.417	C	6	30	7	0	0	1.000
LCS Totals		15	54	16	0	0	1	19	3	7	0	6	0	14	0	0	0	0	1	.00	2	.296	.367	.352	C	14	70	7	0	0	1.000

World Series		Batting																							Fielding						
Year Tm	Age	G	AB	H	2B	3B	HR	TB	R	RBI	GW	TBB	IBB	SO	HBP	SH	SF	SB	CS	SB%	GDP	Avg	OBP	SLG	Pos	G	PO	A	E	DP	FPct
1988 Oak	26	3	11	4	1	0	0	5	0	0	0	0	0	2	0	0	0	0	0	—	0	.364	.364	.455	C	2	11	3	0	0	1.000
1989 Oak	27	4	16	4	0	1	1	9	3	7	0	2	0	1	0	0	0	0	0	—	0	.250	.333	.563	C	4	27	2	0	0	1.000
1990 Oak	28	3	8	1	0	0	0	1	0	0	0	0	0	1	0	0	0	0	0	—	0	.125	.125	.125	C	3	8	1	0	0	1.000
WS Totals		10	35	9	1	1	1	15	3	7	0	2	0	4	0	0	0	0	0	—	0	.257	.297	.429	C	9	46	6	0	0	1.000
Postseason Totals		25	89	25	1	1	2	34	6	14	0	8	0	18	0	0	0	0	1	.00	2	.281	.340	.382	C	23	116	13	0	0	1.000

HARRY STEINFELDT—Harry M. Steinfeldt—Bats: Right; Throws: Right

Ht: 5'9"; Wt: 180 lbs; Born: 9/29/1877 in St. Louis, Missouri; Debut: 4/22/1898; Died: 8/17/1914

World Series		Batting																							Fielding						
Year Tm	Age	G	AB	H	2B	3B	HR	TB	R	RBI	GW	TBB	IBB	SO	HBP	SH	SF	SB	CS	SB%	GDP	Avg	OBP	SLG	Pos	G	PO	A	E	DP	FPct
1906 ChN	29	6	20	5	1	0	0	6	2	2	0	1	0	0	0	3	0	1	1	.00	0	.250	.286	.300	3B	6	4	8	1	0	.923
1907 ChN	30	5	17	8	1	1	0	11	2	2	1	1	0	2	2	1	0	1	0	1.00	0	.471	.550	.647	3B	5	9	6	1	1	.938
1908 ChN	31	5	16	4	0	0	0	4	3	3	1	2	0	5	0	2	1	1	1	.50	0	.250	.316	.250	3B	5	4	11	1	0	.938
1910 ChN	33	5	20	2	1	0	0	3	0	1	0	0	0	4	0	0	0	0	0	—	0	.100	.100	.150	3B	5	2	12	4	0	.778
WS Totals		21	73	19	3	1	0	24	7	8	2	4	0	11	2	6	1	2	2	.50	0	.260	.313	.329	3B	21	19	37	7	1	.889

CASEY STENGEL (HOF 1966-V)—Charles Dillon Stengel—Nickname: The Old Perfessor—B: L; T: L

Ht: 5'11"; Wt: 175 lbs; Born: 7/30/1890 in Kansas City, Mo.; Deb.: 9/17/1912; Died: 9/29/1975

World Series		Batting																							Fielding						
Year Tm	Age	G	AB	H	2B	3B	HR	TB	R	RBI	GW	TBB	IBB	SO	HBP	SH	SF	SB	CS	SB%	GDP	Avg	OBP	SLG	Pos	G	PO	A	E	DP	FPct
1916 Bro	26	4	11	4	0	0	0	4	2	0	0	0	0	1	0	1	0	0	0	—	0	.364	.364	.364	OF	3	3	1	1	0	.800
1922 NYG	32	2	5	2	0	0	0	2	0	0	0	0	0	1	0	0	0	0	0	—	0	.400	.400	.400	OF	2	4	0	0	0	1.000
1923 NYG	33	6	12	5	0	0	2	11	3	4	2	4	0	0	0	0	0	0	0	—	0	.417	.563	.917	OF	6	11	0	0	0	1.000
WS Totals		12	28	11	0	0	2	17	5	4	2	4	0	2	0	1	0	0	0	—	0	.393	.469	.607	OF	11	18	1	1	0	.950

RENNIE STENNETT—Renaldo Antonio Stennett—Bats: Right; Throws: Right

Ht: 5'11"; Wt: 160 lbs; Born: 4/5/1951 in Colon, Panama; Debut: 7/10/1971

LCS		Batting																							Fielding						
Year Tm	Age	G	AB	H	2B	3B	HR	TB	R	RBI	GW	TBB	IBB	SO	HBP	SH	SF	SB	CS	SB%	GDP	Avg	OBP	SLG	Pos	G	PO	A	E	DP	FPct
1972 Pit	21	5	21	6	0	0	0	6	2	1	0	1	0	0	0	0	0	0	1	.00	0	.286	.318	.286	2B	1	1	0	0	0	1.000
																									OF	5	18	1	0	1	1.000
1974 Pit	23	4	16	1	0	0	0	1	1	0	0	1	0	1	0	1	0	0	0	—	1	.063	.118	.063	2B	4	10	10	0	1	1.000
1975 Pit	24	3	14	3	0	0	0	3	0	0	0	0	0	1	0	0	0	0	0	—	0	.214	.214	.214	2B	3	3	8	0	2	1.000
																									SS	1	0	0	0	0	—
1979 Pit	28	1	0	0	0	0	0	0	0	0	0	0	0	0	0	0	0	0	0	—	0	—	—	—	2B	1	0	1	0	0	1.000
LCS Totals		13	51	10	0	0	0	10	3	1	0	2	0	2	0	1	0	0	1	.00	1	.196	.226	.196	2B	9	14	19	0	3	1.000

World Series		Batting																							Fielding						
Year Tm	Age	G	AB	H	2B	3B	HR	TB	R	RBI	GW	TBB	IBB	SO	HBP	SH	SF	SB	CS	SB%	GDP	Avg	OBP	SLG	Pos	G	PO	A	E	DP	FPct
1979 Pit	28	1	1	1	0	0	0	1	0	0	0	0	0	0	0	0	0	0	0	—	0	1.000	1.000	1.000	—						
Postseason Totals		14	52	11	0	0	0	11	3	1	0	2	0	2	0	1	0	0	1	.00	1	.212	.241	.212	2B	9	14	19	0	3	1.000

VERN STEPHENS—Vernon Decatur Stephens—Nicknames: Junior, Buster—Bats: Right; Throws: Right

Ht: 5'10"; Wt: 185 lbs; Born: 10/23/1920 in McAllister, N.M.; Deb.: 9/13/1941; Died: 11/3/1968

World Series		Batting																							Fielding						
Year Tm	Age	G	AB	H	2B	3B	HR	TB	R	RBI	GW	TBB	IBB	SO	HBP	SH	SF	SB	CS	SB%	GDP	Avg	OBP	SLG	Pos	G	PO	A	E	DP	FPct
1944 StL	23	6	22	5	1	0	0	6	2	0	0	3	0	3	0	0	0	0	0	—	0	.227	.320	.273	SS	6	9	19	3	4	.903

JERRY STEPHENSON—Jerry Joseph Stephenson—Throws: Right; Bats: Left

Ht: 6'2"; Wt: 185 lbs; Born: 10/6/1943 in Detroit, Michigan; Debut: 4/14/1963

World Series		Pitching																										
Year Tm	Age	G	GS	CG	GF	IP	BFP	H	R	ER	HR	SH	SF	HB	TBB	IBB	SO	WP	Bk	W	L	Pct	ShO	Sv-Op	Hld	OAvg	OOBP	ERA
1967 Bos	23	1	0	0	0	2.0	10	3	2	2	0	0	1	0	1	0	0	1	0	0	0	—	0	0-0	0	.375	.400	9.00

World Series		Batting																							Fielding						
Year Tm	Age	G	AB	H	2B	3B	HR	TB	R	RBI	GW	TBB	IBB	SO	HBP	SH	SF	SB	CS	SB%	GDP	Avg	OBP	SLG	Pos	G	PO	A	E	DP	FPct
1967 Bos	23	1	0	0	0	0	0	0	0	0	0	0	0	0	0	0	0	0	0	—	0	—	—	—	P	1	0	0	0	0	—

RIGGS STEPHENSON—Jackson Riggs Stephenson—Nickname: Old Hoss—Bats: Right; Throws: Right

Ht: 5'10"; Wt: 185 lbs; Born: 1/5/1898 in Akron, Alabama; Debut: 4/13/1921; Died: 11/15/1985

World Series		Batting																							Fielding						
Year Tm	Age	G	AB	H	2B	3B	HR	TB	R	RBI	GW	TBB	IBB	SO	HBP	SH	SF	SB	CS	SB%	GDP	Avg	OBP	SLG	Pos	G	PO	A	E	DP	FPct
1929 ChN	31	5	19	6	1	0	0	7	3	3	0	2	0	2	0	0	0	0	0	—	2	.316	.381	.368	OF	5	13	1	0	0	1.000
1932 ChN	34	4	18	8	1	0	0	9	2	4	0	0	0	0	0	0	0	0	0	—	1	.444	.444	.500	OF	4	4	0	0	0	1.000
WS Totals		9	37	14	2	0	0	16	5	7	0	2	0	2	0	0	0	0	0	—	3	.378	.410	.432	OF	9	17	1	0	0	1.000

WALTER STEPHENSON—Walter McQueen Stephenson—Nickname: Tarzan—Bats: Right; Throws: Right

Ht: 6'0"; Wt: 180 lbs; Born: 3/27/1911 in Saluda, N.C.; Deb.: 4/29/1935; Died: 7/4/1993

World Series		Batting																							Fielding						
Year Tm	Age	G	AB	H	2B	3B	HR	TB	R	RBI	GW	TBB	IBB	SO	HBP	SH	SF	SB	CS	SB%	GDP	Avg	OBP	SLG	Pos	G	PO	A	E	DP	FPct
1935 ChN	24	1	1	0	0	0	0	0	0	0	0	0	0	1	0	0	0	0	0	—	0	.000	.000	.000	—						

DAVE STEWART—David Keith Stewart—Nicknames: Stew, Smoke—Throws: Right; Bats: Right

Ht: 6'2"; Wt: 200 lbs; Born: 2/19/1957 in Oakland, California; Debut: 9/22/1978

Division Series		Pitching																										
Year Tm	Age	G	GS	CG	GF	IP	BFP	H	R	ER	HR	SH	SF	HB	TBB	IBB	SO	WP	Bk	W	L	Pct	ShO	Sv-Op	Hld	OAvg	OOBP	ERA
1981 LA	24	2	0	0	1	0.2	6	4	3	3	1	0	0	0	0	0	1	0	0	0	2	.000	0	0-0	0	.667	.667	40.50

LCS		Pitching																										
Year Tm	Age	G	GS	CG	GF	IP	BFP	H	R	ER	HR	SH	SF	HB	TBB	IBB	SO	WP	Bk	W	L	Pct	ShO	Sv-Op	Hld	OAvg	OOBP	ERA
1988 Oak	31	2	2	0	0	13.1	55	9	2	2	0	0	0	1	6	0	11	0	0	1	0	1.000	0	0-0	0	.188	.291	1.35
1989 Oak	32	2	2	0	0	16.0	62	13	5	5	3	0	1	0	3	0	9	0	0	2	0	1.000	0	0-0	0	.224	.258	2.81
1990 Oak	33	2	2	0	0	16.0	57	8	2	2	1	1	0	0	2	0	4	0	0	2	0	1.000	0	0-0	0	.148	.179	1.13
1992 Oak	35	2	2	1	0	16.2	66	14	5	5	3	0	0	0	6	0	7	0	0	1	0	1.000	0	0-0	0	.233	.303	2.70
1993 Tor	36	2	2	0	0	13.1	56	8	3	3	0	2	0	1	8	0	8	2	0	2	0	1.000	0	0-0	0	.178	.315	2.03
LCS Totals		10	10	1	0	75.1	592	52	17	17	7	3	1	2	25	0	39	2	0	8	0	1.000	0	0-0	0	.196	.270	2.03

World Series — Pitching

Year Tm	Age	G	GS	CG	GF	IP	BFP	H	R	ER	HR	SH	SF	HB	TBB	IBB	SO	WP	Bk	W	L	Pct	ShO	Sv-Op	Hld	OAvg	OOBP	ERA
1981 LA	24	2	0	0	2	1.2	7	1	0	0	0	0	1	0	2	1	1	0	0	0	0	—	0	0- 0	0	.250	.429	0.00
1988 Oak	31	2	2	0	0	14.1	60	12	7	5	1	0	0	1	5	0	5	1	1	0	1	.000	0	0- 0	0	.222	.300	3.14
1989 Oak	32	2	2	1	0	16.0	61	10	3	3	1	0	0	0	2	0	14	0	0	2	0	1.000	1	0- 0	0	.169	.197	1.69
1990 Oak	33	2	2	1	0	13.0	54	10	6	5	1	1	1	1	6	0	5	0	0	0	2	.000	0	0- 0	0	.222	.321	3.46
1993 Tor	36	2	2	0	0	12.0	55	10	9	9	2	0	0	0	8	0	8	1	1	0	1	.000	0	0- 0	0	.213	.327	6.75
WS Totals		10	8	2	2	57.0	474	43	25	22	5	1	2	2	23	1	33	2	2	2	4	.333	1	0-0	0	.206	.288	3.47
Postseason Totals		22	18	3	3	133.0	1078	99	45	42	13	4	3	4	48	1	73	4	2	10	6	.625	1	0-0	0	.206	.282	2.84

Division Series — Batting / Fielding

Year Tm	Age	G	AB	H	2B	3B	HR	TB	R	RBI	GW	TBB	IBB	SO	HBP	SH	SF	SB	CS	SB%	GDP	Avg	OBP	SLG	Pos	G	PO	A	E	DP	FPct
1981 LA	24	2	0	0	0	0	0	0	0	0	0	0	0	0	0	0	0	0	0	—	0	—	—	—	P	2	0	0	0	0	—

LCS — Batting / Fielding

Year Tm	Age	G	AB	H	2B	3B	HR	TB	R	RBI	GW	TBB	IBB	SO	HBP	SH	SF	SB	CS	SB%	GDP	Avg	OBP	SLG	Pos	G	PO	A	E	DP	FPct
1988 Oak	31	2	0	0	0	0	0	0	0	0	0	0	0	0	0	0	0	0	0	—	0	—	—	—	P	2	0	2	0	0	1.000
1989 Oak	32	2	0	0	0	0	0	0	0	0	0	0	0	0	0	0	0	0	0	—	0	—	—	—	P	2	0	1	0	0	1.000
1990 Oak	33	2	0	0	0	0	0	0	0	0	0	0	0	0	0	0	0	0	0	—	0	—	—	—	P	2	0	3	0	0	1.000
1992 Oak	35	2	0	0	0	0	0	0	0	0	0	0	0	0	0	0	0	0	0	—	0	—	—	—	P	2	1	1	0	0	1.000
1993 Tor	36	2	0	0	0	0	0	0	0	0	0	0	0	0	0	0	0	0	0	—	0	—	—	—	P	2	2	0	0	0	1.000
LCS Totals		10	0	0	0	0	0	0	0	0	0	0	0	0	0	0	0	0	0	—	0	—	—	—	P	10	3	7	0	0	1.000

World Series — Batting / Fielding

Year Tm	Age	G	AB	H	2B	3B	HR	TB	R	RBI	GW	TBB	IBB	SO	HBP	SH	SF	SB	CS	SB%	GDP	Avg	OBP	SLG	Pos	G	PO	A	E	DP	FPct
1981 LA	24	2	0	0	0	0	0	0	0	0	0	0	0	0	0	0	0	0	0	—	0	—	—	—	P	2	0	0	1	0	.000
1988 Oak	31	2	3	0	0	0	0	0	1	0	0	1	0	3	0	0	0	0	0	—	0	.000	.250	.000	P	2	0	1	0	0	1.000
1989 Oak	32	2	3	0	0	0	0	0	0	0	0	0	0	1	0	0	0	0	0	—	0	.000	.000	.000	P	2	3	0	1	0	.750
1990 Oak	33	2	1	0	0	0	0	0	0	0	0	0	0	1	0	0	0	0	0	—	0	.000	.000	.000	P	2	2	1	1	0	.750
1993 Tor	36	2	0	0	0	0	0	0	0	0	0	0	0	0	0	0	0	0	0	—	0	—	—	—	P	2	1	1	0	0	1.000
WS Totals		10	7	0	0	0	0	0	1	0	0	1	0	5	0	0	0	0	0	—	0	.000	.125	.000	P	10	6	3	3	0	.750
Postseason Totals		22	7	0	0	0	0	0	1	0	0	1	0	5	0	0	0	0	0	—	0	.000	.125	.000	P	22	9	10	3	0	.864

JIMMY STEWART—James Franklin Stewart—Bats: Both; Throws: Right

Ht: 6'0"; Wt: 165 lbs; Born: 6/11/1939 in Opelika, Alabama; Debut: 9/3/1963

LCS — Batting / Fielding

Year Tm	Age	G	AB	H	2B	3B	HR	TB	R	RBI	GW	TBB	IBB	SO	HBP	SH	SF	SB	CS	SB%	GDP	Avg	OBP	SLG	Pos	G	PO	A	E	DP	FPct
1970 Cin	31	1	2	0	0	0	0	0	0	0	0	0	0	0	0	0	0	0	0	—	0	.000	.000	.000	OF	1	0	0	0	0	—

World Series — Batting / Fielding

Year Tm	Age	G	AB	H	2B	3B	HR	TB	R	RBI	GW	TBB	IBB	SO	HBP	SH	SF	SB	CS	SB%	GDP	Avg	OBP	SLG	Pos	G	PO	A	E	DP	FPct
1970 Cin	31	2	2	0	0	0	0	0	0	0	0	0	0	1	0	0	0	0	0	—	0	.000	.000	.000	—						
Postseason Totals		3	4	0	0	0	0	0	0	0	0	0	0	1	0	0	0	0	0	—	0	.000	.000	.000	OF	1	0	0	0	0	—

LEFTY STEWART—Walter Cleveland Stewart—Throws: Left; Bats: Right

Ht: 5'10"; Wt: 160 lbs; Born: 9/23/1900 in Sparta, Tennessee; Debut: 4/20/1921; Died: 9/26/1974

World Series — Pitching

Year Tm	Age	G	GS	CG	GF	IP	BFP	H	R	ER	HR	SH	SF	HB	TBB	IBB	SO	WP	Bk	W	L	Pct	ShO	Sv-Op	Hld	OAvg	OOBP	ERA
1933 Was	33	1	1	0	0	2.0	13	6	4	2	1	0	0	0	0	0	0	0	0	0	1	.000	0	0- 0	0	.462	.462	9.00

World Series — Batting / Fielding

Year Tm	Age	G	AB	H	2B	3B	HR	TB	R	RBI	GW	TBB	IBB	SO	HBP	SH	SF	SB	CS	SB%	GDP	Avg	OBP	SLG	Pos	G	PO	A	E	DP	FPct
1933 Was	33	1	1	0	0	0	0	0	0	0	0	0	0	1	0	0	0	0	0	—	0	.000	.000	.000	P	1	0	0	0	0	—

SAMMY STEWART—Samuel Lee Stewart—Throws: Right; Bats: Right

Ht: 6'3"; Wt: 200 lbs; Born: 10/28/1954 in Asheville, North Carolina; Debut: 9/1/1978

LCS — Pitching

Year Tm	Age	G	GS	CG	GF	IP	BFP	H	R	ER	HR	SH	SF	HB	TBB	IBB	SO	WP	Bk	W	L	Pct	ShO	Sv-Op	Hld	OAvg	OOBP	ERA
1983 Bal	28	2	0	0	1	4.1	16	2	0	0	0	0	0	0	1	0	2	0	0	0	0	—	0	1- 1	0	.133	.188	0.00

World Series — Pitching

Year Tm	Age	G	GS	CG	GF	IP	BFP	H	R	ER	HR	SH	SF	HB	TBB	IBB	SO	WP	Bk	W	L	Pct	ShO	Sv-Op	Hld	OAvg	OOBP	ERA
1979 Bal	24	1	0	0	0	2.2	11	4	0	0	0	0	0	0	1	1	0	0	0	0	0	—	0	0- 0	0	.400	.455	0.00
1983 Bal	28	3	0	0	0	5.0	18	2	0	0	0	0	0	0	2	0	6	0	1	0	0	—	0	0- 0	2	.125	.222	0.00
WS Totals		4	0	0	0	7.2	58	6	0	0	0	0	0	0	3	1	6	0	1	0	0	—	0	0-0	2	.231	.310	0.00
Postseason Totals		6	0	0	1	12.0	90	8	0	0	0	0	0	0	4	1	8	0	1	0	0	—	0	1-1	2	.195	.267	0.00

LCS — Batting / Fielding

Year Tm	Age	G	AB	H	2B	3B	HR	TB	R	RBI	GW	TBB	IBB	SO	HBP	SH	SF	SB	CS	SB%	GDP	Avg	OBP	SLG	Pos	G	PO	A	E	DP	FPct
1983 Bal	28	2	0	0	0	0	0	0	0	0	0	0	0	0	0	0	0	0	0	—	0	—	—	—	P	2	2	0	0	0	1.000

World Series — Batting / Fielding

Year Tm	Age	G	AB	H	2B	3B	HR	TB	R	RBI	GW	TBB	IBB	SO	HBP	SH	SF	SB	CS	SB%	GDP	Avg	OBP	SLG	Pos	G	PO	A	E	DP	FPct
1979 Bal	24	1	1	0	0	0	0	0	0	0	0	0	0	1	0	0	0	0	0	—	0	.000	.000	.000	P	1	1	2	0	0	1.000
1983 Bal	28	3	2	0	0	0	0	0	0	0	0	0	0	1	0	0	0	0	0	—	1	.000	.000	.000	P	3	0	0	0	0	—
WS Totals		4	3	0	0	0	0	0	0	0	0	0	0	2	0	0	0	0	0	—	1	.000	.000	.000	P	4	1	2	0	0	1.000
Postseason Totals		6	3	0	0	0	0	0	0	0	0	0	0	2	0	0	0	0	0	—	1	.000	.000	.000	P	6	3	2	0	0	1.000

DAVE STIEB—David Andrew Stieb—Throws: Right; Bats: Right

Ht: 6'0"; Wt: 185 lbs; Born: 7/22/1957 in Santa Ana, California; Debut: 6/29/1979

LCS — Pitching

Year Tm	Age	G	GS	CG	GF	IP	BFP	H	R	ER	HR	SH	SF	HB	TBB	IBB	SO	WP	Bk	W	L	Pct	ShO	Sv-Op	Hld	OAvg	OOBP	ERA
1985 Tor	28	3	3	0	0	20.1	81	11	7	7	1	1	0	1	10	2	18	0	0	1	1	.500	0	0- 0	0	.159	.275	3.10
1989 Tor	32	2	2	0	0	11.1	51	12	8	8	2	1	0	0	6	0	10	0	0	0	2	.000	0	0- 0	0	.273	.360	6.35
LCS Totals		5	5	0	0	31.2	264	23	15	15	3	2	0	1	16	2	28	0	0	1	3	.250	0	0-0	0	.204	.308	4.26

LCS — Batting / Fielding

Year Tm	Age	G	AB	H	2B	3B	HR	TB	R	RBI	GW	TBB	IBB	SO	HBP	SH	SF	SB	CS	SB%	GDP	Avg	OBP	SLG	Pos	G	PO	A	E	DP	FPct
1985 Tor	28	3	0	0	0	0	0	0	0	0	0	0	0	0	0	0	0	0	0	—	0	—	—	—	P	3	1	3	0	0	1.000
1989 Tor	32	2	0	0	0	0	0	0	0	0	0	0	0	0	0	0	0	0	0	—	0	—	—	—	P	2	0	1	0	0	1.000
LCS Totals		5	0	0	0	0	0	0	0	0	0	0	0	0	0	0	0	0	0	—	0	—	—	—	P	5	1	4	0	0	1.000

BOB STINSON—Gorrell Robert Stinson—Bats: Both; Throws: Right

Ht: 5'11"; Wt: 180 lbs; Born: 10/11/1945 in Elkin, North Carolina; Debut: 9/23/1969

LCS — Batting / Fielding

Year Tm	Age	G	AB	H	2B	3B	HR	TB	R	RBI	GW	TBB	IBB	SO	HBP	SH	SF	SB	CS	SB%	GDP	Avg	OBP	SLG	Pos	G	PO	A	E	DP	FPct
1976 KC	30	2	1	0	0	0	0	0	0	0	0	0	0	0	0	0	0	0	0	—	0	.000	.000	.000	C	1	0	0	0	0	—

SNUFFY STIRNWEISS—George Henry Stirnweiss—Bats: Right; Throws: Right

Ht: 5'8"; Wt: 175 lbs; Born: 10/26/1918 in New York, New York; Debut: 4/22/1943; Died: 9/15/1958

World Series — Batting / Fielding

Year Tm	Age	G	AB	H	2B	3B	HR	TB	R	RBI	GW	TBB	IBB	SO	HBP	SH	SF	SB	CS	SB%	GDP	Avg	OBP	SLG	Pos	G	PO	A	E	DP	FPct
1943 NYA	24	1	1	0	0	0	0	0	1	0	0	0	0	0	0	0	0	0	0	—	0	.000	.000	.000	—						
1947 NYA	28	7	27	7	0	1	0	9	3	3	0	8	0	8	0	0	0	0	0	—	0	.259	.429	.333	2B	7	17	18	0	2	1.000
1949 NYA	30	1	0	0	0	0	0	0	0	0	0	0	0	0	0	0	0	0	0	—	0	—	—	—	—						
WS Totals		9	28	7	0	1	0	9	4	3	0	8	0	8	0	0	0	0	0	—	0	.250	.417	.321	2B	7	17	18	0	2	1.000

MILT STOCK—Milton Joseph Stock—Bats: Right; Throws: Right

Ht: 5'8"; Wt: 154 lbs; Born: 7/11/1893 in Chicago, Illinois; Debut: 9/29/1913; Died: 7/16/1977

World Series — Batting / Fielding

Year Tm	Age	G	AB	H	2B	3B	HR	TB	R	RBI	GW	TBB	IBB	SO	HBP	SH	SF	SB	CS	SB%	GDP	Avg	OBP	SLG	Pos	G	PO	A	E	DP	FPct
1915 Phi	22	5	17	2	1	0	0	3	1	0	0	1	0	0	1	1	0	0	0	—	0	.118	.211	.176	3B	5	1	8	0	0	1.000

KEVIN STOCKER—Kevin Douglas Stocker—Bats: Both; Throws: Right

Ht: 6'1"; Wt: 175 lbs; Born: 2/13/1970 in Spokane, Washington; Debut: 7/7/1993

LCS — Batting / Fielding

Year Tm	Age	G	AB	H	2B	3B	HR	TB	R	RBI	GW	TBB	IBB	SO	HBP	SH	SF	SB	CS	SB%	GDP	Avg	OBP	SLG	Pos	G	PO	A	E	DP	FPct
1993 Phi	23	6	22	4	1	0	0	5	0	1	0	2	2	5	0	0	1	0	0	—	0	.182	.240	.227	SS	6	9	14	1	1	.958

World Series — Batting / Fielding

Year Tm	Age	G	AB	H	2B	3B	HR	TB	R	RBI	GW	TBB	IBB	SO	HBP	SH	SF	SB	CS	SB%	GDP	Avg	OBP	SLG	Pos	G	PO	A	E	DP	FPct
1993 Phi	23	6	19	4	1	0	0	5	1	1	0	5	0	5	0	0	0	0	1	.00	0	.211	.375	.263	SS	6	8	13	0	4	1.000
Postseason Totals		12	41	8	2	0	0	10	1	2	0	7	2	10	0	0	1	0	1	.00	0	.195	.306	.244	SS	12	17	27	1	5	.978

TIM STODDARD—Timothy Paul Stoddard—Throws: Right; Bats: Right

Ht: 6'7"; Wt: 230 lbs; Born: 1/24/1953 in East Chicago, Indiana; Debut: 9/7/1975

LCS — Pitching

Year Tm	Age	G	GS	CG	GF	IP	BFP	H	R	ER	HR	SH	SF	HB	TBB	IBB	SO	WP	Bk	W	L	Pct	ShO	Sv-Op	Hld	OAvg	OOBP	ERA
1984 ChN	31	2	0	0	1	2.0	9	1	2	1	0	0	0	0	2	1	2	0	0	0	0	—	0	0- 0	0	.143	.333	4.50

World Series — Pitching

Year Tm	Age	G	GS	CG	GF	IP	BFP	H	R	ER	HR	SH	SF	HB	TBB	IBB	SO	WP	Bk	W	L	Pct	ShO	Sv-Op	Hld	OAvg	OOBP	ERA
1979 Bal	26	4	0	0	2	5.0	21	6	3	3	0	0	0	0	1	0	3	0	0	1	0	1.000	0	0- 0	0	.300	.333	5.40
Postseason Totals		6	0	0	3	7.0	60	7	5	4	0	0	0	0	3	1	5	0	0	1	0	1.000	0	0-0	0	.259	.333	5.14

LCS — Batting / Fielding

Year Tm	Age	G	AB	H	2B	3B	HR	TB	R	RBI	GW	TBB	IBB	SO	HBP	SH	SF	SB	CS	SB%	GDP	Avg	OBP	SLG	Pos	G	PO	A	E	DP	FPct
1984 ChN	31	2	0	0	0	0	0	0	0	0	0	0	0	0	0	0	0	0	0	—	0	—	—	—	P	2	1	1	0	0	1.000

World Series — Batting / Fielding

Year Tm	Age	G	AB	H	2B	3B	HR	TB	R	RBI	GW	TBB	IBB	SO	HBP	SH	SF	SB	CS	SB%	GDP	Avg	OBP	SLG	Pos	G	PO	A	E	DP	FPct
1979 Bal	26	4	1	1	0	0	0	1	0	1	0	0	0	0	0	0	0	0	0	—	0	1.000	1.000	1.000	P	4	1	4	1	0	.833
Postseason Totals		6	1	1	0	0	0	1	0	1	0	0	0	0	0	0	0	0	0	—	0	1.000	1.000	1.000	P	6	2	5	1	0	.875

GEORGE STONE—George Heard Stone—Throws: Left; Bats: Left

Ht: 6'3"; Wt: 205 lbs; Born: 7/9/1946 in Ruston, Louisiana; Debut: 9/15/1967

LCS — Pitching

Year Tm	Age	G	GS	CG	GF	IP	BFP	H	R	ER	HR	SH	SF	HB	TBB	IBB	SO	WP	Bk	W	L	Pct	ShO	Sv-Op	Hld	OAvg	OOBP	ERA
1969 Atl	23	1	0	0	0	1.0	5	2	1	1	0	1	0	0	0	0	0	0	0	0	0	—	0	0- 0	0	.500	.500	9.00
1973 NYN	27	1	1	0	0	6.2	23	3	1	1	1	0	0	0	2	0	4	0	0	0	0	—	0	0- 0	0	.143	.217	1.35
LCS Totals		2	1	0	0	7.2	56	5	2	2	1	1	0	0	2	0	4	0	0	0	0	—	0	0-0	0	.200	.259	2.35

World Series — Pitching

Year Tm	Age	G	GS	CG	GF	IP	BFP	H	R	ER	HR	SH	SF	HB	TBB	IBB	SO	WP	Bk	W	L	Pct	ShO	Sv-Op	Hld	OAvg	OOBP	ERA
1973 NYN	27	2	0	0	2	3.0	14	4	0	0	0	0	0	0	1	0	3	0	0	0	0	—	0	1- 1	0	.308	.357	0.00
Postseason Totals		4	1	0	2	10.2	84	9	2	2	1	1	0	0	3	0	7	0	0	0	0	—	0	1-1	0	.237	.293	1.69

LCS — Batting / Fielding

Year Tm	Age	G	AB	H	2B	3B	HR	TB	R	RBI	GW	TBB	IBB	SO	HBP	SH	SF	SB	CS	SB%	GDP	Avg	OBP	SLG	Pos	G	PO	A	E	DP	FPct
1969 Atl	23	1	1	0	0	0	0	0	0	0	0	0	0	1	0	0	0	0	0	—	0	.000	.000	.000	P	1	1	1	0	0	1.000
1973 NYN	27	1	1	0	0	0	0	0	0	0	0	1	0	1	0	0	0	0	0	—	0	.000	.500	.000	P	1	1	2	0	0	1.000
LCS Totals		2	2	0	0	0	0	0	0	0	0	1	0	2	0	0	0	0	0	—	0	.000	.333	.000	P	2	2	3	0	0	1.000

World Series — Batting / Fielding

Year Tm	Age	G	AB	H	2B	3B	HR	TB	R	RBI	GW	TBB	IBB	SO	HBP	SH	SF	SB	CS	SB%	GDP	Avg	OBP	SLG	Pos	G	PO	A	E	DP	FPct
1973 NYN	27	2	0	0	0	0	0	0	0	0	0	0	0	0	0	0	0	0	0	—	0	—	—	—	P	2	0	0	0	0	—
Postseason Totals		4	2	0	0	0	0	0	0	0	0	1	0	2	0	0	0	0	0	—	0	.000	.333	.000	P	4	2	3	0	0	1.000

STEVE STONE—Steven Michael Stone—Throws: Right; Bats: Right

Ht: 5'10"; Wt: 175 lbs; Born: 7/14/1947 in Euclid, Ohio; Debut: 4/8/1971

World Series — Pitching

Year Tm	Age	G	GS	CG	GF	IP	BFP	H	R	ER	HR	SH	SF	HB	TBB	IBB	SO	WP	Bk	W	L	Pct	ShO	Sv-Op	Hld	OAvg	OOBP	ERA
1979 Bal	32	1	0	0	0	2.0	12	4	2	2	0	0	0	0	2	1	2	0	0	0	0	—	0	0- 0	0	.400	.500	9.00

World Series — Batting / Fielding

Year Tm	Age	G	AB	H	2B	3B	HR	TB	R	RBI	GW	TBB	IBB	SO	HBP	SH	SF	SB	CS	SB%	GDP	Avg	OBP	SLG	Pos	G	PO	A	E	DP	FPct
1979 Bal	32	1	0	0	0	0	0	0	0	0	0	0	0	0	0	0	0	0	0	—	0	—	—	—	P	1	0	0	0	0	—

MEL STOTTLEMYRE—Melvin Leon Stottlemyre—Throws: Right; Bats: Right

Ht: 6'1"; Wt: 178 lbs; Born: 11/13/1941 in Hazleton, Missouri; Debut: 8/12/1964

World Series — Pitching

Year Tm	Age	G	GS	CG	GF	IP	BFP	H	R	ER	HR	SH	SF	HB	TBB	IBB	SO	WP	Bk	W	L	Pct	ShO	Sv-Op	Hld	OAvg	OOBP	ERA
1964 NYA	22	3	3	1	0	20.0	84	18	8	7	0	1	0	0	6	0	12	0	0	1	1	.500	0	0- 0	0	.237	.293	3.15

World Series — Batting / Fielding

Year Tm	Age	G	AB	H	2B	3B	HR	TB	R	RBI	GW	TBB	IBB	SO	HBP	SH	SF	SB	CS	SB%	GDP	Avg	OBP	SLG	Pos	G	PO	A	E	DP	FPct
1964 NYA	22	3	8	1	0	0	0	1	0	0	0	0	0	6	0	0	0	0	0	—	0	.125	.125	.125	P	3	2	5	0	0	1.000

TODD STOTTLEMYRE—Todd Vernon Stottlemyre—Throws: Right; Bats: Left

Ht: 6'3"; Wt: 195 lbs; Born: 5/20/1965 in Sunnyside, Washington; Debut: 4/6/1988

Division Series — Pitching

Year Tm	Age	G	GS	CG	GF	IP	BFP	H	R	ER	HR	SH	SF	HB	TBB	IBB	SO	WP	Bk	W	L	Pct	ShO	Sv-Op	Hld	OAvg	OOBP	ERA
1996 StL	31	1	1	0	0	6.2	28	5	1	1	1	0	0	1	2	0	7	0	0	1	0	1.000	0	0- 0	0	.200	.286	1.35

LCS — Pitching

Year Tm	Age	G	GS	CG	GF	IP	BFP	H	R	ER	HR	SH	SF	HB	TBB	IBB	SO	WP	Bk	W	L	Pct	ShO	Sv-Op	Hld	OAvg	OOBP	ERA
1989 Tor	24	1	1	0	0	5.0	22	7	4	4	1	0	0	0	2	0	3	0	0	0	1	.000	0	0- 0	0	.350	.409	7.20
1991 Tor	26	1	1	0	0	3.2	19	7	4	4	1	0	0	1	1	0	3	0	0	0	1	.000	0	0- 0	0	.412	.474	9.82
1992 Tor	27	1	0	0	0	3.2	14	3	1	1	0	0	0	0	0	0	1	0	0	0	0	—	0	0- 0	0	.214	.214	2.45
1993 Tor	28	1	1	0	0	6.0	26	6	5	5	2	0	0	0	4	0	4	0	1	0	1	.000	0	0- 0	0	.273	.385	7.50
1996 StL	31	3	2	0	1	8.0	43	15	11	11	1	0	0	1	3	0	11	0	0	1	1	.500	0	0-0	0	.385	.442	12.38
LCS Totals		7	5	0	1	26.1	248	38	25	25	5	0	0	2	10	0	22	0	1	1	4	.200	0	0-0	0	.339	.403	8.54

World Series — Pitching

Year Tm	Age	G	GS	CG	GF	IP	BFP	H	R	ER	HR	SH	SF	HB	TBB	IBB	SO	WP	Bk	W	L	Pct	ShO	Sv-Op	Hld	OAvg	OOBP	ERA
1992 Tor	27	4	0	0	1	3.2	14	4	0	0	0	0	0	0	0	0	4	0	0	0	0	—	0	0- 0	1	.286	.286	0.00
1993 Tor	28	1	1	0	0	2.0	13	3	6	6	1	0	0	0	4	0	1	0	0	0	0	—	0	0- 0	0	.333	.538	27.00
WS Totals		5	1	0	1	5.2	54	7	6	6	1	0	0	0	4	0	5	0	0	0	0	—	0	0-0	1	.304	.407	9.53
Postseason Totals		13	7	0	2	38.2	358	50	32	32	7	0	0	3	16	0	34	0	1	2	4	.333	0	0-0	1	.313	.385	7.45

Division Series — Batting / Fielding

Year Tm	Age	G	AB	H	2B	3B	HR	TB	R	RBI	GW	TBB	IBB	SO	HBP	SH	SF	SB	CS	SB%	GDP	Avg	OBP	SLG	Pos	G	PO	A	E	DP	FPct
1996 StL	31	1	2	0	0	0	0	0	0	0	0	0	0	2	0	0	0	0	0	—	0	.000	.000	.000	P	1	0	0	0	0	—

LCS — Batting / Fielding

Year Tm	Age	G	AB	H	2B	3B	HR	TB	R	RBI	GW	TBB	IBB	SO	HBP	SH	SF	SB	CS	SB%	GDP	Avg	OBP	SLG	Pos	G	PO	A	E	DP	FPct
1989 Tor	24	1	0	0	0	0	0	0	0	0	0	0	0	0	0	0	0	0	0	—	0	—	—	—	P	1	0	0	0	0	—
1991 Tor	26	1	0	0	0	0	0	0	0	0	0	0	0	0	0	0	0	0	0	—	0	—	—	—	P	1	1	0	0	0	1.000
1992 Tor	27	1	0	0	0	0	0	0	0	0	0	0	0	0	0	0	0	0	0	—	0	—	—	—	P	1	0	0	0	0	—
1993 Tor	28	1	0	0	0	0	0	0	0	0	0	0	0	0	0	0	0	0	0	—	0	—	—	—	P	1	2	0	0	0	1.000
1996 StL	31	3	2	0	0	0	0	0	0	0	0	0	0	0	0	0	0	0	0	—	0	.000	.000	.000	P	3	0	0	0	0	—
LCS Totals		7	2	0	0	0	0	0	0	0	0	0	0	0	0	0	0	0	0	—	0	.000	.000	.000	P	7	3	0	0	0	1.000

World Series — Batting / Fielding

Year Tm	Age	G	AB	H	2B	3B	HR	TB	R	RBI	GW	TBB	IBB	SO	HBP	SH	SF	SB	CS	SB%	GDP	Avg	OBP	SLG	Pos	G	PO	A	E	DP	FPct
1992 Tor	27	4	0	0	0	0	0	0	0	0	0	0	0	0	0	0	0	0	0	—	0	—	—	—	P	4	0	0	0	0	—
1993 Tor	28	1	0	0	0	0	0	0	0	0	0	1	0	0	0	0	0	0	0	—	0	—	1.000	—	P	1	0	0	0	0	—
WS Totals		5	0	0	0	0	0	0	0	0	0	1	0	0	0	0	0	0	0	—	0	—	1.000	—	P	5	0	0	0	0	—
Postseason Totals		13	4	0	0	0	0	0	0	0	0	1	0	2	0	0	0	0	0	—	0	.000	.200	.000	P	13	3	0	0	0	1.000

LES STRAKER—Lester Paul Straker—Throws: Right; Bats: Right

Ht: 6'1"; Wt: 193 lbs; Born: 10/10/1959 in Ciudad Bolivar, Venezuela; Debut: 4/11/1987

LCS — Pitching

Year Tm	Age	G	GS	CG	GF	IP	BFP	H	R	ER	HR	SH	SF	HB	TBB	IBB	SO	WP	Bk	W	L	Pct	ShO	Sv-Op	Hld	OAvg	OOBP	ERA
1987 Min	27	1	1	0	0	2.2	15	3	5	5	0	0	0	0	4	0	1	0	1	0	0	—	0	0- 0	0	.273	.467	16.88

World Series — Pitching

Year Tm	Age	G	GS	CG	GF	IP	BFP	H	R	ER	HR	SH	SF	HB	TBB	IBB	SO	WP	Bk	W	L	Pct	ShO	Sv-Op	Hld	OAvg	OOBP	ERA
1987 Min	27	2	2	0	0	9.0	39	9	4	4	1	0	0	0	3	0	6	0	1	0	0	—	0	0- 0	0	.250	.308	4.00
Postseason Totals		3	3	0	0	11.2	108	12	9	9	1	0	0	0	7	0	7	0	2	0	0	—	0	0-0	0	.255	.352	6.94

LCS — Batting / Fielding

Year Tm	Age	G	AB	H	2B	3B	HR	TB	R	RBI	GW	TBB	IBB	SO	HBP	SH	SF	SB	CS	SB%	GDP	Avg	OBP	SLG	Pos	G	PO	A	E	DP	FPct
1987 Min	27	1	0	0	0	0	0	0	0	0	0	0	0	0	0	0	0	0	0	—	0	—	—	—	P	1	0	2	0	0	1.000

World Series — Batting / Fielding

Year Tm	Age	G	AB	H	2B	3B	HR	TB	R	RBI	GW	TBB	IBB	SO	HBP	SH	SF	SB	CS	SB%	GDP	Avg	OBP	SLG	Pos	G	PO	A	E	DP	FPct
1987 Min	27	2	2	0	0	0	0	0	0	0	0	0	0	2	0	0	0	0	0	—	0	.000	.000	.000	P	2	1	0	0	0	1.000
Postseason Totals		3	2	0	0	0	0	0	0	0	0	0	0	2	0	0	0	0	0	—	0	.000	.000	.000	P	3	1	2	0	0	1.000

SAMMY STRANG—Samuel Nicklin Strang—Nickname: The Dixie Thrush—Bats: Both; Throws: Right

Ht: 5'8"; Wt: 160 lbs; Born: 12/16/1876 in Chattanooga, Tennessee; Debut: 7/10/1896; Died: 3/13/1932

World Series — Batting / Fielding

Year Tm	Age	G	AB	H	2B	3B	HR	TB	R	RBI	GW	TBB	IBB	SO	HBP	SH	SF	SB	CS	SB%	GDP	Avg	OBP	SLG	Pos	G	PO	A	E	DP	FPct
1905 NYG	28	1	1	0	0	0	0	0	0	0	0	0	0	1	0	0	0	0	0	—	0	.000	.000	.000	—						

DOUG STRANGE—Joseph Douglas Strange—Bats: Both; Throws: Right

Ht: 6'2"; Wt: 170 lbs; Born: 4/13/1964 in Greenville, South Carolina; Debut: 7/13/1989

Division Series — Batting / Fielding

Year Tm	Age	G	AB	H	2B	3B	HR	TB	R	RBI	GW	TBB	IBB	SO	HBP	SH	SF	SB	CS	SB%	GDP	Avg	OBP	SLG	Pos	G	PO	A	E	DP	FPct
1995 Sea	31	2	4	0	0	0	0	0	0	1	0	1	0	1	0	0	0	0	0	—	0	.000	.200	.000	3B	2	0	0	0	0	—

LCS — Batting / Fielding

Year Tm	Age	G	AB	H	2B	3B	HR	TB	R	RBI	GW	TBB	IBB	SO	HBP	SH	SF	SB	CS	SB%	GDP	Avg	OBP	SLG	Pos	G	PO	A	E	DP	FPct
1995 Sea	31	4	4	0	0	0	0	0	0	0	0	0	0	2	0	1	0	0	0	—	0	.000	.000	.000	3B	2	2	3	0	0	1.000
Postseason Totals		6	8	0	0	0	0	0	0	1	0	1	0	3	0	1	0	0	0	—	0	.000	.111	.000	3B	4	2	3	0	0	1.000

DARRYL STRAWBERRY—Darryl Eugene Strawberry—Nickname: Straw—Bats: Left; Throws: Left

Ht: 6'6"; Wt: 190 lbs; Born: 3/12/1962 in Los Angeles, California; Debut: 5/6/1983

Division Series — Batting / Fielding

Year Tm	Age	G	AB	H	2B	3B	HR	TB	R	RBI	GW	TBB	IBB	SO	HBP	SH	SF	SB	CS	SB%	GDP	Avg	OBP	SLG	Pos	G	PO	A	E	DP	FPct
1995 NYA	33	2	2	0	0	0	0	0	0	0	0	0	0	1	0	0	0	0	0	—	0	.000	.000	.000	—						
1996 NYA	34	2	5	0	0	0	0	0	0	0	0	0	0	2	0	0	0	0	0	—	0	.000	.000	.000	—						
DS Totals		4	7	0	0	0	0	0	0	0	0	0	0	3	0	0	0	0	0	—	0	.000	.000	.000	—	0	0	0	0	0	—

LCS — Batting / Fielding

Year Tm	Age	G	AB	H	2B	3B	HR	TB	R	RBI	GW	TBB	IBB	SO	HBP	SH	SF	SB	CS	SB%	GDP	Avg	OBP	SLG	Pos	G	PO	A	E	DP	FPct
1986 NYN	24	6	22	5	1	0	2	12	4	5	0	3	0	12	0	0	1	1	0	1.00	0	.227	.308	.545	OF	6	9	0	0	0	1.000
1988 NYN	26	7	30	9	2	0	1	14	5	6	0	2	0	5	0	0	0	0	1	.00	1	.300	.344	.467	OF	7	11	0	0	0	1.000
1996 NYA	34	4	12	5	0	0	3	14	4	5	0	2	0	2	0	0	0	0	0	—	0	.417	.500	1.167	OF	4	5	0	0	0	1.000
LCS Totals		17	64	19	3	0	6	40	13	16	0	7	0	19	0	0	1	1	1	.50	1	.297	.361	.625	OF	17	25	0	0	0	1.000

World Series — Batting / Fielding

Year Tm	Age	G	AB	H	2B	3B	HR	TB	R	RBI	GW	TBB	IBB	SO	HBP	SH	SF	SB	CS	SB%	GDP	Avg	OBP	SLG	Pos	G	PO	A	E	DP	FPct
1986 NYN	24	7	24	5	1	0	1	9	4	1	0	4	0	6	0	0	0	3	1	.75	0	.208	.321	.375	OF	7	19	0	0	0	1.000
1996 NYA	34	5	16	3	0	0	0	3	0	1	0	4	1	6	0	0	0	0	0	—	0	.188	.350	.188	OF	5	11	0	0	0	1.000
WS Totals		12	40	8	1	0	1	12	4	2	0	8	1	12	0	0	0	3	1	.75	0	.200	.333	.300	OF	12	30	0	0	0	1.000
Postseason Totals		33	111	27	4	0	7	52	17	18	0	15	1	34	0	0	1	4	2	.67	1	.243	.331	.468	OF	29	55	0	0	0	1.000

GEORGE STRICKLAND—George Bevan Strickland—Nickname: Bo—Bats: Right; Throws: Right

Ht: 6'1"; Wt: 175 lbs; Born: 1/10/1926 in New Orleans, Louisiana; Debut: 5/7/1950

World Series — Batting / Fielding

Year Tm	Age	G	AB	H	2B	3B	HR	TB	R	RBI	GW	TBB	IBB	SO	HBP	SH	SF	SB	CS	SB%	GDP	Avg	OBP	SLG	Pos	G	PO	A	E	DP	FPct
1954 Cle	28	3	9	0	0	0	0	0	0	0	0	0	0	2	0	0	0	0	0	—	0	.000	.000	.000	SS	3	6	8	1	1	.933

AMOS STRUNK—Amos Aaron Strunk—Bats: Left; Throws: Left

Ht: 5'11"; Wt: 175 lbs; Born: 1/22/1889 in Philadelphia, Pennsylvania; Debut: 9/24/1908; Died: 7/22/1979

World Series — Batting / Fielding

Year Tm	Age	G	AB	H	2B	3B	HR	TB	R	RBI	GW	TBB	IBB	SO	HBP	SH	SF	SB	CS	SB%	GDP	Avg	OBP	SLG	Pos	G	PO	A	E	DP	FPct
1910 Phi	21	4	18	5	1	1	0	8	2	2	0	2	0	5	0	0	0	0	1	.00	0	.278	.350	.444	OF	4	7	0	1	0	.875
1911 Phi	22	1	0	0	0	0	0	0	0	0	0	0	0	0	0	0	0	0	0	—	0	—	—	—	—						
1913 Phi	24	5	17	2	0	0	0	2	3	0	0	2	1	2	0	1	0	0	0	—	0	.118	.211	.118	OF	5	14	0	0	0	1.000
1914 Phi	25	2	7	2	0	0	0	2	0	0	0	0	0	2	0	0	0	0	0	—	0	.286	.286	.286	OF	2	4	0	0	0	1.000
1918 Bos	29	6	23	4	1	1	0	7	1	0	0	0	0	5	0	1	0	0	1	.00	0	.174	.174	.304	OF	6	8	2	0	0	1.000
WS Totals		18	65	13	2	2	0	19	6	2	0	4	1	14	0	2	0	0	2	.00	0	.200	.246	.292	OF	17	33	2	1	0	.972

DICK STUART—Richard Lee Stuart—Nickname: Dr. Strangeglove—Bats: Right; Throws: Right

Ht: 6'4"; Wt: 212 lbs; Born: 11/7/1932 in San Francisco, California; Debut: 7/10/1958

World Series — Batting / Fielding

Year Tm	Age	G	AB	H	2B	3B	HR	TB	R	RBI	GW	TBB	IBB	SO	HBP	SH	SF	SB	CS	SB%	GDP	Avg	OBP	SLG	Pos	G	PO	A	E	DP	FPct
1960 Pit	27	5	20	3	0	0	0	3	0	0	0	0	0	3	0	0	0	0	0	—	0	.150	.150	.150	1B	5	45	0	0	6	1.000
1966 LA	33	2	2	0	0	0	0	0	0	0	0	0	0	1	0	0	0	0	0	—	0	.000	.000	.000	—						
WS Totals		7	22	3	0	0	0	3	0	0	0	0	0	4	0	0	0	0	0	—	0	.136	.136	.136	1B	5	45	0	0	6	1.000

FRANKLIN STUBBS—Franklin Lee Stubbs—Bats: Left; Throws: Left

Ht: 6'2"; Wt: 215 lbs; Born: 10/21/1960 in Richland, North Carolina; Debut: 4/28/1984

LCS — Batting / Fielding

Year Tm	Age	G	AB	H	2B	3B	HR	TB	R	RBI	GW	TBB	IBB	SO	HBP	SH	SF	SB	CS	SB%	GDP	Avg	OBP	SLG	Pos	G	PO	A	E	DP	FPct
1988 LA	27	4	8	2	0	0	0	2	0	0	0	0	0	4	0	0	0	0	0	—	0	.250	.250	.250	1B	3	16	2	0	2	1.000

World Series — Batting / Fielding

Year Tm	Age	G	AB	H	2B	3B	HR	TB	R	RBI	GW	TBB	IBB	SO	HBP	SH	SF	SB	CS	SB%	GDP	Avg	OBP	SLG	Pos	G	PO	A	E	DP	FPct
1988 LA	27	5	17	5	2	0	0	7	3	2	1	1	0	3	0	0	0	0	0	—	0	.294	.333	.412	1B	5	34	0	0	3	1.000
Postseason Totals		9	25	7	2	0	0	9	3	2	1	1	0	7	0	0	0	0	0	—	0	.280	.308	.360	1B	8	50	2	0	5	1.000

JOHN STUPER—John Anton Stuper—Throws: Right; Bats: Right

Ht: 6'2"; Wt: 200 lbs; Born: 5/9/1957 in Butler, Pennsylvania; Debut: 6/1/1982

LCS — Pitching

Year Tm	Age	G	GS	CG	GF	IP	BFP	H	R	ER	HR	SH	SF	HB	TBB	IBB	SO	WP	Bk	W	L	Pct	ShO	Sv-Op	Hld	OAvg	OOBP	ERA
1982 StL	25	1	1	0	0	6.0	23	4	3	2	0	1	1	0	1	0	4	0	0	0	0	—	0	0- 0	0	.200	.227	3.00

World Series — Pitching

Year Tm	Age	G	GS	CG	GF	IP	BFP	H	R	ER	HR	SH	SF	HB	TBB	IBB	SO	WP	Bk	W	L	Pct	ShO	Sv-Op	Hld	OAvg	OOBP	ERA
1982 StL	25	2	2	1	0	13.0	52	10	5	5	1	0	0	0	5	0	5	3	0	1	0	1.000	0	0- 0	0	.213	.288	3.46
Postseason Totals		3	3	1	0	19.0	150	14	8	7	1	1	1	0	6	0	9	3	0	1	0	1.000	0	0-0	0	.209	.270	3.32

LCS — Batting / Fielding

Year Tm	Age	G	AB	H	2B	3B	HR	TB	R	RBI	GW	TBB	IBB	SO	HBP	SH	SF	SB	CS	SB%	GDP	Avg	OBP	SLG	Pos	G	PO	A	E	DP	FPct
1982 StL	25	1	1	0	0	0	0	0	0	0	0	0	0	0	0	1	0	0	0	—	0	.000	.000	.000	P	1	0	0	0	0	—

World Series — Batting / Fielding

Year Tm	Age	G	AB	H	2B	3B	HR	TB	R	RBI	GW	TBB	IBB	SO	HBP	SH	SF	SB	CS	SB%	GDP	Avg	OBP	SLG	Pos	G	PO	A	E	DP	FPct
1982 StL	25	2	0	0	0	0	0	0	0	0	0	0	0	0	0	0	0	0	0	—	0	—	—	—	P	2	1	1	0	0	1.000
Postseason Totals		3	1	0	0	0	0	0	0	0	0	0	0	0	0	1	0	0	0	—	0	.000	.000	.000	P	3	1	1	0	0	1.000

TOM STURDIVANT—Thomas Virgil Sturdivant—Nicknames: Smoke, Snake—Throws: Right; Bats: Left

Ht: 6'0"; Wt: 170 lbs; Born: 4/28/1930 in Gordon, Kansas; Debut: 4/14/1955

World Series — Pitching

Year Tm	Age	G	GS	CG	GF	IP	BFP	H	R	ER	HR	SH	SF	HB	TBB	IBB	SO	WP	Bk	W	L	Pct	ShO	Sv-Op	Hld	OAvg	OOBP	ERA
1955 NYA	25	2	0	0	2	3.0	16	5	2	2	0	1	0	0	2	1	0	0	0	0	0	—	0	0- 0	0	.385	.467	6.00
1956 NYA	26	2	1	1	0	9.2	43	8	3	3	0	0	0	0	8	0	9	0	0	1	0	1.000	0	0- 0	0	.229	.372	2.79
1957 NYA	27	2	1	0	0	6.0	24	6	4	4	2	2	0	0	1	0	2	0	0	0	0	—	0	0- 0	0	.286	.318	6.00
WS Totals		6	2	1	2	18.2	166	19	9	9	2	3	0	0	11	1	11	0	0	1	0	1.000	0	0-0	0	.275	.375	4.34

World Series — Batting / Fielding

Year Tm	Age	G	AB	H	2B	3B	HR	TB	R	RBI	GW	TBB	IBB	SO	HBP	SH	SF	SB	CS	SB%	GDP	Avg	OBP	SLG	Pos	G	PO	A	E	DP	FPct
1955 NYA	25	2	0	0	0	0	0	0	0	0	0	0	0	0	0	0	0	0	0	—	0	—	—	—	P	2	0	1	0	0	1.000
1956 NYA	26	2	3	1	0	0	0	1	0	0	0	0	0	1	0	0	0	0	0	—	0	.333	.333	.333	P	2	2	0	0	0	1.000
1957 NYA	27	2	1	0	0	0	0	0	0	0	0	0	0	0	0	0	0	0	0	—	0	.000	.000	.000	P	2	0	1	0	0	1.000
WS Totals		6	4	1	0	0	0	1	0	0	0	0	0	1	0	0	0	0	0	—	0	.250	.250	.250	P	6	2	2	0	0	1.000

JOHNNY STURM—John Peter Joseph Sturm—Bats: Left; Throws: Left

Ht: 6'1"; Wt: 185 lbs; Born: 1/23/1916 in St. Louis, Missouri; Debut: 4/15/1941

World Series — Batting / Fielding

Year Tm	Age	G	AB	H	2B	3B	HR	TB	R	RBI	GW	TBB	IBB	SO	HBP	SH	SF	SB	CS	SB%	GDP	Avg	OBP	SLG	Pos	G	PO	A	E	DP	FPct
1941 NYA	25	5	21	6	0	0	0	6	0	2	0	0	0	2	1	0	0	1	1	.50	0	.286	.318	.286	1B	5	48	1	0	5	1.000

BILLY SULLIVAN—William Joseph Sullivan—Bats: Right; Throws: Right

Ht: 5'9"; Wt: 155 lbs; Born: 2/1/1875 in Oakland, Wisconsin; Debut: 9/13/1899; Died: 1/28/1965

World Series — Batting / Fielding

Year Tm	Age	G	AB	H	2B	3B	HR	TB	R	RBI	GW	TBB	IBB	SO	HBP	SH	SF	SB	CS	SB%	GDP	Avg	OBP	SLG	Pos	G	PO	A	E	DP	FPct
1906 ChA	31	6	21	0	0	0	0	0	0	0	0	0	0	9	0	1	0	0	0	—	0	.000	.000	.000	C	6	35	10	2	1	.957

BILLY SULLIVAN—William Joseph Sullivan—Bats: Left; Throws: Right

Ht: 6'0"; Wt: 170 lbs; Born: 10/23/1910 in Chicago, Illinois; Debut: 6/9/1931; Died: 1/4/1994

World Series — Batting / Fielding

Year Tm	Age	G	AB	H	2B	3B	HR	TB	R	RBI	GW	TBB	IBB	SO	HBP	SH	SF	SB	CS	SB%	GDP	Avg	OBP	SLG	Pos	G	PO	A	E	DP	FPct
1940 Det	29	5	13	2	0	0	0	2	3	0	0	5	2	2	0	0	0	0	0	—	0	.154	.389	.154	C	4	23	2	0	0	1.000

HOMER SUMMA—Homer Wayne Summa—Bats: Left; Throws: Right

Ht: 5'10"; Wt: 170 lbs; Born: 11/3/1898 in Gentry, Missouri; Debut: 9/13/1920; Died: 1/29/1966

World Series — Batting / Fielding

Year Tm	Age	G	AB	H	2B	3B	HR	TB	R	RBI	GW	TBB	IBB	SO	HBP	SH	SF	SB	CS	SB%	GDP	Avg	OBP	SLG	Pos	G	PO	A	E	DP	FPct
1929 Phi	30	1	1	0	0	0	0	0	0	0	0	0	0	1	0	0	0	0	0	—	0	.000	.000	.000	—						

CHAMP SUMMERS—John Junior Summers—Bats: Left; Throws: Right

Ht: 6'2"; Wt: 205 lbs; Born: 6/15/1946 in Bremerton, Washington; Debut: 5/4/1974

LCS — Batting / Fielding

Year Tm	Age	G	AB	H	2B	3B	HR	TB	R	RBI	GW	TBB	IBB	SO	HBP	SH	SF	SB	CS	SB%	GDP	Avg	OBP	SLG	Pos	G	PO	A	E	DP	FPct
1984 SD	38	2	2	0	0	0	0	0	0	0	0	0	0	1	0	0	0	0	0	—	0	.000	.000	.000	—						

World Series — Batting / Fielding

Year Tm	Age	G	AB	H	2B	3B	HR	TB	R	RBI	GW	TBB	IBB	SO	HBP	SH	SF	SB	CS	SB%	GDP	Avg	OBP	SLG	Pos	G	PO	A	E	DP	FPct
1984 SD	38	1	1	0	0	0	0	0	0	0	0	0	0	1	0	0	0	0	0	—	0	.000	.000	.000	—						
Postseason Totals		3	3	0	0	0	0	0	0	0	0	0	0	2	0	0	0	0	0	—	0	.000	.000	.000	—	0	0	0	0	0	—

ED SUMMERS—Oron Edgar Summers—Nicknames: Kickapoo Ed, Chief—Throws: Right; Bats: Both

Ht: 6'2"; Wt: 180 lbs; Born: 12/5/1884 in Ladoga, Indiana; Debut: 4/16/1908; Died: 5/12/1953

World Series — Pitching

Year Tm	Age	G	GS	CG	GF	IP	BFP	H	R	ER	HR	SH	SF	HB	TBB	IBB	SO	WP	Bk	W	L	Pct	ShO	Sv-Op	Hld	OAvg	OOBP	ERA
1908 Det	23	2	1	0	1	14.2	66	18	8	7	0	5	1	0	4	0	7	0	0	0	2	.000	0	0- 0	0	.321	.361	4.30
1909 Det	24	2	2	0	0	7.1	41	13	13	7	1	2	0	1	4	0	4	2	0	0	2	.000	0	0- 0	0	.382	.462	8.59
WS Totals		4	3	0	1	22.0	214	31	21	14	1	7	1	1	8	0	11	2	0	0	4	.000	0	0-0	0	.344	.400	5.73

World Series — Batting / Fielding

Year Tm	Age	G	AB	H	2B	3B	HR	TB	R	RBI	GW	TBB	IBB	SO	HBP	SH	SF	SB	CS	SB%	GDP	Avg	OBP	SLG	Pos	G	PO	A	E	DP	FPct
1908 Det	23	2	5	1	0	0	0	1	0	1	0	0	0	2	0	0	0	0	0	—	0	.200	.200	.200	P	2	0	7	0	0	1.000
1909 Det	24	2	3	0	0	0	0	0	0	0	0	0	0	2	0	0	0	0	0	—	0	.000	.000	.000	P	2	0	2	0	0	1.000
WS Totals		4	8	1	0	0	0	1	0	1	0	0	0	4	0	0	0	0	0	—	0	.125	.125	.125	P	4	0	9	0	0	1.000

JIM SUNDBERG—James Howard Sundberg—Bats: Right; Throws: Right

Ht: 6'0"; Wt: 190 lbs; Born: 5/18/1951 in Galesburg, Illinois; Debut: 4/4/1974

LCS — Batting / Fielding

Year Tm	Age	G	AB	H	2B	3B	HR	TB	R	RBI	GW	TBB	IBB	SO	HBP	SH	SF	SB	CS	SB%	GDP	Avg	OBP	SLG	Pos	G	PO	A	E	DP	FPct
1985 KC	34	7	24	4	1	1	1	10	3	6	1	1	0	7	0	0	0	0	0	—	0	.167	.200	.417	C	7	41	2	1	2	.977

World Series — Batting / Fielding

Year Tm	Age	G	AB	H	2B	3B	HR	TB	R	RBI	GW	TBB	IBB	SO	HBP	SH	SF	SB	CS	SB%	GDP	Avg	OBP	SLG	Pos	G	PO	A	E	DP	FPct
1985 KC	34	7	24	6	2	0	0	8	6	1	0	6	0	4	0	0	0	0	0	—	1	.250	.400	.333	C	7	47	3	0	1	1.000
Postseason Totals		14	48	10	3	1	1	18	9	7	1	7	0	11	0	0	0	0	0	—	1	.208	.309	.375	C	14	88	5	1	3	.989

STEVE SUNDRA—Stephen Richard Sundra—Nickname: Smokey—Throws: Right; Bats: Both

Ht: 6'2"; Wt: 190 lbs; Born: 3/27/1910 in Luxor, Pennsylvania; Debut: 4/17/1936; Died: 3/23/1952

World Series — Pitching

Year Tm	Age	G	GS	CG	GF	IP	BFP	H	R	ER	HR	SH	SF	HB	TBB	IBB	SO	WP	Bk	W	L	Pct	ShO	Sv-Op	Hld	OAvg	OOBP	ERA
1939 NYA	29	1	0	0	0	2.2	14	4	3	0	0	0	0	0	1	0	2	0	0	0	0	—	0	0- 0	0	.308	.357	0.00

World Series — Batting / Fielding

Year Tm	Age	G	AB	H	2B	3B	HR	TB	R	RBI	GW	TBB	IBB	SO	HBP	SH	SF	SB	CS	SB%	GDP	Avg	OBP	SLG	Pos	G	PO	A	E	DP	FPct
1939 NYA	29	1	0	0	0	0	0	0	0	0	0	1	0	0	0	0	0	0	0	—	0	—	1.000	—	P	1	0	0	0	0	—

B.J. SURHOFF—William James Surhoff—Bats: Left; Throws: Right

Ht: 6'1"; Wt: 185 lbs; Born: 8/4/1964 in Bronx, New York; Debut: 4/8/1987

Division Series — Batting / Fielding

Year Tm	Age	G	AB	H	2B	3B	HR	TB	R	RBI	GW	TBB	IBB	SO	HBP	SH	SF	SB	CS	SB%	GDP	Avg	OBP	SLG	Pos	G	PO	A	E	DP	FPct
1996 Bal	32	4	13	5	0	0	3	14	3	5	1	0	0	1	0	0	0	0	0	—	0	.385	.385	1.077	OF	3	6	0	0	0	1.000
1997 Bal	33	3	11	3	1	0	0	4	0	2	0	0	0	2	0	0	0	0	0	—	0	.273	.273	.364	OF	3	1	1	0	0	1.000
DS Totals		7	24	8	1	0	3	18	3	7	1	0	0	3	0	0	0	0	0	—	0	.333	.333	.750	OF	6	7	1	0	0	1.000

LCS — Batting / Fielding

Year Tm	Age	G	AB	H	2B	3B	HR	TB	R	RBI	GW	TBB	IBB	SO	HBP	SH	SF	SB	CS	SB%	GDP	Avg	OBP	SLG	Pos	G	PO	A	E	DP	FPct
1996 Bal	32	5	15	4	0	0	0	4	0	2	0	1	0	2	0	0	1	0	0	—	1	.267	.294	.267	OF	5	11	1	0	0	1.000
1997 Bal	33	6	25	5	2	0	0	7	1	1	0	2	0	2	0	0	0	0	0	—	1	.200	.259	.280	1B	1	3	0	0	0	1.000
																									OF	6	10	0	0	0	1.000
LCS Totals		11	40	9	2	0	0	11	1	3	0	3	0	4	0	0	1	0	0	—	2	.225	.273	.275	OF	11	21	1	0	0	1.000
Postseason Totals		18	64	17	3	0	3	29	4	10	1	3	0	7	0	0	1	0	0	—	2	.266	.294	.453	OF	17	28	2	0	0	1.000

RICK SUTCLIFFE—Richard Lee Sutcliffe—Throws: Right; Bats: Left

Ht: 6'7"; Wt: 215 lbs; Born: 6/21/1956 in Independence, Missouri; Debut: 9/29/1976

LCS — Pitching

Year Tm	Age	G	GS	CG	GF	IP	BFP	H	R	ER	HR	SH	SF	HB	TBB	IBB	SO	WP	Bk	W	L	Pct	ShO	Sv-Op	Hld	OAvg	OOBP	ERA
1984 ChN-*C*	28	2	2	0	0	13.1	58	9	6	5	0	1	2	1	8	0	10	0	0	1	1	.500	0	0- 0	0	.196	.316	3.38
1989 ChN	33	1	1	0	0	6.0	26	5	3	3	0	0	0	0	4	2	2	0	1	0	0	—	0	0- 0	0	.227	.346	4.50
LCS Totals		3	3	0	0	19.1	168	14	9	8	0	1	2	1	12	2	12	0	1	1	1	.500	0	0-0	0	.206	.325	3.72

LCS — Batting / Fielding

Year Tm	Age	G	AB	H	2B	3B	HR	TB	R	RBI	GW	TBB	IBB	SO	HBP	SH	SF	SB	CS	SB%	GDP	Avg	OBP	SLG	Pos	G	PO	A	E	DP	FPct
1984 ChN	28	2	6	3	0	0	1	6	1	1	0	0	0	2	0	0	0	0	0	—	0	.500	.500	1.000	P	2	0	0	0	0	—
1989 ChN	33	1	2	1	1	0	0	2	0	0	0	0	0	0	0	1	0	0	0	—	1	.500	.500	1.000	P	1	0	2	0	0	1.000
LCS Totals		3	8	4	1	0	1	8	1	1	0	0	0	2	0	1	0	0	0	—	1	.500	.500	1.000	P	3	0	2	0	0	1.000

Postseason: Register 2231

BRUCE SUTTER—Howard Bruce Sutter—Throws: Right; Bats: Right
Ht: 6'2"; Wt: 190 lbs; Born: 1/8/1953 in Lancaster, Pennsylvania; Debut: 5/9/1976

LCS — Pitching
Year	Tm	Age	G	GS	CG	GF	IP	BFP	H	R	ER	HR	SH	SF	HB	TBB	IBB	SO	WP	Bk	W	L	Pct	ShO	Sv-Op	Hld	OAvg	OOBP	ERA
1982	StL	29	2	0	0	2	4.1	12	0	0	0	0	0	0	0	0	0	1	0	0	1	0	1.000	0	1-1	0	.000	.000	0.00

World Series — Pitching
Year	Tm	Age	G	GS	CG	GF	IP	BFP	H	R	ER	HR	SH	SF	HB	TBB	IBB	SO	WP	Bk	W	L	Pct	ShO	Sv-Op	Hld	OAvg	OOBP	ERA
1982	StL	29	4	0	0	4	7.2	32	6	4	4	0	0	0	0	3	1	6	0	0	1	0	1.000	0	2-2	0	.207	.281	4.70
Postseason Totals			6	0	0	6	12.0	88	6	4	4	0	0	0	0	3	1	7	0	0	2	0	1.000	0	3-3	0	.146	.205	3.00

LCS — Batting / Fielding
Year	Tm	Age	G	AB	H	2B	3B	HR	TB	R	RBI	GW	TBB	IBB	SO	HBP	SH	SF	SB	CS	SB%	GDP	Avg	OBP	SLG	Pos	G	PO	A	E	DP	FPct
1982	StL	29	2	1	0	0	0	0	0	0	0	0	0	0	0	0	0	0	0	0	0	0	.000	.000	.000	P	2	0	2	0	0	1.000

World Series — Batting / Fielding
Year	Tm	Age	G	AB	H	2B	3B	HR	TB	R	RBI	GW	TBB	IBB	SO	HBP	SH	SF	SB	CS	SB%	GDP	Avg	OBP	SLG	Pos	G	PO	A	E	DP	FPct
1982	StL	29	4	0	0	0	0	0	0	0	0	0	0	0	0	0	0	0	0	0	—	0	—	—	—	P	4	0	1	0	0	1.000
Postseason Totals			6	1	0	0	0	0	0	0	0	0	0	0	0	0	0	0	0	0	—	0	.000	.000	.000	P	6	0	3	0	0	1.000

DON SUTTON (HOF 1998-W)—Donald Howard Sutton—Throws: Right; Bats: Right
Ht: 6'1"; Wt: 185 lbs; Born: 4/2/1945 in Clio, Alabama; Debut: 4/14/1966

LCS — Pitching
Year	Tm	Age	G	GS	CG	GF	IP	BFP	H	R	ER	HR	SH	SF	HB	TBB	IBB	SO	WP	Bk	W	L	Pct	ShO	Sv-Op	Hld	OAvg	OOBP	ERA
1974	LA	29	2	2	1	0	17.0	60	7	1	1	1	1	0	1	2	0	13	0	0	2	0	1.000	1	0-0	0	.125	.169	0.53
1977	LA	32	1	1	1	0	9.0	35	9	1	1	0	0	0	0	0	0	4	0	0	1	0	1.000	0	0-0	0	.257	.257	1.00
1978	LA	33	1	1	0	0	5.2	27	7	7	4	1	1	0	0	2	0	5	0	0	0	1	.000	0	0-0	0	.292	.346	6.35
1982	Mil	37	1	1	0	0	7.2	32	8	3	3	1	0	0	0	2	0	4	0	0	1	0	1.000	0	0-0	0	.267	.313	3.52
1986	Cal	41	2	1	0	0	9.2	36	6	2	2	2	1	0	0	1	0	4	0	0	0	0	.000	0	0-0	0	.182	.206	1.86
LCS Totals			7	6	2	0	49.0	380	37	14	11	5	4	0	1	7	0	30	0	0	4	1	.800	1	0-0	0	.208	.242	2.02

World Series — Pitching
Year	Tm	Age	G	GS	CG	GF	IP	BFP	H	R	ER	HR	SH	SF	HB	TBB	IBB	SO	WP	Bk	W	L	Pct	ShO	Sv-Op	Hld	OAvg	OOBP	ERA
1974	LA	29	2	2	0	0	13.0	50	9	4	4	1	0	1	1	3	0	12	1	0	1	0	1.000	0	0-0	0	.200	.260	2.77
1977	LA	32	2	2	1	0	16.0	66	17	7	7	3	2	0	1	1	0	6	0	0	1	0	1.000	0	0-0	0	.274	.297	3.94
1978	LA	33	2	2	0	0	12.0	56	17	10	10	1	0	0	0	4	0	8	1	0	0	2	.000	0	0-0	0	.327	.375	7.50
1982	Mil	37	2	2	0	0	10.1	45	12	11	9	2	1	0	0	1	0	5	0	1	0	1	.000	0	0-0	0	.279	.295	7.84
WS Totals			8	8	1	0	51.1	434	55	32	30	7	3	1	2	9	0	31	2	1	2	3	.400	0	0-0	0	.272	.308	5.26
Postseason Totals			15	14	3	0	100.1	814	92	46	41	12	7	1	3	16	0	61	2	1	6	4	.600	1	0-0	0	.242	.278	3.68

LCS — Batting / Fielding
Year	Tm	Age	G	AB	H	2B	3B	HR	TB	R	RBI	GW	TBB	IBB	SO	HBP	SH	SF	SB	CS	SB%	GDP	Avg	OBP	SLG	Pos	G	PO	A	E	DP	FPct
1974	LA	29	2	7	2	0	0	0	2	0	1	0	1	0	2	0	0	0	0	0	—	0	.286	.375	.286	P	2	2	3	0	1	1.000
1977	LA	32	1	3	0	0	0	0	0	0	0	0	0	0	0	0	0	0	0	0	—	0	.000	.000	.000	P	1	0	2	0	0	1.000
1978	LA	33	1	2	0	0	0	0	0	0	0	0	0	0	2	0	0	0	0	0	—	0	.000	.000	.000	P	1	0	1	0	0	1.000
1982	Mil	37	1	0	0	0	0	0	0	0	0	0	0	0	0	0	0	0	0	0	—	0	—	—	—	P	1	0	1	0	0	1.000
1986	Cal	41	2	0	0	0	0	0	0	0	0	0	0	0	0	0	0	0	0	0	—	0	—	—	—	P	2	1	1	0	0	1.000
LCS Totals			7	12	2	0	0	0	2	0	1	0	1	0	4	0	0	0	0	0	—	0	.167	.231	.167	P	7	3	8	0	1	1.000

World Series — Batting / Fielding
Year	Tm	Age	G	AB	H	2B	3B	HR	TB	R	RBI	GW	TBB	IBB	SO	HBP	SH	SF	SB	CS	SB%	GDP	Avg	OBP	SLG	Pos	G	PO	A	E	DP	FPct
1974	LA	29	2	3	0	0	0	0	0	0	0	0	0	0	2	0	1	0	0	0	—	0	.000	.000	.000	P	2	0	2	0	1	1.000
1977	LA	32	2	6	0	0	0	0	0	0	0	0	1	0	4	0	0	0	0	0	—	0	.000	.143	.000	P	2	1	1	0	0	1.000
1978	LA	33	2	0	0	0	0	0	0	0	0	0	0	0	0	0	0	0	0	0	—	0	—	—	—	P	2	0	0	0	0	—
1982	Mil	37	2	0	0	0	0	0	0	0	0	0	0	0	0	0	0	0	0	0	—	0	—	—	—	P	2	1	3	0	0	1.000
WS Totals			8	9	0	0	0	0	0	0	0	0	1	0	6	0	1	0	0	0	—	0	.000	.100	.000	P	8	2	6	0	1	1.000
Postseason Totals			15	21	2	0	0	0	2	0	1	0	2	0	10	0	1	0	0	0	—	0	.095	.174	.095	P	15	5	14	0	2	1.000

MARK SWEENEY—Mark Patrick Sweeney—Bats: Left; Throws: Left
Ht: 6'1"; Wt: 195 lbs; Born: 10/26/1969 in Framingham, Maine; Debut: 8/4/1995

Division Series — Batting / Fielding
Year	Tm	Age	G	AB	H	2B	3B	HR	TB	R	RBI	GW	TBB	IBB	SO	HBP	SH	SF	SB	CS	SB%	GDP	Avg	OBP	SLG	Pos	G	PO	A	E	DP	FPct
1996	StL	26	1	1	1	0	0	0	1	0	0	0	0	0	0	0	0	0	0	0	—	0	1.000	1.000	1.000	—						

LCS — Batting / Fielding
Year	Tm	Age	G	AB	H	2B	3B	HR	TB	R	RBI	GW	TBB	IBB	SO	HBP	SH	SF	SB	CS	SB%	GDP	Avg	OBP	SLG	Pos	G	PO	A	E	DP	FPct
1996	StL	26	5	4	0	0	0	0	0	1	0	0	0	0	2	0	1	0	0	0	—	0	.000	.000	.000	OF	2	2	0	0	0	1.000
Postseason Totals			6	5	1	0	0	0	1	1	0	0	0	0	2	0	1	0	0	0	—	0	.200	.200	.200	OF	2	2	0	0	0	1.000

BILL SWIFT—William Charles Swift—Throws: Right; Bats: Right
Ht: 6'0"; Wt: 170 lbs; Born: 10/27/1961 in Portland, Maine; Debut: 6/7/1985

Division Series — Pitching
Year	Tm	Age	G	GS	CG	GF	IP	BFP	H	R	ER	HR	SH	SF	HB	TBB	IBB	SO	WP	Bk	W	L	Pct	ShO	Sv-Op	Hld	OAvg	OOBP	ERA
1995	Col	33	1	1	0	0	6.0	24	7	4	4	0	0	0	0	2	0	3	0	0	0	0	—	0	0-0	0	.318	.375	6.00

Division Series — Batting / Fielding
Year	Tm	Age	G	AB	H	2B	3B	HR	TB	R	RBI	GW	TBB	IBB	SO	HBP	SH	SF	SB	CS	SB%	GDP	Avg	OBP	SLG	Pos	G	PO	A	E	DP	FPct
1995	Col	33	1	3	0	0	0	0	0	0	0	0	0	0	2	0	0	0	0	0	—	0	.000	.000	.000	P	1	0	0	0	0	—

BOB SWIFT—Robert Virgil Swift—Bats: Right; Throws: Right
Ht: 5'11"; Wt: 180 lbs; Born: 3/6/1915 in Salina, Kansas; Debut: 4/16/1940; Died: 10/17/1966

World Series — Batting / Fielding
Year	Tm	Age	G	AB	H	2B	3B	HR	TB	R	RBI	GW	TBB	IBB	SO	HBP	SH	SF	SB	CS	SB%	GDP	Avg	OBP	SLG	Pos	G	PO	A	E	DP	FPct
1945	Det	30	3	4	1	0	0	0	1	1	0	0	2	0	0	0	0	0	0	0	—	0	.250	.500	.250	C	3	9	1	0	0	1.000

RON SWOBODA—Ronald Alan Swoboda—Nickname: Rocky—Bats: Right; Throws: Right
Ht: 6'2"; Wt: 195 lbs; Born: 6/30/1944 in Baltimore, Maryland; Debut: 4/12/1965

World Series — Batting / Fielding
Year	Tm	Age	G	AB	H	2B	3B	HR	TB	R	RBI	GW	TBB	IBB	SO	HBP	SH	SF	SB	CS	SB%	GDP	Avg	OBP	SLG	Pos	G	PO	A	E	DP	FPct
1969	NYN	25	4	15	6	1	0	0	7	1	1	1	1	0	3	0	0	0	0	1	.00	0	.400	.438	.467	OF	4	14	0	0	0	1.000

PAT TABLER—Patrick Sean Tabler—Bats: Right; Throws: Right
Ht: 6'3"; Wt: 175 lbs; Born: 2/2/1958 in Hamilton, Ohio; Debut: 8/21/1981

LCS — Batting / Fielding
Year	Tm	Age	G	AB	H	2B	3B	HR	TB	R	RBI	GW	TBB	IBB	SO	HBP	SH	SF	SB	CS	SB%	GDP	Avg	OBP	SLG	Pos	G	PO	A	E	DP	FPct
1991	Tor	33	2	1	0	0	0	0	0	0	0	0	1	0	0	0	0	0	0	0	—	0	.000	.500	.000	—						

World Series — Batting / Fielding
Year	Tm	Age	G	AB	H	2B	3B	HR	TB	R	RBI	GW	TBB	IBB	SO	HBP	SH	SF	SB	CS	SB%	GDP	Avg	OBP	SLG	Pos	G	PO	A	E	DP	FPct
1992	Tor	34	2	2	0	0	0	0	0	0	0	0	0	0	0	0	0	0	0	0	—	0	.000	.000	.000	—						
Postseason Totals			4	3	0	0	0	0	0	0	0	0	1	0	0	0	0	0	0	0	—	0	.000	.250	.000	—						

FRANK TANANA—Frank Daryl Tanana—Throws: Left; Bats: Left
Ht: 6'2"; Wt: 180 lbs; Born: 7/3/1953 in Detroit, Michigan; Debut: 9/9/1973

LCS — Pitching
Year	Tm	Age	G	GS	CG	GF	IP	BFP	H	R	ER	HR	SH	SF	HB	TBB	IBB	SO	WP	Bk	W	L	Pct	ShO	Sv-Op	Hld	OAvg	OOBP	ERA
1979	Cal	26	1	1	0	0	5.0	23	6	2	2	0	0	0	1	2	0	3	0	0	0	0	—	0	0-0	0	.300	.391	3.60
1987	Det	34	1	1	0	0	5.1	29	6	4	3	2	1	1	3	4	0	1	1	0	0	1	.000	0	0-0	0	.300	.464	5.06
LCS Totals			2	2	0	0	10.1	104	12	6	5	2	1	1	4	6	0	4	1	0	0	1	.000	0	0-0	0	.300	.431	4.35

LCS — Batting / Fielding
Year	Tm	Age	G	AB	H	2B	3B	HR	TB	R	RBI	GW	TBB	IBB	SO	HBP	SH	SF	SB	CS	SB%	GDP	Avg	OBP	SLG	Pos	G	PO	A	E	DP	FPct
1979	Cal	26	1	0	0	0	0	0	0	0	0	0	0	0	0	0	0	0	0	0	—	0	—	—	—	P	1	0	0	0	0	—
1987	Det	34	1	0	0	0	0	0	0	0	0	0	0	0	0	0	0	0	0	0	—	0	—	—	—	P	1	0	1	0	0	1.000
LCS Totals			2	0	0	0	0	0	0	0	0	0	0	0	0	0	0	0	0	0	—	0	—	—	—	P	2	0	1	0	0	1.000

LEE TANNEHILL
Lee Ford Tannehill—Bats: Right; Throws: Right
Ht: 5'11"; Wt: 170 lbs; Born: 10/26/1880 in Dayton, Kentucky; Debut: 4/22/1903; Died: 2/16/1938

World Series — Batting / Fielding

Year Tm	Age	G	AB	H	2B	3B	HR	TB	R	RBI	GW	TBB	IBB	SO	HBP	SH	SF	SB	CS	SB%	GDP	Avg	OBP	SLG	Pos	G	PO	A	E	DP	FPct
1906 ChA	25	3	9	1	0	0	0	1	1	0	0	0	0	2	0	0	0	0	0	—	0	.111	.111	.111	SS	3	1	8	0	0	1.000

KEVIN TAPANI
Kevin Ray Tapani—Nickname: Tap—Throws: Right; Bats: Right
Ht: 6'0"; Wt: 180 lbs; Born: 2/18/1964 in Des Moines, Iowa; Debut: 7/4/1989

Pitching

Series	Year Tm	Age	G	GS	CG	GF	IP	BFP	H	R	ER	HR	SH	SF	HB	TBB	IBB	SO	WP	Bk	W	L	Pct	ShO	Sv-Op	Hld	OAvg	OOBP	ERA
Division Series	1995 LA	31	2	0	0	0	0.1	5	0	3	3	0	0	0	0	4	1	1	0	0	0	0	—	0	0-0	0	.000	.800	81.00
LCS	1991 Min	27	2	2	0	0	10.1	48	16	9	9	0	1	0	0	3	0	9	0	0	0	1	.000	0	0-0	0	.364	.404	7.84
World Series	1991 Min	27	2	2	0	0	12.0	50	13	6	6	1	1	2	0	2	0	7	0	0	1	1	.500	0	0-0	0	.289	.306	4.50
Postseason Totals			6	4	0	0	22.2	206	29	18	18	1	2	2	0	9	1	17	0	0	1	2	.333	0	0-0	0	.322	.376	7.15

Batting / Fielding

Series	Year Tm	Age	G	AB	H	2B	3B	HR	TB	R	RBI	GW	TBB	IBB	SO	HBP	SH	SF	SB	CS	SB%	GDP	Avg	OBP	SLG	Pos	G	PO	A	E	DP	FPct
Division Series	1995 LA	31	2	0	0	0	0	0	0	0	0	0	0	0	0	0	0	0	0	0	—	0	—	—	—	P	2	0	0	0	0	
LCS	1991 Min	27	2	0	0	0	0	0	0	0	0	0	0	0	0	0	0	0	0	0	—	0	—	—	—	P	2	3	0	0	0	1.000
World Series	1991 Min	27	2	1	0	0	0	0	0	0	0	0	0	0	0	0	0	0	0	0	—	0	.000	.000	.000	P	2	0	2	0	0	1.000
Postseason Totals			6	1	0	0	0	0	0	0	0	0	0	0	0	0	0	0	0	0	—	0	.000	.000	.000	P	6	3	2	0	0	1.000

TONY TARASCO
Anthony Giacinto Tarasco—Bats: Left; Throws: Right
Ht: 6'1"; Wt: 205 lbs; Born: 12/9/1970 in New York, New York; Debut: 4/30/1993

LCS — Batting / Fielding

Year Tm	Age	G	AB	H	2B	3B	HR	TB	R	RBI	GW	TBB	IBB	SO	HBP	SH	SF	SB	CS	SB%	GDP	Avg	OBP	SLG	Pos	G	PO	A	E	DP	FPct
1993 Atl	22	2	1	0	0	0	0	0	0	0	0	0	0	1	0	0	0	0	0	—	0	.000	.000	.000	OF	2	0	0	0	—	
1996 Bal	25	2	1	0	0	0	0	0	0	0	0	0	0	1	0	0	0	0	0	—	0	.000	.000	.000	OF	2	2	0	0	0	1.000
LCS Totals		4	2	0	0	0	0	0	0	0	0	0	0	0	2	0	0	0	0	0	—	0	.000	.000	.000	OF	4	2	0	0	0	1.000

JOSE TARTABULL
Jose Milages Tartabull—Bats: Left; Throws: Left
Ht: 5'11"; Wt: 165 lbs; Born: 11/27/1938 in Cienfuegos, Cuba; Debut: 4/10/1962

World Series — Batting / Fielding

Year Tm	Age	G	AB	H	2B	3B	HR	TB	R	RBI	GW	TBB	IBB	SO	HBP	SH	SF	SB	CS	SB%	GDP	Avg	OBP	SLG	Pos	G	PO	A	E	DP	FPct
1967 Bos	28	7	13	2	0	0	0	2	1	0	1	1	0	2	0	0	0	0	0	—	0	.154	.214	.154	OF	6	7	0	0	0	1.000

BENNIE TATE
Henry Bennett Tate—Bats: Left; Throws: Right
Ht: 5'8"; Wt: 165 lbs; Born: 12/3/1901 in Whitwell, Tennessee; Debut: 4/29/1924; Died: 10/27/1973

World Series — Batting / Fielding

Year Tm	Age	G	AB	H	2B	3B	HR	TB	R	RBI	GW	TBB	IBB	SO	HBP	SH	SF	SB	CS	SB%	GDP	Avg	OBP	SLG	Pos	G	PO	A	E	DP	FPct
1924 Was	22	3	0	0	0	0	0	0	0	1	0	3	0	0	0	0	0	0	0	—	0	—	1.000	—	—						

EDDIE TAUBENSEE
Edward Kenneth Taubensee—Bats: Left; Throws: Right
Ht: 6'4"; Wt: 205 lbs; Born: 10/31/1968 in Beeville, Texas; Debut: 5/18/1991

LCS — Batting / Fielding

Year Tm	Age	G	AB	H	2B	3B	HR	TB	R	RBI	GW	TBB	IBB	SO	HBP	SH	SF	SB	CS	SB%	GDP	Avg	OBP	SLG	Pos	G	PO	A	E	DP	FPct
1995 Cin	26	2	2	1	0	0	0	1	0	0	0	0	0	0	0	0	0	0	0	—	0	.500	.500	.500	C	1	0	0	0	0	

JULIAN TAVAREZ
Throws: Right; Bats: Right
Ht: 6'2"; Wt: 165 lbs; Born: 5/22/1973 in Santiago, Dominican Republic; Debut: 8/7/1993

Pitching

Series	Year Tm	Age	G	GS	CG	GF	IP	BFP	H	R	ER	HR	SH	SF	HB	TBB	IBB	SO	WP	Bk	W	L	Pct	ShO	Sv-Op	Hld	OAvg	OOBP	ERA
Division Series	1995 Cle	22	3	0	0	0	2.2	13	5	2	2	1	0	0	0	0	0	3	0	0	0	0	—	0	0-1	1	.385	.385	6.75
	1996 Cle	23	2	0	0	2	1.1	6	1	0	0	0	0	0	0	2	0	1	0	0	0	0	—	0	0-0	0	.250	.500	0.00
	1997 SF	24	3	0	0	0	4.0	18	4	2	2	1	0	0	1	2	1	0	0	0	1	0	1.000	0	0-0	0	.267	.389	4.50
DS Totals			8	0	0	2	8.0	74	10	4	4	2	0	0	1	4	1	4	0	0	1	0	1.000	0	0-1	1	.313	.405	4.50
LCS	1995 Cle	22	4	0	0	0	3.1	16	3	1	1	0	0	0	0	1	1	2	0	0	0	1	.000	0	0-0	1	.200	.250	2.70
World Series	1995 Cle	22	5	0	0	1	4.1	17	3	0	0	0	2	0	1	2	0	1	0	0	0	0	—	0	0-0	0	.250	.400	0.00
Postseason Totals			17	0	0	3	15.2	140	16	5	5	2	2	0	2	7	2	7	0	0	0	2	.000	0	0-1	2	.271	.368	2.87

Batting / Fielding

Series	Year Tm	Age	G	AB	H	2B	3B	HR	TB	R	RBI	GW	TBB	IBB	SO	HBP	SH	SF	SB	CS	SB%	GDP	Avg	OBP	SLG	Pos	G	PO	A	E	DP	FPct
Division Series	1995 Cle	22	3	0	0	0	0	0	0	0	0	0	0	0	0	0	0	0	0	0	—	0	—	—	—	P	3	0	0	0	0	
	1996 Cle	23	2	0	0	0	0	0	0	0	0	0	0	0	0	0	0	0	0	0	—	0	—	—	—	P	2	0	0	0	0	
	1997 SF	24	3	0	0	0	0	0	0	0	0	0	0	0	0	0	0	0	0	0	—	0	—	—	—	P	3	0	0	0	0	
DS Totals			8	0	0	0	0	0	0	0	0	0	0	0	0	0	0	0	0	0	—	0	—	—	—	P	8	0	0	0	0	
LCS	1995 Cle	22	4	0	0	0	0	0	0	0	0	0	0	0	0	0	0	0	0	0	—	0	—	—	—	P	4	0	1	0	0	1.000
World Series	1995 Cle	22	5	0	0	0	0	0	0	0	0	0	0	0	0	0	0	0	0	0	—	0	—	—	—	P	5	2	0	0	0	1.000
Postseason Totals			17	0	0	0	0	0	0	0	0	0	0	0	0	0	0	0	0	0	—	0	—	—	—	P	17	2	3	0	0	1.000

FRANK TAVERAS
Franklin Crisostomo Taveras—Bats: Right; Throws: Right
Ht: 6'0"; Wt: 155 lbs; Born: 12/24/1949 in Las Matas de Santa Cruz, Dominican Republic; Debut: 9/25/1971

LCS — Batting / Fielding

Year Tm	Age	G	AB	H	2B	3B	HR	TB	R	RBI	GW	TBB	IBB	SO	HBP	SH	SF	SB	CS	SB%	GDP	Avg	OBP	SLG	Pos	G	PO	A	E	DP	FPct
1974 Pit	24	2	2	0	0	0	0	0	0	0	0	0	0	0	1	0	0	1	0	1.00	0	.000	.333	.000	SS	2	2	1	0	0	1.000
1975 Pit	25	3	7	1	0	0	0	1	0	1	0	1	0	2	0	0	0	0	0	—	0	.143	.250	.143	SS	3	4	6	0	2	1.000
LCS Totals		5	9	1	0	0	0	1	0	1	0	1	0	2	1	0	0	1	0	1.00	0	.111	.273	.111	SS	5	6	7	0	2	1.000

HARRY TAYLOR
James Harry Taylor—Throws: Right; Bats: Right
Ht: 6'1"; Wt: 175 lbs; Born: 5/20/1919 in East Glenn, Indiana; Debut: 9/22/1946

World Series — Pitching

Year Tm	Age	G	GS	CG	GF	IP	BFP	H	R	ER	HR	SH	SF	HB	TBB	IBB	SO	WP	Bk	W	L	Pct	ShO	Sv-Op	Hld	OAvg	OOBP	ERA
1947 Bro	28	1	1	0	0	0.0	4	2	1	0	0	0	0	0	1	0	0	0	0	0	0	—	0	0-0	0	.667	.750	—

World Series — Batting / Fielding

Year Tm	Age	G	AB	H	2B	3B	HR	TB	R	RBI	GW	TBB	IBB	SO	HBP	SH	SF	SB	CS	SB%	GDP	Avg	OBP	SLG	Pos	G	PO	A	E	DP	FPct
1947 Bro	28	1	0	0	0	0	0	0	0	0	0	0	0	0	0	0	0	0	0	—	0	—	—	—	P	1	0	0	0	0	

RON TAYLOR—Ronald Wesley Taylor—Throws: Right; Bats: Right

Ht: 6'1"; Wt: 195 lbs; Born: 12/13/1937 in Toronto, Ontario; Debut: 4/11/1962

LCS — Pitching

Year Tm	Age	G	GS	CG	GF	IP	BFP	H	R	ER	HR	SH	SF	HB	TBB	IBB	SO	WP	Bk	W	L	Pct	ShO	Sv-Op	Hld	OAvg	OOBP	ERA
1969 NYN	31	2	0	0	1	3.1	13	3	0	0	0	0	0	0	0	0	4	0	0	1	0	1.000	0	1- 1	0	.231	.231	0.00

World Series — Pitching

Year Tm	Age	G	GS	CG	GF	IP	BFP	H	R	ER	HR	SH	SF	HB	TBB	IBB	SO	WP	Bk	W	L	Pct	ShO	Sv-Op	Hld	OAvg	OOBP	ERA
1964 StL	26	2	0	0	1	4.2	14	0	0	0	0	0	0	0	1	0	2	0	0	0	0	—	0	1- 1	0	.000	.071	0.00
1969 NYN	31	2	0	0	2	2.1	7	0	0	0	0	0	0	0	1	0	3	0	0	0	0	—	0	1- 1	0	.000	.143	0.00
WS Totals		4	0	0	3	7.0	42	0	0	0	0	0	0	0	2	0	5	0	0	0	0	—	0	2-2	0	.000	.095	0.00
Postseason Totals		6	0	0	4	10.1	68	3	0	0	0	0	0	0	2	0	9	0	0	1	0	1.000	0	3-3	0	.094	.147	0.00

LCS — Batting / Fielding

Year Tm	Age	G	AB	H	2B	3B	HR	TB	R	RBI	GW	TBB	IBB	SO	HBP	SH	SF	SB	CS	SB%	GDP	Avg	OBP	SLG	Pos	G	PO	A	E	DP	FPct
1969 NYN	31	2	0	0	0	0	0	0	0	0	0	0	0	0	0	0	0	0	0	—	0	—	—	—	P	2	1	0	0	0	1.000

World Series — Batting / Fielding

Year Tm	Age	G	AB	H	2B	3B	HR	TB	R	RBI	GW	TBB	IBB	SO	HBP	SH	SF	SB	CS	SB%	GDP	Avg	OBP	SLG	Pos	G	PO	A	E	DP	FPct
1964 StL	26	2	1	0	0	0	0	0	0	0	0	0	0	1	0	0	0	0	0	—	0	.000	.000	.000	P	2	0	2	0	0	1.000
1969 NYN	31	2	0	0	0	0	0	0	0	0	0	0	0	0	0	0	0	0	0	—	0	—	—	—	P	2	0	1	0	0	1.000
WS Totals		4	1	0	0	0	0	0	0	0	0	0	0	1	0	0	0	0	0	—	0	.000	.000	.000	P	4	0	3	0	0	1.000
Postseason Totals		6	1	0	0	0	0	0	0	0	0	0	0	1	0	0	0	0	0	—	0	.000	.000	.000	P	6	1	3	0	0	1.000

TOMMY TAYLOR—Thomas Livingstone Carlto Taylor—Bats: Right; Throws: Right

Ht: 5'8"; Wt: 160 lbs; Born: 9/17/1892 in Mexia, Texas; Debut: 7/9/1924; Died: 4/5/1956

World Series — Batting / Fielding

Year Tm	Age	G	AB	H	2B	3B	HR	TB	R	RBI	GW	TBB	IBB	SO	HBP	SH	SF	SB	CS	SB%	GDP	Avg	OBP	SLG	Pos	G	PO	A	E	DP	FPct
1924 Was	32	3	2	0	0	0	0	0	0	0	0	0	0	2	0	0	0	0	0	—	0	.000	.000	.000	3B	2	0	3	1	0	.750

TONY TAYLOR—Antonio Nemesio Taylor—Bats: Right; Throws: Right

Ht: 5'9"; Wt: 170 lbs; Born: 12/19/1935 in Central Alara, Cuba; Debut: 4/15/1958

LCS — Batting / Fielding

Year Tm	Age	G	AB	H	2B	3B	HR	TB	R	RBI	GW	TBB	IBB	SO	HBP	SH	SF	SB	CS	SB%	GDP	Avg	OBP	SLG	Pos	G	PO	A	E	DP	FPct
1972 Det	36	4	15	2	2	0	0	4	0	0	0	0	0	2	0	0	0	0	0	—	2	.133	.133	.267	2B	4	5	9	0	2	1.000

ZACK TAYLOR—James Wren Taylor—Bats: Right; Throws: Right

Ht: 5'11"; Wt: 180 lbs; Born: 7/27/1898 in Yulee, Florida; Debut: 6/15/1920; Died: 9/19/1974

World Series — Batting / Fielding

Year Tm	Age	G	AB	H	2B	3B	HR	TB	R	RBI	GW	TBB	IBB	SO	HBP	SH	SF	SB	CS	SB%	GDP	Avg	OBP	SLG	Pos	G	PO	A	E	DP	FPct
1929 ChN	31	5	17	3	0	0	0	3	0	3	0	0	0	3	0	0	1	0	0	—	0	.176	.167	.176	C	5	31	4	0	0	1.000

BIRDIE TEBBETTS—George Robert Tebbetts—Bats: Right; Throws: Right

Ht: 5'11"; Wt: 170 lbs; Born: 11/10/1912 in Burlington, Vermont; Debut: 9/16/1936

World Series — Batting / Fielding

Year Tm	Age	G	AB	H	2B	3B	HR	TB	R	RBI	GW	TBB	IBB	SO	HBP	SH	SF	SB	CS	SB%	GDP	Avg	OBP	SLG	Pos	G	PO	A	E	DP	FPct
1940 Det	27	4	11	0	0	0	0	0	0	0	0	0	0	0	0	0	0	0	0	—	0	.000	.000	.000	C	3	13	3	1	1	.941

KENT TEKULVE—Kenton Charles Tekulve—Nickname: Bones—Throws: Right; Bats: Right

Ht: 6'4"; Wt: 180 lbs; Born: 3/5/1947 in Cincinnati, Ohio; Debut: 5/20/1974

LCS — Pitching

Year Tm	Age	G	GS	CG	GF	IP	BFP	H	R	ER	HR	SH	SF	HB	TBB	IBB	SO	WP	Bk	W	L	Pct	ShO	Sv-Op	Hld	OAvg	OOBP	ERA
1975 Pit	28	2	0	0	1	1.1	8	3	1	1	0	0	0	0	1	0	2	0	0	0	0	—	0	0- 0	0	.429	.500	6.75
1979 Pit	32	2	0	0	0	2.2	10	2	1	1	0	0	0	0	2	1	2	1	0	0	0	—	0	0- 1	0	.250	.400	3.38
LCS Totals		4	0	0	1	4.0	36	5	2	2	0	0	0	0	3	1	4	1	0	0	0	—	0	0-1	0	.333	.444	4.50

World Series — Pitching

Year Tm	Age	G	GS	CG	GF	IP	BFP	H	R	ER	HR	SH	SF	HB	TBB	IBB	SO	WP	Bk	W	L	Pct	ShO	Sv-Op	Hld	OAvg	OOBP	ERA
1979 Pit	32	5	0	0	5	9.1	35	4	3	3	0	0	0	0	3	2	10	0	0	0	1	.000	0	3- 4	0	.125	.200	2.89
Postseason Totals		9	0	0	6	13.1	106	9	5	5	0	0	0	0	6	3	14	1	0	0	1	.000	0	3-5	0	.191	.283	3.38

LCS — Batting / Fielding

Year Tm	Age	G	AB	H	2B	3B	HR	TB	R	RBI	GW	TBB	IBB	SO	HBP	SH	SF	SB	CS	SB%	GDP	Avg	OBP	SLG	Pos	G	PO	A	E	DP	FPct
1975 Pit	28	2	0	0	0	0	0	0	0	0	0	0	0	0	0	0	0	0	0	—	0	—	—	—	P	2	0	0	0	0	—
1979 Pit	32	2	1	0	0	0	0	0	0	0	0	0	0	1	0	0	0	0	0	—	0	.000	.000	.000	P	2	0	1	0	0	1.000
LCS Totals		4	1	0	0	0	0	0	0	0	0	0	0	1	0	0	0	0	0	—	0	.000	.000	.000	P	4	0	1	0	0	1.000

World Series — Batting / Fielding

Year Tm	Age	G	AB	H	2B	3B	HR	TB	R	RBI	GW	TBB	IBB	SO	HBP	SH	SF	SB	CS	SB%	GDP	Avg	OBP	SLG	Pos	G	PO	A	E	DP	FPct
1979 Pit	32	5	2	0	0	0	0	0	0	0	0	0	0	0	0	0	0	0	0	—	0	.000	.000	.000	P	5	1	0	0	0	1.000
Postseason Totals		9	3	0	0	0	0	0	0	0	0	0	0	1	0	0	0	0	0	—	0	.000	.000	.000	P	9	1	1	0	0	1.000

GARRY TEMPLETON—Garry Lewis Templeton—Nickname: Jump Steady—Bats: Both; Throws: Right

Ht: 5'11"; Wt: 175 lbs; Born: 3/24/1956 in Lockney, Texas; Debut: 8/9/1976

LCS — Batting / Fielding

Year Tm	Age	G	AB	H	2B	3B	HR	TB	R	RBI	GW	TBB	IBB	SO	HBP	SH	SF	SB	CS	SB%	GDP	Avg	OBP	SLG	Pos	G	PO	A	E	DP	FPct
1984 SD	28	5	15	5	1	0	0	6	2	2	1	2	0	0	0	1	0	1	0	1.00	0	.333	.412	.400	SS	5	18	12	1	5	.968

World Series — Batting / Fielding

Year Tm	Age	G	AB	H	2B	3B	HR	TB	R	RBI	GW	TBB	IBB	SO	HBP	SH	SF	SB	CS	SB%	GDP	Avg	OBP	SLG	Pos	G	PO	A	E	DP	FPct
1984 SD	28	5	19	6	1	0	0	7	1	0	0	0	0	3	0	0	0	0	0	—	0	.316	.316	.368	SS	5	8	11	0	2	1.000
Postseason Totals		10	34	11	2	0	0	13	3	2	1	2	0	3	0	1	0	1	0	1.00	0	.324	.361	.382	SS	10	26	23	1	7	.980

GENE TENACE—Fury Gene Tenace—Bats: Right; Throws: Right

Ht: 6'0"; Wt: 190 lbs; Born: 10/10/1946 in Russellton, Pennsylvania; Debut: 5/29/1969

LCS — Batting / Fielding

Year Tm	Age	G	AB	H	2B	3B	HR	TB	R	RBI	GW	TBB	IBB	SO	HBP	SH	SF	SB	CS	SB%	GDP	Avg	OBP	SLG	Pos	G	PO	A	E	DP	FPct
1971 Oak	24	1	3	0	0	0	0	0	0	0	0	1	0	1	0	0	0	0	0	—	0	.000	.250	.000	C	1	8	0	0	0	1.000
1972 Oak	25	5	17	1	0	0	0	1	1	1	1	3	0	5	0	0	0	0	1	.00	0	.059	.200	.059	C	5	19	3	0	0	1.000
																									2B	2	2	2	1	1	.800
1973 Oak	26	5	17	4	1	0	0	5	3	0	0	2	0	4	1	0	0	0	0	—	0	.235	.350	.294	1B	5	38	3	0	2	1.000
																									C	3	2	0	0	0	1.000
1974 Oak	27	4	11	0	0	0	0	0	1	1	1	4	0	4	0	0	0	1	0	1.00	1	.000	.267	.000	1B	4	35	2	0	3	1.000
1975 Oak	28	3	9	0	0	0	0	0	0	0	0	3	0	2	0	0	0	0	0	—	1	.000	.250	.000	C	3	11	0	0	0	1.000
																									1B	1	8	1	0	3	1.000
LCS Totals		18	57	5	1	0	0	6	5	2	2	13	0	16	1	0	0	1	1	.50	2	.088	.268	.105	C	12	40	3	0	0	1.000

World Series — Batting / Fielding

Year Tm	Age	G	AB	H	2B	3B	HR	TB	R	RBI	GW	TBB	IBB	SO	HBP	SH	SF	SB	CS	SB%	GDP	Avg	OBP	SLG	Pos	G	PO	A	E	DP	FPct
1972 Oak	25	7	23	8	1	0	4	21	5	9	2	2	1	4	0	0	0	0	1	.00	0	.348	.400	.913	C	6	45	4	1	1	.980
																									1B	1	3	1	0	1	1.000
1973 Oak	26	7	19	3	1	0	0	4	0	3	0	11	1	7	0	0	0	0	2	.00	1	.158	.467	.211	1B	7	51	2	2	6	.964
																									C	3	6	0	0	0	1.000
1974 Oak	27	5	9	2	0	0	0	2	0	0	0	3	0	4	0	1	0	0	0	—	1	.222	.417	.222	1B	5	20	1	0	3	1.000
1982 StL	35	5	6	0	0	0	0	0	0	0	0	1	0	2	0	0	0	0	0	—	0	.000	.143	.000	—						
WS Totals		24	57	13	2	0	4	27	5	12	2	17	2	17	0	1	0	0	3	.00	2	.228	.405	.474	1B	13	74	4	2	10	.975
Postseason Totals		42	114	18	3	0	4	33	10	14	4	30	2	33	1	1	0	1	4	.20	4	.158	.338	.289	1B	23	155	10	2	18	.988

WALT TERRELL—Charles Walter Terrell—Throws: Right; Bats: Left

Ht: 6'2"; Wt: 205 lbs; Born: 5/11/1958 in Jeffersonville, Indiana; Debut: 9/8/1982

LCS — Pitching

Year Tm	Age	G	GS	CG	GF	IP	BFP	H	R	ER	HR	SH	SF	HB	TBB	IBB	SO	WP	Bk	W	L	Pct	ShO	Sv-Op	Hld	OAvg	OOBP	ERA
1987 Det	29	1	1	0	0	6.0	28	7	6	6	2	0	0	0	4	0	4	0	0	0	0	—	0	0- 0	0	.292	.393	9.00

LCS		Batting																							Fielding						
Year Tm	Age	G	AB	H	2B	3B	HR	TB	R	RBI	GW	TBB	IBB	SO	HBP	SH	SF	SB	CS	SB%	GDP	Avg	OBP	SLG	Pos	G	PO	A	E	DP	FPct
1987 Det	29	1	0	0	0	0	0	0	0	0	0	0	0	0	0	0	0	0	0	—	0	—	—	—	P	1	0	1	0	0	1.000

BILL TERRY (HOF 1954-W)—William Harold Terry—Nickname: Memphis Bill—Bats: Left; Throws: Left

Ht: 6'1"; Wt: 200 lbs; Born: 10/30/1896 in Atlanta, Georgia; Debut: 9/24/1923; Died: 1/9/1989

World Series		Batting																							Fielding						
Year Tm	Age	G	AB	H	2B	3B	HR	TB	R	RBI	GW	TBB	IBB	SO	HBP	SH	SF	SB	CS	SB%	GDP	Avg	OBP	SLG	Pos	G	PO	A	E	DP	FPct
1924 NYG	27	5	14	6	0	1	1	11	3	1	0	3	1	1	0	0	0	0	0	—	0	.429	.529	.786	1B	4	43	2	0	2	1.000
1933 NYG	36	5	22	6	1	0	1	10	3	1	0	0	0	0	0	0	0	0	0	—	0	.273	.273	.455	1B	5	50	1	0	3	1.000
1936 NYG	39	6	25	6	0	0	0	6	1	4	1	1	0	4	0	1	0	0	0	—	0	.240	.269	.240	1B	6	45	8	0	5	1.000
WS Totals		16	61	18	1	1	2	27	7	6	1	4	1	5	0	1	0	0	0	—	0	.295	.338	.443	1B	15	138	11	0	10	1.000

RALPH TERRY—Ralph Willard Terry—Throws: Right; Bats: Right

Ht: 6'3"; Wt: 195 lbs; Born: 1/9/1936 in Big Cabin, Oklahoma; Debut: 8/6/1956

World Series		Pitching																										
Year Tm	Age	G	GS	CG	GF	IP	BFP	H	R	ER	HR	SH	SF	HB	TBB	IBB	SO	WP	Bk	W	L	Pct	ShO	Sv-Op	Hld	OAvg	OOBP	ERA
1960 NYA	24	2	1	0	1	6.2	29	7	4	4	1	1	0	0	1	0	5	0	0	0	2	.000	0	0- 0	0	.259	.286	5.40
1961 NYA	25	2	2	0	0	9.1	43	12	7	5	2	0	0	0	2	1	7	0	0	0	1	.000	0	0- 0	0	.293	.326	4.82
1962 NYA	26	3	3	2	0	25.0	94	17	5	5	2	3	0	1	2	0	16	0	0	2	1	.667	1	0- 0	0	.193	.220	1.80
1963 NYA	27	1	0	0	0	3.0	12	3	1	1	0	0	0	0	1	1	0	0	0	0	0	—	0	0- 0	0	.273	.333	3.00
1964 NYA	28	1	0	0	1	2.0	7	2	0	0	0	0	0	0	0	0	3	0	0	0	0	—	0	0- 0	0	.286	.286	0.00
WS Totals		9	6	2	2	46.0	370	41	17	15	5	4	0	1	6	2	31	0	0	2	4	.333	1	0-0	0	.236	.265	2.93

World Series		Batting																							Fielding						
Year Tm	Age	G	AB	H	2B	3B	HR	TB	R	RBI	GW	TBB	IBB	SO	HBP	SH	SF	SB	CS	SB%	GDP	Avg	OBP	SLG	Pos	G	PO	A	E	DP	FPct
1960 NYA	24	2	2	0	0	0	0	0	0	0	0	0	0	1	0	0	0	0	0	—	0	.000	.000	.000	P	2	0	3	0	0	1.000
1961 NYA	25	2	3	0	0	0	0	0	0	0	0	0	0	1	0	1	0	0	0	—	0	.000	.000	.000	P	2	1	2	0	0	1.000
1962 NYA	26	3	8	1	0	0	0	1	0	0	0	1	0	6	0	0	0	0	0	—	0	.125	.222	.125	P	3	3	2	0	0	1.000
1963 NYA	27	1	0	0	0	0	0	0	0	0	0	0	0	0	0	0	0	0	0	—	0	—	—	—	P	1	1	1	0	1	1.000
1964 NYA	28	1	0	0	0	0	0	0	0	0	0	0	0	0	0	0	0	0	0	—	0	—	—	—	P	1	0	0	0	0	—
WS Totals		9	13	1	0	0	0	1	0	0	0	1	0	8	0	1	0	0	0	—	0	.077	.143	.077	P	9	5	8	0	1	1.000

JEFF TESREAU—Charles Monroe Tesreau—Throws: Right; Bats: Right

Ht: 6'2"; Wt: 218 lbs; Born: 3/5/1889 in Silver Mine, Missouri; Debut: 4/12/1912; Died: 9/24/1946

World Series		Pitching																										
Year Tm	Age	G	GS	CG	GF	IP	BFP	H	R	ER	HR	SH	SF	HB	TBB	IBB	SO	WP	Bk	W	L	Pct	ShO	Sv-Op	Hld	OAvg	OOBP	ERA
1912 NYG	23	3	3	1	0	23.0	100	19	10	8	1	2	1	1	11	0	15	3	0	1	2	.333	0	0- 0	0	.224	.316	3.13
1913 NYG	24	2	1	0	1	8.1	36	11	7	6	0	0	0	0	1	0	4	0	0	0	1	.000	0	0- 0	0	.314	.333	6.48
1917 NYG	28	1	0	0	1	1.0	3	0	0	0	0	0	0	0	1	0	1	0	0	0	0	—	0	0- 0	0	.000	.333	0.00
WS Totals		6	4	1	2	32.1	278	30	17	14	1	2	1	1	13	0	20	3	0	1	3	.250	0	0-0	0	.246	.321	3.90

World Series		Batting																							Fielding						
Year Tm	Age	G	AB	H	2B	3B	HR	TB	R	RBI	GW	TBB	IBB	SO	HBP	SH	SF	SB	CS	SB%	GDP	Avg	OBP	SLG	Pos	G	PO	A	E	DP	FPct
1912 NYG	23	3	8	3	0	0	0	3	0	2	0	1	0	3	0	0	0	0	1	.00	0	.375	.444	.375	P	3	0	10	0	0	1.000
1913 NYG	24	2	2	0	0	0	0	0	0	0	0	0	0	1	0	0	0	0	0	—	0	.000	.000	.000	P	2	0	1	0	0	1.000
1917 NYG	28	1	0	0	0	0	0	0	0	0	0	0	0	0	0	0	0	0	0	—	0	—	—	—	P	1	0	0	0	0	—
WS Totals		6	10	3	0	0	0	3	0	2	0	1	0	4	0	0	0	0	1	.00	0	.300	.364	.300	P	6	0	11	0	0	1.000

MICKEY TETTLETON—Mickey Lee Tettleton—Bats: Both; Throws: Right

Ht: 6'2"; Wt: 200 lbs; Born: 9/16/1960 in Oklahoma City, Oklahoma; Debut: 6/30/1984

Division Series		Batting																							Fielding						
Year Tm	Age	G	AB	H	2B	3B	HR	TB	R	RBI	GW	TBB	IBB	SO	HBP	SH	SF	SB	CS	SB%	GDP	Avg	OBP	SLG	Pos	G	PO	A	E	DP	FPct
1996 Tex	36	4	12	1	0	0	0	1	1	1	0	5	0	7	0	0	0	0	0	—	0	.083	.353	.083	—						

TIM TEUFEL—Timothy Shawn Teufel—Bats: Right; Throws: Right

Ht: 6'0"; Wt: 175 lbs; Born: 7/7/1958 in Greenwich, Connecticut; Debut: 9/3/1983

LCS		Batting																							Fielding						
Year Tm	Age	G	AB	H	2B	3B	HR	TB	R	RBI	GW	TBB	IBB	SO	HBP	SH	SF	SB	CS	SB%	GDP	Avg	OBP	SLG	Pos	G	PO	A	E	DP	FPct
1986 NYN	28	2	6	1	0	0	0	1	0	0	0	0	0	0	0	0	0	0	0	—	0	.167	.167	.167	2B	2	2	8	0	1	1.000
1988 NYN	30	1	3	0	0	0	0	0	0	0	0	0	0	1	0	0	0	0	0	—	0	.000	.000	.000	2B	1	1	3	0	0	1.000
LCS Totals		3	9	1	0	0	0	1	0	0	0	0	0	1	0	0	0	0	0	—	0	.111	.111	.111	2B	3	3	11	0	1	1.000

World Series		Batting																							Fielding						
Year Tm	Age	G	AB	H	2B	3B	HR	TB	R	RBI	GW	TBB	IBB	SO	HBP	SH	SF	SB	CS	SB%	GDP	Avg	OBP	SLG	Pos	G	PO	A	E	DP	FPct
1986 NYN	28	3	9	4	1	0	1	8	1	1	0	1	0	2	0	0	0	0	0	—	0	.444	.500	.889	2B	3	3	3	1	1	.857
Postseason Totals		6	18	5	1	0	1	9	1	1	0	1	0	3	0	0	0	0	0	—	0	.278	.316	.500	2B	6	6	14	1	2	.952

GEORGE THEODORE—George Basil Theodore—Nickname: Stork—Bats: Right; Throws: Right

Ht: 6'4"; Wt: 190 lbs; Born: 11/13/1947 in Salt Lake City, Utah; Debut: 4/14/1973

World Series		Batting																							Fielding						
Year Tm	Age	G	AB	H	2B	3B	HR	TB	R	RBI	GW	TBB	IBB	SO	HBP	SH	SF	SB	CS	SB%	GDP	Avg	OBP	SLG	Pos	G	PO	A	E	DP	FPct
1973 NYN	25	2	2	0	0	0	0	0	0	0	0	0	0	0	0	0	0	0	0	—	0	.000	.000	.000	OF	1	1	0	0	0	1.000

TOMMY THEVENOW—Thomas Joseph Thevenow—Bats: Right; Throws: Right

Ht: 5'10"; Wt: 155 lbs; Born: 9/6/1903 in Madison, Indiana; Debut: 9/4/1924; Died: 7/29/1957

World Series		Batting																							Fielding						
Year Tm	Age	G	AB	H	2B	3B	HR	TB	R	RBI	GW	TBB	IBB	SO	HBP	SH	SF	SB	CS	SB%	GDP	Avg	OBP	SLG	Pos	G	PO	A	E	DP	FPct
1926 StL	23	7	24	10	1	0	1	14	5	4	1	0	0	1	1	1	0	0	0	—	0	.417	.440	.583	SS	7	9	26	2	5	.946
1928 StL	25	1	0	0	0	0	0	0	0	0	0	0	0	0	0	0	0	0	0	—	0	—	—	—	SS	1	1	0	0	0	1.000
WS Totals		8	24	10	1	0	1	14	5	4	1	0	0	1	1	1	0	0	0	—	0	.417	.440	.583	SS	8	10	26	2	5	.947

BOBBY THIGPEN—Robert Thomas Thigpen—Throws: Right; Bats: Right

Ht: 6'3"; Wt: 195 lbs; Born: 7/17/1963 in Tallahassee, Florida; Debut: 8/6/1986

LCS		Pitching																										
Year Tm	Age	G	GS	CG	GF	IP	BFP	H	R	ER	HR	SH	SF	HB	TBB	IBB	SO	WP	Bk	W	L	Pct	ShO	Sv-Op	Hld	OAvg	OOBP	ERA
1993 Phi	30	2	0	0	1	1.2	7	1	1	1	1	0	0	0	1	0	3	0	0	0	0	—	0	0- 0	0	.167	.286	5.40

World Series		Pitching																										
Year Tm	Age	G	GS	CG	GF	IP	BFP	H	R	ER	HR	SH	SF	HB	TBB	IBB	SO	WP	Bk	W	L	Pct	ShO	Sv-Op	Hld	OAvg	OOBP	ERA
1993 Phi	30	2	0	0	1	2.2	10	1	0	0	0	0	1	1	1	0	0	0	0	0	0	—	0	0- 0	0	.143	.300	0.00
Postseason Totals		4	0	0	2	4.1	34	2	1	1	1	0	1	1	2	0	3	0	0	0	0	—	0	0-0	0	.154	.294	2.08

LCS		Batting																							Fielding						
Year Tm	Age	G	AB	H	2B	3B	HR	TB	R	RBI	GW	TBB	IBB	SO	HBP	SH	SF	SB	CS	SB%	GDP	Avg	OBP	SLG	Pos	G	PO	A	E	DP	FPct
1993 Phi	30	2	0	0	0	0	0	0	0	0	0	0	0	0	0	0	0	0	0	—	0	—	—	—	P	2	0	0	0	0	—

World Series		Batting																							Fielding						
Year Tm	Age	G	AB	H	2B	3B	HR	TB	R	RBI	GW	TBB	IBB	SO	HBP	SH	SF	SB	CS	SB%	GDP	Avg	OBP	SLG	Pos	G	PO	A	E	DP	FPct
1993 Phi	30	2	0	0	0	0	0	0	0	0	0	0	0	0	0	0	0	0	0	—	0	—	—	—	P	2	0	1	0	0	1.000
Postseason Totals		4	0	0	0	0	0	0	0	0	0	0	0	0	0	0	0	0	0	—	0	—	—	—	P	4	0	1	0	0	1.000

BUD THOMAS—Luther Baxter Thomas—Throws: Right; Bats: Right

Ht: 6'0"; Wt: 180 lbs; Born: 9/9/1910 in Faber, Virginia; Debut: 9/13/1932

World Series		Pitching																										
Year Tm	Age	G	GS	CG	GF	IP	BFP	H	R	ER	HR	SH	SF	HB	TBB	IBB	SO	WP	Bk	W	L	Pct	ShO	Sv-Op	Hld	OAvg	OOBP	ERA
1933 Was	23	2	0	0	1	1.1	5	1	0	0	0	0	0	0	0	0	2	0	0	0	0	—	0	0- 0	0	.200	.200	0.00

World Series		Batting																							Fielding						
Year Tm	Age	G	AB	H	2B	3B	HR	TB	R	RBI	GW	TBB	IBB	SO	HBP	SH	SF	SB	CS	SB%	GDP	Avg	OBP	SLG	Pos	G	PO	A	E	DP	FPct
1933 Was	23	2	0	0	0	0	0	0	0	0	0	0	0	0	0	0	0	0	0	—	0	—	—	—	P	2	0	0	0	0	—

DERREL THOMAS—Derrel Osborn Thomas—Bats: Right; Throws: Right

Ht: 6'0"; Wt: 160 lbs; Born: 1/14/1951 in Los Angeles, California; Debut: 9/14/1971

Division Series

Year Tm	Age	G	AB	H	2B	3B	HR	TB	R	RBI	GW	TBB	IBB	SO	HBP	SH	SF	SB	CS	SB%	GDP	Avg	OBP	SLG	Pos	G	PO	A	E	DP	FPct
1981 LA	30	4	2	0	0	0	0	0	1	0	0	0	0	1	0	0	0	0	0	—	0	.000	.000	.000	OF	4	0	0	0	0	—

LCS

Year Tm	Age	G	AB	H	2B	3B	HR	TB	R	RBI	GW	TBB	IBB	SO	HBP	SH	SF	SB	CS	SB%	GDP	Avg	OBP	SLG	Pos	G	PO	A	E	DP	FPct
1981 LA	30	2	1	1	0	0	0	1	2	0	0	0	0	0	0	0	0	0	0	—	0	1.000	1.000	1.000	3B	1	0	0	0	0	—
																									OF	1	1	0	0	0	1.000
1983 LA	32	4	9	4	1	0	0	5	0	0	0	0	0	3	0	0	0	1	0	1.00	0	.444	.444	.556	OF	3	7	0	0	0	1.000
LCS Totals		6	10	5	1	0	0	6	2	0	0	0	0	3	0	0	0	1	0	1.00	0	.500	.500	.600	OF	4	8	0	0	0	1.000

World Series

Year Tm	Age	G	AB	H	2B	3B	HR	TB	R	RBI	GW	TBB	IBB	SO	HBP	SH	SF	SB	CS	SB%	GDP	Avg	OBP	SLG	Pos	G	PO	A	E	DP	FPct
1981 LA	30	5	7	0	0	0	0	0	2	1	0	1	0	2	0	0	0	0	0	—	1	.000	.125	.000	SS	1	1	1	0	1	1.000
																									3B	2	0	0	0	0	—
																									OF	3	3	0	0	0	1.000
Postseason Totals		15	19	5	1	0	0	6	5	1	0	1	0	6	0	0	0	1	0	1.00	1	.263	.300	.316	OF	11	11	0	0	0	1.000

FRANK THOMAS—Frank Edward Thomas—Nickname: Big Hurt—Bats: Right; Throws: Right

Ht: 6'5"; Wt: 240 lbs; Born: 5/27/1968 in Columbus, Georgia; Debut: 8/2/1990

LCS

Year Tm	Age	G	AB	H	2B	3B	HR	TB	R	RBI	GW	TBB	IBB	SO	HBP	SH	SF	SB	CS	SB%	GDP	Avg	OBP	SLG	Pos	G	PO	A	E	DP	FPct
1993 ChA-*M*	25	6	17	6	0	0	1	9	2	3	1	10	2	5	0	0	0	0	0	—	0	.353	.593	.529	1B	4	24	3	0	3	1.000

FRED THOMAS—Frederick Harvey Thomas—Nickname: Tommy—Bats: Right; Throws: Right

Ht: 5'10"; Wt: 160 lbs; Born: 12/19/1892 in Milwaukee, Wisconsin; Debut: 4/22/1918; Died: 1/15/1986

World Series

Year Tm	Age	G	AB	H	2B	3B	HR	TB	R	RBI	GW	TBB	IBB	SO	HBP	SH	SF	SB	CS	SB%	GDP	Avg	OBP	SLG	Pos	G	PO	A	E	DP	FPct
1918 Bos	25	6	17	2	0	0	0	2	0	0	0	1	0	2	0	1	0	0	0	—	0	.118	.167	.118	3B	6	6	10	0	0	1.000

GEORGE THOMAS—George Edward Thomas—Bats: Right; Throws: Right

Ht: 6'3"; Wt: 190 lbs; Born: 11/29/1937 in Minneapolis, Minnesota; Debut: 9/11/1957

World Series

Year Tm	Age	G	AB	H	2B	3B	HR	TB	R	RBI	GW	TBB	IBB	SO	HBP	SH	SF	SB	CS	SB%	GDP	Avg	OBP	SLG	Pos	G	PO	A	E	DP	FPct
1967 Bos	29	2	2	0	0	0	0	0	0	0	0	0	0	1	0	0	0	0	0	—	0	.000	.000	.000	OF	1	1	0	0	0	1.000

GORMAN THOMAS—James Gorman Thomas—Nickname: Stormin' Gorman—Bats: Right; Throws: Right

Ht: 6'2"; Wt: 210 lbs; Born: 12/12/1950 in Charleston, South Carolina; Debut: 4/6/1973

Division Series

Year Tm	Age	G	AB	H	2B	3B	HR	TB	R	RBI	GW	TBB	IBB	SO	HBP	SH	SF	SB	CS	SB%	GDP	Avg	OBP	SLG	Pos	G	PO	A	E	DP	FPct
1981 Mil	30	5	18	2	0	0	1	5	2	1	0	1	0	9	0	0	0	0	0	—	0	.111	.158	.278	OF	3	12	0	0	0	1.000

LCS

Year Tm	Age	G	AB	H	2B	3B	HR	TB	R	RBI	GW	TBB	IBB	SO	HBP	SH	SF	SB	CS	SB%	GDP	Avg	OBP	SLG	Pos	G	PO	A	E	DP	FPct
1982 Mil	31	5	15	1	0	0	1	4	1	3	0	2	0	7	0	0	1	0	1	.00	0	.067	.167	.267	OF	5	13	0	0	0	1.000

World Series

Year Tm	Age	G	AB	H	2B	3B	HR	TB	R	RBI	GW	TBB	IBB	SO	HBP	SH	SF	SB	CS	SB%	GDP	Avg	OBP	SLG	Pos	G	PO	A	E	DP	FPct
1982 Mil	31	7	26	3	0	0	0	3	0	3	1	2	0	7	0	0	0	0	0	—	0	.115	.179	.115	OF	7	15	0	0	0	1.000
Postseason Totals		17	59	6	0	0	2	12	3	7	1	5	0	23	0	0	1	0	1	.00	0	.102	.169	.203	OF	15	40	0	0	0	1.000

IRA THOMAS—Ira Felix Thomas—Bats: Right; Throws: Right

Ht: 6'2"; Wt: 200 lbs; Born: 1/22/1881 in Ballston Spa, New York; Debut: 5/18/1906; Died: 10/11/1958

World Series

Year Tm	Age	G	AB	H	2B	3B	HR	TB	R	RBI	GW	TBB	IBB	SO	HBP	SH	SF	SB	CS	SB%	GDP	Avg	OBP	SLG	Pos	G	PO	A	E	DP	FPct
1908 Det	27	2	4	2	1	0	0	3	0	1	0	1	0	0	0	0	0	0	0	—	0	.500	.600	.750	C	1	9	2	0	0	1.000
1910 Phi	29	4	12	3	0	0	0	3	2	1	0	4	0	1	0	0	0	0	0	—	1	.250	.438	.250	C	4	27	8	1	1	.972
1911 Phi	30	4	12	1	0	0	0	1	1	1	1	1	0	2	0	0	1	0	1	.00	0	.083	.143	.083	C	4	31	4	0	0	1.000
WS Totals		10	28	6	1	0	0	7	3	3	1	6	0	3	0	0	1	0	1	.00	1	.214	.343	.250	C	9	67	14	1	1	.988

MYLES THOMAS—Myles Lewis Thomas—Nickname: Duck Eye—Throws: Right; Bats: Right

Ht: 5'9"; Wt: 170 lbs; Born: 10/22/1897 in State College, Pennsylvania; Debut: 4/18/1926; Died: 12/12/1963

World Series (Pitching)

Year Tm	Age	G	GS	CG	GF	IP	BFP	H	R	ER	HR	SH	SF	HB	TBB	IBB	SO	WP	Bk	W	L	Pct	ShO	Sv-Op	Hld	OAvg	OOBP	ERA
1926 NYA	28	2	0	0	2	3.0	10	3	1	1	0	0	0	1	0	0	0	0	0	0	0	—	0	0-0	0	.333	.400	3.00

World Series

Year Tm	Age	G	AB	H	2B	3B	HR	TB	R	RBI	GW	TBB	IBB	SO	HBP	SH	SF	SB	CS	SB%	GDP	Avg	OBP	SLG	Pos	G	PO	A	E	DP	FPct
1926 NYA	28	2	0	0	0	0	0	0	0	0	0	0	0	0	0	0	0	0	0	—	0	—	—	—	P	2	0	2	0	0	1.000

PINCH THOMAS—Chester David Thomas—Bats: Left; Throws: Right

Ht: 5'9"; Wt: 173 lbs; Born: 1/24/1888 in Camp Point, Illinois; Debut: 4/24/1912; Died: 12/24/1953

World Series

Year Tm	Age	G	AB	H	2B	3B	HR	TB	R	RBI	GW	TBB	IBB	SO	HBP	SH	SF	SB	CS	SB%	GDP	Avg	OBP	SLG	Pos	G	PO	A	E	DP	FPct
1915 Bos	27	2	5	1	0	0	0	1	0	0	0	0	0	0	0	0	0	0	0	—	0	.200	.200	.200	C	2	10	3	0	1	1.000
1916 Bos	28	3	7	1	0	1	0	3	0	0	0	0	0	1	0	1	0	0	0	—	0	.143	.143	.429	C	3	10	4	0	0	1.000
1920 Cle	32	1	0	0	0	0	0	0	0	0	0	0	0	0	0	0	0	0	0	—	0	—	—	—	C	1	1	0	0	0	1.000
WS Totals		6	12	2	0	1	0	4	0	0	0	0	0	1	0	1	0	0	0	—	0	.167	.167	.333	C	6	21	7	0	1	1.000

GARY THOMASSON—Gary Leah Thomasson—Bats: Left; Throws: Left

Ht: 6'1"; Wt: 180 lbs; Born: 7/29/1951 in San Diego, California; Debut: 9/5/1972

LCS

Year Tm	Age	G	AB	H	2B	3B	HR	TB	R	RBI	GW	TBB	IBB	SO	HBP	SH	SF	SB	CS	SB%	GDP	Avg	OBP	SLG	Pos	G	PO	A	E	DP	FPct
1978 NYA	27	3	1	0	0	0	0	0	0	0	0	0	0	0	0	0	0	0	0	—	0	.000	.000	.000	OF	3	2	0	0	0	1.000

World Series

Year Tm	Age	G	AB	H	2B	3B	HR	TB	R	RBI	GW	TBB	IBB	SO	HBP	SH	SF	SB	CS	SB%	GDP	Avg	OBP	SLG	Pos	G	PO	A	E	DP	FPct
1978 NYA	27	3	4	1	0	0	0	1	0	0	0	0	0	1	0	0	0	0	1	.00	0	.250	.250	.250	OF	3	3	0	0	0	1.000
Postseason Totals		6	5	1	0	0	0	1	0	0	0	0	0	1	0	0	0	0	1	.00	0	.200	.200	.200	OF	6	5	0	0	0	1.000

JIM THOME—James Howard Thome—Bats: Left; Throws: Right

Ht: 6'3"; Wt: 200 lbs; Born: 8/27/1970 in Peoria, Illinois; Debut: 9/4/1991

Division Series

Year Tm	Age	G	AB	H	2B	3B	HR	TB	R	RBI	GW	TBB	IBB	SO	HBP	SH	SF	SB	CS	SB%	GDP	Avg	OBP	SLG	Pos	G	PO	A	E	DP	FPct
1995 Cle	25	3	13	2	0	0	1	5	1	3	1	1	0	6	0	0	0	0	0	—	0	.154	.214	.385	3B	3	6	6	0	1	1.000
1996 Cle	26	4	10	3	0	0	0	3	1	0	0	1	0	5	1	0	0	0	0	—	0	.300	.417	.300	3B	4	1	1	0	0	1.000
1997 Cle	27	4	15	3	0	0	0	3	1	1	0	0	0	5	0	1	0	0	0	—	0	.200	.200	.200	1B	4	44	3	0	6	1.000
DS Totals		11	38	8	0	0	1	11	3	4	1	2	0	16	1	1	0	0	0	—	0	.211	.268	.289	3B	7	7	7	0	1	1.000

LCS

Year Tm	Age	G	AB	H	2B	3B	HR	TB	R	RBI	GW	TBB	IBB	SO	HBP	SH	SF	SB	CS	SB%	GDP	Avg	OBP	SLG	Pos	G	PO	A	E	DP	FPct
1995 Cle	25	5	15	4	0	0	2	10	2	5	1	2	0	3	0	0	0	0	0	—	1	.267	.353	.667	3B	5	1	5	1	0	.857
1997 Cle	27	6	14	1	0	0	0	1	3	0	0	5	0	4	0	0	0	0	0	—	0	.071	.316	.071	1B	6	35	2	0	8	1.000
LCS Totals		11	29	5	0	0	2	11	5	5	1	7	0	7	0	0	0	0	0	—	1	.172	.333	.379	1B	6	35	2	0	8	1.000

World Series

Year Tm	Age	G	AB	H	2B	3B	HR	TB	R	RBI	GW	TBB	IBB	SO	HBP	SH	SF	SB	CS	SB%	GDP	Avg	OBP	SLG	Pos	G	PO	A	E	DP	FPct
1995 Cle	25	6	19	4	1	0	1	8	1	2	1	2	0	5	0	0	0	0	0	—	0	.211	.286	.421	3B	6	3	5	1	0	.889
1997 Cle	27	7	28	8	0	1	2	16	8	4	0	5	0	7	0	0	0	0	0	—	2	.286	.394	.571	1B	7	57	5	1	8	.984
WS Totals		13	47	12	1	1	3	24	9	6	1	7	0	12	0	0	0	0	0	—	2	.255	.352	.511	1B	7	57	5	1	8	.984
Postseason Totals		35	114	25	1	1	6	46	17	15	3	16	0	35	1	1	0	0	0	—	3	.219	.321	.404	3B	18	11	17	2	1	.933

DANNY THOMPSON—Danny Leon Thompson—Bats: Right; Throws: Right

Ht: 6'0"; Wt: 183 lbs; Born: 2/1/1947 in Wichita, Kansas; Debut: 6/25/1970; Died: 12/10/1976

LCS — Batting / Fielding

Year Tm	Age	G	AB	H	2B	3B	HR	TB	R	RBI	GW	TBB	IBB	SO	HBP	SH	SF	SB	CS	SB%	GDP	Avg	OBP	SLG	Pos	G	PO	A	E	DP	FPct
1970 Min	23	3	8	1	1	0	0	2	0	0	0	1	0	0	0	0	0	0	0	—	2	.125	.222	.250	2B	3	2	3	1	0	.833

DON THOMPSON—Donald Newlin Thompson—Bats: Left; Throws: Left

Ht: 6'0"; Wt: 185 lbs; Born: 12/28/1923 in Swepsonville, North Carolina; Debut: 4/24/1949

World Series — Batting / Fielding

Year Tm	Age	G	AB	H	2B	3B	HR	TB	R	RBI	GW	TBB	IBB	SO	HBP	SH	SF	SB	CS	SB%	GDP	Avg	OBP	SLG	Pos	G	PO	A	E	DP	FPct
1953 Bro	29	2	0	0	0	0	0	0	0	0	0	0	0	0	0	0	0	0	0	—	0	—	—	—	OF	2	0	1	0	0	1.000

GUS THOMPSON—John Gustav Thompson—Throws: Right; Bats: Right

Ht: 6'2"; Wt: 185 lbs; Born: 6/22/1877 in Humboldt, Iowa; Debut: 8/31/1903; Died: 3/28/1958

World Series — Pitching

Year Tm	Age	G	GS	CG	GF	IP	BFP	H	R	ER	HR	SH	SF	HB	TBB	IBB	SO	WP	Bk	W	L	Pct	ShO	Sv-Op	Hld	OAvg	OOBP	ERA
1903 Pit	26	1	0	0	1	2.0	9	3	1	1	0	0	0	0	0	0	1	0	0	0	0	—	0	0-0	0	.333	.333	4.50

World Series — Batting / Fielding

Year Tm	Age	G	AB	H	2B	3B	HR	TB	R	RBI	GW	TBB	IBB	SO	HBP	SH	SF	SB	CS	SB%	GDP	Avg	OBP	SLG	Pos	G	PO	A	E	DP	FPct
1903 Pit	26	1	1	0	0	0	0	0	0	0	0	0	0	0	0	0	0	0	0	—	0	.000	.000	.000	P	1	0	1	0	0	1.000

HANK THOMPSON—Henry Curtis Thompson—Bats: Left; Throws: Right

Ht: 5'9"; Wt: 174 lbs; Born: 12/8/1925 in Oklahoma City, Oklahoma; Debut: 7/17/1947; Died: 9/30/1969

World Series — Batting / Fielding

Year Tm	Age	G	AB	H	2B	3B	HR	TB	R	RBI	GW	TBB	IBB	SO	HBP	SH	SF	SB	CS	SB%	GDP	Avg	OBP	SLG	Pos	G	PO	A	E	DP	FPct
1951 NYG	25	5	14	2	0	0	0	2	3	0	0	5	0	2	0	0	0	0	0	—	1	.143	.368	.143	OF	5	4	0	2	0	.667
1954 NYG	28	4	11	4	1	0	0	5	6	2	0	7	3	1	0	0	0	0	0	—	0	.364	.611	.455	3B	4	5	12	0	1	1.000
WS Totals		9	25	6	1	0	0	7	9	2	0	12	3	3	0	0	0	0	0	—	1	.240	.486	.280	OF	5	4	0	2	0	.667

JUNIOR THOMPSON—Eugene Earl Thompson—Throws: Right; Bats: Right

Ht: 6'1"; Wt: 185 lbs; Born: 6/7/1917 in Latham, Illinois; Debut: 4/26/1939

World Series — Pitching

Year Tm	Age	G	GS	CG	GF	IP	BFP	H	R	ER	HR	SH	SF	HB	TBB	IBB	SO	WP	Bk	W	L	Pct	ShO	Sv-Op	Hld	OAvg	OOBP	ERA
1939 Cin	22	1	1	0	0	4.2	23	5	7	7	4	0	0	0	4	0	3	1	0	0	1	.000	0	0-0	0	.263	.391	13.50
1940 Cin	23	1	1	0	0	3.1	20	8	6	6	1	1	0	0	4	0	2	0	0	0	1	.000	0	0-0	0	.533	.632	16.20
WS Totals		2	2	0	0	8.0	86	13	13	13	5	1	0	0	8	0	5	1	0	0	2	.000	0	0-0	0	.382	.500	14.63

World Series — Batting / Fielding

Year Tm	Age	G	AB	H	2B	3B	HR	TB	R	RBI	GW	TBB	IBB	SO	HBP	SH	SF	SB	CS	SB%	GDP	Avg	OBP	SLG	Pos	G	PO	A	E	DP	FPct
1939 Cin	22	1	1	1	0	0	0	1	0	0	0	0	0	0	0	1	0	0	0	—	0	1.000	1.000	1.000	P	1	0	0	0	0	—
1940 Cin	23	1	1	0	0	0	0	0	0	0	0	0	0	1	0	0	0	0	0	—	0	.000	.000	.000	P	1	0	1	0	0	1.000
WS Totals		2	2	1	0	0	0	1	0	0	0	0	0	1	0	1	0	0	0	—	0	.500	.500	.500	P	2	0	1	0	0	1.000

MARK THOMPSON—Mark Radford Thompson—Throws: Right; Bats: Right

Ht: 6'2"; Wt: 205 lbs; Born: 4/7/1971 in Russellville, Kentucky; Debut: 7/26/1994

Division Series — Pitching

Year Tm	Age	G	GS	CG	GF	IP	BFP	H	R	ER	HR	SH	SF	HB	TBB	IBB	SO	WP	Bk	W	L	Pct	ShO	Sv-Op	Hld	OAvg	OOBP	ERA
1995 Col	24	1	0	0	1	1.0	3	0	0	0	0	0	0	0	0	0	0	0	0	0	0	—	0	1-1	0	.000	.000	0.00

Division Series — Batting / Fielding

Year Tm	Age	G	AB	H	2B	3B	HR	TB	R	RBI	GW	TBB	IBB	SO	HBP	SH	SF	SB	CS	SB%	GDP	Avg	OBP	SLG	Pos	G	PO	A	E	DP	FPct
1995 Col	24	1	0	0	0	0	0	0	0	0	0	0	0	0	0	0	0	0	0	—	0	—	—	—	P	1	1	0	0	0	1.000

MILT THOMPSON—Milton Bernard Thompson—Bats: Left; Throws: Right

Ht: 5'11"; Wt: 170 lbs; Born: 1/5/1959 in Washington, DC; Debut: 9/4/1984

LCS — Batting / Fielding

Year Tm	Age	G	AB	H	2B	3B	HR	TB	R	RBI	GW	TBB	IBB	SO	HBP	SH	SF	SB	CS	SB%	GDP	Avg	OBP	SLG	Pos	G	PO	A	E	DP	FPct
1993 Phi	34	6	13	3	1	0	0	4	2	0	0	1	1	2	0	0	0	0	0	—	0	.231	.286	.308	OF	5	8	0	1	0	.889

World Series — Batting / Fielding

Year Tm	Age	G	AB	H	2B	3B	HR	TB	R	RBI	GW	TBB	IBB	SO	HBP	SH	SF	SB	CS	SB%	GDP	Avg	OBP	SLG	Pos	G	PO	A	E	DP	FPct
1993 Phi	34	6	16	5	1	1	1	11	3	6	0	1	0	2	0	0	0	0	0	—	1	.313	.353	.688	OF	6	10	0	1	0	.909
Postseason Totals		12	29	8	2	1	1	15	5	6	0	2	1	4	0	0	0	0	0	—	1	.276	.323	.517	OF	11	18	0	2	0	.900

ROBBY THOMPSON—Robert Randall Thompson—Bats: Right; Throws: Right

Ht: 5'11"; Wt: 165 lbs; Born: 5/10/1962 in West Palm Beach, Florida; Debut: 4/8/1986

LCS — Batting / Fielding

Year Tm	Age	G	AB	H	2B	3B	HR	TB	R	RBI	GW	TBB	IBB	SO	HBP	SH	SF	SB	CS	SB%	GDP	Avg	OBP	SLG	Pos	G	PO	A	E	DP	FPct
1987 SF	25	7	20	2	0	1	1	7	4	2	0	5	0	7	1	0	0	2	2	.50	0	.100	.308	.350	2B	6	11	19	1	6	.968
1989 SF	27	5	18	5	0	0	2	11	5	3	1	3	0	2	0	1	0	0	0	—	0	.278	.381	.611	2B	5	10	13	0	4	1.000
LCS Totals		12	38	7	0	1	3	18	9	5	1	8	0	9	1	1	0	2	2	.50	0	.184	.340	.474	2B	11	21	32	1	10	.981

World Series — Batting / Fielding

Year Tm	Age	G	AB	H	2B	3B	HR	TB	R	RBI	GW	TBB	IBB	SO	HBP	SH	SF	SB	CS	SB%	GDP	Avg	OBP	SLG	Pos	G	PO	A	E	DP	FPct
1989 SF	27	4	11	1	0	0	0	1	0	2	0	0	0	4	0	0	1	0	0	—	1	.091	.083	.091	2B	4	4	10	0	2	1.000
Postseason Totals		16	49	8	0	1	3	19	9	7	1	8	0	13	1	1	1	2	2	.50	1	.163	.288	.388	2B	15	25	42	1	12	.985

BOBBY THOMSON—Robert Brown Thomson—Nickname: The Staten Island Scot—Bats: Right; Throws: Right

Ht: 6'2"; Wt: 180 lbs; Born: 10/25/1923 in Glasgow, Scotland; Debut: 9/9/1946

World Series — Batting / Fielding

Year Tm	Age	G	AB	H	2B	3B	HR	TB	R	RBI	GW	TBB	IBB	SO	HBP	SH	SF	SB	CS	SB%	GDP	Avg	OBP	SLG	Pos	G	PO	A	E	DP	FPct
1951 NYG	27	6	21	5	1	0	0	6	1	2	0	5	0	0	0	0	0	0	0	—	0	.238	.385	.286	3B	6	13	15	2	0	.933

DICKIE THON—Richard William Thon—Bats: Right; Throws: Right

Ht: 5'11"; Wt: 160 lbs; Born: 6/20/1958 in South Bend, Indiana; Debut: 5/22/1979

Division Series — Batting / Fielding

Year Tm	Age	G	AB	H	2B	3B	HR	TB	R	RBI	GW	TBB	IBB	SO	HBP	SH	SF	SB	CS	SB%	GDP	Avg	OBP	SLG	Pos	G	PO	A	E	DP	FPct
1981 Hou	23	4	11	2	0	0	0	2	0	0	0	1	0	0	0	0	0	0	0	—	0	.182	.250	.182	SS	4	6	11	1	0	.944

LCS — Batting / Fielding

Year Tm	Age	G	AB	H	2B	3B	HR	TB	R	RBI	GW	TBB	IBB	SO	HBP	SH	SF	SB	CS	SB%	GDP	Avg	OBP	SLG	Pos	G	PO	A	E	DP	FPct
1979 Cal	21	1	0	0	0	0	0	0	1	0	0	0	0	0	0	0	0	0	0	—	0	—	—	—	SS	1	0	0	0	0	—
1986 Hou	28	6	12	3	0	0	1	6	1	1	0	0	0	1	0	0	0	0	0	—	0	.250	.250	.500	SS	6	5	10	0	2	1.000
LCS Totals		7	12	3	0	0	1	6	2	1	0	0	0	1	0	0	0	0	0	—	0	.250	.250	.500	SS	7	5	10	0	2	1.000
Postseason Totals		11	23	5	0	0	1	8	2	1	0	1	0	1	0	0	0	0	0	—	0	.217	.250	.348	SS	11	11	21	1	2	.970

LOU THORNTON—Louis Thornton—Bats: Left; Throws: Right

Ht: 6'2"; Wt: 185 lbs; Born: 4/26/1963 in Montgomery, Alabama; Debut: 4/8/1985

LCS — Batting / Fielding

Year Tm	Age	G	AB	H	2B	3B	HR	TB	R	RBI	GW	TBB	IBB	SO	HBP	SH	SF	SB	CS	SB%	GDP	Avg	OBP	SLG	Pos	G	PO	A	E	DP	FPct
1985 Tor	22	2	0	0	0	0	0	0	1	0	0	0	0	0	0	0	0	0	0	—	0	—	—	—	—						

JIM THORPE—James Francis Thorpe—Bats: Right; Throws: Right

Ht: 6'1"; Wt: 185 lbs; Born: 5/28/1887 in Prague, Oklahoma; Debut: 4/14/1913; Died: 3/28/1953

World Series — Batting / Fielding

Year Tm	Age	G	AB	H	2B	3B	HR	TB	R	RBI	GW	TBB	IBB	SO	HBP	SH	SF	SB	CS	SB%	GDP	Avg	OBP	SLG	Pos	G	PO	A	E	DP	FPct
1917 NYG	30	1	0	0	0	0	0	0	0	0	0	0	0	0	0	0	0	0	0	—	0	—	—	—	—						

MARV THRONEBERRY—Marvin Eugene Throneberry—Nickname: Marvelous Marv—B: L; T: L

Ht: 6'1"; Wt: 190 lbs; Born: 9/2/1933 in Collierville, Tenn.; Deb.: 9/25/1955; Died: 6/23/1994

World Series		Batting																							Fielding						
Year Tm	Age	G	AB	H	2B	3B	HR	TB	R	RBI	GW	TBB	IBB	SO	HBP	SH	SF	SB	CS	SB%	GDP	Avg	OBP	SLG	Pos	G	PO	A	E	DP	FPct
1958 NYA	25	1	1	0	0	0	0	0	0	0	0	0	0	1	0	0	0	0	0	—	0	.000	.000	.000	—						

MARK THURMOND—Mark Anthony Thurmond—Throws: Left; Bats: Left

Ht: 6'0"; Wt: 180 lbs; Born: 9/12/1956 in Houston, Texas; Debut: 5/14/1983

LCS		Pitching																										
Year Tm	Age	G	GS	CG	GF	IP	BFP	H	R	ER	HR	SH	SF	HB	TBB	IBB	SO	WP	Bk	W	L	Pct	ShO	Sv-Op	Hld	OAvg	OOBP	ERA
1984 SD	28	1	1	0	0	3.2	20	7	4	4	0	1	1	0	2	0	1	0	0	0	1	.000	0	0- 0	0	.438	.474	9.82
1987 Det	31	1	0	0	1	0.1	1	0	0	0	0	0	0	0	0	0	0	0	0	0	0	—	0	0- 0	0	.000	.000	0.00
LCS Totals		2	1	0	1	4.0	42	7	4	4	0	1	1	0	2	0	1	0	0	0	1	.000	0	0-0	0	.412	.450	9.00
World Series		Pitching																										
Year Tm	Age	G	GS	CG	GF	IP	BFP	H	R	ER	HR	SH	SF	HB	TBB	IBB	SO	WP	Bk	W	L	Pct	ShO	Sv-Op	Hld	OAvg	OOBP	ERA
1984 SD	28	2	2	0	0	5.1	30	12	6	6	2	0	0	0	3	0	2	0	0	0	1	.000	0	0- 0	0	.444	.500	10.13
Postseason Totals		4	3	0	1	9.1	102	19	10	10	2	1	1	0	5	0	3	0	0	0	2	.000	0	0-0	0	.432	.480	9.64

LCS		Batting																							Fielding						
Year Tm	Age	G	AB	H	2B	3B	HR	TB	R	RBI	GW	TBB	IBB	SO	HBP	SH	SF	SB	CS	SB%	GDP	Avg	OBP	SLG	Pos	G	PO	A	E	DP	FPct
1984 SD	28	1	1	1	0	0	0	1	0	0	0	0	0	0	0	0	0	0	0	—	0	1.000	1.000	1.000	P	1	0	1	0	0	1.000
1987 Det	31	1	0	0	0	0	0	0	0	0	0	0	0	0	0	0	0	0	0	—	0	—	—	—	P	1	0	0	0	0	—
LCS Totals		2	1	1	0	0	0	1	0	0	0	0	0	0	0	0	0	0	0	—	0	1.000	1.000	1.000	P	2	0	1	0	0	1.000
World Series		Batting																							Fielding						
Year Tm	Age	G	AB	H	2B	3B	HR	TB	R	RBI	GW	TBB	IBB	SO	HBP	SH	SF	SB	CS	SB%	GDP	Avg	OBP	SLG	Pos	G	PO	A	E	DP	FPct
1984 SD	28	2	0	0	0	0	0	0	0	0	0	0	0	0	0	0	0	0	0	—	0	—	—	—	P	2	0	2	0	0	1.000
Postseason Totals		4	1	1	0	0	0	1	0	0	0	0	0	0	0	0	0	0	0	—	0	1.000	1.000	1.000	P	4	0	3	0	0	1.000

LUIS TIANT—Luis Clemente Tiant—Throws: Right; Bats: Right

Ht: 6'0"; Wt: 180 lbs; Born: 11/23/1940 in Mariano, Cuba; Debut: 7/19/1964

LCS		Pitching																										
Year Tm	Age	G	GS	CG	GF	IP	BFP	H	R	ER	HR	SH	SF	HB	TBB	IBB	SO	WP	Bk	W	L	Pct	ShO	Sv-Op	Hld	OAvg	OOBP	ERA
1970 Min	29	1	0	0	1	0.2	4	1	2	1	1	0	0	0	0	0	0	0	0	0	0	—	0	0- 0	0	.250	.250	13.50
1975 Bos	34	1	1	1	0	9.0	35	3	1	0	0	0	0	0	3	0	8	0	0	1	0	1.000	0	0- 0	0	.094	.171	0.00
LCS Totals		2	1	1	1	9.2	78	4	3	1	1	0	0	0	3	0	8	0	0	1	0	1.000	0	0-0	0	.111	.179	0.93
World Series		Pitching																										
Year Tm	Age	G	GS	CG	GF	IP	BFP	H	R	ER	HR	SH	SF	HB	TBB	IBB	SO	WP	Bk	W	L	Pct	ShO	Sv-Op	Hld	OAvg	OOBP	ERA
1975 Bos	34	3	3	2	0	25.0	107	25	10	10	1	1	0	0	8	2	12	0	1	2	0	1.000	1	0- 0	0	.255	.311	3.60
Postseason Totals		5	4	3	1	34.2	292	29	13	11	2	1	0	0	11	2	20	0	1	3	0	1.000	1	0-0	0	.216	.276	2.86

LCS		Batting																							Fielding						
Year Tm	Age	G	AB	H	2B	3B	HR	TB	R	RBI	GW	TBB	IBB	SO	HBP	SH	SF	SB	CS	SB%	GDP	Avg	OBP	SLG	Pos	G	PO	A	E	DP	FPct
1970 Min	29	2	0	0	0	0	0	0	0	0	0	0	0	0	0	0	0	0	0	—	0	—	—	—	P	1	0	0	0	0	—
1975 Bos	34	1	0	0	0	0	0	0	0	0	0	0	0	0	0	0	0	0	0	—	0	—	—	—	P	1	0	1	0	0	1.000
LCS Totals		3	0	0	0	0	0	0	0	0	0	0	0	0	0	0	0	0	0	—	0	—	—	—	P	2	0	1	0	0	1.000
World Series		Batting																							Fielding						
Year Tm	Age	G	AB	H	2B	3B	HR	TB	R	RBI	GW	TBB	IBB	SO	HBP	SH	SF	SB	CS	SB%	GDP	Avg	OBP	SLG	Pos	G	PO	A	E	DP	FPct
1975 Bos	34	3	8	2	0	0	0	2	2	0	0	2	0	4	0	1	0	0	0	—	0	.250	.400	.250	P	3	0	4	0	0	1.000
Postseason Totals		6	8	2	0	0	0	2	2	0	0	2	0	4	0	1	0	0	0	—	0	.250	.400	.250	P	5	0	5	0	0	1.000

DICK TIDROW—Richard William Tidrow—Nickname: Dirt—Throws: Right; Bats: Right

Ht: 6'4"; Wt: 210 lbs; Born: 5/14/1947 in San Francisco, California; Debut: 4/18/1972

LCS		Pitching																										
Year Tm	Age	G	GS	CG	GF	IP	BFP	H	R	ER	HR	SH	SF	HB	TBB	IBB	SO	WP	Bk	W	L	Pct	ShO	Sv-Op	Hld	OAvg	OOBP	ERA
1976 NYA	29	3	0	0	2	7.1	33	6	4	3	0	0	2	0	4	0	0	0	0	1	0	1.000	0	0- 0	0	.222	.303	3.68
1977 NYA	30	2	0	0	0	7.0	30	6	3	3	2	0	0	0	3	0	3	0	0	0	0	—	0	0- 0	0	.222	.300	3.86
1978 NYA	31	1	0	0	0	5.2	26	8	3	3	1	0	0	0	2	0	1	0	0	0	0	—	0	0- 0	0	.333	.385	4.76
1983 ChA	36	1	0	0	0	3.0	13	1	1	1	0	0	0	0	3	1	3	0	0	0	0	—	0	0- 0	0	.100	.308	3.00
LCS Totals		7	0	0	2	23.0	204	21	11	10	3	0	2	0	12	1	7	0	0	1	0	1.000	0	0-0	0	.239	.324	3.91
World Series		Pitching																										
Year Tm	Age	G	GS	CG	GF	IP	BFP	H	R	ER	HR	SH	SF	HB	TBB	IBB	SO	WP	Bk	W	L	Pct	ShO	Sv-Op	Hld	OAvg	OOBP	ERA
1976 NYA	29	2	0	0	1	2.1	11	5	2	2	1	0	0	0	1	1	1	0	0	0	0	—	0	0- 0	0	.500	.545	7.71
1977 NYA	30	2	0	0	0	3.2	14	5	2	2	1	0	0	0	0	0	1	0	0	0	0	—	0	0- 0	0	.357	.357	4.91
1978 NYA	31	2	0	0	1	4.2	17	4	1	1	0	0	0	0	0	0	5	0	0	0	0	—	0	0- 0	0	.235	.235	1.93
WS Totals		6	0	0	2	10.2	84	14	5	5	2	0	0	0	1	1	7	0	0	0	0	—	0	0-0	0	.341	.357	4.22
Postseason Totals		13	0	0	4	33.2	288	35	16	15	5	0	2	0	13	2	14	0	0	1	0	1.000	0	0-0	0	.271	.333	4.01

LCS		Batting																							Fielding						
Year Tm	Age	G	AB	H	2B	3B	HR	TB	R	RBI	GW	TBB	IBB	SO	HBP	SH	SF	SB	CS	SB%	GDP	Avg	OBP	SLG	Pos	G	PO	A	E	DP	FPct
1976 NYA	29	3	0	0	0	0	0	0	0	0	0	0	0	0	0	0	0	0	0	—	0	—	—	—	P	3	1	0	0	0	1.000
1977 NYA	30	2	0	0	0	0	0	0	0	0	0	0	0	0	0	0	0	0	0	—	0	—	—	—	P	2	1	2	0	0	1.000
1978 NYA	31	1	0	0	0	0	0	0	0	0	0	0	0	0	0	0	0	0	0	—	0	—	—	—	P	1	0	2	0	0	1.000
1983 ChA	36	1	0	0	0	0	0	0	0	0	0	0	0	0	0	0	0	0	0	—	0	—	—	—	P	1	0	0	0	0	—
LCS Totals		7	0	0	0	0	0	0	0	0	0	0	0	0	0	0	0	0	0	—	0	—	—	—	P	7	2	4	0	0	1.000
World Series		Batting																							Fielding						
Year Tm	Age	G	AB	H	2B	3B	HR	TB	R	RBI	GW	TBB	IBB	SO	HBP	SH	SF	SB	CS	SB%	GDP	Avg	OBP	SLG	Pos	G	PO	A	E	DP	FPct
1976 NYA	29	2	0	0	0	0	0	0	0	0	0	0	0	0	0	0	0	0	0	—	0	—	—	—	P	2	0	0	0	0	—
1977 NYA	30	2	1	0	0	0	0	0	0	0	0	0	0	1	0	0	0	0	0	—	0	.000	.000	.000	P	2	0	1	0	0	1.000
1978 NYA	31	2	0	0	0	0	0	0	0	0	0	0	0	0	0	0	0	0	0	—	0	—	—	—	P	2	0	0	0	0	—
WS Totals		6	1	0	0	0	0	0	0	0	0	0	0	1	0	0	0	0	0	—	0	.000	.000	.000	P	6	0	1	0	0	1.000
Postseason Totals		13	1	0	0	0	0	0	0	0	0	0	0	1	0	0	0	0	0	—	0	.000	.000	.000	P	13	2	5	0	0	1.000

BOB TILLMAN—John Robert Tillman—Bats: Right; Throws: Right

Ht: 6'4"; Wt: 205 lbs; Born: 3/24/1937 in Nashville, Tennessee; Debut: 4/15/1962

LCS		Batting																							Fielding						
Year Tm	Age	G	AB	H	2B	3B	HR	TB	R	RBI	GW	TBB	IBB	SO	HBP	SH	SF	SB	CS	SB%	GDP	Avg	OBP	SLG	Pos	G	PO	A	E	DP	FPct
1969 Atl	32	1	0	0	0	0	0	0	0	0	0	0	0	0	0	0	0	0	0	—	0	—	—	—	C	1	2	0	0	0	1.000

MIKE TIMLIN—Michael August Timlin—Throws: Right; Bats: Right

Ht: 6'4"; Wt: 205 lbs; Born: 3/10/1966 in Midland, Texas; Debut: 4/8/1991

Division Series		Pitching																										
Year Tm	Age	G	GS	CG	GF	IP	BFP	H	R	ER	HR	SH	SF	HB	TBB	IBB	SO	WP	Bk	W	L	Pct	ShO	Sv-Op	Hld	OAvg	OOBP	ERA
1997 Sea	31	1	0	0	0	0.2	6	3	4	4	1	0	0	0	1	1	1	0	0	0	0	—	0	0- 0	0	.600	.667	54.00
LCS		Pitching																										
Year Tm	Age	G	GS	CG	GF	IP	BFP	H	R	ER	HR	SH	SF	HB	TBB	IBB	SO	WP	Bk	W	L	Pct	ShO	Sv-Op	Hld	OAvg	OOBP	ERA
1991 Tor	25	4	0	0	2	5.2	27	5	4	2	1	0	1	0	2	1	5	0	0	0	1	.000	0	0- 1	0	.208	.259	3.18
1992 Tor	26	2	0	0	0	1.1	8	4	1	1	0	0	0	0	0	0	1	0	0	0	0	—	0	0- 0	1	.500	.500	6.75
1993 Tor	27	1	0	0	1	2.1	10	3	1	1	0	0	0	0	0	0	2	0	0	0	0	—	0	0- 0	0	.300	.300	3.86
LCS Totals		7	0	0	3	9.1	90	12	6	4	1	0	1	0	2	1	8	0	0	0	1	.000	0	0-1	1	.286	.311	3.86
World Series		Pitching																										
Year Tm	Age	G	GS	CG	GF	IP	BFP	H	R	ER	HR	SH	SF	HB	TBB	IBB	SO	WP	Bk	W	L	Pct	ShO	Sv-Op	Hld	OAvg	OOBP	ERA
1992 Tor	26	2	0	0	1	1.1	4	0	0	0	0	0	0	0	0	0	0	0	0	0	0	—	0	1- 1	0	.000	.000	0.00
1993 Tor	27	2	0	0	1	2.1	8	2	0	0	0	0	0	0	0	0	4	0	0	0	0	—	0	0- 0	1	.250	.250	0.00
WS Totals		4	0	0	2	3.2	24	2	0	0	0	0	0	0	0	0	4	0	0	0	0	—	0	1-1	1	.167	.167	0.00
Postseason Totals		12	0	0	5	13.2	126	17	10	8	2	0	1	0	3	2	13	0	0	0	1	.000	0	1-2	2	.288	.317	5.27

Division Series		Batting																							Fielding						
Year Tm	Age	G	AB	H	2B	3B	HR	TB	R	RBI	GW	TBB	IBB	SO	HBP	SH	SF	SB	CS	SB%	GDP	Avg	OBP	SLG	Pos	G	PO	A	E	DP	FPct
1997 Sea	31	1	0	0	0	0	0	0	0	0	0	0	0	0	0	0	0	0	0	—	0	—	—	—	P	1	0	0	0	0	—
LCS		**Batting**																							**Fielding**						
Year Tm	Age	G	AB	H	2B	3B	HR	TB	R	RBI	GW	TBB	IBB	SO	HBP	SH	SF	SB	CS	SB%	GDP	Avg	OBP	SLG	Pos	G	PO	A	E	DP	FPct
1991 Tor	25	4	0	0	0	0	0	0	0	0	0	0	0	0	0	0	0	0	0	—	0	—	—	—	P	4	0	2	1	0	.667
1992 Tor	26	2	0	0	0	0	0	0	0	0	0	0	0	0	0	0	0	0	0	—	0	—	—	—	P	2	0	0	0	0	—
1993 Tor	27	1	0	0	0	0	0	0	0	0	0	0	0	0	0	0	0	0	0	—	0	—	—	—	P	1	1	1	0	0	1.000
LCS Totals		7	0	0	0	0	0	0	0	0	0	0	0	0	0	0	0	0	0	—	0	—	—	—	P	7	1	3	1	0	.800
World Series		**Batting**																							**Fielding**						
Year Tm	Age	G	AB	H	2B	3B	HR	TB	R	RBI	GW	TBB	IBB	SO	HBP	SH	SF	SB	CS	SB%	GDP	Avg	OBP	SLG	Pos	G	PO	A	E	DP	FPct
1992 Tor	26	2	0	0	0	0	0	0	0	0	0	0	0	0	0	0	0	0	0	—	0	—	—	—	P	2	0	1	0	0	1.000
1993 Tor	27	2	0	0	0	0	0	0	0	0	0	0	0	0	0	0	0	0	0	—	0	—	—	—	P	2	0	0	0	0	—
WS Totals		4	0	0	0	0	0	0	0	0	0	0	0	0	0	0	0	0	0	—	0	—	—	—	P	4	0	1	0	0	1.000
Postseason Totals		12	0	0	0	0	0	0	0	0	0	0	0	0	0	0	0	0	0	—	0	—	—	—	P	12	1	4	1	0	.833

JOE TINKER (HOF 1946-V)—Joseph Bert Tinker—Bats: Right; Throws: Right

Ht: 5'9"; Wt: 175 lbs; Born: 7/27/1880 in Muscotah, Kansas; Debut: 4/17/1902; Died: 7/27/1948

World Series		Batting																							Fielding						
Year Tm	Age	G	AB	H	2B	3B	HR	TB	R	RBI	GW	TBB	IBB	SO	HBP	SH	SF	SB	CS	SB%	GDP	Avg	OBP	SLG	Pos	G	PO	A	E	DP	FPct
1906 ChN	26	6	18	3	0	0	0	3	4	1	0	2	0	2	0	3	0	3	0	1.00	0	.167	.250	.167	SS	6	10	20	2	0	.938
1907 ChN	27	5	13	2	0	0	0	2	4	1	0	3	0	3	0	2	0	1	0	1.00	0	.154	.313	.154	SS	5	16	23	3	5	.929
1908 ChN	28	5	19	5	0	0	1	8	2	4	1	0	0	2	0	0	0	2	1	.67	0	.263	.263	.421	SS	5	8	20	0	2	1.000
1910 ChN	30	5	18	6	2	0	0	8	2	0	0	2	0	2	0	0	0	1	2	.33	0	.333	.400	.444	SS	5	10	14	2	2	.923
WS Totals		21	68	16	2	0	1	21	12	6	1	7	0	9	0	5	0	7	3	.70	0	.235	.307	.309	SS	21	44	77	7	9	.945

BUD TINNING—Lyle Forest Tinning—Throws: Right; Bats: Both

Ht: 5'11"; Wt: 198 lbs; Born: 3/12/1906 in Pilger, Nebraska; Debut: 4/20/1932; Died: 1/17/1961

World Series		Pitching																										
Year Tm	Age	G	GS	CG	GF	IP	BFP	H	R	ER	HR	SH	SF	HB	TBB	IBB	SO	WP	Bk	W	L	Pct	ShO	Sv-Op	Hld	OAvg	OOBP	ERA
1932 ChN	26	2	0	0	1	2.1	7	0	0	0	0	0	0	0	0	0	3	0	0	0	0	—	0	0-0	0	.000	.000	0.00

World Series		Batting																							Fielding						
Year Tm	Age	G	AB	H	2B	3B	HR	TB	R	RBI	GW	TBB	IBB	SO	HBP	SH	SF	SB	CS	SB%	GDP	Avg	OBP	SLG	Pos	G	PO	A	E	DP	FPct
1932 ChN	26	2	0	0	0	0	0	0	0	0	0	0	0	0	0	0	0	0	0	—	0	—	—	—	P	2	0	1	0	0	1.000

LEE TINSLEY—Lee Owen Tinsley—Bats: Both; Throws: Right

Ht: 5'10"; Wt: 185 lbs; Born: 3/4/1969 in Shelbyville, Kentucky; Debut: 4/6/1993

Division Series		Batting																							Fielding						
Year Tm	Age	G	AB	H	2B	3B	HR	TB	R	RBI	GW	TBB	IBB	SO	HBP	SH	SF	SB	CS	SB%	GDP	Avg	OBP	SLG	Pos	G	PO	A	E	DP	FPct
1995 Bos	26	1	5	0	0	0	0	0	0	0	0	1	1	2	0	0	0	0	0	—	0	.000	.167	.000	OF	1	1	0	0	0	1.000

JOE TIPTON—Joe Hicks Tipton—Bats: Right; Throws: Right

Ht: 5'11"; Wt: 185 lbs; Born: 2/18/1922 in McCaysville, Georgia; Debut: 5/2/1948; Died: 3/1/1994

World Series		Batting																							Fielding						
Year Tm	Age	G	AB	H	2B	3B	HR	TB	R	RBI	GW	TBB	IBB	SO	HBP	SH	SF	SB	CS	SB%	GDP	Avg	OBP	SLG	Pos	G	PO	A	E	DP	FPct
1948 Cle	26	1	1	0	0	0	0	0	0	0	0	0	0	1	0	0	0	0	0	—	0	.000	.000	.000	—						

JIM TOBIN—James Anthony Tobin—Nickname: Abba Dabba—Throws: Right; Bats: Right

Ht: 6'0"; Wt: 185 lbs; Born: 12/27/1912 in Oakland, California; Debut: 4/30/1937; Died: 5/19/1969

World Series		Pitching																										
Year Tm	Age	G	GS	CG	GF	IP	BFP	H	R	ER	HR	SH	SF	HB	TBB	IBB	SO	WP	Bk	W	L	Pct	ShO	Sv-Op	Hld	OAvg	OOBP	ERA
1945 Det	32	1	0	0	0	3.0	14	4	2	2	1	1	0	0	1	0	0	0	0	0	0	—	0	0-0	0	.333	.385	6.00

World Series		Batting																							Fielding						
Year Tm	Age	G	AB	H	2B	3B	HR	TB	R	RBI	GW	TBB	IBB	SO	HBP	SH	SF	SB	CS	SB%	GDP	Avg	OBP	SLG	Pos	G	PO	A	E	DP	FPct
1945 Det	32	1	1	0	0	0	0	0	0	0	0	0	0	0	0	0	0	0	0	—	0	.000	.000	.000	P	1	0	1	0	0	1.000

JIM TODD—James Richard Todd—Throws: Right; Bats: Left

Ht: 6'2"; Wt: 190 lbs; Born: 9/21/1947 in Lancaster, Pennsylvania; Debut: 4/29/1974

LCS		Pitching																										
Year Tm	Age	G	GS	CG	GF	IP	BFP	H	R	ER	HR	SH	SF	HB	TBB	IBB	SO	WP	Bk	W	L	Pct	ShO	Sv-Op	Hld	OAvg	OOBP	ERA
1975 Oak	28	3	0	0	0	1.0	5	3	1	1	0	0	0	0	0	0	0	0	0	0	0	—	0	0-0	0	.600	.600	9.00

LCS		Batting																							Fielding						
Year Tm	Age	G	AB	H	2B	3B	HR	TB	R	RBI	GW	TBB	IBB	SO	HBP	SH	SF	SB	CS	SB%	GDP	Avg	OBP	SLG	Pos	G	PO	A	E	DP	FPct
1975 Oak	28	3	0	0	0	0	0	0	0	0	0	0	0	0	0	0	0	0	0	—	0	—	—	—	P	3	0	0	0	0	—

PHIL TODT—Philip Julius Todt—Nickname: Hook—Bats: Left; Throws: Left

Ht: 6'0"; Wt: 175 lbs; Born: 8/9/1901 in St. Louis, Missouri; Debut: 4/25/1924; Died: 11/15/1973

World Series		Batting																							Fielding						
Year Tm	Age	G	AB	H	2B	3B	HR	TB	R	RBI	GW	TBB	IBB	SO	HBP	SH	SF	SB	CS	SB%	GDP	Avg	OBP	SLG	Pos	G	PO	A	E	DP	FPct
1931 Phi	30	1	0	0	0	0	0	0	0	0	0	1	0	0	0	0	0	0	0	—	0	—	1.000	—	—						

BOBBY TOLAN—Robert Tolan—Bats: Left; Throws: Left

Ht: 5'11"; Wt: 170 lbs; Born: 11/19/1945 in Los Angeles, California; Debut: 9/3/1965

LCS		Batting																							Fielding						
Year Tm	Age	G	AB	H	2B	3B	HR	TB	R	RBI	GW	TBB	IBB	SO	HBP	SH	SF	SB	CS	SB%	GDP	Avg	OBP	SLG	Pos	G	PO	A	E	DP	FPct
1970 Cin	24	3	12	5	0	0	1	8	3	2	1	1	0	1	0	0	0	1	1	.50	0	.417	.462	.667	OF	3	5	0	0	0	1.000
1972 Cin	26	5	21	5	1	1	0	8	3	4	1	0	0	4	0	0	0	0	1	.00	0	.238	.238	.381	OF	5	13	0	0	0	1.000
1976 Phi	30	3	2	0	0	0	0	0	0	0	0	1	1	0	0	0	0	0	0	—	0	.000	.333	.000	1B	1	0	0	0	0	—
																									OF	1	1	0	0	0	1.000
LCS Totals		11	35	10	1	1	1	16	6	6	2	2	1	5	0	0	0	1	2	.33	0	.286	.324	.457	OF	9	19	0	0	0	1.000
World Series		**Batting**																							**Fielding**						
Year Tm	Age	G	AB	H	2B	3B	HR	TB	R	RBI	GW	TBB	IBB	SO	HBP	SH	SF	SB	CS	SB%	GDP	Avg	OBP	SLG	Pos	G	PO	A	E	DP	FPct
1967 StL	21	3	2	0	0	0	0	0	1	0	0	1	0	1	0	0	0	0	0	—	0	.000	.333	.000	—						
1968 StL	22	1	1	0	0	0	0	0	0	0	0	0	0	1	0	0	0	0	0	—	0	.000	.000	.000	—						
1970 Cin	24	5	19	4	1	0	1	8	5	1	0	3	0	2	0	0	0	1	1	.50	0	.211	.318	.421	OF	5	4	0	1	0	.800
1972 Cin	26	7	26	7	1	0	0	8	2	6	0	1	0	4	0	0	0	5	1	.83	0	.269	.296	.308	OF	7	11	0	1	0	.917
WS Totals		16	48	11	2	0	1	16	8	7	0	5	0	8	0	0	0	6	2	.75	0	.229	.302	.333	OF	12	15	0	2	0	.882
Postseason Totals		27	83	21	3	1	2	32	14	13	2	7	1	13	0	0	0	7	4	.64	0	.253	.311	.386	OF	21	34	0	2	0	.944

CHICK TOLSON—Charles Julius Tolson—Nicknames: Toby, Slug—Bats: Right; Throws: Right

Ht: 6'0"; Wt: 185 lbs; Born: 5/3/1895 in Washington, DC; Debut: 7/3/1925; Died: 4/16/1965

World Series		Batting																							Fielding						
Year Tm	Age	G	AB	H	2B	3B	HR	TB	R	RBI	GW	TBB	IBB	SO	HBP	SH	SF	SB	CS	SB%	GDP	Avg	OBP	SLG	Pos	G	PO	A	E	DP	FPct
1929 ChN	34	1	1	0	0	0	0	0	0	0	0	0	0	1	0	0	0	0	0	—	0	.000	.000	.000	—						

DAVE TOMLIN—David Allen Tomlin—Throws: Left; Bats: Left

Ht: 6'2"; Wt: 180 lbs; Born: 6/22/1949 in Maysville, Kentucky; Debut: 9/2/1972

LCS		Pitching																										
Year Tm	Age	G	GS	CG	GF	IP	BFP	H	R	ER	HR	SH	SF	HB	TBB	IBB	SO	WP	Bk	W	L	Pct	ShO	Sv-Op	Hld	OAvg	OOBP	ERA
1973 Cin	24	1	0	0	0	1.2	11	5	3	3	0	0	0	0	1	0	1	0	0	0	0	—	0	0-0	0	.500	.545	16.20
1979 Cin	30	3	0	0	1	3.0	14	3	1	0	0	1	0	0	2	2	3	0	0	0	0	—	0	0-0	0	.273	.385	0.00
LCS Totals		4	0	0	1	4.2	50	8	4	3	0	1	0	0	3	2	4	0	0	0	0	—	0	0-0	0	.381	.458	5.79

LCS		Batting																							Fielding						
Year Tm	Age	G	AB	H	2B	3B	HR	TB	R	RBI	GW	TBB	IBB	SO	HBP	SH	SF	SB	CS	SB%	GDP	Avg	OBP	SLG	Pos	G	PO	A	E	DP	FPct
1973 Cin	24	1	0	0	0	0	0	0	0	0	0	0	0	0	0	0	0	0	0	—	0	—	—	—	P	1	0	0	0	0	—
1979 Cin	30	3	0	0	0	0	0	0	0	0	0	0	0	0	0	0	0	0	0	—	0	—	—	—	P	3	1	1	0	0	1.000
LCS Totals		4	0	0	0	0	0	0	0	0	0	0	0	0	0	0	0	0	0	—	0	—	—	—	P	4	1	1	0	0	1.000

RANDY TOMLIN—Randy Leon Tomlin—Throws: Left; Bats: Left

Ht: 5'11"; Wt: 180 lbs; Born: 6/14/1966 in Bainbridge, Maryland; Debut: 8/6/1990

LCS		Pitching																										
Year Tm	Age	G	GS	CG	GF	IP	BFP	H	R	ER	HR	SH	SF	HB	TBB	IBB	SO	WP	Bk	W	L	Pct	ShO	Sv-Op	Hld	OAvg	OOBP	ERA
1991 Pit	25	1	1	0	0	6.0	26	6	2	2	0	1	0	0	2	0	1	0	0	0	0	—	0	0- 0	0	.261	.320	3.00
1992 Pit	26	2	0	0	0	2.2	13	5	2	2	0	0	0	0	1	0	0	0	0	0	0	—	0	0- 0	0	.417	.462	6.75
LCS Totals		3	1	0	0	8.2	78	11	4	4	0	1	0	0	3	0	1	0	0	0	0	—	0	0-0	0	.314	.368	4.15

LCS		Batting																							Fielding						
Year Tm	Age	G	AB	H	2B	3B	HR	TB	R	RBI	GW	TBB	IBB	SO	HBP	SH	SF	SB	CS	SB%	GDP	Avg	OBP	SLG	Pos	G	PO	A	E	DP	FPct
1991 Pit	25	1	2	0	0	0	0	0	0	0	0	0	0	0	0	0	0	0	0	—	0	.000	.000	.000	P	1	1	0	0	0	1.000
1992 Pit	26	2	0	0	0	0	0	0	0	0	0	0	0	0	0	0	0	0	0	—	0	—	—	—	P	2	0	1	0	0	1.000
LCS Totals		3	2	0	0	0	0	0	0	0	0	0	0	0	0	0	0	0	0	—	0	.000	.000	.000	P	3	1	1	0	0	1.000

FRED TONEY—Fred Alexandra Toney—Throws: Right; Bats: Right

Ht: 6'6"; Wt: 245 lbs; Born: 12/11/1888 in Nashville, Tennessee; Debut: 4/15/1911; Died: 3/11/1953

World Series		Pitching																										
Year Tm	Age	G	GS	CG	GF	IP	BFP	H	R	ER	HR	SH	SF	HB	TBB	IBB	SO	WP	Bk	W	L	Pct	ShO	Sv-Op	Hld	OAvg	OOBP	ERA
1921 NYG	32	2	2	0	0	2.2	18	7	7	7	0	1	0	0	3	0	1	0	0	0	0	—	0	0- 0	0	.500	.588	23.63

World Series		Batting																							Fielding						
Year Tm	Age	G	AB	H	2B	3B	HR	TB	R	RBI	GW	TBB	IBB	SO	HBP	SH	SF	SB	CS	SB%	GDP	Avg	OBP	SLG	Pos	G	PO	A	E	DP	FPct
1921 NYG	32	2	0	0	0	0	0	0	0	0	0	0	0	0	0	0	0	0	0	—	0	—	—	—	P	2	0	1	0	0	1.000

SPECS TOPORCER—George Toporcer—Bats: Left; Throws: Right

Ht: 5'10"; Wt: 165 lbs; Born: 2/9/1899 in New York, New York; Debut: 4/13/1921; Died: 5/17/1989

World Series		Batting																							Fielding						
Year Tm	Age	G	AB	H	2B	3B	HR	TB	R	RBI	GW	TBB	IBB	SO	HBP	SH	SF	SB	CS	SB%	GDP	Avg	OBP	SLG	Pos	G	PO	A	E	DP	FPct
1926 StL	27	1	0	0	0	0	0	0	0	1	0	0	0	0	0	0	1	0	0	—	0	—	.000	—	—						

EARL TORGESON—Clifford Earl Torgeson—Nickname: The Earl of Snohomish—Bats: Left; Throws: Left

Ht: 6'3"; Wt: 180 lbs; Born: 1/1/1924 in Snohomish, Washington; Debut: 4/15/1947; Died: 11/8/1990

World Series		Batting																							Fielding						
Year Tm	Age	G	AB	H	2B	3B	HR	TB	R	RBI	GW	TBB	IBB	SO	HBP	SH	SF	SB	CS	SB%	GDP	Avg	OBP	SLG	Pos	G	PO	A	E	DP	FPct
1948 Bos	24	5	18	7	3	0	0	10	2	1	1	2	0	1	0	0	0	1	0	1.00	0	.389	.450	.556	1B	5	44	5	0	2	1.000
1959 ChA	35	3	1	0	0	0	0	0	1	0	0	1	0	0	0	0	0	0	0	—	0	.000	.500	.000	1B	1	0	0	0	0	—
WS Totals		8	19	7	3	0	0	10	3	1	1	3	0	1	0	0	0	1	0	1.00	0	.368	.455	.526	1B	6	44	5	0	2	1.000

FRANK TORRE—Frank Joseph Torre—Bats: Left; Throws: Left

Ht: 6'4"; Wt: 200 lbs; Born: 12/30/1931 in Brooklyn, New York; Debut: 4/20/1956

World Series		Batting																							Fielding						
Year Tm	Age	G	AB	H	2B	3B	HR	TB	R	RBI	GW	TBB	IBB	SO	HBP	SH	SF	SB	CS	SB%	GDP	Avg	OBP	SLG	Pos	G	PO	A	E	DP	FPct
1957 Mil	25	7	10	3	0	0	2	9	2	3	0	2	0	0	0	0	0	0	0	—	0	.300	.417	.900	1B	7	37	2	0	4	1.000
1958 Mil	26	7	17	3	0	0	0	3	0	1	0	2	0	0	0	1	0	0	0	—	0	.176	.263	.176	1B	5	39	2	2	4	.953
WS Totals		14	27	6	0	0	2	12	2	4	0	4	0	0	0	1	0	0	0	—	0	.222	.323	.444	1B	12	76	4	2	8	.976

MIKE TORREZ—Michael Augustine Torrez—Throws: Right; Bats: Right

Ht: 6'5"; Wt: 220 lbs; Born: 8/28/1946 in Topeka, Kansas; Debut: 9/10/1967

LCS		Pitching																										
Year Tm	Age	G	GS	CG	GF	IP	BFP	H	R	ER	HR	SH	SF	HB	TBB	IBB	SO	WP	Bk	W	L	Pct	ShO	Sv-Op	Hld	OAvg	OOBP	ERA
1977 NYA	31	2	1	0	0	11.0	47	11	5	5	0	1	0	0	5	0	5	0	0	0	1	.000	0	0- 0	0	.268	.348	4.09
World Series		**Pitching**																										
Year Tm	Age	G	GS	CG	GF	IP	BFP	H	R	ER	HR	SH	SF	HB	TBB	IBB	SO	WP	Bk	W	L	Pct	ShO	Sv-Op	Hld	OAvg	OOBP	ERA
1977 NYA	31	2	2	2	0	18.0	73	16	7	5	2	0	0	0	5	0	15	0	0	2	0	1.000	0	0- 0	0	.235	.288	2.50
Postseason Totals		4	3	2	0	29.0	240	27	12	10	2	1	0	0	10	0	20	0	0	2	1	.667	0	0-0	0	.248	.311	3.10

LCS		Batting																							Fielding						
Year Tm	Age	G	AB	H	2B	3B	HR	TB	R	RBI	GW	TBB	IBB	SO	HBP	SH	SF	SB	CS	SB%	GDP	Avg	OBP	SLG	Pos	G	PO	A	E	DP	FPct
1977 NYA	31	2	0	0	0	0	0	0	0	0	0	0	0	0	0	0	0	0	0	—	0	—	—	—	P	2	2	1	0	0	1.000
World Series		**Batting**																							**Fielding**						
Year Tm	Age	G	AB	H	2B	3B	HR	TB	R	RBI	GW	TBB	IBB	SO	HBP	SH	SF	SB	CS	SB%	GDP	Avg	OBP	SLG	Pos	G	PO	A	E	DP	FPct
1977 NYA	31	2	6	0	0	0	0	0	0	0	0	0	0	4	0	1	0	0	0	—	0	.000	.000	.000	P	2	2	3	0	0	1.000
Postseason Totals		4	6	0	0	0	0	0	0	0	0	0	0	4	0	1	0	0	0	—	0	.000	.000	.000	P	4	4	4	0	0	1.000

CESAR TOVAR—Cesar Leonardo Tovar—Nickname: Pepito—Bats: Right; Throws: Right

Ht: 5'9"; Wt: 155 lbs; Born: 7/3/1940 in Caracas, Venezuela; Debut: 4/12/1965; Died: 7/14/1994

LCS		Batting																							Fielding						
Year Tm	Age	G	AB	H	2B	3B	HR	TB	R	RBI	GW	TBB	IBB	SO	HBP	SH	SF	SB	CS	SB%	GDP	Avg	OBP	SLG	Pos	G	PO	A	E	DP	FPct
1969 Min	29	3	13	1	0	0	0	1	0	0	0	1	0	2	0	0	0	1	0	1.00	0	.077	.143	.077	OF	3	10	0	0	0	1.000
1970 Min	30	3	13	5	0	1	0	7	2	1	0	0	0	0	0	0	0	0	0	—	0	.385	.385	.538	2B	1	0	0	0	0	—
																									OF	3	6	0	0	0	1.000
1975 Oak	35	2	2	1	0	0	0	1	2	0	0	1	0	0	0	0	0	0	0	—	0	.500	.667	.500	2B	1	2	2	1	0	.800
LCS Totals		8	28	7	0	1	0	9	4	1	0	2	0	2	0	0	0	1	0	1.00	0	.250	.300	.321	OF	6	16	0	0	0	1.000

BABE TOWNE—Jay King Towne—Bats: Right; Throws: Right

Ht: 5'10"; Wt: 180 lbs; Born: 3/12/1880 in Coon Rapids, Iowa; Debut: 8/1/1906; Died: 10/29/1938

World Series		Batting																							Fielding						
Year Tm	Age	G	AB	H	2B	3B	HR	TB	R	RBI	GW	TBB	IBB	SO	HBP	SH	SF	SB	CS	SB%	GDP	Avg	OBP	SLG	Pos	G	PO	A	E	DP	FPct
1906 ChA	26	1	1	0	0	0	0	0	0	0	0	0	0	0	0	0	0	0	0	—	0	.000	.000	.000	—						

DICK TRACEWSKI—Richard Joseph Tracewski—Nickname: Trixie—Bats: Right; Throws: Right

Ht: 5'11"; Wt: 160 lbs; Born: 2/3/1935 in Eynon, Pennsylvania; Debut: 4/12/1962

World Series		Batting																							Fielding						
Year Tm	Age	G	AB	H	2B	3B	HR	TB	R	RBI	GW	TBB	IBB	SO	HBP	SH	SF	SB	CS	SB%	GDP	Avg	OBP	SLG	Pos	G	PO	A	E	DP	FPct
1963 LA	28	4	13	2	0	0	0	2	1	0	0	1	0	2	0	0	0	0	0	—	0	.154	.214	.154	2B	4	7	7	1	1	.933
1965 LA	30	6	17	2	0	0	0	2	0	0	0	1	0	5	0	0	0	0	1	.00	0	.118	.167	.118	2B	5	11	11	1	4	.957
1968 Det	33	2	0	0	0	0	0	0	1	0	0	0	0	0	0	0	0	0	0	—	0	—	—	—	3B	1	0	0	0	0	—
WS Totals		12	30	4	0	0	0	4	2	0	0	2	0	7	0	0	0	0	1	.00	0	.133	.188	.133	2B	9	18	18	2	5	.947

ALAN TRAMMELL—Alan Stuart Trammell—Bats: Right; Throws: Right

Ht: 6'0"; Wt: 165 lbs; Born: 2/21/1958 in Garden Grove, California; Debut: 9/9/1977

LCS		Batting																							Fielding						
Year Tm	Age	G	AB	H	2B	3B	HR	TB	R	RBI	GW	TBB	IBB	SO	HBP	SH	SF	SB	CS	SB%	GDP	Avg	OBP	SLG	Pos	G	PO	A	E	DP	FPct
1984 Det	26	3	11	4	0	1	1	9	2	3	1	3	0	1	0	0	0	0	0	—	0	.364	.500	.818	SS	3	1	8	0	0	1.000
1987 Det	29	5	20	4	1	0	0	5	3	2	0	1	0	2	0	0	0	0	0	—	2	.200	.238	.250	SS	5	6	9	1	1	.938
LCS Totals		8	31	8	1	1	1	14	5	5	1	4	0	3	0	0	0	0	0	—	2	.258	.343	.452	SS	8	7	17	1	1	.960
World Series		**Batting**																							**Fielding**						
Year Tm	Age	G	AB	H	2B	3B	HR	TB	R	RBI	GW	TBB	IBB	SO	HBP	SH	SF	SB	CS	SB%	GDP	Avg	OBP	SLG	Pos	G	PO	A	E	DP	FPct
1984 Det	26	5	20	9	1	0	2	16	5	6	1	2	0	2	0	1	0	1	1	.50	0	.450	.500	.800	SS	5	8	9	1	0	.944
Postseason Totals		13	51	17	2	1	3	30	10	11	2	6	0	5	0	1	0	1	1	.50	2	.333	.404	.588	SS	13	15	26	2	1	.953

PIE TRAYNOR (HOF 1948-W)—Harold Joseph Traynor—Bats: Right; Throws: Right

Ht: 6'0"; Wt: 170 lbs; Born: 11/11/1899 in Framingham, Massachusetts; Debut: 9/15/1920; Died: 3/16/1972

World Series		Batting																							Fielding						
Year Tm	Age	G	AB	H	2B	3B	HR	TB	R	RBI	GW	TBB	IBB	SO	HBP	SH	SF	SB	CS	SB%	GDP	Avg	OBP	SLG	Pos	G	PO	A	E	DP	FPct
1925 Pit	25	7	26	9	0	2	1	16	2	4	0	3	0	1	0	0	1	1	0	1.00	1	.346	.400	.615	3B	7	6	18	0	2	1.000
1927 Pit	27	4	15	3	1	0	0	4	1	0	0	0	0	1	0	0	0	0	0	—	0	.200	.200	.267	3B	4	5	9	1	1	.933
WS Totals		11	41	12	1	2	1	20	3	4	0	3	0	2	0	0	1	1	0	1.00	1	.293	.333	.488	3B	11	11	27	1	3	.974

JEFF TREADWAY—Hugh Jeffery Treadway—Bats: Left; Throws: Right

Ht: 5'10"; Wt: 170 lbs; Born: 1/22/1963 in Columbus, Georgia; Debut: 9/4/1987

LCS		Batting																							Fielding						
Year Tm	Age	G	AB	H	2B	3B	HR	TB	R	RBI	GW	TBB	IBB	SO	HBP	SH	SF	SB	CS	SB%	GDP	Avg	OBP	SLG	Pos	G	PO	A	E	DP	FPct
1991 Atl	28	1	3	1	0	0	0	1	0	0	0	0	0	0	0	1	0	0	0	—	0	.333	.333	.333	2B	1	2	2	0	1	1.000
1992 Atl	29	3	3	2	0	0	0	2	1	0	0	0	0	1	0	0	0	0	0	—	0	.667	.667	.667	2B	1	0	1	0	0	1.000
LCS Totals		4	6	3	0	0	0	3	1	0	0	0	0	1	0	1	0	0	0	—	0	.500	.500	.500	2B	2	2	3	0	1	1.000
World Series		Batting																							Fielding						
Year Tm	Age	G	AB	H	2B	3B	HR	TB	R	RBI	GW	TBB	IBB	SO	HBP	SH	SF	SB	CS	SB%	GDP	Avg	OBP	SLG	Pos	G	PO	A	E	DP	FPct
1991 Atl	28	3	4	1	0	0	0	1	1	0	0	1	0	2	0	1	0	0	0	—	0	.250	.400	.250	2B	1	1	3	1	1	.800
1992 Atl	29	1	1	0	0	0	0	0	0	0	0	0	0	0	0	0	0	0	0	—	0	.000	.000	.000	—						
WS Totals		4	5	1	0	0	0	1	1	0	0	1	0	2	0	1	0	0	0	—	0	.200	.333	.200	2B	1	1	3	1	1	.800
Postseason Totals		8	11	4	0	0	0	4	2	0	0	1	0	3	0	2	0	0	0	—	0	.364	.417	.364	2B	3	3	6	1	2	.900

TOM TRESH—Thomas Michael Tresh—Bats: Both; Throws: Right

Ht: 6'1"; Wt: 180 lbs; Born: 9/20/1937 in Detroit, Michigan; Debut: 9/3/1961

World Series		Batting																							Fielding						
Year Tm	Age	G	AB	H	2B	3B	HR	TB	R	RBI	GW	TBB	IBB	SO	HBP	SH	SF	SB	CS	SB%	GDP	Avg	OBP	SLG	Pos	G	PO	A	E	DP	FPct
1962 NYA-*RY*	25	7	28	9	1	0	1	13	5	4	1	1	0	4	0	1	0	2	0	1.00	0	.321	.345	.464	OF	7	14	0	0	0	1.000
1963 NYA	26	4	15	3	0	0	1	6	1	2	0	1	0	6	0	0	0	0	0	—	0	.200	.250	.400	OF	4	3	0	0	0	1.000
1964 NYA	27	7	22	6	2	0	2	14	4	7	1	6	2	7	0	0	1	0	0	—	1	.273	.414	.636	OF	7	11	0	0	0	1.000
WS Totals		18	65	18	3	0	4	33	10	13	2	8	2	17	0	1	1	2	0	1.00	1	.277	.351	.508	OF	18	28	0	0	0	1.000

MANNY TRILLO—Jesus Manuel Marcano Trillo—Nickname: Indio—Bats: Right; Throws: Right

Ht: 6'1"; Wt: 150 lbs; Born: 12/25/1950 in Caripito, Venezuela; Debut: 6/28/1973

Division Series		Batting																							Fielding						
Year Tm	Age	G	AB	H	2B	3B	HR	TB	R	RBI	GW	TBB	IBB	SO	HBP	SH	SF	SB	CS	SB%	GDP	Avg	OBP	SLG	Pos	G	PO	A	E	DP	FPct
1981 Phi	30	5	16	3	0	0	0	3	1	1	0	4	2	0	0	0	0	0	0	—	0	.188	.350	.188	2B	5	14	9	0	2	1.000
LCS		Batting																							Fielding						
Year Tm	Age	G	AB	H	2B	3B	HR	TB	R	RBI	GW	TBB	IBB	SO	HBP	SH	SF	SB	CS	SB%	GDP	Avg	OBP	SLG	Pos	G	PO	A	E	DP	FPct
1974 Oak	23	1	0	0	0	0	0	0	1	0	0	0	0	0	0	0	0	0	0	—	0	—	—	—	—						
1980 Phi	29	5	21	8	2	1	0	12	1	4	0	0	0	2	0	2	1	0	0	—	0	.381	.364	.571	2B	5	18	25	1	4	.977
LCS Totals		6	21	8	2	1	0	12	2	4	0	0	0	2	0	2	1	0	0	—	0	.381	.364	.571	2B	5	18	25	1	4	.977
World Series		Batting																							Fielding						
Year Tm	Age	G	AB	H	2B	3B	HR	TB	R	RBI	GW	TBB	IBB	SO	HBP	SH	SF	SB	CS	SB%	GDP	Avg	OBP	SLG	Pos	G	PO	A	E	DP	FPct
1980 Phi	29	6	23	5	2	0	0	7	4	2	1	0	0	0	0	0	1	0	0	—	2	.217	.208	.304	2B	6	14	25	1	6	.975
Postseason Totals		17	60	16	4	1	0	22	7	7	1	4	2	2	0	2	2	0	0	—	2	.267	.303	.367	2B	16	46	59	2	12	.981

DIZZY TROUT—Paul Howard Trout—Throws: Right; Bats: Right

Ht: 6'2"; Wt: 195 lbs; Born: 6/29/1915 in Sandcut, Indiana; Debut: 4/25/1939; Died: 2/28/1972

World Series		Pitching																										
Year Tm	Age	G	GS	CG	GF	IP	BFP	H	R	ER	HR	SH	SF	HB	TBB	IBB	SO	WP	Bk	W	L	Pct	ShO	Sv-Op	Hld	OAvg	OOBP	ERA
1940 Det	25	1	1	0	0	2.0	14	6	3	2	0	0	0	0	1	0	1	0	0	0	1	.000	0	0- 0	0	.462	.500	9.00
1945 Det	30	2	1	1	1	13.2	52	9	2	1	0	2	0	0	3	1	9	0	0	1	1	.500	0	0- 0	0	.191	.240	0.66
WS Totals		3	2	1	1	15.2	132	15	5	3	0	2	0	0	4	1	10	0	0	1	2	.333	0	0-0	0	.250	.297	1.72

World Series		Batting																							Fielding						
Year Tm	Age	G	AB	H	2B	3B	HR	TB	R	RBI	GW	TBB	IBB	SO	HBP	SH	SF	SB	CS	SB%	GDP	Avg	OBP	SLG	Pos	G	PO	A	E	DP	FPct
1940 Det	25	1	1	0	0	0	0	0	0	0	0	0	0	0	0	0	0	0	0	—	0	.000	.000	.000	P	1	0	1	0	0	1.000
1945 Det	30	2	6	1	0	0	0	1	0	0	0	0	0	0	0	0	0	0	0	—	0	.167	.167	.167	P	2	2	5	0	0	1.000
WS Totals		3	7	1	0	0	0	1	0	0	0	0	0	0	0	0	0	0	0	—	0	.143	.143	.143	P	3	2	6	0	0	1.000

STEVE TROUT—Steven Russell Trout—Nickname: Rainbow—Throws: Left; Bats: Left

Ht: 6'4"; Wt: 195 lbs; Born: 7/30/1957 in Detroit, Michigan; Debut: 7/1/1978

LCS		Pitching																										
Year Tm	Age	G	GS	CG	GF	IP	BFP	H	R	ER	HR	SH	SF	HB	TBB	IBB	SO	WP	Bk	W	L	Pct	ShO	Sv-Op	Hld	OAvg	OOBP	ERA
1984 ChN	27	2	1	0	0	9.0	33	5	2	2	0	0	1	0	3	0	3	0	0	1	0	1.000	0	0- 0	0	.172	.242	2.00

LCS		Batting																							Fielding						
Year Tm	Age	G	AB	H	2B	3B	HR	TB	R	RBI	GW	TBB	IBB	SO	HBP	SH	SF	SB	CS	SB%	GDP	Avg	OBP	SLG	Pos	G	PO	A	E	DP	FPct
1984 ChN	27	2	2	1	0	0	0	1	0	0	0	0	0	0	0	1	0	0	0	—	0	.500	.500	.500	P	2	0	1	1	0	.500

BOB TROWBRIDGE—Robert Trowbridge—Throws: Right; Bats: Right

Ht: 6'1"; Wt: 180 lbs; Born: 6/27/1930 in Hudson, New York; Debut: 4/22/1956; Died: 4/3/1980

World Series		Pitching																										
Year Tm	Age	G	GS	CG	GF	IP	BFP	H	R	ER	HR	SH	SF	HB	TBB	IBB	SO	WP	Bk	W	L	Pct	ShO	Sv-Op	Hld	OAvg	OOBP	ERA
1957 Mil	27	1	0	0	0	1.0	8	2	5	5	1	0	0	0	3	0	1	0	0	0	0	—	0	0- 0	0	.400	.625	45.00

World Series		Batting																							Fielding						
Year Tm	Age	G	AB	H	2B	3B	HR	TB	R	RBI	GW	TBB	IBB	SO	HBP	SH	SF	SB	CS	SB%	GDP	Avg	OBP	SLG	Pos	G	PO	A	E	DP	FPct
1957 Mil	27	1	0	0	0	0	0	0	0	0	0	0	0	0	0	0	0	0	0	—	0	—	—	—	P	1	0	0	0	0	—

VIRGIL TRUCKS—Virgil Oliver Trucks—Nickname: Fire—Throws: Right; Bats: Right

Ht: 5'11"; Wt: 198 lbs; Born: 4/26/1917 in Birmingham, Alabama; Debut: 9/27/1941

World Series		Pitching																										
Year Tm	Age	G	GS	CG	GF	IP	BFP	H	R	ER	HR	SH	SF	HB	TBB	IBB	SO	WP	Bk	W	L	Pct	ShO	Sv-Op	Hld	OAvg	OOBP	ERA
1945 Det	28	2	2	1	0	13.1	58	14	5	5	0	2	0	0	5	0	7	0	0	1	0	1.000	0	0- 0	0	.275	.339	3.38

World Series		Batting																							Fielding						
Year Tm	Age	G	AB	H	2B	3B	HR	TB	R	RBI	GW	TBB	IBB	SO	HBP	SH	SF	SB	CS	SB%	GDP	Avg	OBP	SLG	Pos	G	PO	A	E	DP	FPct
1945 Det	28	2	4	0	0	0	0	0	0	0	0	1	0	1	0	0	0	0	0	—	0	.000	.200	.000	P	2	1	1	0	0	1.000

MICHAEL TUCKER—Michael Anthony Tucker—Bats: Left; Throws: Right

Ht: 6'2"; Wt: 185 lbs; Born: 6/25/1971 in South Boston, Virginia; Debut: 4/26/1995

Division Series		Batting																							Fielding						
Year Tm	Age	G	AB	H	2B	3B	HR	TB	R	RBI	GW	TBB	IBB	SO	HBP	SH	SF	SB	CS	SB%	GDP	Avg	OBP	SLG	Pos	G	PO	A	E	DP	FPct
1997 Atl	26	2	6	1	0	0	0	1	0	1	0	0	0	1	0	0	0	0	0	—	0	.167	.167	.167	OF	2	3	0	0	0	1.000
LCS		Batting																							Fielding						
Year Tm	Age	G	AB	H	2B	3B	HR	TB	R	RBI	GW	TBB	IBB	SO	HBP	SH	SF	SB	CS	SB%	GDP	Avg	OBP	SLG	Pos	G	PO	A	E	DP	FPct
1997 Atl	26	5	10	1	0	0	1	4	1	1	0	3	0	4	0	0	0	0	0	—	0	.100	.308	.400	OF	4	5	1	0	1	1.000
Postseason Totals		7	16	2	0	0	1	5	1	2	0	3	0	5	0	0	0	0	0	—	0	.125	.263	.313	OF	6	8	1	0	1	1.000

THURMAN TUCKER—Thurman Lowell Tucker—Nickname: Joe E.—Bats: Left; Throws: Right

Ht: 5'10"; Wt: 165 lbs; Born: 9/26/1917 in Gordon, Texas; Debut: 4/14/1942; Died: 5/7/1993

World Series		Batting																							Fielding						
Year Tm	Age	G	AB	H	2B	3B	HR	TB	R	RBI	GW	TBB	IBB	SO	HBP	SH	SF	SB	CS	SB%	GDP	Avg	OBP	SLG	Pos	G	PO	A	E	DP	FPct
1948 Cle	31	1	3	1	0	0	0	1	1	0	0	1	0	0	0	0	0	0	1	.00	0	.333	.500	.333	OF	1	3	1	0	1	1.000

JOHN TUDOR—John Thomas Tudor—Throws: Left; Bats: Left

Ht: 6'0"; Wt: 185 lbs; Born: 2/2/1954 in Schenectady, New York; Debut: 8/16/1979

LCS		Pitching																										
Year Tm	Age	G	GS	CG	GF	IP	BFP	H	R	ER	HR	SH	SF	HB	TBB	IBB	SO	WP	Bk	W	L	Pct	ShO	Sv-Op	Hld	OAvg	OOBP	ERA
1985 StL	31	2	2	0	0	12.2	52	10	5	4	1	1	0	0	3	1	8	0	0	1	1	.500	0	0- 0	0	.208	.255	2.84
1987 StL	33	2	2	0	0	15.1	65	16	5	3	2	2	0	0	5	2	12	0	0	1	1	.500	0	0- 0	0	.276	.333	1.76
1988 LA	34	1	1	0	0	5.0	24	8	4	4	2	0	0	0	1	0	1	0	0	0	0	—	0	0- 0	0	.348	.375	7.20
LCS Totals		5	5	0	0	33.0	282	34	14	11	5	3	0	0	9	3	21	0	0	2	2	.500	0	0-0	0	.264	.312	3.00
World Series		Pitching																										
Year Tm	Age	G	GS	CG	GF	IP	BFP	H	R	ER	HR	SH	SF	HB	TBB	IBB	SO	WP	Bk	W	L	Pct	ShO	Sv-Op	Hld	OAvg	OOBP	ERA
1985 StL	31	3	3	1	0	18.0	74	15	6	6	1	0	0	1	7	0	14	0	0	2	1	.667	1	0- 0	0	.227	.311	3.00
1987 StL	33	2	2	0	0	11.0	51	15	7	7	1	0	0	0	3	0	8	0	0	1	1	.500	0	0- 0	0	.313	.353	5.73
1988 LA	34	1	1	0	0	1.1	4	0	0	0	0	0	0	0	0	0	1	0	0	0	0	—	0	0- 0	0	.000	.000	0.00
WS Totals		6	6	1	0	30.1	258	30	13	13	2	0	0	1	10	0	23	0	0	3	2	.600	1	0-0	0	.254	.318	3.86
Postseason Totals		11	11	1	0	63.1	540	64	27	24	7	3	0	1	19	3	44	0	0	5	4	.556	1	0-0	0	.259	.315	3.41

LCS		Batting																							Fielding						
Year Tm	Age	G	AB	H	2B	3B	HR	TB	R	RBI	GW	TBB	IBB	SO	HBP	SH	SF	SB	CS	SB%	GDP	Avg	OBP	SLG	Pos	G	PO	A	E	DP	FPct
1985 StL	31	2	4	0	0	0	0	0	1	0	0	1	0	1	0	0	0	0	0	—	1	.000	.200	.000	P	2	0	1	0	0	1.000
1987 StL	33	2	4	0	0	0	0	0	0	0	0	0	0	4	0	0	0	0	0	—	0	.000	.000	.000	P	2	0	4	0	0	1.000
1988 LA	34	1	2	0	0	0	0	0	0	0	0	0	0	2	0	0	0	0	0	—	0	.000	.000	.000	P	1	1	2	0	0	1.000
LCS Totals		5	10	0	0	0	0	0	1	0	0	1	0	7	0	0	0	0	0	—	1	.000	.091	.000	P	5	1	7	0	0	1.000
World Series		Batting																							Fielding						
Year Tm	Age	G	AB	H	2B	3B	HR	TB	R	RBI	GW	TBB	IBB	SO	HBP	SH	SF	SB	CS	SB%	GDP	Avg	OBP	SLG	Pos	G	PO	A	E	DP	FPct
1985 StL	31	3	5	0	0	0	0	0	0	0	0	0	0	4	0	1	0	0	0	—	0	.000	.000	.000	P	3	0	3	0	0	1.000
1987 StL	33	2	2	0	0	0	0	0	0	0	0	0	0	2	0	0	0	0	0	—	0	.000	.000	.000	P	2	0	4	0	0	1.000
1988 LA	34	1	0	0	0	0	0	0	0	0	0	0	0	0	0	0	0	0	0	—	0	—	—	—	P	1	0	0	0	0	—
WS Totals		6	7	0	0	0	0	0	0	0	0	0	0	6	0	1	0	0	0	—	0	.000	.000	.000	P	6	0	7	0	0	1.000
Postseason Totals		11	17	0	0	0	0	0	1	0	0	1	0	13	0	1	0	0	0	—	1	.000	.056	.000	P	11	1	14	0	0	1.000

LEE TUNNELL—Byron Lee Tunnell—Throws: Right; Bats: Right

Ht: 6'1"; Wt: 180 lbs; Born: 10/30/1960 in Tyler, Texas; Debut: 9/4/1982

World Series		Pitching																										
Year Tm	Age	G	GS	CG	GF	IP	BFP	H	R	ER	HR	SH	SF	HB	TBB	IBB	SO	WP	Bk	W	L	Pct	ShO	Sv-Op	Hld	OAvg	OOBP	ERA
1987 StL	26	2	0	0	1	4.1	19	4	2	1	1	0	0	0	2	0	1	0	0	0	0	—	0	0- 0	0	.235	.316	2.08

World Series		Batting																							Fielding						
Year Tm	Age	G	AB	H	2B	3B	HR	TB	R	RBI	GW	TBB	IBB	SO	HBP	SH	SF	SB	CS	SB%	GDP	Avg	OBP	SLG	Pos	G	PO	A	E	DP	FPct
1987 StL	26	2	0	0	0	0	0	0	0	0	0	0	0	0	0	0	0	0	0	—	0	—	—	—	P	2	0	1	0	0	1.000

BOB TURLEY—Robert Lee Turley—Nickname: Bullet Bob—Throws: Right; Bats: Right

Ht: 6'2"; Wt: 215 lbs; Born: 9/19/1930 in Troy, Illinois; Debut: 9/29/1951

World Series		Pitching																										
Year Tm	Age	G	GS	CG	GF	IP	BFP	H	R	ER	HR	SH	SF	HB	TBB	IBB	SO	WP	Bk	W	L	Pct	ShO	Sv-Op	Hld	OAvg	OOBP	ERA
1955 NYA	25	3	1	0	2	5.1	28	7	5	5	1	1	0	1	4	0	7	0	0	0	1	.000	0	0- 0	0	.318	.444	8.44
1956 NYA	26	3	1	1	1	11.0	44	4	1	1	0	1	0	0	8	2	14	0	0	0	1	.000	0	0- 0	0	.114	.279	0.82
1957 NYA	27	3	2	1	1	11.2	47	7	3	3	2	0	0	0	6	0	12	1	0	1	0	1.000	0	0- 0	0	.171	.277	2.31
1958 NYA-*C*	28	4	2	1	2	16.1	64	10	5	5	2	1	0	0	7	1	13	0	0	2	1	.667	1	1- 1	0	.179	.270	2.76
1960 NYA	30	2	2	0	0	9.1	48	15	6	5	1	0	0	1	4	0	0	0	0	1	0	1.000	0	0- 0	0	.349	.417	4.82
WS Totals		15	8	3	6	53.2	462	43	20	19	6	3	0	2	29	3	46	1	0	4	3	.571	1	1-1	0	.218	.325	3.19

World Series		Batting																							Fielding						
Year Tm	Age	G	AB	H	2B	3B	HR	TB	R	RBI	GW	TBB	IBB	SO	HBP	SH	SF	SB	CS	SB%	GDP	Avg	OBP	SLG	Pos	G	PO	A	E	DP	FPct
1955 NYA	25	3	1	0	0	0	0	0	0	0	0	0	0	0	0	0	0	0	0	—	0	.000	.000	.000	P	3	0	1	0	0	1.000
1956 NYA	26	3	4	0	0	0	0	0	0	0	0	0	0	1	0	0	0	0	0	—	0	.000	.000	.000	P	3	0	2	0	0	1.000
1957 NYA	27	3	4	0	0	0	0	0	0	0	0	0	0	2	0	0	0	0	0	—	0	.000	.000	.000	P	3	2	2	0	1	1.000
1958 NYA	28	4	5	1	0	0	0	1	0	2	0	0	0	1	0	1	0	0	0	—	0	.200	.200	.200	P	4	0	1	0	0	1.000
1960 NYA	30	2	4	1	0	0	0	1	0	1	0	0	0	1	0	1	0	0	0	—	0	.250	.250	.250	P	2	0	2	0	0	1.000
WS Totals		15	18	2	0	0	0	2	0	3	0	0	0	5	0	2	0	0	0	—	0	.111	.111	.111	P	15	2	8	0	1	1.000

JIM TURNER—James Riley Turner—Nickname: Milkman Jim—Throws: Right; Bats: Left

Ht: 6'0"; Wt: 185 lbs; Born: 8/6/1903 in Antioch, Tennessee; Debut: 4/30/1937

World Series		Pitching																										
Year Tm	Age	G	GS	CG	GF	IP	BFP	H	R	ER	HR	SH	SF	HB	TBB	IBB	SO	WP	Bk	W	L	Pct	ShO	Sv-Op	Hld	OAvg	OOBP	ERA
1940 Cin	37	1	1	0	0	6.0	25	8	5	5	2	0	0	0	0	0	4	0	0	0	1	.000	0	0- 0	0	.320	.320	7.50
1942 NYA	39	1	0	0	1	1.0	3	0	0	0	0	0	0	0	1	1	0	0	0	0	0	—	0	0- 0	0	.000	.333	0.00
WS Totals		2	1	0	1	7.0	56	8	5	5	2	0	0	0	1	1	4	0	0	0	1	.000	0	0-0	0	.296	.321	6.43

World Series		Batting																							Fielding						
Year Tm	Age	G	AB	H	2B	3B	HR	TB	R	RBI	GW	TBB	IBB	SO	HBP	SH	SF	SB	CS	SB%	GDP	Avg	OBP	SLG	Pos	G	PO	A	E	DP	FPct
1940 Cin	37	1	2	0	0	0	0	0	0	0	0	0	0	0	0	0	0	0	0	—	0	.000	.000	.000	P	1	0	1	0	0	1.000
1942 NYA	39	1	0	0	0	0	0	0	0	0	0	0	0	0	0	0	0	0	0	—	0	—	—	—	P	1	0	0	0	0	—
WS Totals		2	2	0	0	0	0	0	0	0	0	0	0	0	0	0	0	0	0	—	0	.000	.000	.000	P	2	0	1	0	0	1.000

TOM TURNER—Thomas Richard Turner—Bats: Right; Throws: Right

Ht: 6'2"; Wt: 195 lbs; Born: 9/8/1916 in Custer, Oklahoma; Debut: 4/25/1940; Died: 5/14/1986

World Series		Batting																							Fielding						
Year Tm	Age	G	AB	H	2B	3B	HR	TB	R	RBI	GW	TBB	IBB	SO	HBP	SH	SF	SB	CS	SB%	GDP	Avg	OBP	SLG	Pos	G	PO	A	E	DP	FPct
1944 StL	28	1	1	0	0	0	0	0	0	0	0	0	0	0	0	0	0	0	0	—	0	.000	.000	.000	—						

LEFTY TYLER—George Albert Tyler—Throws: Left; Bats: Left

Ht: 6'0"; Wt: 175 lbs; Born: 12/14/1889 in Derry, New Hampshire; Debut: 9/20/1910; Died: 9/29/1953

World Series		Pitching																										
Year Tm	Age	G	GS	CG	GF	IP	BFP	H	R	ER	HR	SH	SF	HB	TBB	IBB	SO	WP	Bk	W	L	Pct	ShO	Sv-Op	Hld	OAvg	OOBP	ERA
1914 Bos	24	1	1	0	0	10.0	41	8	4	4	0	1	1	0	3	1	4	0	0	0	0	—	0	0- 0	0	.222	.275	3.60
1918 ChN	28	3	3	1	0	23.0	92	14	5	3	0	4	0	0	11	0	4	0	0	1	1	.500	0	0- 0	0	.182	.284	1.17
WS Totals		4	4	1	0	33.0	266	22	9	7	0	5	1	0	14	1	8	0	0	1	1	.500	0	0-0	0	.195	.281	1.91

World Series		Batting																							Fielding						
Year Tm	Age	G	AB	H	2B	3B	HR	TB	R	RBI	GW	TBB	IBB	SO	HBP	SH	SF	SB	CS	SB%	GDP	Avg	OBP	SLG	Pos	G	PO	A	E	DP	FPct
1914 Bos	24	1	3	0	0	0	0	0	0	0	0	0	0	1	0	0	0	0	0	—	0	.000	.000	.000	P	1	1	5	0	0	1.000
1918 ChN	28	3	5	1	0	0	0	1	0	2	0	2	0	0	0	0	0	0	0	—	0	.200	.429	.200	P	3	2	9	1	0	.917
WS Totals		4	8	1	0	0	0	1	0	2	0	2	0	1	0	0	0	0	0	—	0	.125	.300	.125	P	4	3	14	1	0	.944

TED UHLAENDER—Theodore Otto Uhlaender—Bats: Left; Throws: Right

Ht: 6'2"; Wt: 190 lbs; Born: 10/21/1940 in Chicago Heights, Illinois; Debut: 9/4/1965

LCS		Batting																							Fielding						
Year Tm	Age	G	AB	H	2B	3B	HR	TB	R	RBI	GW	TBB	IBB	SO	HBP	SH	SF	SB	CS	SB%	GDP	Avg	OBP	SLG	Pos	G	PO	A	E	DP	FPct
1969 Min	28	2	6	1	0	0	0	1	0	0	0	0	0	0	0	0	0	0	0	—	0	.167	.167	.167	OF	2	4	0	1	0	.800
1972 Cin	31	2	2	1	0	0	0	1	0	0	0	0	0	0	0	0	0	0	0	—	0	.500	.500	.500	—						
LCS Totals		4	8	2	0	0	0	2	0	0	0	0	0	0	0	0	0	0	0	—	0	.250	.250	.250	OF	2	4	0	1	0	.800
World Series		Batting																							Fielding						
Year Tm	Age	G	AB	H	2B	3B	HR	TB	R	RBI	GW	TBB	IBB	SO	HBP	SH	SF	SB	CS	SB%	GDP	Avg	OBP	SLG	Pos	G	PO	A	E	DP	FPct
1972 Cin	31	4	4	1	1	0	0	2	0	0	0	0	0	1	0	0	0	0	0	—	0	.250	.250	.500	—						
Postseason Totals		8	12	3	1	0	0	4	0	0	0	0	0	1	0	0	0	0	0	—	0	.250	.250	.333	OF	2	4	0	1	0	.800

GEORGE UHLE—George Ernest Uhle—Nickname: The Bull—Throws: Right; Bats: Right

Ht: 6'0"; Wt: 190 lbs; Born: 9/18/1898 in Cleveland, Ohio; Debut: 4/30/1919; Died: 2/26/1985

World Series		Pitching																										
Year Tm	Age	G	GS	CG	GF	IP	BFP	H	R	ER	HR	SH	SF	HB	TBB	IBB	SO	WP	Bk	W	L	Pct	ShO	Sv-Op	Hld	OAvg	OOBP	ERA
1920 Cle	22	2	0	0	2	3.0	10	1	0	0	0	0	0	0	0	0	3	0	0	0	0	—	0	0- 0	0	.100	.100	0.00

World Series		Batting																							Fielding						
Year Tm	Age	G	AB	H	2B	3B	HR	TB	R	RBI	GW	TBB	IBB	SO	HBP	SH	SF	SB	CS	SB%	GDP	Avg	OBP	SLG	Pos	G	PO	A	E	DP	FPct
1920 Cle	22	2	0	0	0	0	0	0	0	0	0	0	0	0	0	0	0	0	0	—	0	—	—	—	P	2	0	1	0	0	1.000

TOM UNDERWOOD—Thomas Gerald Underwood—Throws: Left; Bats: Right

Ht: 5'11"; Wt: 170 lbs; Born: 12/22/1953 in Kokomo, Indiana; Debut: 8/19/1974

Division Series		Pitching																										
Year Tm	Age	G	GS	CG	GF	IP	BFP	H	R	ER	HR	SH	SF	HB	TBB	IBB	SO	WP	Bk	W	L	Pct	ShO	Sv-Op	Hld	OAvg	OOBP	ERA
1981 Oak	27	1	0	0	0	0.1	1	0	0	0	0	0	0	0	0	0	1	0	0	0	0	—	0	0- 0	1	.000	.000	0.00
LCS		Pitching																										
Year Tm	Age	G	GS	CG	GF	IP	BFP	H	R	ER	HR	SH	SF	HB	TBB	IBB	SO	WP	Bk	W	L	Pct	ShO	Sv-Op	Hld	OAvg	OOBP	ERA
1976 Phi	22	1	0	0	1	0.1	4	1	0	0	0	1	0	0	2	1	0	0	0	0	0	—	0	0- 0	0	1.000	1.000	0.00
1980 NYA	26	2	0	0	2	3.0	12	3	2	0	0	0	0	0	0	0	3	0	0	0	0	—	0	0- 0	0	.250	.250	0.00
1981 Oak	27	2	0	0	2	1.1	8	4	2	2	0	0	0	0	2	0	0	0	0	0	0	—	0	0- 0	0	.667	.750	13.50
LCS Totals		5	0	0	5	4.2	48	8	4	2	0	1	0	0	4	1	3	0	0	0	0	—	0	0-0	0	.421	.522	3.86
Postseason Totals		6	0	0	5	5.0	50	8	4	2	0	1	0	0	4	1	4	0	0	0	0	—	0	0-0	1	.400	.500	3.60

Division Series		Batting																							Fielding						
Year Tm	Age	G	AB	H	2B	3B	HR	TB	R	RBI	GW	TBB	IBB	SO	HBP	SH	SF	SB	CS	SB%	GDP	Avg	OBP	SLG	Pos	G	PO	A	E	DP	FPct
1981 Oak	27	1	0	0	0	0	0	0	0	0	0	0	0	0	0	0	0	0	0	—	0	—	—	—	P	1	0	0	0	0	—
LCS		Batting																							Fielding						
Year Tm	Age	G	AB	H	2B	3B	HR	TB	R	RBI	GW	TBB	IBB	SO	HBP	SH	SF	SB	CS	SB%	GDP	Avg	OBP	SLG	Pos	G	PO	A	E	DP	FPct
1976 Phi	22	1	0	0	0	0	0	0	0	0	0	0	0	0	0	0	0	0	0	—	0	—	—	—	P	1	0	0	0	0	—
1980 NYA	26	2	0	0	0	0	0	0	0	0	0	0	0	0	0	0	0	0	0	—	0	—	—	—	P	2	0	2	0	0	1.000
1981 Oak	27	2	0	0	0	0	0	0	0	0	0	0	0	0	0	0	0	0	0	—	0	—	—	—	P	2	0	0	0	0	—
LCS Totals		5	0	0	0	0	0	0	0	0	0	0	0	0	0	0	0	0	0	—	0	—	—	—	P	5	0	2	0	0	1.000
Postseason Totals		6	0	0	0	0	0	0	0	0	0	0	0	0	0	0	0	0	0	—	0	—	—	—	P	6	0	2	0	0	1.000

DEL UNSER—Delbert Bernard Unser—Bats: Left; Throws: Left

Ht: 6'1"; Wt: 180 lbs; Born: 12/9/1944 in Decatur, Illinois; Debut: 4/10/1968

LCS		Batting																							Fielding						
Year Tm	Age	G	AB	H	2B	3B	HR	TB	R	RBI	GW	TBB	IBB	SO	HBP	SH	SF	SB	CS	SB%	GDP	Avg	OBP	SLG	Pos	G	PO	A	E	DP	FPct
1980 Phi	35	5	5	2	1	0	0	3	2	1	0	0	0	2	0	0	0	0	0	—	0	.400	.400	.600	OF	3	2	0	0	0	1.000
World Series		Batting																							Fielding						
Year Tm	Age	G	AB	H	2B	3B	HR	TB	R	RBI	GW	TBB	IBB	SO	HBP	SH	SF	SB	CS	SB%	GDP	Avg	OBP	SLG	Pos	G	PO	A	E	DP	FPct
1980 Phi	35	3	6	3	2	0	0	5	2	2	0	0	0	1	0	0	0	0	0	—	0	.500	.500	.833	OF	3	1	0	0	0	1.000
Postseason Totals		8	11	5	3	0	0	8	4	3	0	0	0	3	0	0	0	0	0	—	0	.455	.455	.727	OF	6	3	0	0	0	1.000

CECIL UPSHAW—Cecil Lee Upshaw—Throws: Right; Bats: Right

Ht: 6'6"; Wt: 205 lbs; Born: 10/22/1942 in Spearsville, Louisiana; Debut: 10/1/1966; Died: 2/7/1995

LCS		Pitching																										
Year Tm	Age	G	GS	CG	GF	IP	BFP	H	R	ER	HR	SH	SF	HB	TBB	IBB	SO	WP	Bk	W	L	Pct	ShO	Sv-Op	Hld	OAvg	OOBP	ERA
1969 Atl	26	3	0	0	2	6.1	25	5	2	2	1	0	0	0	1	0	4	0	0	0	0	—	0	0-0	0	.208	.240	2.84

LCS		Batting																							Fielding						
Year Tm	Age	G	AB	H	2B	3B	HR	TB	R	RBI	GW	TBB	IBB	SO	HBP	SH	SF	SB	CS	SB%	GDP	Avg	OBP	SLG	Pos	G	PO	A	E	DP	FPct
1969 Atl	26	3	1	0	0	0	0	0	0	0	0	0	0	1	0	0	0	0	0	—	0	.000	.000	.000	P	3	0	1	0	1	1.000

WILLIE UPSHAW—Willie Clay Upshaw—Bats: Left; Throws: Left

Ht: 6'0"; Wt: 185 lbs; Born: 4/27/1957 in Blanco, Texas; Debut: 4/9/1978

LCS		Batting																							Fielding						
Year Tm	Age	G	AB	H	2B	3B	HR	TB	R	RBI	GW	TBB	IBB	SO	HBP	SH	SF	SB	CS	SB%	GDP	Avg	OBP	SLG	Pos	G	PO	A	E	DP	FPct
1985 Tor	28	7	26	6	2	0	0	8	2	1	0	1	0	4	1	0	0	0	0	—	0	.231	.286	.308	1B	7	53	7	1	3	.984

JOSE URIBE—Jose Altagarcia Uribe—Bats: Both; Throws: Right

Ht: 5'10"; Wt: 155 lbs; Born: 1/21/1959 in San Cristobal, Dominican Republic; Debut: 9/13/1984

LCS		Batting																							Fielding						
Year Tm	Age	G	AB	H	2B	3B	HR	TB	R	RBI	GW	TBB	IBB	SO	HBP	SH	SF	SB	CS	SB%	GDP	Avg	OBP	SLG	Pos	G	PO	A	E	DP	FPct
1987 SF	28	7	26	7	1	0	0	8	1	2	1	0	0	4	0	1	0	1	1	.50	0	.269	.269	.308	SS	7	11	20	1	7	.969
1989 SF	30	5	17	4	1	0	0	5	2	1	0	1	0	5	0	0	0	1	0	1.00	0	.235	.278	.294	SS	5	6	9	2	2	.882
LCS Totals		12	43	11	2	0	0	13	3	3	1	1	0	9	0	1	0	2	1	.67	0	.256	.273	.302	SS	12	17	29	3	9	.939
World Series		Batting																							Fielding						
Year Tm	Age	G	AB	H	2B	3B	HR	TB	R	RBI	GW	TBB	IBB	SO	HBP	SH	SF	SB	CS	SB%	GDP	Avg	OBP	SLG	Pos	G	PO	A	E	DP	FPct
1989 SF	30	3	5	1	0	0	0	1	1	0	0	0	0	0	0	0	0	0	0	—	0	.200	.200	.200	SS	3	1	3	0	0	1.000
Postseason Totals		15	48	12	2	0	0	14	4	3	1	1	0	9	0	1	0	2	1	.67	0	.250	.265	.292	SS	15	18	32	3	9	.943

ISMAEL VALDES—Throws: Right; Bats: Right

Ht: 6'3"; Wt: 183 lbs; Born: 8/21/1973 in Victoria, Mexico; Debut: 6/15/1994

Division Series		Pitching																										
Year Tm	Age	G	GS	CG	GF	IP	BFP	H	R	ER	HR	SH	SF	HB	TBB	IBB	SO	WP	Bk	W	L	Pct	ShO	Sv-Op	Hld	OAvg	OOBP	ERA
1995 LA	22	1	1	0	0	7.0	25	3	2	0	1	0	0	0	1	0	6	0	0	0	0	—	0	0-0	0	.125	.160	0.00
1996 LA	23	1	1	0	0	6.1	24	5	3	3	3	0	0	0	0	0	5	0	0	0	1	.000	0	0-0	0	.208	.208	4.26
DS Totals		2	2	0	0	13.1	98	8	5	3	4	0	0	0	1	0	11	0	0	0	1	.000	0	0-0	0	.167	.184	2.03

Division Series		Batting																							Fielding						
Year Tm	Age	G	AB	H	2B	3B	HR	TB	R	RBI	GW	TBB	IBB	SO	HBP	SH	SF	SB	CS	SB%	GDP	Avg	OBP	SLG	Pos	G	PO	A	E	DP	FPct
1995 LA	22	1	3	0	0	0	0	0	0	0	0	0	0	0	0	0	0	0	0	—	0	.000	.000	.000	P	1	0	0	0	0	—
1996 LA	23	1	2	0	0	0	0	0	0	0	0	0	0	0	0	0	0	0	0	—	0	.000	.000	.000	P	1	1	2	0	0	1.000
DS Totals		2	5	0	0	0	0	0	0	0	0	0	0	0	0	0	0	0	0	—	0	.000	.000	.000	P	2	1	2	0	0	1.000

SANDY VALDESPINO—Hilario Valdespino—Bats: Left; Throws: Left

Ht: 5'8"; Wt: 170 lbs; Born: 1/24/1939 in San Jose de las Lajas, Cuba; Debut: 4/12/1965

World Series		Batting																							Fielding						
Year Tm	Age	G	AB	H	2B	3B	HR	TB	R	RBI	GW	TBB	IBB	SO	HBP	SH	SF	SB	CS	SB%	GDP	Avg	OBP	SLG	Pos	G	PO	A	E	DP	FPct
1965 Min	26	5	11	3	1	0	0	4	1	0	0	0	0	1	0	0	0	0	0	—	0	.273	.273	.364	OF	2	6	0	0	0	1.000

JOHN VALENTIN—John William Valentin—Nickname: Val—Bats: Right; Throws: Right

Ht: 6'0"; Wt: 170 lbs; Born: 2/18/1967 in Mineola, New York; Debut: 7/27/1992

Division Series		Batting																							Fielding						
Year Tm	Age	G	AB	H	2B	3B	HR	TB	R	RBI	GW	TBB	IBB	SO	HBP	SH	SF	SB	CS	SB%	GDP	Avg	OBP	SLG	Pos	G	PO	A	E	DP	FPct
1995 Bos	28	3	12	3	1	0	1	7	1	2	0	3	1	1	0	0	0	0	1	.00	0	.250	.400	.583	SS	3	5	5	1	0	.909

FERNANDO VALENZUELA—Throws: Left; Bats: Left

Ht: 5'11"; Wt: 180 lbs; Born: 11/1/1960 in Navojoa, Mexico; Debut: 9/15/1980

Division Series		Pitching																										
Year Tm	Age	G	GS	CG	GF	IP	BFP	H	R	ER	HR	SH	SF	HB	TBB	IBB	SO	WP	Bk	W	L	Pct	ShO	Sv-Op	Hld	OAvg	OOBP	ERA
1981 LA-*CRY*	20	2	2	1	0	17.0	62	10	2	2	0	1	0	0	3	1	10	0	0	1	0	1.000	0	0-0	0	.172	.213	1.06
1996 SD	35	1	0	0	0	0.2	4	0	0	0	0	1	0	0	2	1	0	0	0	0	0	—	0	0-0	0	.000	.667	0.00
DS Totals		3	2	1	0	17.2	132	10	2	2	0	2	0	0	5	2	10	0	0	1	0	1.000	0	0-0	0	.169	.234	1.02
LCS		Pitching																										
Year Tm	Age	G	GS	CG	GF	IP	BFP	H	R	ER	HR	SH	SF	HB	TBB	IBB	SO	WP	Bk	W	L	Pct	ShO	Sv-Op	Hld	OAvg	OOBP	ERA
1981 LA-*CRY*	20	2	2	0	0	14.2	57	10	4	4	0	1	0	0	5	1	10	1	0	1	1	.500	0	0-0	0	.196	.268	2.45
1983 LA	22	1	1	0	0	8.0	33	7	1	1	1	1	0	0	4	0	5	1	0	1	0	1.000	0	0-0	0	.250	.344	1.13
1985 LA	24	2	2	0	0	14.1	63	11	3	3	0	2	0	0	10	2	13	1	0	1	0	1.000	0	0-0	0	.216	.344	1.88
LCS Totals		5	5	0	0	37.0	306	28	8	8	1	4	0	0	19	3	28	3	0	3	1	.750	0	0-0	0	.215	.315	1.95
World Series		Pitching																										
Year Tm	Age	G	GS	CG	GF	IP	BFP	H	R	ER	HR	SH	SF	HB	TBB	IBB	SO	WP	Bk	W	L	Pct	ShO	Sv-Op	Hld	OAvg	OOBP	ERA
1981 LA-*CRY*	20	1	1	1	0	9.0	40	9	4	4	2	1	0	0	7	2	6	0	0	1	0	1.000	0	0-0	0	.281	.410	4.00
Postseason Totals		9	8	2	0	63.2	518	47	14	14	3	7	0	0	31	7	44	3	0	5	1	.833	0	0-0	0	.213	.310	1.98

Division Series		Batting																							Fielding						
Year Tm	Age	G	AB	H	2B	3B	HR	TB	R	RBI	GW	TBB	IBB	SO	HBP	SH	SF	SB	CS	SB%	GDP	Avg	OBP	SLG	Pos	G	PO	A	E	DP	FPct
1981 LA	20	2	4	0	0	0	0	0	0	0	0	0	0	1	0	1	0	0	0	—	0	.000	.000	.000	P	2	0	5	0	0	1.000
1996 SD	35	1	0	0	0	0	0	0	0	0	0	0	0	0	0	0	0	0	0	—	0	—	—	—	P	1	0	1	0	0	1.000
DS Totals		3	4	0	0	0	0	0	0	0	0	0	0	1	0	1	0	0	0	—	0	.000	.000	.000	P	3	0	6	0	0	1.000
LCS		Batting																							Fielding						
Year Tm	Age	G	AB	H	2B	3B	HR	TB	R	RBI	GW	TBB	IBB	SO	HBP	SH	SF	SB	CS	SB%	GDP	Avg	OBP	SLG	Pos	G	PO	A	E	DP	FPct
1981 LA	20	2	5	0	0	0	0	0	0	1	0	0	0	0	0	0	0	0	0	—	0	.000	.000	.000	P	2	0	2	0	0	1.000
1983 LA	22	1	3	0	0	0	0	0	0	0	0	1	0	0	0	0	0	0	0	—	0	.000	.250	.000	P	1	1	0	0	0	1.000
1985 LA	24	2	5	1	0	0	0	1	0	0	0	0	0	0	0	1	0	0	0	—	0	.200	.200	.200	P	2	1	3	1	0	.800
LCS Totals		5	13	1	0	0	0	1	0	1	0	1	0	0	0	1	0	0	0	—	0	.077	.143	.077	P	5	2	5	1	0	.875
World Series		Batting																							Fielding						
Year Tm	Age	G	AB	H	2B	3B	HR	TB	R	RBI	GW	TBB	IBB	SO	HBP	SH	SF	SB	CS	SB%	GDP	Avg	OBP	SLG	Pos	G	PO	A	E	DP	FPct
1981 LA	20	1	3	0	0	0	0	0	0	0	0	1	0	0	0	0	0	0	0	—	0	.000	.250	.000	P	1	0	1	0	0	1.000
Postseason Totals		9	20	1	0	0	0	1	0	1	0	2	0	1	0	2	0	0	0	—	0	.050	.136	.050	P	9	2	12	1	0	.933

DAZZY VANCE (HOF 1955-W)—Clarence Arthur Vance—Throws: Right; Bats: Right

Ht: 6'2"; Wt: 200 lbs; Born: 3/4/1891 in Orient, Iowa; Debut: 4/16/1915; Died: 2/16/1961

World Series — Pitching

Year Tm	Age	G	GS	CG	GF	IP	BFP	H	R	ER	HR	SH	SF	HB	TBB	IBB	SO	WP	Bk	W	L	Pct	ShO	Sv-Op	Hld	OAvg	OOBP	ERA
1934 StL	43	1	0	0	0	1.1	7	2	1	0	0	0	0	0	1	0	3	1	0	0	0	—	0	0-0	0	.333	.429	0.00

World Series — Batting / Fielding

Year Tm	Age	G	AB	H	2B	3B	HR	TB	R	RBI	GW	TBB	IBB	SO	HBP	SH	SF	SB	CS	SB%	GDP	Avg	OBP	SLG	Pos	G	PO	A	E	DP	FPct
1934 StL	43	1	0	0	0	0	0	0	0	0	0	0	0	0	0	0	0	0	0	—	0	—	—	—	P	1	0	0	0	0	—

HY VANDENBERG—Harold Harris Vandenberg—Throws: Right; Bats: Right

Ht: 6'4"; Wt: 220 lbs; Born: 3/17/1907 in Abilene, Kansas; Debut: 6/8/1935; Died: 7/31/1994

World Series — Pitching

Year Tm	Age	G	GS	CG	GF	IP	BFP	H	R	ER	HR	SH	SF	HB	TBB	IBB	SO	WP	Bk	W	L	Pct	ShO	Sv-Op	Hld	OAvg	OOBP	ERA
1945 ChN	38	3	0	0	0	6.0	22	1	0	0	0	1	0	0	3	1	3	0	0	0	0	—	0	0-0	0	.056	.190	0.00

World Series — Batting / Fielding

Year Tm	Age	G	AB	H	2B	3B	HR	TB	R	RBI	GW	TBB	IBB	SO	HBP	SH	SF	SB	CS	SB%	GDP	Avg	OBP	SLG	Pos	G	PO	A	E	DP	FPct
1945 ChN	38	3	1	0	0	0	0	0	0	0	0	0	0	0	0	0	0	0	0	—	0	.000	.000	.000	P	3	1	2	0	0	1.000

JOHNNY VANDER MEER—John Samuel Vander Meer—Nickname: The Dutch Master—T: L; B: B

Ht: 6'1"; Wt: 190 lbs; Born: 11/2/1914 in Prospect Park, N.J.; Deb.: 4/22/1937; Died: 10/6/1997

World Series — Pitching

Year Tm	Age	G	GS	CG	GF	IP	BFP	H	R	ER	HR	SH	SF	HB	TBB	IBB	SO	WP	Bk	W	L	Pct	ShO	Sv-Op	Hld	OAvg	OOBP	ERA
1940 Cin	25	1	0	0	0	3.0	14	2	0	0	0	0	0	0	3	0	2	0	0	0	0	—	0	0-0	0	.182	.357	0.00

World Series — Batting / Fielding

Year Tm	Age	G	AB	H	2B	3B	HR	TB	R	RBI	GW	TBB	IBB	SO	HBP	SH	SF	SB	CS	SB%	GDP	Avg	OBP	SLG	Pos	G	PO	A	E	DP	FPct
1940 Cin	25	1	0	0	0	0	0	0	0	0	0	0	0	0	0	0	0	0	0	—	0	—	—	—	P	1	0	0	0	0	—

JOHN VANDERWAL—John Henry VanderWal—Bats: Left; Throws: Left

Ht: 6'1"; Wt: 180 lbs; Born: 4/29/1966 in Grand Rapids, Michigan; Debut: 9/6/1991

Division Series — Batting / Fielding

Year Tm	Age	G	AB	H	2B	3B	HR	TB	R	RBI	GW	TBB	IBB	SO	HBP	SH	SF	SB	CS	SB%	GDP	Avg	OBP	SLG	Pos	G	PO	A	E	DP	FPct
1995 Col	29	4	4	0	0	0	0	0	0	0	0	0	0	2	0	0	0	0	0	—	1	.000	.000	.000	—						

ANDY VAN SLYKE—Andrew James Van Slyke—Bats: Left; Throws: Right

Ht: 6'1"; Wt: 190 lbs; Born: 12/21/1960 in Utica, New York; Debut: 6/17/1983

LCS — Batting / Fielding

Year Tm	Age	G	AB	H	2B	3B	HR	TB	R	RBI	GW	TBB	IBB	SO	HBP	SH	SF	SB	CS	SB%	GDP	Avg	OBP	SLG	Pos	G	PO	A	E	DP	FPct
1985 StL	24	5	11	1	0	0	0	1	1	1	0	2	1	1	0	0	0	0	0	—	0	.091	.231	.091	OF	5	6	0	0	0	1.000
1990 Pit	29	6	24	5	1	1	0	8	3	3	1	1	0	7	0	0	0	1	0	1.00	0	.208	.240	.333	OF	6	13	1	0	0	1.000
1991 Pit	30	7	25	4	2	0	1	9	3	2	1	5	0	5	0	0	0	1	0	1.00	0	.160	.300	.360	OF	7	18	1	0	0	1.000
1992 Pit	31	7	29	8	3	1	0	13	1	4	1	1	0	5	0	0	1	0	0	—	1	.276	.290	.448	OF	7	20	0	0	0	1.000
LCS Totals		25	89	18	6	2	1	31	8	10	3	9	1	18	0	0	1	2	0	1.00	1	.202	.273	.348	OF	25	57	2	0	0	1.000

World Series — Batting / Fielding

Year Tm	Age	G	AB	H	2B	3B	HR	TB	R	RBI	GW	TBB	IBB	SO	HBP	SH	SF	SB	CS	SB%	GDP	Avg	OBP	SLG	Pos	G	PO	A	E	DP	FPct
1985 StL	24	6	11	1	0	0	0	1	0	0	0	0	0	5	0	0	0	0	0	—	0	.091	.091	.091	OF	6	8	0	0	0	1.000
Postseason Totals		31	100	19	6	2	1	32	8	10	3	9	1	23	0	0	1	2	0	1.00	1	.190	.255	.320	OF	31	65	2	0	0	1.000

GARY VARSHO—Gary Andrew Varsho—Bats: Left; Throws: Right

Ht: 5'11"; Wt: 190 lbs; Born: 6/20/1961 in Marshfield, Wisconsin; Debut: 7/6/1988

LCS — Batting / Fielding

Year Tm	Age	G	AB	H	2B	3B	HR	TB	R	RBI	GW	TBB	IBB	SO	HBP	SH	SF	SB	CS	SB%	GDP	Avg	OBP	SLG	Pos	G	PO	A	E	DP	FPct
1991 Pit	30	2	2	1	0	0	0	1	0	0	0	0	0	1	0	0	0	0	0	—	0	.500	.500	.500	—						
1992 Pit	31	2	2	1	0	0	0	1	0	0	0	0	0	0	0	0	0	0	0	—	0	.500	.500	.500	OF	1	0	0	0	0	—
LCS Totals		4	4	2	0	0	0	2	0	0	0	0	0	1	0	0	0	0	0	—	0	.500	.500	.500	OF	1	0	0	0	0	—

ARKY VAUGHAN (HOF 1985-V)—Joseph Floyd Vaughan—Bats: Left; Throws: Right

Ht: 5'10"; Wt: 175 lbs; Born: 3/9/1912 in Clifty, Arkansas; Debut: 4/17/1932; Died: 8/30/1952

World Series — Batting / Fielding

Year Tm	Age	G	AB	H	2B	3B	HR	TB	R	RBI	GW	TBB	IBB	SO	HBP	SH	SF	SB	CS	SB%	GDP	Avg	OBP	SLG	Pos	G	PO	A	E	DP	FPct
1947 Bro	35	3	2	1	1	0	0	2	0	0	0	1	0	0	0	0	0	0	0	—	0	.500	.667	1.000	—						

GREG VAUGHN—Gregory Lamont Vaughn—Bats: Right; Throws: Right

Ht: 6'0"; Wt: 195 lbs; Born: 7/3/1965 in Sacramento, California; Debut: 8/10/1989

Division Series — Batting / Fielding

Year Tm	Age	G	AB	H	2B	3B	HR	TB	R	RBI	GW	TBB	IBB	SO	HBP	SH	SF	SB	CS	SB%	GDP	Avg	OBP	SLG	Pos	G	PO	A	E	DP	FPct
1996 SD	31	3	3	0	0	0	0	0	0	0	0	0	0	1	0	0	0	0	0	—	0	.000	.000	.000	—						

HIPPO VAUGHN—James Leslie Vaughn—Throws: Left; Bats: Both

Ht: 6'4"; Wt: 215 lbs; Born: 4/9/1888 in Weatherford, Texas; Debut: 6/19/1908; Died: 5/29/1966

World Series — Pitching

Year Tm	Age	G	GS	CG	GF	IP	BFP	H	R	ER	HR	SH	SF	HB	TBB	IBB	SO	WP	Bk	W	L	Pct	ShO	Sv-Op	Hld	OAvg	OOBP	ERA
1918 ChN	30	3	3	3	0	27.0	97	17	3	3	0	3	0	1	5	1	17	0	0	1	2	.333	1	0-0	0	.193	.245	1.00

World Series — Batting / Fielding

Year Tm	Age	G	AB	H	2B	3B	HR	TB	R	RBI	GW	TBB	IBB	SO	HBP	SH	SF	SB	CS	SB%	GDP	Avg	OBP	SLG	Pos	G	PO	A	E	DP	FPct
1918 ChN	30	3	10	0	0	0	0	0	0	0	0	0	0	5	0	0	0	0	0	—	0	.000	.000	.000	P	3	6	11	0	1	1.000

MO VAUGHN—Maurice Samuel Vaughn—Nickname: The Hit Dog—Bats: Left; Throws: Right

Ht: 6'1"; Wt: 225 lbs; Born: 12/15/1967 in Norwalk, Connecticut; Debut: 6/27/1991

Division Series — Batting / Fielding

Year Tm	Age	G	AB	H	2B	3B	HR	TB	R	RBI	GW	TBB	IBB	SO	HBP	SH	SF	SB	CS	SB%	GDP	Avg	OBP	SLG	Pos	G	PO	A	E	DP	FPct
1995 Bos-*M*	27	3	14	0	0	0	0	0	0	0	0	1	0	7	0	0	0	0	0	—	0	.000	.067	.000	1B	3	27	2	0	0	1.000

BOBBY VEACH—Robert Hayes Veach—Bats: Left; Throws: Right

Ht: 5'11"; Wt: 160 lbs; Born: 6/29/1888 in Island, Kentucky; Debut: 8/6/1912; Died: 8/7/1945

World Series — Batting / Fielding

Year Tm	Age	G	AB	H	2B	3B	HR	TB	R	RBI	GW	TBB	IBB	SO	HBP	SH	SF	SB	CS	SB%	GDP	Avg	OBP	SLG	Pos	G	PO	A	E	DP	FPct
1925 Was	37	2	1	0	0	0	0	0	0	1	0	0	0	0	0	0	1	0	0	—	0	.000	.000	.000	—						

BOB VEALE—Robert Andrew Veale—Throws: Left; Bats: Both

Ht: 6'6"; Wt: 212 lbs; Born: 10/28/1935 in Birmingham, Alabama; Debut: 4/16/1962

World Series — Pitching

Year Tm	Age	G	GS	CG	GF	IP	BFP	H	R	ER	HR	SH	SF	HB	TBB	IBB	SO	WP	Bk	W	L	Pct	ShO	Sv-Op	Hld	OAvg	OOBP	ERA
1971 Pit	35	1	0	0	0	0.2	5	1	1	1	0	0	0	0	2	0	0	0	0	0	0	—	0	0-0	0	.333	.600	13.50

World Series — Batting / Fielding

Year Tm	Age	G	AB	H	2B	3B	HR	TB	R	RBI	GW	TBB	IBB	SO	HBP	SH	SF	SB	CS	SB%	GDP	Avg	OBP	SLG	Pos	G	PO	A	E	DP	FPct
1971 Pit	35	1	0	0	0	0	0	0	0	0	0	0	0	0	0	0	0	0	0	—	0	—	—	—	P	1	0	1	0	0	1.000

BUCKY VEIL—Frederick William Veil—Throws: Right; Bats: Right

Ht: 5'10"; Wt: 165 lbs; Born: 8/2/1881 in Tyrone, Pennsylvania; Debut: 4/19/1903; Died: 4/16/1931

World Series — Pitching

Year Tm	Age	G	GS	CG	GF	IP	BFP	H	R	ER	HR	SH	SF	HB	TBB	IBB	SO	WP	Bk	W	L	Pct	ShO	Sv-Op	Hld	OAvg	OOBP	ERA
1903 Pit	22	1	0	0	1	7.0	31	5	1	1	1	2	0	1	5	0	1	0	0	0	0	—	0	0-0	0	.217	.379	1.29

World Series — Batting / Fielding

Year Tm	Age	G	AB	H	2B	3B	HR	TB	R	RBI	GW	TBB	IBB	SO	HBP	SH	SF	SB	CS	SB%	GDP	Avg	OBP	SLG	Pos	G	PO	A	E	DP	FPct
1903 Pit	22	1	2	0	0	0	0	0	0	0	0	0	0	2	0	0	0	0	0	—	0	.000	.000	.000	P	1	0	0	1	0	.000

RANDY VELARDE—Randy Lee Velarde—Bats: Right; Throws: Right

Ht: 6'0"; Wt: 185 lbs; Born: 11/24/1962 in Midland, Texas; Debut: 8/20/1987

Division Series — Batting / Fielding

Year Tm	Age	G	AB	H	2B	3B	HR	TB	R	RBI	GW	TBB	IBB	SO	HBP	SH	SF	SB	CS	SB%	GDP	Avg	OBP	SLG	Pos	G	PO	A	E	DP	FPct
1995 NYA	32	5	17	3	0	0	0	3	3	1	0	6	0	4	1	0	0	0	1	.00	0	.176	.417	.176	2B	4	13	11	0	2	1.000
																									3B	2	1	0	0	0	1.000
																									OF	2	1	0	1	0	.500

OTTO VELEZ—Otoniel Velez—Bats: Right; Throws: Right

Ht: 6'0"; Wt: 170 lbs; Born: 11/29/1950 in Ponce, Puerto Rico; Debut: 9/4/1973

LCS — Batting / Fielding

Year Tm	Age	G	AB	H	2B	3B	HR	TB	R	RBI	GW	TBB	IBB	SO	HBP	SH	SF	SB	CS	SB%	GDP	Avg	OBP	SLG	Pos	G	PO	A	E	DP	FPct
1976 NYA	25	1	1	0	0	0	0	0	0	0	0	0	0	0	0	0	0	0	0	—	0	.000	.000	.000	—						

World Series — Batting / Fielding

Year Tm	Age	G	AB	H	2B	3B	HR	TB	R	RBI	GW	TBB	IBB	SO	HBP	SH	SF	SB	CS	SB%	GDP	Avg	OBP	SLG	Pos	G	PO	A	E	DP	FPct
1976 NYA	25	3	3	0	0	0	0	0	0	0	0	0	0	3	0	0	0	0	0	—	0	.000	.000	.000	—						
Postseason Totals		4	4	0	0	0	0	0	0	0	0	0	0	3	0	0	0	0	0	—	0	.000	.000	.000	—	0	0	0	0	0	—

ROBIN VENTURA—Robin Mark Ventura—Bats: Left; Throws: Right

Ht: 6'1"; Wt: 185 lbs; Born: 7/14/1967 in Santa Maria, California; Debut: 9/12/1989

LCS — Batting / Fielding

Year Tm	Age	G	AB	H	2B	3B	HR	TB	R	RBI	GW	TBB	IBB	SO	HBP	SH	SF	SB	CS	SB%	GDP	Avg	OBP	SLG	Pos	G	PO	A	E	DP	FPct
1993 ChA	26	6	20	4	0	0	1	7	2	5	0	6	2	6	0	0	1	0	0	—	0	.200	.370	.350	3B	6	6	6	1	0	.923
																									1B	1	3	0	0	0	1.000

DARIO VERAS—Dario Antonio Veras—Throws: Right; Bats: Right

Ht: 6'1"; Wt: 155 lbs; Born: 3/13/1973 in Villa Vasquez, Dominican Republic; Debut: 7/31/1996

Division Series — Pitching

Year Tm	Age	G	GS	CG	GF	IP	BFP	H	R	ER	HR	SH	SF	HB	TBB	IBB	SO	WP	Bk	W	L	Pct	ShO	Sv-Op	Hld	OAvg	OOBP	ERA
1996 SD	23	2	0	0	0	1.0	4	1	0	0	0	0	0	0	0	0	1	0	0	0	0	—	0	0-0	0	.250	.250	0.00

Division Series — Batting / Fielding

Year Tm	Age	G	AB	H	2B	3B	HR	TB	R	RBI	GW	TBB	IBB	SO	HBP	SH	SF	SB	CS	SB%	GDP	Avg	OBP	SLG	Pos	G	PO	A	E	DP	FPct
1996 SD	23	2	0	0	0	0	0	0	0	0	0	0	0	0	0	0	0	0	0	—	0	—	—	—	P	2	0	1	0	0	1.000

EMIL VERBAN—Emil Matthew Verban—Nicknames: Dutch, Antelope—Bats: Right; Throws: Right

Ht: 5'11"; Wt: 165 lbs; Born: 8/27/1915 in Lincoln, Illinois; Debut: 4/18/1944; Died: 6/8/1989

World Series — Batting / Fielding

Year Tm	Age	G	AB	H	2B	3B	HR	TB	R	RBI	GW	TBB	IBB	SO	HBP	SH	SF	SB	CS	SB%	GDP	Avg	OBP	SLG	Pos	G	PO	A	E	DP	FPct
1944 StL	29	6	17	7	0	0	0	7	1	2	1	2	1	0	0	0	0	0	0	—	0	.412	.474	.412	2B	6	15	7	0	2	1.000

ZOILO VERSALLES—Zoilo Casanova Versalles—Nickname: Zorro—Bats: Right; Throws: Right

Ht: 5'10"; Wt: 146 lbs; Born: 12/18/1939 in Havana, Cuba; Debut: 8/1/1959; Died: 6/9/1995

World Series — Batting / Fielding

Year Tm	Age	G	AB	H	2B	3B	HR	TB	R	RBI	GW	TBB	IBB	SO	HBP	SH	SF	SB	CS	SB%	GDP	Avg	OBP	SLG	Pos	G	PO	A	E	DP	FPct
1965 Min-*M*	25	7	28	8	1	1	1	14	3	4	1	2	0	7	0	0	0	1	1	.50	0	.286	.333	.500	SS	7	12	12	0	3	1.000

TOM VERYZER—Thomas Martin Veryzer—Bats: Right; Throws: Right

Ht: 6'1"; Wt: 175 lbs; Born: 2/11/1953 in Port Jefferson, New York; Debut: 8/14/1973

LCS — Batting / Fielding

Year Tm	Age	G	AB	H	2B	3B	HR	TB	R	RBI	GW	TBB	IBB	SO	HBP	SH	SF	SB	CS	SB%	GDP	Avg	OBP	SLG	Pos	G	PO	A	E	DP	FPct
1984 ChN	31	3	1	0	0	0	0	0	0	0	0	0	0	0	0	0	0	0	0	—	0	.000	.000	.000	3B	1	0	0	0	0	—
																									SS	2	0	0	0	0	—

FRANK VIOLA—Frank John Viola—Nickname: Sweet Music—Throws: Left; Bats: Left

Ht: 6'4"; Wt: 200 lbs; Born: 4/19/1960 in Hempstead, New York; Debut: 6/6/1982

LCS — Pitching

Year Tm	Age	G	GS	CG	GF	IP	BFP	H	R	ER	HR	SH	SF	HB	TBB	IBB	SO	WP	Bk	W	L	Pct	ShO	Sv-Op	Hld	OAvg	OOBP	ERA
1987 Min	27	2	2	0	0	12.0	56	14	8	7	2	0	0	0	5	0	9	0	0	1	0	1.000	0	0-0	0	.275	.339	5.25

World Series — Pitching

Year Tm	Age	G	GS	CG	GF	IP	BFP	H	R	ER	HR	SH	SF	HB	TBB	IBB	SO	WP	Bk	W	L	Pct	ShO	Sv-Op	Hld	OAvg	OOBP	ERA
1987 Min	27	3	3	0	0	19.1	76	17	8	8	1	0	0	0	3	0	16	0	0	2	1	.667	0	0-0	0	.233	.263	3.72
Postseason Totals		5	5	0	0	31.1	264	31	16	15	3	0	0	0	8	0	25	0	0	3	1	.750	0	0-0	0	.250	.295	4.31

LCS — Batting / Fielding

Year Tm	Age	G	AB	H	2B	3B	HR	TB	R	RBI	GW	TBB	IBB	SO	HBP	SH	SF	SB	CS	SB%	GDP	Avg	OBP	SLG	Pos	G	PO	A	E	DP	FPct
1987 Min	27	2	0	0	0	0	0	0	0	0	0	0	0	0	0	0	0	0	0	—	0	—	—	—	P	2	0	2	0	0	1.000

World Series — Batting / Fielding

Year Tm	Age	G	AB	H	2B	3B	HR	TB	R	RBI	GW	TBB	IBB	SO	HBP	SH	SF	SB	CS	SB%	GDP	Avg	OBP	SLG	Pos	G	PO	A	E	DP	FPct
1987 Min	27	3	1	0	0	0	0	0	0	0	0	0	0	1	0	0	0	0	0	—	0	.000	.000	.000	P	3	1	4	0	0	1.000
Postseason Totals		5	1	0	0	0	0	0	0	0	0	0	0	1	0	0	0	0	0	—	0	.000	.000	.000	P	5	1	6	0	0	1.000

BILL VIRDON—William Charles Virdon—Bats: Left; Throws: Right

Ht: 6'0"; Wt: 175 lbs; Born: 6/9/1931 in Hazel Park, Michigan; Debut: 4/12/1955

World Series — Batting / Fielding

Year Tm	Age	G	AB	H	2B	3B	HR	TB	R	RBI	GW	TBB	IBB	SO	HBP	SH	SF	SB	CS	SB%	GDP	Avg	OBP	SLG	Pos	G	PO	A	E	DP	FPct
1960 Pit	29	7	29	7	3	0	0	10	2	5	1	1	0	3	0	0	0	1	0	1.00	0	.241	.267	.345	OF	7	18	0	1	0	.947

OZZIE VIRGIL—Osvaldo Jose Virgil—Bats: Right; Throws: Right

Ht: 6'1"; Wt: 180 lbs; Born: 12/7/1956 in Mayaguez, Puerto Rico; Debut: 10/5/1980

LCS — Batting / Fielding

Year Tm	Age	G	AB	H	2B	3B	HR	TB	R	RBI	GW	TBB	IBB	SO	HBP	SH	SF	SB	CS	SB%	GDP	Avg	OBP	SLG	Pos	G	PO	A	E	DP	FPct
1983 Phi	26	1	1	0	0	0	0	0	0	0	0	0	0	1	0	0	0	0	0	—	0	.000	.000	.000	—						

World Series — Batting / Fielding

Year Tm	Age	G	AB	H	2B	3B	HR	TB	R	RBI	GW	TBB	IBB	SO	HBP	SH	SF	SB	CS	SB%	GDP	Avg	OBP	SLG	Pos	G	PO	A	E	DP	FPct
1983 Phi	26	3	2	1	0	0	0	1	0	1	0	0	0	0	0	0	0	0	0	—	0	.500	.500	.500	C	1	1	0	0	0	1.000
Postseason Totals		4	3	1	0	0	0	1	0	1	0	0	0	1	0	0	0	0	0	—	0	.333	.333	.333	C	1	1	0	0	0	1.000

JOSE VIZCAINO—Jose Luis Vizcaino—Bats: Both; Throws: Right

Ht: 6'1"; Wt: 150 lbs; Born: 3/26/1968 in San Cristobal, Dominican Republic; Debut: 9/10/1989

Division Series — Batting / Fielding

Year Tm	Age	G	AB	H	2B	3B	HR	TB	R	RBI	GW	TBB	IBB	SO	HBP	SH	SF	SB	CS	SB%	GDP	Avg	OBP	SLG	Pos	G	PO	A	E	DP	FPct
1996 Cle	28	3	12	4	2	0	0	6	1	1	0	1	0	1	0	0	0	0	0	—	0	.333	.385	.500	2B	3	4	3	1	1	.875
1997 SF	29	3	11	2	1	0	0	3	1	0	0	0	0	5	0	1	0	0	0	—	0	.182	.182	.273	SS	3	3	10	0	3	1.000
DS Totals		6	23	6	3	0	0	9	2	1	0	1	0	6	0	1	0	0	0	—	0	.261	.292	.391	2B	3	4	3	1	1	.875

OMAR VIZQUEL—Omar Enrique Vizquel—Bats: Both; Throws: Right

Ht: 5'9"; Wt: 155 lbs; Born: 4/24/1967 in Caracas, Venezuela; Debut: 4/3/1989

Division Series — Batting / Fielding

Year Tm	Age	G	AB	H	2B	3B	HR	TB	R	RBI	GW	TBB	IBB	SO	HBP	SH	SF	SB	CS	SB%	GDP	Avg	OBP	SLG	Pos	G	PO	A	E	DP	FPct
1995 Cle	28	3	12	2	1	0	0	3	2	4	1	2	0	2	0	1	0	1	0	1.00	0	.167	.286	.250	SS	3	4	11	0	0	1.000
1996 Cle	29	4	14	6	1	0	0	7	4	2	0	3	0	4	0	0	1	4	2	.67	0	.429	.500	.500	SS	4	6	10	0	2	1.000
1997 Cle	30	5	18	9	0	0	0	9	3	1	1	2	0	1	0	2	0	4	0	1.00	0	.500	.550	.500	SS	5	12	14	0	4	1.000
DS Totals		12	44	17	2	0	0	19	9	7	2	7	0	7	0	3	1	9	2	.82	0	.386	.462	.432	SS	12	22	35	0	6	1.000

LCS — Batting / Fielding

Year Tm	Age	G	AB	H	2B	3B	HR	TB	R	RBI	GW	TBB	IBB	SO	HBP	SH	SF	SB	CS	SB%	GDP	Avg	OBP	SLG	Pos	G	PO	A	E	DP	FPct
1995 Cle	28	6	23	2	1	0	0	3	2	2	0	5	0	2	0	0	1	3	0	1.00	0	.087	.241	.130	SS	6	9	21	0	3	1.000
1997 Cle	30	6	25	1	0	0	0	1	1	0	0	2	0	10	1	1	0	0	0	—	0	.040	.143	.040	SS	6	16	15	0	8	1.000
LCS Totals		12	48	3	1	0	0	4	3	2	0	7	0	12	1	1	1	3	0	1.00	0	.063	.193	.083	SS	12	25	36	0	11	1.000

World Series — Batting / Fielding

Year Tm	Age	G	AB	H	2B	3B	HR	TB	R	RBI	GW	TBB	IBB	SO	HBP	SH	SF	SB	CS	SB%	GDP	Avg	OBP	SLG	Pos	G	PO	A	E	DP	FPct
1995 Cle	28	6	23	4	0	1	0	6	3	1	0	3	0	5	0	0	0	1	0	1.00	0	.174	.269	.261	SS	6	12	22	0	7	1.000
1997 Cle	30	7	30	7	2	0	0	9	5	1	0	3	0	5	0	0	2	5	0	1.00	0	.233	.303	.300	SS	7	12	17	0	6	1.000
WS Totals		13	53	11	2	1	0	15	8	2	0	6	0	10	0	0	2	6	0	1.00	0	.208	.288	.283	SS	13	24	39	0	13	1.000
Postseason Totals		37	145	31	5	1	0	38	20	11	2	20	0	29	1	6	2	18	2	.90	0	.214	.310	.262	SS	37	71	110	0	30	1.000

BILL VOISELLE
William Symmes Voiselle—Nicknames: Ninety-Six, Big Bill—Throws: Right; Bats: Right   Ht: 6'4"; Wt: 200 lbs; Born: 1/29/1919 in Greenwood, South Carolina; Debut: 9/1/1942

World Series — Pitching

Year Tm	Age	G	GS	CG	GF	IP	BFP	H	R	ER	HR	SH	SF	HB	TBB	IBB	SO	WP	Bk	W	L	Pct	ShO	Sv-Op	Hld	OAvg	OOBP	ERA
1948 Bos	29	2	1	0	0	10.2	42	8	3	3	1	0		1	2	0	2	0	0	0	1	.000	0	0-0	0	.205	.262	2.53

World Series — Batting / Fielding

Year Tm	Age	G	AB	H	2B	3B	HR	TB	R	RBI	GW	TBB	IBB	SO	HBP	SH	SF	SB	CS	SB%	GDP	Avg	OBP	SLG	Pos	G	PO	A	E	DP	FPct
1948 Bos	29	2	2	0	0	0	0	0	0	0	0	0	0	1	0	0	0	0	0	—	0	.000	.000	.000	P	2	1	0	0	0	1.000

ED VOSBERG
Edward John Vosberg—Throws: Left; Bats: Left   Ht: 6'1"; Wt: 190 lbs; Born: 9/28/1961 in Tucson, Arizona; Debut: 9/17/1986

Pitching

Round	Year Tm	Age	G	GS	CG	GF	IP	BFP	H	R	ER	HR	SH	SF	HB	TBB	IBB	SO	WP	Bk	W	L	Pct	ShO	Sv-Op	Hld	OAvg	OOBP	ERA
Division Series	1996 Tex	35	1	0	0	0	0.0	1	1	0	0	0	0	0	0	0	0	0	0	0	0	0	—	0	0-0	0	1.000	1.000	—
LCS	1997 Fla	36	2	0	0	2	2.2	10	2	0	0	0	0	0	0	1	0	3	0	0	0	0	—	0	0-0	0	.222	.300	0.00
World Series	1997 Fla	36	2	0	0	1	3.0	14	3	2	2	0	0	0	0	3	1	2	0	0	0	0	—	0	0-0	0	.273	.429	6.00
Postseason Totals			5	0	0	3	5.2	50	6	2	2	0	0	0	0	4	1	5	0	0	0	0	—	0	0-0	0	.286	.400	3.18

Batting / Fielding

Round	Year Tm	Age	G	AB	H	2B	3B	HR	TB	R	RBI	GW	TBB	IBB	SO	HBP	SH	SF	SB	CS	SB%	GDP	Avg	OBP	SLG	Pos	G	PO	A	E	DP	FPct
Division Series	1996 Tex	35	1	0	0	0	0	0	0	0	0	0	0	0	0	0	0	0	0	0	—	0	—	—	—	P	1	0	0	0	0	—
LCS	1997 Fla	36	2	0	0	0	0	0	0	0	0	0	0	0	0	0	0	0	0	0	—	0	—	—	—	P	2	0	0	0	0	—
World Series	1997 Fla	36	2	0	0	0	0	0	0	0	0	0	0	0	0	0	0	0	0	0	—	0	—	—	—	P	2	1	0	0	0	1.000
Postseason Totals			5	0	0	0	0	0	0	0	0	0	0	0	0	0	0	0	0	0	—	0	—	—	—	P	5	1	0	0	0	1.000

PETE VUCKOVICH
Peter Dennis Vuckovich—Throws: Right; Bats: Right   Ht: 6'4"; Wt: 215 lbs; Born: 10/27/1952 in Johnstown, Pennsylvania; Debut: 8/3/1975

Pitching

Round	Year Tm	Age	G	GS	CG	GF	IP	BFP	H	R	ER	HR	SH	SF	HB	TBB	IBB	SO	WP	Bk	W	L	Pct	ShO	Sv-Op	Hld	OAvg	OOBP	ERA
Division Series	1981 Mil	28	2	1	0	1	5.1	22	2	1	0	0	0	0	0	3	0	4	0	0	1	0	1.000	0	0-0	0	.105	.227	0.00
LCS	1982 Mil-C	29	2	2	1	0	14.1	62	15	7	7	1	4	1	1	7	0	8	0	0	0	0	.000	0	0-0	0	.306	.397	4.40
World Series	1982 Mil-C	29	2	2	0	0	14.0	64	16	9	7	2	0	0	0	5	1	4	0	0	0	1	.000	0	0-0	0	.276	.333	4.50
Postseason Totals			6	5	1	1	33.2	296	33	17	14	3	4	1	1	15	1	16	1	0	1	2	.333	0	0-0	0	.262	.343	3.74

Batting / Fielding

Round	Year Tm	Age	G	AB	H	2B	3B	HR	TB	R	RBI	GW	TBB	IBB	SO	HBP	SH	SF	SB	CS	SB%	GDP	Avg	OBP	SLG	Pos	G	PO	A	E	DP	FPct
Division Series	1981 Mil	28	2	0	0	0	0	0	0	0	0	0	0	0	0	0	0	0	0	0	—	0	—	—	—	P	2	0	1	0	0	1.000
LCS	1982 Mil	29	2	0	0	0	0	0	0	0	0	0	0	0	0	0	0	0	0	0	—	0	—	—	—	P	2	0	3	0	0	1.000
World Series	1982 Mil	29	2	0	0	0	0	0	0	0	0	0	0	0	0	0	0	0	0	0	—	0	—	—	—	P	2	0	2	0	0	1.000
Postseason Totals			6	0	0	0	0	0	0	0	0	0	0	0	0	0	0	0	0	0	—	0	—	—	—	P	6	0	6	0	0	1.000

GEORGE VUKOVICH
George Stephen Vukovich—Bats: Left; Throws: Right   Ht: 6'0"; Wt: 198 lbs; Born: 6/24/1956 in Chicago, Illinois; Debut: 4/13/1980

Batting / Fielding

Round	Year Tm	Age	G	AB	H	2B	3B	HR	TB	R	RBI	GW	TBB	IBB	SO	HBP	SH	SF	SB	CS	SB%	GDP	Avg	OBP	SLG	Pos	G	PO	A	E	DP	FPct
Division Series	1981 Phi	25	5	9	4	0	0	1	7	1	2	1	0	0	3	0	0	0	0	0	—	0	.444	.444	.778	OF	3	6	1	0	0	1.000
LCS	1980 Phi	24	4	3	0	0	0	0	0	0	0	0	0	0	5	0	0	0	0	0	—	0	.000	.000	.000	OF	1	0	0	0	0	—
Postseason Totals			9	12	4	0	0	1	7	1	2	1	0	0	3	0	0	0	0	0	—	0	.333	.333	.583	OF	4	6	1	0	0	1.000

BEN WADE
Benjamin Styron Wade—Throws: Right; Bats: Right   Ht: 6'3"; Wt: 195 lbs; Born: 11/26/1922 in Morehead City, North Carolina; Debut: 4/30/1948

World Series — Pitching

Year Tm	Age	G	GS	CG	GF	IP	BFP	H	R	ER	HR	SH	SF	HB	TBB	IBB	SO	WP	Bk	W	L	Pct	ShO	Sv-Op	Hld	OAvg	OOBP	ERA
1953 Bro	30	2	0	0	1	2.1	12	4	4	4	0	1	0	0	1	0	2	0	0	0	0	—	0	0-0	0	.400	.455	15.43

World Series — Batting / Fielding

Year Tm	Age	G	AB	H	2B	3B	HR	TB	R	RBI	GW	TBB	IBB	SO	HBP	SH	SF	SB	CS	SB%	GDP	Avg	OBP	SLG	Pos	G	PO	A	E	DP	FPct
1953 Bro	30	2	0	0	0	0	0	0	0	0	0	0	0	0	0	0	0	0	0	—	0	—	—	—	P	2	0	0	0	0	—

TERRELL WADE
Hawatha Terrell Wade—Throws: Left; Bats: Left   Ht: 6'3"; Wt: 205 lbs; Born: 1/25/1973 in Rembert, South Carolina; Debut: 9/12/1995

Pitching

Round	Year Tm	Age	G	GS	CG	GF	IP	BFP	H	R	ER	HR	SH	SF	HB	TBB	IBB	SO	WP	Bk	W	L	Pct	ShO	Sv-Op	Hld	OAvg	OOBP	ERA
LCS	1996 Atl	23	1	0	0	0	0.1	1	0	0	0	0	0	0	0	0	0	0	0	1	0	0	—	0	0-0	0	.000	.000	0.00
World Series	1996 Atl	23	2	0	0	0	0.2	3	0	0	0	0	0	0	0	1	0	0	0	0	0	0	—	0	0-0	0	.000	.333	0.00
Postseason Totals			3	0	0	0	1.0	8	0	0	0	0	0	0	0	1	0	1	0	0	0	0	—	0	0-0	0	.000	.250	0.00

Batting / Fielding

Round	Year Tm	Age	G	AB	H	2B	3B	HR	TB	R	RBI	GW	TBB	IBB	SO	HBP	SH	SF	SB	CS	SB%	GDP	Avg	OBP	SLG	Pos	G	PO	A	E	DP	FPct
LCS	1996 Atl	23	1	0	0	0	0	0	0	0	0	0	0	0	0	0	0	0	0	0	—	0	—	—	—	P	1	0	0	0	0	—
World Series	1996 Atl	23	2	0	0	0	0	0	0	0	0	0	0	0	0	0	0	0	0	0	—	0	—	—	—	P	2	0	0	0	0	—
Postseason Totals			3	0	0	0	0	0	0	0	0	0	0	0	0	0	0	0	0	0	—	0	—	—	—	P	3	0	0	0	0	—

BILLY WAGNER—William Edward Wagner—Throws: Left; Bats: Left

Ht: 5'11"; Wt: 180 lbs; Born: 6/25/1971 in Tannersville, Virginia; Debut: 9/13/1995

Year	Tm	Age	G	GS	CG	GF	IP	BFP	H	R	ER	HR	SH	SF	HB	TBB	IBB	SO	WP	Bk	W	L	Pct	ShO	Sv-Op	Hld	OAvg	OOBP	ERA
Division Series															Pitching														
1997	Hou	26	1	0	0	1	1.0	6	3	2	2	0	0	0	0	0	0	2	0	0	0	0	—	0	0-0	0	.500	.500	18.00

Year	Tm	Age	G	AB	H	2B	3B	HR	TB	R	RBI	GW	TBB	IBB	SO	HBP	SH	SF	SB	CS	SB%	GDP	Avg	OBP	SLG	Pos	G	PO	A	E	DP	FPct
Division Series									Batting																	Fielding						
1997	Hou	26	1	0	0	0	0	0	0	0	0	0	0	0	0	0	0	0	0	0	—	0	—	—	—	P	1	0	0	0	0	—

HAL WAGNER—Harold Edward Wagner—Bats: Left; Throws: Right

Ht: 6'0"; Wt: 165 lbs; Born: 7/2/1915 in East Riverton, New Jersey; Debut: 10/3/1937; Died: 8/4/1979

Year	Tm	Age	G	AB	H	2B	3B	HR	TB	R	RBI	GW	TBB	IBB	SO	HBP	SH	SF	SB	CS	SB%	GDP	Avg	OBP	SLG	Pos	G	PO	A	E	DP	FPct
World Series									Batting																	Fielding						
1946	Bos	31	5	13	0	0	0	0	0	0	0	0	0	0	1	0	1	0	0	0	—	0	.000	.000	.000	C	5	20	2	0	0	1.000

HEINIE WAGNER—Charles F. Wagner—Bats: Right; Throws: Right

Ht: 5'9"; Wt: 183 lbs; Born: 9/23/1880 in New York, New York; Debut: 7/1/1902; Died: 3/20/1943

Year	Tm	Age	G	AB	H	2B	3B	HR	TB	R	RBI	GW	TBB	IBB	SO	HBP	SH	SF	SB	CS	SB%	GDP	Avg	OBP	SLG	Pos	G	PO	A	E	DP	FPct
World Series									Batting																	Fielding						
1912	Bos	32	8	30	5	1	0	0	6	1	0	0	3	0	6	0	0	0	1	0	1.00	0	.167	.242	.200	SS	8	25	24	3	1	.942

HONUS WAGNER (HOF 1936-W)—John Peter Wagner—Nickname: The Flying Dutchman—B: R, T: R

Ht: 5'11"; Wt: 200 lbs; Born: 2/24/1874 in Chartiers, Pa.; Deb.: 7/19/1897; Died: 12/6/1955

Year	Tm	Age	G	AB	H	2B	3B	HR	TB	R	RBI	GW	TBB	IBB	SO	HBP	SH	SF	SB	CS	SB%	GDP	Avg	OBP	SLG	Pos	G	PO	A	E	DP	FPct
World Series									Batting																	Fielding						
1903	Pit	29	8	27	6	1	0	0	7	2	3	1	3	0	4	1	1	0	3	1	.75	0	.222	.323	.259	SS	8	12	30	6	4	.875
1909	Pit	35	7	24	8	2	1	0	12	4	6	1	4	0	2	2	0	0	6	2	.75	0	.333	.467	.500	SS	7	13	23	3	1	.923
WS Totals			15	51	14	3	1	0	19	6	9	2	7	0	6	3	1	0	9	3	.75	0	.275	.393	.373	SS	15	25	53	9	5	.897

EDDIE WAITKUS—Edward Stephen Waitkus—Bats: Left; Throws: Left

Ht: 6'0"; Wt: 170 lbs; Born: 9/4/1919 in Cambridge, Massachusetts; Debut: 4/15/1941; Died: 9/15/1972

Year	Tm	Age	G	AB	H	2B	3B	HR	TB	R	RBI	GW	TBB	IBB	SO	HBP	SH	SF	SB	CS	SB%	GDP	Avg	OBP	SLG	Pos	G	PO	A	E	DP	FPct
World Series									Batting																	Fielding						
1950	Phi	31	4	15	4	1	0	0	5	0	0	0	2	0	0	0	1	0	0	0	—	0	.267	.353	.333	1B	4	34	2	0	1	1.000

TIM WAKEFIELD—Timothy Stephen Wakefield—Throws: Right; Bats: Right

Ht: 6'2"; Wt: 195 lbs; Born: 8/2/1966 in Melbourne, Florida; Debut: 7/31/1992

Year	Tm	Age	G	GS	CG	GF	IP	BFP	H	R	ER	HR	SH	SF	HB	TBB	IBB	SO	WP	Bk	W	L	Pct	ShO	Sv-Op	Hld	OAvg	OOBP	ERA
Division Series															Pitching														
1995	Bos	29	1	1	0	0	5.1	27	5	7	7	1	0	0	1	5	0	4	0	0	0	1	.000	0	0-0	0	.238	.407	11.81
LCS															Pitching														
1992	Pit	26	2	2	2	0	18.0	73	14	6	6	4	0	0	0	5	0	7	1	0	2	0	1.000	0	0-0	0	.206	.260	3.00
Postseason Totals			3	3	2	0	23.1	200	19	13	13	5	0	0	1	10	0	11	1	0	2	1	.667	0	0-0	0	.213	.300	5.01

Year	Tm	Age	G	AB	H	2B	3B	HR	TB	R	RBI	GW	TBB	IBB	SO	HBP	SH	SF	SB	CS	SB%	GDP	Avg	OBP	SLG	Pos	G	PO	A	E	DP	FPct
Division Series									Batting																	Fielding						
1995	Bos	29	1	0	0	0	0	0	0	0	0	0	0	0	0	0	0	0	0	0	—	0	—	—	—	P	1	0	0	0	0	—
LCS									Batting																	Fielding						
1992	Pit	26	2	6	0	0	0	0	0	1	0	0	0	0	0	0	2	0	0	0	—	0	.000	.000	.000	P	2	3	2	0	0	1.000
Postseason Totals			3	6	0	0	0	0	0	1	0	0	0	0	0	0	2	0	0	0	—	0	.000	.000	.000	P	3	3	2	0	0	1.000

RUBE WALBERG—George Elvin Walberg—Throws: Left; Bats: Left

Ht: 6'1"; Wt: 190 lbs; Born: 7/27/1896 in Pine City, Minnesota; Debut: 4/29/1923; Died: 10/27/1978

Year	Tm	Age	G	GS	CG	GF	IP	BFP	H	R	ER	HR	SH	SF	HB	TBB	IBB	SO	WP	Bk	W	L	Pct	ShO	Sv-Op	Hld	OAvg	OOBP	ERA
World Series															Pitching														
1929	Phi	33	2	0	0	1	6.1	22	3	1	0	0	0	1	0	0	0	8	0	0	1	0	1.000	0	0-0	0	.143	.136	0.00
1930	Phi	34	1	1	0	0	4.2	18	4	2	2	1	0	0	0	1	0	3	0	0	0	1	.000	0	0-0	0	.235	.278	3.86
1931	Phi	35	2	0	0	1	3.0	12	3	1	1	0	0	0	0	2	0	4	0	0	0	0	—	0	0-0	0	.300	.417	3.00
WS Totals			5	1	0	2	14.0	104	10	4	3	1	0	1	0	3	0	15	0	0	1	1	.500	0	0-0	0	.208	.250	1.93

Year	Tm	Age	G	AB	H	2B	3B	HR	TB	R	RBI	GW	TBB	IBB	SO	HBP	SH	SF	SB	CS	SB%	GDP	Avg	OBP	SLG	Pos	G	PO	A	E	DP	FPct
World Series									Batting																	Fielding						
1929	Phi	33	2	1	0	0	0	0	0	0	0	0	0	0	0	0	0	0	0	0	—	0	.000	.000	.000	P	2	0	1	1	0	.500
1930	Phi	34	1	2	0	0	0	0	0	0	0	0	0	0	1	0	0	0	0	0	—	0	.000	.000	.000	P	1	0	0	0	0	—
1931	Phi	35	2	0	0	0	0	0	0	0	0	0	0	0	0	0	0	0	0	0	—	0	—	—	—	P	2	0	0	0	0	—
WS Totals			5	3	0	0	0	0	0	0	0	0	0	0	1	0	0	0	0	0	—	0	.000	.000	.000	P	5	0	1	1	0	.500

BOB WALK—Robert Vernon Walk—Nickname: Whirlybird—Throws: Right; Bats: Right

Ht: 6'3"; Wt: 185 lbs; Born: 11/26/1956 in Van Nuys, California; Debut: 5/26/1980

Year	Tm	Age	G	GS	CG	GF	IP	BFP	H	R	ER	HR	SH	SF	HB	TBB	IBB	SO	WP	Bk	W	L	Pct	ShO	Sv-Op	Hld	OAvg	OOBP	ERA
LCS															Pitching														
1982	Atl	25	1	0	0	1	1.0	7	2	1	1	0	0	1	0	1	1	1	0	0	0	0	—	0	0-0	0	.400	.429	9.00
1990	Pit	33	2	2	0	0	13.0	50	11	7	7	2	1	1	0	2	0	8	0	0	1	1	.500	0	0-0	0	.239	.265	4.85
1991	Pit	34	3	0	0	1	9.1	35	5	2	2	1	0	0	0	3	1	5	0	1	0	0	—	0	1-1	0	.156	.229	1.93
1992	Pit	35	2	1	1	0	11.2	48	6	5	5	1	0	0	0	7	1	6	0	0	1	0	1.000	0	0-0	0	.146	.271	3.86
LCS Totals			8	3	1	2	35.0	280	24	15	15	4	1	2	0	13	3	20	0	1	2	1	.667	0	1-1	0	.194	.266	3.86
World Series															Pitching														
1980	Phi	23	1	1	0	0	7.0	31	8	6	6	3	0	0	0	3	0	3	1	0	1	0	1.000	0	0-0	0	.286	.355	7.71
Postseason Totals			9	4	1	2	42.0	342	32	21	21	7	1	2	0	16	3	23	1	1	3	1	.750	0	1-1	0	.211	.282	4.50

Year	Tm	Age	G	AB	H	2B	3B	HR	TB	R	RBI	GW	TBB	IBB	SO	HBP	SH	SF	SB	CS	SB%	GDP	Avg	OBP	SLG	Pos	G	PO	A	E	DP	FPct
LCS									Batting																	Fielding						
1982	Atl	25	1	0	0	0	0	0	0	0	0	0	0	0	0	0	0	0	0	0	—	0	—	—	—	P	1	0	0	0	0	—
1990	Pit	33	2	4	0	0	0	0	0	0	0	0	0	0	4	0	0	0	0	0	—	0	.000	.000	.000	P	2	2	1	0	0	1.000
1991	Pit	34	3	2	0	0	0	0	0	0	0	0	0	0	2	0	0	0	0	0	—	0	.000	.000	.000	P	3	0	0	0	0	—
1992	Pit	35	2	5	0	0	0	0	0	0	0	0	0	0	1	0	0	0	0	0	—	0	.000	.000	.000	P	2	1	2	0	0	1.000
LCS Totals			8	11	0	0	0	0	0	0	0	0	0	0	7	0	0	0	0	0	—	0	.000	.000	.000	P	8	3	3	0	0	1.000
World Series									Batting																	Fielding						
1980	Phi	23	1	0	0	0	0	0	0	0	0	0	0	0	0	0	0	0	0	0	—	0	—	—	—	P	1	2	0	0	0	1.000
Postseason Totals			9	11	0	0	0	0	0	0	0	0	0	0	7	0	0	0	0	0	—	0	.000	.000	.000	P	9	5	3	0	0	1.000

BILL WALKER—William Henry Walker—Throws: Left; Bats: Right

Ht: 6'0"; Wt: 175 lbs; Born: 10/7/1903 in East St. Louis, Illinois; Debut: 9/13/1927; Died: 6/14/1966

Year	Tm	Age	G	GS	CG	GF	IP	BFP	H	R	ER	HR	SH	SF	HB	TBB	IBB	SO	WP	Bk	W	L	Pct	ShO	Sv-Op	Hld	OAvg	OOBP	ERA
World Series															Pitching														
1934	StL	30	2	0	0	1	6.1	34	6	7	4	0	3	0	0	6	2	2	0	0	0	2	.000	0	0-0	0	.240	.387	5.68

Year	Tm	Age	G	AB	H	2B	3B	HR	TB	R	RBI	GW	TBB	IBB	SO	HBP	SH	SF	SB	CS	SB%	GDP	Avg	OBP	SLG	Pos	G	PO	A	E	DP	FPct
World Series									Batting																	Fielding						
1934	StL	30	2	2	0	0	0	0	0	0	0	0	0	0	2	0	0	0	0	0	—	0	.000	.000	.000	P	2	0	1	1	0	.500

DIXIE WALKER—Fred Walker—Nickname: The People's Cherce—Bats: Left; Throws: Right

Ht: 6'1"; Wt: 175 lbs; Born: 9/24/1910 in Villa Rica, Georgia; Debut: 4/28/1931; Died: 5/17/1982

Year	Tm	Age	G	AB	H	2B	3B	HR	TB	R	RBI	GW	TBB	IBB	SO	HBP	SH	SF	SB	CS	SB%	GDP	Avg	OBP	SLG	Pos	G	PO	A	E	DP	FPct
World Series									Batting																	Fielding						
1941	Bro	31	5	18	4	2	0	0	6	3	0	0	2	0	1	0	0	0	0	0	—	0	.222	.300	.333	OF	5	14	0	0	0	1.000
1947	Bro	37	7	27	6	1	0	1	10	1	4	0	3	0	1	0	0	0	1	0	1.00	2	.222	.300	.370	OF	7	9	1	0	0	1.000
WS Totals			12	45	10	3	0	1	16	4	4	0	5	0	2	0	0	0	1	0	1.00	2	.222	.300	.356	OF	12	23	1	0	0	1.000

GEE WALKER
—Gerald Holmes Walker—Bats: Right; Throws: Right   Ht: 5'11"; Wt: 188 lbs; Born: 3/19/1908 in Gulfport, Mississippi; Debut: 4/14/1931; Died: 3/20/1981

World Series

Year	Tm	Age	G	AB	H	2B	3B	HR	TB	R	RBI	GW	TBB	IBB	SO	HBP	SH	SF	SB	CS	SB%	GDP	Avg	OBP	SLG	Pos	G	PO	A	E	DP	FPct
1934	Det	26	3	3	1	0	0	0	1	0	1	0	0	0	1	0	0	0	0	1	.00	0	.333	.333	.333	—						
1935	Det	27	3	4	1	0	0	0	1	1	0	0	1	1	0	0	0	0	0	0	—	1	.250	.400	.250	OF	1	0	0	0	0	—
WS Totals			6	7	2	0	0	0	2	1	1	0	1	1	1	0	0	0	0	1	.00	1	.286	.375	.286	OF	1	0	0	0	0	—

GREG WALKER
—Gregory Lee Walker—Bats: Left; Throws: Right   Ht: 6'3"; Wt: 205 lbs; Born: 10/6/1959 in Douglas, Georgia; Debut: 9/18/1982

LCS

Year	Tm	Age	G	AB	H	2B	3B	HR	TB	R	RBI	GW	TBB	IBB	SO	HBP	SH	SF	SB	CS	SB%	GDP	Avg	OBP	SLG	Pos	G	PO	A	E	DP	FPct
1983	ChA	23	2	3	1	0	0	0	1	0	0	0	1	0	2	0	0	0	0	0	—	0	.333	.500	.333	1B	1	7	1	0	2	1.000

HARRY WALKER
—Harry William Walker—Nickname: Harry the Hat—Bats: Left; Throws: Right   Ht: 6'2"; Wt: 175 lbs; Born: 10/22/1916 in Pascagoula, Mississippi; Debut: 9/25/1940

World Series

Year	Tm	Age	G	AB	H	2B	3B	HR	TB	R	RBI	GW	TBB	IBB	SO	HBP	SH	SF	SB	CS	SB%	GDP	Avg	OBP	SLG	Pos	G	PO	A	E	DP	FPct
1942	StL	25	1	1	0	0	0	0	0	0	0	0	0	0	1	0	0	0	0	0	—	0	.000	.000	.000	—						
1943	StL	26	5	18	3	1	0	0	4	0	0	0	0	0	2	0	0	0	0	0	—	0	.167	.167	.222	OF	4	10	0	2	0	.833
1946	StL	30	7	17	7	2	0	0	9	3	6	1	4	2	2	0	0	1	0	1	1.00	0	.412	.524	.529	OF	7	13	0	0	0	1.000
WS Totals			13	36	10	3	0	0	13	3	6	1	4	2	5	0	0	1	0	1	.00	0	.278	.350	.361	OF	11	23	0	2	0	.000

HUB WALKER
—Harvey Willos Walker—Bats: Left; Throws: Right   Ht: 5'10"; Wt: 175 lbs; Born: 8/17/1906 in Gulfport, Mississippi; Debut: 4/15/1931; Died: 11/26/1982

World Series

Year	Tm	Age	G	AB	H	2B	3B	HR	TB	R	RBI	GW	TBB	IBB	SO	HBP	SH	SF	SB	CS	SB%	GDP	Avg	OBP	SLG	Pos	G	PO	A	E	DP	FPct
1945	Det	39	2	2	1	1	0	0	2	1	0	0	0	0	0	0	0	0	0	0	—	1	.500	.500	1.000	—						

LARRY WALKER
—Larry Kenneth Robert Walker—Bats: Left; Throws: Right   Ht: 6'2"; Wt: 185 lbs; Born: 12/1/1966 in Maple Ridge, British Columbia; Debut: 8/16/1989

Division Series

Year	Tm	Age	G	AB	H	2B	3B	HR	TB	R	RBI	GW	TBB	IBB	SO	HBP	SH	SF	SB	CS	SB%	GDP	Avg	OBP	SLG	Pos	G	PO	A	E	DP	FPct
1995	Col	28	4	14	3	0	0	1	6	3	3	0	3	1	4	1	0	0	1	0	1.00	1	.214	.389	.429	OF	4	3	0	0	0	1.000

LUKE WALKER
—James Luke Walker—Nickname: Dixie—Throws: Left; Bats: Left   Ht: 6'2"; Wt: 190 lbs; Born: 9/2/1943 in DeKalb, Texas; Debut: 9/7/1965

LCS — Pitching

Year	Tm	Age	G	GS	CG	GF	IP	BFP	H	R	ER	HR	SH	SF	HB	TBB	IBB	SO	WP	Bk	W	L	Pct	ShO	Sv-Op	Hld	OAvg	OOBP	ERA
1970	Pit	27	1	1	0	0	7.0	27	5	2	1	1	0	0	0	1	1	5	1	0	0	1	.000	0	0-0	0	.192	.222	1.29
1972	Pit	29	1	0	0	0	1.0	6	3	2	2	0	0	1	0	0	0	0	0	0	0	0	—	0	0-0	0	.600	.500	18.00
LCS Totals			2	1	0	0	8.0	66	8	4	3	1	0	1	0	1	1	5	1	0	0	1	.000	0	0-0	0	.258	.273	3.38

World Series — Pitching

Year	Tm	Age	G	GS	CG	GF	IP	BFP	H	R	ER	HR	SH	SF	HB	TBB	IBB	SO	WP	Bk	W	L	Pct	ShO	Sv-Op	Hld	OAvg	OOBP	ERA
1971	Pit	28	1	1	0	0	0.2	6	3	3	3	0	0	2	0	1	0	0	0	0	0	0	—	0	0-0	0	1.000	.667	40.50
Postseason Totals			3	2	0	0	8.2	78	11	7	6	1	0	3	0	2	1	5	1	0	0	1	.000	0	0-0	0	.324	.333	6.23

LCS — Batting

Year	Tm	Age	G	AB	H	2B	3B	HR	TB	R	RBI	GW	TBB	IBB	SO	HBP	SH	SF	SB	CS	SB%	GDP	Avg	OBP	SLG	Pos	G	PO	A	E	DP	FPct
1970	Pit	27	1	2	0	0	0	0	0	0	0	0	0	0	1	0	0	0	0	0	—	0	.000	.000	.000	P	1	0	1	0	0	.000
1972	Pit	29	1	0	0	0	0	0	0	0	0	0	0	0	0	0	0	0	0	0	—	0	.000	.000	.000	P	1	0	0	0	0	—
LCS Totals			2	2	0	0	0	0	0	0	0	0	0	0	1	0	0	0	0	0	—	0	.000	.000	.000	P	2	0	1	0	0	.000

World Series — Batting

Year	Tm	Age	G	AB	H	2B	3B	HR	TB	R	RBI	GW	TBB	IBB	SO	HBP	SH	SF	SB	CS	SB%	GDP	Avg	OBP	SLG	Pos	G	PO	A	E	DP	FPct
1971	Pit	28	1	0	0	0	0	0	0	0	0	0	0	0	0	0	0	0	0	0	—	0	—	—	—	P	1	0	0	0	0	—
Postseason Totals			3	2	0	0	0	0	0	0	0	0	0	0	1	0	0	0	0	0	—	0	.000	.000	.000	P	3	0	1	0	0	.000

RUBE WALKER
—Albert Bluford Walker—Bats: Left; Throws: Right   Ht: 6'0"; Wt: 175 lbs; Born: 5/16/1926 in Lenoir, North Carolina; Debut: 4/20/1948; Died: 12/12/1992

World Series

Year	Tm	Age	G	AB	H	2B	3B	HR	TB	R	RBI	GW	TBB	IBB	SO	HBP	SH	SF	SB	CS	SB%	GDP	Avg	OBP	SLG	Pos	G	PO	A	E	DP	FPct
1956	Bro	30	2	2	0	0	0	0	0	0	0	0	0	0	0	0	0	0	0	0	—	1	.000	.000	.000	—						

TILLY WALKER
—Clarence William Walker—Bats: Right; Throws: Right   Ht: 5'11"; Wt: 165 lbs; Born: 9/4/1887 in Telford, Tennessee; Debut: 4/12/1911; Died: 9/21/1959

World Series

Year	Tm	Age	G	AB	H	2B	3B	HR	TB	R	RBI	GW	TBB	IBB	SO	HBP	SH	SF	SB	CS	SB%	GDP	Avg	OBP	SLG	Pos	G	PO	A	E	DP	FPct
1916	Bos	29	3	11	3	0	1	0	5	1	1	1	1	0	2	0	0	0	0	0	.00	0	.273	.333	.455	OF	3	4	1	0	0	1.000

TIM WALLACH
—Timothy Charles Wallach—Nickname: Eli—Bats: Right; Throws: Right   Ht: 6'3"; Wt: 220 lbs; Born: 9/14/1957 in Huntington Beach, California; Debut: 9/6/1980

Division Series

Year	Tm	Age	G	AB	H	2B	3B	HR	TB	R	RBI	GW	TBB	IBB	SO	HBP	SH	SF	SB	CS	SB%	GDP	Avg	OBP	SLG	Pos	G	PO	A	E	DP	FPct
1981	Mon	24	4	4	1	1	0	0	2	1	0	0	4	1	0	0	0	0	0	0	—	0	.250	.625	.500	OF	3	3	0	0	0	1.000
1995	LA	38	3	12	1	0	0	0	1	0	0	0	1	0	3	0	0	0	0	0	—	0	.083	.154	.083	3B	3	1	2	0	0	1.000
1996	LA	39	3	11	0	0	0	0	0	0	0	0	0	0	1	0	0	0	0	0	—	0	.000	.000	.000	3B	3	2	8	1	1	.909
DS Totals			10	27	2	1	0	0	3	1	0	0	5	1	4	0	0	0	0	0	—	0	.074	.219	.111	3B	6	3	10	1	1	.929

LCS

Year	Tm	Age	G	AB	H	2B	3B	HR	TB	R	RBI	GW	TBB	IBB	SO	HBP	SH	SF	SB	CS	SB%	GDP	Avg	OBP	SLG	Pos	G	PO	A	E	DP	FPct
1981	Mon	24	1	1	0	0	0	0	0	0	0	0	0	0	0	0	0	0	0	0	—	0	.000	.000	.000	—						
Postseason Totals			11	28	2	1	0	0	3	1	0	0	5	1	4	0	0	0	0	0	—	0	.071	.212	.107	3B	6	3	10	1	1	.929

DENNY WALLING
—Dennis Martin Walling—Bats: Left; Throws: Right   Ht: 6'0"; Wt: 180 lbs; Born: 4/17/1954 in Neptune, New Jersey; Debut: 9/7/1975

Division Series

Year	Tm	Age	G	AB	H	2B	3B	HR	TB	R	RBI	GW	TBB	IBB	SO	HBP	SH	SF	SB	CS	SB%	GDP	Avg	OBP	SLG	Pos	G	PO	A	E	DP	FPct
1981	Hou	27	3	6	2	0	0	0	2	0	1	1	0	0	1	0	0	0	0	0	—	0	.333	.333	.333	1B	2	6	2	1	0	.889

LCS

Year	Tm	Age	G	AB	H	2B	3B	HR	TB	R	RBI	GW	TBB	IBB	SO	HBP	SH	SF	SB	CS	SB%	GDP	Avg	OBP	SLG	Pos	G	PO	A	E	DP	FPct
1980	Hou	26	3	9	1	0	0	0	1	2	2	1	1	1	0	0	0	1	0	0	—	0	.111	.182	.111	1B	1	5	0	0	0	1.000
																										OF	2	1	0	0	0	1.000
1986	Hou	32	5	19	3	1	0	0	4	1	2	0	0	0	4	0	0	0	0	0	—	0	.158	.158	.211	3B	5	3	6	0	0	1.000
LCS Totals			8	28	4	1	0	0	5	3	4	1	1	1	4	0	0	1	0	0	—	0	.143	.167	.179	3B	5	3	6	0	0	1.000
Postseason Totals			11	34	6	1	0	0	7	3	5	2	1	1	5	0	0	1	0	0	—	0	.176	.194	.206	3B	5	3	6	0	0	1.000

ED WALSH
(HOF 1946-V)—Edward Augustine Walsh—Nickname: Big Ed—Throws: Right; Bats: Right   Ht: 6'1"; Wt: 193 lbs; Born: 5/14/1881 in Plains, Pennsylvania; Debut: 5/7/1904; Died: 5/26/1959

World Series — Pitching

Year	Tm	Age	G	GS	CG	GF	IP	BFP	H	R	ER	HR	SH	SF	HB	TBB	IBB	SO	WP	Bk	W	L	Pct	ShO	Sv-Op	Hld	OAvg	OOBP	ERA
1906	ChA	25	2	2	1	0	15.0	62	7	6	2	0	2	0	1	6	0	17	1	0	2	0	1.000	1	0-0	0	.132	.233	1.20

World Series — Batting

Year	Tm	Age	G	AB	H	2B	3B	HR	TB	R	RBI	GW	TBB	IBB	SO	HBP	SH	SF	SB	CS	SB%	GDP	Avg	OBP	SLG	Pos	G	PO	A	E	DP	FPct
1906	ChA	25	2	4	0	0	0	0	0	1	0	0	3	0	3	0	0	0	0	0	—	0	.000	.429	.000	P	2	0	4	1	0	.800

JIMMY WALSH—James Charles Walsh—Bats: Left; Throws: Right

Ht: 5'10"; Wt: 170 lbs; Born: 9/22/1885 in Kallila, Ireland; Debut: 8/26/1912; Died: 7/3/1962

World Series — Batting / Fielding

Year Tm	Age	G	AB	H	2B	3B	HR	TB	R	RBI	GW	TBB	IBB	SO	HBP	SH	SF	SB	CS	SB%	GDP	Avg	OBP	SLG	Pos	G	PO	A	E	DP	FPct
1914 Phi	29	3	6	2	1	0	0	3	0	1	0	3	1	1	0	0	0	0	0	—	0	.333	.556	.500	OF	2	2	0	0	0	1.000
1916 Bos	31	1	3	0	0	0	0	0	0	0	0	0	0	0	0	0	0	0	0	—	0	.000	.000	.000	OF	1	1	0	0	0	1.000
WS Totals		4	9	2	1	0	0	3	0	1	0	3	1	1	0	0	0	0	0	—	0	.222	.417	.333	OF	3	3	0	0	0	1.000

BUCKY WALTERS—William Henry Walters—Throws: Right; Bats: Right

Ht: 6'1"; Wt: 180 lbs; Born: 4/19/1909 in Philadelphia, Pennsylvania; Debut: 9/18/1931; Died: 4/20/1991

World Series — Pitching

Year Tm	Age	G	GS	CG	GF	IP	BFP	H	R	ER	HR	SH	SF	HB	TBB	IBB	SO	WP	Bk	W	L	Pct	ShO	Sv-Op	Hld	OAvg	OOBP	ERA
1939 Cin-*M*	30	2	1	1	1	11.0	47	13	9	6	1	2	0	0	1	0	6	0	0	0	2	.000	0	0- 1	0	.295	.311	4.91
1940 Cin	31	2	2	2	0	18.0	66	8	3	3	0	0	0	0	6	0	6	0	0	2	0	1.000	1	0- 0	0	.133	.212	1.50
WS Totals		4	3	3	1	29.0	226	21	12	9	1	2	0	0	7	0	12	0	0	2	2	.500	1	0-1	0	.202	.252	2.79

World Series — Batting / Fielding

Year Tm	Age	G	AB	H	2B	3B	HR	TB	R	RBI	GW	TBB	IBB	SO	HBP	SH	SF	SB	CS	SB%	GDP	Avg	OBP	SLG	Pos	G	PO	A	E	DP	FPct
1939 Cin	30	2	3	0	0	0	0	0	0	0	0	0	0	0	0	0	0	0	0	—	0	.000	.000	.000	P	2	0	3	0	1	1.000
1940 Cin	31	2	7	2	1	0	1	6	2	2	0	0	0	1	0	0	0	0	0	—	0	.286	.286	.857	P	2	0	4	0	0	1.000
WS Totals		4	10	2	1	0	1	6	2	2	0	0	0	1	0	0	0	0	0	—	0	.200	.200	.600	P	4	0	7	0	1	1.000

JEROME WALTON—Jerome O'Terrell Walton—Bats: Right; Throws: Right

Ht: 6'1"; Wt: 175 lbs; Born: 7/8/1965 in Newnan, Georgia; Debut: 4/4/1989

Division Series — Batting / Fielding

Year Tm	Age	G	AB	H	2B	3B	HR	TB	R	RBI	GW	TBB	IBB	SO	HBP	SH	SF	SB	CS	SB%	GDP	Avg	OBP	SLG	Pos	G	PO	A	E	DP	FPct
1995 Cin	30	3	3	0	0	0	0	0	0	0	0	1	0	1	0	0	0	0	0	—	0	.000	.250	.000	OF	3	3	0	0	0	1.000
1997 Bal	32	2	4	0	0	0	0	0	0	0	0	0	0	2	0	0	0	0	0	—	1	.000	.000	.000	1B	2	5	1	0	0	1.000
DS Totals		5	7	0	0	0	0	0	0	0	0	1	0	3	0	0	0	0	0	—	1	.000	.125	.000	OF	3	3	0	0	0	1.000

LCS — Batting / Fielding

Year Tm	Age	G	AB	H	2B	3B	HR	TB	R	RBI	GW	TBB	IBB	SO	HBP	SH	SF	SB	CS	SB%	GDP	Avg	OBP	SLG	Pos	G	PO	A	E	DP	FPct
1989 ChN-*RY*	24	5	22	8	0	0	0	8	4	2	0	2	0	2	0	0	0	0	0	—	0	.364	.417	.364	OF	5	11	0	0	0	1.000
1995 Cin	30	2	7	0	0	0	0	0	0	0	0	0	0	2	0	0	0	0	0	—	1	.000	.000	.000	OF	2	6	0	0	0	1.000
1997 Bal	32	1	0	0	0	0	0	0	0	0	0	0	0	0	0	0	0	0	0	—	0	—	—	—	OF	1	0	0	0	0	—
LCS Totals		8	29	8	0	0	0	8	4	2	0	2	0	4	0	0	0	0	0	—	1	.276	.323	.276	OF	8	17	0	0	0	1.000
Postseason Totals		13	36	8	0	0	0	8	4	2	0	3	0	7	0	0	0	0	0	—	2	.222	.282	.222	OF	11	20	0	0	0	1.000

BILL WAMBSGANSS—William Adolph Wambsganss—Bats: Right; Throws: Right

Ht: 5'11"; Wt: 175 lbs; Born: 3/19/1894 in Cleveland, Ohio; Debut: 8/4/1914; Died: 12/8/1985

World Series — Batting / Fielding

Year Tm	Age	G	AB	H	2B	3B	HR	TB	R	RBI	GW	TBB	IBB	SO	HBP	SH	SF	SB	CS	SB%	GDP	Avg	OBP	SLG	Pos	G	PO	A	E	DP	FPct
1920 Cle	26	7	26	4	0	0	0	4	3	1	0	2	0	1	0	1	0	0	0	—	0	.154	.214	.154	2B	7	20	17	0	4	1.000

LLOYD WANER (HOF 1967-V)—Lloyd James Waner—Nickname: Little Poison—Bats: Left; Throws: Right

Ht: 5'9"; Wt: 150 lbs; Born: 3/16/1906 in Harrah, Oklahoma; Debut: 4/12/1927; Died: 7/22/1982

World Series — Batting / Fielding

Year Tm	Age	G	AB	H	2B	3B	HR	TB	R	RBI	GW	TBB	IBB	SO	HBP	SH	SF	SB	CS	SB%	GDP	Avg	OBP	SLG	Pos	G	PO	A	E	DP	FPct
1927 Pit	21	4	15	6	1	1	0	9	5	0	0	1	0	0	1	1	0	0	0	—	0	.400	.471	.600	OF	4	8	1	2	0	.818

PAUL WANER (HOF 1952-W)—Paul Glee Waner—Nickname: Big Poison—Bats: Left; Throws: Left

Ht: 5'8"; Wt: 153 lbs; Born: 4/16/1903 in Harrah, Oklahoma; Debut: 4/13/1926; Died: 8/29/1965

World Series — Batting / Fielding

Year Tm	Age	G	AB	H	2B	3B	HR	TB	R	RBI	GW	TBB	IBB	SO	HBP	SH	SF	SB	CS	SB%	GDP	Avg	OBP	SLG	Pos	G	PO	A	E	DP	FPct
1927 Pit-*M*	24	4	15	5	1	0	0	6	0	3	0	0	0	1	0	0	2	0	0	—	0	.333	.294	.400	OF	4	8	0	0	0	1.000

AARON WARD—Aaron Lee Ward—Bats: Right; Throws: Right

Ht: 5'10"; Wt: 160 lbs; Born: 8/28/1896 in Bonneville, Arkansas; Debut: 8/14/1917; Died: 1/30/1961

World Series — Batting / Fielding

Year Tm	Age	G	AB	H	2B	3B	HR	TB	R	RBI	GW	TBB	IBB	SO	HBP	SH	SF	SB	CS	SB%	GDP	Avg	OBP	SLG	Pos	G	PO	A	E	DP	FPct
1921 NYA	25	8	26	6	0	0	0	6	1	4	0	2	0	6	0	2	1	0	0	—	0	.231	.276	.231	2B	8	19	32	2	4	.962
1922 NYA	26	5	13	2	0	0	2	8	3	3	0	3	1	3	0	0	1	0	0	—	0	.154	.294	.615	2B	5	13	16	1	4	.967
1923 NYA	27	6	24	10	0	0	1	13	4	2	0	1	0	3	0	0	0	1	0	1.00	0	.417	.440	.542	2B	6	11	26	0	3	1.000
WS Totals		19	63	18	0	0	3	27	8	9	0	6	1	12	0	2	2	1	0	1.00	0	.286	.338	.429	2B	19	43	74	3	11	.975

DUANE WARD—Roy Duane Ward—Throws: Right; Bats: Right

Ht: 6'4"; Wt: 185 lbs; Born: 5/28/1964 in Park View, New Mexico; Debut: 4/12/1986

LCS — Pitching

Year Tm	Age	G	GS	CG	GF	IP	BFP	H	R	ER	HR	SH	SF	HB	TBB	IBB	SO	WP	Bk	W	L	Pct	ShO	Sv-Op	Hld	OAvg	OOBP	ERA
1989 Tor	25	2	0	0	1	3.2	19	6	3	3	0	0	0	0	3	0	5	1	0	0	0	—	0	0- 0	0	.375	.474	7.36
1991 Tor	27	2	0	0	1	4.1	17	4	3	3	0	0	0	0	1	0	6	0	0	0	1	.000	0	1- 1	0	.250	.294	6.23
1992 Tor	28	3	0	0	0	4.0	19	6	3	3	0	1	1	0	1	0	2	0	0	1	0	1.000	0	0- 0	1	.375	.389	6.75
1993 Tor	29	4	0	0	4	4.2	22	4	3	3	2	0	0	1	3	0	8	0	0	0	0	—	0	2- 2	0	.222	.364	5.79
LCS Totals		11	0	0	6	16.2	154	20	12	12	2	1	1	1	8	0	21	1	0	1	1	.500	0	3-3	1	.303	.382	6.48

World Series — Pitching

Year Tm	Age	G	GS	CG	GF	IP	BFP	H	R	ER	HR	SH	SF	HB	TBB	IBB	SO	WP	Bk	W	L	Pct	ShO	Sv-Op	Hld	OAvg	OOBP	ERA
1992 Tor	28	4	0	0	1	3.1	12	1	0	0	0	0	0	0	1	0	6	1	0	2	0	1.000	0	0- 0	2	.091	.167	0.00
1993 Tor	29	4	0	0	4	4.2	17	3	2	1	1	0	0	0	0	0	7	0	0	1	0	1.000	0	2- 2	0	.176	.176	1.93
WS Totals		8	0	0	5	8.0	58	4	2	1	1	0	0	0	1	0	13	1	0	3	0	1.000	0	2-2	2	.143	.172	1.13
Postseason Totals		19	0	0	11	24.2	212	24	14	13	3	1	1	1	9	0	34	2	0	4	1	.800	0	5-5	3	.255	.324	4.74

LCS — Batting / Fielding

Year Tm	Age	G	AB	H	2B	3B	HR	TB	R	RBI	GW	TBB	IBB	SO	HBP	SH	SF	SB	CS	SB%	GDP	Avg	OBP	SLG	Pos	G	PO	A	E	DP	FPct
1989 Tor	25	2	0	0	0	0	0	0	0	0	0	0	0	0	0	0	0	0	0	—	0	—	—	—	P	2	1	0	0	0	1.000
1991 Tor	27	2	0	0	0	0	0	0	0	0	0	0	0	0	0	0	0	0	0	—	0	—	—	—	P	2	0	0	0	0	—
1992 Tor	28	3	0	0	0	0	0	0	0	0	0	0	0	0	0	0	0	0	0	—	0	—	—	—	P	3	1	0	0	0	1.000
1993 Tor	29	4	0	0	0	0	0	0	0	0	0	0	0	0	0	0	0	0	0	—	0	—	—	—	P	4	0	0	0	0	—
LCS Totals		11	0	0	0	0	0	0	0	0	0	0	0	0	0	0	0	0	0	—	0	—	—	—	P	11	2	0	0	0	1.000

World Series — Batting / Fielding

Year Tm	Age	G	AB	H	2B	3B	HR	TB	R	RBI	GW	TBB	IBB	SO	HBP	SH	SF	SB	CS	SB%	GDP	Avg	OBP	SLG	Pos	G	PO	A	E	DP	FPct
1992 Tor	28	4	0	0	0	0	0	0	0	0	0	0	0	0	0	0	0	0	0	—	0	—	—	—	P	4	0	0	0	0	—
1993 Tor	29	4	0	0	0	0	0	0	0	0	0	0	0	0	0	0	0	0	0	—	0	—	—	—	P	4	0	0	0	0	—
WS Totals		8	0	0	0	0	0	0	0	0	0	0	0	0	0	0	0	0	0	—	0	—	—	—	P	8	0	0	0	0	—
Postseason Totals		19	0	0	0	0	0	0	0	0	0	0	0	0	0	0	0	0	0	—	0	—	—	—	P	19	2	0	0	0	1.000

LON WARNEKE—Lonnie Warneke—Nickname: The Arkansas Hummingbird—Throws: Right; Bats: Right

Ht: 6'2"; Wt: 185 lbs; Born: 3/28/1909 in Mt. Ida, Arkansas; Debut: 4/18/1930; Died: 6/23/1976

World Series — Pitching

Year Tm	Age	G	GS	CG	GF	IP	BFP	H	R	ER	HR	SH	SF	HB	TBB	IBB	SO	WP	Bk	W	L	Pct	ShO	Sv-Op	Hld	OAvg	OOBP	ERA
1932 ChN	23	2	1	1	0	10.2	48	15	7	7	1	0	0	0	5	1	8	0	0	0	1	.000	0	0- 0	0	.349	.417	5.91
1935 ChN	26	3	2	1	0	16.2	62	9	1	1	0	0	0	0	4	0	5	0	0	2	0	1.000	1	0- 0	0	.155	.210	0.54
WS Totals		5	3	2	0	27.1	220	24	8	8	1	0	0	0	9	1	13	0	0	2	1	.667	1	0-0	0	.238	.300	2.63

World Series — Batting / Fielding

Year Tm	Age	G	AB	H	2B	3B	HR	TB	R	RBI	GW	TBB	IBB	SO	HBP	SH	SF	SB	CS	SB%	GDP	Avg	OBP	SLG	Pos	G	PO	A	E	DP	FPct
1932 ChN	23	2	4	0	0	0	0	0	0	0	0	0	0	3	0	0	0	0	0	—	0	.000	.000	.000	P	2	1	2	0	1	1.000
1935 ChN	26	3	5	1	0	0	0	1	0	0	0	0	0	0	0	0	0	0	0	—	0	.200	.200	.200	P	3	2	9	0	0	1.000
WS Totals		5	9	1	0	0	0	1	0	0	0	0	0	3	0	0	0	0	0	—	0	.111	.111	.111	P	5	3	11	0	1	1.000

CARL WARWICK—Carl Wayne Warwick—Bats: Right; Throws: Left

Ht: 5'10"; Wt: 170 lbs; Born: 2/27/1937 in Dallas, Texas; Debut: 4/11/1961

World Series		Batting																							Fielding						
Year Tm	Age	G	AB	H	2B	3B	HR	TB	R	RBI	GW	TBB	IBB	SO	HBP	SH	SF	SB	CS	SB%	GDP	Avg	OBP	SLG	Pos	G	PO	A	E	DP	FPct
1964 StL	27	5	4	3	0	0	0	3	2	1	1	1	0	0	0	0	0	0	0	—	0	.750	.800	.750	—						

JIMMY WASDELL—James Charles Wasdell—Bats: Left; Throws: Left

Ht: 5'11"; Wt: 185 lbs; Born: 5/15/1914 in Cleveland, Ohio; Debut: 9/3/1937; Died: 8/6/1983

World Series		Batting																							Fielding						
Year Tm	Age	G	AB	H	2B	3B	HR	TB	R	RBI	GW	TBB	IBB	SO	HBP	SH	SF	SB	CS	SB%	GDP	Avg	OBP	SLG	Pos	G	PO	A	E	DP	FPct
1941 Bro	27	3	5	1	1	0	0	2	0	2	0	0	0	0	0	0	0	0	0	—	0	.200	.200	.400	OF	1	2	0	0	0	1.000

RAY WASHBURN—Ray Clark Washburn—Throws: Right; Bats: Right

Ht: 6'1"; Wt: 205 lbs; Born: 5/31/1938 in Pasco, Washington; Debut: 9/20/1961

World Series		Pitching																										
Year Tm	Age	G	GS	CG	GF	IP	BFP	H	R	ER	HR	SH	SF	HB	TBB	IBB	SO	WP	Bk	W	L	Pct	ShO	Sv-Op	Hld	OAvg	OOBP	ERA
1967 StL	29	2	0	0	0	2.1	9	1	0	0	0	0	0	0	1	1	2	0	0	0	0	—	0	0- 0	0	.125	.222	0.00
1968 StL	30	2	2	0	0	7.1	35	7	8	8	2	0	0	0	7	0	6	0	0	1	1	.500	0	0- 0	0	.250	.400	9.82
1970 Cin	32	1	0	0	0	1.1	8	2	2	2	0	1	0	0	2	0	0	0	0	0	0	—	0	0- 0	0	.400	.571	13.50
WS Totals		5	2	0	0	11.0	104	10	10	10	2	1	0	0	10	1	8	0	0	1	1	.500	0	0-0	0	.244	.392	8.18

World Series		Batting																							Fielding						
Year Tm	Age	G	AB	H	2B	3B	HR	TB	R	RBI	GW	TBB	IBB	SO	HBP	SH	SF	SB	CS	SB%	GDP	Avg	OBP	SLG	Pos	G	PO	A	E	DP	FPct
1967 StL	29	2	0	0	0	0	0	0	0	0	0	0	0	0	0	0	0	0	0	—	0	—	—	—	P	2	0	1	0	0	1.000
1968 StL	30	2	3	0	0	0	0	0	0	0	0	0	0	1	0	0	0	0	0	—	0	.000	.000	.000	P	2	0	1	0	0	1.000
1970 Cin	32	1	0	0	0	0	0	0	0	0	0	0	0	0	0	0	0	0	0	—	0	—	—	—	P	1	1	3	0	0	1.000
WS Totals		5	3	0	0	0	0	0	0	0	0	0	0	1	0	0	0	0	0	—	0	.000	.000	.000	P	5	1	5	0	0	1.000

CLAUDELL WASHINGTON—Bats: Left; Throws: Left

Ht: 6'0"; Wt: 190 lbs; Born: 8/31/1954 in Los Angeles, California; Debut: 7/5/1974

LCS		Batting																							Fielding						
Year Tm	Age	G	AB	H	2B	3B	HR	TB	R	RBI	GW	TBB	IBB	SO	HBP	SH	SF	SB	CS	SB%	GDP	Avg	OBP	SLG	Pos	G	PO	A	E	DP	FPct
1974 Oak	20	4	11	3	1	0	0	4	1	0	0	0	0	0	1	0	0	0	0	—	1	.273	.333	.364	OF	3	11	0	0	0	1.000
1975 Oak	21	3	12	3	1	0	0	4	1	1	0	0	0	2	0	0	0	0	0	—	0	.250	.250	.333	OF	2	1	0	2	0	.333
1982 Atl	28	3	9	3	0	0	0	3	0	0	0	2	1	2	0	0	0	0	1	.00	0	.333	.455	.333	OF	3	5	0	0	0	1.000
LCS Totals		10	32	9	2	0	0	11	2	1	0	2	1	4	1	0	0	0	1	.00	1	.281	.343	.344	OF	8	17	0	2	0	.895
World Series		Batting																							Fielding						
Year Tm	Age	G	AB	H	2B	3B	HR	TB	R	RBI	GW	TBB	IBB	SO	HBP	SH	SF	SB	CS	SB%	GDP	Avg	OBP	SLG	Pos	G	PO	A	E	DP	FPct
1974 Oak	20	5	7	4	0	0	0	4	1	0	0	1	1	1	0	0	0	0	1	.00	0	.571	.625	.571	OF	5	1	0	0	0	1.000
Postseason Totals		15	39	13	2	0	0	15	3	1	0	3	2	5	1	0	0	0	2	.00	1	.333	.395	.385	OF	13	18	0	2	0	.900

HERB WASHINGTON—Herbert Lee Washington—Bats: Right; Throws: Right

Ht: 6'0"; Wt: 170 lbs; Born: 11/16/1951 in Belzonia, Mississippi; Debut: 4/4/1974

LCS		Batting																							Fielding						
Year Tm	Age	G	AB	H	2B	3B	HR	TB	R	RBI	GW	TBB	IBB	SO	HBP	SH	SF	SB	CS	SB%	GDP	Avg	OBP	SLG	Pos	G	PO	A	E	DP	FPct
1974 Oak	22	2	0	0	0	0	0	0	0	0	0	0	0	0	0	0	0	0	2	.00	0	—	—	—	—						
World Series		Batting																							Fielding						
Year Tm	Age	G	AB	H	2B	3B	HR	TB	R	RBI	GW	TBB	IBB	SO	HBP	SH	SF	SB	CS	SB%	GDP	Avg	OBP	SLG	Pos	G	PO	A	E	DP	FPct
1974 Oak	22	3	0	0	0	0	0	0	0	0	0	0	0	0	0	0	0	0	0	—	0	—	—	—	—						
Postseason Totals		5	0	0	0	0	0	0	0	0	0	0	0	0	0	0	0	0	2	.00	0	—	—	—	—	0	0	0	0	0	—

U.L. WASHINGTON—Bats: Both; Throws: Right

Ht: 5'11"; Wt: 175 lbs; Born: 10/27/1953 in Stringtown, Oklahoma; Debut: 9/6/1977

Division Series		Batting																							Fielding						
Year Tm	Age	G	AB	H	2B	3B	HR	TB	R	RBI	GW	TBB	IBB	SO	HBP	SH	SF	SB	CS	SB%	GDP	Avg	OBP	SLG	Pos	G	PO	A	E	DP	FPct
1981 KC	27	3	9	2	0	0	0	2	0	0	0	0	0	1	0	1	0	0	0	—	0	.222	.222	.222	SS	3	6	11	1	1	.944
LCS		Batting																							Fielding						
Year Tm	Age	G	AB	H	2B	3B	HR	TB	R	RBI	GW	TBB	IBB	SO	HBP	SH	SF	SB	CS	SB%	GDP	Avg	OBP	SLG	Pos	G	PO	A	E	DP	FPct
1980 KC	26	3	11	4	1	0	0	5	1	1	0	2	0	3	0	0	0	0	1	.00	0	.364	.462	.455	SS	3	5	7	0	2	1.000
1984 KC	30	2	1	0	0	0	0	0	0	0	0	0	0	1	0	0	0	0	0	—	0	.000	.000	.000	—						
LCS Totals		5	12	4	1	0	0	5	1	1	0	2	0	4	0	0	0	0	1	.00	0	.333	.429	.417	SS	3	5	7	0	2	1.000
World Series		Batting																							Fielding						
Year Tm	Age	G	AB	H	2B	3B	HR	TB	R	RBI	GW	TBB	IBB	SO	HBP	SH	SF	SB	CS	SB%	GDP	Avg	OBP	SLG	Pos	G	PO	A	E	DP	FPct
1980 KC	26	6	22	6	0	0	0	6	1	2	0	0	0	6	0	1	2	0	1	.00	0	.273	.250	.273	SS	6	8	21	1	4	.967
Postseason Totals		14	43	12	1	0	0	13	2	3	0	2	0	11	0	2	2	0	2	.00	0	.279	.298	.302	SS	12	19	39	2	7	.967

GARY WASLEWSKI—Gary Lee Waslewski—Throws: Right; Bats: Right

Ht: 6'4"; Wt: 190 lbs; Born: 7/21/1941 in Meriden, Connecticut; Debut: 6/11/1967

World Series		Pitching																										
Year Tm	Age	G	GS	CG	GF	IP	BFP	H	R	ER	HR	SH	SF	HB	TBB	IBB	SO	WP	Bk	W	L	Pct	ShO	Sv-Op	Hld	OAvg	OOBP	ERA
1967 Bos	26	2	1	0	0	8.1	32	4	2	2	0	0	0	0	2	0	7	0	0	0	0	—	0	0- 0	0	.133	.188	2.16

World Series		Batting																							Fielding						
Year Tm	Age	G	AB	H	2B	3B	HR	TB	R	RBI	GW	TBB	IBB	SO	HBP	SH	SF	SB	CS	SB%	GDP	Avg	OBP	SLG	Pos	G	PO	A	E	DP	FPct
1967 Bos	26	2	1	0	0	0	0	0	0	0	0	0	0	1	1	0	0	0	0	—	0	.000	.500	.000	P	2	2	0	0	0	1.000

JOHN WATHAN—John David Wathan—Nickname: Duke—Bats: Right; Throws: Right

Ht: 6'2"; Wt: 205 lbs; Born: 10/4/1949 in Cedar Rapids, Iowa; Debut: 5/26/1976

Division Series		Batting																							Fielding						
Year Tm	Age	G	AB	H	2B	3B	HR	TB	R	RBI	GW	TBB	IBB	SO	HBP	SH	SF	SB	CS	SB%	GDP	Avg	OBP	SLG	Pos	G	PO	A	E	DP	FPct
1981 KC	31	3	10	3	0	0	0	3	1	0	0	1	0	1	0	0	0	0	0	—	0	.300	.364	.300	C	3	11	3	1	0	.933
LCS		Batting																							Fielding						
Year Tm	Age	G	AB	H	2B	3B	HR	TB	R	RBI	GW	TBB	IBB	SO	HBP	SH	SF	SB	CS	SB%	GDP	Avg	OBP	SLG	Pos	G	PO	A	E	DP	FPct
1976 KC	26	1	0	0	0	0	0	0	0	0	0	0	0	0	0	0	0	0	0	—	0	—	—	—	C	1	0	0	0	0	—
1977 KC	27	4	6	0	0	0	0	0	0	0	0	0	0	3	0	0	0	0	0	—	0	.000	.000	.000	C	1	2	0	0	0	1.000
																									1B	2	17	0	0	0	1.000
1978 KC	28	1	3	0	0	0	0	0	0	0	0	0	0	0	0	0	0	0	0	—	0	.000	.000	.000	1B	1	7	0	0	0	1.000
1980 KC	30	3	6	0	0	0	0	0	1	0	0	3	1	1	0	0	0	0	0	—	0	.000	.333	.000	OF	3	7	0	0	0	1.000
1984 KC	34	1	1	0	0	0	0	0	0	0	0	0	0	0	0	0	0	0	0	—	0	.000	.000	.000	—						
LCS Totals		10	16	0	0	0	0	0	1	0	0	3	1	4	0	0	0	0	0	—	0	.000	.158	.000	1B	3	24	0	0	0	1.000
World Series		Batting																							Fielding						
Year Tm	Age	G	AB	H	2B	3B	HR	TB	R	RBI	GW	TBB	IBB	SO	HBP	SH	SF	SB	CS	SB%	GDP	Avg	OBP	SLG	Pos	G	PO	A	E	DP	FPct
1980 KC	30	3	7	2	0	0	0	2	1	0	0	2	0	1	0	0	1	0	0	—	2	.286	.400	.286	C	2	6	1	0	0	1.000
																									OF	1	1	0	0	0	1.000
1985 KC	35	2	1	0	0	0	0	0	0	0	0	0	0	1	0	0	0	0	0	—	0	.000	.000	.000	—						
WS Totals		5	8	2	0	0	0	2	1	0	0	2	0	2	0	0	1	0	0	—	2	.250	.364	.250	C	2	6	1	0	0	1.000
Postseason Totals		18	34	5	0	0	0	5	3	0	0	6	1	7	0	0	1	0	0	—	2	.147	.268	.147	C	7	19	4	1	0	.958

GEORGE WATKINS—George Archibald Watkins—Bats: Left; Throws: Right

Ht: 6'0"; Wt: 175 lbs; Born: 6/4/1900 in Freestone County, Texas; Debut: 4/15/1930; Died: 6/1/1970

World Series		Batting																							Fielding						
Year Tm	Age	G	AB	H	2B	3B	HR	TB	R	RBI	GW	TBB	IBB	SO	HBP	SH	SF	SB	CS	SB%	GDP	Avg	OBP	SLG	Pos	G	PO	A	E	DP	FPct
1930 StL	30	4	12	2	0	0	1	5	2	1	0	1	0	3	0	0	0	0	0	—	0	.167	.231	.417	OF	4	5	0	1	0	.833
1931 StL	31	5	14	4	1	0	1	8	4	2	0	2	0	1	0	0	0	1	0	1.00	0	.286	.375	.571	OF	5	8	0	0	0	1.000
WS Totals		9	26	6	1	0	2	13	6	3	0	3	0	4	0	0	0	1	0	1.00	0	.231	.310	.500	OF	9	13	0	1	0	.929

BOB WATSON—Robert Jose Watson—Nickname: Bull—Bats: Right; Throws: Right

Ht: 6'0"; Wt: 201 lbs; Born: 4/10/1946 in Los Angeles, California; Debut: 9/9/1966

Division Series		Batting																							Fielding						
Year Tm	Age	G	AB	H	2B	3B	HR	TB	R	RBI	GW	TBB	IBB	SO	HBP	SH	SF	SB	CS	SB%	GDP	Avg	OBP	SLG	Pos	G	PO	A	E	DP	FPct
1981 NYA	35	5	16	7	0	0	0	7	2	1	0	1	0	1	0	0	0	0	0	—	0	.438	.471	.438	1B	5	34	4	1	1	.974
LCS		Batting																							Fielding						
Year Tm	Age	G	AB	H	2B	3B	HR	TB	R	RBI	GW	TBB	IBB	SO	HBP	SH	SF	SB	CS	SB%	GDP	Avg	OBP	SLG	Pos	G	PO	A	E	DP	FPct
1980 NYA	34	3	12	6	3	1	0	11	0	0	0	0	0	0	0	0	0	0	0	—	0	.500	.500	.917	1B	3	28	5	1	2	.971
1981 NYA	35	3	12	3	0	0	0	3	0	1	0	0	0	1	0	0	0	0	0	—	0	.250	.250	.250	1B	3	17	0	0	5	1.000
LCS Totals		6	24	9	3	1	0	14	0	1	0	0	0	1	0	0	0	0	0	—	0	.375	.375	.583	1B	6	45	5	1	7	.980
World Series		Batting																							Fielding						
Year Tm	Age	G	AB	H	2B	3B	HR	TB	R	RBI	GW	TBB	IBB	SO	HBP	SH	SF	SB	CS	SB%	GDP	Avg	OBP	SLG	Pos	G	PO	A	E	DP	FPct
1981 NYA	35	6	22	7	1	0	2	14	2	7	1	3	0	0	0	0	1	0	0	—	0	.318	.385	.636	1B	6	51	0	0	2	1.000
Postseason Totals		17	62	23	4	1	2	35	4	9	1	4	0	2	0	0	1	0	0	—	0	.371	.403	.565	1B	17	130	9	2	10	.986

MULE WATSON—John Reeves Watson—Throws: Right; Bats: Right

Ht: 6'1"; Wt: 185 lbs; Born: 10/15/1896 in Homer, Louisiana; Debut: 7/4/1918; Died: 8/25/1949

World Series		Pitching																										
Year Tm	Age	G	GS	CG	GF	IP	BFP	H	R	ER	HR	SH	SF	HB	TBB	IBB	SO	WP	Bk	W	L	Pct	ShO	Sv-Op	Hld	OAvg	OOBP	ERA
1923 NYG	26	1	1	0	0	2.0	11	4	3	3	0	1	0	0	1	0	1	0	0	0	0	—	0	0-0	0	.444	.500	13.50
1924 NYG	27	1	0	0	1	0.2	2	0	0	0	0	0	0	0	0	0	0	0	0	0	0	—	0	1-1	0	.000	.000	0.00
WS Totals		2	1	0	1	2.2	26	4	3	3	0	1	0	0	1	0	1	0	0	0	0	—	0	1-1	0	.364	.417	10.13

World Series		Batting																							Fielding						
Year Tm	Age	G	AB	H	2B	3B	HR	TB	R	RBI	GW	TBB	IBB	SO	HBP	SH	SF	SB	CS	SB%	GDP	Avg	OBP	SLG	Pos	G	PO	A	E	DP	FPct
1923 NYG	26	1	0	0	0	0	0	0	0	0	0	0	0	0	0	0	0	0	0	—	0	—	—	—	P	1	0	1	0	0	1.000
1924 NYG	27	1	0	0	0	0	0	0	0	0	0	0	0	0	0	0	0	0	0	—	0	—	—	—	P	1	0	0	0	0	—
WS Totals		2	0	0	0	0	0	0	0	0	0	0	0	0	0	0	0	0	0	—	0	—	—	—	P	2	0	1	0	0	1.000

EDDIE WATT—Edward Dean Watt—Throws: Right; Bats: Right

Ht: 5'10"; Wt: 183 lbs; Born: 4/4/1941 in Lamonie, Iowa; Debut: 4/12/1966

LCS		Pitching																										
Year Tm	Age	G	GS	CG	GF	IP	BFP	H	R	ER	HR	SH	SF	HB	TBB	IBB	SO	WP	Bk	W	L	Pct	ShO	Sv-Op	Hld	OAvg	OOBP	ERA
1969 Bal	28	1	0	0	0	2.0	6	0	0	0	0	0	0	0	0	0	2	0	0	0	0	—	0	0-0	0	.000	.000	0.00
1971 Bal	30	1	0	0	1	2.0	7	2	0	0	0	0	0	0	0	0	1	0	0	0	0	—	0	1-1	0	.286	.286	0.00
1973 Bal	32	1	0	0	0	0.1	2	0	0	0	0	1	0	1	0	0	0	0	0	0	0	—	0	0-0	0	—	1.000	0.00
LCS Totals		3	0	0	1	4.1	30	2	0	0	0	1	0	1	0	0	3	0	0	0	0	—	0	1-1	0	.154	.214	0.00
World Series		Pitching																										
Year Tm	Age	G	GS	CG	GF	IP	BFP	H	R	ER	HR	SH	SF	HB	TBB	IBB	SO	WP	Bk	W	L	Pct	ShO	Sv-Op	Hld	OAvg	OOBP	ERA
1969 Bal	28	2	0	0	1	3.0	14	4	2	1	0	0	0	0	0	0	3	0	0	0	1	.000	0	0-0	0	.286	.286	3.00
1970 Bal	29	1	0	0	0	1.0	6	2	1	1	1	0	0	0	1	0	3	0	0	0	1	.000	0	0-1	0	.400	.500	9.00
1971 Bal	30	2	0	0	1	2.1	11	4	1	1	0	0	0	0	0	0	2	0	0	0	1	.000	0	0-0	0	.364	.364	3.86
WS Totals		5	0	0	2	6.1	62	10	4	3	1	0	0	0	1	0	8	0	0	0	3	.000	0	0-1	0	.333	.355	4.26
Postseason Totals		8	0	0	3	10.2	92	12	4	3	1	1	0	1	1	0	11	0	0	0	3	.000	0	1-2	0	.279	.311	2.53

LCS		Batting																							Fielding						
Year Tm	Age	G	AB	H	2B	3B	HR	TB	R	RBI	GW	TBB	IBB	SO	HBP	SH	SF	SB	CS	SB%	GDP	Avg	OBP	SLG	Pos	G	PO	A	E	DP	FPct
1969 Bal	28	1	0	0	0	0	0	0	0	0	0	0	0	0	0	0	0	0	0	—	0	—	—	—	P	1	0	0	0	0	—
1971 Bal	30	1	0	0	0	0	0	0	0	0	0	0	0	0	0	0	0	0	0	—	0	—	—	—	P	1	0	1	0	0	1.000
1973 Bal	32	1	0	0	0	0	0	0	0	0	0	0	0	0	0	0	0	0	0	—	0	—	—	—	P	1	0	1	0	0	1.000
LCS Totals		3	0	0	0	0	0	0	0	0	0	0	0	0	0	0	0	0	0	—	0	—	—	—	P	3	0	2	0	0	1.000
World Series		Batting																							Fielding						
Year Tm	Age	G	AB	H	2B	3B	HR	TB	R	RBI	GW	TBB	IBB	SO	HBP	SH	SF	SB	CS	SB%	GDP	Avg	OBP	SLG	Pos	G	PO	A	E	DP	FPct
1969 Bal	28	2	0	0	0	0	0	0	0	0	0	0	0	0	0	0	0	0	0	—	0	—	—	—	P	2	0	0	1	0	.000
1970 Bal	29	1	0	0	0	0	0	0	0	0	0	0	0	0	0	0	0	0	0	—	0	—	—	—	P	1	0	0	0	0	—
1971 Bal	30	2	0	0	0	0	0	0	0	0	0	0	0	0	0	0	0	0	0	—	0	—	—	—	P	2	0	0	0	0	—
WS Totals		5	0	0	0	0	0	0	0	0	0	0	0	0	0	0	0	0	0	—	0	—	—	—	P	5	0	0	1	0	.000
Postseason Totals		8	0	0	0	0	0	0	0	0	0	0	0	0	0	0	0	0	0	—	0	—	—	—	P	8	0	2	1	0	.667

ROY WEATHERLY—Cyril Roy Weatherly—Nickname: Stormy—Bats: Left; Throws: Right

Ht: 5'6"; Wt: 170 lbs; Born: 2/25/1915 in Warren, Texas; Debut: 6/27/1936; Died: 1/19/1991

World Series		Batting																							Fielding						
Year Tm	Age	G	AB	H	2B	3B	HR	TB	R	RBI	GW	TBB	IBB	SO	HBP	SH	SF	SB	CS	SB%	GDP	Avg	OBP	SLG	Pos	G	PO	A	E	DP	FPct
1943 NYA	28	1	1	0	0	0	0	0	0	0	0	0	0	0	0	0	0	0	0	—	0	.000	.000	.000	—						

DAVE WEATHERS—John David Weathers—Throws: Right; Bats: Right

Ht: 6'3"; Wt: 205 lbs; Born: 9/25/1969 in Lawrenceburg, Tennessee; Debut: 8/2/1991

Division Series		Pitching																										
Year Tm	Age	G	GS	CG	GF	IP	BFP	H	R	ER	HR	SH	SF	HB	TBB	IBB	SO	WP	Bk	W	L	Pct	ShO	Sv-Op	Hld	OAvg	OOBP	ERA
1996 NYA	27	2	0	0	1	5.0	15	1	0	0	0	1	0	0	0	0	5	0	0	1	0	1.000	0	0-0	0	.071	.071	0.00
LCS		Pitching																										
Year Tm	Age	G	GS	CG	GF	IP	BFP	H	R	ER	HR	SH	SF	HB	TBB	IBB	SO	WP	Bk	W	L	Pct	ShO	Sv-Op	Hld	OAvg	OOBP	ERA
1996 NYA	27	2	0	0	1	3.0	12	3	0	0	0	0	0	0	0	0	0	0	0	1	0	1.000	0	0-0	0	.250	.250	0.00
World Series		Pitching																										
Year Tm	Age	G	GS	CG	GF	IP	BFP	H	R	ER	HR	SH	SF	HB	TBB	IBB	SO	WP	Bk	W	L	Pct	ShO	Sv-Op	Hld	OAvg	OOBP	ERA
1996 NYA	27	3	0	0	0	3.0	14	2	1	1	0	0	1	0	3	1	3	0	1	0	0	—	0	0-0	1	.200	.357	3.00
Postseason Totals		7	0	0	2	11.0	82	6	1	1	0	1	1	0	3	1	8	0	1	2	0	1.000	0	0-0	1	.167	.225	0.82

Division Series		Batting																							Fielding						
Year Tm	Age	G	AB	H	2B	3B	HR	TB	R	RBI	GW	TBB	IBB	SO	HBP	SH	SF	SB	CS	SB%	GDP	Avg	OBP	SLG	Pos	G	PO	A	E	DP	FPct
1996 NYA	27	2	0	0	0	0	0	0	0	0	0	0	0	0	0	0	0	0	0	—	0	—	—	—	P	2	0	1	0	0	1.000
LCS		Batting																							Fielding						
Year Tm	Age	G	AB	H	2B	3B	HR	TB	R	RBI	GW	TBB	IBB	SO	HBP	SH	SF	SB	CS	SB%	GDP	Avg	OBP	SLG	Pos	G	PO	A	E	DP	FPct
1996 NYA	27	2	0	0	0	0	0	0	0	0	0	0	0	0	0	0	0	0	0	—	0	—	—	—	P	2	0	0	0	0	—
World Series		Batting																							Fielding						
Year Tm	Age	G	AB	H	2B	3B	HR	TB	R	RBI	GW	TBB	IBB	SO	HBP	SH	SF	SB	CS	SB%	GDP	Avg	OBP	SLG	Pos	G	PO	A	E	DP	FPct
1996 NYA	27	3	0	0	0	0	0	0	0	0	0	0	0	0	0	0	0	0	0	—	0	—	—	—	P	3	0	0	0	0	—
Postseason Totals		7	0	0	0	0	0	0	0	0	0	0	0	0	0	0	0	0	0	—	0	—	—	—	P	7	0	1	0	0	1.000

BUCK WEAVER—George Daniel Weaver—Bats: Right; Throws: Right

Ht: 5'11"; Wt: 170 lbs; Born: 8/18/1890 in Pottstown, Pennsylvania; Debut: 4/11/1912; Died: 1/31/1956

World Series		Batting																							Fielding						
Year Tm	Age	G	AB	H	2B	3B	HR	TB	R	RBI	GW	TBB	IBB	SO	HBP	SH	SF	SB	CS	SB%	GDP	Avg	OBP	SLG	Pos	G	PO	A	E	DP	FPct
1917 ChA	27	6	21	7	1	0	0	8	3	1	0	0	0	2	0	0	0	0	2	.00	1	.333	.333	.381	SS	6	13	14	4	4	.871
1919 ChA	29	8	34	11	4	1	0	17	4	0	0	0	0	2	0	0	0	0	0	—	0	.324	.324	.500	3B	8	9	18	0	0	1.000
WS Totals		14	55	18	5	1	0	25	7	1	0	0	0	4	0	0	0	0	2	.00	1	.327	.327	.455	3B	8	9	18	0	0	1.000

MONTIE WEAVER—Montgomery Morton Weaver—Nickname: Prof—Throws: Right; Bats: Left

Ht: 6'0"; Wt: 170 lbs; Born: 6/15/1906 in Helton, North Carolina; Debut: 9/20/1931; Died: 6/14/1994

World Series		Pitching																										
Year Tm	Age	G	GS	CG	GF	IP	BFP	H	R	ER	HR	SH	SF	HB	TBB	IBB	SO	WP	Bk	W	L	Pct	ShO	Sv-Op	Hld	OAvg	OOBP	ERA
1933 Was	27	1	1	0	0	10.1	45	11	2	2	1	3	0	0	4	1	3	0	0	0	1	.000	0	0-0	0	.289	.357	1.74

World Series		Batting																							Fielding						
Year Tm	Age	G	AB	H	2B	3B	HR	TB	R	RBI	GW	TBB	IBB	SO	HBP	SH	SF	SB	CS	SB%	GDP	Avg	OBP	SLG	Pos	G	PO	A	E	DP	FPct
1933 Was	27	1	4	0	0	0	0	0	0	0	0	0	0	2	0	0	0	0	0	—	0	.000	.000	.000	P	1	1	5	0	0	1.000

SKEETER WEBB—James Laverne Webb—Bats: Right; Throws: Right

Ht: 5'9"; Wt: 150 lbs; Born: 11/4/1909 in Meridian, Mississippi; Debut: 7/20/1932; Died: 7/8/1986

World Series — Batting / Fielding

Year Tm	Age	G	AB	H	2B	3B	HR	TB	R	RBI	GW	TBB	IBB	SO	HBP	SH	SF	SB	CS	SB%	GDP	Avg	OBP	SLG	Pos	G	PO	A	E	DP	FPct
1945 Det	35	7	27	5	0	0	0	5	4	1	0	2	0	1	0	0	0	0	0	—	0	.185	.241	.185	SS	7	9	24	0	3	1.000

LENNY WEBSTER—Leonard Irell Webster—Bats: Right; Throws: Right

Ht: 5'9"; Wt: 185 lbs; Born: 2/10/1965 in New Orleans, Louisiana; Debut: 9/1/1989

Division Series — Batting / Fielding

Year Tm	Age	G	AB	H	2B	3B	HR	TB	R	RBI	GW	TBB	IBB	SO	HBP	SH	SF	SB	CS	SB%	GDP	Avg	OBP	SLG	Pos	G	PO	A	E	DP	FPct
1997 Bal	32	3	6	1	0	0	0	1	1	1	0	1	0	0	0	0	0	0	0	—	1	.167	.286	.167	C	3	20	0	0	0	1.000

LCS — Batting / Fielding

Year Tm	Age	G	AB	H	2B	3B	HR	TB	R	RBI	GW	TBB	IBB	SO	HBP	SH	SF	SB	CS	SB%	GDP	Avg	OBP	SLG	Pos	G	PO	A	E	DP	FPct
1997 Bal	32	4	9	2	0	0	0	2	0	0	0	0	0	1	0	0	0	0	0	—	0	.222	.222	.222	C	3	14	0	2	0	.875
Postseason Totals		7	15	3	0	0	0	3	1	1	0	1	0	1	0	0	0	0	0	—	1	.200	.250	.200	C	6	34	0	2	0	.944

MITCH WEBSTER—Mitchell Dean Webster—Bats: Both; Throws: Left

Ht: 6'0"; Wt: 185 lbs; Born: 5/16/1959 in Larned, Kansas; Debut: 9/2/1983

Division Series — Batting / Fielding

Year Tm	Age	G	AB	H	2B	3B	HR	TB	R	RBI	GW	TBB	IBB	SO	HBP	SH	SF	SB	CS	SB%	GDP	Avg	OBP	SLG	Pos	G	PO	A	E	DP	FPct
1995 LA	36	2	2	0	0	0	0	0	0	0	0	0	0	0	0	0	0	0	0	—	0	.000	.000	.000	—						

LCS — Batting / Fielding

Year Tm	Age	G	AB	H	2B	3B	HR	TB	R	RBI	GW	TBB	IBB	SO	HBP	SH	SF	SB	CS	SB%	GDP	Avg	OBP	SLG	Pos	G	PO	A	E	DP	FPct
1989 ChN	30	3	3	1	0	0	0	1	0	0	0	0	0	0	0	0	0	0	0	—	0	.333	.333	.333	OF	2	0	0	0	0	—
Postseason Totals		5	5	1	0	0	0	1	0	0	0	0	0	0	0	0	0	0	0	—	0	.200	.200	.200	OF	2	0	0	0	0	—

JOHN WEHNER—John Paul Wehner—Bats: Right; Throws: Right

Ht: 6'3"; Wt: 205 lbs; Born: 6/29/1967 in Pittsburgh, Pennsylvania; Debut: 7/17/1991

Division Series — Batting / Fielding

Year Tm	Age	G	AB	H	2B	3B	HR	TB	R	RBI	GW	TBB	IBB	SO	HBP	SH	SF	SB	CS	SB%	GDP	Avg	OBP	SLG	Pos	G	PO	A	E	DP	FPct
1997 Fla	30	1	0	0	0	0	0	0	0	0	0	0	0	0	0	0	0	0	0	—	0	—	—	—	OF	1	0	0	0	0	—

LCS — Batting / Fielding

Year Tm	Age	G	AB	H	2B	3B	HR	TB	R	RBI	GW	TBB	IBB	SO	HBP	SH	SF	SB	CS	SB%	GDP	Avg	OBP	SLG	Pos	G	PO	A	E	DP	FPct
1992 Pit	25	2	2	0	0	0	0	0	0	0	0	0	0	2	0	0	0	0	0	—	0	.000	.000	.000	—						
Postseason Totals		3	2	0	0	0	0	0	0	0	0	0	0	2	0	0	0	0	0	—	0	.000	.000	.000	OF	1	0	0	0	0	—

AL WEIS—Albert John Weis—Bats: Both; Throws: Right

Ht: 6'0"; Wt: 160 lbs; Born: 4/2/1938 in Franklin Square, New York; Debut: 9/15/1962

LCS — Batting / Fielding

Year Tm	Age	G	AB	H	2B	3B	HR	TB	R	RBI	GW	TBB	IBB	SO	HBP	SH	SF	SB	CS	SB%	GDP	Avg	OBP	SLG	Pos	G	PO	A	E	DP	FPct
1969 NYN	31	3	1	0	0	0	0	0	0	0	0	0	0	0	0	0	0	0	0	—	0	.000	.000	.000	2B	3	1	3	0	1	1.000

World Series — Batting / Fielding

Year Tm	Age	G	AB	H	2B	3B	HR	TB	R	RBI	GW	TBB	IBB	SO	HBP	SH	SF	SB	CS	SB%	GDP	Avg	OBP	SLG	Pos	G	PO	A	E	DP	FPct
1969 NYN	31	5	11	5	0	0	1	8	1	3	1	4	2	2	0	0	1	0	0	—	0	.455	.563	.727	2B	5	7	5	1	0	.923
Postseason Totals		8	12	5	0	0	1	8	1	3	1	4	2	2	0	0	1	0	0	—	0	.417	.529	.667	2B	8	8	8	1	1	.941

WALT WEISS—Walter William Weiss—Bats: Both; Throws: Right

Ht: 6'0"; Wt: 175 lbs; Born: 11/28/1963 in Tuxedo, New York; Debut: 7/12/1987

Division Series — Batting / Fielding

Year Tm	Age	G	AB	H	2B	3B	HR	TB	R	RBI	GW	TBB	IBB	SO	HBP	SH	SF	SB	CS	SB%	GDP	Avg	OBP	SLG	Pos	G	PO	A	E	DP	FPct
1995 Col	31	4	12	2	0	0	0	2	1	0	0	3	1	3	1	0	0	1	0	1.00	0	.167	.375	.167	SS	4	6	12	0	4	1.000

LCS — Batting / Fielding

Year Tm	Age	G	AB	H	2B	3B	HR	TB	R	RBI	GW	TBB	IBB	SO	HBP	SH	SF	SB	CS	SB%	GDP	Avg	OBP	SLG	Pos	G	PO	A	E	DP	FPct
1988 Oak-*RY*	24	4	15	5	2	0	0	7	2	2	1	0	0	4	0	0	0	0	0	—	0	.333	.333	.467	SS	4	7	10	0	3	1.000
1989 Oak	25	4	9	1	1	0	0	2	2	0	0	1	0	1	0	1	0	1	0	1.00	0	.111	.200	.222	SS	4	5	10	0	2	1.000
1990 Oak	26	2	7	0	0	0	0	0	2	0	0	2	0	2	0	0	0	0	0	—	0	.000	.222	.000	SS	2	2	7	1	1	.900
1992 Oak	28	3	6	1	0	0	0	1	1	0	0	2	0	1	0	0	0	2	0	1.00	0	.167	.375	.167	SS	3	5	6	0	1	1.000
LCS Totals		13	37	7	3	0	0	10	7	2	1	5	0	8	0	1	0	3	0	1.00	0	.189	.286	.270	SS	13	19	33	1	7	.981

World Series — Batting / Fielding

Year Tm	Age	G	AB	H	2B	3B	HR	TB	R	RBI	GW	TBB	IBB	SO	HBP	SH	SF	SB	CS	SB%	GDP	Avg	OBP	SLG	Pos	G	PO	A	E	DP	FPct
1988 Oak-*RY*	24	5	16	1	0	0	0	1	1	0	0	0	0	2	0	1	0	1	0	1.00	0	.063	.063	.063	SS	5	5	11	1	1	.941
1989 Oak	25	4	15	2	0	0	1	5	3	1	0	2	2	2	0	0	0	0	0	—	0	.133	.235	.333	SS	4	7	8	0	1	1.000
WS Totals		9	31	3	0	0	1	6	4	1	0	2	2	4	0	1	0	1	0	1.00	0	.097	.152	.194	SS	9	12	19	1	2	.969
Postseason Totals		26	80	12	3	0	1	18	12	3	1	10	3	15	1	2	0	5	0	1.00	0	.150	.253	.225	SS	26	37	64	2	13	.981

BOB WELCH—Robert Lynn Welch—Throws: Right; Bats: Right

Ht: 6'3"; Wt: 190 lbs; Born: 11/3/1956 in Detroit, Michigan; Debut: 6/20/1978

Division Series — Pitching

Year Tm	Age	G	GS	CG	GF	IP	BFP	H	R	ER	HR	SH	SF	HB	TBB	IBB	SO	WP	Bk	W	L	Pct	ShO	Sv-Op	Hld	OAvg	OOBP	ERA
1981 LA	24	1	0	0	1	1.0	4	0	0	0	0	0	0	0	1	0	1	0	0	0	0	—	0	0- 0	0	.000	.250	0.00

LCS — Pitching

Year Tm	Age	G	GS	CG	GF	IP	BFP	H	R	ER	HR	SH	SF	HB	TBB	IBB	SO	WP	Bk	W	L	Pct	ShO	Sv-Op	Hld	OAvg	OOBP	ERA
1978 LA	21	1	0	0	1	4.1	16	2	1	1	1	0	0	0	0	0	5	0	0	1	0	1.000	0	0- 0	0	.125	.125	2.08
1981 LA	24	3	0	0	1	1.2	7	2	1	1	0	0	0	0	0	0	2	0	0	0	0	—	0	1- 1	2	.286	.286	5.40
1983 LA	26	1	1	0	0	1.1	6	0	2	1	0	0	0	0	2	0	0	1	0	0	1	.000	0	0- 0	0	.000	.333	6.75
1985 LA	28	1	1	0	0	2.2	18	5	4	2	1	0	0	0	6	3	2	0	0	0	1	.000	0	0- 0	0	.417	.611	6.75
1988 Oak	31	1	1	0	0	1.2	13	6	5	5	1	1	1	0	2	0	0	0	1	0	0	—	0	0- 0	0	.667	.667	27.00
1989 Oak	32	1	1	0	0	5.2	27	8	2	2	0	0	0	0	1	0	4	0	0	1	0	1.000	0	0- 0	0	.308	.333	3.18
1990 Oak-*C*	33	1	1	0	0	7.1	31	6	1	1	0	0	1	0	3	0	4	0	0	1	0	1.000	0	0- 0	0	.222	.290	1.23
1992 Oak	35	1	1	0	0	7.0	29	7	2	2	1	0	0	0	1	0	7	0	0	0	0	—	0	0- 0	0	.250	.276	2.57
LCS Totals		10	6	0	2	31.2	294	36	18	15	4	1	2	0	15	3	24	1	1	3	2	.600	0	1-1	2	.279	.349	4.26

World Series — Pitching

Year Tm	Age	G	GS	CG	GF	IP	BFP	H	R	ER	HR	SH	SF	HB	TBB	IBB	SO	WP	Bk	W	L	Pct	ShO	Sv-Op	Hld	OAvg	OOBP	ERA
1978 LA	21	3	0	0	2	4.1	19	4	3	3	1	0	0	0	2	0	6	0	0	0	1	.000	0	1- 1	0	.235	.316	6.23
1981 LA	24	1	1	0	0	0.0	4	3	2	2	0	0	0	0	1	0	0	0	0	0	0	—	0	0- 0	0	1.000	1.000	—
1988 Oak	31	1	1	0	0	5.0	24	6	1	1	0	1	0	0	3	0	8	0	0	0	0	—	0	0- 0	0	.300	.391	1.80
1990 Oak-*C*	33	1	1	0	0	7.1	31	9	4	4	0	0	0	0	2	0	2	0	0	0	0	—	0	0- 0	0	.310	.355	4.91
WS Totals		6	3	0	2	16.2	156	22	10	10	1	1	0	0	8	0	16	0	0	0	1	.000	0	1-1	0	.319	.390	5.40
Postseason Totals		17	9	0	5	49.1	458	58	28	25	5	2	2	0	24	3	41	1	1	3	3	.500	0	2-2	2	.289	.361	4.56

Division Series — Batting / Fielding

Year Tm	Age	G	AB	H	2B	3B	HR	TB	R	RBI	GW	TBB	IBB	SO	HBP	SH	SF	SB	CS	SB%	GDP	Avg	OBP	SLG	Pos	G	PO	A	E	DP	FPct
1981 LA	24	1	0	0	0	0	0	0	0	0	0	0	0	0	0	0	0	0	0	—	0	—	—	—	P	1	1	0	0	0	1.000

LCS — Batting / Fielding

Year Tm	Age	G	AB	H	2B	3B	HR	TB	R	RBI	GW	TBB	IBB	SO	HBP	SH	SF	SB	CS	SB%	GDP	Avg	OBP	SLG	Pos	G	PO	A	E	DP	FPct
1978 LA	21	1	2	0	0	0	0	0	0	0	0	0	0	1	0	0	0	0	0	—	0	.000	.000	.000	P	1	0	1	0	0	1.000
1981 LA	24	3	0	0	0	0	0	0	0	0	0	0	0	0	0	0	0	0	0	—	0	—	—	—	P	3	0	0	0	0	—
1983 LA	26	1	0	0	0	0	0	0	0	0	0	0	0	0	0	0	0	0	0	—	0	—	—	—	P	1	0	0	0	0	—
1985 LA	28	1	1	0	0	0	0	0	0	0	0	0	0	1	0	0	0	0	0	—	0	.000	.000	.000	P	1	0	0	1	0	.000
1988 Oak	31	1	0	0	0	0	0	0	0	0	0	0	0	0	0	0	0	0	0	—	0	—	—	—	P	1	1	0	0	0	1.000
1989 Oak	32	1	0	0	0	0	0	0	0	0	0	0	0	0	0	0	0	0	0	—	0	—	—	—	P	1	1	0	0	0	1.000
1990 Oak	33	1	0	0	0	0	0	0	0	0	0	0	0	0	0	0	0	0	0	—	0	—	—	—	P	1	0	3	0	0	1.000
1992 Oak	35	1	0	0	0	0	0	0	0	0	0	0	0	0	0	0	0	0	0	—	0	—	—	—	P	1	0	1	0	0	1.000
LCS Totals		10	3	0	0	0	0	0	0	0	0	0	0	2	0	0	0	0	0	—	0	.000	.000	.000	P	10	2	5	1	0	.875

World Series — Batting / Fielding

Year Tm	Age	G	AB	H	2B	3B	HR	TB	R	RBI	GW	TBB	IBB	SO	HBP	SH	SF	SB	CS	SB%	GDP	Avg	OBP	SLG	Pos	G	PO	A	E	DP	FPct
1978 LA	21	3	0	0	0	0	0	0	0	0	0	0	0	0	0	0	0	0	0	—	0	—	—	—	P	3	0	0	0	0	—
1981 LA	24	1	0	0	0	0	0	0	0	0	0	0	0	0	0	0	0	0	0	—	0	—	—	—	P	1	0	0	0	0	—
1988 Oak	31	1	0	0	0	0	0	0	0	0	0	0	0	0	0	0	0	0	0	—	0	—	—	—	P	1	1	1	0	0	1.000
1990 Oak	33	1	3	0	0	0	0	0	0	0	0	0	0	2	0	1	0	0	0	—	0	.000	.000	.000	P	1	0	2	0	0	1.000
WS Totals		6	3	0	0	0	0	0	0	0	0	0	0	2	0	1	0	0	0	—	0	.000	.000	.000	P	6	1	3	0	0	1.000
Postseason Totals		17	6	0	0	0	0	0	0	0	0	0	0	4	0	1	0	0	0	—	0	.000	.000	.000	P	17	4	8	1	0	.923

BOB WELLS—Robert Lee Wells—Throws: Right; Bats: Right

Ht: 6'0"; Wt: 180 lbs; Born: 11/1/1966 in Yakima, Washington; Debut: 5/16/1994

Division Series — Pitching

Year Tm	Age	G	GS	CG	GF	IP	BFP	H	R	ER	HR	SH	SF	HB	TBB	IBB	SO	WP	Bk	W	L	Pct	ShO	Sv-Op	Hld	OAvg	OOBP	ERA
1995 Sea	28	1	0	0	1	1.0	6	2	1	1	0	0	0	0	1	0	0	0	0	0	0	—	0	0- 0	0	.400	.500	9.00
1997 Sea	30	1	0	0	0	1.1	5	1	0	0	0	0	0	0	0	0	1	0	0	0	0	—	0	0- 0	0	.200	.200	0.00
DS Totals		2	0	0	1	2.1	22	3	1	1	0	0	0	0	1	0	1	0	0	0	0	—	0	0-0	0	.300	.364	3.86

LCS — Pitching

Year Tm	Age	G	GS	CG	GF	IP	BFP	H	R	ER	HR	SH	SF	HB	TBB	IBB	SO	WP	Bk	W	L	Pct	ShO	Sv-Op	Hld	OAvg	OOBP	ERA
1995 Sea	28	1	0	0	0	3.0	13	2	1	1	0	0	0	0	2	0	2	0	0	0	0	—	0	0- 0	0	.182	.308	3.00
Postseason Totals		3	0	0	1	5.1	48	5	2	2	0	0	0	0	3	0	3	0	0	0	0	—	0	0-0	0	.238	.333	3.38

Division Series — Batting / Fielding

Year Tm	Age	G	AB	H	2B	3B	HR	TB	R	RBI	GW	TBB	IBB	SO	HBP	SH	SF	SB	CS	SB%	GDP	Avg	OBP	SLG	Pos	G	PO	A	E	DP	FPct
1995 Sea	28	1	0	0	0	0	0	0	0	0	0	0	0	0	0	0	0	0	0	—	0	—	—	—	P	1	0	0	0	0	—
1997 Sea	30	1	0	0	0	0	0	0	0	0	0	0	0	0	0	0	0	0	0	—	0	—	—	—	P	1	0	0	0	0	—
DS Totals		2	0	0	0	0	0	0	0	0	0	0	0	0	0	0	0	0	0	—	0	—	—	—	P	2	0	0	0	0	—

LCS — Batting / Fielding

Year Tm	Age	G	AB	H	2B	3B	HR	TB	R	RBI	GW	TBB	IBB	SO	HBP	SH	SF	SB	CS	SB%	GDP	Avg	OBP	SLG	Pos	G	PO	A	E	DP	FPct
1995 Sea	28	1	0	0	0	0	0	0	0	0	0	0	0	0	0	0	0	0	0	—	0	—	—	—	P	1	0	1	0	0	1.000
Postseason Totals		3	0	0	0	0	0	0	0	0	0	0	0	0	0	0	0	0	0	—	0	—	—	—	P	3	0	1	0	0	1.000

DAVID WELLS—David Lee Wells—Throws: Left; Bats: Left

Ht: 6'3"; Wt: 187 lbs; Born: 5/20/1963 in Torrance, California; Debut: 6/30/1987

Division Series — Pitching

Year Tm	Age	G	GS	CG	GF	IP	BFP	H	R	ER	HR	SH	SF	HB	TBB	IBB	SO	WP	Bk	W	L	Pct	ShO	Sv-Op	Hld	OAvg	OOBP	ERA
1995 Cin	32	1	1	0	0	6.1	28	6	1	0	0	0	0	1	1	0	8	0	0	1	0	1.000	0	0- 0	0	.231	.286	0.00
1996 Bal	33	2	2	0	0	13.2	58	15	7	7	1	1	1	0	4	1	6	0	0	1	0	1.000	0	0- 0	0	.288	.333	4.61
1997 NYA	34	1	1	1	0	9.0	33	5	1	1	0	0	0	0	0	0	1	0	0	1	0	1.000	0	0- 0	0	.152	.152	1.00
DS Totals		4	4	1	0	29.0	238	26	9	8	1	1	1	1	5	1	15	0	0	3	0	1.000	0	0-0	0	.234	.271	2.48

LCS — Pitching

Year Tm	Age	G	GS	CG	GF	IP	BFP	H	R	ER	HR	SH	SF	HB	TBB	IBB	SO	WP	Bk	W	L	Pct	ShO	Sv-Op	Hld	OAvg	OOBP	ERA
1989 Tor	26	1	0	0	0	1.0	5	0	1	0	0	0	0	0	2	0	1	0	0	0	0	—	0	0- 0	0	.000	.400	0.00
1991 Tor	28	4	0	0	1	7.2	31	6	2	2	0	0	0	0	2	1	9	0	0	0	0	—	0	0- 0	0	.207	.258	2.35
1995 Cin	32	1	1	0	0	6.0	27	8	3	3	1	0	0	0	2	0	3	0	0	0	1	.000	0	0- 0	0	.320	.370	4.50
1996 Bal	33	1	1	0	0	6.2	30	8	3	3	0	0	0	1	3	0	6	0	0	1	0	1.000	0	0- 0	0	.308	.400	4.05
LCS Totals		7	2	0	1	21.1	186	22	9	8	1	0	0	1	9	1	19	0	0	1	1	.500	0	0-0	0	.265	.344	3.38

World Series — Pitching

Year Tm	Age	G	GS	CG	GF	IP	BFP	H	R	ER	HR	SH	SF	HB	TBB	IBB	SO	WP	Bk	W	L	Pct	ShO	Sv-Op	Hld	OAvg	OOBP	ERA
1992 Tor	29	4	0	0	1	4.1	15	1	0	0	0	0	1	0	2	0	3	0	0	0	0	—	0	0- 0	1	.083	.200	0.00
Postseason Totals		15	6	1	2	54.2	454	49	18	16	2	1	2	2	16	2	37	0	0	4	1	.800	0	0-0	1	.238	.296	2.63

Division Series — Batting / Fielding

Year Tm	Age	G	AB	H	2B	3B	HR	TB	R	RBI	GW	TBB	IBB	SO	HBP	SH	SF	SB	CS	SB%	GDP	Avg	OBP	SLG	Pos	G	PO	A	E	DP	FPct
1995 Cin	32	1	3	1	0	0	0	1	0	0	0	0	0	1	0	0	0	0	0	—	0	.333	.333	.333	P	1	1	1	0	0	1.000
1996 Bal	33	2	0	0	0	0	0	0	0	0	0	0	0	0	0	0	0	0	0	—	0	—	—	—	P	2	0	3	0	0	1.000
1997 NYA	34	1	0	0	0	0	0	0	0	0	0	0	0	0	0	0	0	0	0	—	0	—	—	—	P	1	0	0	0	0	—
DS Totals		4	3	1	0	0	0	1	0	0	0	0	0	1	0	0	0	0	0	—	0	.333	.333	.333	P	4	1	4	0	0	1.000

LCS — Batting / Fielding

Year Tm	Age	G	AB	H	2B	3B	HR	TB	R	RBI	GW	TBB	IBB	SO	HBP	SH	SF	SB	CS	SB%	GDP	Avg	OBP	SLG	Pos	G	PO	A	E	DP	FPct
1989 Tor	26	1	0	0	0	0	0	0	0	0	0	0	0	0	0	0	0	0	0	—	0	—	—	—	P	1	0	0	0	0	—
1991 Tor	28	4	0	0	0	0	0	0	0	0	0	0	0	0	0	0	0	0	0	—	0	—	—	—	P	4	1	1	0	0	1.000
1995 Cin	32	1	2	1	0	0	0	1	0	0	0	0	0	0	0	0	0	0	0	—	0	.500	.500	.500	P	1	0	0	0	0	—
1996 Bal	33	1	0	0	0	0	0	0	0	0	0	0	0	0	0	0	0	0	0	—	0	—	—	—	P	1	1	0	0	0	1.000
LCS Totals		7	2	1	0	0	0	1	0	0	0	0	0	0	0	0	0	0	0	—	0	.500	.500	.500	P	7	2	1	0	0	1.000

World Series — Batting / Fielding

Year Tm	Age	G	AB	H	2B	3B	HR	TB	R	RBI	GW	TBB	IBB	SO	HBP	SH	SF	SB	CS	SB%	GDP	Avg	OBP	SLG	Pos	G	PO	A	E	DP	FPct
1992 Tor	29	4	0	0	0	0	0	0	0	0	0	0	0	0	0	0	0	0	0	—	0	—	—	—	P	4	0	0	0	0	—
Postseason Totals		15	5	2	0	0	0	2	0	0	0	0	0	1	0	0	0	0	0	—	0	.400	.400	.400	P	15	3	5	0	0	1.000

BUTCH WENSLOFF—Charles William Wensloff—Throws: Right; Bats: Right

Ht: 5'11"; Wt: 185 lbs; Born: 12/3/1915 in Sausalito, California; Debut: 5/2/1943

World Series — Pitching

Year Tm	Age	G	GS	CG	GF	IP	BFP	H	R	ER	HR	SH	SF	HB	TBB	IBB	SO	WP	Bk	W	L	Pct	ShO	Sv-Op	Hld	OAvg	OOBP	ERA
1947 NYA	31	1	0	0	1	2.0	7	0	0	0	0	0	0	0	0	0	0	0	0	0	0	—	0	0- 0	0	.000	.000	0.00

World Series — Batting / Fielding

Year Tm	Age	G	AB	H	2B	3B	HR	TB	R	RBI	GW	TBB	IBB	SO	HBP	SH	SF	SB	CS	SB%	GDP	Avg	OBP	SLG	Pos	G	PO	A	E	DP	FPct
1947 NYA	31	1	0	0	0	0	0	0	0	0	0	0	0	0	0	0	0	0	0	—	0	—	—	—	P	1	0	1	0	0	1.000

BILL WERBER—William Murray Werber—Bats: Right; Throws: Right

Ht: 5'10"; Wt: 170 lbs; Born: 6/20/1908 in Berwyn, Maryland; Debut: 6/25/1930

World Series — Batting / Fielding

Year Tm	Age	G	AB	H	2B	3B	HR	TB	R	RBI	GW	TBB	IBB	SO	HBP	SH	SF	SB	CS	SB%	GDP	Avg	OBP	SLG	Pos	G	PO	A	E	DP	FPct
1939 Cin	31	4	16	4	0	0	0	4	1	2	0	2	0	0	0	0	0	0	1	.00	0	.250	.333	.250	3B	4	3	6	0	0	1.000
1940 Cin	32	7	27	10	4	0	0	14	5	2	0	4	0	2	0	0	0	0	1	.00	1	.370	.452	.519	3B	7	9	16	2	3	.926
WS Totals		11	43	14	4	0	0	18	6	4	0	6	0	2	0	0	0	0	2	.00	1	.326	.408	.419	3B	11	12	22	2	3	.944

DON WERT—Donald Ralph Wert—Bats: Right; Throws: Right

Ht: 5'10"; Wt: 162 lbs; Born: 7/29/1938 in Strasburg, Pennsylvania; Debut: 5/11/1963

World Series — Batting / Fielding

Year Tm	Age	G	AB	H	2B	3B	HR	TB	R	RBI	GW	TBB	IBB	SO	HBP	SH	SF	SB	CS	SB%	GDP	Avg	OBP	SLG	Pos	G	PO	A	E	DP	FPct
1968 Det	30	6	17	2	0	0	0	2	1	2	0	6	1	5	1	0	0	0	0	—	0	.118	.375	.118	3B	6	5	14	0	2	1.000

VIC WERTZ—Victor Woodrow Wertz—Bats: Left; Throws: Right

Ht: 6'0"; Wt: 186 lbs; Born: 2/9/1925 in York, Pennsylvania; Debut: 4/15/1947; Died: 7/7/1983

World Series — Batting / Fielding

Year Tm	Age	G	AB	H	2B	3B	HR	TB	R	RBI	GW	TBB	IBB	SO	HBP	SH	SF	SB	CS	SB%	GDP	Avg	OBP	SLG	Pos	G	PO	A	E	DP	FPct
1954 Cle	29	4	16	8	2	1	1	15	2	3	0	2	0	2	0	0	0	0	0	—	0	.500	.556	.938	1B	4	33	6	1	2	.975

DAVID WEST—David Lee West—Throws: Left; Bats: Left

Ht: 6'6"; Wt: 205 lbs; Born: 9/1/1964 in Memphis, Tennessee; Debut: 9/24/1988

LCS — Pitching

Year Tm	Age	G	GS	CG	GF	IP	BFP	H	R	ER	HR	SH	SF	HB	TBB	IBB	SO	WP	Bk	W	L	Pct	ShO	Sv-Op	Hld	OAvg	OOBP	ERA
1991 Min	27	2	0	0	0	5.2	22	1	0	0	0	1	0	0	4	1	4	2	0	1	0	1.000	0	0- 0	0	.059	.238	0.00
1993 Phi	29	3	0	0	0	2.2	16	5	5	4	0	0	0	0	2	0	5	0	0	0	0	—	0	0- 0	1	.357	.438	13.50
LCS Totals		5	0	0	0	8.1	76	6	5	4	0	1	0	0	6	1	9	2	0	1	0	1.000	0	0-0	1	.194	.324	4.32

World Series — Pitching

Year Tm	Age	G	GS	CG	GF	IP	BFP	H	R	ER	HR	SH	SF	HB	TBB	IBB	SO	WP	Bk	W	L	Pct	ShO	Sv-Op	Hld	OAvg	OOBP	ERA
1991 Min	27	2	0	0	0	0.0	6	2	4	4	1	0	0	0	4	0	0	0	0	0	0	—	0	0- 0	0	1.000	1.000	—
1993 Phi	29	3	0	0	0	1.0	10	5	3	3	0	0	0	1	1	0	0	0	0	0	0	—	0	0- 0	0	.625	.700	27.00
WS Totals		5	0	0	0	1.0	32	7	7	7	1	0	0	1	5	0	0	0	0	0	0	—	0	0-0	0	.700	.813	63.00
Postseason Totals		10	0	0	0	9.1	108	13	12	11	1	1	0	1	11	1	9	2	0	1	0	1.000	0	0-0	1	.317	.472	10.61

LCS — Batting / Fielding

Year Tm	Age	G	AB	H	2B	3B	HR	TB	R	RBI	GW	TBB	IBB	SO	HBP	SH	SF	SB	CS	SB%	GDP	Avg	OBP	SLG	Pos	G	PO	A	E	DP	FPct
1991 Min	27	2	0	0	0	0	0	0	0	0	0	0	0	0	0	0	0	0	0	—	0	—	—	—	P	2	0	0	0	0	—
1993 Phi	29	3	0	0	0	0	0	0	0	0	0	0	0	0	0	0	0	0	0	—	0	—	—	—	P	3	0	1	0	0	1.000
LCS Totals		5	0	0	0	0	0	0	0	0	0	0	0	0	0	0	0	0	0	—	0	—	—	—	P	5	0	1	0	0	1.000

World Series		Batting																							Fielding						
Year Tm	Age	G	AB	H	2B	3B	HR	TB	R	RBI	GW	TBB	IBB	SO	HBP	SH	SF	SB	CS	SB%	GDP	Avg	OBP	SLG	Pos	G	PO	A	E	DP	FPct
1991 Min	27	2	0	0	0	0	0	0	0	0	0	0	0	0	0	0	0	0	0	—	0	—	—	—	P	2	0	0	0	0	—
1993 Phi	29	3	0	0	0	0	0	0	0	0	0	0	0	0	0	0	0	0	0	—	0	—	—	—	P	3	0	0	0	0	—
WS Totals		5	0	0	0	0	0	0	0	0	0	0	0	0	0	0	0	0	0	—	0	—	—	—	P	5	0	0	0	0	—
Postseason Totals		10	0	0	0	0	0	0	0	0	0	0	0	0	0	0	0	0	0	—	0	—	—	—	P	10	0	1	0	0	1.000

WALLY WESTLAKE—Waldon Thomas Westlake—Bats: Right; Throws: Right

Ht: 6'0"; Wt: 186 lbs; Born: 11/8/1920 in Gridley, California; Debut: 4/15/1947

World Series		Batting																							Fielding						
Year Tm	Age	G	AB	H	2B	3B	HR	TB	R	RBI	GW	TBB	IBB	SO	HBP	SH	SF	SB	CS	SB%	GDP	Avg	OBP	SLG	Pos	G	PO	A	E	DP	FPct
1954 Cle	33	2	7	1	0	0	0	1	0	0	0	1	0	3	0	0	0	0	0	—	0	.143	.250	.143	OF	2	6	0	1	0	.857

WES WESTRUM—Wesley Noreen Westrum—Bats: Right; Throws: Right

Ht: 5'11"; Wt: 185 lbs; Born: 11/28/1922 in Clearbrook, Minnesota; Debut: 9/17/1947

World Series		Batting																							Fielding						
Year Tm	Age	G	AB	H	2B	3B	HR	TB	R	RBI	GW	TBB	IBB	SO	HBP	SH	SF	SB	CS	SB%	GDP	Avg	OBP	SLG	Pos	G	PO	A	E	DP	FPct
1951 NYG	28	6	17	4	1	0	0	5	1	0	0	5	0	3	0	0	0	0	0	—	2	.235	.409	.294	C	6	29	2	1	0	.969
1954 NYG	31	4	11	3	0	0	0	3	0	3	0	1	0	3	0	1	2	0	1	.00	0	.273	.286	.273	C	4	23	0	0	0	1.000
WS Totals		10	28	7	1	0	0	8	1	3	0	6	0	6	0	1	2	0	1	.00	2	.250	.361	.286	C	10	52	2	1	0	.982

JOHN WETTELAND—John Karl Wetteland—Throws: Right; Bats: Right

Ht: 6'2", Wt: 195 lbs; Born: 8/21/1966 in San Mateo, California; Debut: 5/31/1989

Division Series		Pitching																										
Year Tm	Age	G	GS	CG	GF	IP	BFP	H	R	ER	HR	SH	SF	HB	TBB	IBB	SO	WP	Bk	W	L	Pct	ShO	Sv-Op	Hld	OAvg	OOBP	ERA
1995 NYA	29	3	0	0	1	4.1	24	8	7	7	2	0	0	1	2	0	5	0	0	0	1	.000	0	0- 0	0	.381	.458	14.54
1996 NYA	30	3	0	0	2	4.0	18	2	0	0	0	2	0	0	4	1	4	0	0	0	0	—	0	2- 2	0	.167	.375	0.00
DS Totals		6	0	0	3	8.1	84	10	7	7	2	2	0	1	6	1	9	0	0	0	1	.000	0	2-2	0	.303	.425	7.56
LCS		Pitching																										
Year Tm	Age	G	GS	CG	GF	IP	BFP	H	R	ER	HR	SH	SF	HB	TBB	IBB	SO	WP	Bk	W	L	Pct	ShO	Sv-Op	Hld	OAvg	OOBP	ERA
1996 NYA	30	4	0	0	3	4.0	15	2	2	2	1	0	0	0	1	0	5	0	0	0	0	—	0	1- 1	0	.143	.200	4.50
World Series		Pitching																										
Year Tm	Age	G	GS	CG	GF	IP	BFP	H	R	ER	HR	SH	SF	HB	TBB	IBB	SO	WP	Bk	W	L	Pct	ShO	Sv-Op	Hld	OAvg	OOBP	ERA
1996 NYA	30	5	0	0	5	4.1	19	4	1	1	0	0	0	0	1	1	6	0	0	0	0	—	0	4- 4	0	.222	.263	2.08
Postseason Totals		15	0	0	11	16.2	152	16	10	10	3	2	0	1	8	2	20	0	0	0	1	.000	0	7-7	0	.246	.338	5.40

Division Series		Batting																							Fielding						
Year Tm	Age	G	AB	H	2B	3B	HR	TB	R	RBI	GW	TBB	IBB	SO	HBP	SH	SF	SB	CS	SB%	GDP	Avg	OBP	SLG	Pos	G	PO	A	E	DP	FPct
1995 NYA	29	3	0	0	0	0	0	0	0	0	0	0	0	0	0	0	0	0	0	—	0	—	—	—	P	3	1	0	0	0	1.000
1996 NYA	30	3	0	0	0	0	0	0	0	0	0	0	0	0	0	0	0	0	0	—	0	—	—	—	P	3	1	2	0	0	1.000
DS Totals		6	0	0	0	0	0	0	0	0	0	0	0	0	0	0	0	0	0	—	0	—	—	—	P	6	2	2	0	0	1.000
LCS		Batting																							Fielding						
Year Tm	Age	G	AB	H	2B	3B	HR	TB	R	RBI	GW	TBB	IBB	SO	HBP	SH	SF	SB	CS	SB%	GDP	Avg	OBP	SLG	Pos	G	PO	A	E	DP	FPct
1996 NYA	30	4	0	0	0	0	0	0	0	0	0	0	0	0	0	0	0	0	0	—	0	—	—	—	P	4	0	0	0	0	—
World Series		Batting																							Fielding						
Year Tm	Age	G	AB	H	2B	3B	HR	TB	R	RBI	GW	TBB	IBB	SO	HBP	SH	SF	SB	CS	SB%	GDP	Avg	OBP	SLG	Pos	G	PO	A	E	DP	FPct
1996 NYA	30	5	0	0	0	0	0	0	0	0	0	0	0	0	0	0	0	0	0	—	0	—	—	—	P	5	0	0	0	0	—
Postseason Totals		15	0	0	0	0	0	0	0	0	0	0	0	0	0	0	0	0	0	—	0	—	—	—	P	15	2	2	0	0	1.000

ZACK WHEAT (HOF 1959-V)—Zachary Davis Wheat—Nickname: Buck—Bats: Left; Throws: Right

Ht: 5'10"; Wt: 170 lbs; Born: 5/23/1888 in Hamilton, Missouri; Debut: 9/11/1909; Died: 3/11/1972

World Series		Batting																							Fielding						
Year Tm	Age	G	AB	H	2B	3B	HR	TB	R	RBI	GW	TBB	IBB	SO	HBP	SH	SF	SB	CS	SB%	GDP	Avg	OBP	SLG	Pos	G	PO	A	E	DP	FPct
1916 Bro	28	5	19	4	0	1	0	6	2	1	0	2	1	2	0	0	0	1	1	.50	0	.211	.286	.316	OF	5	14	0	1	0	.933
1920 Bro	32	7	27	9	2	0	0	11	2	2	2	1	1	2	0	0	0	0	0	—	0	.333	.357	.407	OF	7	15	0	2	0	.882
WS Totals		12	46	13	2	1	0	17	4	3	2	3	2	4	0	0	0	1	1	.50	0	.283	.327	.370	OF	12	29	0	3	0	.906

LARRY WHISENTON—Bats: Left; Throws: Left

Ht: 6'1"; Wt: 190 lbs; Born: 7/3/1956 in St. Louis, Missouri; Debut: 9/17/1977

LCS		Batting																							Fielding						
Year Tm	Age	G	AB	H	2B	3B	HR	TB	R	RBI	GW	TBB	IBB	SO	HBP	SH	SF	SB	CS	SB%	GDP	Avg	OBP	SLG	Pos	G	PO	A	E	DP	FPct
1982 Atl	26	2	2	0	0	0	0	0	0	0	0	0	0	1	0	0	0	0	0	—	0	.000	.000	.000	—						

LOU WHITAKER—Louis Rodman Whitaker—Nickname: Sweet Lou—Bats: Left; Throws: Right

Ht: 5'11"; Wt: 160 lbs; Born: 5/12/1957 in Brooklyn, New York; Debut: 9/9/1977

LCS		Batting																							Fielding						
Year Tm	Age	G	AB	H	2B	3B	HR	TB	R	RBI	GW	TBB	IBB	SO	HBP	SH	SF	SB	CS	SB%	GDP	Avg	OBP	SLG	Pos	G	PO	A	E	DP	FPct
1984 Det	27	3	14	2	0	0	0	2	3	0	0	0	0	3	0	0	0	0	0	—	0	.143	.143	.143	2B	3	5	6	0	0	1.000
1987 Det	30	5	17	3	0	0	1	6	4	1	0	7	0	3	0	0	0	1	0	1.00	0	.176	.417	.353	2B	5	11	14	0	1	1.000
LCS Totals		8	31	5	0	0	1	8	7	1	0	7	0	6	0	0	0	1	0	1.00	0	.161	.316	.258	2B	8	16	20	0	1	1.000
World Series		Batting																							Fielding						
Year Tm	Age	G	AB	H	2B	3B	HR	TB	R	RBI	GW	TBB	IBB	SO	HBP	SH	SF	SB	CS	SB%	GDP	Avg	OBP	SLG	Pos	G	PO	A	E	DP	FPct
1984 Det	27	5	18	5	2	0	0	7	6	0	0	4	0	4	0	1	0	0	0	—	1	.278	.409	.389	2B	5	15	18	0	2	1.000
Postseason Totals		13	49	10	2	0	1	15	13	1	0	11	0	10	0	1	0	1	0	1.00	1	.204	.350	.306	2B	13	31	38	0	3	1.000

BILL WHITE—William DeKova White—Bats: Left; Throws: Left

Ht: 6'0"; Wt: 185 lbs; Born: 1/28/1934 in Lakewood, Florida; Debut: 5/7/1956

World Series		Batting																							Fielding						
Year Tm	Age	G	AB	H	2B	3B	HR	TB	R	RBI	GW	TBB	IBB	SO	HBP	SH	SF	SB	CS	SB%	GDP	Avg	OBP	SLG	Pos	G	PO	A	E	DP	FPct
1964 StL	30	7	27	3	1	0	0	4	2	2	0	2	0	6	0	0	0	1	0	1.00	1	.111	.172	.148	1B	7	62	3	0	4	1.000

DEVON WHITE—Devon Markes White—Nickname: Devo—Bats: Both; Throws: Right

Ht: 6'1"; Wt: 170 lbs; Born: 12/29/1962 in Kingston, Jamaica; Debut: 9/2/1985

Division Series		Batting																							Fielding						
Year Tm	Age	G	AB	H	2B	3B	HR	TB	R	RBI	GW	TBB	IBB	SO	HBP	SH	SF	SB	CS	SB%	GDP	Avg	OBP	SLG	Pos	G	PO	A	E	DP	FPct
1997 Fla	34	3	11	2	0	0	1	5	1	4	1	2	1	3	0	0	0	0	0	—	0	.182	.308	.455	OF	3	3	0	0	0	1.000
LCS		Batting																							Fielding						
Year Tm	Age	G	AB	H	2B	3B	HR	TB	R	RBI	GW	TBB	IBB	SO	HBP	SH	SF	SB	CS	SB%	GDP	Avg	OBP	SLG	Pos	G	PO	A	E	DP	FPct
1986 Cal	23	4	2	1	0	0	0	1	2	0	0	0	0	1	0	0	0	0	1	.00	0	.500	.500	.500	OF	3	3	0	0	0	1.000
1991 Tor	28	5	22	8	1	0	0	9	5	0	0	2	0	3	0	0	0	3	0	1.00	0	.364	.417	.409	OF	5	16	0	0	0	1.000
1992 Tor	29	6	23	8	2	0	0	10	2	2	0	5	0	6	0	0	1	0	4	.00	0	.348	.448	.435	OF	6	16	0	1	0	.941
1993 Tor	30	6	27	12	1	1	1	18	3	2	0	1	0	5	0	0	0	0	1	.00	0	.444	.464	.667	OF	6	15	0	0	0	1.000
1997 Fla	34	6	21	4	1	0	0	5	4	1	0	2	1	7	1	0	0	1	0	1.00	0	.190	.292	.238	OF	6	16	0	0	0	1.000
LCS Totals		27	95	33	5	1	1	43	16	5	0	10	1	22	1	0	1	4	6	.40	0	.347	.411	.453	OF	26	66	0	1	0	.985
World Series		Batting																							Fielding						
Year Tm	Age	G	AB	H	2B	3B	HR	TB	R	RBI	GW	TBB	IBB	SO	HBP	SH	SF	SB	CS	SB%	GDP	Avg	OBP	SLG	Pos	G	PO	A	E	DP	FPct
1992 Tor	29	6	26	6	1	0	0	7	2	2	0	0	0	6	1	0	0	1	0	1.00	0	.231	.259	.269	OF	6	22	1	0	1	1.000
1993 Tor	30	6	24	7	3	2	1	17	8	7	1	4	0	7	0	0	0	1	0	1.00	1	.292	.393	.708	OF	6	16	0	0	0	1.000
1997 Fla	34	7	33	8	3	1	0	13	0	2	0	3	0	10	0	0	0	1	0	1.00	0	.242	.306	.394	OF	7	16	0	0	0	1.000
WS Totals		19	83	21	7	3	1	37	10	11	1	7	0	23	1	0	0	3	0	1.00	1	.253	.319	.446	OF	19	54	1	0	1	1.000
Postseason Totals		49	189	56	12	4	3	85	27	20	2	19	2	48	2	0	1	7	6	.54	1	.296	.365	.450	OF	48	123	1	1	1	.992

DOC WHITE—Guy Harris White—Throws: Left; Bats: Left

Ht: 6'1"; Wt: 150 lbs; Born: 4/9/1879 in Washington, DC; Debut: 4/22/1901; Died: 2/19/1969

World Series		Pitching																										
Year Tm	Age	G	GS	CG	GF	IP	BFP	H	R	ER	HR	SH	SF	HB	TBB	IBB	SO	WP	Bk	W	L	Pct	ShO	Sv-Op	Hld	OAvg	OOBP	ERA
1906 ChA	27	3	2	1	1	15.0	64	12	7	3	0	2	0	1	7	1	4	0	0	1	1	.500	0	1- 1	0	.222	.323	1.80

World Series		Batting																							Fielding						
Year Tm	Age	G	AB	H	2B	3B	HR	TB	R	RBI	GW	TBB	IBB	SO	HBP	SH	SF	SB	CS	SB%	GDP	Avg	OBP	SLG	Pos	G	PO	A	E	DP	FPct
1906 ChA	27	3	3	0	0	0	0	0	0	0	0	1	0	0	0	0	0	0	0	—	0	.000	.250	.000	P	3	1	3	0	0	1.000

ERNIE WHITE—Ernest Daniel White—Throws: Left; Bats: Right

Ht: 5'11"; Wt: 175 lbs; Born: 9/5/1916 in Pacolet Mills, South Carolina; Debut: 5/9/1940; Died: 5/22/1974

World Series		Pitching																										
Year Tm	Age	G	GS	CG	GF	IP	BFP	H	R	ER	HR	SH	SF	HB	TBB	IBB	SO	WP	Bk	W	L	Pct	ShO	Sv-Op	Hld	OAvg	OOBP	ERA
1942 StL	26	1	1	1	0	9.0	33	6	0	0	0	0	0	0	0	0	6	0	0	1	0	1.000	1	0- 0	0	.182	.182	0.00

World Series		Batting																							Fielding						
Year Tm	Age	G	AB	H	2B	3B	HR	TB	R	RBI	GW	TBB	IBB	SO	HBP	SH	SF	SB	CS	SB%	GDP	Avg	OBP	SLG	Pos	G	PO	A	E	DP	FPct
1942 StL	26	1	2	0	0	0	0	0	0	0	0	0	0	0	0	1	0	0	0	—	0	.000	.000	.000	P	1	0	0	0	0	—
1943 StL	27	1	0	0	0	0	0	0	0	0	0	0	0	0	0	0	0	0	0	—	0	—	—	—	—						
WS Totals		2	2	0	0	0	0	0	0	0	0	0	0	0	0	1	0	0	0	—	0	.000	.000	.000	P	1	0	0	0	0	—

FRANK WHITE—Bats: Right; Throws: Right

Ht: 5'11"; Wt: 165 lbs; Born: 9/4/1950 in Greenville, Mississippi; Debut: 6/12/1973

Division Series		Batting																							Fielding						
Year Tm	Age	G	AB	H	2B	3B	HR	TB	R	RBI	GW	TBB	IBB	SO	HBP	SH	SF	SB	CS	SB%	GDP	Avg	OBP	SLG	Pos	G	PO	A	E	DP	FPct
1981 KC	31	3	11	2	0	0	0	2	1	0	0	1	0	1	0	0	0	0	0	—	0	.182	.250	.182	2B	3	5	6	1	1	.917
LCS		**Batting**																							**Fielding**						
Year Tm	Age	G	AB	H	2B	3B	HR	TB	R	RBI	GW	TBB	IBB	SO	HBP	SH	SF	SB	CS	SB%	GDP	Avg	OBP	SLG	Pos	G	PO	A	E	DP	FPct
1976 KC	26	4	8	1	0	0	0	1	2	0	0	0	0	1	0	0	0	0	0	—	0	.125	.125	.125	2B	4	6	11	0	3	1.000
1977 KC	27	5	18	5	1	0	0	6	1	2	0	0	0	4	0	0	0	1	1	.50	0	.278	.263	.333	2B	5	13	16	0	1	1.000
1978 KC	28	4	13	3	0	0	0	3	1	2	0	0	0	0	0	0	0	0	0	—	0	.231	.231	.231	2B	4	8	12	0	3	1.000
1980 KC	30	3	11	6	1	0	1	10	3	3	0	0	0	1	0	0	0	1	0	1.00	0	.545	.545	.909	2B	3	9	10	1	3	.950
1984 KC	34	3	11	1	0	0	0	1	1	0	0	0	0	3	0	0	0	0	0	—	0	.091	.091	.091	2B	3	7	3	0	2	1.000
1985 KC	35	7	25	5	0	0	0	5	1	3	0	1	0	2	0	1	1	0	0	—	1	.200	.222	.200	2B	7	9	28	0	2	1.000
LCS Totals		26	86	21	2	0	1	26	9	10	0	1	0	11	0	1	2	2	1	.67	1	.244	.247	.302	2B	26	52	80	1	14	.992
World Series		**Batting**																							**Fielding**						
Year Tm	Age	G	AB	H	2B	3B	HR	TB	R	RBI	GW	TBB	IBB	SO	HBP	SH	SF	SB	CS	SB%	GDP	Avg	OBP	SLG	Pos	G	PO	A	E	DP	FPct
1980 KC	30	6	25	2	0	0	0	2	0	0	0	1	0	5	0	1	0	1	0	1.00	1	.080	.115	.080	2B	6	13	20	2	6	.943
1985 KC	35	7	28	7	3	0	1	13	4	6	0	3	0	4	0	0	0	1	1	.50	2	.250	.323	.464	2B	7	10	20	0	2	1.000
WS Totals		13	53	9	3	0	1	15	4	6	0	4	0	9	0	1	0	2	1	.67	3	.170	.228	.283	2B	13	23	40	2	8	.969
Postseason Totals		42	150	32	5	0	2	43	14	16	0	6	0	21	0	2	2	4	2	.67	4	.213	.241	.287	2B	42	80	126	4	23	.981

JERRY WHITE—Jerome Cardell White—Bats: Both; Throws: Right

Ht: 5'10"; Wt: 164 lbs; Born: 8/23/1952 in Shirley, Massachusetts; Debut: 9/16/1974

Division Series		Batting																							Fielding						
Year Tm	Age	G	AB	H	2B	3B	HR	TB	R	RBI	GW	TBB	IBB	SO	HBP	SH	SF	SB	CS	SB%	GDP	Avg	OBP	SLG	Pos	G	PO	A	E	DP	FPct
1981 Mon	29	5	18	3	1	0	0	4	3	1	0	2	0	2	0	0	1	3	2	.60	0	.167	.238	.222	OF	5	12	0	0	0	1.000
LCS		**Batting**																							**Fielding**						
Year Tm	Age	G	AB	H	2B	3B	HR	TB	R	RBI	GW	TBB	IBB	SO	HBP	SH	SF	SB	CS	SB%	GDP	Avg	OBP	SLG	Pos	G	PO	A	E	DP	FPct
1981 Mon	29	5	16	5	1	0	1	9	2	3	1	3	1	1	0	0	0	1	0	1.00	0	.313	.421	.563	OF	5	6	0	0	0	1.000
Postseason Totals		10	34	8	2	0	1	13	5	4	1	5	1	3	0	0	1	4	2	.67	0	.235	.325	.382	OF	10	18	0	0	0	1.000

JO-JO WHITE—Joyner Clifford White—Bats: Left; Throws: Right

Ht: 5'11"; Wt: 165 lbs; Born: 6/1/1909 in Red Oak, Georgia; Debut: 4/15/1932; Died: 10/9/1986

World Series		Batting																							Fielding						
Year Tm	Age	G	AB	H	2B	3B	HR	TB	R	RBI	GW	TBB	IBB	SO	HBP	SH	SF	SB	CS	SB%	GDP	Avg	OBP	SLG	Pos	G	PO	A	E	DP	FPct
1934 Det	25	7	23	3	0	0	0	3	6	0	0	8	0	4	1	0	0	1	2	.33	0	.130	.375	.130	OF	7	21	0	1	0	.955
1935 Det	26	5	19	5	0	0	0	5	3	1	1	5	0	7	0	0	0	0	0	—	0	.263	.417	.263	OF	5	12	0	0	0	1.000
WS Totals		12	42	8	0	0	0	8	9	1	1	13	0	11	1	0	0	1	2	.33	0	.190	.393	.190	OF	12	33	0	1	0	.971

ROY WHITE—Roy Hilton White—Bats: Both; Throws: Right

Ht: 5'10"; Wt: 160 lbs; Born: 12/27/1943 in Los Angeles, California; Debut: 9/7/1965

LCS		Batting																							Fielding						
Year Tm	Age	G	AB	H	2B	3B	HR	TB	R	RBI	GW	TBB	IBB	SO	HBP	SH	SF	SB	CS	SB%	GDP	Avg	OBP	SLG	Pos	G	PO	A	E	DP	FPct
1976 NYA	32	5	17	5	3	0	0	8	4	3	0	5	0	1	0	1	0	1	0	1.00	0	.294	.455	.471	OF	5	17	0	0	0	1.000
1977 NYA	33	4	5	2	2	0	0	4	2	0	0	1	0	0	0	0	0	0	0	—	0	.400	.500	.800	OF	1	2	0	1	0	.667
1978 NYA	34	4	16	5	1	0	1	9	5	1	1	1	1	2	0	0	0	0	0	—	1	.313	.353	.563	OF	3	3	0	0	0	1.000
LCS Totals		13	38	12	6	0	1	21	11	4	1	7	1	3	0	1	0	1	0	1.00	1	.316	.422	.553	OF	9	22	0	1	0	.957
World Series		**Batting**																							**Fielding**						
Year Tm	Age	G	AB	H	2B	3B	HR	TB	R	RBI	GW	TBB	IBB	SO	HBP	SH	SF	SB	CS	SB%	GDP	Avg	OBP	SLG	Pos	G	PO	A	E	DP	FPct
1976 NYA	32	4	15	2	0	0	0	2	0	0	0	3	0	0	0	0	0	0	0	—	0	.133	.278	.133	OF	4	14	0	0	0	1.000
1977 NYA	33	2	2	0	0	0	0	0	0	0	0	0	0	0	0	0	0	0	0	—	0	.000	.000	.000	—						
1978 NYA	34	6	24	8	0	0	1	11	9	4	1	4	0	5	0	1	0	2	0	1.00	0	.333	.429	.458	OF	6	15	0	0	0	1.000
WS Totals		12	41	10	0	0	1	13	9	4	1	7	0	5	0	1	0	2	0	1.00	0	.244	.354	.317	OF	10	29	0	0	0	1.000
Postseason Totals		25	79	22	6	0	2	34	20	8	2	14	1	8	0	2	0	3	0	1.00	1	.278	.387	.430	OF	19	51	0	1	0	.981

BURGESS WHITEHEAD—Burgess Urquhart Whitehead—Nickname: Whitey—Bats: R; Throws: R

Ht: 5'10"; Wt: 160 lbs; Born: 6/29/1910 in Tarboro, N.C.; Deb.: 4/30/1933; Died: 11/25/1993

World Series		Batting																							Fielding						
Year Tm	Age	G	AB	H	2B	3B	HR	TB	R	RBI	GW	TBB	IBB	SO	HBP	SH	SF	SB	CS	SB%	GDP	Avg	OBP	SLG	Pos	G	PO	A	E	DP	FPct
1934 StL	24	1	0	0	0	0	0	0	0	0	0	0	0	0	0	0	0	0	0	—	0	—	—	—	SS	1	1	0	0	0	1.000
1936 NYG	26	6	21	1	0	0	0	1	1	3	0	1	0	3	0	0	0	0	1	.00	0	.048	.091	.048	2B	6	14	20	0	5	1.000
1937 NYG	27	5	16	4	2	0	0	6	1	0	0	2	1	0	0	0	0	1	0	1.00	0	.250	.333	.375	2B	5	8	17	1	5	.962
WS Totals		12	37	5	2	0	0	7	2	3	0	3	1	3	0	0	0	1	1	.50	0	.135	.200	.189	2B	11	22	37	1	10	.983

EARL WHITEHILL—Earl Oliver Whitehill—Throws: Left; Bats: Left

Ht: 5'9"; Wt: 174 lbs; Born: 2/7/1900 in Cedar Rapids, Iowa; Debut: 9/15/1923; Died: 10/22/1954

World Series		Pitching																										
Year Tm	Age	G	GS	CG	GF	IP	BFP	H	R	ER	HR	SH	SF	HB	TBB	IBB	SO	WP	Bk	W	L	Pct	ShO	Sv-Op	Hld	OAvg	OOBP	ERA
1933 Was	33	1	1	1	0	9.0	34	5	0	0	0	0	0	0	2	0	2	1	0	1	0	1.000	1	0- 0	0	.156	.206	0.00

World Series		Batting																							Fielding						
Year Tm	Age	G	AB	H	2B	3B	HR	TB	R	RBI	GW	TBB	IBB	SO	HBP	SH	SF	SB	CS	SB%	GDP	Avg	OBP	SLG	Pos	G	PO	A	E	DP	FPct
1933 Was	33	1	3	0	0	0	0	0	0	0	0	0	0	0	0	0	0	0	0	—	0	.000	.000	.000	P	1	0	4	0	0	1.000

GEORGE WHITEMAN—Nickname: Lucky—Bats: Right; Throws: Right

Ht: 5'7"; Wt: 160 lbs; Born: 12/23/1882 in Peoria, Illinois; Debut: 9/13/1907; Died: 2/10/1947

World Series		Batting																							Fielding						
Year Tm	Age	G	AB	H	2B	3B	HR	TB	R	RBI	GW	TBB	IBB	SO	HBP	SH	SF	SB	CS	SB%	GDP	Avg	OBP	SLG	Pos	G	PO	A	E	DP	FPct
1918 Bos	35	6	20	5	0	1	0	7	2	1	0	2	0	1	1	0	0	1	0	1.00	1	.250	.348	.350	OF	6	15	2	1	1	.944

TERRY WHITFIELD—Terry Bertland Whitfield—Bats: Left; Throws: Right

Ht: 6'1"; Wt: 197 lbs; Born: 1/12/1953 in Blythe, California; Debut: 9/29/1974

LCS		Batting																							Fielding						
Year Tm	Age	G	AB	H	2B	3B	HR	TB	R	RBI	GW	TBB	IBB	SO	HBP	SH	SF	SB	CS	SB%	GDP	Avg	OBP	SLG	Pos	G	PO	A	E	DP	FPct
1985 LA	32	1	0	0	0	0	0	0	0	0	0	0	0	0	0	0	0	0	0	—	0	—	—	—	—						

DICK WHITMAN—Dick Corwin Whitman—Bats: Left; Throws: Right

Ht: 5'11"; Wt: 170 lbs; Born: 11/9/1920 in Woodburn, Oregon; Debut: 4/16/1946

World Series		Batting																							Fielding						
Year Tm	Age	G	AB	H	2B	3B	HR	TB	R	RBI	GW	TBB	IBB	SO	HBP	SH	SF	SB	CS	SB%	GDP	Avg	OBP	SLG	Pos	G	PO	A	E	DP	FPct
1949 Bro	28	1	1	0	0	0	0	0	0	0	0	0	0	1	0	0	0	0	0	—	0	.000	.000	.000	—						
1950 Phi	29	3	2	0	0	0	0	0	0	0	0	1	1	0	0	0	0	0	0	—	0	.000	.333	.000	—						
WS Totals		4	3	0	0	0	0	0	0	0	0	1	1	1	0	0	0	0	0	—	0	.000	.250	.000	—	0	0	0	0	0	—

ED WHITSON
Eddie Lee Whitson—Throws: Right; Bats: Right — Ht: 6'3"; Wt: 195 lbs; Born: 5/19/1955 in Johnson City, Tennessee; Debut: 9/4/1977

LCS

Year	Tm	Age	G	GS	CG	GF	IP	BFP	H	R	ER	HR	SH	SF	HB	TBB	IBB	SO	WP	Bk	W	L	Pct	ShO	Sv-Op	Hld	OAvg	OOBP	ERA
1984	SD	29	1	1	0	0	8.0	30	5	1	1	0	0	0	0	2	0	6	0	0	1	0	1.000	0	0-0	0	.179	.233	1.13

World Series

Year	Tm	Age	G	GS	CG	GF	IP	BFP	H	R	ER	HR	SH	SF	HB	TBB	IBB	SO	WP	Bk	W	L	Pct	ShO	Sv-Op	Hld	OAvg	OOBP	ERA
1984	SD	29	1	1	0	0	0.2	7	5	3	3	0	0	1	0	0	0	0	0	0	0	0	—	0	0-0	0	.833	.714	40.50
Postseason Totals			2	2	0	0	8.2	74	10	4	4	0	0	1	0	2	0	6	0	0	1	0	1.000				.294	.324	4.15

LCS

Year	Tm	Age	G	AB	H	2B	3B	HR	TB	R	RBI	GW	TBB	IBB	SO	HBP	SH	SF	SB	CS	SB%	GDP	Avg	OBP	SLG	Pos	G	PO	A	E	DP	FPct
1984	SD	29	1	3	0	0	0	0	0	0	0	0	0	0	1	0	0	0	0	0	—	0	.000	.000	.000	P	1	1	0	0	0	1.000

World Series

Year	Tm	Age	G	AB	H	2B	3B	HR	TB	R	RBI	GW	TBB	IBB	SO	HBP	SH	SF	SB	CS	SB%	GDP	Avg	OBP	SLG	Pos	G	PO	A	E	DP	FPct
1984	SD	29	1	0	0	0	0	0	0	0	0	0	0	0	0	0	0	0	0	0	—	0	—	—	—	P	1	0	0	0	0	—
Postseason Totals			2	3	0	0	0	0	0	0	0	0	0	0	1	0	0	0	0	0	—	0	.000	.000	.000	P	2	1	0	0	0	1.000

ERNIE WHITT
Leo Ernest Whitt—Bats: Left; Throws: Right — Ht: 6'2"; Wt: 200 lbs; Born: 6/13/1952 in Detroit, Michigan; Debut: 9/12/1976

LCS

Year	Tm	Age	G	AB	H	2B	3B	HR	TB	R	RBI	GW	TBB	IBB	SO	HBP	SH	SF	SB	CS	SB%	GDP	Avg	OBP	SLG	Pos	G	PO	A	E	DP	FPct
1985	Tor	33	7	21	4	1	0	0	5	1	2	1	2	0	4	0	0	0	0	0	—	0	.190	.261	.238	C	7	50	3	0	1	1.000
1989	Tor	37	5	16	2	0	0	1	5	1	3	1	2	0	3	0	0	1	0	0	—	0	.125	.211	.313	C	5	32	2	0	0	1.000
LCS Totals			12	37	6	1	0	1	10	2	5	2	4	0	7	0	0	1	0	0	—	0	.162	.238	.270	C	12	82	5	0	1	1.000

POSSUM WHITTED
George Bostic Whitted—Bats: Right; Throws: Right — Ht: 5'8"; Wt: 168 lbs; Born: 2/4/1890 in Durham, North Carolina; Debut: 9/16/1912; Died: 10/16/1962

World Series

Year	Tm	Age	G	AB	H	2B	3B	HR	TB	R	RBI	GW	TBB	IBB	SO	HBP	SH	SF	SB	CS	SB%	GDP	Avg	OBP	SLG	Pos	G	PO	A	E	DP	FPct
1914	Bos	24	4	14	3	0	1	0	5	2	2	0	3	0	1	0	0	0	1	0	1.00	1	.214	.353	.357	OF	4	6	0	0	0	1.000
1915	Phi	25	5	15	1	0	0	0	1	0	1	0	1	0	0	0	0	1	1	0	1.00	0	.067	.125	.067	1B	1	2	0	0	1	1.000
																										OF	5	12	0	0	0	1.000
WS Totals			9	29	4	0	1	0	6	2	3	0	4	0	1	0	1	0	2	0	1.00	1	.138	.242	.207	OF	9	18	0	0	0	1.000

KEMP WICKER
Kemp Caswell Wicker—Throws: Left; Bats: Right — Ht: 5'11"; Wt: 182 lbs; Born: 8/13/1906 in Kernersville, North Carolina; Debut: 8/14/1936; Died: 6/11/1973

World Series

Year	Tm	Age	G	GS	CG	GF	IP	BFP	H	R	ER	HR	SH	SF	HB	TBB	IBB	SO	WP	Bk	W	L	Pct	ShO	Sv-Op	Hld	OAvg	OOBP	ERA
1937	NYA	31	1	0	0	1	1.0	3	0	0	0	0	0	0	0	0	0	0	0	0	0	0	—	0	0-0	0	.000	.000	0.00

World Series

Year	Tm	Age	G	AB	H	2B	3B	HR	TB	R	RBI	GW	TBB	IBB	SO	HBP	SH	SF	SB	CS	SB%	GDP	Avg	OBP	SLG	Pos	G	PO	A	E	DP	FPct
1937	NYA	31	1	0	0	0	0	0	0	0	0	0	0	0	0	0	0	0	0	0	—	0	—	—	—	P	1	0	0	0	0	—

BOB WICKMAN
Robert Joe Wickman—Throws: Right; Bats: Right — Ht: 6'1"; Wt: 207 lbs; Born: 2/6/1969 in Green Bay, Wisconsin; Debut: 8/24/1992

Division Series

Year	Tm	Age	G	GS	CG	GF	IP	BFP	H	R	ER	HR	SH	SF	HB	TBB	IBB	SO	WP	Bk	W	L	Pct	ShO	Sv-Op	Hld	OAvg	OOBP	ERA
1995	NYA	26	3	0	0	0	3.0	14	5	0	0	0	1	1	0	0	0	3	0	0	0	0	—	0	0-0	0	.417	.385	0.00

Division Series

Year	Tm	Age	G	AB	H	2B	3B	HR	TB	R	RBI	GW	TBB	IBB	SO	HBP	SH	SF	SB	CS	SB%	GDP	Avg	OBP	SLG	Pos	G	PO	A	E	DP	FPct
1995	NYA	26	3	0	0	0	0	0	0	0	0	0	0	0	0	0	0	0	0	0	—	0	—	—	—	P	3	0	1	0	0	1.000

CHRIS WIDGER
Christopher Jon Widger—Bats: Right; Throws: Right — Ht: 6'3"; Wt: 195 lbs; Born: 5/21/1971 in Wilmington, Delaware; Debut: 6/23/1995

Division Series

Year	Tm	Age	G	AB	H	2B	3B	HR	TB	R	RBI	GW	TBB	IBB	SO	HBP	SH	SF	SB	CS	SB%	GDP	Avg	OBP	SLG	Pos	G	PO	A	E	DP	FPct
1995	Sea	24	2	3	0	0	0	0	0	0	0	0	0	0	3	0	0	0	0	0	—	0	.000	.000	.000	C	2	14	0	0	0	1.000

LCS

Year	Tm	Age	G	AB	H	2B	3B	HR	TB	R	RBI	GW	TBB	IBB	SO	HBP	SH	SF	SB	CS	SB%	GDP	Avg	OBP	SLG	Pos	G	PO	A	E	DP	FPct
1995	Sea	24	3	1	0	0	0	0	0	0	0	0	0	0	1	0	0	0	0	0	—	0	.000	.000	.000	C	3	7	0	0	0	1.000
Postseason Totals			5	4	0	0	0	0	0	0	0	0	0	0	4	0	0	0	0	0	—	0	.000	.000	.000	C	5	21	0	0	0	1.000

ALAN WIGGINS
Alan Anthony Wiggins—Bats: Both; Throws: Right — Ht: 6'2"; Wt: 160 lbs; Born: 2/17/1958 in Los Angeles, California; Debut: 9/4/1981; Died: 1/6/1991

LCS

Year	Tm	Age	G	AB	H	2B	3B	HR	TB	R	RBI	GW	TBB	IBB	SO	HBP	SH	SF	SB	CS	SB%	GDP	Avg	OBP	SLG	Pos	G	PO	A	E	DP	FPct
1984	SD	26	5	19	6	0	0	0	6	4	1	0	2	0	2	0	1	0	0	1	.00	2	.316	.381	.316	2B	5	11	11	0	3	1.000

World Series

Year	Tm	Age	G	AB	H	2B	3B	HR	TB	R	RBI	GW	TBB	IBB	SO	HBP	SH	SF	SB	CS	SB%	GDP	Avg	OBP	SLG	Pos	G	PO	A	E	DP	FPct
1984	SD	26	5	22	8	1	0	0	9	2	1	0	0	0	2	0	0	0	1	1	.50	0	.364	.364	.409	2B	5	13	6	2	1	.905
Postseason Totals			10	41	14	1	0	0	15	6	2	0	2	0	4	0	1	0	1	2	.33	2	.341	.372	.366	2B	10	24	17	2	4	.953

MILT WILCOX
Milton Edward Wilcox—Throws: Right; Bats: Right — Ht: 6'2"; Wt: 185 lbs; Born: 4/20/1950 in Honolulu, Hawaii; Debut: 9/5/1970

LCS

Year	Tm	Age	G	GS	CG	GF	IP	BFP	H	R	ER	HR	SH	SF	HB	TBB	IBB	SO	WP	Bk	W	L	Pct	ShO	Sv-Op	Hld	OAvg	OOBP	ERA
1970	Cin	20	1	0	0	0	3.0	12	1	0	0	0	0	0	0	2	0	5	0	0	1	0	1.000	0	0-0	0	.100	.250	0.00
1984	Det	34	1	1	0	0	8.0	28	2	0	0	0	0	0	0	2	0	8	0	0	1	0	1.000	0	0-0	0	.077	.143	0.00
LCS Totals			2	1	0	0	11.0	40	3	0	0	0	0	0	0	4	0	13	0	0	2	0	1.000	0	0-0	0	.083	.175	0.00

World Series

Year	Tm	Age	G	GS	CG	GF	IP	BFP	H	R	ER	HR	SH	SF	HB	TBB	IBB	SO	WP	Bk	W	L	Pct	ShO	Sv-Op	Hld	OAvg	OOBP	ERA
1970	Cin	20	2	0	0	0	2.0	9	3	2	2	0	0	0	0	0	0	2	0	0	0	1	.000	0	0-0	0	.333	.333	9.00
1984	Det	34	1	1	0	0	6.0	27	7	1	1	0	0	0	0	2	0	4	0	0	1	0	1.000	0	0-0	0	.280	.333	1.50
WS Totals			3	1	0	0	8.0	72	10	3	3	0	0	0	0	2	0	6	0	0	1	1	.500	0	0-0	0	.294	.333	3.38
Postseason Totals			5	2	0	0	19.0	152	13	3	3	0	0	0	0	6	0	19	0	0	3	1	.750	0	0-0	0	.186	.250	1.42

LCS

Year	Tm	Age	G	AB	H	2B	3B	HR	TB	R	RBI	GW	TBB	IBB	SO	HBP	SH	SF	SB	CS	SB%	GDP	Avg	OBP	SLG	Pos	G	PO	A	E	DP	FPct
1970	Cin	20	1	0	0	0	0	0	0	0	0	0	0	0	0	0	0	0	0	0	—	0	—	—	—	P	1	0	1	0	0	1.000
1984	Det	34	1	0	0	0	0	0	0	0	0	0	0	0	0	0	0	0	0	0	—	0	—	—	—	P	1	2	0	0	0	1.000
LCS Totals			2	0	0	0	0	0	0	0	0	0	0	0	0	0	0	0	0	0	—	0	—	—	—	P	2	2	1	0	0	1.000

World Series

Year	Tm	Age	G	AB	H	2B	3B	HR	TB	R	RBI	GW	TBB	IBB	SO	HBP	SH	SF	SB	CS	SB%	GDP	Avg	OBP	SLG	Pos	G	PO	A	E	DP	FPct
1970	Cin	20	2	0	0	0	0	0	0	0	0	0	0	0	0	0	0	0	0	0	—	0	—	—	—	P	2	0	1	0	0	1.000
1984	Det	34	1	0	0	0	0	0	0	0	0	0	0	0	0	0	0	0	0	0	—	0	—	—	—	P	1	1	1	0	0	1.000
WS Totals			3	0	0	0	0	0	0	0	0	0	0	0	0	0	0	0	0	0	—	0	—	—	—	P	3	1	2	0	0	1.000
Postseason Totals			5	0	0	0	0	0	0	0	0	0	0	0	0	0	0	0	0	0	—	0	—	—	—	P	5	3	3	0	0	1.000

ROB WILFONG
Robert Daniel Wilfong—Bats: Left; Throws: Right — Ht: 6'1"; Wt: 180 lbs; Born: 9/1/1953 in Pasadena, California; Debut: 4/10/1977

LCS

Year	Tm	Age	G	AB	H	2B	3B	HR	TB	R	RBI	GW	TBB	IBB	SO	HBP	SH	SF	SB	CS	SB%	GDP	Avg	OBP	SLG	Pos	G	PO	A	E	DP	FPct
1982	Cal	29	2	1	0	0	0	0	0	0	0	0	0	0	1	0	0	0	0	0	—	0	.000	.000	.000	—						
1986	Cal	33	4	13	4	1	0	0	5	1	2	0	0	0	2	0	0	0	0	0	—	0	.308	.308	.385	2B	4	8	10	0	6	1.000
LCS Totals			6	14	4	1	0	0	5	1	2	0	0	0	3	0	0	0	0	0	—	0	.286	.286	.357	2B	4	8	10	0	6	1.000

HOYT WILHELM (HOF 1985-W)—James Hoyt Wilhelm—Nickname: Old Tilt—Throws: Right; Bats: Right

Ht: 6'0"; Wt: 190 lbs; Born: 7/26/1923 in Huntersville, North Carolina; Debut: 4/19/1952

World Series — Pitching

Year Tm	Age	G	GS	CG	GF	IP	BFP	H	R	ER	HR	SH	SF	HB	TBB	IBB	SO	WP	Bk	W	L	Pct	ShO	Sv-Op	Hld	OAvg	OOBP	ERA
1954 NYG	31	2	0	0	1	2.1	9	1	0	0	0	0	0	0	0	0	3	0	0	0	0	—	0	1- 1	1	.111	.111	0.00

World Series — Batting / Fielding

Year Tm	Age	G	AB	H	2B	3B	HR	TB	R	RBI	GW	TBB	IBB	SO	HBP	SH	SF	SB	CS	SB%	GDP	Avg	OBP	SLG	Pos	G	PO	A	E	DP	FPct
1954 NYG	31	2	1	0	0	0	0	0	0	0	0	0	0	1	0	0	0	0	0	—	0	.000	.000	.000	P	2	0	1	1	0	.500

JOE WILHOIT—Joseph William Wilhoit—Bats: Left; Throws: Right

Ht: 6'2"; Wt: 175 lbs; Born: 12/20/1885 in Hiawatha, Kansas; Debut: 4/12/1916; Died: 9/25/1930

World Series — Batting / Fielding

Year Tm	Age	G	AB	H	2B	3B	HR	TB	R	RBI	GW	TBB	IBB	SO	HBP	SH	SF	SB	CS	SB%	GDP	Avg	OBP	SLG	Pos	G	PO	A	E	DP	FPct
1917 NYG	31	2	1	0	0	0	0	0	0	0	0	1	0	0	0	0	0	0	0	—	0	.000	.500	.000	—						

CURTIS WILKERSON—Curtis Vernon Wilkerson—Bats: Both; Throws: Right

Ht: 5'9"; Wt: 158 lbs; Born: 4/26/1961 in Petersburg, Virginia; Debut: 9/10/1983

LCS — Batting / Fielding

Year Tm	Age	G	AB	H	2B	3B	HR	TB	R	RBI	GW	TBB	IBB	SO	HBP	SH	SF	SB	CS	SB%	GDP	Avg	OBP	SLG	Pos	G	PO	A	E	DP	FPct
1989 ChN	28	3	2	1	0	0	0	1	1	0	0	0	0	0	0	0	0	0	0	—	0	.500	.500	.500	3B	1	0	0	0	0	—
1991 Pit	30	4	4	0	0	0	0	0	0	0	0	0	0	3	0	0	0	0	0	—	0	.000	.000	.000	—						
LCS Totals		7	6	1	0	0	0	1	1	0	0	0	0	3	0	0	0	0	0	—	0	.167	.167	.167	3B	1	0	0	0	0	—

RICK WILKINS—Richard David Wilkins—Bats: Left; Throws: Right

Ht: 6'2"; Wt: 210 lbs; Born: 6/4/1967 in Jacksonville, Florida; Debut: 6/6/1991

Division Series — Batting / Fielding

Year Tm	Age	G	AB	H	2B	3B	HR	TB	R	RBI	GW	TBB	IBB	SO	HBP	SH	SF	SB	CS	SB%	GDP	Avg	OBP	SLG	Pos	G	PO	A	E	DP	FPct
1997 Sea	30	1	0	0	0	0	0	0	0	0	0	1	0	0	0	0	0	0	0	—	0	—	1.000	—	C	1	2	0	0	0	1.000

ROY WILKINSON—Roy Hamilton Wilkinson—Throws: Right; Bats: Right

Ht: 6'1"; Wt: 170 lbs; Born: 5/8/1894 in Canandaigua, New York; Debut: 4/29/1918; Died: 7/2/1956

World Series — Pitching

Year Tm	Age	G	GS	CG	GF	IP	BFP	H	R	ER	HR	SH	SF	HB	TBB	IBB	SO	WP	Bk	W	L	Pct	ShO	Sv-Op	Hld	OAvg	OOBP	ERA
1919 ChA	25	2	0	0	1	7.1	34	9	4	2	0	3	0	1	4	0	3	0	0	0	0	—	0	0- 0	0	.346	.452	2.45

World Series — Batting / Fielding

Year Tm	Age	G	AB	H	2B	3B	HR	TB	R	RBI	GW	TBB	IBB	SO	HBP	SH	SF	SB	CS	SB%	GDP	Avg	OBP	SLG	Pos	G	PO	A	E	DP	FPct
1919 ChA	25	2	2	0	0	0	0	0	0	0	0	0	0	1	0	0	0	0	0	—	0	.000	.000	.000	P	2	0	2	0	0	1.000

TED WILKS—Theodore Wilks—Nickname: Cork—Throws: Right; Bats: Right

Ht: 5'9"; Wt: 178 lbs; Born: 11/13/1915 in Fulton, New York; Debut: 4/25/1944; Died: 8/21/1989

World Series — Pitching

Year Tm	Age	G	GS	CG	GF	IP	BFP	H	R	ER	HR	SH	SF	HB	TBB	IBB	SO	WP	Bk	W	L	Pct	ShO	Sv-Op	Hld	OAvg	OOBP	ERA
1944 StL	28	2	1	0	1	6.1	27	5	4	4	0	0	0	0	3	0	7	0	0	0	1	.000	0	1- 1	0	.208	.296	5.68
1946 StL	30	1	0	0	1	1.0	6	2	1	0	0	0	0	0	0	0	0	0	0	0	0	—	0	0- 0	0	.333	.333	0.00
WS Totals		3	1	0	2	7.1	66	7	5	4	0	0	0	0	3	0	7	0	0	0	1	.000	0	1-1	0	.233	.303	4.91

World Series — Batting / Fielding

Year Tm	Age	G	AB	H	2B	3B	HR	TB	R	RBI	GW	TBB	IBB	SO	HBP	SH	SF	SB	CS	SB%	GDP	Avg	OBP	SLG	Pos	G	PO	A	E	DP	FPct
1944 StL	28	2	2	0	0	0	0	0	0	0	0	0	0	2	0	1	0	0	0	—	0	.000	.000	.000	P	2	0	1	0	0	1.000
1946 StL	30	1	0	0	0	0	0	0	0	0	0	0	0	0	0	0	0	0	0	—	0	—	—	—	P	1	0	1	0	0	1.000
WS Totals		3	2	0	0	0	0	0	0	0	0	0	0	2	0	1	0	0	0	—	0	.000	.000	.000	P	3	0	2	0	0	1.000

JERRY WILLARD—Gerald Duane Willard—Bats: Left; Throws: Right

Ht: 6'2"; Wt: 195 lbs; Born: 3/14/1960 in Oxnard, California; Debut: 4/11/1984

LCS — Batting / Fielding

Year Tm	Age	G	AB	H	2B	3B	HR	TB	R	RBI	GW	TBB	IBB	SO	HBP	SH	SF	SB	CS	SB%	GDP	Avg	OBP	SLG	Pos	G	PO	A	E	DP	FPct
1991 Atl	31	2	2	0	0	0	0	0	0	0	0	0	0	1	0	0	0	0	0	—	0	.000	.000	.000	—						

World Series — Batting / Fielding

Year Tm	Age	G	AB	H	2B	3B	HR	TB	R	RBI	GW	TBB	IBB	SO	HBP	SH	SF	SB	CS	SB%	GDP	Avg	OBP	SLG	Pos	G	PO	A	E	DP	FPct
1991 Atl	31	1	0	0	0	0	0	0	0	1	1	0	0	0	0	0	1	0	0	—	0	—	.000	—	—						
Postseason Totals		3	2	0	0	0	0	0	0	1	1	0	0	1	0	0	1	0	0	—	0	.000	.000	.000	—	0	0	0	0	0	—

ED WILLETT—Robert Edgar Willett—Throws: Right; Bats: Right

Ht: 6'0"; Wt: 183 lbs; Born: 3/7/1884 in Norfolk, Virginia; Debut: 9/5/1906; Died: 5/10/1934

World Series — Pitching

Year Tm	Age	G	GS	CG	GF	IP	BFP	H	R	ER	HR	SH	SF	HB	TBB	IBB	SO	WP	Bk	W	L	Pct	ShO	Sv-Op	Hld	OAvg	OOBP	ERA
1909 Det	25	2	0	0	1	7.2	27	3	1	0	0	0	0	2	0	0	1	0	0	0	0	—	0	0- 0	0	.120	.185	0.00

World Series — Batting / Fielding

Year Tm	Age	G	AB	H	2B	3B	HR	TB	R	RBI	GW	TBB	IBB	SO	HBP	SH	SF	SB	CS	SB%	GDP	Avg	OBP	SLG	Pos	G	PO	A	E	DP	FPct
1909 Det	25	2	2	0	0	0	0	0	0	0	0	0	0	0	0	0	0	0	0	—	0	.000	.000	.000	P	2	1	3	1	0	.800

CARL WILLEY—Carlton Francis Willey—Throws: Right; Bats: Right

Ht: 6'0"; Wt: 175 lbs; Born: 6/6/1931 in Cherryfield, Maine; Debut: 4/30/1958

World Series — Pitching

Year Tm	Age	G	GS	CG	GF	IP	BFP	H	R	ER	HR	SH	SF	HB	TBB	IBB	SO	WP	Bk	W	L	Pct	ShO	Sv-Op	Hld	OAvg	OOBP	ERA
1958 Mil	27	1	0	0	1	1.0	3	0	0	0	0	0	0	0	0	0	2	0	0	0	0	—	0	0- 0	0	.000	.000	0.00

World Series — Batting / Fielding

Year Tm	Age	G	AB	H	2B	3B	HR	TB	R	RBI	GW	TBB	IBB	SO	HBP	SH	SF	SB	CS	SB%	GDP	Avg	OBP	SLG	Pos	G	PO	A	E	DP	FPct
1958 Mil	27	1	0	0	0	0	0	0	0	0	0	0	0	0	0	0	0	0	0	—	0	—	—	—	P	1	0	0	0	0	—

BERNIE WILLIAMS—Bernabe Williams—Bats: Both; Throws: Right

Ht: 6'2"; Wt: 180 lbs; Born: 9/13/1968 in San Juan, Puerto Rico; Debut: 7/7/1991

Division Series — Batting / Fielding

Year Tm	Age	G	AB	H	2B	3B	HR	TB	R	RBI	GW	TBB	IBB	SO	HBP	SH	SF	SB	CS	SB%	GDP	Avg	OBP	SLG	Pos	G	PO	A	E	DP	FPct
1995 NYA	27	5	21	9	2	0	2	17	8	5	1	7	1	3	0	0	0	1	0	1.00	0	.429	.571	.810	OF	5	13	0	0	0	1.000
1996 NYA	28	4	15	7	0	0	3	16	5	5	0	2	0	1	0	0	1	1	1	.50	0	.467	.500	1.067	OF	4	10	0	0	0	1.000
1997 NYA	29	5	17	2	1	0	0	3	3	1	0	4	0	3	1	0	0	0	0	—	1	.118	.318	.176	OF	5	7	0	0	0	1.000
DS Totals		14	53	18	3	0	5	36	16	11	1	13	1	7	1	0	1	2	1	.67	1	.340	.471	.679	OF	14	30	0	0	0	1.000

LCS — Batting / Fielding

Year Tm	Age	G	AB	H	2B	3B	HR	TB	R	RBI	GW	TBB	IBB	SO	HBP	SH	SF	SB	CS	SB%	GDP	Avg	OBP	SLG	Pos	G	PO	A	E	DP	FPct
1996 NYA	28	5	19	9	3	0	2	18	6	6	2	5	1	4	0	0	0	1	0	1.00	0	.474	.583	.947	OF	5	20	0	0	0	1.000

World Series — Batting / Fielding

Year Tm	Age	G	AB	H	2B	3B	HR	TB	R	RBI	GW	TBB	IBB	SO	HBP	SH	SF	SB	CS	SB%	GDP	Avg	OBP	SLG	Pos	G	PO	A	E	DP	FPct
1996 NYA	28	6	24	4	0	0	1	7	3	4	1	3	1	6	0	0	0	1	0	1.00	1	.167	.259	.292	OF	6	15	0	0	0	1.000
Postseason Totals		25	96	31	6	0	8	61	25	21	4	21	3	17	1	0	1	4	1	.80	2	.323	.445	.635	OF	25	65	0	0	0	1.000

BILLY WILLIAMS (HOF 1987-W)—Billy Leo Williams—Bats: Left; Throws: Right

Ht: 6'1"; Wt: 175 lbs; Born: 6/15/1938 in Whistler, Alabama; Debut: 8/6/1959

LCS — Batting / Fielding

Year Tm	Age	G	AB	H	2B	3B	HR	TB	R	RBI	GW	TBB	IBB	SO	HBP	SH	SF	SB	CS	SB%	GDP	Avg	OBP	SLG	Pos	G	PO	A	E	DP	FPct
1975 Oak	37	3	8	0	0	0	0	0	0	0	0	1	0	1	0	0	0	0	0	—	0	.000	.111	.000	—						

DAVEY WILLIAMS—David Carlous Williams—Bats: Right; Throws: Right

Ht: 5'10"; Wt: 160 lbs; Born: 11/2/1927 in Dallas, Texas; Debut: 9/16/1949

World Series		Batting																							Fielding						
Year Tm	Age	G	AB	H	2B	3B	HR	TB	R	RBI	GW	TBB	IBB	SO	HBP	SH	SF	SB	CS	SB%	GDP	Avg	OBP	SLG	Pos	G	PO	A	E	DP	FPct
1951 NYG	23	2	1	0	0	0	0	0	0	0	0	0	0	0	0	0	0	0	0	—	0	.000	.000	.000	—						
1954 NYG	26	4	11	0	0	0	0	0	0	1	0	2	0	2	0	2	0	0	0	—	0	.000	.154	.000	2B	4	10	9	1	2	.950
WS Totals		6	12	0	0	0	0	0	0	1	0	2	0	2	0	2	0	0	0	—	0	.000	.143	.000	2B	4	10	9	1	2	.950

DEWEY WILLIAMS—Dewey Edgar Williams—Nickname: Dee—Bats: Right; Throws: Right

Ht: 6'0"; Wt: 160 lbs; Born: 2/5/1916 in Durham, North Carolina; Debut: 6/28/1944

World Series		Batting																							Fielding						
Year Tm	Age	G	AB	H	2B	3B	HR	TB	R	RBI	GW	TBB	IBB	SO	HBP	SH	SF	SB	CS	SB%	GDP	Avg	OBP	SLG	Pos	G	PO	A	E	DP	FPct
1945 ChN	29	2	2	0	0	0	0	0	0	0	0	0	0	1	0	0	0	0	0	—	0	.000	.000	.000	C	1	1	1	0	0	1.000

DIB WILLIAMS—Edwin Dibrell Williams—Bats: Right; Throws: Right

Ht: 5'11"; Wt: 175 lbs; Born: 1/19/1910 in Greenbrier, Arkansas; Debut: 4/27/1930; Died: 4/2/1992

World Series		Batting																							Fielding						
Year Tm	Age	G	AB	H	2B	3B	HR	TB	R	RBI	GW	TBB	IBB	SO	HBP	SH	SF	SB	CS	SB%	GDP	Avg	OBP	SLG	Pos	G	PO	A	E	DP	FPct
1931 Phi	21	7	25	8	1	0	0	9	2	1	1	2	1	9	0	0	0	0	0	—	0	.320	.370	.360	SS	7	7	24	0	2	1.000

DICK WILLIAMS—Richard Hirschfeld Williams—Bats: Right; Throws: Right

Ht: 6'0"; Wt: 190 lbs; Born: 5/7/1929 in St. Louis, Missouri; Debut: 6/10/1951

World Series		Batting																							Fielding						
Year Tm	Age	G	AB	H	2B	3B	HR	TB	R	RBI	GW	TBB	IBB	SO	HBP	SH	SF	SB	CS	SB%	GDP	Avg	OBP	SLG	Pos	G	PO	A	E	DP	FPct
1953 Bro	24	3	2	1	0	0	0	1	0	0	0	1	0	1	0	0	0	0	0	—	0	.500	.667	.500	—						

EARL WILLIAMS—Earl Craig Williams—Bats: Right; Throws: Right

Ht: 6'3"; Wt: 215 lbs; Born: 7/14/1948 in Newark, New Jersey; Debut: 9/13/1970

LCS		Batting																							Fielding						
Year Tm	Age	G	AB	H	2B	3B	HR	TB	R	RBI	GW	TBB	IBB	SO	HBP	SH	SF	SB	CS	SB%	GDP	Avg	OBP	SLG	Pos	G	PO	A	E	DP	FPct
1973 Bal	25	5	18	5	2	0	1	10	2	4	0	2	0	2	0	0	0	0	0	—	0	.278	.350	.556	C	1	8	0	0	0	1.000
																									1B	4	35	2	0	2	1.000
1974 Bal	26	2	6	0	0	0	0	0	0	0	0	0	0	2	0	0	0	0	0	—	0	.000	.000	.000	1B	2	16	1	1	3	.944
LCS Totals		7	24	5	2	0	1	10	2	4	0	2	0	4	0	0	0	0	0	—	0	.208	.269	.417	1B	6	51	3	1	5	.982

GERALD WILLIAMS—Gerald Floyd Williams—Bats: Right; Throws: Right

Ht: 6'2"; Wt: 190 lbs; Born: 8/10/1966 in New Orleans, Louisiana; Debut: 9/15/1992

Division Series		Batting																							Fielding						
Year Tm	Age	G	AB	H	2B	3B	HR	TB	R	RBI	GW	TBB	IBB	SO	HBP	SH	SF	SB	CS	SB%	GDP	Avg	OBP	SLG	Pos	G	PO	A	E	DP	FPct
1995 NYA	29	5	5	0	0	0	0	0	1	0	0	2	0	3	0	0	0	0	0	—	0	.000	.286	.000	OF	5	7	1	0	1	1.000

LEFTY WILLIAMS—Claude Preston Williams—Throws: Left; Bats: Right

Ht: 5'9"; Wt: 160 lbs; Born: 3/9/1893 in Aurora, Missouri; Debut: 9/17/1913; Died: 11/4/1959

World Series		Pitching																										
Year Tm	Age	G	GS	CG	GF	IP	BFP	H	R	ER	HR	SH	SF	HB	TBB	IBB	SO	WP	Bk	W	L	Pct	ShO	Sv-Op	Hld	OAvg	OOBP	ERA
1917 ChA	24	1	0	0	0	1.0	6	2	1	1	0	0	0	0	0	0	3	0	0	0	0	—	0	0-0	0	.333	.333	9.00
1919 ChA	26	3	3	1	0	16.1	66	12	12	12	0	4	1	0	8	0	4	0	0	0	3	.000	0	0-0	0	.226	.323	6.61
WS Totals		4	3	1	0	17.1	144	14	13	13	0	4	1	0	8	0	7	0	0	0	3	.000	0	0-0	0	.237	.324	6.75

World Series		Batting																							Fielding						
Year Tm	Age	G	AB	H	2B	3B	HR	TB	R	RBI	GW	TBB	IBB	SO	HBP	SH	SF	SB	CS	SB%	GDP	Avg	OBP	SLG	Pos	G	PO	A	E	DP	FPct
1917 ChA	24	1	0	0	0	0	0	0	0	0	0	0	0	0	0	0	0	0	0	—	0	—	—	—	P	1	0	0	1	0	.000
1919 ChA	26	3	5	1	0	0	0	1	0	0	0	0	0	3	0	0	0	0	0	—	0	.200	.200	.200	P	3	1	2	0	0	1.000
WS Totals		4	5	1	0	0	0	1	0	0	0	0	0	3	0	0	0	0	0	—	0	.200	.200	.200	P	4	1	2	1	0	.750

MATT WILLIAMS—Matthew Derrick Williams—Bats: Right; Throws: Right

Ht: 6'2"; Wt: 205 lbs; Born: 11/28/1965 in Bishop, California; Debut: 4/11/1987

Division Series		Batting																							Fielding						
Year Tm	Age	G	AB	H	2B	3B	HR	TB	R	RBI	GW	TBB	IBB	SO	HBP	SH	SF	SB	CS	SB%	GDP	Avg	OBP	SLG	Pos	G	PO	A	E	DP	FPct
1997 Cle	31	5	17	4	1	0	1	8	4	3	0	3	0	3	1	0	0	0	0	—	0	.235	.381	.471	3B	5	2	10	0	1	1.000
LCS		Batting																							Fielding						
Year Tm	Age	G	AB	H	2B	3B	HR	TB	R	RBI	GW	TBB	IBB	SO	HBP	SH	SF	SB	CS	SB%	GDP	Avg	OBP	SLG	Pos	G	PO	A	E	DP	FPct
1989 SF	23	5	20	6	1	0	2	13	2	9	1	0	0	2	1	0	0	0	0	—	0	.300	.333	.650	3B	5	5	12	0	2	1.000
																									SS	1	0	0	0	0	—
1997 Cle	31	6	23	5	1	0	0	6	1	2	0	3	0	7	0	0	0	1	0	1.00	0	.217	.308	.261	3B	6	6	18	2	3	.923
LCS Totals		11	43	11	2	0	2	19	3	11	1	3	0	9	1	0	0	1	0	1.00	0	.256	.319	.442	3B	11	11	30	2	5	.953
World Series		Batting																							Fielding						
Year Tm	Age	G	AB	H	2B	3B	HR	TB	R	RBI	GW	TBB	IBB	SO	HBP	SH	SF	SB	CS	SB%	GDP	Avg	OBP	SLG	Pos	G	PO	A	E	DP	FPct
1989 SF	23	4	16	2	0	0	1	5	1	1	0	0	0	6	0	0	0	0	0	—	0	.125	.125	.313	3B	3	2	6	0	2	1.000
																									SS	4	2	6	0	0	1.000
1997 Cle	31	7	26	10	1	0	1	14	8	3	0	7	0	6	0	0	0	0	0	—	0	.385	.515	.538	3B	7	5	9	0	1	1.000
WS Totals		11	42	12	1	0	2	19	9	4	0	7	0	12	0	0	0	0	0	—	0	.286	.388	.452	3B	10	7	15	0	3	1.000
Postseason Totals		27	102	27	4	0	5	46	16	18	1	13	0	24	2	0	0	1	0	1.00	0	.265	.359	.451	3B	26	20	55	2	9	.974

MITCH WILLIAMS—Mitchell Steven Williams—Nickname: Wild Thing—Throws: Left; Bats: Left

Ht: 6'3"; Wt: 180 lbs; Born: 11/17/1964 in Santa Ana, California; Debut: 4/9/1986

LCS		Pitching																										
Year Tm	Age	G	GS	CG	GF	IP	BFP	H	R	ER	HR	SH	SF	HB	TBB	IBB	SO	WP	Bk	W	L	Pct	ShO	Sv-Op	Hld	OAvg	OOBP	ERA
1989 ChN	24	2	0	0	1	1.0	4	1	0	0	0	0	0	0	0	0	2	0	0	0	0	—	0	0-0	0	.250	.250	0.00
1993 Phi	28	4	0	0	3	5.1	25	6	2	1	0	2	1	0	2	0	5	0	0	2	0	1.000	0	2-4	0	.300	.348	1.69
LCS Totals		6	0	0	4	6.1	58	7	2	1	0	2	1	0	2	0	7	0	0	2	0	1.000	0	2-4	0	.292	.333	1.42
World Series		Pitching																										
Year Tm	Age	G	GS	CG	GF	IP	BFP	H	R	ER	HR	SH	SF	HB	TBB	IBB	SO	WP	Bk	W	L	Pct	ShO	Sv-Op	Hld	OAvg	OOBP	ERA
1993 Phi	28	3	0	0	2	2.2	15	5	6	6	1	0	1	0	4	0	1	0	0	0	2	.000	0	1-3	0	.500	.600	20.25
Postseason Totals		9	0	0	6	9.0	88	12	8	7	1	2	2	0	6	0	8	0	0	2	2	.500	0	3-7	0	.353	.429	7.00

LCS		Batting																							Fielding						
Year Tm	Age	G	AB	H	2B	3B	HR	TB	R	RBI	GW	TBB	IBB	SO	HBP	SH	SF	SB	CS	SB%	GDP	Avg	OBP	SLG	Pos	G	PO	A	E	DP	FPct
1989 ChN	24	2	0	0	0	0	0	0	0	0	0	0	0	0	0	0	0	0	0	—	0	—	—	—	P	2	0	0	0	0	—
1993 Phi	28	4	0	0	0	0	0	0	0	0	0	0	0	0	0	0	0	0	0	—	0	—	—	—	P	4	0	1	1	0	.500
LCS Totals		6	0	0	0	0	0	0	0	0	0	0	0	0	0	0	0	0	0	—	0	—	—	—	P	6	0	1	1	0	.500
World Series		Batting																							Fielding						
Year Tm	Age	G	AB	H	2B	3B	HR	TB	R	RBI	GW	TBB	IBB	SO	HBP	SH	SF	SB	CS	SB%	GDP	Avg	OBP	SLG	Pos	G	PO	A	E	DP	FPct
1993 Phi	28	3	0	0	0	0	0	0	0	0	0	0	0	0	0	0	0	0	0	—	0	—	—	—	P	3	0	1	0	0	1.000
Postseason Totals		9	0	0	0	0	0	0	0	0	0	0	0	0	0	0	0	0	0	—	0	—	—	—	P	9	0	2	1	0	.667

STAN WILLIAMS—Stanley Wilson Williams—Throws: Right; Bats: Right

Ht: 6'5"; Wt: 230 lbs; Born: 9/14/1936 in Enfield, New Hampshire; Debut: 5/17/1958

LCS		Pitching																										
Year Tm	Age	G	GS	CG	GF	IP	BFP	H	R	ER	HR	SH	SF	HB	TBB	IBB	SO	WP	Bk	W	L	Pct	ShO	Sv-Op	Hld	OAvg	OOBP	ERA
1970 Min	34	2	0	0	0	6.0	19	2	0	0	0	0	0	0	1	0	2	0	0	0	0	—	0	0-0	0	.111	.158	0.00
World Series		Pitching																										
Year Tm	Age	G	GS	CG	GF	IP	BFP	H	R	ER	HR	SH	SF	HB	TBB	IBB	SO	WP	Bk	W	L	Pct	ShO	Sv-Op	Hld	OAvg	OOBP	ERA
1959 LA	23	1	0	0	1	2.0	8	0	0	0	0	1	0	0	2	0	1	0	0	0	0	—	0	0-0	0	.000	.286	0.00
1963 NYA	27	1	0	0	0	3.0	10	1	0	0	0	0	0	0	0	0	5	0	0	0	0	—	0	0-0	0	.100	.100	0.00
WS Totals		2	0	0	1	5.0	36	1	0	0	0	1	0	0	2	0	6	0	0	0	0	—	0	0-0	0	.067	.176	0.00
Postseason Totals		4	0	0	1	11.0	74	3	0	0	0	1	0	0	3	0	8	0	0	0	0	—	0	0-0	0	.091	.167	0.00

LCS — Batting / Fielding

Year Tm	Age	G	AB	H	2B	3B	HR	TB	R	RBI	GW	TBB	IBB	SO	HBP	SH	SF	SB	CS	SB%	GDP	Avg	OBP	SLG	Pos	G	PO	A	E	DP	FPct
1970 Min	34	2	0	0	0	0	0	0	0	0	0	1	0	0	0	0	0	0	0	—	0	—	1.000	—	P	2	0	0	0	0	—

World Series — Batting / Fielding

Year Tm	Age	G	AB	H	2B	3B	HR	TB	R	RBI	GW	TBB	IBB	SO	HBP	SH	SF	SB	CS	SB%	GDP	Avg	OBP	SLG	Pos	G	PO	A	E	DP	FPct
1959 LA	23	1	0	0	0	0	0	0	0	0	0	0	0	0	0	0	0	0	0	—	0	—	—	—	P	1	0	0	0	0	—
1963 NYA	27	1	0	0	0	0	0	0	0	0	0	0	0	0	0	0	0	0	0	—	0	—	—	—	P	1	0	0	0	0	—
WS Totals		2	0	0	0	0	0	0	0	0	0	0	0	0	0	0	0	0	0	—	0	—	—	—	P	2	0	0	0	0	—
Postseason Totals		4	0	0	0	0	0	0	0	0	0	1	0	0	0	0	0	0	0	—	0	—	1.000	—	P	4	0	0	0	0	—

TED WILLIAMS (HOF 1966-W)—Theodore Samuel Williams—Nicknames: The Kid, The Splendid Splinter—B: L; T: R

Ht: 6'3"; Wt: 205 lbs; Born: 8/30/1918 in San Diego, Calif.; Deb.: 4/20/1939

World Series — Batting / Fielding

Year Tm	Age	G	AB	H	2B	3B	HR	TB	R	RBI	GW	TBB	IBB	SO	HBP	SH	SF	SB	CS	SB%	GDP	Avg	OBP	SLG	Pos	G	PO	A	E	DP	FPct
1946 Bos-*M*	28	7	25	5	0	0	0	5	2	1	0	5	1	5	0	0	0	0	0	—	0	.200	.333	.200	OF	7	15	2	0	0	1.000

CARL WILLIS—Carl Blake Willis—Throws: Right; Bats: Left

Ht: 6'4"; Wt: 210 lbs; Born: 12/28/1960 in Danville, Virginia; Debut: 6/9/1984

LCS — Pitching

Year Tm	Age	G	GS	CG	GF	IP	BFP	H	R	ER	HR	SH	SF	HB	TBB	IBB	SO	WP	Bk	W	L	Pct	ShO	Sv-Op	Hld	OAvg	OOBP	ERA
1991 Min	30	3	0	0	0	5.1	17	2	0	0	0	0	0	0	0	0	3	0	0	0	0	—	0	0-0	2	.118	.118	0.00

World Series — Pitching

Year Tm	Age	G	GS	CG	GF	IP	BFP	H	R	ER	HR	SH	SF	HB	TBB	IBB	SO	WP	Bk	W	L	Pct	ShO	Sv-Op	Hld	OAvg	OOBP	ERA
1991 Min	30	4	0	0	1	7.0	27	6	4	4	2	1	0	0	2	1	2	0	0	0	0	—	0	0-2	0	.250	.308	5.14
Postseason Totals		7	0	0	1	12.1	88	8	4	4	2	1	0	0	2	1	5	0	0	0	0	—	0	0-2	2	.195	.233	2.92

LCS — Batting / Fielding

Year Tm	Age	G	AB	H	2B	3B	HR	TB	R	RBI	GW	TBB	IBB	SO	HBP	SH	SF	SB	CS	SB%	GDP	Avg	OBP	SLG	Pos	G	PO	A	E	DP	FPct
1991 Min	30	3	0	0	0	0	0	0	0	0	0	0	0	0	0	0	0	0	0	—	0	—	—	—	P	3	0	0	0	0	—

World Series — Batting / Fielding

Year Tm	Age	G	AB	H	2B	3B	HR	TB	R	RBI	GW	TBB	IBB	SO	HBP	SH	SF	SB	CS	SB%	GDP	Avg	OBP	SLG	Pos	G	PO	A	E	DP	FPct
1991 Min	30	4	0	0	0	0	0	0	0	0	0	0	0	0	0	0	0	0	0	—	0	—	—	—	P	4	1	0	0	0	1.000
Postseason Totals		7	0	0	0	0	0	0	0	0	0	0	0	0	0	0	0	0	0	—	0	—	—	—	P	7	1	0	0	0	1.000

RON WILLIS—Ronald Earl Willis—Throws: Right; Bats: Right

Ht: 6'2"; Wt: 185 lbs; Born: 7/12/1943 in Willisville, Tennessee; Debut: 9/20/1966; Died: 11/21/1977

World Series — Pitching

Year Tm	Age	G	GS	CG	GF	IP	BFP	H	R	ER	HR	SH	SF	HB	TBB	IBB	SO	WP	Bk	W	L	Pct	ShO	Sv-Op	Hld	OAvg	OOBP	ERA
1967 StL	24	3	0	0	0	1.0	9	2	4	3	0	0	1	0	4	2	1	0	0	0	0	—	0	0-0	0	.500	.667	27.00
1968 StL	25	3	0	0	1	4.1	18	2	4	4	0	1	0	1	4	1	3	0	0	0	0	—	0	0-0	0	.167	.412	8.31
WS Totals		6	0	0	1	5.1	54	4	8	7	0	1	1	1	8	3	4	0	0	0	0	—	0	0-0	0	.250	.500	11.81

World Series — Batting / Fielding

Year Tm	Age	G	AB	H	2B	3B	HR	TB	R	RBI	GW	TBB	IBB	SO	HBP	SH	SF	SB	CS	SB%	GDP	Avg	OBP	SLG	Pos	G	PO	A	E	DP	FPct
1967 StL	24	3	0	0	0	0	0	0	0	0	0	0	0	0	0	0	0	0	0	—	0	—	—	—	P	3	0	0	0	0	—
1968 StL	25	3	0	0	0	0	0	0	0	0	0	0	0	0	0	0	0	0	0	—	0	—	—	—	P	3	1	0	0	0	1.000
WS Totals		6	0	0	0	0	0	0	0	0	0	0	0	0	0	0	0	0	0	—	0	—	—	—	P	6	1	0	0	0	1.000

VIC WILLIS (HOF 1995-V)—Victor Gazaway Willis—Throws: Right; Bats: Right

Ht: 6'2"; Wt: 185 lbs; Born: 4/12/1876 in Cecil County, Maryland; Debut: 4/20/1898; Died: 8/3/1947

World Series — Pitching

Year Tm	Age	G	GS	CG	GF	IP	BFP	H	R	ER	HR	SH	SF	HB	TBB	IBB	SO	WP	Bk	W	L	Pct	ShO	Sv-Op	Hld	OAvg	OOBP	ERA
1909 Pit	33	2	1	0	1	11.2	49	10	6	4	0	0	0	1	8	0	3	0	0	0	1	.000	0	0-0	0	.250	.388	3.09

World Series — Batting / Fielding

Year Tm	Age	G	AB	H	2B	3B	HR	TB	R	RBI	GW	TBB	IBB	SO	HBP	SH	SF	SB	CS	SB%	GDP	Avg	OBP	SLG	Pos	G	PO	A	E	DP	FPct
1909 Pit	33	2	4	0	0	0	0	0	0	0	0	0	0	1	0	0	0	0	0	—	0	.000	.000	.000	P	2	1	2	0	0	1.000

JIM WILLOUGHBY—James Arthur Willoughby—Throws: Right; Bats: Right

Ht: 6'2"; Wt: 185 lbs; Born: 1/31/1949 in Salinas, California; Debut: 9/5/1971

World Series — Pitching

Year Tm	Age	G	GS	CG	GF	IP	BFP	H	R	ER	HR	SH	SF	HB	TBB	IBB	SO	WP	Bk	W	L	Pct	ShO	Sv-Op	Hld	OAvg	OOBP	ERA
1975 Bos	26	3	0	0	0	6.1	22	3	1	0	0	0	0	1	0	0	2	0	0	0	1	.000	0	0-0	0	.143	.182	0.00

World Series — Batting / Fielding

Year Tm	Age	G	AB	H	2B	3B	HR	TB	R	RBI	GW	TBB	IBB	SO	HBP	SH	SF	SB	CS	SB%	GDP	Avg	OBP	SLG	Pos	G	PO	A	E	DP	FPct
1975 Bos	26	3	0	0	0	0	0	0	0	0	0	0	0	0	0	1	0	0	0	—	0	—	—	—	P	3	1	0	0	0	1.000

MAURY WILLS—Maurice Morning Wills—Bats: Both; Throws: Right

Ht: 5'11"; Wt: 170 lbs; Born: 10/2/1932 in Washington, DC; Debut: 6/6/1959

World Series — Batting / Fielding

Year Tm	Age	G	AB	H	2B	3B	HR	TB	R	RBI	GW	TBB	IBB	SO	HBP	SH	SF	SB	CS	SB%	GDP	Avg	OBP	SLG	Pos	G	PO	A	E	DP	FPct
1959 LA	26	6	20	5	0	0	0	5	2	1	0	0	0	3	0	0	0	1	0	1.00	0	.250	.250	.250	SS	6	10	21	1	3	.969
1963 LA	30	4	15	2	0	0	0	2	1	0	0	1	0	3	0	0	0	1	0	1.00	0	.133	.188	.133	SS	4	5	10	1	0	.938
1965 LA	32	7	30	11	3	0	0	14	3	3	0	1	0	3	0	0	0	3	2	.60	0	.367	.387	.467	SS	7	14	27	0	6	1.000
1966 LA	33	4	13	1	0	0	0	1	0	0	0	3	0	3	0	1	0	1	0	1.00	0	.077	.250	.077	SS	4	11	14	0	3	1.000
WS Totals		21	78	19	3	0	0	22	6	4	0	5	0	12	0	1	0	6	2	.75	0	.244	.289	.282	SS	21	40	72	2	12	.982

ART WILSON—Arthur Earl Wilson—Nickname: Dutch—Bats: Right; Throws: Right

Ht: 5'8"; Wt: 170 lbs; Born: 12/11/1885 in Macon, Illinois; Debut: 9/29/1908; Died: 6/12/1960

World Series — Batting / Fielding

Year Tm	Age	G	AB	H	2B	3B	HR	TB	R	RBI	GW	TBB	IBB	SO	HBP	SH	SF	SB	CS	SB%	GDP	Avg	OBP	SLG	Pos	G	PO	A	E	DP	FPct
1911 NYG	25	1	1	0	0	0	0	0	0	0	0	0	0	0	0	0	0	0	0	—	0	.000	.000	.000	C	1	1	0	0	0	1.000
1912 NYG	26	2	1	1	0	0	0	1	0	0	0	0	0	0	0	0	0	0	0	—	0	1.000	1.000	1.000	C	2	2	1	1	0	.750
1913 NYG	27	3	3	0	0	0	0	0	0	0	0	0	0	2	0	0	0	0	0	—	0	.000	.000	.000	C	3	4	1	0	0	1.000
WS Totals		6	5	1	0	0	0	1	0	0	0	0	0	2	0	0	0	0	0	—	0	.200	.200	.200	C	6	7	2	1	0	.900

CHIEF WILSON—John Owen Wilson—Bats: Left; Throws: Right

Ht: 6'2"; Wt: 185 lbs; Born: 8/21/1883 in Austin, Texas; Debut: 4/15/1908; Died: 2/22/1954

World Series — Batting / Fielding

Year Tm	Age	G	AB	H	2B	3B	HR	TB	R	RBI	GW	TBB	IBB	SO	HBP	SH	SF	SB	CS	SB%	GDP	Avg	OBP	SLG	Pos	G	PO	A	E	DP	FPct
1909 Pit	26	7	27	4	1	0	0	5	2	1	0	0	0	2	0	2	0	1	1	.50	0	.148	.148	.185	OF	7	3	1	1	0	.800

DAN WILSON—Daniel Allen Wilson—Bats: Right; Throws: Right

Ht: 6'3"; Wt: 190 lbs; Born: 3/25/1969 in Arlington Heights, Illinois; Debut: 9/7/1992

Division Series — Batting / Fielding

Year Tm	Age	G	AB	H	2B	3B	HR	TB	R	RBI	GW	TBB	IBB	SO	HBP	SH	SF	SB	CS	SB%	GDP	Avg	OBP	SLG	Pos	G	PO	A	E	DP	FPct
1995 Sea	26	5	17	2	0	0	0	2	0	1	0	2	0	6	0	0	0	0	0	—	1	.118	.211	.118	C	5	34	1	0	1	1.000
1997 Sea	28	4	13	0	0	0	0	0	0	0	0	0	0	9	0	0	0	0	0	—	0	.000	.000	.000	C	4	29	1	0	0	1.000
DS Totals		9	30	2	0	0	0	2	0	1	0	2	0	15	0	0	0	0	0	—	1	.067	.125	.067	C	9	63	2	0	1	1.000

LCS — Batting / Fielding

Year Tm	Age	G	AB	H	2B	3B	HR	TB	R	RBI	GW	TBB	IBB	SO	HBP	SH	SF	SB	CS	SB%	GDP	Avg	OBP	SLG	Pos	G	PO	A	E	DP	FPct
1995 Sea	26	6	16	0	0	0	0	0	0	0	0	0	0	4	0	0	0	0	0	—	0	.000	.000	.000	C	6	35	3	1	0	.974
Postseason Totals		15	46	2	0	0	0	2	0	1	0	2	0	19	0	0	0	0	0	—	1	.043	.083	.043	C	15	98	5	1	1	.990

EARL WILSON—Earl Lawrence Wilson—Throws: Right; Bats: Right

Ht: 6'3"; Wt: 216 lbs; Born: 10/2/1934 in Ponchatoula, Louisiana; Debut: 7/28/1959

World Series — Pitching

Year Tm	Age	G	GS	CG	GF	IP	BFP	H	R	ER	HR	SH	SF	HB	TBB	IBB	SO	WP	Bk	W	L	Pct	ShO	Sv-Op	Hld	OAvg	OOBP	ERA
1968 Det	33	1	1	0	0	4.1	21	4	3	3	0	0	0	0	6	0	3	0	0	0	1	.000	0	0-0	0	.267	.476	6.23

World Series		Batting																							Fielding						
Year Tm	Age	G	AB	H	2B	3B	HR	TB	R	RBI	GW	TBB	IBB	SO	HBP	SH	SF	SB	CS	SB%	GDP	Avg	OBP	SLG	Pos	G	PO	A	E	DP	FPct
1968 Det	33	1	1	0	0	0	0	0	0	0	0	0	0	1	0	0	0	0	0	—	0	.000	.000	.000	P	1	0	2	0	0	1.000

GEORGE WILSON—George Washington Wilson—Nickname: Teddy—Bats: Left; Throws: Right

Ht: 6'1"; Wt: 185 lbs; Born: 8/30/1925 in Cherryville, North Carolina; Debut: 4/15/1952; Died: 10/29/1974

World Series		Batting																							Fielding						
Year Tm	Age	G	AB	H	2B	3B	HR	TB	R	RBI	GW	TBB	IBB	SO	HBP	SH	SF	SB	CS	SB%	GDP	Avg	OBP	SLG	Pos	G	PO	A	E	DP	FPct
1956 NYA	31	1	1	0	0	0	0	0	0	0	0	0	0	1	0	0	0	0	0	—	0	.000	.000	.000	—						

HACK WILSON (HOF 1979-V)—Lewis Robert Wilson—Bats: Right; Throws: Right

Ht: 5'6"; Wt: 190 lbs; Born: 4/26/1900 in Ellwood City, Pennsylvania; Debut: 9/29/1923; Died: 11/23/1948

World Series		Batting																							Fielding						
Year Tm	Age	G	AB	H	2B	3B	HR	TB	R	RBI	GW	TBB	IBB	SO	HBP	SH	SF	SB	CS	SB%	GDP	Avg	OBP	SLG	Pos	G	PO	A	E	DP	FPct
1924 NYG	24	7	30	7	1	0	0	8	1	3	0	1	0	9	0	1	0	0	0	—	2	.233	.258	.267	OF	7	19	1	0	0	1.000
1929 ChN	29	5	17	8	0	1	0	10	2	0	0	4	0	3	0	0	0	0	0	—	0	.471	.571	.588	OF	5	14	0	1	0	.933
WS Totals		12	47	15	1	1	0	18	3	3	0	5	0	12	0	1	0	0	0	—	2	.319	.385	.383	OF	12	33	1	1	0	.971

JIMMIE WILSON—James Wilson—Nickname: Ace—Bats: Right; Throws: Right

Ht: 6'1"; Wt: 200 lbs; Born: 7/23/1900 in Philadelphia, Pennsylvania; Debut: 4/17/1923; Died: 5/31/1947

World Series		Batting																							Fielding						
Year Tm	Age	G	AB	H	2B	3B	HR	TB	R	RBI	GW	TBB	IBB	SO	HBP	SH	SF	SB	CS	SB%	GDP	Avg	OBP	SLG	Pos	G	PO	A	E	DP	FPct
1928 StL	28	3	11	1	1	0	0	2	1	1	0	0	0	3	0	0	0	0	1	.00	1	.091	.091	.182	C	3	14	2	2	0	.889
1930 StL	30	4	15	4	1	0	0	5	0	2	0	0	0	1	0	0	0	0	0	—	0	.267	.267	.333	C	4	23	1	0	0	1.000
1931 StL	31	7	23	5	0	0	0	5	0	2	2	1	0	1	0	0	0	0	1	.00	1	.217	.250	.217	C	7	50	2	1	1	.981
1940 Cin	40	6	17	6	0	0	0	6	2	0	0	1	0	2	0	1	0	1	0	1.00	1	.353	.389	.353	C	6	26	2	0	1	1.000
WS Totals		20	66	16	2	0	0	18	3	5	2	2	0	7	0	1	0	1	2	.33	3	.242	.265	.273	C	20	113	7	3	2	.976

MOOKIE WILSON—William Hayward Wilson—Bats: Both; Throws: Right

Ht: 5'10"; Wt: 170 lbs; Born: 2/9/1956 in Bamberg, South Carolina; Debut: 9/2/1980

LCS		Batting																							Fielding						
Year Tm	Age	G	AB	H	2B	3B	HR	TB	R	RBI	GW	TBB	IBB	SO	HBP	SH	SF	SB	CS	SB%	GDP	Avg	OBP	SLG	Pos	G	PO	A	E	DP	FPct
1986 NYN	30	6	26	3	0	0	0	3	2	1	0	1	0	7	0	0	0	1	0	1.00	1	.115	.148	.115	OF	6	16	1	0	1	1.000
1988 NYN	32	4	13	2	0	0	0	2	2	1	1	2	0	2	0	0	0	0	1	.00	1	.154	.267	.154	OF	3	6	0	0	0	1.000
1989 Tor	33	5	19	5	0	0	0	5	2	2	0	2	0	2	0	0	0	1	0	1.00	0	.263	.333	.263	OF	5	10	0	0	0	1.000
1991 Tor	35	3	8	2	0	0	0	2	1	0	0	1	0	3	0	0	0	1	0	1.00	0	.250	.333	.250	OF	2	4	0	0	0	1.000
LCS Totals		18	66	12	0	0	0	12	7	4	1	6	0	14	0	0	0	3	1	.75	2	.182	.250	.182	OF	16	36	1	0	1	1.000
World Series		Batting																							Fielding						
Year Tm	Age	G	AB	H	2B	3B	HR	TB	R	RBI	GW	TBB	IBB	SO	HBP	SH	SF	SB	CS	SB%	GDP	Avg	OBP	SLG	Pos	G	PO	A	E	DP	FPct
1986 NYN	30	7	26	7	1	0	0	8	3	0	0	1	1	6	1	0	0	3	0	1.00	0	.269	.321	.308	OF	7	13	2	0	0	1.000
Postseason Totals		25	92	19	1	0	0	20	10	4	1	7	1	20	1	0	0	6	1	.86	2	.207	.270	.217	OF	23	49	3	0	1	1.000

NIGEL WILSON—Nigel Edward Wilson—Bats: Left; Throws: Left

Ht: 6'1"; Wt: 185 lbs; Born: 1/12/1970 in Oshawa, Ontario; Debut: 9/8/1993

Division Series		Batting																							Fielding						
Year Tm	Age	G	AB	H	2B	3B	HR	TB	R	RBI	GW	TBB	IBB	SO	HBP	SH	SF	SB	CS	SB%	GDP	Avg	OBP	SLG	Pos	G	PO	A	E	DP	FPct
1996 Cle	26	1	1	0	0	0	0	0	0	0	0	0	0	0	0	0	0	0	0	—	0	.000	.000	.000	—						

STEVE WILSON—Stephen Douglas Wilson—Throws: Left; Bats: Left

Ht: 6'4"; Wt: 205 lbs; Born: 12/13/1964 in Victoria, British Columbia; Debut: 9/16/1988

LCS		Pitching																										
Year Tm	Age	G	GS	CG	GF	IP	BFP	H	R	ER	HR	SH	SF	HB	TBB	IBB	SO	WP	Bk	W	L	Pct	ShO	Sv-Op	Hld	OAvg	OOBP	ERA
1989 ChN	24	2	0	0	1	3.2	16	3	5	2	2	0	0	0	1	0	4	1	0	0	1	.000	0	0-0	0	.200	.250	4.91

LCS		Batting																							Fielding						
Year Tm	Age	G	AB	H	2B	3B	HR	TB	R	RBI	GW	TBB	IBB	SO	HBP	SH	SF	SB	CS	SB%	GDP	Avg	OBP	SLG	Pos	G	PO	A	E	DP	FPct
1989 ChN	24	2	0	0	0	0	0	0	0	0	0	0	0	0	0	0	0	0	0	—	0	—	—	—	P	2	0	1	0	0	1.000

WILLIE WILSON—Willie James Wilson—Bats: Both; Throws: Right

Ht: 6'3"; Wt: 190 lbs; Born: 7/9/1955 in Montgomery, Alabama; Debut: 9/4/1976

Division Series		Batting																							Fielding						
Year Tm	Age	G	AB	H	2B	3B	HR	TB	R	RBI	GW	TBB	IBB	SO	HBP	SH	SF	SB	CS	SB%	GDP	Avg	OBP	SLG	Pos	G	PO	A	E	DP	FPct
1981 KC	26	3	13	4	0	0	0	4	0	1	0	0	0	0	0	0	0	0	0	—	0	.308	.308	.308	OF	3	6	0	0	0	1.000
LCS		Batting																							Fielding						
Year Tm	Age	G	AB	H	2B	3B	HR	TB	R	RBI	GW	TBB	IBB	SO	HBP	SH	SF	SB	CS	SB%	GDP	Avg	OBP	SLG	Pos	G	PO	A	E	DP	FPct
1978 KC	23	3	4	1	0	0	0	1	0	0	0	0	0	2	0	0	0	0	1	.00	0	.250	.250	.250	OF	3	2	0	0	0	1.000
1980 KC	25	3	13	4	2	1	0	8	2	4	1	1	0	2	0	0	0	0	0	—	0	.308	.357	.615	OF	3	6	1	0	0	1.000
1984 KC	29	3	13	2	0	0	0	2	0	0	0	1	0	2	0	0	0	0	1	.00	0	.154	.214	.154	OF	3	10	0	0	0	1.000
1985 KC	30	7	29	9	0	0	1	12	5	2	0	1	0	5	0	1	0	1	1	.50	1	.310	.333	.414	OF	7	12	0	0	0	1.000
1992 Oak	37	6	22	5	1	0	0	6	0	0	0	1	0	5	0	0	0	7	0	1.00	0	.227	.261	.273	OF	6	16	0	0	0	1.000
LCS Totals		22	81	21	3	1	1	29	7	6	1	4	0	16	0	1	0	8	3	.73	1	.259	.294	.358	OF	22	46	1	0	0	1.000
World Series		Batting																							Fielding						
Year Tm	Age	G	AB	H	2B	3B	HR	TB	R	RBI	GW	TBB	IBB	SO	HBP	SH	SF	SB	CS	SB%	GDP	Avg	OBP	SLG	Pos	G	PO	A	E	DP	FPct
1980 KC	25	6	26	4	1	0	0	5	3	0	0	4	0	12	0	0	0	2	0	1.00	0	.154	.267	.192	OF	6	15	1	0	0	1.000
1985 KC	30	7	30	11	0	1	0	13	2	3	0	1	0	4	0	0	0	2	0	1.00	1	.367	.387	.433	OF	7	19	1	0	0	1.000
WS Totals		13	56	15	1	1	0	18	5	3	0	5	0	16	0	0	0	4	0	1.00	1	.268	.328	.321	OF	13	34	2	0	0	1.000
Postseason Totals		38	150	40	4	2	1	51	12	10	1	9	0	32	0	1	0	12	3	.80	2	.267	.308	.340	OF	38	86	3	0	0	1.000

HOOKS WILTSE—George Leroy Wiltse—Throws: Left; Bats: Right

Ht: 6'0"; Wt: 185 lbs; Born: 9/7/1880 in Hamilton, New York; Debut: 4/21/1904; Died: 1/21/1959

World Series		Pitching																										
Year Tm	Age	G	GS	CG	GF	IP	BFP	H	R	ER	HR	SH	SF	HB	TBB	IBB	SO	WP	Bk	W	L	Pct	ShO	Sv-Op	Hld	OAvg	OOBP	ERA
1911 NYG	31	2	0	0	1	3.1	19	8	8	7	0	1	1	0	0	0	2	0	0	0	0	—	0	0-0	0	.471	.444	18.90

World Series		Batting																							Fielding						
Year Tm	Age	G	AB	H	2B	3B	HR	TB	R	RBI	GW	TBB	IBB	SO	HBP	SH	SF	SB	CS	SB%	GDP	Avg	OBP	SLG	Pos	G	PO	A	E	DP	FPct
1911 NYG	31	2	1	0	0	0	0	0	0	0	0	0	0	1	0	0	0	0	0	—	0	.000	.000	.000	P	2	0	2	0	0	1.000
1913 NYG	33	2	2	0	0	0	0	0	0	0	0	0	0	1	0	1	0	0	0	—	0	.000	.000	.000	1B	2	15	2	0	0	1.000
WS Totals		4	3	0	0	0	0	0	0	0	0	0	0	2	0	1	0	0	0	—	0	.000	.000	.000	P	2	0	2	0	0	1.000

DAVE WINFIELD—David Mark Winfield—Bats: Right; Throws: Right

Ht: 6'6"; Wt: 220 lbs; Born: 10/3/1951 in St. Paul, Minnesota; Debut: 6/19/1973

Division Series		Batting																							Fielding						
Year Tm	Age	G	AB	H	2B	3B	HR	TB	R	RBI	GW	TBB	IBB	SO	HBP	SH	SF	SB	CS	SB%	GDP	Avg	OBP	SLG	Pos	G	PO	A	E	DP	FPct
1981 NYA	29	5	20	7	3	0	0	10	2	0	0	1	0	5	0	0	0	0	0	—	0	.350	.381	.500	OF	5	9	1	0	0	1.000
LCS		Batting																							Fielding						
Year Tm	Age	G	AB	H	2B	3B	HR	TB	R	RBI	GW	TBB	IBB	SO	HBP	SH	SF	SB	CS	SB%	GDP	Avg	OBP	SLG	Pos	G	PO	A	E	DP	FPct
1981 NYA	29	3	13	2	1	0	0	3	2	2	1	2	0	2	0	0	0	1	0	1.00	0	.154	.267	.231	OF	3	6	0	0	0	1.000
1992 Tor	40	6	24	6	1	0	2	13	7	3	0	4	1	2	0	0	0	0	0	—	0	.250	.357	.542	—						
LCS Totals		9	37	8	2	0	2	16	9	5	1	6	1	4	0	0	0	1	0	1.00	0	.216	.326	.432	OF	3	6	0	0	0	1.000
World Series		Batting																							Fielding						
Year Tm	Age	G	AB	H	2B	3B	HR	TB	R	RBI	GW	TBB	IBB	SO	HBP	SH	SF	SB	CS	SB%	GDP	Avg	OBP	SLG	Pos	G	PO	A	E	DP	FPct
1981 NYA	29	6	22	1	0	0	0	1	0	1	0	5	0	4	0	0	0	1	0	1.00	0	.045	.222	.045	OF	6	13	0	0	0	1.000
1992 Tor	40	6	22	5	1	0	0	6	0	3	1	2	0	3	0	1	0	0	0	—	0	.227	.292	.273	OF	3	7	0	0	0	1.000
WS Totals		12	44	6	1	0	0	7	0	4	1	7	0	7	0	1	0	1	0	1.00	0	.136	.255	.159	OF	9	20	0	0	0	1.000
Postseason Totals		26	101	21	6	0	2	33	11	9	2	14	1	16	0	1	0	2	0	1.00	0	.208	.304	.327	OF	17	35	1	0	0	1.000

IVY WINGO—Ivey Brown Wingo—Bats: Left; Throws: Right

Ht: 5'10"; Wt: 160 lbs; Born: 7/8/1890 in Gainesville, Georgia; Debut: 4/20/1911; Died: 3/1/1941

World Series		Batting																							Fielding						
Year Tm	Age	G	AB	H	2B	3B	HR	TB	R	RBI	GW	TBB	IBB	SO	HBP	SH	SF	SB	CS	SB%	GDP	Avg	OBP	SLG	Pos	G	PO	A	E	DP	FPct
1919 Cin	29	3	7	4	0	0	0	4	1	1	1	3	0	1	0	1	0	0	1	.00	0	.571	.700	.571	C	3	8	3	0	0	1.000

HERM WINNINGHAM—Herman Son Winningham—Bats: Left; Throws: Right

Ht: 5'11"; Wt: 185 lbs; Born: 12/1/1961 in Orangeburg, South Carolina; Debut: 9/1/1984

LCS		Batting																							Fielding						
Year Tm	Age	G	AB	H	2B	3B	HR	TB	R	RBI	GW	TBB	IBB	SO	HBP	SH	SF	SB	CS	SB%	GDP	Avg	OBP	SLG	Pos	G	PO	A	E	DP	FPct
1990 Cin	28	3	7	2	1	0	0	3	1	1	0	1	0	1	0	0	1	1	1	.50	0	.286	.333	.429	OF	2	7	0	0	0	1.000
World Series		Batting																							Fielding						
Year Tm	Age	G	AB	H	2B	3B	HR	TB	R	RBI	GW	TBB	IBB	SO	HBP	SH	SF	SB	CS	SB%	GDP	Avg	OBP	SLG	Pos	G	PO	A	E	DP	FPct
1990 Cin	28	2	4	2	0	0	0	2	1	0	0	0	0	0	0	0	0	0	0	—	0	.500	.500	.500	OF	1	3	0	0	0	1.000
Postseason Totals		5	11	4	1	0	0	5	2	1	0	1	0	1	0	0	1	1	1	.50	0	.364	.385	.455	OF	3	10	0	0	0	1.000

GEORGE WINTER—George Lovington Winter—Nickname: Sassafrass—Throws: Right; Bats: Unknown

Ht: 5'8"; Wt: 155 lbs; Born: 4/27/1878 in New Providence, Pa.; Deb.: 6/15/1901; Died: 5/26/1951

World Series		Pitching																										
Year Tm	Age	G	GS	CG	GF	IP	BFP	H	R	ER	HR	SH	SF	HB	TBB	IBB	SO	WP	Bk	W	L	Pct	ShO	Sv-Op	Hld	OAvg	OOBP	ERA
1908 Det	30	1	0	0	1	1.0	5	1	1	0	0	0	0	0	1	0	0	0	0	0	0	—	0	0-0	0	.250	.400	0.00

World Series		Batting																							Fielding						
Year Tm	Age	G	AB	H	2B	3B	HR	TB	R	RBI	GW	TBB	IBB	SO	HBP	SH	SF	SB	CS	SB%	GDP	Avg	OBP	SLG	Pos	G	PO	A	E	DP	FPct
1908 Det	30	2	0	0	0	0	0	0	0	0	0	0	0	0	0	0	0	0	0	—	0	—	—	—	P	1	0	0	0	0	—

CASEY WISE—Kendall Cole Wise—Bats: Both; Throws: Right

Ht: 6'0"; Wt: 170 lbs; Born: 9/8/1932 in Lafayette, Indiana; Debut: 4/16/1957

World Series		Batting																							Fielding						
Year Tm	Age	G	AB	H	2B	3B	HR	TB	R	RBI	GW	TBB	IBB	SO	HBP	SH	SF	SB	CS	SB%	GDP	Avg	OBP	SLG	Pos	G	PO	A	E	DP	FPct
1958 Mil	26	2	1	0	0	0	0	0	0	0	0	0	0	1	0	0	0	0	0	—	0	.000	.000	.000	—						

RICK WISE—Richard Charles Wise—Throws: Right; Bats: Right

Ht: 6'1"; Wt: 180 lbs; Born: 9/13/1945 in Jackson, Michigan; Debut: 4/18/1964

LCS		Pitching																										
Year Tm	Age	G	GS	CG	GF	IP	BFP	H	R	ER	HR	SH	SF	HB	TBB	IBB	SO	WP	Bk	W	L	Pct	ShO	Sv-Op	Hld	OAvg	OOBP	ERA
1975 Bos	30	1	1	0	0	7.1	31	6	3	2	0	0	0	0	3	0	2	0	0	1	0	1.000	0	0-0	0	.214	.290	2.45
World Series		Pitching																										
Year Tm	Age	G	GS	CG	GF	IP	BFP	H	R	ER	HR	SH	SF	HB	TBB	IBB	SO	WP	Bk	W	L	Pct	ShO	Sv-Op	Hld	OAvg	OOBP	ERA
1975 Bos	30	2	1	0	1	5.1	24	6	5	5	3	0	0	0	2	0	2	0	0	1	0	1.000	0	0-0	0	.273	.333	8.44
Postseason Totals		3	2	0	1	12.2	110	12	8	7	3	0	0	0	5	0	4	0	0	2	0	1.000	0	0-0	0	.240	.309	4.97

LCS		Batting																							Fielding						
Year Tm	Age	G	AB	H	2B	3B	HR	TB	R	RBI	GW	TBB	IBB	SO	HBP	SH	SF	SB	CS	SB%	GDP	Avg	OBP	SLG	Pos	G	PO	A	E	DP	FPct
1975 Bos	30	1	0	0	0	0	0	0	0	0	0	0	0	0	0	0	0	0	0	—	0	—	—	—	P	1	2	3	0	0	1.000
World Series		Batting																							Fielding						
Year Tm	Age	G	AB	H	2B	3B	HR	TB	R	RBI	GW	TBB	IBB	SO	HBP	SH	SF	SB	CS	SB%	GDP	Avg	OBP	SLG	Pos	G	PO	A	E	DP	FPct
1975 Bos	30	2	2	0	0	0	0	0	0	0	0	0	0	0	0	0	0	0	0	—	0	.000	.000	.000	P	2	0	0	0	0	—
Postseason Totals		3	2	0	0	0	0	0	0	0	0	0	0	0	0	0	0	0	0	—	0	.000	.000	.000	P	3	2	3	0	0	1.000

BOBBY WITT—Robert Andrew Witt—Throws: Right; Bats: Right

Ht: 6'2"; Wt: 190 lbs; Born: 5/11/1964 in Arlington, Virginia; Debut: 4/10/1986

Division Series		Pitching																										
Year Tm	Age	G	GS	CG	GF	IP	BFP	H	R	ER	HR	SH	SF	HB	TBB	IBB	SO	WP	Bk	W	L	Pct	ShO	Sv-Op	Hld	OAvg	OOBP	ERA
1996 Tex	32	1	1	0	0	3.1	16	4	3	3	0	0	0	0	2	0	3	1	0	0	0	—	0	0-0	0	.286	.375	8.10
LCS		Pitching																										
Year Tm	Age	G	GS	CG	GF	IP	BFP	H	R	ER	HR	SH	SF	HB	TBB	IBB	SO	WP	Bk	W	L	Pct	ShO	Sv-Op	Hld	OAvg	OOBP	ERA
1992 Oak	28	1	0	0	1	1.0	6	2	2	2	0	0	1	0	1	0	1	0	0	0	0	—	0	0-0	0	.500	.500	18.00
Postseason Totals		2	1	0	1	4.1	44	6	5	5	0	0	1	0	3	0	4	1	0	0	0	—	0	0-0	0	.333	.409	10.38

Division Series		Batting																							Fielding						
Year Tm	Age	G	AB	H	2B	3B	HR	TB	R	RBI	GW	TBB	IBB	SO	HBP	SH	SF	SB	CS	SB%	GDP	Avg	OBP	SLG	Pos	G	PO	A	E	DP	FPct
1996 Tex	32	1	0	0	0	0	0	0	0	0	0	0	0	0	0	0	0	0	0	—	0	—	—	—	P	1	0	0	0	0	—
LCS		Batting																							Fielding						
Year Tm	Age	G	AB	H	2B	3B	HR	TB	R	RBI	GW	TBB	IBB	SO	HBP	SH	SF	SB	CS	SB%	GDP	Avg	OBP	SLG	Pos	G	PO	A	E	DP	FPct
1992 Oak	28	1	0	0	0	0	0	0	0	0	0	0	0	0	0	0	0	0	0	—	0	—	—	—	P	1	0	0	0	0	—
Postseason Totals		2	0	0	0	0	0	0	0	0	0	0	0	0	0	0	0	0	0	—	0	—	—	—	P	2	0	0	0	0	—

GEORGE WITT—George Adrian Witt—Nickname: Red—Throws: Right; Bats: Right

Ht: 6'3"; Wt: 185 lbs; Born: 11/9/1933 in Long Beach, California; Debut: 9/21/1957

World Series		Pitching																										
Year Tm	Age	G	GS	CG	GF	IP	BFP	H	R	ER	HR	SH	SF	HB	TBB	IBB	SO	WP	Bk	W	L	Pct	ShO	Sv-Op	Hld	OAvg	OOBP	ERA
1960 Pit	26	3	0	0	1	2.2	15	5	0	0	0	0	0	0	2	1	1	1	0	0	0	—	0	0-0	0	.385	.467	0.00

World Series		Batting																							Fielding						
Year Tm	Age	G	AB	H	2B	3B	HR	TB	R	RBI	GW	TBB	IBB	SO	HBP	SH	SF	SB	CS	SB%	GDP	Avg	OBP	SLG	Pos	G	PO	A	E	DP	FPct
1960 Pit	26	3	0	0	0	0	0	0	0	0	0	0	0	0	0	0	0	0	0	—	0	—	—	—	P	3	0	0	0	0	—

MIKE WITT—Michael Atwater Witt—Throws: Right; Bats: Right

Ht: 6'7"; Wt: 185 lbs; Born: 7/20/1960 in Fullerton, California; Debut: 4/11/1981

LCS		Pitching																										
Year Tm	Age	G	GS	CG	GF	IP	BFP	H	R	ER	HR	SH	SF	HB	TBB	IBB	SO	WP	Bk	W	L	Pct	ShO	Sv-Op	Hld	OAvg	OOBP	ERA
1982 Cal	22	1	0	0	0	3.0	13	2	2	2	1	1	0	0	2	0	3	0	0	0	0	—	0	0-0	0	.200	.333	6.00
1986 Cal	26	2	2	1	0	17.2	66	13	5	5	2	0	0	0	2	0	8	0	0	1	0	1.000	0	0-0	0	.203	.227	2.55
LCS Totals		3	2	1	0	20.2	158	15	7	7	3	1	0	0	4	0	11	0	0	1	0	1.000	0	0-0	0	.203	.244	3.05

LCS		Batting																							Fielding						
Year Tm	Age	G	AB	H	2B	3B	HR	TB	R	RBI	GW	TBB	IBB	SO	HBP	SH	SF	SB	CS	SB%	GDP	Avg	OBP	SLG	Pos	G	PO	A	E	DP	FPct
1982 Cal	22	1	0	0	0	0	0	0	0	0	0	0	0	0	0	0	0	0	0	—	0	—	—	—	P	1	0	1	0	0	1.000
1986 Cal	26	2	0	0	0	0	0	0	0	0	0	0	0	0	0	0	0	0	0	—	0	—	—	—	P	2	2	4	0	0	1.000
LCS Totals		3	0	0	0	0	0	0	0	0	0	0	0	0	0	0	0	0	0	—	0	—	—	—	P	3	2	5	0	0	1.000

WHITEY WITT—Lawton Walter Witt—Bats: Left; Throws: Right

Ht: 5'7"; Wt: 150 lbs; Born: 9/28/1895 in Orange, Massachusetts; Debut: 4/12/1916; Died: 7/14/1988

World Series		Batting																							Fielding						
Year Tm	Age	G	AB	H	2B	3B	HR	TB	R	RBI	GW	TBB	IBB	SO	HBP	SH	SF	SB	CS	SB%	GDP	Avg	OBP	SLG	Pos	G	PO	A	E	DP	FPct
1922 NYA	27	5	18	4	1	1	0	7	1	0	0	1	0	2	0	0	0	0	0	—	1	.222	.263	.389	OF	5	7	1	0	0	1.000
1923 NYA	28	6	25	6	2	0	0	8	1	4	0	1	0	1	0	1	0	0	0	—	0	.240	.269	.320	OF	6	18	1	0	0	1.000
WS Totals		11	43	10	3	1	0	15	2	4	0	2	0	3	0	1	0	0	0	—	1	.233	.267	.349	OF	11	25	2	0	0	1.000

MARK WOHLERS—Mark Edward Wohlers—Throws: Right; Bats: Right

Ht: 6'4"; Wt: 207 lbs; Born: 1/23/1970 in Holyoke, Massachusetts; Debut: 8/17/1991

Division Series		Pitching																										
Year Tm	Age	G	GS	CG	GF	IP	BFP	H	R	ER	HR	SH	SF	HB	TBB	IBB	SO	WP	Bk	W	L	Pct	ShO	Sv-Op	Hld	OAvg	OOBP	ERA
1995 Atl	25	3	0	0	2	2.2	16	6	2	2	0	0	0	0	2	1	4	0	0	0	1	.000	0	2-2	0	.429	.500	6.75
1996 Atl	26	3	0	0	3	3.1	11	1	0	0	0	0	0	0	0	0	4	0	0	0	0	—	0	3-3	0	.091	.091	0.00
1997 Atl	27	1	0	0	1	1.0	4	1	0	0	0	0	0	0	0	0	1	0	0	0	0	—	0	0-0	0	.250	.250	0.00
DS Totals		7	0	0	6	7.0	62	8	2	2	0	0	0	0	2	1	9	0	0	0	1	.000	0	5-5	0	.276	.323	2.57

LCS		Pitching																										
Year Tm	Age	G	GS	CG	GF	IP	BFP	H	R	ER	HR	SH	SF	HB	TBB	IBB	SO	WP	Bk	W	L	Pct	ShO	Sv-Op	Hld	OAvg	OOBP	ERA
1991 Atl	21	3	0	0	1	1.2	7	3	0	0	0	1	0	0	1	0	1	0	0	0	0	—	0	0-0	0	.600	.667	0.00
1992 Atl	22	3	0	0	2	3.0	12	2	0	0	0	0	0	0	1	0	2	0	0	0	0	—	0	0-0	0	.182	.250	0.00
1993 Atl	23	4	0	0	4	5.1	21	2	2	2	2	0	0	0	3	1	10	1	0	0	1	.000	0	0-0	0	.111	.238	3.38
1995 Atl	25	4	0	0	3	5.0	17	2	1	1	0	0	1	0	0	0	8	0	0	1	0	1.000	0	0-0	0	.125	.118	1.80
1996 Atl	26	3	0	0	3	3.0	9	0	0	0	0	0	0	0	0	0	4	1	0	0	0	—	0	2-2	0	.000	.000	0.00
1997 Atl	27	1	0	0	1	1.0	4	0	0	0	0	0	0	0	1	0	1	0	0	0	0	—	0	0-0	0	.000	.250	0.00
LCS Totals		18	0	0	14	19.0	140	9	3	3	2	1	1	0	6	1	26	2	0	1	1	.500	0	2-2	0	.145	.217	1.42
World Series		Pitching																										
Year Tm	Age	G	GS	CG	GF	IP	BFP	H	R	ER	HR	SH	SF	HB	TBB	IBB	SO	WP	Bk	W	L	Pct	ShO	Sv-Op	Hld	OAvg	OOBP	ERA
1991 Atl	21	3	0	0	0	1.2	9	2	0	0	0	0	0	0	2	0	1	0	0	0	0	—	0	0-0	0	.286	.444	0.00
1992 Atl	22	2	0	0	0	0.2	3	0	0	0	0	1	0	0	1	1	0	0	0	0	0	—	0	0-0	0	.000	.500	0.00
1995 Atl	25	4	0	0	2	5.0	22	4	1	1	1	0	0	0	3	2	3	0	0	0	0	—	0	2-3	0	.211	.318	1.80
1996 Atl	26	4	0	0	3	4.1	22	7	3	3	1	0	0	0	2	1	4	1	0	0	0	—	0	0-1	0	.350	.409	6.23
WS Totals		13	0	0	5	11.2	112	13	4	4	2	1	0	0	8	4	8	1	0	0	0	—	0	2-4	0	.277	.382	3.09
Postseason Totals		38	0	0	25	37.2	314	30	9	9	4	2	1	0	16	6	43	3	0	1	2	.333	0	9-11	0	.217	.297	2.15

Division Series		Batting																							Fielding						
Year Tm	Age	G	AB	H	2B	3B	HR	TB	R	RBI	GW	TBB	IBB	SO	HBP	SH	SF	SB	CS	SB%	GDP	Avg	OBP	SLG	Pos	G	PO	A	E	DP	FPct
1995 Atl	25	3	0	0	0	0	0	0	0	0	0	0	0	0	0	0	0	0	0	—	0	—	—	—	P	3	0	0	0	0	—
1996 Atl	26	3	0	0	0	0	0	0	0	0	0	0	0	0	0	0	0	0	0	—	0	—	—	—	P	3	0	0	0	0	—
1997 Atl	27	1	0	0	0	0	0	0	0	0	0	0	0	0	0	0	0	0	0	—	0	—	—	—	P	1	0	0	0	0	—
DS Totals		7	0	0	0	0	0	0	0	0	0	0	0	0	0	0	0	0	0	—	0	—	—	—	P	7	0	0	0	0	—
LCS		Batting																							Fielding						
Year Tm	Age	G	AB	H	2B	3B	HR	TB	R	RBI	GW	TBB	IBB	SO	HBP	SH	SF	SB	CS	SB%	GDP	Avg	OBP	SLG	Pos	G	PO	A	E	DP	FPct
1991 Atl	21	3	0	0	0	0	0	0	0	0	0	0	0	0	0	0	0	0	0	—	0	—	—	—	P	3	0	0	0	0	—
1992 Atl	22	3	0	0	0	0	0	0	0	0	0	0	0	0	0	0	0	0	0	—	0	—	—	—	P	3	1	0	0	0	1.000
1993 Atl	23	4	0	0	0	0	0	0	0	0	0	0	0	0	0	0	0	0	0	—	0	—	—	—	P	4	0	0	0	0	—
1995 Atl	25	4	0	0	0	0	0	0	0	0	0	0	0	0	0	0	0	0	0	—	0	—	—	—	P	4	1	0	0	0	1.000
1996 Atl	26	3	1	0	0	0	0	0	0	0	0	0	0	1	0	0	0	0	0	—	0	.000	.000	.000	P	3	0	0	0	0	—
1997 Atl	27	1	0	0	0	0	0	0	0	0	0	0	0	0	0	0	0	0	0	—	0	—	—	—	P	1	0	0	0	0	—
LCS Totals		18	1	0	0	0	0	0	0	0	0	0	0	1	0	0	0	0	0	—	0	.000	.000	.000	P	18	2	0	0	0	1.000
World Series		Batting																							Fielding						
Year Tm	Age	G	AB	H	2B	3B	HR	TB	R	RBI	GW	TBB	IBB	SO	HBP	SH	SF	SB	CS	SB%	GDP	Avg	OBP	SLG	Pos	G	PO	A	E	DP	FPct
1991 Atl	21	3	0	0	0	0	0	0	0	0	0	0	0	0	0	0	0	0	0	—	0	—	—	—	P	3	0	0	0	0	—
1992 Atl	22	2	0	0	0	0	0	0	0	0	0	0	0	0	0	0	0	0	0	—	0	—	—	—	P	2	0	0	0	0	—
1995 Atl	25	4	0	0	0	0	0	0	0	0	0	0	0	0	0	0	0	0	0	—	0	—	—	—	P	4	0	0	0	0	—
1996 Atl	26	4	0	0	0	0	0	0	0	0	0	0	0	0	0	0	0	0	0	—	0	—	—	—	P	4	0	1	0	0	1.000
WS Totals		13	0	0	0	0	0	0	0	0	0	0	0	0	0	0	0	0	0	—	0	—	—	—	P	13	0	1	0	0	1.000
Postseason Totals		38	1	0	0	0	0	0	0	0	0	0	0	1	0	0	0	0	0	—	0	.000	.000	.000	P	38	2	1	0	0	1.000

JIM WOHLFORD—James Eugene Wohlford—Bats: Right; Throws: Right

Ht: 5'11"; Wt: 175 lbs; Born: 2/28/1951 in Visalia, California; Debut: 9/1/1972

LCS		Batting																							Fielding						
Year Tm	Age	G	AB	H	2B	3B	HR	TB	R	RBI	GW	TBB	IBB	SO	HBP	SH	SF	SB	CS	SB%	GDP	Avg	OBP	SLG	Pos	G	PO	A	E	DP	FPct
1976 KC	25	5	11	2	0	0	0	2	3	0	0	3	0	1	0	0	0	2	0	1.00	0	.182	.357	.182	OF	5	7	0	0	0	1.000

BOB WOLCOTT—Robert William Wolcott—Throws: Right; Bats: Right

Ht: 6'0"; Wt: 190 lbs; Born: 9/8/1973 in Huntington Beach, California; Debut: 8/18/1995

LCS		Pitching																										
Year Tm	Age	G	GS	CG	GF	IP	BFP	H	R	ER	HR	SH	SF	HB	TBB	IBB	SO	WP	Bk	W	L	Pct	ShO	Sv-Op	Hld	OAvg	OOBP	ERA
1995 Sea	22	1	1	0	0	7.0	33	8	2	2	1	0	0	0	5	0	2	0	0	1	0	1.000	0	0-0	0	.286	.394	2.57

LCS		Batting																							Fielding						
Year Tm	Age	G	AB	H	2B	3B	HR	TB	R	RBI	GW	TBB	IBB	SO	HBP	SH	SF	SB	CS	SB%	GDP	Avg	OBP	SLG	Pos	G	PO	A	E	DP	FPct
1995 Sea	22	1	0	0	0	0	0	0	0	0	0	0	0	0	0	0	0	0	0	—	0	—	—	—	P	1	1	1	0	0	1.000

JOE WOOD—Nickname: Smokey Joe—Bats: Right; Throws: Right

Ht: 5'11"; Wt: 180 lbs; Born: 10/25/1889 in Kansas City, Missouri; Debut: 8/24/1908; Died: 7/27/1985

World Series		Batting																							Fielding						
Year Tm	Age	G	AB	H	2B	3B	HR	TB	R	RBI	GW	TBB	IBB	SO	HBP	SH	SF	SB	CS	SB%	GDP	Avg	OBP	SLG	Pos	G	PO	A	E	DP	FPct
1912 Bos	22	4	7	2	0	0	0	2	1	1	0	1	0	0	0	0	0	0	0	—	0	.286	.375	.286	P	4	1	6	0	1	1.000
1920 Cle	30	4	10	2	1	0	0	3	2	0	0	1	0	2	0	0	0	0	0	—	0	.200	.273	.300	OF	4	7	0	0	0	1.000
WS Totals		8	17	4	1	0	0	5	3	1	0	2	0	2	0	0	0	0	0	—	0	.235	.316	.294	P	4	1	6	0	1	1.000

World Series		Pitching																										
Year Tm	Age	G	GS	CG	GF	IP	BFP	H	R	ER	HR	SH	SF	HB	TBB	IBB	SO	WP	Bk	W	L	Pct	ShO	Sv-Op	Hld	OAvg	OOBP	ERA
1912 Bos	22	4	3	2	1	22.0	93	27	11	9	0	1	0	1	3	0	21	0	0	3	1	.750	0	0-0	0	.307	.337	3.68

HAL WOODESHICK—Harold Joseph Woodeshick—Throws: Left; Bats: Right

Ht: 6'3"; Wt: 200 lbs; Born: 8/24/1932 in Wilkes-Barre, Pennsylvania; Debut: 9/14/1956

World Series		Pitching																										
Year Tm	Age	G	GS	CG	GF	IP	BFP	H	R	ER	HR	SH	SF	HB	TBB	IBB	SO	WP	Bk	W	L	Pct	ShO	Sv-Op	Hld	OAvg	OOBP	ERA
1967 StL	35	1	0	0	1	1.0	4	1	0	0	0	0	0	0	0	0	0	0	0	0	0	—	0	0-0	0	.250	.250	0.00

World Series		Batting																							Fielding						
Year Tm	Age	G	AB	H	2B	3B	HR	TB	R	RBI	GW	TBB	IBB	SO	HBP	SH	SF	SB	CS	SB%	GDP	Avg	OBP	SLG	Pos	G	PO	A	E	DP	FPct
1967 StL	35	1	0	0	0	0	0	0	0	0	0	0	0	0	0	0	0	0	0	—	0	—	—	—	P	1	0	1	0	0	1.000

GENE WOODLING—Eugene Richard Woodling—Bats: Left; Throws: Right

Ht: 5'9"; Wt: 195 lbs; Born: 8/16/1922 in Akron, Ohio; Debut: 9/23/1943

World Series		Batting																							Fielding						
Year Tm	Age	G	AB	H	2B	3B	HR	TB	R	RBI	GW	TBB	IBB	SO	HBP	SH	SF	SB	CS	SB%	GDP	Avg	OBP	SLG	Pos	G	PO	A	E	DP	FPct
1949 NYA	27	3	10	4	3	0	0	7	4	0	0	3	0	0	0	0	0	0	0	—	0	.400	.538	.700	OF	3	7	0	0	0	1.000
1950 NYA	28	4	14	6	0	0	0	6	2	1	0	2	0	0	0	0	0	0	1	.00	0	.429	.500	.429	OF	4	7	0	1	0	.875
1951 NYA	29	6	18	3	1	1	1	9	6	1	0	5	0	3	0	0	0	0	0	—	0	.167	.348	.500	OF	5	18	0	1	0	.947
1952 NYA	30	7	23	8	1	1	1	14	4	1	0	3	1	3	0	0	0	0	0	—	0	.348	.423	.609	OF	6	18	0	1	0	.947
1953 NYA	31	6	20	6	0	0	1	9	5	3	0	6	1	2	0	0	0	0	0	—	0	.300	.462	.450	OF	6	9	1	0	0	1.000
WS Totals		26	85	27	5	2	3	45	21	6	0	19	2	8	0	0	0	0	1	.00	0	.318	.442	.529	OF	24	59	1	3	0	.952

GARY WOODS—Gary Lee Woods—Bats: Right; Throws: Right

Ht: 6'2"; Wt: 185 lbs; Born: 7/20/1954 in Santa Barbara, California; Debut: 9/14/1976

Division Series		Batting																							Fielding						
Year Tm	Age	G	AB	H	2B	3B	HR	TB	R	RBI	GW	TBB	IBB	SO	HBP	SH	SF	SB	CS	SB%	GDP	Avg	OBP	SLG	Pos	G	PO	A	E	DP	FPct
1981 Hou	27	2	2	0	0	0	0	0	0	0	0	0	0	1	0	0	0	0	0	—	0	.000	.000	.000	—						
LCS		Batting																							Fielding						
Year Tm	Age	G	AB	H	2B	3B	HR	TB	R	RBI	GW	TBB	IBB	SO	HBP	SH	SF	SB	CS	SB%	GDP	Avg	OBP	SLG	Pos	G	PO	A	E	DP	FPct
1980 Hou	26	4	8	2	0	0	0	2	0	1	0	1	0	3	0	0	0	1	0	1.00	0	.250	.333	.250	OF	3	1	0	0	0	1.000
1984 ChN	30	1	1	0	0	0	0	0	0	0	0	0	0	1	0	0	0	0	0	—	0	.000	.000	.000	OF	1	1	0	0	0	1.000
LCS Totals		5	9	2	0	0	0	2	0	1	0	1	0	4	0	0	0	1	0	1.00	0	.222	.300	.222	OF	4	2	0	0	0	1.000
Postseason Totals		7	11	2	0	0	0	2	0	1	0	1	0	5	0	0	0	1	0	1.00	0	.182	.250	.182	OF	4	2	0	0	0	1.000

DICK WOODSON—Richard Lee Woodson—Throws: Right; Bats: Right

Ht: 6'5"; Wt: 205 lbs; Born: 3/30/1945 in Oelwein, Iowa; Debut: 4/8/1969

LCS		Pitching																										
Year Tm	Age	G	GS	CG	GF	IP	BFP	H	R	ER	HR	SH	SF	HB	TBB	IBB	SO	WP	Bk	W	L	Pct	ShO	Sv-Op	Hld	OAvg	OOBP	ERA
1969 Min	24	1	0	0	0	1.2	11	3	2	2	0	0	0	0	3	0	2	0	0	0	0	—	0	0-0	0	.375	.545	10.80
1970 Min	25	1	0	0	0	1.0	6	2	1	1	0	0	0	0	1	0	0	0	0	0	0	—	0	0-0	0	.400	.500	9.00
LCS Totals		2	0	0	0	2.2	34	5	3	3	0	0	0	0	4	0	2	0	0	0	0	—	0	0-0	0	.385	.529	10.13

LCS Year Tm	Age	G	AB	H	2B	3B	HR	TB	R	RBI	GW	TBB	IBB	SO	HBP	SH	SF	SB	CS	SB%	GDP	Avg	OBP	SLG	Pos	G	PO	A	E	DP	FPct
1969 Min	24	1	1	1	0	0	0	1	0	0	0	0	0	0	0	0	0	0	0	—	0	1.000	1.000	1.000	P	1	0	0	0	0	—
1970 Min	25	1	0	0	0	0	0	0	0	0	0	0	0	0	0	0	0	0	0	—	0	—	—	—	P	1	0	0	0	0	—
LCS Totals		2	1	1	0	0	0	1	0	0	0	0	0	0	0	0	0	0	0	—	0	1.000	1.000	1.000	P	2	0	0	0	0	—

TRACY WOODSON—Tracy Michael Woodson—Bats: Right; Throws: Right

Ht: 6'3"; Wt: 215 lbs; Born: 10/5/1962 in Richmond, Virginia; Debut: 4/7/1987

Year Tm	Age	G	AB	H	2B	3B	HR	TB	R	RBI	GW	TBB	IBB	SO	HBP	SH	SF	SB	CS	SB%	GDP	Avg	OBP	SLG	Pos	G	PO	A	E	DP	FPct
LCS																															
1988 LA	25	3	4	1	0	0	0	1	0	0	0	0	0	1	0	0	0	0	0	—	0	.250	.250	.250	1B	3	3	0	0	0	1.000
World Series																															
1988 LA	25	4	4	0	0	0	0	0	0	1	0	0	0	0	0	0	0	0	0	—	0	.000	.000	.000	1B	3	6	1	0	0	1.000
Postseason Totals		7	8	1	0	0	0	1	0	1	0	0	0	1	0	0	0	0	0	—	0	.125	.125	.125	1B	6	9	1	0	0	1.000

WOODY WOODWARD—William Frederick Woodward—Bats: Right; Throws: Right

Ht: 6'2"; Wt: 180 lbs; Born: 9/23/1942 in Miami, Florida; Debut: 9/9/1963

Year Tm	Age	G	AB	H	2B	3B	HR	TB	R	RBI	GW	TBB	IBB	SO	HBP	SH	SF	SB	CS	SB%	GDP	Avg	OBP	SLG	Pos	G	PO	A	E	DP	FPct
LCS																															
1970 Cin	28	3	10	1	0	0	0	1	0	0	0	1	1	0	0	0	0	0	0	—	0	.100	.182	.100	SS	3	5	8	0	0	1.000
																									3B	3	0	1	0	0	1.000
World Series																															
1970 Cin	28	4	5	1	0	0	0	1	0	0	0	0	0	0	0	0	0	0	0	—	0	.200	.200	.200	SS	3	4	5	0	3	1.000
Postseason Totals		7	15	2	0	0	0	2	0	0	0	1	1	0	0	0	0	0	0	—	0	.133	.188	.133	SS	6	9	13	0	3	1.000

RALPH WORKS—Ralph Talmadge Works—Nickname: Judge—Throws: Right; Bats: Left

Ht: 6'2"; Wt: 185 lbs; Born: 3/16/1888 in Payson, Illinois; Debut: 5/1/1909; Died: 8/8/1941

World Series Year Tm	Age	G	GS	CG	GF	IP	BFP	H	R	ER	HR	SH	SF	HB	TBB	IBB	SO	WP	Bk	W	L	Pct	ShO	Sv-Op	Hld	OAvg	OOBP	ERA
1909 Det	21	1	0	0	1	2.0	10	4	2	2	0	0	1	0	0	0	2	0	0	0	0	—	0	0- 0	0	.444	.400	9.00

World Series Year Tm	Age	G	AB	H	2B	3B	HR	TB	R	RBI	GW	TBB	IBB	SO	HBP	SH	SF	SB	CS	SB%	GDP	Avg	OBP	SLG	Pos	G	PO	A	E	DP	FPct
1909 Det	21	1	0	0	0	0	0	0	0	0	0	0	0	0	0	0	0	0	0	—	0	—	—	—	P	1	0	1	0	0	1.000

TIM WORRELL—Timothy Howard Worrell—Throws: Right; Bats: Right

Ht: 6'4"; Wt: 210 lbs; Born: 7/5/1967 in Pasadena, California; Debut: 6/25/1993

Division Series Year Tm	Age	G	GS	CG	GF	IP	BFP	H	R	ER	HR	SH	SF	HB	TBB	IBB	SO	WP	Bk	W	L	Pct	ShO	Sv-Op	Hld	OAvg	OOBP	ERA
1996 SD	29	2	0	0	0	3.2	15	4	1	1	0	0	0	0	1	0	2	0	0	0	0	—	0	0- 1	0	.286	.333	2.45

Division Series Year Tm	Age	G	AB	H	2B	3B	HR	TB	R	RBI	GW	TBB	IBB	SO	HBP	SH	SF	SB	CS	SB%	GDP	Avg	OBP	SLG	Pos	G	PO	A	E	DP	FPct
1996 SD	29	2	0	0	0	0	0	0	0	0	0	0	0	0	0	0	0	0	0	—	0	—	—	—	P	2	0	1	0	0	1.000

TODD WORRELL—Todd Roland Worrell—Throws: Right; Bats: Right

Ht: 6'5"; Wt: 215 lbs; Born: 9/28/1959 in Arcadia, California; Debut: 8/28/1985

Year Tm	Age	G	GS	CG	GF	IP	BFP	H	R	ER	HR	SH	SF	HB	TBB	IBB	SO	WP	Bk	W	L	Pct	ShO	Sv-Op	Hld	OAvg	OOBP	ERA
Division Series																												
1996 LA	37	1	0	0	1	1.0	3	0	0	0	0	0	0	0	1	0	1	0	0	0	0	—	0	0- 0	0	.000	.333	0.00
LCS																												
1985 StL	26	4	0	0	1	6.1	24	4	1	1	1	0	0	0	2	1	3	1	0	1	0	1.000	0	0- 0	1	.182	.250	1.42
1987 StL	28	3	0	0	1	4.1	18	4	1	1	1	0	0	0	1	0	6	0	0	0	0	—	0	1- 1	2	.235	.278	2.08
LCS Totals		7	0	0	2	10.2	84	8	2	2	2	0	0	0	3	1	9	1	0	1	0	1.000	0	1-1	3	.205	.262	1.69
World Series																												
1985 StL	26	3	0	0	2	4.2	20	4	2	2	0	0	0	0	2	1	6	0	0	0	1	.000	0	1- 2	0	.222	.300	3.86
1987 StL	28	4	0	0	4	7.0	31	6	1	1	0	0	0	0	4	0	3	0	0	0	0	—	0	2- 2	0	.222	.323	1.29
WS Totals		7	0	0	6	11.2	102	10	3	3	0	0	0	0	6	1	9	0	0	0	1	.000	0	3-4	0	.222	.314	2.31
Postseason Totals		15	0	0	9	23.1	192	18	5	5	2	0	0	0	10	2	19	1	0	1	1	.500	0	4-5	3	.209	.292	1.93

Year Tm	Age	G	AB	H	2B	3B	HR	TB	R	RBI	GW	TBB	IBB	SO	HBP	SH	SF	SB	CS	SB%	GDP	Avg	OBP	SLG	Pos	G	PO	A	E	DP	FPct
Division Series																															
1996 LA	37	1	0	0	0	0	0	0	0	0	0	0	0	0	0	0	0	0	0	—	0	—	—	—	P	1	0	0	0	0	—
LCS																															
1985 StL	26	4	0	0	0	0	0	0	0	0	0	0	0	0	0	0	0	0	0	—	0	—	—	—	P	4	0	1	0	0	1.000
1987 StL	28	3	1	0	0	0	0	0	0	0	0	0	0	1	0	0	0	0	0	—	0	.000	.000	.000	P	3	0	0	0	0	—
																									OF	1	0	0	0	0	—
LCS Totals		7	1	0	0	0	0	0	0	0	0	0	0	1	0	0	0	0	0	—	0	.000	.000	.000	P	7	0	1	0	0	1.000
World Series																															
1985 StL	26	3	1	0	0	0	0	0	0	0	0	0	0	1	0	0	0	0	0	—	0	.000	.000	.000	P	3	0	1	0	0	1.000
1987 StL	28	4	0	0	0	0	0	0	0	0	0	0	0	0	0	0	0	0	0	—	0	—	—	—	P	4	0	0	0	0	—
WS Totals		7	1	0	0	0	0	0	0	0	0	0	0	1	0	0	0	0	0	—	0	.000	.000	.000	P	7	0	1	0	0	1.000
Postseason Totals		15	2	0	0	0	0	0	0	0	0	0	0	2	0	0	0	0	0	—	0	.000	.000	.000	P	15	0	2	0	0	1.000

AL WORTHINGTON—Allan Fulton Worthington—Throws: Right; Bats: Right

Ht: 6'2"; Wt: 195 lbs; Born: 2/5/1929 in Birmingham, Alabama; Debut: 7/6/1953

Year Tm	Age	G	GS	CG	GF	IP	BFP	H	R	ER	HR	SH	SF	HB	TBB	IBB	SO	WP	Bk	W	L	Pct	ShO	Sv-Op	Hld	OAvg	OOBP	ERA
LCS																												
1969 Min	40	1	0	0	0	1.1	7	3	1	1	0	0	0	0	0	0	1	0	0	0	0	—	0	0- 0	0	.429	.429	6.75
World Series																												
1965 Min	36	2	0	0	0	4.0	16	2	1	0	0	0	0	1	2	0	2	0	0	0	0	—	0	0- 0	0	.154	.313	0.00
Postseason Totals		3	0	0	0	5.1	46	5	2	1	0	0	0	1	2	0	3	0	0	0	0	—	0	0-0	0	.250	.348	1.69

Year Tm	Age	G	AB	H	2B	3B	HR	TB	R	RBI	GW	TBB	IBB	SO	HBP	SH	SF	SB	CS	SB%	GDP	Avg	OBP	SLG	Pos	G	PO	A	E	DP	FPct
LCS																															
1969 Min	40	1	0	0	0	0	0	0	0	0	0	0	0	0	0	0	0	0	0	—	0	—	—	—	P	1	0	0	0	0	—
World Series																															
1965 Min	36	2	0	0	0	0	0	0	0	0	0	0	0	0	0	0	0	0	0	—	0	—	—	—	P	2	1	1	1	0	.667
Postseason Totals		3	0	0	0	0	0	0	0	0	0	0	0	0	0	0	0	0	0	—	0	—	—	—	P	3	1	1	1	0	.667

CHUCK WORTMAN—William Lewis Wortman—Bats: Right; Throws: Right

Ht: 5'7"; Wt: 150 lbs; Born: 1/5/1892 in Baltimore, Maryland; Debut: 7/20/1916; Died: 8/19/1977

World Series Year Tm	Age	G	AB	H	2B	3B	HR	TB	R	RBI	GW	TBB	IBB	SO	HBP	SH	SF	SB	CS	SB%	GDP	Avg	OBP	SLG	Pos	G	PO	A	E	DP	FPct
1918 ChN	26	1	1	0	0	0	0	0	0	0	0	0	0	0	0	0	0	0	0	—	0	.000	.000	.000	2B	1	1	0	0	0	1.000

GLENN WRIGHT—Forest Glenn Wright—Nickname: Buckshot—Bats: Right; Throws: Right

Ht: 5'11"; Wt: 170 lbs; Born: 2/6/1901 in Archie, Missouri; Debut: 4/15/1924; Died: 4/6/1984

World Series Year Tm	Age	G	AB	H	2B	3B	HR	TB	R	RBI	GW	TBB	IBB	SO	HBP	SH	SF	SB	CS	SB%	GDP	Avg	OBP	SLG	Pos	G	PO	A	E	DP	FPct
1925 Pit	24	7	27	5	1	0	1	9	3	3	0	1	0	4	0	0	1	0	0	—	0	.185	.207	.333	SS	7	12	23	2	0	.946
1927 Pit	26	4	13	2	0	0	0	2	1	2	0	0	0	0	0	0	2	0	0	—	1	.154	.133	.154	SS	4	5	13	1	2	.947
WS Totals		11	40	7	1	0	1	11	4	5	0	1	0	4	0	0	3	0	0	—	1	.175	.182	.275	SS	11	17	36	3	2	.946

JARET WRIGHT—Jaret Samuel Wright—Throws: Right; Bats: Right

Ht: 6'2"; Wt: 230 lbs; Born: 12/29/1975 in Anaheim, California; Debut: 6/24/1997

Division Series — Pitching

Year	Tm	Age	G	GS	CG	GF	IP	BFP	H	R	ER	HR	SH	SF	HB	TBB	IBB	SO	WP	Bk	W	L	Pct	ShO	Sv-Op	Hld	OAvg	OOBP	ERA
1997	Cle	21	2	2	0	0	11.1	51	11	6	5	0	0	1	0	7	1	10	0	0	2	0	1.000	0	0- 0	0	.256	.353	3.97

LCS — Pitching

Year	Tm	Age	G	GS	CG	GF	IP	BFP	H	R	ER	HR	SH	SF	HB	TBB	IBB	SO	WP	Bk	W	L	Pct	ShO	Sv-Op	Hld	OAvg	OOBP	ERA
1997	Cle	21	1	1	0	0	3.0	17	6	5	5	3	0	0	0	2	0	3	0	0	0	0	—	0	0- 0	0	.400	.471	15.00

World Series — Pitching

Year	Tm	Age	G	GS	CG	GF	IP	BFP	H	R	ER	HR	SH	SF	HB	TBB	IBB	SO	WP	Bk	W	L	Pct	ShO	Sv-Op	Hld	OAvg	OOBP	ERA
1997	Cle	21	2	2	0	0	12.1	52	7	4	4	2	0	0	0	10	0	12	1	0	1	0	1.000	0	0- 0	0	.167	.327	2.92
Postseason Totals			5	5	0	0	26.2	240	24	15	14	5	0	1	0	19	1	25	1	0	3	0	1.000	0	0-0	0	.240	.358	4.73

Division Series — Batting / Fielding

Year	Tm	Age	G	AB	H	2B	3B	HR	TB	R	RBI	GW	TBB	IBB	SO	HBP	SH	SF	SB	CS	SB%	GDP	Avg	OBP	SLG	Pos	G	PO	A	E	DP	FPct
1997	Cle	21	2	0	0	0	0	0	0	0	0	0	0	0	0	0	0	0	0	0	—	0	—	—	—	P	2	2	3	1	1	.833

LCS — Batting / Fielding

Year	Tm	Age	G	AB	H	2B	3B	HR	TB	R	RBI	GW	TBB	IBB	SO	HBP	SH	SF	SB	CS	SB%	GDP	Avg	OBP	SLG	Pos	G	PO	A	E	DP	FPct
1997	Cle	21	1	0	0	0	0	0	0	0	0	0	0	0	0	0	0	0	0	0	—	0	—	—	—	P	1	0	0	0	0	—

World Series — Batting / Fielding

Year	Tm	Age	G	AB	H	2B	3B	HR	TB	R	RBI	GW	TBB	IBB	SO	HBP	SH	SF	SB	CS	SB%	GDP	Avg	OBP	SLG	Pos	G	PO	A	E	DP	FPct
1997	Cle	21	2	2	0	0	0	0	0	0	0	0	0	0	2	0	1	0	0	0	—	0	.000	.000	.000	P	2	0	1	0	0	1.000
Postseason Totals			5	2	0	0	0	0	0	0	0	0	0	0	2	0	1	0	0	0	—	0	.000	.000	.000	P	5	2	4	1	1	.857

RICK WRONA—Richard James Wrona—Bats: Right; Throws: Right

Ht: 6'1"; Wt: 185 lbs; Born: 12/10/1963 in Tulsa, Oklahoma; Debut: 9/3/1988

LCS — Batting / Fielding

Year	Tm	Age	G	AB	H	2B	3B	HR	TB	R	RBI	GW	TBB	IBB	SO	HBP	SH	SF	SB	CS	SB%	GDP	Avg	OBP	SLG	Pos	G	PO	A	E	DP	FPct
1989	ChN	25	2	5	0	0	0	0	0	0	0	0	0	0	3	0	0	0	0	0	—	0	.000	.000	.000	C	2	9	1	0	0	1.000

JOHN WYATT—John Thomas Wyatt—Throws: Right; Bats: Right

Ht: 5'11"; Wt: 200 lbs; Born: 4/19/1935 in Chicago, Illinois; Debut: 9/8/1961

World Series — Pitching

Year	Tm	Age	G	GS	CG	GF	IP	BFP	H	R	ER	HR	SH	SF	HB	TBB	IBB	SO	WP	Bk	W	L	Pct	ShO	Sv-Op	Hld	OAvg	OOBP	ERA
1967	Bos	32	2	0	0	1	3.2	15	1	2	2	1	0	0	0	3	0	1	0	1	1	0	1.000	0	0- 1	0	.083	.267	4.91

World Series — Batting / Fielding

Year	Tm	Age	G	AB	H	2B	3B	HR	TB	R	RBI	GW	TBB	IBB	SO	HBP	SH	SF	SB	CS	SB%	GDP	Avg	OBP	SLG	Pos	G	PO	A	E	DP	FPct
1967	Bos	32	2	0	0	0	0	0	0	0	0	0	0	0	0	0	0	0	0	0	—	0	—	—	—	P	2	0	0	0	0	—

WHIT WYATT—John Whitlow Wyatt—Throws: Right; Bats: Right

Ht: 6'1"; Wt: 185 lbs; Born: 9/27/1907 in Kensington, Georgia; Debut: 9/16/1929

World Series — Pitching

Year	Tm	Age	G	GS	CG	GF	IP	BFP	H	R	ER	HR	SH	SF	HB	TBB	IBB	SO	WP	Bk	W	L	Pct	ShO	Sv-Op	Hld	OAvg	OOBP	ERA
1941	Bro	34	2	2	2	0	18.0	75	15	5	5	1	0	0	0	10	1	14	1	0	1	1	.500	0	0- 0	0	.231	.333	2.50

World Series — Batting / Fielding

Year	Tm	Age	G	AB	H	2B	3B	HR	TB	R	RBI	GW	TBB	IBB	SO	HBP	SH	SF	SB	CS	SB%	GDP	Avg	OBP	SLG	Pos	G	PO	A	E	DP	FPct
1941	Bro	34	2	6	1	1	0	0	2	1	0	0	0	0	1	0	0	0	0	0	—	1	.167	.167	.333	P	2	1	2	0	0	1.000

JOHN WYCKOFF—John Weldon Wyckoff—Throws: Right; Bats: Right

Ht: 6'1"; Wt: 175 lbs; Born: 2/19/1892 in Williamsport, Pennsylvania; Debut: 4/19/1913; Died: 5/8/1961

World Series — Pitching

Year	Tm	Age	G	GS	CG	GF	IP	BFP	H	R	ER	HR	SH	SF	HB	TBB	IBB	SO	WP	Bk	W	L	Pct	ShO	Sv-Op	Hld	OAvg	OOBP	ERA
1914	Phi	22	1	0	0	1	3.2	14	3	1	1	0	0	0	0	1	0	2	0	0	0	0	—	0	0- 0	0	.231	.286	2.45

World Series — Batting / Fielding

Year	Tm	Age	G	AB	H	2B	3B	HR	TB	R	RBI	GW	TBB	IBB	SO	HBP	SH	SF	SB	CS	SB%	GDP	Avg	OBP	SLG	Pos	G	PO	A	E	DP	FPct
1914	Phi	22	1	1	1	1	0	0	2	0	0	0	0	0	0	0	0	0	0	0	—	0	1.000	1.000	2.000	P	1	1	0	0	0	1.000

EARLY WYNN (HOF 1972-W)—Nickname: Gus—Throws: Right; Bats: Both

Ht: 6'0"; Wt: 190 lbs; Born: 1/6/1920 in Hartford, Alabama; Debut: 9/13/1939

World Series — Pitching

Year	Tm	Age	G	GS	CG	GF	IP	BFP	H	R	ER	HR	SH	SF	HB	TBB	IBB	SO	WP	Bk	W	L	Pct	ShO	Sv-Op	Hld	OAvg	OOBP	ERA
1954	Cle	34	1	1	0	0	7.0	27	4	3	3	1	0	0	0	2	0	5	1	0	0	1	.000	0	0- 0	0	.160	.222	3.86
1959	ChA-*C*	39	3	3	0	0	13.0	62	19	9	8	1	1	0	0	4	0	10	0	0	1	1	.500	0	0- 0	0	.333	.377	5.54
WS Totals			4	4	0	0	20.0	178	23	12	11	2	1	0	0	6	0	15	1	0	1	2	.333	0	0-0	0	.280	.330	4.95

World Series — Batting / Fielding

Year	Tm	Age	G	AB	H	2B	3B	HR	TB	R	RBI	GW	TBB	IBB	SO	HBP	SH	SF	SB	CS	SB%	GDP	Avg	OBP	SLG	Pos	G	PO	A	E	DP	FPct
1954	Cle	34	1	2	1	1	0	0	2	0	0	0	0	0	1	0	1	0	0	0	—	0	.500	.500	1.000	P	1	1	1	0	0	1.000
1959	ChA	39	3	5	1	1	0	0	2	0	1	0	0	0	2	0	0	0	0	0	—	0	.200	.200	.400	P	3	1	3	0	0	1.000
WS Totals			4	7	2	2	0	0	4	0	1	0	0	0	3	0	1	0	0	0	—	0	.286	.286	.571	P	4	2	4	0	0	1.000

JIMMY WYNN—James Sherman Wynn—Nickname: The Toy Cannon—Bats: Right; Throws: Right

Ht: 5'10"; Wt: 160 lbs; Born: 3/12/1942 in Hamilton, Ohio; Debut: 7/10/1963

LCS — Batting / Fielding

Year	Tm	Age	G	AB	H	2B	3B	HR	TB	R	RBI	GW	TBB	IBB	SO	HBP	SH	SF	SB	CS	SB%	GDP	Avg	OBP	SLG	Pos	G	PO	A	E	DP	FPct
1974	LA	32	4	10	2	2	0	0	4	4	2	1	9	2	1	0	0	0	1	0	1.00	0	.200	.579	.400	OF	4	10	0	0	0	1.000

World Series — Batting / Fielding

Year	Tm	Age	G	AB	H	2B	3B	HR	TB	R	RBI	GW	TBB	IBB	SO	HBP	SH	SF	SB	CS	SB%	GDP	Avg	OBP	SLG	Pos	G	PO	A	E	DP	FPct
1974	LA	32	5	16	3	1	0	1	7	1	2	0	4	0	4	0	0	1	0	0	—	0	.188	.333	.438	OF	5	5	0	0	0	1.000
Postseason Totals			9	26	5	3	0	1	11	5	4	1	13	2	5	0	0	1	1	0	1.00	0	.192	.450	.423	OF	9	15	0	0	0	1.000

MARVELL WYNNE—Bats: Left; Throws: Left

Ht: 5'11"; Wt: 175 lbs; Born: 12/17/1959 in Chicago, Illinois; Debut: 6/15/1983

LCS — Batting / Fielding

Year	Tm	Age	G	AB	H	2B	3B	HR	TB	R	RBI	GW	TBB	IBB	SO	HBP	SH	SF	SB	CS	SB%	GDP	Avg	OBP	SLG	Pos	G	PO	A	E	DP	FPct
1989	ChN	29	4	6	1	0	0	0	1	0	0	0	0	0	0	0	0	0	0	0	—	0	.167	.167	.167	OF	2	3	0	0	0	1.000

HANK WYSE—Henry Washington Wyse—Nickname: Hooks—Throws: Right; Bats: Right

Ht: 5'11"; Wt: 185 lbs; Born: 3/1/1918 in Lunsford, Arkansas; Debut: 9/7/1942

World Series — Pitching

Year	Tm	Age	G	GS	CG	GF	IP	BFP	H	R	ER	HR	SH	SF	HB	TBB	IBB	SO	WP	Bk	W	L	Pct	ShO	Sv-Op	Hld	OAvg	OOBP	ERA
1945	ChN	27	3	1	0	1	7.2	35	8	7	6	1	0	0	0	4	0	1	0	0	0	1	.000	0	0- 0	1	.258	.343	7.04

World Series — Batting / Fielding

Year	Tm	Age	G	AB	H	2B	3B	HR	TB	R	RBI	GW	TBB	IBB	SO	HBP	SH	SF	SB	CS	SB%	GDP	Avg	OBP	SLG	Pos	G	PO	A	E	DP	FPct
1945	ChN	27	3	3	0	0	0	0	0	0	0	0	0	0	2	0	0	0	0	0	—	0	.000	.000	.000	P	3	0	0	0	0	—

CARL YASTRZEMSKI (HOF 1989-W)—Carl Michael Yastrzemski—Nickname: Yaz—Bats: Left; Throws: Right

Ht: 5'11"; Wt: 175 lbs; Born: 8/22/1939 in Southampton, New York; Debut: 4/11/1961

LCS — Batting / Fielding

Year	Tm	Age	G	AB	H	2B	3B	HR	TB	R	RBI	GW	TBB	IBB	SO	HBP	SH	SF	SB	CS	SB%	GDP	Avg	OBP	SLG	Pos	G	PO	A	E	DP	FPct
1975	Bos	36	3	11	5	1	0	1	9	4	2	0	1	1	1	0	0	0	0	0	—	0	.455	.500	.818	OF	3	7	2	0	0	1.000

World Series — Batting / Fielding

Year	Tm	Age	G	AB	H	2B	3B	HR	TB	R	RBI	GW	TBB	IBB	SO	HBP	SH	SF	SB	CS	SB%	GDP	Avg	OBP	SLG	Pos	G	PO	A	E	DP	FPct
1967	Bos-*M*	28	7	25	10	2	0	3	21	4	5	1	4	1	1	1	0	0	0	1	.00	1	.400	.500	.840	OF	7	16	2	0	0	1.000
1975	Bos	36	7	29	9	0	0	0	9	7	4	1	4	0	1	0	0	1	0	0	—	1	.310	.382	.310	1B	4	28	0	0	3	1.000
																										OF	4	8	0	0	0	1.000
WS Totals			14	54	19	2	0	3	30	11	9	2	8	1	2	1	0	1	0	1	.00	2	.352	.438	.556	OF	11	24	2	0	0	1.000
Postseason Totals			17	65	24	3	0	4	39	15	11	2	9	2	3	1	0	1	0	1	.00	2	.369	.447	.600	OF	14	31	4	0	0	1.000

EMIL YDE—Emil Ogden Yde—Throws: Left; Bats: Both

Ht: 5'11"; Wt: 165 lbs; Born: 1/28/1900 in Great Lakes, Illinois; Debut: 4/21/1924; Died: 12/4/1968

World Series		Pitching																									
Year Tm	Age	G	GS	CG	GF	IP	BFP	H	R	ER	HR	SH	SF	HB	TBB	IBB	SO	WP	Bk	W	L	Pct	ShO	Sv-Op	Hld	OAvg	OOBP	ERA
1925 Pit	25	1	1	0	0	2.1	14	5	4	3	2	0	0	0	3	0	1	0	0	0	1	.000	0	0-0	0	.455	.571	11.57

World Series		Batting																							Fielding						
Year Tm	Age	G	AB	H	2B	3B	HR	TB	R	RBI	GW	TBB	IBB	SO	HBP	SH	SF	SB	CS	SB%	GDP	Avg	OBP	SLG	Pos	G	PO	A	E	DP	FPct
1925 Pit	25	2	1	0	0	0	0	0	1	0	0	0	0	0	0	0	0	0	0	—	0	.000	.000	.000	P	1	0	0	0	0	—
1927 Pit	27	1	0	0	0	0	0	0	1	0	0	0	0	0	0	0	0	0	0	—	0	—	—	—	—						
WS Totals		3	1	0	0	0	0	0	2	0	0	0	0	0	0	0	0	0	0	—	0	.000	.000	.000	P	1	0	0	0	0	—

STEVE YEAGER—Stephen Wayne Yeager—Bats: Right; Throws: Right

Ht: 6'0"; Wt: 190 lbs; Born: 11/24/1948 in Huntington, West Virginia; Debut: 8/2/1972

Division Series		Batting																							Fielding						
Year Tm	Age	G	AB	H	2B	3B	HR	TB	R	RBI	GW	TBB	IBB	SO	HBP	SH	SF	SB	CS	SB%	GDP	Avg	OBP	SLG	Pos	G	PO	A	E	DP	FPct
1981 LA	32	2	5	2	1	0	0	3	1	0	0	0	0	1	0	0	0	0	0	—	0	.400	.400	.600	C	2	6	0	0	0	1.000
LCS		**Batting**																							**Fielding**						
Year Tm	Age	G	AB	H	2B	3B	HR	TB	R	RBI	GW	TBB	IBB	SO	HBP	SH	SF	SB	CS	SB%	GDP	Avg	OBP	SLG	Pos	G	PO	A	E	DP	FPct
1974 LA	25	3	9	0	0	0	0	0	1	0	0	3	1	3	0	0	0	1	0	1.00	0	.000	.250	.000	C	3	14	1	0	0	1.000
1977 LA	28	4	13	3	0	0	0	3	1	2	0	1	1	3	0	0	0	0	0	—	0	.231	.286	.231	C	4	22	1	0	0	1.000
1978 LA	29	4	13	3	0	0	1	6	2	2	0	2	0	2	0	0	0	1	0	1.00	0	.231	.333	.462	C	4	21	2	0	0	1.000
1981 LA	32	1	2	1	0	0	0	1	1	0	0	0	0	0	0	0	0	0	0	—	0	.500	.500	.500	C	1	2	0	0	0	1.000
1983 LA	34	2	6	1	1	0	0	2	0	0	0	0	0	0	1	0	0	0	0	—	0	.167	.286	.333	C	2	7	1	0	0	1.000
1985 LA	36	1	2	0	0	0	0	0	0	0	0	1	0	1	0	0	0	0	0	—	0	.000	.333	.000	C	1	4	0	0	0	1.000
LCS Totals		15	45	8	1	0	1	12	5	4	0	7	2	9	1	0	0	2	0	1.00	0	.178	.302	.267	C	15	70	5	0	0	1.000
World Series		**Batting**																							**Fielding**						
Year Tm	Age	G	AB	H	2B	3B	HR	TB	R	RBI	GW	TBB	IBB	SO	HBP	SH	SF	SB	CS	SB%	GDP	Avg	OBP	SLG	Pos	G	PO	A	E	DP	FPct
1974 LA	25	4	11	4	1	0	0	5	0	1	1	1	0	4	0	0	0	0	0	—	0	.364	.417	.455	C	4	32	4	1	1	.973
1977 LA	28	6	19	6	1	0	2	13	2	5	0	1	0	1	0	0	1	0	0	—	0	.316	.333	.684	C	6	32	6	0	0	1.000
1978 LA	29	5	13	3	1	0	0	4	2	0	0	1	0	2	0	0	0	0	0	—	0	.231	.286	.308	C	5	23	2	0	0	1.000
1981 LA	32	6	14	4	1	0	2	11	2	4	2	0	0	2	0	0	1	0	0	—	1	.286	.267	.786	C	6	20	0	0	0	1.000
WS Totals		21	57	17	4	0	4	33	6	10	3	3	0	9	0	0	2	0	0	—	1	.298	.323	.579	C	21	107	12	1	1	.992
Postseason Totals		38	107	27	6	0	5	48	12	14	3	10	2	19	1	0	2	2	0	1.00	1	.252	.317	.449	C	38	183	17	1	1	.995

STEVE YERKES—Stephen Douglas Yerkes—Bats: Right; Throws: Right

Ht: 5'9"; Wt: 165 lbs; Born: 5/15/1888 in Hatboro, Pennsylvania; Debut: 9/29/1909; Died: 1/31/1971

World Series		Batting																							Fielding						
Year Tm	Age	G	AB	H	2B	3B	HR	TB	R	RBI	GW	TBB	IBB	SO	HBP	SH	SF	SB	CS	SB%	GDP	Avg	OBP	SLG	Pos	G	PO	A	E	DP	FPct
1912 Bos	24	8	32	8	0	2	0	12	3	4	2	2	0	3	0	1	0	0	0	—	0	.250	.294	.375	2B	8	14	22	1	1	.973

RUDY YORK—Rudolph Preston York—Nickname: The Big Indian—Bats: Right; Throws: Right

Ht: 6'1"; Wt: 209 lbs; Born: 8/17/1913 in Ragland, Alabama; Debut: 8/22/1934; Died: 2/5/1970

World Series		Batting																							Fielding						
Year Tm	Age	G	AB	H	2B	3B	HR	TB	R	RBI	GW	TBB	IBB	SO	HBP	SH	SF	SB	CS	SB%	GDP	Avg	OBP	SLG	Pos	G	PO	A	E	DP	FPct
1940 Det	27	7	26	6	0	1	1	11	3	2	1	4	0	7	0	0	0	0	0	—	1	.231	.333	.423	1B	7	60	2	0	4	1.000
1945 Det	32	7	28	5	1	0	0	6	1	3	0	3	1	4	0	0	0	0	0	—	0	.179	.258	.214	1B	7	67	8	1	3	.987
1946 Bos	33	7	23	6	1	1	2	15	6	5	2	6	3	4	1	0	0	0	0	—	2	.261	.433	.652	1B	7	60	3	1	2	.984
WS Totals		21	77	17	2	2	3	32	10	10	3	13	4	15	1	0	0	0	0	—	3	.221	.341	.416	1B	21	187	13	2	9	.990

NED YOST—Edgar Frederick Yost—Bats: Right; Throws: Right

Ht: 6'1"; Wt: 190 lbs; Born: 8/19/1955 in Eureka, California; Debut: 4/12/1980

World Series		Batting																							Fielding						
Year Tm	Age	G	AB	H	2B	3B	HR	TB	R	RBI	GW	TBB	IBB	SO	HBP	SH	SF	SB	CS	SB%	GDP	Avg	OBP	SLG	Pos	G	PO	A	E	DP	FPct
1982 Mil	27	1	0	0	0	0	0	0	0	0	0	1	0	0	0	0	0	0	0	—	0	—	1.000	—	C	1	1	0	0	0	1.000

CURT YOUNG—Curtis Allen Young—Throws: Left; Bats: Right

Ht: 6'1"; Wt: 175 lbs; Born: 4/16/1960 in Saginaw, Michigan; Debut: 6/24/1983

LCS		Pitching																									
Year Tm	Age	G	GS	CG	GF	IP	BFP	H	R	ER	HR	SH	SF	HB	TBB	IBB	SO	WP	Bk	W	L	Pct	ShO	Sv-Op	Hld	OAvg	OOBP	ERA
1988 Oak	28	1	0	0	0	1.1	5	1	1	0	0	0	0	0	0	0	2	0	0	0	0	—	0	0-0	1	.200	.200	0.00
World Series		**Pitching**																									
Year Tm	Age	G	GS	CG	GF	IP	BFP	H	R	ER	HR	SH	SF	HB	TBB	IBB	SO	WP	Bk	W	L	Pct	ShO	Sv-Op	Hld	OAvg	OOBP	ERA
1990 Oak	30	1	0	0	1	1.0	4	1	0	0	0	0	0	0	0	0	0	0	0	0	0	—	0	0-0	0	.250	.250	0.00
Postseason Totals		2	0	0	1	2.1	18	2	1	0	0	0	0	0	0	0	2	0	0	0	0	—	0	0-0	1	.222	.222	0.00

LCS		Batting																							Fielding						
Year Tm	Age	G	AB	H	2B	3B	HR	TB	R	RBI	GW	TBB	IBB	SO	HBP	SH	SF	SB	CS	SB%	GDP	Avg	OBP	SLG	Pos	G	PO	A	E	DP	FPct
1988 Oak	28	1	0	0	0	0	0	0	0	0	0	0	0	0	0	0	0	0	0	—	0	—	—	—	P	1	0	0	0	0	—
World Series		**Batting**																							**Fielding**						
Year Tm	Age	G	AB	H	2B	3B	HR	TB	R	RBI	GW	TBB	IBB	SO	HBP	SH	SF	SB	CS	SB%	GDP	Avg	OBP	SLG	Pos	G	PO	A	E	DP	FPct
1990 Oak	30	1	0	0	0	0	0	0	0	0	0	0	0	0	0	0	0	0	0	—	0	—	—	—	P	1	0	0	0	0	—
Postseason Totals		2	0	0	0	0	0	0	0	0	0	0	0	0	0	0	0	0	0	—	0	—	—	—	P	2	0	0	0	0	—

CY YOUNG (HOF 1937-W)—Denton True Young—Nickname: Foxy Grandpa—Throws: Right; Bats: Right

Ht: 6'2"; Wt: 210 lbs; Born: 3/29/1867 in Gilmore, Ohio; Debut: 8/6/1890; Died: 11/4/1955

World Series		Pitching																									
Year Tm	Age	G	GS	CG	GF	IP	BFP	H	R	ER	HR	SH	SF	HB	TBB	IBB	SO	WP	Bk	W	L	Pct	ShO	Sv-Op	Hld	OAvg	OOBP	ERA
1903 Bos	36	4	3	3	1	34.0	142	31	14	7	1	3	0	1	4	0	17	0	0	2	1	.667	0	0-0	0	.231	.259	1.85

World Series		Batting																							Fielding						
Year Tm	Age	G	AB	H	2B	3B	HR	TB	R	RBI	GW	TBB	IBB	SO	HBP	SH	SF	SB	CS	SB%	GDP	Avg	OBP	SLG	Pos	G	PO	A	E	DP	FPct
1903 Bos	36	4	15	2	0	1	0	4	1	3	0	0	0	3	0	0	0	0	0	—	1	.133	.133	.267	P	4	0	8	1	0	.889

DMITRI YOUNG—Dmitri Dell Young—Bats: Both; Throws: Right

Ht: 6'2"; Wt: 240 lbs; Born: 10/11/1973 in Vicksburg, Mississippi; Debut: 8/29/1996

LCS		Batting																							Fielding						
Year Tm	Age	G	AB	H	2B	3B	HR	TB	R	RBI	GW	TBB	IBB	SO	HBP	SH	SF	SB	CS	SB%	GDP	Avg	OBP	SLG	Pos	G	PO	A	E	DP	FPct
1996 StL	22	4	7	2	0	1	0	4	1	2	0	0	0	2	0	0	0	0	0	—	0	.286	.286	.571	1B	2	11	1	0	0	1.000

ERIC YOUNG—Eric Orlando Young—Nickname: E.Y.—Bats: Right; Throws: Right

Ht: 5'9"; Wt: 180 lbs; Born: 11/26/1966 in Jacksonville, Florida; Debut: 7/30/1992

Division Series		Batting																							Fielding						
Year Tm	Age	G	AB	H	2B	3B	HR	TB	R	RBI	GW	TBB	IBB	SO	HBP	SH	SF	SB	CS	SB%	GDP	Avg	OBP	SLG	Pos	G	PO	A	E	DP	FPct
1995 Col	28	4	16	7	1	0	1	11	3	2	0	2	1	2	0	0	0	1	0	1.00	0	.438	.500	.688	2B	4	8	13	3	3	.875

MATT YOUNG—Matthew John Young—Throws: Left; Bats: Left

Ht: 6'3"; Wt: 205 lbs; Born: 8/9/1958 in Pasadena, California; Debut: 4/6/1983

LCS		Pitching																									
Year Tm	Age	G	GS	CG	GF	IP	BFP	H	R	ER	HR	SH	SF	HB	TBB	IBB	SO	WP	Bk	W	L	Pct	ShO	Sv-Op	Hld	OAvg	OOBP	ERA
1989 Oak	31	1	0	0	1	0.1	3	0	0	0	0	0	0	0	2	0	0	0	0	0	0	—	0	0-0	0	.000	.667	0.00
World Series		**Pitching**																									
Year Tm	Age	G	GS	CG	GF	IP	BFP	H	R	ER	HR	SH	SF	HB	TBB	IBB	SO	WP	Bk	W	L	Pct	ShO	Sv-Op	Hld	OAvg	OOBP	ERA
1988 Oak	30	1	0	0	0	1.0	4	1	0	0	0	0	0	0	0	0	0	0	0	0	0	—	0	0-0	0	.250	.250	0.00
Postseason Totals		2	0	0	1	1.1	14	1	0	0	0	0	0	0	2	0	0	0	0	0	0	—	0	0-0	0	.200	.429	0.00

LCS		Batting																							Fielding						
Year Tm	Age	G	AB	H	2B	3B	HR	TB	R	RBI	GW	TBB	IBB	SO	HBP	SH	SF	SB	CS	SB%	GDP	Avg	OBP	SLG	Pos	G	PO	A	E	DP	FPct
1989 Oak	31	1	0	0	0	0	0	0	0	0	0	0	0	0	0	0	0	0	0	—	0	—	—	—	P	1	0	0	0	0	—

World Series											Batting														Fielding						
Year Tm	Age	G	AB	H	2B	3B	HR	TB	R	RBI	GW	TBB	IBB	SO	HBP	SH	SF	SB	CS	SB%	GDP	Avg	OBP	SLG	Pos	G	PO	A	E	DP	FPct
1988 Oak	30	1	0	0	0	0	0	0	0	0	0	0	0	0	0	0	0	0	0	—	0	—	—	—	P	1	0	1	0	0	1.000
Postseason Totals		2	0	0	0	0	0	0	0	0	0	0	0	0	0	0	0	0	0	—	0	—	—	—	P	2	0	1	0	0	1.000

ROSS YOUNGS (HOF 1972-V)—Royce Middlebrook Youngs—Nickname: Pep—Bats: Left; Throws: Right

Ht: 5'8"; Wt: 162 lbs; Born: 4/10/1897 in Shiner, Texas; Debut: 9/25/1917; Died: 10/22/1927

World Series											Batting														Fielding						
Year Tm	Age	G	AB	H	2B	3B	HR	TB	R	RBI	GW	TBB	IBB	SO	HBP	SH	SF	SB	CS	SB%	GDP	Avg	OBP	SLG	Pos	G	PO	A	E	DP	FPct
1921 NYG	24	8	25	7	1	1	0	10	3	4	0	7	0	2	0	1	0	2	1	.67	0	.280	.438	.400	OF	8	7	1	0	0	1.000
1922 NYG	25	5	16	6	0	0	0	6	2	2	1	3	1	1	0	0	1	0	1	.00	0	.375	.450	.375	OF	5	9	2	1	1	.917
1923 NYG	26	6	23	8	0	0	1	11	2	3	0	2	0	0	0	0	0	0	1	.00	0	.348	.400	.478	OF	6	5	1	2	0	.750
1924 NYG	27	7	27	5	1	0	0	6	3	1	1	5	2	6	1	0	0	1	1	.50	0	.185	.333	.222	OF	7	8	1	0	0	1.000
WS Totals		26	91	26	2	1	1	33	10	10	2	17	3	9	1	1	1	3	4	.43	0	.286	.400	.363	OF	26	29	5	3	1	.919

ROBIN YOUNT—Robin R. Yount—Bats: Right; Throws: Right

Ht: 6'0"; Wt: 165 lbs; Born: 9/16/1955 in Danville, Illinois; Debut: 4/5/1974

Division Series											Batting														Fielding						
Year Tm	Age	G	AB	H	2B	3B	HR	TB	R	RBI	GW	TBB	IBB	SO	HBP	SH	SF	SB	CS	SB%	GDP	Avg	OBP	SLG	Pos	G	PO	A	E	DP	FPct
1981 Mil	26	5	19	6	0	1	0	8	4	1	0	2	0	2	0	0	1	1	0	1.00	0	.316	.364	.421	SS	5	7	23	1	3	.968
LCS											**Batting**														**Fielding**						
Year Tm	Age	G	AB	H	2B	3B	HR	TB	R	RBI	GW	TBB	IBB	SO	HBP	SH	SF	SB	CS	SB%	GDP	Avg	OBP	SLG	Pos	G	PO	A	E	DP	FPct
1982 Mil-*M*	27	5	16	4	0	0	0	4	1	0	0	5	0	0	0	0	0	0	0	—	2	.250	.429	.250	SS	5	11	12	1	4	.958
World Series											**Batting**														**Fielding**						
Year Tm	Age	G	AB	H	2B	3B	HR	TB	R	RBI	GW	TBB	IBB	SO	HBP	SH	SF	SB	CS	SB%	GDP	Avg	OBP	SLG	Pos	G	PO	A	E	DP	FPct
1982 Mil-*M*	27	7	29	12	3	0	1	18	6	6	0	2	0	2	0	0	0	0	0	—	1	.414	.452	.621	SS	7	20	19	3	1	.929
Postseason Totals		17	64	22	3	1	1	30	11	7	0	9	0	4	0	0	1	1	0	1.00	3	.344	.419	.469	SS	17	38	54	5	8	.948

SAL YVARS—Salvador Anthony Yvars—Bats: Right; Throws: Right

Ht: 5'10"; Wt: 187 lbs; Born: 2/20/1924 in New York, New York; Debut: 9/27/1947

World Series											Batting														Fielding						
Year Tm	Age	G	AB	H	2B	3B	HR	TB	R	RBI	GW	TBB	IBB	SO	HBP	SH	SF	SB	CS	SB%	GDP	Avg	OBP	SLG	Pos	G	PO	A	E	DP	FPct
1951 NYG	27	1	1	0	0	0	0	0	0	0	0	0	0	0	0	0	0	0	0	—	0	.000	.000	.000	—						

CHRIS ZACHARY—William Christopher Zachary—Throws: Right; Bats: Left

Ht: 6'2"; Wt: 200 lbs; Born: 2/19/1944 in Knoxville, Tennessee; Debut: 4/11/1963

LCS															Pitching													
Year Tm	Age	G	GS	CG	GF	IP	BFP	H	R	ER	HR	SH	SF	HB	TBB	IBB	SO	WP	Bk	W	L	Pct	ShO	Sv-Op	Hld	OAvg	OOBP	ERA
1972 Det	28	1	0	0	0	0.0	1	0	1	1	0	0	0	0	1	0	0	2	0	0	0	—	0	0- 0	0	—	1.000	—

LCS											Batting														Fielding						
Year Tm	Age	G	AB	H	2B	3B	HR	TB	R	RBI	GW	TBB	IBB	SO	HBP	SH	SF	SB	CS	SB%	GDP	Avg	OBP	SLG	Pos	G	PO	A	E	DP	FPct
1972 Det	28	1	0	0	0	0	0	0	0	0	0	0	0	0	0	0	0	0	0	—	0	—	—	—	P	1	0	0	0	0	—

TOM ZACHARY—Jonathan Thompson Walton Zachary—Throws: Left; Bats: Left

Ht: 6'1"; Wt: 187 lbs; Born: 5/7/1896 in Graham, North Carolina; Debut: 7/11/1918; Died: 1/24/1969

World Series															Pitching													
Year Tm	Age	G	GS	CG	GF	IP	BFP	H	R	ER	HR	SH	SF	HB	TBB	IBB	SO	WP	Bk	W	L	Pct	ShO	Sv-Op	Hld	OAvg	OOBP	ERA
1924 Was	28	2	2	1	0	17.2	66	13	4	4	0	0	0	0	3	0	3	0	0	1	0	1.000	0	0- 0	0	.206	.242	2.04
1925 Was	29	1	0	0	0	1.2	9	3	2	2	0	1	0	0	1	0	0	0	0	0	0	—	0	0- 0	0	.429	.500	10.80
1928 NYA	32	1	1	1	0	9.0	38	9	3	3	0	1	0	1	1	0	7	0	0	1	0	1.000	0	0- 0	0	.257	.297	3.00
WS Totals		4	3	2	0	28.1	226	25	9	9	0	2	0	1	5	0	10	0	0	2	0	1.000	0	0-0	0	.238	.279	2.86

World Series											Batting														Fielding						
Year Tm	Age	G	AB	H	2B	3B	HR	TB	R	RBI	GW	TBB	IBB	SO	HBP	SH	SF	SB	CS	SB%	GDP	Avg	OBP	SLG	Pos	G	PO	A	E	DP	FPct
1924 Was	28	2	5	0	0	0	0	0	0	0	0	1	0	3	0	0	0	0	0	—	0	.000	.167	.000	P	2	1	4	0	0	1.000
1925 Was	29	1	0	0	0	0	0	0	0	0	0	0	0	0	0	0	0	0	0	—	0	—	—	—	P	1	0	3	0	0	1.000
1928 NYA	32	1	4	0	0	0	0	0	0	0	0	0	0	1	0	0	0	0	0	—	0	.000	.000	.000	P	1	0	1	0	0	1.000
WS Totals		4	9	0	0	0	0	0	0	0	0	1	0	4	0	0	0	0	0	—	0	.000	.100	.000	P	4	1	8	0	0	1.000

PAT ZACHRY—Patrick Paul Zachry—Throws: Right; Bats: Right

Ht: 6'5"; Wt: 180 lbs; Born: 4/24/1952 in Richmond, Texas; Debut: 4/11/1976

LCS															Pitching													
Year Tm	Age	G	GS	CG	GF	IP	BFP	H	R	ER	HR	SH	SF	HB	TBB	IBB	SO	WP	Bk	W	L	Pct	ShO	Sv-Op	Hld	OAvg	OOBP	ERA
1976 Cin-*RY*	24	1	1	0	0	5.0	23	6	2	2	1	2	0	0	3	0	3	0	0	1	0	1.000	0	0- 0	0	.333	.429	3.60
1983 LA	31	2	0	0	2	4.0	18	4	1	1	0	0	0	0	2	0	2	0	0	0	0	—	0	0- 0	0	.250	.333	2.25
LCS Totals		3	1	0	2	9.0	82	10	3	3	1	2	0	0	5	0	5	0	0	1	0	1.000	0	0-0	0	.294	.385	3.00
World Series															**Pitching**													
Year Tm	Age	G	GS	CG	GF	IP	BFP	H	R	ER	HR	SH	SF	HB	TBB	IBB	SO	WP	Bk	W	L	Pct	ShO	Sv-Op	Hld	OAvg	OOBP	ERA
1976 Cin-*RY*	24	1	1	0	0	6.2	30	6	2	2	1	0	0	0	5	0	6	0	0	1	0	1.000	0	0- 0	0	.240	.367	2.70
Postseason Totals		4	2	0	2	15.2	142	16	5	5	2	2	0	0	10	0	11	0	0	2	0	1.000	0	0-0	0	.271	.377	2.87

LCS											Batting														Fielding						
Year Tm	Age	G	AB	H	2B	3B	HR	TB	R	RBI	GW	TBB	IBB	SO	HBP	SH	SF	SB	CS	SB%	GDP	Avg	OBP	SLG	Pos	G	PO	A	E	DP	FPct
1976 Cin	24	1	1	0	0	0	0	0	0	0	0	0	0	0	0	0	0	0	0	—	0	.000	.000	.000	P	1	1	3	0	0	1.000
1983 LA	31	2	0	0	0	0	0	0	0	0	0	0	0	0	0	0	0	0	0	—	0	—	—	—	P	2	1	0	0	0	1.000
LCS Totals		3	1	0	0	0	0	0	0	0	0	0	0	0	0	0	0	0	0	—	0	.000	.000	.000	P	3	2	3	0	0	1.000
World Series											**Batting**														**Fielding**						
Year Tm	Age	G	AB	H	2B	3B	HR	TB	R	RBI	GW	TBB	IBB	SO	HBP	SH	SF	SB	CS	SB%	GDP	Avg	OBP	SLG	Pos	G	PO	A	E	DP	FPct
1976 Cin	24	1	0	0	0	0	0	0	0	0	0	0	0	0	0	0	0	0	0	—	0	—	—	—	P	1	0	2	1	0	.667
Postseason Totals		4	1	0	0	0	0	0	0	0	0	0	0	0	0	0	0	0	0	—	0	.000	.000	.000	P	4	2	5	1	0	.875

GEOFF ZAHN—Geoffrey Clayton Zahn—Throws: Left; Bats: Left

Ht: 6'1"; Wt: 180 lbs; Born: 12/19/1945 in Baltimore, Maryland; Debut: 9/2/1973

LCS															Pitching													
Year Tm	Age	G	GS	CG	GF	IP	BFP	H	R	ER	HR	SH	SF	HB	TBB	IBB	SO	WP	Bk	W	L	Pct	ShO	Sv-Op	Hld	OAvg	OOBP	ERA
1982 Cal	36	1	1	0	0	3.2	16	4	3	3	0	0	2	1	1	0	2	0	0	0	1	.000	0	0- 0	0	.333	.375	7.36

LCS											Batting														Fielding						
Year Tm	Age	G	AB	H	2B	3B	HR	TB	R	RBI	GW	TBB	IBB	SO	HBP	SH	SF	SB	CS	SB%	GDP	Avg	OBP	SLG	Pos	G	PO	A	E	DP	FPct
1982 Cal	36	1	0	0	0	0	0	0	0	0	0	0	0	0	0	0	0	0	0	—	0	—	—	—	P	1	0	0	0	0	—

AL ZARILLA—Allen Lee Zarilla—Nickname: Zeke—Bats: Left; Throws: Right

Ht: 5'11"; Wt: 180 lbs; Born: 5/1/1919 in Los Angeles, California; Debut: 6/30/1943; Died: 9/4/1996

World Series											Batting														Fielding						
Year Tm	Age	G	AB	H	2B	3B	HR	TB	R	RBI	GW	TBB	IBB	SO	HBP	SH	SF	SB	CS	SB%	GDP	Avg	OBP	SLG	Pos	G	PO	A	E	DP	FPct
1944 StL	25	4	10	1	0	0	0	1	1	1	1	0	0	4	0	0	0	0	0	—	1	.100	.100	.100	OF	3	2	0	0	0	1.000

GREG ZAUN—Gregory Owen Zaun—Bats: Both; Throws: Right

Ht: 5'10"; Wt: 170 lbs; Born: 4/14/1971 in Glendale, California; Debut: 6/24/1995

LCS											Batting														Fielding						
Year Tm	Age	G	AB	H	2B	3B	HR	TB	R	RBI	GW	TBB	IBB	SO	HBP	SH	SF	SB	CS	SB%	GDP	Avg	OBP	SLG	Pos	G	PO	A	E	DP	FPct
1997 Fla	26	1	0	0	0	0	0	0	0	0	0	0	0	0	0	0	0	0	0	—	0	—	—	—	C	1	2	0	0	0	1.000
World Series											**Batting**														**Fielding**						
Year Tm	Age	G	AB	H	2B	3B	HR	TB	R	RBI	GW	TBB	IBB	SO	HBP	SH	SF	SB	CS	SB%	GDP	Avg	OBP	SLG	Pos	G	PO	A	E	DP	FPct
1997 Fla	26	2	2	0	0	0	0	0	0	0	0	0	0	0	0	0	0	0	0	—	0	.000	.000	.000	C	1	3	0	0	0	1.000
Postseason Totals		3	2	0	0	0	0	0	0	0	0	0	0	0	0	0	0	0	0	—	0	.000	.000	.000	C	2	5	0	0	0	1.000

JOE ZDEB
Joseph Edmund Zdeb—Nickname: Mad Dog—Bats: Right; Throws: Right

Ht: 5'11"; Wt: 185 lbs; Born: 6/27/1953 in Compton, Illinois; Debut: 4/7/1977

LCS

Year Tm	Age	G	AB	H	2B	3B	HR	TB	R	RBI	GW	TBB	IBB	SO	HBP	SH	SF	SB	CS	SB%	GDP	Avg	OBP	SLG	Pos	G	PO	A	E	DP	FPct
1977 KC	24	4	9	0	0	0	0	0	0	0	0	0	0	2	0	0	0	1	0	1.00	0	.000	.000	.000	OF	4	4	0	0	0	1.000

GEORGE ZEBER
George William Zeber—Bats: Both; Throws: Right

Ht: 5'11"; Wt: 170 lbs; Born: 8/29/1950 in Ellwood City, Pennsylvania; Debut: 5/7/1977

World Series

Year Tm	Age	G	AB	H	2B	3B	HR	TB	R	RBI	GW	TBB	IBB	SO	HBP	SH	SF	SB	CS	SB%	GDP	Avg	OBP	SLG	Pos	G	PO	A	E	DP	FPct
1977 NYA	27	2	2	0	0	0	0	0	0	0	0	0	0	2	0	0	0	0	0	—	0	.000	.000	.000	—						

ROLLIE ZEIDER
Rollie Hubert Zeider—Nickname: Bunions—Bats: Right; Throws: Right

Ht: 5'10"; Wt: 162 lbs; Born: 11/16/1883 in Auburn, Indiana; Debut: 4/14/1910; Died: 9/12/1967

World Series

Year Tm	Age	G	AB	H	2B	3B	HR	TB	R	RBI	GW	TBB	IBB	SO	HBP	SH	SF	SB	CS	SB%	GDP	Avg	OBP	SLG	Pos	G	PO	A	E	DP	FPct
1918 ChN	34	2	0	0	0	0	0	0	0	0	0	2	0	0	0	0	0	0	0	—	0	—	1.000	—	3B	2	1	2	0	0	1.000

TODD ZEILE
Todd Edward Zeile—Bats: Right; Throws: Right

Ht: 6'1"; Wt: 190 lbs; Born: 9/9/1965 in Van Nuys, California; Debut: 8/18/1989

Division Series

Year Tm	Age	G	AB	H	2B	3B	HR	TB	R	RBI	GW	TBB	IBB	SO	HBP	SH	SF	SB	CS	SB%	GDP	Avg	OBP	SLG	Pos	G	PO	A	E	DP	FPct
1996 Bal	31	4	19	5	1	0	0	6	2	0	0	2	0	5	0	0	0	0	0	—	2	.263	.333	.316	3B	4	4	9	2	0	.867

LCS

Year Tm	Age	G	AB	H	2B	3B	HR	TB	R	RBI	GW	TBB	IBB	SO	HBP	SH	SF	SB	CS	SB%	GDP	Avg	OBP	SLG	Pos	G	PO	A	E	DP	FPct
1996 Bal	31	5	22	8	0	0	3	17	3	5	0	2	0	1	0	0	0	0	0	—	0	.364	.417	.773	3B	5	3	7	1	2	.909
Postseason Totals		9	41	13	1	0	3	23	5	5	0	4	0	6	0	0	0	0	0	—	2	.317	.378	.561	3B	9	7	16	3	2	.885

BILL ZEPP
William Clinton Zepp—Throws: Right; Bats: Right

Ht: 6'2"; Wt: 185 lbs; Born: 7/22/1946 in Detroit, Michigan; Debut: 8/12/1969

LCS

Year Tm	Age	G	GS	CG	GF	IP	BFP	H	R	ER	HR	SH	SF	HB	TBB	IBB	SO	WP	Bk	W	L	Pct	ShO	Sv-Op	Hld	OAvg	OOBP	ERA
1970 Min	24	2	0	0	0	1.1	7	2	1	1	1	0	0	0	2	0	2	0	0	0	0	—	0	0-0	0	.400	.571	6.75

LCS

Year Tm	Age	G	AB	H	2B	3B	HR	TB	R	RBI	GW	TBB	IBB	SO	HBP	SH	SF	SB	CS	SB%	GDP	Avg	OBP	SLG	Pos	G	PO	A	E	DP	FPct
1970 Min	24	2	0	0	0	0	0	0	0	0	0	0	0	0	0	0	0	0	0	—	0	—	—	—	P	2	0	0	0	0	—

DON ZIMMER
Donald William Zimmer—Nickname: Popeye—Bats: Right; Throws: Right

Ht: 5'9"; Wt: 165 lbs; Born: 1/17/1931 in Cincinnati, Ohio; Debut: 7/2/1954

World Series

Year Tm	Age	G	AB	H	2B	3B	HR	TB	R	RBI	GW	TBB	IBB	SO	HBP	SH	SF	SB	CS	SB%	GDP	Avg	OBP	SLG	Pos	G	PO	A	E	DP	FPct
1955 Bro	24	4	9	2	0	0	0	2	0	2	0	2	0	5	0	0	1	0	0	—	0	.222	.333	.222	2B	4	4	8	2	3	.857
1959 LA	28	1	1	0	0	0	0	0	0	0	0	0	0	0	0	0	0	0	0	—	0	.000	.000	.000	SS	1	0	1	0	0	1.000
WS Totals		5	10	2	0	0	0	2	0	2	0	2	0	5	0	0	1	0	0	—	0	.200	.308	.200	2B	4	4	8	2	3	.857

HEINIE ZIMMERMAN
Henry Zimmerman—Bats: Right; Throws: Right

Ht: 5'11"; Wt: 176 lbs; Born: 2/9/1887 in New York, New York; Debut: 9/8/1907; Died: 3/14/1969

World Series

Year Tm	Age	G	AB	H	2B	3B	HR	TB	R	RBI	GW	TBB	IBB	SO	HBP	SH	SF	SB	CS	SB%	GDP	Avg	OBP	SLG	Pos	G	PO	A	E	DP	FPct
1907 ChN	20	1	1	0	0	0	0	0	0	0	0	0	0	1	0	0	0	0	0	—	0	.000	.000	.000	2B	1	0	2	0	0	1.000
1910 ChN	23	5	17	4	1	0	0	5	0	2	0	1	0	3	0	1	1	1	1	.50	0	.235	.263	.294	2B	5	11	18	1	1	.967
1917 NYG	30	6	25	3	0	1	0	5	1	0	0	0	0	0	0	0	0	0	1	.00	1	.120	.120	.200	3B	6	9	15	3	0	.889
WS Totals		12	43	7	1	1	0	10	1	2	0	1	0	4	0	1	1	1	2	.33	2	.163	.178	.233	2B	12	11	20	1	1	.969

JERRY ZIMMERMAN
Gerald Robert Zimmerman—Bats: Right; Throws: Right

Ht: 6'2"; Wt: 185 lbs; Born: 9/21/1934 in Omaha, Nebraska; Debut: 4/14/1961

World Series

Year Tm	Age	G	AB	H	2B	3B	HR	TB	R	RBI	GW	TBB	IBB	SO	HBP	SH	SF	SB	CS	SB%	GDP	Avg	OBP	SLG	Pos	G	PO	A	E	DP	FPct
1961 Cin	27	2	0	0	0	0	0	0	0	0	0	0	0	0	0	0	0	0	0	—	0	—	—	—	C	2	4	0	0	0	1.000
1965 Min	31	2	1	0	0	0	0	0	0	0	0	0	0	0	0	0	0	0	0	—	1	.000	.000	.000	C	2	2	1	0	1	1.000
WS Totals		4	1	0	0	0	0	0	0	0	0	0	0	0	0	0	0	0	0	—	1	.000	.000	.000	C	4	6	1	0	1	1.000

RICHIE ZISK
Richard Walter Zisk—Bats: Right; Throws: Right

Ht: 6'1"; Wt: 200 lbs; Born: 2/6/1949 in Brooklyn, New York; Debut: 9/8/1971

LCS

Year Tm	Age	G	AB	H	2B	3B	HR	TB	R	RBI	GW	TBB	IBB	SO	HBP	SH	SF	SB	CS	SB%	GDP	Avg	OBP	SLG	Pos	G	PO	A	E	DP	FPct
1974 Pit	25	3	10	3	0	0	0	3	1	0	0	0	0	3	0	0	0	0	0	—	0	.300	.300	.300	OF	2	2	0	0	0	1.000
1975 Pit	26	3	10	5	1	0	0	6	0	0	0	2	0	2	0	0	0	0	0	—	0	.500	.583	.600	OF	3	8	0	0	0	1.000
LCS Totals		6	20	8	1	0	0	9	1	0	0	2	0	5	0	0	0	0	0	—	0	.400	.455	.450	OF	5	10	0	0	0	1.000

BILL ZUBER
William Henry Zuber—Nickname: Goober—Throws: Right; Bats: Right

Ht: 6'2"; Wt: 195 lbs; Born: 3/26/1913 in Middle Amana, Iowa; Debut: 9/16/1936; Died: 11/2/1982

World Series

Year Tm	Age	G	GS	CG	GF	IP	BFP	H	R	ER	HR	SH	SF	HB	TBB	IBB	SO	WP	Bk	W	L	Pct	ShO	Sv-Op	Hld	OAvg	OOBP	ERA
1946 Bos	33	1	0	0	0	2.0	9	3	1	1	0	0	0	0	1	1	1	0	0	0	0	—	0	0-0	0	.375	.444	4.50

World Series

Year Tm	Age	G	AB	H	2B	3B	HR	TB	R	RBI	GW	TBB	IBB	SO	HBP	SH	SF	SB	CS	SB%	GDP	Avg	OBP	SLG	Pos	G	PO	A	E	DP	FPct
1946 Bos	33	1	0	0	0	0	0	0	0	0	0	0	0	0	0	0	0	0	0	—	0	—	—	—	P	1	0	0	0	0	—

Postseason: Register

20th Century Postseason Batting Leaders—Career

Games

1	Reggie Jackson	77
2	Yogi Berra	75
3	Pete Rose	67
4	Terry Pendleton	66
5	Mickey Mantle	65
6	David Justice	64
7	Lonnie Smith	63
8	Mark Lemke	62
9	Steve Garvey	55
	Jeff Blauser	55
11	Willie McGee	54
	Elston Howard	54
13	Paul Blair	53
	Graig Nettles	53
	Gil McDougald	53
	Hank Bauer	53
17	Phil Rizzuto	52
18	Joe DiMaggio	51
19	4 tied with	50

At-Bats

1	Reggie Jackson	281
2	Pete Rose	268
3	Yogi Berra	259
4	Mark Lemke	232
5	Terry Pendleton	230
	Mickey Mantle	230
7	David Justice	228
8	Steve Garvey	222
9	Lonnie Smith	205
10	Marquis Grissom	204
11	Joe DiMaggio	199
12	Frankie Frisch	197
13	Bill Russell	194
14	Willie McGee	192
15	Roberto Alomar	190
	Gil McDougald	190
17	Devon White	189
18	Fred McGriff	188
	Hank Bauer	188
20	Phil Rizzuto	183

Runs

1	Mickey Mantle	42
2	Reggie Jackson	41
	Yogi Berra	41
4	Babe Ruth	37
5	Fred McGriff	36
	David Justice	36
7	Rickey Henderson	35
8	Marquis Grissom	33
9	Steve Garvey	32
10	George Brett	30
	Pete Rose	30
	Lou Gehrig	30
13	Davey Lopes	29
	Chipper Jones	29
15	Lonnie Smith	28
	Paul Molitor	28
	Ron Gant	28
18	5 tied with	27

Hits

1	Pete Rose	86
2	Reggie Jackson	78
3	Steve Garvey	75
4	Yogi Berra	71
5	Marquis Grissom	67
6	Mark Lemke	63
7	Roberto Alomar	61
8	Mickey Mantle	59
9	Terry Pendleton	58
	Frankie Frisch	58
11	Lonnie Smith	57
	Bill Russell	57
	Fred McGriff	57
14	George Brett	56
	Devon White	56
16	Joe DiMaggio	54
17	Willie McGee	53
	David Justice	53
19	Chipper Jones	50
20	2 tied with	49

Doubles

1	Reggie Jackson	14
	Lonnie Smith	14
	Hal McRae	14
4	Pete Rose	13
5	Terry Pendleton	12
	Devon White	12
7	Rick Dempsey	11
	Tony Fernandez	11
	Javy Lopez	11
	Chipper Jones	11
11	Willie Stargell	10
	Rickey Henderson	10
	Dave Henderson	10
	Cal Ripken Jr.	10
	Fred McGriff	10
	Mark Lemke	10
	Yogi Berra	10
	Frankie Frisch	10
19	10 tied with	9

Triples

1	George Brett	5
2	Rickey Henderson	4
	Devon White	4
	Mariano Duncan	4
	Bill Johnson	4
	Tris Speaker	4
	Tommy Leach	4
8	23 tied with	3

Home Runs

1	Reggie Jackson	18
	Mickey Mantle	18
3	Babe Ruth	15
4	Yogi Berra	12
5	Steve Garvey	11
	Duke Snider	11
7	George Brett	10
	Johnny Bench	10
	Fred McGriff	10
	Lenny Dykstra	10
	Frank Robinson	10
	Lou Gehrig	10
13	Eddie Murray	9
	Manny Ramirez	9
15	David Justice	8
	Bernie Williams	8
	Ryan Klesko	8
	Bill Skowron	8
	Joe DiMaggio	8
20	13 tied with	7

RBI

1	Reggie Jackson	48
2	Mickey Mantle	40
3	Yogi Berra	39
4	Fred McGriff	37
5	Lou Gehrig	35
6	David Justice	33
	Babe Ruth	33
8	Steve Garvey	31
9	Joe DiMaggio	30
10	Bill Skowron	29
11	Ron Cey	27
	Graig Nettles	27
	Ron Gant	27
	Roberto Alomar	27
15	Duke Snider	26
16	Eddie Murray	25
	Sandy Alomar Jr.	25
18	5 tied with	24

Walks

1	David Justice	45
2	Mickey Mantle	43
3	Joe Morgan	38
4	Reggie Jackson	33
	Babe Ruth	33
6	Yogi Berra	32
7	Rickey Henderson	31
8	Gene Tenace	30
	Phil Rizzuto	30
10	Pete Rose	28
11	Eddie Murray	27
	Fred McGriff	27
13	Lou Gehrig	26
14	Ron Cey	25
	Davey Lopes	25
	Mickey Cochrane	25
17	Chipper Jones	24
18	Roberto Alomar	23
	Jim Gilliam	23
20	3 tied with	22

Strikeouts

1	Reggie Jackson	70
2	Mickey Mantle	54
3	Devon White	48
4	Jeff Blauser	45
5	Willie McGee	43
6	David Justice	41
7	Fred McGriff	40
8	Lonnie Smith	38
9	Tony Perez	37
	Mariano Duncan	37
	Marquis Grissom	37
	Elston Howard	37
13	Cesar Geronimo	35
	Dave Henderson	35
	Jim Thome	35
16	Willie Stargell	34
	Darryl Strawberry	34
	Ron Gant	34
19	Gene Tenace	33
	Duke Snider	33

Stolen Bases

1	Rickey Henderson	25
2	Davey Lopes	20
3	Roberto Alomar	18
	Omar Vizquel	18
5	Kenny Lofton	17
6	Joe Morgan	15
7	Lou Brock	14
	Eddie Collins	14
9	Vince Coleman	13
	Ron Gant	13
11	Willie Wilson	12
	Marquis Grissom	12
13	Bert Campaneris	10
	Phil Rizzuto	10
	Frank Chance	10
16	Kirk Gibson	9
	Frankie Frisch	9
	Honus Wagner	9
19	7 tied with	8

Batting Average
(minimum 75 Plate Appearances)

1	Lou Brock	.391
2	Carl Yastrzemski	.369
3	Paul Molitor	.368
4	Will Clark	.364
5	Home Run Baker	.363
6	Lou Gehrig	.361
7	Thurman Munson	.357
8	Derek Jeter	.354
9	Chipper Jones	.352
10	Stan Hack	.348
11	Tony Pena	.338
	Barry Larkin	.338
13	Steve Garvey	.338
14	George Brett	.337
15	Cal Ripken Jr.	.336
16	Marty Barrett	.333
	Billy Martin	.333
18	Al Simmons	.329
19	Marquis Grissom	.328
20	Eddie Collins	.328

On-Base Percentage
(minimum 75 Plate Appearances)

1	Lou Gehrig	.477
2	Babe Ruth	.467
3	Carl Yastrzemski	.447
4	Bernie Williams	.445
5	Gene Woodling	.442
6	Chipper Jones	.435
7	Paul Molitor	.435
8	Lenny Dykstra	.433
9	Will Clark	.430
10	Lou Brock	.424
11	Hank Greenberg	.420
12	Gary Matthews	.413
13	Darren Daulton	.413
14	Cal Ripken Jr.	.411
15	Derek Jeter	.411
16	Stan Hack	.408
17	Enos Slaughter	.406
18	Albert Belle	.405
19	Frank Chance	.402
20	Rickey Henderson	.402

Slugging Percentage
(minimum 75 Plate Appearances)

1	Babe Ruth	.744
2	Lou Gehrig	.731
3	Gary Matthews	.677
4	Lenny Dykstra	.661
5	Al Simmons	.658
6	Lou Brock	.655
7	Bernie Williams	.635
8	George Brett	.627
9	Hank Greenberg	.624
10	Paul Molitor	.615
11	Charlie Keller	.611
12	Carl Yastrzemski	.600
13	Duke Snider	.594
14	Will Clark	.584
15	Chipper Jones	.577
16	Kirk Gibson	.577
17	Brady Anderson	.575
18	Dave Henderson	.570
19	Billy Martin	.566
20	Paul O'Neill	.558

OBP+Slugging
(minimum 75 Plate Appearances)

1	Babe Ruth	1.211
2	Lou Gehrig	1.208
3	Lenny Dykstra	1.094
4	Gary Matthews	1.090
5	Bernie Williams	1.081
6	Lou Brock	1.079
7	Paul Molitor	1.050
8	Carl Yastrzemski	1.047
9	Hank Greenberg	1.044
10	Al Simmons	1.033
11	George Brett	1.023
12	Will Clark	1.015
13	Chipper Jones	1.013
14	Charlie Keller	.978
15	Gene Woodling	.972
16	Albert Belle	.962
17	Paul O'Neill	.958
18	Kirk Gibson	.957
19	Brady Anderson	.955
20	Dave Henderson	.946

Secondary Average
(minimum 75 Plate Appearances)

1	Babe Ruth	.705
2	Albert Belle	.623
3	Lou Gehrig	.588
4	Bernie Williams	.573
5	Kirk Gibson	.564
6	Lenny Dykstra	.563
7	Gary Matthews	.538
8	Rickey Henderson	.524
9	Lou Brock	.483
10	Paul O'Neill	.481
11	Mickey Mantle	.478
12	Hank Greenberg	.471
13	Darren Daulton	.469
14	Joe Morgan	.459
15	Frank Robinson	.452
16	Jose Canseco	.451
17	Brady Anderson	.438
18	Gene Woodling	.435
19	Ryan Klesko	.433
20	Chipper Jones	.430

20th Century Postseason Pitching Leaders—Career

Wins

1	Dave Stewart	10
	John Smoltz	10
	Whitey Ford	10
4	Tom Glavine	9
	Catfish Hunter	9
6	Jim Palmer	8
	Orel Hershiser	8
	Greg Maddux	8
9	Jack Morris	7
	Dave McNally	7
	Bob Gibson	7
	Allie Reynolds	7
	Red Ruffing	7
14	8 tied with	6

Losses

1	Tom Glavine	9
2	Jerry Reuss	8
	Whitey Ford	8
4	Charlie Leibrandt	7
	Greg Maddux	7
6	Steve Carlton	6
	Dave Stewart	6
	Catfish Hunter	6
9	Vida Blue	5
	Doyle Alexander	5
	Dennis Leonard	5
	Doug Drabek	5
	Don Gullett	5
	Schoolboy Rowe	5
	Joe Bush	5
	Rube Marquard	5
	Eddie Plank	5
	Christy Mathewson	5
19	27 tied with	4

Winning Percentage
(minimum 8 decisions)

1	Bob Gibson	.778
	Allie Reynolds	.778
	Red Ruffing	.778
4	John Smoltz	.769
5	Jim Palmer	.727
	Orel Hershiser	.727
7	Burt Hooton	.667
	Tommy John	.667
9	Jack Morris	.636
	Dave McNally	.636
11	Dave Stewart	.625
	Jimmy Key	.625
	Steve Avery	.625
	Vic Raschi	.625
15	Don Sutton	.600
	Catfish Hunter	.600
	Ken Holtzman	.600
	Waite Hoyt	.600
	Chief Bender	.600
20	3 tied with	.556

Games

1	Mark Wohlers	38
2	Rollie Fingers	30
	Rick Honeycutt	30
4	Paul Assenmacher	29
5	Dennis Eckersley	27
6	Tug McGraw	26
7	Mike Stanton	25
8	Jesse Orosco	24
9	Alejandro Pena	23
10	Ron Reed	22
	Dave Stewart	22
	Randy Myers	22
	Catfish Hunter	22
	Clay Carroll	22
	Whitey Ford	22
16	Jose Mesa	21
17	Pedro Borbon	20
	Tom Glavine	20
	John Smoltz	20
	Don Gullett	20

Games Started

1	Whitey Ford	22
2	Tom Glavine	20
	John Smoltz	20
4	Catfish Hunter	19
5	Dave Stewart	18
	Orel Hershiser	18
7	Greg Maddux	17
8	Jim Palmer	15
9	Steve Carlton	14
	Don Sutton	14
11	Tommy John	13
	Jack Morris	13
	Don Gullett	13
14	David Cone	12
	Steve Avery	12
	Ken Holtzman	12
	Dave McNally	12
	Mike Cuellar	12
19	7 tied with	11

Complete Games

1	Christy Mathewson	10
2	Chief Bender	9
3	Bob Gibson	8
	Red Ruffing	8
5	Whitey Ford	7
6	Jim Palmer	6
	Dave McNally	6
	Waite Hoyt	6
	Art Nehf	6
	George Mullin	6
	Eddie Plank	6
12	Jack Morris	5
	Allie Reynolds	5
	George Earnshaw	5
	Carl Mays	5
	Joe Bush	5
	Walter Johnson	5
	Three Finger Brown	5
	Deacon Phillippe	5
	Wild Bill Donovan	5

Shutouts

1	Christy Mathewson	4
2	Whitey Ford	3
	Three Finger Brown	3
4	Scott McGregor	2
	Jim Palmer	2
	Orel Hershiser	2
	Dave McNally	2
	Bob Gibson	2
	Sandy Koufax	2
	Lew Burdette	2
	Allie Reynolds	2
	Wild Bill Hallahan	2
	Art Nehf	2
	Bill Dinneen	2
15	80 tied with	1

Saves

1	Dennis Eckersley	15
2	Rollie Fingers	9
	Mark Wohlers	9
4	Tug McGraw	8
	Goose Gossage	8
	Randy Myers	8
7	John Wetteland	7
8	Jeff Reardon	6
	Jose Mesa	6
10	Ken Dayley	5
	Tom Henke	5
	Rick Aguilera	5
	Duane Ward	5
	Dave Giusti	5
15	Alejandro Pena	4
	Todd Worrell	4
	Robb Nen	4
	Allie Reynolds	4
	Johnny Murphy	4
20	11 tied with	3

Innings Pitched

1	Whitey Ford	146.0
2	John Smoltz	137.2
3	Dave Stewart	133.0
4	Tom Glavine	132.2
5	Catfish Hunter	132.1
6	Orel Hershiser	126.2
7	Jim Palmer	124.1
8	Greg Maddux	117.0
9	Christy Mathewson	101.2
10	Don Sutton	100.1
11	Steve Carlton	99.1
12	Don Gullett	93.0
13	Jack Morris	92.1
14	Dave McNally	90.1
15	Tommy John	88.1
16	Red Ruffing	85.2
17	Mike Cuellar	85.1
18	Chief Bender	85.0
19	Waite Hoyt	83.2
20	Bob Gibson	81.0

Walks

1	Steve Carlton	51
	Tom Glavine	51
3	Jim Palmer	50
	John Smoltz	50
5	Dave Stewart	48
6	Orel Hershiser	40
	David Cone	40
8	Don Gullett	38
9	Catfish Hunter	35
10	Dave McNally	34
	Whitey Ford	34
12	Tug McGraw	33
13	Jack Morris	32
	Allie Reynolds	32
	Art Nehf	32
16	Fernando Valenzuela	31
	Mike Cuellar	31
18	Steve Avery	29
	Bob Turley	29
20	Danny Cox	28

Strikeouts

1	John Smoltz	132
2	Whitey Ford	94
3	Bob Gibson	92
4	Orel Hershiser	91
5	Jim Palmer	90
	Tom Glavine	90
7	Steve Carlton	84
8	Greg Maddux	79
9	Dave Stewart	73
10	Catfish Hunter	70
11	Dave McNally	65
12	Jack Morris	64
13	Nolan Ryan	63
14	Allie Reynolds	62
15	Don Sutton	61
	Sandy Koufax	61
	Red Ruffing	61
18	Steve Avery	60
	Don Gullett	60
20	Chief Bender	59

Strikeouts/9 Innings
(minimum 40 Innings Pitched)

1	Mike Mussina	11.18
2	Bob Gibson	10.22
3	Nolan Ryan	9.66
4	Sandy Koufax	9.63
5	John Smoltz	8.63
6	Tug McGraw	8.25
7	George Earnshaw	8.04
8	Dwight Gooden	7.74
9	Bob Turley	7.71
10	Steve Carlton	7.61
11	Danny Cox	7.56
12	Bob Welch	7.48
13	Tom Seaver	7.44
14	Ron Guidry	7.32
15	David Cone	7.32
16	Roger Clemens	7.28
17	Allie Reynolds	7.22
18	Juan Guzman	7.14
19	Rollie Fingers	7.06
20	Mort Cooper	7.00

ERA
(minimum 40 Innings Pitched)

1	Sandy Koufax	0.95
2	Christy Mathewson	1.06
3	Eddie Plank	1.32
4	Mickey Lolich	1.57
5	Orval Overall	1.58
6	George Earnshaw	1.58
7	Scott McGregor	1.63
8	Stan Coveleski	1.74
9	Lefty Grove	1.75
10	Carl Hubbell	1.79
11	Waite Hoyt	1.83
12	George Mullin	1.86
13	Bob Gibson	1.89
14	Jack Billingham	1.93
15	Herb Pennock	1.95
16	Fernando Valenzuela	1.98
17	Doug Drabek	2.05
18	Walter Johnson	2.16
19	Art Nehf	2.16
20	Carl Mays	2.20

Component ERA
(minimum 40 Innings Pitched)

1	Sandy Koufax	1.32
2	Christy Mathewson	1.36
3	Eddie Plank	1.41
4	George Earnshaw	1.41
5	Deacon Phillippe	1.43
6	Herb Pennock	1.51
7	Nolan Ryan	1.57
8	Stan Coveleski	1.66
9	Bob Gibson	1.68
10	Scott McGregor	1.68
11	Mike Mussina	1.70
12	Jack Billingham	1.74
13	Orval Overall	1.74
14	Carl Mays	1.83
15	Art Nehf	1.84
16	Chief Bender	1.86
17	Lefty Grove	1.87
18	Mickey Lolich	2.04
19	George Mullin	2.13
20	Three Finger Brown	2.14

Opponent Average
(minimum 40 Innings Pitched)

1	Mike Mussina	.170
2	George Earnshaw	.174
3	Sandy Koufax	.180
4	Eddie Plank	.186
5	Art Nehf	.187
6	Nolan Ryan	.188
7	Jack Billingham	.189
8	Bob Gibson	.190
9	Herb Pennock	.195
10	Dave McNally	.201
11	Stan Coveleski	.204
12	Mickey Lolich	.205
13	Orval Overall	.206
14	Dave Stewart	.206
15	Tug McGraw	.207
	Christy Mathewson	.207
17	Scott McGregor	.208
18	Deacon Phillippe	.209
19	Bob Walk	.211
20	Mike Cuellar	.211

Opponent OBP
(minimum 40 Innings Pitched)

1	Sandy Koufax	.223
2	Mike Mussina	.226
3	Herb Pennock	.226
4	Christy Mathewson	.227
5	Deacon Phillippe	.230
6	George Earnshaw	.232
7	Nolan Ryan	.237
8	Stan Coveleski	.238
9	Bob Gibson	.239
10	Scott McGregor	.241
11	Eddie Plank	.243
12	Lefty Grove	.256
13	Mickey Lolich	.257
14	Lew Burdette	.263
15	Carl Hubbell	.265
16	Ralph Terry	.265
17	Chief Bender	.267
18	Warren Spahn	.269
19	Orval Overall	.270
20	Carl Mays	.271

20th Century World Series Batting Leaders—Career

Games

1	Yogi Berra	75
2	Mickey Mantle	65
3	Elston Howard	54
4	Gil McDougald	53
	Hank Bauer	53
6	Phil Rizzuto	52
7	Joe DiMaggio	51
8	Frankie Frisch	50
9	Pee Wee Reese	44
10	Roger Maris	41
	Babe Ruth	41
12	Carl Furillo	40
13	Bill Skowron	39
	Jim Gilliam	39
	Gil Hodges	39
16	Jackie Robinson	38
	Bill Dickey	38
18	Tony Kubek	37
19	3 tied with	36

At-Bats

1	Yogi Berra	259
2	Mickey Mantle	230
3	Joe DiMaggio	199
4	Frankie Frisch	197
5	Gil McDougald	190
6	Hank Bauer	188
7	Phil Rizzuto	183
8	Elston Howard	171
9	Pee Wee Reese	169
10	Roger Maris	152
11	Jim Gilliam	147
12	Tony Kubek	146
13	Bill Dickey	145
14	Jackie Robinson	137
15	Bill Skowron	133
	Duke Snider	133
17	Bobby Richardson	131
	Gil Hodges	131
19	Pete Rose	130
20	3 tied with	129

Runs

1	Mickey Mantle	42
2	Yogi Berra	41
3	Babe Ruth	37
4	Lou Gehrig	30
5	Joe DiMaggio	27
6	Roger Maris	26
7	Elston Howard	25
8	Gil McDougald	23
9	Jackie Robinson	22
10	Reggie Jackson	21
	Hank Bauer	21
	Duke Snider	21
	Gene Woodling	21
	Phil Rizzuto	21
15	Pee Wee Reese	20
	Eddie Collins	20
17	Frank Robinson	19
	Bill Skowron	19
	Bill Dickey	19
20	3 tied with	18

Hits

1	Yogi Berra	71
2	Mickey Mantle	59
3	Frankie Frisch	58
4	Joe DiMaggio	54
5	Hank Bauer	46
	Pee Wee Reese	46
7	Gil McDougald	45
	Phil Rizzuto	45
9	Lou Gehrig	43
10	Elston Howard	42
	Babe Ruth	42
	Eddie Collins	42
13	Bobby Richardson	40
14	Bill Skowron	39
15	Duke Snider	38
16	Bill Dickey	37
	Goose Goslin	37
18	Steve Garvey	36
19	4 tied with	35

Doubles

1	Yogi Berra	10
	Frankie Frisch	10
3	Carl Furillo	9
	Pete Fox	9
	Jack Barry	9
6	Lonnie Smith	8
	Duke Snider	8
	Lou Gehrig	8
9	15 tied with	7

Triples

1	Bill Johnson	4
	Tris Speaker	4
	Tommy Leach	4
4	Dave Concepcion	3
	Tim McCarver	3
	Dan Gladden	3
	Devon White	3
	Mark Lemke	3
	Billy Martin	3
	Hank Bauer	3
	Bobby Brown	3
	Lou Gehrig	3
	Bob Meusel	3
	Frankie Frisch	3
	Freddy Parent	3
	Chick Stahl	3
	Buck Freeman	3
18	34 tied with	2

Home Runs

1	Mickey Mantle	18
2	Babe Ruth	15
3	Yogi Berra	12
4	Duke Snider	11
5	Reggie Jackson	10
	Lou Gehrig	10
7	Frank Robinson	8
	Bill Skowron	8
	Joe DiMaggio	8
10	Gil McDougald	7
	Hank Bauer	7
	Goose Goslin	7
13	Reggie Smith	6
	Lenny Dykstra	6
	Roger Maris	6
	Al Simmons	6
17	7 tied with	5

RBI

1	Mickey Mantle	40
2	Yogi Berra	39
3	Lou Gehrig	35
4	Babe Ruth	33
5	Joe DiMaggio	30
6	Bill Skowron	29
7	Duke Snider	26
8	Reggie Jackson	24
	Gil McDougald	24
	Hank Bauer	24
	Bill Dickey	24
12	Hank Greenberg	22
13	Gil Hodges	21
14	Elston Howard	19
	Billy Martin	19
	Tony Lazzeri	19
	Goose Goslin	19
18	4 tied with	18

Walks

1	Mickey Mantle	43
2	Babe Ruth	33
3	Yogi Berra	32
4	Phil Rizzuto	30
5	Lou Gehrig	26
6	Mickey Cochrane	25
7	Jim Gilliam	23
8	David Justice	22
9	Jackie Robinson	21
10	Gil McDougald	20
11	Gene Woodling	19
	Joe DiMaggio	19
13	Roger Maris	18
	Pee Wee Reese	18
15	Gene Tenace	17
	Gil Hodges	17
	Ross Youngs	17
18	Pete Rose	16
19	5 tied with	15

Strikeouts

1	Mickey Mantle	54
2	Elston Howard	37
3	Duke Snider	33
4	Babe Ruth	30
5	Gil McDougald	29
6	Bill Skowron	26
7	Hank Bauer	25
8	Reggie Jackson	24
	Bob Meusel	24
10	Devon White	23
	Tony Kubek	23
	Frank Robinson	23
	Joe DiMaggio	23
	George Kelly	23
15	Lonnie Smith	22
	Joe Collins	22
	Gil Hodges	22
	Jim Bottomley	22
19	3 tied with	21

Stolen Bases

1	Lou Brock	14
	Eddie Collins	14
3	Davey Lopes	10
	Phil Rizzuto	10
	Frank Chance	10
6	Frankie Frisch	9
	Honus Wagner	9
8	Johnny Evers	8
9	Joe Morgan	7
	Rickey Henderson	7
	Roberto Alomar	7
	Pepper Martin	7
	Joe Tinker	7
14	Vince Coleman	6
	Omar Vizquel	6
	Kenny Lofton	6
	Bobby Tolan	6
	Maury Wills	6
	Jackie Robinson	6
	Jimmy Slagle	6

Batting Average
(minimum 50 Plate Appearances)

1	Paul Molitor	.418
	Pepper Martin	.418
3	Hal McRae	.400
4	Lou Brock	.391
5	Marquis Grissom	.390
6	Thurman Munson	.373
7	George Brett	.373
8	Hank Aaron	.364
9	Home Run Baker	.363
10	Roberto Clemente	.362
11	Lou Gehrig	.361
12	Reggie Jackson	.357
13	Carl Yastrzemski	.352
14	Earle Combs	.350
15	Stan Hack	.348
16	Roberto Alomar	.347
17	Joe Jackson	.345
18	Jimmie Foxx	.344
19	Rickey Henderson	.339
20	2 tied with	.333

On-Base Percentage
(minimum 50 Plate Appearances)

1	Lou Gehrig	.477
2	Paul Molitor	.475
3	Pepper Martin	.467
	Babe Ruth	.467
5	Reggie Jackson	.457
6	Rickey Henderson	.448
7	Earle Combs	.444
8	Gene Woodling	.442
9	Marquis Grissom	.440
10	Hal McRae	.440
11	George Brett	.439
12	Carl Yastrzemski	.438
13	Jimmy Ripple	.433
14	George McQuinn	.431
15	Jimmie Foxx	.425
16	Lou Brock	.424
17	Lenny Dykstra	.424
18	Hank Greenberg	.420
	Hank Gowdy	.420
20	2 tied with	.417

Slugging Percentage
(minimum 50 Plate Appearances)

1	Reggie Jackson	.755
2	Babe Ruth	.744
3	Lou Gehrig	.731
4	Lenny Dykstra	.700
5	Al Simmons	.658
6	Lou Brock	.655
7	Paul Molitor	.636
	Pepper Martin	.636
9	Hank Greenberg	.624
10	Charlie Keller	.611
11	Jimmie Foxx	.609
12	Rickey Henderson	.607
13	Dave Henderson	.606
14	Fred McGriff	.605
15	Hank Aaron	.600
16	Joe Carter	.596
17	Duke Snider	.594
18	Dwight Evans	.580
19	Steve Yeager	.579
20	Willie Stargell	.574

OBP+Slugging
(minimum 50 Plate Appearances)

1	Reggie Jackson	1.212
2	Babe Ruth	1.211
3	Lou Gehrig	1.208
4	Lenny Dykstra	1.124
5	Paul Molitor	1.112
6	Pepper Martin	1.103
7	Lou Brock	1.079
8	Rickey Henderson	1.055
9	Hank Greenberg	1.044
10	Jimmie Foxx	1.034
11	Al Simmons	1.033
12	Hank Aaron	1.017
13	Dave Henderson	1.015
14	Carl Yastrzemski	.993
15	Fred McGriff	.989
16	Charlie Keller	.978
17	Dwight Evans	.977
18	Hal McRae	.973
19	Gene Woodling	.972
20	George Brett	.968

Secondary Average
(minimum 50 Plate Appearances)

1	Babe Ruth	.705
2	Lenny Dykstra	.640
3	Lou Gehrig	.588
4	Rickey Henderson	.571
5	Reggie Jackson	.561
6	Gene Tenace	.544
7	Fred McGriff	.535
8	Lou Brock	.483
9	Eddie Mathews	.480
10	Mickey Mantle	.478
11	Hank Greenberg	.471
12	Joe Morgan	.459
13	Manny Ramirez	.455
14	Darren Daulton	.439
15	Pepper Martin	.436
16	George McQuinn	.436
17	Gene Woodling	.435
18	Frank Robinson	.424
19	Davey Lopes	.422
	Jose Canseco	.422

20th Century World Series Pitching Leaders—Career

Wins

1	Whitey Ford	10
2	Bob Gibson	7
	Allie Reynolds	7
	Red Ruffing	7
5	Lefty Gomez	6
	Waite Hoyt	6
	Chief Bender	6
8	Catfish Hunter	5
	Vic Raschi	5
	Lefty Grove	5
	Herb Pennock	5
	Jack Coombs	5
	Three Finger Brown	5
	Christy Mathewson	5
15	17 tied with	4

Losses

1	Whitey Ford	8
2	Schoolboy Rowe	5
	Joe Bush	5
	Rube Marquard	5
	Eddie Plank	5
	Christy Mathewson	5
7	Charlie Leibrandt	4
	Dave Stewart	4
	Ralph Terry	4
	Don Newcombe	4
	Paul Derringer	4
	Waite Hoyt	4
	Bill Sherdel	4
	Burleigh Grimes	4
	Art Nehf	4
	Carl Mays	4
	Ed Summers	4
	Chief Bender	4
	Three Finger Brown	4
	Wild Bill Donovan	4

Winning Percentage
(minimum 5 decisions)

1	Lefty Gomez	1.000
	Herb Pennock	1.000
	Jack Coombs	1.000
4	Ken Holtzman	.800
	Johnny Podres	.800
	Ed Lopat	.800
	Harry Brecheen	.800
	Tommy Bridges	.800
9	Bob Gibson	.778
	Allie Reynolds	.778
	Red Ruffing	.778
12	Lefty Grove	.714
13	Jack Morris	.667
	Jim Palmer	.667
	Dave McNally	.667
	Don Larsen	.667
	Lew Burdette	.667
	Carl Hubbell	.667
19	Catfish Hunter	.625
	Vic Raschi	.625

Games

1	Whitey Ford	22
2	Rollie Fingers	16
3	Bob Turley	15
	Allie Reynolds	15
5	Clay Carroll	14
6	Mark Wohlers	13
	Clem Labine	13
8	Catfish Hunter	12
	Waite Hoyt	12
	Art Nehf	12
11	Carl Erskine	11
	Vic Raschi	11
	Paul Derringer	11
	Rube Marquard	11
	Christy Mathewson	11
16	8 tied with	10

Games Started

1	Whitey Ford	22
2	Waite Hoyt	11
	Christy Mathewson	11
4	Red Ruffing	10
	Chief Bender	10
6	Catfish Hunter	9
	Bob Gibson	9
	Allie Reynolds	9
	Art Nehf	9
10	Don Sutton	8
	Dave Stewart	8
	Jim Palmer	8
	Bob Turley	8
	Vic Raschi	8
	George Earnshaw	8
	Rube Marquard	8
17	15 tied with	7

Complete Games

1	Christy Mathewson	10
2	Chief Bender	9
3	Bob Gibson	8
	Red Ruffing	8
5	Whitey Ford	7
6	Waite Hoyt	6
	Art Nehf	6
	George Mullin	6
	Eddie Plank	6
10	Allie Reynolds	5
	George Earnshaw	5
	Carl Mays	5
	Joe Bush	5
	Walter Johnson	5
	Three Finger Brown	5
	Deacon Phillippe	5
	Wild Bill Donovan	5
18	15 tied with	4

Shutouts

1	Christy Mathewson	4
2	Whitey Ford	3
	Three Finger Brown	3
4	Bob Gibson	2
	Sandy Koufax	2
	Lew Burdette	2
	Allie Reynolds	2
	Wild Bill Hallahan	2
	Art Nehf	2
	Bill Dinneen	2
11	64 tied with	1

Saves

1	Rollie Fingers	6
2	John Wetteland	4
	Allie Reynolds	4
	Johnny Murphy	4
5	Tug McGraw	3
	Kent Tekulve	3
	Todd Worrell	3
	Will McEnaney	3
	Roy Face	3
	Herb Pennock	3
11	20 tied with	2

Innings Pitched

1	Whitey Ford	146.0
2	Christy Mathewson	101.2
3	Red Ruffing	85.2
4	Chief Bender	85.0
5	Waite Hoyt	83.2
6	Bob Gibson	81.0
7	Art Nehf	79.0
8	Allie Reynolds	77.1
9	Jim Palmer	64.2
10	Catfish Hunter	63.0
11	George Earnshaw	62.2
12	Joe Bush	60.2
13	Vic Raschi	60.1
14	Rube Marquard	58.2
15	George Mullin	58.0
16	Three Finger Brown	57.2
17	Carl Mays	57.1
18	Dave Stewart	57.0
	Sandy Koufax	57.0
20	Burleigh Grimes	56.2

Walks

1	Whitey Ford	34
2	Allie Reynolds	32
	Art Nehf	32
4	Jim Palmer	31
5	Bob Turley	29
6	Paul Derringer	27
	Red Ruffing	27
8	Don Gullett	26
	Burleigh Grimes	26
10	Vic Raschi	25
11	Carl Erskine	24
12	Dave Stewart	23
	Wild Bill Hallahan	23
14	Waite Hoyt	22
15	Jack Coombs	21
	Chief Bender	21
17	Tom Glavine	20
	Joe Bush	20
19	3 tied with	19

Strikeouts

1	Whitey Ford	94
2	Bob Gibson	92
3	Allie Reynolds	62
4	Sandy Koufax	61
	Red Ruffing	61
6	Chief Bender	59
7	George Earnshaw	56
8	Waite Hoyt	49
9	Christy Mathewson	48
10	Bob Turley	46
11	Jim Palmer	44
12	Vic Raschi	43
13	John Smoltz	41
14	Jack Morris	40
15	Don Gullett	37
16	Don Drysdale	36
	Lefty Grove	36
	George Mullin	36
19	8 tied with	35

Strikeouts/9 Innings
(minimum 25 Innings Pitched)

1	Bob Gibson	10.22
2	Sandy Koufax	9.63
3	Steve Carlton	9.09
4	Danny Cox	8.69
5	Roger Craig	8.54
6	John Smoltz	8.39
7	Don Drysdale	8.17
8	Jesse Barnes	8.13
9	Tom Seaver	8.10
10	George Earnshaw	8.04
11	Bob Turley	7.71
12	Orel Hershiser	7.50
13	Ron Guidry	7.31
14	Allie Reynolds	7.22
15	Bill Dinneen	7.20
16	Max Lanier	7.11
17	Monte Pearson	7.07
18	Mickey Lolich	7.00
	Mort Cooper	7.00
20	Jack Morris	6.97

ERA
(minimum 25 Innings Pitched)

1	Jack Billingham	0.36
2	Harry Brecheen	0.83
3	Babe Ruth	0.87
4	Sherry Smith	0.89
5	Sandy Koufax	0.95
6	Hippo Vaughn	1.00
7	Monte Pearson	1.01
8	Christy Mathewson	1.06
9	Babe Adams	1.29
10	Eddie Plank	1.32
11	Rollie Fingers	1.35
12	Wild Bill Hallahan	1.36
13	Jesse Barnes	1.45
14	Orval Overall	1.58
15	George Earnshaw	1.58
16	Spud Chandler	1.62
17	Mickey Lolich	1.67
18	Jesse Haines	1.67
19	Ron Guidry	1.69
20	Max Lanier	1.71

Component ERA
(minimum 25 Innings Pitched)

1	Monte Pearson	1.02
2	Sherry Smith	1.23
3	Hippo Vaughn	1.29
4	Sandy Koufax	1.32
5	Jack Billingham	1.35
6	Christy Mathewson	1.36
7	Eddie Plank	1.41
8	George Earnshaw	1.41
9	Deacon Phillippe	1.43
10	Herb Pennock	1.51
11	Greg Maddux	1.52
12	Scott McGregor	1.62
13	Tom Glavine	1.63
14	Stan Coveleski	1.66
15	Babe Ruth	1.68
16	Bob Gibson	1.68
17	Tiny Bonham	1.72
18	Bucky Walters	1.73
19	Orval Overall	1.74
20	Lefty Tyler	1.79

Opponent Average
(minimum 25 Innings Pitched)

1	Monte Pearson	.151
2	Tom Glavine	.151
3	Jack Billingham	.163
4	Jerry Koosman	.170
5	Sherry Smith	.173
6	George Earnshaw	.174
7	Sandy Koufax	.180
8	Ron Guidry	.180
9	Eddie Plank	.186
10	Babe Ruth	.186
11	Art Nehf	.187
12	Don Larsen	.188
13	Bob Gibson	.190
14	Tiny Bonham	.192
15	Hippo Vaughn	.193
16	Babe Adams	.194
17	Jesse Barnes	.195
	Lefty Tyler	.195
19	Herb Pennock	.195
20	Dave McNally	.198

Opponent OBP
(minimum 25 Innings Pitched)

1	Monte Pearson	.195
2	Sandy Koufax	.223
3	Herb Pennock	.226
4	Scott McGregor	.227
5	Christy Mathewson	.227
6	Deacon Phillippe	.230
7	George Earnshaw	.232
8	Greg Maddux	.235
9	Stan Coveleski	.238
10	Bob Gibson	.239
11	Tom Glavine	.240
12	Eddie Plank	.243
13	Sherry Smith	.243
14	Hippo Vaughn	.245
15	Babe Adams	.245
16	Jack Billingham	.250
17	Bucky Walters	.252
18	Tiny Bonham	.252
19	Tom Seaver	.254
	Jesse Barnes	.254

League Championship Series Batting Leaders—Career

Games

1	Reggie Jackson	45
2	Terry Pendleton	38
3	Ron Gant	31
	Mark Lemke	31
5	Jeff Blauser	29
	David Justice	29
7	Don Baylor	28
	Hal McRae	28
	Pete Rose	28
	Fred McGriff	28
	Roberto Alomar	28
12	George Brett	27
	Richie Hebner	27
	Bob Boone	27
	Joe Morgan	27
	Devon White	27
17	Lonnie Smith	26
	Frank White	26
19	4 tied with	25

At-Bats

1	Reggie Jackson	163
2	Terry Pendleton	135
3	Pete Rose	118
4	Ron Gant	117
5	Roberto Alomar	114
6	Mark Lemke	110
7	Fred McGriff	109
8	George Brett	103
	David Justice	103
10	Don Baylor	96
	Joe Morgan	96
12	Devon White	95
13	Jeff Blauser	92
14	Rickey Henderson	91
15	Steve Garvey	90
16	Willie McGee	89
	Andy Van Slyke	89
18	Bobby Grich	88
	Richie Hebner	88
	Hal McRae	88

Runs

1	George Brett	22
2	Rickey Henderson	18
	Fred McGriff	18
	Jeff Blauser	18
5	Pete Rose	17
	Ron Gant	17
7	Reggie Jackson	16
	Devon White	16
9	Steve Garvey	15
	Willie McGee	15
	David Justice	15
12	Ron Cey	14
	Lenny Dykstra	14
	Roberto Alomar	14
	Chipper Jones	14
16	Don Baylor	13
	Darryl Strawberry	13
18	Dusty Baker	12
	Joe Morgan	12
	Terry Pendleton	12

Hits

1	Pete Rose	45
2	Reggie Jackson	37
3	Roberto Alomar	36
4	George Brett	35
5	Fred McGriff	34
6	Devon White	33
7	Steve Garvey	32
8	Mark Lemke	31
9	Terry Pendleton	30
10	Bill Russell	28
11	Tony Fernandez	27
12	Don Baylor	26
	Bob Boone	26
	Willie McGee	26
15	Richie Hebner	25
	Carney Lansford	25
	Ron Gant	25
	David Justice	25
	Chipper Jones	25
20	3 tied with	24

Doubles

1	Ron Cey	7
	Reggie Jackson	7
	Richie Hebner	7
	Mike Schmidt	7
	Hal McRae	7
	Pete Rose	7
	Fred McGriff	7
	Javy Lopez	7
9	Doug DeCinces	6
	Greg Luzinski	6
	Tony Fernandez	6
	Andy Van Slyke	6
	Mark Lemke	6
	Roy White	6
	Brooks Robinson	6
16	19 tied with	5

Triples

1	George Brett	4
2	Willie McGee	3
	Mariano Duncan	3
	Kenny Lofton	3
5	Davey Lopes	2
	Ozzie Smith	2
	Johnny Bench	2
	Rickey Henderson	2
	Luis Salazar	2
	Andy Van Slyke	2
	Terry Pendleton	2
	Jeff Blauser	2
	Jose Lind	2
14	80 tied with	1

Home Runs

1	George Brett	9
2	Steve Garvey	8
3	Reggie Jackson	6
	Darryl Strawberry	6
5	Sal Bando	5
	Greg Luzinski	5
	Gary Matthews	5
	Graig Nettles	5
	Johnny Bench	5
	Ron Gant	5
11	12 tied with	4

RBI

1	Steve Garvey	21
2	Reggie Jackson	20
3	George Brett	19
	Graig Nettles	19
5	Fred McGriff	18
6	Don Baylor	17
	Ron Gant	17
8	Darryl Strawberry	16
9	Al Oliver	15
	Roberto Alomar	15
11	Ron Cey	14
	Terry Pendleton	14
13	Dusty Baker	13
	Gary Matthews	13
	Tony Perez	13
	Eddie Murray	13
	Mark Lemke	13
	David Justice	13
19	5 tied with	12

Walks

1	Joe Morgan	23
2	Reggie Jackson	17
	Rickey Henderson	17
4	Darrell Porter	16
	David Justice	16
6	Jeff Blauser	15
	Mark Lemke	15
	Roberto Alomar	15
9	Barry Bonds	14
10	Ron Cey	13
	Gene Tenace	13
12	Eddie Murray	12
	Fred McGriff	12
14	Don Baylor	11
	George Brett	11
	Keith Hernandez	11
	Lenny Dykstra	11
	Bobby Bonilla	11
19	7 tied with	10

Strikeouts

1	Reggie Jackson	41
2	Ron Gant	26
3	Cesar Geronimo	24
4	Fred McGriff	23
	Jeff Blauser	23
6	Bobby Grich	22
	Devon White	22
8	Willie McGee	21
	Marquis Grissom	21
10	Greg Luzinski	20
	Mariano Duncan	20
12	Willie Stargell	19
	Darryl Strawberry	19
	Terry Pendleton	19
15	Hal McRae	18
	Mike Marshall	18
	Andy Van Slyke	18
18	5 tied with	17

Stolen Bases

1	Rickey Henderson	16
2	Roberto Alomar	11
3	Davey Lopes	9
4	Willie Wilson	8
	Amos Otis	8
	Joe Morgan	8
	Ron Gant	8
8	Bert Campaneris	6
	Kirk Gibson	6
	Steve Sax	6
	Vince Coleman	6
	Barry Bonds	6
	Kenny Lofton	6
14	Ken Griffey Sr.	5
	Tony Fernandez	5
	Marquis Grissom	5
17	5 tied with	4

Batting Average

(minimum 50 Plate Appearances)

1	Will Clark	.489
2	Mickey Rivers	.386
3	Chipper Jones	.385
4	Pete Rose	.381
5	Dusty Baker	.371
6	Steve Garvey	.356
7	Brooks Robinson	.348
8	Devon White	.347
9	George Brett	.340
10	Javy Lopez	.339
11	Thurman Munson	.339
12	Tony Fernandez	.338
13	Bill Russell	.337
14	Harold Baines	.333
	Tim Raines	.333
16	Cal Ripken Jr.	.328
17	Lenny Dykstra	.323
18	Darrell Porter	.317
19	Carney Lansford	.316
20	Roberto Alomar	.316

On-Base Percentage

(minimum 50 Plate Appearances)

1	Will Clark	.540
2	Dusty Baker	.451
3	Darrell Porter	.450
4	Chipper Jones	.446
5	Lenny Dykstra	.440
6	Pete Rose	.430
7	Mickey Rivers	.417
	Otis Nixon	.417
9	Devon White	.411
10	Cal Ripken Jr.	.409
11	George Brett	.400
	Jose Cruz	.400
	Manny Ramirez	.400
14	Eddie Murray	.397
15	Roberto Alomar	.392
16	Jose Canseco	.389
17	Keith Hernandez	.387
	John Olerud	.387
19	Steve Garvey	.383
20	Rickey Henderson	.382

Slugging Percentage

(minimum 50 Plate Appearances)

1	Will Clark	.844
2	George Brett	.728
3	Steve Garvey	.678
4	Lenny Dykstra	.629
5	Darryl Strawberry	.625
	Javy Lopez	.625
7	Dusty Baker	.597
8	Manny Ramirez	.595
9	Boog Powell	.592
10	Greg Luzinski	.589
11	Chipper Jones	.569
12	Jose Canseco	.568
13	Brady Anderson	.543
14	Pete Rose	.534
15	Johnny Bench	.530
16	Sal Bando	.527
17	Brooks Robinson	.522
18	Dave Henderson	.520
19	Ron Cey	.500
	Thurman Munson	.500

OBP+Slugging

(minimum 50 Plate Appearances)

1	Will Clark	1.384
2	George Brett	1.128
3	Lenny Dykstra	1.069
4	Steve Garvey	1.061
5	Dusty Baker	1.047
6	Chipper Jones	1.015
7	Javy Lopez	1.006
8	Manny Ramirez	.995
9	Darryl Strawberry	.986
10	Pete Rose	.964
11	Boog Powell	.962
12	Jose Canseco	.957
13	Greg Luzinski	.935
14	Brady Anderson	.921
15	Brooks Robinson	.883
16	Eddie Murray	.882
17	Sal Bando	.876
18	Cal Ripken Jr.	.875
19	Mickey Rivers	.873
20	Ron Cey	.868

Secondary Average

(minimum 50 Plate Appearances)

1	Jose Canseco	.568
2	Rickey Henderson	.527
3	Lenny Dykstra	.500
4	George Brett	.495
5	Will Clark	.489
6	Manny Ramirez	.476
7	Kirk Gibson	.475
8	Joe Morgan	.458
9	Brady Anderson	.457
10	Darryl Strawberry	.453
11	Johnny Bench	.446
12	Greg Luzinski	.411
13	Davey Lopes	.408
14	Ron Cey	.402
15	Eddie Murray	.394
16	Boog Powell	.388
17	Dave Henderson	.380
18	Steve Garvey	.378
19	Javy Lopez	.375
20	Barry Bonds	.368

League Championship Series Pitching Leaders—Career

Wins

1	Dave Stewart	8
2	John Smoltz	6
3	Juan Guzman	5
4	Steve Carlton	4
	Bruce Kison	4
	Don Sutton	4
	Tommy John	4
	Jim Palmer	4
	Orel Hershiser	4
	Steve Avery	4
	Catfish Hunter	4
12	10 tied with	3

Losses

1	Jerry Reuss	7
2	Tom Glavine	6
3	Doug Drabek	5
	Greg Maddux	5
5	Doyle Alexander	4
	Todd Stottlemyre	4
7	Gene Garber	3
	Charlie Leibrandt	3
	Dennis Leonard	3
	Dave Stieb	3
	Zane Smith	3
	Alex Fernandez	3
	Catfish Hunter	3
	Ken Holtzman	3
	Don Gullett	3
16	38 tied with	2

Winning Percentage
(minimum 5 decisions)

1	Dave Stewart	1.000
	Juan Guzman	1.000
3	Don Sutton	.800
	Tommy John	.800
	Jim Palmer	.800
	Steve Avery	.800
7	John Smoltz	.750
8	Steve Carlton	.667
9	Bob Welch	.600
	Jack Morris	.600
	Dave McNally	.600
12	Catfish Hunter	.571
13	Dennis Leonard	.400
	Ken Holtzman	.400
	Don Gullett	.400
16	Greg Maddux	.375
17	Tom Glavine	.333
18	Doug Drabek	.286
19	Todd Stottlemyre	.200
20	Jerry Reuss	.000

Games

1	Rick Honeycutt	20
2	Dennis Eckersley	18
	Mark Wohlers	18
4	Tug McGraw	15
5	Jesse Orosco	14
	Randy Myers	14
7	Ron Reed	13
	Alejandro Pena	13
	Dave Giusti	13
10	Tom Henke	12
11	Rollie Fingers	11
	Duane Ward	11
	Steve Avery	11
14	10 tied with	10

Games Started

1	Dave Stewart	10
	Tom Glavine	10
	John Smoltz	10
	Catfish Hunter	10
5	Greg Maddux	9
6	Steve Carlton	8
	Orel Hershiser	8
8	Jerry Reuss	7
	Tommy John	7
	Jim Palmer	7
	Doug Drabek	7
	Steve Avery	7
13	Don Sutton	6
	Bob Welch	6
	Dennis Leonard	6
	Jack Morris	6
	Roger Clemens	6
	Jimmy Key	6
	Don Gullett	6
	Mike Cuellar	6

Complete Games

1	Jim Palmer	5
2	Tommy John	3
	Catfish Hunter	3
4	Mike Scott	2
	Don Sutton	2
	Mike Boddicker	2
	Bruce Hurst	2
	Dennis Leonard	2
	Jack Morris	2
	Danny Cox	2
	Orel Hershiser	2
	Doug Drabek	2
	Tim Wakefield	2
	Ken Holtzman	2
	Dave McNally	2
	Mike Cuellar	2
17	39 tied with	1

Shutouts

1	21 tied with	1

Saves

1	Dennis Eckersley	11
2	Tug McGraw	5
3	Alejandro Pena	4
	Ken Dayley	4
	Randy Myers	4
	Dave Giusti	4
7	Jeff Reardon	3
	Pedro Borbon	3
	Steve Bedrosian	3
	Goose Gossage	3
	Tom Henke	3
	Rick Aguilera	3
	Duane Ward	3
	Jose Mesa	3
15	9 tied with	2

Innings Pitched

1	Dave Stewart	75.1
2	John Smoltz	70.0
3	Catfish Hunter	69.1
4	Tom Glavine	61.2
5	Orel Hershiser	61.0
6	Jim Palmer	59.2
7	Greg Maddux	55.1
8	Steve Carlton	53.2
9	Don Sutton	49.0
10	Doug Drabek	48.1
11	Tommy John	47.2
12	Steve Avery	45.1
13	Mike Cuellar	44.0
14	Nolan Ryan	41.1
15	Jack Morris	40.2
	Don Gullett	40.2
17	Dave McNally	40.1
18	Jimmy Key	38.2
19	Roger Clemens	37.1
20	2 tied with	37.0

Walks

1	Steve Carlton	28
	John Smoltz	28
3	Dave Stewart	25
4	Tom Glavine	22
5	Fernando Valenzuela	19
	Jim Palmer	19
	Greg Maddux	19
	Mike Cuellar	19
9	Juan Guzman	18
	Catfish Hunter	18
11	Jerry Reuss	17
	Orel Hershiser	17
	Steve Avery	17
14	Tug McGraw	16
	Dave Stieb	16
16	Bob Welch	15
	Tommy John	15
	Danny Jackson	15
	David Cone	15
	Dave McNally	15

Strikeouts

1	John Smoltz	67
2	Nolan Ryan	46
	Jim Palmer	46
	Greg Maddux	46
5	Orel Hershiser	42
6	Tom Glavine	41
7	Steve Carlton	39
	Dave Stewart	39
9	Steve Avery	37
	Catfish Hunter	37
11	Doug Drabek	33
12	Mike Mussina	31
13	Don Sutton	30
	Dave McNally	30
15	Dwight Gooden	29
	Roger Clemens	29
17	Fernando Valenzuela	28
	Dave Stieb	28
	Mike Cuellar	28
20	Tommy John	27

Strikeouts/9 Innings
(minimum 25 Innings Pitched)

1	Nolan Ryan	10.02
2	John Candelaria	8.88
3	John Smoltz	8.61
4	Dave Stieb	7.96
5	Todd Stottlemyre	7.52
6	Greg Maddux	7.48
7	Dwight Gooden	7.39
8	Steve Avery	7.35
9	Tug McGraw	7.33
10	Bruce Kison	7.28
11	Vida Blue	7.18
12	Roger Clemens	6.99
13	Jim Palmer	6.94
14	David Cone	6.90
15	Tom Seaver	6.82
	Bob Welch	6.82
17	Fernando Valenzuela	6.81
18	Dave McNally	6.69
19	Dennis Leonard	6.61
20	Steve Carlton	6.54

ERA
(minimum 25 Innings Pitched)

1	Bruce Kison	1.21
2	Gary Nolan	1.35
3	Orel Hershiser	1.62
4	Danny Cox	1.84
5	Fernando Valenzuela	1.95
6	Jim Palmer	1.96
7	Don Sutton	2.02
8	Dave Stewart	2.03
9	Dwight Gooden	2.04
10	Doug Drabek	2.05
11	Ken Holtzman	2.06
12	Tommy John	2.08
13	John Candelaria	2.13
14	Juan Guzman	2.27
15	John Smoltz	2.31
16	Steve Avery	2.38
17	Dock Ellis	2.43
18	Bruce Hurst	2.57
19	Tug McGraw	2.67
20	Paul Splittorff	2.68

Component ERA
(minimum 25 Innings Pitched)

1	Ken Holtzman	1.40
2	Bruce Kison	1.54
3	Nolan Ryan	1.96
4	Don Sutton	1.96
5	Orel Hershiser	2.17
6	Doug Drabek	2.22
7	Steve Avery	2.29
8	Bob Walk	2.31
9	Dave Stewart	2.32
10	Dwight Gooden	2.36
11	Don Gullett	2.40
12	Dennis Eckersley	2.40
13	Mike Cuellar	2.49
14	Vida Blue	2.50
15	Jim Palmer	2.53
16	Gary Nolan	2.60
17	Fernando Valenzuela	2.63
18	John Candelaria	2.80
19	Tug McGraw	2.82
20	Tommy John	2.88

Opponent Average
(minimum 25 Innings Pitched)

1	Bruce Kison	.150
2	Ken Holtzman	.188
3	Bob Walk	.194
4	Dave Stewart	.196
5	John Candelaria	.198
6	Mike Cuellar	.201
7	Dave Stieb	.204
8	Dave McNally	.204
9	Dwight Gooden	.206
10	Don Sutton	.208
11	Juan Guzman	.209
12	Don Gullett	.209
13	Jim Palmer	.211
14	Tug McGraw	.212
15	Fernando Valenzuela	.215
16	Orel Hershiser	.217
17	Nolan Ryan	.218
18	Steve Avery	.219
19	Tom Seaver	.224
20	2 tied with	.225

Opponent OBP
(minimum 25 Innings Pitched)

1	Ken Holtzman	.224
2	Bruce Kison	.239
3	Don Sutton	.242
4	Nolan Ryan	.259
5	Bob Walk	.266
6	John Candelaria	.267
7	Dennis Eckersley	.269
8	Dave Stewart	.270
9	Don Gullett	.272
10	Vida Blue	.276
11	Jim Palmer	.277
12	Dave McNally	.280
13	Catfish Hunter	.280
14	Orel Hershiser	.282
15	Doug Drabek	.284
16	Dwight Gooden	.284
17	Mike Cuellar	.285
18	Gary Nolan	.286
19	Tom Seaver	.290
20	Steve Avery	.292

Postseason Profiles

Hank Aaron

Bats: Right, Throws: Right

Batting	Avg	G	AB	R	H	2B	3B	HR	RBI	BB	SO	HBP	GDP	SB	CS	OBP	Slg
Totals	.362	17	69	11	25	4	1	6	16	5	13	0	2	0	0	.405	.710
Home	.432	9	37	7	16	2	0	4	12	4	4	0	2	0	0	.488	.811
Away	.281	8	32	4	9	2	1	2	4	1	9	0	0	0	0	.303	.594
vs. Left	.375	9	24	0	9	2	1	1	5	1	5	0	1	0	0	.400	.667
vs. Right	.356	17	45	11	16	2	0	5	11	4	8	0	1	0	0	.408	.733
Scoring Pos.	.368	13	19	0	7	1	0	2	10	3	4	0	0	0	0	.455	.737
Close & Late	.400	7	10	1	4	1	0	1	2	0	3	0	0	0	0	.400	.800
None on/out	.250	11	16	0	4	0	1	1	1	1	5	0	0	0	0	.294	.563
None on	.290	16	31	0	9	1	1	2	2	1	6	0	0	0	0	.313	.581
Runners on	.421	16	38	0	16	3	0	4	14	4	7	0	2	0	0	.476	.816
Batting #3	.357	3	14	3	5	2	0	3	7	0	1	0	1	0	0	.357	1.143
Batting #4	.364	14	55	8	20	2	1	3	9	5	12	0	1	0	0	.417	.600

Hit Best Against

	Avg	AB	R	H	2B	3B	HR	RBI	BB	SO	HBP	GDP	SB	CS	OBP	Slg
Don Larsen	.500	8	1	4	0	0	1	2	2	1	0	0	0	0	.600	.875
Whitey Ford	.429	14	1	6	2	0	0	1	1	3	0	0	0	0	.467	.571

Hit Worst Against

	Avg	AB	R	H	2B	3B	HR	RBI	BB	SO	HBP	GDP	SB	CS	OBP	Slg
Bob Turley	.091	11	2	1	0	0	1	1	1	4	0	1	0	0	.167	.364

Babe Adams

Throws: Right, Bats: Left

Pitching	ERA	W	L	Sv	G	GS	IP	BB	SO	Avg	R	H	2B	3B	HR	OBP	Slg
Totals	1.29	3	0	0	4	3	28.0	6	11	.194	5	20	6	0	2	.245	.311
Home	2.00	2	0	0	2	2	18.0	5	10	.182	5	12	2	0	2	.239	.303
Away	0.00	1	0	0	2	1	10.0	1	1	.216	0	8	4	0	0	.256	.324

	Avg	AB	R	H	2B	3B	HR	RBI	BB	SO	HBP	GDP	OBP	Slg
vs. Left	.208	53	0	11	2	0	2	3	5	3	1	0	.288	.358
vs. Right	.180	50	5	9	4	0	0	1	1	8	0	0	.196	.260
Scoring Pos.	.120	25	0	3	0	0	0	1	1	3	0	0	.154	.120
Close & Late	.000	9	0	0	0	0	0	0	1	0	0	0	.100	.000
None on/out	.111	27	0	3	1	0	1	1	2	2	0	0	.172	.259
None on	.200	65	0	13	4	0	2	2	4	8	1	0	.257	.354
Runners on	.184	38	0	7	2	0	0	2	2	3	0	0	.225	.237

Pitched Best Against

	Avg	AB	R	H	2B	3B	HR	RBI	BB	SO	HBP	GDP	SB	CS	OBP	Slg
Donie Bush	.000	8	0	0	0	0	0	0	2	2	1	0	0	1	.273	.000
Ty Cobb	.091	11	2	1	0	0	0	0	1	0	0	0	1	0	.167	.091
George Mullin	.125	8	0	1	0	0	0	0	0	1	0	0	0	0	.125	.125

Pitched Worst Against

	Avg	AB	R	H	2B	3B	HR	RBI	BB	SO	HBP	GDP	SB	CS	OBP	Slg
Davy Jones	.364	11	1	4	0	0	1	1	1	1	0	0	0	0	.417	.636
Sam Crawford	.333	12	2	4	1	0	1	2	0	0	0	0	1	0	.333	.667
Jim Delahanty	.273	11	0	3	1	0	0	1	1	3	0	0	0	0	.333	.364

Rick Aguilera

Throws: Right, Bats: Right

Pitching	ERA	W	L	Sv	G	GS	IP	BB	SO	Avg	R	H	2B	3B	HR	OBP	Slg
Totals	2.63	2	1	5	15	0	24.0	6	17	.250	8	23	3	0	2	.303	.348
Home	2.84	2	0	3	8	0	12.2	3	13	.300	5	15	2	0	1	.352	.400
Away	2.38	0	1	2	7	0	11.1	3	4	.190	3	8	1	0	1	.244	.286

	Avg	AB	R	H	2B	3B	HR	RBI	BB	SO	HBP	GDP	OBP	Slg
vs. Left	.255	47	0	12	1	0	0	4	3	8	1	0	.314	.277
vs. Right	.239	46	6	11	2	0	2	5	3	9	0	0	.286	.413
Scoring Pos.	.375	16	2	6	0	0	0	7	2	2	1	0	.474	.375
Close & Late	.317	41	5	13	1	0	2	6	2	10	0	0	.349	.488
None on/out	.240	25	0	6	0	0	2	2	2	7	0	0	.296	.480
None on	.237	59	0	14	3	0	2	2	4	10	0	0	.286	.390
Runners on	.265	34	2	9	0	0	0	7	2	7	1	0	.324	.265

Pete Alexander

Throws: Right, Bats: Right

Pitching	ERA	W	L	Sv	G	GS	IP	BB	SO	Avg	R	H	2B	3B	HR	OBP	Slg
Totals	3.56	3	2	1	7	5	43.0	12	29	.231	18	36	5	2	3	.282	.346
Home	3.09	1	0	0	2	1	11.2	2	7	.273	4	12	2	0	2	.298	.455
Away	3.73	2	2	1	5	4	31.1	10	22	.214	14	24	3	2	1	.276	.304

	Avg	AB	R	H	2B	3B	HR	RBI	BB	SO	HBP	GDP	OBP	Slg
vs. Left	.198	81	0	16	1	1	3	10	9	8	0	2	.272	.346
vs. Right	.267	75	18	20	4	1	0	6	3	21	0	2	.295	.347
Scoring Pos.	.216	37	0	8	1	0	1	14	3	7	0	2	.262	.324
Close & Late	.276	29	1	8	1	0	0	4	1	5	0	2	.300	.310
None on/out	.341	41	0	14	1	1	1	1	3	6	0	2	.386	.488
None on	.272	92	0	25	3	2	2	2	7	17	0	2	.323	.413
Runners on	.172	64	0	11	2	0	1	14	5	12	0	2	.225	.250

Pitched Best Against

	Avg	AB	R	H	2B	3B	HR	RBI	BB	SO	HBP	GDP	SB	CS	OBP	Slg
Mark Koenig	.000	13	0	0	0	0	0	0	0	2	0	1	0	0	.000	.000
Doc Hoblitzell	.143	7	0	1	0	0	0	1	0	0	0	1	1	0	.125	.143
Jack Barry	.143	7	0	1	0	0	0	0	0	1	0	0	0	0	.143	.143

Pitched Worst Against

	Avg	AB	R	H	2B	3B	HR	RBI	BB	SO	HBP	GDP	SB	CS	OBP	Slg
Duffy Lewis	.625	8	0	5	0	0	0	2	0	2	0	0	0	1	.625	.625
Tris Speaker	.400	5	2	2	0	1	0	0	3	0	0	0	0	0	.625	.800
Bob Meusel	.400	10	3	4	2	1	0	1	1	3	0	0	0	0	.455	.800

Roberto Alomar

Bats: Both, Throws: Right

Batting	Avg	G	AB	R	H	2B	3B	HR	RBI	BB	SO	HBP	GDP	SB	CS	OBP	Slg
Totals	.321	48	190	25	61	9	1	4	27	23	24	0	7	18	2	.391	.442
Home	.319	25	94	10	30	5	0	1	15	12	11	0	3	12	1	.393	.404
Away	.323	23	96	15	31	4	1	3	12	11	13	0	4	6	1	.389	.479
vs. Left	.254	31	59	5	15	4	0	0	8	4	9	0	1	3	1	.292	.322
vs. Right	.351	44	131	20	46	5	1	4	19	19	15	0	6	15	1	.433	.496
Scoring Pos.	.400	40	45	22	18	3	0	2	24	8	7	0	1	9	1	.473	.600
Close & Late	.306	30	36	7	11	2	0	2	5	7	7	0	0	2	1	.409	.528
None on/out	.324	33	37	2	12	3	0	2	2	6	3	0	0	0	0	.419	.568
None on	.290	47	100	2	29	5	0	2	2	14	12	0	0	0	0	.377	.400
Runners on	.356	45	90	23	32	4	1	2	25	9	12	0	7	18	2	.406	.489
Batting #2	.317	27	101	13	32	4	0	3	12	15	11	0	5	10	0	.405	.446
Batting #3	.270	17	74	8	20	4	0	1	12	6	12	0	2	5	1	.317	.365
Batting #6	.500	3	10	2	5	1	0	0	1	2	1	0	0	1	1	.583	.600

Hit Best Against

	Avg	AB	R	H	2B	3B	HR	RBI	BB	SO	HBP	GDP	SB	CS	OBP	Slg
Terry Mulholland	.600	5	2	3	1	0	0	1	0	1	0	0	0	0	.600	.800
Kevin Tapani	.600	5	2	3	0	0	0	3	0	1	0	0	1	0	.600	.600
Jack Morris	.429	7	1	3	0	0	0	0	0	0	0	0	1	0	.429	.429

Hit Worst Against

	Avg	AB	R	H	2B	3B	HR	RBI	BB	SO	HBP	GDP	SB	CS	OBP	Slg
Tom Glavine	.000	7	0	0	0	0	0	0	1	1	0	0	1	0	.125	.000
Jack McDowell	.000	6	2	0	0	0	0	0	3	3	0	0	1	0	.333	.000
Alex Fernandez	.125	8	0	1	0	0	0	1	0	1	0	1	1	0	.125	.125

Brady Anderson

Bats: Left, Throws: Left

Batting	Avg	G	AB	R	H	2B	3B	HR	RBI	BB	SO	HBP	GDP	SB	CS	OBP	Slg
Totals	.300	19	80	16	24	4	0	6	12	10	16	1	0	3	1	.380	.575
Home	.262	10	42	7	11	1	0	3	4	3	12	0	0	0	0	.304	.500
Away	.342	9	38	9	13	3	0	3	8	7	4	1	0	3	1	.457	.658
vs. Left	.258	14	31	6	8	1	0	1	4	4	7	0	0	1	0	.333	.387
vs. Right	.327	16	49	10	16	3	0	5	8	6	9	1	0	2	1	.411	.694
Scoring Pos.	.400	14	10	8	4	2	0	0	5	1	2	1	0	1	0	.462	.600
Close & Late	.471	12	17	3	8	2	0	1	4	2	3	0	0	2	0	.500	.765
None on/out	.265	19	34	3	9	0	0	3	3	4	9	0	0	0	0	.342	.529
None on	.273	19	55	5	15	2	0	5	5	7	12	0	0	0	0	.355	.582
Runners on	.360	18	25	11	9	2	0	1	7	3	4	1	0	3	1	.433	.560
Batting #1	.300	19	80	16	24	4	0	6	12	10	16	1	0	3	1	.380	.575

Hit Best Against

	Avg	AB	R	H	2B	3B	HR	RBI	BB	SO	HBP	GDP	SB	CS	OBP	Slg
Orel Hershiser	.500	6	1	3	0	0	1	1	0	1	0	0	0	0	.500	1.000
Chad Ogea	.429	7	3	3	1	0	1	1	0	2	0	0	0	0	.429	1.000
Jose Mesa	.429	7	0	3	1	0	0	1	0	0	0	0	0	0	.429	.571

Hit Worst Against

	Avg	AB	R	H	2B	3B	HR	RBI	BB	SO	HBP	GDP	SB	CS	OBP	Slg
Andy Pettitte	.143	7	1	1	0	0	1	1	1	1	0	0	0	0	.250	.571

Steve Avery

Throws: Left, Bats: Left

Pitching	ERA	W	L	Sv	G	GS	IP	BB	SO	Avg	R	H	2B	3B	HR	OBP	Slg
Totals	2.90	5	3	0	18	12	77.2	29	60	.219	28	61	14	3	6	.289	.356
Home	2.62	2	1	0	9	5	34.1	13	22	.221	13	27	4	2	2	.290	.336
Away	3.12	3	2	0	9	7	43.1	16	38	.218	15	34	10	1	4	.289	.372

	Avg	AB	R	H	2B	3B	HR	RBI	BB	SO	HBP	GDP	OBP	Slg
vs. Left	.119	59	0	7	3	0	0	4	8	14	0	7	.224	.169
vs. Right	.247	219	0	54	11	3	6	18	21	46	0	7	.307	.406
Scoring Pos.	.191	47	20	9	3	1	0	13	11	10	0	7	.323	.298
Close & Late	.265	34	9	9	2	0	1	2	6	4	0	7	.375	.412
None on/out	.269	78	0	21	4	1	3	3	7	15	0	7	.329	.462
None on	.243	177	7	43	7	1	6	6	17	40	0	7	.309	.395
Runners on	.178	101	21	18	7	2	0	16	12	20	0	7	.256	.287

Pitched Best Against

	Avg	AB	R	H	2B	3B	HR	RBI	BB	SO	HBP	GDP	SB	CS	OBP	Slg
Andy Van Slyke	.000	11	0	0	0	0	0	0	1	2	0	0	0	0	.083	.000
Kent Hrbek	.000	6	0	0	0	0	0	0	0	0	0	1	0	0	.000	.000
Kevin Stocker	.000	5	0	0	0	0	0	0	1	0	0	0	0	0	.167	.000

Pitched Worst Against

	Avg	AB	R	H	2B	3B	HR	RBI	BB	SO	HBP	GDP	SB	CS	OBP	Slg
L. McClendon	.600	5	1	3	2	0	0	2	0	0	0	0	0	0	.600	1.000
Pat Borders	.600	5	0	3	1	0	0	0	0	1	0	0	0	0	.600	.800
Jeff King	.400	5	1	2	2	0	0	1	0	0	0	0	0	0	.400	.800

Dusty Baker

Bats: Right, Throws: Right

Batting	Avg	G	AB	R	H	2B	3B	HR	RBI	BB	SO	HBP	GDP	SB	CS	OBP	Slg
Totals	.282	40	149	23	42	6	0	5	21	12	14	2	3	0	0	.341	.423
Home	.280	20	75	11	21	2	0	3	12	4	9	1	1	0	0	.325	.427
Away	.284	20	74	12	21	4	0	2	9	8	5	1	2	0	0	.357	.419
vs. Left	.320	21	50	0	16	1	0	2	8	8	4	1	0	0	0	.424	.460
vs. Right	.263	40	99	23	26	5	0	3	13	4	10	1	3	0	0	.295	.404
Scoring Pos.	.222	27	36	0	8	1	0	2	15	1	4	1	1	0	0	.256	.417
Close & Late	.300	17	20	2	6	0	0	0	1	0	3	0	0	0	0	.286	.300
None on/out	.345	22	29	0	10	1	0	2	2	2	1	1	0	0	0	.406	.586
None on	.278	39	79	0	22	3	0	2	2	8	7	1	0	0	0	.352	.392
Runners on	.286	37	70	0	20	3	0	3	19	4	7	1	3	0	0	.329	.457
Batting #3	.224	16	58	8	13	3	0	0	5	5	2	1	1	0	0	.292	.276
Batting #5	.214	3	14	3	3	0	0	0	0	0	4	0	0	0	0	.214	.214
Batting #6	.324	20	74	11	24	3	0	4	15	6	8	1	2	0	0	.383	.527

Hit Best Against

	Avg	AB	R	H	2B	3B	HR	RBI	BB	SO	HBP	GDP	SB	CS	OBP	Slg
Steve Carlton	.417	12	3	5	0	0	2	3	4	0	0	0	0	0	.563	.917
Bill Gullickson	.400	5	1	2	1	0	0	1	1	0	1	0	0	0	.571	.600
Don Gullett	.400	5	2	2	0	0	0	1	0	0	1	0	0	0	.500	.400

Hit Worst Against

	Avg	AB	R	H	2B	3B	HR	RBI	BB	SO	HBP	GDP	SB	CS	OBP	Slg
Nolan Ryan	.000	5	1	0	0	0	0	0	1	0	0	1	0	0	.167	.000
Catfish Hunter	.125	8	0	1	0	0	0	0	0	0	0	1	0	0	.125	.125
Tommy John	.167	6	1	1	0	0	0	0	0	1	0	0	0	0	.167	.167

Home Run Baker

Bats: Left, Throws: Right

Batting	Avg	G	AB	R	H	2B	3B	HR	RBI	BB	SO	HBP	GDP	SB	CS	OBP	Slg
Totals	.363	25	91	15	33	7	0	3	18	5	11	0	1	1	5	.392	.538
Home	.308	11	39	6	12	5	0	1	6	3	6	0	0	0	1	.357	.513
Away	.404	14	52	9	21	2	0	2	12	2	5	0	1	1	4	.418	.558
vs. Left	.250	8	24	0	6	1	0	2	8	1	6	0	1	0	0	.280	.542
vs. Right	.403	25	67	15	27	6	0	1	10	4	5	0	0	1	5	.431	.537
Scoring Pos.	.458	18	24	0	11	1	0	2	15	4	3	0	0	1	1	.517	.750
Close & Late	.667	10	12	1	8	1	0	0	2	1	0	0	0	0	0	.692	.750
None on/out	.346	15	26	0	9	3	0	0	0	1	3	0	0	0	0	.370	.462
None on	.300	22	50	0	15	4	0	1	1	1	5	0	0	0	0	.314	.440
Runners on	.439	21	41	0	18	3	0	2	17	4	6	0	1	1	5	.478	.659
Batting #4	.378	20	82	15	31	7	0	3	18	4	11	0	1	1	5	.402	.573

Hit Best Against

	Avg	AB	R	H	2B	3B	HR	RBI	BB	SO	HBP	GDP	SB	CS	OBP	Slg
C. Mathewson	.500	20	4	10	2	0	1	4	1	3	0	0	0	1	.500	.750
Lefty Tyler	.400	5	0	2	1	0	0	2	0	2	0	1	0	0	.400	.600
Rube Marquard	.273	11	2	3	0	0	2	5	0	4	0	0	0	0	.273	.818

Hit Worst Against

	Avg	AB	R	H	2B	3B	HR	RBI	BB	SO	HBP	GDP	SB	CS	OBP	Slg
T. Finger Brown	.111	9	2	1	0	0	0	0	1	1	0	0	0	0	.200	.111

Dave Bancroft

Bats: Both, Throws: Right

Batting	Avg	G	AB	R	H	2B	3B	HR	RBI	BB	SO	HBP	GDP	SB	CS	OBP	Slg
Totals	.172	24	93	10	16	1	0	0	7	6	10	0	1	1	3	.220	.183
Home	.170	13	53	7	9	1	0	0	1	1	5	0	1	0	1	.182	.189
Away	.175	11	40	3	7	0	0	0	6	5	5	0	0	1	2	.267	.175
vs. Left	.083	4	12	0	1	0	0	0	1	0	0	0	0	0	0	.083	.083
vs. Right	.185	24	81	10	15	1	0	0	6	6	10	0	1	1	3	.239	.198
Scoring Pos.	.200	12	15	0	3	0	0	0	7	0	3	0	0	1	1	.188	.200
Close & Late	.333	10	12	1	4	0	0	0	0	0	2	0	0	0	0	.333	.333
None on/out	.103	20	29	0	3	0	0	0	0	0	2	0	0	0	0	.103	.103
None on	.131	24	61	0	8	1	0	0	0	6	5	0	0	0	0	.209	.148
Runners on	.250	20	32	0	8	0	0	0	7	0	5	0	1	1	3	.242	.250
Batting #1	.140	11	43	5	6	0	0	0	3	3	3	0	1	1	0	.196	.140
Batting #2	.200	13	50	5	10	1	0	0	4	3	7	0	0	0	3	.241	.220

Hit Best Against

	Avg	AB	R	H	2B	3B	HR	RBI	BB	SO	HBP	GDP	SB	CS	OBP	Slg
Rube Foster	.375	8	1	3	0	0	0	0	0	2	0	0	0	1	.375	.375
Bob Shawkey	.313	16	1	5	0	0	0	2	0	1	0	0	0	1	.313	.313

Hit Worst Against

	Avg	AB	R	H	2B	3B	HR	RBI	BB	SO	HBP	GDP	SB	CS	OBP	Slg
Herb Pennock	.000	8	0	0	0	0	0	0	0	0	0	0	0	0	.000	.000
Waite Hoyt	.063	16	5	1	0	0	0	1	2	3	0	0	1	0	.167	.063
Joe Bush	.143	14	1	2	0	0	0	0	0	1	0	1	0	0	.143	.143

Sal Bando

Bats: Right, Throws: Right

Batting	Avg	G	AB	R	H	2B	3B	HR	RBI	BB	SO	HBP	GDP	SB	CS	OBP	Slg
Totals	.245	44	159	21	39	9	1	5	13	18	32	2	2	0	1	.328	.409
Home	.250	21	76	9	19	3	1	2	7	9	17	1	2	0	0	.333	.395
Away	.241	23	83	12	20	6	0	3	6	9	15	1	0	0	1	.323	.422
vs. Left	.260	28	77	0	20	5	1	3	6	12	13	0	0	0	0	.360	.468
vs. Right	.232	44	82	21	19	4	0	2	7	6	19	2	2	0	0	.297	.354
Scoring Pos.	.176	28	34	0	6	1	1	1	9	4	10	1	1	0	0	.275	.353
Close & Late	.250	25	24	1	6	0	0	1	4	3	5	1	1	0	0	.357	.375
None on/out	.353	28	34	0	12	2	0	2	2	3	3	1	1	0	0	.421	.588
None on	.289	43	97	0	28	7	0	4	4	13	14	1	0	0	0	.378	.485
Runners on	.177	37	62	0	11	2	1	1	9	5	18	1	2	0	1	.246	.290
Batting #3	.222	23	81	15	18	3	1	4	10	13	21	2	0	0	0	.340	.432
Batting #5	.240	13	50	5	12	3	0	1	2	2	7	0	2	0	0	.269	.360
Batting #7	.357	4	14	1	5	3	0	0	1	2	2	0	0	0	1	.438	.571

Hit Best Against

	Avg	AB	R	H	2B	3B	HR	RBI	BB	SO	HBP	GDP	SB	CS	OBP	Slg
Dave McNally	.500	8	4	4	1	0	3	4	2	0	0	0	0	0	.600	1.750
Tom Seaver	.286	7	2	2	1	0	0	0	0	2	0	0	0	0	.286	.429
Mickey Lolich	.250	8	0	2	0	0	0	0	0	0	0	0	0	0	.250	.250

Hit Worst Against

	Avg	AB	R	H	2B	3B	HR	RBI	BB	SO	HBP	GDP	SB	CS	OBP	Slg
Jack Billingham	.000	5	0	0	0	0	0	0	0	2	0	1	0	0	.000	.000
Jon Matlack	.125	8	1	1	0	0	0	0	1	1	0	0	0	0	.222	.125
Mike Cuellar	.154	13	2	2	1	0	0	0	2	2	0	0	0	0	.267	.231

Hank Bauer

Bats: Right, Throws: Right

Batting	Avg	G	AB	R	H	2B	3B	HR	RBI	BB	SO	HBP	GDP	SB	CS	OBP	Slg
Totals	.245	53	188	21	46	2	3	7	24	8	25	1	2	1	3	.279	.399
Home	.245	26	94	13	23	2	2	4	16	4	15	0	0	0	1	.276	.436
Away	.245	27	94	8	23	0	1	3	8	4	10	1	2	1	2	.283	.362
vs. Left	.189	20	53	0	10	1	2	2	9	2	5	1	0	0	1	.232	.396
vs. Right	.267	53	135	21	36	1	1	5	15	6	20	0	2	1	2	.298	.400
Scoring Pos.	.184	30	38	0	7	1	1	0	12	2	4	0	0	0	0	.225	.263
Close & Late	.280	21	25	3	7	0	1	1	3	1	3	0	0	0	0	.308	.480
None on/out	.292	42	65	0	19	1	0	2	2	3	11	0	0	0	0	.324	.400
None on	.257	47	113	0	29	1	0	4	4	6	19	0	0	0	0	.294	.372
Runners on	.227	45	75	0	17	1	3	3	20	2	6	1	2	1	3	.256	.440
Batting #1	.309	23	94	11	29	2	0	6	16	3	18	0	2	1	3	.330	.521
Batting #3	.225	10	40	7	9	0	1	1	2	2	4	1	0	0	0	.279	.350
Batting #5	.250	4	12	1	3	0	0	0	1	0	1	0	0	0	0	.250	.250
Batting #7	.120	10	25	1	3	0	1	0	4	2	2	0	0	0	0	.185	.200

Hit Best Against

	Avg	AB	R	H	2B	3B	HR	RBI	BB	SO	HBP	GDP	SB	CS	OBP	Slg
Don Newcombe	.500	6	1	3	0	0	0	0	0	0	0	0	1	0	.500	.500
Clem Labine	.429	7	1	3	0	0	0	0	1	1	0	0	0	0	.500	.429
Russ Meyer	.400	5	0	2	0	0	0	0	0	1	0	0	0	0	.400	.400

Hit Worst Against

	Avg	AB	R	H	2B	3B	HR	RBI	BB	SO	HBP	GDP	SB	CS	OBP	Slg
Joe Black	.000	7	0	0	0	0	0	1	0	1	0	0	0	0	.000	.000
Jim Konstanty	.000	6	0	0	0	0	0	1	0	0	0	0	0	0	.000	.000
Johnny Podres	.000	6	1	0	0	0	0	0	0	1	1	0	0	0	.143	.000

Don Baylor

Bats: Right, Throws: Right

Batting	Avg	G	AB	R	H	2B	3B	HR	RBI	BB	SO	HBP	GDP	SB	CS	OBP	Slg
Totals	.273	38	121	17	33	5	1	4	21	13	21	5	4	0	1	.362	.430
Home	.309	19	55	9	17	3	1	1	10	7	11	2	2	0	1	.394	.455
Away	.242	19	66	8	16	2	0	3	11	6	10	3	2	0	0	.333	.409
vs. Left	.292	23	48	2	14	2	1	1	7	4	9	2	3	0	1	.364	.438
vs. Right	.260	38	73	15	19	3	0	3	14	9	12	3	1	0	0	.360	.425
Scoring Pos.	.382	26	34	0	13	1	1	2	18	5	8	1	0	0	0	.452	.647
Close & Late	.318	23	22	1	7	2	0	2	9	3	3	1	1	0	1	.423	.682
None on/out	.208	21	24	0	5	1	0	0	0	1	5	3	0	0	0	.321	.250
None on	.190	31	63	0	12	3	0	1	1	6	10	4	0	0	0	.301	.286
Runners on	.362	34	58	0	21	2	1	3	20	7	11	1	4	0	1	.426	.586
Batting #4	.263	5	19	3	5	0	1	1	7	1	2	0	0	0	0	.286	.526
Batting #5	.278	22	79	13	22	5	0	3	12	10	13	5	4	0	1	.394	.456
Batting #6	.333	5	15	1	5	0	0	0	1	2	4	0	0	0	0	.412	.333

Hit Best Against

	Avg	AB	R	H	2B	3B	HR	RBI	BB	SO	HBP	GDP	SB	CS	OBP	Slg
Vida Blue	.400	5	2	2	0	0	0	0	2	0	0	0	0	1	.571	.400
Catfish Hunter	.400	5	0	2	0	0	0	0	0	1	0	0	0	0	.400	.400
Don Sutton	.250	8	0	2	2	0	0	1	1	2	0	0	0	0	.333	.500

Hit Worst Against

	Avg	AB	R	H	2B	3B	HR	RBI	BB	SO	HBP	GDP	SB	CS	OBP	Slg
Ken Holtzman	.000	8	0	0	0	0	0	0	0	3	0	1	0	0	.000	.000
Bruce Hurst	.000	5	0	0	0	0	0	0	1	2	0	0	0	0	.167	.000
Pete Vuckovich	.167	6	0	1	0	0	0	0	1	0	0	1	0	0	.286	.167

Albert Belle

Bats: Right, Throws: Right

Batting	Avg	G	AB	R	H	2B	3B	HR	RBI	BB	SO	HBP	GDP	SB	CS	OBP	Slg
Totals	.230	18	61	10	14	2	0	6	14	17	15	1	0	1	1	.405	.557
Home	.250	9	32	7	8	1	0	4	11	9	8	1	0	1	0	.429	.656
Away	.207	9	29	3	6	1	0	2	3	8	7	0	0	0	1	.378	.448
vs. Left	.211	9	19	2	4	1	0	1	1	6	5	1	0	0	1	.423	.421
vs. Right	.238	15	42	8	10	1	0	5	13	11	10	0	0	1	0	.396	.619
Scoring Pos.	.286	13	14	4	4	1	0	2	9	7	4	0	0	0	0	.524	.786
Close & Late	.273	10	11	3	3	0	0	3	6	3	3	1	0	0	0	.467	1.091
None on/out	.133	13	15	1	2	0	0	1	1	3	4	1	0	0	0	.316	.333
None on	.158	18	38	3	6	1	0	3	3	5	10	1	0	0	0	.273	.421
Runners on	.348	17	23	7	8	1	0	3	11	12	5	0	0	1	1	.571	.783
Batting #4	.230	18	61	10	14	2	0	6	14	17	15	1	0	1	1	.405	.557

Hit Best Against

	Avg	AB	R	H	2B	3B	HR	RBI	BB	SO	HBP	GDP	SB	CS	OBP	Slg
Randy Johnson	.333	6	0	2	1	0	0	0	0	1	0	0	0	0	.333	.500

Hit Worst Against

	Avg	AB	R	H	2B	3B	HR	RBI	BB	SO	HBP	GDP	SB	CS	OBP	Slg
David Wells	.000	5	0	0	0	0	0	0	1	0	0	0	0	0	.167	.000
Greg Maddux	.200	5	2	1	0	0	1	2	1	1	0	0	0	0	.333	.800

Johnny Bench

Bats: Right, Throws: Right

Batting	Avg	G	AB	R	H	2B	3B	HR	RBI	BB	SO	HBP	GDP	SB	CS	OBP	Slg
Totals	.266	45	169	27	45	8	3	10	20	18	29	0	4	6	2	.335	.527
Home	.351	22	77	17	27	4	3	7	12	11	12	0	2	3	1	.427	.753
Away	.196	23	92	10	18	4	0	3	8	7	17	0	2	3	1	.253	.337
vs. Left	.237	21	59	0	14	4	1	1	3	5	10	0	1	3	1	.292	.390
vs. Right	.282	45	110	27	31	4	2	9	17	13	19	0	3	3	1	.358	.600
Scoring Pos.	.214	36	42	0	9	2	0	2	10	9	6	0	1	3	0	.346	.405
Close & Late	.200	19	20	2	4	0	0	2	4	7	2	0	0	2	1	.407	.500
None on/out	.356	32	45	0	16	3	1	3	3	3	6	0	0	0	0	.396	.667
None on	.275	44	102	0	28	6	2	7	7	5	20	0	0	0	0	.308	.578
Runners on	.254	40	67	0	17	2	1	3	13	13	9	0	4	6	2	.370	.448
Batting #3	.120	6	25	3	3	1	0	0	0	2	6	0	0	1	0	.185	.160
Batting #4	.244	25	90	14	22	3	1	4	8	12	15	0	1	4	0	.330	.433
Batting #5	.296	7	27	3	8	2	1	3	5	3	5	0	0	0	1	.367	.778
Batting #6	.333	3	12	3	4	1	0	1	1	1	2	0	1	1	0	.385	.667
Batting #7	.533	4	15	4	8	1	1	2	6	0	1	0	2	0	1	.533	1.133

Hit Best Against

	Avg	AB	R	H	2B	3B	HR	RBI	BB	SO	HBP	GDP	SB	CS	OBP	Slg
Ken Holtzman	.800	5	2	4	1	0	0	0	1	0	0	0	1	0	.833	1.000
Dock Ellis	.556	9	2	5	0	0	0	0	2	0	0	1	2	0	.636	.556
Tom Seaver	.429	7	1	3	1	0	1	1	1	1	0	0	0	0	.500	1.000

Hit Worst Against

	Avg	AB	R	H	2B	3B	HR	RBI	BB	SO	HBP	GDP	SB	CS	OBP	Slg
B. Moon Odom	.000	5	0	0	0	0	0	0	0	2	0	0	0	0	.000	.000
Luis Tiant	.167	12	0	2	1	0	0	2	0	3	0	0	0	0	.167	.250
Steve Blass	.167	6	0	1	0	0	0	0	1	0	0	0	0	0	.286	.167

Chief Bender

Throws: Right, Bats: Right

Pitching	ERA	W	L	Sv	G	GS	IP	BB	SO	Avg	R	H	2B	3B	HR	OBP	Slg
Totals	2.44	6	4	0	10	10	85.0	21	59	.212	28	64	13	5	1	.267	.298
Home	2.83	4	1	0	5	5	41.1	9	25	.203	16	30	5	4	1	.252	.311
Away	2.06	2	3	0	5	5	43.2	12	34	.221	12	34	8	1	0	.281	.286

	Avg	AB	R	H	2B	3B	HR	RBI	BB	SO	HBP	GDP	OBP	Slg
vs. Left	.226	93	0	21	4	2	0	8	8	20	0	2	.287	.312
vs. Right	.206	209	28	43	9	3	1	18	13	39	2	2	.258	.292
Scoring Pos.	.212	66	0	14	1	3	1	23	4	15	0	2	.254	.364
Close & Late	.210	62	3	13	5	2	1	11	4	10	0	2	.258	.403
None on/out	.215	79	0	17	5	1	0	0	6	10	1	2	.279	.304
None on	.217	180	0	39	9	1	0	0	13	32	2	2	.277	.278
Runners on	.205	122	0	25	4	4	1	26	8	27	0	2	.252	.328

Pitched Best Against

	Avg	AB	R	H	2B	3B	HR	RBI	BB	SO	HBP	GDP	SB	CS	OBP	Slg
Harry Steinfeldt	.000	7	0	0	0	0	0	0	0	2	0	0	0	0	.000	.000
Fred Snodgrass	.000	11	1	0	0	0	0	1	1	3	1	0	0	2	.143	.000
Dan McGann	.000	6	0	0	0	0	0	0	1	5	0	0	0	0	.143	.000

Pitched Worst Against

	Avg	AB	R	H	2B	3B	HR	RBI	BB	SO	HBP	GDP	SB	CS	OBP	Slg
Wildfire Schulte	.500	6	2	3	1	0	0	0	2	2	0	0	0	3	.625	.667
R. Bresnahan	.375	8	0	3	2	0	0	0	0	0	0	0	0	0	.375	.625
George Burns	.375	8	2	3	2	0	0	2	0	1	0	0	1	0	.375	.625

Yogi Berra

Bats: Left, Throws: Right

Batting	Avg	G	AB	R	H	2B	3B	HR	RBI	BB	SO	HBP	GDP	SB	CS	OBP	Slg
Totals	.274	75	259	41	71	10	0	12	39	32	17	3	5	0	2	.359	.452
Home	.263	36	118	14	31	7	0	5	15	12	11	1	2	0	2	.336	.449
Away	.284	39	141	27	40	3	0	7	24	20	6	2	3	0	0	.378	.454
vs. Left	.323	30	62	0	20	4	0	1	5	7	1	0	0	0	1	.386	.435
vs. Right	.259	75	197	41	51	6	0	11	34	25	16	3	5	0	1	.351	.457
Scoring Pos.	.232	48	56	0	13	2	0	3	26	11	4	0	3	0	0	.353	.429
Close & Late	.242	33	33	3	8	3	0	0	3	4	0	1	0	0	0	.342	.333
None on/out	.328	49	61	0	20	4	0	3	3	4	4	1	0	0	0	.379	.541
None on	.261	73	138	0	36	6	0	6	6	16	8	2	0	0	0	.346	.435
Runners on	.289	71	121	0	35	4	0	6	33	16	9	1	5	0	2	.374	.471
Batting #3	.177	16	62	8	11	1	0	1	4	4	5	0	0	0	0	.227	.242
Batting #4	.352	30	108	21	38	7	0	7	21	14	5	3	1	0	2	.440	.611
Batting #5	.265	18	68	9	18	2	0	3	12	7	6	0	3	0	0	.333	.426
Batting #6	.143	6	14	1	2	0	0	0	1	5	0	0	1	0	0	.350	.143

Hit Best Against

	Avg	AB	R	H	2B	3B	HR	RBI	BB	SO	HBP	GDP	SB	CS	OBP	Slg
Clem Labine	.643	14	3	0	[illegible]	0	1	6	1	1	0	0	0	0	.667	1.000
Billy Loes	.444	9	2	4	0	0	1	1	0	1	1	0	0	1	.500	.778
Dave Koslo	.429	7	1	3	1	0	0	0	0	0	0	0	0	0	.429	.571

Hit Worst Against

	Avg	AB	R	H	2B	3B	HR	RBI	BB	SO	HBP	GDP	SB	CS	OBP	Slg
Joe Black	.000	9	0	0	0	0	0	0	0	1	0	1	0	0	.000	.000
Hal Gregg	.000	5	0	0	0	0	0	0	0	1	0	0	0	0	.000	.000
Sal Maglie	.111	9	1	1	0	0	0	0	1	0	0	0	0	0	.200	.111

Jack Billingham

Throws: Right, Bats: Right

Pitching	ERA	W	L	Sv	G	GS	IP	BB	SO	Avg	R	H	2B	3B	HR	OBP	Slg
Totals	1.93	2	1	1	10	6	42.0	15	32	.189	11	28	6	0	0	.273	.230
Home	0.57	1	0	0	3	2	15.2	4	11	.100	2	5	1	0	0	.167	.120
Away	2.73	1	1	1	7	4	26.1	11	21	.235	9	23	5	0	0	.324	.286

	Avg	AB	R	H	2B	3B	HR	RBI	BB	SO	HBP	GDP	OBP	Slg
vs. Left	.232	56	0	13	4	0	0	3	10	6	1	2	.358	.304
vs. Right	.160	94	11	15	2	0	0	7	5	26	1	2	.210	.181
Scoring Pos.	.265	34	0	9	1	0	0	9	7	5	0	2	.390	.294
Close & Late	.059	17	0	1	0	0	0	1	0	3	0	2	.059	.059
None on/out	.154	39	0	6	4	0	0	0	2	11	1	2	.214	.256
None on	.121	91	0	11	4	0	0	0	7	21	2	2	.200	.165
Runners on	.288	59	0	17	2	0	0	10	8	11	0	2	.373	.322

Pitched Best Against

	Avg	AB	R	H	2B	3B	HR	RBI	BB	SO	HBP	GDP	SB	CS	OBP	Slg
Bert Campaneris	.000	6	0	0	0	0	0	0	1	1	0	0	0	0	.143	.000
Matty Alou	.000	5	0	0	0	0	0	0	0	0	0	0	0	0	.000	.000
Sal Bando	.000	5	0	0	0	0	0	0	0	2	0	1	0	0	.000	.000

Pitched Worst Against

	Avg	AB	R	H	2B	3B	HR	RBI	BB	SO	HBP	GDP	SB	CS	OBP	Slg
Rico Petrocelli	.400	5	0	2	0	0	0	1	0	2	0	0	0	0	.400	.400
Cleon Jones	.333	6	1	2	1	0	0	1	0	2	0	1	0	0	.333	.500
Wayne Garrett	.286	7	1	2	1	0	0	0	0	0	0	0	0	0	.286	.429

Vida Blue

Throws: Left, Bats: Both

Pitching	ERA	W	L	Sv	G	GS	IP	BB	SO	Avg	R	H	2B	3B	HR	OBP	Slg
Totals	4.31	1	5	2	17	10	64.2	23	47	.228	31	55	13	1	6	.293	.365
Home	5.21	0	0	0	6	3	19.0	12	9	.232	11	16	2	0	3	.341	.391
Away	3.94	1	5	2	11	7	45.2	11	38	.227	20	39	11	1	3	.272	.355

	Avg	AB	R	H	2B	3B	HR	RBI	BB	SO	HBP	GDP	OBP	Slg
vs. Left	.259	58	0	15	3	0	2	6	5	16	0	2	.317	.414
vs. Right	.217	184	31	40	10	1	4	21	18	31	0	2	.284	.348
Scoring Pos.	.326	46	0	15	5	0	1	19	7	5	0	2	.400	.500
Close & Late	.344	32	3	11	4	0	1	10	6	5	0	2	.447	.563
None on/out	.191	68	0	13	5	0	1	1	3	16	0	2	.225	.309
None on	.186	156	0	29	8	0	3	3	15	35	0	2	.257	.295
Runners on	.302	86	0	26	5	1	3	24	8	12	0	2	.354	.488

Pitched Best Against

	Avg	AB	R	H	2B	3B	HR	RBI	BB	SO	HBP	GDP	SB	CS	OBP	Slg
Bill Buckner	.000	6	0	0	0	0	0	0	0	1	0	0	0	0	.000	.000
Felix Millan	.000	6	0	0	0	0	0	0	0	1	0	0	0	0	.000	.000
Davey Lopes	.000	5	1	0	0	0	0	0	2	1	0	0	0	1	.286	.000

Pitched Worst Against

	Avg	AB	R	H	2B	3B	HR	RBI	BB	SO	HBP	GDP	SB	CS	OBP	Slg
Cleon Jones	.800	5	3	4	1	0	1	1	1	0	0	0	0	0	.833	1.600
Bobby Tolan	.500	6	1	3	1	0	0	2	0	1	0	0	1	0	.500	.667
Steve Garvey	.500	6	1	3	0	0	0	1	0	0	0	0	0	0	.500	.500

Bert Blyleven

Throws: Right, Bats: Right

Pitching	ERA	W	L	Sv	G	GS	IP	BB	SO	Avg	R	H	2B	3B	HR	OBP	Slg
Totals	2.47	5	1	0	8	6	47.1	8	36	.239	15	43	5	0	5	.277	.350
Home	1.98	4	0	0	4	3	27.1	3	26	.238	8	24	2	0	3	.260	.347
Away	3.15	1	1	0	4	3	20.0	5	10	.241	7	19	3	0	2	.299	.354

	Avg	AB	R	H	2B	3B	HR	RBI	BB	SO	HBP	GDP	OBP	Slg
vs. Left	.254	71	0	18	2	0	3	6	6	12	2	2	.325	.408
vs. Right	.229	109	15	25	3	0	2	9	2	24	0	2	.243	.312
Scoring Pos.	.135	37	0	5	1	0	0	7	2	10	0	2	.175	.162
Close & Late	.333	9	1	3	0	0	0	1	0	1	0	2	.333	.333
None on/out	.224	49	0	11	1	0	1	1	1	11	0	2	.240	.306
None on	.248	113	0	28	3	0	3	3	5	19	1	2	.286	.354
Runners on	.224	67	0	15	2	0	2	12	3	17	1	2	.264	.343

Pitched Best Against

	Avg	AB	R	H	2B	3B	HR	RBI	BB	SO	HBP	GDP	SB	CS	OBP	Slg
Tom Herr	.000	6	0	0	0	0	0	0	0	0	0	0	0	0	.000	.000
Willie McGee	.000	6	0	0	0	0	0	0	0	4	0	0	0	0	.000	.000
Dan Driessen	.000	9	1	0	0	0	0	0	1	2	0	0	0	0	.100	.000

Pitched Worst Against

	Avg	AB	R	H	2B	3B	HR	RBI	BB	SO	HBP	GDP	SB	CS	OBP	Slg
Curt Ford	.600	5	1	3	0	0	0	2	1	0	0	0	0	0	.667	.600
Jose Oquendo	.500	6	0	3	0	0	0	0	0	1	0	0	0	1	.500	.500
Tony Pena	.500	6	0	3	0	0	0	2	0	1	0	0	0	0	.500	.500

Wade Boggs

Bats: Left, Throws: Right

Batting	Avg	G	AB	R	H	2B	3B	HR	RBI	BB	SO	HBP	GDP	SB	CS	OBP	Slg
Totals	.273	39	154	15	42	9	1	2	16	16	20	0	6	0	0	.337	.383
Home	.244	21	82	9	20	3	1	2	8	7	10	0	3	0	0	.300	.378
Away	.306	18	72	6	22	6	0	0	8	9	10	0	3	0	0	.378	.389
vs. Left	.265	24	34	0	9	1	0	0	5	5	5	0	1	0	0	.350	.294
vs. Right	.275	39	120	15	33	8	1	2	11	11	15	0	5	0	0	.333	.408
Scoring Pos.	.212	31	33	4	7	2	0	0	12	4	6	0	2	0	0	.282	.273
Close & Late	.192	23	26	3	5	1	0	0	3	5	4	0	2	0	0	.313	.231
None on/out	.216	28	37	0	8	2	1	0	0	4	4	0	0	0	0	.293	.324
None on	.258	37	89	1	23	5	1	1	1	11	12	0	0	0	0	.340	.371
Runners on	.292	36	65	6	19	4	0	1	15	5	8	0	6	0	0	.333	.400
Batting #1	.253	20	87	10	22	6	1	1	9	12	11	0	3	0	0	.340	.379
Batting #2	.158	9	38	1	6	2	0	0	1	1	5	0	1	0	0	.179	.211
Batting #3	.500	6	22	3	11	1	0	1	3	2	4	0	1	0	0	.520	.682

Hit Best Against

	Avg	AB	R	H	2B	3B	HR	RBI	BB	SO	HBP	GDP	SB	CS	OBP	Slg
Kirk McCaskill	.600	5	3	3	0	1	0	0	1	0	0	0	0	0	.667	1.000
Bob Welch	.600	5	1	3	0	0	0	2	0	1	0	0	0	0	.500	.600
Dave Stewart	.455	11	1	5	0	0	1	1	1	4	0	0	0	0	.500	.727

Hit Worst Against

	Avg	AB	R	H	2B	3B	HR	RBI	BB	SO	HBP	GDP	SB	CS	OBP	Slg
Andy Benes	.000	6	1	0	0	0	0	0	1	2	0	0	0	0	.143	.000
Ron Darling	.111	9	0	1	0	0	0	1	0	1	0	0	0	0	.111	.111
Greg Maddux	.143	7	0	1	0	0	0	0	0	0	0	1	0	0	.143	.143

Barry Bonds

Bats: Left, Throws: Left

Batting	Avg	G	AB	R	H	2B	3B	HR	RBI	BB	SO	HBP	GDP	SB	CS	OBP	Slg
Totals	.200	23	80	10	16	4	0	1	5	14	16	1	1	7	0	.323	.288
Home	.162	11	37	4	6	2	0	0	2	6	8	1	1	5	0	.295	.216
Away	.233	12	43	6	10	2	0	1	3	8	8	0	0	2	0	.346	.349
vs. Left	.208	22	48	6	10	1	0	1	4	9	9	1	1	4	0	.339	.292
vs. Right	.188	15	32	4	6	3	0	0	1	5	7	0	0	3	0	.297	.281
Scoring Pos.	.095	15	21	6	2	2	0	0	4	4	5	0	0	1	0	.231	.190
Close & Late	.222	16	18	1	4	2	0	0	1	2	1	0	1	2	0	.300	.333
None on/out	.429	19	21	1	9	1	0	1	1	3	4	0	0	0	0	.500	.619
None on	.286	23	42	1	12	2	0	1	1	6	9	1	0	0	0	.388	.405
Runners on	.105	22	38	9	4	2	0	0	4	8	7	0	1	7	0	.255	.158
Batting #3	.250	3	12	0	3	2	0	0	2	0	3	0	0	1	0	.231	.417
Batting #4	.261	7	23	5	6	1	0	1	2	6	4	1	0	1	0	.433	.435
Batting #5	.156	13	45	5	7	1	0	0	1	8	9	0	1	5	0	.283	.178

Hit Best Against

	Avg	AB	R	H	2B	3B	HR	RBI	BB	SO	HBP	GDP	SB	CS	OBP	Slg
Steve Avery	.333	12	2	4	1	0	0	1	0	3	0	1	2	0	.333	.417

Hit Worst Against

	Avg	AB	R	H	2B	3B	HR	RBI	BB	SO	HBP	GDP	SB	CS	OBP	Slg
Tom Glavine	.111	9	1	1	0	0	1	1	1	1	1	0	0	0	.273	.444
John Smoltz	.167	12	1	2	1	0	0	0	4	2	0	0	1	0	.375	.250
Jose Rijo	.200	5	1	1	0	0	0	0	1	2	0	0	0	0	.333	.200

Bobby Bonilla

Bats: Both, Throws: Right

Batting	Avg	G	AB	R	H	2B	3B	HR	RBI	BB	SO	HBP	GDP	SB	CS	OBP	Slg
Totals	.217	38	143	16	31	5	0	5	19	20	25	0	6	0	2	.313	.357
Home	.284	21	74	9	21	3	0	4	13	11	8	0	1	0	1	.376	.486
Away	.145	17	69	7	10	2	0	1	6	9	17	0	5	0	1	.244	.217
vs. Left	.226	25	62	4	14	3	0	1	8	8	6	0	2	0	1	.314	.323
vs. Right	.210	29	81	12	17	2	0	4	11	12	19	0	4	0	1	.312	.383
Scoring Pos.	.250	29	36	13	9	0	0	2	15	8	4	0	3	0	0	.386	.417
Close & Late	.273	20	22	3	6	3	0	1	1	6	4	0	1	0	0	.429	.545
None on/out	.297	29	37	2	11	3	0	2	2	7	9	0	0	0	0	.409	.541
None on	.219	37	73	2	16	5	0	2	2	10	14	0	0	0	0	.313	.370
Runners on	.214	36	70	14	15	0	0	3	17	10	11	0	6	0	2	.313	.343
Batting #4	.243	28	103	10	25	5	0	1	11	15	13	0	6	0	2	.339	.320
Batting #5	.114	9	35	5	4	0	0	3	7	5	10	0	0	0	0	.225	.371

Hit Best Against

	Avg	AB	R	H	2B	3B	HR	RBI	BB	SO	HBP	GDP	SB	CS	OBP	Slg
Greg Maddux	.600	5	2	3	1	0	0	1	1	2	0	0	0	0	.667	.800
Jose Mesa	.400	5	0	2	1	0	0	2	0	2	0	0	0	0	.400	.600
Tom Glavine	.364	11	1	4	1	0	0	4	3	1	0	1	0	0	.500	.455

Hit Worst Against

	Avg	AB	R	H	2B	3B	HR	RBI	BB	SO	HBP	GDP	SB	CS	OBP	Slg
Andy Pettitte	.000	7	0	0	0	0	0	0	0	0	0	0	0	0	.000	.000
Denny Neagle	.000	5	0	0	0	0	0	0	0	1	0	0	0	0	.000	.000
Chad Ogea	.000	5	0	0	0	0	0	0	0	0	0	0	0	0	.000	.000

Bob Boone

Bats: Right, Throws: Right

Batting	Avg	G	AB	R	H	2B	3B	HR	RBI	BB	SO	HBP	GDP	SB	CS	OBP	Slg
Totals	.311	36	106	12	33	2	0	2	13	7	8	1	1	0	1	.353	.387
Home	.392	19	51	7	20	2	0	1	7	4	3	0	1	0	1	.429	.490
Away	.236	17	55	5	13	0	0	1	6	3	5	1	0	0	0	.283	.291
vs. Left	.350	10	20	0	7	0	0	1	1	1	2	0	1	0	0	.381	.500
vs. Right	.302	36	86	12	26	2	0	1	12	6	6	1	0	0	1	.347	.360
Scoring Pos.	.333	21	24	0	8	2	0	0	11	2	4	0	1	0	0	.357	.417
Close & Late	.333	23	21	1	7	0	0	0	1	2	2	0	1	0	0	.375	.333
None on/out	.333	16	21	0	7	0	0	2	2	2	1	0	0	0	0	.391	.619
None on	.293	33	58	0	17	0	0	2	2	3	3	1	0	0	0	.339	.397
Runners on	.333	30	48	0	16	2	0	0	11	4	5	0	1	0	1	.370	.375
Batting #7	.273	7	22	1	6	0	0	0	1	1	1	0	0	0	0	.304	.273
Batting #8	.343	10	35	4	12	0	0	1	4	2	4	0	0	0	0	.378	.429
Batting #9	.318	16	44	7	14	2	0	1	8	4	3	1	0	0	0	.373	.432

Hit Best Against

	Avg	AB	R	H	2B	3B	HR	RBI	BB	SO	HBP	GDP	SB	CS	OBP	Slg
Roger Clemens	.556	9	2	5	0	0	0	1	1	1	1	0	0	0	.636	.556
Bruce Hurst	.500	6	1	3	0	0	1	1	0	1	0	0	0	0	.500	1.000
Nolan Ryan	.500	6	1	3	0	0	0	2	0	0	0	0	0	0	.500	.500

Hit Worst Against

	Avg	AB	R	H	2B	3B	HR	RBI	BB	SO	HBP	GDP	SB	CS	OBP	Slg
Oil Can Boyd	.167	6	1	1	0	0	0	0	0	1	0	0	0	0	.167	.167
Renie Martin	.200	5	0	1	0	0	0	0	0	0	0	0	0	0	.200	.200

Jim Bottomley

Bats: Left, Throws: Left

Batting	Avg	G	AB	R	H	2B	3B	HR	RBI	BB	SO	HBP	GDP	SB	CS	OBP	Slg
Totals	.200	24	90	8	18	5	1	1	10	7	22	0	0	0	1	.258	.311
Home	.133	12	45	2	6	2	1	0	4	3	13	0	0	0	0	.188	.222
Away	.267	12	45	6	12	3	0	1	6	4	9	0	0	0	1	.327	.400
vs. Left	.135	12	37	0	5	1	1	0	5	1	8	0	0	0	0	.158	.216
vs. Right	.245	24	53	8	13	4	0	1	5	6	14	0	0	0	1	.322	.377
Scoring Pos.	.231	18	26	0	6	2	1	0	9	3	4	0	0	0	0	.310	.385
Close & Late	.000	9	7	0	0	0	0	0	0	2	2	0	0	0	0	.222	.000
None on/out	.200	18	20	0	4	1	0	0	0	2	5	0	0	0	0	.273	.250
None on	.220	24	50	0	11	3	0	1	1	4	15	0	0	0	0	.278	.340
Runners on	.175	21	40	0	7	2	1	0	9	3	7	0	0	0	1	.233	.275
Batting #4	.208	20	77	7	16	5	1	1	10	5	19	0	0	0	1	.256	.338
Batting #6	.154	4	13	1	2	0	0	0	0	2	3	0	0	0	0	.267	.154

Hit Best Against

	Avg	AB	R	H	2B	3B	HR	RBI	BB	SO	HBP	GDP	SB	CS	OBP	Slg
Urban Shocker	.400	5	1	2	0	0	0	2	0	0	0	0	0	0	.400	.400
Waite Hoyt	.375	16	2	6	0	0	1	1	3	2	0	0	0	0	.474	.563
Herb Pennock	.375	8	1	3	1	0	0	1	0	2	0	0	0	0	.375	.500

Hit Worst Against

	Avg	AB	R	H	2B	3B	HR	RBI	BB	SO	HBP	GDP	SB	CS	OBP	Slg
G. Earnshaw	.000	18	0	0	0	0	0	0	3	9	0	0	0	0	.143	.000
Lefty Grove	.050	20	1	1	0	0	0	1	1	3	0	0	0	0	.095	.050

Larry Bowa

Bats: Both, Throws: Right

Batting	Avg	G	AB	R	H	2B	3B	HR	RBI	BB	SO	HBP	GDP	SB	CS	OBP	Slg
Totals	.254	32	118	11	30	4	0	0	6	9	5	0	2	4	1	.307	.288
Home	.250	16	56	5	14	2	0	0	4	5	3	0	1	1	1	.311	.286
Away	.258	16	62	6	16	2	0	0	2	4	2	0	1	3	0	.303	.290
vs. Left	.242	14	33	0	8	1	0	0	1	1	2	0	1	1	0	.265	.273
vs. Right	.259	32	85	11	22	3	0	0	5	8	3	0	1	3	1	.323	.294
Scoring Pos.	.333	18	21	0	7	1	0	0	6	8	1	0	0	0	0	.517	.381
Close & Late	.368	18	19	2	7	1	0	0	1	4	0	0	0	3	0	.478	.421
None on/out	.211	24	38	0	8	2	0	0	0	1	2	0	0	0	0	.231	.263
None on	.263	30	80	0	21	3	0	0	0	1	4	0	0	0	0	.272	.300
Runners on	.237	27	38	0	9	1	0	0	6	8	1	0	2	4	1	.370	.263
Batting #2	.229	8	35	4	8	0	0	0	1	2	2	0	1	0	0	.270	.229
Batting #7	.250	10	36	2	9	1	0	0	1	3	3	0	0	1	1	.308	.278
Batting #8	.277	14	47	5	13	3	0	0	4	4	0	0	1	3	0	.333	.340

Hit Best Against

	Avg	AB	R	H	2B	3B	HR	RBI	BB	SO	HBP	GDP	SB	CS	OBP	Slg
Dennis Leonard	.600	5	1	3	0	0	0	1	0	0	0	0	2	0	.600	.600
Renie Martin	.400	5	1	2	0	0	0	0	0	0	0	0	1	0	.400	.400
Nolan Ryan	.333	6	1	2	0	0	0	0	0	2	0	0	0	0	.333	.333

Hit Worst Against

	Avg	AB	R	H	2B	3B	HR	RBI	BB	SO	HBP	GDP	SB	CS	OBP	Slg
Tommy John	.000	11	1	0	0	0	0	0	0	1	0	1	0	0	.000	.000
D. Quisenberry	.000	6	0	0	0	0	0	0	0	0	0	0	0	0	.000	.000
Steve Rogers	.000	6	0	0	0	0	0	0	0	0	0	0	0	0	.000	.000

Harry Brecheen

Throws: Left, Bats: Left

Pitching	ERA	W	L	Sv	G	GS	IP	BB	SO	Avg	R	H	2B	3B	HR	OBP	Slg
Totals	0.83	4	1	0	7	3	32.2	12	18	.241	3	28	3	1	0	.313	.284
Home	0.82	3	1	0	4	2	22.0	7	13	.211	2	16	2	1	0	.277	.263
Away	0.84	1	0	0	3	1	10.2	5	5	.300	1	12	1	0	0	.378	.325

	Avg	AB	R	H	2B	3B	HR	RBI	BB	SO	HBP	GDP	OBP	Slg
vs. Left	.243	37	0	9	1	0	0	1	6	10	0	2	.349	.270
vs. Right	.241	79	3	19	2	1	0	4	6	8	0	2	.294	.291
Scoring Pos.	.130	23	0	3	1	0	0	5	5	4	0	2	.286	.174
Close & Late	.192	26	1	5	2	0	0	4	3	3	0	2	.276	.269
None on/out	.241	29	0	7	1	1	0	0	2	4	0	2	.290	.345
None on	.297	64	0	19	2	1	0	0	5	10	0	2	.348	.359
Runners on	.173	52	0	9	1	0	0	5	7	8	0	2	.271	.192

Pitched Best Against

	Avg	AB	R	H	2B	3B	HR	RBI	BB	SO	HBP	GDP	SB	CS	OBP	Slg
Roy Partee	.000	6	0	0	0	0	0	0	0	1	0	0	0	0	.000	.000
Leon Culberson	.000	5	0	0	0	0	0	0	0	2	0	0	0	0	.000	.000
Johnny Pesky	.125	8	0	1	0	0	0	0	1	2	0	0	0	0	.222	.125

Pitched Worst Against

	Avg	AB	R	H	2B	3B	HR	RBI	BB	SO	HBP	GDP	SB	CS	OBP	Slg
Bobby Doerr	.375	8	0	3	0	0	0	1	0	0	0	0	0	0	.375	.375
Dom DiMaggio	.333	9	0	3	1	0	0	2	0	1	0	2	0	0	.333	.444
Rudy York	.286	7	1	2	0	1	0	0	2	0	0	2	0	0	.444	.571

George Brett

Bats: Left, Throws: Right

Batting	Avg	G	AB	R	H	2B	3B	HR	RBI	BB	SO	HBP	GDP	SB	CS	OBP	Slg
Totals	.337	43	166	30	56	8	5	10	23	17	20	0	4	2	3	.397	.627
Home	.341	23	91	17	31	5	4	4	12	6	9	0	2	2	2	.378	.615
Away	.333	20	75	13	25	3	1	6	11	11	11	0	2	0	1	.419	.640
vs. Left	.296	29	54	0	16	1	2	1	5	8	10	0	1	1	0	.387	.444
vs. Right	.357	43	112	30	40	7	3	9	18	9	10	0	3	1	3	.402	.714
Scoring Pos.	.200	28	30	0	6	0	1	2	11	7	3	0	1	1	0	.342	.467
Close & Late	.400	18	20	2	8	1	0	2	6	2	6	0	0	0	1	.455	.750
None on/out	.455	27	33	0	15	3	2	2	2	4	1	0	0	0	0	.514	.848
None on	.379	43	103	0	39	7	2	7	7	8	13	0	0	0	0	.423	.689
Runners on	.270	40	63	0	17	1	3	3	16	9	7	0	4	2	3	.356	.524
Batting #1	.429	3	14	6	6	0	1	3	3	0	1	0	0	0	0	.429	1.214
Batting #3	.319	38	144	23	46	7	4	7	20	17	19	0	4	2	2	.389	.569

Hit Best Against

	Avg	AB	R	H	2B	3B	HR	RBI	BB	SO	HBP	GDP	SB	CS	OBP	Slg
Doyle Alexander	.800	5	5	4	1	0	3	4	1	0	0	0	0	0	.833	2.800
Catfish Hunter	.667	9	3	6	0	0	3	3	0	0	0	0	0	1	.667	1.667
Steve Carlton	.600	5	0	3	0	0	0	0	1	0	0	1	0	0	.667	.600

Hit Worst Against

	Avg	AB	R	H	2B	3B	HR	RBI	BB	SO	HBP	GDP	SB	CS	OBP	Slg
Dick Tidrow	.000	8	0	0	0	0	0	0	0	0	0	0	0	0	.000	.000
Danny Cox	.167	6	1	1	1	0	0	1	0	1	0	1	0	0	.167	.333

Lou Brock

Bats: Left, Throws: Left

Batting	Avg	G	AB	R	H	2B	3B	HR	RBI	BB	SO	HBP	GDP	SB	CS	OBP	Slg
Totals	.391	21	87	16	34	7	2	4	13	5	10	0	0	14	3	.424	.655
Home	.349	11	43	7	15	3	1	2	5	2	6	0	0	4	1	.378	.605
Away	.432	10	44	9	19	4	1	2	8	3	4	0	0	10	2	.468	.705
vs. Left	.409	8	22	0	9	3	0	1	4	2	3	0	0	2	2	.458	.682
vs. Right	.385	21	65	16	25	4	2	3	9	3	7	0	0	12	1	.412	.646
Scoring Pos.	.357	12	14	0	5	2	0	0	8	0	0	0	0	2	1	.357	.500
Close & Late	.375	8	8	1	3	1	0	1	3	1	1	0	0	2	0	.444	.875
None on/out	.371	20	35	0	13	2	2	2	2	2	5	0	0	0	0	.405	.714
None on	.377	20	61	0	23	4	2	3	3	4	8	0	0	0	0	.415	.656
Runners on	.423	19	26	0	11	3	0	1	10	1	2	0	0	14	3	.444	.654
Batting #1	.439	14	57	14	25	5	2	3	8	5	7	0	0	14	3	.484	.754
Batting #2	.300	7	30	2	9	2	0	1	5	0	3	0	0	0	0	.300	.467

Hit Best Against

	Avg	AB	R	H	2B	3B	HR	RBI	BB	SO	HBP	GDP	SB	CS	OBP	Slg
Jose Santiago	1.000	5	3	5	0	0	0	0	0	0	0	0	2	0	1.000	1.000
Mickey Lolich	.455	11	2	5	2	0	0	0	2	2	0	0	2	2	.538	.636
Jim Bouton	.375	8	0	3	1	0	0	0	0	0	0	0	0	0	.375	.500

Hit Worst Against

	Avg	AB	R	H	2B	3B	HR	RBI	BB	SO	HBP	GDP	SB	CS	OBP	Slg
Jim Lonborg	.167	12	1	2	1	0	0	0	0	1	0	0	2	0	.167	.250
Al Downing	.200	5	1	1	0	0	1	1	0	0	0	0	0	0	.200	.800
Denny McLain	.222	9	1	2	0	0	1	1	0	1	0	0	1	0	.222	.556

Three Finger Brown

Throws: Right, Bats: Both

Pitching	ERA	W	L	Sv	G	GS	IP	BB	SO	Avg	R	H	2B	3B	HR	OBP	Slg
Totals	2.81	5	4	0	9	7	57.2	13	35	.231	26	50	13	1	0	.278	.301
Home	2.25	1	2	0	3	2	20.0	4	15	.189	9	14	5	1	0	.231	.284
Away	3.11	4	2	0	6	5	37.2	9	20	.254	17	36	8	0	0	.303	.310

	Avg	AB	R	H	2B	3B	HR	RBI	BB	SO	HBP	GDP	OBP	Slg
vs. Left	.254	114	0	29	8	0	0	12	7	20	0	2	.298	.325
vs. Right	.204	103	26	21	5	1	0	7	6	15	1	2	.255	.272
Scoring Pos.	.317	63	0	20	8	0	0	19	1	9	0	2	.328	.444
Close & Late	.214	42	3	9	4	0	0	3	1	5	0	2	.233	.310
None on/out	.167	54	0	9	1	1	0	0	3	9	0	2	.211	.222
None on	.183	120	0	22	4	1	0	0	10	21	1	2	.252	.233
Runners on	.289	97	0	28	9	0	0	19	3	14	0	2	.310	.381

Pitched Best Against

	Avg	AB	R	H	2B	3B	HR	RBI	BB	SO	HBP	GDP	SB	CS	OBP	Slg
G. Schaefer	.000	7	0	0	0	0	0	0	0	2	0	0	0	0	.000	.000
Billy Sullivan	.000	7	0	0	0	0	0	0	0	2	0	0	0	0	.000	.000
Boss Schmidt	.000	5	0	0	0	0	0	0	0	0	0	0	0	0	.000	.000

Pitched Worst Against

	Avg	AB	R	H	2B	3B	HR	RBI	BB	SO	HBP	GDP	SB	CS	OBP	Slg
Eddie Collins	.556	9	2	5	3	0	0	3	1	0	0	0	4	0	.600	.889
George Davis	.400	5	2	2	1	0	0	3	0	1	0	0	0	1	.400	.600
Harry Davis	.375	8	2	3	2	0	0	2	1	1	0	0	0	0	.444	.625

Jay Buhner

Bats: Right, Throws: Right

Batting	Avg	G	AB	R	H	2B	3B	HR	RBI	BB	SO	HBP	GDP	SB	CS	OBP	Slg
Totals	.350	15	60	9	21	3	0	6	10	7	18	0	1	0	1	.418	.700
Home	.355	8	31	6	11	1	0	3	5	3	10	0	1	0	0	.412	.677
Away	.345	7	29	3	10	2	0	3	5	4	8	0	0	0	1	.424	.724
vs. Left	.143	5	7	1	1	0	0	1	1	1	2	0	0	0	1	.250	.571
vs. Right	.377	15	53	8	20	3	0	5	9	6	16	0	1	0	0	.441	.717
Scoring Pos.	.235	10	17	3	4	0	0	1	5	0	8	0	0	0	0	.235	.412
Close & Late	.471	9	17	2	8	2	0	1	3	1	4	0	0	0	0	.500	.765
None on/out	.417	9	12	1	5	0	0	1	1	0	3	0	0	0	0	.417	.667
None on	.433	14	30	5	13	2	0	5	5	5	7	0	0	0	0	.514	1.000
Runners on	.267	14	30	4	8	1	0	1	5	2	11	0	1	0	1	.313	.400
Batting #6	.360	13	50	9	18	2	0	6	10	6	14	0	1	0	0	.429	.760

Hit Best Against

	Avg	AB	R	H	2B	3B	HR	RBI	BB	SO	HBP	GDP	SB	CS	OBP	Slg
David Cone	.375	8	0	3	0	0	0	1	0	2	0	0	0	0	.375	.375

Hit Worst Against

	Avg	AB	R	H	2B	3B	HR	RBI	BB	SO	HBP	GDP	SB	CS	OBP	Slg
Orel Hershiser	.000	6	0	0	0	0	0	0	0	3	0	0	0	0	.000	.000
Dennis Martinez	.200	5	2	1	1	0	0	0	1	2	0	0	0	0	.333	.400

Lew Burdette

Throws: Right, Bats: Right

Pitching	ERA	W	L	Sv	G	GS	IP	BB	SO	Avg	R	H	2B	3B	HR	OBP	Slg
Totals	2.92	4	2	0	6	6	49.1	8	25	.232	19	43	5	0	6	.263	.357
Home	2.77	2	1	0	3	3	26.0	3	13	.226	11	21	2	0	4	.247	.376
Away	3.09	2	1	0	3	3	23.1	5	12	.239	8	22	3	0	2	.278	.337

	Avg	AB	R	H	2B	3B	HR	RBI	BB	SO	HBP	GDP	OBP	Slg
vs. Left	.196	97	0	19	3	0	2	5	6	15	0	1	.240	.289
vs. Right	.270	89	19	24	2	0	4	11	2	10	0	1	.286	.427
Scoring Pos.	.182	33	0	6	1	0	1	10	4	1	0	1	.263	.303
Close & Late	.321	28	2	9	1	0	2	6	0	3	0	1	.321	.571
None on/out	.327	52	0	17	1	0	4	4	3	7	0	1	.364	.577
None on	.239	117	0	28	3	0	4	4	4	19	0	1	.264	.368
Runners on	.217	69	0	15	2	0	2	12	4	6	0	1	.257	.333

Pitched Best Against

	Avg	AB	R	H	2B	3B	HR	RBI	BB	SO	HBP	GDP	SB	CS	OBP	Slg
Harry Simpson	.000	7	0	0	0	0	0	0	0	2	0	1	0	0	.000	.000
Yogi Berra	.143	21	3	3	2	0	0	1	2	0	0	2	0	0	.217	.238
Jerry Lumpe	.167	12	0	2	0	0	0	0	0	2	0	0	0	0	.167	.167

Pitched Worst Against

	Avg	AB	R	H	2B	3B	HR	RBI	BB	SO	HBP	GDP	SB	CS	OBP	Slg
Jerry Coleman	.444	9	0	4	0	0	0	1	1	0	0	0	0	0	.500	.444
Elston Howard	.333	9	3	3	0	0	0	2	1	3	0	0	1	0	.400	.333
Mickey Mantle	.294	17	3	5	0	0	2	3	2	2	0	0	0	1	.368	.647

Joe Bush

Throws: Right, Bats: Right

Pitching	ERA	W	L	Sv	G	GS	IP	BB	SO	Avg	R	H	2B	3B	HR	OBP	Slg
Totals	2.67	2	5	1	9	6	60.2	20	18	.231	20	49	7	3	2	.299	.321
Home	1.02	1	1	1	4	1	17.2	4	5	.125	2	7	1	1	1	.183	.232
Away	3.35	1	4	0	5	5	43.0	16	13	.269	18	42	6	2	1	.339	.353

	Avg	AB	R	H	2B	3B	HR	RBI	BB	SO	HBP	GDP	OBP	Slg
vs. Left	.212	99	0	21	2	1	1	6	11	7	0	5	.288	.283
vs. Right	.246	114	20	28	5	2	1	13	9	11	1	5	.306	.351
Scoring Pos.	.310	42	0	13	2	0	0	17	5	2	0	5	.375	.357
Close & Late	.286	49	5	14	2	0	1	8	3	3	0	5	.321	.388
None on/out	.175	57	0	10	2	1	1	1	5	5	0	5	.242	.298
None on	.201	134	0	27	3	3	2	2	13	14	0	5	.272	.313
Runners on	.278	79	0	22	4	0	0	17	7	4	1	5	.341	.329

Pitched Best Against

	Avg	AB	R	H	2B	3B	HR	RBI	BB	SO	HBP	GDP	SB	CS	OBP	Slg
Possum Whitted	.000	5	0	0	0	0	0	0	0	1	0	0	0	0	.000	.000
Ross Youngs	.000	11	2	0	0	0	0	0	4	1	0	0	0	1	.267	.000
Dave Bancroft	.143	14	1	2	0	0	0	0	0	1	0	1	0	0	.143	.143

Pitched Worst Against

	Avg	AB	R	H	2B	3B	HR	RBI	BB	SO	HBP	GDP	SB	CS	OBP	Slg
Johnny Evers	.600	5	0	3	0	0	0	0	0	0	0	0	1	0	[illegible]	.600
Hank Gowdy	.429	7	1	3	2	0	1	2	1	0	0	0	0	0	.500	1.143
Heine Groh	.385	13	1	5	0	1	0	0	1	1	0	0	0	1	.429	.538

Roy Campanella

Bats: Right, Throws: Right

Batting	Avg	G	AB	R	H	2B	3B	HR	RBI	BB	SO	HBP	GDP	SB	CS	OBP	Slg
Totals	.237	32	114	14	27	5	0	4	12	12	20	1	1	0	2	.310	.386
Home	.302	17	63	12	19	4	0	4	9	5	10	0	1	0	1	.348	.556
Away	.157	15	51	2	8	1	0	0	3	7	10	1	0	0	1	.267	.176
vs. Left	.195	16	41	0	8	1	0	1	4	4	4	0	0	0	1	.261	.293
vs. Right	.260	32	73	14	19	4	0	3	8	8	16	1	1	0	1	.337	.438
Scoring Pos.	.192	24	26	0	5	0	0	0	7	4	5	0	1	0	0	.281	.192
Close & Late	.211	16	19	1	4	0	0	1	2	0	5	0	0	0	0	.211	.368
None on/out	.353	24	34	0	12	3	0	1	1	2	2	1	0	0	0	.405	.529
None on	.246	32	69	0	17	5	0	3	3	6	10	1	0	0	0	.316	.449
Runners on	.222	29	45	0	10	0	0	1	9	6	10	0	1	0	2	.302	.289
Batting #4	.250	9	36	4	9	3	0	2	5	3	5	0	0	0	0	.308	.500
Batting #5	.281	9	32	6	9	0	0	1	2	3	4	1	1	0	1	.361	.375
Batting #7	.273	3	11	1	3	1	0	0	2	0	2	0	0	0	0	.250	.364
Batting #8	.192	9	26	3	5	1	0	1	3	6	6	0	0	0	0	.333	.346

Hit Best Against

	Avg	AB	R	H	2B	3B	HR	RBI	BB	SO	HBP	GDP	SB	CS	OBP	Slg
Tom Sturdivant	.600	5	0	3	1	0	0	1	2	1	0	0	0	0	.714	.800
Vic Raschi	.333	15	2	5	1	0	1	2	2	1	0	0	0	0	.412	.600
Johnny Kucks	.333	6	1	2	2	0	0	0	0	0	0	0	0	0	.333	.667

Hit Worst Against

	Avg	AB	R	H	2B	3B	HR	RBI	BB	SO	HBP	GDP	SB	CS	OBP	Slg
Bob Turley	.125	8	1	1	0	0	1	2	0	5	0	0	0	0	.125	.500
Whitey Ford	.143	14	1	2	0	0	0	2	2	3	0	0	0	1	.235	.143
Allie Reynolds	.143	14	0	2	0	0	0	0	2	5	1	1	0	1	.294	.143

Bert Campaneris

Bats: Right, Throws: Right

Batting	Avg	G	AB	R	H	2B	3B	HR	RBI	BB	SO	HBP	GDP	SB	CS	OBP	Slg
Totals	.243	37	144	15	35	4	1	3	11	6	20	4	1	10	4	.290	.347
Home	.234	19	77	9	18	2	1	2	7	3	13	3	1	6	2	.286	.364
Away	.254	18	67	6	17	2	0	1	4	3	7	1	0	4	2	.296	.328
vs. Left	.274	22	73	0	20	1	1	3	8	2	9	2	1	6	2	.308	.438
vs. Right	.211	37	71	15	15	3	0	0	3	4	11	2	0	4	2	.273	.254
Scoring Pos.	.296	24	27	0	8	0	0	1	9	1	7	0	1	4	0	.310	.407
Close & Late	.320	22	25	3	8	0	0	1	3	0	5	0	0	4	0	.308	.440
None on/out	.209	35	67	0	14	1	0	2	2	2	8	2	0	0	0	.254	.313
None on	.252	36	103	0	26	4	1	2	2	5	13	4	0	0	0	.313	.369
Runners on	.220	33	41	0	9	0	0	1	9	1	7	0	1	10	4	.233	.293
Batting #1	.233	32	129	14	30	3	1	3	7	5	20	4	1	9	3	.283	.341
Batting #2	.455	3	11	0	5	1	0	0	4	1	0	0	0	1	1	.462	.545

Hit Best Against

	Avg	AB	R	H	2B	3B	HR	RBI	BB	SO	HBP	GDP	SB	CS	OBP	Slg
Gary Nolan	.400	5	0	2	0	0	0	0	0	0	0	0	0	1	.400	.400
Mike Cuellar	.313	16	1	5	0	0	1	3	0	1	0	0	1	2	.313	.500
Don Sutton	.286	7	0	2	1	0	0	0	0	2	0	0	0	0	.286	.429

Hit Worst Against

	Avg	AB	R	H	2B	3B	HR	RBI	BB	SO	HBP	GDP	SB	CS	OBP	Slg
Jack Billingham	.000	6	0	0	0	0	0	0	1	1	0	0	0	0	.143	.000
Jon Matlack	.125	8	2	1	0	0	1	2	0	1	1	0	1	0	.222	.500
Jim Palmer	.143	14	0	2	1	0	0	0	2	1	0	0	1	0	.250	.214

Jose Canseco

Bats: Right, Throws: Right

Batting	Avg	G	AB	R	H	2B	3B	HR	RBI	BB	SO	HBP	GDP	SB	CS	OBP	Slg
Totals	.186	29	102	15	19	1	0	7	18	19	27	1	2	5	3	.317	.402
Home	.070	14	43	4	3	1	0	1	2	11	15	0	0	2	2	.259	.163
Away	.271	15	59	11	16	0	0	6	16	8	12	1	2	3	1	.362	.576
vs. Left	.318	14	22	2	7	0	0	4	5	3	3	0	1	0	1	.400	.864
vs. Right	.150	28	80	13	12	1	0	3	13	16	24	1	1	5	2	.296	.275
Scoring Pos.	.167	26	36	8	6	0	0	2	12	8	10	0	0	2	1	.311	.333
Close & Late	.167	15	18	2	3	0	0	1	3	3	6	0	2	2	0	.273	.333
None on/out	.267	13	15	0	4	0	0	1	1	2	2	0	0	0	0	.353	.467
None on	.176	27	51	1	9	1	0	4	4	6	13	0	0	0	0	.263	.431
Runners on	.196	27	51	9	10	0	0	3	14	13	14	1	2	5	3	.364	.373
Batting #3	.218	24	87	15	19	1	0	7	18	16	24	1	2	5	2	.343	.471
Batting #4	.000	4	14	0	0	0	0	0	0	2	2	0	0	0	0	.125	.000

Hit Best Against

	Avg	AB	R	H	2B	3B	HR	RBI	BB	SO	HBP	GDP	SB	CS	OBP	Slg
Bruce Hurst	.333	6	2	2	0	0	2	2	0	1	0	1	0	0	.333	1.333

Hit Worst Against

	Avg	AB	R	H	2B	3B	HR	RBI	BB	SO	HBP	GDP	SB	CS	OBP	Slg
Orel Hershiser	.000	11	0	0	0	0	0	0	0	3	0	0	0	0	.000	.000
Scott Garrelts	.200	5	1	1	0	0	0	0	0	2	0	0	0	0	.200	.200
Roger Clemens	.200	5	1	1	0	0	1	2	2	0	0	0	0	0	.429	.800

Rod Carew

Bats: Left, Throws: Right

Batting	Avg	G	AB	R	H	2B	3B	HR	RBI	BB	SO	HBP	GDP	SB	CS	OBP	Slg
Totals	.220	14	50	6	11	4	0	0	1	5	9	0	0	2	2	.291	.300
Home	.136	6	22	1	3	1	0	0	0	0	4	0	0	1	0	.136	.182
Away	.286	8	28	5	8	3	0	0	1	5	5	0	0	1	2	.394	.393
vs. Left	.167	5	18	0	3	1	0	0	0	1	5	0	0	0	0	.211	.222
vs. Right	.250	14	32	6	8	3	0	0	1	4	4	0	0	2	2	.333	.344
Scoring Pos.	.000	4	5	0	0	0	0	0	1	1	1	0	0	0	0	.167	.000
Close & Late	.200	8	10	0	2	1	0	0	1	2	1	0	0	0	1	.333	.300
None on/out	.143	10	14	0	2	1	0	0	0	0	3	0	0	0	0	.143	.214
None on	.270	14	37	0	10	3	0	0	0	4	7	0	0	0	0	.341	.351
Runners on	.077	12	13	0	1	1	0	0	1	1	2	0	0	2	2	.143	.154
Batting #2	.148	7	27	2	4	1	0	0	0	5	5	0	0	1	1	.281	.185

Hit Best Against

	Avg	AB	R	H	2B	3B	HR	RBI	BB	SO	HBP	GDP	SB	CS	OBP	Slg
Jim Palmer	.300	10	1	3	1	0	0	0	0	1	0	0	0	1	.300	.400

Hit Worst Against

	Avg	AB	R	H	2B	3B	HR	RBI	BB	SO	HBP	GDP	SB	CS	OBP	Slg
Pete Vuckovich	.000	6	0	0	0	0	0	0	2	1	0	0	0	0	.250	.000

Steve Carlton

Throws: Left, Bats: Left

Pitching	ERA	W	L	Sv	G	GS	IP	BB	SO	Avg	R	H	2B	3B	HR	OBP	Slg
Totals	3.26	6	6	0	16	14	99.1	51	84	.262	40	[illegible]	[illegible]	4	7	[illegible]	[illegible]
Home	3.06	4	5	0	11	9	64.2	34	58	.257	26	61	10	2	5	.350	.380
Away	3.63	2	1	0	5	5	34.2	17	26	.269	14	35	9	2	2	.351	.415

	Avg	AB	R	H	2B	3B	HR	RBI	BB	SO	HBP	GDP	OBP	Slg
vs. Left	.232	56	0	13	1	1	0	4	12	21	0	2	.368	.286
vs. Right	.266	312	40	83	18	3	7	30	39	61	1	2	.346	.410
Scoring Pos.	.167	96	0	16	5	0	1	25	22	28	1	2	.320	.250
Close & Late	.412	17	3	7	1	0	1	8	4	0	0	2	.500	.647
None on/out	.323	93	0	30	5	2	1	1	12	21	0	2	.400	.452
None on	.302	212	0	64	12	4	5	5	21	45	0	2	.365	.467
Runners on	.205	156	0	32	7	0	2	29	30	37	1	2	.332	.288

Pitched Best Against

	Avg	AB	R	H	2B	3B	HR	RBI	BB	SO	HBP	GDP	SB	CS	OBP	Slg
Ken Landreaux	.000	6	0	0	0	0	0	0	0	3	0	0	0	0	.000	.000
Glenn Burke	.000	5	0	0	0	0	0	0	0	1	0	0	0	0	.000	.000
Jerry Manuel	.000	5	0	0	0	0	0	0	1	2	0	0	0	0	.167	.000

Pitched Worst Against

	Avg	AB	R	H	2B	3B	HR	RBI	BB	SO	HBP	GDP	SB	CS	OBP	Slg
George Brett	.600	5	0	3	0	0	0	0	1	0	0	1	0	0	.667	.600
Steve Sax	.571	7	0	4	0	0	0	0	0	0	0	0	0	2	.571	.571
Steve Garvey	.500	10	2	5	1	0	1	2	0	0	0	0	0	0	.500	.900

Clay Carroll

Throws: Right, Bats: Right

Pitching	ERA	W	L	Sv	G	GS	IP	BB	SO	Avg	R	H	2B	3B	HR	OBP	Slg
Totals	1.39	4	2	2	22	0	32.1	13	22	.214	5	24	3	0	1	.296	.268
Home	1.13	1	1	0	9	0	16.0	10	11	.163	2	8	2	0	1	.305	.265
Away	1.65	3	1	2	13	0	16.1	3	11	.254	3	16	1	0	0	.288	.270

	Avg	AB	R	H	2B	3B	HR	RBI	BB	SO	HBP	GDP	OBP	Slg
vs. Left	.270	37	0	10	1	0	1	3	7	5	0	1	.386	.378
vs. Right	.187	75	5	14	2	0	0	9	6	17	0	1	.247	.213
Scoring Pos.	.258	31	0	8	0	0	0	11	5	7	0	1	.361	.258
Close & Late	.196	56	2	11	2	0	0	5	11	9	0	1	.328	.232
None on/out	.125	24	0	3	1	0	0	0	4	4	0	1	.250	.167
None on	.161	62	0	10	2	0	1	1	8	13	0	1	.257	.242
Runners on	.280	50	0	14	1	0	0	11	5	9	0	1	.345	.300

Pitched Worst Against

	Avg	AB	R	H	2B	3B	HR	RBI	BB	SO	HBP	GDP	SB	CS	OBP	Slg
Dave Johnson	.400	5	0	2	1	0	0	1	0	1	0	0	0	0	.400	.600

Gary Carter

Bats: Right, Throws: Right

Batting	Avg	G	AB	R	H	2B	3B	HR	RBI	BB	SO	HBP	GDP	SB	CS	OBP	Slg
Totals	.280	30	118	11	33	8	1	4	21	8	15	0	2	0	0	.320	.466
Home	.228	15	57	5	13	1	1	1	9	4	5	0	0	0	0	.274	.333
Away	.328	15	61	6	20	7	0	3	12	4	10	0	2	0	0	.364	.590
vs. Left	.237	14	38	0	9	1	1	0	3	4	3	0	0	0	0	.310	.316
vs. Right	.300	30	80	11	24	7	0	4	18	4	12	0	2	0	0	.326	.538
Scoring Pos.	.297	27	37	0	11	4	1	2	18	4	6	0	2	0	0	.349	.622
Close & Late	.412	15	17	0	7	2	0	0	6	2	2	0	0	0	0	.429	.529
None on/out	.286	23	35	0	10	3	0	0	0	1	2	0	0	0	0	.306	.371
None on	.250	28	64	0	16	3	0	2	2	3	6	0	0	0	0	.284	.391
Runners on	.315	29	54	0	17	5	1	2	19	5	9	0	2	0	0	.361	.556
Batting #4	.297	23	91	11	27	7	0	4	17	7	12	0	2	0	0	.340	.505
Batting #7	.158	5	19	0	3	1	0	0	3	1	2	0	0	0	0	.200	.211

Hit Best Against

	Avg	AB	R	H	2B	3B	HR	RBI	BB	SO	HBP	GDP	SB	CS	OBP	Slg
Burt Hooton	.400	5	1	2	0	0	0	0	2	0	0	0	0	0	.571	.400
Steve Carlton	.333	6	0	2	1	0	0	1	1	0	0	0	0	0	.429	.500
F. Valenzuela	.333	6	0	2	0	0	0	0	1	2	0	0	0	0	.429	.333

Hit Worst Against

	Avg	AB	R	H	2B	3B	HR	RBI	BB	SO	HBP	GDP	SB	CS	OBP	Slg
Mike Scott	.000	8	0	0	0	0	0	0	0	4	0	0	0	0	.000	.000
Bob Knepper	.000	6	1	0	0	0	0	0	0	0	0	0	0	0	.000	.000
Roger Clemens	.000	5	0	0	0	0	0	0	0	1	0	0	0	0	.000	.000

Joe Carter

Bats: Right, Throws: Right

Batting	Avg	G	AB	R	H	2B	3B	HR	RBI	BB	SO	HBP	GDP	SB	CS	OBP	Slg
Totals	.252	29	119	15	30	5	0	6	20	7	20	0	1	2	1	.282	.445
Home	.207	15	58	6	12	1	0	5	14	5	13	0	1	1	0	.262	.483
Away	.295	14	61	9	18	4	0	1	6	2	7	0	0	1	1	.303	.410
vs. Left	.258	15	31	4	8	1	0	4	10	2	2	0	0	0	0	.278	.677
vs. Right	.250	28	88	11	22	4	0	2	10	5	18	0	1	2	1	.284	.364
Scoring Pos.	.297	23	37	10	11	1	0	2	15	2	12	0	0	1	0	.295	.486
Close & Late	.300	16	20	2	6	2	0	1	3	2	1	0	0	1	0	.364	.550
None on/out	.182	18	22	1	4	1	0	1	1	2	2	0	0	0	0	.250	.364

Batting	Avg	G	AB	R	H	2B	3B	HR	RBI	BB	SO	HBP	GDP	SB	CS	OBP	Slg
None on	.207	27	58	3	12	3	0	3	3	5	7	0	0	0	0	.270	.414
Runners on	.295	28	61	12	18	2	0	3	17	2	13	0	1	2	1	.294	.475
Batting #3	.239	17	67	7	16	4	0	4	10	6	11	0	1	2	1	.293	.478
Batting #4	.269	12	52	8	14	1	0	2	10	1	9	0	0	0	0	.268	.404

Hit Best Against

	Avg	AB	R	H	2B	3B	HR	RBI	BB	SO	HBP	GDP	SB	CS	OBP	Slg
Kevin Tapani	.333	6	0	2	1	0	0	2	0	0	0	0	0	1	.333	.500
Jack Morris	.286	7	2	2	1	0	0	0	0	2	0	0	0	0	.286	.429

Hit Worst Against

	Avg	AB	R	H	2B	3B	HR	RBI	BB	SO	HBP	GDP	SB	CS	OBP	Slg
Alex Fernandez	.125	8	0	1	0	0	0	0	0	2	0	0	0	0	.125	.125
Dave Stewart	.143	7	0	1	0	0	0	0	1	1	0	0	0	0	.250	.143
Tom Glavine	.143	7	1	1	0	0	1	1	1	0	0	0	0	0	.250	.571

Orlando Cepeda

Bats: Right, Throws: Right

Batting	Avg	G	AB	R	H	2B	3B	HR	RBI	BB	SO	HBP	GDP	SB	CS	OBP	Slg
Totals	.207	22	87	6	18	5	0	3	12	3	13	1	2	1	2	.242	.368
Home	.261	12	46	3	12	4	0	0	5	1	7	1	1	1	1	.292	.348
Away	.146	10	41	3	6	1	0	3	7	2	6	0	1	0	1	.186	.390
vs. Left	.286	8	28	0	8	2	0	1	6	1	5	0	1	0	1	.310	.464
vs. Right	.169	22	59	6	10	3	0	2	6	2	8	1	1	1	1	.210	.322
Scoring Pos.	.222	17	27	0	6	1	0	2	9	2	1	0	2	0	0	.276	.481
Close & Late	.231	11	13	0	3	0	0	1	3	0	3	0	0	0	0	.231	.462
None on/out	.263	13	19	0	5	1	0	0	0	0	4	0	0	0	0	.263	.316
None on	.211	22	38	0	8	2	0	0	0	1	9	1	0	0	0	.250	.263
Runners on	.204	22	49	0	10	3	0	3	12	2	4	0	2	1	2	.235	.449
Batting #4	.175	14	57	3	10	2	0	2	7	2	7	0	1	0	1	.203	.316
Batting #5	.267	8	30	3	8	3	0	1	5	1	6	1	1	1	1	.313	.467

Hit Best Against

	Avg	AB	R	H	2B	3B	HR	RBI	BB	SO	HBP	GDP	SB	CS	OBP	Slg
Whitey Ford	.300	10	1	3	1	0	0	2	0	1	0	1	0	1	.300	.400
Mickey Lolich	.273	11	1	3	0	0	1	3	1	2	0	0	0	0	.333	.545

Hit Worst Against

	Avg	AB	R	H	2B	3B	HR	RBI	BB	SO	HBP	GDP	SB	CS	OBP	Slg
Jim Lonborg	.000	10	0	0	0	0	0	0	0	1	0	0	0	0	.000	.000
Jose Santiago	.000	6	0	0	0	0	0	0	0	2	0	1	0	0	.000	.000
Denny McLain	.222	9	0	2	0	0	0	0	0	1	0	0	0	0	.222	.222

Ron Cey

Bats: Right, Throws: Right

Batting	Avg	G	AB	R	H	2B	3B	HR	RBI	BB	SO	HBP	GDP	SB	CS	OBP	Slg
Totals	.261	45	161	22	42	8	0	7	27	25	29	1	2	1	0	.362	.441
Home	.301	21	73	15	22	5	0	5	18	13	11	1	1	1	0	.414	.575
Away	.227	24	88	7	20	3	0	2	9	12	18	0	1	0	0	.317	.330
vs. Left	.309	26	68	0	21	5	0	4	13	11	12	0	2	0	0	.400	.559
vs. Right	.226	45	93	22	21	3	0	3	14	14	17	1	0	1	0	.333	.355
Scoring Pos.	.314	32	35	0	11	0	0	4	22	6	5	0	1	0	0	.405	.657
Close & Late	.208	21	24	2	5	1	0	1	4	2	3	1	0	0	0	.296	.375
None on/out	.304	35	46	0	14	2	0	1	1	7	11	0	0	0	0	.396	.413
None on	.280	45	93	0	26	6	0	3	3	14	19	0	0	0	0	.374	.441
Runners on	.235	43	68	0	16	2	0	4	24	11	10	1	2	1	0	.346	.441
Batting #4	.273	13	44	7	12	2	0	2	10	6	11	1	1	1	0	.365	.455
Batting #5	.274	20	73	10	20	3	0	3	14	11	10	0	0	0	0	.369	.438
Batting #6	.250	11	40	5	10	3	0	2	3	8	6	0	1	0	0	.375	.475

Hit Best Against

	Avg	AB	R	H	2B	3B	HR	RBI	BB	SO	HBP	GDP	SB	CS	OBP	Slg
Catfish Hunter	.400	10	2	4	0	0	2	6	0	1	0	0	0	0	.400	1.000
Bill Gullickson	.400	5	1	2	1	0	0	1	2	1	0	0	0	0	.571	.600
Steve Carlton	.375	8	3	3	0	0	1	5	3	2	0	1	0	0	.545	.750

Hit Worst Against

	Avg	AB	R	H	2B	3B	HR	RBI	BB	SO	HBP	GDP	SB	CS	OBP	Slg
Dick Tidrow	.000	5	0	0	0	0	0	0	0	1	0	0	0	0	.000	.000
Goose Gossage	.000	6	0	0	0	0	0	0	0	2	1	0	0	0	.143	.000
Don Gullett	.000	5	0	0	0	0	0	1	1	2	0	0	0	0	.143	.000

Chris Chambliss

Bats: Left, Throws: Right

Batting	Avg	G	AB	R	H	2B	3B	HR	RBI	BB	SO	HBP	GDP	SB	CS	OBP	Slg
Totals	.281	30	114	12	32	4	1	3	15	5	14	1	3	2	0	.314	.412
Home	.232	15	56	8	13	3	0	3	10	4	8	0	2	2	0	.279	.446
Away	.328	15	58	4	19	1	1	0	5	1	6	1	1	0	0	.350	.379
vs. Left	.364	22	55	0	20	2	1	1	9	1	5	1	1	1	0	.379	.491
vs. Right	.203	30	59	12	12	2	0	2	6	4	9	0	2	1	0	.254	.339
Scoring Pos.	.240	18	25	0	6	0	0	1	11	3	1	0	1	1	0	.310	.360
Close & Late	.250	17	20	1	5	0	0	1	2	1	2	0	1	0	0	.286	.400
None on/out	.333	20	33	0	11	2	0	1	1	1	4	1	0	0	0	.371	.485
None on	.258	28	62	0	16	2	1	1	1	1	8	1	0	0	0	.281	.371
Runners on	.308	26	52	0	16	2	0	2	14	4	6	0	3	2	0	.351	.462
Batting #4	.333	6	24	3	8	2	0	1	5	1	2	0	0	1	0	.346	.542
Batting #5	.295	11	44	6	13	1	1	2	7	0	3	1	2	1	0	.311	.500
Batting #6	.474	5	19	2	9	1	0	0	3	1	4	0	1	0	0	.500	.526
Batting #7	.074	8	27	1	2	0	0	0	0	3	5	0	0	0	0	.167	.074

Hit Best Against

	Avg	AB	R	H	2B	3B	HR	RBI	BB	SO	HBP	GDP	SB	CS	OBP	Slg
Larry Gura	.667	9	2	6	0	1	0	1	0	2	0	0	0	0	.667	.889
Andy Hassler	.500	6	2	3	1	0	1	2	0	1	0	0	0	0	.500	1.167
Don Sutton	.444	9	1	4	0	0	0	1	1	0	0	0	0	0	.500	.444

Hit Worst Against

	Avg	AB	R	H	2B	3B	HR	RBI	BB	SO	HBP	GDP	SB	CS	OBP	Slg
Dennis Leonard	.091	11	0	1	0	0	0	1	0	5	0	0	0	0	.091	.091
Tommy John	.111	9	1	1	0	0	0	1	0	1	0	1	0	0	.111	.111
Paul Splittorff	.167	12	0	2	0	0	0	2	1	1	0	0	0	0	.214	.167

Frank Chance

Bats: Right, Throws: Right

Batting	Avg	G	AB	R	H	2B	3B	HR	RBI	BB	SO	HBP	GDP	SB	CS	OBP	Slg
Totals	.310	20	71	11	22	3	1	0	6	8	6	3	0	10	2	.402	.380
Home	.297	11	37	5	11	3	1	0	4	5	4	1	0	5	0	.395	.432
Away	.324	9	34	6	11	0	0	0	2	3	2	2	0	5	2	.410	.324
vs. Left	.222	7	18	0	4	1	0	0	0	2	1	1	0	2	1	.333	.278
vs. Right	.340	20	53	11	18	2	1	0	6	6	5	2	0	8	1	.426	.415
Scoring Pos.	.346	18	26	0	9	0	1	0	6	3	2	1	0	4	1	.433	.423
Close & Late	.600	8	10	2	6	0	1	0	3	1	1	0	0	1	0	.636	.800
None on/out	.316	15	19	0	6	1	0	0	0	3	1	1	0	0	0	.435	.368
None on	.306	18	36	0	11	3	0	0	0	5	3	2	0	0	0	.419	.389
Runners on	.314	19	35	0	11	0	1	0	6	3	3	1	0	10	2	.385	.371
Batting #3	.214	4	14	3	3	1	0	0	0	3	2	1	0	3	1	.389	.286
Batting #4	.333	16	57	8	19	2	1	0	6	5	4	2	0	7	1	.406	.404

Hit Best Against

	Avg	AB	R	H	2B	3B	HR	RBI	BB	SO	HBP	GDP	SB	CS	OBP	Slg
Ed Summers	.500	6	2	3	0	0	0	0	1	0	0	0	1	0	.571	.500
George Mullin	.429	7	1	3	0	0	0	1	1	0	0	0	3	0	.500	.429
Jack Coombs	.400	10	1	4	1	0	0	2	0	2	0	0	0	0	.400	.500

Hit Worst Against

	Avg	AB	R	H	2B	3B	HR	RBI	BB	SO	HBP	GDP	SB	CS	OBP	Slg
Doc White	.000	5	1	0	0	0	0	0	1	1	1	0	1	1	.286	.000
Ed Walsh	.200	5	0	1	1	0	0	0	1	0	1	0	0	0	.429	.400

Spud Chandler

Throws: Right, Bats: Right

Pitching	ERA	W	L	Sv	G	GS	IP	BB	SO	Avg	R	H	2B	3B	HR	OBP	Slg
Totals	1.62	2	2	1	6	4	33.1	9	16	.235	8	28	2	0	0	.289	.252
Home	1.64	1	2	0	3	3	22.0	4	8	.187	6	14	2	0	0	.228	.213
Away	1.59	1	0	1	3	1	11.1	5	8	.318	2	14	0	0	0	.388	.318

	Avg	AB	R	H	2B	3B	HR	RBI	BB	SO	HBP	GDP	OBP	Slg
vs. Left	.200	55	0	11	0	0	0	3	3	10	0	1	.241	.200
vs. Right	.266	64	8	17	2	0	0	5	6	6	0	1	.329	.297
Scoring Pos.	.250	28	0	7	1	0	0	8	5	6	0	1	.364	.286
Close & Late	.286	21	0	6	0	0	0	1	0	2	0	1	.286	.286
None on/out	.226	31	0	7	0	0	0	0	3	3	0	1	.294	.226
None on	.205	73	0	15	0	0	0	0	3	9	0	1	.237	.205
Runners on	.283	46	0	13	2	0	0	8	6	7	0	1	.365	.326

Pitched Best Against

	Avg	AB	R	H	2B	3B	HR	RBI	BB	SO	HBP	GDP	SB	CS	OBP	Slg
Johnny Hopp	.000	7	0	0	0	0	0	0	0	1	0	0	0	0	.000	.000
Debs Garms	.000	5	0	0	0	0	0	0	0	2	0	0	0	0	.000	.000
Stan Musial	.182	11	0	2	0	0	0	0	1	2	0	0	0	1	.250	.182

Pitched Worst Against

	Avg	AB	R	H	2B	3B	HR	RBI	BB	SO	HBP	GDP	SB	CS	OBP	Slg
Ray Sanders	.429	7	1	3	0	0	0	0	1	1	0	0	0	0	.500	.429
Marty Marion	.333	9	0	3	1	0	0	1	0	0	0	1	0	0	.333	.444
Whitey Kurowski	.333	9	1	3	0	0	0	0	1	0	0	1	0	0	.400	.333

Eddie Cicotte

Throws: Right, Bats: Both

Pitching	ERA	W	L	Sv	G	GS	IP	BB	SO	Avg	R	H	2B	3B	HR	OBP	Slg
Totals	2.22	2	3	0	6	5	44.2	7	20	.247	14	42	5	3	0	.279	.312
Home	0.75	1	1	0	3	2	24.0	2	7	.227	5	20	2	1	0	.244	.273
Away	3.92	1	2	0	3	3	20.2	5	13	.268	9	22	3	2	0	.315	.354

	Avg	AB	R	H	2B	3B	HR	RBI	BB	SO	HBP	GDP	OBP	Slg
vs. Left	.281	96	0	27	4	2	0	11	5	11	1	0	.324	.365
vs. Right	.203	74	14	15	1	1	0	4	2	9	0	0	.221	.243
Scoring Pos.	.302	43	0	13	3	1	0	15	0	4	0	0	.295	.419
Close & Late	.286	7	0	2	0	0	0	0	0	1	0	0	.286	.286
None on/out	.195	41	0	8	0	2	0	0	2	7	1	0	.250	.293
None on	.242	95	0	23	2	2	0	0	5	11	1	0	.287	.305
Runners on	.253	75	0	19	3	1	0	15	2	9	0	0	.269	.320

Pitched Best Against

	Avg	AB	R	H	2B	3B	HR	RBI	BB	SO	HBP	GDP	SB	CS	OBP	Slg
Art Fletcher	.000	11	0	0	0	0	0	0	0	1	0	0	0	0	.000	.000
Edd Roush	.000	8	0	0	0	0	0	0	1	0	0	0	1	0	.111	.000
Benny Kauff	.091	11	0	1	0	0	0	1	0	1	0	0	1	1	.091	.091

Pitched Worst Against

	Avg	AB	R	H	2B	3B	HR	RBI	BB	SO	HBP	GDP	SB	CS	OBP	Slg
Ivy Wingo	.667	6	1	4	0	0	0	1	3	0	0	0	0	1	.778	.667
Dave Robertson	.636	11	1	7	1	1	0	1	0	0	0	0	1	0	.636	.909
Greasy Neale	.333	9	1	3	1	0	0	1	0	1	0	0	0	0	.333	.444

Will Clark

Bats: Left, Throws: Left

Batting	Avg	G	AB	R	H	2B	3B	HR	RBI	BB	SO	HBP	GDP	SB	CS	OBP	Slg
Totals	.364	20	77	14	28	6	1	3	11	9	13	0	2	1	0	.430	.584
Home	.385	10	39	7	15	4	1	0	3	3	9	0	1	0	0	.429	.538
Away	.342	10	38	7	13	2	0	3	8	6	4	0	1	1	0	.432	.632
vs. Left	.320	15	25	0	8	1	0	1	5	6	5	0	0	1	0	.452	.480
vs. Right	.385	20	52	14	20	5	1	2	6	3	8	0	2	0	0	.418	.635
Scoring Pos.	.235	14	17	1	4	1	0	1	8	5	2	0	1	0	0	.409	.471
Close & Late	.300	9	10	0	3	1	0	0	2	2	1	0	0	0	0	.417	.400
None on/out	.333	16	21	0	7	1	1	0	0	0	2	0	0	0	0	.333	.476
None on	.409	20	44	0	18	3	1	1	1	4	8	0	0	0	0	.458	.591
Runners on	.303	20	33	0	10	3	0	2	10	5	5	0	2	1	0	.395	.576
Batting #3	.472	9	36	10	17	4	1	2	8	3	5	0	0	0	0	.513	.806
Batting #5	.125	4	16	1	2	0	0	0	0	3	2	0	1	0	0	.263	.125
Batting #6	.353	5	17	3	6	1	0	1	3	3	4	0	0	1	0	.450	.588

Hit Best Against

	Avg	AB	R	H	2B	3B	HR	RBI	BB	SO	HBP	GDP	SB	CS	OBP	Slg
Greg Maddux	1.000	5	4	5	2	0	2	6	0	0	0	0	0	0	1.000	2.600
Dave Stewart	.429	7	1	3	1	0	0	0	0	1	0	0	0	0	.429	.571
John Tudor	.400	5	1	2	0	0	1	2	2	1	0	0	0	0	.571	1.000

Hit Worst Against

	Avg	AB	R	H	2B	3B	HR	RBI	BB	SO	HBP	GDP	SB	CS	OBP	Slg
Mike Moore	.167	6	1	1	0	0	0	0	0	1	0	0	0	0	.167	.167

Fred Clarke

Bats: Left, Throws: Right

Batting	Avg	G	AB	R	H	2B	3B	HR	RBI	BB	SO	HBP	GDP	SB	CS	OBP	Slg
Totals	.245	15	53	10	13	2	1	2	9	6	8	1	0	4	0	.328	.434
Home	.259	7	27	6	7	1	1	2	6	1	2	0	0	2	0	.286	.593
Away	.231	8	26	4	6	1	0	0	3	5	6	1	0	2	0	.364	.269
vs. Right	.245	15	53	10	13	2	1	2	9	6	8	1	0	4	0	.328	.434
Scoring Pos.	.231	11	13	0	3	1	0	1	8	2	2	0	0	1	0	.313	.538
Close & Late	.333	5	6	0	2	1	0	1	5	0	0	0	0	1	0	.333	1.000
None on/out	.143	7	7	0	1	0	1	0	0	1	1	0	0	0	0	.250	.429
None on	.226	15	31	0	7	0	1	1	1	4	5	0	0	0	0	.314	.387
Runners on	.273	14	22	0	6	2	0	1	8	2	3	1	0	4	0	.346	.500
Batting #2	.265	8	34	3	9	2	1	0	2	1	5	0	0	1	0	.286	.382
Batting #3	.211	7	19	7	4	0	0	2	7	5	3	1	0	3	0	.385	.526

Hit Best Against

	Avg	AB	R	H	2B	3B	HR	RBI	BB	SO	HBP	GDP	SB	CS	OBP	Slg
Bill Dinneen	.313	16	1	5	1	0	0	2	1	4	0	0	1	0	.353	.375

Hit Worst Against

	Avg	AB	R	H	2B	3B	HR	RBI	BB	SO	HBP	GDP	SB	CS	OBP	Slg
George Mullin	.182	11	4	2	0	0	1	2	2	3	0	0	1	0	.308	.455
Cy Young	.188	16	2	3	0	1	0	0	0	1	0	0	0	0	.188	.313

Roger Clemens

Throws: Right, Bats: Right

Pitching	ERA	W	L	Sv	G	GS	IP	BB	SO	Avg	R	H	2B	3B	HR	OBP	Slg
Totals	3.88	1	2	0	9	9	55.2	19	45	.234	26	49	5	0	2	.304	.287
Home	3.62	1	1	0	4	4	27.1	8	20	.231	12	24	3	0	1	.298	.288
Away	4.13	0	1	0	5	5	28.1	11	25	.238	14	25	2	0	1	.310	.286

	Avg	AB	R	H	2B	3B	HR	RBI	BB	SO	HBP	GDP	OBP	Slg
vs. Left	.214	103	0	22	4	0	0	6	12	25	0	3	.296	.252
vs. Right	.255	106	20	27	1	0	2	11	7	20	2	3	.313	.321
Scoring Pos.	.256	39	3	10	2	0	0	14	2	7	0	3	.293	.308
Close & Late	.250	16	1	4	0	0	1	3	0	3	0	3	.250	.438
None on/out	.207	58	0	12	1	0	1	1	3	15	0	3	.246	.276
None on	.173	127	0	22	3	0	1	1	14	31	2	3	.266	.220
Runners on	.329	82	6	27	2	0	1	16	5	14	0	3	.368	.390

Pitched Best Against

	Avg	AB	R	H	2B	3B	HR	RBI	BB	SO	HBP	GDP	SB	CS	OBP	Slg
Gary Carter	.000	5	0	0	0	0	0	0	0	1	0	0	0	0	.000	.000
Lenny Dykstra	.000	5	0	0	0	0	0	0	0	3	0	0	0	0	.000	.000
Reggie Jackson	.000	10	0	0	0	0	0	0	1	2	0	0	0	0	.091	.000

Pitched Worst Against

	Avg	AB	R	H	2B	3B	HR	RBI	BB	SO	HBP	GDP	SB	CS	OBP	Slg
Bob Boone	.556	9	2	5	0	0	0	1	1	1	1	0	0	0	.636	.556
Gary Pettis	.444	9	2	4	0	0	0	1	1	1	0	0	0	1	.500	.444
Keith Hernandez	.400	5	0	2	0	0	0	1	1	0	0	0	0	0	.500	.400

Roberto Clemente

Bats: Right, Throws: Right

Batting	Avg	G	AB	R	H	2B	3B	HR	RBI	BB	SO	HBP	GDP	SB	CS	OBP	Slg
Totals	.318	26	107	8	34	3	1	3	14	6	21	0	1	0	0	.354	.449
Home	.278	13	54	3	15	0	0	0	9	2	10	0	1	0	0	.304	.278
Away	.358	13	53	5	19	3	1	3	5	4	11	0	0	0	0	.404	.623
vs. Left	.317	15	41	0	13	1	0	2	5	2	4	0	1	0	0	.349	.488
vs. Right	.318	26	66	8	21	2	1	1	9	4	17	0	0	0	0	.357	.424
Scoring Pos.	.471	16	17	0	8	0	0	0	11	4	3	0	0	0	0	.571	.471
Close & Late	.118	17	17	2	2	0	0	0	1	3	2	0	0	0	0	.250	.118
None on/out	.238	17	21	0	5	1	0	1	1	0	4	0	0	0	0	.238	.429
None on	.324	24	68	0	22	3	1	3	3	1	14	0	0	0	0	.333	.529
Runners on	.308	21	39	0	12	0	0	0	11	5	7	0	1	0	0	.386	.308
Batting #3	.323	24	99	7	32	3	1	3	12	6	21	0	0	0	0	.362	.465

Hit Best Against

	Avg	AB	R	H	2B	3B	HR	RBI	BB	SO	HBP	GDP	SB	CS	OBP	Slg
Jim Palmer	.444	9	1	4	1	1	1	1	0	0	0	0	0	0	.444	1.111
Dave McNally	.429	7	0	3	1	0	0	1	0	0	0	0	0	0	.429	.571
Whitey Ford	.375	8	0	3	0	0	0	0	0	1	0	0	0	0	.375	.375

Hit Worst Against

	Avg	AB	R	H	2B	3B	HR	RBI	BB	SO	HBP	GDP	SB	CS	OBP	Slg
Don Gullett	.167	6	0	1	0	0	0	0	0	1	0	0	0	0	.167	.167
Gary Nolan	.167	6	0	1	1	0	0	0	1	3	0	0	0	0	.286	.333

Ty Cobb

Bats: Left, Throws: Right

Batting	Avg	G	AB	R	H	2B	3B	HR	RBI	BB	SO	HBP	GDP	SB	CS	OBP	Slg
Totals	.262	17	65	7	17	4	1	0	9	3	7	2	1	4	3	.314	.354
Home	.235	9	34	3	8	3	1	0	6	1	6	1	0	0	2	.278	.382
Away	.290	8	31	4	9	1	0	0	3	2	1	1	1	4	1	.353	.323
vs. Left	.556	3	9	0	5	2	0	0	4	0	0	2	1	0	1	.636	.778
vs. Right	.214	17	56	7	12	2	1	0	5	3	7	0	0	4	2	.254	.286
Scoring Pos.	.364	16	22	0	8	3	0	0	9	2	2	1	1	2	2	.440	.500
Close & Late	.375	6	8	1	3	1	0	0	3	0	0	1	0	0	0	.444	.500
None on/out	.286	13	14	0	4	1	0	0	0	1	3	0	0	0	0	.333	.357
None on	.242	16	33	0	8	1	1	0	0	1	3	1	0	0	0	.286	.333
Runners on	.281	17	32	0	9	3	0	0	9	2	4	1	1	4	3	.343	.375
Batting #3	.231	7	26	3	6	3	0	0	5	2	2	1	0	2	1	.310	.346
Batting #4	.282	10	39	4	11	1	1	0	4	1	5	1	1	2	2	.317	.359

Hit Best Against

	Avg	AB	R	H	2B	3B	HR	RBI	BB	SO	HBP	GDP	SB	CS	OBP	Slg
Jack Pfiester	.571	7	1	4	1	0	0	2	0	0	1	1	0	0	.625	.714
Ed Reulbach	.444	9	1	4	0	0	0	1	0	1	0	0	2	1	.444	.444
Nick Maddox	.400	5	0	2	1	0	0	2	0	1	0	0	0	0	.400	.600

Hit Worst Against

	Avg	AB	R	H	2B	3B	HR	RBI	BB	SO	HBP	GDP	SB	CS	OBP	Slg
Babe Adams	.091	11	2	1	0	0	0	0	1	0	0	0	1	0	.167	.091
T. Finger Brown	.125	8	1	1	0	0	0	0	0	3	0	0	0	0	.125	.125
Orval Overall	.133	15	1	2	0	1	0	1	1	1	0	0	0	0	.188	.267

Mickey Cochrane

Bats: Left, Throws: Right

Batting	Avg	G	AB	R	H	2B	3B	HR	RBI	BB	SO	HBP	GDP	SB	CS	OBP	Slg
Totals	.245	31	110	17	27	4	0	2	7	25	8	0	3	0	1	.382	.336
Home	.286	16	56	9	16	3	0	2	6	11	4	0	0	0	1	.397	.446
Away	.204	15	54	8	11	1	0	0	1	14	4	0	3	0	0	.368	.222
vs. Left	.208	10	24	0	5	1	0	0	1	8	3	0	0	0	0	.406	.250
vs. Right	.256	31	86	17	22	3	0	2	6	17	5	0	3	0	1	.375	.360
Scoring Pos.	.176	21	17	0	3	0	0	0	3	7	1	0	0	0	0	.400	.176
Close & Late	.278	15	18	3	5	0	0	0	0	2	1	0	0	0	0	.350	.278
None on/out	.250	19	20	0	5	0	0	0	0	3	1	0	0	0	0	.348	.250
None on	.254	31	67	0	17	2	0	2	2	16	6	0	0	0	0	.398	.373
Runners on	.233	28	43	0	10	2	0	0	5	9	2	0	3	0	1	.358	.279
Batting #2	.250	13	52	5	13	2	0	0	2	8	4	0	1	0	0	.350	.288
Batting #3	.241	18	58	12	14	2	0	2	5	17	4	0	2	0	1	.408	.379

Hit Best Against

	Avg	AB	R	H	2B	3B	HR	RBI	BB	SO	HBP	GDP	SB	CS	OBP	Slg
Paul Derringer	.500	6	2	3	0	0	0	1	1	0	0	0	0	0	.571	.500
Charlie Root	.429	7	1	3	2	0	0	1	1	0	0	0	0	0	.500	.714
Larry French	.429	7	2	3	0	0	0	0	0	1	0	0	0	0	.429	.429

Hit Worst Against

	Avg	AB	R	H	2B	3B	HR	RBI	BB	SO	HBP	GDP	SB	CS	OBP	Slg
Syl Johnson	.000	5	0	0	0	0	0	0	1	0	0	0	0	0	.167	.000
Burleigh Grimes	.154	13	2	2	0	0	1	1	3	3	0	0	0	1	.313	.385
Dizzy Dean	.167	12	0	2	0	0	0	0	0	0	0	1	0	0	.167	.167

Eddie Collins

Bats: Left, Throws: Right

Batting	Avg	G	AB	R	H	2B	3B	HR	RBI	BB	SO	HBP	GDP	SB	CS	OBP	Slg
Totals	.328	34	128	20	42	7	2	0	11	10	11	1	0	14	4	.376	.414
Home	.333	16	57	10	19	4	0	0	4	4	7	1	0	6	1	.387	.404
Away	.324	18	71	10	23	3	2	0	7	6	4	0	0	8	3	.367	.423
vs. Left	.350	15	40	0	14	1	1	0	4	5	1	0	0	3	2	.404	.425
vs. Right	.318	34	88	20	28	6	1	0	7	5	10	1	0	11	2	.362	.409
Scoring Pos.	.261	24	23	0	6	2	0	0	10	3	1	0	0	5	1	.321	.348
Close & Late	.375	15	16	4	6	0	0	0	1	2	0	0	0	2	0	.444	.375
None on/out	.214	20	28	0	6	2	1	0	0	2	2	0	0	0	0	.267	.357
None on	.322	34	87	0	28	3	1	0	0	7	8	1	0	0	0	.379	.379
Runners on	.341	29	41	0	14	4	1	0	11	3	3	0	0	14	4	.370	.488
Batting #2	.226	8	31	2	7	1	0	0	1	1	2	1	0	1	1	.265	.258
Batting #3	.361	26	97	18	35	6	2	0	10	9	9	0	0	13	3	.411	.464

Hit Best Against

	Avg	AB	R	H	2B	3B	HR	RBI	BB	SO	HBP	GDP	SB	CS	OBP	Slg
T. Finger Brown	.556	9	2	5	3	0	0	3	1	0	0	0	4	0	.600	.889
Rube Marquard	.500	8	3	4	1	1	0	0	2	0	0	0	2	0	.600	.875
Rube Benton	.429	7	1	3	0	0	0	0	0	0	0	0	0	0	.429	.429

Hit Worst Against

	Avg	AB	R	H	2B	3B	HR	RBI	BB	SO	HBP	GDP	SB	CS	OBP	Slg
Jimmy Ring	.000	5	0	0	0	0	0	0	0	0	1	0	0	0	.167	.000
Dick Rudolph	.143	7	0	1	0	0	0	0	1	1	0	0	0	0	.250	.143
Dutch Ruether	.167	6	0	1	0	0	0	1	0	0	0	0	0	1	.143	.167

Earle Combs

Bats: Left, Throws: Right

Batting	Avg	G	AB	R	H	2B	3B	HR	RBI	BB	SO	HBP	GDP	SB	CS	OBP	Slg
Totals	.350	16	60	17	21	3	0	1	9	10	7	1	1	0	0	.444	.450
Home	.419	8	31	9	13	2	0	0	4	5	1	0	1	0	0	.500	.484
Away	.276	8	29	8	8	1	0	1	5	5	6	1	0	0	0	.389	.414
vs. Left	.400	6	10	0	4	1	0	0	3	4	1	1	0	0	0	.600	.500
vs. Right	.340	16	50	17	17	2	0	1	6	6	6	0	1	0	0	.404	.440
Scoring Pos.	.417	11	12	0	5	1	0	0	8	2	0	1	1	0	0	.500	.500
Close & Late	.400	6	5	1	2	0	0	0	2	1	1	0	0	0	0	.500	.400
None on/out	.407	15	27	0	11	0	0	1	1	6	4	0	0	0	0	.515	.519
None on	.340	15	47	0	16	2	0	1	1	7	6	0	0	0	0	.426	.447
Runners on	.385	11	13	0	5	1	0	0	8	3	1	1	1	0	0	.500	.462
Batting #1	.350	15	60	17	21	3	0	1	8	10	7	1	1	0	0	.451	.450

Hit Best Against

	Avg	AB	R	H	2B	3B	HR	RBI	BB	SO	HBP	GDP	SB	CS	OBP	Slg
Jesse Haines	.429	7	0	3	0	0	0	0	1	1	0	0	0	0	.500	.429
Pete Alexander	.333	9	0	3	1	0	0	2	1	0	0	0	0	0	.364	.444
Bill Sherdel	.286	7	1	2	0	0	0	0	2	0	0	0	0	0	.444	.286

Dave Concepcion

Bats: Right, Throws: Right

Batting	Avg	G	AB	R	H	2B	3B	HR	RBI	BB	SO	HBP	GDP	SB	CS	OBP	Slg
Totals	.297	35	101	13	30	4	3	2	13	6	12	1	2	7	3	.333	.455
Home	.348	17	46	7	16	2	2	1	6	3	6	1	1	5	2	.385	.543
Away	.255	18	55	6	14	2	1	1	7	3	6	0	1	2	1	.288	.382
vs. Left	.289	17	38	0	11	1	0	1	5	3	5	0	0	3	0	.326	.395
vs. Right	.302	35	63	13	19	3	3	1	8	3	7	1	2	4	3	.338	.492
Scoring Pos.	.333	22	27	0	9	2	0	0	10	5	4	0	1	3	1	.400	.407
Close & Late	.250	18	20	2	5	0	0	0	2	0	1	0	1	2	2	.238	.250
None on/out	.320	19	25	0	8	0	1	1	1	1	4	0	0	0	0	.346	.520
None on	.295	29	61	0	18	2	2	2	2	1	6	1	0	0	0	.317	.492
Runners on	.300	27	40	0	12	2	1	0	11	5	6	0	2	7	3	.354	.400
Batting #3	.429	4	14	1	6	1	0	0	0	0	3	0	1	0	1	.429	.500
Batting #6	.304	6	23	3	7	0	0	1	2	1	3	0	0	3	0	.333	.435
Batting #7	.217	6	23	5	5	2	0	1	3	1	1	1	0	2	0	.269	.435
Batting #8	.280	10	25	3	7	0	2	0	5	3	2	0	0	1	1	.333	.440
Batting #9	.313	7	16	1	5	1	0	0	3	1	3	0	0	1	1	.353	.500

Hit Best Against

	Avg	AB	R	H	2B	3B	HR	RBI	BB	SO	HBP	GDP	SB	CS	OBP	Slg
John Candelaria	.333	6	2	2	0	0	1	1	0	1	0	0	0	0	.333	.833

Hit Worst Against

	Avg	AB	R	H	2B	3B	HR	RBI	BB	SO	HBP	GDP	SB	CS	OBP	Slg
Luis Tiant	.083	12	1	1	0	0	0	1	0	1	0	0	0	0	.083	.167
Bill Lee	.167	6	0	1	0	0	0	0	0	0	0	0	0	0	.167	.167
Catfish Hunter	.200	5	0	1	0	0	0	1	0	2	0	0	1	0	.200	.200

2280 Postseason: Player Profiles

David Cone

Throws: Right, Bats: Left

Pitching	ERA	W	L	Sv	G	GS	IP	BB	SO	Avg	R	H	2B	3B	HR	OBP	Slg
Totals	4.67	4	3	0	13	12	71.1	40	58	.250	41	69	7	2	9	.348	.388
Home	5.29	2	1	0	6	5	32.1	18	27	.250	19	31	3	2	6	.350	.452
Away	4.15	2	2	0	7	7	39.0	22	31	.250	22	38	4	0	3	.347	.336

	Avg	AB	R	H	2B	3B	HR	RBI	BB	SO	HBP	GDP	OBP	Slg
vs. Left	.219	151	0	33	4	1	5	17	28	28	0	3	.339	.358
vs. Right	.288	125	6	36	3	1	4	19	12	30	2	3	.360	.424
Scoring Pos.	.271	70	13	19	1	0	2	25	14	17	1	3	.395	.371
Close & Late	.235	17	5	4	0	0	2	4	5	4	0	3	.409	.588
None on/out	.191	68	0	13	2	1	1	1	10	13	0	3	.295	.294
None on	.205	161	14	33	6	2	3	3	21	31	1	3	.301	.323
Runners on	.313	115	21	36	1	0	6	33	19	27	1	3	.412	.478

Pitched Best Against

	Avg	AB	R	H	2B	3B	HR	RBI	BB	SO	HBP	GDP	SB	CS	OBP	Slg
Vince Coleman	.000	8	0	0	0	0	0	0	0	1	0	0	0	0	.000	.000
John Shelby	.000	6	0	0	0	0	0	0	0	4	0	0	0	0	.000	.000
Kirk Gibson	.000	6	0	0	0	0	0	0	1	0	0	0	0	0	.143	.000

Pitched Worst Against

	Avg	AB	R	H	2B	3B	HR	RBI	BB	SO	HBP	GDP	SB	CS	OBP	Slg
M. Grissom	.600	5	1	3	0	1	0	0	0	1	0	0	0	0	.600	1.000
Deion Sanders	.600	5	2	3	1	0	0	0	1	0	0	0	4	0	.667	.800
Edgar Martinez	.571	7	1	4	1	0	0	0	1	0	0	0	0	0	.625	.714

Jack Coombs

Throws: Right, Bats: Both

Pitching	ERA	W	L	Sv	G	GS	IP	BB	SO	Avg	R	H	2B	3B	HR	OBP	Slg
Totals	2.70	5	0	0	6	6	53.1	21	34	.225	18	41	13	1	1	.304	.324
Home	3.52	2	0	0	2	2	15.1	10	6	.278	6	15	4	1	1	.385	.444
Away	2.37	3	0	0	4	4	38.0	11	28	.203	12	26	9	0	0	.268	.273

	Avg	AB	R	H	2B	3B	HR	RBI	BB	SO	HBP	GDP	OBP	Slg
vs. Left	.309	55	0	17	5	1	1	7	8	6	0	1	.397	.491
vs. Right	.186	129	18	24	8	0	0	8	13	28	1	1	.260	.248
Scoring Pos.	.176	51	0	9	3	0	0	13	7	13	1	1	.274	.235
Close & Late	.150	40	0	6	2	0	0	6	8	9	0	1	.286	.200
None on/out	.196	46	0	9	5	0	0	0	8	4	0	1	.315	.304
None on	.245	106	0	26	9	0	1	1	12	18	0	1	.322	.358
Runners on	.192	78	0	15	4	1	0	14	9	16	1	1	.275	.269

Pitched Best Against

	Avg	AB	R	H	2B	3B	HR	RBI	BB	SO	HBP	GDP	SB	CS	OBP	Slg
Red Murray	.000	6	0	0	0	0	0	0	1	3	0	0	0	1	.143	.000
Fred Snodgrass	.000	6	0	0	0	0	0	0	1	3	0	0	0	0	.143	.000
Fred Merkle	.000	5	1	0	0	0	0	0	2	1	1	0	0	1	.375	.000

Pitched Worst Against

	Avg	AB	R	H	2B	3B	HR	RBI	BB	SO	HBP	GDP	SB	CS	OBP	Slg
Jimmy Sheckard	.500	6	4	3	2	0	0	0	6	0	0	0	0	0	.750	.833
Joe Tinker	.417	12	1	5	2	0	0	0	1	1	0	0	1	1	.462	.583
Frank Chance	.400	10	1	4	1	0	0	2	0	2	0	0	0	0	.400	.500

Stan Coveleski

Throws: Right, Bats: Right

Pitching	ERA	W	L	Sv	G	GS	IP	BB	SO	Avg	R	H	2B	3B	HR	OBP	Slg
Totals	1.74	3	2	0	5	5	41.1	7	11	.204	9	31	2	0	2	.238	.257
Home	1.85	2	1	0	3	3	24.1	5	5	.213	5	19	1	0	0	.253	.225
Away	1.59	1	1	0	2	2	17.0	2	6	.190	4	12	1	0	2	.215	.302

	Avg	AB	R	H	2B	3B	HR	RBI	BB	SO	HBP	GDP	OBP	Slg
vs. Left	.280	50	0	14	2	0	0	1	1	2	0	0	.294	.320
vs. Right	.167	102	9	17	0	0	2	8	6	9	0	0	.211	.225
Scoring Pos.	.185	27	0	5	0	0	1	7	3	0	0	0	.258	.296
Close & Late	.190	21	4	4	0	0	1	5	2	0	0	0	.261	.333
None on/out	.146	41	0	6	1	0	0	0	1	3	0	0	.167	.171
None on	.200	100	0	20	1	0	1	1	3	9	0	0	.223	.240
Runners on	.212	52	0	11	1	0	1	8	4	2	0	0	.263	.288

Pitched Best Against

	Avg	AB	R	H	2B	3B	HR	RBI	BB	SO	HBP	GDP	SB	CS	OBP	Slg
Hi Myers	.000	11	0	0	0	0	0	0	0	1	0	0	0	0	.000	.000
Vic Aldridge	.000	6	0	0	0	0	0	0	0	0	0	1	0	0	.000	.000
Otto Miller	.000	5	0	0	0	0	0	0	0	1	0	2	0	0	.000	.000

Pitched Worst Against

	Avg	AB	R	H	2B	3B	HR	RBI	BB	SO	HBP	GDP	SB	CS	OBP	Slg
Max Carey	.571	7	2	4	0	0	0	0	1	1	0	0	1	0	.625	.571
Kiki Cuyler	.500	6	2	3	0	0	1	3	1	0	0	0	0	0	.571	1.000
Earl Smith	.500	6	0	3	0	0	0	0	0	1	0	1	0	0	.500	.500

Sam Crawford

Bats: Left, Throws: Left

Batting	Avg	G	AB	R	H	2B	3B	HR	RBI	BB	SO	HBP	GDP	SB	CS	OBP	Slg
Totals	.232	17	69	7	16	5	0	1	8	2	6	0	2	1	0	.254	.348
Home	.167	9	36	2	6	3	0	0	2	2	3	0	1	0	0	.211	.250
Away	.303	8	33	5	10	2	0	1	6	0	3	0	1	1	0	.303	.455
vs. Left	.200	3	10	0	2	0	0	0	1	0	1	0	0	0	0	.200	.200
vs. Right	.237	17	59	7	14	5	0	1	7	2	5	0	2	1	0	.262	.373
Scoring Pos.	.105	14	19	0	2	0	0	0	5	0	3	0	0	1	0	.105	.105
Close & Late	.125	7	8	1	1	0	0	0	3	0	2	0	0	0	0	.125	.125
None on/out	.250	11	12	0	3	1	0	0	0	2	1	0	0	0	0	.357	.333
None on	.235	17	34	0	8	3	0	1	1	2	2	0	0	0	0	.278	.412
Runners on	.229	16	35	0	8	2	0	0	7	0	4	0	2	1	0	.229	.286
Batting #3	.220	10	41	3	9	2	0	0	4	1	5	0	1	0	0	.238	.268
Batting #4	.250	7	28	4	7	3	0	1	4	1	1	0	1	1	0	.276	.464

Hit Best Against

	Avg	AB	R	H	2B	3B	HR	RBI	BB	SO	HBP	GDP	SB	CS	OBP	Slg
Babe Adams	.333	12	2	4	1	0	1	2	0	0	0	0	1	0	.333	.667
T. Finger Brown	.333	9	0	3	2	0	0	0	0	0	0	1	0	0	.333	.556
Orval Overall	.250	16	2	4	0	0	0	2	1	2	0	0	0	0	.294	.250

Hit Worst Against

	Avg	AB	R	H	2B	3B	HR	RBI	BB	SO	HBP	GDP	SB	CS	OBP	Slg
Nick Maddox	.000	5	0	0	0	0	0	1	0	0	0	0	0	0	.000	.000
Ed Reulbach	.111	9	0	1	0	0	0	0	0	2	0	0	0	0	.111	.111
Jack Pfiester	.143	7	1	1	0	0	0	1	0	1	0	0	0	0	.143	.143

Frankie Crosetti

Bats: Right, Throws: Right

Batting	Avg	G	AB	R	H	2B	3B	HR	RBI	BB	SO	HBP	GDP	SB	CS	OBP	Slg
Totals	.174	29	115	16	20	5	1	1	11	14	20	1	2	1	1	.269	.261
Home	.179	15	56	7	10	2	1	0	7	5	13	0	0	1	1	.246	.250
Away	.169	14	59	9	10	3	0	1	4	9	7	1	2	0	0	.290	.271
vs. Left	.179	14	39	0	7	3	0	0	1	2	3	0	2	1	0	.220	.256
vs. Right	.171	29	76	16	13	2	1	1	10	12	17	1	0	0	1	.292	.263
Scoring Pos.	.172	20	29	0	5	1	1	0	9	6	3	0	1	0	0	.314	.276
Close & Late	.375	9	8	4	3	1	0	1	4	2	1	0	0	0	0	.500	.875
None on/out	.182	26	44	0	8	2	0	0	0	5	9	0	0	0	0	.265	.227
None on	.143	29	70	0	10	3	0	0	0	7	16	1	0	0	0	.231	.186
Runners on	.222	26	45	0	10	2	1	1	11	7	4	0	2	1	1	.327	.378
Batting #1	.184	21	87	11	16	4	1	1	10	11	15	1	1	0	1	.283	.287
Batting #2	.154	4	13	3	2	0	0	0	1	1	2	0	0	1	0	.214	.154
Batting #8	.133	4	15	2	2	1	0	0	0	2	3	0	1	0	0	.235	.200

Hit Best Against

	Avg	AB	R	H	2B	3B	HR	RBI	BB	SO	HBP	GDP	SB	CS	OBP	Slg
Dizzy Dean	.400	5	1	2	1	0	1	4	0	0	0	0	0	0	.400	1.200
Mort Cooper	.375	8	1	3	0	0	0	0	0	2	0	0	0	0	.375	.375
Carl Hubbell	.286	14	3	4	2	0	0	0	1	0	0	1	0	0	.333	.429

Hit Worst Against

	Avg	AB	R	H	2B	3B	HR	RBI	BB	SO	HBP	GDP	SB	CS	OBP	Slg
Paul Derringer	.000	7	0	0	0	0	0	0	0	1	0	0	0	0	.000	.000
Cliff Melton	.000	6	0	0	0	0	0	0	0	1	0	0	0	0	.000	.000
Lon Warneke	.000	5	0	0	0	0	0	0	0	1	0	0	0	0	.000	.000

Mike Cuellar

Throws: Left, Bats: Left

Pitching	ERA	W	L	Sv	G	GS	IP	BB	SO	Avg	R	H	2B	3B	HR	OBP	Slg
Totals	2.85	4	4	0	12	12	85.1	31	56	.211	32	66	18	0	7	.280	.335
Home	1.89	3	2	0	6	6	47.2	16	29	.154	11	25	9	0	2	.228	.247
Away	4.06	1	2	0	6	6	37.2	15	27	.272	21	41	9	0	5	.337	.430

	Avg	AB	R	H	2B	3B	HR	RBI	BB	SO	HBP	GDP	OBP	Slg
vs. Left	.196	46	0	9	5	0	2	3	9	13	0	2	.327	.435
vs. Right	.213	267	32	57	13	0	5	28	22	43	0	2	.271	.318
Scoring Pos.	.226	62	0	14	2	0	1	23	7	7	0	2	.296	.306
Close & Late	.250	40	4	10	2	0	3	9	3	8	0	2	.295	.525
None on/out	.225	89	0	20	7	0	4	4	4	15	0	2	.258	.438
None on	.205	200	0	41	12	0	5	5	16	37	0	2	.264	.340
Runners on	.221	113	0	25	6	0	2	26	15	19	0	2	.308	.327

Pitched Best Against

	Avg	AB	R	H	2B	3B	HR	RBI	BB	SO	HBP	GDP	SB	CS	OBP	Slg
Ed Charles	.000	7	0	0	0	0	0	0	0	2	0	0	0	0	.000	.000
Steve Blass	.000	6	0	0	0	0	0	0	0	0	0	0	0	0	.000	.000
Leo Cardenas	.000	5	0	0	0	0	0	0	0	0	0	0	0	0	.000	.000

Pitched Worst Against

	Avg	AB	R	H	2B	3B	HR	RBI	BB	SO	HBP	GDP	SB	CS	OBP	Slg
Tony Oliva	.667	6	3	4	3	0	1	2	0	0	0	0	0	0	.667	1.667
Jose Pagan	.500	6	0	3	2	0	0	2	0	0	0	0	0	0	.500	.833
M. Sanguillen	.500	6	1	3	1	0	0	0	0	0	0	0	0	0	.500	.667

Kiki Cuyler

Bats: Right, Throws: Right

Batting	Avg	G	AB	R	H	2B	3B	HR	RBI	BB	SO	HBP	GDP	SB	CS	OBP	Slg
Totals	.281	16	64	9	18	5	1	2	12	2	14	1	0	1	3	.313	.484
Home	.258	8	31	3	8	3	0	2	7	1	9	0	0	0	1	.281	.548
Away	.303	8	33	6	10	2	1	0	5	1	5	1	0	1	2	.343	.424
vs. Left	.091	6	11	0	1	0	1	0	0	0	2	0	0	0	0	.091	.273
vs. Right	.321	16	53	9	17	5	0	2	12	2	12	1	0	1	3	.357	.528
Scoring Pos.	.333	10	21	0	7	2	0	1	10	2	5	1	0	0	1	.417	.571
Close & Late	.231	11	13	1	3	1	0	1	5	0	2	1	0	0	0	.286	.538
None on/out	.375	5	8	0	3	1	0	0	0	0	2	0	0	0	0	.375	.500
None on	.321	13	28	0	9	2	1	1	1	0	5	0	0	0	0	.321	.571
Runners on	.250	15	36	0	9	3	0	1	11	2	9	1	0	1	3	.308	.417
Batting #3	.273	11	44	5	12	4	1	2	8	1	7	1	0	1	2	.304	.545
Batting #5	.300	5	20	4	6	1	0	0	4	1	7	0	0	0	1	.333	.350

Hit Best Against

	Avg	AB	R	H	2B	3B	HR	RBI	BB	SO	HBP	GDP	SB	CS	OBP	Slg
Stan Coveleski	.500	6	2	3	0	0	1	3	1	0	0	0	0	0	.571	1.000
Howard Ehmke	.333	6	2	2	1	0	0	0	0	2	0	0	0	1	.333	.500
Walter Johnson	.250	12	0	3	2	0	0	3	0	4	0	0	0	1	.250	.417

Hit Worst Against

	Avg	AB	R	H	2B	3B	HR	RBI	BB	SO	HBP	GDP	SB	CS	OBP	Slg
Alex Ferguson	.143	7	1	1	1	0	0	0	0	0	0	0	0	0	.143	.286
G. Earnshaw	.167	6	0	1	0	0	0	2	1	3	0	0	0	0	.286	.167
Red Ruffing	.200	5	1	1	0	0	0	0	0	2	0	0	1	0	.200	.200

Al Dark

Bats: Right, Throws: Right

Batting	Avg	G	AB	R	H	2B	3B	HR	RBI	BB	SO	HBP	GDP	SB	CS	OBP	Slg
Totals	.323	16	65	9	21	4	0	1	4	3	6	0	2	0	0	.353	.431
Home	.344	8	32	4	11	3	0	0	1	1	1	0	2	0	0	.364	.438
Away	.303	8	33	5	10	1	0	1	3	2	5	0	0	0	0	.343	.424
vs. Left	.273	7	22	0	6	1	0	0	0	0	2	0	1	0	0	.273	.318
vs. Right	.349	16	43	9	15	3	0	1	4	3	4	0	1	0	0	.391	.488
Scoring Pos.	.333	9	9	0	3	0	0	1	4	0	1	0	1	0	0	.333	.667
Close & Late	.143	6	7	0	1	0	0	0	0	0	1	0	1	0	0	.143	.143
None on/out	.429	10	14	0	6	1	0	0	0	0	2	0	0	0	0	.429	.500
None on	.304	16	46	0	14	4	0	0	0	3	4	0	0	0	0	.347	.391
Runners on	.368	13	19	0	7	0	0	1	4	0	2	0	2	0	0	.368	.526
Batting #2	.323	16	65	9	21	4	0	1	4	3	6	0	2	0	0	.353	.431

Hit Best Against

	Avg	AB	R	H	2B	3B	HR	RBI	BB	SO	HBP	GDP	SB	CS	OBP	Slg
Allie Reynolds	.500	8	2	4	3	0	1	3	0	1	0	1	0	0	.500	1.250
Bob Lemon	.400	15	3	6	0	0	0	0	1	1	0	1	0	0	.438	.400
Ed Lopat	.375	8	1	3	0	0	0	0	0	0	0	0	0	0	.375	.375

Hit Worst Against

	Avg	AB	R	H	2B	3B	HR	RBI	BB	SO	HBP	GDP	SB	CS	OBP	Slg
Bob Feller	.143	7	1	1	0	0	0	0	0	0	0	0	0	0	.143	.143

Andre Dawson

Bats: Right, Throws: Right

Batting	Avg	G	AB	R	H	2B	3B	HR	RBI	BB	SO	HBP	GDP	SB	CS	OBP	Slg
Totals	.186	15	59	3	11	1	1	0	3	3	16	1	3	2	0	.238	.237
Home	.185	7	27	1	5	0	1	0	0	2	9	0	1	1	0	.241	.259
Away	.188	8	32	2	6	1	0	0	3	1	7	1	2	1	0	.235	.219
vs. Left	.263	8	19	0	5	0	1	0	0	1	5	0	1	0	0	.300	.368
vs. Right	.150	15	40	3	6	1	0	0	3	2	11	1	2	2	0	.209	.175
Scoring Pos.	.211	12	19	0	4	1	0	0	3	2	7	0	1	0	0	.286	.263
Close & Late	.100	8	10	0	1	0	0	0	0	0	1	0	1	0	0	.100	.100
None on/out	.375	7	8	0	3	0	1	0	0	0	2	0	0	0	0	.375	.625
None on	.250	13	28	0	7	0	1	0	0	1	7	1	0	0	0	.300	.321
Runners on	.129	13	31	0	4	1	0	0	3	2	9	0	3	2	0	.182	.161
Batting #3	.225	10	40	3	9	0	1	0	0	1	10	0	2	2	0	.244	.275
Batting #5	.105	5	19	0	2	1	0	0	3	2	6	1	1	0	0	.227	.158

Hit Best Against

	Avg	AB	R	H	2B	3B	HR	RBI	BB	SO	HBP	GDP	SB	CS	OBP	Slg
Steve Carlton	.286	7	1	2	0	1	0	0	0	4	0	0	0	0	.286	.571

Hit Worst Against

	Avg	AB	R	H	2B	3B	HR	RBI	BB	SO	HBP	GDP	SB	CS	OBP	Slg
Burt Hooton	.000	7	0	0	0	0	0	0	0	3	0	1	0	0	.000	.000
F. Valenzuela	.143	7	1	1	0	0	0	0	0	1	0	1	0	0	.143	.143
Scott Garrelts	.200	5	0	1	1	0	0	1	1	0	0	0	0	0	.333	.400

Ken Dayley

Throws: Left, Bats: Left

Pitching	ERA	W	L	Sv	G	GS	IP	BB	SO	Avg	R	H	2B	3B	HR	OBP	Slg
Totals	0.44	1	0	5	16	0	20.2	6	15	.092	1	6	1	0	1	.181	.154
Home	0.00	0	0	4	7	0	10.2	3	7	.118	0	4	0	0	0	.189	.118
Away	0.90	1	0	1	9	0	10.0	3	8	.065	1	2	1	0	1	.147	.194

	Avg	AB	R	H	2B	3B	HR	RBI	BB	SO	HBP	GDP	OBP	Slg
vs. Left	.077	13	0	1	0	0	0	0	3	3	0	0	.250	.077
vs. Right	.096	52	1	5	1	0	1	4	3	12	1	0	.161	.173
Scoring Pos.	.083	12	0	1	0	0	1	4	0	2	0	0	.083	.333
Close & Late	.083	12	0	1	0	0	0	0	1	2	0	0	.154	.083
None on/out	.063	16	0	1	0	0	0	0	1	5	1	0	.167	.063
None on	.095	42	0	4	1	0	0	0	5	12	1	0	.208	.119
Runners on	.087	23	0	2	0	0	1	4	1	3	0	0	.125	.217

Dizzy Dean

Throws: Right, Bats: Right

Pitching	ERA	W	L	Sv	G	GS	IP	BB	SO	Avg	R	H	2B	3B	HR	OBP	Slg
Totals	2.88	2	2	0	5	4	34.1	6	19	.217	12	28	6	0	4	.257	.357
Home	4.50	0	2	0	2	2	16.0	4	8	.220	9	13	3	0	3	.281	.424
Away	1.47	2	0	0	3	2	18.1	2	11	.214	3	15	3	0	1	.236	.300

	Avg	AB	R	H	2B	3B	HR	RBI	BB	SO	HBP	GDP	OBP	Slg
vs. Left	.227	75	0	17	1	0	1	3	5	6	1	0	.284	.280
vs. Right	.204	54	12	11	5	0	3	11	1	13	0	0	.218	.463
Scoring Pos.	.200	25	0	5	2	0	0	7	0	8	0	0	.200	.280
Close & Late	.250	16	2	4	0	0	2	4	0	4	0	0	.250	.625
None on/out	.294	34	0	10	2	0	1	1	2	2	0	0	.333	.441
None on	.208	77	0	16	2	0	2	2	5	8	1	0	.265	.312
Runners on	.231	52	0	12	4	0	2	12	1	11	0	0	.245	.423

Pitched Best Against

	Avg	AB	R	H	2B	3B	HR	RBI	BB	SO	HBP	GDP	SB	CS	OBP	Slg
Marv Owen	.000	11	0	0	0	0	0	0	0	3	0	0	0	0	.000	.000
Red Rolfe	.000	5	0	0	0	0	0	0	0	2	0	0	0	0	.000	.000
Jo-Jo White	.000	7	1	0	0	0	0	0	4	2	1	0	0	0	.417	.000

Pitched Worst Against

	Avg	AB	R	H	2B	3B	HR	RBI	BB	SO	HBP	GDP	SB	CS	OBP	Slg
C. Gehringer	.417	12	1	5	0	0	1	2	0	0	0	0	0	0	.417	.667
Frankie Crosetti	.400	5	1	2	1	0	1	4	0	0	0	0	0	0	.400	1.200
Billy Rogell	.333	12	1	4	0	0	0	0	0	2	0	0	1	0	.333	.333

Bucky Dent

Bats: Right, Throws: Right

Batting	Avg	G	AB	R	H	2B	3B	HR	RBI	BB	SO	HBP	GDP	SB	CS	OBP	Slg
Totals	.277	24	83	4	23	2	0	0	15	4	4	0	2	0	0	.310	.301
Home	.243	11	37	3	9	1	0	0	3	3	2	0	1	0	0	.300	.270
Away	.304	13	46	1	14	1	0	0	12	1	2	0	1	0	0	.319	.326
vs. Left	.316	16	38	0	12	1	0	0	7	1	0	0	2	0	0	.333	.342
vs. Right	.244	24	45	4	11	1	0	0	8	3	4	0	0	0	0	.292	.267
Scoring Pos.	.385	17	26	0	10	1	0	0	14	2	3	0	1	0	0	.429	.423
Close & Late	.357	10	14	1	5	0	0	0	6	0	0	0	0	0	0	.357	.357
None on/out	.273	11	11	0	3	0	0	0	0	1	0	0	0	0	0	.333	.273
None on	.190	23	42	0	8	0	0	0	0	2	0	0	0	0	0	.227	.190
Runners on	.366	19	41	0	15	2	0	0	15	2	4	0	2	0	0	.395	.415
Batting #8	.227	7	22	0	5	0	0	0	2	2	2	0	0	0	0	.292	.227
Batting #9	.302	15	53	4	16	2	0	0	13	2	2	0	1	0	0	.327	.340

Hit Best Against

	Avg	AB	R	H	2B	3B	HR	RBI	BB	SO	HBP	GDP	SB	CS	OBP	Slg
Larry Gura	.500	8	1	4	1	0	0	3	0	0	0	1	0	0	.500	.625
Don Sutton	.417	12	1	5	0	0	0	4	0	0	0	0	0	0	.417	.417
Charlie Hough	.400	5	0	2	1	0	0	1	0	1	0	0	0	0	.400	.600

Hit Worst Against

	Avg	AB	R	H	2B	3B	HR	RBI	BB	SO	HBP	GDP	SB	CS	OBP	Slg
Paul Splittorff	.083	12	0	1	0	0	0	0	0	0	0	1	0	0	.083	.083
Dennis Leonard	.100	10	0	1	0	0	0	1	0	1	0	0	0	0	.100	.100
Burt Hooton	.167	6	1	1	0	0	0	0	1	2	0	0	0	0	.286	.167

Paul Derringer

Throws: Right, Bats: Right

Pitching	ERA	W	L	Sv	G	GS	IP	BB	SO	Avg	R	H	2B	3B	HR	OBP	Slg
Totals	3.42	2	4	0	11	7	52.2	27	30	.227	26	45	7	2	3	.320	.328
Home	4.19	1	3	0	8	5	34.1	20	18	.256	22	34	5	0	3	.353	.361
Away	1.96	1	1	0	3	2	18.1	7	12	.169	4	11	2	2	0	.250	.262

	Avg	AB	R	H	2B	3B	HR	RBI	BB	SO	HBP	GDP	OBP	Slg
vs. Left	.202	89	0	18	2	1	2	7	14	14	0	2	.311	.315
vs. Right	.243	111	26	27	5	1	1	22	13	16	0	2	.323	.333
Scoring Pos.	.302	43	0	13	3	0	0	23	19	5	0	2	.516	.372
Close & Late	.200	20	3	4	0	1	2	3	1	3	0	2	.238	.600
None on/out	.189	53	0	10	1	0	1	1	1	8	0	2	.204	.264
None on	.195	123	0	24	3	1	2	2	6	21	0	2	.233	.285
Runners on	.273	77	0	21	4	1	1	27	21	9	0	2	.429	.390

Pitched Best Against

	Avg	AB	R	H	2B	3B	HR	RBI	BB	SO	HBP	GDP	SB	CS	OBP	Slg
Frankie Crosetti	.000	7	0	0	0	0	0	0	0	1	0	0	0	0	.000	.000
Red Rolfe	.000	7	0	0	0	0	0	0	0	0	0	0	0	0	.000	.000
Bing Miller	.000	6	0	0	0	0	0	0	0	2	0	0	0	0	.000	.000

Pitched Worst Against

	Avg	AB	R	H	2B	3B	HR	RBI	BB	SO	HBP	GDP	SB	CS	OBP	Slg
Hank Greenberg	.500	10	2	5	2	0	0	1	2	1	0	0	0	0	.583	.700
M. Cochrane	.500	6	2	3	0	0	0	1	1	0	0	0	0	0	.571	.500
Jimmie Foxx	.500	6	1	3	0	0	0	2	0	1	0	0	0	0	.500	.500

Bill Dickey

Bats: Left, Throws: Right

Batting	Avg	G	AB	R	H	2B	3B	HR	RBI	BB	SO	HBP	GDP	SB	CS	OBP	Slg
Totals	.255	38	145	19	37	1	1	5	24	15	12	1	4	1	1	.329	.379
Home	.250	19	68	3	17	1	0	1	11	5	7	1	1	0	1	.311	.309
Away	.260	19	77	16	20	0	1	4	13	10	5	0	3	1	0	.345	.442
vs. Left	.205	20	44	0	9	0	0	1	5	2	5	0	2	0	0	.239	.273
vs. Right	.277	38	101	19	28	1	1	4	19	13	7	1	2	1	1	.365	.426
Scoring Pos.	.318	30	44	0	14	0	1	1	18	6	5	1	2	0	0	.412	.432
Close & Late	.188	15	16	3	3	0	0	1	3	3	0	0	0	0	0	.316	.375
None on/out	.160	22	25	0	4	0	0	1	1	4	3	0	0	0	0	.276	.280
None on	.192	36	78	0	15	0	0	3	3	5	6	0	0	0	0	.241	.308
Runners on	.328	36	67	0	22	1	1	2	21	10	6	1	4	1	1	.423	.463
Batting #5	.182	17	66	11	12	0	1	4	15	7	9	0	1	0	0	.260	.394
Batting #6	.333	16	60	7	20	1	0	1	9	7	3	1	3	1	1	.412	.400
Batting #7	.263	5	19	1	5	0	0	0	0	1	0	0	0	0	0	.300	.263

Hit Best Against

	Avg	AB	R	H	2B	3B	HR	RBI	BB	SO	HBP	GDP	SB	CS	OBP	Slg
Bill Lee	.800	5	1	4	0	0	0	1	0	0	0	0	1	0	.800	.800
Lon Warneke	.600	5	0	3	0	0	0	2	1	0	0	1	0	1	.667	.600
Paul Derringer	.286	7	1	2	0	0	1	2	0	1	0	0	0	0	.286	.714

Hit Worst Against

	Avg	AB	R	H	2B	3B	HR	RBI	BB	SO	HBP	GDP	SB	CS	OBP	Slg
F. Fitzsimmons	.000	7	0	0	0	0	0	0	1	0	0	0	0	0	.125	.000
Carl Hubbell	.071	14	1	1	0	0	0	1	0	2	0	0	0	0	.071	.071
Whit Wyatt	.125	8	1	1	0	0	0	0	0	1	0	0	0	0	.125	.125

Joe DiMaggio

Bats: Right, Throws: Right

Batting	Avg	G	AB	R	H	2B	3B	HR	RBI	BB	SO	HBP	GDP	SB	CS	OBP	Slg
Totals	.271	51	199	27	54	6	0	8	30	19	23	1	7	0	0	.336	.422
Home	.233	25	90	7	21	4	0	0	4	9	10	1	4	0	0	.310	.278
Away	.303	26	109	20	33	2	0	8	26	10	13	0	3	0	0	.358	.541
vs. Left	.275	21	51	0	14	0	0	2	7	5	5	0	1	0	0	.339	.392
vs. Right	.270	51	148	27	40	6	0	6	23	14	18	1	6	0	0	.335	.432
Scoring Pos.	.255	40	55	0	14	2	0	0	18	10	8	0	6	0	0	.364	.291
Close & Late	.385	25	26	4	10	1	0	2	6	4	0	0	2	0	0	.467	.654
None on/out	.255	32	47	0	12	1	0	1	1	3	6	1	0	0	0	.314	.340
None on	.299	49	97	0	29	4	0	4	4	5	10	1	0	0	0	.340	.464
Runners on	.245	48	102	0	25	2	0	4	26	14	13	0	7	0	0	.333	.382
Batting #3	.313	11	48	5	15	3	0	1	7	1	6	0	1	0	0	.320	.438
Batting #4	.258	40	151	22	39	3	0	7	23	18	17	1	6	0	0	.341	.417

Hit Best Against

	Avg	AB	R	H	2B	3B	HR	RBI	BB	SO	HBP	GDP	SB	CS	OBP	Slg
Hugh Casey	.500	6	1	3	0	0	0	1	0	0	0	2	0	0	.500	.500
Bucky Walters	.500	6	2	3	0	0	0	1	0	0	0	1	0	0	.500	.500
Mort Cooper	.429	7	2	3	0	0	0	1	0	0	0	0	0	0	.429	.429

Hit Worst Against

	Avg	AB	R	H	2B	3B	HR	RBI	BB	SO	HBP	GDP	SB	CS	OBP	Slg
Bill Lee	.000	6	0	0	0	0	0	0	0	1	0	0	0	0	.000	.000
Hal Gregg	.000	5	0	0	0	0	0	0	1	1	0	0	0	0	.167	.000
Dave Koslo	.000	5	1	0	0	0	0	0	2	0	0	0	0	0	.286	.000

Wild Bill Donovan

Throws: Right, Bats: Right

Pitching	ERA	W	L	Sv	G	GS	IP	BB	SO	Avg	R	H	2B	3B	HR	OBP	Slg
Totals	2.88	1	4	0	6	6	50.0	17	33	.240	21	41	6	1	1	.321	.304
Home	3.00	0	3	0	3	3	21.0	11	7	.284	10	19	2	0	0	.395	.313
Away	2.79	1	1	0	3	3	29.0	6	26	.212	11	22	4	1	1	.268	.298

	Avg	AB	R	H	2B	3B	HR	RBI	BB	SO	HBP	GDP	OBP	Slg
vs. Left	.257	70	0	18	1	1	0	10	4	5	1	2	.303	.300
vs. Right	.223	103	21	23	5	0	1	8	13	27	3	2	.328	.301
Scoring Pos.	.235	51	0	12	2	1	0	15	6	11	0	2	.310	.314
Close & Late	.219	32	3	7	0	0	1	4	1	6	2	2	.286	.313
None on/out	.178	45	0	8	1	0	0	0	4	8	1	2	.260	.200
None on	.237	97	0	23	2	0	0	0	10	18	3	2	.327	.258
Runners on	.237	76	0	18	4	1	1	18	7	14	1	2	.306	.355

Pitched Best Against

	Avg	AB	R	H	2B	3B	HR	RBI	BB	SO	HBP	GDP	SB	CS	OBP	Slg
Chief Wilson	.000	6	1	0	0	0	0	0	0	0	0	0	0	0	.000	.000
Solly Hofman	.143	7	1	1	0	0	0	0	0	3	0	0	0	0	.143	.143
Joe Tinker	.182	11	3	2	0	0	1	2	1	3	0	0	0	0	.250	.455

Pitched Worst Against

	Avg	AB	R	H	2B	3B	HR	RBI	BB	SO	HBP	GDP	SB	CS	OBP	Slg
Bill Abstein	.400	5	1	2	1	0	0	0	1	3	0	0	0	1	.500	.600
Johnny Evers	.375	16	3	6	1	0	0	2	0	1	0	0	2	2	.375	.438
Dots Miller	.333	6	0	2	1	0	0	1	0	1	0	0	0	0	.333	.500

Doug Drabek

Throws: Right, Bats: Right

Pitching	ERA	W	L	Sv	G	GS	IP	BB	SO	Avg	R	H	2B	3B	HR	OBP	Slg
Totals	2.05	2	5	0	7	7	48.1	14	33	.225	16	40	12	0	1	.284	.309
Home	1.63	2	2	0	4	4	27.2	8	16	.238	7	24	5	0	0	.291	.287
Away	2.61	0	3	0	3	3	20.2	6	17	.208	9	16	7	0	1	.274	.338

	Avg	AB	R	H	2B	3B	HR	RBI	BB	SO	HBP	GDP	OBP	Slg
vs. Left	.239	109	0	26	7	0	0	7	9	17	1	0	.300	.303
vs. Right	.203	69	0	14	5	0	1	4	5	16	0	0	.257	.319
Scoring Pos.	.222	45	15	10	3	0	0	9	5	8	0	0	.294	.289
Close & Late	.270	37	5	10	6	0	0	2	4	10	0	0	.341	.432
None on/out	.255	47	0	12	5	0	0	0	3	11	1	0	.314	.362
None on	.236	106	1	25	8	0	1	1	8	21	1	0	.296	.340
Runners on	.208	72	15	15	4	0	0	10	6	12	0	0	.266	.264

Pitched Best Against

	Avg	AB	R	H	2B	3B	HR	RBI	BB	SO	HBP	GDP	SB	CS	OBP	Slg
Joe Oliver	.000	5	0	0	0	0	0	0	0	1	0	0	0	0	.000	.000
Terry Pendleton	.063	16	1	1	1	0	0	0	1	3	0	0	0	0	.118	.125
Eric Davis	.125	8	0	1	0	0	0	0	0	5	0	0	0	0	.125	.125

Pitched Worst Against

	Avg	AB	R	H	2B	3B	HR	RBI	BB	SO	HBP	GDP	SB	CS	OBP	Slg
Barry Larkin	.429	7	2	3	2	0	0	1	1	0	0	1	1	0	.500	.714
Otis Nixon	.400	10	1	4	0	0	0	1	0	0	0	0	1	0	.400	.400
Paul O'Neill	.375	8	0	3	1	0	0	2	0	1	0	0	1	0	.375	.500

Dave Dravecky

Throws: Left, Bats: Right

Pitching	ERA	W	L	Sv	G	GS	IP	BB	SO	Avg	R	H	2B	3B	HR	OBP	Slg
Totals	0.35	1	1	0	7	2	25.2	5	24	.146	1	12	1	1	0	.193	.183
Home	0.00	0	0	0	3	0	5.1	0	5	.059	0	1	0	0	0	.059	.059
Away	0.44	1	1	0	4	2	20.1	5	19	.169	1	11	1	1	0	.225	.215

	Avg	AB	R	H	2B	3B	HR	RBI	BB	SO	HBP	GDP	OBP	Slg
vs. Left	.077	13	0	1	1	0	0	0	0	10	0	3	.077	.154
vs. Right	.159	69	1	11	0	1	0	1	5	14	0	3	.213	.188
Scoring Pos.	.083	12	0	1	0	0	0	1	0	4	0	3	.077	.083
Close & Late	.000	9	0	0	0	0	0	0	0	2	0	3	.000	.000
None on/out	.143	21	0	3	1	1	0	0	4	5	0	3	.280	.286
None on	.153	59	0	9	1	1	0	0	5	18	0	3	.219	.203
Runners on	.130	23	0	3	0	0	0	1	0	6	0	3	.125	.130

Pitched Best Against

	Avg	AB	R	H	2B	3B	HR	RBI	BB	SO	HBP	GDP	SB	CS	OBP	Slg
Terry Pendleton	.000	6	0	0	0	0	0	0	0	3	0	0	0	0	.000	.000
Vince Coleman	.000	6	0	0	0	0	0	0	1	2	0	0	0	0	.143	.000
Ozzie Smith	.000	6	0	0	0	0	0	0	1	1	0	1	0	0	.143	.000

Pitched Worst Against

	Avg	AB	R	H	2B	3B	HR	RBI	BB	SO	HBP	GDP	SB	CS	OBP	Slg
Jim Lindeman	.500	6	0	3	0	0	0	0	0	0	0	0	0	0	.500	.500
Tom Herr	.429	7	0	3	0	0	0	0	0	0	0	0	0	0	.429	.429

Don Drysdale

Throws: Right, Bats: Right

Pitching	ERA	W	L	Sv	G	GS	IP	BB	SO	Avg	R	H	2B	3B	HR	OBP	Slg
Totals	2.95	3	3	0	7	6	39.2	12	36	.247	17	36	2	0	8	.308	.425
Home	2.33	3	1	0	4	4	27.0	9	26	.237	7	23	0	0	4	.308	.361
Away	4.26	0	2	0	3	2	12.2	3	10	.265	10	13	2	0	4	.308	.551

	Avg	AB	R	H	2B	3B	HR	RBI	BB	SO	HBP	GDP	OBP	Slg
vs. Left	.214	70	0	15	1	0	2	3	7	15	1	1	.295	.314
vs. Right	.273	77	17	21	1	0	6	13	5	21	0	1	.317	.519
Scoring Pos.	.238	21	0	5	0	0	1	7	3	6	0	1	.333	.381
Close & Late	.222	18	0	4	0	0	0	0	0	5	0	1	.222	.222
None on/out	.175	40	0	7	2	0	0	0	2	11	0	1	.214	.225
None on	.240	104	0	25	2	0	5	5	7	21	0	1	.288	.404
Runners on	.256	43	0	11	0	0	3	11	5	15	1	1	.347	.465

Pitched Best Against

	Avg	AB	R	H	2B	3B	HR	RBI	BB	SO	HBP	GDP	SB	CS	OBP	Slg
Jimmie Hall	.000	6	0	0	0	0	0	0	0	5	0	0	0	0	.000	.000
Tony Oliva	.167	6	1	1	0	0	1	1	0	0	0	0	0	0	.167	.667
Don Mincher	.200	5	2	1	0	0	1	1	1	3	0	0	0	0	.333	.800

Pitched Worst Against

	Avg	AB	R	H	2B	3B	HR	RBI	BB	SO	HBP	GDP	SB	CS	OBP	Slg
Frank Robinson	.400	5	2	2	0	0	2	3	0	1	0	0	0	0	.400	1.600
Frank Quilici	.400	5	1	2	1	0	0	1	0	0	0	0	0	0	.400	.600
Luis Aparicio	.375	8	0	3	0	0	0	0	1	1	0	0	0	2	.444	.375

Lenny Dykstra

Bats: Left, Throws: Left

Batting	Avg	G	AB	R	H	2B	3B	HR	RBI	BB	SO	HBP	GDP	SB	CS	OBP	Slg
Totals	.321	32	112	27	36	6	1	10	19	20	23	2	0	5	0	.433	.661
Home	.255	16	51	14	13	3	0	5	10	10	17	0	0	2	0	.377	.608
Away	.377	16	61	13	23	3	1	5	9	10	6	2	0	3	0	.479	.705
vs. Left	.345	12	29	4	10	2	1	2	4	3	7	0	0	1	0	.406	.690
vs. Right	.313	32	83	23	26	4	0	8	15	17	16	2	0	4	0	.441	.651
Scoring Pos.	.400	22	15	10	6	0	0	4	11	5	4	1	0	0	0	.571	1.200
Close & Late	.333	14	15	5	5	0	0	3	6	4	3	0	0	1	0	.474	.933
None on/out	.259	29	54	1	14	4	1	2	2	8	10	0	0	0	0	.355	.481
None on	.238	30	80	3	19	6	1	4	4	15	17	1	0	0	0	.365	.488
Runners on	.531	27	32	11	17	0	0	6	15	5	6	1	0	5	0	.605	1.094
Batting #1	.320	25	100	23	32	6	0	9	16	16	20	2	0	5	0	.424	.650

Hit Best Against

	Avg	AB	R	H	2B	3B	HR	RBI	BB	SO	HBP	GDP	SB	CS	OBP	Slg
Tim Belcher	.500	6	3	3	2	0	1	3	2	0	0	0	0	0	.625	1.333
Mike Scott	.286	7	0	2	0	0	0	0	1	1	0	0	1	0	.375	.286

Hit Worst Against

	Avg	AB	R	H	2B	3B	HR	RBI	BB	SO	HBP	GDP	SB	CS	OBP	Slg
Roger Clemens	.000	5	0	0	0	0	0	0	0	3	0	0	0	0	.000	.000
Bruce Hurst	.125	8	0	1	0	0	0	0	1	4	0	0	0	0	.222	.125
Nolan Ryan	.143	7	1	1	0	0	0	0	0	2	0	0	0	0	.143	.143

George Earnshaw

Throws: Right, Bats: Right

Pitching	ERA	W	L	Sv	G	GS	IP	BB	SO	Avg	R	H	2B	3B	HR	OBP	Slg
Totals	1.58	3	3	0	8	8	62.2	17	56	.174	14	39	12	1	2	.232	.263
Home	0.75	3	1	0	4	4	36.0	7	32	.150	5	19	7	1	1	.194	.244
Away	2.70	0	2	0	4	4	26.2	10	24	.206	9	20	5	0	1	.280	.289

	Avg	AB	R	H	2B	3B	HR	RBI	BB	SO	HBP	GDP	OBP	Slg
vs. Left	.145	62	0	9	3	0	0	1	4	17	0	1	.197	.194
vs. Right	.184	163	14	30	9	1	2	11	13	39	0	1	.244	.288
Scoring Pos.	.136	44	0	6	1	0	0	9	7	12	0	1	.255	.159
Close & Late	.167	18	1	3	2	0	0	2	4	3	0	1	.318	.278
None on/out	.153	59	0	9	2	1	0	0	5	11	0	1	.219	.220
None on	.196	148	0	29	11	1	1	1	8	34	0	1	.237	.304
Runners on	.130	77	0	10	1	0	1	11	9	22	0	1	.221	.182

Pitched Best Against

	Avg	AB	R	H	2B	3B	HR	RBI	BB	SO	HBP	GDP	SB	CS	OBP	Slg
Taylor Douthit	.000	11	0	0	0	0	0	0	0	1	0	0	0	0	.000	.000
Jake Flowers	.000	5	0	0	0	0	0	0	0	0	0	0	0	0	.000	.000
Jim Bottomley	.000	18	0	0	0	0	0	0	3	9	0	0	0	0	.143	.000

Pitched Worst Against

	Avg	AB	R	H	2B	3B	HR	RBI	BB	SO	HBP	GDP	SB	CS	OBP	Slg
Pepper Martin	.500	8	2	4	2	0	0	0	1	1	0	0	4	0	.556	.750
Rogers Hornsby	.429	7	2	3	1	0	0	1	0	4	0	0	0	0	.429	.571
Andy High	.375	8	3	3	0	0	0	0	0	0	0	0	0	0	.375	.375

Dennis Eckersley

Throws: Right, Bats: Right

Pitching	ERA	W	L	Sv	G	GS	IP	BB	SO	Avg	R	H	2B	3B	HR	OBP	Slg
Totals	2.83	1	3	15	27	1	35.0	3	21	.256	11	34	5	0	2	.270	.338
Home	1.17	1	0	7	13	0	15.1	1	11	.228	2	13	1	0	1	.241	.298
Away	4.12	0	3	8	14	1	19.2	2	10	.276	9	21	4	0	1	.291	.368

	Avg	AB	R	H	2B	3B	HR	RBI	BB	SO	HBP	GDP	OBP	Slg
vs. Left	.306	62	0	19	2	0	2	12	3	6	0	1	.338	.435
vs. Right	.211	71	6	15	3	0	0	4	0	15	0	1	.208	.254
Scoring Pos.	.303	33	5	10	1	0	2	15	1	7	0	1	.314	.515
Close & Late	.297	64	5	19	1	0	2	12	2	11	0	1	.313	.406
None on/out	.233	30	0	7	1	0	0	0	1	4	0	1	.258	.267
None on	.244	78	0	19	4	0	0	0	2	12	0	1	.263	.295
Runners on	.273	55	5	15	1	0	2	16	1	9	0	1	.281	.400

Pitched Best Against

	Avg	AB	R	H	2B	3B	HR	RBI	BB	SO	HBP	GDP	SB	CS	OBP	Slg
Kelly Gruber	.200	5	0	1	0	0	0	1	0	0	0	0	0	0	.167	.200

Pitched Worst Against

	Avg	AB	R	H	2B	3B	HR	RBI	BB	SO	HBP	GDP	SB	CS	OBP	Slg
Tony Gwynn	.600	5	1	3	1	0	0	0	0	0	0	0	0	0	.600	.800

Dwight Evans

Bats: Right, Throws: Right

Batting	Avg	G	AB	R	H	2B	3B	HR	RBI	BB	SO	HBP	GDP	SB	CS	OBP	Slg
Totals	.239	32	113	11	27	7	1	4	19	15	20	1	1	0	1	.333	.425
Home	.200	17	60	6	12	5	0	1	7	7	13	1	0	0	1	.294	.333
Away	.283	15	53	5	15	2	1	3	12	8	7	0	1	0	0	.377	.528
vs. Left	.207	14	29	0	6	2	1	0	4	4	3	0	1	0	0	.303	.345
vs. Right	.250	32	84	11	21	5	0	4	15	11	17	1	0	0	1	.344	.452
Scoring Pos.	.281	23	32	0	9	3	1	0	13	7	7	0	1	0	1	.410	.438
Close & Late	.263	19	19	1	5	1	0	1	8	3	3	0	0	0	0	.364	.474
None on/out	.222	17	27	0	6	2	0	1	1	1	6	0	0	0	0	.250	.407
None on	.177	31	62	0	11	4	0	2	2	6	11	1	0	0	0	.261	.339
Runners on	.314	27	51	0	16	3	1	2	17	9	9	0	1	0	1	.417	.529
Batting #5	.333	4	15	3	5	2	0	2	7	3	2	0	1	0	0	.444	.867
Batting #6	.228	16	57	3	13	2	0	1	7	7	9	0	0	0	0	.313	.316
Batting #7	.233	9	30	3	7	2	1	1	5	4	6	1	0	0	1	.343	.467

Hit Best Against

	Avg	AB	R	H	2B	3B	HR	RBI	BB	SO	HBP	GDP	SB	CS	OBP	Slg
Dwight Gooden	.600	5	1	3	0	0	1	3	1	1	0	0	0	0	.667	1.200
Kirk McCaskill	.333	6	0	2	1	0	0	3	0	0	0	0	0	0	.333	.500
Don Gullett	.286	7	1	2	0	0	0	1	1	0	0	0	0	0	.375	.286

Hit Worst Against

	Avg	AB	R	H	2B	3B	HR	RBI	BB	SO	HBP	GDP	SB	CS	OBP	Slg
Mike Witt	.000	8	0	0	0	0	0	0	0	2	0	0	0	0	.000	.000
Dave Stewart	.091	11	0	1	1	0	0	0	1	4	0	0	0	0	.167	.182
Ron Darling	.143	7	1	1	0	0	1	1	1	0	0	0	0	0	.250	.571

Johnny Evers

Bats: Left, Throws: Right

Batting	Avg	G	AB	R	H	2B	3B	HR	RBI	BB	SO	HBP	GDP	SB	CS	OBP	Slg
Totals	.316	20	76	11	24	4	0	0	6	4	8	0	0	8	5	.350	.368
Home	.333	10	36	3	12	2	0	0	4	3	4	0	0	5	2	.385	.389
Away	.300	10	40	8	12	2	0	0	2	1	4	0	0	3	3	.317	.350
vs. Left	.348	9	23	0	8	3	0	0	2	1	3	0	0	0	2	.375	.478
vs. Right	.302	20	53	11	16	1	0	0	4	3	5	0	0	8	3	.339	.321
Scoring Pos.	.462	13	13	0	6	2	0	0	6	2	1	0	0	4	2	.533	.615
Close & Late	.333	6	9	0	3	0	0	0	1	1	0	0	0	0	2	.400	.333
None on/out	.111	14	18	0	2	0	0	0	0	1	2	0	0	0	0	.158	.111
None on	.224	19	49	0	11	1	0	0	0	2	6	0	0	0	0	.255	.245
Runners on	.481	18	27	0	13	3	0	0	6	2	2	0	0	8	5	.517	.593
Batting #2	.389	9	36	7	14	1	0	0	4	3	4	0	0	3	3	.436	.417
Batting #6	.350	5	20	2	7	2	0	0	1	0	1	0	0	3	1	.350	.450
Batting #7	.150	6	20	2	3	1	0	0	1	1	3	0	0	2	1	.190	.200

Hit Best Against

	Avg	AB	R	H	2B	3B	HR	RBI	BB	SO	HBP	GDP	SB	CS	OBP	Slg
Joe Bush	.600	5	0	3	0	0	0	0	0	0	0	0	1	0	.600	.600
W. Bill Donovan	.375	16	3	6	1	0	0	2	0	1	0	0	2	2	.375	.438

Hit Worst Against

	Avg	AB	R	H	2B	3B	HR	RBI	BB	SO	HBP	GDP	SB	CS	OBP	Slg
Ed Walsh	.000	5	0	0	0	0	0	0	1	2	0	0	0	1	.167	.000
Nick Altrock	.167	6	0	1	0	0	0	1	0	1	0	0	0	1	.167	.167
Ed Summers	.167	6	1	1	0	0	0	0	0	1	0	0	0	0	.167	.167

Red Faber
Throws: Right, Bats: Both

Pitching	ERA	W	L	Sv	G	GS	IP	BB	SO	Avg	R	H	2B	3B	HR	OBP	Slg
Totals	2.33	3	1	0	4	3	27.0	3	9	.221	7	21	1	1	1	.260	.284
Home	1.64	2	0	0	2	1	11.0	1	2	.216	2	8	0	0	0	.237	.216
Away	2.81	1	1	0	2	2	16.0	2	7	.224	5	13	1	1	1	.274	.328

	Avg	AB	R	H	2B	3B	HR	RBI	BB	SO	HBP	GDP	OBP	Slg
vs. Left	.235	34	0	8	1	0	1	1	1	4	2	1	.297	.353
vs. Right	.213	61	7	13	0	1	0	5	2	5	0	1	.238	.246
Scoring Pos.	.211	19	0	4	0	1	0	5	0	1	1	1	.250	.316
Close & Late	.000	12	0	0	0	0	0	0	0	2	0	1	.000	.000
None on/out	.231	26	0	6	0	0	0	0	0	6	1	1	.259	.231
None on	.250	60	0	15	1	0	1	1	2	7	1	1	.286	.317
Runners on	.171	35	0	6	0	1	0	5	1	2	1	1	.216	.229

Pitched Best Against

	Avg	AB	R	H	2B	3B	HR	RBI	BB	SO	HBP	GDP	SB	CS	OBP	Slg
H. Zimmerman	.000	12	0	0	0	0	0	0	0	0	0	0	0	0	.000	.000
Benny Kauff	.083	12	1	1	0	0	1	1	0	1	0	0	0	0	.083	.333
Bill Rariden	.125	8	1	1	0	0	0	1	1	1	0	1	0	0	.222	.125

Pitched Worst Against

	Avg	AB	R	H	2B	3B	HR	RBI	BB	SO	HBP	GDP	SB	CS	OBP	Slg
Dave Robertson	.400	10	2	4	0	0	0	0	0	0	1	0	0	0	.455	.400
Art Fletcher	.333	12	1	4	0	0	0	0	0	0	0	0	0	0	.333	.333
Walter Holke	.300	10	1	3	1	0	0	0	0	2	1	0	0	1	.364	.400

Tony Fernandez
Bats: Both, Throws: Right

Batting	Avg	G	AB	R	H	2B	3B	HR	RBI	BB	SO	HBP	GDP	SB	CS	OBP	Slg
Totals	.327	43	150	13	49	11	0	1	23	10	16	2	3	5	1	.367	.420
Home	.338	23	77	8	26	7	0	0	10	6	9	1	2	3	1	.379	.429
Away	.315	20	73	5	23	4	0	1	13	4	7	1	1	2	0	.354	.411
vs. Left	.400	29	60	2	24	7	0	0	11	3	6	1	2	0	0	.431	.517
vs. Right	.278	37	90	11	25	4	0	1	12	7	10	1	1	5	1	.327	.356
Scoring Pos.	.351	30	37	4	13	3	0	0	21	5	5	2	1	2	0	.417	.432
Close & Late	.333	25	30	3	10	4	0	1	3	2	3	1	1	1	0	.394	.567
None on/out	.310	31	42	0	13	3	0	0	0	1	1	0	0	0	0	.326	.381
None on	.349	40	83	1	29	6	0	1	1	4	7	0	0	0	0	.379	.458
Runners on	.299	38	67	4	20	5	0	0	22	6	9	2	3	5	1	.354	.373
Batting #2	.400	2	10	1	4	0	0	1	3	0	1	0	0	0	0	.400	.700
Batting #5	.350	5	20	6	7	3	0	0	1	1	2	0	0	5	0	.381	.500
Batting #7	.267	13	45	3	12	1	0	0	9	5	8	2	1	0	1	.365	.289
Batting #8	.275	11	40	1	11	4	0	0	6	2	2	0	1	0	0	.295	.375
Batting #9	.333	7	24	2	8	2	0	0	2	1	2	0	1	0	0	.346	.417

Hit Best Against

	Avg	AB	R	H	2B	3B	HR	RBI	BB	SO	HBP	GDP	SB	CS	OBP	Slg
Danny Jackson	.500	6	0	3	0	0	0	0	0	0	0	0	0	0	.500	.500
Andy Benes	.400	5	0	2	1	0	0	0	0	0	0	1	0	0	.400	.600
Jack McDowell	.400	5	0	2	0	0	0	0	0	1	0	0	0	0	.400	.400

Hit Worst Against

	Avg	AB	R	H	2B	3B	HR	RBI	BB	SO	HBP	GDP	SB	CS	OBP	Slg
Curt Schilling	.000	5	0	0	0	0	0	1	1	1	0	0	0	1	.167	.000

Rollie Fingers
Throws: Right, Bats: Right

Pitching	ERA	W	L	Sv	G	GS	IP	BB	SO	Avg	R	H	2B	3B	HR	OBP	Slg
Totals	2.35	4	4	9	30	0	57.1	17	45	.245	20	50	4	1	5	.311	.348
Home	2.30	2	3	3	15	0	31.1	7	25	.243	13	28	3	1	3	.293	.365
Away	2.42	2	1	6	15	0	26.0	10	20	.247	7	22	1	0	2	.333	.326

	Avg	AB	R	H	2B	3B	HR	RBI	BB	SO	HBP	GDP	OBP	Slg
vs. Left	.263	80	0	21	2	1	1	5	9	10	1	2	.344	.350
vs. Right	.234	124	20	29	2	0	4	11	8	34	2	2	.289	.347
Scoring Pos.	.174	69	0	12	0	0	0	10	5	20	1	2	.237	.174
Close & Late	.270	100	8	27	3	1	3	12	5	23	1	2	.308	.410
None on/out	.348	46	0	16	1	0	3	3	4	8	0	2	.400	.565
None on	.313	96	0	30	3	1	5	5	12	17	2	2	.400	.521
Runners on	.185	108	0	20	1	0	0	11	5	27	1	2	.226	.194

Pitched Best Against

	Avg	AB	R	H	2B	3B	HR	RBI	BB	SO	HBP	GDP	SB	CS	OBP	Slg
Denis Menke	.000	6	0	0	0	0	0	0	0	3	0	0	0	0	.000	.000
Wayne Garrett	.000	5	0	0	0	0	0	0	0	2	0	1	0	0	.000	.000
Felix Millan	.000	5	0	0	0	0	0	0	0	0	0	0	0	0	.000	.000

Pitched Worst Against

	Avg	AB	R	H	2B	3B	HR	RBI	BB	SO	HBP	GDP	SB	CS	OBP	Slg
Bud Harrelson	.400	5	1	2	1	0	0	0	1	1	0	0	0	0	.500	.600
B. Robinson	.400	5	0	2	1	0	0	1	0	0	0	0	0	0	.400	.600
Don Hahn	.400	5	0	2	0	0	0	0	0	1	0	0	0	0	.400	.400

Carlton Fisk
Bats: Right, Throws: Right

Batting	Avg	G	AB	R	H	2B	3B	HR	RBI	BB	SO	HBP	GDP	SB	CS	OBP	Slg
Totals	.259	14	54	9	14	2	0	2	6	8	12	0	1	1	0	.355	.407
Home	.267	8	30	6	8	2	0	1	4	5	6	0	0	0	0	.371	.433
Away	.250	6	24	3	6	0	0	1	2	3	6	0	1	1	0	.333	.375
vs. Left	.241	12	29	0	7	2	0	0	0	3	5	0	0	1	0	.313	.310
vs. Right	.280	14	25	9	7	0	0	2	6	5	7	0	1	0	0	.400	.520
Scoring Pos.	.231	11	13	0	3	0	0	0	4	4	4	0	0	1	0	.412	.231
Close & Late	.250	9	8	1	2	0	0	1	2	3	2	0	1	0	0	.455	.625
None on/out	.357	9	14	0	5	1	0	2	2	0	3	0	0	0	0	.357	.857
None on	.259	14	27	0	7	2	0	2	2	3	6	0	0	0	0	.333	.556
Runners on	.259	14	27	0	7	0	0	0	4	5	6	0	1	1	0	.375	.259
Batting #2	.176	4	17	0	3	1	0	0	0	1	3	0	0	0	0	.222	.235
Batting #4	.297	10	37	9	11	1	0	2	6	7	9	0	1	1	0	.409	.486

Hit Worst Against

	Avg	AB	R	H	2B	3B	HR	RBI	BB	SO	HBP	GDP	SB	CS	OBP	Slg
Ken Holtzman	.000	5	1	0	0	0	0	0	0	0	0	0	0	0	.000	.000
Don Gullett	.125	8	0	1	0	0	0	0	1	3	0	0	0	0	.222	.125

Whitey Ford
Throws: Left, Bats: Left

Pitching	ERA	W	L	Sv	G	GS	IP	BB	SO	Avg	R	H	2B	3B	HR	OBP	Slg
Totals	2.71	10	8	0	22	22	146.0	34	94	.240	51	132	20	4	8	.286	.335
Home	1.77	7	2	0	11	11	86.2	22	58	.209	23	66	12	3	4	.262	.304
Away	4.10	3	6	0	11	11	59.1	12	36	.283	28	66	8	1	4	.319	.378

	Avg	AB	R	H	2B	3B	HR	RBI	BB	SO	HBP	GDP	OBP	Slg
vs. Left	.191	136	0	26	6	1	3	15	7	38	0	9	.228	.316
vs. Right	.257	413	51	106	14	3	5	28	27	56	3	9	.305	.341
Scoring Pos.	.255	106	0	27	3	0	4	38	6	20	0	9	.282	.396
Close & Late	.143	42	2	6	2	0	0	4	3	4	1	9	.208	.190
None on/out	.239	142	0	34	6	1	3	3	12	23	0	9	.299	.359
None on	.252	329	0	83	13	4	4	4	19	56	1	9	.295	.353
Runners on	.223	220	0	49	7	0	4	39	15	38	2	9	.273	.309

Pitched Best Against

	Avg	AB	R	H	2B	3B	HR	RBI	BB	SO	HBP	GDP	SB	CS	OBP	Slg
Ed Bailey	.000	6	0	0	0	0	0	0	0	2	0	0	0	0	.000	.000
Vada Pinson	.000	6	0	0	0	0	0	0	0	0	0	0	0	0	.000	.000
Maury Wills	.000	5	0	0	0	0	0	0	1	3	0	0	0	0	.167	.000

Pitched Worst Against

	Avg	AB	R	H	2B	3B	HR	RBI	BB	SO	HBP	GDP	SB	CS	OBP	Slg
Carl Furillo	.563	16	2	9	3	0	1	3	1	2	1	0	0	0	.611	.938
Frank Howard	.500	6	2	3	1	0	1	1	0	0	0	0	0	0	.500	1.167
Jose Pagan	.500	8	0	4	0	0	0	1	0	0	0	0	0	0	.500	.500

George Foster
Bats: Right, Throws: Right

Batting	Avg	G	AB	R	H	2B	3B	HR	RBI	BB	SO	HBP	GDP	SB	CS	OBP	Slg
Totals	.289	23	76	11	22	2	0	3	12	8	13	0	1	2	3	.353	.434
Home	.343	13	35	8	12	0	0	2	5	6	4	0	1	2	1	.429	.514
Away	.244	10	41	3	10	2	0	1	7	2	9	0	0	0	2	.279	.366
vs. Left	.304	10	23	0	7	0	0	2	3	3	4	0	0	1	0	.385	.565
vs. Right	.283	23	53	11	15	2	0	1	9	5	9	0	1	1	3	.339	.377
Scoring Pos.	.250	17	24	0	6	2	0	0	8	2	7	0	0	0	0	.296	.333
Close & Late	.286	12	14	1	4	1	0	0	3	2	2	0	0	0	1	.353	.357
None on/out	.316	14	19	0	6	0	0	1	1	0	3	0	0	0	0	.316	.474
None on	.275	20	40	0	11	0	0	2	2	5	6	0	0	0	0	.356	.425
Runners on	.306	20	36	0	11	2	0	1	10	3	7	0	1	2	3	.350	.444
Batting #4	.200	3	10	1	2	0	0	1	2	4	3	0	0	0	0	.429	.500
Batting #5	.286	10	35	6	10	0	0	2	4	1	7	0	1	1	1	.297	.457
Batting #6	.323	8	31	4	10	2	0	0	6	3	3	0	0	1	2	.382	.387

Hit Best Against

	Avg	AB	R	H	2B	3B	HR	RBI	BB	SO	HBP	GDP	SB	CS	OBP	Slg
Luis Tiant	.417	12	1	5	1	0	0	2	0	0	0	0	0	1	.417	.500
Bill Lee	.333	6	0	2	0	0	0	0	0	1	0	0	0	0	.333	.333

Jimmie Foxx
Bats: Right, Throws: Right

Batting	Avg	G	AB	R	H	2B	3B	HR	RBI	BB	SO	HBP	GDP	SB	CS	OBP	Slg
Totals	.344	18	64	11	22	3	1	4	11	9	10	0	3	0	0	.425	.609
Home	.286	9	28	5	8	2	1	1	3	7	5	0	2	0	0	.429	.536
Away	.389	9	36	6	14	1	0	3	8	2	5	0	1	0	0	.421	.667
vs. Left	.444	4	9	0	4	0	0	0	0	4	0	0	0	0	0	.615	.444
vs. Right	.327	18	55	11	18	3	1	4	11	5	10	0	3	0	0	.383	.636
Scoring Pos.	.267	14	15	0	4	0	0	1	6	4	2	0	0	0	0	.421	.467
Close & Late	.364	9	11	3	4	0	0	2	4	1	1	0	1	0	0	.417	.909
None on/out	.467	12	15	0	7	1	0	0	0	4	1	0	0	0	0	.579	.533
None on	.394	17	33	0	13	2	1	2	2	4	7	0	0	0	0	.459	.697
Runners on	.290	16	31	0	9	1	0	2	9	5	3	0	3	0	0	.389	.516
Batting #5	.344	18	64	11	22	3	1	4	11	9	10	0	3	0	0	.425	.609

Hit Best Against

	Avg	AB	R	H	2B	3B	HR	RBI	BB	SO	HBP	GDP	SB	CS	OBP	Slg
Charlie Root	.500	6	2	3	0	0	1	1	0	0	0	0	0	0	.500	1.000
Paul Derringer	.500	6	1	3	0	0	0	2	0	1	0	0	0	0	.500	.500
W. Bill Hallahan	.444	9	0	4	0	0	0	0	4	0	0	0	0	0	.615	.444

Hit Worst Against

	Avg	AB	R	H	2B	3B	HR	RBI	BB	SO	HBP	GDP	SB	CS	OBP	Slg
Guy Bush	.000	5	0	0	0	0	0	0	0	1	0	0	0	0	.000	.000
Pat Malone	.200	5	1	1	0	0	1	3	1	0	0	2	0	0	.333	.800
Burleigh Grimes	.231	13	2	3	0	1	1	2	2	6	0	0	0	0	.333	.615

Frankie Frisch
Bats: Both, Throws: Right

Batting	Avg	G	AB	R	H	2B	3B	HR	RBI	BB	SO	HBP	GDP	SB	CS	OBP	Slg
Totals	.294	50	197	16	58	10	3	0	9	12	9	1	3	9	3	.335	.376
Home	.354	25	96	10	34	3	2	0	5	6	5	1	3	2	2	.390	.427
Away	.238	25	101	6	24	7	1	0	4	6	4	0	0	7	1	.280	.327
vs. Left	.340	20	50	0	17	3	1	0	1	2	3	0	1	0	0	.365	.440
vs. Right	.279	50	147	16	41	7	2	0	8	10	6	1	2	9	3	.325	.354
Scoring Pos.	.190	32	42	0	8	1	0	0	9	3	2	1	0	2	0	.250	.214
Close & Late	.259	24	27	2	7	1	1	0	0	2	3	0	1	2	0	.310	.370
None on/out	.250	29	36	0	9	0	1	0	0	2	1	0	0	0	0	.289	.306
None on	.313	48	112	0	35	8	3	0	0	5	5	0	0	0	0	.342	.438
Runners on	.271	45	85	0	23	2	0	0	9	7	4	1	3	9	3	.326	.294
Batting #2	.333	7	30	1	10	4	1	0	0	4	1	1	0	1	0	.429	.533
Batting #3	.288	42	163	15	47	6	2	0	9	8	8	0	3	8	3	.318	.350

Hit Best Against

	Avg	AB	R	H	2B	3B	HR	RBI	BB	SO	HBP	GDP	SB	CS	OBP	Slg
Herb Pennock	.625	8	2	5	0	1	0	0	0	0	0	0	0	0	.625	.875
Tom Zachary	.444	9	2	4	2	0	0	0	2	0	0	0	0	0	.545	.667
Bob Shawkey	.417	12	4	5	0	0	0	0	2	1	0	0	2	0	.500	.417

Hit Worst Against

	Avg	AB	R	H	2B	3B	HR	RBI	BB	SO	HBP	GDP	SB	CS	OBP	Slg
Schoolboy Rowe	.111	9	0	1	0	0	0	0	0	0	0	0	0	0	.111	.111
G. Earnshaw	.150	20	0	3	2	0	0	0	1	0	0	0	2	0	.190	.250
G. Mogridge	.167	6	0	1	0	0	0	0	0	0	0	0	0	0	.167	.167

Carl Furillo

Bats: Right, Throws: Right

Batting	Avg	G	AB	R	H	2B	3B	HR	RBI	BB	SO	HBP	GDP	SB	CS	OBP	Slg
Totals	.268	40	127	13	34	9	0	2	13	13	15	1	5	0	0	.338	.386
Home	.221	21	68	7	15	3	0	0	7	6	11	0	3	0	0	.280	.265
Away	.322	19	59	6	19	6	0	2	6	7	4	1	2	0	0	.403	.525
vs. Left	.383	20	47	0	18	6	0	1	4	4	3	1	1	0	0	.442	.574
vs. Right	.200	40	80	13	16	3	0	1	9	9	12	0	4	0	0	.278	.275
Scoring Pos.	.222	23	27	0	6	1	0	0	9	5	2	0	2	0	0	.333	.259
Close & Late	.231	21	26	1	6	0	0	1	6	1	1	0	2	0	0	.259	.346
None on/out	.364	25	33	0	12	4	0	1	1	2	3	0	0	0	0	.400	.576
None on	.274	36	73	0	20	6	0	1	1	7	10	1	0	0	0	.346	.397
Runners on	.259	35	54	0	14	3	0	1	12	6	5	0	5	0	0	.328	.370
Batting #5	.313	10	32	4	10	2	0	1	4	4	5	1	2	0	0	.395	.469
Batting #6	.250	5	16	0	4	2	0	0	3	1	2	0	1	0	0	.294	.375
Batting #7	.275	15	51	7	14	3	0	1	4	4	4	0	2	0	0	.327	.392
Batting #8	.133	6	15	0	2	0	0	0	0	3	3	0	0	0	0	.278	.133

Hit Best Against

	Avg	AB	R	H	2B	3B	HR	RBI	BB	SO	HBP	GDP	SB	CS	OBP	Slg
Whitey Ford	.563	16	2	9	3	0	1	3	1	2	1	0	0	0	.611	.938
Joe Page	.375	8	1	3	1	0	0	1	1	0	0	0	0	0	.444	.500
Ed Lopat	.300	10	2	3	2	0	0	0	0	0	0	1	0	0	.300	.500

Hit Worst Against

	Avg	AB	R	H	2B	3B	HR	RBI	BB	SO	HBP	GDP	SB	CS	OBP	Slg
Bob Turley	.125	8	1	1	0	0	0	0	0	2	0	0	0	0	.125	.125
Tommy Byrne	.143	7	0	1	0	0	0	0	2	0	0	0	0	0	.333	.143
Allie Reynolds	.154	13	1	2	0	0	1	2	3	1	0	0	0	0	.313	.385

Gary Gaetti

Bats: Right, Throws: Right

Batting	Avg	G	AB	R	H	2B	3B	HR	RBI	BB	SO	HBP	GDP	SB	CS	OBP	Slg
Totals	.256	22	82	11	21	3	1	5	16	4	16	2	1	2	0	.303	.500
Home	.333	11	39	9	13	3	0	4	7	4	7	0	0	1	0	.395	.718
Away	.186	11	43	2	8	0	1	1	9	0	9	2	1	1	0	.217	.302
vs. Left	.200	11	25	2	5	1	0	0	2	0	5	1	1	2	0	.222	.240
vs. Right	.281	21	57	9	16	2	1	5	14	4	11	1	0	0	0	.339	.614
Scoring Pos.	.238	16	21	2	5	0	1	2	12	3	3	0	1	0	0	.320	.619
Close & Late	.333	13	12	1	4	0	1	1	8	1	2	1	0	0	0	.429	.750
None on/out	.286	16	21	0	6	0	0	1	1	0	2	1	0	0	0	.318	.429
None on	.260	21	50	0	13	2	0	3	3	0	13	1	0	0	0	.275	.480
Runners on	.250	18	32	2	8	1	1	2	13	4	3	1	1	2	0	.342	.531
Batting #4	.167	6	24	2	4	2	0	0	2	1	2	1	0	2	0	.222	.250
Batting #5	.293	16	58	9	17	1	1	5	14	3	14	1	1	0	0	.339	.603

Hit Best Against

	Avg	AB	R	H	2B	3B	HR	RBI	BB	SO	HBP	GDP	SB	CS	OBP	Slg
John Smoltz	.600	5	0	3	0	0	0	0	1	1	0	0	0	0	.667	.600
Tom Glavine	.400	5	0	2	0	0	0	0	0	1	0	0	0	0	.400	.400
Greg Maddux	.286	7	1	2	0	0	1	4	0	1	0	0	0	0	.286	.714

Hit Worst Against

	Avg	AB	R	H	2B	3B	HR	RBI	BB	SO	HBP	GDP	SB	CS	OBP	Slg
John Tudor	.167	6	1	1	1	0	0	1	0	1	0	0	0	0	.167	.333

Ron Gant

Bats: Right, Throws: Right

Batting	Avg	G	AB	R	H	2B	3B	HR	RBI	BB	SO	HBP	GDP	SB	CS	OBP	Slg
Totals	.230	48	178	28	41	7	1	7	27	15	34	3	5	13	1	.298	.399
Home	.233	24	86	15	20	3	1	5	17	10	17	1	1	7	1	.316	.465
Away	.228	24	92	13	21	4	0	2	10	5	17	2	4	6	0	.280	.337
vs. Left	.289	22	45	9	13	4	0	3	10	6	11	1	3	4	1	.377	.578
vs. Right	.211	44	133	19	28	3	1	4	17	9	23	2	2	9	0	.269	.338
Scoring Pos.	.170	41	47	19	8	3	1	1	19	3	10	1	4	2	0	.226	.340
Close & Late	.171	28	35	5	6	1	0	1	4	3	7	0	2	4	0	.231	.286
None on/out	.258	29	31	2	8	1	0	2	2	1	6	0	0	0	0	.281	.484
None on	.274	47	95	4	26	4	0	4	4	8	16	2	0	0	0	.343	.442
Runners on	.181	47	83	24	15	3	1	3	23	7	18	1	5	13	1	.247	.349
Batting #3	.234	34	137	20	32	6	1	5	19	9	27	3	3	8	1	.293	.401
Batting #5	.364	3	11	1	4	0	0	0	2	1	1	0	0	2	0	.417	.364
Batting #6	.179	9	28	7	5	1	0	2	6	5	6	0	2	2	0	.294	.429

Hit Best Against

	Avg	AB	R	H	2B	3B	HR	RBI	BB	SO	HBP	GDP	SB	CS	OBP	Slg
Zane Smith	.500	6	0	3	0	0	0	0	0	0	1	0	4	0	.571	.500
Tom Glavine	.444	9	2	4	0	0	2	4	0	2	0	0	0	0	.444	1.111
Greg Maddux	.400	10	2	4	1	0	0	1	0	3	1	0	0	0	.455	.500

Hit Worst Against

	Avg	AB	R	H	2B	3B	HR	RBI	BB	SO	HBP	GDP	SB	CS	OBP	Slg
Scott Erickson	.000	6	0	0	0	0	0	0	0	0	0	0	0	0	.000	.000
John Smoltz	.100	10	0	1	0	0	0	0	0	1	0	0	0	0	.100	.100
Tim Wakefield	.167	6	1	1	0	0	1	1	1	1	0	1	0	0	.286	.667

Steve Garvey

Bats: Right, Throws: Right

Batting	Avg	G	AB	R	H	2B	3B	HR	RBI	BB	SO	HBP	GDP	SB	CS	OBP	Slg
Totals	.338	55	222	32	75	8	3	11	31	8	32	0	4	2	2	.361	.550
Home	.376	27	109	21	41	4	1	6	16	2	20	0	3	1	1	.387	.596
Away	.301	28	113	11	34	4	2	5	15	6	12	0	1	1	1	.336	.504
vs. Left	.400	27	80	0	32	5	0	7	14	2	12	0	1	0	0	.415	.725
vs. Right	.303	55	142	32	43	3	3	4	17	6	19	0	3	2	2	.331	.451
Scoring Pos.	.213	43	61	0	13	0	2	2	16	5	11	0	3	0	0	.273	.377
Close & Late	.370	21	27	3	10	1	0	2	5	0	5	0	0	1	1	.370	.630
None on/out	.326	35	46	0	15	0	0	2	2	1	5	0	0	0	0	.340	.457
None on	.371	50	116	0	43	5	1	5	5	3	15	0	0	0	0	.387	.560
Runners on	.302	51	106	0	32	3	2	6	26	5	16	0	4	2	2	.333	.538
Batting #3	.321	13	53	5	17	4	0	1	9	2	7	0	2	0	0	.345	.453
Batting #4	.341	32	132	20	45	3	2	9	19	3	19	0	2	1	1	.356	.598
Batting #5	.351	10	37	7	13	1	1	1	3	3	5	0	0	1	1	.400	.514

Hit Best Against

	Avg	AB	R	H	2B	3B	HR	RBI	BB	SO	HBP	GDP	SB	CS	OBP	Slg
L. Christenson	.600	5	3	3	0	1	1	3	0	1	0	0	0	0	.600	1.600
Don Gullett	.500	6	2	3	1	0	0	0	1	1	0	0	0	0	.571	.667
Tommy John	.500	6	0	3	0	0	0	0	0	1	0	0	0	0	.500	.500

Hit Worst Against

	Avg	AB	R	H	2B	3B	HR	RBI	BB	SO	HBP	GDP	SB	CS	OBP	Slg
Ray Burris	.143	7	0	1	0	0	0	0	0	1	0	1	0	0	.143	.143
Rollie Fingers	.200	5	0	1	0	0	0	0	0	1	0	0	0	0	.200	.200
Catfish Hunter	.200	10	0	2	0	0	0	0	0	1	0	0	0	0	.200	.200

Lou Gehrig

Bats: Left, Throws: Left

Batting	Avg	G	AB	R	H	2B	3B	HR	RBI	BB	SO	HBP	GDP	SB	CS	OBP	Slg
Totals	.361	34	119	30	43	8	3	10	35	26	17	2	1	0	1	.477	.731
Home	.322	17	59	14	19	3	1	4	16	10	7	0	1	0	0	.420	.610
Away	.400	17	60	16	24	5	2	6	19	16	10	2	0	0	1	.525	.850
vs. Left	.297	20	37	0	11	3	1	3	13	9	7	2	0	0	0	.458	.676
vs. Right	.390	34	82	30	32	5	2	7	22	17	10	0	1	0	1	.485	.756
Scoring Pos.	.270	27	37	0	10	2	1	2	24	12	5	2	0	0	0	.462	.541
Close & Late	.444	11	9	1	4	0	0	1	1	3	1	1	0	0	0	.615	.778
None on/out	.375	20	24	0	9	2	0	3	3	4	3	0	0	0	0	.464	.833
None on	.404	31	57	0	23	6	1	6	6	7	8	0	0	0	0	.469	.860
Runners on	.323	34	62	0	20	2	2	4	29	19	9	2	1	0	1	.482	.613
Batting #4	.378	23	82	25	31	6	3	10	31	19	10	2	1	0	1	.495	.890
Batting #5	.324	11	37	5	12	2	0	0	4	7	7	0	0	0	0	.432	.378

Hit Best Against

	Avg	AB	R	H	2B	3B	HR	RBI	BB	SO	HBP	GDP	SB	CS	OBP	Slg
Lon Warneke	.800	5	3	4	1	0	0	1	0	0	0	1	0	0	.800	1.000
Bill Sherdel	.500	10	2	5	2	0	1	4	5	1	0	0	0	0	.667	1.000
Jesse Haines	.444	9	2	4	0	0	2	3	3	0	0	0	0	0	.583	1.111

Hit Worst Against

	Avg	AB	R	H	2B	3B	HR	RBI	BB	SO	HBP	GDP	SB	CS	OBP	Slg
Carl Hubbell	.167	12	3	2	0	0	2	3	1	3	1	0	0	0	.286	.667
Bill Lee	.200	5	1	1	0	0	0	0	1	2	0	0	0	0	.333	.200
F. Fitzsimmons	.200	5	1	1	0	0	1	2	0	0	0	0	0	0	.200	.800

Charlie Gehringer

Bats: Left, Throws: Right

Batting	Avg	G	AB	R	H	2B	3B	HR	RBI	BB	SO	HBP	GDP	SB	CS	OBP	Slg
Totals	.321	20	81	12	26	4	0	1	7	7	1	0	3	2	0	.375	.407
Home	.333	10	39	6	13	1	0	0	4	5	0	0	2	1	0	.409	.359
Away	.310	10	42	6	13	3	0	1	3	2	1	0	1	1	0	.341	.452
vs. Left	.333	6	15	0	5	1	0	0	2	3	0	0	0	1	0	.444	.400
vs. Right	.318	20	66	12	21	3	0	1	5	4	1	0	3	1	0	.357	.409
Scoring Pos.	.412	13	17	0	7	1	0	0	6	2	0	0	0	0	0	.474	.471
Close & Late	.333	7	9	2	3	1	0	0	0	1	0	0	0	2	0	.400	.444
None on/out	.429	14	14	0	6	0	0	1	1	2	0	0	0	0	0	.500	.643
None on	.316	18	38	0	12	1	0	1	1	5	1	0	0	0	0	.395	.421
Runners on	.326	18	43	0	14	3	0	0	6	2	0	0	3	2	0	.356	.395
Batting #3	.321	20	81	12	26	4	0	1	7	7	1	0	3	2	0	.375	.407

Hit Best Against

	Avg	AB	R	H	2B	3B	HR	RBI	BB	SO	HBP	GDP	SB	CS	OBP	Slg
Tex Carleton	.600	5	1	3	1	0	0	1	1	1	0	0	1	0	.667	.800
Bill Lee	.600	5	2	3	1	0	0	0	0	0	0	0	0	0	.600	.800
Dizzy Dean	.417	12	1	5	0	0	1	2	0	0	0	0	0	0	.417	.667

Hit Worst Against

	Avg	AB	R	H	2B	3B	HR	RBI	BB	SO	HBP	GDP	SB	CS	OBP	Slg
Lon Warneke	.000	6	0	0	0	0	0	0	1	0	0	0	0	0	.143	.000
Bucky Walters	.125	8	1	1	0	0	0	1	0	0	0	1	0	0	.125	.125
Paul Derringer	.222	9	0	2	0	0	0	0	0	0	0	2	0	0	.222	.222

Bob Gibson

Throws: Right, Bats: Right

Pitching	ERA	W	L	Sv	G	GS	IP	BB	SO	Avg	R	H	2B	3B	HR	OBP	Slg
Totals	1.89	7	2	0	9	9	81.0	17	92	.190	19	55	9	2	6	.239	.297
Home	2.66	3	2	0	5	5	44.0	9	49	.213	13	35	6	1	3	.257	.317
Away	0.97	4	0	0	4	4	37.0	8	43	.159	6	20	3	1	3	.215	.270

	Avg	AB	R	H	2B	3B	HR	RBI	BB	SO	HBP	GDP	OBP	Slg
vs. Left	.183	126	0	23	2	1	3	11	11	29	1	3	.254	.286
vs. Right	.195	164	19	32	7	1	3	7	6	63	1	3	.227	.305
Scoring Pos.	.216	37	0	8	2	1	2	14	4	11	0	3	.286	.486
Close & Late	.154	39	3	6	0	1	1	6	1	9	0	3	.175	.282
None on/out	.158	76	0	12	2	1	0	0	7	23	0	3	.229	.211
None on	.203	192	0	39	5	1	4	4	12	60	0	3	.250	.302
Runners on	.163	98	0	16	4	1	2	14	5	32	2	3	.217	.286

Pitched Best Against

	Avg	AB	R	H	2B	3B	HR	RBI	BB	SO	HBP	GDP	SB	CS	OBP	Slg
Jerry Adair	.000	8	0	0	0	0	0	0	0	3	0	0	0	0	.000	.000
Ken Harrelson	.000	7	0	0	0	0	0	0	0	2	0	1	0	0	.000	.000
Joe Foy	.000	5	0	0	0	0	0	0	1	2	0	0	0	0	.167	.000

Pitched Worst Against

	Avg	AB	R	H	2B	3B	HR	RBI	BB	SO	HBP	GDP	SB	CS	OBP	Slg
B. Richardson	.500	14	2	7	1	0	0	1	0	2	0	1	0	0	.500	.571
Don Wert	.400	5	0	2	0	0	0	1	1	2	0	0	0	0	.500	.400
Jose Tartabull	.400	5	0	2	0	0	0	0	0	1	0	0	0	0	.400	.400

Kirk Gibson

Bats: Left, Throws: Left

Batting	Avg	G	AB	R	H	2B	3B	HR	RBI	BB	SO	HBP	GDP	SB	CS	OBP	Slg
Totals	.282	21	78	13	22	2	0	7	21	12	19	1	0	9	1	.380	.577
Home	.297	12	37	6	11	1	0	3	12	9	8	1	0	7	0	.438	.568
Away	.268	9	41	7	11	1	0	4	9	3	11	0	0	2	1	.318	.585
vs. Left	.261	12	23	0	6	0	0	2	5	3	5	0	0	2	0	.346	.522
vs. Right	.291	21	55	13	16	2	0	5	16	9	14	1	0	7	1	.394	.600
Scoring Pos.	.304	19	23	1	7	1	0	3	16	4	5	1	0	2	0	.414	.739
Close & Late	.222	13	18	2	4	0	0	3	7	0	6	0	0	0	0	.222	.722
None on/out	.267	14	15	0	4	1	0	0	0	2	2	0	0	0	0	.353	.333
None on	.237	20	38	0	9	1	0	3	3	8	8	0	0	0	0	.370	.500
Runners on	.325	21	40	1	13	1	0	4	18	4	11	1	0	9	1	.391	.650
Batting #3	.273	20	77	12	21	2	0	6	19	12	19	1	0	9	1	.374	.532

Hit Best Against

	Avg	AB	R	H	2B	3B	HR	RBI	BB	SO	HBP	GDP	SB	CS	OBP	Slg
Bert Blyleven	.400	5	1	2	1	0	0	0	1	2	0	0	1	0	.500	.600
Frank Viola	.333	6	2	2	0	0	1	2	1	2	0	0	0	0	.429	.833

Hit Worst Against	Avg	AB	R	H	2B	3B	HR	RBI	BB	SO	HBP	GDP	SB	CS	OBP	Slg
Dwight Gooden	.000	7	0	0	0	0	0	0	1	4	0	0	0	0	.125	.000
David Cone	.000	6	0	0	0	0	0	0	1	0	0	0	0	0	.143	.000

Jim Gilliam

Bats: Both, Throws: Right

Batting	Avg	G	AB	R	H	2B	3B	HR	RBI	BB	SO	HBP	GDP	SB	CS	OBP	Slg
Totals	.211	39	147	15	31	5	0	2	12	23	9	2	4	4	4	.326	.286
Home	.271	20	70	11	19	5	0	1	10	15	2	2	1	3	2	.414	.386
Away	.156	19	77	4	12	0	0	1	2	8	7	0	3	1	2	.235	.195
vs. Left	.170	22	53	0	9	1	0	1	5	6	2	0	3	0	0	.254	.245
vs. Right	.234	39	94	15	22	4	0	1	7	17	7	2	1	4	4	.363	.309
Scoring Pos.	.207	28	29	0	6	1	0	0	9	8	2	0	0	0	1	.378	.241
Close & Late	.118	16	17	3	2	0	0	0	0	4	1	0	1	1	1	.286	.118
None on/out	.183	37	60	0	11	1	0	1	1	7	6	0	0	0	0	.269	.250
None on	.218	39	101	0	22	3	0	2	2	13	7	2	0	0	0	.319	.307
Runners on	.196	35	46	0	9	2	0	0	10	10	2	0	4	4	4	.339	.239
Batting #1	.230	26	100	10	23	4	0	2	9	17	8	1	2	4	3	.347	.330
Batting #2	.178	12	45	5	8	1	0	0	2	4	1	1	2	0	1	.260	.200

Hit Best Against	Avg	AB	R	H	2B	3B	HR	RBI	BB	SO	HBP	GDP	SB	CS	OBP	Slg
Bob Shaw	.571	7	1	4	0	0	0	0	1	0	0	0	1	0	.625	.571
Jim Kaat	.250	8	1	2	0	0	0	1	0	0	0	0	0	0	.250	.250
Hit Worst Against																
Johnny Kucks	.000	6	0	0	0	0	0	0	0	0	0	0	1	0	.000	.000
Ed Lopat	.000	5	0	0	0	0	0	0	0	0	0	0	0	0	.000	.000
Mudcat Grant	.091	11	1	1	0	0	0	0	1	0	0	0	0	0	.167	.091

Tom Glavine

Throws: Left, Bats: Left

Pitching	ERA	W	L	Sv	G	GS	IP	BB	SO	Avg	R	H	2B	3B	HR	OBP	Slg
Totals	3.05	9	9	0	20	20	132.2	51	90	.214	50	102	24	4	13	.296	.363
Home	3.09	9	4	0	13	13	84.1	35	63	.201	31	60	13	2	5	.289	.308
Away	2.98	0	5	0	7	7	48.1	16	27	.236	19	42	11	2	8	.310	.455

	Avg	AB	R	H	2B	3B	HR	RBI	BB	SO	HBP	GDP	OBP	Slg
vs. Left	.202	89	0	18	5	1	4	11	5	20	3	9	.268	.416
vs. Right	.216	388	0	84	19	3	9	36	46	70	2	9	.303	.351
Scoring Pos.	.227	97	35	22	5	1	3	32	20	18	2	9	.370	.392
Close & Late	.216	51	2	11	3	0	1	2	3	7	0	9	.259	.333
None on/out	.289	135	0	39	5	3	7	7	9	23	0	9	.333	.526
None on	.220	295	7	65	15	3	8	8	27	60	2	9	.290	.373
Runners on	.203	182	43	37	9	1	5	39	24	30	3	9	.306	.346

Pitched Best Against	Avg	AB	R	H	2B	3B	HR	RBI	BB	SO	HBP	GDP	SB	CS	OBP	Slg
Dan Gladden	.000	7	0	0	0	0	0	0	0	1	0	0	0	0	.000	.000
Brian Jordan	.000	6	0	0	0	0	0	0	0	0	0	1	0	0	.000	.000
Roberto Alomar	.000	7	0	0	0	0	0	0	1	1	0	0	1	0	.125	.000
Pitched Worst Against																
Pat Borders	.500	6	1	3	0	0	1	1	0	0	0	0	0	0	.500	1.000
Royce Clayton	.500	6	1	3	0	0	0	0	0	0	0	0	0	1	.500	.500
Ron Gant	.444	9	2	4	0	0	2	4	0	2	0	0	0	0	.444	1.111

Lefty Gomez

Throws: Left, Bats: Left

Pitching	ERA	W	L	Sv	G	GS	IP	BB	SO	Avg	R	H	2B	3B	HR	OBP	Slg
Totals	2.68	6	0	0	7	7	50.1	15	31	.263	17	51	9	1	2	.316	.351
Home	1.00	2	0	0	2	2	18.0	2	10	.227	3	15	3	1	0	.250	.303
Away	3.62	4	0	0	5	5	32.1	13	21	.281	14	36	6	0	2	.348	.375

	Avg	AB	R	H	2B	3B	HR	RBI	BB	SO	HBP	GDP	OBP	Slg
vs. Left	.295	61	0	18	1	0	2	7	2	8	0	1	.317	.410
vs. Right	.248	133	17	33	8	1	0	7	13	23	0	1	.315	.323
Scoring Pos.	.171	41	0	7	2	0	0	11	4	9	0	1	.244	.220
Close & Late	.158	19	0	3	0	0	0	0	2	3	0	1	.238	.158
None on/out	.354	48	0	17	3	0	0	0	3	6	0	1	.392	.417
None on	.324	105	0	34	7	1	1	1	5	12	0	1	.355	.438
Runners on	.191	89	0	17	2	0	1	13	10	19	0	1	.273	.247

Pitched Best Against	Avg	AB	R	H	2B	3B	HR	RBI	BB	SO	HBP	GDP	SB	CS	OBP	Slg
Harry Danning	.000	5	0	0	0	0	0	0	0	3	0	0	0	0	.000	.000
Billy Jurges	.000	6	0	0	0	0	0	0	0	0	0	0	0	0	.000	.000
Gus Mancuso	.111	9	2	1	1	0	0	0	2	1	0	1	0	0	.273	.222
Pitched Worst Against																
Jimmy Ripple	.429	7	1	3	0	0	0	0	1	0	0	0	0	0	.500	.429
Dick Bartell	.385	13	3	5	2	0	0	1	4	1	0	0	0	0	.529	.538
Bill Terry	.375	8	0	3	0	0	0	2	0	1	0	0	0	0	.375	.375

Dwight Gooden

Throws: Right, Bats: Right

Pitching	ERA	W	L	Sv	G	GS	IP	BB	SO	Avg	R	H	2B	3B	HR	OBP	Slg
Totals	3.06	0	3	0	8	7	50.0	20	43	.251	19	48	5	2	5	.326	.377
Home	3.86	0	1	0	3	3	23.1	9	19	.250	11	22	2	0	3	.320	.375
Away	2.36	0	2	0	5	4	26.2	11	24	.252	8	26	3	2	2	.331	.379

	Avg	AB	R	H	2B	3B	HR	RBI	BB	SO	HBP	GDP	OBP	Slg
vs. Left	.266	109	0	29	4	0	2	11	10	25	0	2	.322	.358
vs. Right	.232	82	18	19	1	2	3	9	10	18	2	2	.330	.402
Scoring Pos.	.183	60	1	11	1	0	0	13	8	18	1	2	.282	.200
Close & Late	.273	22	1	6	1	0	1	3	1	4	0	2	.304	.455
None on/out	.327	49	0	16	4	1	3	3	7	11	0	2	.411	.633
None on	.267	105	0	28	4	2	3	3	11	23	0	2	.336	.429
Runners on	.233	86	1	20	1	0	2	17	9	20	2	2	.313	.314

Pitched Best Against	Avg	AB	R	H	2B	3B	HR	RBI	BB	SO	HBP	GDP	SB	CS	OBP	Slg
Jeff Hamilton	.000	8	0	0	0	0	0	0	0	2	0	0	0	0	.000	.000
Rich Gedman	.000	5	0	0	0	0	0	0	0	2	0	0	0	0	.000	.000
Kirk Gibson	.000	7	0	0	0	0	0	0	1	4	0	0	0	0	.125	.000

Pitched Worst Against	Avg	AB	R	H	2B	3B	HR	RBI	BB	SO	HBP	GDP	SB	CS	OBP	Slg
Dwight Evans	.600	5	1	3	0	0	1	3	1	1	0	0	0	0	.667	1.200
Jim Rice	.600	5	2	3	0	1	0	0	1	1	0	0	0	0	.667	1.000
Marty Barrett	.600	5	0	3	0	0	0	1	1	0	0	0	0	0	.667	.600

Joe Gordon

Bats: Right, Throws: Right

Batting	Avg	G	AB	R	H	2B	3B	HR	RBI	BB	SO	HBP	GDP	SB	CS	OBP	Slg
Totals	.243	29	103	12	25	5	1	4	16	12	17	0	1	2	0	.322	.427
Home	.245	15	49	8	12	0	0	3	7	8	8	0	0	1	0	.351	.429
Away	.241	14	54	4	13	5	1	1	9	4	9	0	1	1	0	.293	.426
vs. Left	.125	13	24	0	3	1	0	1	2	2	6	0	0	0	0	.192	.292
vs. Right	.278	29	79	12	22	4	1	3	14	10	11	0	1	2	0	.360	.468
Scoring Pos.	.400	19	25	0	10	2	0	0	12	3	5	0	0	1	0	.464	.480
Close & Late	.200	13	10	0	2	1	0	0	3	3	4	0	0	0	0	.385	.300
None on/out	.167	22	30	0	5	1	0	1	1	1	4	0	0	0	0	.194	.300
None on	.226	29	62	0	14	3	1	4	4	5	8	0	0	0	0	.284	.500
Runners on	.268	25	41	0	11	2	0	0	12	7	9	0	1	2	0	.375	.317
Batting #4	.182	6	22	3	4	0	0	1	2	1	2	0	0	1	0	.217	.318
Batting #5	.200	4	15	2	3	1	0	1	2	1	3	0	0	0	0	.250	.467
Batting #6	.118	4	17	1	2	1	0	0	0	0	6	0	0	0	0	.118	.176
Batting #7	.294	11	34	3	10	1	1	1	6	9	3	0	1	0	0	.442	.471
Batting #8	.400	4	15	3	6	2	0	1	6	1	3	0	0	1	0	.438	.733

Hit Best Against	Avg	AB	R	H	2B	3B	HR	RBI	BB	SO	HBP	GDP	SB	CS	OBP	Slg
Max Lanier	.250	8	2	2	1	0	1	1	1	2	0	0	0	0	.333	.750
Johnny Beazley	.250	8	0	2	1	0	0	0	0	3	0	0	0	0	.250	.375
Hit Worst Against																
Mort Cooper	.083	12	0	1	0	0	0	0	1	3	0	0	0	0	.154	.083
Johnny Sain	.143	7	0	1	0	0	0	0	0	1	0	0	1	0	.143	.143
Paul Derringer	.167	6	1	1	0	0	0	0	0	1	0	0	0	0	.167	.167

Goose Goslin

Bats: Left, Throws: Right

Batting	Avg	G	AB	R	H	2B	3B	HR	RBI	BB	SO	HBP	GDP	SB	CS	OBP	Slg
Totals	.287	32	129	16	37	6	0	7	19	12	14	0	0	0	3	.348	.496
Home	.254	17	71	4	18	4	0	3	10	4	10	0	0	0	2	.293	.437
Away	.328	15	58	12	19	2	0	4	9	8	4	0	0	0	1	.409	.569
vs. Left	.250	14	44	0	11	2	0	3	8	3	7	0	0	0	1	.298	.500
vs. Right	.306	32	85	16	26	4	0	4	11	9	6	0	0	0	2	.372	.494
Scoring Pos.	.303	22	33	0	10	1	0	3	15	6	2	0	0	0	0	.410	.606
Close & Late	.333	20	27	1	9	2	0	0	4	2	3	0	0	0	0	.379	.407
None on/out	.355	23	31	0	11	1	0	1	1	2	2	0	0	0	0	.394	.484
None on	.304	31	69	0	21	4	0	4	4	4	8	0	0	0	0	.342	.536
Runners on	.267	29	60	0	16	2	0	3	15	8	5	0	0	0	3	.353	.450
Batting #2	.250	5	20	2	5	1	0	1	1	1	3	0	0	0	0	.286	.450
Batting #3	.308	7	26	6	8	1	0	3	6	3	2	0	0	0	0	.379	.692
Batting #4	.302	15	63	8	19	4	0	3	10	5	7	0	0	0	2	.353	.508
Batting #5	.250	5	20	0	5	0	0	0	2	3	1	0	0	0	1	.348	.250

Hit Best Against	Avg	AB	R	H	2B	3B	HR	RBI	BB	SO	HBP	GDP	SB	CS	OBP	Slg
Virgil Barnes	.667	6	1	4	1	0	1	4	0	1	0	0	0	1	.667	1.333
Bill Lee	.600	5	2	3	0	0	0	2	1	0	0	0	0	0	.667	.600
Johnny Morrison	.600	5	2	3	0	0	0	0	0	1	0	0	0	0	.600	.600
Hit Worst Against																
Lon Warneke	.000	5	0	0	0	0	0	0	1	0	0	0	0	0	.167	.000
Art Nehf	.100	10	0	1	0	0	0	0	0	2	0	0	0	1	.100	.100
Carl Hubbell	.125	8	0	1	0	0	0	0	0	1	0	0	0	0	.125	.125

Goose Gossage

Throws: Right, Bats: Right

Pitching	ERA	W	L	Sv	G	GS	IP	BB	SO	Avg	R	H	2B	3B	HR	OBP	Slg
Totals	2.87	2	1	8	19	0	31.1	7	29	.188	10	21	2	0	3	.246	.286
Home	3.00	2	1	6	11	0	18.0	5	16	.200	6	13	2	0	1	.264	.277
Away	2.70	0	0	2	8	0	13.1	2	13	.170	4	8	0	0	2	.220	.298

	Avg	AB	R	H	2B	3B	HR	RBI	BB	SO	HBP	GDP	OBP	Slg
vs. Left	.191	47	0	9	0	0	2	8	3	15	1	1	.255	.319
vs. Right	.182	66	10	12	2	0	1	5	4	14	1	1	.236	.258
Scoring Pos.	.269	26	0	7	0	0	2	11	1	5	0	1	.286	.500
Close & Late	.200	60	5	12	1	0	3	13	5	14	1	1	.269	.367
None on/out	.130	23	0	3	1	0	0	0	3	6	0	1	.231	.174
None on	.164	61	0	10	1	0	1	1	5	17	1	1	.239	.230
Runners on	.212	52	0	11	1	0	2	12	2	12	1	1	.250	.346

Pitched Best Against	Avg	AB	R	H	2B	3B	HR	RBI	BB	SO	HBP	GDP	SB	CS	OBP	Slg
Ron Cey	.000	6	0	0	0	0	0	0	0	2	1	0	0	0	.143	.000
Bill Russell	.000	5	0	0	0	0	0	0	0	0	0	1	0	0	.000	.000

Hank Greenberg

Bats: Right, Throws: Right

Batting	Avg	G	AB	R	H	2B	3B	HR	RBI	BB	SO	HBP	GDP	SB	CS	OBP	Slg
Totals	.318	23	85	17	27	7	2	5	22	13	19	2	4	1	0	.420	.624
Home	.302	12	43	8	13	1	1	4	12	5	10	2	2	0	0	.400	.651
Away	.333	11	42	9	14	6	1	1	10	8	9	0	2	1	0	.440	.595
vs. Left	.333	6	12	0	4	2	0	1	4	2	3	0	1	0	0	.429	.750
vs. Right	.315	23	73	17	23	5	2	4	18	11	16	2	3	1	0	.419	.603
Scoring Pos.	.360	21	25	0	9	4	0	2	16	5	7	0	2	1	0	.467	.760
Close & Late	.273	11	11	1	3	1	1	0	2	3	2	0	1	0	0	.429	.545
None on/out	.333	15	24	0	8	1	1	0	0	1	5	0	0	0	0	.360	.458
None on	.300	21	40	0	12	1	1	2	2	5	9	0	0	0	0	.378	.525
Runners on	.333	22	45	0	15	6	1	3	20	8	10	2	4	1	0	.455	.711
Batting #4	.304	19	69	15	21	5	2	5	17	12	14	2	4	0	0	.422	.652
Batting #6	.375	4	16	2	6	2	0	0	5	1	5	0	0	1	0	.412	.500

Hit Best Against	Avg	AB	R	H	2B	3B	HR	RBI	BB	SO	HBP	GDP	SB	CS	OBP	Slg
Paul Derringer	.500	10	2	5	2	0	0	1	2	1	0	0	0	0	.583	.700
Hank Borowy	.333	6	1	2	1	0	0	1	1	1	1	1	0	0	.500	.500
Dizzy Dean	.273	11	3	3	0	0	1	2	1	5	0	0	0	0	.333	.545

Hit Worst Against	Avg	AB	R	H	2B	3B	HR	RBI	BB	SO	HBP	GDP	SB	CS	OBP	Slg
Claude Passeau	.000	7	1	0	0	0	0	1	1	1	0	0	0	0	.125	.000
Bucky Walters	.167	6	0	1	1	0	0	1	2	1	0	1	0	0	.375	.333

Bobby Grich

Bats: Right, Throws: Right

Batting	Avg	G	AB	R	H	2B	3B	HR	RBI	BB	SO	HBP	GDP	SB	CS	OBP	Slg
Totals	.182	24	88	5	16	3	0	3	9	5	22	3	1	0	0	.247	.318
Home	.190	11	42	2	8	1	0	1	4	3	12	1	0	0	0	.261	.286
Away	.174	13	46	3	8	2	0	2	5	2	10	2	1	0	0	.235	.348
vs. Left	.219	11	32	0	7	0	0	1	4	0	6	0	1	0	0	.212	.313
vs. Right	.161	24	56	5	9	3	0	2	5	5	16	3	0	0	0	.266	.321
Scoring Pos.	.200	13	15	0	3	0	0	1	5	3	4	2	0	0	0	.381	.400
Close & Late	.150	17	20	1	3	0	0	1	3	1	4	0	1	0	0	.182	.300
None on/out	.118	14	17	0	2	0	0	1	1	0	1	0	0	0	0	.118	.294
None on	.154	24	52	0	8	2	0	1	1	1	10	1	0	0	0	.185	.250
Runners on	.222	23	36	0	8	1	0	2	8	4	12	2	1	0	0	.326	.417
Batting #2	.150	4	20	1	3	0	0	1	2	0	6	0	0	0	0	.150	.300
Batting #3	.316	5	19	3	6	2	0	1	3	1	2	0	1	0	0	.350	.579
Batting #6	.300	3	10	0	3	0	0	0	1	0	0	0	0	0	0	.273	.300
Batting #7	.100	9	30	0	3	1	0	0	1	2	9	2	0	0	0	.206	.133

Hit Best Against	Avg	AB	R	H	2B	3B	HR	RBI	BB	SO	HBP	GDP	SB	CS	OBP	Slg
Bruce Hurst	.429	7	1	3	0	0	1	2	0	2	0	0	0	0	.429	.857

Hit Worst Against	Avg	AB	R	H	2B	3B	HR	RBI	BB	SO	HBP	GDP	SB	CS	OBP	Slg
Roger Clemens	.000	6	0	0	0	0	0	0	0	4	1	0	0	0	.143	.000
Ken Holtzman	.111	9	0	1	0	0	0	0	0	1	0	1	0	0	.111	.111
Vida Blue	.125	8	0	1	0	0	0	0	0	2	0	1	0	0	.125	.125

Ken Griffey Jr.

Bats: Left, Throws: Left

Batting	Avg	G	AB	R	H	2B	3B	HR	RBI	BB	SO	HBP	GDP	SB	CS	OBP	Slg
Totals	.305	15	59	11	18	2	0	6	11	7	11	1	0	5	1	.382	.644
Home	.310	8	29	6	9	1	0	3	4	5	6	1	0	3	1	.429	.655
Away	.300	7	30	5	9	1	0	3	7	2	5	0	0	2	0	.333	.633
vs. Left	.273	7	11	1	3	0	0	1	3	1	2	0	0	1	0	.308	.545
vs. Right	.313	14	48	10	15	2	0	5	8	6	9	1	0	4	1	.400	.667
Scoring Pos.	.200	14	10	5	2	1	0	0	4	3	4	1	0	2	0	.400	.300
Close & Late	.455	8	11	6	5	1	0	3	5	1	1	1	0	0	0	.500	1.364
None on/out	.250	8	12	2	3	0	0	2	2	0	2	0	0	0	0	.250	.750
None on	.278	15	36	5	10	1	0	5	5	4	6	0	0	0	0	.350	.722
Runners on	.348	15	23	6	8	1	0	1	6	3	5	1	0	5	1	.429	.522
Batting #3	.305	15	59	11	18	2	0	6	11	7	11	1	0	5	1	.382	.644

Hit Best Against	Avg	AB	R	H	2B	3B	HR	RBI	BB	SO	HBP	GDP	SB	CS	OBP	Slg
Orel Hershiser	.500	6	1	3	1	0	1	2	1	0	0	0	0	0	.571	1.167
David Cone	.375	8	3	3	0	0	3	4	0	1	0	0	0	0	.375	1.500

Hit Worst Against	Avg	AB	R	H	2B	3B	HR	RBI	BB	SO	HBP	GDP	SB	CS	OBP	Slg
Mike Mussina	.000	6	0	0	0	0	0	0	0	1	0	0	0	0	.000	.000

Ken Griffey Sr.

Bats: Left, Throws: Left

Batting	Avg	G	AB	R	H	2B	3B	HR	RBI	BB	SO	HBP	GDP	SB	CS	OBP	Slg
Totals	.240	20	75	11	18	5	2	0	11	6	8	1	1	8	0	.301	.360
Home	.200	9	35	5	7	2	0	0	7	1	4	1	1	5	0	.237	.257
Away	.275	11	40	6	11	3	2	0	4	5	4	0	0	3	0	.356	.450
vs. Left	.333	13	27	0	9	1	1	0	5	4	6	0	0	4	0	.419	.444
vs. Right	.188	20	48	11	9	4	1	0	6	2	2	1	1	4	0	.231	.313
Scoring Pos.	.316	15	19	0	6	2	1	0	10	2	4	1	0	3	0	.391	.526
Close & Late	.357	11	14	4	5	2	0	0	2	1	1	0	0	1	0	.400	.500
None on/out	.278	14	18	0	5	0	0	0	0	1	1	0	0	0	0	.316	.278
None on	.225	19	40	0	9	2	1	0	0	4	2	0	0	0	0	.295	.325
Runners on	.257	18	35	0	9	3	1	0	11	2	6	1	1	8	0	.308	.400
Batting #2	.213	11	47	6	10	1	2	0	6	4	3	0	0	4	0	.269	.319
Batting #7	.333	6	21	5	7	3	0	0	5	2	4	0	1	4	0	.391	.476

Hit Best Against	Avg	AB	R	H	2B	3B	HR	RBI	BB	SO	HBP	GDP	SB	CS	OBP	Slg
Luis Tiant	.364	11	2	4	2	1	0	3	1	0	0	0	0	0	.417	.727

Hit Worst Against	Avg	AB	R	H	2B	3B	HR	RBI	BB	SO	HBP	GDP	SB	CS	OBP	Slg
Tom Seaver	.167	6	0	1	1	0	0	0	0	1	1	0	0	0	.286	.333
Bill Lee	.200	5	1	1	0	0	0	0	1	1	0	0	0	0	.333	.200

Burleigh Grimes

Throws: Right, Bats: Right

Pitching	ERA	W	L	Sv	G	GS	IP	BB	SO	Avg	R	H	2B	3B	HR	OBP	Slg
Totals	4.29	3	4	0	9	7	56.2	26	28	.234	28	49	6	4	8	.321	.416
Home	2.60	2	1	0	4	3	27.2	13	15	.225	8	23	3	0	3	.313	.343
Away	5.90	1	3	0	5	4	29.0	13	13	.243	20	26	3	4	5	.328	.486

	Avg	AB	R	H	2B	3B	HR	RBI	BB	SO	HBP	GDP	OBP	Slg
vs. Left	.241	108	0	26	3	3	3	12	17	13	1	2	.349	.407
vs. Right	.228	101	28	23	3	1	5	16	9	15	0	2	.288	.426
Scoring Pos.	.261	46	0	12	2	1	2	18	8	3	1	2	.375	.478
Close & Late	.281	32	3	9	0	1	2	7	7	3	0	2	.410	.531
None on/out	.180	50	0	9	2	0	1	1	9	11	0	2	.305	.280
None on	.218	124	0	27	3	3	3	3	16	21	0	2	.307	.363
Runners on	.259	85	0	22	3	1	5	25	10	7	1	2	.340	.494

Pitched Best Against	Avg	AB	R	H	2B	3B	HR	RBI	BB	SO	HBP	GDP	SB	CS	OBP	Slg
Joe Sewell	.000	11	0	0	0	0	0	0	0	0	0	1	0	0	.000	.000
Lefty Grove	.000	5	0	0	0	0	0	0	0	3	0	0	0	0	.000	.000
Max Bishop	.000	13	1	0	0	0	0	0	3	5	0	0	0	0	.188	.000

Pitched Worst Against	Avg	AB	R	H	2B	3B	HR	RBI	BB	SO	HBP	GDP	SB	CS	OBP	Slg
Tris Speaker	.500	8	1	4	1	1	0	1	2	0	0	0	0	0	.600	.875
C. Jamieson	.455	11	2	5	1	0	0	1	1	0	0	0	1	0	.500	.545
Doc Johnston	.429	7	1	3	0	0	0	0	2	0	0	0	1	2	.556	.429

Marquis Grissom

Bats: Right, Throws: Right

Batting	Avg	G	AB	R	H	2B	3B	HR	RBI	BB	SO	HBP	GDP	SB	CS	OBP	Slg
Totals	.328	48	204	33	67	7	3	5	19	10	37	1	2	12	3	.363	.466
Home	.327	24	98	15	32	3	2	1	7	6	17	1	1	7	1	.371	.429
Away	.330	24	106	18	35	4	1	4	12	4	20	0	1	5	2	.355	.500
vs. Left	.381	27	63	12	24	2	0	2	6	4	7	0	1	6	1	.418	.508
vs. Right	.305	46	141	21	43	5	3	3	13	6	30	1	1	6	2	.338	.447
Scoring Pos.	.317	39	41	27	13	2	0	1	14	5	6	0	0	6	1	.391	.439
Close & Late	.289	29	38	6	11	2	1	1	4	3	12	0	1	3	0	.341	.474
None on/out	.366	42	71	1	26	3	2	1	1	0	14	1	0	0	0	.375	.507
None on	.305	48	131	3	40	4	3	3	3	5	28	1	0	0	0	.336	.450
Runners on	.370	44	73	30	27	3	0	2	16	5	9	0	2	12	3	.410	.493
Batting #1	.345	30	139	23	48	6	2	4	13	4	22	1	1	9	2	.368	.504
Batting #8	.412	5	17	3	7	1	0	0	1	2	3	0	0	0	0	.474	.471
Batting #9	.250	13	48	7	12	0	1	1	5	4	12	0	1	3	1	.308	.354

Hit Best Against	Avg	AB	R	H	2B	3B	HR	RBI	BB	SO	HBP	GDP	SB	CS	OBP	Slg
T. Stottlemyre	.800	5	4	4	0	0	1	2	0	0	0	0	1	0	.800	1.400
David Cone	.600	5	1	3	0	1	0	0	0	1	0	0	0	0	.600	1.000
D. Osborne	.600	5	2	3	0	0	0	0	0	1	0	0	0	0	.600	.600

Hit Worst Against	Avg	AB	R	H	2B	3B	HR	RBI	BB	SO	HBP	GDP	SB	CS	OBP	Slg
Jeff Nelson	.000	6	0	0	0	0	0	0	0	0	0	0	0	0	.000	.000
Mike Mussina	.000	5	0	0	0	0	0	0	0	5	0	0	0	0	.000	.000
Andy Benes	.111	9	1	1	1	0	0	0	0	1	0	0	0	0	.111	.222

Lefty Grove

Throws: Left, Bats: Left

Pitching	ERA	W	L	Sv	G	GS	IP	BB	SO	Avg	R	H	2B	3B	HR	OBP	Slg
Totals	1.75	5	2	1	8	5	51.1	6	36	.236	12	46	8	1	0	.256	.287
Home	2.84	1	1	1	3	2	19.0	2	11	.267	6	20	4	0	0	.278	.320
Away	1.11	4	1	0	5	3	32.1	4	25	.217	6	26	4	1	0	.242	.267

	Avg	AB	R	H	2B	3B	HR	RBI	BB	SO	HBP	GDP	OBP	Slg
vs. Left	.077	26	0	2	0	0	0	1	1	4	0	3	.111	.077
vs. Right	.260	169	12	44	8	1	0	10	5	31	0	3	.278	.320
Scoring Pos.	.225	40	0	9	1	0	0	11	0	7	0	3	.214	.250
Close & Late	.154	26	0	4	0	0	0	0	1	7	0	3	.185	.154
None on/out	.120	50	0	6	1	0	0	0	1	10	0	3	.137	.140
None on	.200	120	0	24	6	1	0	0	5	21	0	3	.232	.267
Runners on	.293	75	0	22	2	0	0	11	1	14	0	3	.295	.320

Pitched Best Against	Avg	AB	R	H	2B	3B	HR	RBI	BB	SO	HBP	GDP	SB	CS	OBP	Slg
Taylor Douthit	.000	9	0	0	0	0	0	1	0	1	0	0	0	0	.000	.000
Ray Blades	.000	8	1	0	0	0	0	0	2	3	0	0	0	0	.200	.000
Jim Bottomley	.050	20	1	1	0	0	0	1	1	3	0	0	0	0	.095	.050

Pitched Worst Against	Avg	AB	R	H	2B	3B	HR	RBI	BB	SO	HBP	GDP	SB	CS	OBP	Slg
Burleigh Grimes	.571	7	0	4	0	0	0	2	0	1	0	0	0	0	.571	.571
Pepper Martin	.455	11	2	5	2	0	0	1	1	1	0	0	1	0	.500	.636
Charlie Gelbert	.444	18	2	8	1	1	0	2	1	4	0	0	0	0	.474	.611

Pedro Guerrero

Bats: Right, Throws: Right

Batting	Avg	G	AB	R	H	2B	3B	HR	RBI	BB	SO	HBP	GDP	SB	CS	OBP	Slg
Totals	.225	26	89	7	20	4	2	4	16	13	19	2	5	3	0	.333	.449
Home	.282	13	39	4	11	2	1	3	10	10	10	2	0	3	0	.442	.615
Away	.180	13	50	3	9	2	1	1	6	3	9	0	5	0	0	.226	.320
vs. Left	.207	14	29	0	6	2	0	2	4	6	6	1	0	1	0	.361	.483
vs. Right	.233	26	60	7	14	2	2	2	12	7	13	1	5	2	0	.319	.433
Scoring Pos.	.318	20	22	0	7	1	2	0	11	8	5	0	1	0	0	.484	.545
Close & Late	.077	14	13	0	1	0	0	0	1	3	3	0	1	0	0	.250	.077
None on/out	.200	16	20	0	4	2	0	0	0	4	4	0	0	0	0	.238	.300
None on	.191	25	47	0	9	3	0	3	3	3	9	1	0	0	0	.255	.447
Runners on	.262	25	42	0	11	1	2	1	13	10	10	1	5	3	0	.407	.452
Batting #3	.214	4	14	1	3	1	0	0	2	2	0	0	1	0	0	.294	.286
Batting #4	.278	6	18	2	5	1	1	0	4	6	5	1	0	2	0	.480	.444
Batting #6	.186	12	43	4	8	1	1	4	10	3	11	1	2	1	0	.255	.535
Batting #7	.273	3	11	0	3	0	0	0	0	1	2	0	2	0	0	.333	.273

Hit Worst Against	Avg	AB	R	H	2B	3B	HR	RBI	BB	SO	HBP	GDP	SB	CS	OBP	Slg
Bill Gullickson	.000	6	0	0	0	0	0	0	0	2	0	1	0	0	.000	.000
Tommy John	.000	5	0	0	0	0	0	0	0	0	0	0	0	0	.000	.000
Nolan Ryan	.000	5	0	0	0	0	0	0	1	2	0	0	1	0	.167	.000

Ron Guidry

Throws: Left, Bats: Left

Pitching	ERA	W	L	Sv	G	GS	IP	BB	SO	Avg	R	H	2B	3B	HR	OBP	Slg
Totals	3.02	5	2	0	10	10	62.2	25	51	.229	21	52	12	2	5	.302	.366
Home	1.70	4	0	0	5	5	37.0	14	27	.203	7	26	3	1	2	.278	.289
Away	4.91	1	2	0	5	5	25.2	11	24	.263	14	26	9	1	3	.333	.465

	Avg	AB	R	H	2B	3B	HR	RBI	BB	SO	HBP	GDP	OBP	Slg
vs. Left	.262	42	0	11	2	2	1	5	6	11	0	0	.347	.476
vs. Right	.220	186	21	41	10	0	4	15	19	40	0	0	.290	.339
Scoring Pos.	.222	45	0	10	1	0	1	15	5	8	0	0	.283	.311
Close & Late	.063	16	1	1	0	0	1	1	1	3	0	0	.118	.250
None on/out	.167	60	0	10	3	1	0	0	5	12	0	0	.231	.250
None on	.245	143	0	35	10	1	4	4	16	33	0	0	.321	.413
Runners on	.200	85	0	17	2	1	1	16	9	18	0	0	.268	.282

Pitched Best Against	Avg	AB	R	H	2B	3B	HR	RBI	BB	SO	HBP	GDP	SB	CS	OBP	Slg
John Wathan	.000	5	1	0	0	0	0	0	2	2	0	0	0	0	.286	.000
Al Cowens	.111	9	0	1	0	0	0	2	0	3	0	0	0	0	.111	.111
Reggie Smith	.125	8	0	1	0	0	0	0	1	2	0	0	0	0	.222	.125

Pitched Worst Against	Avg	AB	R	H	2B	3B	HR	RBI	BB	SO	HBP	GDP	SB	CS	OBP	Slg
Frank White	.500	8	0	4	1	0	0	2	0	1	0	0	0	1	.500	.625
George Brett	.364	11	3	4	1	2	0	1	1	1	0	0	0	0	.417	.818
Amos Otis	.364	11	2	4	2	0	0	0	0	1	0	0	1	0	.364	.545

Don Gullett

Throws: Left, Bats: Right

Pitching	ERA	W	L	Sv	G	GS	IP	BB	SO	Avg	R	H	2B	3B	HR	OBP	Slg
Totals	3.77	4	5	2	20	13	93.0	38	60	.230	41	78	12	5	5	.310	.339
Home	3.35	3	2	1	9	7	45.2	19	29	.221	17	36	5	3	2	.309	.325
Away	4.18	1	3	1	11	6	47.1	19	31	.239	24	42	7	2	3	.311	.352

	Avg	AB	R	H	2B	3B	HR	RBI	BB	SO	HBP	GDP	OBP	Slg
vs. Left	.241	116	0	28	5	2	2	14	10	14	2	1	.308	.371
vs. Right	.223	224	41	50	7	3	3	18	28	46	1	1	.310	.321
Scoring Pos.	.295	61	0	18	4	1	1	24	9	13	0	1	.365	.443
Close & Late	.240	50	2	12	2	0	0	3	6	10	0	1	.321	.280
None on/out	.180	89	0	16	3	1	0	0	7	14	2	1	.255	.236
None on	.184	212	0	39	5	3	2	2	24	41	3	1	.276	.264
Runners on	.305	128	0	39	7	2	3	30	14	19	0	1	.363	.461

Pitched Best Against

	Avg	AB	R	H	2B	3B	HR	RBI	BB	SO	HBP	GDP	SB	CS	OBP	Slg
Gene Alley	.000	5	0	0	0	0	0	0	0	1	0	0	0	0	.000	.000
Ron Cey	.000	5	0	0	0	0	0	1	1	2	0	0	0	0	.143	.000
Carlton Fisk	.125	8	0	1	0	0	0	0	1	3	0	0	0	0	.222	.125

Pitched Worst Against

	Avg	AB	R	H	2B	3B	HR	RBI	BB	SO	HBP	GDP	SB	CS	OBP	Slg
Richie Hebner	.556	9	2	5	2	0	0	2	0	0	0	0	0	0	.556	.778
Steve Garvey	.500	6	2	3	1	0	0	0	1	1	0	0	0	0	.571	.667
Dusty Baker	.400	5	2	2	0	0	0	1	0	0	1	0	0	0	.500	.400

Juan Guzman

Throws: Right, Bats: Right

Pitching	ERA	W	L	Sv	G	GS	IP	BB	SO	Avg	R	H	2B	3B	HR	OBP	Slg
Totals	2.44	5	1	0	8	8	51.2	27	41	.221	17	42	5	1	1	.324	.274
Home	2.33	2	0	0	4	4	27.0	8	27	.208	8	21	1	1	1	.266	.267
Away	2.55	3	1	0	4	4	24.2	19	14	.236	9	21	4	0	0	.382	.281

	Avg	AB	R	H	2B	3B	HR	RBI	BB	SO	HBP	GDP	OBP	Slg
vs. Left	.217	115	0	25	4	0	0	10	19	19	1	3	.333	.252
vs. Right	.227	75	0	17	1	1	1	6	8	22	1	3	.310	.307
Scoring Pos.	.254	59	13	15	1	0	0	15	10	16	1	3	.371	.271
Close & Late	.182	11	1	2	0	0	0	1	1	2	0	3	.250	.182
None on/out	.222	45	0	10	3	0	0	0	7	8	0	3	.327	.289
None on	.200	100	2	20	4	1	1	1	14	17	0	3	.298	.290
Runners on	.244	90	15	22	1	0	0	15	13	24	2	3	.352	.256

Pitched Best Against

	Avg	AB	R	H	2B	3B	HR	RBI	BB	SO	HBP	GDP	SB	CS	OBP	Slg
R. Henderson	.000	7	0	0	0	0	0	0	0	2	0	0	0	0	.000	.000
Jim Eisenreich	.000	6	0	0	0	0	0	0	0	1	0	0	0	0	.000	.000
Robin Ventura	.000	6	0	0	0	0	0	0	1	2	0	0	0	0	.143	.000

Pitched Worst Against

	Avg	AB	R	H	2B	3B	HR	RBI	BB	SO	HBP	GDP	SB	CS	OBP	Slg
John Kruk	.600	5	1	3	0	0	0	3	1	1	0	0	0	0	.667	.600
Terry Steinbach	.600	5	0	3	0	0	0	1	1	2	0	0	0	0	.667	.600
Willie Wilson	.600	5	0	3	0	0	0	0	1	1	0	0	3	0	.667	.600

Tony Gwynn

Bats: Left, Throws: Left

Batting	Avg	G	AB	R	H	2B	3B	HR	RBI	BB	SO	HBP	GDP	SB	CS	OBP	Slg
Totals	.314	13	51	7	16	4	0	0	4	4	6	0	0	2	2	.357	.392
Home	.429	6	21	5	9	2	0	0	3	4	3	0	0	1	2	.500	.524
Away	.233	7	30	2	7	2	0	0	1	0	3	0	0	1	0	.233	.300
vs. Left	.182	6	11	0	2	1	0	0	0	0	3	0	0	0	0	.182	.273
vs. Right	.350	13	40	7	14	3	0	0	4	4	3	0	0	2	2	.400	.425
Scoring Pos.	.154	10	13	0	2	1	0	0	4	1	1	0	0	1	0	.200	.231
Close & Late	.333	9	9	2	3	1	0	0	2	1	0	0	0	0	1	.400	.444
None on/out	.500	8	10	0	5	1	0	0	0	0	1	0	0	0	0	.500	.600
None on	.387	13	31	0	12	3	0	0	0	1	4	0	0	0	0	.406	.484
Runners on	.200	11	20	0	4	1	0	0	4	3	2	0	0	2	2	.292	.250
Batting #2	.314	13	51	7	16	4	0	0	4	4	6	0	0	2	2	.357	.392

Hit Best Against

	Avg	AB	R	H	2B	3B	HR	RBI	BB	SO	HBP	GDP	SB	CS	OBP	Slg
D. Eckersley	.600	5	1	3	1	0	0	0	0	0	0	0	0	0	.600	.800
Jack Morris	.333	6	0	2	0	0	0	0	2	0	0	0	1	1	.500	.333
Rick Sutcliffe	.286	7	2	2	1	0	0	2	0	1	0	0	0	0	.286	.429

Stan Hack

Bats: Left, Throws: Right

Batting	Avg	G	AB	R	H	2B	3B	HR	RBI	BB	SO	HBP	GDP	SB	CS	OBP	Slg
Totals	.348	18	69	6	24	5	1	0	5	7	6	0	3	1	3	.408	.449
Home	.324	10	37	5	12	1	0	0	5	4	3	0	3	1	2	.390	.351
Away	.375	8	32	1	12	4	1	0	0	3	3	0	0	0	1	.429	.563
vs. Left	.167	6	18	0	3	0	0	0	1	1	3	0	1	0	1	.211	.167
vs. Right	.412	18	51	6	21	5	1	0	4	6	3	0	2	1	2	.474	.549
Scoring Pos.	.250	13	12	0	3	0	0	0	4	0	0	0	1	0	0	.250	.250
Close & Late	.250	9	12	0	3	1	1	0	1	1	1	0	2	0	0	.308	.500
None on/out	.409	16	22	0	9	1	1	0	0	6	2	0	0	0	0	.536	.545
None on	.444	17	45	0	20	4	1	0	0	7	5	0	0	0	0	.519	.578
Runners on	.167	17	24	0	4	1	0	0	5	0	1	0	3	1	3	.167	.208
Batting #1	.404	11	47	4	19	4	0	0	5	5	4	0	2	0	3	.462	.489
Batting #7	.227	7	22	2	5	1	1	0	0	2	2	0	1	1	0	.292	.364

Hit Best Against

	Avg	AB	R	H	2B	3B	HR	RBI	BB	SO	HBP	GDP	SB	CS	OBP	Slg
Virgil Trucks	1.000	5	1	5	1	0	0	2	2	0	0	0	0	0	1.000	1.200
Red Ruffing	.556	9	0	5	0	0	0	1	0	0	0	1	0	1	.556	.556
Tommy Bridges	.375	8	0	3	1	1	0	0	1	0	0	0	0	0	.444	.750

Hit Worst Against

	Avg	AB	R	H	2B	3B	HR	RBI	BB	SO	HBP	GDP	SB	CS	OBP	Slg
Hal Newhouser	.100	10	0	1	0	0	0	1	1	2	0	0	0	1	.182	.100
Schoolboy Rowe	.125	8	1	1	0	0	0	0	1	1	0	0	0	0	.222	.125

Jesse Haines

Throws: Right, Bats: Right

Pitching	ERA	W	L	Sv	G	GS	IP	BB	SO	Avg	R	H	2B	3B	HR	OBP	Slg
Totals	1.67	3	1	0	6	4	32.1	16	12	.211	9	24	1	0	3	.308	.298
Home	1.46	2	1	0	4	3	24.2	10	10	.188	7	16	0	0	2	.274	.259
Away	2.35	1	0	0	2	1	7.2	6	2	.276	2	8	1	0	1	.400	.414

	Avg	AB	R	H	2B	3B	HR	RBI	BB	SO	HBP	GDP	OBP	Slg
vs. Left	.228	57	0	13	0	0	3	5	10	4	0	0	.343	.386
vs. Right	.193	57	9	11	1	0	0	3	6	8	0	0	.270	.211
Scoring Pos.	.130	23	0	3	0	0	0	3	4	3	0	0	.259	.130
Close & Late	.000	17	0	0	0	0	0	0	3	2	0	0	.150	.000
None on/out	.286	28	0	8	0	0	1	1	5	2	0	0	.394	.393
None on	.274	62	0	17	0	0	2	2	9	7	0	0	.366	.371
Runners on	.135	52	0	7	1	0	1	6	7	5	0	0	.237	.212

Pitched Best Against

	Avg	AB	R	H	2B	3B	HR	RBI	BB	SO	HBP	GDP	SB	CS	OBP	Slg
Tony Lazzeri	.000	10	1	0	0	0	0	0	1	3	0	2	1	0	.091	.000
Mark Koenig	.100	10	0	1	0	0	0	0	0	1	0	1	0	0	.100	.100
Bob Meusel	.100	10	1	1	0	0	0	0	2	1	0	0	1	0	.250	.100

Pitched Worst Against

	Avg	AB	R	H	2B	3B	HR	RBI	BB	SO	HBP	GDP	SB	CS	OBP	Slg
Joe Dugan	.500	6	1	3	0	0	0	0	0	0	0	0	0	1	.500	.500
Lou Gehrig	.444	9	2	4	0	0	2	3	3	0	0	0	0	0	.583	1.111
Earle Combs	.429	7	0	3	0	0	0	0	1	1	0	0	0	0	.500	.429

Wild Bill Hallahan

Throws: Left, Bats: Right

Pitching	ERA	W	L	Sv	G	GS	IP	BB	SO	Avg	R	H	2B	3B	HR	OBP	Slg
Totals	1.36	3	1	1	7	5	39.2	23	27	.201	6	29	7	0	0	.315	.250
Home	0.44	2	0	1	4	2	20.1	15	15	.174	1	12	2	0	0	.321	.203
Away	2.33	1	1	0	3	3	19.1	8	12	.227	5	17	5	0	0	.310	.293

	Avg	AB	R	H	2B	3B	HR	RBI	BB	SO	HBP	GDP	OBP	Slg
vs. Left	.188	48	0	9	2	0	0	2	9	6	1	0	.328	.229
vs. Right	.208	96	6	20	5	0	0	4	14	20	0	0	.309	.260
Scoring Pos.	.128	39	0	5	3	0	0	5	4	11	0	0	.209	.205
Close & Late	.214	28	0	6	0	0	0	2	3	5	0	0	.290	.214
None on/out	.216	37	0	8	1	0	0	0	3	2	0	0	.275	.243
None on	.213	75	0	16	3	0	0	0	11	11	1	0	.322	.253
Runners on	.188	69	0	13	4	0	0	6	12	15	0	0	.309	.246

Pitched Best Against

	Avg	AB	R	H	2B	3B	HR	RBI	BB	SO	HBP	GDP	SB	CS	OBP	Slg
Joe Boley	.000	6	0	0	0	0	0	0	0	1	0	0	0	0	.000	.000
Jimmy Dykes	.100	10	1	1	0	0	0	0	4	2	0	0	0	0	.357	.100
Mule Haas	.111	9	0	1	0	0	0	0	0	3	0	0	0	0	.111	.111

Pitched Worst Against

	Avg	AB	R	H	2B	3B	HR	RBI	BB	SO	HBP	GDP	SB	CS	OBP	Slg
Jimmie Foxx	.444	9	0	4	0	0	0	0	4	0	0	0	0	0	.615	.444
Jimmy Moore	.400	5	0	2	0	0	0	0	0	0	0	0	0	0	.400	.400
Al Simmons	.385	13	1	5	2	0	0	0	0	2	0	1	0	0	.385	.538

Bucky Harris

Bats: Right, Throws: Right

Batting	Avg	G	AB	R	H	2B	3B	HR	RBI	BB	SO	HBP	GDP	SB	CS	OBP	Slg
Totals	.232	14	56	7	13	2	0	2	7	2	7	1	1	0	2	.271	.375
Home	.333	7	27	4	9	2	0	2	7	2	1	0	1	0	2	.379	.630
Away	.138	7	29	3	4	0	0	0	0	0	6	1	0	0	0	.167	.138
vs. Left	.250	7	20	0	5	0	0	1	4	2	1	0	0	0	1	.318	.400
vs. Right	.222	14	36	7	8	2	0	1	3	0	6	1	1	0	1	.243	.361
Scoring Pos.	.300	8	10	0	3	1	0	0	5	0	0	0	0	0	1	.300	.400
Close & Late	.444	8	9	1	4	1	0	0	3	0	1	0	0	0	0	.444	.556
None on/out	.333	7	9	0	3	1	0	0	0	1	0	1	0	0	0	.455	.444
None on	.182	14	33	0	6	1	0	2	2	2	5	1	0	0	0	.250	.394
Runners on	.304	12	23	0	7	1	0	0	5	0	2	0	1	0	2	.304	.348
Batting #2	.232	14	56	7	13	2	0	2	7	2	7	1	1	0	2	.271	.375

Hit Best Against

	Avg	AB	R	H	2B	3B	HR	RBI	BB	SO	HBP	GDP	SB	CS	OBP	Slg
Virgil Barnes	.714	7	3	5	2	0	1	3	0	2	0	0	0	0	.714	1.429
Art Nehf	.300	10	0	3	0	0	0	3	0	0	0	0	0	1	.300	.300
Jack Bentley	.250	8	1	2	0	0	1	1	1	1	0	0	0	0	.333	.625

Hit Worst Against

	Avg	AB	R	H	2B	3B	HR	RBI	BB	SO	HBP	GDP	SB	CS	OBP	Slg
Vic Aldridge	.000	7	0	0	0	0	0	0	0	1	0	0	0	0	.000	.000
Ray Kremer	.143	7	1	1	0	0	0	0	0	1	0	1	0	0	.143	.143

Gabby Hartnett

Bats: Right, Throws: Right

Batting	Avg	G	AB	R	H	2B	3B	HR	RBI	BB	SO	HBP	GDP	SB	CS	OBP	Slg
Totals	.241	16	54	3	13	2	1	2	3	1	11	0	2	0	0	.255	.426
Home	.172	9	29	2	5	0	1	2	2	0	4	0	1	0	0	.172	.448
Away	.320	7	25	1	8	2	0	0	1	1	7	0	1	0	0	.346	.400
vs. Left	.111	5	9	0	1	0	0	0	0	1	3	0	0	0	0	.200	.111
vs. Right	.267	16	45	3	12	2	1	2	3	0	8	0	2	0	0	.267	.489
Scoring Pos.	.071	10	14	0	1	0	0	0	1	0	4	0	1	0	0	.071	.071
Close & Late	.250	6	4	0	1	0	0	0	0	0	1	0	0	0	0	.250	.250
None on/out	.300	11	20	0	6	1	0	2	2	0	3	0	0	0	0	.300	.650
None on	.303	13	33	0	10	2	1	2	2	0	4	0	0	0	0	.303	.606
Runners on	.143	14	21	0	3	0	0	0	1	1	7	0	2	0	0	.182	.143
Batting #4	.292	6	24	1	7	0	0	1	2	0	3	0	2	0	0	.292	.417
Batting #6	.091	3	11	0	1	0	1	0	0	0	2	0	0	0	0	.091	.273
Batting #7	.313	4	16	2	5	2	0	1	1	1	3	0	0	0	0	.353	.625

Hit Best Against

	Avg	AB	R	H	2B	3B	HR	RBI	BB	SO	HBP	GDP	SB	CS	OBP	Slg
Red Ruffing	.375	8	1	3	2	1	0	0	0	3	0	0	0	0	.375	.875
Tommy Bridges	.375	8	0	3	0	0	0	0	0	1	0	1	0	0	.375	.375
Schoolboy Rowe	.333	9	0	3	0	0	0	1	0	1	0	0	0	0	.333	.333

Hit Worst Against

	Avg	AB	R	H	2B	3B	HR	RBI	BB	SO	HBP	GDP	SB	CS	OBP	Slg
Lefty Gomez	.167	6	0	1	0	0	0	0	1	1	0	0	0	0	.286	.167

Billy Hatcher

Bats: Right, Throws: Right

Batting	Avg	G	AB	R	H	2B	3B	HR	RBI	BB	SO	HBP	GDP	SB	CS	OBP	Slg
Totals	.404	14	52	12	21	5	1	2	6	5	4	1	1	3	1	.466	.654
Home	.448	7	29	8	13	4	1	1	4	3	4	0	0	1	0	.500	.759
Away	.348	7	23	4	8	1	0	1	2	2	0	1	1	2	1	.423	.522
vs. Left	.474	7	19	3	9	1	0	2	4	2	1	0	0	0	0	.524	.842
vs. Right	.364	14	33	9	12	4	1	0	2	3	3	1	1	3	1	.432	.545

Batting	Avg	G	AB	R	H	2B	3B	HR	RBI	BB	SO	HBP	GDP	SB	CS	OBP	Slg
Scoring Pos.	.375	9	8	6	3	1	0	0	2	2	0	0	0	0	0	.500	.500
Close & Late	.375	8	8	1	3	0	1	0	1	2	2	0	0	0	0	.500	.625
None on/out	.286	9	14	0	4	1	1	0	0	1	3	0	0	0	0	.333	.500
None on	.394	14	33	0	13	2	1	1	1	3	4	1	0	0	0	.459	.606
Runners on	.421	12	19	8	8	3	0	1	5	2	0	0	1	3	1	.476	.737
Batting #2	.425	11	40	9	17	4	1	1	4	4	2	1	1	2	1	.489	.650

Hit Best Against	Avg	AB	R	H	2B	3B	HR	RBI	BB	SO	HBP	GDP	SB	CS	OBP	Slg
Zane Smith	.800	5	2	4	1	0	1	2	0	0	0	0	0	0	.800	1.600
Bobby Ojeda	.250	8	2	2	0	0	0	0	0	1	0	0	0	0	.250	.250

Hit Worst Against	Avg	AB	R	H	2B	3B	HR	RBI	BB	SO	HBP	GDP	SB	CS	OBP	Slg
Bob Walk	.000	5	0	0	0	0	0	0	0	1	0	0	0	0	.000	.000
Dwight Gooden	.167	6	0	1	0	0	0	0	2	1	0	0	1	0	.375	.167

Dave Henderson

Bats: Right, Throws: Right

Batting	Avg	G	AB	R	H	2B	3B	HR	RBI	BB	SO	HBP	GDP	SB	CS	OBP	Slg
Totals	.298	36	121	24	36	10	1	7	20	14	35	3	2	1	0	.376	.570
Home	.238	19	63	11	15	5	1	2	9	7	22	1	1	1	0	.315	.444
Away	.362	17	58	13	21	5	0	5	11	7	13	2	1	0	0	.441	.707
vs. Left	.290	18	31	2	9	4	0	0	3	4	5	1	0	0	0	.389	.419
vs. Right	.300	35	90	22	27	6	1	7	17	10	30	2	2	1	0	.371	.622
Scoring Pos.	.292	26	24	7	7	4	0	0	11	5	8	2	0	0	0	.412	.458
Close & Late	.471	17	17	2	8	1	0	2	7	3	6	0	0	0	0	.500	.882
None on/out	.341	24	44	1	15	4	0	4	4	4	11	1	0	0	0	.408	.705
None on	.313	33	80	2	25	5	1	5	5	5	21	1	0	0	0	.360	.588
Runners on	.268	29	41	7	11	5	0	2	15	9	14	2	2	1	0	.400	.537
Batting #2	.295	11	44	4	13	4	0	1	5	4	15	0	1	0	0	.354	.455
Batting #5	.313	9	32	10	10	4	0	3	5	6	8	1	1	0	0	.436	.719
Batting #7	.438	4	16	4	7	0	0	2	3	1	2	1	0	0	0	.500	.813
Batting #8	.222	8	18	5	4	1	1	1	6	3	6	0	0	0	0	.304	.556

Hit Best Against	Avg	AB	R	H	2B	3B	HR	RBI	BB	SO	HBP	GDP	SB	CS	OBP	Slg
Tim Belcher	.667	6	1	4	1	0	0	1	0	1	0	0	0	0	.667	.833
Bruce Hurst	.500	6	0	3	1	0	0	2	0	1	0	0	0	0	.500	.667
Dwight Gooden	.400	5	2	2	0	1	1	1	0	2	0	0	0	0	.400	1.400

Hit Worst Against	Avg	AB	R	H	2B	3B	HR	RBI	BB	SO	HBP	GDP	SB	CS	OBP	Slg
Orel Hershiser	.000	6	0	0	0	0	0	0	2	3	0	0	0	0	.250	.000
Ron Darling	.167	6	1	1	0	0	0	0	1	2	1	0	0	0	.375	.167
Bobby Ojeda	.200	5	1	1	0	0	0	0	1	1	0	0	0	0	.333	.200

Rickey Henderson

Bats: Right, Throws: Left

Batting	Avg	G	AB	R	H	2B	3B	HR	RBI	BB	SO	HBP	GDP	SB	CS	OBP	Slg
Totals	.288	44	170	35	49	10	4	5	17	31	24	2	1	25	5	.402	.482
Home	.353	20	68	18	24	2	1	1	3	19	13	1	0	17	4	.500	.456
Away	.245	24	102	17	25	8	3	4	14	12	11	1	1	8	1	.328	.500
vs. Left	.396	25	48	7	19	5	2	3	10	10	5	0	0	10	2	.500	.771
vs. Right	.246	43	122	28	30	5	2	2	7	21	19	2	1	15	3	.363	.369
Scoring Pos.	.250	36	40	21	10	0	2	2	14	3	7	1	1	10	2	.311	.500
Close & Late	.333	21	21	4	7	0	0	0	3	5	1	0	0	2	1	.444	.333
None on/out	.261	44	69	3	18	4	1	3	3	16	8	0	0	0	0	.400	.478
None on	.282	44	110	3	31	9	2	3	3	24	16	1	0	0	0	.415	.482
Runners on	.300	43	60	21	18	1	2	2	14	7	8	1	1	25	5	.377	.483
Batting #1	.288	44	170	35	49	10	4	5	17	31	24	2	1	25	5	.402	.482

Hit Best Against	Avg	AB	R	H	2B	3B	HR	RBI	BB	SO	HBP	GDP	SB	CS	OBP	Slg
T. Stottlemyre	.667	6	3	4	0	0	1	1	2	0	0	0	3	0	.750	1.167
Scott Garrelts	.400	5	0	2	1	0	0	1	0	1	0	0	0	0	.400	.600
Danny Jackson	.400	5	2	2	0	0	0	0	0	0	0	0	1	0	.400	.400

Hit Worst Against	Avg	AB	R	H	2B	3B	HR	RBI	BB	SO	HBP	GDP	SB	CS	OBP	Slg
Juan Guzman	.000	7	0	0	0	0	0	0	0	2	0	0	0	0	.000	.000
Alex Fernandez	.000	7	1	0	0	0	0	0	1	2	0	0	0	0	.125	.000
Terry Mulholland	.000	5	0	0	0	0	0	0	1	1	0	0	0	1	.167	.000

Tom Henke

Throws: Right, Bats: Right

Pitching	ERA	W	L	Sv	G	GS	IP	BB	SO	Avg	R	H	2B	3B	HR	OBP	Slg
Totals	1.83	2	0	5	15	0	19.2	9	15	.152	4	10	0	0	1	.263	.197
Home	2.61	1	0	2	8	0	10.1	5	12	.171	3	6	0	0	1	.275	.257
Away	0.96	1	0	3	7	0	9.1	4	3	.129	1	4	0	0	0	.250	.129

	Avg	AB	R	H	2B	3B	HR	RBI	BB	SO	HBP	GDP	OBP	Slg
vs. Left	.235	34	0	8	0	0	1	5	5	6	0	0	.333	.324
vs. Right	.063	32	3	2	0	0	0	1	4	9	1	0	.189	.063
Scoring Pos.	.211	19	1	4	0	0	0	5	2	3	0	0	.286	.211
Close & Late	.167	48	2	8	0	0	0	5	6	9	1	0	.273	.167
None on/out	.250	16	0	4	0	0	1	1	1	3	0	0	.294	.438
None on	.161	31	0	5	0	0	1	1	5	7	1	0	.297	.258
Runners on	.143	35	1	5	0	0	0	5	4	8	0	0	.231	.143

Pitched Best Against	Avg	AB	R	H	2B	3B	HR	RBI	BB	SO	HBP	GDP	SB	CS	OBP	Slg
Mark McGwire	.000	5	0	0	0	0	0	0	0	1	0	0	0	0	.000	.000

Pitched Worst Against	Avg	AB	R	H	2B	3B	HR	RBI	BB	SO	HBP	GDP	SB	CS	OBP	Slg
Willie Wilson	.333	6	2	2	0	0	0	0	0	0	0	0	1	0	.333	.333

Billy Herman

Bats: Right, Throws: Right

Batting	Avg	G	AB	R	H	2B	3B	HR	RBI	BB	SO	HBP	GDP	SB	CS	OBP	Slg
Totals	.242	18	66	9	16	3	1	1	7	4	9	0	1	0	0	.286	.364
Home	.226	9	31	4	7	2	1	0	1	2	4	0	0	0	0	.273	.355
Away	.257	9	35	5	9	1	0	1	6	2	5	0	1	0	0	.297	.371
vs. Left	.231	6	13	0	3	1	0	0	0	1	5	0	0	0	0	.286	.308
vs. Right	.245	18	53	9	13	2	1	1	7	3	4	0	1	0	0	.286	.377
Scoring Pos.	.333	12	15	0	5	1	0	0	5	0	2	0	0	0	0	.333	.400
Close & Late	.222	9	9	0	2	0	0	0	3	0	1	0	0	0	0	.222	.222
None on/out	.263	14	19	0	5	2	1	0	0	1	4	0	0	0	0	.300	.474
None on	.194	17	36	0	7	2	1	0	0	3	4	0	0	0	0	.256	.306
Runners on	.300	16	30	0	9	1	0	1	7	1	5	0	1	0	0	.323	.433
Batting #1	.222	4	18	5	4	1	0	0	1	1	3	0	0	0	0	.263	.278
Batting #2	.250	13	48	4	12	2	1	1	6	3	6	0	1	0	0	.294	.396

Hit Best Against	Avg	AB	R	H	2B	3B	HR	RBI	BB	SO	HBP	GDP	SB	CS	OBP	Slg
Tommy Bridges	.500	8	1	4	0	0	1	5	0	1	0	1	0	0	.500	.875
Schoolboy Rowe	.250	8	2	2	1	1	0	1	0	0	0	0	0	0	.250	.625
Lefty Gomez	.250	8	2	2	1	0	0	0	0	4	0	0	0	0	.250	.375

Hit Worst Against	Avg	AB	R	H	2B	3B	HR	RBI	BB	SO	HBP	GDP	SB	CS	OBP	Slg
Red Ruffing	.235	17	2	4	0	0	0	1	1	0	0	0	0	0	.278	.235

Keith Hernandez

Bats: Left, Throws: Left

Batting	Avg	G	AB	R	H	2B	3B	HR	RBI	BB	SO	HBP	GDP	SB	CS	OBP	Slg
Totals	.265	30	117	13	31	3	1	2	21	20	19	0	3	1	0	.370	.359
Home	.246	16	61	7	15	0	0	1	11	12	8	0	0	0	0	.365	.295
Away	.286	14	56	6	16	3	1	1	10	8	11	0	3	1	0	.375	.429
vs. Left	.333	11	33	0	11	3	0	0	8	4	2	0	0	1	0	.395	.424
vs. Right	.238	30	84	13	20	0	1	2	13	16	17	0	3	0	0	.360	.333
Scoring Pos.	.289	26	38	0	11	3	1	1	19	12	6	0	0	0	0	.451	.500
Close & Late	.222	16	18	0	4	2	0	0	4	7	5	0	0	0	0	.440	.333
None on/out	.267	14	15	0	4	0	0	0	0	2	1	0	0	0	0	.353	.267
None on	.175	29	57	0	10	0	0	0	0	6	10	0	0	0	0	.254	.175
Runners on	.350	28	60	0	21	3	1	2	21	14	9	0	3	1	0	.467	.533
Batting #3	.257	27	105	10	27	3	1	2	20	18	16	0	3	1	0	.363	.362
Batting #4	.333	3	12	3	4	0	0	0	1	2	3	0	0	0	0	.429	.333

Hit Best Against	Avg	AB	R	H	2B	3B	HR	RBI	BB	SO	HBP	GDP	SB	CS	OBP	Slg
Nolan Ryan	.429	7	1	3	0	1	0	2	0	1	0	0	0	0	.429	.714
Roger Clemens	.400	5	0	2	0	0	0	1	1	0	0	0	0	0	.500	.400
Pascual Perez	.400	5	1	2	0	0	0	1	0	1	0	0	0	0	.400	.400

Hit Worst Against	Avg	AB	R	H	2B	3B	HR	RBI	BB	SO	HBP	GDP	SB	CS	OBP	Slg
Mike Scott	.125	8	0	1	0	0	0	0	0	3	0	0	0	0	.125	.125
Don Sutton	.167	6	1	1	0	0	1	2	0	0	0	0	0	0	.167	.667
Pete Vuckovich	.167	6	0	1	0	0	0	0	1	1	0	0	0	0	.286	.167

Orel Hershiser

Throws: Right, Bats: Right

Pitching	ERA	W	L	Sv	G	GS	IP	BB	SO	Avg	R	H	2B	3B	HR	OBP	Slg
Totals	2.70	8	3	1	19	18	126.2	40	91	.222	43	102	15	0	8	.291	.307
Home	1.96	6	1	0	11	11	82.2	19	58	.222	20	66	11	0	2	.276	.279
Away	4.09	2	2	1	8	7	44.0	21	33	.222	23	36	4	0	6	.316	.358

	Avg	AB	R	H	2B	3B	HR	RBI	BB	SO	HBP	GDP	OBP	Slg
vs. Left	.244	271	0	66	13	0	5	20	31	47	4	3	.328	.347
vs. Right	.191	188	11	36	2	0	3	14	9	43	1	3	.232	.250
Scoring Pos.	.240	96	24	23	6	0	2	28	8	20	2	3	.306	.365
Close & Late	.175	40	1	7	1	0	0	4	8	8	0	3	.313	.200
None on/out	.244	127	0	31	3	0	5	5	10	21	0	3	.299	.386
None on	.222	288	7	64	8	0	6	6	21	59	3	3	.282	.313
Runners on	.222	171	25	38	7	0	2	28	19	31	2	3	.304	.298

Pitched Best Against	Avg	AB	R	H	2B	3B	HR	RBI	BB	SO	HBP	GDP	SB	CS	OBP	Slg
K. McReynolds	.000	11	0	0	0	0	0	0	0	3	0	0	0	0	.000	.000
Howard Johnson	.000	7	1	0	0	0	0	0	0	1	0	0	0	0	.000	.000
Andy Van Slyke	.000	6	0	0	0	0	0	0	1	0	0	0	0	0	.143	.000

Pitched Worst Against	Avg	AB	R	H	2B	3B	HR	RBI	BB	SO	HBP	GDP	SB	CS	OBP	Slg
Charles Johnson	.600	5	2	3	0	0	1	2	0	1	0	0	0	0	.600	1.200
Gregg Jefferies	.545	11	1	6	1	0	0	0	1	0	0	0	0	0	.583	.636
Ken Griffey Jr.	.500	6	1	3	1	0	1	2	1	0	0	0	0	0	.571	1.167

Gil Hodges

Bats: Right, Throws: Right

Batting	Avg	G	AB	R	H	2B	3B	HR	RBI	BB	SO	HBP	GDP	SB	CS	OBP	Slg
Totals	.267	39	131	15	35	2	1	5	21	17	22	0	4	1	1	.349	.412
Home	.314	20	70	11	22	2	1	4	16	8	13	0	1	0	0	.385	.543
Away	.213	19	61	4	13	0	0	1	5	9	9	0	3	1	1	.310	.262
vs. Left	.231	18	39	0	9	0	0	1	5	8	5	0	0	1	1	.362	.308
vs. Right	.283	39	92	15	26	2	1	4	16	9	17	0	4	0	0	.343	.457
Scoring Pos.	.346	23	26	0	9	2	0	2	17	5	5	0	1	1	0	.438	.654
Close & Late	.300	21	20	1	6	0	0	2	4	1	4	0	2	0	1	.333	.600
None on/out	.194	27	31	0	6	0	0	2	2	5	3	0	0	0	0	.306	.387
None on	.200	37	75	0	15	0	1	2	2	7	14	0	0	0	0	.268	.307
Runners on	.357	35	56	0	20	2	0	3	19	10	8	0	4	1	1	.448	.554
Batting #5	.306	14	49	8	15	2	1	2	10	6	6	0	0	0	0	.382	.510
Batting #6	.340	14	53	5	18	0	0	3	10	4	7	0	1	1	1	.379	.509
Batting #7	.053	7	19	0	1	0	0	0	1	3	6	0	3	0	0	.182	.053

Hit Best Against	Avg	AB	R	H	2B	3B	HR	RBI	BB	SO	HBP	GDP	SB	CS	OBP	Slg
Don Larsen	.500	6	2	3	0	0	1	2	0	1	0	0	0	0	.500	1.000
Bob Shaw	.429	7	0	3	0	1	0	0	0	1	0	0	0	0	.429	.714
Johnny Sain	.333	6	0	2	0	0	0	0	0	1	0	0	0	0	.333	.333

Hit Worst Against	Avg	AB	R	H	2B	3B	HR	RBI	BB	SO	HBP	GDP	SB	CS	OBP	Slg
Johnny Kucks	.000	5	0	0	0	0	0	0	0	0	0	0	0	0	.000	.000
Bob Turley	.000	6	0	0	0	0	0	0	1	1	0	0	0	0	.143	.000
Allie Reynolds	.071	14	1	1	0	0	1	2	1	3	0	3	0	0	.133	.286

Ken Holtzman

Throws: Left, Bats: Right

Pitching	ERA	W	L	Sv	G	GS	IP	BB	SO	Avg	R	H	2B	3B	HR	OBP	Slg
Totals	2.30	6	4	0	13	12	70.1	18	39	.231	22	61	12	2	2	.280	.314
Home	1.61	5	1	0	7	7	50.1	9	27	.194	10	35	7	2	1	.233	.272
Away	4.05	1	3	0	6	5	20.0	9	12	.310	12	26	5	0	1	.376	.405

	Avg	AB	R	H	2B	3B	HR	RBI	BB	SO	HBP	GDP	OBP	Slg
vs. Left	.286	63	0	18	3	0	1	6	2	7	0	1	.308	.381
vs. Right	.214	201	22	43	9	2	1	9	16	32	0	1	.272	.294
Scoring Pos.	.178	45	0	8	2	1	1	14	4	11	0	1	.245	.333
Close & Late	.160	25	0	4	1	0	0	0	1	2	0	1	.192	.200
None on/out	.236	72	0	17	4	0	0	0	4	11	0	1	.276	.292
None on	.229	166	0	38	8	1	1	1	10	24	0	1	.273	.307
Runners on	.235	98	0	23	4	1	1	14	8	15	0	1	.292	.327

Pitched Best Against	Avg	AB	R	H	2B	3B	HR	RBI	BB	SO	HBP	GDP	SB	CS	OBP	Slg
Davey Lopes	.000	7	1	0	0	0	0	0	0	3	0	0	0	0	.000	.000
Pete Rose	.000	7	0	0	0	0	0	0	0	0	0	0	0	0	.000	.000
M. Rettenmund	.000	5	0	0	0	0	0	0	0	2	0	0	0	0	.000	.000

Pitched Worst Against	Avg	AB	R	H	2B	3B	HR	RBI	BB	SO	HBP	GDP	SB	CS	OBP	Slg
Johnny Bench	.800	5	2	4	1	0	0	0	1	0	0	0	1	0	.833	1.000
Tony Perez	.600	5	0	3	0	0	0	0	0	1	0	0	0	0	.600	.600
Steve Garvey	.500	6	1	3	0	0	0	0	0	1	0	0	0	0	.500	.500

Harry Hooper

Bats: Left, Throws: Right

Batting	Avg	G	AB	R	H	2B	3B	HR	RBI	BB	SO	HBP	GDP	SB	CS	OBP	Slg
Totals	.293	24	92	13	27	3	2	2	6	11	11	1	0	3	5	.371	.435
Home	.235	13	51	7	12	2	1	0	2	4	6	0	0	2	0	.286	.314
Away	.366	11	41	6	15	1	1	2	4	7	5	1	0	1	5	.469	.585
vs. Left	.214	12	42	0	9	1	0	1	1	3	4	1	0	0	4	.283	.310
vs. Right	.360	24	50	13	18	2	2	1	5	8	7	0	0	3	1	.441	.540
Scoring Pos.	.278	14	18	0	5	1	0	0	3	2	3	0	0	0	1	.333	.333
Close & Late	.316	16	19	3	6	1	0	1	3	0	3	0	0	0	0	.300	.526
None on/out	.351	24	37	0	13	1	1	1	1	5	4	0	0	0	0	.429	.514
None on	.303	24	66	0	20	2	1	2	2	7	7	0	0	0	0	.370	.455
Runners on	.269	21	26	0	7	1	1	0	4	4	4	1	0	3	5	.375	.385
Batting #1	.293	24	92	13	27	3	2	2	6	11	11	1	0	3	5	.371	.435

Hit Best Against	Avg	AB	R	H	2B	3B	HR	RBI	BB	SO	HBP	GDP	SB	CS	OBP	Slg
Erskine Mayer	.600	5	2	3	0	0	1	1	2	2	0	0	0	0	.714	1.200
Jeff Tesreau	.429	7	1	3	1	0	0	2	3	3	0	0	0	0	.545	.571
C. Mathewson	.357	14	2	5	1	1	0	0	0	0	0	0	2	0	.357	.571

Hit Worst Against	Avg	AB	R	H	2B	3B	HR	RBI	BB	SO	HBP	GDP	SB	CS	OBP	Slg
Lefty Tyler	.111	9	0	1	0	0	0	0	1	0	0	0	0	1	.200	.111
Rube Marquard	.154	13	1	2	1	0	0	0	1	2	0	0	0	0	.214	.231
Sherry Smith	.167	6	0	1	0	0	0	0	0	0	0	0	0	0	.167	.167

Burt Hooton

Throws: Right, Bats: Right

Pitching	ERA	W	L	Sv	G	GS	IP	BB	SO	Avg	R	H	2B	3B	HR	OBP	Slg
Totals	3.17	6	3	0	11	11	59.2	27	33	.243	24	55	7	1	4	.325	.336
Home	1.77	3	0	0	3	3	20.1	7	9	.233	4	17	4	0	1	.309	.329
Away	3.89	3	3	0	8	8	39.1	20	24	.248	20	38	3	1	3	.333	.340

	Avg	AB	R	H	2B	3B	HR	RBI	BB	SO	HBP	GDP	OBP	Slg
vs. Left	.250	124	0	31	5	0	2	12	12	16	1	2	.321	.339
vs. Right	.235	102	24	24	2	1	2	9	15	16	0	2	.331	.333
Scoring Pos.	.196	46	0	9	2	0	0	15	10	13	0	2	.333	.239
Close & Late	.100	10	0	1	0	0	0	0	2	1	0	2	.250	.100
None on/out	.290	62	0	18	1	1	1	1	7	6	0	2	.362	.387
None on	.273	132	0	36	5	1	2	2	12	15	0	2	.333	.371
Runners on	.202	94	0	19	2	0	2	19	15	17	1	2	.315	.287

Pitched Best Against	Avg	AB	R	H	2B	3B	HR	RBI	BB	SO	HBP	GDP	SB	CS	OBP	Slg
Andre Dawson	.000	7	0	0	0	0	0	0	0	3	0	1	0	0	.000	.000
Larry Parrish	.000	6	0	0	0	0	0	0	0	0	0	0	0	0	.000	.000
Dave Winfield	.000	5	0	0	0	0	0	0	1	0	0	0	0	0	.167	.000

Pitched Worst Against	Avg	AB	R	H	2B	3B	HR	RBI	BB	SO	HBP	GDP	SB	CS	OBP	Slg
Jerry White	.600	5	0	3	1	0	0	0	1	0	0	0	1	0	.667	.800
Rodney Scott	.500	6	0	3	0	0	0	0	1	0	0	0	1	0	.571	.500
Roy White	.429	7	3	3	0	0	0	1	0	0	0	0	2	0	.429	.429

Rogers Hornsby

Bats: Right, Throws: Right

Batting	Avg	G	AB	R	H	2B	3B	HR	RBI	BB	SO	HBP	GDP	SB	CS	OBP	Slg
Totals	.245	12	49	6	12	2	1	0	5	3	10	0	1	1	0	.288	.327
Home	.190	5	21	2	4	0	0	0	1	1	6	0	1	1	0	.227	.190
Away	.286	7	28	4	8	2	1	0	4	2	4	0	0	0	0	.333	.429
vs. Left	.125	7	16	0	2	0	0	0	0	1	1	0	1	0	0	.176	.125
vs. Right	.303	12	33	6	10	2	1	0	5	2	9	0	0	1	0	.343	.424
Scoring Pos.	.300	9	10	0	3	0	0	0	5	1	2	0	0	1	0	.364	.300
Close & Late	.500	2	2	0	1	0	0	0	0	0	0	0	1	0	0	.500	.500
None on/out	.222	6	9	0	2	0	0	0	0	0	1	0	0	0	0	.222	.222
None on	.276	12	29	0	8	2	1	0	0	1	5	0	0	0	0	.300	.414
Runners on	.200	11	20	0	4	0	0	0	5	2	5	0	1	1	0	.273	.200
Batting #3	.245	12	49	6	12	2	1	0	5	3	10	0	1	1	0	.288	.327

Hit Best Against	Avg	AB	R	H	2B	3B	HR	RBI	BB	SO	HBP	GDP	SB	CS	OBP	Slg
G. Earnshaw	.429	7	2	3	1	0	0	1	0	4	0	0	0	0	.429	.571
Waite Hoyt	.375	8	1	3	0	0	0	1	0	2	0	0	1	0	.375	.375

Hit Worst Against	Avg	AB	R	H	2B	3B	HR	RBI	BB	SO	HBP	GDP	SB	CS	OBP	Slg
Howard Ehmke	.000	6	0	0	0	0	0	0	0	2	0	0	0	0	.000	.000
Herb Pennock	.111	9	0	1	0	0	0	0	0	0	0	1	0	0	.111	.111

Elston Howard

Bats: Right, Throws: Right

Batting	Avg	G	AB	R	H	2B	3B	HR	RBI	BB	SO	HBP	GDP	SB	CS	OBP	Slg
Totals	.246	54	171	25	42	7	1	5	19	12	37	3	6	1	0	.306	.386
Home	.205	25	73	8	15	2	0	2	7	6	18	1	2	0	0	.275	.315
Away	.276	29	98	17	27	5	1	3	12	6	19	2	4	1	0	.330	.439
vs. Left	.265	29	68	0	18	2	1	2	5	7	7	1	5	0	0	.342	.412
vs. Right	.233	54	103	25	24	5	0	3	14	5	30	2	1	1	0	.282	.369

Batting	Avg	G	AB	R	H	2B	3B	HR	RBI	BB	SO	HBP	GDP	SB	CS	OBP	Slg
Scoring Pos.	.289	31	38	0	11	0	0	1	13	7	8	1	2	0	0	.413	.368
Close & Late	.276	23	29	2	8	0	0	2	8	0	7	1	3	0	0	.300	.483
None on/out	.244	30	45	0	11	3	1	2	2	1	12	0	0	0	0	.261	.489
None on	.255	44	98	0	25	7	1	2	2	4	21	0	0	0	0	.284	.408
Runners on	.233	46	73	0	17	0	0	3	17	8	16	3	6	1	0	.333	.356
Batting #4	.167	4	12	2	2	0	0	1	2	0	0	0	0	0	0	.167	.417
Batting #5	.333	13	48	13	16	3	0	0	3	6	12	1	2	1	0	.418	.396
Batting #6	.225	20	71	8	16	4	0	3	10	4	13	1	4	0	0	.276	.408
Batting #8	.111	9	27	0	3	0	0	0	1	1	6	0	0	0	0	.143	.111

Hit Best Against	Avg	AB	R	H	2B	3B	HR	RBI	BB	SO	HBP	GDP	SB	CS	OBP	Slg
Roger Craig	.600	5	0	3	1	0	0	1	2	2	0	0	0	0	.714	.800
Don Newcombe	.400	5	2	2	0	0	2	3	0	1	0	0	0	0	.400	1.600
Clem Labine	.400	5	2	2	0	0	0	1	0	0	0	0	0	0	.400	.400

Hit Worst Against	Avg	AB	R	H	2B	3B	HR	RBI	BB	SO	HBP	GDP	SB	CS	OBP	Slg
Jack Sanford	.000	6	0	0	0	0	0	0	0	3	0	0	0	0	.000	.000
Bob Gibson	.133	15	1	2	1	0	0	0	0	5	1	0	0	0	.188	.200
Johnny Podres	.182	11	0	2	0	0	0	0	0	1	0	0	0	0	.182	.182

Waite Hoyt

Throws: Right, Bats: Right

Pitching	ERA	W	L	Sv	G	GS	IP	BB	SO	Avg	R	H	2B	3B	HR	OBP	Slg
Totals	1.83	6	4	0	12	11	83.2	22	49	.260	28	81	13	1	2	.304	.328
Home	1.74	2	3	0	6	6	41.1	13	21	.188	12	27	3	1	2	.253	.264
Away	1.91	4	1	0	6	5	42.1	9	28	.323	16	54	10	0	0	.348	.383

	Avg	AB	R	H	2B	3B	HR	RBI	BB	SO	HBP	GDP	OBP	Slg
vs. Left	.252	143	0	36	5	0	1	8	16	17	1	2	.323	.308
vs. Right	.268	168	28	45	8	1	1	17	6	32	0	2	.287	.345
Scoring Pos.	.246	65	0	16	2	1	1	24	2	12	0	2	.240	.354
Close & Late	.108	37	0	4	0	0	0	3	2	10	0	2	.150	.108
None on/out	.286	77	0	22	5	0	0	0	6	14	1	2	.345	.351
None on	.297	165	0	49	9	0	1	1	16	23	1	2	.363	.370
Runners on	.219	146	0	32	4	1	1	24	6	26	0	2	.238	.281

Pitched Best Against	Avg	AB	R	H	2B	3B	HR	RBI	BB	SO	HBP	GDP	SB	CS	OBP	Slg
Wattie Holm	.000	6	0	0	0	0	0	1	0	1	0	0	0	0	.000	.000
Bill Sherdel	.000	5	0	0	0	0	0	0	0	2	0	0	0	0	.000	.000
Jimmie Wilson	.000	5	0	0	0	0	0	0	0	0	0	0	0	1	.000	.000

Pitched Worst Against	Avg	AB	R	H	2B	3B	HR	RBI	BB	SO	HBP	GDP	SB	CS	OBP	Slg
Heine Groh	.667	6	2	4	0	1	0	2	0	0	0	0	0	0	.667	1.000
T. Thevenow	.667	6	1	4	1	0	0	3	0	1	0	0	0	0	.667	.833
J. Rawlings	.455	11	0	5	3	0	0	0	0	0	0	0	0	0	.455	.727

Carl Hubbell

Throws: Left, Bats: Right

Pitching	ERA	W	L	Sv	G	GS	IP	BB	SO	Avg	R	H	2B	3B	HR	OBP	Slg
Totals	1.79	4	2	0	6	6	50.1	12	32	.214	18	40	4	1	3	.265	.294
Home	1.00	3	0	0	3	3	27.0	4	22	.184	6	18	2	1	2	.223	.286
Away	2.70	1	2	0	3	3	23.1	8	10	.247	12	22	2	0	1	.309	.303

	Avg	AB	R	H	2B	3B	HR	RBI	BB	SO	HBP	GDP	OBP	Slg
vs. Left	.195	87	0	17	0	1	3	10	6	15	1	2	.255	.322
vs. Right	.228	101	18	23	4	0	0	5	6	17	0	2	.271	.267
Scoring Pos.	.250	40	0	10	0	0	1	13	4	3	1	2	.333	.325
Close & Late	.207	29	0	6	0	0	0	2	4	5	1	2	.324	.207
None on/out	.229	48	0	11	3	0	1	1	4	12	0	2	.288	.354
None on	.205	112	0	23	4	1	2	2	5	21	0	2	.239	.313
Runners on	.224	76	0	17	0	0	1	13	7	11	1	2	.298	.263

Pitched Best Against	Avg	AB	R	H	2B	3B	HR	RBI	BB	SO	HBP	GDP	SB	CS	OBP	Slg
Ossie Bluege	.000	7	0	0	0	0	0	0	0	3	0	0	0	0	.000	.000
Heinie Manush	.000	6	1	0	0	0	0	0	1	1	0	0	0	0	.143	.000
Bill Dickey	.071	14	1	1	0	0	0	1	0	2	0	0	0	0	.071	.071

Pitched Worst Against	Avg	AB	R	H	2B	3B	HR	RBI	BB	SO	HBP	GDP	SB	CS	OBP	Slg
Red Rolfe	.462	13	3	6	0	1	0	1	1	1	0	0	0	0	.500	.615
Jake Powell	.375	8	1	3	1	0	0	0	0	1	0	0	0	1	.375	.500
Buddy Myer	.375	8	1	3	0	0	0	0	1	1	0	0	0	0	.444	.375

Catfish Hunter

Throws: Right, Bats: Right

Pitching	ERA	W	L	Sv	G	GS	IP	BB	SO	Avg	R	H	2B	3B	HR	OBP	Slg
Totals	3.26	9	6	1	22	19	132.1	35	70	.231	49	114	21	4	21	.282	.418
Home	4.30	3	3	0	9	9	52.1	13	20	.241	25	48	12	2	13	.291	.518
Away	2.59	6	3	1	13	10	80.0	22	50	.224	24	66	9	2	8	.277	.350

	Avg	AB	R	H	2B	3B	HR	RBI	BB	SO	HBP	GDP	OBP	Slg
vs. Left	.224	210	0	47	8	3	12	18	20	30	0	5	.290	.462
vs. Right	.237	283	49	67	13	1	9	27	15	40	1	5	.277	.385
Scoring Pos.	.193	83	0	16	2	1	2	22	11	15	0	5	.281	.313
Close & Late	.196	46	2	9	2	0	1	4	4	5	0	5	.260	.304
None on/out	.302	139	0	42	9	2	8	8	9	10	1	5	.349	.568
None on	.245	323	0	79	18	3	16	16	21	43	1	5	.293	.467
Runners on	.206	170	0	35	3	1	5	29	14	27	0	5	.263	.324

Pitched Best Against	Avg	AB	R	H	2B	3B	HR	RBI	BB	SO	HBP	GDP	SB	CS	OBP	Slg
Cleon Jones	.000	6	0	0	0	0	0	0	0	1	0	0	0	0	.000	.000
Rick Monday	.000	6	0	0	0	0	0	0	0	2	0	0	0	0	.000	.000
Tom Seaver	.000	5	0	0	0	0	0	0	0	2	0	0	0	0	.000	.000

Pitched Worst Against	Avg	AB	R	H	2B	3B	HR	RBI	BB	SO	HBP	GDP	SB	CS	OBP	Slg
George Brett	.667	9	3	6	0	0	3	3	0	0	0	0	0	1	.667	1.667
Ellie Hendricks	.500	6	2	3	0	0	1	1	1	2	0	0	0	0	.571	1.000
Tony Perez	.500	10	1	5	1	0	0	1	2	0	0	0	0	0	.583	.600

2290 Postseason: Player Profiles

Bruce Hurst

Throws: Left, Bats: Left

Pitching	ERA	W	L	Sv	G	GS	IP	BB	SO	Avg	R	H	2B	3B	HR	OBP	Slg
Totals	2.29	3	2	0	7	7	51.0	12	37	.242	14	46	7	0	6	.287	.374
Home	1.67	2	1	0	3	3	27.0	4	17	.260	6	27	4	0	3	.287	.385
Away	3.00	1	1	0	4	4	24.0	8	20	.221	8	19	3	0	3	.287	.360

	Avg	AB	R	H	2B	3B	HR	RBI	BB	SO	HBP	GDP	OBP	Slg
vs. Left	.189	37	0	7	0	0	1	3	3	11	0	1	.250	.270
vs. Right	.255	153	14	39	7	0	5	11	9	26	0	1	.296	.399
Scoring Pos.	.175	40	0	7	1	0	1	9	3	8	0	1	.233	.275
Close & Late	.143	21	1	3	1	0	0	2	1	5	0	1	.182	.190
None on/out	.240	50	0	12	3	0	2	2	3	9	0	1	.283	.420
None on	.274	113	0	31	6	0	5	5	8	21	0	1	.322	.460
Runners on	.195	77	0	15	1	0	1	9	4	16	0	1	.235	.247

Pitched Best Against

	Avg	AB	R	H	2B	3B	HR	RBI	BB	SO	HBP	GDP	SB	CS	OBP	Slg
G. Hendrick	.000	6	0	0	0	0	0	0	0	1	0	0	0	0	.000	.000
Don Baylor	.000	5	0	0	0	0	0	0	1	2	0	0	0	0	.167	.000
Mark McGwire	.000	5	0	0	0	0	0	0	1	2	0	0	0	0	.167	.000

Pitched Worst Against

	Avg	AB	R	H	2B	3B	HR	RBI	BB	SO	HBP	GDP	SB	CS	OBP	Slg
Bob Boone	.500	6	1	3	0	0	1	1	0	1	0	0	0	0	.500	1.000
Dave Henderson	.500	6	0	3	1	0	0	2	0	1	0	0	0	0	.500	.667
Tim Teufel	.444	9	1	4	1	0	1	1	1	2	0	0	0	0	.500	.889

Joe Jackson

Bats: Left, Throws: Right

Batting	Avg	G	AB	R	H	2B	3B	HR	RBI	BB	SO	HBP	GDP	SB	CS	OBP	Slg
Totals	.345	14	55	9	19	3	0	1	8	2	2	0	0	1	1	.368	.455
Home	.407	7	27	6	11	2	0	1	5	1	1	0	0	1	1	.429	.593
Away	.286	7	28	3	8	1	0	0	3	1	1	0	0	0	0	.310	.321
vs. Left	.310	8	29	0	9	1	0	0	3	0	1	0	0	0	0	.310	.345
vs. Right	.385	14	26	9	10	2	0	1	5	2	1	0	0	1	1	.429	.577
Scoring Pos.	.316	12	19	0	6	1	0	0	7	1	1	0	0	0	0	.350	.368
Close & Late	.500	8	8	0	4	1	0	0	2	1	0	0	0	0	0	.556	.625
None on/out	.455	9	11	0	5	2	0	0	0	1	0	0	0	0	0	.500	.636
None on	.417	13	24	0	10	2	0	1	1	1	1	0	0	0	0	.440	.625
Runners on	.290	14	31	0	9	1	0	0	7	1	1	0	0	1	1	.313	.323
Batting #4	.345	14	55	9	19	3	0	1	8	2	2	0	0	1	1	.368	.455

Hit Best Against

	Avg	AB	R	H	2B	3B	HR	RBI	BB	SO	HBP	GDP	SB	CS	OBP	Slg
Slim Sallee	.533	15	2	8	1	0	0	2	0	1	0	0	0	0	.533	.600
Jimmy Ring	.400	5	0	2	1	0	0	0	1	1	0	0	0	0	.500	.600

Hit Worst Against

	Avg	AB	R	H	2B	3B	HR	RBI	BB	SO	HBP	GDP	SB	CS	OBP	Slg
Rube Benton	.000	7	1	0	0	0	0	0	0	0	0	0	0	0	.000	.000
Dutch Ruether	.143	7	2	1	0	0	0	1	0	0	0	0	0	0	.143	.143
Ferdie Schupp	.200	5	1	1	0	0	0	0	0	0	0	0	0	0	.200	.200

Reggie Jackson

Bats: Left, Throws: Left

Batting	Avg	G	AB	R	H	2B	3B	HR	RBI	BB	SO	HBP	GDP	SB	CS	OBP	Slg
Totals	.278	77	281	41	78	14	1	18	48	33	70	3	4	5	1	.358	.527
Home	.275	38	138	19	38	5	1	9	27	15	34	2	0	3	1	.353	.522
Away	.280	39	143	22	40	9	0	9	21	18	36	1	4	2	0	.364	.531
vs. Left	.244	49	123	0	30	7	1	6	22	15	33	1	4	2	0	.329	.463
vs. Right	.304	77	158	41	48	7	0	12	26	18	37	2	0	3	1	.382	.576
Scoring Pos.	.193	57	83	0	16	3	0	3	24	9	22	1	1	2	0	.277	.337
Close & Late	.256	39	43	2	11	3	0	1	8	3	8	1	1	0	0	.319	.395
None on/out	.410	50	61	0	25	3	1	5	5	7	13	0	0	0	0	.471	.738
None on	.313	69	134	0	42	6	1	10	10	18	33	1	0	0	0	.399	.597
Runners on	.245	72	147	0	36	8	0	8	38	15	37	2	4	5	1	.321	.463
Batting #3	.200	8	30	4	6	1	0	3	3	3	9	0	1	0	0	.273	.533
Batting #4	.292	66	240	37	70	13	1	15	43	30	57	3	3	5	1	.376	.542

Hit Best Against

	Avg	AB	R	H	2B	3B	HR	RBI	BB	SO	HBP	GDP	SB	CS	OBP	Slg
Tug McGraw	.667	6	2	4	1	1	0	2	1	0	0	0	0	0	.714	1.167
Tommy John	.556	9	3	5	0	0	1	3	1	2	0	0	0	0	.600	.889
Oil Can Boyd	.429	7	1	3	1	0	0	2	0	1	0	0	0	0	.429	.571

Hit Worst Against

	Avg	AB	R	H	2B	3B	HR	RBI	BB	SO	HBP	GDP	SB	CS	OBP	Slg
Dave McNally	.000	10	0	0	0	0	0	0	0	3	0	0	0	0	.000	.000
Jerry Koosman	.000	5	0	0	0	0	0	0	0	2	0	1	0	0	.000	.000
Larry Gura	.000	7	0	0	0	0	0	0	2	2	0	0	0	0	.222	.000

Travis Jackson

Bats: Right, Throws: Right

Batting	Avg	G	AB	R	H	2B	3B	HR	RBI	BB	SO	HBP	GDP	SB	CS	OBP	Slg
Totals	.149	19	67	7	10	1	0	0	4	3	10	0	3	1	0	.183	.164
Home	.167	9	30	5	5	0	0	0	4	0	3	0	0	1	0	.161	.167
Away	.135	10	37	2	5	1	0	0	0	3	7	0	3	0	0	.200	.162
vs. Left	.130	9	23	0	3	1	0	0	0	1	0	0	1	0	0	.167	.174
vs. Right	.159	19	44	7	7	0	0	0	4	2	10	0	2	1	0	.191	.159
Scoring Pos.	.071	12	14	0	1	0	0	0	4	1	2	0	0	0	0	.125	.071
Close & Late	.133	13	15	1	2	0	0	0	1	0	2	0	2	0	0	.125	.133
None on/out	.462	11	13	0	6	0	0	0	0	0	2	0	0	0	0	.462	.462
None on	.229	19	35	0	8	1	0	0	0	1	6	0	0	0	0	.250	.257
Runners on	.063	16	32	0	2	0	0	0	4	2	4	0	3	1	0	.114	.063
Batting #6	.222	5	18	3	4	1	0	0	2	1	3	0	1	0	0	.263	.278
Batting #7	.074	7	27	3	2	0	0	0	1	1	4	0	2	1	0	.103	.074
Batting #8	.190	6	21	1	4	0	0	0	1	1	3	0	0	0	0	.227	.190

Hit Best Against

	Avg	AB	R	H	2B	3B	HR	RBI	BB	SO	HBP	GDP	SB	CS	OBP	Slg
Lefty Gomez	.286	7	1	2	0	0	0	0	0	0	0	0	0	0	.286	.286

Hit Worst Against

	Avg	AB	R	H	2B	3B	HR	RBI	BB	SO	HBP	GDP	SB	CS	OBP	Slg
Firpo Marberry	.000	6	1	0	0	0	0	0	0	2	0	0	0	0	.000	.000
Tom Zachary	.000	6	0	0	0	0	0	0	0	0	0	1	0	0	.000	.000
G. Mogridge	.000	5	0	0	0	0	0	0	0	0	0	0	0	0	.000	.000

Derek Jeter

Bats: Right, Throws: Right

Batting	Avg	G	AB	R	H	2B	3B	HR	RBI	BB	SO	HBP	GDP	SB	CS	OBP	Slg
Totals	.354	20	82	18	29	4	0	3	5	7	18	1	1	4	0	.411	.512
Home	.432	9	37	8	16	1	0	3	4	2	8	1	1	2	0	.475	.703
Away	.289	11	45	10	13	3	0	0	1	5	10	0	0	2	0	.360	.356
vs. Left	.471	7	17	2	8	0	0	0	0	1	5	0	0	0	0	.500	.471
vs. Right	.323	19	65	16	21	4	0	3	5	6	13	1	1	4	0	.389	.523
Scoring Pos.	.250	17	16	13	4	0	0	0	2	1	4	0	0	0	0	.294	.250
Close & Late	.611	12	18	6	11	1	0	0	1	0	3	0	0	0	0	.611	.833
None on/out	.462	18	26	1	12	1	0	1	1	2	5	1	0	0	0	.517	.615
None on	.429	20	49	3	21	4	0	3	3	6	10	1	0	0	0	.500	.694
Runners on	.242	19	33	15	8	0	0	0	2	1	8	0	1	4	0	.265	.242
Batting #1	.267	7	30	6	8	1	0	0	1	1	8	0	1	2	0	.290	.300
Batting #2	.344	8	32	10	11	2	0	2	2	6	9	0	0	1	0	.447	.594
Batting #9	.500	5	20	2	10	1	0	1	2	0	1	1	0	1	0	.524	.700

Hit Best Against

	Avg	AB	R	H	2B	3B	HR	RBI	BB	SO	HBP	GDP	SB	CS	OBP	Slg
Scott Erickson	.667	6	1	4	0	0	0	0	0	0	0	0	2	0	.667	.667
Orel Hershiser	.429	7	1	3	1	0	0	0	0	0	0	0	0	0	.429	.571
Greg Maddux	.333	6	1	2	0	0	0	1	0	1	1	1	1	0	.429	.333

Hit Worst Against

	Avg	AB	R	H	2B	3B	HR	RBI	BB	SO	HBP	GDP	SB	CS	OBP	Slg
John Smoltz	.000	6	1	0	0	0	0	0	1	1	0	0	0	0	.143	.000
Jaret Wright	.000	5	1	0	0	0	0	0	1	4	0	0	0	0	.167	.000

Tommy John

Throws: Left, Bats: Right

Pitching	ERA	W	L	Sv	G	GS	IP	BB	SO	Avg	R	H	2B	3B	HR	OBP	Slg
Totals	2.65	6	3	0	14	13	88.1	24	48	.245	36	82	9	0	6	.302	.325
Home	2.95	4	2	0	9	9	58.0	13	31	.259	26	59	8	0	6	.307	.373
Away	2.08	2	1	0	5	4	30.1	11	17	.215	10	23	1	0	0	.292	.224

	Avg	AB	R	H	2B	3B	HR	RBI	BB	SO	HBP	GDP	OBP	Slg
vs. Left	.210	100	0	21	4	0	1	9	4	16	1	4	.248	.280
vs. Right	.260	235	36	61	5	0	5	21	20	32	3	4	.324	.345
Scoring Pos.	.224	67	0	15	1	0	0	21	9	12	0	4	.312	.239
Close & Late	.353	34	4	12	0	0	2	10	0	4	0	4	.343	.529
None on/out	.279	86	0	24	2	0	2	2	8	15	1	4	.347	.372
None on	.255	192	0	49	6	0	3	3	13	30	4	4	.316	.333
Runners on	.231	143	0	33	3	0	3	27	11	18	0	4	.284	.315

Pitched Best Against

	Avg	AB	R	H	2B	3B	HR	RBI	BB	SO	HBP	GDP	SB	CS	OBP	Slg
Larry Bowa	.000	11	1	0	0	0	0	0	0	1	0	1	0	0	.000	.000
Ben Oglivie	.000	6	0	0	0	0	0	0	0	1	0	0	0	0	.000	.000
Pedro Guerrero	.000	5	0	0	0	0	0	0	0	0	0	0	0	0	.000	.000

Pitched Worst Against

	Avg	AB	R	H	2B	3B	HR	RBI	BB	SO	HBP	GDP	SB	CS	OBP	Slg
Reggie Jackson	.556	9	3	5	0	0	1	3	1	2	0	0	0	0	.600	.889
Steve Garvey	.500	6	0	3	0	0	0	0	0	1	0	0	0	0	.500	.500
Paul Molitor	.444	9	2	4	0	0	1	1	1	2	0	0	0	1	.500	.778

Randy Johnson

Throws: Left, Bats: Right

Pitching	ERA	W	L	Sv	G	GS	IP	BB	SO	Avg	R	H	2B	3B	HR	OBP	Slg
Totals	3.52	2	3	0	6	5	38.1	14	45	.225	17	31	4	1	5	.292	.377
Home	4.43	2	2	0	4	3	22.1	10	26	.250	12	20	3	0	3	.330	.400
Away	2.25	0	1	0	2	2	16.0	4	19	.190	5	11	1	1	2	.238	.345

	Avg	AB	R	H	2B	3B	HR	RBI	BB	SO	HBP	GDP	OBP	Slg
vs. Left	.292	24	0	7	0	1	0	3	0	13	0	0	.292	.375
vs. Right	.211	114	0	24	4	0	5	12	14	32	0	0	.292	.377
Scoring Pos.	.267	30	6	8	0	0	0	9	3	8	0	0	.314	.267
Close & Late	.190	21	2	4	1	0	0	2	3	8	0	0	.292	.238
None on/out	.135	37	0	5	1	1	1	1	3	13	0	0	.200	.297
None on	.178	90	9	16	3	1	5	5	9	32	0	0	.253	.400
Runners on	.313	48	8	15	1	0	0	10	5	13	0	0	.364	.333

Pitched Best Against

	Avg	AB	R	H	2B	3B	HR	RBI	BB	SO	HBP	GDP	SB	CS	OBP	Slg
Omar Vizquel	.000	7	0	0	0	0	0	1	0	0	0	0	0	0	.000	.000
Eddie Murray	.000	6	0	0	0	0	0	0	0	1	0	0	0	0	.000	.000
Manny Ramirez	.000	6	0	0	0	0	0	0	0	3	0	0	0	0	.000	.000

Pitched Worst Against

	Avg	AB	R	H	2B	3B	HR	RBI	BB	SO	HBP	GDP	SB	CS	OBP	Slg
Cal Ripken Jr.	.571	7	0	4	0	0	0	1	0	0	0	0	0	0	.571	.571
Carlos Baerga	.500	8	1	4	0	0	1	1	0	2	0	0	0	0	.500	.875
Kenny Lofton	.500	8	2	4	0	1	0	2	0	3	0	0	2	0	.500	.750

Walter Johnson

Throws: Right, Bats: Right

Pitching	ERA	W	L	Sv	G	GS	IP	BB	SO	Avg	R	H	2B	3B	HR	OBP	Slg
Totals	2.16	3	3	0	6	5	50.0	15	35	.298	20	56	11	3	4	.356	.452
Home	1.08	2	1	0	3	2	25.0	11	19	.264	4	23	2	1	2	.343	.379
Away	3.24	1	2	0	3	3	25.0	4	16	.327	16	33	9	2	2	.367	.515

	Avg	AB	R	H	2B	3B	HR	RBI	BB	SO	HBP	GDP	OBP	Slg
vs. Left	.394	66	0	26	8	2	2	7	8	6	3	3	.481	.667
vs. Right	.244	123	20	30	3	1	2	13	7	29	0	3	.280	.333
Scoring Pos.	.260	50	0	13	4	1	0	14	5	11	1	3	.328	.380
Close & Late	.327	52	5	17	4	2	0	8	9	11	0	3	.413	.481
None on/out	.340	47	0	16	1	0	2	2	5	7	1	3	.415	.489
None on	.374	91	0	34	6	2	3	3	8	15	2	3	.436	.582
Runners on	.224	98	0	22	5	1	1	17	7	20	1	3	.278	.327

Pitched Best Against

	Avg	AB	R	H	2B	3B	HR	RBI	BB	SO	HBP	GDP	SB	CS	OBP	Slg
Glenn Wright	.083	12	0	1	0	0	0	0	0	2	0	0	0	0	.083	.083
Travis Jackson	.125	8	1	1	0	0	0	1	1	2	0	1	0	0	.200	.125
Eddie Moore	.167	12	3	2	1	0	0	1	1	0	0	1	0	0	.231	.250

Pitched Worst Against

	Avg	AB	R	H	2B	3B	HR	RBI	BB	SO	HBP	GDP	SB	CS	OBP	Slg
Art Nehf	.600	5	1	3	0	0	0	0	0	0	0	0	0	0	.600	.600
Bill Terry	.571	7	2	4	0	1	1	1	3	0	0	0	0	0	.700	1.286
Max Carey	.500	10	3	5	3	0	0	2	1	1	2	0	2	1	.615	.800

Andruw Jones

Bats: Right, Throws: Right

Batting	Avg	G	AB	R	H	2B	3B	HR	RBI	BB	SO	HBP	GDP	SB	CS	OBP	Slg
Totals	.326	22	43	8	14	1	0	3	11	9	10	1	0	1	2	.453	.558
Home	.304	11	23	5	7	1	0	1	5	5	5	0	0	1	2	.429	.478
Away	.350	11	20	3	7	0	0	2	6	4	5	1	0	0	0	.480	.650
vs. Left	.350	12	20	3	7	0	0	1	5	7	2	1	0	1	1	.536	.500
vs. Right	.304	14	23	5	7	1	0	2	6	2	8	0	0	0	1	.360	.609
Scoring Pos.	.500	12	14	7	7	1	0	2	9	4	2	0	0	0	0	.611	1.000
Close & Late	.250	7	8	1	2	0	0	0	0	0	3	0	0	0	0	.250	.250
None on/out	.400	10	10	0	4	0	0	0	0	0	2	1	0	0	0	.455	.400
None on	.227	14	22	0	5	0	0	0	0	3	6	1	0	0	0	.346	.227
Runners on	.429	15	21	8	9	1	0	3	11	6	4	0	0	1	2	.556	.905
Batting #6	.400	8	20	2	8	1	0	0	3	5	4	0	0	1	1	.520	.450
Batting #7	.300	7	20	5	6	0	0	3	8	2	5	1	0	0	1	.391	.750

Chipper Jones

Bats: Both, Throws: Right

Batting	Avg	G	AB	R	H	2B	3B	HR	RBI	BB	SO	HBP	GDP	SB	CS	OBP	Slg
Totals	.352	39	142	29	50	11	0	7	23	24	18	0	3	5	1	.435	.577
Home	.371	20	70	15	26	3	0	4	12	15	11	0	1	4	0	.471	.586
Away	.333	19	72	14	24	8	0	3	11	9	7	0	2	1	1	.398	.569
vs. Left	.393	33	56	9	22	4	0	0	5	13	6	0	2	4	0	.500	.464
vs. Right	.326	35	86	20	28	7	0	7	18	11	12	0	1	1	1	.390	.651
Scoring Pos.	.241	33	29	20	7	2	0	1	15	10	3	0	1	2	0	.395	.414
Close & Late	.333	22	21	7	7	2	0	1	1	7	2	0	1	1	1	.500	.571
None on/out	.417	28	36	2	15	4	0	2	2	4	4	0	0	0	0	.475	.694
None on	.373	38	83	4	31	7	0	4	4	10	11	0	0	0	0	.441	.602
Runners on	.322	37	59	25	19	4	0	3	19	14	7	0	3	5	1	.429	.542
Batting #3	.352	39	142	29	50	11	0	7	23	24	18	0	3	5	1	.435	.577

Hit Best Against

	Avg	AB	R	H	2B	3B	HR	RBI	BB	SO	HBP	GDP	SB	CS	OBP	Slg
Dennis Martinez	.800	5	0	4	1	0	0	1	0	0	0	0	0	0	.667	1.000
Andy Benes	.750	8	2	6	1	0	0	0	1	0	0	0	0	0	.778	.875
Pete Schourek	.500	6	1	3	0	0	0	0	1	1	0	0	0	0	.571	.500

Hit Worst Against

	Avg	AB	R	H	2B	3B	HR	RBI	BB	SO	HBP	GDP	SB	CS	OBP	Slg
Kevin Brown	.143	7	1	1	0	0	1	1	1	0	0	0	0	0	.250	.571
Orel Hershiser	.167	6	0	1	1	0	0	0	0	2	0	0	0	0	.167	.333

David Justice

Bats: Left, Throws: Left

Batting	Avg	G	AB	R	H	2B	3B	HR	RBI	BB	SO	HBP	GDP	SB	CS	OBP	Slg
Totals	.232	64	228	36	53	7	0	8	33	45	41	1	2	3	2	.359	.368
Home	.273	31	110	26	30	5	0	6	21	24	22	0	2	3	1	.400	.482
Away	.195	33	118	10	23	2	0	2	12	21	19	1	0	0	1	.319	.263
vs. Left	.209	47	86	9	18	3	0	1	13	11	18	1	0	0	0	.303	.279
vs. Right	.246	57	142	27	35	4	0	7	20	34	23	0	2	3	2	.390	.423
Scoring Pos.	.225	56	71	24	16	2	0	0	23	19	13	1	1	0	0	.387	.254
Close & Late	.174	36	46	4	8	0	0	0	7	7	9	0	1	1	0	.278	.174
None on/out	.260	43	50	5	13	1	0	5	5	9	13	0	0	0	0	.373	.580
None on	.239	62	117	6	28	5	0	6	6	20	22	0	0	0	0	.350	.436
Runners on	.225	61	111	30	25	2	0	2	27	25	19	1	2	3	2	.367	.297
Batting #4	.230	34	122	22	28	3	0	6	21	27	27	0	1	3	2	.369	.402
Batting #5	.224	28	98	13	22	3	0	2	10	18	13	1	1	0	0	.345	.316

Hit Best Against

	Avg	AB	R	H	2B	3B	HR	RBI	BB	SO	HBP	GDP	SB	CS	OBP	Slg
Tim Wakefield	.444	9	2	4	0	0	2	3	0	0	0	0	0	0	.444	1.111
Mike Mussina	.400	5	0	2	1	0	0	0	1	1	0	0	0	0	.500	.600
Danny Jackson	.400	5	0	2	0	0	0	0	0	0	0	0	0	0	.400	.400

Hit Worst Against

	Avg	AB	R	H	2B	3B	HR	RBI	BB	SO	HBP	GDP	SB	CS	OBP	Slg
Curt Schilling	.000	5	0	0	0	0	0	1	1	2	0	0	0	0	.143	.000
Al Leiter	.000	5	1	0	0	0	0	0	1	2	0	0	0	0	.167	.000
Zane Smith	.143	7	1	1	0	0	0	0	0	3	0	0	0	0	.143	.143

Al Kaline

Bats: Right, Throws: Right

Batting	Avg	G	AB	R	H	2B	3B	HR	RBI	BB	SO	HBP	GDP	SB	CS	OBP	Slg
Totals	.333	12	48	9	16	2	0	3	9	2	9	1	0	0	0	.373	.563
Home	.364	6	22	3	8	1	0	1	4	2	3	0	0	0	0	.417	.545
Away	.308	6	26	6	8	1	0	2	5	0	6	1	0	0	0	.333	.577
vs. Left	.625	6	8	0	5	0	0	1	3	1	0	0	0	0	0	.667	1.000
vs. Right	.275	12	40	9	11	2	0	2	6	1	9	1	0	0	0	.310	.475
Scoring Pos.	.500	5	8	0	4	0	0	1	7	0	0	0	0	0	0	.500	.875
Close & Late	.375	7	8	1	3	0	0	1	3	0	1	0	0	0	0	.375	.750
None on/out	.500	7	6	0	3	0	0	0	0	1	0	1	0	0	0	.625	.500
None on	.303	12	33	0	10	1	0	2	2	2	6	1	0	0	0	.361	.515
Runners on	.400	9	15	0	6	1	0	1	7	0	3	0	0	0	0	.400	.667
Batting #2	.188	4	16	2	3	0	0	1	1	1	2	0	0	0	0	.235	.375
Batting #3	.406	8	32	7	13	2	0	2	8	1	7	1	0	0	0	.441	.656

Hit Best Against

	Avg	AB	R	H	2B	3B	HR	RBI	BB	SO	HBP	GDP	SB	CS	OBP	Slg
Ray Washburn	.400	5	2	2	0	0	1	3	0	1	0	0	0	0	.400	1.000
Bob Gibson	.250	12	0	3	2	0	0	0	0	5	0	0	0	0	.250	.417

Hit Worst Against

	Avg	AB	R	H	2B	3B	HR	RBI	BB	SO	HBP	GDP	SB	CS	OBP	Slg
Catfish Hunter	.000	6	0	0	0	0	0	0	1	1	0	0	0	0	.143	.000
Nelson Briles	.167	6	0	1	0	0	0	0	0	1	0	0	0	0	.167	.167
B. Moon Odom	.167	6	0	1	0	0	0	0	0	1	0	0	0	0	.167	.167

Charlie Keller

Bats: Left, Throws: Right

Batting	Avg	G	AB	R	H	2B	3B	HR	RBI	BB	SO	HBP	GDP	SB	CS	OBP	Slg
Totals	.306	19	72	18	22	3	2	5	18	7	11	0	2	1	0	.367	.611
Home	.243	10	37	8	9	1	2	1	7	3	4	0	1	0	0	.300	.459
Away	.371	9	35	10	13	2	0	4	11	4	7	0	1	1	0	.436	.771
vs. Left	.125	7	16	0	2	0	0	0	0	3	4	0	1	1	0	.263	.125
vs. Right	.357	19	56	18	20	3	2	5	18	4	7	0	1	0	0	.400	.750
Scoring Pos.	.500	10	14	0	7	1	1	2	12	2	1	0	1	0	0	.563	1.143
Close & Late	.583	10	12	4	7	1	2	2	7	0	0	0	0	1	0	.583	1.500
None on/out	.278	13	18	0	5	1	0	1	1	1	2	0	0	0	0	.316	.500
None on	.250	18	40	0	10	1	1	1	1	4	8	0	0	0	0	.318	.400
Runners on	.375	17	32	0	12	2	1	4	17	3	3	0	2	1	0	.429	.875
Batting #3	.438	4	16	8	7	1	1	3	6	1	2	0	0	0	0	.471	1.188
Batting #4	.222	5	18	3	4	0	1	0	2	2	5	0	1	1	0	.300	.333
Batting #5	.324	9	34	7	11	2	0	2	10	4	4	0	1	0	0	.395	.559

Hit Best Against

	Avg	AB	R	H	2B	3B	HR	RBI	BB	SO	HBP	GDP	SB	CS	OBP	Slg
Bucky Walters	.500	6	3	3	1	0	0	1	0	0	0	0	0	0	.500	.667
Johnny Beazley	.375	8	1	3	0	0	1	2	0	0	0	0	0	0	.375	.750
Whit Wyatt	.286	7	2	2	0	0	0	1	1	1	0	1	0	0	.375	.286

Hit Worst Against

	Avg	AB	R	H	2B	3B	HR	RBI	BB	SO	HBP	GDP	SB	CS	OBP	Slg
Max Lanier	.000	7	0	0	0	0	0	0	2	3	0	1	0	0	.222	.000
Mort Cooper	.214	14	3	3	0	1	1	5	0	4	0	0	0	0	.214	.571

George Kelly

Bats: Right, Throws: Right

Batting	Avg	G	AB	R	H	2B	3B	HR	RBI	BB	SO	HBP	GDP	SB	CS	OBP	Slg
Totals	.248	26	101	11	25	2	0	1	12	5	23	0	9	0	2	.280	.297
Home	.300	13	50	4	15	1	0	0	5	2	13	0	2	0	1	.327	.320
Away	.196	13	51	7	10	1	0	1	7	3	10	0	7	0	1	.236	.275
vs. Left	.273	8	22	0	6	1	0	0	2	2	3	0	1	0	0	.333	.318
vs. Right	.241	26	79	11	19	1	0	1	10	3	20	0	8	0	2	.265	.291
Scoring Pos.	.208	17	24	0	5	0	0	0	10	2	8	0	2	0	0	.259	.208
Close & Late	.174	20	23	1	4	0	0	0	5	2	6	0	5	0	0	.231	.174
None on/out	.333	22	27	0	9	1	0	1	1	2	7	0	0	0	0	.379	.481
None on	.313	25	48	0	15	2	0	1	1	2	11	0	0	0	0	.340	.417
Runners on	.189	25	53	0	10	0	0	0	11	3	12	0	9	0	2	.228	.189
Batting #4	.290	7	31	7	9	1	0	1	4	1	8	0	2	0	0	.303	.419
Batting #5	.233	8	30	3	7	1	0	0	5	3	10	0	3	0	1	.303	.267
Batting #6	.278	5	18	0	5	0	0	0	2	0	3	0	1	0	1	.278	.278
Batting #7	.182	6	22	1	4	0	0	0	1	1	2	0	3	0	0	.217	.182

Hit Best Against

	Avg	AB	R	H	2B	3B	HR	RBI	BB	SO	HBP	GDP	SB	CS	OBP	Slg
Tom Zachary	.429	7	2	3	0	0	0	2	1	0	0	1	0	0	.500	.429
Bob Shawkey	.417	12	0	5	0	0	0	5	1	1	0	0	0	1	.462	.417
Joe Bush	.364	11	0	4	0	0	0	2	1	1	0	2	0	0	.417	.364

Hit Worst Against

	Avg	AB	R	H	2B	3B	HR	RBI	BB	SO	HBP	GDP	SB	CS	OBP	Slg
Carl Mays	.067	15	1	1	1	0	0	0	0	3	0	3	0	0	.067	.133
Herb Pennock	.125	8	0	1	0	0	0	0	0	2	0	0	0	0	.125	.125
Walter Johnson	.182	11	2	2	0	0	1	2	0	5	0	1	0	0	.167	.455

Jimmy Key

Throws: Left, Bats: Right

Pitching	ERA	W	L	Sv	G	GS	IP	BB	SO	Avg	R	H	2B	3B	HR	OBP	Slg
Totals	3.15	5	3	0	14	11	68.2	17	35	.275	25	71	15	1	5	.326	.399
Home	3.77	3	2	0	8	8	43.0	11	20	.310	18	52	13	1	3	.362	.452
Away	2.10	2	1	0	6	3	25.2	6	15	.211	7	19	2	0	2	.258	.300

	Avg	AB	R	H	2B	3B	HR	RBI	BB	SO	HBP	GDP	OBP	Slg
vs. Left	.190	42	0	8	0	0	1	7	2	6	1	1	.239	.262
vs. Right	.292	216	8	63	15	1	4	18	15	29	3	1	.343	.426
Scoring Pos.	.156	64	12	10	1	0	1	17	7	7	2	1	.250	.219
Close & Late	.143	21	2	3	1	0	0	2	0	3	0	1	.143	.190
None on/out	.299	67	0	20	5	1	1	1	4	12	1	1	.347	.448
None on	.279	154	3	43	11	1	2	2	8	26	2	1	.323	.403
Runners on	.269	104	14	28	4	0	3	23	9	9	2	1	.331	.394

Pitched Best Against

	Avg	AB	R	H	2B	3B	HR	RBI	BB	SO	HBP	GDP	SB	CS	OBP	Slg
Terry Steinbach	.000	5	0	0	0	0	0	0	0	0	0	0	0	0	.000	.000
Terry Pendleton	.125	8	1	1	1	0	0	0	0	0	0	1	0	1	.125	.250
David Justice	.167	6	0	1	0	0	0	0	0	2	1	0	0	0	.286	.167

Pitched Worst Against

	Avg	AB	R	H	2B	3B	HR	RBI	BB	SO	HBP	GDP	SB	CS	OBP	Slg
Frank White	.600	5	1	3	0	0	0	0	0	0	0	0	0	0	.600	.600
M. Grissom	.500	10	1	5	1	0	0	1	0	0	0	0	1	0	.500	.600
Hal McRae	.400	5	0	2	0	0	0	0	0	0	0	0	0	0	.400	.400

Harmon Killebrew

Bats: Right, Throws: Right

Batting	Avg	G	AB	R	H	2B	3B	HR	RBI	BB	SO	HBP	GDP	SB	CS	OBP	Slg
Totals	.250	13	40	6	10	1	0	3	6	14	10	0	1	0	0	.444	.500
Home	.333	7	24	4	8	1	0	2	5	5	5	0	0	0	0	.448	.625
Away	.125	6	16	2	2	0	0	1	1	9	5	0	1	0	0	.440	.313
vs. Left	.259	10	27	0	7	0	0	2	5	10	4	0	1	0	0	.459	.481
vs. Right	.231	13	13	6	3	1	0	1	1	4	6	0	0	0	0	.412	.538
Scoring Pos.	.500	9	6	0	3	0	0	0	2	3	1	0	0	0	0	.667	.500
Close & Late	.000	4	3	0	0	0	0	0	0	3	0	0	0	0	0	.500	.000
None on/out	.154	12	13	0	2	0	0	1	1	4	6	0	0	0	0	.353	.385
None on	.208	13	24	0	5	1	0	2	2	9	8	0	0	0	0	.424	.500
Runners on	.313	12	16	0	5	0	0	1	4	5	2	0	1	0	0	.476	.500
Batting #3	.231	4	13	3	3	0	0	2	4	6	3	0	1	0	0	.474	.692
Batting #4	.259	9	27	3	7	1	0	1	2	8	7	0	1	0	0	.429	.407

Hit Best Against

	Avg	AB	R	H	2B	3B	HR	RBI	BB	SO	HBP	GDP	SB	CS	OBP	Slg
Sandy Koufax	.444	9	0	4	0	0	0	1	1	1	0	0	0	0	.500	.444
Mike Cuellar	.400	5	2	2	0	0	1	2	1	0	0	1	0	0	.500	1.000

Hit Worst Against

	Avg	AB	R	H	2B	3B	HR	RBI	BB	SO	HBP	GDP	SB	CS	OBP	Slg
Claude Osteen	.000	6	0	0	0	0	0	0	1	0	0	0	0	0	.143	.000
Dave McNally	.167	6	1	1	0	0	1	2	3	2	0	0	0	0	.444	.667
Jim Palmer	.167	6	1	1	1	0	0	0	2	3	0	0	0	0	.375	.333

Bruce Kison

Throws: Right, Bats: Right

Pitching	ERA	W	L	Sv	G	GS	IP	BB	SO	Avg	R	H	2B	3B	HR	OBP	Slg
Totals	1.98	5	1	0	10	4	36.1	16	27	.153	10	19	3	0	3	.264	.250
Home	0.86	3	0	0	4	1	21.0	2	16	.116	2	8	1	0	1	.176	.174
Away	3.52	2	1	0	6	3	15.1	14	11	.200	8	11	2	0	2	.357	.345

	Avg	AB	R	H	2B	3B	HR	RBI	BB	SO	HBP	GDP	OBP	Slg
vs. Left	.104	48	0	5	1	0	1	3	6	8	0	3	.200	.188
vs. Right	.184	76	10	14	2	0	2	6	10	19	3	3	.303	.289
Scoring Pos.	.167	18	0	3	0	0	1	6	6	3	0	3	.360	.333
Close & Late	.125	8	0	1	0	0	0	0	2	1	1	3	.364	.125
None on/out	.118	34	0	4	1	0	0	0	4	9	0	3	.211	.147
None on	.155	84	0	13	3	0	1	1	7	21	3	3	.245	.226
Runners on	.150	40	0	6	0	0	2	8	9	6	0	3	.300	.300

Pitched Best Against

	Avg	AB	R	H	2B	3B	HR	RBI	BB	SO	HBP	GDP	SB	CS	OBP	Slg
Cecil Cooper	.000	7	0	0	0	0	0	0	0	3	0	0	0	0	.000	.000
Ted Simmons	.000	5	0	0	0	0	0	1	0	1	0	0	0	0	.000	.000
Gorman Thomas	.000	5	0	0	0	0	0	0	0	3	0	0	0	0	.000	.000

Pitched Worst Against

	Avg	AB	R	H	2B	3B	HR	RBI	BB	SO	HBP	GDP	SB	CS	OBP	Slg
Paul Molitor	.667	6	2	4	1	0	1	2	1	1	0	0	1	0	.714	1.333
Charlie Moore	.400	5	1	2	0	0	0	0	0	1	0	0	0	0	.400	.400

Ryan Klesko

Bats: Left, Throws: Left

Batting	Avg	G	AB	R	H	2B	3B	HR	RBI	BB	SO	HBP	GDP	SB	CS	OBP	Slg
Totals	.247	36	97	17	24	2	0	8	15	15	30	0	3	1	1	.348	.515
Home	.204	19	49	7	10	1	0	3	8	8	17	0	1	1	0	.316	.408
Away	.292	17	48	10	14	1	0	5	7	7	13	0	2	1	1	.382	.625
vs. Left	.129	21	31	1	4	0	0	0	1	2	11	0	1	0	1	.182	.129
vs. Right	.303	33	66	16	20	2	0	8	14	13	19	0	2	1	0	.418	.697
Scoring Pos.	.273	24	22	10	6	1	0	2	9	7	3	0	2	0	0	.448	.591
Close & Late	.353	17	17	6	6	0	0	2	3	4	6	0	0	1	0	.476	.706
None on/out	.348	19	23	3	8	1	0	3	3	2	6	0	0	0	0	.400	.783
None on	.280	32	50	6	14	1	0	6	6	6	14	0	0	0	0	.357	.660
Runners on	.213	31	47	11	10	1	0	2	9	9	16	0	3	1	1	.339	.362
Batting #5	.217	16	46	6	10	1	0	5	10	8	18	0	2	1	0	.333	.565
Batting #6	.414	11	29	9	12	1	0	3	5	4	6	0	1	0	0	.485	.759
Batting #7	.125	6	16	1	2	0	0	0	0	3	4	0	0	0	1	.263	.125

Hit Best Against

	Avg	AB	R	H	2B	3B	HR	RBI	BB	SO	HBP	GDP	SB	CS	OBP	Slg
Kevin Brown	.333	6	1	2	0	0	1	2	1	1	0	0	0	0	.429	.833

Hit Worst Against

	Avg	AB	R	H	2B	3B	HR	RBI	BB	SO	HBP	GDP	SB	CS	OBP	Slg
Pete Schourek	.000	5	0	0	0	0	0	0	1	3	0	0	0	1	.167	.000
Orel Hershiser	.200	5	1	1	0	0	0	0	0	2	0	0	0	0	.200	.200

Sandy Koufax

Throws: Left, Bats: Right

Pitching	ERA	W	L	Sv	G	GS	IP	BB	SO	Avg	R	H	2B	3B	HR	OBP	Slg
Totals	0.95	4	3	0	8	7	57.0	11	61	.180	10	36	4	1	2	.223	.240
Home	0.87	2	2	0	4	4	31.0	4	26	.194	6	21	2	1	1	.223	.259
Away	1.04	2	1	0	4	3	26.0	7	35	.163	4	15	2	0	1	.222	.217

	Avg	AB	R	H	2B	3B	HR	RBI	BB	SO	HBP	GDP	OBP	Slg
vs. Left	.148	61	0	9	1	0	0	2	1	19	0	0	.161	.164
vs. Right	.194	139	10	27	3	1	2	5	10	42	0	0	.248	.273
Scoring Pos.	.231	26	0	6	2	0	0	4	2	5	0	0	.286	.308
Close & Late	.125	24	0	3	0	0	1	2	0	9	0	0	.125	.250
None on/out	.175	57	0	10	0	1	0	0	0	22	0	0	.175	.211
None on	.172	134	0	23	2	1	1	1	7	43	0	0	.213	.224
Runners on	.197	66	0	13	2	0	1	6	4	18	0	0	.243	.273

Pitched Best Against

	Avg	AB	R	H	2B	3B	HR	RBI	BB	SO	HBP	GDP	SB	CS	OBP	Slg
Hector Lopez	.000	5	0	0	0	0	0	0	0	1	0	0	0	0	.000	.000
Bob Allison	.000	9	0	0	0	0	0	0	1	7	0	0	0	0	.100	.000
Zoilo Versalles	.091	11	1	1	0	0	0	0	0	4	0	0	0	0	.091	.091

Pitched Worst Against

	Avg	AB	R	H	2B	3B	HR	RBI	BB	SO	HBP	GDP	SB	CS	OBP	Slg
Luis Aparicio	.571	7	0	4	1	0	0	1	0	1	0	0	0	1	.571	.714
H. Killebrew	.444	9	0	4	0	0	0	1	1	1	0	0	0	0	.500	.444
Elston Howard	.375	8	0	3	0	0	0	0	0	1	0	0	0	0	.375	.375

Tony Kubek

Bats: Left, Throws: Right

Batting	Avg	G	AB	R	H	2B	3B	HR	RBI	BB	SO	HBP	GDP	SB	CS	OBP	Slg
Totals	.240	37	146	16	35	2	0	2	10	5	23	1	3	0	3	.268	.295
Home	.206	17	63	3	13	2	0	0	1	3	12	0	0	0	1	.242	.238
Away	.265	20	83	13	22	0	0	2	9	2	11	1	3	0	2	.287	.337
vs. Left	.228	21	57	0	13	1	0	0	4	1	10	0	2	0	0	.241	.246
vs. Right	.247	37	89	16	22	1	0	2	6	4	12	1	1	0	3	.284	.326
Scoring Pos.	.185	22	27	0	5	0	0	1	9	2	4	0	2	0	0	.233	.296
Close & Late	.267	14	15	2	4	0	0	0	1	0	0	0	2	0	0	.267	.267
None on/out	.238	24	42	0	10	0	0	0	0	1	7	1	0	0	0	.273	.238
None on	.270	35	100	0	27	1	0	1	1	1	14	1	0	0	0	.284	.310
Runners on	.174	30	46	0	8	1	0	1	9	4	8	0	3	0	3	.235	.261
Batting #1	.311	14	61	7	19	1	0	0	2	1	6	0	3	0	3	.323	.328
Batting #2	.200	12	50	9	10	1	0	2	6	2	9	1	0	0	0	.245	.340
Batting #8	.111	9	27	0	3	0	0	0	2	2	7	0	0	0	0	.167	.111

Hit Best Against

	Avg	AB	R	H	2B	3B	HR	RBI	BB	SO	HBP	GDP	SB	CS	OBP	Slg
Billy O'Dell	.600	5	1	3	0	0	0	0	0	1	0	0	0	0	.600	.600
Vern Law	.333	9	1	3	1	0	0	0	1	1	0	0	0	0	.400	.444
Billy Pierce	.286	7	0	2	1	0	0	1	0	0	0	0	0	0	.286	.429

Hit Worst Against

	Avg	AB	R	H	2B	3B	HR	RBI	BB	SO	HBP	GDP	SB	CS	OBP	Slg
Sandy Koufax	.125	8	1	1	0	0	0	0	0	3	0	1	0	0	.125	.125
Warren Spahn	.133	15	1	2	0	0	0	0	0	2	0	1	0	0	.133	.133
Jim O'Toole	.167	6	0	1	0	0	0	1	1	1	0	0	0	0	.286	.167

Carney Lansford

Bats: Right, Throws: Right

Batting	Avg	G	AB	R	H	2B	3B	HR	RBI	BB	SO	HBP	GDP	SB	CS	OBP	Slg
Totals	.305	33	128	17	39	3	0	2	18	10	10	0	3	4	1	.355	.375
Home	.284	17	67	7	19	1	0	1	9	3	3	0	2	3	1	.314	.343
Away	.328	16	61	10	20	2	0	1	9	7	7	0	1	1	0	.397	.410

Batting	Avg	G	AB	R	H	2B	3B	HR	RBI	BB	SO	HBP	GDP	SB	CS	OBP	Slg
vs. Left	.360	15	25	1	9	1	0	0	4	3	1	0	1	1	0	.429	.400
vs. Right	.291	33	103	16	30	2	0	2	14	7	9	0	2	3	1	.336	.369
Scoring Pos.	.417	27	36	8	15	2	0	1	17	5	3	0	0	1	0	.488	.556
Close & Late	.300	16	20	2	6	1	0	0	3	0	0	0	0	0	0	.300	.350
None on/out	.269	18	26	0	7	1	0	0	0	1	3	0	0	0	0	.296	.308
None on	.284	30	74	1	21	1	0	1	1	1	7	0	0	0	0	.293	.338
Runners on	.333	32	54	8	18	2	0	1	17	9	3	0	3	4	1	.429	.426
Batting #1	.250	5	20	4	5	1	0	1	2	2	3	0	0	0	1	.318	.450
Batting #2	.284	18	67	9	19	1	0	1	11	8	5	0	3	3	0	.360	.343
Batting #5	.350	5	20	3	7	1	0	0	3	0	2	0	0	1	0	.350	.400
Batting #6	.333	3	12	0	4	0	0	0	1	0	0	0	0	0	0	.333	.333

Hit Best Against

	Avg	AB	R	H	2B	3B	HR	RBI	BB	SO	HBP	GDP	SB	CS	OBP	Slg
Jose Rijo	.500	6	0	3	0	0	0	1	0	0	0	0	1	0	.500	.500
Mike Boddicker	.400	5	1	2	0	0	1	2	0	0	0	0	0	1	.400	1.000
T. Stottlemyre	.400	5	1	2	0	0	0	1	0	0	0	0	0	0	.400	.400

Hit Worst Against

	Avg	AB	R	H	2B	3B	HR	RBI	BB	SO	HBP	GDP	SB	CS	OBP	Slg
Jack Morris	.167	6	0	1	0	0	0	1	0	0	0	1	0	0	.167	.167

Barry Larkin

Bats: Right, Throws: Right

Batting	Avg	G	AB	R	H	2B	3B	HR	RBI	BB	SO	HBP	GDP	SB	CS	OBP	Slg
Totals	.338	17	71	11	24	5	2	0	3	7	4	0	2	8	1	.397	.465
Home	.394	8	33	7	13	3	1	0	0	4	0	0	1	6	0	.459	.545
Away	.289	9	38	4	11	2	1	0	3	3	4	0	1	2	1	.341	.395
vs. Left	.417	5	12	2	5	1	1	0	0	1	0	0	0	0	0	.462	.667
vs. Right	.322	17	59	9	19	4	1	0	3	6	4	0	2	8	1	.385	.424
Scoring Pos.	.333	15	12	9	4	1	1	0	3	1	1	0	0	3	0	.385	.583
Close & Late	.455	9	11	1	5	2	0	0	2	0	0	0	0	1	0	.455	.636
None on/out	.458	17	24	0	11	4	1	0	0	5	2	0	0	0	0	.552	.708
None on	.377	17	53	0	20	4	1	0	0	6	3	0	0	0	0	.441	.491
Runners on	.222	16	18	11	4	1	1	0	3	1	1	0	2	8	1	.263	.389
Batting #1	.300	10	40	8	12	3	1	0	2	5	1	0	2	3	0	.378	.425
Batting #2	.387	7	31	3	12	2	1	0	1	2	3	0	0	5	1	.424	.516

Hit Best Against

	Avg	AB	R	H	2B	3B	HR	RBI	BB	SO	HBP	GDP	SB	CS	OBP	Slg
Doug Drabek	.429	7	2	3	2	0	0	1	1	0	0	1	1	0	.500	.714

Hit Worst Against

	Avg	AB	R	H	2B	3B	HR	RBI	BB	SO	HBP	GDP	SB	CS	OBP	Slg
Zane Smith	.200	5	1	1	0	0	0	0	0	0	0	0	0	0	.200	.200

Don Larsen

Throws: Right, Bats: Right

Pitching	ERA	W	L	Sv	G	GS	IP	BB	SO	Avg	R	H	2B	3B	HR	OBP	Slg
Totals	2.75	4	2	0	10	6	36.0	19	24	.188	16	24	2	0	3	.298	.273
Home	1.40	2	1	0	4	3	19.1	5	17	.152	4	10	1	0	0	.208	.167
Away	4.32	2	1	0	6	3	16.2	14	7	.226	12	14	1	0	3	.380	.387

	Avg	AB	R	H	2B	3B	HR	RBI	BB	SO	HBP	GDP	OBP	Slg
vs. Left	.203	59	0	12	2	0	0	4	15	10	0	1	.365	.237
vs. Right	.174	69	16	12	0	0	3	8	4	14	2	1	.234	.304
Scoring Pos.	.091	22	0	2	1	0	0	6	8	3	2	1	.353	.136
Close & Late	.100	10	0	1	0	0	0	0	1	1	1	1	.250	.100
None on/out	.265	34	0	9	0	0	1	1	5	4	0	1	.359	.353
None on	.185	81	0	15	0	0	1	1	7	17	0	1	.250	.222
Runners on	.191	47	0	9	2	0	2	11	12	7	2	1	.365	.362

Pitched Best Against

	Avg	AB	R	H	2B	3B	HR	RBI	BB	SO	HBP	GDP	SB	CS	OBP	Slg
Pee Wee Reese	.000	6	0	0	0	0	0	0	0	1	0	0	0	0	.000	.000
Jackie Robinson	.000	6	0	0	0	0	0	0	0	0	1	0	0	0	.000	.000
Duke Snider	.000	5	0	0	0	0	0	0	1	1	0	0	0	0	.167	.000

Pitched Worst Against

	Avg	AB	R	H	2B	3B	HR	RBI	BB	SO	HBP	GDP	SB	CS	OBP	Slg
Gil Hodges	.500	6	2	3	0	0	1	2	0	1	0	0	0	0	.500	1.000
Hank Aaron	.500	8	1	4	0	0	1	2	2	1	0	0	0	0	.600	.875
R. Schoendienst	.444	9	1	4	0	0	0	0	0	0	0	0	0	0	.444	.444

Tony Lazzeri

Bats: Right, Throws: Right

Batting	Avg	G	AB	R	H	2B	3B	HR	RBI	BB	SO	HBP	GDP	SB	CS	OBP	Slg
Totals	.262	32	107	16	28	3	1	4	19	12	19	1	2	2	1	.333	.421
Home	.176	15	51	6	9	0	0	1	4	3	11	0	0	0	1	.222	.235
Away	.339	17	56	10	19	3	1	3	15	9	8	1	2	2	0	.420	.589
vs. Left	.324	16	34	0	11	0	1	1	2	2	5	1	0	1	0	.368	.471
vs. Right	.233	32	73	16	17	3	0	3	17	10	14	0	2	1	1	.318	.397
Scoring Pos.	.250	27	32	0	8	0	0	2	16	7	4	0	0	2	1	.357	.438
Close & Late	.273	12	11	0	3	1	0	0	2	1	3	0	1	0	0	.308	.364
None on/out	.417	20	24	0	10	2	1	1	1	1	5	0	0	0	0	.440	.708
None on	.240	30	50	0	12	2	1	1	1	5	12	1	0	0	0	.321	.380
Runners on	.281	29	57	0	16	1	0	3	18	7	7	0	2	2	1	.343	.456
Batting #5	.294	4	17	4	5	0	0	2	5	2	1	0	0	0	0	.368	.647
Batting #6	.226	15	53	5	12	3	0	0	3	3	10	0	2	2	1	.254	.283
Batting #8	.379	10	29	7	11	0	1	2	9	6	5	1	0	0	0	.500	.655

Hit Best Against

	Avg	AB	R	H	2B	3B	HR	RBI	BB	SO	HBP	GDP	SB	CS	OBP	Slg
Bill Sherdel	.417	12	0	5	0	0	0	1	0	1	0	0	1	0	.385	.417
Lon Warneke	.400	5	1	2	0	0	1	2	0	0	0	0	0	0	.400	1.000
Hal Schumacher	.400	5	1	2	0	0	0	2	3	1	0	0	0	0	.625	.400

Hit Worst Against

	Avg	AB	R	H	2B	3B	HR	RBI	BB	SO	HBP	GDP	SB	CS	OBP	Slg
Jesse Haines	.000	10	1	0	0	0	0	0	1	3	0	2	1	0	.091	.000
Carl Hubbell	.091	11	0	1	0	0	0	0	1	3	0	0	0	0	.167	.091
Pete Alexander	.182	11	2	2	1	0	0	1	0	2	0	0	0	1	.182	.273

Mark Lemke

Bats: Both, Throws: Right

Batting	Avg	G	AB	R	H	2B	3B	HR	RBI	BB	SO	HBP	GDP	SB	CS	OBP	Slg
Totals	.272	62	232	22	63	10	3	1	24	22	27	0	5	0	1	.335	.353
Home	.316	31	114	11	36	6	3	0	19	14	19	0	5	0	1	.391	.421
Away	.229	31	118	11	27	4	0	1	5	8	8	0	0	0	0	.278	.288

Batting	Avg	G	AB	R	H	2B	3B	HR	RBI	BB	SO	HBP	GDP	SB	CS	OBP	Slg
vs. Left	.268	36	71	8	19	5	1	0	9	4	7	0	1	0	0	.307	.366
vs. Right	.273	59	161	14	44	5	2	1	15	18	20	0	4	0	1	.346	.348
Scoring Pos.	.345	42	55	19	19	5	1	0	22	6	6	0	1	0	0	.410	.473
Close & Late	.182	32	44	3	8	0	1	0	2	4	5	0	0	0	0	.250	.227
None on/out	.250	39	48	1	12	1	0	1	1	4	10	0	0	0	0	.308	.333
None on	.243	60	136	1	33	3	1	1	1	13	18	0	0	0	0	.309	.301
Runners on	.313	55	96	21	30	7	2	0	23	9	9	0	5	0	1	.371	.427
Batting #2	.263	29	114	13	30	5	0	1	11	9	10	0	3	0	1	.317	.333
Batting #7	.333	9	33	4	11	2	3	0	5	6	3	0	1	0	0	.436	.576
Batting #8	.267	21	75	5	20	3	0	0	7	7	13	0	1	0	0	.329	.307
Batting #9	.200	3	10	0	2	0	0	0	1	0	1	0	0	0	0	.200	.200

Hit Best Against

	Avg	AB	R	H	2B	3B	HR	RBI	BB	SO	HBP	GDP	SB	CS	OBP	Slg
T. Stottlemyre	.667	6	2	4	1	0	0	0	1	1	0	0	0	0	.714	.833
Danny Jackson	.667	6	1	4	1	0	0	3	0	0	0	0	0	0	.667	.833
Zane Smith	.667	6	0	4	1	0	0	1	0	0	0	0	0	0	.667	.833

Hit Worst Against

	Avg	AB	R	H	2B	3B	HR	RBI	BB	SO	HBP	GDP	SB	CS	OBP	Slg
Andy Pettitte	.000	5	0	0	0	0	0	0	0	2	0	0	0	0	.000	.000
David Wells	.000	5	0	0	0	0	0	0	0	0	0	1	0	0	.000	.000
Bob Walk	.000	7	0	0	0	0	0	0	1	1	0	0	0	0	.125	.000

Bob Lemon

Throws: Right, Bats: Left

Pitching	ERA	W	L	Sv	G	GS	IP	BB	SO	Avg	R	H	2B	3B	HR	OBP	Slg
Totals	3.94	2	2	0	4	4	29.2	15	17	.286	15	32	4	0	1	.367	.348
Home	11.25	0	1	0	1	1	4.0	3	5	.389	6	7	2	0	0	.455	.500
Away	2.81	2	1	0	3	3	25.2	12	12	.266	9	25	2	0	1	.349	.319

	Avg	AB	R	H	2B	3B	HR	RBI	BB	SO	HBP	GDP	OBP	Slg
vs. Left	.318	44	0	14	1	0	1	5	7	5	0	4	.412	.409
vs. Right	.265	68	15	18	3	0	0	4	8	12	0	4	.338	.309
Scoring Pos.	.241	29	0	7	1	0	1	9	5	2	0	4	.343	.379
Close & Late	.200	15	2	3	1	0	1	3	4	2	0	4	.368	.467
None on/out	.321	28	0	9	0	0	0	0	4	7	0	4	.406	.321
None on	.276	58	0	16	1	0	0	0	7	10	0	4	.354	.293
Runners on	.296	54	0	16	3	0	1	9	8	7	0	4	.381	.407

Pitched Best Against

	Avg	AB	R	H	2B	3B	HR	RBI	BB	SO	HBP	GDP	SB	CS	OBP	Slg
Marv Rickert	.000	7	0	0	0	0	0	0	0	1	0	1	0	0	.000	.000
Davey Williams	.000	6	0	0	0	0	0	0	0	0	0	0	0	0	.000	.000
Whitey Lockman	.125	8	1	1	0	0	0	0	0	1	0	0	0	0	.125	.125

Pitched Worst Against

	Avg	AB	R	H	2B	3B	HR	RBI	BB	SO	HBP	GDP	SB	CS	OBP	Slg
Don Mueller	.625	8	2	5	0	0	0	1	0	1	0	0	0	0	.625	.625
Glenn Elliott	.571	7	1	4	0	0	0	1	1	1	0	1	0	0	.625	.571
Mike McCormick	.429	7	0	3	0	0	0	1	0	2	0	0	0	0	.429	.429

Freddy Lindstrom

Bats: Right, Throws: Right

Batting	Avg	G	AB	R	H	2B	3B	HR	RBI	BB	SO	HBP	GDP	SB	CS	OBP	Slg
Totals	.289	11	45	1	13	3	0	0	4	4	7	0	1	0	3	.347	.356
Home	.455	5	22	1	10	2	0	0	4	2	1	0	1	0	2	.500	.545
Away	.130	6	23	0	3	1	0	0	0	2	6	0	0	0	1	.200	.174
vs. Left	.333	4	12	0	4	1	0	0	0	2	1	0	0	0	0	.429	.417
vs. Right	.273	11	33	1	9	2	0	0	4	2	6	0	1	0	3	.314	.333
Scoring Pos.	.364	9	11	0	4	1	0	0	4	0	1	0	1	0	1	.364	.455
Close & Late	.286	5	7	0	2	1	0	0	1	0	1	0	0	0	0	.286	.429
None on/out	.200	11	15	0	3	1	0	0	0	2	3	0	0	0	0	.294	.267
None on	.233	11	30	0	7	2	0	0	0	3	6	0	0	0	0	.303	.300
Runners on	.400	9	15	0	6	1	0	0	4	1	1	0	1	0	3	.438	.467
Batting #1	.333	7	30	1	10	2	0	0	4	3	6	0	0	0	2	.394	.400
Batting #3	.200	4	15	0	3	1	0	0	0	1	1	0	1	0	1	.250	.267

Hit Best Against

	Avg	AB	R	H	2B	3B	HR	RBI	BB	SO	HBP	GDP	SB	CS	OBP	Slg
G. Mogridge	.600	5	1	3	1	0	0	0	1	0	0	0	0	0	.667	.800
Schoolboy Rowe	.400	5	0	2	1	0	0	0	0	0	0	0	0	1	.400	.600
Walter Johnson	.364	11	0	4	0	0	0	2	0	2	0	0	0	2	.364	.364

Hit Worst Against

	Avg	AB	R	H	2B	3B	HR	RBI	BB	SO	HBP	GDP	SB	CS	OBP	Slg
Tom Zachary	.143	7	0	1	0	0	0	0	1	1	0	0	0	0	.250	.143

Kenny Lofton

Bats: Left, Throws: Left

Batting	Avg	G	AB	R	H	2B	3B	HR	RBI	BB	SO	HBP	GDP	SB	CS	OBP	Slg
Totals	.233	28	120	19	28	2	3	0	5	12	22	1	2	17	3	.306	.300
Home	.188	15	64	12	12	2	1	0	3	8	14	1	1	9	2	.284	.250
Away	.286	13	56	7	16	0	2	0	2	4	8	0	1	8	1	.333	.357
vs. Left	.154	20	52	5	8	0	1	0	3	4	17	0	1	6	0	.214	.192
vs. Right	.294	23	68	14	20	2	2	0	2	8	5	1	1	11	3	.372	.382
Scoring Pos.	.217	25	23	18	5	0	0	0	5	5	8	0	0	8	0	.345	.217
Close & Late	.273	18	22	5	6	0	0	0	1	5	5	1	0	6	1	.429	.273
None on/out	.217	28	46	0	10	2	2	0	0	2	7	1	0	0	0	.265	.348
None on	.235	28	81	0	19	2	3	0	0	6	10	1	0	0	0	.295	.333
Runners on	.231	28	39	19	9	0	0	0	5	6	12	0	2	17	3	.326	.231
Batting #1	.233	28	120	19	28	2	3	0	5	12	22	1	2	17	3	.306	.300

Hit Best Against

	Avg	AB	R	H	2B	3B	HR	RBI	BB	SO	HBP	GDP	SB	CS	OBP	Slg
Randy Johnson	.500	8	2	4	0	1	0	2	0	3	0	0	2	0	.500	.750

Hit Worst Against

	Avg	AB	R	H	2B	3B	HR	RBI	BB	SO	HBP	GDP	SB	CS	OBP	Slg
Tom Glavine	.000	6	0	0	0	0	0	0	0	0	0	0	2	0	.000	.000
Al Leiter	.000	5	0	0	0	0	0	0	0	2	0	1	0	0	.000	.000
Kevin Brown	.125	8	1	1	0	0	0	1	0	2	0	0	1	0	.125	.125

Ed Lopat

Throws: Left, Bats: Left

Pitching	ERA	W	L	Sv	G	GS	IP	BB	SO	Avg	R	H	2B	3B	HR	OBP	Slg
Totals	2.60	4	1	0	7	7	52.0	12	19	.256	16	51	6	1	0	.299	.296
Home	2.62	2	1	0	4	4	34.1	10	9	.256	10	33	4	1	0	.309	.302
Away	2.55	2	0	0	3	3	17.2	2	10	.257	6	18	2	0	0	.278	.286

	Avg	AB	R	H	2B	3B	HR	RBI	BB	SO	HBP	GDP	OBP	Slg
vs. Left	.188	48	0	9	0	0	0	2	0	9	0	2	.188	.188
vs. Right	.276	152	16	42	6	1	0	10	12	10	0	2	.329	.329
Scoring Pos.	.213	47	0	10	1	0	0	12	5	2	0	2	.288	.234
Close & Late	.281	32	3	9	0	0	0	3	3	0	0	2	.343	.281
None on/out	.245	53	0	13	2	0	0	0	1	7	0	2	.259	.283
None on	.270	115	0	31	5	1	0	0	6	13	0	2	.306	.330
Runners on	.235	85	0	20	1	0	0	12	6	6	0	2	.286	.247

Pitched Best Against

	Avg	AB	R	H	2B	3B	HR	RBI	BB	SO	HBP	GDP	SB	CS	OBP	Slg
Jim Gilliam	.000	5	0	0	0	0	0	0	0	0	0	0	0	0	.000	.000
Preacher Roe	.000	5	0	0	0	0	0	0	0	2	0	0	0	0	.000	.000
Eddie Stanky	.000	7	0	0	0	0	0	0	1	0	0	0	0	0	.125	.000

Pitched Worst Against

	Avg	AB	R	H	2B	3B	HR	RBI	BB	SO	HBP	GDP	SB	CS	OBP	Slg
Monte Irvin	.625	8	1	5	0	0	0	0	0	0	0	0	1	0	.625	.625
Pee Wee Reese	.538	13	2	7	1	1	0	1	2	0	0	0	0	0	.600	.769
Jackie Robinson	.417	12	3	5	0	0	0	2	2	0	0	0	0	0	.500	.417

Davey Lopes

Bats: Right, Throws: Right

Batting	Avg	G	AB	R	H	2B	3B	HR	RBI	BB	SO	HBP	GDP	SB	CS	OBP	Slg
Totals	.238	50	181	29	43	3	3	6	22	25	23	0	2	20	3	.330	.387
Home	.239	25	88	15	21	1	2	4	14	12	12	0	1	11	2	.330	.432
Away	.237	25	93	14	22	2	1	2	8	13	11	0	1	9	1	.330	.344
vs. Left	.164	29	73	0	12	1	1	1	5	14	9	0	1	3	2	.299	.247
vs. Right	.287	50	108	29	31	2	2	5	17	11	14	0	1	17	1	.353	.481
Scoring Pos.	.424	33	33	0	14	0	2	4	20	8	5	0	0	4	0	.537	.909
Close & Late	.214	23	28	2	6	1	0	0	2	4	5	0	2	4	0	.313	.250
None on/out	.193	45	83	0	16	2	1	2	2	9	9	0	0	0	0	.272	.313
None on	.192	48	130	0	25	3	1	2	2	15	16	0	0	0	0	.276	.277
Runners on	.353	40	51	0	18	0	2	4	20	10	7	0	2	20	3	.459	.667
Batting #1	.242	45	178	28	43	3	3	6	22	24	23	0	1	20	3	.332	.393

Hit Best Against

	Avg	AB	R	H	2B	3B	HR	RBI	BB	SO	HBP	GDP	SB	CS	OBP	Slg
Catfish Hunter	.417	12	2	5	0	0	1	2	1	0	0	0	3	0	.462	.667
L. Christenson	.400	5	2	2	1	0	1	2	0	0	0	0	0	0	.400	1.200
Don Gullett	.333	6	2	2	0	1	0	0	1	2	0	0	0	0	.429	.667

Hit Worst Against

	Avg	AB	R	H	2B	3B	HR	RBI	BB	SO	HBP	GDP	SB	CS	OBP	Slg
Ken Holtzman	.000	7	1	0	0	0	0	0	0	3	0	0	0	0	.000	.000
Vida Blue	.000	5	1	0	0	0	0	0	2	1	0	0	0	1	.286	.000
Mike Torrez	.125	8	0	1	0	0	0	0	1	1	0	0	1	0	.222	.125

Javy Lopez

Bats: Right, Throws: Right

Batting	Avg	G	AB	R	H	2B	3B	HR	RBI	BB	SO	HBP	GDP	SB	CS	OBP	Slg
Totals	.291	35	117	18	34	11	0	5	20	11	18	2	3	2	1	.351	.513
Home	.302	18	53	9	16	5	0	2	12	7	6	2	1	2	1	.391	.509
Away	.281	17	64	9	18	6	0	3	8	4	12	0	2	0	0	.314	.516
vs. Left	.342	19	38	6	13	4	0	1	5	7	5	0	2	0	0	.426	.526
vs. Right	.266	33	79	12	21	7	0	4	15	4	13	2	1	2	1	.310	.506
Scoring Pos.	.250	30	36	15	9	3	0	3	18	4	5	0	2	1	0	.295	.583
Close & Late	.240	17	25	3	6	0	0	2	6	0	5	2	1	0	0	.296	.480
None on/out	.304	20	23	1	7	1	0	1	1	2	2	0	0	0	0	.360	.478
None on	.310	33	58	2	18	5	0	2	2	4	8	2	0	0	0	.375	.500
Runners on	.271	31	59	16	16	6	0	3	18	7	10	0	3	2	1	.329	.525
Batting #5	.257	10	35	8	9	3	0	1	6	6	8	0	2	0	0	.349	.429
Batting #6	.347	13	49	8	17	6	0	2	6	4	6	1	0	2	0	.393	.592
Batting #7	.250	11	32	2	8	2	0	2	8	1	4	1	1	0	1	.294	.500

Hit Best Against

	Avg	AB	R	H	2B	3B	HR	RBI	BB	SO	HBP	GDP	SB	CS	OBP	Slg
Pete Schourek	.500	6	0	3	0	0	0	0	0	0	0	0	0	0	.500	.500

Hit Worst Against

	Avg	AB	R	H	2B	3B	HR	RBI	BB	SO	HBP	GDP	SB	CS	OBP	Slg
Kevin Brown	.000	7	0	0	0	0	0	0	0	3	0	0	0	0	.000	.000
Andy Benes	.143	7	1	1	0	0	1	2	0	0	0	0	0	0	.143	.571

Greg Luzinski

Bats: Right, Throws: Right

Batting	Avg	G	AB	R	H	2B	3B	HR	RBI	BB	SO	HBP	GDP	SB	CS	OBP	Slg
Totals	.244	23	82	10	20	6	1	5	12	7	25	3	1	1	0	.326	.524
Home	.222	12	45	6	10	2	1	2	5	2	17	2	1	0	0	.286	.444
Away	.270	11	37	4	10	4	0	3	7	5	8	1	0	1	0	.372	.622
vs. Left	.280	12	25	0	7	2	0	2	5	4	9	0	0	1	0	.379	.600
vs. Right	.228	23	57	10	13	4	1	3	7	3	16	3	1	0	0	.302	.491
Scoring Pos.	.176	13	17	0	3	3	0	0	3	1	3	1	1	0	0	.263	.353
Close & Late	.308	11	13	1	4	2	0	0	2	1	4	0	0	0	0	.357	.462
None on/out	.333	16	21	0	7	1	1	1	1	2	9	1	0	0	0	.417	.619
None on	.250	22	40	0	10	2	1	2	2	5	16	2	0	0	0	.362	.500
Runners on	.238	21	42	0	10	4	0	3	10	2	9	1	1	1	0	.289	.548
Batting #4	.267	21	75	10	20	6	1	5	12	7	21	2	1	1	0	.345	.573

Hit Best Against

	Avg	AB	R	H	2B	3B	HR	RBI	BB	SO	HBP	GDP	SB	CS	OBP	Slg
Tommy John	.375	8	2	3	0	0	1	2	2	1	0	0	1	0	.500	.750
Nolan Ryan	.333	6	1	2	1	0	0	1	0	4	0	0	0	0	.333	.500
Don Sutton	.286	7	0	2	1	0	0	0	0	0	0	0	0	0	.286	.429

Fred Lynn

Bats: Left, Throws: Left

Batting	Avg	G	AB	R	H	2B	3B	HR	RBI	BB	SO	HBP	GDP	SB	CS	OBP	Slg
Totals	.407	15	54	8	22	4	0	2	13	5	8	0	2	0	0	.450	.593
Home	.400	8	30	4	12	1	0	2	7	3	3	0	2	0	0	.455	.633
Away	.417	7	24	4	10	3	0	0	6	2	5	0	0	0	0	.444	.542
vs. Left	.360	11	25	0	9	2	0	0	3	2	5	0	0	0	0	.407	.440
vs. Right	.448	15	29	8	13	2	0	2	10	3	3	0	2	0	0	.485	.724
Scoring Pos.	.600	12	15	0	9	3	0	1	11	3	2	0	0	0	0	.632	1.000
Close & Late	.333	7	6	0	2	2	0	0	2	1	0	0	0	0	0	.429	.667
None on/out	.333	12	15	0	5	0	0	1	1	1	4	0	0	0	0	.375	.533
None on	.321	15	28	0	9	0	0	1	1	2	5	0	0	0	0	.367	.429

Batting	Avg	G	AB	R	H	2B	3B	HR	RBI	BB	SO	HBP	GDP	SB	CS	OBP	Slg
Runners on	.500	14	26	0	13	4	0	1	12	3	3	0	2	0	0	.533	.769
Batting #4	.571	4	14	3	8	2	0	0	4	2	2	0	1	0	0	.625	.714
Batting #5	.306	10	36	4	11	2	0	1	8	3	5	0	1	0	0	.350	.444

Hit Best Against

	Avg	AB	R	H	2B	3B	HR	RBI	BB	SO	HBP	GDP	SB	CS	OBP	Slg
Pete Vuckovich	.714	7	1	5	0	0	0	2	0	0	0	1	0	0	.714	.714
Don Gullett	.375	8	0	3	1	0	0	1	1	2	0	0	0	0	.444	.500

Hit Worst Against

	Avg	AB	R	H	2B	3B	HR	RBI	BB	SO	HBP	GDP	SB	CS	OBP	Slg
Ken Holtzman	.200	5	1	1	0	0	0	0	0	0	0	0	0	0	.200	.200

Greg Maddux

Throws: Right, Bats: Right

Pitching	ERA	W	L	Sv	G	GS	IP	BB	SO	Avg	R	H	2B	3B	HR	OBP	Slg
Totals	3.08	8	7	0	17	17	117.0	26	79	.243	56	107	19	2	9	.292	.357
Home	2.83	5	3	0	8	8	57.1	9	41	.244	30	54	7	0	5	.279	.344
Away	3.32	3	4	0	9	9	59.2	17	38	.242	26	53	12	2	4	.304	.370

	Avg	AB	R	H	2B	3B	HR	RBI	BB	SO	HBP	GDP	OBP	Slg
vs. Left	.228	215	0	49	8	1	4	20	13	34	2	8	.277	.330
vs. Right	.258	225	12	58	11	1	5	32	13	45	3	8	.306	.382
Scoring Pos.	.272	92	21	25	8	2	5	46	13	16	2	8	.367	.565
Close & Late	.277	47	4	13	2	0	1	6	3	10	1	8	.327	.383
None on/out	.172	116	0	20	3	0	0	0	2	22	2	8	.200	.198
None on	.238	277	14	66	10	0	2	2	11	50	3	8	.275	.296
Runners on	.252	163	30	41	9	2	7	50	15	29	2	8	.319	.460

Pitched Best Against

	Avg	AB	R	H	2B	3B	HR	RBI	BB	SO	HBP	GDP	SB	CS	OBP	Slg
Jim Eisenreich	.000	6	0	0	0	0	0	0	0	1	0	0	0	0	.000	.000
Devon White	.000	6	1	0	0	0	0	0	0	4	1	0	1	0	.143	.000
Larry Walker	.000	5	1	0	0	0	0	0	1	2	0	1	0	0	.167	.000

Pitched Worst Against

	Avg	AB	R	H	2B	3B	HR	RBI	BB	SO	HBP	GDP	SB	CS	OBP	Slg
Will Clark	1.000	5	4	5	2	0	2	6	0	0	0	0	0	0	1.000	2.600
Vinny Castilla	.833	6	2	5	1	0	2	3	0	0	0	1	0	0	.833	2.000
Eric Young	.714	7	1	5	1	0	0	0	1	1	0	0	1	0	.750	.857

Bill Madlock

Bats: Right, Throws: Right

Batting	Avg	G	AB	R	H	2B	3B	HR	RBI	BB	SO	HBP	GDP	SB	CS	OBP	Slg
Totals	.308	17	65	8	20	2	0	4	12	7	6	0	3	3	2	.375	.523
Home	.538	7	26	6	14	2	0	2	7	4	3	0	2	1	1	.600	.846
Away	.154	10	39	2	6	0	0	2	5	3	3	0	1	2	1	.214	.308
vs. Left	.280	10	25	0	7	1	0	2	4	3	3	0	0	2	0	.357	.560
vs. Right	.325	17	40	8	13	1	0	2	8	4	3	0	3	1	2	.386	.500
Scoring Pos.	.353	12	17	0	6	0	0	0	7	5	1	0	2	0	0	.500	.353
Close & Late	.182	9	11	0	2	0	0	0	0	1	1	0	1	0	0	.250	.182
None on/out	.154	9	13	0	2	0	0	1	1	0	0	0	0	0	0	.154	.385
None on	.237	17	38	0	9	1	0	3	3	1	4	0	0	0	0	.256	.500
Runners on	.407	16	27	0	11	1	0	1	9	6	2	0	3	3	2	.515	.556
Batting #3	.308	3	13	2	4	1	0	0	2	0	1	0	0	1	0	.308	.385
Batting #4	.364	3	11	3	4	0	0	3	5	0	1	0	1	0	0	.364	1.182
Batting #6	.333	10	36	3	12	1	0	1	5	7	1	0	2	2	2	.442	.444

Hit Best Against

	Avg	AB	R	H	2B	3B	HR	RBI	BB	SO	HBP	GDP	SB	CS	OBP	Slg
Joaquin Andujar	.500	6	1	3	0	0	1	3	0	2	0	0	0	0	.500	1.000
Mike Flanagan	.500	6	0	3	0	0	0	1	1	0	0	0	0	0	.571	.500
John Tudor	.333	6	3	2	1	0	1	1	0	0	0	0	1	0	.333	1.000

Hit Worst Against

	Avg	AB	R	H	2B	3B	HR	RBI	BB	SO	HBP	GDP	SB	CS	OBP	Slg
Scott McGregor	.143	7	0	1	0	0	0	1	1	1	0	0	0	0	.250	.143

Mickey Mantle

Bats: Both, Throws: Right

Batting	Avg	G	AB	R	H	2B	3B	HR	RBI	BB	SO	HBP	GDP	SB	CS	OBP	Slg
Totals	.257	65	230	42	59	6	2	18	40	43	54	0	2	3	4	.374	.535
Home	.250	29	92	14	23	2	2	5	8	22	17	0	0	2	3	.395	.478
Away	.261	36	138	28	36	4	0	13	32	21	37	0	2	1	1	.358	.572
vs. Left	.272	34	81	0	22	2	1	7	16	13	10	0	1	1	1	.372	.580
vs. Right	.248	65	149	42	37	4	1	11	24	30	44	0	1	2	3	.374	.510
Scoring Pos.	.262	47	42	0	11	0	0	4	20	13	12	0	1	1	1	.436	.548
Close & Late	.344	31	32	5	11	0	1	4	9	3	7	0	1	0	1	.400	.781
None on/out	.254	45	63	0	16	1	1	5	5	6	16	0	0	0	0	.319	.540
None on	.235	62	132	0	31	3	2	9	9	25	31	0	0	0	0	.357	.492
Runners on	.286	62	98	0	28	3	0	9	31	18	23	0	2	3	4	.397	.592
Batting #1	.200	3	10	1	2	0	0	0	1	2	3	0	0	0	0	.333	.200
Batting #3	.309	26	97	19	30	3	1	9	14	19	16	0	1	1	2	.422	.639
Batting #4	.223	29	103	19	23	3	1	7	19	19	29	0	1	2	0	.344	.476
Batting #5	.211	5	19	3	4	0	0	2	6	3	6	0	0	0	1	.318	.526

Hit Best Against

	Avg	AB	R	H	2B	3B	HR	RBI	BB	SO	HBP	GDP	SB	CS	OBP	Slg
Don Bessent	.600	5	0	3	1	0	0	0	0	1	0	0	0	0	.600	.800
Curt Simmons	.400	5	1	2	1	0	1	1	1	1	0	0	0	0	.500	1.200
Sal Maglie	.333	6	2	2	0	0	2	3	2	1	0	1	0	0	.500	1.333

Hit Worst Against

	Avg	AB	R	H	2B	3B	HR	RBI	BB	SO	HBP	GDP	SB	CS	OBP	Slg
Billy O'Dell	.000	5	0	0	0	0	0	0	1	2	0	0	1	0	.167	.000
Johnny Podres	.100	10	1	1	0	0	1	1	0	0	0	1	0	0	.100	.400
Bob Gibson	.100	10	3	1	0	0	1	4	2	5	0	0	0	0	.250	.400

Roger Maris

Bats: Left, Throws: Right

Batting	Avg	G	AB	R	H	2B	3B	HR	RBI	BB	SO	HBP	GDP	SB	CS	OBP	Slg
Totals	.217	41	152	26	33	5	0	6	18	18	21	0	3	0	0	.298	.368
Home	.149	19	67	10	10	1	0	2	7	5	7	0	3	0	0	.208	.254
Away	.271	22	85	16	23	4	0	4	11	13	14	0	0	0	0	.364	.459
vs. Left	.157	22	51	0	8	1	0	3	7	3	12	0	1	0	0	.204	.353
vs. Right	.248	41	101	26	25	4	0	3	11	15	9	0	2	0	0	.342	.376
Scoring Pos.	.135	27	37	0	5	2	0	0	11	7	7	0	0	0	0	.267	.189
Close & Late	.261	20	23	2	6	1	0	1	4	0	4	0	0	0	0	.261	.435
None on/out	.250	19	16	0	4	0	0	1	1	5	0	0	0	0	0	.429	.438
None on	.228	38	79	0	18	0	0	6	6	10	9	0	0	0	0	.315	.456
Runners on	.205	38	73	0	15	5	0	0	12	8	12	0	3	0	0	.280	.274
Batting #3	.248	28	113	21	28	4	0	4	12	12	15	0	2	0	0	.317	.389
Batting #5	.143	9	28	4	4	1	0	1	5	5	3	0	0	0	0	.273	.286

Hit Best Against

	Avg	AB	R	H	2B	3B	HR	RBI	BB	SO	HBP	GDP	SB	CS	OBP	Slg
Jim Lonborg	.444	9	1	4	0	0	1	2	0	0	0	0	0	0	.400	.778
Jose Santiago	.400	5	1	2	1	0	0	4	1	0	0	0	0	0	.500	.600
Billy O'Dell	.333	6	1	2	1	0	0	2	0	1	0	0	0	0	.333	.500

Hit Worst Against

	Avg	AB	R	H	2B	3B	HR	RBI	BB	SO	HBP	GDP	SB	CS	OBP	Slg
Jack Sanford	.000	9	0	0	0	0	0	0	1	0	0	0	0	0	.100	.000
Jim O'Toole	.000	6	1	0	0	0	0	0	1	1	0	0	0	0	.143	.000
Curt Simmons	.143	7	1	1	0	0	1	1	0	2	0	0	0	0	.143	.571

Rube Marquard

Throws: Left, Bats: Both

Pitching	ERA	W	L	Sv	G	GS	IP	BB	SO	Avg	R	H	2B	3B	HR	OBP	Slg
Totals	3.07	2	5	0	11	8	58.2	15	35	.240	28	52	14	4	4	.288	.396
Home	3.67	1	3	0	5	5	27.0	7	13	.277	17	28	6	2	3	.324	.465
Away	2.56	1	2	0	6	3	31.2	8	22	.207	11	24	8	2	1	.256	.336

	Avg	AB	R	H	2B	3B	HR	RBI	BB	SO	HBP	GDP	OBP	Slg
vs. Left	.211	71	0	15	3	2	1	6	7	9	0	0	.282	.352
vs. Right	.253	146	28	37	11	2	3	21	8	26	0	0	.290	.418
Scoring Pos.	.278	54	0	15	4	1	4	26	3	6	0	0	.310	.611
Close & Late	.143	14	1	2	2	0	0	2	1	0	0	0	.200	.286
None on/out	.214	56	0	12	3	1	0	0	3	9	0	0	.254	.304
None on	.223	130	0	29	6	3	0	0	11	27	0	0	.284	.315
Runners on	.264	87	0	23	8	1	4	27	4	8	0	0	.293	.517

Pitched Best Against

	Avg	AB	R	H	2B	3B	HR	RBI	BB	SO	HBP	GDP	SB	CS	OBP	Slg
Heinie Wagner	.000	8	0	0	0	0	0	0	0	2	0	0	1	0	.000	.000
Chief Bender	.000	5	0	0	0	0	0	0	0	1	0	0	0	0	.000	.000
Tris Speaker	.091	11	0	1	0	0	0	0	1	1	0	0	1	0	.167	.091

Pitched Worst Against

	Avg	AB	R	H	2B	3B	HR	RBI	BB	SO	HBP	GDP	SB	CS	OBP	Slg
Eddie Collins	.500	8	3	4	1	1	0	0	2	0	0	0	2	0	.600	.875
Tilly Walker	.500	6	1	3	0	1	0	1	0	2	0	0	0	1	.500	.833
Jake Stahl	.500	8	1	4	1	0	0	0	0	1	0	0	0	1	.500	.625

Billy Martin

Bats: Right, Throws: Right

Batting	Avg	G	AB	R	H	2B	3B	HR	RBI	BB	SO	HBP	GDP	SB	CS	OBP	Slg
Totals	.333	28	99	15	33	2	3	5	19	5	15	1	4	1	5	.371	.566
Home	.364	14	44	6	16	1	2	2	9	3	6	1	2	1	4	.417	.614
Away	.309	14	55	9	17	1	1	3	10	2	9	0	2	0	1	.333	.527
vs. Left	.188	9	16	0	3	0	0	1	1	3	3	1	0	0	1	.350	.375
vs. Right	.361	28	83	15	30	2	3	4	18	2	12	0	4	1	4	.376	.602
Scoring Pos.	.346	20	26	0	9	0	1	2	15	3	3	0	0	0	1	.414	.654
Close & Late	.300	11	10	2	3	0	0	0	1	0	0	0	1	1	0	.300	.300
None on/out	.300	17	20	0	6	0	1	1	1	1	4	0	0	0	0	.333	.550
None on	.373	25	51	0	19	1	2	3	3	2	9	1	0	0	0	.407	.647
Runners on	.292	26	48	0	14	1	1	2	16	3	6	0	4	1	5	.333	.479
Batting #2	.333	3	12	2	4	0	0	0	0	1	4	0	0	0	0	.385	.333
Batting #6	.345	7	29	3	10	1	1	2	6	0	4	0	2	0	1	.345	.655
Batting #7	.400	11	35	8	14	1	2	2	9	2	5	0	2	1	3	.432	.714
Batting #8	.217	7	23	2	5	0	0	1	4	2	2	1	0	0	1	.308	.348

Hit Best Against

	Avg	AB	R	H	2B	3B	HR	RBI	BB	SO	HBP	GDP	SB	CS	OBP	Slg
Don Newcombe	.667	6	2	4	0	1	0	0	0	1	0	0	0	1	.667	1.000
Russ Meyer	.600	5	1	3	0	0	1	2	0	1	0	0	0	1	.600	1.200
Roger Craig	.429	7	2	3	0	0	1	2	0	0	0	1	0	0	.429	.857

Hit Worst Against

	Avg	AB	R	H	2B	3B	HR	RBI	BB	SO	HBP	GDP	SB	CS	OBP	Slg
Johnny Podres	.125	8	0	1	0	0	0	0	1	1	0	0	0	0	.222	.125
Don Bessent	.200	5	0	1	0	0	0	1	0	2	0	1	0	1	.200	.200
Joe Black	.222	9	0	2	0	0	0	0	0	2	0	0	0	0	.222	.222

Pepper Martin

Bats: Right, Throws: Right

Batting	Avg	G	AB	R	H	2B	3B	HR	RBI	BB	SO	HBP	GDP	SB	CS	OBP	Slg
Totals	.418	15	55	14	23	7	1	1	9	5	6	0	0	7	2	.467	.636
Home	.417	8	24	5	10	4	1	0	2	4	2	0	0	4	1	.500	.667
Away	.419	7	31	9	13	3	0	1	7	1	4	0	0	3	1	.438	.613
vs. Left	.429	8	14	0	6	2	0	0	3	3	2	0	0	1	2	.529	.571
vs. Right	.415	15	41	14	17	5	1	1	6	2	4	0	0	6	0	.442	.659
Scoring Pos.	.462	9	13	0	6	1	0	1	9	2	2	0	0	4	1	.533	.769
Close & Late	.333	6	6	1	2	1	0	0	0	1	1	0	0	1	0	.429	.500
None on/out	.625	12	16	0	10	2	1	0	0	1	1	0	0	0	0	.647	.875
None on	.412	14	34	0	14	5	1	0	0	2	4	0	0	0	0	.444	.618
Runners on	.429	14	21	0	9	2	0	1	9	3	2	0	0	7	2	.500	.667
Batting #1	.355	7	31	8	11	3	1	0	4	3	3	0	0	2	1	.412	.516
Batting #4	.300	3	10	1	3	0	0	1	4	2	1	0	0	1	1	.417	.600
Batting #6	.643	4	14	4	9	4	0	0	1	0	2	0	0	4	0	.643	.929

Hit Best Against

	Avg	AB	R	H	2B	3B	HR	RBI	BB	SO	HBP	GDP	SB	CS	OBP	Slg
Tommy Bridges	.556	9	4	5	2	1	0	0	0	0	0	0	1	0	.556	1.000
G. Earnshaw	.500	8	2	4	2	0	0	0	1	1	0	0	4	0	.556	.750
Lefty Grove	.455	11	2	5	2	0	0	1	1	1	0	0	1	0	.500	.636

Eddie Mathews

Bats: Left, Throws: Right

Batting	Avg	G	AB	R	H	2B	3B	HR	RBI	BB	SO	HBP	GDP	SB	CS	OBP	Slg
Totals	.200	16	50	7	10	5	0	1	7	15	17	0	1	1	0	.385	.360
Home	.240	8	25	6	6	2	0	1	4	11	8	0	0	1	0	.472	.440
Away	.160	8	25	1	4	3	0	0	3	4	9	0	1	0	0	.276	.280
vs. Left	.143	8	14	0	2	1	0	0	1	6	6	0	0	0	0	.400	.214
vs. Right	.222	16	36	7	8	4	0	1	6	9	11	0	1	1	0	.378	.417
Scoring Pos.	.286	10	14	0	4	2	0	1	7	4	5	0	0	0	0	.444	.643
Close & Late	.167	5	6	1	1	0	0	1	2	0	3	0	0	0	0	.167	.667
None on/out	.000	12	7	0	0	0	0	0	0	6	3	0	0	0	0	.462	.000
None on	.154	16	26	0	4	2	0	0	0	10	9	0	0	0	0	.389	.231
Runners on	.250	13	24	0	6	3	0	1	7	5	8	0	1	1	0	.379	.500
Batting #3	.196	13	46	7	9	5	0	1	7	11	16	0	1	1	0	.351	.370

Hit Worst Against

	Avg	AB	R	H	2B	3B	HR	RBI	BB	SO	HBP	GDP	SB	CS	OBP	Slg
Don Larsen	.167	6	1	1	1	0	0	2	3	4	0	0	0	0	.444	.333
Bob Turley	.182	11	0	2	1	0	0	0	4	3	0	0	0	0	.400	.273
Whitey Ford	.182	11	2	2	1	0	0	1	5	5	0	0	0	0	.438	.273

Christy Mathewson

Throws: Right, Bats: Right

Pitching	ERA	W	L	Sv	G	GS	IP	BB	SO	Avg	R	H	2B	3B	HR	OBP	Slg
Totals	1.06	5	5	0	11	11	101.2	10	48	.207	22	76	19	4	1	.227	.288
Home	0.95	2	2	0	4	4	38.0	2	14	.203	7	27	4	0	1	.212	.256
Away	1.13	3	3	0	7	7	63.2	8	34	.209	15	49	15	4	0	.236	.306

	Avg	AB	R	H	2B	3B	HR	RBI	BB	SO	HBP	GDP	OBP	Slg
vs. Left	.257	109	0	28	3	2	0	5	5	15	1	1	.293	.321
vs. Right	.185	259	22	48	16	2	1	15	5	33	0	1	.199	.274
Scoring Pos.	.162	74	0	12	3	2	0	18	5	11	0	1	.205	.257
Close & Late	.186	70	3	13	3	0	0	5	3	6	0	1	.216	.229
None on/out	.210	100	0	21	5	1	0	0	2	13	0	1	.225	.280
None on	.223	242	0	54	14	2	1	1	3	33	1	1	.236	.310
Runners on	.175	126	0	22	5	2	0	19	7	15	0	1	.212	.246

Pitched Best Against

	Avg	AB	R	H	2B	3B	HR	RBI	BB	SO	HBP	GDP	SB	CS	OBP	Slg
Hugh Bedient	.000	6	0	0	0	0	0	0	0	0	0	0	0	0	.000	.000
Stuffy McInnis	.000	6	0	0	0	0	0	1	0	1	0	0	0	0	.000	.000
Bill Carrigan	.000	5	0	0	0	0	0	0	0	0	0	0	0	0	.000	.000

Pitched Worst Against

	Avg	AB	R	H	2B	3B	HR	RBI	BB	SO	HBP	GDP	SB	CS	OBP	Slg
H. Run Baker	.500	20	4	10	2	0	1	4	1	3	0	0	0	1	.500	.750
Tris Speaker	.417	12	2	5	0	1	0	2	1	1	0	0	0	0	.462	.583
Harry Hooper	.357	14	2	5	1	1	0	0	0	0	0	0	2	0	.357	.571

Gary Matthews

Bats: Right, Throws: Right

Batting	Avg	G	AB	R	H	2B	3B	HR	RBI	BB	SO	HBP	GDP	SB	CS	OBP	Slg
Totals	.323	19	65	12	21	0	1	7	15	10	9	0	3	2	1	.413	.677
Home	.400	10	35	9	14	0	0	6	14	5	5	0	1	1	0	.475	.914
Away	.233	9	30	3	7	0	1	1	1	5	4	0	2	1	1	.343	.400
vs. Left	.231	11	26	0	6	0	0	4	7	3	2	0	1	0	0	.310	.692
vs. Right	.385	19	39	12	15	0	1	3	8	7	7	0	2	2	1	.478	.667
Scoring Pos.	.227	15	22	0	5	0	0	2	10	4	4	0	2	0	0	.346	.500
Close & Late	.000	9	9	0	0	0	0	0	0	1	2	0	1	0	0	.100	.000
None on/out	.500	13	16	0	8	0	0	4	4	1	2	0	0	0	0	.529	1.250
None on	.429	19	35	0	15	0	1	5	5	6	4	0	0	0	0	.512	.914
Runners on	.200	18	30	0	6	0	0	2	10	4	5	0	3	2	1	.294	.400
Batting #3	.211	6	19	4	4	0	1	2	5	6	4	0	2	1	1	.400	.632
Batting #5	.410	11	39	7	16	0	0	4	9	3	3	0	1	1	0	.452	.718

Hit Best Against

	Avg	AB	R	H	2B	3B	HR	RBI	BB	SO	HBP	GDP	SB	CS	OBP	Slg
Steve Rogers	.250	8	0	2	0	1	0	0	0	0	0	1	0	0	.250	.500

Hit Worst Against

	Avg	AB	R	H	2B	3B	HR	RBI	BB	SO	HBP	GDP	SB	CS	OBP	Slg
Scott McGregor	.143	7	0	1	0	0	0	0	0	1	0	0	0	0	.143	.143
Jerry Reuss	.167	6	1	1	0	0	1	3	0	0	0	0	0	0	.167	.667

Carl Mays

Throws: Right, Bats: Left

Pitching	ERA	W	L	Sv	G	GS	IP	BB	SO	Avg	R	H	2B	3B	HR	OBP	Slg
Totals	2.20	3	4	1	8	7	57.1	8	17	.232	16	47	9	3	0	.271	.305
Home	3.08	1	2	1	4	3	26.1	4	3	.237	9	22	3	1	0	.276	.290
Away	1.45	2	2	0	4	4	31.0	4	14	.227	7	25	6	2	0	.267	.318

	Avg	AB	R	H	2B	3B	HR	RBI	BB	SO	HBP	GDP	OBP	Slg
vs. Left	.228	79	0	18	2	1	0	3	5	4	0	1	.274	.278
vs. Right	.234	124	16	29	7	2	0	14	3	13	3	1	.269	.323
Scoring Pos.	.293	41	0	12	1	1	0	16	3	7	1	1	.356	.366
Close & Late	.273	22	3	6	2	0	0	5	0	3	0	1	.273	.364
None on/out	.167	54	0	9	1	1	0	0	2	2	1	1	.211	.222
None on	.215	130	0	28	6	2	0	0	5	8	2	1	.255	.292
Runners on	.260	73	0	19	3	1	0	17	3	9	1	1	.299	.329

Pitched Best Against

	Avg	AB	R	H	2B	3B	HR	RBI	BB	SO	HBP	GDP	SB	CS	OBP	Slg
Phil Douglas	.000	7	0	0	0	0	0	0	0	2	0	0	0	0	.000	.000
C. Hollocher	.000	7	0	0	0	0	0	0	0	1	0	0	0	0	.000	.000
George Kelly	.067	15	1	1	0	0	0	0	0	3	0	3	0	0	.067	.133

Pitched Worst Against

	Avg	AB	R	H	2B	3B	HR	RBI	BB	SO	HBP	GDP	SB	CS	OBP	Slg
Charlie Pick	.429	7	1	3	1	0	0	0	0	0	0	0	1	0	.429	.571
George Burns	.333	12	0	4	3	0	0	2	0	1	0	0	0	0	.333	.583
J. Rawlings	.333	9	2	3	0	0	0	1	0	0	1	0	0	0	.400	.333

Willie Mays

Bats: Right, Throws: Right

Batting	Avg	G	AB	R	H	2B	3B	HR	RBI	BB	SO	HBP	GDP	SB	CS	OBP	Slg
Totals	.247	25	89	12	22	5	0	1	10	10	12	0	4	3	0	.323	.337
Home	.268	13	41	7	11	3	0	1	6	7	5	0	4	2	0	.375	.415
Away	.229	12	48	5	11	2	0	0	4	3	7	0	0	1	0	.275	.271
vs. Left	.296	12	27	0	8	0	0	0	1	2	3	0	1	1	0	.345	.296
vs. Right	.226	25	62	12	14	5	0	1	9	8	9	0	3	2	0	.314	.355
Scoring Pos.	.300	20	30	0	9	2	0	1	10	3	3	0	2	0	0	.364	.467
Close & Late	.385	11	13	1	5	2	0	1	3	2	0	0	1	2	0	.467	.769
None on/out	.318	18	22	0	7	2	0	0	0	2	4	0	0	0	0	.375	.409
None on	.256	22	43	0	11	2	0	0	0	5	7	0	0	0	0	.333	.302
Runners on	.239	24	46	0	11	3	0	1	10	5	5	0	4	3	0	.314	.370
Batting #3	.265	9	34	4	9	4	0	1	4	3	6	0	0	1	0	.324	.471
Batting #4	.276	8	29	6	8	1	0	0	4	5	4	0	1	2	0	.382	.310
Batting #7	.154	3	13	0	2	0	0	0	1	0	1	0	3	0	0	.154	.154

Hit Best Against

	Avg	AB	R	H	2B	3B	HR	RBI	BB	SO	HBP	GDP	SB	CS	OBP	Slg
Vic Raschi	.600	5	1	3	0	0	0	1	0	0	0	0	0	0	.600	.600
Whitey Ford	.444	9	2	4	0	0	0	1	1	1	0	1	0	0	.500	.444

Hit Worst Against

	Avg	AB	R	H	2B	3B	HR	RBI	BB	SO	HBP	GDP	SB	CS	OBP	Slg
Allie Reynolds	.000	7	0	0	0	0	0	0	0	0	0	3	0	0	.000	.000
Ed Lopat	.000	6	0	0	0	0	0	0	1	1	0	0	0	0	.143	.000
Ralph Terry	.091	11	0	1	1	0	0	0	0	2	0	0	0	0	.091	.182

Tim McCarver

Bats: Left, Throws: Right

Batting	Avg	G	AB	R	H	2B	3B	HR	RBI	BB	SO	HBP	GDP	SB	CS	OBP	Slg
Totals	.273	28	88	13	24	2	3	2	12	13	9	0	0	1	1	.359	.432
Home	.244	16	45	5	11	1	2	0	4	4	5	0	0	1	0	.294	.356
Away	.302	12	43	8	13	1	1	2	8	9	4	0	0	0	1	.423	.512
vs. Left	.200	12	25	0	5	1	1	0	1	4	5	0	0	0	0	.310	.320
vs. Right	.302	28	63	13	19	1	2	2	11	9	4	0	0	1	1	.378	.476
Scoring Pos.	.267	19	15	0	4	0	0	2	11	6	3	0	0	1	1	.435	.667
Close & Late	.300	11	10	0	3	0	0	1	4	2	0	0	0	0	0	.417	.600
None on/out	.346	19	26	0	9	1	0	0	0	3	2	0	0	0	0	.414	.385
None on	.288	25	59	0	17	2	2	0	0	5	5	0	0	0	0	.344	.390
Runners on	.241	24	29	0	7	0	1	2	12	8	4	0	0	1	1	.385	.517
Batting #5	.244	11	41	6	10	1	2	1	6	3	3	0	0	0	1	.289	.439
Batting #6	.370	8	27	3	10	0	0	1	5	5	2	0	0	1	0	.455	.481
Batting #7	.235	6	17	4	4	1	1	0	1	5	4	0	0	0	0	.409	.412

Hit Best Against

	Avg	AB	R	H	2B	3B	HR	RBI	BB	SO	HBP	GDP	SB	CS	OBP	Slg
Denny McLain	.571	7	2	4	0	2	0	1	1	1	0	0	0	0	.625	1.143
Jim Bouton	.500	6	1	3	0	0	0	0	2	0	0	0	0	0	.625	.500
Mel Stottlemyre	.250	8	1	2	0	0	0	1	1	1	0	0	1	0	.333	.250

Hit Worst Against

	Avg	AB	R	H	2B	3B	HR	RBI	BB	SO	HBP	GDP	SB	CS	OBP	Slg
Jim Lonborg	.111	9	1	1	1	0	0	0	0	0	0	0	0	0	.111	.222
Mickey Lolich	.200	10	0	2	0	0	0	0	2	1	0	0	0	0	.333	.200

Gil McDougald

Bats: Right, Throws: Right

Batting	Avg	G	AB	R	H	2B	3B	HR	RBI	BB	SO	HBP	GDP	SB	CS	OBP	Slg
Totals	.237	53	190	23	45	4	1	7	24	20	29	1	2	2	1	.310	.379
Home	.163	26	92	8	15	2	0	1	7	7	16	1	1	0	1	.228	.217
Away	.306	27	98	15	30	2	1	6	17	13	13	0	1	2	0	.384	.531
vs. Left	.268	22	56	0	15	2	0	1	5	4	7	1	0	0	0	.328	.357
vs. Right	.224	53	134	23	30	2	1	6	19	16	22	0	2	2	1	.303	.388
Scoring Pos.	.289	34	38	0	11	1	0	2	18	4	3	1	1	0	0	.356	.474
Close & Late	.360	23	25	2	9	0	0	1	1	2	3	0	1	0	0	.407	.480
None on/out	.239	38	46	0	11	0	1	3	3	5	8	0	0	0	0	.314	.478
None on	.214	52	126	0	27	2	1	5	5	14	20	0	0	0	0	.293	.365
Runners on	.281	44	64	0	18	2	0	2	19	6	9	1	2	2	1	.342	.406
Batting #1	.156	8	32	2	5	0	0	0	2	4	1	0	0	0	0	.250	.156
Batting #2	.280	13	50	5	14	2	0	2	4	2	9	0	0	0	0	.308	.440
Batting #3	.350	6	20	1	7	0	0	0	1	4	2	0	0	0	0	.458	.350
Batting #5	.250	6	20	5	5	0	0	0	3	4	3	0	0	1	1	.360	.250
Batting #6	.150	5	20	2	3	1	0	1	5	0	4	1	0	0	0	.190	.350
Batting #7	.239	14	46	7	11	1	1	4	9	5	9	0	2	1	0	.308	.565

Hit Best Against

	Avg	AB	R	H	2B	3B	HR	RBI	BB	SO	HBP	GDP	SB	CS	OBP	Slg
Johnny Podres	.444	9	0	4	0	0	0	0	0	1	0	0	0	0	.444	.444
Billy Loes	.400	10	2	4	0	0	1	3	2	1	0	0	0	0	.500	.700
Warren Spahn	.350	20	2	7	0	0	1	2	1	2	0	0	0	0	.381	.500

Hit Worst Against

	Avg	AB	R	H	2B	3B	HR	RBI	BB	SO	HBP	GDP	SB	CS	OBP	Slg
Sal Maglie	.000	9	0	0	0	0	0	0	1	4	0	0	0	0	.100	.000
Preacher Roe	.125	8	1	1	0	0	0	0	0	1	1	0	0	0	.222	.125
Dave Koslo	.143	7	1	1	1	0	0	1	0	0	0	0	0	0	.143	.286

Willie McGee

Bats: Both, Throws: Right

Batting	Avg	G	AB	R	H	2B	3B	HR	RBI	BB	SO	HBP	GDP	SB	CS	OBP	Slg
Totals	.276	54	192	27	53	8	3	4	23	7	43	0	3	8	6	.302	.411
Home	.267	27	90	13	24	5	1	1	11	5	25	0	1	3	3	.305	.378
Away	.284	27	102	14	29	3	2	3	12	2	18	0	2	5	3	.298	.441
vs. Left	.290	26	62	1	18	3	1	1	6	3	16	0	0	1	1	.323	.419
vs. Right	.269	50	130	26	35	5	2	3	17	4	27	0	3	7	5	.291	.408
Scoring Pos.	.246	40	57	5	14	1	1	1	20	4	11	0	1	2	1	.295	.351
Close & Late	.174	20	23	1	4	0	0	0	4	1	3	0	1	3	0	.208	.174
None on/out	.240	34	50	0	12	4	1	0	0	3	11	0	0	0	0	.283	.360
None on	.302	47	116	0	35	7	2	3	3	3	27	0	0	0	0	.319	.474
Runners on	.237	48	76	5	18	1	1	1	20	4	16	0	3	8	6	.275	.316
Batting #1	.333	9	33	6	11	3	0	1	5	3	5	0	0	2	3	.389	.515
Batting #2	.206	16	63	7	13	2	0	0	2	3	13	0	2	4	2	.242	.238
Batting #5	.348	12	46	3	16	2	1	0	5	0	13	0	0	0	1	.348	.435
Batting #7	.281	8	32	7	9	1	2	1	7	0	8	0	0	0	0	.281	.531
Batting #8	.273	3	11	4	3	0	0	2	4	1	1	0	1	2	0	.333	.818

Hit Best Against

	Avg	AB	R	H	2B	3B	HR	RBI	BB	SO	HBP	GDP	SB	CS	OBP	Slg
Les Straker	.600	5	1	3	1	0	0	0	0	0	0	0	0	0	.600	.800
Rick Reuschel	.600	5	1	3	0	0	0	1	0	0	0	0	0	1	.600	.600
Pete Vuckovich	.500	6	3	3	0	0	2	4	1	0	0	0	0	0	.571	1.500

Hit Worst Against

	Avg	AB	R	H	2B	3B	HR	RBI	BB	SO	HBP	GDP	SB	CS	OBP	Slg
Bert Blyleven	.000	6	0	0	0	0	0	0	0	4	0	0	0	0	.000	.000
Dave Dravecky	.000	5	0	0	0	0	0	0	0	2	0	0	0	0	.000	.000
F. Valenzuela	.000	5	1	0	0	0	0	0	2	4	0	0	0	0	.286	.000

2296 Postseason: Player Profiles

Tug McGraw

Throws: Left, Bats: Right

Pitching	ERA	W	L	Sv	G	GS	IP	BB	SO	Avg	R	H	2B	3B	HR	OBP	Slg
Totals	2.24	3	3	8	26	0	52.1	33	48	.207	15	38	6	2	1	.326	.277
Home	1.61	1	0	5	14	0	28.0	17	25	.194	5	19	3	0	1	.310	.255
Away	2.96	2	3	3	12	0	24.1	16	23	.221	10	19	3	2	0	.343	.302

	Avg	AB	R	H	2B	3B	HR	RBI	BB	SO	HBP	GDP	OBP	Slg
vs. Left	.340	47	0	16	2	2	0	7	8	9	0	1	.429	.468
vs. Right	.159	138	15	22	4	0	1	9	25	38	1	1	.289	.210
Scoring Pos.	.220	59	0	13	3	0	0	15	17	16	0	1	.380	.271
Close & Late	.226	115	5	26	3	1	0	11	21	29	0	1	.338	.270
None on/out	.239	46	0	11	2	2	1	1	5	10	0	1	.314	.435
None on	.198	101	0	20	3	2	1	1	11	23	1	1	.283	.297
Runners on	.214	84	0	18	3	0	0	15	22	24	0	1	.367	.250

Pitched Best Against

	Avg	AB	R	H	2B	3B	HR	RBI	BB	SO	HBP	GDP	SB	CS	OBP	Slg
Jesus Alou	.000	5	0	0	0	0	0	1	0	0	0	0	0	0	.000	.000
Ray Fosse	.000	5	0	0	0	0	0	0	0	1	0	0	0	0	.000	.000
Bert Campaneris	.200	5	1	1	0	0	0	0	0	2	1	0	1	0	.333	.200

Pitched Worst Against

	Avg	AB	R	H	2B	3B	HR	RBI	BB	SO	HBP	GDP	SB	CS	OBP	Slg
Reggie Jackson	.667	6	2	4	1	1	0	2	1	0	0	0	0	0	.714	1.167
Joe Morgan	.400	5	1	2	1	1	0	0	2	1	0	0	1	0	.571	1.000

Scott McGregor

Throws: Left, Bats: Both

Pitching	ERA	W	L	Sv	G	GS	IP	BB	SO	Avg	R	H	2B	3B	HR	OBP	Slg
Totals	1.63	3	3	0	6	6	49.2	8	26	.208	10	37	9	1	3	.241	.320
Home	1.99	0	3	0	3	3	22.2	5	10	.207	6	17	4	0	3	.253	.366
Away	1.33	3	0	0	3	3	27.0	3	16	.208	4	20	5	1	0	.230	.281

	Avg	AB	R	H	2B	3B	HR	RBI	BB	SO	HBP	GDP	OBP	Slg
vs. Left	.435	46	0	20	6	1	2	4	1	7	0	4	.438	.739
vs. Right	.129	132	10	17	3	0	1	5	7	19	0	4	.173	.174
Scoring Pos.	.100	30	0	3	1	0	0	5	3	1	0	4	.176	.133
Close & Late	.125	24	1	3	1	0	1	1	1	3	0	4	.160	.292
None on/out	.265	49	0	13	2	0	1	1	2	9	0	4	.294	.367
None on	.244	119	0	29	7	1	2	2	4	20	0	4	.268	.370
Runners on	.136	59	0	8	2	0	1	7	4	6	0	4	.188	.220

Pitched Best Against

	Avg	AB	R	H	2B	3B	HR	RBI	BB	SO	HBP	GDP	SB	CS	OBP	Slg
Bo Diaz	.000	5	0	0	0	0	0	0	1	0	0	0	0	0	.167	.000
Mike Schmidt	.000	7	0	0	0	0	0	0	0	2	0	0	0	0	.000	.000
Ivan DeJesus	.000	6	0	0	0	0	0	0	0	1	0	1	0	0	.000	.000

Pitched Worst Against

	Avg	AB	R	H	2B	3B	HR	RBI	BB	SO	HBP	GDP	SB	CS	OBP	Slg
Willie Stargell	.750	8	3	6	3	0	1	2	0	1	0	0	0	0	.750	1.500
Joe Morgan	.500	6	1	3	0	1	1	1	1	1	0	0	0	1	.571	1.333
Omar Moreno	.500	8	1	4	2	0	0	0	0	1	0	0	0	0	.500	.750

Fred McGriff

Bats: Left, Throws: Left

Batting	Avg	G	AB	R	H	2B	3B	HR	RBI	BB	SO	HBP	GDP	SB	CS	OBP	Slg
Totals	.303	50	188	36	57	10	1	10	37	27	40	0	4	1	1	.385	.527
Home	.286	26	98	21	28	4	1	5	17	13	15	0	3	0	0	.369	.500
Away	.322	24	90	15	29	6	0	5	20	14	25	0	1	1	1	.402	.556
vs. Left	.338	41	80	14	27	6	0	3	19	10	16	0	1	0	0	.402	.525
vs. Right	.278	45	108	22	30	4	1	7	18	17	24	0	3	1	1	.373	.528
Scoring Pos.	.373	44	51	27	19	0	0	2	24	13	9	0	1	0	0	.478	.490
Close & Late	.257	29	35	7	9	1	0	1	5	4	7	0	1	1	0	.333	.371
None on/out	.314	38	51	3	16	6	1	3	3	4	10	0	0	0	0	.364	.647
None on	.261	47	92	6	24	8	1	6	6	11	22	0	0	0	0	.340	.565
Runners on	.344	46	96	29	33	2	0	4	31	16	18	0	4	1	1	.426	.490
Batting #3	.143	5	21	1	3	0	0	0	3	0	4	0	0	0	0	.143	.143
Batting #4	.323	45	167	35	54	10	1	10	34	27	36	0	4	1	1	.411	.575

Hit Best Against

	Avg	AB	R	H	2B	3B	HR	RBI	BB	SO	HBP	GDP	SB	CS	OBP	Slg
Rick Honeycutt	.400	5	2	2	0	0	2	4	0	1	0	0	0	0	.400	1.600
Danny Jackson	.333	6	1	2	1	0	0	0	0	2	0	0	0	0	.333	.500
Curt Schilling	.286	7	0	2	0	0	0	0	0	3	0	0	0	0	.286	.286

Hit Worst Against

	Avg	AB	R	H	2B	3B	HR	RBI	BB	SO	HBP	GDP	SB	CS	OBP	Slg
Dave Stewart	.000	8	0	0	0	0	0	0	0	1	0	0	0	0	.000	.000
Dennis Martinez	.000	5	0	0	0	0	0	0	0	1	0	1	0	0	.000	.000
Andy Benes	.143	7	1	1	0	0	0	1	0	1	0	1	0	0	.143	.143

Mark McGwire

Bats: Right, Throws: Right

Batting	Avg	G	AB	R	H	2B	3B	HR	RBI	BB	SO	HBP	GDP	SB	CS	OBP	Slg
Totals	.228	32	114	12	26	2	0	4	13	16	27	2	3	0	0	.331	.351
Home	.273	16	55	8	15	2	0	3	6	7	16	2	0	0	0	.375	.473
Away	.186	16	59	4	11	0	0	1	7	9	11	0	3	0	0	.290	.237
vs. Left	.278	12	18	3	5	0	0	0	2	4	5	0	1	0	0	.391	.278
vs. Right	.219	31	96	9	21	2	0	4	11	12	22	2	2	0	0	.318	.365
Scoring Pos.	.185	20	27	3	5	1	0	0	8	8	5	0	1	0	0	.361	.222
Close & Late	.200	15	20	1	4	0	0	1	3	1	6	0	0	0	0	.238	.350
None on/out	.167	22	30	0	5	0	0	2	2	3	11	1	0	0	0	.265	.367
None on	.246	30	65	1	16	1	0	3	3	6	21	1	0	0	0	.319	.400
Runners on	.204	28	49	4	10	1	0	1	10	10	6	1	3	0	0	.344	.286
Batting #4	.270	10	37	4	10	1	0	1	5	5	9	0	1	0	0	.349	.378
Batting #5	.178	13	45	4	8	0	0	2	5	8	10	2	2	0	0	.327	.311
Batting #6	.350	5	20	2	7	1	0	1	1	0	5	0	0	0	0	.350	.550
Batting #7	.083	4	12	2	1	0	0	0	2	3	3	0	0	0	0	.267	.083

Hit Best Against

	Avg	AB	R	H	2B	3B	HR	RBI	BB	SO	HBP	GDP	SB	CS	OBP	Slg
T. Stottlemyre	.600	5	1	3	1	0	0	1	0	0	0	0	0	0	.600	.800
Mike Boddicker	.400	5	2	2	0	0	1	1	0	2	1	0	0	0	.500	1.000
Dave Stieb	.333	6	2	2	0	0	1	1	0	1	0	0	0	0	.333	.833

Hit Worst Against

	Avg	AB	R	H	2B	3B	HR	RBI	BB	SO	HBP	GDP	SB	CS	OBP	Slg
Tom Henke	.000	5	0	0	0	0	0	0	0	1	0	0	0	0	.000	.000
Jose Rijo	.000	6	0	0	0	0	0	0	0	1	0	0	0	0	.000	.000
Bruce Hurst	.000	5	0	0	0	0	0	0	1	2	0	0	0	0	.167	.000

Dave McNally

Throws: Left, Bats: Right

Pitching	ERA	W	L	Sv	G	GS	IP	BB	SO	Avg	R	H	2B	3B	HR	OBP	Slg
Totals	2.49	7	4	0	14	12	90.1	34	65	.201	30	65	9	3	12	.278	.358
Home	1.88	6	2	0	9	7	62.1	18	48	.177	16	39	6	1	5	.238	.282
Away	3.86	1	2	0	5	5	28.0	16	17	.250	14	26	3	2	7	.355	.519

	Avg	AB	R	H	2B	3B	HR	RBI	BB	SO	HBP	GDP	OBP	Slg
vs. Left	.085	59	0	5	1	0	1	1	4	15	0	3	.143	.153
vs. Right	.226	266	30	60	8	3	11	26	30	50	1	3	.305	.402
Scoring Pos.	.164	67	0	11	1	2	1	13	7	14	0	3	.240	.284
Close & Late	.161	56	2	9	1	0	1	5	6	7	0	3	.238	.232
None on/out	.312	93	0	29	3	1	9	9	9	23	1	3	.379	.656
None on	.218	202	0	44	7	1	9	9	22	45	1	3	.298	.396
Runners on	.171	123	0	21	2	2	3	18	12	20	0	3	.243	.293

Pitched Best Against

	Avg	AB	R	H	2B	3B	HR	RBI	BB	SO	HBP	GDP	SB	CS	OBP	Slg
Bud Harrelson	.000	7	0	0	0	0	0	0	1	2	0	0	0	0	.125	.000
Cleon Jones	.000	6	1	0	0	0	0	0	0	0	1	0	0	0	.143	.000
Willie Stargell	.000	6	0	0	0	0	0	0	2	2	0	0	0	0	.250	.000

Pitched Worst Against

	Avg	AB	R	H	2B	3B	HR	RBI	BB	SO	HBP	GDP	SB	CS	OBP	Slg
Sal Bando	.500	8	4	4	1	0	3	4	2	0	0	0	0	0	.600	1.750
Al Weis	.500	6	1	3	0	0	1	2	1	1	0	0	0	0	.571	1.000
Joe Rudi	.500	10	1	5	1	1	1	2	0	0	0	0	0	0	.500	1.100

Hal McRae

Bats: Right, Throws: Right

Batting	Avg	G	AB	R	H	2B	3B	HR	RBI	BB	SO	HBP	GDP	SB	CS	OBP	Slg
Totals	.292	48	144	14	42	14	1	1	15	12	23	4	0	1	6	.356	.424
Home	.304	26	69	7	21	10	0	0	7	8	10	2	0	0	3	.383	.449
Away	.280	22	75	7	21	4	1	1	8	4	13	2	0	1	3	.329	.400
vs. Left	.328	30	58	0	19	5	0	1	7	4	8	1	0	1	2	.381	.466
vs. Right	.267	48	86	14	23	9	1	0	8	8	15	3	0	0	4	.340	.395
Scoring Pos.	.231	30	26	0	6	1	0	0	11	7	3	1	0	0	0	.378	.269
Close & Late	.200	23	25	1	5	2	0	0	2	2	2	1	0	0	0	.286	.280
None on/out	.270	29	37	0	10	7	0	0	0	1	6	1	0	0	0	.308	.459
None on	.311	39	90	0	28	11	1	0	0	4	18	2	0	0	0	.354	.456
Runners on	.259	43	54	0	14	3	0	1	15	8	5	2	0	1	6	.358	.370
Batting #2	.364	9	33	7	12	3	0	1	3	5	3	0	0	1	2	.447	.545
Batting #4	.302	13	43	2	13	3	0	0	4	3	10	2	0	0	3	.375	.372
Batting #5	.269	7	26	3	7	4	1	0	2	1	3	1	0	0	1	.310	.500
Batting #6	.229	11	35	2	8	4	0	0	4	2	5	0	0	0	0	.263	.343

Hit Best Against

	Avg	AB	R	H	2B	3B	HR	RBI	BB	SO	HBP	GDP	SB	CS	OBP	Slg
Doyle Alexander	.667	6	0	4	2	0	0	2	0	1	0	0	0	0	.667	1.000
Mike Torrez	.600	5	2	3	2	0	0	0	0	0	0	0	0	0	.600	1.000
Dick Tidrow	.429	7	1	3	0	1	0	0	2	0	0	0	0	1	.556	.714

Hit Worst Against

	Avg	AB	R	H	2B	3B	HR	RBI	BB	SO	HBP	GDP	SB	CS	OBP	Slg
Catfish Hunter	.200	10	1	2	1	0	0	2	0	3	0	0	0	0	.182	.300

Jose Mesa

Throws: Right, Bats: Right

Pitching	ERA	W	L	Sv	G	GS	IP	BB	SO	Avg	R	H	2B	3B	HR	OBP	Slg
Totals	3.49	2	1	6	21	0	28.1	9	24	.313	11	36	5	1	4	.365	.478
Home	3.79	2	1	3	13	0	19.0	5	15	.333	8	26	5	0	2	.373	.474
Away	2.89	0	0	3	8	0	9.1	4	9	.270	3	10	0	1	2	.349	.486

	Avg	AB	R	H	2B	3B	HR	RBI	BB	SO	HBP	GDP	OBP	Slg
vs. Left	.349	63	0	22	4	1	2	9	6	10	0	0	.400	.540
vs. Right	.269	52	0	14	1	0	2	6	3	14	1	0	.321	.404
Scoring Pos.	.267	30	5	8	1	0	1	12	3	6	1	0	.343	.400
Close & Late	.289	83	9	24	3	0	2	8	7	20	1	0	.348	.398
None on/out	.308	26	0	8	0	0	2	2	3	5	0	0	.379	.538
None on	.375	56	3	21	4	1	3	3	5	10	0	0	.426	.643
Runners on	.254	59	8	15	1	0	1	12	4	14	1	0	.308	.322

Pitched Worst Against

	Avg	AB	R	H	2B	3B	HR	RBI	BB	SO	HBP	GDP	SB	CS	OBP	Slg
Brady Anderson	.429	7	0	3	1	0	0	1	0	0	0	0	0	0	.429	.571
Bobby Bonilla	.400	5	0	2	1	0	0	2	0	2	0	0	0	0	.400	.600

Paul Molitor

Bats: Right, Throws: Right

Batting	Avg	G	AB	R	H	2B	3B	HR	RBI	BB	SO	HBP	GDP	SB	CS	OBP	Slg
Totals	.368	29	117	28	43	5	3	6	22	12	15	2	2	3	2	.435	.615
Home	.241	14	54	11	13	3	1	2	7	8	7	0	1	2	1	.339	.444
Away	.476	15	63	17	30	2	2	4	15	4	8	2	1	1	1	.522	.762
vs. Left	.324	15	37	8	12	0	2	3	6	3	7	1	1	1	1	.390	.676
vs. Right	.388	28	80	20	31	5	1	3	16	9	8	1	1	2	1	.456	.588
Scoring Pos.	.571	22	21	13	12	1	2	1	14	7	2	1	0	1	0	.690	.952
Close & Late	.333	15	15	4	5	0	0	1	1	2	3	0	0	1	1	.412	.533
None on/out	.366	26	41	0	15	3	0	1	1	1	6	0	0	0	0	.381	.512
None on	.297	29	74	2	22	4	0	3	3	4	10	0	0	0	0	.333	.473
Runners on	.488	25	43	15	21	1	3	3	19	8	5	2	2	3	2	.585	.860
Batting #1	.314	17	70	11	22	1	0	3	9	6	12	0	2	2	2	.368	.457
Batting #3	.563	4	16	8	9	1	2	2	5	2	1	0	0	1	0	.611	1.250
Batting #6	.387	8	31	9	12	3	1	1	8	4	2	2	0	0	0	.486	.645

Hit Best Against

	Avg	AB	R	H	2B	3B	HR	RBI	BB	SO	HBP	GDP	SB	CS	OBP	Slg
Jack McDowell	.800	5	3	4	1	0	1	3	1	0	0	0	0	0	.833	1.600
Bruce Kison	.667	6	2	4	1	0	1	2	1	1	0	0	0	0	.714	1.333
Terry Mulholland	.600	5	3	3	0	1	1	2	1	0	0	0	0	0	.667	1.600

Hit Worst Against

	Avg	AB	R	H	2B	3B	HR	RBI	BB	SO	HBP	GDP	SB	CS	OBP	Slg
Dave Righetti	.000	5	0	0	0	0	0	0	0	2	0	0	0	0	.000	.000

Joe Morgan

Bats: Left, Throws: Right

Batting	Avg	G	AB	R	H	2B	3B	HR	RBI	BB	SO	HBP	GDP	SB	CS	OBP	Slg
Totals	.182	50	181	26	33	9	3	5	13	38	19	0	2	15	4	.323	.348
Home	.153	27	98	11	15	3	3	2	6	19	11	0	1	9	2	.288	.306
Away	.217	23	83	15	18	6	0	3	7	19	8	0	1	6	2	.363	.398

Batting	Avg	G	AB	R	H	2B	3B	HR	RBI	BB	SO	HBP	GDP	SB	CS	OBP	Slg
vs. Left	.217	37	83	0	18	6	2	3	10	17	9	0	1	6	2	.347	.446
vs. Right	.153	50	98	26	15	3	1	2	3	21	10	0	1	9	2	.303	.265
Scoring Pos.	.171	33	35	0	6	1	0	0	7	14	2	0	0	3	0	.400	.200
Close & Late	.290	32	31	4	9	4	1	1	4	11	2	0	0	1	1	.476	.581
None on/out	.169	37	59	0	10	2	1	1	1	10	7	0	0	0	0	.290	.288
None on	.195	48	113	0	22	6	3	5	5	21	13	0	0	0	0	.321	.434
Runners on	.162	44	68	0	11	3	0	0	8	17	6	0	2	15	4	.326	.206
Batting #1	.176	9	34	4	6	0	1	2	2	4	4	0	0	1	2	.263	.412
Batting #2	.177	26	96	13	17	7	0	2	7	17	11	0	2	9	2	.301	.313
Batting #3	.196	15	51	9	10	2	2	1	4	17	4	0	0	5	0	.391	.373

Hit Best Against

	Avg	AB	R	H	2B	3B	HR	RBI	BB	SO	HBP	GDP	SB	CS	OBP	Slg
Scott McGregor	.500	6	1	3	0	1	1	1	1	1	0	0	0	1	.571	1.333
Tug McGraw	.400	5	1	2	1	1	0	0	2	1	0	0	1	0	.571	1.000
Luis Tiant	.273	11	2	3	1	0	0	0	2	0	0	0	0	0	.385	.364

Hit Worst Against

	Avg	AB	R	H	2B	3B	HR	RBI	BB	SO	HBP	GDP	SB	CS	OBP	Slg
Dock Ellis	.000	5	0	0	0	0	0	0	0	1	0	0	0	0	.000	.000
Jerry Reuss	.000	7	1	0	0	0	0	0	2	0	0	0	3	0	.222	.000
Ken Holtzman	.143	7	0	1	1	0	0	0	0	1	0	0	0	0	.143	.286

Jack Morris

Throws: Right, Bats: Right

Pitching	ERA	W	L	Sv	G	GS	IP	BB	SO	Avg	R	H	2B	3B	HR	OBP	Slg
Totals	3.80	7	4	0	13	13	92.1	32	64	.241	39	83	18	1	9	.304	.377
Home	3.80	4	2	0	6	6	45.0	11	28	.240	19	40	8	0	6	.287	.395
Away	3.80	3	2	0	7	7	47.1	21	36	.242	20	43	10	1	3	.320	.360

	Avg	AB	R	H	2B	3B	HR	RBI	BB	SO	HBP	GDP	OBP	Slg
vs. Left	.258	178	0	46	8	1	6	16	17	30	0	4	.321	.416
vs. Right	.222	167	11	37	10	0	3	21	15	34	0	4	.286	.335
Scoring Pos.	.216	88	14	19	7	0	2	29	14	18	0	4	.320	.364
Close & Late	.161	31	2	5	1	0	1	2	1	5	0	4	.188	.290
None on/out	.232	95	0	22	2	1	3	3	4	12	0	4	.263	.368
None on	.226	221	9	50	8	1	6	6	13	44	0	4	.269	.353
Runners on	.266	124	19	33	10	0	3	31	19	20	0	4	.361	.419

Pitched Best Against

	Avg	AB	R	H	2B	3B	HR	RBI	BB	SO	HBP	GDP	SB	CS	OBP	Slg
Bobby Brown	.000	7	0	0	0	0	0	0	0	2	0	0	0	0	.000	.000
Garry Templeton	.000	7	0	0	0	0	0	0	0	3	0	0	0	0	.000	.000
C. Martinez	.000	6	0	0	0	0	0	0	0	3	0	0	0	0	.000	.000

Pitched Worst Against

	Avg	AB	R	H	2B	3B	HR	RBI	BB	SO	HBP	GDP	SB	CS	OBP	Slg
Harold Baines	.667	6	3	4	1	0	1	2	0	0	0	1	0	0	.667	1.333
Otis Nixon	.600	5	2	3	1	0	0	0	1	0	0	0	3	0	.667	.800
Pat Borders	.500	6	0	3	1	0	0	2	0	0	0	0	0	0	.500	.667

George Mullin

Throws: Right, Bats: Right

Pitching	ERA	W	L	Sv	G	GS	IP	BB	SO	Avg	R	H	2B	3B	HR	OBP	Slg
Totals	1.86	3	3	0	7	6	58.0	15	36	.218	22	46	7	3	1	.278	.294
Home	2.18	2	1	0	4	3	33.0	10	18	.205	12	25	4	2	0	.265	.270
Away	1.44	1	2	0	3	3	25.0	5	18	.236	10	21	3	1	1	.296	.326

	Avg	AB	R	H	2B	3B	HR	RBI	BB	SO	HBP	GDP	OBP	Slg
vs. Left	.175	80	0	14	1	0	1	5	6	15	0	2	.233	.225
vs. Right	.242	132	22	32	6	3	0	13	9	21	3	2	.303	.333
Scoring Pos.	.190	58	0	11	3	2	0	17	6	15	1	2	.273	.310
Close & Late	.083	12	0	1	0	0	0	0	0	3	0	2	.083	.083
None on/out	.148	54	0	8	1	0	0	0	4	7	0	2	.207	.167
None on	.208	130	0	27	4	1	1	1	8	16	1	2	.259	.277
Runners on	.232	82	0	19	3	2	0	17	7	20	2	2	.304	.317

Pitched Best Against

	Avg	AB	R	H	2B	3B	HR	RBI	BB	SO	HBP	GDP	SB	CS	OBP	Slg
Babe Adams	.000	6	0	0	0	0	0	0	0	0	0	0	0	0	.000	.000
Johnny Kling	.091	11	1	1	0	0	0	0	0	1	0	1	0	0	.091	.091
Jimmy Sheckard	.091	11	0	1	1	0	0	1	0	3	0	1	0	1	.091	.182

Pitched Worst Against

	Avg	AB	R	H	2B	3B	HR	RBI	BB	SO	HBP	GDP	SB	CS	OBP	Slg
Jimmy Slagle	.429	7	2	3	0	0	0	2	2	2	0	0	3	1	.556	.429
Frank Chance	.429	7	1	3	0	0	0	1	1	0	0	0	3	0	.500	.429
Joe Tinker	.375	8	1	3	0	0	0	1	2	1	0	0	1	1	.500	.375

Thurman Munson

Bats: Right, Throws: Right

Batting	Avg	G	AB	R	H	2B	3B	HR	RBI	BB	SO	HBP	GDP	SB	CS	OBP	Slg
Totals	.357	30	129	19	46	9	0	3	22	5	19	0	4	1	1	.378	.496
Home	.516	15	62	11	32	5	0	2	15	4	7	0	0	1	1	.545	.694
Away	.209	15	67	8	14	4	0	1	7	1	12	0	4	0	0	.217	.313
vs. Left	.357	21	56	0	20	5	0	1	8	2	6	0	3	1	0	.379	.500
vs. Right	.356	30	73	19	26	4	0	2	14	3	12	0	1	0	1	.377	.493
Scoring Pos.	.441	21	34	0	15	4	0	0	16	2	4	0	1	0	0	.459	.559
Close & Late	.316	15	19	1	6	2	0	1	7	2	3	0	0	0	0	.364	.579
None on/out	.316	17	19	0	6	1	0	0	0	2	3	0	0	0	0	.381	.368
None on	.313	30	67	0	21	3	0	1	1	2	12	0	0	0	0	.333	.403
Runners on	.403	30	62	0	25	6	0	2	21	3	6	0	4	1	1	.424	.597
Batting #2	.100	2	10	0	1	0	0	0	0	0	0	0	1	0	0	.100	.100
Batting #3	.378	28	119	19	45	9	0	3	22	5	18	0	3	1	1	.400	.529

Hit Best Against

	Avg	AB	R	H	2B	3B	HR	RBI	BB	SO	HBP	GDP	SB	CS	OBP	Slg
Andy Hassler	.571	7	2	4	1	0	0	1	0	1	0	0	0	0	.571	.714
Burt Hooton	.400	10	3	4	1	0	0	2	1	1	0	0	0	0	.455	.500
Charlie Hough	.400	5	0	2	1	0	0	3	0	2	0	0	0	0	.400	.600

Hit Worst Against

	Avg	AB	R	H	2B	3B	HR	RBI	BB	SO	HBP	GDP	SB	CS	OBP	Slg
Tommy John	.222	9	3	2	1	0	0	1	2	3	0	1	1	0	.364	.333

Eddie Murray

Bats: Both, Throws: Right

Batting	Avg	G	AB	R	H	2B	3B	HR	RBI	BB	SO	HBP	GDP	SB	CS	OBP	Slg
Totals	.258	44	159	21	41	3	1	9	25	27	27	0	2	3	1	.366	.459
Home	.238	23	80	8	19	3	1	5	15	12	16	0	1	1	1	.337	.488
Away	.278	21	79	13	22	0	0	4	10	15	11	0	1	2	0	.394	.430
vs. Left	.173	24	52	2	9	0	0	4	7	9	11	0	1	0	0	.295	.404
vs. Right	.299	39	107	19	32	3	1	5	18	18	16	0	1	3	1	.400	.486
Scoring Pos.	.279	32	43	4	12	1	0	3	15	11	9	0	1	1	0	.426	.512
Close & Late	.261	21	23	0	6	0	0	0	1	7	3	0	0	0	1	.433	.261
None on/out	.222	31	36	1	8	0	0	3	3	5	8	0	0	0	0	.317	.472
None on	.190	43	79	1	15	1	1	3	3	13	15	0	0	0	0	.304	.342
Runners on	.325	41	80	7	26	2	0	6	22	14	12	0	2	3	1	.426	.575
Batting #4	.250	21	76	14	19	1	0	6	15	14	14	0	2	2	1	.367	.500
Batting #5	.226	14	53	5	12	1	1	2	7	8	7	0	0	0	0	.328	.396
Batting #7	.333	9	30	2	10	1	0	1	3	5	6	0	0	1	0	.429	.467

Hit Best Against

	Avg	AB	R	H	2B	3B	HR	RBI	BB	SO	HBP	GDP	SB	CS	OBP	Slg
John Denny	.333	6	0	2	0	0	0	0	0	0	0	0	0	0	.333	.333

Hit Worst Against

	Avg	AB	R	H	2B	3B	HR	RBI	BB	SO	HBP	GDP	SB	CS	OBP	Slg
Jim Bibby	.000	5	0	0	0	0	0	0	0	4	0	1	0	0	.000	.000
Randy Johnson	.000	6	0	0	0	0	0	0	0	1	0	0	0	0	.000	.000
Greg Maddux	.000	5	0	0	0	0	0	0	1	0	0	0	0	0	.167	.000

Stan Musial

Bats: Left, Throws: Left

Batting	Avg	G	AB	R	H	2B	3B	HR	RBI	BB	SO	HBP	GDP	SB	CS	OBP	Slg
Totals	.256	23	86	9	22	7	1	1	8	12	4	0	1	1	2	.347	.395
Home	.186	11	43	1	8	2	0	0	3	3	4	0	1	0	0	.239	.233
Away	.326	12	43	8	14	5	1	1	5	9	0	0	0	1	2	.442	.558
vs. Left	.333	5	12	0	4	1	0	0	1	1	1	0	0	0	0	.385	.417
vs. Right	.243	23	74	9	18	6	1	1	7	11	3	0	1	1	2	.341	.392
Scoring Pos.	.263	18	19	0	5	3	0	0	6	6	0	0	0	0	1	.440	.421
Close & Late	.273	10	11	1	3	0	0	0	1	1	0	0	0	0	0	.333	.273
None on/out	.190	18	21	0	4	0	0	0	0	2	0	0	0	0	0	.261	.190
None on	.220	23	59	0	13	3	1	0	0	4	3	0	0	0	0	.270	.305
Runners on	.333	20	27	0	9	4	0	1	8	8	1	0	1	1	2	.486	.593
Batting #3	.265	18	68	7	18	6	1	1	6	8	4	0	1	1	1	.342	.426
Batting #4	.222	5	18	2	4	1	0	0	2	4	0	0	0	0	1	.364	.278

Hit Best Against

	Avg	AB	R	H	2B	3B	HR	RBI	BB	SO	HBP	GDP	SB	CS	OBP	Slg
Hank Borowy	.400	5	2	2	0	0	0	0	1	0	0	0	0	0	.500	.400
D. Galehouse	.333	6	0	2	1	0	0	0	1	0	0	1	0	0	.429	.500
Tex Hughson	.250	8	1	2	2	0	0	3	0	1	0	0	0	0	.250	.500

Hit Worst Against

	Avg	AB	R	H	2B	3B	HR	RBI	BB	SO	HBP	GDP	SB	CS	OBP	Slg
Nels Potter	.000	5	0	0	0	0	0	0	0	0	0	0	0	0	.000	.000
Red Ruffing	.000	7	0	0	0	0	0	0	1	0	0	0	0	0	.125	.000
Mickey Harris	.167	6	1	1	0	0	0	1	0	1	0	0	0	0	.167	.167

Mike Mussina

Throws: Right, Bats: Right

Pitching	ERA	W	L	Sv	G	GS	IP	BB	SO	Avg	R	H	2B	3B	HR	OBP	Slg
Totals	2.53	2	1	0	6	6	42.2	11	53	.170	13	26	7	0	5	.226	.314
Home	2.38	1	1	0	3	3	22.2	7	23	.141	6	11	3	0	2	.212	.256
Away	2.70	1	0	0	3	3	20.0	4	30	.200	7	15	4	0	3	.241	.373

	Avg	AB	R	H	2B	3B	HR	RBI	BB	SO	HBP	GDP	OBP	Slg
vs. Left	.176	74	0	13	5	0	0	2	7	22	0	1	.247	.243
vs. Right	.165	79	0	13	2	0	5	10	4	31	0	1	.205	.380
Scoring Pos.	.185	27	7	5	1	0	1	8	0	5	0	1	.185	.333
Close & Late	.261	23	1	6	2	0	1	4	4	4	0	1	.370	.478
None on/out	.095	42	0	4	1	0	2	2	3	15	0	1	.156	.262
None on	.137	102	4	14	4	0	4	4	11	41	0	1	.221	.294
Runners on	.235	51	9	12	3	0	1	8	0	12	0	1	.235	.353

Pitched Best Against

	Avg	AB	R	H	2B	3B	HR	RBI	BB	SO	HBP	GDP	SB	CS	OBP	Slg
S. Alomar Jr.	.000	9	0	0	0	0	0	0	0	3	0	0	0	0	.000	.000
M. Grissom	.000	5	0	0	0	0	0	0	0	5	0	0	0	0	.000	.000
Brian Giles	.000	5	0	0	0	0	0	0	1	4	0	0	0	0	.167	.000

Pitched Worst Against

	Avg	AB	R	H	2B	3B	HR	RBI	BB	SO	HBP	GDP	SB	CS	OBP	Slg
David Justice	.400	5	0	2	1	0	0	0	1	1	0	0	0	0	.500	.600
Edgar Martinez	.333	6	2	2	0	0	2	2	0	1	0	0	0	0	.333	1.333

Randy Myers

Throws: Left, Bats: Left

Pitching	ERA	W	L	Sv	G	GS	IP	BB	SO	Avg	R	H	2B	3B	HR	OBP	Slg
Totals	1.30	2	2	8	22	0	27.2	11	27	.160	4	15	4	0	1	.248	.234
Home	0.00	1	0	5	11	0	15.1	8	14	.082	0	4	1	0	0	.211	.102
Away	2.92	1	2	3	11	0	12.1	3	13	.244	4	11	3	0	1	.292	.378

	Avg	AB	R	H	2B	3B	HR	RBI	BB	SO	HBP	GDP	OBP	Slg
vs. Left	.125	24	0	3	0	0	0	0	3	6	0	1	.222	.125
vs. Right	.171	70	0	12	4	0	1	4	8	21	0	1	.256	.271
Scoring Pos.	.105	19	3	2	1	0	0	2	4	7	0	1	.261	.158
Close & Late	.182	55	4	10	2	0	1	3	9	13	0	1	.297	.273
None on/out	.208	24	1	5	0	0	1	1	1	6	0	1	.240	.333
None on	.172	58	1	10	2	0	1	1	5	17	0	1	.238	.259
Runners on	.139	36	3	5	2	0	0	3	6	10	0	1	.262	.194

Pitched Best Against

	Avg	AB	R	H	2B	3B	HR	RBI	BB	SO	HBP	GDP	SB	CS	OBP	Slg
Omar Vizquel	.000	5	0	0	0	0	0	0	0	2	0	0	0	0	.000	.000

Art Nehf

Throws: Left, Bats: Left

Pitching	ERA	W	L	Sv	G	GS	IP	BB	SO	Avg	R	H	2B	3B	HR	OBP	Slg
Totals	2.16	4	4	0	12	9	79.0	32	28	.187	23	50	7	1	2	.273	.243
Home	3.24	1	2	0	5	4	33.1	7	14	.194	13	21	3	1	1	.242	.269
Away	1.38	3	2	0	7	5	45.2	25	14	.182	10	29	4	0	1	.293	.226

	Avg	AB	R	H	2B	3B	HR	RBI	BB	SO	HBP	GDP	OBP	Slg
vs. Left	.172	87	0	15	1	1	2	8	12	17	0	4	.273	.276
vs. Right	.193	181	23	35	6	0	0	12	20	11	1	4	.272	.227
Scoring Pos.	.125	48	0	6	0	0	1	17	12	4	0	4	.281	.188
Close & Late	.255	47	4	12	2	0	1	9	5	1	1	4	.327	.362
None on/out	.133	75	0	10	2	0	0	0	5	9	0	4	.188	.160
None on	.182	176	0	32	4	1	1	1	18	20	1	4	.262	.233
Runners on	.196	92	0	18	3	0	1	19	14	8	0	4	.291	.261

Pitched Best Against

	Avg	AB	R	H	2B	3B	HR	RBI	BB	SO	HBP	GDP	SB	CS	OBP	Slg
Mike McNally	.000	5	1	0	0	0	0	0	1	0	0	0	0	1	.167	.000
Muddy Ruel	.000	5	0	0	0	0	0	0	2	0	0	0	0	0	.286	.000
Wally Pipp	.095	21	0	2	0	0	0	2	2	2	0	0	0	0	.174	.095

Pitched Worst Against

	Avg	AB	R	H	2B	3B	HR	RBI	BB	SO	HBP	GDP	SB	CS	OBP	Slg
Sam Rice	.333	9	0	3	0	0	0	1	1	1	0	0	1	0	.400	.333
R. Peckinpaugh	.313	16	1	5	1	0	0	1	4	0	0	1	1	0	.450	.375
Bucky Harris	.300	10	0	3	0	0	0	3	0	0	0	0	0	1	.300	.300

Graig Nettles

Bats: Left, Throws: Right

Batting	Avg	G	AB	R	H	2B	3B	HR	RBI	BB	SO	HBP	GDP	SB	CS	OBP	Slg
Totals	.225	53	182	17	41	5	1	5	27	19	21	1	5	0	2	.295	.346
Home	.258	30	93	11	24	2	0	4	15	16	10	1	1	0	2	.363	.409
Away	.191	23	89	6	17	3	1	1	12	3	11	0	4	0	0	.213	.281
vs. Left	.183	36	71	0	13	2	0	3	14	7	9	0	3	0	1	.250	.338
vs. Right	.252	53	111	17	28	3	1	2	13	12	12	1	2	0	1	.323	.351
Scoring Pos.	.220	38	50	0	11	3	1	1	22	7	7	0	1	0	1	.290	.380
Close & Late	.333	24	24	0	8	2	0	0	6	1	3	0	2	0	0	.346	.417
None on/out	.316	26	38	0	12	0	0	2	2	2	4	0	0	0	0	.350	.474
None on	.247	49	89	0	22	2	0	3	3	8	12	0	0	0	0	.309	.371
Runners on	.204	48	93	0	19	3	1	2	24	11	9	1	5	0	2	.282	.323
Batting #2	.154	3	13	0	2	0	0	0	1	0	1	0	0	0	0	.154	.154
Batting #4	.192	9	26	3	5	0	0	0	4	6	1	0	0	0	0	.314	.192
Batting #5	.227	5	22	3	5	0	1	0	1	0	4	0	1	0	0	.227	.318
Batting #6	.243	31	107	9	26	5	0	4	19	13	13	1	3	0	2	.325	.402
Batting #7	.182	3	11	2	2	0	0	1	2	0	2	0	1	0	0	.182	.455

Hit Best Against

	Avg	AB	R	H	2B	3B	HR	RBI	BB	SO	HBP	GDP	SB	CS	OBP	Slg
Dennis Leonard	.455	11	3	5	0	1	2	3	1	3	0	0	0	0	.500	1.182
Steve Mingori	.400	5	2	2	0	0	1	1	0	0	0	0	0	0	.400	1.000
Jack Morris	.333	6	1	2	0	0	0	0	1	0	0	0	0	0	.429	.333

Hit Worst Against

	Avg	AB	R	H	2B	3B	HR	RBI	BB	SO	HBP	GDP	SB	CS	OBP	Slg
Rick Sutcliffe	.000	5	0	0	0	0	0	1	0	1	0	0	0	0	.000	.000
Andy Hassler	.000	5	0	0	0	0	0	0	2	2	0	0	0	0	.286	.000
Paul Splittorff	.067	15	0	1	1	0	0	0	0	1	0	0	0	0	.067	.133

Tony Oliva

Bats: Left, Throws: Right

Batting	Avg	G	AB	R	H	2B	3B	HR	RBI	BB	SO	HBP	GDP	SB	CS	OBP	Slg
Totals	.314	13	51	7	16	5	0	3	5	2	10	0	1	1	0	.340	.588
Home	.333	7	27	4	9	4	0	1	2	1	4	0	0	0	0	.357	.593
Away	.292	6	24	3	7	1	0	2	3	1	6	0	1	1	0	.320	.583
vs. Left	.265	10	34	0	9	4	0	2	4	2	8	0	1	1	0	.306	.559
vs. Right	.412	13	17	7	7	1	0	1	1	0	2	0	0	0	0	.412	.647
Scoring Pos.	.111	6	9	0	1	1	0	0	1	0	1	0	1	0	0	.111	.222
Close & Late	.200	3	5	1	1	0	0	1	2	1	2	0	0	0	0	.333	.800
None on/out	.400	8	15	0	6	2	0	1	1	0	2	0	0	0	0	.400	.733
None on	.382	13	34	0	13	4	0	2	2	1	6	0	0	0	0	.400	.676
Runners on	.176	11	17	0	3	1	0	1	3	1	4	0	1	1	0	.222	.412
Batting #3	.265	9	34	3	9	2	0	1	2	1	8	0	1	0	0	.286	.412
Batting #4	.412	4	17	4	7	3	0	2	3	1	2	0	0	1	0	.444	.941

Hit Best Against

	Avg	AB	R	H	2B	3B	HR	RBI	BB	SO	HBP	GDP	SB	CS	OBP	Slg
Mike Cuellar	.667	6	3	4	3	0	1	2	0	0	0	0	0	0	.667	1.667
Jim Palmer	.500	8	1	4	1	0	0	0	0	2	0	0	0	0	.500	.625
Claude Osteen	.286	7	0	2	0	0	0	0	0	1	0	1	0	0	.286	.286

Hit Worst Against

	Avg	AB	R	H	2B	3B	HR	RBI	BB	SO	HBP	GDP	SB	CS	OBP	Slg
Sandy Koufax	.111	9	1	1	1	0	0	1	1	5	0	0	0	0	.200	.222
Don Drysdale	.167	6	1	1	0	0	1	1	0	0	0	0	0	0	.167	.667

Al Oliver

Bats: Left, Throws: Left

Batting	Avg	G	AB	R	H	2B	3B	HR	RBI	BB	SO	HBP	GDP	SB	CS	OBP	Slg
Totals	.228	28	92	8	21	5	1	3	17	8	14	1	0	0	0	.297	.402
Home	.222	13	45	5	10	2	1	3	12	3	6	1	0	0	0	.286	.511
Away	.234	15	47	3	11	3	0	0	5	5	8	0	0	0	0	.308	.298
vs. Left	.120	14	25	0	3	0	1	1	3	6	5	0	0	0	0	.290	.320
vs. Right	.269	28	67	8	18	5	0	2	14	2	8	1	0	0	0	.300	.433
Scoring Pos.	.379	21	29	0	11	2	1	1	13	3	4	1	0	0	0	.455	.621
Close & Late	.353	14	17	0	6	2	0	0	6	1	5	0	0	0	0	.389	.471
None on/out	.308	11	13	0	4	2	0	0	0	0	1	0	0	0	0	.308	.462
None on	.109	25	46	0	5	2	0	0	0	3	5	0	0	0	0	.163	.152
Runners on	.348	25	46	0	16	3	1	3	17	5	8	1	0	0	0	.423	.652
Batting #2	.238	6	21	4	5	1	1	1	3	2	4	0	0	0	0	.304	.524
Batting #3	.160	7	25	2	4	0	0	1	3	4	2	0	0	0	0	.276	.280
Batting #5	.238	12	42	2	10	3	0	1	8	2	6	1	0	0	0	.289	.381

Hit Best Against

	Avg	AB	R	H	2B	3B	HR	RBI	BB	SO	HBP	GDP	SB	CS	OBP	Slg
Don Gullett	.300	10	2	3	0	1	1	3	0	1	0	0	0	0	.300	.800

Hit Worst Against

	Avg	AB	R	H	2B	3B	HR	RBI	BB	SO	HBP	GDP	SB	CS	OBP	Slg
Don Sutton	.000	7	0	0	0	0	0	0	0	2	0	0	0	0	.000	.000
Gary Nolan	.111	9	1	1	0	0	1	2	1	1	0	0	0	0	.200	.444
Jim Palmer	.125	8	1	1	1	0	0	0	0	2	0	0	0	0	.125	.250

Paul O'Neill

Bats: Left, Throws: Left

Batting	Avg	G	AB	R	H	2B	3B	HR	RBI	BB	SO	HBP	GDP	SB	CS	OBP	Slg
Totals	.288	32	104	15	30	7	0	7	20	20	14	0	4	2	0	.400	.558
Home	.241	16	54	5	13	4	0	2	7	10	7	0	1	1	0	.354	.426
Away	.340	16	50	10	17	3	0	5	13	10	7	0	3	1	0	.450	.700
vs. Left	.273	15	22	2	6	0	0	2	2	4	5	0	2	0	0	.385	.545
vs. Right	.293	29	82	13	24	7	0	5	18	16	9	0	2	2	0	.404	.561
Scoring Pos.	.214	25	28	9	6	3	0	1	11	10	5	0	0	1	0	.410	.429
Close & Late	.250	14	16	1	4	1	0	1	2	4	4	0	0	0	0	.381	.500
None on/out	.308	14	13	0	4	1	0	0	0	1	4	0	0	0	0	.357	.385
None on	.370	28	54	3	20	4	0	3	3	6	6	0	0	0	0	.433	.611
Runners on	.200	30	50	12	10	3	0	4	17	14	8	0	4	2	0	.369	.500
Batting #3	.324	19	71	13	23	4	0	6	17	14	8	0	0	2	0	.430	.634
Batting #6	.154	5	13	0	2	1	0	0	0	2	2	0	0	0	0	.267	.231
Batting #7	.250	6	16	2	4	1	0	1	2	4	3	0	4	0	0	.400	.500

Hit Best Against

	Avg	AB	R	H	2B	3B	HR	RBI	BB	SO	HBP	GDP	SB	CS	OBP	Slg
Bob Walk	.500	6	1	3	1	0	1	2	0	0	0	0	0	0	.500	1.167
Andy Benes	.400	5	2	2	0	0	1	2	1	1	0	0	0	0	.500	1.000
Doug Drabek	.375	8	0	3	1	0	0	2	0	1	0	0	1	0	.375	.500

Hit Worst Against

	Avg	AB	R	H	2B	3B	HR	RBI	BB	SO	HBP	GDP	SB	CS	OBP	Slg
Scott Erickson	.000	5	0	0	0	0	0	0	0	0	0	1	0	0	.000	.000
Dave Stewart	.000	5	0	0	0	0	0	1	0	2	0	0	0	0	.000	.000
Orel Hershiser	.200	5	1	1	1	0	0	1	0	0	0	0	0	0	.200	.400

Mel Ott

Bats: Left, Throws: Right

Batting	Avg	G	AB	R	H	2B	3B	HR	RBI	BB	SO	HBP	GDP	SB	CS	OBP	Slg
Totals	.295	16	61	8	18	2	0	4	10	8	9	0	1	0	1	.377	.525
Home	.393	8	28	6	11	2	0	3	8	6	3	0	0	0	1	.500	.786
Away	.212	8	33	2	7	0	0	1	2	2	6	0	1	0	0	.257	.303
vs. Left	.250	7	20	0	5	1	0	3	8	3	4	0	0	0	0	.348	.750
vs. Right	.317	16	41	8	13	1	0	1	2	5	5	0	1	0	1	.391	.415
Scoring Pos.	.273	11	11	0	3	1	0	0	4	3	2	0	1	0	0	.429	.364
Close & Late	.400	9	10	1	4	0	0	1	1	2	0	0	0	0	0	.500	.700
None on/out	.250	12	16	0	4	1	0	0	0	2	3	0	0	0	0	.333	.313
None on	.289	15	38	0	11	1	0	2	2	3	5	0	0	0	0	.341	.474
Runners on	.304	14	23	0	7	1	0	2	8	5	4	0	1	0	1	.429	.609
Batting #3	.200	5	20	1	4	0	0	1	3	1	4	0	0	0	0	.238	.350
Batting #4	.364	9	33	6	12	1	0	2	4	6	5	0	1	0	1	.462	.576

Hit Best Against

	Avg	AB	R	H	2B	3B	HR	RBI	BB	SO	HBP	GDP	SB	CS	OBP	Slg
Bump Hadley	.600	5	0	3	0	0	0	0	0	0	0	1	0	0	.600	.600
Red Ruffing	.444	9	3	4	1	0	0	1	2	0	0	0	0	0	.545	.556

Hit Worst Against

	Avg	AB	R	H	2B	3B	HR	RBI	BB	SO	HBP	GDP	SB	CS	OBP	Slg
Monte Pearson	.125	8	0	1	0	0	0	0	0	2	0	0	0	0	.125	.125
Lefty Gomez	.214	14	2	3	1	0	2	5	2	2	0	0	0	0	.313	.714

Orval Overall

Throws: Right, Bats: Both

Pitching	ERA	W	L	Sv	G	GS	IP	BB	SO	Avg	R	H	2B	3B	HR	OBP	Slg
Totals	1.58	3	1	0	8	5	51.1	15	35	.206	11	37	5	1	0	.270	.244
Home	1.14	1	0	0	3	2	23.2	5	15	.205	5	17	2	0	0	.250	.229
Away	1.95	2	1	0	5	3	27.2	10	20	.206	6	20	3	1	0	.287	.258

	Avg	AB	R	H	2B	3B	HR	RBI	BB	SO	HBP	GDP	OBP	Slg
vs. Left	.204	108	0	22	3	1	0	9	10	13	1	0	.277	.250
vs. Right	.208	72	11	15	2	0	0	4	5	21	0	0	.260	.236
Scoring Pos.	.231	52	0	12	1	0	0	13	5	14	0	0	.298	.250
Close & Late	.200	20	2	4	0	0	0	4	0	4	1	0	.238	.200
None on/out	.178	45	0	8	2	0	0	0	6	8	0	0	.275	.222
None on	.175	103	0	18	3	1	0	0	10	16	0	0	.248	.223
Runners on	.247	77	0	19	2	0	0	13	5	18	1	0	.301	.273

Pitched Best Against

	Avg	AB	R	H	2B	3B	HR	RBI	BB	SO	HBP	GDP	SB	CS	OBP	Slg
Charley O'Leary	.000	15	0	0	0	0	0	0	0	4	0	0	0	0	.000	.000
Billy Sullivan	.000	5	0	0	0	0	0	0	0	2	0	0	0	0	.000	.000
W. Bill Donovan	.000	11	0	0	0	0	0	0	1	3	0	0	1	0	.083	.000

Pitched Worst Against

	Avg	AB	R	H	2B	3B	HR	RBI	BB	SO	HBP	GDP	SB	CS	OBP	Slg
George Rohe	.600	5	0	3	0	0	0	1	1	0	0	0	0	0	.667	.600
Davy Jones	.500	6	2	3	0	0	0	0	3	0	0	0	2	0	.667	.500
Ed Hahn	.400	5	1	2	0	0	0	0	0	0	0	0	0	0	.400	.400

Jim Palmer

Throws: Right, Bats: Right

Pitching	ERA	W	L	Sv	G	GS	IP	BB	SO	Avg	R	H	2B	3B	HR	OBP	Slg
Totals	2.61	8	3	0	17	15	124.1	50	90	.220	36	101	18	4	10	.298	.342
Home	2.52	3	2	0	9	9	75.0	29	61	.225	21	62	8	3	5	.301	.331
Away	2.74	5	1	0	8	6	49.1	21	29	.212	15	39	10	1	5	.293	.359

	Avg	AB	R	H	2B	3B	HR	RBI	BB	SO	HBP	GDP	OBP	Slg
vs. Left	.225	209	0	47	5	0	4	12	24	50	1	2	.305	.306
vs. Right	.216	250	36	54	13	4	6	22	26	40	1	2	.291	.372
Scoring Pos.	.170	100	0	17	5	0	2	24	12	31	1	2	.259	.280
Close & Late	.182	66	2	12	0	0	1	5	4	13	0	2	.225	.227
None on/out	.159	113	0	18	3	0	2	2	13	14	1	2	.252	.239
None on	.232	267	0	62	9	3	8	8	33	39	1	2	.319	.378
Runners on	.203	192	0	39	9	1	2	26	17	51	1	2	.268	.292

Pitched Best Against

	Avg	AB	R	H	2B	3B	HR	RBI	BB	SO	HBP	GDP	SB	CS	OBP	Slg
Dave Cash	.000	9	0	0	0	0	0	0	0	0	0	0	0	0	.000	.000
Tony Perez	.000	7	1	0	0	0	0	0	2	2	0	0	0	0	.222	.000
Bernie Carbo	.000	5	0	0	0	0	0	0	2	2	0	0	0	1	.286	.000

Pitched Worst Against

	Avg	AB	R	H	2B	3B	HR	RBI	BB	SO	HBP	GDP	SB	CS	OBP	Slg
Phil Garner	.600	5	1	3	1	0	0	0	1	0	1	0	0	0	.714	.800
Lee May	.500	6	2	3	0	0	1	3	1	0	0	0	0	0	.571	1.000
M. Sanguillen	.500	8	0	4	0	0	0	0	0	1	0	0	0	0	.500	.500

Dave Parker

Bats: Left, Throws: Right

Batting	Avg	G	AB	R	H	2B	3B	HR	RBI	BB	SO	HBP	GDP	SB	CS	OBP	Slg
Totals	.234	30	111	11	26	5	0	3	11	7	24	2	3	1	1	.287	.360
Home	.193	15	57	6	11	4	0	2	8	2	15	0	1	1	0	.213	.368
Away	.278	15	54	5	15	1	0	1	3	5	9	2	2	0	1	.361	.352
vs. Left	.235	15	34	0	8	2	0	1	3	2	13	2	1	1	1	.308	.382
vs. Right	.234	30	77	11	18	3	0	2	8	5	11	0	2	0	0	.277	.351
Scoring Pos.	.133	21	30	1	4	1	0	0	6	2	6	1	0	0	0	.200	.167
Close & Late	.294	15	17	2	5	1	0	0	2	1	4	0	0	0	1	.333	.353
None on/out	.280	20	25	1	7	0	0	2	2	1	6	0	0	0	0	.308	.520
None on	.241	29	58	1	14	2	0	3	3	5	16	1	0	0	0	.313	.431
Runners on	.226	28	53	1	12	3	0	0	8	2	8	1	3	1	1	.259	.283
Batting #3	.333	11	45	5	15	3	0	1	7	4	10	1	2	1	1	.385	.467
Batting #4	.200	10	40	3	8	2	0	1	3	2	8	0	0	0	0	.238	.325
Batting #5	.143	4	14	0	2	0	0	0	0	0	4	0	0	0	0	.143	.143

Hit Best Against

	Avg	AB	R	H	2B	3B	HR	RBI	BB	SO	HBP	GDP	SB	CS	OBP	Slg
Mike Flanagan	.625	8	2	5	1	0	0	0	0	2	0	0	0	1	.625	.750
Orel Hershiser	.375	8	0	3	0	0	0	0	0	2	0	0	0	0	.375	.375
Jim Palmer	.333	6	0	2	0	0	0	1	1	1	0	0	0	0	.429	.333

Hit Worst Against

	Avg	AB	R	H	2B	3B	HR	RBI	BB	SO	HBP	GDP	SB	CS	OBP	Slg
Scott McGregor	.000	7	0	0	0	0	0	1	0	3	0	0	0	0	.000	.000
Dave Stieb	.167	6	0	1	0	0	0	1	0	0	0	0	0	0	.167	.167

Monte Pearson

Throws: Right, Bats: Right

Pitching	ERA	W	L	Sv	G	GS	IP	BB	SO	Avg	R	H	2B	3B	HR	OBP	Slg
Totals	1.01	4	0	0	4	4	35.2	7	28	.151	5	19	2	0	1	.195	.190
Home	1.00	3	0	0	3	3	27.0	5	24	.147	4	14	1	0	1	.190	.189
Away	1.04	1	0	0	1	1	8.2	2	4	.161	1	5	1	0	0	.212	.194

	Avg	AB	R	H	2B	3B	HR	RBI	BB	SO	HBP	GDP	OBP	Slg
vs. Left	.218	55	0	12	2	0	0	3	5	10	0	0	.283	.255
vs. Right	.099	71	5	7	0	0	1	2	2	18	0	0	.123	.141
Scoring Pos.	.100	20	0	2	0	0	0	3	1	4	0	0	.143	.100
Close & Late	.167	12	0	2	1	0	0	2	2	1	0	0	.286	.250
None on/out	.121	33	0	4	1	0	0	0	3	5	0	0	.194	.152
None on	.161	87	0	14	1	0	1	1	3	18	0	0	.189	.207
Runners on	.128	39	0	5	1	0	0	4	4	10	0	0	.209	.154

Pitched Best Against

	Avg	AB	R	H	2B	3B	HR	RBI	BB	SO	HBP	GDP	SB	CS	OBP	Slg
B. Whitehead	.000	6	0	0	0	0	0	0	0	0	0	0	0	0	.000	.000
Dick Bartell	.125	8	1	1	0	0	0	0	0	2	0	0	0	0	.125	.125
Mel Ott	.125	8	0	1	0	0	0	0	0	2	0	0	0	0	.125	.125

Pitched Worst Against

	Avg	AB	R	H	2B	3B	HR	RBI	BB	SO	HBP	GDP	SB	CS	OBP	Slg
Jimmy Ripple	.375	8	1	3	0	0	0	1	0	0	0	0	0	1	.375	.375
Jo-Jo Moore	.286	7	0	2	0	0	0	0	1	1	0	0	0	1	.375	.286

Alejandro Pena

Throws: Right, Bats: Right

Pitching	ERA	W	L	Sv	G	GS	IP	BB	SO	Avg	R	H	2B	3B	HR	OBP	Slg
Totals	2.03	4	3	4	23	0	31.0	14	28	.211	7	23	6	0	2	.304	.321
Home	0.71	1	0	2	9	0	12.2	2	11	.196	1	9	0	0	1	.229	.261
Away	2.95	3	3	2	14	0	18.1	12	17	.222	6	14	6	0	1	.351	.365

	Avg	AB	R	H	2B	3B	HR	RBI	BB	SO	HBP	GDP	OBP	Slg
vs. Left	.234	47	0	11	2	0	1	6	10	14	0	1	.362	.340
vs. Right	.194	62	4	12	4	0	1	4	4	14	1	1	.254	.306
Scoring Pos.	.143	35	3	5	3	0	0	7	10	13	1	1	.340	.229
Close & Late	.216	74	5	16	6	0	1	7	13	21	1	1	.341	.338
None on/out	.308	26	0	8	3	0	1	1	2	6	0	1	.357	.538
None on	.263	57	0	15	3	0	1	1	4	14	0	1	.311	.368
Runners on	.154	52	3	8	3	0	1	9	10	14	1	1	.297	.269

Terry Pendleton

Bats: Both, Throws: Right

Batting	Avg	G	AB	R	H	2B	3B	HR	RBI	BB	SO	HBP	GDP	SB	CS	OBP	Slg
Totals	.252	66	230	26	58	12	3	3	23	12	30	0	4	2	2	.288	.370
Home	.250	32	104	13	26	7	2	1	13	7	13	0	1	0	0	.295	.385
Away	.254	34	126	13	32	5	1	2	10	5	17	0	3	2	2	.282	.357
vs. Left	.284	37	81	8	23	6	2	0	11	4	10	0	4	1	2	.318	.407
vs. Right	.235	61	149	18	35	6	1	3	12	8	20	0	0	1	0	.272	.349
Scoring Pos.	.271	44	59	12	16	5	0	0	19	4	9	0	2	1	0	.313	.356
Close & Late	.300	36	40	2	12	3	1	0	3	4	6	0	2	1	0	.364	.425
None on/out	.267	34	45	0	12	3	0	0	0	3	8	0	0	0	0	.313	.333
None on	.242	58	132	2	32	5	3	2	2	6	17	0	0	0	0	.275	.371
Runners on	.265	60	98	14	26	7	0	1	21	6	13	0	4	2	2	.305	.367
Batting #2	.327	11	49	7	16	4	1	2	4	3	2	0	2	0	0	.365	.571
Batting #3	.191	17	68	4	13	4	0	0	5	2	10	0	1	0	0	.211	.250
Batting #5	.308	6	13	3	4	1	0	0	2	1	3	0	0	0	0	.357	.385
Batting #6	.281	16	64	9	18	0	1	1	6	1	8	0	0	2	1	.292	.359
Batting #7	.227	8	22	2	5	2	1	0	6	4	4	0	0	0	0	.346	.409

Hit Best Against

	Avg	AB	R	H	2B	3B	HR	RBI	BB	SO	HBP	GDP	SB	CS	OBP	Slg
Tommy Greene	.600	5	1	3	0	0	0	2	0	0	0	0	0	0	.600	.600
C. Leibrandt	.429	7	1	3	1	0	0	3	0	0	0	0	0	0	.429	.571
F. Valenzuela	.429	7	1	3	1	0	0	0	0	1	0	0	0	1	.429	.571

Hit Worst Against

	Avg	AB	R	H	2B	3B	HR	RBI	BB	SO	HBP	GDP	SB	CS	OBP	Slg
Curt Schilling	.000	7	0	0	0	0	0	0	0	1	0	0	0	0	.000	.000
Dave Dravecky	.000	6	0	0	0	0	0	0	0	3	0	0	0	0	.000	.000
Doug Drabek	.063	16	1	1	1	0	0	0	1	3	0	0	0	0	.118	.125

Herb Pennock

Throws: Left, Bats: Both

Pitching	ERA	W	L	Sv	G	GS	IP	BB	SO	Avg	R	H	2B	3B	HR	OBP	Slg
Totals	1.95	5	0	3	10	5	55.1	8	24	.195	12	39	5	1	3	.226	.275
Home	0.86	2	0	0	3	2	21.0	3	5	.129	2	9	2	0	0	.164	.157
Away	2.62	3	0	3	7	3	34.1	5	19	.231	10	30	3	1	3	.259	.338

	Avg	AB	R	H	2B	3B	HR	RBI	BB	SO	HBP	GDP	OBP	Slg
vs. Left	.213	47	0	10	2	0	1	4	0	9	0	2	.213	.319
vs. Right	.190	153	12	29	3	1	2	8	8	15	0	2	.230	.261
Scoring Pos.	.200	40	0	8	0	0	0	8	1	5	0	2	.220	.200
Close & Late	.159	44	1	7	2	0	0	3	3	3	0	2	.213	.205
None on/out	.222	54	0	12	2	1	2	2	2	6	0	2	.250	.407
None on	.195	128	0	25	4	1	3	3	6	15	0	2	.231	.313
Runners on	.194	72	0	14	1	0	0	9	2	9	0	2	.216	.208

Pitched Best Against

	Avg	AB	R	H	2B	3B	HR	RBI	BB	SO	HBP	GDP	SB	CS	OBP	Slg
Billy Southworth	.000	8	0	0	0	0	0	0	0	0	0	0	0	0	.000	.000
Bill Sherdel	.000	5	0	0	0	0	0	0	0	2	0	0	0	0	.000	.000
Wattie Holm	.000	7	0	0	0	0	0	0	1	1	0	0	0	0	.125	.000

Pitched Worst Against

	Avg	AB	R	H	2B	3B	HR	RBI	BB	SO	HBP	GDP	SB	CS	OBP	Slg
Frankie Frisch	.625	8	2	5	0	1	0	0	0	0	0	0	0	0	.625	.875
Ross Youngs	.500	8	1	4	0	0	1	3	0	0	0	0	0	0	.500	.875
Bob O'Farrell	.429	7	0	3	0	0	0	1	1	0	0	0	0	0	.500	.429

Tony Perez

Bats: Right, Throws: Right

Batting	Avg	G	AB	R	H	2B	3B	HR	RBI	BB	SO	HBP	GDP	SB	CS	OBP	Slg
Totals	.238	47	172	16	41	6	0	6	24	14	37	0	3	1	2	.291	.378
Home	.313	23	83	11	26	2	0	4	14	7	15	0	0	1	1	.363	.482
Away	.169	24	89	5	15	4	0	2	10	7	22	0	3	0	1	.224	.281
vs. Left	.226	24	62	0	14	0	0	3	8	3	11	0	2	0	0	.258	.371
vs. Right	.245	47	110	16	27	6	0	3	16	11	26	0	1	1	2	.309	.382
Scoring Pos.	.220	37	50	0	11	1	0	2	18	3	12	0	1	0	0	.250	.360
Close & Late	.310	22	29	2	9	1	0	0	4	2	3	0	1	0	1	.344	.345
None on/out	.283	35	46	0	13	3	0	0	0	4	13	0	0	0	0	.340	.348
None on	.222	44	99	0	22	4	0	3	3	8	24	0	0	0	0	.280	.354
Runners on	.260	45	73	0	19	2	0	3	21	6	13	0	3	1	2	.305	.411
Batting #3	.136	11	44	4	6	2	0	2	3	4	6	0	2	0	0	.208	.318
Batting #4	.227	18	66	7	15	1	0	2	13	5	15	0	0	1	1	.274	.333
Batting #5	.317	16	60	5	19	3	0	2	8	5	16	0	0	0	1	.364	.467

Hit Best Against

	Avg	AB	R	H	2B	3B	HR	RBI	BB	SO	HBP	GDP	SB	CS	OBP	Slg
Ken Holtzman	.600	5	0	3	0	0	0	0	0	1	0	0	0	0	.600	.600
Catfish Hunter	.500	10	1	5	1	0	0	1	2	0	0	0	0	0	.583	.600
Dave Giusti	.500	6	0	3	1	0	0	1	0	2	0	0	0	0	.500	.667

Hit Worst Against

	Avg	AB	R	H	2B	3B	HR	RBI	BB	SO	HBP	GDP	SB	CS	OBP	Slg
Jim Palmer	.000	7	1	0	0	0	0	0	2	2	0	0	0	0	.222	.000
Luis Tiant	.083	12	0	1	0	0	0	0	0	5	0	0	0	0	.083	.083
Dock Ellis	.111	9	0	1	1	0	0	0	1	1	0	0	0	0	.200	.222

Lou Piniella

Bats: Right, Throws: Right

Batting	Avg	G	AB	R	H	2B	3B	HR	RBI	BB	SO	HBP	GDP	SB	CS	OBP	Slg
Totals	.305	44	141	15	43	7	0	3	19	2	10	1	4	2	0	.317	.418
Home	.277	23	65	4	18	3	0	1	11	1	4	0	2	2	0	.284	.369
Away	.329	21	76	11	25	4	0	2	8	1	6	1	2	0	0	.346	.461
vs. Left	.354	36	79	0	28	5	0	2	11	2	5	1	2	0	0	.378	.494
vs. Right	.242	44	62	15	15	2	0	1	8	0	5	0	2	2	0	.238	.323
Scoring Pos.	.353	29	34	0	12	1	0	1	16	0	2	0	2	0	0	.343	.471
Close & Late	.286	16	21	0	6	0	0	0	2	0	2	0	0	0	0	.286	.286
None on/out	.371	24	35	0	13	2	0	0	0	0	2	0	0	0	0	.371	.429
None on	.303	37	76	0	23	4	0	2	2	2	6	1	0	0	0	.329	.434
Runners on	.308	36	65	0	20	3	0	1	17	0	4	0	4	2	0	.303	.400
Batting #3	.200	2	10	2	2	0	0	0	0	0	1	0	0	0	0	.200	.200
Batting #4	.389	11	36	6	14	4	0	1	4	0	2	0	1	1	0	.389	.583
Batting #5	.279	19	61	6	17	2	0	1	10	0	3	1	3	1	0	.290	.361
Batting #7	.208	8	24	1	5	1	0	1	3	2	4	0	0	0	0	.259	.375

Hit Best Against

	Avg	AB	R	H	2B	3B	HR	RBI	BB	SO	HBP	GDP	SB	CS	OBP	Slg
Jerry Reuss	.667	6	1	4	1	0	0	2	0	0	0	0	0	0	.667	.833
Tommy John	.333	9	2	3	0	0	0	2	0	0	1	0	0	0	.400	.333
Burt Hooton	.333	9	0	3	0	0	0	1	0	0	0	1	0	0	.333	.333

Hit Worst Against

	Avg	AB	R	H	2B	3B	HR	RBI	BB	SO	HBP	GDP	SB	CS	OBP	Slg
F. Valenzuela	.200	5	1	1	0	0	0	0	0	1	0	1	0	0	.200	.200
Dennis Leonard	.222	9	1	2	1	0	0	1	0	2	0	0	0	0	.222	.333
Don Sutton	.231	13	1	3	0	0	0	0	0	1	0	0	1	0	.231	.231

Eddie Plank

Throws: Left, Bats: Left

Pitching	ERA	W	L	Sv	G	GS	IP	BB	SO	Avg	R	H	2B	3B	HR	OBP	Slg
Totals	1.32	2	5	0	7	6	54.2	11	32	.186	11	36	6	0	0	.243	.216
Home	1.70	1	3	0	4	4	37.0	8	25	.215	8	29	4	0	0	.279	.244
Away	0.51	1	2	0	3	2	17.2	3	7	.119	3	7	2	0	0	.159	.153

	Avg	AB	R	H	2B	3B	HR	RBI	BB	SO	HBP	GDP	OBP	Slg
vs. Left	.174	46	0	8	1	0	0	1	1	8	1	2	.208	.196
vs. Right	.189	148	11	28	5	0	0	10	10	24	3	2	.253	.223
Scoring Pos.	.190	42	0	8	1	0	0	11	3	6	1	2	.255	.214
Close & Late	.216	37	4	8	2	0	0	5	3	4	1	2	.286	.270
None on/out	.118	51	0	6	1	0	0	0	3	10	1	2	.182	.137
None on	.177	124	0	22	4	0	0	0	5	22	2	2	.221	.210
Runners on	.200	70	0	14	2	0	0	11	6	10	2	2	.278	.229

Pitched Best Against

	Avg	AB	R	H	2B	3B	HR	RBI	BB	SO	HBP	GDP	SB	CS	OBP	Slg
Ted Cather	.000	5	0	0	0	0	0	0	0	1	0	0	0	0	.000	.000
George Burns	.000	7	0	0	0	0	0	0	1	3	0	0	0	0	.125	.000
Tillie Shafer	.000	7	1	0	0	0	0	0	1	0	0	0	0	1	.125	.000

Pitched Worst Against

	Avg	AB	R	H	2B	3B	HR	RBI	BB	SO	HBP	GDP	SB	CS	OBP	Slg
Fred Snodgrass	.600	5	0	3	0	0	0	0	0	1	1	0	0	0	.667	.600
C. Mathewson	.500	8	1	4	0	0	0	1	1	1	0	0	0	0	.556	.500
Larry McLean	.429	7	0	3	0	0	0	1	0	0	0	0	0	0	.429	.429

Johnny Podres

Throws: Left, Bats: Left

Pitching	ERA	W	L	Sv	G	GS	IP	BB	SO	Avg	R	H	2B	3B	HR	OBP	Slg
Totals	2.11	4	1	0	6	6	38.1	13	18	.206	14	29	7	1	3	.282	.333
Home	2.31	1	1	0	2	2	11.2	4	6	.190	8	8	1	1	2	.277	.405
Away	2.03	3	0	0	4	4	26.2	9	12	.212	6	21	6	0	1	.284	.303

	Avg	AB	R	H	2B	3B	HR	RBI	BB	SO	HBP	GDP	OBP	Slg
vs. Left	.125	32	0	4	1	0	2	5	3	3	0	1	.200	.344
vs. Right	.229	109	14	25	6	1	1	3	10	15	2	1	.306	.330
Scoring Pos.	.125	32	0	4	0	0	1	5	2	6	0	1	.176	.219
Close & Late	.143	14	0	2	0	1	0	1	0	2	0	1	.143	.286
None on/out	.225	40	0	9	4	0	2	2	2	1	0	1	.262	.475
None on	.225	89	0	20	7	0	2	2	8	11	1	1	.296	.371
Runners on	.173	52	0	9	0	1	1	6	5	7	1	1	.259	.269

Pitched Best Against

	Avg	AB	R	H	2B	3B	HR	RBI	BB	SO	HBP	GDP	SB	CS	OBP	Slg
Bob Cerv	.000	8	0	0	0	0	0	0	0	3	0	0	0	0	.000	.000
Hank Bauer	.000	6	1	0	0	0	0	0	0	1	1	0	0	0	.143	.000
Mickey Mantle	.100	10	1	1	0	0	1	1	0	0	0	1	0	0	.100	.400

Pitched Worst Against

	Avg	AB	R	H	2B	3B	HR	RBI	BB	SO	HBP	GDP	SB	CS	OBP	Slg
Gil McDougald	.444	9	0	4	0	0	0	0	0	1	0	0	0	0	.444	.444
Phil Rizzuto	.400	5	2	2	0	0	0	0	4	0	0	0	0	0	.667	.400
Luis Aparicio	.400	5	1	2	1	0	0	0	0	0	0	0	0	0	.400	.600

Boog Powell

Bats: Left, Throws: Right

Batting	Avg	G	AB	R	H	2B	3B	HR	RBI	BB	SO	HBP	GDP	SB	CS	OBP	Slg
Totals	.262	33	126	17	33	4	0	6	18	12	17	0	6	0	0	.324	.437
Home	.217	18	69	9	15	1	0	3	7	6	9	0	2	0	0	.280	.362
Away	.316	15	57	8	18	3	0	3	11	6	8	0	4	0	0	.375	.526
vs. Left	.300	17	30	0	9	2	0	0	6	3	8	0	1	0	0	.353	.367
vs. Right	.250	33	96	17	24	2	0	6	12	9	9	0	5	0	0	.314	.458
Scoring Pos.	.381	17	21	0	8	2	0	0	10	3	1	0	1	0	0	.440	.476
Close & Late	.333	15	15	2	5	1	0	0	3	5	1	0	2	0	0	.500	.400
None on/out	.208	21	24	0	5	1	0	2	2	2	2	0	0	0	0	.269	.500
None on	.222	33	72	0	16	2	0	4	4	6	10	0	0	0	0	.282	.417
Runners on	.315	30	54	0	17	2	0	2	14	6	7	0	6	0	0	.377	.463
Batting #3	.213	13	47	11	10	0	0	5	9	9	7	0	3	0	0	.339	.532
Batting #4	.320	12	50	5	16	3	0	1	6	3	7	0	1	0	0	.358	.440
Batting #5	.269	7	26	1	7	1	0	0	2	0	3	0	2	0	0	.269	.308

Hit Best Against

	Avg	AB	R	H	2B	3B	HR	RBI	BB	SO	HBP	GDP	SB	CS	OBP	Slg
Bob Moose	.400	5	1	2	0	0	0	0	0	0	0	0	0	0	.400	.400
Tom Seaver	.286	7	0	2	0	0	0	0	0	1	0	0	0	0	.286	.286

Hit Worst Against

	Avg	AB	R	H	2B	3B	HR	RBI	BB	SO	HBP	GDP	SB	CS	OBP	Slg
Steve Blass	.000	8	0	0	0	0	0	0	0	3	0	0	0	0	.000	.000
Jerry Koosman	.143	7	0	1	0	0	0	0	1	2	0	0	0	0	.250	.143
Catfish Hunter	.154	13	3	2	0	0	2	3	0	1	0	1	0	0	.154	.615

Kirby Puckett

Bats: Right, Throws: Right

Batting	Avg	G	AB	R	H	2B	3B	HR	RBI	BB	SO	HBP	GDP	SB	CS	OBP	Slg
Totals	.309	24	97	16	30	3	2	5	16	8	17	1	1	3	1	.361	.536
Home	.286	12	46	8	13	2	1	1	7	5	9	0	1	2	1	.346	.435
Away	.333	12	51	8	17	1	1	4	9	3	8	1	0	1	0	.375	.627
vs. Left	.368	18	38	7	14	1	1	3	7	3	5	0	1	2	0	.405	.684
vs. Right	.271	21	59	9	16	2	1	2	9	5	12	1	0	1	1	.333	.441
Scoring Pos.	.222	21	27	4	6	0	0	0	8	5	6	1	1	0	1	.343	.222
Close & Late	.267	15	15	4	4	1	0	1	3	4	3	1	0	1	0	.450	.533
None on/out	.391	18	23	3	9	0	0	3	3	1	2	0	0	0	0	.417	.783
None on	.364	23	55	4	20	1	1	5	5	1	9	0	0	0	0	.375	.691
Runners on	.238	24	42	4	10	2	1	0	11	7	8	1	1	3	1	.346	.333
Batting #3	.312	23	93	15	29	3	2	4	15	6	15	1	1	3	1	.353	.516

Hit Best Against

	Avg	AB	R	H	2B	3B	HR	RBI	BB	SO	HBP	GDP	SB	CS	OBP	Slg
John Tudor	.600	5	2	3	0	0	0	1	1	0	0	0	1	0	.667	.600
Steve Avery	.400	5	2	2	0	1	1	3	0	2	0	0	0	0	.333	1.400
Tom Candiotti	.400	5	1	2	0	0	1	1	0	1	0	0	0	0	.400	1.000

Hit Worst Against

	Avg	AB	R	H	2B	3B	HR	RBI	BB	SO	HBP	GDP	SB	CS	OBP	Slg
Tom Glavine	.167	6	1	1	0	0	0	0	0	1	0	1	0	0	.167	.167
John Smoltz	.200	5	0	1	0	0	0	0	1	1	0	0	0	0	.333	.200

Dan Quisenberry

Throws: Right, Bats: Right

Pitching	ERA	W	L	Sv	G	GS	IP	BB	SO	Avg	R	H	2B	3B	HR	OBP	Slg
Totals	3.21	3	4	3	18	0	28.0	9	8	.287	14	29	6	1	0	.339	.366
Home	2.76	2	2	2	10	0	16.1	4	4	.276	6	16	4	0	0	.317	.345
Away	3.86	1	2	1	8	0	11.2	5	4	.302	8	13	2	1	0	.367	.395

	Avg	AB	R	H	2B	3B	HR	RBI	BB	SO	HBP	GDP	OBP	Slg
vs. Left	.327	49	0	16	4	0	0	9	6	1	0	1	.400	.408
vs. Right	.245	53	14	13	2	1	0	8	3	7	0	1	.276	.321
Scoring Pos.	.238	42	0	10	2	0	0	13	7	1	0	1	.333	.286
Close & Late	.318	66	9	21	6	0	0	16	5	6	0	1	.356	.409
None on/out	.450	20	0	9	0	1	0	0	2	2	0	1	.500	.550
None on	.326	43	0	14	0	1	0	0	2	5	0	1	.356	.372
Runners on	.254	59	0	15	6	0	0	17	7	3	0	1	.324	.356

Pitched Best Against

	Avg	AB	R	H	2B	3B	HR	RBI	BB	SO	HBP	GDP	SB	CS	OBP	Slg
Larry Bowa	.000	6	0	0	0	0	0	0	0	0	0	0	0	0	.000	.000
Garry Maddox	.000	5	0	0	0	0	0	0	1	0	0	0	0	0	.167	.000
Manny Trillo	.167	6	0	1	0	0	0	1	0	0	0	0	0	0	.167	.167

Tim Raines

Bats: Both, Throws: Right

Batting	Avg	G	AB	R	H	2B	3B	HR	RBI	BB	SO	HBP	GDP	SB	CS	OBP	Slg
Totals	.286	29	112	17	32	5	0	1	5	11	9	0	3	3	3	.347	.357
Home	.241	14	58	7	14	2	0	1	4	4	6	0	2	1	2	.286	.328
Away	.333	15	54	10	18	3	0	0	1	7	3	0	1	2	1	.410	.389
vs. Left	.276	13	29	3	8	1	0	0	1	6	4	0	2	0	1	.400	.310
vs. Right	.289	25	83	14	24	4	0	1	4	5	5	0	1	3	2	.326	.373
Scoring Pos.	.267	22	15	14	4	0	0	0	3	3	2	0	0	0	0	.368	.267
Close & Late	.273	16	22	3	6	0	0	0	0	2	1	0	2	0	0	.333	.273
None on/out	.279	25	43	0	12	3	0	0	0	4	4	0	0	0	0	.340	.349
None on	.292	27	72	0	21	4	0	0	0	7	6	0	0	0	0	.354	.347
Runners on	.275	25	40	16	11	1	0	1	5	4	3	0	3	3	3	.333	.375
Batting #1	.288	24	104	15	30	5	0	1	5	9	8	0	3	3	3	.342	.365

Hit Best Against

	Avg	AB	R	H	2B	3B	HR	RBI	BB	SO	HBP	GDP	SB	CS	OBP	Slg
F. Valenzuela	.429	7	1	3	1	0	0	1	0	1	0	0	0	1	.429	.571
Juan Guzman	.286	7	0	2	0	0	0	1	0	1	0	0	1	1	.286	.286

Hit Worst Against

	Avg	AB	R	H	2B	3B	HR	RBI	BB	SO	HBP	GDP	SB	CS	OBP	Slg
Burt Hooton	.125	8	0	1	0	0	0	0	0	1	0	0	0	0	.125	.125
Orel Hershiser	.167	6	0	1	0	0	0	1	0	1	0	0	0	0	.143	.167
Dave Stewart	.200	5	2	1	0	0	0	0	2	1	0	0	0	0	.429	.200

Manny Ramirez

Bats: Right, Throws: Right

Batting	Avg	G	AB	R	H	2B	3B	HR	RBI	BB	SO	HBP	GDP	SB	CS	OBP	Slg
Totals	.215	37	135	17	29	4	0	9	18	19	29	2	8	1	0	.316	.444
Home	.208	19	72	9	15	4	0	4	9	11	14	1	3	1	0	.321	.431
Away	.222	18	63	8	14	0	0	5	9	8	15	1	5	0	0	.311	.460
vs. Left	.208	22	48	7	10	3	0	3	8	7	10	0	2	0	0	.309	.458
vs. Right	.218	32	87	10	19	1	0	6	10	12	19	2	6	1	0	.320	.437
Scoring Pos.	.179	26	28	8	5	1	0	0	7	5	7	1	4	0	0	.306	.214
Close & Late	.138	22	29	2	4	0	0	0	0	8	11	0	0	1	0	.324	.138
None on/out	.233	22	30	4	7	1	0	4	4	5	5	0	0	0	0	.343	.667
None on	.234	35	77	7	18	2	0	7	7	10	15	1	0	0	0	.330	.532
Runners on	.190	34	58	10	11	2	0	2	11	9	14	1	8	1	0	.300	.328
Batting #3	.191	18	68	8	13	2	0	4	12	11	13	1	5	0	0	.305	.397
Batting #6	.286	10	35	5	10	2	0	3	3	4	10	0	1	0	0	.359	.600
Batting #7	.188	9	32	4	6	0	0	2	3	4	6	1	2	1	0	.297	.375

Hit Best Against

	Avg	AB	R	H	2B	3B	HR	RBI	BB	SO	HBP	GDP	SB	CS	OBP	Slg
L. Hernandez	.400	5	1	2	0	0	1	1	2	0	0	0	0	0	.571	1.000
David Wells	.400	10	3	4	2	0	1	1	0	0	0	0	0	0	.400	.900
Scott Erickson	.333	9	1	3	1	0	1	1	0	1	0	0	0	0	.333	.778

Hit Worst Against

	Avg	AB	R	H	2B	3B	HR	RBI	BB	SO	HBP	GDP	SB	CS	OBP	Slg
Randy Johnson	.000	6	0	0	0	0	0	0	0	3	0	0	0	0	.000	.000
Greg Maddux	.167	6	0	1	0	0	0	1	0	3	0	0	0	0	.167	.167
Andy Pettitte	.167	6	1	1	1	0	0	2	0	1	0	1	0	0	.167	.333

Willie Randolph

Bats: Right, Throws: Right

Batting	Avg	G	AB	R	H	2B	3B	HR	RBI	BB	SO	HBP	GDP	SB	CS	OBP	Slg
Totals	.222	47	162	19	36	6	1	4	14	20	15	0	5	3	1	.304	.346
Home	.238	24	84	11	20	3	0	2	9	10	10	0	2	3	0	.316	.345
Away	.205	23	78	8	16	3	1	2	5	10	5	0	3	0	1	.292	.346
vs. Left	.234	30	64	1	15	2	0	0	1	14	3	0	2	0	1	.372	.266
vs. Right	.214	46	98	18	21	4	1	4	13	6	12	0	2	3	0	.255	.398
Scoring Pos.	.162	30	37	1	6	0	0	0	9	6	1	0	2	0	0	.267	.162
Close & Late	.091	24	22	2	2	1	0	0	3	3	1	0	1	0	0	.192	.136
None on/out	.234	32	47	0	11	3	1	1	1	6	5	0	0	0	0	.321	.404
None on	.257	45	105	0	27	5	1	4	4	11	12	0	0	0	0	.328	.438
Runners on	.158	38	57	1	9	1	0	0	10	9	3	0	4	3	1	.265	.175
Batting #1	.261	12	46	4	12	3	1	2	4	10	7	0	0	1	1	.393	.500
Batting #2	.179	7	28	6	5	2	0	1	2	3	2	0	0	0	0	.250	.357
Batting #8	.197	19	61	6	12	1	0	0	5	6	4	0	3	2	0	.265	.213
Batting #9	.333	6	18	2	6	0	0	1	3	0	2	0	1	0	0	.333	.500

Hit Best Against

	Avg	AB	R	H	2B	3B	HR	RBI	BB	SO	HBP	GDP	SB	CS	OBP	Slg
Mark Littell	.400	5	0	2	0	0	0	2	0	1	0	0	1	0	.333	.400
Larry Gura	.364	11	1	4	1	0	0	0	0	1	0	1	0	0	.364	.455
Burt Hooton	.300	10	3	3	1	0	1	1	2	1	0	0	1	0	.417	.700

Hit Worst Against

	Avg	AB	R	H	2B	3B	HR	RBI	BB	SO	HBP	GDP	SB	CS	OBP	Slg
Jerry Reuss	.000	5	0	0	0	0	0	0	1	0	0	0	0	0	.167	.000
Jose Rijo	.167	6	0	1	0	0	0	0	0	0	0	0	0	0	.167	.167

Vic Raschi

Throws: Right, Bats: Right

Pitching	ERA	W	L	Sv	G	GS	IP	BB	SO	Avg	R	H	2B	3B	HR	OBP	Slg
Totals	2.24	5	3	0	11	8	60.1	25	43	.229	21	52	10	1	5	.308	.348
Home	0.60	1	1	0	3	2	15.0	6	6	.245	2	13	3	1	0	.322	.340
Away	2.78	4	2	0	8	6	45.1	19	37	.224	19	39	7	0	5	.304	.351

	Avg	AB	R	H	2B	3B	HR	RBI	BB	SO	HBP	GDP	OBP	Slg
vs. Left	.216	74	0	16	4	1	3	6	7	15	0	1	.284	.419
vs. Right	.234	154	21	36	6	0	2	15	18	28	1	1	.318	.312
Scoring Pos.	.220	50	0	11	1	0	2	18	7	9	0	1	.316	.360
Close & Late	.308	26	1	8	0	0	2	5	2	3	0	1	.357	.538
None on/out	.241	58	0	14	5	0	1	1	5	12	1	1	.313	.379
None on	.228	136	0	31	9	1	3	3	13	28	1	1	.300	.375
Runners on	.228	92	0	21	1	0	2	18	12	15	0	1	.317	.304

Pitched Best Against

	Avg	AB	R	H	2B	3B	HR	RBI	BB	SO	HBP	GDP	SB	CS	OBP	Slg
Marv Rackley	.000	5	0	0	0	0	0	0	0	2	0	0	0	0	.000	.000
S. Jorgensen	.143	7	1	1	1	0	0	0	1	0	0	0	0	0	.250	.286
Carl Furillo	.167	12	0	2	1	0	0	2	2	4	0	1	0	0	.286	.250

Pitched Worst Against

	Avg	AB	R	H	2B	3B	HR	RBI	BB	SO	HBP	GDP	SB	CS	OBP	Slg
Willie Mays	.600	5	1	3	0	0	0	1	0	0	0	0	0	0	.600	.600
Whitey Lockman	.500	6	1	3	1	0	1	3	0	0	0	1	0	0	.500	1.167
Hank Thompson	.400	5	1	2	0	0	0	0	1	1	0	1	0	0	.500	.400

Postseason: Player Profiles 2301

Jeff Reardon

Throws: Right, Bats: Right

Pitching	ERA	W	L	Sv	G	GS	IP	BB	SO	Avg	R	H	2B	3B	HR	OBP	Slg
Totals	4.57	2	3	6	18	0	21.2	8	14	.253	11	21	1	0	5	.319	.446
Home	3.00	2	1	3	10	0	12.0	6	6	.175	4	7	1	0	1	.283	.275
Away	6.52	0	2	3	8	0	9.2	2	8	.326	7	14	0	0	4	.356	.605

	Avg	AB	R	H	2B	3B	HR	RBI	BB	SO	HBP	GDP	OBP	Slg
vs. Left	.300	30	0	9	1	0	3	7	4	6	1	0	.389	.633
vs. Right	.226	53	7	12	0	0	2	8	4	8	0	0	.276	.340
Scoring Pos.	.222	27	2	6	1	0	0	7	2	5	0	0	.258	.259
Close & Late	.178	45	4	8	1	0	3	10	6	9	1	0	.278	.400
None on/out	.389	18	0	7	0	0	1	1	0	3	0	0	.389	.556
None on	.262	42	2	11	0	0	2	2	4	6	0	0	.326	.405
Runners on	.244	41	2	10	1	0	3	13	4	8	1	0	.313	.488

Pee Wee Reese

Bats: Right, Throws: Right

Batting	Avg	G	AB	R	H	2B	3B	HR	RBI	BB	SO	HBP	GDP	SB	CS	OBP	Slg
Totals	.272	44	169	20	46	3	2	2	16	18	17	1	2	5	3	.346	.349
Home	.218	23	87	10	19	1	0	2	11	11	8	1	1	1	0	.313	.299
Away	.329	21	82	10	27	2	2	0	5	7	9	0	1	4	3	.382	.402
vs. Left	.357	21	56	0	20	2	2	1	3	3	4	1	2	1	0	.400	.518
vs. Right	.230	44	113	20	26	1	0	1	13	15	13	0	0	4	3	.320	.265
Scoring Pos.	.314	24	35	0	11	0	0	0	14	3	3	0	1	1	0	.368	.314
Close & Late	.409	20	22	2	9	0	0	1	2	4	1	0	1	3	0	.500	.545
None on/out	.200	30	35	0	7	2	0	1	1	4	2	1	0	0	0	.300	.343
None on	.269	41	104	0	28	3	2	2	2	13	11	1	0	0	0	.356	.394
Runners on	.277	36	65	0	18	0	0	0	14	5	6	0	2	5	3	.329	.277
Batting #1	.250	7	28	2	7	1	0	1	3	1	0	1	1	1	0	.300	.393
Batting #2	.267	31	120	14	32	2	2	1	11	15	16	0	1	2	2	.348	.342
Batting #7	.429	4	14	3	6	0	0	0	2	2	1	0	0	1	1	.500	.429

Hit Best Against

	Avg	AB	R	H	2B	3B	HR	RBI	BB	SO	HBP	GDP	SB	CS	OBP	Slg
Ed Lopat	.538	13	2	7	1	1	0	1	2	0	0	0	0	0	.600	.769
Tommy Byrne	.500	8	3	4	1	0	1	1	0	1	1	0	0	0	.556	1.000
Allie Reynolds	.429	21	4	9	1	0	0	1	2	1	0	0	2	2	.478	.476

Hit Worst Against

	Avg	AB	R	H	2B	3B	HR	RBI	BB	SO	HBP	GDP	SB	CS	OBP	Slg
Don Larsen	.000	6	0	0	0	0	0	0	0	1	0	0	0	0	.000	.000
Bill Bevens	.000	5	0	0	0	0	0	1	0	1	0	0	1	0	.000	.000
Bob Turley	.000	5	1	0	0	0	0	0	1	2	0	0	0	0	.167	.000

Jerry Reuss

Throws: Left, Bats: Left

Pitching	ERA	W	L	Sv	G	GS	IP	BB	SO	Avg	R	H	2B	3B	HR	OBP	Slg
Totals	3.59	2	8	0	11	11	62.2	25	25	.234	31	57	7	0	5	.305	.324
Home	0.82	2	2	0	4	4	33.0	13	16	.167	3	20	3	0	1	.248	.217
Away	6.67	0	6	0	7	7	29.2	12	9	.298	28	37	4	0	4	.360	.427

	Avg	AB	R	H	2B	3B	HR	RBI	BB	SO	HBP	GDP	OBP	Slg
vs. Left	.192	52	0	10	3	0	0	2	3	9	0	0	.236	.250
vs. Right	.245	192	31	47	4	0	5	24	22	16	0	0	.322	.344
Scoring Pos.	.230	61	0	14	2	0	3	22	9	4	0	0	.329	.410
Close & Late	.182	33	0	6	1	0	0	0	3	7	0	0	.250	.212
None on/out	.150	60	0	9	1	0	0	0	5	6	0	0	.215	.167
None on	.222	144	0	32	3	0	1	1	13	17	0	0	.287	.264
Runners on	.250	100	0	25	4	0	4	25	12	8	0	0	.330	.410

Pitched Best Against

	Avg	AB	R	H	2B	3B	HR	RBI	BB	SO	HBP	GDP	SB	CS	OBP	Slg
Rick Cerone	.000	5	0	0	0	0	0	0	0	0	1	0	0	0	.000	.000
Tony Scott	.000	7	0	0	0	0	0	0	1	2	0	0	0	1	.125	.000
Willie Randolph	.000	5	0	0	0	0	0	0	1	0	0	0	0	0	.167	.000

Pitched Worst Against

	Avg	AB	R	H	2B	3B	HR	RBI	BB	SO	HBP	GDP	SB	CS	OBP	Slg
Mike Schmidt	.667	6	3	4	1	0	1	2	1	0	0	0	0	0	.714	1.333
Lou Piniella	.667	6	1	4	1	0	0	2	0	0	0	0	0	0	.667	.833
Jose Cruz	.571	7	0	4	0	0	0	0	1	1	0	0	1	0	.625	.571

Allie Reynolds

Throws: Right, Bats: Right

Pitching	ERA	W	L	Sv	G	GS	IP	BB	SO	Avg	R	H	2B	3B	HR	OBP	Slg
Totals	2.79	7	2	4	15	9	77.1	32	62	.226	25	61	16	2	8	.310	.389
Home	3.56	4	1	1	8	6	43.0	21	36	.242	18	38	8	1	6	.335	.420
Away	1.83	3	1	3	7	3	34.1	11	26	.204	7	23	8	1	2	.274	.345

	Avg	AB	R	H	2B	3B	HR	RBI	BB	SO	HBP	GDP	OBP	Slg
vs. Left	.186	86	0	16	7	0	4	10	11	21	0	9	.278	.407
vs. Right	.245	184	25	45	9	2	4	13	21	41	1	9	.325	.380
Scoring Pos.	.174	69	0	12	3	0	2	15	7	16	0	9	.250	.304
Close & Late	.160	50	0	8	1	0	1	4	2	14	0	9	.192	.240
None on/out	.179	67	0	12	1	0	3	3	11	20	1	9	.304	.328
None on	.260	150	0	39	12	2	4	4	22	38	1	9	.358	.447
Runners on	.183	120	0	22	4	0	4	19	10	24	0	9	.246	.317

Pitched Best Against

	Avg	AB	R	H	2B	3B	HR	RBI	BB	SO	HBP	GDP	SB	CS	OBP	Slg
Willie Mays	.000	7	0	0	0	0	0	0	0	0	3	0	0	0	.000	.000
Dick Sisler	.000	5	0	0	0	0	0	0	0	2	0	0	0	0	.000	.000
Hank Thompson	.000	5	2	0	0	0	0	0	3	0	0	0	0	0	.375	.000

Pitched Worst Against

	Avg	AB	R	H	2B	3B	HR	RBI	BB	SO	HBP	GDP	SB	CS	OBP	Slg
Monte Irvin	.750	8	1	6	0	1	0	1	0	1	0	0	1	1	.750	1.000
Al Dark	.500	8	2	4	3	0	1	3	0	1	0	1	0	0	.500	1.250
Pee Wee Reese	.429	21	4	9	1	0	0	1	2	1	0	0	2	2	.478	.476

Jim Rice

Bats: Right, Throws: Right

Batting	Avg	G	AB	R	H	2B	3B	HR	RBI	BB	SO	HBP	GDP	SB	CS	OBP	Slg
Totals	.225	18	71	14	16	2	1	2	7	9	21	0	2	0	0	.313	.366
Home	.235	9	34	7	8	1	1	2	6	4	9	0	1	0	0	.316	.500
Away	.216	9	37	7	8	1	0	0	1	5	12	0	1	0	0	.310	.243
vs. Left	.143	9	14	0	2	0	0	1	3	3	8	0	0	0	0	.294	.357
vs. Right	.246	18	57	14	14	2	1	1	4	6	13	0	2	0	0	.317	.368
Scoring Pos.	.056	13	18	0	1	0	0	1	5	3	2	0	2	0	0	.190	.222
Close & Late	.455	9	11	1	5	1	0	0	0	1	3	0	1	0	0	.500	.545
None on/out	.280	15	25	0	7	1	1	0	0	3	8	0	0	0	0	.357	.400
None on	.237	17	38	0	9	1	1	0	0	4	16	0	0	0	0	.310	.316
Runners on	.212	16	33	0	7	1	0	2	7	5	5	0	2	0	0	.316	.424
Batting #4	.241	14	58	14	14	2	1	2	6	7	17	0	2	0	0	.323	.414
Batting #5	.091	3	11	0	1	0	0	0	1	1	3	0	0	0	0	.167	.091

Hit Best Against

	Avg	AB	R	H	2B	3B	HR	RBI	BB	SO	HBP	GDP	SB	CS	OBP	Slg
Roger McDowell	.600	5	2	3	1	0	0	0	0	0	0	0	0	0	.600	.800
Dwight Gooden	.600	5	2	3	0	1	0	0	1	1	0	0	0	0	.667	1.000

Hit Worst Against

	Avg	AB	R	H	2B	3B	HR	RBI	BB	SO	HBP	GDP	SB	CS	OBP	Slg
Mike Witt	.125	8	1	1	0	0	0	0	0	3	0	0	0	0	.125	.125
Kirk McCaskill	.167	6	2	1	0	0	0	1	0	2	0	0	0	0	.167	.167
Ron Darling	.200	5	1	1	0	0	0	0	3	1	0	0	0	0	.500	.200

Sam Rice

Bats: Left, Throws: Right

Batting	Avg	G	AB	R	H	2B	3B	HR	RBI	BB	SO	HBP	GDP	SB	CS	OBP	Slg
Totals	.302	15	63	7	19	0	0	0	4	3	3	0	1	2	0	.333	.302
Home	.344	7	32	4	11	0	0	0	2	1	1	0	1	2	0	.364	.344
Away	.258	8	31	3	8	0	0	0	2	2	2	0	0	0	0	.303	.258
vs. Left	.300	7	20	0	6	0	0	0	1	1	3	0	0	2	0	.333	.300
vs. Right	.302	15	43	7	13	0	0	0	3	2	0	0	1	0	0	.333	.302
Scoring Pos.	.118	12	17	0	2	0	0	0	4	0	1	0	0	0	0	.118	.118
Close & Late	.357	8	14	0	5	0	0	0	1	0	0	0	1	1	0	.357	.357
None on/out	.250	11	16	0	4	0	0	0	0	1	2	0	0	0	0	.294	.250
None on	.359	15	39	0	14	0	0	0	0	3	2	0	0	0	0	.405	.359
Runners on	.208	14	24	0	5	0	0	0	4	0	1	0	1	2	0	.208	.208
Batting #1	.364	7	33	5	12	0	0	0	3	0	1	0	0	0	0	.364	.364
Batting #3	.207	7	29	2	6	0	0	0	1	3	2	0	1	2	0	.281	.207

Hit Best Against

	Avg	AB	R	H	2B	3B	HR	RBI	BB	SO	HBP	GDP	SB	CS	OBP	Slg
Vic Aldridge	.455	11	2	5	0	0	0	1	0	0	0	0	0	0	.455	.455
Art Nehf	.333	9	0	3	0	0	0	1	1	1	0	0	1	0	.400	.333
Jack Bentley	.250	8	1	2	0	0	0	0	0	1	0	0	1	0	.250	.250

Hit Worst Against

	Avg	AB	R	H	2B	3B	HR	RBI	BB	SO	HBP	GDP	SB	CS	OBP	Slg
Virgil Barnes	.000	6	0	0	0	0	0	0	0	0	0	1	0	0	.000	.000
Ray Kremer	.200	10	1	2	0	0	0	0	0	0	0	0	0	0	.200	.200

Bobby Richardson

Bats: Right, Throws: Right

Batting	Avg	G	AB	R	H	2B	3B	HR	RBI	BB	SO	HBP	GDP	SB	CS	OBP	Slg
Totals	.305	36	131	16	40	6	2	1	15	5	7	0	2	2	1	.331	.405
Home	.304	17	56	4	17	2	0	1	8	2	5	0	1	0	1	.328	.393
Away	.307	19	75	12	23	4	2	0	7	3	2	0	1	2	0	.333	.413
vs. Left	.291	20	55	0	16	4	0	0	2	1	4	0	0	1	1	.304	.364
vs. Right	.316	36	76	16	24	2	2	1	13	4	3	0	2	1	0	.350	.434
Scoring Pos.	.417	14	24	0	10	2	2	1	15	0	3	0	1	0	0	.417	.792
Close & Late	.313	16	16	1	5	0	0	0	3	0	1	0	0	1	0	.313	.313
None on/out	.361	23	36	0	13	0	0	0	0	1	0	0	0	0	0	.378	.361
None on	.294	32	85	0	25	2	0	0	0	4	4	0	0	0	0	.326	.318
Runners on	.326	26	46	0	15	4	2	1	15	1	3	0	2	2	1	.340	.565
Batting #1	.393	6	28	4	11	1	0	0	0	0	0	0	0	1	1	.393	.429
Batting #2	.270	19	74	6	20	3	0	0	3	4	6	0	2	1	0	.308	.311
Batting #7	.167	4	12	1	2	0	0	1	6	0	1	0	0	0	0	.167	.417
Batting #8	.438	4	16	5	7	2	2	0	6	1	0	0	0	0	0	.471	.813

Hit Best Against

	Avg	AB	R	H	2B	3B	HR	RBI	BB	SO	HBP	GDP	SB	CS	OBP	Slg
Jim O'Toole	.714	7	0	5	1	0	0	0	0	0	0	0	0	1	.714	.857
Bob Gibson	.500	14	2	7	1	0	0	1	0	2	0	1	0	0	.500	.571
Curt Simmons	.429	7	0	3	0	0	0	0	0	0	0	0	1	0	.429	.429

Hit Worst Against

	Avg	AB	R	H	2B	3B	HR	RBI	BB	SO	HBP	GDP	SB	CS	OBP	Slg
Billy Pierce	.000	7	0	0	0	0	0	0	0	0	0	0	0	0	.000	.000
Bob Purkey	.167	6	0	1	0	0	0	0	0	0	0	0	1	0	.167	.167
Jack Sanford	.200	10	2	2	0	0	0	0	2	0	0	0	0	0	.333	.200

Cal Ripken Jr.

Bats: Right, Throws: Right

Batting	Avg	G	AB	R	H	2B	3B	HR	RBI	BB	SO	HBP	GDP	SB	CS	OBP	Slg
Totals	.336	28	110	14	37	10	0	1	8	12	22	2	1	0	0	.411	.455
Home	.360	14	50	5	18	5	0	1	7	6	9	1	0	0	0	.439	.520
Away	.317	14	60	9	19	5	0	0	1	6	13	1	1	0	0	.388	.400
vs. Left	.286	22	42	1	12	4	0	0	2	8	11	0	1	0	0	.400	.381
vs. Right	.368	26	68	13	25	6	0	1	6	4	11	2	0	0	0	.419	.500
Scoring Pos.	.421	18	19	6	8	0	0	1	8	5	3	1	0	0	0	.560	.579
Close & Late	.263	14	19	2	5	2	0	0	1	3	3	0	0	0	0	.364	.368
None on/out	.320	18	25	0	8	2	0	0	0	2	6	0	0	0	0	.370	.400
None on	.264	27	72	0	19	4	0	0	0	5	18	1	0	0	0	.321	.319
Runners on	.474	21	38	7	18	6	0	1	8	7	4	1	1	0	0	.565	.711
Batting #3	.273	9	33	7	9	2	0	0	2	5	7	1	1	0	0	.385	.333
Batting #5	.417	3	12	0	5	0	0	0	1	1	2	0	0	0	0	.462	.417
Batting #6	.354	16	65	7	23	8	0	1	5	6	13	1	0	0	0	.417	.523

Hit Best Against

	Avg	AB	R	H	2B	3B	HR	RBI	BB	SO	HBP	GDP	SB	CS	OBP	Slg
Randy Johnson	.571	7	0	4	0	0	0	1	0	0	0	0	0	0	.571	.571
Charles Nagy	.500	12	2	6	1	0	1	3	1	3	0	0	0	0	.538	.833
Chad Ogea	.400	5	0	2	1	0	0	0	1	1	0	0	0	0	.500	.600

Mickey Rivers

Bats: Left, Throws: Left

Batting	Avg	G	AB	R	H	2B	3B	HR	RBI	BB	SO	HBP	GDP	SB	CS	OBP	Slg
Totals	.308	29	120	14	37	4	1	0	4	4	9	0	0	4	3	.331	.358
Home	.356	15	59	7	21	1	1	0	1	2	4	0	0	2	2	.377	.407
Away	.262	14	61	7	16	3	0	0	3	2	5	0	0	2	1	.286	.311
vs. Left	.386	20	57	0	22	4	0	0	4	1	4	0	0	1	2	.397	.456
vs. Right	.238	29	63	14	15	0	1	0	0	3	4	0	0	3	1	.273	.270

Batting	Avg	G	AB	R	H	2B	3B	HR	RBI	BB	SO	HBP	GDP	SB	CS	OBP	Slg
Scoring Pos.	.130	16	23	0	3	0	0	0	4	0	2	0	0	1	0	.130	.130
Close & Late	.429	11	14	2	6	0	0	0	1	0	1	0	0	0	0	.429	.429
None on/out	.365	29	52	0	19	2	1	0	0	2	2	0	0	0	0	.389	.442
None on	.333	29	78	0	26	4	1	0	0	4	4	0	0	0	0	.366	.410
Runners on	.262	22	42	0	11	0	0	0	4	0	4	0	0	4	3	.262	.262
Batting #1	.308	29	120	14	37	4	1	0	4	4	8	0	0	4	3	.331	.358

Hit Best Against

	Avg	AB	R	H	2B	3B	HR	RBI	BB	SO	HBP	GDP	SB	CS	OBP	Slg
Larry Gura	.538	13	4	7	1	0	0	2	1	1	0	0	0	0	.571	.615
Paul Splittorff	.538	13	3	7	1	0	0	0	0	1	0	0	1	0	.538	.615
Andy Hassler	.286	7	1	2	0	0	0	0	0	0	0	0	0	1	.286	.286

Hit Worst Against

	Avg	AB	R	H	2B	3B	HR	RBI	BB	SO	HBP	GDP	SB	CS	OBP	Slg
Dennis Leonard	.182	11	1	2	0	1	0	0	2	0	0	0	0	0	.308	.364
Don Sutton	.200	15	0	3	0	0	0	0	0	0	0	0	0	1	.200	.200

Phil Rizzuto

Bats: Right, Throws: Right

Batting	Avg	G	AB	R	H	2B	3B	HR	RBI	BB	SO	HBP	GDP	SB	CS	OBP	Slg
Totals	.246	52	183	21	45	3	0	2	8	30	11	1	2	10	3	.355	.295
Home	.286	26	91	10	26	2	0	1	3	10	3	0	1	5	0	.356	.341
Away	.207	26	92	11	19	1	0	1	5	20	8	1	1	5	3	.354	.250
vs. Left	.308	22	39	0	12	2	0	1	3	9	1	0	1	4	0	.438	.436
vs. Right	.229	52	144	21	33	1	0	1	5	21	10	1	1	6	3	.331	.257
Scoring Pos.	.139	31	36	0	5	1	0	0	5	6	2	0	1	2	1	.262	.167
Close & Late	.130	23	23	0	3	0	0	0	0	3	2	0	0	0	0	.231	.130
None on/out	.348	33	46	0	16	2	0	1	1	8	2	1	0	0	0	.455	.457
None on	.270	50	111	0	30	2	0	1	1	18	6	1	0	0	0	.377	.315
Runners on	.208	48	72	0	15	1	0	1	7	12	5	0	2	10	3	.321	.264
Batting #1	.250	15	56	6	14	0	0	1	2	10	2	0	1	5	0	.364	.304
Batting #2	.218	14	55	7	12	1	0	1	3	7	5	1	0	0	2	.317	.291
Batting #7	.214	3	14	0	3	1	0	0	1	1	0	0	0	0	0	.267	.286
Batting #8	.276	20	58	8	16	1	0	0	2	12	4	0	1	5	1	.400	.293

Hit Best Against

	Avg	AB	R	H	2B	3B	HR	RBI	BB	SO	HBP	GDP	SB	CS	OBP	Slg
Hal Gregg	.500	6	1	3	0	0	0	1	0	0	0	0	1	0	.500	.500
Johnny Podres	.400	5	2	2	0	0	0	0	4	0	0	0	0	0	.667	.400
Johnny Beazley	.375	8	1	3	0	0	1	1	1	1	0	0	1	0	.444	.750

Hit Worst Against

	Avg	AB	R	H	2B	3B	HR	RBI	BB	SO	HBP	GDP	SB	CS	OBP	Slg
Don Newcombe	.125	8	0	1	0	0	0	0	0	1	0	0	0	0	.125	.125
Hugh Casey	.125	8	0	1	0	0	0	0	1	0	0	0	0	0	.222	.125
Jim Konstanty	.167	6	0	1	0	0	0	0	0	0	0	0	0	0	.167	.167

Bob Robertson

Bats: Right, Throws: Right

Batting	Avg	G	AB	R	H	2B	3B	HR	RBI	BB	SO	HBP	GDP	SB	CS	OBP	Slg
Totals	.283	21	53	10	15	2	0	6	12	6	10	0	0	0	0	.356	.660
Home	.227	9	22	4	5	1	0	3	5	3	3	0	0	0	0	.320	.682
Away	.323	12	31	6	10	1	0	3	7	3	7	0	0	0	0	.382	.645
vs. Left	.348	9	23	0	8	2	0	5	10	2	5	0	0	0	0	.400	1.087
vs. Right	.233	21	30	10	7	0	0	1	2	4	5	0	0	0	0	.324	.333
Scoring Pos.	.222	13	18	0	4	0	0	2	8	1	4	0	0	0	0	.263	.556
Close & Late	.364	12	11	1	4	0	0	1	4	1	3	0	0	0	0	.417	.636
None on/out	.286	11	14	0	4	1	0	2	2	3	2	0	0	0	0	.412	.786
None on	.379	14	29	0	11	2	0	4	4	4	4	0	0	0	0	.455	.862
Runners on	.167	14	24	0	4	0	0	2	8	2	6	0	0	0	0	.231	.417
Batting #5	.368	5	19	7	7	2	0	5	9	2	5	0	0	0	0	.429	1.263
Batting #6	.222	7	27	3	6	0	0	1	2	2	4	0	0	0	0	.276	.333

Hit Best Against

	Avg	AB	R	H	2B	3B	HR	RBI	BB	SO	HBP	GDP	SB	CS	OBP	Slg
Jim Palmer	.333	6	0	2	0	0	0	1	2	3	0	0	0	0	.500	.333
Gaylord Perry	.286	7	0	2	0	0	0	0	0	0	0	0	0	0	.286	.286

Hit Worst Against

	Avg	AB	R	H	2B	3B	HR	RBI	BB	SO	HBP	GDP	SB	CS	OBP	Slg
Mike Cuellar	.143	7	1	1	0	0	1	3	0	3	0	0	0	0	.143	.571
Dave McNally	.200	5	2	1	0	0	1	1	1	2	0	0	0	0	.333	.800

Brooks Robinson

Bats: Right, Throws: Right

Batting	Avg	G	AB	R	H	2B	3B	HR	RBI	BB	SO	HBP	GDP	SB	CS	OBP	Slg
Totals	.303	39	145	17	44	8	0	5	21	6	9	0	3	0	2	.323	.462
Home	.361	20	72	8	26	3	0	2	11	5	4	0	1	0	2	.397	.486
Away	.247	19	73	9	18	5	0	3	10	1	5	0	2	0	0	.247	.438
vs. Left	.233	21	43	0	10	2	0	0	3	2	1	0	1	0	1	.261	.279
vs. Right	.333	39	102	17	34	6	0	5	18	4	8	0	2	0	1	.349	.539
Scoring Pos.	.313	22	32	0	10	1	0	0	16	2	4	0	1	0	1	.316	.344
Close & Late	.500	17	20	1	10	1	0	1	6	1	1	0	0	0	1	.478	.700
None on/out	.289	29	38	0	11	2	0	2	2	0	2	0	0	0	0	.289	.500
None on	.300	38	90	0	27	6	0	5	5	3	5	0	0	0	0	.323	.533
Runners on	.309	31	55	0	17	2	0	0	16	3	4	0	3	0	2	.323	.345
Batting #4	.214	4	14	2	3	0	0	1	1	1	0	0	0	0	0	.267	.429
Batting #5	.327	13	52	6	17	2	0	2	7	0	5	0	0	0	2	.315	.481
Batting #6	.308	18	65	7	20	5	0	1	10	4	4	0	2	0	0	.338	.431
Batting #7	.286	4	14	2	4	1	0	1	3	1	0	0	1	0	0	.333	.571

Hit Best Against

	Avg	AB	R	H	2B	3B	HR	RBI	BB	SO	HBP	GDP	SB	CS	OBP	Slg
Jim Perry	.667	6	1	4	0	0	0	1	0	1	0	0	0	1	.571	.667
Gary Nolan	.600	5	2	3	0	0	2	3	0	0	0	0	0	0	.600	1.800
Bob Moose	.600	5	1	3	0	0	0	1	0	0	0	0	0	0	.600	.600

Hit Worst Against

	Avg	AB	R	H	2B	3B	HR	RBI	BB	SO	HBP	GDP	SB	CS	OBP	Slg
Tom Seaver	.000	6	0	0	0	0	0	1	0	0	0	0	0	0	.000	.000
Ken Holtzman	.000	6	0	0	0	0	0	0	1	0	0	0	0	0	.143	.000
Jerry Koosman	.143	7	0	1	0	0	0	1	0	0	0	0	0	0	.143	.143

Frank Robinson

Bats: Right, Throws: Right

Batting	Avg	G	AB	R	H	2B	3B	HR	RBI	BB	SO	HBP	GDP	SB	CS	OBP	Slg
Totals	.238	35	126	25	30	5	1	10	19	20	32	3	1	0	0	.356	.532
Home	.261	19	69	13	18	4	0	6	11	8	20	2	0	0	0	.354	.580
Away	.211	16	57	12	12	1	1	4	8	12	12	1	1	0	0	.357	.474
vs. Left	.226	20	31	0	7	1	1	3	5	11	9	1	0	0	0	.442	.613
vs. Right	.242	35	95	25	23	4	0	7	14	9	23	2	1	0	0	.321	.505
Scoring Pos.	.174	21	23	0	4	1	0	1	6	5	5	1	0	0	0	.345	.348
Close & Late	.125	12	16	1	2	2	0	0	1	2	8	0	1	0	0	.222	.250
None on/out	.188	26	32	0	6	0	1	2	2	5	8	0	0	0	0	.297	.438
None on	.241	34	79	0	19	3	1	6	6	15	19	1	0	0	0	.368	.532
Runners on	.234	31	47	0	11	2	0	4	13	5	13	2	1	0	0	.333	.532
Batting #3	.264	15	53	11	14	2	1	6	10	13	11	0	0	0	0	.409	.679
Batting #4	.219	20	73	14	16	3	0	4	9	7	21	3	1	0	0	.313	.425

Hit Best Against

	Avg	AB	R	H	2B	3B	HR	RBI	BB	SO	HBP	GDP	SB	CS	OBP	Slg
Don Drysdale	.400	5	2	2	0	0	2	3	0	1	0	0	0	0	.400	1.600
Jim Perry	.400	5	2	2	0	0	1	1	2	2	0	0	0	0	.571	1.000
Bob Miller	.400	5	1	2	0	0	0	0	1	1	0	0	0	0	.500	.400

Hit Worst Against

	Avg	AB	R	H	2B	3B	HR	RBI	BB	SO	HBP	GDP	SB	CS	OBP	Slg
Bob Moose	.000	5	0	0	0	0	0	0	0	3	0	0	0	0	.000	.000
Tom Seaver	.143	7	1	1	0	0	0	0	0	1	0	0	0	0	.143	.143
Jerry Koosman	.167	6	1	1	0	0	1	1	2	1	0	0	0	0	.375	.667

Jackie Robinson

Bats: Right, Throws: Right

Batting	Avg	G	AB	R	H	2B	3B	HR	RBI	BB	SO	HBP	GDP	SB	CS	OBP	Slg
Totals	.234	38	137	22	32	7	1	2	12	21	14	0	5	6	0	.335	.343
Home	.257	20	74	10	19	2	0	2	9	10	6	0	4	1	0	.345	.365
Away	.206	18	63	12	13	5	1	0	3	11	8	0	1	5	0	.324	.317
vs. Left	.238	18	42	0	10	1	1	1	4	7	3	0	1	2	0	.347	.381
vs. Right	.232	38	95	22	22	6	0	1	8	14	11	0	4	4	0	.330	.326
Scoring Pos.	.222	33	45	0	10	1	0	0	10	5	3	0	3	4	0	.300	.244
Close & Late	.278	17	18	1	5	0	0	0	3	3	2	0	1	2	0	.381	.278
None on/out	.167	27	30	0	5	2	0	2	2	6	3	0	0	0	0	.306	.433
None on	.270	37	63	0	17	6	1	2	2	14	9	0	0	0	0	.403	.492
Runners on	.203	36	74	0	15	1	0	0	10	7	5	0	5	6	0	.272	.216
Batting #2	.400	3	10	2	4	1	0	0	1	2	1	0	0	2	0	.500	.500
Batting #3	.276	7	29	4	8	2	0	0	4	1	3	0	0	2	0	.300	.345
Batting #4	.181	21	72	10	13	2	0	2	5	16	9	0	3	1	0	.330	.292
Batting #7	.269	7	26	6	7	2	1	0	2	2	1	0	2	1	0	.321	.423

Hit Best Against

	Avg	AB	R	H	2B	3B	HR	RBI	BB	SO	HBP	GDP	SB	CS	OBP	Slg
Bob Turley	.500	6	1	3	0	0	0	2	1	0	0	0	0	0	.571	.500
Ed Lopat	.417	12	3	5	0	0	0	2	2	0	0	0	0	0	.500	.417
Tom Morgan	.400	5	2	2	0	0	0	0	0	0	0	0	0	0	.400	.400

Hit Worst Against

	Avg	AB	R	H	2B	3B	HR	RBI	BB	SO	HBP	GDP	SB	CS	OBP	Slg
Don Larsen	.000	6	0	0	0	0	0	0	0	0	0	1	0	0	.000	.000
Joe Page	.000	7	1	0	0	0	0	0	1	1	0	0	0	0	.125	.000
Johnny Kucks	.000	6	0	0	0	0	0	0	1	1	0	1	0	0	.143	.000

Steve Rogers

Throws: Right, Bats: Right

Pitching	ERA	W	L	Sv	G	GS	IP	BB	SO	Avg	R	H	2B	3B	HR	OBP	Slg
Totals	0.98	3	1	0	4	3	27.2	4	11	.238	3	24	1	1	2	.267	.327
Home	1.45	2	1	0	3	2	18.2	3	9	.261	3	18	1	1	2	.292	.391
Away	0.00	1	0	0	1	1	9.0	1	2	.188	0	6	0	0	0	.212	.188

	Avg	AB	R	H	2B	3B	HR	RBI	BB	SO	HBP	GDP	OBP	Slg
vs. Left	.154	39	0	6	1	0	1	1	2	5	0	1	.195	.256
vs. Right	.290	62	3	18	0	1	1	2	2	5	0	1	.313	.371
Scoring Pos.	.067	15	0	1	0	0	0	1	2	2	0	1	.176	.067
Close & Late	.250	12	1	3	0	0	1	1	0	3	0	1	.250	.500
None on/out	.276	29	0	8	0	0	1	1	0	4	0	1	.276	.379
None on	.261	69	0	18	1	1	2	2	1	6	0	1	.271	.391
Runners on	.188	32	0	6	0	0	0	1	3	4	0	1	.257	.188

Pitched Best Against

	Avg	AB	R	H	2B	3B	HR	RBI	BB	SO	HBP	GDP	SB	CS	OBP	Slg
Larry Bowa	.000	6	0	0	0	0	0	0	0	0	0	0	0	0	.000	.000
Pedro Guerrero	.000	5	0	0	0	0	0	0	0	2	0	2	0	0	.000	.000
Mike Schmidt	.143	7	0	1	0	0	0	0	1	1	0	1	0	0	.250	.143

Pitched Worst Against

	Avg	AB	R	H	2B	3B	HR	RBI	BB	SO	HBP	GDP	SB	CS	OBP	Slg
Pete Rose	.429	7	0	3	1	0	0	0	1	0	0	1	0	0	.500	.571
Steve Garvey	.400	5	0	2	0	0	0	0	0	0	0	0	0	0	.400	.400
Lonnie Smith	.375	8	0	3	0	0	0	0	0	1	0	0	0	1	.375	.375

Red Rolfe

Bats: Left, Throws: Right

Batting	Avg	G	AB	R	H	2B	3B	HR	RBI	BB	SO	HBP	GDP	SB	CS	OBP	Slg
Totals	.284	28	116	17	33	4	1	0	6	9	9	0	1	1	2	.336	.336
Home	.241	13	54	6	13	1	0	0	3	4	4	0	0	1	1	.293	.259
Away	.323	15	62	11	20	3	1	0	3	5	5	0	1	0	1	.373	.403
vs. Left	.364	9	22	0	8	0	1	0	1	3	2	0	0	0	0	.440	.455
vs. Right	.266	28	94	17	25	4	0	0	5	6	7	0	1	1	2	.310	.309
Scoring Pos.	.261	18	23	0	6	0	0	0	6	1	1	0	1	0	1	.292	.261
Close & Late	.100	11	10	1	1	0	0	0	0	1	2	0	0	0	0	.182	.100
None on/out	.263	15	19	0	5	1	0	0	0	2	0	0	0	0	0	.333	.316
None on	.320	28	75	0	24	4	1	0	0	4	7	0	0	0	0	.354	.400
Runners on	.220	26	41	0	9	0	0	0	6	5	2	0	1	1	2	.304	.220
Batting #2	.284	28	116	17	33	4	1	0	6	9	9	0	1	1	2	.336	.336

Hit Best Against

	Avg	AB	R	H	2B	3B	HR	RBI	BB	SO	HBP	GDP	SB	CS	OBP	Slg
Mort Cooper	.500	6	3	3	1	0	0	0	1	2	0	0	0	0	.571	.667
Carl Hubbell	.462	13	3	6	0	1	0	1	1	1	0	0	0	0	.500	.615
Hal Schumacher	.444	9	3	4	2	0	0	0	2	1	0	0	0	1	.545	.667

Hit Worst Against

	Avg	AB	R	H	2B	3B	HR	RBI	BB	SO	HBP	GDP	SB	CS	OBP	Slg
Paul Derringer	.000	7	0	0	0	0	0	0	0	0	0	0	0	0	.000	.000
Dizzy Dean	.000	5	0	0	0	0	0	0	0	2	0	0	0	0	.000	.000
Whit Wyatt	.125	8	0	1	0	0	0	0	1	0	0	0	0	1	.222	.125

Pete Rose

Bats: Both, Throws: Right

Batting	Avg	G	AB	R	H	2B	3B	HR	RBI	BB	SO	HBP	GDP	SB	CS	OBP	Slg
Totals	.321	67	268	30	86	13	2	5	22	28	22	2	3	2	5	.388	.440
Home	.311	33	122	13	38	5	1	1	7	18	8	1	0	0	4	.401	.393
Away	.329	34	146	17	48	8	1	4	15	10	14	1	3	2	1	.376	.479
vs. Left	.277	38	101	0	28	3	1	1	6	8	6	0	1	1	1	.330	.356
vs. Right	.347	67	167	30	58	10	1	4	16	20	16	2	2	1	4	.421	.491
Scoring Pos.	.333	43	42	0	14	3	0	0	15	15	4	0	1	0	0	.500	.405
Close & Late	.421	37	38	6	16	0	0	2	11	11	0	1	0	0	0	.560	.579
None on/out	.298	58	104	0	31	5	1	1	1	4	8	1	0	0	0	.330	.394
None on	.326	67	193	0	63	9	2	4	4	12	17	2	0	0	0	.372	.456
Runners on	.307	61	75	0	23	4	0	1	18	16	5	0	3	2	5	.424	.400
Batting #1	.315	45	184	19	58	9	2	4	16	21	15	1	1	1	3	.386	.451
Batting #2	.337	21	83	11	28	4	0	1	6	7	7	1	2	1	2	.396	.422

Hit Best Against	Avg	AB	R	H	2B	3B	HR	RBI	BB	SO	HBP	GDP	SB	CS	OBP	Slg
Nolan Ryan	.600	5	0	3	0	0	0	1	2	1	0	0	0	1	.714	.600
Dock Ellis	.500	10	1	5	0	0	0	1	1	0	0	1	0	0	.545	.500
Bill Lee	.500	8	0	4	0	0	0	1	0	1	0	0	0	0	.500	.500

Hit Worst Against	Avg	AB	R	H	2B	3B	HR	RBI	BB	SO	HBP	GDP	SB	CS	OBP	Slg
Ken Holtzman	.000	7	0	0	0	0	0	0	0	0	0	0	0	0	.000	.000
Larry Gura	.000	6	0	0	0	0	0	0	0	0	0	0	0	0	.000	.000
Mike Cuellar	.167	6	1	1	1	0	0	0	0	0	0	0	0	0	.167	.333

Joe Rudi

Bats: Right, Throws: Right

Batting	Avg	G	AB	R	H	2B	3B	HR	RBI	BB	SO	HBP	GDP	SB	CS	OBP	Slg
Totals	.257	38	140	8	36	6	1	3	15	13	20	1	2	0	1	.323	.379
Home	.273	18	66	5	18	2	1	1	10	4	11	1	2	0	1	.319	.379
Away	.243	20	74	3	18	4	0	2	5	9	9	0	0	0	0	.325	.378
vs. Left	.290	25	69	0	20	4	1	2	10	8	8	0	0	0	1	.359	.464
vs. Right	.225	38	71	8	16	2	0	1	5	5	12	1	2	0	0	.286	.296
Scoring Pos.	.357	28	28	0	10	0	1	0	12	8	4	0	1	0	0	.486	.429
Close & Late	.227	18	22	1	5	0	0	1	5	1	4	0	1	0	0	.261	.364
None on/out	.258	20	31	0	8	0	0	2	2	1	3	0	0	0	0	.281	.452
None on	.244	37	90	0	22	5	0	3	3	3	14	1	0	0	0	.277	.400
Runners on	.280	35	50	0	14	1	1	0	12	10	6	0	2	0	1	.393	.340
Batting #2	.250	15	56	4	14	3	0	1	7	7	5	0	0	0	1	.333	.357
Batting #3	.268	11	41	2	11	1	0	1	3	3	9	1	0	0	0	.326	.366
Batting #5	.229	10	35	1	8	0	1	1	5	3	5	0	2	0	0	.289	.371

Hit Best Against	Avg	AB	R	H	2B	3B	HR	RBI	BB	SO	HBP	GDP	SB	CS	OBP	Slg
Mike Marshall	.600	5	1	3	0	0	1	3	0	0	0	1	0	0	.600	1.200
Dave McNally	.500	10	1	5	1	1	1	2	0	0	0	0	0	0	.500	1.100
Tom Seaver	.429	7	1	3	1	0	0	1	1	1	0	0	0	0	.500	.571

Hit Worst Against	Avg	AB	R	H	2B	3B	HR	RBI	BB	SO	HBP	GDP	SB	CS	OBP	Slg
Mickey Lolich	.000	8	0	0	0	0	0	1	0	2	0	0	0	0	.000	.000
Gary Nolan	.000	5	0	0	0	0	0	0	0	0	0	0	0	0	.000	.000
Jim Palmer	.000	9	0	0	0	0	0	0	2	3	0	0	0	0	.182	.000

Red Ruffing

Throws: Right, Bats: Right

Pitching	ERA	W	L	Sv	G	GS	IP	BB	SO	Avg	R	H	2B	3B	HR	OBP	Slg
Totals	2.52	7	2	0	10	10	85.2	27	61	.231	32	74	10	4	4	.291	.325
Home	2.25	5	1	0	7	7	60.0	17	43	.226	21	51	9	2	3	.280	.323
Away	3.16	2	1	0	3	3	25.2	10	18	.245	11	23	1	2	1	.317	.330

	Avg	AB	R	H	2B	3B	HR	RBI	BB	SO	HBP	GDP	OBP	Slg
vs. Left	.223	130	0	29	4	1	1	7	18	23	0	2	.318	.292
vs. Right	.237	190	32	45	6	3	3	21	9	38	0	2	.271	.347
Scoring Pos.	.243	70	0	17	1	2	2	25	6	17	0	2	.303	.400
Close & Late	.227	66	3	15	0	2	2	13	6	7	0	2	.292	.379
None on/out	.294	85	0	25	7	0	1	1	2	11	0	2	.310	.412
None on	.237	190	0	45	9	1	2	2	12	32	0	2	.282	.326
Runners on	.223	130	0	29	1	3	2	26	15	29	0	2	.303	.323

Pitched Best Against	Avg	AB	R	H	2B	3B	HR	RBI	BB	SO	HBP	GDP	SB	CS	OBP	Slg
Johnny Hopp	.000	7	0	0	0	0	0	0	0	1	0	0	0	0	.000	.000
Frank Demaree	.000	7	1	0	0	0	0	0	1	1	0	0	0	0	.125	.000
Stan Musial	.000	7	0	0	0	0	0	0	1	0	0	0	0	0	.125	.000

Pitched Worst Against	Avg	AB	R	H	2B	3B	HR	RBI	BB	SO	HBP	GDP	SB	CS	OBP	Slg
R. Stephenson	.600	5	0	3	0	0	0	0	0	0	0	0	0	0	.600	.600
Stan Hack	.556	9	0	5	0	0	0	1	0	0	0	1	0	1	.556	.556
Phil Cavarretta	.500	8	1	4	1	0	0	0	0	1	0	0	0	0	.500	.625

Bill Russell

Bats: Right, Throws: Right

Batting	Avg	G	AB	R	H	2B	3B	HR	RBI	BB	SO	HBP	GDP	SB	CS	OBP	Slg
Totals	.294	49	194	14	57	5	3	0	18	11	15	0	5	3	3	.332	.351
Home	.337	24	95	8	32	3	0	0	10	3	8	0	2	1	1	.357	.368
Away	.253	25	99	6	25	2	3	0	8	8	7	0	3	2	2	.308	.333
vs. Left	.235	28	81	0	19	1	2	0	9	5	5	0	3	0	2	.279	.296
vs. Right	.336	49	113	14	38	4	1	0	9	6	10	0	2	3	1	.370	.389
Scoring Pos.	.349	32	43	0	15	1	1	0	16	6	6	0	1	2	0	.429	.419
Close & Late	.242	27	33	1	8	0	0	0	3	1	5	0	2	0	0	.265	.242
None on/out	.308	31	39	0	12	1	0	0	0	0	3	0	0	0	0	.308	.333
None on	.250	48	116	0	29	3	1	0	0	4	7	0	0	0	0	.275	.293
Runners on	.359	43	78	0	28	2	2	0	18	7	8	0	5	3	3	.412	.436
Batting #2	.271	28	118	11	32	3	2	0	8	5	11	0	2	2	3	.301	.331
Batting #7	.349	11	43	2	15	1	1	0	7	3	3	0	2	1	0	.391	.419
Batting #8	.303	10	33	1	10	1	0	0	3	3	1	0	1	0	0	.361	.333

Hit Best Against	Avg	AB	R	H	2B	3B	HR	RBI	BB	SO	HBP	GDP	SB	CS	OBP	Slg
Ron Reed	.600	5	1	3	1	0	0	0	1	0	0	0	1	0	.667	.800
Dave Giusti	.600	5	1	3	0	0	0	3	0	0	0	0	0	0	.600	.600
Ray Burris	.571	7	0	4	0	1	0	0	0	0	0	0	0	0	.571	.857

Hit Worst Against	Avg	AB	R	H	2B	3B	HR	RBI	BB	SO	HBP	GDP	SB	CS	OBP	Slg
Goose Gossage	.000	5	0	0	0	0	0	0	0	0	0	1	0	0	.000	.000
Nolan Ryan	.000	6	0	0	0	0	0	0	0	0	0	0	0	0	.000	.000
Mike Torrez	.000	7	0	0	0	0	0	0	1	1	0	0	0	0	.125	.000

Babe Ruth

Bats: Left, Throws: Left

Batting	Avg	G	AB	R	H	2B	3B	HR	RBI	BB	SO	HBP	GDP	SB	CS	OBP	Slg
Totals	.326	41	129	37	42	5	2	15	33	33	30	2	3	4	5	.467	.744
Home	.306	21	62	18	19	4	2	4	12	19	10	0	1	4	1	.469	.629
Away	.343	20	67	19	23	1	0	11	21	14	20	2	2	0	4	.464	.851
vs. Left	.286	22	49	0	14	3	1	5	12	13	16	0	2	2	2	.435	.694
vs. Right	.350	41	80	37	28	2	1	10	21	20	14	2	1	2	3	.485	.775
Scoring Pos.	.294	30	34	0	10	0	1	2	18	8	10	1	0	2	1	.432	.529
Close & Late	.000	18	16	1	0	0	0	0	0	4	3	0	1	0	1	.200	.000
None on/out	.444	21	18	0	8	2	0	2	2	6	4	0	0	0	0	.583	.889
None on	.391	39	69	0	27	5	1	11	11	17	16	1	0	0	0	.517	.971
Runners on	.250	37	60	0	15	0	1	4	22	16	14	1	3	4	5	.410	.483
Batting #3	.350	35	117	37	41	5	1	15	30	33	26	2	3	4	5	.497	.795

Hit Best Against	Avg	AB	R	H	2B	3B	HR	RBI	BB	SO	HBP	GDP	SB	CS	OBP	Slg
Phil Douglas	.429	7	1	3	0	0	1	2	1	3	0	0	0	0	.500	.857
Bill Sherdel	.417	12	5	5	2	0	2	2	3	2	0	1	0	0	.533	1.083
Jesse Haines	.375	8	3	3	0	0	1	1	4	0	0	0	0	0	.583	.750

Hit Worst Against	Avg	AB	R	H	2B	3B	HR	RBI	BB	SO	HBP	GDP	SB	CS	OBP	Slg
Sherry Smith	.000	5	0	0	0	0	0	1	0	2	0	0	0	0	.000	.000
Jesse Barnes	.167	6	1	1	1	0	0	0	2	2	0	0	0	1	.375	.333
Pete Alexander	.200	10	3	2	0	0	1	1	3	1	0	0	1	1	.385	.500

Pitching	ERA	W	L	Sv	G	GS	IP	BB	SO	Avg	R	H	2B	3B	HR	OBP	Slg
Totals	0.87	3	0	0	3	3	31.0	10	8	.186	3	19	1	0	1	.265	.225
Home	1.23	2	0	0	2	2	22.0	9	4	.186	3	13	1	0	1	.278	.243
Away	0.00	1	0	0	1	1	9.0	1	4	.188	0	6	0	0	0	.235	.188

	Avg	AB	R	H	2B	3B	HR	RBI	BB	SO	HBP	GDP	OBP	Slg
vs. Left	.135	37	0	5	1	0	0	1	3	4	1	0	.220	.162
vs. Right	.215	65	3	14	0	0	1	2	7	4	0	0	.292	.262
Scoring Pos.	.125	16	0	2	0	0	0	2	1	0	0	0	.176	.125
Close & Late	.125	32	0	4	0	0	0	2	3	2	0	0	.200	.125
None on/out	.179	28	0	5	0	0	0	0	4	3	0	0	.281	.179
None on	.188	69	0	13	1	0	1	1	7	8	1	0	.273	.246
Runners on	.182	33	0	6	0	0	0	2	3	0	0	0	.250	.182

Pitched Best Against	Avg	AB	R	H	2B	3B	HR	RBI	BB	SO	HBP	GDP	SB	CS	OBP	Slg
C. Hollocher	.000	7	0	0	0	0	0	1	0	0	0	0	0	0	.000	.000
Bill Killefer	.000	6	1	0	0	0	0	0	1	0	0	1	0	0	.143	.000
Jake Daubert	.000	5	0	0	0	0	0	0	1	1	0	0	0	0	.167	.000

Pitched Worst Against	Avg	AB	R	H	2B	3B	HR	RBI	BB	SO	HBP	GDP	SB	CS	OBP	Slg
Charlie Pick	.400	5	0	2	0	0	0	0	0	1	0	0	0	0	.400	.400
Fred Merkle	.333	6	0	2	0	0	0	0	2	0	0	0	0	0	.500	.333
Charlie Deal	.333	6	0	2	0	0	0	0	0	0	0	0	0	0	.333	.333

Nolan Ryan

Throws: Right, Bats: Right

Pitching	ERA	W	L	Sv	G	GS	IP	BB	SO	Avg	R	H	2B	3B	HR	OBP	Slg
Totals	3.07	2	2	1	9	7	58.2	14	63	.188	23	39	4	1	3	.237	.260
Home	4.15	2	1	1	5	3	30.1	7	30	.196	14	21	1	1	2	.243	.280
Away	1.91	0	1	0	4	4	28.1	7	33	.178	9	18	3	0	1	.229	.238

	Avg	AB	R	H	2B	3B	HR	RBI	BB	SO	HBP	GDP	OBP	Slg
vs. Left	.207	92	0	19	0	1	1	8	8	32	0	1	.267	.261
vs. Right	.172	116	23	20	4	0	2	11	6	31	0	1	.211	.259
Scoring Pos.	.323	31	0	10	2	1	0	14	3	6	0	1	.361	.452
Close & Late	.265	34	1	9	0	0	0	1	3	7	0	1	.324	.265
None on/out	.105	57	0	6	1	0	0	0	2	17	0	1	.136	.123
None on	.130	146	0	19	1	0	2	2	8	50	0	1	.175	.178
Runners on	.323	62	0	20	3	1	1	17	6	13	0	1	.371	.452

Pitched Best Against	Avg	AB	R	H	2B	3B	HR	RBI	BB	SO	HBP	GDP	SB	CS	OBP	Slg
Bill Russell	.000	6	0	0	0	0	0	0	0	0	0	0	0	0	.000	.000
Dusty Baker	.000	5	1	0	0	0	0	0	1	0	0	1	0	0	.167	.000
Pedro Guerrero	.000	5	0	0	0	0	0	0	1	2	0	0	1	0	.167	.000

Pitched Worst Against	Avg	AB	R	H	2B	3B	HR	RBI	BB	SO	HBP	GDP	SB	CS	OBP	Slg
Pete Rose	.600	5	0	3	0	0	0	1	2	1	0	0	0	1	.714	.600
Manny Trillo	.600	5	1	3	0	0	0	0	0	0	0	0	0	0	.600	.600
Bob Boone	.500	6	1	3	0	0	0	2	0	0	0	0	0	0	.500	.500

Wally Schang

Bats: Both, Throws: Right

Batting	Avg	G	AB	R	H	2B	3B	HR	RBI	BB	SO	HBP	GDP	SB	CS	OBP	Slg
Totals	.287	32	94	8	27	4	2	1	9	11	20	0	1	1	2	.362	.404
Home	.308	15	39	3	12	2	1	0	5	8	8	0	0	0	2	.426	.410
Away	.273	17	55	5	15	2	1	1	4	3	12	0	1	1	0	.310	.400
vs. Left	.270	16	37	0	10	1	1	0	5	4	5	0	1	1	1	.341	.351
vs. Right	.298	32	57	8	17	3	1	1	4	7	15	0	0	0	1	.375	.439
Scoring Pos.	.250	17	16	0	4	0	1	0	7	3	5	0	0	0	1	.368	.375
Close & Late	.500	15	14	2	7	1	0	0	0	2	1	0	0	1	0	.563	.571
None on/out	.217	18	23	0	5	0	0	0	0	3	6	0	0	0	0	.308	.217
None on	.236	32	55	0	13	2	0	1	1	8	13	0	0	0	0	.333	.327
Runners on	.359	27	39	0	14	2	2	0	8	3	7	0	1	1	2	.405	.513
Batting #6	.250	6	20	0	5	1	0	0	1	0	5	0	0	1	0	.250	.300
Batting #7	.318	6	22	3	7	1	0	0	0	1	2	0	1	0	0	.348	.364
Batting #8	.275	19	51	4	14	2	2	1	8	10	13	0	0	0	2	.393	.451

Hit Best Against	Avg	AB	R	H	2B	3B	HR	RBI	BB	SO	HBP	GDP	SB	CS	OBP	Slg
Phil Douglas	.444	9	1	4	0	1	0	1	1	2	0	0	0	0	.500	.667
Hippo Vaughn	.400	5	0	2	0	0	0	1	0	3	0	0	1	0	.400	.400
Hugh McQuillan	.375	8	0	3	0	0	0	0	0	1	0	0	0	0	.375	.375

Hit Worst Against	Avg	AB	R	H	2B	3B	HR	RBI	BB	SO	HBP	GDP	SB	CS	OBP	Slg
Dick Rudolph	.000	5	0	0	0	0	0	0	0	3	0	0	0	0	.000	.000
Art Nehf	.211	19	1	4	1	0	0	0	1	1	0	1	0	0	.250	.263

Mike Schmidt

Bats: Right, Throws: Right

Batting	Avg	G	AB	R	H	2B	3B	HR	RBI	BB	SO	HBP	GDP	SB	CS	OBP	Slg
Totals	.236	36	140	19	33	9	0	4	16	15	26	0	1	1	1	.304	.386
Home	.243	19	70	11	17	5	0	1	8	9	11	0	1	0	0	.321	.357
Away	.229	17	70	8	16	4	0	3	8	6	15	0	0	1	1	.286	.414
vs. Left	.250	17	44	0	11	3	0	2	5	4	6	0	0	0	1	.306	.455
vs. Right	.229	36	96	19	22	6	0	2	11	11	20	0	1	1	0	.303	.354
Scoring Pos.	.138	24	29	0	4	1	0	0	8	4	5	0	1	0	0	.222	.172
Close & Late	.185	20	27	1	5	1	0	0	4	1	6	0	0	0	0	.207	.222
None on/out	.296	20	27	0	8	4	0	1	1	2	6	0	0	0	0	.345	.556
None on	.253	36	79	0	20	5	0	2	2	7	15	0	0	0	0	.314	.392
Runners on	.213	34	61	0	13	4	0	2	14	8	11	0	1	1	1	.292	.377
Batting #3	.225	25	102	14	23	5	0	3	11	9	21	0	0	1	0	.286	.363
Batting #4	.304	7	23	4	7	2	0	1	4	4	3	0	1	0	0	.393	.522

Hit Best Against

	Avg	AB	R	H	2B	3B	HR	RBI	BB	SO	HBP	GDP	SB	CS	OBP	Slg
Jerry Reuss	.667	6	3	4	1	0	1	2	1	0	0	0	0	0	.714	1.333
Larry Gura	.333	6	1	2	0	0	1	2	0	0	0	0	0	0	.333	.833

Hit Worst Against

	Avg	AB	R	H	2B	3B	HR	RBI	BB	SO	HBP	GDP	SB	CS	OBP	Slg
Scott McGregor	.000	7	0	0	0	0	0	0	0	2	0	0	0	0	.000	.000
Tommy John	.100	10	2	1	0	0	0	0	1	1	0	0	0	0	.182	.100
Steve Rogers	.143	7	0	1	0	0	0	0	1	1	0	1	0	0	.250	.143

Red Schoendienst

Bats: Both, Throws: Right

Batting	Avg	G	AB	R	H	2B	3B	HR	RBI	BB	SO	HBP	GDP	SB	CS	OBP	Slg
Totals	.269	19	78	8	21	5	1	0	3	2	4	0	1	1	1	.288	.359
Home	.318	11	44	6	14	5	0	0	2	2	2	0	0	1	0	.348	.432
Away	.206	8	34	2	7	0	1	0	1	0	2	0	1	0	1	.206	.265
vs. Left	.174	10	23	0	4	1	1	0	1	1	2	0	1	0	0	.208	.304
vs. Right	.309	19	55	8	17	4	0	0	2	1	2	0	0	1	1	.321	.382
Scoring Pos.	.250	13	16	0	4	0	0	0	3	1	1	0	1	1	0	.294	.250
Close & Late	.250	9	8	0	2	0	0	0	1	1	0	0	0	1	0	.333	.250
None on/out	.344	18	32	0	11	3	1	0	0	0	2	0	0	0	0	.344	.500
None on	.275	19	51	0	14	3	1	0	0	0	3	0	0	0	0	.275	.373
Runners on	.259	18	27	0	7	2	0	0	3	2	1	0	1	1	1	.310	.333
Batting #1	.242	16	66	6	16	3	1	0	3	2	4	0	1	1	1	.265	.318
Batting #2	.417	3	12	2	5	2	0	0	0	0	0	0	0	0	0	.417	.583

Hit Best Against

	Avg	AB	R	H	2B	3B	HR	RBI	BB	SO	HBP	GDP	SB	CS	OBP	Slg
Bob Turley	.444	9	1	4	1	0	0	1	0	0	0	0	0	0	.444	.556
Don Larsen	.444	9	1	4	0	0	0	0	0	0	0	0	0	0	.444	.444
Tex Hughson	.375	8	2	3	0	0	0	0	0	0	0	0	1	0	.375	.375

Hit Worst Against

	Avg	AB	R	H	2B	3B	HR	RBI	BB	SO	HBP	GDP	SB	CS	OBP	Slg
Joe Dobson	.200	5	0	1	0	0	0	0	0	2	0	0	0	1	.200	.200
Mickey Harris	.200	5	1	1	1	0	0	0	0	0	0	0	0	0	.200	.400
Whitey Ford	.214	14	2	3	0	1	0	1	1	1	0	1	0	0	.267	.357

Tom Seaver

Throws: Right, Bats: Right

Pitching	ERA	W	L	Sv	G	GS	IP	BB	SO	Avg	R	H	2B	3B	HR	OBP	Slg
Totals	2.77	3	3	0	8	8	61.2	16	51	.221	20	51	15	1	6	.273	.372
Home	1.57	2	0	0	4	4	34.1	10	27	.203	7	25	6	1	1	.257	.293
Away	4.28	1	3	0	4	4	27.1	6	24	.241	13	26	9	0	5	.291	.463

	Avg	AB	R	H	2B	3B	HR	RBI	BB	SO	HBP	GDP	OBP	Slg
vs. Left	.224	107	0	24	8	1	3	9	8	27	1	0	.282	.402
vs. Right	.218	124	20	27	7	0	3	11	8	24	1	0	.265	.347
Scoring Pos.	.182	44	0	8	4	0	0	12	6	15	1	0	.273	.273
Close & Late	.200	30	2	6	0	0	2	4	2	7	0	0	.242	.400
None on/out	.154	65	0	10	3	0	3	3	1	14	0	0	.167	.338
None on	.232	151	0	35	9	1	6	6	7	31	1	0	.270	.424
Runners on	.200	80	0	16	6	0	0	14	9	20	1	0	.277	.275

Pitched Best Against

	Avg	AB	R	H	2B	3B	HR	RBI	BB	SO	HBP	GDP	SB	CS	OBP	Slg
B. Robinson	.000	6	0	0	0	0	0	1	0	0	0	0	0	0	.000	.000
Catfish Hunter	.000	5	0	0	0	0	0	0	0	3	0	0	0	0	.000	.000
Dave Johnson	.000	5	1	0	0	0	0	0	1	1	0	0	0	1	.167	.000

Pitched Worst Against

	Avg	AB	R	H	2B	3B	HR	RBI	BB	SO	HBP	GDP	SB	CS	OBP	Slg
Johnny Bench	.429	7	1	3	1	0	1	1	1	1	0	0	0	0	.500	1.000
Joe Rudi	.429	7	1	3	1	0	0	1	1	1	0	0	0	0	.500	.571
Pete Rose	.375	8	2	3	1	0	1	1	1	1	0	0	0	0	.444	.875

Al Simmons

Bats: Right, Throws: Right

Batting	Avg	G	AB	R	H	2B	3B	HR	RBI	BB	SO	HBP	GDP	SB	CS	OBP	Slg
Totals	.329	19	73	15	24	6	0	6	17	6	9	0	2	0	0	.375	.658
Home	.385	10	39	10	15	5	0	4	7	1	3	0	1	0	0	.390	.821
Away	.265	9	34	5	9	1	0	2	10	5	6	0	1	0	0	.359	.471
vs. Left	.385	4	13	0	5	2	0	0	0	0	2	0	1	0	0	.385	.538
vs. Right	.317	19	60	15	19	4	0	6	17	6	7	0	1	0	0	.373	.683
Scoring Pos.	.286	13	14	0	4	1	0	0	7	3	3	0	1	0	0	.389	.357
Close & Late	.308	10	13	2	4	2	0	1	2	0	0	0	0	0	0	.286	.692
None on/out	.316	13	19	0	6	1	0	2	2	1	2	0	0	0	0	.350	.684
None on	.371	18	35	0	13	3	0	3	3	2	3	0	0	0	0	.405	.714
Runners on	.289	18	38	0	11	3	0	3	14	4	6	0	2	0	0	.349	.605
Batting #4	.333	18	69	14	23	5	0	6	17	6	9	0	2	0	0	.382	.667

Hit Best Against

	Avg	AB	R	H	2B	3B	HR	RBI	BB	SO	HBP	GDP	SB	CS	OBP	Slg
Pat Malone	.500	6	2	3	1	0	0	2	1	1	0	0	0	0	.571	.667
W. Bill Hallahan	.385	13	1	5	2	0	0	0	0	2	0	1	0	0	.385	.538
Syl Johnson	.286	7	1	2	1	0	1	2	0	1	0	1	0	0	.286	.857

Hit Worst Against

	Avg	AB	R	H	2B	3B	HR	RBI	BB	SO	HBP	GDP	SB	CS	OBP	Slg
Charlie Root	.167	6	1	1	0	0	1	1	0	2	0	0	0	0	.167	.667
Paul Derringer	.200	5	1	1	0	0	1	4	2	1	0	0	0	0	.429	.800
Burleigh Grimes	.214	14	2	3	0	0	2	3	2	1	0	0	0	0	.313	.643

Ted Simmons

Bats: Both, Throws: Right

Batting	Avg	G	AB	R	H	2B	3B	HR	RBI	BB	SO	HBP	GDP	SB	CS	OBP	Slg
Totals	.186	17	59	6	11	1	0	3	8	8	9	0	1	0	0	.279	.356
Home	.154	8	26	2	4	0	0	0	3	5	5	0	0	0	0	.281	.154
Away	.212	9	33	4	7	1	0	3	5	3	4	0	1	0	0	.278	.515
vs. Left	.308	11	26	0	8	1	0	1	4	5	5	0	0	0	0	.419	.462
vs. Right	.091	17	33	6	3	0	0	2	4	3	4	0	1	0	0	.162	.273
Scoring Pos.	.200	11	15	0	3	1	0	0	4	4	4	0	1	0	0	.350	.267
Close & Late	.400	6	5	1	2	1	0	1	3	2	2	0	0	0	0	.571	1.200
None on/out	.095	16	21	0	2	0	0	0	0	3	3	0	0	0	0	.208	.095
None on	.200	17	35	0	7	0	0	2	2	3	4	0	0	0	0	.263	.371
Runners on	.167	15	24	0	4	1	0	1	6	5	5	0	1	0	0	.300	.333
Batting #4	.186	17	59	6	11	1	0	3	8	8	9	0	1	0	0	.279	.356

Hit Best Against

	Avg	AB	R	H	2B	3B	HR	RBI	BB	SO	HBP	GDP	SB	CS	OBP	Slg
Tommy John	.429	7	3	3	0	0	1	2	2	1	0	0	0	0	.556	.857

Hit Worst Against

	Avg	AB	R	H	2B	3B	HR	RBI	BB	SO	HBP	GDP	SB	CS	OBP	Slg
Bruce Kison	.000	5	0	0	0	0	0	1	0	1	0	0	0	0	.000	.000
Joaquin Andujar	.167	6	0	1	0	0	0	0	0	0	0	0	0	0	.167	.167
Ron Guidry	.200	5	0	1	0	0	0	1	0	1	0	0	0	0	.200	.200

Bill Skowron

Bats: Right, Throws: Right

Batting	Avg	G	AB	R	H	2B	3B	HR	RBI	BB	SO	HBP	GDP	SB	CS	OBP	Slg
Totals	.293	39	133	19	39	4	1	8	29	6	26	1	5	0	0	.326	.519
Home	.236	17	55	7	13	2	1	3	8	2	12	1	2	0	0	.276	.473
Away	.333	22	78	12	26	2	0	5	21	4	14	0	3	0	0	.361	.551
vs. Left	.340	23	50	0	17	3	0	4	11	5	7	0	2	0	0	.400	.640
vs. Right	.265	39	83	19	22	1	1	4	18	1	19	1	3	0	0	.279	.446
Scoring Pos.	.313	31	48	0	15	0	0	3	24	2	7	1	2	0	0	.346	.500
Close & Late	.222	13	18	0	4	0	0	1	4	0	3	0	0	0	0	.222	.389
None on/out	.355	25	31	0	11	3	0	2	2	2	5	0	0	0	0	.394	.645
None on	.308	31	65	0	20	4	1	5	5	3	16	0	0	0	0	.338	.631
Runners on	.279	36	68	0	19	0	0	3	24	3	10	1	5	0	0	.315	.412
Batting #5	.217	6	23	3	5	1	0	2	5	1	5	0	0	0	0	.250	.522
Batting #6	.373	15	59	12	22	3	0	5	16	1	11	0	3	0	0	.377	.678
Batting #7	.256	12	39	2	10	0	1	1	7	4	8	1	2	0	0	.341	.385

Hit Best Against

	Avg	AB	R	H	2B	3B	HR	RBI	BB	SO	HBP	GDP	SB	CS	OBP	Slg
Vern Law	.625	8	3	5	1	0	2	3	0	1	0	0	0	0	.625	1.500
Johnny Podres	.375	8	1	3	2	0	0	0	0	1	0	0	0	0	.375	.625
Warren Spahn	.273	11	1	3	0	0	1	1	1	1	0	0	0	0	.333	.545

Hit Worst Against

	Avg	AB	R	H	2B	3B	HR	RBI	BB	SO	HBP	GDP	SB	CS	OBP	Slg
Billy Pierce	.000	5	0	0	0	0	0	0	0	1	0	0	0	0	.000	.000
Jack Sanford	.167	6	1	1	0	0	0	0	0	3	0	0	0	0	.167	.167
Roy Face	.200	5	1	1	0	0	0	0	0	1	0	0	0	0	.200	.200

Enos Slaughter

Bats: Left, Throws: Right

Batting	Avg	G	AB	R	H	2B	3B	HR	RBI	BB	SO	HBP	GDP	SB	CS	OBP	Slg
Totals	.291	27	79	17	23	3	1	3	8	15	8	1	2	1	1	.406	.468
Home	.211	14	38	7	8	2	1	1	4	13	6	0	0	0	0	.412	.395
Away	.366	13	41	10	15	1	0	2	4	2	2	1	2	1	1	.400	.537
vs. Left	.111	6	9	0	1	0	0	0	1	1	2	0	0	0	0	.200	.111
vs. Right	.314	27	70	17	22	3	1	3	7	14	6	1	2	1	1	.430	.514
Scoring Pos.	.200	17	20	0	4	0	0	1	6	5	2	0	0	0	0	.346	.350
Close & Late	.308	12	13	3	4	1	0	0	1	1	1	0	1	0	0	.357	.385
None on/out	.316	18	19	0	6	0	0	2	2	2	2	0	0	0	0	.381	.632
None on	.333	25	45	0	15	2	1	2	2	9	5	1	0	0	0	.455	.556
Runners on	.235	21	34	0	8	1	0	1	6	6	3	0	2	1	1	.341	.353
Batting #2	.385	3	13	4	5	0	0	0	1	0	0	0	0	0	0	.357	.385
Batting #3	.238	7	21	4	5	1	0	1	2	5	2	0	1	0	0	.385	.429
Batting #4	.368	5	19	5	7	1	1	1	1	2	2	1	0	1	0	.455	.684
Batting #5	.261	8	23	3	6	1	0	1	4	7	3	0	1	0	1	.433	.435

Hit Best Against

	Avg	AB	R	H	2B	3B	HR	RBI	BB	SO	HBP	GDP	SB	CS	OBP	Slg
Sal Maglie	.429	7	1	3	0	0	0	0	1	0	0	0	0	0	.500	.429
Red Ruffing	.333	6	1	2	0	0	1	1	2	1	0	1	0	0	.500	.833
Lew Burdette	.273	11	1	3	1	0	0	0	1	2	0	1	0	1	.333	.364

Hit Worst Against

	Avg	AB	R	H	2B	3B	HR	RBI	BB	SO	HBP	GDP	SB	CS	OBP	Slg
Boo Ferriss	.167	6	0	1	0	0	0	0	0	2	0	0	0	0	.167	.167
Mickey Harris	.200	5	0	1	0	0	0	1	0	1	0	0	0	0	.200	.200
Tiny Bonham	.200	5	1	1	1	0	0	0	0	0	0	0	0	0	.200	.400

Lonnie Smith

Bats: Right, Throws: Right

Batting	Avg	G	AB	R	H	2B	3B	HR	RBI	BB	SO	HBP	GDP	SB	CS	OBP	Slg
Totals	.278	63	205	28	57	14	2	4	17	16	38	4	2	8	9	.341	.424
Home	.302	32	96	16	29	7	0	3	8	8	17	3	0	5	5	.370	.469
Away	.257	31	109	12	28	7	2	1	9	8	21	1	2	3	4	.314	.385
vs. Left	.227	19	44	4	10	2	0	1	1	5	12	1	0	4	4	.320	.341
vs. Right	.292	60	161	24	47	12	2	3	16	11	26	3	2	4	5	.347	.447
Scoring Pos.	.286	42	42	6	12	3	0	1	14	7	5	1	0	3	2	.392	.429
Close & Late	.417	31	24	3	10	2	0	1	2	7	7	1	1	0	1	.563	.625
None on/out	.300	48	80	1	24	6	1	1	1	7	15	1	0	0	0	.364	.438
None on	.277	55	137	3	38	10	2	3	3	8	26	3	0	0	0	.331	.445
Runners on	.279	55	68	7	19	4	0	1	14	8	12	1	2	8	9	.359	.382
Batting #1	.288	42	160	21	46	12	0	3	10	14	29	2	2	8	9	.352	.419
Batting #3	.273	3	11	1	3	0	0	0	1	0	1	1	0	0	0	.308	.273
Batting #6	.273	3	11	3	3	2	1	0	0	1	2	0	0	0	0	.333	.636

Hit Best Against

	Avg	AB	R	H	2B	3B	HR	RBI	BB	SO	HBP	GDP	SB	CS	OBP	Slg
Pete Vuckovich	.500	8	3	4	2	1	0	1	0	0	0	0	0	0	.500	1.000
Dennis Lamp	.400	5	0	2	1	0	0	1	0	2	0	0	0	0	.400	.600
Danny Cox	.375	8	0	3	1	0	0	0	0	0	0	0	0	0	.375	.500

Hit Worst Against

	Avg	AB	R	H	2B	3B	HR	RBI	BB	SO	HBP	GDP	SB	CS	OBP	Slg
Doyle Alexander	.000	6	0	0	0	0	0	0	0	2	0	0	0	0	.000	.000
Kevin Tapani	.000	6	0	0	0	0	0	0	0	1	0	0	0	0	.000	.000
John Tudor	.125	8	1	1	0	0	0	0	1	3	0	0	1	1	.222	.125

Ozzie Smith

Bats: Both, Throws: Right

Batting	Avg	G	AB	R	H	2B	3B	HR	RBI	BB	SO	HBP	GDP	SB	CS	OBP	Slg
Totals	.236	42	144	14	34	1	2	1	10	20	9	0	3	6	1	.325	.292
Home	.250	21	72	9	18	1	1	1	6	12	5	0	1	4	1	.353	.333
Away	.222	21	72	5	16	0	1	0	4	8	4	0	2	2	0	.296	.250
vs. Left	.151	22	53	2	8	1	0	0	1	10	4	0	3	2	1	.286	.170
vs. Right	.286	41	91	12	26	0	2	1	9	10	5	0	0	4	0	.350	.363
Scoring Pos.	.235	31	34	1	8	0	0	0	8	10	1	0	2	3	0	.391	.235
Close & Late	.350	20	20	2	7	0	1	1	3	2	0	0	0	1	0	.409	.600
None on/out	.111	24	27	0	3	0	1	0	0	5	3	0	0	0	0	.250	.185
None on	.207	41	92	0	19	1	1	1	1	9	7	0	0	0	0	.277	.272
Runners on	.288	36	52	1	15	0	1	0	9	11	2	0	3	6	1	.400	.327
Batting #1	.118	5	17	1	2	0	0	0	0	3	1	0	1	0	0	.250	.118
Batting #2	.207	23	82	10	17	0	2	1	6	10	8	0	1	3	1	.290	.293
Batting #8	.500	6	20	0	10	1	0	0	3	4	0	0	0	2	0	.560	.550
Batting #9	.200	8	25	3	5	0	0	0	1	3	0	0	1	1	0	.286	.200

Hit Best Against

	Avg	AB	R	H	2B	3B	HR	RBI	BB	SO	HBP	GDP	SB	CS	OBP	Slg
Orel Hershiser	.429	7	0	3	0	0	0	0	0	1	0	0	0	0	.429	.429
F. Valenzuela	.400	5	1	2	0	0	0	0	1	0	0	0	1	0	.500	.400
Pete Vuckovich	.333	6	1	2	0	0	0	1	1	0	0	0	0	0	.429	.333

Hit Worst Against

	Avg	AB	R	H	2B	3B	HR	RBI	BB	SO	HBP	GDP	SB	CS	OBP	Slg
C. Leibrandt	.000	7	0	0	0	0	0	0	1	0	0	1	0	0	.125	.000
Mike Caldwell	.000	6	1	0	0	0	0	0	1	0	0	1	0	0	.143	.000
Danny Jackson	.000	5	0	0	0	0	0	0	2	0	0	0	1	0	.286	.000

Reggie Smith

Bats: Both, Throws: Right

Batting	Avg	G	AB	R	H	2B	3B	HR	RBI	BB	SO	HBP	GDP	SB	CS	OBP	Slg
Totals	.234	32	107	17	25	3	1	6	17	10	20	1	3	1	3	.303	.449
Home	.182	15	55	9	10	0	1	2	6	4	9	0	1	0	2	.237	.327
Away	.294	15	51	8	15	3	0	4	10	6	10	1	2	1	1	.379	.588
vs. Left	.162	15	37	0	6	0	0	0	3	5	7	0	0	1	1	.256	.162
vs. Right	.271	32	70	17	19	3	1	6	14	5	13	1	3	0	2	.329	.600
Scoring Pos.	.333	21	21	0	7	0	0	1	9	2	5	1	1	0	0	.400	.476
Close & Late	.063	14	16	0	1	1	0	0	0	1	4	0	1	0	1	.118	.125
None on/out	.150	18	20	0	3	0	0	1	1	2	1	0	0	0	0	.227	.300
None on	.188	27	64	0	12	2	0	3	3	6	12	0	0	0	0	.257	.359
Runners on	.302	29	43	0	13	1	1	3	14	4	8	1	3	1	3	.367	.581
Batting #3	.215	20	79	14	17	2	1	4	12	8	16	1	3	1	2	.295	.418
Batting #5	.200	3	10	1	2	0	0	1	1	2	1	0	0	0	0	.333	.500
Batting #6	.273	3	11	2	3	1	0	1	2	0	0	0	0	0	0	.273	.636

Hit Best Against

	Avg	AB	R	H	2B	3B	HR	RBI	BB	SO	HBP	GDP	SB	CS	OBP	Slg
Nelson Briles	.400	5	1	2	0	0	1	1	0	0	0	0	0	0	.400	1.000
Catfish Hunter	.333	9	4	3	1	0	1	2	0	1	0	1	0	0	.333	.778
Mike Torrez	.286	7	3	2	0	0	1	1	1	1	0	2	0	0	.375	.714

Hit Worst Against

	Avg	AB	R	H	2B	3B	HR	RBI	BB	SO	HBP	GDP	SB	CS	OBP	Slg
Bob Gibson	.111	9	0	1	0	0	0	0	1	2	0	0	0	1	.200	.111
Ron Guidry	.125	8	0	1	0	0	0	0	1	2	0	0	0	0	.222	.125
Steve Carlton	.154	13	2	2	0	0	0	0	1	2	0	0	0	0	.214	.154

John Smoltz

Throws: Right, Bats: Right

Pitching	ERA	W	L	Sv	G	GS	IP	BB	SO	Avg	R	H	2B	3B	HR	OBP	Slg
Totals	2.35	10	3	0	20	20	137.2	50	132	.214	41	110	24	3	8	.286	.320
Home	2.44	3	2	0	9	9	62.2	21	64	.226	21	53	12	1	6	.291	.363
Away	2.28	7	1	0	11	11	75.0	29	68	.204	20	57	12	2	2	.282	.283

	Avg	AB	R	H	2B	3B	HR	RBI	BB	SO	HBP	GDP	OBP	Slg
vs. Left	.206	262	0	54	10	2	3	19	32	63	2	2	.295	.294
vs. Right	.223	251	0	56	14	1	5	18	18	69	0	2	.275	.347
Scoring Pos.	.206	107	29	22	5	0	1	25	12	28	0	2	.281	.280
Close & Late	.250	52	6	13	3	0	1	4	3	8	0	2	.291	.365
None on/out	.182	132	0	24	5	1	2	2	13	37	1	2	.260	.280
None on	.207	309	10	64	14	2	6	6	28	87	1	2	.275	.324
Runners on	.225	204	31	46	10	1	2	31	22	45	1	2	.301	.314

Pitched Best Against

	Avg	AB	R	H	2B	3B	HR	RBI	BB	SO	HBP	GDP	SB	CS	OBP	Slg
Jeff King	.000	9	1	0	0	0	0	0	0	1	0	0	0	0	.000	.000
Ozzie Smith	.000	8	0	0	0	0	0	0	0	1	0	0	0	0	.000	.000
Doug Drabek	.000	5	0	0	0	0	0	0	1	3	0	0	0	0	.167	.000

Pitched Worst Against

	Avg	AB	R	H	2B	3B	HR	RBI	BB	SO	HBP	GDP	SB	CS	OBP	Slg
Pat Borders	.600	5	1	3	2	0	0	2	1	0	0	0	0	0	.667	1.000
Gary Gaetti	.600	5	0	3	0	0	0	0	1	1	0	0	0	0	.667	.600
Brian Harper	.500	6	1	3	1	0	0	0	0	0	0	0	0	0	.500	.667

Duke Snider

Bats: Left, Throws: Right

Batting	Avg	G	AB	R	H	2B	3B	HR	RBI	BB	SO	HBP	GDP	SB	CS	OBP	Slg
Totals	.286	36	133	21	38	8	0	11	26	13	33	1	2	1	0	.351	.594
Home	.379	18	66	16	25	5	0	8	17	10	14	0	1	0	0	.461	.818
Away	.194	18	67	5	13	3	0	3	9	3	19	1	1	1	0	.236	.373
vs. Left	.213	18	47	0	10	2	0	2	9	0	16	0	1	1	0	.208	.383
vs. Right	.326	36	86	21	28	6	0	9	17	13	17	1	1	0	0	.420	.709
Scoring Pos.	.370	22	27	0	10	2	0	4	17	6	3	0	1	0	0	.471	.889
Close & Late	.286	12	14	0	4	1	0	0	2	2	4	1	0	0	0	.412	.357
None on/out	.357	21	28	0	10	2	0	4	4	0	7	0	0	0	0	.357	.857
None on	.270	34	74	0	20	4	0	6	6	3	19	1	0	0	0	.308	.568
Runners on	.305	33	59	0	18	4	0	5	20	10	14	0	2	1	0	.400	.627
Batting #3	.299	28	107	18	32	6	0	9	20	10	29	1	2	0	0	.361	.607
Batting #6	.333	3	12	2	4	2	0	1	4	1	3	0	0	1	0	.385	.750

Hit Best Against

	Avg	AB	R	H	2B	3B	HR	RBI	BB	SO	HBP	GDP	SB	CS	OBP	Slg
Johnny Sain	.800	5	1	4	1	0	1	3	0	0	1	0	0	0	.833	1.600
Johnny Kucks	.571	7	1	4	0	0	1	3	0	0	0	0	0	0	.571	1.000
Bob Turley	.400	5	0	2	1	0	0	0	3	3	0	0	0	0	.625	.600

Hit Worst Against

	Avg	AB	R	H	2B	3B	HR	RBI	BB	SO	HBP	GDP	SB	CS	OBP	Slg
Don Larsen	.000	5	0	0	0	0	0	0	1	1	0	0	0	0	.167	.000
Ed Lopat	.143	14	1	2	0	0	0	0	0	2	0	1	1	0	.143	.143
Allie Reynolds	.188	16	2	3	2	0	1	2	1	5	0	0	0	0	.235	.500

Warren Spahn

Throws: Left, Bats: Left

Pitching	ERA	W	L	Sv	G	GS	IP	BB	SO	Avg	R	H	2B	3B	HR	OBP	Slg
Totals	3.05	4	3	0	8	6	56.0	13	32	.225	19	47	7	2	5	.269	.349
Home	4.00	2	2	0	5	4	36.0	9	18	.266	16	37	4	1	5	.309	.417
Away	1.35	2	1	0	3	2	20.0	4	14	.143	3	10	3	1	0	.189	.214

	Avg	AB	R	H	2B	3B	HR	RBI	BB	SO	HBP	GDP	OBP	Slg
vs. Left	.219	64	0	14	2	0	0	3	8	13	0	0	.301	.250
vs. Right	.228	145	19	33	5	2	5	14	5	19	0	0	.253	.393
Scoring Pos.	.231	39	0	9	1	0	1	11	2	6	0	0	.262	.333
Close & Late	.208	48	3	10	0	1	2	5	2	14	0	0	.240	.375
None on/out	.211	57	0	12	4	0	1	1	1	8	0	0	.224	.333
None on	.219	137	0	30	6	1	3	3	7	21	0	0	.257	.343
Runners on	.236	72	0	17	1	1	2	14	6	11	0	0	.291	.361

Pitched Best Against

	Avg	AB	R	H	2B	3B	HR	RBI	BB	SO	HBP	GDP	SB	CS	OBP	Slg
Whitey Ford	.000	6	1	0	0	0	0	0	2	2	0	0	0	0	.250	.000
Andy Carey	.125	16	0	2	1	0	0	1	0	2	0	0	0	0	.125	.188
Tony Kubek	.133	15	1	2	0	0	0	0	0	2	0	1	0	0	.133	.133

Pitched Worst Against

	Avg	AB	R	H	2B	3B	HR	RBI	BB	SO	HBP	GDP	SB	CS	OBP	Slg
Lou Boudreau	.600	5	1	3	2	0	0	1	0	0	0	0	0	0	.600	1.000
Jerry Coleman	.500	6	1	3	1	0	0	0	0	0	0	0	0	0	.500	.667
Larry Doby	.400	5	0	2	1	0	0	1	0	2	0	0	0	0	.400	.600

Tris Speaker

Bats: Left, Throws: Left

Batting	Avg	G	AB	R	H	2B	3B	HR	RBI	BB	SO	HBP	GDP	SB	CS	OBP	Slg
Totals	.306	20	72	12	22	3	4	0	3	11	4	0	1	1	4	.398	.458
Home	.375	11	40	9	15	0	3	0	3	6	1	0	0	0	1	.457	.525
Away	.219	9	32	3	7	3	1	0	0	5	3	0	1	1	3	.324	.375
vs. Left	.174	8	23	0	4	1	0	0	0	2	2	0	0	1	0	.240	.217
vs. Right	.367	20	49	12	18	2	4	0	3	9	2	0	1	0	4	.466	.571
Scoring Pos.	.250	17	16	0	4	0	1	0	3	5	0	0	1	0	1	.429	.375
Close & Late	.400	10	10	0	4	1	0	0	1	1	1	0	0	0	0	.455	.500
None on/out	.100	9	10	0	1	0	0	0	0	1	0	0	0	0	0	.182	.100
None on	.341	20	41	0	14	3	3	0	0	5	3	0	0	0	0	.413	.561
Runners on	.258	20	31	0	8	0	1	0	3	6	1	0	1	1	4	.378	.323
Batting #3	.306	20	72	12	22	3	4	0	3	11	4	0	1	1	4	.398	.458

Hit Best Against

	Avg	AB	R	H	2B	3B	HR	RBI	BB	SO	HBP	GDP	SB	CS	OBP	Slg
Burleigh Grimes	.500	8	1	4	1	1	0	1	2	0	0	0	0	0	.600	.875
C. Mathewson	.417	12	2	5	0	1	0	2	1	1	0	0	0	0	.462	.583
Pete Alexander	.400	5	2	2	0	1	0	0	3	0	0	0	0	0	.625	.800

Hit Worst Against

	Avg	AB	R	H	2B	3B	HR	RBI	BB	SO	HBP	GDP	SB	CS	OBP	Slg
Rube Marquard	.091	11	0	1	0	0	0	0	1	1	0	0	1	0	.167	.091
Jeff Tesreau	.200	10	2	2	0	1	0	0	2	1	0	1	0	1	.333	.400

Mike Stanton

Throws: Left, Bats: Left

Pitching	ERA	W	L	Sv	G	GS	IP	BB	SO	Avg	R	H	2B	3B	HR	OBP	Slg
Totals	0.64	1	1	1	25	0	28.0	14	26	.207	4	19	2	0	1	.306	.261
Home	0.75	1	0	0	12	0	12.0	6	10	.244	2	10	2	0	1	.340	.366
Away	0.56	0	1	1	13	0	16.0	8	16	.176	2	9	0	0	0	.279	.176

	Avg	AB	R	H	2B	3B	HR	RBI	BB	SO	HBP	GDP	OBP	Slg
vs. Left	.133	30	0	4	0	0	0	1	4	14	0	2	.229	.133
vs. Right	.242	62	0	15	2	0	1	2	10	12	0	2	.342	.323
Scoring Pos.	.000	29	3	0	0	0	0	2	7	11	0	2	.184	.000
Close & Late	.200	65	1	13	1	0	1	2	8	20	0	2	.284	.262
None on/out	.440	25	0	11	0	0	0	0	1	6	0	2	.462	.440
None on	.347	49	1	17	2	0	1	1	4	12	0	2	.396	.449
Runners on	.047	43	3	2	0	0	0	2	10	14	0	2	.218	.047

Pitched Best Against

	Avg	AB	R	H	2B	3B	HR	RBI	BB	SO	HBP	GDP	SB	CS	OBP	Slg
Barry Bonds	.200	5	1	1	0	0	0	0	2	1	0	0	0	0	.429	.200
Brian Harper	.200	5	0	1	0	0	0	0	0	1	0	0	0	0	.200	.200

Willie Stargell

Bats: Left, Throws: Left

Batting	Avg	G	AB	R	H	2B	3B	HR	RBI	BB	SO	HBP	GDP	SB	CS	OBP	Slg
Totals	.278	36	133	18	37	10	0	7	20	17	34	1	3	0	0	.359	.511
Home	.339	16	56	9	19	6	0	2	7	7	11	0	1	0	0	.406	.554
Away	.234	20	77	9	18	4	0	5	13	10	23	1	2	0	0	.326	.481
vs. Left	.266	24	64	0	17	7	0	4	12	6	19	0	1	0	0	.324	.563
vs. Right	.290	36	69	18	20	3	0	3	8	11	15	1	2	0	0	.390	.464
Scoring Pos.	.158	28	38	0	6	2	0	2	13	6	12	1	3	0	0	.277	.368
Close & Late	.333	19	21	1	7	3	0	1	4	4	4	0	0	0	0	.423	.619
None on/out	.333	27	36	0	12	1	0	3	3	2	7	0	0	0	0	.368	.611
None on	.373	34	67	0	25	6	0	4	4	4	13	0	0	0	0	.408	.642
Runners on	.182	34	66	0	12	4	0	3	16	13	21	1	3	0	0	.317	.379
Batting #4	.259	30	108	12	28	7	0	5	15	17	29	1	2	0	0	.362	.463
Batting #5	.471	4	17	5	8	3	0	2	5	0	3	0	1	0	0	.444	1.000

Hit Best Against

	Avg	AB	R	H	2B	3B	HR	RBI	BB	SO	HBP	GDP	SB	CS	OBP	Slg
Scott McGregor	.750	8	3	6	3	0	1	2	0	1	0	0	0	0	.750	1.500
Don Sutton	.429	7	1	3	0	0	1	1	0	2	0	0	0	0	.429	.857
Gary Nolan	.300	10	0	3	1	0	0	0	0	3	0	0	0	0	.300	.400

Hit Worst Against

	Avg	AB	R	H	2B	3B	HR	RBI	BB	SO	HBP	GDP	SB	CS	OBP	Slg
Dave McNally	.000	6	0	0	0	0	0	0	2	2	0	0	0	0	.250	.000
Gaylord Perry	.000	6	0	0	0	0	0	0	1	2	1	0	0	0	.250	.000
Mike Flanagan	.143	7	1	1	0	0	1	3	0	2	0	0	0	0	.125	.571

Dave Stewart

Throws: Right, Bats: Right

Pitching	ERA	W	L	Sv	G	GS	IP	BB	SO	Avg	R	H	2B	3B	HR	OBP	Slg
Totals	2.77	10	6	0	22	18	133.0	48	73	.206	45	99	13	0	13	.282	.315
Home	2.50	5	3	0	9	9	68.1	24	33	.194	22	48	7	0	4	.265	.270
Away	3.06	5	3	0	13	9	64.2	24	40	.220	23	51	6	0	9	.300	.362

	Avg	AB	R	H	2B	3B	HR	RBI	BB	SO	HBP	GDP	OBP	Slg
vs. Left	.208	259	0	54	6	0	6	24	25	34	1	7	.279	.301
vs. Right	.204	221	10	45	7	0	7	16	23	39	3	7	.286	.330
Scoring Pos.	.176	85	14	15	0	0	3	27	11	17	1	7	.270	.282
Close & Late	.347	49	11	17	2	0	2	9	2	3	1	7	.377	.510
None on/out	.190	126	0	24	4	0	3	3	15	17	1	7	.282	.294
None on	.211	304	16	64	11	0	8	8	34	45	2	7	.294	.326
Runners on	.199	176	19	35	2	0	5	32	14	28	2	7	.262	.295

Pitched Best Against

	Avg	AB	R	H	2B	3B	HR	RBI	BB	SO	HBP	GDP	SB	CS	OBP	Slg
Fred McGriff	.000	8	0	0	0	0	0	0	0	1	0	0	0	0	.000	.000
Todd Benzinger	.000	7	0	0	0	0	0	0	0	1	0	1	0	0	.000	.000
Marty Barrett	.000	5	1	0	0	0	0	0	1	0	0	0	0	0	.167	.000

Pitched Worst Against

	Avg	AB	R	H	2B	3B	HR	RBI	BB	SO	HBP	GDP	SB	CS	OBP	Slg
Devon White	.667	6	0	4	1	0	0	1	2	0	0	0	0	1	.750	.833
Chris Sabo	.600	5	0	3	1	0	0	0	1	1	0	0	0	1	.667	.800
Dave Winfield	.571	7	3	4	1	0	2	2	1	0	0	0	0	0	.625	1.571

Darryl Strawberry

Bats: Left, Throws: Left

Batting	Avg	G	AB	R	H	2B	3B	HR	RBI	BB	SO	HBP	GDP	SB	CS	OBP	Slg
Totals	.243	33	111	17	27	4	0	7	18	15	34	0	1	4	2	.331	.468
Home	.184	16	49	6	9	1	0	4	11	7	17	0	1	3	0	.286	.449
Away	.290	17	62	11	18	3	0	3	7	8	17	0	0	1	2	.366	.484
vs. Left	.250	17	36	0	9	0	0	2	8	2	13	0	0	1	0	.289	.417
vs. Right	.240	32	75	17	18	4	0	5	10	13	21	0	1	3	2	.348	.493
Scoring Pos.	.219	22	32	1	7	2	0	2	12	4	8	0	1	0	0	.297	.469
Close & Late	.333	19	21	3	7	2	0	1	3	4	2	0	1	1	0	.440	.571
None on/out	.188	27	32	1	6	1	0	2	2	5	9	0	0	0	0	.297	.406
None on	.219	30	64	2	14	2	0	4	4	7	24	0	0	0	0	.296	.438
Runners on	.277	29	47	2	13	2	0	3	14	8	10	0	1	4	2	.375	.511
Batting #4	.300	7	30	5	9	2	0	1	6	2	5	0	1	0	1	.344	.467
Batting #5	.204	14	49	8	10	2	0	3	6	8	19	0	0	4	1	.310	.429
Batting #6	.250	12	32	4	8	0	0	3	6	5	10	0	0	0	0	.351	.531

Hit Best Against

	Avg	AB	R	H	2B	3B	HR	RBI	BB	SO	HBP	GDP	SB	CS	OBP	Slg
Bob Knepper	.333	6	1	2	0	0	1	3	0	3	0	0	0	0	.333	.833
Orel Hershiser	.250	12	2	3	2	0	0	2	0	1	0	1	0	0	.250	.417

Hit Worst Against

	Avg	AB	R	H	2B	3B	HR	RBI	BB	SO	HBP	GDP	SB	CS	OBP	Slg
John Smoltz	.000	5	0	0	0	0	0	0	1	1	0	0	0	0	.167	.000
Bruce Hurst	.111	9	0	1	0	0	0	0	1	3	0	0	1	0	.200	.111
Mike Scott	.143	7	0	1	0	0	0	0	0	4	0	0	1	0	.143	.143

Don Sutton

Throws: Right, Bats: Right

Pitching	ERA	W	L	Sv	G	GS	IP	BB	SO	Avg	R	H	2B	3B	HR	OBP	Slg
Totals	3.68	6	4	0	15	14	100.1	16	61	.242	46	92	17	1	12	.278	.387
Home	3.19	5	2	0	8	8	59.1	9	39	.238	24	53	12	0	6	.270	.372
Away	4.39	1	2	0	7	6	41.0	7	22	.248	22	39	5	1	6	.287	.408

	Avg	AB	R	H	2B	3B	HR	RBI	BB	SO	HBP	GDP	OBP	Slg
vs. Left	.277	206	0	57	10	1	7	24	11	29	2	1	.320	.437
vs. Right	.201	174	46	35	7	0	5	14	5	32	1	1	.227	.328
Scoring Pos.	.250	64	0	16	6	0	3	26	4	5	0	1	.290	.484
Close & Late	.368	38	2	14	6	0	0	6	1	4	0	1	.385	.526
None on/out	.269	104	0	28	2	1	4	4	5	19	1	1	.309	.423
None on	.252	242	0	61	7	1	9	9	10	44	3	1	.290	.401
Runners on	.225	138	0	31	10	0	3	29	6	17	0	1	.255	.362

Pitched Best Against

	Avg	AB	R	H	2B	3B	HR	RBI	BB	SO	HBP	GDP	SB	CS	OBP	Slg
Al Oliver	.000	7	0	0	0	0	0	0	0	2	0	0	0	0	.000	.000
Rennie Stennett	.000	7	0	0	0	0	0	0	0	1	0	1	0	0	.000	.000
Bill North	.000	6	1	0	0	0	0	0	0	1	0	1	1	0	.000	.000

Pitched Worst Against

	Avg	AB	R	H	2B	3B	HR	RBI	BB	SO	HBP	GDP	SB	CS	OBP	Slg
Brian Doyle	.500	6	2	3	1	0	0	2	0	0	0	0	0	0	.500	.667
Ted Sizemore	.500	6	2	3	0	0	0	1	0	0	0	1	0	0	.500	.500
Chris Chambliss	.444	9	1	4	0	0	0	1	1	0	0	0	0	0	.500	.444

Gene Tenace

Bats: Right, Throws: Right

Batting	Avg	G	AB	R	H	2B	3B	HR	RBI	BB	SO	HBP	GDP	SB	CS	OBP	Slg
Totals	.158	42	114	10	18	3	0	4	14	30	33	1	4	1	4	.338	.289
Home	.140	22	57	8	8	1	0	2	5	16	18	1	1	1	3	.338	.263
Away	.175	20	57	2	10	2	0	2	9	14	15	0	3	0	1	.338	.316
vs. Left	.115	24	52	0	6	0	0	1	5	16	17	0	1	1	2	.324	.173
vs. Right	.194	42	62	10	12	3	0	3	9	14	16	1	3	0	2	.351	.387
Scoring Pos.	.200	21	30	0	6	2	0	1	10	8	7	0	1	0	2	.368	.367
Close & Late	.167	22	24	2	4	0	0	0	1	6	6	0	1	0	0	.333	.167
None on/out	.174	22	23	0	4	1	0	0	0	6	11	1	0	0	0	.367	.217
None on	.150	37	60	0	9	1	0	2	2	20	22	1	0	0	0	.370	.267
Runners on	.167	35	54	0	9	2	0	2	12	10	11	0	4	1	4	.297	.315
Batting #5	.143	14	42	3	6	2	0	0	3	14	14	1	2	0	2	.368	.190
Batting #6	.130	9	23	1	3	0	0	0	1	7	7	0	2	1	0	.333	.130
Batting #7	.163	14	43	6	7	0	0	4	8	8	9	0	0	0	2	.294	.442

Hit Worst Against

	Avg	AB	R	H	2B	3B	HR	RBI	BB	SO	HBP	GDP	SB	CS	OBP	Slg
Jon Matlack	.000	6	0	0	0	0	0	1	1	2	0	0	0	0	.143	.000
Mickey Lolich	.000	8	1	0	0	0	0	0	0	2	0	0	0	0	.000	.000
Dave McNally	.000	5	0	0	0	0	0	0	1	3	0	0	0	0	.167	.000

Bill Terry

Bats: Left, Throws: Left

Batting	Avg	G	AB	R	H	2B	3B	HR	RBI	BB	SO	HBP	GDP	SB	CS	OBP	Slg
Totals	.295	16	61	7	18	1	1	2	6	4	5	0	0	0	0	.338	.443
Home	.357	8	28	5	10	1	1	0	2	2	1	0	0	0	0	.400	.464
Away	.242	8	33	2	8	0	0	2	4	2	4	0	0	0	0	.286	.424
vs. Left	.235	6	17	0	4	0	0	0	2	0	2	0	0	0	0	.235	.235
vs. Right	.318	16	44	7	14	1	1	2	4	4	3	0	0	0	0	.375	.523
Scoring Pos.	.267	10	15	0	4	0	0	0	4	1	1	0	0	0	0	.313	.267
Close & Late	.154	11	13	1	2	0	0	0	2	2	0	0	0	0	0	.267	.154
None on/out	.333	11	12	0	4	0	0	0	0	1	2	0	0	0	0	.385	.333
None on	.294	16	34	0	10	0	1	2	2	1	2	0	0	0	0	.314	.529
Runners on	.296	14	27	0	8	1	0	0	4	3	3	0	0	0	0	.367	.333
Batting #3	.255	11	47	4	12	1	0	1	5	1	4	0	0	0	0	.271	.340
Batting #5	.462	4	13	3	6	0	1	1	1	3	1	0	0	0	0	.563	.846

Hit Best Against

	Avg	AB	R	H	2B	3B	HR	RBI	BB	SO	HBP	GDP	SB	CS	OBP	Slg
Walter Johnson	.571	7	2	4	0	1	1	1	3	0	0	0	0	0	.700	1.286
G. Crowder	.500	6	1	3	1	0	0	0	0	0	0	0	0	0	.500	.667
Montie Weaver	.400	5	1	2	0	0	1	1	0	0	0	0	0	0	.400	1.000

Ralph Terry

Throws: Right, Bats: Right

Pitching	ERA	W	L	Sv	G	GS	IP	BB	SO	Avg	R	H	2B	3B	HR	OBP	Slg
Totals	2.93	2	4	0	9	6	46.0	6	31	.236	17	41	7	3	5	.265	.397
Home	2.96	1	2	0	5	3	27.1	5	22	.238	11	25	5	2	2	.273	.381
Away	2.89	1	2	0	4	3	18.2	1	9	.232	6	16	2	1	3	.254	.420

	Avg	AB	R	H	2B	3B	HR	RBI	BB	SO	HBP	GDP	OBP	Slg
vs. Left	.214	70	0	15	4	1	2	9	4	9	0	0	.257	.386
vs. Right	.250	104	17	26	3	2	3	7	2	22	1	0	.271	.404
Scoring Pos.	.296	27	0	8	2	1	1	10	2	2	0	0	.345	.556
Close & Late	.308	26	2	8	2	0	2	3	0	8	0	0	.308	.615
None on/out	.265	49	0	13	1	0	3	3	1	7	0	0	.280	.469
None on	.226	115	0	26	3	2	3	3	4	20	1	0	.258	.365
Runners on	.254	59	0	15	4	1	2	13	2	11	0	0	.279	.458

Pitched Best Against

	Avg	AB	R	H	2B	3B	HR	RBI	BB	SO	HBP	GDP	SB	CS	OBP	Slg
Jim Davenport	.000	10	0	0	0	0	0	0	0	4	0	0	0	0	.000	.000
Vada Pinson	.000	6	0	0	0	0	0	0	0	1	0	0	0	0	.000	.000
Willie Mays	.091	11	0	1	1	0	0	0	0	2	0	0	0	0	.091	.182

Pitched Worst Against

	Avg	AB	R	H	2B	3B	HR	RBI	BB	SO	HBP	GDP	SB	CS	OBP	Slg
Eddie Kasko	.500	6	1	3	0	0	0	0	0	2	0	0	0	0	.500	.500
Jack Sanford	.429	7	0	3	0	0	0	0	0	2	0	0	0	0	.429	.429
Felipe Alou	.300	10	0	3	0	1	0	0	0	2	0	0	0	0	.300	.500

Jim Thome

Bats: Left, Throws: Right

Batting	Avg	G	AB	R	H	2B	3B	HR	RBI	BB	SO	HBP	GDP	SB	CS	OBP	Slg
Totals	.219	35	114	17	25	1	1	6	15	16	35	1	3	0	0	.321	.404
Home	.222	18	54	10	12	1	1	4	9	11	17	0	0	0	0	.354	.500
Away	.217	17	60	7	13	0	0	2	6	5	18	1	3	0	0	.288	.317
vs. Left	.162	21	37	4	6	0	0	1	3	4	14	1	1	0	0	.262	.243
vs. Right	.247	30	77	13	19	1	1	5	12	12	21	0	2	0	0	.348	.481
Scoring Pos.	.214	28	28	11	6	0	0	1	7	6	12	1	1	0	0	.371	.321
Close & Late	.208	20	24	2	5	0	0	0	1	4	6	0	1	0	0	.321	.208
None on/out	.036	25	28	0	1	1	0	0	0	3	10	0	0	0	0	.129	.071
None on	.203	33	59	2	12	1	1	2	2	7	16	0	0	0	0	.288	.356
Runners on	.236	31	55	15	13	0	0	4	13	9	19	1	3	0	0	.354	.455
Batting #3	.300	3	10	1	3	0	0	0	0	1	5	1	0	0	0	.417	.300
Batting #4	.158	6	19	2	3	0	0	0	0	4	5	0	0	0	0	.304	.158
Batting #6	.218	14	55	7	12	0	1	4	10	5	16	0	1	0	0	.283	.473
Batting #7	.208	8	24	5	5	0	0	1	3	4	7	0	2	0	0	.321	.333

Hit Best Against

	Avg	AB	R	H	2B	3B	HR	RBI	BB	SO	HBP	GDP	SB	CS	OBP	Slg
L. Hernandez	.333	6	3	2	0	1	1	1	1	0	0	0	0	0	.429	1.167
Greg Maddux	.333	6	0	2	0	0	0	1	0	0	0	0	0	0	.333	.333
Scott Erickson	.250	8	2	2	0	0	0	0	1	3	0	0	0	0	.333	.250

Hit Worst Against

	Avg	AB	R	H	2B	3B	HR	RBI	BB	SO	HBP	GDP	SB	CS	OBP	Slg
Tom Glavine	.000	6	0	0	0	0	0	0	0	3	0	0	0	0	.000	.000
Mike Mussina	.000	6	1	0	0	0	0	0	3	4	0	0	0	0	.333	.000

Luis Tiant

Throws: Right, Bats: Right

Pitching	ERA	W	L	Sv	G	GS	IP	BB	SO	Avg	R	H	2B	3B	HR	OBP	Slg
Totals	2.86	3	0	0	5	4	34.2	11	20	.216	13	29	7	2	2	.276	.343
Home	2.45	2	0	0	4	3	25.2	7	16	.200	9	20	4	1	2	.252	.320
Away	4.00	1	0	0	1	1	9.0	4	4	.265	4	9	3	1	0	.342	.412

	Avg	AB	R	H	2B	3B	HR	RBI	BB	SO	HBP	GDP	OBP	Slg
vs. Left	.277	65	0	18	4	2	1	6	9	5	0	0	.365	.446
vs. Right	.159	69	13	11	3	0	1	8	2	15	0	0	.183	.246
Scoring Pos.	.206	34	0	7	3	2	1	12	3	5	0	0	.270	.500
Close & Late	.261	23	2	6	3	0	0	3	2	2	0	0	.320	.391
None on/out	.250	32	0	8	0	0	1	1	3	3	0	0	.314	.344
None on	.227	75	0	17	2	0	1	1	6	10	0	0	.284	.293
Runners on	.203	59	0	12	5	2	1	13	5	10	0	0	.266	.407

Pitched Best Against

	Avg	AB	R	H	2B	3B	HR	RBI	BB	SO	HBP	GDP	SB	CS	OBP	Slg
Tony Perez	.083	12	0	1	0	0	0	0	0	5	0	0	0	0	.083	.083
D. Concepcion	.083	12	1	1	1	0	0	1	0	1	0	0	0	0	.083	.167
Johnny Bench	.167	12	0	2	1	0	0	2	0	3	0	0	0	0	.167	.250

Pitched Worst Against

	Avg	AB	R	H	2B	3B	HR	RBI	BB	SO	HBP	GDP	SB	CS	OBP	Slg
Cesar Geronimo	.556	9	1	5	0	1	1	2	2	1	0	0	0	0	.636	1.111
George Foster	.417	12	1	5	1	0	0	2	0	0	0	0	0	1	.417	.500
Ken Griffey Sr.	.364	11	2	4	2	1	0	3	1	0	0	0	0	0	.417	.727

Joe Tinker

Bats: Right, Throws: Right

Batting	Avg	G	AB	R	H	2B	3B	HR	RBI	BB	SO	HBP	GDP	SB	CS	OBP	Slg
Totals	.235	21	68	12	16	2	0	1	6	7	9	0	0	7	3	.307	.309
Home	.167	11	36	5	6	1	0	1	3	3	8	0	0	2	2	.231	.278
Away	.313	10	32	7	10	1	0	0	3	4	1	0	0	5	1	.389	.344
vs. Left	.133	7	15	0	2	0	0	0	0	1	0	0	0	0	0	.188	.133
vs. Right	.264	21	53	12	14	2	0	1	6	6	9	0	0	7	3	.339	.358
Scoring Pos.	.125	15	16	0	2	0	0	0	4	2	3	0	0	5	0	.222	.125
Close & Late	.375	11	8	1	3	0	0	1	3	1	2	0	0	1	0	.444	.750
None on/out	.200	19	25	0	5	0	0	0	0	1	3	0	0	0	0	.231	.200
None on	.238	21	42	0	10	2	0	0	0	4	5	0	0	0	0	.304	.286
Runners on	.231	19	26	0	6	0	0	1	6	3	4	0	0	7	3	.310	.346
Batting #6	.167	6	18	4	3	0	0	0	1	2	2	0	0	3	0	.250	.167
Batting #7	.297	10	37	4	11	2	0	1	4	2	4	0	0	3	3	.333	.432
Batting #8	.154	5	13	4	2	0	0	0	1	3	3	0	0	1	0	.313	.154

Hit Best Against

	Avg	AB	R	H	2B	3B	HR	RBI	BB	SO	HBP	GDP	SB	CS	OBP	Slg
Jack Coombs	.417	12	1	5	2	0	0	0	1	1	0	0	1	1	.462	.583
George Mullin	.375	8	1	3	0	0	0	1	2	1	0	0	1	1	.500	.375
Doc White	.333	6	1	2	0	0	0	0	1	0	0	0	0	0	.429	.333

Hit Worst Against

	Avg	AB	R	H	2B	3B	HR	RBI	BB	SO	HBP	GDP	SB	CS	OBP	Slg
Ed Walsh	.000	6	1	0	0	0	0	0	0	2	0	0	1	0	.000	.000
Chief Bender	.167	6	1	1	0	0	0	0	1	1	0	0	0	1	.286	.167
W. Bill Donovan	.182	11	3	2	0	0	1	2	1	3	0	0	0	0	.250	.455

Alan Trammell

Bats: Right, Throws: Right

Batting	Avg	G	AB	R	H	2B	3B	HR	RBI	BB	SO	HBP	GDP	SB	CS	OBP	Slg
Totals	.333	13	51	10	17	2	1	3	11	6	5	0	2	1	1	.404	.588
Home	.308	7	26	6	8	1	0	2	7	4	1	0	1	0	0	.400	.577
Away	.360	6	25	4	9	1	1	1	4	2	4	0	1	1	1	.407	.600
vs. Left	.400	8	15	0	6	2	1	1	3	4	1	0	0	0	0	.526	.867
vs. Right	.306	13	36	10	11	0	0	2	8	2	4	0	2	1	1	.342	.472
Scoring Pos.	.462	9	13	0	6	0	0	1	6	3	1	0	0	0	0	.563	.692
Close & Late	.111	9	9	1	1	1	0	0	0	0	1	0	1	0	0	.111	.222
None on/out	.143	7	7	0	1	0	0	1	1	0	0	0	0	0	0	.143	.571
None on	.208	12	24	0	5	0	0	1	1	3	4	0	0	0	0	.296	.333
Runners on	.444	12	27	0	12	2	1	2	10	3	1	0	2	1	1	.500	.815
Batting #2	.419	8	31	7	13	1	1	3	9	5	3	0	0	1	1	.500	.806
Batting #4	.200	5	20	3	4	1	0	0	2	1	2	0	2	0	0	.238	.250

Hit Best Against

	Avg	AB	R	H	2B	3B	HR	RBI	BB	SO	HBP	GDP	SB	CS	OBP	Slg
Frank Viola	.333	6	1	2	1	0	0	0	1	0	0	0	0	0	.429	.500

Hit Worst Against

	Avg	AB	R	H	2B	3B	HR	RBI	BB	SO	HBP	GDP	SB	CS	OBP	Slg
Andy Hawkins	.000	5	0	0	0	0	0	0	0	2	0	0	0	0	.000	.000
Bert Blyleven	.167	6	1	1	0	0	0	1	0	1	0	1	0	0	.167	.167

John Tudor

Throws: Left, Bats: Left

Pitching	ERA	W	L	Sv	G	GS	IP	BB	SO	Avg	R	H	2B	3B	HR	OBP	Slg
Totals	3.41	5	4	0	11	11	63.1	19	44	.259	27	64	10	3	7	.315	.409
Home	2.55	3	2	0	5	5	35.1	9	26	.255	12	35	5	1	4	.301	.394
Away	4.50	2	2	0	6	6	28.0	10	18	.264	15	29	5	2	3	.331	.427

	Avg	AB	R	H	2B	3B	HR	RBI	BB	SO	HBP	GDP	OBP	Slg
vs. Left	.393	28	0	11	0	0	2	5	2	8	0	0	.433	.607
vs. Right	.242	219	27	53	10	3	5	17	17	36	1	0	.300	.384
Scoring Pos.	.208	53	0	11	1	1	1	12	9	9	1	0	.333	.321
Close & Late	.067	15	0	1	0	0	0	0	1	5	1	0	.176	.067
None on/out	.352	71	0	25	5	1	3	3	2	13	0	0	.370	.577
None on	.255	149	0	38	8	2	3	3	9	28	0	0	.297	.396
Runners on	.265	98	0	26	2	1	4	19	10	16	1	0	.339	.429

Pitched Best Against

	Avg	AB	R	H	2B	3B	HR	RBI	BB	SO	HBP	GDP	SB	CS	OBP	Slg
Kent Hrbek	.000	5	0	0	0	0	0	0	0	1	0	0	0	0	.000	.000
Frank White	.000	8	1	0	0	0	0	0	1	0	0	0	0	0	.111	.000
Greg Gagne	.000	5	1	0	0	0	0	0	1	0	0	0	0	0	.167	.000

Pitched Worst Against

	Avg	AB	R	H	2B	3B	HR	RBI	BB	SO	HBP	GDP	SB	CS	OBP	Slg
Kirby Puckett	.600	5	2	3	0	0	0	1	1	0	0	0	1	0	.667	.600
Jeffrey Leonard	.571	7	2	4	0	0	1	1	1	2	0	0	0	0	.625	1.000
Dan Gladden	.500	6	1	3	0	1	0	0	0	0	0	0	0	0	.500	.833

Bob Turley

Throws: Right, Bats: Right

Pitching	ERA	W	L	Sv	G	GS	IP	BB	SO	Avg	R	H	2B	3B	HR	OBP	Slg
Totals	3.19	4	3	1	15	8	53.2	29	46	.218	20	43	7	0	6	.325	.345
Home	0.90	2	0	0	3	2	20.0	6	19	.149	2	10	1	0	2	.219	.254
Away	4.54	2	3	1	12	6	33.2	23	27	.254	18	33	6	0	4	.374	.392

	Avg	AB	R	H	2B	3B	HR	RBI	BB	SO	HBP	GDP	OBP	Slg
vs. Left	.276	87	0	24	3	0	3	7	21	15	1	1	.422	.414
vs. Right	.173	110	20	19	4	0	3	8	8	31	1	1	.235	.291
Scoring Pos.	.214	42	0	9	1	0	0	7	7	6	0	1	.327	.238
Close & Late	.186	43	2	8	1	0	0	3	5	6	0	1	.271	.209
None on/out	.240	50	0	12	3	0	3	3	8	14	1	1	.356	.480
None on	.231	108	0	25	4	0	4	4	18	29	1	1	.346	.380
Runners on	.202	89	0	18	3	0	2	11	11	17	1	1	.297	.303

Pitched Best Against

	Avg	AB	R	H	2B	3B	HR	RBI	BB	SO	HBP	GDP	SB	CS	OBP	Slg
Bill Virdon	.000	6	0	0	0	0	0	0	0	0	0	0	0	0	.000	.000
Johnny Logan	.000	12	0	0	0	0	0	0	1	5	0	0	0	0	.077	.000
Gil Hodges	.000	6	0	0	0	0	0	0	1	1	0	0	0	0	.143	.000

Pitched Worst Against

	Avg	AB	R	H	2B	3B	HR	RBI	BB	SO	HBP	GDP	SB	CS	OBP	Slg
Don Hoak	.600	5	1	3	2	0	0	1	0	0	0	0	0	0	.600	1.000
Smoky Burgess	.600	5	0	3	0	0	0	0	1	0	0	0	0	0	.667	.600
Rocky Nelson	.500	6	2	3	0	0	1	2	0	0	0	0	0	0	.500	1.000

Fernando Valenzuela

Throws: Left, Bats: Left

Pitching	ERA	W	L	Sv	G	GS	IP	BB	SO	Avg	R	H	2B	3B	HR	OBP	Slg
Totals	1.98	5	1	0	9	8	63.2	31	44	.213	14	47	11	0	3	.310	.303
Home	2.31	4	1	0	6	5	39.0	18	25	.246	10	34	6	0	3	.333	.355
Away	1.46	1	0	0	3	3	24.2	13	19	.157	4	13	5	0	0	.271	.217

	Avg	AB	R	H	2B	3B	HR	RBI	BB	SO	HBP	GDP	OBP	Slg
vs. Left	.162	37	0	6	2	0	0	1	5	9	0	1	.262	.216
vs. Right	.222	185	14	41	9	0	3	11	26	34	0	1	.318	.319
Scoring Pos.	.163	49	0	8	2	0	0	8	15	8	0	1	.359	.204
Close & Late	.229	35	0	8	2	0	0	2	9	3	0	1	.386	.286
None on/out	.230	61	0	14	5	0	2	2	6	8	0	1	.299	.410
None on	.228	145	0	33	9	0	2	2	12	30	0	1	.287	.331
Runners on	.182	77	0	14	2	0	1	10	19	13	0	1	.344	.247

Pitched Best Against

	Avg	AB	R	H	2B	3B	HR	RBI	BB	SO	HBP	GDP	SB	CS	OBP	Slg
Jose Cruz	.000	8	0	0	0	0	0	0	0	2	0	0	0	0	.000	.000
Jerry Mumphrey	.000	5	0	0	0	0	0	0	0	1	0	0	0	0	.000	.000
Phil Garner	.000	7	0	0	0	0	0	0	1	2	0	0	0	0	.125	.000

Pitched Worst Against

	Avg	AB	R	H	2B	3B	HR	RBI	BB	SO	HBP	GDP	SB	CS	OBP	Slg
Terry Pendleton	.429	7	1	3	1	0	0	0	0	1	0	0	0	1	.429	.571
Tim Raines	.429	7	1	3	1	0	0	1	0	1	0	0	0	1	.429	.571
Ozzie Smith	.400	5	1	2	0	0	0	0	1	0	0	0	1	0	.500	.400

Omar Vizquel

Bats: Both, Throws: Right

Batting	Avg	G	AB	R	H	2B	3B	HR	RBI	BB	SO	HBP	GDP	SB	CS	OBP	Slg
Totals	.214	37	145	20	31	5	1	0	11	20	29	1	0	18	2	.310	.262
Home	.263	19	76	13	20	2	1	0	8	11	16	0	0	9	1	.352	.316
Away	.159	18	69	7	11	3	0	0	3	9	13	1	0	9	1	.263	.203
vs. Left	.208	27	53	8	11	1	0	0	6	9	8	1	0	7	2	.323	.226
vs. Right	.217	32	92	12	20	4	1	0	5	11	21	0	0	11	0	.301	.283
Scoring Pos.	.171	31	35	16	6	2	0	0	10	6	4	0	0	8	0	.279	.229
Close & Late	.176	22	34	1	6	0	0	0	1	3	9	0	0	4	1	.243	.176
None on/out	.161	27	31	0	5	1	0	0	0	5	6	0	0	0	0	.278	.194
None on	.220	36	91	0	20	3	0	0	0	11	22	1	0	0	0	.311	.253
Runners on	.204	35	54	20	11	2	1	0	11	9	7	0	0	18	2	.308	.278
Batting #1	.100	2	10	0	1	0	0	0	0	0	2	0	0	2	0	.100	.100
Batting #2	.203	31	123	16	25	4	1	0	10	18	26	1	0	13	1	.308	.252

Hit Best Against

	Avg	AB	R	H	2B	3B	HR	RBI	BB	SO	HBP	GDP	SB	CS	OBP	Slg
Kevin Brown	.600	5	2	3	2	0	0	0	1	0	0	0	1	0	.667	1.000
David Wells	.571	7	1	4	1	0	0	2	2	1	0	0	2	2	.600	.714
Andy Pettitte	.400	5	3	2	0	0	0	0	0	0	0	0	1	0	.400	.400

Hit Worst Against

	Avg	AB	R	H	2B	3B	HR	RBI	BB	SO	HBP	GDP	SB	CS	OBP	Slg
Randy Johnson	.000	7	0	0	0	0	0	1	0	0	0	0	0	0	.000	.000
Randy Myers	.000	5	0	0	0	0	0	0	0	2	0	0	0	0	.000	.000
Scott Erickson	.000	8	0	0	0	0	0	0	1	2	0	0	1	0	.111	.000

Honus Wagner

Bats: Right, Throws: Right

Batting	Avg	G	AB	R	H	2B	3B	HR	RBI	BB	SO	HBP	GDP	SB	CS	OBP	Slg
Totals	.275	15	51	6	14	3	1	0	9	7	6	3	0	9	3	.393	.373
Home	.261	7	23	2	6	1	0	0	2	2	4	2	0	4	2	.370	.304
Away	.286	8	28	4	8	2	1	0	7	5	2	1	0	5	1	.412	.429
vs. Right	.275	15	51	6	14	3	1	0	9	7	6	3	0	9	3	.393	.373
Scoring Pos.	.263	15	19	0	5	1	1	0	9	5	3	1	0	5	1	.440	.421
Close & Late	.000	4	2	0	0	0	0	0	0	1	0	0	0	1	0	.333	.000
None on/out	.133	11	15	0	2	1	0	0	0	1	1	0	0	0	0	.188	.200
None on	.167	13	24	0	4	2	0	0	0	1	2	2	0	0	0	.259	.250
Runners on	.370	15	27	0	10	1	1	0	9	6	4	1	0	9	3	.500	.481
Batting #4	.275	15	51	6	14	3	1	0	9	7	6	3	0	9	3	.393	.373

Hit Best Against

	Avg	AB	R	H	2B	3B	HR	RBI	BB	SO	HBP	GDP	SB	CS	OBP	Slg
Bill Dinneen	.286	14	0	4	0	0	0	1	1	2	0	0	2	1	.333	.286
George Mullin	.250	12	2	3	2	1	0	4	2	1	1	0	0	0	.400	.583

Hit Worst Against

	Avg	AB	R	H	2B	3B	HR	RBI	BB	SO	HBP	GDP	SB	CS	OBP	Slg
Cy Young	.167	12	2	2	1	0	0	2	2	2	1	0	1	0	.333	.250
W. Bill Donovan	.200	5	0	1	0	0	0	0	1	1	0	0	1	1	.333	.200

Bob Watson

Bats: Right, Throws: Right

Batting	Avg	G	AB	R	H	2B	3B	HR	RBI	BB	SO	HBP	GDP	SB	CS	OBP	Slg
Totals	.371	17	62	4	23	4	1	2	9	4	2	0	0	0	0	.403	.565
Home	.406	9	32	2	13	1	1	1	6	2	2	0	0	0	0	.441	.594
Away	.333	8	30	2	10	3	0	1	3	2	0	0	0	0	0	.364	.533
vs. Left	.385	12	26	0	10	3	0	2	5	2	0	0	0	0	0	.429	.731
vs. Right	.361	17	36	4	13	1	1	0	4	2	2	0	0	0	0	.385	.444
Scoring Pos.	.333	13	15	0	5	0	0	1	8	0	1	0	0	0	0	.313	.533
Close & Late	.375	8	8	0	3	1	0	0	1	0	0	0	0	0	0	.375	.500
None on/out	.348	14	23	0	8	1	1	1	1	1	0	0	0	0	0	.375	.609
None on	.378	16	37	0	14	3	1	1	1	2	0	0	0	0	0	.410	.595
Runners on	.360	15	25	0	9	1	0	1	8	2	2	0	0	0	0	.393	.520
Batting #3	.500	3	12	0	6	3	1	0	0	0	0	0	0	0	0	.500	.917
Batting #5	.267	4	15	2	4	1	0	2	4	2	0	0	0	0	0	.353	.733
Batting #7	.357	8	28	2	10	0	0	0	2	1	2	0	0	0	0	.379	.357

Hit Worst Against

	Avg	AB	R	H	2B	3B	HR	RBI	BB	SO	HBP	GDP	SB	CS	OBP	Slg
Burt Hooton	.167	6	0	1	0	0	0	0	0	0	0	0	0	0	.167	.167

David Wells

Throws: Left, Bats: Left

Pitching	ERA	W	L	Sv	G	GS	IP	BB	SO	Avg	R	H	2B	3B	HR	OBP	Slg
Totals	2.63	4	1	0	15	6	54.2	16	37	.238	18	49	11	1	2	.296	.330
Home	2.84	2	0	0	6	2	19.0	2	18	.250	7	19	5	0	1	.275	.355
Away	2.52	2	1	0	9	4	35.2	14	19	.231	11	30	6	1	1	.308	.315

	Avg	AB	R	H	2B	3B	HR	RBI	BB	SO	HBP	GDP	OBP	Slg
vs. Left	.244	41	0	10	3	0	0	4	2	10	1	3	.295	.317
vs. Right	.236	165	1	39	8	1	2	13	14	27	1	3	.297	.333
Scoring Pos.	.200	45	5	9	1	0	1	16	6	12	1	3	.296	.289
Close & Late	.357	14	1	5	0	0	0	2	0	3	0	3	.357	.357
None on/out	.231	52	0	12	3	1	1	1	3	8	1	3	.286	.385
None on	.250	116	5	29	6	1	1	1	9	18	1	3	.310	.345
Runners on	.222	90	12	20	5	0	1	16	7	19	1	3	.280	.311

Pitched Best Against

	Avg	AB	R	H	2B	3B	HR	RBI	BB	SO	HBP	GDP	SB	CS	OBP	Slg
Mark Lemke	.000	5	0	0	0	0	0	0	0	0	0	1	0	0	.000	.000
Albert Belle	.000	5	0	0	0	0	0	0	1	0	0	0	0	0	.167	.000
Kevin Seitzer	.091	11	0	1	0	0	0	0	0	2	0	0	0	0	.091	.091

Pitched Worst Against

	Avg	AB	R	H	2B	3B	HR	RBI	BB	SO	HBP	GDP	SB	CS	OBP	Slg
Omar Vizquel	.571	7	1	4	1	0	0	2	2	1	0	0	2	2	.600	.714
Manny Ramirez	.400	10	3	4	2	0	1	1	0	0	0	0	0	0	.400	.900
M. Grissom	.333	6	0	2	0	0	0	0	0	0	0	0	0	0	.333	.333

John Wetteland

Throws: Right, Bats: Right

Pitching	ERA	W	L	Sv	G	GS	IP	BB	SO	Avg	R	H	2B	3B	HR	OBP	Slg
Totals	5.40	0	1	7	15	0	16.2	8	20	.246	10	16	2	0	3	.338	.415
Home	3.86	0	0	1	6	0	9.1	2	13	.308	4	12	2	0	1	.341	.436
Away	7.36	0	1	6	9	0	7.1	6	7	.154	6	4	0	0	2	.333	.385

	Avg	AB	R	H	2B	3B	HR	RBI	BB	SO	HBP	GDP	OBP	Slg
vs. Left	.237	38	0	9	1	0	2	4	4	11	1	0	.326	.421
vs. Right	.259	27	0	7	1	0	1	6	4	9	0	0	.355	.407
Scoring Pos.	.227	22	7	5	0	0	2	9	2	7	1	0	.320	.500
Close & Late	.265	49	6	13	2	0	2	7	6	15	1	0	.357	.429
None on/out	.182	11	0	2	0	0	0	0	5	5	0	0	.438	.182
None on	.286	28	2	8	2	0	1	1	5	8	0	0	.394	.464
Runners on	.216	37	8	8	0	0	2	9	3	12	1	0	.293	.378

Devon White

Bats: Both, Throws: Right

Batting	Avg	G	AB	R	H	2B	3B	HR	RBI	BB	SO	HBP	GDP	SB	CS	OBP	Slg
Totals	.296	49	189	27	56	12	4	3	20	19	48	2	1	7	6	.365	.450
Home	.255	27	98	12	25	5	2	1	5	11	23	1	1	4	4	.333	.378
Away	.341	22	91	15	31	7	2	2	15	8	25	1	0	3	2	.400	.527
vs. Left	.292	30	65	10	19	6	1	2	11	3	14	1	0	1	1	.333	.508
vs. Right	.298	46	124	17	37	6	3	1	9	16	34	1	1	6	5	.380	.419
Scoring Pos.	.387	34	31	22	12	2	2	1	17	7	9	0	0	2	0	.487	.677
Close & Late	.242	24	33	4	8	1	1	1	5	1	8	1	0	0	0	.286	.424
None on/out	.266	40	64	0	17	3	0	0	0	2	16	1	0	0	0	.299	.313
None on	.301	46	123	2	37	8	2	2	2	7	30	2	0	0	0	.348	.447
Runners on	.288	44	66	23	19	4	2	1	18	12	18	0	1	7	6	.392	.455
Batting #1	.262	29	122	12	32	7	1	0	6	10	32	2	0	6	4	.326	.336
Batting #2	.373	12	51	11	19	4	3	2	9	5	12	0	1	1	1	.429	.686
Batting #8	.250	5	12	2	3	1	0	1	5	2	3	0	0	0	0	.357	.583

Hit Best Against

	Avg	AB	R	H	2B	3B	HR	RBI	BB	SO	HBP	GDP	SB	CS	OBP	Slg
Kevin Tapani	.800	5	3	4	1	0	0	0	1	1	0	0	2	0	.833	1.000
Dave Stewart	.667	6	0	4	1	0	0	1	2	0	0	0	0	1	.750	.833
Chad Ogea	.571	7	0	4	1	0	0	0	0	1	0	0	1	0	.571	.714

Hit Worst Against

	Avg	AB	R	H	2B	3B	HR	RBI	BB	SO	HBP	GDP	SB	CS	OBP	Slg
Jaret Wright	.000	6	0	0	0	0	0	0	0	4	0	0	0	0	.000	.000
Greg Maddux	.000	6	1	0	0	0	0	0	0	4	1	0	1	0	.143	.000
Mike Moore	.000	5	1	0	0	0	0	0	1	2	0	0	0	1	.167	.000

Frank White

Bats: Right, Throws: Right

Batting	Avg	G	AB	R	H	2B	3B	HR	RBI	BB	SO	HBP	GDP	SB	CS	OBP	Slg
Totals	.213	42	150	14	32	5	0	2	16	6	21	0	4	4	2	.241	.287
Home	.214	23	84	7	18	4	0	0	9	4	9	0	2	3	1	.244	.262
Away	.212	19	66	7	14	1	0	2	7	2	12	0	2	1	1	.235	.318
vs. Left	.294	25	51	0	15	2	0	1	3	2	5	0	1	0	1	.321	.392
vs. Right	.172	42	99	14	17	3	0	1	13	4	15	0	3	4	1	.200	.232
Scoring Pos.	.231	27	39	0	9	4	0	0	13	3	3	0	4	0	0	.273	.333
Close & Late	.200	14	15	0	3	0	0	0	1	2	2	0	0	1	0	.294	.200
None on/out	.135	29	37	0	5	0	0	0	0	1	6	0	0	0	0	.158	.135
None on	.173	39	81	0	14	1	0	1	1	2	16	0	0	0	0	.193	.222
Runners on	.261	37	69	0	18	4	0	1	15	4	4	0	4	4	2	.293	.362
Batting #2	.083	6	24	1	2	0	0	0	0	2	4	0	0	0	0	.154	.083
Batting #4	.250	7	28	4	7	3	0	1	6	3	4	0	2	1	1	.323	.464
Batting #5	.400	3	10	1	4	0	0	0	2	1	0	0	0	0	0	.417	.400
Batting #7	.182	8	22	3	4	0	0	0	0	0	4	0	0	0	0	.182	.182
Batting #8	.182	3	11	0	2	0	0	0	1	0	1	0	0	1	0	.182	.182
Batting #9	.277	13	47	5	13	2	0	1	7	0	6	0	1	2	1	.271	.383

Hit Best Against

	Avg	AB	R	H	2B	3B	HR	RBI	BB	SO	HBP	GDP	SB	CS	OBP	Slg
Danny Cox	.600	5	0	3	1	0	0	1	1	1	0	0	1	1	.667	.800
Jimmy Key	.600	5	1	3	0	0	0	0	0	0	0	0	0	0	.600	.600
Ron Guidry	.500	8	0	4	1	0	0	2	0	1	0	0	0	1	.500	.625

Hit Worst Against

	Avg	AB	R	H	2B	3B	HR	RBI	BB	SO	HBP	GDP	SB	CS	OBP	Slg
Dave Stieb	.000	8	0	0	0	0	0	0	0	1	0	1	0	0	.000	.000
John Tudor	.000	8	1	0	0	0	0	0	1	0	0	0	0	0	.111	.000
Steve Carlton	.167	6	0	1	0	0	0	0	0	1	0	1	0	0	.167	.167

Bernie Williams

Bats: Both, Throws: Right

Batting	Avg	G	AB	R	H	2B	3B	HR	RBI	BB	SO	HBP	GDP	SB	CS	OBP	Slg
Totals	.323	25	96	25	31	6	0	8	21	21	17	1	2	4	1	.445	.635
Home	.317	11	41	7	13	4	0	1	8	11	6	1	0	1	0	.472	.488
Away	.327	14	55	18	18	2	0	7	13	10	11	0	2	3	1	.424	.745
vs. Left	.409	16	22	6	9	0	0	4	6	8	3	1	2	1	1	.581	.955
vs. Right	.297	24	74	19	22	6	0	4	15	13	14	0	0	3	0	.398	.541
Scoring Pos.	.333	23	27	16	9	1	0	1	12	6	1	0	0	0	1	.441	.481
Close & Late	.391	17	23	7	9	3	0	3	7	6	4	0	1	0	0	.500	.913
None on/out	.421	16	19	4	8	0	0	4	4	4	3	0	0	0	0	.522	1.053
None on	.333	24	48	6	16	3	0	6	6	12	10	1	0	0	0	.475	.771
Runners on	.313	25	48	19	15	3	0	2	15	9	7	0	2	4	1	.414	.500
Batting #2	.429	5	21	8	9	2	0	2	5	7	3	0	0	1	0	.571	.810
Batting #3	.353	13	51	13	18	3	0	6	14	8	11	0	1	3	1	.433	.765
Batting #4	.167	7	24	4	4	1	0	0	2	6	3	1	1	0	0	.355	.208

Hit Best Against

	Avg	AB	R	H	2B	3B	HR	RBI	BB	SO	HBP	GDP	SB	CS	OBP	Slg
Scott Erickson	.333	6	1	2	2	0	0	1	1	2	0	0	0	0	.429	.667
Greg Maddux	.286	7	0	2	0	0	0	1	0	0	0	0	0	0	.286	.286

Hit Worst Against

	Avg	AB	R	H	2B	3B	HR	RBI	BB	SO	HBP	GDP	SB	CS	OBP	Slg
John Smoltz	.000	6	0	0	0	0	0	0	1	3	0	0	0	0	.143	.000

Matt Williams

Bats: Right, Throws: Right

Batting	Avg	G	AB	R	H	2B	3B	HR	RBI	BB	SO	HBP	GDP	SB	CS	OBP	Slg
Totals	.265	27	102	16	27	4	0	5	18	13	24	2	0	1	0	.359	.451
Home	.302	14	53	9	16	2	0	3	12	8	9	0	0	0	0	.393	.509
Away	.224	13	49	7	11	2	0	2	6	5	15	2	0	1	0	.321	.388
vs. Left	.333	15	27	5	9	1	0	2	7	6	7	0	0	1	0	.455	.593
vs. Right	.240	26	75	11	18	3	0	3	11	7	17	2	0	0	0	.321	.400
Scoring Pos.	.300	20	20	9	6	1	0	1	10	7	7	1	0	0	0	.500	.500
Close & Late	.267	14	15	2	4	0	0	1	3	5	3	0	0	0	0	.450	.467
None on/out	.294	21	34	0	10	2	0	0	0	4	8	0	0	0	0	.368	.353
None on	.259	26	54	1	14	2	0	1	1	6	14	1	0	0	0	.344	.352
Runners on	.271	25	48	13	13	2	0	4	17	7	10	1	0	1	0	.375	.563
Batting #4	.286	4	14	3	4	0	0	1	3	3	2	0	0	1	0	.412	.500
Batting #5	.274	16	62	10	17	2	0	3	12	7	16	1	0	0	0	.357	.452
Batting #6	.231	7	26	3	6	2	0	1	3	3	6	1	0	0	0	.333	.423

Hit Best Against

	Avg	AB	R	H	2B	3B	HR	RBI	BB	SO	HBP	GDP	SB	CS	OBP	Slg
Andy Pettitte	.400	5	2	2	0	0	1	3	1	1	0	0	0	0	.500	1.000
Kevin Brown	.400	5	3	2	0	0	0	0	0	0	0	0	0	0	.400	.400

Hit Worst Against

	Avg	AB	R	H	2B	3B	HR	RBI	BB	SO	HBP	GDP	SB	CS	OBP	Slg
Dave Stewart	.143	7	1	1	0	0	1	1	0	3	0	0	0	0	.143	.571
Scott Erickson	.167	6	0	1	0	0	0	0	0	1	0	0	0	0	.167	.167
Mike Mussina	.167	6	0	1	0	0	0	1	0	3	0	0	0	0	.167	.167

Maury Wills

Bats: Both, Throws: Right

Batting	Avg	G	AB	R	H	2B	3B	HR	RBI	BB	SO	HBP	GDP	SB	CS	OBP	Slg
Totals	.244	21	78	6	19	3	0	0	4	5	12	0	0	6	2	.289	.282
Home	.257	10	35	4	9	3	0	0	2	3	4	0	0	5	1	.316	.343
Away	.233	11	43	2	10	0	0	0	2	2	8	0	0	1	1	.267	.233
vs. Left	.208	11	24	0	5	2	0	0	1	3	5	0	0	2	0	.296	.292
vs. Right	.259	21	54	6	14	1	0	0	3	2	7	0	0	4	2	.286	.278
Scoring Pos.	.294	9	17	0	5	1	0	0	4	0	1	0	0	1	0	.294	.353
Close & Late	.375	9	8	1	3	0	0	0	1	1	1	0	0	0	0	.444	.375
None on/out	.310	20	29	0	9	2	0	0	0	2	6	0	0	0	0	.355	.379
None on	.231	21	52	0	12	2	0	0	0	4	11	0	0	0	0	.286	.269
Runners on	.269	16	26	0	7	1	0	0	4	1	1	0	0	6	2	.296	.308
Batting #1	.241	15	58	4	14	3	0	0	3	5	9	0	0	5	2	.302	.293
Batting #8	.250	6	20	2	5	0	0	0	1	0	3	0	0	1	0	.250	.250

Hit Best Against

	Avg	AB	R	H	2B	3B	HR	RBI	BB	SO	HBP	GDP	SB	CS	OBP	Slg
Early Wynn	.500	6	1	3	0	0	0	1	0	1	0	0	1	0	.500	.500
Mudcat Grant	.417	12	1	5	0	0	0	1	0	2	0	0	1	1	.417	.417
Jim Kaat	.250	8	1	2	1	0	0	0	0	1	0	0	0	0	.250	.375

Hit Worst Against

	Avg	AB	R	H	2B	3B	HR	RBI	BB	SO	HBP	GDP	SB	CS	OBP	Slg
Whitey Ford	.000	5	0	0	0	0	0	0	1	3	0	0	0	0	.167	.000
Bob Shaw	.200	5	0	1	0	0	0	0	0	0	0	0	0	0	.200	.200

Hack Wilson

Bats: Right, Throws: Right

Batting	Avg	G	AB	R	H	2B	3B	HR	RBI	BB	SO	HBP	GDP	SB	CS	OBP	Slg
Totals	.319	12	47	3	15	1	1	0	3	5	12	0	2	0	0	.385	.383
Home	.222	5	18	1	4	1	0	0	2	2	4	0	1	0	0	.300	.278
Away	.379	7	29	2	11	0	1	0	1	3	8	0	1	0	0	.438	.448
vs. Left	.294	6	17	0	5	0	0	0	2	0	3	0	1	0	0	.294	.294
vs. Right	.333	12	30	3	10	1	1	0	1	5	9	0	1	0	0	.429	.433
Scoring Pos.	.182	10	11	0	2	1	0	0	3	3	2	0	2	0	0	.357	.273
Close & Late	.556	7	9	0	5	1	0	0	2	1	3	0	1	0	0	.600	.667
None on/out	.385	10	13	0	5	0	1	0	0	1	2	0	0	0	0	.429	.538
None on	.333	12	24	0	8	0	1	0	0	1	5	0	0	0	0	.360	.417
Runners on	.304	12	23	0	7	1	0	0	3	4	7	0	2	0	0	.407	.348
Batting #4	.471	5	17	2	8	0	1	0	0	4	3	0	0	0	0	.571	.588
Batting #6	.233	7	30	1	7	1	0	0	3	1	9	0	2	0	0	.258	.267

Hit Best Against

	Avg	AB	R	H	2B	3B	HR	RBI	BB	SO	HBP	GDP	SB	CS	OBP	Slg
Firpo Marberry	.400	5	1	2	1	0	0	1	0	2	0	1	0	0	.400	.600
Tom Zachary	.375	8	0	3	0	0	0	1	0	2	0	1	0	0	.375	.375

Hit Worst Against

	Avg	AB	R	H	2B	3B	HR	RBI	BB	SO	HBP	GDP	SB	CS	OBP	Slg
G. Mogridge	.000	5	0	0	0	0	0	1	0	0	0	0	0	0	.000	.000
Howard Ehmke	.167	6	0	1	0	0	0	0	0	2	0	0	0	0	.167	.167
Walter Johnson	.200	10	0	2	0	0	0	0	1	5	0	0	0	0	.273	.200

Willie Wilson

Bats: Both, Throws: Right

Batting	Avg	G	AB	R	H	2B	3B	HR	RBI	BB	SO	HBP	GDP	SB	CS	OBP	Slg
Totals	.267	38	150	12	40	4	2	1	10	9	32	0	2	12	3	.308	.340
Home	.273	20	77	6	21	2	1	0	6	6	9	0	1	4	2	.325	.325
Away	.260	18	73	6	19	2	1	1	4	3	23	0	1	8	1	.289	.356
vs. Left	.227	21	44	0	10	2	1	1	6	6	13	0	0	2	1	.320	.386
vs. Right	.283	38	106	12	30	2	1	0	4	3	19	0	2	10	2	.303	.321
Scoring Pos.	.206	27	34	0	7	1	2	1	10	2	9	0	0	5	1	.250	.441
Close & Late	.130	20	23	2	3	0	0	0	0	3	2	0	0	4	1	.231	.130
None on/out	.245	32	49	0	12	1	0	0	0	2	9	0	0	0	0	.275	.265
None on	.237	36	93	0	22	2	0	0	0	6	22	0	0	0	0	.283	.258
Runners on	.316	34	57	0	18	2	2	1	10	3	10	0	2	12	3	.350	.474
Batting #1	.215	15	65	5	14	3	1	0	5	6	16	0	0	2	1	.282	.292
Batting #2	.328	15	61	7	20	0	1	1	5	2	9	0	2	3	1	.349	.410
Batting #7	.250	5	20	0	5	1	0	0	0	1	5	0	0	7	0	.286	.300

Hit Best Against

	Avg	AB	R	H	2B	3B	HR	RBI	BB	SO	HBP	GDP	SB	CS	OBP	Slg
Doyle Alexander	.600	5	2	3	0	0	0	0	1	1	0	0	0	1	.667	.600
Juan Guzman	.600	5	0	3	0	0	0	0	1	1	0	0	3	0	.667	.600
Danny Cox	.500	6	1	3	0	0	0	0	0	0	0	1	1	0	.500	.500

Hit Worst Against

	Avg	AB	R	H	2B	3B	HR	RBI	BB	SO	HBP	GDP	SB	CS	OBP	Slg
Dennis Lamp	.000	5	0	0	0	0	0	0	0	0	0	0	0	0	.000	.000
Steve Carlton	.143	7	1	1	0	0	0	0	1	5	0	0	1	0	.250	.143
Steve McCatty	.200	5	0	1	0	0	0	1	0	0	0	0	0	0	.200	.200

Dave Winfield

Bats: Right, Throws: Right

Batting	Avg	G	AB	R	H	2B	3B	HR	RBI	BB	SO	HBP	GDP	SB	CS	OBP	Slg
Totals	.208	26	101	11	21	6	0	2	9	14	16	0	0	2	0	.304	.327
Home	.176	14	51	6	9	4	0	1	4	8	8	0	0	1	0	.288	.314
Away	.240	12	50	5	12	2	0	1	5	6	8	0	0	1	0	.321	.340
vs. Left	.294	15	34	0	10	3	0	0	2	5	7	0	0	1	0	.385	.382
vs. Right	.164	26	67	11	11	3	0	2	7	9	9	0	0	1	0	.263	.299
Scoring Pos.	.160	21	25	5	4	2	0	0	7	5	4	0	0	0	0	.300	.240
Close & Late	.263	14	19	4	5	3	0	0	4	1	5	0	0	0	0	.300	.421
None on/out	.200	20	25	1	5	0	0	1	1	2	4	0	0	0	0	.259	.320
None on	.245	26	53	2	13	3	0	2	2	5	9	0	0	0	0	.310	.415
Runners on	.167	25	48	5	8	3	0	0	7	9	7	0	0	2	0	.298	.229
Batting #3	.182	14	55	4	10	4	0	0	3	8	11	0	0	2	0	.286	.255
Batting #4	.239	12	46	7	11	2	0	2	6	6	5	0	0	0	0	.327	.413

Hit Best Against

	Avg	AB	R	H	2B	3B	HR	RBI	BB	SO	HBP	GDP	SB	CS	OBP	Slg
Dave Stewart	.571	7	3	4	1	0	2	2	1	0	0	0	0	0	.625	1.571
John Smoltz	.286	7	0	2	0	0	0	1	0	1	0	0	0	0	.286	.286

Hit Worst Against

	Avg	AB	R	H	2B	3B	HR	RBI	BB	SO	HBP	GDP	SB	CS	OBP	Slg
Matt Keough	.000	5	0	0	0	0	0	0	0	2	0	0	0	0	.000	.000
Burt Hooton	.000	5	0	0	0	0	0	0	1	0	0	0	0	0	.167	.000
Jerry Reuss	.167	6	0	1	0	0	0	0	0	3	0	0	0	0	.167	.167

Mark Wohlers

Throws: Right, Bats: Right

Pitching	ERA	W	L	Sv	G	GS	IP	BB	SO	Avg	R	H	2B	3B	HR	OBP	Slg
Totals	2.15	1	2	9	38	0	37.2	16	43	.217	9	30	4	0	4	.297	.333
Home	3.10	0	2	5	21	0	20.1	10	18	.221	7	17	2	0	2	.307	.325
Away	1.04	1	0	4	17	0	17.1	6	25	.213	2	13	2	0	2	.284	.344

	Avg	AB	R	H	2B	3B	HR	RBI	BB	SO	HBP	GDP	OBP	Slg
vs. Left	.171	70	0	12	2	0	2	4	9	26	0	0	.263	.286
vs. Right	.265	68	0	18	2	0	2	8	7	17	0	0	.333	.382
Scoring Pos.	.176	34	3	6	1	0	1	9	9	7	0	0	.341	.294
Close & Late	.193	88	5	17	2	0	2	8	13	26	0	0	.297	.284
None on/out	.242	33	0	8	2	0	1	1	3	13	0	0	.306	.394
None on	.250	80	6	20	3	0	3	3	6	27	0	0	.302	.400
Runners on	.172	58	3	10	1	0	1	9	10	16	0	0	.290	.241

Todd Worrell

Throws: Right, Bats: Right

Pitching	ERA	W	L	Sv	G	GS	IP	BB	SO	Avg	R	H	2B	3B	HR	OBP	Slg
Totals	1.93	1	1	4	15	0	23.1	10	19	.209	5	18	7	3	2	.292	.430
Home	0.00	0	0	2	8	0	11.0	4	11	.158	0	6	5	2	0	.238	.395
Away	3.65	1	1	2	7	0	12.1	6	8	.250	5	12	2	1	2	.333	.458

	Avg	AB	R	H	2B	3B	HR	RBI	BB	SO	HBP	GDP	OBP	Slg
vs. Left	.194	31	0	6	2	1	1	3	3	9	0	1	.265	.419
vs. Right	.218	55	5	12	5	2	1	6	7	10	0	1	.306	.436
Scoring Pos.	.148	27	0	4	1	1	0	6	6	4	0	1	.303	.259
Close & Late	.209	43	3	9	2	2	1	7	7	6	0	1	.320	.419
None on/out	.238	21	0	5	2	1	1	1	0	5	0	1	.238	.571
None on	.234	47	0	11	5	2	2	2	3	12	0	1	.280	.553
Runners on	.179	39	0	7	2	1	0	7	7	7	0	1	.304	.282

Carl Yastrzemski

Bats: Left, Throws: Right

Batting	Avg	G	AB	R	H	2B	3B	HR	RBI	BB	SO	HBP	GDP	SB	CS	OBP	Slg
Totals	.369	17	65	15	24	3	0	4	11	9	3	1	2	0	1	.447	.600
Home	.400	10	40	12	16	1	0	4	9	6	1	0	0	0	0	.478	.725
Away	.320	7	25	3	8	2	0	0	2	3	2	1	2	0	1	.400	.400
vs. Left	.333	12	30	0	10	0	0	2	8	2	3	0	1	0	0	.364	.533
vs. Right	.400	17	35	15	14	3	0	2	3	7	0	1	1	0	1	.512	.657
Scoring Pos.	.308	12	13	0	4	0	0	1	7	3	1	0	1	0	0	.412	.538
Close & Late	.429	7	7	0	3	1	0	0	1	1	0	0	0	0	0	.500	.571
None on/out	.385	11	13	0	5	1	0	2	2	1	0	0	0	0	0	.429	.923
None on	.400	17	35	0	14	3	0	2	2	6	2	1	0	0	0	.500	.657
Runners on	.333	17	30	0	10	0	0	2	9	3	1	0	2	0	1	.382	.533
Batting #3	.369	17	65	15	24	3	0	4	11	9	3	1	2	0	1	.447	.600

Hit Best Against

	Avg	AB	R	H	2B	3B	HR	RBI	BB	SO	HBP	GDP	SB	CS	OBP	Slg
Ken Holtzman	.500	6	2	3	0	0	0	0	0	1	0	0	0	0	.500	.500
Don Gullett	.333	9	3	3	0	0	0	3	1	0	0	0	0	0	.364	.333
Bob Gibson	.273	11	0	3	1	0	0	0	1	0	0	0	0	0	.333	.364

Steve Yeager

Bats: Right, Throws: Right

Batting	Avg	G	AB	R	H	2B	3B	HR	RBI	BB	SO	HBP	GDP	SB	CS	OBP	Slg
Totals	.252	38	107	12	27	6	0	5	14	10	19	1	1	2	0	.317	.449
Home	.245	17	49	5	12	2	0	2	8	3	7	0	1	1	0	.278	.408
Away	.259	21	58	7	15	4	0	3	6	7	12	1	0	1	0	.348	.483
vs. Left	.231	30	65	0	15	4	0	3	8	8	12	1	0	0	0	.320	.431
vs. Right	.286	38	42	12	12	2	0	2	6	2	7	0	1	2	0	.311	.476
Scoring Pos.	.200	27	30	0	6	0	0	1	10	2	4	1	1	0	0	.257	.300
Close & Late	.200	12	10	1	2	1	0	1	2	2	1	0	0	0	0	.308	.600
None on/out	.214	21	28	0	6	1	0	0	0	1	6	0	0	0	0	.241	.250
None on	.267	32	60	0	16	5	0	4	4	6	14	0	0	0	0	.333	.550
Runners on	.234	33	47	0	11	1	0	1	10	4	5	1	1	2	0	.296	.319
Batting #8	.244	27	78	8	19	2	0	4	13	8	15	0	0	2	0	.307	.423
Batting #9	.231	5	13	2	3	1	0	0	0	1	2	0	1	0	0	.286	.308

Hit Best Against

	Avg	AB	R	H	2B	3B	HR	RBI	BB	SO	HBP	GDP	SB	CS	OBP	Slg
Mike Torrez	.429	7	0	3	1	0	0	0	0	1	0	0	0	0	.429	.571
Ken Holtzman	.400	5	0	2	1	0	0	0	0	1	0	0	0	0	.400	.600
Vida Blue	.400	5	0	2	0	0	0	1	1	2	0	0	0	0	.500	.400

Hit Worst Against

	Avg	AB	R	H	2B	3B	HR	RBI	BB	SO	HBP	GDP	SB	CS	OBP	Slg
Steve Carlton	.154	13	1	2	1	0	0	0	0	4	1	0	0	0	.214	.231
Don Gullett	.200	5	1	1	0	0	1	3	1	0	0	0	0	0	.333	.800

Cy Young

Throws: Right, Bats: Right

Pitching	ERA	W	L	Sv	G	GS	IP	BB	SO	Avg	R	H	2B	3B	HR	OBP	Slg
Totals	1.85	2	1	0	4	3	34.0	4	17	.231	14	31	3	6	1	.259	.366
Home	2.25	0	1	0	2	1	16.0	3	7	.238	9	15	2	3	1	.284	.413
Away	1.50	2	0	0	2	2	18.0	1	10	.225	5	16	1	3	0	.236	.324

	Avg	AB	R	H	2B	3B	HR	RBI	BB	SO	HBP	GDP	OBP	Slg
vs. Left	.222	63	0	14	0	1	1	6	2	9	0	1	.246	.302
vs. Right	.236	72	14	17	3	5	0	6	2	7	1	1	.267	.417
Scoring Pos.	.194	36	0	7	0	1	0	11	2	5	1	1	.256	.250
Close & Late	.267	15	0	4	0	1	0	3	0	2	0	1	.267	.400
None on/out	.152	33	0	5	2	1	0	0	0	5	0	1	.152	.273
None on	.269	78	0	21	3	5	1	1	1	9	0	1	.278	.474
Runners on	.175	57	0	10	0	1	0	11	3	7	1	1	.230	.211

Pitched Best Against

	Avg	AB	R	H	2B	3B	HR	RBI	BB	SO	HBP	GDP	SB	CS	OBP	Slg
G. Beaumont	.118	17	2	2	0	0	0	0	0	1	0	0	0	0	.118	.118
Claude Ritchey	.133	15	2	2	0	0	0	2	1	4	0	0	1	0	.188	.133
Honus Wagner	.167	12	2	2	1	0	0	2	2	2	1	0	1	0	.333	.250

Pitched Worst Against

	Avg	AB	R	H	2B	3B	HR	RBI	BB	SO	HBP	GDP	SB	CS	OBP	Slg
Tommy Leach	.375	16	1	6	0	3	0	3	0	3	0	1	0	1	.375	.750
Jimmy Sebring	.375	16	2	6	0	0	1	4	0	1	0	0	0	1	.375	.563
Kitty Bransfield	.267	15	3	4	0	2	0	0	0	1	0	0	1	0	.267	.533

Ross Youngs

Bats: Left, Throws: Right

Batting	Avg	G	AB	R	H	2B	3B	HR	RBI	BB	SO	HBP	GDP	SB	CS	OBP	Slg
Totals	.286	26	91	10	26	2	1	1	10	17	9	1	0	3	4	.400	.363
Home	.378	13	45	8	17	1	1	1	8	6	3	1	0	1	0	.453	.511
Away	.196	13	46	2	9	1	0	0	2	11	6	0	0	2	4	.351	.217
vs. Left	.227	8	22	0	5	0	0	1	3	2	2	0	0	0	0	.292	.364
vs. Right	.304	26	69	10	21	2	1	0	7	15	7	1	0	3	4	.430	.362
Scoring Pos.	.227	18	22	0	5	0	1	0	9	5	3	1	0	1	1	.379	.318
Close & Late	.250	14	12	2	3	2	0	0	2	4	0	0	0	1	1	.412	.417
None on/out	.348	17	23	0	8	0	0	1	1	3	2	0	0	0	0	.423	.478
None on	.409	23	44	0	18	1	0	1	1	7	4	0	0	0	0	.490	.500
Runners on	.170	24	47	0	8	1	1	0	9	10	5	1	0	3	4	.322	.234
Batting #3	.185	7	27	3	5	1	0	0	1	5	6	1	0	1	1	.333	.222
Batting #4	.313	14	48	5	15	1	1	1	7	9	2	0	0	2	2	.421	.438
Batting #5	.375	5	16	2	6	0	0	0	2	3	1	0	0	0	1	.450	.375

Hit Best Against

	Avg	AB	R	H	2B	3B	HR	RBI	BB	SO	HBP	GDP	SB	CS	OBP	Slg
Herb Pennock	.500	8	1	4	0	0	1	3	0	0	0	0	0	0	.500	.875
Bob Shawkey	.400	10	2	4	0	0	0	1	3	2	0	0	0	0	.538	.400
Sad Sam Jones	.400	5	0	2	0	0	0	0	0	0	0	0	0	0	.400	.400

Hit Worst Against

	Avg	AB	R	H	2B	3B	HR	RBI	BB	SO	HBP	GDP	SB	CS	OBP	Slg
Joe Bush	.000	11	2	0	0	0	0	0	4	1	0	0	0	1	.267	.000
G. Mogridge	.000	5	2	0	0	0	0	0	2	2	0	0	0	0	.286	.000
Tom Zachary	.125	8	1	1	0	0	0	0	0	0	0	0	0	0	.125	.125

Robin Yount

Bats: Right, Throws: Right

Batting	Avg	G	AB	R	H	2B	3B	HR	RBI	BB	SO	HBP	GDP	SB	CS	OBP	Slg
Totals	.344	17	64	11	22	3	1	1	7	9	4	0	3	1	0	.419	.469
Home	.346	8	26	6	9	1	0	1	4	7	2	0	3	1	0	.471	.500
Away	.342	9	38	5	13	2	1	0	3	2	2	0	0	0	0	.375	.447
vs. Left	.391	9	23	0	9	0	1	0	1	2	2	0	1	1	0	.423	.478
vs. Right	.317	17	41	11	13	3	0	1	6	7	2	0	1	0	0	.417	.463
Scoring Pos.	.308	13	13	0	4	1	0	0	6	3	0	0	0	0	0	.412	.385
Close & Late	.375	8	8	3	3	0	0	1	3	1	0	0	0	0	0	.444	.750
None on/out	.222	8	9	0	2	1	0	0	0	1	0	0	0	0	0	.300	.333
None on	.316	16	38	0	12	1	1	1	1	6	3	0	0	0	0	.409	.474
Runners on	.385	16	26	0	10	2	0	0	6	3	1	0	2	1	0	.433	.462
Batting #2	.344	17	64	11	22	3	1	1	7	9	4	0	2	1	0	.419	.469

Hit Best Against

	Avg	AB	R	H	2B	3B	HR	RBI	BB	SO	HBP	GDP	SB	CS	OBP	Slg
Bob Forsch	.875	8	3	7	2	0	1	3	0	0	0	0	0	0	.875	1.500
Dave Righetti	.400	5	1	2	0	1	0	0	0	2	0	0	0	0	.400	.800
Tommy John	.300	10	1	3	0	0	0	0	0	0	0	1	0	0	.300	.300

Hit Worst Against

	Avg	AB	R	H	2B	3B	HR	RBI	BB	SO	HBP	GDP	SB	CS	OBP	Slg
Joaquin Andujar	.167	6	0	1	0	0	0	0	0	0	0	1	0	0	.167	.167
Bruce Kison	.167	6	0	1	0	0	0	0	1	0	0	0	0	0	.286	.167
John Stuper	.167	6	1	1	1	0	0	1	1	0	0	0	0	0	.286	.333

1884 Providence Grays (NL) 3, New York Metropolitans (AA) 0

The National League's Providence Grays met the American Association champion New York Metropolitans in the first postseason series touted as an interleague championship. In the bottom of the first inning of Game 1, Providence got two runs off New York hurler Tim Keefe on a pair of hit batsmen, a pair of wild pitches and a passed ball. Old Hoss Radbourn needed nothing more, and finished with a two-hit shutout for a 6-0 Providence victory. Radbourn and Keefe hooked up again the very next day. Providence third baseman Jerry Denny socked a three-run homer in the top of the fifth, and the game was called on account of darkness in the top of the eighth, with the Grays taking a 3-1 victory. The Grays had won the three-game Series, but the players had been promised the profits from the final two games of the Series, so Game 3 was played anyway. It was little more than an exhibition, as Keefe umpired. Providence ran up an 11-2 lead before both clubs agreed to call it a day after seven innings.

Game 1 — October 23 at New York

	1 2 3	4 5 6	7 8 9	R	H	E
Metropolitans	0 0 0	0 0 0	0 0 0	0	2	0
Grays	2 0 1	0 0 0	3 0 x	6	5	2

W—Radbourn (1-0). L—Keefe (0-1). A—2500.

Game 2 — October 24 at New York

	1 2 3	4 5 6 7	R	H	E
Grays	0 0 0	0 3 0 0	3	5	4
Metropolitans	0 0 0	0 1 0 0	1	3	1

W—Radbourn (2-0). L—Keefe (0-2). HR—Denny (1). A—1000.

Game 3 — October 25 at New York

	1 2 3	4 5 6	R	H	E
Grays	1 2 0	0 4 4	11	9	3
Metropolitans	0 0 0	0 1 1	2	6	9

W—Radbourn (3-0). L—Becannon (0-1). A—300.

Batting

Grays	G	AB	R	H	RBI	2B	3B	HR	BB	SO	SB	Avg
Cliff Carroll, of	3	10	2	1	1	0	0	0	1	1	0	.100
Jerry Denny, 3b	3	9	3	4	2	0	1	1	0	3	0	.444
Jack Farrell, 2b	3	9	3	4	0	2	0	0	0	0	1	.444
Barney Gilligan, c	3	9	3	4	2	2	0	0	0	1	0	.444
Paul Hines, of	3	8	5	2	1	0	0	0	3	0	2	.250
Arthur Irwin, ss	3	9	2	2	2	0	1	0	0	2	0	.222
Old Hoss Radbourn, p	3	10	1	1	2	0	0	0	1	3	0	.100
Paul Radford, of	3	7	1	0	1	0	0	0	0	1	0	.000
Joe Start, 1b	3	10	0	1	1	0	0	0	0	2	0	.100
Totals	3	81	20	19	12	4	2	1	5	13	3	.235

Metropolitans	G	AB	R	H	RBI	2B	3B	HR	BB	SO	SB	Avg
Buck Becannon, p	1	2	0	1	0	0	0	0	0	0	0	.500
Steve Brady, of	3	10	1	0	0	0	0	0	0	1	0	.000
Dude Esterbrook, 3b	3	10	0	3	0	1	0	0	0	3	1	.300
Tom Forster, 2b	1	3	0	0	0	0	0	0	0	1	0	.000
Bill Holbert, c	1	2	0	0	0	0	0	0	0	1	0	.000
Tim Keefe, p	2	5	0	1	0	0	0	0	0	4	0	.200
Ed Kennedy, of	3	7	0	0	0	0	0	0	0	2	0	.000
Candy Nelson, ss	3	10	0	1	0	0	0	0	0	1	0	.100
Dave Orr, 1b	3	9	0	1	0	0	0	0	0	0	0	.111
Charlie Reipschlager, c	2	5	1	0	0	0	0	0	0	1	0	.000
Chief Roseman, of	3	9	1	3	1	0	0	0	0	1	0	.333
Dasher Troy, 2b	2	5	0	1	1	0	0	0	0	1	0	.200
Totals	3	77	3	11	2	1	0	0	0	16	1	.143

Pitching

Grays	G	GS	CG	ShO	IP	H	R	ER	BB	SO	W-L	Sv	ERA
Old Hoss Radbourn	3	3	3	1	22.0	11	3	0	0	16	3-0	0	0.00
Totals	3	3	3	1	22.0	11	3	0	0	16	3-0	0	0.00

Metropolitans	G	GS	CG	ShO	IP	H	R	ER	BB	SO	W-L	Sv	ERA
Buck Becannon	1	1	1	0	6.0	9	11	7	2	1	0-1	0	10.50
Tim Keefe	2	2	2	0	15.0	10	9	6	3	12	0-2	0	3.60
Totals	3	3	3	0	21.0	19	20	13	5	13	0-3	0	5.57

1885 Chicago White Stockings (NL) 3, St. Louis Browns (AA) 3

This is the World Series that settled absolutely nothing. St. Louis' Bob Caruthers held a 5-1 lead into the late innings of the opener, but Fred Pfeffer capped a Chicago rally with a game-tying three-run homer in the eighth, just before the game was called due to darkness—still tied, 5-5. In Game 2, the crowd overran the field and caused the game to be forfeited to Chicago after umpire Dave Sullivan twice reversed himself on an errant call. Caruthers contributed a key triple and pitched St. Louis to a 7-4 victory in Game 3. The Browns took the fourth game 3-2 when Bill Gleason scored from second on an infield groundout in the bottom of the eighth. John Clarkson pitched the White Stockings to a 9-2 win in Game 5. Before the start of Game 6, it was announced that the seventh game alone would decide the championship. Then Chicago's Jim McCormick went out and tossed a two-hitter for a 9-2 win. Clarkson was slated to pitch for Chicago in the finale, but McCormick was forced to go when Clarkson showed up late. St. Louis pounded McCormick and came away with a 13-4 victory. Everyone regarded them as champions except their owner, Chris Von Der Ahe, who called the series a tie and pocketed the players' prize money.

Game 1 — October 14 at Chicago

	1	2	3	4	5	6	7	8	R	H	E
Browns	0	1	0	4	0	0	0	0	5	7	2
White Stockings	0	0	0	1	0	0	0	4	5	5	10

HR—Pfeffer (1). A—2000.

Game 2 — October 15 at St Louis

	1	2	3	4	5	6	R	H	E
White Stockings	1	1	0	0	0	3	5	6	5
Browns	3	0	0	1	0	0	4	2	4

W—McCormick (1-0). L—Foutz (0-1). A—2000.

Game 3 — October 16 at St Louis

	1	2	3	4	5	6	7	8	9	R	H	E
White Stockings	1	1	1	0	0	0	0	0	1	4	8	7
Browns	5	0	0	0	0	2	0	0	x	7	8	4

W—Caruthers (1-0). L—Clarkson (0-1). A—3000.

Game 4 — October 17 at St Louis

	1	2	3	4	5	6	7	8	9	R	H	E
White Stockings	0	0	0	0	2	0	0	0	0	2	8	3
Browns	0	0	1	0	0	0	0	2	x	3	6	7

W—Foutz (1-1). L—McCormick (1-1). HR—Dalrymple (1). A—3000.

Game 5 — October 22 at Pittsburgh

	1	2	3	4	5	6	7	R	H	E
White Stockings	4	0	0	1	1	0	3	9	7	1
Browns	0	1	0	0	0	0	1	2	4	7

W—Clarkson (1-1). L—Foutz (1-2). A—500.

Game 6 — October 23 at Cincinnati

	1	2	3	4	5	6	7	8	9	R	H	E
White Stockings	2	0	0	1	1	1	0	4	0	9	11	7
Browns	0	0	2	0	0	0	0	0	0	2	2	7

W—McCormick (2-1). L—Caruthers (1-1). A—1500.

Game 7 — October 24 at Cincinnati

	1	2	3	4	5	6	7	8	R	H	E
White Stockings	2	0	0	0	2	0	0	0	4	9	9
Browns	0	0	4	6	2	1	0	x	13	13	5

W—Foutz (2-2). L—McCormick (2-2). A—1200.

Batting

White Stockings	G	AB	R	H	RBI	2B	3B	HR	BB	SO	SB	Avg
Cap Anson, 1b	7	26	8	11	—	1	1	0	2	—	—	.423
Tom Burns, ss-4, 3b-3	7	25	3	2	—	0	1	0	0	—	—	.080
John Clarkson, p-3, of-2	5	13	1	2	—	1	0	0	0	—	—	.154
Abner Dalrymple, of	7	26	4	7	—	2	0	1	2	—	—	.269
Silver Flint, c	4	14	0	2	—	0	0	0	0	—	—	.143
George Gore, of	1	3	1	0	—	0	0	0	1	—	—	.000
Bug Holliday, of	1	4	0	0	—	0	0	0	0	—	—	.000
King Kelly, of-4, c-3	7	26	9	9	—	3	1	0	2	—	—	.346
Jim McCormick, p	4	17	1	3	—	0	0	0	0	—	—	.176
Fred Pfeffer, 2b	7	27	5	11	—	2	0	1	0	—	—	.407
Billy Sunday, of	6	22	5	6	—	2	0	0	2	—	—	.273
Ned Williamson, 3b-4, ss-3	7	23	1	2	—	0	0	0	4	—	—	.087
Totals	7	226	38	55	0	11	3	2	13	0	0	.243

Browns	G	AB	R	H	RBI	2B	3B	HR	BB	SO	SB	Avg
Sam Barkley, 2b	7	23	3	2	—	0	0	0	2	—	—	.087
Doc Bushong, c	4	13	1	2	—	0	0	0	0	—	—	.154
Bob Caruthers, p-3, of-2	5	15	1	3	—	0	1	0	1	—	—	.200
Charlie Comiskey, 1b	7	24	6	7	—	0	0	0	0	—	—	.292
Dave Foutz, p	4	12	1	2	—	0	0	0	0	—	—	.167
Bill Gleason, ss	7	26	5	6	—	2	0	0	1	—	—	.231
Arlie Latham, 3b	7	22	5	7	—	3	0	0	2	—	—	.318
Hugh Nicol, of	1	2	0	0	—	0	0	0	0	—	—	.000
Tip O'Neill, of	7	24	4	5	—	0	0	0	0	—	—	.208
Yank Robinson, of-4, c-3	7	23	5	4	—	0	1	0	1	—	—	.174
Curt Welch, of	7	27	5	4	—	1	1	0	0	—	—	.148
Totals	7	211	36	42	0	6	3	0	7	0	0	.199

Pitching

White Stockings	G	GS	CG	ShO	IP	H	R	ER	BB	SO	W-L	Sv	ERA
John Clarkson	3	3	3	0	23.0	19	14	4	3	20	1-1	0	1.57
Jim McCormick	4	4	4	0	29.0	23	22	6	4	14	2-2	0	1.86
Totals	7	7	7	0	52.0	42	36	10	7	34	3-3	0	1.73

Browns	G	GS	CG	ShO	IP	H	R	ER	BB	SO	W-L	Sv	ERA
Bob Caruthers	3	3	3	0	26.0	25	18	7	4	16	1-1	0	2.42
Dave Foutz	4	4	4	0	29.1	30	20	2	9	14	2-2	0	0.61
Totals	7	7	7	0	55.1	55	38	9	13	30	3-3	0	1.46

1886 St. Louis Browns (AA) 4, Chicago White Stockings (NL) 2

For the second year in a row, the Browns and the White Stockings took part in a Series rife with controversy. John Clarkson tossed a five-hitter as the White Sox took the opener, 6-0. St. Louis' Tip O'Neill legged out a pair of inside-the-park homers in Game 2 as the Browns cruised to a 12-0 victory. Bob Caruthers tossed eight one-hit innings before the growing shadows caused the game to be called. Caruthers started again the next day, but the White Stockings pounded him for an 11-4 victory. The fourth game was a back-and-forth affair. The Browns went ahead in the bottom of the eighth when Chicago shortstop Ned Williamson dropped a popup, and darkness brought the game to a close after seven innings with St. Louis ahead, 8-5. The White Stockings quite probably threw the fifth game in order to extend the Series and boost the receipts. Shortstop Ned Williamson took the mound, and when the Browns batted him around, he was replaced by outfielder Jimmy Ryan. St. Louis won, 10-3. The White Stockings played to win in Game 6, and took a 3-0 lead into the bottom of the eighth. But St. Louis rallied, and Arlie Latham tied the game with a two-run triple. In the bottom of the 10th, Curt Welch singled, moved up on a single and a sacrifice, and scored the winning run on a wild pitch to give the Browns the championship. Welch's play became known as the "$15,000 slide," a reference to the winner's total share.

Game 1 — October 18 at Chicago

	1	2	3	4	5	6	7	8	9	R	H	E
Browns	0	0	0	0	0	0	0	0	0	0	5	3
White Stockings	2	0	0	0	1	0	3	x		6	10	4

W—Clarkson (1-0). L—Foutz (0-1). A—6000.

Game 2 — October 19 at Chicago

	1	2	3	4	5	6	7	8	R	H	E
Browns	2	0	0	2	3	0	5	0	12	13	2
White Stockings	0	0	0	0	0	0	0		0	2	10

W—Caruthers (1-0). L—McCormick (0-1). HR—O'Neill 2 (2). A—8000.

Game 3 — October 20 at Chicago

	1	2	3	4	5	6	7	8	R	H	E
White Stockings	2	0	0	1	1	2	3	2	11	9	2
Browns	0	1	0	0	0	2	0	1	4	9	7

W—Clarkson (2-0). L—Caruthers (1-1). HR—Gore (1), Kelly (1). A—6000.

Game 4 — October 21 at St Louis

	1	2	3	4	5	6	7	R	H	E
White Stockings	3	0	0	0	0	2	0	5	6	4
Browns	0	1	1	0	3	3	x	8	7	4

W—Foutz (1-1). L—Clarkson (2-1). A—8000.

Game 5 — October 22 at St Louis

	1	2	3	4	5	6	7	8	R	H	E
White Stockings	0	1	1	1	0	0	0	0	3	3	3
Browns	2	1	4	0	0	3	0	x	10	11	3

W—Hudson (1-0). L—Williamson (0-1). A—10000.

Game 6 — October 23 at St Louis

	1	2	3	4	5	6	7	8	9	10	R	H	E
White Stockings	0	1	0	1	0	1	0	0	0	0	3	6	2
Browns	0	0	0	0	0	0	0	3	0	1	4	5	3

W—Caruthers (2-1). L—Clarkson (2-2). HR—Pfeffer (1). A—8000.

Batting

Browns	G	AB	R	H	RBI	2B	3B	HR	BB	SO	SB	Avg
Doc Bushong, c	6	16	4	3	2	1	0	0	4	5	0	.188
Bob Caruthers, p-3, of-3	6	24	6	6	5	1	2	0	1	4	1	.250
Charlie Comiskey, 1b	6	24	2	7	2	1	0	0	0	4	0	.292
Dave Foutz, p-2, of-2	4	15	2	3	3	1	1	0	0	3	0	.200
Bill Gleason, ss	6	24	3	5	5	0	0	0	1	3	0	.208
Nat Hudson, p-1, of-1	2	6	1	1	0	0	1	0	1	3	0	.167
Arlie Latham, 3b-6, c-1	6	23	4	4	3	0	1	0	3	4	2	.174
Tip O'Neill, of	6	20	4	8	5	0	2	2	4	5	2	.400
Yank Robinson, 2b	6	19	5	6	3	1	1	0	2	3	2	.316
Curt Welch, of	6	20	7	7	1	2	0	0	3	4	2	.350
Totals	6	191	38	50	29	7	8	2	19	38	9	.262

Batting

White Stockings	G	AB	R	H	RBI	2B	3B	HR	BB	SO	SB	Avg
Cap Anson, 1b-6, c-2	6	21	3	5	1	1	0	0	4	0	1	.238
Tom Burns, 3b-6, of-1	6	21	2	6	1	2	1	0	0	2	0	.286
John Clarkson, p-4, of-1	4	15	0	1	1	0	0	0	0	2	1	.067
Abner Dalrymple, of	6	21	2	4	2	1	1	0	0	5	1	.190
Silver Flint, c	1	3	0	0	1	0	0	0	0	1	0	.000
George Gore, of	6	23	4	4	2	0	0	1	3	3	0	.174
King Kelly, c-5, ss-2, 1b-1, 3b-1	6	24	4	5	1	0	0	1	2	2	1	.208
Jim McCormick, p	1	3	0	0	0	0	0	0	0	0	0	.000
Fred Pfeffer, 2b	6	21	7	6	4	0	0	1	2	1	2	.286
Jimmy Ryan, of-6, p-1, ss-1	6	20	4	5	2	1	0	0	1	1	1	.250
Ned Williamson, ss-6, p-2, c-1, of-1	6	18	2	1	3	0	1	0	4	5	1	.056
Totals	6	190	28	37	18	5	3	3	15	22	8	.195

Pitching

Browns	G	GS	CG	ShO	IP	H	R	ER	BB	SO	W-L	Sv	ERA
Bob Caruthers	3	3	3	1	26.0	18	14	7	6	12	2-1	0	2.42
Dave Foutz	2	2	2	0	15.0	16	11	6	6	7	1-1	0	3.60
Nat Hudson	1	1	1	0	7.0	3	3	2	3	3	1-0	0	2.57
Totals	6	6	6	1	48.0	37	28	15	15	22	4-2	0	2.81

Pitching

White Stockings	G	GS	CG	ShO	IP	H	R	ER	BB	SO	W-L	Sv	ERA
John Clarkson	4	4	3	1	31.1	25	15	7	12	28	2-2	0	2.01
Jim McCormick	1	1	1	0	8.0	13	12	6	2	4	0-1	0	6.75
Jimmy Ryan	1	0	0	0	5.0	8	8	5	4	4	0-0	0	9.00
Ned Williamson	2	1	0	0	2.0	4	3	1	1	2	0-1	0	4.50
Totals	6	6	4	1	46.1	50	38	19	19	38	2-4	0	3.69

1887 Detroit Wolverines (NL) 10, St. Louis Browns (AA) 5

The Wolverines downed the Browns in the longest World Series of all time. The Series was effectively over after Game 11, when the Tigers won their eighth game, but the clubs continued on until 15 matches were in the books. Bob Caruthers pitched a four-hitter as the Browns took the opener, 6-1. Pete Conway pitched the Wolverines to a 5-3 win in Game 2 to even the Series. Game 3 was the turning point of the Series. Caruthers took a 1-0 lead into the bottom of the eighth. With two out and no one on base, Caruthers fielded Charlie Ganzel's apparent inning-ending grounder but threw wildly to first. Jack Rowe followed with a topper toward third. Caruthers cut it off but threw it into right field, and Ganzel scored when Charlie Comiskey's return throw got past third baseman Arlie Latham. Detroit scored the winning run in the bottom of the 13th thanks to St. Louis' shoddy defensive play, and the Wolverines went on to take six of the next eight games. Lady Baldwin won four of five decisions for the Wolverines, while Sam Thompson led their offense with a .362 average in 61 at-bats.

Game 1 — October 10 at St Louis

	1	2	3	4	5	6	7	8	9	R	H	E
Browns	2	0	0	0	4	0	0	0	0	6	12	0
Wolverines	0	0	0	0	0	0	0	0	1	1	4	5

W—Caruthers (1-0). L—Getzien (0-1). A—4208.

Game 2 — October 11 at St Louis

	1	2	3	4	5	6	7	8	9	R	H	E
Wolverines	0	2	2	0	0	0	1	0	0	5	10	2
Browns	0	0	0	0	0	0	1	2	0	3	8	7

W—Conway (1-0). L—Foutz (0-1). A—6408.

Game 3 — October 12 at Detroit

	1	2	3	4	5	6	7	8	9	10	11	12	13	R	H	E
Browns	0	1	0	0	0	0	0	0	0	0	0	0	0	1	13	7
Wolverines	0	0	0	0	0	0	0	1	0	0	0	0	1	2	6	1

W—Getzien (1-1). L—Caruthers (1-1). A—4509.

Game 4 — October 13 at Pittsburgh

	1	2	3	4	5	6	7	8	9	R	H	E
Wolverines	4	1	0	0	1	2	0	0	0	8	11	1
Browns	0	0	0	0	0	0	0	0	0	0	2	6

W—Baldwin (1-0). L—King (0-1). A—2447.

Game 5 — October 14 at Brooklyn

	1	2	3	4	5	6	7	8	9	R	H	E
Browns	2	0	0	0	0	2	1	0	0	5	5	4
Wolverines	0	0	0	0	2	0	0	0	0	2	7	5

W—Caruthers (2-1). L—Conway (1-1). A—6796.

Game 6 — October 15 at New York

	1	2	3	4	5	6	7	8	9	R	H	E
Wolverines	3	3	0	0	0	0	0	0	3	9	12	1
Browns	0	0	0	0	0	0	0	0	0	0	2	8

W—Getzien (2-1). L—Foutz (0-2). A—5797.

Game 7 — October 17 at Philadelphia

	1	2	3	4	5	6	7	8	9	R	H	E
Browns	0	0	0	0	0	0	0	0	1	1	8	1
Wolverines	0	3	0	0	0	0	0	0	x	3	6	1

W—Baldwin (2-0). L—Caruthers (2-2). HR—O'Neill (1). A—6478.

Game 8 — October 18 at Boston

	1	2	3	4	5	6	7	8	9	R	H	E
Wolverines	0	3	1	0	0	3	2	0	0	9	13	2
Browns	1	0	0	0	0	1	0	0	0	2	8	5

W—Getzien (3-1). L—Caruthers (2-3). HR—Thompson 2 (2). A—2891.

Game 9 — October 19 at Philadelphia

	1	2	3	4	5	6	7	8	9	R	H	E
Browns	0	0	0	1	0	1	0	0	0	2	9	2
Wolverines	0	0	0	1	0	0	2	1	x	4	6	3

W—Conway (2-1). L—King (0-2). A—2389.

Game 10 — Oct. 21 at Washington D.C.

	1	2	3	4	5	6	7	8	9	R	H	E
Wolverines	2	0	0	0	1	0	0	0	1	4	8	3
Browns	2	0	0	3	1	4	1	x		11	16	5

W—Caruthers (3-3). L—Getzien (3-2). HR—Latham (1), Richardson (1), Welch (1). A—1261.

Game 11 — October 21 at Baltimore

	1	2	3	4	5	6	7	8	9	R	H	E
Browns	1	1	0	0	1	0	0	0	0	3	2	7
Wolverines	1	0	0	3	4	4	1	0	x	13	14	7

W—Baldwin (3-0). L—Foutz (0-3). HR—Twitchell (1). A—2707.

Game 12 — October 22 at Brooklyn

	1	2	3	4	5	6	7	R	H	E
Wolverines	0	0	0	1	0	0	0	1	5	3
Browns	4	1	0	0	0	0	x	5	10	2

W—King (1-2). L—Conway (2-2). A—1138.

Game 13 — October 24 at Detroit

	1	2	3	4	5	6	7	8	9	R	H	E
Wolverines	0	2	0	1	0	0	1	2	0	6	12	3
Browns	1	0	0	0	1	0	0	0	1	3	4	5

W—Baldwin (4-0). L—Caruthers (3-4). A—3389.

Game 14 — October 25 at Chicago

	1	2	3	4	5	6	7	8	9	R	H	E
Browns	0	0	0	0	2	1	0	0		3	10	5
Wolverines	3	0	0	0	1	0	0	0	x	4	4	4

W—Getzien (4-2). L—King (1-3). A—378.

Game 15 — October 26 at St Louis

	1	2	3	4	5	6	R	H	E
Browns	3	4	0	1	1	0	9	11	5
Wolverines	0	1	1	0	0	0	2	8	7

W—Caruthers (4-4). L—Baldwin (4-1). A—659.

Batting

Wolverines	G	AB	R	H	RBI	2B	3B	HR	BB	SO	SB	Avg
Lady Baldwin, p	5	17	1	4	1	1	0	0	2	2	1	.235
Charlie Bennett, c-10, 1b-3	11	42	6	11	9	2	1	0	3	5	5	.262
Dan Brouthers, 1b	1	3	0	2	0	0	0	0	0	0	0	.667
Pete Conway, p	4	12	0	0	0	0	0	0	0	2	0	.000
Fred Dunlap, 2b	11	40	5	6	1	0	1	0	0	4	4	.150
Charlie Ganzel, 1b-10, c-7	14	58	5	13	2	1	0	0	1	2	3	.224
Charlie Getzien, p	6	20	5	6	2	2	0	0	3	6	1	.300
Ned Hanlon, of	15	50	5	11	4	1	1	0	5	1	7	.220
Hardy Richardson, of-10, 2b-5, 3b-1	15	66	12	13	4	5	2	1	9	7	1	.197
Jack Rowe, ss	15	63	12	21	7	1	1	0	2	5	5	.333
Sy Sutcliffe, 1b-3, c-1	4	11	1	1	0	0	0	0	1	1	1	.091
Sam Thompson, of	15	58	8	21	7	2	0	2	3	3	5	.362
Larry Twitchell, of	6	20	5	5	3	1	0	1	0	1	1	.250
Deacon White, 3b-14, 1b-1	15	58	8	12	3	1	1	0	2	0	2	.207
Totals	15	518	73	126	43	17	7	4	23	37	42	.243

Browns	G	AB	R	H	RBI	2B	3B	HR	BB	SO	SB	Avg
Jack Boyle, c	6	24	1	5	1	0	0	0	0	4	0	.208
Doc Bushong, c	9	29	3	7	1	0	0	0	4	1	0	.241
Bob Caruthers, p-8, of-3	10	46	2	11	3	0	0	1	1	3	3	.239
Charlie Comiskey, 1b-14, of-1	15	62	8	19	2	2	0	0	1	1	4	.306
Dave Foutz, of-11, p-3, 1b-1	15	59	4	10	1	2	1	0	2	3	0	.169
Bill Gleason, ss	13	49	3	8	1	0	0	0	3	2	1	.163
Silver King, p	4	14	0	1	0	0	0	0	0	3	0	.071
Arlie Latham, 3b	15	58	12	17	1	1	0	0	9	2	15	.293
Harry Lyons, ss	2	7	3	2	0	0	0	0	0	1	0	.286
Tip O'Neill, of	15	65	7	13	5	2	1	1	0	2	0	.200
Yank Robinson, 2b	15	46	5	15	4	5	1	0	10	6	4	.326
Curt Welch, of	15	58	6	12	6	3	1	1	0	2	1	.207
Totals	15	517	54	120	25	15	4	2	31	27	28	.232

Pitching

Wolverines	G	GS	CG	ShO	IP	H	R	ER	BB	SO	W-L	Sv	ERA
Lady Baldwin	5	5	5	1	42.0	28	16	7	10	4	4-1	0	1.50
Pete Conway	4	4	4	0	33.0	31	15	11	6	10	2-2	0	3.00
Charlie Getzien	6	6	6	1	58.0	61	23	16	15	17	4-2	0	2.48
Totals	15	15	15	2	133.0	120	54	34	31	31	10-5	0	2.30

Browns	G	GS	CG	ShO	IP	H	R	ER	BB	SO	W-L	Sv	ERA
Bob Caruthers	8	8	8	0	71.2	64	29	17	12	19	4-4	0	2.13
Dave Foutz	3	3	3	0	26.0	36	27	10	9	6	0-3	0	3.46
Silver King	4	4	4	0	31.0	26	17	7	2	21	1-3	0	2.03
Totals	15	15	15	0	128.2	126	73	34	23	46	5-10	0	2.38

1888 New York Giants (NL) 6, St. Louis Browns (AA) 4

New York Giants ace Tim Keefe bested St. Louis Browns hurler Silver King in the opener of the 1888 World Series, 2-1. The Giants scored the eventual go-ahead run in the bottom of the third when Mike Tiernan lit out for second, St. Louis catcher Jack Boyle threw the ball into center field and outfielder Harry Lyons let it roll through his legs as Tiernan trotted home. Elton Chamberlin twirled a five-hit shutout in Game 2 to give St. Louis a 3-0 win. Keefe outdueled King again in Game 3 as New York prevailed, 4-2. New York went up three games to one with a 6-3 victory in Game 4. King took a 4-1 lead into the bottom of the eighth inning of the fifth game before the Browns unraveled. The Giants rallied and scored the go-ahead run when Yank Robinson and Harry Lyons collided in short center field on a fly ball that should have ended the inning. Darkness abbreviated the Giants' 6-4 victory. The Giants closed to within one game of the championship with a crushing 12-5 victory in Game 6. Chamberlin was staked to an early 4-0 lead, but suddenly lost his effectiveness in the top of the sixth, allowing 11 runs in the final three frames. St. Louis stayed alive with a come-from-behind, 7-5 victory in Game 7. Shortstop Bill White capped an eighth-inning rally by doubling in the go-ahead runs. The next day, Buck Ewing gave the Giants an early lead with a solo homer and a three-run triple, and the Giants tallied six more in the top of the ninth to turn a close game into a championship-clinching 11-3 rout. The final three games were played as exhibitions.

Game 1 — October 16 at New York

	1	2	3	4	5	6	7	8	9	R	H	E
Browns	0	0	1	0	0	0	0	0	0	1	3	5
Giants	0	1	1	0	0	0	0	x		2	2	4

W—Keefe (1-0). L—King (0-1). A—4876.

Game 2 — October 17 at New York

	1	2	3	4	5	6	7	8	9	R	H	E
Browns	0	1	0	0	0	0	0	0	2	3	7	4
Giants	0	0	0	0	0	0	0	0	0	0	6	1

W—Chamberlin (1-0). L—Welch (0-1). A—5575.

Game 3 — October 18 at New York

	1	2	3	4	5	6	7	8	9	R	H	E
Browns	0	0	0	0	0	0	0	1	1	2	5	5
Giants	2	0	0	1	0	0	1	0	x	4	5	2

W—Keefe (2-0). L—King (0-2). A—5780.

Game 4 — October 19 at Brooklyn

	1	2	3	4	5	6	7	8	9	R	H	E
Giants	1	0	4	0	1	0	0	0	0	6	8	2
Browns	0	0	1	0	0	0	0	2	0	3	7	4

W—Crane (1-0). L—Chamberlin (1-1). A—3062.

Game 5 — October 20 at New York

	1	2	3	4	5	6	7	8	R	H	E
Browns	0	0	3	0	0	1	0	0	4	5	5
Giants	1	0	0	0	0	0	0	5	6	9	2

W—Keefe (3-0). L—King (0-3). A—9124.

Game 6 — October 22 at Philadelphia

	1	2	3	4	5	6	7	8	R	H	E
Giants	0	0	0	1	0	3	3	5	12	13	5
Browns	3	0	1	0	0	0	0	1	5	3	7

W—Welch (1-1). L—Chamberlin (1-2). A—3281.

Game 7 — October 24 at St Louis

	1	2	3	4	5	6	7	8	R	H	E
Giants	0	3	0	0	2	0	0		5	11	3
Browns	0	0	0	3	0	0	0	4	7	8	3

W—King (1-3). L—Crane (1-1). A—4624.

Game 8 — October 25 at St Louis

	1	2	3	4	5	6	7	8	9	R	H	E
Giants	1	0	3	1	0	0	0	0	6	11	12	2
Browns	0	0	0	1	0	0	1	1	0	3	5	6

W—Keefe (4-0). L—Chamberlin (1-3). HR—Ewing (1), Tiernan (1). A—4865.

Game 9 — October 26 at St Louis

	1	2	3	4	5	6	7	8	9	10	R	H	E
Browns	1	4	0	0	2	0	2	0	2	3	14	15	4
Giants	0	3	5	0	0	0	1	2	0	0	11	14	5

W—Devlin (0-0). L—George (0-1). HR—O'Neill (1). A—711.

Game 10 — October 27 at St Louis

	1	2	3	4	5	6	7	8	9	R	H	E
Browns	0	1	0	5	0	5	4	2	1	18	17	3
Giants	3	1	0	0	0	0	0	2	1	7	13	8

W—Chamberlin (2-3). L—Titcomb (0-1). HR—George (1), McCarthy (1), O'Neill (2). A—412.

Batting

Giants	G	AB	R	H	RBI	2B	3B	HR	BB	SO	SB	Avg
Willard Brown, c	2	8	1	3	0	1	0	0	0	0	0	.375
Roger Connor, 1b	7	23	7	7	3	1	2	0	4	0	4	.304
Ed Crane, p	2	7	1	1	2	0	0	0	0	1	0	.143
Buck Ewing, c-6, 1b-1	7	26	5	9	6	0	2	1	1	3	5	.346
Bill George, p-1, 1b-1	2	9	2	3	4	1	0	1	0	2	0	.333
George Gore, of-2, 3b-1	3	11	5	5	0	1	0	0	2	2	2	.455
Gil Hatfield, p-1, 2b-1, ss-1	2	8	2	2	1	0	0	0	1	2	1	.250
Tim Keefe, p	4	11	2	1	0	0	0	0	2	2	1	.091
Pat Murphy, c	3	10	1	1	1	0	0	0	0	0	0	.100
Jim O'Rourke, of-7, 1b-2, ss-1	10	36	4	8	1	0	0	0	4	2	3	.222
Danny Richardson, 2b	9	36	6	6	6	2	0	0	3	5	3	.167
Mike Slattery, of-10, 2b-1	10	39	6	8	5	2	0	0	5	6	6	.205
Mike Tiernan, of	10	38	8	13	6	0	1	8	2	5		.342
Cannonball Titcomb, p-1, of-1	1	4	1	2	1	1	0	0	0	0	0	.500
Monte Ward, ss	8	29	4	11	6	1	0	0	1	0	6	.379
Mickey Welch, p	2	7	2	2	1	0	0	0	0	0	0	.286
Art Whitney, 3b-9, of-1	10	37	7	12	12	0	1	0	1	4	2	.324
Totals	10	339	64	94	55	10	5	3	27	30	38	.277

Browns	G	AB	R	H	RBI	2B	3B	HR	BB	SO	SB	Avg
Jack Boyle, c-4, of-1	4	16	4	7	4	0	1	0	2	2	3	.438
Elton Chamberlin, p	5	13	3	0	0	0	0	0	4	3	1	.000
Charlie Comiskey, 1b-10, of-1	10	41	6	11	3	1	1	0	1	1	4	.268
Jim Devlin, p	1	3	0	0	0	0	0	0	0	0	0	.000
Ed Herr, of	3	11	2	1	0	0	0	0	0	5	1	.091
Silver King, p	5	15	1	1	0	0	0	0	1	6	0	.067
Arlie Latham, 3b	10	40	10	10	3	0	0	0	5	6	11	.250
Harry Lyons, of	5	17	0	2	1	0	0	0	1	5	0	.118
Tommy McCarthy, of	10	41	10	10	9	1	0	1	0	0	6	.244
Jocko Milligan, c-8, 1b-1	8	25	5	10	4	2	1	0	3	3	0	.400
Tip O'Neill, of	10	37	8	9	11	1	0	2	6	3	0	.243
Yank Robinson, 2b	10	36	7	9	7	2	1	0	6	12	2	.250
Bill White, ss	10	35	4	5	4	1	0	0	3	6	1	.143
Totals	10	330	60	75	46	8	4	3	32	52	29	.227

Pitching

Giants	G	GS	CG	ShO	IP	H	R	ER	BB	SO	W-L	Sv	ERA
Ed Crane	2	2	2	0	17.0	15	10	4	6	12	1-1	0	2.12
Bill George	1	1	1	0	10.0	15	14	8	3	4	0-1	0	7.20
Gil Hatfield	1	0	0	0	5.0	12	12	7	3	2	0-0	0	12.60
Tim Keefe	4	4	4	0	35.0	18	10	2	9	30	4-0	0	0.51
Cannonball Titcomb	1	1	0	0	4.0	5	6	3	2	2	0-1	0	6.75
Mickey Welch	2	2	2	0	17.0	10	8	5	9	2	1-1	0	2.65
Totals	10	10	9	0	88.0	75	60	29	32	52	6-4	0	2.97

Browns	G	GS	CG	ShO	IP	H	R	ER	BB	SO	W-L	Sv	ERA
Elton Chamberlin	5	5	5	1	44.0	52	36	26	16	13	2-3	0	5.32
Jim Devlin	1	0	0	0	7.0	5	3	2	2	5	1-0	0	2.57
Silver King	5	5	4	0	35.0	37	25	9	9	12	1-3	0	2.31
Totals	10	10	9	1	86.0	94	64	37	27	30	4-6	0	3.87

1889 New York Giants (NL) 6,
Brooklyn Bridegrooms (AA) 3

The 1889 Series was the first intracity matchup, as the Brooklyn Bridegrooms faced the New York Giants. Brooklyn took an early 5-0 lead on New York's Tim Keefe in Game 1, but the Giants came back to take the lead in the seventh. Brooklyn came back to take a 12-10 lead in the bottom of the eighth, just before the game was called due to darkness (many thought that the timing of the call was more than just a fortunate coincidence). The Giants' skill on the basepaths resulted in a 6-2 victory in Game 2. Brooklyn took the third game, 8-7, on another fortuitous decision by the umpire. The game was called with the Giants trailing by a run with out and the bases loaded in the top of the ninth. Brooklyn led Game 4 7-2 until the Giants tied it with five in their half of the sixth. Darkness fell, but the umpires delayed calling the game long enough to allow Brooklyn to score the go-ahead runs for a 10-7 win. Ed Crane notched a two-run homer and pitched New York to an 11-3 win in the fifth game. Brooklyn's Adonis Terry was within one out of a 1-0 shutout victory in Game 6. Then Monte Ward singled, stole second and third, and scored on a single by Roger Connor. Jack Slattery scored all the way from second on an infield groundout in the 11th to give the New Yorkers a 2-1 win and tie the Series at three games apiece. Brooklyn pounded New York starter Tom Lovett in Game 7, and held on for an 11-7 victory. The Giants' onslaught continued in Game 8 as they posted a 16-7 victory to come within a game of winning the Series. The ninth game was tied 2-2 in the bottom of the seventh, and New York's Buck Ewing was batting with two out and Slattery on second base. Ewing struck out on a high pitch, but the ball got away from the catcher and went all the way to the backstop. Incredibly, Slattery scored all the way from second with the eventual winning run.

Game 1 — October 18 at New York

	1	2	3	4	5	6	7	8	R	H	E
Giants	0	2	0	2	1	0	5	0	10	12	2
Bridegrooms	5	1	0	0	0	2	4		12	16	3

W—Terry (1-0). L—Keefe (0-1). HR—Collins (1), Richardson (1). A—8848.

Game 2 — October 19 at Brooklyn

	1	2	3	4	5	6	7	8	9	R	H	E
Giants	1	1	1	1	2	0	0	0	0	6	10	4
Bridegrooms	1	1	0	0	0	0	0	0	0	2	4	8

W—Crane (1-0). L—Caruthers (0-1). A—16172.

Game 3 — October 22 at New York

	1	2	3	4	5	6	7	8	R	H	E
Giants	2	0	0	0	3	2	0	0	7	15	2
Bridegrooms	0	2	3	1	2	0	0	x	8	12	3

W—Hughes (1-0). L—Welch (0-1). HR—Corkhill (1), O'Rourke (1). A—5181.

Game 4 — October 23 at Brooklyn

	1	2	3	4	5	6	R	H	E
Giants	0	0	1	1	0	5	7	9	8
Bridegrooms	2	0	2	0	3	3	10	7	1

W—Terry (2-0). L—Crane (1-1). HR—Burns (1). A—3045.

Game 5 — October 24 at Brooklyn

	1	2	3	4	5	6	7	8	9	R	H	E
Giants	0	0	4	0	4	0	0	2	1	11	12	2
Bridegrooms	0	0	0	1	1	1	0	0	0	3	8	2

W—Crane (2-1). L—Caruthers (0-2). HR—Brown (1), Crane (1), Richardson (2). A—2901.

Game 6 — October 25 at New York

	1	2	3	4	5	6	7	8	9	10	11	R	H	E
Bridegrooms	0	1	0	0	0	0	0	0	0	0	0	1	6	4
Giants	0	0	0	0	0	0	0	0	1	0	1	2	7	1

W—O'Day (1-0). L—Terry (2-1). A—2556.

Game 7 — October 26 at New York

	1	2	3	4	5	6	7	8	9	R	H	E
Bridegrooms	0	0	4	0	3	0	0	0	0	7	5	3
Giants	1	8	0	0	0	1	1	0	x	11	14	4

W—Crane (3-1). L—Lovett (0-1). HR—O'Rourke (2), Richardson (3). A—3312.

Game 8 — October 28 at Brooklyn

	1	2	3	4	5	6	7	8	9	R	H	E
Giants	5	4	1	2	0	3	0	0	1	16	15	4
Bridegrooms	2	0	0	0	0	0	0	2	3	7	5	4

W—Crane (4-1). L—Terry (2-2). HR—Burns (2), Foutz (1), Tiernan (1). A—2584.

Game 9 — October 29 at New York

	1	2	3	4	5	6	7	8	9	R	H	E
Bridegrooms	2	0	0	0	0	0	0	0	0	2	4	2
Giants	1	0	0	0	1	0	1	0	x	3	8	5

W—O'Day (2-0). L—Terry (2-3). A—3067.

Batting

Giants	G	AB	R	H	RBI	2B	3B	HR	BB	SO	SB	Avg
Willard Brown, c	1	5	3	3	2	0	0	1	0	0	0	.600
Roger Connor, 1b	9	35	9	12	12	2	2	0	3	2	8	.343
Ed Crane, p	5	18	3	5	5	1	1	1	1	2	0	.278
Buck Ewing, c	8	36	5	9	7	4	0	0	2	5	1	.250
George Gore, of	5	21	5	7	1	1	1	0	3	0	2	.333
Tim Keefe, p	2	4	1	2	0	1	0	0	1	1	0	.500
Hank O'Day, p	3	6	0	1	0	0	0	0	2	2	0	.167
Jim O'Rourke, of	9	36	7	14	7	2	2	2	2	2	3	.389
Danny Richardson, 2b	9	35	8	11	8	1	1	3	3	5	3	.314
Mike Slattery, of	4	16	6	3	1	0	0	0	3	1	1	.188
Mike Tiernan, of	9	38	12	11	5	1	1	1	5	3	3	.289
Monte Ward, ss	9	36	10	15	7	0	1	0	5	2	10	.417
Mickey Welch, p	1	3	0	1	0	1	0	0	0	1	0	.333
Art Whitney, 3b	9	35	4	8	3	2	1	0	1	0	0	.229
Totals	9	324	73	102	58	16	10	8	31	26	31	.315

Bridegrooms	G	AB	R	H	RBI	2B	3B	HR	BB	SO	SB	Avg
Oyster Burns, of	9	35	8	8	11	3	0	2	5	6	0	.229
Doc Bushong, c	3	8	0	0	0	0	0	0	1	0	0	.000
Bob Caruthers, p	4	8	1	2	1	0	0	0	3	3	0	.250
Bob Clark, c	4	12	3	5	3	2	0	0	2	2	0	.417
Hub Collins, 2b	9	35	13	13	7	2	3	0	1	7	5	.371
Pop Corkhill, of	9	24	5	5	5	1	0	1	6	2	1	.208
Jumbo Davis, ss	1	4	0	0	0	0	0	0	0	0	0	.000
Dave Foutz, 1b-9, p-1	9	35	7	10	9	2	0	1	4	2	3	.286
Mickey Hughes, p	1	3	1	1	0	1	0	0	1	2	0	.333
Tom Lovett, p	1	1	0	0	0	0	0	0	0	0	0	.000
Darby O'Brien, of	9	31	8	5	4	0	1	0	12	6	6	.161
George Pinckney, 3b	9	31	8	8	3	2	0	0	4	2	2	.258
Germany Smith, ss	8	29	2	5	2	1	0	0	3	2	2	.172
Adonis Terry, p-5, 1b-1	5	18	1	3	1	0	0	0	1	1	1	.167
Joe Visner, c-3, of-2	5	16	2	2	0	1	0	0	2	3	0	.125
Totals	9	290	52	67	41	17	2	5	51	36	21	.231

Pitching

Giants	G	GS	CG	ShO	IP	H	R	ER	BB	SO	W-L	Sv	ERA
Ed Crane	5	5	4	0	38.2	29	29	16	32	19	4-1	0	3.72
Tim Keefe	2	1	1	0	11.0	17	12	10	2	4	0-1	1	8.18
Hank O'Day	3	2	2	0	23.0	10	3	3	14	12	2-0	0	1.17
Mickey Welch	1	1	0	0	5.0	11	8	5	3	1	0-1	0	9.00
Totals	9	9	7	0	77.2	67	52	34	51	36	6-3	1	3.94

Bridegrooms	G	GS	CG	ShO	IP	H	R	ER	BB	SO	W-L	Sv	ERA
Bob Caruthers	4	2	2	0	24.0	28	19	10	6	6	0-2	0	3.75
Dave Foutz	1	0	0	0	5.0	5	4	4	2	2	0-0	0	7.20
Mickey Hughes	1	1	0	0	7.0	14	7	6	3	1	1-0	0	7.71
Tom Lovett	1	1	0	0	3.0	8	9	8	2	1	0-1	0	24.00
Adonis Terry	5	5	4	0	37.2	47	34	25	18	14	2-3	0	5.97
Totals	9	9	6	0	76.2	102	73	53	31	26	3-6	1	6.22

1890 Brooklyn Bridegrooms (NL) 3, Louisville Colonels (AA) 3

The American Association's Louisville Cyclones met the National League champion Brooklyn Bridegrooms in the 1890 World Series. Adonis Terry tossed a two-hitter in the opener, leading Brooklyn to a 9-0 victory. Six Louisville errors led to eight unearned runs. Germany Smith's two-run single in the top of the fourth keyed Brooklyn's 5-3 victory in Game 2. It was decided in the middle of Game 3 that only eight innings would be played. Brooklyn seemed to be on the verge of taking a three-games-to-none lead in the Series when they took 7-4 lead into the bottom of the eighth. But Louisville rallied and ultimately scored the tying run on Terry's wild pitch. The game ended in a 7-7 tie. Game 4 was tied at four apiece when Louisville's Tim Shinnick tripled to lead off the bottom of the seventh. A moment later, he scored the go-ahead run on an infield groundout, and the Cyclones held on for a 5-4 victory. After the Series shifted to Brooklyn's Washington Park, the Bridegrooms notched a 7-2 victory in Game 5 behind Tom Lovett's five-hit pitching. Louisville staved off elimination with a 9-8 win in the sixth game as Red Ehret quelled a late Brooklyn rally in a nick of time. The next day, Ehret tossed a four-hitter, turning back the Bridegrooms, 6-2. Due to cold weather and poor attendance, the clubs decided to postpone the remainder of the Series until the following spring. The Series never was resumed, however, leaving the clubs tied with three wins and one tie apiece.

Game 1 — October 17 at Louisville

	1	2	3	4	5	6	7	8	R	H	E
Bridegrooms	3	0	0	0	3	0	3	0	9	11	1
Colonels	0	0	0	0	0	0	0	0	0	2	6

W—Terry (1-0). L—Stratton (0-1). A—5600.

Game 2 — October 18 at Louisville

	1	2	3	4	5	6	7	8	9	R	H	E
Bridegrooms	0	2	0	2	0	1	0	0	0	5	5	3
Colonels	1	0	1	0	0	0	0	0	1	3	6	5

W—Lovett (1-0). L—Daily (0-1). A—2860.

Game 3 — October 20 at Louisville

	1	2	3	4	5	6	7	8	R	H	E
Bridegrooms	0	2	0	1	3	0	1	0	7	10	2
Colonels	0	0	1	0	1	2	0	3	7	11	3

A—2500.

Game 4 — October 21 at Louisville

	1	2	3	4	5	6	7	8	9	R	H	E
Bridegrooms	0	3	1	0	0	0	0	0	0	4	7	2
Colonels	3	0	1	0	0	0	1	0	x	5	9	2

W—Ehret (1-0). L—Lovett (1-1). A—1050.

Game 5 — October 25 at Brooklyn

	1	2	3	4	5	6	7	8	9	R	H	E
Colonels	0	1	0	0	1	0	0	0	0	2	5	6
Bridegrooms	2	1	0	2	0	0	2	0	x	7	7	0

W—Lovett (2-1). L—Daily (0-2). HR—Burns (1). A—1000.

Game 6 — October 27 at Brooklyn

	1	2	3	4	5	6	7	8	9	R	H	E
Colonels	0	1	2	1	0	1	2	2	0	9	13	3
Bridegrooms	1	0	0	0	0	4	0	3	0	8	12	3

W—Stratton (1-1). L—Terry (1-1). A—600.

Game 7 — October 28 at Brooklyn

	1	2	3	4	5	6	7	8	9	R	H	E
Colonels	1	0	3	0	0	0	0	2	0	6	8	3
Bridegrooms	2	0	0	0	0	0	0	0	0	2	4	1

W—Ehret (2-0). L—Lovett (2-2). A—300.

Batting

Bridegrooms	G	AB	R	H	RBI	2B	3B	HR	BB	SO	SB	Avg
Oyster Burns, of-4, 3b-3	7	27	6	6	5	2	0	1	3	4	0	.222
Doc Bushong, c	2	6	0	0	0	0	0	0	0	1	0	.000
Bob Caruthers, of	2	6	0	0	0	0	0	0	2	0	0	.000
Bob Clark, c	1	3	2	2	1	0	1	0	0	0	0	.667
Hub Collins, 2b	7	29	7	9	1	0	1	0	3	0	2	.310
Tom Daly, c-6, 1b-1	6	22	1	4	3	2	0	0	0	4	2	.182
Patsy Donovan, of	5	17	5	8	3	1	0	0	2	1	3	.471
Dave Foutz, 1b-7, of-1	7	30	6	9	4	2	1	0	0	1	1	.300
Tom Lovett, p-4, of-1	5	15	0	1	0	0	0	0	0	4	0	.067
Darby O'Brien, of	6	24	3	3	3	0	1	0	1	5	3	.125
George Pinckney, 3b	4	14	4	5	3	0	2	0	2	1	1	.357
Germany Smith, ss	7	29	3	8	7	0	2	0	0	3	1	.276
Adonis Terry, p-3, of-3	6	20	5	1	0	1	0	0	6	3	1	.050
Totals	7	242	42	56	30	8	8	1	19	27	14	.231

Colonels	G	AB	R	H	RBI	2B	3B	HR	BB	SO	SB	Avg
Ned Bligh, c	2	3	0	0	0	0	0	0	0	1	0	.000
Ed Daily, of-4, p-2	6	22	1	3	3	1	1	0	1	2	2	.136
Red Ehret, p	3	7	1	3	0	0	0	0	0	0	0	.429
Charlie Hamburg, of	7	26	3	7	2	1	0	0	0	3	0	.269
George Meakim, p	1	2	0	1	0	0	0	0	0	0	0	.500
Harry Raymond, ss-5, 3b-3	7	27	5	4	1	1	1	0	2	5	1	.148
John Ryan, c	6	19	0	1	2	0	0	0	0	1	1	.053
Tim Shinnick, 2b	7	24	3	7	3	1	1	0	2	2	2	.292
Scott Stratton, p-3, of-1	4	9	4	2	0	1	0	0	2	1	3	.222
Harry Taylor, 1b	7	30	6	9	2	1	0	0	2	3	3	.300
Phil Tomney, ss	3	5	1	1	0	0	0	0	3	1	0	.200
Farmer Weaver, of	7	27	4	7	4	1	0	0	1	2	5	.259
Pete Weckbecker, c	1	4	0	0	0	0	0	0	0	1	0	.000
Chicken Wolf, 3b-5, of-3	7	25	4	9	8	3	1	0	3	0	2	.360
Totals	7	230	32	54	25	10	5	0	16	22	19	.235

Pitching

Bridegrooms	G	GS	CG	ShO	IP	H	R	ER	BB	SO	W-L	Sv	ERA
Tom Lovett	4	4	4	0	35.0	29	16	11	6	14	2-2	0	2.83
Adonis Terry	3	3	3	1	25.0	25	16	10	10	8	1-1	0	3.60
Totals	7	7	7	1	60.0	54	32	21	16	22	3-3	0	3.15

Colonels	G	GS	CG	ShO	IP	H	R	ER	BB	SO	W-L	Sv	ERA
Ed Daily	2	2	2	0	17.0	12	12	5	8	5	0-2	0	2.65
Red Ehret	3	2	2	0	20.0	12	9	3	6	13	2-0	1	1.35
George Meakim	1	0	0	0	4.0	6	4	0	1	1	0-0	0	0.00
Scott Stratton	3	3	1	0	19.0	26	17	5	4	8	1-1	0	2.37
Totals	7	7	5	0	60.0	56	42	13	19	27	3-3	1	1.95

1892 Boston Beaneaters (NL) 5, Cleveland Spiders (NL) 0

In 1892, the National League was the only remaining major league. The NL split its season into two halves and announced that the winners of each half would play for the championship. The Boston Beaneaters won the first half, and in the second half, they finished only three games behind the first-place Cleveland Spiders. Cleveland opened at home with Cy Young, as Boston countered with hard-hitting hurler Jack Stivetts. The two matched zeroes as the shadows grew. Cleveland nearly won it in the ninth when Jesse Burkett tried to score from second on a forceout, but second baseman Joe Quinn's peg cut him down at the plate. The game was called after 11 innings, ending as a scoreless tie. Each hurler went the distance. Boston's John Clarkson downed Cleveland 4-3 in Game 2, stranding the tying run on third base in the ninth. Stivetts pitched Boston to a 3-2 victory in Game 3. He also doubled and scored the eventual winning run in the bottom of the seventh. Kid Nichols made his first appearance in Game 4, blanking the Spiders, 4-0. Two errors by Boston shortstop Herman Long and a three-run homer by Clarkson gave the Spiders an early 6-0 lead in Game 5. But Boston exploded for nine runs in the middle three innings, and took a 12-7 decision to move to within a game of the championship. Young, hampered by a sore arm, was ineffective in Game 6, and the Beaneaters turned back the Spiders with an 8-3 victory.

Game 1 — October 17 at Cleveland

	1	2	3	4	5	6	7	8	9	10	11	R	H	E
Spiders	0	0	0	0	0	0	0	0	0	0	0	0	4	1
Beaneaters	0	0	0	0	0	0	0	0	0	0	0	0	6	0

A—6000.

Game 2 — October 18 at Cleveland

	1	2	3	4	5	6	7	8	9	R	H	E
Beaneaters	1	0	1	0	1	0	0	1	0	4	10	2
Spiders	0	0	1	1	0	0	0	0	1	3	10	2

W—Staley (1-0). L—Clarkson (0-1). A—6700.

Game 3 — October 19 at Cleveland

	1	2	3	4	5	6	7	8	9	R	H	E
Spiders	2	0	0	0	0	0	0	0	0	2	8	0
Beaneaters	1	1	0	0	0	0	1	0	x	3	9	2

W—Stivetts (1-0). L—Young (0-1). A—5000.

Game 4 — October 21 at Boston

	1	2	3	4	5	6	7	8	9	R	H	E
Spiders	0	0	0	0	0	0	0	0	0	0	7	3
Beaneaters	0	0	2	0	0	2	0	0	x	4	6	0

W—Nichols (1-0). L—Cuppy (0-1). HR—Duffy (1). A—6547.

Game 5 — October 22 at Boston

	1	2	3	4	5	6	7	8	9	R	H	E
Spiders	0	6	0	0	1	0	0	0	0	7	9	4
Beaneaters	0	0	0	3	2	4	3	0	x	12	14	3

W—Stivetts (2-0). L—Clarkson (0-2). HR—Clarkson (1), Tucker (1). A—3466.

Game 6 — October 24 at Boston

	1	2	3	4	5	6	7	8	9	R	H	E
Spiders	0	0	3	0	0	0	0	0	0	3	10	5
Beaneaters	0	0	2	2	1	1	1	1	x	8	11	5

W—Nichols (2-0). L—Young (0-2). HR—Bennett (1). A—2300.

Batting

Beaneaters	G	AB	R	H	RBI	2B	3B	HR	BB	SO	SB	Avg
Charlie Bennett, c	2	7	2	2	1	0	0	1	0	2	1	.286
Hugh Duffy, of	6	26	3	12	9	3	2	1	1	0	3	.462
Charlie Ganzel, c	2	8	1	4	2	0	0	0	1	0	0	.500
King Kelly, c	2	8	0	0	0	0	0	0	0	2	1	.000
Herman Long, ss	6	27	4	6	1	0	0	0	0	0	2	.222
Bobby Lowe, of	6	23	8	3	0	0	0	0	1	2	1	.130
Tommy McCarthy, of	6	21	2	8	2	2	0	0	6	1	3	.381
Billy Nash, 3b	6	24	3	4	4	0	0	0	2	3	2	.167
Kid Nichols, p	2	7	1	2	2	0	0	0	0	1	1	.286
Joe Quinn, 2b	6	21	2	6	4	1	1	0	1	2	0	.286
Harry Staley, p	1	4	0	0	0	0	0	0	0	3	0	.000
Jack Stivetts, p	3	12	3	3	1	1	1	0	0	2	0	.250
Tommy Tucker, 1b	6	23	2	6	2	0	0	1	0	1	0	.261
Totals	6	211	31	56	28	7	4	3	12	19	14	.265

Spiders	G	AB	R	H	RBI	2B	3B	HR	BB	SO	SB	Avg
Jesse Burkett, of	6	25	3	8	1	1	0	0	0	2	4	.320
Cupid Childs, 2b	6	22	3	9	0	0	2	0	5	1	0	.409
John Clarkson, p	2	8	1	2	3	0	0	1	0	1	0	.250
Nig Cuppy, p	1	3	0	0	0	0	0	0	0	2	0	.000
George Davis, 3b	3	6	0	1	0	0	0	0	0	1	0	.167
Jimmy McAleer, of	6	22	0	4	1	0	0	0	2	2	1	.182
Ed McKean, ss	6	25	2	11	6	0	0	0	1	3	0	.440
Jack O'Connor, of	6	22	1	3	0	0	0	0	2	3	0	.136
Patsy Tebeau, 3b	5	18	1	0	0	0	0	0	0	2	1	.000
Jake Virtue, 1b	6	24	1	3	0	0	0	0	2	5	1	.125
Cy Young, p	3	11	1	1	0	0	0	0	0	5	0	.091
Chief Zimmer, c	6	23	2	6	2	1	1	0	0	3	0	.261
Totals	6	209	15	48	13	2	3	1	12	30	7	.230

Pitching

Beaneaters	G	GS	CG	ShO	IP	H	R	ER	BB	SO	W-L	Sv	ERA
Kid Nichols	2	2	2	1	18.0	17	3	2	4	13	2-0	0	1.00
Harry Staley	1	1	1	0	9.0	10	3	3	1	0	1-0	0	3.00
Jack Stivetts	3	3	3	1	29.0	21	9	3	7	17	2-0	0	0.93
Totals	6	6	6	2	56.0	48	15	8	12	30	5-0	0	1.29

Spiders	G	GS	CG	ShO	IP	H	R	ER	BB	SO	W-L	Sv	ERA
John Clarkson	2	2	2	0	17.0	24	16	10	5	9	0-2	0	5.29
Nig Cuppy	1	1	1	0	8.0	6	4	1	4	1	0-1	0	1.13
Cy Young	3	3	3	1	27.0	26	11	9	3	9	0-2	0	3.00
Totals	6	6	6	1	52.0	56	31	20	12	19	0-5	0	3.46

1894 New York Giants (NL) 4, Baltimore Orioles (NL) 0

Beginning in 1894, the National League scheduled a postseason championship series between the regular season's first- and second-place clubs. The winner was to be awarded the Temple Cup, an ornate silver loving cup. The first-place Baltimore Orioles were matched up against the runner-up New York Giants. Amos Rusie overpowered the Orioles in Game 1 as the Giants prevailed, 4-1. Game 2 was tied 5-5 in the top of the ninth when Baltimore shortstop Hughie Jennings muffed a double-play grounder, loading the bases. Mike Tiernan cleared the bases with a triple, and the Giants took a 9-6 decision. Rusie shut down the Orioles again in Game 3 for another 4-1 Giants victory. Rusie fanned nine and even drove in the go-ahead run with a fifth-inning groundout. The Orioles, who had all but tossed in the towel, started journeyman Bill Hawke in Game 4, and the Giants rolled to a Series-clinching 16-3 victory. First baseman Jack Doyle led the Giants with 10 hits in 17 at-bats.

Game 1 — October 4 at Baltimore

	1	2	3	4	5	6	7	8	9	R	H	E
Giants	0	0	0	0	1	1	1	1	0	4	13	2
Orioles	0	0	0	0	0	0	0	0	1	1	7	1

W—Rusie (1-0). L—Esper (0-1). A—9000.

Game 2 — October 5 at Baltimore

	1	2	3	4	5	6	7	8	9	R	H	E
Giants	0	0	4	0	0	0	0	1	4	9	14	3
Orioles	0	2	2	0	0	0	1	0	1	6	7	2

W—Meekin (1-0). L—Gleason (0-1). A—11000.

Game 3 — October 6 at New York

	1	2	3	4	5	6	7	8	9	R	H	E
Orioles	0	0	0	1	0	0	0	0	0	1	7	4
Giants	1	0	0	0	1	2	0	0	x	4	10	4

W—Rusie (2-0). L—Hemming (0-1). A—22000.

Game 4 — October 8 at New York

	1	2	3	4	5	6	7	8	R	H	E
Orioles	2	0	1	0	0	0	0	0	3	6	3
Giants	1	0	1	3	5	1	5	x	16	20	4

W—Meekin (2-0). L—Hawke (0-1). A—12000.

Batting

Giants	G	AB	R	H	RBI	2B	3B	HR	BB	SO	SB	Avg
Eddie Burke, of	4	18	3	7	2	1	0	0	1	0	1	.389
George Davis, 3b	4	16	5	5	5	2	2	0	2	0	2	.313
Jack Doyle, 1b	4	17	4	10	6	1	1	0	1	1	6	.588
Duke Farrell, c	4	15	5	6	2	0	0	0	1	1	1	.400
Shorty Fuller, ss	4	14	4	4	2	0	0	0	2	0	1	.286
Jouett Meekin, p	2	9	2	5	3	0	0	0	0	1	0	.556
Yale Murphy, of	1	1	0	0	0	0	0	0	0	0	0	.000
Amos Rusie, p	2	7	1	3	1	1	0	0	0	1	0	.429
Mike Tiernan, of	4	17	5	5	3	0	1	0	2	2	0	.294
George Van Haltren, of	4	14	3	7	0	1	1	0	2	2	2	.500
Monte Ward, 2b	4	17	1	5	6	0	0	0	0	0	0	.294
Totals	**4**	**145**	**33**	**57**	**30**	**6**	**5**	**0**	**11**	**8**	**13**	**.393**

Orioles	G	AB	R	H	RBI	2B	3B	HR	BB	SO	SB	Avg
Frank Bonner, ss-1, of-1	2	5	0	0	0	0	0	0	0	2	0	.000
Steve Brodie, of	4	15	2	0	0	0	0	0	0	2	1	.000
Dan Brouthers, 1b	4	16	2	3	0	0	0	0	1	0	3	.188
Duke Esper, p	1	2	0	0	0	0	0	0	1	1	0	.000
Kid Gleason, p	2	5	0	1	1	0	1	0	0	1	0	.200
Bill Hawke, p	1	2	0	0	0	0	0	0	0	1	0	.000
George Hemming, p	1	3	0	0	0	0	0	0	1	1	0	.000
Hughie Jennings, ss	4	14	0	2	1	0	0	0	0	2	0	.143
Willie Keeler, of	3	12	1	3	1	0	0	0	1	0	0	.250
Joe Kelley, of	4	15	2	5	0	1	1	0	3	2	1	.333
John McGraw, 3b	4	16	2	4	2	0	0	0	0	1	1	.250
Heinie Reitz, 2b	4	15	1	4	4	0	0	0	1	3	1	.333
Wilbert Robinson, c	4	15	1	4	1	0	0	0	1	1	1	.267
Totals	**4**	**135**	**11**	**27**	**10**	**1**	**2**	**0**	**11**	**15**	**8**	**.200**

Pitching

Giants	G	GS	CG	ShO	IP	H	R	ER	BB	SO	W-L	Sv	ERA
Jouett Meekin	2	2	2	0	17.0	13	9	3	8	6	2-0	0	1.59
Amos Rusie	2	2	2	0	18.0	14	2	1	3	9	2-0	0	0.50
Totals	**4**	**4**	**4**	**0**	**35.0**	**27**	**11**	**4**	**11**	**15**	**4-0**	**0**	**1.03**

Orioles	G	GS	CG	ShO	IP	H	R	ER	BB	SO	W-L	Sv	ERA
Duke Esper	1	1	1	0	9.0	13	4	4	1	3	0-1	0	4.00
Kid Gleason	2	1	1	0	13.0	25	20	14	6	3	0-1	0	9.69
Bill Hawke	1	1	0	0	4.0	9	5	4	1	0	0-1	0	9.00
George Hemming	1	1	1	0	8.0	10	4	1	3	2	0-1	0	1.13
Totals	**4**	**4**	**3**	**0**	**34.0**	**57**	**33**	**23**	**11**	**8**	**0-4**	**0**	**6.09**

1895 Cleveland Spiders (NL) 4, Baltimore Orioles (NL) 1

The Baltimore Orioles topped the National League regular-season standings for the second straight year in 1895, and the second-place Cleveland Spiders were their foes in the Temple Cup games. The lead exchanged hands several times in the opener. The Orioles went ahead 4-3 in the top of the ninth when John McGraw delivered a two-out RBI single. But in the bottom of the frame, the Giants tied it back up before loading the bases with none out. After a forceout at home, Chief Zimmer sent a double-play grounder to second. But second baseman Kid Gleason's relay to first was late, and Cupid Childs came home with the winning run for Cleveland. The Spiders tallied three runs in the first inning of Game 2, and took a 7-2 decision behind Nig Cuppy's five-hit pitching. In Game 3, Cleveland put together a three-run first inning once again, and Cy Young cruised to a 7-1 victory. Baltimore's Duke Esper tossed a five-hit shutout in Game 4, but the Spiders came back to wrap up the Series in the fifth game. The game was scoreless until Young began a three-run rally with a leadoff double in the seventh inning. Young closed out the 5-2 victory to give Cleveland the championship.

Game 1 — October 2 at Cleveland

	1	2	3	4	5	6	7	8	9	R	H	E
Orioles	0	0	0	0	0	1	0	2	1	4	12	0
Spiders	0	0	0	0	1	1	0	1	2	5	14	3

W—Young (1-0). L—McMahon (0-1). A—8000.

Game 2 — October 3 at Cleveland

	1	2	3	4	5	6	7	8	9	R	H	E
Orioles	0	1	0	0	0	1	0	0	0	2	5	4
Spiders	3	0	0	0	1	2	1	0	x	7	10	5

W—Cuppy (1-0). L—Hoffer (0-1). A—10000.

Game 3 — October 5 at Cleveland

	1	2	3	4	5	6	7	8	9	R	H	E
Orioles	0	0	0	0	0	0	0	1	0	1	7	1
Spiders	3	0	0	0	0	0	3	1	x	7	13	1

W—Young (2-0). L—McMahon (0-2). A—12000.

Game 4 — October 7 at Baltimore

	1	2	3	4	5	6	7	8	9	R	H	E
Spiders	0	0	0	0	0	0	0	0	0	0	5	1
Orioles	0	1	2	0	0	0	2	0	x	5	9	1

W—Esper (1-0). L—Cuppy (1-1). A—9100.

Game 5 — October 8 at Baltimore

	1	2	3	4	5	6	7	8	9	R	H	E
Spiders	0	0	0	0	0	0	3	2	0	5	11	3
Orioles	0	0	0	0	0	0	1	0	1	2	9	5

W—Young (3-0). L—Hoffer (0-2). A—5000.

Batting

Spiders	G	AB	R	H	RBI	2B	3B	HR	BB	SO	SB	Avg
Harry Blake, of	5	20	1	5	2	3	0	0	0	2	0	.250
Jesse Burkett, of	5	20	3	9	2	2	0	0	0	0	1	.450
Cupid Childs, 2b	5	21	4	4	2	1	0	0	1	0	1	.190
Nig Cuppy, p	2	6	1	1	1	0	0	0	0	0	0	.167
Jimmy McAleer, of	5	21	2	6	2	0	0	0	0	0	1	.286
Chippy McGarr, 3b	5	19	3	7	1	2	0	0	1	0	2	.368
Ed McKean, ss	5	20	2	6	4	1	1	0	3	0	1	.300
Patsy Tebeau, 1b	5	21	3	6	3	1	0	0	1	1	0	.286
Cy Young, p	3	12	3	3	1	1	0	0	0	1	0	.250
Chief Zimmer, c	4	18	2	6	3	2	0	0	3	4	0	.333
Totals	**5**	**178**	**24**	**53**	**21**	**14**	**1**	**0**	**9**	**8**	**6**	**.298**

Orioles	G	AB	R	H	RBI	2B	3B	HR	BB	SO	SB	Avg
Steve Brodie, of	5	20	1	4	2	0	0	0	0	0	0	.200
Scoops Carey, 1b	5	19	0	5	1	1	0	0	0	0	0	.263
Boileryard Clarke, c	2	7	1	2	0	0	0	0	0	0	2	.286
Duke Esper, p	1	3	0	0	0	0	0	0	1	2	0	.000
Kid Gleason, 2b	5	19	0	2	0	0	0	0	0	1	0	.105
Bill Hoffer, p	2	7	0	0	0	0	0	0	0	2	0	.000
Hughie Jennings, ss	5	19	3	7	2	2	0	0	1	0	1	.368
Willie Keeler, of	5	17	3	4	1	0	0	0	3	1	0	.235
Joe Kelley, of	5	19	1	7	5	0	0	0	1	1	1	.368
John McGraw, 3b	5	20	4	8	1	2	0	0	2	0	2	.400
Sadie McMahon, p	2	7	0	0	0	0	0	0	0	0	0	.000
Wilbert Robinson, c	3	12	1	3	0	1	0	0	0	1	0	.250
Totals	**5**	**169**	**14**	**42**	**12**	**6**	**0**	**0**	**8**	**8**	**6**	**.249**

Pitching

Spiders	G	GS	CG	ShO	IP	H	R	ER	BB	SO	W-L	Sv	ERA
Nig Cuppy	2	2	2	0	17.0	14	7	6	4	6	1-1	0	3.18
Cy Young	3	3	3	0	27.0	28	7	7	4	2	3-0	0	2.33
Totals	**5**	**5**	**5**	**0**	**44.0**	**42**	**14**	**13**	**8**	**8**	**4-1**	**0**	**2.67**

Orioles	G	GS	CG	ShO	IP	H	R	ER	BB	SO	W-L	Sv	ERA
Duke Esper	1	1	1	0	9.0	5	0	0	0	3	1-0	0	0.00
Bill Hoffer	2	2	2	0	17.0	21	12	8	6	4	0-2	0	4.24
Sadie McMahon	2	2	2	0	16.2	27	12	11	3	2	0-2	0	5.94
Totals	**5**	**5**	**5**	**1**	**42.2**	**53**	**24**	**19**	**9**	**9**	**1-4**	**0**	**4.01**

1896 Baltimore Orioles (NL) 4, Cleveland Spiders (NL) 0

For the second straight year, the Baltimore Orioles and Cleveland Indians finished first and second, respectively, in the National League race. Baltimore's John McGraw led off the opener with a line drive off the wrist of Cleveland pitcher Cy Young. The Orioles went on to notch 12 more hits off Young and rolled to a 7-1 victory. Baltimore jumped out to a 6-0 lead in Game 2, and cruised to a 7-2 decision behind the seven-hit pitching of Joe Corbett. Baltimore held a 3-2 lead in Game 3 before tallying three runs in the top of the eighth on the way to a 6-2 victory. Corbett finished off the four-game sweep with a masterful four-hit shutout, and also notched three hits in the 5-0 Baltimore victory. Willie Keeler and Joe Kelley each notched eight hits in 17 at-bats for the Orioles.

Game 1
October 2 at Baltimore

	1	2	3	4	5	6	7	8	9	R	H	E
Orioles	0	0	2	0	0	1	3	1	0	7	13	1
Spiders	0	0	0	0	0	1	0	0	0	1	5	4

W—Hoffer (1-0). L—Young (0-1). A—4000.

Game 3
October 5 at Baltimore

	1	2	3	4	5	6	7	8	9	R	H	E
Orioles	0	1	1	0	0	1	0	3	0	6	8	2
Spiders	0	0	1	0	1	0	0	0	0	2	10	2

W—Hoffer (2-0). L—Cuppy (0-1). A—2000.

Game 4
October 8 at Cleveland

	1	2	3	4	5	6	7	8	9	R	H	E
Spiders	0	0	0	0	0	0	0	0	0	0	4	2
Orioles	0	0	0	0	0	0	2	3	x	5	11	1

W—Corbett (2-0). L—Cuppy (0-2). A—1500.

Game 2
October 3 at Baltimore

	1	2	3	4	5	6	7	8	R	H	E
Orioles	4	0	2	0	1	0	0	0	7	10	3
Spiders	0	0	1	0	0	1	0	0	2	7	3

W—Corbett (1-0). L—Wallace (0-1). A—3100.

Batting

Orioles	G	AB	R	H	RBI	2B	3B	HR	BB	SO	SB	Avg
Steve Brodie, of	4	15	1	1	3	0	0	0	0	0	1	.067
Joe Corbett, p	2	6	1	3	0	1	0	0	1	1	0	.500
Jack Doyle, 1b	4	17	3	5	4	1	0	0	0	0	2	.294
Bill Hoffer, p	2	7	1	2	0	0	2	0	0	1	0	.286
Hughie Jennings, ss	4	15	5	5	3	2	0	0	1	2	1	.333
Willie Keeler, of	4	17	4	8	4	1	2	0	0	0	1	.471
Joe Kelley, of	4	17	3	8	4	1	0	0	0	1	2	.471
John McGraw, 3b	4	15	4	4	1	0	0	0	0	0	4	.267
Joe Quinn, 3b	1	3	1	0	0	0	0	0	0	0	0	.000
Heinie Reitz, 2b	4	15	1	2	2	0	0	0	1	0	0	.133
Wilbert Robinson, c	4	15	1	4	2	1	0	0	0	3	0	.267
Totals	4	142	25	42	23	7	4	0	3	8	11	.296

Batting

Spiders	G	AB	R	H	RBI	2B	3B	HR	BB	SO	SB	Avg
Harry Blake, of	4	14	1	1	0	0	0	0	1	1	1	.071
Jesse Burkett, of	4	15	1	5	0	0	0	0	2	3	0	.333
Cupid Childs, 2b	4	13	2	3	0	0	0	0	4	0	1	.231
Nig Cuppy, p	2	7	0	1	0	0	0	0	0	1	0	.143
Jimmy McAleer, of	4	15	0	2	1	0	0	0	1	2	1	.133
Chippy McGarr, 3b	4	16	0	1	0	0	0	0	0	3	2	.063
Ed McKean, ss	4	16	0	5	1	1	1	0	1	2	1	.313
Jack O'Connor, 1b	4	14	1	4	0	0	0	0	1	2	0	.286
Patsy Tebeau, 1b	1	1	0	0	0	0	0	0	0	0	0	.000
Bobby Wallace, ph-2, p-1	3	5	0	1	0	0	0	0	0	0	0	.200
Cy Young, p	1	3	0	0	0	0	0	0	0	0	0	.000
Chief Zimmer, c	4	14	0	3	1	1	0	0	2	6	0	.214
Totals	4	133	5	26	4	2	1	0	12	20	6	.195

Pitching

Orioles	G	GS	CG	ShO	IP	H	R	ER	BB	SO	W-L	Sv	ERA
Joe Corbett	2	2	2	1	18.0	11	2	1	7	10	2-0	0	0.50
Bill Hoffer	2	2	2	0	18.0	15	3	3	5	10	2-0	0	1.50
Totals	4	4	4	1	36.0	26	5	4	12	20	4-0	0	1.00

Pitching

Spiders	G	GS	CG	ShO	IP	H	R	ER	BB	SO	W-L	Sv	ERA
Nig Cuppy	2	2	2	0	17.0	19	11	9	0	4	0-2	0	4.76
Bobby Wallace	1	1	1	0	8.0	10	7	4	2	4	0-1	0	4.50
Cy Young	1	1	1	0	9.0	13	7	6	1	0	0-1	0	6.00
Totals	4	4	4	0	34.0	42	25	19	3	8	0-4	0	5.03

1897 Baltimore Orioles (NL) 4, Boston Beaneaters (NL) 1

The Boston Beaneaters edged the Baltimore Orioles by two games for the National League pennant in 1897. The first game of their Temple Cup series was a wild affair. Baltimore batted around in the top of the first, tallying four runs, but Boston came right back with three of their own in the bottom half. The lead changed hands several times before Boston struck for five in the bottom of the sixth to go in front 11-10. Boston starter Kid Nichols had to leave the game with a sore arm, though, and Baltimore came back with two in the top of the seventh to go back up by a run. But Boston tied it in the bottom of the eighth before Marty Bergen laid down a perfect squeeze to bring home the go-ahead run, and Boston hung on to win, 13-12. Game 2 featured more of the same. Baltimore jumped out to a 4-0 lead, fell behind 8-5, and went back on top 11-8—all before five innings were in the books. Orioles pitcher Joe Corbett survived 16 Boston hits and prevailed, 13-11. Corbett led his own club at the plate with four hits. Bill Hoffer pitched Baltimore to a seven-inning, 8-3 victory in Game 3. The Orioles came out swinging in Game 4, battering Boston starter Jack Stivetts for 11 runs in two innings. The Beaneaters began to chip away at the Orioles' lead, though, and drew to within three runs by the top of the eighth. Hugh Duffy's sacrifice fly and Jimmy Collins' RBI single made it a one-run game. The Beaneaters put the winning runs on base in the ninth, but Chick Stahl popped out with the bases loaded to end the game, as Baltimore took a 12-11 decision. Boston fielded a laughable lineup for the finale, sending rookie Charlie Hickman to the mound. Baltimore defeated the Beaneaters with ease, winning the championship with a 9-3 victory.

Game 1
October 4 at Boston

	1 2 3	4 5 6	7 8 9	R	H	E
Orioles	4 0 1	0 2 3	2 0 0	12	20	4
Beaneaters	3 0 0	1 2 5	0 2 x	13	12	4

W—Lewis (1-0). L—Nops (0-1). A—9600.

Game 2
October 5 at Boston

	1 2 3	4 5 6	7 8 9	R	H	E
Orioles	1 3 0	1 6 0	1 1 0	13	17	2
Beaneaters	0 0 2	6 2 0	1 0 0	11	16	3

W—Corbett (1-0). L—Klobedanz (0-1). HR—Clarke (1), Corbett (1), Long (1), Reitz (1). A—6500.

Game 3
October 6 at Boston

	1 2 3	4 5 6 7	R	H	E
Orioles	0 4 4	0 0 0 0	8	9	2
Beaneaters	0 0 3	0 0 0 0	3	10	2

W—Hoffer (1-0). L—Lewis (1-1). A—5000.

Game 4
October 9 at Baltimore

	1 2 3	4 5 6	7 8 9	R	H	E
Beaneaters	0 0 0	0 2 4	3 2 0	11	16	3
Orioles	6 5 0	0 0 1	0 0 x	12	14	3

W—Nops (1-1). L—Stivetts (0-1). A—2500.

Game 5
October 11 at Baltimore

	1 2 3	4 5 6	7 8 9	R	H	E
Beaneaters	0 2 0	0 0 0	0 0 1	3	15	3
Orioles	0 2 3	0 0 0	2 2 x	9	13	2

W—Hoffer (2-0). L—Hickman (0-1). A—700.

Batting

Orioles	G	AB	R	H	RBI	2B	3B	HR	BB	SO	SB	Avg
Frank Bowerman, c-1, 1b-1	2	8	2	4	4	0	1	0	0	0	0	.500
Boileryard Clarke, c	4	16	5	9	4	1	1	1	1	0	0	.563
Joe Corbett, p	2	6	2	4	2	1	0	1	0	1	0	.667
Jack Doyle, 1b	5	19	7	10	9	2	0	0	0	1	2	.526
Bill Hoffer, p	2	8	2	2	0	1	0	0	0	0	0	.250
Hughie Jennings, ss	5	22	5	7	3	2	0	0	4	0	0	.318
Willie Keeler, of	5	23	5	9	2	2	0	0	4	0	0	.391
Joe Kelley, of	4	16	7	5	5	3	0	0	5	0	0	.313
John McGraw, 3b	5	20	6	6	6	1	1	0	7	0	0	.300
Jerry Nops, p	2	7	0	2	1	0	0	0	1	5	0	.286
Tom O'Brien, of	1	5	2	2	0	1	0	0	0	0	0	.400
Heinie Reitz, 2b	5	20	4	5	4	1	0	1	2	0	0	.250
Jake Stenzel, of	5	21	7	8	3	1	1	0	2	0	2	.381
Totals	**5**	**191**	**54**	**73**	**43**	**16**	**4**	**3**	**26**	**7**	**4**	**.382**

Beaneaters	G	AB	R	H	RBI	2B	3B	HR	BB	SO	SB	Avg
Marty Bergen, c	1	4	0	2	1	0	0	0	0	1	1	.500
Jimmy Collins, 3b	5	22	2	4	4	0	0	0	1	0	0	.182
Hugh Duffy, of	5	21	6	11	7	2	0	0	1	0	0	.524
Billy Hamilton, of	4	16	6	8	2	1	0	0	5	3	2	.500
Charlie Hickman, p-1, of-1	1	4	0	1	1	1	0	0	0	0	0	.250
Fred Klobedanz, p	2	5	3	5	0	0	0	0	0	0	0	1.000
Fred Lake, c	1	3	0	0	0	0	0	0	0	1	0	.000
Ted Lewis, p	3	6	1	3	1	1	0	0	1	0	0	.500
Herman Long, ss	5	21	4	6	5	1	1	1	2	2	1	.286
Bobby Lowe, 2b	5	23	6	9	6	2	0	0	1	0	1	.391
Kid Nichols, p	1	3	0	0	1	0	0	0	0	0	0	.000
Chick Stahl, of	5	21	6	8	6	1	0	0	3	2	2	.381
Jack Stivetts, p-2, of-1	3	7	1	0	0	0	0	0	1	0	1	.000
Jim Sullivan, p	1	1	0	0	0	0	0	0	0	0	0	.000
Fred Tenney, 1b	5	21	4	6	2	0	0	0	4	1	2	.286
George Yeager, c	3	12	2	6	2	1	1	0	2	0	0	.500
Totals	**5**	**190**	**41**	**69**	**38**	**10**	**2**	**1**	**21**	**10**	**10**	**.363**

Pitching

Orioles	G	GS	CG	ShO	IP	H	R	ER	BB	SO	W-L	Sv	ERA
Joe Corbett	2	1	1	0	12.0	21	16	12	8	5	1-0	0	9.00
Bill Hoffer	2	2	2	0	16.0	25	6	6	4	2	2-0	0	3.38
Jerry Nops	2	2	1	0	14.0	23	19	20	9	3	1-1	0	12.86
Totals	**5**	**5**	**4**	**0**	**42.0**	**69**	**41**	**38**	**21**	**10**	**4-1**	**0**	**8.14**

Beaneaters	G	GS	CG	ShO	IP	H	R	ER	BB	SO	W-L	Sv	ERA
Charlie Hickman	1	1	0	0	5.0	7	5	2	2	0	0-1	0	3.60
Fred Klobedanz	2	1	0	0	8.2	12	9	9	8	0	0-1	0	9.35
Ted Lewis	3	1	0	0	12.0	18	11	8	9	4	1-1	0	6.00
Kid Nichols	1	1	0	0	6.0	14	10	8	0	3	0-0	0	12.00
Jack Stivetts	2	1	0	0	6.1	16	15	13	7	0	0-1	0	18.47
Jim Sullivan	1	0	0	0	3.0	6	4	1	0	0	0-0	0	3.00
Totals	**5**	**5**	**0**	**0**	**41.0**	**73**	**54**	**41**	**26**	**7**	**1-4**	**0**	**9.00**

1900 Brooklyn Superbas (NL) 3, Pittsburgh Pirates (NL) 1

The Brooklyn Superbas won the National League pennant, but Pittsburgh Pirates fans believed their club to be superior. The *Pittsburgh Chronicle-Telegraph* pledged a silver cup to the winner of a five-game postseason series. Brooklyn's Joe McGinnity bested Pittsburgh's Rube Waddell in the opener. McGinnity had a shutout going until Pittsburgh tallied a pair of unearned runs in the bottom of the ninth. Frank Kitson's four-hit pitching combined with six Pittsburgh errors to give the Superbas a 4-2 victory in Game 2. Pittsburgh came back to take Game 3 10-0 as Deacon Phillippe tossed a six-hitter. McGinnity wrapped it up by downing Pittsburgh 6-1 the next day. The Pirates didn't manage to score an earned run off McGinnity in either of his two victories.

Game 1 — October 15 at Pittsburgh

	1	2	3	4	5	6	7	8	9	R	H	E
Superbas	0	0	3	1	0	1	0	0	0	5	13	1
Pirates	0	0	0	0	0	0	0	0	2	2	5	4

W—McGinnity (1-0). L—Waddell (0-1). A—4000.

Game 3 — October 17 at Pittsburgh

	1	2	3	4	5	6	7	8	9	R	H	E
Superbas	0	0	0	0	0	0	0	0	0	0	6	3
Pirates	3	1	0	0	2	0	1	3	x	10	13	1

W—Phillippe (1-0). L—Howell (0-1). A—2500.

Game 4 — October 18 at Pittsburgh

	1	2	3	4	5	6	7	8	9	R	H	E
Superbas	1	0	0	3	1	1	0	0	0	6	8	0
Pirates	0	0	0	0	0	1	0	0	0	1	9	3

W—McGinnity (2-0). L—Leever (0-2). A—2335.

Game 2 — October 16 at Pittsburgh

	1	2	3	4	5	6	7	8	9	R	H	E
Superbas	0	1	0	0	0	3	0	0	0	4	7	0
Pirates	0	0	0	1	0	0	1	0	0	2	4	6

W—Kitson (1-0). L—Leever (0-1). A—1800.

Batting

Superbas	G	AB	R	H	RBI	2B	3B	HR	BB	SO	SB	Avg
Lave Cross, 3b	4	18	2	5	1	0	1	0	0	0	1	.278
Bill Dahlen, ss	4	17	3	3	2	0	1	0	0	3	1	.176
Tom Daly, 2b	4	13	2	2	1	1	0	0	3	1	0	.154
Duke Farrell, c	2	8	0	3	1	0	0	0	0	0	1	.375
Harry Howell, p	1	3	0	0	0	0	0	0	0	2	0	.000
Hughie Jennings, 1b	4	18	1	3	2	1	0	0	1	1	0	.167
Fielder Jones, of	4	18	3	5	4	0	0	0	1	1	1	.278
Willie Keeler, of	4	17	0	6	0	0	0	0	1	0	0	.353
Joe Kelley, of	4	17	2	3	1	0	0	0	2	3	0	.176
Frank Kitson, p	1	3	0	0	0	0	0	0	1	2	0	.000
Joe McGinnity, p	2	7	1	1	1	0	0	0	0	2	0	.143
Deacon McGuire, c	2	8	1	3	0	1	0	0	0	1	0	.375
Totals	4	147	15	34	13	3	2	0	9	16	4	.231

Pirates	G	AB	R	H	RBI	2B	3B	HR	BB	SO	SB	Avg
Ginger Beaumont, of	4	15	2	4	1	0	0	0	1	0	1	.267
Bones Ely, ss	4	14	1	4	0	1	0	0	1	1	2	.286
Tommy Leach, of	4	17	4	3	1	0	0	0	1	2	0	.176
Sam Leever, p	2	4	0	1	0	0	0	0	0	1	1	.250
Tom O'Brien, 1b	4	16	1	2	2	1	0	0	1	0	0	.125
Jack O'Connor, c	2	4	0	1	1	0	0	0	1	0	0	.250
Deacon Phillippe, p	1	4	1	0	0	0	0	0	0	1	0	.000
Claude Ritchey, 2b	4	15	3	5	1	1	0	0	1	0	0	.333
Pop Schriver, ph	1	1	0	0	0	0	0	0	0	0	0	.000
Rube Waddell, p	2	5	0	1	0	0	0	0	0	1	0	.200
Honus Wagner, of	4	15	2	6	3	1	0	0	1	2	2	.400
Jimmy Williams, 3b	4	14	0	3	0	0	0	0	1	0	0	.214
Chief Zimmer, c	3	9	1	1	1	0	0	0	0	2	1	.111
Totals	4	133	15	31	10	4	0	0	6	10	7	.233

Pitching

Superbas	G	GS	CG	ShO	IP	H	R	ER	BB	SO	W-L	Sv	ERA
Harry Howell	1	1	1	0	8.0	13	10	3	2	3	0-1	0	3.38
Frank Kitson	1	1	1	0	9.0	4	2	1	1	2	1-0	0	1.00
Joe McGinnity	2	2	2	0	18.0	14	3	0	3	5	2-0	0	0.00
Totals	4	4	4	0	35.0	31	15	4	6	10	3-1	0	1.03

Pirates	G	GS	CG	ShO	IP	H	R	ER	BB	SO	W-L	Sv	ERA
Sam Leever	2	2	1	0	13.0	13	8	2	4	4	0-2	0	1.38
Deacon Phillippe	1	1	1	1	9.0	6	0	0	2	5	1-0	0	0.00
Rube Waddell	2	1	1	0	14.0	15	7	3	3	7	0-1	0	1.93
Totals	4	4	3	1	36.0	34	15	5	9	16	1-3	0	1.25

All-Star Games

Box Scores

For every All-Star Game, we provide a summary and detailed box score.

Player Register

For each position player who has appeared in an All-Star Game, we list his career hitting statistics in 23 categories. These are broken down into American League and National League stats if he played for both leagues in the All-Star Game. We also show six fielding statistics for each position he played.

Pitcher Register

For each pitcher who had appeared in an All-Star Game, we provide his career pitching statistics in 15 categories. As with the hitters, these are broken down into American League and National League stats if he played for both leagues in the All-Star Game.

Leaders

We list the top 20 career totals in 16 batting and 16 pitching categories. Minimums for the percentage categories are 10 plate appearances for hitters and two decisions (winning percentage only) or seven innings for pitchers.

Absentee Players

We detail every player who was selected to play in an All-Star Game but didn't make an appearance, along with the reason he didn't play.

Abbreviations & Formulas

A complete list of team and statistical abbreviations are listed in the back of the book, along with an appendix explaining formulas and the availability of certain statistics.

All-Star Game Box Scores

July 6, 1933
Chicago (Comiskey Park)

Naturally, Babe Ruth captured the spotlight in the very first All-Star Game. His two-run homer in the third gave the AL a 3-0 lead, and his running catch of Chick Hafey's eighth-inning line drive was the game's defensive highlight. Lefty Gomez started for the AL, tossing three scoreless innings and driving in the game's first run. Frankie Frisch homered for the Nationals, and Pepper Martin's single accounted for the other NL run. Lefthanders Carl Hubbell and Lefty Grove kept the final innings scoreless.

National League	AB	R	H	RBI	BB	K
Pepper Martin, 3b, StL	4	0	0	1	0	1
Frankie Frisch, 2b, StL	4	1	2	1	0	0
Chuck Klein, rf, Phi	4	0	1	0	0	0
Paul Waner, rf, Pit	0	0	0	0	0	0
Chick Hafey, lf, Cin	4	0	1	0	0	0
Bill Terry, 1b, NYG	4	0	2	0	0	0
Wally Berger, cf, Bos	4	0	0	0	0	0
Dick Bartell, ss, Phi	2	0	0	0	0	1
Pie Traynor, ph, Pit	1	0	1	0	0	0
Carl Hubbell, p, NYG	0	0	0	0	0	0
Tony Cuccinello, ph, Bro	1	0	0	0	0	1
Jimmie Wilson, c, StL	1	0	0	0	0	0
Lefty O'Doul, ph, NYG	1	0	0	0	0	0
Gabby Hartnett, c, ChN	1	0	0	0	0	1
Wild Bill Hallahan, p, StL	1	0	0	0	0	0
Lon Warneke, p, ChN	1	1	1	0	0	0
Woody English, ph-ss, ChN	1	0	0	0	0	0
TOTALS	34	2	8	2	0	4

American League	AB	R	H	RBI	BB	K
Ben Chapman, lf-rf, NYA	5	0	1	0	0	1
Charlie Gehringer, 2b, Det	3	1	0	0	2	0
Babe Ruth, rf, NYA	4	1	2	2	0	2
Sammy West, cf, StL	0	0	0	0	0	0
Lou Gehrig, 1b, NYA	2	0	0	0	2	1
Al Simmons, cf-lf, ChA	4	0	1	0	0	0
Jimmy Dykes, 3b, ChA	3	1	2	0	1	0
Joe Cronin, ss, Was	3	1	1	0	1	0
Rick Ferrell, c, Bos	3	0	0	0	0	0
Lefty Gomez, p, NYA	1	0	1	1	0	0
General Crowder, p, Was	1	0	0	0	0	0
Earl Averill, ph, Cle	1	0	1	1	0	0
Lefty Grove, p, Phi	1	0	0	0	0	0
TOTALS	31	4	9	4	6	4

	1	2	3	4	5	6	7	8	9		R	H	E
NL	0	0	0	0	0	2	0	0	0		2	8	0
AL	0	1	2	0	0	1	0	0	x		4	9	1

E—Gehrig. DP—NL 1 (Bartell to Frisch to Terry), AL 1 (Dykes to Gehrig). LOB—NL 5, AL 10. Scoring Position—NL 0-for-5, AL 2-for-10. 2B—Traynor. 3B—Warneke. HR—Frisch, Ruth. S—Ferrell. GDP—Simmons. SB—Gehringer.

National League	IP	H	R	ER	BB	K
Wild Bill Hallahan, StL (L)	2.0	2	3	3	5	1
Lon Warneke, ChN	4.0	6	1	1	0	2
Carl Hubbell, NYG	2.0	1	0	0	1	1

American League	IP	H	R	ER	BB	K
Lefty Gomez, NYA (W)	3.0	2	0	0	0	1
General Crowder, Was	3.0	3	2	2	0	0
Lefty Grove, Phi (S)	3.0	3	0	0	0	3

Hallahan pitched to three batters in the 3rd.

Time—2:05. Attendance—47,595. Umpires—HP, Dinneen. 1B, Klem. 2B, McGowan. 3B, Rigler.

July 10, 1934
New York (Polo Grounds)

Carl Hubbell created a legend for himself by fanning Babe Ruth, Lou Gehrig, Jimmie Foxx, Al Simmons and Joe Cronin in order. Still, the AL battled back for eight runs in the fourth and fifth, as Earl Averill drove in three with a double and a triple. Mel Harder finished with five scoreless innings, as the AL topped the NL, 9-7. Three of the NL's runs came on a homer by Joe Medwick, and teammate Frankie Frisch accounted for another run with a solo shot.

American League	AB	R	H	RBI	BB	K
Charlie Gehringer, 2b, Det	3	0	2	0	3	0
Heinie Manush, lf, Was	2	0	0	0	1	0
Red Ruffing, p, NYA	1	0	1	2	0	0
Mel Harder, p, Cle	2	0	0	0	0	1
Babe Ruth, rf, NYA	2	1	0	0	2	1
Ben Chapman, rf, NYA	2	0	1	0	0	0
Lou Gehrig, 1b, NYA	4	1	0	0	1	3
Jimmie Foxx, 3b, Phi	5	1	2	1	0	2
Al Simmons, cf-lf, ChA	5	3	3	1	0	1
Joe Cronin, ss, Was	5	1	2	2	0	1
Bill Dickey, c, NYA	2	1	1	0	2	1
Mickey Cochrane, c, Det	1	0	0	0	0	0
Lefty Gomez, p, NYA	1	0	0	0	0	1
Earl Averill, ph-cf, Cle	4	1	2	3	0	1
Sammy West, cf, StL	0	0	0	0	0	0
TOTALS	39	9	14	9	9	12

National League	AB	R	H	RBI	BB	K
Frankie Frisch, 2b, StL	3	3	2	1	1	0
Billy Herman, 2b, ChN	2	0	1	0	0	0
Pie Traynor, 3b, Pit	5	2	2	1	0	0
Joe Medwick, lf, StL	2	1	1	3	0	1
Chuck Klein, ph-lf, ChN	3	0	1	0	0	0
Kiki Cuyler, rf, ChN	2	0	0	0	0	0
Mel Ott, ph-rf, NYG	2	0	0	0	0	1
Wally Berger, cf, Bos	2	0	0	0	0	1
Paul Waner, ph-cf, Pit	2	0	0	0	0	0
Bill Terry, 1b, NYG	3	0	1	0	1	0
Travis Jackson, ss, NYG	2	0	0	0	0	0
Arky Vaughan, ph-ss, Pit	2	0	0	0	0	1
Gabby Hartnett, c, ChN	2	0	0	0	0	0
Al Lopez, c, Bro	2	0	0	0	0	1
Carl Hubbell, p, NYG	0	0	0	0	0	0
Lon Warneke, p, ChN	0	0	0	0	0	0
Van Lingle Mungo, p, Bro	0	0	0	0	0	0
Pepper Martin, ph, StL	0	1	0	0	1	0
Dizzy Dean, p, StL	1	0	0	0	0	0
Fred Frankhouse, p, Bos	1	0	0	0	0	0
TOTALS	36	7	8	6	3	5

	1	2	3	4	5	6	7	8	9		R	H	E
AL	0	0	0	2	6	1	0	0	0		9	14	1
NL	1	0	3	0	3	0	0	0	0		7	8	1

E—Berger, Gehrig. DP—NL 1 (Lopez to Vaughan). LOB—AL 12, NL 5. Scoring Position—AL 6-for-18, NL 3-for-8. 2B—Foxx, Simmons 2, Cronin, Herman, Averill. 3B—Averill, Chapman. HR—Frisch, Medwick. SB—Gehringer, Manush, Traynor, Ott.

American League	IP	H	R	ER	BB	K
Lefty Gomez, NYA	3.0	3	4	4	1	3
Red Ruffing, NYA	1.0	4	3	3	1	0
Mel Harder, Cle (W)	5.0	1	0	0	1	2

National League	IP	H	R	ER	BB	K
Carl Hubbell, NYG	3.0	2	0	0	2	6
Lon Warneke, ChN	1.0	3	4	4	3	1
Van Lingle Mungo, Bro (L)	1.0	4	4	4	2	1
Dizzy Dean, StL	3.0	5	1	1	1	4
Fred Frankhouse, Bos	1.0	0	0	0	1	0

Warneke pitched to two batters in the 5th. Ruffing pitched to four batters in the 5th.

Time—2:44. Attendance—48,363. Umpires—HP, Pfirman. 1B, Owens. 2B, Stark. 3B, Moriarty.

July 8, 1935
Cleveland (Municipal Stadium)

Jimmie Foxx drove in three runs with a homer and a single, and Lefty Gomez pitched six strong innings as the AL beat the NL for the third straight year, 4-1. Mel Harder threw three scoreless innings to close out the contest. Combined with the five scoreless frames he'd recorded the year before, this gave him an All-Star-record of eight straight scoreless innings. The NL got its only run in the top of the fourth when Arky Vaughan doubled and Bill Terry drove him in with a single.

National League	AB	R	H	RBI	BB	K
Pepper Martin, 3b, StL	4	0	1	0	0	2
Arky Vaughan, ss, Pit	3	1	1	0	1	0
Mel Ott, rf, NYG	4	0	0	0	0	1
Joe Medwick, lf, StL	3	0	0	0	1	1
Bill Terry, 1b, NYG	3	0	1	1	0	0
Ripper Collins, 1b, StL	1	0	0	0	0	0
Wally Berger, cf, Bos	2	0	0	0	0	1
Jo-Jo Moore, ph-cf, NYG	2	0	0	0	0	0
Billy Herman, 2b, ChN	3	0	0	0	0	0
Jimmie Wilson, c, Phi	3	0	1	0	0	0
Burgess Whitehead, pr, StL	0	0	0	0	0	0
Gabby Hartnett, c, ChN	0	0	0	0	0	0
Bill Walker, p, StL	0	0	0	0	0	0
Gus Mancuso, ph, NYG	1	0	0	0	0	0
Hal Schumacher, p, NYG	1	0	0	0	0	0
Paul Waner, ph, Pit	1	0	0	0	0	0
Paul Derringer, p, Cin	0	0	0	0	0	0
Dizzy Dean, p, StL	0	0	0	0	0	0
TOTALS	31	1	4	1	2	5

American League	AB	R	H	RBI	BB	K
Joe Vosmik, rf, Cle	4	1	1	0	0	0
Charlie Gehringer, 2b, Det	3	0	2	0	1	0
Lou Gehrig, 1b, NYA	3	1	0	0	1	0
Jimmie Foxx, 3b, Phi	3	1	2	3	1	1
Ossie Bluege, 3b, Was	0	0	0	0	0	0
Bob Johnson, lf, Phi	4	0	0	0	0	3
Ben Chapman, lf, NYA	0	0	0	0	0	0
Al Simmons, cf, ChA	4	0	2	0	0	2
Doc Cramer, cf, Phi	0	0	0	0	0	0
Rollie Hemsley, c, StL	4	1	1	0	0	0
Joe Cronin, ss, Bos	4	0	0	1	0	1
Lefty Gomez, p, NYA	2	0	0	0	0	1
Mel Harder, p, Cle	1	0	0	0	0	1
TOTALS	32	4	8	4	3	9

	1	2	3	4	5	6	7	8	9		R	H	E
NL	0	0	0	1	0	0	0	0	0		1	4	1
AL	2	1	0	0	1	0	0	0	x		4	8	0

E—Martin. LOB—NL 5, AL 7. Scoring Position—NL 1-for-7, AL 1-for-7. 2B—Vaughan, Wilson, Gehringer, Simmons. 3B—Hemsley. HR—Foxx. SB—Martin.

National League	IP	H	R	ER	BB	K
Bill Walker, StL (L)	2.0	2	3	3	1	2
Hal Schumacher, NYG	4.0	4	1	1	1	5
Paul Derringer, Cin	1.0	1	0	0	0	1
Dizzy Dean, StL	1.0	1	0	0	1	1

American League	IP	H	R	ER	BB	K
Lefty Gomez, NYA (W)	6.0	3	1	1	2	4
Mel Harder, Cle (S)	3.0	1	0	0	0	1

Time—2:06. Attendance—69,831. Umpires—HP, Ormsby. 1B, Magerkurth. 2B, Geisel. 3B, Sears.

July 7, 1936
Boston (Braves Field)

The National League won its first All-Star Game by the score of 4-3, as a rookie named Joe DiMaggio made a crucial error and failed to come up with another clean catch. In the bottom of the second, Gabby Hartnett lined the ball to center, and ended up with an RBI triple when DiMaggio failed to make a shoestring catch. Hartnett subsequently scored to give the NL a 2-0 advantage. After Augie Galan homered in the fifth to make it 3-0, DiMaggio misplayed Billy Herman's single, leading to the NL's fourth run when Medwick drove in Herman with a single.

American League	AB	R	H	RBI	BB	K
Luke Appling, ss, ChA	4	0	1	2	1	0
Charlie Gehringer, 2b, Det	3	0	2	0	2	0
Joe DiMaggio, rf, NYA	5	0	0	0	0	0
Lou Gehrig, 1b, NYA	2	1	1	1	2	0
Earl Averill, cf, Cle	3	0	0	0	0	0
Ben Chapman, cf, Was	1	0	0	0	0	0
Rick Ferrell, c, Bos	2	0	0	0	0	2
Bill Dickey, ph-c, NYA	2	0	0	0	0	0
Rip Radcliff, lf, ChA	2	0	1	0	0	0
Goose Goslin, lf, Det	1	1	1	0	1	0
Mike Higgins, 3b, Phi	2	0	0	0	0	2
Jimmie Foxx, ph-3b, Bos	2	1	1	0	0	1
Lefty Grove, p, Bos	1	0	0	0	0	1
Schoolboy Rowe, p, Det	1	0	0	0	0	0
George Selkirk, ph, NYA	0	0	0	0	1	0
Mel Harder, p, Cle	0	0	0	0	0	0
Frankie Crosetti, ph, NYA	1	0	0	0	0	1
TOTALS	32	3	7	3	7	7

National League	AB	R	H	RBI	BB	K
Augie Galan, cf, ChN	4	1	1	1	0	2
Billy Herman, 2b, ChN	3	1	2	0	1	0
Ripper Collins, 1b, StL	2	0	0	0	2	0
Joe Medwick, lf, StL	4	0	1	1	0	0
Frank Demaree, rf, ChN	3	1	0	0	0	0
Mel Ott, ph-rf, NYG	1	0	1	0	0	0
Gabby Hartnett, c, ChN	4	1	1	1	0	0
Pinky Whitney, 3b, Phi	3	0	1	1	0	1
Lew Riggs, ph-3b, Cin	1	0	0	0	0	0
Leo Durocher, ss, StL	3	0	1	0	0	1
Dizzy Dean, p, StL	1	0	0	0	0	1
Carl Hubbell, p, NYG	1	0	0	0	0	0
Curt Davis, p, ChN	0	0	0	0	0	0
Lon Warneke, p, ChN	1	0	0	0	0	0
TOTALS	31	4	9	4	3	6

	1	2	3	4	5	6	7	8	9		R	H	E
AL	0	0	0	0	0	0	3	0	0		3	7	1
NL	0	2	0	0	2	0	0	0	x		4	9	0

E—DiMaggio. DP—AL 1 (Higgins to Gehringer to Gehrig), NL 1 (Whitney to Herman to Collins). LOB—AL 9, NL 6. Scoring Position—AL 1-for-6, NL 1-for-3. 2B—Gehringer. 3B—Hartnett. HR—Gehrig, Galan. GDP—DiMaggio, Demaree.

American League	IP	H	R	ER	BB	K
Lefty Grove, Bos (L)	3.0	3	2	2	2	2
Schoolboy Rowe, Det	3.0	4	2	1	1	2
Mel Harder, Cle	2.0	2	0	0	0	2

National League	IP	H	R	ER	BB	K
Dizzy Dean, StL (W)	3.0	0	0	0	2	3
Carl Hubbell, NYG	3.0	2	0	0	1	2
Curt Davis, ChN	0.2	4	3	3	1	0
Lon Warneke, ChN (S)	2.1	1	0	0	3	2

PB—Hartnett. Time—2:00. Attendance—25,556. Umpires—HP, Reardon. 1B, Summers. 2B, Stewart. 3B, Kolls.

July 7, 1937
Washington (Griffith Stadium)

Five New York Yankees needed little help from the rest of the American Leaguers in defeating the National League, 8-3. Lou Gehrig had a double, a homer and four RBI; Bill Dickey singled, doubled, and drove in a run; Red Rolfe hit a single and a triple and scored a pair of runs; and Joe DiMaggio singled and scored a run. Lefty Gomez started and won the game, throwing three shutout innings. Joe Medwick laced two doubles and two singles for the Nationals.

National League	AB	R	H	RBI	BB	K
Paul Waner, rf, Pit	5	0	0	1	0	0
Billy Herman, 2b, ChN	5	1	2	0	0	0
Arky Vaughan, 3b, Pit	5	0	2	0	0	0
Joe Medwick, lf, StL	5	1	4	1	0	0
Frank Demaree, cf, ChN	5	0	1	0	0	0
Johnny Mize, 1b, StL	4	0	0	1	0	0
Gabby Hartnett, c, ChN	3	1	1	0	0	0
Burgess Whitehead, pr, NYG	0	0	0	0	0	0
Gus Mancuso, c, NYG	1	0	0	0	0	0
Dick Bartell, ss, NYG	4	0	1	0	0	0
Dizzy Dean, p, StL	1	0	0	0	0	0
Carl Hubbell, p, NYG	0	0	0	0	0	0
Cy Blanton, p, Pit	0	0	0	0	0	0
Mel Ott, ph, NYG	1	0	1	0	0	0
Lee Grissom, p, Cin	0	0	0	0	0	0
Ripper Collins, ph, ChN	1	0	1	0	0	0
Van Lingle Mungo, p, Bro	0	0	0	0	0	0
Jo-Jo Moore, ph, NYG	1	0	0	0	0	0
Bucky Walters, p, Phi	0	0	0	0	0	0
TOTALS	41	3	13	3	0	0

American League	AB	R	H	RBI	BB	K
Red Rolfe, 3b, NYA	4	2	2	1	0	0
Charlie Gehringer, 2b, Det	5	1	3	1	0	0
Joe DiMaggio, rf, NYA	4	1	1	0	1	2
Lou Gehrig, 1b, NYA	4	1	2	4	0	2
Earl Averill, cf, Cle	3	0	1	0	1	1
Joe Cronin, ss, Bos	4	1	1	0	0	0
Bill Dickey, c, NYA	3	1	2	1	1	0
Sammy West, lf, StL	4	1	1	0	0	0
Lefty Gomez, p, NYA	1	0	0	0	0	1
Tommy Bridges, p, Det	1	0	0	0	0	0
Jimmie Foxx, ph, Bos	1	0	0	0	0	0
Mel Harder, p, Cle	1	0	0	0	0	0
TOTALS	35	8	13	8	4	7

	1	2	3	4	5	6	7	8	9		R	H	E
NL	0	0	0	1	1	1	0	0	0		3	13	0
AL	0	0	2	3	1	2	0	0	x		8	13	2

E—Rolfe 2. DP—NL 1 (Bartell to Mize). LOB—NL 11, AL 7. Scoring Position—NL 2-for-10, AL 4-for-10. 2B—Medwick 2, Gehrig, Cronin, Dickey, Ott. 3B—Rolfe. HR—Gehrig.

National League	IP	H	R	ER	BB	K
Dizzy Dean, StL (L)	3.0	4	2	2	1	2
Carl Hubbell, NYG	0.2	3	3	3	1	1
Cy Blanton, Pit	0.1	0	0	0	0	0
Lee Grissom, Cin	1.0	2	1	1	0	2
Van Lingle Mungo, Bro	2.0	2	2	2	2	1
Bucky Walters, Phi	1.0	2	0	0	0	0

American League	IP	H	R	ER	BB	K
Lefty Gomez, NYA (W)	3.0	1	0	0	0	0
Tommy Bridges, Det	3.0	7	3	3	0	0
Mel Harder, Cle (S)	3.0	5	0	0	0	0

Time—2:30. Attendance—31,391. Umpires—HP, McGowan. 1B, Pinelli. 2B, Quinn. 3B, Barr.

July 6, 1938
Cincinnati (Crosley Field)

The pitching of Johnny Vander Meer and Bill Lee helped the National League defeat the American League, 4-1. Each hurler allowed only one hit in three innings of shutout ball. Meanwhile, the National League scored against each of the AL's three pitchers, Lefty Gomez, Johnny Allen and Lefty Grove. Gomez started for the AL for the fifth time. Ernie Lombardi had two singles and an RBI for the Nationals, while Joe Cronin recorded a single, a double and an RBI for the Americans.

American League	AB	R	H	RBI	BB	K
Mike Kreevich, lf, ChA	2	0	0	0	0	0
Doc Cramer, ph-lf, Bos	2	0	0	0	0	0
Charlie Gehringer, 2b, Det	3	0	1	0	1	0
Earl Averill, cf, Cle	4	0	0	0	0	0
Jimmie Foxx, 1b-3b, Bos	4	0	1	0	0	1
Joe DiMaggio, rf, NYA	4	1	1	0	0	1
Bill Dickey, c, NYA	4	0	1	0	0	0
Joe Cronin, ss, Bos	3	0	2	1	1	0
Buddy Lewis, 3b, Was	1	0	0	0	0	0
Lou Gehrig, ph-1b, NYA	3	0	1	0	0	0
Lefty Gomez, p, NYA	1	0	0	0	0	0
Johnny Allen, p, Cle	1	0	0	0	0	0
Rudy York, ph, Det	1	0	0	0	0	1
Lefty Grove, p, Bos	0	0	0	0	0	0
Bob Johnson, ph, Phi	1	0	0	0	0	1
TOTALS	34	1	7	1	2	5

National League	AB	R	H	RBI	BB	K
Stan Hack, 3b, ChN	4	1	1	0	0	1
Billy Herman, 2b, ChN	4	0	0	0	0	2
Ival Goodman, rf, Cin	3	0	0	0	0	1
Joe Medwick, lf, StL	4	0	1	1	0	0
Mel Ott, cf, NYG	4	1	1	0	0	1
Ernie Lombardi, c, Cin	4	0	2	1	0	0
Frank McCormick, 1b, Cin	4	1	1	0	0	0
Leo Durocher, ss, Bro	3	1	1	0	0	1
Johnny Vander Meer, p, Cin	0	0	0	0	0	0
Hank Leiber, ph, NYG	1	0	0	0	0	0
Bill Lee, p, ChN	1	0	0	0	0	0
Mace Brown, p, Pit	1	0	0	0	0	1
TOTALS	33	4	8	2	0	7

	1	2	3	4	5	6	7	8	9		R	H	E
AL	0	0	0	0	0	0	0	0	1		1	7	4
NL	1	0	0	1	0	0	2	0	x		4	8	0

E—DiMaggio, Dickey, Cronin, Foxx. LOB—AL 8, NL 6. Scoring Position—AL 1-for-8, NL 1-for-7. 2B—Dickey, Cronin. 3B—Ott. SB—DiMaggio, Goodman.

American League	IP	H	R	ER	BB	K
Lefty Gomez, NYA (L)	3.0	2	1	0	0	1
Johnny Allen, Cle	3.0	2	1	1	0	3
Lefty Grove, Bos	2.0	4	2	0	0	3

National League	IP	H	R	ER	BB	K
J. Vander Meer, Cin (W)	3.0	1	0	0	0	1
Bill Lee, ChN	3.0	1	0	0	1	2
Mace Brown, Pit (S)	3.0	5	1	1	1	2

HBP—Goodman by Allen. Time—1:58. Attendance—27,067. Umpires—HP, Ballanfant. 1B, Basil. 2B, Klem. 3B, Geisel.

July 11, 1939
New York (Yankee Stadium)

With six New York Yankees in the starting lineup, the American League triumphed, 3-1. Not surprisingly, several Yankees made key contributions. George Selkirk tied the game, 1-1, with an RBI single in the bottom of the fourth, Joe DiMaggio hit a tremendous solo homer in the fifth, and Tommy Bridges got the victory after tossing 2.1 scoreless innings. Twenty-year-old Bob Feller worked out of a jam in the sixth and finished out the game with 3.2 one-hit innings.

National League	AB	R	H	RBI	BB	K
Stan Hack, 3b, ChN	4	0	1	0	1	3
Lonny Frey, 2b, Cin	4	0	1	1	0	0
Ival Goodman, rf, Cin	1	0	0	0	1	0
Billy Herman, ph, ChN	1	0	0	0	0	1
Terry Moore, cf, StL	1	0	0	0	0	0
Frank McCormick, 1b, Cin	4	0	0	0	0	0
Ernie Lombardi, c, Cin	4	0	2	0	0	0
Joe Medwick, lf, StL	4	0	0	0	0	1
Mel Ott, cf-rf, NYG	4	0	2	0	0	0
Arky Vaughan, ss, Pit	3	1	1	0	1	0
Paul Derringer, p, Cin	1	0	0	0	0	1
Dolph Camilli, ph, Bro	1	0	0	0	0	1
Bill Lee, p, ChN	0	0	0	0	0	0
Babe Phelps, ph, Bro	1	0	0	0	0	0
Lou Fette, p, Bos	0	0	0	0	0	0
Johnny Mize, ph, StL	1	0	0	0	0	1
TOTALS	34	1	7	1	3	9

American League	AB	R	H	RBI	BB	K
Doc Cramer, rf, Bos	4	0	1	0	0	1
Red Rolfe, 3b, NYA	4	0	1	0	0	0
Joe DiMaggio, cf, NYA	4	1	1	1	0	0
Bill Dickey, c, NYA	3	1	0	0	1	0
Hank Greenberg, 1b, Det	3	1	1	0	1	0
Joe Cronin, ss, Bos	4	0	1	0	0	1
George Selkirk, lf, NYA	2	0	1	1	2	0
Joe Gordon, 2b, NYA	4	0	0	0	0	1
Red Ruffing, p, NYA	0	0	0	0	0	0
Myril Hoag, ph, StL	1	0	0	0	0	0
Tommy Bridges, p, Det	1	0	0	0	0	1
Bob Feller, p, Cle	1	0	0	0	0	1
TOTALS	31	3	6	2	4	6

	1	2	3	4	5	6	7	8	9		R	H	E
NL	0	0	1	0	0	0	0	0	0		1	7	1
AL	0	0	0	2	1	0	0	0	x		3	6	1

E—Vaughan, Cronin. DP—AL 1 (Gordon to Cronin to Greenberg). LOB—NL 9, AL 8. Scoring Position—NL 2-for-5, AL 1-for-6. 2B—Frey. HR—DiMaggio. GDP—Vaughan.

National League	IP	H	R	ER	BB	K
Paul Derringer, Cin	3.0	2	0	0	0	1
Bill Lee, ChN (L)	3.0	3	3	2	3	4
Lou Fette, Bos	2.0	1	0	0	1	1

American League	IP	H	R	ER	BB	K
Red Ruffing, NYA	3.0	4	1	1	1	4
Tommy Bridges, Det (W)	2.1	2	0	0	1	3
Bob Feller, Cle (S)	3.2	1	0	0	1	2

Time—1:55. Attendance—62,892. Umpires—HP, Hubbard. 1B, Goetz. 2B, Rommel. 3B, Magerkurth.

July 9, 1940
St. Louis (Sportsman's Park)

Boston Bees outfielder Max West blasted a three-run homer before the National League had even made its first out of the game, and the Senior Circuit blanked the AL squad, 4-0. Cincinnati's Paul Derringer and Bucky Walters each tossed two scoreless frames for the Nationals, while Billy Herman shone at the plate with three hits in three at-bats. Luke Appling was responsible for two of the AL's three safeties. Bobo Newsom was the AL's only effective pitcher, allowing only one hit over three scoreless frames.

American League	AB	R	H	RBI	BB	K
Cecil Travis, 3b, Was	3	0	0	0	0	0
Ken Keltner, 3b, Cle	1	0	0	0	0	1
Ted Williams, lf, Bos	2	0	0	0	1	0
Lou Finney, rf, Bos	0	0	0	0	1	0
Charlie Keller, rf, NYA	2	0	0	0	0	1
Hank Greenberg, lf, Det	2	0	0	0	0	0
Joe DiMaggio, cf, NYA	4	0	0	0	0	0
Jimmie Foxx, 1b, Bos	3	0	0	0	0	1
Luke Appling, ss, ChA	3	0	2	0	0	0
Lou Boudreau, ss, Cle	0	0	0	0	0	0
Bill Dickey, c, NYA	1	0	0	0	0	0
Frankie Hayes, c, Phi	1	0	0	0	0	0
Rollie Hemsley, c, Cle	1	0	0	0	0	0
Joe Gordon, 2b, NYA	2	0	0	0	0	2
Ray Mack, ph-2b, Cle	1	0	0	0	0	1
Red Ruffing, p, NYA	1	0	0	0	0	0
Bobo Newsom, p, Det	1	0	1	0	0	0
Bob Feller, p, Cle	1	0	0	0	0	1
TOTALS	29	0	3	0	2	7

National League	AB	R	H	RBI	BB	K
Arky Vaughan, ss, Pit	3	1	1	0	0	1
Eddie Miller, ss, Bos	1	0	0	0	0	1
Billy Herman, 2b, ChN	3	1	3	0	0	0
Pete Coscarart, 2b, Bro	1	0	0	0	0	1
Max West, rf, Bos	1	1	1	3	0	0
Bill Nicholson, rf, ChN	2	0	0	0	0	0
Mel Ott, rf, NYG	0	1	0	0	1	0
Johnny Mize, 1b, StL	2	0	0	0	0	0
Frank McCormick, 1b, Cin	1	0	0	0	0	0
Ernie Lombardi, c, Cin	2	0	1	0	0	0
Babe Phelps, c, Bro	0	0	0	0	1	0
Harry Danning, c, NYG	1	0	1	1	0	0
Joe Medwick, lf, Bro	2	0	0	0	0	0
Jo-Jo Moore, lf, NYG	2	0	0	0	0	0
Cookie Lavagetto, 3b, Bro	2	0	0	0	0	0
Pinky May, 3b, Phi	1	0	0	0	0	0
Terry Moore, cf, StL	3	0	0	0	1	1
Paul Derringer, p, Cin	1	0	0	0	0	1
Bucky Walters, p, Cin	0	0	0	0	0	0
Whit Wyatt, p, Bro	1	0	0	0	0	1
Larry French, p, ChN	0	0	0	0	0	0
Carl Hubbell, p, NYG	0	0	0	0	0	0
TOTALS	29	4	7	4	3	6

	1	2	3	4	5	6	7	8	9		R	H	E
AL	0	0	0	0	0	0	0	0	0		0	3	1
NL	3	0	0	0	0	0	0	1	x		4	7	0

E—Hemsley. DP—NL 1 (Coscarart to Miller to McCormick). LOB—AL 4, NL 7. Scoring Position—AL 0-for-2, NL 2-for-8. 2B—Appling. HR—West. S—McCormick, French. GDP—Travis.

American League	IP	H	R	ER	BB	K
Red Ruffing, NYA (L)	3.0	5	3	3	0	2
Bobo Newsom, Det	3.0	1	0	0	1	1
Bob Feller, Cle	2.0	1	1	1	2	3

National League	IP	H	R	ER	BB	K
Paul Derringer, Cin (W)	2.0	1	0	0	1	3
Bucky Walters, Cin	2.0	0	0	0	0	0
Whit Wyatt, Bro	2.0	1	0	0	0	1
Larry French, ChN	2.0	1	0	0	0	2
Carl Hubbell, NYG	1.0	0	0	0	1	1

HBP—May by Feller. Time—1:53. Attendance—32,373. Umpires—HP, Reardon. 1B, Pipgras. 2B, Stewart. 3B, Basil.

July 8, 1941
Detroit (Briggs Stadium)

Ted Williams launched the most famous home run in All-Star history, a game-winning, two-out, three-run homer off Claude Passeau in the bottom of the ninth, propelling the American League to a 7-5 victory. Until then, the hero of the game had been Pittsburgh's Arky Vaughan with a single and a pair of two-run homers. Bob Feller fanned four in three shutout innings. Two of the DiMaggio brothers played for the Junior circuit: Joe had a double and scored three runs, while Dom laced an RBI single in his only at-bat.

National League	AB	R	H	RBI	BB	K
Stan Hack, 3b, ChN	2	0	1	0	1	1
Cookie Lavagetto, ph-3b, Bro	1	0	0	0	0	0
Terry Moore, lf, StL	5	0	0	1	0	1
Pete Reiser, cf, Bro	4	0	0	0	0	2
Johnny Mize, 1b, StL	4	1	1	0	0	0
Frank McCormick, 1b, Cin	0	0	0	0	0	0
Bill Nicholson, rf, ChN	1	0	0	0	0	1
Bob Elliott, rf, Pit	1	0	0	0	0	0
Enos Slaughter, rf, StL	2	1	1	0	0	1
Arky Vaughan, ss, Pit	4	2	3	4	0	0
Eddie Miller, ss, Bos	0	0	0	0	0	0
Lonny Frey, 2b, Cin	1	0	1	0	0	0
Billy Herman, ph-2b, Bro	3	0	2	0	0	0
Mickey Owen, c, Bro	1	0	0	0	0	0
Al Lopez, c, Pit	1	0	0	0	0	0
Harry Danning, c, NYG	1	0	0	0	0	0
Whit Wyatt, p, Bro	0	0	0	0	0	0
Mel Ott, ph, NYG	1	0	0	0	0	1
Paul Derringer, p, Cin	0	0	0	0	0	0
Bucky Walters, p, Cin	1	1	1	0	0	0
Joe Medwick, ph, Bro	1	0	0	0	0	0
Claude Passeau, p, ChN	1	0	0	0	0	0
TOTALS	35	5	10	5	1	7

American League	AB	R	H	RBI	BB	K
Bobby Doerr, 2b, Bos	3	0	0	0	0	1
Joe Gordon, 2b, NYA	2	1	1	0	0	0
Cecil Travis, 3b, Was	4	1	1	0	1	0
Joe DiMaggio, cf, NYA	4	3	1	1	1	0
Ted Williams, lf, Bos	4	1	2	4	1	1
Jeff Heath, rf, Cle	2	0	0	0	1	1
Dom DiMaggio, rf, Bos	1	0	1	1	0	0
Joe Cronin, ss, Bos	2	0	0	0	0	1
Lou Boudreau, ss, Cle	2	0	2	1	0	0
Rudy York, 1b, Det	3	0	1	0	0	0
Jimmie Foxx, 1b, Bos	1	0	0	0	0	1
Bill Dickey, c, NYA	3	0	1	0	0	0
Frankie Hayes, c, Phi	1	0	0	0	0	0
Bob Feller, p, Cle	0	0	0	0	0	0
Roy Cullenbine, ph, StL	1	0	0	0	0	0
Thornton Lee, p, ChA	1	0	0	0	0	0
Sid Hudson, p, Was	0	0	0	0	0	0
Charlie Keller, ph, NYA	1	0	0	0	0	1
Eddie Smith, p, ChA	0	0	0	0	0	0
Ken Keltner, ph, Cle	1	1	1	0	0	0
TOTALS	36	7	11	7	4	6

	1	2	3	4	5	6	7	8	9		R	H	E
NL	0	0	0	0	0	1	2	2	0		5	10	2
AL	0	0	0	1	0	1	0	1	4		7	11	3

E—Reiser 2, Williams, Smith, Heath. DP—NL 1 (Frey to Vaughan to Mize), AL 1 (York to Cronin). LOB—NL 6, AL 7. Scoring Position—NL 2-for-8, AL 4-for-12. 2B—Mize, Travis, Joe DiMaggio, Williams, Herman, Walters. HR—Vaughan 2, Williams. S—Hack, Lopez. GDP—Reiser, Heath.

National League	IP	H	R	ER	BB	K
Whit Wyatt, Bro	2.0	0	0	0	1	0
Paul Derringer, Cin	2.0	2	1	0	1	0
Bucky Walters, Cin	2.0	3	1	1	2	2
C. Passeau, ChN (BS; L)	2.2	6	5	5	1	3

American League	IP	H	R	ER	BB	K
Bob Feller, Cle	3.0	1	0	0	4	4
Thornton Lee, ChA	3.0	4	1	1	0	0
Sid Hudson, Was (BS)	1.0	3	2	2	1	1
Eddie Smith, ChA (W)	2.0	2	2	2	0	2

Time—2:23. Attendance—54,674. Umpires—HP, Summers. 1B, Jorda. 2B, Grieve. 3B, Pinelli.

July 6, 1942
New York (Polo Grounds)

Lou Boudreau hit the second pitch of the game into the Polo Grounds' upper deck, and later in the same inning, Rudy York launched a two-run homer to give the American League all the runs it would need in a 3-1 victory. Spud Chandler threw four innings of shutout ball for the Junior Circuit, and Johnny Vander Meer fanned four in three scoreless frames for the Senior Circuit. Joe DiMaggio went 2-for-4 while no other batter in the contest logged more than one safety.

American League	AB	R	H	RBI	BB	K
Lou Boudreau, ss, Cle	4	1	1	1	0	0
Tommy Henrich, rf, NYA	4	1	1	0	0	1
Ted Williams, lf, Bos	4	0	1	0	0	0
Joe DiMaggio, cf, NYA	4	0	2	0	0	0
Rudy York, 1b, Det	4	1	1	2	0	1
Joe Gordon, 2b, NYA	4	0	0	0	0	3
Ken Keltner, 3b, Cle	4	0	0	0	0	1
Birdie Tebbetts, c, Det	4	0	0	0	0	2
Spud Chandler, p, NYA	1	0	0	0	0	0
Bob Johnson, ph, Phi	1	0	1	0	0	0
Al Benton, p, Det	1	0	0	0	0	0
TOTALS	35	3	7	3	0	8

National League	AB	R	H	RBI	BB	K
Jimmy Brown, 2b, StL	2	0	0	0	0	0
Billy Herman, 2b, Bro	1	0	0	0	0	0
Arky Vaughan, 3b, Bro	2	0	0	0	1	0
Bob Elliott, 3b, Pit	1	0	1	0	0	0
Pete Reiser, cf, Bro	3	0	1	0	0	0
Terry Moore, cf, StL	1	0	0	0	0	0
Johnny Mize, 1b, NYG	2	0	0	0	0	0
Frank McCormick, 1b, Cin	2	0	0	0	0	0
Mel Ott, rf, NYG	4	0	0	0	0	2
Joe Medwick, lf, Bro	2	0	0	0	0	0
Enos Slaughter, lf, StL	2	0	1	0	0	0
Walker Cooper, c, StL	2	0	1	0	0	0
Ernie Lombardi, c, Bos	1	0	0	0	1	0
Eddie Miller, ss, Bos	2	0	0	0	0	1
Pee Wee Reese, ss, Bro	1	0	0	0	0	0
Mort Cooper, p, StL	0	0	0	0	0	0
Willard Marshall, ph, NYG	1	0	0	0	0	0
Johnny Vander Meer, p, Cin	0	0	0	0	0	0
Danny Litwhiler, ph, Phi	1	0	1	0	0	0
Claude Passeau, p, ChN	0	0	0	0	0	0
Mickey Owen, ph, Bro	1	1	1	1	0	0
Bucky Walters, p, Cin	0	0	0	0	0	0
TOTALS	31	1	6	1	2	3

	1	2	3	4	5	6	7	8	9		R	H	E
AL	3	0	0	0	0	0	0	0	0		3	7	0
NL	0	0	0	0	0	0	0	1	0		1	6	1

E—Brown. DP—AL 2 (Gordon to Boudreau to York; Boudreau to York). LOB—AL 5, NL 6. Scoring Position—AL 1-for-5, NL 0-for-2. 2B—Henrich. HR—Boudreau, York, Owen. GDP—Brown, Vaughan.

American League	IP	H	R	ER	BB	K
Spud Chandler, NYA (W)	4.0	2	0	0	0	2
Al Benton, Det (S)	5.0	4	1	1	2	1

National League	IP	H	R	ER	BB	K
Mort Cooper, StL (L)	3.0	4	3	3	0	2
Johnny Vander Meer, Cin	3.0	2	0	0	0	4
Claude Passeau, ChN	2.0	1	0	0	0	1
Bucky Walters, Cin	1.0	0	0	0	0	1

PB—Tebbetts. HBP—Brown by Chandler. Time—2:07. Attendance—34,178. Umpires—HP, Ballanfant. 1B, Stewart. 2B, Barlick. 3B, McGowan.

July 13, 1943
Philadelphia (Shibe Park)

A three-run homer by Bobby Doerr in the second inning propelled the American League to a 5-3 victory. Vince DiMaggio upheld the family honor with a single, a triple and a homer, and Stan Hack laced three singles in five trips for the Nationals. Hal Newhouser contributed three scoreless innings, while Al Javery was the most effective of the National League hurlers, working two clean frames. Johnny Vander Meer fanned six batters in 2.2 innings.

National League	AB	R	H	RBI	BB	K
Stan Hack, 3b, ChN	5	1	3	0	0	0
Billy Herman, 2b, Bro	5	0	2	0	0	0
Stan Musial, lf-rf, StL	4	0	1	1	0	0
Bill Nicholson, rf, ChN	2	0	0	0	0	0
Augie Galan, ph-lf, Bro	1	0	0	0	1	0
Elbie Fletcher, 1b, Pit	2	0	0	0	0	0
Babe Dahlgren, ph-1b, Phi	2	0	0	0	0	0
Walker Cooper, c, StL	2	0	1	0	0	0
Ernie Lombardi, ph-c, NYG	2	0	0	0	0	0
Harry Walker, cf, StL	1	0	0	0	0	0
Vince DiMaggio, ph-cf, Pit	3	2	3	1	0	0
Marty Marion, ss, StL	2	0	0	0	0	0
Mel Ott, ph, NYG	1	0	0	0	0	1
Eddie Miller, ss, Cin	1	0	0	0	0	0
Mort Cooper, p, StL	1	0	0	0	0	0
Johnny Vander Meer, p, Cin	1	0	0	0	0	1
Rip Sewell, p, Pit	0	0	0	0	0	0
Dixie Walker, ph, Bro	1	0	0	1	0	0
Al Javery, p, Bos	0	0	0	0	0	0
Lonny Frey, ph, Cin	1	0	0	0	0	0
TOTALS	37	3	10	3	1	3

American League	AB	R	H	RBI	BB	K
George Case, rf, Was	2	1	0	0	1	1
Ken Keltner, 3b, Cle	4	1	1	0	0	3
Dick Wakefield, lf, Det	4	0	2	1	0	1
Bob Johnson, lf, Was	0	0	0	0	0	0
Vern Stephens, ss, StL	3	0	1	0	0	1
Dick Siebert, 1b, Phi	1	0	0	0	0	0
Rudy York, ph-1b, Det	3	0	1	0	0	2
Chet Laabs, cf, StL	3	1	0	0	1	1
Jake Early, c, Was	2	1	0	0	1	1
Bobby Doerr, 2b, Bos	4	1	2	3	0	0
Dutch Leonard, p, Was	1	0	1	0	0	0
Hal Newhouser, p, Det	1	0	0	0	0	0
Jeff Heath, ph, Cle	1	0	0	0	0	0
Tex Hughson, p, Bos	0	0	0	0	0	0
TOTALS	29	5	8	4	3	10

	1	2	3	4	5	6	7	8	9		R	H	E
NL	1	0	0	0	0	0	1	0	1		3	10	3
AL	0	3	1	0	1	0	0	0	x		5	8	1

E—Stephens, Hack, Herman 2. DP—NL 3 (Hack to Herman to Fletcher; Vander Meer to Marion to Herman; Miller to Herman to Dahlgren), AL 1 (Stephens to Doerr to York). LOB—NL 8, AL 6. Scoring Position—NL 0-for-7, AL 2-for-7. 2B—Musial, Keltner, Wakefield. 3B—DiMaggio. HR—Doerr, DiMaggio. S—Stephens, Early. GDP—Case, Laabs, Newhouser, Dahlgren.

National League	IP	H	R	ER	BB	K
Mort Cooper, StL (L)	2.1	4	4	4	2	1
Johnny Vander Meer, Cin	2.2	2	1	0	1	6
Rip Sewell, Pit	1.0	0	0	0	0	0
Al Javery, Bos	2.0	2	0	0	0	3

American League	IP	H	R	ER	BB	K
Dutch Leonard, Was (W)	3.0	2	1	1	0	0
Hal Newhouser, Det	3.0	3	0	0	1	1
Tex Hughson, Bos (S)	3.0	5	2	2	0	2

HBP—Case by MCooper. Time—2:07. Attendance—31,938. Umpires—HP, Rommel. 1B, Conlan. 2B, Rue. 3B, Dunn.

July 11, 1944
Pittsburgh (Forbes Field)

The National League triumphed, 7-1, after getting off to a slow start. Hank Borowy started for the AL and held the Nationals scoreless for three innings. Borowy even drove in a run before departing with a 1-0 lead. The NL came back to score seven runs after the fourth inning. Whitey Kurowski doubled in two runs, and Phil Cavarretta reached base an All-Star-record five times with a triple, a single and three walks. Tex Hughson took the loss for the Americans.

American League	AB	R	H	RBI	BB	K
Thurman Tucker, cf, ChA	4	0	0	0	0	0
Stan Spence, rf, Was	4	0	2	0	0	0
George McQuinn, 1b, StL	4	0	1	0	0	1
Vern Stephens, ss, StL	4	0	1	0	0	1
Bob Johnson, lf, Bos	3	0	0	0	1	1
Ken Keltner, 3b, Cle	4	1	1	0	0	0
Bobby Doerr, 2b, Bos	3	0	0	0	0	1
Rollie Hemsley, c, NYA	2	0	0	0	0	0
Frankie Hayes, c, Phi	1	0	0	0	0	1
Hank Borowy, p, NYA	1	0	1	1	0	0
Tex Hughson, p, Bos	1	0	0	0	0	0
Bob Muncrief, p, StL	0	0	0	0	0	0
Mike Higgins, ph, Det	1	0	0	0	0	0
Hal Newhouser, p, Det	0	0	0	0	0	0
Bobo Newsom, p, Phi	0	0	0	0	0	0
TOTALS	32	1	6	1	1	5

National League	AB	R	H	RBI	BB	K
Augie Galan, lf, Bro	4	1	1	1	1	0
Phil Cavarretta, 1b, ChN	2	1	2	0	3	0
Stan Musial, cf-rf, StL	4	1	1	1	0	0
Walker Cooper, c, StL	5	1	2	1	0	1
Ray Mueller, c, Cin	0	0	0	0	0	0
Dixie Walker, rf, Bro	4	0	2	1	0	0
Vince DiMaggio, cf, Pit	0	0	0	0	0	0
Bob Elliott, 3b, Pit	3	0	0	0	0	0
Whitey Kurowski, 3b, StL	1	0	1	2	0	0
Connie Ryan, 2b, Bos	4	1	2	0	0	0
Marty Marion, ss, StL	3	1	0	0	0	2
Bucky Walters, p, Cin	0	0	0	0	0	0
Mel Ott, ph, NYG	1	0	0	0	0	0
Ken Raffensberger, p, Phi	0	0	0	0	0	0
Bill Nicholson, ph, ChN	1	1	1	1	0	0
Rip Sewell, p, Pit	1	0	0	0	0	1
Joe Medwick, ph, NYG	0	0	0	0	0	0
Jim Tobin, p, Bos	0	0	0	0	0	0
TOTALS	33	7	12	7	4	4

	1	2	3	4	5	6	7	8	9		R	H	E
AL	0	1	0	0	0	0	0	0	0		1	6	3
NL	0	0	0	0	4	0	2	1	x		7	12	1

E—Ryan, Doerr, McQuinn, Hayes. DP—AL 1 (Spence to Hemsley), NL 1 (Marion to Ryan to Cavarretta). LOB—AL 5, NL 9. Scoring Position—AL 1-for-5, NL 6-for-16. 2B—Nicholson, Kurowski. 3B—Cavarretta. S—Musial, Marion, Medwick. GDP—Keltner. SB—Ryan.

American League	IP	H	R	ER	BB	K
Hank Borowy, NYA	3.0	3	0	0	1	0
Tex Hughson, Bos (L)	1.2	5	4	3	1	2
Bob Muncrief, StL	1.1	1	0	0	0	1
Hal Newhouser, Det	1.2	3	3	2	2	1
Bobo Newsom, Phi	0.1	0	0	0	0	0

National League	IP	H	R	ER	BB	K
Bucky Walters, Cin	3.0	5	1	1	0	1
Ken Raffensberger, Phi (W)	2.0	1	0	0	0	2
Rip Sewell, Pit	3.0	0	0	0	1	2
Jim Tobin, Bos	1.0	0	0	0	0	0

WP—Muncrief. Time—2:11. Attendance—29,589. Umpires—HP, Barr. 1B, Hubbard. 2B, Sears. 3B, Berry.

July 9, 1946
Boston (Fenway Park)

After a one-year hiatus because of World War II, the All-Star Game returned. The American League trounced the National League, 12-0, in the most lopsided affair in All-Star Game history. Ted Williams had a field day before the hometown fans at Fenway Park, slugging two home runs—including one off Rip Sewell's "eephus" pitch—as well as a pair of singles. Williams also drew a walk, and finished the day with four runs scored and five RBI. Bob Feller, Hal Newhouser and Jack Kramer threw three shutout innings apiece for the Americans, allowing just three hits all together.

National League	AB	R	H	RBI	BB	K
Red Schoendienst, 2b, StL	2	0	0	0	0	0
Frankie Gustine, ph-2b, Pit	1	0	0	0	1	1
Stan Musial, lf, StL	2	0	0	0	0	0
Del Ennis, ph-lf, Phi	2	0	0	0	0	2
Johnny Hopp, cf, Bos	2	0	1	0	0	0
Peanuts Lowrey, ph-cf, ChN	2	0	1	0	0	0
Dixie Walker, rf, Bro	3	0	0	0	0	0
Enos Slaughter, rf, StL	1	0	0	0	0	0
Whitey Kurowski, 3b, StL	3	0	0	0	0	2
Emil Verban, ph, Phi	1	0	0	0	0	0
Johnny Mize, 1b, NYG	1	0	0	0	0	0
Frank McCormick, ph-1b, Phi	1	0	0	0	0	0
Phil Cavarretta, ph-1b, ChN	1	0	0	0	0	1
Walker Cooper, c, NYG	1	0	1	0	0	0
Phil Masi, c, Bos	2	0	0	0	0	0
Marty Marion, ss, StL	3	0	0	0	0	2
Claude Passeau, p, ChN	1	0	0	0	0	1
Kirby Higbe, p, Bro	1	0	0	0	0	0
Ewell Blackwell, p, Cin	0	0	0	0	0	0
Ray Lamanno, c, Cin	1	0	0	0	0	0
Rip Sewell, p, Pit	0	0	0	0	0	0
TOTALS	31	0	3	0	1	10

American League	AB	R	H	RBI	BB	K
Dom DiMaggio, cf, Bos	2	0	1	0	0	0
Stan Spence, cf, Was	0	1	0	0	1	0
Sam Chapman, cf, Phi	2	0	0	1	0	0
Johnny Pesky, ss, Bos	2	0	0	0	0	0
Vern Stephens, ss, StL	3	1	2	2	0	0
Ted Williams, lf, Bos	4	4	4	5	1	0
Charlie Keller, rf, NYA	4	2	1	2	1	1
Bobby Doerr, 2b, Bos	2	0	0	0	0	0
Joe Gordon, 2b, NYA	2	0	1	2	0	0
Mickey Vernon, 1b, Was	2	0	0	0	0	0
Rudy York, 1b, Bos	2	0	1	0	0	0
Ken Keltner, 3b, Cle	0	0	0	0	1	0
Snuffy Stirnweiss, 3b, NYA	3	1	1	0	0	1
Frankie Hayes, c, Cle	1	0	0	0	0	0
Buddy Rosar, c, Phi	2	1	1	0	0	0
Hal Wagner, c, Bos	1	0	0	0	0	0
Bob Feller, p, Cle	0	0	0	0	0	0
Luke Appling, ph, ChA	1	0	0	0	0	0
Hal Newhouser, p, Det	1	1	1	0	0	0
Bill Dickey, ph, NYA	1	0	0	0	0	1
Jack Kramer, p, StL	1	1	1	0	0	0
TOTALS	36	12	14	12	4	3

	1	2	3	4	5	6	7	8	9	R	H	E
NL	0	0	0	0	0	0	0	0	0	0	3	0
AL	2	0	0	1	3	0	2	4	x	12	14	1

E—Pesky. DP—NL 2 (Marion to Mize; Schoendienst to Marion to Mize). LOB—NL 5, AL 4. Scoring Position—NL 0-for-2, AL 4-for-8. 2B—Stephens, Gordon. HR—Williams 2, Keller. GDP—Pesky.

National League	IP	H	R	ER	BB	K
Claude Passeau, ChN (L)	3.0	2	2	2	2	0
Kirby Higbe, Bro	1.1	5	4	4	1	2
Ewell Blackwell, Cin	2.2	3	2	2	1	1
Rip Sewell, Pit	1.0	4	4	4	0	0

American League	IP	H	R	ER	BB	K
Bob Feller, Cle (W)	3.0	2	0	0	0	3
Hal Newhouser, Det	3.0	1	0	0	0	4
Jack Kramer, StL (S)	3.0	0	0	0	1	3

WP—Blackwell. Time—2:19. Attendance—34,906. Umpires— HP, Summers. 1B, Boggess. 2B, Rommel. 3B, Goetz.

July 8, 1947
Chicago (Wrigley Field)

Pinch-hitter Stan Spence drove in the go-ahead run with a seventh-inning RBI single as the American League edged the National League, 2-1. Starting pitcher Hal Newhouser tossed three scoreless frames for the Americans before Johnny Mize homered off Spec Shea in the bottom of the fourth to give the Senior Circuit a 1-0 lead. In the top of the sixth, Luke Appling lined a pinch-hit single, and ultimately scored the tying run on a double-play groundout. In the following frame, Bobby Doerr singled and stole second. National League pitcher Johnny Sain tried to pick him off, but his throw hit Doerr, and advanced to third. Spence delivered the decisive blow later in the inning. Shea was credited with the victory, becoming the first rookie pitcher to win an All-Star Game.

American League	AB	R	H	RBI	BB	K
George Kell, 3b, Det	4	0	0	0	0	2
Bill Johnson, 3b, NYA	0	0	0	0	0	0
Buddy Lewis, rf, Was	2	0	0	0	0	0
Luke Appling, ph, ChA	1	1	1	0	0	0
Tommy Henrich, rf, NYA	1	0	0	0	0	1
Ted Williams, lf, Bos	4	0	2	0	0	1
Joe DiMaggio, cf, NYA	3	0	1	0	1	0
Lou Boudreau, ss, Cle	4	0	0	0	0	1
George McQuinn, 1b, NYA	4	0	0	0	0	1
Joe Gordon, 2b, Cle	2	0	1	0	0	1
Bobby Doerr, 2b, Bos	2	1	1	0	0	0
Buddy Rosar, c, Phi	4	0	0	0	0	1
Hal Newhouser, p, Det	1	0	0	0	0	0
Spec Shea, p, NYA	1	0	0	0	0	0
Stan Spence, ph, Was	1	0	1	1	0	0
Walt Masterson, p, Was	0	0	0	0	0	0
Joe Page, p, NYA	0	0	0	0	0	0
TOTALS	34	2	8	1	1	8

National League	AB	R	H	RBI	BB	K
Harry Walker, cf, Phi	2	0	0	0	0	1
Andy Pafko, cf, ChN	2	0	1	0	0	0
Dixie Walker, rf, Bro	2	0	0	0	0	0
Willard Marshall, rf, NYG	1	0	0	0	0	1
Walker Cooper, c, NYG	3	0	0	0	0	1
Bruce Edwards, c, Bro	0	0	0	0	0	0
Phil Cavarretta, ph-1b, ChN	1	0	0	0	0	1
Johnny Mize, 1b, NYG	3	1	2	1	1	0
Phil Masi, pr-c, Bos	0	0	0	0	0	0
Enos Slaughter, lf, StL	3	0	0	0	1	0
Frankie Gustine, 3b, Pit	2	0	0	0	0	0
Whitey Kurowski, 3b, StL	2	0	0	0	0	0
Marty Marion, ss, StL	2	0	1	0	0	0
Pee Wee Reese, ss, Bro	1	0	0	0	0	1
Emil Verban, 2b, Phi	2	0	0	0	0	0
Eddie Stanky, 2b, Bro	2	0	0	0	0	0
Ewell Blackwell, p, Cin	0	0	0	0	0	0
Bert Haas, ph, Cin	1	0	0	0	0	0
Harry Brecheen, p, StL	0	0	0	0	0	0
Johnny Sain, p, Bos	0	0	0	0	0	0
Stan Musial, ph, StL	1	0	0	0	0	0
Warren Spahn, p, Bos	0	0	0	0	0	0
Schoolboy Rowe, ph, Phi	1	0	0	0	0	0
TOTALS	32	1	5	1	4	6

	1	2	3	4	5	6	7	8	9	R	H	E
AL	0	0	0	0	0	1	1	0	0	2	8	0
NL	0	0	0	1	0	0	0	0	0	1	5	1

E—Sain. DP—NL 1 (Reese to Stanky to Mize). LOB—AL 6, NL 8. Scoring Position—AL 2-for-12, NL 0-for-2. 2B—Williams, Gordon. HR—Mize. GDP—DiMaggio. SB—Doerr.

American League	IP	H	R	ER	BB	K
Hal Newhouser, Det	3.0	1	0	0	0	2
Spec Shea, NYA (W)	3.0	3	1	1	2	2
Walt Masterson, Was	1.2	0	0	0	1	2
Joe Page, NYA (S)	1.1	1	0	0	1	0

National League	IP	H	R	ER	BB	K
Ewell Blackwell, Cin	3.0	1	0	0	0	4
Harry Brecheen, StL	3.0	5	1	1	0	2
Johnny Sain, Bos (L)	1.0	2	1	1	0	1
Warren Spahn, Bos	2.0	0	0	0	1	1

WP—Blackwell. PB—Cooper. Time—2:19. Attendance— 41,123. Umpires—HP, Conlan. 1B, Boyer. 2B, Henline. 3B, Passarella.

July 13, 1948
St. Louis (Sportsman's Park)

Vic Raschi tossed three scoreless innings and singled in the go-ahead runs as the American League triumphed over the National League, 5-2. Raschi's bases-loaded single in the fourth plated Ken Keltner and George McQuinn, breaking a 2-2 tie. Ewell Blackwell threw three shutout innings for the Nationals, and Joe Coleman worked three perfect innings for the Americans. Stan Musial's two-run blast onto Sportsman's Park's right-field roof gave the NL a 2-0 lead in the top of the first, but Hoot Evers' solo shot in the second and Lou Boudreau's sacrifice fly in the third tied it up before Raschi put the AL ahead for good in the fourth.

National League	AB	R	H	RBI	BB	K
Richie Ashburn, cf, Phi	4	1	2	0	0	1
Ralph Kiner, lf, Pit	1	0	0	0	0	0
Red Schoendienst, 2b, StL	4	0	0	0	0	1
Bill Rigney, 2b, NYG	0	0	0	0	0	0
Stan Musial, lf-cf, StL	4	1	2	2	1	1
Johnny Mize, 1b, NYG	4	0	1	0	0	0
Enos Slaughter, rf, StL	2	0	1	0	1	0
Tommy Holmes, rf, Bos	1	0	0	0	0	0
Andy Pafko, 3b, ChN	2	0	0	0	0	0
Bob Elliott, 3b, Bos	2	0	1	0	0	0
Walker Cooper, c, NYG	2	0	0	0	0	0
Phil Masi, c, Bos	2	0	0	0	0	0
Pee Wee Reese, ss, Bro	2	0	0	0	0	0
Buddy Kerr, ss, NYG	2	0	0	0	0	1
Ralph Branca, p, Bro	1	0	0	0	0	0
Frankie Gustine, ph, Pit	1	0	0	0	0	0
Johnny Schmitz, p, ChN	0	0	0	0	0	0
Johnny Sain, p, Bos	0	0	0	0	0	0
Eddie Waitkus, ph, ChN	0	0	0	0	1	0
Ewell Blackwell, p, Cin	0	0	0	0	0	0
Bobby Thomson, ph, NYG	1	0	0	0	0	1
TOTALS	35	2	8	2	4	7

American League	AB	R	H	RBI	BB	K
Pat Mullin, rf, Det	1	0	0	0	1	1
Joe DiMaggio, ph, NYA	1	0	0	1	0	0
Al Zarilla, rf, StL	2	0	0	0	0	0
Tommy Henrich, lf, NYA	3	0	0	0	1	2
Lou Boudreau, ss, Cle	2	0	0	1	0	0
Vern Stephens, ss, Bos	2	0	0	0	0	1
Joe Gordon, 2b, Cle	2	0	0	0	0	0
Bobby Doerr, 2b, Bos	2	0	0	0	0	1
Hoot Evers, cf, Det	4	1	1	1	0	1
Ken Keltner, 3b, Cle	3	1	1	0	1	0
George McQuinn, 1b, NYA	4	1	2	0	0	0
Buddy Rosar, c, Phi	1	0	0	0	0	0
Birdie Tebbetts, c, Bos	1	1	0	0	2	1
Walt Masterson, p, Was	0	0	0	0	0	0
Mickey Vernon, ph, Was	1	0	0	0	0	1
Vic Raschi, p, NYA	1	0	1	2	0	0
Ted Williams, ph, Bos	0	0	0	0	1	0
Hal Newhouser, pr, Det	0	0	0	0	0	0
Joe Coleman, p, Phi	0	0	0	0	0	0
TOTALS	29	5	6	5	7	7

	1	2	3	4	5	6	7	8	9	R	H	E
NL	2	0	0	0	0	0	0	0	0	2	8	0
AL	0	1	1	3	0	0	0	0	x	5	6	0

LOB—NL 10, AL 8. Scoring Position—NL 1-for-7, AL 1-for-11. HR—Musial, Evers. S—Coleman. SB—Ashburn, Mullin, McQuinn, Vernon.

National League	IP	H	R	ER	BB	K
Ralph Branca, Bro	3.0	1	2	2	3	3
Johnny Schmitz, ChN (L)	0.1	3	3	3	1	0
Johnny Sain, Bos	1.2	0	0	0	0	0
Ewell Blackwell, Cin	3.0	2	0	0	3	1

American League	IP	H	R	ER	BB	K
Walt Masterson, Was	3.0	5	2	2	1	1
Vic Raschi, NYA (W)	3.0	3	0	0	1	3
Joe Coleman, Phi (S)	3.0	0	0	0	2	3

WP—Masterson. Time—2:27. Attendance—34,009. Umpires—HP, Berry. 1B, Stewart. 2B, Paparella. 3B, Reardon.

July 12, 1949
Brooklyn (Ebbets Field)

The American League outscored the National League 11-7 without the aid of a single home run. Joe DiMaggio drove in three runs with a double and a single, while his brother Dom scored twice and also logged a double and a single. Stan Musial was the NL's hitting star with a pair of singles and a home run. Jackie Robinson, Don Newcombe, Roy Campanella and Larry Doby became the first black players to participate in an All-Star Game. Robinson doubled and scored three runs. Newcombe was the game's losing pitcher, although he drove in a run and was robbed of a possible extra-base hit when Ted Williams snagged his bases-loaded liner in the second.

American League	AB	R	H	RBI	BB	K
Dom DiMaggio, rf-cf, Bos	5	2	2	1	0	1
Vic Raschi, p, NYA	1	0	0	0	0	0
George Kell, 3b, Det	3	2	2	0	1	0
Bob Dillinger, pr-3b, StL	1	2	1	1	0	0
Ted Williams, lf, Bos	2	1	0	0	2	1
Dale Mitchell, lf, Cle	1	0	1	1	0	0
Joe DiMaggio, cf, NYA	4	1	2	3	0	0
Larry Doby, pr-rf-cf, Cle	1	0	0	0	0	0
Eddie Joost, ss, Phi	2	1	1	2	1	0
Vern Stephens, ss, Bos	2	0	0	0	0	1
Eddie Robinson, 1b, Was	5	1	1	1	0	0
Billy Goodman, 1b, Bos	0	0	0	0	0	0
Cass Michaels, 2b, ChA	2	0	0	0	1	0
Joe Gordon, 2b, Cle	2	1	1	0	0	1
Birdie Tebbetts, c, Bos	2	0	2	1	0	0
Yogi Berra, c, NYA	3	0	0	0	0	0
Mel Parnell, p, Bos	1	0	0	0	0	1
Virgil Trucks, p, Det	1	0	0	0	0	0
Lou Brissie, p, Phi	1	0	0	0	0	0
Vic Wertz, ph-rf, Det	2	0	0	0	0	0
TOTALS	41	11	13	10	5	5

National League	AB	R	H	RBI	BB	K
Pee Wee Reese, ss, Bro	5	0	0	0	1	0
Jackie Robinson, 2b, Bro	4	3	1	0	1	0
Stan Musial, cf-rf, StL	4	1	3	2	1	0
Ralph Kiner, lf, Pit	5	1	1	2	0	0
Johnny Mize, 1b, NYG	2	0	1	0	0	1
Gil Hodges, pr-1b, Bro	3	1	1	0	0	0
Willard Marshall, rf, NYG	1	1	0	0	2	0
Vern Bickford, p, Bos	0	0	0	0	0	0
Bobby Thomson, ph, NYG	1	0	0	0	0	0
Howie Pollet, p, StL	0	0	0	0	0	0
Ewell Blackwell, p, Cin	0	0	0	0	0	0
Enos Slaughter, ph, StL	1	0	0	0	0	0
Preacher Roe, p, Bro	0	0	0	0	0	0
Eddie Kazak, 3b, StL	2	0	2	1	0	0
Sid Gordon, 3b, NYG	2	0	1	0	1	0
Andy Seminick, c, Phi	1	0	0	0	0	0
Roy Campanella, c, Bro	2	0	0	0	1	1
Warren Spahn, p, Bos	0	0	0	0	0	0
Don Newcombe, p, Bro	0	0	0	1	0	0
Red Schoendienst, ph, StL	1	0	1	0	0	0
George Munger, p, StL	0	0	0	0	0	0
Andy Pafko, ph-cf, ChN	2	0	1	0	1	0
TOTALS	36	7	12	6	8	3

	1	2	3	4	5	6	7	8	9	R	H	E
AL	4	0	0	2	0	2	3	0	0	11	13	1
NL	2	1	2	0	0	2	0	0	0	7	12	4

E—Campanella, Mitchell, Marshall, Reese, Mize. DP—AL 2 (Michaels to Joost to ERobinson; Joost to Michaels to ERobinson), NL 1 (JRobinson to Reese to Hodges). LOB—AL 8, NL 12. Scoring Position—AL 7-for-19, NL 3-for-11. 2B—DDiMaggio, JDiMaggio, Tebbetts, JRobinson, JGordon, SGordon, Mitchell. HR—Musial, Kiner. SF—Newcombe. GDP—Reese, Kiner, Brissie. SB—Kell.

American League	IP	H	R	ER	BB	K
Mel Parnell, Bos	1.0	3	3	3	1	1
Virgil Trucks, Det (W)	2.0	3	2	2	2	0
Lou Brissie, Phi	3.0	5	2	2	2	1
Vic Raschi, NYA (S)	3.0	1	0	0	3	1

National League	IP	H	R	ER	BB	K
Warren Spahn, Bos	1.1	4	4	0	2	3
Don Newcombe, Bro (L)	2.2	3	2	2	1	0
George Munger, StL	1.0	0	0	0	1	0
Vern Bickford, Bos	1.0	2	2	2	1	0
Howie Pollet, StL	1.0	4	3	3	0	0
Ewell Blackwell, Cin	1.0	0	0	0	0	2
Preacher Roe, Bro	1.0	0	0	0	0	0

Parnell pitched to three batters in the 2nd.

HBP—Seminick by Parnell. Time—3:04. Attendance—32,577. Umpires—HP, Barlick. 1B, Hubbard. 2B, Gore. 3B, Summers.

July 11, 1950
Chicago (Comiskey Park)

The Senior Circuit scored a 14-inning 4-3 victory in one of the most gripping All-Star games ever played. The decisive blow came off the bat of switch-hitting St. Louis second baseman Red Schoendienst in the top of the 14th. Schoendienst's solo shot put the NL on top for good and marked the keystoner's first career home run batting righthanded. In the first inning, Boston left fielder Ted Williams fractured his left elbow in a collision with Comiskey Park's left field wall while hauling in Ralph Kiner's long fly. Although Williams stayed in the game and later contributed an RBI single, he was forced to undergo an operation two days later to repair the damage. The injury would affect him for the rest of his career. Kiner played a prominent role later in the contest, when his ninth-inning game-tying homer sent the game into extra innings. The most impressive mound performance was turned in by the Giants' Larry Jansen, who struck out six and allowed only one hit over five innings of shutout ball.

National League	AB	R	H	RBI	BB	K
Puddin' Head Jones, 3b, Phi	7	0	1	0	0	0
Ralph Kiner, lf, Pit	6	1	2	1	0	1
Stan Musial, 1b, StL	5	0	0	0	1	0
Jackie Robinson, 2b, Bro	4	1	1	0	0	0
Johnny Wyrostek, ph-rf, Cin	2	0	0	0	0	0
Enos Slaughter, cf-rf, StL	4	1	2	1	1	0
Red Schoendienst, 2b, StL	1	1	1	1	0	0
Hank Sauer, rf, ChN	2	0	0	1	0	0
Andy Pafko, cf, ChN	4	0	2	0	0	0
Roy Campanella, c, Bro	6	0	0	0	0	2
Marty Marion, ss, StL	2	0	0	0	0	0
Jim Konstanty, p, Phi	0	0	0	0	0	0
Larry Jansen, p, NYG	2	0	0	0	0	1
Duke Snider, ph, Bro	1	0	0	0	0	0
Ewell Blackwell, p, Cin	1	0	0	0	0	1
Robin Roberts, p, Phi	1	0	0	0	0	1
Don Newcombe, p, Bro	0	0	0	0	0	0
Dick Sisler, ph, Phi	1	0	1	0	0	0
Pee Wee Reese, pr-ss, Bro	3	0	0	0	1	1
TOTALS	52	4	10	4	3	7

American League	AB	R	H	RBI	BB	K
Phil Rizzuto, ss, NYA	6	0	2	0	0	1
Larry Doby, cf, Cle	6	1	2	0	0	2
George Kell, 3b, Det	6	0	0	2	0	1
Ted Williams, lf, Bos	4	0	1	1	0	1
Dom DiMaggio, lf, Bos	2	0	0	0	0	0
Walt Dropo, 1b, Bos	3	0	1	0	0	0
Ferris Fain, ph-1b, Phi	3	0	1	0	0	0
Hoot Evers, rf, Det	2	0	0	0	1	1
Joe DiMaggio, rf, NYA	3	0	0	0	0	0
Yogi Berra, c, NYA	2	0	0	0	0	0
Jim Hegan, pr-c, Cle	3	0	0	0	0	3
Bobby Doerr, 2b, Bos	3	0	0	0	0	0
Jerry Coleman, 2b, NYA	2	0	0	0	0	2
Vic Raschi, p, NYA	0	0	0	0	0	0
Cass Michaels, ph, Was	1	1	1	0	0	0
Bob Lemon, p, Cle	0	1	0	0	1	0
Art Houtteman, p, Det	1	0	0	0	0	1
Allie Reynolds, p, NYA	1	0	0	0	0	0
Tommy Henrich, ph, NYA	1	0	0	0	0	0
Ted Gray, p, Det	0	0	0	0	0	0
Bob Feller, p, Cle	0	0	0	0	0	0
TOTALS	49	3	8	3	2	12

	1	2	3	4	5	6	7	8	9	10	11	12	13	14	R	H	E
NL	0	2	0	0	0	0	0	0	1	0	0	0	0	1	4	10	0
AL	0	0	1	0	2	0	0	0	0	0	0	0	0	0	3	8	1

E—Coleman. DP—AL 1 (Rizzuto to Doerr to Dropo). LOB—NL 9, AL 6. Scoring Position—NL 0-for-7, AL 2-for-10. 2B—Kiner, Doby, Michaels. 3B—Slaughter, Dropo. HR—Kiner, Schoendienst. GDP—Jones, JDiMaggio.

National League	IP	H	R	ER	BB	K
Robin Roberts, Phi	3.0	3	1	1	1	1
Don Newcombe, Bro	2.0	3	2	2	1	1
Jim Konstanty, Phi	1.0	0	0	0	0	2
Larry Jansen, NYG	5.0	1	0	0	0	6
Ewell Blackwell, Cin (W)	3.0	1	0	0	0	2

American League	IP	H	R	ER	BB	K
Vic Raschi, NYA	3.0	2	2	2	0	1
Bob Lemon, Cle	3.0	1	0	0	0	2
Art Houtteman, Det (BS)	3.0	3	1	1	1	0
Allie Reynolds, NYA	3.0	1	0	0	1	2
Ted Gray, Det (L)	1.1	3	1	1	0	1
Bob Feller, Cle	0.2	0	0	0	1	1

WP—Roberts. PB—Hegan. Time—3:19. Attendance—46,127. Umpires—HP, McGowan. 1B, Pinelli. 2B, Rommel. 3B, Conlan.

July 10, 1951
Detroit (Briggs Stadium)

The National League won 8-3 in a slugfest that featured six home runs, twice as many as any previous midsummer classic. The NL's Stan Musial and Ralph Kiner provided two of the Senior Circuit's four longballs, while Richie Ashburn's all-around play earned rave reviews. The Phillies' center fielder lashed the first pitch of the game for a double. He moved to third on a short flyball to right and proceeded to score the game's first run when Stan Musial stole second base and Nellie Fox dropped the throw from catcher Yogi Berra. In the bottom of the second, Ashburn gunned down Ferris Fain at the plate to prevent the AL from taking a 2-1 lead. He also pulled off the most spectacular fielding play of the game when he hauled in Wertz' long flyball at the center-field wall in the sixth. The catch likely prevented a home run. Brooklyn's Jackie Robinson also contributed a pair of hits, one of them on a daring and perfectly placed squeeze bunt with two out in the seventh.

National League	AB	R	H	RBI	BB	K
Richie Ashburn, cf, Phi	4	2	2	0	1	0
Duke Snider, cf, Bro	0	0	0	0	0	0
Al Dark, ss, NYG	5	0	1	0	0	0
Pee Wee Reese, ss, Bro	0	0	0	0	0	0
Stan Musial, lf-rf-lf, StL	4	1	2	1	1	0
Wally Westlake, lf, StL	0	0	0	0	0	0
Jackie Robinson, 2b, Bro	4	1	2	1	1	0
Red Schoendienst, 2b, StL	0	0	0	0	0	0
Gil Hodges, 1b, Bro	5	2	2	2	0	1
Bob Elliott, 3b, Bos	2	1	1	2	0	0
Puddin' Head Jones, 3b, Phi	2	0	0	0	1	1
Del Ennis, rf, Phi	2	0	0	0	0	1
Ralph Kiner, lf, Pit	2	1	1	1	0	0
Johnny Wyrostek, rf, Cin	1	0	0	0	0	0
Roy Campanella, c, Bro	4	0	0	0	0	0
Robin Roberts, p, Phi	0	0	0	0	0	0
Enos Slaughter, ph, StL	1	0	0	0	0	0
Sal Maglie, p, NYG	1	0	0	0	0	0
Don Newcombe, p, Bro	2	0	1	0	0	0
Ewell Blackwell, p, Cin	0	0	0	0	0	0
TOTALS	39	8	12	7	4	3

American League	AB	R	H	RBI	BB	K
Dom DiMaggio, cf, Bos	5	0	1	0	0	2
Nellie Fox, 2b, ChA	3	0	1	0	0	0
Bobby Doerr, ph-2b, Bos	1	0	1	0	1	0
George Kell, 3b, Det	3	1	1	1	1	1
Ted Williams, lf, Bos	3	0	1	0	1	1
Jim Busby, lf, ChA	0	0	0	0	0	0
Yogi Berra, c, NYA	4	1	1	0	0	0
Vic Wertz, rf, Det	3	1	1	1	0	0
Phil Rizzuto, ss, NYA	1	0	0	0	0	0
Ferris Fain, 1b, Phi	3	0	1	1	0	1
Eddie Robinson, ph-1b, ChA	1	0	0	0	0	0
Chico Carrasquel, ss, ChA	2	0	1	0	0	0
Minnie Minoso, ph-rf, ChA	2	0	0	0	0	0
Ned Garver, p, StL	1	0	0	0	0	1
Ed Lopat, p, NYA	0	0	0	0	0	0
Larry Doby, ph, Cle	1	0	0	0	0	0
Fred Hutchinson, p, Det	0	0	0	0	0	0
Vern Stephens, ph, Bos	1	0	0	0	0	1
Mel Parnell, p, Bos	0	0	0	0	0	0
Bob Lemon, p, Cle	0	0	0	0	0	0
Jim Hegan, ph, Cle	1	0	1	0	0	0
TOTALS	35	3	10	3	3	7

	1	2	3	4	5	6	7	8	9	R	H	E
NL	1	0	0	3	0	2	1	1	0	8	12	1
AL	0	1	0	1	1	0	0	0	0	3	10	2

E—Fox, Robinson, Berra. DP—NL 1 (Campanella to JRobinson), AL 1 (Berra to Kell). LOB—NL 8, AL 9. Scoring Position—NL 1-for-11, AL 1-for-8. 2B—Ashburn, Hegan. 3B—Williams, Fain. HR—Musial, Hodges, Elliott, Kell, Wertz, Kiner. S—Kell. SB—Musial. CS—Musial, DDiMaggio.

National League	IP	H	R	ER	BB	K
Robin Roberts, Phi	2.0	4	1	1	1	1
Sal Maglie, NYG (W)	3.0	3	2	2	1	1
Don Newcombe, Bro	3.0	2	0	0	0	3
Ewell Blackwell, Cin	1.0	1	0	0	1	2

American League	IP	H	R	ER	BB	K
Ned Garver, StL	3.0	1	1	0	1	1
Ed Lopat, NYA (L)	1.0	3	3	3	0	0
Fred Hutchinson, Det	3.0	3	3	3	2	0
Mel Parnell, Bos	1.0	3	1	1	0	1
Bob Lemon, Cle	1.0	2	0	0	1	1

PB—Campanella. Time—2:41. Attendance—52,075. Umpires—HP, Passarella. 1B, Robb. 2B, Hurley. 3B, Jorda.

July 8, 1952
Philadelphia (Shibe Park)

In the first rain-shortened All-Star Game ever, the NL won a five-inning affair by the score of 3-2. Once again, the NL did its damage via the longball, scoring all three of its runs on homers. Jackie Robinson connected for a solo shot in the first inning, and Hank Sauer sent a mammoth two-run blast onto Shibe Park's left-field roof in the fourth. The strongest mound performances came from a pair of hometown southpaws, Curt Simmons of the Phillies and the Athletics' Bobby Shantz. Simmons allowed only one hit over three innings of shutout ball, and Shantz struck out the side in the fifth. Only the rain prevented Shantz from attempting to tie Carl Hubbell's All-Star Game record of five straight strikeouts. Rain fell steadily throughout the game, which was finally called after a 56-minute delay.

American League	AB	R	H	RBI	BB	K
Dom DiMaggio, cf, Bos	2	0	1	0	1	1
Larry Doby, cf, Cle	0	0	0	0	0	0
Hank Bauer, rf, NYA	3	0	1	0	0	1
Jackie Jensen, rf, Was	0	0	0	0	0	0
Dale Mitchell, lf, Cle	1	0	0	0	0	1
Minnie Minoso, ph-lf, ChA	1	1	1	0	0	0
Al Rosen, 3b, Cle	1	1	0	0	1	0
Yogi Berra, c, NYA	2	0	0	0	0	0
Eddie Robinson, 1b, ChA	2	0	1	1	0	1
Bobby Avila, 2b, Cle	2	0	1	1	0	0
Phil Rizzuto, ss, NYA	2	0	0	0	0	0
Vic Raschi, p, NYA	0	0	0	0	0	0
Gil McDougald, ph, NYA	1	0	0	0	0	0
Bob Lemon, p, Cle	1	0	0	0	0	0
Bobby Shantz, p, Phi	0	0	0	0	0	0
TOTALS	18	2	5	2	2	4

National League	AB	R	H	RBI	BB	K
Whitey Lockman, 1b, NYG	3	0	0	0	0	1
Jackie Robinson, 2b, Bro	3	1	1	1	0	1
Stan Musial, cf, StL	2	1	0	0	0	2
Hank Sauer, lf, ChN	2	1	1	2	0	1
Roy Campanella, c, Bro	1	0	0	0	1	0
Enos Slaughter, rf, StL	2	0	1	0	0	0
Bobby Thomson, 3b, NYG	2	0	0	0	0	0
Granny Hamner, ss, Phi	1	0	0	0	1	0
Curt Simmons, p, Phi	0	0	0	0	0	0
Pee Wee Reese, ph, Bro	1	0	0	0	0	0
Bob Rush, p, ChN	1	0	0	0	0	0
TOTALS	18	3	3	3	2	6

```
        1 2 3 4 5        R H E
AL      0 0 0 2 0        2 5 0
NL      1 0 0 2 x        3 3 0
```

DP—NL 1 (Hamner to JRobinson to Lockman). LOB—AL 3, NL 3. Scoring Position—AL 2-for-5, NL 0-for-2. 2B—DiMaggio, Slaughter, Minoso. HR—JRobinson, Sauer. GDP—Rizzuto. CS—Bauer.

American League	IP	H	R	ER	BB	K
Vic Raschi, NYA	2.0	1	1	1	0	3
Bob Lemon, Cle (L)	2.0	2	2	2	2	0
Bobby Shantz, Phi	1.0	0	0	0	0	3

National League	IP	H	R	ER	BB	K
Curt Simmons, Phi	3.0	1	0	0	1	3
Bob Rush, ChN (W)	2.0	4	2	2	1	1

HBP—Musial by Lemon. Time—1:29. Attendance—32,785. Umpires—HP, Barlick. 1B, Berry. 2B, Boggess. 3B, Summers.

July 14, 1953
Cincinnati (Crosley Field)

Four National League hurlers held the American League to just five hits as the NL rolled to an easy 5-1 victory. NL starter Robin Roberts worked three scoreless innings, and Warren Spahn and Curt Simmons followed with two scoreless frames apiece. Enos Slaughter was the offensive star with two hits, two runs, a walk and a stolen base. He also made the defensive play of the day, a diving, rolling catch of Harvey Kuenn's liner into the right-field corner. Pee Wee Reese chipped in a double, a single and two RBI.

American League	AB	R	H	RBI	BB	K
Billy Goodman, 2b, Bos	2	0	0	0	1	0
Nellie Fox, 2b, ChA	1	0	0	0	0	0
Mickey Vernon, 1b, Was	3	0	0	0	0	2
Ferris Fain, 1b, ChA	1	1	1	0	0	0
Hank Bauer, rf, NYA	2	0	0	0	1	1
Johnny Mize, ph, NYA	1	0	1	0	0	0
Mickey Mantle, cf, NYA	2	0	0	0	1	0
Billy Hunter, pr, StL	0	0	0	0	0	0
Larry Doby, cf, Cle	1	0	0	0	0	0
Al Rosen, 3b, Cle	4	0	0	0	0	0
Gus Zernial, lf, Phi	2	0	1	0	0	1
Minnie Minoso, ph, ChA	2	0	2	1	0	0
Yogi Berra, c, NYA	4	0	0	0	0	0
Chico Carrasquel, ss, ChA	2	0	0	0	0	0
George Kell, ph, Bos	1	0	0	0	0	0
Phil Rizzuto, ss, NYA	0	0	0	0	0	0
Billy Pierce, p, ChA	1	0	0	0	0	1
Allie Reynolds, p, NYA	0	0	0	0	0	0
Harvey Kuenn, p, Det	1	0	0	0	0	0
Mike Garcia, p, Cle	0	0	0	0	0	0
Eddie Robinson, ph, Phi	1	0	0	0	0	0
Satchel Paige, p, StL	0	0	0	0	0	0
TOTALS	31	1	5	1	3	5

National League	AB	R	H	RBI	BB	K
Pee Wee Reese, ss, Bro	4	0	2	2	0	0
Granny Hamner, ss, Phi	0	0	0	0	0	0
Red Schoendienst, 2b, StL	3	0	0	0	0	0
Davey Williams, 2b, NYG	0	0	0	0	1	0
Stan Musial, lf, StL	4	0	2	0	0	1
Ted Kluszewski, 1b, Cin	3	0	1	0	0	0
Gil Hodges, pr-1b, Bro	1	0	0	0	0	0
Roy Campanella, c, Bro	4	1	1	0	0	1
Eddie Mathews, 3b, Mil	3	1	0	0	0	0
Gus Bell, cf, Cin	3	0	0	0	0	0
Duke Snider, ph-cf, Bro	0	1	0	0	1	0
Enos Slaughter, rf, StL	3	2	2	1	1	0
Robin Roberts, p, Phi	0	0	0	0	0	0
Ralph Kiner, ph, ChN	1	0	0	0	0	1
Warren Spahn, p, Mil	0	0	0	0	0	0
Richie Ashburn, ph, Phi	1	0	1	1	0	0
Curt Simmons, p, Phi	0	0	0	0	0	0
Jackie Robinson, ph, Bro	1	0	0	0	0	0
Murry Dickson, p, Pit	1	0	1	1	0	0
TOTALS	32	5	10	5	3	3

```
        1 2 3 4 5 6 7 8 9        R H E
AL      0 0 0 0 0 0 0 0 1        1 5 0
NL      0 0 0 0 2 0 1 2 x        5 10 0
```

DP—AL 1 (Carrasquel to Vernon), NL 1 (Campanella to Reese). LOB—AL 6, NL 7. Scoring Position—AL 1-for-5, NL 5-for-10. 2B—Reese. GDP—Mathews. SB—Slaughter. CS—Goodman.

American League	IP	H	R	ER	BB	K
Billy Pierce, ChA	3.0	1	0	0	0	1
Allie Reynolds, NYA (L)	2.0	2	2	2	1	0
Mike Garcia, Cle	2.0	4	1	1	1	2
Satchel Paige, StL	1.0	3	2	2	1	0

National League	IP	H	R	ER	BB	K
Robin Roberts, Phi	3.0	1	0	0	1	2
Warren Spahn, Mil (W)	2.0	0	0	0	1	2
Curt Simmons, Phi	2.0	1	0	0	1	1
Murry Dickson, Pit (S)	2.0	3	1	1	0	0

HBP—Mathews by Reynolds. Time—2:19. Attendance—30,846. Umpires—HP, Conlan. 1B, Stevens. 2B, Donatelli. 3B, McKinley.

July 13, 1954
Cleveland (Municipal Stadium)

The National and American League squads combined to launch six home runs, but it was Nellie Fox' eighth-inning Texas League single that gave the AL an 11-9 win. With the score tied 9-9, the sacks full, and two out in the eighth, Fox sent a hump-backed liner over second, just out of the reach of shortstop Alvin Dark to score Mickey Mantle and Yogi Berra with the eventual winning runs. Earlier in the inning, Larry Doby's solo homer had tied the score. Al Rosen homered twice and drove in five runs for the Americans, while Ted Kluszewski notched an RBI single and a two-run homer for the Nationals.

National League	AB	R	H	RBI	BB	K
Granny Hamner, 2b, Phi	3	0	0	0	0	0
Red Schoendienst, 2b, StL	2	0	0	0	0	0
Al Dark, ss, NYG	5	0	1	0	0	0
Duke Snider, cf-rf, Bro	4	2	3	0	1	0
Stan Musial, rf-lf, StL	5	1	2	0	0	0
Ted Kluszewski, 1b, Cin	4	2	2	3	0	0
Gil Hodges, 1b, Bro	1	0	0	0	0	0
Ray Jablonski, 3b, StL	3	1	1	1	0	0
Randy Jackson, 3b, ChN	2	0	0	0	0	0
Jackie Robinson, lf, Bro	2	1	1	2	0	0
Willie Mays, cf, NYG	2	1	1	0	0	0
Roy Campanella, c, Bro	3	0	1	0	1	1
Smoky Burgess, c, Phi	0	0	0	0	0	0
Robin Roberts, p, Phi	1	0	0	0	0	0
Don Mueller, ph, NYG	1	0	1	1	0	0
Johnny Antonelli, p, NYG	0	0	0	0	0	0
Frank Thomas, ph, Pit	1	0	0	0	0	1
Warren Spahn, p, Mil	0	0	0	0	0	0
Marv Grissom, p, NYG	0	0	0	0	0	0
Gus Bell, ph, Cin	1	1	1	2	0	0
Gene Conley, p, Mil	0	0	0	0	0	0
Carl Erskine, p, Bro	0	0	0	0	0	0
TOTALS	40	9	14	9	2	2

American League	AB	R	H	RBI	BB	K
Minnie Minoso, lf-rf, ChA	4	1	2	0	1	0
Jimmy Piersall, rf, Bos	0	0	0	0	0	0
Bobby Avila, 2b, Cle	3	1	3	2	0	0
Bob Keegan, p, ChA	0	0	0	0	0	0
Dean Stone, p, Was	0	0	0	0	0	0
Larry Doby, ph-cf, Cle	1	1	1	1	0	0
Mickey Mantle, cf, NYA	5	1	2	0	0	1
Virgil Trucks, p, ChA	0	0	0	0	0	0
Yogi Berra, c, NYA	4	2	2	0	1	0
Al Rosen, 1b-3b, Cle	4	2	3	5	1	1
Ray Boone, 3b, Det	4	1	1	1	0	0
Mickey Vernon, ph-1b, Was	1	0	0	0	0	1
Hank Bauer, rf, NYA	2	0	1	0	0	1
Bob Porterfield, p, Was	1	0	0	0	0	0
Nellie Fox, ph-2b, ChA	2	0	1	2	0	1
Chico Carrasquel, ss, ChA	5	1	1	0	0	2
Whitey Ford, p, NYA	1	0	0	0	0	1
Sandy Consuegra, p, ChA	0	0	0	0	0	0
Bob Lemon, p, Cle	0	0	0	0	0	0
Ted Williams, ph-lf, Bos	2	1	0	0	1	2
Irv Noren, lf, NYA	0	0	0	0	0	0
TOTALS	39	11	17	11	4	10

```
        1 2 3 4 5 6 7 8 9        R H E
NL      0 0 0 5 2 0 0 2 0        9 14 0
AL      0 0 4 1 2 1 0 3 x       11 17 1
```

E—Minoso. DP—AL 1 (Avila to Carrasquel to Rosen). LOB—NL 6, AL 9. Scoring Position—NL 5-for-11, AL 5-for-12. 2B—Snider, Robinson, Mueller. HR—Kluszewski, Rosen 2, Boone, Bell, Doby. SF—Avila. GDP—Kluszewski. CS—Schoendienst.

National League	IP	H	R	ER	BB	K
Robin Roberts, Phi	3.0	5	4	4	2	5
Johnny Antonelli, NYG	2.0	4	3	3	0	2
Warren Spahn, Mil	0.2	4	1	1	1	0
Marv Grissom, NYG	1.1	0	0	0	0	2
Gene Conley, Mil (BS; L)	0.1	3	3	3	1	0
Carl Erskine, Bro	0.2	1	0	0	1	0

American League	IP	H	R	ER	BB	K
Whitey Ford, NYA	3.0	1	0	0	1	0
Sandy Consuegra, ChA	0.1	5	5	5	0	0
Bob Lemon, Cle	0.2	1	0	0	0	0
Bob Porterfield, Was	3.0	4	2	2	0	1
Bob Keegan, ChA (BS)	0.2	3	2	2	0	1
Dean Stone, Was (W)	0.1	0	0	0	0	0
Virgil Trucks, ChA (S)	1.0	0	0	0	0	0

Time—3:10. Attendance—68,751. Umpires—HP, Rommel. 1B, Ballanfant. 2B, Honochick. 3B, Stewart.

All-Star Games: Box Scores

July 12, 1955
Milwaukee (County Stadium)

Stan Musial's 12th-inning homer gave the National League a 6-5 victory. The dinger came on the first pitch of the inning from Frank Sullivan. The American League had jumped out to a 4-0 lead after one inning, with three of the runs coming on a homer by Mickey Mantle. In the sixth inning, Mickey Vernon's RBI groundout made it 5-0 Americans, but the Nationals got two back in the seventh on an RBI single by Johnny Logan and an error by Chico Carrasquel. The NL tied it up in the following inning on RBI singles by Randy Jackson and Hank Aaron and an error by Al Rosen. Gene Conley got the win after striking out the side in the top of the 12th.

American League	AB	R	H	RBI	BB	K
Harvey Kuenn, ss, Det	3	1	1	0	0	0
Chico Carrasquel, ss, ChA	3	0	2	0	0	0
Nellie Fox, 2b, ChA	3	1	1	0	0	0
Bobby Avila, 2b, Cle	1	0	0	0	1	1
Ted Williams, lf, Bos	3	1	1	0	1	0
Al Smith, lf, Cle	1	0	0	0	1	1
Mickey Mantle, cf, NYA	6	1	2	3	0	1
Yogi Berra, c, NYA	6	1	1	0	0	0
Al Kaline, rf, Det	4	0	1	0	1	2
Mickey Vernon, 1b, Was	5	0	1	1	1	2
Jim Finigan, 3b, KCA	3	0	0	0	0	1
Al Rosen, 3b, Cle	2	0	0	0	1	2
Billy Pierce, p, ChA	0	0	0	0	0	0
Jackie Jensen, ph, Bos	1	0	0	0	0	0
Early Wynn, p, Cle	0	0	0	0	0	0
Vic Power, ph, KCA	1	0	0	0	0	0
Whitey Ford, p, NYA	1	0	0	0	0	1
Frank Sullivan, p, Bos	1	0	0	0	0	1
TOTALS	44	5	10	4	6	12

National League	AB	R	H	RBI	BB	K
Red Schoendienst, 2b, StL	6	0	2	0	0	0
Del Ennis, lf, Phi	1	0	0	0	0	1
Stan Musial, ph-lf, StL	4	1	1	1	1	1
Duke Snider, cf, Bro	2	0	0	0	0	1
Willie Mays, cf, NYG	3	2	2	0	0	1
Ted Kluszewski, 1b, Cin	5	1	2	0	0	0
Eddie Mathews, 3b, Mil	2	0	0	0	0	0
Randy Jackson, 3b, ChN	3	1	1	1	0	1
Don Mueller, rf, NYG	2	0	1	0	0	0
Hank Aaron, pr-rf, Mil	2	1	2	1	1	0
Ernie Banks, ss, ChN	2	0	0	0	0	1
Johnny Logan, ss, Mil	3	0	1	1	0	1
Del Crandall, c, Mil	1	0	0	0	0	0
Smoky Burgess, ph-c, Cin	1	0	0	0	0	0
Stan Lopata, ph-c, Phi	3	0	0	0	0	1
Robin Roberts, p, Phi	0	0	0	0	0	0
Frank Thomas, ph, Pit	1	0	0	0	0	0
Harvey Haddix, p, StL	0	0	0	0	0	0
Gil Hodges, ph, Bro	1	0	1	0	0	0
Don Newcombe, p, Bro	0	0	0	0	0	0
Gene Baker, ph, ChN	1	0	0	0	0	0
Sam Jones, p, ChN	0	0	0	0	0	0
Joe Nuxhall, p, Cin	2	0	0	0	0	0
Gene Conley, p, Mil	0	0	0	0	0	0
TOTALS	45	6	13	4	2	8

	1 2 3	4 5 6	7 8 9	10 11 12	R	H	E
AL	4 0 0	0 0 1	0 0 0	0 0 0	5	10	2
NL	0 0 0	0 0 0	2 3 0	0 0 1	6	13	1

E—Mathews, Carrasquel, Rosen. DP—AL 1 (Wynn to Carrasquel to Vernon), NL 1 (Kluszewski to Banks to Roberts). LOB—AL 12, NL 8. Scoring Position—AL 1-for-11, NL 4-for-11. 2B—Kaline, Kluszewski. HR—Mantle, Musial. S—Pierce, Avila. GDP—Berra, Musial.

American League	IP	H	R	ER	BB	K
Billy Pierce, ChA	3.0	1	0	0	0	3
Early Wynn, Cle	3.0	3	0	0	0	1
Whitey Ford, NYA	1.2	5	5	3	1	0
Frank Sullivan, Bos (BS; L)	3.1	4	1	1	1	4

National League	IP	H	R	ER	BB	K
Robin Roberts, Phi	3.0	4	4	4	1	0
Harvey Haddix, StL	3.0	3	1	1	0	2
Don Newcombe, Bro	1.0	1	0	0	0	1
Sam Jones, ChN	0.2	0	0	0	2	1
Joe Nuxhall, Cin	3.1	2	0	0	3	5
Gene Conley, Mil (W)	1.0	0	0	0	0	3

Sullivan pitched to one batter in the 12th.

WP—Roberts. PB—Crandall. HBP—Kaline by Jones. Time—3:17. Attendance—45,314. Umpires—HP, Barlick. 1B, Soar. 2B, Boggess. 3B, Summers.

July 10, 1956
Washington (Griffith Stadium)

Ken Boyer starred at the plate and in the field as the National League overpowered the American League for a 7-3 victory. Boyer rapped out three singles in five trips to the plate and made three standout plays at the hot corner. In the bottom of the first, Boyer dove to his left to spear a hot smash off the bat of Harvey Kuenn. In the fifth inning, he victimized Kuenn a second time, backhanding his grounder down the third base line and recovering in time to throw him out at first. Three Reds players figured prominently in the NL's winning cause: Ted Kluszewski had a pair of doubles in two at-bats, and keystone combo Johnny Temple and Roy McMillan had two hits apiece.

National League	AB	R	H	RBI	BB	K
Johnny Temple, 2b, Cin	4	1	2	1	1	2
Frank Robinson, lf, Cin	2	0	0	0	0	2
Duke Snider, ph-cf, Bro	3	0	0	0	0	1
Stan Musial, rf-lf, StL	4	1	1	1	0	1
Hank Aaron, lf, Mil	1	0	0	0	0	0
Ken Boyer, 3b, StL	5	1	3	1	0	0
Gus Bell, cf, Cin	1	0	0	0	0	1
Willie Mays, ph-cf-rf, NYG	3	2	1	2	1	2
Dale Long, 1b, Pit	2	0	0	0	0	2
Ted Kluszewski, ph-1b, Cin	2	1	2	1	0	0
Ed Bailey, c, Cin	3	0	0	0	1	0
Roy Campanella, c, Bro	0	0	0	0	0	0
Roy McMillan, ss, Cin	3	1	2	0	1	0
Bob Friend, p, Pit	0	0	0	0	0	0
Rip Repulski, ph, StL	1	0	0	0	0	0
Warren Spahn, p, Mil	1	0	0	0	0	0
Johnny Antonelli, p, NYG	1	0	0	0	0	1
TOTALS	36	7	11	6	4	12

American League	AB	R	H	RBI	BB	K
Harvey Kuenn, ss, Det	5	0	1	0	0	0
Nellie Fox, 2b, ChA	4	1	2	0	0	0
Ted Williams, lf, Bos	4	1	1	2	0	1
Mickey Mantle, cf, NYA	4	1	1	1	0	3
Yogi Berra, c, NYA	2	0	2	0	0	0
Sherm Lollar, ph-c, ChA	2	0	1	0	0	0
Al Kaline, rf, Det	3	0	1	0	0	0
Jimmy Piersall, rf, Bos	1	0	0	0	0	0
Mickey Vernon, 1b, Bos	2	0	0	0	0	0
Vic Power, ph-1b, KCA	2	0	1	0	0	0
George Kell, 3b, Bal	4	0	1	0	0	0
Billy Pierce, p, ChA	0	0	0	0	0	0
Harry Simpson, ph, KCA	1	0	0	0	0	1
Whitey Ford, p, NYA	0	0	0	0	0	0
Jim Wilson, p, ChA	0	0	0	0	0	0
Billy Martin, ph, NYA	1	0	0	0	0	0
Tom Brewer, p, Bos	0	0	0	0	0	0
Ray Boone, ph, Det	1	0	0	0	0	0
Herb Score, p, Cle	0	0	0	0	0	0
Early Wynn, p, Cle	0	0	0	0	0	0
Roy Sievers, ph, Was	1	0	0	0	0	0
TOTALS	37	3	11	3	0	5

	1 2 3	4 5 6	7 8 9	R	H	E
NL	0 0 1	2 1 1	2 0 0	7	11	0
AL	0 0 0	0 0 3	0 0 0	3	11	0

DP—NL 1 (McMillan to Temple to Kluszewski). LOB—NL 7, AL 7. Scoring Position—NL 3-for-9, AL 0-for-5. 2B—Kluszewski 2. HR—Musial, Williams, Mantle, Mays. S—Friend. GDP—Kell. SB—Temple. CS—Boyer.

National League	IP	H	R	ER	BB	K
Bob Friend, Pit (W)	3.0	3	0	0	0	3
Warren Spahn, Mil	2.0	4	3	3	0	1
Johnny Antonelli, NYG (S)	4.0	4	0	0	0	1

American League	IP	H	R	ER	BB	K
Billy Pierce, ChA (L)	3.0	2	1	1	1	5
Whitey Ford, NYA	1.0	3	2	2	1	2
Jim Wilson, ChA	1.0	2	1	1	0	1
Tom Brewer, Bos	2.0	4	3	3	1	2
Herb Score, Cle	1.0	0	0	0	1	1
Early Wynn, Cle	1.0	0	0	0	0	1

Spahn pitched to three batters in the 6th.

WP—Brewer 2. Time—2:45. Attendance—28,843. Umpires—HP, Berry. 1B, Pinelli. 2B, Hurley. 3B, Gore.

July 9, 1957
St. Louis (Busch Stadium)

The American League held on to beat the National League, 6-5, thanks to Minnie Minoso's clutch fielding in the bottom of the ninth. The NL had cut the lead to 6-4, and had runners on first and second with one out when Ernie Banks singled to left. Hank Foiles scored on the play to cut the margin to a single run, but Minoso came up throwing and nailed Gus Bell trying to advance to third. Gil Hodges followed with a liner to left, but Minoso made a running catch to end the game and preserve the win. Minoso also had an RBI double in his only at-bat.

American League	AB	R	H	RBI	BB	K
Harvey Kuenn, ss, Det	2	0	0	1	1	0
Gil McDougald, ss, NYA	2	1	0	0	0	0
Nellie Fox, 2b, ChA	4	0	0	0	0	0
Al Kaline, rf, Det	5	1	2	2	0	0
Mickey Mantle, cf, NYA	4	1	1	0	1	1
Ted Williams, lf, Bos	3	1	0	0	1	0
Minnie Minoso, lf, ChA	1	0	1	1	0	0
Vic Wertz, 1b, Cle	2	0	1	1	0	0
Bill Skowron, 1b, NYA	3	1	2	0	0	0
Yogi Berra, c, NYA	3	0	1	1	1	0
George Kell, 3b, Bal	2	0	0	0	0	0
Frank Malzone, 3b, Bos	2	0	0	0	0	0
Jim Bunning, p, Det	1	0	0	0	0	0
Charlie Maxwell, ph, Det	1	0	1	0	0	0
Billy Loes, p, Bal	1	0	0	0	0	0
Early Wynn, p, Cle	0	0	0	0	0	0
Billy Pierce, p, ChA	1	1	1	0	0	0
Don Mossi, p, Cle	0	0	0	0	0	0
Bob Grim, p, NYA	0	0	0	0	0	0
TOTALS	37	6	10	6	4	1

National League	AB	R	H	RBI	BB	K
Johnny Temple, 2b, Cin	2	0	0	0	0	1
Red Schoendienst, ph-2b, Mil	2	0	0	0	0	0
Hank Aaron, rf, Mil	4	0	1	0	0	1
Stan Musial, 1b, StL	3	1	1	0	1	0
Willie Mays, cf, NYG	4	2	2	1	0	1
Ed Bailey, c, Cin	3	1	1	0	0	0
Hank Foiles, ph, Pit	1	1	1	0	0	0
Frank Robinson, lf, Cin	2	0	1	0	0	0
Gus Bell, ph-lf, Cin	1	0	1	2	1	0
Don Hoak, 3b, Cin	1	0	0	0	0	0
Eddie Mathews, ph-3b, Mil	3	0	0	0	0	1
Roy McMillan, ss, Cin	1	0	0	0	0	0
Ernie Banks, ph-ss, ChN	3	0	1	1	0	1
Curt Simmons, p, Phi	0	0	0	0	0	0
Lew Burdette, p, Mil	1	0	0	0	0	0
Jack Sanford, p, Phi	0	0	0	0	0	0
Wally Moon, ph, StL	1	0	0	0	0	0
Larry Jackson, p, StL	0	0	0	0	0	0
Gino Cimoli, ph, Bro	1	0	0	0	0	1
Clem Labine, p, Bro	0	0	0	0	0	0
Gil Hodges, ph, Bro	1	0	0	0	0	0
TOTALS	34	5	9	4	2	6

	1 2 3	4 5 6	7 8 9	R	H	E
AL	0 2 0	0 0 1	0 0 3	6	10	0
NL	0 0 0	0 0 0	2 0 3	5	9	1

E—Schoendienst. DP—AL 1 (Malzone to Fox to Skowron). LOB—AL 9, NL 4. Scoring Position—AL 3-for-10, NL 2-for-8. 2B—Musial, Skowron, Bell, Minoso. 3B—Mays. S—Fox. GDP—Banks.

American League	IP	H	R	ER	BB	K
Jim Bunning, Det (W)	3.0	0	0	0	0	1
Billy Loes, Bal	3.0	3	0	0	0	1
Early Wynn, Cle	0.1	3	2	2	0	0
Billy Pierce, ChA	1.2	2	3	3	2	3
Don Mossi, Cle	0.2	1	0	0	0	1
Bob Grim, NYA (S)	0.1	0	0	0	0	0

National League	IP	H	R	ER	BB	K
Curt Simmons, Phi (L)	1.0	2	2	2	2	0
Lew Burdette, Mil	4.0	2	0	0	1	0
Jack Sanford, Phi	1.0	2	1	1	0	0
Larry Jackson, StL	2.0	1	0	0	1	0
Clem Labine, Bro	1.0	3	3	1	0	1

Simmons pitched to four batters in the 2nd. Pierce pitched to five batters in the 9th.

WP—Sanford, Pierce. Time—2:43. Attendance—30,693. Umpires—HP, Dascoli. 1B, Napp. 2B, Dixon. 3B, Stevens.

July 8, 1958
Baltimore (Memorial Stadium)

The American League edged the National League 4-3, as neither team was able to notch a single extra-base hit. Willie Mays led off the game with a single off the third-base bag. After moving to third on a single by Stan Musial, Mays scored the game's first run on Hank Aaron's sacrifice fly. Gil McDougald's pinch-hit RBI single in the sixth plated the eventual game-winner. Billy O'Dell of the host Orioles tossed three perfect innings for the Americans, and Turk Farrell fanned four in two shutout innings.

National League	AB	R	H	RBI	BB	K
Willie Mays, cf, SF	4	2	1	0	0	0
Bob Skinner, lf, Pit	3	0	1	1	0	0
Lee Walls, ph-lf, ChN	1	0	0	0	0	0
Stan Musial, 1b, StL	4	1	1	0	0	0
Hank Aaron, rf, Mil	2	0	0	1	1	0
Ernie Banks, ss, ChN	3	0	0	0	0	1
Frank Thomas, 3b, Pit	3	0	1	0	1	0
Bill Mazeroski, 2b, Pit	4	0	0	0	0	1
Del Crandall, c, Mil	4	0	0	0	0	0
Warren Spahn, p, Mil	0	0	0	0	1	0
Don Blasingame, ph, StL	1	0	0	0	0	0
Bob Friend, p, Pit	0	0	0	0	0	0
Larry Jackson, p, StL	0	0	0	0	0	0
Johnny Logan, ph, Mil	1	0	0	0	0	0
Turk Farrell, p, Phi	0	0	0	0	0	0
TOTALS	30	3	4	2	3	2

American League	AB	R	H	RBI	BB	K
Nellie Fox, 2b, ChA	4	1	2	1	0	0
Mickey Mantle, cf, NYA	2	0	1	0	2	0
Jackie Jensen, rf, Bos	4	0	0	1	0	1
Bob Cerv, lf, KCA	2	0	1	0	1	0
Billy O'Dell, p, Bal	0	0	0	0	0	0
Bill Skowron, 1b, NYA	4	0	0	0	0	1
Frank Malzone, 3b, Bos	4	1	1	0	0	1
Gus Triandos, c, Bal	2	0	1	0	0	0
Yogi Berra, ph-c, NYA	2	0	0	0	0	0
Luis Aparicio, ss, ChA	2	1	0	0	0	0
Ted Williams, ph-lf, Bos	2	0	0	0	0	0
Al Kaline, lf, Det	0	0	0	0	0	0
Bob Turley, p, NYA	0	0	0	0	0	0
Ray Narleski, p, Cle	1	0	1	0	0	0
Mickey Vernon, ph, Cle	1	1	1	0	0	0
Early Wynn, p, ChA	0	0	0	0	0	0
Gil McDougald, ph-ss, NYA	1	0	1	1	0	0
TOTALS	31	4	9	3	3	4

	1	2	3	4	5	6	7	8	9		R	H	E
NL	2	1	0	0	0	0	0	0	0		3	4	2
AL	1	1	0	0	1	1	0	0	x		4	9	2

E—Banks, Triandos, Thomas, Fox. DP—NL 3 (Thomas to Mazeroski to Musial; Banks to Mazeroski to Musial; Banks to Mazeroski to Musial), AL 1 (Malzone to Fox to Skowron). LOB—NL 5, AL 7. Scoring Position—NL 1-for-3, AL 2-for-8. S—O'Dell. SF—Aaron. GDP—Mazeroski, Fox, Jensen, Skowron. SB—Mays.

National League	IP	H	R	ER	BB	K
Warren Spahn, Mil	3.0	5	2	1	0	0
Bob Friend, Pit (L)	2.1	4	2	1	2	0
Larry Jackson, StL	0.2	0	0	0	0	0
Turk Farrell, Phi	2.0	0	0	0	1	4

American League	IP	H	R	ER	BB	K
Bob Turley, NYA	1.2	3	3	3	2	0
Ray Narleski, Cle	3.1	1	0	0	1	0
Early Wynn, ChA (W)	1.0	0	0	0	0	0
Billy O'Dell, Bal (S)	3.0	0	0	0	0	2

WP—Turley. HBP—Banks by Turley. Time—2:13. Attendance—48,829. Umpires—HP, Rommel. 1B, Gorman. 2B, McKinley. 3B, Conlan.

July 7, 1959
Pittsburgh (Forbes Field)

Willie Mays tripled in the winning run in the bottom of the eighth as the National League prevailed, 5-4. May's blast followed Hank Aaron's game-tying single off Whitey Ford. The NL had fallen behind, 4-3, after a three-run American League uprising in the top of the eighth. Gus Triandos had capped the three-run rally with a bases-loaded double. Eddie Mathews and Al Kaline each notched solo homers in the contest, while Don Drysdale fanned four batters in three perfect innings.

American League	AB	R	H	RBI	BB	K
Minnie Minoso, lf, Cle	5	0	0	0	0	2
Nellie Fox, 2b, ChA	5	1	2	0	0	1
Al Kaline, cf, Det	3	1	1	1	0	1
Harvey Kuenn, cf, Det	1	1	0	0	1	0
Bill Skowron, 1b, NYA	3	0	2	0	0	0
Vic Power, 1b, Cle	1	1	1	1	0	0
Rocky Colavito, rf, Cle	3	0	1	0	0	1
Ted Williams, ph, Bos	0	0	0	0	1	0
Gil McDougald, pr-ss, NYA	0	0	0	0	0	0
Gus Triandos, c, Bal	4	0	1	2	0	0
Mickey Mantle, pr-rf, NYA	0	0	0	0	0	0
Harmon Killebrew, 3b, Was	3	0	0	0	0	1
Jim Bunning, p, Det	0	0	0	0	0	0
Pete Runnels, ph, Bos	0	0	0	0	0	0
Roy Sievers, ph, Was	0	0	0	0	1	0
Whitey Ford, p, NYA	0	0	0	0	0	0
Bud Daley, p, KCA	0	0	0	0	0	0
Luis Aparicio, ss, ChA	3	0	0	0	0	1
Sherm Lollar, ph-c, ChA	1	0	0	0	0	0
Early Wynn, p, ChA	1	0	0	0	0	1
Ryne Duren, p, NYA	1	0	0	0	0	0
Frank Malzone, 3b, Bos	2	0	0	0	0	0
TOTALS	36	4	8	4	3	9

National League	AB	R	H	RBI	BB	K
Johnny Temple, 2b, Cin	2	0	0	0	0	0
Stan Musial, ph, StL	1	0	0	0	0	0
Roy Face, p, Pit	0	0	0	0	0	0
Johnny Antonelli, p, SF	0	0	0	0	0	0
Ken Boyer, ph-3b, StL	1	1	1	0	0	0
Eddie Mathews, 3b, Mil	3	1	1	1	0	1
Dick Groat, p, Pit	0	0	0	0	0	0
Don Elston, p, ChN	0	0	0	0	0	0
Hank Aaron, rf, Mil	4	1	2	1	0	1
Willie Mays, cf, SF	4	0	1	1	0	1
Ernie Banks, ss, ChN	3	1	2	0	1	1
Orlando Cepeda, 1b, SF	4	0	0	0	0	0
Wally Moon, lf, LA	2	0	0	0	1	2
Del Crandall, c, Mil	3	1	1	1	0	1
Don Drysdale, p, LA	1	0	0	0	0	1
Lew Burdette, p, Mil	1	0	0	0	0	0
Bill Mazeroski, 2b, Pit	1	0	1	1	0	0
TOTALS	30	5	9	5	2	9

	1	2	3	4	5	6	7	8	9		R	H	E
AL	0	0	0	1	0	0	0	3	0		4	8	0
NL	1	0	0	0	0	0	2	2	x		5	9	1

E—Mathews. DP—AL 1 (Aparicio to Skowron). LOB—AL 8, NL 4. Scoring Position—AL 2-for-6, NL 3-for-10. 2B—Triandos, Banks 2. 3B—Mays. HR—Kaline, Mathews. S—Groat. GDP—Cepeda.

American League	IP	H	R	ER	BB	K
Early Wynn, ChA	3.0	2	1	1	1	3
Ryne Duren, NYA	3.0	1	0	0	1	4
Jim Bunning, Det	1.0	3	2	2	0	1
Whitey Ford, NYA (BS; L)	0.1	3	2	2	0	0
Bud Daley, KCA	0.2	0	0	0	0	1

National League	IP	H	R	ER	BB	K
Don Drysdale, LA	3.0	0	0	0	0	4
Lew Burdette, Mil	3.0	4	1	1	0	2
Roy Face, Pit	1.2	3	3	3	2	2
Johnny Antonelli, SF (W)	0.1	0	0	0	0	0
Don Elston, ChN (S)	1.0	1	0	0	0	1

WP—Elston. Time—2:33. Attendance—35,277. Umpires—HP, Barlick. 1B, Runge. 2B, Donatelli. 3B, Paparella.

August 3, 1959
Los Angeles (LA Coliseum)

The American League won 5-3 in a battle of longballs, as two All-Star Games were held in the same year for the first time. Frank Malzone went deep in the second, and Yogi Berra socked a two-run homer in the third to give the AL a 3-1 lead. Frank Robinson and Jim Gilliam each hit solo shots for the Nationals, but Rocky Colavito's eighth-inning homer accounted for the AL's fifth and final run. Robinson had two singles in addition to his circuit shot.

American League	AB	R	H	RBI	BB	K
Pete Runnels, 1b, Bos	3	0	0	0	1	2
Vic Power, 1b, Cle	1	0	0	0	0	0
Nellie Fox, 2b, ChA	4	1	2	1	1	0
Ted Williams, lf, Bos	3	0	0	0	0	1
Al Kaline, lf-cf, Det	2	0	0	0	0	1
Yogi Berra, c, NYA	3	1	1	2	0	2
Sherm Lollar, c, ChA	0	0	0	0	1	0
Mickey Mantle, cf, NYA	3	0	1	0	1	1
Billy O'Dell, p, Bal	0	0	0	0	0	0
Cal McLish, p, Cle	0	0	0	0	0	0
Roger Maris, rf, KCA	2	0	0	0	0	1
Rocky Colavito, rf, Cle	2	1	1	1	0	1
Frank Malzone, 3b, Bos	4	1	1	1	0	0
Luis Aparicio, ss, ChA	3	0	0	0	1	1
Jerry Walker, p, Bal	1	0	0	0	0	0
Gene Woodling, ph, Bal	1	0	0	0	0	0
Early Wynn, p, ChA	0	0	0	0	0	0
Hoyt Wilhelm, p, Bal	0	0	0	0	0	0
Tony Kubek, ph-lf, NYA	1	1	0	0	1	1
TOTALS	33	5	6	5	6	12

National League	AB	R	H	RBI	BB	K
Johnny Temple, 2b, Cin	2	1	1	0	0	0
Jim Gilliam, ph-3b, LA	2	1	1	1	1	0
Ken Boyer, 3b, StL	2	0	0	0	1	0
Charlie Neal, 2b, LA	1	0	0	0	0	0
Hank Aaron, rf, Mil	3	0	0	1	0	0
Willie Mays, cf, SF	4	0	0	0	0	0
Ernie Banks, ss, ChN	4	0	0	0	0	2
Stan Musial, 1b, StL	0	0	0	0	1	0
Frank Robinson, 1b, Cin	3	1	3	1	0	0
Wally Moon, lf, LA	2	0	0	0	2	0
Del Crandall, c, Mil	2	0	1	0	0	0
Hal Smith, c, StL	2	0	0	0	0	1
Don Drysdale, p, LA	0	0	0	0	0	0
Eddie Mathews, ph, Mil	1	0	0	0	0	1
Gene Conley, p, Phi	0	0	0	0	0	0
Joe Cunningham, ph, StL	1	0	0	0	0	0
Vada Pinson, pr, Cin	0	0	0	0	0	0
Sam Jones, p, SF	0	0	0	0	0	0
Dick Groat, p, Pit	1	0	0	0	0	0
Roy Face, p, Pit	0	0	0	0	0	0
Smoky Burgess, ph, Pit	1	0	0	0	0	0
TOTALS	31	3	6	3	5	4

	1	2	3	4	5	6	7	8	9		R	H	E
AL	0	1	2	0	0	0	1	1	0		5	6	0
NL	1	0	0	0	0	1	0	1	0	0		3	6	3

E—Robinson, Banks, Jones. DP—AL 1 (Runnels). LOB—AL 7, NL 7. Scoring Position—AL 1-for-6, NL 0-for-5. 2B—Temple. HR—Berra, Malzone, Robinson, Colavito, Gilliam. SF—Aaron. SB—Aparicio. CS—Mantle.

American League	IP	H	R	ER	BB	K
Jerry Walker, Bal (W)	3.0	2	1	1	1	1
Early Wynn, ChA	2.0	1	1	1	3	1
Hoyt Wilhelm, Bal	1.0	1	0	0	0	0
Billy O'Dell, Bal	1.0	1	1	1	0	0
Cal McLish, Cle (S)	2.0	1	0	0	1	2

National League	IP	H	R	ER	BB	K
Don Drysdale, LA (L)	3.0	4	3	3	3	5
Gene Conley, Phi	2.0	0	0	0	1	2
Sam Jones, SF	2.0	1	1	0	2	3
Roy Face, Pit	2.0	1	1	0	2	2

Time—2:42. Attendance—55,105. Umpires—HP, Jackowski. 1B, Berry. 2B, Venzon. 3B, Summers.

July 11, 1960

Kansas City (Municipal Stadium)

The National League jumped out to a 5-0 lead after three innings and held on to win, 5-3. Ernie Banks' two-run homer in the first inning and Del Crandall's solo shot in the second put the NL in front. Banks doubled and scored in the third for the Senior Circuit's final run. Al Kaline had a two-run homer, and Willie Mays notched a single, a double and a triple. NL starter Bob Friend allowed only one hit over three scoreless frames.

National League	AB	R	H	RBI	BB	K
Willie Mays, cf, SF	4	1	3	0	0	0
Vada Pinson, cf, Cin	1	0	0	0	0	1
Bob Skinner, lf, Pit	4	1	1	1	0	1
Orlando Cepeda, lf, SF	1	0	0	0	0	1
Eddie Mathews, 3b, Mil	4	0	0	0	0	0
Ken Boyer, 3b, StL	0	0	0	0	1	0
Hank Aaron, rf, Mil	4	0	0	0	0	0
Roberto Clemente, rf, Pit	1	0	0	0	0	0
Ernie Banks, ss, ChN	4	2	2	2	0	0
Dick Groat, ss, Pit	0	0	0	0	0	0
Joe Adcock, 1b, Mil	3	0	2	0	0	0
Bill White, pr-1b, StL	1	0	0	0	0	1
Bill Mazeroski, 2b, Pit	2	0	1	1	0	0
Stan Musial, ph, StL	1	0	1	0	0	0
Tony Taylor, pr, Phi	0	0	0	0	0	0
Charlie Neal, 2b, LA	0	0	0	0	0	0
Del Crandall, c, Mil	3	1	2	1	0	0
Smoky Burgess, c, Pit	1	0	0	0	0	0
Bob Friend, p, Pit	2	0	0	0	0	2
Mike McCormick, p, SF	1	0	0	0	0	0
Roy Face, p, Pit	0	0	0	0	0	0
Norm Larker, ph, LA	1	0	0	0	0	0
Bob Buhl, p, Mil	0	0	0	0	0	0
Vern Law, p, Pit	0	0	0	0	0	0
TOTALS	38	5	12	5	1	6

American League	AB	R	H	RBI	BB	K
Minnie Minoso, lf, ChA	3	0	0	0	0	0
Jim Lemon, lf, Was	1	0	0	0	1	1
Frank Malzone, 3b, Bos	3	0	0	0	0	0
Brooks Robinson, 3b, Bal	2	0	0	0	0	0
Roger Maris, rf, NYA	2	0	0	0	0	1
Harvey Kuenn, rf, Cle	3	1	1	0	0	0
Mickey Mantle, cf, NYA	0	0	0	0	2	0
Al Kaline, cf, Det	2	2	1	2	0	0
Bill Skowron, 1b, NYA	3	0	1	0	0	2
Frank Lary, p, Det	0	0	0	0	0	0
Sherm Lollar, ph, ChA	1	0	0	0	0	0
Bud Daley, p, KCA	0	0	0	0	0	0
Yogi Berra, c, NYA	2	0	0	0	0	0
Elston Howard, c, NYA	1	0	0	0	1	1
Pete Runnels, 2b, Bos	1	0	0	0	1	0
Nellie Fox, 2b, ChA	2	0	1	1	0	0
Ron Hansen, ss, Bal	2	0	1	0	0	1
Luis Aparicio, ss, ChA	2	0	0	0	0	0
Bill Monbouquette, p, Bos	0	0	0	0	0	0
Ted Williams, ph, Bos	1	0	0	0	0	0
Chuck Estrada, p, Bal	0	0	0	0	0	0
Jim Coates, p, NYA	0	0	0	0	0	0
Al Smith, ph, ChA	1	0	0	0	0	0
Gary Bell, p, Cle	0	0	0	0	0	0
Jim Gentile, ph-1b, Bal	2	0	1	0	0	1
TOTALS	34	3	6	3	5	7

	1 2 3	4 5 6	7 8 9	R	H	E
NL	3 1 1	0 0 0	0 0 0	5	12	4
AL	0 0 0	0 0 1	0 2 0	3	6	1

E—Neal, Daley, Mathews 2, Burgess. DP—NL 1 (Banks to Mazeroski to White), AL 1 (Malzone to Skowron). LOB—NL 8, AL 9. Scoring Position—NL 5-for-12, AL 1-for-7. 2B—Mays, Banks, Adcock. 3B—Mays. HR—Banks, Crandall, Kaline. GDP—Crandall, Aparicio. SB—Skinner.

National League	IP	H	R	ER	BB	K
Bob Friend, Pit (W)	3.0	1	0	0	1	2
Mike McCormick, SF	2.1	3	1	0	3	2
Roy Face, Pit	1.2	0	0	0	0	2
Bob Buhl, Mil	1.1	2	2	1	1	1
Vern Law, Pit (S)	0.2	0	0	0	0	0

American League	IP	H	R	ER	BB	K
Bill Monbouquette, Bos (L)	2.0	5	4	4	0	2
Chuck Estrada, Bal	1.0	4	1	1	0	1
Jim Coates, NYA	2.0	2	0	0	0	0
Gary Bell, Cle	2.0	0	0	0	0	0
Frank Lary, Det	1.0	1	0	0	0	1
Bud Daley, KCA	1.0	0	0	0	1	2

Balk—Friend. WP—Friend. HBP—Mazeroski by Coates. Time—2:39. Attendance—30,619. Umpires—HP, Honochick. 1B, Gorman. 2B, Chylak. 3B, Boggess.

July 13, 1960

New York (Yankee Stadium)

Two days after their 5-3 win in the first All-Star Game, the Nationals completed the sweep with a 6-0 victory. Willie Mays had another three-hit day, lacing two singles and a solo homer. Eddie Mathews and Ken Boyer each contributed two-run homers, and Stan Musial added a blast into Yankee Stadium's upper deck with the bases empty in the seventh. Vern Law, Johnny Podres and Stan Williams each tossed two hitless frames for the Senior Circuit.

National League	AB	R	H	RBI	BB	K
Willie Mays, cf, SF	4	1	3	1	0	0
Vada Pinson, cf, Cin	0	0	0	0	1	0
Bob Skinner, lf, Pit	3	0	1	0	0	1
Orlando Cepeda, lf, SF	2	0	0	0	0	0
Hank Aaron, rf, Mil	3	0	0	0	0	0
Roberto Clemente, ph-rf, Pit	0	0	0	0	1	0
Ernie Banks, ss, ChN	3	0	1	0	0	0
Dick Groat, ph-ss, Pit	1	0	0	0	0	0
Joe Adcock, 1b, Mil	2	1	1	0	0	1
Bill White, 1b, StL	1	0	0	0	0	0
Norm Larker, ph-1b, LA	0	1	0	0	1	0
Eddie Mathews, 3b, Mil	3	1	1	2	0	0
Ken Boyer, 3b, StL	1	1	1	2	0	0
Bill Mazeroski, 2b, Pit	2	0	0	0	0	0
Charlie Neal, 2b, LA	1	0	0	0	0	0
Tony Taylor, 2b, Phi	1	0	1	0	0	0
Del Crandall, c, Mil	2	0	0	0	0	0
Stan Williams, p, LA	0	0	0	0	0	0
Stan Musial, ph, StL	1	1	1	1	0	0
Ed Bailey, c, Cin	1	0	0	0	0	0
Vern Law, p, Pit	1	0	0	0	0	0
Johnny Podres, p, LA	0	0	0	0	0	0
Smoky Burgess, ph-c, Pit	2	0	0	0	0	1
Larry Jackson, p, StL	0	0	0	0	0	0
Bill Henry, p, Cin	0	0	0	0	0	0
Lindy McDaniel, p, StL	0	0	0	0	0	0
TOTALS	34	6	10	6	3	3

American League	AB	R	H	RBI	BB	K
Minnie Minoso, lf, ChA	2	0	0	0	1	1
Ted Williams, ph, Bos	1	0	1	0	0	0
Brooks Robinson, pr-3b, Bal	1	0	0	0	0	0
Pete Runnels, 2b, Bos	2	0	0	0	1	1
Gerry Staley, p, ChA	0	0	0	0	0	0
Al Kaline, ph-lf, Det	1	0	1	0	1	0
Roger Maris, rf, NYA	4	0	0	0	1	0
Mickey Mantle, cf, NYA	4	0	1	0	0	1
Bill Skowron, 1b, NYA	1	0	1	0	1	0
Vic Power, 1b, Cle	2	0	0	0	0	0
Yogi Berra, c, NYA	2	0	0	0	0	1
Sherm Lollar, c, ChA	2	0	1	0	0	0
Frank Malzone, 3b, Bos	2	0	0	0	1	0
Frank Lary, p, Det	0	0	0	0	0	0
Al Smith, ph, ChA	1	0	0	0	0	0
Gary Bell, p, Cle	0	0	0	0	0	0
Ron Hansen, ss, Bal	4	0	2	0	0	0
Whitey Ford, p, NYA	0	0	0	0	0	0
Harvey Kuenn, ph, Cle	1	0	0	0	0	0
Early Wynn, p, ChA	0	0	0	0	0	0
Nellie Fox, ph-2b, ChA	3	0	1	0	0	0
TOTALS	33	0	8	0	6	4

	1 2 3	4 5 6	7 8 9	R	H	E
NL	0 2 1	0 0 0	1 0 2	6	10	0
AL	0 0 0	0 0 0	0 0 0	0	8	0

DP—NL 2 (Law to Banks to Adcock; Banks to Neal to White), AL 1 (Fox to Hansen to Power). LOB—NL 5, AL 12. Scoring Position—NL 0-for-4, AL 0-for-6. 2B—Lollar. HR—Mays, Mathews, Musial, Boyer. S—Henry. GDP—Minoso, Berra, Groat. SB—Mays. CS—Mays.

National League	IP	H	R	ER	BB	K
Vern Law, Pit (W)	2.0	1	0	0	0	1
Johnny Podres, LA	2.0	1	0	0	3	1
Stan Williams, LA	2.0	2	0	0	1	2
Larry Jackson, StL	1.0	1	0	0	2	0
Bill Henry, Cin	1.0	2	0	0	0	0
Lindy McDaniel, StL	1.0	1	0	0	0	0

American League	IP	H	R	ER	BB	K
Whitey Ford, NYA (L)	3.0	5	3	3	0	1
Early Wynn, ChA	2.0	0	0	0	0	2
Gerry Staley, ChA	2.0	2	1	1	0	0
Frank Lary, Det	1.0	1	0	0	1	0
Gary Bell, Cle	1.0	2	2	2	2	0

Time—2:42. Attendance—38,362. Umpires—HP, Chylak. 1B, Boggess. 2B, Honochick. 3B, Gorman.

July 11, 1961

San Francisco (Candlestick Park)

Roberto Clemente's RBI single capped the National League's 10-inning, come-from-behind, 5-4 victory. The Nationals held a 3-1 lead and had limited the Americans to just one hit through eight innings. As near gale-force winds whipped through Candlestick Park, the AL squad pushed across a run and put men on first and second. Reliever Stu Miller was summoned from the bullpen, and subsequently committed a costly balk amid the relentless gust. Rocky Colavito sent a grounder to Ken Boyer, who bobbled it as Al Kaline scored the tying run. In the 10th, Boyer's wild throw enabled Nellie Fox to score the go-ahead run, but the Nationals countered in the bottom of the frame with Willie Mays' RBI double and Clemente's game-winning single.

American League	AB	R	H	RBI	BB	K
Johnny Temple, 2b, Cle	3	0	0	0	0	0
Jim Gentile, ph-1b, Bal	2	0	0	0	0	2
Norm Cash, 1b, Det	4	0	1	0	0	2
Nellie Fox, pr-2b, ChA	0	2	0	0	1	0
Mickey Mantle, cf, NYA	3	0	0	0	0	2
Al Kaline, cf, Det	2	1	1	1	0	0
Roger Maris, rf, NYA	4	0	1	0	1	2
Rocky Colavito, lf, Det	4	0	0	1	0	0
Tony Kubek, ss, NYA	4	0	0	0	0	1
John Romano, c, Cle	3	0	0	0	0	1
Yogi Berra, ph-c, NYA	1	0	0	0	0	0
Elston Howard, c, NYA	0	0	0	0	0	0
Brooks Robinson, 3b, Bal	2	0	0	0	0	0
Jim Bunning, p, Det	0	0	0	0	0	0
Jackie Brandt, ph, Bal	1	0	0	0	0	1
Dick Howser, 3b, KCA	1	0	0	0	0	0
Whitey Ford, p, NYA	1	0	0	0	0	0
Frank Lary, p, Det	0	0	0	0	0	0
Dick Donovan, p, Was	0	0	0	0	0	0
Harmon Killebrew, ph-3b, Min	2	1	1	1	0	0
Mike Fornieles, p, Bos	0	0	0	0	0	0
Hoyt Wilhelm, p, Bal	1	0	0	0	0	1
TOTALS	38	4	4	3	2	12

National League	AB	R	H	RBI	BB	K
Maury Wills, ss, LA	5	0	1	0	0	0
Eddie Mathews, 3b, Mil	2	0	0	0	0	0
Bob Purkey, p, Cin	0	0	0	0	0	0
Stan Musial, ph, StL	1	0	0	0	0	0
Mike McCormick, p, SF	0	0	0	0	0	0
George Altman, ph, ChN	1	1	1	1	0	0
Roy Face, p, Pit	0	0	0	0	0	0
Sandy Koufax, p, LA	0	0	0	0	0	0
Stu Miller, p, SF	0	0	0	0	0	0
Hank Aaron, ph, Mil	1	1	1	0	0	0
Willie Mays, cf, SF	5	2	2	1	0	1
Orlando Cepeda, lf, SF	3	0	0	0	0	0
Frank Robinson, lf, Cin	1	0	1	0	0	0
Roberto Clemente, rf, Pit	4	1	2	2	0	1
Bill White, 1b, StL	3	0	1	1	0	1
Frank Bolling, 2b, Mil	3	0	0	0	0	1
Don Zimmer, 2b, ChN	1	0	0	0	0	0
Smoky Burgess, c, Pit	4	0	1	0	0	0
Warren Spahn, p, Mil	0	0	0	0	0	0
Dick Stuart, ph, Pit	1	0	1	0	0	0
Ken Boyer, 3b, StL	2	0	0	0	1	2
TOTALS	37	5	11	5	1	6

	1 2 3	4 5 6	7 8 9	10	R	H	E
AL	0 0 0	0 0 1	0 0 2	1	4	4	2
NL	0 1 0	1 0 0	0 1 0	2	5	11	5

E—Cepeda, Gentile, Kubek, Boyer 2, Zimmer, Burgess. LOB—AL 6, NL 9. Scoring Position—AL 1-for-9, NL 3-for-11. 2B—Cash, Mays, Stuart. 3B—Clemente. HR—Killebrew, Altman. SF—Clemente, White. SB—FRobinson.

American League	IP	H	R	ER	BB	K
Whitey Ford, NYA	3.0	2	1	1	0	2
Frank Lary, Det	0.0	0	1	0	0	0
Dick Donovan, Was	2.0	4	0	0	0	1
Jim Bunning, Det	2.0	0	0	0	0	2
Mike Fornieles, Bos	0.1	2	1	1	0	0
Hoyt Wilhelm, Bal (L)	1.2	3	2	2	1	1

National League	IP	H	R	ER	BB	K
Warren Spahn, Mil	3.0	0	0	0	0	3
Bob Purkey, Cin	2.0	0	0	0	0	1
Mike McCormick, SF	3.0	1	1	1	1	3
Roy Face, Pit	0.1	2	2	2	0	1
Sandy Koufax, LA	0.0	1	0	0	0	0
Stu Miller, SF (BS; W)	1.2	0	1	0	1	4

Lary pitched to one batter in the 4th. Koufax pitched to one batter in the 9th. Wilhelm pitched to five batters in the 10th.

Balk—Miller. PB—Howard. HBP—FRobinson by Wilhelm. Time—2:53. Attendance—44,115. Umpires—HP, Landes. 1B, Umont. 2B, Crawford. 3B, Runge.

July 31, 1961
Boston (Fenway Park)

A downpour at Fenway Park resulted in the only tie game in All-Star history. Rocky Colavito's first-inning homer off Bob Purkey gave the Americans a 1-0 lead. The lead held until the top of the sixth, when AL shortstop Luis Aparicio failed to charge Eddie Kasko's slow-hit grounder, enabling the NL to load the bases with two outs. On the very next play, Bill White tied the game with a sharp grounder up the middle, but Aparicio made a fantastic stop to hold Orlando Cepeda at third base. The game was called after nine innings.

National League	AB	R	H	RBI	BB	K
Maury Wills, ss, LA	2	0	1	0	0	0
Hank Aaron, rf, Mil	2	0	0	0	0	0
Stu Miller, p, SF	0	0	0	0	0	0
Eddie Mathews, 3b, Mil	3	1	0	0	1	1
Willie Mays, cf, SF	3	0	1	0	1	0
Orlando Cepeda, lf, SF	3	0	0	0	0	0
Roberto Clemente, rf, Pit	2	0	0	0	0	0
Eddie Kasko, ss, Cin	1	0	1	0	0	0
Ernie Banks, ph-ss, ChN	1	0	0	0	0	1
Bill White, 1b, StL	4	0	2	1	0	0
Frank Bolling, 2b, Mil	4	0	0	0	0	0
Smoky Burgess, c, Pit	1	0	0	0	0	1
John Roseboro, c, LA	3	0	0	0	0	3
Bob Purkey, p, Cin	0	0	0	0	0	0
Dick Stuart, ph, Pit	1	0	0	0	0	0
Art Mahaffey, p, Phi	0	0	0	0	0	0
Stan Musial, ph, StL	1	0	0	0	0	0
Sandy Koufax, p, LA	0	0	0	0	0	0
George Altman, ph-rf, ChN	1	0	0	0	0	0
TOTALS	32	1	5	1	2	7

American League	AB	R	H	RBI	BB	K
Norm Cash, 1b, Det	4	0	0	0	0	1
Rocky Colavito, lf, Det	4	1	1	1	0	0
Al Kaline, rf, Det	4	0	2	0	0	0
Mickey Mantle, cf, NYA	3	0	0	0	1	2
John Romano, c, Cle	1	0	0	0	0	0
Roger Maris, ph, NYA	1	0	0	0	0	0
Elston Howard, c, NYA	2	0	0	0	0	0
Luis Aparicio, ss, ChA	2	0	0	0	1	1
Roy Sievers, ph, ChA	1	0	0	0	0	0
Johnny Temple, 2b, Cle	2	0	0	0	1	1
Brooks Robinson, 3b, Bal	3	0	1	0	0	1
Jim Bunning, p, Det	1	0	0	0	0	0
Don Schwall, p, Bos	1	0	0	0	0	0
Camilo Pascual, p, Min	1	0	0	0	0	0
TOTALS	30	1	4	1	3	8

	1	2	3	4	5	6	7	8	9		R	H	E
NL	0	0	0	0	0	1	0	0	0		1	5	1
AL	1	0	0	0	0	0	0	0	0		1	4	0

E—Bolling. DP—NL 2 (Bolling to Kasko to White; White to Kasko to Bolling). LOB—NL 7, AL 5. Scoring Position—NL 2-for-9, AL 0-for-5. 2B—White. HR—Colavito. GDP—Temple, Schwall. SB—Kaline.

National League	IP	H	R	ER	BB	K
Bob Purkey, Cin	2.0	1	1	1	2	2
Art Mahaffey, Phi	2.0	0	0	0	1	0
Sandy Koufax, LA	2.0	2	0	0	0	1
Stu Miller, SF	3.0	1	0	0	0	5

American League	IP	H	R	ER	BB	K
Jim Bunning, Det	3.0	0	0	0	0	1
Don Schwall, Bos	3.0	5	1	1	1	2
Camilo Pascual, Min	3.0	0	0	0	1	4

PB—Burgess. HBP—Cepeda by Schwall. Time—2:27. Attendance—31,851. Umpires—HP, Napp. 1B, Secory. 2B, Flaherty. 3B, Sudol.

July 10, 1962
Washington (RFK Stadium)

The American League was unable to contain Maury Wills as the National League notched a 3-1 victory. After Stan Musial led off the top of the sixth with a single, Wills went in to pinch-run and promptly swiped second base without a throw. Dick Groat followed with a single to score Wills with the first run of the game. Wills' only at-bat of the game produced a leadoff single in the top of the eighth. He was able to advance to third on Jim Davenport's single when he deked right fielder Rocky Colavito into throwing to second instead of third. Wills proceeded to score on a short foul fly to right field. Roberto Clemente had three hits in three trips for the Senior Circuit.

National League	AB	R	H	RBI	BB	K
Dick Groat, ss, Pit	3	1	1	1	0	0
Jim Davenport, 3b, SF	1	0	1	0	0	0
Roberto Clemente, rf, Pit	3	0	3	0	0	0
Felipe Alou, rf, SF	0	0	0	1	0	0
Willie Mays, cf, SF	3	0	0	0	1	0
Orlando Cepeda, 1b, SF	3	0	0	1	0	1
Bob Purkey, p, Cin	0	0	0	0	0	0
Johnny Callison, ph, Phi	1	0	1	0	0	0
Bob Shaw, p, Mil	0	0	0	0	0	0
Tommy Davis, lf, LA	4	0	0	0	0	0
Ken Boyer, 3b, StL	2	0	0	0	0	1
Ernie Banks, 1b, ChN	2	0	0	0	0	0
Del Crandall, c, Mil	4	0	0	0	0	0
Bill Mazeroski, 2b, Pit	2	0	0	0	0	0
Frank Bolling, 2b, Mil	2	0	0	0	0	0
Don Drysdale, p, LA	1	0	0	0	0	1
Juan Marichal, p, SF	0	0	0	0	0	0
Stan Musial, ph, StL	1	0	1	0	0	0
Maury Wills, pr-ss, LA	1	2	1	0	0	0
TOTALS	33	3	8	3	1	3

American League	AB	R	H	RBI	BB	K
Rich Rollins, 3b, Min	2	1	1	0	0	0
Brooks Robinson, 3b, Bal	0	0	0	0	0	1
Billy Moran, 2b, LAA	3	0	1	0	0	1
Bobby Richardson, 2b, NYA	1	0	0	0	0	0
Roger Maris, cf, NYA	2	0	1	1	0	1
Jim Landis, cf, ChA	1	0	0	0	0	1
Mickey Mantle, rf, NYA	1	0	0	0	1	1
Rocky Colavito, pr-lf, Det	1	0	0	1	0	0
Jim Gentile, 1b, Bal	3	0	0	0	1	1
Leon Wagner, lf-rf, LAA	4	0	0	0	0	0
Earl Battey, c, Min	2	0	0	0	0	0
John Romano, c, Cle	2	0	1	0	0	0
Luis Aparicio, ss, ChA	4	0	1	0	0	0
Jim Bunning, p, Det	0	0	0	0	0	0
Lee Thomas, ph, LAA	1	0	0	0	0	0
Camilo Pascual, p, Min	1	0	0	0	0	0
Dick Donovan, p, Cle	0	0	0	0	0	0
Norm Siebern, ph, KCA	1	0	0	0	0	0
Milt Pappas, p, Bal	0	0	0	0	0	0
TOTALS	29	1	4	1	3	5

	1	2	3	4	5	6	7	8	9		R	H	E
NL	0	0	0	0	0	2	0	1	0		3	8	0
AL	0	0	0	0	0	1	0	0	0		1	4	0

DP—NL 1 (Cepeda to Groat to Drysdale), AL 1 (Battey to Rollins). LOB—NL 5, AL 7. Scoring Position—NL 1-for-9, AL 0-for-5. 2B—Clemente. 3B—Aparicio. SF—Maris, Alou. GDP—Battey. SB—Mays, Wills. CS—Clemente.

National League	IP	H	R	ER	BB	K
Don Drysdale, LA	3.0	1	0	0	1	3
Juan Marichal, SF (W)	2.0	0	0	0	1	0
Bob Purkey, Cin	2.0	2	1	1	0	1
Bob Shaw, Mil (S)	2.0	1	0	0	1	1

American League	IP	H	R	ER	BB	K
Jim Bunning, Det	3.0	1	0	0	0	2
Camilo Pascual, Min (L)	3.0	4	2	2	1	1
Dick Donovan, Cle	2.0	3	1	1	0	0
Milt Pappas, Bal	1.0	0	0	0	0	0

HBP—Rollins by Drysdale, BRobinson by Shaw. Time—2:23. Attendance—45,480. Umpires—HP, Hurley. 1B, Donatelli. 2B, Stewart. 3B, Venzon.

July 30, 1962
Chicago (Wrigley Field)

The American League overpowered the National League, winning 9-4 on homers from Leon Wagner, Pete Runnels and Rocky Colavito. Wagner's homer was one of his three hits, and Colavito drove in four of the Junior Circuit's runs with a three-run homer and a sacrifice fly. Willie Mays and Dick Groat had two hits apiece for the Nationals. Johnny Podres tossed two scoreless innings, and doubled and scored in his only at-bat.

American League	AB	R	H	RBI	BB	K
Rich Rollins, 3b, Min	3	0	1	0	0	0
Brooks Robinson, 3b, Bal	1	1	0	0	1	0
Billy Moran, 2b, LAA	4	0	1	0	0	0
Yogi Berra, ph, NYA	1	0	0	0	0	0
Bobby Richardson, pr-2b, NYA	0	1	0	0	0	0
Roger Maris, cf, NYA	4	2	1	1	1	0
Rocky Colavito, rf, Det	4	1	1	4	0	1
Jim Gentile, 1b, Bal	4	0	1	0	1	1
Earl Battey, c, Min	2	1	0	0	1	0
Al Kaline, pr, Det	0	1	0	0	0	0
Elston Howard, c, NYA	2	0	0	0	0	2
Leon Wagner, lf, LAA	4	1	3	2	0	0
Lee Thomas, lf, LAA	0	0	0	0	0	0
Luis Aparicio, ss, ChA	2	0	0	0	0	1
Tom Tresh, ss, NYA	2	0	1	1	0	0
Dave Stenhouse, p, Was	0	0	0	0	0	0
Pete Runnels, ph, Bos	1	1	1	1	0	0
Ray Herbert, p, ChA	1	0	0	0	0	1
Hank Aguirre, p, Det	2	0	0	0	0	2
Milt Pappas, p, Bal	0	0	0	0	0	0
TOTALS	37	9	10	9	4	8

National League	AB	R	H	RBI	BB	K
Dick Groat, ss, Pit	3	0	2	2	0	0
Maury Wills, ss, LA	1	0	0	0	0	0
Roberto Clemente, rf, Pit	2	0	0	0	0	1
Frank Robinson, rf, Cin	3	0	0	0	0	0
Willie Mays, cf, SF	2	0	2	0	0	0
Hank Aaron, cf, Mil	2	0	0	0	0	0
Orlando Cepeda, 1b, SF	1	0	0	0	1	0
Ernie Banks, 1b, ChN	2	1	1	0	0	0
Tommy Davis, lf, LA	1	0	0	0	0	0
Stan Musial, ph-lf, StL	2	0	0	0	0	0
Billy Williams, lf, ChN	1	0	1	0	0	0
Ken Boyer, 3b, StL	3	0	1	0	0	0
Eddie Mathews, 3b, Mil	1	0	0	0	0	1
Del Crandall, c, Mil	1	0	0	0	0	0
John Roseboro, c, LA	3	1	1	1	0	1
Bill Mazeroski, 2b, Pit	1	0	0	0	0	0
George Altman, ph, ChN	1	0	0	0	0	0
Bob Gibson, p, StL	0	0	0	0	0	0
Turk Farrell, p, Hou	0	0	0	0	0	0
Richie Ashburn, ph, NYN	1	1	1	0	0	0
Juan Marichal, p, SF	0	0	0	0	0	0
Johnny Callison, ph, Phi	0	0	0	0	1	0
Johnny Podres, p, LA	1	1	1	0	0	0
Art Mahaffey, p, Phi	0	0	0	0	0	0
Frank Bolling, 2b, Mil	3	0	1	0	0	0
TOTALS	35	4	10	4	2	3

	1	2	3	4	5	6	7	8	9		R	H	E
AL	0	0	1	2	0	1	3	0	2		9	10	0
NL	0	1	0	0	0	0	1	1	1		4	10	4

E—Davis, Groat, Mathews 2. DP—AL 2 (Aparicio to Moran to Gentile; Moran to Aparicio to Gentile). LOB—AL 6, NL 7. Scoring Position—AL 2-for-3, NL 1-for-6. 2B—Maris, Podres, Bolling, Tresh.—Banks. HR—Colavito, Wagner, Runnels, Roseboro. SF—Colavito. GDP—Cepeda, Roseboro.

American League	IP	H	R	ER	BB	K
Dave Stenhouse, Was	2.0	3	1	1	1	1
Ray Herbert, ChA (W)	3.0	3	0	0	0	0
Hank Aguirre, Det	3.0	3	2	2	0	2
Milt Pappas, Bal	1.0	1	1	1	1	0

National League	IP	H	R	ER	BB	K
Johnny Podres, LA	2.0	2	0	0	0	2
Art Mahaffey, Phi (L)	2.0	2	3	3	1	1
Bob Gibson, StL	2.0	1	1	1	2	1
Turk Farrell, Hou	1.0	3	3	3	1	2
Juan Marichal, SF	2.0	2	2	1	0	2

WP—Stenhouse, Marichal 2. HBP—Groat by Stenhouse. Time—2:28. Attendance—38,359. Umpires—HP, Conlan. 1B, McKinley. 2B, Burkhart. 3B, Rice.

July 9, 1963
Cleveland (Cleveland Stadium)

With the All-Star Game returning to a once-per-year format, Willie Mays' all-around play led the National League to a 5-3 victory. Mays scored the first run of the contest in the second inning when he walked, stole second, and came home on Dick Groat's single. In the following frame, he laced an RBI single, stole second, and scored on Ed Bailey's RBI single to put the NL ahead, 3-1. He also notched an RBI groundout in the fifth, and made the best defensive play of the day, hauling in Joe Pepitone's long eighth-inning drive at the center-field fence. The NL staff held the AL to just six hits.

National League	AB	R	H	RBI	BB	K
Tommy Davis, lf, LA	3	1	1	0	1	0
Duke Snider, ph-lf, NYN	1	0	0	0	0	1
Hank Aaron, rf, Mil	4	1	0	0	0	0
Bill White, 1b, StL	4	1	1	0	0	0
Willie Mays, cf, SF	3	2	1	2	1	1
Roberto Clemente, cf, Pit	0	0	0	0	0	0
Ed Bailey, c, SF	1	0	1	1	1	0
Stan Musial, ph, StL	1	0	0	0	0	0
Ray Culp, p, Phi	0	0	0	0	0	0
Ron Santo, 3b, ChN	1	0	1	1	0	0
Ken Boyer, 3b, StL	3	0	0	0	0	0
Hal Woodeshick, p, Hou	0	0	0	0	0	0
Willie McCovey, ph, SF	1	0	0	0	0	1
Don Drysdale, p, LA	0	0	0	0	0	0
Dick Groat, ss, StL	4	0	1	1	0	1
Julian Javier, 2b, StL	4	0	0	0	0	2
Jim O'Toole, p, Cin	1	0	0	0	0	0
Larry Jackson, p, ChN	1	0	0	0	0	0
Johnny Edwards, c, Cin	2	0	0	0	0	0
TOTALS	34	5	6	5	3	6

American League	AB	R	H	RBI	BB	K
Nellie Fox, 2b, ChA	3	0	1	0	0	1
Bobby Richardson, 2b, NYA	2	0	0	0	0	0
Albie Pearson, cf, LAA	4	1	2	0	0	1
Tom Tresh, cf, NYA	0	0	0	0	0	0
Al Kaline, rf, Det	3	0	0	0	0	1
Bob Allison, rf, Min	1	0	0	0	1	0
Frank Malzone, 3b, Bos	3	1	1	1	0	0
Jim Bouton, p, NYA	0	0	0	0	0	0
Juan Pizarro, p, ChA	0	0	0	0	0	0
Harmon Killebrew, ph, Min	1	0	0	0	0	1
Dick Radatz, p, Bos	0	0	0	0	0	0
Leon Wagner, lf, LAA	3	1	2	0	0	0
Elston Howard, c, NYA	1	0	0	0	0	1
Earl Battey, c, Min	2	0	1	1	0	0
Carl Yastrzemski, ph-lf, Bos	2	0	0	0	0	1
Joe Pepitone, 1b, NYA	4	0	0	0	0	2
Zoilo Versalles, ss, Min	1	0	1	0	1	0
Luis Aparicio, ss, Bal	1	0	0	0	0	0
Ken McBride, p, LAA	1	0	1	1	0	0
Jim Bunning, p, Det	0	0	0	0	0	0
Brooks Robinson, 3b, Bal	2	0	2	0	0	0
TOTALS	34	3	11	3	1	9

	1	2	3	4	5	6	7	8	9		R	H	E
NL	0	1	2	0	1	0	0	1	0		5	6	0
AL	0	1	2	0	0	0	0	0	0		3	11	1

E—Richardson. DP—NL 2 (Davis to Bailey; Groat to Javier to White). LOB—NL 5, AL 7. Scoring Position—NL 4-for-9, AL 3-for-10. 2B—Pearson. S—Bunning. GDP—Richardson 2. SB—White, Mays 2.

National League	IP	H	R	ER	BB	K
Jim O'Toole, Cin	2.0	4	1	1	0	1
Larry Jackson, ChN (W)	2.0	4	2	2	0	3
Ray Culp, Phi	1.0	1	0	0	0	0
Hal Woodeshick, Hou	2.0	1	0	0	1	3
Don Drysdale, LA (S)	2.0	1	0	0	0	2

American League	IP	H	R	ER	BB	K
Ken McBride, LAA	3.0	4	3	3	2	1
Jim Bunning, Det (L)	2.0	0	1	0	1	0
Jim Bouton, NYA	1.0	0	0	0	0	0
Juan Pizarro, ChA	1.0	0	0	0	0	0
Dick Radatz, Bos	2.0	2	1	1	0	5

HBP—Versalles by O'Toole. Time—2:20. Attendance—44,160. Umpires—HP, Soar. 1B, Jackowski. 2B, Smith. 3B, Pryor.

July 7, 1964
New York (Shea Stadium)

After the American League took a one-run lead into the bottom of the ninth, Johnny Callison's two-out, three-run homer gave the National League a 7-4 victory. Willie Mays led off the inning with a walk and subsequently stole second. Orlando Cepeda followed with a single to right, and Mays scored the tying run when Joe Pepitone uncorked a poor throw to the plate. After two outs and a walk, Callison struck the winning blow. Billy Williams and Ken Boyer each added solo shots for the Nationals, while Brooks Robinson had a triple, a single and two RBI for the Americans.

American League	AB	R	H	RBI	BB	K
Jim Fregosi, ss, LAA	4	1	1	1	0	1
Tony Oliva, rf, Min	4	0	0	0	0	1
Dick Radatz, p, Bos	1	0	0	0	0	1
Mickey Mantle, cf, NYA	4	1	1	0	0	2
Jimmie Hall, cf, Min	0	0	0	0	0	0
Harmon Killebrew, lf, Min	4	1	3	1	0	0
Chuck Hinton, lf, Was	0	0	0	0	0	0
Bob Allison, 1b, Min	3	0	0	0	1	2
Joe Pepitone, pr-1b, NYA	0	0	0	0	0	0
Brooks Robinson, 3b, Bal	4	0	2	2	0	0
Bobby Richardson, 2b, NYA	4	0	1	0	0	1
Elston Howard, c, NYA	3	1	0	0	0	2
Dean Chance, p, LAA	1	0	0	0	0	0
John Wyatt, p, KCA	0	0	0	0	0	0
Norm Siebern, ph, Bal	1	0	0	0	0	0
Camilo Pascual, p, Min	0	0	0	0	0	0
Rocky Colavito, ph-rf, KCA	2	0	1	0	0	0
TOTALS	35	4	9	4	1	10

National League	AB	R	H	RBI	BB	K
Roberto Clemente, rf, Pit	3	1	1	0	0	1
Chris Short, p, Phi	0	0	0	0	0	0
Turk Farrell, p, Hou	0	0	0	0	0	0
Bill White, 1b, StL	1	0	0	0	0	1
Juan Marichal, p, SF	0	0	0	0	0	0
Dick Groat, ss, StL	3	0	1	1	0	1
Leo Cardenas, pr-ss, Cin	1	0	0	0	0	0
Billy Williams, lf, ChN	4	1	1	1	0	0
Willie Mays, cf, SF	3	1	0	0	1	0
Orlando Cepeda, 1b, SF	4	0	1	1	0	0
Curt Flood, pr, StL	0	1	0	0	0	0
Ken Boyer, 3b, StL	4	1	2	1	0	1
Joe Torre, c, Mil	2	0	0	0	0	0
Johnny Edwards, c, Cin	1	1	0	0	1	1
Ron Hunt, 2b, NYN	3	0	1	0	0	1
Hank Aaron, ph, Mil	1	0	0	0	0	1
Don Drysdale, p, LA	0	0	0	0	0	0
Willie Stargell, ph, Pit	1	0	0	0	0	0
Jim Bunning, p, Phi	0	0	0	0	0	0
Johnny Callison, ph-rf, Phi	3	1	1	3	0	0
TOTALS	34	7	8	7	2	8

	1	2	3	4	5	6	7	8	9		R	H	E
AL	1	0	0	0	0	2	1	0	0		4	9	0
NL	0	0	0	2	1	0	0	0	4		7	8	0

LOB—AL 7, NL 3. Scoring Position—AL 2-for-11, NL 2-for-7. 2B—Groat, Colavito. 3B—Robinson. HR—Williams, Boyer, Callison. SF—Fregosi. SB—Mays.

American League	IP	H	R	ER	BB	K
Dean Chance, LAA	3.0	2	0	0	0	2
John Wyatt, KCA	1.0	2	2	2	0	0
Camilo Pascual, Min	2.0	2	1	1	0	1
Dick Radatz, Bos (BS; L)	2.2	2	4	4	2	5

National League	IP	H	R	ER	BB	K
Don Drysdale, LA	3.0	2	1	0	0	3
Jim Bunning, Phi	2.0	2	0	0	0	4
Chris Short, Phi (BS)	1.0	3	2	2	0	1
Turk Farrell, Hou	2.0	2	1	1	1	0
Juan Marichal, SF (W)	1.0	0	0	0	0	1

WP—Drysdale. PB—Torre. HBP—Howard by Farrell. Time—2:37. Attendance—50,850. Umpires—HP, Sudol. 1B, Paparella. 2B, Secory. 3B, Chylak.

July 13, 1965
Minnesota (Metropolitan Stadium)

Teammates Willie Mays and Juan Marichal led the National League to a 6-5 victory. Mays homered, walked twice and scored the deciding run, while Marichal threw three shutout innings, allowing only one hit and facing the minimum nine batters. Two-run homers by Joe Torre and Willie Stargell gave the NL a 5-0 lead after two, but the AL pulled even in the bottom of the fifth with two-run shots from Dick McAuliffe and Harmon Killebrew. The Nationals went ahead for good in the top of the seventh when Mays scored on Ron Santo's dribbler up the middle.

National League	AB	R	H	RBI	BB	K
Willie Mays, cf, SF	3	2	1	1	2	1
Hank Aaron, rf, Mil	5	0	1	0	0	1
Willie Stargell, lf, Pit	3	2	2	2	0	1
Roberto Clemente, ph-lf, Pit	2	0	0	0	0	0
Dick Allen, 3b, Phi	3	0	1	0	0	1
Ron Santo, 3b, ChN	2	0	1	1	0	0
Joe Torre, c, Mil	4	1	1	2	0	0
Ernie Banks, 1b, ChN	4	0	2	0	0	1
Pete Rose, 2b, Cin	2	0	0	0	1	2
Maury Wills, ss, LA	4	0	1	0	0	0
Leo Cardenas, ss, Cin	0	0	0	0	0	0
Juan Marichal, p, SF	1	1	1	0	0	0
Cookie Rojas, ph, Phi	1	0	0	0	0	0
Jim Maloney, p, Cin	0	0	0	0	0	0
Don Drysdale, p, LA	0	0	0	0	0	0
Frank Robinson, ph, Cin	1	0	0	0	0	1
Sandy Koufax, p, LA	0	0	0	0	0	0
Turk Farrell, p, Hou	0	0	0	0	0	0
Billy Williams, ph, ChN	1	0	0	0	0	0
Bob Gibson, p, StL	0	0	0	0	0	0
TOTALS	36	6	11	6	3	7

American League	AB	R	H	RBI	BB	K
Dick McAuliffe, ss, Det	3	2	2	2	0	0
Sam McDowell, p, Cle	0	0	0	0	0	0
Tony Oliva, ph-rf, Min	2	0	1	0	0	0
Brooks Robinson, 3b, Bal	4	1	1	0	0	1
Max Alvis, 3b, Cle	1	0	0	0	0	0
Harmon Killebrew, 1b, Min	3	1	1	2	2	1
Rocky Colavito, rf, Cle	4	0	1	1	0	0
Eddie Fisher, p, ChA	0	0	0	0	0	0
Joe Pepitone, ph, NYA	1	0	0	0	0	1
Willie Horton, lf, Det	3	0	0	1	1	1
Felix Mantilla, 2b, Bos	2	0	0	0	0	0
Bobby Richardson, 2b, NYA	2	0	0	0	0	0
Vic Davalillo, cf, Cle	2	0	1	0	0	0
Zoilo Versalles, ss, Min	1	0	0	0	1	0
Earl Battey, c, Min	2	0	0	0	0	0
Bill Freehan, c, Det	1	0	1	0	1	0
Milt Pappas, p, Bal	0	0	0	0	0	0
Mudcat Grant, p, Min	2	0	0	0	0	0
Al Kaline, ph, Det	1	0	0	0	0	0
Pete Richert, p, Was	0	0	0	0	0	0
Jimmie Hall, ph-cf, Min	2	1	0	0	1	1
TOTALS	34	5	8	5	6	5

	1	2	3	4	5	6	7	8	9		R	H	E
NL	3	2	0	0	0	0	1	0	0		6	11	0
AL	0	0	0	1	4	0	0	0	0		5	8	0

DP—NL 1 (Wills to Rose to Banks), AL 2 (BRobinson to Mantilla to Killebrew; McDowell to Richardson to Killebrew). LOB—NL 7, AL 8. Scoring Position—NL 2-for-9, AL 1-for-8. 2B—Oliva. HR—Mays, Stargell, Torre, McAuliffe, Killebrew. S—Rose. GDP—Aaron, Torre, Battey.

National League	IP	H	R	ER	BB	K
Juan Marichal, SF	3.0	1	0	0	0	0
Jim Maloney, Cin	1.2	5	5	5	2	1
Don Drysdale, LA	0.1	0	0	0	0	0
Sandy Koufax, LA (W)	1.0	0	0	0	2	1
Turk Farrell, Hou	1.0	0	0	0	1	0
Bob Gibson, StL (S)	2.0	2	0	0	1	3

American League	IP	H	R	ER	BB	K
Milt Pappas, Bal	1.0	4	3	3	1	0
Mudcat Grant, Min	2.0	2	2	2	1	3
Pete Richert, Was	2.0	1	0	0	0	2
Sam McDowell, Cle (L)	2.0	3	1	1	1	2
Eddie Fisher, ChA	2.0	1	0	0	0	0

WP—Maloney. Time—2:45. Attendance—46,706. Umpires—HP, Stevens. 1B, Weyer. 2B, DiMuro. 3B, Williams.

July 12, 1966
St. Louis (Busch Stadium)

In the oppressive St. Louis heat, the National League prevailed 2-1 in 10 innings. Hometown hero Tim McCarver opened the 10th inning with a single, moved to second on Ron Hunt's sacrifice bunt, and came home to score the winning run on Maury Wills' RBI single. Brooks Robinson starred for the Americans, collecting two singles and a triple in four trips to the plate. The Orioles' third sacker also set an All-Star Game record by handling eight chances flawlessly. Denny McLain threw three perfect innings for the AL, striking out three.

American League	AB	R	H	RBI	BB	K
Dick McAuliffe, ss, Det	3	0	0	0	0	1
Mel Stottlemyre, p, NYA	0	0	0	0	0	0
Rocky Colavito, ph, Cle	1	0	0	0	0	0
Sonny Siebert, p, Cle	0	0	0	0	0	0
Pete Richert, p, Was	0	0	0	0	0	0
Al Kaline, cf, Det	4	0	1	0	0	0
Tommie Agee, cf, ChA	0	0	0	0	0	0
Frank Robinson, lf, Bal	4	0	0	0	0	1
Tony Oliva, rf, Min	4	0	0	0	0	0
Brooks Robinson, 3b, Bal	4	1	3	0	0	0
George Scott, 1b, Bos	2	0	0	0	0	0
Norm Cash, ph-1b, Det	2	0	0	0	0	0
Bill Freehan, c, Det	2	0	1	0	0	0
Earl Battey, c, Min	1	0	0	0	1	1
Bobby Knoop, 2b, Cal	2	0	0	0	0	1
Bobby Richardson, ph-2b, NYA	2	0	0	0	0	0
Denny McLain, p, Det	1	0	0	0	0	1
Jim Kaat, p, Min	0	0	0	0	0	0
Harmon Killebrew, ph, Min	1	0	1	0	0	0
Jim Fregosi, pr-ss, Cal	2	0	0	0	0	1
TOTALS	35	1	6	0	1	6

National League	AB	R	H	RBI	BB	K
Willie Mays, cf, SF	4	1	1	0	0	1
Roberto Clemente, rf, Pit	4	0	2	0	0	0
Hank Aaron, lf, Atl	4	0	0	0	0	1
Willie McCovey, 1b, SF	3	0	0	0	1	0
Ron Santo, 3b, ChN	4	0	1	1	0	0
Joe Torre, c, Atl	3	0	0	0	0	1
Tim McCarver, c, StL	1	1	1	0	0	0
Jim Lefebvre, 2b, LA	2	0	0	0	0	0
Ron Hunt, 2b, NYN	1	0	0	0	0	0
Leo Cardenas, ss, Cin	2	0	0	0	0	0
Willie Stargell, ph, Pit	1	0	0	0	0	0
Maury Wills, ss, LA	1	0	1	1	0	0
Sandy Koufax, p, LA	0	0	0	0	0	0
Curt Flood, ph, StL	1	0	0	0	0	0
Jim Bunning, p, Phi	0	0	0	0	0	0
Dick Allen, ph, Phi	1	0	0	0	0	1
Juan Marichal, p, SF	0	0	0	0	0	0
Jim Ray Hart, ph, SF	1	0	0	0	0	1
Gaylord Perry, p, SF	0	0	0	0	0	0
TOTALS	33	2	6	2	1	5

	1	2	3	4	5	6	7	8	9	10	R	H	E
AL	0	1	0	0	0	0	0	0	0	0	1	6	0
NL	0	0	0	1	0	0	0	0	0	1	2	6	0

DP—NL 1 (McCovey to Cardenas). LOB—AL 5, NL 5. Scoring Position—AL 0-for-6, NL 2-for-7. 2B—Clemente. 3B—BRobinson. S—Hunt. GDP—Cash.

American League	IP	H	R	ER	BB	K
Denny McLain, Det	3.0	0	0	0	0	3
Jim Kaat, Min	2.0	3	1	1	0	1
Mel Stottlemyre, NYA	2.0	1	0	0	1	0
Sonny Siebert, Cle	2.0	0	0	0	0	1
Pete Richert, Was (L)	0.1	2	1	1	0	0

National League	IP	H	R	ER	BB	K
Sandy Koufax, LA	3.0	1	1	1	0	1
Jim Bunning, Phi	2.0	1	0	0	0	2
Juan Marichal, SF	3.0	3	0	0	0	2
Gaylord Perry, SF (W)	2.0	1	0	0	1	1

WP—Koufax, Perry. Time—2:19. Attendance—49,936. Umpires—HP, Barlick. 1B, Umont. 2B, Vargo. 3B, Honochick.

July 11, 1967
Anaheim (Anaheim Stadium)

Tony Perez' home run in the 15th inning gave the National League a 2-1 win in the longest game in All-Star history. Dick Allen gave the NL a 1-0 edge with a solo homer in the second inning, and the AL tied it in the sixth on Brooks Robinson' circuit shot. Ferguson Jenkins tied an All-Star Game record with six strikeouts in three innings. Boston Carl Yastrzemski had three hits and reached base five times. National League hurlers fanned 17 batters while American League pitchers registered 13 whiffs to set an all-time combined strikeout record.

National League	AB	R	H	RBI	BB	K
Lou Brock, lf, StL	2	0	0	0	0	0
Willie Mays, ph-cf, SF	4	0	0	0	0	1
Roberto Clemente, rf, Pit	6	0	1	0	0	4
Hank Aaron, cf-lf, Atl	6	0	1	0	0	0
Orlando Cepeda, 1b, StL	6	0	0	0	0	1
Dick Allen, 3b, Phi	4	1	1	1	0	3
Tony Perez, 3b, Cin	2	1	1	1	0	1
Joe Torre, c, Atl	2	0	0	0	0	0
Tom Haller, c, SF	1	0	0	0	0	0
Ernie Banks, ph, ChN	1	0	1	0	0	0
Tim McCarver, c, StL	2	0	2	0	0	0
Bill Mazeroski, 2b, Pit	4	0	0	0	0	0
Don Drysdale, p, LA	0	0	0	0	0	0
Tommy Helms, ph, Cin	1	0	0	0	0	0
Tom Seaver, p, NYN	0	0	0	0	0	0
Gene Alley, ss, Pit	5	0	0	0	0	3
Juan Marichal, p, SF	1	0	0	0	0	0
Fergie Jenkins, p, ChN	1	0	0	0	0	0
Bob Gibson, p, StL	0	0	0	0	0	0
Jimmy Wynn, ph, Hou	1	0	1	0	0	0
Chris Short, p, Phi	0	0	0	0	0	0
Rusty Staub, ph, Hou	1	0	1	0	0	0
Mike Cuellar, p, Hou	0	0	0	0	0	0
Pete Rose, ph-2b, Cin	1	0	0	0	0	0
TOTALS	51	2	9	2	0	13

American League	AB	R	H	RBI	BB	K
Brooks Robinson, 3b, Bal	6	1	1	1	0	1
Rod Carew, 2b, Min	3	0	0	0	0	1
Dick McAuliffe, 2b, Det	3	0	0	0	0	0
Tony Oliva, cf, Min	6	0	2	0	0	3
Harmon Killebrew, 1b, Min	6	0	0	0	0	2
Tony Conigliaro, rf, Bos	6	0	0	0	0	2
Carl Yastrzemski, lf, Bos	4	0	3	0	2	1
Bill Freehan, c, Det	5	0	0	0	0	2
Rico Petrocelli, ss, Bos	1	0	0	0	0	0
Jim McGlothlin, p, Cal	0	0	0	0	0	0
Mickey Mantle, ph, NYA	1	0	0	0	0	1
Gary Peters, p, ChA	0	0	0	0	0	0
Don Mincher, ph, Cal	1	0	1	0	0	0
Tommie Agee, pr, ChA	0	0	0	0	0	0
Al Downing, p, NYA	0	0	0	0	0	0
Max Alvis, ph, Cle	1	0	0	0	0	0
Catfish Hunter, p, KCA	1	0	0	0	0	1
Ken Berry, ph, ChA	1	0	0	0	0	1
Dean Chance, p, Min	0	0	0	0	0	0
Jim Fregosi, ph-ss, Cal	4	0	1	0	0	2
TOTALS	49	1	8	1	2	17

	1	2	3	4	5	6	7	8	9	10	11	12	13	14	15	R	H	E
NL	0	1	0	0	0	0	0	0	0	0	0	0	0	0	1	2	9	0
AL	0	0	0	0	0	1	0	0	0	0	0	0	0	0	0	1	8	0

DP—NL 2 (Torre to Mazeroski; McCarver to Rose), AL 2 (BRobinson to Carew to Killebrew; McAuliffe to Killebrew). LOB—NL 5, AL 7. Scoring Position—NL 0-for-6, AL 0-for-5. 2B—Yastrzemski, McCarver. HR—Allen, BRobinson, Perez. S—Mazeroski, Freehan, Fregosi. GDP—Cepeda. SB—Aaron. CS—Oliva 2.

National League	IP	H	R	ER	BB	K
Juan Marichal, SF	3.0	1	0	0	0	3
Fergie Jenkins, ChN	3.0	3	1	1	0	6
Bob Gibson, StL	2.0	2	0	0	0	2
Chris Short, Phi	2.0	0	0	0	1	1
Mike Cuellar, Hou	2.0	1	0	0	0	2
Don Drysdale, LA (W)	2.0	1	0	0	0	2
Tom Seaver, NYN (S)	1.0	0	0	0	1	1

American League	IP	H	R	ER	BB	K
Dean Chance, Min	3.0	2	1	1	0	1
Jim McGlothlin, Cal	2.0	1	0	0	0	2
Gary Peters, ChA	3.0	0	0	0	0	4
Al Downing, NYA	2.0	2	0	0	0	2
Catfish Hunter, KCA (L)	5.0	4	1	1	0	4

Time—3:41. Attendance—46,309. Umpires—HP, Runge. 1B, Secory. 2B, DiMuro. 3B, Burkhart.

July 9, 1968
Houston (Astrodome)

In the Year of the Pitcher, not a single run scored in the final eight innings of the All-Star Game, as the National League prevailed,1-0. Willie Mays scored the only run of the game in the bottom of the first on a double-play groundout by teammate Willie McCovey. Twins slugger Harmon Killebrew tore his hamstring when he stretched to take a throw at first base in the third inning. National League hurlers struck out 11 without walking a batter and retired 20 consecutive hitters at one point. Tom Seaver fanned five in only two innings of work.

American League	AB	R	H	RBI	BB	K
Jim Fregosi, ss, Cal	3	0	1	0	0	1
Bert Campaneris, ss, Oak	1	0	0	0	0	0
Rod Carew, 2b, Min	3	0	0	0	0	0
Dave Johnson, 2b, Bal	1	0	0	0	0	1
Carl Yastrzemski, cf-lf, Bos	4	0	0	0	0	2
Frank Howard, rf, Was	2	0	0	0	0	1
Tony Oliva, rf, Min	1	0	1	0	0	0
Willie Horton, lf, Det	2	0	0	0	0	0
Joe Azcue, c, Cle	1	0	0	0	0	1
Duane Josephson, c, ChA	0	0	0	0	0	0
Harmon Killebrew, 1b, Min	1	0	0	0	0	0
Boog Powell, 1b, Bal	2	0	0	0	0	2
Bill Freehan, c, Det	2	0	0	0	0	1
Denny McLain, p, Det	0	0	0	0	0	0
Sam McDowell, p, Cle	0	0	0	0	0	0
Mickey Mantle, ph, NYA	1	0	0	0	0	1
Mel Stottlemyre, p, NYA	0	0	0	0	0	0
Tommy John, p, ChA	0	0	0	0	0	0
Brooks Robinson, 3b, Bal	2	0	0	0	0	0
Don Wert, 3b, Det	1	0	1	0	0	0
Luis Tiant, p, Cle	0	0	0	0	0	0
Ken Harrelson, ph, Bos	1	0	0	0	0	0
Blue Moon Odom, p, Oak	0	0	0	0	0	0
Rick Monday, cf, Oak	2	0	0	0	0	1
TOTALS	30	0	3	0	0	11

National League	AB	R	H	RBI	BB	K
Willie Mays, cf, SF	4	1	1	0	0	1
Curt Flood, lf, StL	1	0	0	0	2	0
Matty Alou, lf, Pit	1	0	1	0	0	0
Julian Javier, 2b, StL	0	0	0	0	0	0
Willie McCovey, 1b, SF	4	0	0	0	0	3
Hank Aaron, rf, Atl	3	0	1	0	1	2
Ron Santo, 3b, ChN	2	0	1	0	2	0
Tony Perez, 3b, Cin	0	0	0	0	0	0
Tommy Helms, 2b, Cin	3	0	1	0	1	0
Ron Reed, p, Atl	0	0	0	0	0	0
Jerry Koosman, p, NYN	0	0	0	0	0	0
Jerry Grote, c, NYN	2	0	0	0	0	1
Steve Carlton, p, StL	0	0	0	0	0	0
Rusty Staub, ph, Hou	1	0	0	0	0	0
Tom Seaver, p, NYN	0	0	0	0	0	0
Felipe Alou, lf, Atl	0	0	0	0	0	0
Don Kessinger, ss, ChN	2	0	0	0	0	1
Billy Williams, ph, ChN	1	0	0	0	0	0
Leo Cardenas, ss, Cin	0	0	0	0	0	0
Don Drysdale, p, LA	1	0	0	0	0	0
Juan Marichal, p, SF	0	0	0	0	0	0
Tom Haller, ph-c, LA	2	0	0	0	0	1
Johnny Bench, c, Cin	0	0	0	0	0	0
TOTALS	27	1	5	0	6	9

	1	2	3	4	5	6	7	8	9	R	H	E
AL	0	0	0	0	0	0	0	0	0	0	3	1
NL	1	0	0	0	0	0	0	0	x	1	5	0

E—Killebrew. DP—AL 2 (Carew to Fregosi to Killebrew; Johnson to Powell). LOB—AL 3, NL 8. Scoring Position—AL 0-for-5, NL 0-for-9. 2B—Fregosi, Helms, Oliva, Wert. GDP—McCovey, Helms. SB—Aaron.

American League	IP	H	R	ER	BB	K
Luis Tiant, Cle (L)	2.0	2	1	0	2	2
Blue Moon Odom, Oak	2.0	0	0	0	2	2
Denny McLain, Det	2.0	1	0	0	2	1
Sam McDowell, Cle	1.0	1	0	0	0	3
Mel Stottlemyre, NYA	0.1	0	0	0	0	1
Tommy John, ChA	0.2	1	0	0	0	0

National League	IP	H	R	ER	BB	K
Don Drysdale, LA (W)	3.0	1	0	0	0	0
Juan Marichal, SF	2.0	0	0	0	0	3
Steve Carlton, StL	1.0	0	0	0	0	1
Tom Seaver, NYN	2.0	2	0	0	0	5
Ron Reed, Atl	0.2	0	0	0	0	1
Jerry Koosman, NYN (S)	0.1	0	0	0	0	1

WP—Tiant. Time—2:10. Attendance—48,321. Umpires—HP, Crawford. 1B, Napp. 2B, Steiner. 3B, Kinnamon.

July 23, 1969
Washington (RFK Stadium)

Willie McCovey blasted two home runs and drove in three runs as the National League breezed to a 9-3 victory. Johnny Bench had a single, a homer and two RBI, and he could have had more. In the sixth, he lined a pitch deep to left, but Carl Yastrzemski leapt high above the wall to take away a sure home run. Among the AL's six hits were two longballs, one apiece by Frank Howard and Bill Freehan. Blue Moon Odom was racked for five hits and five runs in only one-third of an inning. Mel Stottlemyre had to fill in as the AL starting pitcher after Denny McLain arrived late due to a dental appointment.

National League	AB	R	H	RBI	BB	K
Matty Alou, cf, Pit	4	1	2	0	1	1
Don Kessinger, ss, ChN	3	0	0	0	0	0
Willie Mays, ph, SF	1	0	0	0	0	0
Denis Menke, ss, Hou	1	0	0	0	0	1
Hank Aaron, rf, Atl	4	1	1	0	0	1
Bill Singer, p, LA	0	0	0	0	0	0
Glenn Beckert, 2b, ChN	1	0	0	0	0	0
Willie McCovey, 1b, SF	4	2	2	3	0	1
Lee May, 1b, Cin	1	0	0	0	0	1
Ron Santo, 3b, ChN	3	0	0	0	1	0
Tony Perez, 3b, Cin	1	0	0	0	0	1
Cleon Jones, lf, NYN	4	2	2	0	0	0
Pete Rose, lf, Cin	1	0	0	0	0	0
Johnny Bench, c, Cin	3	2	2	2	1	0
Randy Hundley, c, ChN	1	0	0	0	0	1
Felix Millan, 2b, Atl	4	1	1	2	0	1
Jerry Koosman, p, NYN	0	0	0	0	0	0
Larry Dierker, p, Hou	0	0	0	0	0	0
Phil Niekro, p, Atl	0	0	0	0	0	0
Steve Carlton, p, StL	2	0	1	1	0	1
Bob Gibson, p, StL	0	0	0	0	0	0
Ernie Banks, ph, ChN	1	0	0	0	0	0
Roberto Clemente, rf, Pit	1	0	0	0	0	1
TOTALS	40	9	11	8	3	10

American League	AB	R	H	RBI	BB	K
Rod Carew, 2b, Min	3	0	0	0	0	0
Mike Andrews, 2b, Bos	1	0	0	0	0	0
Reggie Jackson, cf-rf, Oak	2	0	0	0	1	0
Carl Yastrzemski, lf, Bos	1	0	0	0	0	0
Frank Robinson, rf, Bal	2	0	0	0	0	1
Paul Blair, cf, Bal	2	0	0	0	0	0
Boog Powell, 1b, Bal	4	0	1	0	0	1
Frank Howard, lf, Was	1	1	1	1	1	0
Reggie Smith, pr-lf-rf, Bos	2	1	0	0	0	0
Sal Bando, 3b, Oak	3	0	1	0	0	0
Sam McDowell, p, Cle	0	0	0	0	0	0
Ray Culp, p, Bos	0	0	0	0	0	0
Roy White, ph, NYA	1	0	0	0	0	1
Rico Petrocelli, ss, Bos	3	0	1	0	0	1
Jim Fregosi, ss, Cal	1	0	0	0	0	0
Bill Freehan, c, Det	2	1	2	2	0	0
John Roseboro, c, Min	1	0	0	0	0	0
Carlos May, ph, ChA	1	0	0	0	0	1
Mel Stottlemyre, p, NYA	0	0	0	0	0	0
Blue Moon Odom, p, Oak	0	0	0	0	0	0
Darold Knowles, p, Was	0	0	0	0	0	0
Harmon Killebrew, ph, Min	1	0	0	0	0	0
Denny McLain, p, Det	0	0	0	0	0	0
Don Mincher, ph, Sea	1	0	0	0	0	1
Dave McNally, p, Bal	0	0	0	0	0	0
Brooks Robinson, 3b, Bal	1	0	0	0	0	1
TOTALS	33	3	6	3	2	7

	1 2 3	4 5 6	7 8 9	R	H	E
NL	1 2 5	1 0 0	0 0 0	9	11	0
AL	0 1 1	1 0 0	0 0 0	3	6	2

E—Petrocelli, Howard. LOB—NL 7, AL 5. Scoring Position—NL 2-for-8, AL 1-for-6. 2B—Millan, Carlton, Petrocelli. HR—McCovey 2, Bench, Howard, Freehan.

National League	IP	H	R	ER	BB	K
Steve Carlton, StL (W)	3.0	2	2	2	1	2
Bob Gibson, StL	1.0	2	1	1	1	2
Bill Singer, LA	2.0	0	0	0	0	2
Jerry Koosman, NYN	1.2	1	0	0	0	1
Larry Dierker, Hou	0.1	1	0	0	0	0
Phil Niekro, Atl	1.0	0	0	0	0	2

American League	IP	H	R	ER	BB	K
Mel Stottlemyre, NYA (L)	2.0	4	3	2	0	1
Blue Moon Odom, Oak	0.1	5	5	4	0	0
Darold Knowles, Was	0.2	0	0	0	0	0
Denny McLain, Det	1.0	1	1	1	2	2
Dave McNally, Bal	2.0	1	0	0	1	1
Sam McDowell, Cle	2.0	0	0	0	0	4
Ray Culp, Bos	1.0	0	0	0	0	2

WP—Stottlemyre. Time—2:38. Attendance—45,259. Umpires—HP, Flaherty. 1B, Donatelli. 2B, Stewart. 3B, Gorman.

July 14, 1970
Cincinnati (Riverfront Stadium)

Pete Rose bowled over catcher Ray Fosse to score the winning run for the National League in the bottom of the 12th inning. The collision helped to crystallize the public image of Rose, and it also quite possibly helped to destroy Fosse's career. The Americans took a 4-1 lead into the ninth when the NL mounted a three-run rally. No one scored until the bottom of the 12th, when Rose lined a two-out single and moved to second on Billy Grabarkewitz' base hit. Jim Hickman lined a single to center, and Rose came around from second to score the game-winner. The win was the NL's eighth straight.

American League	AB	R	H	RBI	BB	K
Luis Aparicio, ss, ChA	6	0	0	0	0	2
Carl Yastrzemski, cf-1b, Bos	6	1	4	1	0	0
Frank Robinson, rf-lf, Bal	3	0	0	0	0	2
Willie Horton, lf, Det	2	1	2	0	1	0
Boog Powell, 1b, Bal	3	0	0	0	0	0
Amos Otis, cf, KC	3	0	0	0	0	0
Harmon Killebrew, 3b, Min	2	0	1	0	0	1
Tommy Harper, pr, Mil	0	0	0	0	0	0
Brooks Robinson, 3b, Bal	3	1	2	2	0	0
Frank Howard, lf, Was	2	0	0	0	0	1
Tony Oliva, rf, Min	2	0	1	0	1	0
Dave Johnson, 2b, Bal	5	0	1	0	0	1
Clyde Wright, p, Cal	0	0	0	0	0	0
Bill Freehan, c, Det	1	0	0	0	0	0
Ray Fosse, c, Cle	2	1	1	1	1	0
Jim Palmer, p, Bal	1	0	0	0	0	0
Sam McDowell, p, Cle	0	0	0	0	0	0
Alex Johnson, ph, Cal	1	0	0	0	0	0
Jim Perry, p, Min	0	0	0	0	0	0
Jim Fregosi, ph, Cal	1	0	0	0	0	0
Catfish Hunter, p, Oak	0	0	0	0	0	0
Fritz Peterson, p, NYA	0	0	0	0	0	0
Mel Stottlemyre, p, NYA	0	0	0	0	0	0
Sandy Alomar, 2b, Cal	1	0	0	0	0	0
TOTALS	44	4	12	4	3	7

National League	AB	R	H	RBI	BB	K
Willie Mays, cf, SF	3	0	0	0	0	1
Gaylord Perry, p, SF	0	0	0	0	0	0
Willie McCovey, ph-1b, SF	2	0	1	1	0	0
Claude Osteen, pr-p, LA	0	0	0	0	0	0
Joe Torre, ph, StL	1	0	0	0	0	0
Dick Allen, 1b, StL	3	0	0	0	1	1
Bob Gibson, p, StL	0	0	0	0	0	0
Roberto Clemente, ph-rf, Pit	1	0	0	1	0	0
Hank Aaron, rf, Atl	2	0	0	0	0	0
Pete Rose, rf-lf, Cin	3	1	1	0	1	2
Tony Perez, 3b, Cin	3	0	0	0	0	2
Billy Grabarkewitz, 3b, LA	3	0	1	0	0	0
Rico Carty, lf, Atl	1	0	0	0	1	0
Jim Hickman, lf-1b, ChN	4	0	1	1	0	2
Johnny Bench, c, Cin	3	0	0	0	0	3
Dick Dietz, c, SF	2	1	1	1	0	0
Don Kessinger, ss, ChN	2	0	2	0	0	0
Bud Harrelson, ss, NYN	3	2	2	0	0	0
Glenn Beckert, 2b, ChN	2	0	0	0	0	0
Cito Gaston, cf, SD	2	0	0	0	1	0
Tom Seaver, p, NYN	0	0	0	0	0	0
Rusty Staub, ph, Mon	1	0	0	0	0	0
Jim Merritt, p, Cin	0	0	0	0	0	0
Denis Menke, ph-2b, Hou	0	0	0	0	1	0
Joe Morgan, 2b, Hou	2	1	1	0	0	0
TOTALS	43	5	10	4	5	11

	1 2 3	4 5 6	7 8 9	10 11 12	R	H	E
AL	0 0 0	0 0 1	1 2 0	0 0 0	4	12	0
NL	0 0 0	0 0 0	1 0 3	0 0 1	5	10	0

DP—AL 1 (Aparicio to Yastrzemski), NL 1 (Harrelson to Morgan to Hickman). LOB—AL 9, NL 10. Scoring Position—AL 3-for-10, NL 2-for-9. 2B—Yastrzemski, Oliva. 3B—Robinson. HR—Dietz. S—McDowell. SF—Fosse, Clemente. GDP—Otis, McCovey. CS—Harper.

American League	IP	H	R	ER	BB	K
Jim Palmer, Bal	3.0	1	0	0	1	3
Sam McDowell, Cle	3.0	1	0	0	3	3
Jim Perry, Min	2.0	1	1	1	1	3
Catfish Hunter, Oak	0.1	3	3	3	0	0
Fritz Peterson, NYA	0.0	1	0	0	0	0
Mel Stottlemyre, NYA (BS)	1.2	0	0	0	0	2
Clyde Wright, Cal (L)	1.2	3	1	1	0	0

National League	IP	H	R	ER	BB	K
Tom Seaver, NYN	3.0	1	0	0	0	4
Jim Merritt, Cin	2.0	1	0	0	0	1
Gaylord Perry, SF	2.0	4	2	2	1	0
Bob Gibson, StL	2.0	3	2	2	1	2
Claude Osteen, LA (W)	3.0	3	0	0	1	0

Peterson pitched to one batter in the 9th.

HBP—Menke by JPerry. Time—3:19. Attendance—51,838. Umpires—HP, Barlick. 1B, Rice. 2B, Secory. 3B, Haller.

July 13, 1971
Detroit (Tiger Stadium)

The American League broke its eight-game losing streak, topping the National League 6-4. Vida Blue fell behind 3-0 after surrendering homers to Johnny Bench and Hank Aaron, but Reggie Jackson brought the AL back to within a run with a gigantic blast off the light tower transformer of Tiger Stadium. It was one of the longest shots in the history of All-Star competition. Later in the same inning, Frank Robinson put the AL ahead for good with a two-run shot into the right-field seats. Robinson's teammates, pitchers Jim Palmer and Mike Cuellar, combined to toss four innings of scoreless relief.

National League	AB	R	H	RBI	BB	K
Willie Mays, cf, SF	2	0	0	0	0	0
Roberto Clemente, rf, Pit	2	1	1	1	0	1
Felix Millan, 2b, Atl	0	0	0	0	0	0
Hank Aaron, rf, Atl	2	1	1	1	0	0
Lee May, 1b, Cin	1	0	0	0	1	0
Joe Torre, 3b, StL	3	0	0	0	0	1
Ron Santo, ph-3b, ChN	1	0	0	0	0	0
Willie Stargell, lf, Pit	2	1	0	0	0	2
Lou Brock, ph, StL	1	0	0	0	0	0
Willie McCovey, 1b, SF	2	0	0	0	0	1
Juan Marichal, p, SF	0	0	0	0	0	0
Don Kessinger, ss, ChN	2	0	0	0	0	0
Johnny Bench, c, Cin	4	1	2	2	0	0
Glenn Beckert, 2b, ChN	3	0	0	0	0	0
Pete Rose, rf, Cin	0	0	0	0	0	0
Bud Harrelson, ss, NYN	2	0	0	0	0	0
Fergie Jenkins, p, ChN	0	0	0	0	0	0
Nate Colbert, ph, SD	1	0	0	0	0	1
Don Wilson, p, Hou	0	0	0	0	0	0
Dock Ellis, p, Pit	1	0	0	0	0	1
Willie Davis, cf, LA	1	0	1	0	0	0
Bobby Bonds, ph-cf, SF	1	0	0	0	0	1
TOTALS	31	4	5	4	1	8

American League	AB	R	H	RBI	BB	K
Rod Carew, 2b, Min	1	1	0	0	2	0
Cookie Rojas, 2b, KC	1	0	0	0	0	0
Bobby Murcer, cf, NYA	3	0	1	0	0	1
Mike Cuellar, p, Bal	0	0	0	0	0	0
Don Buford, ph, Bal	1	0	0	0	0	1
Mickey Lolich, p, Det	0	0	0	0	0	0
Carl Yastrzemski, lf, Bos	3	0	0	0	1	0
Frank Robinson, rf, Bal	2	1	1	2	0	0
Al Kaline, rf, Det	2	1	1	0	0	1
Norm Cash, 1b, Det	2	0	0	0	0	2
Harmon Killebrew, 1b, Min	2	1	1	2	0	0
Brooks Robinson, 3b, Bal	3	0	1	0	0	0
Bill Freehan, c, Det	3	0	0	0	0	0
Thurman Munson, c, NYA	0	0	0	0	0	0
Luis Aparicio, ss, Bos	3	1	1	0	0	0
Vida Blue, p, Oak	0	0	0	0	0	0
Reggie Jackson, ph, Oak	1	1	1	2	0	0
Jim Palmer, p, Bal	0	0	0	0	0	0
Frank Howard, ph, Was	1	0	0	0	0	0
Amos Otis, cf, KC	1	0	0	0	0	0
TOTALS	29	6	7	6	3	5

	1 2 3	4 5 6	7 8 9	R	H	E
NL	0 2 1	0 0 0	0 1 0	4	5	0
AL	0 0 4	0 0 2	0 0 x	6	7	0

DP—NL 2 (Beckert to Kessinger to May; Santo to Millan to May), AL 1 (BRobinson to Rojas to Killebrew). LOB—NL 2, AL 2. Scoring Position—NL 0-for-0, AL 0-for-1. HR—Aaron, Bench, FRobinson, Jackson, Clemente, Killebrew. GDP—Torre, Aparicio, Killebrew.

National League	IP	H	R	ER	BB	K
Dock Ellis, Pit (L)	3.0	4	4	4	1	2
Juan Marichal, SF	2.0	0	0	0	1	1
Fergie Jenkins, ChN	1.0	3	2	2	0	0
Don Wilson, Hou	2.0	0	0	0	1	2

American League	IP	H	R	ER	BB	K
Vida Blue, Oak (W)	3.0	2	3	3	0	3
Jim Palmer, Bal	2.0	1	0	0	0	2
Mike Cuellar, Bal	2.0	1	0	0	1	2
Mickey Lolich, Det (S)	2.0	1	1	1	0	1

HBP—Stargell by Blue. Time—2:05. Attendance—53,559. Umpires—HP, Umont. 1B, Pryor. 2B, O'Donnell. 3B, Harvey.

July 25, 1972

Atlanta (Atlanta-Fulton County Stadium)

The National League narrowly averted a loss, scoring the tying run in the bottom of the ninth and the winning run in the bottom of the 10th. The AL scored first on an RBI single by Rod Carew in the third. The lead held until the sixth, when Hank Aaron blasted a two-out, two-run homer for a 2-1 NL lead. The AL took back the lead with a pinch-hit two-run homer off the bat of Cookie Rojas in the top of the eighth. In the bottom of the ninth, Lee May plated the tying run with an RBI groundout. In the following inning, Joe Morgan capped the NL's comeback with an RBI single. Tug McGraw got the win for the Nationals while Dave McNally took the loss for the Americans.

American League	AB	R	H	RBI	BB	K
Rod Carew, 2b, Min	2	0	1	1	1	0
Cookie Rojas, ph-2b, KC	1	1	1	2	0	0
Bobby Murcer, cf, NYA	3	0	0	0	0	0
Richie Scheinblum, rf, KC	1	0	0	0	0	0
Reggie Jackson, rf-cf, Oak	4	0	2	0	0	1
Dick Allen, 1b, ChA	3	0	0	0	0	0
Norm Cash, 1b, Det	1	0	0	0	0	1
Carl Yastrzemski, lf, Bos	3	0	0	0	0	1
Joe Rudi, lf, Oak	1	0	1	0	0	0
Bobby Grich, ss, Bal	4	0	0	0	0	2
Brooks Robinson, 3b, Bal	2	0	0	0	0	0
Sal Bando, 3b, Oak	2	0	0	0	0	0
Bill Freehan, c, Det	1	1	0	0	1	0
Carlton Fisk, c, Bos	2	1	1	0	0	1
Jim Palmer, p, Bal	0	0	0	0	0	0
Mickey Lolich, p, Det	1	0	0	0	0	1
Gaylord Perry, p, Cle	0	0	0	0	0	0
Reggie Smith, ph, Bos	1	0	0	0	0	1
Wilbur Wood, p, ChA	0	0	0	0	0	0
Lou Piniella, ph, KC	1	0	0	0	0	0
Dave McNally, p, Bal	0	0	0	0	0	0
TOTALS	33	3	6	3	2	8

National League	AB	R	H	RBI	BB	K
Joe Morgan, 2b, Cin	4	0	1	1	1	0
Willie Mays, cf, NYN	2	0	0	0	0	1
Cesar Cedeno, cf, Hou	2	1	1	0	0	1
Hank Aaron, rf, Atl	3	1	1	2	0	1
Al Oliver, rf, Pit	1	0	0	0	0	0
Willie Stargell, lf, Pit	1	0	0	0	1	0
Billy Williams, lf, ChN	2	1	1	0	0	0
Johnny Bench, c, Cin	2	0	1	0	0	0
Manny Sanguillen, c, Pit	2	0	1	0	0	0
Lee May, 1b, Hou	4	0	1	1	0	0
Joe Torre, 3b, StL	3	0	1	0	0	1
Ron Santo, 3b, ChN	1	0	0	0	0	0
Don Kessinger, ss, ChN	2	0	0	0	0	0
Steve Carlton, p, Phi	0	0	0	0	0	0
Bill Stoneman, p, Mon	1	0	0	0	0	1
Tug McGraw, p, NYN	0	0	0	0	0	0
Nate Colbert, ph, SD	0	1	0	0	1	0
Bob Gibson, p, StL	0	0	0	0	0	0
Steve Blass, p, Pit	0	0	0	0	0	0
Glenn Beckert, ph, ChN	1	0	0	0	0	0
Don Sutton, p, LA	0	0	0	0	0	0
Chris Speier, ss, SF	2	0	0	0	0	0
TOTALS	33	4	8	4	3	5

	1	2	3	4	5	6	7	8	9	10	R	H	E
AL	0	0	1	0	0	0	0	2	0	0	3	6	0
NL	0	0	0	0	0	2	0	0	1	1	4	8	0

DP—AL 2 (Carew to Allen; Bando to Rojas to Cash), NL 2 (LMay; LMay to Speier). LOB—AL 3, NL 5. Scoring Position—AL 1-for-3, NL 1-for-4. 2B—Jackson, Rudi. HR—Aaron, Rojas. S—Palmer, Speier. GDP—Murcer, Bench, Santo. SB—Morgan.

American League	IP	H	R	ER	BB	K
Jim Palmer, Bal	3.0	1	0	0	1	2
Mickey Lolich, Det	2.0	1	0	0	0	1
Gaylord Perry, Cle (BS)	2.0	3	2	2	0	1
Wilbur Wood, ChA (BS)	2.0	2	1	1	1	1
Dave McNally, Bal (L)	0.1	1	1	1	1	0

National League	IP	H	R	ER	BB	K
Bob Gibson, StL	2.0	1	0	0	0	0
Steve Blass, Pit	1.0	1	1	1	1	0
Don Sutton, LA	2.0	1	0	0	0	2
Steve Carlton, Phi	1.0	0	0	0	1	0
Bill Stoneman, Mon (BS)	2.0	2	2	2	0	2
Tug McGraw, NYN (W)	2.0	1	0	0	0	4

Time—2:26. Attendance—53,107. Umpires—HP, Landes. 1B, DiMuro. 2B, Weyer. 3B, Neudecker.

July 24, 1973

Kansas City (Royals Stadium)

The National League overpowered the American League, winning 7-1 on the strength of home runs from Willie Davis, Johnny Bench and Bobby Bonds. Six different NL hurlers combined to hold the Junior Circuit scoreless over the final seven frames. The Oakland A's boasted the AL's starting pitcher (Catfish Hunter), leadoff hitter (Bert Campaneris) and cleanup hitter (Reggie Jackson).

National League	AB	R	H	RBI	BB	K
Pete Rose, lf, Cin	3	1	0	0	1	0
Wayne Twitchell, p, Phi	0	0	0	0	0	0
Dave Giusti, p, Pit	0	0	0	0	0	0
Manny Mota, ph-lf, LA	1	0	0	0	0	0
Jim Brewer, p, LA	0	0	0	0	0	0
Joe Morgan, 2b, Cin	3	2	1	0	1	0
Dave Johnson, 2b, Atl	1	0	0	0	0	0
Cesar Cedeno, cf, Hou	3	0	1	1	0	2
Bill Russell, ss, LA	2	0	0	0	0	0
Hank Aaron, 1b, Atl	2	0	1	1	0	0
Joe Torre, 1b-3b, StL	3	0	0	0	0	0
Billy Williams, rf, ChN	2	0	1	0	0	0
Bobby Bonds, rf, SF	2	1	2	2	0	0
Johnny Bench, c, Cin	3	1	1	1	0	0
Ted Simmons, ph-c, StL	1	0	0	0	0	1
Ron Santo, 3b, ChN	1	1	1	0	2	0
Nate Colbert, ph, SD	1	0	0	0	0	0
Ron Fairly, 1b, Mon	0	0	0	0	0	0
Chris Speier, ss, SF	2	0	0	0	0	1
Willie Stargell, ph-lf, Pit	1	0	0	0	0	1
Willie Mays, ph, NYN	1	0	0	0	0	1
Tom Seaver, p, NYN	0	0	0	0	0	0
Bob Watson, lf, Hou	0	0	0	0	0	0
Rick Wise, p, StL	0	0	0	0	0	0
Darrell Evans, ph, Atl	0	0	0	0	1	0
Claude Osteen, p, LA	0	0	0	0	0	0
Don Sutton, p, LA	0	0	0	0	0	0
Willie Davis, ph-cf, LA	2	1	2	2	0	0
TOTALS	34	7	10	7	5	6

American League	AB	R	H	RBI	BB	K
Bert Campaneris, ss, Oak	3	0	0	0	0	2
Ed Brinkman, ss, Det	1	0	0	0	0	0
Rod Carew, 2b, Min	3	0	0	0	0	0
Cookie Rojas, 2b, KC	0	0	0	0	1	0
John Mayberry, 1b, KC	3	0	1	0	1	0
Reggie Jackson, rf, Oak	4	1	1	0	0	1
Paul Blair, cf, Bal	0	0	0	0	0	0
Amos Otis, cf, KC	2	0	2	1	0	0
Dave May, cf-rf, Mil	2	0	0	0	0	0
Bobby Murcer, lf, NYA	3	0	0	0	1	0
Carlton Fisk, c, Bos	2	0	0	0	0	0
Thurman Munson, c, NYA	2	0	0	0	0	1
Brooks Robinson, 3b, Bal	2	0	0	0	0	0
Sal Bando, 3b, Oak	1	0	0	0	0	0
Dave Nelson, 3b, Tex	0	0	0	0	0	0
Willie Horton, ph, Det	1	0	0	0	0	1
Catfish Hunter, p, Oak	0	0	0	0	0	0
Ken Holtzman, p, Oak	0	0	0	0	0	0
Bert Blyleven, p, Min	0	0	0	0	0	0
Buddy Bell, ph, Cle	1	0	1	0	0	0
Bill Singer, p, Cal	0	0	0	0	0	0
Pat Kelly, ph, ChA	1	0	0	0	0	0
Nolan Ryan, p, Cal	0	0	0	0	0	0
Jim Spencer, ph, Tex	1	0	0	0	0	0
Sparky Lyle, p, NYA	0	0	0	0	0	0
Rollie Fingers, p, Oak	0	0	0	0	0	0
TOTALS	32	1	5	1	3	5

	1	2	3	4	5	6	7	8	9	R	H	E
NL	0	0	2	1	2	2	0	0	0	7	10	0
AL	0	1	0	0	0	0	0	0	0	1	5	0

DP—AL 1 (Rojas to Brinkman to Mayberry). LOB—NL 6, AL 7. Scoring Position—NL 3-for-8, AL 1-for-10. 2B—Morgan, Mayberry, Jackson, Bonds. 3B—Bell. HR—Bench, Bonds, Davis. S—Osteen. GDP—Morgan. SB—Otis.

National League	IP	H	R	ER	BB	K
Rick Wise, StL (W)	2.0	2	1	1	0	1
Claude Osteen, LA	2.0	2	0	0	1	1
Don Sutton, LA	1.0	0	0	0	0	1
Wayne Twitchell, Phi	1.0	1	0	0	0	1
Dave Giusti, Pit	1.0	0	0	0	0	0
Tom Seaver, NYN	1.0	0	0	0	1	0
Jim Brewer, LA	1.0	0	0	0	1	2

American League	IP	H	R	ER	BB	K
Catfish Hunter, Oak	1.1	1	0	0	0	1
Ken Holtzman, Oak	0.2	1	0	0	0	0
Bert Blyleven, Min (L)	1.0	2	2	2	2	0
Bill Singer, Cal	2.0	3	3	3	1	2
Nolan Ryan, Cal	2.0	2	2	2	2	2
Sparky Lyle, NYA	1.0	1	0	0	0	1
Rollie Fingers, Oak	1.0	0	0	0	0	0

PB—Fisk. Time—2:45. Attendance—40,849. Umpires—HP, Chylak. 1B, Burkhart. 2B, Barnett. 3B, Williams.

July 23, 1974

Pittsburgh (Three Rivers Stadium)

Steve Garvey, the second write-in candidate in history to be picked to start in an All-Star Game, starred at bat and in the field as the National League breezed past the American League, 7-2. In the second inning, Garvey singled and scored the first run of the game on a double by teammate Ron Cey. The Americans took a 2-1 lead in the top of the third and threatened to extend their lead when Bobby Murcer strode to the plate with two out and runners on first and second. He hit a smash toward right field, but Garvey went to his right, made a great stop, and threw to Andy Messersmith covering to end the inning. In the fourth, Garvey doubled in the tying run before Cey's RBI groundout put the Senior Circuit ahead for good. Later, Don Kessinger added an RBI triple and Reggie Smith homered.

American League	AB	R	H	RBI	BB	K
Rod Carew, 2b, Min	1	1	0	0	1	0
Bobby Grich, 2b, Bal	3	0	1	0	0	0
Bert Campaneris, ss, Oak	4	0	0	0	0	2
Reggie Jackson, rf, Oak	3	0	0	0	1	2
Dick Allen, 1b, ChA	2	0	1	1	0	1
Carl Yastrzemski, 1b, Bos	1	0	0	0	1	0
Bobby Murcer, cf, NYA	2	0	0	0	0	0
George Hendrick, cf, Cle	2	0	1	0	0	0
Jeff Burroughs, lf, Tex	0	0	0	0	2	0
Joe Rudi, lf, Oak	2	0	0	0	0	1
Brooks Robinson, 3b, Bal	3	0	0	0	0	0
John Mayberry, ph, KC	1	0	0	0	0	0
Rollie Fingers, p, Oak	0	0	0	0	0	0
Thurman Munson, c, NYA	3	1	1	0	1	0
Gaylord Perry, p, Cle	0	0	0	0	0	0
Al Kaline, ph, Det	1	0	0	0	0	0
Luis Tiant, p, Bos	0	0	0	0	0	0
Frank Robinson, ph, Cal	1	0	0	0	0	0
Catfish Hunter, p, Oak	0	0	0	0	0	0
Dave Chalk, 3b, Cal	1	0	0	0	0	1
TOTALS	30	2	4	1	6	7

National League	AB	R	H	RBI	BB	K
Pete Rose, lf, Cin	2	0	0	0	0	1
Ken Brett, p, Pit	0	0	0	0	0	0
Lou Brock, ph, StL	1	1	1	0	0	0
Reggie Smith, rf, StL	2	1	1	1	0	0
Joe Morgan, 2b, Cin	2	0	1	1	0	1
Dave Cash, ph-2b, Phi	1	0	0	0	0	0
Hank Aaron, rf, Atl	2	0	0	0	0	0
Cesar Cedeno, cf, Hou	2	0	0	0	0	1
Johnny Bench, c, Cin	3	1	2	0	1	1
Jerry Grote, c, NYN	0	0	0	0	0	0
Jimmy Wynn, cf-rf, LA	3	1	1	0	0	0
Jon Matlack, p, NYN	0	0	0	0	0	0
John Grubb, lf, SD	1	0	0	0	0	0
Steve Garvey, 1b, LA	4	1	2	1	0	1
Ron Cey, 3b, LA	2	0	1	2	0	0
Mike Schmidt, ph-3b, Phi	0	1	0	0	2	0
Larry Bowa, ss, Phi	2	0	0	0	0	0
Tony Perez, ph, Cin	1	0	0	0	0	1
Don Kessinger, ss, ChN	1	1	1	1	0	0
Andy Messersmith, p, LA	0	0	0	0	0	0
Ralph Garr, ph-lf, Atl	3	0	0	0	0	1
Lynn McGlothen, p, StL	0	0	0	0	0	0
Mike Marshall, p, LA	1	0	0	0	0	0
TOTALS	33	7	10	6	3	7

	1	2	3	4	5	6	7	8	9	R	H	E
AL	0	0	2	0	0	0	0	0	0	2	4	1
NL	0	1	0	2	1	0	1	2	x	7	10	1

E—Bench, Munson. LOB—AL 8, NL 6. Scoring Position—AL 1-for-4, NL 1-for-6. 2B—Munson, Morgan, Garvey, Cey. 3B—Kessinger. HR—Smith. S—Perry. SF—Morgan. SB—Carew, Brock.

American League	IP	H	R	ER	BB	K
Gaylord Perry, Cle	3.0	3	1	1	0	4
Luis Tiant, Bos (L)	2.0	4	3	2	1	0
Catfish Hunter, Oak	2.0	2	1	1	1	3
Rollie Fingers, Oak	1.0	1	2	2	1	0

National League	IP	H	R	ER	BB	K
Andy Messersmith, LA	3.0	2	2	2	3	4
Ken Brett, Pit (W)	2.0	1	0	0	1	0
Jon Matlack, NYN	1.0	1	0	0	1	0
Lynn McGlothen, StL	1.0	0	0	0	0	1
Mike Marshall, LA (S)	2.0	0	0	0	1	2

WP—Fingers. Time—2:37. Attendance—50,706. Umpires—HP, Sudol. 1B, Frantz. 2B, Vargo. 3B, Anthony.

July 15, 1975
Milwaukee (County Stadium)

Bill Madlock bounced a two-run single through the drawn-in infield in the top of the ninth, propelling the National League to a 6-3 win over the American League. The Nationals broke on top first with solo homers from Steve Garvey and Jimmy Wynn in the second inning. In the third, Lou Brock singled, went to second on a balk, stole third, and scored on a single by Johnny Bench. Carl Yastrzemski tied it up with a three-run homer off Tom Seaver in the bottom of the sixth. It remained tied until Madlock's two-run single. Pete Rose followed with a sacrifice fly to account for the final run.

National League	AB	R	H	RBI	BB	K
Pete Rose, rf-lf, Cin	4	0	2	1	0	0
Gary Carter, lf, Mon	0	0	0	0	0	0
Lou Brock, lf, StL	3	1	1	0	0	0
Bobby Murcer, rf, SF	2	0	0	0	0	0
Randy Jones, p, SD	0	0	0	0	0	0
Joe Morgan, 2b, Cin	4	0	1	0	0	0
Dave Cash, 2b, Phi	1	0	0	0	0	0
Johnny Bench, c, Cin	4	0	1	1	0	0
Steve Garvey, 1b, LA	3	1	2	1	0	0
Tony Perez, ph-1b, Cin	1	0	0	0	0	1
Jimmy Wynn, cf, LA	2	1	1	1	0	0
Reggie Smith, cf-rf, StL	2	1	1	0	0	0
Ron Cey, 3b, LA	3	0	1	0	0	0
Tom Seaver, p, NYN	0	0	0	0	0	0
Jon Matlack, p, NYN	0	0	0	0	0	0
Al Oliver, ph-cf, Pit	1	1	1	0	0	0
Dave Concepcion, ss, Cin	2	0	1	0	0	1
Greg Luzinski, ph, Phi	1	0	0	0	0	1
Larry Bowa, ss, Phi	0	1	0	0	0	0
Jerry Reuss, p, Pit	1	0	0	0	0	0
Bob Watson, ph, Hou	1	0	0	0	0	0
Don Sutton, p, LA	0	0	0	0	0	0
Bill Madlock, 3b, ChN	2	0	1	2	0	0
TOTALS	37	6	13	6	0	3

American League	AB	R	H	RBI	BB	K
Bobby Bonds, cf, NYA	3	0	0	0	0	1
George Scott, 1b, Mil	2	0	0	0	0	2
Rod Carew, 2b, Min	5	0	1	0	0	1
Thurman Munson, c, NYA	2	0	1	0	0	0
Claudell Washington, pr-cf-lf, Oak	1	0	1	0	0	0
Reggie Jackson, rf, Oak	3	0	1	0	0	2
Bucky Dent, ss, ChA	1	0	0	0	0	1
Joe Rudi, lf, Oak	3	0	1	0	0	0
George Hendrick, pr-rf, Cle	1	1	1	0	0	0
Graig Nettles, 3b, NYA	4	0	1	0	0	1
Gene Tenace, 1b-c, Oak	3	1	0	0	1	1
Bert Campaneris, ss, Oak	2	0	2	0	0	0
Fred Lynn, ph-cf, Bos	2	0	0	0	0	1
Vida Blue, p, Oak	0	0	0	0	0	0
Hank Aaron, ph, Mil	1	0	0	0	0	0
Steve Busby, p, KC	0	0	0	0	0	0
Mike Hargrove, ph, Tex	1	0	0	0	0	0
Jim Kaat, p, ChA	0	0	0	0	0	0
Carl Yastrzemski, ph, Bos	1	1	1	3	0	0
Catfish Hunter, p, NYA	0	0	0	0	0	0
Goose Gossage, p, ChA	0	0	0	0	0	0
Hal McRae, ph, KC	1	0	0	0	0	0
TOTALS	36	3	10	3	1	10

	1 2 3	4 5 6	7 8 9	R	H	E
NL	0 2 1	0 0 0	0 0 3	6	13	1
AL	0 0 0	0 0 3	0 0 0	3	10	1

E—Concepcion, Tenace. LOB—NL 6, AL 8. Scoring Position—NL 2-for-7, AL 1-for-8. 2B—Oliver. HR—Garvey, Wynn, Yastrzemski. SF—Rose. SB—Brock, Nettles, Washington, Hendrick. CS—Concepcion, Washington.

National League	IP	H	R	ER	BB	K
Jerry Reuss, Pit	3.0	3	0	0	0	2
Don Sutton, LA	2.0	3	0	0	0	1
Tom Seaver, NYN (BS)	1.0	2	3	3	1	2
Jon Matlack, NYN (W)	2.0	2	0	0	0	4
Randy Jones, SD (S)	1.0	0	0	0	0	1

American League	IP	H	R	ER	BB	K
Vida Blue, Oak	2.0	5	2	2	0	1
Steve Busby, KC	2.0	4	1	1	0	0
Jim Kaat, ChA	2.0	0	0	0	0	0
Catfish Hunter, NYA (L)	2.0	3	2	2	0	2
Goose Gossage, ChA	1.0	1	1	1	0	0

Hunter pitched to two batters in the 9th.

Balk—Busby. PB—Bench. HBP—Bowa by Gossage, Munson by Reuss. Time—2:35. Attendance—51,480. Umpires—HP, Haller. 1B, Pelekoudas. 2B, Springstead. 3B, Froemming.

July 13, 1976
Philadelphia (Veterans Stadium)

The National League easily turned back its American League foes, 7-1, in a game that was one-sided right from the start. In the bottom of the first, Steve Garvey tripled in Pete Rose and subsequently scored on a groundout. The NL got two more in the third on a two-run homer from George Foster. The American League got its only run in the following inning on a circuit shot by Fred Lynn, but the NL tacked on three more in the bottom of the eighth, with two coming on a homer by Cesar Cedeno. Randy Jones tossed three scoreless innings and combined with four other pitchers to five-hit the AL squad. Rookie sensation Mark Fidrych took the loss.

American League	AB	R	H	RBI	BB	K
Ron LeFlore, lf, Det	2	0	1	0	0	1
Carl Yastrzemski, lf, Bos	2	0	0	0	0	0
Rod Carew, 1b, Min	3	0	0	0	1	0
George Brett, 3b, KC	2	0	0	0	1	0
Don Money, 3b, Mil	1	0	0	0	0	0
Thurman Munson, c, NYA	2	0	0	0	0	0
Carlton Fisk, c, Bos	1	0	0	0	0	0
Chris Chambliss, ph, NYA	1	0	0	0	0	0
Fred Lynn, cf, Bos	3	1	1	1	0	1
Amos Otis, ph, KC	1	0	0	0	0	1
Toby Harrah, ss, Tex	2	0	0	0	0	0
Mark Belanger, ss, Bal	1	0	0	0	0	0
Freddie Patek, ss, KC	0	0	0	0	0	0
Rusty Staub, rf, Det	2	0	2	0	0	0
Luis Tiant, p, Bos	0	0	0	0	0	0
Butch Wynegar, ph, Min	0	0	0	0	1	0
Frank Tanana, p, Cal	0	0	0	0	0	0
Bobby Grich, 2b, Bal	2	0	0	0	0	0
Phil Garner, 2b, Oak	1	0	0	0	0	1
Mark Fidrych, p, Det	0	0	0	0	0	0
Hal McRae, ph, KC	1	0	0	0	0	0
Catfish Hunter, p, NYA	0	0	0	0	0	0
Mickey Rivers, ph-rf, NYA	2	0	1	0	0	1
TOTALS	29	1	5	1	3	5

National League	AB	R	H	RBI	BB	K
Pete Rose, 3b, Cin	3	1	2	0	0	0
Al Oliver, rf-lf, Pit	1	0	0	0	0	0
Steve Garvey, 1b, LA	3	1	1	1	0	0
Dave Cash, 2b, Phi	1	1	1	0	0	0
Joe Morgan, 2b, Cin	3	1	1	0	0	0
Tony Perez, 1b, Cin	0	0	0	0	1	0
George Foster, cf-rf, Cin	3	1	1	3	0	0
John Montefusco, p, SF	0	0	0	0	0	0
Bill Russell, ss, LA	1	0	0	0	0	0
Greg Luzinski, lf, Phi	3	0	0	0	0	0
Ken Griffey Sr., rf, Cin	1	1	1	1	0	0
Johnny Bench, c, Cin	2	0	1	0	0	1
Cesar Cedeno, cf, Hou	2	1	1	2	0	1
Dave Kingman, rf, NYN	2	0	0	0	0	1
Bob Boone, c, Phi	2	0	0	0	0	0
Dave Concepcion, ss, Cin	2	0	1	0	0	0
Larry Bowa, ss, Phi	1	0	0	0	0	0
Rick Rhoden, p, LA	0	0	0	0	0	0
Ron Cey, 3b, LA	0	0	0	0	0	0
Randy Jones, p, SD	1	0	0	0	0	1
Tom Seaver, p, NYN	1	0	0	0	0	1
Mike Schmidt, 3b, Phi	1	0	0	0	0	0
Ken Forsch, p, Hou	0	0	0	0	0	0
TOTALS	33	7	10	7	1	5

	1 2 3	4 5 6	7 8 9	R	H	E
AL	0 0 0	1 0 0	0 0 0	1	5	0
NL	2 0 2	0 0 0	0 3 x	7	10	0

DP—AL 1 (Money to Garner to Carew), NL 3 (Morgan to Concepcion to Garvey; Morgan to Bowa to Garvey; Cash to Russell to Perez). LOB—AL 4, NL 3. Scoring Position—AL 0-for-1, NL 1-for-9. 3B—Rose, Garvey. HR—Lynn, Foster, Cedeno. GDP—Carew, Grich, Yastrzemski, Russell. SB—Carew.

American League	IP	H	R	ER	BB	K
Mark Fidrych, Det (L)	2.0	4	2	2	0	1
Catfish Hunter, NYA	2.0	2	2	2	0	3
Luis Tiant, Bos	2.0	1	0	0	0	1
Frank Tanana, Cal	2.0	3	3	3	1	0

National League	IP	H	R	ER	BB	K
Randy Jones, SD (W)	3.0	2	0	0	1	1
Tom Seaver, NYN	2.0	2	1	1	0	1
John Montefusco, SF	2.0	0	0	0	2	2
Rick Rhoden, LA	1.0	1	0	0	0	0
Ken Forsch, Hou	1.0	0	0	0	0	1

PB—Munson. Time—2:12. Attendance—63,974. Umpires—HP, Wendelstedt. 1B, Neudecker. 2B, Olsen. 3B, Denkinger.

July 19, 1977
New York (Yankee Stadium)

The National League nicked Jim Palmer for four runs in the top of the first and held on to win, 7-5. Joe Morgan led off the game with a homer off Palmer, and after George Foster doubled in a run, Greg Luzinski went deep for a 4-0 NL lead. Steve Garvey reached Palmer for a third-inning homer before the Baltimore righthander was pulled. Richie Zisk later cracked a two-run double, and George Scott added a two-run homer, but it was too little, too late for the American League. Dave Winfield had a single, a double and two RBI for the Nationals.

National League	AB	R	H	RBI	BB	K
Joe Morgan, 2b, Cin	4	1	1	1	0	1
Manny Trillo, 2b, ChN	1	0	0	0	0	1
Steve Garvey, 1b, LA	3	1	1	1	0	2
Willie Montanez, 1b, Atl	2	0	0	0	0	1
Dave Parker, rf, Pit	3	1	1	0	0	1
Garry Templeton, ss, StL	1	1	1	0	0	0
George Foster, cf, Cin	3	1	1	1	0	1
Jerry Morales, cf, ChN	0	1	0	0	0	0
Greg Luzinski, lf, Phi	2	1	1	2	0	0
Dave Winfield, lf, SD	2	0	2	2	0	0
Ron Cey, 3b, LA	2	0	0	0	1	1
Tom Seaver, p, Cin	0	0	0	0	0	0
Reggie Smith, ph, LA	1	0	1	0	0	0
Mike Schmidt, pr, Phi	0	0	0	0	0	0
Rick Reuschel, p, ChN	0	0	0	0	0	0
John Stearns, c, NYN	0	0	0	0	0	0
Johnny Bench, c, Cin	2	0	0	0	0	1
Gary Lavelle, p, SF	0	0	0	0	0	0
Pete Rose, ph-3b, Cin	2	0	0	0	0	0
Dave Concepcion, ss, Cin	1	0	0	0	1	0
Ellis Valentine, rf, Mon	1	0	0	0	1	0
Don Sutton, p, LA	0	0	0	0	0	0
Ted Simmons, c, StL	3	0	0	0	0	0
Goose Gossage, p, Pit	0	0	0	0	0	0
TOTALS	33	7	9	7	3	9

American League	AB	R	H	RBI	BB	K
Rod Carew, 1b, Min	3	1	1	0	0	0
George Scott, 1b, Bos	2	1	1	2	0	0
Willie Randolph, 2b, NYA	5	0	1	1	0	2
George Brett, 3b, KC	2	0	0	0	1	0
Bill Campbell, p, Bos	0	0	0	0	0	0
Ron Fairly, ph, Tor	1	0	0	0	0	1
Sparky Lyle, p, NYA	0	0	0	0	0	0
Thurman Munson, ph, NYA	1	0	0	0	0	1
Carl Yastrzemski, cf, Bos	2	0	0	0	0	1
Fred Lynn, cf, Bos	1	1	0	0	1	0
Richie Zisk, lf, ChA	3	0	2	2	0	1
Ken Singleton, rf, Bal	0	0	0	0	0	0
Reggie Jackson, rf, NYA	2	0	1	0	0	1
Jim Rice, rf-lf, Bos	2	0	1	0	0	0
Carlton Fisk, c, Bos	2	0	0	0	0	1
Butch Wynegar, c, Min	2	1	1	0	0	0
Rick Burleson, ss, Bos	2	0	0	0	0	0
Bert Campaneris, ss, Tex	1	1	0	0	1	1
Jim Palmer, p, Bal	0	0	0	0	0	0
Jim Kern, p, Cle	0	0	0	0	0	0
Ruppert Jones, ph, Sea	1	0	0	0	0	0
Dennis Eckersley, p, Cle	0	0	0	0	0	0
Larry Hisle, ph, Min	1	0	0	0	0	0
Dave LaRoche, p, Cal	0	0	0	0	0	0
Graig Nettles, 3b, NYA	2	0	0	0	0	1
TOTALS	35	5	8	5	3	10

	1 2 3	4 5 6	7 8 9	R	H	E
NL	4 0 1	0 0 0	0 2 0	7	9	1
AL	0 0 0	0 0 2	1 0 2	5	8	0

E—Templeton. DP—NL 1 (Montanez to Templeton), AL 1 (Randolph to Scott). LOB—NL 4, AL 7. Scoring Position—NL 2-for-7, AL 2-for-7. 2B—Foster, Zisk, Winfield, Templeton. HR—Morgan, Garvey, Luzinski, Scott. S—Sutton. GDP—Wynegar, Rose. CS—Concepcion.

National League	IP	H	R	ER	BB	K
Don Sutton, LA (W)	3.0	1	0	0	1	4
Gary Lavelle, SF	2.0	1	0	0	0	2
Tom Seaver, Cin	2.0	4	3	2	1	2
Rick Reuschel, ChN	1.0	1	0	0	0	0
Goose Gossage, Pit	1.0	1	2	2	1	2

American League	IP	H	R	ER	BB	K
Jim Palmer, Bal (L)	2.0	5	5	5	1	3
Jim Kern, Cle	1.0	0	0	0	0	2
Dennis Eckersley, Cle	2.0	0	0	0	0	1
Dave LaRoche, Cal	1.0	1	0	0	1	0
Bill Campbell, Bos	1.0	0	0	0	1	2
Sparky Lyle, NYA	2.0	3	2	2	0	1

Palmer pitched to one batter in the 3rd.

WP—Palmer, Lyle. HBP—Morales by Lyle, Singleton by Reuschel. Time—2:34. Attendance—56,683. Umpires—HP, Kunkel. 1B, Harvey. 2B, Phillips. 3B, Stello.

July 11, 1978
San Diego (San Diego Stadium)

The National League tallied four runs in the bottom of the eighth to grab a 7-3 victory. The game was knotted at three going into the eighth when Goose Gossage took the mound for the Americans. Steve Garvey greeted him with a triple and scored on a wild pitch to put the NL on top, 4-3. Bob Boone later laced a two-run single to center, and Davey Lopes capped the scoring with an RBI single. Rod Carew had two triples and scored two runs for the AL, while NL relievers combined to toss six scoreless frames.

American League	AB	R	H	RBI	BB	K
Rod Carew, 1b, Min	4	2	2	0	0	0
George Brett, 3b, KC	3	1	2	2	0	0
Goose Gossage, p, NYA	0	0	0	0	0	0
Jim Rice, lf, Bos	4	0	0	0	0	2
Chet Lemon, lf, ChA	0	0	0	0	0	0
Richie Zisk, rf, Tex	2	0	1	0	1	1
Dwight Evans, rf, Bos	1	0	0	0	0	1
Carlton Fisk, c, Bos	2	0	0	1	0	0
Jim Sundberg, c, Tex	0	0	0	0	0	0
Jason Thompson, ph, Det	1	0	0	0	0	0
Fred Lynn, cf, Bos	4	0	1	0	0	1
Don Money, 2b, Mil	2	0	0	0	0	1
Frank White, 2b, KC	1	0	0	0	0	0
Darrell Porter, ph, KC	1	0	0	0	0	0
Freddie Patek, ss, KC	3	0	1	0	0	1
Jim Palmer, p, Bal	1	0	0	0	0	0
Matt Keough, p, Oak	0	0	0	0	0	0
Roy Howell, ph, Tor	1	0	0	0	0	0
Lary Sorensen, p, Mil	0	0	0	0	0	0
Larry Hisle, ph, Mil	1	0	1	0	0	0
Jim Kern, p, Cle	0	0	0	0	0	0
Ron Guidry, p, NYA	0	0	0	0	0	0
Graig Nettles, 3b, NYA	0	0	0	0	0	0
TOTALS	31	3	8	3	1	7

National League	AB	R	H	RBI	BB	K
Pete Rose, 3b, Cin	4	0	1	0	0	0
Davey Lopes, pr-2b, LA	1	0	1	1	0	0
Joe Morgan, 2b, Cin	3	1	0	0	1	1
Jack Clark, rf, SF	1	0	0	0	0	1
George Foster, cf, Cin	2	1	0	0	2	1
Greg Luzinski, lf, Phi	2	0	1	1	1	0
Rollie Fingers, p, SD	0	0	0	0	0	0
Willie Stargell, ph, Pit	1	0	0	0	0	0
Bruce Sutter, p, ChN	0	0	0	0	0	0
Phil Niekro, p, Atl	0	0	0	0	0	0
Steve Garvey, 1b, LA	3	1	2	2	1	0
Ted Simmons, c, StL	3	0	1	0	0	1
Dave Concepcion, ss, Cin	0	1	0	0	1	0
Rick Monday, rf, LA	2	0	0	0	0	0
Steve Rogers, p, Mon	0	0	0	0	0	0
Dave Winfield, lf, SD	2	1	1	0	0	0
Larry Bowa, ss, Phi	3	1	2	0	0	0
Bob Boone, c, Phi	1	1	1	2	0	0
Biff Pocoroba, c, Atl	0	0	0	0	0	0
Vida Blue, p, SF	0	0	0	0	0	0
Reggie Smith, ph-rf, LA	3	0	0	0	0	2
Ron Cey, 3b, LA	1	0	0	0	0	0
TOTALS	32	7	10	6	6	6

	1 2 3	4 5 6	7 8 9	R	H	E
AL	2 0 1	0 0 0	0 0 0	3	8	1
NL	0 0 3	0 0 0	0 4 x	7	10	0

E—Lemon. DP—AL 1 (Brett to Money to Carew). LOB—AL 4, NL 7. Scoring Position—AL 1-for-6, NL 4-for-10. 2B—Brett, Rose. 3B—Carew 2, Garvey. SF—Brett, Fisk. GDP—Monday. SB—Brett, Bowa. CS—Carew, Zisk, Lopes.

American League	IP	H	R	ER	BB	K
Jim Palmer, Bal	2.2	3	3	3	4	4
Matt Keough, Oak	0.1	1	0	0	0	0
Lary Sorensen, Mil	3.0	1	0	0	0	0
Jim Kern, Cle	0.2	1	0	0	1	1
Ron Guidry, NYA	0.1	0	0	0	0	0
Goose Gossage, NYA (L)	1.0	4	4	4	1	1

National League	IP	H	R	ER	BB	K
Vida Blue, SF	3.0	5	3	3	1	2
Steve Rogers, Mon	2.0	2	0	0	0	2
Rollie Fingers, SD	2.0	1	0	0	0	1
Bruce Sutter, ChN (W)	1.2	0	0	0	0	2
Phil Niekro, Atl	0.1	0	0	0	0	0

WP—Rogers, Gossage. PB—Sundberg. Time—2:37. Attendance—51,549. Umpires—HP, Pryor. 1B, Chylak. 2B, Tata. 3B, Deegan.

July 17, 1979
Seattle (Kingdome)

The National League won 7-6 on a bases-loaded walk by Lee Mazzilli in the top of the ninth inning. After Jim Kern had walked the bases full with two out, Ron Guidry was brought in to face Mazzilli, but couldn't get the ball over. One inning earlier, Mazzilli had tied the game with a pinch-hit solo homer. The defensive star of the game was Dave Parker, who nailed two American League runners on the bases.

National League	AB	R	H	RBI	BB	K
Davey Lopes, 2b, LA	3	0	1	0	0	1
Joe Morgan, ph-2b, Cin	1	1	0	0	1	1
Dave Parker, rf, Pit	3	0	1	1	1	1
Steve Garvey, 1b, LA	2	1	0	0	1	0
Gaylord Perry, p, SD	0	0	0	0	0	0
Joe Sambito, p, Hou	0	0	0	0	0	0
Craig Reynolds, ss, Hou	2	0	0	0	0	0
Mike Schmidt, 3b, Phi	3	2	2	1	0	0
Ron Cey, 3b, LA	1	0	0	0	1	0
Larry Parrish, 3b, Mon	0	0	0	0	0	0
George Foster, lf, Cin	1	0	1	1	0	0
Gary Matthews, lf, Atl	2	0	0	0	0	0
Lee Mazzilli, ph-cf, NYN	1	1	1	2	1	0
Dave Winfield, cf-lf, SD	5	1	1	1	0	1
Bob Boone, c, Phi	2	1	1	0	0	0
Gary Carter, c, Mon	2	0	1	1	0	0
Larry Bowa, ss, Phi	2	0	0	0	1	0
Mike LaCoss, p, Cin	0	0	0	0	0	0
Keith Hernandez, ph, StL	1	0	0	0	0	1
Bruce Sutter, p, ChN	0	0	0	0	0	0
Steve Carlton, p, Phi	0	0	0	0	0	0
Lou Brock, ph, StL	1	0	1	0	0	0
Joaquin Andujar, p, Hou	0	0	0	0	0	0
Jack Clark, ph, SF	1	0	0	0	0	0
Steve Rogers, p, Mon	0	0	0	0	0	0
Pete Rose, ph-1b, Phi	2	0	0	0	0	0
TOTALS	35	7	10	7	6	5

American League	AB	R	H	RBI	BB	K
Roy Smalley, ss, Min	3	0	0	0	1	0
Bobby Grich, 2b, Cal	1	0	0	0	0	1
George Brett, 3b, KC	3	1	0	0	1	0
Graig Nettles, 3b, NYA	1	0	1	0	0	0
Don Baylor, lf, Cal	4	2	2	1	0	0
Jim Kern, p, Tex	0	0	0	0	0	0
Ron Guidry, p, NYA	0	0	0	0	0	0
Ken Singleton, ph, Bal	1	0	0	0	0	0
Jim Rice, rf-lf, Bos	5	0	1	0	0	2
Fred Lynn, cf, Bos	1	1	1	2	0	0
Chet Lemon, cf, ChA	2	1	0	0	1	1
Carl Yastrzemski, 1b, Bos	3	0	2	1	0	0
Rick Burleson, pr-ss, Bos	2	1	0	0	0	1
Darrell Porter, c, KC	3	0	1	0	0	0
Brian Downing, c, Cal	1	0	1	0	0	0
Frank White, 2b, KC	2	0	0	0	0	0
Bruce Bochte, ph-1b, Sea	1	0	1	1	0	0
Nolan Ryan, p, Cal	0	0	0	0	0	0
Cecil Cooper, ph, Mil	0	0	0	0	1	0
Bob Stanley, p, Bos	0	0	0	0	0	0
Steve Kemp, ph, Det	1	0	0	0	0	0
Mark Clear, p, Cal	0	0	0	0	0	0
Reggie Jackson, ph-rf, NYA	1	0	0	0	1	0
TOTALS	35	6	10	5	5	5

	1 2 3	4 5 6	7 8 9	R	H	E
NL	2 1 1	0 0 1	0 1 1	7	10	1
AL	3 0 2	0 0 1	0 0 0	6	10	0

E—Schmidt. DP—AL 2 (Brett to White to Yastrzemski; White to Smalley to Yastrzemski). LOB—NL 8, AL 9. Scoring Position—NL 3-for-11, AL 4-for-12. 2B—Schmidt, Foster, Winfield, Baylor, Rice, Porter. 3B—Schmidt. HR—Lynn, Mazzilli. S—Bochte. SF—Parker. GDP—Boone, Rose.

National League	IP	H	R	ER	BB	K
Steve Carlton, Phi	1.0	2	3	3	1	0
Joaquin Andujar, Hou	2.0	2	2	1	1	0
Steve Rogers, Mon	2.0	0	0	0	0	2
Gaylord Perry, SD	0.0	3	1	1	0	0
Joe Sambito, Hou	0.2	0	0	0	1	0
Mike LaCoss, Cin	1.1	1	0	0	0	0
Bruce Sutter, ChN (W)	2.0	2	0	0	2	3

American League	IP	H	R	ER	BB	K
Nolan Ryan, Cal	2.0	5	3	3	1	2
Bob Stanley, Bos	2.0	1	1	1	0	0
Mark Clear, Cal	2.0	2	1	1	1	0
Jim Kern, Tex (BS; L)	2.2	2	2	2	3	3
Ron Guidry, NYA	0.1	0	0	0	1	0

Perry pitched to three batters in the 6th.

Balk—Kern. WP—Andujar. HBP—Lemon by Andujar. Time—3:11. Attendance—58,905. Umpires—HP, Maloney. 1B, Weyer. 2B, Bremigan. 3B, Williams.

July 8, 1980
Los Angeles (Dodger Stadium)

Steve Stone and Tommy John held the National League hitless for the first 4.2 innings, but Ken Griffey broke it up with a home run off Tommy John, and the NL went on to win, 4-2. Fred Lynn's two-run homer in the top of the fifth had given the AL a 2-0 lead, but the NL got one back on Griffey's shot and went ahead 3-2 in the following frame. The NL took advantage of two Dave Stieb wild pitches and a passed ball to score its final run in the bottom of the seventh. It was the NL's ninth straight win and 17th in the last 18 games.

American League	AB	R	H	RBI	BB	K
Willie Randolph, 2b, NYA	4	0	2	0	0	0
Dave Stieb, p, Tor	0	0	0	0	0	0
Alan Trammell, ss, Det	0	0	0	0	0	0
Rod Carew, 1b, Cal	2	1	2	0	1	0
Cecil Cooper, 1b, Mil	1	0	0	0	0	0
Fred Lynn, cf, Bos	3	1	1	2	0	1
Al Bumbry, cf, Bal	1	0	0	0	0	0
Reggie Jackson, rf, NYA	2	0	1	0	1	1
Ken Landreaux, pr-rf, Min	1	0	0	0	0	0
Ben Oglivie, lf, Mil	2	0	0	0	1	1
Al Oliver, lf, Tex	1	0	0	0	0	0
Goose Gossage, p, NYA	0	0	0	0	0	0
Carlton Fisk, c, Bos	2	0	0	0	0	2
Darrell Porter, c, KC	1	0	0	0	0	1
Rickey Henderson, lf, Oak	1	0	0	0	0	0
Graig Nettles, 3b, NYA	2	0	0	0	0	0
Buddy Bell, 3b, Tex	2	0	0	0	0	1
Bucky Dent, ss, NYA	2	0	1	0	0	1
Tommy John, p, NYA	1	0	0	0	0	1
Ed Farmer, p, ChA	0	0	0	0	0	0
Bobby Grich, 2b, Cal	0	0	0	0	1	0
Steve Stone, p, Bal	1	0	0	0	0	1
Robin Yount, ss, Mil	2	0	0	0	0	0
Lance Parrish, c, Det	1	0	0	0	0	1
TOTALS	32	2	7	2	4	11

National League	AB	R	H	RBI	BB	K
Davey Lopes, 2b, LA	1	0	0	0	0	0
Phil Garner, 2b, Pit	2	1	1	0	1	1
Reggie Smith, cf, LA	2	0	0	0	0	0
George Hendrick, cf, StL	2	0	1	1	0	0
Bruce Sutter, p, ChN	0	0	0	0	0	0
Dave Parker, rf, Pit	2	0	0	0	0	1
Dave Winfield, rf, SD	2	0	0	1	0	0
Steve Garvey, 1b, LA	2	0	0	0	0	0
Keith Hernandez, ph-1b, StL	2	0	2	0	0	0
Johnny Bench, c, Cin	1	0	0	0	0	0
John Stearns, c, NYN	1	0	0	0	0	0
Pete Rose, ph, Phi	1	0	0	0	0	0
Jim Bibby, p, Pit	0	0	0	0	0	0
Dale Murphy, cf, Atl	1	0	0	0	0	0
Dave Kingman, lf, ChN	1	0	0	0	0	1
Ken Griffey Sr., lf, Cin	3	1	2	1	0	0
Ken Reitz, 3b, StL	2	0	0	0	0	0
Jerry Reuss, p, LA	0	0	0	0	0	0
Dave Concepcion, ss, Cin	1	1	0	0	0	0
Bill Russell, ss, LA	2	0	0	0	0	0
Gary Carter, c, Mon	1	0	0	0	0	0
J.R. Richard, p, Hou	0	0	0	0	0	0
Bob Welch, p, LA	1	0	0	0	0	1
Ray Knight, 3b, Cin	1	1	1	0	1	0
TOTALS	31	4	7	3	2	4

	1 2 3	4 5 6	7 8 9	R	H	E
AL	0 0 0	0 2 0	0 0 0	2	7	2
NL	0 0 0	0 1 2	1 0 x	4	7	0

E—Randolph 2. DP—AL 1 (Randolph to Yount to Cooper), NL 1 (Concepcion to Garner to Hernandez). LOB—AL 7, NL 5. Scoring Position—AL 0-for-5, NL 2-for-7. 2B—Carew. HR—Lynn, Griffey Sr.. GDP—Cooper, Rose. SB—Carew, Garner, Knight.

American League	IP	H	R	ER	BB	K
Steve Stone, Bal	3.0	0	0	0	0	3
Tommy John, NYA (L)	2.1	4	3	3	0	1
Ed Farmer, ChA	0.2	1	0	0	0	0
Dave Stieb, Tor	1.0	1	1	0	2	0
Goose Gossage, NYA	1.0	1	0	0	0	0

National League	IP	H	R	ER	BB	K
J.R. Richard, Hou	2.0	1	0	0	2	3
Bob Welch, LA	3.0	5	2	2	1	4
Jerry Reuss, LA (W)	1.0	0	0	0	0	3
Jim Bibby, Pit	1.0	1	0	0	0	0
Bruce Sutter, ChN (S)	2.0	0	0	0	1	1

WP—Welch, Stieb 2. PB—Porter. Time—2:33. Attendance—56,088. Umpires—HP, Kibler. 1B, Barnett. 2B, Colosi. 3B, McKean.

August 9, 1981
Cleveland (Cleveland Stadium)

After a 50-day strike, the All-Star Game finally took place on August 9, and Mike Schmidt quickly showed everyone how fun the game could be. His two-run homer in the top of the eighth inning gave the National League a come-from-behind, 5-4 victory, thrilling the 72,086 fans jammed into Cleveland's Municipal Stadium. Gary Carter hit a pair of home runs for the Nationals.

National League	AB	R	H	RBI	BB	K
Pete Rose, 1b, Phi	3	0	1	0	0	0
Burt Hooton, p, LA	0	0	0	0	0	0
Dick Ruthven, p, Phi	0	0	0	0	0	0
Pedro Guerrero, ph, LA	1	0	0	0	0	1
Vida Blue, p, SF	0	0	0	0	0	0
Bill Madlock, 3b, Pit	1	0	0	0	0	0
Dave Concepcion, ss, Cin	3	0	0	0	0	1
Ozzie Smith, ss, SD	0	0	0	0	2	0
Dave Parker, rf, Pit	3	1	1	1	0	1
Mike Easler, rf, Pit	1	1	0	0	1	0
Mike Schmidt, 3b, Phi	4	1	2	2	0	1
Nolan Ryan, p, Hou	0	0	0	0	0	0
Phil Garner, 2b, Pit	0	0	0	0	0	0
George Foster, lf, Cin	2	0	0	0	0	0
Dusty Baker, lf, LA	2	0	1	0	0	0
Tim Raines, pr-lf, Mon	0	0	0	0	0	0
Andre Dawson, cf, Mon	4	0	1	0	0	1
Gary Carter, c, Mon	3	2	2	2	0	0
Bruce Benedict, c, Atl	1	0	0	0	0	1
Davey Lopes, 2b, LA	0	0	0	0	1	0
Manny Trillo, 2b, Phi	2	0	0	0	0	0
Bill Buckner, ph, ChN	1	0	0	0	0	0
Bruce Sutter, p, StL	0	0	0	0	0	0
Fernando Valenzuela, p, LA	0	0	0	0	0	0
Joel Youngblood, ph, NYN	1	0	0	0	0	0
Tom Seaver, p, Cin	0	0	0	0	0	0
Bob Knepper, p, Hou	0	0	0	0	0	0
Terry Kennedy, ph, SD	1	0	0	0	0	0
Steve Garvey, 1b, LA	2	0	1	0	0	0
TOTALS	35	5	9	5	4	6

American League	AB	R	H	RBI	BB	K
Rod Carew, 1b, Cal	3	0	1	0	0	1
Eddie Murray, ph-1b, Bal	2	0	0	0	0	0
Willie Randolph, 2b, NYA	3	0	1	0	0	1
Ted Simmons, ph, Mil	1	0	1	1	0	0
Frank White, pr-2b, KC	1	0	0	0	0	0
George Brett, 3b, KC	3	0	0	0	0	2
Mike Norris, p, Oak	0	0	0	0	0	0
Al Oliver, ph, Tex	1	0	0	0	0	0
Ron Davis, p, NYA	0	0	0	0	0	0
Rollie Fingers, p, Mil	0	0	0	0	0	0
Dave Stieb, p, Tor	1	0	0	0	0	1
Dave Winfield, cf, NYA	4	0	0	0	1	0
Ken Singleton, lf, Bal	3	2	2	1	0	0
Rick Burleson, ss, Cal	1	0	0	0	0	0
Reggie Jackson, rf, NYA	1	0	0	0	0	0
Dwight Evans, ph-rf, Bos	2	1	1	0	1	0
Carlton Fisk, c, ChA	3	1	1	0	0	1
Bo Diaz, c, Cle	1	0	0	0	0	1
Bucky Dent, ss, NYA	2	0	2	0	0	0
Fred Lynn, ph, Cal	1	0	1	1	0	0
Tony Armas, lf, Oak	1	0	0	0	0	1
Jack Morris, p, Det	0	0	0	0	0	0
Tom Paciorek, ph, Sea	1	0	1	0	0	0
Len Barker, p, Cle	0	0	0	0	0	0
Gorman Thomas, ph, Mil	1	0	0	0	0	0
Ken Forsch, p, Cal	0	0	0	0	0	0
Buddy Bell, 3b, Tex	1	0	0	1	0	0
TOTALS	37	4	11	4	2	8

	1 2 3	4 5 6	7 8 9	R	H	E
NL	0 0 0	0 1 1	1 2 0	5	9	1
AL	0 1 0	0 0 3	0 0 0	4	11	1

E—Schmidt, Fingers. LOB—NL 7, AL 9. Scoring Position—NL 0-for-8, AL 3-for-11. 2B—Schmidt, Dent, Garvey. HR—Parker, Schmidt, Carter 2, Singleton. SF—Bell. SB—Dawson, OSmith. CS—Carew.

National League	IP	H	R	ER	BB	K
Fernando Valenzuela, LA	1.0	2	0	0	0	0
Tom Seaver, Cin	1.0	3	1	1	0	1
Bob Knepper, Hou	2.0	1	0	0	2	3
Burt Hooton, LA	1.2	5	3	3	0	1
Dick Ruthven, Phi	0.1	0	0	0	0	0
Vida Blue, SF (W)	1.0	0	0	0	0	1
Nolan Ryan, Hou	1.0	0	0	0	0	1
Bruce Sutter, StL (S)	1.0	0	0	0	0	1

American League	IP	H	R	ER	BB	K
Jack Morris, Det	2.0	2	0	0	1	2
Len Barker, Cle	2.0	0	0	0	0	1
Ken Forsch, Cal	1.0	1	1	1	0	0
Mike Norris, Oak	1.0	2	1	1	0	1
Ron Davis, NYA	1.0	1	1	1	0	1
Rollie Fingers, Mil (BS; L)	0.1	2	2	2	2	0
Dave Stieb, Tor	1.2	1	0	0	1	1

WP—Blue. Time—2:59. Attendance—72,086. Umpires—HP, Haller. 1B, Vargo. 2B, DiMuro. 3B, Engel.

July 13, 1982
Montreal (Stade Olympique)

Dave Concepcion hit a two-run homer and National League hurlers fanned 10 American League hitters en route to a 4-1 NL victory. Concepcion's blast came with two out in the bottom of the second off Dennis Eckersley and gave the NL a lead it would never relinquish. Ruppert Jones tripled and scored on a sacrifice fly in the following inning, and Al Oliver doubled and scored the final run of the game in the bottom of the sixth. The American League's only run came in the top of the first when Rickey Henderson singled, moved up on a single and a wild pitch, and came home on a sacrifice fly. Henderson had three hits for the Americans.

American League	AB	R	H	RBI	BB	K
Rickey Henderson, lf, Oak	4	1	3	0	1	0
Fred Lynn, cf, Cal	2	0	0	0	0	0
Willie Wilson, cf, KC	2	0	0	0	0	1
Kent Hrbek, ph, Min	1	0	0	0	0	0
George Brett, 3b, KC	2	0	2	0	0	0
Buddy Bell, ph-3b, Tex	3	0	0	0	0	2
Reggie Jackson, rf, Cal	1	0	0	1	0	0
Dave Winfield, rf, NYA	2	0	1	0	0	0
Cecil Cooper, 1b, Mil	2	0	1	0	0	1
Eddie Murray, ph-1b, Bal	1	0	0	0	1	0
Robin Yount, ss, Mil	3	0	0	0	1	1
Bobby Grich, 2b, Cal	1	0	0	0	1	1
Carl Yastrzemski, ph, Bos	1	0	0	0	0	1
Dan Quisenberry, p, KC	0	0	0	0	0	0
Hal McRae, ph, KC	0	0	0	0	1	0
Rollie Fingers, p, Mil	0	0	0	0	0	0
Carlton Fisk, c, ChA	2	0	0	0	0	1
Lance Parrish, c, Det	2	0	1	0	0	0
Dennis Eckersley, p, Bos	1	0	0	0	0	0
Andre Thornton, ph, Cle	1	0	0	0	0	1
Jim Clancy, p, Tor	0	0	0	0	0	0
Floyd Bannister, p, Sea	0	0	0	0	0	0
Frank White, 2b, KC	1	0	0	0	0	1
Ben Oglivie, ph, Mil	1	0	0	0	0	0
TOTALS	33	1	8	1	5	10

National League	AB	R	H	RBI	BB	K
Tim Raines, lf, Mon	1	0	0	0	1	1
Steve Carlton, p, Phi	0	0	0	0	0	0
Bob Horner, ph, Atl	1	0	0	0	0	0
Mario Soto, p, Cin	0	0	0	0	0	0
Jason Thompson, ph, Pit	1	0	0	0	0	0
Fernando Valenzuela, p, LA	0	0	0	0	0	0
Greg Minton, p, SF	0	0	0	0	0	0
Steve Howe, p, LA	0	0	0	0	0	0
Tom Hume, p, Cin	0	0	0	0	0	0
Pete Rose, 1b, Phi	1	0	0	1	0	0
Al Oliver, 1b, Mon	2	1	2	0	0	0
Andre Dawson, cf, Mon	4	0	1	0	0	0
Mike Schmidt, 3b, Phi	1	0	0	0	0	0
Ray Knight, 3b, Hou	3	0	0	0	0	1
Gary Carter, c, Mon	3	0	1	1	0	0
Tony Pena, pr-c, Pit	1	0	0	0	0	0
John Stearns, c, NYN	0	0	0	0	0	0
Dale Murphy, rf, Atl	2	1	0	0	1	0
Dave Concepcion, ss, Cin	3	1	1	2	0	0
Ozzie Smith, pr-ss, StL	0	0	0	0	0	0
Manny Trillo, 2b, Phi	2	0	1	0	0	0
Steve Sax, pr-2b, LA	1	0	1	0	0	0
Steve Rogers, p, Mon	0	0	0	0	0	0
Ruppert Jones, ph, SD	1	1	1	0	0	0
Dusty Baker, lf, LA	2	0	0	0	0	0
Lonnie Smith, lf, StL	0	0	0	0	0	0
TOTALS	29	4	8	4	2	2

	1 2 3	4 5 6	7 8 9	R	H	E
AL	1 0 0	0 0 0	0 0 0	1	8	2
NL	0 2 1	0 0 1	0 0 x	4	8	1

E—Bell, Henderson, Sax. DP—NL 1 (Carlton to Concepcion to Rose). LOB—AL 11, NL 4. Scoring Position—AL 2-for-10, NL 1-for-7. 2B—Parrish, Oliver. 3B—Jones. HR—Concepcion. SF—Jackson, Rose. GDP—Wilson. SB—Henderson, Raines, Pena. CS—Sax, Oliver, OSmith.

American League	IP	H	R	ER	BB	K
Dennis Eckersley, Bos (L)	3.0	2	3	3	2	1
Jim Clancy, Tor	1.0	0	0	0	0	0
Floyd Bannister, Sea	1.0	1	0	0	0	0
Dan Quisenberry, KC	2.0	3	1	1	0	1
Rollie Fingers, Mil	1.0	2	0	0	0	0

National League	IP	H	R	ER	BB	K
Steve Rogers, Mon (W)	3.0	4	1	1	0	2
Steve Carlton, Phi	2.0	1	0	0	2	4
Mario Soto, Cin	2.0	3	0	0	0	4
Fernando Valenzuela, LA	0.2	0	0	0	2	0
Greg Minton, SF	0.2	0	0	0	1	0
Steve Howe, LA	0.1	0	0	0	0	0
Tom Hume, Cin (S)	0.1	0	0	0	0	0

WP—Rogers. Time—2:53. Attendance—59,057. Umpires—HP, Harvey. 1B, Springstead. 2B, McSherry. 3B, McKeon.

July 6, 1983
Chicago (Comiskey Park)

After losing 19 of the previous 20 All-Star Games, the last thing anyone expected was a 13-3 breakout victory for the American League. Fred Lynn put the AL well on its way with his homer in the bottom of the third with the bases loaded, the first grand slam in All-Star history. The slam capped a seven-run inning and gave the AL a 9-1 lead. Atlee Hammaker was the victim of the outburst, absorbing all seven runs in only two-thirds of an inning. AL starter Dave Stieb tossed three hitless innings.

National League	AB	R	H	RBI	BB	K
Steve Sax, 2b, LA	3	1	1	1	0	0
Glenn Hubbard, 2b, Atl	1	0	1	0	0	0
Tim Raines, lf, Mon	3	0	0	0	0	1
Bill Madlock, ph-3b, Pit	1	0	0	0	0	0
Andre Dawson, cf, Mon	3	0	0	0	0	1
Dave Dravecky, p, SD	0	0	0	0	0	0
Pascual Perez, p, Atl	0	0	0	0	0	0
Jesse Orosco, p, NYN	0	0	0	0	0	0
Johnny Bench, ph, Cin	1	0	0	0	0	0
Lee Smith, p, ChN	0	0	0	0	0	0
Al Oliver, 1b, Mon	2	1	1	0	1	0
Darrell Evans, 1b, SF	1	0	0	0	0	0
Dale Murphy, rf, Atl	3	0	1	1	0	1
Pedro Guerrero, 3b-lf, LA	1	0	0	0	0	1
Mike Schmidt, 3b, Phi	3	0	0	0	0	1
Bruce Benedict, c, Atl	1	0	1	0	0	0
Gary Carter, c, Mon	2	0	0	0	0	0
Leon Durham, rf, ChN	2	0	0	0	0	1
Ozzie Smith, ss, StL	2	1	1	0	0	0
Willie McGee, cf, StL	2	0	1	0	0	0
Mario Soto, p, Cin	1	0	0	0	0	0
Atlee Hammaker, p, SF	0	0	0	0	0	0
Bill Dawley, p, Hou	0	0	0	0	0	0
Dickie Thon, ph-ss, Hou	3	0	1	0	0	0
TOTALS	35	3	8	2	1	6

American League	AB	R	H	RBI	BB	K
Rod Carew, 1b, Cal	3	2	2	1	1	0
Eddie Murray, 1b, Bal	2	0	0	0	0	0
Robin Yount, ss, Mil	2	1	0	1	1	1
Cal Ripken Jr., ss, Bal	0	0	0	0	1	0
Fred Lynn, cf, Cal	3	1	1	4	1	2
Willie Wilson, cf, KC	1	0	1	1	0	0
Jim Rice, lf, Bos	4	1	2	1	0	0
Ben Oglivie, rf, Mil	1	0	0	0	0	1
Matt Young, p, Sea	0	0	0	0	0	0
Dan Quisenberry, p, KC	0	0	0	0	0	0
George Brett, 3b, KC	4	2	2	1	0	1
Ted Simmons, c, Mil	2	0	0	0	0	0
Lance Parrish, c, Det	2	0	0	0	0	1
Cecil Cooper, ph, Mil	1	1	1	0	0	0
Bob Boone, c, Cal	0	0	0	0	0	0
Dave Winfield, rf, NYA	3	2	3	1	0	0
Ron Kittle, lf-rf, ChA	2	1	1	0	0	1
Manny Trillo, 2b, Cle	3	1	1	0	0	0
Lou Whitaker, ph-2b, Det	1	1	1	2	0	0
Dave Stieb, p, Tor	0	0	0	0	0	0
Doug DeCinces, ph, Cal	1	0	0	0	0	0
Rick Honeycutt, p, Tex	0	0	0	0	0	0
Gary Ward, ph, Min	1	0	0	0	0	0
Bob Stanley, p, Bos	0	0	0	0	0	0
Carl Yastrzemski, ph, Bos	1	0	0	0	0	1
Rickey Henderson, lf, Oak	1	0	0	1	0	0
TOTALS	38	13	15	13	4	8

	1 2 3	4 5 6	7 8 9	R	H	E
NL	1 0 0	1 1 0	0 0 0	3	8	3
AL	1 1 7	0 0 0	2 2 x	13	15	2

E—Carew, Guerrero, Schmidt, Sax, Stieb. DP—AL 2 (Yount to Trillo to Carew; Brett to Trillo). LOB—NL 6, AL 9. Scoring Position—NL 2-for-9, AL 5-for-17. 2B—Oliver, Brett, Winfield, Wilson. 3B—Brett, Whitaker. HR—Lynn, Rice. S—Stieb. SF—Yount, Brett, Whitaker. GDP—Raines, Schmidt. SB—Sax, Raines.

National League	IP	H	R	ER	BB	K
Mario Soto, Cin (L)	2.0	2	2	0	2	2
Atlee Hammaker, SF	0.2	6	7	7	1	0
Bill Dawley, Hou	1.1	1	0	0	0	1
Dave Dravecky, SD	2.0	1	0	0	0	2
Pascual Perez, Atl	0.2	3	2	2	1	1
Jesse Orosco, NYN	0.1	0	0	0	0	1
Lee Smith, ChN	1.0	2	2	1	0	1

American League	IP	H	R	ER	BB	K
Dave Stieb, Tor (W)	3.0	0	1	0	1	4
Rick Honeycutt, Tex	2.0	5	2	2	0	0
Bob Stanley, Bos	2.0	2	0	0	0	0
Matt Young, Sea	1.0	0	0	0	0	1
Dan Quisenberry, KC	1.0	1	0	0	0	1

PB—Benedict. Time—3:05. Attendance—43,801. Umpires—HP, Maloney. 1B, Wendelstedt. 2B, Hendry. 3B, Quick.

July 10, 1984
San Francisco (Candlestick Park)

The 1984 Midsummer Classic was, quite simply, the All-K Game. National League hurlers registered 11 strikeouts, barely edging the American League staff's total of 10 whiffs. The NL's 3-1 victory was somewhat overshadowed by the masterful pitching performances. In the fourth inning, Fernando Valenzuela struck out the side. In the following inning, Valenzuela was replaced by Dwight Gooden, who proceeded to also strike out the side. In the seventh, Bill Caudill extracted a measure of revenge for the AL, fanning the side himself. Steve Garvey scored the game's first run in the bottom of the first when Dale Murphy singled and Dave Winfield's peg home was dropped by catcher Lance Parrish. In the top of the second, George Brett tied it up with a solo shot off Charlie Lea, but Gary Carter answered with a circuit clout of his own in the bottom of the frame.

American League	AB	R	H	RBI	BB	K
Lou Whitaker, 2b, Det	3	0	2	0	0	0
Damaso Garcia, 2b, Tor	1	0	0	0	0	0
Rod Carew, 1b, Cal	2	0	0	0	0	1
Eddie Murray, 1b, Bal	2	0	1	0	0	1
Cal Ripken Jr., ss, Bal	3	0	0	0	0	0
Alfredo Griffin, ss, Tor	0	0	0	0	0	0
Don Mattingly, ph, NYA	1	0	0	0	0	0
Dave Winfield, lf-rf, NYA	4	0	1	0	0	1
Reggie Jackson, rf, Cal	2	0	0	0	0	1
Rickey Henderson, lf-cf, Oak	2	0	0	0	0	1
George Brett, 3b, KC	3	1	1	1	0	1
Bill Caudill, p, Oak	0	0	0	0	0	0
Willie Hernandez, p, Det	0	0	0	0	0	0
Lance Parrish, c, Det	2	0	0	0	0	2
Jim Sundberg, c, Mil	1	0	0	0	0	0
Chet Lemon, cf, Det	2	0	1	0	0	1
Jim Rice, ph-lf, Bos	1	0	0	0	0	1
Dave Stieb, p, Tor	0	0	0	0	0	0
Andre Thornton, ph, Cle	1	0	1	0	0	0
Jack Morris, p, Det	0	0	0	0	0	0
Alvin Davis, ph, Sea	1	0	0	0	0	1
Rich Dotson, p, ChA	0	0	0	0	0	0
Buddy Bell, 3b, Tex	1	0	0	0	0	0
TOTALS	32	1	7	1	0	11

National League	AB	R	H	RBI	BB	K
Tony Gwynn, lf, SD	3	0	1	0	0	1
Tim Raines, lf, Mon	1	0	0	0	0	1
Ryne Sandberg, 2b, ChN	4	0	1	0	0	1
Steve Garvey, 1b, SD	3	1	1	0	0	0
Keith Hernandez, 1b, NYN	1	0	0	0	0	1
Dale Murphy, cf, Atl	3	1	2	1	1	0
Mike Schmidt, 3b, Phi	3	0	0	0	0	2
Tim Wallach, 3b, Mon	1	0	0	0	0	0
Darryl Strawberry, rf, NYN	2	0	1	0	0	1
Claudell Washington, rf, Atl	2	0	1	0	0	1
Gary Carter, c, Mon	2	1	1	1	1	0
Jody Davis, c, ChN	1	0	0	0	0	0
Goose Gossage, p, SD	0	0	0	0	0	0
Ozzie Smith, ss, StL	3	0	0	0	0	0
Charlie Lea, p, Mon	0	0	0	0	0	0
Chili Davis, ph, SF	1	0	0	0	0	0
Fernando Valenzuela, p, LA	0	0	0	0	0	0
Jerry Mumphrey, ph, Hou	1	0	0	0	0	1
Dwight Gooden, p, NYN	0	0	0	0	0	0
Bob Brenly, ph, SF	1	0	0	0	0	1
Mario Soto, p, Cin	0	0	0	0	0	0
Tony Pena, c, Pit	0	0	0	0	0	0
TOTALS	32	3	8	2	2	10

	1 2 3	4 5 6	7 8 9	R	H	E
AL	0 1 0	0 0 0	0 0 0	1	7	2
NL	1 1 0	0 0 0	0 1 x	3	8	0

E—Jackson, Parrish. DP—NL 1 (Garvey to Carter). LOB—AL 4, NL 7. Scoring Position—AL 0-for-8, NL 1-for-10. 2B—Whitaker, Winfield, Murray, Washington. HR—Brett, Murphy, Carter. GDP—Carew. SB—Gwynn, Sandberg, Strawberry, OSmith. CS—Lemon.

American League	IP	H	R	ER	BB	K
Dave Stieb, Tor (L)	2.0	3	2	1	0	2
Jack Morris, Det	2.0	2	0	0	1	2
Rich Dotson, ChA	2.0	2	0	0	1	2
Bill Caudill, Oak	1.0	0	0	0	0	3
Willie Hernandez, Det	1.0	1	1	1	0	1

National League	IP	H	R	ER	BB	K
Charlie Lea, Mon (W)	2.0	3	1	1	0	2
Fernando Valenzuela, LA	2.0	2	0	0	0	3
Dwight Gooden, NYN	2.0	1	0	0	0	3
Mario Soto, Cin	2.0	0	0	0	0	1
Goose Gossage, SD (S)	1.0	1	0	0	0	2

Time—2:29. Attendance—57,756. Umpires—HP, Weyer. 1B, Clark. 2B, Rennert. 3B, Merrill.

July 16, 1985
Minnesota (Metrodome)

LaMarr Hoyt and four other National League pitchers combined to five-hit the American League squad en route to a 6-1 NL triumph. The Americans drew first blood, as Rickey Henderson singled, stole second, moved to third on a wild throw by catcher Terry Kennedy, and scored on a sacrifice fly by George Brett. Kennedy made amends by grounding an RBI single to tie the game in the following frame. Steve Garvey put the NL on top for good with an RBI single in the top of the third. Later, a two-run single by Ozzie Virgil and a two-run double by Willie McGee padded the lead.

National League	AB	R	H	RBI	BB	K
Tony Gwynn, lf, SD	1	0	0	0	0	0
Jose Cruz, lf, Hou	1	0	0	0	2	0
Tim Raines, ph-lf, Mon	0	1	0	0	1	0
Tom Herr, 2b, StL	3	1	1	0	0	0
Nolan Ryan, p, Hou	1	0	0	0	0	1
Tony Pena, c, Pit	1	0	0	0	0	1
Steve Garvey, 1b, SD	3	0	1	1	0	0
Jack Clark, 1b, StL	1	0	0	0	1	0
Dale Murphy, cf, Atl	3	0	1	0	0	1
Willie McGee, cf, StL	2	0	1	2	0	0
Darryl Strawberry, rf, NYN	1	2	1	0	1	0
Dave Parker, rf, Cin	2	0	0	0	0	1
Graig Nettles, 3b, SD	2	0	0	0	0	0
Tim Wallach, 3b, Mon	2	1	1	0	1	1
Terry Kennedy, c, SD	2	0	1	1	0	0
Ozzie Virgil, c, Phi	1	0	1	2	0	0
Fernando Valenzuela, p, LA	0	0	0	0	0	0
Pete Rose, ph, Cin	1	0	0	0	0	0
Jeff Reardon, p, Mon	0	0	0	0	0	0
Glenn Wilson, ph, Phi	1	0	0	0	0	1
Goose Gossage, p, SD	0	0	0	0	0	0
Ozzie Smith, ss, StL	4	0	0	0	0	0
LaMarr Hoyt, p, SD	1	0	0	0	0	1
Garry Templeton, ph, SD	1	0	1	0	0	0
Ryne Sandberg, 2b, ChN	1	1	0	0	1	1
TOTALS	35	6	9	6	7	8

American League	AB	R	H	RBI	BB	K
Rickey Henderson, cf, NYA	3	1	1	0	0	1
Paul Molitor, 3b-cf, Mil	1	0	0	0	0	1
Lou Whitaker, 2b, Det	2	0	0	0	0	0
Damaso Garcia, 2b, Tor	2	0	1	0	0	0
George Brett, 3b, KC	1	0	0	1	1	0
Phil Bradley, cf, Sea	1	0	0	0	0	1
Dan Petry, p, Det	0	0	0	0	0	0
Willie Hernandez, p, Det	0	0	0	0	0	0
Eddie Murray, 1b, Bal	3	0	0	0	0	0
Tom Brunansky, rf, Min	1	0	0	0	0	0
Cal Ripken Jr., ss, Bal	3	0	1	0	0	0
Alan Trammell, ss, Det	1	0	0	0	0	0
Dave Winfield, rf, NYA	3	0	1	0	0	0
Donnie Moore, p, Cal	0	0	0	0	0	0
Wade Boggs, 3b, Bos	0	0	0	0	1	0
Jim Rice, lf, Bos	3	0	0	0	1	2
Carlton Fisk, c, ChA	2	0	0	0	0	0
Ernie Whitt, c, Tor	0	0	0	0	0	0
Gary Ward, ph, Tex	1	0	0	0	0	0
Rich Gedman, c, Bos	1	0	0	0	0	1
Jack Morris, p, Det	0	0	0	0	0	0
Jimmy Key, p, Tor	0	0	0	0	0	0
Harold Baines, ph, ChA	1	0	1	0	0	0
Bert Blyleven, p, Cle	0	0	0	0	0	0
Cecil Cooper, ph, Mil	0	0	0	0	1	0
Dave Stieb, p, Tor	0	0	0	0	0	0
Don Mattingly, 1b, NYA	1	0	0	0	0	0
TOTALS	30	1	5	1	4	6

	1 2 3	4 5 6	7 8 9	R	H	E
NL	0 1 1	0 2 0	0 0 2	6	9	1
AL	1 0 0	0 0 0	0 0 0	1	5	0

E—Kennedy. DP—NL 1 (Pena to Sandberg to Reardon to Wallach). LOB—NL 10, AL 7. Scoring Position—NL 4-for-11, AL 0-for-7. 2B—Herr, Murphy, Wallach, McGee. SF—Brett. SB—Strawberry, Henderson, Winfield, Cruz, Garcia.

National League	IP	H	R	ER	BB	K
LaMarr Hoyt, SD (W)	3.0	2	1	0	0	0
Nolan Ryan, Hou	3.0	2	0	0	2	2
Fernando Valenzuela, LA	1.0	0	0	0	1	1
Jeff Reardon, Mon	1.0	1	0	0	0	1
Goose Gossage, SD	1.0	0	0	0	1	2

American League	IP	H	R	ER	BB	K
Jack Morris, Det (L)	2.2	5	2	2	1	1
Jimmy Key, Tor	0.1	0	0	0	0	0
Bert Blyleven, Cle	2.0	3	2	2	1	1
Dave Stieb, Tor	1.0	0	0	0	1	2
Donnie Moore, Cal	2.0	0	0	0	0	1
Dan Petry, Det	0.1	0	2	2	3	1
Willie Hernandez, Det	0.2	1	0	0	1	2

WP—Valenzuela. HBP—Strawberry by Blyleven. Time—2:54. Attendance—54,960. Umpires—HP, McCoy. 1B, Kibler. 2B, Bremigan. 3B, Williams.

July 15, 1986
Houston (Astrodome)

Roger Clemens tossed three perfect innings and Lou Whitaker hit a two-run homer as the American League triumphed, 3-2. Whitaker's blast came off National League starter and loser Dwight Gooden. Whitaker was later replaced by Frank White, who hit a solo shot off Mike Scott in the seventh to make it 3-0, Americans. Steve Sax' RBI single in the bottom of the eighth drew the Nationals to within a run, but they could get no closer, as Dave Righetti and Don Aase combined to get the final four outs for the AL. Fernando Valenzuela tied an All-Star Game record by fanning five straight hitters in the fourth and fifth innings. National League pitchers tied a record with 12 strikeouts overall, and the two clubs combined for only 10 hits.

American League	AB	R	H	RBI	BB	K
Kirby Puckett, cf, Min	3	0	1	0	1	0
Rickey Henderson, lf, NYA	3	0	0	0	0	1
Lloyd Moseby, lf, Tor	0	0	0	0	1	0
Wade Boggs, 3b, Bos	3	0	1	0	0	0
Brook Jacoby, ph-3b, Cle	1	0	0	0	0	1
Lance Parrish, c, Det	3	0	0	0	0	0
Jim Rice, ph, Bos	1	0	0	0	0	1
Rich Gedman, c, Bos	0	0	0	0	0	0
Wally Joyner, 1b, Cal	1	0	0	0	0	0
Don Mattingly, ph-1b, NYA	3	0	0	0	0	2
Cal Ripken Jr., ss, Bal	4	0	0	0	0	2
Tony Fernandez, ss, Tor	0	0	0	0	0	0
Dave Winfield, rf, NYA	1	1	1	0	0	0
Jesse Barfield, ph-rf, Tor	3	0	0	0	0	2
Lou Whitaker, 2b, Det	2	1	1	2	0	1
Frank White, ph-2b, KC	2	1	1	1	0	0
Roger Clemens, p, Bos	1	0	0	0	0	1
Teddy Higuera, p, Mil	1	0	0	0	0	1
Harold Baines, ph, ChA	1	0	0	0	0	0
Charlie Hough, p, Tex	0	0	0	0	0	0
Dave Righetti, p, NYA	0	0	0	0	0	0
Don Aase, p, Bal	0	0	0	0	0	0
TOTALS	33	3	5	3	2	12

National League	AB	R	H	RBI	BB	K
Tony Gwynn, lf, SD	3	0	0	0	0	1
Steve Sax, 2b, LA	1	0	1	1	0	0
Ryne Sandberg, 2b, ChN	3	0	0	0	0	2
Mike Scott, p, Hou	0	0	0	0	0	0
Sid Fernandez, p, NYN	0	0	0	0	0	0
Glenn Davis, ph, Hou	1	0	0	0	0	0
Mike Krukow, p, SF	0	0	0	0	0	0
Keith Hernandez, 1b, NYN	4	0	0	0	0	0
Gary Carter, c, NYN	3	0	0	0	0	0
Jody Davis, c, ChN	1	0	1	0	0	0
Tony Pena, pr, Pit	0	0	0	0	0	0
Darryl Strawberry, rf, NYN	2	0	1	0	0	1
Dave Parker, rf, Cin	2	0	1	0	0	0
Mike Schmidt, 3b, Phi	1	0	0	0	1	0
Chris Brown, 3b, SF	2	1	1	0	0	0
Dale Murphy, cf, Atl	2	0	0	0	0	0
Chili Davis, cf, SF	1	0	0	0	0	1
Ozzie Smith, ss, StL	1	0	0	0	0	0
Hubie Brooks, ph-ss, Mon	2	1	0	0	0	1
Dwight Gooden, p, NYN	0	0	0	0	0	0
Kevin Bass, ph, Hou	1	0	0	0	0	0
Fernando Valenzuela, p, LA	0	0	0	0	0	0
Tim Raines, ph-lf, Mon	2	0	0	0	0	1
TOTALS	32	2	5	1	1	7

	1 2 3	4 5 6	7 8 9	R	H	E
AL	0 2 0	0 0 0	1 0 0	3	5	0
NL	0 0 0	0 0 0	0 2 0	2	5	1

E—Sandberg. LOB—AL 5, NL 4. Scoring Position—AL 1-for-6, NL 1-for-8. 2B—Winfield, Brown. HR—Whitaker, White. GDP—Brown. SB—Puckett, Moseby, Sax.

American League	IP	H	R	ER	BB	K
Roger Clemens, Bos (W)	3.0	0	0	0	0	2
Teddy Higuera, Mil	3.0	1	0	0	1	2
Charlie Hough, Tex	1.2	2	2	1	0	3
Dave Righetti, NYA	0.2	2	0	0	0	0
Don Aase, Bal (S)	0.2	0	0	0	0	0

National League	IP	H	R	ER	BB	K
Dwight Gooden, NYN (L)	3.0	3	2	2	0	2
Fernando Valenzuela, LA	3.0	1	0	0	0	5
Mike Scott, Hou	1.0	1	1	1	0	2
Sid Fernandez, NYN	1.0	0	0	0	2	3
Mike Krukow, SF	1.0	0	0	0	0	0

Balk—Gooden, Hough. PB—Gedman. Time—2:28. Attendance—45,774. Umpires—HP, Froemming. 1B, Palermo. 2B, Runge. 3B, Reed.

July 14, 1987

Oakland (Oakland-Alameda Coliseum)

The National and American League squads played scoreless ball for 12 innings, before Tim Raines hit a two-run triple in the top of the 13th to give the NL a 2-0 victory. The AL almost won it in the bottom of the ninth, but NL reliever Steve Bedrosian snared a wild throw behind first base and pegged the ball to catcher Ozzie Virgil, who survived a violent collision to tag out Dave Winfield at the plate.

National League	AB	R	H	RBI	BB	K
Eric Davis, lf, Cin	3	0	0	0	0	1
Tim Raines, lf, Mon	3	0	3	2	0	0
Ryne Sandberg, 2b, ChN	2	0	0	0	0	0
Juan Samuel, 2b, Phi	4	0	0	0	0	1
Andre Dawson, cf-rf, ChN	3	0	1	0	0	1
Rick Reuschel, p, Pit	0	0	0	0	0	0
Jeffrey Leonard, rf, SF	2	0	0	0	0	0
Mike Schmidt, 3b, Phi	2	0	1	0	0	0
Tim Wallach, 3b, Mon	3	0	0	0	0	2
Jack Clark, 1b, StL	3	0	0	0	0	2
Keith Hernandez, 1b, NYN	2	0	1	0	0	1
Darryl Strawberry, rf, NYN	2	0	0	0	0	0
Bo Diaz, c, Cin	1	0	0	0	0	0
Ozzie Virgil, c, Atl	2	1	1	0	0	0
Gary Carter, c, NYN	1	0	0	0	1	0
Orel Hershiser, p, LA	0	0	0	0	0	0
Dale Murphy, rf, Atl	1	0	0	0	0	0
John Franco, p, Cin	0	0	0	0	0	0
Steve Bedrosian, p, Phi	0	0	0	0	0	0
Pedro Guerrero, ph, LA	1	0	0	0	0	0
Lee Smith, p, ChN	1	0	0	0	0	1
Sid Fernandez, p, NYN	0	0	0	0	0	0
Ozzie Smith, ss, StL	2	0	0	0	0	0
Hubie Brooks, ss, Mon	3	1	1	0	0	1
Mike Scott, p, Hou	0	0	0	0	0	0
Tony Gwynn, ph, SD	1	0	0	0	0	0
Rick Sutcliffe, p, ChN	0	0	0	0	0	0
Willie McGee, cf, StL	4	0	0	0	0	0
TOTALS	46	2	8	2	1	10

American League	AB	R	H	RBI	BB	K
Rickey Henderson, cf, NYA	3	0	1	0	0	0
Mark McGwire, 1b, Oak	3	0	0	0	0	1
Don Mattingly, 1b, NYA	1	0	0	0	2	0
Kevin Seitzer, 3b, KC	2	0	0	0	1	0
Wade Boggs, 3b, Bos	3	0	0	0	0	0
Mark Langston, p, Sea	0	0	0	0	0	0
Dan Plesac, p, Mil	0	0	0	0	0	0
Harold Baines, ph, ChA	1	0	0	0	0	0
Dave Righetti, p, NYA	0	0	0	0	0	0
Tom Henke, p, Tor	0	0	0	0	0	0
Larry Parrish, ph, Tex	1	0	1	0	0	0
Jay Howell, p, Oak	0	0	0	0	0	0
Pat Tabler, ph, Cle	1	0	0	0	0	1
George Bell, lf, Tor	3	0	0	0	0	0
Matt Nokes, c, Det	2	0	0	0	0	0
Dave Winfield, rf-lf, NYA	5	0	1	0	1	0
Cal Ripken Jr., ss, Bal	2	0	1	0	0	0
Tony Fernandez, ss, Tor	2	0	0	0	0	1
Terry Kennedy, c, Bal	2	0	0	0	0	1
Dwight Evans, rf, Bos	2	0	2	0	1	0
Willie Randolph, 2b, NYA	1	0	0	0	0	0
Harold Reynolds, 2b, Sea	3	0	0	0	0	0
Bret Saberhagen, p, KC	0	0	0	0	0	0
Alan Trammell, ph, Det	1	0	0	0	0	0
Jack Morris, p, Det	0	0	0	0	0	0
Kirby Puckett, ph-cf, Min	4	0	0	0	0	3
TOTALS	42	0	6	0	5	7

	1	2	3	4	5	6	7	8	9	10	11	12	13	R	H	E
NL	0	0	0	0	0	0	0	0	0	0	0	0	2	2	8	2
AL	0	0	0	0	0	0	0	0	0	0	0	0	0	0	6	1

E—OSmith, Scott, McGwire. DP—NL 2 (Clark to OSmith; Hernandez to Brooks to Bedrosian to Virgil). LOB—NL 6, AL 11. Scoring Position—NL 1-for-6, AL 0-for-8. 2B—Dawson, Winfield. 3B—Raines. S—Reynolds, TFernandez, Nokes. SB—Raines. CS—Schmidt.

National League	IP	H	R	ER	BB	K
Mike Scott, Hou	2.0	1	0	0	0	1
Rick Sutcliffe, ChN	2.0	1	0	0	1	0
Orel Hershiser, LA	2.0	1	0	0	1	0
Rick Reuschel, Pit	1.1	1	0	0	0	1
John Franco, Cin	0.2	0	0	0	0	0
Steve Bedrosian, Phi	1.0	0	0	0	2	0
Lee Smith, ChN (W)	3.0	2	0	0	0	4
Sid Fernandez, NYN (S)	1.0	0	0	0	1	1

American League	IP	H	R	ER	BB	K
Bret Saberhagen, KC	3.0	1	0	0	0	0
Jack Morris, Det	2.0	1	0	0	1	2
Mark Langston, Sea	2.0	0	0	0	0	3
Dan Plesac, Mil	1.0	0	0	0	0	1
Dave Righetti, NYA	0.1	1	0	0	0	0
Tom Henke, Tor	2.2	2	0	0	0	1
Jay Howell, Oak (L)	2.0	3	2	2	0	3

Time—3:39. Attendance—49,671. Umpires—HP, Denkinger. 1B, Stello. 2B, Voltaggio. 3B, West.

July 12, 1988

Cincinnati (Riverfront Stadium)

The Americans beat the Nationals 2-1 in a game that featured only 11 base hits. The biggest one was a homer by Oakland catcher Terry Steinbach in the top of the third inning. Steinbach, who entered the game with a .217 batting average, clouted the circuit shot off NL starting pitcher Dwight Gooden. In the following frame, he hit a sacrifice fly to score Dave Winfield with the AL's only other run. Dennis Eckersley, one of five Oakland players to participate in the game, pitched a perfect ninth inning for a save.

American League	AB	R	H	RBI	BB	K
Rickey Henderson, cf, NYA	2	0	1	0	1	0
Carney Lansford, 3b, Oak	1	0	0	0	0	0
Paul Molitor, 2b, Mil	3	0	0	0	0	1
Kirby Puckett, cf, Min	1	0	0	0	0	0
Wade Boggs, 3b, Bos	3	0	1	0	0	0
Harold Reynolds, 2b, Sea	1	0	0	0	0	0
Jose Canseco, lf-rf, Oak	4	0	0	0	0	1
Dave Winfield, rf, NYA	3	1	1	0	0	0
Dave Stieb, p, Tor	0	0	0	0	0	0
Jeff Russell, p, Tex	0	0	0	0	0	0
Doug Jones, p, Cle	0	0	0	0	0	0
Dan Plesac, p, Mil	0	0	0	0	0	0
George Brett, ph, KC	1	0	0	0	0	0
Kurt Stillwell, ss, KC	0	0	0	0	0	0
Cal Ripken Jr., ss, Bal	3	0	0	0	1	0
Dennis Eckersley, p, Oak	0	0	0	0	0	0
Mark McGwire, 1b, Oak	2	0	1	0	0	1
Don Mattingly, 1b, NYA	2	0	0	0	0	0
Terry Steinbach, c, Oak	1	1	1	2	0	0
Mike Greenwell, lf, Bos	1	0	0	0	0	0
Frank Viola, p, Min	0	0	0	0	0	0
Gary Gaetti, ph, Min	1	0	0	0	0	0
Roger Clemens, p, Bos	0	0	0	0	0	0
Johnny Ray, ph, Cal	1	0	0	0	0	0
Mark Gubicza, p, KC	0	0	0	0	0	0
Tim Laudner, c, Min	1	0	1	0	0	0
TOTALS	31	2	6	2	2	3

National League	AB	R	H	RBI	BB	K
Vince Coleman, lf, StL	2	1	1	0	0	0
Andres Galarraga, 1b, Mon	2	0	0	0	0	1
Ryne Sandberg, 2b, ChN	4	0	1	0	0	2
Todd Worrell, p, StL	0	0	0	0	0	0
Andre Dawson, cf, ChN	2	0	1	0	0	0
Willie McGee, pr-cf, StL	2	0	0	0	0	0
Darryl Strawberry, rf, NYN	4	0	1	0	0	1
Bobby Bonilla, 3b, Pit	4	0	0	0	0	0
Will Clark, 1b, SF	2	0	0	0	0	0
David Cone, p, NYN	0	0	0	0	0	0
Barry Larkin, ss, Cin	2	0	0	0	0	1
Gary Carter, c, NYN	3	0	1	0	0	1
Chris Sabo, pr, Cin	0	0	0	0	0	0
Lance Parrish, c, Phi	1	0	0	0	0	0
Ozzie Smith, ss, StL	2	0	0	0	0	1
Kevin Gross, p, Phi	0	0	0	0	0	0
Mark Davis, p, SD	0	0	0	0	0	0
Bob Walk, p, Pit	0	0	0	0	0	0
Rafael Palmeiro, ph-lf, ChN	0	0	0	0	1	0
Dwight Gooden, p, NYN	0	0	0	0	0	0
Gerald Perry, ph, Atl	1	0	0	0	0	0
Bob Knepper, p, Hou	0	0	0	0	0	0
Andy Van Slyke, lf, Pit	2	0	0	0	0	0
Orel Hershiser, p, LA	0	0	0	0	0	0
Vance Law, 2b, ChN	0	0	0	0	0	0
TOTALS	33	1	5	0	1	7

	1	2	3	4	5	6	7	8	9	R	H	E
AL	0	0	1	1	0	0	0	0	0	2	6	2
NL	0	0	0	1	0	0	0	0	0	1	5	0

E—Mattingly, Steinbach. DP—NL 1 (Clark to Smith). LOB—AL 5, NL 6. Scoring Position—AL 1-for-4, NL 0-for-5. 2B—Winfield, Laudner. HR—Steinbach. SF—Steinbach. GDP—Molitor. SB—Coleman, Sabo.

American League	IP	H	R	ER	BB	K
Frank Viola, Min (W)	2.0	0	0	0	0	1
Roger Clemens, Bos	1.0	0	0	0	0	1
Mark Gubicza, KC	2.0	3	1	1	0	2
Dave Stieb, Tor	1.0	1	0	0	0	0
Jeff Russell, Tex	1.0	1	0	0	1	0
Doug Jones, Cle	0.2	0	0	0	0	1
Dan Plesac, Mil	0.1	0	0	0	0	1
Dennis Eckersley, Oak (S)	1.0	0	0	0	0	1

National League	IP	H	R	ER	BB	K
Dwight Gooden, NYN (L)	3.0	3	1	1	1	1
Bob Knepper, Hou	1.0	2	1	1	1	0
David Cone, NYN	1.0	0	0	0	0	1
Kevin Gross, Phi	1.0	0	0	0	0	1
Mark Davis, SD	0.2	1	0	0	0	0
Bob Walk, Pit	0.1	0	0	0	0	0
Orel Hershiser, LA	1.0	0	0	0	0	0
Todd Worrell, StL	1.0	0	0	0	0	0

Balk—Gooden. WP—Gubicza. Time—2:26. Attendance—55,837. Umpires—HP, Pulli. 1B, Barnett. 2B, Tata. 3B, Ford.

July 11, 1989

Anaheim (Anaheim Stadium)

Bo Jackson might not have been the most well-suited hitter in the world to handle the AL's leadoff duties, but he made manager Tony La Russa look like a genius for batting him first when he led off the bottom of the first inning with a home run. Wade Boggs followed with another longball, which tied the game after the NL had scored a pair in the top of the first. In the very next inning, Jackson's RBI groundout gave the AL a lead it would never relinquish. Forty-two-year-old Nolan Ryan became the oldest pitcher in history to win an All-Star Game, striking out three in two scoreless innings. For the first time, the DH was used in All-Star Game play.

National League	AB	R	H	RBI	BB	K
Ozzie Smith, ss, StL	4	0	1	0	0	0
Tony Gwynn, rf, SD	2	1	1	0	1	1
Andre Dawson, rf, ChN	1	0	0	0	0	0
Will Clark, 1b, SF	2	0	0	0	0	1
Glenn Davis, 1b, Hou	1	1	1	0	1	0
Kevin Mitchell, lf, SF	4	1	2	1	0	2
Vince Coleman, pr-lf, StL	0	0	0	0	0	0
Eric Davis, cf, Cin	2	0	0	0	1	0
Von Hayes, cf, Phi	1	0	1	1	0	0
Howard Johnson, 3b, NYN	3	0	1	1	0	1
Tim Wallach, 3b, Mon	1	0	0	0	0	0
Pedro Guerrero, dh, StL	2	0	0	0	0	0
Bobby Bonilla, ph-dh, Pit	2	0	2	0	0	0
Ryne Sandberg, 2b, ChN	3	0	0	0	0	2
Willie Randolph, 2b, LA	1	0	0	0	0	0
Benito Santiago, c, SD	1	0	0	0	0	1
Mike Scioscia, c, LA	1	0	0	0	0	0
Tony Pena, ph-c, StL	2	0	0	0	0	0
TOTALS	33	3	9	3	3	8

American League	AB	R	H	RBI	BB	K
Bo Jackson, lf, KC	4	1	2	2	0	1
Mike Greenwell, lf, Bos	0	0	0	0	0	0
Wade Boggs, 3b, Bos	3	1	1	1	0	0
Gary Gaetti, 3b, Min	1	0	0	0	0	1
Kirby Puckett, cf, Min	3	1	1	0	0	0
Devon White, cf, Cal	1	0	0	0	0	0
Harold Baines, dh, ChA	3	1	1	1	0	1
Jeffrey Leonard, ph-dh, Sea	1	0	0	0	0	1
Julio Franco, 2b, Tex	3	0	1	0	0	0
Don Mattingly, 1b, NYA	1	0	1	0	0	0
Cal Ripken Jr., ss, Bal	3	0	1	0	0	0
Tony Fernandez, pr-ss, Tor	1	0	0	0	0	0
Ruben Sierra, rf, Tex	3	1	2	1	1	0
Mark McGwire, 1b, Oak	3	0	1	0	0	0
Steve Sax, 2b, NYA	1	0	0	0	0	0
Terry Steinbach, c, Oak	3	0	1	0	0	0
Mickey Tettleton, c, Bal	1	0	0	0	0	1
TOTALS	35	5	12	5	1	5

	1	2	3	4	5	6	7	8	9	R	H	E
NL	2	0	0	0	0	0	0	1	0	3	9	1
AL	2	1	2	0	0	0	0	0	x	5	12	0

E—Santiago. DP—AL 1 (Fernandez to Sax to Mattingly). LOB—NL 6, AL 7. Scoring Position—NL 3-for-8, AL 2-for-11. 2B—Ripken Jr., Mattingly. HR—Jackson, Boggs. GDP—EDavis, Pena. SB—Gwynn, EDavis, Johnson, Jackson. CS—Smith.

National League	IP	H	R	ER	BB	K
Rick Reuschel, SF	1.0	3	2	2	0	0
John Smoltz, Atl (L)	1.0	2	1	1	0	0
Rick Sutcliffe, ChN	1.0	4	2	2	0	0
Tim Burke, Mon	2.0	2	0	0	0	1
Mark Davis, SD	1.0	0	0	0	0	2
Jay Howell, LA	1.0	1	0	0	0	1
Mitch Williams, ChN	1.0	0	0	0	1	1

American League	IP	H	R	ER	BB	K
Dave Stewart, Oak	1.0	3	2	2	2	0
Nolan Ryan, Tex (W)	2.0	1	0	0	0	3
Mark Gubicza, KC	1.0	0	0	0	0	1
Mike Moore, Oak	1.0	0	0	0	0	1
Greg Swindell, Cle	1.2	2	0	0	0	3
Jeff Russell, Tex	1.0	1	1	1	1	0
Dan Plesac, Mil	0.0	1	0	0	0	0
Doug Jones, Cle (S)	1.1	1	0	0	0	0

Plesac pitched to one batter in the 8th.

WP—Sutcliffe. Time—2:48. Attendance—64,036. Umpires—HP, Evans. 1B, Engle. 2B, Cooney. 3B, Crawford.

July 10, 1990
Chicago (Wrigley Field)

The American League held the National League to two hits en route to a 2-0 victory. The game was scoreless until Julio Franco hit a two-run double off Rob Dibble in the seventh inning to account for the game's only runs. Six AL hurlers combined to blank the NL on two hits and two walks, retiring 16 NL hitters in a row at one point. The rainy, windy conditions turned Wrigley Field into a pitcher's paradise. Franco's decisive blow followed a 68-minute rain delay. The AL won its third straight All-Star Game, something it hadn't done in over 40 years.

American League	AB	R	H	RBI	BB	K
Rickey Henderson, lf, Oak	3	0	0	0	0	1
Ozzie Guillen, ss, ChA	2	0	0	0	0	0
Wade Boggs, 3b, Bos	2	0	2	0	1	0
Kelly Gruber, pr-3b, Tor	1	0	0	0	1	0
Jose Canseco, rf, Oak	4	0	0	0	1	1
Cal Ripken Jr., ss, Bal	2	0	0	0	0	0
George Bell, ph-lf, Tor	2	0	0	0	0	1
Ken Griffey Jr., cf, Sea	2	0	0	0	1	0
Kirby Puckett, ph-cf, Min	1	0	1	0	0	0
Mark McGwire, 1b, Oak	2	0	0	0	0	2
Cecil Fielder, ph-1b, Det	1	0	0	0	1	0
Sandy Alomar Jr., c, Cle	3	1	2	0	0	0
Bobby Thigpen, p, ChA	0	0	0	0	0	0
Alan Trammell, ph, Det	1	0	0	0	0	0
Chuck Finley, p, Cal	0	0	0	0	0	0
Dennis Eckersley, p, Oak	0	0	0	0	0	0
Steve Sax, 2b, NYA	1	0	0	0	1	0
Bret Saberhagen, p, KC	0	0	0	0	0	0
Lance Parrish, ph-c, Cal	1	1	1	0	1	0
Bob Welch, p, Oak	0	0	0	0	0	0
Brook Jacoby, ph, Cle	1	0	0	0	0	0
Dave Stieb, p, Tor	0	0	0	0	0	0
Julio Franco, ph-2b, Tex	3	0	1	2	0	0
TOTALS	32	2	7	2	7	5

National League	AB	R	H	RBI	BB	K
Lenny Dykstra, cf, Phi	4	0	1	0	0	0
Ryne Sandberg, 2b, ChN	3	0	0	0	0	0
Roberto Alomar, 2b, SD	1	0	0	0	0	0
Will Clark, 1b, SF	3	0	1	0	0	0
Randy Myers, p, Cin	0	0	0	0	0	0
John Franco, p, NYN	0	0	0	0	0	0
Matt Williams, ph, SF	1	0	0	0	0	1
Kevin Mitchell, lf, SF	2	0	0	0	0	1
Frank Viola, p, NYN	0	0	0	0	0	0
Tim Wallach, 3b, Mon	2	0	0	0	0	0
Andre Dawson, rf, ChN	2	0	0	0	0	1
Darryl Strawberry, rf, NYN	1	0	0	0	0	1
Chris Sabo, 3b, Cin	2	0	0	0	0	0
Dave Smith, p, Hou	0	0	0	0	0	0
Jeff Brantley, p, SF	0	0	0	0	0	0
Rob Dibble, p, Cin	0	0	0	0	0	0
Bobby Bonilla, 1b, Pit	1	0	0	0	0	0
Mike Scioscia, c, LA	2	0	0	0	0	1
Greg Olson, ph-c, Atl	1	0	0	0	0	1
Ozzie Smith, ss, StL	1	0	0	0	0	0
Dennis Martinez, p, Mon	0	0	0	0	0	0
Barry Bonds, lf, Pit	1	0	0	0	1	0
Jack Armstrong, p, Cin	0	0	0	0	0	0
Ramon Martinez, p, LA	0	0	0	0	0	0
Tony Gwynn, ph, SD	0	0	0	0	1	0
Barry Larkin, pr-ss, Cin	0	0	0	0	0	0
Shawon Dunston, ss, ChN	2	0	0	0	0	0
TOTALS	29	0	2	0	2	6

	1 2 3	4 5 6	7 8 9	R	H	E
AL	0 0 0	0 0 0	2 0 0	2	7	0
NL	0 0 0	0 0 0	0 0 0	0	2	1

E—Strawberry. DP—NL 2 (Sandberg to Larkin to Clark; Strawberry to Scioscia). LOB—AL 10, NL 4. Scoring Position—AL 1-for-10, NL 0-for-1. 2B—JuFranco. GDP—Sax. SB—Canseco, Sax, Larkin, Gruber 2.

American League	IP	H	R	ER	BB	K
Bob Welch, Oak	2.0	1	0	0	0	1
Dave Stieb, Tor	2.0	0	0	0	1	1
Bret Saberhagen, KC (W)	2.0	0	0	0	0	1
Bobby Thigpen, ChA	1.0	0	0	0	0	1
Chuck Finley, Cal	1.0	0	0	0	1	1
Dennis Eckersley, Oak (S)	1.0	1	0	0	0	1

National League	IP	H	R	ER	BB	K
Jack Armstrong, Cin	2.0	1	0	0	0	2
Ramon Martinez, LA	1.0	0	0	0	2	1
Dennis Martinez, Mon	1.0	0	0	0	0	1
Frank Viola, NYN	1.0	1	0	0	0	0
Dave Smith, Hou	0.2	1	0	0	2	1
Jeff Brantley, SF (L)	0.1	2	2	2	0	0
Rob Dibble, Cin	1.0	1	0	0	1	0
Randy Myers, Cin	1.0	1	0	0	2	0
John Franco, NYN	1.0	0	0	0	0	0

Brantley pitched to two batters in the 7th.

Time—2:53. Attendance—39,071. Umpires—HP, Montague. 1B, Phillips. 2B, Rippley. 3B, Johnson.

July 9, 1991
Toronto (SkyDome)

Cal Ripken launched a three-run homer off ex-teammate Dennis Martinez to lead the AL to a 4-2 victory. Andre Dawson homered off Roger Clemens in the fourth inning, his first RBI in eight All-Star appearances, but for the most part, NL bats remained unable to solve AL pitching. Bobby Bonilla's first-inning RBI single off the ankle of Jack Morris accounted for the only other NL run. Harold Baines drove in a run for the AL with a seventh-inning sacrifice fly, and Ken Griffey Jr. had two singles in three at-bats. Montreal's Dennis Martinez took the loss for the NL, while another Canadian club's representative, Toronto's Jimmy Key, picked up the victory for the AL.

National League	AB	R	H	RBI	BB	K
Tony Gwynn, cf, SD	4	1	2	0	0	0
Brett Butler, pr-cf, LA	1	0	0	0	0	0
Ryne Sandberg, 2b, ChN	3	0	1	0	0	0
Juan Samuel, 2b, LA	1	0	1	0	0	0
Will Clark, 1b, SF	2	0	1	0	1	0
Eddie Murray, 1b, LA	1	0	0	0	0	1
Bobby Bonilla, dh, Pit	4	0	2	1	0	1
Andre Dawson, rf, ChN	2	1	1	1	0	0
Felix Jose, rf, StL	2	0	1	0	0	0
Ivan Calderon, lf, Mon	2	0	1	0	0	0
Paul O'Neill, ph-lf, Cin	2	0	0	0	0	1
Chris Sabo, 3b, Cin	2	0	0	0	0	0
Howard Johnson, ph-3b, NYN	2	0	0	0	0	1
Benito Santiago, c, SD	3	0	0	0	0	1
Craig Biggio, c, Hou	1	0	0	0	0	0
Ozzie Smith, ss, StL	1	0	0	0	1	0
Barry Larkin, ss, Cin	1	0	0	0	0	0
George Bell, ph, ChN	1	0	0	0	0	1
TOTALS	35	2	10	2	2	6

American League	AB	R	H	RBI	BB	K
Rickey Henderson, lf, Oak	2	1	1	0	0	0
Joe Carter, lf, Tor	1	1	1	0	1	0
Wade Boggs, 3b, Bos	2	1	1	0	1	0
Paul Molitor, ph-3b, Mil	0	0	0	0	0	0
Cal Ripken Jr., ss, Bal	3	1	2	3	0	0
Ozzie Guillen, ph-ss, ChA	0	0	0	0	0	0
Cecil Fielder, 1b, Det	3	0	0	0	0	1
Rafael Palmeiro, ph-1b, Tex	0	0	0	0	1	0
Danny Tartabull, dh, KC	2	0	0	0	0	1
Harold Baines, ph-dh, Oak	1	0	0	1	0	0
Dave Henderson, rf, Oak	2	0	0	0	0	1
Ruben Sierra, ph-rf, Tex	2	0	0	0	0	2
Ken Griffey Jr., cf, Sea	3	0	2	0	0	0
Kirby Puckett, cf, Min	1	0	0	0	0	0
Sandy Alomar Jr., c, Cle	2	0	0	0	0	0
Carlton Fisk, c, ChA	2	0	1	0	0	1
Roberto Alomar, 2b, Tor	4	0	0	0	0	0
TOTALS	30	4	8	4	3	6

	1 2 3	4 5 6	7 8 9	R	H	E
NL	1 0 0	1 0 0	0 0 0	2	10	0
AL	0 0 3	0 0 0	1 0 x	4	8	0

DP—AL 2 (Boggs to Alomar to Fielder; Boggs to Alomar to Fielder). LOB—NL 8, AL 8. Scoring Position—NL 1-for-10, AL 1-for-5. 2B—Sandberg. HR—Dawson, Ripken Jr. S—Guillen. SF—Baines. GDP—Gwynn, Dawson. SB—Calderon.

National League	IP	H	R	ER	BB	K
Tom Glavine, Atl	2.0	1	0	0	1	3
Dennis Martinez, Mon (L)	2.0	4	3	3	0	0
Frank Viola, NYN	1.0	0	0	0	1	0
Pete Harnisch, Hou	1.0	2	0	0	0	1
John Smiley, Pit	0.0	1	1	1	0	0
Rob Dibble, Cin	1.0	0	0	0	1	1
Mike Morgan, LA	1.0	0	0	0	0	1

American League	IP	H	R	ER	BB	K
Jack Morris, Min	2.0	4	1	1	0	1
Jimmy Key, Tor (W)	1.0	1	0	0	0	1
Roger Clemens, Bos	1.0	1	1	1	0	0
Jack McDowell, ChA	2.0	1	0	0	2	0
Jeff Reardon, Bos	0.2	1	0	0	0	0
Rick Aguilera, Min	1.1	2	0	0	0	3
Dennis Eckersley, Oak (S)	1.0	0	0	0	0	1

Smiley pitched to two batters in the 7th.

Reached, Catcher's Interference—Molitor by Biggio. Time—3:04. Attendance—52,383. Umpires—HP, Brinkman. 1B, McSherry. 2B, Kaiser. 3B, Quick.

July 14, 1992
San Diego (Jack Murphy Stadium)

The American League beat up on National League starter Tom Glavine on the way to a decisive 13-6 victory. The Junior Circuit notched its baker's dozen by way of 19 base hits. The first five AL pitchers tossed a scoreless inning each as the AL scoring machine broke into double figures before the NL even got on the board.

American League	AB	R	H	RBI	BB	K
Roberto Alomar, 2b, Tor	3	1	1	0	0	0
Carlos Baerga, 2b, Cle	1	1	1	1	0	0
Charles Nagy, p, Cle	1	1	1	0	0	0
Jeff Montgomery, p, KC	0	0	0	0	0	0
Rick Aguilera, p, Min	1	0	0	0	0	1
Dennis Eckersley, p, Oak	0	0	0	0	0	0
Wade Boggs, 3b, Bos	3	1	1	0	0	1
Robin Ventura, 3b, ChA	2	1	2	1	0	0
Kirby Puckett, lf, Min	3	1	1	0	0	1
Roger Clemens, p, Bos	0	0	0	0	0	0
Ruben Sierra, rf, Tex	2	2	1	2	0	0
Joe Carter, rf, Tor	3	1	2	1	0	0
Travis Fryman, ss, Det	1	1	1	1	1	0
Mark McGwire, 1b, Oak	3	1	1	2	0	0
Paul Molitor, ph-1b, Mil	2	0	1	0	0	1
Cal Ripken Jr., ss, Bal	3	0	1	1	0	0
Mike Mussina, p, Bal	0	0	0	0	0	0
Roberto Kelly, cf, NYA	2	0	1	2	0	1
Ken Griffey Jr., cf, Sea	3	2	3	2	0	0
Ivan Rodriguez, c, Tex	2	0	0	0	0	1
Sandy Alomar Jr., c, Cle	3	0	1	0	0	0
Mark Langston, p, Cal	0	0	0	0	0	0
Chuck Knoblauch, ph-2b, Min	1	0	0	0	1	0
Kevin Brown, p, Tex	1	0	0	0	0	1
Jack McDowell, p, ChA	0	0	0	0	0	0
Edgar Martinez, ph, Sea	1	0	0	0	0	0
Juan Guzman, p, Tor	0	0	0	0	0	0
Brady Anderson, lf, Bal	3	0	0	0	0	0
TOTALS	44	13	19	13	2	7

National League	AB	R	H	RBI	BB	K
Ozzie Smith, ss, StL	3	0	1	0	0	1
Tony Fernandez, ss, SD	2	1	1	0	0	0
Tony Gwynn, rf, SD	2	0	0	0	1	0
John Kruk, rf, Phi	2	1	2	0	0	0
Barry Bonds, lf, Pit	3	1	1	0	0	0
Bip Roberts, lf, Cin	2	1	2	2	0	0
Fred McGriff, 1b, SD	3	0	2	1	0	0
Dennis Martinez, p, Mon	0	0	0	0	0	0
Doug Jones, p, Hou	0	0	0	0	0	0
Tom Pagnozzi, ph, StL	1	0	0	0	0	0
Norm Charlton, p, Cin	1	0	0	0	0	1
Terry Pendleton, 3b, Atl	2	0	1	0	0	0
Bob Tewksbury, p, StL	0	0	0	0	0	0
John Smoltz, p, Atl	0	0	0	0	0	0
Will Clark, ph-1b, SF	2	1	1	3	0	1
Andy Van Slyke, cf, Pit	2	0	0	0	0	0
Ron Gant, ph-cf, Atl	2	0	0	0	0	0
Ryne Sandberg, 2b, ChN	2	0	0	0	0	1
Craig Biggio, 2b, Hou	2	0	0	0	0	1
Benito Santiago, c, SD	1	0	0	0	0	1
Darren Daulton, c, Phi	3	1	0	0	0	0
Tom Glavine, p, Atl	0	0	0	0	0	0
Greg Maddux, p, ChN	0	0	0	0	0	0
Larry Walker, ph, Mon	1	0	1	0	0	0
David Cone, p, NYN	0	0	0	0	0	0
Gary Sheffield, 3b, SD	2	0	0	0	0	0
Mike Sharperson, 3b, LA	1	0	0	0	0	1
TOTALS	39	6	12	6	1	7

	1 2 3	4 5 6	7 8 9	R	H	E
AL	4 1 1	0 0 4	0 3 0	13	19	1
NL	1 0 0	0 0 1	0 3 2	6	12	1

E—Molitor, Kruk. DP—AL 1 (Baerga to Ripken Jr. to McGwire). LOB—AL 6, NL 7. Scoring Position—AL 10-for-17, NL 4-for-9. 2B—Griffey Jr., OSmith, Bonds, Baerga, Ventura, Kelly. HR—Griffey Jr., Sierra, Clark. GDP—Van Slyke. SB—RAlomar 2.

American League	IP	H	R	ER	BB	K
Kevin Brown, Tex (W)	1.0	0	0	0	0	1
Jack McDowell, ChA	1.0	0	0	0	0	0
Juan Guzman, Tor	1.0	2	0	0	1	2
Roger Clemens, Bos	1.0	2	0	0	0	0
Mike Mussina, Bal	1.0	0	0	0	0	0
Mark Langston, Cal	1.0	2	1	1	0	1
Charles Nagy, Cle	1.0	0	0	0	0	1
Jeff Montgomery, KC	0.2	2	2	2	0	0
Rick Aguilera, Min	0.2	1	1	1	0	0
Dennis Eckersley, Oak	0.2	3	2	0	0	2

National League	IP	H	R	ER	BB	K
Tom Glavine, Atl (L)	1.2	9	5	5	0	2
Greg Maddux, ChN	1.1	1	1	1	0	0
David Cone, NYN	1.0	0	0	0	0	1
Bob Tewksbury, StL	1.2	4	4	4	1	0
John Smoltz, Atl	0.1	0	0	0	0	0
Dennis Martinez, Mon	1.0	0	0	0	1	1
Doug Jones, Hou	1.0	4	3	3	0	2
Norm Charlton, Cin	1.0	0	0	0	0	1

Time—2:55. Attendance—59,372. Umpires—HP, Harvey. 1B, Garcia. 2B, Wendelstedt. 3B, Kosc.

July 13, 1993
Baltimore (Camden Yards)

The relentless American League squad scored against five different National League pitchers en route to a 9-3 triumph. Gary Sheffield hit a two-run homer in the first inning, and Barry Bonds doubled twice and scored a pair of runs, but the rest of the Nationals combined for only three hits. Randy Johnson tossed two hitless innings for the AL, and fanned John Kruk in one of the most memorable All-Star at-bats ever. After Johnson's first pitch to Kruk sailed over the batter's head to the backstop, Kruk decided it was in his best interests to find a way out of the batter's box as quickly as possible. He accomplished that by flailing weakly at the next three pitches while striding toward the dugout and out of harm's way. On the third strike, he took one big step as he swung and just kept walking. Kirby Puckett led the AL stars with a homer and an RBI double.

National League	AB	R	H	RBI	BB	K
Marquis Grissom, cf, Mon	3	0	0	0	0	1
Roberto Kelly, cf, Cin	1	0	0	0	0	1
Barry Bonds, lf, SF	3	2	2	0	0	0
Bobby Bonilla, lf, NYN	1	0	1	0	0	0
Gary Sheffield, 3b, Fla	3	1	2	2	0	0
Dave Hollins, 3b, Phi	1	0	1	0	0	0
John Kruk, 1b, Phi	3	0	0	0	0	2
Andres Galarraga, 1b, Col	1	0	0	0	0	0
Barry Larkin, ss, Cin	2	0	0	1	0	1
Jeff Blauser, ss, Atl	1	0	0	0	0	1
Mark Grace, dh, ChN	3	0	0	0	0	0
Gregg Jefferies, ph, StL	1	0	0	0	0	1
David Justice, rf, Atl	3	0	1	0	0	0
Tony Gwynn, rf, SD	1	0	0	0	0	0
Darren Daulton, c, Phi	3	0	0	0	0	1
Mike Piazza, c, LA	1	0	0	0	0	1
Ryne Sandberg, 2b, ChN	1	0	0	0	1	0
Jay Bell, 2b, Pit	1	0	0	0	0	0
TOTALS	33	3	7	3	1	9

American League	AB	R	H	RBI	BB	K
Roberto Alomar, 2b, Tor	3	1	1	1	0	0
Carlos Baerga, 2b, Cle	2	1	0	0	0	1
Paul Molitor, dh, Tor	1	0	0	0	1	0
Albert Belle, ph-dh, Cle	1	2	1	1	1	0
Frank Thomas, ph-dh, ChA	1	0	1	0	0	0
Ken Griffey Jr., cf, Sea	3	1	1	1	0	1
Devon White, cf, Tor	2	1	1	1	0	0
Joe Carter, rf, Tor	3	0	1	0	0	1
Juan Gonzalez, rf, Tex	1	0	0	0	1	1
John Olerud, 1b, Tor	2	0	0	0	0	0
Cecil Fielder, 1b, Det	1	0	0	0	0	0
Kirby Puckett, lf, Min	3	1	2	2	0	0
Greg Vaughn, lf, Mil	1	1	1	0	0	0
Cal Ripken Jr., ss, Bal	3	0	0	0	0	1
Travis Fryman, ss, Det	1	0	0	0	0	0
Wade Boggs, 3b, NYA	1	0	0	0	1	0
Scott Cooper, 3b, Bos	2	0	0	0	0	1
Ivan Rodriguez, c, Tex	2	1	1	0	0	0
Terry Steinbach, c, Oak	2	0	1	1	0	1
TOTALS	35	9	11	7	4	7

	1 2 3	4 5 6	7 8 9	R	H	E
NL	2 0 0	0 0 1	0 0 0	3	7	2
AL	0 1 1	0 3 3	1 0 x	9	11	0

E—Blauser, Justice. LOB—NL 5, AL 7. Scoring Position—NL 2-for-6, AL 4-for-9. 2B—Bonds 2, Puckett, Rodriguez, White, Steinbach, Hollins. HR—Sheffield, Alomar, Puckett. SF—Larkin. SB—White.

National League	IP	H	R	ER	BB	K
Terry Mulholland, Phi	2.0	1	1	1	2	0
Andy Benes, SD	2.0	2	1	1	0	2
John Burkett, SF (L)	0.2	4	3	3	0	1
Steve Avery, Atl	1.0	1	3	0	1	1
John Smoltz, Atl	0.1	0	0	0	1	0
Rod Beck, SF	1.0	2	1	1	0	1
Bryan Harvey, Fla	1.0	1	0	0	0	2

American League	IP	H	R	ER	BB	K
Mark Langston, Cal	2.0	3	2	2	1	2
Randy Johnson, Sea	2.0	0	0	0	0	1
Jack McDowell, ChA (W)	1.0	0	0	0	0	0
Jimmy Key, NYA	1.0	2	1	1	0	1
Jeff Montgomery, KC	1.0	0	0	0	0	1
Rick Aguilera, Min	1.0	2	0	0	0	2
Duane Ward, Tor	1.0	0	0	0	0	2

WP—Smoltz 2. HBP—Fielder by Burkett. Time—2:49. Attendance—48,147. Umpires—HP, McKean. 1B, Davidson. 2B, Reilly. 3B, Darling.

July 12, 1994
Pittsburgh (Three Rivers Stadium)

Fred McGriff saved the NL from defeat with a game-tying, pinch-hit two-run homer in the bottom of the ninth, and Moises Alou doubled in Tony Gwynn in the bottom of the 10th to give the NL an 8-7 comeback victory. There were 27 hits in the game, including two by Gwynn, who scored twice and drove in two runs.

American League	AB	R	H	RBI	BB	K
Roberto Alomar, 2b, Tor	3	1	1	0	0	0
Chuck Knoblauch, 2b, Min	3	1	0	0	0	2
Wade Boggs, 3b, NYA	3	1	1	0	0	2
Scott Cooper, 3b, Bos	2	1	1	1	0	0
Ken Griffey Jr., cf, Sea	3	0	2	1	0	0
Kenny Lofton, cf, Cle	2	0	1	2	0	1
Frank Thomas, 1b, ChA	2	1	2	1	1	0
Will Clark, 1b, Tex	2	0	2	0	0	0
Joe Carter, lf, Tor	3	1	0	0	0	0
Albert Belle, lf, Cle	2	0	0	0	0	0
Kirby Puckett, rf, Min	3	0	1	1	0	0
Ruben Sierra, rf, Oak	2	0	1	0	0	0
Cal Ripken Jr., ss, Bal	5	0	1	0	0	2
Ivan Rodriguez, c, Tex	5	1	2	0	0	1
Jimmy Key, p, NYA	0	0	0	0	0	0
Paul Molitor, ph, Tor	1	0	0	0	0	0
David Cone, p, KC	0	0	0	0	0	0
Chili Davis, ph, Cal	1	0	0	0	0	0
Mike Mussina, p, Bal	0	0	0	0	0	0
Randy Johnson, p, Sea	0	0	0	0	0	0
Mickey Tettleton, ph, Det	0	0	0	0	1	0
Pat Hentgen, p, Tor	0	0	0	0	0	0
Paul O'Neill, ph, NYA	1	0	0	0	0	0
Wilson Alvarez, p, ChA	0	0	0	0	0	0
Lee Smith, p, Bal	0	0	0	0	0	0
Travis Fryman, ph, Det	1	0	0	0	0	0
Jason Bere, p, ChA	0	0	0	0	0	0
TOTALS	44	7	15	6	2	8

National League	AB	R	H	RBI	BB	K
Gregg Jefferies, 1b, StL	1	2	1	0	0	0
Ken Hill, p, Mon	0	0	0	0	0	0
Dante Bichette, ph, Col	1	0	1	0	0	0
Doug Drabek, p, Hou	0	0	0	0	0	0
John Hudek, p, Hou	0	0	0	0	0	0
Danny Jackson, p, Phi	0	0	0	0	0	0
Wil Cordero, ss, Mon	2	0	0	0	0	0
Tony Gwynn, cf-rf, SD	5	2	2	2	0	0
Barry Bonds, lf, SF	3	0	0	1	0	2
Moises Alou, lf, Mon	1	0	1	1	0	0
Mike Piazza, c, LA	4	0	1	1	0	0
Darrin Fletcher, c, Mon	0	0	0	0	0	0
Matt Williams, 3b, SF	3	0	0	0	0	2
Ken Caminiti, 3b, Hou	1	0	0	0	0	0
David Justice, rf, Atl	2	0	0	0	0	0
Marquis Grissom, cf, Mon	1	1	1	1	1	0
Mariano Duncan, 2b, Phi	1	0	0	0	0	0
Carlos Garcia, 2b, Pit	2	0	1	0	0	0
Craig Biggio, 2b, Hou	1	1	0	0	0	0
Ozzie Smith, ss, StL	3	0	1	0	0	0
Rod Beck, p, SF	0	0	0	0	0	0
Randy Myers, p, ChN	0	0	0	0	0	0
Fred McGriff, ph-1b, Atl	1	1	1	2	0	0
Greg Maddux, p, Atl	0	0	0	0	0	0
Jeff Bagwell, ph-1b, Hou	4	1	2	0	0	1
Doug Jones, p, Phi	0	0	0	0	0	0
TOTALS	36	8	12	8	1	5

	1 2 3	4 5 6	7 8 9	10	R	H	E
AL	1 0 0	0 0 3	3 0 0	0	7	15	0
NL	1 0 3	0 0 1	0 0 2	1	8	12	1

E—Williams. DP—AL 1 (Ripken Jr. to Clark), NL 1 (Maddux to Jefferies). LOB—AL 9, NL 4. Scoring Position—AL 5-for-14, NL 2-for-4. 2B—Griffey Jr., Ripken Jr., Jefferies, Gwynn, Cooper, Alou. HR—Grissom, McGriff. SF—Bonds. GDP—Cordero. SB—RAlomar, Lofton, Clark.

American League	IP	H	R	ER	BB	K
Jimmy Key, NYA	2.0	1	1	1	0	1
David Cone, KC	2.0	4	3	3	0	3
Mike Mussina, Bal	1.0	1	0	0	0	1
Randy Johnson, Sea	1.0	2	1	1	0	0
Pat Hentgen, Tor	1.0	1	0	0	0	0
Wilson Alvarez, ChA	1.0	0	0	0	0	0
Lee Smith, Bal (BS)	1.0	1	2	2	1	0
Jason Bere, ChA (L)	0.0	2	1	1	0	0

National League	IP	H	R	ER	BB	K
Greg Maddux, Atl	3.0	3	1	1	0	2
Ken Hill, Mon	2.0	0	0	0	1	0
Doug Drabek, Hou (BS)	0.2	4	3	1	0	1
John Hudek, Hou	0.2	1	2	2	1	1
Danny Jackson, Phi (BS)	0.0	3	1	1	0	0
Rod Beck, SF	1.2	1	0	0	0	1
Randy Myers, ChN	1.0	1	0	0	0	1
Doug Jones, Phi (W)	1.0	2	0	0	0	2

Jackson pitched to three batters in the 7th. Bere pitched to two batters in the 10th.

HBP—Jefferies by Cone. Time—3:14. Attendance—59,568. Umpires—HP, Runge. 1B, Shulock. 2B, Layne. 3B, Roe.

July 11, 1995
Texas (The Ballpark at Arlington)

Jeff Conine, the only NL position player not to appear in the preceding year's All-Star Game, entered the game in the eighth inning with the score tied 2-2. He made the most of his long-awaited opportunity, blasting a home run into the left-field seats to provide the margin of victory in the Senior Circuit's 3-2 win. Conine's shot was one of only three hits by the NL -- each of them home runs. Craig Biggio and Mike Piazza also parked round-trippers. Randy Johnson, Kevin Appier and Dennis Martinez combined to no-hit the NL for 5.2 innings before Biggio's blast with two outs in the sixth. Carlos Baerga went 3-for-3 with a run scored for the AL.

National League	AB	R	H	RBI	BB	K
Lenny Dykstra, cf, Phi	2	0	0	0	1	0
Sammy Sosa, cf, ChN	1	0	0	0	0	0
Tony Gwynn, rf, SD	2	0	0	0	0	0
Reggie Sanders, rf, Cin	1	0	0	0	0	1
Raul Mondesi, rf, LA	1	0	0	0	0	0
Barry Bonds, lf, SF	3	0	0	0	0	1
Dante Bichette, lf, Col	1	0	0	0	0	1
Mike Piazza, c, LA	3	1	1	1	0	0
Darren Daulton, c, Phi	0	0	0	0	0	0
Fred McGriff, 1b, Atl	3	0	0	0	0	2
Mark Grace, 1b, ChN	0	0	0	0	0	0
Ron Gant, dh, Cin	2	0	0	0	0	1
Jeff Conine, ph-dh, Fla	1	1	1	1	0	0
Barry Larkin, ss, Cin	3	0	0	0	0	0
Jose Offerman, ss, LA	0	0	0	0	0	0
Vinny Castilla, 3b, Col	2	0	0	0	0	1
Bobby Bonilla, 3b, NYN	1	0	0	0	0	1
Craig Biggio, 2b, Hou	2	1	1	1	0	0
Mickey Morandini, 2b, Phi	1	0	0	0	0	1
TOTALS	29	3	3	3	1	9

American League	AB	R	H	RBI	BB	K
Kenny Lofton, cf, Cle	3	0	0	0	0	1
Jim Edmonds, ph-cf, Cal	1	0	0	0	0	1
Carlos Baerga, 2b, Cle	3	1	3	0	0	0
Roberto Alomar, pr-2b, Tor	1	0	0	0	0	0
Edgar Martinez, dh, Sea	3	0	0	0	0	1
Tino Martinez, ph-dh, Sea	1	0	1	0	0	0
Frank Thomas, 1b, ChA	2	1	1	2	0	0
Mo Vaughn, 1b, Bos	2	0	0	0	0	2
Albert Belle, lf, Cle	3	0	0	0	0	1
Paul O'Neill, lf, NYA	1	0	0	0	0	0
Cal Ripken Jr., ss, Bal	3	0	2	0	0	0
Gary DiSarcina, pr-ss, Cal	1	0	0	0	0	0
Wade Boggs, 3b, NYA	2	0	1	0	0	0
Kevin Seitzer, ph-3b, Mil	2	0	0	0	0	0
Kirby Puckett, rf, Min	2	0	0	0	0	1
Manny Ramirez, ph-rf, Cle	0	0	0	0	2	0
Ivan Rodriguez, c, Tex	3	0	0	0	0	1
Mike Stanley, c, NYA	1	0	0	0	0	0
TOTALS	34	2	8	2	2	8

	1 2 3	4 5 6	7 8 9	R	H	E
NL	0 0 0	0 0 1	1 1 0	3	3	0
AL	0 0 0	2 0 0	0 0 0	2	8	0

LOB—NL 0, AL 7. Scoring Position—NL 0-for-0, AL 0-for-8. 2B—Baerga. HR—Piazza, Biggio, Thomas, Conine. SB—RAlomar. CS—Dykstra, Baerga.

National League	IP	H	R	ER	BB	K
Hideo Nomo, LA	2.0	1	0	0	0	3
John Smiley, Cin	2.0	2	2	2	0	0
Tyler Green, Phi	1.0	2	0	0	0	1
Denny Neagle, Pit	1.0	1	0	0	0	1
Carlos Perez, Mon	0.1	1	0	0	1	0
Heathcliff Slocumb, Phi (W)	1.0	1	0	0	0	2
Tom Henke, StL	0.2	0	0	0	0	1
Randy Myers, ChN (S)	1.0	0	0	0	1	0

American League	IP	H	R	ER	BB	K
Randy Johnson, Sea	2.0	0	0	0	1	3
Kevin Appier, KC	2.0	0	0	0	0	1
Dennis Martinez, Cle	2.0	1	1	1	0	0
Kenny Rogers, Tex (BS)	1.0	1	1	1	0	2
Steve Ontiveros, Oak (L)	0.2	1	1	1	0	1
David Wells, Det	0.1	0	0	0	0	1
Jose Mesa, Cle	1.0	0	0	0	0	1

Time—2:40. Attendance—50,920. Umpires—HP, Merrill. 1B, Williams. 2B, Clark. 3B, Winters.

July 9, 1996
Philadelphia (Veterans Stadium)

Mike Piazza had a happy homecoming, driving in two runs with a homer and a double at Philadelphia's Veterans Stadium in the NL's 6-0 victory. Piazza, who grew up in nearby Norristown, launched a 445-foot blast in the second inning to give the NL a 2-0 advantage.

American League	AB	R	H	RBI	BB	K
Kenny Lofton, cf, Cle	3	0	2	0	0	0
Joe Carter, cf, Tor	1	0	1	0	0	0
Wade Boggs, 3b, NYA	3	0	0	0	0	0
Travis Fryman, ph-3b, Det	1	0	0	0	0	1
Roberto Alomar, 2b, Bal	3	0	1	0	0	0
Chuck Knoblauch, 2b, Min	1	0	1	0	0	0
Albert Belle, lf, Cle	4	0	0	0	0	3
Mo Vaughn, 1b, Bos	3	0	1	0	0	0
Mark McGwire, 1b, Oak	1	0	1	0	0	0
Ivan Rodriguez, c, Tex	2	0	0	0	0	1
Sandy Alomar Jr., ph-c, Cle	2	0	0	0	0	0
Cal Ripken Jr., ss, Bal	3	0	0	0	0	0
Troy Percival, p, Cal	0	0	0	0	0	0
Roberto Hernandez, p, ChA	0	0	0	0	0	0
Dan Wilson, ph, Sea	1	0	0	0	0	0
Brady Anderson, rf, Bal	2	0	0	0	0	0
Roger Pavlik, p, Tex	0	0	0	0	0	0
Alex Rodriguez, ph-ss, Sea	1	0	0	0	0	0
Charles Nagy, p, Cle	0	0	0	0	0	0
Edgar Martinez, ph, Sea	1	0	0	0	0	0
Chuck Finley, p, Cal	0	0	0	0	0	0
Jay Buhner, ph-rf, Sea	2	0	0	0	0	0
TOTALS	34	0	7	0	0	5

National League	AB	R	H	RBI	BB	K
Lance Johnson, cf, NYN	4	1	3	0	0	0
Barry Larkin, ss, Cin	3	1	1	0	0	0
Ozzie Smith, ss, StL	1	0	0	0	0	0
Barry Bonds, lf, SF	3	0	1	1	0	0
Pedro Martinez, p, Mon	0	0	0	0	0	0
Gary Sheffield, rf, Fla	1	0	0	0	0	0
Fred McGriff, 1b, Atl	2	0	0	0	0	2
Tom Glavine, p, Atl	0	0	0	0	0	0
Ken Caminiti, 3b, SD	2	1	1	1	0	0
Todd Worrell, p, LA	0	0	0	0	0	0
Jason Kendall, c, Pit	0	0	0	0	0	0
Mike Piazza, c, LA	3	1	2	2	0	1
Todd Hundley, c, NYN	1	0	0	0	0	0
Mark Wohlers, p, Atl	0	0	0	0	0	0
Al Leiter, p, Fla	0	0	0	0	0	0
Dante Bichette, rf, Col	3	1	1	0	0	1
Steve Trachsel, p, ChN	0	0	0	0	0	0
Mark Grudzielanek, 3b, Mon	1	0	0	0	0	0
Chipper Jones, 3b, Atl	2	1	1	0	0	0
Ricky Bottalico, p, Phi	0	0	0	0	0	0
Ellis Burks, lf, Col	2	0	1	0	0	1
Craig Biggio, 2b, Hou	3	0	0	1	0	1
Eric Young, pr-2b, Col	1	0	0	0	0	0
John Smoltz, p, Atl	0	0	0	0	0	0
Henry Rodriguez, ph, Mon	1	0	1	1	0	0
Kevin Brown, p, Fla	0	0	0	0	0	0
Jeff Bagwell, 1b, Hou	2	0	0	0	0	0
TOTALS	35	6	12	6	0	8

	1	2	3	4	5	6	7	8	9		R	H	E
AL	0	0	0	0	0	0	0	0	0		0	7	0
NL	1	2	1	0	0	2	0	0	x		6	12	1

E—Caminiti. DP—AL 1 (IRodriguez to Ripken Jr.), NL 1 (Smith to Young to Bagwell). LOB—AL 7, NL 5. Scoring Position—AL 1-for-10, NL 2-for-12. 2B—MVaughn, Johnson, Piazza, Bichette. 3B—Burks. HR—Piazza, Caminiti. GDP—SAlomar Jr. SB—Lofton 2, Johnson. CS—Johnson, Bonds.

American League	IP	H	R	ER	BB	K
Charles Nagy, Cle (L)	2.0	4	3	3	0	1
Chuck Finley, Cal	2.0	3	1	1	0	4
Roger Pavlik, Tex	2.0	3	2	2	0	2
Troy Percival, Cal	1.0	1	0	0	0	1
Roberto Hernandez, ChA	1.0	1	0	0	0	0

National League	IP	H	R	ER	BB	K
John Smoltz, Atl (W)	2.0	2	0	0	0	1
Kevin Brown, Fla	1.0	0	0	0	0	0
Tom Glavine, Atl	1.0	0	0	0	0	1
Ricky Bottalico, Phi	1.0	0	0	0	0	1
Pedro Martinez, Mon	1.0	2	0	0	0	1
Steve Trachsel, ChN	1.0	0	0	0	0	0
Todd Worrell, LA	1.0	2	0	0	0	1
Mark Wohlers, Atl	0.2	1	0	0	0	0
Al Leiter, Fla	0.1	0	0	0	0	0

WP—Pavlik. Time—2:35. Attendance—62,670. Umpires—HP, Marsh. 1B. McCoy. 2B. Reliford. 3B. Brinkman.

July 8, 1997
Cleveland (Jacobs Field)

Hometown hero Sandy Alomar thrilled the Cleveland crowd with a two-run homer in the bottom of the seventh, providing the margin of victory in the AL's 3-1 triumph. Edgar Martinez' solo homer gave the AL a 1-0 lead in the bottom of the second, and five AL hurlers protected it until Jose Rosado surrendered a solo shot to Javy Lopez in the top of the seventh. In the second inning, AL lefthander Randy Johnson revived memories of his All-Star confrontation with John Kruk when he sailed a pitch over the head of former teammate Larry Walker, who'd drawn criticism for sitting out a game against Johnson earlier in the season. After Johnson buzzed him, Walker, a lefthanded hitter, stuck his batting helmet on backwards and stepped back in batting righthanded. After taking a pitch from that side, he reverted to his natural side and worked a walk.

National League	AB	R	H	RBI	BB	K
Craig Biggio, 2b, Hou	3	0	0	0	0	1
Tony Womack, 2b, Pit	1	0	0	0	0	0
Tony Gwynn, dh, SD	3	0	0	0	0	0
Andres Galarraga, ph-dh, Col	1	0	0	0	0	1
Barry Bonds, lf, SF	2	0	0	0	1	1
Steve Finley, lf, SD	1	0	0	0	0	1
Mike Piazza, c, LA	1	0	0	0	1	0
Javy Lopez, c, Atl	1	1	1	1	0	0
Charles Johnson, c, Fla	1	0	0	0	0	1
Jeff Bagwell, 1b, Hou	3	0	0	0	0	0
Mark Grace, 1b, ChN	1	0	0	0	0	0
Larry Walker, rf, Col	1	0	0	0	1	0
Moises Alou, rf, Fla	2	0	1	0	0	0
Ken Caminiti, 3b, SD	2	0	0	0	0	0
Chipper Jones, 3b, Atl	1	0	0	0	0	0
Ray Lankford, cf, StL	2	0	0	0	1	1
Jeff Blauser, ss, Atl	2	0	1	0	0	0
Royce Clayton, ss, StL	1	0	0	0	0	1
TOTALS	29	1	3	1	4	7

American League	AB	R	H	RBI	BB	K
Brady Anderson, lf-rf, Bal	4	0	2	0	0	0
Alex Rodriguez, ss, Sea	3	0	1	0	0	2
Nomar Garciaparra, ss, Bos	1	0	0	0	0	0
Ken Griffey Jr., cf, Sea	4	0	0	0	0	2
Tino Martinez, 1b, NYA	2	0	0	0	0	0
Mark McGwire, 1b, Oak	2	0	0	0	0	2
Edgar Martinez, dh, Sea	2	1	2	1	0	0
Jim Thome, ph-dh, Cle	1	0	0	0	0	0
Paul O'Neill, rf, NYA	2	0	0	0	0	1
Bernie Williams, lf, NYA	0	1	0	0	1	0
Cal Ripken Jr., 3b, Bal	2	0	1	0	0	0
Joey Cora, pr-2b, Sea	1	0	0	0	0	0
Chuck Knoblauch, 2b, Min	0	0	0	0	0	0
Ivan Rodriguez, c, Tex	2	0	0	0	0	0
Sandy Alomar Jr., c, Cle	1	1	1	2	0	0
Roberto Alomar, 2b, Bal	2	0	0	0	0	0
Jeff Cirillo, 3b, Mil	1	0	0	0	0	1
TOTALS	30	3	7	3	1	8

	1	2	3	4	5	6	7	8	9		R	H	E
NL	0	0	0	0	0	0	1	0	0		1	3	0
AL	0	1	0	0	0	0	2	0	x		3	7	0

LOB—NL 5, AL 4. Scoring Position—NL 0-for-4, AL 1-for-5. 2B—Anderson. HR—EMartinez, Lopez, SAlomar Jr. SB—Bonds. CS—EMartinez.

National League	IP	H	R	ER	BB	K
Greg Maddux, Atl	2.0	2	1	1	0	0
Curt Schilling, Phi	2.0	2	0	0	0	3
Kevin Brown, Fla	1.0	1	0	0	0	0
Pedro Martinez, Mon	1.0	0	0	0	0	2
Shawn Estes, SF (L)	1.0	1	2	2	1	1
Bobby Jones, NYN	1.0	1	0	0	0	2

American League	IP	H	R	ER	BB	K
Randy Johnson, Sea	2.0	0	0	0	1	2
Roger Clemens, Tor	1.0	1	0	0	0	0
David Cone, NYA	1.0	0	0	0	2	0
Justin Thompson, Det	1.0	0	0	0	0	1
Pat Hentgen, Tor	1.0	0	0	0	0	1
Jose Rosado, KC (BS; W)	1.0	2	1	1	1	1
Randy Myers, Bal	1.0	0	0	0	0	2
Mariano Rivera, NYA (S)	1.0	0	0	0	0	0

WP—Schilling, Estes. PB—Lopez. Time—2:36. Attendance—44,916. Umpires—HP, Barnett. 1B. Davis. 2B. Coble. 3B. Kellogg.

All-Star Games: Box Scores

All-Star Game Player Register

										Batting															Fielding						
		G	AB	H	2B	3B	HR	TB	R	RBI	TBB	IBB	SO	HBP	SH	SF	SB	CS	SB%	GDP	Avg	OBP	SLG	Pos	G	PO	A	E	DP	FPct
Hank Aaron	NL	23	66	13	0	0	2	19	7	8	3	0	8	0	0	2	2	0	1.00	1	.197	.225	.288	OF	20	20	1	0	0	1.000
	AL	1	1	0	0	0	0	0	0	0	0	0	0	0	0	0	0	0	—	0	.000	.000	.000	—	0	0	0	0	0	—
	Tot	24	67	13	0	0	2	19	7	8	3	0	8	0	0	2	2	0	1.00	1	.194	.222	.284	OF	20	20	1	0	0	1.000
Joe Adcock	NL	2	5	3	1	0	0	4	1	0	0	0	1	0	0	0	0	0	—	0	.600	.600	.800	1B	2	6	0	0	1	1.000
Tommie Agee	AL	2	0	0	0	0	0	0	0	0	0	0	0	0	0	0	0	0	—	0	—	—	—	OF	1	1	0	0	0	1.000
Dick Allen	NL	4	11	2	0	0	1	5	1	1	1	0	6	0	0	0	0	0	—	0	.182	.250	.455	3B	2	0	3	0	0	1.000
	AL	2	5	1	0	0	0	1	0	1	0	0	1	0	0	0	0	0	—	0	.200	.200	.200	1B	2	6	0	0	1	1.000
	Tot	6	16	3	0	0	1	6	1	2	1	0	7	0	0	0	0	0	—	0	.188	.235	.375	1B	3	10	0	0	1	1.000
Gene Alley	NL	1	5	0	0	0	0	0	0	0	0	0	3	0	0	0	0	0	—	0	.000	.000	.000	SS	1	1	3	0	0	1.000
Bob Allison	AL	2	4	0	0	0	0	0	0	0	1	0	3	0	0	0	0	0	—	0	.000	.200	.000	1B	1	9	0	0	0	1.000
Roberto Alomar	AL	7	19	4	0	0	1	7	3	1	0	0	0	0	0	0	4	0	1.00	0	.211	.211	.368	2B	7	3	15	0	2	1.000
	NL	1	1	0	0	0	0	0	0	0	0	0	0	0	0	0	0	0	—	0	.000	.000	.000	2B	1	1	2	0	0	1.000
	Tot	8	20	4	0	0	1	7	3	1	0	0	0	0	0	0	4	0	1.00	0	.200	.200	.350	2B	8	4	17	0	2	1.000
Sandy Alomar	AL	1	1	0	0	0	0	0	0	0	0	0	0	0	0	0	0	0	—	0	.000	.000	.000	2B	1	0	2	0	0	1.000
Sandy Alomar Jr.	AL	5	11	4	0	0	1	7	2	2	0	0	0	0	0	0	0	0	—	1	.364	.364	.636	C	5	13	0	0	0	1.000
Felipe Alou	NL	2	0	0	0	0	0	0	0	1	0	0	0	0	0	1	0	0	—	0	—	.000	—	OF	2	0	0	0	0	—
Matty Alou	NL	2	5	3	0	0	0	3	1	0	1	0	1	0	0	0	0	0	—	0	.600	.667	.600	OF	2	6	0	0	0	1.000
Moises Alou	NL	2	3	2	1	0	0	3	0	1	0	0	0	0	0	0	0	0	—	0	.667	.667	1.000	OF	2	1	0	0	0	1.000
George Altman	NL	3	3	1	0	0	1	4	1	1	0	0	0	0	0	0	0	0	—	0	.333	.333	1.333	OF	1	0	0	0	0	—
Max Alvis	AL	2	2	0	0	0	0	0	0	0	0	0	0	0	0	0	0	0	—	0	.000	.000	.000	3B	1	0	0	0	0	—
Brady Anderson	AL	3	9	2	1	0	0	3	0	0	0	0	0	0	0	0	0	0	—	0	.222	.222	.333	OF	3	2	0	0	0	1.000
Mike Andrews	AL	1	1	0	0	0	0	0	0	0	0	0	0	0	0	0	0	0	—	0	.000	.000	.000	2B	1	0	0	0	0	—
Luis Aparicio	AL	10	28	2	0	1	0	4	2	0	2	0	6	0	0	0	1	0	1.00	2	.071	.133	.143	SS	10	15	20	0	4	1.000
Luke Appling	AL	4	9	4	1	0	0	5	1	2	1	0	0	0	0	0	0	0	—	0	.444	.500	.556	SS	2	2	2	0	0	1.000
Tony Armas	AL	1	1	0	0	0	0	0	0	0	0	0	1	0	0	0	0	0	—	0	.000	.000	.000	OF	1	0	0	0	0	—
Richie Ashburn	NL	4	10	6	1	0	0	7	4	1	1	0	1	0	0	0	1	0	1.00	0	.600	.636	.700	OF	2	5	1	0	0	1.000
Earl Averill	AL	5	15	4	1	1	0	7	1	4	1	0	3	0	0	0	0	0	—	0	.267	.313	.467	OF	4	11	1	0	0	1.000
Bobby Avila	AL	3	6	4	0	0	0	4	1	3	1	0	1	0	1	1	0	0	—	0	.667	.625	.667	2B	3	2	3	0	1	1.000
Joe Azcue	AL	1	1	0	0	0	0	0	0	0	0	0	1	0	0	0	0	0	—	0	.000	.000	.000	C	1	5	0	0	0	1.000
Carlos Baerga	AL	3	6	4	2	0	0	6	3	1	0	0	1	0	0	0	0	1	.00	0	.667	.667	1.000	2B	3	2	4	0	1	1.000
Jeff Bagwell	NL	3	9	2	0	0	0	2	1	0	0	0	2	0	0	0	0	0	—	0	.222	.222	.222	1B	3	16	3	0	1	1.000
Ed Bailey	NL	4	8	2	0	0	0	2	1	1	2	0	0	0	0	0	0	0	—	0	.250	.400	.250	C	4	9	2	0	1	1.000
Harold Baines	AL	5	7	2	0	0	0	2	1	2	0	0	1	0	0	1	0	0	—	0	.286	.250	.286	—	0	0	0	0	0	—
Dusty Baker	NL	2	4	1	0	0	0	1	0	0	0	0	0	0	0	0	0	0	—	0	.250	.250	.250	OF	2	2	0	0	0	1.000
Sal Bando	AL	3	6	1	0	0	0	1	0	0	0	0	0	0	0	0	0	0	—	0	.167	.167	.167	3B	3	1	3	0	1	1.000
Ernie Banks	NL	13	33	10	3	1	1	18	4	3	1	0	8	1	0	0	0	0	—	1	.303	.343	.545	SS	8	11	14	2	6	.926
Jesse Barfield	AL	1	3	0	0	0	0	0	0	0	0	0	2	0	0	0	0	0	—	0	.000	.000	.000	OF	1	2	0	0	0	1.000
Dick Bartell	NL	2	6	1	0	0	0	1	0	0	0	0	1	0	0	0	0	0	—	0	.167	.167	.167	SS	2	2	6	0	2	1.000
Earl Battey	AL	5	9	1	0	0	0	1	1	1	2	0	1	0	0	0	0	0	—	2	.111	.273	.111	C	5	12	2	0	1	1.000
Hank Bauer	AL	3	7	2	0	0	0	2	0	0	1	0	3	0	0	0	0	1	.00	0	.286	.375	.286	OF	3	6	0	0	0	1.000
Don Baylor	AL	1	4	2	1	0	0	3	2	1	0	0	0	0	0	0	0	0	—	0	.500	.500	.750	OF	1	1	0	0	0	1.000
Glenn Beckert	NL	4	7	0	0	0	0	0	0	0	0	0	0	0	0	0	0	0	—	0	.000	.000	.000	2B	3	2	6	0	1	1.000
Mark Belanger	AL	1	1	0	0	0	0	0	0	0	0	0	0	0	0	0	0	0	—	0	.000	.000	.000	SS	1	1	1	0	0	1.000
Buddy Bell	AL	5	8	1	0	1	0	3	0	1	0	0	3	0	0	1	0	0	—	0	.125	.111	.375	3B	4	1	6	1	0	.875
George Bell	AL	2	5	0	0	0	0	0	0	0	0	0	1	0	0	0	0	0	—	0	.000	.000	.000	OF	2	3	0	0	0	1.000
	NL	1	1	0	0	0	0	0	0	0	0	0	1	0	0	0	0	0	—	0	.000	.000	.000	—	0	0	0	0	0	—
	Tot	3	6	0	0	0	0	0	0	0	0	0	2	0	0	0	0	0	—	0	.000	.000	.000	OF	2	3	0	0	0	1.000
Gus Bell	NL	4	6	2	1	0	1	6	1	4	1	0	1	0	0	0	0	0	—	0	.333	.429	1.000	OF	3	6	0	0	0	1.000
Jay Bell	NL	1	1	0	0	0	0	0	0	0	0	0	0	0	0	0	0	0	—	0	.000	.000	.000	2B	1	1	1	0	0	1.000
Albert Belle	AL	4	10	1	0	0	0	1	2	1	1	0	4	0	0	0	0	0	—	0	.100	.182	.100	OF	3	3	0	0	0	1.000
Johnny Bench	NL	12	28	10	0	0	3	19	5	6	2	0	6	0	0	0	0	0	—	1	.357	.400	.679	C	11	49	2	1	0	.981
Bruce Benedict	NL	2	2	1	0	0	0	1	0	0	0	0	1	0	0	0	0	0	—	0	.500	.500	.500	C	2	8	0	0	0	1.000
Wally Berger	NL	3	8	0	0	0	0	0	0	0	0	0	2	0	0	0	0	0	—	0	.000	.000	.000	OF	3	5	0	1	0	.833
Yogi Berra	AL	15	41	8	0	0	1	11	5	3	2	0	3	0	0	0	0	0	—	2	.195	.233	.268	C	14	61	7	1	1	.986
Dante Bichette	NL	3	5	2	1	0	0	3	1	0	0	0	2	0	0	0	0	0	—	0	.400	.400	.600	OF	2	2	0	0	0	1.000
Craig Biggio	NL	6	12	1	0	0	1	4	2	2	0	0	3	0	0	0	0	0	—	0	.083	.083	.333	2B	5	5	9	0	0	1.000
Paul Blair	AL	2	2	0	0	0	0	0	0	0	0	0	0	0	0	0	0	0	—	0	.000	.000	.000	OF	2	3	0	0	0	1.000
Jeff Blauser	NL	2	3	1	0	0	0	1	0	0	0	0	1	0	0	0	0	0	—	0	.333	.333	.333	SS	2	2	3	1	0	.833
Ossie Bluege	AL	1	0	0	0	0	0	0	0	0	0	0	0	0	0	0	0	0	—	0	—	—	—	3B	1	0	0	0	0	—
Bruce Bochte	AL	1	1	1	0	0	0	1	0	1	0	0	0	0	1	0	0	0	—	0	1.000	1.000	1.000	1B	1	2	0	0	0	1.000
Wade Boggs	AL	12	28	9	0	0	1	12	4	1	4	1	3	0	0	0	0	0	—	0	.321	.406	.429	3B	12	5	17	0	2	1.000
Frank Bolling	NL	4	12	1	1	0	0	2	0	0	0	0	1	0	0	0	0	0	—	0	.083	.083	.167	2B	4	8	9	1	2	.944
Barry Bonds	NL	7	18	4	3	0	0	7	3	2	2	0	4	0	0	1	1	1	.50	0	.222	.286	.389	OF	7	11	0	0	0	1.000
Bobby Bonds	NL	2	3	2	1	0	1	6	1	2	0	0	1	0	0	0	0	0	—	0	.667	.667	2.000	OF	2	0	0	0	0	—
	AL	1	3	0	0	0	0	0	0	0	0	0	1	0	0	0	0	0	—	0	.000	.000	.000	OF	1	0	1	0	0	1.000
	Tot	3	6	2	1	0	1	6	1	2	0	0	2	0	0	0	0	0	—	0	.333	.333	1.000	OF	3	0	1	0	0	1.000
Bobby Bonilla	NL	6	13	5	0	0	0	5	0	1	0	0	2	0	0	0	0	0	—	0	.385	.385	.385	3B	2	0	2	0	0	1.000
Bob Boone	NL	3	5	2	0	0	0	2	2	2	0	0	0	0	0	0	0	0	—	1	.400	.400	.400	C	3	8	1	0	0	1.000
	AL	1	0	0	0	0	0	0	0	0	0	0	0	0	0	0	0	0	—	0	—	—	—	C	1	1	0	0	0	1.000
	Tot	4	5	2	0	0	0	2	2	2	0	0	0	0	0	0	0	0	—	1	.400	.400	.400	C	4	9	1	0	0	1.000
Ray Boone	AL	2	5	1	0	0	1	4	1	1	0	0	0	0	0	0	0	0	—	0	.200	.200	.800	3B	1	1	3	0	0	1.000
Lou Boudreau	AL	5	12	4	0	0	1	7	1	3	0	0	1	0	0	0	0	0	—	0	.333	.333	.583	SS	5	10	10	0	2	1.000
Larry Bowa	NL	5	8	2	0	0	0	2	2	0	1	0	0	1	0	0	1	0	1.00	0	.250	.400	.250	SS	5	9	8	0	1	1.000
Ken Boyer	NL	10	23	8	0	0	2	14	4	4	3	0	4	0	0	0	0	1	.00	0	.348	.423	.609	3B	10	7	9	2	0	.889
Phil Bradley	AL	1	1	0	0	0	0	0	0	0	0	0	1	0	0	0	0	0	—	0	.000	.000	.000	OF	1	1	0	0	0	1.000
George Brett	AL	10	24	7	2	1	1	14	5	5	4	0	4	0	0	3	1	0	1.00	0	.292	.355	.583	3B	9	9	13	0	3	1.000
Ed Brinkman	AL	1	1	0	0	0	0	0	0	0	0	0	0	0	0	0	0	0	—	0	.000	.000	.000	SS	1	1	1	0	1	1.000
Lou Brock	NL	5	8	3	0	0	0	3	2	0	0	0	0	0	0	0	2	0	1.00	0	.375	.375	.375	OF	2	3	0	0	0	1.000
Hubie Brooks	NL	2	5	1	0	0	0	1	2	0	0	0	2	0	0	0	0	0	—	0	.200	.200	.200	SS	2	2	2	0	1	1.000
Chris Brown	NL	1	2	1	1	0	0	2	1	0	0	0	0	0	0	0	0	0	—	1	.500	.500	1.000	3B	1	1	0	0	0	1.000
Jimmy Brown	NL	1	2	0	0	0	0	0	0	0	0	0	0	1	0	0	0	0	—	1	.000	.333	.000	2B	1	1	0	1	0	.500

		Batting																						Fielding					
		G	AB	H	2B	3B	HR	TB	R	RBI	TBB	IBB	SO	HBP	SH	SF	SB	CS	SB%	GDP	Avg	OBP	SLG	Pos	G	PO	A	E	DP	FPct
Tom Brunansky	AL	1	1	0	0	0	0	0	0	0	0	0	0	0	0	0	0	0	—	0	.000	.000	.000	OF	1	0	0	0	0	—
Jay Buhner	AL	1	2	0	0	0	0	0	0	0	0	0	0	0	0	0	0	0	—	0	.000	.000	.000	OF	1	1	0	0	0	1.000
Al Bumbry	AL	1	1	0	0	0	0	0	0	0	0	0	0	0	0	0	0	0	—	0	.000	.000	.000	OF	1	2	0	0	0	1.000
Smoky Burgess	NL	7	10	1	0	0	0	1	0	0	0	0	2	0	0	0	0	0	—	0	.100	.100	.100	C	6	23	0	2	0	.920
Ellis Burks	NL	1	2	1	0	1	0	3	0	0	0	0	1	0	0	0	0	0	—	0	.500	.500	1.500	OF	1	1	0	0	0	1.000
Rick Burleson	AL	3	5	0	0	0	0	0	1	0	0	0	1	0	0	0	0	0	—	0	.000	.000	.000	SS	3	1	4	0	0	1.000
Jeff Burroughs	AL	1	0	0	0	0	0	0	0	0	2	0	0	0	0	0	0	0	—	0	—	1.000	—	OF	1	1	0	0	0	1.000
Jim Busby	AL	1	0	0	0	0	0	0	0	0	0	0	0	0	0	0	0	0	—	0	—	—	—	OF	1	0	0	0	0	—
Brett Butler	NL	1	1	0	0	0	0	0	0	0	0	0	0	0	0	0	0	0	—	0	.000	.000	.000	OF	1	0	0	0	0	—
Ivan Calderon	NL	1	2	1	0	0	0	1	0	0	0	0	0	0	0	0	1	0	1.00	0	.500	.500	.500	OF	1	1	0	0	0	1.000
Johnny Callison	NL	3	4	2	0	0	1	5	1	3	1	0	0	0	0	0	0	0	—	0	.500	.600	1.250	OF	1	0	0	0	0	—
Ken Caminiti	NL	3	5	1	0	0	1	4	1	1	0	0	1	0	0	0	0	0	—	0	.200	.200	.800	3B	3	0	0	1	0	.000
Roy Campanella	NL	7	20	2	0	0	0	2	1	0	3	1	5	0	0	0	0	0	—	0	.100	.217	.100	C	7	45	6	1	2	.981
Bert Campaneris	AL	5	11	2	0	0	0	2	1	0	1	0	5	0	0	0	0	0	—	0	.182	.250	.182	SS	5	7	8	0	0	1.000
Jose Canseco	AL	2	8	0	0	0	0	0	0	0	1	0	2	0	0	0	1	0	1.00	0	.000	.111	.000	OF	2	4	0	0	0	1.000
Leo Cardenas	NL	4	3	0	0	0	0	0	0	0	0	0	1	0	0	0	0	0	—	0	.000	.000	.000	SS	4	3	3	0	1	1.000
Rod Carew	AL	15	41	10	1	2	0	15	8	2	7	1	4	0	0	0	3	2	.60	2	.244	.354	.366	2B	8	15	15	0	3	1.000
Chico Carrasquel	AL	4	12	4	0	0	0	4	1	0	0	0	2	0	0	0	0	0	—	0	.333	.333	.333	SS	4	7	11	1	3	.947
Gary Carter	NL	10	20	6	0	0	3	15	3	5	2	0	1	0	0	0	0	0	—	0	.300	.364	.750	C	9	44	2	0	1	1.000
Joe Carter	AL	5	11	5	0	0	0	5	3	1	1	0	1	0	0	0	0	0	—	0	.455	.500	.455	OF	5	5	0	0	0	1.000
Rico Carty	NL	1	1	0	0	0	0	0	0	0	1	0	0	0	0	0	0	0	—	0	.000	.500	.000	OF	1	0	0	0	0	—
George Case	AL	1	2	0	0	0	0	0	1	0	1	0	1	1	0	0	0	0	—	1	.000	.500	.000	OF	1	0	0	0	0	—
Dave Cash	NL	3	3	1	0	0	0	1	1	0	0	0	0	0	0	0	0	0	—	0	.333	.333	.333	2B	3	1	2	0	1	1.000
Norm Cash	AL	5	13	1	1	0	0	2	0	0	0	0	6	0	0	0	0	0	—	1	.077	.077	.154	1B	5	31	1	0	1	1.000
Vinny Castilla	NL	1	2	0	0	0	0	0	0	0	0	0	1	0	0	0	0	0	—	0	.000	.000	.000	3B	1	0	0	0	0	—
Phil Cavarretta	NL	3	4	2	0	1	0	4	1	0	3	0	2	0	0	0	0	0	—	0	.500	.714	1.000	1B	3	14	0	0	1	1.000
Cesar Cedeno	NL	4	9	3	0	0	1	6	2	3	0	0	5	0	0	0	0	0	—	0	.333	.333	.667	OF	4	6	0	0	0	1.000
Orlando Cepeda	NL	9	27	1	0	0	0	1	0	2	1	0	3	1	0	0	0	0	—	3	.037	.103	.037	1B	5	22	2	0	1	1.000
Bob Cerv	AL	1	2	1	0	0	0	1	0	0	1	1	0	0	0	0	0	0	—	0	.500	.667	.500	OF	1	4	0	0	0	1.000
Ron Cey	NL	6	9	2	1	0	0	3	0	2	2	0	1	0	0	0	0	0	—	0	.222	.364	.333	3B	6	3	2	0	0	1.000
Dave Chalk	AL	1	1	0	0	0	0	0	0	0	0	0	1	0	0	0	0	0	—	0	.000	.000	.000	3B	1	0	0	0	0	—
Ben Chapman	AL	4	8	2	0	1	0	4	0	0	0	0	1	0	0	0	0	0	—	0	.250	.250	.500	OF	4	1	1	0	0	1.000
Sam Chapman	AL	1	2	0	0	0	0	0	0	1	0	0	0	0	0	0	0	0	—	0	.000	.000	.000	OF	1	1	0	0	0	1.000
Jeff Cirillo	AL	1	1	0	0	0	0	0	0	0	0	0	1	0	0	0	0	0	—	0	.000	.000	.000	3B	1	0	0	0	0	—
Jack Clark	NL	4	6	0	0	0	0	0	0	0	1	0	3	0	0	0	0	0	—	0	.000	.143	.000	1B	2	11	1	0	1	1.000
Will Clark	NL	5	11	3	0	0	1	6	1	3	1	0	2	0	0	0	0	0	—	0	.273	.333	.545	1B	5	18	1	0	2	1.000
	AL	1	2	2	0	0	0	2	0	0	0	0	0	0	0	0	1	0	1.00	0	1.000	1.000	1.000	1B	1	7	0	0	1	1.000
	Tot	6	13	5	0	0	1	8	1	3	1	0	2	0	0	0	1	0	1.00	0	.385	.429	.615	1B	6	25	1	0	3	1.000
Royce Clayton	NL	1	1	0	0	0	0	0	0	0	0	0	1	0	0	0	0	0	—	0	.000	.000	.000	SS	1	0	1	0	0	1.000
Roberto Clemente	NL	14	31	10	2	1	1	17	3	4	1	0	9	0	0	2	0	1	.00	0	.323	.324	.548	OF	14	20	0	0	0	1.000
Mickey Cochrane	AL	1	1	0	0	0	0	0	0	0	0	0	0	0	0	0	0	0	—	0	.000	.000	.000	C	1	1	1	0	0	1.000
Rocky Colavito	AL	9	25	6	1	0	3	16	3	8	1	0	3	0	0	1	0	0	—	0	.240	.259	.640	OF	8	9	0	0	0	1.000
Jerry Coleman	AL	1	2	0	0	0	0	0	0	0	0	0	2	0	0	0	0	0	—	0	.000	.000	.000	2B	1	0	0	1	0	.000
Vince Coleman	NL	2	2	1	0	0	0	1	1	0	0	0	0	0	0	0	1	0	1.00	0	.500	.500	.500	OF	2	3	0	0	0	1.000
Ripper Collins	NL	3	4	1	0	0	0	1	0	0	2	0	0	0	0	0	0	0	—	0	.250	.500	.250	1B	2	11	1	0	1	1.000
Dave Concepcion	NL	7	12	3	0	0	1	6	3	2	2	0	2	0	0	0	0	2	.00	0	.250	.357	.500	SS	7	7	8	1	3	.938
Tony Conigliaro	AL	1	6	0	0	0	0	0	0	0	0	0	2	0	0	0	0	0	—	0	.000	.000	.000	OF	1	4	0	0	0	1.000
Jeff Conine	NL	1	1	1	0	0	1	4	1	1	0	0	0	0	0	0	0	0	—	0	1.000	1.000	4.000	—	0	0	0	0	0	—
Cecil Cooper	AL	5	4	2	0	0	0	2	1	0	2	0	1	0	0	0	0	0	—	1	.500	.667	.500	1B	2	11	0	0	1	1.000
Scott Cooper	AL	2	4	1	1	0	0	2	1	1	0	0	1	0	0	0	0	0	—	0	.250	.250	.500	3B	2	1	2	0	0	1.000
Walker Cooper	NL	6	15	5	0	0	0	5	1	1	0	0	2	0	0	0	0	0	—	0	.333	.333	.333	C	6	28	3	0	0	1.000
Joey Cora	AL	1	1	0	0	0	0	0	0	0	0	0	0	0	0	0	0	0	—	0	.000	.000	.000	2B	1	0	1	0	0	1.000
Wil Cordero	NL	1	2	0	0	0	0	0	0	0	0	0	0	0	0	0	0	0	—	1	.000	.000	.000	SS	1	1	1	0	1	1.000
Pete Coscarart	NL	1	1	0	0	0	0	0	0	0	0	0	1	0	0	0	0	0	—	0	.000	.000	.000	2B	1	0	2	0	1	1.000
Doc Cramer	AL	3	6	1	0	0	0	1	0	0	0	0	1	0	0	0	0	0	—	0	.167	.167	.167	OF	3	3	0	0	0	1.000
Del Crandall	NL	8	20	4	0	0	1	7	2	2	0	0	1	0	0	0	0	0	—	1	.200	.200	.350	C	8	38	1	0	0	1.000
Joe Cronin	AL	7	25	7	3	0	0	10	3	4	2	0	4	0	0	0	0	0	—	0	.280	.333	.400	SS	7	13	25	2	2	.950
Jose Cruz	NL	1	1	0	0	0	0	0	0	0	2	0	0	0	0	0	1	0	1.00	0	.000	.667	.000	OF	1	2	0	0	0	1.000
Kiki Cuyler	NL	1	2	0	0	0	0	0	0	0	0	0	0	0	0	0	0	0	—	0	.000	.000	.000	OF	1	2	0	0	0	1.000
Babe Dahlgren	NL	1	2	0	0	0	0	0	0	0	0	0	0	0	0	0	0	0	—	1	.000	.000	.000	1B	1	3	0	0	1	1.000
Harry Danning	NL	2	2	1	0	0	0	1	0	1	0	0	0	0	0	0	0	0	—	0	.500	.500	.500	C	2	9	0	0	0	1.000
Al Dark	NL	2	10	2	0	0	0	2	0	0	0	0	0	0	0	0	0	0	—	0	.200	.200	.200	SS	2	1	4	0	0	1.000
Darren Daulton	NL	3	6	0	0	0	0	0	1	0	0	0	1	0	0	0	0	0	—	0	.000	.000	.000	C	3	12	0	0	0	1.000
Vic Davalillo	AL	1	2	1	0	0	0	1	0	0	0	0	0	0	0	0	0	0	—	0	.500	.500	.500	OF	1	1	0	0	0	1.000
Jim Davenport	NL	1	1	1	0	0	0	1	0	0	0	0	0	0	0	0	0	0	—	0	1.000	1.000	1.000	3B	1	0	1	0	0	1.000
Chili Davis	NL	2	2	0	0	0	0	0	0	0	0	0	1	0	0	0	0	0	—	0	.000	.000	.000	OF	1	0	0	0	0	—
	AL	1	1	0	0	0	0	0	0	0	0	0	0	0	0	0	0	0	—	0	.000	.000	.000	—	0	0	0	0	0	—
	Tot	3	3	0	0	0	0	0	0	0	0	0	1	0	0	0	0	0	—	0	.000	.000	.000	OF	1	0	0	0	0	—
Eric Davis	NL	2	5	0	0	0	0	0	0	0	1	0	1	0	0	0	1	0	1.00	1	.000	.167	.000	OF	2	2	0	0	0	1.000
Glenn Davis	NL	2	2	1	0	0	0	1	1	0	1	0	0	0	0	0	0	0	—	0	.500	.667	.500	1B	1	7	0	0	0	1.000
Jody Davis	NL	2	2	1	0	0	0	1	0	0	0	0	0	0	0	0	0	0	—	0	.500	.500	.500	C	2	4	0	0	0	1.000
Tommy Davis	NL	3	8	1	0	0	0	1	1	0	1	0	0	0	0	0	0	0	—	0	.125	.222	.125	OF	3	4	2	1	1	.857
Willie Davis	NL	2	3	3	0	0	1	6	1	2	0	0	0	0	0	0	0	0	—	0	1.000	1.000	2.000	OF	2	3	0	0	0	1.000
Andre Dawson	NL	8	21	5	1	0	1	9	1	1	0	0	4	0	0	0	1	0	1.00	1	.238	.238	.429	OF	8	16	0	0	0	1.000
Frank Demaree	NL	2	8	2	0	0	0	2	1	0	0	0	0	0	0	0	0	0	—	1	.250	.250	.250	OF	2	4	1	0	0	1.000
Bucky Dent	AL	3	5	3	1	0	0	4	0	0	0	0	2	0	0	0	0	0	—	0	.600	.600	.800	SS	3	0	4	0	0	1.000
Bo Diaz	AL	1	1	0	0	0	0	0	0	0	0	0	1	0	0	0	0	0	—	0	.000	.000	.000	C	1	2	0	0	0	1.000
	NL	1	1	0	0	0	0	0	0	0	0	0	0	0	0	0	0	0	—	0	.000	.000	.000	C	1	1	0	0	0	1.000
	Tot	2	2	0	0	0	0	0	0	0	0	0	1	0	0	0	0	0	—	0	.000	.000	.000	C	2	3	0	0	0	1.000
Bill Dickey	AL	8	19	5	2	0	0	7	3	1	4	0	2	0	0	0	0	0	—	0	.263	.391	.368	C	7	32	2	1	0	.971
Dick Dietz	NL	1	2	1	0	0	1	4	1	1	0	0	0	0	0	0	0	0	—	0	.500	.500	2.000	C	1	2	0	0	0	1.000
Bob Dillinger	AL	1	1	1	0	0	0	1	2	1	0	0	0	0	0	0	0	0	—	0	1.000	1.000	1.000	3B	1	0	2	0	0	1.000
Dom DiMaggio	AL	6	17	6	2	0	0	8	2	2	1	0	4	0	0	0	0	1	.00	0	.353	.389	.471	OF	6	7	0	0	0	1.000
Joe DiMaggio	AL	11	40	9	2	0	1	14	7	6	3	0	3	0	0	0	1	0	1.00	3	.225	.279	.350	OF	10	13	1	2	0	.875

		G	AB	H	2B	3B	HR	TB	R	RBI	TBB	IBB	SO	HBP	SH	SF	SB	CS	SB%	GDP	Avg	OBP	SLG	Pos	G	PO	A	E	DP	FPct
		Batting																						Fielding						
Vince DiMaggio	NL	2	3	3	0	1	1	8	2	1	0	0	0	0	0	0	0	0	—	0	1.000	1.000	2.667	OF	2	1	0	0	0	1.000
Gary DiSarcina	AL	1	1	0	0	0	0	0	0	0	0	0	0	0	0	0	0	0	—	0	.000	.000	.000	SS	1	0	0	0	0	—
Larry Doby	AL	6	10	3	1	0	1	7	2	1	0	0	2	0	0	0	0	0	—	0	.300	.300	.700	OF	5	12	1	0	0	1.000
Bobby Doerr	AL	8	20	4	0	0	1	7	2	3	1	0	3	0	0	0	1	0	1.00	0	.200	.238	.350	2B	8	10	14	1	2	.960
Brian Downing	AL	1	1	1	0	0	0	1	0	0	0	0	0	0	0	0	0	0	—	0	1.000	1.000	1.000	C	1	3	0	0	0	1.000
Walt Dropo	AL	1	3	1	0	1	0	3	0	0	0	0	0	0	0	0	0	0	—	0	.333	.333	1.000	1B	1	8	1	0	1	1.000
Mariano Duncan	NL	1	1	0	0	0	0	0	0	0	0	0	0	0	0	0	0	0	—	0	.000	.000	.000	2B	1	0	2	0	0	1.000
Shawon Dunston	NL	1	2	0	0	0	0	0	0	0	0	0	0	0	0	0	0	0	—	0	.000	.000	.000	SS	1	0	0	0	0	—
Leon Durham	NL	1	2	0	0	0	0	0	0	0	0	0	1	0	0	0	0	0	—	0	.000	.000	.000	OF	1	0	0	0	0	—
Leo Durocher	NL	2	6	2	0	0	0	2	1	0	0	0	2	0	0	0	0	0	—	0	.333	.333	.333	SS	2	4	3	0	0	1.000
Jimmy Dykes	AL	1	3	2	0	0	0	2	1	0	1	0	0	0	0	0	0	0	—	0	.667	.750	.667	3B	1	2	4	0	1	1.000
Lenny Dykstra	NL	2	6	1	0	0	0	1	0	0	1	0	0	0	0	0	0	1	.00	0	.167	.286	.167	OF	2	4	0	0	0	1.000
Jake Early	AL	1	2	0	0	0	0	0	1	0	1	0	1	0	1	0	0	0	—	0	.000	.333	.000	C	1	3	0	0	0	1.000
Mike Easler	NL	1	1	0	0	0	0	0	1	0	1	0	0	0	0	0	0	0	—	0	.000	.500	.000	OF	1	0	0	0	0	—
Jim Edmonds	AL	1	1	0	0	0	0	0	0	0	0	0	1	0	0	0	0	0	—	0	.000	.000	.000	OF	1	0	0	0	0	—
Bruce Edwards	NL	1	0	0	0	0	0	0	0	0	0	0	0	0	0	0	0	0	—	0	—	—	—	C	1	2	0	0	0	1.000
Johnny Edwards	NL	2	3	0	0	0	0	0	1	0	1	1	1	0	0	0	0	0	—	0	.000	.250	.000	C	2	10	0	0	0	1.000
Bob Elliott	NL	5	9	3	0	0	1	6	1	2	0	0	0	0	0	0	0	0	—	0	.333	.333	.667	3B	4	2	6	0	0	1.000
Woody English	NL	1	1	0	0	0	0	0	0	0	0	0	0	0	0	0	0	0	—	0	.000	.000	.000	SS	1	0	0	0	0	—
Del Ennis	NL	3	5	0	0	0	0	0	0	0	0	0	4	0	0	0	0	0	—	0	.000	.000	.000	OF	3	1	0	0	0	1.000
Darrell Evans	NL	2	1	0	0	0	0	0	0	0	1	0	0	0	0	0	0	0	—	0	.000	.500	.000	1B	1	2	1	0	0	1.000
Dwight Evans	AL	3	5	3	0	0	0	3	1	0	2	0	1	0	0	0	0	0	—	0	.600	.714	.600	OF	3	7	0	0	0	1.000
Hoot Evers	AL	2	6	1	0	0	1	4	1	1	1	0	2	0	0	0	0	0	—	0	.167	.286	.667	OF	2	1	0	0	0	1.000
Ferris Fain	AL	3	7	3	0	1	0	5	1	1	0	0	1	0	0	0	0	0	—	0	.429	.429	.714	1B	3	8	2	0	0	1.000
Ron Fairly	NL	1	0	0	0	0	0	0	0	0	0	0	0	0	0	0	0	0	—	0	—	—	—	1B	1	4	0	0	0	1.000
	AL	1	1	0	0	0	0	0	0	0	0	0	1	0	0	0	0	0	—	0	.000	.000	.000	—	0	0	0	0	0	—
	Tot	2	1	0	0	0	0	0	0	0	0	0	1	0	0	0	0	0	—	0	.000	.000	.000	1B	1	4	0	0	0	1.000
Tony Fernandez	AL	3	3	0	0	0	0	0	0	0	0	0	1	0	1	0	0	0	—	0	.000	.000	.000	SS	3	3	5	0	2	1.000
	NL	1	2	1	0	0	0	1	1	0	0	0	0	0	0	0	0	0	—	0	.500	.500	.500	SS	1	3	0	0	0	1.000
	Tot	4	5	1	0	0	0	1	1	0	0	0	1	0	1	0	0	0	—	0	.200	.200	.200	SS	4	6	5	0	2	1.000
Rick Ferrell	AL	2	5	0	0	0	0	0	0	0	0	0	2	0	1	0	0	0	—	0	.000	.000	.000	C	2	8	0	0	0	1.000
Cecil Fielder	AL	3	5	0	0	0	0	0	0	0	1	0	1	1	0	0	0	0	—	0	.000	.286	.000	1B	3	13	3	0	2	1.000
Jim Finigan	AL	1	3	0	0	0	0	0	0	0	0	0	1	0	0	0	0	0	—	0	.000	.000	.000	3B	1	2	0	0	0	1.000
Steve Finley	NL	1	1	0	0	0	0	0	0	0	0	0	1	0	0	0	0	0	—	0	.000	.000	.000	OF	1	1	0	0	0	1.000
Lou Finney	AL	1	0	0	0	0	0	0	0	0	1	0	0	0	0	0	0	0	—	0	—	1.000	—	OF	1	0	0	0	0	—
Carlton Fisk	AL	10	20	3	0	0	0	3	2	1	0	0	7	0	0	1	0	0	—	0	.150	.143	.150	C	10	34	1	0	0	1.000
Darrin Fletcher	NL	1	0	0	0	0	0	0	0	0	0	0	0	0	0	0	0	0	—	0	—	—	—	C	1	3	0	0	0	1.000
Elbie Fletcher	NL	1	2	0	0	0	0	0	0	0	0	0	0	0	0	0	0	0	—	0	.000	.000	.000	1B	1	3	0	0	1	1.000
Curt Flood	NL	3	2	0	0	0	0	0	1	0	2	0	0	0	0	0	0	0	—	0	.000	.500	.000	OF	1	1	0	0	0	1.000
Ray Fosse	AL	1	2	1	0	0	0	1	1	1	1	0	0	0	0	1	0	0	—	0	.500	.500	.500	C	1	7	0	0	0	1.000
George Foster	NL	5	11	3	2	0	1	8	3	5	2	1	2	0	0	0	0	0	—	0	.273	.385	.727	OF	5	4	0	0	0	1.000
Nellie Fox	AL	13	38	14	0	0	0	14	7	5	2	0	3	0	1	0	0	0	—	1	.368	.400	.368	2B	13	25	14	2	3	.951
Jimmie Foxx	AL	7	19	6	1	0	1	10	3	4	1	0	7	0	0	0	0	0	—	0	.316	.350	.526	3B	4	1	4	1	0	.833
Julio Franco	AL	2	6	2	1	0	0	3	0	2	0	0	0	0	0	0	0	0	—	0	.333	.333	.500	2B	2	2	1	0	0	1.000
Bill Freehan	AL	8	17	4	0	0	1	7	2	2	2	0	3	0	1	0	0	0	—	0	.235	.316	.412	C	8	42	1	0	0	1.000
Jim Fregosi	AL	6	15	3	1	0	0	4	1	1	0	0	5	0	1	1	0	0	—	0	.200	.188	.267	SS	5	7	11	0	1	1.000
Lonny Frey	NL	3	6	2	1	0	0	3	0	1	0	0	0	0	0	0	0	0	—	0	.333	.333	.500	2B	2	1	7	0	1	1.000
Frankie Frisch	NL	2	7	4	0	0	2	10	4	2	1	0	0	0	0	0	0	0	—	0	.571	.625	1.429	2B	2	5	4	0	1	1.000
Travis Fryman	AL	4	4	1	0	0	0	1	1	1	1	0	1	0	0	0	0	0	—	0	.250	.400	.250	SS	2	1	4	0	0	1.000
Gary Gaetti	AL	2	2	0	0	0	0	0	0	0	0	0	1	0	0	0	0	0	—	0	.000	.000	.000	3B	1	1	0	0	0	1.000
Augie Galan	NL	3	9	2	0	0	1	5	2	2	2	0	2	0	0	0	0	0	—	0	.222	.364	.556	OF	3	4	0	0	0	1.000
Andres Galarraga	NL	3	4	0	0	0	0	0	0	0	0	0	2	0	0	0	0	0	—	0	.000	.000	.000	1B	2	6	0	0	0	1.000
Ron Gant	NL	2	4	0	0	0	0	0	0	0	0	0	1	0	0	0	0	0	—	0	.000	.000	.000	OF	1	1	0	0	0	1.000
Carlos Garcia	NL	1	2	1	0	0	0	1	0	0	0	0	0	0	0	0	0	0	—	0	.500	.500	.500	2B	1	0	1	0	0	1.000
Damaso Garcia	AL	2	3	1	0	0	0	1	0	0	0	0	0	0	0	0	1	0	1.00	0	.333	.333	.333	2B	2	1	3	0	0	1.000
Nomar Garciaparra	AL	1	1	0	0	0	0	0	0	0	0	0	0	0	0	0	0	0	—	0	.000	.000	.000	SS	1	1	0	0	0	1.000
Phil Garner	NL	2	2	1	0	0	0	1	1	0	1	0	1	0	0	0	1	0	1.00	0	.500	.667	.500	2B	2	1	3	0	1	1.000
	AL	1	1	0	0	0	0	0	0	0	0	0	1	0	0	0	0	0	—	0	.000	.000	.000	2B	1	1	1	0	1	1.000
	Tot	3	3	1	0	0	0	1	1	0	1	0	2	0	0	0	1	0	1.00	0	.333	.500	.333	2B	3	2	4	0	2	1.000
Ralph Garr	NL	1	3	0	0	0	0	0	0	0	0	0	1	0	0	0	0	0	—	0	.000	.000	.000	OF	1	0	0	0	0	—
Steve Garvey	NL	10	28	11	2	2	2	23	7	7	2	0	3	0	0	0	0	0	—	0	.393	.433	.821	1B	10	49	6	0	3	1.000
Cito Gaston	NL	1	2	0	0	0	0	0	0	0	1	0	0	0	0	0	0	0	—	0	.000	.333	.000	OF	1	2	0	0	0	1.000
Rich Gedman	AL	2	1	0	0	0	0	0	0	0	0	0	1	0	0	0	0	0	—	0	.000	.000	.000	C	2	5	1	0	0	1.000
Lou Gehrig	AL	6	18	4	1	0	2	11	4	5	6	0	6	0	0	0	0	0	—	0	.222	.417	.611	1B	6	54	2	2	2	.966
Charlie Gehringer	AL	6	20	10	2	0	0	12	2	1	9	1	0	0	0	0	2	0	1.00	0	.500	.655	.600	2B	6	10	15	0	1	1.000
Jim Gentile	AL	4	11	2	0	0	0	2	0	0	2	0	5	0	0	0	0	0	—	0	.182	.308	.182	1B	4	20	0	1	2	.952
Jim Gilliam	NL	1	2	1	0	0	1	4	1	1	1	0	0	0	0	0	0	0	—	0	.500	.667	2.000	3B	1	0	0	0	0	—
Juan Gonzalez	AL	1	1	0	0	0	0	0	0	0	1	0	1	0	0	0	0	0	—	0	.000	.500	.000	OF	1	1	0	0	0	1.000
Billy Goodman	AL	2	2	0	0	0	0	0	0	0	1	0	0	0	0	0	0	1	.00	0	.000	.333	.000	1B	1	1	1	0	0	1.000
Ival Goodman	NL	2	4	0	0	0	0	0	0	0	1	1	1	1	0	0	1	0	1.00	0	.000	.333	.000	OF	2	2	0	0	0	1.000
Joe Gordon	AL	8	20	4	3	0	0	7	2	2	0	0	8	0	0	0	0	0	—	0	.200	.200	.350	2B	8	11	20	0	2	1.000
Sid Gordon	NL	1	2	1	1	0	0	2	0	0	1	0	0	0	0	0	0	0	—	0	.500	.667	1.000	3B	1	0	4	0	0	1.000
Goose Goslin	AL	1	1	1	0	0	0	1	1	0	1	0	0	0	0	0	0	0	—	0	1.000	1.000	1.000	OF	1	1	0	0	0	1.000
Billy Grabarkewitz	NL	1	3	1	0	0	0	1	0	0	0	0	0	0	0	0	0	0	—	0	.333	.333	.333	3B	1	0	1	0	0	1.000
Mark Grace	NL	3	4	0	0	0	0	0	0	0	0	0	0	0	0	0	0	0	—	0	.000	.000	.000	1B	2	2	0	0	0	1.000
Hank Greenberg	AL	2	5	1	0	0	0	1	1	0	1	0	0	0	0	0	0	0	—	0	.200	.333	.200	1B	1	7	1	0	1	1.000
Mike Greenwell	AL	2	1	0	0	0	0	0	0	0	0	0	0	0	0	0	0	0	—	0	.000	.000	.000	OF	2	2	0	0	0	1.000
Bobby Grich	AL	6	11	1	0	0	0	1	0	0	2	0	4	0	0	0	0	0	—	1	.091	.231	.091	2B	5	5	6	0	0	1.000
Ken Griffey Jr.	AL	6	18	8	2	0	1	13	3	4	1	1	3	0	0	0	0	0	—	0	.444	.474	.722	OF	6	9	0	0	0	1.000
Ken Griffey Sr.	NL	2	4	3	0	0	1	6	2	2	0	0	0	0	0	0	0	0	—	0	.750	.750	1.500	OF	2	1	0	0	0	1.000
Alfredo Griffin	AL	1	0	0	0	0	0	0	0	0	0	0	0	0	0	0	0	0	—	0	—	—	—	SS	1	0	1	0	0	1.000
Marquis Grissom	NL	2	4	1	0	0	1	4	1	1	1	0	1	0	0	0	0	0	—	0	.250	.400	1.000	OF	2	2	1	0	0	1.000
Dick Groat	NL	8	15	5	1	0	0	6	1	5	0	0	2	1	1	0	0	0	—	1	.333	.375	.400	SS	6	8	10	1	3	.947
Jerry Grote	NL	2	2	0	0	0	0	0	0	0	0	0	1	0	0	0	0	0	—	0	.000	.000	.000	C	2	4	0	0	0	1.000

All-Star Games: Player Register 2351

		Batting																						Fielding						
		G	AB	H	2B	3B	HR	TB	R	RBI	TBB	IBB	SO	HBP	SH	SF	SB	CS	SB%	GDP	Avg	OBP	SLG	Pos	G	PO	A	E	DP	FPct
John Grubb	NL	1	1	0	0	0	0	0	0	0	0	0	0	0	0	0	0	0	—	0	.000	.000	.000	OF	1	0	0	0	0	—
Kelly Gruber	AL	1	1	0	0	0	0	0	0	0	1	0	0	0	0	0	2	0	1.00	0	.000	.500	.000	3B	1	0	1	0	0	1.000
Mark Grudzielanek	NL	1	1	0	0	0	0	0	0	0	0	0	0	0	0	0	0	0	—	0	.000	.000	.000	3B	1	0	0	0	0	—
Pedro Guerrero	NL	4	5	0	0	0	0	0	0	0	0	0	2	0	0	0	0	0	—	0	.000	.000	.000	3B	1	0	0	0	0	—
Ozzie Guillen	AL	2	2	0	0	0	0	0	0	0	0	0	0	0	1	0	0	0	—	0	.000	.000	.000	SS	2	1	2	0	0	1.000
Frankie Gustine	NL	3	4	0	0	0	0	0	0	0	1	0	2	0	0	0	0	0	—	0	.000	.200	.000	2B	1	1	1	0	0	1.000
Tony Gwynn	NL	12	27	6	1	0	0	7	4	2	3	0	3	0	0	0	2	0	1.00	1	.222	.300	.259	OF	9	13	2	0	0	1.000
Stan Hack	NL	4	15	6	0	0	0	6	2	0	2	0	5	0	1	0	0	0	—	0	.400	.471	.400	3B	4	5	5	1	1	.909
Chick Hafey	NL	1	4	1	0	0	0	1	0	0	0	0	0	0	0	0	0	0	—	0	.250	.250	.250	OF	1	0	0	0	0	—
Jimmie Hall	AL	2	2	0	0	0	0	0	1	0	1	0	1	0	0	0	0	0	—	0	.000	.333	.000	OF	2	0	0	0	0	—
Tom Haller	NL	2	3	0	0	0	0	0	0	0	0	0	1	0	0	0	0	0	—	0	.000	.000	.000	C	2	13	0	0	0	1.000
Granny Hamner	NL	3	4	0	0	0	0	0	0	0	1	1	0	0	0	0	0	0	—	0	.000	.200	.000	SS	2	1	3	0	1	1.000
Ron Hansen	AL	2	6	3	0	0	0	3	0	0	0	0	1	0	0	0	0	0	—	0	.500	.500	.500	SS	2	2	4	0	1	1.000
Toby Harrah	AL	1	2	0	0	0	0	0	0	0	0	0	0	0	0	0	0	0	—	0	.000	.000	.000	SS	1	0	0	0	0	—
Bud Harrelson	NL	2	5	2	0	0	0	2	2	0	0	0	0	0	0	0	0	0	—	0	.400	.400	.400	SS	2	1	6	0	1	1.000
Gabby Hartnett	NL	5	10	2	0	1	0	4	2	1	0	0	1	0	0	0	0	0	—	0	.200	.200	.400	C	5	27	0	0	0	1.000
Frankie Hayes	AL	4	4	0	0	0	0	0	0	0	0	0	1	0	0	0	0	0	—	0	.000	.000	.000	C	4	10	0	1	0	.909
Von Hayes	NL	1	1	1	0	0	0	1	0	1	0	0	0	0	0	0	0	0	—	0	1.000	1.000	1.000	OF	1	0	0	0	0	—
Jeff Heath	AL	2	3	0	0	0	0	0	0	0	1	0	1	0	0	0	0	0	—	1	.000	.250	.000	OF	1	1	0	1	0	.500
Jim Hegan	AL	2	4	1	1	0	0	2	0	0	0	0	3	0	0	0	0	0	—	0	.250	.250	.500	C	1	7	1	0	0	1.000
Tommy Helms	NL	2	4	1	1	0	0	2	0	0	1	0	0	0	0	0	0	0	—	1	.250	.400	.500	2B	1	1	2	0	0	1.000
Rollie Hemsley	AL	3	7	1	0	1	0	3	1	0	0	0	0	0	0	0	0	0	—	0	.143	.143	.429	C	3	10	0	1	1	.909
Dave Henderson	AL	1	2	0	0	0	0	0	0	0	0	0	1	0	0	0	0	0	—	0	.000	.000	.000	OF	1	2	0	0	0	1.000
Rickey Henderson	AL	10	24	7	0	0	0	7	3	1	2	0	4	0	0	0	2	0	1.00	0	.292	.346	.292	OF	10	9	0	1	0	.900
George Hendrick	AL	2	3	2	0	0	0	2	1	0	0	0	0	0	0	0	1	0	1.00	0	.667	.667	.667	OF	2	3	0	0	0	1.000
	NL	1	2	1	0	0	0	1	0	1	0	0	0	0	0	0	0	0	—	0	.500	.500	.500	OF	1	0	0	0	0	—
	Tot	3	5	3	0	0	0	3	1	1	0	0	0	0	0	0	1	0	1.00	0	.600	.600	.600	OF	3	3	0	0	0	1.000
Tommy Henrich	AL	4	9	1	1	0	0	2	1	0	1	0	4	0	0	0	0	0	—	0	.111	.200	.222	OF	3	6	0	0	0	1.000
Billy Herman	NL	10	30	13	2	0	0	15	3	0	1	0	3	0	0	0	0	0	—	0	.433	.452	.500	2B	8	14	21	2	4	.946
Keith Hernandez	NL	5	10	3	0	0	0	3	0	0	0	0	3	0	0	0	0	0	—	0	.300	.300	.300	1B	4	15	2	0	2	1.000
Tom Herr	NL	1	3	1	1	0	0	2	1	0	0	0	0	0	0	0	0	0	—	0	.333	.333	.667	2B	1	0	1	0	0	1.000
Jim Hickman	NL	1	4	1	0	0	0	1	0	1	0	0	2	0	0	0	0	0	—	0	.250	.250	.250	1B	1	4	1	0	1	1.000
Mike Higgins	AL	2	3	0	0	0	0	0	0	0	0	0	2	0	0	0	0	0	—	0	.000	.000	.000	3B	1	0	1	0	1	1.000
Chuck Hinton	AL	1	0	0	0	0	0	0	0	0	0	0	0	0	0	0	0	0	—	0	—	—	—	OF	1	0	0	0	0	—
Don Hoak	NL	1	1	0	0	0	0	0	0	0	0	0	0	0	0	0	0	0	—	0	.000	.000	.000	3B	1	1	0	0	0	1.000
Gil Hodges	NL	6	12	4	0	0	1	7	3	2	0	0	1	0	0	0	0	0	—	0	.333	.333	.583	1B	4	16	3	0	1	1.000
Dave Hollins	NL	1	1	1	1	0	0	2	0	0	0	0	0	0	0	0	0	0	—	0	1.000	1.000	2.000	3B	1	1	0	0	0	1.000
Tommy Holmes	NL	1	1	0	0	0	0	0	0	0	0	0	0	0	0	0	0	0	—	0	.000	.000	.000	OF	1	1	0	0	0	1.000
Johnny Hopp	NL	1	2	1	0	0	0	1	0	0	0	0	0	0	0	0	0	0	—	0	.500	.500	.500	OF	1	0	0	0	0	—
Willie Horton	AL	4	8	2	0	0	0	2	1	0	2	1	2	0	0	0	0	0	—	0	.250	.400	.250	OF	3	4	0	0	0	1.000
Elston Howard	AL	6	9	0	0	0	0	0	1	0	1	0	7	1	0	0	0	0	—	0	.000	.182	.000	C	6	26	0	0	0	1.000
Frank Howard	AL	4	6	1	0	0	1	4	1	1	1	0	2	0	0	0	0	0	—	0	.167	.286	.667	OF	3	0	0	1	0	.000
Dick Howser	AL	1	1	0	0	0	0	0	0	0	0	0	0	0	0	0	0	0	—	0	.000	.000	.000	3B	1	0	1	0	0	1.000
Glenn Hubbard	NL	1	1	1	0	0	0	1	0	0	0	0	0	0	0	0	0	0	—	0	1.000	1.000	1.000	2B	1	0	0	0	0	—
Randy Hundley	NL	1	1	0	0	0	0	0	0	0	0	0	1	0	0	0	0	0	—	0	.000	.000	.000	C	1	3	0	0	0	1.000
Todd Hundley	NL	1	1	0	0	0	0	0	0	0	0	0	0	0	0	0	0	0	—	0	.000	.000	.000	C	1	1	0	0	0	1.000
Ron Hunt	NL	2	4	1	0	0	0	1	0	0	0	0	1	0	1	0	0	0	—	0	.250	.250	.250	2B	2	1	1	0	0	1.000
Ray Jablonski	NL	1	3	1	0	0	0	1	1	1	0	0	0	0	0	0	0	0	—	0	.333	.333	.333	3B	1	0	1	0	0	1.000
Bo Jackson	AL	1	4	2	0	0	1	5	1	2	0	0	1	0	0	0	1	0	1.00	0	.500	.500	1.250	OF	1	2	0	0	0	1.000
Randy Jackson	NL	2	5	1	0	0	0	1	1	1	0	0	1	0	0	0	0	0	—	0	.200	.200	.200	3B	2	1	1	0	0	1.000
Reggie Jackson	AL	12	26	7	2	0	1	12	2	3	4	1	9	0	0	1	0	0	—	0	.269	.355	.462	OF	11	15	0	1	0	.938
Travis Jackson	NL	1	2	0	0	0	0	0	0	0	0	0	1	0	0	0	0	0	—	0	.000	.000	.000	SS	1	0	1	0	0	1.000
Brook Jacoby	AL	2	2	0	0	0	0	0	0	0	0	0	1	0	0	0	0	0	—	0	.000	.000	.000	3B	1	1	1	0	0	1.000
Julian Javier	NL	2	4	0	0	0	0	0	0	0	0	0	2	0	0	0	0	0	—	0	.000	.000	.000	2B	2	4	1	0	1	1.000
Gregg Jefferies	NL	2	2	1	1	0	0	2	2	0	0	0	1	1	0	0	0	0	—	0	.500	.667	1.000	1B	1	6	0	0	1	1.000
Jackie Jensen	AL	3	5	0	0	0	0	0	0	1	0	0	1	0	0	0	0	0	—	1	.000	.000	.000	OF	2	1	0	0	0	1.000
Bill Johnson	AL	1	0	0	0	0	0	0	0	0	0	0	0	0	0	0	0	0	—	0	—	—	—	3B	1	0	0	0	0	—
Bob Johnson	AL	5	9	1	0	0	0	1	0	0	1	0	5	0	0	0	0	0	—	0	.111	.200	.111	OF	3	7	1	0	0	1.000
Charles Johnson	NL	1	1	0	0	0	0	0	0	0	0	0	1	0	0	0	0	0	—	0	.000	.000	.000	C	1	2	0	0	0	1.000
Dave Johnson	AL	2	6	1	0	0	0	1	0	0	0	0	2	0	0	0	0	0	—	0	.167	.167	.167	2B	2	6	2	0	1	1.000
	NL	1	1	0	0	0	0	0	0	0	0	0	0	0	0	0	0	0	—	0	.000	.000	.000	2B	1	1	1	0	0	1.000
	Tot	3	7	1	0	0	0	1	0	0	0	0	2	0	0	0	0	0	—	0	.143	.143	.143	2B	3	7	3	0	1	1.000
Howard Johnson	NL	2	5	1	0	0	0	1	0	1	0	0	2	0	0	0	1	0	1.00	0	.200	.200	.200	3B	2	0	0	0	0	—
Lance Johnson	NL	1	4	3	1	0	0	4	1	0	0	0	0	0	0	0	1	1	.50	0	.750	.750	1.000	OF	1	5	0	0	0	1.000
Chipper Jones	NL	2	3	1	0	0	0	1	1	0	0	0	0	0	0	0	0	0	—	0	.333	.333	.333	3B	2	1	2	0	0	1.000
Cleon Jones	NL	1	4	2	0	0	0	2	2	0	0	0	0	0	0	0	0	0	—	0	.500	.500	.500	OF	1	3	0	0	0	1.000
Puddin' Head Jones	NL	2	9	1	0	0	0	1	0	0	1	0	1	0	0	0	0	0	—	1	.111	.200	.111	3B	2	5	3	0	1	1.000
Eddie Joost	AL	1	2	1	0	0	0	1	1	2	1	0	0	0	0	0	0	0	—	0	.500	.667	.500	SS	1	2	2	0	2	1.000
Felix Jose	NL	1	2	1	0	0	0	1	0	0	0	0	0	0	0	0	0	0	—	0	.500	.500	.500	OF	1	1	0	0	0	1.000
Duane Josephson	AL	1	0	0	0	0	0	0	0	0	0	0	0	0	0	0	0	0	—	0	—	—	—	C	1	0	0	0	0	—
Wally Joyner	AL	1	1	0	0	0	0	0	0	0	0	0	0	0	0	0	0	0	—	0	.000	.000	.000	1B	1	3	1	0	0	1.000
David Justice	NL	2	5	1	0	0	0	1	0	0	0	0	0	0	0	0	0	0	—	0	.200	.200	.200	OF	2	2	0	1	0	.667
Al Kaline	AL	16	37	12	1	0	2	19	7	6	2	0	6	1	0	0	1	0	1.00	0	.324	.375	.514	OF	13	21	1	0	0	1.000
Eddie Kasko	NL	1	1	1	0	0	0	1	0	0	0	0	0	0	0	0	0	0	—	0	1.000	1.000	1.000	SS	1	2	4	0	2	1.000
Eddie Kazak	NL	1	2	2	0	0	0	2	0	1	0	0	0	0	0	0	0	0	—	0	1.000	1.000	1.000	3B	1	0	1	0	0	1.000
George Kell	AL	7	23	4	0	0	1	7	3	3	2	0	4	0	1	0	1	0	1.00	1	.174	.240	.304	3B	6	6	9	0	1	1.000
Charlie Keller	AL	3	7	1	0	0	1	4	2	2	1	0	3	0	0	0	0	0	—	0	.143	.250	.571	OF	2	5	0	0	0	1.000
Roberto Kelly	AL	1	2	1	1	0	0	2	0	2	0	0	1	0	0	0	0	0	—	0	.500	.500	1.000	OF	1	1	0	0	0	1.000
	NL	1	1	0	0	0	0	0	0	0	0	0	1	0	0	0	0	0	—	0	.000	.000	.000	OF	1	0	1	0	0	1.000
	Tot	2	3	1	1	0	0	2	0	2	0	0	2	0	0	0	0	0	—	0	.333	.333	.667	OF	2	1	1	0	0	1.000
Ken Keltner	AL	7	17	4	1	0	0	5	4	0	2	0	5	0	0	0	0	0	—	1	.235	.316	.294	3B	6	5	14	0	0	1.000
Jason Kendall	NL	1	0	0	0	0	0	0	0	0	0	0	0	0	0	0	0	0	—	0	—	—	—	C	1	0	0	0	0	—
Terry Kennedy	AL	1	2	0	0	0	0	0	0	0	0	0	1	0	0	0	0	0	—	0	.000	.000	.000	C	1	3	1	0	0	1.000
	NL	2	3	1	0	0	0	1	0	1	0	0	0	0	0	0	0	0	—	0	.333	.333	.333	C	1	0	0	1	0	.000

		Batting																						Fielding						
		G	AB	H	2B	3B	HR	TB	R	RBI	TBB	IBB	SO	HBP	SH	SF	SB	CS	SB%	GDP	Avg	OBP	SLG	Pos	G	PO	A	E	DP	FPct
	Tot	3	5	1	0	0	0	1	0	1	0	0	1	0	0	0	0	0	—	0	.200	.200	.200	C	2	3	1	1	0	.800
Buddy Kerr	NL	1	2	0	0	0	0	0	0	0	0	0	1	0	0	0	0	0	—	0	.000	.000	.000	SS	1	1	0	0	0	1.000
Don Kessinger	NL	6	12	3	0	1	0	5	1	1	0	0	1	0	0	0	0	0	—	0	.250	.250	.417	SS	6	3	3	0	1	1.000
Harmon Killebrew	AL	11	26	8	0	0	3	17	4	6	2	0	6	0	0	0	0	0	—	1	.308	.357	.654	1B	4	30	2	1	6	.970
Ralph Kiner	NL	5	15	4	1	0	3	14	3	4	0	0	2	0	0	0	0	0	—	1	.267	.267	.933	OF	4	6	0	0	0	1.000
Dave Kingman	NL	2	3	0	0	0	0	0	0	0	0	0	2	0	0	0	0	0	—	0	.000	.000	.000	OF	2	1	0	0	0	1.000
Ron Kittle	AL	1	2	1	0	0	0	1	1	0	0	0	1	0	0	0	0	0	—	0	.500	.500	.500	OF	1	1	0	0	0	1.000
Chuck Klein	NL	2	7	2	0	0	0	2	0	1	0	0	0	0	0	0	0	0	—	0	.286	.286	.286	OF	2	4	0	0	0	1.000
Ted Kluszewski	NL	4	14	7	3	0	1	13	4	4	0	0	0	0	0	0	0	0	—	1	.500	.500	.929	1B	4	21	1	0	2	1.000
Ray Knight	NL	2	4	1	0	0	0	1	1	0	1	0	1	0	0	0	1	0	1.00	0	.250	.400	.250	3B	2	1	5	0	0	1.000
Chuck Knoblauch	AL	4	5	1	0	0	0	1	1	0	1	0	2	0	0	0	0	0	—	0	.200	.333	.200	2B	4	5	4	0	0	1.000
Bobby Knoop	AL	1	2	0	0	0	0	0	0	0	0	0	1	0	0	0	0	0	—	0	.000	.000	.000	2B	1	3	1	0	0	1.000
Mike Kreevich	AL	1	2	0	0	0	0	0	0	0	0	0	0	0	0	0	0	0	—	0	.000	.000	.000	OF	1	1	0	0	0	1.000
John Kruk	NL	2	5	2	0	0	0	2	1	0	0	0	2	0	0	0	0	0	—	0	.400	.400	.400	1B	1	7	0	0	0	1.000
Tony Kubek	AL	2	5	0	0	0	0	0	1	0	1	0	2	0	0	0	0	0	—	0	.000	.167	.000	SS	1	1	2	1	0	.750
Harvey Kuenn	AL	7	16	3	0	0	0	3	3	1	2	0	0	0	0	0	0	0	—	0	.188	.278	.188	SS	3	3	4	0	0	1.000
Whitey Kurowski	NL	3	6	1	1	0	0	2	0	2	0	0	3	0	0	0	0	0	—	0	.167	.167	.333	3B	3	2	3	0	0	1.000
Chet Laabs	AL	1	3	0	0	0	0	0	1	0	1	0	1	0	0	0	0	0	—	1	.000	.250	.000	OF	1	7	0	0	0	1.000
Jim Landis	AL	1	1	0	0	0	0	0	0	0	0	0	1	0	0	0	0	0	—	0	.000	.000	.000	OF	1	2	0	0	0	1.000
Ken Landreaux	AL	1	1	0	0	0	0	0	0	0	0	0	0	0	0	0	0	0	—	0	.000	.000	.000	OF	1	1	0	0	0	1.000
Ray Lankford	NL	1	2	0	0	0	0	0	0	0	1	0	1	0	0	0	0	0	—	0	.000	.333	.000	OF	1	0	0	0	0	—
Carney Lansford	AL	1	1	0	0	0	0	0	0	0	0	0	0	0	0	0	0	0	—	0	.000	.000	.000	3B	1	0	1	0	0	1.000
Norm Larker	NL	2	1	0	0	0	0	0	1	0	1	0	0	0	0	0	0	0	—	0	.000	.500	.000	1B	1	3	0	0	0	1.000
Barry Larkin	NL	6	11	1	0	0	0	1	1	1	0	0	2	0	0	1	1	0	1.00	0	.091	.083	.091	SS	6	5	11	0	1	1.000
Tim Laudner	AL	1	1	1	1	0	0	2	0	0	0	0	0	0	0	0	0	0	—	0	1.000	1.000	2.000	C	1	3	0	0	0	1.000
Cookie Lavagetto	NL	2	3	0	0	0	0	0	0	0	0	0	0	0	0	0	0	0	—	0	.000	.000	.000	3B	2	0	1	0	0	1.000
Vance Law	NL	1	0	0	0	0	0	0	0	0	0	0	0	0	0	0	0	0	—	0	—	—	—	2B	1	0	0	0	0	—
Jim Lefebvre	NL	1	2	0	0	0	0	0	0	0	0	0	0	0	0	0	0	0	—	0	.000	.000	.000	2B	1	2	0	0	0	1.000
Ron LeFlore	AL	1	2	1	0	0	0	1	0	0	0	0	1	0	0	0	0	0	—	0	.500	.500	.500	OF	1	2	0	0	0	1.000
Chet Lemon	AL	3	4	1	0	0	0	1	1	0	1	0	2	1	0	0	0	1	.00	0	.250	.500	.250	OF	3	2	0	1	0	.667
Jim Lemon	AL	1	1	0	0	0	0	0	0	0	1	0	1	0	0	0	0	0	—	0	.000	.500	.000	OF	1	1	0	0	0	1.000
Jeffrey Leonard	AL	1	1	0	0	0	0	0	0	0	0	0	1	0	0	0	0	0	—	0	.000	.000	.000	—	0	0	0	0	0	—
	NL	1	2	0	0	0	0	0	0	0	0	0	0	0	0	0	0	0	—	0	.000	.000	.000	OF	1	0	0	0	0	—
	Tot	2	3	0	0	0	0	0	0	0	0	0	1	0	0	0	0	0	—	0	.000	.000	.000	OF	1	0	0	0	0	—
Buddy Lewis	AL	2	3	0	0	0	0	0	0	0	0	0	0	0	0	0	0	0	—	0	.000	.000	.000	3B	1	0	1	0	0	1.000
Whitey Lockman	NL	1	3	0	0	0	0	0	0	0	0	0	1	0	0	0	0	0	—	0	.000	.000	.000	1B	1	5	0	0	1	1.000
Kenny Lofton	AL	3	8	3	0	0	0	3	0	2	0	0	2	0	0	0	3	0	1.00	0	.375	.375	.375	OF	3	1	0	0	0	1.000
Johnny Logan	NL	2	4	1	0	0	0	1	0	1	0	0	1	0	0	0	0	0	—	0	.250	.250	.250	SS	1	1	1	0	0	1.000
Sherm Lollar	AL	5	6	2	1	0	0	3	0	0	1	0	0	0	0	0	0	0	—	0	.333	.429	.500	C	4	7	0	0	0	1.000
Ernie Lombardi	NL	5	13	5	0	0	0	5	0	1	1	0	0	0	0	0	0	0	—	0	.385	.429	.385	C	5	19	0	0	0	1.000
Dale Long	NL	1	2	0	0	0	0	0	0	0	0	0	2	0	0	0	0	0	—	0	.000	.000	.000	1B	1	6	0	0	0	1.000
Stan Lopata	NL	1	3	0	0	0	0	0	0	0	0	0	1	0	0	0	0	0	—	0	.000	.000	.000	C	1	10	0	0	0	1.000
Davey Lopes	NL	4	5	2	0	0	0	2	0	1	1	0	1	0	0	0	0	1	.00	0	.400	.500	.400	2B	4	5	4	0	0	1.000
Al Lopez	NL	2	3	0	0	0	0	0	0	0	0	0	1	0	1	0	0	0	—	0	.000	.000	.000	C	2	8	1	0	1	1.000
Javy Lopez	NL	1	1	1	0	0	1	4	1	1	0	0	0	0	0	0	0	0	—	0	1.000	1.000	4.000	C	1	4	1	0	0	1.000
Peanuts Lowrey	NL	1	2	1	0	0	0	1	0	0	0	0	0	0	0	0	0	0	—	0	.500	.500	.500	OF	1	3	0	0	0	1.000
Greg Luzinski	NL	4	8	2	0	0	1	5	1	3	1	0	1	0	0	0	0	0	—	0	.250	.333	.625	OF	3	0	0	0	0	—
Fred Lynn	AL	9	20	6	0	0	4	18	5	10	2	0	6	0	0	0	0	0	—	0	.300	.364	.900	OF	8	9	0	0	0	1.000
Ray Mack	AL	1	1	0	0	0	0	0	0	0	0	0	1	0	0	0	0	0	—	0	.000	.000	.000	2B	1	0	0	0	0	—
Bill Madlock	NL	3	4	1	0	0	0	1	0	2	0	0	0	0	0	0	0	0	—	0	.250	.250	.250	3B	3	0	1	0	0	1.000
Frank Malzone	AL	7	20	3	0	0	1	6	3	2	1	0	1	0	0	0	0	0	—	0	.150	.190	.300	3B	7	6	14	0	3	1.000
Gus Mancuso	NL	2	2	0	0	0	0	0	0	0	0	0	0	0	0	0	0	0	—	0	.000	.000	.000	C	1	1	0	0	0	1.000
Felix Mantilla	AL	1	2	0	0	0	0	0	0	0	0	0	0	0	0	0	0	0	—	0	.000	.000	.000	2B	1	1	1	0	1	1.000
Mickey Mantle	AL	16	43	10	0	0	2	16	5	4	9	0	17	0	0	0	0	1	.00	0	.233	.365	.372	OF	14	28	0	0	0	1.000
Heinie Manush	AL	1	2	0	0	0	0	0	0	0	1	0	0	0	0	0	1	0	1.00	0	.000	.333	.000	OF	1	0	0	0	0	—
Marty Marion	NL	5	12	1	0	0	0	1	1	0	0	0	4	0	1	0	0	0	—	0	.083	.083	.083	SS	5	8	14	0	4	1.000
Roger Maris	AL	7	19	2	1	0	0	3	2	2	3	0	5	0	0	1	0	0	—	0	.105	.217	.158	OF	6	11	0	0	0	1.000
Willard Marshall	NL	3	3	0	0	0	0	0	1	0	3	0	1	0	0	0	0	0	—	0	.000	.500	.000	OF	2	4	0	1	0	.800
Pepper Martin	NL	3	8	1	0	0	0	1	1	1	1	0	3	0	0	0	1	0	1.00	0	.125	.222	.125	3B	2	0	3	1	0	.750
Edgar Martinez	AL	4	7	2	0	0	1	5	1	1	0	0	1	0	0	0	0	1	.00	0	.286	.286	.714	—	0	0	0	0	0	—
Tino Martinez	AL	2	3	1	0	0	0	1	0	0	0	0	0	0	0	0	0	0	—	0	.333	.333	.333	1B	1	10	0	0	0	1.000
Phil Masi	NL	3	4	1	0	0	0	1	0	0	0	0	0	0	0	0	0	0	—	0	.250	.250	.250	C	3	8	1	0	0	1.000
Eddie Mathews	NL	10	25	2	0	0	2	8	4	3	1	0	5	1	0	0	0	0	—	1	.080	.148	.320	3B	9	4	7	6	0	.647
Gary Matthews	NL	1	2	0	0	0	0	0	0	0	0	0	0	0	0	0	0	0	—	0	.000	.000	.000	OF	1	2	0	0	0	1.000
Don Mattingly	AL	6	9	1	1	0	0	2	0	0	2	0	2	0	0	0	0	0	—	0	.111	.273	.222	1B	5	27	1	1	3	.966
Dave May	AL	1	2	0	0	0	0	0	0	0	0	0	0	0	0	0	0	0	—	0	.000	.000	.000	OF	1	0	0	0	0	—
Lee May	NL	3	6	1	0	0	0	1	0	1	1	0	1	0	0	0	0	0	—	0	.167	.286	.167	1B	3	22	2	0	4	1.000
Pinky May	NL	1	1	0	0	0	0	0	0	0	0	0	0	1	0	0	0	0	—	0	.000	.500	.000	3B	1	0	0	0	0	—
John Mayberry	AL	2	4	1	1	0	0	2	0	0	1	0	0	0	0	0	0	0	—	0	.250	.400	.500	1B	1	8	0	0	1	1.000
Willie Mays	NL	24	75	23	2	3	3	40	20	9	7	0	14	0	0	0	6	1	.86	0	.307	.366	.533	OF	22	55	0	0	0	1.000
Bill Mazeroski	NL	7	16	2	0	0	0	2	0	2	0	0	1	1	1	0	0	0	—	1	.125	.176	.125	2B	7	15	8	0	5	1.000
Lee Mazzilli	NL	1	1	1	0	0	1	4	1	2	1	0	0	0	0	0	0	0	—	0	1.000	1.000	4.000	OF	1	0	0	0	0	—
Dick McAuliffe	AL	3	9	2	0	0	1	5	2	2	0	0	1	0	0	0	0	0	—	0	.222	.222	.556	SS	2	4	1	0	0	1.000
Tim McCarver	NL	2	3	3	1	0	0	4	1	0	0	0	0	0	0	0	0	0	—	0	1.000	1.000	1.333	C	2	8	1	0	1	1.000
Frank McCormick	NL	6	12	1	0	0	0	1	1	0	0	0	1	0	1	0	0	0	—	0	.083	.083	.083	1B	6	24	2	0	1	1.000
Willie McCovey	NL	6	16	3	0	0	2	9	2	4	1	1	6	0	0	0	0	0	—	2	.188	.235	.563	1B	5	27	1	0	1	1.000
Gil McDougald	AL	4	4	1	0	0	0	1	1	1	0	0	0	0	0	0	0	0	—	0	.250	.250	.250	SS	3	1	3	0	0	1.000
Willie McGee	NL	4	10	2	1	0	0	3	0	2	0	0	0	0	0	0	0	0	—	0	.200	.200	.300	OF	4	6	0	0	0	1.000
Fred McGriff	NL	4	9	3	0	0	1	6	1	3	0	0	4	0	0	0	0	0	—	0	.333	.333	.667	1B	4	14	2	0	0	1.000
Mark McGwire	AL	7	16	4	0	0	0	4	1	2	0	0	6	0	0	0	0	0	—	0	.250	.250	.250	1B	7	37	1	1	1	.974
Roy McMillan	NL	2	4	2	0	0	0	2	1	0	1	0	0	0	0	0	0	0	—	0	.500	.600	.500	SS	2	3	5	0	1	1.000
George McQuinn	AL	3	12	3	0	0	0	3	1	0	0	0	2	0	0	0	1	0	1.00	0	.250	.250	.250	1B	3	28	2	1	0	.968
Joe Medwick	NL	10	27	7	2	0	1	12	2	6	1	0	3	0	1	0	0	0	—	0	.259	.286	.444	OF	8	6	0	0	0	1.000
Denis Menke	NL	2	1	0	0	0	0	0	0	0	1	0	1	1	0	0	0	0	—	0	.000	.667	.000	2B	1	2	1	0	0	1.000

		Batting																						Fielding						
		G	AB	H	2B	3B	HR	TB	R	RBI	TBB	IBB	SO	HBP	SH	SF	SB	CS	SB%	GDP	Avg	OBP	SLG	Pos	G	PO	A	E	DP	FPct
Cass Michaels	AL	2	3	1	1	0	0	2	1	0	1	0	0	0	0	0	0	0	—	0	.333	.500	.667	2B	1	1	3	0	2	1.000
Felix Millan	NL	2	4	1	1	0	0	2	1	2	0	0	1	0	0	0	0	0	—	0	.250	.250	.500	2B	2	2	2	0	1	1.000
Eddie Miller	NL	4	4	0	0	0	0	0	0	0	0	0	3	0	0	0	0	0	—	0	.000	.000	.000	SS	4	4	4	0	2	1.000
Minnie Minoso	AL	8	20	6	2	0	0	8	2	2	2	0	3	0	0	0	0	0	—	1	.300	.364	.400	OF	8	5	2	1	0	.875
Dale Mitchell	AL	2	2	1	1	0	0	2	0	1	0	0	1	0	0	0	0	0	—	0	.500	.500	1.000	OF	2	2	0	1	0	.667
Kevin Mitchell	NL	2	6	2	0	0	0	2	1	1	0	0	3	0	0	0	0	0	—	0	.333	.333	.333	OF	2	1	0	0	0	1.000
Johnny Mize	NL	9	23	5	1	0	1	9	2	2	1	0	3	0	0	0	0	0	—	0	.217	.250	.391	1B	8	43	1	1	5	.978
	AL	1	1	1	0	0	0	1	0	0	0	0	0	0	0	0	0	0	—	0	1.000	1.000	1.000	—	0	0	0	0	0	—
	Tot	10	24	6	1	0	1	10	2	2	1	0	3	0	0	0	0	0	—	0	.250	.280	.417	1B	8	43	1	1	5	.978
Paul Molitor	AL	6	8	1	0	0	0	1	0	0	1	0	3	0	0	0	0	0	—	1	.125	.222	.125	3B	2	0	0	0	0	—
Rick Monday	AL	1	2	0	0	0	0	0	0	0	0	0	1	0	0	0	0	0	—	0	.000	.000	.000	OF	1	0	0	0	0	—
	NL	1	2	0	0	0	0	0	0	0	0	0	0	0	0	0	0	0	—	1	.000	.000	.000	OF	1	1	0	0	0	1.000
	Tot	2	4	0	0	0	0	0	0	0	0	0	1	0	0	0	0	0	—	1	.000	.000	.000	OF	2	1	0	0	0	1.000
Raul Mondesi	NL	1	1	0	0	0	0	0	0	0	0	0	0	0	0	0	0	0	—	0	.000	.000	.000	OF	1	2	0	0	0	1.000
Don Money	AL	2	3	0	0	0	0	0	0	0	0	0	1	0	0	0	0	0	—	0	.000	.000	.000	2B	1	1	1	0	1	1.000
Willie Montanez	NL	1	2	0	0	0	0	0	0	0	0	0	1	0	0	0	0	0	—	0	.000	.000	.000	1B	1	6	1	0	1	1.000
Wally Moon	NL	3	5	0	0	0	0	0	0	0	3	0	2	0	0	0	0	0	—	0	.000	.375	.000	OF	2	2	0	0	0	1.000
Jo-Jo Moore	NL	4	5	0	0	0	0	0	0	0	0	0	0	0	0	0	0	0	—	0	.000	.000	.000	OF	2	2	0	0	0	1.000
Terry Moore	NL	4	10	0	0	0	0	0	0	1	1	0	2	0	0	0	0	0	—	0	.000	.091	.000	OF	4	3	0	0	0	1.000
Jerry Morales	NL	1	0	0	0	0	0	0	1	0	0	0	0	1	0	0	0	0	—	0	—	1.000	—	OF	1	1	0	0	0	1.000
Billy Moran	AL	2	7	2	0	0	0	2	0	0	0	0	1	0	0	0	0	0	—	0	.286	.286	.286	2B	2	1	4	0	2	1.000
Mickey Morandini	NL	1	1	0	0	0	0	0	0	0	0	0	1	0	0	0	0	0	—	0	.000	.000	.000	2B	1	0	1	0	0	1.000
Joe Morgan	NL	9	26	7	2	0	1	12	7	3	4	0	4	0	0	1	1	0	1.00	1	.269	.355	.462	2B	9	15	19	0	3	1.000
Lloyd Moseby	AL	1	0	0	0	0	0	0	0	0	1	0	0	0	0	0	1	0	1.00	0	—	1.000	—	OF	1	0	0	0	0	—
Manny Mota	NL	1	1	0	0	0	0	0	0	0	0	0	0	0	0	0	0	0	—	0	.000	.000	.000	OF	1	0	0	0	0	—
Don Mueller	NL	2	3	2	1	0	0	3	0	1	0	0	0	0	0	0	0	0	—	0	.667	.667	1.000	OF	1	0	0	0	0	—
Ray Mueller	NL	1	0	0	0	0	0	0	0	0	0	0	0	0	0	0	0	0	—	0	—	—	—	C	1	0	0	0	0	—
Pat Mullin	AL	1	1	0	0	0	0	0	0	0	1	0	1	0	0	0	1	0	1.00	0	.000	.500	.000	OF	1	0	0	0	0	—
Thurman Munson	AL	6	10	2	1	0	0	3	1	0	1	0	2	1	0	0	0	0	—	0	.200	.333	.300	C	5	18	2	1	0	.952
Bobby Murcer	AL	4	11	1	0	0	0	1	0	0	1	0	1	0	0	0	0	0	—	1	.091	.167	.091	OF	4	2	1	0	0	1.000
	NL	1	2	0	0	0	0	0	0	0	0	0	0	0	0	0	0	0	—	0	.000	.000	.000	OF	1	1	0	0	0	1.000
	Tot	5	13	1	0	0	0	1	0	0	1	0	1	0	0	0	0	0	—	1	.077	.143	.077	OF	5	3	1	0	0	1.000
Dale Murphy	NL	7	15	4	1	0	1	8	2	2	2	0	2	0	0	0	0	0	—	0	.267	.353	.533	OF	7	6	0	0	0	1.000
Eddie Murray	AL	5	10	1	1	0	0	2	0	0	1	0	1	0	0	0	0	0	—	0	.100	.182	.200	1B	5	18	3	0	0	1.000
	NL	1	1	0	0	0	0	0	0	0	0	0	1	0	0	0	0	0	—	0	.000	.000	.000	1B	1	3	0	0	0	1.000
	Tot	6	11	1	1	0	0	2	0	0	1	0	2	0	0	0	0	0	—	0	.091	.167	.182	1B	6	21	3	0	0	1.000
Stan Musial	NL	24	63	20	2	0	6	40	11	10	7	1	7	1	1	0	1	1	.50	1	.317	.394	.635	OF	12	15	3	0	0	1.000
Charlie Neal	NL	3	2	0	0	0	0	0	0	0	0	0	0	0	0	0	0	0	—	0	.000	.000	.000	2B	3	1	4	1	1	.833
Dave Nelson	AL	1	0	0	0	0	0	0	0	0	0	0	0	0	0	0	0	0	—	0	—	—	—	3B	1	1	0	0	0	1.000
Graig Nettles	AL	5	9	2	0	0	0	2	0	0	0	0	2	0	0	0	1	0	1.00	0	.222	.222	.222	3B	5	3	7	0	0	1.000
	NL	1	2	0	0	0	0	0	0	0	0	0	0	0	0	0	0	0	—	0	.000	.000	.000	3B	1	0	1	0	0	1.000
	Tot	6	11	2	0	0	0	2	0	0	0	0	2	0	0	0	1	0	1.00	0	.182	.182	.182	3B	6	3	8	0	0	1.000
Bill Nicholson	NL	4	6	1	1	0	0	2	1	1	0	0	1	0	0	0	0	0	—	0	.167	.167	.333	OF	3	2	0	0	0	1.000
Matt Nokes	AL	1	2	0	0	0	0	0	0	0	0	0	0	0	1	0	0	0	—	0	.000	.000	.000	C	1	8	0	0	0	1.000
Irv Noren	AL	1	0	0	0	0	0	0	0	0	0	0	0	0	0	0	0	0	—	0	—	—	—	OF	1	0	0	0	0	—
Jose Offerman	NL	1	0	0	0	0	0	0	0	0	0	0	0	0	0	0	0	0	—	0	—	—	—	SS	1	0	0	0	0	—
Ben Oglivie	AL	3	4	0	0	0	0	0	0	0	1	0	2	0	0	0	0	0	—	0	.000	.200	.000	OF	2	1	0	0	0	1.000
John Olerud	AL	1	2	0	0	0	0	0	0	0	0	0	0	0	0	0	0	0	—	0	.000	.000	.000	1B	1	4	0	0	0	1.000
Tony Oliva	AL	6	19	5	3	0	0	8	0	0	1	0	4	0	0	0	0	2	.00	0	.263	.300	.421	OF	6	6	0	0	0	1.000
Al Oliver	NL	5	7	4	3	0	0	7	3	0	1	0	0	0	0	0	0	1	.00	0	.571	.625	1.000	OF	3	1	0	0	0	1.000
	AL	2	2	0	0	0	0	0	0	0	0	0	0	0	0	0	0	0	—	0	.000	.000	.000	OF	1	0	0	0	0	—
	Tot	7	9	4	3	0	0	7	3	0	1	0	0	0	0	0	0	1	.00	0	.444	.500	.778	OF	4	1	0	0	0	1.000
Greg Olson	NL	1	1	0	0	0	0	0	0	0	0	0	1	0	0	0	0	0	—	0	.000	.000	.000	C	1	0	0	0	0	—
Paul O'Neill	AL	3	4	0	0	0	0	0	0	0	0	0	1	0	0	0	0	0	—	0	.000	.000	.000	OF	2	1	0	0	0	1.000
	NL	1	2	0	0	0	0	0	0	0	0	0	1	0	0	0	0	0	—	0	.000	.000	.000	OF	1	0	0	0	0	—
	Tot	4	6	0	0	0	0	0	0	0	0	0	2	0	0	0	0	0	—	0	.000	.000	.000	OF	3	1	0	0	0	1.000
Amos Otis	AL	4	7	2	0	0	0	2	0	1	0	0	1	0	0	0	1	0	1.00	1	.286	.286	.286	OF	3	2	0	0	0	1.000
Mel Ott	NL	11	23	5	1	1	0	8	2	0	1	0	6	0	0	0	1	0	1.00	0	.217	.250	.348	OF	7	9	1	0	0	1.000
Mickey Owen	NL	2	2	1	0	0	1	4	1	1	0	0	0	0	0	0	0	0	—	0	.500	.500	2.000	C	1	0	0	0	0	—
Andy Pafko	NL	4	10	4	0	0	0	4	0	0	1	0	1	0	0	0	0	0	—	0	.400	.455	.400	OF	3	8	0	0	0	1.000
Rafael Palmeiro	AL	1	0	0	0	0	0	0	0	0	1	1	0	0	0	0	0	0	—	0	—	1.000	—	1B	1	2	0	0	0	1.000
	NL	1	0	0	0	0	0	0	0	0	1	0	0	0	0	0	0	0	—	0	—	1.000	—	OF	1	1	0	0	0	1.000
	Tot	2	0	0	0	0	0	0	0	0	2	1	0	0	0	0	0	0	—	0	—	1.000	—	1B	1	2	0	0	0	1.000
Dave Parker	NL	6	15	4	0	0	1	7	2	2	1	1	5	0	0	1	0	0	—	0	.267	.294	.467	OF	6	4	2	0	0	1.000
Lance Parrish	AL	6	11	2	1	0	0	3	1	0	1	0	4	0	0	0	0	0	—	0	.182	.250	.273	C	6	13	4	1	0	.944
	NL	1	1	0	0	0	0	0	0	0	0	0	0	0	0	0	0	0	—	0	.000	.000	.000	C	1	0	0	0	0	—
	Tot	7	12	2	1	0	0	3	1	0	1	0	4	0	0	0	0	0	—	0	.167	.231	.250	C	7	13	4	1	0	.944
Larry Parrish	NL	1	0	0	0	0	0	0	0	0	0	0	0	0	0	0	0	0	—	0	—	—	—	3B	1	0	0	0	0	—
	AL	1	1	1	0	0	0	1	0	0	0	0	0	0	0	0	0	0	—	0	1.000	1.000	1.000	—	0	0	0	0	0	—
	Tot	2	1	1	0	0	0	1	0	0	0	0	0	0	0	0	0	0	—	0	1.000	1.000	1.000	3B	1	0	0	0	0	—
Freddie Patek	AL	2	3	1	0	0	0	1	0	0	0	0	1	0	0	0	0	0	—	0	.333	.333	.333	SS	2	1	2	0	0	1.000
Albie Pearson	AL	1	4	2	1	0	0	3	1	0	0	0	1	0	0	0	0	0	—	0	.500	.500	.750	OF	1	4	0	0	0	1.000
Tony Pena	NL	5	4	0	0	0	0	0	0	0	0	0	1	0	0	0	1	0	1.00	1	.000	.000	.000	C	4	11	1	0	1	1.000
Terry Pendleton	NL	1	2	1	0	0	0	1	0	0	0	0	0	0	0	0	0	0	—	0	.500	.500	.500	3B	1	0	2	0	0	1.000
Joe Pepitone	AL	3	5	0	0	0	0	0	0	0	0	0	3	0	0	0	0	0	—	0	.000	.000	.000	1B	2	9	0	0	0	1.000
Tony Perez	NL	7	8	1	0	0	1	4	1	1	1	0	6	0	0	0	0	0	—	0	.125	.222	.500	3B	4	2	6	0	0	1.000
Johnny Pesky	AL	1	2	0	0	0	0	0	0	0	0	0	0	0	0	0	0	0	—	1	.000	.000	.000	SS	1	1	0	1	0	.500
Rico Petrocelli	AL	2	4	1	1	0	0	2	0	0	0	0	1	0	0	0	0	0	—	0	.250	.250	.500	SS	2	1	4	1	0	.833
Babe Phelps	NL	2	1	0	0	0	0	0	0	0	1	0	0	0	0	0	0	0	—	0	.000	.500	.000	C	1	1	0	0	0	1.000
Mike Piazza	NL	5	12	4	1	0	2	11	2	4	1	0	2	0	0	0	0	0	—	0	.333	.385	.917	C	5	21	1	0	0	1.000
Jimmy Piersall	AL	2	1	0	0	0	0	0	0	0	0	0	0	0	0	0	0	0	—	0	.000	.000	.000	OF	2	1	0	0	0	1.000
Vada Pinson	NL	3	1	0	0	0	0	0	0	0	1	0	1	0	0	0	0	0	—	0	.000	.500	.000	OF	2	1	0	0	0	1.000
Biff Pocoroba	NL	1	0	0	0	0	0	0	0	0	0	0	0	0	0	0	0	0	—	0	—	—	—	C	1	0	0	0	0	—
Darrell Porter	AL	3	5	1	1	0	0	2	0	0	0	0	1	0	0	0	0	0	—	0	.200	.200	.400	C	2	2	1	0	0	1.000

		Batting																						Fielding						
		G	AB	H	2B	3B	HR	TB	R	RBI	TBB	IBB	SO	HBP	SH	SF	SB	CS	SB%	GDP	Avg	OBP	SLG	Pos	G	PO	A	E	DP	FPct
Boog Powell	AL	3	9	1	0	0	0	1	0	0	0	0	3	0	0	0	0	0	—	0	.111	.111	.111	1B	3	16	1	0	1	1.000
Vic Power	AL	5	7	2	0	0	0	2	1	1	0	0	0	0	0	0	0	0	—	0	.286	.286	.286	1B	4	15	1	0	1	1.000
Kirby Puckett	AL	10	24	7	1	0	1	11	3	3	1	0	5	0	0	0	1	0	1.00	0	.292	.320	.458	OF	10	14	0	0	0	1.000
Rip Radcliff	AL	1	2	1	0	0	0	1	0	0	0	0	0	0	0	0	0	0	—	0	.500	.500	.500	OF	1	2	0	0	0	1.000
Tim Raines	NL	7	10	3	0	1	0	5	1	2	2	0	4	0	0	0	3	0	1.00	1	.300	.417	.500	OF	7	9	0	0	0	1.000
Manny Ramirez	AL	1	0	0	0	0	0	0	0	0	2	0	0	0	0	0	0	0	—	0	—	1.000	—	OF	1	2	0	0	0	1.000
Willie Randolph	AL	4	13	4	0	0	0	4	0	1	0	0	3	0	0	0	0	0	—	0	.308	.308	.308	2B	4	2	15	2	2	.895
	NL	1	1	0	0	0	0	0	0	0	0	0	0	0	0	0	0	0	—	0	.000	.000	.000	2B	1	0	0	0	0	—
	Tot	5	14	4	0	0	0	4	0	1	0	0	3	0	0	0	0	0	—	0	.286	.286	.286	2B	5	2	15	2	2	.895
Pee Wee Reese	NL	8	17	2	1	0	0	3	0	2	3	0	3	0	0	0	0	0	—	1	.118	.250	.176	SS	7	8	14	1	3	.957
Pete Reiser	NL	2	7	1	0	0	0	1	0	0	0	0	2	0	0	0	0	0	—	1	.143	.143	.143	OF	2	9	0	2	0	.818
Ken Reitz	NL	1	2	0	0	0	0	0	0	0	0	0	0	0	0	0	0	0	—	0	.000	.000	.000	3B	1	1	0	0	0	1.000
Craig Reynolds	NL	1	2	0	0	0	0	0	0	0	0	0	0	0	0	0	0	0	—	0	.000	.000	.000	SS	1	0	1	0	0	1.000
Harold Reynolds	AL	2	4	0	0	0	0	0	0	0	0	0	0	0	1	0	0	0	—	0	.000	.000	.000	2B	2	5	5	0	0	1.000
Jim Rice	AL	7	20	4	1	0	1	8	1	1	1	0	8	0	0	0	0	0	—	0	.200	.238	.400	OF	6	9	0	0	0	1.000
Bobby Richardson	AL	6	11	1	0	0	0	1	1	0	0	0	1	0	0	0	0	0	—	2	.091	.091	.091	2B	6	6	7	1	1	.929
Lew Riggs	NL	1	1	0	0	0	0	0	0	0	0	0	1	0	0	0	0	0	—	0	.000	.000	.000	3B	1	0	0	0	0	—
Bill Rigney	NL	1	0	0	0	0	0	0	0	0	1	0	0	0	0	0	0	0	—	0	—	1.000	—	2B	1	2	0	0	0	1.000
Cal Ripken Jr.	AL	15	42	10	2	0	1	15	1	4	2	0	5	0	0	0	0	0	—	0	.238	.273	.357	SS	14	13	20	0	3	1.000
Mickey Rivers	AL	1	2	1	0	0	0	1	0	0	0	0	1	0	0	0	0	0	—	0	.500	.500	.500	OF	1	2	0	0	0	1.000
Phil Rizzuto	AL	4	9	2	0	0	0	2	0	0	0	0	1	0	0	0	0	0	—	1	.222	.222	.222	SS	4	5	4	0	1	1.000
Bip Roberts	NL	1	2	2	0	0	0	2	1	2	0	0	0	0	0	0	0	0	—	0	1.000	1.000	1.000	OF	1	0	0	0	0	—
Brooks Robinson	AL	18	45	13	0	3	1	22	5	5	1	0	4	1	0	0	0	0	—	0	.289	.319	.489	3B	18	11	32	0	3	1.000
Eddie Robinson	AL	4	9	2	0	0	0	2	1	2	0	0	1	0	0	0	0	0	—	0	.222	.222	.222	1B	3	9	1	0	2	1.000
Frank Robinson	NL	6	12	5	0	0	1	8	1	1	0	0	3	1	0	0	1	0	1.00	0	.417	.462	.667	OF	4	9	0	0	0	1.000
	AL	5	12	1	0	0	1	4	1	2	0	0	4	0	0	0	0	0	—	0	.083	.083	.333	OF	4	5	0	0	0	1.000
	Tot	11	24	6	0	0	2	12	2	3	0	0	7	1	0	0	1	0	1.00	0	.250	.280	.500	OF	8	14	0	0	0	1.000
Jackie Robinson	NL	6	18	6	2	0	1	11	7	4	2	0	1	0	0	0	0	0	—	0	.333	.400	.611	2B	4	9	6	1	3	.938
Alex Rodriguez	AL	2	4	1	0	0	0	1	0	0	0	0	2	0	0	0	0	0	—	0	.250	.250	.250	SS	2	0	1	0	0	1.000
Ivan Rodriguez	AL	6	16	3	1	0	0	4	2	0	0	0	4	0	0	0	0	0	—	0	.188	.188	.250	C	6	27	4	0	1	1.000
Cookie Rojas	AL	3	2	1	0	0	1	4	1	2	1	0	0	0	0	0	0	0	—	0	.500	.667	2.000	2B	3	5	3	0	3	1.000
	NL	1	1	0	0	0	0	0	0	0	0	0	0	0	0	0	0	0	—	0	.000	.000	.000	—	0	0	0	0	0	—
	Tot	4	3	1	0	0	1	4	1	2	1	0	0	0	0	0	0	0	—	0	.333	.500	1.333	2B	3	5	3	0	3	1.000
Red Rolfe	AL	2	8	3	0	1	0	5	2	2	1	0	0	0	0	0	0	0	—	0	.375	.444	.625	3B	2	1	2	2	0	.600
Rich Rollins	AL	2	5	2	0	0	0	2	1	0	0	0	0	1	0	0	0	0	—	0	.400	.500	.400	3B	2	1	4	0	1	1.000
John Romano	AL	3	6	1	0	0	0	1	0	0	0	0	1	0	0	0	0	0	—	0	.167	.167	.167	C	3	9	0	0	0	1.000
Buddy Rosar	AL	3	7	1	0	0	0	1	1	0	0	0	1	0	0	0	0	0	—	0	.143	.143	.143	C	3	12	0	0	0	1.000
Pete Rose	NL	16	33	7	1	1	0	10	3	2	3	0	5	0	1	2	0	0	—	3	.212	.263	.303	OF	6	11	0	0	0	1.000
John Roseboro	NL	2	6	1	0	0	1	4	1	1	0	0	4	0	0	0	0	0	—	1	.167	.167	.667	C	2	12	0	0	0	1.000
	AL	1	1	0	0	0	0	0	0	0	0	0	0	0	0	0	0	0	—	0	.000	.000	.000	C	1	6	0	0	0	1.000
	Tot	3	7	1	0	0	1	4	1	1	0	0	4	0	0	0	0	0	—	1	.143	.143	.571	C	3	18	0	0	0	1.000
Al Rosen	AL	4	11	3	0	0	2	9	3	5	3	0	3	0	0	0	0	0	—	0	.273	.429	.818	3B	4	5	5	1	0	.909
Joe Rudi	AL	3	6	2	1	0	0	3	0	0	0	0	1	0	0	0	0	0	—	0	.333	.333	.500	OF	3	6	0	0	0	1.000
Pete Runnels	AL	5	7	1	0	0	1	4	1	1	3	0	3	0	0	0	0	0	—	0	.143	.400	.571	2B	2	0	2	0	0	1.000
Bill Russell	NL	3	5	0	0	0	0	0	0	0	0	0	0	0	0	0	0	0	—	1	.000	.000	.000	SS	3	1	6	0	1	1.000
Babe Ruth	AL	2	6	2	0	0	1	5	2	2	2	0	3	0	0	0	0	0	—	0	.333	.500	.833	OF	2	1	0	0	0	1.000
Connie Ryan	NL	1	4	2	0	0	0	2	1	0	0	0	0	0	0	0	1	0	1.00	0	.500	.500	.500	2B	1	4	4	1	1	.889
Chris Sabo	NL	3	4	0	0	0	0	0	0	0	0	0	0	0	0	0	1	0	1.00	0	.000	.000	.000	3B	2	1	2	0	0	1.000
Juan Samuel	NL	2	5	1	0	0	0	1	0	0	0	0	1	0	0	0	0	0	—	0	.200	.200	.200	2B	2	9	3	0	0	1.000
Ryne Sandberg	NL	10	26	3	1	0	0	4	1	0	2	0	9	0	0	0	1	0	1.00	0	.115	.179	.154	2B	10	9	21	1	2	.968
Reggie Sanders	NL	1	1	0	0	0	0	0	0	0	0	0	1	0	0	0	0	0	—	0	.000	.000	.000	OF	1	0	0	0	0	—
Manny Sanguillen	NL	1	2	1	0	0	0	1	0	0	0	0	0	0	0	0	0	0	—	0	.500	.500	.500	C	1	6	0	0	0	1.000
Benito Santiago	NL	3	5	0	0	0	0	0	0	0	0	0	3	0	0	0	0	0	—	0	.000	.000	.000	C	3	7	0	1	0	.875
Ron Santo	NL	8	15	5	0	0	0	5	1	3	5	0	0	0	0	0	0	0	—	1	.333	.500	.333	3B	8	7	6	0	1	1.000
Hank Sauer	NL	2	4	1	0	0	1	4	1	3	0	0	1	0	0	0	0	0	—	0	.250	.250	1.000	OF	2	1	0	0	0	1.000
Steve Sax	NL	3	5	3	0	0	0	3	1	2	0	0	0	0	0	0	2	1	.67	0	.600	.600	.600	2B	3	4	1	2	0	.714
	AL	2	2	0	0	0	0	0	0	0	1	0	0	0	0	0	1	0	1.00	1	.000	.333	.000	2B	2	1	4	0	1	1.000
	Tot	5	7	3	0	0	0	3	1	2	1	0	0	0	0	0	3	1	.75	1	.429	.500	.429	2B	5	5	5	2	1	.833
Richie Scheinblum	AL	1	1	0	0	0	0	0	0	0	0	0	0	0	0	0	0	0	—	0	.000	.000	.000	OF	1	1	0	0	0	1.000
Mike Schmidt	NL	10	18	5	2	1	1	12	4	3	3	0	4	0	0	0	0	1	.00	1	.278	.381	.667	3B	9	1	9	3	0	.769
Red Schoendienst	NL	9	21	4	0	0	1	7	1	1	0	0	0	0	0	0	0	1	.00	0	.190	.190	.333	2B	8	5	9	1	2	.933
Mike Scioscia	NL	2	3	0	0	0	0	0	0	0	0	0	1	0	0	0	0	0	—	0	.000	.000	.000	C	2	9	0	0	1	1.000
George Scott	AL	3	6	1	0	0	1	4	1	2	0	0	2	0	0	0	0	0	—	0	.167	.167	.667	1B	3	13	1	0	1	1.000
Kevin Seitzer	AL	2	4	0	0	0	0	0	0	0	1	0	0	0	0	0	0	0	—	0	.000	.200	.000	3B	2	0	0	0	0	—
George Selkirk	AL	2	2	1	0	0	0	1	0	1	3	1	0	0	0	0	0	0	—	0	.500	.800	.500	OF	1	0	0	0	0	—
Andy Seminick	NL	1	1	0	0	0	0	0	0	0	0	0	0	1	0	0	0	0	—	0	.000	.500	.000	C	1	3	0	0	0	1.000
Mike Sharperson	NL	1	1	0	0	0	0	0	0	0	0	0	1	0	0	0	0	0	—	0	.000	.000	.000	3B	1	0	0	0	0	—
Gary Sheffield	NL	3	6	2	0	0	1	5	1	2	0	0	0	0	0	0	0	0	—	0	.333	.333	.833	3B	2	1	2	0	0	1.000
Dick Siebert	AL	1	1	0	0	0	0	0	0	0	0	0	0	0	0	0	0	0	—	0	.000	.000	.000	1B	1	3	1	0	0	1.000
Ruben Sierra	AL	4	9	4	0	0	1	7	3	3	1	0	2	0	0	0	0	0	—	0	.444	.500	.778	OF	4	3	0	0	0	1.000
Al Simmons	AL	3	13	6	3	0	0	9	3	1	0	0	3	0	0	0	0	0	—	1	.462	.462	.692	OF	3	9	0	0	0	1.000
Ted Simmons	NL	3	7	1	0	0	0	1	0	0	0	0	2	0	0	0	0	0	—	0	.143	.143	.143	C	3	10	2	0	0	1.000
	AL	2	3	1	0	0	0	1	0	1	0	0	0	0	0	0	0	0	—	0	.333	.333	.333	C	1	4	0	0	0	1.000
	Tot	5	10	2	0	0	0	2	0	1	0	0	2	0	0	0	0	0	—	0	.200	.200	.200	C	4	14	2	0	0	1.000
Ken Singleton	AL	3	4	2	0	0	1	5	2	1	0	0	0	1	0	0	0	0	—	0	.500	.600	1.250	OF	2	0	0	0	0	—
Bob Skinner	NL	3	10	3	0	0	0	3	1	2	0	0	2	0	0	0	1	0	1.00	0	.300	.300	.300	OF	3	5	0	0	0	1.000
Bill Skowron	AL	5	14	6	1	0	0	7	1	0	1	0	3	0	0	0	0	0	—	1	.429	.467	.500	1B	5	31	1	0	4	1.000
Enos Slaughter	NL	10	21	8	1	1	0	11	4	2	4	0	2	0	0	0	1	0	1.00	0	.381	.480	.524	OF	8	11	0	0	0	1.000
Roy Smalley	AL	1	3	0	0	0	0	0	0	0	1	1	0	0	0	0	0	0	—	0	.000	.250	.000	SS	1	2	2	0	1	1.000
Al Smith	AL	3	3	0	0	0	0	0	0	0	1	0	1	0	0	0	0	0	—	0	.000	.250	.000	OF	1	0	0	0	0	—
Hal Smith	NL	1	2	0	0	0	0	0	0	0	0	0	1	0	0	0	0	0	—	0	.000	.000	.000	C	1	5	0	0	0	1.000
Lonnie Smith	NL	1	0	0	0	0	0	0	0	0	0	0	0	0	0	0	0	0	—	0	—	—	—	OF	1	1	0	0	0	1.000
Ozzie Smith	NL	14	27	4	1	0	0	5	1	0	3	0	2	0	0	0	2	2	.50	0	.148	.233	.185	SS	14	16	23	1	3	.975
Reggie Smith	NL	5	10	3	0	0	1	6	2	1	0	0	2	0	0	0	0	0	—	0	.300	.300	.600	OF	4	3	0	0	0	1.000

All-Star Games: Player Register 2355

		Batting																						Fielding						
		G	AB	H	2B	3B	HR	TB	R	RBI	TBB	IBB	SO	HBP	SH	SF	SB	CS	SB%	GDP	Avg	OBP	SLG	Pos	G	PO	A	E	DP	FPct
	AL	2	3	0	0	0	0	0	1	0	0	0	1	0	0	0	0	0	—	0	.000	.000	.000	OF	1	0	0	0	0	—
	Tot	7	13	3	0	0	1	6	3	1	0	0	3	0	0	0	0	0	—	0	.231	.231	.462	OF	5	3	0	0	0	1.000
Duke Snider	NL	7	11	3	1	0	0	4	3	0	2	0	3	0	0	0	0	0	—	0	.273	.385	.364	OF	6	7	0	0	0	1.000
Sammy Sosa	NL	1	1	0	0	0	0	0	0	0	0	0	0	0	0	0	0	0	—	0	.000	.000	.000	OF	1	2	0	0	0	1.000
Chris Speier	NL	2	4	0	0	0	0	0	0	0	0	0	1	0	1	0	0	0	—	0	.000	.000	.000	SS	2	2	6	0	1	1.000
Stan Spence	AL	3	5	3	0	0	0	3	1	1	1	1	0	0	0	0	0	0	—	0	.600	.667	.600	OF	2	3	1	0	1	1.000
Eddie Stanky	NL	1	2	0	0	0	0	0	0	0	0	0	0	0	0	0	0	0	—	0	.000	.000	.000	2B	1	2	2	0	1	1.000
Mike Stanley	AL	1	1	0	0	0	0	0	0	0	0	0	0	0	0	0	0	0	—	0	.000	.000	.000	C	1	3	0	0	0	1.000
Willie Stargell	NL	7	10	2	0	0	1	5	3	2	1	0	4	1	0	0	0	0	—	0	.200	.333	.500	OF	4	4	0	0	0	1.000
Rusty Staub	AL	1	2	2	0	0	0	2	0	0	0	0	0	0	0	0	0	0	—	0	1.000	1.000	1.000	OF	1	1	0	0	0	1.000
	NL	3	3	1	0	0	0	1	0	0	0	0	0	0	0	0	0	0	—	0	.333	.333	.333	—	0	0	0	0	0	—
	Tot	4	5	3	0	0	0	3	0	0	0	0	0	0	0	0	0	0	—	0	.600	.600	.600	OF	1	1	0	0	0	1.000
John Stearns	NL	3	1	0	0	0	0	0	0	0	0	0	0	0	0	0	0	0	—	0	.000	.000	.000	C	3	7	0	0	0	1.000
Terry Steinbach	AL	3	6	3	1	0	1	7	1	3	0	0	1	0	0	1	0	0	—	0	.500	.429	1.167	C	3	15	2	1	0	.944
Vern Stephens	AL	6	15	5	1	0	0	6	1	2	0	0	5	0	1	0	0	0	—	0	.333	.333	.400	SS	5	5	7	1	1	.923
Kurt Stillwell	AL	1	0	0	0	0	0	0	0	0	0	0	0	0	0	0	0	0	—	0	—	—	—	SS	1	1	0	0	0	1.000
Snuffy Stirnweiss	AL	1	3	1	0	0	0	1	1	0	0	0	1	0	0	0	0	0	—	0	.333	.333	.333	3B	1	0	0	0	0	—
Darryl Strawberry	NL	6	12	4	0	0	0	4	2	0	1	0	4	1	0	0	2	0	1.00	0	.333	.429	.333	OF	6	11	1	1	1	.923
Jim Sundberg	AL	2	1	0	0	0	0	0	0	0	0	0	0	0	0	0	0	0	—	0	.000	.000	.000	C	2	8	1	0	0	1.000
Danny Tartabull	AL	1	2	0	0	0	0	0	0	0	0	0	1	0	0	0	0	0	—	0	.000	.000	.000	—	0	0	0	0	0	—
Tony Taylor	NL	2	1	1	0	0	0	1	0	0	0	0	0	0	0	0	0	0	—	0	1.000	1.000	1.000	2B	1	2	1	0	0	1.000
Birdie Tebbetts	AL	3	7	2	1	0	0	3	1	1	2	0	3	0	0	0	0	0	—	0	.286	.444	.429	C	3	11	2	0	0	1.000
Johnny Temple	NL	4	10	3	1	0	0	4	2	1	1	0	3	0	0	0	1	0	1.00	0	.300	.364	.400	2B	4	7	7	0	1	1.000
	AL	2	5	0	0	0	0	0	0	0	1	0	1	0	0	0	0	0	—	1	.000	.167	.000	2B	2	3	5	0	0	1.000
	Tot	6	15	3	1	0	0	4	2	1	2	0	4	0	0	0	1	0	1.00	1	.200	.294	.267	2B	6	10	12	0	1	1.000
Garry Templeton	NL	2	2	2	1	0	0	3	1	0	0	0	0	0	0	0	0	0	—	0	1.000	1.000	1.500	SS	1	1	2	1	1	.750
Gene Tenace	AL	1	3	0	0	0	0	0	1	0	1	0	1	0	0	0	0	0	—	0	.000	.250	.000	C	1	2	0	1	0	.667
Bill Terry	NL	3	10	4	0	0	0	4	0	1	1	0	0	0	0	0	0	0	—	0	.400	.455	.400	1B	3	16	3	0	1	1.000
Mickey Tettleton	AL	2	1	0	0	0	0	0	0	0	1	0	1	0	0	0	0	0	—	0	.000	.500	.000	C	1	2	0	0	0	1.000
Frank Thomas	NL	3	5	1	0	0	0	1	0	0	1	0	1	0	0	0	0	0	—	0	.200	.333	.200	3B	1	1	3	1	1	.800
Frank Thomas	AL	3	5	4	0	0	1	7	2	3	1	0	0	0	0	0	0	0	—	0	.800	.833	1.400	1B	2	11	1	0	0	1.000
Lee Thomas	AL	2	1	0	0	0	0	0	0	0	0	0	0	0	0	0	0	0	—	0	.000	.000	.000	OF	1	1	0	0	0	1.000
Jim Thome	AL	1	1	0	0	0	0	0	0	0	0	0	0	0	0	0	0	0	—	0	.000	.000	.000	—	0	0	0	0	0	—
Bobby Thomson	NL	3	4	0	0	0	0	0	0	0	0	0	1	0	0	0	0	0	—	0	.000	.000	.000	3B	1	1	1	0	0	1.000
Dickie Thon	NL	1	3	1	0	0	0	1	0	0	0	0	0	0	0	0	0	0	—	0	.333	.333	.333	SS	1	0	2	0	0	1.000
Joe Torre	NL	8	21	2	0	0	1	5	1	2	0	0	3	0	0	0	0	0	—	2	.095	.095	.238	C	4	19	2	0	1	1.000
Alan Trammell	AL	4	3	0	0	0	0	0	0	0	0	0	0	0	0	0	0	0	—	0	.000	.000	.000	SS	2	0	0	0	0	—
Cecil Travis	AL	2	7	1	1	0	0	2	1	0	1	0	0	0	0	0	0	0	—	1	.143	.250	.286	3B	2	1	2	0	0	1.000
Pie Traynor	NL	2	6	3	1	0	0	4	2	1	0	0	0	0	0	0	1	0	1.00	0	.500	.500	.667	3B	1	1	0	0	0	1.000
Tom Tresh	AL	2	2	1	1	0	0	2	0	1	0	0	0	0	0	0	0	0	—	0	.500	.500	1.000	SS	1	0	4	0	0	1.000
Gus Triandos	AL	2	6	2	1	0	0	3	0	2	0	0	0	0	0	0	0	0	—	0	.333	.333	.500	C	2	9	0	1	0	.900
Manny Trillo	NL	3	5	1	0	0	0	1	0	0	0	0	1	0	0	0	0	0	—	0	.200	.200	.200	2B	3	1	3	0	0	1.000
	AL	1	3	1	0	0	0	1	1	0	0	0	0	0	0	0	0	0	—	0	.333	.333	.333	2B	1	3	1	0	2	1.000
	Tot	4	8	2	0	0	0	2	1	0	0	0	1	0	0	0	0	0	—	0	.250	.250	.250	2B	4	4	4	0	2	1.000
Thurman Tucker	AL	1	4	0	0	0	0	0	0	0	0	0	0	0	0	0	0	0	—	0	.000	.000	.000	OF	1	4	0	0	0	1.000
Ellis Valentine	NL	1	1	0	0	0	0	0	0	0	1	0	0	0	0	0	0	0	—	0	.000	.500	.000	OF	1	0	0	0	0	—
Andy Van Slyke	NL	2	4	0	0	0	0	0	0	0	0	0	0	0	0	0	0	0	—	1	.000	.000	.000	OF	2	2	0	0	0	1.000
Arky Vaughan	NL	7	22	8	1	0	2	15	5	4	3	0	1	0	0	0	0	0	—	2	.364	.440	.682	SS	5	11	6	1	2	.944
Greg Vaughn	AL	1	1	1	0	0	0	1	1	0	0	0	0	0	0	0	0	0	—	0	1.000	1.000	1.000	OF	1	0	0	0	0	—
Mo Vaughn	AL	2	5	1	1	0	0	2	0	0	0	0	2	0	0	0	0	0	—	0	.200	.200	.400	1B	2	9	1	0	0	1.000
Robin Ventura	AL	1	2	2	1	0	0	3	1	1	0	0	0	0	0	0	0	0	—	0	1.000	1.000	1.500	3B	1	1	1	0	0	1.000
Emil Verban	NL	2	3	0	0	0	0	0	0	0	0	0	0	0	0	0	0	0	—	0	.000	.000	.000	2B	1	0	0	0	0	—
Mickey Vernon	AL	7	14	2	0	0	0	2	2	1	2	0	5	0	0	0	1	0	1.00	0	.143	.250	.143	1B	5	21	1	0	2	1.000
Zoilo Versalles	AL	2	2	1	0	0	0	1	0	0	2	0	0	1	0	0	0	0	—	0	.500	.800	.500	SS	2	0	4	0	0	1.000
Ozzie Virgil	NL	2	3	2	0	0	0	2	1	2	0	0	0	0	0	0	0	0	—	0	.667	.667	.667	C	2	10	0	0	1	1.000
Joe Vosmik	AL	1	4	1	0	0	0	1	1	0	0	0	0	0	0	0	0	0	—	0	.250	.250	.250	OF	1	1	0	0	0	1.000
Hal Wagner	AL	1	1	0	0	0	0	0	0	0	0	0	0	0	0	0	0	0	—	0	.000	.000	.000	C	1	4	0	0	0	1.000
Leon Wagner	AL	3	11	5	0	0	1	8	2	2	0	0	0	0	0	0	0	0	—	0	.455	.455	.727	OF	3	6	0	0	0	1.000
Dick Wakefield	AL	1	4	2	1	0	0	3	0	1	0	0	1	0	0	0	0	0	—	0	.500	.500	.750	OF	1	3	0	0	0	1.000
Dixie Walker	NL	4	10	2	0	0	0	2	0	2	0	0	0	0	0	0	0	0	—	0	.200	.200	.200	OF	3	2	0	0	0	1.000
Harry Walker	NL	2	3	0	0	0	0	0	0	0	0	0	1	0	0	0	0	0	—	0	.000	.000	.000	OF	2	2	0	0	0	1.000
Larry Walker	NL	2	2	1	0	0	0	1	0	0	1	0	0	0	0	0	0	0	—	0	.500	.667	.500	OF	1	0	0	0	0	—
Tim Wallach	NL	5	9	1	1	0	0	2	1	0	1	1	3	0	0	0	0	0	—	0	.111	.200	.222	3B	5	1	3	0	1	1.000
Lee Walls	NL	1	1	0	0	0	0	0	0	0	0	0	0	0	0	0	0	0	—	0	.000	.000	.000	OF	1	0	0	0	0	—
Paul Waner	NL	4	8	0	0	0	0	0	0	1	0	0	1	0	0	0	0	0	—	0	.000	.000	.000	OF	3	1	0	0	0	1.000
Claudell Washington	AL	1	1	1	0	0	0	1	0	0	0	0	0	0	0	0	1	1	.50	0	1.000	1.000	1.000	OF	1	1	0	0	0	1.000
	NL	1	2	1	1	0	0	2	0	0	0	0	1	0	0	0	0	0	—	0	.500	.500	1.000	OF	1	1	0	0	0	1.000
	Tot	2	3	2	1	0	0	3	0	0	0	0	1	0	0	0	1	1	.50	0	.667	.667	1.000	OF	2	2	0	0	0	1.000
Bob Watson	NL	2	1	0	0	0	0	0	0	0	0	0	0	0	0	0	0	0	—	0	.000	.000	.000	OF	1	0	0	0	0	—
Don Wert	AL	1	1	1	1	0	0	2	0	0	0	0	0	0	0	0	0	0	—	0	1.000	1.000	2.000	3B	1	1	0	0	0	1.000
Vic Wertz	AL	3	7	2	0	0	1	5	1	2	0	0	0	0	0	0	0	0	—	0	.286	.286	.714	OF	2	2	0	0	0	1.000
Max West	NL	1	1	1	0	0	1	4	1	3	0	0	0	0	0	0	0	0	—	0	1.000	1.000	4.000	OF	1	0	0	0	0	—
Sammy West	AL	3	4	1	0	0	0	1	1	0	0	0	0	0	0	0	0	0	—	0	.250	.250	.250	OF	3	6	0	0	0	1.000
Wally Westlake	NL	1	0	0	0	0	0	0	0	0	0	0	0	0	0	0	0	0	—	0	—	—	—	OF	1	0	0	0	0	—
Lou Whitaker	AL	4	8	4	1	1	1	10	2	4	0	0	1	0	0	1	0	0	—	0	.500	.444	1.250	2B	4	2	9	0	0	1.000
Bill White	NL	6	14	4	1	0	0	5	1	2	0	0	3	0	0	1	1	0	1.00	0	.286	.267	.357	1B	5	29	5	0	6	1.000
Devon White	AL	2	3	1	1	0	0	2	1	1	0	0	0	0	0	0	1	0	1.00	0	.333	.333	.667	OF	2	1	0	0	0	1.000
Frank White	AL	5	7	1	0	0	1	4	1	1	0	0	1	0	0	0	0	0	—	0	.143	.143	.571	2B	5	7	6	0	3	1.000
Pinky Whitney	NL	1	3	1	0	0	0	1	0	1	0	0	1	0	0	0	0	0	—	0	.333	.333	.333	3B	1	0	2	0	1	1.000
Ernie Whitt	AL	1	0	0	0	0	0	0	0	0	0	0	0	0	0	0	0	0	—	0	—	—	—	C	1	2	0	0	0	1.000
Bernie Williams	AL	1	0	0	0	0	0	0	1	0	1	0	0	0	0	0	0	0	—	0	—	1.000	—	OF	1	1	0	0	0	1.000
Billy Williams	NL	6	11	3	0	0	1	6	2	2	0	0	0	0	0	0	0	0	—	0	.273	.273	.545	OF	4	3	0	0	0	1.000
Davey Williams	NL	1	0	0	0	0	0	0	0	0	1	0	0	0	0	0	0	0	—	0	—	1.000	—	2B	1	2	0	0	0	1.000
Matt Williams	NL	2	4	0	0	0	0	0	0	0	0	0	3	0	0	0	0	0	—	0	.000	.000	.000	3B	1	0	1	1	0	.500

		G	AB	H	2B	3B	HR	TB	R	RBI	TBB	IBB	SO	HBP	SH	SF	SB	CS	SB%	GDP	Avg	OBP	SLG	Pos	G	PO	A	E	DP	FPct
					Batting																				Fielding					

Batting / Fielding

Name	Lg	G	AB	H	2B	3B	HR	TB	R	RBI	TBB	IBB	SO	HBP	SH	SF	SB	CS	SB%	GDP	Avg	OBP	SLG	Pos	G	PO	A	E	DP	FPct
Ted Williams	AL	18	46	14	2	1	4	30	10	12	11	0	10	0	0	0	0	0	—	0	.304	.439	.652	OF	14	24	0	1	0	.960
Maury Wills	NL	6	14	5	0	0	0	5	2	1	0	0	0	0	0	0	1	0	1.00	0	.357	.357	.357	SS	6	5	9	0	1	1.000
Jimmie Wilson	NL	2	4	1	1	0	0	2	0	0	0	0	0	0	0	0	0	0	—	0	.250	.250	.500	C	2	10	0	0	0	1.000
Willie Wilson	AL	2	3	1	1	0	0	2	0	1	0	0	1	0	0	0	0	0	—	1	.333	.333	.667	OF	2	3	0	0	0	1.000
Dave Winfield	AL	8	25	9	5	0	0	14	4	1	2	0	1	0	0	0	1	0	1.00	0	.360	.407	.560	OF	8	8	2	0	0	1.000
	NL	4	11	4	2	0	0	6	2	4	0	0	1	0	0	0	0	0	—	0	.364	.364	.545	OF	4	7	0	0	0	1.000
	Tot	12	36	13	7	0	0	20	6	5	2	0	2	0	0	0	1	0	1.00	0	.361	.395	.556	OF	12	15	2	0	0	1.000
Tony Womack	NL	1	1	0	0	0	0	0	0	0	0	0	0	0	0	0	0	0	—	0	.000	.000	.000	2B	1	1	0	0	0	1.000
Butch Wynegar	AL	2	2	1	0	0	0	1	1	0	1	0	0	0	0	0	0	0	—	1	.500	.667	.500	C	1	3	0	0	0	1.000
Jimmy Wynn	NL	3	6	3	0	0	1	6	2	1	0	0	0	0	0	0	0	0	—	0	.500	.500	1.000	OF	2	1	0	0	0	1.000
Johnny Wyrostek	NL	2	3	0	0	0	0	0	0	0	0	0	0	0	0	0	0	0	—	0	.000	.000	.000	OF	2	0	0	0	0	—
Carl Yastrzemski	AL	14	34	10	2	0	1	15	2	5	4	0	8	0	0	0	0	0	—	1	.294	.368	.441	OF	9	8	0	0	0	1.000
Rudy York	AL	5	13	4	0	0	1	7	1	2	0	0	4	0	0	0	0	0	—	0	.308	.308	.538	1B	4	26	5	0	4	1.000
Eric Young	NL	1	1	0	0	0	0	0	0	0	0	0	0	0	0	0	0	0	—	0	.000	.000	.000	2B	1	2	1	0	1	1.000
Robin Yount	AL	3	7	0	0	0	0	0	1	1	2	1	2	0	0	1	0	0	—	0	.000	.200	.000	SS	3	3	5	0	2	1.000
Al Zarilla	AL	1	2	0	0	0	0	0	0	0	0	0	0	0	0	0	0	0	—	0	.000	.000	.000	OF	1	2	0	0	0	1.000
Gus Zernial	AL	1	2	1	0	0	0	1	0	0	0	0	1	0	0	0	0	0	—	0	.500	.500	.500	OF	1	1	0	0	0	1.000
Don Zimmer	NL	1	1	0	0	0	0	0	0	0	0	0	0	0	0	0	0	0	—	0	.000	.000	.000	2B	1	0	0	1	0	.000
Richie Zisk	AL	2	5	3	1	0	0	4	0	2	1	0	2	0	0	0	0	1	.00	0	.600	.667	.800	OF	2	0	0	0	0	—

		G	GS	GF	IP	BFP	H	R	ER	HR	SH	SF	HB	TBB	IBB	SO	WP	Bk	W	L	Pct	Sv-Op	OAvg	OOBP	ERA
Don Aase	AL	1	0	1	0.2	1	0	0	0	0	0	0	0	0	0	0	0	0	0	0	—	1-1	.000	.000	0.00
Rick Aguilera	AL	3	0	0	3.0	14	5	1	1	1	0	0	0	0	0	5	0	0	0	0	—	0-0	.357	.357	3.00
Hank Aguirre	AL	1	0	0	3.0	12	3	2	2	0	0	0	0	0	0	2	0	0	0	0	—	0-0	.250	.250	6.00
Johnny Allen	AL	1	0	0	3.0	12	2	1	1	0	0	0	1	0	0	3	0	0	0	0	—	0-0	.182	.250	3.00
Wilson Alvarez	AL	1	0	0	1.0	3	0	0	0	0	0	0	0	0	0	0	0	0	0	0	—	0-0	.000	.000	0.00
Joaquin Andujar	NL	1	0	0	2.0	11	2	2	1	0	0	0	1	1	0	0	1	0	0	0	—	0-0	.222	.364	4.50
Johnny Antonelli	NL	3	0	1	6.1	27	8	3	3	1	0	1	0	1	0	3	0	0	1	0	1.000	1-1	.320	.333	4.26
Kevin Appier	AL	1	0	0	2.0	6	0	0	0	0	0	0	0	0	0	1	0	0	0	0	—	0-0	.000	.000	0.00
Jack Armstrong	NL	1	1	0	2.0	7	1	0	0	0	0	0	0	0	0	1	0	0	0	0	—	0-0	.143	.143	0.00
Steve Avery	NL	1	0	0	1.0	6	1	3	0	0	0	0	0	1	0	1	0	0	0	0	—	0-0	.200	.333	0.00
Floyd Bannister	AL	1	0	0	1.0	3	1	0	0	0	0	0	0	0	0	0	0	0	0	0	—	0-0	.333	.333	0.00
Len Barker	AL	1	0	0	2.0	6	0	0	0	0	0	0	0	0	0	1	0	0	0	0	—	0-0	.000	.000	0.00
Rod Beck	NL	2	0	0	2.2	10	3	1	1	0	0	0	0	0	0	2	0	0	0	0	—	0-0	.300	.300	3.38
Steve Bedrosian	NL	1	0	0	1.0	4	0	0	0	0	1	0	0	2	0	0	0	0	0	0	—	0-0	.000	.667	0.00
Gary Bell	AL	2	0	1	3.0	13	2	2	2	1	1	0	0	2	0	0	0	0	0	0	—	0-0	.200	.333	6.00
Andy Benes	NL	1	0	0	2.0	8	2	1	1	1	0	0	0	0	0	2	0	0	0	0	—	0-0	.250	.250	4.50
Al Benton	AL	1	0	1	5.0	20	4	1	1	1	0	0	0	2	0	1	0	0	0	0	—	1-1	.222	.300	1.80
Jason Bere	AL	1	0	1	0.0	2	2	1	1	0	0	0	0	0	0	0	0	0	0	1	.000	0-0	1.000	1.000	—
Jim Bibby	NL	1	0	0	1.0	3	1	0	0	0	0	0	0	0	0	0	0	0	0	0	—	0-0	.333	.333	0.00
Vern Bickford	NL	1	0	0	1.0	6	2	2	2	0	0	0	0	1	0	0	0	0	0	0	—	0-0	.400	.500	18.00
Ewell Blackwell	NL	6	1	3	13.2	53	8	2	2	0	1	0	0	5	0	12	2	0	1	0	1.000	0-0	.170	.250	1.32
Cy Blanton	NL	1	0	0	0.1	1	0	0	0	0	0	0	0	0	0	1	0	0	0	0	—	0-0	.000	.000	0.00
Steve Blass	NL	1	0	0	1.0	4	1	1	1	0	1	0	0	1	0	0	0	0	0	0	—	0-0	.500	.667	9.00
Vida Blue	AL	2	2	0	5.0	22	7	5	5	4	0	0	1	0	0	4	0	0	1	0	1.000	0-0	.333	.364	9.00
	NL	2	1	0	4.0	18	5	3	3	0	0	2	0	1	0	3	1	0	1	0	1.000	0-0	.333	.333	6.75
	Tot	4	3	0	9.0	40	12	8	8	4	0	2	1	1	0	7	1	0	2	0	1.000	0-0	.333	.350	8.00
Bert Blyleven	AL	2	0	0	3.0	16	5	4	4	0	0	0	0	3	0	1	0	0	0	1	.000	0-0	.417	.563	12.00
Hank Borowy	AL	1	1	0	3.0	12	3	0	0	0	0	0	0	1	0	0	0	0	0	0	—	0-0	.273	.333	0.00
Ricky Bottalico	NL	1	0	0	1.0	4	0	0	0	0	0	0	0	0	0	1	0	0	0	0	—	0-0	.000	.000	0.00
Jim Bouton	AL	1	0	0	1.0	3	0	0	0	0	0	0	0	0	0	0	0	0	0	0	—	0-0	.000	.000	0.00
Ralph Branca	NL	1	1	0	3.0	13	1	2	2	1	0	0	0	3	0	3	0	0	0	0	—	0-0	.100	.308	6.00
Jeff Brantley	NL	1	0	0	0.1	3	2	2	2	0	0	0	0	0	0	0	0	0	0	1	.000	0-0	.667	.667	54.00
Harry Brecheen	NL	1	0	0	3.0	13	5	1	1	0	0	0	0	0	0	2	0	0	0	0	—	0-0	.385	.385	3.00
Ken Brett	NL	1	0	0	2.0	8	1	0	0	0	0	0	0	1	0	0	0	0	1	0	1.000	0-0	.143	.250	0.00
Jim Brewer	NL	1	0	1	1.0	4	0	0	0	0	0	0	0	1	0	2	0	0	0	0	—	0-0	.000	.250	0.00
Tom Brewer	AL	1	0	0	2.0	11	4	3	3	1	0	0	0	1	0	2	2	0	0	0	—	0-0	.400	.455	13.50
Tommy Bridges	AL	2	0	0	5.1	28	9	3	3	0	0	0	0	1	0	3	0	0	1	0	1.000	0-0	.333	.357	5.06
Lou Brissie	AL	1	0	0	3.0	16	5	2	2	1	0	0	0	2	1	1	0	0	0	0	—	0-0	.357	.438	6.00
Kevin Brown	NL	2	0	0	2.0	7	1	0	0	0	0	0	0	0	0	1	0	0	0	0	—	0-0	.143	.143	0.00
	AL	1	1	0	1.0	3	0	0	0	0	0	0	0	0	0	1	0	0	1	0	1.000	0-0	.000	.000	0.00
	Tot	3	1	0	3.0	10	1	0	0	0	0	0	0	0	0	1	0	0	1	0	1.000	0-0	.100	.100	0.00
Mace Brown	NL	1	0	1	3.0	15	5	1	1	0	0	0	0	1	0	2	0	0	0	0	—	1-1	.357	.400	3.00
Bob Buhl	NL	1	0	0	1.1	8	2	2	1	1	0	0	0	1	0	1	0	0	0	0	—	0-0	.286	.375	6.75
Jim Bunning	AL	6	3	0	14.0	47	4	3	2	0	0	0	0	1	0	7	0	0	1	1	.500	0-0	.087	.106	1.29
	NL	2	0	0	4.0	15	3	0	0	0	0	0	0	0	0	6	0	0	0	0	—	0-0	.200	.200	0.00
	Tot	8	3	0	18.0	62	7	3	2	0	0	0	0	1	0	13	0	0	1	1	.500	0-0	.115	.129	1.00
Lew Burdette	NL	2	0	0	7.0	29	6	1	1	1	0	0	0	1	0	2	0	0	0	0	—	0-0	.214	.241	1.29
Tim Burke	NL	1	0	0	2.0	8	2	0	0	0	0	0	0	0	0	1	0	0	0	0	—	0-0	.250	.250	0.00
John Burkett	NL	1	0	0	0.2	7	4	3	3	0	0	0	1	0	0	1	0	0	0	1	.000	0-0	.667	.714	40.50
Steve Busby	AL	1	0	0	2.0	9	4	1	1	0	0	0	0	0	0	0	1	0	0	0	—	0-0	.444	.444	4.50
Bill Campbell	AL	1	0	0	1.0	4	0	0	0	0	0	0	0	0	0	2	0	0	0	0	—	0-0	.000	.250	0.00
Steve Carlton	NL	5	2	0	8.0	32	5	5	5	3	0	0	0	5	0	7	0	0	1	0	1.000	0-0	.185	.313	5.63
Bill Caudill	AL	1	0	0	1.0	3	0	0	0	0	0	0	0	0	0	3	0	0	0	0	—	0-0	.000	.000	0.00
Dean Chance	AL	2	2	0	6.0	22	4	1	1	1	0	0	0	0	0	3	0	0	0	0	—	0-0	.182	.182	1.50
Spud Chandler	AL	1	1	0	4.0	14	2	0	0	0	0	0	0	0	0	1	0	0	1	0	1.000	0-0	.154	.214	0.00
Norm Charlton	NL	1	0	1	1.0	3	0	0	0	0	0	0	0	0	0	1	0	0	0	0	—	0-0	.000	.000	0.00
Jim Clancy	AL	1	0	0	1.0	3	0	0	0	0	0	0	0	0	0	0	0	0	0	0	—	0-0	.000	.000	0.00
Mark Clear	AL	1	0	0	2.0	8	2	1	1	0	0	0	0	1	0	0	0	0	0	0	—	0-0	.286	.375	4.50
Roger Clemens	AL	5	1	0	7.0	24	4	1	1	1	0	0	0	0	0	3	0	0	1	0	1.000	0-0	.167	.167	1.29
Jim Coates	AL	1	0	0	2.0	8	2	0	0	0	0	0	1	0	0	0	0	0	0	0	—	0-0	.286	.375	0.00
Joe Coleman	AL	1	0	1	3.0	11	0	0	0	0	0	0	0	2	0	3	0	0	0	0	—	1-1	.000	.182	0.00
David Cone	AL	2	0	0	3.0	15	4	3	3	0	0	0	1	2	0	3	0	0	0	0	—	0-0	.333	.467	9.00
	NL	2	0	0	2.0	6	0	0	0	0	0	0	0	0	0	2	0	0	0	0	—	0-0	.000	.000	0.00
	Tot	4	0	0	5.0	21	4	3	3	0	0	0	1	2	0	5	0	0	0	0	—	0-0	.222	.333	5.40
Gene Conley	NL	3	0	1	3.1	15	3	3	3	1	0	0	0	2	0	5	0	0	1	1	.500	0-1	.231	.333	8.10
Sandy Consuegra	AL	1	0	0	0.1	6	5	5	5	0	0	0	0	0	0	0	0	0	0	0	—	0-0	.833	.833	135.00
Mort Cooper	NL	2	2	0	5.1	26	8	7	7	3	1	0	1	2	0	3	0	0	0	2	.000	0-0	.364	.440	11.81
General Crowder	AL	1	0	0	3.0	12	3	2	2	1	0	0	0	0	0	0	0	0	0	0	—	0-0	.250	.250	6.00
Mike Cuellar	AL	1	0	0	2.0	7	1	0	0	0	0	0	0	1	0	2	0	0	0	0	—	0-0	.167	.286	0.00
	NL	1	0	0	2.0	7	1	0	0	0	0	0	0	0	0	2	0	0	0	0	—	0-0	.143	.143	0.00
	Tot	2	0	0	4.0	14	2	0	0	0	0	0	0	1	0	4	0	0	0	0	—	0-0	.154	.214	0.00
Ray Culp	AL	1	0	1	1.0	3	0	0	0	0	0	0	0	0	0	2	0	0	0	0	—	0-0	.000	.000	0.00
	NL	1	0	0	1.0	4	1	0	0	0	0	0	0	0	0	0	0	0	0	0	—	0-0	.250	.250	0.00
	Tot	2	0	1	2.0	7	1	0	0	0	0	0	0	0	0	2	0	0	0	0	—	0-0	.143	.143	0.00
Bud Daley	AL	2	0	2	1.2	6	0	0	0	0	0	0	0	1	0	3	0	0	0	0	—	0-0	.000	.167	0.00
Curt Davis	NL	1	0	0	0.2	7	4	3	3	1	0	0	0	1	0	0	0	0	0	0	—	0-0	.667	.714	40.50
Mark Davis	NL	2	0	0	1.2	6	1	0	0	0	0	0	0	0	0	2	0	0	0	0	—	0-0	.167	.167	0.00
Ron Davis	AL	1	0	0	1.0	4	1	1	1	1	0	0	0	0	0	1	0	0	0	0	—	0-0	.250	.250	9.00
Bill Dawley	NL	1	0	0	1.1	5	1	0	0	0	0	0	0	0	0	0	0	0	0	0	—	0-0	.200	.200	0.00
Dizzy Dean	NL	4	2	1	10.0	41	10	3	3	1	0	0	0	5	0	10	0	0	1	1	.500	0-0	.278	.366	2.70
Paul Derringer	NL	4	2	0	8.0	31	6	1	1	0	0	0	0	1	0	6	0	0	1	0	1.000	0-0	.200	.226	1.13
Rob Dibble	NL	2	0	0	2.0	8	1	0	0	0	1	1	0	2	1	1	0	0	0	0	—	0-0	.250	.429	0.00

		G	GS	GF	IP	BFP	H	R	ER	HR	SH	SF	HB	TBB	IBB	SO	WP	Bk	W	L	Pct	Sv-Op	OAvg	OOBP	ERA
Murry Dickson	NL	1	0	1	2.0	9	3	1	1	0	0	0	0	0	0	0	0	0	0	0	—	1-1	.333	.333	4.50
Larry Dierker	NL	1	0	0	0.1	2	1	0	0	0	0	0	0	0	0	0	0	0	0	0	—	0-0	.500	.500	0.00
Dick Donovan	AL	2	0	0	4.0	19	7	1	1	0	0	2	0	0	0	1	0	0	0	0	—	0-0	.412	.368	2.25
Rich Dotson	AL	1	0	0	2.0	9	2	0	0	0	0	0	0	1	0	2	0	0	0	0	—	0-0	.250	.333	0.00
Al Downing	AL	1	0	0	2.0	8	2	0	0	0	0	0	0	0	0	2	0	0	0	0	—	0-0	.250	.250	0.00
Doug Drabek	NL	1	0	0	0.2	6	4	3	1	0	0	0	0	0	0	1	0	0	0	0	—	0-1	.667	.667	13.50
Dave Dravecky	NL	1	0	0	2.0	7	1	0	0	0	0	0	0	0	0	2	0	0	0	0	—	0-0	.143	.143	0.00
Don Drysdale	NL	8	5	1	19.1	69	10	4	3	2	0	0	1	4	0	19	1	0	2	1	.667	1-1	.156	.217	1.40
Ryne Duren	AL	1	0	0	3.0	10	1	0	0	0	0	0	0	1	0	4	0	0	0	0	—	0-0	.111	.200	0.00
Dennis Eckersley	AL	6	1	4	8.2	35	6	5	3	1	0	1	0	2	0	7	0	0	0	1	.000	3-3	.188	.229	3.12
Dock Ellis	NL	1	1	0	3.0	14	4	4	4	2	0	0	0	1	0	2	0	0	0	1	.000	0-0	.308	.357	12.00
Don Elston	NL	1	0	1	1.0	4	1	0	0	0	0	0	0	0	0	1	1	0	0	0	—	1-1	.250	.250	0.00
Carl Erskine	NL	1	0	1	0.2	3	1	0	0	0	0	0	0	0	0	1	0	0	0	0	—	0-0	.333	.333	0.00
Shawn Estes	NL	1	0	0	1.0	5	1	2	2	1	0	0	0	1	0	1	1	0	0	1	.000	0-0	.250	.400	18.00
Chuck Estrada	AL	1	0	0	1.0	7	4	1	1	0	0	0	0	0	0	1	0	0	0	0	—	0-0	.571	.571	9.00
Roy Face	NL	4	0	1	5.2	24	6	6	6	1	0	0	0	2	0	7	0	0	0	0	—	0-0	.273	.333	9.53
Ed Farmer	AL	1	0	0	0.2	3	1	0	0	0	0	0	0	0	0	0	0	0	0	0	—	0-0	.333	.333	0.00
Turk Farrell	NL	4	0	1	6.0	28	5	4	4	1	1	1	1	4	0	7	0	0	0	0	—	0-0	.238	.370	6.00
Bob Feller	AL	5	2	3	12.1	46	5	1	1	0	2	0	1	4	0	13	0	0	1	0	1.000	1-1	.128	.227	0.73
Sid Fernandez	NL	2	0	1	2.0	9	0	0	0	0	0	0	0	3	0	4	0	0	0	0	—	1-1	.000	.333	0.00
Lou Fette	NL	1	0	1	2.0	8	1	0	0	0	0	0	0	1	0	1	0	0	0	0	—	0-0	.143	.250	0.00
Mark Fidrych	AL	1	1	0	2.0	10	4	2	2	0	0	0	0	0	0	1	0	0	0	1	.000	0-0	.400	.400	9.00
Rollie Fingers	AL	4	0	3	3.1	16	5	4	4	1	0	0	0	3	0	0	1	0	0	1	.000	0-1	.385	.500	10.80
	NL	1	0	0	2.0	6	1	0	0	0	0	0	0	0	0	1	0	0	0	0	—	0-0	.167	.167	0.00
	Tot	5	0	3	5.1	22	6	4	4	1	0	0	0	3	0	1	1	0	0	1	.000	0-1	.316	.409	6.75
Chuck Finley	AL	2	0	0	3.0	12	3	1	1	0	0	0	0	1	0	5	0	0	0	0	—	0-0	.273	.333	3.00
Eddie Fisher	AL	1	0	1	2.0	8	1	0	0	0	1	0	0	0	0	0	0	0	0	0	—	0-0	.143	.143	0.00
Whitey Ford	AL	6	3	0	12.0	57	19	13	11	3	1	1	0	3	0	5	0	0	0	2	.000	0-1	.365	.393	8.25
Mike Fornieles	AL	1	0	0	0.1	3	2	1	1	1	0	0	0	0	0	0	0	0	0	0	—	0-0	.667	.667	27.00
Ken Forsch	AL	1	0	0	1.0	4	1	1	1	1	0	0	0	0	0	0	0	0	0	0	—	0-0	.250	.250	9.00
	NL	1	0	1	1.0	3	0	0	0	0	0	0	0	0	0	1	0	0	0	0	—	0-0	.000	.000	0.00
	Tot	2	0	1	2.0	7	1	1	1	1	0	0	0	0	0	1	0	0	0	0	—	0-0	.143	.143	4.50
John Franco	NL	2	0	1	1.2	5	0	0	0	0	0	0	0	0	0	0	0	0	0	0	—	0-0	.000	.000	0.00
Fred Frankhouse	NL	1	0	1	1.0	4	0	0	0	0	0	0	0	1	0	0	0	0	0	0	—	0-0	.000	.250	0.00
Larry French	NL	1	0	0	2.0	7	1	0	0	0	0	0	0	0	0	2	0	0	0	0	—	0-0	.143	.143	0.00
Bob Friend	NL	3	2	0	8.1	37	8	2	1	0	0	0	0	3	1	5	1	1	2	1	.667	0-0	.235	.297	1.08
Mike Garcia	AL	1	0	0	2.0	10	4	1	1	0	0	0	0	1	0	2	0	0	0	0	—	0-0	.444	.500	4.50
Ned Garver	AL	1	1	0	3.0	11	1	1	0	0	0	0	0	1	0	1	0	0	0	0	—	0-0	.100	.182	0.00
Bob Gibson	NL	6	1	1	11.0	48	11	4	4	0	1	0	0	5	0	10	0	0	0	0	—	1-1	.262	.340	3.27
Dave Giusti	NL	1	0	0	1.0	3	0	0	0	0	0	0	0	0	0	0	0	0	0	0	—	0-0	.000	.000	0.00
Tom Glavine	NL	3	2	0	4.2	24	10	5	5	0	0	0	0	1	0	6	0	0	0	1	.000	0-0	.435	.458	9.64
Lefty Gomez	AL	5	5	0	18.0	68	11	6	5	2	0	0	0	3	0	9	0	0	3	1	.750	0-0	.169	.206	2.50
Dwight Gooden	NL	3	2	0	8.0	32	7	3	3	2	0	0	0	1	0	6	0	2	0	2	.000	0-0	.226	.250	3.38
Goose Gossage	AL	3	0	3	3.0	16	6	5	5	0	0	1	1	1	0	1	1	0	0	1	.000	0-0	.462	.500	15.00
	NL	3	0	3	3.0	13	2	2	2	1	0	0	0	2	0	6	0	0	0	0	—	1-1	.182	.308	6.00
	Tot	6	0	6	6.0	29	8	7	7	1	0	1	1	3	0	7	1	0	0	1	.000	1-1	.333	.414	10.50
Mudcat Grant	AL	1	0	0	2.0	8	2	2	2	1	0	0	0	1	0	3	0	0	0	0	—	0-0	.286	.375	9.00
Ted Gray	AL	1	0	0	1.1	7	3	1	1	1	0	0	0	0	0	1	0	0	0	1	.000	0-0	.429	.429	6.75
Tyler Green	NL	1	0	0	1.0	5	2	0	0	0	0	0	0	0	0	1	0	0	0	0	—	0-0	.400	.400	0.00
Bob Grim	AL	1	0	1	0.1	1	0	0	0	0	0	0	0	0	0	0	0	0	0	0	—	1-1	.000	.000	0.00
Lee Grissom	NL	1	0	0	1.0	5	2	1	1	0	0	0	0	0	0	2	0	0	0	0	—	0-0	.400	.400	9.00
Marv Grissom	NL	1	0	0	1.1	4	0	0	0	0	0	0	0	0	0	2	0	0	0	0	—	0-0	.000	.000	0.00
Kevin Gross	NL	1	0	0	1.0	3	0	0	0	0	0	0	0	0	0	1	0	0	0	0	—	0-0	.000	.000	0.00
Lefty Grove	AL	3	1	2	8.0	35	10	4	2	0	0	0	0	2	0	8	0	0	0	1	.000	1-1	.303	.343	2.25
Mark Gubicza	AL	2	0	0	3.0	12	3	1	1	0	0	0	0	0	0	3	1	0	0	0	—	0-0	.250	.250	3.00
Ron Guidry	AL	2	0	1	0.2	3	0	0	0	0	0	0	0	1	0	0	0	0	0	0	—	0-0	.000	.333	0.00
Juan Guzman	AL	1	0	0	1.0	6	2	0	0	0	0	0	0	1	0	2	0	0	0	0	—	0-0	.400	.500	0.00
Harvey Haddix	NL	1	0	0	3.0	12	3	1	1	0	0	0	0	0	0	2	0	0	0	0	—	0-0	.250	.250	3.00
Wild Bill Hallahan	NL	1	1	0	2.0	13	2	3	3	1	0	0	0	5	0	1	0	0	0	1	.000	0-0	.250	.538	13.50
Atlee Hammaker	NL	1	0	0	0.2	9	6	7	7	2	0	0	0	1	1	0	0	0	0	0	—	0-0	.750	.778	94.50
Mel Harder	AL	4	0	4	13.0	50	9	0	0	0	0	0	0	1	0	5	0	0	1	0	1.000	2-2	.184	.200	0.00
Pete Harnisch	NL	1	0	0	1.0	5	2	0	0	0	0	0	0	0	0	1	0	0	0	0	—	0-0	.400	.400	0.00
Bryan Harvey	NL	1	0	1	1.0	4	1	0	0	0	0	0	0	0	0	2	0	0	0	0	—	0-0	.250	.250	0.00
Tom Henke	AL	1	0	0	2.2	10	2	0	0	0	0	0	0	0	0	1	0	0	0	0	—	0-0	.200	.200	0.00
	NL	1	0	0	0.2	2	0	0	0	0	0	0	0	0	0	1	0	0	0	0	—	0-0	.000	.000	0.00
	Tot	2	0	0	3.1	12	2	0	0	0	0	0	0	0	0	2	0	0	0	0	—	0-0	.167	.167	0.00
Bill Henry	NL	1	0	0	1.0	5	2	0	0	0	0	0	0	0	0	0	0	0	0	0	—	0-0	.400	.400	0.00
Pat Hentgen	AL	2	0	0	2.0	6	1	0	0	0	0	0	0	0	0	0	0	0	0	0	—	0-0	.167	.167	0.00
Ray Herbert	AL	1	0	0	3.0	10	3	0	0	0	0	0	0	0	0	0	0	0	1	0	1.000	0-0	.300	.300	0.00
Roberto Hernandez	AL	1	0	1	1.0	4	1	0	0	0	0	0	0	0	0	0	0	0	0	0	—	0-0	.250	.250	0.00
Willie Hernandez	AL	2	0	2	1.2	8	2	1	1	1	0	0	0	1	1	3	0	0	0	0	—	0-0	.286	.375	5.40
Orel Hershiser	NL	2	0	0	3.0	11	1	0	0	0	0	0	0	1	0	0	0	0	0	0	—	0-0	.100	.182	0.00
Kirby Higbe	NL	1	0	3	1.1	10	5	4	4	1	0	0	0	1	1	2	0	0	0	0	—	0-0	.556	.600	27.00
Teddy Higuera	AL	1	0	0	3.0	11	1	0	0	0	0	0	0	1	0	2	0	0	0	0	—	0-0	.100	.182	0.00
Ken Hill	NL	1	0	0	2.0	7	0	0	0	0	0	0	0	1	0	0	0	0	0	0	—	0-0	.000	.143	0.00
Ken Holtzman	AL	1	0	0	0.2	3	1	0	0	0	0	0	0	0	0	0	0	0	0	0	—	0-0	.333	.333	0.00
Rick Honeycutt	AL	1	0	0	2.0	9	5	2	2	0	0	0	0	0	0	0	0	0	0	0	—	0-0	.556	.556	9.00
Burt Hooton	NL	1	0	0	1.2	10	5	3	3	0	0	1	0	0	0	1	0	0	0	0	—	0-0	.556	.500	16.20
Charlie Hough	AL	1	0	0	1.2	8	2	2	1	0	0	0	0	0	0	3	0	1	0	0	—	0-0	.250	.250	5.40
Art Houtteman	AL	1	0	0	3.0	13	3	1	1	1	0	0	0	1	0	0	0	0	0	0	—	0-1	.250	.308	3.00
Steve Howe	NL	1	0	0	0.1	1	0	0	0	0	0	0	0	0	0	0	0	0	0	0	—	0-0	.000	.000	0.00
Jay Howell	AL	1	0	1	2.0	9	3	2	2	0	0	0	0	0	0	3	0	0	0	1	.000	0-0	.333	.333	9.00
	NL	1	0	0	1.0	4	1	0	0	0	0	0	0	0	0	1	0	0	0	0	—	0-0	.250	.250	0.00
	Tot	2	0	1	3.0	13	4	2	2	0	0	0	0	0	0	4	0	0	0	1	.000	0-0	.308	.308	6.00
LaMarr Hoyt	NL	1	1	0	3.0	11	2	1	0	0	0	0	1	0	0	0	0	0	1	0	1.000	0-0	.200	.182	0.00

Name		G	GS	GF	IP	BFP	H	R	ER	HR	SH	SF	HB	TBB	IBB	SO	WP	BK	W	L	Pct	SV-Up	OAvg	OOBP	ERA
Carl Hubbell	NL	5	1	2	9.2	43	8	3	3	0	0	0	0	6	0	11	0	0	0	0	—	0-0	.216	.326	2.79
John Hudek	NL	1	0	0	0.2	4	1	2	2	0	0	0	0	1	0	1	0	0	0	0	—	0-0	.333	.500	27.00
Sid Hudson	AL	1	0	0	1.0	7	3	2	2	1	1	0	0	1	0	1	0	0	0	0	—	0-1	.600	.667	18.00
Tex Hughson	AL	2	0	1	4.2	25	10	6	5	1	0	0	0	1	0	4	0	0	0	1	.000	1-1	.417	.440	9.64
Tom Hume	NL	1	0	1	0.1	1	0	0	0	0	0	0	0	0	0	0	0	0	0	0	—	1-1	.000	.000	0.00
Catfish Hunter	AL	6	1	1	12.2	53	15	9	9	4	1	0	0	1	0	13	0	0	0	2	.000	0-0	.294	.308	6.39
Fred Hutchinson	AL	1	0	0	3.0	15	3	3	3	1	0	0	0	2	0	0	0	0	0	0	—	0-0	.231	.333	9.00
Danny Jackson	NL	1	0	0	0.0	3	3	1	1	0	0	0	0	0	0	0	0	0	0	0	—	0-1	1.000	1.000	—
Larry Jackson	NL	4	0	0	5.2	25	6	2	2	0	1	0	0	3	0	3	0	0	1	0	1.000	0-0	.286	.375	3.18
Larry Jansen	NL	1	0	0	5.0	16	1	0	0	0	0	0	0	0	0	6	0	0	0	0	—	0-0	.063	.063	0.00
Al Javery	NL	1	0	1	2.0	8	2	0	0	0	0	0	0	0	0	3	0	0	0	0	—	0-0	.250	.250	0.00
Fergie Jenkins	NL	2	0	0	4.0	16	6	3	3	2	0	0	0	0	0	6	0	0	0	0	—	0-0	.375	.375	6.75
Tommy John	AL	2	0	1	3.0	13	5	3	3	1	0	0	0	0	0	1	0	0	0	1	.000	0-0	.385	.385	9.00
Randy Johnson	AL	4	2	0	7.0	23	2	1	1	1	0	0	0	2	0	6	0	0	0	0	—	0-0	.095	.174	1.29
Bobby Jones	NL	1	0	1	1.0	4	1	0	0	0	0	0	0	0	0	2	0	0	0	0	—	0-0	.250	.250	0.00
Doug Jones	AL	2	0	1	2.0	7	1	0	0	0	0	0	0	0	0	1	0	0	0	0	—	1-1	.143	.143	0.00
	NL	2	0	1	2.0	12	6	3	3	0	0	0	0	0	0	4	0	0	1	0	1.000	0-0	.500	.500	13.50
	Tot	4	0	2	4.0	19	7	3	3	0	0	0	0	0	0	5	0	0	1	0	1.000	1-1	.368	.368	6.75
Randy Jones	NL	2	1	1	4.0	14	2	0	0	0	0	0	0	1	0	2	0	0	1	0	1.000	1-1	.154	.214	0.00
Sam Jones	NL	2	0	0	2.2	15	1	1	0	0	0	0	1	4	0	4	0	0	0	0	—	0-0	.100	.400	0.00
Jim Kaat	AL	2	0	0	4.0	15	3	1	1	0	0	0	0	0	0	1	0	0	0	0	—	0-0	.200	.200	2.25
Bob Keegan	AL	1	0	0	0.2	6	3	2	2	1	0	0	0	0	0	1	0	0	0	1	.000	0-1	.500	.500	27.00
Matt Keough	AL	1	0	0	0.1	2	1	0	0	0	0	0	0	0	0	0	0	0	0	0	—	0-0	.500	.500	0.00
Jim Kern	AL	3	0	0	4.1	20	3	2	2	1	0	0	0	4	2	6	0	1	0	1	.000	0-1	.188	.350	4.15
Jimmy Key	AL	4	1	0	4.1	17	4	2	2	0	0	2	0	0	0	3	0	0	1	0	1.000	0-0	.267	.235	4.15
Bob Knepper	NL	2	0	0	3.0	15	3	1	1	0	0	1	0	3	0	3	0	0	0	0	—	0-0	.273	.400	3.00
Darold Knowles	AL	1	0	0	0.2	2	0	0	0	0	0	0	0	0	0	0	0	0	0	0	—	0-0	.000	.000	0.00
Jim Konstanty	NL	1	0	0	1.0	3	0	0	0	0	0	0	0	0	0	2	0	0	0	0	—	0-0	.000	.000	0.00
Jerry Koosman	NL	2	0	1	2.0	7	1	0	0	0	0	0	0	0	0	2	0	0	0	0	—	1-1	.143	.143	0.00
Sandy Koufax	NL	4	1	0	6.0	23	4	1	1	0	0	0	0	2	0	3	1	0	1	0	1.000	0-0	.190	.261	1.50
Jack Kramer	AL	1	0	1	3.0	10	0	0	0	0	0	0	0	1	0	3	0	0	0	0	—	1-1	.000	.100	0.00
Mike Krukow	NL	1	0	0	1.0	3	0	0	0	0	0	0	0	0	0	0	0	0	0	0	—	0-0	.000	.000	0.00
Clem Labine	NL	1	0	1	1.0	7	3	3	1	0	1	0	0	0	0	1	0	0	0	0	—	0-0	.500	.500	9.00
Mike LaCoss	NL	1	0	0	1.1	4	1	0	0	0	0	0	0	0	0	0	0	0	0	0	—	0-0	.250	.250	0.00
Mark Langston	AL	3	1	0	5.0	21	5	3	3	1	0	0	0	1	0	6	0	0	0	0	—	0-0	.250	.286	5.40
Dave LaRoche	AL	1	0	0	1.0	5	1	0	0	0	0	0	0	1	0	0	0	0	0	0	—	0-0	.250	.400	0.00
Frank Lary	AL	3	0	0	2.0	9	2	1	0	0	0	0	0	1	0	1	0	0	0	0	—	0-0	.250	.333	0.00
Gary Lavelle	NL	1	0	0	2.0	7	1	0	0	0	0	0	0	0	0	2	0	0	0	0	—	0-0	.143	.143	0.00
Vern Law	NL	2	1	1	2.2	8	1	0	0	0	0	0	0	0	0	1	0	0	1	0	1.000	1-1	.125	.125	0.00
Charlie Lea	NL	1	1	0	2.0	8	3	1	1	1	0	0	0	0	0	2	0	0	1	0	1.000	0-0	.375	.375	4.50
Bill Lee	NL	2	0	0	6.0	27	4	3	2	1	0	0	0	4	1	6	0	0	0	1	.000	0-0	.174	.296	3.00
Thornton Lee	AL	1	0	0	3.0	13	4	1	1	0	1	0	0	0	0	0	0	0	0	0	—	0-0	.333	.333	3.00
Al Leiter	NL	1	0	1	0.1	1	0	0	0	0	0	0	0	0	0	0	0	0	0	0	—	0-0	.000	.000	0.00
Bob Lemon	AL	4	0	1	6.2	28	6	2	2	1	0	0	1	3	1	3	0	0	0	1	.000	0-0	.250	.357	2.70
Dutch Leonard	AL	1	1	0	3.0	12	2	1	1	0	0	0	0	0	0	0	0	0	1	0	1.000	0-0	.167	.167	3.00
Billy Loes	AL	1	0	0	3.0	11	3	0	0	0	0	0	0	0	0	1	0	0	0	0	—	0-0	.273	.273	0.00
Mickey Lolich	AL	2	0	1	4.0	14	2	1	1	1	0	0	0	0	0	2	0	0	0	0	—	1-1	.143	.143	2.25
Ed Lopat	AL	1	0	0	1.0	6	3	3	3	2	0	0	0	0	0	0	0	0	0	1	.000	0-0	.500	.500	27.00
Sparky Lyle	AL	2	0	1	3.0	13	4	2	2	0	0	0	1	0	0	2	1	0	0	0	—	0-0	.333	.385	6.00
Greg Maddux	NL	3	2	0	6.1	24	6	3	3	2	0	0	0	0	0	5	0	0	0	0	—	0-0	.250	.250	4.26
Sal Maglie	NL	1	0	0	3.0	14	3	2	2	2	1	0	0	1	0	1	0	0	1	0	1.000	0-0	.250	.308	6.00
Art Mahaffey	NL	2	0	0	4.0	17	2	3	3	2	0	0	0	2	0	1	0	0	0	1	.000	0-0	.133	.235	6.75
Jim Maloney	NL	1	0	0	1.2	12	5	5	5	2	0	0	0	2	0	1	1	0	0	0	—	0-0	.500	.583	27.00
Juan Marichal	NL	8	2	2	18.0	62	7	2	1	0	0	1	0	2	0	12	2	0	2	0	1.000	0-0	.119	.145	0.50
Mike Marshall	NL	1	0	1	2.0	7	0	0	0	0	0	0	0	1	0	2	0	0	0	0	—	1-1	.000	.143	0.00
Dennis Martinez	NL	3	0	0	4.0	17	4	3	3	1	0	0	0	1	0	2	0	0	0	1	.000	0-0	.250	.294	6.75
	AL	1	0	0	2.0	7	1	1	1	1	0	0	0	0	0	0	0	0	0	0	—	0-0	.143	.143	4.50
	Tot	4	0	0	6.0	24	5	4	4	2	0	0	0	1	0	2	0	0	0	1	.000	0-0	.217	.250	6.00
Pedro Martinez	NL	2	0	0	2.0	8	2	0	0	0	0	0	0	0	0	3	0	0	0	0	—	0-0	.250	.250	0.00
Ramon Martinez	NL	1	0	0	1.0	5	0	0	0	0	0	0	0	2	1	1	0	0	0	0	—	0-0	.000	.400	0.00
Walt Masterson	AL	2	1	0	4.2	21	5	2	2	1	0	0	0	2	0	3	1	0	0	0	—	0-0	.263	.333	3.86
Jon Matlack	NL	2	0	0	3.0	12	3	0	0	0	0	0	0	1	0	4	0	0	1	0	1.000	0-0	.273	.333	0.00
Ken McBride	AL	1	1	0	3.0	15	4	3	3	0	0	0	0	2	0	1	0	0	0	0	—	0-0	.308	.400	9.00
Mike McCormick	NL	2	0	0	5.1	24	4	2	1	1	0	0	0	4	0	5	0	0	0	0	—	0-0	.200	.333	1.69
Lindy McDaniel	NL	1	0	1	1.0	4	1	0	0	0	0	0	0	0	0	0	0	0	0	0	—	0-0	.250	.250	0.00
Jack McDowell	AL	3	0	0	4.0	14	1	0	0	0	0	0	0	2	0	0	0	0	1	0	1.000	0-0	.083	.214	0.00
Sam McDowell	AL	4	0	0	8.0	32	5	1	1	0	0	0	0	4	0	12	0	0	0	1	.000	0-0	.179	.281	1.13
Lynn McGlothen	NL	1	0	0	1.0	3	0	0	0	0	0	0	0	0	0	1	0	0	0	0	—	0-0	.000	.000	0.00
Jim McGlothlin	AL	1	0	0	2.0	6	1	0	0	0	0	0	0	0	0	2	0	0	0	0	—	0-0	.167	.167	0.00
Tug McGraw	NL	1	0	1	2.0	7	1	0	0	0	0	0	0	0	0	4	0	0	1	0	1.000	0-0	.143	.143	0.00
Denny McLain	AL	3	1	0	6.0	24	2	1	1	1	0	0	0	4	0	6	0	0	0	0	—	0-0	.100	.250	1.50
Cal McLish	AL	1	0	1	2.0	8	1	0	0	0	0	0	0	1	0	2	0	0	0	0	—	1-1	.143	.250	0.00
Dave McNally	AL	2	0	1	2.1	11	2	1	1	0	1	0	0	2	0	1	0	0	0	1	.000	0-0	.250	.400	3.86
Jim Merritt	NL	1	0	0	2.0	6	1	0	0	0	0	0	0	0	0	2	0	0	0	0	—	0-0	.167	.167	0.00
Jose Mesa	AL	1	0	1	1.0	3	0	0	0	0	0	0	0	0	0	1	0	0	0	0	—	0-0	.000	.000	0.00
Andy Messersmith	NL	1	1	0	3.0	14	2	2	2	0	1	0	0	3	0	4	0	0	0	0	—	0-0	.200	.385	6.00
Stu Miller	NL	2	0	2	4.2	19	1	1	0	0	0	0	0	1	0	9	0	1	1	0	1.000	0-1	.056	.105	0.00
Greg Minton	NL	1	0	0	0.2	3	0	0	0	0	0	0	0	1	0	0	0	0	0	0	—	0-0	.000	.333	0.00
Bill Monbouquette	AL	1	1	0	2.0	11	5	4	4	2	0	0	0	0	0	2	0	0	0	1	.000	0-0	.455	.455	18.00
John Montefusco	NL	1	0	0	2.0	8	0	0	0	0	0	0	0	2	0	2	0	0	0	0	—	0-0	.000	.250	0.00
Jeff Montgomery	AL	2	0	0	1.2	7	2	2	2	0	0	0	0	1	0	1	0	0	0	0	—	0-0	.286	.286	10.80
Donnie Moore	AL	1	0	0	2.0	6	0	0	0	0	0	0	0	0	0	1	0	0	0	0	—	0-0	.000	.000	0.00
Mike Moore	AL	1	0	0	1.0	3	0	0	0	0	0	0	0	0	0	1	0	0	0	0	—	0-0	.000	.000	0.00
Mike Morgan	NL	1	0	1	1.0	3	0	0	0	0	0	0	0	1	0	0	0	0	0	0	—	0-0	.000	.000	0.00
Jack Morris	AL	5	3	0	10.2	48	14	3	3	0	0	0	0	4	0	8	0	0	0	1	.000	0-0	.318	.375	2.53

		G	GS	GF	IP	BFP	H	R	ER	HR	SH	SF	HB	TBB	IBB	SO	WP	Bk	W	L	Pct	Sv-Op	OAvg	OOBP	ERA
Don Mossi	AL	1	0	0	0.2	2	1	0	0	0	0	0	0	0	0	1	0	0	0	0	—	0-0	.500	.500	0.00
Terry Mulholland	NL	1	1	0	2.0	9	1	1	1	1	0	0	0	2	0	0	0	0	0	0	—	0-0	.143	.333	4.50
Bob Muncrief	AL	1	0	0	1.1	5	1	0	0	0	1	0	0	0	0	1	1	0	0	0	—	0-0	.250	.250	0.00
George Munger	NL	1	0	0	1.0	3	0	0	0	0	0	0	0	1	0	0	0	0	0	0	—	0-0	.000	.333	0.00
Van Lingle Mungo	NL	2	0	0	3.0	17	6	6	6	0	0	0	0	4	1	2	0	0	0	1	.000	0-0	.462	.588	18.00
Mike Mussina	AL	2	0	0	2.0	7	1	0	0	0	0	0	0	0	0	1	0	0	0	0	—	0-0	.143	.143	0.00
Randy Myers	NL	3	0	1	3.0	14	2	0	0	0	0	0	0	3	0	1	0	0	0	0	—	1-1	.182	.357	0.00
	AL	1	0	0	1.0	3	0	0	0	0	0	0	0	0	0	2	0	0	0	0	—	0-0	.000	.000	0.00
	Tot	4	0	1	4.0	17	2	0	0	0	0	0	0	3	0	3	0	0	0	0	—	1-1	.143	.294	0.00
Charles Nagy	AL	2	1	0	3.0	13	4	3	3	1	0	0	0	0	0	2	0	0	0	1	.000	0-0	.308	.308	9.00
Ray Narleski	AL	1	0	0	3.1	12	1	0	0	0	0	0	0	1	0	0	0	0	0	0	—	0-0	.091	.167	0.00
Denny Neagle	NL	1	0	0	1.0	4	1	0	0	0	0	0	0	0	0	1	0	0	0	0	—	0-0	.250	.250	0.00
Don Newcombe	NL	4	0	0	8.2	37	9	4	4	0	0	0	0	2	0	5	0	0	0	1	.000	0-0	.257	.297	4.15
Hal Newhouser	AL	4	1	0	10.2	43	8	3	2	0	2	0	0	3	0	8	0	0	0	0	—	0-0	.211	.268	1.69
Bobo Newsom	AL	2	0	1	3.1	12	1	0	0	0	0	0	0	1	0	1	0	0	0	0	—	0-0	.091	.167	0.00
Phil Niekro	NL	2	0	2	1.1	4	0	0	0	0	0	0	0	0	0	2	0	0	0	0	—	0-0	.000	.000	0.00
Hideo Nomo	NL	1	1	0	2.0	6	1	0	0	0	0	0	0	0	0	3	0	0	0	0	—	0-0	.167	.167	0.00
Mike Norris	AL	1	0	0	1.0	5	2	1	1	1	0	0	0	0	0	1	0	0	0	0	—	0-0	.400	.400	9.00
Joe Nuxhall	NL	1	0	0	3.1	15	2	0	0	0	1	0	0	3	0	5	0	0	0	0	—	0-0	.182	.357	0.00
Billy O'Dell	AL	2	0	1	4.0	13	1	1	1	1	0	0	0	0	0	2	0	0	0	0	—	1-1	.077	.077	2.25
Blue Moon Odom	AL	2	0	0	2.1	15	5	5	4	1	0	0	0	2	0	2	0	0	0	0	—	0-0	.385	.467	15.43
Steve Ontiveros	AL	1	0	0	0.2	3	1	1	1	1	0	0	0	0	0	1	0	0	0	1	.000	0-0	.333	.333	13.50
Jesse Orosco	NL	1	0	0	0.1	1	0	0	0	0	0	0	0	0	0	1	0	0	0	0	—	0-0	.000	.000	0.00
Claude Osteen	NL	2	0	1	5.0	21	5	0	0	0	0	0	0	2	1	1	0	0	1	0	1.000	0-0	.263	.333	0.00
Jim O'Toole	NL	1	1	0	2.0	10	4	1	1	0	0	0	1	0	0	1	0	0	0	0	—	0-0	.444	.500	4.50
Joe Page	AL	1	0	1	1.1	6	1	0	0	0	0	0	0	0	0	0	0	0	0	0	—	1-1	.200	.333	0.00
Satchel Paige	AL	1	0	1	1.0	6	3	2	2	0	0	0	0	1	0	0	0	0	0	0	—	0-0	.600	.667	18.00
Jim Palmer	AL	5	4	0	12.2	53	11	8	8	3	1	0	0	7	0	14	1	0	0	1	.000	0-0	.244	.346	5.68
Milt Pappas	AL	3	1	2	3.0	16	5	4	4	3	0	0	0	2	0	0	0	0	0	0	—	0-0	.357	.438	12.00
Mel Parnell	AL	2	1	0	2.0	14	6	4	4	2	0	0	1	1	0	2	0	0	0	0	—	0-0	.500	.571	18.00
Camilo Pascual	AL	3	0	1	8.0	31	6	3	3	0	0	0	0	2	0	6	0	0	0	1	.000	0-0	.207	.258	3.38
Claude Passeau	NL	3	1	1	7.2	33	9	7	7	2	0	0	0	3	0	4	0	0	0	2	.000	0-1	.300	.364	8.22
Roger Pavlik	AL	1	0	0	2.0	9	3	2	2	1	0	0	0	0	0	2	0	0	0	0	—	0-0	.333	.333	9.00
Troy Percival	AL	1	0	0	1.0	4	1	0	0	0	0	0	0	0	0	1	0	0	0	0	—	0-0	.250	.250	0.00
Carlos Perez	NL	1	0	0	0.1	3	1	0	0	0	0	0	0	1	0	0	0	0	0	0	—	0-0	.500	.667	0.00
Pascual Perez	NL	1	0	0	0.2	6	3	2	2	0	0	0	0	1	0	1	0	0	0	0	—	0-0	.600	.667	27.00
Gaylord Perry	NL	3	0	1	4.0	22	8	3	3	0	1	1	0	2	0	1	1	0	1	0	1.000	0-0	.444	.476	6.75
	AL	2	1	0	5.0	21	6	3	3	1	0	0	0	0	0	5	0	0	0	0	—	0-1	.286	.286	5.40
	Tot	5	1	1	9.0	43	14	6	6	1	1	1	0	2	0	6	1	0	1	0	1.000	0-1	.359	.381	6.00
Jim Perry	AL	1	0	0	2.0	8	1	1	1	0	0	0	1	1	0	3	0	0	0	0	—	0-0	.167	.375	4.50
Gary Peters	AL	1	0	0	3.0	9	0	0	0	0	0	0	0	0	0	4	0	0	0	0	—	0-0	.000	.000	0.00
Fritz Peterson	AL	1	0	0	0.0	1	1	0	0	0	0	0	0	0	0	0	0	0	0	0	—	0-0	1.000	1.000	—
Dan Petry	AL	1	0	0	0.1	4	0	2	2	0	0	0	0	3	0	1	0	0	0	0	—	0-0	.000	.750	54.00
Billy Pierce	AL	4	3	0	10.2	39	6	4	4	0	1	0	0	3	0	12	1	0	0	1	.000	0-0	.171	.237	3.38
Juan Pizarro	AL	1	0	0	1.0	3	0	0	0	0	0	0	0	0	0	0	0	0	0	0	—	0-0	.000	.000	0.00
Dan Plesac	AL	3	0	0	1.1	5	1	0	0	0	0	0	0	0	0	2	0	0	0	0	—	0-0	.200	.200	0.00
Johnny Podres	NL	2	1	0	4.0	18	3	0	0	0	0	0	0	3	0	3	0	0	0	0	—	0-0	.200	.333	0.00
Howie Pollet	NL	1	0	0	1.0	7	4	3	3	0	0	0	0	0	0	0	0	0	0	0	—	0-0	.571	.571	27.00
Bob Porterfield	AL	1	0	0	3.0	13	4	2	2	1	0	0	0	0	0	1	0	0	0	0	—	0-0	.308	.308	6.00
Bob Purkey	NL	3	1	0	6.0	24	3	2	2	1	0	1	0	2	0	4	0	0	0	0	—	0-0	.143	.208	3.00
Dan Quisenberry	AL	2	0	1	3.0	13	4	1	1	0	0	0	0	0	0	2	0	0	0	0	—	0-0	.308	.308	3.00
Dick Radatz	AL	2	0	2	4.2	20	4	5	5	1	0	0	0	2	1	10	0	0	0	1	.000	0-1	.222	.300	9.64
Ken Raffensberger	NL	1	0	0	2.0	7	1	0	0	0	0	0	0	0	0	2	0	0	1	0	1.000	0-0	.143	.143	0.00
Vic Raschi	AL	4	2	1	11.0	44	7	3	3	1	0	0	0	4	0	8	0	0	1	0	1.000	1-1	.175	.250	2.45
Jeff Reardon	AL	1	0	0	0.2	3	1	0	0	0	0	0	0	0	0	0	0	0	0	0	—	0-0	.333	.333	0.00
	NL	1	0	0	1.0	3	1	0	0	0	0	0	0	0	0	1	0	0	0	0	—	0-0	.333	.333	0.00
	Tot	2	0	0	1.2	6	2	0	0	0	0	0	0	0	0	1	0	0	0	0	—	0-0	.333	.333	0.00
Ron Reed	NL	1	0	0	0.2	2	0	0	0	0	0	0	0	0	0	1	0	0	0	0	—	0-0	.000	.000	0.00
Rick Reuschel	NL	3	1	0	3.1	15	5	2	2	2	1	0	1	0	0	1	0	0	0	0	—	0-0	.385	.429	5.40
Jerry Reuss	NL	2	1	0	4.0	17	3	0	0	0	0	0	1	0	0	5	0	0	1	0	1.000	0-0	.188	.235	0.00
Allie Reynolds	AL	2	0	0	5.0	22	3	2	2	0	0	0	1	2	1	2	0	0	0	1	.000	0-0	.158	.273	3.60
Rick Rhoden	NL	1	0	0	1.0	3	1	0	0	0	0	0	0	0	0	0	0	0	0	0	—	0-0	.333	.333	0.00
J.R. Richard	NL	1	1	0	2.0	9	1	0	0	0	0	0	0	2	0	3	0	0	0	0	—	0-0	.143	.333	0.00
Pete Richert	AL	2	0	1	2.1	10	3	1	1	0	1	0	0	0	0	2	0	0	0	1	.000	0-0	.333	.333	3.86
Dave Righetti	AL	2	0	0	1.0	6	3	0	0	0	0	0	0	0	0	0	0	0	0	0	—	0-0	.500	.500	0.00
Mariano Rivera	AL	1	0	1	1.0	3	0	0	0	0	0	0	0	0	0	1	0	0	0	0	—	1-1	.000	.000	0.00
Robin Roberts	NL	5	5	0	14.0	62	17	10	10	3	1	0	0	6	0	9	2	0	0	0	—	0-0	.309	.377	6.43
Preacher Roe	NL	1	0	1	1.0	3	0	0	0	0	0	0	0	0	0	0	0	0	0	0	—	0-0	.000	.000	0.00
Kenny Rogers	AL	1	0	0	1.0	4	1	1	1	1	0	0	0	0	0	2	0	0	0	0	—	0-1	.250	.250	9.00
Steve Rogers	NL	3	1	0	7.0	27	6	1	1	0	0	1	0	0	0	6	2	0	1	0	1.000	0-0	.231	.222	1.29
Jose Rosado	AL	1	0	0	1.0	6	2	1	1	1	0	0	0	1	0	1	0	0	1	0	1.000	0-1	.400	.500	9.00
Schoolboy Rowe	AL	1	0	0	3.0	13	4	2	1	1	0	0	0	1	0	2	0	0	0	0	—	0-0	.333	.385	3.00
Red Ruffing	AL	3	2	0	7.0	36	13	7	7	1	0	0	0	2	1	6	0	0	0	1	.000	0-0	.382	.417	9.00
Bob Rush	NL	1	0	1	2.0	9	4	2	2	0	0	0	0	1	0	1	0	0	1	0	1.000	0-0	.500	.556	9.00
Jeff Russell	AL	2	0	0	2.0	10	2	1	1	0	0	0	0	2	0	0	0	0	0	0	—	0-0	.250	.400	4.50
Dick Ruthven	NL	1	0	0	0.1	1	0	0	0	0	0	0	0	0	0	0	0	0	0	0	—	0-0	.000	.000	0.00
Nolan Ryan	AL	3	1	0	6.0	28	8	5	5	1	0	1	0	3	0	7	0	0	1	0	1.000	0-0	.333	.393	7.50
	NL	2	0	0	4.0	16	2	0	0	0	0	0	0	2	0	3	0	0	0	0	—	0-0	.143	.250	0.00
	Tot	5	1	0	10.0	44	10	5	5	1	0	1	0	5	0	10	0	0	1	0	1.000	0-0	.263	.341	4.50
Bret Saberhagen	AL	2	1	0	5.0	16	1	0	0	0	0	0	0	0	0	1	0	0	1	0	1.000	0-0	.063	.063	0.00
Johnny Sain	NL	2	0	0	2.2	10	2	1	1	0	0	0	0	0	0	4	0	0	0	1	.000	0-0	.200	.200	3.38
Joe Sambito	NL	1	0	0	0.2	3	0	0	0	0	0	0	0	0	0	0	0	0	0	0	—	0-0	.000	.333	0.00
Jack Sanford	NL	1	0	0	1.0	5	2	1	1	0	0	0	0	0	0	1	0	0	0	0	—	0-0	.400	.400	9.00
Curt Schilling	NL	1	0	0	2.0	7	2	0	0	0	0	0	0	0	0	3	1	0	0	0	—	0-0	.286	.286	0.00
Johnny Schmitz	NL	1	0	0	0.1	5	3	3	3	0	0	0	0	1	0	0	0	0	0	1	.000	0-0	.750	.800	81.00

All-Star Games: Pitcher Register

		G	GS	GF	IP	DFP	H	R	ER	HR	SH	SF	HB	TBB	IBB	SO	WP	Bk	W	L	Pct	Sv-Op	OAvg	OOBP	ERA
Hal Schumacher	NL	1	0	0	4.0	17	4	1	1	0	0	0	0	1	0	5	0	0	0	0	—	0-0	.250	.294	2.25
Don Schwall	AL	1	0	0	3.0	16	5	1	1	0	0	0	1	1	0	2	0	0	0	0	—	0-0	.357	.438	3.00
Herb Score	AL	1	0	0	1.0	4	0	0	0	0	0	0	0	1	0	1	0	0	0	0	—	0-0	.000	.250	0.00
Mike Scott	NL	2	1	0	3.0	11	2	1	1	1	0	0	0	0	0	3	0	0	0	0	—	0-0	.182	.182	3.00
Tom Seaver	NL	8	1	1	13.0	57	14	8	7	3	0	0	0	4	0	16	0	0	0	0	—	1-2	.264	.316	4.85
Rip Sewell	NL	3	0	1	5.0	20	4	4	4	1	1	0	0	1	0	2	0	0	0	0	—	0-0	.222	.263	7.20
Bobby Shantz	AL	1	0	1	1.0	3	0	0	0	0	0	0	0	0	0	3	0	0	0	0	—	0-0	.000	.000	0.00
Bob Shaw	NL	1	0	1	2.0	9	1	0	0	0	0	0	1	1	0	1	0	0	0	0	—	1-1	.143	.333	0.00
Spec Shea	AL	1	0	0	3.0	14	3	1	1	1	0	0	0	2	0	2	0	0	1	0	1.000	0-0	.250	.357	3.00
Chris Short	NL	2	0	0	3.0	13	3	2	2	0	1	0	0	1	0	2	0	0	0	1	.000	0-1	.273	.333	6.00
Sonny Siebert	AL	1	0	0	2.0	6	0	0	0	0	0	0	0	0	0	1	0	0	0	0	—	0-0	.000	.000	0.00
Curt Simmons	NL	3	2	0	6.0	26	4	2	2	0	0	0	0	4	0	4	0	0	0	1	.000	0-0	.182	.308	3.00
Bill Singer	AL	1	0	0	2.0	10	3	3	3	2	1	0	0	1	0	2	0	0	0	0	—	0-0	.375	.444	13.50
	NL	1	0	0	2.0	6	0	0	0	0	0	0	0	0	0	0	0	0	0	0	—	0-0	.000	.000	0.00
	Tot	2	0	0	4.0	16	3	3	3	2	1	0	0	1	0	2	0	0	0	0	—	0-0	.214	.267	6.75
Heathcliff Slocumb	NL	1	0	0	1.0	4	1	0	0	0	0	0	0	0	0	2	0	0	1	0	1.000	0-0	.250	.250	0.00
John Smiley	NL	2	0	0	2.0	10	3	3	3	1	0	0	0	0	0	0	0	0	0	0	—	0-0	.333	.333	13.50
Dave Smith	NL	1	0	0	0.2	5	1	0	0	0	0	0	0	2	1	1	0	0	0	0	—	0-0	.333	.600	0.00
Eddie Smith	AL	1	0	1	2.0	9	2	2	2	1	0	0	0	0	0	2	0	0	1	0	1.000	0-0	.222	.222	9.00
Lee Smith	NL	2	0	1	4.0	17	4	2	1	0	1	1	0	0	0	5	0	0	1	0	1.000	0-0	.267	.250	2.25
	AL	1	0	0	1.0	5	1	2	2	1	0	0	0	1	0	0	0	0	0	1	—	0-1	.250	.400	18.00
	Tot	3	0	1	5.0	22	5	4	3	1	1	1	0	1	0	5	0	0	1	0	1.000	0-1	.263	.286	5.40
John Smoltz	NL	4	1	0	3.2	16	5	1	1	0	0	0	0	1	0	1	2	0	1	1	.500	0-0	.333	.375	2.45
Lary Sorensen	AL	1	0	0	3.0	10	1	0	0	0	0	0	0	0	0	0	0	0	0	0	—	0-0	.100	.100	0.00
Mario Soto	NL	3	1	0	6.0	27	5	2	0	0	1	2	0	2	1	7	0	0	0	1	.000	0-0	.227	.269	0.00
Warren Spahn	NL	7	3	1	14.0	65	17	10	5	2	0	0	0	5	0	10	0	0	1	0	1.000	0-0	.283	.338	3.21
Gerry Staley	AL	1	0	0	2.0	8	2	1	1	1	0	0	0	0	0	0	0	0	0	0	—	0-0	.250	.250	4.50
Bob Stanley	AL	2	0	0	4.0	15	3	1	1	0	0	0	0	0	0	0	0	0	0	0	—	0-0	.200	.200	2.25
Dave Stenhouse	AL	1	1	0	2.0	11	3	1	1	0	0	0	1	1	0	1	1	0	0	0	—	0-0	.333	.455	4.50
Dave Stewart	AL	1	1	0	1.0	7	3	2	2	0	0	0	0	2	0	0	1	0	0	0	—	0-0	.600	.714	18.00
Dave Stieb	AL	7	2	1	11.2	49	6	4	1	1	0	0	0	6	0	10	2	0	1	1	.500	0-0	.140	.245	0.77
Dean Stone	AL	1	0	0	0.1	0	0	0	0	0	0	0	0	0	0	0	0	0	1	0	1.000	0-0	—		0.00
Steve Stone	AL	1	1	0	3.0	9	0	0	0	0	0	0	0	0	0	3	0	0	0	0	—	0-0	.000	.000	0.00
Bill Stoneman	NL	1	0	0	2.0	8	2	2	2	1	0	0	0	0	0	2	0	0	0	1	—	0-1	.250	.250	9.00
Mel Stottlemyre	AL	4	1	0	6.0	25	5	3	2	1	0	1	0	1	1	4	1	0	0	1	.000	0-1	.217	.240	3.00
Frank Sullivan	AL	1	0	1	3.1	15	4	1	1	1	0	0	0	1	0	4	0	0	0	1	.000	0-1	.286	.333	2.70
Rick Sutcliffe	NL	2	0	0	3.0	16	5	2	2	0	0	0	0	1	0	1	0	0	0	0	—	0-0	.333	.375	6.00
Bruce Sutter	NL	4	0	3	6.2	24	2	0	0	0	1	0	0	3	1	7	0	0	2	0	1.000	2-2	.100	.217	0.00
Don Sutton	NL	4	1	0	8.0	29	5	0	0	0	0	0	0	1	0	7	0	0	1	0	1.000	0-0	.179	.207	0.00
Greg Swindell	NL	1	0	0	1.2	6	2	0	0	0	0	0	0	0	0	3	0	0	0	0	—	0-0	.333	.333	0.00
Frank Tanana	AL	1	0	1	2.0	9	3	3	3	1	0	0	0	1	0	0	0	0	0	0	—	0-0	.375	.444	13.50
Bob Tewksbury	NL	1	0	0	1.2	10	4	4	4	1	0	0	0	1	0	0	0	0	0	0	—	0-0	.444	.500	21.60
Bobby Thigpen	AL	1	0	0	1.0	3	0	0	0	0	0	0	0	0	0	1	0	0	0	0	—	0-0	.000	.000	0.00
Justin Thompson	AL	1	0	0	1.0	3	0	0	0	0	0	0	0	0	0	1	0	0	0	0	—	0-0	.000	.000	0.00
Luis Tiant	AL	3	1	0	6.0	27	7	4	2	0	0	1	0	3	0	3	1	0	0	2	.000	0-0	.304	.370	3.00
Jim Tobin	NL	1	0	1	1.0	3	0	0	0	0	0	0	0	0	0	0	0	0	0	0	—	0-0	.000	.000	0.00
Steve Trachsel	NL	1	0	0	1.0	3	0	0	0	0	0	0	0	0	0	0	0	0	0	0	—	0-0	.000	.000	0.00
Virgil Trucks	AL	2	0	1	3.0	13	3	2	2	0	0	1	0	3	0	4	0	0	1	0	1.000	1-1	.333	.462	6.00
Bob Turley	AL	1	1	0	1.2	11	3	3	3	0	0	1	1	2	0	1	0	0	0	0	—	0-0	.429	.545	16.20
Wayne Twitchell	NL	1	0	0	1.0	4	1	0	0	0	0	0	0	0	0	1	0	0	0	0	—	0-0	.250	.250	0.00
Fernando Valenzuela	NL	5	1	0	7.2	29	5	0	0	0	0	0	0	3	0	9	1	0	0	0	—	0-0	.192	.276	0.00
Johnny Vander Meer	NL	3	1	0	8.2	32	5	1	0	0	0	0	0	1	0	11	0	0	1	0	1.000	0-0	.161	.188	0.00
Frank Viola	NL	2	0	0	2.0	7	1	0	0	0	0	0	0	1	0	0	0	0	0	0	—	0-0	.167	.286	0.00
	AL	1	1	0	2.0	6	0	0	0	0	0	0	0	0	0	1	0	0	1	0	1.000	0-0	.000	.000	0.00
	Tot	3	1	0	4.0	13	1	0	0	0	0	0	0	1	0	1	0	0	1	0	1.000	0-0	.083	.154	0.00
Bob Walk	NL	1	0	0	0.1	1	0	0	0	0	0	0	0	0	0	0	0	0	0	0	—	0-0	.000	.000	0.00
Bill Walker	NL	1	1	0	2.0	9	2	3	3	1	0	0	0	1	0	2	0	0	0	1	.000	0-0	.250	.333	13.50
Jerry Walker	AL	1	1	0	3.0	11	2	1	1	0	0	1	0	1	0	1	0	0	1	0	1.000	0-0	.222	.273	3.00
Bucky Walters	NL	5	1	2	9.0	39	10	2	2	0	0	0	0	2	0	4	0	0	0	0	—	0-0	.270	.308	2.00
Duane Ward	AL	1	0	1	1.0	3	0	0	0	0	0	0	0	0	0	2	0	0	0	0	—	0-0	.000	.000	0.00
Lon Warneke	NL	3	0	1	7.1	37	10	5	5	0	1	0	0	6	0	5	0	0	0	0	—	1-1	.333	.444	6.14
Bob Welch	AL	1	1	0	2.0	7	1	0	0	0	0	0	0	0	0	1	0	0	0	0	—	0-0	.143	.143	0.00
	NL	1	0	0	3.0	14	5	2	2	1	0	0	0	1	0	4	1	0	0	0	—	0-0	.385	.429	6.00
	Tot	2	1	0	5.0	21	6	2	2	1	0	0	0	1	0	5	1	0	0	0	—	0-0	.300	.333	3.60
David Wells	AL	1	0	0	0.1	1	0	0	0	0	0	0	0	0	0	1	0	0	0	0	—	0-0	.000	.000	0.00
Hoyt Wilhelm	AL	2	0	1	2.2	14	4	2	2	0	0	0	1	1	0	1	0	0	0	1	.000	0-0	.333	.429	6.75
Mitch Williams	NL	1	0	1	1.0	3	0	0	0	0	0	0	0	1	0	1	0	0	0	0	—	0-0	.000	.333	0.00
Stan Williams	NL	1	0	0	2.0	8	2	0	0	0	0	0	0	1	0	2	0	0	0	0	—	0-0	.286	.375	0.00
Don Wilson	NL	1	0	1	2.0	6	0	0	0	0	0	0	0	1	0	2	0	0	0	0	—	0-0	.000	.167	0.00
Jim Wilson	AL	1	0	0	1.0	5	2	1	1	0	0	0	0	0	0	1	0	0	0	0	—	0-0	.400	.400	9.00
Rick Wise	NL	1	1	0	2.0	8	2	1	1	0	0	0	0	0	0	1	0	0	1	0	1.000	0-0	.250	.250	4.50
Mark Wohlers	NL	1	0	0	0.2	2	1	0	0	0	0	0	0	0	0	0	0	0	0	0	—	0-0	.500	.500	0.00
Wilbur Wood	AL	1	0	0	2.0	8	2	1	1	0	0	0	0	0	0	1	0	0	0	1	—	0-0	.286	.375	4.50
Hal Woodeshick	NL	1	0	0	2.0	7	1	0	0	0	0	0	0	1	0	3	0	0	0	0	—	0-0	.167	.286	0.00
Todd Worrell	NL	2	0	1	2.0	8	2	0	0	0	0	0	0	0	0	1	0	0	0	0	—	0-0	.250	.250	0.00
Clyde Wright	AL	1	0	1	1.2	8	3	1	1	0	0	0	0	0	0	0	0	0	0	1	.000	0-0	.375	.375	5.40
John Wyatt	AL	1	0	0	1.0	5	2	2	2	2	0	0	0	0	0	0	0	0	0	0	—	0-0	.400	.400	18.00
Whit Wyatt	NL	2	1	0	4.0	12	1	0	0	0	0	0	0	1	0	1	0	0	0	0	—	0-0	.091	.167	0.00
Early Wynn	AL	7	1	1	12.1	49	9	4	4	2	0	0	0	4	0	8	0	0	1	0	1.000	0-0	.200	.265	2.92
Matt Young	AL	1	0	0	1.0	3	0	0	0	0	0	0	0	0	0	1	0	0	0	0	—	0-0	.000	.000	0.00

All-Star Game Batting Leaders—Career

Games

1	Hank Aaron	24
	Willie Mays	24
	Stan Musial	24
4	Brooks Robinson	18
	Ted Williams	18
6	Pete Rose	16
	Al Kaline	16
	Mickey Mantle	16
9	Rod Carew	15
	Cal Ripken Jr.	15
	Yogi Berra	15
12	Ozzie Smith	14
	Carl Yastrzemski	14
	Roberto Clemente	14
15	Ernie Banks	13
	Nellie Fox	13
17	5 tied with	12

At-Bats

1	Willie Mays	75
2	Hank Aaron	67
3	Stan Musial	63
4	Ted Williams	46
5	Brooks Robinson	45
6	Mickey Mantle	43
7	Cal Ripken Jr.	42
8	Rod Carew	41
	Yogi Berra	41
10	Joe DiMaggio	40
11	Nellie Fox	38
12	Al Kaline	37
13	Dave Winfield	36
14	Carl Yastrzemski	34
15	Pete Rose	33
	Ernie Banks	33
17	Roberto Clemente	31
18	Billy Herman	30
19	4 tied with	28

Runs

1	Willie Mays	20
2	Stan Musial	11
3	Ted Williams	10
4	Rod Carew	8
5	Steve Garvey	7
	Joe Morgan	7
	Hank Aaron	7
	Al Kaline	7
	Nellie Fox	7
	Jackie Robinson	7
	Joe DiMaggio	7
12	Dave Winfield	6
13	George Brett	5
	Fred Lynn	5
	Johnny Bench	5
	Brooks Robinson	5
	Mickey Mantle	5
	Yogi Berra	5
	Arky Vaughan	5
20	13 tied with	4

Hits

1	Willie Mays	23
2	Stan Musial	20
3	Nellie Fox	14
	Ted Williams	14
5	Dave Winfield	13
	Brooks Robinson	13
	Hank Aaron	13
	Billy Herman	13
9	Al Kaline	12
10	Steve Garvey	11
11	Rod Carew	10
	Carl Yastrzemski	10
	Johnny Bench	10
	Cal Ripken Jr.	10
	Roberto Clemente	10
	Ernie Banks	10
	Mickey Mantle	10
	Charlie Gehringer	10
19	Wade Boggs	9
	Joe DiMaggio	9

Doubles

1	Dave Winfield	7
2	Al Oliver	3
	Barry Bonds	3
	Tony Oliva	3
	Ernie Banks	3
	Ted Kluszewski	3
	Joe Gordon	3
	Joe Cronin	3
	Al Simmons	3
10	22 tied with	2

Triples

1	Brooks Robinson	3
	Willie Mays	3
3	Rod Carew	2
	Steve Garvey	2
5	25 tied with	1

Home Runs

1	Stan Musial	6
2	Fred Lynn	4
	Ted Williams	4
4	Gary Carter	3
	Johnny Bench	3
	Rocky Colavito	3
	Harmon Killebrew	3
	Willie Mays	3
	Ralph Kiner	3
10	13 tied with	2

RBI

1	Ted Williams	12
2	Fred Lynn	10
	Stan Musial	10
4	Willie Mays	9
5	Rocky Colavito	8
	Hank Aaron	8
7	Steve Garvey	7
8	Johnny Bench	6
	Harmon Killebrew	6
	Al Kaline	6
	Joe DiMaggio	6
	Joe Medwick	6
13	10 tied with	5

Walks

1	Ted Williams	11
2	Mickey Mantle	9
	Charlie Gehringer	9
4	Rod Carew	7
	Willie Mays	7
	Stan Musial	7
7	Lou Gehrig	6
8	Ron Santo	5
9	George Brett	4
	Reggie Jackson	4
	Carl Yastrzemski	4
	Joe Morgan	4
	Wade Boggs	4
	Enos Slaughter	4
	Bill Dickey	4
16	17 tied with	3

Strikeouts

1	Mickey Mantle	17
2	Willie Mays	14
3	Ted Williams	10
4	Reggie Jackson	9
	Ryne Sandberg	9
	Roberto Clemente	9
7	Jim Rice	8
	Carl Yastrzemski	8
	Hank Aaron	8
	Ernie Banks	8
	Joe Gordon	8
12	Carlton Fisk	7
	Dick Allen	7
	Frank Robinson	7
	Elston Howard	7
	Stan Musial	7
	Jimmie Foxx	7
18	11 tied with	6

Stolen Bases

1	Willie Mays	6
2	Roberto Alomar	4
3	Rod Carew	3
	Tim Raines	3
	Steve Sax	3
	Kenny Lofton	3
7	Ozzie Smith	2
	Rickey Henderson	2
	Tony Gwynn	2
	Darryl Strawberry	2
	Kelly Gruber	2
	Lou Brock	2
	Hank Aaron	2
	Charlie Gehringer	2
15	51 tied with	1

Batting Average

(minimum 10 Plate Appearances)

1	Richie Ashburn	.600
2	Ted Kluszewski	.500
	Charlie Gehringer	.500
4	Al Simmons	.462
5	Joe Carter	.455
	Leon Wagner	.455
7	Al Oliver	.444
	Ruben Sierra	.444
	Ken Griffey Jr.	.444
	Luke Appling	.444
11	Billy Herman	.433
12	Bill Skowron	.429
13	Andy Pafko	.400
	Stan Hack	.400
	Bill Terry	.400
16	Steve Garvey	.393
17	Bobby Bonilla	.385
	Will Clark	.385
	Ernie Lombardi	.385
20	Enos Slaughter	.381

On-Base Percentage

(minimum 10 Plate Appearances)

1	Charlie Gehringer	.655
2	Richie Ashburn	.636
3	Al Oliver	.500
	Joe Carter	.500
	Ruben Sierra	.500
	Ron Santo	.500
	Ted Kluszewski	.500
	Luke Appling	.500
9	Enos Slaughter	.480
10	Ken Griffey Jr.	.474
11	Stan Hack	.471
12	Bill Skowron	.467
13	Al Simmons	.462
14	Leon Wagner	.455
	Andy Pafko	.455
	Bill Terry	.455
17	Billy Herman	.452
18	Arky Vaughan	.440
19	Ted Williams	.439
20	Steve Garvey	.433

Slugging Percentage

(minimum 10 Plate Appearances)

1	Ralph Kiner	.933
2	Ted Kluszewski	.929
3	Mike Piazza	.917
4	Fred Lynn	.900
5	Steve Garvey	.821
6	Al Rosen	.818
7	Al Oliver	.778
	Ruben Sierra	.778
9	Gary Carter	.750
10	George Foster	.727
	Leon Wagner	.727
12	Ken Griffey Jr.	.722
13	Richie Ashburn	.700
	Larry Doby	.700
15	Al Simmons	.692
16	Arky Vaughan	.682
17	Johnny Bench	.679
18	Mike Schmidt	.667
19	Harmon Killebrew	.654
20	Ted Williams	.652

OBP+Slugging

(minimum 10 Plate Appearances)

1	Ted Kluszewski	1.429
2	Richie Ashburn	1.336
3	Mike Piazza	1.301
4	Al Oliver	1.278
	Ruben Sierra	1.278
6	Fred Lynn	1.264
7	Charlie Gehringer	1.255
	Steve Garvey	1.255
9	Al Rosen	1.247
10	Ralph Kiner	1.200
11	Ken Griffey Jr.	1.196
12	Leon Wagner	1.182
13	Al Simmons	1.154
14	Arky Vaughan	1.122
15	Gary Carter	1.114
16	George Foster	1.112
17	Ted Williams	1.091
18	Johnny Bench	1.079
19	Luke Appling	1.056

Secondary Average

(minimum 10 Plate Appearances)

1	Pete Runnels	.857
2	Al Rosen	.818
3	Lou Gehrig	.722
4	Fred Lynn	.700
	Tim Raines	.700
6	Mike Piazza	.667
	Ralph Kiner	.667
8	Charlie Gehringer	.650
9	George Foster	.636
10	Ted Williams	.587
11	Mike Schmidt	.556
	Augie Galan	.556
13	Gary Carter	.550
14	George Brett	.500
	Steve Garvey	.500
16	Arky Vaughan	.455
17	Al Oliver	.444
	Ruben Sierra	.444
	Stan Musial	.444
20	Rocky Colavito	.440

All-Star Game Pitching Leaders—Career

Wins

1	Lefty Gomez	3
2	Vida Blue	2
	Bruce Sutter	2
	Juan Marichal	2
	Don Drysdale	2
	Bob Friend	2
7	54 tied with	1

Losses

1	Luis Tiant	2
	Dwight Gooden	2
	Catfish Hunter	2
	Whitey Ford	2
	Mort Cooper	2
	Claude Passeau	2
7	55 tied with	1

Winning Percentage

(minimum 2 decisions)

1	Vida Blue	1.000
	Bruce Sutter	1.000
	Juan Marichal	1.000
4	Lefty Gomez	.750
5	Don Drysdale	.667
	Bob Friend	.667
7	Dave Stieb	.500
	John Smoltz	.500
	Jim Bunning	.500
	Gene Conley	.500
	Dizzy Dean	.500
12	Luis Tiant	.000
	Dwight Gooden	.000
	Catfish Hunter	.000
	Whitey Ford	.000
	Mort Cooper	.000
	Claude Passeau	.000

Games

1	Tom Seaver	8
	Juan Marichal	8
	Don Drysdale	8
	Jim Bunning	8
5	Dave Stieb	7
	Warren Spahn	7
	Early Wynn	7
8	Dennis Eckersley	6
	Goose Gossage	6
	Catfish Hunter	6
	Bob Gibson	6
	Whitey Ford	6
	Ewell Blackwell	6
14	13 tied with	5

Games Started

1	Don Drysdale	5
	Robin Roberts	5
	Lefty Gomez	5
4	Jim Palmer	4
5	Vida Blue	3
	Jack Morris	3
	Jim Bunning	3
	Whitey Ford	3
	Billy Pierce	3
	Warren Spahn	3
11	16 tied with	2

Saves

1	Dennis Eckersley	3
2	Bruce Sutter	2
	Mel Harder	2
4	33 tied with	1

Innings Pitched

1	Don Drysdale	19.1
2	Juan Marichal	18.0
	Jim Bunning	18.0
	Lefty Gomez	18.0
5	Robin Roberts	14.0
	Warren Spahn	14.0
7	Ewell Blackwell	13.2
8	Tom Seaver	13.0
	Mel Harder	13.0
10	Jim Palmer	12.2
	Catfish Hunter	12.2
12	Early Wynn	12.1
	Bob Feller	12.1
14	Whitey Ford	12.0
15	Dave Stieb	11.2
16	Bob Gibson	11.0
	Vic Raschi	11.0
18	Jack Morris	10.2
	Billy Pierce	10.2
	Hal Newhouser	10.2

Hits

1	Whitey Ford	19
2	Robin Roberts	17
	Warren Spahn	17
4	Catfish Hunter	15
5	Gaylord Perry	14
	Tom Seaver	14
	Jack Morris	14
8	Red Ruffing	13
9	Vida Blue	12
10	Jim Palmer	11
	Bob Gibson	11
	Lefty Gomez	11
13	Nolan Ryan	10
	Tom Glavine	10
	Don Drysdale	10
	Tex Hughson	10
	Bucky Walters	10
	Dizzy Dean	10
	Lon Warneke	10
	Lefty Grove	10

Home Runs

1	Vida Blue	4
	Catfish Hunter	4
3	Steve Carlton	3
	Tom Seaver	3
	Jim Palmer	3
	Milt Pappas	3
	Whitey Ford	3
	Robin Roberts	3
	Mort Cooper	3
10	20 tied with	2

Walks

1	Jim Palmer	7
2	Dave Stieb	6
	Robin Roberts	6
	Lon Warneke	6
	Carl Hubbell	6
6	Steve Carlton	5
	Nolan Ryan	5
	Bob Gibson	5
	Ewell Blackwell	5
	Warren Spahn	5
	Dizzy Dean	5
	Wild Bill Hallahan	5
13	15 tied with	4

Strikeouts

1	Don Drysdale	19
2	Tom Seaver	16
3	Jim Palmer	14
4	Catfish Hunter	13
	Jim Bunning	13
	Bob Feller	13
7	Sam McDowell	12
	Juan Marichal	12
	Billy Pierce	12
	Ewell Blackwell	12
11	Johnny Vander Meer	11
	Carl Hubbell	11
13	Nolan Ryan	10
	Dave Stieb	10
	Dick Radatz	10
	Bob Gibson	10
	Warren Spahn	10
	Dizzy Dean	10
19	4 tied with	9

Strikeouts/9 Innings

(minimum 7 Innings Pitched)

1	Sam McDowell	13.50
2	Johnny Vander Meer	11.42
3	Tom Seaver	11.08
4	Fernando Valenzuela	10.57
5	Carl Hubbell	10.24
6	Billy Pierce	10.13
7	Jim Palmer	9.95
8	Bob Feller	9.49
9	Catfish Hunter	9.24
10	Nolan Ryan	9.00
	Dizzy Dean	9.00
	Lefty Grove	9.00
13	Don Drysdale	8.84
14	Bob Gibson	8.18
15	Ewell Blackwell	7.90
16	Steve Carlton	7.88
	Don Sutton	7.88
18	4 tied with	7.71

ERA

(minimum 7 Innings Pitched)

1	Don Sutton	0.00
	Fernando Valenzuela	0.00
	Johnny Vander Meer	0.00
	Mel Harder	0.00
5	Juan Marichal	0.50
6	Bob Feller	0.73
7	Dave Stieb	0.77
8	Jim Bunning	1.00
9	Bob Friend	1.08
10	Sam McDowell	1.13
	Paul Derringer	1.13
12	Steve Rogers	1.29
	Roger Clemens	1.29
	Randy Johnson	1.29
	Lew Burdette	1.29
16	Ewell Blackwell	1.32
17	Don Drysdale	1.40
18	Hal Newhouser	1.69
19	Bucky Walters	2.00
20	Lefty Grove	2.25

Component ERA

(minimum 7 Innings Pitched)

1	Jim Bunning	0.41
2	Juan Marichal	0.49
3	Johnny Vander Meer	0.90
4	Randy Johnson	0.97
5	Bob Feller	1.00
6	Don Sutton	1.07
7	Mel Harder	1.10
8	Roger Clemens	1.11
9	Billy Pierce	1.22
10	Paul Derringer	1.38
11	Ewell Blackwell	1.42
12	Don Drysdale	1.43
13	Steve Rogers	1.44
14	Lefty Gomez	1.46
15	Camilo Pascual	1.71
16	Hal Newhouser	1.73
17	Fernando Valenzuela	1.79
18	Dave Stieb	1.80
19	Dennis Eckersley	1.88
20	Sam McDowell	1.92

Opponent Average

(minimum 7 Innings Pitched)

1	Randy Johnson	.095
2	Jim Bunning	.115
3	Juan Marichal	.119
4	Bob Feller	.128
5	Dave Stieb	.140
6	Don Drysdale	.156
7	Johnny Vander Meer	.161
8	Roger Clemens	.167
9	Lefty Gomez	.169
10	Ewell Blackwell	.170
11	Billy Pierce	.171
12	Vic Raschi	.175
13	Don Sutton	.179
	Sam McDowell	.179
15	Mel Harder	.184
16	Steve Carlton	.185
17	Dennis Eckersley	.188
18	Fernando Valenzuela	.192
19	Early Wynn	.200
	Paul Derringer	.200

Opponent OBP

(minimum 7 Innings Pitched)

1	Jim Bunning	.129
2	Juan Marichal	.145
3	Roger Clemens	.167
4	Randy Johnson	.174
5	Johnny Vander Meer	.188
6	Mel Harder	.200
7	Lefty Gomez	.206
8	Don Sutton	.207
9	Don Drysdale	.217
10	Steve Rogers	.222
11	Paul Derringer	.226
12	Bob Feller	.227
13	Dennis Eckersley	.229
14	Billy Pierce	.237
15	Lew Burdette	.241
16	Dave Stieb	.245
17	Dwight Gooden	.250
	Vic Raschi	.250
	Ewell Blackwell	.250
20	Camilo Pascual	.258

All-Star Players Who Didn't Play

Year	Player, Pos, Team	Lg	Reason
1933	Bill Dickey, c, NYA	AL	Manager's decision
	Wes Ferrell, p, Cle	AL	Manager's decision
	Jimmie Foxx, 1b, Phi	AL	Manager's decision
	Oral Hildebrand, p, Cle	AL	Manager's decision
	Tony Lazzeri, 2b, NYA	AL	Manager's decision
	Hal Schumacher, p, NYG	NL	Manager's decision
1934	Tommy Bridges, p, Det	AL	Manager's decision
	Jimmy Dykes, 3b, ChA	AL	Manager's decision
	Rick Ferrell, c, Bos	AL	Manager's decision
	Mike Higgins, 3b, Phi	AL	Manager's decision
	Jack Russell, p, Was	AL	Manager's decision
	Jo-Jo Moore, of, NYG	NL	Injured
1935	Earl Averill, of, Cle	AL	Injured
	Tommy Bridges, p, Det	AL	Manager's decision
	Mickey Cochrane, c, Det	AL	Manager's decision
	Rick Ferrell, c, Bos	AL	Manager's decision
	Lefty Grove, p, Bos	AL	Manager's decision
	Buddy Myer, 2b, Was	AL	Manager's decision
	Schoolboy Rowe, p, Det	AL	Manager's decision
	Sammy West, of, StL	AL	Manager's decision
	Frankie Frisch, 2b, StL	NL	Manager's decision
	Carl Hubbell, p, NYG	NL	Manager's decision
1936	Tommy Bridges, p, Det	AL	Injured
	Lefty Gomez, p, NYA	AL	Manager's decision
	Rollie Hemsley, c, StL	AL	Manager's decision
	Vern Kennedy, p, ChA	AL	Manager's decision
	Monte Pearson, p, NYA	AL	Manager's decision
	Wally Berger, of, Bos	NL	Manager's decision
	Ernie Lombardi, c, Cin	NL	Manager's decision
	Stu Martin, 2b, StL	NL	Manager's decision
	Jo-Jo Moore, of, NYG	NL	Manager's decision
	Van Lingle Mungo, p, Bro	NL	Manager's decision
	Gus Suhr, 1b, Pit	NL	Manager's decision
	Arky Vaughan, ss, Pit	NL	Manager's decision
1937	Beau Bell, of, StL	AL	Manager's decision
	Harlond Clift, 3b, StL	AL	Manager's decision
	Doc Cramer, of, Bos	AL	Manager's decision
	Rick Ferrell, c, Was	AL	Manager's decision
	Wes Ferrell, p, Was	AL	Manager's decision
	Hank Greenberg, 1b, Det	AL	Manager's decision
	Lefty Grove, p, Bos	AL	Manager's decision
	Johnny Murphy, p, NYA	AL	Manager's decision
	Buddy Myer, 2b, Was	AL	Manager's decision
	Luke Sewell, c, ChA	AL	Manager's decision
	Monty Stratton, p, ChA	AL	Injured
	Gee Walker, of, Det	AL	Injured
	Billy Jurges, ss, ChN	NL	Manager's decision
	Ernie Lombardi, c, Cin	NL	Manager's decision
	Pepper Martin, of, StL	NL	Manager's decision
1938	Bob Feller, p, Cle	AL	Manager's decision
	Rick Ferrell, c, Was	AL	Manager's decision
	Hank Greenberg, 1b, Det	AL	Injured
	Vern Kennedy, p, Det	AL	Manager's decision
	Johnny Murphy, p, NYA	AL	Manager's decision
	Bobo Newsom, p, StL	AL	Manager's decision
	Red Rolfe, 3b, NYA	AL	Manager's decision
	Red Ruffing, p, NYA	AL	Manager's decision
	Cecil Travis, ss, Was	AL	Manager's decision
	Tony Cuccinello, 2b, Bos	NL	Manager's decision
	Harry Danning, c, NYG	NL	Manager's decision
	Paul Derringer, p, Cin	NL	Manager's decision
	Gabby Hartnett, c, ChN	NL	Manager's decision
	Carl Hubbell, p, NYG	NL	Manager's decision
	Cookie Lavagetto, 3b, Bro	NL	Manager's decision
	Hersh Martin, of, Phi	NL	Manager's decision
	Jo-Jo Moore, of, NYG	NL	Manager's decision
	Babe Phelps, c, Bro	NL	Injured
	Jim Turner, p, Bos	NL	Manager's decision
	Arky Vaughan, ss, Pit	NL	Manager's decision
	Lloyd Waner, of, Pit	NL	Manager's decision
1939	Luke Appling, ss, ChA	AL	Manager's decision
	George Case, of, Was	AL	Manager's decision
	Frankie Crosetti, ss, NYA	AL	Manager's decision
	Jimmie Foxx, 1b, Bos	AL	Manager's decision
	Lou Gehrig, 1b, NYA	AL	Manager's decision
	Lefty Gomez, p, NYA	AL	Manager's decision
	Lefty Grove, p, Bos	AL	Manager's decision
	Frankie Hayes, c, Phi	AL	Manager's decision
	Rollie Hemsley, c, Cle	AL	Manager's decision
	Bob Johnson, of, Phi	AL	Manager's decision
	Ted Lyons, p, ChA	AL	Manager's decision
	George McQuinn, 1b, StL	AL	Manager's decision
	Johnny Murphy, p, NYA	AL	Manager's decision
	Bobo Newsom, p, Det	AL	Manager's decision
	Morrie Arnovich, of, Phi	NL	Manager's decision
	Harry Danning, c, NYG	NL	Manager's decision
	Curt Davis, p, StL	NL	Manager's decision
	Billy Jurges, ss, NYG	NL	Manager's decision
	Cookie Lavagetto, 3b, Bro	NL	Manager's decision
	Johnny Vander Meer, p, Cin	NL	Manager's decision
	Bucky Walters, p, Cin	NL	Manager's decision
	Lon Warneke, p, StL	NL	Manager's decision
	Whit Wyatt, p, Bro	NL	Manager's decision
1940	Tommy Bridges, p, Det	AL	Manager's decision
	Doc Cramer, of, Bos	AL	Manager's decision
	Bob Johnson, of, Phi	AL	Manager's decision
	Dutch Leonard, p, Was	AL	Manager's decision
	George McQuinn, 1b, StL	AL	Manager's decision
	Al Milnar, p, Cle	AL	Manager's decision
	Monte Pearson, p, NYA	AL	Manager's decision
	Red Rolfe, 3b, NYA	AL	Injured
	Leo Durocher, ss, Bro	NL	Manager's decision
	Kirby Higbe, p, Phi	NL	Manager's decision
	Billy Jurges, ss, NYG	NL	Injured
	Hank Leiber, of, ChN	NL	Injured
	Hugh Mulcahy, p, Phi	NL	Manager's decision
1941	Luke Appling, ss, ChA	AL	Manager's decision
	Al Benton, p, Det	AL	Manager's decision
	Red Ruffing, p, NYA	AL	Manager's decision
	Marius Russo, p, NYA	AL	Manager's decision
	Birdie Tebbetts, c, Det	AL	Manager's decision
	Cy Blanton, p, Phi	NL	Manager's decision
	Dolph Camilli, 1b, Bro	NL	Injured
	Carl Hubbell, p, NYG	NL	Manager's decision
	Hank Leiber, of, ChN	NL	Injured
	Lon Warneke, p, StL	NL	Manager's decision
1942	Jim Bagby Jr., p, Cle	AL	Manager's decision
	Tiny Bonham, p, NYA	AL	Manager's decision
	Bill Dickey, c, NYA	AL	Injured
	Dom DiMaggio, of, Bos	AL	Manager's decision

Year	Player, Pos, Team	Lg	Reason	Year	Player, Pos, Team	Lg	Reason
	Bobby Doerr, 2b, Bos	AL	Manager's decision		Boo Ferriss, p, Bos	AL	Game cancelled
	Sid Hudson, p, Was	AL	Manager's decision		Hank Greenberg, of, Det	AL	Game cancelled
	Tex Hughson, p, Bos	AL	Manager's decision		Oscar Grimes, 3b, NYA	AL	Game cancelled
	George McQuinn, 1b, StL	AL	Manager's decision		Steve Gromek, p, Cle	AL	Game cancelled
	Hal Newhouser, p, Det	AL	Manager's decision		Frankie Hayes, c, Cle	AL	Game cancelled
	Phil Rizzuto, ss, NYA	AL	Manager's decision		Jeff Heath, of, Cle	AL	Game cancelled
	Buddy Rosar, c, NYA	AL	Manager's decision		Bob Johnson, of, Bos	AL	Game cancelled
	Red Ruffing, p, NYA	AL	Manager's decision		Jack Kramer, p, StL	AL	Game cancelled
	Eddie Smith, p, ChA	AL	Manager's decision		Thornton Lee, p, ChA	AL	Game cancelled
	Stan Spence, of, Was	AL	Manager's decision		Dutch Leonard, p, Was	AL	Game cancelled
	Hal Wagner, c, Phi	AL	Manager's decision		Eddie Mayo, 2b, Det	AL	Game cancelled
	Paul Derringer, p, Cin	NL	Injured		George McQuinn, 1b, StL	AL	Game cancelled
	Carl Hubbell, p, NYG	NL	Manager's decision		Wally Moses, of, ChA	AL	Game cancelled
	Cliff Melton, p, NYG	NL	Injured		Hal Newhouser, p, Det	AL	Game cancelled
	Ray Starr, p, Cin	NL	Manager's decision		Allie Reynolds, p, Cle	AL	Game cancelled
	Whit Wyatt, p, Bro	NL	Manager's decision		Vern Stephens, ss, StL	AL	Game cancelled
1943	Luke Appling, ss, ChA	AL	Manager's decision		Snuffy Stirnweiss, 2b, NYA	AL	Game cancelled
	Jim Bagby Jr., p, Cle	AL	Manager's decision		Mike Tresh, c, ChA	AL	Game cancelled
	Tiny Bonham, p, NYA	AL	Manager's decision		Red Barrett, p, StL	NL	Game cancelled
	Lou Boudreau, ss, Cle	AL	Manager's decision		Phil Cavarretta, 1b, ChN	NL	Game cancelled
	Spud Chandler, p, NYA	AL	Manager's decision		Mort Cooper, p, Bos	NL	Game cancelled
	Bill Dickey, c, NYA	AL	Manager's decision		Bob Elliott, 3b, Pit	NL	Game cancelled
	Joe Gordon, 2b, NYA	AL	Manager's decision		Hal Gregg, p, Bro	NL	Game cancelled
	Oscar Judd, p, Bos	AL	Manager's decision		Stan Hack, 3b, ChN	NL	Game cancelled
	Charlie Keller, of, NYA	AL	Injured		Tommy Holmes, of, Bos	NL	Game cancelled
	Johnny Lindell, of, NYA	AL	Manager's decision		Don Johnson, 2b, ChN	NL	Game cancelled
	Buddy Rosar, c, Cle	AL	Manager's decision		Whitey Kurowski, 3b, StL	NL	Game cancelled
	Al Smith, p, Cle	AL	Manager's decision		Ernie Lombardi, c, NYG	NL	Game cancelled
	Ace Adams, p, NYG	NL	Manager's decision		Marty Marion, ss, StL	NL	Game cancelled
	Whitey Kurowski, 3b, StL	NL	Manager's decision		Phil Masi, c, Bos	NL	Game cancelled
	Max Lanier, p, StL	NL	Manager's decision		Frank McCormick, 1b, Cin	NL	Game cancelled
	Frank McCormick, 1b, Cin	NL	Injured		Van Lingle Mungo, p, NYG	NL	Game cancelled
	Mickey Owen, c, Bro	NL	Manager's decision		Bill Nicholson, of, ChN	NL	Game cancelled
	Claude Passeau, p, ChN	NL	Manager's decision		Ken O'Dea, c, StL	NL	Game cancelled
	Howie Pollet, p, StL	NL	Injured		Mel Ott, of, NYG	NL	Game cancelled
1944	Lou Boudreau, ss, Cle	AL	Manager's decision		Andy Pafko, of, ChN	NL	Game cancelled
	George Case, of, Was	AL	Injured		Claude Passeau, p, ChN	NL	Game cancelled
	Roy Cullenbine, of, Cle	AL	Manager's decision		Preacher Roe, p, Pit	NL	Game cancelled
	Rick Ferrell, c, Was	AL	Manager's decision		Goody Rosen, of, Bro	NL	Game cancelled
	Pete Fox, of, Bos	AL	Manager's decision		Rip Sewell, p, Pit	NL	Game cancelled
	Orval Grove, p, ChA	AL	Manager's decision		Emil Verban, 2b, StL	NL	Game cancelled
	Oris Hockett, of, Cle	AL	Manager's decision		Dixie Walker, of, Bro	NL	Game cancelled
	Dutch Leonard, p, Was	AL	Manager's decision		Hank Wyse, p, ChN	NL	Game cancelled
	Joe Page, p, NYA	AL	Manager's decision	1946	Spud Chandler, p, NYA	AL	Manager's decision
	Dizzy Trout, p, Det	AL	Manager's decision		Joe DiMaggio, of, NYA	AL	Manager's decision
	Rudy York, 1b, Det	AL	Manager's decision		Boo Ferriss, p, Bos	AL	Manager's decision
	Nate Andrews, p, Bos	NL	Manager's decision		Mickey Harris, p, Bos	AL	Manager's decision
	Al Javery, p, Bos	NL	Manager's decision		Mort Cooper, p, Bos	NL	Manager's decision
	Don Johnson, 2b, ChN	NL	Manager's decision		Eddie Miller, ss, Cin	NL	Injured
	Max Lanier, p, StL	NL	Injured		Howie Pollet, p, StL	NL	Manager's decision
	Frank McCormick, 1b, Cin	NL	Manager's decision		Pee Wee Reese, ss, Bro	NL	Injured
	Eddie Miller, ss, Cin	NL	Injured		Pete Reiser, of, Bro	NL	Manager's decision
	George Munger, p, StL	NL	Injured		Johnny Schmitz, p, ChN	NL	Manager's decision
	Mickey Owen, c, Bro	NL	Manager's decision	1947	Spud Chandler, p, NYA	AL	Manager's decision
	Bill Voiselle, p, NYG	NL	Manager's decision		Bob Feller, p, Cle	AL	Injured
	Frankie Zak, ss, Pit	NL	Manager's decision		Jim Hegan, c, Cle	AL	Manager's decision
1945	Hank Borowy, p, NYA	AL	Game cancelled		Charlie Keller, of, NYA	AL	Injured
	Lou Boudreau, ss, Cle	AL	Game cancelled		Jack Kramer, p, StL	AL	Manager's decision
	George Case, of, Was	AL	Game cancelled		Pat Mullin, of, Det	AL	Manager's decision
	Russ Christopher, p, Phi	AL	Game cancelled		Aaron Robinson, c, NYA	AL	Manager's decision
	Tony Cuccinello, 3b, ChA	AL	Game cancelled		Dizzy Trout, p, Det	AL	Manager's decision
	Nick Etten, 1b, NYA	AL	Game cancelled		Early Wynn, p, Was	AL	Manager's decision
	Rick Ferrell, c, Was	AL	Game cancelled		Rudy York, 1b, ChA	AL	Manager's decision

Year	Player, Pos, Team	Lg	Reason
	Ralph Branca, p, Bro	NL	Manager's decision
	Bob Elliott, 3b, Bos	NL	Injured
	Eddie Miller, ss, Cin	NL	Injured
	George Munger, p, StL	NL	Manager's decision
1948	Yogi Berra, c, NYA	AL	Manager's decision
	Joe Dobson, p, Bos	AL	Manager's decision
	Bob Feller, p, Cle	AL	Injured
	Joe Haynes, p, ChA	AL	Manager's decision
	George Kell, 3b, Det	AL	Manager's decision
	Bob Lemon, p, Cle	AL	Manager's decision
	Joe Page, p, NYA	AL	Manager's decision
	Harry Brecheen, p, StL	NL	Manager's decision
	Sid Gordon, 3b, NYG	NL	Manager's decision
	Marty Marion, ss, StL	NL	Injured
	Clyde McCullough, c, ChN	NL	Manager's decision
	Elmer Riddle, p, Pit	NL	Manager's decision
	Eddie Stanky, 2b, Bos	NL	Injured
1949	Jim Hegan, c, Cle	AL	Manager's decision
	Tommy Henrich, of, NYA	AL	Manager's decision
	Alex Kellner, p, Phi	AL	Manager's decision
	Bob Lemon, p, Cle	AL	Manager's decision
	Allie Reynolds, p, NYA	AL	Manager's decision
	Ralph Branca, p, Bro	NL	Manager's decision
	Walker Cooper, c, Cin	NL	Manager's decision
	Marty Marion, ss, StL	NL	Manager's decision
	Eddie Waitkus, 1b, Phi	NL	Manager's decision
1950	Tommy Byrne, p, NYA	AL	Manager's decision
	Sherm Lollar, c, StL	AL	Manager's decision
	Ray Scarborough, p, ChA	AL	Manager's decision
	Vern Stephens, ss, Bos	AL	Manager's decision
	Walker Cooper, c, Bos	NL	Manager's decision
	Gil Hodges, 1b, Bro	NL	Manager's decision
	Preacher Roe, p, Bro	NL	Manager's decision
	Bob Rush, p, ChN	NL	Manager's decision
	Warren Spahn, p, Bos	NL	Manager's decision
	Eddie Stanky, 2b, NYG	NL	Manager's decision
	Johnny Wyrostek, of, Cin	NL	Manager's decision
1951	Joe DiMaggio, of, NYA	AL	Manager's decision
	Randy Gumpert, p, ChA	AL	Manager's decision
	Connie Marrero, p, Was	AL	Manager's decision
	Bobby Shantz, p, Phi	AL	Manager's decision
	Bruce Edwards, c, ChN	NL	Manager's decision
	Larry Jansen, p, NYG	NL	Manager's decision
	Dutch Leonard, p, ChN	NL	Manager's decision
	Preacher Roe, p, Bro	NL	Manager's decision
	Warren Spahn, p, Bos	NL	Manager's decision
1952	Ferris Fain, 1b, Phi	AL	Manager's decision
	Nellie Fox, 2b, ChA	AL	Manager's decision
	Mike Garcia, p, Cle	AL	Manager's decision
	Jim Hegan, c, Cle	AL	Manager's decision
	Eddie Joost, ss, Phi	AL	Manager's decision
	George Kell, 3b, Bos	AL	Injured
	Mickey Mantle, of, NYA	AL	Manager's decision
	Satchel Paige, p, StL	AL	Manager's decision
	Allie Reynolds, p, NYA	AL	Manager's decision
	Vic Wertz, of, Det	AL	Manager's decision
	Eddie Yost, 3b, Was	AL	Manager's decision
	Toby Atwell, c, ChN	NL	Manager's decision
	Al Dark, ss, NYG	NL	Manager's decision
	Carl Furillo, of, Bro	NL	Manager's decision
	Grady Hatton, 2b, Cin	NL	Manager's decision
	Gil Hodges, 1b, Bro	NL	Manager's decision
	Monte Irvin, of, NYG	NL	Manager's decision
	Ralph Kiner, of, Pit	NL	Manager's decision
	Sal Maglie, p, NYG	NL	Manager's decision
	Robin Roberts, p, Phi	NL	Manager's decision
	Preacher Roe, p, Bro	NL	Manager's decision
	Red Schoendienst, 2b, StL	NL	Manager's decision
	Duke Snider, of, Bro	NL	Manager's decision
	Warren Spahn, p, Bos	NL	Manager's decision
	Gerry Staley, p, StL	NL	Manager's decision
	Wes Westrum, c, NYG	NL	Manager's decision
1953	Bob Lemon, p, Cle	AL	Manager's decision
	Johnny Sain, p, NYA	AL	Manager's decision
	Sammy White, c, Bos	AL	Manager's decision
	Ted Williams, of, Bos	AL	Manager's decision
	Del Crandall, c, Mil	NL	Injured
	Carl Furillo, of, Bro	NL	Manager's decision
	Harvey Haddix, p, StL	NL	Manager's decision
	Clyde McCullough, c, ChN	NL	Manager's decision
	Del Rice, c, StL	NL	Injured
	Gerry Staley, p, StL	NL	Manager's decision
	Wes Westrum, c, NYG	NL	Manager's decision
	Hoyt Wilhelm, p, NYG	NL	Manager's decision
1954	Ferris Fain, 1b, ChA	AL	Injured
	Jim Finigan, 3b, Phi	AL	Manager's decision
	Mike Garcia, p, Cle	AL	Injured
	George Kell, 3b, ChA	AL	Injured
	Harvey Kuenn, ss, Det	AL	Manager's decision
	Sherm Lollar, c, ChA	AL	Manager's decision
	Allie Reynolds, p, NYA	AL	Injured
	Bob Turley, p, Bal	AL	Manager's decision
	Del Crandall, c, Mil	NL	Manager's decision
	Harvey Haddix, p, StL	NL	Injured
	Pee Wee Reese, ss, Bro	NL	Manager's decision
	Jim Wilson, p, Mil	NL	Manager's decision
1955	Larry Doby, of, Cle	AL	Manager's decision
	Dick Donovan, p, ChA	AL	Manager's decision
	Billy Hoeft, p, Det	AL	Manager's decision
	Sherm Lollar, c, ChA	AL	Manager's decision
	Herb Score, p, Cle	AL	Manager's decision
	Bob Turley, p, NYA	AL	Manager's decision
	Jim Wilson, p, Bal	AL	Manager's decision
	Luis Arroyo, p, StL	NL	Manager's decision
	Roy Campanella, c, Bro	NL	Injured
1956	Johnny Kucks, p, NYA	AL	Manager's decision
	Charlie Maxwell, of, Det	AL	Manager's decision
	Gil McDougald, ss, NYA	AL	Manager's decision
	Ray Narleski, p, Cle	AL	Injured
	Frank Sullivan, p, Bos	AL	Manager's decision
	Ernie Banks, ss, ChN	NL	Manager's decision
	Del Crandall, c, Mil	NL	Injured
	Jim Gilliam, 2b, Bro	NL	Manager's decision
	Clem Labine, p, Bro	NL	Manager's decision
	Brooks Lawrence, p, Cin	NL	Manager's decision
	Stan Lopata, c, Phi	NL	Manager's decision
	Eddie Mathews, 3b, Mil	NL	Manager's decision
	Joe Nuxhall, p, Cin	NL	Manager's decision
	Robin Roberts, p, Phi	NL	Manager's decision
1957	Joe DeMaestri, ss, KCA	AL	Manager's decision
	Elston Howard, of, NYA	AL	Manager's decision
	Bobby Richardson, 2b, NYA	AL	Manager's decision
	Bobby Shantz, p, NYA	AL	Manager's decision
	Roy Sievers, of, Was	AL	Manager's decision
	Gus Triandos, c, Bal	AL	Manager's decision
	Johnny Antonelli, p, NYG	NL	Manager's decision

All-Star Games: Absentee Players

Year	Player, Pos, Team	Lg	Reason
	Johnny Logan, ss, Mil	NL	Manager's decision
	Hal Smith, c, StL	NL	Manager's decision
	Warren Spahn, p, Mil	NL	Manager's decision
1958	Rocky Bridges, ss, Was	AL	Manager's decision
	Ryne Duren, p, NYA	AL	Manager's decision
	Whitey Ford, p, NYA	AL	Manager's decision
	Elston Howard, c, NYA	AL	Manager's decision
	Tony Kubek, ss, NYA	AL	Manager's decision
	Harvey Kuenn, of, Det	AL	Manager's decision
	Sherm Lollar, c, ChA	AL	Manager's decision
	Billy Pierce, p, ChA	AL	Manager's decision
	Johnny Antonelli, p, SF	NL	Manager's decision
	Richie Ashburn, of, Phi	NL	Manager's decision
	George Crowe, 1b, Cin	NL	Manager's decision
	Eddie Mathews, 3b, Mil	NL	Manager's decision
	Don McMahon, p, Mil	NL	Manager's decision
	Walt Moryn, of, ChN	NL	Manager's decision
	Johnny Podres, p, LA	NL	Manager's decision
	Bob Purkey, p, Cin	NL	Manager's decision
	John Roseboro, c, LA	NL	Manager's decision
	Bob Schmidt, c, SF	NL	Manager's decision
1959	Bob Allison, of, Was (2nd game)	AL	Manager's decision
	Yogi Berra, c, NYA (1st game)	AL	Manager's decision
	Bud Daley, p, KCA (2nd game)	AL	Manager's decision
	Ryne Duren, p, NYA (2nd game)	AL	Manager's decision
	Elston Howard, 1b, NYA (2nd game)	AL	Manager's decision
	Harmon Killebrew, 3b, Was (2nd game)	AL	Manager's decision
	Harvey Kuenn, of, Det (2nd game)	AL	Injured
	Gil McDougald, 2b, NYA (2nd game)	AL	Injured
	Minnie Minoso, of, Cle (2nd game)	AL	Manager's decision
	Camilo Pascual, p, Was (2nd game)	AL	Injured
	Billy Pierce, p, ChA (1st game)	AL	Manager's decision
	Pedro Ramos, p, Was (2nd game)	AL	Manager's decision
	Bobby Richardson, 2b, NYA (2nd game)	AL	Manager's decision
	Roy Sievers, 1b, Was (2nd game)	AL	Manager's decision
	Bill Skowron, 1b, NYA (2nd game)	AL	Injured
	Gus Triandos, c, Bal (2nd game)	AL	Injured
	Hoyt Wilhelm, p, Bal (1st game)	AL	Manager's decision
	Johnny Antonelli, p, SF (2nd game)	NL	Manager's decision
	Lew Burdette, p, Mil (2nd game)	NL	Manager's decision
	Smoky Burgess, c, Pit (1st game)	NL	Manager's decision
	Orlando Cepeda, 1b, SF (2nd game)	NL	Injured
	Gene Conley, p, Phi (1st game)	NL	Manager's decision
	Joe Cunningham, of, StL (1st game)	NL	Manager's decision
	Don Elston, p, ChN (2nd game)	NL	Manager's decision
	Johnny Logan, ss, Mil (2nd game)	NL	Manager's decision
	Bill Mazeroski, 2b, Pit (2nd game)	NL	Manager's decision
	Vinegar Bend Mizell, p, StL (1st game)	NL	Injured
	Vada Pinson, of, Cin (2nd game)	NL	Manager's decision
	Frank Robinson, 1b, Cin (2nd game)	NL	Manager's decision
	Hal Smith, c, StL (1st game)	NL	Manager's decision
	Warren Spahn, p, Mil (1st game)	NL	Manager's decision
	Bill White, of, StL (1st game)	NL	Manager's decision
	Bill White, of, StL (2nd game)	NL	Injured
1960	Luis Aparicio, ss, ChA (2nd game)	AL	Manager's decision
	Jim Coates, p, NYA (2nd game)	AL	Manager's decision
	Bud Daley, p, KCA (2nd game)	AL	Manager's decision
	Chuck Estrada, p, Bal (2nd game)	AL	Manager's decision
	Whitey Ford, p, NYA (1st game)	AL	Manager's decision
	Jim Gentile, 1b, Bal (2nd game)	AL	Manager's decision
	Elston Howard, c, NYA (2nd game)	AL	Manager's decision
	Jim Lemon, of, Was (2nd game)	AL	Manager's decision
	Bill Monbouquette, p, Bos (2nd game)	AL	Manager's decision
	Camilo Pascual, p, Was (1st game)	AL	Injured
	Vic Power, 1b, Cle (1st game)	AL	Manager's decision
	Gerry Staley, p, ChA (1st game)	AL	Manager's decision
	Dick Stigman, p, Cle (1st game)	AL	Manager's decision
	Dick Stigman, p, Cle (2nd game)	AL	Manager's decision
	Early Wynn, p, ChA (1st game)	AL	Manager's decision
	Ed Bailey, c, Cin (1st game)	NL	Manager's decision
	Bob Buhl, p, Mil (2nd game)	NL	Manager's decision
	Roy Face, p, Pit (2nd game)	NL	Manager's decision
	Bob Friend, p, Pit (2nd game)	NL	Manager's decision
	Bill Henry, p, Cin (1st game)	NL	Manager's decision
	Larry Jackson, p, StL (1st game)	NL	Manager's decision
	Mike McCormick, p, SF (2nd game)	NL	Manager's decision
	Lindy McDaniel, p, StL (1st game)	NL	Manager's decision
	Johnny Podres, p, LA (1st game)	NL	Manager's decision
	Stan Williams, p, LA (1st game)	NL	Manager's decision
1961	Luis Arroyo, p, NYA (2nd game)	AL	Manager's decision
	Yogi Berra, of, NYA (2nd game)	AL	Manager's decision
	Jackie Brandt, of, Bal (2nd game)	AL	Manager's decision
	Dick Donovan, p, Was (2nd game)	AL	Manager's decision
	Ryne Duren, p, LAA (1st game)	AL	Manager's decision
	Whitey Ford, p, NYA (2nd game)	AL	Manager's decision
	Nellie Fox, 2b, ChA (2nd game)	AL	Manager's decision
	Tito Francona, of, Cle (2nd game)	AL	Manager's decision
	Jim Gentile, 1b, Bal (2nd game)	AL	Manager's decision
	Dick Howser, ss, KCA (2nd game)	AL	Manager's decision
	Harmon Killebrew, 1b, Min (2nd game)	AL	Manager's decision
	Tony Kubek, ss, NYA (2nd game)	AL	Injured
	Barry Latman, p, Cle (2nd game)	AL	Manager's decision
	Ken McBride, p, LAA (2nd game)	AL	Manager's decision
	Jim Perry, p, Cle (1st game)	AL	Manager's decision
	Billy Pierce, p, ChA (1st game)	AL	Manager's decision
	Bill Skowron, 1b, NYA (2nd game)	AL	Manager's decision
	Hoyt Wilhelm, p, Bal (2nd game)	AL	Manager's decision
	Ed Bailey, c, SF (2nd game)	NL	Manager's decision
	Ken Boyer, 3b, StL (2nd game)	NL	Manager's decision
	Don Drysdale, p, LA (2nd game)	NL	Manager's decision
	Roy Face, p, Pit (2nd game)	NL	Manager's decision
	Joey Jay, p, Cin (1st game)	NL	Manager's decision
	Joey Jay, p, Cin (2nd game)	NL	Manager's decision
	Eddie Kasko, ss, Cin (1st game)	NL	Manager's decision
	Art Mahaffey, p, Phi (1st game)	NL	Manager's decision
	Mike McCormick, p, SF (2nd game)	NL	Manager's decision
	Frank Robinson, of, Cin (2nd game)	NL	Manager's decision
	John Roseboro, c, LA (2nd game)	NL	Manager's decision
	Warren Spahn, p, Mil (2nd game)	NL	Manager's decision
	Don Zimmer, 2b, ChN (2nd game)	NL	Manager's decision
1962	Hank Aguirre, p, Det (1st game)	AL	Manager's decision
	Jim Bunning, p, Det (2nd game)	AL	Manager's decision
	Dick Donovan, p, Cle (2nd game)	AL	Manager's decision
	Elston Howard, c, NYA (1st game)	AL	Manager's decision
	Jim Kaat, p, Min (2nd game)	AL	Manager's decision
	Jim Landis, of, ChA (2nd game)	AL	Injured
	Mickey Mantle, of, NYA (2nd game)	AL	Manager's decision
	Ken McBride, p, LAA (2nd game)	AL	Injured
	Bill Monbouquette, p, Bos (1st game)	AL	Manager's decision
	Camilo Pascual, p, Min (2nd game)	AL	Manager's decision
	John Romano, c, Cle (2nd game)	AL	Manager's decision
	Norm Siebern, 1b, KCA (2nd game)	AL	Manager's decision
	Dave Stenhouse, p, Was (1st game)	AL	Manager's decision
	Ralph Terry, p, NYA (1st game)	AL	Manager's decision
	Ralph Terry, p, NYA (2nd game)	AL	Manager's decision
	Tom Tresh, ss, NYA (1st game)	AL	Manager's decision

Year	Player, Pos, Team	Lg	Reason	Year	Player, Pos, Team	Lg	Reason
	Hoyt Wilhelm, p, Bal (1st game)	AL	Injured		Claude Raymond, p, Hou	NL	Manager's decision
	Hank Aaron, of, Mil (1st game)	NL	Injured		Phil Regan, p, LA	NL	Manager's decision
	Felipe Alou, of, SF (2nd game)	NL	Injured		Bob Veale, p, Pit	NL	Manager's decision
	Richie Ashburn, of, NYN (1st game)	NL	Manager's decision	1967	Paul Casanova, c, Was	AL	Manager's decision
	Ken Boyer, 3b, LA (2nd game)	NL	Injured		Andy Etchebarren, c, Bal	AL	Manager's decision
	Jim Davenport, 3b, SF (2nd game)	NL	Manager's decision		Steve Hargan, p, Cle	AL	Manager's decision
	Turk Farrell, p, Hou (1st game)	NL	Manager's decision		Joe Horlen, p, ChA	AL	Manager's decision
	Bob Gibson, p, StL (1st game)	NL	Manager's decision		Al Kaline, of, Det	AL	Injured
	Sandy Koufax, p, LA (1st game)	NL	Manager's decision		Jim Lonborg, p, Bos	AL	Manager's decision
	Bob Purkey, p, Cin (2nd game)	NL	Manager's decision		Frank Robinson, of, Bal	AL	Injured
	John Roseboro, c, LA (1st game)	NL	Manager's decision		Denny Lemaster, p, Atl	NL	Injured
	Warren Spahn, p, Mil (1st game)	NL	Manager's decision		Claude Osteen, p, LA	NL	Manager's decision
	Warren Spahn, p, Mil (2nd game)	NL	Manager's decision	1968	Gary Bell, p, Bos	AL	Manager's decision
1963	Steve Barber, p, Bal	AL	Injured		Jose Santiago, p, Bos	AL	Injured
	Mudcat Grant, p, Cle	AL	Manager's decision		Gene Alley, ss, Pit	NL	Injured
	Don Leppert, c, Was	AL	Manager's decision		Woodie Fryman, p, Phi	NL	Manager's decision
	Mickey Mantle, of, NYA	AL	Injured		Bob Gibson, p, StL	NL	Manager's decision
	Bill Monbouquette, p, Bos	AL	Manager's decision		Pete Rose, of, Cin	NL	Injured
	Norm Siebern, 1b, KCA	AL	Manager's decision	1969	Mike Hegan, of, Sea	AL	Injured
	Orlando Cepeda, 1b, SF	NL	Manager's decision		Dave Johnson, 2b, Bal	AL	Injured
	Sandy Koufax, p, LA	NL	Manager's decision		Mickey Lolich, p, Det	AL	Manager's decision
	Juan Marichal, p, SF	NL	Manager's decision		Tony Oliva, of, Min	AL	Injured
	Bill Mazeroski, 2b, Pit	NL	Injured		Ellie Rodriguez, c, KC	AL	Manager's decision
	Warren Spahn, p, Mil	NL	Manager's decision		Chris Cannizzaro, c, SD	NL	Manager's decision
	Joe Torre, c, Mil	NL	Manager's decision		Grant Jackson, p, Phi	NL	Manager's decision
	Maury Wills, ss, LA	NL	Manager's decision		Juan Marichal, p, SF	NL	Manager's decision
1964	Luis Aparicio, ss, Bal	AL	Injured		Tom Seaver, p, NYN	NL	Manager's decision
	Eddie Bressoud, ss, Bos	AL	Manager's decision		Rusty Staub, of, Mon	NL	Manager's decision
	Whitey Ford, p, NYA	AL	Manager's decision	1970	Rod Carew, 2b, Min	AL	Injured
	Bill Freehan, c, Det	AL	Manager's decision		Mike Cuellar, p, Bal	AL	Manager's decision
	Al Kaline, of, Det	AL	Injured		Dave McNally, p, Bal	AL	Manager's decision
	Jack Kralick, p, Cle	AL	Manager's decision		Jerry Moses, c, Bos	AL	Manager's decision
	Jerry Lumpe, 2b, Det	AL	Manager's decision		Roy White, of, NYA	AL	Manager's decision
	Frank Malzone, 3b, Bos	AL	Manager's decision		Joe Hoerner, p, Phi	NL	Manager's decision
	Gary Peters, p, ChA	AL	Manager's decision		Felix Millan, 2b, Atl	NL	Injured
	Juan Pizarro, p, ChA	AL	Manager's decision		Wayne Simpson, p, Cin	NL	Manager's decision
	Smoky Burgess, c, Pit	NL	Manager's decision		Hoyt Wilhelm, p, Atl	NL	Manager's decision
	Dick Ellsworth, p, ChN	NL	Manager's decision	1971	Leo Cardenas, ss, Min	AL	Manager's decision
	Sandy Koufax, p, LA	NL	Manager's decision		Dave Duncan, c, Oak	AL	Manager's decision
	Bill Mazeroski, 2b, Pit	NL	Manager's decision		Ray Fosse, c, Cle	AL	Injured
	Ron Santo, 3b, ChN	NL	Manager's decision		Sam McDowell, p, Cle	AL	Injured
1965	Elston Howard, c, NYA	AL	Manager's decision		Bill Melton, 3b, ChA	AL	Manager's decision
	Mickey Mantle, of, NYA	AL	Injured		Andy Messersmith, p, Cal	AL	Manager's decision
	John O'Donoghue, p, KCA	AL	Manager's decision		Tony Oliva, of, Min	AL	Injured
	Bill Skowron, 1b, ChA	AL	Injured		Marty Pattin, p, Mil	AL	Manager's decision
	Mel Stottlemyre, p, NYA	AL	Manager's decision		Jim Perry, p, Min	AL	Manager's decision
	Carl Yastrzemski, of, Bos	AL	Injured		Boog Powell, 1b, Bal	AL	Injured
	Johnny Callison, of, Phi	NL	Manager's decision		Sonny Siebert, p, Bos	AL	Manager's decision
	Johnny Edwards, c, Cin	NL	Manager's decision		Wilbur Wood, p, ChA	AL	Manager's decision
	Sammy Ellis, p, Cin	NL	Manager's decision		Steve Carlton, p, StL	NL	Manager's decision
	Ed Kranepool, 1b, NYN	NL	Manager's decision		Clay Carroll, p, Cin	NL	Manager's decision
	Bob Veale, p, Pit	NL	Manager's decision		Larry Dierker, p, Hou	NL	Injured
1966	Steve Barber, p, Bal	AL	Manager's decision		Manny Sanguillen, c, Pit	NL	Manager's decision
	Gary Bell, p, Cle	AL	Manager's decision		Tom Seaver, p, NYN	NL	Manager's decision
	Andy Etchebarren, c, Bal	AL	Manager's decision		Rusty Staub, of, Mon	NL	Manager's decision
	Catfish Hunter, p, KCA	AL	Manager's decision		Rick Wise, p, Phi	NL	Manager's decision
	Sam McDowell, p, Cle	AL	Injured	1972	Luis Aparicio, ss, Bos	AL	Injured
	Carl Yastrzemski, of, Bos	AL	Manager's decision		Bert Campaneris, ss, Oak	AL	Manager's decision
	Felipe Alou, 1b, Atl	NL	Manager's decision		Joe Coleman, p, Det	AL	Injured
	Bob Gibson, p, StL	NL	Injured		Pat Dobson, p, Bal	AL	Manager's decision
	Tom Haller, c, SF	NL	Manager's decision		Toby Harrah, ss, Tex	AL	Injured
	Billy McCool, p, Cin	NL	Manager's decision		Ken Holtzman, p, Oak	AL	Manager's decision
	Joe Morgan, 2b, Hou	NL	Injured		Catfish Hunter, p, Oak	AL	Manager's decision

Year	Player, Pos, Team	Lg	Reason	Year	Player, Pos, Team	Lg	Reason
	Carlos May, of, ChA	AL	Manager's decision		Jim Slaton, p, Mil	AL	Manager's decision
	Amos Otis, of, KC	AL	Injured		Frank Tanana, p, Cal	AL	Injured
	Freddie Patek, ss, KC	AL	Injured		Jason Thompson, 1b, Det	AL	Manager's decision
	Ellie Rodriguez, c, Mil	AL	Manager's decision		Joaquin Andujar, p, Hou	NL	Manager's decision
	Nolan Ryan, p, Cal	AL	Manager's decision		John Candelaria, p, Pit	NL	Manager's decision
	Lou Brock, of, StL	NL	Manager's decision		Steve Carlton, p, Phi	NL	Manager's decision
	Clay Carroll, p, Cin	NL	Manager's decision		Ken Griffey Sr., of, Cin	NL	Manager's decision
	Roberto Clemente, of, Pit	NL	Injured		Bruce Sutter, p, ChN	NL	Injured
	Fergie Jenkins, p, ChN	NL	Manager's decision	1978	Rick Burleson, ss, Bos	AL	Injured
	Gary Nolan, p, Cin	NL	Injured		Mike Flanagan, p, Bal	AL	Manager's decision
	Tom Seaver, p, NYN	NL	Manager's decision		Reggie Jackson, of, NYA	AL	Injured
	Ted Simmons, c, StL	NL	Manager's decision		Thurman Munson, c, NYA	AL	Injured
1973	Dick Allen, 1b, ChA	AL	Injured		Eddie Murray, 1b, Bal	AL	Manager's decision
	Jim Colborn, p, Mil	AL	Manager's decision		Jerry Remy, 2b, Bos	AL	Manager's decision
	Bill Freehan, c, Det	AL	Manager's decision		Craig Reynolds, ss, Sea	AL	Manager's decision
	Bill Lee, p, Bos	AL	Manager's decision		Frank Tanana, p, Cal	AL	Manager's decision
	Carl Yastrzemski, 1b, Bos	AL	Injured		Carl Yastrzemski, of, Bos	AL	Injured
	Dave Concepcion, ss, Cin	NL	Injured		Johnny Bench, c, Cin	NL	Injured
1974	Sal Bando, 3b, Oak	AL	Injured		Jeff Burroughs, of, Atl	NL	Manager's decision
	Steve Busby, p, KC	AL	Manager's decision		Ross Grimsley, p, Mon	NL	Manager's decision
	Mike Cuellar, p, Bal	AL	Manager's decision		Tommy John, p, LA	NL	Manager's decision
	Carlton Fisk, c, Bos	AL	Injured		Terry Puhl, of, Hou	NL	Manager's decision
	Ed Herrmann, c, ChA	AL	Manager's decision		Tom Seaver, p, Cin	NL	Manager's decision
	John Hiller, p, Det	AL	Manager's decision		Pat Zachry, p, NYN	NL	Manager's decision
	Don Money, 3b, Mil	AL	Manager's decision	1979	Rod Carew, 1b, Cal	AL	Injured
	Darrell Porter, c, Mil	AL	Manager's decision		Tommy John, p, NYA	AL	Manager's decision
	Cookie Rojas, 2b, KC	AL	Manager's decision		Dave Lemanczyk, p, Tor	AL	Manager's decision
	Jim Sundberg, c, Tex	AL	Manager's decision		Sid Monge, p, Cle	AL	Manager's decision
	Wilbur Wood, p, ChA	AL	Manager's decision		Jeff Newman, c, Oak	AL	Manager's decision
	Buzz Capra, p, Atl	NL	Manager's decision		Don Stanhouse, p, Bal	AL	Manager's decision
	Steve Carlton, p, Phi	NL	Manager's decision		Johnny Bench, c, Cin	NL	Injured
	Steve Rogers, p, Mon	NL	Manager's decision		Dave Concepcion, ss, Cin	NL	Injured
	Ted Simmons, c, StL	NL	Manager's decision		Dave Kingman, of, ChN	NL	Injured
	Chris Speier, ss, SF	NL	Manager's decision		Joe Niekro, p, Hou	NL	Manager's decision
1975	Dave Chalk, 3b, Cal	AL	Manager's decision		Ted Simmons, c, StL	NL	Injured
	Rollie Fingers, p, Oak	AL	Manager's decision		John Stearns, c, NYN	NL	Manager's decision
	Bill Freehan, c, Det	AL	Manager's decision		Garry Templeton, ss, StL	NL	Manager's decision
	Toby Harrah, ss, Tex	AL	Manager's decision	1980	George Brett, 3b, KC	AL	Injured
	Jorge Orta, 2b, ChA	AL	Injured		Tom Burgmeier, p, Bos	AL	Manager's decision
	Jim Palmer, p, Bal	AL	Manager's decision		Larry Gura, p, KC	AL	Manager's decision
	Nolan Ryan, p, Cal	AL	Manager's decision		Rick Honeycutt, p, Sea	AL	Manager's decision
	Mike Marshall, p, LA	NL	Manager's decision		Paul Molitor, 2b, Mil	AL	Injured
	Tug McGraw, p, Phi	NL	Manager's decision		Jorge Orta, of, Cle	AL	Manager's decision
	Andy Messersmith, p, LA	NL	Manager's decision		Jim Rice, of, Bos	AL	Injured
	Phil Niekro, p, Atl	NL	Manager's decision		Vida Blue, p, SF	NL	Injured
	Manny Sanguillen, c, Pit	NL	Manager's decision		Steve Carlton, p, Phi	NL	Manager's decision
1976	Rollie Fingers, p, Oak	AL	Manager's decision		Jose Cruz, of, Hou	NL	Manager's decision
	Goose Gossage, p, ChA	AL	Manager's decision		Mike Schmidt, 3b, Phi	NL	Injured
	Dave LaRoche, p, Cle	AL	Manager's decision		Kent Tekulve, p, Pit	NL	Manager's decision
	Sparky Lyle, p, NYA	AL	Manager's decision		Ed Whitson, p, SF	NL	Manager's decision
	Willie Randolph, 2b, NYA	AL	Injured	1981	Britt Burns, p, ChA	AL	Manager's decision
	Bill Travers, p, Mil	AL	Manager's decision		Doug Corbett, p, Min	AL	Manager's decision
	Woodie Fryman, p, Mon	NL	Manager's decision		Goose Gossage, p, NYA	AL	Injured
	Jon Matlack, p, NYN	NL	Manager's decision		Scott McGregor, p, Bal	AL	Manager's decision
	Bake McBride, of, StL	NL	Manager's decision		Steve Carlton, p, Phi	NL	Manager's decision
	Andy Messersmith, p, Atl	NL	Injured	1982	Rod Carew, 1b, Cal	AL	Injured
	Dick Ruthven, p, Atl	NL	Manager's decision		Mark Clear, p, Bos	AL	Manager's decision
	Steve Swisher, c, ChN	NL	Manager's decision		Goose Gossage, p, NYA	AL	Manager's decision
1977	Vida Blue, p, Oak	AL	Injured		Ron Guidry, p, NYA	AL	Manager's decision
	Mark Fidrych, p, Det	AL	Injured		Toby Harrah, 3b, Cle	AL	Manager's decision
	Wayne Gross, 3b, Oak	AL	Manager's decision		Leon Durham, of, ChN	NL	Manager's decision
	Don Money, 2b, Mil	AL	Injured		Phil Niekro, p, Atl	NL	Manager's decision
	Nolan Ryan, p, Cal	AL	Manager's decision	1983	Ron Guidry, p, NYA	AL	Injured

Year	Player, Pos, Team	Lg	Reason	Year	Player, Pos, Team	Lg	Reason
	Reggie Jackson, dh, Cal	AL	Injured	1990	Ellis Burks, of, Bos	AL	Injured
	Aurelio Lopez, p, Det	AL	Manager's decision		Roger Clemens, p, Bos	AL	Manager's decision
	Tippy Martinez, p, Bal	AL	Manager's decision		Randy Johnson, p, Sea	AL	Manager's decision
	Rick Sutcliffe, p, Cle	AL	Manager's decision		Doug Jones, p, Cle	AL	Manager's decision
	George Hendrick, 1b, StL	NL	Manager's decision		Gregg Olson, p, Bal	AL	Manager's decision
	Terry Kennedy, c, SD	NL	Manager's decision		Dave Parker, dh, Mil	AL	Manager's decision
	Gary Lavelle, p, SF	NL	Manager's decision		Neal Heaton, p, Pit	NL	Manager's decision
	Steve Rogers, p, Mon	NL	Manager's decision		Benito Santiago, c, SD	NL	Injured
	Fernando Valenzuela, p, LA	NL	Manager's decision	1991	Julio Franco, 2b, Tex	AL	Manager's decision
1984	Tony Armas, of, Bos	AL	Manager's decision		Bryan Harvey, p, Cal	AL	Manager's decision
	Mike Boddicker, p, Bal	AL	Manager's decision		Mark Langston, p, Cal	AL	Manager's decision
	Dave Engle, c, Min	AL	Manager's decision		Mark McGwire, 1b, Oak	AL	Injured
	Phil Niekro, p, NYA	AL	Manager's decision		Scott Sanderson, p, NYA	AL	Manager's decision
	Dan Quisenberry, p, KC	AL	Manager's decision		Tom Browning, p, Cin	NL	Manager's decision
	Alan Trammell, ss, Det	AL	Injured		John Kruk, 1b, Phi	NL	Manager's decision
	Joaquin Andujar, p, StL	NL	Injured		Lee Smith, p, StL	NL	Manager's decision
	Al Holland, p, Phi	NL	Manager's decision		Darryl Strawberry, of, LA	NL	Injured
	Mike Marshall, of, LA	NL	Manager's decision	1992	Jose Canseco, of, Oak	AL	Injured
	Jesse Orosco, p, NYN	NL	Manager's decision		Lee Smith, p, StL	NL	Manager's decision
	Rafael Ramirez, ss, Atl	NL	Manager's decision	1993	Pat Hentgen, p, Tor	AL	Manager's decision
	Juan Samuel, 2b, Phi	NL	Manager's decision		Mike Mussina, p, Bal	AL	Manager's decision
	Bruce Sutter, p, StL	NL	Manager's decision		Tom Glavine, p, Atl	NL	Manager's decision
1985	Jay Howell, p, Oak	AL	Manager's decision		Darryl Kile, p, Hou	NL	Manager's decision
	Lance Parrish, c, Det	AL	Injured		Lee Smith, p, StL	NL	Manager's decision
	Joaquin Andujar, p, StL	NL	Manager's decision		Robby Thompson, 2b, SF	NL	Injured
	Gary Carter, c, NYN	NL	Injured		Andy Van Slyke, of, Pit	NL	Injured
	Ron Darling, p, NYN	NL	Manager's decision	1994	Ricky Bones, p, Mil	AL	Manager's decision
	Scott Garrelts, p, SF	NL	Manager's decision		Jeff Conine, of, Fla	NL	Manager's decision
	Dwight Gooden, p, NYN	NL	Manager's decision		Lenny Dykstra, of, Phi	NL	Injured
	Pedro Guerrero, of, LA	NL	Injured		Barry Larkin, ss, Cin	NL	Injured
1986	George Brett, 3b, KC	AL	Injured		Jose Rijo, p, Cin	NL	Injured
	Jose Canseco, of, Oak	AL	Manager's decision		Bret Saberhagen, p, NYN	NL	Manager's decision
	Willie Hernandez, p, Det	AL	Manager's decision	1995	Chuck Finley, p, Cal	AL	Manager's decision
	Eddie Murray, 1b, Bal	AL	Manager's decision		Ken Griffey Jr., of, Sea	AL	Injured
	Jim Presley, 3b, Sea	AL	Manager's decision		Erik Hanson, p, Bos	AL	Manager's decision
	Ken Schrom, p, Cle	AL	Manager's decision		Lee Smith, p, Cal	AL	Manager's decision
	Mike Witt, p, Cal	AL	Manager's decision		Ozzie Smith, ss, StL	NL	Injured
	John Franco, p, Cin	NL	Manager's decision		Matt Williams, 3b, SF	NL	Injured
	Shane Rawley, p, Phi	NL	Manager's decision		Todd Worrell, p, LA	NL	Manager's decision
	Jeff Reardon, p, Mon	NL	Manager's decision	1996	Ken Griffey Jr., of, Sea	AL	Injured
	Rick Rhoden, p, Pit	NL	Manager's decision		Jose Mesa, p, Cle	AL	Manager's decision
	Dave Smith, p, Hou	NL	Manager's decision		Jeff Montgomery, p, KC	AL	Manager's decision
1987	Bruce Hurst, p, Bos	AL	Manager's decision		Andy Pettitte, p, NYA	AL	Manager's decision
	Lou Whitaker, 2b, Det	AL	Injured		Frank Thomas, 1b, ChA	AL	Injured
	Mike Witt, p, Cal	AL	Manager's decision		Greg Vaughn, of, Mil	AL	Manager's decision
1988	Doyle Alexander, p, Det	AL	Manager's decision		John Wetteland, p, NYA	AL	Manager's decision
	Ozzie Guillen, ss, ChA	AL	Injured		Tony Gwynn, of, SD	NL	Injured
	Jeff Reardon, p, Min	AL	Manager's decision		Greg Maddux, p, Atl	NL	Manager's decision
	Alan Trammell, ss, Det	AL	Injured		Matt Williams, 3b, SF	NL	Injured
	Shawon Dunston, ss, ChN	NL	Manager's decision	1997	Albert Belle, of, ChA	AL	Manager's decision
	Danny Jackson, p, Cin	NL	Manager's decision		Jason Dickson, p, Ana	AL	Manager's decision
	Greg Maddux, p, ChN	NL	Manager's decision		David Justice, of, Cle	AL	Injured
	Robby Thompson, 2b, SF	NL	Injured		Jimmy Key, p, Bal	AL	Injured
1989	Jose Canseco, of, Oak	AL	Injured		Mike Mussina, p, Bal	AL	Manager's decision
	Chuck Finley, p, Cal	AL	Manager's decision		Frank Thomas, 1b, ChA	AL	Injured
	Kelly Gruber, 3b, Tor	AL	Manager's decision		Rod Beck, p, SF	NL	Manager's decision
	Mike Henneman, p, Det	AL	Manager's decision		Tom Glavine, p, Atl	NL	Manager's decision
	John Franco, p, Cin	NL	Manager's decision		Todd Hundley, c, NYN	NL	Injured
	Orel Hershiser, p, LA	NL	Manager's decision		Darryl Kile, p, Hou	NL	Manager's decision
	Barry Larkin, ss, Cin	NL	Manager's decision		Barry Larkin, ss, Cin	NL	Injured
	Mike Schmidt, 3b, Phi	NL	Injured		Kenny Lofton, of, Atl	NL	Injured
	Mike Scott, p, Hou	NL	Injured		Denny Neagle, p, Atl	NL	Manager's decision
	Darryl Strawberry, of, NYN	NL	Injured				

Awards

Hall Of Fame

From the first Hall of Fame elections in 1936 to the present, we list the complete voting for each year by player, along with his position and his basic statistics (italics indicate an incomplete total). We also provide a listing by person that show his yearly vote totals, with boldface indicating that he was inducted. Finally, we show the yearly winners of the Ford C. Frick (broadcasters) and J.G. Taylor Spink (writers) awards.

Yearly Voting

Baseball's official awards are the Most Valuable Player (1911-1914, 1922-1923 in the American League, 1924-1928, 1929 in the National League, 1931-1997 in both), Cy Young (1956-1997), Rookie of the Year (1947-1997) and Manager of the Year (1983-1997). For each year, we provide the complete voting, including first-place votes (italics indicate an incomplete total), total points and award share (percentage of total possible points). Basic statistics for each person receiving a vote also are listed. For Gold Gloves (1957-1997), we list the winner at each of the position along with his basic statistics.

Share Leaders

Bill James created the award share to measure the support a player received in voting during his career. This section lists the top 200 leaders in the Most Valuable Player balloting, the top 100 in Cy Young voting and all 65 men who have received Manager of the Year votes. Each person's awards won and total first-place votes (italic indicate an incomplete total) also are shown.

Postseason

We list all of baseball's official awards—World Series MVP (1955-1993, 1995-1997), National League Championship Series MVP (1977-1993, 1995-1997) and American League Championship Series MVP (1980-1993, 1995-1997)—and basic statistics for the winners.

STATS Retroactive

For each league that lacked an official baseball award winner in a season, either because the award didn't exist or encompassed more than one league, Jim Callis chose a STATS award winner. We list them by award, along with their basic statistics. Besides the four awards mentioned above, we also include World Series MVP, 19th Century World Series MVP, League Championship MVP and Division Series MVP when they weren't officially chosen by baseball.

STATS Retroactive All-Stars

For each league season, Jim Callis also picked an all-star team consisting of eight position players (including three outfielders, rather than left, center and right fielders) and a varying number of pitchers. The number of starting pitchers each year roughly parallels the number of main starters used by each team. One relief pitcher per year is chosen starting in 1924, when Washington's Firpo Marberry became the first hurler to accumulate 15 saves in one season. A designated hitter also is selected for each American League season since 1973, when the DH rule first came into play. Basic statistics are included for each all-star (italics indicate an incomplete total). After the yearly listings of all-stars, we also rank the top 25 players with the most selections overall, consecutively and at each position.

Abbreviations & Formulas

A complete list of team and statistical abbreviations are listed in the back of the book, along with an appendix explaining formulas and the availability of certain statistics.

1936

Veterans

Player, Position	Stats	Votes
Cap Anson, 1b	.329-97-1879	40
Buck Ewing, c	.303-71-883	40
Willie Keeler, of	.341-33-810	33
Cy Young, p	511-316, 2.63	32
Ed Delahanty, of	.346-101-1464	22
John McGraw, 3b	.334-13-462 (Manager)	17
Herman Long, ss	.277-91-1054	16
Old Hoss Radbourn, p	309-195, 2.67	16
King Kelly, of	.308-69-950	15
Amos Rusie, p	245-174, 3.07	12
Hughie Jennings, ss	.311-18-840	11
Fred Clarke, of	.312-67-1015	9
Jimmy Collins, 3b	.294-65-983	8
Charlie Comiskey, 1b	.264-29-735 (Executive)	6
Jerry Denny, 3b	.260-74-667	6
Bill Lange, of	.330-39-578	6
Wilbert Robinson, c	.273-18-722 (Manager)	6
Harry Stovey, of	.288-122-760	6
George Wright, ss	.256-2-132 (Pioneer)	6
John Clarkson, p	328-177, 2.81	5
Honus Wagner, ss	.327-101-1732	5
Hugh Duffy, of	.324-106-1302	4
Ross Barnes, ss	.319-2-111	3
Charlie Bennett, c	.256-55-533	3
Kid Nichols, p	361-208, 2.95	3
Monte Ward, ss	.275-26-867	3
Dan Brouthers, 1b	.342-106-1296	2
Fred Dunlap, 2b	.292-41-366	2
Jack Glasscock, ss	.290-27-825	2
Billy Hamilton, of	.344-40-736	2
Nap Lajoie, 2b	.338-82-1599	2
Bobby Lowe, 2b	.273-71-984	2
Ned Williamson, 3b	.255-64-667	2
Doug Allison, c	.232-0-28	1
Joe Battin, 3b	.218-3-81	1
Jake Beckley, 1b	.308-86-1575	1
Tommy Bond, p	193-115, 2.25	1
Jesse Burkett, of	.338-75-952	1
Lou Criger, c	.221-11-342	1
Bill Dahlen, ss	.272-84-1233	1
Jake Daubert, 1b	.303-56-722	1
Jack Doyle, 1b	.299-26-968	1
Tim Keefe, p	341-225, 2.62	1
Matt Kilroy, p	141-133, 3.47	1
Arlie Latham, 3b	.269-27-562	1
Jimmy McAleer, of	.253-12-469	1
Tommy McCarthy, of	.292-44-735	1
Cal McVey, 1b	.328-3-169	1
Charlie Pabor, p	National Association	1
Lip Pike, of	.304-5-88	1
Jack Remsen, of	.233-5-86	1
Hardy Richardson, 2b	.299-70-822	1
Fred Tenney, 1b	.294-22-688	1
George Van Haltren, of	.316-69-1014	1
Bobby Wallace, ss	.268-34-1121	1
Deacon White, 3b	.303-18-756	1

Needed for election: 59

1936

BBWAA

Player, Position	Stats	Votes
Ty Cobb, of	.366-117-1933	222
Babe Ruth, of	.342-714-2210	215
Honus Wagner, ss	.327-101-1732	215
Christy Mathewson, p	373-188, 2.13	205
Walter Johnson, p	417-279, 2.17	189
Nap Lajoie, 2b	.338-82-1599	146
Tris Speaker, of	.345-117-1537	133
Cy Young, p	511-316, 2.63	111
Rogers Hornsby, 2b	.358-301-1584	105
Mickey Cochrane, c	.320-119-832	80
George Sisler, 1b	.340-102-1175	77
Eddie Collins, 2b	.333-47-1300	60
Jimmy Collins, 3b	.294-65-983	58
Pete Alexander, p	373-208, 2.56	55
Lou Gehrig, 1b	.340-493-1995	51
Roger Bresnahan, c	.279-26-530	47
Willie Keeler, of	.341-33-810	40
Rube Waddell, p	193-143, 2.16	33
Jimmie Foxx, 1b	.325-534-1921	21
Ed Walsh, p	195-126, 1.81	20
Ed Delahanty, of	.346-101-1464	17
Pie Traynor, 3b	.320-58-1273	16
Frankie Frisch, 2b	.316-105-1244	14
Lefty Grove, p	300-141, 3.06	12
Hal Chase, 1b	.291-57-941	11
Ross Youngs, of	.322-42-592	10
Bill Terry, 1b	.341-154-1078	9
Johnny Kling, c	.272-20-513	8
Lou Criger, c	.221-11-342	7
Three Finger Brown, p	239-129, 2.06	6
Johnny Evers, 2b	.270-12-538	6
Frank Chance, 1b	.296-20-596	5
John McGraw, 3b	.334-13-462 (Manager)	4
Ray Schalk, c	.253-11-594	4
Al Simmons, of	.334-307-1827	4
Chief Bender, p	212-127, 2.45	2
Joe Jackson, of	.356-54-785	2
Edd Roush, of	.323-68-981	2
Home Run Baker, 3b	.307-96-987	1
Bill Bradley, 3b	.271-34-552	1
Fred Clarke, of	.312-67-1015	1
Sam Crawford, of	.309-97-1525	1
Kid Elberfeld, ss	.271-10-535	1
Connie Mack, c	.245-5-265 (Manager)	1
Rube Marquard, p	201-177, 3.08	1
Nap Rucker, p	134-134, 2.42	1
Dazzy Vance, p	197-140, 3.24	1

Needed for election: 170

1937

BBWAA

Player, Position	Stats	Votes
Nap Lajoie, 2b	**.338-82-1599**	**168**
Tris Speaker, of	**.345-117-1537**	**165**
Cy Young, p	**511-316, 2.63**	**153**
Pete Alexander, p	373-208, 2.56	125
Eddie Collins, 2b	.333-47-1300	115
Willie Keeler, of	.341-33-810	115
George Sisler, 1b	.340-102-1175	106
Ed Delahanty, of	.346-101-1464	70
Rube Waddell, p	193-143, 2.16	67
Jimmy Collins, 3b	.294-65-983	66
Ed Walsh, p	195-126, 1.81	56
Rogers Hornsby, 2b	.358-301-1584	53
Frank Chance, 1b	.296-20-596	49
Johnny Evers, 2b	.270-12-538	44
Roger Bresnahan, c	.279-26-530	43
John McGraw, 3b	.334-13-462 (Manager)	35
Three Finger Brown, p	239-129, 2.06	31
Rabbit Maranville, ss	.258-28-884	25
Ray Schalk, c	.253-11-594	24
Eddie Plank, p	326-194, 2.35	23
Fred Clarke, of	.312-67-1015	22
Johnny Kling, c	.272-20-513	20
Hal Chase, 1b	.291-57-941	18
Chief Bender, p	212-127, 2.45	17
Lou Criger, c	.221-11-342	16
Ross Youngs, of	.322-42-592	16
Herb Pennock, p	241-162, 3.61	15
Joe Tinker, ss	.262-31-782	15
Home Run Baker, 3b	.307-96-987	13
Rube Marquard, p	201-177, 3.08	13
Joe Wood, of	.283-23-325	13
Joe McGinnity, p	246-142, 2.66	12
Addie Joss, p	160-97, 1.89	11
Nap Rucker, p	134-134, 2.42	11
Harry Heilmann, of	.342-183-1539	10
Edd Roush, of	.323-68-981	10
Dazzy Vance, p	197-140, 3.24	10
Babe Adams, p	194-140, 2.75	8
Hugh Duffy, of	.324-106-1302	7
Jimmy Archer, c	.249-16-296	6
Max Carey, of	.285-70-800	6
Mike Donlin, of	.333-51-543	6
Harry Hooper, of	.281-75-817	6
Bill Bradley, 3b	.271-34-552	5
Bill Carrigan, c	.257-6-235	5
Sam Crawford, of	.309-97-1525	5
Miller Huggins, 2b	.265-9-318	5
Wilbert Robinson, c	.273-18-722	5
Fred Tenney, 1b	.294-22-688	5
Zack Wheat, of	.317-132-1248	5
Earle Combs, of	.325-58-628	4
Clark Griffith, p	237-146, 3.31 (Executive)	4
Hughie Jennings, ss	.311-18-840	4
Nick Altrock, p	84-74, 2.67	3
Dave Bancroft, ss	.279-32-591	3
George Burns, of	.287-41-611	3
Wild Bill Donovan, p	186-139, 2.69	3
Red Faber, p	254-213, 3.15	3
Duffy Lewis, of	.284-38-793	3
Art Nehf, p	184-120, 3.20	3
Roger Peckinpaugh, ss	.259-48-739	3
Marty Bergen, c	.265-10-176	2
Ping Bodie, of	.275-43-516	2
Jack Coombs, p	158-110, 2.78	2
Gavy Cravath, of	.287-119-719	2
Jake Daubert, 1b	.303-56-722	2
Larry Doyle, 2b	.290-74-793	2
Art Fletcher, ss	.277-32-675	2
Hank Gowdy, c	.270-21-322	2
Hans Lobert, 3b	.274-32-482	2
Sherry Magee, of	.291-83-1176	2
Ossee Schreckengost, c	.271-9-338	2
Everett Scott, ss	.249-20-549	2
Ted Breitenstein, p	160-170, 4.04	1
Jesse Burkett, of	.338-75-952	1
Donie Bush, ss	.250-9-436	1
Jack Chesbro, p	198-132, 2.68	1
Bill Cissell, 2b	.267-29-423	1
Shano Collins, of	.264-22-705	1
Red Dooin, c	.240-10-344	1
Joe Dugan, 3b	.280-42-571	1
Kid Elberfeld, ss	.271-10-535	1
Cy Falkenberg, p	130-123, 2.68	1
Kid Gleason, 2b	.261-15-823	1
Burleigh Grimes, p	270-212, 3.52	1
Heine Groh, 3b	.292-26-566	1
Bill Hinchman, of	.261-20-369	1
Joe Judge, 1b	.298-71-1034	1
Dickie Kerr, p	53-34, 3.84	1
Tommy Leach, of	.269-62-810	1
Sam Leever, p	195-100, 2.47	1
Herman Long, ss	.277-91-1054	1
Dolf Luque, p	193-179, 3.24	1
Stuffy McInnis, 1b	.308-20-1060	1
Larry McLean, c	.262-6-298	1
Bob Meusel, of	.309-156-1067	1
Hack Miller, of	.323-38-205	1
Pat Moran, c	.235-18-262	1
Danny Murphy, 2b	.290-44-702	1
Red Murray, of	.270-37-579	1
Dode Paskert, of	.268-41-577	1
Bugs Raymond, p	45-57, 2.49	1
Eppa Rixey, p	266-251, 3.15	1
Dick Rudolph, p	121-108, 2.66	1
Amos Rusie, p	245-174, 3.07	1

Wildfire Schulte, of	.270-92-792	1
Joe Sewell, ss	.312-49-1051	1
Harry Steinfeldt, 3b	.267-27-762	1
Gabby Street, c	.208-2-105	1
Billy Sullivan, c	.212-21-378	1
Bobby Veach, of	.310-64-1166	1
Bobby Wallace, ss	.268-34-1121	1
Hack Wilson, of	.307-244-1062	1
Needed for election: 151		

1938

BBWAA

Player, Position	Stats	Votes
Pete Alexander, p	**373-208, 2.56**	**212**
George Sisler, 1b	.340-102-1175	179
Willie Keeler, of	.341-33-810	177
Eddie Collins, 2b	.333-47-1300	175
Rube Waddell, p	193-143, 2.16	148
Frank Chance, 1b	.296-20-596	133
Ed Delahanty, of	.346-101-1464	132
Ed Walsh, p	195-126, 1.81	110
Johnny Evers, 2b	.270-12-538	91
Jimmy Collins, 3b	.294-65-983	79
Rabbit Maranville, ss	.258-28-884	73
Roger Bresnahan, c	.279-26-530	67
Fred Clarke, of	.312-67-1015	63
Three Finger Brown, p	239-129, 2.06	54
Miller Huggins, 2b	.265-9-318	48
Rogers Hornsby, 2b	.358-301-1584	46
Ray Schalk, c	.253-11-594	45
Ross Youngs, of	.322-42-592	40
Eddie Plank, p	326-194, 2.35	38
Herb Pennock, p	241-162, 3.61	37
Joe McGinnity, p	246-142, 2.66	36
Chief Bender, p	212-127, 2.45	33
Home Run Baker, 3b	.307-96-987	32
Johnny Kling, c	.272-20-513	26
Hugh Duffy, of	.324-106-1302	24
Hughie Jennings, ss	.311-18-840	23
Addie Joss, p	160-97, 1.89	18
Wilbert Robinson, c	.273-18-722 (Manager)	17
Joe Tinker, ss	.262-31-782	16
Harry Heilmann, of	.342-183-1539	14
Nap Rucker, p	134-134, 2.42	12
Babe Adams, p	194-140, 2.75	11
Sam Crawford, of	.309-97-1525	11
Lou Criger, c	.221-11-342	11
Clark Griffith, p	237-146, 3.31 (Executive)	10
Rube Marquard, p	201-177, 3.08	10
Dazzy Vance, p	197-140, 3.24	10
Edd Roush, of	.323-68-981	9
Hank Gowdy, c	.270-21-322	8
Amos Rusie, p	245-174, 3.07	8
Fred Tenney, 1b	.294-22-688	8
Nick Altrock, p	84-74, 2.67	7
Jimmy Archer, c	.249-16-296	7
Earle Combs, of	.325-58-628	7
Bill Terry, 1b	.341-154-1078	7
Bobby Wallace, ss	.268-34-1121	7
Zack Wheat, of	.317-132-1248	7
Max Carey, of	.285-70-800	6
Joe Wood, of	.283-23-325	6
Mike Donlin, of	.333-51-543	5
Duffy Lewis, of	.284-38-793	5
Art Nehf, p	184-120, 3.20	5
Bill Carrigan, c	.257-6-235	4
Bill Dinneen, p	170-177, 3.01	4
Larry Doyle, 2b	.290-74-793	4
Harry Hooper, of	.281-75-817	4
Stuffy McInnis, 1b	.308-20-1060	4
Jack Barry, ss	.243-10-429	3
George Burns, of	.287-41-611	3
Art Fletcher, ss	.277-32-675	3
Heine Groh, 3b	.292-26-566	3
Dickie Kerr, p	53-34, 3.84	3
Kid Nichols, p	361-208, 2.95	3

Pie Traynor, 3b	.320-58-1273	3
Dave Bancroft, ss	.279-32-591	2
Bill Bradley, 3b	.271-34-552	2
Jesse Burkett, of	.338-75-952	2
Jack Chesbro, p	198-132, 2.68	2
Jack Coombs, p	158-110, 2.78	2
Gavy Cravath, of	.287-119-719	2
Kid Elberfeld, ss	.271-10-535	2
Eddie Foster, 3b	.264-6-446	2
Joe Judge, 1b	.298-71-1034	2
Sherry Magee, of	.291-83-1176	2
Roger Peckinpaugh, ss	.259-48-739	2
Eppa Rixey, p	266-251, 3.15	2
Ossee Schreckengost, c	.271-9-338	2
Everett Scott, ss	.249-20-549	2
Casey Stengel, of	.284-60-535 (Manager)	2
Ginger Beaumont, of	.311-39-617	1
Marty Bergen, c	.265-10-176	1
Ray Chapman, ss	.278-17-364	1
Andy Coakley, p	58-59, 2.35	1
Wilbur Cooper, p	216-178, 2.89	1
Stan Coveleski, p	215-142, 2.88	1
Doc Crandall, p	2.92, 24 saves	1
Walton Cruise, of	.277-30-272	1
Bill Dahlen, ss	.272-84-1233	1
Jake Daubert, 1b	.303-56-722	1
Wild Bill Donovan, p	186-139, 2.69	1
Red Dooin, c	.240-10-344	1
Joe Dugan, 3b	.280-42-571	1
Howard Ehmke, p	166-166, 3.75	1
Red Faber, p	254-213, 3.15	1
Elmer Flick, of	.313-48-756	1
Kid Gleason, 2b	.261-15-823	1
Eddie Grant, 3b	.249-5-277	1
Burleigh Grimes, p	270-212, 3.52	1
Bucky Harris, 2b	.274-9-506 (Manager)	1
Buck Herzog, 2b	.259-20-445	1
Charlie Irwin, 3b	.267-16-488	1
Arlie Latham, 3b	.269-27-562	1
Hans Lobert, 3b	.274-32-482	1
Herman Long, ss	.277-91-1054	1
Dolf Luque, p	193-179, 3.24	1
Firpo Marberry, p	3.63, 101 saves	1
Bob Meusel, of	.309-156-1067	1
Clyde Milan, of	.285-17-617	1
Pat Moran, c	.235-18-262	1
Red Murray, of	.270-37-579	1
Hub Perdue, p	51-64, 3.85	1
Sam Rice, of	.322-34-1078	1
Jimmy Sheckard, of	.274-56-813	1
Urban Shocker, p	187-117, 3.16	1
Jake Stahl, 1b	.260-31-437	1
Gabby Street, c	.208-2-105	1
Ira Thomas, c	.242-3-155	1
Cy Williams, of	.292-251-1005	1
Chief Zimmer, c	.269-26-625	1
Needed for election: 197		

1939

BBWAA

Player, Position	Stats	Votes
George Sisler, 1b	**.340-102-1175**	**235**
Eddie Collins, 2b	**.333-47-1300**	**213**
Willie Keeler, of	**.341-33-810**	**207**
Rube Waddell, p	193-143, 2.16	179
Rogers Hornsby, 2b	.358-301-1584	176
Frank Chance, 1b	.296-20-596	158
Ed Delahanty, of	.346-101-1464	145
Ed Walsh, p	195-126, 1.81	132
Johnny Evers, 2b	.270-12-538	107
Miller Huggins, 2b	.265-9-318	97
Rabbit Maranville, ss	.258-28-884	82
Jimmy Collins, 3b	.294-65-983	72
Roger Bresnahan, c	.279-26-530	67
Fred Clarke, of	.312-67-1015	59
Three Finger Brown, p	239-129, 2.06	54

Wilbert Robinson, c	.273-18-722 (Manager)	46
Chief Bender, p	212-127, 2.45	40
Herb Pennock, p	241-162, 3.61	40
Ray Schalk, c	.253-11-594	35
Hugh Duffy, of	.324-106-1302	34
Ross Youngs, of	.322-42-592	34
Hughie Jennings, ss	.311-18-840	33
Joe McGinnity, p	246-142, 2.66	32
Home Run Baker, 3b	.307-96-987	30
Mickey Cochrane, c	.320-119-832	28
Addie Joss, p	160-97, 1.89	28
Eddie Plank, p	326-194, 2.35	28
Frankie Frisch, 2b	.316-105-1244	26
Clark Griffith, p	237-146, 3.31 (Executive)	20
Bill Terry, 1b	.341-154-1078	16
Dazzy Vance, p	197-140, 3.24	15
Johnny Kling, c	.272-20-513	14
Nap Rucker, p	134-134, 2.42	13
Joe Tinker, ss	.262-31-782	12
Babe Adams, p	194-140, 2.75	11
Pie Traynor, 3b	.320-58-1273	10
Harry Heilmann, of	.342-183-1539	8
Edd Roush, of	.323-68-981	8
Max Carey, of	.285-70-800	7
Bill Dinneen, p	170-177, 3.01	7
Kid Nichols, p	361-208, 2.95	7
Nick Altrock, p	84-74, 2.67	6
Jack Chesbro, p	198-132, 2.68	6
Sam Crawford, of	.309-97-1525	6
Duffy Lewis, of	.284-38-793	6
Amos Rusie, p	245-174, 3.07	6
Casey Stengel, of	.284-60-535 (Manager)	6
Mike Donlin, of	.333-51-543	5
Harry Hooper, of	.281-75-817	5
Dickie Kerr, p	53-34, 3.84	5
Bobby Wallace, ss	.268-34-1121	5
Hank Gowdy, c	.270-21-322	4
Rube Marquard, p	201-177, 3.08	4
Stuffy McInnis, 1b	.308-20-1060	4
Zack Wheat, of	.317-132-1248	4
Jimmy Archer, c	.249-16-296	3
Earle Combs, of	.325-58-628	3
Red Faber, p	254-213, 3.15	3
Fred Tenney, 1b	.294-22-688	3
Donie Bush, ss	.250-9-436	2
Bill Carrigan, c	.257-6-235	2
Gavy Cravath, of	.287-119-719	2
Lou Criger, c	.221-11-342	2
Wild Bill Donovan, p	186-139, 2.69	2
Buck Ewing, c	.303-71-883	2
Eddie Grant, 3b	.249-5-277	2
Hans Lobert, 3b	.274-32-482	2
Ossee Schreckengost, c	.271-9-338	2
Joe Wood, of	.283-23-325	2
Dave Bancroft, ss	.279-32-591	1
Jack Barry, ss	.243-10-429	1
Marty Bergen, c	.265-10-176	1
Bill Bradley, 3b	.271-34-552	1
George Burns, of	.287-41-611	1
Wilbur Cooper, p	216-178, 2.89	1
Lave Cross, 3b	.292-47-1371	1
Jake Daubert, 1b	.303-56-722	1
Larry Doyle, 2b	.290-74-793	1
Art Fletcher, ss	.277-32-675	1
Chick Fraser, p	176-213, 3.68	1
Kid Gleason, 2b	.261-15-823	1
Burleigh Grimes, p	270-212, 3.52	1
Charlie Grimm, 1b	.290-79-1078	1
Noodles Hahn, p	130-94, 2.55	1
Jesse Haines, p	210-158, 3.64	1
Bucky Harris, 2b	.274-9-506 (Manager)	1
Waite Hoyt, p	237-182, 3.59	1
Charlie Irwin, 3b	.267-16-488	1
Sad Sam Jones, p	229-217, 3.84	1
Joe Kelley, of	.317-65-1194	1
Otto Knabe, 2b	.247-8-365	1
Tommy Leach, of	.269-62-810	1
Herman Long, ss	.277-91-1054	1
Dolf Luque, p	193-179, 3.24	1
Sherry Magee, of	.291-83-1176	1

Pat Moran, c	.235-18-262	1
Art Nehf, p	184-120, 3.20	1
Roger Peckinpaugh, ss	.259-48-739	1
Heinie Peitz, c	.271-16-560	1
Hub Perdue, p	51-64, 3.85	1
Deacon Phillippe, p	189-109, 2.59	1
Al Schacht, p	4.48, 2 saves	1
Everett Scott, ss	.249-20-549	1
Urban Shocker, p	187-117, 3.16	1
Jake Stahl, 1b	.260-31-437	1
Harry Steinfeldt, 3b	.267-27-762	1
Gabby Street, c	.208-2-105	1
Hack Wilson, of	.307-244-1062	1

Needed for election: 206

1939

BBWAA Special Election

Player, Position	Stats	Votes
Lou Gehrig, 1b	.340-493-1995	—

Needed for election: —

1942

BBWAA

Player, Position	Stats	Votes
Rogers Hornsby, 2b	.358-301-1584	182
Frank Chance, 1b	.296-20-596	136
Rube Waddell, p	193-143, 2.16	126
Ed Walsh, p	195-126, 1.81	113
Miller Huggins, 2b	.265-9-318	111
Ed Delahanty, of	.346-101-1464	104
Johnny Evers, 2b	.270-12-538	91
Wilbert Robinson, c	.273-18-722 (Manager)	89
Mickey Cochrane, c	.320-119-832	88
Frankie Frisch, 2b	.316-105-1244	84
Hugh Duffy, of	.324-106-1302	77
Herb Pennock, p	241-162, 3.61	72
Clark Griffith, p	237-146, 3.31 (Executive)	71
Jimmy Collins, 3b	.294-65-983	68
Rabbit Maranville, ss	.258-28-884	66
Hughie Jennings, ss	.311-18-840	64
Three Finger Brown, p	239-129, 2.06	63
Eddie Plank, p	326-194, 2.35	63
Joe McGinnity, p	246-142, 2.66	59
Fred Clarke, of	.312-67-1015	58
Roger Bresnahan, c	.279-26-530	57
Chief Bender, p	212-127, 2.45	55
Ray Schalk, c	.253-11-594	53
Pie Traynor, 3b	.320-58-1273	45
Ross Youngs, of	.322-42-592	44
Home Run Baker, 3b	.307-96-987	39
Dazzy Vance, p	197-140, 3.24	37
Bill Terry, 1b	.341-154-1078	36
Joe Tinker, ss	.262-31-782	36
Addie Joss, p	160-97, 1.89	33
Johnny Kling, c	.272-20-513	15
Nap Rucker, p	134-134, 2.42	15
Babe Adams, p	194-140, 2.75	11
Hank Gowdy, c	.270-21-322	8
Kid Nichols, p	361-208, 2.95	5
Jesse Burkett, of	.338-75-952	4
Harry Heilmann, of	.342-183-1539	4
Eddie Grant, 3b	.249-5-277	3
Zack Wheat, of	.317-132-1248	3
Donie Bush, ss	.250-9-436	2
Sam Crawford, of	.309-97-1525	2
Pepper Martin, of	.298-59-501	2
Roger Peckinpaugh, ss	.259-48-739	2
Bobby Wallace, ss	.268-34-1121	2
Ginger Beaumont, of	.311-39-617	1
Jake Beckley, 1b	.308-86-1575	1
Joe Boley, ss	.269-7-227	1
Bill Bradley, 3b	.271-34-552	1
Lave Cross, 3b	.292-47-1371	1
Bill Dinneen, p	170-177, 3.01	1
Jack Dunn, 3b	.245-1-164 (Executive)	1
Kid Elberfeld, ss	.271-10-535	1
Red Faber, p	254-213, 3.15	1
Billy Hamilton, of	.344-40-736	1
Babe Herman, of	.324-181-997	1
Waite Hoyt, p	237-182, 3.59	1
Joe Kelley, of	.317-65-1194	1
Dickie Kerr, p	53-34, 3.84	1
Arlie Latham, 3b	.269-27-562	1
Bobby Lowe, 2b	.273-71-984	1
Sherry Magee, of	.291-83-1176	1
Deacon Phillippe, p	189-109, 2.59	1
Edd Roush, of	.323-68-981	1
Amos Rusie, p	245-174, 3.07	1
Germany Schaefer, 2b	.257-9-308	1
Everett Scott, ss	.249-20-549	1
Harry Steinfeldt, 3b	.267-27-762	1
Fred Tenney, 1b	.294-22-688	1
Bill Wambsganss, 2b	.259-7-519	1
Hack Wilson, of	.307-244-1062	1
Joe Wood, of	.283-23-325	1

Needed for election: 175

1945

BBWAA

Player, Position	Stats	Votes
Frank Chance, 1b	.296-20-596	179
Rube Waddell, p	193-143, 2.16	154
Ed Walsh, p	195-126, 1.81	137
Johnny Evers, 2b	.270-12-538	134
Roger Bresnahan, c	.279-26-530	133
Miller Huggins, 2b	.265-9-318	133
Mickey Cochrane, c	.320-119-832	125
Jimmy Collins, 3b	.294-65-983	121
Ed Delahanty, of	.346-101-1464	111
Clark Griffith, p	237-146, 3.31 (Executive)	108
Frankie Frisch, 2b	.316-105-1244	101
Hughie Jennings, ss	.311-18-840	92
Wilbert Robinson, c	.273-18-722 (Manager)	81
Pie Traynor, 3b	.320-58-1273	81
Hugh Duffy, of	.324-106-1302	64
Fred Clarke, of	.312-67-1015	53
Rabbit Maranville, ss	.258-28-884	51
Joe Tinker, ss	.262-31-782	49
Three Finger Brown, p	239-129, 2.06	46
Herb Pennock, p	241-162, 3.61	45
Joe McGinnity, p	246-142, 2.66	44
Chief Bender, p	212-127, 2.45	40
Eddie Plank, p	326-194, 2.35	33
Ray Schalk, c	.253-11-594	33
Bill Terry, 1b	.341-154-1078	32
Lefty Grove, p	300-141, 3.06	28
Home Run Baker, 3b	.307-96-987	26
Carl Hubbell, p	253-154, 2.98	24
Addie Joss, p	160-97, 1.89	23
Ross Youngs, of	.322-42-592	22
Dazzy Vance, p	197-140, 3.24	18
Dizzy Dean, p	150-83, 3.02	17
Bill Dickey, c	.313-202-1209	17
Johnny Kling, c	.272-20-513	12
Charlie Gehringer, 2b	.320-184-1427	10
Nap Rucker, p	134-134, 2.42	10
Babe Adams, p	194-140, 2.75	7
Lefty Gomez, p	189-102, 3.34	7
Harry Heilmann, of	.342-183-1539	5
Kid Nichols, p	361-208, 2.95	5
Edd Roush, of	.323-68-981	5
Sam Crawford, of	.309-97-1525	4
Ted Lyons, p	260-230, 3.67	4
Bill Carrigan, c	.257-6-235	3
Wild Bill Donovan, p	186-139, 2.69	3
Hank Gowdy, c	.270-21-322	3
Hank Greenberg, 1b	.313-331-1276	3
Bobby Wallace, ss	.268-34-1121	3
Jesse Burkett, of	.338-75-952	2
Kid Elberfeld, ss	.271-10-535	2
Eddie Grant, 3b	.249-5-277	2
Gabby Hartnett, c	.297-236-1179	2
Bobby Lowe, 2b	.273-71-984	2
Bill McKechnie, 3b	.251-8-240 (Manager)	2
Deacon Phillippe, p	189-109, 2.59	2
Casey Stengel, of	.284-60-535 (Manager)	2
Zack Wheat, of	.317-132-1248	2
Ginger Beaumont, of	.311-39-617	1
Donie Bush, ss	.250-9-436	1
Howie Camnitz, p	133-107, 2.75	1
Max Carey, of	.285-70-800	1
Earle Combs, of	.325-58-628	1
Wid Conroy, 3b	.248-22-452	1
Harry Davis, 1b	.276-75-952	1
Joe DiMaggio, of	.325-361-1537	1
Bill Dinneen, p	170-177, 3.01	1
Mike Donlin, of	.333-51-543	1
Jack Dunn, 3b	.245-1-164 (Executive)	1
Kid Gleason, 2b	.261-15-823	1
Joe Gordon, 2b	.268-253-975	1
Charlie Grimm, 1b	.290-79-1078	1
Heine Groh, 3b	.292-26-566	1
Dickie Kerr, p	53-34, 3.84	1
Tony Lazzeri, 2b	.292-178-1191	1
Duffy Lewis, of	.284-38-793	1
Herman Long, ss	.277-91-1054	1
Sherry Magee, of	.291-83-1176	1
Pepper Martin, of	.298-59-501	1
Bob Meusel, of	.309-156-1067	1
Pat Moran, c	.235-18-262	1
Van Lingle Mungo, p	120-115, 3.47	1
Danny Murphy, 2b	.290-44-702	1
Claude Ritchey, 2b	.273-18-673	1
Eppa Rixey, p	266-251, 3.15	1
Charlie Root, p	201-160, 3.59	1
Amos Rusie, p	245-174, 3.07	1
Cy Seymour, of	.303-52-799	1
Jimmy Sheckard, of	.274-56-813	1
Billy Southworth, of	.297-52-561	1
Bill Sweeney, 2b	.272-11-389	1
Johnny Vander Meer, p	119-121, 3.44	1
Cy Williams, of	.292-251-1005	1
Steve Yerkes, 2b	.269-6-254	1

Needed for election: 186

1946

BBWAA

Player, Position	Stats	Votes
Frank Chance, 1b	.296-20-596	144
Johnny Evers, 2b	.270-12-538	130
Miller Huggins, 2b	.265-9-318	129
Rube Waddell, p	193-143, 2.16	122
Ed Walsh, p	195-126, 1.81	115
Frankie Frisch, 2b	.316-105-1244	104
Carl Hubbell, p	253-154, 2.98	101
Mickey Cochrane, c	.320-119-832	80
Clark Griffith, p	237-146, 3.31 (Executive)	73
Lefty Grove, p	300-141, 3.06	71
Pie Traynor, 3b	.320-58-1273	65
Three Finger Brown, p	239-129, 2.06	56
Joe Tinker, ss	.262-31-782	55
Joe McGinnity, p	246-142, 2.66	53
Rabbit Maranville, ss	.258-28-884	50
Charlie Gehringer, 2b	.320-184-1427	43
Herb Pennock, p	241-162, 3.61	41
Dizzy Dean, p	150-83, 3.02	40
Bill Dickey, c	.313-202-1209	40
Home Run Baker, 3b	.307-96-987	39
Chief Bender, p	212-127, 2.45	39
Ray Schalk, c	.253-11-594	36
Eddie Plank, p	326-194, 2.35	34
Bill Terry, 1b	.341-154-1078	31
Dazzy Vance, p	197-140, 3.24	31
Jimmie Foxx, 1b	.325-534-1921	26
Ross Youngs, of	.322-42-592	25

Harry Heilmann, of	.342-183-1539	23
Johnny Kling, c	.272-20-513	20
Addie Joss, p	160-97, 1.89	14
Nap Rucker, p	134-134, 2.42	13
Edd Roush, of	.323-68-981	11
Sam Crawford, of	.309-97-1525	9
Babe Adams, p	194-140, 2.75	6
Lou Criger, c	.221-11-342	6
Rube Marquard, p	201-177, 3.08	6
Zack Wheat, of	.317-132-1248	6
Joe Wood, of	.283-23-325	5
Wild Bill Donovan, p	186-139, 2.69	4
Lefty Gomez, p	189-102, 3.34	4
Paul Waner, of	.333-113-1309	4
Ted Lyons, p	260-230, 3.67	3
Jesse Burkett, of	.338-75-952	2
Donie Bush, ss	.250-9-436	2
Jack Coombs, p	158-110, 2.78	2
Harry Davis, 1b	.276-75-952	2
Gabby Hartnett, c	.297-236-1179	2
Joe Jackson, of	.356-54-785	2
Bill McKechnie, 3b	.251-8-240 (Manager)	2
Dave Bancroft, ss	.279-32-591	1
Ginger Beaumont, of	.311-39-617	1
Bill Bradley, 3b	.271-34-552	1
Jack Chesbro, p	198-132, 2.68	1
John Clarkson, p	328-177, 2.81	1
Gavy Cravath, of	.287-119-719	1
Bill Dinneen, p	170-177, 3.01	1
Jack Dunn, 3b	.245-1-164 (Executive)	1
Eddie Grant, 3b	.249-5-277	1
Charlie Grimm, 1b	.290-79-1078	1
Waite Hoyt, p	237-182, 3.59	1
Fielder Jones, of	.285-21-631	1
Bill Killefer, c	.238-4-240	1
Otto Knabe, 2b	.247-8-365	1
Herman Long, ss	.277-91-1054	1
Sherry Magee, of	.291-83-1176	1
Pepper Martin, of	.298-59-501	1
Kid Nichols, p	361-208, 2.95	1
Deacon Phillippe, p	189-109, 2.59	1
Muddy Ruel, c	.275-4-532	1
Jimmy Sheckard, of	.274-56-813	1
Al Simmons, of	.334-307-1827	1
Billy Southworth, of	.297-52-561	1
Tully Sparks, p	121-136, 2.79	1
Billy Sullivan, c	.212-21-378	1
Jesse Tannehill, p	197-116, 2.79	1
Fred Tenney, 1b	.294-22-688	1
Needed for election: 198		

1946

BBWAA Runoff

Player, Position	Stats	Votes
Frank Chance, 1b	.296-20-596	150
Johnny Evers, 2b	.270-12-538	110
Miller Huggins, 2b	.265-9-318	106
Ed Walsh, p	195-126, 1.81	106
Rube Waddell, p	193-143, 2.16	87
Clark Griffith, p	237-146, 3.31 (Executive)	82
Carl Hubbell, p	253-154, 2.98	75
Frankie Frisch, 2b	.316-105-1244	67
Mickey Cochrane, c	.320-119-832	65
Lefty Grove, p	300-141, 3.06	61
Pie Traynor, 3b	.320-58-1273	53
Three Finger Brown, p	239-129, 2.06	48
Joe McGinnity, p	246-142, 2.66	47
Dizzy Dean, p	150-83, 3.02	45
Joe Tinker, ss	.262-31-782	45
Home Run Baker, 3b	.307-96-987	36
Chief Bender, p	212-127, 2.45	35
Bill Dickey, c	.313-202-1209	32
Rabbit Maranville, ss	.258-28-884	29
Charlie Gehringer, 2b	.320-184-1427	23
Herb Pennock, p	241-162, 3.61	16
Needed for election: 152		

1947

BBWAA

Player, Position	Stats	Votes
Carl Hubbell, p	**253-154, 2.98**	**140**
Frankie Frisch, 2b	**.316-105-1244**	**136**
Mickey Cochrane, c	**.320-119-832**	**128**
Lefty Grove, p	**300-141, 3.06**	**123**
Pie Traynor, 3b	.320-58-1273	119
Charlie Gehringer, 2b	.320-184-1427	105
Rabbit Maranville, ss	.258-28-884	91
Dizzy Dean, p	150-83, 3.02	88
Herb Pennock, p	241-162, 3.61	86
Chief Bender, p	212-127, 2.45	72
Harry Heilmann, of	.342-183-1539	65
Ray Schalk, c	.253-11-594	50
Dazzy Vance, p	197-140, 3.24	50
Home Run Baker, 3b	.307-96-987	49
Bill Terry, 1b	.341-154-1078	46
Zack Wheat, of	.317-132-1248	37
Ross Youngs, of	.322-42-592	36
Joe Wood, of	.283-23-325	29
Edd Roush, of	.323-68-981	25
Babe Adams, p	194-140, 2.75	22
Rube Marquard, p	201-177, 3.08	18
Jimmie Foxx, 1b	.325-534-1921	10
Joe Cronin, ss	.301-170-1424	6
Al Simmons, of	.334-307-1827	6
Art Fletcher, ss	.277-32-675	3
Gavy Cravath, of	.287-119-719	2
Gabby Hartnett, c	.297-236-1179	2
Eppa Rixey, p	266-251, 3.15	2
Terry Turner, ss	.253-8-528	2
Eddie Dyer, p	4.75, 3 saves	1
Charlie Gelbert, ss	.267-17-350	1
Lefty Gomez, p	189-102, 3.34	1
Hank Gowdy, c	.270-21-322	1
Jesse Haines, p	210-158, 3.64	1
Bubbles Hargrave, c	.310-29-376	1
George Kelly, 1b	.297-148-1020	1
Tony Lazzeri, 2b	.292-178-1191	1
Everett Scott, ss	.249-20-549	1
Needed for election: 121		

1948

BBWAA

Player, Position	Stats	Votes
Herb Pennock, p	**241-162, 3.61**	**94**
Pie Traynor, 3b	**.320-58-1273**	**93**
Al Simmons, of	.334-307-1827	60
Charlie Gehringer, 2b	.320-184-1427	52
Bill Terry, 1b	.341-154-1078	52
Paul Waner, of	.333-113-1309	51
Jimmie Foxx, 1b	.325-534-1921	50
Dizzy Dean, p	150-83, 3.02	40
Harry Heilmann, of	.342-183-1539	40
Bill Dickey, c	.313-202-1209	39
Rabbit Maranville, ss	.258-28-884	38
Gabby Hartnett, c	.297-236-1179	33
Joe Cronin, ss	.301-170-1424	25
Dazzy Vance, p	197-140, 3.24	23
Ray Schalk, c	.253-11-594	22
Tony Lazzeri, 2b	.292-178-1191	21
Ross Youngs, of	.322-42-592	19
Edd Roush, of	.323-68-981	17
Lefty Gomez, p	189-102, 3.34	16
Ted Lyons, p	260-230, 3.67	15
Zack Wheat, of	.317-132-1248	15
Max Carey, of	.285-70-800	9
Jimmie Wilson, c	.284-32-621	8
Burleigh Grimes, p	270-212, 3.52	7
Waite Hoyt, p	237-182, 3.59	7
Pepper Martin, of	.298-59-501	7
Earle Combs, of	.325-58-628	6
Charlie Grimm, 1b	.290-79-1078	6

Rube Marquard, p	201-177, 3.08	6
Bob Meusel, of	.309-156-1067	6
Chief Bender, p	212-127, 2.45	5
Jimmy Dykes, 3b	.280-108-1071	5
Travis Jackson, ss	.291-135-929	5
Stuffy McInnis, 1b	.308-20-1060	5
Eppa Rixey, p	266-251, 3.15	5
Joe Wood, of	.283-23-325	5
Babe Adams, p	194-140, 2.75	4
Home Run Baker, 3b	.307-96-987	4
Dave Bancroft, ss	.279-32-591	4
Jim Bottomley, 1b	.310-219-1422	4
Miller Huggins, 2b	.265-9-318	4
Lefty O'Doul, of	.349-113-542	4
Red Ruffing, p	273-225, 3.80	4
Kiki Cuyler, of	.321-128-1065	3
Joe Dugan, 3b	.280-42-571	3
George Earnshaw, p	127-93, 4.38	3
Red Faber, p	254-213, 3.15	3
Art Fletcher, ss	.277-32-675	3
Bucky Harris, 2b	.274-9-506 (Manager)	3
Hank Gowdy, c	.270-21-322	3
Chuck Klein, of	.320-300-1201	3
Eddie Rommel, p	3.54, 29 saves	3
Charlie Root, p	201-160, 3.59	3
Everett Scott, ss	.249-20-549	3
Ossie Bluege, 3b	.272-43-848	2
Jack Coombs, p	158-110, 2.78	2
Wilbur Cooper, p	216-178, 2.89	2
Stan Coveleski, p	215-142, 2.88	2
Freddie Fitzsimmons, p	217-146, 3.51	2
Stan Hack, 3b	.301-57-642	2
Jesse Haines, p	210-158, 3.64	2
Babe Herman, of	.324-181-997	2
Harry Hooper, of	.281-75-817	2
George Kelly, 1b	.297-148-1020	2
Johnny Kling, c	.272-20-513	2
Steve O'Neill, c	.263-13-537	2
Jack Quinn, p	247-218, 3.28	2
Al Schacht, p	4.48, 2 saves	2
Hack Wilson, of	.307-244-1062	2
Glenn Wright, ss	.294-94-723	2
Dick Bartell, ss	.284-79-710	1
Carson Bigbee, of	.287-17-324	1
Leon Cadore, p	68-72, 3.14	1
Dolph Camilli, 1b	.277-239-950	1
Spud Davis, c	.308-77-647	1
Paul Derringer, p	223-212, 3.46	1
Leo Durocher, ss	.247-24-567 (Manager)	1
Wes Ferrell, p	193-128, 4.04	1
Lew Fonseca, 1b	.316-31-485	1
Goose Goslin, of	.316-248-1609	1
Heine Groh, 3b	.292-26-566	1
Chick Hafey, of	.317-164-833	1
Wild Bill Hallahan, p	102-94, 4.03	1
Billy Herman, 2b	.304-47-839	1
Bob Johnson, of	.296-288-1283	1
Ray Kremer, p	143-85, 3.76	1
Heinie Manush, of	.330-110-1173	1
Joe Medwick, of	.324-205-1383	1
Dots Miller, p	.263-32-715	1
Hugh Mulcahy, p	45-89, 4.49	1
Van Lingle Mungo, p	120-115, 3.47	1
Joe Oeschger, p	82-116, 3.81	1
Sam Rice, of	.322-34-1078	1
Wally Schang, c	.284-59-710	1
Hal Schumacher, p	158-121, 3.36	1
George Selkirk, of	.290-108-576	1
Hank Severeid, c	.289-17-539	1
Joe Sewell, ss	.312-49-1051	1
Luke Sewell, c	.259-20-696	1
Bill Sherdel, p	165-146, 3.72	1
Urban Shocker, p	187-117, 3.16	1
Earl Smith, c	.303-46-355	1
Sherry Smith, p	114-118, 3.32	1
Casey Stengel, of	.284-60-535 (Manager)	1
Sammy West, of	.299-75-838	1
Cy Williams, of	.292-251-1005	1
Needed for election: 91		

1949

BBWAA

Player, Position	Stats	Votes
Charlie Gehringer, 2b	.320-184-1427	102
Mel Ott, of	.304-511-1860	94
Al Simmons, of	.334-307-1827	89
Dizzy Dean, p	150-83, 3.02	88
Jimmie Foxx, 1b	.325-534-1921	85
Bill Terry, 1b	.341-154-1078	81
Paul Waner, of	.333-113-1309	73
Hank Greenberg, 1b	.313-331-1276	67
Bill Dickey, c	.313-202-1209	65
Harry Heilmann, of	.342-183-1539	59
Rabbit Maranville, ss	.258-28-884	58
Gabby Hartnett, c	.297-236-1179	35
Joe Cronin, ss	.301-170-1424	33
Dazzy Vance, p	197-140, 3.24	33
Ted Lyons, p	260-230, 3.67	29
Ray Schalk, c	.253-11-594	24
Hack Wilson, of	.307-244-1062	24
Red Ruffing, p	273-225, 3.80	22
Tony Lazzeri, 2b	.292-178-1191	20
Ross Youngs, of	.322-42-592	20
Lefty Gomez, p	189-102, 3.34	17
Pepper Martin, of	.298-59-501	16
Zack Wheat, of	.317-132-1248	15
Edd Roush, of	.323-68-981	14
Max Carey, of	.285-70-800	12
Bucky Harris, 2b	.274-9-506 (Manager)	11
Hank Gowdy, c	.270-21-322	10
Charlie Grimm, 1b	.290-79-1078	10
Chuck Klein, of	.320-300-1201	9
Jim Bottomley, 1b	.310-219-1422	8
Burleigh Grimes, p	270-212, 3.52	8
Stuffy McInnis, 1b	.308-20-1060	8
Jimmy Dykes, 3b	.280-108-1071	7
Waite Hoyt, p	237-182, 3.59	7
Billy Southworth, of	.297-52-561	7
Earle Combs, of	.325-58-628	6
Red Faber, p	254-213, 3.15	6
Travis Jackson, ss	.291-135-929	6
Steve O'Neill, c	.263-13-537	6
Jimmie Wilson, c	.284-32-621	6
Babe Adams, p	194-140, 2.75	5
Dave Bancroft, ss	.279-32-591	5
Babe Herman, of	.324-181-997	5
Wilbur Cooper, p	216-178, 2.89	4
Kiki Cuyler, of	.321-128-1065	4
Goose Goslin, of	.316-248-1609	4
Stan Hack, 3b	.301-57-642	4
Mel Harder, p	223-186, 3.80	4
Rube Marquard, p	201-177, 3.08	4
Lefty O'Doul, of	.349-113-542	4
Eppa Rixey, p	266-251, 3.15	4
Stan Coveleski, p	215-142, 2.88	3
Bob Meusel, of	.309-156-1067	3
Sam Rice, of	.322-34-1078	3
Everett Scott, ss	.249-20-549	3
Casey Stengel, of	.284-60-535 (Manager)	3
Lloyd Waner, of	.316-27-598	3
Chief Bender, p	212-127, 2.45	2
Joe Dugan, 3b	.280-42-571	2
George Earnshaw, p	127-93, 4.38	2
Freddie Fitzsimmons, p	217-146, 3.51	2
Charlie Gelbert, ss	.267-17-350	2
Chick Hafey, of	.317-164-833	2
Jesse Haines, p	210-158, 3.64	2
Billy Jurges, ss	.258-43-656	2
Red Lucas, p	157-135, 3.71	2
Eddie Rommel, p	3.54, 29 saves	2
Urban Shocker, p	187-117, 3.16	2
Lon Warneke, p	192-121, 3.18	2
Cy Williams, of	.292-251-1005	2
Earl Averill, of	.318-238-1165	1
Ossie Bluege, 3b	.272-43-848	1
Ping Bodie, of	.275-43-516	1
George Burns, of	.287-41-611	1
Ben Chapman, of	.302-90-977	1
Spud Davis, c	.308-77-647	1
Leo Durocher, ss	.247-24-567 (Manager)	1
Howard Ehmke, p	166-166, 3.75	1
Wes Ferrell, p	193-128, 4.04	1
Art Fletcher, ss	.277-32-675	1
Joe Judge, 1b	.298-71-1034	1
George Kelly, 1b	.297-148-1020	1
Dickie Kerr, p	53-34, 3.84	1
Freddy Lindstrom, 3b	.311-103-779	1
Al Lopez, c	.261-51-652 (Manager)	1
Heinie Manush, of	.330-110-1173	1
Buddy Myer, 2b	.303-38-850	1
Art Nehf, p	184-120, 3.20	1
Roger Peckinpaugh, ss	.259-48-739	1
Hub Pruett, p	4.63, 13 saves	1
Jimmy Ring, p	118-149, 4.12	1
Charlie Root, p	201-160, 3.59	1
George Selkirk, of	.290-108-576	1
Bill Sherdel, p	165-146, 3.72	1
Fred Toney, p	137-102, 2.69	1
Bill Werber, 3b	.271-78-539	1
Whitey Witt, of	.287-18-302	1
Glenn Wright, ss	.294-94-723	1

Needed for election: 115

1949

BBWAA Runoff

Player, Position	Stats	Votes
Charlie Gehringer, 2b	**.320-184-1427**	**159**
Mel Ott, of	.304-511-1860	128
Jimmie Foxx, 1b	.325-534-1921	89
Dizzy Dean, p	150-83, 3.02	81
Al Simmons, of	.334-307-1827	76
Paul Waner, of	.333-113-1309	63
Harry Heilmann, of	.342-183-1539	52
Bill Terry, 1b	.341-154-1078	48
Hank Greenberg, 1b	.313-331-1276	44
Bill Dickey, c	.313-202-1209	39
Rabbit Maranville, ss	.258-28-884	39
Ray Schalk, c	.253-11-594	17
Joe Cronin, ss	.301-170-1424	16
Dazzy Vance, p	197-140, 3.24	15
Ted Lyons, p	260-230, 3.67	14
Hack Wilson, of	.307-244-1062	12
Ross Youngs, of	.322-42-592	11
Gabby Hartnett, c	.297-236-1179	7
Tony Lazzeri, 2b	.292-178-1191	6
Red Ruffing, p	273-225, 3.80	4

Needed for election: 141 (one player maximum)

1950

BBWAA

Player, Position	Stats	Votes
Mel Ott, of	.304-511-1860	115
Bill Terry, 1b	.341-154-1078	105
Jimmie Foxx, 1b	.325-534-1921	103
Paul Waner, of	.333-113-1309	95
Al Simmons, of	.334-307-1827	90
Harry Heilmann, of	.342-183-1539	87
Dizzy Dean, p	150-83, 3.02	85
Bill Dickey, c	.313-202-1209	78
Rabbit Maranville, ss	.258-28-884	66
Hank Greenberg, 1b	.313-331-1276	64
Gabby Hartnett, c	.297-236-1179	54
Dazzy Vance, p	197-140, 3.24	52
Ted Lyons, p	260-230, 3.67	42
Joe Cronin, ss	.301-170-1424	33
Tony Lazzeri, 2b	.292-178-1191	21
Lefty Gomez, p	189-102, 3.34	18
Zack Wheat, of	.317-132-1248	17
Ross Youngs, of	.322-42-592	17
Edd Roush, of	.323-68-981	16
Ray Schalk, c	.253-11-594	16
Hack Wilson, of	.307-244-1062	16
Max Carey, of	.285-70-800	14
Chuck Klein, of	.320-300-1201	14
Charlie Grimm, 1b	.290-79-1078	13
Red Ruffing, p	273-225, 3.80	12
Kiki Cuyler, of	.321-128-1065	11
Jesse Haines, p	210-158, 3.64	11
Waite Hoyt, p	237-182, 3.59	11
Dave Bancroft, ss	.279-32-591	9
Red Faber, p	254-213, 3.15	9
Lefty O'Doul, of	.349-113-542	9
Cy Williams, of	.292-251-1005	9
Jim Bottomley, 1b	.310-219-1422	8
Stan Hack, 3b	.301-57-642	8
Pepper Martin, of	.298-59-501	7
Red Rolfe, 3b	.289-69-497	7
Babe Adams, p	194-140, 2.75	6
Chief Bender, p	212-127, 2.45	6
Hank Gowdy, c	.270-21-322	6
Burleigh Grimes, p	270-212, 3.52	6
Travis Jackson, ss	.291-135-929	6
Eppa Rixey, p	266-251, 3.15	6
Home Run Baker, 3b	.307-96-987	4
Chick Hafey, of	.317-164-833	4
Bucky Harris, 2b	.274-9-506 (Manager)	4
Bob O'Farrell, c	.273-51-549	4
Muddy Ruel, c	.275-4-532	4
Bucky Walters, p	198-160, 3.30	4
Jimmie Wilson, c	.284-32-621	4
Earle Combs, of	.325-58-628	3
Ernie Lombardi, c	.306-190-990	3
Everett Scott, ss	.249-20-549	3
Casey Stengel, of	.284-60-535 (Manager)	3
George Burns, of	.287-41-611	2
Spud Chandler, p	109-43, 2.84	2
Jimmy Dykes, 3b	.280-108-1071	2
George Earnshaw, p	127-93, 4.38	2
Lew Fonseca, 1b	.316-31-485	2
Goose Goslin, of	.316-248-1609	2
Heine Groh, 3b	.292-26-566	2
Mel Harder, p	223-186, 3.80	2
Babe Herman, of	.324-181-997	2
Mike Higgins, 3b	.292-140-1075	2
Harry Hooper, of	.281-75-817	2
Miller Huggins, 2b	.265-9-318	2
Bob Meusel, of	.309-156-1067	2
Art Nehf, p	184-120, 3.20	2
Tommy Thevenow, ss	.247-2-456	2
Glenn Wright, ss	.294-94-723	2
Stan Coveleski, p	215-142, 2.88	1
Frankie Crosetti, ss	.245-98-649	1
Paul Derringer, p	223-212, 3.46	1
Jewel Ens, 2b	.290-1-24	1
Freddie Fitzsimmons, p	217-146, 3.51	1
Art Fletcher, ss	.277-32-675	1
Charlie Gelbert, ss	.267-17-350	1
Mike Gonzalez, c	.253-13-263	1
Red Lucas, p	157-135, 3.71	1
Dolf Luque, p	193-179, 3.24	1
Sherry Magee, of	.291-83-1176	1
Firpo Marberry, p	3.63, 101 saves	1
Stuffy McInnis, 1b	.308-20-1060	1
Bill McKechnie, 3b	.251-8-240 (Manager)	1
Clyde Milan, of	.285-17-617	1
Jo-Jo Moore, of	.298-79-513	1
Terry Moore, of	.280-80-513	1
Steve O'Neill, c	.263-13-537	1
Hub Pruett, p	4.63, 13 saves	1
Sam Rice, of	.322-34-1078	1
Eddie Rommel, p	3.54, 29 saves	1
Charlie Root, p	201-160, 3.59	1
Wally Schang, c	.284-59-710	1
George Selkirk, of	.290-108-576	1
Bill Sherdel, p	165-146, 3.72	1
Billy Southworth, of	.297-52-561	1
Bill Wambsganss, 2b	.259-7-519	1
Lloyd Waner, of	.316-27-598	1
Bill Werber, 3b	.271-78-539	1
Joe Wood, of	.283-23-325	1

Needed for election: 126

1951

BBWAA

Player, Position	Stats	Votes
Mel Ott, of	**.304-511-1860**	**197**
Jimmie Foxx, 1b	**.325-534-1921**	**179**
Paul Waner, of	.333-113-1309	162
Harry Heilmann, of	.342-183-1539	153
Bill Terry, 1b	.341-154-1078	148
Dizzy Dean, p	150-83, 3.02	145
Bill Dickey, c	.313-202-1209	118
Al Simmons, of	.334-307-1827	116
Rabbit Maranville, ss	.258-28-884	110
Ted Lyons, p	260-230, 3.67	71
Dazzy Vance, p	197-140, 3.24	70
Hank Greenberg, 1b	.313-331-1276	67
Gabby Hartnett, c	.297-236-1179	57
Joe Cronin, ss	.301-170-1424	44
Ray Schalk, c	.253-11-594	37
Chief Bender, p	212-127, 2.45	35
Ross Youngs, of	.322-42-592	34
Max Carey, of	.285-70-800	27
Tony Lazzeri, 2b	.292-178-1191	27
Hank Gowdy, c	.270-21-322	26
Lefty Gomez, p	189-102, 3.34	23
Edd Roush, of	.323-68-981	21
Hack Wilson, of	.307-244-1062	21
Pepper Martin, of	.298-59-501	19
Zack Wheat, of	.317-132-1248	19
Chuck Klein, of	.320-300-1201	15
Waite Hoyt, p	237-182, 3.59	13
Lefty O'Doul, of	.349-113-542	13
Babe Adams, p	194-140, 2.75	12
Dave Bancroft, ss	.279-32-591	9
Charlie Grimm, 1b	.290-79-1078	9
Bucky Harris, 2b	.274-9-506 (Manager)	9
Red Ruffing, p	273-225, 3.80	9
Home Run Baker, 3b	.307-96-987	8
Kiki Cuyler, of	.321-128-1065	8
Red Faber, p	254-213, 3.15	8
Bill McKechnie, 3b	.251-8-240 (Manager)	8
Casey Stengel, of	.284-60-535 (Manager)	8
Cy Williams, of	.292-251-1005	7
Jim Bottomley, 1b	.310-219-1422	6
Red Rolfe, 3b	.289-69-497	6
Burleigh Grimes, p	270-212, 3.52	5
Eppa Rixey, p	266-251, 3.15	5
Joe Wood, of	.283-23-325	5
Art Fletcher, ss	.277-32-675	4
Travis Jackson, ss	.291-135-929	4
Art Nehf, p	184-120, 3.20	4
Al Schacht, p	4.48, 2 saves	4
Billy Southworth, of	.297-52-561	4
Jimmy Dykes, 3b	.280-108-1071	3
Stan Hack, 3b	.301-57-642	3
Harry Hooper, of	.281-75-817	3
Dickie Kerr, p	53-34, 3.84	3
Ernie Lombardi, c	.306-190-990	3
Rube Marquard, p	201-177, 3.08	3
Stuffy McInnis, 1b	.308-20-1060	3
Steve O'Neill, c	.263-13-537	3
Duffy Lewis, of	.284-38-793	2
Sherry Magee, of	.291-83-1176	2
Everett Scott, ss	.249-20-549	2
George Selkirk, of	.290-108-576	2
Jimmie Wilson, c	.284-32-621	2
Dick Bartell, ss	.284-79-710	1
Spud Chandler, p	109-43, 2.84	1
Jack Coombs, p	158-110, 2.78	1
Wilbur Cooper, p	216-178, 2.89	1
Jake Daubert, 1b	.303-56-722	1
Paul Derringer, p	223-212, 3.46	1
Howard Ehmke, p	166-166, 3.75	1
Charlie Gelbert, ss	.267-17-350	1
Chick Hafey, of	.317-164-833	1
Mel Harder, p	223-186, 3.80	1
Babe Herman, of	.324-181-997	1
Mike Higgins, 3b	.292-140-1075	1
Tim Jordan, 1b	.261-32-232	1
Clyde Milan, of	.285-17-617	1
Satchel Paige, p	3.29, 32 saves	1
Hub Pruett, p	4.63, 13 saves	1
Sam Rice, of	.322-34-1078	1
Eddie Rommel, p	3.54, 29 saves	1
Dick Rudolph, p	121-108, 2.66	1
Muddy Ruel, c	.275-4-532	1
Bill Sherdel, p	165-146, 3.72	1
Lloyd Waner, of	.316-27-598	1
Glenn Wright, ss	.294-94-723	1

Needed for election: 170

1952

BBWAA

Player, Position	Stats	Votes
Harry Heilmann, of	**.342-183-1539**	**203**
Paul Waner, of	**.333-113-1309**	**195**
Bill Terry, 1b	.341-154-1078	155
Dizzy Dean, p	150-83, 3.02	152
Al Simmons, of	.334-307-1827	141
Bill Dickey, c	.313-202-1209	139
Rabbit Maranville, ss	.258-28-884	133
Dazzy Vance, p	197-140, 3.24	105
Ted Lyons, p	260-230, 3.67	101
Gabby Hartnett, c	.297-236-1179	77
Hank Greenberg, 1b	.313-331-1276	75
Chief Bender, p	212-127, 2.45	70
Joe Cronin, ss	.301-170-1424	48
Ray Schalk, c	.253-11-594	44
Max Carey, of	.285-70-800	36
Hank Gowdy, c	.270-21-322	34
Ross Youngs, of	.322-42-592	34
Pepper Martin, of	.298-59-501	31
Zack Wheat, of	.317-132-1248	30
Lefty Gomez, p	189-102, 3.34	29
Tony Lazzeri, 2b	.292-178-1191	29
Casey Stengel, of	.284-60-535 (Manager)	27
Edd Roush, of	.323-68-981	24
Hack Wilson, of	.307-244-1062	21
Chuck Klein, of	.320-300-1201	19
Lefty O'Doul, of	.349-113-542	19
Bucky Harris, 2b	.274-9-506 (Manager)	12
Waite Hoyt, p	237-182, 3.59	12
Dave Bancroft, ss	.279-32-591	11
Duffy Lewis, of	.284-38-793	11
Kiki Cuyler, of	.321-128-1065	10
Mel Harder, p	223-186, 3.80	10
Steve O'Neill, c	.263-13-537	10
Red Ruffing, p	273-225, 3.80	10
Babe Adams, p	194-140, 2.75	9
Red Faber, p	254-213, 3.15	9
Burleigh Grimes, p	270-212, 3.52	9
Dickie Kerr, p	53-34, 3.84	9
Rube Marquard, p	201-177, 3.08	9
Jim Bottomley, 1b	.310-219-1422	7
Jimmie Wilson, c	.284-32-621	7
Charlie Grimm, 1b	.290-79-1078	6
Jimmy Dykes, 3b	.280-108-1071	5
Tommy Henrich, of	.282-183-795	4
Red Rolfe, 3b	.289-69-497	4
Everett Scott, ss	.249-20-549	4
Cy Williams, of	.292-251-1005	4
Babe Herman, of	.324-181-997	3
Art Nehf, p	184-120, 3.20	3
Eppa Rixey, p	266-251, 3.15	3
Bucky Walters, p	198-160, 3.30	3
Earl Averill, of	.318-238-1165	2
Wilbur Cooper, p	216-178, 2.89	2
Al Lopez, c	.261-51-652 (Manager)	2
Roger Peckinpaugh, ss	.259-48-739	2
Eddie Rommel, p	3.54, 29 saves	2
Lloyd Waner, of	.316-27-598	2
Ben Chapman, of	.302-90-977	1
Earle Combs, of	.325-58-628	1
Frankie Crosetti, ss	.245-98-649	1
Leo Durocher, ss	.247-24-567 (Manager)	1
Howard Ehmke, p	166-166, 3.75	1
Mike Gonzalez, c	.253-13-263	1
Chick Hafey, of	.317-164-833	1
Travis Jackson, ss	.291-135-929	1
Dolf Luque, p	193-179, 3.24	1
Bob Meusel, of	.309-156-1067	1
Clyde Milan, of	.285-17-617	1
Hub Pruett, p	4.63, 13 saves	1
Sam Rice, of	.322-34-1078	1
Muddy Ruel, c	.275-4-532	1
George Selkirk, of	.290-108-576	1
Billy Southworth, of	.297-52-561	1
Bill Werber, 3b	.271-78-539	1
Glenn Wright, ss	.294-94-723	1

Needed for election: 176

1953

BBWAA

Player, Position	Stats	Votes
Dizzy Dean, p	**150-83, 3.02**	**209**
Al Simmons, of	**.334-307-1827**	**199**
Bill Terry, 1b	.341-154-1078	191
Bill Dickey, c	.313-202-1209	179
Rabbit Maranville, ss	.258-28-884	164
Dazzy Vance, p	197-140, 3.24	150
Ted Lyons, p	260-230, 3.67	139
Joe DiMaggio, of	.325-361-1537	117
Chief Bender, p	212-127, 2.45	104
Gabby Hartnett, c	.297-236-1179	104
Hank Greenberg, 1b	.313-331-1276	80
Joe Cronin, ss	.301-170-1424	69
Casey Stengel, of	.284-60-535 (Manager)	61
Hank Gowdy, c	.270-21-322	58
Max Carey, of	.285-70-800	55
Ray Schalk, c	.253-11-594	52
Pepper Martin, of	.298-59-501	43
Hack Wilson, of	.307-244-1062	43
Lefty Gomez, p	189-102, 3.34	35
Edd Roush, of	.323-68-981	32
Zack Wheat, of	.317-132-1248	32
Ross Youngs, of	.322-42-592	31
Tony Lazzeri, 2b	.292-178-1191	28
Red Ruffing, p	273-225, 3.80	24
Bucky Harris, 2b	.274-9-506 (Manager)	21
Duffy Lewis, of	.284-38-793	20
Rube Marquard, p	201-177, 3.08	19
Kiki Cuyler, of	.321-128-1065	18
Babe Adams, p	194-140, 2.75	17
Waite Hoyt, p	237-182, 3.59	14
Dickie Kerr, p	53-34, 3.84	13
Steve O'Neill, c	.263-13-537	13
Lefty O'Doul, of	.349-113-542	11
Dave Bancroft, ss	.279-32-591	10
Jim Bottomley, 1b	.310-219-1422	10
Tommy Henrich, of	.282-183-795	10
Bucky Walters, p	198-160, 3.30	10
Jimmie Wilson, c	.284-32-621	10
Wilbur Cooper, p	216-178, 2.89	9
Red Faber, p	254-213, 3.15	9
Burleigh Grimes, p	270-212, 3.52	9
Charlie Grimm, 1b	.290-79-1078	9
Mel Harder, p	223-186, 3.80	8
Muddy Ruel, c	.275-4-532	8
Jimmy Dykes, 3b	.280-108-1071	5
Red Rolfe, 3b	.289-69-497	5
Everett Scott, ss	.249-20-549	5
Jesse Haines, p	210-158, 3.64	4
Art Nehf, p	184-120, 3.20	4
Cy Williams, of	.292-251-1005	4
Earle Combs, of	.325-58-628	3
Howard Ehmke, p	166-166, 3.75	3
Sam Rice, of	.322-34-1078	3
Eppa Rixey, p	266-251, 3.15	3
Glenn Wright, ss	.294-94-723	3
Luke Appling, ss	.310-45-1116	2

Player, Position	Stats	Votes
Bobby Doerr, 2b	.288-223-1247	2
Chick Hafey, of	.317-164-833	2
Babe Herman, of	.324-181-997	2
Travis Jackson, ss	.291-135-929	2
Al Lopez, c	.261-51-652 (Manager)	2
Roger Peckinpaugh, ss	.259-48-739	2
Billy Southworth, of	.297-52-561	2
Nick Altrock, p	84-74, 2.67	1
Donie Bush, ss	.250-9-436	1
Mike Gonzalez, c	.253-13-263	1
Charlie Keller, of	.286-189-760	1
Johnny Kling, c	.272-20-513	1
Bill Lange, of	.330-39-578	1
Dolf Luque, p	193-179, 3.24	1
Clyde Milan, of	.285-17-617	1
Terry Moore, of	.280-80-513	1
Charley O'Leary, ss	.226-3-213	1
Hub Pruett, p	4.63, 13 saves	1
Dave Robertson, of	.287-47-364	1
Eddie Rommel, p	3.54, 29 saves	1
Germany Schaefer, 2b	.257-9-308	1
George Selkirk, of	.290-108-576	1
Bill Sherdel, p	165-146, 3.72	1
Arky Vaughan, ss	.318-96-926	1
Bill Wambsganss, 2b	.259-7-519	1
Needed for election: 198		

1954

BBWAA

Player, Position	Stats	Votes
Rabbit Maranville, ss	**.258-28-884**	**209**
Bill Dickey, c	**.313-202-1209**	**202**
Bill Terry, 1b	**.341-154-1078**	**195**
Joe DiMaggio, of	.325-361-1537	175
Ted Lyons, p	260-230, 3.67	170
Dazzy Vance, p	197-140, 3.24	158
Gabby Hartnett, c	.297-236-1179	151
Hank Greenberg, 1b	.313-331-1276	97
Joe Cronin, ss	.301-170-1424	85
Max Carey, of	.285-70-800	55
Ray Schalk, c	.253-11-594	54
Edd Roush, of	.323-68-981	52
Hank Gowdy, c	.270-21-322	51
Hack Wilson, of	.307-244-1062	48
Lefty Gomez, p	189-102, 3.34	38
Ross Youngs, of	.322-42-592	34
Zack Wheat, of	.317-132-1248	33
Tony Lazzeri, 2b	.292-178-1191	30
Red Ruffing, p	273-225, 3.80	29
Kiki Cuyler, of	.321-128-1065	20
Duffy Lewis, of	.284-38-793	20
Jim Bottomley, 1b	.310-219-1422	16
Rube Marquard, p	201-177, 3.08	15
Waite Hoyt, p	237-182, 3.59	14
Babe Adams, p	194-140, 2.75	13
Dickie Kerr, p	53-34, 3.84	13
Red Faber, p	254-213, 3.15	12
Chuck Klein, of	.320-300-1201	11
Dave Bancroft, ss	.279-32-591	10
Sam Rice, of	.322-34-1078	9
Jimmie Wilson, c	.284-32-621	8
Wilbur Cooper, p	216-178, 2.89	7
Art Nehf, p	184-120, 3.20	7
Jesse Haines, p	210-158, 3.64	6
Eppa Rixey, p	266-251, 3.15	5
Muddy Ruel, c	.275-4-532	5
Howard Ehmke, p	166-166, 3.75	4
Everett Scott, ss	.249-20-549	4
Bill Wambsganss, 2b	.259-7-519	4
Cy Williams, of	.292-251-1005	4
Clyde Milan, of	.285-17-617	3
Nick Altrock, p	84-74, 2.67	2
Chick Hafey, of	.317-164-833	2
Arky Vaughan, ss	.318-96-926	2
Lu Blue, 1b	.287-44-692	1
Ossie Bluege, 3b	.272-43-848	1

Player, Position	Stats	Votes
Goose Goslin, of	.316-248-1609	1
Heine Groh, 3b	.292-26-566	1
Babe Herman, of	.324-181-997	1
Travis Jackson, ss	.291-135-929	1
Roger Peckinpaugh, ss	.259-48-739	1
Joe Sewell, ss	.312-49-1051	1
Glenn Wright, ss	.294-94-723	1
Needed for election: 189		

1955

BBWAA

Player, Position	Stats	Votes
Joe DiMaggio, of	**.325-361-1537**	**223**
Ted Lyons, p	**260-230, 3.67**	**217**
Dazzy Vance, p	**197-140, 3.24**	**205**
Gabby Hartnett, c	**.297-236-1179**	**195**
Hank Greenberg, 1b	.313-331-1276	157
Joe Cronin, ss	.301-170-1424	135
Max Carey, of	.285-70-800	119
Ray Schalk, c	.253-11-594	113
Edd Roush, of	.323-68-981	97
Hank Gowdy, c	.270-21-322	90
Hack Wilson, of	.307-244-1062	81
Lefty Gomez, p	189-102, 3.34	71
Tony Lazzeri, 2b	.292-178-1191	66
Red Ruffing, p	273-225, 3.80	60
Zack Wheat, of	.317-132-1248	51
Ross Youngs, of	.322-42-592	48
Kiki Cuyler, of	.321-128-1065	35
Rube Marquard, p	201-177, 3.08	35
Duffy Lewis, of	.284-38-793	34
Waite Hoyt, p	237-182, 3.59	33
Sam Rice, of	.322-34-1078	28
Red Faber, p	254-213, 3.15	27
Jim Bottomley, 1b	.310-219-1422	26
Dickie Kerr, p	53-34, 3.84	25
Chuck Klein, of	.320-300-1201	25
Babe Adams, p	194-140, 2.75	24
Dave Bancroft, ss	.279-32-591	19
Jimmie Wilson, c	.284-32-621	13
Wilbur Cooper, p	216-178, 2.89	11
Muddy Ruel, c	.275-4-532	11
Jesse Haines, p	210-158, 3.64	10
Howard Ehmke, p	166-166, 3.75	8
Eppa Rixey, p	266-251, 3.15	8
Everett Scott, ss	.249-20-549	8
Goose Goslin, of	.316-248-1609	7
Art Nehf, p	184-120, 3.20	7
Clyde Milan, of	.285-17-617	6
Heine Groh, 3b	.292-26-566	5
Babe Herman, of	.324-181-997	5
Travis Jackson, ss	.291-135-929	5
Bill Wambsganss, 2b	.259-7-519	5
Chick Hafey, of	.317-164-833	4
Arky Vaughan, ss	.318-96-926	4
Glenn Wright, ss	.294-94-723	4
Luke Appling, ss	.310-45-1116	3
Burleigh Grimes, p	270-212, 3.52	3
Cy Williams, of	.292-251-1005	3
Earl Averill, of	.318-238-1165	2
George Earnshaw, p	127-93, 4.38	2
Joe Judge, 1b	.298-71-1034	2
Bob Meusel, of	.309-156-1067	2
Johnny Allen, p	142-75, 3.75	1
Charlie Berry, c	.267-23-256	1
Max Bishop, 2b	.271-41-379	1
Earle Combs, of	.325-58-628	1
Jake Daubert, 1b	.303-56-722	1
Paul Derringer, p	223-212, 3.46	1
Jimmy Dykes, 3b	.280-108-1071	1
Joe Gordon, 2b	.268-253-975	1
Mule Haas, of	.292-43-496	1
Sad Sam Jones, p	229-217, 3.84	1
Roger Peckinpaugh, ss	.259-48-739	1
Hal Schumacher, p	158-121, 3.36	1
Joe Sewell, ss	.312-49-1051	1

Player, Position	Stats	Votes
Bill Sherdel, p	105-140, 3.72	1
Needed for election: 189		

1956

BBWAA

Player, Position	Stats	Votes
Hank Greenberg, 1b	**.313-331-1276**	**164**
Joe Cronin, ss	**.301-170-1424**	**152**
Red Ruffing, p	273-225, 3.80	97
Edd Roush, of	.323-68-981	91
Lefty Gomez, p	189-102, 3.34	89
Hack Wilson, of	.307-244-1062	74
Max Carey, of	.285-70-800	65
Tony Lazzeri, 2b	.292-178-1191	64
Kiki Cuyler, of	.321-128-1065	55
Hank Gowdy, c	.270-21-322	49
Sam Rice, of	.322-34-1078	45
Chuck Klein, of	.320-300-1201	44
Jim Bottomley, 1b	.310-219-1422	42
Waite Hoyt, p	237-182, 3.59	37
Red Faber, p	254-213, 3.15	34
Joe Medwick, of	.324-205-1383	31
Eppa Rixey, p	266-251, 3.15	27
Goose Goslin, of	.316-248-1609	26
Zack Wheat, of	.317-132-1248	26
Burleigh Grimes, p	270-212, 3.52	25
Ross Youngs, of	.322-42-592	19
Lloyd Waner, of	.316-27-598	18
Jimmie Wilson, c	.284-32-621	17
Chick Hafey, of	.317-164-833	16
Muddy Ruel, c	.275-4-532	16
Dave Bancroft, ss	.279-32-591	15
Luke Appling, ss	.310-45-1116	14
Earle Combs, of	.325-58-628	14
Jesse Haines, p	210-158, 3.64	14
Travis Jackson, ss	.291-135-929	14
Heinie Manush, of	.330-110-1173	13
Paul Derringer, p	223-212, 3.46	12
Babe Herman, of	.324-181-997	11
Cy Williams, of	.292-251-1005	11
Arky Vaughan, ss	.318-96-926	9
Howard Ehmke, p	166-166, 3.75	8
Ernie Lombardi, c	.306-190-990	8
Wes Ferrell, p	193-128, 4.04	7
Pepper Martin, of	.298-59-501	7
Bobby Doerr, 2b	.288-223-1247	5
Lefty O'Doul, of	.349-113-542	5
Bucky Walters, p	198-160, 3.30	5
Doc Cramer, of	.296-37-842	4
Joe Gordon, 2b	.268-253-975	4
Earl Averill, of	.318-238-1165	3
Tommy Bridges, p	194-138, 3.57	3
George Earnshaw, p	127-93, 4.38	3
Freddie Fitzsimmons, p	217-146, 3.51	3
Freddy Lindstrom, 3b	.311-103-779	3
Frank McCormick, 1b	.299-128-954	3
Red Rolfe, 3b	.289-69-497	3
Joe Sewell, ss	.312-49-1051	3
Johnny Vander Meer, p	119-121, 3.44	3
Glenn Wright, ss	.294-94-723	3
Ossie Bluege, 3b	.272-43-848	2
Lou Boudreau, ss	.295-68-789	2
Guy Bush, p	176-136, 3.86	2
Mort Cooper, p	128-75, 2.97	2
Hughie Critz, 2b	.268-38-531	2
Lew Fonseca, 1b	.316-31-485	2
Tommy Henrich, of	.282-183-795	2
Billy Herman, 2b	.304-47-839	2
Joe Judge, 1b	.298-71-1034	2
Charlie Keller, of	.286-189-760	2
George Kelly, 1b	.297-148-1020	2
Hal Schumacher, p	158-121, 3.36	2
Riggs Stephenson, of	.336-63-773	2
Jim Tobin, p	105-112, 3.45	2
Wally Berger, of	.300-242-898	1
Max Bishop, 2b	.271-41-379	1

Dolph Camilli, 1b	.277-239-950	1
Spud Chandler, p	109-43, 2.84	1
Frankie Crosetti, ss	.245-98-649	1
Tony Cuccinello, 2b	.280-94-884	1
Joe Dugan, 3b	.280-42-571	1
Leo Durocher, ss	.247-24-567 (Manager)	1
Jimmy Dykes, 3b	.280-108-1071	1
Rick Ferrell, c	.281-28-734	1
Mule Haas, of	.292-43-496	1
Stan Hack, 3b	.301-57-642	1
Wild Bill Hallahan, p	102-94, 4.03	1
Bob Johnson, of	.296-288-1283	1
Sad Sam Jones, p	229-217, 3.84	1
Joe Kuhel, 1b	.277-131-1049	1
Al Lopez, c	.261-51-652 (Manager)	1
Dolf Luque, p	193-179, 3.24	1
Marty Marion, ss	.263-36-624	1
Bob Meusel, of	.309-156-1067	1
Johnny Mostil, of	.301-23-376	1
Allie Reynolds, p	182-107, 3.30	1
Phil Rizzuto, ss	.273-38-563	1
Al Schacht, p	4.48, 2 saves	1
Wally Schang, c	.284-59-710	1
Everett Scott, ss	.249-20-549	1
Bill Sherdel, p	165-146, 3.72	1
Earl Smith, c	.303-46-355	1
Gus Suhr, 1b	.279-84-818	1
Jim Turner, p	69-60, 3.22	1
George Uhle, p	200-166, 3.99	1
Bill Wambsganss, 2b	.259-7-519	1
Burgess Whitehead, 2b	.266-17-245	1
Earl Whitehill, p	218-185, 4.36	1
Ken Williams, of	.319-196-913	1

Needed for election: 145

1958

BBWAA

Player, Position	Stats	Votes
Max Carey, of	.285-70-800	136
Edd Roush, of	.323-68-981	112
Red Ruffing, p	273-225, 3.80	99
Hack Wilson, of	.307-244-1062	94
Kiki Cuyler, of	.321-128-1065	90
Sam Rice, of	.322-34-1078	90
Tony Lazzeri, 2b	.292-178-1191	80
Luke Appling, ss	.310-45-1116	77
Lefty Gomez, p	189-102, 3.34	76
Burleigh Grimes, p	270-212, 3.52	71
Red Faber, p	254-213, 3.15	68
Lou Boudreau, ss	.295-68-789	64
Jim Bottomley, 1b	.310-219-1422	57
Joe Medwick, of	.324-205-1383	50
Pepper Martin, of	.298-59-501	46
Hank Gowdy, c	.270-21-322	45
Bucky Harris, 2b	.274-9-506 (Manager)	45
Dave Bancroft, ss	.279-32-591	43
Lloyd Waner, of	.316-27-598	39
Waite Hoyt, p	237-182, 3.59	37
Chuck Klein, of	.320-300-1201	36
Johnny Vander Meer, p	119-121, 3.44	35
Earle Combs, of	.325-58-628	34
Stan Coveleski, p	215-142, 2.88	34
Al Lopez, c	.261-51-652 (Manager)	34
Bucky Walters, p	198-160, 3.30	33
Eppa Rixey, p	266-251, 3.15	32
Leo Durocher, ss	.247-24-567 (Manager)	28
Lefty O'Doul, of	.349-113-542	27
Jimmy Dykes, 3b	.280-108-1071	26
Goose Goslin, of	.316-248-1609	26
Charlie Grimm, 1b	.290-79-1078	26
Bobby Doerr, 2b	.288-223-1247	25
Jesse Haines, p	210-158, 3.64	22
Heinie Manush, of	.330-110-1173	22
Nick Altrock, p	84-74, 2.67	20
Billy Southworth, of	.297-52-561	18
Freddie Fitzsimmons, p	217-146, 3.51	16

Paul Derringer, p	223-212, 3.46	15
Dolf Luque, p	193-179, 3.24	15
Earl Averill, of	.318-238-1165	14
Babe Herman, of	.324-181-997	13
Art Nehf, p	184-120, 3.20	13
Red Rolfe, 3b	.289-69-497	13
Chick Hafey, of	.317-164-833	12
Terry Moore, of	.280-80-513	12
Schoolboy Rowe, p	158-101, 3.87	12
Tommy Bridges, p	194-138, 3.57	11
Joe Gordon, 2b	.268-253-975	11
Tommy Henrich, of	.282-183-795	11
Travis Jackson, ss	.291-135-929	11
Steve O'Neill, c	.263-13-537	10
Muddy Ruel, c	.275-4-532	10
Joe Judge, 1b	.298-71-1034	9
Charlie Keller, of	.286-189-760	9
Jack Quinn, p	247-218, 3.28	9
Wally Schang, c	.284-59-710	8
Birdie Tebbetts, c	.270-38-469	8
Glenn Wright, ss	.294-94-723	8
Howard Ehmke, p	166-166, 3.75	7
Billy Herman, 2b	.304-47-839	7
Eddie Rommel, p	3.54, 29 saves	7
Stan Hack, 3b	.301-57-642	6
Mel Harder, p	223-186, 3.80	6
Mike Higgins, 3b	.292-140-1075	6
Carl Mays, p	207-126, 2.92	6
Pete Reiser, of	.295-58-368	6
Charlie Root, p	201-160, 3.59	6
Arky Vaughan, ss	.318-96-926	6
Cy Williams, of	.292-251-1005	6
Joe Bush, p	196-183, 3.51	5
Frankie Crosetti, ss	.245-98-649	5
Joe Dugan, 3b	.280-42-571	5
Orval Grove, p	63-73, 3.78	5
Freddy Lindstrom, 3b	.311-103-779	5
Firpo Marberry, p	3.63, 101 saves	5
Bob Meusel, of	.309-156-1067	5
Max Bishop, 2b	.271-41-379	4
Dolph Camilli, 1b	.277-239-950	4
Cookie Lavagetto, 3b	.269-40-486	4
Ernie Lombardi, c	.306-190-990	4
Urban Shocker, p	187-117, 3.16	4
George Uhle, p	200-166, 3.99	4
Moe Berg, c	.243-6-206	3
Charlie Berry, c	.267-23-256	3
Mort Cooper, p	128-75, 2.97	3
Tony Cuccinello, 2b	.280-94-884	3
Bill Doak, p	169-157, 2.98	3
Lew Fonseca, 1b	.316-31-485	3
Mike Gonzalez, c	.253-13-263	3
Frankie Gustine, 2b	.265-38-480	3
Willie Kamm, 3b	.281-29-826	3
Bob O'Farrell, c	.273-51-549	3
Luke Sewell, c	.259-20-696	3
Bill Werber, 3b	.271-78-539	3
Jimmie Wilson, c	.284-32-621	3
Wally Berger, of	.300-242-898	2
Ossie Bluege, 3b	.272-43-848	2
Doc Cramer, of	.296-37-842	2
Tommy Holmes, of	.302-88-581	2
George Kelly, 1b	.297-148-1020	2
Ray Kremer, p	143-85, 3.76	2
Freddy Leach, of	.307-72-509	2
Marty McManus, 2b	.289-120-996	2
Lee Meadows, p	188-180, 3.38	2
Van Lingle Mungo, p	120-115, 3.47	2
Cy Perkins, c	.259-30-409	2
Bill Sherdel, p	165-146, 3.72	2
Lon Warneke, p	192-121, 3.18	2
Earl Whitehill, p	218-185, 4.36	2
Sparky Adams, 2b	.286-9-394	1
Jimmy Austin, 3b	.246-13-390	1
Dick Bartell, ss	.284-79-710	1
Larry Benton, p	127-128, 4.03	1
Ray Blades, of	.301-50-340	1
George Case, of	.282-21-377	1
Sam Chapman, of	.266-180-773	1
Watty Clark, p	111-97, 3.66	1

General Crowder, p	167-115, 4.12	1
Harry Danning, c	.285-57-397	1
Curt Davis, p	158-131, 3.42	1
Jumbo Elliott, p	63-74, 4.24	1
Rick Ferrell, c	.281-28-734	1
George Grantham, 2b	.302-105-712	1
Mule Haas, of	.292-43-496	1
Wild Bill Hallahan, p	102-94, 4.03	1
Bubbles Hargrave, c	.310-29-376	1
Billy Jurges, ss	.258-43-656	1
Ken Keltner, 3b	.276-163-852	1
Red Kress, ss	.286-89-799	1
Red Lucas, p	157-135, 3.71	1
Gus Mancuso, c	.265-53-543	1
Bing Miller, of	.312-117-990	1
Wally Moses, of	.291-89-679	1
Johnny Mostil, of	.301-23-376	1
Charley O'Leary, ss	.226-3-213	1
Monte Pearson, p	100-61, 4.00	1
Wally Pipp, 1b	.281-90-996	1
Hal Schumacher, p	158-121, 3.36	1
Jack Scott, p	103-109, 3.85	1
Joe Sewell, ss	.312-49-1051	1
Rip Sewell, p	143-97, 3.48	1
Riggs Stephenson, of	.336-63-773	1
Gus Suhr, 1b	.279-84-818	1
Clyde Sukeforth, c	.264-2-96	1
Rube Walberg, p	155-141, 4.17	1
Harry Walker, of	.296-10-214	1
Ken Williams, of	.319-196-913	1
Whit Wyatt, p	106-95, 3.79	1
Pep Young, 2b	.262-32-347	1
Tom Zachary, p	186-191, 3.73	1

Needed for election: 200

1960

BBWAA

Player, Position	Stats	Votes
Edd Roush, of	.323-68-981	146
Sam Rice, of	.322-34-1078	143
Eppa Rixey, p	266-251, 3.15	142
Burleigh Grimes, p	270-212, 3.52	92
Jim Bottomley, 1b	.310-219-1422	89
Red Ruffing, p	273-225, 3.80	86
Red Faber, p	254-213, 3.15	83
Luke Appling, ss	.310-45-1116	72
Kiki Cuyler, of	.321-128-1065	72
Hack Wilson, of	.307-244-1062	72
Tony Lazzeri, 2b	.292-178-1191	59
Lefty Gomez, p	189-102, 3.34	51
Johnny Mize, 1b	.312-359-1337	45
Lefty O'Doul, of	.349-113-542	45
Earle Combs, of	.325-58-628	43
Hank Gowdy, c	.270-21-322	38
Joe Medwick, of	.324-205-1383	38
Chuck Klein, of	.320-300-1201	37
Marty Marion, ss	.263-36-624	37
Lou Boudreau, ss	.295-68-789	35
Bucky Harris, 2b	.274-9-506 (Manager)	31
Johnny Vander Meer, p	119-121, 3.44	31
Dave Bancroft, ss	.279-32-591	30
Goose Goslin, of	.316-248-1609	30
Chick Hafey, of	.317-164-833	29
Waite Hoyt, p	237-182, 3.59	29
Pepper Martin, of	.298-59-501	29
Jimmy Dykes, 3b	.280-108-1071	27
Al Lopez, c	.261-51-652 (Manager)	26
Allie Reynolds, p	182-107, 3.30	24
Joe Sewell, ss	.312-49-1051	23
Lloyd Waner, of	.316-27-598	22
Jesse Haines, p	210-158, 3.64	20
Heinie Manush, of	.330-110-1173	20
Bucky Walters, p	198-160, 3.30	19
Nick Altrock, p	84-74, 2.67	18
Glenn Wright, ss	.294-94-723	18
Bobby Doerr, 2b	.288-223-1247	15

Player, Position	Stats	Votes
Joe Judge, 1b	.298-71-1034	15
Freddie Fitzsimmons, p	217-146, 3.51	13
Charlie Grimm, 1b	.290-79-1078	13
Howard Ehmke, p	166-166, 3.75	12
Mel Harder, p	223-186, 3.80	12
Eddie Rommel, p	3.54, 29 saves	12
Earl Averill, of	.318-238-1165	11
Joe Gordon, 2b	.268-253-975	11
Travis Jackson, ss	.291-135-929	11
Wally Schang, c	.284-59-710	11
Hal Schumacher, p	158-121, 3.36	11
Cy Williams, of	.292-251-1005	11
Leo Durocher, ss	.247-24-567 (Manager)	10
Tommy Henrich, of	.282-183-795	10
Bob Meusel, of	.309-156-1067	10
Red Rolfe, 3b	.289-69-497	10
Arky Vaughan, ss	.318-96-926	10
Muddy Ruel, c	.275-4-532	9
Frankie Crosetti, ss	.245-98-649	8
Paul Derringer, p	223-212, 3.46	8
Joe Dugan, 3b	.280-42-571	8
Wes Ferrell, p	193-128, 4.04	8
Pete Reiser, of	.295-58-368	8
Harry Brecheen, p	133-92, 2.92	7
Orval Grove, p	63-73, 3.78	7
Babe Herman, of	.324-181-997	7
Charlie Keller, of	.286-189-760	7
Terry Moore, of	.280-80-513	7
Stan Hack, 3b	.301-57-642	6
Freddy Lindstrom, 3b	.311-103-779	6
Ernie Lombardi, c	.306-190-990	6
Bing Miller, of	.312-117-990	6
Bobo Newsom, p	211-222, 3.98	6
Jimmie Wilson, c	.284-32-621	6
Moe Berg, c	.243-6-206	5
Max Bishop, 2b	.271-41-379	5
George Kelly, 1b	.297-148-1020	5
Tommy Bridges, p	194-138, 3.57	4
Dom DiMaggio, of	.298-87-618	4
Dolf Luque, p	193-179, 3.24	4
Riggs Stephenson, of	.336-63-773	4
George Uhle, p	200-166, 3.99	4
Lon Warneke, p	192-121, 3.18	4
Ossie Bluege, 3b	.272-43-848	3
Dolph Camilli, 1b	.277-239-950	3
Lew Fonseca, 1b	.316-31-485	3
Mike Higgins, 3b	.292-140-1075	3
Red Kress, ss	.286-89-799	3
Bob O'Farrell, c	.273-51-549	3
Schoolboy Rowe, p	158-101, 3.87	3
Luke Sewell, c	.259-20-696	3
Eddie Stanky, 2b	.268-29-364	3
Earl Whitehill, p	218-185, 4.36	3
Hank Edwards, of	.280-51-276	2
Bob Elliott, 3b	.289-170-1195	2
Mike Gonzalez, c	.253-13-263	2
Wild Bill Hallahan, p	102-94, 4.03	2
Tommy Holmes, of	.302-88-581	2
Cookie Lavagetto, 3b	.269-40-486	2
Dutch Leonard, p	191-181, 3.25	2
Firpo Marberry, p	3.63, 101 saves	2
Marty McManus, 2b	.289-120-996	2
Van Lingle Mungo, p	120-115, 3.47	2
Jack Quinn, p	247-218, 3.28	2
Charlie Root, p	201-160, 3.59	2
Bill Sherdel, p	165-146, 3.72	2
Sparky Adams, 2b	.286-9-394	1
Dick Bartell, ss	.284-79-710	1
Ray Blades, of	.301-50-340	1
George Case, of	.282-21-377	1
Mort Cooper, p	128-75, 2.97	1
Doc Cramer, of	.296-37-842	1
General Crowder, p	167-115, 4.12	1
Harry Danning, c	.285-57-397	1
Rick Ferrell, c	.281-28-734	1
Heine Groh, 3b	.292-26-566	1
Mule Haas, of	.292-43-496	1
Bubbles Hargrave, c	.310-29-376	1
Addie Joss, p	160-97, 1.89	1
Willie Kamm, 3b	.281-29-826	1
Ken Keltner, 3b	.276-163-852	1
Freddy Leach, of	.307-72-509	1
Hans Lobert, 3b	.274-32-482	1
Wally Moses, of	.291-89-679	1
Bill Nicholson, of	.268-235-948	1
Charley O'Leary, ss	.226-3-213	1
Johnny Pesky, ss	.307-17-404	1
Preacher Roe, p	127-84, 3.43	1
Sibby Sisti, 2b	.244-27-260	1
Gus Suhr, 1b	.279-84-818	1
Birdie Tebbetts, c	.270-38-469	1
Rube Walberg, p	155-141, 4.17	1
Tom Zachary, p	186-191, 3.73	1

Needed for election: 202

1962

BBWAA

Player, Position	Stats	Votes
Bob Feller, p	**266-162, 3.25**	**150**
Jackie Robinson, 2b	**.311-137-734**	**124**
Sam Rice, of	.322-34-1078	81
Red Ruffing, p	273-225, 3.80	72
Eppa Rixey, p	266-251, 3.15	49
Luke Appling, ss	.310-45-1116	48
Phil Rizzuto, ss	.273-38-563	44
Burleigh Grimes, p	270-212, 3.52	43
Hack Wilson, of	.307-244-1062	39
Joe Medwick, of	.324-205-1383	34
Kiki Cuyler, of	.321-128-1065	31
Red Faber, p	254-213, 3.15	30
Jim Bottomley, 1b	.310-219-1422	20
Lefty Gomez, p	189-102, 3.34	20
Waite Hoyt, p	237-182, 3.59	18
Chuck Klein, of	.320-300-1201	18
Marty Marion, ss	.263-36-624	16
Heinie Manush, of	.330-110-1173	15
Allie Reynolds, p	182-107, 3.30	15
Goose Goslin, of	.316-248-1609	14
Johnny Mize, 1b	.312-359-1337	14
Lefty O'Doul, of	.349-113-542	13
Lou Boudreau, ss	.295-68-789	12
Al Lopez, c	.261-51-652 (Manager)	11
Bobby Doerr, 2b	.288-223-1247	10
Tony Lazzeri, 2b	.292-178-1191	8
Chick Hafey, of	.317-164-833	7
Mel Harder, p	223-186, 3.80	7
Freddy Lindstrom, 3b	.311-103-779	7
Earle Combs, of	.325-58-628	6
Jimmy Dykes, 3b	.280-108-1071	6
Pepper Martin, of	.298-59-501	6
Arky Vaughan, ss	.318-96-926	6
Ralph Kiner, of	.279-369-1015	5
Ernie Lombardi, c	.306-190-990	5
Johnny Vander Meer, p	119-121, 3.44	5
Bucky Walters, p	198-160, 3.30	5
Lloyd Waner, of	.316-27-598	5
Joe Gordon, 2b	.268-253-975	4
Billy Herman, 2b	.304-47-839	4
Hal Newhouser, p	207-150, 3.06	4
Jimmie Wilson, c	.284-32-621	4
Earl Averill, of	.318-238-1165	3
Jesse Haines, p	210-158, 3.64	3
Tommy Henrich, of	.282-183-795	3
Bobo Newsom, p	211-222, 3.98	3
Phil Cavarretta, 1b	.293-95-920	2
Spud Chandler, p	109-43, 2.84	2
Dom DiMaggio, of	.298-87-618	2
Charlie Grimm, 1b	.290-79-1078	2
Firpo Marberry, p	3.63, 101 saves	2
Lon Warneke, p	192-121, 3.18	2
Tommy Bridges, p	194-138, 3.57	2
George Case, of	.282-21-377	1
Billy Cox, 3b	.262-66-351	1
Doc Cramer, of	.296-37-842	1
Leo Durocher, ss	.247-24-567 (Manager)	1
Bob Elliott, 3b	.289-170-1195	1
Wes Ferrell, p	193-128, 4.04	1
Freddie Fitzsimmons, p	217-146, 3.51	1
Fred Hutchinson, p	95-71, 3.73	1
Travis Jackson, ss	.291-135-929	1
Charlie Keller, of	.286-189-760	1
George Kelly, 1b	.297-148-1020	1
Frank McCormick, 1b	.299-128-954	1
Terry Moore, of	.280-80-513	1
Vic Raschi, p	132-66, 3.72	1
Preacher Roe, p	127-84, 3.43	1
Red Rolfe, 3b	.289-69-497	1
Johnny Sain, p	139-116, 3.49	1
Hal Schumacher, p	158-121, 3.36	1
Luke Sewell, c	.259-20-696	1
Rip Sewell, p	143-97, 3.48	1
Riggs Stephenson, of	.336-63-773	1
Dixie Walker, of	.306-105-1023	1
Glenn Wright, ss	.294-94-723	1
Rudy York, 1b	.275-277-1152	1

Needed for election: 120

1964

BBWAA

Player, Position	Stats	Votes
Luke Appling, ss	.310-45-1116	142
Red Ruffing, p	273-225, 3.80	141
Roy Campanella, c	.276-242-856	115
Joe Medwick, of	.324-205-1383	108
Pee Wee Reese, ss	.269-126-885	73
Lou Boudreau, ss	.295-68-789	68
Al Lopez, c	.261-51-652 (Manager)	57
Chuck Klein, of	.320-300-1201	56
Johnny Mize, 1b	.312-359-1337	54
Mel Harder, p	223-186, 3.80	51
Johnny Vander Meer, p	119-121, 3.44	51
Marty Marion, ss	.263-36-624	50
Lloyd Waner, of	.316-27-598	47
Phil Rizzuto, ss	.273-38-563	45
Allie Reynolds, p	182-107, 3.30	35
Bucky Walters, p	198-160, 3.30	35
George Kell, 3b	.306-78-870	33
Ernie Lombardi, c	.306-190-990	33
Ralph Kiner, of	.279-369-1015	31
Joe Gordon, 2b	.268-253-975	30
Billy Herman, 2b	.304-47-839	26
Hal Newhouser, p	207-150, 3.06	26
Bobby Doerr, 2b	.288-223-1247	24
Bob Lemon, p	207-128, 3.23	24
Phil Cavarretta, 1b	.293-95-920	22
Pepper Martin, of	.298-59-501	19
Bobo Newsom, p	211-222, 3.98	17
Arky Vaughan, ss	.318-96-926	17
Tommy Bridges, p	194-138, 3.57	15
Leo Durocher, ss	.247-24-567 (Manager)	15
Terry Moore, of	.280-80-513	14
Tommy Henrich, of	.282-183-795	13
Sal Maglie, p	119-62, 3.15	13
Lon Warneke, p	192-121, 3.18	13
Doc Cramer, of	.296-37-842	12
Dom DiMaggio, of	.298-87-618	12
Charlie Keller, of	.286-189-760	12
Fred Hutchinson, p	95-71, 3.73	10
Hal Schumacher, p	158-121, 3.36	10
Rudy York, 1b	.275-277-1152	10
Vic Raschi, p	132-66, 3.72	8
Spud Chandler, p	109-43, 2.84	6
Frank McCormick, 1b	.299-128-954	6
Dixie Walker, of	.306-105-1023	6
Bob Elliott, 3b	.289-170-1195	4
Virgil Trucks, p	177-135, 3.39	4
Ellis Kinder, p	3.43, 102 saves	3
Johnny Sain, p	139-116, 3.49	3
George Case, of	.282-21-377	2
Art Houtteman, p	87-91, 4.14	2
Wes Westrum, c	.217-96-315	2
Jim Wilson, p	86-89, 4.01	2

Steve Gromek, p	123-108, 3.41	1
Bob Kuzava, p	4.05, 13 saves	1
Eddie Miksis, 2b	.236-44-228	1
Ron Northey, of	.276-108-513	1
Rip Sewell, p	143-97, 3.48	1
Roy Smalley, ss	.227-61-305	1
Dizzy Trout, p	170-161, 3.23	1

Needed for election: 151

1964

BBWAA Runoff

Player, Position	Stats	Votes
Luke Appling, ss	**.310-45-1116**	**189**
Red Ruffing, p	273-225, 3.80	184
Roy Campanella, c	.276-242-856	138
Joe Medwick, of	.324-205-1383	130
Pee Wee Reese, ss	.269-126-885	47
Lou Boudreau, ss	.295-68-789	43
Al Lopez, c	.261-51-652 (Manager)	34
Johnny Vander Meer, p	119-121, 3.44	20
Chuck Klein, of	.320-300-1201	18
Marty Marion, ss	.263-36-624	17
Mel Harder, p	223-186, 3.80	14
Johnny Mize, 1b	.312-359-1337	12
Lloyd Waner, of	.316-27-598	12
Phil Rizzuto, ss	.273-38-563	11
Billy Herman, 2b	.304-47-839	9
Ernie Lombardi, c	.306-190-990	9
George Kell, 3b	.306-78-870	8
Bucky Walters, p	198-160, 3.30	8
Allie Reynolds, p	182-107, 3.30	6
Arky Vaughan, ss	.318-96-926	6
Bobby Doerr, 2b	.288-223-1247	5
Pepper Martin, of	.298-59-501	5
Ralph Kiner, of	.279-369-1015	3
Bob Lemon, p	207-128, 3.23	3
Hal Newhouser, p	207-150, 3.06	3
Leo Durocher, ss	.247-24-567 (Manager)	2
Tommy Bridges, p	194-138, 3.57	1
Phil Cavarretta, 1b	.293-95-920	1
Joe Gordon, 2b	.268-253-975	1
Bobo Newsom, p	211-222, 3.98	1

Needed for election: 169 (one player maximum)

1966

BBWAA

Player, Position	Stats	Votes
Ted Williams, of	**.344-521-1839**	**282**
Red Ruffing, p	273-225, 3.80	208
Roy Campanella, c	.276-242-856	197
Joe Medwick, of	.324-205-1383	187
Lou Boudreau, ss	.295-68-789	115
Al Lopez, c	.261-51-652 (Manager)	109
Enos Slaughter, of	.300-169-1304	100
Pee Wee Reese, ss	.269-126-885	95
Marty Marion, ss	.263-36-624	86
Johnny Mize, 1b	.312-359-1337	81
Ralph Kiner, of	.279-369-1015	74
Johnny Vander Meer, p	119-121, 3.44	72
Allie Reynolds, p	182-107, 3.30	60
Bucky Walters, p	198-160, 3.30	56
Phil Rizzuto, ss	.273-38-563	54
Arky Vaughan, ss	.318-96-926	36
Mel Harder, p	223-186, 3.80	34
Ernie Lombardi, c	.306-190-990	34
Hal Newhouser, p	207-150, 3.06	32
Joe Gordon, 2b	.268-253-975	31
Bobby Doerr, 2b	.288-223-1247	30
George Kell, 3b	.306-78-870	29
Billy Herman, 2b	.304-47-839	28
Bobo Newsom, p	211-222, 3.98	25
Bob Lemon, p	207-128, 3.23	21
Mickey Vernon, 1b	.286-172-1311	20

Al Dark, ss	.289-126-757	17
Tommy Bridges, p	194-138, 3.57	16
Bobby Thomson, of	.270-264-1026	12
Phil Cavarretta, 1b	.293-95-920	9
Larry Doby, of	.283-253-970	7
Don Newcombe, p	149-90, 3.56	7
Carl Erskine, p	122-78, 4.00	6
Jim Hegan, c	.228-92-525	5
Gil McDougald, 2b	.276-112-576	5
Grady Hatton, 3b	.254-91-533	4
Whitey Lockman, 1b	.279-114-563	4
Hank Sauer, of	.266-288-876	4
Del Ennis, of	.284-288-1284	3
Carl Furillo, of	.299-192-1058	2
Marv Grissom, p	3.41, 58 saves	2
Morrie Martin, p	4.29, 15 saves	2
Andy Pafko, of	.285-213-976	2
Del Rice, c	.237-79-441	2
Bobby Adams, 3b	.269-37-303	1
Chico Carrasquel, ss	.258-55-474	1
Jim Hearn, p	109-89, 3.81	1
Solly Hemus, ss	.273-51-263	1
Bob Porterfield, p	87-97, 3.79	1

Needed for election: 227

1967

BBWAA

Player, Position	Stats	Votes
Joe Medwick, of	.324-205-1383	212
Red Ruffing, p	273-225, 3.80	212
Roy Campanella, c	.276-242-856	204
Lou Boudreau, ss	.295-68-789	143
Ralph Kiner, of	.279-369-1015	124
Enos Slaughter, of	.300-169-1304	123
Al Lopez, c	.261-51-652 (Manager)	114
Marty Marion, ss	.263-36-624	90
Johnny Mize, 1b	.312-359-1337	89
Pee Wee Reese, ss	.269-126-885	89
Johnny Vander Meer, p	119-121, 3.44	87
Allie Reynolds, p	182-107, 3.30	77
Phil Rizzuto, ss	.273-38-563	71
Joe Gordon, 2b	.268-253-975	66
Bucky Walters, p	198-160, 3.30	65
Hal Newhouser, p	207-150, 3.06	62
Billy Herman, 2b	.304-47-839	59
Mel Harder, p	223-186, 3.80	52
Arky Vaughan, ss	.318-96-926	46
Ernie Lombardi, c	.306-190-990	43
George Kell, 3b	.306-78-870	40
Al Dark, ss	.289-126-757	38
Bobby Doerr, 2b	.288-223-1247	35
Bob Lemon, p	207-128, 3.23	35
Hank Bauer, of	.277-164-703	23
Bobo Newsom, p	211-222, 3.98	19
Don Newcombe, p	149-90, 3.56	18
Phil Cavarretta, 1b	.293-95-920	15
Mickey Vernon, 1b	.286-172-1311	14
Larry Doby, of	.283-253-970	10
Bobby Thomson, of	.270-264-1026	10
Ted Kluszewski, 1b	.298-279-1028	9
Gil McDougald, 2b	.276-112-576	4
Jackie Jensen, of	.279-199-929	3
Terry Moore, of	.280-80-513	3
Del Ennis, of	.284-288-1284	2
Carl Furillo, of	.299-192-1058	2
Jim Hegan, c	.228-92-525	2
Earl Torgeson, 1b	.265-149-740	2
Elmer Valo, of	.282-58-601	2
Clint Courtney, c	.268-38-313	1
Walt Dropo, 1b	.270-152-704	1
Ned Garver, p	129-157, 3.73	1
Grady Hatton, 3b	.254-91-533	1
Jim Hearn, p	109-89, 3.81	1
Billy Martin, 2b	.257-64-333	1
Andy Pafko, of	.285-213-976	1

Needed for election: 219

1967

BBWAA Runoff

Player, Position	Stats	Votes
Red Ruffing, p	**273-225, 3.80**	**266**
Joe Medwick, of	.324-205-1383	248
Roy Campanella, c	.276-242-856	170
Lou Boudreau, ss	.295-68-789	68
Al Lopez, c	.261-51-652 (Manager)	50
Enos Slaughter, of	.300-169-1304	48
Ralph Kiner, of	.279-369-1015	41
Johnny Vander Meer, p	119-121, 3.44	35
Ernie Lombardi, c	.306-190-990	25
Bucky Walters, p	198-160, 3.30	24
Marty Marion, ss	.263-36-624	22
Allie Reynolds, p	182-107, 3.30	19
Arky Vaughan, ss	.318-96-926	19
Pee Wee Reese, ss	.269-126-885	16
Bobby Doerr, 2b	.288-223-1247	15
Mel Harder, p	223-186, 3.80	14
Billy Herman, 2b	.304-47-839	14
Johnny Mize, 1b	.312-359-1337	14
Phil Rizzuto, ss	.273-38-563	14
Joe Gordon, 2b	.268-253-975	13
Hal Newhouser, p	207-150, 3.06	13
George Kell, 3b	.306-78-870	11
Hank Bauer, of	.277-164-703	9
Al Dark, ss	.289-126-757	7
Bob Lemon, p	207-128, 3.23	7
Bobo Newsom, p	211-222, 3.98	6
Phil Cavarretta, 1b	.293-95-920	4
Don Newcombe, p	149-90, 3.56	2
Mickey Vernon, 1b	.286-172-1311	2
Larry Doby, of	.283-253-970	1
Bobby Thomson, of	.270-264-1026	1

Needed for election: 230 (one player maximum)

1968

BBWAA

Player, Position	Stats	Votes
Joe Medwick, of	**.324-205-1383**	**240**
Roy Campanella, c	.276-242-856	205
Lou Boudreau, ss	.295-68-789	146
Enos Slaughter, of	.300-169-1304	129
Ralph Kiner, of	.279-369-1015	118
Johnny Mize, 1b	.312-359-1337	103
Allie Reynolds, p	182-107, 3.30	95
Marty Marion, ss	.263-36-624	89
Arky Vaughan, ss	.318-96-926	82
Pee Wee Reese, ss	.269-126-885	81
Johnny Vander Meer, p	119-121, 3.44	79
Joe Gordon, 2b	.268-253-975	77
Phil Rizzuto, ss	.273-38-563	74
Hal Newhouser, p	207-150, 3.06	67
Bucky Walters, p	198-160, 3.30	67
Bobby Doerr, 2b	.288-223-1247	48
George Kell, 3b	.306-78-870	47
Bob Lemon, p	207-128, 3.23	47
Al Dark, ss	.289-126-757	36
Terry Moore, of	.280-80-513	33
Phil Cavarretta, 1b	.293-95-920	23
Tommy Henrich, of	.282-183-795	22
Bobo Newsom, p	211-222, 3.98	22
Mickey Vernon, 1b	.286-172-1311	22
Frankie Crosetti, ss	.245-98-649	15
Ted Kluszewski, 1b	.298-279-1028	14
Bobby Thomson, of	.270-264-1026	13
Charlie Keller, of	.286-189-760	11
Sal Maglie, p	119-62, 3.15	11
Carl Erskine, p	122-78, 4.00	9
Don Newcombe, p	149-90, 3.56	9
Walker Cooper, c	.285-173-812	8
Dom DiMaggio, of	.298-87-618	8
Johnny Sain, p	139-116, 3.49	7
Richie Ashburn, of	.308-29-586	6

Schoolboy Rowe, p	158-101, 3.87	6
Dixie Walker, of	.306-105-1023	6
Ewell Blackwell, p	82-78, 3.30	5
Dutch Leonard, p	191-181, 3.25	5
Gil McDougald, 2b	.276-112-576	4
Wally Moses, of	.291-89-679	4
Harry Brecheen, p	133-92, 2.92	3
Jackie Jensen, of	.279-199-929	3
Frank McCormick, 1b	.299-128-954	3
Augie Galan, of	.287-100-830	2
Ed Lopat, p	166-112, 3.21	2
Preacher Roe, p	127-84, 3.43	2
Vic Raschi, p	132-66, 3.72	1
Needed for election: 213		

1969

BBWAA

Player, Position	Stats	Votes
Stan Musial, of	**.331-475-1951**	**317**
Roy Campanella, c	**.276-242-856**	**270**
Lou Boudreau, ss	.295-68-789	218
Ralph Kiner, of	.279-369-1015	137
Enos Slaughter, of	.300-169-1304	128
Johnny Mize, 1b	.312-359-1337	116
Marty Marion, ss	.263-36-624	112
Allie Reynolds, p	182-107, 3.30	98
Joe Gordon, 2b	.268-253-975	97
Johnny Vander Meer, p	119-121, 3.44	95
Early Wynn, p	300-244, 3.54	95
Pee Wee Reese, ss	.269-126-885	89
Gil Hodges, 1b	.273-370-1274	82
Hal Newhouser, p	207-150, 3.06	82
Phil Rizzuto, ss	.273-38-563	78
Red Schoendienst, 2b	.289-84-773	65
Bobby Doerr, 2b	.288-223-1247	62
George Kell, 3b	.306-78-870	60
Bob Lemon, p	207-128, 3.23	56
Tommy Henrich, of	.282-183-795	50
Al Dark, ss	.289-126-757	48
Phil Cavarretta, 1b	.293-95-920	37
Bobo Newsom, p	211-222, 3.98	32
Mickey Vernon, 1b	.286-172-1311	21
Bucky Walters, p	198-160, 3.30	20
Schoolboy Rowe, p	158-101, 3.87	17
Charlie Keller, of	.286-189-760	14
Dom DiMaggio, of	.298-87-618	13
Ewell Blackwell, p	82-78, 3.30	11
Ted Kluszewski, 1b	.298-279-1028	11
Richie Ashburn, of	.308-29-586	10
Dixie Walker, of	.306-105-1023	9
Johnny Sain, p	139-116, 3.49	8
Minnie Minoso, of	.298-186-1023	6
Bobby Thomson, of	.270-264-1026	6
Walker Cooper, c	.285-173-812	5
Carl Erskine, p	122-78, 4.00	4
Dutch Leonard, p	191-181, 3.25	4
Wally Moses, of	.291-89-679	4
Mort Cooper, p	128-75, 2.97	3
Gil McDougald, 2b	.276-112-576	3
Don Newcombe, p	149-90, 3.56	3
Vic Raschi, p	132-66, 3.72	3
Harry Brecheen, p	133-92, 2.92	2
Ed Lopat, p	166-112, 3.21	2
Jackie Jensen, of	.279-199-929	1
Needed for election: 255		

1970

BBWAA

Player, Position	Stats	Votes
Lou Boudreau, ss	**.295-68-789**	**232**
Ralph Kiner, of	.279-369-1015	167
Gil Hodges, 1b	.273-370-1274	145
Early Wynn, p	300-244, 3.54	140

Enos Slaughter, of	.300-169-1304	133
Johnny Mize, 1b	.312-359-1337	126
Marty Marion, ss	.263-36-624	120
Pee Wee Reese, ss	.269-126-885	97
Red Schoendienst, 2b	.289-84-773	97
George Kell, 3b	.306-78-870	90
Allie Reynolds, p	182-107, 3.30	89
Johnny Vander Meer, p	119-121, 3.44	88
Hal Newhouser, p	207-150, 3.06	80
Joe Gordon, 2b	.268-253-975	79
Phil Rizzuto, ss	.273-38-563	79
Bobby Doerr, 2b	.288-223-1247	75
Bob Lemon, p	207-128, 3.23	70
Tommy Henrich, of	.282-183-795	62
Al Dark, ss	.289-126-757	55
Phil Cavarretta, 1b	.293-95-920	51
Duke Snider, of	.295-407-1333	51
Bucky Walters, p	198-160, 3.30	29
Dom DiMaggio, of	.298-87-618	15
Ewell Blackwell, p	82-78, 3.30	14
Bobo Newsom, p	211-222, 3.98	12
Richie Ashburn, of	.308-29-586	11
Mickey Vernon, 1b	.286-172-1311	10
Walker Cooper, c	.285-173-812	9
Johnny Sain, p	139-116, 3.49	9
Ted Kluszewski, 1b	.298-279-1028	8
Charlie Keller, of	.286-189-760	7
Bobby Shantz, p	3.38, 48 saves	7
Dutch Leonard, p	191-181, 3.25	5
Wally Moses, of	.291-89-679	5
Don Newcombe, p	149-90, 3.56	5
Billy Pierce, p	211-169, 3.27	5
Bobby Thomson, of	.270-264-1026	4
Harry Brecheen, p	133-92, 2.92	3
Augie Galan, of	.287-100-830	3
Carl Erskine, p	122-78, 4.00	2
Carl Furillo, of	.299-192-1058	2
Vic Wertz, of	.277-266-1178	2
Jackie Jensen, of	.279-199-929	1
Ed Lopat, p	166-112, 3.21	1
Gil McDougald, 2b	.276-112-576	1
Preacher Roe, p	127-84, 3.43	1
Needed for election: 225		

1971

BBWAA

Player, Position	Stats	Votes
Yogi Berra, c	.285-358-1430	242
Early Wynn, p	300-244, 3.54	240
Ralph Kiner, of	.279-369-1015	212
Gil Hodges, 1b	.273-370-1274	180
Enos Slaughter, of	.300-169-1304	165
Johnny Mize, 1b	.312-359-1337	157
Pee Wee Reese, ss	.269-126-885	127
Marty Marion, ss	.263-36-624	123
Red Schoendienst, 2b	.289-84-773	123
Allie Reynolds, p	182-107, 3.30	110
George Kell, 3b	.306-78-870	105
Johnny Vander Meer, p	119-121, 3.44	98
Hal Newhouser, p	207-150, 3.06	94
Phil Rizzuto, ss	.273-38-563	92
Bob Lemon, p	207-128, 3.23	90
Duke Snider, of	.295-407-1333	89
Phil Cavarretta, 1b	.293-95-920	83
Bobby Doerr, 2b	.288-223-1247	78
Al Dark, ss	.289-126-757	54
Nellie Fox, 2b	.288-35-790	39
Bobo Newsom, p	211-222, 3.98	17
Dom DiMaggio, of	.298-87-618	15
Charlie Keller, of	.286-189-760	14
Mickey Vernon, 1b	.286-172-1311	12
Johnny Sain, p	139-116, 3.49	11
Richie Ashburn, of	.308-29-586	10
Harvey Haddix, p	136-113, 3.63	10
Ted Kluszewski, 1b	.298-279-1028	9
Don Newcombe, p	149-90, 3.56	8

Harry Brecheen, p	133-92, 2.92	7
Walker Cooper, c	.285-173-812	7
Wally Moses, of	.291-89-679	7
Billy Pierce, p	211-169, 3.27	7
Carl Furillo, of	.299-192-1058	5
Bobby Shantz, p	3.38, 48 saves	5
Ed Lopat, p	166-112, 3.21	4
Gil McDougald, 2b	.276-112-576	4
Roy Sievers, 1b	.267-318-1147	4
Bobby Thomson, of	.270-264-1026	4
Carl Erskine, p	122-78, 4.00	3
Dutch Leonard, p	191-181, 3.25	3
Preacher Roe, p	127-84, 3.43	3
Jackie Jensen, of	.279-199-929	2
Wally Moon, of	.289-142-661	2
Vic Power, 1b	.284-126-658	2
Vic Raschi, p	132-66, 3.72	2
Vic Wertz, of	.277-266-1178	2
Bill Bruton, of	.273-94-545	1
Needed for election: 270		

1972

BBWAA

Player, Position	Stats	Votes
Sandy Koufax, p	**165-87, 2.76**	**344**
Yogi Berra, c	**.285-358-1430**	**339**
Early Wynn, p	**300-244, 3.54**	**301**
Ralph Kiner, of	.279-369-1015	235
Gil Hodges, 1b	.273-370-1274	161
Johnny Mize, 1b	.312-359-1337	157
Enos Slaughter, of	.300-169-1304	149
Pee Wee Reese, ss	.269-126-885	129
Marty Marion, ss	.263-36-624	120
Bob Lemon, p	207-128, 3.23	117
George Kell, 3b	.306-78-870	115
Allie Reynolds, p	182-107, 3.30	105
Red Schoendienst, 2b	.289-84-773	104
Phil Rizzuto, ss	.273-38-563	103
Hal Newhouser, p	207-150, 3.06	92
Duke Snider, of	.295-407-1333	84
Nellie Fox, 2b	.288-35-790	64
Phil Cavarretta, 1b	.293-95-920	61
Al Dark, ss	.289-126-757	55
Dom DiMaggio, of	.298-87-618	36
Bobo Newsom, p	211-222, 3.98	31
Charlie Keller, of	.286-189-760	24
Johnny Sain, p	139-116, 3.49	21
Mickey Vernon, 1b	.286-172-1311	12
Richie Ashburn, of	.308-29-586	11
Ted Kluszewski, 1b	.298-279-1028	10
Bobby Thomson, of	.270-264-1026	10
Harvey Haddix, p	136-113, 3.63	9
Roy McMillan, ss	.243-68-594	9
Bobby Shantz, p	3.38, 48 saves	9
Walker Cooper, c	.285-173-812	8
Bobby Richardson, 2b	.266-34-390	8
Don Newcombe, p	149-90, 3.56	7
Harry Brecheen, p	133-92, 2.92	5
Dutch Leonard, p	191-181, 3.25	5
Carl Erskine, p	122-78, 4.00	4
Gil McDougald, 2b	.276-112-576	4
Billy Pierce, p	211-169, 3.27	4
Vic Raschi, p	132-66, 3.72	4
Vic Wertz, of	.277-266-1178	4
Vic Power, 1b	.284-126-658	3
Roy Sievers, 1b	.267-318-1147	3
Carl Furillo, of	.299-192-1058	2
Ed Lopat, p	166-112, 3.21	2
Preacher Roe, p	127-84, 3.43	2
Jackie Jensen, of	.279-199-929	1
Needed for election: 297		

1973

BBWAA Special Election

Player, Position	Stats	Votes
Roberto Clemente, of	.317-240-1305	393

Needed for election: 318

1973

BBWAA

Player, Position	Stats	Votes
Warren Spahn, p	363-245, 3.09	316
Whitey Ford, p	236-106, 2.75	255
Ralph Kiner, of	.279-369-1015	235
Gil Hodges, 1b	.273-370-1274	218
Robin Roberts, p	286-245, 3.41	213
Bob Lemon, p	207-128, 3.23	177
Johnny Mize, 1b	.312-359-1337	157
Enos Slaughter, of	.300-169-1304	145
Marty Marion, ss	.263-36-624	127
Pee Wee Reese, ss	.269-126-885	126
George Kell, 3b	.306-78-870	114
Phil Rizzuto, ss	.273-38-563	111
Duke Snider, of	.295-407-1333	101
Red Schoendienst, 2b	.289-84-773	96
Allie Reynolds, p	182-107, 3.30	93
Hal Newhouser, p	207-150, 3.06	79
Phil Cavarretta, 1b	.293-95-920	73
Nellie Fox, 2b	.288-35-790	73
Al Dark, ss	.289-126-757	53
Johnny Sain, p	139-116, 3.49	47
Dom DiMaggio, of	.298-87-618	43
Bobo Newsom, p	211-222, 3.98	33
Richie Ashburn, of	.308-29-586	25
Mickey Vernon, 1b	.286-172-1311	23
Ted Kluszewski, 1b	.298-279-1028	14
Lew Burdette, p	203-144, 3.66	12
Don Newcombe, p	149-90, 3.56	11
Vern Law, p	162-147, 3.77	9
Walker Cooper, c	.285-173-812	8
Dick Groat, ss	.286-39-707	7
Vic Raschi, p	132-66, 3.72	7
Dutch Leonard, p	191-181, 3.25	6
Roy McMillan, ss	.243-68-594	5
Bobby Shantz, p	3.38, 48 saves	5
Curt Simmons, p	193-183, 3.54	5
Carl Erskine, p	122-78, 4.00	4
Billy Pierce, p	211-169, 3.27	4
Harry Brecheen, p	133-92, 2.92	3
Bobby Thomson, of	.270-264-1026	3
Gil McDougald, 2b	.276-112-576	2
Bobby Richardson, 2b	.266-34-390	2
Vic Wertz, of	.277-266-1178	2
Smoky Burgess, c	.295-126-673	1
Harvey Haddix, p	136-113, 3.63	1

Needed for election: 285

1974

BBWAA

Player, Position	Stats	Votes
Mickey Mantle, of	.298-536-1509	322
Whitey Ford, p	236-106, 2.75	284
Robin Roberts, p	286-245, 3.41	224
Ralph Kiner, of	.279-369-1015	215
Gil Hodges, 1b	.273-370-1274	198
Bob Lemon, p	207-128, 3.23	190
Enos Slaughter, of	.300-169-1304	145
Pee Wee Reese, ss	.269-126-885	141
Eddie Mathews, 3b	.271-512-1453	118
Phil Rizzuto, ss	.273-38-563	111
Duke Snider, of	.295-407-1333	111
Red Schoendienst, 2b	.289-84-773	110
Allie Reynolds, p	182-107, 3.30	101

Player, Position	Stats	Votes
George Kell, 3b	.306-78-870	94
Nellie Fox, 2b	.288-35-790	79
Roger Maris, of	.260-275-851	78
Hal Newhouser, p	207-150, 3.06	73
Phil Cavarretta, 1b	.293-95-920	61
Richie Ashburn, of	.308-29-586	56
Al Dark, ss	.289-126-757	54
Johnny Sain, p	139-116, 3.49	51
Don Larsen, p	3.78, 23 saves	29
Ted Kluszewski, 1b	.298-279-1028	28
Mickey Vernon, 1b	.286-172-1311	27
Elston Howard, c	.274-167-762	19
Carl Erskine, p	122-78, 4.00	11
Walker Cooper, c	.285-173-812	9
Harvey Haddix, p	136-113, 3.63	8
Lew Burdette, p	203-144, 3.66	7
Don Newcombe, p	149-90, 3.56	7
Bobby Thomson, of	.270-264-1026	6
Vern Law, p	162-147, 3.77	5
Bobby Richardson, 2b	.266-34-390	5
Dick Groat, ss	.286-39-707	4
Roy McMillan, ss	.243-68-594	4
Billy Pierce, p	211-169, 3.27	4
Vic Raschi, p	132-66, 3.72	3
Bobby Shantz, p	3.38, 48 saves	3
Curt Simmons, p	193-183, 3.54	3
Bill Virdon, of	.267-91-502	3
Smoky Burgess, c	.295-126-673	2
Rocky Colavito, of	.266-374-1159	2
Vic Wertz, of	.277-266-1178	2

Needed for election: 274

1975

BBWAA

Player, Position	Stats	Votes
Ralph Kiner, of	.279-369-1015	273
Robin Roberts, p	286-245, 3.41	263
Bob Lemon, p	207-128, 3.23	233
Gil Hodges, 1b	.273-370-1274	188
Enos Slaughter, of	.300-169-1304	177
Hal Newhouser, p	207-150, 3.06	155
Pee Wee Reese, ss	.269-126-885	154
Eddie Mathews, 3b	.271-512-1453	148
Phil Cavarretta, 1b	.293-95-920	129
Duke Snider, of	.295-407-1333	129
Johnny Sain, p	139-116, 3.49	123
Phil Rizzuto, ss	.273-38-563	117
George Kell, 3b	.306-78-870	114
Red Schoendienst, 2b	.289-84-773	94
Richie Ashburn, of	.308-29-586	76
Don Drysdale, p	209-166, 2.95	76
Nellie Fox, 2b	.288-35-790	76
Roger Maris, of	.260-275-851	70
Al Dark, ss	.289-126-757	48
Vic Raschi, p	132-66, 3.72	37
Ted Kluszewski, 1b	.298-279-1028	33
Elston Howard, c	.274-167-762	23
Don Larsen, p	3.78, 23 saves	23
Mickey Vernon, 1b	.286-172-1311	22
Walker Cooper, c	.285-173-812	13
Lew Burdette, p	203-144, 3.66	11
Don Newcombe, p	149-90, 3.56	11
Bobby Thomson, of	.270-264-1026	10
Ken Boyer, 3b	.287-282-1141	9
Harvey Haddix, p	136-113, 3.63	8
Will White, p	229-166, 2.28	7
Vern Law, p	162-147, 3.77	6
Vic Wertz, of	.277-266-1178	5
Dick Groat, ss	.286-39-707	4
Johnny Podres, p	148-116, 3.68	3
Rocky Colavito, of	.266-374-1159	1
Bill Virdon, of	.267-91-502	1

Needed for election: 272

1976

BBWAA

Player, Position	Stats	Votes
Robin Roberts, p	286-245, 3.41	337
Bob Lemon, p	207-128, 3.23	305
Gil Hodges, 1b	.273-370-1274	233
Enos Slaughter, of	.300-169-1304	197
Eddie Mathews, 3b	.271-512-1453	189
Pee Wee Reese, ss	.269-126-885	186
Nellie Fox, 2b	.288-35-790	174
Duke Snider, of	.295-407-1333	159
Phil Rizzuto, ss	.273-38-563	149
George Kell, 3b	.306-78-870	129
Red Schoendienst, 2b	.289-84-773	129
Don Drysdale, p	209-166, 2.95	114
Roger Maris, of	.260-275-851	87
Richie Ashburn, of	.308-29-586	85
Al Dark, ss	.289-126-757	62
Walker Cooper, c	.285-173-812	56
Elston Howard, c	.274-167-762	55
Mickey Vernon, 1b	.286-172-1311	52
Ted Kluszewski, 1b	.298-279-1028	50
Don Larsen, p	3.78, 23 saves	47
Roy Face, p	3.48, 193 saves	23
Lew Burdette, p	203-144, 3.66	21
Don Newcombe, p	149-90, 3.56	21
Ken Boyer, 3b	.287-282-1141	15
Del Crandall, c	.254-179-657	15
Vern Law, p	162-147, 3.77	9
Bobby Thomson, of	.270-264-1026	9
Harvey Haddix, p	136-113, 3.63	8
Dick Groat, ss	.286-39-707	7
Will White, p	229-166, 2.28	7
Vic Wertz, of	.277-266-1178	5
Johnny Podres, p	148-116, 3.68	2

Needed for election: 291

1977

BBWAA

Player, Position	Stats	Votes
Ernie Banks, 1b	.274-512-1636	321
Eddie Mathews, 3b	.271-512-1453	239
Gil Hodges, 1b	.273-370-1274	224
Enos Slaughter, of	.300-169-1304	222
Duke Snider, of	.295-407-1333	212
Don Drysdale, p	209-166, 2.95	197
Pee Wee Reese, ss	.269-126-885	163
Nellie Fox, 2b	.288-35-790	152
Jim Bunning, p	224-184, 3.27	146
George Kell, 3b	.306-78-870	141
Richie Ashburn, of	.308-29-586	139
Red Schoendienst, 2b	.289-84-773	105
Lew Burdette, p	203-144, 3.66	85
Roger Maris, of	.260-275-851	72
Al Dark, ss	.289-126-757	66
Harvey Kuenn, of	.303-87-671	57
Ted Kluszewski, 1b	.298-279-1028	55
Mickey Vernon, 1b	.286-172-1311	52
Walker Cooper, c	.285-173-812	45
Elston Howard, c	.274-167-762	43
Don Newcombe, p	149-90, 3.56	43
Don Larsen, p	3.78, 23 saves	39
Roy Face, p	3.48, 193 saves	33
Curt Flood, of	.293-85-636	16
Ken Boyer, 3b	.287-282-1141	14
Bobby Thomson, of	.270-264-1026	10
Del Crandall, c	.254-179-657	8
Harvey Haddix, p	136-113, 3.63	7
Vern Law, p	162-147, 3.77	5
Dick Groat, ss	.286-39-707	4
Vic Wertz, of	.277-266-1178	4
Will White, p	229-166, 2.28	4
Camilo Pascual, p	174-170, 3.63	3
Johnny Podres, p	148-116, 3.68	3

Needed for election: 288

1978

BBWAA

Player, Position	Stats	Votes
Eddie Mathews, 3b	**.271-512-1453**	**301**
Enos Slaughter, of	.300-169-1304	261
Duke Snider, of	.295-407-1333	254
Gil Hodges, 1b	.273-370-1274	226
Don Drysdale, p	209-166, 2.95	219
Jim Bunning, p	224-184, 3.27	181
Pee Wee Reese, ss	.269-126-885	169
Richie Ashburn, of	.308-29-586	158
Hoyt Wilhelm, p	2.52, 227 saves	158
Nellie Fox, 2b	.288-35-790	149
Red Schoendienst, 2b	.289-84-773	130
Maury Wills, ss	.281-20-458	115
Roger Maris, of	.260-275-851	83
Lew Burdette, p	203-144, 3.66	76
Mickey Vernon, 1b	.286-172-1311	66
Al Dark, ss	.289-126-757	60
Harvey Kuenn, of	.303-87-671	58
Ted Kluszewski, 1b	.298-279-1028	51
Don Newcombe, p	149-90, 3.56	48
Elston Howard, c	.274-167-762	41
Don Larsen, p	3.78, 23 saves	32
Roy Face, p	3.48, 193 saves	27
Bill Mazeroski, 2b	.260-138-853	23
Ken Boyer, 3b	.287-282-1141	18
Curt Flood, of	.293-85-636	8
Harvey Haddix, p	136-113, 3.63	7
Del Crandall, c	.254-179-657	6
Vern Law, p	162-147, 3.77	6
Bobby Thomson, of	.270-264-1026	5
Vic Wertz, of	.277-266-1178	4
Dick Groat, ss	.286-39-707	3
Jim Maloney, p	134-84, 3.19	2
Clete Boyer, 3b	.242-162-654	1
Denny McLain, p	131-91, 3.39	1
Camilo Pascual, p	174-170, 3.63	1

Needed for election: 285

1979

BBWAA

Player, Position	Stats	Votes
Willie Mays, of	**.302-660-1903**	**409**
Duke Snider, of	.295-407-1333	308
Enos Slaughter, of	.300-169-1304	297
Gil Hodges, 1b	.273-370-1274	242
Don Drysdale, p	209-166, 2.95	233
Nellie Fox, 2b	.288-35-790	174
Hoyt Wilhelm, p	2.52, 227 saves	168
Maury Wills, ss	.281-20-458	166
Red Schoendienst, 2b	.289-84-773	159
Jim Bunning, p	224-184, 3.27	147
Richie Ashburn, of	.308-29-586	130
Roger Maris, of	.260-275-851	127
Luis Aparicio, ss	.262-83-791	120
Mickey Vernon, 1b	.286-172-1311	88
Al Dark, ss	.289-126-757	80
Harvey Kuenn, of	.303-87-671	63
Ted Kluszewski, 1b	.298-279-1028	58
Lew Burdette, p	203-144, 3.66	53
Don Larsen, p	3.78, 23 saves	53
Don Newcombe, p	149-90, 3.56	52
Bill Mazeroski, 2b	.260-138-853	36
Roy Face, p	3.48, 193 saves	35
Elston Howard, c	.274-167-762	30
Ken Boyer, 3b	.287-282-1141	20
Curt Flood, of	.293-85-636	14
Bobby Thomson, of	.270-264-1026	11
Del Crandall, c	.254-179-657	9
Vern Law, p	162-147, 3.77	9
Harvey Haddix, p	136-113, 3.63	8
Frank Howard, of	.273-382-1119	6
Ron Perranoski, p	2.79, 179 saves	6
Milt Pappas, p	209-164, 3.40	5
Clete Boyer, 3b	.242-162-654	3
Denny McLain, p	131-91, 3.39	3
Jim Maloney, p	134-84, 3.19	2
Johnny Callison, of	.264-226-840	1
Hal Lanier, ss	.228-8-273	1
Chris Short, p	135-132, 3.43	1

Needed for election: 324

1980

BBWAA

Player, Position	Stats	Votes
Al Kaline, of	**.297-399-1583**	**340**
Duke Snider, of	**.295-407-1333**	**333**
Don Drysdale, p	209-166, 2.95	238
Gil Hodges, 1b	.273-370-1274	230
Hoyt Wilhelm, p	2.52, 227 saves	209
Jim Bunning, p	224-184, 3.27	177
Red Schoendienst, 2b	.289-84-773	164
Nellie Fox, 2b	.288-35-790	161
Maury Wills, ss	.281-20-458	146
Richie Ashburn, of	.308-29-586	134
Luis Aparicio, ss	.262-83-791	124
Roger Maris, of	.260-275-851	111
Mickey Vernon, 1b	.286-172-1311	96
Harvey Kuenn, of	.303-87-671	83
Lew Burdette, p	203-144, 3.66	66
Don Newcombe, p	149-90, 3.56	59
Ted Kluszewski, 1b	.298-279-1028	50
Orlando Cepeda, 1b	.297-379-1365	48
Al Dark, ss	.289-126-757	43
Bill Mazeroski, 2b	.260-138-853	33
Don Larsen, p	3.78, 23 saves	31
Elston Howard, c	.274-167-762	29
Roy Face, p	3.48, 193 saves	21
Ron Santo, 3b	.277-342-1331	15
Norm Cash, 1b	.271-377-1103	6
Matty Alou, of	.307-31-427	5
Felipe Alou, of	.286-206-852	3
Mel Stottlemyre, p	164-139, 2.97	3
Steve Blass, p	103-76, 3.63	2
Jim Hickman, of	.252-159-560	1
Sonny Jackson, ss	.251-7-162	1
Don McMahon, p	2.96, 153 saves	1

Needed for election: 289

1981

BBWAA

Player, Position	Stats	Votes
Bob Gibson, p	**251-174, 2.91**	**337**
Don Drysdale, p	209-166, 2.95	243
Gil Hodges, 1b	.273-370-1274	241
Harmon Killebrew, 1b	.256-573-1584	239
Hoyt Wilhelm, p	2.52, 227 saves	238
Juan Marichal, p	243-142, 2.89	233
Nellie Fox, 2b	.288-35-790	168
Red Schoendienst, 2b	.289-84-773	166
Jim Bunning, p	224-184, 3.27	164
Maury Wills, ss	.281-20-458	163
Richie Ashburn, of	.308-29-586	142
Roger Maris, of	.260-275-851	94
Harvey Kuenn, of	.303-87-671	93
Elston Howard, c	.274-167-762	83
Orlando Cepeda, 1b	.297-379-1365	77
Thurman Munson, c	.292-113-701	62
Ted Kluszewski, 1b	.298-279-1028	56
Luis Aparicio, ss	.262-83-791	48
Lew Burdette, p	203-144, 3.66	48
Bill Mazeroski, 2b	.260-138-853	38
Don Larsen, p	3.78, 23 saves	33
Roy Face, p	3.48, 193 saves	23
Vada Pinson, of	.286-256-1170	18
Jim Perry, p	215-174, 3.45	6
Dave McNally, p	184-119, 3.24	5
Claude Osteen, p	196-195, 3.30	2
Glenn Beckert, 2b	.283-22-360	1
Gates Brown, of	.257-84-322	1
Leo Cardenas, ss	.257-118-689	1
Lindy McDaniel, p	3.45, 172 saves	1
Jim Northrup, of	.267-153-610	1
Sonny Siebert, p	140-114, 3.21	1

Needed for election: 301

1982

BBWAA

Player, Position	Stats	Votes
Hank Aaron, of	**.305-755-2297**	**406**
Frank Robinson, of	**.294-586-1812**	**370**
Juan Marichal, p	243-142, 2.89	305
Harmon Killebrew, 1b	.256-573-1584	246
Hoyt Wilhelm, p	2.52, 227 saves	236
Don Drysdale, p	209-166, 2.95	233
Gil Hodges, 1b	.273-370-1274	205
Luis Aparicio, ss	.262-83-791	174
Jim Bunning, p	224-184, 3.27	138
Red Schoendienst, 2b	.289-84-773	135
Nellie Fox, 2b	.288-35-790	127
Richie Ashburn, of	.308-29-586	126
Billy Williams, of	.290-426-1475	97
Maury Wills, ss	.281-20-458	91
Roger Maris, of	.260-275-851	69
Tony Oliva, of	.304-220-947	63
Harvey Kuenn, of	.303-87-671	62
Lew Burdette, p	203-144, 3.66	43
Orlando Cepeda, 1b	.297-379-1365	42
Elston Howard, c	.274-167-762	40
Don Larsen, p	3.78, 23 saves	32
Bill Mazeroski, 2b	.260-138-853	28
Thurman Munson, c	.292-113-701	26
Roy Face, p	3.48, 193 saves	22
Vada Pinson, of	.286-256-1170	6
Tommy Davis, of	.294-153-1052	5
Dave McNally, p	184-119, 3.24	5
Lindy McDaniel, p	3.45, 172 saves	3
Rico Petrocelli, ss	.251-210-773	3
Jim Brewer, p	3.07, 132 saves	2
Bill Freehan, c	.262-200-758	2
Leo Cardenas, ss	.257-118-689	1

Needed for election: 312

1983

BBWAA

Player, Position	Stats	Votes
Brooks Robinson, 3b	**.267-268-1357**	**344**
Juan Marichal, p	**243-142, 2.89**	**313**
Harmon Killebrew, 1b	.256-573-1584	269
Luis Aparicio, ss	.262-83-791	252
Hoyt Wilhelm, p	2.52, 227 saves	243
Don Drysdale, p	209-166, 2.95	242
Gil Hodges, 1b	.273-370-1274	237
Nellie Fox, 2b	.288-35-790	173
Billy Williams, of	.290-426-1475	153
Red Schoendienst, 2b	.289-84-773	146
Jim Bunning, p	224-184, 3.27	138
Harvey Kuenn, of	.303-87-671	77
Maury Wills, ss	.281-20-458	77
Tony Oliva, of	.304-220-947	75
Roger Maris, of	.260-275-851	69
Orlando Cepeda, 1b	.297-379-1365	59
Bill Mazeroski, 2b	.260-138-853	48
Lew Burdette, p	203-144, 3.66	43
Roy Face, p	3.48, 193 saves	32
Elston Howard, c	.274-167-762	32
Don Larsen, p	3.78, 23 saves	22
Joe Torre, c	.297-252-1185	20
Thurman Munson, c	.292-113-701	18

Player, Position	Stats	Votes
Dick Allen, 1b	.292-351-1119	14
Vada Pinson, of	.286-256-1170	12
Jim Perry, p	215-174, 3.45	7
Boog Powell, 1b	.266-339-1187	5
Ray Sadecki, p	135-131, 3.78	2
Dave Giusti, p	3.60, 145 saves	1
Tommy Helms, 2b	.269-34-477	1
Felix Millan, 2b	.279-22-403	1
Needed for election: 281		

1984

BBWAA

Player, Position	Stats	Votes
Luis Aparicio, ss	**.262-83-791**	**341**
Harmon Killebrew, 1b	**.256-573-1584**	**335**
Don Drysdale, p	**209-166, 2.95**	**316**
Hoyt Wilhelm, p	2.52, 227 saves	290
Nellie Fox, 2b	.288-35-790	246
Billy Williams, of	.290-426-1475	202
Jim Bunning, p	224-184, 3.27	201
Orlando Cepeda, 1b	.297-379-1365	124
Tony Oliva, of	.304-220-947	124
Roger Maris, of	.260-275-851	107
Harvey Kuenn, of	.303-87-671	106
Maury Wills, ss	.281-20-458	104
Lew Burdette, p	203-144, 3.66	97
Bill Mazeroski, 2b	.260-138-853	74
Roy Face, p	3.48, 193 saves	65
Elston Howard, c	.274-167-762	45
Joe Torre, c	.297-252-1185	45
Thurman Munson, c	.292-113-701	29
Don Larsen, p	3.78, 23 saves	25
Wilbur Wood, p	3.24, 57 saves	14
Jim Fregosi, ss	.265-151-706	4
Jim Bouton, p	3.57, 6 saves	3
Dave Johnson, 2b	.261-136-609	3
Mickey Stanley, of	.248-117-500	2
Bob Bailey, 3b	.257-189-773	1
Clay Carroll, p	2.94, 143 saves	1
Needed for election: 303		

1985

BBWAA

Player, Position	Stats	Votes
Hoyt Wilhelm, p	**2.52, 227 saves**	**331**
Lou Brock, of	**.293-149-900**	**315**
Nellie Fox, 2b	.288-35-790	295
Billy Williams, of	.290-426-1475	252
Jim Bunning, p	224-184, 3.27	214
Catfish Hunter, p	224-166, 3.26	212
Roger Maris, of	.260-275-851	128
Harvey Kuenn, of	.303-87-671	125
Orlando Cepeda, 1b	.297-379-1365	114
Tony Oliva, of	.304-220-947	114
Maury Wills, ss	.281-20-458	93
Bill Mazeroski, 2b	.260-138-853	87
Lew Burdette, p	203-144, 3.66	82
Mickey Lolich, p	217-191, 3.44	78
Ken Boyer, 3b	.287-282-1141	68
Roy Face, p	3.48, 193 saves	62
Elston Howard, c	.274-167-762	54
Ron Santo, 3b	.277-342-1331	53
Joe Torre, c	.297-252-1185	44
Don Larsen, p	3.78, 23 saves	32
Thurman Munson, c	.292-113-701	32
Dick Allen, 1b	.292-351-1119	28
Curt Flood, of	.293-85-636	28
Vada Pinson, of	.286-256-1170	19
Wilbur Wood, p	3.24, 57 saves	16
Harvey Haddix, p	136-113, 3.63	15
Dave McNally, p	184-119, 3.24	7
Ken Holtzman, p	174-150, 3.49	4
Ron Fairly, 1b	.266-215-1044	3

Player, Position	Stats	Votes
Jim Lonborg, p	157-137, 3.86	3
Andy Messersmith, p	130-99, 2.86	3
Don Kessinger, ss	.252-14-527	2
Denny McLain, p	131-91, 3.39	2
Jesus Alou, of	.280-32-377	1
Rico Carty, of	.299-204-890	1
Dock Ellis, p	138-119, 3.46	1
Needed for election: 297		

1986

BBWAA

Player, Position	Stats	Votes
Willie McCovey, 1b	**.270-521-1555**	**346**
Billy Williams, of	.290-426-1475	315
Catfish Hunter, p	224-166, 3.26	289
Jim Bunning, p	224-184, 3.27	279
Roger Maris, of	.260-275-851	177
Tony Oliva, of	.304-220-947	154
Orlando Cepeda, 1b	.297-379-1365	152
Harvey Kuenn, of	.303-87-671	144
Maury Wills, ss	.281-20-458	124
Bill Mazeroski, 2b	.260-138-853	100
Lew Burdette, p	203-144, 3.66	96
Ken Boyer, 3b	.287-282-1141	95
Minnie Minoso, of	.298-186-1023	89
Mickey Lolich, p	217-191, 3.44	86
Roy Face, p	3.48, 193 saves	74
Ron Santo, 3b	.277-342-1331	64
Joe Torre, c	.297-252-1185	60
Elston Howard, c	.274-167-762	51
Curt Flood, of	.293-85-636	45
Vada Pinson, of	.286-256-1170	43
Dick Allen, 1b	.292-351-1119	41
Thurman Munson, c	.292-113-701	35
Don Larsen, p	3.78, 23 saves	33
Wilbur Wood, p	3.24, 57 saves	23
Tim McCarver, c	.271-97-645	16
Dave McNally, p	184-119, 3.24	12
John Hiller, p	2.83, 125 saves	11
Paul Blair, of	.250-134-620	8
J.R. Richard, p	107-71, 3.15	7
Ken Holtzman, p	174-150, 3.49	5
Willie Horton, of	.273-325-1163	4
Jim Lonborg, p	157-137, 3.86	3
Andy Messersmith, p	130-99, 2.86	3
Dave Cash, 2b	.283-21-426	2
Manny Sanguillen, c	.296-65-585	2
Jack Billingham, p	145-113, 3.83	1
Jose Cardenal, of	.275-138-775	1
Bud Harrelson, ss	.236-7-267	1
George Scott, 1b	.268-271-1051	1
Needed for election: 319		

1987

BBWAA

Player, Position	Stats	Votes
Billy Williams, of	**.290-426-1475**	**354**
Catfish Hunter, p	**224-166, 3.26**	**315**
Jim Bunning, p	224-184, 3.27	289
Orlando Cepeda, 1b	.297-379-1365	179
Roger Maris, of	.260-275-851	176
Tony Oliva, of	.304-220-947	160
Harvey Kuenn, of	.303-87-671	144
Bill Mazeroski, 2b	.260-138-853	125
Maury Wills, ss	.281-20-458	113
Ken Boyer, 3b	.287-282-1141	96
Lew Burdette, p	203-144, 3.66	96
Mickey Lolich, p	217-191, 3.44	84
Minnie Minoso, of	.298-186-1023	82
Roy Face, p	3.48, 193 saves	78
Ron Santo, 3b	.277-342-1331	78
Dick Allen, 1b	.292-351-1119	55
Curt Flood, of	.293-85-636	50

Player, Position	Stats	Votes
Vada Pinson, of	.286-256-1170	48
Joe Torre, c	.297-252-1185	47
Elston Howard, c	.274-167-762	44
Don Larsen, p	3.78, 23 saves	30
Thurman Munson, c	.292-113-701	28
Wilbur Wood, p	3.24, 57 saves	26
Bobby Bonds, of	.268-332-1024	24
Mike Marshall, p	3.14, 188 saves	6
Sal Bando, 3b	.254-242-1039	3
Needed for election: 310		

1988

BBWAA

Player, Position	Stats	Votes
Willie Stargell, of	**.282-475-1540**	**352**
Jim Bunning, p	224-184, 3.27	317
Tony Oliva, of	.304-220-947	202
Orlando Cepeda, 1b	.297-379-1365	199
Roger Maris, of	.260-275-851	184
Harvey Kuenn, of	.303-87-671	168
Bill Mazeroski, 2b	.260-138-853	143
Luis Tiant, p	229-172, 3.30	132
Maury Wills, ss	.281-20-458	127
Ken Boyer, 3b	.287-282-1141	109
Mickey Lolich, p	217-191, 3.44	109
Ron Santo, 3b	.277-342-1331	108
Minnie Minoso, of	.298-186-1023	90
Roy Face, p	3.48, 193 saves	79
Vada Pinson, of	.286-256-1170	67
Joe Torre, c	.297-252-1185	60
Sparky Lyle, p	2.88, 238 saves	56
Elston Howard, c	.274-167-762	53
Dick Allen, 1b	.292-351-1119	52
Curt Flood, of	.293-85-636	48
Thurman Munson, c	.292-113-701	32
Don Larsen, p	3.78, 23 saves	31
Wilbur Wood, p	3.24, 57 saves	30
Bobby Bonds, of	.268-332-1024	27
Manny Mota, of	.304-31-438	18
Mark Belanger, ss	.228-20-389	16
Bill Lee, p	119-90, 3.62	3
Reggie Smith, of	.287-314-1092	3
Lee May, 1b	.267-354-1244	2
Al Hrabosky, p	3.10, 97 saves	1
Needed for election: 321		

1989

BBWAA

Player, Position	Stats	Votes
Johnny Bench, c	**.267-389-1376**	**431**
Carl Yastrzemski, of	**.285-452-1844**	**423**
Gaylord Perry, p	314-265, 3.11	304
Jim Bunning, p	224-184, 3.27	283
Fergie Jenkins, p	284-226, 3.34	234
Orlando Cepeda, 1b	.297-379-1365	176
Tony Oliva, of	.304-220-947	135
Bill Mazeroski, 2b	.260-138-853	134
Harvey Kuenn, of	.303-87-671	115
Maury Wills, ss	.281-20-458	95
Jim Kaat, p	283-237, 3.45	87
Ron Santo, 3b	.277-342-1331	75
Ken Boyer, 3b	.287-282-1141	62
Minnie Minoso, of	.298-186-1023	59
Roy Face, p	3.48, 193 saves	47
Mickey Lolich, p	217-191, 3.44	47
Luis Tiant, p	229-172, 3.30	47
Joe Torre, c	.297-252-1185	40
Dick Allen, 1b	.292-351-1119	35
Vada Pinson, of	.286-256-1170	33
Thurman Munson, c	.292-113-701	31
Bobby Bonds, of	.268-332-1024	29
Curt Flood, of	.293-85-636	27
Sparky Lyle, p	2.88, 238 saves	25

Awards: Hall Of Fame

Bert Campaneris, ss	.259-79-646	14
Wilbur Wood, p	3.24, 57 saves	14
Manny Mota, of	.304-31-438	9
Bobby Murcer, of	.277-252-1043	3
Don Money, 3b	.261-176-729	1
Gene Tenace, c	.241-201-674	1
Needed for election: 336		

Al Oliver, of	.303-219-1326	19
Sparky Lyle, p	2.88, 238 saves	15
Larry Bowa, ss	.260-15-525	11
Jerry Koosman, p	222-209, 3.36	4
Jeff Burroughs, of	.261-240-882	1
Mike Hargrove, 1b	.290-80-686	1
Richie Hebner, 3b	.276-203-890	1
Burt Hooton, p	151-136, 3.38	1
Mike Jorgensen, 1b	.243-95-426	1
John Lowenstein, of	.253-116-441	1
Ellis Valentine, of	.278-123-474	1
Needed for election: 333		

Bill Madlock, 3b	.305-163-860	19
Pete Rose, of	.303-160-1314	14
Ron Cey, 3b	.261-316-1139	8
Doug DeCinces, 3b	.259-237-879	2
Davey Lopes, 2b	.263-155-614	2
Andre Thornton, dh	.254-253-895	2
Bill Campbell, p	3.54, 126 saves	1
Needed for election: 318		

1990

BBWAA

Player, Position	Stats	Votes
Jim Palmer, p	**268-152, 2.86**	**411**
Joe Morgan, 2b	**.271-268-1133**	**363**
Gaylord Perry, p	314-265, 3.11	320
Fergie Jenkins, p	284-226, 3.34	296
Jim Bunning, p	224-184, 3.27	257
Orlando Cepeda, 1b	.297-379-1365	211
Tony Oliva, of	.304-220-947	142
Bill Mazeroski, 2b	.260-138-853	131
Harvey Kuenn, of	.303-87-671	107
Ron Santo, 3b	.277-342-1331	96
Maury Wills, ss	.281-20-458	95
Jim Kaat, p	283-237, 3.45	79
Ken Boyer, 3b	.287-282-1141	78
Dick Allen, 1b	.292-351-1119	58
Joe Torre, c	.297-252-1185	55
Minnie Minoso, of	.298-186-1023	51
Roy Face, p	3.48, 193 saves	50
Luis Tiant, p	229-172, 3.30	42
Vada Pinson, of	.286-256-1170	36
Curt Flood, of	.293-85-636	35
Thurman Munson, c	.292-113-701	33
Bobby Bonds, of	.268-332-1024	30
Mickey Lolich, p	217-191, 3.44	27
Sparky Lyle, p	2.88, 238 saves	25
Tug McGraw, p	3.14, 180 saves	6
Bucky Dent, ss	.247-40-423	3
Bob Watson, 1b	.295-184-989	3
Rick Monday, of	.264-241-775	2
Lou Piniella, of	.291-102-766	2
Mickey Rivers, of	.295-61-499	2
Jim Bibby, p	111-101, 3.76	1
Greg Luzinski, of	.276-307-1128	1
Jerry Remy, 2b	.275-7-329	1
Mike Torrez, p	185-160, 3.96	1
Needed for election: 333		

1992

BBWAA

Player, Position	Stats	Votes
Tom Seaver, p	**311-205, 2.86**	**425**
Rollie Fingers, p	**2.90, 341 saves**	**349**
Orlando Cepeda, 1b	.297-379-1365	246
Tony Perez, 1b	.279-379-1652	215
Bill Mazeroski, 2b	.260-138-853	182
Tony Oliva, of	.304-220-947	175
Ron Santo, 3b	.277-342-1331	136
Jim Kaat, p	283-237, 3.45	114
Maury Wills, ss	.281-20-458	110
Ken Boyer, 3b	.287-282-1141	71
Dick Allen, 1b	.292-351-1119	69
Minnie Minoso, of	.298-186-1023	69
Joe Torre, c	.297-252-1185	62
Luis Tiant, p	229-172, 3.30	50
Mickey Lolich, p	217-191, 3.44	45
Curt Flood, of	.293-85-636	42
Pete Rose, of	.303-160-1314	41
Bobby Bonds, of	.268-332-1024	40
Vada Pinson, of	.286-256-1170	36
Thurman Munson, c	.292-113-701	32
Rusty Staub, of	.279-292-1466	26
George Foster, of	.274-348-1239	24
Vida Blue, p	200 161, 3.26	23
Bobby Grich, 2b	.266-224-864	11
Dusty Baker, of	.278-242-1013	4
Dave Kingman, of	.236-442-1210	3
Bill Russell, ss	.263-46-627	3
Cesar Cedeno, of	.285-199-976	2
Steve Yeager, c	.228-102-410	2
Toby Harrah, 3b	.264-195-918	1
Dennis Leonard, p	144-106, 3.70	1
Needed for election: 323		

1994

BBWAA

Player, Position	Stats	Votes
Steve Carlton, p	**329-244, 3.22**	**436**
Orlando Cepeda, 1b	.297-379-1365	335
Phil Niekro, p	318-274, 3.35	273
Tony Perez, 1b	.279-379-1652	263
Don Sutton, p	324-256, 3.26	259
Steve Garvey, 1b	.294-272-1308	166
Tony Oliva, of	.304-220-947	158
Ron Santo, 3b	.277-342-1331	150
Bruce Sutter, p	2.83, 300 saves	109
Jim Kaat, p	283-237, 3.45	98
Dick Allen, 1b	.292-351-1119	66
Ken Boyer, 3b	.287-282-1141	56
Joe Torre, c	.297-252-1185	53
Vada Pinson, of	.286-256-1170	46
Minnie Minoso, of	.298-186-1023	45
Luis Tiant, p	229-172, 3.30	42
Curt Flood, of	.293-85-636	40
Graig Nettles, 3b	.248-390-1314	38
Bobby Bonds, of	.268-332-1024	37
Rusty Staub, of	.279-292-1466	36
Dave Concepcion, ss	.267-101-950	31
Thurman Munson, c	.292-113-701	31
Ron Guidry, p	170-91, 3.29	24
Mickey Lolich, p	217-191, 3.44	23
Pete Rose, of	.303-160-1314	19
Ted Simmons, c	.285-248-1389	17
George Foster, of	.274-348-1239	16
Vida Blue, p	209-161, 3.26	14
Don Baylor, dh	.260-338-1276	12
Joe Niekro, p	221-204, 3.59	6
Jose Cruz, of	.284-165-1077	2
Phil Garner, 2b	.260-109-738	2
Larry Parrish, 3b	.263-256-992	2
Ray Knight, 3b	.271-84-595	1
Needed for election: 342		

1991

BBWAA

Player, Position	Stats	Votes
Rod Carew, 1b	**.328-92-1015**	**401**
Gaylord Perry, p	**314-265, 3.11**	**342**
Fergie Jenkins, p	**284-226, 3.34**	**334**
Rollie Fingers, p	2.90, 341 saves	291
Jim Bunning, p	224-184, 3.27	282
Orlando Cepeda, 1b	.297-379-1365	192
Tony Oliva, of	.304-220-947	160
Bill Mazeroski, 2b	.260-138-853	142
Ron Santo, 3b	.277-342-1331	116
Harvey Kuenn, of	.303-87-671	110
Jim Kaat, p	283-237, 3.45	62
Maury Wills, ss	.281-20-458	61
Dick Allen, 1b	.292-351-1119	59
Ken Boyer, 3b	.287-282-1141	58
Joe Torre, c	.297-252-1185	41
Bobby Bonds, of	.268-332-1024	39
Minnie Minoso, of	.298-186-1023	38
Mickey Lolich, p	217-191, 3.44	33
Luis Tiant, p	229-172, 3.30	32
Vada Pinson, of	.286-256-1170	30
Thurman Munson, c	.292-113-701	28
Rusty Staub, of	.279-292-1466	28
Curt Flood, of	.293-85-636	23

1993

BBWAA

Player, Position	Stats	Votes
Reggie Jackson, of	**.262-563-1702**	**396**
Phil Niekro, p	318-274, 3.35	278
Orlando Cepeda, 1b	.297-379-1365	252
Tony Perez, 1b	.279-379-1652	233
Steve Garvey, 1b	.294-272-1308	176
Tony Oliva, of	.304-220-947	157
Ron Santo, 3b	.277-342-1331	155
Jim Kaat, p	283-237, 3.45	125
Dick Allen, 1b	.292-351-1119	70
Ken Boyer, 3b	.287-282-1141	69
Minnie Minoso, of	.298-186-1023	67
Joe Torre, c	.297-252-1185	63
Luis Tiant, p	229-172, 3.30	62
Bobby Bonds, of	.268-332-1024	45
Mickey Lolich, p	217-191, 3.44	43
Thurman Munson, c	.292-113-701	40
Vada Pinson, of	.286-256-1170	38
Vida Blue, p	209-161, 3.26	37
Curt Flood, of	.293-85-636	36
Rusty Staub, of	.279-292-1466	32
George Foster, of	.274-348-1239	29

1995

BBWAA

Player, Position	Stats	Votes
Mike Schmidt, 3b	**.267-548-1595**	**444**
Phil Niekro, p	318-274, 3.35	286
Don Sutton, p	324-256, 3.26	264
Tony Perez, 1b	.279-379-1652	259
Steve Garvey, 1b	.294-272-1308	196
Tony Oliva, of	.304-220-947	149
Ron Santo, 3b	.277-342-1331	139
Jim Rice, of	.298-382-1451	137
Bruce Sutter, p	2.83, 300 saves	137
Jim Kaat, p	283-237, 3.45	100
Tommy John, p	288-231, 3.34	98
Dick Allen, 1b	.292-351-1119	72
Minnie Minoso, of	.298-186-1023	66
Curt Flood, of	.293-85-636	59
Joe Torre, c	.297-252-1185	50
Luis Tiant, p	229-172, 3.30	45
Dave Concepcion, ss	.267-101-950	43
Bobby Bonds, of	.268-332-1024	35
Vada Pinson, of	.286-256-1170	32
Thurman Munson, c	.292-113-701	30
Graig Nettles, 3b	.248-390-1314	28
Vida Blue, p	209-161, 3.26	26

Player, Position	Stats	Votes
Mickey Lolich, p	217-191, 3.44	26
Ron Guidry, p	170-91, 3.29	25
Rusty Staub, of	.279-292-1466	23
George Foster, of	.274-348-1239	19
Don Baylor, dh	.260-338-1276	12
Buddy Bell, 3b	.279-201-1106	8
Darrell Evans, 3b	.248-414-1354	8
Kent Tekulve, p	2.85, 184 saves	6
Bob Forsch, p	168-136, 3.76	2
Willie Hernandez, p	3.38, 147 saves	2
Mike Krukow, p	124-117, 3.90	1
Chris Speier, ss	.246-112-720	1
Jim Sundberg, c	.248-95-624	1

Needed for election: 345

1996

BBWAA

Player, Position	Stats	Votes
Phil Niekro, p	318-274, 3.35	321
Tony Perez, 1b	.279-379-1652	309
Don Sutton, p	324-256, 3.26	300
Steve Garvey, 1b	.294-272-1308	175
Ron Santo, 3b	.277-342-1331	174
Tony Oliva, of	.304-220-947	170
Jim Rice, of	.298-382-1451	166
Bruce Sutter, p	2.83, 300 saves	137
Tommy John, p	288-231, 3.34	102
Jim Kaat, p	283-237, 3.45	91
Dick Allen, 1b	.292-351-1119	89
Curt Flood, of	.293-85-636	71
Luis Tiant, p	229-172, 3.30	64
Dave Concepcion, ss	.267-101-950	63
Minnie Minoso, of	.298-186-1023	62
Vada Pinson, of	.286-256-1170	51
Joe Torre, c	.297-252-1185	50
Ron Guidry, p	170-91, 3.29	37
Graig Nettles, 3b	.248-390-1314	37
Mickey Lolich, p	217-191, 3.44	33
Bobby Bonds, of	.268-332-1024	24
Bob Boone, c	.254-105-826	24
Rusty Staub, of	.279-292-1466	24
Dan Quisenberry, p	2.76, 244 saves	18
Frank White, 2b	.255-160-886	18
Bill Buckner, 1b	.289-174-1208	10
Jerry Reuss, p	220-191, 3.64	2
John Tudor, p	117-72, 3.12	2
Chet Lemon, of	.273-215-884	1

Needed for election: 353

1997

BBWAA

Player, Position	Stats	Votes
Phil Niekro, p	**318-274, 3.35**	**380**
Don Sutton, p	324-256, 3.26	346
Tony Perez, 1b	.279-379-1652	312
Ron Santo, 3b	.277-342-1331	186
Jim Rice, of	.298-382-1451	178
Steve Garvey, 1b	.294-272-1308	167
Bruce Sutter, p	2.83, 300 saves	130
Jim Kaat, p	283-237, 3.45	107
Joe Torre, c	.297-252-1185	105
Tommy John, p	288-231, 3.34	97
Minnie Minoso, of	.298-186-1023	84
Dave Parker, of	.290-339-1493	84
Dick Allen, 1b	.292-351-1119	79
Dave Concepcion, ss	.267-101-950	60
Luis Tiant, p	229-172, 3.30	53
Keith Hernandez, 1b	.296-162-1071	45
Mickey Lolich, p	217-191, 3.44	34
Ron Guidry, p	170-91, 3.29	31
Bob Boone, c	.254-105-826	28
Dwight Evans, of	.272-385-1384	28
Ken Griffey Sr., of	.296-152-859	22

Player, Position	Stats	Votes
Fred Lynn, of	.283-306-1111	22
Graig Nettles, 3b	.248-390-1314	22
Bobby Bonds, of	.268-332-1024	20
Rusty Staub, of	.279-292-1466	18
Rick Reuschel, p	214-191, 3.37	2
Mike Scott, p	124-108, 3.54	2
Garry Templeton, ss	.271-70-728	2
Terry Kennedy, c	.264-113-628	1
Terry Puhl, of	.280-62-435	1

Needed for election: 355

1998

BBWAA

Player, Position	Stats	Votes
Don Sutton, p	**324-256, 3.26**	**386**
Tony Perez, 1b	.279-379-1652	321
Ron Santo, 3b	.277-342-1331	204
Jim Rice, of	.298-382-1451	203
Gary Carter, c	.262-324-1225	200
Steve Garvey, 1b	.294-272-1308	195
Bruce Sutter, p	2.83, 300 saves	147
Tommy John, p	288-231, 3.34	129
Jim Kaat, p	283-237, 3.45	129
Dave Parker, of	.290-339-1493	116
Bert Blyleven, p	287-250, 3.31	83
Dave Concepcion, ss	.267-101-950	80
Minnie Minoso, of	.298-186-1023	76
Luis Tiant, p	229-172, 3.30	62
Keith Hernandez, 1b	.296-162-1071	51
Dwight Evans, of	.272-385-1384	49
Mickey Lolich, p	217-191, 3.44	39
Ron Guidry, p	170-91, 3.29	37
Bob Boone, c	.254-105-826	26
Jack Clark, of	.267-340-1180	7
Willie Randolph, 2b	.276-54-687	5
Carney Lansford, 3b	.290-151-874	3
Brian Downing, dh	.267-275-1073	2
Mike Flanagan, p	167-143, 3.90	2
Rick Dempsey, c	.233-96-471	1

Needed for election: 355

Hall of Fame Voting—By Person

Hank Aaron
.305-755-2297 in 3298 G

Year	Votes	Pct.
1982	**406**	**98**

Babe Adams
194-140, 2.75 in 482 G

Year	Votes	Pct.
1937	8	4
1938	11	4
1939	11	4
1942	11	5
1945	7	3
1946	6	2
1947	22	14
1948	4	3
1949	5	3
1950	6	4
1951	12	5
1952	9	4
1953	17	6
1954	13	5
1955	24	10

Bobby Adams
.269-37-303 in 1281 G

Year	Votes	Pct.
1966	1	0

Sparky Adams
.286-9-394 in 1424 G

Year	Votes	Pct.
1958	1	0
1960	1	0

Pete Alexander
373-208, 2.56 in 696 G

Year	Votes	Pct.
1936	55	24
1937	125	62
1938	**212**	**81**

Dick Allen
.292-351-1119 in 1749 G

Year	Votes	Pct.
1983	14	4
1985	28	7
1986	41	10
1987	55	13
1988	52	12
1989	35	8
1990	58	13
1991	59	13
1992	69	16
1993	70	17
1994	66	15
1995	72	16
1996	89	19
1997	79	17

Johnny Allen
142-75, 3.75 in 352 G

Year	Votes	Pct.
1955	1	0

Doug Allison
.232-0-28 in 94 G

Year	Votes	Pct.
1936 Veterans	1	1

Felipe Alou
.286-206-852 in 2082 G

Year	Votes	Pct.
1980	3	1

Jesus Alou
.280-32-377 in 1380 G

Year	Votes	Pct.
1985	1	0

Matty Alou
.307-31-427 in 1667 G

Year	Votes	Pct.
1980	5	1

Walter Alston
.000-0-0 in 1 G (Manager)

Year		
1983	Veterans Committee	

Nick Altrock
84-74, 2.67 in 218 G

Year	Votes	Pct.
1937	3	1
1938	7	3
1939	6	2
1953	1	0
1954	2	1
1958	20	8
1960	18	7

Cap Anson
.329-97-1879 in 2276 G

Year	Votes	Pct.
1936 Veterans	40	51
1939	Committee on Old-Timers	

Luis Aparicio
.262-83-791 in 2599 G

Year	Votes	Pct.
1979	120	28
1980	124	32
1981	48	12
1982	174	42
1983	252	67
1984	**341**	**85**

Luke Appling
.310-45-1116 in 2422 G

Year	Votes	Pct.
1953	2	1
1955	3	1
1956	14	7
1958	77	29
1960	72	27
1962	48	30
1964	142	71
1964 Runoff	**189**	**84**

Jimmy Archer
.249-16-296 in 847 G

Year	Votes	Pct.
1937	6	3
1938	7	3
1939	3	1

Richie Ashburn
.308-29-586 in 2189 G

Year	Votes	Pct.
1968	6	2
1969	10	3
1970	11	4
1971	10	3
1972	11	3
1973	25	7
1974	56	15
1975	76	21
1976	85	22
1977	139	36
1978	158	42
1979	130	30
1980	134	35
1981	142	35
1982	126	30
1995	Veterans Committee	

Jimmy Austin
.246-13-390 in 1580 G

Year	Votes	Pct.
1958	1	0

Earl Averill
.318-238-1165 in 1669 G

Year	Votes	Pct.
1949	1	1
1952	2	1
1955	2	1
1956	3	2
1958	14	5
1960	11	4
1962	3	2
1975	Committee on Veterans	

Bob Bailey
.257-189-773 in 1931 G

Year	Votes	Pct.
1984	1	0

Dusty Baker
.278-242-1013 in 2039 G

Year	Votes	Pct.
1992	4	1

Home Run Baker
.307-96-987 in 1575 G

Year	Votes	Pct.
1936	1	0
1937	13	6
1938	32	12
1939	30	11
1942	39	17
1945	26	11
1946	39	15
1946 Runoff	36	18
1947	49	30
1948	4	3
1950	4	2
1951	8	4
1955	Committee on Veterans	

Dave Bancroft
.279-32-591 in 1913 G

Year	Votes	Pct.
1937	3	1
1938	2	1
1939	1	0
1946	1	0
1948	4	3
1949	5	3
1950	9	5
1951	9	4
1952	11	5
1953	10	4
1954	10	4
1955	19	8
1956	15	8
1958	43	16
1960	30	11
1971	Committee on Veterans	

Sal Bando
.254-242-1039 in 2019 G

Year	Votes	Pct.
1987	3	1

Ernie Banks
.274-512-1636 in 2528 G

Year	Votes	Pct.
1977	**321**	**84**

Al Barlick
Umpire

Year		
1989	Veterans Committee	

Ross Barnes
.319-2-111 in 234 G

Year	Votes	Pct.
1936 Veterans	3	4

Ed Barrow
Executive

Year	Votes	Pct.
1953	Committee on Veterans	

Jack Barry
.243-10-429 in 1223 G

Year	Votes	Pct.
1938	3	1
1939	1	0

Dick Bartell
.284-79-710 in 2016 G

Year	Votes	Pct.
1948	1	1
1951	1	0
1958	1	0
1960	1	0

Joe Battin
.218-3-81 in 360 G

Year	Votes	Pct.
1936 Veterans	1	1

Hank Bauer
.277-164-703 in 1544 G

Year	Votes	Pct.
1967	23	8
1967 Runoff	9	3

Don Baylor
.260-338-1276 in 2292 G

Year	Votes	Pct.
1994	12	3
1995	12	3

Ginger Beaumont
.311-39-617 in 1463 G

Year	Votes	Pct.
1938	1	0
1942	1	0
1945	1	0
1946	1	0

Glenn Beckert
.283-22-360 in 1320 G

Year	Votes	Pct.
1981	1	0

Jake Beckley
.308-86-1575 in 2386 G

Year	Votes	Pct.
1936 Veterans	1	1
1942	1	0
1971	Committee on Veterans	

Mark Belanger
.228-20-389 in 2016 G

Year	Votes	Pct.
1988	16	4

Buddy Bell
.279-201-1106 in 2405 G

Year	Votes	Pct.
1995	8	2

Cool Papa Bell
Negro Leaguer

Year		
1974	Special Committee on Negro Leagues	

Johnny Bench

.267-389-1376 in 2158 G

Year	Votes	Pct.
1989	**431**	**96**

Chief Bender

212-127, 2.45 in 459 G

Year	Votes	Pct.
1936	2	1
1937	17	8
1938	33	13
1939	40	15
1942	55	24
1945	40	16
1946	39	15
1946 Runoff	35	17
1947	72	45
1948	5	4
1949	2	1
1950	6	4
1951	35	15
1952	70	30
1953	104	39
1953	**Committee on Veterans**	

Charlie Bennett

.256-55-533 in 1062 G

Year	Votes	Pct.
1936 Veterans	3	4

Larry Benton

127-128, 4.03 in 455 G

Year	Votes	Pct.
1958	1	0

Moe Berg

.243-6-206 in 663 G

Year	Votes	Pct.
1958	3	1
1960	5	2

Marty Bergen

.265-10-176 in 344 G

Year	Votes	Pct.
1937	2	1
1938	1	0
1939	1	0

Wally Berger

.300-242-898 in 1350 G

Year	Votes	Pct.
1956	1	1
1958	2	1

Yogi Berra

.285-358-1430 in 2120 G

Year	Votes	Pct.
1971	242	67
1972	**339**	**86**

Charlie Berry

.267-23-256 in 709 G

Year	Votes	Pct.
1955	1	0
1958	3	1

Jim Bibby

111-101, 3.76 in 340 G

Year	Votes	Pct.
1990	1	0

Carson Bigbee

.287-17-324 in 1147 G

Year	Votes	Pct.
1948	1	1

Jack Billingham

145-113, 3.83 in 476 G

Year	Votes	Pct.
1986	1	0

Max Bishop

.271-41-379 in 1338 G

Year	Votes	Pct.
1955	1	0
1956	1	1
1958	4	2
1960	5	2

Ewell Blackwell

82-78, 3.30 in 236 G

Year	Votes	Pct.
1968	5	2
1969	11	3
1970	14	5

Ray Blades

.301-50-340 in 767 G

Year	Votes	Pct.
1958	1	0
1960	1	0

Paul Blair

.250-134-620 in 1947 G

Year	Votes	Pct.
1986	8	2

Steve Blass

103-76, 3.63 in 282 G

Year	Votes	Pct.
1980	2	1

Lu Blue

.287-44-692 in 1615 G

Year	Votes	Pct.
1954	1	0

Vida Blue

209-161, 3.26 in 502 G

Year	Votes	Pct.
1992	23	5
1993	37	9
1994	14	3
1995	26	6

Ossie Bluege

.272-43-848 in 1867 G

Year	Votes	Pct.
1948	2	2
1949	1	1
1954	1	0
1956	2	1
1958	2	1
1960	3	1

Bert Blyleven

287-250, 3.31 in 692 G

Year	Votes	Pct.
1998	83	18

Ping Bodie

.275-43-516 in 1049 G

Year	Votes	Pct.
1937	2	1
1949	1	1

Joe Boley

.269-7-227 in 540 G

Year	Votes	Pct.
1942	1	0

Tommy Bond

193-115, 2.25 in 322 G

Year	Votes	Pct.
1936 Veterans	1	1

Bobby Bonds

.268-332-1024 in 1849 G

Year	Votes	Pct.
1987	24	6
1988	27	6
1989	29	6
1990	30	7
1991	39	9
1992	40	9
1993	45	11
1994	37	8
1995	35	8
1996	24	5
1997	20	4

Bob Boone

.254-105-826 in 2264 G

Year	Votes	Pct.
1996	24	5
1997	28	6
1998	26	5

Jim Bottomley

.310-219-1422 in 1991 G

Year	Votes	Pct.
1948	4	3
1949	8	5
1950	8	5
1951	6	3
1952	7	3
1953	10	4
1954	16	6
1955	26	10
1956	42	22
1958	57	21
1960	89	33
1962	20	13
1974	**Committee on Veterans**	

Lou Boudreau

.295-68-789 in 1646 G

Year	Votes	Pct.
1956	2	1
1958	64	24
1960	35	13
1962	12	8
1964	68	34
1964 Runoff	43	19
1966	115	38
1967	143	49
1967 Runoff	68	22
1968	146	52
1969	218	64
1970	**232**	**77**

Jim Bouton

3.57, 6 saves in 304 G

Year	Votes	Pct.
1984	3	1

Larry Bowa

.260-15-525 in 2247 G

Year	Votes	Pct.
1991	11	2

Clete Boyer

.242-162-654 in 1725 G

Year	Votes	Pct.
1978	1	0
1979	3	1

Ken Boyer

.287-282-1141 in 2034 G

Year	Votes	Pct.
1975	9	2
1976	15	4
1977	14	4
1978	18	5
1979	20	5
1985	68	17
1986	95	22
1987	96	23
1988	109	26
1989	62	14
1990	78	18
1991	58	13
1992	71	17
1993	69	16
1994	56	12

Bill Bradley

.271-34-552 in 1460 G

Year	Votes	Pct.
1936	1	0
1937	5	2
1938	2	1
1939	1	0
1942	1	0
1946	1	0

Harry Brecheen

133-92, 2.92 in 318 G

Year	Votes	Pct.
1960	7	3
1968	3	1
1969	2	1
1970	3	1
1971	7	2
1972	5	1
1973	3	1

Ted Breitenstein

160-170, 4.04 in 379 G

Year	Votes	Pct.
1937	1	0

Roger Bresnahan

.279-26-530 in 1446 G

Year	Votes	Pct.
1936	47	21
1937	43	21
1938	67	26
1939	67	24
1942	57	24
1945	133	54
1945	**Committee on Old-Timers**	

Jim Brewer

3.07, 132 saves in 584 G

Year	Votes	Pct.
1982	2	0

Tommy Bridges

194-138, 3.57 in 424 G

Year	Votes	Pct.
1956	3	2
1958	11	4
1960	4	1
1962	1	1
1964	15	7
1964 Runoff	1	0
1966	16	5

Lou Brock

.293-149-900 in 2616 G

Year	Votes	Pct.
1985	**315**	**80**

Dan Brouthers

.342-106-1296 in 1673 G

Year	Votes	Pct.
1936 Veterans	2	3
1945	**Committee on Old-Timers**	

Gates Brown

.257-84-322 in 1051 G

Year	Votes	Pct.
1981	1	0

Three Finger Brown

239-129, 2.06 in 481 G

Year	Votes	Pct.
1936	6	3
1937	31	15
1938	54	21
1939	54	20
1942	63	27
1945	46	19
1946	56	21
1946 Runoff	48	24
1949	**Committee on Old-Timers**	

Bill Bruton
.273-94-545 in 1610 G

Year	Votes	Pct.
1971	1	0

Bill Buckner
.289-174-1208 in 2517 G

Year	Votes	Pct.
1996	10	2

Morgan Bulkeley
Executive

Year	
1937	Centennial Commission

Jim Bunning
224-184, 3.27 in 591 G

Year	Votes	Pct.
1977	146	38
1978	181	48
1979	147	34
1980	177	46
1981	164	41
1982	138	33
1983	138	37
1984	201	50
1985	214	54
1986	279	66
1987	289	70
1988	317	74
1989	283	63
1990	257	58
1991	282	64
1996	Veterans Committee	

Lew Burdette
203-144, 3.66 in 626 G

Year	Votes	Pct.
1973	12	3
1974	7	2
1975	11	3
1976	21	5
1977	85	22
1978	76	20
1979	53	12
1980	66	17
1981	48	12
1982	43	10
1983	43	11
1984	97	24
1985	82	21
1986	96	23
1987	96	23

Smoky Burgess
.295-126-673 in 1691 G

Year	Votes	Pct.
1973	1	0
1974	2	1

Jesse Burkett
.338-75-952 in 2067 G

Year	Votes	Pct.
1936 Veterans	1	1
1937	1	0
1938	2	1
1942	4	2
1945	2	1
1946	2	1
1946	Committee on Old-Timers	

George Burns
.287-41-611 in 1853 G

Year	Votes	Pct.
1937	3	1
1938	3	1
1939	1	0
1949	1	1
1950	2	1

Jeff Burroughs
.261-240-882 in 1689 G

Year	Votes	Pct.
1991	1	0

Donie Bush
.250-9-436 in 1946 G

Year	Votes	Pct.
1937	1	0
1939	2	1
1942	2	1
1945	1	0
1946	2	1
1953	1	0

Guy Bush
176-136, 3.86 in 542 G

Year	Votes	Pct.
1956	2	1

Joe Bush
196-183, 3.51 in 489 G

Year	Votes	Pct.
1958	5	2

Leon Cadore
68-72, 3.14 in 192 G

Year	Votes	Pct.
1948	1	1

Johnny Callison
.264-226-840 in 1886 G

Year	Votes	Pct.
1979	1	0

Dolph Camilli
.277-239-950 in 1490 G

Year	Votes	Pct.
1948	1	1
1956	1	1
1958	4	2
1960	3	1

Howie Camnitz
133-107, 2.75 in 326 G

Year	Votes	Pct.
1945	1	0

Roy Campanella
.276-242-856 in 1215 G

Year	Votes	Pct.
1964	115	57
1964 Runoff	138	61
1966	197	65
1967	204	70
1967 Runoff	170	56
1968	205	72
1969	270	79

Bert Campaneris
.259-79-646 in 2328 G

Year	Votes	Pct.
1989	14	3

Bill Campbell
3.54, 126 saves in 700 G

Year	Votes	Pct.
1993	1	0

Jose Cardenal
.275-138-775 in 2017 G

Year	Votes	Pct.
1986	1	0

Leo Cardenas
.257-118-689 in 1941 G

Year	Votes	Pct.
1981	1	0
1982	1	0

Rod Carew
.328-92-1015 in 2469 G

Year	Votes	Pct.
1991	**401**	**91**

Max Carey
.285-70-800 in 2476 G

Year	Votes	Pct.
1937	6	3
1938	6	2
1939	7	3
1945	1	0
1948	9	7
1949	12	8
1950	14	8
1951	27	12
1952	36	15
1953	55	21
1954	55	22
1955	119	47
1956	65	34
1958	136	51
1961	Committee on Veterans	

Steve Carlton
329-244, 3.22 in 741 G

Year	Votes	Pct.
1994	**436**	**96**

Chico Carrasquel
.258-55-474 in 1325 G

Year	Votes	Pct.
1966	1	0

Bill Carrigan
.257-6-235 in 706 G

Year	Votes	Pct.
1937	5	2
1938	4	2
1939	2	1
1945	3	1

Clay Carroll
2.94, 143 saves in 731 G

Year	Votes	Pct.
1984	1	0

Gary Carter
.262-324-1225 in 2296 G

Year	Votes	Pct.
1998	200	42

Alexander Cartwright
Pioneer

Year	
1938	Centennial Commission

Rico Carty
.299-204-890 in 1651 G

Year	Votes	Pct.
1985	1	0

George Case
.282-21-377 in 1226 G

Year	Votes	Pct.
1958	1	0
1960	1	0
1962	1	1
1964	2	1

Dave Cash
.283-21-426 in 1422 G

Year	Votes	Pct.
1986	2	0

Norm Cash
.271-377-1103 in 2089 G

Year	Votes	Pct.
1980	6	2

Phil Cavarretta
.293-95-920 in 2030 G

Year	Votes	Pct.
1962	2	1
1964	22	11
1964 Runoff	1	0
1966	9	3
1967	15	5
1967 Runoff	4	1
1968	23	8
1969	37	11
1970	51	17
1971	83	23
1972	61	15
1973	73	19
1974	61	17
1975	129	36

Cesar Cedeno
.285-199-976 in 2006 G

Year	Votes	Pct.
1992	2	0

Orlando Cepeda
.297-379-1365 in 2124 G

Year	Votes	Pct.
1980	48	12
1981	77	19
1982	42	10
1983	59	16
1984	124	31
1985	114	29
1986	152	36
1987	179	43
1988	199	47
1989	176	39
1990	211	48
1991	192	43
1992	246	57
1993	252	60
1994	335	74

Ron Cey
.261-316-1139 in 2073 G

Year	Votes	Pct.
1993	8	2

Henry Chadwick
Pioneer

Year	
1938	Centennial Commission

Frank Chance
.296-20-596 in 1286 G

Year	Votes	Pct.
1936	5	2
1937	49	24
1938	133	51
1939	158	58
1942	136	58
1945	179	72
1946	144	55
1946 Runoff	150	74
1946	Committee on Old-Timers	

Happy Chandler
Executive

Year	
1982	Veterans Committee

Spud Chandler
109-43, 2.84 in 211 G

Year	Votes	Pct.
1950	2	1
1951	1	0
1956	1	1
1962	2	1
1964	6	3

Ben Chapman
.302-90-977 in 1717 G

Year	Votes	Pct.
1949	1	1
1952	1	0

Ray Chapman
.278-17-364 in 1051 G

Year	Votes	Pct.
1938	1	0

Sam Chapman
.266-180-773 in 1368 G

Year	Votes	Pct.
1958	1	0

Oscar Charleston
Negro Leaguer

Year		
1976	Special Committee on Negro Leagues	

Hal Chase
.291-57-941 in 1917 G

Year	Votes	Pct.
1936	11	5
1937	18	9

Jack Chesbro
198-132, 2.68 in 392 G

Year	Votes	Pct.
1937	1	0
1938	2	1
1939	6	2
1946	1	0
1946	Committee on Old-Timers	

Bill Cissell
.267-29-423 in 956 G

Year	Votes	Pct.
1937	1	0

Jack Clark
.267-340-1180 in 1994 G

Year	Votes	Pct.
1998	7	1

Watty Clark
111-97, 3.66 in 355 G

Year	Votes	Pct.
1958	1	0

Fred Clarke
.312-67-1015 in 2242 G

Year	Votes	Pct.
1936 Veterans	9	12
1936	1	0
1937	22	11
1938	63	24
1939	59	22
1942	58	25
1945	53	21
1945	Committee on Old-Timers	

John Clarkson
328-177, 2.81 in 531 G

Year	Votes	Pct.
1936 Veterans	5	6
1946	1	0
1963	Committee on Veterans	

Roberto Clemente
.317-240-1305 in 2433 G

Year	Votes	Pct.
1973 Special	393	93

Andy Coakley
58-59, 2.35 in 150 G

Year	Votes	Pct.
1938	1	0

Ty Cobb
.366-117-1933 in 3034 G

Year	Votes	Pct.
1936	**222**	**98**

Mickey Cochrane
.320-119-832 in 1482 G

Year	Votes	Pct.
1936	80	35
1939	28	10
1942	88	38
1945	125	51
1946	80	30
1946 Runoff	65	32
1947	**128**	**80**

Rocky Colavito
.266-374-1159 in 1841 G

Year	Votes	Pct.
1974	2	1
1975	1	0

Eddie Collins
.333-47-1300 in 2826 G

Year	Votes	Pct.
1936	60	27
1937	115	57
1938	175	67
1939	**213**	**78**

Jimmy Collins
.294-65-983 in 1728 G

Year	Votes	Pct.
1936 Veterans	8	10
1936	58	26
1937	66	33
1938	79	30
1939	72	26
1942	68	29
1945	121	49
1945	Committee on Old-Timers	

Shano Collins
.264-22-705 in 1799 G

Year	Votes	Pct.
1937	1	0

Earle Combs
.325-58-628 in 1455 G

Year	Votes	Pct.
1937	4	2
1938	7	3
1939	3	1
1945	1	0
1948	6	5
1949	6	4
1950	3	2
1952	1	0
1953	3	1
1955	1	0
1956	14	7
1958	34	13
1960	43	16
1962	6	4
1970	Committee on Veterans	

Charlie Comiskey
.264-29-735 in 1390 G (Executive)

Year	Votes	Pct.
1936 Veterans	6	8
1939	Committee on Old-Timers	

Dave Concepcion
.267-101-950 in 2488 G

Year	Votes	Pct.
1994	31	7
1995	43	9
1996	63	13
1997	60	13
1998	80	17

Jocko Conlan
.263-0-31 in 128 G (Umpire)

Year		
1974	Committee on Veterans	

Tom Connolly
Umpire

Year		
1953	Committee on Veterans	

Roger Connor
.317-138-1322 in 1997 G

Year		
1976	Committee on Veterans	

Wid Conroy
.248-22-452 in 1375 G

Year	Votes	Pct.
1945	1	0

Jack Coombs
158-110, 2.78 in 355 G

Year	Votes	Pct.
1937	2	1
1938	2	1
1946	2	1
1948	2	2
1951	1	0

Mort Cooper
128-75, 2.97 in 295 G

Year	Votes	Pct.
1956	2	1
1958	3	1
1960	1	0
1969	3	1

Walker Cooper
.285-173-812 in 1473 G

Year	Votes	Pct.
1968	8	3
1969	5	1
1970	9	3
1971	7	2
1972	8	2
1973	8	2
1974	9	2
1975	13	4
1976	56	14
1977	45	12

Wilbur Cooper
216-178, 2.89 in 517 G

Year	Votes	Pct.
1938	1	0
1939	1	0
1948	2	2
1949	4	3
1951	1	0
1952	2	1
1953	9	3
1954	7	3
1955	11	4

Clint Courtney
.268-38-313 in 946 G

Year	Votes	Pct.
1967	1	0

Stan Coveleski
215-142, 2.88 in 450 G

Year	Votes	Pct.
1938	1	0
1948	2	2
1949	3	2
1950	1	1
1958	34	13
1969	Committee on Veterans	

Billy Cox
.262-66-351 in 1058 G

Year	Votes	Pct.
1962	1	1

Doc Cramer
.296-37-842 in 2239 G

Year	Votes	Pct.
1956	4	2
1958	2	1
1960	1	0
1962	1	1
1964	12	6

Del Crandall
.254-179-657 in 1573 G

Year	Votes	Pct.
1976	15	4
1977	8	2
1978	6	2
1979	9	2

Doc Crandall
2.92, 24 saves in 302 G

Year	Votes	Pct.
1938	1	0

Gavy Cravath
.287-119-719 in 1221 G

Year	Votes	Pct.
1937	2	1
1938	2	1
1939	2	1
1946	1	0
1947	2	1

Sam Crawford
.309-97-1525 in 2517 G

Year	Votes	Pct.
1936	1	0
1937	5	2
1938	11	4
1939	6	2
1942	2	1
1945	4	2
1946	9	3
1957	Committee on Veterans	

Lou Criger
.221-11-342 in 1012 G

Year	Votes	Pct.
1936 Veterans	1	1
1936	7	3
1937	16	8
1938	11	4
1939	2	1
1946	6	2

Hughie Critz
.268-38-531 in 1478 G

Year	Votes	Pct.
1956	2	1

Joe Cronin
.301-170-1424 in 2124 G

Year	Votes	Pct.
1947	6	4
1948	25	21
1949	33	22
1949 Runoff	16	9
1950	33	20
1951	44	19
1952	48	21
1953	69	26
1954	85	34
1955	135	54
1956	**152**	**79**

Frankie Crosetti

.245-98-649 in 1683 G

Year	Votes	Pct.
1950	1	1
1952	1	0
1956	1	1
1958	5	2
1960	8	3
1968	15	5

Lave Cross

.292-47-1371 in 2275 G

Year	Votes	Pct.
1939	1	0
1942	1	0

General Crowder

167-115, 4.12 in 402 G

Year	Votes	Pct.
1958	1	0
1960	1	0

Walton Cruise

.277-30-272 in 736 G

Year	Votes	Pct.
1938	1	0

Jose Cruz

.284-165-1077 in 2353 G

Year	Votes	Pct.
1994	2	0

Tony Cuccinello

.280-94-884 in 1704 G

Year	Votes	Pct.
1956	1	1
1958	3	1

Candy Cummings

21-22, 2.78 in 43 G (Pioneer)

Year		
1939	Committee on Old-Timers	

Kiki Cuyler

.321-128-1065 in 1879 G

Year	Votes	Pct.
1948	3	2
1949	4	3
1950	11	7
1951	8	4
1952	10	4
1953	18	7
1954	20	8
1955	35	14
1956	55	28
1958	90	34
1960	72	27
1962	31	19
1968	Committee on Veterans	

Bill Dahlen

.272-84-1233 in 2443 G

Year	Votes	Pct.
1936 Veterans	1	1
1938	1	0

Ray Dandridge

Negro Leaguer

Year		
1987	Veterans Committee	

Harry Danning

.285-57-397 in 890 G

Year	Votes	Pct.
1958	1	0
1960	1	0

Al Dark

.289-126-757 in 1828 G

Year	Votes	Pct.
1966	17	6

Year	Votes	Pct.
1967	38	13
1967 Runoff	7	2
1968	36	13
1969	48	14
1970	55	18
1971	54	15
1972	55	14
1973	53	14
1974	54	15
1975	48	13
1976	62	16
1977	66	17
1978	60	16
1979	80	19
1980	43	11

Jake Daubert

.303-56-722 in 2014 G

Year	Votes	Pct.
1936 Veterans	1	1
1937	2	1
1938	1	0
1939	1	0
1951	1	0
1955	1	0

Curt Davis

158-131, 3.42 in 429 G

Year	Votes	Pct.
1958	1	0

George Davis

.295-73-1437 in 2368 G

Year		
1998	Veterans Committee	

Harry Davis

.276-75-952 in 1755 G

Year	Votes	Pct.
1945	1	0
1946	2	1

Spud Davis

.308-77-647 in 1458 G

Year	Votes	Pct.
1948	1	1
1949	1	1

Tommy Davis

.294-153-1052 in 1999 G

Year	Votes	Pct.
1982	5	1

Leon Day

Negro Leaguer

Year		
1995	Veterans Committee	

Dizzy Dean

150-83, 3.02 in 317 G

Year	Votes	Pct.
1945	17	7
1946	40	15
1946 Runoff	45	22
1947	88	55
1948	40	33
1949	88	58
1949 Runoff	81	43
1950	85	51
1951	145	64
1952	152	65
1953	**209**	**79**

Doug DeCinces

.259-237-879 in 1649 G

Year	Votes	Pct.
1993	2	0

Ed Delahanty

.346-101-1464 in 1835 G

Year	Votes	Pct.
1936 Veterans	22	28
1936	17	8
1937	70	35
1938	132	50
1939	145	53
1942	104	45
1945	111	45
1945	**Committee on Old-Timers**	

Rick Dempsey

.233-96-471 in 1766 G

Year	Votes	Pct.
1998	1	0

Jerry Denny

.260-74-667 in 1237 G

Year	Votes	Pct.
1936 Veterans	6	8

Bucky Dent

.247-40-423 in 1392 G

Year	Votes	Pct.
1990	3	1

Paul Derringer

223-212, 3.46 in 579 G

Year	Votes	Pct.
1948	1	1
1950	1	1
1951	1	0
1955	1	0
1956	12	6
1958	15	6
1960	8	3

Bill Dickey

.313-202-1209 in 1789 G

Year	Votes	Pct.
1945	17	7
1946	40	15
1946 Runoff	32	16
1948	39	32
1949	65	42
1949 Runoff	39	21
1950	78	47
1951	118	52
1952	139	59
1953	179	68
1954	**202**	**80**

Martin Dihigo

Negro Leaguer

Year		
1977	Special Committee on Negro Leagues	

Dom DiMaggio

.298-87-618 in 1399 G

Year	Votes	Pct.
1960	4	1
1962	2	1
1964	12	6
1968	8	3
1969	13	4
1970	15	5
1971	15	4
1972	36	9
1973	43	11

Joe DiMaggio

.325-361-1537 in 1736 G

Year	Votes	Pct.
1945	1	0
1953	117	44
1954	175	69
1955	**223**	**89**

Bill Dinneen

170-177, 3.01 in 391 G

Year	Votes	Pct.
1938	4	2
1939	7	3
1942	1	0
1945	1	0
1946	1	0

Bill Doak

169-157, 2.98 in 453 G

Year	Votes	Pct.
1958	3	1

Larry Doby

.283-253-970 in 1533 G

Year	Votes	Pct.
1966	7	2
1967	10	3
1967 Runoff	1	0
1998	**Veterans Committee**	

Bobby Doerr

.288-223-1247 in 1865 G

Year	Votes	Pct.
1953	2	1
1956	5	3
1958	25	9
1960	15	6
1962	10	6
1964	24	12
1964 Runoff	5	2
1966	30	10
1967	35	12
1967 Runoff	15	5
1968	48	17
1969	62	18
1970	75	25
1971	78	22
1986	**Veterans Committee**	

Mike Donlin

.333-51-543 in 1049 G

Year	Votes	Pct.
1937	6	3
1938	5	2
1939	5	2
1945	1	0

Wild Bill Donovan

186-139, 2.69 in 378 G

Year	Votes	Pct.
1937	3	1
1938	1	0
1939	2	1
1945	3	1
1946	4	2

Red Dooin

.240-10-344 in 1286 G

Year	Votes	Pct.
1937	1	0
1938	1	0

Brian Downing

.267-275-1073 in 2344 G

Year	Votes	Pct.
1998	2	0

Jack Doyle

.299-26-968 in 1564 G

Year	Votes	Pct.
1936 Veterans	1	1

Larry Doyle

.290-74-793 in 1766 G

Year	Votes	Pct.
1937	2	1
1938	4	2
1939	1	0

Walt Dropo
.270-152-704 in 1288 G

Year	Votes	Pct.
1967	1	0

Don Drysdale
209-166, 2.95 in 518 G

Year	Votes	Pct.
1975	76	21
1976	114	29
1977	197	51
1978	219	58
1979	233	54
1980	238	62
1981	243	61
1982	233	56
1983	242	65
1984	**316**	**78**

Hugh Duffy
.324-106-1302 in 1737 G

Year	Votes	Pct.
1936 Veterans	4	5
1937	7	3
1938	24	9
1939	34	12
1942	77	33
1945	64	26
1945	**Committee on Old-Timers**	

Joe Dugan
.280-42-571 in 1447 G

Year	Votes	Pct.
1937	1	0
1938	1	0
1948	3	2
1949	2	1
1956	1	1
1958	5	2
1960	8	3

Fred Dunlap
.292-41-*366* in 965 G

Year	Votes	Pct.
1936 Veterans	2	3

Jack Dunn
.245-1-164 in 490 G (Executive)

Year	Votes	Pct.
1942	1	0
1945	1	0
1946	1	0

Leo Durocher
.247-24-567 in 1637 G (Manager)

Year	Votes	Pct.
1948	1	1
1949	1	1
1952	1	0
1956	1	1
1958	28	11
1960	10	4
1962	1	1
1964	15	7
1964 Runoff	2	1
1994	**Veterans Committee**	

Eddie Dyer
4.75, 3 saves in 69 G

Year	Votes	Pct.
1947	1	1

Jimmy Dykes
.280-108-1071 in 2282 G

Year	Votes	Pct.
1948	5	4
1949	7	5
1950	2	1
1951	3	1
1952	5	2
1953	5	2
1955	1	0
1956	1	1
1958	26	10
1960	27	10
1962	6	4

George Earnshaw
127-93, 4.38 in 319 G

Year	Votes	Pct.
1948	3	2
1949	2	1
1950	2	1
1955	2	1
1956	3	2

Hank Edwards
.280-51-276 in 735 G

Year	Votes	Pct.
1960	2	1

Howard Ehmke
166-166, 3.75 in 427 G

Year	Votes	Pct.
1938	1	0
1949	1	1
1951	1	0
1952	1	0
1953	3	1
1954	4	2
1955	8	3
1956	8	4
1958	7	3
1960	12	4

Kid Elberfeld
.271-10-535 in 1292 G

Year	Votes	Pct.
1936	1	0
1937	1	0
1938	2	1
1942	1	0
1945	2	1

Bob Elliott
.289-170-1195 in 1978 G

Year	Votes	Pct.
1960	2	1
1962	1	1
1964	4	2

Jumbo Elliott
63-74, 4.24 in 252 G

Year	Votes	Pct.
1958	1	0

Dock Ellis
138-119, 3.46 in 345 G

Year	Votes	Pct.
1985	1	0

Del Ennis
.284-288-1284 in 1903 G

Year	Votes	Pct.
1966	3	1
1967	2	1

Jewel Ens
.290-1-24 in 67 G

Year	Votes	Pct.
1950	1	1

Carl Erskine
122-78, 4.00 in 335 G

Year	Votes	Pct.
1966	6	2
1968	9	3
1969	4	1
1970	2	1
1971	3	1
1972	4	1
1973	4	1
1974	11	3

Billy Evans
Umpire

Year		
1973	**Committee on Veterans**	

Darrell Evans
.248-414-1354 in 2687 G

Year	Votes	Pct.
1995	8	2

Dwight Evans
.272-385-1384 in 2606 G

Year	Votes	Pct.
1997	28	6
1998	49	10

Johnny Evers
.270-12-538 in 1784 G

Year	Votes	Pct.
1936	6	3
1937	44	22
1938	91	35
1939	107	39
1942	91	39
1945	134	54
1946	130	49
1946 Runoff	110	54
1946	**Committee on Old-Timers**	

Buck Ewing
.303-71-883 in 1315 G

Year	Votes	Pct.
1936 Veterans	40	51
1939	2	1
1939	**Committee on Old-Timers**	

Red Faber
254-213, 3.15 in 669 G

Year	Votes	Pct.
1937	3	1
1938	1	0
1939	3	1
1942	1	0
1948	3	2
1949	6	4
1950	9	5
1951	8	4
1952	9	4
1953	9	3
1954	12	5
1955	27	11
1956	34	18
1958	68	26
1960	83	31
1962	30	19
1964	**Committee on Veterans**	

Roy Face
3.48, 193 saves in 848 G

Year	Votes	Pct.
1976	23	6
1977	33	9
1978	27	7
1979	35	8
1980	21	5
1981	23	6
1982	22	5
1983	32	9
1984	65	16
1985	62	16
1986	74	17
1987	78	19
1988	79	19
1989	47	11
1990	50	11

Ron Fairly
.266-215-1044 in 2442 G

Year	Votes	Pct.
1985	3	1

Cy Falkenberg
130-123, 2.68 in 330 G

Year	Votes	Pct.
1937	1	0

Bob Feller
266-162, 3.25 in 570 G

Year	Votes	Pct.
1962	**150**	**94**

Rick Ferrell
.281-28-734 in 1884 G

Year	Votes	Pct.
1956	1	1
1958	1	0
1960	1	0
1984	**Veterans Committee**	

Wes Ferrell
193-128, 4.04 in 374 G

Year	Votes	Pct.
1948	1	1
1949	1	1
1956	7	4
1960	8	3
1962	1	1

Rollie Fingers
2.90, 341 saves in 944 G

Year	Votes	Pct.
1991	291	66
1992	**349**	**81**

Freddie Fitzsimmons
217-146, 3.51 in 513 G

Year	Votes	Pct.
1948	2	2
1949	2	1
1950	1	1
1956	3	2
1958	16	6
1960	13	5
1962	1	1

Mike Flanagan
167-143, 3.90 in 526 G

Year	Votes	Pct.
1998	2	0

Art Fletcher
.277-32-675 in 1533 G

Year	Votes	Pct.
1937	2	1
1938	3	1
1939	1	0
1947	3	2
1948	3	2
1949	1	1
1950	1	1
1951	4	2

Elmer Flick
.313-48-756 in 1482 G

Year	Votes	Pct.
1938	1	0
1963	**Committee on Veterans**	

Curt Flood
.293-85-636 in 1759 G

Year	Votes	Pct.
1977	16	4
1978	8	2
1979	14	3
1985	28	7
1986	45	11
1987	50	12
1988	48	11
1989	27	6
1990	35	8
1991	23	5
1992	42	10
1993	36	9
1994	40	9
1995	59	13
1996	71	15

Lew Fonseca

.316-31-485 in 937 G

Year	Votes	Pct.
1948	1	1
1950	2	1
1956	2	1
1958	3	1
1960	3	1

Whitey Ford

236-106, 2.75 in 498 G

Year	Votes	Pct.
1973	255	67
1974	**284**	**78**

Bob Forsch

168-136, 3.76 in 498 G

Year	Votes	Pct.
1995	2	0

Eddie Foster

.264-6-446 in 1500 G

Year	Votes	Pct.
1938	2	1

George Foster

.274-348-1239 in 1977 G

Year	Votes	Pct.
1992	24	6
1993	29	7
1994	16	4
1995	19	4

Rube Foster

Negro Leaguer

Year		
1981		Veterans Committee

Willie Foster

Negro Leaguer

Year		
1996		Veterans Committee

Nellie Fox

.288-35-790 in 2367 G

Year	Votes	Pct.
1971	39	11
1972	64	16
1973	73	19
1974	79	22
1975	76	21
1976	174	45
1977	152	40
1978	149	39
1979	174	40
1980	161	42
1981	168	42
1982	127	31
1983	173	46
1984	246	61
1985	295	75
1997		**Veterans Committee**

Jimmie Foxx

.325-534-1921 in 2317 G

Year	Votes	Pct.
1936	21	9
1946	26	10
1947	10	6
1948	50	41
1949	85	56
1949 Runoff	89	48
1950	103	62
1951	**179**	**79**

Chick Fraser

176-213, 3.68 in 433 G

Year	Votes	Pct.
1939	1	0

Bill Freehan

.262-200-758 in 1774 G

Year	Votes	Pct.
1982	2	0

Jim Fregosi

.265-151-706 in 1902 G

Year	Votes	Pct.
1984	4	1

Ford Frick

Executive

Year		
1970		Committee on Veterans

Frankie Frisch

.316-105-1244 in 2311 G

Year	Votes	Pct.
1936	14	6
1939	26	9
1942	84	36
1945	101	41
1946	104	40
1946 Runoff	67	33
1947	**136**	**84**

Carl Furillo

.299-192-1058 in 1806 G

Year	Votes	Pct.
1966	2	1
1967	2	1
1970	2	1
1971	5	1
1972	2	1

Augie Galan

.287-100-830 in 1742 G

Year	Votes	Pct.
1968	2	1
1970	3	1

Pud Galvin

360-308, 2.87 in 697 G

Year		
1965		Committee on Veterans

Phil Garner

.260-109-738 in 1860 G

Year	Votes	Pct.
1994	2	0

Ned Garver

129-157, 3.73 in 402 G

Year	Votes	Pct.
1967	1	0

Steve Garvey

.294-272-1308 in 2332 G

Year	Votes	Pct.
1993	176	42
1994	166	36
1995	196	43
1996	175	37
1997	167	35
1998	195	41

Lou Gehrig

.340-493-1995 in 2164 G

Year	Votes	Pct.
1936	51	23
1939 Special	—	—

Charlie Gehringer

.320-184-1427 in 2323 G

Year	Votes	Pct.
1945	10	4
1946	43	16
1946 Runoff	23	11
1947	105	65
1948	52	43
1949	102	67
1949 Runoff	**159**	**85**

Charlie Gelbert

.267-17-350 in 876 G

Year	Votes	Pct.
1947	1	1
1949	2	1
1950	1	1
1951	1	0

Bob Gibson

251-174, 2.91 in 528 G

Year	Votes	Pct.
1981	**337**	**84**

Josh Gibson

Negro Leaguer

Year		
1972		Special Committee on Negro Leagues

Warren Giles

Executive

Year		
1979		Veterans Committee

Dave Giusti

3.60, 145 saves in 668 G

Year	Votes	Pct.
1983	1	0

Jack Glasscock

.290-27-825 in 1736 G

Year	Votes	Pct.
1936 Veterans	2	3

Kid Gleason

.261-15-823 in 1966 G

Year	Votes	Pct.
1937	1	0
1938	1	0
1939	1	0
1945	1	0

Lefty Gomez

189-102, 3.34 in 368 G

Year	Votes	Pct.
1945	7	3
1946	4	2
1947	1	1
1948	16	13
1949	17	11
1950	18	11
1951	23	10
1952	29	12
1953	35	13
1954	38	15
1955	71	28
1956	89	46
1958	76	29
1960	51	19
1962	20	13
1972		**Committee on Veterans**

Mike Gonzalez

.253-13-263 in 1042 G

Year	Votes	Pct.
1950	1	1
1952	1	0
1953	1	0
1958	3	1
1960	2	1

Joe Gordon

.268-253-975 in 1566 G

Year	Votes	Pct.
1945	1	0
1955	1	0
1956	4	2
1958	11	4
1960	11	4
1962	4	3
1964	30	15

1964 Runoff	1	0
1966	31	10
1967	66	23
1967 Runoff	13	4
1968	77	27
1969	97	29
1970	79	26

Goose Goslin

.316-248-1609 in 2287 G

Year	Votes	Pct.
1948	1	1
1949	4	3
1950	2	1
1954	1	0
1955	7	3
1956	26	13
1958	26	10
1960	30	11
1962	14	9
1968		**Committee on Veterans**

Hank Gowdy

.270-21-322 in 1050 G

Year	Votes	Pct.
1937	2	1
1938	8	3
1939	4	1
1942	8	3
1945	3	1
1947	1	1
1948	3	2
1949	10	7
1950	6	4
1951	26	12
1952	34	15
1953	58	22
1954	51	20
1955	90	36
1956	49	25
1958	45	17
1960	38	14

Eddie Grant

.249-5-277 in 990 G

Year	Votes	Pct.
1938	1	0
1939	2	1
1942	3	1
1945	2	1
1946	1	0

George Grantham

.302-105-712 in 1444 G

Year	Votes	Pct.
1958	1	0

Hank Greenberg

.313-331-1276 in 1394 G

Year	Votes	Pct.
1945	3	1
1949	67	44
1949 Runoff	44	24
1950	64	38
1951	67	30
1952	75	32
1953	80	30
1954	97	38
1955	157	63
1956	**164**	**85**

Bobby Grich

.266-224-864 in 2008 G

Year	Votes	Pct.
1992	11	3

Ken Griffey Sr.

.296-152-859 in 2097 G

Year	Votes	Pct.
1997	22	5

Clark Griffith

237-146, 3.31 in 452 G (Executive)

Year	Votes	Pct.
1937	4	2
1938	10	4
1939	20	7
1942	71	30
1945	108	44
1946	73	28
1946 Runoff	82	41
1946	**Committee on Old-Timers**	

Burleigh Grimes

270-212, 3.52 in 616 G

Year	Votes	Pct.
1937	1	0
1938	1	0
1939	1	0
1948	7	6
1949	8	5
1950	6	4
1951	5	2
1952	9	4
1953	9	3
1955	3	1
1956	25	13
1958	71	27
1960	92	34
1962	43	27
1964	**Committee on Veterans**	

Charlie Grimm

.290-79-1078 in 2166 G

Year	Votes	Pct.
1939	1	0
1945	1	0
1946	1	0
1948	6	5
1949	10	7
1950	13	8
1951	9	4
1952	6	3
1953	9	3
1958	26	10
1960	13	5
1962	2	1

Marv Grissom

3.41, 58 saves in 356 G

Year	Votes	Pct.
1966	2	1

Dick Groat

.286-39-707 in 1929 G

Year	Votes	Pct.
1973	7	2
1974	4	1
1975	4	1
1976	7	2
1977	4	1
1978	3	1

Heine Groh

.292-26-566 in 1676 G

Year	Votes	Pct.
1937	1	0
1938	3	1
1945	1	0
1948	1	1
1950	2	1
1954	1	0
1955	5	2
1960	1	0

Steve Gromek

123-108, 3.41 in 447 G

Year	Votes	Pct.
1964	1	0

Lefty Grove

300-141, 3.06 in 616 G

Year	Votes	Pct.
1936	12	5
1945	28	11
1946	71	27
1946 Runoff	61	30
1947	**123**	**76**

Orval Grove

63-73, 3.78 in 207 G

Year	Votes	Pct.
1958	5	2
1960	7	3

Ron Guidry

170-91, 3.29 in 368 G

Year	Votes	Pct.
1994	24	5
1995	25	5
1996	37	8
1997	31	7
1998	37	8

Frankie Gustine

.265-38-480 in 1261 G

Year	Votes	Pct.
1958	3	1

Mule Haas

.292-43-496 in 1168 G

Year	Votes	Pct.
1955	1	0
1956	1	1
1958	1	0
1960	1	0

Stan Hack

.301-57-642 in 1938 G

Year	Votes	Pct.
1948	2	2
1949	4	3
1950	8	5
1951	3	1
1956	1	1
1958	6	2
1960	6	2

Harvey Haddix

136-113, 3.63 in 453 G

Year	Votes	Pct.
1971	10	3
1972	9	2
1973	1	0
1974	8	2
1975	8	2
1976	8	2
1977	7	2
1978	7	2
1979	8	2
1985	15	4

Chick Hafey

.317-164-833 in 1283 G

Year	Votes	Pct.
1948	1	1
1949	2	1
1950	4	2
1951	1	0
1952	1	0
1953	2	1
1954	2	1
1955	4	2
1956	16	8
1958	12	5
1960	29	11
1962	7	4
1971	**Committee on Veterans**	

Noodles Hahn

130-94, 2.55 in 243 G

Year	Votes	Pct.
1939	1	0

Jesse Haines

210-158, 3.64 in 555 G

Year	Votes	Pct.
1939	1	0
1947	1	1
1948	2	2
1949	2	1
1950	11	7
1953	4	2
1954	6	2
1955	10	4
1956	14	7
1958	22	8
1960	20	7
1962	3	2
1970	**Committee on Veterans**	

Wild Bill Hallahan

102-94, 4.03 in 324 G

Year	Votes	Pct.
1948	1	1
1956	1	1
1958	1	0
1960	2	1

Billy Hamilton

.344-40-736 in 1591 G

Year	Votes	Pct.
1936 Veterans	2	3
1942	1	0
1961	**Committee on Veterans**	

Ned Hanlon

.260-30-517 in 1267 G (Manager)

Year		
1996	**Veterans Committee**	

Mel Harder

223-186, 3.80 in 582 G

Year	Votes	Pct.
1949	4	3
1950	2	1
1951	1	0
1952	10	4
1953	8	3
1958	6	2
1960	12	4
1962	7	4
1964	51	25
1964 Runoff	14	6
1966	34	11
1967	52	18
1967 Runoff	14	5

Bubbles Hargrave

.310-29-376 in 852 G

Year	Votes	Pct.
1947	1	1
1958	1	0
1960	1	0

Mike Hargrove

.290-80-686 in 1666 G

Year	Votes	Pct.
1991	1	0

Toby Harrah

.264-195-918 in 2155 G

Year	Votes	Pct.
1992	1	0

Bud Harrelson

.236-7-267 in 1533 G

Year	Votes	Pct.
1986	1	0

Will Harridge

Executive

Year		
1972	**Committee on Veterans**	

Bucky Harris

.274-9-506 in 1264 G (Manager)

Year	Votes	Pct.
1938	1	0
1939	1	0
1948	3	2
1949	11	7
1950	4	2
1951	9	4
1952	12	5
1953	21	8
1958	45	17
1960	31	12
1975	**Committee on Veterans**	

Gabby Hartnett

.297-236-1179 in 1990 G

Year	Votes	Pct.
1945	2	1
1946	2	1
1947	2	1
1948	33	27
1949	35	23
1949 Runoff	7	4
1950	54	32
1951	57	25
1952	77	33
1953	104	39
1954	151	60
1955	**195**	**78**

Grady Hatton

.254-91-533 in 1312 G

Year	Votes	Pct.
1966	4	1
1967	1	0

Jim Hearn

109-89, 3.81 in 396 G

Year	Votes	Pct.
1966	1	0
1967	1	0

Richie Hebner

.276-203-890 in 1908 G

Year	Votes	Pct.
1991	1	0

Jim Hegan

.228-92-525 in 1666 G

Year	Votes	Pct.
1966	5	2
1967	2	1

Harry Heilmann

.342-183-1539 in 2148 G

Year	Votes	Pct.
1937	10	5
1938	14	5
1939	8	3
1942	4	2
1945	5	2
1946	23	9
1947	65	40
1948	40	33
1949	59	39
1949 Runoff	52	28
1950	87	52
1951	153	68
1952	**203**	**87**

Tommy Helms

.269-34-477 in 1435 G

Year	Votes	Pct.
1983	1	0

Solly Hemus
.273-51-263 in 961 G

Year	Votes	Pct.
1966	1	0

Tommy Henrich
.282-183-795 in 1284 G

Year	Votes	Pct.
1952	4	2
1953	10	4
1956	2	1
1958	11	4
1960	10	4
1962	3	2
1964	13	6
1968	22	8
1969	50	15
1970	62	21

Babe Herman
.324-181-997 in 1552 G

Year	Votes	Pct.
1942	1	0
1948	2	2
1949	5	3
1950	2	1
1951	1	0
1952	3	1
1953	2	1
1954	1	0
1955	5	2
1956	11	6
1958	13	5
1960	7	3

Billy Herman
.304-47-839 in 1922 G

Year	Votes	Pct.
1948	1	1
1956	2	1
1958	7	3
1962	4	3
1964	26	13
1964 Runoff	9	4
1966	28	9
1967	59	20
1967 Runoff	14	5
1975	**Committee on Veterans**	

Keith Hernandez
.296-162-1071 in 2088 G

Year	Votes	Pct.
1997	45	10
1998	51	11

Willie Hernandez
3.38, 147 saves in 744 G

Year	Votes	Pct.
1995	2	0

Buck Herzog
.259-20-445 in 1493 G

Year	Votes	Pct.
1938	1	0

Jim Hickman
.252-159-560 in 1421 G

Year	Votes	Pct.
1980	1	0

Mike Higgins
.292-140-1075 in 1802 G

Year	Votes	Pct.
1950	2	1
1951	1	0
1958	6	2
1960	3	1

John Hiller
2.83, 125 saves in 545 G

Year	Votes	Pct.
1986	11	3

Bill Hinchman
.261-20-369 in 908 G

Year	Votes	Pct.
1937	1	0

Gil Hodges
.273-370-1274 in 2071 G

Year	Votes	Pct.
1969	82	24
1970	145	48
1971	180	50
1972	161	41
1973	218	57
1974	198	54
1975	188	52
1976	233	60
1977	224	58
1978	226	60
1979	242	56
1980	230	60
1981	241	60
1982	205	49
1983	237	63

Tommy Holmes
.302-88-581 in 1320 G

Year	Votes	Pct.
1958	2	1
1960	2	1

Ken Holtzman
174-150, 3.49 in 451 G

Year	Votes	Pct.
1985	4	1
1986	5	1

Harry Hooper
.281-75-817 in 2308 G

Year	Votes	Pct.
1937	6	3
1938	4	2
1939	5	2
1948	2	2
1950	2	1
1951	3	1
1971	**Committee on Veterans**	

Burt Hooton
151-136, 3.38 in 480 G

Year	Votes	Pct.
1991	1	0

Rogers Hornsby
.358-301-1584 in 2259 G

Year	Votes	Pct.
1936	105	46
1937	53	26
1938	46	18
1939	176	64
1942	**182**	**78**

Willie Horton
.273-325-1163 in 2028 G

Year	Votes	Pct.
1986	4	1

Art Houtteman
87-91, 4.14 in 325 G

Year	Votes	Pct.
1964	2	1

Elston Howard
.274-167-762 in 1605 G

Year	Votes	Pct.
1974	19	5
1975	23	6
1976	55	14
1977	43	11
1978	41	11
1979	30	7
1980	29	8

	83	21
1981	83	21
1982	40	10
1983	32	9
1984	45	11
1985	54	14
1986	51	12
1987	44	11
1988	53	12

Frank Howard
.273-382-1119 in 1895 G

Year	Votes	Pct.
1979	6	1

Waite Hoyt
237-182, 3.59 in 674 G

Year	Votes	Pct.
1939	1	0
1942	1	0
1946	1	0
1948	7	6
1949	7	5
1950	11	7
1951	13	6
1952	12	5
1953	14	5
1954	14	6
1955	33	13
1956	37	19
1958	37	14
1960	29	11
1962	18	11
1969	**Committee on Veterans**	

Al Hrabosky
3.10, 97 saves in 545 G

Year	Votes	Pct.
1988	1	0

Cal Hubbard
Umpire

Year		
1976	**Committee on Veterans**	

Carl Hubbell
253-154, 2.98 in 535 G

Year	Votes	Pct.
1945	24	10
1946	101	38
1946 Runoff	75	37
1947	**140**	**87**

Miller Huggins
.265-9-318 in 1586 G (Manager)

Year	Votes	Pct.
1937	5	2
1938	48	18
1939	97	35
1942	111	48
1945	133	54
1946	129	49
1946 Runoff	106	52
1948	4	3
1950	2	1
1964	**Committee on Veterans**	

William Hulbert
Executive

Year		
1995	**Veterans Committee**	

Catfish Hunter
224-166, 3.26 in 500 G

Year	Votes	Pct.
1985	212	54
1986	289	68
1987	**315**	**76**

Fred Hutchinson
95-71, 3.73 in 242 G

Year	Votes	Pct.
1962	1	1
1964	10	5

Monte Irvin
.293-99-443 in 764 G (Negro Leaguer)

Year		
1973	**Special Committee on Negro Leagues**	

Charlie Irwin
.267-16-488 in 989 G

Year	Votes	Pct.
1938	1	0
1939	1	0

Joe Jackson
.356-54-785 in 1330 G

Year	Votes	Pct.
1936	2	1
1946	2	1

Reggie Jackson
.262-563-1702 in 2820 G

Year	Votes	Pct.
1993	**396**	**94**

Sonny Jackson
.251-7-162 in 936 G

Year	Votes	Pct.
1980	1	0

Travis Jackson
.291-135-929 in 1656 G

Year	Votes	Pct.
1948	5	4
1949	6	4
1950	6	4
1951	4	2
1952	1	0
1953	2	1
1954	1	0
1955	5	2
1956	14	7
1958	11	4
1960	11	4
1962	1	1
1982	**Veterans Committee**	

Fergie Jenkins
284-226, 3.34 in 664 G

Year	Votes	Pct.
1989	234	52
1990	296	67
1991	**334**	**75**

Hughie Jennings
.311-18-840 in 1285 G

Year	Votes	Pct.
1936 Veterans	11	14
1937	4	2
1938	23	9
1939	33	12
1942	64	27
1945	92	37
1945	**Committee on Old-Timers**	

Jackie Jensen
.279-199-929 in 1438 G

Year	Votes	Pct.
1967	3	1
1968	3	1
1969	1	0
1970	1	0
1971	2	1
1972	1	0

Tommy John
288-231, 3.34 in 760 G

Year	Votes	Pct.
1995	98	21
1996	102	22
1997	97	21
1998	129	27

Ban Johnson
Executive

Year		
1937		Centennial Commission

Bob Johnson
.296-288-1283 in 1863 G

Year	Votes	Pct.
1948	1	1
1956	1	1

Dave Johnson
.261-136-609 in 1435 G

Year	Votes	Pct.
1984	3	1

Judy Johnson
Negro Leaguer

Year		
1975		Special Committee on Negro Leagues

Walter Johnson
417-279, 2.17 in 802 G

Year	Votes	Pct.
1936	189	84

Fielder Jones
.285-21-631 in 1788 G

Year	Votes	Pct.
1946	1	0

Sad Sam Jones
229-217, 3.84 in 647 G

Year	Votes	Pct.
1939	1	0
1955	1	0
1956	1	1

Tim Jordan
.261-32-232 in 540 G

Year	Votes	Pct.
1951	1	0

Mike Jorgensen
.243-95-426 in 1633 G

Year	Votes	Pct.
1991	1	0

Addie Joss
160-97, 1.89 in 286 G

Year	Votes	Pct.
1937	11	5
1938	18	7
1939	28	10
1942	33	14
1945	23	9
1946	14	5
1960	1	0
1978		Veterans Committee

Joe Judge
.298-71-1034 in 2171 G

Year	Votes	Pct.
1937	1	0
1938	2	1
1949	1	1
1955	2	1
1956	2	1
1958	9	3
1960	15	6

Billy Jurges
.258-43-656 in 1816 G

Year	Votes	Pct.
1949	2	1
1958	1	0

Jim Kaat
283-237, 3.45 in 898 G

Year	Votes	Pct.
1989	87	19
1990	79	18
1991	62	14
1992	114	27
1993	125	30
1994	98	22
1995	100	22
1996	91	19
1997	107	23
1998	129	27

Al Kaline
.297-399-1583 in 2834 G

Year	Votes	Pct.
1980	340	88

Willie Kamm
.281-29-826 in 1692 G

Year	Votes	Pct.
1958	3	1
1960	1	0

Tim Keefe
341-225, 2.62 in 599 G

Year	Votes	Pct.
1936 Veterans	1	1
1964		Committee on Veterans

Willie Keeler
.341-33-810 in 2123 G

Year	Votes	Pct.
1936 Veterans	33	42
1936	40	18
1937	115	57
1938	177	68
1939	207	76

George Kell
.306-78-870 in 1795 G

Year	Votes	Pct.
1964	33	16
1964 Runoff	8	4
1966	29	10
1967	40	14
1967 Runoff	11	4
1968	47	17
1969	60	18
1970	90	30
1971	105	29
1972	115	29
1973	114	30
1974	94	26
1975	114	31
1976	129	33
1977	141	37
1983		Veterans Committee

Charlie Keller
.286-189-760 in 1170 G

Year	Votes	Pct.
1953	1	0
1956	2	1
1958	9	3
1960	7	3
1962	1	1
1964	12	6
1968	11	4
1969	14	4
1970	7	2
1971	14	4
1972	24	6

Joe Kelley
.317-65-1194 in 1842 G

Year	Votes	Pct.
1939	1	0
1942	1	0
1971		Committee on Veterans

George Kelly
.297-148-1020 in 1622 G

Year	Votes	Pct.
1947	1	1
1948	2	2
1949	1	1
1956	2	1
1958	2	1
1960	5	2
1962	1	1
1973		Committee on Veterans

King Kelly
.308-69-950 in 1455 G

Year	Votes	Pct.
1936 Veterans	15	19
1945		Committee on Old-Timers

Ken Keltner
.276-163-852 in 1526 G

Year	Votes	Pct.
1958	1	0
1960	1	0

Terry Kennedy
.264-113-628 in 1491 G

Year	Votes	Pct.
1997	1	0

Dickie Kerr
53-34, 3.84 in 140 G

Year	Votes	Pct.
1937	1	0
1938	3	1
1939	5	2
1942	1	0
1945	1	0
1949	1	1
1951	3	1
1952	9	4
1953	13	5
1954	13	5
1955	25	10

Don Kessinger
.252-14-527 in 2078 G

Year	Votes	Pct.
1985	2	1

Harmon Killebrew
.256-573-1584 in 2435 G

Year	Votes	Pct.
1981	239	60
1982	246	59
1983	269	72
1984	335	83

Bill Killefer
.238-4-240 in 1035 G

Year	Votes	Pct.
1946	1	0

Matt Kilroy
141-133, 3.47 in 303 G

Year	Votes	Pct.
1936 Veterans	1	1

Ellis Kinder
3.43, 102 saves in 484 G

Year	Votes	Pct.
1964	3	1

Ralph Kiner
.279-369-1015 in 1472 G

Year	Votes	Pct.
1962	5	3
1964	31	15
1964 Runoff	3	1
1966	74	25
1967	124	42
1967 Runoff	41	13
1968	118	42
1969	137	40
1970	167	56
1971	212	59
1972	235	59
1973	235	62
1974	215	59
1975	273	75

Dave Kingman
.236-442-1210 in 1941 G

Year	Votes	Pct.
1992	3	1

Chuck Klein
.320-300-1201 in 1753 G

Year	Votes	Pct.
1948	3	2
1949	9	6
1950	14	8
1951	15	7
1952	19	8
1954	11	4
1955	25	10
1956	44	23
1958	36	14
1960	37	14
1962	18	11
1964	56	28
1964 Runoff	18	8
1980		Veterans Committee

Bill Klem
Umpire

Year		
1953		Committee on Veterans

Johnny Kling
.272-20-513 in 1260 G

Year	Votes	Pct.
1936	8	4
1937	20	10
1938	26	10
1939	14	5
1942	15	6
1945	12	5
1946	20	8
1948	2	2
1953	1	0

Ted Kluszewski
.298-279-1028 in 1718 G

Year	Votes	Pct.
1967	9	3
1968	14	5
1969	11	3
1970	8	3
1971	9	3
1972	10	3
1973	14	4
1974	28	8
1975	33	9
1976	50	13
1977	55	14
1978	51	13
1979	58	13
1980	50	13
1981	56	14

Otto Knabe
.247-8-365 in 1279 G

Year	Votes	Pct.
1939	1	0
1946	1	0

Ray Knight
.271-84-595 in 1495 G

Year	Votes	Pct.
1994	1	0

Jerry Koosman
222-209, 3.36 in 612 G

Year	Votes	Pct.
1991	4	1

Sandy Koufax
165-87, 2.76 in 397 G

Year	Votes	Pct.
1972	**344**	**87**

Ray Kremer
143-85, 3.76 in 308 G

Year	Votes	Pct.
1948	1	1
1958	2	1

Red Kress
.286-89-799 in 1391 G

Year	Votes	Pct.
1958	1	0
1960	3	1

Mike Krukow
124-117, 3.90 in 369 G

Year	Votes	Pct.
1995	1	0

Harvey Kuenn
.303-87-671 in 1833 G

Year	Votes	Pct.
1977	57	15
1978	58	15
1979	63	15
1980	83	22
1981	93	23
1982	62	15
1983	77	21
1984	106	26
1985	125	32
1986	144	34
1987	144	35
1988	168	39
1989	115	26
1990	107	24
1991	110	25

Joe Kuhel
.277-131-1049 in 2104 G

Year	Votes	Pct.
1956	1	1

Bob Kuzava
4.05, 13 saves in 213 G

Year	Votes	Pct.
1964	1	0

Nap Lajoie
.338-82-1599 in 2480 G

Year	Votes	Pct.
1936 Veterans	2	3
1936	146	65
1937	**168**	**84**

Kenesaw Landis
Executive

Year		
1944	**Committee on Old-Timers**	

Bill Lange
.330-39-578 in 811 G

Year	Votes	Pct.
1936 Veterans	6	8
1953	1	0

Hal Lanier
.228-8-273 in 1196 G

Year	Votes	Pct.
1979	1	0

Carney Lansford
.290-151-874 in 1862 G

Year	Votes	Pct.
1998	3	1

Don Larsen
3.78, 23 saves in 412 G

Year	Votes	Pct.
1974	29	8
1975	23	6
1976	47	12
1977	39	10
1978	32	8
1979	53	12
1980	31	8
1981	33	8
1982	32	8
1983	22	6
1984	25	6
1985	32	8
1986	33	8
1987	30	7
1988	31	7

Tom Lasorda
6.48, 1 save in 26 G (Manager)

Year		
1997	**Veterans Committee**	

Arlie Latham
.269-27-562 in 1627 G

Year	Votes	Pct.
1936 Veterans	1	1
1938	1	0
1942	1	0

Cookie Lavagetto
.269-40-486 in 1043 G

Year	Votes	Pct.
1958	4	2
1960	2	1

Vern Law
162-147, 3.77 in 483 G

Year	Votes	Pct.
1973	9	2
1974	5	1
1975	6	1
1976	9	2
1977	5	1
1978	6	2
1979	9	2

Tony Lazzeri
.292-178-1191 in 1740 G

Year	Votes	Pct.
1945	1	0
1947	1	1
1948	21	17
1949	20	13
1949 Runoff	6	3
1950	21	13
1951	27	12
1952	29	12
1953	28	11
1954	30	12
1955	66	26
1956	64	33
1958	80	30
1960	59	22
1962	8	5
1991	**Veterans Committee**	

Freddy Leach
.307-72-509 in 991 G

Year	Votes	Pct.
1958	2	1
1960	1	0

Tommy Leach
.269-62-810 in 2156 G

Year	Votes	Pct.
1937	1	0
1939	1	0

Bill Lee
119-90, 3.62 in 416 G

Year	Votes	Pct.
1988	3	1

Sam Leever
195-100, 2.47 in 388 G

Year	Votes	Pct.
1937	1	0

Bob Lemon
207-128, 3.23 in 460 G

Year	Votes	Pct.
1964	24	12
1964 Runoff	3	1
1966	21	7
1967	35	12
1967 Runoff	7	2
1968	47	17
1969	56	16
1970	70	23
1971	90	25
1972	117	30
1973	177	47
1974	190	52
1975	233	64
1976	**305**	**79**

Chet Lemon
.273-215-884 in 1988 G

Year	Votes	Pct.
1996	1	0

Buck Leonard
Negro Leaguer

Year		
1972	**Special Committee on Negro Leagues**	

Dennis Leonard
144-106, 3.70 in 312 G

Year	Votes	Pct.
1992	1	0

Dutch Leonard
191-181, 3.25 in 640 G

Year	Votes	Pct.
1960	2	1
1968	5	2
1969	4	1
1970	5	2
1971	3	1
1972	5	1
1973	6	2

Duffy Lewis
.284-38-793 in 1459 G

Year	Votes	Pct.
1937	3	1
1938	5	2
1939	6	2
1945	1	0
1951	2	1
1952	11	5
1953	20	8
1954	20	8
1955	34	14

Freddy Lindstrom
.311-103-779 in 1438 G

Year	Votes	Pct.
1949	1	1
1956	3	2
1958	5	2
1960	6	2
1962	7	4
1976	**Committee on Veterans**	

Pop Lloyd
Negro Leaguer

Year		
1977	**Special Committee on Negro Leagues**	

Hans Lobert
.274-32-482 in 1317 G

Year	Votes	Pct.
1937	2	1
1938	1	0
1939	2	1
1960	1	0

Whitey Lockman
.279-114-563 in 1666 G

Year	Votes	Pct.
1966	4	1

Mickey Lolich
217-191, 3.44 in 586 G

Year	Votes	Pct.
1985	78	20
1986	86	20
1987	84	20
1988	109	26
1989	47	11
1990	27	6
1991	33	7
1992	45	10
1993	43	10
1994	23	5
1995	26	6
1996	33	7
1997	34	7
1998	39	8

Ernie Lombardi
.306-190-990 in 1853 G

Year	Votes	Pct.
1950	3	2
1951	3	1
1956	8	4
1958	4	2
1960	6	2
1962	5	3
1964	33	16
1964 Runoff	9	4
1966	34	11
1967	43	15
1967 Runoff	25	8
1986	**Veterans Committee**	

Jim Lonborg
157-137, 3.86 in 425 G

Year	Votes	Pct.
1985	3	1
1986	3	1

Herman Long
.277-91-1054 in 1874 G

Year	Votes	Pct.
1936 Veterans	16	21
1937	1	0
1938	1	0
1939	1	0
1945	1	0
1946	1	0

Ed Lopat

166-112, 3.21 in 340 G

Year	Votes	Pct.
1968	2	1
1969	2	1
1970	1	0
1971	4	1
1972	2	1

Davey Lopes

.263-155-614 in 1812 G

Year	Votes	Pct.
1993	2	0

Al Lopez

.261-51-652 in 1950 G (Manager)

Year	Votes	Pct.
1949	1	1
1952	2	1
1953	2	1
1956	1	1
1958	34	13
1960	26	10
1962	11	7
1964	57	28
1964 Runoff	34	15
1966	109	36
1967	114	39
1967 Runoff	50	16
1977	Committee on Veterans	

Bobby Lowe

.273-71-984 in 1820 G

Year	Votes	Pct.
1936 Veterans	2	3
1942	1	0
1945	2	1

John Lowenstein

.253-116-441 in 1368 G

Year	Votes	Pct.
1991	1	0

Red Lucas

157-135, 3.71 in 396 G

Year	Votes	Pct.
1949	2	1
1950	1	1
1958	1	0

Dolf Luque

193-179, 3.24 in 550 G

Year	Votes	Pct.
1937	1	0
1938	1	0
1939	1	0
1950	1	1
1952	1	0
1953	1	0
1956	1	1
1958	15	6
1960	4	1

Greg Luzinski

.276-307-1128 in 1821 G

Year	Votes	Pct.
1990	1	0

Sparky Lyle

2.88, 238 saves in 899 G

Year	Votes	Pct.
1988	56	13
1989	25	6
1990	25	6
1991	15	3

Fred Lynn

.283-306-1111 in 1969 G

Year	Votes	Pct.
1997	22	5

Ted Lyons

260-230, 3.67 in 594 G

Year	Votes	Pct.
1945	4	2
1946	3	1
1948	15	12
1949	29	19
1949 Runoff	14	7
1950	42	25
1951	71	31
1952	101	43
1953	139	53
1954	170	67
1955	**217**	**86**

Connie Mack

.245-5-265 in 723 G (Manager)

Year	Votes	Pct.
1936	1	0
1937	Centennial Commission	

Larry MacPhail

Executive

Year		
1978	Veterans Committee	

Lee MacPhail

Executive

Year		
1998	Veterans Committee	

Bill Madlock

.305-163-860 in 1806 G

Year	Votes	Pct.
1993	19	4

Sherry Magee

.291-83-1176 in 2087 G

Year	Votes	Pct.
1937	2	1
1938	2	1
1939	1	0
1942	1	0
1945	1	0
1946	1	0
1950	1	1
1951	2	1

Sal Maglie

119-62, 3.15 in 303 G

Year	Votes	Pct.
1964	13	6
1968	11	4

Jim Maloney

134-84, 3.19 in 302 G

Year	Votes	Pct.
1978	2	1
1979	2	0

Gus Mancuso

.265-53-543 in 1460 G

Year	Votes	Pct.
1958	1	0

Mickey Mantle

.298-536-1509 in 2401 G

Year	Votes	Pct.
1974	322	88

Heinie Manush

.330-110-1173 in 2009 G

Year	Votes	Pct.
1948	1	1
1949	1	1
1956	13	7
1958	22	8
1960	20	7
1962	15	9
1964	Committee on Veterans	

Rabbit Maranville

.258-28-884 in 2670 G

Year	Votes	Pct.
1937	25	12
1938	73	28
1939	82	30
1942	66	28
1945	51	21
1946	50	19
1946 Runoff	29	14
1947	91	57
1948	38	31
1949 Runoff	39	21
1950	66	40
1951	110	49
1952	133	57
1953	164	62
1954	**209**	**83**

Firpo Marberry

3.63, 101 saves in 551 G

Year	Votes	Pct.
1938	1	0
1950	1	1
1958	5	2
1960	2	1
1962	2	1

Juan Marichal

243-142, 2.89 in 471 G

Year	Votes	Pct.
1981	233	58
1982	305	73
1983	**313**	**84**

Marty Marion

.263-36-624 in 1572 G

Year	Votes	Pct.
1956	1	1
1960	37	14
1962	16	10
1964	50	25
1964 Runoff	17	8
1966	86	28
1967	90	31
1967 Runoff	22	7
1968	89	31
1969	112	33
1970	120	40
1971	123	34
1972	120	30
1973	127	33

Roger Maris

.260-275-851 in 1463 G

Year	Votes	Pct.
1974	78	21
1975	70	19
1976	87	22
1977	72	19
1978	83	22
1979	127	29
1980	111	29
1981	94	23
1982	69	17
1983	69	18
1984	107	27
1985	128	32
1986	177	42
1987	176	43
1988	184	43

Rube Marquard

201-177, 3.08 in 536 G

Year	Votes	Pct.
1936	1	0
1937	13	6
1938	10	4
1939	4	1
1946	6	2

Year	Votes	Pct.
1947	18	11
1948	6	5
1949	4	3
1951	3	1
1952	9	4
1953	19	7
1954	15	6
1955	35	14
1971	Committee on Veterans	

Mike Marshall

3.14, 188 saves in 723 G

Year	Votes	Pct.
1987	6	1

Billy Martin

.257-64-333 in 1021 G

Year	Votes	Pct.
1967	1	0

Morrie Martin

4.29, 15 saves in 250 G

Year	Votes	Pct.
1966	2	1

Pepper Martin

.298-59-501 in 1189 G

Year	Votes	Pct.
1942	2	1
1945	1	0
1946	1	0
1948	7	6
1949	16	10
1950	7	4
1951	19	8
1952	31	13
1953	43	16
1956	7	4
1958	46	17
1960	29	11
1962	6	4
1964	19	9
1964 Runoff	5	2

Eddie Mathews

.271-512-1453 in 2391 G

Year	Votes	Pct.
1974	118	32
1975	148	41
1976	189	49
1977	239	62
1978	**301**	**79**

Christy Mathewson

373-188, 2.13 in 635 G

Year	Votes	Pct.
1936	**205**	**91**

Lee May

.267-354-1244 in 2071 G

Year	Votes	Pct.
1988	2	0

Carl Mays

207-126, 2.92 in 490 G

Year	Votes	Pct.
1958	6	2

Willie Mays

.302-660-1903 in 2992 G

Year	Votes	Pct.
1979	**409**	**95**

Bill Mazeroski
.260-138-853 in 2163 G

Year	Votes	Pct.
1978	23	6
1979	36	8
1980	33	9
1981	38	9
1982	28	7
1983	48	13
1984	74	18
1985	87	22
1986	100	24
1987	125	30
1988	143	33
1989	134	30
1990	131	30
1991	142	32
1992	182	42

Jimmy McAleer
.253-12-469 in 1020 G

Year	Votes	Pct.
1936 Veterans	1	1

Joe McCarthy
Manager

Year		
1957	Committee on Veterans	

Tommy McCarthy
.292-44-735 in 1275 G

Year	Votes	Pct.
1936 Veterans	1	1
1946	Committee on Old-Timers	

Tim McCarver
.271-97-645 in 1909 G

Year	Votes	Pct.
1986	16	4

Frank McCormick
.299-128-954 in 1534 G

Year	Votes	Pct.
1956	3	2
1962	1	1
1964	6	3
1968	3	1

Willie McCovey
.270-521-1555 in 2588 G

Year	Votes	Pct.
1986	346	81

Lindy McDaniel
3.45, 172 saves in 987 G

Year	Votes	Pct.
1981	1	0
1982	3	1

Gil McDougald
.276-112-576 in 1336 G

Year	Votes	Pct.
1966	5	2
1967	4	1
1968	4	1
1969	3	1
1970	1	0
1971	4	1
1972	4	1
1973	2	1
1974	3	1

Joe McGinnity
246-142, 2.66 in 465 G

Year	Votes	Pct.
1937	12	6
1938	36	14
1939	32	12
1942	59	25
1945	44	18
1946	53	20
1946 Runoff	47	23
1946	Committee on Old-Timers	

Bill McGowan
Umpire

Year		
1992	Veterans Committee	

John McGraw
.334-13-462 in 1099 G (Manager)

Year	Votes	Pct.
1936 Veterans	17	22
1936	4	2
1937	35	17
1937	Centennial Commission	

Tug McGraw
3.14, 180 saves in 824 G

Year	Votes	Pct.
1990	6	1

Stuffy McInnis
.308-20-1060 in 2128 G

Year	Votes	Pct.
1937	1	0
1938	4	2
1939	4	1
1948	5	4
1949	8	5
1950	1	1
1951	3	1

Bill McKechnie
.251-8-240 in 845 G (Manager)

Year	Votes	Pct.
1945	2	1
1946	2	1
1950	1	1
1951	8	4
1962	Committee on Veterans	

Denny McLain
131-91, 3.39 in 280 G

Year	Votes	Pct.
1978	1	0
1979	3	1
1985	2	1

Larry McLean
.262-6-298 in 862 G

Year	Votes	Pct.
1937	1	0

Don McMahon
2.96, 153 saves in 874 G

Year	Votes	Pct.
1980	1	0

Marty McManus
.289-120-996 in 1831 G

Year	Votes	Pct.
1958	2	1
1960	2	1

Roy McMillan
.243-68-594 in 2093 G

Year	Votes	Pct.
1972	9	2
1973	5	1
1974	4	1

Dave McNally
184-119, 3.24 in 424 G

Year	Votes	Pct.
1981	5	1
1982	5	1
1985	7	2
1986	12	3

Cal McVey
.328-3-169 in 265 G

Year	Votes	Pct.
1936 Veterans	1	1

Lee Meadows
188-180, 3.38 in 490 G

Year	Votes	Pct.
1958	2	1

Joe Medwick
.324-205-1383 in 1984 G

Year	Votes	Pct.
1948	1	1
1956	31	16
1958	50	19
1960	38	14
1962	34	21
1964	108	54
1964 Runoff	130	58
1966	187	62
1967	212	73
1967 Runoff	248	81
1968	240	85

Andy Messersmith
130-99, 2.86 in 344 G

Year	Votes	Pct.
1985	3	1
1986	3	1

Bob Meusel
.309-156-1067 in 1407 G

Year	Votes	Pct.
1937	1	0
1938	1	0
1945	1	0
1948	6	5
1949	3	2
1950	2	1
1952	2	1
1955	2	1
1956	1	1
1958	5	2
1960	10	4

Eddie Miksis
.236-44-228 in 1042 G

Year	Votes	Pct.
1964	1	0

Clyde Milan
.285-17-617 in 1981 G

Year	Votes	Pct.
1938	1	0
1950	1	1
1951	1	0
1952	1	0
1953	1	0
1954	3	1
1955	6	2

Felix Millan
.279-22-403 in 1480 G

Year	Votes	Pct.
1983	1	0

Bing Miller
.312-117-990 in 1821 G

Year	Votes	Pct.
1958	1	0
1960	6	2

Dots Miller
.263-32-715 in 1589 G

Year	Votes	Pct.
1948	1	1

Hack Miller
.323-38-205 in 349 G

Year	Votes	Pct.
1937	1	0

Minnie Minoso
.298-186-1023 in 1835 G

Year	Votes	Pct.
1969	6	2
1986	89	21
1987	82	20
1988	90	21
1989	59	13
1990	51	11
1991	38	9
1992	69	16
1993	67	16
1994	45	10
1995	66	14
1996	62	13
1997	84	18
1998	76	16

Johnny Mize
.312-359-1337 in 1884 G

Year	Votes	Pct.
1960	45	17
1962	14	9
1964	54	27
1964 Runoff	12	5
1966	81	27
1967	89	30
1967 Runoff	14	5
1968	103	36
1969	116	34
1970	126	42
1971	157	44
1972	157	40
1973	157	41
1981	Veterans Committee	

Rick Monday
.264-241-775 in 1986 G

Year	Votes	Pct.
1990	2	0

Don Money
.261-176-729 in 1720 G

Year	Votes	Pct.
1989	1	0

Wally Moon
.289-142-661 in 1457 G

Year	Votes	Pct.
1971	2	1

Jo-Jo Moore
.298-79-513 in 1335 G

Year	Votes	Pct.
1950	1	1

Terry Moore
.280-80-513 in 1298 G

Year	Votes	Pct.
1950	1	1
1953	1	0
1958	12	5
1960	7	3
1962	1	1
1964	14	7
1967	3	1
1968	33	12

Pat Moran
.235-18-262 in 818 G (Manager)

Year	Votes	Pct.
1937	1	0
1938	1	0
1939	1	0
1945	1	0

Joe Morgan
.271-268-1133 in 2649 G

Year	Votes	Pct.
1990	363	82

Wally Moses
.291-89-679 in 2012 G

Year	Votes	Pct.
1958	1	0
1960	1	0
1968	4	1
1969	4	1
1970	5	2
1971	7	2

Johnny Mostil
.301-23-376 in 972 G

Year	Votes	Pct.
1956	1	1
1958	1	0

Manny Mota
.304-31-438 in 1536 G

Year	Votes	Pct.
1988	18	4
1989	9	2

Hugh Mulcahy
45-89, 4.49 in 220 G

Year	Votes	Pct.
1948	1	1

Van Lingle Mungo
120-115, 3.47 in 364 G

Year	Votes	Pct.
1945	1	0
1948	1	1
1958	2	1
1960	2	1

Thurman Munson
.292-113-701 in 1423 G

Year	Votes	Pct.
1981	62	15
1982	26	6
1983	18	5
1984	29	7
1985	32	8
1986	35	8
1987	28	7
1988	32	7
1989	31	7
1990	33	7
1991	28	6
1992	32	7
1993	40	9
1994	31	7
1995	30	7

Bobby Murcer
.277-252-1043 in 1908 G

Year	Votes	Pct.
1989	3	1

Danny Murphy
.290-44-702 in 1495 G

Year	Votes	Pct.
1937	1	0
1945	1	0

Red Murray
.270-37-579 in 1264 G

Year	Votes	Pct.
1937	1	0
1938	1	0

Stan Musial
.331-475-1951 in 3026 G

Year	Votes	Pct.
1969	**317**	**93**

Buddy Myer
.303-38-850 in 1923 G

Year	Votes	Pct.
1949	1	1

Art Nehf
184-120, 3.20 in 451 G

Year	Votes	Pct.
1937	3	1
1938	5	2
1939	1	0
1949	1	1
1950	2	1
1951	4	2
1952	3	1
1953	4	2
1954	7	3
1955	7	3
1958	13	5

Graig Nettles
.248-390-1314 in 2700 G

Year	Votes	Pct.
1994	38	8
1995	28	6
1996	37	8
1997	22	5

Don Newcombe
149-90, 3.56 in 344 G

Year	Votes	Pct.
1966	7	2
1967	18	6
1967 Runoff	2	1
1968	9	3
1969	3	1
1970	5	2
1971	8	2
1972	7	2
1973	11	3
1974	7	2
1975	11	3
1976	21	5
1977	43	11
1978	48	13
1979	52	12
1980	59	15

Hal Newhouser
207-150, 3.06 in 488 G

Year	Votes	Pct.
1962	4	3
1964	26	13
1964 Runoff	3	1
1966	32	11
1967	62	21
1967 Runoff	13	4
1968	67	24
1969	82	24
1970	80	27
1971	94	26
1972	92	23
1973	79	21
1974	73	20
1975	155	43
1992	**Veterans Committee**	

Bobo Newsom
211-222, 3.98 in 600 G

Year	Votes	Pct.
1960	6	2
1962	3	2
1964	17	8
1964 Runoff	1	0
1966	25	8
1967	19	7
1967 Runoff	6	2
1968	22	8
1969	32	9
1970	12	4
1971	17	5
1972	31	8
1973	33	9

Kid Nichols
361-208, 2.95 in 620 G

Year	Votes	Pct.
1936 Veterans	3	4
1938	3	1
1939	7	3
1942	5	2
1945	5	2
1946	1	0
1949	**Committee on Old-Timers**	

Bill Nicholson
.268-235-948 in 1677 G

Year	Votes	Pct.
1960	1	0

Joe Niekro
221-204, 3.59 in 702 G

Year	Votes	Pct.
1994	6	1

Phil Niekro
318-274, 3.35 in 864 G

Year	Votes	Pct.
1993	278	66
1994	273	60
1995	286	62
1996	321	68
1997	**380**	**80**

Ron Northey
.276-108-513 in 1084 G

Year	Votes	Pct.
1964	1	0

Jim Northrup
.267-153-610 in 1392 G

Year	Votes	Pct.
1981	1	0

Lefty O'Doul
.349-113-542 in 970 G

Year	Votes	Pct.
1948	4	3
1949	4	3
1950	9	5
1951	13	6
1952	19	8
1953	11	4
1956	5	3
1958	27	10
1960	45	17
1962	13	8

Bob O'Farrell
.273-51-549 in 1492 G

Year	Votes	Pct.
1950	4	2
1958	3	1
1960	3	1

Charley O'Leary
.226-3-213 in 955 G

Year	Votes	Pct.
1953	1	0
1958	1	0
1960	1	0

Steve O'Neill
.263-13-537 in 1586 G

Year	Votes	Pct.
1948	2	2
1949	6	4
1950	1	1
1951	3	1
1952	10	4
1953	13	5
1958	10	4

Jim O'Rourke
.310-51-1010 in 1774 G

Year		
1945	**Committee on Old-Timers**	

Joe Oeschger
82-116, 3.81 in 365 G

Year	Votes	Pct.
1948	1	1

Tony Oliva
.304-220-947 in 1676 G

Year	Votes	Pct.
1982	63	15
1983	75	20
1984	124	31
1985	114	29
1986	154	36
1987	160	39
1988	202	47
1989	135	30
1990	142	32
1991	160	36
1992	175	41
1993	157	37
1994	158	35
1995	149	32
1996	170	36

Al Oliver
.303-219-1326 in 2368 G

Year	Votes	Pct.
1991	19	4

Claude Osteen
196-195, 3.30 in 541 G

Year	Votes	Pct.
1981	2	0

Mel Ott
.304-511-1860 in 2730 G

Year	Votes	Pct.
1949	94	61
1949 Runoff	128	68
1950	115	69
1951	**197**	**87**

Charlie Pabor
National Association

Year	Votes	Pct.
1936 Veterans	1	1

Andy Pafko
.285-213-976 in 1852 G

Year	Votes	Pct.
1966	2	1
1967	1	0

Satchel Paige
3.29, 32 saves in 179 G (Negro Leaguer)

Year	Votes	Pct.
1951	1	0
1971	**Special Committee on Negro Leagues**	

Jim Palmer
268-152, 2.86 in 558 G

Year	Votes	Pct.
1990	**411**	**93**

Milt Pappas
209-164, 3.40 in 520 G

Year	Votes	Pct.
1979	5	1

Dave Parker
.290-339-1493 in 2466 G

Year	Votes	Pct.
1997	84	18
1998	116	25

Larry Parrish
.263-256-992 in 1891 G

Year	Votes	Pct.
1994	2	0

Camilo Pascual
174-170, 3.63 in 529 G

Year	Votes	Pct.
1977	3	1
1978	1	0

Dode Paskert
.268-41-577 in 1716 G

Year	Votes	Pct.
1937	1	0

Monte Pearson
100-61, 4.00 in 224 G

Year	Votes	Pct.
1958	1	0

Roger Peckinpaugh
.259-48-739 in 2012 G

Year	Votes	Pct.
1937	3	1
1938	2	1
1939	1	0
1942	2	1
1949	1	1
1952	2	1
1953	2	1
1954	1	0
1955	1	0

Heinie Peitz
.271-16-560 in 1234 G

Year	Votes	Pct.
1939	1	0

Herb Pennock
241-162, 3.61 in 617 G

Year	Votes	Pct.
1937	15	7
1938	37	14
1939	40	15
1942	72	31
1945	45	18
1946	41	16
1946 Runoff	16	8
1947	86	53
1948	**94**	**78**

Hub Perdue
51-64, 3.85 in 161 G

Year	Votes	Pct.
1938	1	0
1939	1	0

Tony Perez
.279-379-1652 in 2777 G

Year	Votes	Pct.
1992	215	50
1993	233	55
1994	263	58
1995	259	56
1996	309	66
1997	312	66
1998	321	68

Cy Perkins
.259-30-409 in 1171 G

Year	Votes	Pct.
1958	2	1

Ron Perranoski
2.79, 179 saves in 737 G

Year	Votes	Pct.
1979	6	1

Gaylord Perry
314-265, 3.11 in 777 G

Year	Votes	Pct.
1989	304	68
1990	320	72
1991	**342**	**77**

Jim Perry
215-174, 3.45 in 630 G

Year	Votes	Pct.
1981	6	1
1983	7	2

Johnny Pesky
.307-17-404 in 1270 G

Year	Votes	Pct.
1960	1	0

Rico Petrocelli
.251-210-773 in 1553 G

Year	Votes	Pct.
1982	3	1

Deacon Phillippe
189-109, 2.59 in 372 G

Year	Votes	Pct.
1939	1	0
1942	1	0
1945	2	1
1946	1	0

Billy Pierce
211-169, 3.27 in 585 G

Year	Votes	Pct.
1970	5	2
1971	7	2
1972	4	1
1973	4	1
1974	4	1

Lip Pike
.304-5-88 in 163 G

Year	Votes	Pct.
1936 Veterans	1	1

Lou Piniella
.291-102-766 in 1747 G

Year	Votes	Pct.
1990	2	0

Vada Pinson
.286-256-1170 in 2469 G

Year	Votes	Pct.
1981	18	4
1982	6	1
1983	12	3
1985	19	5
1986	43	10
1987	48	12
1988	67	16
1989	33	7
1990	36	8
1991	30	7
1992	36	8
1993	38	9
1994	46	10
1995	32	7
1996	51	11

Wally Pipp
.281-90-996 in 1872 G

Year	Votes	Pct.
1958	1	0

Eddie Plank
326-194, 2.35 in 623 G

Year	Votes	Pct.
1937	23	11
1938	38	15
1939	28	10
1942	63	27
1945	33	13
1946	34	13
1946	**Committee on Old-Timers**	

Johnny Podres
148-116, 3.68 in 440 G

Year	Votes	Pct.
1975	3	1
1976	2	1
1977	3	1

Bob Porterfield
87-97, 3.79 in 318 G

Year	Votes	Pct.
1966	1	0

Boog Powell
.266-339-1187 in 2042 G

Year	Votes	Pct.
1983	5	1

Vic Power
.284-126-658 in 1627 G

Year	Votes	Pct.
1971	2	1
1972	3	1

Hub Pruett
4.63, 13 saves in 211 G

Year	Votes	Pct.
1949	1	1
1950	1	1
1951	1	0
1952	1	0
1953	1	0

Terry Puhl
.280-62-435 in 1531 G

Year	Votes	Pct.
1997	1	0

Jack Quinn
247-218, 3.28 in 755 G

Year	Votes	Pct.
1948	2	2
1958	9	3
1960	2	1

Dan Quisenberry
2.76, 244 saves in 674 G

Year	Votes	Pct.
1996	18	4

Old Hoss Radbourn
309-195, 2.67 in 528 G

Year	Votes	Pct.
1936 Veterans	16	21
1939	**Committee on Old-Timers**	

Willie Randolph
.276-54-687 in 2202 G

Year	Votes	Pct.
1998	5	1

Vic Raschi
132-66, 3.72 in 269 G

Year	Votes	Pct.
1962	1	1
1964	8	4
1968	1	0
1969	3	1
1971	2	1
1972	4	1
1973	7	2
1974	3	1
1975	37	10

Bugs Raymond
45-57, 2.49 in 136 G

Year	Votes	Pct.
1937	1	0

Pee Wee Reese
.269-126-885 in 2166 G

Year	Votes	Pct.
1964	73	36
1964 Runoff	47	21
1966	95	31
1967	89	30
1967 Runoff	16	5
1968	81	29
1969	89	26
1970	97	32
1971	127	35
1972	129	33
1973	126	33
1974	141	39
1975	154	43
1976	186	48
1977	163	43
1978	169	45
1984	**Veterans Committee**	

Pete Reiser
.295-58-368 in 861 G

Year	Votes	Pct.
1958	6	2
1960	8	3

Jack Remsen
.233-5-86 in 341 G

Year	Votes	Pct.
1936 Veterans	1	1

Jerry Remy
.275-7-329 in 1154 G

Year	Votes	Pct.
1990	1	0

Rick Reuschel
214-191, 3.37 in 557 G

Year	Votes	Pct.
1997	2	0

Jerry Reuss
220-191, 3.64 in 628 G

Year	Votes	Pct.
1996	2	0

Allie Reynolds
182-107, 3.30 in 434 G

Year	Votes	Pct.
1956	1	1
1960	24	9
1962	15	9
1964	35	17
1964 Runoff	6	3
1966	60	20
1967	77	26
1967 Runoff	19	6
1968	95	34
1969	98	29
1970	89	30
1971	110	31
1972	105	27
1973	93	24
1974	101	28

Del Rice
.237-79-441 in 1309 G

Year	Votes	Pct.
1966	2	1

Jim Rice
.298-382-1451 in 2089 G

Year	Votes	Pct.
1995	137	30
1996	166	35
1997	178	38
1998	203	43

Sam Rice

.322-34-1078 in 2404 G

Year	Votes	Pct.
1938	1	0
1948	1	1
1949	3	2
1950	1	1
1951	1	0
1952	1	0
1953	3	1
1954	9	4
1955	28	11
1956	45	23
1958	90	34
1960	143	53
1962	81	51
1963	**Committee on Veterans**	

J.R. Richard

107-71, 3.15 in 238 G

Year	Votes	Pct.
1986	7	2

Bobby Richardson

.266-34-390 in 1412 G

Year	Votes	Pct.
1972	8	2
1973	2	1
1974	5	1

Hardy Richardson

.299-70-822 in 1331 G

Year	Votes	Pct.
1936 Veterans	1	1

Branch Rickey

.239-3-39 in 120 G (Executive)

Year		
1967	**Committee on Veterans**	

Jimmy Ring

118-149, 4.12 in 389 G

Year	Votes	Pct.
1949	1	1

Claude Ritchey

.273-18-673 in 1671 G

Year	Votes	Pct.
1945	1	0

Mickey Rivers

.295-61-499 in 1467 G

Year	Votes	Pct.
1990	2	0

Eppa Rixey

266-251, 3.15 in 692 G

Year	Votes	Pct.
1937	1	0
1938	2	1
1945	1	0
1947	2	1
1948	5	4
1949	4	3
1950	6	4
1951	5	2
1952	3	1
1953	3	1
1954	5	2
1955	8	3
1956	27	14
1958	32	12
1960	142	53
1962	49	31
1963	**Committee on Veterans**	

Phil Rizzuto

.273-38-563 in 1661 G

Year	Votes	Pct.
1956	1	1
1962	44	28
1964	45	22
1964 Runoff	11	5
1966	54	18
1967	71	24
1967 Runoff	14	5
1968	74	26
1969	78	23
1970	79	26
1971	92	26
1972	103	26
1973	111	29
1974	111	30
1975	117	32
1976	149	38
1994	**Veterans Committee**	

Robin Roberts

286-245, 3.41 in 676 G

Year	Votes	Pct.
1973	213	56
1974	224	61
1975	263	73
1976	**337**	**87**

Dave Robertson

.287-47-364 in 804 G

Year	Votes	Pct.
1953	1	0

Brooks Robinson

.267-268-1357 in 2896 G

Year	Votes	Pct.
1983	**344**	**92**

Frank Robinson

.294-586-1812 in 2808 G

Year	Votes	Pct.
1982	**370**	**89**

Jackie Robinson

.311-137-734 in 1382 G

Year	Votes	Pct.
1962	**124**	**78**

Wilbert Robinson

.273-18-722 in 1371 G (Manager)

Year	Votes	Pct.
1936 Veterans	6	8
1937	5	2
1938	17	6
1939	46	17
1942	89	38
1945	81	33
1945	**Committee on Old-Timers**	

Preacher Roe

127-84, 3.43 in 333 G

Year	Votes	Pct.
1960	1	0
1962	1	1
1968	2	1
1970	1	0
1971	3	1
1972	2	1

Bullet Joe Rogan

Negro Leaguer

Year		
1998	**Veterans Committee**	

Red Rolfe

.289-69-497 in 1175 G

Year	Votes	Pct.
1950	7	4
1951	6	3
1952	4	2
1953	5	2
1956	3	2
1958	13	5
1960	10	4
1962	1	1

Eddie Rommel

3.54, 29 saves in 500 G

Year	Votes	Pct.
1948	3	2
1949	2	1
1950	1	1
1951	1	0
1952	2	1
1953	1	0
1958	7	3
1960	12	4

Charlie Root

201-160, 3.59 in 632 G

Year	Votes	Pct.
1945	1	0
1948	3	2
1949	1	1
1950	1	1
1958	6	2
1960	2	1

Pete Rose

.303-160-1314 in 3562 G

Year	Votes	Pct.
1992	41	10
1993	14	3
1994	19	4

Edd Roush

.323-68-981 in 1967 G

Year	Votes	Pct.
1936	2	1
1937	10	5
1938	9	3
1939	8	3
1942	1	0
1945	5	2
1946	11	4
1947	25	16
1948	17	14
1949	14	9
1950	16	10
1951	21	9
1952	24	10
1953	32	12
1954	52	21
1955	97	39
1956	91	47
1958	112	42
1960	146	54
1986	**Committee on Veterans**	

Schoolboy Rowe

158-101, 3.87 in 382 G

Year	Votes	Pct.
1958	12	5
1960	3	1
1968	6	2
1969	17	5

Nap Rucker

134-134, 2.42 in 336 G

Year	Votes	Pct.
1936	1	0
1937	11	5
1938	12	5
1939	13	5
1942	15	6
1945	10	4
1946	13	5

Dick Rudolph

121-108, 2.66 in 279 G

Year	Votes	Pct.
1937	1	0
1951	1	0

Muddy Ruel

.275-4-532 in 1470 G

Year	Votes	Pct.
1946	1	0
1950	4	2
1951	1	0
1952	1	0
1953	8	3
1954	5	2
1955	11	4
1956	16	8
1958	10	4
1960	9	3

Red Ruffing

273-225, 3.80 in 624 G

Year	Votes	Pct.
1948	4	3
1949	22	14
1949 Runoff	4	2
1950	12	7
1951	9	4
1952	10	4
1953	24	9
1954	29	12
1955	60	24
1956	97	50
1958	99	37
1960	86	32
1962	72	45
1964	141	70
1964 Runoff	184	82
1966	208	69
1967	212	73
1967 Runoff	**266**	**87**

Amos Rusie

245-174, 3.07 in 462 G

Year	Votes	Pct.
1936 Veterans	12	15
1937	1	0
1938	8	3
1939	6	2
1942	1	0
1945	1	0
1977	**Committee on Veterans**	

Bill Russell

.263-46-627 in 2181 G

Year	Votes	Pct.
1992	3	1

Babe Ruth

.342-714-2210 in 2503 G

Year	Votes	Pct.
1936	215	95

Ray Sadecki

135-131, 3.78 in 563 G

Year	Votes	Pct.
1983	2	1

Johnny Sain

139-116, 3.49 in 412 G

Year	Votes	Pct.
1962	1	1
1964	3	1
1968	7	2
1969	8	2
1970	9	3
1971	11	3
1972	21	5
1973	47	12
1974	51	14
1975	123	34

Manny Sanguillen

.296-65-585 in 1448 G

Year	Votes	Pct.
1986	2	0

Ron Santo

.277-342-1331 in 2243 G

Year	Votes	Pct.
1980	15	4
1985	53	13
1986	64	15
1987	78	19
1988	108	25
1989	75	17
1990	96	22
1991	116	26
1992	136	32
1993	155	37
1994	150	33
1995	139	30
1996	174	37
1997	186	39
1998	204	43

Hank Sauer

.266-288-876 in 1399 G

Year	Votes	Pct.
1966	4	1

Al Schacht

4.48, 2 saves in 53 G

Year	Votes	Pct.
1939	1	0
1948	2	2
1951	4	2
1956	1	1

Germany Schaefer

.257-9-308 in 1143 G

Year	Votes	Pct.
1942	1	0
1953	1	0

Ray Schalk

.253-11-594 in 1760 G

Year	Votes	Pct.
1936	4	2
1937	24	12
1938	45	17
1909	35	13
1942	53	23
1945	33	13
1946	36	14
1947	50	31
1948	22	18
1949	24	16
1949 Runoff	17	9
1950	16	10
1951	37	16
1952	44	19
1953	52	20
1954	54	21
1955	113	45
1955	**Committee on Veterans**	

Wally Schang

.284-59-710 in 1840 G

Year	Votes	Pct.
1948	1	1
1950	1	1
1956	1	1
1958	8	3
1960	11	4

Mike Schmidt

.267-548-1595 in 2404 G

Year	Votes	Pct.
1995	**444**	**97**

Red Schoendienst

.289-84-773 in 2216 G

Year	Votes	Pct.
1969	65	19
1970	97	32
1971	123	34
1972	104	26
1973	96	25
1974	110	30
1975	94	26

Year	Votes	Pct.
1976	129	33
1977	105	27
1978	130	34
1979	159	37
1980	164	43
1981	166	41
1982	135	33
1983	146	39
1989	**Veterans Committee**	

Ossee Schreckengost

.271-9-338 in 893 G

Year	Votes	Pct.
1937	2	1
1938	2	1
1939	2	1

Wildfire Schulte

.270-92-792 in 1806 G

Year	Votes	Pct.
1937	1	0

Hal Schumacher

158-121, 3.36 in 391 G

Year	Votes	Pct.
1948	1	1
1955	1	0
1956	2	1
1958	1	0
1960	11	4
1962	1	1
1964	10	5

Everett Scott

.249-20-549 in 1654 G

Year	Votes	Pct.
1937	2	1
1938	2	1
1939	1	0
1942	1	0
1947	1	1
1948	3	2
1949	3	2
1950	3	2
1951	2	1
1952	4	2
1953	5	2
1954	4	2
1955	8	3
1956	1	1

George Scott

.268-271-1051 in 2034 G

Year	Votes	Pct.
1986	1	0

Jack Scott

103-109, 3.85 in 356 G

Year	Votes	Pct.
1958	1	0

Mike Scott

124-108, 3.54 in 347 G

Year	Votes	Pct.
1997	2	0

Tom Seaver

311-205, 2.86 in 656 G

Year	Votes	Pct.
1992	**425**	**99**

George Selkirk

.290-108-576 in 846 G

Year	Votes	Pct.
1948	1	1
1949	1	1
1950	1	1
1951	2	1
1952	1	0
1953	1	0

Hank Severeid

.289-17-539 in 1390 G

Year	Votes	Pct.
1948	1	1

Joe Sewell

.312-49-1051 in 1903 G

Year	Votes	Pct.
1937	1	0
1948	1	1
1954	1	0
1955	1	0
1956	3	2
1958	1	0
1960	23	9
1977	**Committee on Veterans**	

Luke Sewell

.259-20-696 in 1630 G

Year	Votes	Pct.
1948	1	1
1958	3	1
1960	3	1
1962	1	1

Rip Sewell

143-97, 3.48 in 390 G

Year	Votes	Pct.
1958	1	0
1962	1	1
1964	1	0

Cy Seymour

.303-52-799 in 1528 G

Year	Votes	Pct.
1945	1	0

Bobby Shantz

3.38, 48 saves in 537 G

Year	Votes	Pct.
1970	7	2
1971	5	1
1972	9	2
1973	5	1
1974	3	1

Jimmy Sheckard

.274-56-813 in 2122 G

Year	Votes	Pct.
1938	1	0
1945	1	0
1946	1	0

Bill Sherdel

165-146, 3.72 in 514 G

Year	Votes	Pct.
1948	1	1
1949	1	1
1950	1	1
1951	1	0
1953	1	0
1955	1	0
1956	1	1
1958	2	1
1960	2	1

Urban Shocker

187-117, 3.16 in 411 G

Year	Votes	Pct.
1938	1	0
1939	1	0
1948	1	1
1949	2	1
1958	4	2

Chris Short

135-132, 3.43 in 501 G

Year	Votes	Pct.
1979	1	0

Sonny Siebert

140-114, 3.21 in 399 G

Year	Votes	Pct.
1981	1	0

Roy Sievers

.267-318-1147 in 1887 G

Year	Votes	Pct.
1971	4	1
1972	3	1

Al Simmons

.334-307-1827 in 2215 G

Year	Votes	Pct.
1936	4	2
1946	1	0
1947	6	4
1948	60	50
1949	89	58
1949 Runoff	76	41
1950	90	54
1951	116	51
1952	141	60
1953	**199**	**75**

Curt Simmons

193-183, 3.54 in 569 G

Year	Votes	Pct.
1973	5	1
1974	3	1

Ted Simmons

.285-248-1389 in 2456 G

Year	Votes	Pct.
1994	17	4

George Sisler

.340-102-1175 in 2055 G

Year	Votes	Pct.
1936	77	34
1937	106	53
1938	179	68
1939	**235**	**86**

Sibby Sisti

.244-27-260 in 1016 G

Year	Votes	Pct.
1960	1	0

Enos Slaughter

.300-169-1304 in 2380 G

Year	Votes	Pct.
1966	100	33
1967	123	42
1967 Runoff	48	16
1968	129	46
1969	128	38
1970	133	44
1971	165	46
1972	149	38
1973	145	38
1974	145	40
1975	177	49
1976	197	51
1977	222	58
1978	261	69
1979	297	69
1985	**Veterans Committee**	

Roy Smalley

.227-61-305 in 872 G

Year	Votes	Pct.
1964	1	0

Earl Smith

.303-46-355 in 860 G

Year	Votes	Pct.
1948	1	1
1956	1	1

Reggie Smith

.287-314-1092 in 1987 G

Year	Votes	Pct.
1988	3	1

Sherry Smith

114-118, 3.32 in 373 G

Year	Votes	Pct.
1948	1	1

Duke Snider
.295-407-1333 in 2143 G

Year	Votes	Pct.
1970	51	17
1971	89	25
1972	84	21
1973	101	27
1974	111	30
1975	129	36
1976	159	41
1977	212	55
1978	254	67
1979	308	71
1980	**333**	**86**

Billy Southworth
.297-52-561 in 1192 G

Year	Votes	Pct.
1945	1	0
1946	1	0
1949	7	5
1950	1	1
1951	4	2
1952	1	0
1953	2	1
1958	18	7

Warren Spahn
363-245, 3.09 in 750 G

Year	Votes	Pct.
1973	**316**	**83**

Al Spalding
48-12, 1.78 in 65 G (Pioneer)

Year		
1939	**Committee on Old-Timers**	

Tully Sparks
121-136, 2.79 in 313 G

Year	Votes	Pct.
1946	1	0

Tris Speaker
.345-117-1537 in 2789 G

Year	Votes	Pct.
1936	133	59
1937	**165**	**82**

Chris Speier
.246-112-720 in 2260 G

Year	Votes	Pct.
1995	1	0

Jake Stahl
.260-31-437 in 981 G

Year	Votes	Pct.
1938	1	0
1939	1	0

Eddie Stanky
.268-29-364 in 1259 G

Year	Votes	Pct.
1960	3	1

Mickey Stanley
.248-117-500 in 1516 G

Year	Votes	Pct.
1984	2	0

Willie Stargell
.282-475-1540 in 2360 G

Year	Votes	Pct.
1988	**352**	**82**

Rusty Staub
.279-292-1466 in 2951 G

Year	Votes	Pct.
1991	28	6
1992	26	6
1993	32	8
1994	36	8
1995	23	5
1996	24	5
1997	18	4

Harry Steinfeldt
.267-27-762 in 1646 G

Year	Votes	Pct.
1937	1	0
1939	1	0
1942	1	0

Casey Stengel
.284-60-535 in 1277 G (Manager)

Year	Votes	Pct.
1938	2	1
1939	6	2
1945	2	1
1948	1	1
1949	3	2
1950	3	2
1951	8	4
1952	27	12
1953	61	23
1966	**Committee on Veterans**	

Riggs Stephenson
.336-63-773 in 1310 G

Year	Votes	Pct.
1956	2	1
1958	1	0
1960	4	1
1962	1	1

Mel Stottlemyre
164-139, 2.97 in 360 G

Year	Votes	Pct.
1980	3	1

Harry Stovey
.288-122-760 in 1486 G

Year	Votes	Pct.
1936 Veterans	6	8

Gabby Street
.208-2-105 in 503 G

Year	Votes	Pct.
1937	1	0
1938	1	0
1939	1	0

Gus Suhr
.279-84-818 in 1435 G

Year	Votes	Pct.
1956	1	1
1958	1	0
1960	1	0

Clyde Sukeforth
.264-2-96 in 486 G

Year	Votes	Pct.
1958	1	0

Billy Sullivan
.212-21-378 in 1146 G

Year	Votes	Pct.
1937	1	0
1946	1	0

Jim Sundberg
.248-95-624 in 1962 G

Year	Votes	Pct.
1995	1	0

Bruce Sutter
2.83, 300 saves in 661 G

Year	Votes	Pct.
1994	109	24
1995	137	30
1996	137	29
1997	130	27
1998	147	31

Don Sutton
324-256, 3.26 in 774 G

Year	Votes	Pct.
1994	259	57
1995	264	57
1996	300	64
1997	346	73
1998	**386**	**82**

Bill Sweeney
.272-11-389 in 1039 G

Year	Votes	Pct.
1945	1	0

Jesse Tannehill
197-116, 2.79 in 358 G

Year	Votes	Pct.
1946	1	0

Birdie Tebbetts
.270-38-469 in 1162 G

Year	Votes	Pct.
1958	8	3
1960	1	0

Kent Tekulve
2.85, 184 saves in 1050 G

Year	Votes	Pct.
1995	6	1

Garry Templeton
.271-70-728 in 2079 G

Year	Votes	Pct.
1997	2	0

Gene Tenace
.241-201-674 in 1555 G

Year	Votes	Pct.
1989	1	0

Fred Tenney
.294-22-688 in 1994 G

Year	Votes	Pct.
1936 Veterans	1	1
1937	5	2
1938	8	3
1939	3	1
1942	1	0
1946	1	0

Bill Terry
.341-154-1078 in 1721 G

Year	Votes	Pct.
1936	9	4
1938	7	3
1939	16	6
1942	36	15
1945	32	13
1946	31	12
1947	46	29
1948	52	43
1949	81	53
1949 Runoff	48	26
1950	105	63
1951	148	65
1952	155	66
1953	191	72
1954	**195**	**77**

Tommy Thevenow
.247-2-456 in 1229 G

Year	Votes	Pct.
1950	2	1

Ira Thomas
.242-3-155 in 481 G

Year	Votes	Pct.
1938	1	0

Sam Thompson
.331-127-1299 in 1407 G

Year		
1974	**Committee on Veterans**	

Bobby Thomson
.270-264-1026 in 1779 G

Year	Votes	Pct.
1966	12	4
1967	10	3
1967 Runoff	1	0
1968	13	5
1969	6	2
1970	4	1
1971	4	1
1972	10	3
1973	3	1
1974	6	2
1975	10	3
1976	9	2
1977	10	3
1978	5	1
1979	11	3

Andre Thornton
.254-253-895 in 1565 G

Year	Votes	Pct.
1993	2	0

Luis Tiant
229-172, 3.30 in 573 G

Year	Votes	Pct.
1988	132	31
1989	47	11
1990	42	9
1991	32	7
1992	50	12
1993	62	15
1994	42	9
1995	45	10
1996	64	14
1997	53	11
1998	62	13

Joe Tinker
.262-31-782 in 1803 G

Year	Votes	Pct.
1937	15	7
1938	16	6
1939	12	4
1942	36	15
1945	49	20
1946	55	21
1946 Runoff	45	22
1946	**Committee on Old-Timers**	

Jim Tobin
105-112, 3.45 in 287 G

Year	Votes	Pct.
1956	2	1

Fred Toney
137-102, 2.69 in 336 G

Year	Votes	Pct.
1949	1	1

Earl Torgeson
.265-149-740 in 1668 G

Year	Votes	Pct.
1967	2	1

Joe Torre
.297-252-1185 in 2209 G

Year	Votes	Pct.
1983	20	5
1984	45	11
1985	44	11
1986	60	14
1987	47	11
1988	60	14
1989	40	9
1990	55	12
1991	41	9
1992	62	14
1993	63	15
1994	53	12
1995	50	11
1996	50	11
1997	105	22

Mike Torrez
185-160, 3.96 in 494 G

Year	Votes	Pct.
1990	1	0

Pie Traynor
.320-58-1273 in 1941 G

Year	Votes	Pct.
1936	16	7
1938	3	1
1939	10	4
1942	45	19
1945	81	33
1946	65	25
1946 Runoff	53	26
1947	119	74
1948	**93**	**77**

Dizzy Trout
170-161, 3.23 in 521 G

Year	Votes	Pct.
1964	1	0

Virgil Trucks
177-135, 3.39 in 517 G

Year	Votes	Pct.
1964	4	2

John Tudor
117-72, 3.12 in 281 G

Year	Votes	Pct.
1996	2	0

Jim Turner
69-60, 3.22 in 231 G

Year	Votes	Pct.
1956	1	1

Terry Turner
.253-8-528 in 1665 G

Year	Votes	Pct.
1947	2	1

George Uhle
200-166, 3.99 in 513 G

Year	Votes	Pct.
1956	1	1
1958	4	2
1960	4	1

Ellis Valentine
.278-123-474 in 894 G

Year	Votes	Pct.
1991	1	0

Elmer Valo
.282-58-601 in 1806 G

Year	Votes	Pct.
1967	2	1

George Van Haltren
.316-69-1014 in 1984 G

Year	Votes	Pct.
1936 Veterans	1	1

Dazzy Vance
197-140, 3.24 in 442 G

Year	Votes	Pct.
1936	1	0
1937	10	5
1938	10	4
1939	15	5
1942	37	16
1945	18	7
1946	31	12
1947	50	31
1948	23	19
1949	33	22
1949 Runoff	15	8
1950	52	31
1951	70	31
1952	105	45
1953	150	57
1954	158	63
1955	**205**	**82**

Johnny Vander Meer
119-121, 3.44 in 346 G

Year	Votes	Pct.
1945	1	0
1956	3	2
1958	35	13
1960	31	12
1962	5	3
1964	51	25
1964 Runoff	20	9
1966	72	24
1967	87	30
1967 Runoff	35	11
1968	79	28
1969	95	28
1970	88	29
1971	98	27

Arky Vaughan
.318-96-926 in 1817 G

Year	Votes	Pct.
1953	1	0
1954	2	1
1955	4	2
1956	9	5
1958	6	2
1960	10	4
1962	6	4
1964	17	8
1964 Runoff	6	3
1966	36	12
1967	46	16
1967 Runoff	19	6
1968	82	29
1985		**Veterans Committee**

Bobby Veach
.310-64-1166 in 1822 G

Year	Votes	Pct.
1937	1	0

Bill Veeck
Executive

Year		
1991		**Veterans Committee**

Mickey Vernon
.286-172-1311 in 2409 G

Year	Votes	Pct.
1966	20	7
1967	14	5
1967 Runoff	2	1
1968	22	8
1969	21	6
1970	10	3
1971	12	3
1972	12	3
1973	23	6
1974	27	7
1975	22	6
1976	52	13
1977	52	14
1978	66	17
1979	88	20
1980	96	25

Bill Virdon
.267-91-502 in 1583 G

Year	Votes	Pct.
1974	3	1
1975	1	0

Rube Waddell
193-143, 2.16 in 407 G

Year	Votes	Pct.
1936	33	15
1937	67	33
1938	148	56
1939	179	65
1942	126	54
1945	154	62
1946	122	46
1946 Runoff	87	43
1946		**Committee on Old-Timers**

Honus Wagner
.327-101-1732 in 2792 G

Year	Votes	Pct.
1936 Veterans	5	6
1936	**215**	**95**

Rube Walberg
155-141, 4.17 in 544 G

Year	Votes	Pct.
1958	1	0
1960	1	0

Dixie Walker
.306-105-1023 in 1905 G

Year	Votes	Pct.
1962	1	1
1964	6	3
1968	6	2
1969	9	3

Harry Walker
.296-10-214 in 807 G

Year	Votes	Pct.
1958	1	0

Bobby Wallace
.268-34-1121 in 2383 G

Year	Votes	Pct.
1936 Veterans	1	1
1937	1	0
1938	7	3
1939	5	2
1942	2	1
1945	3	1
1953		**Committee on Veterans**

Ed Walsh
195-126, 1.81 in 431 G

Year	Votes	Pct.
1936	20	9
1937	56	28
1938	110	42
1939	132	48
1942	113	48
1945	137	55
1946	115	44
1946 Runoff	106	52
1946		**Committee on Old-Timers**

Bucky Walters
198-160, 3.30 in 428 G

Year	Votes	Pct.
1950	4	2
1952	3	1
1953	10	4
1956	5	3
1958	33	12
1960	19	7
1962	5	3
1964	35	17
1964 Runoff	8	4
1966	56	19
1967	65	22
1967 Runoff	24	8
1968	67	24
1969	20	6
1970	29	10

Bill Wambsganss
.259-7-519 in 1492 G

Year	Votes	Pct.
1942	1	0
1950	1	1
1953	1	0
1954	4	2
1955	5	2
1956	1	1

Lloyd Waner
.316-27-598 in 1993 G

Year	Votes	Pct.
1949	3	2
1950	1	1
1951	1	0
1952	2	1
1956	18	9
1958	39	15
1960	22	8
1962	5	3
1964	47	23
1964 Runoff	12	5
1967		**Committee on Veterans**

Paul Waner
.333-113-1309 in 2549 G

Year	Votes	Pct.
1946	4	2
1948	51	42
1949	73	48
1949 Runoff	63	34
1950	95	57
1951	162	72
1952	**195**	**83**

Monte Ward
.275-26-867 in 1825 G

Year	Votes	Pct.
1936 Veterans	3	4
1964		**Committee on Veterans**

Lon Warneke
192-121, 3.18 in 445 G

Year	Votes	Pct.
1949	2	1
1958	2	1
1960	4	1
1962	2	1
1964	13	6

Bob Watson
.295-184-989 in 1832 G

Year	Votes	Pct.
1990	3	1

Earl Weaver
Manager

Year		
1996		**Veterans Committee**

George Weiss
Executive

Year		
1971		**Committee on Veterans**

Mickey Welch
309-211, 2.71 in 564 G

Year		
1973		**Committee on Veterans**

Willie Wells
Negro Leaguer

Year		
1997		**Veterans Committee**

Bill Werber
.271-78-539 in 1295 G

Year	Votes	Pct.
1949	1	1
1950	1	1
1952	1	0
1958	3	1

Vic Wertz

.277-266-1178 in 1862 G

Year	Votes	Pct.
1970	2	1
1971	2	1
1972	4	1
1973	2	1
1974	2	1
1975	5	1
1976	5	1
1977	4	1
1978	4	1

Sammy West

.299-75-838 in 1753 G

Year	Votes	Pct.
1948	1	1

Wes Westrum

.217-96-315 in 919 G

Year	Votes	Pct.
1964	2	1

Zack Wheat

.317-132-1248 in 2410 G

Year	Votes	Pct.
1937	5	2
1938	7	3
1939	4	1
1942	3	1
1945	2	1
1946	6	2
1947	37	23
1948	15	12
1949	15	10
1950	17	10
1951	19	8
1952	30	13
1953	32	12
1954	33	13
1955	51	20
1956	26	13
1959	**Committee on Veterans**	

Deacon White

.303-18-756 in 1299 G

Year	Votes	Pct.
1936 Veterans	1	1

Frank White

.255-160-886 in 2324 G

Year	Votes	Pct.
1996	18	4

Will White

229-166, 2.28 in 403 G

Year	Votes	Pct.
1975	7	2
1976	7	2
1977	4	1

Burgess Whitehead

.266-17-245 in 924 G

Year	Votes	Pct.
1956	1	1

Earl Whitehill

218-185, 4.36 in 541 G

Year	Votes	Pct.
1956	1	1
1958	2	1
1960	3	1

Hoyt Wilhelm

2.52, 227 saves in 1070 G

Year	Votes	Pct.
1978	158	42
1979	168	39
1980	209	54
1981	238	59
1982	236	57
1983	243	65
1984	290	72
1985	**331**	**84**

Billy Williams

.290-426-1475 in 2488 G

Year	Votes	Pct.
1982	97	23
1983	153	41
1984	202	50
1985	252	64
1986	315	74
1987	**354**	**86**

Cy Williams

.292-251-1005 in 2002 G

Year	Votes	Pct.
1938	1	0
1945	1	0
1948	1	1
1949	2	1
1950	9	5
1951	7	3
1952	4	2
1953	4	2
1954	4	2
1955	3	1
1956	11	6
1958	6	2
1960	11	4

Ken Williams

.319-196-913 in 1397 G

Year	Votes	Pct.
1956	1	1
1958	1	0

Ted Williams

.344-521-1839 in 2292 G

Year	Votes	Pct.
1966	**282**	**93**

Ned Williamson

.255-64-667 in 1201 G

Year	Votes	Pct.
1936 Veterans	2	3

Vic Willis

249-205, 2.63 in 513 G

Year		
1995	**Veterans Committee**	

Maury Wills

.281-20-458 in 1942 G

Year	Votes	Pct.
1978	115	30
1979	166	38
1980	146	38
1981	163	41
1982	91	22
1983	77	21
1984	104	26
1985	93	24
1986	124	29
1987	113	27
1988	127	30
1989	95	21
1990	95	21
1991	61	14
1992	110	26

Hack Wilson

.307-244-1062 in 1348 G

Year	Votes	Pct.
1937	1	0
1939	1	0
1942	1	0
1948	2	2
1949	24	16
1949 Runoff	12	6
1950	16	10
1951	21	9
1952	21	9
1953	43	16
1954	48	19
1955	81	32
1956	74	38
1958	94	35
1960	72	27
1962	39	24
1979	**Veterans Committee**	

Jim Wilson

86-89, 4.01 in 257 G

Year	Votes	Pct.
1964	2	1

Jimmie Wilson

.284-32-621 in 1525 G

Year	Votes	Pct.
1948	8	7
1949	6	4
1950	4	2
1951	2	1
1952	7	3
1953	10	4
1954	8	3
1955	13	5
1956	17	9
1958	3	1
1960	6	2
1962	4	3

Whitey Witt

.287-18-302 in 1139 G

Year	Votes	Pct.
1949	1	1

Joe Wood

116-57, 2.03 in 225 G

Year	Votes	Pct.
1937	13	6
1938	6	2
1939	2	1
1942	1	0
1946	5	2
1947	29	18
1948	5	4
1950	1	1
1951	5	2

Wilbur Wood

3.24, 57 saves in 651 G

Year	Votes	Pct.
1984	14	3
1985	16	4
1986	23	5
1987	26	6
1988	30	7
1989	14	3

George Wright

.256-2-132 in 329 G (Pioneer)

Year	Votes	Pct.
1936	6	8
1937	**Centennial Commission**	

Glenn Wright

.294-94-723 in 1119 G

Year	Votes	Pct.
1948	2	2
1949	1	1
1950	2	1
1951	1	0
1952	1	0
1953	3	1
1954	1	0
1955	4	2
1956	3	2
1958	8	3
1960	18	7
1962	1	1

Harry Wright

.000-0-0 in 2 G (Pioneer)

Year		
1953	**Committee on Veterans**	

Whit Wyatt

106-95, 3.79 in 360 G

Year	Votes	Pct.
1958	1	0

Early Wynn

300-244, 3.54 in 691 G

Year	Votes	Pct.
1969	95	28
1970	140	47
1971	240	67
1972	**301**	**76**

Carl Yastrzemski

.285-452-1844 in 3308 G

Year	Votes	Pct.
1989	**423**	**95**

Tom Yawkey

Executive

Year		
1980	**Veterans Committee**	

Steve Yeager

.228-102-410 in 1269 G

Year	Votes	Pct.
1992	2	0

Steve Yerkes

.269-6-254 in 711 G

Year	Votes	Pct.
1945	1	0

Rudy York

.275-277-1152 in 1603 G

Year	Votes	Pct.
1962	1	1
1964	10	5

Cy Young

511-316, 2.63 in 906 G

Year	Votes	Pct.
1936 Veterans	32	41
1936	111	49
1937	**153**	**76**

Pep Young

.262-32-347 in 730 G

Year	Votes	Pct.
1958	1	0

Ross Youngs

.322-42-592 in 1211 G

Year	Votes	Pct.
1936	10	4
1937	16	8
1938	40	15
1939	34	12
1942	44	19
1945	22	9
1946	25	10
1947	36	22
1948	19	16
1949	20	13
1949 Runoff	11	6
1950	17	10
1951	34	15
1952	34	15
1953	31	12
1954	34	13
1955	48	19
1956	19	10
1972	**Committee on Veterans**	

Tom Zachary

186-191, 3.73 in 533 G

Year	Votes	Pct.
1958	1	0
1960	1	0

Chief Zimmer

.269-26-625 in 1280 G

Year	Votes	Pct.
1938	1	0

Writers and Broadcasters in the Hall of Fame

Ford C. Frick Award

Year	Broadcaster	Year	Broadcaster	Year	Broadcaster	Year	Broadcaster
1978	Mel Allen	1982	Vin Scully	1988	Lindsey Nelson	1994	Bob Murphy
	Red Barber	1983	Jack Brickhouse	1989	Harry Caray	1995	Bob Wolff
1979	Bob Elson	1984	Curt Gowdy	1990	By Saam	1996	Herb Carneal
1980	Russ Hodges	1985	Buck Canel	1991	Joe Garagiola	1997	Jimmy Dudley
1981	Ernie Harwell	1986	Bob Prince	1992	Milo Hamilton	1998	Jaime Jarrin
		1987	Jack Buck	1993	Chuck Thompson		

J.G. Taylor Spink Award

Year	Writer	Year	Writer	Year	Writer	Year	Writer
1962	J.G. Taylor Spink	1973	J. Roy Stockton		Dick Young	1988	Bob Hunter
1963	Ring Lardner		Warren Brown	1979	Bob Broeg		Ray Kelly
1964	Hugh Fullerton		John Drebinger		Tommy Holmes	1989	Jerome Holtzman
1965	Charles Dryden		John F. Kieran	1980	Joe Reichler	1990	Phil Collier
1966	Grantland Rice	1974	John Carmichael		Milton Richman	1991	Ritter Collett
1967	Damon Runyon		James Isaminger	1981	Bob Addie	1992	Leonard Koppett
1968	H.G. Salsinger	1975	Tom Meany		Allen Lewis		Bus Saidt
1969	Sid Mercer		Shirley Povich	1982	Si Burick	1993	Wendell Smith
1970	Heywood C. Broun	1976	Harold Kaese	1983	Ken Smith	1995	Joseph Durso
1971	Frank Graham		Red Smith	1984	Joe McGuff	1996	Charley Feeney
1972	Dan Daniel	1977	Gordon Cobbledick	1985	Earl Lawson	1997	Sam Lacy
	Fred Lieb		Edgar Munzel	1986	Jack Lang		
		1978	Tim Murnane	1987	Jim Murray		

1911

American League

MVP

Player, Pos, Team	Stats	1st Pl	Pts	Share
Ty Cobb, of, Det	.420-8-127	8.0	64.0	1.00
Ed Walsh, p, ChA	27-18, 2.22	0.0	35.0	0.55
Eddie Collins, 2b, Phi	.365-3-73	0.0	32.0	0.50
Joe Jackson, of, Cle	.408-7-83	0.0	28.0	0.44
Walter Johnson, p, Was	25-13, 1.90	0.0	19.0	0.30
Birdie Cree, of, NYA	.348-4-88	0.0	16.0	0.25
Tris Speaker, of, Bos	.334-8-80	0.0	16.0	0.25
Ira Thomas, c, Phi	.273-0-39	0.0	12.0	0.19
Clyde Milan, of, Was	.315-3-35	0.0	10.0	0.16
Vean Gregg, p, Cle	23-7, 1.80	0.0	9.0	0.14
Home Run Baker, 3b, Phi	.334-11-115	0.0	8.0	0.13
Jack Coombs, p, Phi	28-12, 3.53	0.0	6.0	0.09
Nap Lajoie, 1b, Cle	.365-2-60	0.0	5.0	0.08
John Knight, ss, NYA	.268-3-62	0.0	4.0	0.06
Sam Crawford, of, Det	.378-7-115	0.0	4.0	0.06
Bris Lord, of, Phi	.310-3-55	0.0	4.0	0.06
Donie Bush, ss, Det	.232-1-36	0.0	4.0	0.06
Russ Ford, p, NYA	22-11, 2.27	0.0	3.0	0.05
Jack Barry, ss, Phi	.265-1-63	0.0	3.0	0.05
Jimmy Austin, 3b, StL	.261-2-45	0.0	2.0	0.03
Frank LaPorte, 2b, StL	.314-2-82	0.0	2.0	0.03
Stuffy McInnis, 1b, Phi	.321-3-77	0.0	1.0	0.02
George McBride, ss, Was	.235-0-59	0.0	1.0	0.02

National League

MVP

Player, Pos, Team	Stats	1st Pl	Pts	Share
Wildfire Schulte, of, ChN	.300-21-107	0.0	29.0	0.45
Christy Mathewson, p, NYG	26-13, 1.99	0.0	25.0	0.39
Larry Doyle, 2b, NYG	.310-13-77	0.0	23.0	0.36
Honus Wagner, ss, Pit	.334-9-89	0.0	23.0	0.36
Pete Alexander, p, Phi	28-13, 2.57	0.0	23.0	0.36
Miller Huggins, 2b, StL	.261-1-24	0.0	21.0	0.33
Fred Merkle, 1b, NYG	.283-12-84	0.0	19.0	0.30
Rube Marquard, p, NYG	24-7, 2.50	0.0	19.0	0.30
Jake Daubert, 1b, Bro	.307-5-45	0.0	16.0	0.25
Joe Tinker, ss, ChN	.278-4-69	0.0	11.0	0.17
Chief Meyers, c, NYG	.332-1-61	0.0	11.0	0.17
Jimmy Sheckard, of, ChN	.276-4-50	0.0	9.0	0.14
Mike Mitchell, of, Cin	.291-2-84	0.0	9.0	0.14
Mickey Doolan, ss, Phi	.238-1-49	0.0	6.0	0.09
Bob Harmon, p, StL	23-16, 3.13	0.0	6.0	0.09
Jimmy Archer, c, ChN	.253-4-41	0.0	5.0	0.08
Hans Lobert, 3b, Phi	.285-9-72	0.0	4.0	0.06
George Gibson, c, Pit	.209-0-19	0.0	4.0	0.06
Three Finger Brown, p, ChN	21-11, 2.80	0.0	4.0	0.06
Bob Bescher, of, Cin	.275-1-44	0.0	4.0	0.06
Bill Sweeney, 2b, Bos	.314-3-63	0.0	3.0	0.05
Otto Knabe, 2b, Phi	.237-1-42	0.0	2.0	0.03
Ed Konetchy, 1b, StL	.289-6-88	0.0	2.0	0.03
Doc Hoblitzell, 1b, Cin	.289-11-91	0.0	2.0	0.03
Jimmy Walsh, of, Phi	.270-1-31	0.0	2.0	0.03
Josh Devore, of, NYG	.280-3-50	0.0	2.0	0.03
Fred Luderus, 1b, Phi	.301-16-99	0.0	1.0	0.02
Johnny Kling, c, ChN-Bos	.212-3-29	0.0	1.0	0.02
Babe Adams, p, Pit	22-12, 2.33	0.0	1.0	0.02
Nap Rucker, p, Bro	22-18, 2.74	0.0	1.0	0.02

1912

American League

MVP

Player, Pos, Team	Stats	1st Pl	Pts	Share
Tris Speaker, of, Bos	.383-10-90	0.0	59.0	0.92
Ed Walsh, p, ChA	27-17, 2.15	0.0	30.0	0.47
Walter Johnson, p, Was	33-12, 1.39	0.0	28.0	0.44
Clyde Milan, of, Was	.306-1-79	0.0	23.0	0.36
Joe Wood, p, Bos	34-5, 1.91	0.0	22.0	0.34
Eddie Collins, 2b, Phi	.348-0-64	0.0	18.0	0.28
Home Run Baker, 3b, Phi	.347-10-130	0.0	17.0	0.27
Ty Cobb, of, Det	.410-7-83	0.0	17.0	0.27
Joe Jackson, of, Cle	.395-3-90	0.0	16.0	0.25
Heinie Wagner, ss, Bos	.274-2-68	0.0	12.0	0.19
Chick Gandil, 1b, Was	.305-2-81	0.0	7.0	0.11
Burt Shotton, of, StL	.290-2-40	0.0	6.0	0.09
Del Pratt, 2b, StL	.302-5-69	0.0	5.0	0.08
Eddie Foster, 3b, Was	.285-2-70	0.0	4.0	0.06
Larry Gardner, 3b, Bos	.315-3-86	0.0	4.0	0.06
Sam Crawford, of, Det	.325-4-109	0.0	4.0	0.06
Jack Barry, ss, Phi	.261-0-55	0.0	4.0	0.06
Bill Carrigan, c, Bos	.263-0-24	0.0	3.0	0.05
George Moriarty, 3b, Det	.248-0-54	0.0	3.0	0.05
Joe Birmingham, of, Cle	.255-1-45	0.0	2.0	0.03
Danny Moeller, of, Was	.276-6-46	0.0	1.0	0.02
George McBride, ss, Was	.226-1-52	0.0	1.0	0.02
Stuffy McInnis, 1b, Phi	.327-3-101	0.0	1.0	0.02
Bert Daniels, of, NYA	.274-2-41	0.0	1.0	0.02

National League

MVP

Player, Pos, Team	Stats	1st Pl	Pts	Share
Larry Doyle, 2b, NYG	.330-10-90	0.0	48.0	0.75
Honus Wagner, ss, Pit	.324-7-102	0.0	43.0	0.67
Chief Meyers, c, NYG	.358-6-54	0.0	25.0	0.39
Joe Tinker, ss, ChN	.282-0-75	0.0	23.0	0.36
Bob Bescher, of, Cin	.281-4-38	0.0	17.0	0.27
Bill Sweeney, 2b, Bos	.344-1-100	0.0	16.0	0.25
Heinie Zimmerman, 3b, ChN	.372-14-99	0.0	16.0	0.25
Rube Marquard, p, NYG	26-11, 2.57	0.0	13.0	0.20
Chief Wilson, of, Pit	.300-11-95	0.0	13.0	0.20
Jake Daubert, 1b, Bro	.308-3-66	0.0	13.0	0.20
Otto Knabe, 2b, Phi	.282-0-46	0.0	10.0	0.16
Ed Konetchy, 1b, StL	.314-8-82	0.0	8.0	0.13
Christy Mathewson, p, NYG	23-12, 2.12	0.0	8.0	0.13
Dode Paskert, of, Phi	.315-2-43	0.0	6.0	0.09
Jeff Tesreau, p, NYG	17-7, 1.96	0.0	6.0	0.09
Red Murray, of, NYG	.277-3-92	0.0	5.0	0.08
Miller Huggins, 2b, StL	.304-0-29	0.0	5.0	0.08
Armando Marsans, of, Cin	.317-1-38	0.0	4.0	0.06
Fred Merkle, 1b, NYG	.309-11-84	0.0	4.0	0.06
Johnny Evers, 2b, ChN	.341-1-63	0.0	3.0	0.05
Claude Hendrix, p, Pit	24-9, 2.59	0.0	3.0	0.05
Jimmy Archer, c, ChN	.283-5-58	0.0	1.0	0.02
Pete Alexander, p, Phi	19-17, 2.81	0.0	1.0	0.02

1913

American League

MVP

Player, Pos, Team	Stats	1st Pl	Pts	Share
Walter Johnson, p, Was	36-7, 1.14	0.0	54.0	0.84
Joe Jackson, of, Cle	.373-7-71	0.0	43.0	0.67
Eddie Collins, 2b, Phi	.345-3-73	0.0	30.0	0.47
Tris Speaker, of, Bos	.363-3-71	0.0	26.0	0.41
Home Run Baker, 3b, Phi	.336-12-117	0.0	21.0	0.33
Chick Gandil, 1b, Was	.318-1-72	0.0	14.0	0.22
Stuffy McInnis, 1b, Phi	.326-4-90	0.0	12.0	0.19
Wally Schang, c, Phi	.266-3-30	0.0	11.0	0.17
Clyde Milan, of, Was	.301-3-54	0.0	8.0	0.13
Jack Barry, ss, Phi	.275-3-85	0.0	8.0	0.13
Nap Lajoie, 2b, Cle	.335-1-68	0.0	7.0	0.11
Donie Bush, ss, Det	.251-1-40	0.0	6.0	0.09
Heinie Wagner, ss, Bos	.227-2-34	0.0	6.0	0.09
Reb Russell, p, ChA	22-16, 1.91	0.0	5.0	0.08
Burt Shotton, of, StL	.297-1-28	0.0	5.0	0.08
George McBride, ss, Was	.214-1-52	0.0	5.0	0.08
Jim Scott, p, ChA	20-20, 1.90	0.0	5.0	0.08
George Stovall, 1b, StL	.287-1-24	0.0	5.0	0.08
Sam Crawford, of, Det	.316-9-83	0.0	5.0	0.08
Ty Cobb, of, Det	.390-4-67	0.0	3.0	0.05
Ray Schalk, c, ChA	.244-1-38	0.0	3.0	0.05
Chief Bender, p, Phi	2.20, 13 saves	0.0	2.0	0.03
Terry Turner, 3b, Cle	.247-0-44	0.0	2.0	0.03
Steve O'Neill, c, Cle	.295-0-29	0.0	1.0	0.02
Harry Hooper, of, Bos	.288-4-40	0.0	1.0	0.02

National League

MVP

Player, Pos, Team	Stats	1st Pl	Pts	Share
Jake Daubert, 1b, Bro	.350-2-52	0.0	50.0	0.78
Gavy Cravath, of, Phi	.341-19-128	0.0	40.0	0.63
Rabbit Maranville, ss, Bos	.247-2-48	0.0	23.0	0.36
Christy Mathewson, p, NYG	25-11, 2.06	0.0	21.0	0.33
Chief Meyers, c, NYG	.312-3-47	0.0	20.0	0.31
Vic Saier, 1b, ChN	.289-14-92	0.0	15.0	0.23
Larry Cheney, p, ChN	21-14, 2.57	0.0	12.0	0.19
Dots Miller, 1b, Pit	.272-7-90	0.0	11.0	0.17
Honus Wagner, ss, Pit	.300-3-56	0.0	11.0	0.17
Johnny Evers, 2b, ChN	.285-3-49	0.0	10.0	0.16
Tom Seaton, p, Phi	27-12, 2.60	0.0	9.0	0.14
Art Fletcher, ss, NYG	.297-4-71	0.0	7.0	0.11
Jimmy Archer, c, ChN	.266-2-44	0.0	6.0	0.09
Bill Sweeney, 2b, Bos	.257-0-47	0.0	6.0	0.09
Jim Viox, 2b, Pit	.317-2-65	0.0	6.0	0.09
Larry Doyle, 2b, NYG	.280-5-73	0.0	5.0	0.08
Tillie Shafer, 3b, NYG	.287-5-52	0.0	5.0	0.08
Red Murray, of, NYG	.267-2-59	0.0	4.0	0.06
Heinie Zimmerman, 3b, ChN	.313-9-95	0.0	4.0	0.06
Otto Knabe, 2b, Phi	.263-2-53	0.0	4.0	0.06
Babe Adams, p, Pit	21-10, 2.15	0.0	3.0	0.05
George Cutshaw, 2b, Bro	.267-7-80	0.0	3.0	0.05
George Burns, of, NYG	.286-2-54	0.0	2.0	0.03
Armando Marsans, of, Cin	.297-0-38	0.0	2.0	0.03
Bert Humphries, p, ChN	16-4, 2.69	0.0	2.0	0.03
Three Finger Brown, p, Cin	2.91, 6 saves	0.0	1.0	0.02

1914

American League

MVP

Player, Pos, Team	Stats	1st Pl	Pts	Share
Eddie Collins, 2b, Phi	.344-2-85	7.0	63.0	0.98
Sam Crawford, of, Det	.314-8-104	0.0	35.0	0.55
Donie Bush, ss, Det	.252-0-32	0.0	17.0	0.27
Home Run Baker, 3b, Phi	.319-9-89	0.0	17.0	0.27
Joe Jackson, of, Cle	.338-3-53	0.0	15.0	0.23
Ray Schalk, c, ChA	.270-0-36	0.0	13.0	0.20
Eddie Foster, 3b, Was	.282-2-50	0.0	11.0	0.17
Buck Weaver, ss, ChA	.246-2-28	0.0	11.0	0.17
Stuffy McInnis, 1b, Phi	.314-1-95	0.0	11.0	0.17
Del Pratt, 2b, StL	.283-5-65	0.0	10.0	0.16
Wally Schang, c, Phi	.287-3-45	0.0	10.0	0.16
Tris Speaker, of, Bos	.338-4-90	0.0	9.0	0.14
Tilly Walker, of, StL	.298-6-78	0.0	9.0	0.14
Ty Cobb, of, Det	.368-2-57	0.0	7.0	0.11
Everett Scott, ss, Bos	.239-2-37	0.0	7.0	0.11
Jack Barry, ss, Phi	.242-0-42	0.0	6.0	0.09
Dutch Leonard, p, Bos	19-5, 1.00	0.0	6.0	0.09
Eddie Plank, p, Phi	15-7, 2.87	0.0	5.0	0.08
George McBride, ss, Was	.203-0-24	0.0	5.0	0.08
Duffy Lewis, of, Bos	.278-2-79	0.0	4.0	0.06
Harry Hooper, of, Bos	.258-1-41	0.0	4.0	0.06
Fritz Maisel, 3b, NYA	.239-2-47	0.0	3.0	0.05
Roger Peckinpaugh, ss, NYA	.223-3-51	0.0	2.0	0.03
Clyde Milan, of, Was	.295-1-39	0.0	2.0	0.03
Sam Agnew, c, StL	.212-0-16	0.0	2.0	0.03
Roy Hartzell, of, NYA	.233-1-32	0.0	2.0	0.03
Eddie Cicotte, p, ChA	11-16, 2.04	0.0	1.0	0.02
George Moriarty, 3b, Det	.254-1-40	0.0	1.0	0.02

National League

MVP

Player, Pos, Team	Stats	1st Pl	Pts	Share
Johnny Evers, 2b, Bos	.279-1-40	0.0	50.0	0.78
Rabbit Maranville, ss, Bos	.246-4-78	0.0	44.0	0.69
Bill James, p, Bos	26-7, 1.90	0.0	33.0	0.52
George Burns, of, NYG	.303-3-60	0.0	31.0	0.48
Dots Miller, 1b, StL	.290-4-88	0.0	18.0	0.28
Jeff Tesreau, p, NYG	26-10, 2.37	0.0	15.0	0.23
Dick Rudolph, p, Bos	26-10, 2.35	0.0	14.0	0.22
Sherry Magee, of, Phi	.314-15-103	0.0	14.0	0.22
Zack Wheat, of, Bro	.319-9-89	0.0	10.0	0.16
Pete Alexander, p, Phi	27-15, 2.38	0.0	9.0	0.14
Roger Bresnahan, c, ChN	.278-0-24	0.0	6.0	0.09
Lee Magee, of, StL	.284-2-40	0.0	6.0	0.09
Bill Doak, p, StL	19-6, 1.72	0.0	5.0	0.08
Jim Viox, 2b, Pit	.265-1-57	0.0	5.0	0.08
Art Fletcher, ss, NYG	.286-2-79	0.0	5.0	0.08
Christy Mathewson, p, NYG	24-13, 3.00	0.0	4.0	0.06
Vic Saier, 1b, ChN	.240-18-72	0.0	4.0	0.06
Butch Schmidt, 1b, Bos	.285-1-71	0.0	4.0	0.06
Jake Daubert, 1b, Bro	.329-6-45	0.0	4.0	0.06
Lew McCarty, c, Bro	.254-1-30	0.0	3.0	0.05
Heine Groh, 2b, Cin	.288-2-32	0.0	2.0	0.03
Tommy Clarke, c, Cin	.262-2-25	0.0	1.0	0.02
Gavy Cravath, of, Phi	.299-19-100	0.0	1.0	0.02

1922

American League

MVP

Player, Pos, Team	Stats	1st Pl	Pts	Share
George Sisler, 1b, StL	.420-8-105	0.0	59.0	0.92
Eddie Rommel, p, Phi	27-13, 3.28	0.0	31.0	0.48
Ray Schalk, c, ChA	.281-4-60	0.0	26.0	0.41
Joe Bush, p, NYA	26-7, 3.31	0.0	19.0	0.30
Eddie Collins, 2b, ChA	.324-1-69	0.0	18.0	0.28
Johnny Bassler, c, Det	.323-0-41	0.0	13.0	0.20
Steve O'Neill, c, Cle	.311-2-65	0.0	13.0	0.20
Joe Judge, 1b, Was	.294-10-81	0.0	12.0	0.19
Wally Pipp, 1b, NYA	.329-9-90	0.0	12.0	0.19
Lu Blue, 1b, Det	.300-6-45	0.0	11.0	0.17
Chick Galloway, ss, Phi	.324-6-69	0.0	10.0	0.16
Harry Heilmann, of, Det	.356-21-92	0.0	8.0	0.13
Del Pratt, 2b, Bos	.301-6-86	0.0	7.0	0.11
Wally Schang, c, NYA	.319-1-53	0.0	7.0	0.11
Bob Meusel, of, NYA	.319-16-84	0.0	6.0	0.09
Everett Scott, ss, NYA	.269-3-45	0.0	6.0	0.09
Walter Johnson, p, Was	15-16, 2.99	0.0	5.0	0.08
Urban Shocker, p, StL	24-17, 2.97	0.0	5.0	0.08
Charlie Jamieson, of, Cle	.323-3-57	0.0	4.0	0.06
Joe Sewell, ss, Cle	.299-2-83	0.0	4.0	0.06
George Burns, 1b, Bos	.306-12-73	0.0	2.0	0.03
Jimmy Dykes, 3b, Phi	.275-12-68	0.0	2.0	0.03
Bucky Harris, 2b, Was	.269-2-40	0.0	2.0	0.03
Roger Peckinpaugh, ss, Was	.254-2-48	0.0	2.0	0.03
Bill Wambsganss, 2b, Cle	.262-0-47	0.0	2.0	0.03
George Cutshaw, 2b, Det	.267-2-61	0.0	1.0	0.02
Cy Perkins, c, Phi	.267-6-69	0.0	1.0	0.02

1923

American League

MVP

Player, Pos, Team	Stats	1st Pl	Pts	Share
Babe Ruth, of, NYA	.393-41-131	8.0	64.0	1.00
Eddie Collins, 2b, ChA	.360-5-67	0.0	37.0	0.58
Harry Heilmann, of, Det	.403-18-115	0.0	31.0	0.48
Wally Gerber, ss, StL	.281-1-62	0.0	20.0	0.31
Joe Sewell, ss, Cle	.353-3-109	0.0	20.0	0.31
Charlie Jamieson, of, Cle	.345-2-51	0.0	19.0	0.30
Johnny Bassler, c, Det	.298-0-49	0.0	17.0	0.27
Chick Galloway, ss, Phi	.278-2-62	0.0	13.0	0.20
George Uhle, p, Cle	26-16, 3.77	0.0	13.0	0.20
George Burns, 1b, Bos	.328-7-82	0.0	8.0	0.13

Howard Ehmke, p, Bos	20-17, 3.78	0.0	7.0	0.11
Muddy Ruel, c, Was	.316-0-54	0.0	7.0	0.11
Roger Peckinpaugh, ss, Was	.264-2-62	0.0	6.0	0.09
Urban Shocker, p, StL	20-12, 3.41	0.0	5.0	0.08
Joe Judge, 1b, Was	.314-2-63	0.0	4.0	0.06
Marty McManus, 2b, StL	.309-15-94	0.0	4.0	0.06
Ken Williams, of, StL	.357-29-91	0.0	4.0	0.06
Joe Harris, of, Bos	.335-13-76	0.0	3.0	0.05
Bucky Harris, 2b, Was	.282-2-70	0.0	3.0	0.05
Joe Hauser, 1b, Phi	.307-17-94	0.0	1.0	0.02
Walter Johnson, p, Was	17-12, 3.48	0.0	1.0	0.02
Cy Perkins, c, Phi	.270-2-65	0.0	1.0	0.02

1924

American League

MVP

Player, Pos, Team	Stats	1st Pl	Pts	Share
Walter Johnson, p, Was	23-7, 2.72	0.0	55.0	0.86
Eddie Collins, 2b, ChA	.349-6-86	0.0	49.0	0.77
Charlie Jamieson, of, Cle	.359-3-54	0.0	25.0	0.39
Herb Pennock, p, NYA	21-9, 2.83	0.0	24.0	0.38
Johnny Bassler, c, Det	.346-1-68	0.0	22.0	0.34
Hank Severeid, c, StL	.308-4-48	0.0	17.0	0.27
Joe Hauser, 1b, Phi	.288-27-115	0.0	13.0	0.20
Baby Doll Jacobson, of, StL	.318-19-97	0.0	11.0	0.17
Harry Heilmann, of, Det	.346-10-114	0.0	9.0	0.14
Joe Sewell, ss, Cle	.316-4-104	0.0	9.0	0.14
Muddy Ruel, c, Was	.283-0-57	0.0	7.0	0.11
Wally Schang, c, NYA	.292-5-52	0.0	7.0	0.11
Al Simmons, of, Phi	.308-8-102	0.0	7.0	0.11
Wally Pipp, 1b, NYA	.295-9-113	0.0	6.0	0.09
Howard Ehmke, p, Bos	19-17, 3.46	0.0	5.0	0.08
Ira Flagstead, of, Bos	.307-5-43	0.0	5.0	0.08
Wally Gerber, ss, StL	.272-0-55	0.0	4.0	0.06
Earl Whitehill, p, Det	17-9, 3.86	0.0	4.0	0.06
Lu Blue, 1b, Det	.311-2-50	0.0	3.0	0.05
Ike Boone, of, Bos	.333-13-96	0.0	2.0	0.03
Joe Harris, 1b, Bos	.301-3-77	0.0	2.0	0.03
Chick Galloway, ss, Phi	.276-2-48	0.0	1.0	0.02
Ken Williams, of, StL	.324-18-84	0.0	1.0	0.02

National League

MVP

Player, Pos, Team	Stats	1st Pl	Pts	Share
Dazzy Vance, p, Bro	28-6, 2.16	0.0	74.0	0.93
Rogers Hornsby, 2b, StL	.424-25-94	0.0	62.0	0.78
Frankie Frisch, 2b, NYG	.328-7-69	0.0	40.0	0.50
Zack Wheat, of, Bro	.375-14-97	0.0	40.0	0.50
Ross Youngs, of, NYG	.356-10-74	0.0	35.0	0.44
George Kelly, 2b, NYG	.324-21-136	0.0	34.0	0.43
Rabbit Maranville, 2b, Pit	.266-2-71	0.0	33.0	0.41
Kiki Cuyler, of, Pit	.354-9-85	0.0	25.0	0.31
Jack Fournier, 1b, Bro	.334-27-116	0.0	21.0	0.26
Edd Roush, of, Cin	.348-3-72	0.0	12.0	0.15
Glenn Wright, ss, Pit	.287-7-111	0.0	10.0	0.13
Andy High, 2b, Bro	.328-6-61	0.0	9.0	0.11
Babe Pinelli, 3b, Cin	.306-0-70	0.0	7.0	0.09
Rube Bressler, 1b, Cin	.347-4-49	0.0	6.0	0.08
Gabby Hartnett, c, ChN	.299-16-67	0.0	5.0	0.06
Burleigh Grimes, p, Bro	22-13, 3.82	0.0	5.0	0.06
Jim Bottomley, 1b, StL	.316-14-111	0.0	4.0	0.05
Jimmy Johnston, ss, Bro	.298-2-29	0.0	3.0	0.04
Max Carey, of, Pit	.297-8-55	0.0	3.0	0.04
Travis Jackson, ss, NYG	.302-11-76	0.0	3.0	0.04
Emil Yde, p, Pit	16-3, 2.83	0.0	2.0	0.03
Cy Williams, of, Phi	.328-24-93	0.0	1.0	0.01
Eppa Rixey, p, Cin	15-14, 2.76	0.0	1.0	0.01
Pete Alexander, p, ChN	12-5, 3.03	0.0	1.0	0.01
Hank DeBerry, c, Bro	.243-3-26	0.0	1.0	0.01

1925

American League

MVP

Player, Pos, Team	Stats	1st Pl	Pts	Share
Roger Peckinpaugh, ss, Was	.294-4-64	0.0	45.0	0.70
Al Simmons, of, Phi	.384-24-129	0.0	41.0	0.64
Joe Sewell, ss, Cle	.336-1-98	0.0	21.0	0.33
Harry Heilmann, of, Det	.393-13-134	0.0	20.0	0.31
Harry Rice, of, StL	.359-11-47	0.0	18.0	0.28
Earl Sheely, 1b, ChA	.315-9-111	0.0	17.0	0.27
Ira Flagstead, of, Bos	.280-6-61	0.0	10.0	0.16
Baby Doll Jacobson, of, StL	.341-15-76	0.0	10.0	0.16
Johnny Mostil, of, ChA	.299-2-50	0.0	10.0	0.16
Ossie Bluege, 3b, Was	.287-4-79	0.0	8.0	0.13
Mickey Cochrane, c, Phi	.331-6-55	0.0	8.0	0.13
Lu Blue, 1b, Det	.306-3-94	0.0	7.0	0.11
Stan Coveleski, p, Was	20-5, 2.84	0.0	7.0	0.11
Willie Kamm, 3b, ChA	.279-6-83	0.0	7.0	0.11
Eddie Rommel, p, Phi	21-10, 3.69	0.0	7.0	0.11
Ray Schalk, c, ChA	.274-0-52	0.0	7.0	0.11
Al Wingo, of, Det	.370-5-68	0.0	7.0	0.11
Earle Combs, of, NYA	.342-3-61	0.0	6.0	0.09
Bob Meusel, of, NYA	.290-33-138	0.0	6.0	0.09
Ted Lyons, p, ChA	21-11, 3.26	0.0	5.0	0.08
George Burns, 1b, Cle	.336-6-79	0.0	4.0	0.06
Marty McManus, 2b, StL	.288-13-90	0.0	4.0	0.06
Herb Pennock, p, NYA	16-17, 2.96	0.0	4.0	0.06
Benny Bengough, c, NYA	.258-0-23	0.0	2.0	0.03
Howard Ehmke, p, Bos	9-20, 3.73	0.0	2.0	0.03
Lou Gehrig, 1b, NYA	.295-20-68	0.0	2.0	0.03
Ike Boone, of, Bos	.330-9-68	0.0	1.0	0.02
Joe Dugan, 3b, NYA	.292-0-31	0.0	1.0	0.02
Phil Todt, 1b, Bos	.278-11-75	0.0	1.0	0.02

National League

MVP

Player, Pos, Team	Stats	1st Pl	Pts	Share
Rogers Hornsby, 2b, StL	.403-39-143	0.0	73.0	0.91
Kiki Cuyler, of, Pit	.357-18-102	0.0	61.0	0.76
George Kelly, 2b, NYG	.309-20-99	0.0	52.0	0.65
Glenn Wright, ss, Pit	.308-18-121	0.0	43.0	0.54
Dazzy Vance, p, Bro	22-9, 3.53	0.0	42.0	0.53
Dave Bancroft, ss, Bos	.319-2-49	0.0	41.0	0.51
Jim Bottomley, 1b, StL	.367-21-128	0.0	28.0	0.35
Pie Traynor, 3b, Pit	.320-6-106	0.0	27.0	0.34
Frankie Frisch, 3b, NYG	.331-11-48	0.0	13.0	0.16
Edd Roush, of, Cin	.339-8-83	0.0	12.0	0.15
Max Carey, of, Pit	.343-5-44	0.0	11.0	0.14
Irish Meusel, of, NYG	.328-21-111	0.0	6.0	0.08
Dolf Luque, p, Cin	16-18, 2.63	0.0	5.0	0.06
Charlie Grimm, 1b, ChN	.306-10-76	0.0	5.0	0.06
Zack Wheat, of, Bro	.359-14-103	0.0	4.0	0.05
Pete Donohue, p, Cin	21-14, 3.08	0.0	4.0	0.05
Bubbles Hargrave, c, Cin	.300-2-33	0.0	4.0	0.05
George Harper, of, Phi	.349-18-97	0.0	3.0	0.04
Heinie Sand, ss, Phi	.278-3-55	0.0	3.0	0.04
Doc Gautreau, 2b, Bos	.262-0-23	0.0	2.0	0.03
Vic Aldridge, p, Pit	15-7, 3.63	0.0	1.0	0.01

1926

American League

MVP

Player, Pos, Team	Stats	1st Pl	Pts	Share
George Burns, 1b, Cle	.358-4-114	0.0	63.0	0.98
Johnny Mostil, of, ChA	.328-4-42	0.0	33.0	0.52
Herb Pennock, p, NYA	23-11, 3.62	0.0	32.0	0.50
Sam Rice, of, Was	.337-3-76	0.0	18.0	0.28
Harry Heilmann, of, Det	.367-9-103	0.0	16.0	0.25
Heinie Manush, of, Det	.378-14-86	0.0	16.0	0.25
Al Simmons, of, Phi	.343-19-109	0.0	16.0	0.25
Lefty Grove, p, Phi	13-13, 2.51	0.0	12.0	0.19
Goose Goslin, of, Was	.354-17-108	0.0	9.0	0.14
Lou Gehrig, 1b, NYA	.313-16-112	0.0	7.0	0.11

Player, Pos, Team	Stats	1st Pl	Pts	Share
Tony Lazzeri, 2b, NYA	.275-18-114	0.0	7.0	0.11
Bibb Falk, of, ChA	.345-8-108	0.0	6.0	0.09
Bob Fothergill, of, Det	.367-3-73	0.0	6.0	0.09
Ski Melillo, 2b, StL	.255-1-30	0.0	6.0	0.09
Harry Rice, of, StL	.313-9-59	0.0	6.0	0.09
Ossie Bluege, 3b, Was	.271-3-65	0.0	5.0	0.08
Phil Todt, 1b, Bos	.255-7-69	0.0	5.0	0.08
Mickey Cochrane, c, Phi	.273-8-47	0.0	4.0	0.06
Joe Judge, 1b, Was	.291-7-92	0.0	4.0	0.06
Marty McManus, 3b, StL	.284-9-68	0.0	4.0	0.06
Bob Meusel, of, NYA	.315-12-81	0.0	3.0	0.05
Topper Rigney, ss, Bos	.270-4-53	0.0	3.0	0.05
Ira Flagstead, of, Bos	.299-3-31	0.0	2.0	0.03
Wally Gerber, ss, StL	.270-0-42	0.0	2.0	0.03
Tom Zachary, p, StL	14-15, 3.60	0.0	2.0	0.03
Baby Doll Jacobson, of, StL-Bos	.299-8-90	0.0	1.0	0.02

National League

MVP

Player, Pos, Team	Stats	1st Pl	Pts	Share
Bob O'Farrell, c, StL	.293-7-68	0.0	79.0	0.99
Hughie Critz, 2b, Cin	.270-3-79	0.0	60.0	0.75
Ray Kremer, p, Pit	20-6, 2.61	0.0	32.0	0.40
Tommy Thevenow, ss, StL	.256-2-63	0.0	30.0	0.38
Hack Wilson, of, ChN	.321-21-109	0.0	25.0	0.31
Les Bell, 3b, StL	.325-17-100	0.0	24.0	0.30
Bubbles Hargrave, c, Cin	.353-6-62	0.0	24.0	0.30
Flint Rhem, p, StL	20-7, 3.21	0.0	20.0	0.25
Freddy Lindstrom, 3b, NYG	.302-9-76	0.0	17.0	0.21
Dave Bancroft, ss, Bos	.311-1-44	0.0	17.0	0.21
Hal Carlson, p, Phi	17-12, 3.23	0.0	16.0	0.20
Paul Waner, of, Pit	.336-8-79	0.0	15.0	0.19
Pie Traynor, 3b, Pit	.317-3-92	0.0	14.0	0.18
Wally Pipp, 1b, Cin	.291-6-99	0.0	12.0	0.15
Eddie Brown, of, Bos	.328-2-84	0.0	10.0	0.13
Babe Herman, 1b, Bro	.319-11-81	0.0	8.0	0.10
Charlie Root, p, ChN	18-17, 2.82	0.0	8.0	0.10
Rogers Hornsby, 2b, StL	.317-11-93	0.0	7.0	0.09
Johnny Butler, ss, Bro	.269-1-68	0.0	5.0	0.06
Billy Southworth, of, NYG-StL	.320-16-99	0.0	5.0	0.06
Pete Alexander, p, ChN-StL	12-10, 3.05	0.0	5.0	0.06
Carl Mays, p, Cin	19-12, 3.14	0.0	4.0	0.05
George Kelly, 1b, NYG	.303-13-80	0.0	2.0	0.03
Curt Walker, of, Cin	.306-6-78	0.0	1.0	0.01

1927

American League

MVP

Player, Pos, Team	Stats	1st Pl	Pts	Share
Lou Gehrig, 1b, NYA	.373-47-175	7.0	56.0	0.88
Harry Heilmann, of, Det	.398-14-120	0.0	35.0	0.55
Ted Lyons, p, ChA	22-14, 2.84	0.0	34.0	0.53
Mickey Cochrane, c, Phi	.338-12-80	0.0	18.0	0.28
Al Simmons, of, Phi	.392-15-108	0.0	18.0	0.28
Goose Goslin, of, Was	.334-13-120	0.0	15.0	0.23
Muddy Ruel, c, Was	.308-1-52	0.0	15.0	0.23
Jimmy Dykes, 1b, Phi	.324-3-60	0.0	14.0	0.22
Luke Sewell, c, Cle	.294-0-53	0.0	13.0	0.20
Joe Sewell, ss, Cle	.316-1-92	0.0	9.0	0.14
Tony Lazzeri, 2b, NYA	.309-18-102	1.0	8.0	0.13
Bobby Reeves, ss, Was	.255-1-39	0.0	7.0	0.11
Frank O'Rourke, 3b, StL	.268-1-39	0.0	6.0	0.09
Jackie Tavener, ss, Det	.274-5-59	0.0	6.0	0.09
Hod Lisenbee, p, Was	18-9, 3.57	0.0	5.0	0.08
Bing Miller, of, StL	.325-5-75	0.0	5.0	0.08
Alex Metzler, of, ChA	.319-3-61	0.0	4.0	0.06
Ira Flagstead, of, Bos	.285-4-69	0.0	3.0	0.05
Charlie Jamieson, of, Cle	.309-0-36	0.0	3.0	0.05
Wally Schang, c, StL	.319-5-42	0.0	3.0	0.05
Fred Schulte, of, StL	.317-3-34	0.0	3.0	0.05
Willis Hudlin, p, Cle	18-12, 4.01	0.0	2.0	0.03
Bill Regan, 2b, Bos	.274-2-66	0.0	2.0	0.03
Jack Rothrock, ss, Bos	.259-1-36	0.0	2.0	0.03
Slim Harriss, p, Bos	14-21, 4.18	0.0	1.0	0.02
Phil Todt, 1b, Bos	.236-6-52	0.0	1.0	0.02

National League

MVP

Player, Pos, Team	Stats	1st Pl	Pts	Share
Paul Waner, of, Pit	.380-9-131	0.0	72.0	0.90
Frankie Frisch, 2b, StL	.337-10-78	0.0	66.0	0.83
Rogers Hornsby, 2b, NYG	.361-26-125	0.0	54.0	0.68
Charlie Root, p, ChN	26-15, 3.76	0.0	46.0	0.58
Travis Jackson, ss, NYG	.318-14-98	0.0	42.0	0.53
Lloyd Waner, of, Pit	.355-2-27	0.0	25.0	0.31
Pie Traynor, 3b, Pit	.342-5-106	0.0	18.0	0.23
Jesse Haines, p, StL	24-10, 2.72	0.0	16.0	0.20
Ray Kremer, p, Pit	19-8, 2.47	0.0	14.0	0.18
Gabby Hartnett, c, ChN	.294-10-80	0.0	12.0	0.15
Red Lucas, p, Cin	18-11, 3.38	0.0	10.0	0.13
Hack Wilson, of, ChN	.318-30-129	0.0	9.0	0.11
Bill Terry, 1b, NYG	.326-20-121	0.0	6.0	0.08
Jim Bottomley, 1b, StL	.303-19-124	0.0	6.0	0.08
Bubbles Hargrave, c, Cin	.308-0-35	0.0	6.0	0.08
Jakie May, p, Cin	15-12, 3.51	0.0	6.0	0.08
Cy Williams, of, Phi	.274-30-98	0.0	6.0	0.08
Doc Farrell, ss, NYG-Bos	.316-4-92	0.0	4.0	0.05
Burleigh Grimes, p, NYG	19-8, 3.54	0.0	4.0	0.05
Max Carey, of, Bro	.266-1-54	0.0	3.0	0.04
Riggs Stephenson, of, ChN	.344-7-82	0.0	3.0	0.04
Pete Alexander, p, StL	21-10, 2.52	0.0	3.0	0.04
Carmen Hill, p, Pit	22-11, 3.24	0.0	2.0	0.03
Jesse Petty, p, Bro	13-18, 2.98	0.0	2.0	0.03
Dutch Ulrich, p, Phi	8-11, 3.17	0.0	2.0	0.03
Chick Hafey, of, StL	.329-18-63	0.0	1.0	0.01

1928

American League

MVP

Player, Pos, Team	Stats	1st Pl	Pts	Share
Mickey Cochrane, c, Phi	.293-10-57	0.0	53.0	0.83
Heinie Manush, of, StL	.378-13-108	0.0	51.0	0.80
Joe Judge, 1b, Was	.306-3-93	0.0	27.0	0.42
Tony Lazzeri, 2b, NYA	.332-10-82	0.0	27.0	0.42
Willie Kamm, 3b, ChA	.308-1-84	0.0	15.0	0.23
Goose Goslin, of, Was	.379-17-102	0.0	13.0	0.20
Earle Combs, of, NYA	.310-7-56	0.0	13.0	0.20
Charlie Gehringer, 2b, Det	.320-6-74	0.0	12.0	0.19
Buddy Myer, 3b, Bos	.313-1-44	0.0	11.0	0.17
Waite Hoyt, p, NYA	23-7, 3.36	0.0	8.0	0.13
Jimmie Foxx, 3b, Phi	.328-13-79	0.0	7.0	0.11
Joe Sewell, ss, Cle	.323-4-70	0.0	6.0	0.09
Luke Sewell, c, Cle	.270-3-52	0.0	6.0	0.09
Ira Flagstead, of, Bos	.290-1-39	0.0	5.0	0.08
Ed Morris, p, Bos	19-15, 3.53	0.0	4.0	0.06
Harry Heilmann, of, Det	.328-14-107	0.0	4.0	0.06
Carl Lind, 2b, Cle	.294-1-54	0.0	4.0	0.06
Bill Cissell, ss, ChA	.260-1-60	0.0	4.0	0.06
Tommy Thomas, p, ChA	17-16, 3.08	0.0	4.0	0.06
Ownie Carroll, p, Det	16-12, 3.27	0.0	3.0	0.05
Harry Rice, of, Det	.302-6-81	0.0	3.0	0.05
Lew Fonseca, 1b, Cle	.327-3-36	0.0	2.0	0.03
Ted Lyons, p, ChA	15-14, 3.98	0.0	2.0	0.03
Johnny Hodapp, 3b, Cle	.323-2-73	0.0	2.0	0.03
Alex Metzler, of, ChA	.304-3-55	0.0	1.0	0.02
Bill Regan, 2b, Bos	.264-7-75	0.0	1.0	0.02

National League

MVP

Player, Pos, Team	Stats	1st Pl	Pts	Share
Jim Bottomley, 1b, StL	.325-31-136	0.0	76.0	0.95
Freddy Lindstrom, 3b, NYG	.358-14-107	0.0	70.0	0.88
Burleigh Grimes, p, Pit	25-14, 2.99	0.0	53.0	0.66
Larry Benton, p, NYG	25-9, 2.73	0.0	37.0	0.46
Hughie Critz, 2b, Cin	.296-5-52	0.0	37.0	0.46
Pie Traynor, 3b, Pit	.337-3-124	0.0	28.0	0.35
Hack Wilson, of, ChN	.313-31-120	0.0	21.0	0.26
Shanty Hogan, c, NYG	.333-10-71	0.0	17.0	0.21
Travis Jackson, ss, NYG	.270-14-77	0.0	16.0	0.20
Rabbit Maranville, ss, StL	.240-1-34	0.0	14.0	0.18
Dazzy Vance, p, Bro	22-10, 2.09	0.0	13.0	0.16
Chick Hafey, of, StL	.337-27-111	0.0	11.0	0.14
Rogers Hornsby, 2b, Bos	.387-21-94	0.0	10.0	0.13
Gabby Hartnett, c, ChN	.302-14-57	0.0	6.0	0.08
Paul Waner, of, Pit	.370-6-86	0.0	5.0	0.06
Lance Richbourg, of, Bos	.337-2-52	0.0	5.0	0.06
Taylor Douthit, of, StL	.295-3-43	0.0	5.0	0.06
Del Bissonette, 1b, Bro	.320-25-106	0.0	3.0	0.04
Jake Flowers, 2b, Bro	.274-2-44	0.0	3.0	0.04
Jimmie Wilson, c, Phi-StL	.264-2-63	0.0	3.0	0.04
Pinky Whitney, 3b, Phi	.301-10-103	0.0	3.0	0.04
Hod Ford, ss, Cin	.241-0-54	0.0	2.0	0.03
Fresco Thompson, 2b, Phi	.287-3-50	0.0	1.0	0.01

1929

National League

MVP

Player, Pos, Team	Stats	1st Pl	Pts	Share
Rogers Hornsby, 2b, ChN	.380-39-149	3.0	60.0	0.75
Lefty O'Doul, of, Phi	.398-32-122	0.0	54.0	0.68
Bill Terry, 1b, NYG	.372-14-117	0.0	48.0	0.60
Burleigh Grimes, p, Pit	17-7, 3.13	0.0	35.0	0.44
Lloyd Waner, of, Pit	.353-5-74	0.0	30.0	0.38
Red Lucas, p, Cin	19-12, 3.60	0.0	29.0	0.36
Pie Traynor, 3b, Pit	.356-4-108	0.0	27.0	0.34
Hack Wilson, of, ChN	.345-39-159	0.0	24.0	0.30
Babe Herman, of, Bro	.381-21-113	0.0	24.0	0.30
Guy Bush, p, ChN	18-7, 3.66	0.0	16.0	0.20
Chuck Klein, of, Phi	.356-43-145	0.0	15.0	0.19
Mel Ott, of, NYG	.328-42-151	0.0	15.0	0.19
Taylor Douthit, of, StL	.336-9-62	0.0	14.0	0.18
Charlie Grimm, 1b, ChN	.298-10-91	0.0	13.0	0.16
Travis Jackson, ss, NYG	.294-21-94	0.0	8.0	0.10
Rabbit Maranville, ss, Bos	.284-0-55	0.0	8.0	0.10
Hughie Critz, 2b, Cin	.247-1-50	0.0	5.0	0.06
Bernie Friberg, 2b, Phi	.301-7-55	0.0	4.0	0.05
Pat Malone, p, ChN	22-10, 3.57	0.0	3.0	0.04
Frankie Frisch, 2b, StL	.334-5-74	0.0	2.0	0.03
Pinky Whitney, 3b, Phi	.327-8-115	0.0	2.0	0.03
Johnny Frederick, of, Bro	.328-24-75	0.0	2.0	0.03
Riggs Stephenson, of, ChN	.362-17-110	0.0	1.0	0.01
Zack Taylor, c, Bos-ChN	.266-1-41	0.0	1.0	0.01

1931

American League

MVP

Player, Pos, Team	Stats	1st Pl	Pts	Share
Lefty Grove, p, Phi	31-4, 2.06	0.0	78.0	0.98
Lou Gehrig, 1b, NYA	.341-46-184	0.0	59.0	0.74
Al Simmons, of, Phi	.390-22-128	0.0	51.0	0.64
Earl Averill, of, Cle	.333-32-143	0.0	43.0	0.54
Babe Ruth, of, NYA	.373-46-163	0.0	40.0	0.50
Earl Webb, of, Bos	.333-14-103	0.0	22.0	0.28
Joe Cronin, ss, Was	.306-12-126	0.0	18.0	0.23
Ski Melillo, 2b, StL	.306-2-75	0.0	17.0	0.21
Sammy West, of, Was	.333-3-91	0.0	16.0	0.20
Mickey Cochrane, c, Phi	.349-17-89	0.0	16.0	0.20
George Earnshaw, p, Phi	21-7, 3.67	0.0	12.0	0.15
Wes Ferrell, p, Cle	22-12, 3.75	0.0	12.0	0.15
Firpo Marberry, p, Was	16-4, 3.45	0.0	11.0	0.14
Hal Rhyne, ss, Bos	.273-0-51	0.0	10.0	0.13
Ben Chapman, of, NYA	.315-17-122	0.0	7.0	0.09
John Stone, of, Det	.327-10-76	0.0	6.0	0.08
Charlie Gehringer, 2b, Det	.311-4-53	0.0	4.0	0.05
Lu Blue, 1b, ChA	.304-1-62	0.0	4.0	0.05
Red Kress, 3b, StL	.311-16-114	0.0	3.0	0.04
Carl Reynolds, of, ChA	.290-6-77	0.0	2.0	0.03
Lefty Stewart, p, StL	14-17, 4.40	0.0	2.0	0.03
Goose Goslin, of, StL	.328-24-105	0.0	2.0	0.03
Danny MacFayden, p, Bos	16-12, 4.02	0.0	2.0	0.03
Tom Oliver, of, Bos	.276-0-70	0.0	2.0	0.03
Jimmie Foxx, 1b, Phi	.291-30-120	0.0	1.0	0.01

National League

MVP

Player, Pos, Team	Stats	1st Pl	Pts	Share
Frankie Frisch, 2b, StL	.311-4-82	*0.0*	65.0	0.81
Chuck Klein, of, Phi	.337-31-121	*0.0*	55.0	0.69
Bill Terry, 1b, NYG	.349-9-112	*0.0*	53.0	0.66
Woody English, ss, ChN	.319-2-53	*0.0*	30.0	0.38
Chick Hafey, of, StL	.349-16-95	*0.0*	29.0	0.36
Jimmie Wilson, c, StL	.274-0-51	*0.0*	28.0	0.35
Travis Jackson, ss, NYG	.310-5-71	*0.0*	24.0	0.30
Charlie Grimm, 1b, ChN	.331-4-66	*0.0*	21.0	0.26
Sparky Adams, 3b, StL	.293-1-40	*0.0*	18.0	0.23
Ed Brandt, p, Bos	18-11, 2.92	*0.0*	15.0	0.19
Rabbit Maranville, ss, Bos	.260-0-33	*0.0*	15.0	0.19
Kiki Cuyler, of, ChN	.330-9-88	*0.0*	14.0	0.18
Pie Traynor, 3b, Pit	.298-2-103	*0.0*	12.0	0.15
Red Lucas, p, Cin	14-13, 3.59	*0.0*	10.0	0.13
Lloyd Waner, of, Pit	.314-4-57	0.0	8.0	0.10
Jim Bottomley, 1b, StL	.348-9-75	0.0	8.0	0.10
Jumbo Elliott, p, Phi	19-14, 4.27	0.0	6.0	0.08
Jack Quinn, p, Bro	2.66, 15 saves	0.0	6.0	0.08
Neal Finn, 2b, Bro	.274-0-45	0.0	5.0	0.06
Watty Clark, p, Bro	14-10, 3.20	0.0	3.0	0.04
Paul Derringer, p, StL	18-8, 3.36	0.0	3.0	0.04
Charlie Root, p, ChN	17-14, 3.48	0.0	3.0	0.04
Dick Bartell, ss, Phi	.289-0-34	0.0	2.0	0.03
Johnny Vergez, 3b, NYG	.278-13-81	0.0	2.0	0.03
Freddie Fitzsimmons, p, NYG	18-11, 3.05	0.0	1.0	0.01
Lefty O'Doul, of, Bro	.336-7-75	0.0	1.0	0.01
Glenn Wright, ss, Bro	.284-9-32	0.0	1.0	0.01
Tony Cuccinello, 2b, Cin	.315-2-93	0.0	1.0	0.01
Charlie Gelbert, ss, StL	.289-1-62	0.0	1.0	0.01

1932

American League

MVP

Player, Pos, Team	Stats	1st Pl	Pts	Share
Jimmie Foxx, 1b, Phi	.364-58-169	*5.0*	75.0	0.94
Lou Gehrig, 1b, NYA	.349-34-151	*0.0*	55.0	0.69
Heinie Manush, of, Was	.342-14-116	*0.0*	41.0	0.51
Earl Averill, of, Cle	.314-32-124	*0.0*	37.0	0.46
Lefty Gomez, p, NYA	24-7, 4.21	*0.0*	27.0	0.34
Joe Cronin, ss, Was	.318-6-116	*0.0*	26.0	0.33
Babe Ruth, of, NYA	.341-41-137	*0.0*	26.0	0.33
Tony Lazzeri, 2b, NYA	.300-15-113	*0.0*	21.0	0.26
Al Simmons, of, Phi	.322-35-151	*0.0*	13.0	0.16
Charlie Gehringer, 2b, Det	.298-19-107	*0.0*	13.0	0.16
Dale Alexander, 1b, Det-Bos	.367-8-60	*0.0*	10.0	0.13
Bill Cissell, 2b, ChA-Cle	.315-7-98	*0.0*	10.0	0.13
Rick Ferrell, c, StL	.315-2-65	0.0	9.0	0.11
Lefty Grove, p, Phi	25-10, 2.84	0.0	8.0	0.10
Johnny Allen, p, NYA	17-4, 3.70	0.0	8.0	0.10
Bill Dickey, c, NYA	.310-15-84	0.0	8.0	0.10
Goose Goslin, of, StL	.299-17-104	0.0	7.0	0.09
Montie Weaver, p, Was	22-10, 4.08	0.0	6.0	0.08
Harry Davis, 1b, Det	.269-4-74	0.0	5.0	0.06
Dave Harris, of, Was	.327-6-29	0.0	5.0	0.06
Wes Ferrell, p, Cle	23-13, 3.66	0.0	5.0	0.06
Jim Levey, ss, StL	.280-4-63	0.0	5.0	0.06
Ted Lyons, p, ChA	10-15, 3.28	0.0	5.0	0.06
Billy Sullivan, 1b, ChA	.316-1-45	0.0	3.0	0.04
Eric McNair, ss, Phi	.285-18-95	0.0	3.0	0.04
Smead Jolley, of, ChA-Bos	.312-18-106	0.0	3.0	0.04
General Crowder, p, Was	26-13, 3.33	0.0	2.0	0.03
Marty McManus, 2b, Bos	.235-5-24	0.0	2.0	0.03
Gee Walker, of, Det	.323-8-78	0.0	1.0	0.01
Joe Sewell, 3b, NYA	.272-11-68	0.0	1.0	0.01

National League

MVP

Player, Pos, Team	Stats	1st Pl	Pts	Share
Chuck Klein, of, Phi	.348-38-137	*6.0*	78.0	0.98
Lon Warneke, p, ChN	22-6, 2.37	*0.0*	68.0	0.85
Lefty O'Doul, of, Bro	.368-21-90	*0.0*	58.0	0.73
Paul Waner, of, Pit	.341-8-82	*0.0*	37.0	0.46
Riggs Stephenson, of, ChN	.324-4-85	*0.0*	32.0	0.40
Bill Terry, 1b, NYG	.350-28-117	*0.0*	25.0	0.31
Don Hurst, 1b, Phi	.339-24-143	*0.0*	24.0	0.30
Pie Traynor, 3b, Pit	.329-2-68	*0.0*	17.0	0.21
Billy Herman, 2b, ChN	.314-1-51	*0.0*	16.0	0.20
Mel Ott, of, NYG	.318-38-123	*0.0*	15.0	0.19
Bob Brown, p, Bos	14-7, 3.30	*0.0*	10.0	0.13
Babe Herman, of, Cin	.326-16-87	0.0	8.0	0.10
Lloyd Waner, of, Pit	.333-2-38	0.0	6.0	0.08
Wally Berger, of, Bos	.307-17-73	0.0	6.0	0.08
Ernie Orsatti, of, StL	.336-2-44	0.0	6.0	0.08
Hack Wilson, of, Bro	.297-23-123	0.0	6.0	0.08
Rabbit Maranville, 2b, Bos	.235-0-37	0.0	5.0	0.06
Jimmie Wilson, c, StL	.248-2-28	0.0	5.0	0.06
Tony Cuccinello, 2b, Bro	.281-12-77	0.0	4.0	0.05
Dizzy Dean, p, StL	18-15, 3.30	0.0	4.0	0.05
Frankie Frisch, 2b, StL	.292-3-60	0.0	3.0	0.04
Ripper Collins, 1b, StL	.279-21-91	0.0	3.0	0.04
Arky Vaughan, ss, Pit	.318-4-61	0.0	1.0	0.01
Guy Bush, p, ChN	19-11, 3.21	0.0	1.0	0.01

1933

American League

MVP

Player, Pos, Team	Stats	1st Pl	Pts	Share
Jimmie Foxx, 1b, Phi	.356-48-163	4.0	74.0	0.93
Joe Cronin, ss, Was	.309-5-118	2.0	62.0	0.78
Heinie Manush, of, Was	.336-5-95	2.0	54.0	0.68
Lou Gehrig, 1b, NYA	.334-32-139	0.0	39.0	0.49
Lefty Grove, p, Phi	24-8, 3.20	0.0	35.0	0.44
Charlie Gehringer, 2b, Det	.325-12-105	0.0	32.0	0.40
General Crowder, p, Was	24-15, 3.97	0.0	28.0	0.35
Al Simmons, of, ChA	.331-14-119	0.0	19.0	0.24
Earl Whitehill, p, Was	22-8, 3.33	0.0	18.0	0.23
Ski Melillo, 2b, StL	.292-3-79	0.0	12.0	0.15
Sammy West, of, StL	.300-11-48	0.0	11.0	0.14
Rick Ferrell, c, StL-Bos	.290-4-77	0.0	9.0	0.11
Bill Dickey, c, NYA	.318-14-97	0.0	9.0	0.11
Tony Lazzeri, 2b, NYA	.294-18-104	0.0	6.0	0.08
Joe Kuhel, 1b, Was	.322-11-107	0.0	5.0	0.06
Earl Averill, of, Cle	.301-11-92	0.0	5.0	0.06
Buddy Myer, 2b, Was	.302-4-61	0.0	5.0	0.06
Mickey Cochrane, c, Phi	.322-15-60	0.0	5.0	0.06
Bob Johnson, of, Phi	.290-21-93	0.0	5.0	0.06
Ben Chapman, of, NYA	.312-9-98	0.0	4.0	0.05
Max Bishop, 2b, Phi	.294-4-42	0.0	1.0	0.01
Luke Appling, ss, ChA	.322-6-85	0.0	1.0	0.01
Willie Kamm, 3b, Cle	.282-1-47	0.0	1.0	0.01

National League

MVP

Player, Pos, Team	Stats	1st Pl	Pts	Share
Carl Hubbell, p, NYG	23-12, 1.66	*0.0*	77.0	0.96
Chuck Klein, of, Phi	.368-28-120	*0.0*	48.0	0.60
Wally Berger, of, Bos	.313-27-106	*0.0*	44.0	0.55
Bill Terry, 1b, NYG	.322-6-58	*0.0*	35.0	0.44
Pepper Martin, 3b, StL	.316-8-57	*0.0*	31.0	0.39
Gus Mancuso, c, NYG	.264-6-56	*0.0*	24.0	0.30
Dizzy Dean, p, StL	20-18, 3.04	*0.0*	23.0	0.29
Pie Traynor, 3b, Pit	.304-1-82	*0.0*	20.0	0.25
Blondy Ryan, ss, NYG	.238-3-48	*0.0*	19.0	0.24
Al Lopez, c, Bro	.301-3-41	*0.0*	18.0	0.23
Ben Cantwell, p, Bos	20-10, 2.62	*0.0*	18.0	0.23
Hal Schumacher, p, NYG	19-12, 2.16	*0.0*	11.0	0.14
Rabbit Maranville, 2b, Bos	.218-0-38	*0.0*	11.0	0.14
Guy Bush, p, ChN	20-12, 2.75	*0.0*	11.0	0.14
Larry French, p, Pit	18-13, 2.72	*0.0*	10.0	0.13
Frankie Frisch, 2b, StL	.303-4-66	0.0	7.0	0.09
Jim Bottomley, 1b, Cin	.250-13-83	0.0	6.0	0.08
Joe Medwick, of, StL	.306-18-98	0.0	5.0	0.06
Gabby Hartnett, c, ChN	.276-16-88	0.0	5.0	0.06
Lon Warneke, p, ChN	18-13, 2.00	0.0	4.0	0.05
Red Lucas, p, Cin	10-16, 3.40	0.0	3.0	0.04
Dick Bartell, ss, Phi	.271-1-37	0.0	3.0	0.04
Arky Vaughan, ss, Pit	.314-9-97	0.0	2.0	0.03
Randy Moore, of, Bos	.302-8-70	0.0	2.0	0.03
Spud Davis, c, Phi	.349-9-65	0.0	1.0	0.01
Chick Hafey, of, Cin	.303-7-62	0.0	1.0	0.01
Dolf Luque, p, NYG	2.69, 4 saves	0.0	1.0	0.01

1934

American League

MVP

Player, Pos, Team	Stats	1st Pl	Pts	Share
Mickey Cochrane, c, Det	.320-2-76	*0.0*	67.0	0.84
Charlie Gehringer, 2b, Det	.356-11-127	*0.0*	65.0	0.81
Lefty Gomez, p, NYA	26-5, 2.33	*0.0*	60.0	0.75
Schoolboy Rowe, p, Det	24-8, 3.45	*0.0*	59.0	0.74
Lou Gehrig, 1b, NYA	.363-49-165	*0.0*	54.0	0.68
Hank Greenberg, 1b, Det	.339-26-139	*0.0*	29.0	0.36
Hal Trosky, 1b, Cle	.330-35-142	*0.0*	18.0	0.23
Wes Ferrell, p, Bos	14-5, 3.63	*0.0*	16.0	0.20
Marv Owen, 3b, Det	.317-8-96	*0.0*	13.0	0.16
Jimmie Foxx, 1b, Phi	.334-44-130	*0.0*	11.0	0.14
Al Simmons, of, ChA	.344-18-104	0.0	9.0	0.11
Bill Werber, 3b, Bos	.321-11-67	0.0	8.0	0.10
Roy Johnson, of, Bos	.320-7-119	0.0	8.0	0.10
Goose Goslin, of, Det	.305-13-100	0.0	6.0	0.08
Sammy West, of, StL	.326-9-55	0.0	5.0	0.06
Mel Harder, p, Cle	20-12, 2.61	0.0	4.0	0.05
Mike Higgins, 3b, Phi	.330-16-90	0.0	3.0	0.04
Earl Averill, of, Cle	.313-31-113	0.0	3.0	0.04
Bill Knickerbocker, ss, Cle	.317-4-67	0.0	2.0	0.03

National League

MVP

Player, Pos, Team	Stats	1st Pl	Pts	Share
Dizzy Dean, p, StL	30-7, 2.66	*6.0*	78.0	0.98
Paul Waner, of, Pit	.362-14-90	*0.0*	50.0	0.63
Jo-Jo Moore, of, NYG	.331-15-61	*0.0*	42.0	0.53
Travis Jackson, ss, NYG	.268-16-101	*0.0*	39.0	0.49
Mel Ott, of, NYG	.326-35-135	*0.0*	37.0	0.46
Ripper Collins, 1b, StL	.333-35-128	*0.0*	32.0	0.40
Bill Terry, 1b, NYG	.354-8-83	*0.0*	30.0	0.38
Curt Davis, p, Phi	19-17, 2.95	*0.0*	18.0	0.23
Paul Dean, p, StL	19-11, 3.43	*0.0*	16.0	0.20
Hal Schumacher, p, NYG	23-10, 3.18	*0.0*	16.0	0.20
Carl Hubbell, p, NYG	21-12, 2.30	*0.0*	16.0	0.20
Wally Berger, of, Bos	.298-34-121	*0.0*	13.0	0.16
Lon Warneke, p, ChN	22-10, 3.21	*0.0*	10.0	0.13
Gabby Hartnett, c, ChN	.299-22-90	0.0	9.0	0.11
Gordon Slade, ss, Cin	.285-4-52	0.0	5.0	0.06
Kiki Cuyler, of, ChN	.338-6-69	0.0	4.0	0.05
Benny Frey, p, Cin	11-16, 3.52	0.0	4.0	0.05
Fred Frankhouse, p, Bos	17-9, 3.20	0.0	4.0	0.05
Buzz Boyle, of, Bro	.305-7-48	0.0	4.0	0.05
Billy Herman, 2b, ChN	.303-3-42	0.0	4.0	0.05
Frankie Frisch, 2b, StL	.305-3-75	0.0	4.0	0.05
Waite Hoyt, p, Pit	2.93, 5 saves	0.0	2.0	0.03
Al Lopez, c, Bro	.273-7-54	0.0	1.0	0.01
Van Lingle Mungo, p, Bro	18-16, 3.37	0.0	1.0	0.01
Arky Vaughan, ss, Pit	.333-12-94	0.0	1.0	0.01

1935

American League

MVP

Player, Pos, Team	Stats	1st Pl	Pts	Share
Hank Greenberg, 1b, Det	.328-36-170	8.0	80.0	1.00
Wes Ferrell, p, Bos	25-14, 3.52	0.0	62.0	0.78
Joe Vosmik, of, Cle	.348-10-110	0.0	39.0	0.49
Buddy Myer, 2b, Was	.349-5-100	0.0	36.0	0.45
Lou Gehrig, 1b, NYA	.329-30-119	0.0	29.0	0.36
Charlie Gehringer, 2b, Det	.330-19-108	0.0	26.0	0.33
Mickey Cochrane, c, Det	.319-5-47	0.0	24.0	0.30
Doc Cramer, of, Phi	.332-3-70	0.0	18.0	0.23
Moose Solters, of, Bos-StL	.319-18-112	0.0	16.0	0.20
Rollie Hemsley, c, StL	.290-0-48	0.0	16.0	0.20
Jimmie Foxx, 1b, Phi	.346-36-115	0.0	11.0	0.14
Tommy Bridges, p, Det	21-10, 3.51	0.0	11.0	0.14
Ted Lyons, p, ChA	15-8, 3.02	0.0	10.0	0.13
Lefty Grove, p, Bos	20-12, 2.70	0.0	8.0	0.10
Zeke Bonura, 1b, ChA	.295-21-92	0.0	7.0	0.09
Luke Appling, ss, ChA	.307-1-71	0.0	7.0	0.09

2414

Awards: Yearly Voting

Player, Pos, Team	Stats	1st Pl	Pts	Share
Luke Sewell, c, ChA	.285-2-67	0.0	7.0	0.09
Johnny Allen, p, NYA	13-6, 3.61	0.0	5.0	0.06
John Whitehead, p, ChA	13-13, 3.72	0.0	4.0	0.05
Mike Higgins, 3b, Phi	.296-23-94	0.0	3.0	0.04
Johnny Marcum, p, Phi	17-12, 4.08	0.0	3.0	0.04
Eldon Auker, p, Det	18-7, 3.83	0.0	2.0	0.03
Mel Harder, p, Cle	22-11, 3.29	0.0	2.0	0.03
Lyn Lary, ss, Was-StL	.268-2-42	0.0	1.0	0.01

National League

MVP

Player, Pos, Team	Stats	1st Pl	Pts	Share
Gabby Hartnett, c, ChN	.344-13-91	0.0	75.0	0.94
Dizzy Dean, p, StL	28-12, 3.04	0.0	66.0	0.83
Arky Vaughan, ss, Pit	.385-19-99	0.0	45.0	0.56
Billy Herman, 2b, ChN	.341-7-83	0.0	38.0	0.48
Joe Medwick, of, StL	.353-23-126	0.0	37.0	0.46
Carl Hubbell, p, NYG	23-12, 3.27	0.0	20.0	0.25
Wally Berger, of, Bos	.295-34-130	0.0	20.0	0.25
Bill Terry, 1b, NYG	.341-6-64	0.0	20.0	0.25
Augie Galan, of, ChN	.314-12-79	0.0	18.0	0.23
Pepper Martin, 3b, StL	.299-9-54	0.0	16.0	0.20
Hank Leiber, of, NYG	.331-22-107	0.0	11.0	0.14
Lon Warneke, p, ChN	20-13, 3.06	0.0	9.0	0.11
Ernie Lombardi, c, Cin	.343-12-64	0.0	8.0	0.10
Frankie Frisch, 2b, StL	.294-1-55	0.0	7.0	0.09
Cy Blanton, p, Pit	18-13, 2.58	0.0	5.0	0.06
Johnny Moore, of, Phi	.323-19-93	0.0	5.0	0.06
Ethan Allen, of, Phi	.307-8-63	0.0	4.0	0.05
Gus Mancuso, c, NYG	.298-5-56	0.0	4.0	0.05
Paul Derringer, p, Cin	22-13, 3.51	0.0	4.0	0.05
Mel Ott, of, NYG	.322-31-114	0.0	3.0	0.04
Paul Dean, p, StL	19-12, 3.37	0.0	2.0	0.03
Ripper Collins, 1b, StL	.313-23-122	0.0	2.0	0.03
Curt Davis, p, Phi	16-14, 3.66	0.0	2.0	0.03
Paul Waner, of, Pit	.321-11-78	0.0	1.0	0.01
Bill Lee, p, ChN	20-6, 2.96	0.0	1.0	0.01
Travis Jackson, 3b, NYG	.301-9-80	0.0	1.0	0.01
Dolph Camilli, 1b, Phi	.261-25-83	0.0	1.0	0.01

1936

American League

MVP

Player, Pos, Team	Stats	1st Pl	Pts	Share
Lou Gehrig, 1b, NYA	.354-49-152	0.0	73.0	0.91
Luke Appling, ss, ChA	.388-6-128	0.0	65.0	0.81
Earl Averill, of, Cle	.378-28-126	0.0	48.0	0.60
Charlie Gehringer, 2b, Det	.354-15-116	0.0	39.0	0.49
Bill Dickey, c, NYA	.362-22-107	0.0	29.0	0.36
Vern Kennedy, p, ChA	21-9, 4.63	0.0	27.0	0.34
Joe Kuhel, 1b, Was	.321-16-118	0.0	27.0	0.34
Joe DiMaggio, of, NYA	.323-29-125	0.0	26.0	0.33
Tommy Bridges, p, Det	23-11, 3.60	0.0	25.0	0.31
Hal Trosky, 1b, Cle	.343-42-162	0.0	19.0	0.24
Jimmie Foxx, 1b, Bos	.338-41-143	0.0	16.0	0.20
Gee Walker, of, Det	.353-12-93	0.0	14.0	0.18
Beau Bell, of, StL	.344-11-123	0.0	10.0	0.13
Wally Moses, of, Phi	.345-7-66	0.0	7.0	0.09
Lefty Grove, p, Bos	17-12, 2.81	0.0	5.0	0.06
Jimmy Dykes, 3b, ChA	.267-7-60	0.0	3.0	0.04
Rip Radcliff, of, ChA	.335-8-82	0.0	3.0	0.04
Sammy West, of, StL	.278-7-70	0.0	2.0	0.03
Zeke Bonura, 1b, ChA	.330-12-138	0.0	1.0	0.01
Eric McNair, ss, Bos	.285-4-74	0.0	1.0	0.01

National League

MVP

Player, Pos, Team	Stats	1st Pl	Pts	Share
Carl Hubbell, p, NYG	26-6, 2.31	6.0	60.0	0.75
Dizzy Dean, p, StL	24-13, 3.17	0.0	53.0	0.66
Billy Herman, 2b, ChN	.334-5-93	0.0	37.0	0.46
Joe Medwick, of, StL	.351-18-138	0.0	30.0	0.38
Paul Waner, of, Pit	.373-5-94	0.0	29.0	0.36
Mel Ott, of, NYG	.328-33-135	0.0	28.0	0.35
Frank Demaree, of, ChN	.350-16-96	0.0	17.0	0.21

Player, Pos, Team	Stats	1st Pl	Pts	Share
Gus Mancuso, c, NYG	.301-9-63	0.0	13.0	0.16
Danny MacFayden, p, Bos	17-13, 2.87	0.0	12.0	0.15
Leo Durocher, ss, StL	.286-1-58	0.0	8.0	0.10
Paul Derringer, p, Cin	19-19, 4.02	0.0	6.0	0.08
Gabby Hartnett, c, ChN	.307-7-64	0.0	6.0	0.08
Burgess Whitehead, 2b, NYG	.278-4-47	0.0	6.0	0.08
Al Lopez, c, Bos	.242-7-50	0.0	5.0	0.06
Van Lingle Mungo, p, Bro	18-19, 3.35	0.0	5.0	0.06
Wally Berger, of, Bos	.288-25-91	0.0	4.0	0.05
Dolph Camilli, 1b, Phi	.315-28-102	0.0	4.0	0.05
Babe Phelps, c, Bro	.367-5-57	0.0	3.0	0.04
Dick Bartell, ss, NYG	.298-8-42	0.0	2.0	0.03
Ernie Lombardi, c, Cin	.333-12-68	0.0	1.0	0.01
Terry Moore, of, StL	.264-5-47	0.0	1.0	0.01

1937

American League

MVP

Player, Pos, Team	Stats	1st Pl	Pts	Share
Charlie Gehringer, 2b, Det	.371-14-96	6.0	78.0	0.98
Joe DiMaggio, of, NYA	.346-46-167	2.0	74.0	0.93
Hank Greenberg, 1b, Det	.337-40-183	0.0	48.0	0.60
Lou Gehrig, 1b, NYA	.351-37-159	0.0	42.0	0.53
Luke Sewell, c, ChA	.269-1-61	0.0	22.0	0.28
Bill Dickey, c, NYA	.332-29-133	0.0	22.0	0.28
Joe Cronin, ss, Bos	.307-18-110	0.0	19.0	0.24
Red Ruffing, p, NYA	20-7, 2.98	0.0	18.0	0.23
Lefty Gomez, p, NYA	21-11, 2.33	0.0	14.0	0.18
Mike Kreevich, of, ChA	.302-12-73	0.0	13.0	0.16
Cecil Travis, ss, Was	.344-3-66	0.0	12.0	0.15
Wally Moses, of, Phi	.320-25-86	0.0	12.0	0.15
Johnny Allen, p, Cle	15-1, 2.55	0.0	11.0	0.14
Harlond Clift, 3b, StL	.306-29-118	0.0	11.0	0.14
Rip Radcliff, of, ChA	.325-4-79	0.0	10.0	0.13
Buddy Lewis, 3b, Was	.314-10-79	0.0	7.0	0.09
Luke Appling, ss, ChA	.317-4-77	0.0	5.0	0.06
Beau Bell, of, StL	.340-14-117	0.0	5.0	0.06
Earl Averill, of, Cle	.299-21-92	0.0	4.0	0.05
Lyn Lary, ss, Cle	.290-8-77	0.0	4.0	0.05
Roxie Lawson, p, Det	18-7, 5.26	0.0	4.0	0.05
Gee Walker, of, Det	.335-18-113	0.0	3.0	0.04
Rudy York, c, Det	.307-35-103	0.0	1.0	0.01
Pete Fox, of, Det	.331-12-82	0.0	1.0	0.01

National League

MVP

Player, Pos, Team	Stats	1st Pl	Pts	Share
Joe Medwick, of, StL	.374-31-154	2.0	70.0	0.88
Gabby Hartnett, c, ChN	.354-12-82	3.0	68.0	0.85
Carl Hubbell, p, NYG	22-8, 3.20	1.0	52.0	0.65
Jim Turner, p, Bos	20-11, 2.38	0.0	30.0	0.38
Lou Fette, p, Bos	20-10, 2.88	0.0	29.0	0.36
Dick Bartell, ss, NYG	.306-14-62	1.0	26.0	0.33
Mel Ott, of, NYG	.294-31-95	0.0	24.0	0.30
Paul Waner, of, Pit	.354-2-74	0.0	21.0	0.26
Billy Herman, 2b, ChN	.335-8-65	0.0	19.0	0.24
Johnny Mize, 1b, StL	.364-25-113	0.0	18.0	0.23
Cliff Melton, p, NYG	20-9, 2.61	0.0	17.0	0.21
Charlie Root, p, ChN	3.38, 5 saves	0.0	15.0	0.19
Pinky Whitney, 3b, Phi	.341-8-79	0.0	13.0	0.16
Harry Danning, c, NYG	.288-8-51	1.0	10.0	0.13
Frank Demaree, of, ChN	.324-17-115	0.0	9.0	0.11
Lon Warneke, p, StL	18-11, 4.53	0.0	6.0	0.08
Billy Jurges, ss, ChN	.298-1-65	0.0	4.0	0.05
Johnny Cooney, of, Bro	.293-0-37	0.0	4.0	0.05
Billy Myers, ss, Cin	.251-7-43	0.0	2.0	0.03
Lee Grissom, p, Cin	12-17, 3.26	0.0	2.0	0.03
Heinie Manush, of, Bro	.333-4-73	0.0	1.0	0.01

1938

American League

MVP

Player, Pos, Team	Stats	1st Pl	Pts	Share
Jimmie Foxx, 1b, Bos	.349-50-175	19.0	305.0	0.91
Bill Dickey, c, NYA	.313-27-115	3.0	196.0	0.58
Hank Greenberg, 1b, Det	.315-58-146	0.0	162.0	0.48
Red Ruffing, p, NYA	21-7, 3.31	0.0	146.0	0.43
Bobo Newsom, p, StL	20-16, 5.08	0.0	111.0	0.33
Joe DiMaggio, of, NYA	.324-32-140	0.0	106.0	0.32
Joe Cronin, ss, Bos	.325-17-94	0.0	92.0	0.27
Earl Averill, of, Cle	.330-14-93	0.0	34.0	0.10
Cecil Travis, ss, Was	.335-5-67	0.0	33.0	0.10
Charlie Gehringer, 2b, Det	.306-20-107	0.0	27.0	0.08
Jeff Heath, of, Cle	.343-21-112	0.0	24.0	0.07
Joe Gordon, 2b, NYA	.255-25-97	0.0	23.0	0.07
Hal Trosky, 1b, Cle	.334-19-110	0.0	22.0	0.07
Ken Keltner, 3b, Cle	.276-26-113	0.0	16.0	0.05
Monty Stratton, p, ChA	15-9, 4.01	0.0	15.0	0.04
Mel Harder, p, Cle	17-10, 3.83	0.0	14.0	0.04
Bob Johnson, of, Phi	.313-30-113	0.0	13.0	0.04
Harlond Clift, 3b, StL	.290-34-118	0.0	11.0	0.03
Lou Gehrig, 1b, NYA	.295-29-114	0.0	10.0	0.03
Pete Fox, of, Det	.293-7-96	0.0	9.0	0.03
Joe Vosmik, of, Bos	.324-9-86	0.0	7.0	0.02
George McQuinn, 1b, StL	.324-12-82	0.0	7.0	0.02
Lefty Grove, p, Bos	14-4, 3.08	0.0	7.0	0.02
Buddy Lewis, 3b, Was	.296-12-91	0.0	5.0	0.01
Red Rolfe, 3b, NYA	.311-10-80	0.0	5.0	0.01
Buddy Myer, 2b, Was	.336-6-71	0.0	5.0	0.01
Earle Brucker, c, Phi	.374-3-35	0.0	5.0	0.01
Johnny Allen, p, Cle	14-8, 4.19	0.0	3.0	0.01
Frankie Crosetti, ss, NYA	.263-9-55	0.0	2.0	0.01
Lefty Gomez, p, NYA	18-12, 3.35	0.0	1.0	0.00
Doc Cramer, of, Bos	.301-0-71	0.0	1.0	0.00

National League

MVP

Player, Pos, Team	Stats	1st Pl	Pts	Share
Ernie Lombardi, c, Cin	.342-19-95	10.0	229.0	0.68
Bill Lee, p, ChN	22-9, 2.66	5.0	166.0	0.49
Arky Vaughan, ss, Pit	.322-7-68	0.0	163.0	0.49
Mel Ott, 3b, NYG	.311-36-116	0.0	132.0	0.39
Frank McCormick, 1b, Cin	.327-5-106	0.0	130.0	0.39
Johnny Rizzo, of, Pit	.301-23-111	0.0	96.0	0.29
Stan Hack, 3b, ChN	.320-4-67	0.0	87.0	0.26
Paul Derringer, p, Cin	21-14, 2.93	0.0	70.0	0.21
Mace Brown, p, Pit	3.80, 5 saves	0.0	62.0	0.18
Gabby Hartnett, c, ChN	.274-10-59	0.0	61.0	0.18
Joe Medwick, of, StL	.322-21-122	0.0	55.0	0.16
Johnny Mize, 1b, StL	.337-27-102	0.0	28.0	0.08
Tony Cuccinello, 2b, Bos	.265-9-76	0.0	23.0	0.07
Pep Young, 2b, Pit	.278-4-79	0.0	19.0	0.06
Clay Bryant, p, ChN	19-11, 3.10	0.0	16.0	0.05
Harry Danning, c, NYG	.306-9-60	0.0	13.0	0.04
Ival Goodman, of, Cin	.292-30-92	0.0	11.0	0.03
Johnny Vander Meer, p, Cin	15-10, 3.12	0.0	6.0	0.02
Leo Durocher, ss, Bro	.219-1-56	0.0	6.0	0.02
Dick Coffman, p, NYG	3.48, 12 saves	0.0	6.0	0.02
Al Lopez, c, Bos	.267-1-14	0.0	5.0	0.01
Lloyd Waner, of, Pit	.313-5-57	0.0	5.0	0.01
Debs Garms, of, Bos	.315-0-47	0.0	5.0	0.01
Dolph Camilli, 1b, Bro	.251-24-100	0.0	5.0	0.01
Charlie Root, p, ChN	2.86, 8 saves	0.0	3.0	0.01
Jo-Jo Moore, of, NYG	.302-11-56	0.0	3.0	0.01
Johnny Hudson, 2b, Bro	.261-2-37	0.0	3.0	0.01
Hugh Mulcahy, p, Phi	10-20, 4.61	0.0	3.0	0.01
Lee Handley, 3b, Pit	.268-6-51	0.0	2.0	0.01
Lon Warneke, p, StL	13-8, 3.97	0.0	1.0	0.00
Freddie Fitzsimmons, p, Bro	11-8, 3.02	0.0	1.0	0.00
Hersh Martin, of, Phi	.298-3-39	0.0	1.0	0.00

1939

American League

MVP

Player, Pos, Team	Stats	1st Pl	Pts	Share
Joe DiMaggio, of, NYA	.381-30-126	15.0	280.0	0.83
Jimmie Foxx, 1b, Bos	.360-35-105	1.0	170.0	0.51
Bob Feller, p, Cle	24-9, 2.85	3.0	155.0	0.46
Ted Williams, of, Bos	.327-31-145	0.0	126.0	0.38
Red Ruffing, p, NYA	21-7, 2.93	0.0	116.0	0.35
Bill Dickey, c, NYA	.302-24-105	3.0	110.0	0.33
Dutch Leonard, p, Was	20-8, 3.54	1.0	71.0	0.21
Bob Johnson, of, Phi	.338-23-114	0.0	52.0	0.15
Joe Gordon, 2b, NYA	.284-28-111	0.0	43.0	0.13
Mike Kreevich, of, ChA	.323-5-77	1.0	38.0	0.11
Clint Brown, p, ChA	3.88, 18 saves	0.0	34.0	0.10
Ken Keltner, 3b, Cle	.325-13-97	0.0	26.0	0.08
George McQuinn, 1b, StL	.316-20-94	0.0	24.0	0.07
Charlie Gehringer, 2b, Det	.325-16-86	0.0	21.0	0.06
Lefty Grove, p, Bos	15-4, 2.54	0.0	17.0	0.05
Joe Cronin, ss, Bos	.308-19-107	0.0	15.0	0.04
Ted Lyons, p, ChA	14-6, 2.76	0.0	13.0	0.04
Hank Greenberg, 1b, Det	.312-33-112	0.0	12.0	0.04
Bobo Newsom, p, StL-Det	20-11, 3.58	0.0	11.0	0.03
Johnny Rigney, p, ChA	15-8, 3.70	0.0	9.0	0.03
Joe Kuhel, 1b, ChA	.300-15-56	0.0	8.0	0.02
Charlie Keller, of, NYA	.334-11-83	0.0	7.0	0.02
Jeff Heath, of, Cle	.292-14-69	0.0	7.0	0.02
Gee Walker, of, ChA	.291-13-111	0.0	7.0	0.02
Frankie Hayes, c, Phi	.283-20-83	0.0	7.0	0.02
Tommy Bridges, p, Det	17-7, 3.50	0.0	7.0	0.02
Red Rolfe, 3b, NYA	.329-14-80	0.0	6.0	0.02
Barney McCosky, of, Det	.311-4-58	0.0	6.0	0.02
Eric McNair, 3b, ChA	.324-7-82	0.0	5.0	0.01
Hal Trosky, 1b, Cle	.335-25-104	0.0	4.0	0.01
George Case, of, Was	.302-2-35	0.0	3.0	0.01
Myril Hoag, of, StL	.295-10-75	0.0	3.0	0.01
Rudy York, c, Det	.307-20-68	0.0	1.0	0.00
Luke Appling, ss, ChA	.314-0-56	0.0	1.0	0.00

National League

MVP

Player, Pos, Team	Stats	1st Pl	Pts	Share
Bucky Walters, p, Cin	27-11, 2.29	18.0	303.0	0.90
Johnny Mize, 1b, StL	.349-28-108	1.0	178.0	0.53
Paul Derringer, p, Cin	25-7, 2.93	2.0	174.0	0.52
Frank McCormick, 1b, Cin	.332-18-128	2.0	159.0	0.47
Curt Davis, p, StL	22-16, 3.63	0.0	106.0	0.32
Jimmy Brown, ss, StL	.298-3-51	1.0	99.0	0.29
Joe Medwick, of, StL	.332-14-117	0.0	81.0	0.24
Leo Durocher, ss, Bro	.277-1-34	0.0	52.0	0.15
Harry Danning, c, NYG	.313-16-74	0.0	33.0	0.10
Luke Hamlin, p, Bro	20-13, 3.64	0.0	32.0	0.10
Mel Ott, of, NYG	.308-27-80	0.0	21.0	0.06
Billy Jurges, ss, NYG	.285-6-63	0.0	20.0	0.06
Dolph Camilli, 1b, Bro	.290-26-104	0.0	20.0	0.06
Billy Myers, ss, Cin	.281-9-56	0.0	18.0	0.05
Stan Hack, 3b, ChN	.298-8-56	0.0	17.0	0.05
Augie Galan, of, ChN	.304-6-71	0.0	15.0	0.04
Terry Moore, of, StL	.295-17-77	0.0	15.0	0.04
Morrie Arnovich, of, Phi	.324-5-67	0.0	10.0	0.03
Lonny Frey, 2b, Cin	.291-11-55	0.0	8.0	0.02
Bill Lee, p, ChN	19-15, 3.44	0.0	8.0	0.02
Enos Slaughter, of, StL	.320-12-86	0.0	8.0	0.02
Bill Werber, 3b, Cin	.289-5-57	0.0	6.0	0.02
Max West, of, Bos	.285-19-82	0.0	5.0	0.01
Gabby Hartnett, c, ChN	.278-12-59	0.0	5.0	0.01
Ival Goodman, of, Cin	.323-7-84	0.0	4.0	0.01
Buddy Hassett, 1b, Bos	.308-2-60	0.0	4.0	0.01
Pete Coscarart, 2b, Bro	.277-4-43	0.0	4.0	0.01
Elbie Fletcher, 1b, Bos-Pit	.290-12-77	0.0	4.0	0.01
Cookie Lavagetto, 3b, Bro	.300-10-87	0.0	3.0	0.01
Bob Bowman, p, StL	2.60, 9 saves	0.0	2.0	0.01
Eddie Miller, ss, Bos	.267-4-31	0.0	1.0	0.00
Billy Herman, 2b, ChN	.307-7-70	0.0	1.0	0.00

1940

American League

MVP

Player, Pos, Team	Stats	1st Pl	Pts	Share
Hank Greenberg, of, Det	.340-41-150	16.0	292.0	0.87
Bob Feller, p, Cle	27-11, 2.61	6.0	222.0	0.66
Joe DiMaggio, of, NYA	.352-31-133	0.0	151.0	0.45
Bobo Newsom, p, Det	21-5, 2.83	1.0	120.0	0.36
Lou Boudreau, ss, Cle	.295-9-101	1.0	119.0	0.35
Jimmie Foxx, 1b, Bos	.297-36-119	0.0	110.0	0.33
Schoolboy Rowe, p, Det	16-3, 3.46	0.0	62.0	0.18
Rudy York, 1b, Det	.316-33-134	0.0	61.0	0.18
Rip Radcliff, of, StL	.342-7-81	0.0	55.0	0.16
Luke Appling, ss, ChA	.348-0-79	0.0	54.0	0.16
Roy Weatherly, of, Cle	.303-12-59	0.0	34.0	0.10
Dick Bartell, ss, Det	.233-7-53	0.0	26.0	0.08
Joe Kuhel, 1b, ChA	.280-27-94	0.0	18.0	0.05
Sid Hudson, p, Was	17-16, 4.57	0.0	16.0	0.05
Ted Williams, of, Bos	.344-23-113	0.0	16.0	0.05
Barney McCosky, of, Det	.340-4-57	0.0	11.0	0.03
Tiny Bonham, p, NYA	9-3, 1.90	0.0	8.0	0.02
Wally Judnich, of, StL	.303-24-89	0.0	6.0	0.02
Johnny Babich, p, Phi	14-13, 3.73	0.0	5.0	0.01
Mike Tresh, c, ChA	.281-1-64	0.0	4.0	0.01
Frankie Hayes, c, Phi	.308-16-70	0.0	4.0	0.01
Ray Mack, 2b, Cle	.283-12-69	0.0	4.0	0.01
Joe Gordon, 2b, NYA	.281-30-103	0.0	3.0	0.01
Cecil Travis, 3b, Was	.322-2-76	0.0	3.0	0.01
Bob Kennedy, 3b, ChA	.252-3-52	0.0	3.0	0.01
Charlie Gehringer, 2b, Det	.313-10-81	0.0	3.0	0.01
Rollie Hemsley, c, Cle	.267-4-42	0.0	2.0	0.01
Ted Lyons, p, ChA	12-8, 3.24	0.0	2.0	0.01
Lou Finney, of, Bos	.320-5-73	0.0	1.0	0.00
Eldon Auker, p, StL	16-11, 3.96	0.0	1.0	0.00

National League

MVP

Player, Pos, Team	Stats	1st Pl	Pts	Share
Frank McCormick, 1b, Cin	.309-19-127	16.0	274.0	0.82
Johnny Mize, 1b, StL	.314-43-137	6.0	209.0	0.62
Bucky Walters, p, Cin	22-10, 2.48	0.0	146.0	0.43
Paul Derringer, p, Cin	20-12, 3.06	1.0	121.0	0.36
Freddie Fitzsimmons, p, Bro	16-2, 2.81	0.0	84.0	0.25
Dixie Walker, of, Bro	.308-6-66	0.0	71.0	0.21
Harry Danning, c, NYG	.300-13-91	0.0	64.0	0.19
Stan Hack, 3b, ChN	.317-8-40	0.0	61.0	0.18
Ernie Lombardi, c, Cin	.319-14-74	1.0	38.0	0.11
Bill Werber, 3b, Cin	.277-12-48	0.0	36.0	0.11
Johnny Cooney, of, Bos	.318-0-21	0.0	31.0	0.09
Dolph Camilli, 1b, Bro	.287-23-96	0.0	30.0	0.09
Eddie Miller, ss, Bos	.276-14-79	0.0	28.0	0.08
Debs Garms, 3b, Pit	.355-5-57	0.0	28.0	0.08
Arky Vaughan, ss, Pit	.300-7-95	0.0	27.0	0.08
Claude Passeau, p, ChN	20-13, 2.50	0.0	26.0	0.08
Joe Beggs, p, Cin	2.00, 7 saves	0.0	19.0	0.06
Terry Moore, of, StL	.304-17-64	0.0	18.0	0.05
Elbie Fletcher, 1b, Pit	.273-16-104	0.0	16.0	0.05
Bill Nicholson, of, ChN	.297-25-98	0.0	12.0	0.04
Kirby Higbe, p, Phi	14-19, 3.72	0.0	10.0	0.03
Bama Rowell, 2b, Bos	.305-3-58	0.0	10.0	0.03
Al Lopez, c, Bos-Pit	.273-3-41	0.0	9.0	0.03
Maurice Van Robays, of, Pit	.273-11-116	0.0	8.0	0.02
Rip Sewell, p, Pit	16-5, 2.80	0.0	7.0	0.02
Pee Wee Reese, ss, Bro	.272-5-28	0.0	6.0	0.02
Max West, of, Bos	.261-7-72	0.0	6.0	0.02
Babe Young, 1b, NYG	.286-17-101	0.0	6.0	0.02
Whit Wyatt, p, Bro	15-14, 3.46	0.0	3.0	0.01
Johnny Rizzo, of, Pit-Cin-Phi	.283-24-72	0.0	3.0	0.01
Pinky May, 3b, Phi	.293-1-48	0.0	3.0	0.01
Hugh Mulcahy, p, Phi	13-22, 3.60	0.0	3.0	0.01
Pepper Martin, of, StL	.316-3-39	0.0	2.0	0.01
Frankie Gustine, 2b, Pit	.281-1-55	0.0	1.0	0.00

1941

American League

MVP

Player, Pos, Team	Stats	1st Pl	Pts	Share
Joe DiMaggio, of, NYA	.357-30-125	15.0	291.0	0.87
Ted Williams, of, Bos	.406-37-120	8.0	254.0	0.76
Bob Feller, p, Cle	25-13, 3.15	0.0	174.0	0.52
Thornton Lee, p, ChA	22-11, 2.37	1.0	144.0	0.43
Charlie Keller, of, NYA	.298-33-122	0.0	126.0	0.38
Cecil Travis, ss, Was	.359-7-101	0.0	101.0	0.30
Joe Gordon, 2b, NYA	.276-24-87	0.0	60.0	0.18
Jeff Heath, of, Cle	.340-24-123	0.0	37.0	0.11
Dick Newsome, p, Bos	19-10, 4.13	0.0	32.0	0.10
Roy Cullenbine, of, StL	.317-9-98	0.0	29.0	0.09
Joe Cronin, ss, Bos	.311-16-95	0.0	26.0	0.08
Sam Chapman, of, Phi	.322-25-106	0.0	25.0	0.07
Bill Dickey, c, NYA	.284-7-71	0.0	18.0	0.05
Tommy Henrich, of, NYA	.277-31-85	0.0	16.0	0.05
Barney McCosky, of, Det	.324-3-55	0.0	12.0	0.04
Ted Lyons, p, ChA	12-10, 3.70	0.0	12.0	0.04
Dick Siebert, 1b, Phi	.334-5-79	0.0	10.0	0.03
Lou Boudreau, ss, Cle	.257-10-56	0.0	10.0	0.03
Al Benton, p, Det	2.97, 7 saves	0.0	8.0	0.02
Phil Rizzuto, ss, NYA	.307-3-46	0.0	7.0	0.02
Dutch Leonard, p, Was	18-13, 3.45	0.0	7.0	0.02
Bruce Campbell, of, Det	.275-15-93	0.0	4.0	0.01
Rudy York, 1b, Det	.259-27-111	0.0	3.0	0.01
Frankie Hayes, c, Phi	.280-12-63	0.0	3.0	0.01
Taffy Wright, of, ChA	.322-10-97	0.0	2.0	0.01
Red Ruffing, p, NYA	15-6, 3.54	0.0	2.0	0.01
Eldon Auker, p, StL	14-15, 5.50	0.0	1.0	0.00
Mike Higgins, 3b, Det	.298-11-73	0.0	1.0	0.00
Dom DiMaggio, of, Bos	.283-8-58	0.0	1.0	0.00

National League

MVP

Player, Pos, Team	Stats	1st Pl	Pts	Share
Dolph Camilli, 1b, Bro	.285-34-120	*19.0*	300.0	0.89
Pete Reiser, of, Bro	.343-14-76	*2.0*	183.0	0.54
Whit Wyatt, p, Bro	22-10, 2.34	*0.0*	151.0	0.45
Jimmy Brown, 3b, StL	.306-3-56	*1.0*	107.0	0.32
Elmer Riddle, p, Cin	19-4, 2.24	*0.0*	98.0	0.29
Ernie White, p, StL	17-7, 2.40	*0.0*	77.0	0.23
Kirby Higbe, p, Bro	22-9, 3.14	*0.0*	64.0	0.19
Johnny Hopp, of, StL	.303-4-50	*0.0*	61.0	0.18
Johnny Mize, 1b, StL	.317-16-100	*0.0*	48.0	0.14
Dixie Walker, of, Bro	.311-9-71	*1.0*	34.0	0.10
Billy Herman, 2b, ChN-Bro	.285-3-41	*0.0*	27.0	0.08
Terry Moore, of, StL	.294-6-68	*0.0*	26.0	0.08
Stan Hack, 3b, ChN	.317-7-45	*0.0*	26.0	0.08
Elbie Fletcher, 1b, Pit	.288-11-74	*0.0*	22.0	0.07
Johnny Cooney, of, Bos	.319-0-29	*0.0*	20.0	0.06
Bill Nicholson, of, ChN	.254-26-98	*0.0*	16.0	0.05
Gus Mancuso, c, StL	.229-2-37	*0.0*	14.0	0.04
Creepy Crespi, 2b, StL	.279-4-46	0.0	13.0	0.04
Mel Ott, of, NYG	.286-27-90	0.0	12.0	0.04
Enos Slaughter, of, StL	.311-13-76	0.0	12.0	0.04
Babe Young, 1b, NYG	.265-25-104	0.0	10.0	0.03
Vince DiMaggio, of, Pit	.267-21-100	0.0	10.0	0.03
Jim Tobin, p, Bos	12-12, 3.10	0.0	10.0	0.03
Al Lopez, c, Pit	.265-5-43	0.0	8.0	0.02
Marty Marion, ss, StL	.252-3-58	0.0	8.0	0.02
Mort Cooper, p, StL	13-9, 3.91	0.0	8.0	0.02
Lon Warneke, p, StL	17-9, 3.15	0.0	7.0	0.02
Nick Etten, 1b, Phi	.311-14-79	0.0	6.0	0.02
Bucky Walters, p, Cin	19-15, 2.83	0.0	6.0	0.02
Babe Dahlgren, 1b, Bos-ChN	.267-23-89	0.0	6.0	0.02
Bill Werber, 3b, Cin	.239-4-46	0.0	6.0	0.02
Estel Crabtree, of, StL	.341-5-28	0.0	5.0	0.01
Johnny Rucker, of, NYG	.288-1-42	0.0	4.0	0.01
Danny Litwhiler, of, Phi	.305-18-66	0.0	3.0	0.01
Harry Danning, c, NYG	.244-7-56	0.0	2.0	0.01
Carl Hubbell, p, NYG	11-9, 3.57	0.0	2.0	0.01
Cookie Lavagetto, 3b, Bro	.277-1-78	0.0	2.0	0.01
Arky Vaughan, ss, Pit	.316-6-38	0.0	2.0	0.01

1942

American League

MVP

Player, Pos, Team	Stats	1st Pl	Pts	Share
Joe Gordon, 2b, NYA	.322-18-103	12.0	270.0	0.80
Ted Williams, of, Bos	.356-36-137	9.0	249.0	0.74
Johnny Pesky, ss, Bos	.331-2-51	2.0	143.0	0.43
Vern Stephens, ss, StL	.294-14-92	1.0	140.0	0.42
Tiny Bonham, p, NYA	21-5, 2.27	0.0	102.0	0.30
Tex Hughson, p, Bos	22-6, 2.59	0.0	92.0	0.27
Joe DiMaggio, of, NYA	.305-21-114	0.0	86.0	0.26
Stan Spence, of, Was	.323-4-79	0.0	65.0	0.19
Phil Marchildon, p, Phi	17-14, 4.20	0.0	39.0	0.12
Lou Boudreau, ss, Cle	.283-2-58	0.0	34.0	0.10
Bobby Doerr, 2b, Bos	.290-15-102	0.0	24.0	0.07
Ted Lyons, p, ChA	14-6, 2.10	0.0	23.0	0.07
George Case, of, Was	.320-5-43	0.0	17.0	0.05
Ken Keltner, 3b, Cle	.287-6-78	0.0	15.0	0.04
Charlie Keller, of, NYA	.292-26-108	0.0	15.0	0.04
Wally Judnich, of, StL	.313-17-82	0.0	14.0	0.04
Bill Dickey, c, NYA	.295-2-37	0.0	12.0	0.04
Don Gutteridge, 2b, StL	.255-1-50	0.0	12.0	0.04
Phil Rizzuto, ss, NYA	.284-4-68	0.0	9.0	0.03
Chet Laabs, of, StL	.275-27-99	0.0	9.0	0.03
Rick Ferrell, c, StL	.223-0-26	0.0	8.0	0.02
Hank Borowy, p, NYA	15-4, 2.52	0.0	8.0	0.02
Jim Bagby Jr., p, Cle	17-9, 2.96	0.0	6.0	0.02
Taffy Wright, of, ChA	.333-0-47	0.0	6.0	0.02
Tony Lupien, 1b, Bos	.281-3-70	0.0	4.0	0.01
Les Fleming, 1b, Cle	.292-14-82	0.0	4.0	0.01
Spud Chandler, p, NYA	16-5, 2.38	0.0	3.0	0.01
Rudy York, 1b, Det	.260-21-90	0.0	3.0	0.01
Barney McCosky, of, Det	.293-7-50	0.0	1.0	0.00

National League

MVP

Player, Pos, Team	Stats	1st Pl	Pts	Share
Mort Cooper, p, StL	22-7, 1.78	13.0	263.0	0.78
Enos Slaughter, of, StL	.318-13-98	6.0	200.0	0.60
Mel Ott, of, NYG	.295-30-93	4.0	190.0	0.57
Mickey Owen, c, Bro	.259-0-44	0.0	103.0	0.31
Johnny Mize, 1b, NYG	.305-26-110	0.0	97.0	0.29
Pete Reiser, of, Bro	.310-10-64	0.0	91.0	0.27
Marty Marion, ss, StL	.276-0-54	1.0	81.0	0.24
Dolph Camilli, 1b, Bro	.252-26-109	0.0	42.0	0.13
Bob Elliott, 3b, Pit	.296-9-89	0.0	39.0	0.12
Claude Passeau, p, ChN	19-14, 2.68	0.0	33.0	0.10
Walker Cooper, c, StL	.281-7-65	0.0	28.0	0.08
Stan Musial, of, StL	.315-10-72	0.0	26.0	0.08
Ernie Lombardi, c, Bos	.330-11-46	0.0	24.0	0.07
Johnny Beazley, p, StL	21-6, 2.13	0.0	24.0	0.07
Jimmy Brown, 2b, StL	.256-1-71	0.0	24.0	0.07
Whit Wyatt, p, Bro	19-7, 2.73	0.0	22.0	0.07
Joe Medwick, of, Bro	.300-4-96	0.0	20.0	0.06
Terry Moore, of, StL	.288-6-49	0.0	15.0	0.04
Bill Nicholson, of, ChN	.294-21-78	0.0	14.0	0.04
Stan Hack, 3b, ChN	.300-6-39	0.0	11.0	0.03
Johnny Vander Meer, p, Cin	18-12, 2.43	0.0	11.0	0.03
Tommy Hughes, p, Phi	12-18, 3.06	0.0	10.0	0.03
Ray Starr, p, Cin	15-13, 2.67	0.0	9.0	0.03
Larry French, p, Bro	1.83, 0 saves	0.0	7.0	0.02
Pee Wee Reese, ss, Bro	.255-3-53	0.0	6.0	0.02
Whitey Kurowski, 3b, StL	.254-9-42	0.0	6.0	0.02
Ray Lamanno, c, Cin	.264-12-43	0.0	4.0	0.01
Max West, 1b, Bos	.254-16-56	0.0	4.0	0.01
Lonny Frey, 2b, Cin	.266-2-39	0.0	4.0	0.01
Frank McCormick, 1b, Cin	.277-13-89	0.0	4.0	0.01
Al Javery, p, Bos	12-16, 3.03	0.0	3.0	0.01
Eddie Miller, ss, Bos	.243-6-47	0.0	1.0	0.00

1943

American League

MVP

Player, Pos, Team	Stats	1st Pl	Pts	Share
Spud Chandler, p, NYA	20-4, 1.64	12.0	246.0	0.73
Luke Appling, ss, ChA	.328-3-80	5.0	215.0	0.64
Rudy York, 1b, Det	.271-34-118	1.0	152.0	0.45
Bill Johnson, 3b, NYA	.280-5-94	3.0	135.0	0.40
Bob Johnson, of, Was	.265-7-63	1.0	116.0	0.35
Dick Wakefield, of, Det	.316-7-79	0.0	72.0	0.21
Nick Etten, 1b, NYA	.271-14-107	0.0	61.0	0.18
Bill Dickey, c, NYA	.351-4-33	2.0	58.0	0.17
Vern Stephens, ss, StL	.289-22-91	0.0	49.0	0.15
Lou Boudreau, ss, Cle	.286-3-67	0.0	40.0	0.12
Dizzy Trout, p, Det	20-12, 2.48	0.0	38.0	0.11
George Case, of, Was	.294-1-52	0.0	37.0	0.11
Charlie Keller, of, NYA	.271-31-86	0.0	31.0	0.09
Bobby Doerr, 2b, Bos	.270-16-75	0.0	21.0	0.06
Al Smith, p, Cle	17-7, 2.55	0.0	19.0	0.06
Jerry Priddy, 2b, Was	.271-4-62	0.0	17.0	0.05
Oris Hockett, of, Cle	.276-2-51	0.0	14.0	0.04
Don Gutteridge, 2b, StL	.273-1-36	0.0	13.0	0.04
Early Wynn, p, Was	18-12, 2.91	0.0	13.0	0.04
Jim Bagby Jr., p, Cle	17-14, 3.10	0.0	11.0	0.03
Doc Cramer, of, Det	.300-1-43	0.0	8.0	0.02
Mike Higgins, 3b, Det	.277-10-84	0.0	8.0	0.02
Chet Laabs, of, StL	.250-17-85	0.0	6.0	0.02
Jake Early, c, Was	.258-5-60	0.0	6.0	0.02
Joe Gordon, 2b, NYA	.249-17-69	0.0	4.0	0.01
Roger Wolff, p, Phi	10-15, 3.54	0.0	4.0	0.01
Skeeter Newsome, ss, Bos	.265-1-22	0.0	3.0	0.01
Joe Cronin, 3b, Bos	.312-5-29	0.0	3.0	0.01
Jesse Flores, p, Phi	12-14, 3.11	0.0	3.0	0.01
Gordon Maltzberger, p, ChA	2.46, 14 saves	0.0	3.0	0.01
Frankie Crosetti, ss, NYA	.233-2-20	0.0	2.0	0.01
Ken Keltner, 3b, Cle	.260-4-39	0.0	2.0	0.01
Pete Fox, of, Bos	.288-2-44	0.0	1.0	0.00
Ralph Hodgin, 3b, ChA	.314-1-50	0.0	1.0	0.00
Johnny Murphy, p, NYA	2.51, 8 saves	0.0	1.0	0.00
Dick Siebert, 1b, Phi	.251-1-72	0.0	1.0	0.00
Jim Tabor, 3b, Bos	.242-13-85	0.0	1.0	0.00
Hal Wagner, c, Phi	.239-1-26	0.0	1.0	0.00

National League

MVP

Player, Pos, Team	Stats	1st Pl	Pts	Share
Stan Musial, of, StL	.357-13-81	13.0	267.0	0.79
Walker Cooper, c, StL	.318-9-81	5.0	192.0	0.57
Bill Nicholson, of, ChN	.309-29-128	5.0	181.0	0.54
Billy Herman, 2b, Bro	.330-2-100	0.0	140.0	0.42
Mort Cooper, p, StL	21-8, 2.30	0.0	130.0	0.39
Rip Sewell, p, Pit	21-9, 2.54	0.0	127.0	0.38
Elmer Riddle, p, Cin	21-11, 2.66	0.0	68.0	0.20
Bob Elliott, 3b, Pit	.315-7-101	0.0	52.0	0.15
Frank McCormick, 1b, Cin	.303-8-59	0.0	26.0	0.08
Eddie Miller, ss, Cin	.224-2-71	0.0	24.0	0.07
Clyde Shoun, p, Cin	3.06, 7 saves	1.0	24.0	0.07
Mickey Witek, 2b, NYG	.314-6-55	0.0	21.0	0.06
Marty Marion, ss, StL	.280-1-52	0.0	20.0	0.06
Schoolboy Rowe, p, Phi	14-8, 2.94	0.0	18.0	0.05
Whit Wyatt, p, Bro	14-5, 2.49	0.0	15.0	0.04
Arky Vaughan, ss, Bro	.305-5-66	0.0	15.0	0.04
Ray Mueller, c, Cin	.260-8-52	0.0	12.0	0.04
Al Javery, p, Bos	17-16, 3.21	0.0	12.0	0.04
Stan Hack, 3b, ChN	.289-3-35	0.0	10.0	0.03
Mel Ott, of, NYG	.234-18-47	0.0	9.0	0.03
Elbie Fletcher, 1b, Pit	.283-9-70	0.0	7.0	0.02
Ace Adams, p, NYG	2.82, 9 saves	0.0	7.0	0.02
Lou Klein, 2b, StL	.287-7-62	0.0	6.0	0.02
Augie Galan, of, Bro	.287-9-67	0.0	5.0	0.01
Dixie Walker, of, Bro	.302-5-71	0.0	5.0	0.01
Jim Tobin, p, Bos	14-14, 2.74	0.0	5.0	0.01
Dick Bartell, 3b, NYG	.270-5-28	0.0	5.0	0.01
Phil Cavarretta, 1b, ChN	.291-8-73	0.0	4.0	0.01
Tommy Holmes, of, Bos	.270-5-41	0.0	2.0	0.01
Ron Northey, of, Phi	.278-16-68	0.0	2.0	0.01
Babe Dahlgren, 1b, Phi	.287-5-56	0.0	2.0	0.01
Hi Bithorn, p, ChN	18-12, 2.60	0.0	1.0	0.00
Bucky Walters, p, Cin	15-15, 3.54	0.0	1.0	0.00
Lonny Frey, 2b, Cin	.263-2-43	0.0	1.0	0.00

1944

American League

MVP

Player, Pos, Team	Stats	1st Pl	Pts	Share
Hal Newhouser, p, Det	29-9, 2.22	7.0	236.0	0.70
Dizzy Trout, p, Det	27-14, 2.12	10.0	232.0	0.69
Vern Stephens, ss, StL	.293-20-109	4.0	193.0	0.57
Snuffy Stirnweiss, 2b, NYA	.319-8-43	1.0	129.0	0.38
Dick Wakefield, of, Det	.355-12-53	2.0	128.0	0.38
Lou Boudreau, ss, Cle	.327-3-67	0.0	84.0	0.25
Bobby Doerr, 2b, Bos	.325-15-81	0.0	75.0	0.22
Stan Spence, of, Was	.316-18-100	0.0	56.0	0.17
Nels Potter, p, StL	19-7, 2.83	0.0	52.0	0.15
Bob Johnson, of, Bos	.324-17-106	0.0	51.0	0.15
Mark Christman, 3b, StL	.271-6-83	0.0	27.0	0.08
Tex Hughson, p, Bos	18-5, 2.26	0.0	22.0	0.07
Doc Cramer, of, Det	.292-2-42	0.0	14.0	0.04
Frankie Hayes, c, Phi	.248-13-78	0.0	13.0	0.04
Pete Fox, of, Bos	.315-1-64	0.0	12.0	0.04
Jack Kramer, p, StL	17-13, 2.49	0.0	9.0	0.03
Johnny Lindell, of, NYA	.300-18-103	0.0	8.0	0.02
Paul Richards, c, Det	.237-3-37	0.0	8.0	0.02
Don Gutteridge, 2b, StL	.245-3-36	0.0	7.0	0.02
Mike Higgins, 3b, Det	.297-7-76	0.0	7.0	0.02
George McQuinn, 1b, StL	.250-11-72	0.0	7.0	0.02
George Kell, 3b, Phi	.268-0-44	0.0	6.0	0.02
Roy Cullenbine, of, Cle	.284-16-80	0.0	5.0	0.01
Nick Etten, 1b, NYA	.293-22-91	0.0	5.0	0.01
Rudy York, 1b, Det	.276-18-98	0.0	5.0	0.01
Rollie Hemsley, c, NYA	.268-2-26	0.0	4.0	0.01
Mike Kreevich, of, StL	.301-5-44	0.0	4.0	0.01
Wally Moses, of, ChA	.280-3-34	0.0	4.0	0.01
Eddie Mayo, 2b, Det	.249-5-63	0.0	3.0	0.01
Dick Siebert, 1b, Phi	.306-6-52	0.0	3.0	0.01
Hank Borowy, p, NYA	17-12, 2.64	0.0	2.0	0.01
Frankie Crosetti, ss, NYA	.239-5-30	0.0	2.0	0.01
Ralph Hodgin, 3b, ChA	.295-1-51	0.0	2.0	0.01
Bob Muncrief, p, StL	13-8, 3.08	0.0	1.0	0.00

National League

MVP

Player, Pos, Team	Stats	1st Pl	Pts	Share
Marty Marion, ss, StL	.267-6-63	7.0	190.0	0.57
Bill Nicholson, of, ChN	.287-33-122	4.0	189.0	0.56
Dixie Walker, of, Bro	.357-13-91	3.0	145.0	0.43
Stan Musial, of, StL	.347-12-94	3.0	136.0	0.40
Bucky Walters, p, Cin	23-8, 2.40	0.0	107.0	0.32
Bill Voiselle, p, NYG	21-16, 3.02	3.0	107.0	0.32
Ray Mueller, c, Cin	.286-10-73	2.0	85.0	0.25
Walker Cooper, c, StL	.317-13-72	1.0	72.0	0.21
Mort Cooper, p, StL	22-7, 2.46	0.0	63.0	0.19
Bob Elliott, 3b, Pit	.297-10-108	0.0	57.0	0.17
Rip Sewell, p, Pit	21-12, 3.18	0.0	49.0	0.15
Babe Dahlgren, 1b, Pit	.289-12-101	1.0	33.0	0.10
Frank McCormick, 1b, Cin	.305-20-102	0.0	32.0	0.10
Phil Cavarretta, 1b, ChN	.321-5-82	0.0	27.0	0.08
Ray Sanders, 1b, StL	.295-12-102	0.0	25.0	0.07
Mel Ott, of, NYG	.288-26-82	0.0	20.0	0.06
Jim Tobin, p, Bos	18-19, 3.01	0.0	13.0	0.04
Johnny Hopp, of, StL	.336-11-72	0.0	10.0	0.03
Ron Northey, of, Phi	.288-22-104	0.0	10.0	0.03
Joe Medwick, of, NYG	.337-7-85	0.0	9.0	0.03
Johnny Barrett, of, Pit	.269-7-83	0.0	8.0	0.02
Eddie Miller, ss, Cin	.209-4-55	0.0	7.0	0.02
Tommy Holmes, of, Bos	.309-13-73	0.0	6.0	0.02
Ted Wilks, p, StL	17-4, 2.64	0.0	4.0	0.01
Tony Lupien, 1b, Phi	.283-5-52	0.0	3.0	0.01
Stan Hack, 3b, ChN	.282-3-32	0.0	2.0	0.01
Max Lanier, p, StL	17-12, 2.65	0.0	2.0	0.01
Connie Ryan, 2b, Bos	.295-4-25	0.0	2.0	0.01
Augie Galan, of, Bro	.318-12-93	0.0	1.0	0.00
Whitey Kurowski, 3b, StL	.270-20-87	0.0	1.0	0.00
Jim Russell, of, Pit	.312-8-66	0.0	1.0	0.00

1945

American League

MVP

Player, Pos, Team	Stats	1st Pl	Pts	Share
Hal Newhouser, p, Det	25-9, 1.81	9.0	236.0	0.70
Eddie Mayo, 2b, Det	.285-10-54	7.0	164.0	0.49
Snuffy Stirnweiss, 2b, NYA	.309-10-64	4.0	161.0	0.48
Boo Ferriss, p, Bos	21-10, 2.96	2.0	148.0	0.44
George Myatt, 2b, Was	.296-1-39	1.0	98.0	0.29
Vern Stephens, ss, StL	.289-24-89	0.0	94.0	0.28
Roger Wolff, p, Was	20-10, 2.12	0.0	78.0	0.23
Lou Boudreau, ss, Cle	.307-3-48	0.0	70.0	0.21
George Case, of, Was	.294-1-31	0.0	60.0	0.18
Paul Richards, c, Det	.256-3-32	0.0	35.0	0.10
Mike Tresh, c, ChA	.249-0-47	0.0	33.0	0.10
Joe Kuhel, 1b, Was	.285-2-75	1.0	29.0	0.09
Roy Cullenbine, of, Cle-Det	.272-18-93	0.0	26.0	0.08
Hank Greenberg, of, Det	.311-13-60	0.0	25.0	0.07
Nick Etten, 1b, NYA	.285-18-111	0.0	21.0	0.06
Tony Cuccinello, 3b, ChA	.308-2-49	0.0	18.0	0.05
Dizzy Trout, p, Det	18-15, 3.14	0.0	17.0	0.05
Dutch Leonard, p, Was	17-7, 2.13	0.0	16.0	0.05
Roy Schalk, 2b, ChA	.248-1-65	0.0	13.0	0.04
Jeff Heath, of, Cle	.305-15-61	0.0	10.0	0.03
George Binks, of, Was	.278-6-81	0.0	9.0	0.03
Bob Muncrief, p, StL	13-4, 2.72	0.0	8.0	0.02
Al Benton, p, Det	13-8, 2.02	0.0	6.0	0.02
Rick Ferrell, c, Was	.266-1-38	0.0	6.0	0.02
Bob Johnson, of, Bos	.280-12-74	0.0	6.0	0.02
Mark Christman, 3b, StL	.277-4-34	0.0	5.0	0.01
Bobby Estalella, of, Phi	.299-8-52	0.0	5.0	0.01
Frankie Hayes, c, Phi-Cle	.234-9-57	0.0	5.0	0.01
Doc Cramer, of, Det	.275-6-58	0.0	4.0	0.01
Wally Moses, of, ChA	.295-2-50	0.0	4.0	0.01
Eddie Lake, ss, Bos	.279-11-51	0.0	2.0	0.01
Russ Christopher, p, Phi	13-13, 3.17	0.0	1.0	0.00
Skeeter Newsome, 2b, Bos	.290-1-48	0.0	1.0	0.00
Rudy York, 1b, Det	.264-18-87	0.0	1.0	0.00

National League

MVP

Player, Pos, Team	Stats	1st Pl	Pts	Share
Phil Cavarretta, 1b, ChN	.355-6-97	15.0	279.0	0.83
Tommy Holmes, of, Bos	.352-28-117	3.0	175.0	0.52
Red Barrett, p, Bos-StL	23-12, 3.00	1.0	151.0	0.45
Andy Pafko, of, ChN	.298-12-110	4.0	131.0	0.39
Whitey Kurowski, 3b, StL	.323-21-102	0.0	90.0	0.27
Hank Borowy, p, ChN	11-2, 2.13	1.0	84.0	0.25
Hank Wyse, p, ChN	22-10, 2.68	0.0	72.0	0.21
Marty Marion, ss, StL	.277-1-59	0.0	69.0	0.21
Dixie Walker, of, Bro	.300-8-124	0.0	66.0	0.20
Goody Rosen, of, Bro	.325-12-75	0.0	56.0	0.17
Stan Hack, 3b, ChN	.323-2-43	0.0	42.0	0.13
Harry Brecheen, p, StL	15-4, 2.52	0.0	31.0	0.09
Mel Ott, of, NYG	.308-21-79	0.0	22.0	0.07
Augie Galan, 1b, Bro	.307-9-92	0.0	18.0	0.05
Johnny Hopp, of, StL	.289-3-44	0.0	17.0	0.05
Bob Elliott, 3b, Pit	.290-8-108	0.0	15.0	0.04
Luis Olmo, of, Bro	.313-10-110	0.0	13.0	0.04
Buster Adams, of, Phi-StL	.287-22-109	0.0	12.0	0.04
Claude Passeau, p, ChN	17-9, 2.46	0.0	9.0	0.03
Johnny Barrett, of, Pit	.256-15-67	0.0	8.0	0.02
Ed Heusser, p, Cin	11-16, 3.71	0.0	7.0	0.02
Don Johnson, 2b, ChN	.302-2-58	0.0	7.0	0.02
Buddy Kerr, ss, NYG	.249-4-40	0.0	7.0	0.02
Frank McCormick, 1b, Cin	.276-10-81	0.0	6.0	0.02
Bill Salkeld, c, Pit	.311-15-52	0.0	6.0	0.02
Peanuts Lowrey, of, ChN	.283-7-89	0.0	5.0	0.01
Ace Adams, p, NYG	3.42, 15 saves	0.0	4.0	0.01
Andy Karl, p, Phi	2.99, 15 saves	0.0	4.0	0.01
Hal Gregg, p, Bro	18-13, 3.47	0.0	2.0	0.01
Al Lopez, c, Pit	.218-0-18	0.0	2.0	0.01
Phil Masi, c, Bos	.272-7-46	0.0	2.0	0.01
Eddie Miller, ss, Cin	.238-13-49	0.0	2.0	0.01
Vince DiMaggio, of, Phi	.257-19-84	0.0	1.0	0.00
Eddie Stanky, 2b, Bro	.258-1-39	0.0	1.0	0.00

1946

American League

MVP

Player, Pos, Team	Stats	1st Pl	Pts	Share
Ted Williams, of, Bos	.342-38-123	9.0	224.0	0.67
Hal Newhouser, p, Det	26-9, 1.94	3.0	197.0	0.59
Bobby Doerr, 2b, Bos	.271-18-116	5.0	158.0	0.47
Johnny Pesky, ss, Bos	.335-2-55	2.0	141.0	0.42
Mickey Vernon, 1b, Was	.353-8-85	1.0	134.0	0.40
Bob Feller, p, Cle	26-15, 2.18	1.0	105.0	0.31
Boo Ferriss, p, Bos	25-6, 3.25	1.0	94.0	0.28
Hank Greenberg, 1b, Det	.277-44-127	2.0	91.0	0.27
Dom DiMaggio, of, Bos	.316-7-73	0.0	56.0	0.17
Lou Boudreau, ss, Cle	.293-6-62	0.0	37.0	0.11
Rudy York, 1b, Bos	.276-17-119	0.0	28.0	0.08
Luke Appling, ss, ChA	.309-1-55	0.0	26.0	0.08
Tex Hughson, p, Bos	20-11, 2.75	0.0	19.0	0.06
Earl Caldwell, p, ChA	2.08, 8 saves	0.0	18.0	0.05
Charlie Keller, of, NYA	.275-30-101	0.0	17.0	0.05
George Kell, 3b, Phi-Det	.322-4-52	0.0	12.0	0.04
Spud Chandler, p, NYA	20-8, 2.10	0.0	12.0	0.04
Aaron Robinson, c, NYA	.297-16-64	0.0	12.0	0.04
Bobo Newsom, p, Phi-Was	14-13, 2.93	0.0	6.0	0.02
Vern Stephens, ss, StL	.307-14-64	0.0	6.0	0.02
Joe DiMaggio, of, NYA	.290-25-95	0.0	6.0	0.02
Phil Marchildon, p, Phi	13-16, 3.49	0.0	5.0	0.01
Buddy Rosar, c, Phi	.283-2-47	0.0	4.0	0.01
Stan Spence, of, Was	.292-16-87	0.0	4.0	0.01
Johnny Berardino, 2b, StL	.265-5-68	0.0	2.0	0.01
Tommy Henrich, of, NYA	.251-19-83	0.0	1.0	0.00
Hal Wagner, c, Bos	.230-6-52	0.0	1.0	0.00

National League

MVP

Player, Pos, Team	Stats	1st Pl	Pts	Share
Stan Musial, 1b, StL	.365-16-103	22.0	319.0	0.95
Dixie Walker, of, Bro	.319-9-116	0.0	159.0	0.47
Enos Slaughter, of, StL	.300-18-130	2.0	144.0	0.43
Howie Pollet, p, StL	21-10, 2.10	0.0	116.0	0.35
Johnny Sain, p, Bos	20-14, 2.21	0.0	95.0	0.28
Pee Wee Reese, ss, Bro	.284-5-60	0.0	79.0	0.24
Eddie Stanky, 2b, Bro	.273-0-36	0.0	67.0	0.20
Del Ennis, of, Phi	.313-17-73	0.0	61.0	0.18
Pete Reiser, of, Bro	.277-11-73	0.0	58.0	0.17
Phil Cavarretta, of, ChN	.294-8-78	0.0	49.0	0.15
Buddy Kerr, ss, NYG	.249-6-40	0.0	37.0	0.11
Johnny Hopp, 1b, Bos	.333-3-48	0.0	34.0	0.10
Eddie Waitkus, 1b, ChN	.304-4-55	0.0	21.0	0.06
Bruce Edwards, c, Bro	.267-1-25	0.0	20.0	0.06
Kirby Higbe, p, Bro	17-8, 3.03	0.0	18.0	0.05
Harry Brecheen, p, StL	15-15, 2.49	0.0	14.0	0.04
Johnny Mize, 1b, NYG	.337-22-70	0.0	14.0	0.04
Grady Hatton, 3b, Cin	.271-14-69	0.0	12.0	0.04
Tommy Holmes, of, Bos	.310-6-79	0.0	11.0	0.03
Jim Tabor, 3b, Phi	.268-10-50	0.0	10.0	0.03
Emil Verban, 2b, StL-Phi	.274-0-34	0.0	10.0	0.03
Harry Walker, of, StL	.237-3-27	0.0	9.0	0.03
Schoolboy Rowe, p, Phi	11-4, 2.12	0.0	8.0	0.02
Phil Masi, c, Bos	.267-3-62	0.0	7.0	0.02
Johnny Vander Meer, p, Cin	10-12, 3.17	0.0	7.0	0.02
Red Schoendienst, 2b, StL	.281-0-34	0.0	6.0	0.02
Billy Cox, ss, Pit	.290-2-36	0.0	5.0	0.01
Frankie Gustine, 2b, Pit	.259-8-52	0.0	4.0	0.01
Marty Marion, ss, StL	.233-3-46	0.0	4.0	0.01
Ralph Kiner, of, Pit	.247-23-81	0.0	3.0	0.01
Whitey Kurowski, 3b, StL	.301-14-89	0.0	3.0	0.01
Ray Mueller, c, Cin	.254-8-48	0.0	3.0	0.01
Johnny Schmitz, p, ChN	11-11, 2.61	0.0	3.0	0.01
Peanuts Lowrey, of, ChN	.257-4-54	0.0	2.0	0.01
Frank McCormick, 1b, Phi	.284-11-66	0.0	2.0	0.01
Carl Furillo, of, Bro	.284-3-35	0.0	1.0	0.00
Oscar Judd, p, Phi	11-12, 3.53	0.0	1.0	0.00

1947

American League

MVP

Player, Pos, Team	Stats	1st Pl	Pts	Share
Joe DiMaggio, of, NYA	.315-20-97	8.0	202.0	0.60
Ted Williams, of, Bos	.343-32-114	3.0	201.0	0.60
Lou Boudreau, ss, Cle	.307-4-67	1.0	168.0	0.50
Joe Page, p, NYA	2.48, 17 saves	7.0	167.0	0.50
George Kell, 3b, Det	.320-5-93	0.0	132.0	0.39
George McQuinn, 1b, NYA	.304-13-80	3.0	77.0	0.23
Joe Gordon, 2b, Cle	.272-29-93	0.0	59.0	0.18
Bob Feller, p, Cle	20-11, 2.68	0.0	58.0	0.17
Phil Marchildon, p, Phi	19-9, 3.22	0.0	47.0	0.14
Luke Appling, ss, ChA	.306-8-49	0.0	43.0	0.13
Barney McCosky, of, Phi	.328-1-52	0.0	35.0	0.10
Eddie Joost, ss, Phi	.206-13-64	2.0	35.0	0.10
Tommy Henrich, of, NYA	.287-16-98	0.0	33.0	0.10
Spec Shea, p, NYA	14-5, 3.07	0.0	23.0	0.07
Yogi Berra, c, NYA	.280-11-54	0.0	18.0	0.05
Allie Reynolds, p, NYA	19-8, 3.20	0.0	18.0	0.05
Bob Dillinger, 3b, StL	.294-3-37	0.0	13.0	0.04
Johnny Pesky, ss, Bos	.324-0-39	0.0	11.0	0.03
Ferris Fain, 1b, Phi	.291-7-71	0.0	9.0	0.03
Bill Johnson, 3b, NYA	.285-10-95	0.0	9.0	0.03
Stan Spence, of, Was	.279-16-73	0.0	9.0	0.03
Fred Hutchinson, p, Det	18-10, 3.03	0.0	8.0	0.02
Early Wynn, p, Was	17-15, 3.64	0.0	7.0	0.02
Bobby Doerr, 2b, Bos	.258-17-95	0.0	6.0	0.02
Buddy Rosar, c, Phi	.259-1-33	0.0	6.0	0.02
Mark Christman, ss, Was	.222-1-33	0.0	4.0	0.01
Bill McCahan, p, Phi	10-5, 3.32	0.0	4.0	0.01
Dale Mitchell, of, Cle	.316-1-34	0.0	4.0	0.01
Roy Cullenbine, 1b, Det	.224-24-78	0.0	3.0	0.01
Joe Dobson, p, Bos	18-8, 2.95	0.0	3.0	0.01
Jeff Heath, of, StL	.251-27-85	0.0	1.0	0.00
Ed Lopat, p, ChA	16-13, 2.81	0.0	1.0	0.00
Vern Stephens, ss, StL	.279-15-83	0.0	1.0	0.00
Taffy Wright, of, ChA	.324-4-54	0.0	1.0	0.00

National League

MVP

Player, Pos, Team	Stats	1st Pl	Pts	Share
Bob Elliott, 3b, Bos	.317-22-113	9.0	205.0	0.61
Ewell Blackwell, p, Cin	22-8, 2.47	2.0	175.0	0.52
Johnny Mize, 1b, NYG	.302-51-138	2.0	144.0	0.43
Bruce Edwards, c, Bro	.295-9-80	4.0	140.0	0.42
Jackie Robinson, 1b, Bro	.297-12-48	1.0	106.0	0.32
Ralph Kiner, of, Pit	.313-51-127	0.0	101.0	0.30
Larry Jansen, p, NYG	21-5, 3.16	1.0	91.0	0.27
Pee Wee Reese, ss, Bro	.284-12-73	2.0	80.0	0.24
Whitey Kurowski, 3b, StL	.310-27-104	0.0	45.0	0.13
Harry Walker, of, StL-Phi	.363-1-41	0.0	45.0	0.13
Ralph Branca, p, Bro	21-12, 2.67	0.0	40.0	0.12
Hugh Casey, p, Bro	3.99, 18 saves	0.0	37.0	0.11
Eddie Stanky, 2b, Bro	.252-3-53	0.0	32.0	0.10
Dutch Leonard, p, Phi	17-12, 2.68	1.0	32.0	0.10
Warren Spahn, p, Bos	21-10, 2.33	0.0	26.0	0.08
Johnny Sain, p, Bos	21-12, 3.52	0.0	20.0	0.06
Willard Marshall, of, NYG	.291-36-107	1.0	20.0	0.06
Walker Cooper, c, NYG	.305-35-122	0.0	19.0	0.06
Dixie Walker, of, Bro	.306-9-94	1.0	14.0	0.04
Enos Slaughter, of, StL	.294-10-86	0.0	12.0	0.04
Stan Musial, 1b, StL	.312-19-95	0.0	12.0	0.04
Emil Verban, 2b, Phi	.285-0-42	0.0	9.0	0.03
Phil Cavarretta, of, ChN	.314-2-63	0.0	6.0	0.02
Peanuts Lowrey, 3b, ChN	.281-5-37	0.0	2.0	0.01
Eddie Miller, ss, Cin	.268-19-87	0.0	2.0	0.01
Andy Pafko, of, ChN	.302-13-66	0.0	1.0	0.00

Rookie of the Year

Player, Pos, Team	Stats	1st Pl	Pts	Share
Jackie Robinson, 1b, Bro	.297-12-48	*0.0*	129.0	0.78
Larry Jansen, p, NYG	21-5, 3.16	*0.0*	105.0	0.64
Spec Shea	14-5, 3.07	*0.0*	67.0	0.41
Ferris Fain	.291-7-71	*0.0*	43.0	0.26
Frankie Baumholtz, of, Cin	.283-5-45	*0.0*	42.0	0.25

1948

American League

MVP

Player, Pos, Team	Stats	1st Pl	Pts	Share
Lou Boudreau, ss, Cle	.355-18-106	22.0	324.0	0.96
Joe DiMaggio, of, NYA	.320-39-155	2.0	213.0	0.63
Ted Williams, of, Bos	.369-25-127	0.0	171.0	0.51
Vern Stephens, ss, Bos	.269-29-137	0.0	121.0	0.36
Bob Lemon, p, Cle	20-14, 2.82	0.0	101.0	0.30
Joe Gordon, 2b, Cle	.280-32-124	0.0	63.0	0.19
Tommy Henrich, of, NYA	.308-25-100	0.0	63.0	0.19
Gene Bearden, p, Cle	20-7, 2.43	0.0	52.0	0.15
Hal Newhouser, p, Det	21-12, 3.01	0.0	48.0	0.14
Eddie Joost, ss, Phi	.250-16-55	0.0	39.0	0.12
Hank Majeski, 3b, Phi	.310-12-120	0.0	23.0	0.07
Birdie Tebbetts, c, Bos	.280-5-68	0.0	23.0	0.07
Vic Raschi, p, NYA	19-8, 3.84	0.0	23.0	0.07
Ken Keltner, 3b, Cle	.297-31-119	0.0	18.0	0.05
Jerry Priddy, 2b, StL	.296-8-79	0.0	16.0	0.05
George Kell, 3b, Det	.304-2-44	0.0	14.0	0.04
Hoot Evers, of, Det	.314-10-103	0.0	13.0	0.04
Al Zarilla, of, StL	.329-12-74	0.0	11.0	0.03
Bobby Doerr, 2b, Bos	.285-27-111	0.0	10.0	0.03
Bob Dillinger, 3b, StL	.321-2-44	0.0	10.0	0.03
Jim Hegan, c, Cle	.248-14-61	0.0	10.0	0.03
Luke Appling, 3b, ChA	.314-0-47	0.0	8.0	0.02
Bob Feller, p, Cle	19-15, 3.56	0.0	6.0	0.02
Lou Brissie, p, Phi	14-10, 4.13	0.0	5.0	0.01
Ferris Fain, 1b, Phi	.281-7-88	0.0	5.0	0.01
Joe Dobson, p, Bos	16-10, 3.56	0.0	5.0	0.01
Billy Goodman, 1b, Bos	.310-1-66	0.0	4.0	0.01
Barney McCosky, of, Phi	.326-0-46	0.0	4.0	0.01
Yogi Berra, c, NYA	.305-14-98	0.0	3.0	0.01
Dom DiMaggio, of, Bos	.285-9-87	0.0	3.0	0.01
Larry Doby, of, Cle	.301-14-66	0.0	3.0	0.01
Cliff Fannin, p, StL	10-14, 4.17	0.0	2.0	0.01
Pat Mullin, of, Det	.288-23-80	0.0	1.0	0.00
Phil Rizzuto, ss, NYA	.252-6-50	0.0	1.0	0.00

National League

MVP

Player, Pos, Team	Stats	1st Pl	Pts	Share
Stan Musial, of, StL	.376-39-131	18.0	303.0	0.90
Johnny Sain, p, Bos	24-15, 2.60	5.0	223.0	0.66
Al Dark, ss, Bos	.322-3-48	1.0	174.0	0.52
Sid Gordon, 3b, NYG	.299-30-107	0.0	72.0	0.21
Harry Brecheen, p, StL	20-7, 2.24	0.0	61.0	0.18
Pee Wee Reese, ss, Bro	.274-9-75	0.0	60.0	0.18
Ralph Kiner, of, Pit	.265-40-123	0.0	55.0	0.16
Enos Slaughter, of, StL	.321-11-90	0.0	55.0	0.16
Danny Murtaugh, 2b, Pit	.290-1-71	0.0	52.0	0.15
Stan Rojek, ss, Pit	.290-4-51	0.0	51.0	0.15
Richie Ashburn, of, Phi	.333-2-40	0.0	48.0	0.14
Johnny Schmitz, p, ChN	18-13, 2.64	0.0	37.0	0.11
Bob Elliott, 3b, Bos	.283-23-100	0.0	33.0	0.10
Warren Spahn, p, Bos	15-12, 3.71	0.0	31.0	0.09
Jackie Robinson, 2b, Bro	.296-12-85	0.0	30.0	0.09
Andy Pafko, 3b, ChN	.312-26-101	0.0	25.0	0.07
Johnny Mize, 1b, NYG	.289-40-125	0.0	22.0	0.07
Rex Barney, p, Bro	15-13, 3.10	0.0	15.0	0.04
Johnny Vander Meer, p, Cin	17-14, 3.41	0.0	13.0	0.04
Johnny Wyrostek, of, Cin	.273-17-76	0.0	9.0	0.03
Ralph Branca, p, Bro	14-9, 3.51	0.0	8.0	0.02
Roy Campanella, c, Bro	.258-9-45	0.0	8.0	0.02
Bob Chesnes, p, Pit	14-6, 3.57	0.0	8.0	0.02
Phil Cavarretta, 1b, ChN	.278-3-40	0.0	6.0	0.02
Eddie Miller, ss, Phi	.246-14-61	0.0	4.0	0.01
Del Ennis, of, Phi	.290-30-95	0.0	3.0	0.01
Grady Hatton, 3b, Cin	.240-9-44	0.0	3.0	0.01
Larry Jansen, p, NYG	18-12, 3.61	0.0	2.0	0.01
Dixie Walker, of, Pit	.316-2-54	0.0	2.0	0.01
Gil Hodges, 1b, Bro	.249-11-70	0.0	1.0	0.00
Whitey Lockman, of, NYG	.286-18-59	0.0	1.0	0.00
Hank Sauer, of, Cin	.260-35-97	0.0	1.0	0.00

Rookie of the Year

Player, Pos, Team	Stats	1st Pl	Pts	Share
Al Dark, ss, Bos	.322-3-48	27.0	27.0	0.56
Gene Bearden	20-7, 2.43	8.0	8.0	0.17
Richie Ashburn, of, Phi	.333-2-40	7.0	7.0	0.15
Lou Brissie	14-10, 4.13	3.0	3.0	0.06
Billy Goodman	.310-1-66	3.0	3.0	0.06

1949

American League

MVP

Player, Pos, Team	Stats	1st Pl	Pts	Share
Ted Williams, of, Bos	.343-43-159	13.0	272.0	0.81
Phil Rizzuto, ss, NYA	.275-5-65	5.0	175.0	0.52
Joe Page, p, NYA	2.59, 27 saves	3.0	166.0	0.49
Mel Parnell, p, Bos	25-7, 2.77	1.0	151.0	0.45
Ellis Kinder, p, Bos	23-6, 3.36	0.0	122.0	0.36
Tommy Henrich, of, NYA	.287-24-85	1.0	121.0	0.36
Vern Stephens, ss, Bos	.290-39-159	1.0	100.0	0.30
George Kell, 3b, Det	.343-3-59	0.0	80.0	0.24
Bob Lemon, p, Cle	22-10, 2.99	0.0	57.0	0.17
Vic Wertz, of, Det	.304-20-133	0.0	51.0	0.15
Vic Raschi, p, NYA	21-10, 3.34	0.0	19.0	0.06
Joe DiMaggio, of, NYA	.346-14-67	0.0	18.0	0.05
Eddie Joost, ss, Phi	.263-23-81	0.0	11.0	0.03
Lou Boudreau, ss, Cle	.284-4-60	0.0	10.0	0.03
Yogi Berra, c, NYA	.277-20-91	0.0	9.0	0.03
Dom DiMaggio, of, Bos	.307-8-60	0.0	7.0	0.02
Bobby Doerr, 2b, Bos	.309-18-109	0.0	7.0	0.02
Alex Kellner, p, Phi	20-12, 3.75	0.0	6.0	0.02
Eddie Robinson, 1b, Was	.294-18-78	0.0	6.0	0.02
Roy Sievers, of, StL	.306-16-91	0.0	6.0	0.02
Birdie Tebbetts, c, Bos	.270-5-48	0.0	6.0	0.02
Luke Appling, ss, ChA	.301-5-58	0.0	3.0	0.01
Art Houtteman, p, Det	15-10, 3.71	0.0	3.0	0.01
Jerry Priddy, 2b, StL	.290-11-63	0.0	3.0	0.01
Virgil Trucks, p, Det	19-11, 2.81	0.0	3.0	0.01
Dale Mitchell, of, Cle	.317-3-56	0.0	2.0	0.01
Allie Reynolds, p, NYA	17-6, 4.00	0.0	2.0	0.01

Rookie of the Year

Pitcher, Pos, Team	Stats	1st Pl	Pts	Share
Roy Sievers, of, StL	.306-16-91	10.0	10.0	0.45
Alex Kellner, p, Phi	20-12, 3.75	5.0	5.0	0.23
Jerry Coleman, 2b, NYA	.275-2-42	4.0	4.0	0.18
Bob Kuzava, p, ChA	10-6, 4.02	1.0	1.0	0.05
Johnny Groth, of, Det	.293-11-73	1.0	1.0	0.05
Mike Garcia, p, Cle	2.36, 2 saves	1.0	1.0	0.05

National League

MVP

Player, Pos, Team	Stats	1st Pl	Pts	Share
Jackie Robinson, 2b, Bro	.342-16-124	12.0	264.0	0.79
Stan Musial, of, StL	.338-36-123	5.0	226.0	0.67
Enos Slaughter, of, StL	.336-13-96	2.0	181.0	0.54
Ralph Kiner, of, Pit	.310-54-127	0.0	133.0	0.40
Pee Wee Reese, ss, Bro	.279-16-73	2.0	118.0	0.35
Carl Furillo, of, Bro	.322-18-106	2.0	68.0	0.20
Warren Spahn, p, Bos	21-14, 3.07	0.0	60.0	0.18
Don Newcombe, p, Bro	17-8, 3.17	0.0	55.0	0.16
Ken Heintzelman, p, Phi	17-10, 3.02	1.0	48.0	0.14
Red Schoendienst, 2b, StL	.297-3-54	0.0	30.0	0.09
Gil Hodges, 1b, Bro	.285-23-115	0.0	29.0	0.09
Howie Pollet, p, StL	20-9, 2.77	0.0	29.0	0.09
Del Ennis, of, Phi	.302-25-110	0.0	28.0	0.08
Bobby Thomson, of, NYG	.309-27-109	0.0	25.0	0.07
Roy Campanella, c, Bro	.287-22-82	0.0	22.0	0.07
Preacher Roe, p, Bro	15-6, 2.79	0.0	21.0	0.06
Granny Hamner, ss, Phi	.263-6-53	0.0	9.0	0.03
Whitey Lockman, of, NYG	.301-11-65	0.0	9.0	0.03
Russ Meyer, p, Phi	17-8, 3.08	0.0	8.0	0.02
Ken Raffensberger, p, Cin	18-17, 3.39	0.0	8.0	0.02
Hank Sauer, of, Cin-ChN	.275-31-99	0.0	8.0	0.02
Ted Wilks, p, StL	3.73, 9 saves	0.0	8.0	0.02
Richie Ashburn, of, Phi	.284-1-37	0.0	6.0	0.02
Johnny Schmitz, p, ChN	11-13, 4.35	0.0	6.0	0.02
Al Dark, ss, Bos	.276-3-53	0.0	3.0	0.01
Marty Marion, ss, StL	.272-5-70	0.0	3.0	0.01
Puddin' Head Jones, 3b, Phi	.244-19-77	0.0	2.0	0.01
Willard Marshall, of, NYG	.307-12-70	0.0	2.0	0.01
Earl Torgeson, 1b, Bos	.260-4-19	0.0	2.0	0.01
Sid Gordon, 3b, NYG	.284-26-90	0.0	1.0	0.00
Dick Sisler, 1b, Phi	.289-7-50	0.0	1.0	0.00

Rookie of the Year

Pitcher, Pos, Team	Stats	1st Pl	Pts	Share
Don Newcombe, p, Bro	17-8, 3.17	21.0	21.0	0.88
Del Crandall, c, Bos	.263-4-34	3.0	3.0	0.13

1950

American League

MVP

Player, Pos, Team	Stats	1st Pl	Pts	Share
Phil Rizzuto, ss, NYA	.324-7-66	16.0	284.0	0.88
Billy Goodman, of, Bos	.354-4-68	4.0	180.0	0.56
Yogi Berra, c, NYA	.322-28-124	3.0	146.0	0.45
George Kell, 3b, Det	.340-8-101	0.0	127.0	0.39
Bob Lemon, p, Cle	23-11, 3.84	0.0	102.0	0.32
Walt Dropo, 1b, Bos	.322-34-144	0.0	75.0	0.23
Vic Raschi, p, NYA	21-8, 4.00	0.0	63.0	0.20
Larry Doby, of, Cle	.326-25-102	0.0	57.0	0.18
Joe DiMaggio, of, NYA	.301-32-122	0.0	54.0	0.17
Vic Wertz, of, Det	.308-27-123	0.0	50.0	0.16
Hoot Evers, of, Det	.323-21-103	0.0	38.0	0.12
Chico Carrasquel, ss, ChA	.282-4-46	0.0	21.0	0.07
Dizzy Trout, p, Det	13-5, 3.75	0.0	21.0	0.07
Dom DiMaggio, of, Bos	.328-7-70	0.0	17.0	0.05
Irv Noren, of, Was	.295-14-98	0.0	16.0	0.05
Bobby Doerr, 2b, Bos	.294-27-120	0.0	15.0	0.05
Johnny Mize, 1b, NYA	.277-25-72	0.0	11.0	0.03
Jerry Priddy, 2b, Det	.277-13-75	0.0	11.0	0.03
Al Rosen, 3b, Cle	.287-37-116	0.0	11.0	0.03
Eddie Yost, 3b, Was	.295-11-58	0.0	8.0	0.02
Mel Parnell, p, Bos	18-10, 3.61	0.0	7.0	0.02
Whitey Ford, p, NYA	9-1, 2.81	0.0	7.0	0.02
Ted Williams, of, Bos	.317-28-97	0.0	7.0	0.02
Ned Garver, p, StL	13-18, 3.39	0.0	6.0	0.02
Vern Stephens, ss, Bos	.295-30-144	0.0	6.0	0.02
Art Houtteman, p, Det	19-12, 3.54	0.0	6.0	0.02
Sherm Lollar, c, StL	.280-13-65	0.0	4.0	0.01
Ed Lopat, p, NYA	18-8, 3.47	0.0	3.0	0.01
Ken Wood, of, StL	.225-13-62	0.0	2.0	0.01
Sam Dente, ss, Was	.239-2-59	0.0	1.0	0.00
Dave Philley, of, ChA	.242-14-80	0.0	1.0	0.00

Rookie of the Year

Pitcher, Pos, Team	Stats	1st Pl	Pts	Share
Walt Dropo, 1b, Bos	.322-34-144	15.0	15.0	0.65
Whitey Ford, p, NYA	9-1, 2.81	6.0	6.0	0.26
Chico Carrasquel, ss, ChA	.282-4-46	2.0	2.0	0.09

National League

MVP

Player, Pos, Team	Stats	1st Pl	Pts	Share
Jim Konstanty, p, Phi	2.66, 22 saves	18.0	286.0	0.85
Stan Musial, of, StL	.346-28-109	1.0	158.0	0.47
Eddie Stanky, 2b, NYG	.300-8-51	2.0	144.0	0.43
Del Ennis, of, Phi	.311-31-126	0.0	104.0	0.31
Ralph Kiner, of, Pit	.272-47-118	1.0	91.0	0.27
Granny Hamner, ss, Phi	.270-11-82	2.0	79.0	0.24
Robin Roberts, p, Phi	20-11, 3.02	0.0	68.0	0.20
Gil Hodges, 1b, Bro	.283-32-113	0.0	55.0	0.16
Duke Snider, of, Bro	.321-31-107	0.0	53.0	0.16
Sal Maglie, p, NYG	2.71, 1 saves	0.0	51.0	0.15
Ewell Blackwell, p, Cin	17-15, 2.97	0.0	41.0	0.12
Andy Pafko, of, ChN	.304-36-92	0.0	38.0	0.11
Roy Campanella, c, Bro	.281-31-89	0.0	29.0	0.09
Andy Seminick, c, Phi	.288-24-68	0.0	25.0	0.07
Jackie Robinson, 2b, Bro	.328-14-81	0.0	23.0	0.07
Curt Simmons, p, Phi	17-8, 3.40	0.0	22.0	0.07
Preacher Roe, p, Bro	19-11, 3.30	0.0	15.0	0.04
Ted Kluszewski, 1b, Cin	.307-25-111	0.0	14.0	0.04
Warren Spahn, p, Bos	21-17, 3.16	0.0	14.0	0.04
Don Newcombe, p, Bro	19-11, 3.70	0.0	14.0	0.04
Johnny Sain, p, Bos	20-13, 3.94	0.0	12.0	0.04
Sid Gordon, of, Bos	.304-27-103	0.0	11.0	0.03
Jim Hearn, p, StL-NYG	11-4, 2.49	0.0	10.0	0.03
Pee Wee Reese, ss, Bro	.260-11-52	0.0	8.0	0.02

Eddie Waitkus, 1b, Phi	.284-2-44	0.0	8.0	0.02
Bob Elliott, 3b, Bos	.305-24-107	0.0	8.0	0.02
Earl Torgeson, 1b, Bos	.290-23-87	0.0	6.0	0.02
Sam Jethroe, of, Bos	.273-18-58	0.0	6.0	0.02
Hank Sauer, of, ChN	.274-32-103	0.0	5.0	0.01
Vern Bickford, p, Bos	19-14, 3.47	0.0	4.0	0.01
Carl Furillo, of, Bro	.305-18-106	0.0	4.0	0.01
Wes Westrum, c, NYG	.236-23-71	0.0	3.0	0.01
Dick Sisler, of, Phi	.296-13-83	0.0	2.0	0.01
Hank Thompson, 3b, NYG	.289-20-91	0.0	2.0	0.01
Larry Jansen, p, NYG	19-13, 3.01	0.0	2.0	0.01
Puddin' Head Jones, 3b, Phi	.267-25-88	0.0	1.0	0.00

Rookie of the Year

Pitcher, Pos, Team	Stats	1st Pl	Pts	Share
Sam Jethroe, of, Bos	.273-18-58	11.0	11.0	0.48
Bob Miller, p, Phi	11-6, 3.57	5.0	5.0	0.22
Danny O'Connell, ss, Pit	.292-8-32	4.0	4.0	0.17
Bubba Church, p, Phi	8-6, 2.73	2.0	2.0	0.09
Bill Serena, 3b, ChN	.239-17-61	1.0	1.0	0.04

1951

American League

MVP

Player, Pos, Team	Stats	1st Pl	Pts	Share
Yogi Berra, c, NYA	.294-27-88	6.0	184.0	0.55
Ned Garver, p, StL	20-12, 3.73	6.0	157.0	0.47
Allie Reynolds, p, NYA	17-8, 3.05	6.0	125.0	0.37
Minnie Minoso, of, Cle-ChA	.326-10-76	1.0	120.0	0.36
Bob Feller, p, Cle	22-8, 3.50	0.0	118.0	0.35
Ferris Fain, 1b, Phi	.344-6-57	1.0	103.0	0.31
Ellis Kinder, p, Bos	2.55, 14 saves	2.0	66.0	0.20
Vic Raschi, p, NYA	21-10, 3.27	0.0	64.0	0.19
Gil McDougald, 3b, NYA	.306-14-63	0.0	63.0	0.19
Bobby Avila, 2b, Cle	.304-10-58	0.0	49.0	0.15
Phil Rizzuto, ss, NYA	.274-2-43	1.0	47.0	0.14
Ed Lopat, p, NYA	21-9, 2.91	1.0	44.0	0.13
Ted Williams, of, Bos	.318-30-126	0.0	35.0	0.10
Eddie Joost, ss, Phi	.289-19-78	0.0	32.0	0.10
George Kell, 3b, Det	.319-2-59	0.0	30.0	0.09
Early Wynn, p, Cle	20-13, 3.02	0.0	20.0	0.06
Nellie Fox, 2b, ChA	.313-4-55	0.0	25.0	0.07
Billy Goodman, 1b, Bos	.297-0-50	0.0	21.0	0.06
Dom DiMaggio, of, Bos	.296-12-72	0.0	16.0	0.05
Gus Zernial, of, ChA-Phi	.268-33-129	0.0	15.0	0.04
Bobby Shantz, p, Phi	18-10, 3.94	0.0	14.0	0.04
Mike Garcia, p, Cle	20-13, 3.15	0.0	11.0	0.03
Gil Coan, of, Was	.303-9-62	0.0	8.0	0.02
Mel Parnell, p, Bos	18-11, 3.26	0.0	7.0	0.02
Eddie Robinson, 1b, ChA	.282-29-117	0.0	7.0	0.02
Gene Woodling, of, NYA	.281-15-71	0.0	5.0	0.01
Johnny Pesky, ss, Bos	.313-3-41	0.0	5.0	0.01
Irv Noren, of, Was	.279-8-86	0.0	4.0	0.01
Dale Mitchell, of, Cle	.290-11-62	0.0	4.0	0.01
Virgil Trucks, p, Det	4.33, 1 saves	0.0	2.0	0.01
Eddie Yost, 3b, Was	.283-12-65	0.0	2.0	0.01
Jim Busby, of, ChA	.283-5-68	0.0	2.0	0.01
Johnny Mize, 1b, NYA	.259-10-49	0.0	2.0	0.01

Rookie of the Year

Pitcher, Pos, Team	Stats	1st Pl	Pts	Share
Gil McDougald, 3b, NYA	.306-14-63	13.0	13.0	0.54
Minnie Minoso, of, Cle-ChA	.326-10-76	11.0	11.0	0.46

National League

MVP

Player, Pos, Team	Stats	1st Pl	Pts	Share
Roy Campanella, c, Bro	.325-33-108	11.0	243.0	0.72
Stan Musial, of, StL	.355-32-108	2.0	191.0	0.57
Monte Irvin, of, NYG	.312-24-121	5.0	166.0	0.49
Sal Maglie, p, NYG	23-6, 2.93	1.0	153.0	0.46
Preacher Roe, p, Bro	22-3, 3.04	2.0	138.0	0.41
Jackie Robinson, 2b, Bro	.338-19-88	1.0	92.0	0.27
Richie Ashburn, of, Phi	.344-4-63	0.0	69.0	0.21
Bobby Thomson, of, NYG	.293-32-101	1.0	62.0	0.18
Murry Dickson, p, Pit	20-16, 4.02	1.0	59.0	0.18
Ralph Kiner, of, Pit	.309-42-109	0.0	49.0	0.15
Warren Spahn, p, Bos	22-14, 2.98	0.0	45.0	0.13
Al Dark, ss, NYG	.303-14-69	0.0	30.0	0.09
Robin Roberts, p, Phi	21-15, 3.03	0.0	27.0	0.08
Larry Jansen, p, NYG	23-11, 3.04	0.0	26.0	0.08
Pee Wee Reese, ss, Bro	.286-10-84	0.0	15.0	0.04
Gil Hodges, 1b, Bro	.268-40-103	0.0	10.0	0.03
Sid Gordon, of, Bos	.287-29-109	0.0	10.0	0.03
Ken Raffensberger, p, Cin	16-17, 3.44	0.0	8.0	0.02
Johnny Wyrostek, of, Cin	.311-2-61	0.0	6.0	0.02
Ewell Blackwell, p, Cin	16-15, 3.44	0.0	6.0	0.02
Carl Furillo, of, Bro	.295-16-91	0.0	6.0	0.02
Don Newcombe, p, Bro	20-9, 3.28	0.0	3.0	0.01
Phil Cavarretta, 1b, ChN	.311-6-28	0.0	1.0	0.00
Hank Sauer, of, ChN	.263-30-89	0.0	1.0	0.00

Rookie of the Year

Pitcher, Pos, Team	Stats	1st Pl	Pts	Share
Willie Mays, of, NYG	.274-20-68	18.0	18.0	0.75
Chet Nichols, p, Bos	11-8, 2.88	4.0	4.0	0.17
Clem Labine, p, Bro	2.20, 0 saves	2.0	2.0	0.08

1952

American League

MVP

Player, Pos, Team	Stats	1st Pl	Pts	Share
Bobby Shantz, p, Phi	24-7, 2.48	16.0	280.0	0.83
Allie Reynolds, p, NYA	20-8, 2.06	4.0	183.0	0.54
Mickey Mantle, of, NYA	.311-23-87	3.0	143.0	0.43
Yogi Berra, c, NYA	.273-30-98	0.0	104.0	0.31
Early Wynn, p, Cle	23-12, 2.90	0.0	99.0	0.29
Ferris Fain, 1b, Phi	.327-2-59	0.0	66.0	0.20
Nellie Fox, 2b, ChA	.296-0-39	1.0	59.0	0.18
Bob Lemon, p, Cle	22-11, 2.50	0.0	58.0	0.17
Mike Garcia, p, Cle	22-11, 2.37	0.0	52.0	0.15
Al Rosen, 3b, Cle	.302-28-105	0.0	51.0	0.15
Eddie Robinson, 1b, ChA	.296-22-104	0.0	47.0	0.14
Larry Doby, of, Cle	.276-32-104	0.0	46.0	0.14
Luke Easter, 1b, Cle	.263-31-97	0.0	40.0	0.12
Phil Rizzuto, ss, NYA	.254-2-43	0.0	33.0	0.10
Eddie Joost, ss, Phi	.244-20-75	0.0	20.0	0.06
Billy Goodman, 2b, Bos	.306-4-56	0.0	18.0	0.05
Satchel Paige, p, StL	3.07, 10 saves	0.0	12.0	0.04
Jackie Jensen, of, NYA-Was	.280-10-82	0.0	12.0	0.04
Vic Raschi, p, NYA	16-6, 2.78	0.0	12.0	0.04
Dale Mitchell, of, Cle	.323-5-58	0.0	11.0	0.03
Hank Bauer, of, NYA	.293-17-74	0.0	10.0	0.03
Gene Woodling, of, NYA	.309-12-63	0.0	10.0	0.03
Pete Runnels, ss, Was	.285-1-64	0.0	8.0	0.02
Clint Courtney, c, StL	.286-5-50	0.0	7.0	0.02
Dick Gernert, 1b, Bos	.243-19-67	0.0	6.0	0.02
Walt Dropo, 1b, Bos-Det	.276-29-97	0.0	5.0	0.01
Saul Rogovin, p, ChA	14-9, 3.85	0.0	4.0	0.01
Sammy White, c, Bos	.281-10-49	0.0	4.0	0.01
Bobby Avila, 2b, Cle	.300-7-45	0.0	3.0	0.01
Billy Pierce, p, ChA	15-12, 2.57	0.0	3.0	0.01
Johnny Sain, p, NYA	3.46, 7 saves	0.0	3.0	0.01
Bobby Young, 2b, StL	.247-4-39	0.0	3.0	0.01
Joe Collins, 1b, NYA	.280-18-59	0.0	2.0	0.01
Connie Marrero, p, Was	11-8, 2.88	0.0	1.0	0.00
Bob Porterfield, p, Was	13-14, 2.72	0.0	1.0	0.00

Rookie of the Year

Pitcher, Pos, Team	Stats	1st Pl	Pts	Share
Harry Byrd, p, Phi	15-15, 3.31	9.0	9.0	0.38
Clint Courtney, c, StL	.286-5-50	8.0	8.0	0.33
Sammy White, c, Bos	.281-10-49	7.0	7.0	0.29

National League

MVP

Player, Pos, Team	Stats	1st Pl	Pts	Share
Hank Sauer, of, ChN	.270-37-121	8.0	226.0	0.67
Robin Roberts, p, Phi	28-7, 2.59	7.0	211.0	0.63
Joe Black, p, Bro	2.15, 15 saves	8.0	208.0	0.62
Hoyt Wilhelm, p, NYG	2.43, 11 saves	0.0	133.0	0.40
Stan Musial, of, StL	.336-21-91	0.0	127.0	0.38
Enos Slaughter, of, StL	.300-11-101	0.0	92.0	0.27
Jackie Robinson, 2b, Bro	.308-19-75	0.0	31.0	0.09
Pee Wee Reese, ss, Bro	.272-6-58	0.0	29.0	0.09
Duke Snider, of, Bro	.303-21-92	1.0	29.0	0.09
Roy Campanella, c, Bro	.269-22-97	0.0	25.0	0.07
Red Schoendienst, 2b, StL	.303-7-67	0.0	25.0	0.07
Al Dark, ss, NYG	.301-14-73	0.0	24.0	0.07
Murry Dickson, p, Pit	14-21, 3.57	0.0	22.0	0.07
Del Ennis, of, Phi	.289-20-107	0.0	18.0	0.05
Whitey Lockman, 1b, NYG	.290-13-58	0.0	18.0	0.05
Bobby Thomson, 3b, NYG	.270-24-108	0.0	17.0	0.05
Frankie Baumholtz, of, ChN	.325-4-35	0.0	16.0	0.05
Ted Kluszewski, 1b, Cin	.320-16-86	0.0	16.0	0.05
Gil Hodges, 1b, Bro	.254-32-102	0.0	15.0	0.04
Roy McMillan, ss, Cin	.244-7-57	0.0	15.0	0.04
Eddie Mathews, 3b, Bos	.242-25-58	0.0	13.0	0.04
Bobby Adams, 3b, Cin	.283-6-48	0.0	9.0	0.03
Billy Cox, 3b, Bro	.259-6-34	0.0	8.0	0.02
Warren Hacker, p, ChN	15-9, 2.58	0.0	8.0	0.02
Ralph Kiner, of, Pit	.244-37-87	0.0	8.0	0.02
Sal Maglie, p, NYG	18-8, 2.92	0.0	8.0	0.02
Ken Raffensberger, p, Cin	17-13, 2.81	0.0	8.0	0.02
Warren Spahn, p, Bos	14-19, 2.98	0.0	8.0	0.02
Preacher Roe, p, Bro	11-2, 3.12	0.0	7.0	0.02
Sid Gordon, of, Bos	.289-25-75	0.0	6.0	0.02
Granny Hamner, ss, Phi	.275-17-87	0.0	5.0	0.01
Solly Hemus, ss, StL	.268-15-52	0.0	5.0	0.01
Monte Irvin, of, NYG	.310-4-21	0.0	5.0	0.01
George Shuba, of, Bro	.305-9-40	0.0	5.0	0.01
Eddie Yuhas, p, StL	2.72, 6 saves	0.0	5.0	0.01
Al Brazle, p, StL	2.72, 16 saves	0.0	3.0	0.01
Johnny Logan, ss, Bos	.283-4-42	0.0	3.0	0.01
Toby Atwell, c, ChN	.290-2-31	0.0	2.0	0.01
Catfish Metkovich, 1b, Pit	.271-7-41	0.0	2.0	0.01
Walker Cooper, c, Bos	.235-10-55	0.0	1.0	0.00

Rookie of the Year

Pitcher, Pos, Team	Stats	1st Pl	Pts	Share
Joe Black, p, Bro	2.15, 15 saves	19.0	19.0	0.79
Hoyt Wilhelm, p, NYG	2.43, 11 saves	3.0	3.0	0.13
Dick Groat, ss, Pit	.284-1-29	1.0	1.0	0.04
Eddie Mathews, 3b, Bos	.242-25-58	1.0	1.0	0.04

1953

American League

MVP

Player, Pos, Team	Stats	1st Pl	Pts	Share
Al Rosen, 3b, Cle	.336-43-145	24.0	336.0	1.00
Yogi Berra, c, NYA	.296-27-108	0.0	167.0	0.50
Mickey Vernon, 1b, Was	.337-15-115	0.0	162.0	0.48
Minnie Minoso, of, ChA	.313-15-104	0.0	100.0	0.30
Virgil Trucks, p, StL-ChA	20-10, 2.93	0.0	81.0	0.24
Phil Rizzuto, ss, NYA	.271-2-54	0.0	76.0	0.23
Bob Porterfield, p, Was	22-10, 3.35	0.0	64.0	0.19
Ray Boone, 3b, Cle-Det	.296-26-114	0.0	59.0	0.18
Jimmy Piersall, of, Bos	.272-3-52	0.0	56.0	0.17
Billy Pierce, p, ChA	18-12, 2.72	0.0	55.0	0.16
Ellis Kinder, p, Bos	1.85, 27 saves	0.0	41.0	0.12
Hank Bauer, of, NYA	.304-10-57	0.0	37.0	0.11
Allie Reynolds, p, NYA	3.41, 13 saves	0.0	37.0	0.11
Mel Parnell, p, Bos	21-8, 3.06	0.0	27.0	0.08
Harvey Kuenn, ss, Det	.308-2-48	0.0	23.0	0.07
Bob Lemon, p, Cle	21-15, 3.36	0.0	22.0	0.07
Ed Lopat, p, NYA	16-4, 2.42	0.0	18.0	0.05
Gus Zernial, of, Phi	.284-42-108	0.0	16.0	0.05
Dave Philley, of, Phi	.303-9-59	0.0	11.0	0.03
Whitey Ford, p, NYA	18-6, 3.00	0.0	8.0	0.02
Billy Goodman, 2b, Bos	.313-2-41	0.0	5.0	0.01
Mickey Mantle, of, NYA	.295-21-92	0.0	4.0	0.01
Gene Woodling, of, NYA	.306-10-58	0.0	3.0	0.01
Eddie Yost, 3b, Was	.272-9-45	0.0	3.0	0.01
Billy Martin, 2b, NYA	.257-15-75	0.0	2.0	0.01
Chico Carrasquel, ss, ChA	.279-2-47	0.0	1.0	0.00
George Kell, 3b, Bos	.307-12-73	0.0	1.0	0.00
Ted Williams, of, Bos	.407-13-34	0.0	1.0	0.00

Rookie of the Year

Pitcher, Pos, Team	Stats	1st Pl	Pts	Share
Harvey Kuenn, ss, Det	.308-2-48	23.0	23.0	0.96
Tom Umphlett, of, Bos	.283-3-59	1.0	1.0	0.04

National League

MVP

Player, Pos, Team	Stats	1st Pl	Pts	Share
Roy Campanella, c, Bro	.312-41-142	17.0	297.0	0.88
Eddie Mathews, 3b, Mil	.302-47-135	3.0	216.0	0.64
Duke Snider, of, Bro	.336-42-126	1.0	157.0	0.47
Red Schoendienst, 2b, StL	.342-15-79	2.0	155.0	0.46
Warren Spahn, p, Mil	23-7, 2.10	0.0	120.0	0.36
Robin Roberts, p, Phi	23-16, 2.75	1.0	106.0	0.32
Ted Kluszewski, 1b, Cin	.316-40-108	0.0	69.0	0.21
Stan Musial, of, StL	.337-30-113	0.0	62.0	0.18
Carl Erskine, p, Bro	20-6, 3.54	0.0	54.0	0.16
Carl Furillo, of, Bro	.344-21-92	0.0	54.0	0.16
Pee Wee Reese, ss, Bro	.271-13-61	0.0	27.0	0.08
Jackie Robinson, of, Bro	.329-12-95	0.0	19.0	0.06
Del Ennis, of, Phi	.285-29-125	0.0	14.0	0.04
Gil Hodges, 1b, Bro	.302-31-122	0.0	13.0	0.04
Monte Irvin, of, NYG	.329-21-97	0.0	11.0	0.03
Danny O'Connell, 3b, Pit	.294-7-55	0.0	10.0	0.03
Harvey Haddix, p, StL	20-9, 3.06	0.0	9.0	0.03
Frank Thomas, of, Pit	.255-30-102	0.0	6.0	0.02
Richie Ashburn, of, Phi	.330-2-57	0.0	5.0	0.01
Gus Bell, of, Cin	.300-30-105	0.0	3.0	0.01
Johnny Logan, ss, Mil	.273-11-73	0.0	3.0	0.01
Ruben Gomez, p, NYG	13-11, 3.40	0.0	2.0	0.01
Granny Hamner, 2b, Phi	.276-21-92	0.0	2.0	0.01
Del Crandall, c, Mil	.272-15-51	0.0	1.0	0.00
Hank Thompson, 3b, NYG	.302-24-74	0.0	1.0	0.00

Rookie of the Year

Pitcher, Pos, Team	Stats	1st Pl	Pts	Share
Jim Gilliam, 2b, Bro	.278-6-63	11.0	11.0	0.46
Harvey Haddix, p, StL	20-9, 3.06	4.0	4.0	0.17
Ray Jablonski, 3b, StL	.268-21-112	3.0	3.0	0.13
Rip Repulski, of, StL	.275-15-66	2.0	2.0	0.08
Bill Bruton, of, Mil	.250-1-41	2.0	2.0	0.08
Fred Baczewski, p, ChN-Cin	11-4, 3.64	1.0	1.0	0.04
Jim Greengrass, of, Cin	.285-20-100	1.0	1.0	0.04

1954

American League

MVP

Player, Pos, Team	Stats	1st Pl	Pts	Share
Yogi Berra, c, NYA	.307-22-125	7.0	230.0	0.68
Larry Doby, of, Cle	.272-32-126	5.0	210.0	0.63
Bobby Avila, 2b, Cle	.341-15-67	5.0	203.0	0.60
Minnie Minoso, of, ChA	.320-19-116	2.0	186.0	0.55
Bob Lemon, p, Cle	23-7, 2.72	5.0	179.0	0.53
Early Wynn, p, Cle	23-11, 2.73	0.0	72.0	0.21
Ted Williams, of, Bos	.345-29-89	0.0	65.0	0.19
Harvey Kuenn, ss, Det	.306-5-48	0.0	37.0	0.11
Mickey Vernon, 1b, Was	.290-20-97	0.0	30.0	0.09
Nellie Fox, 2b, ChA	.319-2-47	0.0	30.0	0.09
Bob Grim, p, NYA	20-6, 3.26	0.0	25.0	0.07
Jim Finigan, 3b, Phi	.302-7-51	0.0	19.0	0.06
Virgil Trucks, p, ChA	19-12, 2.79	0.0	19.0	0.06
Jackie Jensen, of, Bos	.276-25-117	0.0	17.0	0.05
Mickey Mantle, of, NYA	.300-27-102	0.0	16.0	0.05
Irv Noren, of, NYA	.319-12-66	0.0	16.0	0.05
Al Rosen, 3b, Cle	.300-24-102	0.0	16.0	0.05
Jim Busby, of, Was	.298-7-80	0.0	7.0	0.02
Joe Coleman, p, Bal	13-17, 3.50	0.0	6.0	0.02
Billy Goodman, 2b, Bos	.303-1-36	0.0	6.0	0.02
Mike Garcia, p, Cle	19-8, 2.64	0.0	6.0	0.02
Jim Hegan, c, Cle	.234-11-40	0.0	5.0	0.01
Hank Bauer, of, NYA	.294-12-54	0.0	4.0	0.01
Al Kaline, of, Det	.276-4-43	0.0	4.0	0.01
Bob Turley, p, Bal	14-15, 3.46	0.0	4.0	0.01
Steve Gromek, p, Det	18-16, 2.74	0.0	1.0	0.00
Cal Abrams, of, Bal	.293-6-25	0.0	1.0	0.00
Ray Boone, 3b, Det	.295-20-85	0.0	1.0	0.00
Roy Sievers, of, Was	.232-24-102	0.0	1.0	0.00

Rookie of the Year

Pitcher, Pos, Team	Stats	1st Pl	Pts	Share
Bob Grim, p, NYA	20-6, 3.26	15.0	15.0	0.63
Jim Finigan, 3b, Phi	.302-7-51	8.0	8.0	0.33
Al Kaline, of, Det	.276-4-43	1.0	1.0	0.04

National League

MVP

Player, Pos, Team	Stats	1st Pl	Pts	Share
Willie Mays, of, NYG	.345-41-110	16.0	283.0	0.84
Ted Kluszewski, 1b, Cin	.326-49-141	7.0	217.0	0.65
Johnny Antonelli, p, NYG	21-7, 2.30	0.0	154.0	0.46
Duke Snider, of, Bro	.341-40-130	0.0	135.0	0.40
Al Dark, ss, NYG	.293-20-70	1.0	110.0	0.33
Stan Musial, of, StL	.330-35-126	0.0	97.0	0.29
Robin Roberts, p, Phi	23-15, 2.97	0.0	70.0	0.21
Joe Adcock, 1b, Mil	.308-23-87	0.0	60.0	0.18
Pee Wee Reese, ss, Bro	.309-10-69	0.0	53.0	0.16
Gil Hodges, 1b, Bro	.304-42-130	0.0	40.0	0.12
Warren Spahn, p, Mil	21-12, 3.14	0.0	38.0	0.11
Don Mueller, of, NYG	.342-4-71	0.0	30.0	0.09
Red Schoendienst, 2b, StL	.315-5-79	0.0	24.0	0.07
Frank Thomas, of, Pit	.298-23-94	0.0	24.0	0.07
Hoyt Wilhelm, p, NYG	2.10, 7 saves	0.0	17.0	0.05
Ernie Banks, ss, ChN	.275-19-79	0.0	14.0	0.04
Del Crandall, c, Mil	.242-21-64	0.0	13.0	0.04
Johnny Logan, ss, Mil	.275-8-66	0.0	9.0	0.03
Eddie Mathews, 3b, Mil	.290-40-103	0.0	5.0	0.01
Granny Hamner, 2b, Phi	.299-13-89	0.0	5.0	0.01
Richie Ashburn, of, Phi	.313-1-41	0.0	5.0	0.01
Sal Maglie, p, NYG	14-6, 3.26	0.0	4.0	0.01
Gene Conley, p, Mil	14-9, 2.96	0.0	3.0	0.01
Marv Grissom, p, NYG	2.35, 19 saves	0.0	2.0	0.01
Roy McMillan, ss, Cin	.250-4-42	0.0	2.0	0.01
Dusty Rhodes, of, NYG	.341-15-50	0.0	1.0	0.00
Hank Sauer, of, ChN	.288-41-103	0.0	1.0	0.00

Rookie of the Year

Pitcher, Pos, Team	Stats	1st Pl	Pts	Share
Wally Moon, of, StL	.304-12-76	17.0	17.0	0.71
Ernie Banks, ss, ChN	.275-19-79	4.0	4.0	0.17
Gene Conley, p, Mil	14-9, 2.96	2.0	2.0	0.08
Hank Aaron, of, Mil	.280-13-69	1.0	1.0	0.04

1955

American League

MVP

Player, Pos, Team	Stats	1st Pl	Pts	Share
Yogi Berra, c, NYA	.272-27-108	7.0	218.0	0.65
Al Kaline, of, Det	.340-27-102	4.0	201.0	0.60
Al Smith, of, Cle	.306-22-77	7.0	200.0	0.60
Ted Williams, of, Bos	.356-28-83	1.0	143.0	0.43
Mickey Mantle, of, NYA	.306-37-99	0.0	113.0	0.34
Ray Narleski, p, Cle	3.71, 19 saves	1.0	90.0	0.27
Nellie Fox, 2b, ChA	.311-6-59	0.0	84.0	0.25
Hank Bauer, of, NYA	.278-20-53	1.0	64.0	0.19
Vic Power, 1b, KCA	.319-19-76	1.0	53.0	0.16
Jackie Jensen, of, Bos	.275-26-116	0.0	39.0	0.12
Sherm Lollar, c, ChA	.261-16-61	0.0	37.0	0.11
Gil McDougald, 2b, NYA	.285-13-53	2.0	34.0	0.10
Billy Klaus, ss, Bos	.283-7-60	0.0	27.0	0.08
Tommy Byrne, p, NYA	16-5, 3.15	0.0	24.0	0.07
Whitey Ford, p, NYA	18-7, 2.63	0.0	21.0	0.06
Ray Boone, 3b, Det	.284-20-116	0.0	16.0	0.05
Roy Sievers, of, Was	.271-25-106	0.0	9.0	0.03
Harvey Kuenn, ss, Det	.306-8-62	0.0	8.0	0.02
Billy Pierce, p, ChA	15-10, 1.97	0.0	8.0	0.02
Dave Philley, of, Cle-Bal	.299-8-50	0.0	6.0	0.02
Early Wynn, p, Cle	17-11, 2.82	0.0	6.0	0.02
Elmer Valo, of, KCA	.364-3-37	0.0	5.0	0.01
Mickey Vernon, 1b, Was	.301-14-85	0.0	4.0	0.01
Billy Hoeft, p, Det	16-7, 2.99	0.0	1.0	0.00
Don Mossi, p, Cle	2.42, 9 saves	0.0	1.0	0.00
Frank Sullivan, p, Bos	18-13, 2.91	0.0	1.0	0.00
Gus Triandos, 1b, Bal	.277-12-65	0.0	1.0	0.00
Jose Valdivielso, ss, Was	.221-2-28	0.0	1.0	0.00
Sammy White, c, Bos	.261-11-64	0.0	1.0	0.00

Rookie of the Year

Pitcher, Pos, Team	Stats	1st Pl	Pts	Share
Herb Score, p, Cle	16-10, 2.85	18.0	18.0	0.75
Billy Klaus, ss, Bos	.283-7-60	5.0	5.0	0.21
Norm Zauchin, 1b, Bos	.239-27-93	1.0	1.0	0.04

National League

MVP

Player, Pos, Team	Stats	1st Pl	Pts	Share
Roy Campanella, c, Bro	.318-32-107	8.0	226.0	0.67
Duke Snider, of, Bro	.309-42-136	8.0	221.0	0.66
Ernie Banks, ss, ChN	.295-44-117	6.0	195.0	0.58
Willie Mays, of, NYG	.319-51-127	0.0	165.0	0.49
Robin Roberts, p, Phi	23-14, 3.28	1.0	159.0	0.47
Ted Kluszewski, 1b, Cin	.314-47-113	0.0	111.0	0.33
Don Newcombe, p, Bro	20-5, 3.20	0.0	89.0	0.26
Stan Musial, 1b, StL	.319-33-108	0.0	46.0	0.14
Hank Aaron, of, Mil	.314-27-106	0.0	36.0	0.11
Pee Wee Reese, ss, Bro	.282-10-61	1.0	36.0	0.11
Johnny Logan, ss, Mil	.297-13-83	0.0	24.0	0.07
Wally Post, of, Cin	.309-40-109	0.0	23.0	0.07
Del Ennis, of, Phi	.296-29-120	0.0	21.0	0.06
Richie Ashburn, of, Phi	.338-3-42	0.0	17.0	0.05
Clem Labine, p, Bro	3.24, 11 saves	0.0	11.0	0.03
Bob Friend, p, Pit	2.83, 2 saves	0.0	10.0	0.03
Del Crandall, c, Mil	.236-26-62	0.0	8.0	0.02
Eddie Mathews, 3b, Mil	.289-41-101	0.0	6.0	0.02
Dale Long, 1b, Pit	.291-16-79	0.0	3.0	0.01
Jack Meyer, p, Phi	3.43, 16 saves	0.0	3.0	0.01
Gene Baker, 2b, ChN	.268-11-52	0.0	2.0	0.01
Carl Furillo, of, Bro	.314-26-95	0.0	2.0	0.01
Vern Law, p, Pit	10-10, 3.81	0.0	1.0	0.00
Frank Thomas, of, Pit	.245-25-72	0.0	1.0	0.00

Rookie of the Year

Pitcher, Pos, Team	Stats	1st Pl	Pts	Share
Bill Virdon, of, StL	.281-17-68	15.0	15.0	0.63
Jack Meyer, p, Phi	3.43, 16 saves	7.0	7.0	0.29
Don Bessent, p, Bro	2.70, 3 saves	2.0	2.0	0.08

1956

American League

MVP

Player, Pos, Team	Stats	1st Pl	Pts	Share
Mickey Mantle, of, NYA	.353-52-130	24.0	336.0	1.00
Yogi Berra, c, NYA	.298-30-105	0.0	186.0	0.55
Al Kaline, of, Det	.314-27-128	0.0	142.0	0.42
Harvey Kuenn, ss, Det	.332-12-88	0.0	80.0	0.24
Billy Pierce, p, ChA	20-9, 3.32	0.0	75.0	0.22
Ted Williams, of, Bos	.345-24-82	0.0	70.0	0.21
Bob Nieman, of, ChA-Bal	.320-14-68	0.0	55.0	0.16
Gil McDougald, ss, NYA	.311-13-56	0.0	55.0	0.16
Vic Wertz, 1b, Cle	.264-32-106	0.0	45.0	0.13
Bob Lemon, p, Cle	20-14, 3.03	0.0	40.0	0.12
Harry Simpson, of, KCA	.293-21-105	0.0	37.0	0.11
Whitey Ford, p, NYA	19-6, 2.47	0.0	33.0	0.10
Early Wynn, p, Cle	20-9, 2.72	0.0	32.0	0.10
Jimmy Piersall, of, Bos	.293-14-87	0.0	28.0	0.08
Nellie Fox, 2b, ChA	.296-4-52	0.0	28.0	0.08
Sherm Lollar, c, ChA	.293-11-75	0.0	27.0	0.08
Frank Lary, p, Det	21-13, 3.15	0.0	24.0	0.07
Pete Runnels, 1b, Was	.310-8-76	0.0	24.0	0.07
Herb Score, p, Cle	20-9, 2.53	0.0	18.0	0.05
Jackie Jensen, of, Bos	.315-20-97	0.0	15.0	0.04
Mickey Vernon, 1b, Bos	.310-15-84	0.0	14.0	0.04
Tom Brewer, p, Bos	19-9, 3.50	0.0	11.0	0.03
Hank Bauer, of, NYA	.241-26-84	0.0	8.0	0.02
Charlie Maxwell, of, Det	.326-28-87	0.0	8.0	0.02
Luis Aparicio, ss, ChA	.266-3-56	0.0	7.0	0.02
Gus Triandos, c, Bal	.279-21-88	0.0	6.0	0.02
Frank Bolling, 2b, Det	.281-7-45	0.0	3.0	0.01
Minnie Minoso, of, ChA	.316-21-88	0.0	3.0	0.01
Vic Power, 1b, KCA	.309-14-63	0.0	3.0	0.01
Johnny Kucks, p, NYA	18-9, 3.85	0.0	2.0	0.01
Roy Sievers, of, Was	.253-29-95	0.0	1.0	0.00

Rookie of the Year

Pitcher, Pos, Team	Stats	1st Pl	Pts	Share
Luis Aparicio, ss, ChA	.266-3-56	22.0	22.0	0.92
Tito Francona, of, Bal	.258-9-57	1.0	1.0	0.04
Rocky Colavito, of, Cle	.276-21-65	1.0	1.0	0.04

National League

MVP

Player, Pos, Team	Stats	1st Pl	Pts	Share
Don Newcombe, p, Bro	27-7, 3.06	8.0	223.0	0.66
Sal Maglie, p, Bro	13-5, 2.87	4.0	183.0	0.54
Hank Aaron, of, Mil	.328-26-92	0.0	146.0	0.43
Warren Spahn, p, Mil	20-11, 2.78	1.0	126.0	0.38
Jim Gilliam, 2b, Bro	.300-6-43	4.0	103.0	0.31
Roy McMillan, ss, Cin	.263-3-62	3.0	96.0	0.29
Frank Robinson, of, Cin	.290-38-83	0.0	79.0	0.24
Pee Wee Reese, ss, Bro	.257-9-46	3.0	71.0	0.21
Stan Musial, 1b, StL	.310-27-109	0.0	62.0	0.18
Duke Snider, of, Bro	.292-43-101	1.0	55.0	0.16
Joe Adcock, 1b, Mil	.291-38-103	0.0	54.0	0.16
Bob Friend, p, Pit	17-17, 3.46	0.0	38.0	0.11
Hersh Freeman, p, Cin	3.40, 18 saves	0.0	25.0	0.07
Johnny Antonelli, p, NYG	20-13, 2.86	0.0	18.0	0.05
Ted Kluszewski, 1b, Cin	.302-35-102	0.0	18.0	0.05
Jackie Robinson, 3b, Bro	.275-10-43	0.0	17.0	0.05
Willie Mays, of, NYG	.296-36-84	0.0	14.0	0.04
Ed Bailey, c, Cin	.300-28-75	0.0	13.0	0.04
Bill Virdon, of, StL-Pit	.319-10-46	0.0	13.0	0.04
Stan Lopata, c, Phi	.267-32-95	0.0	11.0	0.03
Carl Furillo, of, Bro	.289-21-83	0.0	9.0	0.03
Lew Burdette, p, Mil	19-10, 2.70	0.0	8.0	0.02
Bob Buhl, p, Mil	18-8, 3.32	0.0	7.0	0.02
Robin Roberts, p, Phi	19-18, 4.45	0.0	7.0	0.02
Brooks Lawrence, p, Cin	19-10, 3.99	0.0	6.0	0.02
Dale Long, 1b, Pit	.263-27-91	0.0	4.0	0.01
Wally Moon, of, StL	.298-16-68	0.0	3.0	0.01
Ernie Banks, ss, ChN	.297-28-85	0.0	2.0	0.01
Ken Boyer, 3b, StL	.306-26-98	0.0	2.0	0.01
Clem Labine, p, Bro	3.35, 19 saves	0.0	1.0	0.00
Johnny Logan, ss, Mil	.281-15-46	0.0	1.0	0.00
Richie Ashburn, of, Phi	.303-3-50	0.0	1.0	0.00

Cy Young

Pitcher, Team	Stats	1st Pl	Pts	Share
Don Newcombe, Bro	27-7, 3.06	10.0	10.0	0.63
Sal Maglie, Cle-Bro	13-5, 2.89	4.0	4.0	0.25
Warren Spahn, Mil	20-11, 2.78	1.0	1.0	0.06
Whitey Ford, NYA	19-6, 2.47	1.0	1.0	0.06

Rookie of the Year

Pitcher, Pos, Team	Stats	1st Pl	Pts	Share
Frank Robinson, of, Cin	.290-38-83	24.0	24.0	1.00

1957

American League

MVP

Player, Pos, Team	Stats	1st Pl	Pts	Share
Mickey Mantle, of, NYA	.365-34-94	6.0	233.0	0.69
Ted Williams, of, Bos	.388-38-87	5.0	209.0	0.62
Roy Sievers, of, Was	.301-42-114	4.0	205.0	0.61
Nellie Fox, 2b, ChA	.317-6-61	5.0	193.0	0.57
Gil McDougald, ss, NYA	.289-13-62	4.0	165.0	0.49
Vic Wertz, 1b, Cle	.282-28-105	0.0	61.0	0.18
Frank Malzone, 3b, Bos	.292-15-103	0.0	58.0	0.17
Minnie Minoso, of, ChA	.310-12-103	0.0	55.0	0.16
Jim Bunning, p, Det	20-8, 2.69	0.0	46.0	0.14
Al Kaline, of, Det	.295-23-90	0.0	40.0	0.12
Billy Pierce, p, ChA	20-12, 3.26	0.0	35.0	0.10
Billy Gardner, 2b, Bal	.262-6-55	0.0	22.0	0.07
Dick Donovan, p, ChA	16-6, 2.77	0.0	19.0	0.06
Yogi Berra, c, NYA	.251-24-82	0.0	18.0	0.05
Gene Woodling, of, Cle	.321-19-78	0.0	13.0	0.04
Bob Grim, p, NYA	2.63, 19 saves	0.0	9.0	0.03
Bob Boyd, 1b, Bal	.318-4-34	0.0	9.0	0.03
Charlie Maxwell, of, Det	.276-24-82	0.0	5.0	0.01
Woodie Held, of, NYA-KCA	.239-20-50	0.0	4.0	0.01
Whitey Ford, p, NYA	11-5, 2.57	0.0	4.0	0.01
Vic Power, 1b, KCA	.259-14-42	0.0	3.0	0.01
Jimmy Piersall, of, Bos	.261-19-63	0.0	2.0	0.01
Bill Skowron, 1b, NYA	.304-17-88	0.0	2.0	0.01
Harvey Kuenn, ss, Det	.277-9-44	0.0	2.0	0.01
Sherm Lollar, c, ChA	.256-11-70	0.0	2.0	0.01
Tony Kubek, of, NYA	.297-3-39	0.0	1.0	0.00
Bobby Shantz, p, NYA	11-5, 2.45	0.0	1.0	0.00

Rookie of the Year

Pitcher, Pos, Team	Stats	1st Pl	Pts	Share
Tony Kubek, of, NYA	.297-3-39	23.0	23.0	0.96
Frank Malzone, 3b, Bos	.292-15-103	1.0	1.0	0.04

Gold Gloves

Player, Pos, Team	Rng	LRng	FPct	LFPct
Bobby Shantz, p, NYA	—	—	.986	.963
Sherm Lollar, c, ChA	—	—	.998	.991
Nellie Fox, 2b, ChA	5.85	4.84	.986	.980
Frank Malzone, 3b, Bos	3.41	2.77	.954	.951
Al Kaline, of, Det	2.29	1.97	.985	.980
Minnie Minoso, of, ChA	1.99	1.97	.984	.980

National League

MVP

Player, Pos, Team	Stats	1st Pl	Pts	Share
Hank Aaron, of, Mil	.322-44-132	9.0	239.0	0.71
Stan Musial, 1b, StL	.351-29-102	5.0	230.0	0.68
Red Schoendienst, 2b, NYG-Mil	.309-15-65	8.0	221.0	0.66
Willie Mays, of, NYG	.333-35-97	1.0	174.0	0.52
Warren Spahn, p, Mil	21-11, 2.69	1.0	131.0	0.39
Ernie Banks, ss, ChN	.285-43-102	0.0	60.0	0.18
Gil Hodges, 1b, Bro	.299-27-98	0.0	54.0	0.16
Eddie Mathews, 3b, Mil	.292-32-94	0.0	45.0	0.13
Frank Robinson, of, Cin	.322-29-75	0.0	42.0	0.13
Jack Sanford, p, Phi	19-8, 3.08	0.0	39.0	0.12
Don Hoak, 3b, Cin	.293-19-89	0.0	31.0	0.09
Don Blasingame, 2b, StL	.271-8-58	0.0	26.0	0.08
Ed Bouchee, 1b, Phi	.293-17-76	0.0	26.0	0.08
Bob Buhl, p, Mil	18-7, 2.74	0.0	15.0	0.04
Del Ennis, of, StL	.286-24-105	0.0	13.0	0.04
Dick Groat, ss, Pit	.315-7-54	0.0	13.0	0.04
Al Dark, ss, StL	.290-4-64	0.0	12.0	0.04
Duke Snider, of, Bro	.274-40-92	0.0	10.0	0.03
Frank Thomas, 1b, Pit	.290-23-89	0.0	8.0	0.02
Don Drysdale, p, Bro	17-9, 2.69	0.0	8.0	0.02
Roy McMillan, ss, Cin	.272-1-55	0.0	6.0	0.02
Dick Drott, p, ChN	15-11, 3.58	0.0	6.0	0.02
Granny Hamner, 2b, Phi	.227-10-62	0.0	3.0	0.01
Lew Burdette, p, Mil	17-9, 3.72	0.0	2.0	0.01
Johnny Logan, ss, Mil	.273-10-49	0.0	1.0	0.00
Harry Anderson, of, Phi	.268-17-61	0.0	1.0	0.00

Cy Young

Pitcher, Team	Stats	1st Pl	Pts	Share
Warren Spahn, Mil	21-11, 2.69	15.0	15.0	0.94
Dick Donovan, ChA	16-6, 2.77	1.0	1.0	0.06

Rookie of the Year

Pitcher, Pos, Team	Stats	1st Pl	Pts	Share
Jack Sanford, p, Phi	19-8, 3.08	16.0	16.0	0.67
Ed Bouchee, 1b, Phi	.293-17-76	4.0	4.0	0.17
Dick Drott, p, ChN	15-11, 3.58	3.0	3.0	0.13
Bob Hazle, of, Mil	.403-7-27	1.0	1.0	0.04

Gold Gloves

Player, Pos, Team	Rng	LRng	FPct	LFPct
Gil Hodges, 1b, Bro	—	—	.990	.990
Roy McMillan, ss, Cin	4.44	4.35	.977	.958
Willie Mays, of, NYG	2.91	2.07	.980	.980

1958

American League

MVP

Player, Pos, Team	Stats	1st Pl	Pts	Share
Jackie Jensen, of, Bos	.286-35-122	9.0	233.0	0.69
Bob Turley, p, NYA	21-7, 2.97	7.0	191.0	0.57
Rocky Colavito, of, Cle	.303-41-113	4.0	181.0	0.54
Bob Cerv, of, KCA	.305-38-104	3.0	164.0	0.49
Mickey Mantle, of, NYA	.304-42-97	0.0	127.0	0.38
Roy Sievers, of, Was	.295-39-108	0.0	95.0	0.28
Ted Williams, of, Bos	.328-26-85	0.0	89.0	0.26
Nellie Fox, 2b, ChA	.300-0-49	1.0	88.0	0.26
Sherm Lollar, c, ChA	.273-20-84	0.0	57.0	0.17
Pete Runnels, 2b, Bos	.322-8-59	0.0	29.0	0.09
Gus Triandos, c, Bal	.245-30-79	0.0	27.0	0.08
Dick Hyde, p, Was	1.75, 18 saves	0.0	26.0	0.08
Harvey Kuenn, of, Det	.319-8-54	0.0	24.0	0.07
Cal McLish, p, Cle	16-8, 2.99	0.0	18.0	0.05
Vic Power, 1b, KCA-Cle	.312-16-80	0.0	15.0	0.04
Frank Bolling, 2b, Det	.269-14-75	0.0	10.0	0.03
Elston Howard, c, NYA	.314-11-66	0.0	9.0	0.03
Yogi Berra, c, NYA	.266-22-90	0.0	6.0	0.02
Minnie Minoso, of, Cle	.302-24-80	0.0	6.0	0.02
Al Kaline, of, Det	.313-16-85	0.0	5.0	0.01
Gil McDougald, 2b, NYA	.250-14-65	0.0	5.0	0.01
Ryne Duren, p, NYA	2.02, 20 saves	0.0	4.0	0.01
Frank Lary, p, Det	16-15, 2.90	0.0	3.0	0.01
Jack Harshman, p, Bal	12-15, 2.89	0.0	2.0	0.01
Dick Donovan, p, ChA	15-14, 3.01	0.0	1.0	0.00
Frank Malzone, 3b, Bos	.295-15-87	0.0	1.0	0.00

Cy Young

Pitcher, Team	Stats	1st Pl	Pts	Share
Bob Turley, NYA	21-7, 2.97	5.0	5.0	0.33
Warren Spahn, Mil	22-11, 3.07	4.0	4.0	0.27
Bob Friend, Pit	22-14, 3.68	3.0	3.0	0.20
Lew Burdette, Mil	20-10, 2.91	3.0	3.0	0.20

Rookie of the Year

Pitcher, Pos, Team	Stats	1st Pl	Pts	Share
Albie Pearson, of, Was	.275-3-33	14.0	14.0	0.58
Ryne Duren, p, NYA	2.02, 20 saves	7.0	7.0	0.29
Gary Bell, p, Cle	12-10, 3.31	3.0	3.0	0.13

Gold Gloves

Player, Pos, Team	Rng	LRng	FPct	LFPct
Bobby Shantz, p, NYA	—	—	1.000	.963
Sherm Lollar, c, ChA	—	—	.987	.990
Vic Power, 1b, KCA-Cle	—	—	.992	.991
Frank Bolling, 2b, Det	5.11	4.68	.985	.978
Frank Malzone, 3b, Bos	3.34	2.59	.950	.951
Luis Aparicio, ss, ChA	5.19	4.17	.973	.964
Al Kaline, of, Det	2.34	1.94	.994	.982
Jimmy Piersall, of, Bos	2.58	1.94	.985	.982
Norm Siebern, of, NYA	2.01	1.94	.982	.982

National League

MVP

Player, Pos, Team	Stats	1st Pl	Pts	Share
Ernie Banks, ss, ChN	.313-47-129	16.0	283.0	0.84
Willie Mays, of, SF	.347-29-96	3.0	185.0	0.55
Hank Aaron, of, Mil	.326-30-95	0.0	166.0	0.49
Frank Thomas, 3b, Pit	.281-35-109	2.0	143.0	0.43
Warren Spahn, p, Mil	22-11, 3.07	1.0	108.0	0.32
Bob Friend, p, Pit	22-14, 3.68	0.0	98.0	0.29
Richie Ashburn, of, Phi	.350-2-33	0.0	62.0	0.18
Bill Mazeroski, 2b, Pit	.275-19-68	1.0	61.0	0.18
Orlando Cepeda, 1b, SF	.312-25-96	0.0	57.0	0.17
Del Crandall, c, Mil	.272-18-63	0.0	48.0	0.14
Lew Burdette, p, Mil	20-10, 2.91	0.0	47.0	0.14
Stan Musial, 1b, StL	.337-17-62	0.0	39.0	0.12
Ken Boyer, 3b, StL	.307-23-90	0.0	31.0	0.09
Johnny Temple, 2b, Cin	.306-3-47	0.0	26.0	0.08
Bob Skinner, of, Pit	.321-13-70	1.0	18.0	0.05
Wes Covington, of, Mil	.330-24-74	0.0	16.0	0.05
Roy Face, p, Pit	2.89, 20 saves	0.0	8.0	0.02
Harry Anderson, of, Phi	.301-23-97	0.0	5.0	0.01
Jim Gilliam, of, LA	.261-2-43	0.0	4.0	0.01
Bob Purkey, p, Cin	17-11, 3.60	0.0	4.0	0.01
Frank Robinson, of, Cin	.269-31-83	0.0	4.0	0.01
Joe Adcock, 1b, Mil	.275-19-54	0.0	2.0	0.01
Carl Furillo, of, LA	.290-18-83	0.0	1.0	0.00

Rookie of the Year

Pitcher, Pos, Team	Stats	1st Pl	Pts	Share
Orlando Cepeda, 1b, SF	.312-25-96	21.0	21.0	1.00

Gold Gloves

Player, Pos, Team	Rng	LRng	FPct	LFPct
Harvey Haddix, p, Cin	—	—	.973	.955
Del Crandall, c, Mil	—	—	.990	.988
Gil Hodges, 1b, LA	—	—	.992	.990
Bill Mazeroski, 2b, Pit	5.53	4.76	.980	.975
Ken Boyer, 3b, StL	3.51	2.86	.962	.952
Roy McMillan, ss, Cin	4.63	4.57	.980	.964
Hank Aaron, of, Mil	2.07	1.95	.984	.980
Willie Mays, of, SF	2.95	1.95	.980	.980
Frank Robinson, of, Cin	2.33	1.95	.991	.980

1959

American League

MVP

Player, Pos, Team	Stats	1st Pl	Pts	Share
Nellie Fox, 2b, ChA	.306-2-70	16.0	295.0	0.88
Luis Aparicio, ss, ChA	.257-6-51	8.0	255.0	0.76
Early Wynn, p, ChA	22-10, 3.17	0.0	123.0	0.37
Rocky Colavito, of, Cle	.257-42-111	0.0	117.0	0.35
Tito Francona, of, Cle	.363-20-79	0.0	102.0	0.30
Al Kaline, of, Det	.327-27-94	0.0	84.0	0.25
Jim Landis, of, ChA	.272-5-60	0.0	66.0	0.20
Harvey Kuenn, of, Det	.353-9-71	0.0	64.0	0.19
Sherm Lollar, c, ChA	.265-22-84	0.0	44.0	0.13
Jackie Jensen, of, Bos	.277-28-112	0.0	40.0	0.12
Cal McLish, p, Cle	19-8, 3.63	0.0	35.0	0.10
Yogi Berra, c, NYA	.284-19-69	0.0	26.0	0.08
Minnie Minoso, of, Cle	.302-21-92	0.0	26.0	0.08
Frank Malzone, 3b, Bos	.280-19-92	0.0	24.0	0.07
Harmon Killebrew, 3b, Was	.242-42-105	0.0	21.0	0.06
Gene Woodling, of, Bal	.300-14-77	0.0	18.0	0.05
Mickey Mantle, of, NYA	.285-31-75	0.0	13.0	0.04
Bobby Richardson, 2b, NYA	.301-2-33	0.0	11.0	0.03
Camilo Pascual, p, Was	17-10, 2.64	0.0	9.0	0.03
Bob Shaw, p, ChA	18-6, 2.69	0.0	8.0	0.02
Gus Triandos, c, Bal	.216-25-73	0.0	8.0	0.02
Bud Daley, p, KCA	16-13, 3.16	0.0	7.0	0.02
Vic Power, 1b, Cle	.289-10-60	0.0	5.0	0.01
Bill Tuttle, of, KCA	.300-7-43	0.0	5.0	0.01
Jim Lemon, of, Was	.279-33-100	0.0	4.0	0.01
Pete Runnels, 2b, Bos	.314-6-57	0.0	2.0	0.01
Ted Williams, of, Bos	.254-10-43	0.0	2.0	0.01
Bob Allison, of, Was	.261-30-85	0.0	1.0	0.00
Gerry Staley, p, ChA	2.24, 14 saves	0.0	1.0	0.00

Cy Young

Pitcher, Team	Stats	1st Pl	Pts	Share
Early Wynn, ChA	22-10, 3.17	13.0	13.0	0.81
Sam Jones, SF	21-15, 2.83	2.0	2.0	0.13
Bob Shaw, ChA	18-6, 2.69	1.0	1.0	0.06

Rookie of the Year

Pitcher, Pos, Team	Stats	1st Pl	Pts	Share
Bob Allison, of, Was	.261-30-85	18.0	18.0	0.75
Jim Perry, p, Cle	2.65, 4 saves	5.0	5.0	0.21
Russ Snyder, of, KCA	.313-3-21	1.0	1.0	0.04

Gold Gloves

Player, Pos, Team	Rng	LRng	FPct	LFPct
Bobby Shantz, p, NYA	—	—	.933	.956
Sherm Lollar, c, ChA	—	—	.993	.989
Vic Power, 1b, Cle	—	—	.995	.990
Nellie Fox, 2b, ChA	5.24	4.73	.988	.976
Frank Malzone, 3b, Bos	3.19	2.72	.953	.952
Luis Aparicio, ss, ChA	4.88	3.97	.970	.959
Jackie Jensen, of, Bos	2.21	1.97	.982	.980
Al Kaline, of, Det	2.71	1.97	.989	.980
Minnie Minoso, of, Cle	2.22	1.97	.985	.980

National League

MVP

Player, Pos, Team	Stats	1st Pl	Pts	Share
Ernie Banks, ss, ChN	.304-45-143	10.5	232.5	0.75
Eddie Mathews, 3b, Mil	.306-46-114	5.5	189.5	0.61
Hank Aaron, of, Mil	.355-39-123	2.0	174.0	0.56
Wally Moon, of, LA	.302-19-74	4.0	161.0	0.52
Sam Jones, p, SF	21-15, 2.83	0.0	130.0	0.42
Willie Mays, of, SF	.313-34-104	0.0	85.0	0.28
Roy Face, p, Pit	2.70, 10 saves	0.0	67.0	0.22
Charlie Neal, 2b, LA	.287-19-83	0.0	64.0	0.21
Frank Robinson, 1b, Cin	.311-36-125	0.0	52.0	0.17
Ken Boyer, 3b, StL	.309-28-94	0.0	37.0	0.12
Del Crandall, c, Mil	.257-21-72	0.0	27.0	0.09
Lew Burdette, p, Mil	21-15, 4.07	0.0	14.0	0.05
Roger Craig, p, LA	11-5, 2.06	0.0	12.0	0.04
Joe Cunningham, of, StL	.345-7-60	0.0	12.0	0.04
Vada Pinson, of, Cin	.316-20-84	0.0	11.0	0.04
Johnny Temple, 2b, Cin	.311-8-67	0.0	8.0	0.03
Don Hoak, 3b, Pit	.294-8-65	0.0	6.0	0.02
Gil Hodges, 1b, LA	.276-25-80	0.0	4.0	0.01
Orlando Cepeda, 1b, SF	.317-27-105	0.0	3.0	0.01

Player, Pos, Team	Stats	1st Pl	Pts	Share
Vern Law, p, Pit	18-9, 2.98	0.0	3.0	0.01
Warren Spahn, p, Mil	21-15, 2.96	0.0	3.0	0.01
Gene Conley, p, Phi	12-7, 3.00	0.0	1.0	0.00
Willie McCovey, 1b, SF	.354-13-38	0.0	1.0	0.00
Duke Snider, of, LA	.308-23-88	0.0	1.0	0.00

Rookie of the Year

Pitcher, Pos, Team	Stats	1st Pl	Pts	Share
Willie McCovey, 1b, SF	.354-13-38	24.0	24.0	1.00

Gold Gloves

Player, Pos, Team	Rng	LRng	FPct	LFPct
Harvey Haddix, p, Pit	—	—	1.000	.954
Del Crandall, c, Mil	—	—	.994	.989
Gil Hodges, 1b, LA	—	—	.992	.988
Charlie Neal, 2b, LA	5.29	4.78	.989	.976
Ken Boyer, 3b, StL	3.03	2.66	.956	.950
Roy McMillan, ss, Cin	5.04	4.53	.974	.966
Hank Aaron, of, Mil	1.80	1.90	.982	.977
Jackie Brandt, of, SF	1.60	1.90	.984	.977
Willie Mays, of, SF	2.44	1.90	.984	.977

1960

American League

MVP

Player, Pos, Team	Stats	1st Pl	Pts	Share
Roger Maris, of, NYA	.283-39-112	8.0	225.0	0.67
Mickey Mantle, of, NYA	.275-40-94	10.0	222.0	0.66
Brooks Robinson, 3b, Bal	.294-14-88	3.0	211.0	0.63
Minnie Minoso, of, ChA	.311-20-105	2.0	141.0	0.42
Ron Hansen, ss, Bal	.255-22-86	1.0	110.0	0.33
Al Smith, of, ChA	.315-12-72	0.0	73.0	0.22
Roy Sievers, 1b, ChA	.295-28-93	0.0	58.0	0.17
Earl Battey, c, Was	.270-15-60	0.0	57.0	0.17
Bill Skowron, 1b, NYA	.309-26-91	0.0	56.0	0.17
Jim Lemon, of, Was	.269-38-100	0.0	36.0	0.11
Tony Kubek, ss, NYA	.273-14-62	0.0	29.0	0.09
Chuck Estrada, p, Bal	18-11, 3.58	0.0	28.0	0.08
Ted Williams, of, Bos	.316-29-72	0.0	25.0	0.07
Vic Wertz, 1b, Bos	.282-19-103	0.0	22.0	0.07
Yogi Berra, c, NYA	.276-15-62	0.0	21.0	0.06
Jim Gentile, 1b, Bal	.292-21-98	0.0	21.0	0.06
Pete Runnels, 2b, Bos	.320-2-35	0.0	18.0	0.05
Nellie Fox, 2b, ChA	.289-2-59	0.0	11.0	0.03
Vic Power, 1b, Cle	.288-10-84	0.0	11.0	0.03
Steve Barber, p, Bal	10-7, 3.22	0.0	7.0	0.02
Luis Aparicio, ss, ChA	.277-2-61	0.0	6.0	0.02
Jim Perry, p, Cle	18-10, 3.62	0.0	6.0	0.02
Gerry Staley, p, ChA	2.42, 10 saves	0.0	4.0	0.01
Jim Bunning, p, Det	11-14, 2.79	0.0	3.0	0.01
Gene Woodling, of, Bal	.283-11-62	0.0	3.0	0.01
Harvey Kuenn, of, Cle	.308-9-54	0.0	3.0	0.01
Bud Daley, p, KCA	16-16, 4.56	0.0	3.0	0.01
Mike Fornieles, p, Bos	2.64, 14 saves	0.0	2.0	0.01
Charlie Maxwell, of, Det	.237-24-81	0.0	2.0	0.01
Jimmy Piersall, of, Cle	.282-18-66	0.0	2.0	0.01

Rookie of the Year

Pitcher, Pos, Team	Stats	1st Pl	Pts	Share
Ron Hansen, ss, Bal	.255-22-86	22.0	22.0	0.92
Chuck Estrada, p, Bal	18-11, 3.58	1.0	1.0	0.04
Jim Gentile, 1b, Bal	.292-21-98	1.0	1.0	0.04

Gold Gloves

Player, Pos, Team	Rng	LRng	FPct	LFPct
Bobby Shantz, p, NYA	—	—	1.000	.967
Earl Battey, c, Was	—	—	.982	.987
Vic Power, 1b, Cle	—	—	.996	.991
Nellie Fox, 2b, ChA	5.77	4.66	.985	.979
Brooks Robinson, 3b, Bal	3.28	2.72	.977	.952
Luis Aparicio, ss, ChA	5.59	4.37	.979	.960
Jim Landis, of, ChA	2.60	1.95	.985	.982
Roger Maris, of, NYA	2.05	1.95	.985	.982
Minnie Minoso, of, ChA	1.92	1.95	.980	.982

National League

MVP

Player, Pos, Team	Stats	1st Pl	Pts	Share
Dick Groat, ss, Pit	.325-2-50	16.0	276.0	0.90
Don Hoak, 3b, Pit	.282-16-79	5.0	162.0	0.53
Willie Mays, of, SF	.319-29-103	0.0	115.0	0.37
Ernie Banks, ss, ChN	.271-41-117	0.0	100.0	0.32
Lindy McDaniel, p, StL	2.09, 26 saves	0.0	95.0	0.31
Ken Boyer, 3b, StL	.304-32-97	0.0	80.0	0.26
Vern Law, p, Pit	20-9, 3.08	0.0	80.0	0.26
Roberto Clemente, of, Pit	.314-16-94	1.0	62.0	0.20
Ernie Broglio, p, StL	2.74, 0 saves	0.0	58.0	0.19
Eddie Mathews, 3b, Mil	.277-39-124	0.0	52.0	0.17
Hank Aaron, of, Mil	.292-40-126	0.0	49.0	0.16
Roy Face, p, Pit	2.90, 24 saves	0.0	47.0	0.15
Del Crandall, c, Mil	.294-19-77	0.0	31.0	0.10
Warren Spahn, p, Mil	21-10, 3.50	0.0	27.0	0.09
Norm Larker, 1b, LA	.323-5-78	0.0	21.0	0.07
Stan Musial, of, StL	.275-17-63	0.0	18.0	0.06
Maury Wills, ss, LA	.295-0-27	0.0	7.0	0.02
Vada Pinson, of, Cin	.287-20-61	0.0	6.0	0.02
Joe Adcock, 1b, Mil	.298-25-91	0.0	5.0	0.02
Smoky Burgess, c, Pit	.294-7-39	0.0	2.0	0.01
Frank Robinson, 1b, Cin	.297-31-83	0.0	2.0	0.01
Larry Sherry, p, LA	3.79, 7 saves	0.0	2.0	0.01
Pancho Herrera, 1b, Phi	.281-17-71	0.0	1.0	0.00

Cy Young

Pitcher, Team	Stats	1st Pl	Pts	Share
Vern Law, Pit	20-9, 3.08	8.0	8.0	0.57
Warren Spahn, Mil	21-10, 3.50	4.0	4.0	0.29
Ernie Broglio, StL	2.74, 0 saves	1.0	1.0	0.07
Lindy McDaniel, StL	2.09, 26 saves	1.0	1.0	0.07

Rookie of the Year

Pitcher, Pos, Team	Stats	1st Pl	Pts	Share
Frank Howard, of, LA	.268-23-77	12.0	12.0	0.55
Pancho Herrera, 1b, Phi	.281-17-71	4.0	4.0	0.18
Art Mahaffey, p, Phi	7-3, 2.31	3.0	3.0	0.14
Ron Santo, 3b, ChN	.251-9-44	2.0	2.0	0.09
Tommy Davis, of, LA	.276-11-44	1.0	1.0	0.05

Gold Gloves

Player, Pos, Team	Rng	LRng	FPct	LFPct
Harvey Haddix, p, Pit	—	—	.982	.962
Del Crandall, c, Mil	—	—	.988	.986
Bill White, 1b, StL	—	—	.990	.990
Bill Mazeroski, 2b, Pit	5.71	4.48	.989	.974
Ken Boyer, 3b, StL	3.01	2.61	.959	.952
Ernie Banks, ss, ChN	4.94	4.23	.977	.960
Hank Aaron, of, Mil	2.18	1.92	.982	.978
Willie Mays, of, SF	2.66	1.92	.981	.978
Wally Moon, of, LA	1.65	1.92	.986	.978

1961

American League

MVP

Player, Pos, Team	Stats	1st Pl	Pts	Share
Roger Maris, of, NYA	.269-61-142	7.0	202.0	0.72
Mickey Mantle, of, NYA	.317-54-128	6.0	198.0	0.71
Jim Gentile, 1b, Bal	.302-46-141	5.0	157.0	0.56
Norm Cash, 1b, Det	.361-41-132	1.0	151.0	0.54
Whitey Ford, p, NYA	25-4, 3.21	0.0	102.0	0.36
Luis Arroyo, p, NYA	2.19, 29 saves	1.0	95.0	0.34
Frank Lary, p, Det	23-9, 3.24	0.0	53.0	0.19
Rocky Colavito, of, Det	.290-45-140	0.0	51.0	0.18
Al Kaline, of, Det	.324-19-82	0.0	35.0	0.13
Elston Howard, c, NYA	.348-21-77	0.0	30.0	0.11
Harmon Killebrew, 1b, Min	.288-46-122	0.0	29.0	0.10
Luis Aparicio, ss, ChA	.272-6-45	0.0	16.0	0.06
Jimmy Piersall, of, Cle	.322-6-40	0.0	10.0	0.04
Steve Barber, p, Bal	18-12, 3.33	0.0	7.0	0.03
Don Schwall, p, Bos	15-7, 3.22	0.0	7.0	0.03
Norm Siebern, 1b, KCA	.296-18-98	0.0	7.0	0.03
Dick Donovan, p, Was	10-10, 2.40	0.0	5.0	0.02
Bubba Phillips, 3b, Cle	.264-18-72	0.0	5.0	0.02
Brooks Robinson, 3b, Bal	.287-7-61	0.0	4.0	0.01
Chuck Schilling, 2b, Bos	.259-5-62	0.0	4.0	0.01
Tom Morgan, p, LAA	2.36, 10 saves	0.0	3.0	0.01

Al Smith, 3b, ChA	.278-28-93	0.0	3.0	0.01
Yogi Berra, of, NYA	.271-22-61	0.0	2.0	0.01
Bobby Richardson, 2b, NYA	.261-3-49	0.0	1.0	0.00
John Romano, c, Cle	.299-21-80	0.0	1.0	0.00
Lee Thomas, of, NYA-LAA	.285-24-70	0.0	1.0	0.00
Hoyt Wilhelm, p, Bal	2.30, 18 saves	0.0	1.0	0.00

Cy Young

Pitcher, Team	Stats	1st Pl	Pts	Share
Whitey Ford, NYA	25-4, 3.21	9.0	9.0	0.53
Warren Spahn, Mil	21-13, 3.02	6.0	6.0	0.35
Frank Lary, Det	23-9, 3.24	2.0	2.0	0.12

Rookie of the Year

Pitcher, Pos, Team	Stats	1st Pl	Pts	Share
Don Schwall, p, Bos	15-7, 3.22	7.0	7.0	0.35
Dick Howser, ss, KCA	.280-3-45	6.0	6.0	0.30
Floyd Robinson, of, ChA	.310-11-59	2.0	2.0	0.10
Chuck Schilling, 2b, Bos	.259-5-62	2.0	2.0	0.10
Lee Thomas, of, NYA-LAA	.285-24-70	2.0	2.0	0.10
Jake Wood, 2b, Det	.258-11-69	1.0	1.0	0.05

Gold Gloves

Player, Pos, Team	Rng	LRng	FPct	LFPct
Frank Lary, p, Det	—	—	.989	.953
Earl Battey, c, Min	—	—	.993	.989
Vic Power, 1b, Cle	—	—	.994	.990
Bobby Richardson, 2b, NYA	4.90	4.72	.978	.978
Brooks Robinson, 3b, Bal	2.96	2.79	.972	.950
Luis Aparicio, ss, ChA	4.81	4.37	.962	.956
Al Kaline, of, Det	2.63	1.98	.990	.977
Jim Landis, of, ChA	2.86	1.98	.988	.977
Jimmy Piersall, of, Cle	2.81	1.98	.991	.977

National League

MVP

Player, Pos, Team	Stats	1st Pl	Pts	Share
Frank Robinson, of, Cin	.323-37-124	15.0	219.0	0.98
Orlando Cepeda, 1b, SF	.311-46-142	0.0	117.0	0.52
Vada Pinson, of, Cin	.343-16-87	0.0	104.0	0.46
Roberto Clemente, of, Pit	.351-23-89	0.0	81.0	0.36
Joey Jay, p, Cin	21-10, 3.53	1.0	74.0	0.33
Willie Mays, of, SF	.308-40-123	0.0	70.0	0.31
Ken Boyer, 3b, StL	.329-24-95	0.0	43.0	0.19
Hank Aaron, of, Mil	.327-34-120	0.0	39.0	0.17
Maury Wills, ss, LA	.282-1-31	0.0	36.0	0.16
Jim O'Toole, p, Cin	19-9, 3.10	0.0	31.0	0.14
Warren Spahn, p, Mil	21-13, 3.02	0.0	31.0	0.14
Stu Miller, p, SF	2.66, 17 saves	0.0	26.0	0.12
Wally Moon, of, LA	.328-17-88	0.0	22.0	0.10
George Altman, of, ChN	.303-27-96	0.0	9.0	0.04
Johnny Podres, p, LA	18-5, 3.74	0.0	9.0	0.04
Roy McMillan, ss, Mil	.220-7-48	0.0	8.0	0.04
Eddie Mathews, 3b, Mil	.306-32-91	0.0	7.0	0.03
Sandy Koufax, p, LA	18-13, 3.52	0.0	5.0	0.02
John Roseboro, c, LA	.251-18-59	0.0	4.0	0.02
Jim Brosnan, p, Cin	3.04, 16 saves	0.0	3.0	0.01
Joe Torre, c, Mil	.278-10-42	0.0	2.0	0.01
Larry Jackson, p, StL	14-11, 3.75	0.0	1.0	0.00
Jerry Lynch, of, Cin	.315-13-50	0.0	1.0	0.00
Bobby Malkmus, 2b, Phi	.231-7-31	0.0	1.0	0.00
Dick Stuart, 1b, Pit	.301-35-117	0.0	1.0	0.00

Rookie of the Year

Pitcher, Pos, Team	Stats	1st Pl	Pts	Share
Billy Williams, of, ChN	.278-25-86	10.0	10.0	0.63
Joe Torre, c, Mil	.278-10-42	5.0	5.0	0.31
Jack Curtis, p, ChN	10-13, 4.89	1.0	1.0	0.06

Gold Gloves

Player, Pos, Team	Rng	LRng	FPct	LFPct
Bobby Shantz, p, Pit	—	—	1.000	.959
John Roseboro, c, LA	—	—	.986	.985
Bill White, 1b, StL	—	—	.989	.990
Bill Mazeroski, 2b, Pit	6.02	4.89	.975	.976
Ken Boyer, 3b, StL	3.03	2.60	.951	.948
Maury Wills, ss, LA	4.60	4.28	.959	.959
Roberto Clemente, of, Pit	1.97	1.86	.969	.977
Willie Mays, of, SF	2.56	1.86	.980	.977
Vada Pinson, of, Cin	2.68	1.86	.976	.977

1962

American League

MVP

Player, Pos, Team	Stats	1st Pl	Pts	Share
Mickey Mantle, of, NYA	.321-30-89	13.0	234.0	0.84
Bobby Richardson, 2b, NYA	.302-8-59	5.0	152.0	0.54
Harmon Killebrew, of, Min	.243-48-126	1.0	99.0	0.35
Leon Wagner, of, LAA	.268-37-107	0.0	85.0	0.30
Dick Donovan, p, Cle	20-10, 3.59	0.0	64.0	0.23
Al Kaline, of, Det	.304-29-94	0.0	58.0	0.21
Norm Siebern, 1b, KCA	.308-25-117	0.0	53.0	0.19
Rich Rollins, 3b, Min	.298-16-96	0.0	47.0	0.17
Brooks Robinson, 3b, Bal	.303-23-86	0.0	41.0	0.15
Floyd Robinson, of, ChA	.312-11-109	0.0	33.0	0.12
Lee Thomas, 1b, LAA	.290-26-104	0.0	32.0	0.11
Tom Tresh, ss, NYA	.286-20-93	1.0	30.0	0.11
Billy Moran, 2b, LAA	.282-17-74	0.0	28.0	0.10
Ralph Terry, p, NYA	23-12, 3.19	0.0	19.0	0.07
Camilo Pascual, p, Min	20-11, 3.32	0.0	14.0	0.05
Rocky Colavito, of, Det	.273-37-112	0.0	13.0	0.05
Hank Aguirre, p, Det	16-8, 2.21	0.0	10.0	0.04
Joe Cunningham, 1b, ChA	.295-8-70	0.0	9.0	0.03
Pete Runnels, 1b, Bos	.326-10-60	0.0	9.0	0.03
Carl Yastrzemski, of, Bos	.296-19-94	0.0	9.0	0.03
Vic Power, 1b, Min	.290-16-63	0.0	8.0	0.03
Dick Radatz, p, Bos	2.24, 24 saves	0.0	8.0	0.03
Jim Bunning, p, Det	19-10, 3.59	0.0	8.0	0.03
Zoilo Versalles, ss, Min	.241-17-67	0.0	8.0	0.03
Jerry Lumpe, 2b, KCA	.301-10-83	0.0	7.0	0.03
Eddie Bressoud, ss, Bos	.277-14-68	0.0	6.0	0.02
Bob Rodgers, c, LAA	.258-6-61	0.0	6.0	0.02
Whitey Ford, p, NYA	17-8, 2.90	0.0	6.0	0.02
Ray Herbert, p, ChA	20-9, 3.27	0.0	5.0	0.02
Chuck Hinton, of, Was	.310-17-75	0.0	5.0	0.02
Frank Malzone, 3b, Bos	.283-21-95	0.0	3.0	0.01
Norm Cash, 1b, Det	.243-39-89	0.0	3.0	0.01
Al Smith, 3b, ChA	.292-16-82	0.0	1.0	0.00

Rookie of the Year

Pitcher, Pos, Team	Stats	1st Pl	Pts	Share
Tom Tresh, ss, NYA	.286-20-93	13.0	13.0	0.65
Bob Rodgers, c, LAA	.258-6-61	4.0	4.0	0.20
Bernie Allen, 2b, Min	.269-12-64	1.0	1.0	0.05
Dean Chance, p, LAA	2.96, 8 saves	1.0	1.0	0.05
Dick Radatz, p, Bos	2.24, 24 saves	1.0	1.0	0.05

Gold Gloves

Player, Pos, Team	Rng	LRng	FPct	LFPct
Jim Kaat, p, Min	—	—	.967	.958
Earl Battey, c, Min	—	—	.991	.989
Vic Power, 1b, Min	—	—	.993	.990
Bobby Richardson, 2b, NYA	5.16	4.87	.982	.980
Brooks Robinson, 3b, Bal	3.10	2.79	.979	.952
Luis Aparicio, ss, ChA	4.82	4.47	.973	.962
Al Kaline, of, Det	2.33	1.92	.983	.980
Jim Landis, of, ChA	2.51	1.92	.995	.980
Mickey Mantle, of, NYA	1.86	1.92	.978	.980

National League

MVP

Player, Pos, Team	Stats	1st Pl	Pts	Share
Maury Wills, ss, LA	.299-6-48	8.0	209.0	0.75
Willie Mays, of, SF	.304-49-141	7.0	202.0	0.72
Tommy Davis, of, LA	.346-27-153	3.0	175.0	0.63
Frank Robinson, of, Cin	.342-39-136	2.0	164.0	0.59
Don Drysdale, p, LA	25-9, 2.83	0.0	85.0	0.30
Hank Aaron, of, Mil	.323-45-128	0.0	72.0	0.26
Jack Sanford, p, SF	24-7, 3.43	0.0	62.0	0.22
Bob Purkey, p, Cin	23-5, 2.81	0.0	33.0	0.12
Frank Howard, of, LA	.296-31-119	0.0	32.0	0.11
Stan Musial, of, StL	.330-19-82	0.0	19.0	0.07
Jose Pagan, ss, SF	.259-7-57	0.0	13.0	0.05
Don Demeter, 3b, Phi	.307-29-107	0.0	12.0	0.04
Felipe Alou, of, SF	.316-25-98	0.0	10.0	0.04
Bill White, 1b, StL	.324-20-102	0.0	10.0	0.04
Orlando Cepeda, 1b, SF	.306-35-114	0.0	9.0	0.03
Dick Groat, ss, Pit	.294-2-61	0.0	7.0	0.03
Roberto Clemente, of, Pit	.312-10-74	0.0	6.0	0.02
Ernie Banks, 1b, ChN	.269-37-104	0.0	5.0	0.02
Ken Boyer, 3b, StL	.291-24-98	0.0	5.0	0.02
Johnny Callison, of, Phi	.300-23-83	0.0	5.0	0.02
Harvey Kuenn, of, SF	.304-10-68	0.0	5.0	0.02
Juan Marichal, p, SF	18-11, 3.36	0.0	4.0	0.01
Bob Skinner, of, Pit	.302-20-75	0.0	4.0	0.01
Jim Davenport, 3b, SF	.297-14-58	0.0	3.0	0.01
Sandy Koufax, p, LA	14-7, 2.54	0.0	3.0	0.01
Del Crandall, c, Mil	.297-8-45	0.0	2.0	0.01
Art Mahaffey, p, Phi	19-14, 3.94	0.0	2.0	0.01
Ed Roebuck, p, LA	3.09, 9 saves	0.0	2.0	0.01
Eddie Kasko, 3b, Cin	.278-4-41	0.0	1.0	0.00
Eddie Mathews, 3b, Mil	.265-29-90	0.0	1.0	0.00

Cy Young

Pitcher, Team	Stats	1st Pl	Pts	Share
Don Drysdale, LA	25-9, 2.83	14.0	14.0	0.70
Jack Sanford, SF	24-7, 3.43	4.0	4.0	0.20
Bob Purkey, Cin	23-5, 2.81	1.0	1.0	0.05
Billy Pierce, SF	16-6, 3.49	1.0	1.0	0.05

Rookie of the Year

Pitcher, Pos, Team	Stats	1st Pl	Pts	Share
Ken Hubbs, 2b, ChN	.260-5-49	19.0	19.0	0.95
Donn Clendenon, 1b, Pit	.302-7-28	1.0	1.0	0.05

Gold Gloves

Player, Pos, Team	Rng	LRng	FPct	LFPct
Bobby Shantz, p, Hou-StL	—	—	.972	.948
Del Crandall, c, Mil	—	—	.994	.987
Bill White, 1b, StL	—	—	.993	.990
Ken Hubbs, 2b, ChN	5.36	4.68	.983	.974
Jim Davenport, 3b, SF	2.70	2.56	.953	.949
Maury Wills, ss, LA	4.78	4.43	.956	.963
Roberto Clemente, of, Pit	2.03	1.79	.973	.974
Willie Mays, of, SF	2.70	1.79	.991	.974
Bill Virdon, of, Pit	2.38	1.79	.976	.974

1963

American League

MVP

Player, Pos, Team	Stats	1st Pl	Pts	Share
Elston Howard, c, NYA	.287-28-85	15.0	248.0	0.89
Al Kaline, of, Det	.312-27-101	1.0	148.0	0.53
Whitey Ford, p, NYA	24-7, 2.74	3.0	125.0	0.45
Harmon Killebrew, of, Min	.258-45-96	0.0	85.0	0.30
Dick Radatz, p, Bos	1.97, 25 saves	0.0	84.0	0.30
Carl Yastrzemski, of, Bos	.321-14-68	0.0	81.0	0.29
Earl Battey, c, Min	.285-26-84	0.0	57.0	0.20
Gary Peters, p, ChA	19-8, 2.33	0.0	55.0	0.20
Pete Ward, 3b, ChA	.295-22-84	0.0	52.0	0.19
Bobby Richardson, 2b, NYA	.265-3-48	0.0	43.0	0.15
Tom Tresh, of, NYA	.269-25-71	1.0	38.0	0.14
Camilo Pascual, p, Min	21-9, 2.46	0.0	29.0	0.10
Dick Stuart, 1b, Bos	.261-42-118	0.0	25.0	0.09
Albie Pearson, of, LAA	.304-6-47	0.0	22.0	0.08
Bob Allison, of, Min	.271-35-91	0.0	15.0	0.05
Jim Bouton, p, NYA	21-7, 2.53	0.0	11.0	0.04
Max Alvis, 3b, Cle	.274-22-67	0.0	10.0	0.04
Joe Pepitone, 1b, NYA	.271-27-89	0.0	10.0	0.04
Leon Wagner, of, LAA	.291-26-90	0.0	9.0	0.03
Stu Miller, p, Bal	2.24, 27 saves	0.0	9.0	0.03
Wayne Causey, ss, KCA	.280-8-44	0.0	5.0	0.02
Rich Rollins, 3b, Min	.307-16-61	0.0	5.0	0.02
Luis Aparicio, ss, Bal	.250-5-45	0.0	3.0	0.01
Bill Dailey, p, Min	1.99, 21 saves	0.0	3.0	0.01
Jim Fregosi, ss, LAA	.287-9-50	0.0	3.0	0.01
Nellie Fox, 2b, ChA	.260-2-42	0.0	2.0	0.01
Tony Kubek, ss, NYA	.257-7-44	0.0	1.0	0.00
Floyd Robinson, of, ChA	.283-13-71	0.0	1.0	0.00
Norm Siebern, 1b, KCA	.272-16-83	0.0	1.0	0.00

Rookie of the Year

Pitcher, Pos, Team	Stats	1st Pl	Pts	Share
Gary Peters, p, ChA	19-8, 2.33	10.0	10.0	0.50
Pete Ward, 3b, ChA	.295-22-84	6.0	6.0	0.30
Jimmie Hall, of, Min	.260-33-80	4.0	4.0	0.20

Gold Gloves

Player, Pos, Team	Rng	LRng	FPct	LFPct
Jim Kaat, p, Min	—	—	.984	.955
Elston Howard, c, NYA	—	—	.994	.989

Vic Power, 1b, Min	—	—	.992	.990
Bobby Richardson, 2b, NYA	5.06	4.68	.984	.980
Brooks Robinson, 3b, Bal	3.02	2.85	.976	.947
Zoilo Versalles, ss, Min	4.71	4.56	.961	.965
Al Kaline, of, Det	1.87	1.91	.992	.981
Jim Landis, of, ChA	2.18	1.91	.993	.981
Carl Yastrzemski, of, Bos	1.99	1.91	.980	.981

National League

MVP

Player, Pos, Team	Stats	1st Pl	Pts	Share
Sandy Koufax, p, LA	25-5, 1.88	14.0	237.0	0.85
Dick Groat, ss, StL	.319-6-73	4.0	190.0	0.68
Hank Aaron, of, Mil	.319-44-130	1.0	135.0	0.48
Ron Perranoski, p, LA	1.67, 21 saves	0.0	130.0	0.46
Willie Mays, of, SF	.314-38-103	0.0	102.0	0.36
Jim Gilliam, 2b, LA	.282-6-49	1.0	62.0	0.22
Bill White, 1b, StL	.304-27-109	0.0	56.0	0.20
Tommy Davis, of, LA	.326-16-88	0.0	41.0	0.15
Ron Santo, 3b, ChN	.297-25-99	0.0	41.0	0.15
Vada Pinson, of, Cin	.313-22-106	0.0	32.0	0.11
Juan Marichal, p, SF	25-8, 2.41	0.0	31.0	0.11
Warren Spahn, p, Mil	23-7, 2.60	0.0	30.0	0.11
Ken Boyer, 3b, StL	.285-24-111	0.0	19.0	0.07
Roberto Clemente, of, Pit	.320-17-76	0.0	12.0	0.04
Johnny Callison, of, Phi	.284-26-78	0.0	11.0	0.04
Tony Taylor, 2b, Phi	.281-5-49	0.0	10.0	0.04
Willie McCovey, of, SF	.280-44-102	0.0	9.0	0.03
Maury Wills, ss, LA	.302-0-34	0.0	9.0	0.03
Dick Ellsworth, p, ChN	22-10, 2.11	0.0	7.0	0.03
Jim Maloney, p, Cin	23-7, 2.77	0.0	7.0	0.03
Don Demeter, of, Phi	.258-22-83	0.0	3.0	0.01
Don Drysdale, p, LA	19-17, 2.63	0.0	3.0	0.01
Tony Gonzalez, of, Phi	.306-4-66	0.0	2.0	0.01
Curt Flood, of, StL	.302-5-63	0.0	1.0	0.00

Cy Young

Pitcher, Team	Stats	1st Pl	Pts	Share
Sandy Koufax, LA	25-5, 1.88	20.0	20.0	1.00

Rookie of the Year

Pitcher, Pos, Team	Stats	1st Pl	Pts	Share
Pete Rose, 2b, Cin	.273-6-41	17.0	17.0	0.85
Ron Hunt, 2b, NYN	.272-10-42	2.0	2.0	0.10
Ray Culp, p, Phi	14-11, 2.97	1.0	1.0	0.05

Gold Gloves

Player, Pos, Team	Rng	LRng	FPct	LFPct
Bobby Shantz, p, StL	—	—	.969	.951
Johnny Edwards, c, Cin	—	—	.995	.986
Bill White, 1b, StL	—	—	.991	.989
Bill Mazeroski, 2b, Pit	6.13	4.59	.984	.974
Ken Boyer, 3b, StL	2.65	2.54	.925	.941
Bobby Wine, ss, Phi	4.39	4.22	.971	.961
Roberto Clemente, of, Pit	1.66	1.75	.958	.977
Curt Flood, of, StL	2.61	1.75	.988	.977
Willie Mays, of, SF	2.57	1.75	.981	.977

1964

American League

MVP

Player, Pos, Team	Stats	1st Pl	Pts	Share
Brooks Robinson, 3b, Bal	.317-28-118	18.0	269.0	0.96
Mickey Mantle, of, NYA	.303-35-111	2.0	171.0	0.61
Elston Howard, c, NYA	.313-15-84	0.0	124.0	0.44
Tony Oliva, of, Min	.323-32-94	0.0	99.0	0.35
Dean Chance, p, LAA	20-9, 1.65	0.0	97.0	0.35
Pete Ward, 3b, ChA	.282-23-94	0.0	67.5	0.24
Bill Freehan, c, Det	.300-18-80	0.0	44.0	0.16
Gary Peters, p, ChA	20-8, 2.50	0.0	44.0	0.16
Dick Radatz, p, Bos	2.29, 29 saves	0.0	37.0	0.13
Harmon Killebrew, of, Min	.270-49-111	0.0	31.0	0.11
Boog Powell, of, Bal	.290-39-99	0.0	28.0	0.10
Wally Bunker, p, Bal	19-5, 2.69	0.0	23.0	0.08
Jim Fregosi, ss, LAA	.277-18-72	0.0	21.0	0.08
Al Kaline, of, Det	.293-17-68	0.0	17.0	0.06
Floyd Robinson, of, ChA	.301-11-59	0.0	14.0	0.05
Ron Hansen, ss, ChA	.261-20-68	0.0	10.0	0.04
Bobby Richardson, 2b, NYA	.267-4-50	0.0	9.0	0.03
Leon Wagner, of, Cle	.253-31-100	0.0	9.0	0.03
Juan Pizarro, p, ChA	19-9, 2.56	0.0	8.0	0.03
Hoyt Wilhelm, p, ChA	1.99, 27 saves	0.0	8.0	0.03
Joe Horlen, p, ChA	13-9, 1.88	0.0	7.0	0.03
Whitey Ford, p, NYA	17-6, 2.13	0.0	7.0	0.03
Bob Allison, 1b, Min	.287-32-86	0.0	5.0	0.02
Rocky Colavito, of, KCA	.274-34-102	0.0	5.0	0.02
Mel Stottlemyre, p, NYA	9-3, 2.06	0.0	4.0	0.01
Roger Maris, of, NYA	.281-26-71	0.0	4.0	0.01
Wayne Causey, ss, KCA	.281-8-49	0.0	4.0	0.01
Luis Aparicio, ss, Bal	.266-10-37	0.0	3.5	0.01
Dick Stuart, 1b, Bos	.279-33-114	0.0	3.0	0.01
Eddie Bressoud, ss, Bos	.293-15-55	0.0	2.0	0.01
Claude Osteen, p, Was	15-13, 3.33	0.0	2.0	0.01
Dave Wickersham, p, Det	19-12, 3.44	0.0	2.0	0.01
Don Lock, of, Was	.248-28-80	0.0	1.0	0.00

Cy Young

Pitcher, Team	Stats	1st Pl	Pts	Share
Dean Chance, LAA	20-9, 1.65	17.0	17.0	0.85
Larry Jackson, ChN	24-11, 3.14	2.0	2.0	0.10
Sandy Koufax, LA	19-5, 1.74	1.0	1.0	0.05

Rookie of the Year

Pitcher, Pos, Team	Stats	1st Pl	Pts	Share
Tony Oliva, of, Min	.323-32-94	19.0	19.0	0.95
Wally Bunker, p, Bal	19-5, 2.69	1.0	1.0	0.05

Gold Gloves

Player, Pos, Team	Rng	LRng	FPct	LFPct
Jim Kaat, p, Min	—	—	.928	.957
Elston Howard, c, NYA	—	—	.998	.990
Vic Power, 1b, Min-LAA	—	—	.998	.991
Bobby Richardson, 2b, NYA	5.16	4.54	.982	.980
Brooks Robinson, 3b, Bal	2.94	2.76	.972	.954
Luis Aparicio, ss, Bal	4.81	4.55	.979	.968
Vic Davalillo, of, Cle	2.50	1.79	.986	.980
Al Kaline, of, Det	2.09	1.79	.990	.980
Jim Landis, of, ChA	1.88	1.79	.995	.980

National League

MVP

Player, Pos, Team	Stats	1st Pl	Pts	Share
Ken Boyer, 3b, StL	.295-24-119	14.0	243.0	0.87
Johnny Callison, of, Phi	.274-31-104	2.0	187.0	0.67
Bill White, 1b, StL	.303-21-102	2.0	106.5	0.38
Frank Robinson, of, Cin	.306-29-96	0.0	98.0	0.35
Joe Torre, c, Mil	.321-20-109	1.0	85.0	0.30
Willie Mays, of, SF	.296-47-111	0.0	66.0	0.24
Dick Allen, 3b, Phi	.318-29-91	0.0	63.0	0.23
Ron Santo, 3b, ChN	.313-30-114	0.0	59.0	0.21
Roberto Clemente, of, Pit	.339-12-87	0.0	56.0	0.20
Lou Brock, of, ChN-StL	.315-14-58	1.0	40.0	0.14
Curt Flood, of, StL	.311-5-46	0.0	38.0	0.14
Larry Jackson, p, ChN	24-11, 3.14	0.0	26.0	0.09
Jim Bunning, p, Phi	19-8, 2.63	0.0	23.0	0.08
Hank Aaron, of, Mil	.328-24-95	0.0	22.0	0.08
Juan Marichal, p, SF	21-8, 2.48	0.0	14.0	0.05
Sammy Ellis, p, Cin	2.57, 14 saves	0.0	13.0	0.05
Sandy Koufax, p, LA	19-5, 1.74	0.0	7.5	0.03
Vada Pinson, of, Cin	.266-23-84	0.0	6.0	0.02
Jim Ray Hart, 3b, SF	.286-31-81	0.0	6.0	0.02
Billy Williams, of, ChN	.312-33-98	0.0	6.0	0.02
Ruben Amaro, ss, Phi	.264-4-34	0.0	5.0	0.02
Tommy Davis, of, LA	.275-14-86	0.0	4.0	0.01
Bob Gibson, p, StL	19-12, 3.01	0.0	2.0	0.01
Chris Short, p, Phi	17-9, 2.20	0.0	2.0	0.01
Ron Hunt, 2b, NYN	.303-6-42	0.0	1.0	0.00
Barney Schultz, p, StL	1.64, 14 saves	0.0	1.0	0.00

Rookie of the Year

Pitcher, Pos, Team	Stats	1st Pl	Pts	Share
Dick Allen, 3b, Phi	.318-29-91	18.0	18.0	0.90
Rico Carty, of, Mil	.330-22-88	1.0	1.0	0.05
Jim Ray Hart, 3b, SF	.286-31-81	1.0	1.0	0.05

Gold Gloves

Player, Pos, Team	Rng	LRng	FPct	LFPct
Bobby Shantz, p, StL-ChN-Phi	—	—	.971	.953
Johnny Edwards, c, Cin	—	—	.992	.988
Bill White, 1b, StL	—	—	.996	.990
Bill Mazeroski, 2b, Pit	5.49	4.61	.975	.973
Ron Santo, 3b, ChN	3.25	2.60	.963	.941
Ruben Amaro, ss, Phi	4.20	4.32	.971	.963
Roberto Clemente, of, Pit	1.96	1.72	.968	.973
Curt Flood, of, StL	2.48	1.72	.988	.973
Willie Mays, of, SF	2.45	1.72	.984	.973

1965

American League

MVP

Player, Pos, Team	Stats	1st Pl	Pts	Share
Zoilo Versalles, ss, Min	.273-19-77	19.0	275.0	0.98
Tony Oliva, of, Min	.321-16-98	1.0	174.0	0.62
Brooks Robinson, 3b, Bal	.297-18-80	0.0	150.0	0.54
Eddie Fisher, p, ChA	2.40, 24 saves	0.0	122.0	0.44
Rocky Colavito, of, Cle	.287-26-108	0.0	89.0	0.32
Mudcat Grant, p, Min	21-7, 3.30	0.0	74.0	0.26
Stu Miller, p, Bal	1.89, 24 saves	0.0	45.0	0.16
Willie Horton, of, Det	.273-29-104	0.0	24.0	0.09
Tom Tresh, of, NYA	.279-26-74	0.0	23.0	0.08
Earl Battey, c, Min	.297-6-60	0.0	22.0	0.08
Don Wert, 3b, Det	.261-12-54	0.0	22.0	0.08
Carl Yastrzemski, of, Bos	.312-20-72	0.0	22.0	0.08
Jimmie Hall, of, Min	.285-20-86	0.0	19.0	0.07
Mel Stottlemyre, p, NYA	20-9, 2.63	0.0	17.0	0.06
Harmon Killebrew, 1b, Min	.269-25-75	0.0	15.0	0.05
Al Kaline, of, Det	.281-18-72	0.0	9.0	0.03
Jerry Adair, 2b, Bal	.259-7-66	0.0	7.0	0.03
Ron Hansen, ss, ChA	.235-11-66	0.0	7.0	0.03
Sam McDowell, p, Cle	17-11, 2.18	0.0	7.0	0.03
Bobby Richardson, 2b, NYA	.247-6-47	0.0	6.0	0.02
Vic Davalillo, of, Cle	.301-5-40	0.0	5.0	0.02
Jim Fregosi, ss, Cal	.277-15-64	0.0	5.0	0.02
Fred Whitfield, 1b, Cle	.293-26-90	0.0	5.0	0.02
Bobby Knoop, 2b, Cal	.269-7-43	0.0	4.0	0.01
Don Buford, 2b, ChA	.283-10-47	0.0	3.0	0.01
Mickey Mantle, of, NYA	.255-19-46	0.0	3.0	0.01
Pete Richert, p, Was	15-12, 2.60	0.0	3.0	0.01
Floyd Robinson, of, ChA	.265-14-66	0.0	3.0	0.01
Bert Campaneris, ss, KCA	.270-6-42	0.0	2.0	0.01
Frank Howard, of, Was	.289-21-84	0.0	2.0	0.01
Ron Kline, p, Was	2.63, 29 saves	0.0	2.0	0.01
Felix Mantilla, 2b, Bos	.275-18-92	0.0	2.0	0.01
Norm Cash, 1b, Det	.266-30-82	0.0	1.0	0.00
Tony Conigliaro, of, Bos	.269-32-82	0.0	1.0	0.00

Rookie of the Year

Pitcher, Pos, Team	Stats	1st Pl	Pts	Share
Curt Blefary, of, Bal	.260-22-70	12.0	12.0	0.60
Marcelino Lopez, p, Cal	14-13, 2.93	8.0	8.0	0.40

Gold Gloves

Player, Pos, Team	Rng	LRng	FPct	LFPct
Jim Kaat, p, Min	—	—	.929	.951
Bill Freehan, c, Det	—	—	.996	.988
Joe Pepitone, 1b, NYA	—	—	.997	.991
Bobby Richardson, 2b, NYA	4.91	4.38	.981	.978
Brooks Robinson, 3b, Bal	3.08	2.87	.967	.960
Zoilo Versalles, ss, Min	4.59	4.38	.950	.962
Al Kaline, of, Det	1.74	1.78	.985	.978
Tom Tresh, of, NYA	1.91	1.78	.970	.978
Carl Yastrzemski, of, Bos	1.79	1.78	.987	.978

National League

MVP

Player, Pos, Team	Stats	1st Pl	Pts	Share
Willie Mays, of, SF	.317-52-112	9.0	224.0	0.80
Sandy Koufax, p, LA	26-8, 2.04	6.0	177.0	0.63
Maury Wills, ss, LA	.286-0-33	5.0	164.0	0.59
Deron Johnson, 3b, Cin	.287-32-130	0.0	108.0	0.39
Don Drysdale, p, LA	23-12, 2.77	0.0	77.0	0.28
Pete Rose, 2b, Cin	.312-11-81	0.0	67.0	0.24
Hank Aaron, of, Mil	.318-32-89	0.0	58.0	0.21
Roberto Clemente, of, Pit	.329-10-65	0.0	56.0	0.20
Juan Marichal, p, SF	22-13, 2.13	0.0	26.0	0.09
Willie McCovey, 1b, SF	.276-39-92	0.0	25.0	0.09
Joe Torre, c, Mil	.291-27-80	0.0	23.0	0.08
Billy Williams, of, ChN	.315-34-108	0.0	21.0	0.08
Frank Linzy, p, SF	1.43, 21 saves	0.0	16.0	0.06
Willie Stargell, of, Pit	.272-27-107	0.0	15.0	0.05
Curt Flood, of, StL	.310-11-83	0.0	13.0	0.05

Jim Ray Hart, 3b, SF	.299-23-96	0.0	13.0	0.05
Vern Law, p, Pit	17-9, 2.15	0.0	12.0	0.04
Frank Robinson, of, Cin	.296-33-113	0.0	11.0	0.04
Ron Santo, 3b, ChN	.285-33-101	0.0	11.0	0.04
Eddie Mathews, 3b, Mil	.251-32-95	0.0	8.0	0.03
Leo Cardenas, ss, Cin	.287-11-57	0.0	7.0	0.03
Jim Maloney, p, Cin	20-9, 2.54	0.0	7.0	0.03
Jim Lefebvre, 2b, LA	.250-12-69	0.0	7.0	0.03
Johnny Callison, of, Phi	.262-32-101	0.0	6.0	0.02
Lou Johnson, of, LA	.259-12-58	0.0	6.0	0.02
Cookie Rojas, 2b, Phi	.303-3-42	0.0	5.0	0.02
John Roseboro, c, LA	.233-8-57	0.0	5.0	0.02
Dick Allen, 3b, Phi	.302-20-85	0.0	4.0	0.01
Tony Cloninger, p, Mil	24-11, 3.29	0.0	4.0	0.01
Jim Gilliam, 3b, LA	.280-4-39	0.0	3.0	0.01
Joe Morgan, 2b, Hou	.271-14-40	0.0	1.0	0.00

Cy Young

Pitcher, Team	Stats	1st Pl	Pts	Share
Sandy Koufax, LA	26-8, 2.04	20.0	20.0	1.00

Rookie of the Year

Pitcher, Pos, Team	Stats	1st Pl	Pts	Share
Jim Lefebvre, 2b, LA	.250-12-69	13.0	13.0	0.65
Joe Morgan, 2b, Hou	.271-14-40	4.0	4.0	0.20
Frank Linzy, p, SF	1.43, 21 saves	3.0	3.0	0.15

Gold Gloves

Player, Pos, Team	Rng	LRng	FPct	LFPct
Bob Gibson, p, StL	—	—	.952	.956
Joe Torre, c, Mil	—	—	.991	.988
Bill White, 1b, StL	—	—	.992	.990
Bill Mazeroski, 2b, Pit	5.74	4.71	.988	.974
Ron Santo, 3b, ChN	3.22	2.47	.957	.951
Leo Cardenas, ss, Cin	4.72	4.20	.975	.964
Roberto Clemente, of, Pit	2.10	1.75	.968	.975
Curt Flood, of, StL	2.36	1.75	.986	.975
Willie Mays, of, SF	2.32	1.75	.983	.975

1966

American League

MVP

Player, Pos, Team	Stats	1st Pl	Pts	Share
Frank Robinson, of, Bal	.316-49-122	20.0	280.0	1.00
Brooks Robinson, 3b, Bal	.269-23-100	0.0	153.0	0.55
Boog Powell, 1b, Bal	.287-34-109	0.0	122.0	0.44
Harmon Killebrew, 3b, Min	.281-39-110	0.0	96.0	0.34
Jim Kaat, p, Min	25-13, 2.75	0.0	84.0	0.30
Tony Oliva, of, Min	.307-25-87	0.0	71.0	0.25
Al Kaline, of, Det	.288-29-88	0.0	66.0	0.24
Tommie Agee, of, ChA	.273-22-86	0.0	63.0	0.23
Luis Aparicio, ss, Bal	.276-6-41	0.0	51.0	0.18
Bert Campaneris, ss, KCA	.267-5-42	0.0	36.0	0.13
Stu Miller, p, Bal	2.25, 18 saves	0.0	27.0	0.10
Norm Cash, 1b, Det	.279-32-93	0.0	23.0	0.08
Jack Aker, p, KCA	1.99, 32 saves	0.0	22.0	0.08
Earl Wilson, p, Bos-Det	18-11, 3.07	0.0	13.0	0.05
Denny McLain, p, Det	20-14, 3.92	0.0	12.0	0.04
Bill Freehan, c, Det	.234-12-46	0.0	9.0	0.03
Andy Etchebarren, c, Bal	.221-11-50	0.0	7.0	0.03
Bobby Knoop, 2b, Cal	.232-17-72	0.0	6.0	0.02
Mickey Mantle, of, NYA	.288-23-56	0.0	5.0	0.02
Tom Tresh, of, NYA	.233-27-68	0.0	5.0	0.02
Jack Sanford, p, Cal	3.83, 5 saves	0.0	4.0	0.01
Rick Reichardt, of, Cal	.288-16-44	0.0	4.0	0.01
Fred Valentine, of, Was	.276-16-59	0.0	4.0	0.01
Willie Horton, of, Det	.262-27-100	0.0	4.0	0.01
Leon Wagner, of, Cle	.279-23-66	0.0	4.0	0.01
Pete Richert, p, Was	14-14, 3.37	0.0	3.0	0.01
Joe Pepitone, 1b, NYA	.255-31-83	0.0	2.0	0.01
Tony Conigliaro, of, Bos	.265-28-93	0.0	1.0	0.00
Sonny Siebert, p, Cle	16-8, 2.80	0.0	1.0	0.00
Carl Yastrzemski, of, Bos	.278-16-80	0.0	1.0	0.00
Jim Fregosi, ss, Cal	.252-13-67	0.0	1.0	0.00

Rookie of the Year

Pitcher, Pos, Team	Stats	1st Pl	Pts	Share
Tommie Agee, of, ChA	.273-22-86	16.0	16.0	0.80
Jim Nash, p, KCA	12-1, 2.06	2.0	2.0	0.10
Dave Johnson, 2b, Bal	.257-7-56	1.0	1.0	0.05
George Scott, 1b, Bos	.245-27-90	1.0	1.0	0.05

Gold Gloves

Player, Pos, Team	Rng	LRng	FPct	LFPct
Jim Kaat, p, Min	—	—	.956	.952
Bill Freehan, c, Det	—	—	.996	.988
Joe Pepitone, 1b, NYA	—	—	.995	.991
Bobby Knoop, 2b, Cal	5.40	4.38	.981	.975
Brooks Robinson, 3b, Bal	3.10	2.80	.976	.954
Luis Aparicio, ss, Bal	4.93	4.41	.978	.960
Tommie Agee, of, ChA	2.44	1.82	.982	.982
Al Kaline, of, Det	2.10	1.82	.993	.982
Tony Oliva, of, Min	2.16	1.82	.972	.982

National League

MVP

Player, Pos, Team	Stats	1st Pl	Pts	Share
Roberto Clemente, of, Pit	.317-29-119	8.0	218.0	0.78
Sandy Koufax, p, LA	27-9, 1.73	9.0	208.0	0.74
Willie Mays, of, SF	.288-37-103	0.0	111.0	0.40
Dick Allen, 3b, Phi	.317-40-110	1.0	107.0	0.38
Felipe Alou, 1b, Atl	.327-31-74	2.0	83.0	0.30
Juan Marichal, p, SF	25-6, 2.23	0.0	74.0	0.26
Phil Regan, p, LA	1.62, 21 saves	0.0	66.0	0.24
Hank Aaron, of, Atl	.279-44-127	0.0	57.0	0.20
Matty Alou, of, Pit	.342-2-27	0.0	36.0	0.13
Pete Rose, 2b, Cin	.313-16-70	0.0	31.0	0.11
Gene Alley, ss, Pit	.299-7-43	0.0	24.0	0.09
Ron Santo, 3b, ChN	.312-30-94	0.0	23.0	0.08
John Roseboro, c, LA	.276-9-53	0.0	22.0	0.08
Orlando Cepeda, 1b, SF-StL	.301-20-73	0.0	22.0	0.08
Willie Stargell, of, Pit	.315-33-102	0.0	19.0	0.07
Joe Torre, c, Atl	.315-36-101	0.0	18.0	0.06
Willie McCovey, 1b, SF	.295-36-96	0.0	12.0	0.04
Jim Lefebvre, 2b, LA	.274-24-74	0.0	8.0	0.03
Gaylord Perry, p, SF	21-8, 2.99	0.0	8.0	0.03
Curt Flood, of, StL	.267-10-78	0.0	7.0	0.03
Maury Wills, ss, LA	.273-1-39	0.0	5.0	0.02
Rusty Staub, of, Hou	.280-13-81	0.0	4.0	0.01
Bill Mazeroski, 2b, Pit	.262-16-82	0.0	3.0	0.01
Glenn Beckert, 2b, ChN	.287-1-59	0.0	3.0	0.01
Jim Maloney, p, Cin	16-8, 2.80	0.0	3.0	0.01
Bill White, 1b, Phi	.276-22-103	0.0	3.0	0.01
Lou Brock, of, StL	.285-15-46	0.0	2.0	0.01
Bob Shaw, p, SF-NYN	12-14, 4.29	0.0	1.0	0.00
Chris Short, p, Phi	20-10, 3.54	0.0	1.0	0.00
Willie Davis, of, LA	.284-11-61	0.0	1.0	0.00

Cy Young

Pitcher, Team	Stats	1st Pl	Pts	Share
Sandy Koufax, LA	27-9, 1.73	20.0	20.0	1.00

Rookie of the Year

Pitcher, Pos, Team	Stats	1st Pl	Pts	Share
Tommy Helms, 3b, Cin	.284-9-49	12.0	12.0	0.60
Sonny Jackson, ss, Hou	.292-3-25	3.0	3.0	0.15
Tito Fuentes, ss, SF	.261-9-40	2.0	2.0	0.10
Randy Hundley, c, ChN	.236-19-63	1.0	1.0	0.05
Cleon Jones, of, NYN	.275-8-57	1.0	1.0	0.05
Larry Jaster, p, StL	11-5, 3.26	1.0	1.0	0.05

Gold Gloves

Player, Pos, Team	Rng	LRng	FPct	LFPct
Bob Gibson, p, StL	—	—	.964	.947
John Roseboro, c, LA	—	—	.993	.987
Bill White, 1b, Phi	—	—	.994	.989
Bill Mazeroski, 2b, Pit	5.86	4.68	.992	.978
Ron Santo, 3b, ChN	3.56	2.66	.956	.954
Gene Alley, ss, Pit	4.94	4.43	.979	.964
Roberto Clemente, of, Pit	2.18	1.78	.965	.974
Curt Flood, of, StL	2.49	1.78	1.000	.974
Willie Mays, of, SF	2.52	1.78	.982	.974

1967

American League

MVP

Player, Pos, Team	Stats	1st Pl	Pts	Share
Carl Yastrzemski, of, Bos	.326-44-121	19.0	275.0	0.98
Harmon Killebrew, 1b, Min	.269-44-113	0.0	161.0	0.58
Bill Freehan, c, Det	.282-20-74	0.0	137.0	0.49
Joe Horlen, p, ChA	19-7, 2.06	0.0	91.0	0.33
Al Kaline, of, Det	.308-25-78	0.0	88.0	0.31
Jim Lonborg, p, Bos	22-9, 3.16	0.0	82.0	0.29
Jim Fregosi, ss, Cal	.290-9-56	0.0	70.0	0.25
Cesar Tovar, of, Min	.267-6-47	1.0	70.0	0.25
Gary Peters, p, ChA	16-11, 2.28	0.0	37.0	0.13
George Scott, 1b, Bos	.303-19-82	0.0	33.0	0.12
Frank Robinson, of, Bal	.311-30-94	0.0	31.0	0.11
Earl Wilson, p, Det	22-11, 3.27	0.0	20.0	0.07
Dean Chance, p, Min	20-14, 2.73	0.0	19.0	0.07
Ron Hansen, ss, ChA	.233-8-51	0.0	13.0	0.05
Jerry Adair, 2b, ChA-Bos	.271-3-35	0.0	11.0	0.04
Paul Blair, of, Bal	.293-11-64	0.0	9.0	0.03
Rico Petrocelli, ss, Bos	.259-17-66	0.0	7.0	0.03
Elston Howard, c, NYA-Bos	.178-4-28	0.0	7.0	0.03
Tony Oliva, of, Min	.289-17-83	0.0	6.0	0.02
Jim Kaat, p, Min	16-13, 3.04	0.0	4.0	0.01
Paul Casanova, c, Was	.248-9-53	0.0	3.0	0.01
Don Mincher, 1b, Cal	.273-25-76	0.0	3.0	0.01
Mickey Lolich, p, Det	14-13, 3.04	0.0	2.0	0.01
Minnie Rojas, p, Cal	2.52, 27 saves	0.0	1.0	0.00

Cy Young

Pitcher, Team	Stats	1st Pl	Pts	Share
Jim Lonborg, Bos	22-9, 3.16	18.0	18.0	0.90
Joe Horlen, ChA	19-7, 2.06	2.0	2.0	0.10

Rookie of the Year

Pitcher, Pos, Team	Stats	1st Pl	Pts	Share
Rod Carew, 2b, Min	.292-8-51	19.0	19.0	0.95
Reggie Smith, of, Bos	.246-15-61	1.0	1.0	0.05

Gold Gloves

Player, Pos, Team	Rng	LRng	FPct	LFPct
Jim Kaat, p, Min	—	—	.952	.957
Bill Freehan, c, Det	—	—	.992	.989
George Scott, 1b, Bos	—	—	.987	.991
Bobby Knoop, 2b, Cal	4.83	4.19	.986	.979
Brooks Robinson, 3b, Bal	3.49	2.72	.980	.955
Jim Fregosi, ss, Cal	4.59	4.11	.965	.963
Paul Blair, of, Bal	2.62	1.76	.985	.980
Al Kaline, of, Det	1.78	1.76	.983	.980
Carl Yastrzemski, of, Bos	1.93	1.76	.978	.980

National League

MVP

Player, Pos, Team	Stats	1st Pl	Pts	Share
Orlando Cepeda, 1b, StL	.325-25-111	20.0	280.0	1.00
Tim McCarver, c, StL	.295-14-69	0.0	136.0	0.49
Roberto Clemente, of, Pit	.357-23-110	0.0	129.0	0.46
Ron Santo, 3b, ChN	.300-31-98	0.0	103.0	0.37
Hank Aaron, of, Atl	.307-39-109	0.0	79.0	0.28
Mike McCormick, p, SF	22-10, 2.85	0.0	73.0	0.26
Lou Brock, of, StL	.299-21-76	0.0	49.0	0.18
Tony Perez, 3b, Cin	.290-26-102	0.0	43.0	0.15
Julian Javier, 2b, StL	.281-14-64	0.0	41.0	0.15
Pete Rose, of, Cin	.301-12-76	0.0	40.0	0.14
Jimmy Wynn, of, Hou	.249-37-107	0.0	29.0	0.10
Fergie Jenkins, p, ChN	20-13, 2.80	0.0	26.0	0.09
Curt Flood, of, StL	.335-5-50	0.0	24.0	0.09
Ernie Banks, 1b, ChN	.276-23-95	0.0	22.0	0.08
Nelson Briles, p, StL	2.43, 6 saves	0.0	20.0	0.07
Rusty Staub, of, Hou	.333-10-74	0.0	12.0	0.04
Dick Hughes, p, StL	16-6, 2.67	0.0	10.0	0.04
Jim Ray Hart, 3b, SF	.289-29-99	0.0	10.0	0.04
Dick Allen, 3b, Phi	.307-23-77	0.0	9.0	0.03
Ted Abernathy, p, Cin	1.27, 28 saves	0.0	8.0	0.03
Clete Boyer, 3b, Atl	.245-26-96	0.0	6.0	0.02
Bob Gibson, p, StL	13-7, 2.98	0.0	5.0	0.02
Randy Hundley, c, ChN	.267-14-60	0.0	5.0	0.02
Jim Bunning, p, Phi	17-15, 2.29	0.0	5.0	0.02
Tom Seaver, p, NYN	16-13, 2.76	0.0	5.0	0.02
Tommy Davis, of, NYN	.302-16-73	0.0	3.0	0.01
Gene Alley, ss, Pit	.287-6-55	0.0	3.0	0.01
Tony Gonzalez, of, Phi	.339-9-59	0.0	3.0	0.01
Willie McCovey, 1b, SF	.276-31-91	0.0	2.0	0.01

Cy Young

Pitcher, Team	Stats	1st Pl	Pts	Share
Mike McCormick, SF	22-10, 2.85	18.0	18.0	0.90
Fergie Jenkins, ChN	20-13, 2.80	1.0	1.0	0.05
Jim Bunning, Phi	17-15, 2.29	1.0	1.0	0.05

Rookie of the Year

Pitcher, Pos, Team	Stats	1st Pl	Pts	Share
Tom Seaver, p, NYN	16-13, 2.76	11.0	11.0	0.55
Dick Hughes, p, StL	16-6, 2.67	6.0	6.0	0.30
Gary Nolan, p, Cin	14-8, 2.58	3.0	3.0	0.15

Gold Gloves

Player, Pos, Team	Rng	LRng	FPct	LFPct
Bob Gibson, p, StL	—	—	1.000	.960
Randy Hundley, c, ChN	—	—	.996	.990
Wes Parker, 1b, LA	—	—	.996	.991
Bill Mazeroski, 2b, Pit	5.61	4.63	.981	.976
Ron Santo, 3b, ChN	3.60	2.75	.957	.950
Gene Alley, ss, Pit	5.18	4.31	.967	.963
Roberto Clemente, of, Pit	1.75	1.80	.966	.976
Curt Flood, of, StL	2.52	1.80	.988	.976
Willie Mays, of, SF	2.09	1.80	.976	.976

1968

American League

MVP

Player, Pos, Team	Stats	1st Pl	Pts	Share
Denny McLain, p, Det	31-6, 1.96	20.0	280.0	1.00
Bill Freehan, c, Det	.263-25-84	0.0	161.0	0.58
Ken Harrelson, of, Bos	.275-35-109	0.0	103.0	0.37
Willie Horton, of, Det	.285-36-85	0.0	102.0	0.36
Dave McNally, p, Bal	22-10, 1.95	0.0	78.0	0.28
Luis Tiant, p, Cle	21-9, 1.60	0.0	78.0	0.28
Dick McAuliffe, 2b, Det	.249-16-56	0.0	71.0	0.25
Frank Howard, of, Was	.274-44-106	0.0	63.0	0.23
Carl Yastrzemski, of, Bos	.301-23-74	0.0	50.0	0.18
Mel Stottlemyre, p, NYA	21-12, 2.45	0.0	43.0	0.15
Bert Campaneris, ss, Oak	.276-4-38	0.0	39.0	0.14
Roy White, of, NYA	.267-17-62	0.0	17.0	0.06
Jim Northrup, of, Det	.264-21-90	0.0	15.0	0.05
Luis Aparicio, ss, ChA	.264-4-36	0.0	13.0	0.05
Jim Fregosi, ss, Cal	.244-9-49	0.0	11.0	0.04
Don Buford, of, Bal	.282-15-46	0.0	11.0	0.04
Brooks Robinson, 3b, Bal	.253-17-75	0.0	8.0	0.03
Reggie Jackson, of, Oak	.250-29-74	0.0	8.0	0.03
Tony Oliva, of, Min	.289-18-68	0.0	5.0	0.02
Danny Cater, 1b, Oak	.290-6-62	0.0	5.0	0.02
Mike Andrews, 2b, Bos	.271-7-45	0.0	4.0	0.01
Boog Powell, 1b, Bal	.249-22-85	0.0	4.0	0.01
Cesar Tovar, of, Min	.272-6-47	0.0	3.0	0.01
Norm Cash, 1b, Det	.263-25-63	0.0	3.0	0.01
Mickey Stanley, of, Det	.259-11-60	0.0	2.0	0.01
Wilbur Wood, p, ChA	1.87, 16 saves	0.0	2.0	0.01
Ted Uhlaender, of, Min	.283-7-52	0.0	1.0	0.00

Cy Young

Pitcher, Team	Stats	1st Pl	Pts	Share
Denny McLain, Det	31-6, 1.96	20.0	20.0	1.00

Rookie of the Year

Pitcher, Pos, Team	Stats	1st Pl	Pts	Share
Stan Bahnsen, p, NYA	17-12, 2.05	17.0	17.0	0.85
Del Unser, of, Was	.230-1-30	3.0	3.0	0.15

Gold Gloves

Player, Pos, Team	Rng	LRng	FPct	LFPct
Jim Kaat, p, Min	—	—	.976	.957
Bill Freehan, c, Det	—	—	.994	.990
George Scott, 1b, Bos	—	—	.987	.989
Bobby Knoop, 2b, Cal	5.13	4.34	.981	.977
Brooks Robinson, 3b, Bal	3.22	2.67	.970	.951
Luis Aparicio, ss, ChA	5.22	4.08	.977	.962
Reggie Smith, of, Bos	2.57	1.80	.985	.981
Mickey Stanley, of, Det	2.34	1.80	1.000	.981
Carl Yastrzemski, of, Bos	2.02	1.80	.991	.981

National League

MVP

Player, Pos, Team	Stats	1st Pl	Pts	Share
Bob Gibson, p, StL	22-9, 1.12	14.0	242.0	0.86
Pete Rose, of, Cin	.335-10-49	6.0	205.0	0.73
Willie McCovey, 1b, SF	.293-36-105	0.0	135.0	0.48
Curt Flood, of, StL	.301-5-60	0.0	116.0	0.41
Juan Marichal, p, SF	26-9, 2.43	0.0	93.0	0.33
Lou Brock, of, StL	.279-6-51	0.0	73.0	0.26
Mike Shannon, 3b, StL	.266-15-79	0.0	55.0	0.20
Billy Williams, of, ChN	.288-30-98	0.0	48.0	0.17
Glenn Beckert, 2b, ChN	.294-4-37	0.0	40.0	0.14
Felipe Alou, of, Atl	.317-11-57	0.0	33.0	0.12
Matty Alou, of, Pit	.332-0-52	0.0	32.0	0.11
Hank Aaron, of, Atl	.287-29-86	0.0	19.0	0.07
Willie Mays, of, SF	.289-23-79	0.0	14.0	0.05
Ernie Banks, 1b, ChN	.246-32-83	0.0	14.0	0.05
Jerry Koosman, p, NYN	19-12, 2.08	0.0	14.0	0.05
Johnny Bench, c, Cin	.275-15-82	0.0	11.0	0.04
Phil Regan, p, LA-ChN	2.27, 25 saves	0.0	7.0	0.03
Fergie Jenkins, p, ChN	20-15, 2.63	0.0	6.0	0.02
Tony Perez, 3b, Cin	.282-18-92	0.0	5.0	0.02
Nelson Briles, p, StL	19-11, 2.81	0.0	4.0	0.01
Dal Maxvill, ss, StL	.253-1-24	0.0	4.0	0.01
Steve Blass, p, Pit	18-6, 2.12	0.0	3.0	0.01
Tom Haller, c, LA	.285-4-53	0.0	3.0	0.01
Ron Santo, 3b, ChN	.246-26-98	0.0	2.0	0.01
Clay Carroll, p, Atl-Cin	2.69, 17 saves	0.0	1.0	0.00
Tommy Helms, 2b, Cin	.288-2-47	0.0	1.0	0.00

Cy Young

Pitcher, Team	Stats	1st Pl	Pts	Share
Bob Gibson, StL	22-9, 1.12	20.0	20.0	1.00

Rookie of the Year

Pitcher, Pos, Team	Stats	1st Pl	Pts	Share
Johnny Bench, c, Cin	.275-15-82	10.5	10.5	0.50
Jerry Koosman, p, NYN	19-12, 2.08	9.5	9.5	0.45

Gold Gloves

Player, Pos, Team	Rng	LRng	FPct	LFPct
Bob Gibson, p, StL	—	—	.980	.958
Johnny Bench, c, Cin	—	—	.991	.990
Wes Parker, 1b, LA	—	—	.999	.992
Glenn Beckert, 2b, ChN	5.27	4.74	.977	.977
Ron Santo, 3b, ChN	3.14	2.72	.971	.954
Dal Maxvill, ss, StL	4.57	4.50	.969	.962
Roberto Clemente, of, Pit	2.34	1.82	.984	.975
Curt Flood, of, StL	2.66	1.82	.983	.975
Willie Mays, of, SF	2.17	1.82	.978	.975

1969

American League

MVP

Player, Pos, Team	Stats	1st Pl	Pts	Share
Harmon Killebrew, 3b, Min	.276-49-140	16.0	294.0	0.88
Boog Powell, 1b, Bal	.304-37-121	6.0	227.0	0.68
Frank Robinson, of, Bal	.308-32-100	2.0	162.0	0.48
Frank Howard, of, Was	.296-48-111	0.0	115.0	0.34
Reggie Jackson, of, Oak	.275-47-118	0.0	110.0	0.33
Denny McLain, p, Det	24-9, 2.80	0.0	85.0	0.25
Rico Petrocelli, ss, Bos	.297-40-97	0.0	71.0	0.21
Mike Cuellar, p, Bal	23-11, 2.38	0.0	55.0	0.16
Jim Perry, p, Min	20-6, 2.82	0.0	40.0	0.12
Rod Carew, 2b, Min	.332-8-56	0.0	30.0	0.09
Paul Blair, of, Bal	.285-26-76	0.0	28.0	0.08
Leo Cardenas, ss, Min	.280-10-70	0.0	27.0	0.08
Ron Perranoski, p, Min	2.11, 31 saves	0.0	25.0	0.07
Dave McNally, p, Bal	20-7, 3.22	0.0	25.0	0.07
Tony Oliva, of, Min	.309-24-101	0.0	21.0	0.06
Sal Bando, 3b, Oak	.281-31-113	0.0	18.0	0.05
Cesar Tovar, of, Min	.288-11-52	0.0	9.0	0.03
Mel Stottlemyre, p, NYA	20-14, 2.82	0.0	8.0	0.02
Carl Yastrzemski, of, Bos	.255-40-111	0.0	8.0	0.02
Ed Brinkman, ss, Was	.266-2-43	0.0	7.0	0.02
Jim Fregosi, ss, Cal	.260-12-47	0.0	7.0	0.02
Reggie Smith, of, Bos	.309-25-93	0.0	6.0	0.02
Del Unser, of, Was	.286-7-57	0.0	5.0	0.01
Brooks Robinson, 3b, Bal	.234-23-84	0.0	5.0	0.01
Mike Epstein, 1b, Was	.278-30-85	0.0	4.0	0.01
Mike Andrews, 2b, Bos	.293-15-59	0.0	3.0	0.01
Dick Bosman, p, Was	14-5, 2.19	0.0	3.0	0.01
Bill Freehan, c, Det	.262-16-49	0.0	3.0	0.01
Tommy Harper, 2b, Sea	.235-9-41	0.0	2.0	0.01
Andy Messersmith, p, Cal	16-11, 2.52	0.0	2.0	0.01
Rich Reese, 1b, Min	.322-16-69	0.0	2.0	0.01
Ken Tatum, p, Cal	1.36, 22 saves	0.0	2.0	0.01
Roy White, of, NYA	.290-7-74	0.0	2.0	0.01
Mark Belanger, ss, Bal	.287-2-50	0.0	2.0	0.01
Dick Green, 2b, Oak	.275-12-64	0.0	1.0	0.00
Jim Northrup, of, Det	.295-25-66	0.0	1.0	0.00
Lou Piniella, of, KC	.282-11-68	0.0	1.0	0.00

Cy Young

Pitcher, Team	Stats	1st Pl	Pts	Share
Mike Cuellar, Bal	23-11, 2.38	10.0	10.0	0.42
Denny McLain, Det	24-9, 2.80	10.0	10.0	0.42
Jim Perry, Min	20-6, 2.82	3.0	3.0	0.13
Dave McNally, Bal	20-7, 3.22	1.0	1.0	0.04

Rookie of the Year

Pitcher, Pos, Team	Stats	1st Pl	Pts	Share
Lou Piniella, of, KC	.282-11-68	9.0	9.0	0.38
Mike Nagy, p, Bos	12-2, 3.11	6.0	6.0	0.25
Carlos May, of, ChA	.281-18-62	5.0	5.0	0.21
Ken Tatum, p, Cal	1.36, 22 saves	4.0	4.0	0.17

Gold Gloves

Player, Pos, Team	Rng	LRng	FPct	LFPct
Jim Kaat, p, Min	—	—	.826	.951
Bill Freehan, c, Det	—	—	.992	.987
Joe Pepitone, 1b, NYA	—	—	.995	.992
Dave Johnson, 2b, Bal	5.10	4.58	.984	.976
Brooks Robinson, 3b, Bal	3.42	2.74	.976	.955
Mark Belanger, ss, Bal	4.73	4.43	.968	.966
Paul Blair, of, Bal	2.81	1.84	.988	.978
Mickey Stanley, of, Det	1.90	1.84	.985	.978
Carl Yastrzemski, of, Bos	1.84	1.84	.985	.978

National League

MVP

Player, Pos, Team	Stats	1st Pl	Pts	Share
Willie McCovey, 1b, SF	.320-45-126	11.0	265.0	0.79
Tom Seaver, p, NYN	25-7, 2.21	11.0	243.0	0.72
Hank Aaron, of, Atl	.300-44-97	2.0	188.0	0.56
Pete Rose, of, Cin	.348-16-82	0.0	127.0	0.38
Ron Santo, 3b, ChN	.289-29-123	0.0	124.0	0.37
Tommie Agee, of, NYN	.271-26-76	0.0	89.0	0.26
Cleon Jones, of, NYN	.340-12-75	0.0	82.0	0.24
Roberto Clemente, of, Pit	.345-19-91	0.0	51.0	0.15
Phil Niekro, p, Atl	23-13, 2.56	0.0	47.0	0.14
Tony Perez, 3b, Cin	.294-37-122	0.0	28.0	0.08
Maury Wills, ss, Mon-LA	.274-4-47	0.0	17.0	0.05
Ernie Banks, 1b, ChN	.253-23-106	0.0	15.0	0.04
Rico Carty, of, Atl	.342-16-58	0.0	12.0	0.04
Johnny Bench, c, Cin	.293-26-90	0.0	12.0	0.04
Don Kessinger, ss, ChN	.273-4-53	0.0	8.0	0.02
Tony Gonzalez, of, SD-Atl	.269-12-58	0.0	8.0	0.02
Ron Hunt, 2b, SF	.262-3-41	0.0	8.0	0.02
Denis Menke, ss, Hou	.269-10-90	0.0	8.0	0.02
Wayne Granger, p, Cin	2.80, 27 saves	0.0	8.0	0.02
Jimmy Wynn, of, Hou	.269-33-87	0.0	8.0	0.02
Willie Davis, of, LA	.311-11-59	0.0	7.0	0.02
Willie Stargell, of, Pit	.307-29-92	0.0	7.0	0.02
Juan Marichal, p, SF	21-11, 2.10	0.0	6.0	0.02
Billy Williams, of, ChN	.293-21-95	0.0	6.0	0.02
Jerry Koosman, p, NYN	17-9, 2.28	0.0	6.0	0.02
Joe Torre, 1b, StL	.289-18-101	0.0	6.0	0.02
Matty Alou, of, Pit	.331-1-48	0.0	6.0	0.02
Larry Dierker, p, Hou	20-13, 2.33	0.0	6.0	0.02
Tom Haller, c, LA	.263-6-39	0.0	3.0	0.01
Bob Gibson, p, StL	20-13, 2.18	0.0	2.0	0.01
Bobby Bonds, of, SF	.259-32-90	0.0	2.0	0.01
Randy Hundley, c, ChN	.255-18-64	0.0	2.0	0.01
Lee May, 1b, Cin	.278-38-110	0.0	2.0	0.01
Ted Sizemore, 2b, LA	.271-4-46	0.0	2.0	0.01
Wes Parker, 1b, LA	.278-13-68	0.0	2.0	0.01
Johnny Edwards, c, Hou	.232-6-50	0.0	1.0	0.00
Rusty Staub, of, Mon	.302-29-79	0.0	1.0	0.00
Orlando Cepeda, 1b, Atl	.257-22-88	0.0	1.0	0.00

Cy Young

Pitcher, Team	Stats	1st Pl	Pts	Share
Tom Seaver, NYN	25-7, 2.21	23.0	23.0	0.96
Phil Niekro, Atl	23-13, 2.56	1.0	1.0	0.04

Rookie of the Year

Pitcher, Pos, Team	Stats	1st Pl	Pts	Share
Ted Sizemore, 2b, LA	.271-4-46	14.0	14.0	0.58
Coco Laboy, 3b, Mon	.258-18-83	3.0	3.0	0.13
Al Oliver, 1b, Pit	.285-17-70	3.0	3.0	0.13
Bob Didier, c, Atl	.256-0-32	2.0	2.0	0.08
Larry Hisle, of, Phi	.266-20-56	2.0	2.0	0.08

Gold Gloves

Player, Pos, Team	Rng	LRng	FPct	LFPct
Bob Gibson, p, StL	—	—	.946	.958
Johnny Bench, c, Cin	—	—	.992	.989
Wes Parker, 1b, LA	—	—	.995	.992
Felix Millan, 2b, Atl	5.04	4.65	.980	.974
Clete Boyer, 3b, Atl	2.94	2.63	.965	.946
Don Kessinger, ss, ChN	5.15	4.21	.976	.963
Roberto Clemente, of, Pit	1.78	1.75	.980	.973
Curt Flood, of, StL	2.47	1.75	.989	.973
Pete Rose, of, Cin	2.09	1.75	.988	.973

1970

American League

MVP

Player, Pos, Team	Stats	1st Pl	Pts	Share
Boog Powell, 1b, Bal	.297-35-114	11.0	234.0	0.70
Tony Oliva, of, Min	.325-23-107	5.0	157.0	0.47
Harmon Killebrew, 3b, Min	.271-41-113	1.0	152.0	0.45
Carl Yastrzemski, 1b, Bos	.329-40-102	2.0	136.0	0.40
Frank Howard, of, Was	.283-44-126	1.0	91.0	0.27
Tommy Harper, 3b, Mil	.296-31-82	1.0	78.0	0.23
Brooks Robinson, 3b, Bal	.276-18-94	2.0	75.0	0.22
Alex Johnson, of, Cal	.329-14-86	0.0	70.0	0.21
Jim Perry, p, Min	24-12, 3.04	0.0	63.0	0.19
Frank Robinson, of, Bal	.306-25-78	0.0	60.0	0.18
Mike Cuellar, p, Bal	24-8, 3.48	0.0	45.0	0.13
Jim Fregosi, ss, Cal	.278-22-82	0.0	35.0	0.10
Luis Aparicio, ss, ChA	.313-5-43	0.0	35.0	0.10
Ron Perranoski, p, Min	2.43, 34 saves	1.0	35.0	0.10
Roy White, of, NYA	.296-22-94	0.0	25.0	0.07
Dave McNally, p, Bal	24-9, 3.22	0.0	22.0	0.07
Sam McDowell, p, Cle	20-12, 2.92	0.0	22.0	0.07
Cesar Tovar, of, Min	.300-10-54	0.0	16.0	0.05
Thurman Munson, c, NYA	.302-6-53	0.0	15.0	0.04
Don Buford, of, Bal	.272-17-66	0.0	12.0	0.04
Clyde Wright, p, Cal	22-12, 2.83	0.0	8.0	0.02
Lindy McDaniel, p, NYA	2.01, 29 saves	0.0	8.0	0.02
Ray Fosse, c, Cle	.307-18-61	0.0	7.0	0.02
Bert Campaneris, ss, Oak	.279-22-64	0.0	5.0	0.01
Jim Palmer, p, Bal	20-10, 2.71	0.0	4.0	0.01
Reggie Smith, of, Bos	.303-22-74	0.0	3.0	0.01
Sal Bando, 3b, Oak	.263-20-75	0.0	1.0	0.00
Tony Horton, 1b, Cle	.269-17-59	0.0	1.0	0.00
Bob Oliver, 1b, KC	.260-27-99	0.0	1.0	0.00

Cy Young

Pitcher, Team	Stats	1st Pl	Pts	Share
Jim Perry, Min	24-12, 3.04	6.0	55.0	0.46
Dave McNally, Bal	24-9, 3.22	5.0	47.0	0.39
Sam McDowell, Cle	20-12, 2.92	4.0	45.0	0.38
Mike Cuellar, Bal	24-8, 3.48	6.0	44.0	0.37
Jim Palmer, Bal	20-10, 2.71	1.0	11.0	0.09
Clyde Wright, Cal	22-12, 2.83	1.0	9.0	0.08
Ron Perranoski, Min	2.43, 34 saves	1.0	5.0	0.04

Rookie of the Year

Pitcher, Pos, Team	Stats	1st Pl	Pts	Share
Thurman Munson, c, NYA	.302-6-53	23.0	23.0	0.96
Roy Foster, of, Cle	.268-23-60	1.0	1.0	0.04

Gold Gloves

Player, Pos, Team	Rng	LRng	FPct	LFPct
Jim Kaat, p, Min	—	—	.935	.951
Ray Fosse, c, Cle	—	—	.989	.988
Jim Spencer, 1b, Cal	—	—	.995	.991
Dave Johnson, 2b, Bal	5.16	4.64	.990	.979
Brooks Robinson, 3b, Bal	3.06	2.67	.966	.949
Luis Aparicio, ss, ChA	5.03	4.39	.976	.967
Ken Berry, of, ChA	2.46	1.85	.988	.980
Paul Blair, of, Bal	2.95	1.85	.990	.980
Mickey Stanley, of, Det	2.42	1.85	1.000	.980

National League

MVP

Player, Pos, Team	Stats	1st Pl	Pts	Share
Johnny Bench, c, Cin	.293-45-148	22.0	326.0	0.97
Billy Williams, of, ChN	.322-42-129	2.0	218.0	0.65
Tony Perez, 3b, Cin	.317-40-129	0.0	149.0	0.44
Bob Gibson, p, StL	23-7, 3.12	0.0	110.0	0.33
Wes Parker, 1b, LA	.319-10-111	0.0	91.0	0.27
Dave Giusti, p, Pit	3.06, 26 saves	0.0	72.0	0.21
Pete Rose, of, Cin	.316-15-52	0.0	54.0	0.16
Jim Hickman, of, ChN	.315-32-115	0.0	52.0	0.15
Willie McCovey, 1b, SF	.289-39-126	0.0	47.0	0.14
Rico Carty, of, Atl	.366-25-101	0.0	43.0	0.13
Manny Sanguillen, c, Pit	.325-7-61	0.0	36.0	0.11
Roberto Clemente, of, Pit	.352-14-60	0.0	33.0	0.10
Donn Clendenon, 1b, NYN	.288-22-97	0.0	26.0	0.08
Gaylord Perry, p, SF	23-13, 3.20	0.0	24.0	0.07
Willie Stargell, of, Pit	.264-31-85	0.0	20.0	0.06
Bobby Tolan, of, Cin	.316-16-80	0.0	17.0	0.05
Hank Aaron, of, Atl	.298-38-118	0.0	16.0	0.05
Joe Torre, c, StL	.325-21-100	0.0	15.0	0.04
Tommie Agee, of, NYN	.286-24-75	0.0	13.0	0.04
Bud Harrelson, ss, NYN	.243-1-42	0.0	10.0	0.03
Fergie Jenkins, p, ChN	22-16, 3.39	0.0	8.0	0.02
Jim Merritt, p, Cin	20-12, 4.08	0.0	8.0	0.02
Don Kessinger, ss, ChN	.266-1-39	0.0	6.0	0.02
Cito Gaston, of, SD	.318-29-93	0.0	5.0	0.01
Deron Johnson, 1b, Phi	.256-27-93	0.0	4.0	0.01
Luke Walker, p, Pit	3.04, 3 saves	0.0	4.0	0.01
Carl Morton, p, Mon	18-11, 3.60	0.0	3.0	0.01
Bob Robertson, 1b, Pit	.287-27-82	0.0	3.0	0.01
Tom Seaver, p, NYN	18-12, 2.82	0.0	2.0	0.01
Wayne Granger, p, Cin	2.66, 35 saves	0.0	1.0	0.00

Cy Young

Pitcher, Team	Stats	1st Pl	Pts	Share
Bob Gibson, StL	23-7, 3.12	23.0	118.0	0.98
Gaylord Perry, SF	23-13, 3.20	1.0	51.0	0.43
Fergie Jenkins, ChN	22-16, 3.39	0.0	16.0	0.13
Dave Giusti, Pit	3.06, 26 saves	0.0	8.0	0.07
Jim Merritt, Cin	20-12, 4.08	0.0	8.0	0.07
Gary Nolan, Cin	18-7, 3.27	0.0	5.0	0.04
Tom Seaver, NYN	18-12, 2.82	0.0	4.0	0.03
Wayne Granger, Cin	2.66, 35 saves	0.0	3.0	0.03
Carl Morton, Mon	18-11, 3.60	0.0	2.0	0.02
Luke Walker, Pit	3.04, 3 saves	0.0	1.0	0.01

Rookie of the Year

Pitcher, Pos, Team	Stats	1st Pl	Pts	Share
Carl Morton, p, Mon	18-11, 3.60	11.0	11.0	0.46
Bernie Carbo, of, Cin	.310-21-63	8.0	8.0	0.33
Larry Bowa, ss, Phi	.250-0-34	3.0	3.0	0.13
Wayne Simpson, p, Cin	14-3, 3.02	1.0	1.0	0.04
Cesar Cedeno, of, Hou	.310-7-42	1.0	1.0	0.04

Gold Gloves

Player, Pos, Team	Rng	LRng	FPct	LFPct
Bob Gibson, p, StL	—	—	.931	.951
Johnny Bench, c, Cin	—	—	.986	.987
Wes Parker, 1b, LA	—	—	.996	.992
Tommy Helms, 2b, Cin	5.14	4.67	.983	.979
Doug Rader, 3b, Hou	3.27	2.58	.966	.945
Don Kessinger, ss, ChN	4.92	4.23	.972	.965
Tommie Agee, of, NYN	2.52	1.78	.967	.976
Roberto Clemente, of, Pit	1.93	1.78	.966	.976
Pete Rose, of, Cin	1.99	1.78	.997	.976

1971

American League

MVP

Player, Pos, Team	Stats	1st Pl	Pts	Share
Vida Blue, p, Oak	24-8, 1.82	14.0	268.0	0.80
Sal Bando, 3b, Oak	.271-24-94	4.0	182.0	0.54
Frank Robinson, of, Bal	.281-28-99	2.0	170.0	0.51
Brooks Robinson, 3b, Bal	.272-20-92	3.0	163.0	0.49
Mickey Lolich, p, Det	25-14, 2.92	1.0	155.0	0.46
Freddie Patek, ss, KC	.267-6-36	0.0	77.0	0.23
Bobby Murcer, of, NYA	.331-25-94	0.0	72.0	0.21
Amos Otis, of, KC	.301-15-79	0.0	67.0	0.20
Wilbur Wood, p, ChA	22-13, 1.91	0.0	54.0	0.16
Tony Oliva, of, Min	.337-22-81	0.0	36.0	0.11
Dave McNally, p, Bal	21-5, 2.89	0.0	26.0	0.08
Norm Cash, 1b, Det	.283-32-91	0.0	21.0	0.06
Bill Melton, 3b, ChA	.269-33-86	0.0	18.0	0.05
Reggie Jackson, of, Oak	.277-32-80	0.0	15.0	0.04
Cookie Rojas, 2b, KC	.300-6-59	0.0	15.0	0.04
Ken Sanders, p, Mil	1.91, 31 saves	0.0	13.0	0.04
Pat Dobson, p, Bal	20-8, 2.90	0.0	9.0	0.03
Reggie Smith, of, Bos	.283-30-96	0.0	9.0	0.03
Dave Johnson, 2b, Bal	.282-18-72	0.0	8.0	0.02
Merv Rettenmund, of, Bal	.318-11-75	0.0	8.0	0.02
Harmon Killebrew, 1b, Min	.254-28-119	0.0	5.0	0.01
Jim Palmer, p, Bal	20-9, 2.68	0.0	5.0	0.01
Leo Cardenas, ss, Min	.264-18-75	0.0	5.0	0.01
Mike Cuellar, p, Bal	20-9, 3.08	0.0	4.0	0.01
Cesar Tovar, of, Min	.311-1-45	0.0	4.0	0.01
George Scott, 1b, Bos	.263-24-78	0.0	3.0	0.01
Don Buford, of, Bal	.290-19-54	0.0	2.0	0.01
Catfish Hunter, p, Oak	21-11, 2.96	0.0	1.0	0.00
Graig Nettles, 3b, Cle	.261-28-86	0.0	1.0	0.00

Cy Young

Pitcher, Team	Stats	1st Pl	Pts	Share
Vida Blue, Oak	24-8, 1.82	14.0	98.0	0.82
Mickey Lolich, Det	25-14, 2.92	9.0	85.0	0.71
Wilbur Wood, ChA	22-13, 1.91	1.0	23.0	0.19
Dave McNally, Bal	21-5, 2.89	0.0	8.0	0.07
Dick Drago, KC	17-11, 2.98	0.0	1.0	0.01
Andy Messersmith, Cal	20-13, 2.99	0.0	1.0	0.01

Rookie of the Year

Pitcher, Pos, Team	Stats	1st Pl	Pts	Share
Chris Chambliss, 1b, Cle	.275-9-48	11.0	11.0	0.46
Bill Parsons, p, Mil	13-17, 3.20	5.0	5.0	0.21
Angel Mangual, of, Oak	.286-4-30	4.0	4.0	0.17
Doug Griffin, 2b, Bos	.244-3-27	3.0	3.0	0.13
Paul Splittorff, p, KC	8-9, 2.68	1.0	1.0	0.04

Gold Gloves

Player, Pos, Team	Rng	LRng	FPct	LFPct
Jim Kaat, p, Min	—	—	.982	.958
Ray Fosse, c, Cle	—	—	.988	.988
George Scott, 1b, Bos	—	—	.992	.992
Dave Johnson, 2b, Bal	5.20	4.76	.984	.980
Brooks Robinson, 3b, Bal	3.11	2.74	.968	.956
Mark Belanger, ss, Bal	4.85	4.27	.978	.965
Paul Blair, of, Bal	2.43	1.96	.991	.982
Amos Otis, of, KC	2.88	1.96	.990	.982
Carl Yastrzemski, of, Bos	2.03	1.96	.993	.982

National League

MVP

Player, Pos, Team	Stats	1st Pl	Pts	Share
Joe Torre, 3b, StL	.363-24-137	21.0	318.0	0.95
Willie Stargell, of, Pit	.295-48-125	3.0	222.0	0.66
Hank Aaron, 1b, Atl	.327-47-118	0.0	180.0	0.54
Bobby Bonds, of, SF	.288-33-102	0.0	139.0	0.41
Roberto Clemente, of, Pit	.341-13-86	0.0	87.0	0.26
Maury Wills, ss, LA	.281-3-44	0.0	74.0	0.22
Fergie Jenkins, p, ChN	24-13, 2.77	0.0	71.0	0.21
Manny Sanguillen, c, Pit	.319-7-81	0.0	49.0	0.15
Tom Seaver, p, NYN	20-10, 1.76	0.0	46.0	0.14
Al Downing, p, LA	20-9, 2.68	0.0	36.0	0.11
Glenn Beckert, 2b, ChN	.342-2-42	0.0	35.0	0.10
Lee May, 1b, Cin	.278-39-98	0.0	28.0	0.08
Lou Brock, of, StL	.313-7-61	0.0	20.0	0.06
Dave Giusti, p, Pit	2.93, 30 saves	0.0	16.0	0.05
Willie McCovey, 1b, SF	.277-18-70	0.0	15.0	0.04
Ted Simmons, c, StL	.304-7-77	0.0	13.0	0.04
Willie Davis, of, LA	.309-10-74	0.0	13.0	0.04
Jerry Johnson, p, SF	2.97, 18 saves	0.0	12.0	0.04
Willie Mays, of, SF	.271-18-61	0.0	11.0	0.03
Rusty Staub, of, Mon	.311-19-97	0.0	11.0	0.03
Billy Williams, of, ChN	.301-28-93	0.0	10.0	0.03
Bud Harrelson, ss, NYN	.252-0-32	0.0	4.0	0.01
Bob Gibson, p, StL	16-13, 3.04	0.0	3.0	0.01
Ralph Garr, of, Atl	.343-9-44	0.0	1.0	0.00
Dave Roberts, p, SD	14-17, 2.10	0.0	1.0	0.00
Pete Rose, of, Cin	.304-13-44	0.0	1.0	0.00

Cy Young

Pitcher, Team	Stats	1st Pl	Pts	Share
Fergie Jenkins, ChN	24-13, 2.77	17.0	97.0	0.81
Tom Seaver, NYN	20-10, 1.76	6.0	61.0	0.51
Al Downing, LA	20-9, 2.68	1.0	40.0	0.33
Dock Ellis, Pit	19-9, 3.06	0.0	9.0	0.08
Bob Gibson, StL	16-13, 3.04	0.0	3.0	0.03
Jerry Johnson, SF	2.97, 18 saves	0.0	2.0	0.02
Dave Roberts, SD	14-17, 2.10	0.0	2.0	0.02
Juan Marichal, SF	18-11, 2.94	0.0	1.0	0.01
Bill Stoneman, Mon	17-16, 3.15	0.0	1.0	0.01

Rookie of the Year

Pitcher, Pos, Team	Stats	1st Pl	Pts	Share
Earl Williams, c, Atl	.260-33-87	18.0	18.0	0.75
Willie Montanez, of, Phi	.255-30-99	6.0	6.0	0.25

Gold Gloves

Player, Pos, Team	Rng	LRng	FPct	LFPct
Bob Gibson, p, StL	—	—	.942	.954
Johnny Bench, c, Cin	—	—	.988	.988
Wes Parker, 1b, LA	—	—	.996	.992
Tommy Helms, 2b, Cin	5.79	4.86	.990	.978
Doug Rader, 3b, Hou	2.73	2.32	.946	.949
Bud Harrelson, ss, NYN	4.99	4.46	.978	.968
Bobby Bonds, of, SF	2.20	1.92	.994	.979
Roberto Clemente, of, Pit	2.24	1.92	.993	.979
Willie Davis, of, LA	2.62	1.92	.981	.979

1972

American League

MVP

Player, Pos, Team	Stats	1st Pl	Pts	Share
Dick Allen, 1b, ChA	.308-37-113	21.0	321.0	0.96
Joe Rudi, of, Oak	.305-19-75	1.0	164.0	0.49
Sparky Lyle, p, NYA	1.92, 35 saves	1.0	158.0	0.47
Carlton Fisk, c, Bos	.293-22-61	0.0	96.0	0.29
Bobby Murcer, of, NYA	.292-33-96	0.0	89.0	0.26
Gaylord Perry, p, Cle	24-16, 1.92	0.0	88.0	0.26
Wilbur Wood, p, ChA	24-17, 2.51	0.0	78.0	0.23
Luis Tiant, p, Bos	1.91, 3 saves	0.0	70.5	0.21
Ed Brinkman, ss, Det	.203-6-49	0.0	62.0	0.18
Mickey Lolich, p, Det	22-14, 2.50	1.0	60.0	0.18
Catfish Hunter, p, Oak	21-7, 2.04	0.0	57.0	0.17
John Mayberry, 1b, KC	.298-25-100	0.0	27.0	0.08
Jim Palmer, p, Bal	21-10, 2.07	0.0	21.0	0.06
Bobby Grich, ss, Bal	.278-12-50	0.0	16.0	0.05
Rod Carew, 2b, Min	.318-0-51	0.0	16.0	0.05
Bert Campaneris, ss, Oak	.240-8-32	0.0	11.0	0.03
Mike Epstein, 1b, Oak	.270-26-70	0.0	11.0	0.03
Luis Aparicio, ss, Bos	.257-3-39	0.0	9.5	0.03
Rico Petrocelli, 3b, Bos	.240-15-75	0.0	9.0	0.03
Reggie Jackson, of, Oak	.265-25-75	0.0	9.0	0.03
Carlos May, of, ChA	.308-12-68	0.0	6.0	0.02
George Scott, 1b, Mil	.266-20-88	0.0	6.0	0.02
Danny Thompson, ss, Min	.276-4-48	0.0	5.0	0.01
Al Kaline, of, Det	.313-10-32	0.0	4.0	0.01
Tommy Harper, of, Bos	.254-14-49	0.0	4.0	0.01
Bill Freehan, c, Det	.262-10-56	0.0	3.0	0.01
Ken McMullen, 3b, Cal	.269-9-34	0.0	3.0	0.01
Brooks Robinson, 3b, Bal	.250-8-64	0.0	3.0	0.01
Reggie Smith, of, Bos	.270-21-74	0.0	3.0	0.01
Sal Bando, 3b, Oak	.236-15-77	0.0	2.0	0.01
Nolan Ryan, p, Cal	19-16, 2.28	0.0	2.0	0.01
Amos Otis, of, KC	.293-11-54	0.0	1.0	0.00
Lou Piniella, of, KC	.312-11-72	0.0	1.0	0.00

Cy Young

Pitcher, Team	Stats	1st Pl	Pts	Share
Gaylord Perry, Cle	24-16, 1.92	9.0	64.0	0.53
Wilbur Wood, ChA	24-17, 2.51	7.0	58.0	0.48
Mickey Lolich, Det	22-14, 2.50	3.0	27.0	0.23
Catfish Hunter, Oak	21-7, 2.04	2.0	26.0	0.22
Jim Palmer, Bal	21-10, 2.07	2.0	20.0	0.17
Luis Tiant, Bos	1.91, 3 saves	1.0	16.0	0.13
Sparky Lyle, NYA	1.92, 35 saves	0.0	3.0	0.03
Nolan Ryan, Cal	19-16, 2.28	0.0	2.0	0.02

Rookie of the Year

Pitcher, Pos, Team	Stats	1st Pl	Pts	Share
Carlton Fisk, c, Bos	.293-22-61	24.0	24.0	1.00

Gold Gloves

Player, Pos, Team	Rng	LRng	FPct	LFPct
Jim Kaat, p, Min	—	—	.923	.950
Carlton Fisk, c, Bos	—	—	.984	.985
George Scott, 1b, Mil	—	—	.992	.991
Doug Griffin, 2b, Bos	5.05	4.42	.978	.977
Brooks Robinson, 3b, Bal	3.04	2.71	.977	.955
Ed Brinkman, ss, Det	4.67	4.51	.990	.967
Ken Berry, of, Cal	2.46	1.91	1.000	.983
Paul Blair, of, Bal	2.50	1.91	.991	.983
Bobby Murcer, of, NYA	2.60	1.91	.992	.983

National League

MVP

Player, Pos, Team	Stats	1st Pl	Pts	Share
Johnny Bench, c, Cin	.270-40-125	11.0	263.0	0.78
Billy Williams, of, ChN	.333-37-122	5.0	211.0	0.63
Willie Stargell, 1b, Pit	.293-33-112	2.0	201.0	0.60
Joe Morgan, 2b, Cin	.292-16-73	5.0	197.0	0.59
Steve Carlton, p, Phi	27-10, 1.97	1.0	124.0	0.37
Cesar Cedeno, of, Hou	.320-22-82	0.0	112.0	0.33
Al Oliver, of, Pit	.312-12-89	0.0	52.0	0.15
Nate Colbert, 1b, SD	.250-38-111	0.0	45.0	0.13
Lee May, 1b, Hou	.284-29-98	0.0	30.0	0.09
Ted Simmons, c, StL	.303-16-96	0.0	22.0	0.07
Mike Marshall, p, Mon	1.78, 18 saves	0.0	22.0	0.07
Pete Rose, of, Cin	.307-6-57	0.0	19.0	0.06
Roberto Clemente, of, Pit	.312-10-60	0.0	16.0	0.05
Clay Carroll, p, Cin	2.25, 37 saves	0.0	16.0	0.05
Lou Brock, of, StL	.311-3-42	0.0	13.0	0.04
Hank Aaron, 1b, Atl	.265-34-77	0.0	12.0	0.04
Manny Sanguillen, c, Pit	.298-7-71	0.0	12.0	0.04
Steve Blass, p, Pit	19-8, 2.49	0.0	9.0	0.03
Ralph Garr, of, Atl	.325-12-53	0.0	7.0	0.02
Gene Clines, of, Pit	.334-0-17	0.0	6.0	0.02
Bobby Tolan, of, Cin	.283-8-82	0.0	6.0	0.02
Dusty Baker, of, Atl	.321-17-76	0.0	5.0	0.01
Manny Mota, of, LA	.323-5-48	0.0	4.0	0.01
Dave Kingman, 3b, SF	.225-29-83	0.0	3.0	0.01
Tug McGraw, p, NYN	1.70, 27 saves	0.0	2.0	0.01
Rusty Staub, of, NYN	.293-9-38	0.0	2.0	0.01
Tom Seaver, p, NYN	21-12, 2.92	0.0	2.0	0.01
Jose Cardenal, of, ChN	.291-17-70	0.0	1.0	0.00
Fergie Jenkins, p, ChN	20-12, 3.20	0.0	1.0	0.00
Chris Speier, ss, SF	.269-15-71	0.0	1.0	0.00

Cy Young

Pitcher, Team	Stats	1st Pl	Pts	Share
Steve Carlton, Phi	27-10, 1.97	24.0	120.0	1.00
Steve Blass, Pit	19-8, 2.49	0.0	35.0	0.29
Fergie Jenkins, ChN	20-12, 3.20	0.0	23.0	0.19
Mike Marshall, Mon	1.78, 18 saves	0.0	8.0	0.07
Gary Nolan, Cin	15-5, 1.99	0.0	6.0	0.05
Tom Seaver, NYN	21-12, 2.92	0.0	6.0	0.05
Clay Carroll, Cin	2.25, 37 saves	0.0	6.0	0.05
Don Sutton, LA	19-9, 2.08	0.0	6.0	0.05
Bob Gibson, StL	19-11, 2.46	0.0	3.0	0.03
Milt Pappas, ChN	17-7, 2.77	0.0	3.0	0.03

Rookie of the Year

Pitcher, Pos, Team	Stats	1st Pl	Pts	Share
Jon Matlack, p, NYN	15-10, 2.32	19.0	19.0	0.79
Dave Rader, c, SF	.259-6-41	4.0	4.0	0.17
John Milner, of, NYN	.238-17-38	1.0	1.0	0.04

Gold Gloves

Player, Pos, Team	Rng	LRng	FPct	LFPct
Bob Gibson, p, StL	—	—	.983	.950
Johnny Bench, c, Cin	—	—	.992	.987
Wes Parker, 1b, LA	—	—	.997	.992
Felix Millan, 2b, Atl	5.10	4.88	.987	.978
Doug Rader, 3b, Hou	3.02	2.55	.958	.945
Larry Bowa, ss, Phi	4.71	4.48	.987	.967
Cesar Cedeno, of, Hou	2.58	1.96	.981	.978
Roberto Clemente, of, Pit	2.17	1.96	1.000	.978
Willie Davis, of, LA	2.62	1.96	.987	.978

1973

American League

MVP

Player, Pos, Team	Stats	1st Pl	Pts	Share
Reggie Jackson, of, Oak	.293-32-117	24.0	336.0	1.00
Jim Palmer, p, Bal	22-9, 2.40	0.0	172.0	0.51
Amos Otis, of, KC	.300-26-93	0.0	112.0	0.33
Rod Carew, 2b, Min	.350-6-62	0.0	83.0	0.25
John Hiller, p, Det	1.44, 38 saves	0.0	83.0	0.25
Sal Bando, 3b, Oak	.287-29-98	0.0	83.0	0.25
John Mayberry, 1b, KC	.278-26-100	0.0	76.0	0.23
Dave May, of, Mil	.303-25-93	0.0	65.0	0.19
Bobby Murcer, of, NYA	.304-22-95	0.0	53.0	0.16
Tommy Davis, dh, Bal	.306-7-89	0.0	47.0	0.14
Catfish Hunter, p, Oak	21-5, 3.34	0.0	47.0	0.14
Thurman Munson, c, NYA	.301-20-74	0.0	43.0	0.13
Tommy Harper, of, Bos	.281-17-71	0.0	33.0	0.10
George Scott, 1b, Mil	.306-24-107	0.0	25.0	0.07
Orlando Cepeda, dh, Bos	.289-20-86	0.0	21.0	0.06
Frank Robinson, of, Cal	.266-30-97	0.0	21.0	0.06
Nolan Ryan, p, Cal	21-16, 2.87	0.0	20.0	0.06
Carlton Fisk, c, Bos	.246-26-71	0.0	16.0	0.05
Bobby Grich, 2b, Bal	.251-12-50	0.0	9.0	0.03
Carl Yastrzemski, 1b, Bos	.296-19-95	0.0	9.0	0.03
Mark Belanger, ss, Bal	.226-0-27	0.0	8.0	0.02
Deron Johnson, dh, Oak	.246-19-81	0.0	8.0	0.02
John Briggs, of, Mil	.246-18-57	0.0	6.0	0.02
Joe Coleman, p, Det	23-15, 3.53	0.0	6.0	0.02
Cookie Rojas, 2b, KC	.276-6-69	0.0	5.0	0.01
Bert Blyleven, p, Min	20-17, 2.52	0.0	4.0	0.01
Gaylord Perry, p, Cle	19-19, 3.38	0.0	4.0	0.01
Bert Campaneris, ss, Oak	.250-4-46	0.0	4.0	0.01
Vida Blue, p, Oak	20-9, 3.28	0.0	3.0	0.01
Carlos May, dh, ChA	.268-20-96	0.0	3.0	0.01
Willie Horton, of, Det	.316-17-53	0.0	3.0	0.01
Bill North, of, Oak	.285-5-34	0.0	3.0	0.01
Paul Blair, of, Bal	.280-10-64	0.0	2.0	0.01
Dave Nelson, 2b, Tex	.286-7-48	0.0	2.0	0.01
Dick Allen, 1b, ChA	.316-16-41	0.0	1.0	0.00

Cy Young

Pitcher, Team	Stats	1st Pl	Pts	Share
Jim Palmer, Bal	22-9, 2.40	14.0	88.0	0.73
Nolan Ryan, Cal	21-16, 2.87	9.0	62.0	0.52
Catfish Hunter, Oak	21-5, 3.34	1.0	52.0	0.43
John Hiller, Det	1.44, 38 saves	0.0	6.0	0.05
Wilbur Wood, ChA	24-20, 3.46	0.0	3.0	0.03
Jim Colborn, Mil	20-12, 3.18	0.0	2.0	0.02
Vida Blue, Oak	20-9, 3.28	0.0	1.0	0.01
Bert Blyleven, Min	20-17, 2.52	0.0	1.0	0.01
Gaylord Perry, Cle	19-19, 3.38	0.0	1.0	0.01

Rookie of the Year

Pitcher, Pos, Team	Stats	1st Pl	Pts	Share
Al Bumbry, of, Bal	.337-7-34	13.5	13.5	0.54
Pedro Garcia, 2b, Mil	.245-15-54	3.0	3.0	0.13
Darrell Porter, c, Mil	.254-16-67	2.0	2.0	0.08
Steve Busby, p, KC	16-15, 4.23	2.0	2.0	0.08
Doc Medich, p, NYA	14-9, 2.95	2.0	2.0	0.08
Rich Coggins, of, Bal	.319-7-41	1.5	1.5	0.04

Gold Gloves

Player, Pos, Team	Rng	LRng	FPct	LFPct
Jim Kaat, p, Min-ChA	—	—	.973	.951
Thurman Munson, c, NYA	—	—	.984	.985
George Scott, 1b, Mil	—	—	.994	.992
Bobby Grich, 2b, Bal	5.80	4.67	.995	.980
Brooks Robinson, 3b, Bal	3.14	2.68	.970	.950
Mark Belanger, ss, Bal	5.01	4.43	.971	.963
Paul Blair, of, Bal	2.66	2.02	.990	.979
Amos Otis, of, KC	2.52	2.02	.986	.979
Mickey Stanley, of, Det	2.74	2.02	.993	.979

National League

MVP

Player, Pos, Team	Stats	1st Pl	Pts	Share
Pete Rose, of, Cin	.338-5-64	12.0	274.0	0.82
Willie Stargell, of, Pit	.299-44-119	10.0	250.0	0.74
Bobby Bonds, of, SF	.283-39-96	1.0	174.0	0.52
Joe Morgan, 2b, Cin	.290-26-82	1.0	102.0	0.30

Mike Marshall, p, Mon	2.66, 31 saves	0.0	93.0	0.28
Lou Brock, of, StL	.297-7-63	0.0	65.0	0.19
Tony Perez, 1b, Cin	.314-27-101	0.0	59.0	0.18
Tom Seaver, p, NYN	19-10, 2.08	0.0	57.0	0.17
Ken Singleton, of, Mon	.302-23-103	0.0	52.0	0.15
Johnny Bench, c, Cin	.253-25-104	0.0	41.0	0.12
Cesar Cedeno, of, Hou	.320-25-70	0.0	39.0	0.12
Hank Aaron, of, Atl	.301-40-96	0.0	35.0	0.10
Dave Johnson, 2b, Atl	.270-43-99	0.0	34.0	0.10
Ted Simmons, c, StL	.310-13-91	0.0	20.0	0.06
Tug McGraw, p, NYN	3.87, 25 saves	0.0	17.0	0.05
Felix Millan, 2b, NYN	.290-3-37	0.0	12.0	0.04
Willie Davis, of, LA	.285-16-77	0.0	12.0	0.04
Darrell Evans, 3b, Atl	.281-41-104	0.0	11.0	0.03
Lee May, 1b, Hou	.270-28-105	0.0	9.0	0.03
Tito Fuentes, 2b, SF	.277-6-63	0.0	8.0	0.02
Bob Watson, of, Hou	.312-16-94	0.0	7.0	0.02
Joe Ferguson, c, LA	.263-25-88	0.0	7.0	0.02
Jose Cardenal, of, ChN	.303-11-68	0.0	6.0	0.02
Jack Billingham, p, Cin	19-10, 3.04	0.0	6.0	0.02
Al Oliver, of, Pit	.292-20-99	0.0	6.0	0.02
Ron Hunt, 2b, Mon	.309-0-18	0.0	5.0	0.01
Ron Bryant, p, SF	24-12, 3.53	0.0	5.0	0.01
Garry Maddox, of, SF	.319-11-76	0.0	3.0	0.01
Bud Harrelson, ss, NYN	.258-0-20	0.0	2.0	0.01
Billy Williams, of, ChN	.288-20-86	0.0	2.0	0.01
Greg Luzinski, of, Phi	.285-29-97	0.0	2.0	0.01
Bill Russell, ss, LA	.265-4-56	0.0	1.0	0.00

Cy Young

Pitcher, Team	Stats	1st Pl	Pts	Share
Tom Seaver, NYN	19-10, 2.08	10.0	71.0	0.59
Mike Marshall, Mon	2.66, 31 saves	9.0	54.0	0.45
Ron Bryant, SF	24-12, 3.53	3.0	50.0	0.42
Jack Billingham, Cin	19-10, 3.04	2.0	30.0	0.25
Don Sutton, LA	18-10, 2.42	0.0	7.0	0.06
Fred Norman, SD-Cin	13-13, 3.60	0.0	3.0	0.03
Dave Giusti, Pit	2.37, 20 saves	0.0	1.0	0.01

Rookie of the Year

Pitcher, Pos, Team	Stats	1st Pl	Pts	Share
Gary Matthews, of, SF	.300-12-58	11.0	11.0	0.46
Steve Rogers, p, Mon	10-5, 1.54	3.5	3.5	0.13
Bob Boone, c, Phi	.261-10-61	2.0	2.0	0.08
Elias Sosa, p, SF	3.28, 18 saves	2.0	2.0	0.08
Dan Driessen, 3b, Cin	.301-4-47	2.0	2.0	0.08
Ron Cey, 3b, LA	.245-15-80	1.0	1.0	0.04
Davey Lopes, 2b, LA	.275-6-37	1.0	1.0	0.04
John Grubb, of, SD	.311-8-37	1.0	1.0	0.04
Richie Zisk, of, Pit	.324-10-54	0.5	0.5	0.00

Gold Gloves

Player, Pos, Team	Rng	LRng	FPct	LFPct
Bob Gibson, p, StL	—	—	.946	.950
Johnny Bench, c, Cin	—	—	.995	.987
Mike Jorgensen, 1b, Mon	—	—	.995	.992
Joe Morgan, 2b, Cin	5.56	4.91	.990	.980
Doug Rader, 3b, Hou	2.83	2.49	.945	.946
Roger Metzger, ss, Hou	4.43	4.31	.982	.961
Bobby Bonds, of, SF	2.27	1.96	.970	.977
Cesar Cedeno, of, Hou	2.70	1.96	.981	.977
Willie Davis, of, LA	2.40	1.96	.980	.977

1974

American League

MVP

Player, Pos, Team	Stats	1st Pl	Pts	Share
Jeff Burroughs, of, Tex	.301-25-118	10.0	248.0	0.74
Joe Rudi, of, Oak	.293-22-99	5.5	161.5	0.48
Sal Bando, 3b, Oak	.243-22-103	3.5	143.5	0.43
Reggie Jackson, of, Oak	.289-29-93	1.0	119.0	0.35
Fergie Jenkins, p, Tex	25-12, 2.82	3.0	118.0	0.35
Catfish Hunter, p, Oak	25-12, 2.49	1.0	107.0	0.32
Rod Carew, 2b, Min	.364-3-55	0.0	70.0	0.21
Elliott Maddox, of, NYA	.303-3-45	0.0	59.0	0.18
Bobby Grich, 2b, Bal	.263-19-82	0.0	49.0	0.15
Mike Cuellar, p, Bal	22-10, 3.11	0.0	42.0	0.13
Luis Tiant, p, Bos	22-13, 2.92	0.0	41.0	0.12
Brooks Robinson, 3b, Bal	.288-7-59	0.0	30.0	0.09
Paul Blair, of, Bal	.261-17-62	0.0	27.0	0.08
Nolan Ryan, p, Cal	22-16, 2.89	0.0	24.0	0.07
Bert Campaneris, ss, Oak	.290-2-41	0.0	23.0	0.07
Rollie Fingers, p, Oak	2.65, 18 saves	0.0	21.0	0.06
Gaylord Perry, p, Cle	21-13, 2.51	0.0	18.0	0.05
Carl Yastrzemski, 1b, Bos	.301-15-79	0.0	14.0	0.04
Ken Henderson, of, ChA	.292-20-95	0.0	12.0	0.04
John Hiller, p, Det	2.64, 13 saves	0.0	11.0	0.03
Lenny Randle, 3b, Tex	.302-1-49	0.0	10.0	0.03
Bobby Murcer, of, NYA	.274-10-88	0.0	10.0	0.03
Lou Piniella, of, NYA	.305-9-70	0.0	8.0	0.02
Dick Allen, 1b, ChA	.301-32-88	0.0	8.0	0.02
Sparky Lyle, p, NYA	1.66, 15 saves	0.0	7.0	0.02
Thurman Munson, c, NYA	.261-13-60	0.0	6.0	0.02
Tommy Davis, dh, Bal	.289-11-84	0.0	6.0	0.02
Mark Belanger, ss, Bal	.225-5-36	0.0	6.0	0.02
Don Money, 3b, Mil	.283-15-65	0.0	5.0	0.01
Tom Murphy, p, Mil	1.90, 20 saves	0.0	3.0	0.01
Hal McRae, dh, KC	.310-15-88	0.0	3.0	0.01
Steve Busby, p, KC	22-14, 3.39	0.0	3.0	0.01
George Scott, 1b, Mil	.281-17-82	0.0	2.0	0.01
Pat Dobson, p, NYA	19-15, 3.07	0.0	1.0	0.00

Cy Young

Pitcher, Team	Stats	1st Pl	Pts	Share
Catfish Hunter, Oak	25-12, 2.49	12.0	90.0	0.75
Fergie Jenkins, Tex	25-12, 2.82	10.0	75.0	0.63
Nolan Ryan, Cal	22-16, 2.89	1.0	28.0	0.23
Luis Tiant, Bos	22-13, 2.92	0.0	8.0	0.07
Gaylord Perry, Cle	21-13, 2.51	1.0	8.0	0.07
Mike Cuellar, Bal	22-10, 3.11	0.0	6.0	0.05
John Hiller, Det	2.64, 13 saves	0.0	1.0	0.01

Rookie of the Year

Pitcher, Pos, Team	Stats	1st Pl	Pts	Share
Mike Hargrove, 1b, Tex	.323-4-66	16.5	16.5	0.67
Bucky Dent, ss, ChA	.274-5-45	3.0	3.0	0.13
George Brett, 3b, KC	.282-2-47	2.0	2.0	0.08
Rick Burleson, ss, Bos	.284-4-44	1.5	1.5	0.04
Jim Sundberg, c, Tex	.247-3-36	1.0	1.0	0.04

Gold Gloves

Player, Pos, Team	Rng	LRng	FPct	LFPct
Jim Kaat, p, ChA	—	—	.959	.947
Thurman Munson, c, NYA	—	—	.974	.983
George Scott, 1b, Mil	—	—	.992	.992
Bobby Grich, 2b, Bal	5.86	4.56	.979	.975
Brooks Robinson, 3b, Bal	3.43	2.77	.967	.954
Mark Belanger, ss, Bal	5.13	4.24	.984	.965
Paul Blair, of, Bal	3.01	2.12	.985	.980
Amos Otis, of, KC	3.03	2.12	.986	.980
Joe Rudi, of, Oak	1.72	2.12	.984	.980

National League

MVP

Player, Pos, Team	Stats	1st Pl	Pts	Share
Steve Garvey, 1b, LA	.312-21-111	13.0	270.0	0.80
Lou Brock, of, StL	.306-3-48	8.0	233.0	0.69
Mike Marshall, p, LA	2.42, 21 saves	1.0	146.0	0.43
Johnny Bench, c, Cin	.280-33-129	0.0	141.0	0.42
Jimmy Wynn, of, LA	.271-32-108	2.0	137.0	0.41
Mike Schmidt, 3b, Phi	.282-36-116	0.0	136.0	0.40
Al Oliver, of, Pit	.321-11-85	0.0	87.0	0.26
Joe Morgan, 2b, Cin	.293-22-67	0.0	72.0	0.21
Richie Zisk, of, Pit	.313-17-100	0.0	54.0	0.16
Willie Stargell, of, Pit	.301-25-96	0.0	43.0	0.13
Reggie Smith, of, StL	.309-23-100	0.0	39.0	0.12
Ralph Garr, of, Atl	.353-11-54	0.0	11.0	0.03
Ted Simmons, c, StL	.272-20-103	0.0	7.0	0.02
Dave Cash, 2b, Phi	.300-2-58	0.0	6.0	0.02
Dave Concepcion, ss, Cin	.281-14-82	0.0	5.0	0.01
Jack Billingham, p, Cin	19-11, 3.94	0.0	4.0	0.01
Cesar Cedeno, of, Hou	.269-26-102	0.0	4.0	0.01
Al Hrabosky, p, StL	2.95, 9 saves	0.0	4.0	0.01
Andy Messersmith, p, LA	20-6, 2.59	0.0	4.0	0.01
Buzz Capra, p, Atl	16-8, 2.28	0.0	3.0	0.01
Lynn McGlothen, p, StL	16-12, 2.69	0.0	2.0	0.01
Bake McBride, of, StL	.309-6-56	0.0	2.0	0.01
Richie Hebner, 3b, Pit	.291-18-68	0.0	2.0	0.01
Rennie Stennett, 2b, Pit	.291-7-56	0.0	2.0	0.01
Bill Buckner, of, LA	.314-7-58	0.0	1.0	0.00
Ron Cey, 3b, LA	.262-18-97	0.0	1.0	0.00

Cy Young

Pitcher, Team	Stats	1st Pl	Pts	Share
Mike Marshall, LA	2.42, 21 saves	17.0	96.0	0.80
Andy Messersmith, LA	20-6, 2.59	5.0	66.0	0.55
Phil Niekro, Atl	20-13, 2.38	1.0	15.0	0.13
Don Sutton, LA	19-9, 3.23	1.0	12.0	0.10
Al Hrabosky, StL	2.95, 9 saves	0.0	9.0	0.08
Jack Billingham, Cin	19-11, 3.94	0.0	8.0	0.07
Don Gullett, Cin	17-11, 3.04	0.0	5.0	0.04
Clay Carroll, Cin	2.15, 6 saves	0.0	2.0	0.02
Dave Giusti, Pit	3.32, 12 saves	0.0	1.0	0.01
Buzz Capra, Atl	16-8, 2.28	0.0	1.0	0.01
Lynn McGlothen, StL	16-12, 2.69	0.0	1.0	0.01

Rookie of the Year

Pitcher, Pos, Team	Stats	1st Pl	Pts	Share
Bake McBride, of, StL	.309-6-56	16.0	16.0	0.67
Greg Gross, of, Hou	.314-0-36	7.0	7.0	0.29
Bill Madlock, 3b, ChN	.313-9-54	1.0	1.0	0.04

Gold Gloves

Player, Pos, Team	Rng	LRng	FPct	LFPct
Andy Messersmith, p, LA	—	—	.873	.944
Johnny Bench, c, Cin	—	—	.993	.985
Steve Garvey, 1b, LA	—	—	.995	.991
Joe Morgan, 2b, Cin	5.13	4.64	.982	.973
Doug Rader, 3b, Hou	3.13	2.64	.965	.948
Dave Concepcion, ss, Cin	4.84	4.26	.963	.961
Bobby Bonds, of, SF	2.14	1.96	.966	.979
Cesar Cedeno, of, Hou	2.91	1.96	.993	.979
Cesar Geronimo, of, Cin	2.54	1.96	.987	.979

1975

American League

MVP

Player, Pos, Team	Stats	1st Pl	Pts	Share
Fred Lynn, of, Bos	.331-21-105	22.0	326.0	0.97
John Mayberry, 1b, KC	.291-34-106	0.0	157.0	0.47
Jim Rice, of, Bos	.309-22-102	0.0	154.0	0.46
Rollie Fingers, p, Oak	2.98, 24 saves	2.0	129.0	0.38
Reggie Jackson, of, Oak	.253-36-104	0.0	118.0	0.35
Jim Palmer, p, Bal	23-11, 2.09	0.0	82.0	0.24
Thurman Munson, c, NYA	.318-12-102	0.0	69.0	0.21
George Scott, 1b, Mil	.285-36-109	0.0	64.5	0.19
Rod Carew, 2b, Min	.359-14-80	0.0	54.5	0.16
Ken Singleton, of, Bal	.300-15-55	0.0	44.0	0.13
George Brett, 3b, KC	.308-11-89	0.0	37.5	0.11
Catfish Hunter, p, NYA	23-14, 2.58	0.0	31.0	0.09
Rick Burleson, ss, Bos	.252-6-62	0.0	28.0	0.08
Claudell Washington, of, Oak	.308-10-77	0.0	22.0	0.07
Toby Harrah, ss, Tex	.293-20-93	0.0	16.0	0.05
Mike Torrez, p, Bal	20-9, 3.06	0.0	12.0	0.04
Goose Gossage, p, ChA	1.84, 26 saves	0.0	11.0	0.03
Paul Lindblad, p, Oak	2.72, 7 saves	0.0	7.0	0.02
Gene Tenace, c, Oak	.255-29-87	0.0	7.0	0.02
Boog Powell, 1b, Cle	.297-27-86	0.0	6.5	0.02
Don Baylor, of, Bal	.282-25-76	0.0	6.0	0.02
Bert Campaneris, ss, Oak	.265-4-46	0.0	6.0	0.02
Bill Lee, p, Bos	17-9, 3.95	0.0	5.0	0.01
Jim Todd, p, Oak	2.29, 12 saves	0.0	5.0	0.01
Denny Doyle, 2b, Cal-Bos	.298-4-36	0.0	5.0	0.01
Rick Wise, p, Bos	19-12, 3.95	0.0	4.0	0.01
Joe Rudi, 1b, Oak	.278-21-75	0.0	3.0	0.01
Jim Kaat, p, ChA	20-14, 3.11	0.0	2.0	0.01
Lee May, 1b, Bal	.262-20-99	0.0	2.0	0.01
Bobby Bonds, of, NYA	.270-32-85	0.0	1.0	0.00
Carl Yastrzemski, 1b, Bos	.269-14-60	0.0	1.0	0.00

Cy Young

Pitcher, Team	Stats	1st Pl	Pts	Share
Jim Palmer, Bal	23-11, 2.09	15.0	98.0	0.82
Catfish Hunter, NYA	23-14, 2.58	7.0	74.0	0.62
Rollie Fingers, Oak	2.98, 24 saves	2.0	25.0	0.21
Frank Tanana, Cal	16-9, 2.62	0.0	7.0	0.06
Jim Kaat, ChA	20-14, 3.11	0.0	7.0	0.06
Vida Blue, Oak	22-11, 3.01	0.0	2.0	0.02
Goose Gossage, ChA	1.84, 26 saves	0.0	2.0	0.02
Rick Wise, Bos	19-12, 3.95	0.0	1.0	0.01

Rookie of the Year

Pitcher, Pos, Team	Stats	1st Pl	Pts	Share
Fred Lynn, of, Bos	.331-21-105	23.5	23.5	0.96
Jim Rice, of, Bos	.309-22-102	0.5	0.5	0.00

Gold Gloves

Player, Pos, Team	Rng	LRng	FPct	LFPct
Jim Kaat, p, ChA	—	—	.982	.940
Thurman Munson, c, NYA	—	—	.972	.983
George Scott, 1b, Mil	—	—	.989	.990
Bobby Grich, 2b, Bal	6.05	4.73	.977	.975
Brooks Robinson, 3b, Bal	2.95	2.81	.979	.954
Mark Belanger, ss, Bal	5.05	4.09	.978	.959
Paul Blair, of, Bal	2.43	2.10	.991	.979
Fred Lynn, of, Bos	2.88	2.10	.983	.979
Joe Rudi, of, Oak	1.66	2.10	1.000	.979

National League

MVP

Player, Pos, Team	Stats	1st Pl	Pts	Share
Joe Morgan, 2b, Cin	.327-17-94	21.5	321.5	0.96
Greg Luzinski, of, Phi	.300-34-120	0.0	154.0	0.46
Dave Parker, of, Pit	.308-25-101	0.0	120.0	0.36
Johnny Bench, c, Cin	.283-28-110	0.0	117.0	0.35
Pete Rose, 3b, Cin	.317-7-74	2.5	114.0	0.34
Ted Simmons, c, StL	.332-18-100	0.0	103.0	0.31
Willie Stargell, 1b, Pit	.295-22-90	0.0	69.0	0.21
Al Hrabosky, p, StL	1.66, 22 saves	0.0	66.0	0.20
Tom Seaver, p, NYN	22-9, 2.38	0.0	65.0	0.19
Randy Jones, p, SD	20-12, 2.24	0.0	54.0	0.16
Steve Garvey, 1b, LA	.319-18-95	0.0	50.0	0.15
Bill Madlock, 3b, ChN	.354-7-64	0.0	45.0	0.13
Dave Cash, 2b, Phi	.305-4-57	0.0	26.0	0.08
Rusty Staub, of, NYN	.282-19-105	0.0	20.0	0.06
Tony Perez, 1b, Cin	.282-20-109	0.0	18.0	0.05
Mike Schmidt, 3b, Phi	.249-38-95	0.0	16.0	0.05
Manny Sanguillen, c, Pit	.328-9-58	0.0	16.0	0.05
Ron Cey, 3b, LA	.283-25-101	0.0	11.5	0.03
Dave Kingman, of, NYN	.231-36-88	0.0	9.0	0.03
Bob Watson, 1b, Hou	.324-18-85	0.0	8.0	0.02
Lou Brock, of, StL	.309-3-47	0.0	6.0	0.02
Larry Bowa, ss, Phi	.305-2-38	0.0	3.0	0.01
Jerry Reuss, p, Pit	18-11, 2.54	0.0	2.0	0.01
Andy Messersmith, p, LA	19-14, 2.29	0.0	1.0	0.00
Willie Montanez, 1b, Phi-SF	.302-10-101	0.0	1.0	0.00

Cy Young

Pitcher, Team	Stats	1st Pl	Pts	Share
Tom Seaver, NYN	22-9, 2.38	15.0	98.0	0.82
Randy Jones, SD	20-12, 2.24	7.0	80.0	0.67
Al Hrabosky, StL	1.66, 22 saves	2.0	33.0	0.28
John Montefusco, SF	15-9, 2.88	0.0	2.0	0.02
Don Gullett, Cin	15-4, 2.42	0.0	1.0	0.01
Andy Messersmith, LA	19-14, 2.29	0.0	1.0	0.01
Don Sutton, LA	16-13, 2.87	0.0	1.0	0.01

Rookie of the Year

Pitcher, Pos, Team	Stats	1st Pl	Pts	Share
John Montefusco, p, SF	15-9, 2.88	12.0	12.0	0.50
Gary Carter, of, Mon	.270-17-68	9.0	9.0	0.38
Larry Parrish, 3b, Mon	.274-10-65	1.0	1.0	0.04
Rawly Eastwick, p, Cin	2.60, 22 saves	1.0	1.0	0.04
Manny Trillo, 2b, ChN	.248-7-70	1.0	1.0	0.04

Gold Gloves

Player, Pos, Team	Rng	LRng	FPct	LFPct
Andy Messersmith, p, LA	—	—	.915	.946
Johnny Bench, c, Cin	—	—	.989	.985
Steve Garvey, 1b, LA	—	—	.995	.990
Joe Morgan, 2b, Cin	5.50	4.92	.986	.975
Ken Reitz, 3b, StL	2.52	2.58	.946	.945
Dave Concepcion, ss, Cin	5.25	4.21	.977	.963
Cesar Cedeno, of, Hou	2.52	2.01	.982	.978
Cesar Geronimo, of, Cin	2.84	2.01	.993	.978
Garry Maddox, of, SF-Phi	3.07	2.01	.985	.978

1976

American League

MVP

Player, Pos, Team	Stats	1st Pl	Pts	Share
Thurman Munson, c, NYA	.302-17-105	18.0	304.0	0.90
George Brett, 3b, KC	.333-7-67	2.0	217.0	0.65
Mickey Rivers, of, NYA	.312-8-67	1.0	179.5	0.53
Hal McRae, dh, KC	.332-8-73	0.0	99.0	0.29
Chris Chambliss, 1b, NYA	.293-17-96	0.0	71.5	0.21
Rod Carew, 1b, Min	.331-9-90	1.0	71.0	0.21
Amos Otis, of, KC	.279-18-86	1.0	58.0	0.17
Bill Campbell, p, Min	3.01, 20 saves	0.0	56.0	0.17
Lee May, 1b, Bal	.258-25-109	0.0	51.0	0.15
Jim Palmer, p, Bal	22-13, 2.51	0.0	47.0	0.14
Mark Fidrych, p, Det	19-9, 2.34	1.0	41.0	0.12
Joe Rudi, of, Oak	.270-13-94	0.0	35.0	0.10
Sal Bando, 3b, Oak	.240-27-84	0.0	31.0	0.09
Carl Yastrzemski, 1b, Bos	.267-21-102	0.0	26.0	0.08
Frank Tanana, p, Cal	19-10, 2.43	0.0	19.0	0.06
Reggie Jackson, of, Bal	.277-27-91	0.0	17.0	0.05
Graig Nettles, 3b, NYA	.254-32-93	0.0	17.0	0.05
Gene Tenace, 1b, Oak	.249-22-66	0.0	13.0	0.04
Rollie Fingers, p, Oak	2.47, 20 saves	0.0	12.0	0.04
Vida Blue, p, Oak	18-13, 2.35	0.0	10.0	0.03
Ed Figueroa, p, NYA	19-10, 3.02	0.0	9.0	0.03
Sparky Lyle, p, NYA	2.26, 23 saves	0.0	8.0	0.02
Ron LeFlore, of, Det	.316-4-39	0.0	6.0	0.02
Mark Littell, p, KC	2.08, 16 saves	0.0	5.0	0.01
Rico Carty, dh, Cle	.310-13-83	0.0	5.0	0.01
Roy White, of, NYA	.286-14-65	0.0	3.0	0.01
Luis Tiant, p, Bos	21-12, 3.06	0.0	3.0	0.01
John Mayberry, 1b, KC	.232-13-95	0.0	1.0	0.00
Butch Wynegar, c, Min	.260-10-69	0.0	1.0	0.00

Cy Young

Pitcher, Team	Stats	1st Pl	Pts	Share
Jim Palmer, Bal	22-13, 2.51	19.0	108.0	0.90
Mark Fidrych, Det	19-9, 2.34	5.0	51.0	0.43
Frank Tanana, Cal	19-10, 2.43	0.0	18.0	0.15
Ed Figueroa, NYA	19-10, 3.02	0.0	12.0	0.10
Luis Tiant, Bos	21-12, 3.06	0.0	10.0	0.08
Vida Blue, Oak	18-13, 2.35	0.0	8.0	0.07
Bill Campbell, Min	3.01, 20 saves	0.0	7.0	0.06
Rollie Fingers, Oak	2.47, 20 saves	0.0	1.0	0.01
Wayne Garland, Bal	20-7, 2.67	0.0	1.0	0.01

Rookie of the Year

Pitcher, Pos, Team	Stats	1st Pl	Pts	Share
Mark Fidrych, p, Det	19-9, 2.34	22.0	22.0	0.92
Butch Wynegar, c, Min	.260-10-69	2.0	2.0	0.08

Gold Gloves

Player, Pos, Team	Rng	LRng	FPct	LFPct
Jim Palmer, p, Bal	—	—	.987	.950
Jim Sundberg, c, Tex	—	—	.991	.981
George Scott, 1b, Mil	—	—	.991	.992
Bobby Grich, 2b, Bal	5.64	4.64	.985	.975
Aurelio Rodriguez, 3b, Det	3.13	2.64	.978	.953
Mark Belanger, ss, Bal	5.12	4.40	.982	.967
Dwight Evans, of, Bos	2.34	2.21	.994	.981
Rick Manning, of, Cle	2.70	2.21	.987	.981
Joe Rudi, of, Oak	2.10	2.21	.989	.981

National League

MVP

Player, Pos, Team	Stats	1st Pl	Pts	Share
Joe Morgan, 2b, Cin	.320-27-111	19.0	311.0	0.93
George Foster, of, Cin	.306-29-121	5.0	221.0	0.66
Mike Schmidt, 3b, Phi	.262-38-107	0.0	179.0	0.53
Pete Rose, 3b, Cin	.323-10-63	0.0	131.0	0.39
Garry Maddox, of, Phi	.330-6-68	0.0	98.0	0.29
Bill Madlock, 3b, ChN	.339-15-84	0.0	51.0	0.15
Steve Garvey, 1b, LA	.317-13-80	0.0	51.0	0.15
Greg Luzinski, of, Phi	.304-21-95	0.0	49.0	0.15
Ken Griffey Sr., of, Cin	.336-6-74	0.0	49.0	0.15
Randy Jones, p, SD	22-14, 2.74	0.0	48.0	0.14
Bob Watson, 1b, Hou	.313-16-102	0.0	38.0	0.11
Al Oliver, of, Pit	.323-12-61	0.0	30.0	0.09
Rawly Eastwick, p, Cin	2.09, 26 saves	0.0	26.0	0.08
Jerry Koosman, p, NYN	21-10, 2.69	0.0	20.0	0.06
Steve Carlton, p, Phi	20-7, 3.13	0.0	16.0	0.05
Dave Cash, 2b, Phi	.284-1-56	0.0	15.0	0.04
J.R. Richard, p, Hou	20-15, 2.75	0.0	12.0	0.04
Rick Monday, of, ChN	.272-32-77	0.0	11.0	0.03
Dave Kingman, of, NYN	.238-37-86	0.0	11.0	0.03
Dave Parker, of, Pit	.313-13-90	0.0	10.0	0.03
Bill Robinson, of, Pit	.303-21-64	0.0	9.0	0.03
Don Sutton, p, LA	21-10, 3.06	0.0	7.0	0.02
Ron Cey, 3b, LA	.277-23-80	0.0	6.0	0.02
Willie Montanez, 1b, SF-Atl	.317-11-84	0.0	4.0	0.01
Lou Brock, of, StL	.301-4-67	0.0	3.0	0.01
Cesar Cedeno, of, Hou	.297-18-83	0.0	3.0	0.01
Cesar Geronimo, of, Cin	.307-2-49	0.0	3.0	0.01
Richie Zisk, of, Pit	.289-21-89	0.0	3.0	0.01
Larry Bowa, ss, Phi	.248-0-49	0.0	1.0	0.00

Cy Young

Pitcher, Team	Stats	1st Pl	Pts	Share
Randy Jones, SD	22-14, 2.74	15.0	96.0	0.80
Jerry Koosman, NYN	21-10, 2.69	7.0	69.5	0.58
Don Sutton, LA	21-10, 3.06	1.0	25.5	0.21
Steve Carlton, Phi	20-7, 3.13	0.0	11.0	0.09
Rawly Eastwick, Cin	2.09, 26 saves	0.0	6.0	0.05
Jon Matlack, NYN	17-10, 2.95	1.0	5.0	0.04
J.R. Richard, Hou	20-15, 2.75	0.0	2.0	0.02
Tom Seaver, NYN	14-11, 2.59	0.0	1.0	0.01

Rookie of the Year

Pitcher, Pos, Team	Stats	1st Pl	Pts	Share
Butch Metzger, p, SD	2.92, 16 saves	11.0	11.0	0.46
Pat Zachry, p, Cin	14-7, 2.74	11.0	11.0	0.46
Heity Cruz, 3b, StL	.228-13-71	2.0	2.0	0.08

Gold Gloves

Player, Pos, Team	Rng	LRng	FPct	LFPct
Jim Kaat, p, Phi	—	—	.949	.950
Johnny Bench, c, Cin	—	—	.997	.986
Steve Garvey, 1b, LA	—	—	.998	.991
Joe Morgan, 2b, Cin	5.09	4.93	.981	.975
Mike Schmidt, 3b, Phi	3.23	2.61	.961	.952
Dave Concepcion, ss, Cin	5.40	4.48	.968	.964
Cesar Cedeno, of, Hou	2.66	2.03	.980	.979
Cesar Geronimo, of, Cin	2.67	2.03	.985	.979
Garry Maddox, of, Phi	3.13	2.03	.989	.979

1977

American League

MVP

Player, Pos, Team	Stats	1st Pl	Pts	Share
Rod Carew, 1b, Min	.388-14-100	12.0	273.0	0.70
Al Cowens, of, KC	.312-23-112	4.0	217.0	0.55
Ken Singleton, of, Bal	.328-24-99	3.0	200.0	0.51
Jim Rice, dh, Bos	.320-39-114	1.0	163.0	0.42
Graig Nettles, 3b, NYA	.255-37-107	2.0	112.0	0.29
Sparky Lyle, p, NYA	2.17, 26 saves	1.0	79.0	0.20
Thurman Munson, c, NYA	.308-18-100	1.0	70.0	0.18
Reggie Jackson, of, NYA	.286-32-110	1.0	67.0	0.17
Carlton Fisk, c, Bos	.315-26-102	1.0	67.0	0.17
Bill Campbell, p, Bos	2.96, 31 saves	0.0	65.0	0.17
Mickey Rivers, of, NYA	.326-12-69	0.0	59.0	0.15
Larry Hisle, of, Min	.302-28-119	1.0	54.0	0.14
George Brett, 3b, KC	.312-22-88	0.0	51.0	0.13
Richie Zisk, of, ChA	.290-30-101	0.0	34.0	0.09
Jim Sundberg, c, Tex	.291-6-65	0.0	30.0	0.08
Bobby Bonds, of, Cal	.264-37-115	0.0	28.0	0.07
Carl Yastrzemski, of, Bos	.296-28-102	1.0	25.0	0.06
Ron Guidry, p, NYA	16-7, 2.82	0.0	11.0	0.03
Jim Palmer, p, Bal	20-11, 2.91	0.0	9.0	0.02
Ron LeFlore, of, Det	.325-16-57	0.0	7.0	0.02
Jason Thompson, 1b, Det	.270-31-105	0.0	6.0	0.02
Rick Burleson, ss, Bos	.293-3-52	0.0	5.0	0.01
Butch Hobson, 3b, Bos	.265-30-112	0.0	4.0	0.01
Nolan Ryan, p, Cal	19-16, 2.77	0.0	3.0	0.01
George Scott, 1b, Bos	.269-33-95	0.0	3.0	0.01
Hal McRae, dh, KC	.298-21-92	0.0	3.0	0.01
Lyman Bostock, of, Min	.336-14-90	0.0	2.0	0.01
Tom Johnson, p, Min	3.13, 15 saves	0.0	2.0	0.01
Chris Chambliss, 1b, NYA	.287-17-90	0.0	1.0	0.00
Oscar Gamble, dh, ChA	.297-31-83	0.0	1.0	0.00
Dennis Leonard, p, KC	20-12, 3.04	0.0	1.0	0.00

Cy Young

Pitcher, Team	Stats	1st Pl	Pts	Share
Sparky Lyle, NYA	2.17, 26 saves	9.0	56.5	0.40
Jim Palmer, Bal	20-11, 2.91	6.0	48.0	0.34
Nolan Ryan, Cal	19-16, 2.77	6.0	46.0	0.33
Dennis Leonard, KC	20-12, 3.04	5.0	45.0	0.32
Bill Campbell, Bos	2.96, 31 saves	1.0	25.5	0.18
Dave Goltz, Min	20-11, 3.36	1.0	19.0	0.14
Ron Guidry, NYA	16-7, 2.82	0.0	5.0	0.04
Dave Rozema, Det	15-7, 3.09	0.0	4.0	0.03
Frank Tanana, Cal	15-9, 2.54	0.0	3.0	0.02

Rookie of the Year

Pitcher, Pos, Team	Stats	1st Pl	Pts	Share
Eddie Murray, dh, Bal	.283-27-88	12.5	12.5	0.43
Mitchell Page, of, Oak	.307-21-75	9.5	9.5	0.32
Bump Wills, 2b, Tex	.287-9-62	4.0	4.0	0.14
Dave Rozema, p, Det	15-7, 3.09	2.0	2.0	0.07

Gold Gloves

Player, Pos, Team	Rng	LRng	FPct	LFPct
Jim Palmer, p, Bal	—	—	.971	.948
Jim Sundberg, c, Tex	—	—	.994	.986
Jim Spencer, 1b, ChA	—	—	.991	.990
Frank White, 2b, KC	4.89	4.76	.989	.978
Graig Nettles, 3b, NYA	2.90	2.73	.974	.957
Mark Belanger, ss, Bal	4.65	4.07	.985	.963
Juan Beniquez, of, Tex	2.61	2.03	.988	.978
Al Cowens, of, KC	2.02	2.03	.982	.978
Carl Yastrzemski, of, Bos	2.16	2.03	1.000	.978

National League

MVP

Player, Pos, Team	Stats	1st Pl	Pts	Share
George Foster, of, Cin	.320-52-149	15.0	291.0	0.87
Greg Luzinski, of, Phi	.309-39-130	9.0	255.0	0.76
Dave Parker, of, Pit	.338-21-88	0.0	156.0	0.46
Reggie Smith, of, LA	.307-32-87	0.0	112.0	0.33
Steve Carlton, p, Phi	23-10, 2.64	0.0	100.0	0.30
Steve Garvey, 1b, LA	.297-33-115	0.0	98.0	0.29
Bruce Sutter, p, ChN	1.34, 31 saves	0.0	68.0	0.20
Ron Cey, 3b, LA	.241-30-110	0.0	60.0	0.18
Ted Simmons, c, StL	.318-21-95	0.0	58.0	0.17
Mike Schmidt, 3b, Phi	.274-38-101	0.0	48.0	0.14
Bill Robinson, 1b, Pit	.304-26-104	0.0	34.0	0.10
Tommy John, p, LA	20-7, 2.78	0.0	33.0	0.10
Garry Templeton, ss, StL	.322-8-79	0.0	20.0	0.06
Rollie Fingers, p, SD	2.99, 35 saves	0.0	17.0	0.05
Pete Rose, 3b, Cin	.311-9-64	0.0	15.0	0.04
Jeff Burroughs, of, Atl	.271-41-114	0.0	9.0	0.03
Al Oliver, of, Pit	.308-19-82	0.0	9.0	0.03
John Candelaria, p, Pit	20-5, 2.34	0.0	8.0	0.02
Rennie Stennett, 2b, Pit	.336-5-51	0.0	7.0	0.02
Willie McCovey, 1b, SF	.280-28-86	0.0	5.0	0.01
Johnny Bench, c, Cin	.275-31-109	0.0	3.0	0.01
Rick Reuschel, p, ChN	20-10, 2.79	0.0	3.0	0.01
Ellis Valentine, of, Mon	.293-25-76	0.0	3.0	0.01
Tug McGraw, p, Phi	2.62, 9 saves	0.0	2.0	0.01
Larry Bowa, ss, Phi	.280-4-41	0.0	1.0	0.00
Tom Seaver, p, NYN-Cin	21-6, 2.58	0.0	1.0	0.00

Cy Young

Pitcher, Team	Stats	1st Pl	Pts	Share
Steve Carlton, Phi	23-10, 2.64	17.0	104.0	0.87
Tommy John, LA	20-7, 2.78	3.0	54.0	0.45
Tom Seaver, NYN-Cin	21-6, 2.58	2.0	18.0	0.15
Rick Reuschel, ChN	20-10, 2.79	1.0	18.0	0.15
John Candelaria, Pit	20-5, 2.34	1.0	17.0	0.14
Bruce Sutter, ChN	1.34, 31 saves	0.0	5.0	0.04

Rookie of the Year

Pitcher, Pos, Team	Stats	1st Pl	Pts	Share
Andre Dawson, of, Mon	.282-19-65	10.0	10.0	0.42
Steve Henderson, of, NYN	.297-12-65	9.0	9.0	0.38
Gene Richards, of, SD	.290-5-32	4.0	4.0	0.17
Floyd Bannister, p, Hou	8-9, 4.04	1.0	1.0	0.04

Gold Gloves

Player, Pos, Team	Rng	LRng	FPct	LFPct
Jim Kaat, p, Phi	—	—	.897	.950
Johnny Bench, c, Cin	—	—	.987	.985
Steve Garvey, 1b, LA	—	—	.995	.991
Joe Morgan, 2b, Cin	4.70	4.47	.993	.977
Mike Schmidt, 3b, Phi	3.37	2.54	.964	.956
Dave Concepcion, ss, Cin	4.94	4.30	.986	.963
Cesar Geronimo, of, Cin	2.61	1.93	.992	.978
Garry Maddox, of, Phi	2.83	1.93	.977	.978
Dave Parker, of, Pit	2.63	1.93	.965	.978

1978

American League

MVP

Player, Pos, Team	Stats	1st Pl	Pts	Share
Jim Rice, of, Bos	.315-46-139	20.0	352.0	0.90
Ron Guidry, p, NYA	25-3, 1.74	8.0	291.0	0.74
Larry Hisle, of, Mil	.290-34-115	0.0	201.0	0.51
Amos Otis, of, KC	.298-22-96	0.0	90.0	0.23
Rusty Staub, dh, Det	.273-24-121	0.0	88.0	0.22
Graig Nettles, 3b, NYA	.276-27-93	0.0	86.0	0.22
Don Baylor, dh, Cal	.255-34-99	0.0	51.0	0.13
Eddie Murray, 1b, Bal	.285-27-95	0.0	50.0	0.13
Carlton Fisk, c, Bos	.284-20-88	0.0	49.0	0.13
Darrell Porter, c, KC	.265-18-78	0.0	48.0	0.12
Rod Carew, 1b, Min	.333-5-70	0.0	46.0	0.12
Mike Caldwell, p, Mil	22-9, 2.36	0.0	41.0	0.10
Goose Gossage, p, NYA	2.01, 27 saves	0.0	39.0	0.10
Al Oliver, of, Tex	.324-14-89	0.0	26.5	0.07
Jim Sundberg, c, Tex	.278-6-58	0.0	24.0	0.06
Ron LeFlore, of, Det	.297-12-62	0.0	21.0	0.05
Reggie Jackson, of, NYA	.274-27-97	0.0	18.0	0.05
Carl Yastrzemski, of, Bos	.277-17-81	0.0	17.0	0.04
George Brett, 3b, KC	.294-9-62	0.0	14.0	0.04
Andre Thornton, 1b, Cle	.262-33-105	0.0	12.5	0.03
Lou Piniella, of, NYA	.314-6-69	0.0	11.0	0.03
Thurman Munson, c, NYA	.297-6-71	0.0	9.0	0.02
Lyman Bostock, of, Cal	.296-5-71	0.0	8.0	0.02
Larry Gura, p, KC	16-4, 2.72	0.0	8.0	0.02
Fred Lynn, of, Bos	.298-22-82	0.0	6.0	0.02
Mickey Rivers, of, NYA	.265-11-48	0.0	6.0	0.02
Bob Stanley, p, Bos	2.60, 10 saves	0.0	6.0	0.02
Dave LaRoche, p, Cal	2.82, 25 saves	0.0	6.0	0.02
Don Money, 1b, Mil	.293-14-54	0.0	5.0	0.01
Willie Randolph, 2b, NYA	.279-3-42	0.0	5.0	0.01
Dennis Eckersley, p, Bos	20-8, 2.99	0.0	4.0	0.01
Hal McRae, dh, KC	.273-16-72	0.0	4.0	0.01
Leon Roberts, of, Sea	.301-22-92	0.0	3.0	0.01
Rich Gale, p, KC	14-8, 3.09	0.0	2.0	0.01
Ken Singleton, of, Bal	.293-20-81	0.0	2.0	0.01
Rick Burleson, ss, Bos	.248-5-49	0.0	1.0	0.00
Frank Tanana, p, Cal	18-12, 3.65	0.0	1.0	0.00

Cy Young

Pitcher, Team	Stats	1st Pl	Pts	Share
Ron Guidry, NYA	25-3, 1.74	28.0	140.0	1.00
Mike Caldwell, Mil	22-9, 2.36	0.0	76.0	0.54
Jim Palmer, Bal	21-12, 2.46	0.0	14.0	0.10
Dennis Eckersley, Bos	20-8, 2.99	0.0	10.0	0.07
Goose Gossage, NYA	2.01, 27 saves	0.0	4.0	0.01
Fergie Jenkins, Tex	18-8, 3.04	0.0	2.0	0.01
Ed Figueroa, NYA	20-9, 2.99	0.0	1.0	0.01
Larry Gura, KC	16-4, 2.72	0.0	1.0	0.01
Dennis Leonard, KC	21-17, 3.33	0.0	1.0	0.01
Mike Marshall, Min	2.45, 21 saves	0.0	1.0	0.01
Paul Splittorff, KC	19-13, 3.40	0.0	1.0	0.01
Bob Stanley, Bos	2.60, 10 saves	0.0	1.0	0.01

Rookie of the Year

Pitcher, Pos, Team	Stats	1st Pl	Pts	Share
Lou Whitaker, 2b, Det	.285-3-58	21.0	21.0	0.75
Paul Molitor, 2b, Mil	.273-6-45	3.0	3.0	0.11
Carney Lansford, 3b, Cal	.294-8-52	2.0	2.0	0.07
Rich Gale, p, KC	14-8, 3.09	1.0	1.0	0.04
Alan Trammell, ss, Det	.268-2-34	1.0	1.0	0.04

Gold Gloves

Player, Pos, Team	Rng	LRng	FPct	LFPct
Jim Palmer, p, Bal	—	—	.972	.954
Jim Sundberg, c, Tex	—	—	.997	.983
Chris Chambliss, 1b, NYA	—	—	.997	.992
Frank White, 2b, KC	5.07	4.74	.978	.980
Graig Nettles, 3b, NYA	2.74	2.59	.975	.954
Mark Belanger, ss, Bal	4.43	4.19	.985	.964
Dwight Evans, of, Bos	2.25	2.13	.982	.979
Fred Lynn, of, Bos	2.81	2.13	.984	.979
Rick Miller, of, Cal	2.81	2.13	.989	.979

National League

MVP

Player, Pos, Team	Stats	1st Pl	Pts	Share
Dave Parker, of, Pit	.334-30-117	21.0	320.0	0.95
Steve Garvey, 1b, LA	.316-21-113	0.0	194.0	0.58
Larry Bowa, ss, Phi	.294-3-43	3.0	189.0	0.56
Reggie Smith, of, LA	.295-29-93	0.0	164.0	0.49
Jack Clark, of, SF	.306-25-98	0.0	107.0	0.32
George Foster, of, Cin	.281-40-120	0.0	104.0	0.31
Greg Luzinski, of, Phi	.265-35-101	0.0	48.0	0.14
Gaylord Perry, p, SD	21-6, 2.73	0.0	45.0	0.13
Willie Stargell, 1b, Pit	.295-28-97	0.0	39.0	0.12
Dave Winfield, of, SD	.308-24-97	0.0	37.0	0.11
Pete Rose, 3b, Cin	.302-7-52	0.0	35.0	0.10
Vida Blue, p, SF	18-10, 2.79	0.0	33.0	0.10
Kent Tekulve, p, Pit	2.33, 31 saves	0.0	23.0	0.07
Rollie Fingers, p, SD	2.52, 37 saves	0.0	16.0	0.05
Burt Hooton, p, LA	19-10, 2.71	0.0	15.0	0.04
Davey Lopes, 2b, LA	.278-17-58	0.0	12.0	0.04
Phil Niekro, p, Atl	19-18, 2.88	0.0	8.0	0.02
Bill Buckner, 1b, ChN	.323-5-74	0.0	8.0	0.02
Jeff Burroughs, of, Atl	.301-23-77	0.0	7.0	0.02
Bruce Sutter, p, ChN	3.18, 27 saves	0.0	5.0	0.01
Garry Maddox, of, Phi	.288-11-68	0.0	4.0	0.01
Enos Cabell, 3b, Hou	.295-7-71	0.0	2.0	0.01
Bob Boone, c, Phi	.283-12-62	0.0	1.0	0.00

Cy Young

Pitcher, Team	Stats	1st Pl	Pts	Share
Gaylord Perry, SD	21-6, 2.73	22.0	116.0	0.97
Burt Hooton, LA	19-10, 2.71	0.0	38.0	0.32
Vida Blue, SF	18-10, 2.79	1.0	17.0	0.14
J.R. Richard, Hou	18-11, 3.11	1.0	13.0	0.11
Kent Tekulve, Pit	2.33, 31 saves	0.0	12.0	0.10
Phil Niekro, Atl	19-18, 2.88	0.0	10.0	0.08
Ross Grimsley, Mon	20-11, 3.05	0.0	7.0	0.06
Rollie Fingers, SD	2.52, 37 saves	0.0	1.0	0.01
Tommy John, LA	17-10, 3.30	0.0	1.0	0.01
Don Robinson, Pit	14-6, 3.47	0.0	1.0	0.01

Rookie of the Year

Pitcher, Pos, Team	Stats	1st Pl	Pts	Share
Bob Horner, 3b, Atl	.266-23-63	12.5	12.5	0.50
Ozzie Smith, ss, SD	.258-1-46	8.5	8.5	0.33
Don Robinson, p, Pit	14-6, 3.47	3.0	3.0	0.13

Gold Gloves

Player, Pos, Team	Rng	LRng	FPct	LFPct
Phil Niekro, p, Atl	—	—	.976	.951
Bob Boone, c, Phi	—	—	.991	.985
Keith Hernandez, 1b, StL	—	—	.994	.992
Davey Lopes, 2b, LA	5.18	4.34	.974	.977
Mike Schmidt, 3b, Phi	3.04	2.53	.963	.952
Larry Bowa, ss, Phi	4.65	4.25	.986	.966
Garry Maddox, of, Phi	2.93	1.95	.983	.980
Dave Parker, of, Pit	2.14	1.95	.960	.980
Ellis Valentine, of, Mon	2.19	1.95	.970	.980

1979

American League

MVP

Player, Pos, Team	Stats	1st Pl	Pts	Share
Don Baylor, of, Cal	.296-36-139	20.0	347.0	0.89
Ken Singleton, of, Bal	.295-35-111	3.0	241.0	0.61
George Brett, 3b, KC	.329-23-107	2.0	226.0	0.58
Fred Lynn, of, Bos	.333-39-122	0.0	160.5	0.41
Jim Rice, of, Bos	.325-39-130	0.0	124.0	0.32
Mike Flanagan, p, Bal	23-9, 3.08	3.0	100.0	0.26
Gorman Thomas, of, Mil	.244-45-123	0.0	87.0	0.22
Bobby Grich, 2b, Cal	.294-30-101	0.0	58.0	0.15
Darrell Porter, c, KC	.291-20-112	0.0	52.0	0.13
Buddy Bell, 3b, Tex	.299-18-101	0.0	48.0	0.12
Eddie Murray, 1b, Bal	.295-25-99	0.0	25.5	0.06
Jim Kern, p, Tex	1.57, 29 saves	0.0	25.0	0.06
Mike Marshall, p, Min	2.65, 32 saves	0.0	25.0	0.06
Brian Downing, c, Cal	.326-12-75	0.0	24.0	0.06
Sixto Lezcano, of, Mil	.321-28-101	0.0	18.0	0.05
Roy Smalley, ss, Min	.271-24-95	0.0	16.0	0.04
Willie Wilson, of, KC	.315-6-49	0.0	15.0	0.04

Steve Kemp, of, Det	.318-26-105	0.0	15.0	0.04
Mark Clear, p, Cal	3.63, 14 saves	0.0	12.0	0.03
Paul Molitor, 2b, Mil	.322-9-62	0.0	8.0	0.02
Rick Burleson, ss, Bos	.278-5-60	0.0	7.0	0.02
Tommy John, p, NYA	21-9, 2.96	0.0	5.0	0.01
Cecil Cooper, 1b, Mil	.308-24-106	0.0	4.0	0.01
Reggie Jackson, of, NYA	.297-29-89	0.0	3.0	0.01
Willie Horton, dh, Sea	.279-29-106	0.0	3.0	0.01
Dan Ford, of, Cal	.290-21-101	0.0	1.0	0.00
Ron Guidry, p, NYA	18-8, 2.78	0.0	1.0	0.00
Mike Hargrove, of, Cle	.325-10-56	0.0	1.0	0.00

Cy Young

Pitcher, Team	Stats	1st Pl	Pts	Share
Mike Flanagan, Bal	23-9, 3.08	26.0	136.0	0.97
Tommy John, NYA	21-9, 2.96	1.0	51.0	0.36
Ron Guidry, NYA	18-8, 2.78	1.0	26.0	0.19
Jim Kern, Tex	1.57, 29 saves	0.0	25.0	0.18
Mike Marshall, Min	2.65, 32 saves	0.0	7.0	0.05
Jerry Koosman, Min	20-13, 3.38	0.0	5.0	0.04
Dennis Eckersley, Bos	17-10, 2.99	0.0	1.0	0.01
Aurelio Lopez, Det	2.41, 21 saves	0.0	1.0	0.01

Rookie of the Year

Pitcher, Pos, Team	Stats	1st Pl	Pts	Share
John Castino, 3b, Min	.285-5-52	7.0	7.0	0.25
Alfredo Griffin, ss, Tor	.287-2-31	7.0	7.0	0.25
Mark Clear, p, Cal	3.63, 14 saves	5.0	5.0	0.18
Ron Davis, p, NYA	2.85, 9 saves	3.0	3.0	0.11
Ross Baumgarten, p, ChA	13-8, 3.54	3.0	3.0	0.11
Pat Putnam, 1b, Tex	.277-18-64	3.0	3.0	0.11

Gold Gloves

Player, Pos, Team	Rng	LRng	FPct	LFPct
Jim Palmer, p, Bal	—	—	1.000	.949
Jim Sundberg, c, Tex	—	—	.995	.982
Cecil Cooper, 1b, Mil	—	—	.993	.992
Frank White, 2b, KC	5.19	4.80	.982	.978
Buddy Bell, 3b, Tex	3.24	2.66	.969	.953
Rick Burleson, ss, Bos	5.20	4.10	.980	.965
Dwight Evans, of, Bos	2.16	2.13	.988	.981
Sixto Lezcano, of, Mil	2.16	2.13	.986	.981
Fred Lynn, of, Bos	2.73	2.13	.987	.981

National League

MVP

Player, Pos, Team	Stats	1st Pl	Pts	Share
Willie Stargell, 1b, Pit	.281-32-82	10.0	216.0	0.64
Keith Hernandez, 1b, StL	.344-11-105	4.0	216.0	0.64
Dave Winfield, of, SD	.308-34-118	4.0	155.0	0.46
Larry Parrish, 3b, Mon	.307-30-82	0.0	128.0	0.38
Ray Knight, 3b, Cin	.318-10-79	2.0	82.0	0.24
Joe Niekro, p, Hou	21-11, 3.00	1.0	75.5	0.22
Bruce Sutter, p, ChN	2.22, 37 saves	0.0	69.0	0.21
Kent Tekulve, p, Pit	2.75, 31 saves	1.0	64.0	0.19
Dave Concepcion, ss, Cin	.281-16-84	0.0	63.0	0.19
Dave Parker, of, Pit	.310-25-94	0.0	56.0	0.17
Dave Kingman, of, ChN	.288-48-115	0.0	53.0	0.16
George Foster, of, Cin	.302-30-98	0.0	34.0	0.10
Mike Schmidt, 3b, Phi	.253-45-114	0.0	32.0	0.10
Steve Garvey, 1b, LA	.315-28-110	0.0	30.0	0.09
Omar Moreno, of, Pit	.282-8-69	0.0	23.0	0.07
Pete Rose, 1b, Phi	.331-4-59	0.0	23.0	0.07
Gary Carter, c, Mon	.283-22-75	1.0	15.0	0.04
Bill Madlock, 3b, SF-Pit	.298-14-85	1.0	14.0	0.04
J.R. Richard, p, Hou	18-13, 2.71	0.0	12.0	0.04
Phil Niekro, p, Atl	21-20, 3.39	0.0	11.5	0.03
Joe Sambito, p, Hou	1.77, 22 saves	0.0	9.0	0.03
Tom Seaver, p, Cin	16-6, 3.14	0.0	9.0	0.03
Johnny Bench, c, Cin	.276-22-80	0.0	7.0	0.02
Andre Dawson, of, Mon	.275-25-92	0.0	6.0	0.02
Garry Templeton, ss, StL	.314-9-62	0.0	5.0	0.01
Gary Matthews, of, Atl	.304-27-90	0.0	4.0	0.01
Dave Collins, of, Cin	.318-3-35	0.0	3.0	0.01
Bob Horner, 3b, Atl	.314-33-98	0.0	1.0	0.00

Cy Young

Pitcher, Team	Stats	1st Pl	Pts	Share
Bruce Sutter, ChN	2.22, 37 saves	10.0	72.0	0.60
Joe Niekro, Hou	21-11, 3.00	9.0	66.0	0.55
J.R. Richard, Hou	18-13, 2.71	4.0	41.0	0.34
Tom Seaver, Cin	16-6, 3.14	0.0	20.0	0.17
Kent Tekulve, Pit	2.75, 31 saves	1.0	14.0	0.12
Phil Niekro, Atl	21-20, 3.39	0.0	3.0	0.03

Rookie of the Year

Pitcher, Pos, Team	Stats	1st Pl	Pts	Share
Rick Sutcliffe, p, LA	17-10, 3.46	20.0	20.0	0.83
Jeffrey Leonard, of, Hou	.290-0-47	3.0	3.0	0.13
Scot Thompson, of, ChN	.289-2-29	1.0	1.0	0.04

Gold Gloves

Player, Pos, Team	Rng	LRng	FPct	LFPct
Phil Niekro, p, Atl	—	—	.989	.951
Bob Boone, c, Phi	—	—	.988	.985
Keith Hernandez, 1b, StL	—	—	.995	.992
Manny Trillo, 2b, Phi	5.41	4.55	.985	.979
Mike Schmidt, 3b, Phi	3.03	2.50	.954	.951
Dave Concepcion, ss, Cin	5.26	4.51	.967	.965
Garry Maddox, of, Phi	3.19	2.00	.996	.979
Dave Parker, of, Pit	2.25	2.00	.960	.979
Dave Winfield, of, SD	2.28	2.00	.986	.979

1980

American League

MVP

Player, Pos, Team	Stats	1st Pl	Pts	Share
George Brett, 3b, KC	.390-24-118	17.0	335.0	0.85
Reggie Jackson, of, NYA	.300-41-111	5.0	234.0	0.60
Goose Gossage, p, NYA	2.27, 33 saves	4.0	218.0	0.56
Willie Wilson, of, KC	.326-3-49	1.0	169.0	0.43
Cecil Cooper, 1b, Mil	.352-25-122	0.0	160.0	0.41
Eddie Murray, 1b, Bal	.300-32-116	0.0	106.0	0.27
Rick Cerone, c, NYA	.277-14-85	1.0	77.0	0.20
Dan Quisenberry, p, KC	3.09, 33 saves	0.0	76.5	0.19
Steve Stone, p, Bal	25-7, 3.23	0.0	53.0	0.14
Rickey Henderson, of, Oak	.303-9-53	0.0	51.0	0.13
Al Oliver, of, Tex	.319-19-117	0.0	31.5	0.08
Tony Armas, of, Oak	.279-35-109	0.0	29.0	0.07
Al Bumbry, of, Bal	.318-9-53	0.0	27.0	0.07
Ben Oglivie, of, Mil	.304-41-118	0.0	27.0	0.07
Willie Randolph, 2b, NYA	.294-7-46	0.0	10.0	0.03
Mike Norris, p, Oak	22-9, 2.53	0.0	10.0	0.03
Robin Yount, ss, Mil	.293-23-87	0.0	8.0	0.02
Mickey Rivers, of, Tex	.333-7-60	0.0	7.0	0.02
Buddy Bell, 3b, Tex	.329-17-83	0.0	7.0	0.02
Alan Trammell, ss, Det	.300-9-65	0.0	6.0	0.02
Ken Singleton, of, Bal	.304-24-104	0.0	4.0	0.01
Tony Perez, 1b, Bos	.275-25-105	0.0	2.0	0.01
Miguel Dilone, of, Cle	.341-0-40	0.0	2.0	0.01
Fred Lynn, of, Bos	.301-12-61	0.0	1.0	0.00
John Wathan, c, KC	.305-6-58	0.0	1.0	0.00

Cy Young

Pitcher, Team	Stats	1st Pl	Pts	Share
Steve Stone, Bal	25-7, 3.23	13.0	100.0	0.71
Mike Norris, Oak	22-9, 2.53	13.0	91.0	0.65
Goose Gossage, NYA	2.27, 33 saves	2.0	37.5	0.26
Tommy John, NYA	22-9, 3.43	0.0	14.0	0.10
Dan Quisenberry, KC	3.09, 33 saves	0.0	7.5	0.05
Larry Gura, KC	18-10, 2.95	0.0	1.0	0.01
Scott McGregor, Bal	20-8, 3.32	0.0	1.0	0.01

Rookie of the Year

Pitcher, Pos, Team	Stats	1st Pl	Pts	Share
Joe Charboneau, of, Cle	.289-23-87	15.0	102.0	0.73
Dave Stapleton, 2b, Bos	.321-7-45	3.0	40.0	0.29
Doug Corbett, p, Min	1.98, 23 saves	3.0	38.0	0.27
Damaso Garcia, 2b, Tor	.278-4-46	3.0	35.0	0.25
Britt Burns, p, ChA	15-13, 2.84	4.0	33.0	0.24
Ricky Peters, of, Det	.291-2-42	0.0	3.0	0.02
Rich Dotson, p, ChA	12-10, 4.27	0.0	1.0	0.01

Gold Gloves

Player, Pos, Team	Rng	LRng	FPct	LFPct
Mike Norris, p, Oak	—	—	.963	.957
Jim Sundberg, c, Tex	—	—	.993	.986
Cecil Cooper, 1b, Mil	—	—	.997	.992
Frank White, 2b, KC	5.51	4.91	.988	.981
Buddy Bell, 3b, Tex	3.39	2.59	.981	.951
Alan Trammell, ss, Det	4.42	4.26	.980	.963
Fred Lynn, of, Bos	2.85	2.15	.994	.979
Dwayne Murphy, of, Oak	3.29	2.15	.990	.979
Willie Wilson, of, KC	3.09	2.15	.988	.979

National League

MVP

Player, Pos, Team	Stats	1st Pl	Pts	Share
Mike Schmidt, 3b, Phi	.286-48-121	24.0	336.0	1.00
Gary Carter, c, Mon	.264-29-101	0.0	193.0	0.57
Jose Cruz, of, Hou	.302-11-91	0.0	166.0	0.49
Dusty Baker, of, LA	.294-29-97	0.0	138.0	0.41
Steve Carlton, p, Phi	24-9, 2.34	0.0	134.0	0.40
Steve Garvey, 1b, LA	.304-26-106	0.0	131.0	0.39
Andre Dawson, of, Mon	.308-17-87	0.0	72.0	0.21
George Hendrick, of, StL	.302-25-109	0.0	50.0	0.15
Bob Horner, 3b, Atl	.268-35-89	0.0	42.0	0.13
Bake McBride, of, Phi	.309-9-87	0.0	32.0	0.10
Keith Hernandez, 1b, StL	.321-16-99	0.0	29.0	0.09
Dale Murphy, of, Atl	.281-33-89	0.0	23.0	0.07
Cesar Cedeno, of, Hou	.309-10-73	0.0	14.0	0.04
Jim Bibby, p, Pit	19-6, 3.32	0.0	11.0	0.03
Bill Buckner, 1b, ChN	.324-10-68	0.0	11.0	0.03
Tug McGraw, p, Phi	1.46, 20 saves	0.0	10.0	0.03
Johnny Bench, c, Cin	.250-24-68	0.0	7.0	0.02
Jack Clark, of, SF	.284-22-82	0.0	6.0	0.02
Joe Niekro, p, Hou	20-12, 3.55	0.0	3.0	0.01
Mike Easler, of, Pit	.338-21-74	0.0	2.0	0.01
Jerry Reuss, p, LA	18-6, 2.51	0.0	2.0	0.01
Ken Griffey Sr., of, Cin	.294-13-85	0.0	1.0	0.00
Ron LeFlore, of, Mon	.257-4-39	0.0	1.0	0.00
Gene Richards, of, SD	.301-4-41	0.0	1.0	0.00
Rodney Scott, 2b, Mon	.224-0-46	0.0	1.0	0.00

Cy Young

Pitcher, Team	Stats	1st Pl	Pts	Share
Steve Carlton, Phi	24-9, 2.34	23.0	118.0	0.98
Jerry Reuss, LA	18-6, 2.51	1.0	55.0	0.46
Jim Bibby, Pit	19-6, 3.32	0.0	28.0	0.23
Joe Niekro, Hou	20-12, 3.55	0.0	11.0	0.09
Tug McGraw, Phi	1.46, 20 saves	0.0	1.0	0.01
Steve Rogers, Mon	16-11, 2.98	0.0	1.0	0.01
Joe Sambito, Hou	2.19, 17 saves	0.0	1.0	0.01
Mario Soto, Cin	3.07, 4 saves	0.0	1.0	0.01

Rookie of the Year

Pitcher, Pos, Team	Stats	1st Pl	Pts	Share
Steve Howe, p, LA	2.66, 17 saves	12.0	80.0	0.67
Bill Gullickson, p, Mon	10-5, 3.00	5.0	53.0	0.44
Lonnie Smith, of, Phi	.339-3-20	4.0	49.0	0.41
Ron Oester, 2b, Cin	.277-2-20	1.0	16.0	0.13
Dave Smith, p, Hou	1.93, 10 saves	2.0	13.0	0.11
Jeff Reardon, p, NYN	2.61, 6 saves	0.0	2.0	0.02
Al Holland, p, SF	1.75, 7 saves	0.0	1.0	0.01
Leon Durham, of, StL	.271-8-42	0.0	1.0	0.01
Bob Walk, p, Phi	11-7, 4.57	0.0	1.0	0.01

Gold Gloves

Player, Pos, Team	Rng	LRng	FPct	LFPct
Phil Niekro, p, Atl	—	—	.983	.952
Gary Carter, c, Mon	—	—	.993	.983
Keith Hernandez, 1b, StL	—	—	.995	.992
Doug Flynn, 2b, NYN	5.10	4.71	.991	.980
Mike Schmidt, 3b, Phi	3.15	2.39	.946	.948
Ozzie Smith, ss, SD	5.75	4.30	.974	.966
Andre Dawson, of, Mon	2.88	1.98	.986	.980
Garry Maddox, of, Phi	2.88	1.98	.976	.980
Dave Winfield, of, SD	1.84	1.98	.987	.980

1981

American League

MVP

Player, Pos, Team	Stats	1st Pl	Pts	Share
Rollie Fingers, p, Mil	1.04, 28 saves	15.0	319.0	0.81
Rickey Henderson, of, Oak	.319-6-35	12.0	308.0	0.79
Dwight Evans, of, Bos	.296-22-71	0.0	140.0	0.36
Tony Armas, of, Oak	.261-22-76	1.0	139.0	0.35
Eddie Murray, 1b, Bal	.294-22-78	0.0	137.0	0.35
Carney Lansford, 3b, Bos	.336-4-52	0.0	109.0	0.28
Dave Winfield, of, NYA	.294-13-68	0.0	98.0	0.25
Cecil Cooper, 1b, Mil	.320-12-60	0.0	96.0	0.24
Goose Gossage, p, NYA	0.77, 20 saves	0.0	62.0	0.16
Tom Paciorek, of, Sea	.326-14-66	0.0	46.0	0.12
Dwayne Murphy, of, Oak	.251-15-60	0.0	45.0	0.11

Kirk Gibson, of, Det	.328-9-40	0.0	40.0	0.10
Steve McCatty, p, Oak	14-7, 2.33	0.0	22.0	0.06
Bobby Grich, 2b, Cal	.304-22-61	0.0	19.0	0.05
Jack Morris, p, Det	14-7, 3.05	0.0	17.0	0.04
Al Oliver, dh, Tex	.309-4-55	0.0	8.0	0.02
Robin Yount, ss, Mil	.273-10-49	0.0	7.0	0.02
Buddy Bell, 3b, Tex	.294-10-64	0.0	7.0	0.02
Bill Almon, ss, ChA	.301-4-41	0.0	6.0	0.02
Jerry Mumphrey, of, NYA	.307-6-32	0.0	5.0	0.01
Mike Hargrove, 1b, Cle	.317-2-49	0.0	4.0	0.01
Alan Trammell, ss, Det	.258-2-31	0.0	4.0	0.01
Ken Singleton, of, Bal	.278-13-49	0.0	3.0	0.01
Steve Kemp, of, Det	.277-9-49	0.0	3.0	0.01
Dennis Martinez, p, Bal	14-5, 3.32	0.0	3.0	0.01
Greg Luzinski, dh, ChA	.265-21-62	0.0	3.0	0.01
Dave Stieb, p, Tor	11-10, 3.19	0.0	1.0	0.00
George Brett, 3b, KC	.314-6-43	0.0	1.0	0.00

Cy Young

Pitcher, Team	Stats	1st Pl	Pts	Share
Rollie Fingers, Mil	1.04, 28 saves	22.0	126.0	0.90
Steve McCatty, Oak	14-7, 2.33	6.0	84.5	0.60
Jack Morris, Det	14-7, 3.05	0.0	21.0	0.15
Pete Vuckovich, Mil	14-4, 3.55	0.0	8.5	0.06
Dennis Martinez, Bal	14-5, 3.32	0.0	3.5	0.02
Goose Gossage, NYA	0.77, 20 saves	0.0	3.0	0.02
Ron Guidry, NYA	11-5, 2.76	0.0	2.5	0.01
Britt Burns, ChA	10-6, 2.64	0.0	2.0	0.01
Larry Gura, KC	11-8, 2.72	0.0	1.0	0.01

Rookie of the Year

Pitcher, Pos, Team	Stats	1st Pl	Pts	Share
Dave Righetti, p, NYA	8-4, 2.05	23.0	127.0	0.91
Rich Gedman, c, Bos	.288-5-26	5.0	64.0	0.46
Bobby Ojeda, p, Bos	6-2, 3.12	0.0	36.0	0.26
Mike Jones, p, KC	6-3, 3.21	0.0	8.0	0.06
Dave Engle, of, Min	.258-5-32	0.0	4.5	0.03
Mike Witt, p, Cal	8-9, 3.28	0.0	4.0	0.03
Shooty Babitt, 2b, Oak	.256-0-14	0.0	4.0	0.03
George Bell, of, Tor	.233-5-12	0.0	2.0	0.01
Gary Ward, of, Min	.264-3-29	0.0	1.5	0.01
Brad Havens, p, Min	3-6, 3.58	0.0	1.0	0.01

Gold Gloves

Player, Pos, Team	Rng	LRng	FPct	LFPct
Mike Norris, p, Oak	—	—	.976	.963
Jim Sundberg, c, Tex	—	—	.996	.987
Mike Squires, 1b, ChA	—	—	.992	.993
Frank White, 2b, KC	5.26	4.93	.988	.982
Buddy Bell, 3b, Tex	3.61	2.52	.961	.950
Alan Trammell, ss, Det	5.03	4.19	.983	.967
Dwight Evans, of, Bos	2.48	2.16	.993	.983
Rickey Henderson, of, Oak	3.12	2.16	.979	.983
Dwayne Murphy, of, Oak	3.13	2.16	.985	.983

National League

MVP

Player, Pos, Team	Stats	1st Pl	Pts	Share
Mike Schmidt, 3b, Phi	.316-31-91	21.0	321.0	0.96
Andre Dawson, of, Mon	.302-24-64	2.0	215.0	0.64
George Foster, of, Cin	.295-22-90	0.0	146.0	0.43
Dave Concepcion, ss, Cin	.306-5-67	0.0	108.0	0.32
Fernando Valenzuela, p, LA	13-7, 2.48	1.0	90.0	0.27
Gary Carter, c, Mon	.251-16-68	0.0	77.0	0.23
Dusty Baker, of, LA	.320-9-49	0.0	65.0	0.19
Bruce Sutter, p, StL	2.62, 25 saves	0.0	59.0	0.18
Steve Carlton, p, Phi	13-4, 2.42	0.0	41.0	0.12
Tom Seaver, p, Cin	14-2, 2.54	0.0	35.0	0.10
Pete Rose, 1b, Phi	.325-0-33	0.0	35.0	0.10
Bill Buckner, 1b, ChN	.311-10-75	0.0	35.0	0.10
Gary Matthews, of, Phi	.301-9-67	0.0	31.0	0.09
Jose Cruz, of, Hou	.267-13-55	0.0	25.0	0.07
George Hendrick, of, StL	.284-18-61	0.0	25.0	0.07
Nolan Ryan, p, Hou	11-5, 1.69	0.0	23.0	0.07
Bill Madlock, 3b, Pit	.341-6-45	0.0	20.0	0.06
Art Howe, 3b, Hou	.296-3-36	0.0	16.0	0.05
Tim Raines, of, Mon	.304-5-37	0.0	15.0	0.04
Rick Camp, p, Atl	1.78, 17 saves	0.0	9.0	0.03
Keith Hernandez, 1b, StL	.306-8-48	0.0	9.0	0.03
Tom Herr, 2b, StL	.268-0-46	0.0	7.0	0.02
Greg Minton, p, SF	2.88, 21 saves	0.0	4.0	0.01
Warren Cromartie, 1b, Mon	.304-6-42	0.0	3.0	0.01
Steve Garvey, 1b, LA	.283-10-64	0.0	1.0	0.00
Milt May, c, SF	.310-2-33	0.0	1.0	0.00

Cy Young

Pitcher, Team	Stats	1st Pl	Pts	Share
Fernando Valenzuela, LA	13-7, 2.48	8.0	70.0	0.58
Tom Seaver, Cin	14-2, 2.54	8.0	67.0	0.56
Steve Carlton, Phi	13-4, 2.42	5.0	50.0	0.42
Nolan Ryan, Hou	11-5, 1.69	3.0	28.0	0.23
Bruce Sutter, StL	2.62, 25 saves	0.0	1.0	0.01

Rookie of the Year

Pitcher, Pos, Team	Stats	1st Pl	Pts	Share
Fernando Valenzuela, p, LA	13-7, 2.48	17.5	107.0	0.89
Tim Raines, of, Mon	.304-5-37	6.5	85.0	0.71
Hubie Brooks, 3b, NYN	.307-4-38	0.0	8.5	0.07
Bruce Berenyi, p, Cin	9-6, 3.50	0.0	5.0	0.04
Juan Bonilla, 2b, SD	.290-1-25	0.0	5.0	0.04
Tony Pena, c, Pit	.300-2-17	0.0	4.0	0.03
Mookie Wilson, of, NYN	.271-3-14	0.0	1.5	0.01

Gold Gloves

Player, Pos, Team	Rng	LRng	FPct	LFPct
Steve Carlton, p, Phi	—	—	1.000	.959
Gary Carter, c, Mon	—	—	.993	.983
Keith Hernandez, 1b, StL	—	—	.997	.992
Manny Trillo, 2b, Phi	5.65	4.72	.987	.982
Mike Schmidt, 3b, Phi	3.20	2.47	.956	.948
Ozzie Smith, ss, SD	5.84	4.44	.976	.960
Dusty Baker, of, LA	1.87	2.02	.990	.980
Andre Dawson, of, Mon	3.27	2.02	.980	.980
Garry Maddox, of, Phi	2.76	2.02	.977	.980

1982

American League

MVP

Player, Pos, Team	Stats	1st Pl	Pts	Share
Robin Yount, ss, Mil	.331-29-114	27.0	385.0	0.98
Eddie Murray, 1b, Bal	.316-32-110	0.0	228.0	0.58
Doug DeCinces, 3b, Cal	.301-30-97	0.0	178.0	0.45
Hal McRae, dh, KC	.308-27-133	0.0	175.0	0.45
Cecil Cooper, 1b, Mil	.313-32-121	0.0	152.0	0.39
Reggie Jackson, of, Cal	.275-39-101	1.0	107.0	0.27
Dwight Evans, of, Bos	.292-32-98	0.0	57.0	0.15
Gorman Thomas, of, Mil	.245-39-112	0.0	44.5	0.11
Dan Quisenberry, p, KC	2.57, 35 saves	0.0	39.0	0.10
Rickey Henderson, of, Oak	.267-10-51	0.0	38.0	0.10
Dave Winfield, of, NYA	.280-37-106	0.0	33.0	0.08
Paul Molitor, 3b, Mil	.302-19-71	0.0	29.5	0.07
Lance Parrish, c, Det	.284-32-87	0.0	26.0	0.07
Brian Downing, of, Cal	.281-28-84	0.0	22.0	0.06
Willie Wilson, of, KC	.332-3-46	0.0	16.0	0.04
Rollie Fingers, p, Mil	2.60, 29 saves	0.0	12.0	0.03
Bob Boone, c, Cal	.256-7-58	0.0	12.0	0.03
Pete Vuckovich, p, Mil	18-6, 3.34	0.0	11.0	0.03
Jim Rice, of, Bos	.309-24-97	0.0	10.0	0.03
Toby Harrah, 3b, Cle	.304-25-78	0.0	9.0	0.02
Harold Baines, of, ChA	.271-25-105	0.0	9.0	0.02
George Brett, 3b, KC	.301-21-82	0.0	9.0	0.02
Don Baylor, dh, Cal	.263-24-93	0.0	8.0	0.02
Andre Thornton, dh, Cle	.273-32-116	0.0	8.0	0.02
Bob Stanley, p, Bos	3.10, 14 saves	0.0	6.0	0.02
Jim Palmer, p, Bal	15-5, 3.13	0.0	5.0	0.01
Damaso Garcia, 2b, Tor	.310-5-42	0.0	5.0	0.01
Rod Carew, 1b, Cal	.319-3-44	0.0	5.0	0.01
Bill Caudill, p, Sea	2.35, 26 saves	0.0	4.0	0.01
Buddy Bell, 3b, Tex	.296-13-67	0.0	3.0	0.01
Cal Ripken Jr., ss, Bal	.264-28-93	0.0	3.0	0.01
Carney Lansford, 3b, Bos	.301-11-63	0.0	1.0	0.00
Rick Sutcliffe, p, Cle	14-8, 2.96	0.0	1.0	0.00
Gary Ward, of, Min	.289-28-91	0.0	1.0	0.00

Cy Young

Pitcher, Team	Stats	1st Pl	Pts	Share
Pete Vuckovich, Mil	18-6, 3.34	14.0	87.0	0.62
Jim Palmer, Bal	15-5, 3.13	4.0	59.0	0.42
Dan Quisenberry, KC	2.57, 35 saves	4.0	40.0	0.29
Dave Stieb, Tor	17-14, 3.25	5.0	36.0	0.26
Rick Sutcliffe, Cle	14-8, 2.96	1.0	14.0	0.10
Geoff Zahn, Cal	18-8, 3.73	0.0	7.0	0.05
Bob Stanley, Bos	3.10, 14 saves	0.0	4.0	0.03
Bill Caudill, Sea	2.35, 26 saves	0.0	4.0	0.03
Dan Petry, Det	15-9, 3.22	0.0	1.0	0.01

Rookie of the Year

Pitcher, Pos, Team	Stats	1st Pl	Pts	Share
Cal Ripken Jr., ss, Bal	.264-28-93	24.0	132.0	0.94
Kent Hrbek, 1b, Min	.301-23-92	4.0	90.0	0.64
Wade Boggs, 1b, Bos	.349-5-44	0.0	10.5	0.07
Ed Vande Berg, p, Sea	2.37, 5 saves	0.0	9.0	0.06
Gary Gaetti, 3b, Min	.230-25-84	0.0	4.0	0.03
Dave Hostetler, 1b, Tex	.232-22-67	0.0	3.0	0.02
Von Hayes, of, Cle	.250-14-82	0.0	2.0	0.01
Jesse Barfield, of, Tor	.246-18-58	0.0	1.5	0.01

Gold Gloves

Player, Pos, Team	Rng	LRng	FPct	LFPct
Ron Guidry, p, NYA	—	—	1.000	.958
Bob Boone, c, Cal	—	—	.989	.988
Eddie Murray, 1b, Bal	—	—	.997	.992
Frank White, 2b, KC	5.21	4.70	.978	.981
Buddy Bell, 3b, Tex	3.63	2.62	.976	.954
Robin Yount, ss, Mil	4.82	4.17	.969	.965
Dwight Evans, of, Bos	2.20	2.15	.973	.982
Dwayne Murphy, of, Oak	3.17	2.15	.983	.982
Dave Winfield, of, NYA	2.19	2.15	.974	.982

National League

MVP

Player, Pos, Team	Stats	1st Pl	Pts	Share
Dale Murphy, of, Atl	.281-36-109	14.0	283.0	0.84
Lonnie Smith, of, StL	.307-8-69	8.0	218.0	0.65
Pedro Guerrero, of, LA	.304-32-100	0.0	175.0	0.52
Al Oliver, 1b, Mon	.331-22-109	0.0	175.0	0.52
Bruce Sutter, p, StL	2.90, 36 saves	2.0	134.0	0.40
Mike Schmidt, 3b, Phi	.280-35-87	0.0	54.0	0.16
Jack Clark, of, SF	.274-27-103	0.0	53.0	0.16
Greg Minton, p, SF	1.83, 30 saves	0.0	44.0	0.13
Steve Carlton, p, Phi	23-11, 3.10	0.0	41.0	0.12
Bill Buckner, 1b, ChN	.306-15-105	0.0	38.0	0.11
Bill Madlock, 3b, Pit	.319-19-95	0.0	37.0	0.11
Gary Carter, c, Mon	.293-29-97	0.0	35.0	0.10
Ozzie Smith, ss, StL	.248-2-43	0.0	25.0	0.07
George Hendrick, of, StL	.282-19-104	0.0	20.0	0.06
Terry Kennedy, c, SD	.295-21-97	0.0	20.0	0.06
Joe Morgan, 2b, SF	.289-14-61	0.0	17.0	0.05
Keith Hernandez, 1b, StL	.299-7-94	0.0	12.0	0.04
Jason Thompson, 1b, Pit	.284-31-101	0.0	12.0	0.04
Gene Garber, p, Atl	2.34, 30 saves	0.0	6.0	0.02
Joaquin Andujar, p, StL	15-10, 2.47	0.0	6.0	0.02
Fernando Valenzuela, p, LA	19-13, 2.87	0.0	3.0	0.01
Andre Dawson, of, Mon	.301-23-83	0.0	3.0	0.01
Chris Chambliss, 1b, Atl	.270-20-86	0.0	2.0	0.01
Gary Matthews, of, Phi	.281-19-83	0.0	2.0	0.01
Ray Knight, 1b, Hou	.294-6-70	0.0	1.0	0.00

Cy Young

Pitcher, Team	Stats	1st Pl	Pts	Share
Steve Carlton, Phi	23-11, 3.10	20.0	112.0	0.93
Steve Rogers, Mon	19-8, 2.40	1.0	29.0	0.24
Fernando Valenzuela, LA	19-13, 2.87	1.0	25.5	0.21
Bruce Sutter, StL	2.90, 36 saves	2.0	25.0	0.21
Phil Niekro, Atl	17-4, 3.61	0.0	18.0	0.15
Greg Minton, SF	1.83, 30 saves	0.0	4.0	0.03
Joaquin Andujar, StL	15-10, 2.47	0.0	1.0	0.01
Gene Garber, Atl	2.34, 30 saves	0.0	1.0	0.01
Mario Soto, Cin	14-13, 2.79	0.0	0.5	0.00

Rookie of the Year

Pitcher, Pos, Team	Stats	1st Pl	Pts	Share
Steve Sax, 2b, LA	.282-4-47	9.0	63.0	0.53
Johnny Ray, 2b, Pit	.281-7-63	6.0	57.0	0.48
Willie McGee, of, StL	.296-4-56	5.0	39.0	0.33
Chili Davis, of, SF	.261-19-76	3.0	32.0	0.27
Luis DeLeon, p, SD	2.03, 15 saves	0.0	10.0	0.08
Ryne Sandberg, 3b, ChN	.271-7-54	1.0	9.0	0.08
Steve Bedrosian, p, Atl	2.42, 11 saves	0.0	4.0	0.03
Dave LaPoint, p, StL	3.42, 0 saves	0.0	1.0	0.01
Eric Show, p, SD	2.64, 3 saves	0.0	1.0	0.01

Gold Gloves

Player, Pos, Team	Rng	LRng	FPct	LFPct
Phil Niekro, p, Atl	—	—	.982	.952
Gary Carter, c, Mon	—	—	.991	.985
Keith Hernandez, 1b, StL	—	—	.994	.992
Manny Trillo, 2b, Phi	5.26	4.75	.994	.978
Mike Schmidt, 3b, Phi	2.93	2.43	.950	.951
Ozzie Smith, ss, StL	5.86	4.38	.984	.967

Andre Dawson, of, Mon	2.90	1.91	.982	.978
Garry Maddox, of, Phi	2.35	1.91	.992	.978
Dale Murphy, of, Atl	2.55	1.91	.979	.978

1983

American League

MVP

Player, Pos, Team	Stats	1st Pl	Pts	Share
Cal Ripken Jr., ss, Bal	.318-27-102	15.0	322.0	0.82
Eddie Murray, 1b, Bal	.306-33-111	10.0	290.0	0.74
Carlton Fisk, c, ChA	.289-26-86	3.0	209.0	0.53
Jim Rice, of, Bos	.305-39-126	0.0	150.0	0.38
Cecil Cooper, 1b, Mil	.307-30-126	0.0	123.0	0.31
Dan Quisenberry, p, KC	1.94, 45 saves	0.0	107.5	0.27
Dave Winfield, of, NYA	.283-32-116	0.0	85.0	0.22
Lou Whitaker, 2b, Det	.320-12-72	0.0	84.0	0.21
Lance Parrish, c, Det	.269-27-114	0.0	66.0	0.17
Harold Baines, of, ChA	.280-20-99	0.0	49.0	0.13
Willie Upshaw, 1b, Tor	.306-27-104	0.0	41.5	0.10
Wade Boggs, 3b, Bos	.361-5-74	0.0	25.0	0.06
LaMarr Hoyt, p, ChA	24-10, 3.66	0.0	24.5	0.06
Lloyd Moseby, of, Tor	.315-18-81	0.0	21.0	0.05
Bob Stanley, p, Bos	2.85, 33 saves	0.0	11.5	0.03
Alan Trammell, ss, Det	.319-14-66	0.0	11.0	0.03
Greg Luzinski, dh, ChA	.255-32-95	0.0	9.0	0.02
Robin Yount, ss, Mil	.308-17-80	0.0	6.0	0.02
Ted Simmons, c, Mil	.308-13-108	0.0	4.0	0.01
Rich Dotson, p, ChA	22-7, 3.23	0.0	3.5	0.01
Rudy Law, of, ChA	.283-3-34	0.0	2.0	0.01
Ron Guidry, p, NYA	21-9, 3.42	0.0	2.0	0.01
Jack Morris, p, Det	20-13, 3.34	0.0	2.0	0.01
Julio Cruz, 2b, Sea-ChA	.252-3-52	0.0	1.0	0.00
Rickey Henderson, of, Oak	.292-9-48	0.0	1.0	0.00
George Wright, of, Tex	.276-18-80	0.0	1.0	0.00
Tippy Martinez, p, Bal	2.35, 21 saves	0.0	0.5	0.00

Cy Young

Pitcher, Team	Stats	1st Pl	Pts	Share
LaMarr Hoyt, ChA	24-10, 3.66	17.0	116.0	0.83
Dan Quisenberry, KC	1.94, 45 saves	9.0	81.0	0.58
Jack Morris, Det	20-13, 3.34	2.0	38.0	0.27
Rich Dotson, ChA	22-7, 3.23	0.0	9.0	0.06
Ron Guidry, NYA	21-9, 3.42	0.0	5.0	0.04
Scott McGregor, Bal	18-7, 3.18	0.0	3.0	0.02

Rookie of the Year

Pitcher, Pos, Team	Stats	1st Pl	Pts	Share
Ron Kittle, of, ChA	.254-35-100	15.0	104.0	0.74
Julio Franco, ss, Cle	.273-8-80	8.0	78.0	0.56
Mike Boddicker, p, Bal	16-8, 2.77	5.0	70.0	0.50

Manager of the Year

Manager, Team	Stats	1st Pl	Pts	Share
Tony La Russa, ChA	99-63, 1st W	17.0	17.0	0.61
Joe Altobelli, Bal	98-64, 1st E	7.0	7.0	0.25
Bobby Cox, Tor	89-73, 4th E	4.0	4.0	0.14

Gold Gloves

Player, Pos, Team	Rng	LRng	FPct	LFPct
Ron Guidry, p, NYA	—	—	1.000	.958
Lance Parrish, c, Det	—	—	.995	.986
Eddie Murray, 1b, Bal	—	—	.993	.992
Lou Whitaker, 2b, Det	4.66	4.77	.983	.981
Buddy Bell, 3b, Tex	3.29	2.57	.967	.955
Alan Trammell, ss, Det	4.31	4.15	.979	.963
Dwight Evans, of, Bos	2.30	2.16	.987	.981
Dwayne Murphy, of, Oak	3.00	2.16	.979	.981
Dave Winfield, of, NYA	2.11	2.16	.978	.981

National League

MVP

Player, Pos, Team	Stats	1st Pl	Pts	Share
Dale Murphy, of, Atl	.302-36-121	21.0	318.0	0.95
Andre Dawson, of, Mon	.299-32-113	1.0	213.0	0.63
Mike Schmidt, 3b, Phi	.255-40-109	1.0	191.0	0.57
Pedro Guerrero, 3b, LA	.298-32-103	1.0	182.0	0.54
Tim Raines, of, Mon	.298-11-71	0.0	83.0	0.25
Jose Cruz, of, Hou	.318-14-92	0.0	76.0	0.23
Dickie Thon, ss, Hou	.286-20-79	0.0	67.0	0.20
Bill Madlock, 3b, Pit	.323-12-68	0.0	45.0	0.13
Al Holland, p, Phi	2.26, 25 saves	0.0	42.0	0.13
Terry Kennedy, c, SD	.284-17-98	0.0	37.0	0.11
George Hendrick, 1b, StL	.318-18-97	0.0	33.0	0.10
Tony Pena, c, Pit	.301-15-70	0.0	25.0	0.07
John Denny, p, Phi	19-6, 2.37	0.0	24.0	0.07
Mario Soto, p, Cin	17-13, 2.70	0.0	16.0	0.05
Darrell Evans, 1b, SF	.277-30-82	0.0	16.0	0.05
Rafael Ramirez, ss, Atl	.297-7-58	0.0	15.0	0.04
Jesse Orosco, p, NYN	1.47, 17 saves	0.0	14.0	0.04
Lee Smith, p, ChN	1.65, 29 saves	0.0	8.5	0.02
Al Oliver, 1b, Mon	.300-8-84	0.0	3.0	0.01
Jeffrey Leonard, of, SF	.279-21-87	0.0	2.0	0.01
Lonnie Smith, of, StL	.321-8-45	0.0	1.5	0.00
Jody Davis, c, ChN	.271-24-84	0.0	1.0	0.00
Keith Hernandez, 1b, StL-NYN	.297-12-63	0.0	1.0	0.00
Bob Horner, 3b, Atl	.303-20-68	0.0	1.0	0.00
Ozzie Smith, ss, StL	.243-3-50	0.0	1.0	0.00

Cy Young

Pitcher, Team	Stats	1st Pl	Pts	Share
John Denny, Phi	19-6, 2.37	20.0	103.0	0.86
Mario Soto, Cin	17-13, 2.70	2.0	61.0	0.51
Jesse Orosco, NYN	1.47, 17 saves	1.0	19.0	0.16
Steve Rogers, Mon	17-12, 3.23	1.0	15.0	0.13
Larry McWilliams, Pit	15-8, 3.25	0.0	7.0	0.06
Al Holland, Phi	2.26, 25 saves	0.0	4.0	0.03
Craig McMurtry, Atl	15-9, 3.08	0.0	3.0	0.03
Bob Welch, LA	15-12, 2.65	0.0	2.0	0.02
Nolan Ryan, Hou	14-9, 2.98	0.0	1.0	0.01
Lee Smith, ChN	1.65, 29 saves	0.0	1.0	0.01

Rookie of the Year

Pitcher, Pos, Team	Stats	1st Pl	Pts	Share
Darryl Strawberry, of, NYN	.257-26-74	18.0	106.0	0.88
Craig McMurtry, p, Atl	15-9, 3.08	6.0	49.0	0.41
Mel Hall, of, ChN	.283-17-56	0.0	32.0	0.27
Gary Redus, of, Cin	.247-17-51	0.0	8.0	0.07
Bill Doran, 2b, Hou	.271-8-39	0.0	7.0	0.06
Frank DiPino, p, Hou	2.65, 20 saves	0.0	6.0	0.05
Greg Brock, 1b, LA	.224-20-66	0.0	3.0	0.03
Jose DeLeon, p, Pit	7-3, 2.83	0.0	3.0	0.03
Mark Thurmond, p, SD	7-3, 2.65	0.0	1.0	0.01
Lee Tunnell, p, Pit	11-6, 3.65	0.0	1.0	0.01

Manager of the Year

Manager, Team	Stats	1st Pl	Pts	Share
Tom Lasorda, LA	91-71, 1st W	10.0	10.0	0.42
Bob Lillis, Hou	85-77, 3rd W	9.0	9.0	0.38
Chuck Tanner, Pit	84-78, 2nd E	4.0	4.0	0.17
Paul Owens, Phi	47-30, 1st E	1.0	1.0	0.04

Gold Gloves

Player, Pos, Team	Rng	LRng	FPct	LFPct
Phil Niekro, p, Atl	—	—	.955	.952
Tony Pena, c, Pit	—	—	.992	.984
Keith Hernandez, 1b, StL-NYN	—	—	.992	.992
Ryne Sandberg, 2b, ChN	5.74	4.46	.986	.978
Mike Schmidt, 3b, Phi	2.87	2.29	.959	.949
Ozzie Smith, ss, StL	5.21	4.16	.975	.967
Andre Dawson, of, Mon	2.81	1.92	.980	.980
Willie McGee, of, StL	2.70	1.92	.987	.980
Dale Murphy, of, Atl	2.39	1.92	.985	.980

1984

American League

MVP

Player, Pos, Team	Stats	1st Pl	Pts	Share
Willie Hernandez, p, Det	1.92, 32 saves	16.0	306.0	0.78
Kent Hrbek, 1b, Min	.311-27-107	5.0	247.0	0.63
Dan Quisenberry, p, KC	2.64, 44 saves	5.0	235.0	0.60
Eddie Murray, 1b, Bal	.306-29-110	2.0	197.0	0.50
Don Mattingly, 1b, NYA	.343-23-110	0.0	113.0	0.29
Kirk Gibson, of, Det	.282-27-91	0.0	96.0	0.24
Tony Armas, of, Bos	.268-43-123	0.0	87.5	0.22
Dave Winfield, of, NYA	.340-19-100	0.0	83.0	0.21
Alan Trammell, ss, Det	.314-14-69	0.0	76.5	0.19
Willie Wilson, of, KC	.301-2-44	0.0	61.0	0.16
Dwight Evans, of, Bos	.295-32-104	0.0	39.0	0.10
Alvin Davis, 1b, Sea	.284-27-116	0.0	26.0	0.07
Jim Rice, of, Bos	.280-28-122	0.0	10.0	0.03
Harold Baines, of, ChA	.304-29-94	0.0	10.0	0.03
Dave Kingman, dh, Oak	.268-35-118	0.0	10.0	0.03
Lance Parrish, c, Det	.237-33-98	0.0	8.0	0.02
Willie Upshaw, 1b, Tor	.278-19-84	0.0	8.0	0.02
Brian Downing, of, Cal	.275-23-91	0.0	6.0	0.02
Steve Balboni, 1b, KC	.244-28-77	0.0	5.0	0.01
George Bell, of, Tor	.292-26-87	0.0	5.0	0.01
Andre Thornton, dh, Cle	.271-33-99	0.0	5.0	0.01
Buddy Bell, 3b, Tex	.315-11-83	0.0	4.0	0.01
Dave Stieb, p, Tor	16-8, 2.83	0.0	4.0	0.01
Lloyd Moseby, of, Tor	.280-18-92	0.0	4.0	0.01
Juan Beniquez, of, Cal	.336-8-39	0.0	2.0	0.01
Mike Boddicker, p, Bal	20-11, 2.79	0.0	2.0	0.01
Doyle Alexander, p, Tor	17-6, 3.13	0.0	1.0	0.00
Cal Ripken Jr., ss, Bal	.304-27-86	0.0	1.0	0.00

Cy Young

Pitcher, Team	Stats	1st Pl	Pts	Share
Willie Hernandez, Det	1.92, 32 saves	12.0	88.0	0.63
Dan Quisenberry, KC	2.64, 44 saves	9.0	71.0	0.51
Bert Blyleven, Cle	19-7, 2.87	4.0	45.0	0.32
Mike Boddicker, Bal	20-11, 2.79	3.0	41.0	0.29
Dan Petry, Det	18-8, 3.24	0.0	3.0	0.02
Frank Viola, Min	18-12, 3.21	0.0	2.0	0.01
Jack Morris, Det	19-11, 3.60	0.0	1.0	0.01
Dave Stieb, Tor	16-8, 2.83	0.0	1.0	0.01

Rookie of the Year

Pitcher, Pos, Team	Stats	1st Pl	Pts	Share
Alvin Davis, 1b, Sea	.284-27-116	25.0	134.0	0.96
Mark Langston, p, Sea	17-10, 3.40	3.0	82.0	0.59
Kirby Puckett, of, Min	.296-0-31	0.0	23.0	0.16
Tim Teufel, 2b, Min	.262-14-61	0.0	5.0	0.04
Mike Young, of, Bal	.252-17-52	0.0	3.0	0.02
Roger Clemens, p, Bos	9-4, 4.32	0.0	2.0	0.01
Mark Gubicza, p, KC	10-14, 4.05	0.0	1.0	0.01
Al Nipper, p, Bos	11-6, 3.89	0.0	1.0	0.01
Ron Romanick, p, Cal	12-12, 3.76	0.0	1.0	0.01

Manager of the Year

Manager, Team	Stats	1st Pl	Pts	Share
Sparky Anderson, Det	104-58, 1st E	13.0	96.0	0.69
Dick Howser, KC	84-78, 1st W	11.0	95.0	0.68
Billy Gardner, Min	81-81, 2nd W	4.0	48.0	0.34
Bobby Cox, Tor	89-73, 2nd E	0.0	9.0	0.06
John McNamara, Cal	81-81, 2nd W	0.0	4.0	0.03

Gold Gloves

Player, Pos, Team	Rng	LRng	FPct	LFPct
Ron Guidry, p, NYA	—	—	1.000	.958
Lance Parrish, c, Det	—	—	.991	.987
Eddie Murray, 1b, Bal	—	—	.992	.991
Lou Whitaker, 2b, Det	4.89	4.45	.979	.980
Buddy Bell, 3b, Tex	3.07	2.19	.958	.950
Alan Trammell, ss, Det	4.33	3.93	.980	.962
Dwight Evans, of, Bos	1.98	2.17	.994	.983
Dwayne Murphy, of, Oak	3.19	2.17	.988	.983
Dave Winfield, of, NYA	2.21	2.17	.994	.983

National League

MVP

Player, Pos, Team	Stats	1st Pl	Pts	Share
Ryne Sandberg, 2b, ChN	.314-19-84	22.0	326.0	0.97
Keith Hernandez, 1b, NYN	.311-15-94	1.0	195.0	0.58
Tony Gwynn, of, SD	.351-5-71	1.0	184.0	0.55
Rick Sutcliffe, p, ChN	16-1, 2.69	0.0	151.0	0.45
Gary Matthews, of, ChN	.291-14-82	0.0	70.0	0.21
Bruce Sutter, p, StL	1.54, 45 saves	0.0	67.0	0.20
Mike Schmidt, 3b, Phi	.277-36-106	0.0	55.5	0.16
Jose Cruz, of, Hou	.312-12-95	0.0	53.0	0.16
Dale Murphy, of, Atl	.290-36-100	0.0	52.5	0.15
Jody Davis, c, ChN	.256-19-94	0.0	49.0	0.15
Tim Raines, of, Mon	.309-8-60	0.0	41.0	0.12
Leon Durham, 1b, ChN	.279-23-96	0.0	38.0	0.11
Goose Gossage, p, SD	2.90, 25 saves	0.0	34.0	0.10
Gary Carter, c, Mon	.294-27-106	0.0	32.0	0.10
Dwight Gooden, p, NYN	17-9, 2.60	0.0	28.0	0.08
Alan Wiggins, 2b, SD	.258-3-34	0.0	14.0	0.04
Ron Cey, 3b, ChN	.240-25-97	0.0	6.0	0.02
Kevin McReynolds, of, SD	.278-20-75	0.0	6.0	0.02
Bob Dernier, of, ChN	.278-3-32	0.0	6.0	0.02
Steve Garvey, 1b, SD	.284-8-86	0.0	5.0	0.01
Bob Brenly, c, SF	.291-20-80	0.0	1.0	0.00

Juan Samuel, 2b, Phi	.272-15-69	0.0	1.0	0.00
Jeffrey Leonard, of, SF	.302-21-86	0.0	1.0	0.00

Cy Young

Pitcher, Team	Stats	1st Pl	Pts	Share
Rick Sutcliffe, ChN	16-1, 2.69	24.0	120.0	1.00
Dwight Gooden, NYN	17-9, 2.60	0.0	45.0	0.38
Bruce Sutter, StL	1.54, 45 saves	0.0	33.5	0.28
Joaquin Andujar, StL	20-14, 3.34	0.0	12.5	0.10
Goose Gossage, SD	2.90, 25 saves	0.0	3.0	0.03
Mario Soto, Cin	18-7, 3.53	0.0	2.0	0.02

Rookie of the Year

Pitcher, Pos, Team	Stats	1st Pl	Pts	Share
Dwight Gooden, p, NYN	17-9, 2.60	23.0	118.0	0.98
Juan Samuel, 2b, Phi	.272-15-69	1.0	67.0	0.56
Orel Hershiser, p, LA	2.66, 2 saves	0.0	15.0	0.13
Dan Gladden, of, SF	.351-4-31	0.0	9.0	0.08
Ron Darling, p, NYN	12-9, 3.81	0.0	3.0	0.03
Carmelo Martinez, of, SD	.250-13-66	0.0	2.0	0.02
Jeff Stone, of, Phi	.362-1-15	0.0	1.0	0.01
Terry Pendleton, 3b, StL	.324-1-33	0.0	1.0	0.01

Manager of the Year

Manager, Team	Stats	1st Pl	Pts	Share
Jim Frey, ChN	96-65, 1st E	16.0	101.0	0.84
Davey Johnson, NYN	90-72, 2nd E	4.0	72.0	0.60
Dick Williams, SD	92-70, 1st W	4.0	41.0	0.34
Bob Lillis, Hou	80-82, 2nd W	0.0	2.0	0.02

Gold Gloves

Player, Pos, Team	Rng	LRng	FPct	LFPct
Joaquin Andujar, p, StL	—	—	.958	.954
Tony Pena, c, Pit	—	—	.991	.986
Keith Hernandez, 1b, NYN	—	—	.994	.992
Ryne Sandberg, 2b, ChN	5.54	4.71	.993	.979
Mike Schmidt, 3b, Phi	2.86	2.36	.941	.943
Ozzie Smith, ss, StL	5.40	3.98	.982	.965
Andre Dawson, of, Mon	2.30	1.91	.975	.979
Bob Dernier, of, ChN	2.57	1.91	.986	.979
Dale Murphy, of, Atl	2.37	1.91	.987	.979

1985

American League

MVP

Player, Pos, Team	Stats	1st Pl	Pts	Share
Don Mattingly, 1b, NYA	.324-35-145	23.0	367.0	0.94
George Brett, 3b, KC	.335-30-112	5.0	274.0	0.70
Rickey Henderson, of, NYA	.314-24-72	0.0	174.0	0.44
Wade Boggs, 3b, Bos	.368-8-78	0.0	159.0	0.41
Eddie Murray, 1b, Bal	.297-31-124	0.0	130.0	0.33
Donnie Moore, p, Cal	1.92, 31 saves	0.0	96.0	0.24
Jesse Barfield, of, Tor	.289-27-84	0.0	88.0	0.22
George Bell, of, Tor	.275-28-95	0.0	84.0	0.21
Harold Baines, of, ChA	.309-22-113	0.0	49.0	0.13
Bret Saberhagen, p, KC	20-6, 2.87	0.0	45.0	0.11
Dan Quisenberry, p, KC	2.37, 37 saves	0.0	39.0	0.10
Dave Winfield, of, NYA	.275-26-114	0.0	35.0	0.09
Carlton Fisk, c, ChA	.238-37-107	0.0	29.0	0.07
Darrell Evans, 1b, Det	.248-40-94	0.0	17.0	0.04
Ron Guidry, p, NYA	22-6, 3.27	0.0	15.0	0.04
Phil Bradley, of, Sea	.300-26-88	0.0	12.0	0.03
Cal Ripken Jr., ss, Bal	.282-26-110	0.0	9.0	0.02
Kirk Gibson, of, Det	.287-29-97	0.0	7.0	0.02
Steve Balboni, 1b, KC	.243-36-88	0.0	6.0	0.02
Tom Henke, p, Tor	2.03, 13 saves	0.0	5.0	0.01
Dennis Lamp, p, Tor	3.32, 2 saves	0.0	3.0	0.01
Kirby Puckett, of, Min	.288-4-74	0.0	3.0	0.01
Doyle Alexander, p, Tor	17-10, 3.45	0.0	3.0	0.01
Damaso Garcia, 2b, Tor	.282-8-65	0.0	2.0	0.01
Rich Gedman, c, Bos	.295-18-80	0.0	1.0	0.00

Cy Young

Pitcher, Team	Stats	1st Pl	Pts	Share
Bret Saberhagen, KC	20-6, 2.87	23.0	127.0	0.91
Ron Guidry, NYA	22-6, 3.27	4.0	88.0	0.63
Dan Quisenberry, KC	2.37, 37 saves	0.0	9.0	0.06
Bert Blyleven, Cle-Min	17-16, 3.16	1.0	9.0	0.06
Charlie Leibrandt, KC	17-9, 2.69	0.0	7.0	0.05
Doyle Alexander, Tor	17-10, 3.45	0.0	5.0	0.04
Britt Burns, ChA	18-11, 3.96	0.0	2.0	0.01
Dave Stieb, Tor	14-13, 2.48	0.0	2.0	0.01
Donnie Moore, Cal	1.92, 31 saves	0.0	2.0	0.01
Mike Moore, Sea	17-10, 3.46	0.0	1.0	0.01

Rookie of the Year

Pitcher, Pos, Team	Stats	1st Pl	Pts	Share
Ozzie Guillen, ss, ChA	.273-1-33	16.0	101.0	0.72
Teddy Higuera, p, Mil	15-8, 3.90	9.0	67.0	0.48
Ernest Riles, ss, Mil	.286-5-45	0.0	29.0	0.21
Oddibe McDowell, of, Tex	.239-18-42	1.0	25.0	0.18
Stew Cliburn, p, Cal	2.09, 6 saves	1.0	16.0	0.11
Brian Fisher, p, NYA	2.38, 14 saves	0.0	7.0	0.05
Tom Henke, p, Tor	2.03, 13 saves	1.0	5.0	0.04
Mark Salas, c, Min	.300-9-41	0.0	2.0	0.01

Manager of the Year

Manager, Team	Stats	1st Pl	Pts	Share
Bobby Cox, Tor	99-62, 1st E	16.0	104.0	0.74
Dick Howser, KC	91-71, 1st W	4.0	66.0	0.47
Gene Mauch, Cal	90-72, 2nd W	8.0	57.0	0.41
Billy Martin, NYA	91-54, 2nd E	0.0	19.0	0.14
Jackie Moore, Oak	77-85, 4th W	0.0	4.0	0.03
Tony La Russa, ChA	85-77, 3rd W	0.0	1.0	0.01
John McNamara, Bos	81-81, 5th E	0.0	1.0	0.01

Gold Gloves

Player, Pos, Team	Rng	LRng	FPct	LFPct
Ron Guidry, p, NYA	—	—	.976	.953
Lance Parrish, c, Det	—	—	.993	.987
Don Mattingly, 1b, NYA	—	—	.995	.991
Lou Whitaker, 2b, Det	4.85	4.48	.985	.982
George Brett, 3b, KC	2.93	2.38	.967	.953
Alfredo Griffin, ss, Oak	4.43	3.93	.960	.964
Dwight Evans, of, Bos	1.97	2.10	.990	.982
Dwayne Murphy, of, Oak	2.92	2.10	.989	.982
Gary Pettis, of, Cal	3.12	2.10	.990	.982
Dave Winfield, of, NYA	2.16	2.10	.991	.982

National League

MVP

Player, Pos, Team	Stats	1st Pl	Pts	Share
Willie McGee, of, StL	.353-10-82	14.0	280.0	0.83
Dave Parker, of, Cin	.312-34-125	6.0	220.0	0.65
Pedro Guerrero, of, LA	.320-33-87	3.0	208.0	0.62
Dwight Gooden, p, NYN	24-4, 1.53	1.0	162.0	0.48
Tom Herr, 2b, StL	.302-8-110	0.0	119.0	0.35
Gary Carter, c, NYN	.281-32-100	0.0	116.0	0.35
Dale Murphy, of, Atl	.300-37-111	0.0	63.0	0.19
Keith Hernandez, 1b, NYN	.309-10-91	0.0	61.0	0.18
John Tudor, p, StL	21-8, 1.93	0.0	61.0	0.18
Jack Clark, 1b, StL	.281-22-87	0.0	20.0	0.06
Vince Coleman, of, StL	.267-1-40	0.0	16.0	0.05
Tim Raines, of, Mon	.320-11-41	0.0	15.0	0.04
Ryne Sandberg, 2b, ChN	.305-26-83	0.0	14.0	0.04
Mike Marshall, of, LA	.293-28-95	0.0	11.0	0.03
Hubie Brooks, ss, Mon	.269-13-100	0.0	11.0	0.03
Orel Hershiser, p, LA	19-3, 2.03	0.0	9.0	0.03
Keith Moreland, of, ChN	.307-14-106	0.0	8.0	0.02
Ozzie Smith, ss, StL	.276-6-54	0.0	5.0	0.01
Mike Scioscia, c, LA	.296-7-53	0.0	5.0	0.01
Jeff Reardon, p, Mon	3.18, 41 saves	0.0	4.0	0.01
Jose Cruz, of, Hou	.300-9-79	0.0	2.0	0.01
Bill Doran, 2b, Hou	.287-14-59	0.0	2.0	0.01
Mariano Duncan, ss, LA	.244-6-39	0.0	1.0	0.00
Tony Gwynn, of, SD	.317-6-46	0.0	1.0	0.00
Fernando Valenzuela, p, LA	17-10, 2.45	0.0	1.0	0.00
Glenn Wilson, of, Phi	.275-14-102	0.0	1.0	0.00

Cy Young

Pitcher, Team	Stats	1st Pl	Pts	Share
Dwight Gooden, NYN	24-4, 1.53	24.0	120.0	1.00
John Tudor, StL	21-8, 1.93	0.0	65.0	0.54
Orel Hershiser, LA	19-3, 2.03	0.0	17.0	0.14
Joaquin Andujar, StL	21-12, 3.40	0.0	6.0	0.05
Fernando Valenzuela, LA	17-10, 2.45	0.0	4.0	0.03
Tom Browning, Cin	20-9, 3.55	0.0	3.0	0.03
Jeff Reardon, Mon	3.18, 41 saves	0.0	1.0	0.01

Rookie of the Year

Pitcher, Pos, Team	Stats	1st Pl	Pts	Share
Vince Coleman, of, StL	.267-1-40	24.0	120.0	1.00
Tom Browning, p, Cin	20-9, 3.55	0.0	72.0	0.60
Mariano Duncan, ss, LA	.244-6-39	0.0	9.0	0.08
Chris Brown, 3b, SF	.271-16-61	0.0	7.0	0.06
Glenn Davis, 1b, Hou	.271-20-64	0.0	3.0	0.03
Roger McDowell, p, NYN	2.83, 17 saves	0.0	2.0	0.02
Joe Orsulak, of, Pit	.300-0-21	0.0	2.0	0.02
Joe Hesketh, p, Mon	10-5, 2.49	0.0	1.0	0.01

Manager of the Year

Manager, Team	Stats	1st Pl	Pts	Share
Whitey Herzog, StL	101-61, 1st E	11.0	86.0	0.72
Pete Rose, Cin	89-72, 2nd W	10.0	85.0	0.71
Tom Lasorda, LA	95-67, 1st W	3.0	39.0	0.33
Davey Johnson, NYN	98-64, 2nd E	0.0	4.0	0.03
Buck Rodgers, Mon	84-77, 3rd E	0.0	2.0	0.02

Gold Gloves

Player, Pos, Team	Rng	LRng	FPct	LFPct
Rick Reuschel, p, Pit	—	—	1.000	.953
Tony Pena, c, Pit	—	—	.988	.987
Keith Hernandez, 1b, NYN	—	—	.997	.993
Ryne Sandberg, 2b, ChN	5.58	4.82	.986	.982
Tim Wallach, 3b, Mon	3.45	2.47	.967	.948
Ozzie Smith, ss, StL	5.15	4.26	.983	.963
Andre Dawson, of, Mon	1.96	1.88	.973	.979
Willie McGee, of, StL	2.64	1.88	.978	.979
Dale Murphy, of, Atl	2.12	1.88	.980	.979

1986

American League

MVP

Player, Pos, Team	Stats	1st Pl	Pts	Share
Roger Clemens, p, Bos	24-4, 2.48	19.0	339.0	0.86
Don Mattingly, 1b, NYA	.352-31-113	5.0	258.0	0.66
Jim Rice, of, Bos	.324-20-110	4.0	241.0	0.61
George Bell, of, Tor	.309-31-108	0.0	125.0	0.32
Jesse Barfield, of, Tor	.289-40-108	0.0	107.0	0.27
Kirby Puckett, of, Min	.328-31-96	0.0	105.0	0.27
Wade Boggs, 3b, Bos	.357-8-71	0.0	87.0	0.22
Wally Joyner, 1b, Cal	.290-22-100	0.0	74.0	0.19
Joe Carter, of, Cle	.302-29-121	0.0	72.0	0.18
Dave Righetti, p, NYA	2.45, 46 saves	0.0	71.0	0.18
Doug DeCinces, 3b, Cal	.256-26-96	0.0	56.0	0.14
Mike Witt, p, Cal	18-10, 2.84	0.0	34.0	0.09
Don Baylor, dh, Bos	.238-31-94	0.0	32.0	0.08
Tony Fernandez, ss, Tor	.310-10-65	0.0	17.0	0.04
Teddy Higuera, p, Mil	20-11, 2.79	0.0	7.0	0.02
Gary Gaetti, 3b, Min	.287-34-108	0.0	6.0	0.02
Pete O'Brien, 1b, Tex	.290-23-90	0.0	5.0	0.01
Scott Fletcher, ss, Tex	.300-3-50	0.0	5.0	0.01
Marty Barrett, 2b, Bos	.286-4-60	0.0	5.0	0.01
Jose Canseco, of, Oak	.240-33-117	0.0	3.0	0.01
Jim Presley, 3b, Sea	.265-27-107	0.0	2.0	0.01
Dick Schofield, ss, Cal	.249-13-57	0.0	1.0	0.00

Cy Young

Pitcher, Team	Stats	1st Pl	Pts	Share
Roger Clemens, Bos	24-4, 2.48	28.0	140.0	1.00
Teddy Higuera, Mil	20-11, 2.79	0.0	42.0	0.30
Mike Witt, Cal	18-10, 2.84	0.0	35.0	0.25
Dave Righetti, NYA	2.45, 46 saves	0.0	20.0	0.14
Jack Morris, Det	21-8, 3.27	0.0	13.0	0.09
Mark Eichhorn, Tor	1.72, 10 saves	0.0	2.0	0.01

Rookie of the Year

Pitcher, Pos, Team	Stats	1st Pl	Pts	Share
Jose Canseco, of, Oak	.240-33-117	16.0	110.0	0.79
Wally Joyner, 1b, Cal	.290-22-100	12.0	98.0	0.70
Mark Eichhorn, p, Tor	1.72, 10 saves	0.0	23.0	0.16
Cory Snyder, of, Cle	.272-24-69	0.0	16.0	0.11
Danny Tartabull, of, Sea	.270-25-96	0.0	4.0	0.03
Ruben Sierra, of, Tex	.264-16-55	0.0	1.0	0.01

Manager of the Year

Manager, Team	Stats	1st Pl	Pts	Share
John McNamara, Bos	95-66, 1st E	13.0	95.0	0.68
Bobby Valentine, Tex	87-75, 2nd W	12.0	90.0	0.64

Gene Mauch, Cal	92-70, 1st W	2.0	44.0	0.31
Pat Corrales, Cle	84-78, 5th E	1.0	18.0	0.13
Lou Piniella, NYA	90-72, 2nd E	0.0	5.0	0.04

Gold Gloves

Player, Pos, Team	Rng	LRng	FPct	LFPct
Ron Guidry, p, NYA	—	—	.968	.957
Bob Boone, c, Cal	—	—	.988	.989
Don Mattingly, 1b, NYA	—	—	.996	.991
Frank White, 2b, KC	5.00	4.34	.987	.981
Gary Gaetti, 3b, Min	2.90	2.37	.956	.948
Tony Fernandez, ss, Tor	4.53	3.94	.983	.967
Jesse Barfield, of, Tor	2.47	2.06	.992	.980
Gary Pettis, of, Cal	3.08	2.06	.985	.980
Kirby Puckett, of, Min	2.73	2.06	.986	.980

National League

MVP

Player, Pos, Team	Stats	1st Pl	Pts	Share
Mike Schmidt, 3b, Phi	.290-37-119	15.0	287.0	0.85
Glenn Davis, 1b, Hou	.265-31-101	6.0	231.0	0.69
Gary Carter, c, NYN	.255-24-105	1.0	181.0	0.54
Keith Hernandez, 1b, NYN	.310-13-83	2.0	179.0	0.53
Dave Parker, of, Cin	.273-31-116	0.0	144.0	0.43
Tim Raines, of, Mon	.334-9-62	0.0	99.0	0.29
Kevin Bass, of, Hou	.311-20-79	0.0	73.0	0.22
Von Hayes, 1b, Phi	.305-19-98	0.0	41.0	0.12
Tony Gwynn, of, SD	.329-14-59	0.0	34.0	0.10
Mike Scott, p, Hou	18-10, 2.22	0.0	33.0	0.10
Bill Doran, 2b, Hou	.276-6-37	0.0	32.0	0.10
Eric Davis, of, Cin	.277-27-71	0.0	21.0	0.06
Steve Sax, 2b, LA	.332-6-56	0.0	13.0	0.04
Ray Knight, 3b, NYN	.298-11-76	0.0	9.0	0.03
Mike Krukow, p, SF	20-9, 3.05	0.0	8.0	0.02
Todd Worrell, p, StL	2.08, 36 saves	0.0	7.0	0.02
Roger McDowell, p, NYN	3.02, 22 saves	0.0	5.0	0.01
Dave Smith, p, Hou	2.73, 33 saves	0.0	5.0	0.01
Fernando Valenzuela, p, LA	21-11, 3.14	0.0	4.0	0.01
Lenny Dykstra, of, NYN	.295-8-45	0.0	4.0	0.01
Bobby Ojeda, p, NYN	18-5, 2.57	0.0	2.0	0.01
Dale Murphy, of, Atl	.265-29-83	0.0	2.0	0.01
Candy Maldonado, of, SF	.252-18-85	0.0	2.0	0.01

Cy Young

Pitcher, Team	Stats	1st Pl	Pts	Share
Mike Scott, Hou	18-10, 2.22	15.0	98.0	0.82
Fernando Valenzuela, LA	21-11, 3.14	9.0	88.0	0.73
Mike Krukow, SF	20-9, 3.05	0.0	15.0	0.13
Bobby Ojeda, NYN	18-5, 2.57	0.0	9.0	0.08
Ron Darling, NYN	15-6, 2.81	0.0	2.0	0.02
Rick Rhoden, Pit	15-12, 2.84	0.0	2.0	0.02
Dwight Gooden, NYN	17-6, 2.84	0.0	1.0	0.01
Sid Fernandez, NYN	16-6, 3.52	0.0	1.0	0.01

Rookie of the Year

Pitcher, Pos, Team	Stats	1st Pl	Pts	Share
Todd Worrell, p, StL	2.08, 36 saves	23.0	118.0	0.98
Robby Thompson, 2b, SF	.271-7-47	0.0	46.0	0.38
Kevin Mitchell, of, NYN	.277-12-43	1.0	22.0	0.18
Charlie Kerfeld, p, Hou	2.59, 7 saves	0.0	17.0	0.14
Will Clark, 1b, SF	.287-11-41	0.0	5.0	0.04
Barry Bonds, of, Pit	.223-16-48	0.0	4.0	0.03
Jim Deshaies, p, Hou	12-5, 3.25	0.0	1.0	0.01
Barry Larkin, ss, Cin	.283-3-19	0.0	1.0	0.01
Bruce Ruffin, p, Phi	9-4, 2.46	0.0	1.0	0.01
John Kruk, of, SD	.309-4-38	0.0	1.0	0.01

Manager of the Year

Manager, Team	Stats	1st Pl	Pts	Share
Hal Lanier, Hou	96-66, 1st W	19.0	108.0	0.90
Davey Johnson, NYN	108-54, 1st E	3.0	62.0	0.52
Roger Craig, SF	83-79, 3rd W	2.0	42.0	0.35
John Felske, Phi	86-75, 2nd E	0.0	3.0	0.03
Jim Leyland, Pit	64-98, 6th E	0.0	1.0	0.01

Gold Gloves

Player, Pos, Team	Rng	LRng	FPct	LFPct
Fernando Valenzuela, p, LA	—	—	.987	.955
Jody Davis, c, ChN	—	—	.992	.985
Keith Hernandez, 1b, NYN	—	—	.996	.992
Ryne Sandberg, 2b, ChN	5.24	4.54	.994	.980
Mike Schmidt, 3b, Phi	2.40	2.20	.980	.946
Ozzie Smith, ss, StL	4.74	3.96	.978	.963
Tony Gwynn, of, SD	2.23	1.82	.989	.979
Willie McGee, of, StL	2.76	1.82	.991	.979
Dale Murphy, of, Atl	1.94	1.82	.981	.979

1987

American League

MVP

Player, Pos, Team	Stats	1st Pl	Pts	Share
George Bell, of, Tor	.308-47-134	16.0	332.0	0.85
Alan Trammell, ss, Det	.343-28-105	12.0	311.0	0.79
Kirby Puckett, of, Min	.332-28-99	0.0	201.0	0.51
Dwight Evans, 1b, Bos	.305-34-123	0.0	127.0	0.32
Paul Molitor, dh, Mil	.353-16-75	0.0	125.0	0.32
Mark McGwire, 1b, Oak	.289-49-118	0.0	109.0	0.28
Don Mattingly, 1b, NYA	.327-30-115	0.0	92.0	0.23
Tony Fernandez, ss, Tor	.322-5-67	0.0	79.0	0.20
Wade Boggs, 3b, Bos	.363-24-89	0.0	64.0	0.16
Gary Gaetti, 3b, Min	.257-31-109	0.0	47.0	0.12
Jeff Reardon, p, Min	4.48, 31 saves	0.0	37.0	0.09
Darrell Evans, 1b, Det	.257-34-99	0.0	21.0	0.05
Doyle Alexander, p, Det	9-0, 1.53	0.0	17.0	0.04
Tom Henke, p, Tor	2.49, 34 saves	0.0	17.0	0.04
Wally Joyner, 1b, Cal	.285-34-117	0.0	17.0	0.04
Kent Hrbek, 1b, Min	.285-34-90	0.0	11.0	0.03
Danny Tartabull, of, KC	.309-34-101	0.0	10.0	0.03
Robin Yount, of, Mil	.312-21-103	0.0	8.0	0.02
Roger Clemens, p, Bos	20-9, 2.97	0.0	7.0	0.02
Jack Morris, p, Det	18-11, 3.38	0.0	5.0	0.01
Kevin Seitzer, 3b, KC	.323-15-83	0.0	5.0	0.01
Ruben Sierra, of, Tex	.263-30-109	0.0	5.0	0.01
Jose Canseco, of, Oak	.257-31-113	0.0	4.0	0.01
Matt Nokes, c, Det	.289-32-87	0.0	1.0	0.00

Cy Young

Pitcher, Team	Stats	1st Pl	Pts	Share
Roger Clemens, Bos	20-9, 2.97	21.0	124.0	0.89
Jimmy Key, Tor	17-8, 2.76	4.0	64.0	0.46
Dave Stewart, Oak	20-13, 3.68	2.0	32.0	0.23
Doyle Alexander, Det	9-0, 1.53	1.0	8.0	0.06
Mark Langston, Sea	19-13, 3.84	0.0	7.0	0.05
Teddy Higuera, Mil	18-10, 3.85	0.0	5.0	0.04
Frank Viola, Min	17-10, 2.90	0.0	5.0	0.04
Jeff Reardon, Min	4.48, 31 saves	0.0	4.0	0.03
Jack Morris, Det	18-11, 3.38	0.0	3.0	0.02

Rookie of the Year

Pitcher, Pos, Team	Stats	1st Pl	Pts	Share
Mark McGwire, 1b, Oak	.289-49-118	28.0	140.0	1.00
Kevin Seitzer, 3b, KC	.323-15-83	0.0	64.0	0.46
Matt Nokes, c, Det	.289-32-87	0.0	32.0	0.23
Mike Greenwell, of, Bos	.328-19-89	0.0	9.0	0.06
Devon White, of, Cal	.263-24-87	0.0	5.0	0.04
Mike Henneman, p, Det	2.98, 7 saves	0.0	1.0	0.01
Nelson Liriano, 2b, Tor	.241-2-10	0.0	1.0	0.01

Manager of the Year

Manager, Team	Stats	1st Pl	Pts	Share
Sparky Anderson, Det	98-64, 1st E	11.0	90.0	0.64
Tom Trebelhorn, Mil	91-71, 3rd E	7.0	78.0	0.56
Tom Kelly, Min	85-77, 1st W	10.0	74.0	0.53
Tony La Russa, Oak	81-81, 3rd W	0.0	8.0	0.06
Doc Edwards, Cle	30-45, 7th E	0.0	1.0	0.01
Lou Piniella, NYA	89-73, 4th E	0.0	1.0	0.01

Gold Gloves

Player, Pos, Team	Rng	LRng	FPct	LFPct
Mark Langston, p, Sea	—	—	.961	.955
Bob Boone, c, Cal	—	—	.983	.988
Don Mattingly, 1b, NYA	—	—	.996	.992
Frank White, 2b, KC	5.12	4.48	.987	.980
Gary Gaetti, 3b, Min	2.63	2.31	.973	.952
Tony Fernandez, ss, Tor	4.56	4.02	.979	.970
Jesse Barfield, of, Tor	2.27	2.00	.992	.980
Kirby Puckett, of, Min	2.37	2.00	.986	.980
Dave Winfield, of, NYA	1.79	2.00	.989	.980

National League

MVP

Player, Pos, Team	Stats	1st Pl	Pts	Share
Andre Dawson, of, ChN	.287-49-137	11.0	269.0	0.80
Ozzie Smith, ss, StL	.303-0-75	9.0	193.0	0.57
Jack Clark, 1b, StL	.286-35-106	3.0	186.0	0.55
Tim Wallach, 3b, Mon	.298-26-123	1.0	165.0	0.49
Will Clark, 1b, SF	.308-35-91	0.0	128.0	0.38
Darryl Strawberry, of, NYN	.284-39-104	0.0	95.0	0.28
Tim Raines, of, Mon	.330-18-68	0.0	80.0	0.24
Tony Gwynn, of, SD	.370-7-54	0.0	75.0	0.22
Eric Davis, of, Cin	.293-37-100	0.0	73.0	0.22
Howard Johnson, 3b, NYN	.265-36-99	0.0	42.0	0.13
Dale Murphy, of, Atl	.295-44-105	0.0	34.0	0.10
Vince Coleman, of, StL	.289-3-43	0.0	20.0	0.06
Juan Samuel, 2b, Phi	.272-28-100	0.0	19.0	0.06
Mike Schmidt, 3b, Phi	.293-35-113	0.0	13.0	0.04
Pedro Guerrero, of, LA	.338-27-89	0.0	12.0	0.04
Steve Bedrosian, p, Phi	2.83, 40 saves	0.0	6.0	0.02
Milt Thompson, of, Phi	.302-7-43	0.0	4.0	0.01
Bill Doran, 2b, Hou	.283-16-79	0.0	1.0	0.00
Terry Pendleton, 3b, StL	.286-12-96	0.0	1.0	0.00

Cy Young

Pitcher, Team	Stats	1st Pl	Pts	Share
Steve Bedrosian, Phi	2.83, 40 saves	9.0	57.0	0.48
Rick Sutcliffe, ChN	18-10, 3.68	4.0	55.0	0.46
Rick Reuschel, Pit-SF	13-9, 3.09	8.0	54.0	0.45
Orel Hershiser, LA	16-16, 3.06	2.0	14.0	0.12
Nolan Ryan, Hou	8-16, 2.76	0.0	12.0	0.10
Dwight Gooden, NYN	15-7, 3.21	1.0	12.0	0.10
Mike Scott, Hou	16-13, 3.23	0.0	9.0	0.08
Bob Welch, LA	15-9, 3.22	0.0	3.0	0.03

Rookie of the Year

Pitcher, Pos, Team	Stats	1st Pl	Pts	Share
Benito Santiago, c, SD	.300-18-79	24.0	120.0	1.00
Mike Dunne, p, Pit	13-6, 3.03	0.0	66.0	0.55
Joe Magrane, p, StL	9-7, 3.54	0.0	10.0	0.08
Casey Candaele, 2b, Mon	.272-1-23	0.0	9.0	0.08
Gerald Young, of, Hou	.321-1-15	0.0	7.0	0.06
Chris James, of, Phi	.293-17-54	0.0	1.0	0.01
Les Lancaster, p, ChN	8-3, 4.90	0.0	1.0	0.01
Greg Mathews, p, StL	11-11, 3.73	0.0	1.0	0.01
Randy Myers, p, NYN	3.96, 6 saves	0.0	1.0	0.01

Manager of the Year

Manager, Team	Stats	1st Pl	Pts	Share
Buck Rodgers, Mon	91-71, 3rd E	13.0	92.0	0.77
Roger Craig, SF	90-72, 1st W	6.0	65.0	0.54
Whitey Herzog, StL	95-67, 1st E	5.0	54.0	0.45
Davey Johnson, NYN	92-70, 2nd E	0.0	3.0	0.03
Jim Leyland, Pit	80-82, 4th E	0.0	2.0	0.02

Gold Gloves

Player, Pos, Team	Rng	LRng	FPct	LFPct
Rick Reuschel, p, Pit-SF	—	—	.969	.955
Mike LaValliere, c, Pit	—	—	.992	.987
Keith Hernandez, 1b, NYN	—	—	.993	.991
Ryne Sandberg, 2b, ChN	5.11	4.44	.985	.982
Terry Pendleton, 3b, StL	3.08	2.34	.949	.951
Ozzie Smith, ss, StL	4.82	3.89	.987	.965
Eric Davis, of, Cin	3.05	1.83	.990	.981
Andre Dawson, of, ChN	1.86	1.83	.986	.981
Tony Gwynn, of, SD	1.99	1.83	.981	.981

1988

American League

MVP

Player, Pos, Team	Stats	1st Pl	Pts	Share
Jose Canseco, of, Oak	.307-42-124	28.0	392.0	1.00
Mike Greenwell, of, Bos	.325-22-119	0.0	242.0	0.62
Kirby Puckett, of, Min	.356-24-121	0.0	219.0	0.56
Dave Winfield, of, NYA	.322-25-107	0.0	164.0	0.42
Dennis Eckersley, p, Oak	2.35, 45 saves	0.0	156.0	0.40
Wade Boggs, 3b, Bos	.366-5-58	0.0	107.0	0.27
Alan Trammell, ss, Det	.311-15-69	0.0	62.0	0.16
Paul Molitor, 3b, Mil	.312-13-60	0.0	50.0	0.13
Dwight Evans, of, Bos	.293-21-111	0.0	49.0	0.13

Frank Viola, p, Min	24-7, 2.64	0.0	39.0	0.10
Robin Yount, of, Mil	.306-13-91	0.0	34.0	0.09
George Brett, 1b, KC	.306-24-103	0.0	29.0	0.07
Dave Henderson, of, Oak	.304-24-94	0.0	28.0	0.07
Bruce Hurst, p, Bos	18-6, 3.66	0.0	15.0	0.04
Doug Jones, p, Cle	2.27, 37 saves	0.0	11.0	0.03
Jeff Reardon, p, Min	2.47, 42 saves	0.0	11.0	0.03
Fred McGriff, 1b, Tor	.282-34-82	0.0	9.0	0.02
Rickey Henderson, of, NYA	.305-6-50	0.0	8.0	0.02
Mark McGwire, 1b, Oak	.260-32-99	0.0	6.0	0.02
Joe Carter, of, Cle	.271-27-98	0.0	5.0	0.01
Lee Smith, p, Bos	2.80, 29 saves	0.0	4.0	0.01
Gary Gaetti, 3b, Min	.301-28-88	0.0	3.0	0.01
Dan Plesac, p, Mil	2.41, 30 saves	0.0	3.0	0.01
Dave Stewart, p, Oak	21-12, 3.23	0.0	3.0	0.01
Julio Franco, 2b, Cle	.303-10-54	0.0	2.0	0.01
Tony Fernandez, ss, Tor	.287-5-70	0.0	1.0	0.00

Cy Young

Pitcher, Team	Stats	1st Pl	Pts	Share
Frank Viola, Min	24-7, 2.64	27.0	138.0	0.99
Dennis Eckersley, Oak	2.35, 45 saves	1.0	52.0	0.37
Mark Gubicza, KC	20-8, 2.70	0.0	26.0	0.19
Dave Stewart, Oak	21-12, 3.23	0.0	16.0	0.11
Bruce Hurst, Bos	18-6, 3.66	0.0	12.0	0.09
Roger Clemens, Bos	18-12, 2.93	0.0	8.0	0.06

Rookie of the Year

Pitcher, Pos, Team	Stats	1st Pl	Pts	Share
Walt Weiss, ss, Oak	.250-3-39	17.0	103.0	0.74
Bryan Harvey, p, Cal	2.13, 17 saves	3.0	49.0	0.35
Jody Reed, ss, Bos	.293-1-28	6.0	48.0	0.34
Don August, p, Mil	13-7, 3.09	0.0	22.0	0.16
Dave Gallagher, of, ChA	.303-5-31	2.0	18.0	0.13
Melido Perez, p, ChA	12-10, 3.79	0.0	9.0	0.06
Mike Schooler, p, Sea	3.54, 15 saves	0.0	2.0	0.01
Cecil Espy, of, Tex	.248-2-39	0.0	1.0	0.01

Manager of the Year

Manager, Team	Stats	1st Pl	Pts	Share
Tony La Russa, Oak	104-58, 1st W	15.0	103.0	0.74
Joe Morgan, Bos	46-31, 1st E	9.0	89.0	0.64
Sparky Anderson, Det	88-74, 2nd E	3.0	37.0	0.26
Tom Trebelhorn, Mil	87-75, 3rd E	1.0	15.0	0.11
Tom Kelly, Min	91-71, 2nd W	0.0	6.0	0.04
Jim Fregosi, ChA	71-90, 5th W	0.0	1.0	0.01
Lou Piniella, NYA	45-48, 5th E	0.0	1.0	0.01

Gold Gloves

Player, Pos, Team	Rng	LRng	FPct	LFPct
Mark Langston, p, Sea	—	—	.933	.961
Bob Boone, c, Cal	—	—	.986	.989
Don Mattingly, 1b, NYA	—	—	.993	.992
Harold Reynolds, 2b, Sea	4.90	4.40	.977	.982
Gary Gaetti, 3b, Min	2.56	2.36	.977	.954
Tony Fernandez, ss, Tor	4.66	4.14	.981	.971
Gary Pettis, of, Det	2.90	2.14	.987	.979
Kirby Puckett, of, Min	2.92	2.14	.994	.979
Devon White, of, Cal	3.20	2.14	.976	.979

National League

MVP

Player, Pos, Team	Stats	1st Pl	Pts	Share
Kirk Gibson, of, LA	.290-25-76	13.0	272.0	0.81
Darryl Strawberry, of, NYN	.269-39-101	7.0	236.0	0.70
Kevin McReynolds, of, NYN	.288-27-99	4.0	162.0	0.48
Andy Van Slyke, of, Pit	.288-25-100	0.0	160.0	0.48
Will Clark, 1b, SF	.282-29-109	0.0	135.0	0.40
Orel Hershiser, p, LA	23-8, 2.26	0.0	111.0	0.33
Andres Galarraga, 1b, Mon	.302-29-92	0.0	105.0	0.31
Glenn Davis, 1b, Hou	.271-30-99	0.0	72.0	0.21
Danny Jackson, p, Cin	23-8, 2.73	0.0	41.0	0.12
David Cone, p, NYN	20-3, 2.22	0.0	37.0	0.11
Tony Gwynn, of, SD	.313-7-70	0.0	29.0	0.09
John Franco, p, Cin	1.57, 39 saves	0.0	23.0	0.07
Eric Davis, of, Cin	.273-26-93	0.0	14.0	0.04
Bobby Bonilla, 3b, Pit	.274-24-100	0.0	7.0	0.02
Andre Dawson, of, ChN	.303-24-79	0.0	6.0	0.02
Randy Myers, p, NYN	1.72, 26 saves	0.0	3.0	0.01
Brett Butler, of, SF	.287-6-43	0.0	2.0	0.01
Steve Sax, 2b, LA	.277-5-57	0.0	1.0	0.00

Cy Young

Pitcher, Team	Stats	1st Pl	Pts	Share
Orel Hershiser, LA	23-8, 2.26	24.0	120.0	1.00
Danny Jackson, Cin	23-8, 2.73	0.0	54.0	0.45
David Cone, NYN	20-3, 2.22	0.0	42.0	0.35

Rookie of the Year

Pitcher, Pos, Team	Stats	1st Pl	Pts	Share
Chris Sabo, 3b, Cin	.271-11-44	11.0	79.0	0.66
Mark Grace, 1b, ChN	.296-7-57	7.0	61.0	0.51
Tim Belcher, p, LA	12-6, 2.91	3.0	35.0	0.29
Ron Gant, 2b, Atl	.259-19-60	1.0	22.0	0.18
Roberto Alomar, 2b, SD	.266-9-41	2.0	11.0	0.09
Damon Berryhill, c, ChN	.259-7-38	0.0	3.0	0.03
Gregg Jefferies, 3b, NYN	.321-6-17	0.0	3.0	0.03
Ricky Jordan, 1b, Phi	.308-11-43	0.0	2.0	0.02

Manager of the Year

Manager, Team	Stats	1st Pl	Pts	Share
Tom Lasorda, LA	94-67, 1st W	19.0	101.0	0.84
Jim Leyland, Pit	85-75, 2nd E	1.0	50.0	0.42
Davey Johnson, NYN	100-60, 1st E	2.0	38.0	0.32
Jack McKeon, SD	67-48, 3rd W	2.0	27.0	0.23

Gold Gloves

Player, Pos, Team	Rng	LRng	FPct	LFPct
Orel Hershiser, p, LA	—	—	.939	.955
Benito Santiago, c, SD	—	—	.985	.987
Keith Hernandez, 1b, NYN	—	—	.998	.991
Ryne Sandberg, 2b, ChN	5.31	4.58	.987	.980
Tim Wallach, 3b, Mon	2.95	2.35	.962	.947
Ozzie Smith, ss, StL	5.02	3.99	.972	.967
Eric Davis, of, Cin	2.32	1.98	.981	.982
Andre Dawson, of, ChN	1.86	1.98	.989	.982
Andy Van Slyke, of, Pit	2.75	1.98	.991	.982

1989

American League

MVP

Player, Pos, Team	Stats	1st Pl	Pts	Share
Robin Yount, of, Mil	.318-21-103	8.0	256.0	0.65
Ruben Sierra, of, Tex	.306-29-119	6.0	228.0	0.58
Cal Ripken Jr., ss, Bal	.257-21-93	6.0	216.0	0.55
George Bell, of, Tor	.297-18-104	4.0	205.0	0.52
Dennis Eckersley, p, Oak	1.56, 33 saves	3.0	116.0	0.30
Fred McGriff, 1b, Tor	.269-36-92	0.0	96.0	0.24
Kirby Puckett, of, Min	.339-9-85	0.0	84.0	0.21
Bret Saberhagen, p, KC	23-6, 2.16	0.0	82.0	0.21
Rickey Henderson, of, NYA-Oak	.274-12-57	0.0	67.0	0.17
Bo Jackson, of, KC	.256-32-105	0.0	46.0	0.12
Dave Parker, dh, Oak	.264-22-97	0.0	44.0	0.11
Gregg Olson, p, Bal	1.69, 27 saves	0.0	35.0	0.09
Bert Blyleven, p, Cal	17-5, 2.73	0.0	32.0	0.08
Dave Stewart, p, Oak	21-9, 3.32	0.0	30.0	0.08
Don Mattingly, 1b, NYA	.303-23-113	0.0	25.0	0.06
Joe Carter, of, Cle	.243-35-105	0.0	23.0	0.06
Carney Lansford, 3b, Oak	.336-2-52	1.0	20.0	0.05
Nick Esasky, 1b, Bos	.277-30-108	0.0	19.0	0.05
Tony Fernandez, ss, Tor	.257-11-64	0.0	9.0	0.02
Mike Moore, p, Oak	19-11, 2.61	0.0	6.0	0.02
Wade Boggs, 3b, Bos	.330-3-54	0.0	3.0	0.01
Steve Sax, 2b, NYA	.315-5-63	0.0	3.0	0.01
Alvin Davis, 1b, Sea	.305-21-95	0.0	2.0	0.01
Nolan Ryan, p, Tex	16-10, 3.20	0.0	2.0	0.01
Chili Davis, of, Cal	.271-22-90	0.0	1.0	0.00
Mark McGwire, 1b, Oak	.231-33-95	0.0	1.0	0.00
Mookie Wilson, of, Tor	.298-2-17	0.0	1.0	0.00

Cy Young

Pitcher, Team	Stats	1st Pl	Pts	Share
Bret Saberhagen, KC	23-6, 2.16	27.0	138.0	0.99
Dave Stewart, Oak	21-9, 3.32	1.0	80.0	0.57
Mike Moore, Oak	19-11, 2.61	0.0	10.0	0.07
Bert Blyleven, Cal	17-5, 2.73	0.0	9.0	0.06
Nolan Ryan, Tex	16-10, 3.20	0.0	5.0	0.04
Jeff Ballard, Bal	18-8, 3.43	0.0	3.0	0.02
Dennis Eckersley, Oak	1.56, 33 saves	0.0	3.0	0.02
Gregg Olson, Bal	1.69, 27 saves	0.0	3.0	0.02
Jeff Russell, Tex	1.98, 38 saves	0.0	1.0	0.01

Rookie of the Year

Pitcher, Pos, Team	Stats	1st Pl	Pts	Share
Gregg Olson, p, Bal	1.69, 27 saves	26.0	136.0	0.97
Tom Gordon, p, KC	3.64, 1 saves	1.0	67.0	0.48
Ken Griffey Jr., of, Sea	.264-16-61	1.0	21.0	0.15
Craig Worthington, 3b, Bal	.247-15-70	0.0	16.0	0.11
Jim Abbott, p, Cal	12-12, 3.92	0.0	10.0	0.07
Kevin Brown, p, Tex	12-9, 3.35	0.0	2.0	0.01

Manager of the Year

Manager, Team	Stats	1st Pl	Pts	Share
Frank Robinson, Bal	87-75, 2nd E	23.0	125.0	0.89
Cito Gaston, Tor	77-49, 1st E	3.0	62.0	0.44
Tony La Russa, Oak	99-63, 1st W	2.0	51.0	0.36
Doug Rader, Cal	91-71, 3rd W	0.0	13.0	0.09
John Wathan, KC	92-70, 2nd W	0.0	1.0	0.01

Gold Gloves

Player, Pos, Team	Rng	LRng	FPct	LFPct
Bret Saberhagen, p, KC	—	—	.934	.960
Bob Boone, c, KC	—	—	.991	.989
Don Mattingly, 1b, NYA	—	—	.995	.993
Harold Reynolds, 2b, Sea	5.41	4.51	.980	.981
Gary Gaetti, 3b, Min	2.84	2.34	.973	.943
Tony Fernandez, ss, Tor	5.25	4.11	.992	.971
Gary Pettis, of, Det	2.74	2.12	.988	.980
Kirby Puckett, of, Min	2.87	2.12	.991	.980
Devon White, of, Cal	2.86	2.12	.989	.980

National League

MVP

Player, Pos, Team	Stats	1st Pl	Pts	Share
Kevin Mitchell, of, SF	.291-47-125	20.0	314.0	0.93
Will Clark, 1b, SF	.333-23-111	3.0	225.0	0.67
Pedro Guerrero, 1b, StL	.311-17-117	1.0	190.0	0.57
Ryne Sandberg, 2b, ChN	.290-30-76	0.0	157.0	0.47
Howard Johnson, 3b, NYN	.287-36-101	0.0	153.0	0.46
Mark Davis, p, SD	1.85, 44 saves	0.0	76.0	0.23
Glenn Davis, 1b, Hou	.269-34-89	0.0	64.0	0.19
Tony Gwynn, of, SD	.336-4-62	0.0	57.0	0.17
Eric Davis, of, Cin	.281-34-101	0.0	44.0	0.13
Mitch Williams, p, ChN	2.64, 36 saves	0.0	41.0	0.12
Lonnie Smith, of, Atl	.315-21-79	0.0	34.0	0.10
Jack Clark, 1b, SD	.242-26-94	0.0	16.0	0.05
Jerome Walton, of, ChN	.293-5-46	0.0	14.0	0.04
Mark Grace, 1b, ChN	.314-13-79	0.0	9.0	0.03
Mike Scott, p, Hou	20-10, 3.10	0.0	6.0	0.02
Bobby Bonilla, 3b, Pit	.281-24-86	0.0	5.0	0.01
Brett Butler, of, SF	.283-4-36	0.0	3.0	0.01
Tim Raines, of, Mon	.286-9-60	0.0	3.0	0.01
Milt Thompson, of, StL	.290-4-68	0.0	3.0	0.01
Scott Garrelts, p, SF	14-5, 2.28	0.0	2.0	0.01

Cy Young

Pitcher, Team	Stats	1st Pl	Pts	Share
Mark Davis, SD	1.85, 44 saves	19.0	107.0	0.89
Mike Scott, Hou	20-10, 3.10	4.0	65.0	0.54
Greg Maddux, ChN	19-12, 2.95	0.0	17.0	0.14
Joe Magrane, StL	18-9, 2.91	0.0	7.0	0.06
Orel Hershiser, LA	15-15, 2.31	1.0	7.0	0.06
Tim Belcher, LA	15-12, 2.82	0.0	4.0	0.03
Scott Garrelts, SF	14-5, 2.28	0.0	4.0	0.03
Rick Reuschel, SF	17-8, 2.94	0.0	3.0	0.03
Mike Bielecki, ChN	18-7, 3.14	0.0	1.0	0.01
Mitch Williams, ChN	2.64, 36 saves	0.0	1.0	0.01

Rookie of the Year

Pitcher, Pos, Team	Stats	1st Pl	Pts	Share
Jerome Walton, of, ChN	.293-5-46	22.0	116.0	0.97
Dwight Smith, of, ChN	.324-9-52	2.0	68.0	0.57
Gregg Jefferies, 2b, NYN	.258-12-56	0.0	18.0	0.15
Derek Lilliquist, p, Atl	8-10, 3.97	0.0	6.0	0.05
Andy Benes, p, SD	6-3, 3.51	0.0	3.0	0.03
Charlie Hayes, 3b, SF-Phi	.257-8-43	0.0	3.0	0.03
Greg Harris, p, SD	2.60, 6 saves	0.0	2.0	0.02

Manager of the Year

Manager, Team	Stats	1st Pl	Pts	Share
Don Zimmer, ChN	93-69, 1st E	23.0	118.0	0.98
Roger Craig, SF	92-70, 1st W	1.0	62.0	0.52
Whitey Herzog, StL	86-76, 3rd E	0.0	31.0	0.26
Art Howe, Hou	86-76, 3rd W	0.0	4.0	0.03
Jack McKeon, SD	89-73, 2nd W	0.0	1.0	0.01

Gold Gloves

Player, Pos, Team	Rng	LRng	FPct	LFPct
Ron Darling, p, NYN	—	—	.929	.947
Benito Santiago, c, SD	—	—	.975	.986
Andres Galarraga, 1b, Mon	—	—	.992	.992
Ryne Sandberg, 2b, ChN	4.90	4.43	.992	.981
Terry Pendleton, 3b, StL	3.14	2.25	.971	.943
Ozzie Smith, ss, StL	4.52	3.88	.976	.966
Eric Davis, of, Cin	2.40	1.96	.984	.981
Tony Gwynn, of, SD	2.33	1.96	.984	.981
Andy Van Slyke, of, Pit	2.82	1.96	.989	.981

1990

American League

MVP

Player, Pos, Team	Stats	1st Pl	Pts	Share
Rickey Henderson, of, Oak	.325-28-61	14.0	317.0	0.81
Cecil Fielder, 1b, Det	.277-51-132	10.0	286.0	0.73
Roger Clemens, p, Bos	21-6, 1.93	3.0	212.0	0.54
Kelly Gruber, 3b, Tor	.274-31-118	0.0	175.0	0.45
Bobby Thigpen, p, ChA	1.83, 57 saves	0.0	170.0	0.43
Dennis Eckersley, p, Oak	0.61, 48 saves	1.0	112.0	0.29
George Brett, 1b, KC	.329-14-87	0.0	60.0	0.15
Dave Stewart, p, Oak	22-11, 2.56	0.0	56.0	0.14
Bob Welch, p, Oak	27-6, 2.95	0.0	54.0	0.14
Fred McGriff, 1b, Tor	.300-35-88	0.0	30.0	0.08
Mark McGwire, 1b, Oak	.235-39-108	0.0	29.0	0.07
Jose Canseco, of, Oak	.274-37-101	0.0	26.0	0.07
Ellis Burks, of, Bos	.296-21-89	0.0	25.0	0.06
Rafael Palmeiro, 1b, Tex	.319-14-89	0.0	22.0	0.06
Carlton Fisk, c, ChA	.285-18-65	0.0	16.0	0.04
Dave Parker, dh, Mil	.289-21-92	0.0	11.0	0.03
Ozzie Guillen, ss, ChA	.279-1-58	0.0	10.0	0.03
Jody Reed, 2b, Bos	.289-5-51	0.0	9.0	0.02
Alan Trammell, ss, Det	.304-14-89	0.0	7.0	0.02
Ken Griffey Jr., of, Sea	.300-22-80	0.0	7.0	0.02
Tony Pena, c, Bos	.263-7-56	0.0	6.0	0.02
Wade Boggs, 3b, Bos	.302-6-63	0.0	5.0	0.01
Doug Jones, p, Cle	2.56, 43 saves	0.0	3.0	0.01
Cal Ripken Jr., ss, Bal	.250-21-84	0.0	2.0	0.01
Nolan Ryan, p, Tex	13-9, 3.44	0.0	1.0	0.00
Dave Stieb, p, Tor	18-6, 2.93	0.0	1.0	0.00

Cy Young

Pitcher, Team	Stats	1st Pl	Pts	Share
Bob Welch, Oak	27-6, 2.95	15.0	107.0	0.76
Roger Clemens, Bos	21-6, 1.93	8.0	77.0	0.55
Dave Stewart, Oak	22-11, 2.56	3.0	43.0	0.31
Bobby Thigpen, ChA	1.83, 57 saves	2.0	20.0	0.14
Dennis Eckersley, Oak	0.61, 48 saves	0.0	2.0	0.01
Dave Stieb, Tor	18-6, 2.93	0.0	2.0	0.01
Chuck Finley, Cal	18-9, 2.40	0.0	1.0	0.01

Rookie of the Year

Pitcher, Pos, Team	Stats	1st Pl	Pts	Share
Sandy Alomar Jr., c, Cle	.290-9-66	28.0	140.0	1.00
Kevin Maas, 1b, NYA	.252-21-41	0.0	47.0	0.34
Kevin Appier, p, KC	12-8, 2.76	0.0	31.0	0.22
John Olerud, dh, Tor	.265-14-48	0.0	13.0	0.09
Kevin Tapani, p, Min	12-8, 4.07	0.0	9.0	0.06
Travis Fryman, 3b, Det	.297-9-27	0.0	5.0	0.04
Robin Ventura, 3b, ChA	.249-5-54	0.0	3.0	0.02
Ben McDonald, p, Bal	8-5, 2.43	0.0	2.0	0.01
Alex Cole, of, Cle	.300-0-13	0.0	1.0	0.01
Scott Radinsky, p, ChA	4.82, 4 saves	0.0	1.0	0.01

Manager of the Year

Manager, Team	Stats	1st Pl	Pts	Share
Jeff Torborg, ChA	94-68, 2nd W	23.0	128.0	0.91
Tony La Russa, Oak	103-59, 1st W	4.0	72.0	0.51
Joe Morgan, Bos	88-74, 1st E	1.0	28.0	0.20
Sparky Anderson, Det	79-83, 3rd E	0.0	12.0	0.09
Cito Gaston, Tor	86-76, 2nd E	0.0	6.0	0.04
Bobby Valentine, Tex	83-79, 3rd W	0.0	4.0	0.03
Jim Lefebvre, Sea	77-85, 5th W	0.0	1.0	0.01
Doug Rader, Cal	80-82, 4th W	0.0	1.0	0.01

Gold Gloves

Player, Pos, Team	Rng	LRng	FPct	LFPct
Mike Boddicker, p, Bos	—	—	.966	.953
Sandy Alomar Jr., c, Cle	—	—	.981	.991
Mark McGwire, 1b, Oak	—	—	.997	.992
Harold Reynolds, 2b, Sea	5.18	4.53	.978	.984
Kelly Gruber, 3b, Tor	2.78	2.32	.955	.944
Ozzie Guillen, ss, ChA	4.57	4.00	.977	.973
Ellis Burks, of, Bos	2.31	2.04	.994	.981
Ken Griffey Jr., of, Sea	2.24	2.04	.980	.981
Gary Pettis, of, Tex	2.30	2.04	.993	.981

National League

MVP

Player, Pos, Team	Stats	1st Pl	Pts	Share
Barry Bonds, of, Pit	.301-33-114	23.0	331.0	0.99
Bobby Bonilla, of, Pit	.280-32-120	1.0	212.0	0.63
Darryl Strawberry, of, NYN	.277-37-108	0.0	167.0	0.50
Ryne Sandberg, 2b, ChN	.306-40-100	0.0	151.0	0.45
Eddie Murray, 1b, LA	.330-26-95	0.0	123.0	0.37
Matt Williams, 3b, SF	.277-33-122	0.0	95.0	0.28
Barry Larkin, ss, Cin	.301-7-67	0.0	82.0	0.24
Doug Drabek, p, Pit	22-6, 2.76	0.0	59.0	0.18
Lenny Dykstra, of, Phi	.325-9-60	0.0	41.0	0.12
Tim Wallach, 3b, Mon	.296-21-98	0.0	36.0	0.11
Kevin Mitchell, of, SF	.290-35-93	0.0	20.0	0.06
Eric Davis, of, Cin	.260-24-86	0.0	12.0	0.04
Chris Sabo, 3b, Cin	.270-25-71	0.0	11.0	0.03
Ron Gant, of, Atl	.303-32-84	0.0	10.0	0.03
Dwight Gooden, p, NYN	19-7, 3.83	0.0	10.0	0.03
Ramon Martinez, p, LA	20-6, 2.92	0.0	9.0	0.03
Joe Carter, of, SD	.232-24-115	0.0	7.0	0.02
Randy Myers, p, Cin	2.08, 31 saves	0.0	7.0	0.02
Paul O'Neill, of, Cin	.270-16-78	0.0	6.0	0.02
Jose Rijo, p, Cin	14-8, 2.70	0.0	6.0	0.02
Andre Dawson, of, ChN	.310-27-100	0.0	6.0	0.02
Dave Magadan, 1b, NYN	.328-6-72	0.0	4.0	0.01
Benito Santiago, c, SD	.270-11-53	0.0	3.0	0.01
Brett Butler, of, SF	.309-3-44	0.0	2.0	0.01
David Justice, 1b, Atl	.282-28-78	0.0	2.0	0.01
Pedro Guerrero, 1b, StL	.281-13-80	0.0	2.0	0.01
Kal Daniels, of, LA	.296-27-94	0.0	1.0	0.00
Andy Van Slyke, of, Pit	.284-17-77	0.0	1.0	0.00

Cy Young

Pitcher, Team	Stats	1st Pl	Pts	Share
Doug Drabek, Pit	22-6, 2.76	23.0	118.0	0.98
Ramon Martinez, LA	20-6, 2.92	1.0	70.0	0.58
Frank Viola, NYN	20-12, 2.67	0.0	19.0	0.16
Dwight Gooden, NYN	19-7, 3.83	0.0	8.0	0.07
Randy Myers, Cin	2.08, 31 saves	0.0	1.0	0.01

Rookie of the Year

Pitcher, Pos, Team	Stats	1st Pl	Pts	Share
David Justice, 1b, Atl	.282-28-78	23.0	118.0	0.98
Delino DeShields, 2b, Mon	.289-4-45	1.0	60.0	0.50
Hal Morris, 1b, Cin	.340-7-36	0.0	13.0	0.11
John Burkett, p, SF	14-7, 3.79	0.0	12.0	0.10
Mike Harkey, p, ChN	12-6, 3.26	0.0	7.0	0.06
Todd Zeile, c, StL	.244-15-57	0.0	4.0	0.03
Marquis Grissom, of, Mon	.257-3-29	0.0	1.0	0.01
Larry Walker, of, Mon	.241-19-51	0.0	1.0	0.01

Manager of the Year

Manager, Team	Stats	1st Pl	Pts	Share
Jim Leyland, Pit	95-67, 1st E	17.0	99.0	0.83
Lou Piniella, Cin	91-71, 1st W	3.0	49.0	0.41
Buck Rodgers, Mon	85-77, 3rd E	3.0	32.0	0.27
Tom Lasorda, LA	86-76, 2nd W	1.0	32.0	0.27
Roger Craig, SF	85-77, 3rd W	0.0	2.0	0.02
Bud Harrelson, NYN	71-49, 2nd E	0.0	2.0	0.02

Gold Gloves

Player, Pos, Team	Rng	LRng	FPct	LFPct
Greg Maddux, p, ChN	—	—	1.000	.957
Benito Santiago, c, SD	—	—	.980	.987
Andres Galarraga, 1b, Mon	—	—	.993	.992
Ryne Sandberg, 2b, ChN	4.85	4.28	.989	.983
Tim Wallach, 3b, Mon	2.71	2.31	.954	.947
Ozzie Smith, ss, StL	4.21	4.00	.980	.967
Barry Bonds, of, Pit	2.35	2.01	.983	.981
Tony Gwynn, of, SD	2.40	2.01	.985	.981
Andy Van Slyke, of, Pit	2.50	2.01	.976	.981

1991

American League

MVP

Player, Pos, Team	Stats	1st Pl	Pts	Share
Cal Ripken Jr., ss, Bal	.323-34-114	15.0	318.0	0.81
Cecil Fielder, 1b, Det	.261-44-133	9.0	286.0	0.73
Frank Thomas, dh, ChA	.318-32-109	1.0	181.0	0.46
Jose Canseco, of, Oak	.266-44-122	0.0	145.0	0.37
Joe Carter, of, Tor	.273-33-108	1.0	136.0	0.35
Roberto Alomar, 2b, Tor	.295-9-69	2.0	128.0	0.33
Kirby Puckett, of, Min	.319-15-89	0.0	78.0	0.20
Ruben Sierra, of, Tex	.307-25-116	0.0	63.0	0.16
Ken Griffey Jr., of, Sea	.327-22-100	0.0	62.0	0.16
Roger Clemens, p, Bos	18-10, 2.62	0.0	57.0	0.15
Paul Molitor, dh, Mil	.325-17-75	0.0	51.0	0.13
Danny Tartabull, of, KC	.316-31-100	0.0	32.0	0.08
Jack Morris, p, Min	18-12, 3.43	0.0	29.0	0.07
Chili Davis, dh, Min	.277-29-93	0.0	21.0	0.05
Julio Franco, 2b, Tex	.341-15-78	0.0	17.0	0.04
Devon White, of, Tor	.282-17-60	0.0	15.0	0.04
Scott Erickson, p, Min	20-8, 3.18	0.0	12.0	0.03
Rick Aguilera, p, Min	2.35, 42 saves	0.0	11.0	0.03
Rafael Palmeiro, 1b, Tex	.322-26-88	0.0	6.0	0.02
Robin Ventura, 3b, ChA	.284-23-100	0.0	3.0	0.01
Dave Henderson, of, Oak	.276-25-85	0.0	1.0	0.00

Cy Young

Pitcher, Team	Stats	1st Pl	Pts	Share
Roger Clemens, Bos	18-10, 2.62	21.0	119.0	0.85
Scott Erickson, Min	20-8, 3.18	3.0	56.0	0.40
Jim Abbott, Cal	18-11, 2.89	0.0	26.0	0.19
Jack Morris, Min	18-12, 3.43	3.0	17.0	0.12
Bryan Harvey, Cal	1.60, 46 saves	0.0	10.0	0.07
Mark Langston, Cal	19-8, 3.00	0.0	7.0	0.05
Kevin Tapani, Min	16-9, 2.99	1.0	6.0	0.04
Bill Gullickson, Det	20-9, 3.90	0.0	5.0	0.04
Jack McDowell, ChA	17-10, 3.41	0.0	3.0	0.02
Duane Ward, Tor	2.77, 23 saves	0.0	3.0	0.02

Rookie of the Year

Pitcher, Pos, Team	Stats	1st Pl	Pts	Share
Chuck Knoblauch, 2b, Min	.281-1-50	26.0	136.0	0.97
Juan Guzman, p, Tor	10-3, 2.99	1.0	68.0	0.49
Milt Cuyler, of, Det	.257-3-33	1.0	22.0	0.16
Ivan Rodriguez, c, Tex	.264-3-27	0.0	10.0	0.07
Rich DeLucia, p, Sea	12-13, 5.09	0.0	7.0	0.05
Mike Timlin, p, Tor	3.16, 3 saves	0.0	2.0	0.01
Mark Whiten, of, Tor-Cle	.243-9-45	0.0	2.0	0.01
Doug Henry, p, Mil	1.00, 15 saves	0.0	1.0	0.01
Leo Gomez, 3b, Bal	.233-16-45	0.0	1.0	0.01
Brent Mayne, c, KC	.251-3-31	0.0	1.0	0.01
Charles Nagy, p, Cle	10-15, 4.13	0.0	1.0	0.01
Phil Plantier, of, Bos	.331-11-35	0.0	1.0	0.01

Manager of the Year

Manager, Team	Stats	1st Pl	Pts	Share
Tom Kelly, Min	95-67, 1st W	27.0	138.0	0.99
Sparky Anderson, Det	84-78, 2nd E	1.0	50.0	0.36
Cito Gaston, Tor	72-57, 1st E	0.0	17.0	0.12
Jim Lefebvre, Sea	83-79, 5th W	0.0	16.0	0.11
Joe Morgan, Bos	84-78, 2nd E	0.0	16.0	0.11
Jeff Torborg, ChA	87-75, 2nd W	0.0	6.0	0.04
Bobby Valentine, Tex	85-77, 3rd W	0.0	3.0	0.02
Hal McRae, KC	66-58, 6th W	0.0	3.0	0.02
Tony La Russa, Oak	84-78, 4th W	0.0	2.0	0.01
Stump Merrill, NYA	71-91, 5th E	0.0	1.0	0.01

Gold Gloves

Player, Pos, Team	Rng	LRng	FPct	LFPct
Mark Langston, p, Cal	—	—	.942	.956
Tony Pena, c, Bos	—	—	.995	.990
Don Mattingly, 1b, NYA	—	—	.996	.992
Roberto Alomar, 2b, Tor	4.88	4.44	.981	.981
Robin Ventura, 3b, ChA	2.79	2.33	.959	.955
Cal Ripken Jr., ss, Bal	4.91	3.95	.986	.971
Ken Griffey Jr., of, Sea	2.47	2.03	.989	.983
Kirby Puckett, of, Min	2.54	2.03	.985	.983
Devon White, of, Tor	2.87	2.03	.998	.983

National League

MVP

Player, Pos, Team	Stats	1st Pl	Pts	Share
Terry Pendleton, 3b, Atl	.319-22-86	12.0	274.0	0.82
Barry Bonds, of, Pit	.292-25-116	10.0	259.0	0.77
Bobby Bonilla, of, Pit	.302-18-100	1.0	191.0	0.57
Will Clark, 1b, SF	.301-29-116	0.0	118.0	0.35
Howard Johnson, 3b, NYN	.259-38-117	0.0	112.0	0.33
Ron Gant, of, Atl	.251-32-105	0.0	110.0	0.33
Brett Butler, of, LA	.296-2-38	1.0	103.0	0.31
Lee Smith, p, StL	2.34, 47 saves	0.0	89.0	0.26
Darryl Strawberry, of, LA	.265-28-99	0.0	76.0	0.23
Fred McGriff, 1b, SD	.278-31-106	0.0	23.0	0.07
Tom Glavine, p, Atl	20-11, 2.55	0.0	16.0	0.05
David Justice, of, Atl	.275-21-87	0.0	11.0	0.03
Jay Bell, ss, Pit	.270-16-67	0.0	11.0	0.03
Andre Dawson, of, ChN	.272-31-104	0.0	5.0	0.01
John Smiley, p, Pit	20-8, 3.08	0.0	5.0	0.01
Tony Gwynn, of, SD	.317-4-62	0.0	4.0	0.01
John Kruk, 1b, Phi	.294-21-92	0.0	2.0	0.01
Ryne Sandberg, 2b, ChN	.291-26-100	0.0	2.0	0.01
Barry Larkin, ss, Cin	.302-20-69	0.0	2.0	0.01
Dennis Martinez, p, Mon	14-11, 2.39	0.0	1.0	0.00
Chris Sabo, 3b, Cin	.301-26-88	0.0	1.0	0.00
Ozzie Smith, ss, StL	.285-3-50	0.0	1.0	0.00

Cy Young

Pitcher, Team	Stats	1st Pl	Pts	Share
Tom Glavine, Atl	20-11, 2.55	19.0	110.0	0.92
Lee Smith, StL	2.34, 47 saves	4.0	60.0	0.50
John Smiley, Pit	20-8, 3.08	0.0	26.0	0.22
Jose Rijo, Cin	15-6, 2.51	1.0	13.0	0.11
Dennis Martinez, Mon	14-11, 2.39	0.0	4.0	0.03
Steve Avery, Atl	18-8, 3.38	0.0	1.0	0.01
Andy Benes, SD	15-11, 3.03	0.0	1.0	0.01
Mitch Williams, Phi	2.34, 30 saves	0.0	1.0	0.01

Rookie of the Year

Pitcher, Pos, Team	Stats	1st Pl	Pts	Share
Jeff Bagwell, 1b, Hou	.294-15-82	23.0	118.0	0.98
Orlando Merced, 1b, Pit	.275-10-50	1.0	53.0	0.44
Ray Lankford, of, StL	.251-9-69	0.0	28.0	0.23
Brian Hunter, 1b, Atl	.251-12-50	0.0	7.0	0.06
Bret Barberie, ss, Mon	.353-2-18	0.0	3.0	0.03
Wes Chamberlain, of, Phi	.240-13-50	0.0	3.0	0.03
Chuck McElroy, p, ChN	1.95, 3 saves	0.0	3.0	0.03
Mike Stanton, p, Atl	2.88, 7 saves	0.0	1.0	0.01

Manager of the Year

Manager, Team	Stats	1st Pl	Pts	Share
Bobby Cox, Atl	94-68, 1st W	13.0	96.0	0.80
Jim Leyland, Pit	98-64, 1st E	9.0	74.0	0.62
Joe Torre, StL	84-78, 2nd E	2.0	41.0	0.34
Tom Lasorda, LA	93-69, 2nd W	0.0	5.0	0.04

Gold Gloves

Player, Pos, Team	Rng	LRng	FPct	LFPct
Greg Maddux, p, ChN	—	—	.978	.955
Tom Pagnozzi, c, StL	—	—	.991	.988
Will Clark, 1b, SF	—	—	.997	.992
Ryne Sandberg, 2b, ChN	4.98	4.28	.995	.982
Matt Williams, 3b, SF	2.74	2.31	.964	.950
Ozzie Smith, ss, StL	4.21	3.88	.987	.966
Barry Bonds, of, Pit	2.23	1.88	.991	.983
Tony Gwynn, of, SD	2.23	1.88	.990	.983
Andy Van Slyke, of, Pit	2.08	1.88	.996	.983

1992

American League

MVP

Player, Pos, Team	Stats	1st Pl	Pts	Share
Dennis Eckersley, p, Oak	1.91, 51 saves	15.0	306.0	0.78
Kirby Puckett, of, Min	.329-19-110	3.0	209.0	0.53
Joe Carter, of, Tor	.264-34-119	4.0	201.0	0.51
Mark McGwire, 1b, Oak	.268-42-104	1.0	155.0	0.40
Dave Winfield, dh, Tor	.290-26-108	2.0	141.0	0.36
Roberto Alomar, 2b, Tor	.310-8-76	3.0	118.0	0.30
Mike Devereaux, of, Bal	.276-24-107	0.0	109.0	0.28
Frank Thomas, 1b, ChA	.323-24-115	0.0	108.0	0.28
Cecil Fielder, 1b, Det	.244-35-124	0.0	83.0	0.21
Paul Molitor, dh, Mil	.320-12-89	0.0	63.0	0.16
Carlos Baerga, 2b, Cle	.312-20-105	0.0	31.0	0.08
Edgar Martinez, 3b, Sea	.343-18-73	0.0	29.0	0.07
Jack Morris, p, Tor	21-6, 4.04	0.0	18.0	0.05
Roger Clemens, p, Bos	18-11, 2.41	0.0	16.0	0.04
Brady Anderson, of, Bal	.271-21-80	0.0	16.0	0.04
Juan Gonzalez, of, Tex	.260-43-109	0.0	15.0	0.04
Ken Griffey Jr., of, Sea	.308-27-103	0.0	13.0	0.03
Pat Listach, ss, Mil	.290-1-47	0.0	8.0	0.02
Jack McDowell, p, ChA	20-10, 3.18	0.0	5.0	0.01
George Bell, dh, ChA	.255-25-112	0.0	3.0	0.01
Mike Bordick, 2b, Oak	.300-3-48	0.0	2.0	0.01
Mike Mussina, p, Bal	18-5, 2.54	0.0	2.0	0.01
Albert Belle, dh, Cle	.260-34-112	0.0	1.0	0.00

Cy Young

Pitcher, Team	Stats	1st Pl	Pts	Share
Dennis Eckersley, Oak	1.91, 51 saves	19.0	107.0	0.76
Jack McDowell, ChA	20-10, 3.18	2.0	51.0	0.36
Roger Clemens, Bos	18-11, 2.41	4.0	48.0	0.34
Mike Mussina, Bal	18-5, 2.54	2.0	26.0	0.19
Jack Morris, Tor	21-6, 4.04	1.0	10.0	0.07
Kevin Brown, Tex	21-11, 3.32	0.0	9.0	0.06
Charles Nagy, Cle	17-10, 2.96	0.0	1.0	0.01

Rookie of the Year

Pitcher, Pos, Team	Stats	1st Pl	Pts	Share
Pat Listach, ss, Mil	.290-1-47	20.0	122.0	0.87
Kenny Lofton, of, Cle	.285-5-42	7.0	85.0	0.61
Dave Fleming, p, Sea	17-10, 3.39	0.0	23.0	0.16
Cal Eldred, p, Mil	11-2, 1.79	1.0	22.0	0.16

Manager of the Year

Manager, Team	Stats	1st Pl	Pts	Share
Tony La Russa, Oak	96-66, 1st W	25.0	132.0	0.94
Phil Garner, Mil	92-70, 2nd E	2.0	76.0	0.54
Johnny Oates, Bal	89-73, 3rd E	0.0	27.0	0.19
Cito Gaston, Tor	96-66, 1st E	1.0	13.0	0.09
Mike Hargrove, Cle	76-86, 4th E	0.0	4.0	0.03

Gold Gloves

Player, Pos, Team	Rng	LRng	FPct	LFPct
Mark Langston, p, Cal	—	—	.941	.953
Ivan Rodriguez, c, Tex	—	—	.983	.989
Don Mattingly, 1b, NYA	—	—	.997	.993
Roberto Alomar, 2b, Tor	4.43	4.60	.993	.983
Robin Ventura, 3b, ChA	3.27	2.40	.957	.950
Cal Ripken, ss, Bal	4.52	4.13	.984	.969
Ken Griffey Jr., of, Sea	2.68	2.17	.997	.983
Kirby Puckett, of, Min	2.70	2.17	.993	.983
Devon White, of, Tor	2.97	2.17	.985	.983

National League

MVP

Player, Pos, Team	Stats	1st Pl	Pts	Share
Barry Bonds, of, Pit	.311-34-103	18.0	304.0	0.90
Terry Pendleton, 3b, Atl	.311-21-105	4.0	232.0	0.69
Gary Sheffield, 3b, SD	.330-33-100	2.0	204.0	0.61
Andy Van Slyke, of, Pit	.324-14-89	0.0	145.0	0.43
Larry Walker, of, Mon	.301-23-93	0.0	111.0	0.33
Darren Daulton, c, Phi	.270-27-109	0.0	100.0	0.30
Fred McGriff, 1b, SD	.286-35-104	0.0	100.0	0.30
Bip Roberts, of, Cin	.323-4-45	0.0	64.0	0.19
Marquis Grissom, of, Mon	.276-14-66	0.0	54.0	0.16
Tom Glavine, p, Atl	20-8, 2.76	0.0	18.0	0.05
Greg Maddux, p, ChN	20-11, 2.18	0.0	14.0	0.04
Ryne Sandberg, 2b, ChN	.304-26-87	0.0	12.0	0.04
Barry Larkin, ss, Cin	.304-12-78	0.0	12.0	0.04
Doug Jones, p, Hou	1.85, 36 saves	0.0	8.0	0.02
John Kruk, 1b, Phi	.323-10-70	0.0	8.0	0.02
Mark Grace, 1b, ChN	.307-9-79	0.0	6.0	0.02
Delino DeShields, 2b, Mon	.292-7-56	0.0	6.0	0.02
Ray Lankford, of, StL	.293-20-86	0.0	5.0	0.01
Jeff Bagwell, 1b, Hou	.273-18-96	0.0	4.0	0.01
Dave Hollins, 3b, Phi	.270-27-93	0.0	3.0	0.01
Brett Butler, of, LA	.309-3-39	0.0	2.0	0.01
Ozzie Smith, ss, StL	.295-0-31	0.0	2.0	0.01
Otis Nixon, of, Atl	.294-2-22	0.0	1.0	0.00
John Wetteland, p, Mon	2.92, 37 saves	0.0	1.0	0.00

Cy Young

Pitcher, Team	Stats	1st Pl	Pts	Share
Greg Maddux, ChN	20-11, 2.18	20.0	112.0	0.93
Tom Glavine, Atl	20-8, 2.76	4.0	78.0	0.65
Bob Tewksbury, StL	16-5, 2.16	0.0	22.0	0.18
Lee Smith, StL	3.12, 43 saves	0.0	3.0	0.03
Doug Drabek, Pit	15-11, 2.77	0.0	1.0	0.01

Rookie of the Year

Pitcher, Pos, Team	Stats	1st Pl	Pts	Share
Eric Karros, 1b, LA	.257-20-88	22.0	116.0	0.97
Moises Alou, of, Mon	.282-9-56	0.0	30.0	0.25
Tim Wakefield, p, Pit	8-1, 2.15	2.0	29.0	0.24
Reggie Sanders, of, Cin	.270-12-36	0.0	23.0	0.19
Donovan Osborne, p, StL	11-9, 3.77	0.0	12.0	0.10
Mike Perez, p, StL	1.84, 0 saves	0.0	2.0	0.02
Ben Rivera, p, Atl-Phi	3.07, 0 saves	0.0	1.0	0.01
Frank Seminara, p, SD	9-4, 3.68	0.0	1.0	0.01
Brian Williams, p, Hou	7-6, 3.92	0.0	1.0	0.01
Mark Wohlers, p, Atl	2.55, 4 saves	0.0	1.0	0.01

Manager of the Year

Manager, Team	Stats	1st Pl	Pts	Share
Jim Leyland, Pit	96-66, 1st E	20.0	109.0	0.91
Felipe Alou, Mon	70-55, 2nd E	3.0	65.0	0.54
Bobby Cox, Atl	98-64, 1st W	1.0	29.0	0.24
Art Howe, Hou	81-81, 4th W	0.0	9.0	0.08
Lou Piniella, Cin	90-72, 2nd W	0.0	4.0	0.03

Gold Gloves

Player, Pos, Team	Rng	LRng	FPct	LFPct
Greg Maddux, p, ChN	—	—	.969	.954
Tom Pagnozzi, c, StL	—	—	.999	.991
Mark Grace, 1b, ChN	—	—	.998	.993
Jose Lind, 2b, Pit	5.51	4.27	.992	.981
Terry Pendleton, 3b, Atl	2.90	2.29	.960	.952
Ozzie Smith, ss, StL	4.94	3.86	.985	.969
Barry Bonds, of, Pit	2.26	1.96	.991	.983
Andy Van Slyke, of, Pit	2.81	1.96	.989	.983
Larry Walker, of, Mon	2.05	1.96	.993	.983

1993

American League

MVP

Player, Pos, Team	Stats	1st Pl	Pts	Share
Frank Thomas, 1b, ChA	.317-41-128	28.0	392.0	1.00
Paul Molitor, dh, Tor	.332-22-111	0.0	209.0	0.53
John Olerud, 1b, Tor	.363-24-107	0.0	198.0	0.51
Juan Gonzalez, of, Tex	.310-46-118	0.0	185.0	0.47
Ken Griffey Jr., of, Sea	.309-45-109	0.0	182.0	0.46
Roberto Alomar, 2b, Tor	.326-17-93	0.0	102.0	0.26
Albert Belle, of, Cle	.290-38-129	0.0	81.0	0.21
Rafael Palmeiro, 1b, Tex	.295-37-105	0.0	52.0	0.13
Jack McDowell, p, ChA	22-10, 3.37	0.0	51.0	0.13
Carlos Baerga, 2b, Cle	.321-21-114	0.0	50.0	0.13
Jimmy Key, p, NYA	18-6, 3.00	0.0	29.0	0.07
Joe Carter, of, Tor	.254-33-121	0.0	25.0	0.06
Mike Stanley, c, NYA	.305-26-84	0.0	15.0	0.04
Jeff Montgomery, p, KC	2.27, 45 saves	0.0	15.0	0.04
Kenny Lofton, of, Cle	.325-1-42	0.0	11.0	0.03
Tony Phillips, of, Det	.313-7-57	0.0	10.0	0.03
Chris Hoiles, c, Bal	.310-29-82	0.0	10.0	0.03
Mo Vaughn, 1b, Bos	.297-29-101	0.0	8.0	0.02
Don Mattingly, 1b, NYA	.291-17-86	0.0	7.0	0.02
Cal Ripken Jr., ss, Bal	.257-24-90	0.0	7.0	0.02
Alex Fernandez, p, ChA	18-9, 3.13	0.0	4.0	0.01
Duane Ward, p, Tor	2.13, 45 saves	0.0	3.0	0.01
Greg Gagne, ss, KC	.280-10-57	0.0	3.0	0.01
Kevin Appier, p, KC	18-8, 2.56	0.0	1.0	0.00
Cecil Fielder, 1b, Det	.267-30-117	0.0	1.0	0.00
Randy Johnson, p, Sea	19-8, 3.24	0.0	1.0	0.00

Cy Young

Pitcher, Team	Stats	1st Pl	Pts	Share
Jack McDowell, ChA	22-10, 3.37	21.0	124.0	0.89
Randy Johnson, Sea	19-8, 3.24	6.0	75.0	0.54
Kevin Appier, KC	18-8, 2.56	1.0	30.0	0.21
Jimmy Key, NYA	18-6, 3.00	0.0	14.0	0.10
Duane Ward, Tor	2.13, 45 saves	0.0	5.0	0.04
Pat Hentgen, Tor	19-9, 3.87	0.0	3.0	0.02
Juan Guzman, Tor	14-3, 3.99	0.0	1.0	0.01

Rookie of the Year

Pitcher, Pos, Team	Stats	1st Pl	Pts	Share
Tim Salmon, of, Cal	.283-31-95	28.0	140.0	1.00
Jason Bere, p, ChA	12-5, 3.47	0.0	59.0	0.42
Aaron Sele, p, Bos	7-2, 2.74	0.0	19.0	0.14
Wayne Kirby, of, Cle	.269-6-60	0.0	12.0	0.09
Rich Amaral, 2b, Sea	.290-1-44	0.0	8.0	0.06
Brent Gates, 2b, Oak	.290-7-69	0.0	7.0	0.05
Troy Neel, dh, Oak	.290-19-63	0.0	5.0	0.04
Jerry Dipoto, p, Cle	2.40, 11 saves	0.0	1.0	0.01
David Hulse, of, Tex	.290-1-29	0.0	1.0	0.01

Manager of the Year

Manager, Team	Stats	1st Pl	Pts	Share
Gene Lamont, ChA	94-68, 1st W	8.0	72.0	0.51
Buck Showalter, NYA	88-74, 2nd E	7.0	63.0	0.45
Cito Gaston, Tor	95-67, 1st E	6.0	49.0	0.35
Kevin Kennedy, Tex	86-76, 2nd W	3.0	28.0	0.20
Lou Piniella, Sea	82-80, 4th W	3.0	24.0	0.17
Mike Hargrove, Cle	76-86, 6th E	1.0	10.0	0.07
Johnny Oates, Bal	85-77, 3rd E	0.0	5.0	0.04
Butch Hobson, Bos	80-82, 5th E	0.0	1.0	0.01

Gold Gloves

Player, Pos, Team	Rng	LRng	FPct	LFPct
Mark Langston, p, Cal	—	—	.966	.953
Ivan Rodriguez, c, Tex	—	—	.991	.991
Don Mattingly, 1b, NYA	—	—	.998	.993
Roberto Alomar, 2b, Tor	4.59	4.54	.980	.981
Robin Ventura, 3b, ChA	2.52	2.31	.965	.951
Omar Vizquel, ss, Sea	4.65	4.13	.980	.973
Ken Griffey Jr., of, Sea	2.33	2.09	.991	.983
Kenny Lofton, of, Cle	2.83	2.09	.979	.983
Devon White, of, Tor	2.79	2.09	.993	.983

National League

MVP

Player, Pos, Team	Stats	1st Pl	Pts	Share
Barry Bonds, of, SF	.336-46-123	24.0	372.0	0.95
Lenny Dykstra, of, Phi	.305-19-66	4.0	267.0	0.68
David Justice, of, Atl	.270-40-120	0.0	183.0	0.47
Fred McGriff, 1b, SD-Atl	.291-37-101	0.0	177.0	0.45
Ron Gant, of, Atl	.274-36-117	0.0	176.0	0.45
Matt Williams, 3b, SF	.294-38-110	0.0	103.0	0.26
Darren Daulton, c, Phi	.257-24-105	0.0	79.0	0.20
Marquis Grissom, of, Mon	.298-19-95	0.0	66.0	0.17
Mike Piazza, c, LA	.318-35-112	0.0	49.0	0.13
Andres Galarraga, 1b, Col	.370-22-98	0.0	45.0	0.11
Gregg Jefferies, 1b, StL	.342-16-83	0.0	28.0	0.07
Rod Beck, p, SF	2.16, 48 saves	0.0	23.0	0.06
Greg Maddux, p, Atl	20-10, 2.36	0.0	17.0	0.04
Bryan Harvey, p, Fla	1.70, 45 saves	0.0	14.0	0.04
Robby Thompson, 2b, SF	.312-19-65	0.0	11.0	0.03
Jeff Blauser, ss, Atl	.305-15-73	0.0	9.0	0.02
John Kruk, 1b, Phi	.316-14-85	0.0	9.0	0.02
Mark Grace, 1b, ChN	.325-14-98	0.0	8.0	0.02
Jay Bell, ss, Pit	.310-9-51	0.0	4.0	0.01
Jeff Bagwell, 1b, Hou	.320-20-88	0.0	3.0	0.01
Tony Gwynn, of, SD	.358-7-59	0.0	2.0	0.01
Randy Myers, p, ChN	3.11, 53 saves	0.0	2.0	0.01
Jose Rijo, p, Cin	14-9, 2.48	0.0	2.0	0.01
John Burkett, p, SF	22-7, 3.65	0.0	1.0	0.00
Tom Glavine, p, Atl	22-6, 3.20	0.0	1.0	0.00
John Wetteland, p, Mon	1.37, 43 saves	0.0	1.0	0.00

Cy Young

Pitcher, Team	Stats	1st Pl	Pts	Share
Greg Maddux, Atl	20-10, 2.36	22.0	119.0	0.85
Bill Swift, SF	21-8, 2.82	2.0	61.0	0.44
Tom Glavine, Atl	22-6, 3.20	4.0	49.0	0.35
John Burkett, SF	22-7, 3.65	0.0	9.0	0.06
Jose Rijo, Cin	14-9, 2.48	0.0	8.0	0.06
Tommy Greene, Phi	16-4, 3.42	0.0	2.0	0.01
Mark Portugal, Hou	18-4, 2.77	0.0	2.0	0.01
Bryan Harvey, Fla	1.70, 45 saves	0.0	1.0	0.01
Randy Myers, ChN	3.11, 53 saves	0.0	1.0	0.01

Rookie of the Year

Pitcher, Pos, Team	Stats	1st Pl	Pts	Share
Mike Piazza, c, LA	.318-35-112	28.0	140.0	1.00
Greg McMichael, p, Atl	2.06, 19 saves	0.0	40.0	0.29
Jeff Conine, of, Fla	.292-12-79	0.0	31.0	0.22
Chuck Carr, of, Fla	.267-4-41	0.0	18.0	0.13
Al Martin, of, Pit	.281-18-64	0.0	6.0	0.04
Kevin Stocker, ss, Phi	.324-2-31	0.0	4.0	0.03
Wil Cordero, ss, Mon	.248-10-58	0.0	3.0	0.02
Kirk Rueter, p, Mon	8-0, 2.73	0.0	3.0	0.02
Carlos Garcia, 2b, Pit	.269-12-47	0.0	2.0	0.01
Pedro Martinez, p, LA	2.61, 2 saves	0.0	2.0	0.01
Steve Cooke, p, Pit	10-10, 3.89	0.0	1.0	0.01
Ricky Gutierrez, ss, SD	.251-5-26	0.0	1.0	0.01
Armando Reynoso, p, Col	12-11, 4.00	0.0	1.0	0.01

Manager of the Year

Manager, Team	Stats	1st Pl	Pts	Share
Dusty Baker, SF	103-59, 2nd W	15.0	105.0	0.75
Jim Fregosi, Phi	97-65, 1st E	11.0	92.0	0.66
Felipe Alou, Mon	94-68, 2nd E	2.0	27.0	0.19
Bobby Cox, Atl	104-58, 1st W	0.0	27.0	0.19
Don Baylor, Col	67-95, 6th W	0.0	1.0	0.01

Gold Gloves

Player, Pos, Team	Rng	LRng	FPct	LFPct
Greg Maddux, p, Atl	—	—	.933	.953
Kirt Manwaring, c, SF	—	—	.998	.989
Mark Grace, 1b, ChN	—	—	.997	.992
Robby Thompson, 2b, SF	5.13	4.49	.988	.980
Matt Williams, 3b, SF	2.66	2.31	.970	.945
Jay Bell, ss, Pit	5.08	4.04	.986	.965
Barry Bonds, of, SF	2.02	2.00	.984	.979
Marquis Grissom, of, Mon	2.70	2.00	.984	.979
Larry Walker, of, Mon	2.17	2.00	.979	.979

1994

American League

MVP

Player, Pos, Team	Stats	1st Pl	Pts	Share
Frank Thomas, 1b, ChA	.353-38-101	24.0	372.0	0.95
Ken Griffey Jr., of, Sea	.323-40-90	3.0	233.0	0.59
Albert Belle, of, Cle	.357-36-101	0.0	225.0	0.57
Kenny Lofton, of, Cle	.349-12-57	1.0	181.0	0.46
Paul O'Neill, of, NYA	.359-21-83	0.0	150.0	0.38
Jimmy Key, p, NYA	17-4, 3.27	0.0	102.0	0.26
Kirby Puckett, of, Min	.317-20-112	0.0	100.0	0.26
Julio Franco, dh, ChA	.319-20-98	0.0	49.0	0.13
David Cone, p, KC	16-5, 2.94	0.0	40.0	0.10
Joe Carter, of, Tor	.271-27-103	0.0	35.0	0.09
Jose Canseco, dh, Tex	.282-31-90	0.0	27.0	0.07
Cal Ripken Jr., ss, Bal	.315-13-75	0.0	24.0	0.06
Wade Boggs, 3b, NYA	.342-11-55	0.0	19.0	0.05
Lee Smith, p, Bal	3.29, 33 saves	0.0	18.0	0.05
Will Clark, 1b, Tex	.329-13-80	0.0	17.0	0.04
Rafael Palmeiro, 1b, Bal	.319-23-76	0.0	11.0	0.03
Mo Vaughn, 1b, Bos	.310-26-82	0.0	10.0	0.03
Don Mattingly, 1b, NYA	.304-6-51	0.0	9.0	0.02
Paul Molitor, dh, Tor	.341-14-75	0.0	9.0	0.02
Chuck Knoblauch, 2b, Min	.312-5-51	0.0	8.0	0.02
Mike Mussina, p, Bal	16-5, 3.06	0.0	8.0	0.02
Chili Davis, dh, Cal	.311-26-84	0.0	3.0	0.01
Jason Bere, p, ChA	12-2, 3.81	0.0	1.0	0.00
Ruben Sierra, of, Oak	.268-23-92	0.0	1.0	0.00

Cy Young

Pitcher, Team	Stats	1st Pl	Pts	Share
David Cone, KC	16-5, 2.94	15.0	108.0	0.77
Jimmy Key, NYA	17-4, 3.27	10.0	96.0	0.69
Randy Johnson, Sea	13-6, 3.19	2.0	24.0	0.17
Mike Mussina, Bal	16-5, 3.06	1.0	23.0	0.16
Lee Smith, Bal	3.29, 33 saves	0.0	1.0	0.01

Rookie of the Year

Pitcher, Pos, Team	Stats	1st Pl	Pts	Share
Bob Hamelin, dh, KC	.282-24-65	25.0	134.0	0.96
Manny Ramirez, of, Cle	.269-17-60	0.0	44.0	0.31
Rusty Greer, of, Tex	.314-10-46	3.0	42.0	0.30
Darren Hall, p, Tor	3.41, 17 saves	0.0	9.0	0.06
Chris Gomez, ss, Det	.257-8-53	0.0	6.0	0.04
Bill Risley, p, Sea	3.44, 0 saves	0.0	6.0	0.04
Brian Anderson, p, Cal	7-5, 5.22	0.0	4.0	0.03
Jeffrey Hammonds, of, Bal	.296-8-31	0.0	4.0	0.03
Jim Edmonds, of, Cal	.273-5-37	0.0	2.0	0.01
Jose Valentin, ss, Mil	.239-11-46	0.0	1.0	0.01

Manager of the Year

Manager, Team	Stats	1st Pl	Pts	Share
Buck Showalter, NYA	70-43, 1st E	24.0	132.0	0.94
Mike Hargrove, Cle	66-47, 2nd C	4.0	86.0	0.61
Gene Lamont, ChA	67-46, 1st C	0.0	17.0	0.12
Tony La Russa, Oak	51-63, 2nd W	0.0	10.0	0.07
Hal McRae, KC	64-51, 3rd C	0.0	6.0	0.04
Butch Hobson, Bos	54-61, 4th E	0.0	1.0	0.01

Gold Gloves

Player, Pos, Team	Rng	LRng	FPct	LFPct
Mark Langston, p, Cal	—	—	.938	.956
Ivan Rodriguez, c, Tex	—	—	.992	.991
Don Mattingly, 1b, NYA	—	—	.998	.992
Roberto Alomar, 2b, Tor	4.25	4.48	.991	.981
Wade Boggs, 3b, NYA	2.73	2.34	.962	.948
Omar Vizquel, ss, Cle	4.59	4.22	.981	.969
Ken Griffey Jr., of, Sea	2.30	2.09	.983	.982
Kenny Lofton, of, Cle	2.58	2.09	.993	.982
Devon White, of, Tor	2.77	2.09	.978	.982

National League

MVP

Player, Pos, Team	Stats	1st Pl	Pts	Share
Jeff Bagwell, 1b, Hou	.368-39-116	28.0	392.0	1.00
Matt Williams, 3b, SF	.267-43-96	0.0	281.0	0.72
Moises Alou, of, Mon	.339-22-78	0.0	183.0	0.47
Barry Bonds, of, SF	.312-37-81	0.0	144.0	0.37
Greg Maddux, p, Atl	16-6, 1.56	0.0	133.0	0.34
Mike Piazza, c, LA	.319-24-92	0.0	121.0	0.31
Tony Gwynn, of, SD	.394-12-64	0.0	112.0	0.29
Fred McGriff, 1b, Atl	.318-34-94	0.0	96.0	0.24
Kevin Mitchell, of, Cin	.326-30-77	0.0	86.0	0.22
Andres Galarraga, 1b, Col	.319-31-85	0.0	42.0	0.11
Larry Walker, of, Mon	.322-19-86	0.0	23.0	0.06
Ken Hill, p, Mon	16-5, 3.32	0.0	22.0	0.06
Marquis Grissom, of, Mon	.288-11-45	0.0	22.0	0.06
Dante Bichette, of, Col	.304-27-95	0.0	19.0	0.05
Hal Morris, 1b, Cin	.335-10-78	0.0	18.0	0.05
Craig Biggio, 2b, Hou	.318-6-56	0.0	17.0	0.04
Gregg Jefferies, 1b, StL	.325-12-55	0.0	5.0	0.01
Jeff Conine, of, Fla	.319-18-82	0.0	4.0	0.01
Tim Wallach, 3b, LA	.280-23-78	0.0	4.0	0.01
John Franco, p, NYN	2.70, 30 saves	0.0	3.0	0.01
Bret Boone, 2b, Cin	.320-12-68	0.0	2.0	0.01
Andy Benes, p, SD	6-14, 3.86	0.0	1.0	0.00
Brett Butler, of, LA	.314-8-33	0.0	1.0	0.00
Bret Saberhagen, p, NYN	14-4, 2.74	0.0	1.0	0.00

Cy Young

Pitcher, Team	Stats	1st Pl	Pts	Share
Greg Maddux, Atl	16-6, 1.56	28.0	140.0	1.00
Ken Hill, Mon	16-5, 3.32	0.0	56.0	0.40
Bret Saberhagen, NYN	14-4, 2.74	0.0	42.0	0.30
Marvin Freeman, Col	10-2, 2.80	0.0	4.0	0.03
Doug Drabek, Hou	12-6, 2.84	0.0	4.0	0.03
Danny Jackson, Phi	14-6, 3.26	0.0	3.0	0.02
John Franco, NYN	2.70, 30 saves	0.0	2.0	0.01
Rod Beck, SF	2.77, 28 saves	0.0	1.0	0.01

Rookie of the Year

Pitcher, Pos, Team	Stats	1st Pl	Pts	Share
Raul Mondesi, of, LA	.306-16-56	28.0	140.0	1.00
John Hudek, p, Hou	2.97, 16 saves	0.0	27.0	0.19
Ryan Klesko, of, Atl	.278-17-47	0.0	25.0	0.18
Steve Trachsel, p, ChN	9-7, 3.21	0.0	22.0	0.16
Cliff Floyd, 1b, Mon	.281-4-41	0.0	10.0	0.07
Joey Hamilton, p, SD	9-6, 2.98	0.0	10.0	0.07
William VanLandingham, p, SF	8-2, 3.54	0.0	9.0	0.06
Hector Carrasco, p, Cin	2.24, 6 saves	0.0	3.0	0.02
Bobby Jones, p, NYN	12-7, 3.15	0.0	3.0	0.02
Javy Lopez, c, Atl	.245-13-35	0.0	2.0	0.01
Shane Reynolds, p, Hou	3.05, 0 saves	0.0	1.0	0.01

Manager of the Year

Manager, Team	Stats	1st Pl	Pts	Share
Felipe Alou, Mon	74-40, 1st E	27.0	138.0	0.99
Davey Johnson, Cin	66-48, 1st C	0.0	51.0	0.36
Terry Collins, Hou	66-49, 2nd C	0.0	31.0	0.22
Dallas Green, NYN	55-58, 3rd E	1.0	12.0	0.09
Tom Lasorda, LA	58-56, 1st W	0.0	8.0	0.06
Don Baylor, Col	53-64, 3rd W	0.0	8.0	0.06
Bobby Cox, Atl	68-46, 2nd E	0.0	3.0	0.02
Dusty Baker, SF	55-60, 2nd W	0.0	1.0	0.01

Gold Gloves

Player, Pos, Team	Rng	LRng	FPct	LFPct
Greg Maddux, p, Atl	—	—	.935	.958
Tom Pagnozzi, c, StL	—	—	.998	.991
Jeff Bagwell, 1b, Hou	—	—	.991	.992
Craig Biggio, 2b, Hou	4.98	4.56	.988	.981
Matt Williams, 3b, SF	2.85	2.24	.963	.951
Barry Larkin, ss, Cin	4.45	4.05	.980	.966
Barry Bonds, of, SF	1.86	1.90	.986	.980
Marquis Grissom, of, Mon	3.01	1.90	.985	.980
Darren Lewis, of, SF	2.51	1.90	.993	.980

1995

American League

MVP

Player, Pos, Team	Stats	1st Pl	Pts	Share
Mo Vaughn, 1b, Bos	.300-39-126	12.0	308.0	0.79
Albert Belle, of, Cle	.317-50-126	11.0	300.0	0.77
Edgar Martinez, dh, Sea	.356-29-113	4.0	244.0	0.62
Jose Mesa, p, Cle	1.13, 46 saves	1.0	130.0	0.33
Jay Buhner, of, Sea	.262-40-121	0.0	120.0	0.31
Randy Johnson, p, Sea	18-2, 2.48	0.0	111.0	0.28
Tim Salmon, of, Cal	.330-34-105	0.0	110.0	0.28
Frank Thomas, 1b, ChA	.308-40-111	0.0	86.0	0.22
John Valentin, ss, Bos	.298-27-102	0.0	57.0	0.15
Gary Gaetti, 3b, KC	.261-35-96	0.0	45.0	0.11
Rafael Palmeiro, 1b, Bal	.310-39-104	0.0	34.0	0.09
Manny Ramirez, of, Cle	.308-31-107	0.0	30.0	0.08
Tim Wakefield, p, Bos	16-8, 2.95	0.0	20.0	0.05
Jim Edmonds, of, Cal	.290-33-107	0.0	18.0	0.05
Paul O'Neill, of, NYA	.300-22-96	0.0	14.0	0.04

Cy Young

Pitcher, Team	Stats	1st Pl	Pts	Share
Randy Johnson, Sea	18-2, 2.48	26.0	136.0	0.97
Jose Mesa, Cle	1.13, 46 saves	2.0	54.0	0.39
Tim Wakefield, Bos	16-8, 2.95	0.0	29.0	0.21
David Cone, Tor-NYA	18-8, 3.57	0.0	18.0	0.13
Mike Mussina, Bal	19-9, 3.29	0.0	14.0	0.10
Charles Nagy, Cle	16-6, 4.55	0.0	1.0	0.01

Rookie of the Year

Pitcher, Pos, Team	Stats	1st Pl	Pts	Share
Marty Cordova, of, Min	.277-24-84	13.0	105.0	0.75
Garret Anderson, of, Cal	.321-16-69	13.0	99.0	0.71
Andy Pettitte, p, NYA	12-9, 4.17	1.0	16.0	0.11
Troy Percival, p, Cal	1.95, 3 saves	1.0	13.0	0.09
Shawn Green, of, Tor	.288-15-54	0.0	8.0	0.06
Ray Durham, 2b, ChA	.257-7-51	0.0	3.0	0.02
Julian Tavarez, p, Cle	2.44, 0 saves	0.0	3.0	0.02
Jon Nunnally, of, KC	.244-14-42	0.0	2.0	0.01
Tom Goodwin, of, KC	.288-4-28	0.0	1.0	0.01
Brad Radke, p, Min	11-14, 5.32	0.0	1.0	0.01
Steve Sparks, p, Mil	9-11, 4.63	0.0	1.0	0.01

Manager of the Year

Manager, Team	Stats	1st Pl	Pts	Share
Lou Piniella, Sea	79-66, 1st W	9.0	86.0	0.61
Kevin Kennedy, Bos	86-58, 1st E	11.0	74.0	0.53
Mike Hargrove, Cle	100-44, 1st C	8.0	71.0	0.51
Buck Showalter, NYA	79-65, 2nd E	0.0	8.0	0.06
Marcel Lachemann, Cal	78-67, 2nd W	0.0	5.0	0.04
Phil Garner, Mil	65-79, 4th C	0.0	4.0	0.03
Bob Boone, KC	70-74, 2nd C	0.0	3.0	0.02
Johnny Oates, Tex	74-70, 3rd W	0.0	1.0	0.01

Gold Gloves

Player, Pos, Team	Rng	LRng	FPct	LFPct
Mark Langston, p, Cal	—	—	.938	.960
Ivan Rodriguez, c, Tex	—	—	.990	.990
J.T. Snow, 1b, Cal	—	—	.997	.993
Roberto Alomar, 2b, Tor	4.99	4.34	.994	.981
Wade Boggs, 3b, NYA	2.24	2.19	.981	.952
Omar Vizquel, ss, Cle	4.52	4.16	.986	.974
Ken Griffey Jr., of, Sea	2.79	1.99	.990	.983
Kenny Lofton, of, Cle	2.27	1.99	.970	.983
Devon White, of, Tor	2.71	1.99	.989	.983

National League

MVP

Player, Pos, Team	Stats	1st Pl	Pts	Share
Barry Larkin, ss, Cin	.319-15-66	11.0	281.0	0.72
Dante Bichette, of, Col	.340-40-128	6.0	251.0	0.64
Greg Maddux, p, Atl	19-2, 1.63	7.0	249.0	0.64
Mike Piazza, c, LA	.346-32-93	3.0	214.0	0.55
Eric Karros, 1b, LA	.298-32-105	0.0	135.0	0.34
Reggie Sanders, of, Cin	.306-28-99	0.0	120.0	0.31
Larry Walker, of, Col	.306-36-101	0.0	88.0	0.22
Sammy Sosa, of, ChN	.268-36-119	0.0	81.0	0.21
Tony Gwynn, of, SD	.368-9-90	0.0	72.0	0.18
Craig Biggio, 2b, Hou	.302-22-77	0.0	58.0	0.15
Ron Gant, of, Cin	.276-29-88	1.0	31.0	0.08
Barry Bonds, of, SF	.294-33-104	0.0	21.0	0.05
Mark Grace, 1b, ChN	.326-16-92	0.0	14.0	0.04
Derek Bell, of, Hou	.334-8-86	0.0	12.0	0.03
Jeff Bagwell, 1b, Hou	.290-21-87	0.0	5.0	0.01
Charlie Hayes, 3b, Phi	.276-11-85	0.0	4.0	0.01
Andres Galarraga, 1b, Col	.280-31-106	0.0	4.0	0.01
Chipper Jones, 3b, Atl	.265-23-86	0.0	3.0	0.01
Vinny Castilla, 3b, Col	.309-32-90	0.0	3.0	0.01
Fred McGriff, 1b, Atl	.280-27-93	0.0	2.0	0.01
Pete Schourek, p, Cin	18-7, 3.22	0.0	2.0	0.01
Jeff Conine, of, Fla	.302-25-105	0.0	1.0	0.00
Tom Henke, p, StL	1.82, 36 saves	0.0	1.0	0.00

Cy Young

Pitcher, Team	Stats	1st Pl	Pts	Share
Greg Maddux, Atl	19-2, 1.63	28.0	140.0	1.00
Pete Schourek, Cin	18-7, 3.22	0.0	55.0	0.39
Tom Glavine, Atl	16-7, 3.08	0.0	30.0	0.21
Hideo Nomo, LA	13-6, 2.54	0.0	19.0	0.14
Ramon Martinez, LA	17-7, 3.66	0.0	8.0	0.06

Rookie of the Year

Pitcher, Pos, Team	Stats	1st Pl	Pts	Share
Hideo Nomo, p, LA	13-6, 2.54	18.0	118.0	0.84
Chipper Jones, 3b, Atl	.265-23-86	10.0	104.0	0.74
Quilvio Veras, 2b, Fla	.261-5-32	0.0	14.0	0.10
Jason Isringhausen, p, NYN	9-2, 2.81	0.0	4.0	0.03
John Mabry, 1b, StL	.307-5-41	0.0	4.0	0.03
Carlos Perez, p, Mon	10-8, 3.69	0.0	4.0	0.03
Chad Fonville, 2b, Mon-LA	.278-0-16	0.0	1.0	0.01
Brian Hunter, of, Hou	.302-2-28	0.0	1.0	0.01
Charles Johnson, c, Fla	.251-11-39	0.0	1.0	0.01
Ismael Valdes, p, LA	13-11, 3.05	0.0	1.0	0.01

Manager of the Year

Manager, Team	Stats	1st Pl	Pts	Share
Don Baylor, Col	77-67, 2nd W	19.0	122.0	0.87
Davey Johnson, Cin	85-59, 1st C	8.0	89.0	0.64
Bobby Cox, Atl	90-54, 1st E	1.0	20.0	0.14
Terry Collins, Hou	76-68, 2nd C	0.0	11.0	0.08
Jim Riggleman, ChN	73-71, 3rd C	0.0	6.0	0.04
Dallas Green, NYN	69-75, 2nd E	0.0	3.0	0.02
Bruce Bochy, SD	70-74, 3rd W	0.0	1.0	0.01

Gold Gloves

Player, Pos, Team	Rng	LRng	FPct	LFPct
Greg Maddux, p, Atl	—	—	1.000	.956
Charles Johnson, c, Fla	—	—	.992	.989
Mark Grace, 1b, ChN	—	—	.995	.993
Craig Biggio, 2b, Hou	5.09	4.58	.986	.984
Ken Caminiti, 3b, SD	2.78	2.33	.936	.946
Barry Larkin, ss, Cin	4.10	3.97	.980	.968
Steve Finley, of, SD	2.17	1.82	.977	.979
Marquis Grissom, of, Atl	2.34	1.82	.994	.979
Raul Mondesi, of, LA	2.16	1.82	.980	.979

1996

American League

MVP

Player, Pos, Team	Stats	1st Pl	Pts	Share
Juan Gonzalez, of, Tex	.314-47-144	11.0	290.0	0.74
Alex Rodriguez, ss, Sea	.358-36-123	10.0	287.0	0.73
Albert Belle, of, Cle	.311-48-148	2.0	228.0	0.58
Ken Griffey Jr., of, Sea	.303-49-140	4.0	188.0	0.48
Mo Vaughn, 1b, Bos	.326-44-143	0.0	184.0	0.47
Rafael Palmeiro, 1b, Bal	.289-39-142	0.0	104.0	0.27
Mark McGwire, 1b, Oak	.312-52-113	0.0	100.0	0.26
Frank Thomas, 1b, ChA	.349-40-134	0.0	88.0	0.22
Brady Anderson, of, Bal	.297-50-110	0.0	53.0	0.14
Ivan Rodriguez, c, Tex	.300-19-86	1.0	52.0	0.13
Kenny Lofton, of, Cle	.317-14-67	0.0	34.0	0.09
Mariano Rivera, p, NYA	2.09, 5 saves	0.0	27.0	0.07
Paul Molitor, dh, Min	.341-9-113	0.0	19.0	0.05
Andy Pettitte, p, NYA	21-8, 3.87	0.0	11.0	0.03
Jim Thome, 3b, Cle	.311-38-116	0.0	9.0	0.02
Chuck Knoblauch, 2b, Min	.341-13-72	0.0	8.0	0.02
Jay Buhner, of, Sea	.271-44-138	0.0	6.0	0.02
Bernie Williams, of, NYA	.305-29-102	0.0	6.0	0.02
John Wetteland, p, NYA	2.83, 43 saves	0.0	4.0	0.01
Roberto Alomar, 2b, Bal	.328-22-94	0.0	3.0	0.01
Terry Steinbach, c, Oak	.272-35-100	0.0	1.0	0.00

Cy Young

Pitcher, Team	Stats	1st Pl	Pts	Share
Pat Hentgen, Tor	20-10, 3.22	16.0	110.0	0.79
Andy Pettitte, NYA	21-8, 3.87	11.0	104.0	0.74
Mariano Rivera, NYA	2.09, 5 saves	1.0	18.0	0.13
Charles Nagy, Cle	17-5, 3.41	0.0	12.0	0.09
Mike Mussina, Bal	19-11, 4.81	0.0	5.0	0.04
Alex Fernandez, ChA	16-10, 3.45	0.0	1.0	0.01
Roberto Hernandez, ChA	1.91, 38 saves	0.0	1.0	0.01
Ken Hill, Tex	16-10, 3.63	0.0	1.0	0.01

Rookie of the Year

Pitcher, Pos, Team	Stats	1st Pl	Pts	Share
Derek Jeter, ss, NYA	.314-10-78	28.0	140.0	1.00
James Baldwin, p, ChA	11-6, 4.42	0.0	64.0	0.46
Tony Clark, 1b, Det	.250-27-72	0.0	30.0	0.21
Rocky Coppinger, p, Bal	10-6, 5.18	0.0	6.0	0.04
Jose Rosado, p, KC	8-6, 3.21	0.0	6.0	0.04
Darin Erstad, of, Cal	.284-4-20	0.0	3.0	0.02
Tony Batista, 2b, Oak	.298-6-25	0.0	1.0	0.01
Tim Crabtree, p, Tor	2.54, 1 saves	0.0	1.0	0.01
Jeff D'Amico, p, Mil	6-6, 5.44	0.0	1.0	0.01

Manager of the Year

Manager, Team	Stats	1st Pl	Pts	Share
Johnny Oates, Tex	90-72, 1st W	12.0	89.0	0.64
Joe Torre, NYA	92-70, 1st E	10.0	89.0	0.64
Lou Piniella, Sea	85-76, 2nd W	3.0	50.0	0.25
Mike Hargrove, Cle	99-62, 1st C	2.0	22.0	0.16
Buddy Bell, Det	53-109, 5th E	1.0	5.0	0.04
Davey Johnson, Bal	88-74, 2nd E	0.0	4.0	0.03
Tom Kelly, Min	78-84, 4th C	0.0	4.0	0.03
Art Howe, Oak	78-84, 3rd W	0.0	3.0	0.02
Kevin Kennedy, Bos	85-77, 3rd E	0.0	1.0	0.01

Gold Gloves

Player, Pos, Team	Rng	LRng	FPct	LFPct
Mike Mussina, p, Bal	—	—	1.000	.960
Ivan Rodriguez, c, Tex	—	—	.989	.990
J.T. Snow, 1b, Cal	—	—	.993	.992
Roberto Alomar, 2b, Bal	5.13	4.33	.985	.980
Robin Ventura, 3b, ChA	2.48	2.18	.974	.956
Omar Vizquel, ss, Cle	4.49	4.19	.971	.971
Jay Buhner, of, Sea	1.83	2.02	.989	.983
Ken Griffey Jr., of, Sea	2.81	2.02	.990	.983
Kenny Lofton, of, Cle	2.56	2.02	.975	.983

National League

MVP

Player, Pos, Team	Stats	1st Pl	Pts	Share
Ken Caminiti, 3b, SD	.326-40-130	28.0	392.0	1.00
Mike Piazza, c, LA	.336-36-105	0.0	237.0	0.60
Ellis Burks, of, Col	.344-40-128	0.0	186.0	0.47

Chipper Jones, 3b, Atl	.309-30-110	0.0	158.0	0.40
Barry Bonds, of, SF	.308-42-129	0.0	132.0	0.34
Andres Galarraga, 1b, Col	.304-47-150	0.0	112.0	0.29
Gary Sheffield, of, Fla	.314-42-120	0.0	112.0	0.29
Brian Jordan, of, StL	.310-17-104	0.0	69.0	0.18
Jeff Bagwell, 1b, Hou	.315-31-120	0.0	59.0	0.15
Steve Finley, of, SD	.298-30-95	0.0	38.0	0.10
John Smoltz, p, Atl	24-8, 2.94	0.0	33.0	0.08
Barry Larkin, ss, Cin	.298-33-89	0.0	29.0	0.07
Marquis Grissom, of, Atl	.308-23-74	0.0	23.0	0.06
Bernard Gilkey, of, NYN	.317-30-117	0.0	13.0	0.03
Sammy Sosa, of, ChN	.273-40-100	0.0	12.0	0.03
Eric Karros, 1b, LA	.260-34-111	0.0	10.0	0.03
Henry Rodriguez, of, Mon	.276-36-103	0.0	9.0	0.02
Todd Hundley, c, NYN	.259-41-112	0.0	7.0	0.02
Lance Johnson, of, NYN	.333-9-69	0.0	7.0	0.02
Dante Bichette, of, Col	.313-31-141	0.0	6.0	0.02
Todd Worrell, p, LA	3.03, 44 saves	0.0	3.0	0.01
Kevin Brown, p, Fla	17-11, 1.89	0.0	2.0	0.01
Trevor Hoffman, p, SD	2.25, 42 saves	0.0	2.0	0.01
Moises Alou, of, Mon	.281-21-96	0.0	1.0	0.00

Cy Young

Pitcher, Team	Stats	1st Pl	Pts	Share
John Smoltz, Atl	24-8, 2.94	26.0	136.0	0.97
Kevin Brown, Fla	17-11, 1.89	2.0	88.0	0.63
Andy Benes, StL	18-10, 3.83	0.0	9.0	0.06
Hideo Nomo, LA	16-11, 3.19	0.0	5.0	0.04
Trevor Hoffman, SD	2.25, 42 saves	0.0	3.0	0.02
Greg Maddux, Atl	15-11, 2.72	0.0	3.0	0.02
Todd Worrell, LA	3.03, 44 saves	0.0	3.0	0.02
Denny Neagle, Pit-Atl	16-9, 3.50	0.0	2.0	0.01
Jeff Fassero, Mon	15-11, 3.30	0.0	1.0	0.01
Al Leiter, Fla	16-12, 2.93	0.0	1.0	0.01
Shane Reynolds, Hou	16-10, 3.65	0.0	1.0	0.01

Rookie of the Year

Pitcher, Pos, Team	Stats	1st Pl	Pts	Share
Todd Hollandsworth, of, LA	.291-12-59	15.0	105.0	0.75
Edgar Renteria, ss, Fla	.309-5-31	10.0	84.0	0.60
Jason Kendall, c, Pit	.300-3-42	1.0	30.0	0.21
F.P. Santangelo, of, Mon	.277-7-56	1.0	15.0	0.11
Rey Ordonez, ss, NYN	.257-1-30	1.0	7.0	0.05
Jermaine Dye, of, Atl	.281-12-37	0.0	6.0	0.04
Alan Benes, p, StL	13-10, 4.90	0.0	5.0	0.04

Manager of the Year

Manager, Team	Stats	1st Pl	Pts	Share
Bruce Bochy, SD	91-71, 1st W	10.0	76.0	0.54
Felipe Alou, Mon	88-74, 2nd E	8.0	74.0	0.53
Tony La Russa, StL	88-74, 1st C	7.0	69.0	0.49
Bobby Cox, Atl	96-66, 1st E	3.0	24.0	0.17
Bill Russell, LA	49-37, 2nd W	0.0	6.0	0.04
Terry Collins, Hou	82-80, 2nd C	0.0	3.0	0.02

Gold Gloves

Player, Pos, Team	Rng	LRng	FPct	LFPct
Greg Maddux, p, Atl	—	—	.991	.954
Charles Johnson, c, Fla	—	—	.995	.989
Mark Grace, 1b, ChN	—	—	.997	.992
Craig Biggio, 2b, Hou	4.94	4.40	.988	.981
Ken Caminiti, 3b, SD	2.85	2.21	.954	.948
Barry Larkin, ss, Cin	4.34	3.99	.975	.967
Barry Bonds, of, SF	1.95	1.80	.980	.978
Steve Finley, of, SD	2.45	1.80	.982	.978
Marquis Grissom, of, Atl	2.20	1.80	.997	.978

1997

American League

MVP

Player, Pos, Team	Stats	1st Pl	Pts	Share
Ken Griffey Jr., of, Sea	.304-56-147	28.0	392.0	1.00
Tino Martinez, 1b, NYA	.296-44-141	0.0	248.0	0.63
Frank Thomas, 1b, ChA	.347-35-125	0.0	172.0	0.44
Randy Myers, p, Bal	1.51, 45 saves	0.0	128.0	0.33
David Justice, of, Cle	.329-33-101	0.0	90.0	0.23
Jim Thome, 1b, Cle	.286-40-102	0.0	89.0	0.23
Tim Salmon, of, Ana	.296-33-129	0.0	84.0	0.21
Nomar Garciaparra, ss, Bos	.306-30-98	0.0	83.0	0.21
Juan Gonzalez, dh, Tex	.296-42-131	0.0	66.0	0.17
Roger Clemens, p, Tor	21-7, 2.05	0.0	56.0	0.14
Randy Johnson, p, Sea	20-4, 2.28	0.0	42.0	0.11
Paul O'Neill, of, NYA	.324-21-117	0.0	37.0	0.09
Rafael Palmeiro, 1b, Bal	.254-38-110	0.0	36.0	0.09
Edgar Martinez, dh, Sea	.330-28-108	0.0	22.0	0.06
Sandy Alomar Jr., c, Cle	.324-21-83	0.0	22.0	0.06
Ivan Rodriguez, c, Tex	.313-20-77	0.0	16.0	0.04
Bernie Williams, of, NYA	.328-21-100	0.0	14.0	0.04
Tony Clark, 1b, Det	.276-32-117	0.0	13.0	0.03
Jay Buhner, of, Sea	.243-40-109	0.0	12.0	0.03
Doug Jones, p, Mil	2.02, 36 saves	0.0	5.0	0.01
Arthur Rhodes, p, Bal	3.02, 1 saves	0.0	5.0	0.01
Roberto Alomar, 2b, Bal	.333-14-60	0.0	4.0	0.01
Rusty Greer, of, Tex	.321-26-87	0.0	4.0	0.01
Derek Jeter, ss, NYA	.291-10-70	0.0	3.0	0.01
Mariano Rivera, p, NYA	1.88, 43 saves	0.0	2.0	0.01
Brad Radke, p, Min	20-10, 3.87	0.0	2.0	0.01
Deivi Cruz, ss, Det	.241-2-40	0.0	2.0	0.01
Mo Vaughn, 1b, Bos	.315-35-96	0.0	2.0	0.01
Jeromy Burnitz, of, Mil	.281-27-85	0.0	1.0	0.00

Cy Young

Pitcher, Team	Stats	1st Pl	Pts	Share
Roger Clemens, Tor	21-7, 2.05	25.0	134.0	0.96
Randy Johnson, Sea	20-4, 2.28	2.0	77.0	0.55
Brad Radke, Min	20-10, 3.87	2.0	17.0	0.12
Randy Myers, Bal	1.51, 45 saves	1.0	14.0	0.10
Andy Pettitte, NYA	18-7, 2.88	0.0	9.0	0.06
Mike Mussina, Bal	15-8, 3.20	0.0	1.0	0.01

Rookie of the Year

Pitcher, Pos, Team	Stats	1st Pl	Pts	Share
Nomar Garciaparra, ss, Bos	.306-30-98	28.0	140.0	1.00
Jose Cruz Jr., of, Sea-Tor	.248-26-68	0.0	61.0	0.44
Jason Dickson, p, Ana	13-9, 4.29	0.0	27.0	0.19
Deivi Cruz, ss, Det	.241-2-40	0.0	12.0	0.09
Jaret Wright, p, Cle	8-3, 4.38	0.0	7.0	0.05
Mike Cameron, of, ChA	.259-14-55	0.0	5.0	0.04

Manager of the Year

Manager, Team	Stats	1st Pl	Pts	Share
Davey Johnson, Bal	98-64, 1st E	10.0	88.0	0.63
Buddy Bell, Det	79-83, 3rd E	4.0	50.0	0.36
Phil Garner, Mil	78-83, 3rd C	5.0	42.0	0.30
Lou Piniella, Sea	90-72, 1st W	3.0	30.0	0.21
Terry Collins, Ana	84-78, 2nd W	4.0	24.0	0.17
Mike Hargrove, Cle	86-75, 1st C	2.0	13.0	0.09
Joe Torre, NYA	96-66, 2nd E	0.0	5.0	0.04

Gold Gloves

Player, Pos, Team	Rng	LRng	FPct	LFPct
Mike Mussina, p, Bal	—	—	1.000	.955
Ivan Rodriguez, c, Tex	—	—	.992	.991
Rafael Palmeiro, 1b, Bal	—	—	.993	.992
Chuck Knoblauch, 2b, Min	4.62	4.33	.985	.980
Matt Williams, 3b, Cle	2.58	2.32	.970	.953
Omar Vizquel, ss, Cle	4.43	4.05	.985	.974
Jim Edmonds, of, Ana	2.79	2.02	.985	.982
Ken Griffey Jr., of, Sea	2.59	2.02	.985	.982
Bernie Williams, of, NYA	2.13	2.02	.993	.982

National League

MVP

Player, Pos, Team	Stats	1st Pl	Pts	Share
Larry Walker, of, Col	.366-49-130	22.0	359.0	0.92
Mike Piazza, c, LA	.362-40-124	3.0	263.0	0.67
Jeff Bagwell, 1b, Hou	.286-43-135	3.0	233.0	0.59
Craig Biggio, 2b, Hou	.309-22-81	0.0	157.0	0.40
Barry Bonds, of, SF	.291-40-101	0.0	123.0	0.31
Tony Gwynn, of, SD	.372-17-119	0.0	113.0	0.29
Andres Galarraga, 1b, Col	.318-41-140	0.0	85.0	0.22
Jeff Kent, 2b, SF	.250-29-121	0.0	80.0	0.20
Chipper Jones, 3b, Atl	.295-21-111	0.0	70.0	0.18
Moises Alou, of, Fla	.292-23-115	0.0	60.0	0.15
Charles Johnson, c, Fla	.250-19-63	0.0	22.0	0.06
Greg Maddux, p, Atl	19-4, 2.20	0.0	16.0	0.04
Edgardo Alfonzo, 3b, NYN	.315-10-72	0.0	10.0	0.03
Curt Schilling, p, Phi	17-11, 2.97	0.0	9.0	0.02
Raul Mondesi, of, LA	.310-30-87	0.0	8.0	0.02
Pedro Martinez, p, Mon	17-8, 1.90	0.0	6.0	0.02
Mark McGwire, 1b, StL	.253-24-42	0.0	6.0	0.02
Ray Lankford, of, StL	.295-31-98	0.0	6.0	0.02
Sammy Sosa, of, ChN	.251-36-119	0.0	5.0	0.01
Kevin Young, 1b, Pit	.300-18-74	0.0	5.0	0.01
Jeff Blauser, ss, Atl	.308-17-70	0.0	4.0	0.01
Vinny Castilla, 3b, Col	.304-40-113	0.0	3.0	0.01
Darryl Kile, p, Hou	19-7, 2.57	0.0	3.0	0.01
Rod Beck, p, SF	3.47, 37 saves	0.0	2.0	0.01
Tony Womack, 2b, Pit	.278-6-50	0.0	2.0	0.01
Kenny Lofton, of, Atl	.333-5-48	0.0	1.0	0.00
J.T. Snow, 1b, SF	.281-28-104	0.0	1.0	0.00

Cy Young

Pitcher, Team	Stats	1st Pl	Pts	Share
Pedro Martinez, Mon	17-8, 1.90	25.0	134.0	0.96
Greg Maddux, Atl	19-4, 2.20	3.0	75.0	0.54
Denny Neagle, Atl	20-5, 2.97	0.0	24.0	0.17
Curt Schilling, Phi	17-11, 2.97	0.0	12.0	0.09
Darryl Kile, Hou	19-7, 2.57	0.0	7.0	0.05

Rookie of the Year

Pitcher, Pos, Team	Stats	1st Pl	Pts	Share
Scott Rolen, 3b, Phi	.283-21-92	28.0	140.0	1.00
Livan Hernandez, p, Fla	9-3, 3.18	0.0	25.0	0.18
Matt Morris, p, StL	12-9, 3.19	0.0	25.0	0.18
Rich Loiselle, p, Pit	3.10, 29 saves	0.0	22.0	0.16
Andruw Jones, of, Atl	.231-18-70	0.0	15.0	0.11
Vladimir Guerrero, of, Mon	.302-11-40	0.0	9.0	0.06
Jose Guillen, of, Pit	.267-14-70	0.0	4.0	0.03
Brett Tomko, p, Cin	11-7, 3.43	0.0	4.0	0.03
Jeremi Gonzalez, p, ChN	11-9, 4.25	0.0	3.0	0.02
Tony Womack, 2b, Pit	.278-6-50	0.0	3.0	0.02
Kevin Orie, 3b, ChN	.275-8-44	0.0	1.0	0.01
Neifi Perez, ss, Col	.291-5-31	0.0	1.0	0.01

Manager of the Year

Manager, Team	Stats	1st Pl	Pts	Share
Dusty Baker, SF	90-72, 1st W	17.0	110.0	0.79
Gene Lamont, Pit	79-83, 2nd C	10.0	92.0	0.66
Larry Dierker, Hou	84-78, 1st C	1.0	34.0	0.24
Bobby Valentine, NYN	88-74, 3rd E	0.0	7.0	0.05
Bobby Cox, Atl	101-61, 1st E	0.0	6.0	0.04
Terry Francona, Phi	68-94, 5th E	0.0	2.0	0.01
Jim Leyland, Fla	92-70, 2nd E	0.0	1.0	0.01

Gold Gloves

Player, Pos, Team	Rng	LRng	FPct	LFPct
Greg Maddux, p, Atl	—	—	.956	.953
Charles Johnson, c, Fla	—	—	1.000	.990
J.T. Snow, 1b, SF	—	—	.995	.993
Craig Biggio, 2b, Hou	5.28	4.31	.979	.981
Ken Caminiti, 3b, SD	2.86	2.19	.941	.946
Rey Ordonez, ss, NYN	4.46	3.85	.983	.973
Barry Bonds, of, SF	1.89	1.77	.984	.980
Raul Mondesi, of, LA	2.19	1.77	.989	.980
Larry Walker, of, Col	1.62	1.77	.992	.980

Award Share Leaders—Career

MVP

	Player	Won	1st Pl	Share
1	Stan Musial	3	69.0	6.97
2	Ted Williams	2	48.0	6.43
3	Willie Mays	2	36.0	6.01
4	Mickey Mantle	3	64.0	5.77
5	Hank Aaron	1	14.0	5.51
6	Joe DiMaggio	3	*42.0*	5.44
7	Lou Gehrig	2	*7.0*	5.43
8	Mike Schmidt	3	61.0	4.97
9	Frank Robinson	2	41.0	4.84
10	Barry Bonds	3	75.0	4.68
11	Jimmie Foxx	3	*29.0*	4.20
12	Yogi Berra	3	23.0	4.00
13	Eddie Collins	1	*7.0*	3.86
14	Hank Greenberg	2	*26.0*	3.69
15	Pete Rose	1	20.5	3.69
16	Brooks Robinson	1	26.0	3.68
17	Frank Thomas	2	53.0	3.57
18	Charlie Gehringer	1	*6.0*	3.55
19	Eddie Murray	0	12.0	3.33
20	Rogers Hornsby	2	*3.0*	3.33
21	George Brett	1	26.0	3.31
22	Willie Stargell	1	25.0	3.30
23	Reggie Jackson	1	32.0	3.28
24	Harmon Killebrew	1	18.0	3.25
25	Dave Parker	1	27.0	3.19
26	Jim Rice	1	25.0	3.14
27	Joe Morgan	2	46.5	3.04
28	Al Kaline	0	5.0	2.93
29	Ernie Banks	2	32.5	2.92
30	Paul Waner	1	*0.0*	2.88
31	Roberto Clemente	1	9.0	2.82
32	Carl Hubbell	2	7.0	2.82
33	Dizzy Dean	1	6.0	2.80
34	Johnny Bench	2	33.0	2.77
35	Ken Griffey Jr.	1	35.0	2.75
36	Mel Ott	0	*4.0*	2.73
37	Bill Terry	0	*0.0*	2.71
38	Mickey Cochrane	2	*0.0*	2.70
39	Lou Boudreau	1	24.0	2.67
40	Frankie Frisch	1	*0.0*	2.59
41	Kirby Puckett	0	3.0	2.55
42	Walter Johnson	2	*0.0*	2.53
43	Roy Campanella	3	36.0	2.53
44	Gabby Hartnett	1	*3.0*	2.52
45	Bob Feller	0	10.0	2.49
46	Steve Garvey	1	13.0	2.47
47	Johnny Mize	0	*9.0*	2.47
48	Rickey Henderson	1	26.0	2.46
49	Chuck Klein	1	*6.0*	2.45
50	Warren Spahn	0	3.0	2.45
51	Al Simmons	0	*0.0*	2.43
52	Nellie Fox	1	23.0	2.43
53	George Foster	1	20.0	2.37
54	Andre Dawson	1	14.0	2.37
55	Dale Murphy	2	35.0	2.31
56	Cal Ripken Jr.	2	36.0	2.30
57	Pedro Guerrero	0	5.0	2.29
58	Sandy Koufax	1	29.0	2.28
59	Joe Medwick	1	*2.0*	2.27
60	Mike Piazza	0	6.0	2.26
61	Carl Yastrzemski	1	22.0	2.25
62	Heinie Manush	0	*2.0*	2.25
63	Don Mattingly	1	28.0	2.22
64	Dave Winfield	0	6.0	2.20
65	Hal Newhouser	2	19.0	2.13
66	Albert Belle	0	13.0	2.13
67	Rabbit Maranville	0	*0.0*	2.12
68	Vern Stephens	0	6.0	2.11
69	Enos Slaughter	0	10.0	2.10
70	Keith Hernandez	1	7.0	2.09
71	Pie Traynor	0	*0.0*	2.04
72	Bill Dickey	0	*8.0*	2.02
73	Luke Appling	0	5.0	2.02
74	Ryne Sandberg	1	22.0	1.97
75	Duke Snider	0	11.0	1.97
76	Joe Cronin	0	*2.0*	1.97
77	Boog Powell	1	17.0	1.94
78	Lefty Grove	1	*0.0*	1.93
79	Gary Carter	0	2.0	1.93
80	Robin Roberts	0	9.0	1.93
81	Billy Herman	0	*0.0*	1.93
82	George Bell	1	20.0	1.92
83	Harry Heilmann	0	*0.0*	1.92
84	Phil Rizzuto	1	22.0	1.92
85	Tony Gwynn	0	1.0	1.91
86	Tony Oliva	0	6.0	1.90
87	Minnie Minoso	0	5.0	1.90
88	Frank McCormick	1	*18.0*	1.88
89	Orlando Cepeda	1	20.0	1.88
90	Earl Averill	0	*0.0*	1.85
91	Will Clark	0	3.0	1.85
92	Maury Wills	1	13.0	1.84
93	Babe Ruth	1	*8.0*	1.83
94	Robin Yount	2	35.0	1.80
95	Rod Carew	1	13.0	1.79
96	Jeff Bagwell	1	31.0	1.78
97	Dennis Eckersley	1	19.0	1.77
98	Roger Clemens	1	22.0	1.75
99	Pee Wee Reese	0	8.0	1.75
100	Jackie Robinson	1	14.0	1.73
101	Tris Speaker	1	*0.0*	1.72
102	Darryl Strawberry	0	7.0	1.71
103	Eddie Mathews	0	8.5	1.70
104	Bob Lemon	0	5.0	1.68
105	Bucky Walters	1	18.0	1.68
106	Cecil Fielder	0	19.0	1.67
107	Travis Jackson	0	*0.0*	1.66
108	Willie McCovey	1	11.0	1.65
109	Dick Groat	1	20.0	1.64
110	Dick Allen	1	22.0	1.64
111	Ken Boyer	1	14.0	1.62
112	Dazzy Vance	1	*0.0*	1.61
113	Jim Bottomley	1	*0.0*	1.60
114	Billy Williams	0	7.0	1.60
115	Lou Brock	0	9.0	1.60
116	Joe Jackson	0	*0.0*	1.59
117	Joe Gordon	1	*12.0*	1.56
118	Greg Luzinski	0	9.0	1.54
119	Larry Walker	1	22.0	1.53
120	Jose Canseco	1	28.0	1.52
121	Terry Pendleton	1	16.0	1.51
122	Thurman Munson	1	19.0	1.50
123	Elston Howard	1	15.0	1.49
124	Dixie Walker	0	*5.0*	1.48
125	Joe Torre	1	22.0	1.47
126	Rocky Colavito	0	4.0	1.45
127	Paul Molitor	0	0.0	1.44
128	Ken Singleton	0	6.0	1.43
129	Rollie Fingers	1	17.0	1.42
130	Ty Cobb	1	*8.0*	1.42
131	Juan Gonzalez	1	11.0	1.42
132	Lefty O'Doul	0	*0.0*	1.41
133	Fred McGriff	0	0.0	1.41
134	Roger Maris	2	15.0	1.41
135	Fred Lynn	1	22.0	1.40
136	Tom Seaver	0	11.0	1.39
137	Mort Cooper	1	13.0	1.38
138	Red Schoendienst	0	10.0	1.37
139	Sal Bando	0	7.5	1.37
140	Cecil Cooper	0	0.0	1.36
141	Steve Carlton	0	1.0	1.36
142	Ted Kluszewski	0	7.0	1.32
143	Ralph Kiner	0	1.0	1.31
144	Mo Vaughn	1	12.0	1.31
145	Kiki Cuyler	0	*0.0*	1.30
146	Jake Daubert	1	*0.0*	1.30
147	Denny McLain	1	20.0	1.30
148	Joe Carter	0	5.0	1.29
149	Carlton Fisk	0	4.0	1.28
150	Hughie Critz	0	*0.0*	1.28
151	Bill Freehan	0	0.0	1.27
152	Dan Quisenberry	0	5.0	1.27
153	Lefty Gomez	0	*0.0*	1.27
154	Matt Williams	0	0.0	1.26
155	Paul Derringer	0	*3.0*	1.25
156	Al Oliver	0	0.0	1.25
157	Dolph Camilli	1	*19.0*	1.24
158	Luis Aparicio	0	8.0	1.24
159	Lon Warneke	0	0.0	1.24
160	Bobby Bonilla	0	2.0	1.24
161	Al Rosen	1	24.0	1.23
162	Bob Gibson	1	14.0	1.23
163	Arky Vaughan	0	*0.0*	1.23
164	Bill Nicholson	0	*9.0*	1.23
165	Ron Santo	0	0.0	1.22
166	Alan Trammell	0	12.0	1.22
167	Bob Elliott	1	9.0	1.22
168	Kevin Mitchell	1	20.0	1.21
169	George Kell	0	0.0	1.21
170	Burleigh Grimes	0	*0.0*	1.21
171	George Burns	1	*0.0*	1.20
	Honus Wagner	0	*0.0*	1.20
173	Bruce Sutter	0	2.0	1.20
	Wade Boggs	0	0.0	1.20
175	Sal Maglie	0	5.0	1.19
176	Larry Doyle	1	*0.0*	1.19
	Wes Ferrell	0	*0.0*	1.19
178	Kirk Gibson	1	13.0	1.17
179	Jack Clark	0	3.0	1.15
180	Don Newcombe	1	8.0	1.14
181	Don Baylor	1	20.0	1.14
182	Early Wynn	0	0.0	1.13
183	Roy Sievers	0	4.0	1.12
184	Marty Marion	1	8.0	1.12
185	Phil Cavarretta	1	15.0	1.11
186	Greg Maddux	0	7.0	1.10
187	George Kelly	0	*0.0*	1.10
188	Glenn Davis	0	6.0	1.09
189	Joe Sewell	0	*0.0*	1.09
190	Wally Berger	0	0.0	1.09
	Freddy Lindstrom	0	*0.0*	1.09
192	Allie Reynolds	0	10.0	1.09
193	Joe Rudi	0	6.5	1.08
194	Barry Larkin	1	11.0	1.08
195	Whitey Ford	0	3.0	1.08
196	Hack Wilson	0	*0.0*	1.06
197	Jackie Jensen	1	9.0	1.06
198	Dwight Evans	0	0.0	1.05
199	Al Dark	0	2.0	1.05
200	Johnny Sain	0	5.0	1.05

Cy Young

	Player	Won	1st Pl	Share
1	Roger Clemens	4	107.0	4.64
2	Greg Maddux	4	101.0	4.48
3	Steve Carlton	4	89.0	4.29
4	Tom Seaver	3	64.0	3.84
5	Jim Palmer	3	61.0	3.57
6	Sandy Koufax	3	61.0	3.05
7	Randy Johnson	1	36.0	2.23
8	Bret Saberhagen	2	50.0	2.19
9	Tom Glavine	1	27.0	2.13
10	Bob Gibson	2	43.0	2.03
11	Catfish Hunter	1	22.0	2.02
12	Gaylord Perry	2	33.0	2.00
13	Warren Spahn	1	30.0	1.91
14	Ron Guidry	1	33.0	1.90
15	Fergie Jenkins	1	28.0	1.82
16	Fernando Valenzuela	1	18.0	1.56
17	Rick Sutcliffe	1	29.0	1.56
18	Dwight Gooden	1	25.0	1.55
19	Dan Quisenberry	0	22.0	1.49
20	Nolan Ryan	0	19.0	1.47
21	Randy Jones	1	22.0	1.47
22	Mike Scott	1	19.0	1.43
23	Denny McLain	2	30.0	1.42
24	Mike Marshall	1	26.0	1.37
25	Orel Hershiser	1	27.0	1.32
26	Jack McDowell	1	23.0	1.27
27	Dennis Eckersley	1	20.0	1.25
28	David Cone	1	15.0	1.25
29	Jimmy Key	0	14.0	1.24
30	Dave Stewart	0	6.0	1.22
31	Frank Viola	1	27.0	1.19
32	Bruce Sutter	1	12.0	1.14
33	Rollie Fingers	1	24.0	1.13
34	Vida Blue	1	15.0	1.05
35	Doug Drabek	1	23.0	1.02
36	Mike Flanagan	1	26.0	0.97
	John Smoltz	1	26.0	0.97
38	Pedro Martinez	1	25.0	0.96
39	Mickey Lolich	0	12.0	0.93
40	Tommy John	0	4.0	0.92
41	Jim Lonborg	1	18.0	0.90
	Mike McCormick	1	18.0	0.90
43	Mark Davis	1	19.0	0.89
44	John Denny	1	20.0	0.86
45	Dean Chance	1	17.0	0.85
46	Mike Cuellar	1	16.0	0.83
47	LaMarr Hoyt	1	17.0	0.83
48	Early Wynn	1	13.0	0.81
49	Pat Hentgen	1	16.0	0.81
	Andy Pettitte	0	11.0	0.81
51	Bob Welch	1	15.0	0.81
52	Jack Morris	0	6.0	0.74
53	Steve Stone	1	13.0	0.71
54	Don Drysdale	1	14.0	0.70
	Wilbur Wood	0	8.0	0.70
56	Kevin Brown	0	2.0	0.69
57	Pete Vuckovich	1	14.0	0.68
58	Mike Norris	0	13.0	0.65
59	Joe Niekro	0	9.0	0.64
60	Ramon Martinez	0	1.0	0.64
61	Willie Hernandez	1	12.0	0.63
62	Don Newcombe	1	10.0	0.63
	Rick Reuschel	0	9.0	0.63
64	Jerry Koosman	0	7.0	0.61
65	Steve McCatty	0	6.0	0.60
66	Whitey Ford	1	10.0	0.59
67	Jim Perry	1	9.0	0.58
68	Vern Law	1	8.0	0.57
69	Andy Messersmith	0	5.0	0.57
70	Mike Caldwell	0	0.0	0.54
71	John Tudor	0	0.0	0.54
72	Lee Smith	0	4.0	0.54
73	Mario Soto	0	2.0	0.54
74	Dave McNally	0	6.0	0.50
75	Mike Mussina	0	3.0	0.49
76	Steve Bedrosian	1	9.0	0.48
77	Danny Jackson	0	0.0	0.47
78	J.R. Richard	0	5.0	0.47
79	Bert Blyleven	0	5.0	0.46
	Jerry Reuss	0	1.0	0.46
81	Bill Swift	0	2.0	0.44
82	Don Sutton	0	2.0	0.43
83	Sparky Lyle	1	9.0	0.43
84	Mark Fidrych	0	5.0	0.43
	Phil Niekro	0	2.0	0.43
86	Ron Bryant	0	3.0	0.42
87	Ken Hill	0	0.0	0.41
88	Scott Erickson	0	3.0	0.40
89	Pete Schourek	0	0.0	0.39
90	Jose Mesa	0	2.0	0.39
91	Sam McDowell	0	4.0	0.38
	Steve Rogers	0	2.0	0.38
93	Goose Gossage	0	2.0	0.36
94	Al Hrabosky	0	2.0	0.35
95	Teddy Higuera	0	0.0	0.34
96	Bob Turley	1	5.0	0.33
	Al Downing	0	1.0	0.33
98	Dennis Leonard	0	5.0	0.33
99	Jack Billingham	0	2.0	0.32
	Burt Hooton	0	0.0	0.32

Manager of the Year

	Manager	Won	1st Pl	Share
1	Tony La Russa	3	70.0	3.81
2	Davey Johnson	1	27.0	3.15
3	Jim Leyland	2	47.0	2.80
4	Bobby Cox	2	38.0	2.56
5	Felipe Alou	1	40.0	2.25
6	Sparky Anderson	2	28.0	2.04
7	Tom Lasorda	2	33.0	1.95
8	Lou Piniella	1	21.0	1.74
9	Tom Kelly	1	37.0	1.59
10	Dusty Baker	2	32.0	1.54
11	Mike Hargrove	0	17.0	1.47
12	Buck Showalter	1	31.0	1.45
13	Roger Craig	0	9.0	1.43
14	Whitey Herzog	1	16.0	1.43
15	Gene Lamont	1	18.0	1.29
16	Dick Howser	0	15.0	1.15
17	Cito Gaston	0	10.0	1.05
18	Buck Rodgers	1	16.0	1.05
19	Joe Torre	1	12.0	1.01
20	Don Zimmer	1	23.0	0.98
21	Jeff Torborg	1	23.0	0.96
22	Joe Morgan	0	10.0	0.95
23	Don Baylor	1	19.0	0.94
24	Hal Lanier	1	19.0	0.90
25	Frank Robinson	1	23.0	0.89
26	Johnny Oates	1	12.0	0.87
	Phil Garner	0	7.0	0.87
28	Jim Frey	1	16.0	0.84
29	Bobby Valentine	0	12.0	0.74
30	Kevin Kennedy	0	14.0	0.74
31	Gene Mauch	0	10.0	0.72
32	John McNamara	1	13.0	0.71
33	Pete Rose	0	10.0	0.71
34	Jim Fregosi	0	11.0	0.66
	Tom Trebelhorn	0	8.0	0.66
36	Bruce Bochy	1	10.0	0.55
37	Terry Collins	0	4.0	0.49
38	Buddy Bell	0	5.0	0.39
39	Bob Lillis	0	9.0	0.39
40	Billy Gardner	0	4.0	0.34
41	Dick Williams	0	4.0	0.34
42	Joe Altobelli	0	7.0	0.25
43	Larry Dierker	0	1.0	0.24
44	Jack McKeon	0	2.0	0.23
45	Chuck Tanner	0	4.0	0.17
46	Billy Martin	0	0.0	0.14
47	Art Howe	0	0.0	0.13
48	Pat Corrales	0	1.0	0.13
49	Jim Lefebvre	0	0.0	0.12
50	Dallas Green	0	1.0	0.11
51	Doug Rader	0	0.0	0.10
52	Hal McRae	0	0.0	0.06
53	Jim Riggleman	0	0.0	0.04
	Bill Russell	0	0.0	0.04
55	Paul Owens	0	1.0	0.04
56	Marcel Lachemann	0	0.0	0.04
57	Jackie Moore	0	0.0	0.03
58	John Felske	0	0.0	0.03
59	Bob Boone	0	0.0	0.02
60	Bud Harrelson	0	0.0	0.02
61	Butch Hobson	0	0.0	0.01
	Terry Francona	0	0.0	0.01
63	Doc Edwards	0	0.0	0.01
	Stump Merrill	0	0.0	0.01
	John Wathan	0	0.0	0.01

Postseason Awards

World Series MVP

Year	Player, Pos, Tm	Lg	Stats
1955	Johnny Podres, p, Bro	NL	2-0, 1.00
1956	Don Larsen, p, NYA	AL	1-0, 0.00
1957	Lew Burdette, p, Mil	NL	3-0, 0.67
1958	Bob Turley, p, NYA	AL	2-1, 2.76
1959	Larry Sherry, p, LA	NL	0.71, 2 saves
1960	Bobby Richardson, 2b, NYA	AL	.367-1-12
1961	Whitey Ford, p, NYA	AL	2-0, 0.00
1962	Ralph Terry, p, NYA	AL	2-1, 1.80
1963	Sandy Koufax, p, LA	NL	2-0, 1.50
1964	Bob Gibson, p, StL	NL	2-1, 3.00
1965	Sandy Koufax, p, LA	NL	2-1, 0.38
1966	Frank Robinson, of, Bal	AL	.286-2-3
1967	Bob Gibson, p, StL	NL	3-0, 1.00
1968	Mickey Lolich, p, Det	AL	3-0, 1.67
1969	Donn Clendenon, 1b, NYN	NL	.357-3-4
1970	Brooks Robinson, 3b, Bal	AL	.429-2-6
1971	Roberto Clemente, of, Pit	NL	.414-2-4
1972	Gene Tenace, c, Oak	AL	.348-4-9
1973	Reggie Jackson, of, Oak	AL	.310-1-6
1974	Rollie Fingers, p, Oak	AL	1.93, 2 saves
1975	Pete Rose, 3b, Cin	NL	.370-0-2
1976	Johnny Bench, c, Cin	NL	.533-2-6
1977	Reggie Jackson, of, NYA	AL	.450-5-8
1978	Bucky Dent, ss, NYA	AL	.417-0-7
1979	Willie Stargell, 1b, Pit	NL	.400-3-7
1980	Mike Schmidt, 3b, Phi	NL	.381-2-7
1981	Ron Cey, 3b, LA	NL	.350-1-6
	Pedro Guerrero, of, LA	NL	.333-2-7
	Steve Yeager, c, LA	NL	.286-2-4
1982	Darrell Porter, c, StL	NL	.286-1-5
1983	Rick Dempsey, c, Bal	AL	.385-1-2
1984	Alan Trammell, ss, Det	AL	.450-2-6
1985	Bret Saberhagen, p, KC	AL	2-0, 0.50
1986	Ray Knight, 3b, NYN	NL	.391-1-5
1987	Frank Viola, p, Min	AL	2-1, 3.72
1988	Orel Hershiser, p, LA	NL	2-0, 1.00
1989	Dave Stewart, p, Oak	AL	2-0, 1.69
1990	Jose Rijo, p, Cin	NL	2-0, 0.59
1991	Jack Morris, p, Min	AL	2-0, 1.17
1992	Pat Borders, c, Tor	AL	.450-1-3
1993	Paul Molitor, dh, Tor	AL	.500-2-8
1995	Tom Glavine, p, Atl	NL	2-0, 1.29
1996	John Wetteland, p, NYA	AL	2.08, 4 saves
1997	Livan Hernandez, p, Fla	NL	2-0, 5.27

League Championship MVP

Year	Player, Pos, Tm	Lg	Stats
1977	Dusty Baker, of, LA	NL	.357-2-8
1978	Steve Garvey, 1b, LA	NL	.389-4-7
1979	Willie Stargell, 1b, Pit	NL	.455-2-6
1980	Frank White, 2b, KC	AL	.545-1-3
	Manny Trillo, 2b, Phi	NL	.381-0-4
1981	Graig Nettles, 3b, NYA	AL	.500-1-9
	Burt Hooton, p, LA	NL	2-0, 0.00
1982	Fred Lynn, of, Cal	AL	.611-1-5
	Darrell Porter, c, StL	NL	.556-0-1
1983	Mike Boddicker, p, Bal	AL	1-0, 0.00
	Gary Matthews, of, Phi	NL	.429-3-8
1984	Kirk Gibson, of, Det	AL	.417-1-2
	Steve Garvey, 1b, SD	NL	.400-1-7
1985	George Brett, 3b, KC	AL	.348-3-5
	Ozzie Smith, ss, StL	NL	.435-1-3
1986	Marty Barrett, 2b, Bos	AL	.367-0-5
	Mike Scott, p, Hou	NL	2-0, 0.50
1987	Gary Gaetti, 3b, Min	AL	.300-2-5
	Jeffrey Leonard, of, SF	NL	.417-4-5
1988	Dennis Eckersley, p, Oak	AL	0.00, 4 saves
	Orel Hershiser, p, LA	NL	1-0, 1.09
1989	Rickey Henderson, of, Oak	AL	.400-2-5
	Will Clark, 1b, SF	NL	.650-2-8
1990	Dave Stewart, p, Oak	AL	2-0, 1.13
	Rob Dibble, p, Cin	NL	0.00, 1 saves
	Randy Myers, p, Cin	NL	0.00, 3 saves
1991	Kirby Puckett, of, Min	AL	.429-2-6
	Steve Avery, p, Atl	NL	2-0, 0.00
1992	Roberto Alomar, 2b, Tor	AL	.423-2-4
	John Smoltz, p, Atl	NL	2-0, 2.66
1993	Dave Stewart, p, Tor	AL	2-0, 2.03
	Curt Schilling, p, Phi	NL	0-0, 1.69
1995	Orel Hershiser, p, Cle	AL	2-0, 1.29
	Mike Devereaux, of, Atl	NL	.308-1-5
1996	Bernie Williams, of, NYA	AL	.474-2-6
	Javy Lopez, c, Atl	NL	.542-2-6
1997	Marquis Grissom, of, Cle	AL	.261-1-4
	Livan Hernandez, p, Fla	NL	2-0, 0.84

STATS Retroactive Awards

MVP

In making the MVP and other retroactive award choices, we didn't try to guess what the voting trends might have been in a particular era. We concentrated on individual statistics (offensive and defensive) and team performance. Not surprisingly, Babe Ruth did particularly well, winning nine retroactive MVPs, including five in a row. Rogers Hornsby and Honus Wagner garnered seven each, with Wagner taking five straight. Ty Cobb collected five. Dan Brouthers won in both the American Association and National League and totaled three overall, tying Ed Delahanty. Because the American and National Leagues had restrictive qualifications for its 1920s MVPs, we weigh in with retroactive choices for those years as well.

Year	Player, Pos, Tm	Lg	Stats
1876	Ross Barnes, 2b, ChN	NL	.429-1-59
1877	Deacon White, 1b, Bos	NL	.387-2-49
1878	Paul Hines, of, Prv	NL	.358-4-50
1879	Monte Ward, p, Prv	NL	47-19, 2.15
1880	George Gore, of, ChN	NL	.360-2-47
1881	Cap Anson, 1b, ChN	NL	.399-1-82
1882	Dan Brouthers, 1b, Buf	NL	.368-6-63
	Pete Browning, 2b, Lou	AA	.378-5——
1883	Jim Whitney, p, Bos	NL	37-21, 2.24
	Harry Stovey, 1b, Phi	AA	.302-14——
1884	Old Hoss Radbourn, p, Prv	NL	59-12, 1.38
	Fred Dunlap, 2b, StL	UA	.412-13——
	Guy Hecker, p, Lou	AA	52-20, 1.80
1885	John Clarkson, p, ChN	NL	53-16, 1.85
	Bob Caruthers, p, STL	AA	40-13, 2.07
1886	King Kelly, of, ChN	NL	.388-4-79
	Bob Caruthers, p-of, STL	AA	30-14, 2.32
1887	Sam Thompson, of, Det	NL	.372-11-166
	Tip O'Neill, of, STL	AA	.435-14-123
1888	Cap Anson, 1b, ChN	NL	.344-12-84
	Silver King, p, STL	AA	45-21, 1.64
1889	John Clarkson, p, Bos	NL	49-19, 2.73
	Tommy Tucker, 1b, Bal	AA	.372-5-99
1890	Oyster Burns, of, Bro	NL	.284-13-128
	Roger Connor, 1b, NY	PL	.349-14-103
	Chicken Wolf, of, Lou	AA	.363-4-98
1891	Billy Hamilton, of, Phi	NL	.340-2-60
	Dan Brouthers, 1b, Bos	AA	.350-5-109
1892	Dan Brouthers, 1b, Bro	NL	.335-5-124
1893	Ed Delahanty, of, Phi	NL	.368-19-146
1894	Hugh Duffy, of, Bos	NL	.440-18-145
1895	Hughie Jennings, ss, Bal	NL	.386-4-125
1896	Hughie Jennings, ss, Bal	NL	.401-0-121
1897	George Davis, ss, NYG	NL	.353-10-136
1898	Billy Hamilton, of, Bos	NL	.369-3-50
1899	Ed Delahanty, of, Phi	NL	.410-9-137
1900	Honus Wagner, of, Pit	NL	.381-4-100
1901	Nap Lajoie, 2b, Phi	AL	.426-14-125
	Honus Wagner, ss, Pit	NL	.353-6-126
1902	Ed Delahanty, of, Was	AL	.376-10-93
	Honus Wagner, of, Pit	NL	.330-3-91
1903	Nap Lajoie, 2b, Cle	AL	.344-7-93
	Honus Wagner, ss, Pit	NL	.355-5-101
1904	Jack Chesbro, p, NYA	AL	41-12, 1.82
	Honus Wagner, ss, Pit	NL	.349-4-75
1905	Rube Waddell, p, Phi	AL	27-10, 1.48
	Christy Mathewson, p, NYG	NL	31-9, 1.28
1906	George Stone, of, StL	AL	.358-6-71

Year	Player, Pos, Tm	Lg	Stats
	Frank Chance, 1b, ChN	NL	.319-3-71
1907	Ty Cobb, of, Det	AL	.350-5-119
	Honus Wagner, ss, Pit	NL	.350-6-82
1908	Ed Walsh, p, ChA	AL	40-15, 1.42
	Christy Mathewson, p, NYG	NL	37-11, 1.43
1909	Ty Cobb, of, Det	AL	.377-9-107
	Honus Wagner, ss, Pit	NL	.339-5-100
1910	Ty Cobb, of, Det	AL	.383-8-91
	Sherry Magee, of, Phi	NL	.331-6-123
1914	Benny Kauff, of, Ind	FL	.370-8-95
1915	Ty Cobb, of, Det	AL	.369-3-99
	Pete Alexander, p, Phi	NL	31-10, 1.22
	Benny Kauff, of, Bro	FL	.342-12-83
1916	Tris Speaker, of, Cle	AL	.386-2-79
	Pete Alexander, p, Phi	NL	33-12, 1.55
1917	Ty Cobb, of, Det	AL	.383-6-102
	Rogers Hornsby, ss, StL	NL	.327-8-66
1918	Babe Ruth, of, Bos	AL	.300-11-66
	Hippo Vaughn, p, ChN	NL	22-10, 1.74
1919	Babe Ruth, of, Bos	AL	.322-29-114
	Heine Groh, 3b, Cin	NL	.310-5-63
1920	Babe Ruth, of, NYA	AL	.376-54-137
	Rogers Hornsby, 2b, StL	NL	.370-9-94
1921	Babe Ruth, of, NYA	AL	.378-59-171
	Rogers Hornsby, 2b, StL	NL	.397-21-126
1922	George Sisler, 1b, StL	AL	.420-8-105
	Rogers Hornsby, 2b, StL	NL	.401-42-152
1923	Babe Ruth, of, NYA	AL	.393-41-131
	Dolf Luque, p, Cin	NL	27-8, 1.93
1924	Babe Ruth, of, NYA	AL	.378-46-121
	Rogers Hornsby, 2b, StL	NL	.424-25-94
1925	Al Simmons, of, Phi	AL	.384-24-129
	Rogers Hornsby, 2b, StL	NL	.403-39-143
1926	Babe Ruth, of, NYA	AL	.372-47-146
	Hack Wilson, of, ChN	NL	.321-21-109
1927	Babe Ruth, of, NYA	AL	.356-60-164
	Paul Waner, of, Pit	NL	.380-9-131
1928	Babe Ruth, of, NYA	AL	.323-54-142
	Jim Bottomley, 1b, StL	NL	.325-31-136
1929	Jimmie Foxx, 1b, Phi	AL	.354-33-117
	Rogers Hornsby, 2b, ChN	NL	.380-39-149
1930	Lefty Grove, p, Phi	AL	28-5, 2.54
	Hack Wilson, of, ChN	NL	.356-56-190

Cy Young

A more appropriate name might be the Walter Johnson Award or the Christy Mathewson Award, as those two Hall of Famers tied for the lead with seven retroactive Cy Young Awards. Johnson took five straight at one point, while Mathewson had a four-year run. Young himself won six (three in each league), the same total as Lefty Grove, who captured his consecutively. Four-time winners included Pete Alexander, Bob Feller and Warren Spahn. Any pitcher who won his league's official Most Valuable Player Award automatically was named the retroactive Cy Young Award winner for that year.

Year	Player, Tm	Lg	Stats
1876	Al Spalding, ChN	NL	47-12, 1.75
1877	Tommy Bond, Bos	NL	40-17, 2.11
1878	Tommy Bond, Bos	NL	40-19, 2.06
1879	Monte Ward, Prv	NL	47-19, 2.15
1880	Larry Corcoran, ChN	NL	43-14, 1.95
1881	Larry Corcoran, ChN	NL	31-14, 2.31
1882	Jim McCormick, Cle	NL	36-30, 2.37
	Will White, Cin	AA	40-12, 1.54

Year	Player, Tm	Lg	Stats
1883	Old Hoss Radbourn, Prv	NL	48-25, 2.05
	Will White, Cin	AA	43-22, 2.09
1884	Old Hoss Radbourn, Prv	NL	59-12, 1.38
	Jim McCormick, Cin	UA	21-3, 1.54
	Guy Hecker, Lou	AA	52-20, 1.80
1885	John Clarkson, ChN	NL	53-16, 1.85
	Bob Caruthers, STL	AA	40-13, 2.07
1886	Lady Baldwin, Det	NL	42-13, 2.24
	Dave Foutz, STL	AA	41-16, 2.11
1887	John Clarkson, ChN	NL	38-21, 3.08
	Matt Kilroy, Bal	AA	46-19, 3.07
1888	Tim Keefe, NYG	NL	35-12, 1.74
	Silver King, STL	AA	45-21, 1.64
1889	John Clarkson, Bos	NL	49-19, 2.73
	Bob Caruthers, Bro	AA	40-11, 3.13
1890	Bill Hutchison, ChN	NL	42-25, 2.70
	Silver King, Chi	PL	30-22, 2.69
	Scott Stratton, Lou	AA	34-14, 2.36
1891	Bill Hutchison, ChN	NL	44-19, 2.81
	George Haddock, Bos	AA	34-11, 2.49
1892	Cy Young, Cle	NL	36-12, 1.93
1893	Cy Young, Cle	NL	34-16, 3.36
1894	Amos Rusie, NYG	NL	36-13, 2.78
1895	Cy Young, Cle	NL	35-10, 3.24
1896	Kid Nichols, Bos	NL	30-14, 2.83
1897	Kid Nichols, Bos	NL	31-11, 2.64
1898	Kid Nichols, Bos	NL	31-12, 2.13
1899	Vic Willis, Bos	NL	27-8, 2.50
1900	Joe McGinnity, NYG	NL	28-8, 2.94
1901	Cy Young, Bos	AL	33-10, 1.62
	Deacon Phillippe, Pit	NL	22-12, 2.22
1902	Cy Young, Bos	AL	32-11, 2.15
	Jack Taylor, ChN	NL	23-11, 1.33
1903	Cy Young, Bos	AL	28-9, 2.08
	Christy Mathewson, NYG	NL	30-13, 2.26
1904	Jack Chesbro, NYA	AL	41-12, 1.82
	Joe McGinnity, NYG	NL	35-8, 1.61
1905	Rube Waddell, Phi	AL	27-10, 1.48
	Christy Mathewson, NYG	NL	31-9, 1.28
1906	Al Orth, NYA	AL	27-17, 2.34
	Three Finger Brown, ChN	NL	26-6, 1.04
1907	Addie Joss, Cle	AL	27-11, 1.83
	Orval Overall, ChN	NL	23-8, 1.68
1908	Ed Walsh, ChA	AL	40-15, 1.42
	Christy Mathewson, NYG	NL	37-11, 1.43
1909	George Mullin, Det	AL	29-8, 2.22
	Christy Mathewson, NYG	NL	25-6, 1.14
1910	Jack Coombs, Phi	AL	31-9, 1.30
	Christy Mathewson, NYG	NL	27-9, 1.89
1911	Walter Johnson, Was	AL	25-13, 1.90
	Christy Mathewson, NYG	NL	26-13, 1.99
1912	Walter Johnson, Was	AL	33-12, 1.39
	Rube Marquard, NYG	NL	26-11, 2.57
1913	Walter Johnson, Was	AL	36-7, 1.14
	Christy Mathewson, NYG	NL	25-11, 2.06
1914	Walter Johnson, Was	AL	28-18, 1.72
	Bill James, Bos	NL	26-7, 1.90
	Claude Hendrix, Chi	FL	29-11, 1.69
1915	Walter Johnson, Was	AL	27-13, 1.55
	Pete Alexander, Phi	NL	31-10, 1.22
	George McConnell, Chi	FL	25-10, 2.20
1916	Babe Ruth, Bos	AL	23-12, 1.75
	Pete Alexander, Phi	NL	33-12, 1.55
1917	Eddie Cicotte, ChA	AL	28-12, 1.53
	Pete Alexander, Phi	NL	30-13, 1.83
1918	Walter Johnson, Was	AL	23-13, 1.27
	Hippo Vaughn, ChN	NL	22-10, 1.74
1919	Eddie Cicotte, ChA	AL	29-7, 1.82

	Hippo Vaughn, ChN	NL	21-14, 1.79
1920	Jim Bagby, Cle	AL	31-12, 2.89
	Pete Alexander, ChN	NL	27-14, 1.91
1921	Red Faber, ChA	AL	25-15, 2.48
	Burleigh Grimes, Bro	NL	22-13, 2.83
1922	Urban Shocker, StL	AL	24-17, 2.97
	Wilbur Cooper, Pit	NL	23-14, 3.18
1923	George Uhle, Cle	AL	26-16, 3.77
	Dolf Luque, Cin	NL	27-8, 1.93
1924	Walter Johnson, Was	AL	23-7, 2.72
	Dazzy Vance, Bro	NL	28-6, 2.16
1925	Stan Coveleski, Was	AL	20-5, 2.84
	Eppa Rixey, Cin	NL	21-11, 2.88
1926	George Uhle, Cle	AL	27-11, 2.83
	Ray Kremer, Pit	NL	20-6, 2.61
1927	Waite Hoyt, NYA	AL	22-7, 2.63
	Jesse Haines, StL	NL	24-10, 2.72
1928	Lefty Grove, Phi	AL	24-8, 2.58
	Larry Benton, NYG	NL	25-9, 2.73
1929	Lefty Grove, Phi	AL	20-6, 2.81
	Pat Malone, ChN	NL	22-10, 3.57
1930	Lefty Grove, Phi	AL	28-5, 2.54
	Pat Malone, ChN	NL	20-9, 3.94
1931	Lefty Grove, Phi	AL	31-4, 2.06
	Ed Brandt, Bos	NL	18-11, 2.92
1932	Lefty Grove, Phi	AL	25-10, 2.84
	Lon Warneke, ChN	NL	22-6, 2.37
1933	Lefty Grove, Phi	AL	24-8, 3.20
	Carl Hubbell, NYG	NL	23-12, 1.66
1934	Lefty Gomez, NYA	AL	26-5, 2.33
	Dizzy Dean, StL	NL	30-7, 2.66
1935	Wes Ferrell, Bos	AL	25-14, 3.52
	Dizzy Dean, StL	NL	28-12, 3.04
1936	Tommy Bridges, Det	AL	23-11, 3.60
	Carl Hubbell, NYG	NL	26-6, 2.31
1937	Lefty Gomez, NYA	AL	21-11, 2.33
	Cliff Melton, NYG	NL	20-9, 2.61
1938	Red Ruffing, NYA	AL	21-7, 3.31
	Bill Lee, ChN	NL	22-9, 2.66
1939	Bob Feller, Cle	AL	24-9, 2.85
	Bucky Walters, Cin	NL	27-11, 2.29
1940	Bob Feller, Cle	AL	27-11, 2.61
	Bucky Walters, Cin	NL	22-10, 2.48
1941	Bob Feller, Cle	AL	25-13, 3.15
	Whit Wyatt, Bro	NL	22-10, 2.34
1942	Tex Hughson, Bos	AL	22-6, 2.59
	Mort Cooper, StL	NL	22-7, 1.78
1943	Spud Chandler, NYA	AL	20-4, 1.64
	Mort Cooper, StL	NL	21-8, 2.30
1944	Hal Newhouser, Det	AL	29-9, 2.22
	Bucky Walters, Cin	NL	23-8, 2.40
1945	Hal Newhouser, Det	AL	25-9, 1.81
	Hank Wyse, ChN	NL	22-10, 2.68
1946	Hal Newhouser, Det	AL	26-9, 1.94
	Howie Pollet, StL	NL	21-10, 2.10
1947	Bob Feller, Cle	AL	20-11, 2.68
	Ewell Blackwell, Cin	NL	22-8, 2.47
1948	Gene Bearden, Cle	AL	20-7, 2.43
	Johnny Sain, Bos	NL	24-15, 2.60
1949	Mel Parnell, Bos	AL	25-7, 2.77
	Warren Spahn, Bos	NL	21-14, 3.07
1950	Bob Lemon, Cle	AL	23-11, 3.84
	Jim Konstanty, Phi	NL	2.66, 22 saves
1951	Ed Lopat, NYA	AL	21-9, 2.91
	Sal Maglie, NYG	NL	23-6, 2.93
1952	Bobby Shantz, Phi	AL	24-7, 2.48
	Robin Roberts, Phi	NL	28-7, 2.59
1953	Virgil Trucks, ChA	AL	20-10, 2.93
	Warren Spahn, Mil	NL	23-7, 2.10
1954	Bob Lemon, Cle	AL	23-7, 2.72
	Johnny Antonelli, NYG	NL	21-7, 2.30

1955	Whitey Ford, NYA	AL	18-7, 2.63
	Robin Roberts, Phi	NL	23-14, 3.28
1956	Herb Score, Cle	AL	20-9, 2.53
1957	Jim Bunning, Det	AL	20-8, 2.69
1958	Warren Spahn, Mil	NL	22-11, 3.07
1959	Sam Jones, SF	NL	21-15, 2.83
1960	Chuck Estrada, Bal	AL	18-11, 3.58
1961	Warren Spahn, Mil	NL	21-13, 3.02
1962	Ralph Terry, NYA	AL	23-12, 3.19
1963	Dick Radatz, Bos	AL	1.97, 25 saves
1964	Sandy Koufax, LA	NL	19-5, 1.74
1965	Sam McDowell, Cle	AL	17-11, 2.18
1966	Jim Kaat, Min	AL	25-13, 2.75

Rookie of the Year

Eighteen of the retroactive Rookies of the Year are Hall of Famers, starting with Elmer Flick in 1898. Pete Browning and Benny Kauff were the only players to win retroactive MVP and Rookie of the Year Awards in the same season. Gene Bearden, Larry Corcoran and Cliff Melton were the only three pitchers to pull off the retroactive Cy Young-Rookie of the Year double in the same season. Two teams produced three consecutive winners: the 1921-23 Cubs (Ray Grimes, Hack Miller, George Grantham) and the 1925-27 Yankees (Earle Combs, Tony Lazzeri, Wilcy Moore). Players were considered rookie-eligible if they hadn't exceeded the modern standards of 130 career at-bats or 50 innings pitched in the major leagues. Players with significant National Association experience weren't considered for early National League Rookie of the Year awards.

Year	Player, Pos, Tm	Lg	Stats
1876	Charley Jones, of, Cin	NL	.286-4-38
1877	Terry Larkin, p, Har	NL	29-25, 2.14
1878	Will White, p, Cin	NL	30-21, 1.79
1879	John O'Rourke, of, Bos	NL	.341-6-62
1880	Larry Corcoran, p, ChN	NL	43-14, 1.95
1881	Jim Whitney, p, Bos	NL	31-33, 2.48
1882	Mike Muldoon, 3b, Cle	NL	.246-6-45
	Pete Browning, 2b, Lou	AA	.378-5——
1883	Charlie Buffinton, of, Bos	NL	.238-1-26
	Steve Brady, 1b, NY	AA	.271-0——
1884	Alex McKinnon, 1b, NYG	NL	.272-4-73
	Harry Moore, of, Was	UA	.336-1——
	Dave Orr, 1b, NY	AA	.354-9——
1885	Ed Daily, p, Phi	NL	26-23, 2.21
	Norm Baker, p, Lou	AA	13-12, 3.40
1886	Jocko Flynn, p, ChN	NL	23-6, 2.24
	Matt Kilroy, p, Bal	AA	29-34, 3.37
1887	Billy O'Brien, 1b, WaN	NL	.278-19-73
	Mike Griffin, of, Bal	AA	.301-3-94
1888	Dummy Hoy, of, WaN	NL	.274-2-29
	Mickey Hughes, p, Bro	AA	25-13, 2.13
1889	Patsy Tebeau, 3b, Cle	NL	.282-8-76
	Jesse Duryea, p, Cin	AA	32-19, 2.56
1890	Billy Rhines, p, Cin	NL	28-17, 1.95
	Bill Joyce, 3b, Bro	PL	.252-1-78
	Cupid Childs, 2b, Syr	AA	.345-2-89
1891	Bill Dahlen, 3b, ChN	NL	.260-9-76
	Jim Canavan, ss, Cin	AA	.238-10-87
1892	Nig Cuppy, p, Cle	NL	28-13, 2.51
1893	Heinie Reitz, 2b, Bal	NL	.286-1-76
1894	Jimmy Bannon, of, Bos	NL	.336-13-114
1895	Bill Hoffer, p, Bal	NL	31-6, 3.21
1896	Gene DeMontreville, ss, Was	NL	.343-8-77
1897	Chick Stahl, of, Bos	NL	.354-4-97

1898	Elmer Flick, of, Phi	NL	.302-8-81
1899	Jimmy Williams, 3b, Pit	NL	.355-9-116
1900	Jimmy Barrett, of, Cin	NL	.316-5-42
1901	Socks Seybold, of, Phi	AL	.334-8-90
	Christy Mathewson, p, NYG	NL	20-17, 2.41
1902	Patsy Dougherty, of, Bos	AL	.342-0-34
	Homer Smoot, of, StL	NL	.311-3-48
1903	Charlie Carr, 1b, Det	AL	.281-2-79
	Jake Weimer, p, ChN	NL	20-8, 2.30
1904	Fred Glade, p, StL	AL	18-15, 2.27
	Harry Lumley, of, Bro	NL	.279-9-78
1905	George Stone, of, StL	AL	.296-7-52
	Ed Reulbach, p, ChN	NL	18-14, 1.42
1906	Claude Rossman, 1b, Cle	AL	.308-1-53
	Jack Pfiester, p, ChN	NL	20-8, 1.51
1907	Glenn Liebhardt, p, Cle	AL	18-14, 2.09
	Mike Mitchell, of, Cin	NL	.292-3-47
1908	Ed Summers, p, Det	AL	24-12, 1.64
	George McQuillan, p, Phi	NL	23-17, 1.53
1909	Home Run Baker, 3b, Phi	AL	.305-4-85
	Doc Hoblitzell, 1b, Cin	NL	.308-4-67
1910	Russ Ford, p, NYA	AL	26-6, 1.65
	King Cole, p, ChN	NL	20-4, 1.80
1911	Joe Jackson, of, Cle	AL	.408-7-83
	Pete Alexander, p, Phi	NL	28-13, 2.57
1912	Del Pratt, 2b, StL	AL	.302-5-69
	Larry Cheney, p, ChN	NL	26-10, 2.85
1913	Reb Russell, p, ChA	AL	22-16, 1.91
	Jim Viox, 2b, Pit	NL	.317-2-65
1914	George Burns, 1b, Det	AL	.291-5-57
	Jeff Pfeffer, p, Bro	NL	23-12, 1.97
	Benny Kauff, of, Ind	FL	.370-8-95
1915	Babe Ruth, p, Bos	AL	18-8, 2.44
	Dave Bancroft, ss, StL	NL	.254-7-30
	Ernie Johnson, ss, STL	FL	.240-7-67
1916	Jim Bagby, p, Cle	AL	16-16, 2.61
	Rogers Hornsby, 3b, StL	NL	.313-6-65
1917	Joe Harris, 1b, Cle	AL	.304-0-65
	Walter Holke, 1b, NYG	NL	.277-2-55
1918	Scott Perry, p, Phi	AL	20-19, 1.98
	Charlie Hollocher, ss, ChN	NL	.316-2-38
1919	Ira Flagstead, of, Det	AL	.331-5-41
	Verne Clemons, c, StL	NL	.264-2-22
1920	Bob Meusel, of, NYA	AL	.328-11-83
	Pat Duncan, of, Cin	NL	.295-2-83
1921	Joe Sewell, ss, Cle	AL	.318-4-91
	Ray Grimes, 1b, ChN	NL	.321-6-79
1922	Herman Pillette, p, Det	AL	19-12, 2.85
	Hack Miller, of, ChN	NL	.352-12-78
1923	Willie Kamm, 3b, ChA	AL	.292-6-87
	George Grantham, 2b, ChN	NL	.281-8-70
1924	Firpo Marberry, p, Was	AL	3.09, 15 saves
	Glenn Wright, ss, Pit	NL	.287-7-111
1925	Earle Combs, of, NYA	AL	.342-3-61
	Jimmy Welsh, of, Bos	NL	.312-7-63
1926	Tony Lazzeri, 2b, NYA	AL	.275-18-114
	Paul Waner, of, Pit	NL	.336-8-79
1927	Wilcy Moore, p, NYA	AL	2.28, 13 saves
	Lloyd Waner, of, Pit	NL	.355-2-27
1928	Red Kress, ss, StL	AL	.273-3-81
	Del Bissonette, 1b, Bro	NL	.320-25-106
1929	Dale Alexander, 1b, Det	AL	.343-25-137
	Johnny Frederick, of, Bro	NL	.328-24-75
1930	Ben Chapman, 3b, NYA	AL	.316-10-81
	Wally Berger, of, Bos	NL	.310-38-119
1931	Joe Vosmik, of, Cle	AL	.320-7-117
	Paul Derringer, p, StL	NL	18-8, 3.36
1932	Johnny Allen, p, NYA	AL	17-4, 3.70
	Billy Herman, 2b, ChN	NL	.314-1-51
1933	Mike Higgins, 3b, Phi	AL	.314-13-99
	Joe Medwick, of, StL	NL	.306-18-98

Year	Player	Lg	Stats
1934	Hal Trosky, 1b, Cle	AL	.330-35-142
	Curt Davis, p, Phi	NL	19-17, 2.95
1935	Jake Powell, of, Was	AL	.312-6-98
	Cy Blanton, p, Pit	NL	18-13, 2.58
1936	Joe DiMaggio, of, NYA	AL	.323-29-125
	Johnny Mize, 1b, StL	NL	.329-19-93
1937	Rudy York, c, Det	AL	.307-35-103
	Cliff Melton, p, NYG	NL	20-9, 2.61
1938	Jeff Heath, of, Cle	AL	.343-21-112
	Johnny Rizzo, of, Pit	NL	.301-23-111
1939	Ted Williams, of, Bos	AL	.327-31-145
	Bob Bowman, p, StL	NL	2.60, 9 saves
1940	Wally Judnich, of, StL	AL	.303-24-89
	Babe Young, 1b, NYG	NL	.286-17-101
1941	Phil Rizzuto, ss, NYA	AL	.307-3-46
	Elmer Riddle, p, Cin	NL	19-4, 2.24
1942	Johnny Pesky, ss, Bos	AL	.331-2-51
	Johnny Beazley, p, StL	NL	21-6, 2.13
1943	Dick Wakefield, of, Det	AL	.316-7-79
	Lou Klein, 2b, StL	NL	.287-7-62
1944	Joe Berry, p, Phi	AL	1.94, 12 saves
	Bill Voiselle, p, NYG	NL	21-16, 3.02
1945	Boo Ferriss, p, Bos	AL	21-10, 2.96
	Ken Burkhart, p, StL	NL	18-8, 2.90
1946	Hoot Evers, of, Det	AL	.266-4-33
	Del Ennis, of, Phi	NL	.313-17-73
1947	Ferris Fain, 1b, Phi	AL	.291-7-71
1948	Gene Bearden, p, Cle	AL	20-7, 2.43

Manager of the Year

The 14 Hall of Famers primarily honored for their managerial abilities combined to win 57 retroactive Manager of the Year Awards, led by Connie Mack and Casey Stengel with seven each. Stengel received three consecutive awards, the only skipper to do so. John McGraw was the only six-time winner, while Cap Anson, Joe McCarthy and Bill McKechnie each earned five selections. McKechnie and Billy Martin each were honored with four different teams. Four men—Lou Boudreau, Frank Chance, Mickey Cochrane and Fred Dunlap—won MVP and Manager of the Year Awards in the same season.

Year	Manager, Tm	Lg	Stats
1876	Al Spalding, ChN	NL	52-14, 1st
1877	Harry Wright, Bos	NL	42-18, 1st
1878	Cal McVey, Cin	NL	37-23, 2nd
1879	George Wright, Prv	NL	59-25, 1st
1880	Cap Anson, ChN	NL	67-17, 1st
1881	Jim O'Rourke, Buf	NL	45-38, 3rd
1882	Cap Anson, ChN	NL	55-29, 1st
	Pop Snyder, Cin	AA	55-25, 1st
1883	John Morrill, Bos	NL	33-11, 1st
	Lon Knight, Phi	AA	66-32, 1st
1884	Frank Bancroft, Prv	NL	84-28, 1st
	Fred Dunlap, STL	UA	66-16, 1st
	Jim Mutrie, NY	AA	75-32, 1st
1885	Cap Anson, ChN	NL	87-25, 1st
	Charlie Comiskey, STL	AA	79-33, 1st
1886	Bill Watkins, Det	NL	87-36, 2nd
	Horace Phillips, Pit	AA	80-57, 2nd
1887	Bill Watkins, Det	NL	79-45, 1st
	Billy Barnie, Bal	AA	77-58, 3rd
1888	Jim Mutrie, NYG	NL	84-47, 1st
	Charlie Comiskey, STL	AA	92-43, 1st
1889	Jim Hart, Bos	NL	83-45, 2nd
	Bill McGunnigle, Bro	AA	93-44, 1st
1890	Cap Anson, ChN	NL	84-53, 2nd

Year	Manager, Tm	Lg	Stats
	King Kelly, Bos	PL	81-48, 1st
	Jack Chapman, Lou	AA	88-44, 1st
1891	Frank Selee, Bos	NL	87-51, 1st
	Billy Barnie, Bal	AA	71-64, 4th
1892	Patsy Tebeau, Cle	NL	93-56, 2nd
1893	Frank Selee, Bos	NL	86-43, 1st
1894	Ned Hanlon, Bal	NL	89-39, 1st
1895	Cap Anson, ChN	NL	72-58, 4th
1896	Ned Hanlon, Bal	NL	90-39, 1st
1897	Frank Selee, Bos	NL	93-39, 1st
1898	Tom Burns, ChN	NL	85-65, 4th
1899	Bill Shettsline, Phi	NL	94-58, 3rd
1900	Ned Hanlon, Bro	NL	82-54, 1st
1901	Clark Griffith, ChA	AL	83-53, 1st
	Fred Clarke, Pit	NL	90-49, 1st
1902	Connie Mack, Phi	AL	83-53, 1st
	Fred Clarke, Pit	NL	103-36, 1st
1903	Jimmy Collins, Bos	AL	91-47, 1st
	John McGraw, NYG	NL	84-55, 2nd
1904	Fielder Jones, ChA	AL	66-47, 3rd
	John McGraw, NYG	NL	106-47, 1st
1905	Connie Mack, Phi	AL	92-56, 1st
	Hugh Duffy, Phi	NL	83-69, 4th
1906	Clark Griffith, NYA	AL	90-61, 2nd
	Frank Chance, ChN	NL	116-36, 1st
1907	Hughie Jennings, Det	AL	92-58, 1st
	Frank Chance, ChN	NL	107-45, 1st
1908	Jimmy McAleer, StL	AL	83-69, 4th
	John McGraw, NYG	NL	98-56, 2nd
1909	Connie Mack, Phi	AL	95-58, 2nd
	Fred Clarke, Pit	NL	110-42, 1st
1910	Connie Mack, Phi	AL	102-48, 1st
	Frank Chance, ChN	NL	104-50, 1st
1911	George Stovall, Cle	AL	74-62, 3rd
	John McGraw, NYG	NL	99-54, 1st
1912	Jake Stahl, Bos	AL	105-47, 1st
	John McGraw, NYG	NL	103-48, 1st
1913	Joe Birmingham, Cle	AL	86-66, 3rd
	Red Dooin, Phi	NL	88-63, 2nd
1914	Bill Carrigan, Bos	AL	91-62, 2nd
	George Stallings, Bos	NL	94-59, 1st
	Bill Phillips, Ind	FL	88-65, 1st
1915	Hughie Jennings, Det	AL	100-54, 2nd
	Pat Moran, Phi	NL	90-62, 1st
	Joe Tinker, Chi	FL	86-66, 1st
1916	Fielder Jones, StL	AL	79-75, 5th
	Wilbert Robinson, Bro	NL	94-60, 1st
1917	Pants Rowland, ChA	AL	100-54, 1st
	Miller Huggins, StL	NL	82-70, 3rd
1918	Ed Barrow, Bos	AL	75-51, 1st
	Fred Mitchell, ChN	NL	84-45, 1st
1919	Kid Gleason, ChA	AL	88-52, 1st
	Pat Moran, Cin	NL	96-44, 1st
1920	Tris Speaker, Cle	AL	98-56, 1st
	Wilbert Robinson, Bro	NL	93-61, 1st
1921	George McBride, Was	AL	80-73, 4th
	Branch Rickey, StL	NL	87-66, 3rd
1922	Lee Fohl, StL	AL	93-61, 2nd
	John McGraw, NYG	NL	93-61, 1st
1923	Miller Huggins, NYA	AL	98-54, 1st
	Pat Moran, Cin	NL	91-63, 2nd
1924	Bucky Harris, Was	AL	92-62, 1st
	Wilbert Robinson, Bro	NL	92-62, 2nd
1925	Connie Mack, Phi	AL	88-64, 2nd
	Bill McKechnie, Pit	NL	95-58, 1st
1926	Miller Huggins, NYA	AL	91-63, 1st
	Rogers Hornsby, StL	NL	89-65, 1st
1927	Miller Huggins, NYA	AL	110-44, 1st
	Donie Bush, Pit	NL	94-60, 1st
1928	Dan Howley, StL	AL	82-72, 3rd
	Bill McKechnie, StL	NL	95-59, 1st

Year	Manager, Tm	Lg	Stats
1929	Roger Peckinpaugh, Cle	AL	81-71, 3rd
	Joe McCarthy, ChN	NL	98-54, 1st
1930	Walter Johnson, Was	AL	94-60, 2nd
	Gabby Street, StL	NL	92-62, 1st
1931	Connie Mack, Phi	AL	107-45, 1st
	Gabby Street, StL	NL	101-53, 1st
1932	Joe McCarthy, NYA	AL	107-47, 1st
	George Gibson, Pit	NL	86-68, 2nd
1933	Joe Cronin, Was	AL	99-53, 1st
	Bill Terry, NYG	NL	91-61, 1st
1934	Mickey Cochrane, Det	AL	101-53, 1st
	Frank Frisch, StL	NL	95-58, 1st
1935	Jimmy Dykes, ChA	AL	74-78, 5th
	Charlie Grimm, ChN	NL	100-54, 1st
1936	Joe McCarthy, NYA	AL	102-51, 1st
	Bill McKechnie, Bos	NL	71-83, 6th
1937	Joe McCarthy, NYA	AL	102-52, 1st
	Bill Terry, NYG	NL	95-57, 1st
1938	Joe Cronin, Bos	AL	88-61, 2nd
	Gabby Hartnett, ChN	NL	44-27, 1st
1939	Jimmy Dykes, ChA	AL	85-69, 4th
	Bill McKechnie, Cin	NL	97-57, 1st
1940	Del Baker, Det	AL	90-64, 1st
	Bill McKechnie, Cin	NL	100-53, 1st
1941	Joe McCarthy, NYA	AL	101-53, 1st
	Leo Durocher, Bro	NL	100-54, 1st
1942	Luke Sewell, StL	AL	82-69, 3rd
	Billy Southworth, StL	NL	106-48, 1st
1943	Ossie Bluege, Was	AL	84-69, 2nd
	Frank Frisch, Pit	NL	80-74, 4th
1944	Luke Sewell, StL	AL	89-65, 1st
	Billy Southworth, StL	NL	105-49, 1st
1945	Steve O'Neill, Det	AL	88-65, 1st
	Charlie Grimm, ChN	NL	98-56, 1st
1946	Joe Cronin, Bos	AL	104-50, 1st
	Eddie Dyer, StL	NL	98-58, 1st
1947	Connie Mack, Phi	AL	78-76, 5th
	Burt Shotton, Bro	NL	92-60, 1st
1948	Lou Boudreau, Cle	AL	97-58, 1st
	Billy Southworth, Bos	NL	91-62, 1st
1949	Casey Stengel, NYA	AL	97-57, 1st
	Eddie Sawyer, Phi	NL	81-73, 3rd
1950	Casey Stengel, NYA	AL	98-56, 1st
	Eddie Sawyer, Phi	NL	91-63, 1st
1951	Paul Richards, ChA	AL	81-73, 4th
	Leo Durocher, NYG	NL	98-59, 1st
1952	Bucky Harris, Was	AL	78-76, 5th
	Phil Cavarretta, ChN	NL	77-77, 5th
1953	Casey Stengel, NYA	AL	99-52, 1st
	Chuck Dressen, Bro	NL	105-49, 1st
1954	Al Lopez, Cle	AL	111-43, 1st
	Leo Durocher, NYG	NL	97-57, 1st
1955	Pinky Higgins, Bos	AL	84-70, 4th
	Walter Alston, Bro	NL	98-55, 1st
1956	Casey Stengel, NYA	AL	97-57, 1st
	Birdie Tebbetts, Cin	NL	91-63, 3rd
1957	Casey Stengel, NYA	AL	98-56, 1st
	Fred Haney, Mil	NL	95-59, 1st
1958	Casey Stengel, NYA	AL	92-62, 1st
	Danny Murtaugh, Pit	NL	84-70, 2nd
1959	Al Lopez, ChA	AL	94-60, 1st
	Walter Alston, LA	NL	88-68, 1st
1960	Casey Stengel, NYA	AL	97-57, 1st
	Danny Murtaugh, Pit	NL	95-59, 1st
1961	Bob Scheffing, Det	AL	101-61, 2nd
	Fred Hutchinson, Cin	NL	93-61, 1st
1962	Bill Rigney, LAA	AL	86-76, 3rd
	Alvin Dark, SF	NL	103-62, 1st
1963	Ralph Houk, NYA	AL	104-57, 1st
	Bob Kennedy, ChN	NL	82-80, 7th
1964	Hank Bauer, Bal	AL	97-65, 3rd

	Player, Pos, Tm	Lg	Record, Finish
	Johnny Keane, StL	NL	93-69, 1st
1965	Sam Mele, Min	AL	102-60, 1st
	Walter Alston, LA	NL	97-65, 1st
1966	Hank Bauer, Bal	AL	97-63, 1st
	Walter Alston, LA	NL	95-67, 1st
1967	Dick Williams, Bos	AL	92-70, 1st
	Red Schoendienst, StL	NL	101-60, 1st
1968	Mayo Smith, Det	AL	103-59, 1st
	Red Schoendienst, StL	NL	97-65, 1st
1969	Billy Martin, Min	AL	97-65, 1st W
	Gil Hodges, NYN	NL	100-62, 1st W
1970	Earl Weaver, Bal	AL	108-54, 1st E
	Sparky Anderson, Cin	NL	102-60, 1st W
1971	Dick Williams, Oak	AL	101-60, 1st W
	Red Schoendienst, StL	NL	90-72, 2nd E
1972	Chuck Tanner, ChA	AL	87-67, 2nd W
	Sparky Anderson, Cin	NL	95-59, 1st W
1973	Earl Weaver, Bal	AL	97-65, 1st E
	Gene Mauch, Mon	NL	79-83, 4th E
1974	Billy Martin, Tex	AL	84-76, 2nd W
	Walter Alston, LA	NL	102-60, 1st W
1975	Darrell Johnson, Bos	AL	95-65, 1st E
	Sparky Anderson, Cin	NL	108-54, 1st W
1976	Billy Martin, NYA	AL	97-62, 1st E
	Danny Ozark, Phi	NL	101-61, 1st E
1977	Bob Lemon, ChA	AL	90-72, 3rd W
	Tom Lasorda, LA	NL	98-64, 1st W
1978	Bob Lemon, NYA	AL	48-20, 1st E
	Roger Craig, SD	NL	84-78, 4th W
1979	Earl Weaver, Bal	AL	102-57, 1st E
	Dick Williams, Mon	NL	95-65, 2nd E
1980	Dick Howser, NYA	AL	103-59, 1st E
	Bill Virdon, Hou	NL	93-70, 1st W
1981	Billy Martin, Oak	AL	64-45, 1st W
	Whitey Herzog, StL	NL	59-43, 1st E
1982	Harvey Kuenn, Mil	AL	72-43, 1st W
	Joe Torre, Atl	NL	89-73, 1st W

World Series MVP

Six different players won retroactive World Series MVP Awards twice each, while just three garnered the honor while playing for the losing team. Home Run Baker, Lou Gehrig, Charlie Keller, Pepper Martin, Allie Reynolds, Babe Ruth were the two-time winners, with Reynolds the lone player to capture it in consecutive years. Ruth also was one of five players to pull the MVP- World Series MVP double in the same season (he did it twice), joined by Spud Chandler, Jimmie Foxx, Carl Hubbell and Christy Mathewson. Joe Harris, Waite Hoyt and Duke Snider were the retroactive World Series MVPs who didn't earn a championship as well. Statistically speaking, Joe Jackson was the top performer in the 1919 World Series, but we couldn't justify picking him as the MVP.

Year	Player, Pos, Tm	Lg	Stats
1903	Bill Dinneen, p, Bos	AL	3-1, 2.06
1905	Christy Mathewson, p, NYG	NL	3-0, 0.00
1906	George Davis, ss, ChA	AL	.308-0-6
1907	Jimmy Slagle, of, ChN	NL	.273-0-4
1908	Three Finger Brown, p, ChN	NL	2-0, 0.00
1909	Babe Adams, p, Pit	NL	3-0, 1.33
1910	Danny Murphy, of, Phi	AL	.350-1-9
1911	Home Run Baker, 3b, Phi	AL	.375-2-5

Year	Player, Pos, Tm	Lg	Stats
1912	Joe Wood, p, Bos	AL	3-1, 3.68
1913	Home Run Baker, 3b, Phi	AL	.450-1-7
1914	Hank Gowdy, c, Bos	NL	.545-1-3
1915	Duffy Lewis, of, Bos	AL	.444-1-5
1916	Ernie Shore, p, Bos	NL	2-0, 1.53
1917	Red Faber, p, ChA	AL	3-1, 2.33
1918	Carl Mays, p, Bos	AL	2-0, 1.00
1919	Hod Eller, p, Cin	NL	2-0, 2.00
1920	Stan Coveleski, p, Cle	AL	3-0, 0.67
1921	Waite Hoyt, p, NYA	AL	2-1, 0.00
1922	Irish Meusel, of, NYG	NL	.250-1-7
1923	Babe Ruth, of, NYA	AL	.368-3-3
1924	Goose Goslin, of, Was	AL	.344-3-7
1925	Joe Harris, of, Was	AL	.440-3-6
1926	Pete Alexander, p, StL	NL	2-0, 1.33
1927	Babe Ruth, of, NYA	AL	.400-2-7
1928	Lou Gehrig, 1b, NYA	AL	.545-4-9
1929	Jimmie Foxx, 1b, Phi	AL	.350-2-5
1930	George Earnshaw, p, Phi	AL	2-0, 0.72
1931	Pepper Martin, 3b, StL	NL	.500-1-5
1932	Lou Gehrig, 1b, NYA	AL	.529-3-8
1933	Carl Hubbell, p, NYG	NL	2-0, 0.00
1934	Pepper Martin, 3b, StL	NL	.355-0-4
1935	Charlie Gehringer, 2b, Det	AL	.375-0-4
1936	Jake Powell, of, NYA	AL	.455-1-5
1937	Lefty Gomez, p, NYA	AL	2-0, 1.50
1938	Joe Gordon, 2b, NYA	AL	.400-1-6
1939	Charlie Keller, of, NYA	AL	.438-3-6
1940	Jimmy Ripple, of, Cin	NL	.333-1-6
1941	Charlie Keller, of, NYA	AL	.389-0-5
1942	Johnny Beazley, p, StL	NL	2-0, 2.50
1943	Spud Chandler, p, NYA	AL	2-0, 0.50
1944	Mort Cooper, p, StL	NL	1-1, 1.13
1945	Hank Greenberg, of, Det	AL	.304-2-7
1946	Harry Brecheen, p, StL	NL	3-0, 0.45
1947	Johnny Lindell, of, NYA	AL	.500-0-7
1948	Gene Bearden, p, Cle	AL	1-0, 0.00
1949	Allie Reynolds, p, NYA	AL	1-0, 0.00
1950	Allie Reynolds, p, NYA	AL	1-0, 0.87
1951	Ed Lopat, p, NYA	AL	2-0, 0.50
1952	Duke Snider, of, Bro	NL	.345-4-8
1953	Billy Martin, 2b, NYA	AL	.500-2-8
1954	Dusty Rhodes, of, NYG	NL	.667-2-7

19th Century WS MVP

Lost in the shadow of the World Series are the several 19th-century championships. The first was the American Association-National League World Series of 1884-90, and the NL had three more postseason series after the AA folded. There was the World Series of 1892, which matched split- season champions; the Temple Cups of 1894-97, which matched the first- and second-place teams; and the Chronicle-Telegraph Cup of 1900, which did the same. Jack Doyle was the only two-time recipient of the retroactive 19th-century championship MVP Awards, while Bob Caruthers and Old Hoss Radbourn won it in the same season that they were retroactive MVPs.

Year	Player, Pos, Tm	Lg	Stats
1884	Old Hoss Radbourn, p, Prv	NL	3-0, 0.00
1885	Cap Anson, 1b, ChN	NL	.423-0—
1886	Bob Caruthers, p, STL	AA	2-1, 2.42
1887	Lady Baldwin, p, Det	NL	4-1, 1.50

Year	Player, Pos, Tm	Lg	Stats
1888	Tim Keefe, p, NYG	NL	4-0, 0.51
1889	Monte Ward, ss, NYG	NL	.417-0-7
1890	Red Ehret, p, Lou	AA	2-0, 1.35
1892	Hugh Duffy, of, Bos	NL	.462-1-9
1894	Jack Doyle, 1b, NYG	NL	.588-0-6
1895	Cy Young, p, Cle	NL	3-0, 2.33
1896	Willie Keeler, of, Bal	NL	.471-0-4
1897	Jack Doyle, 1b, Bal	NL	.526-0-9
1900	Joe McGinnity, p, Bro	NL	2-0, 0.00

League Championship MVP

Boog Powell is the only player to grab two retroactive League Championship Series MVP Awards, narrowly edging teammate Brooks Robinson in both cases.

Year	Player, Pos, Tm	Lg	Stats
1969	Dave McNally, p, Bal	AL	1-0, 0.00
	Ken Boswell, 2b, NYN	NL	.333-2-5
1970	Boog Powell, 1b, Bal	AL	.429-1-6
	Bobby Tolan, of, Cin	NL	.417-1-2
1971	Boog Powell, 1b, Bal	AL	.300-2-3
	Bob Robertson, 1b, Pit	NL	.438-4-6
1972	Blue Moon Odom, p, Oak	AL	2-0, 0.00
	Johnny Bench, c, Cin	NL	.333-1-2
1973	Catfish Hunter, p, Oak	AL	2-0, 1.65
	Tom Seaver, p, NYN	NL	1-1, 1.62
1974	Vida Blue, p, Oak	AL	1-0, 0.00
	Don Sutton, p, LA	NL	2-0, 0.53
1975	Carl Yastrzemski, of, Bos	AL	.455-1-2
	Tony Perez, 1b, Cin	NL	.417-1-4
1976	Chris Chambliss, 1b, NYA	AL	.524-2-8
	Pete Rose, 3b, Cin	NL	.429-0-2
1977	Sparky Lyle, p, NYA	AL	2-0, 0.96
1978	Reggie Jackson, of, NYA	AL	.462-2-6
1979	Eddie Murray, 1b, Bal	AL	.417-1-5

Division Series MVP

Several players have contracts awarding them bonuses if they win the Division Series MVP Award. Problem is, the honor doesn't exist (unless you count our retroactive selections). Juan Gonzalez and Paul O'Neill both were named retroactive winners despite playing for losing clubs.

Year	Player, Pos, Tm	Lg	Stats
1981	Goose Gossage, p, NYA	AL	0.00, 3 saves
	Dwayne Murphy, of, Oak	AL	.545-1-2
	Jerry Reuss, p, LA	NL	1-0, 0.00
	Steve Rogers, p, Mon	NL	2-0, 0.51
1995	Edgar Martinez, dh, Sea	AL	.571-2-10
	Eddie Murray, dh, Cle	AL	.385-1-3
	Marquis Grissom, of, Atl	NL	.524-3-4
	Hal Morris, 1b, Cin	NL	.500-0-2
1996	Juan Gonzalez, of, Tex	AL	.438-5-9
	B.J. Surhoff, of, Bal	AL	.385-3-5
	Ron Gant, of, StL	NL	.400-1-4
	Mark Wohlers, p, Atl	NL	0.00, 3 saves
1997	Mike Mussina, p, Bal	AL	2-0, 1.93
	Paul O'Neill, of, NYA	AL	.421-2-7
	Chipper Jones, 3b, Atl	NL	.500-1-2
	Gary Sheffield, of, Fla	NL	.556-1-1

STATS Retroactive All-Star Teams

1876 National League

Pos	Player, Team	Stats
C	Deacon White, ChN	.343-1-60
1B	Cal McVey, ChN	.347-1-53
2B	Ross Barnes, ChN	.429-1-59
3B	Cap Anson, ChN	.356-2-59
SS	John Peters, ChN	.351-1-47
OF	George Hall, PhN	.366-5-45
OF	Paul Hines, ChN	.331-2-59
OF	Jim O'Rourke, Bos	.327-2-43
SP	Al Spalding, ChN	47-12, 1.75

1877 National League

Pos	Player, Team	Stats
C	Cal McVey, ChN	.368-0-36
1B	Deacon White, Bos	.387-2-49
2B	Joe Gerhardt, Lou	.304-1-35
3B	Cap Anson, ChN	.337-0-32
SS	John Peters, ChN	.317-0-41
OF	John Cassidy, Har	.378-0-27
OF	Charley Jones, Cin-ChN	.313-2-38
OF	Jim O'Rourke, Bos	.362-0-23
SP	Tommy Bond, Bos	40-17, 2.11

1878 National League

Pos	Player, Team	Stats
C	Lew Brown, Prv	.305-1-43
1B	Joe Start, ChN	.351-1-27
2B	Jack Burdock, Bos	.260-0-25
3B	Cal McVey, Cin	.306-2-25
SS	Bob Ferguson, ChN	.351-0-39
OF	Cap Anson, ChN	.341-0-40
OF	Paul Hines, Prv	.358-4-50
OF	Orator Shaffer, Ind	.338-0-30
SP	Tommy Bond, Bos	40-19, 2.06

1879 National League

Pos	Player, Team	Stats
C	Deacon White, Cin	.330-1-52
1B	Joe Start, Prv	.319-2-37
2B	Jack Farrell, Syr-Prv	.295-1-26
3B	King Kelly, Cin	.348-2-47
SS	George Wright, Prv	.276-1-42
OF	Paul Hines, Prv	.357-2-52
OF	Charley Jones, Bos	.315-9-62
OF	John O'Rourke, Bos	.341-6-62
SP	Monte Ward, Prv	47-19, 2.15

1880 National League

Pos	Player, Team	Stats
C	John Clapp, Cin	.282-1-20
1B	Cap Anson, ChN	.337-1-74
2B	Fred Dunlap, Cle	.276-4-30
3B	Roger Connor, Try	.332-3-47
SS	Tom Burns, ChN	.309-0-43
OF	Abner Dalrymple, ChN	.330-0-36
OF	George Gore, ChN	.360-2-47
OF	Harry Stovey, Wor	.265-6-28
SP	Larry Corcoran, ChN	43-14, 1.95

1881 National League

Pos	Player, Team	Stats
C	Charlie Bennett, Det	.301-7-64
1B	Cap Anson, ChN	.399-1-82
2B	Fred Dunlap, Cle	.325-3-24
3B	Jim O'Rourke, Buf	.302-0-30
SS	Tom Burns, ChN	.278-4-42
OF	Dan Brouthers, Buf	.319-8-45
OF	King Kelly, ChN	.323-2-55
OF	Tom York, Prv	.304-2-47
SP	Larry Corcoran, ChN	31-14, 2.31

1882 National League

Pos	Player, Team	Stats
C	Charlie Bennett, Det	.301-5-51
1B	Dan Brouthers, Buf	.368-6-63
2B	Hardy Richardson, Buf	.271-2-57
3B	Ned Williamson, ChN	.282-3-60
SS	King Kelly, ChN	.305-1-55
OF	Abner Dalrymple, ChN	.295-1-36
OF	George Gore, ChN	.319-3-51
OF	Paul Hines, Prv	.309-4-34
SP	Jim McCormick, Cle	36-30, 2.37
SP	Jim Whitney, Bos	24-21, 2.64

1882 American Assoc.

Pos	Player, Team	Stats
C	Jack O'Brien, Phi	.303-3-37
1B	Guy Hecker, Lou	.276-3—
2B	Pete Browning, Lou	.378-5—
3B	Hick Carpenter, Cin	.342-1-62
SS	Bill Gleason, STL	.288-1—
OF	Joe Sommer, Cin	.288-1-29
OF	Ed Swartwood, Pit	.329-4—
OF	Chicken Wolf, Lou	.299-0—
SP	Tony Mullane, Lou	30-24, 1.88
SP	Will White, Cin	40-12, 1.54

1883 National League

Pos	Player, Team	Stats
C	Buck Ewing, NYG	.303-10-41
1B	Dan Brouthers, Buf	.374-3-97
2B	Jack Burdock, Bos	.330-5-88
3B	Ezra Sutton, Bos	.324-3-73
SS	Tom Burns, ChN	.294-2-67
OF	George Gore, ChN	.334-2-52
OF	Jim O'Rourke, Buf	.328-1-38
OF	George Wood, Det	.302-5-47
SP	Old Hoss Radbourn, Prv	48-25, 2.05
SP	Jim Whitney, Bos	37-21, 2.24

1883 American Assoc.

Pos	Player, Team	Stats
C	Ed Whiting, Lou	.292-2—
1B	Harry Stovey, Phi	.302-14—
2B	Pop Smith, Col	.262-4—
3B	Hick Carpenter, Cin	.296-3—
SS	Mike Moynahan, Phi	.308-1—
OF	Pete Browning, Lou	.338-4—
OF	Charley Jones, Cin	.294-10—
OF	John O'Rourke, NY	.270-2—
SP	Tim Keefe, NY	41-27, 2.41
SP	Will White, Cin	43-22, 2.09

1884 National League

Pos	Player, Team	Stats
C	Jack Rowe, Buf	.315-4-61
1B	Dan Brouthers, Buf	.327-14-79
2B	Fred Pfeffer, ChN	.289-25-101
3B	Ned Williamson, ChN	.278-27-84
SS	Jack Glasscock, Cle	.249-1-22
OF	Paul Hines, Prv	.302-3-41
OF	King Kelly, ChN	.354-13-95
OF	Jim O'Rourke, Buf	.347-5-63
SP	Pud Galvin, Buf	46-22, 1.99
SP	Old Hoss Radbourn, Prv	59-12, 1.38

1884 Union Assoc.

Pos	Player, Team	Stats
C	Eddie Fusselback, Bal	.284-1—
1B	Jumbo Schoeneck, Chi-Pit-Bal	.308-2—
2B	Fred Dunlap, STL	.412-13—
3B	Jack Gleason, STL	.324-4—
SS	Jack Glasscock, Cin	.419-2—
OF	Buster Hoover, Phi	.364-0—
OF	Harry Moore, Was	.336-1—
OF	Orator Shaffer, STL	.360-2—
SP	Jim McCormick, Cin	21-3, 1.54
SP	Billy Taylor, STL	25-4, 1.68

1884 American Assoc.

Pos	Player, Team	Stats
C	Jim Keenan, Ind	.293-3—
1B	John Reilly, Cin	.339-11—
2B	Sam Barkley, Tol	.306-1—
3B	Pete Browning, Lou	.336-4—
SS	Frank Fennelly, WaD-Cin	.311-4—
OF	Charley Jones, Cin	.314-7—
OF	Fred Lewis, STL	.323-0—
OF	Chief Roseman, NY	.298-4—
SP	Guy Hecker, Lou	52-20, 1.80
SP	Tim Keefe, NY	37-17, 2.26

1885 National League

Pos	Player, Team	Stats
C	Buck Ewing, NYG	.304-6-63
1B	Roger Connor, NYG	.371-1-65
2B	Hardy Richardson, Buf	.319-6-44
3B	Ezra Sutton, Bos	.313-4-47
SS	Sam Wise, Bos	.283-4-46
OF	Abner Dalrymple, ChN	.274-11-61
OF	George Gore, ChN	.313-5-57
OF	King Kelly, ChN	.288-9-75
SP	John Clarkson, ChN	53-16, 1.85
SP	Mickey Welch, NYG	44-11, 1.66

1885 American Assoc.

Pos	Player, Team	Stats
C	Fred Carroll, Pit	.268-0-30
1B	Harry Stovey, Phi	.315-13-75
2B	Sam Barkley, STL	.268-3-53
3B	Hick Carpenter, Cin	.277-2-61
SS	Frank Fennelly, Cin	.273-10-89
OF	Pete Browning, Lou	.362-9-73
OF	Charley Jones, Cin	.322-5-35
OF	Henry Larkin, Phi	.329-8-88
SP	Bob Caruthers, STL	40-13, 2.07
SP	Ed Morris, Pit	39-24, 2.35

1886 National League

Pos	Player, Team	Stats
C	Buck Ewing, NYG	.309-4-31
1B	Cap Anson, ChN	.371-10-147
2B	Fred Pfeffer, ChN	.264-7-95
3B	Tom Burns, ChN	.276-3-65
SS	Jack Glasscock, StL	.325-3-40
OF	George Gore, ChN	.304-6-63
OF	King Kelly, ChN	.388-4-79
OF	Hardy Richardson, Det	.351-11-61
SP	Lady Baldwin, Det	42-13, 2.24
SP	John Clarkson, ChN	36-17, 2.41
SP	Tim Keefe, NYG	42-20, 2.53

1886 American Assoc.

Pos	Player, Team	Stats
C	Fred Carroll, Pit	.288-5-64
1B	Dave Orr, NY	.338-7-91
2B	Bid McPhee, Cin	.268-8-70
3B	Arlie Latham, STL	.301-1-47
SS	Frank Fennelly, Cin	.249-6-72
OF	Pete Browning, Lou	.340-2-68
OF	Tip O'Neill, STL	.328-3-107
OF	Harry Stovey, Phi	.294-7-59
SP	Bob Caruthers, STL	30-14, 2.32
SP	Dave Foutz, STL	41-16, 2.11
SP	Ed Morris, Pit	41-20, 2.45

1887 National League

Pos	Player, Team	Stats
C	Jack Clements, Phi	.280-1-47
1B	Dan Brouthers, Det	.338-12-101
2B	Hardy Richardson, Det	.328-8-94
3B	Jerry Denny, Ind	.324-11-97
SS	Sam Wise, Bos	.334-9-92
OF	King Kelly, Bos	.322-8-63
OF	Sam Thompson, Det	.372-11-166
OF	George Wood, Phi	.289-14-66
SP	Dan Casey, Phi	28-13, 2.86
SP	John Clarkson, ChN	38-21, 3.08
SP	Tim Keefe, NYG	35-19, 3.10

1887 American Assoc.

Pos	Player, Team	Stats
C	Kid Baldwin, Cin	.253-1-57
1B	Charlie Comiskey, STL	.335-4-103
2B	Yank Robinson, STL	.305-1-74
3B	Denny Lyons, Phi	.367-6-102
SS	Oyster Burns, Bal	.341-9-99
OF	Pete Browning, Lou	.402-4-118
OF	Dave Foutz, STL	.357-4-108
OF	Tip O'Neill, STL	.435-14-123
SP	Bob Caruthers, STL	29-9, 3.30
SP	Matt Kilroy, Bal	46-19, 3.07
SP	Elmer Smith, Cin	34-17, 2.94

1888 National League

Pos	Player, Team	Stats
C	King Kelly, Bos	.318-9-71
1B	Cap Anson, ChN	.344-12-84
2B	Fred Pfeffer, ChN	.250-8-57
3B	Jerry Denny, Ind	.261-12-63
SS	Ned Williamson, ChN	.250-8-73
OF	Dick Johnston, Bos	.296-12-68
OF	Jimmy Ryan, ChN	.332-16-64
OF	Mike Tiernan, NYG	.293-9-52
SP	Charlie Buffinton, Phi	28-17, 1.91
SP	Tim Keefe, NYG	35-12, 1.74
SP	Mickey Welch, NYG	26-19, 1.93

1888 American Assoc.

Pos	Player, Team	Stats
C	Jim Keenan, Cin	.233-1-40
1B	John Reilly, Cin	.321-13-103
2B	Yank Robinson, STL	.231-3-53
3B	Denny Lyons, Phi	.296-6-83
SS	Ed McKean, Cle	.299-6-68
OF	Pete Browning, Lou	.313-3-72
OF	Tip O'Neill, STL	.335-5-98
OF	Harry Stovey, Phi	.287-9-65
SP	Bob Caruthers, Bro	29-15, 2.39
SP	Silver King, STL	45-21, 1.64
SP	Ed Seward, Phi	35-19, 2.01

1889 National League

Pos	Player, Team	Stats
C	Buck Ewing, NYG	.327-4-87
1B	Dan Brouthers, Bos	.373-7-118
2B	Hardy Richardson, Bos	.304-6-79
3B	Jerry Denny, Ind	.282-18-112
SS	Jack Glasscock, Ind	.352-7-85
OF	Jimmy Ryan, ChN	.307-17-72
OF	Sam Thompson, Phi	.296-20-111
OF	Mike Tiernan, NYG	.335-10-73
SP	Charlie Buffinton, Phi	28-16, 3.24
SP	John Clarkson, Bos	49-19, 2.73
SP	Mickey Welch, NYG	27-12, 3.02

1889 American Assoc.

Pos	Player, Team	Stats
C	Jocko Milligan, STL	.366-12-76
1B	Tommy Tucker, Bal	.372-5-99
2B	Lou Bierbauer, Phi	.304-7-105
3B	Denny Lyons, Phi	.329-9-82
SS	Herman Long, KC	.275-3-60
OF	Bug Holliday, Cin	.321-19-104
OF	Tip O'Neill, STL	.335-9-110
OF	Harry Stovey, Phi	.308-19-119
SP	Bob Caruthers, Bro	40-11, 3.13
SP	Elton Chamberlin, STL	32-15, 2.97
SP	Jesse Duryea, Cin	32-19, 2.56

1890 National League

Pos	Player, Team	Stats
C	Jack Clements, Phi	.315-7-74
1B	Cap Anson, ChN	.312-7-107
2B	Hub Collins, Bro	.278-3-69
3B	George Pinckney, Bro	.309-7-83
SS	Jack Glasscock, NYG	.336-1-66
OF	Oyster Burns, Bro	.284-13-128
OF	Sam Thompson, Phi	.313-4-102
OF	Mike Tiernan, NYG	.304-13-59
SP	Kid Gleason, Phi	38-17, 2.63
SP	Bill Hutchison, ChN	42-25, 2.70
SP	Billy Rhines, Cin	28-17, 1.95

1890 Players' League

Pos	Player, Team	Stats
C	Buck Ewing, NY	.338-8-72
1B	Roger Connor, NY	.349-14-103
2B	Lou Bierbauer, Bro	.306-7-99
3B	Patsy Tebeau, Cle	.300-5-74
SS	Monte Ward, Bro	.337-4-60
OF	Pete Browning, Cle	.373-5-93
OF	Jim O'Rourke, NY	.360-9-115
OF	Hardy Richardson, Bos	.326-13-146
SP	Mark Baldwin, Chi	34-24, 3.31
SP	Silver King, Chi	30-22, 2.69
SP	Old Hoss Radbourn, Bos	27-12, 3.31

1890 American Assoc.

Pos	Player, Team	Stats
C	Jack O'Connor, CoC	.324-2-66
1B	Perry Werden, Tol	.295-6-72
2B	Cupid Childs, Syr	.345-2-89
3B	Denny Lyons, Phi	.354-7-73
SS	Phil Tomney, Lou	.277-1-58
OF	Spud Johnson, CoC	.346-1-113
OF	Tommy McCarthy, STL	.350-6-69
OF	Chicken Wolf, Lou	.363-4-98
SP	Sadie McMahon, Phi-Bal	36-21, 3.27
SP	Jack Stivetts, STL	27-21, 3.52
SP	Scott Stratton, Lou	34-14, 2.36

1891 National League

Pos	Player, Team	Stats
C	Jack Clements, Phi	.310-4-75
1B	Cap Anson, ChN	.291-8-120
2B	Cupid Childs, Cle	.281-2-83
3B	Arlie Latham, Cin	.272-7-53
SS	Herman Long, Bos	.282-9-75
OF	Billy Hamilton, Phi	.340-2-60
OF	Harry Stovey, Bos	.279-16-95
OF	Mike Tiernan, NYG	.306-16-73
SP	Bill Hutchison, ChN	44-19, 2.81
SP	Kid Nichols, Bos	30-17, 2.39
SP	Amos Rusie, NYG	33-20, 2.55

1891 American Assoc.

Pos	Player, Team	Stats
C	Jocko Milligan, Phi	.303-11-106
1B	Dan Brouthers, Bos	.350-5-109
2B	Jack Crooks, CoC	.245-0-46
3B	Duke Farrell, Bos	.302-12-110
SS	Paul Radford, Bos	.259-0-65
OF	Tom Brown, Bos	.321-5-71
OF	Hugh Duffy, Bos	.336-9-110
OF	Tip O'Neill, STL	.321-10-95
SP	George Haddock, Bos	34-11, 2.49
SP	Sadie McMahon, Bal	35-24, 2.81
SP	Jack Stivetts, STL	33-22, 2.86

1892 National League

Pos	Player, Team	Stats
C	Jack Doyle, Cle-NYG	.297-6-69
1B	Dan Brouthers, Bro	.335-5-124
2B	Cupid Childs, Cle	.317-3-53
3B	Bill Joyce, Bro	.245-6-45
SS	Bill Dahlen, ChN	.291-5-58
OF	Oyster Burns, Bro	.315-4-96
OF	Ed Delahanty, Phi	.306-6-91
OF	Billy Hamilton, Phi	.330-3-53
SP	Kid Nichols, Bos	35-16, 2.84
SP	Jack Stivetts, Bos	35-16, 3.03
SP	Cy Young, Cle	36-12, 1.93

1893 National League

Pos	Player, Team	Stats
C	Jack Clements, Phi	.285-17-80
1B	Roger Connor, NYG	.305-11-105
2B	Cupid Childs, Cle	.326-3-65
3B	George Davis, NYG	.355-11-119
SS	Ed McKean, Cle	.310-4-133
OF	Ed Delahanty, Phi	.368-19-146
OF	Billy Hamilton, Phi	.380-5-44
OF	Sam Thompson, Phi	.370-11-126
SP	Frank Killen, Pit	36-14, 3.64
SP	Kid Nichols, Bos	34-14, 3.52
SP	Cy Young, Cle	34-16, 3.36

1894 National League

Pos	Player, Team	Stats
C	Wilbert Robinson, Bal	.353-1-98
1B	Dan Brouthers, Bal	.347-9-128
2B	Bobby Lowe, Bos	.346-17-115
3B	Bill Joyce, Was	.355-17-89
SS	Bill Dahlen, ChN	.357-15-107
OF	Hugh Duffy, Bos	.440-18-145
OF	Billy Hamilton, Phi	.404-4-87
OF	Sam Thompson, Phi	.407-13-141
SP	Sadie McMahon, Bal	25-8, 4.21
SP	Jouett Meekin, NYG	33-9, 3.70
SP	Amos Rusie, NYG	36-13, 2.78

1895 National League

Pos	Player, Team	Stats
C	Jack Clements, Phi	.394-13-75
1B	Ed Cartwright, Was	.331-3-90
2B	Bid McPhee, Cin	.299-1-75
3B	Bill Joyce, Was	.312-17-95
SS	Hughie Jennings, Bal	.386-4-125
OF	Jesse Burkett, Cle	.409-5-83
OF	Ed Delahanty, Phi	.404-11-106
OF	Sam Thompson, Phi	.392-18-165
SP	Pink Hawley, Pit	31-22, 3.18
SP	Bill Hoffer, Bal	31-6, 3.21
SP	Cy Young, Cle	35-10, 3.24

1896 National League

Pos	Player, Team	Stats
C	Deacon McGuire, Was	.321-2-70
1B	Jack Doyle, Bal	.339-1-101
2B	Cupid Childs, Cle	.355-1-106
3B	Bill Joyce, Was-NYG	.333-13-94
SS	Hughie Jennings, Bal	.401-0-121
OF	Jesse Burkett, Cle	.410-6-72
OF	Ed Delahanty, Phi	.397-13-126
OF	Joe Kelley, Bal	.364-8-100
SP	Bill Hoffer, Bal	25-7, 3.38
SP	Kid Nichols, Bos	30-14, 2.83
SP	Cy Young, Cle	28-15, 3.24

1897 National League

Pos	Player, Team	Stats
C	Deacon McGuire, Was	.343-4-53
1B	Nap Lajoie, Phi	.361-9-127
2B	Cupid Childs, Cle	.338-1-61
3B	Jimmy Collins, Bos	.346-6-132
SS	George Davis, NYG	.353-10-136
OF	Fred Clarke, Lou	.390-6-67
OF	Billy Hamilton, Bos	.343-3-61
OF	Willie Keeler, Bal	.424-0-74
SP	Joe Corbett, Bal	24-8, 3.11
SP	Kid Nichols, Bos	31-11, 2.64
SP	Amos Rusie, NYG	28-10, 2.54

1898 National League

Pos	Player, Team	Stats
C	Mike Grady, NYG	.296-3-49
1B	Dan McGann, Bal	.301-5-106
2B	Nap Lajoie, Phi	.324-6-127
3B	John McGraw, Bal	.342-0-53
SS	Hughie Jennings, Bal	.328-1-87
OF	Ed Delahanty, Phi	.334-4-92
OF	Elmer Flick, Phi	.302-8-81
OF	Billy Hamilton, Bos	.369-3-50
SP	Clark Griffith, ChN	24-10, 1.88
SP	Doc McJames, Bal	27-15, 2.36
SP	Kid Nichols, Bos	31-12, 2.13
SP	Cy Young, Cle	25-13, 2.53

1899 National League

Pos	Player, Team	Stats
C	Mike Grady, NYG	.334-2-54
1B	Jake Beckley, Cin	.333-3-99
2B	Nap Lajoie, Phi	.378-6-70
3B	John McGraw, Bal	.391-1-33
SS	Bobby Wallace, StL	.295-12-108
OF	Jesse Burkett, StL	.396-7-71
OF	Ed Delahanty, Phi	.410-9-137
OF	Buck Freeman, Was	.318-25-122
SP	Jim Hughes, Bro	28-6, 2.68
SP	Joe McGinnity, Bal	28-16, 2.68
SP	Vic Willis, Bos	27-8, 2.50
SP	Cy Young, StL	26-16, 2.58

1900 National League

Pos	Player, Team	Stats
C	Ed McFarland, Phi	.305-0-38
1B	Jake Beckley, Cin	.341-2-94
2B	Nap Lajoie, Phi	.337-7-92
3B	John McGraw, StL	.344-2-33
SS	George Davis, NYG	.319-3-61
OF	Jesse Burkett, StL	.363-7-68
OF	Elmer Flick, Phi	.367-11-110
OF	Honus Wagner, Pit	.381-4-100
SP	Bill Dinneen, Bos	20-14, 3.12
SP	Joe McGinnity, Bro	28-8, 2.94
SP	Deacon Phillippe, Pit	20-13, 2.84
SP	Jesse Tannehill, Pit	20-6, 2.88

1901 American League

Pos	Player, Team	Stats
C	Ossee Schreckengost, Bos	.304-0-38
1B	Buck Freeman, Bos	.339-12-114
2B	Nap Lajoie, Phi	.426-14-125
3B	Jimmy Collins, Bos	.332-6-94
SS	Kid Elberfeld, Det	.308-3-76
OF	Mike Donlin, Bal	.340-5-67
OF	Fielder Jones, ChA	.311-2-65
OF	Socks Seybold, Phi	.334-8-90
SP	Clark Griffith, ChA	24-7, 2.67
SP	Roscoe Miller, Det	23-13, 2.95
SP	Roy Patterson, ChA	20-16, 3.37
SP	Cy Young, Bos	33-10, 1.62

1901 National League

Pos	Player, Team	Stats
C	Deacon McGuire, Bro	.296-0-40
1B	Joe Kelley, Bro	.307-4-65
2B	Tom Daly, Bro	.315-3-90
3B	Otto Krueger, StL	.275-2-79
SS	Honus Wagner, Pit	.353-6-126
OF	Jesse Burkett, StL	.376-10-75
OF	Ed Delahanty, Phi	.354-8-108
OF	Jimmy Sheckard, Bro	.354-11-104
SP	Wild Bill Donovan, Bro	25-15, 2.77
SP	Noodles Hahn, Cin	22-19, 2.71
SP	Al Orth, Phi	20-12, 2.27
SP	Deacon Phillippe, Pit	22-12, 2.22

1902 American League

Pos	Player, Team	Stats
C	Ossee Schreckengost, Cle-Phi	.327-2-52
1B	Charlie Hickman, Bos-Cle	.361-11-110
2B	Nap Lajoie, Phi-Cle	.378-7-65
3B	Lave Cross, Phi	.342-0-108
SS	George Davis, ChA	.299-3-93
OF	Ed Delahanty, Was	.376-10-93
OF	Buck Freeman, Bos	.309-11-121
OF	Socks Seybold, Phi	.316-16-97
SP	Bill Bernhard, Phi-Cle	18-5, 2.15
SP	Red Donahue, StL	22-11, 2.76
SP	Rube Waddell, Phi	24-7, 2.05
SP	Cy Young, Bos	32-11, 2.15

1902 National League

Pos	Player, Team	Stats
C	Johnny Kling, ChN	.285-0-57
1B	Jake Beckley, Cin	.330-5-69
2B	Heinie Peitz, Cin	.315-1-60
3B	Tommy Leach, Pit	.278-6-85
SS	Bill Dahlen, Bro	.264-2-74
OF	Ginger Beaumont, Pit	.357-0-67
OF	Fred Clarke, Pit	.316-2-53
OF	Honus Wagner, Pit	.330-3-91
SP	Jack Chesbro, Pit	28-6, 2.17
SP	Noodles Hahn, Cin	23-12, 1.77
SP	Jesse Tannehill, Pit	20-6, 1.95
SP	Jack Taylor, ChN	23-11, 1.33

1903 American League

Pos	Player, Team	Stats
C	Harry Bemis, Cle	.261-1-41
1B	Charlie Hickman, Cle	.295-12-97
2B	Nap Lajoie, Cle	.344-7-93
3B	Bill Bradley, Cle	.313-6-68
SS	Freddy Parent, Bos	.304-4-80
OF	Sam Crawford, Det	.335-4-89
OF	Patsy Dougherty, Bos	.331-4-59
OF	Buck Freeman, Bos	.287-13-104
SP	Bill Dinneen, Bos	21-13, 2.26
SP	Earl Moore, Cle	19-9, 1.74
SP	Eddie Plank, Phi	23-16, 2.38
SP	Cy Young, Bos	28-9, 2.08

1903 National League

Pos	Player, Team	Stats
C	Johnny Kling, ChN	.297-3-68
1B	Frank Chance, ChN	.327-2-81
2B	Claude Ritchey, Pit	.287-0-59
3B	Harry Steinfeldt, Cin	.312-6-83
SS	Honus Wagner, Pit	.355-5-101
OF	Roger Bresnahan, NYG	.350-4-55
OF	Fred Clarke, Pit	.351-5-70
OF	Mike Donlin, Cin	.351-7-67
SP	Sam Leever, Pit	25-7, 2.06
SP	Christy Mathewson, NYG	30-13, 2.26
SP	Joe McGinnity, NYG	31-20, 2.43
SP	Deacon Phillippe, Pit	25-9, 2.43

1904 American League

Pos	Player, Team	Stats
C	Joe Sugden, StL	.267-0-30
1B	Harry Davis, Phi	.309-10-62
2B	Nap Lajoie, Cle	.376-5-102
3B	Bill Bradley, Cle	.300-6-83
SS	Freddy Parent, Bos	.291-6-77
OF	Elmer Flick, Cle	.306-6-56
OF	Willie Keeler, NYA	.343-2-40
OF	Chick Stahl, Bos	.290-3-67
SP	Jack Chesbro, NYA	41-12, 1.82
SP	Eddie Plank, Phi	26-17, 2.17
SP	Rube Waddell, Phi	25-19, 1.62
SP	Cy Young, Bos	26-16, 1.97

1904 National League

Pos	Player, Team	Stats
C	Mike Grady, StL	.313-5-43
1B	Frank Chance, ChN	.310-6-49
2B	Miller Huggins, Cin	.263-2-30
3B	Art Devlin, NYG	.281-1-66
SS	Honus Wagner, Pit	.349-4-75
OF	Mike Donlin, Cin-NYG	.329-3-52
OF	Harry Lumley, Bro	.279-9-78
OF	Cy Seymour, Cin	.313-5-58
SP	Jack Harper, Cin	23-9, 2.30
SP	Christy Mathewson, NYG	33-12, 2.03
SP	Joe McGinnity, NYG	35-8, 1.61
SP	Kid Nichols, StL	21-13, 2.02

1905 American League

Pos	Player, Team	Stats
C	Ossee Schreckengost, Phi	.272-0-45
1B	Harry Davis, Phi	.282-8-83
2B	Danny Murphy, Phi	.278-6-71
3B	Jimmy Collins, Bos	.276-4-65
SS	George Davis, ChA	.278-1-55
OF	Sam Crawford, Det	.297-6-75
OF	Elmer Flick, Cle	.306-4-64
OF	George Stone, StL	.296-7-52
SP	Nick Altrock, ChA	23-12, 1.88
SP	Ed Killian, Det	23-14, 2.27
SP	Eddie Plank, Phi	24-12, 2.26
SP	Rube Waddell, Phi	27-10, 1.48

1905 National League

Pos	Player, Team	Stats
C	Roger Bresnahan, NYG	.302-0-46
1B	Frank Chance, ChN	.316-2-70
2B	Miller Huggins, Cin	.273-1-38
3B	Ernie Courtney, Phi	.275-2-77
SS	Honus Wagner, Pit	.363-6-101
OF	Mike Donlin, NYG	.356-7-80
OF	Cy Seymour, Cin	.377-8-121
OF	John Titus, Phi	.308-2-89
SP	Red Ames, NYG	22-8, 2.74
SP	Christy Mathewson, NYG	31-9, 1.28
SP	Deacon Phillippe, Pit	20-13, 2.19
SP	Ed Reulbach, ChN	18-14, 1.42

1906 American League

Pos	Player, Team	Stats
C	Ossee Schreckengost, Phi	.284-1-41
1B	Harry Davis, Phi	.292-12-96
2B	Nap Lajoie, Cle	.355-0-91
3B	Frank LaPorte, NYA	.264-2-54
SS	George Davis, ChA	.277-0-80
OF	Elmer Flick, Cle	.311-1-62
OF	Socks Seybold, Phi	.316-5-59
OF	George Stone, StL	.358-6-71
SP	Addie Joss, Cle	21-9, 1.72
SP	Al Orth, NYA	27-17, 2.34
SP	Bob Rhoads, Cle	22-10, 1.80
SP	Doc White, ChA	18-6, 1.52

1906 National League

Pos	Player, Team	Stats
C	Roger Bresnahan, NYG	.281-0-43
1B	Frank Chance, ChN	.319-3-71
2B	Sammy Strang, NYG	.319-4-49
3B	Harry Steinfeldt, ChN	.327-3-83
SS	Honus Wagner, Pit	.339-2-71
OF	Harry Lumley, Bro	.324-9-61
OF	Sherry Magee, Phi	.282-6-67
OF	Roy Thomas, Phi	.254-0-16
SP	Three Finger Brown, ChN	26-6, 1.04
SP	Joe McGinnity, NYG	27-12, 2.25
SP	Jack Pfiester, ChN	20-8, 1.51
SP	Vic Willis, Pit	23-13, 1.73

1907 American League

Pos	Player, Team	Stats
C	Nig Clarke, Cle	.269-3-33
1B	Harry Davis, Phi	.266-8-87
2B	Nap Lajoie, Cle	.299-2-63
3B	Jimmy Collins, Bos-Phi	.279-0-45
SS	Kid Elberfeld, NYA	.271-0-51
OF	Ty Cobb, Det	.350-5-119
OF	Sam Crawford, Det	.323-4-81
OF	Elmer Flick, Cle	.302-3-58
SP	Wild Bill Donovan, Det	25-4, 2.19
SP	Addie Joss, Cle	27-11, 1.83
SP	Ed Killian, Det	25-13, 1.78
SP	Ed Walsh, ChA	24-18, 1.60

1907 National League

Pos	Player, Team	Stats
C	Roger Bresnahan, NYG	.253-4-38
1B	Frank Chance, ChN	.293-1-49
2B	Ed Abbaticchio, Pit	.262-2-82
3B	Dave Brain, Bos	.279-10-56
SS	Honus Wagner, Pit	.350-6-82
OF	Fred Clarke, Pit	.289-2-59
OF	Tommy Leach, Pit	.303-4-43
OF	Sherry Magee, Phi	.328-4-85
SP	Three Finger Brown, ChN	20-6, 1.39
SP	Christy Mathewson, NYG	24-12, 2.00
SP	Orval Overall, ChN	23-8, 1.68
SP	Tully Sparks, Phi	22-8, 2.00

1908 American League

Pos	Player, Team	Stats
C	Boss Schmidt, Det	.265-1-38
1B	Claude Rossman, Det	.294-2-71
2B	Nap Lajoie, Cle	.289-2-74
3B	Hobe Ferris, StL	.270-2-74
SS	Germany Schaefer, Det	.259-3-52
OF	Ty Cobb, Det	.324-4-108
OF	Sam Crawford, Det	.311-7-80
OF	Doc Gessler, Bos	.308-3-63
SP	Addie Joss, Cle	24-11, 1.16
SP	Ed Summers, Det	24-12, 1.64
SP	Ed Walsh, ChA	40-15, 1.42
SP	Cy Young, Bos	21-11, 1.26

1908 National League

Pos	Player, Team	Stats
C	Roger Bresnahan, NYG	.283-1-54
1B	Frank Chance, ChN	.272-2-55
2B	Johnny Evers, ChN	.300-0-37
3B	Hans Lobert, Cin	.293-4-63
SS	Honus Wagner, Pit	.354-10-109
OF	Fred Clarke, Pit	.265-2-53
OF	Mike Donlin, NYG	.334-6-106
OF	Sherry Magee, Phi	.283-2-57
SP	Three Finger Brown, ChN	29-9, 1.47
SP	Nick Maddox, Pit	23-8, 2.28
SP	Christy Mathewson, NYG	37-11, 1.43
SP	Ed Reulbach, ChN	24-7, 2.03

1909 American League

Pos	Player, Team	Stats
C	Bill Carrigan, Bos	.296-1-36
1B	Jake Stahl, Bos	.294-6-60
2B	Eddie Collins, Phi	.346-3-56
3B	Home Run Baker, Phi	.305-4-85
SS	Donie Bush, Det	.273-0-33
OF	Ty Cobb, Det	.377-9-107
OF	Sam Crawford, Det	.314-6-97
OF	Tris Speaker, Bos	.309-7-77
SP	Chief Bender, Phi	18-8, 1.66
SP	Harry Krause, Phi	18-8, 1.39
SP	George Mullin, Det	29-8, 2.22
SP	Eddie Plank, Phi	19-10, 1.76

1909 National League

Pos	Player, Team	Stats
C	George Gibson, Pit	.265-2-52
1B	Ed Konetchy, StL	.286-4-80
2B	Larry Doyle, NYG	.302-6-49
3B	Harry Steinfeldt, ChN	.252-2-59
SS	Honus Wagner, Pit	.339-5-100
OF	Fred Clarke, Pit	.287-3-68
OF	Moose McCormick, NYG	.291-3-27
OF	Mike Mitchell, Cin	.310-4-86
SP	Three Finger Brown, ChN	27-9, 1.31
SP	Howie Camnitz, Pit	25-6, 1.62
SP	Christy Mathewson, NYG	25-6, 1.14
SP	Orval Overall, ChN	20-11, 1.42

1910 American League

Pos	Player, Team	Stats
C	Ted Easterly, Cle	.306-0-55
1B	Jake Stahl, Bos	.271-10-77
2B	Nap Lajoie, Cle	.384-4-76
3B	Home Run Baker, Phi	.283-2-74
SS	John Knight, NYA	.312-3-45
OF	Ty Cobb, Det	.383-8-91
OF	Danny Murphy, Phi	.300-4-64
OF	Tris Speaker, Bos	.340-7-65
SP	Chief Bender, Phi	23-5, 1.58
SP	Jack Coombs, Phi	31-9, 1.30
SP	Russ Ford, NYA	26-6, 1.65
SP	Walter Johnson, Was	25-17, 1.36

1910 National League

Pos	Player, Team	Stats
C	Larry McLean, Cin	.298-2-71
1B	Ed Konetchy, StL	.302-3-78
2B	Larry Doyle, NYG	.285-8-69
3B	Bobby Byrne, Pit	.296-2-52
SS	Honus Wagner, Pit	.320-4-81
OF	Solly Hofman, ChN	.325-3-86
OF	Sherry Magee, Phi	.331-6-123
OF	Wildfire Schulte, ChN	.301-10-68
SP	Three Finger Brown, ChN	25-13, 1.86
SP	King Cole, ChN	20-4, 1.80
SP	Christy Mathewson, NYG	27-9, 1.89
SP	Earl Moore, Phi	22-15, 2.58

1911 American League

Pos	Player, Team	Stats
C	Oscar Stanage, Det	.264-3-51
1B	Jim Delahanty, Det	.339-3-94
2B	Eddie Collins, Phi	.365-3-73
3B	Home Run Baker, Phi	.334-11-115
SS	Donie Bush, Det	.232-1-36
OF	Ty Cobb, Det	.420-8-127
OF	Sam Crawford, Det	.378-7-115
OF	Joe Jackson, Cle	.408-7-83
SP	Vean Gregg, Cle	23-7, 1.80
SP	Walter Johnson, Was	25-13, 1.90
SP	Eddie Plank, Phi	23-8, 2.10
SP	Ed Walsh, ChA	27-18, 2.22

1911 National League

Pos	Player, Team	Stats
C	Chief Meyers, NYG	.332-1-61
1B	Ed Konetchy, StL	.289-6-88
2B	Larry Doyle, NYG	.310-13-77
3B	Hans Lobert, Phi	.285-9-72
SS	Honus Wagner, Pit	.334-9-89
OF	Sherry Magee, Phi	.288-15-94
OF	Wildfire Schulte, ChN	.300-21-107
OF	Jimmy Sheckard, ChN	.276-4-50
SP	Babe Adams, Pit	22-12, 2.33
SP	Pete Alexander, Phi	28-13, 2.57
SP	Rube Marquard, NYG	24-7, 2.50
SP	Christy Mathewson, NYG	26-13, 1.99

1912 American League

Pos	Player, Team	Stats
C	Jack Lapp, Phi	.292-1-35
1B	Stuffy McInnis, Phi	.327-3-101
2B	Eddie Collins, Phi	.348-0-64
3B	Home Run Baker, Phi	.347-10-130
SS	Heinie Wagner, Bos	.274-2-68
OF	Ty Cobb, Det	.410-7-83
OF	Joe Jackson, Cle	.395-3-90
OF	Tris Speaker, Bos	.383-10-90
SP	Walter Johnson, Was	33-12, 1.39
SP	Eddie Plank, Phi	26-6, 2.22
SP	Ed Walsh, ChA	27-17, 2.15
SP	Joe Wood, Bos	34-5, 1.91

1912 National League

Pos	Player, Team	Stats
C	Chief Meyers, NYG	.358-6-54
1B	Ed Konetchy, StL	.314-8-82
2B	Larry Doyle, NYG	.330-10-90
3B	Heinie Zimmerman, ChN	.372-14-99
SS	Honus Wagner, Pit	.324-7-102
OF	Dode Paskert, Phi	.315-2-43
OF	John Titus, Phi-Bos	.309-5-70
OF	Chief Wilson, Pit	.300-11-95
SP	Larry Cheney, ChN	26-10, 2.85
SP	Claude Hendrix, Pit	24-9, 2.59
SP	Rube Marquard, NYG	26-11, 2.57
SP	Christy Mathewson, NYG	23-12, 2.12

1913 American League

Pos	Player, Team	Stats
C	Jeff Sweeney, NYA	.265-2-40
1B	Stuffy McInnis, Phi	.326-4-90
2B	Eddie Collins, Phi	.345-3-73
3B	Home Run Baker, Phi	.336-12-117
SS	Jack Barry, Phi	.275-3-85
OF	Ty Cobb, Det	.390-4-67
OF	Joe Jackson, Cle	.373-7-71
OF	Tris Speaker, Bos	.363-3-71
SP	Chief Bender, Phi	21-10, 2.20
SP	Cy Falkenberg, Cle	23-10, 2.22
SP	Walter Johnson, Was	36-7, 1.14
SP	Reb Russell, ChA	22-16, 1.91

1913 National League

Pos	Player, Team	Stats
C	Chief Meyers, NYG	.312-3-47
1B	Jake Daubert, Bro	.350-2-52
2B	Jim Viox, Pit	.317-2-65
3B	Heinie Zimmerman, ChN	.313-9-95
SS	Joe Tinker, Cin	.317-1-57
OF	Gavy Cravath, Phi	.341-19-128
OF	Tommy Leach, ChN	.287-6-32
OF	Sherry Magee, Phi	.306-11-70
SP	Rube Marquard, NYG	23-10, 2.50
SP	Christy Mathewson, NYG	25-11, 2.06
SP	Tom Seaton, Phi	27-12, 2.60
SP	Jeff Tesreau, NYG	22-13, 2.17

1914 American League

Pos	Player, Team	Stats
C	Wally Schang, Phi	.287-3-45
1B	Stuffy McInnis, Phi	.314-1-95
2B	Eddie Collins, Phi	.344-2-85
3B	Home Run Baker, Phi	.319-9-89
SS	Donie Bush, Det	.252-0-32
OF	Ty Cobb, Det	.368-2-57
OF	Sam Crawford, Det	.314-8-104
OF	Tris Speaker, Bos	.338-4-90
SP	Chief Bender, Phi	17-3, 2.26
SP	Harry Coveleski, Det	22-12, 2.49
SP	Walter Johnson, Was	28-18, 1.72
SP	Dutch Leonard, Bos	19-5, 1.00

1914 National League

Pos	Player, Team	Stats
C	Chief Meyers, NYG	.286-1-55
1B	Jake Daubert, Bro	.329-6-45
2B	Johnny Evers, Bos	.279-1-40
3B	Heinie Zimmerman, ChN	.296-4-87
SS	Rabbit Maranville, Bos	.246-4-78
OF	Joe Connolly, Bos	.306-9-65
OF	Gavy Cravath, Phi	.299-19-100
OF	Sherry Magee, Phi	.314-15-103
SP	Pete Alexander, Phi	27-15, 2.38
SP	Bill James, Bos	26-7, 1.90
SP	Dick Rudolph, Bos	26-10, 2.35
SP	Jeff Tesreau, NYG	26-10, 2.37

1914 Federal League

Pos	Player, Team	Stats
C	Art Wilson, Chi	.291-10-64
1B	Fred Beck, Chi	.279-11-77
2B	Duke Kenworthy, KC	.317-15-91
3B	Ed Lennox, Pit	.312-11-84
SS	Baldy Louden, Buf	.313-6-63
OF	Steve Evans, Bro	.348-12-96
OF	Benny Kauff, Ind	.370-8-95
OF	Dutch Zwilling, Chi	.313-16-95
SP	Cy Falkenberg, Ind	25-16, 2.22
SP	Russ Ford, Buf	21-6, 1.82
SP	Claude Hendrix, Chi	29-11, 1.69
SP	Jack Quinn, Bal	26-14, 2.60

1915 American League

Pos	Player, Team	Stats
C	Ray Schalk, ChA	.266-1-54
1B	Jack Fournier, ChA	.322-5-77
2B	Eddie Collins, ChA	.332-4-77
3B	Ossie Vitt, Det	.250-1-48
SS	Ray Chapman, Cle	.270-3-67
OF	Ty Cobb, Det	.369-3-99
OF	Tris Speaker, Bos	.322-0-69
OF	Bobby Veach, Det	.313-3-112
SP	Walter Johnson, Was	27-13, 1.55
SP	Jim Scott, ChA	24-11, 2.03
SP	Ernie Shore, Bos	19-8, 1.64
SP	Joe Wood, Bos	15-5, 1.49

1915 National League

Pos	Player, Team	Stats
C	Frank Snyder, StL	.298-2-55
1B	Fred Luderus, Phi	.315-7-62
2B	Larry Doyle, NYG	.320-4-70
3B	Heine Groh, Cin	.290-3-50
SS	Buck Herzog, Cin	.264-1-42
OF	Gavy Cravath, Phi	.285-24-115
OF	Tommy Griffith, Cin	.307-4-85
OF	Bill Hinchman, Pit	.307-5-77
SP	Pete Alexander, Phi	31-10, 1.22
SP	Al Mamaux, Pit	21-8, 2.04
SP	Erskine Mayer, Phi	21-15, 2.36
SP	Fred Toney, Cin	15-6, 1.58

1915 Federal League

Pos	Player, Team	Stats
C	Art Wilson, Chi	.305-7-31
1B	Ed Konetchy, Pit	.314-10-93
2B	Lee Magee, Bro	.323-4-49
3B	George Perring, KC	.259-7-67
SS	Jimmy Esmond, New	.258-5-62
OF	Steve Evans, Bro-Bal	.308-4-67
OF	Benny Kauff, Bro	.342-12-83
OF	Dutch Zwilling, Chi	.286-13-94
SP	Nick Cullop, KC	22-11, 2.44
SP	Dave Davenport, STL	22-18, 2.20
SP	George McConnell, Chi	25-10, 2.20
SP	Eddie Plank, STL	21-11, 2.08

1916 American League

Pos	Player, Team	Stats
C	Les Nunamaker, NYA	.296-0-28
1B	Wally Pipp, NYA	.262-12-93
2B	Eddie Collins, ChA	.308-0-52
3B	Larry Gardner, Bos	.308-2-62
SS	Roger Peckinpaugh, NYA	.255-4-58
OF	Ty Cobb, Det	.371-5-68
OF	Joe Jackson, ChA	.341-3-78
OF	Tris Speaker, Cle	.386-2-79
SP	Harry Coveleski, Det	21-11, 1.97
SP	Walter Johnson, Was	25-20, 1.90
SP	Babe Ruth, Bos	23-12, 1.75
SP	Bob Shawkey, NYA	24-14, 2.21

1916 National League

Pos	Player, Team	Stats
C	Ivy Wingo, Cin	.245-2-40
1B	Hal Chase, Cin	.339-4-82
2B	Larry Doyle, NYG-ChN	.278-3-54
3B	Rogers Hornsby, StL	.313-6-65
SS	Art Fletcher, NYG	.286-3-66
OF	Gavy Cravath, Phi	.283-11-70
OF	Bill Hinchman, Pit	.315-4-76
OF	Zack Wheat, Bro	.312-9-73
SP	Pete Alexander, Phi	33-12, 1.55
SP	Larry Cheney, Bro	18-12, 1.92
SP	Jeff Pfeffer, Bro	25-11, 1.92
SP	Eppa Rixey, Phi	22-10, 1.85

1917 American League

Pos	Player, Team	Stats
C	Wally Schang, Phi	.285-3-36
1B	George Sisler, StL	.353-2-52
2B	Eddie Collins, ChA	.289-0-67
3B	Home Run Baker, NYA	.282-6-71
SS	Ray Chapman, Cle	.302-2-36
OF	Ty Cobb, Det	.383-6-102
OF	Tris Speaker, Cle	.352-2-60
OF	Bobby Veach, Det	.319-8-103
SP	Jim Bagby, Cle	23-13, 1.96
SP	Eddie Cicotte, ChA	28-12, 1.53
SP	Carl Mays, Bos	22-9, 1.74
SP	Babe Ruth, Bos	24-13, 2.01

1917 National League

Pos	Player, Team	Stats
C	Ivy Wingo, Cin	.266-2-39
1B	Hal Chase, Cin	.277-4-86
2B	Larry Doyle, ChN	.254-6-61
3B	Heine Groh, Cin	.304-1-53
SS	Rogers Hornsby, StL	.327-8-66
OF	George Burns, NYG	.302-5-45
OF	Gavy Cravath, Phi	.280-12-83
OF	Edd Roush, Cin	.341-4-67
SP	Pete Alexander, Phi	30-13, 1.83
SP	Ferdie Schupp, NYG	21-7, 1.95
SP	Fred Toney, Cin	24-16, 2.20
SP	Hippo Vaughn, ChN	23-13, 2.01

1918 American League

Pos	Player, Team	Stats
C	Steve O'Neill, Cle	.242-1-35
1B	George Burns, Phi	.352-6-70
2B	Eddie Collins, ChA	.276-2-30
3B	Home Run Baker, NYA	.306-6-62
SS	Ray Chapman, Cle	.267-1-32
OF	Ty Cobb, Det	.382-3-64
OF	Babe Ruth, Bos	.300-11-66
OF	Tris Speaker, Cle	.318-0-61
SP	Stan Coveleski, Cle	22-13, 1.82
SP	Walter Johnson, Was	23-13, 1.27
SP	Carl Mays, Bos	21-13, 2.21
SP	Scott Perry, Phi	20-19, 1.98

1918 National League

Pos	Player, Team	Stats
C	Mike Gonzalez, StL	.252-3-20
1B	Sherry Magee, Cin	.298-2-76
2B	George Cutshaw, Pit	.285-5-68
3B	Heine Groh, Cin	.320-1-37
SS	Rogers Hornsby, StL	.281-5-60
OF	George Burns, NYG	.290-4-51
OF	Dode Paskert, ChN	.286-2-59
OF	Edd Roush, Cin	.333-5-62
SP	Wilbur Cooper, Pit	19-14, 2.11
SP	Burleigh Grimes, Bro	19-9, 2.14
SP	Lefty Tyler, ChN	19-8, 2.00
SP	Hippo Vaughn, ChN	22-10, 1.74

1919 American League

Pos	Player, Team	Stats
C	Wally Schang, Bos	.306-0-55
1B	George Sisler, StL	.352-10-83
2B	Eddie Collins, ChA	.319-4-80
3B	Buck Weaver, ChA	.296-3-75
SS	Roger Peckinpaugh, NYA	.305-7-33
OF	Ty Cobb, Det	.384-1-70
OF	Joe Jackson, ChA	.351-7-96
OF	Babe Ruth, Bos	.322-29-114
SP	Eddie Cicotte, ChA	29-7, 1.82
SP	Stan Coveleski, Cle	24-12, 2.52
SP	Walter Johnson, Was	20-14, 1.49
SP	Allen Sothoron, StL	20-13, 2.20

Awards: STATS Retroactive All-Stars

1919 National League

Pos	Player, Team	Stats
C	Ivy Wingo, Cin	.273-0-27
1B	Fred Luderus, Phi	.293-5-49
2B	Larry Doyle, NYG	.289-7-52
3B	Heine Groh, Cin	.310-5-63
SS	Rabbit Maranville, Bos	.267-5-43
OF	George Burns, NYG	.303-2-46
OF	Hi Myers, Bro	.307-5-73
OF	Edd Roush, Cin	.321-4-71
SP	Jesse Barnes, NYG	25-9, 2.40
SP	Dutch Ruether, Cin	19-6, 1.82
SP	Slim Sallee, Cin	21-7, 2.06
SP	Hippo Vaughn, ChN	21-14, 1.79

1920 American League

Pos	Player, Team	Stats
C	Steve O'Neill, Cle	.321-3-55
1B	George Sisler, StL	.407-19-122
2B	Eddie Collins, ChA	.372-3-76
3B	Larry Gardner, Cle	.310-3-118
SS	Ray Chapman, Cle	.303-3-49
OF	Joe Jackson, ChA	.382-12-121
OF	Babe Ruth, NYA	.376-54-137
OF	Tris Speaker, Cle	.388-8-107
SP	Jim Bagby, Cle	31-12, 2.89
SP	Stan Coveleski, Cle	24-14, 2.49
SP	Carl Mays, NYA	26-11, 3.06
SP	Bob Shawkey, NYA	20-13, 2.45

1920 National League

Pos	Player, Team	Stats
C	Verne Clemons, StL	.281-1-36
1B	George Kelly, NYG	.266-11-94
2B	Rogers Hornsby, StL	.370-9-94
3B	Milt Stock, StL	.319-0-76
SS	Dave Bancroft, Phi-NYG	.299-0-36
OF	Edd Roush, Cin	.339-4-90
OF	Zack Wheat, Bro	.328-9-73
OF	Ross Youngs, NYG	.351-6-78
SP	Pete Alexander, ChN	27-14, 1.91
SP	Wilbur Cooper, Pit	24-15, 2.39
SP	Burleigh Grimes, Bro	23-11, 2.22
SP	Fred Toney, NYG	21-11, 2.65

1921 American League

Pos	Player, Team	Stats
C	Wally Schang, NYA	.316-6-55
1B	George Sisler, StL	.371-12-104
2B	Del Pratt, Bos	.324-5-100
3B	Larry Gardner, Cle	.319-3-115
SS	Joe Sewell, Cle	.318-4-91
OF	Ty Cobb, Det	.389-12-101
OF	Harry Heilmann, Det	.394-19-139
OF	Babe Ruth, NYA	.378-59-171
SP	Red Faber, ChA	25-15, 2.48
SP	Sad Sam Jones, Bos	23-16, 3.22
SP	Carl Mays, NYA	27-9, 3.05
SP	Urban Shocker, StL	27-12, 3.55

1921 National League

Pos	Player, Team	Stats
C	Frank Snyder, NYG	.320-8-45
1B	George Kelly, NYG	.308-23-122
2B	Rogers Hornsby, StL	.397-21-126
3B	Frankie Frisch, NYG	.341-8-100
SS	Dave Bancroft, NYG	.318-6-67
OF	Austin McHenry, StL	.350-17-102
OF	Irish Meusel, Phi-NYG	.343-14-87
OF	Ross Youngs, NYG	.327-3-102
SP	Wilbur Cooper, Pit	22-14, 3.25
SP	Burleigh Grimes, Bro	22-13, 2.83
SP	Art Nehf, NYG	20-10, 3.63
SP	Eppa Rixey, Cin	19-18, 2.78

1922 American League

Pos	Player, Team	Stats
C	Steve O'Neill, Cle	.311-2-65
1B	George Sisler, StL	.420-8-105
2B	Marty McManus, StL	.312-11-109
3B	Jimmy Dykes, Phi	.275-12-68
SS	Joe Sewell, Cle	.299-2-83
OF	Ty Cobb, Det	.401-4-99
OF	Babe Ruth, NYA	.315-35-96
OF	Ken Williams, StL	.332-39-155
SP	Joe Bush, NYA	26-7, 3.31
SP	Red Faber, ChA	21-17, 2.80
SP	Eddie Rommel, Phi	27-13, 3.28
SP	Urban Shocker, StL	24-17, 2.97

1922 National League

Pos	Player, Team	Stats
C	Bob O'Farrell, ChN	.324-4-60
1B	Ray Grimes, ChN	.354-14-99
2B	Rogers Hornsby, StL	.401-42-152
3B	Milt Stock, StL	.305-5-79
SS	Dave Bancroft, NYG	.321-4-60
OF	Carson Bigbee, Pit	.350-5-99
OF	Max Carey, Pit	.329-10-70
OF	Irish Meusel, NYG	.331-16-132
SP	Wilbur Cooper, Pit	23-14, 3.18
SP	Pete Donohue, Cin	18-9, 3.12
SP	Eppa Rixey, Cin	25-13, 3.53
SP	Dutch Ruether, Bro	21-12, 3.53

1923 American League

Pos	Player, Team	Stats
C	Muddy Ruel, Was	.316-0-54
1B	Joe Hauser, Phi	.307-17-94
2B	Eddie Collins, ChA	.360-5-67
3B	Willie Kamm, ChA	.292-6-87
SS	Joe Sewell, Cle	.353-3-109
OF	Harry Heilmann, Det	.403-18-115
OF	Babe Ruth, NYA	.393-41-131
OF	Tris Speaker, Cle	.380-17-130
SP	Waite Hoyt, NYA	17-9, 3.02
SP	Herb Pennock, NYA	19-6, 3.33
SP	Urban Shocker, StL	20-12, 3.41
SP	George Uhle, Cle	26-16, 3.77

1923 National League

Pos	Player, Team	Stats
C	Bubbles Hargrave, Cin	.333-10-78
1B	Jack Fournier, Bro	.351-22-102
2B	Rogers Hornsby, StL	.384-17-83
3B	Pie Traynor, Pit	.338-12-101
SS	Dave Bancroft, NYG	.304-1-31
OF	Edd Roush, Cin	.351-6-88
OF	Cy Williams, Phi	.293-41-114
OF	Ross Youngs, NYG	.336-3-87
SP	Pete Alexander, ChN	22-12, 3.19
SP	Dolf Luque, Cin	27-8, 1.93
SP	Johnny Morrison, Pit	25-13, 3.49
SP	Eppa Rixey, Cin	20-15, 2.80

1924 American League

Pos	Player, Team	Stats
C	Glenn Myatt, Cle	.342-8-73
1B	Joe Hauser, Phi	.288-27-115
2B	Eddie Collins, ChA	.349-6-86
3B	Joe Dugan, NYA	.302-3-56
SS	Joe Sewell, Cle	.316-4-104
OF	Goose Goslin, Was	.344-12-129
OF	Harry Heilmann, Det	.346-10-114
OF	Babe Ruth, NYA	.378-46-121
SP	Walter Johnson, Was	23-7, 2.72
SP	Herb Pennock, NYA	21-9, 2.83
SP	Sloppy Thurston, ChA	20-14, 3.80
SP	Tom Zachary, Was	15-9, 2.75
RP	Firpo Marberry, Was	3.09, 15 saves

1924 National League

Pos	Player, Team	Stats
C	Gabby Hartnett, ChN	.299-16-67
1B	Jack Fournier, Bro	.334-27-116
2B	Rogers Hornsby, StL	.424-25-94
3B	Pie Traynor, Pit	.294-5-82
SS	Glenn Wright, Pit	.287-7-111
OF	Kiki Cuyler, Pit	.354-9-85
OF	Zack Wheat, Bro	.375-14-97
OF	Ross Youngs, NYG	.356-10-74
SP	Ray Kremer, Pit	18-10, 3.19
SP	Carl Mays, Cin	20-9, 3.15
SP	Dazzy Vance, Bro	28-6, 2.16
SP	Emil Yde, Pit	16-3, 2.83
RP	Claude Jonnard, NYG	2.41, 5 saves

1925 American League

Pos	Player, Team	Stats
C	Mickey Cochrane, Phi	.331-6-55
1B	George Sisler, StL	.345-12-105
2B	Eddie Collins, ChA	.346-3-80
3B	Sammy Hale, Phi	.345-8-63
SS	Joe Sewell, Cle	.336-1-98
OF	Ty Cobb, Det	.378-12-102
OF	Harry Heilmann, Det	.393-13-134
OF	Al Simmons, Phi	.384-24-129
SP	Ted Blankenship, ChA	17-8, 3.16
SP	Stan Coveleski, Was	20-5, 2.84
SP	Walter Johnson, Was	20-7, 3.07
SP	Ted Lyons, ChA	21-11, 3.26
RP	Firpo Marberry, Was	3.47, 15 saves

1925 National League

Pos	Player, Team	Stats
C	Gabby Hartnett, ChN	.289-24-67
1B	Jack Fournier, Bro	.350-22-130
2B	Rogers Hornsby, StL	.403-39-143
3B	Pie Traynor, Pit	.320-6-106
SS	Glenn Wright, Pit	.308-18-121
OF	Ray Blades, StL	.342-12-57
OF	Kiki Cuyler, Pit	.357-18-102
OF	Zack Wheat, Bro	.359-14-103
SP	Pete Donohue, Cin	21-14, 3.08
SP	Lee Meadows, Pit	19-10, 3.67
SP	Eppa Rixey, Cin	21-11, 2.88
SP	Dazzy Vance, Bro	22-9, 3.53
RP	Jakie May, Cin	3.87, 2 saves

1926 American League

Pos	Player, Team	Stats
C	Wally Schang, StL	.330-8-50
1B	Lou Gehrig, NYA	.313-16-112
2B	Tony Lazzeri, NYA	.275-18-114
3B	Marty McManus, StL	.284-9-68
SS	Joe Sewell, Cle	.324-4-85
OF	Goose Goslin, Was	.354-17-108
OF	Harry Heilmann, Det	.367-9-103
OF	Babe Ruth, NYA	.372-47-146
SP	Ted Lyons, ChA	18-16, 3.01
SP	Herb Pennock, NYA	23-11, 3.62
SP	Urban Shocker, NYA	19-11, 3.38
SP	George Uhle, Cle	27-11, 2.83
RP	Firpo Marberry, Was	3.00, 22 saves

1926 National League

Pos	Player, Team	Stats
C	Bob O'Farrell, StL	.293-7-68
1B	Jim Bottomley, StL	.299-19-120
2B	Rogers Hornsby, StL	.317-11-93
3B	Les Bell, StL	.325-17-100
SS	Travis Jackson, NYG	.327-8-51
OF	Kiki Cuyler, Pit	.321-8-92
OF	Paul Waner, Pit	.336-8-79
OF	Hack Wilson, ChN	.321-21-109
SP	Pete Donohue, Cin	20-14, 3.37
SP	Ray Kremer, Pit	20-6, 2.61
SP	Carl Mays, Cin	19-12, 3.14
SP	Flint Rhem, StL	20-7, 3.21
RP	Jakie May, Cin	3.22, 3 saves

1927 American League

Pos	Player, Team	Stats
C	Mickey Cochrane, Phi	.338-12-80
1B	Lou Gehrig, NYA	.373-47-175
2B	Tony Lazzeri, NYA	.309-18-102
3B	Sammy Hale, Phi	.313-5-81
SS	Joe Sewell, Cle	.316-1-92
OF	Harry Heilmann, Det	.398-14-120
OF	Babe Ruth, NYA	.356-60-164
OF	Al Simmons, Phi	.392-15-108
SP	Lefty Grove, Phi	20-13, 3.19
SP	Waite Hoyt, NYA	22-7, 2.63
SP	Ted Lyons, ChA	22-14, 2.84
SP	Urban Shocker, NYA	18-6, 2.84
RP	Wilcy Moore, NYA	2.28, 13 saves

1927 National League

Pos	Player, Team	Stats
C	Gabby Hartnett, ChN	.294-10-80
1B	Bill Terry, NYG	.326-20-121
2B	Rogers Hornsby, NYG	.361-26-125
3B	Pie Traynor, Pit	.342-5-106
SS	Travis Jackson, NYG	.318-14-98
OF	Chick Hafey, StL	.329-18-63
OF	Paul Waner, Pit	.380-9-131
OF	Hack Wilson, ChN	.318-30-129
SP	Pete Alexander, StL	21-10, 2.52
SP	Jesse Haines, StL	24-10, 2.72
SP	Ray Kremer, Pit	19-8, 2.47
SP	Charlie Root, ChN	26-15, 3.76
RP	George Mogridge, Bos	3.70, 5 saves

1928 American League

Pos	Player, Team	Stats
C	Mickey Cochrane, Phi	.293-10-57
1B	Lou Gehrig, NYA	.374-27-142
2B	Charlie Gehringer, Det	.320-6-74
3B	Jimmie Foxx, Phi	.328-13-79
SS	Joe Sewell, Cle	.323-4-70
OF	Goose Goslin, Was	.379-17-102
OF	Heinie Manush, StL	.378-13-108
OF	Babe Ruth, NYA	.323-54-142
SP	Lefty Grove, Phi	24-8, 2.58
SP	Waite Hoyt, NYA	23-7, 3.36
SP	Herb Pennock, NYA	17-6, 2.56
SP	George Pipgras, NYA	24-13, 3.38
RP	Eddie Rommel, Phi	3.06, 4 saves

1928 National League

Pos	Player, Team	Stats
C	Gabby Hartnett, ChN	.302-14-57
1B	Jim Bottomley, StL	.325-31-136
2B	Rogers Hornsby, Bos	.387-21-94
3B	Freddy Lindstrom, NYG	.358-14-107
SS	Travis Jackson, NYG	.270-14-77
OF	Chick Hafey, StL	.337-27-111
OF	Paul Waner, Pit	.370-6-86
OF	Hack Wilson, ChN	.313-31-120
SP	Larry Benton, NYG	25-9, 2.73
SP	Burleigh Grimes, Pit	25-14, 2.99
SP	Bill Sherdel, StL	21-10, 2.86
SP	Dazzy Vance, Bro	22-10, 2.09
RP	Joe Dawson, Pit	3.29, 3 saves

1929 American League

Pos	Player, Team	Stats
C	Mickey Cochrane, Phi	.331-7-95
1B	Jimmie Foxx, Phi	.354-33-117
2B	Charlie Gehringer, Det	.339-13-106
3B	Marty McManus, Det	.280-18-90
SS	Red Kress, StL	.305-9-107
OF	Harry Heilmann, Det	.344-15-120
OF	Babe Ruth, NYA	.345-46-154
OF	Al Simmons, Phi	.365-34-157
SP	George Earnshaw, Phi	24-8, 3.29
SP	Wes Ferrell, Cle	21-10, 3.60
SP	Lefty Grove, Phi	20-6, 2.81
SP	Firpo Marberry, Was	19-12, 3.06
RP	Bill Shores, Phi	3.60, 7 saves

1929 National League

Pos	Player, Team	Stats
C	Jimmie Wilson, StL	.325-4-71
1B	Jim Bottomley, StL	.314-29-137
2B	Rogers Hornsby, ChN	.380-39-149
3B	Pie Traynor, Pit	.356-4-108
SS	Travis Jackson, NYG	.294-21-94
OF	Lefty O'Doul, Phi	.398-32-122
OF	Mel Ott, NYG	.328-42-151
OF	Hack Wilson, ChN	.345-39-159
SP	Burleigh Grimes, Pit	17-7, 3.13
SP	Red Lucas, Cin	19-12, 3.60
SP	Pat Malone, ChN	22-10, 3.57
SP	Charlie Root, ChN	19-6, 3.47
RP	Johnny Morrison, Bro	4.48, 8 saves

1930 American League

Pos	Player, Team	Stats
C	Mickey Cochrane, Phi	.357-10-85
1B	Lou Gehrig, NYA	.379-41-174
2B	Charlie Gehringer, Det	.330-16-98
3B	Marty McManus, Det	.320-9-89
SS	Joe Cronin, Was	.346-13-126
OF	Goose Goslin, Was-StL	.308-37-138
OF	Babe Ruth, NYA	.359-49-153
OF	Al Simmons, Phi	.381-36-165
SP	Wes Ferrell, Cle	25-13, 3.31
SP	Lefty Grove, Phi	28-5, 2.54
SP	Ted Lyons, ChA	22-15, 3.78
SP	Lefty Stewart, StL	20-12, 3.45
RP	Jack Quinn, Phi	4.42, 6 saves

1930 National League

Pos	Player, Team	Stats
C	Gabby Hartnett, ChN	.339-37-122
1B	Bill Terry, NYG	.401-23-129
2B	Frankie Frisch, StL	.346-10-114
3B	Freddy Lindstrom, NYG	.379-22-106
SS	Glenn Wright, Bro	.321-22-126
OF	Babe Herman, Bro	.393-35-130
OF	Chuck Klein, Phi	.386-40-170
OF	Hack Wilson, ChN	.356-56-190
SP	Freddie Fitzsimmons, NYG	19-7, 4.25
SP	Carl Hubbell, NYG	17-12, 3.87
SP	Pat Malone, ChN	20-9, 3.94
SP	Dazzy Vance, Bro	17-15, 2.61
RP	Hi Bell, StL	3.90, 8 saves

1931 American League

Pos	Player, Team	Stats
C	Mickey Cochrane, Phi	.349-17-89
1B	Lou Gehrig, NYA	.341-46-184
2B	Max Bishop, Phi	.294-5-37
3B	Red Kress, StL	.311-16-114
SS	Joe Cronin, Was	.306-12-126
OF	Earl Averill, Cle	.333-32-143
OF	Babe Ruth, NYA	.373-46-163
OF	Al Simmons, Phi	.390-22-128
SP	George Earnshaw, Phi	21-7, 3.67
SP	Wes Ferrell, Cle	22-12, 3.75
SP	Lefty Gomez, NYA	21-9, 2.63
SP	Lefty Grove, Phi	31-4, 2.06
RP	Bump Hadley, Was	3.06, 8 saves

1931 National League

Pos	Player, Team	Stats
C	Gabby Hartnett, ChN	.282-8-70
1B	Bill Terry, NYG	.349-9-112
2B	Frankie Frisch, StL	.311-4-82
3B	Pie Traynor, Pit	.298-2-103
SS	Woody English, ChN	.319-2-53
OF	Chick Hafey, StL	.349-16-95
OF	Chuck Klein, Phi	.337-31-121
OF	Mel Ott, NYG	.292-29-115
SP	Ed Brandt, Bos	18-11, 2.92
SP	Freddie Fitzsimmons, NYG	18-11, 3.05
SP	Wild Bill Hallahan, StL	19-9, 3.29
SP	Heinie Meine, Pit	19-13, 2.98
RP	Jack Quinn, Bro	2.66, 15 saves

1932 American League

Pos	Player, Team	Stats
C	Mickey Cochrane, Phi	.293-23-112
1B	Jimmie Foxx, Phi	.364-58-169
2B	Tony Lazzeri, NYA	.300-15-113
3B	Willie Kamm, Cle	.286-3-83
SS	Joe Cronin, Was	.318-6-116
OF	Earl Averill, Cle	.314-32-124
OF	Babe Ruth, NYA	.341-41-137
OF	Al Simmons, Phi	.322-35-151
SP	General Crowder, Was	26-13, 3.33
SP	Wes Ferrell, Cle	23-13, 3.66
SP	Lefty Grove, Phi	25-10, 2.84
SP	Red Ruffing, NYA	18-7, 3.09
RP	Firpo Marberry, Was	4.01, 13 saves

1932 National League

Pos	Player, Team	Stats
C	Spud Davis, Phi	.336-14-70
1B	Bill Terry, NYG	.350-28-117
2B	Billy Herman, ChN	.314-1-51
3B	Pinky Whitney, Phi	.298-13-124
SS	Dick Bartell, Phi	.308-1-53
OF	Chuck Klein, Phi	.348-38-137
OF	Lefty O'Doul, Bro	.368-21-90
OF	Mel Ott, NYG	.318-38-123
SP	Guy Bush, ChN	19-11, 3.21
SP	Dizzy Dean, StL	18-15, 3.30
SP	Carl Hubbell, NYG	18-11, 2.50
SP	Lon Warneke, ChN	22-6, 2.37
RP	Ben Cantwell, Bos	2.96, 5 saves

1933 American League

Pos	Player, Team	Stats
C	Mickey Cochrane, Phi	.322-15-60
1B	Jimmie Foxx, Phi	.356-48-163
2B	Charlie Gehringer, Det	.325-12-105
3B	Mike Higgins, Phi	.314-13-99
SS	Joe Cronin, Was	.309-5-118
OF	Bob Johnson, Phi	.290-21-93
OF	Babe Ruth, NYA	.301-34-103
OF	Al Simmons, ChA	.331-14-119
SP	General Crowder, Was	24-15, 3.97
SP	Lefty Gomez, NYA	16-10, 3.18
SP	Lefty Grove, Phi	24-8, 3.20
SP	Earl Whitehill, Was	22-8, 3.33
RP	Jack Russell, Was	2.69, 13 saves

1933 National League

Pos	Player, Team	Stats
C	Gabby Hartnett, ChN	.276-16-88
1B	Ripper Collins, StL	.310-10-68
2B	Frankie Frisch, StL	.303-4-66
3B	Pepper Martin, StL	.316-8-57
SS	Arky Vaughan, Pit	.314-9-97
OF	Wally Berger, Bos	.313-27-106
OF	Chuck Klein, Phi	.368-28-120
OF	Mel Ott, NYG	.283-23-103
SP	Ben Cantwell, Bos	20-10, 2.62
SP	Carl Hubbell, NYG	23-12, 1.66
SP	Hal Schumacher, NYG	19-12, 2.16
SP	Lon Warneke, ChN	18-13, 2.00
RP	Hi Bell, NYG	2.05, 5 saves

1934 American League

Pos	Player, Team	Stats
C	Mickey Cochrane, Det	.320-2-76
1B	Lou Gehrig, NYA	.363-49-165
2B	Charlie Gehringer, Det	.356-11-127
3B	Bill Werber, Bos	.321-11-67
SS	Billy Rogell, Det	.296-3-100
OF	Earl Averill, Cle	.313-31-113
OF	Bob Johnson, Phi	.307-34-92
OF	Al Simmons, ChA	.344-18-104
SP	Tommy Bridges, Det	22-11, 3.67
SP	Lefty Gomez, NYA	26-5, 2.33
SP	Mel Harder, Cle	20-12, 2.61
SP	Schoolboy Rowe, Det	24-8, 3.45
RP	Jack Russell, Was	4.17, 7 saves

Awards: STATS Retroactive All-Stars

1934 National League

Pos	Player, Team	Stats
C	Gabby Hartnett, ChN	.299-22-90
1B	Ripper Collins, StL	.333-35-128
2B	Frankie Frisch, StL	.305-3-75
3B	Pepper Martin, StL	.289-5-49
SS	Arky Vaughan, Pit	.333-12-94
OF	Wally Berger, Bos	.298-34-121
OF	Mel Ott, NYG	.326-35-135
OF	Paul Waner, Pit	.362-14-90
SP	Curt Davis, Phi	19-17, 2.95
SP	Dizzy Dean, StL	30-7, 2.66
SP	Carl Hubbell, NYG	21-12, 2.30
SP	Hal Schumacher, NYG	23-10, 3.18
RP	Dolf Luque, NYG	3.83, 7 saves

1935 American League

Pos	Player, Team	Stats
C	Mickey Cochrane, Det	.319-5-47
1B	Hank Greenberg, Det	.328-36-170
2B	Buddy Myer, Was	.349-5-100
3B	Odell Hale, Cle	.304-16-101
SS	Luke Appling, ChA	.307-1-71
OF	Pete Fox, Det	.321-15-73
OF	Bob Johnson, Phi	.299-28-109
OF	Joe Vosmik, Cle	.348-10-110
SP	Tommy Bridges, Det	21-10, 3.51
SP	Wes Ferrell, Bos	25-14, 3.52
SP	Lefty Grove, Bos	20-12, 2.70
SP	Mel Harder, Cle	22-11, 3.29
RP	Johnny Murphy, NYA	4.08, 5 saves

1935 National League

Pos	Player, Team	Stats
C	Gabby Hartnett, ChN	.344-13-91
1B	Ripper Collins, StL	.313-23-122
2B	Billy Herman, ChN	.341-7-83
3B	Stan Hack, ChN	.311-4-64
SS	Arky Vaughan, Pit	.385-19-99
OF	Wally Berger, Bos	.295-34-130
OF	Joe Medwick, StL	.353-23-126
OF	Mel Ott, NYG	.322-31-114
SP	Cy Blanton, Pit	18-13, 2.58
SP	Dizzy Dean, StL	28-12, 3.04
SP	Carl Hubbell, NYG	23-12, 3.27
SP	Bill Lee, ChN	20-6, 2.96
RP	Syl Johnson, Phi	3.56, 6 saves

1936 American League

Pos	Player, Team	Stats
C	Bill Dickey, NYA	.362-22-107
1B	Lou Gehrig, NYA	.354-49-152
2B	Charlie Gehringer, Det	.354-15-116
3B	Harlond Clift, StL	.302-20-73
SS	Luke Appling, ChA	.388-6-128
OF	Earl Averill, Cle	.378-28-126
OF	Joe DiMaggio, NYA	.323-29-125
OF	Goose Goslin, Det	.315-24-125
SP	Johnny Allen, Cle	20-10, 3.44
SP	Tommy Bridges, Det	23-11, 3.60
SP	Lefty Grove, Bos	17-12, 2.81
SP	Red Ruffing, NYA	20-12, 3.85
RP	Pat Malone, NYA	3.81, 9 saves

1936 National League

Pos	Player, Team	Stats
C	Ernie Lombardi, Cin	.333-12-68
1B	Dolph Camilli, Phi	.315-28-102
2B	Billy Herman, ChN	.334-5-93
3B	Stan Hack, ChN	.298-6-78
SS	Arky Vaughan, Pit	.335-9-78
OF	Joe Medwick, StL	.351-18-138
OF	Mel Ott, NYG	.328-33-135
OF	Paul Waner, Pit	.373-5-94
SP	Dizzy Dean, StL	24-13, 3.17
SP	Larry French, ChN	18-9, 3.39
SP	Carl Hubbell, NYG	26-6, 2.31
SP	Danny MacFayden, Bos	17-13, 2.87
RP	Bob Smith, Bos	3.77, 8 saves

1937 American League

Pos	Player, Team	Stats
C	Bill Dickey, NYA	.332-29-133
1B	Lou Gehrig, NYA	.351-37-159
2B	Charlie Gehringer, Det	.371-14-96
3B	Harlond Clift, StL	.306-29-118
SS	Joe Cronin, Bos	.307-18-110
OF	Earl Averill, Cle	.299-21-92
OF	Joe DiMaggio, NYA	.346-46-167
OF	Bob Johnson, Phi	.306-25-108
SP	Johnny Allen, Cle	15-1, 2.55
SP	Lefty Gomez, NYA	21-11, 2.33
SP	Lefty Grove, Bos	17-9, 3.02
SP	Red Ruffing, NYA	20-7, 2.98
RP	Clint Brown, ChA	3.42, 18 saves

1937 National League

Pos	Player, Team	Stats
C	Gabby Hartnett, ChN	.354-12-82
1B	Johnny Mize, StL	.364-25-113
2B	Billy Herman, ChN	.335-8-65
3B	Pinky Whitney, Phi	.341-8-79
SS	Dick Bartell, NYG	.306-14-62
OF	Frank Demaree, ChN	.324-17-115
OF	Joe Medwick, StL	.374-31-154
OF	Mel Ott, NYG	.294-31-95
SP	Lou Fette, Bos	20-10, 2.88
SP	Carl Hubbell, NYG	22-8, 3.20
SP	Cliff Melton, NYG	20-9, 2.61
SP	Jim Turner, Bos	20-11, 2.38
RP	Charlie Root, ChN	3.38, 5 saves

1938 American League

Pos	Player, Team	Stats
C	Rudy York, Det	.298-33-127
1B	Jimmie Foxx, Bos	.349-50-175
2B	Charlie Gehringer, Det	.306-20-107
3B	Harlond Clift, StL	.290-34-118
SS	Joe Cronin, Bos	.325-17-94
OF	Earl Averill, Cle	.330-14-93
OF	Joe DiMaggio, NYA	.324-32-140
OF	Jeff Heath, Cle	.343-21-112
SP	Bob Feller, Cle	17-11, 4.08
SP	Lefty Gomez, NYA	18-12, 3.35
SP	Mel Harder, Cle	17-10, 3.83
SP	Red Ruffing, NYA	21-7, 3.31
RP	Johnny Murphy, NYA	4.24, 11 saves

1938 National League

Pos	Player, Team	Stats
C	Ernie Lombardi, Cin	.342-19-95
1B	Johnny Mize, StL	.337-27-102
2B	Billy Herman, ChN	.277-1-56
3B	Mel Ott, NYG	.311-36-116
SS	Arky Vaughan, Pit	.322-7-68
OF	Ival Goodman, Cin	.292-30-92
OF	Joe Medwick, StL	.322-21-122
OF	Johnny Rizzo, Pit	.301-23-111
SP	Clay Bryant, ChN	19-11, 3.10
SP	Paul Derringer, Cin	21-14, 2.93
SP	Bill Lee, ChN	22-9, 2.66
SP	Johnny Vander Meer, Cin	15-10, 3.12
RP	Dick Coffman, NYG	3.48, 12 saves

1939 American League

Pos	Player, Team	Stats
C	Bill Dickey, NYA	.302-24-105
1B	Jimmie Foxx, Bos	.360-35-105
2B	Charlie Gehringer, Det	.325-16-86
3B	Red Rolfe, NYA	.329-14-80
SS	Joe Cronin, Bos	.308-19-107
OF	Joe DiMaggio, NYA	.381-30-126
OF	Bob Johnson, Phi	.338-23-114
OF	Ted Williams, Bos	.327-31-145
SP	Bob Feller, Cle	24-9, 2.85
SP	Lefty Grove, Bos	15-4, 2.54
SP	Dutch Leonard, Was	20-8, 3.54
SP	Red Ruffing, NYA	21-7, 2.93
RP	Clint Brown, ChA	3.88, 18 saves

1939 National League

Pos	Player, Team	Stats
C	Harry Danning, NYG	.313-16-74
1B	Johnny Mize, StL	.349-28-108
2B	Billy Herman, ChN	.307-7-70
3B	Cookie Lavagetto, Bro	.300-10-87
SS	Arky Vaughan, Pit	.306-6-62
OF	Hank Leiber, ChN	.310-24-88
OF	Joe Medwick, StL	.332-14-117
OF	Mel Ott, NYG	.308-27-80
SP	Hugh Casey, Bro	15-10, 2.93
SP	Curt Davis, StL	22-16, 3.63
SP	Paul Derringer, Cin	25-7, 2.93
SP	Bucky Walters, Cin	27-11, 2.29
RP	Bob Bowman, StL	2.60, 9 saves

1940 American League

Pos	Player, Team	Stats
C	Frankie Hayes, Phi	.308-16-70
1B	Rudy York, Det	.316-33-134
2B	Joe Gordon, NYA	.281-30-103
3B	Harlond Clift, StL	.273-20-87
SS	Joe Cronin, Bos	.285-24-111
OF	Joe DiMaggio, NYA	.352-31-133
OF	Hank Greenberg, Det	.340-41-150
OF	Ted Williams, Bos	.344-23-113
SP	Bob Feller, Cle	27-11, 2.61
SP	Al Milnar, Cle	18-10, 3.27
SP	Bobo Newsom, Det	21-5, 2.83
SP	Schoolboy Rowe, Det	16-3, 3.46
RP	Johnny Murphy, NYA	3.69, 9 saves

1940 National League

Pos	Player, Team	Stats
C	Ernie Lombardi, Cin	.319-14-74
1B	Johnny Mize, StL	.314-43-137
2B	Lonny Frey, Cin	.266-8-54
3B	Debs Garms, Pit	.355-5-57
SS	Arky Vaughan, Pit	.300-7-95
OF	Bill Nicholson, ChN	.297-25-98
OF	Mel Ott, NYG	.289-19-79
OF	Enos Slaughter, StL	.306-17-73
SP	Paul Derringer, Cin	20-12, 3.06
SP	Freddie Fitzsimmons, Bro	16-2, 2.81
SP	Claude Passeau, ChN	20-13, 2.50
SP	Bucky Walters, Cin	22-10, 2.48
RP	Joe Beggs, Cin	2.00, 7 saves

1941 American League

Pos	Player, Team	Stats
C	Frankie Hayes, Phi	.280-12-63
1B	Jimmie Foxx, Bos	.300-19-105
2B	Joe Gordon, NYA	.276-24-87
3B	Ken Keltner, Cle	.269-23-84
SS	Cecil Travis, Was	.359-7-101
OF	Joe DiMaggio, NYA	.357-30-125
OF	Charlie Keller, NYA	.298-33-122
OF	Ted Williams, Bos	.406-37-120
SP	Bob Feller, Cle	25-13, 3.15
SP	Thornton Lee, ChA	22-11, 2.37
SP	Dutch Leonard, Was	18-13, 3.45
SP	Marius Russo, NYA	14-10, 3.09
RP	Johnny Murphy, NYA	1.98, 15 saves

1941 National League

Pos	Player, Team	Stats
C	Ernie Lombardi, Cin	.264-10-60
1B	Dolph Camilli, Bro	.285-34-120
2B	Billy Herman, ChN-Bro	.285-3-41
3B	Stan Hack, ChN	.317-7-45
SS	Arky Vaughan, Pit	.316-6-38
OF	Joe Medwick, Bro	.318-18-88
OF	Mel Ott, NYG	.286-27-90
OF	Pete Reiser, Bro	.343-14-76
SP	Kirby Higbe, Bro	22-9, 3.14
SP	Elmer Riddle, Cin	19-4, 2.24
SP	Bucky Walters, Cin	19-15, 2.83
SP	Whit Wyatt, Bro	22-10, 2.34
RP	Hugh Casey, Bro	3.89, 7 saves

1942 American League

Pos	Player, Team	Stats
C	Bill Dickey, NYA	.295-2-37
1B	Les Fleming, Cle	.292-14-82
2B	Joe Gordon, NYA	.322-18-103
3B	Harlond Clift, StL	.274-7-55
SS	Johnny Pesky, Bos	.331-2-51
OF	Joe DiMaggio, NYA	.305-21-114
OF	Charlie Keller, NYA	.292-26-108
OF	Ted Williams, Bos	.356-36-137
SP	Tiny Bonham, NYA	21-5, 2.27
SP	Spud Chandler, NYA	16-5, 2.38
SP	Tex Hughson, Bos	22-6, 2.59
SP	Ted Lyons, ChA	14-6, 2.10
RP	Joe Haynes, ChA	2.62, 6 saves

1942 National League

Pos	Player, Team	Stats
C	Ernie Lombardi, Bos	.330-11-46
1B	Johnny Mize, NYG	.305-26-110
2B	Lonny Frey, Cin	.266-2-39
3B	Stan Hack, ChN	.300-6-39
SS	Pee Wee Reese, Bro	.255-3-53
OF	Stan Musial, StL	.315-10-72
OF	Mel Ott, NYG	.295-30-93
OF	Enos Slaughter, StL	.318-13-98
SP	Johnny Beazley, StL	21-6, 2.13
SP	Mort Cooper, StL	22-7, 1.78
SP	Johnny Vander Meer, Cin	18-12, 2.43
SP	Whit Wyatt, Bro	19-7, 2.73
RP	Ace Adams, NYG	1.84, 11 saves

1943 American League

Pos	Player, Team	Stats
C	Jake Early, Was	.258-5-60
1B	Rudy York, Det	.271-34-118
2B	Joe Gordon, NYA	.249-17-69
3B	Bill Johnson, NYA	.280-5-94
SS	Luke Appling, ChA	.328-3-80
OF	Jeff Heath, Cle	.274-18-79
OF	Charlie Keller, NYA	.271-31-86
OF	Dick Wakefield, Det	.316-7-79
SP	Tiny Bonham, NYA	15-8, 2.27
SP	Spud Chandler, NYA	20-4, 1.64
SP	Al Smith, Cle	17-7, 2.55
SP	Dizzy Trout, Det	20-12, 2.48
RP	Gordon Maltzberger, ChA	2.46, 14 saves

1943 National League

Pos	Player, Team	Stats
C	Walker Cooper, StL	.318-9-81
1B	Phil Cavarretta, ChN	.291-8-73
2B	Billy Herman, Bro	.330-2-100
3B	Bob Elliott, Pit	.315-7-101
SS	Arky Vaughan, Bro	.305-5-66
OF	Augie Galan, Bro	.287-9-67
OF	Stan Musial, StL	.357-13-81
OF	Bill Nicholson, ChN	.309-29-128
SP	Mort Cooper, StL	21-8, 2.30
SP	Max Lanier, StL	15-7, 1.90
SP	Elmer Riddle, Cin	21-11, 2.66
SP	Rip Sewell, Pit	21-9, 2.54
RP	Ace Adams, NYG	2.82, 9 saves

1944 American League

Pos	Player, Team	Stats
C	Frankie Hayes, Phi	.248-13-78
1B	Nick Etten, NYA	.293-22-91
2B	Bobby Doerr, Bos	.325-15-81
3B	Ken Keltner, Cle	.295-13-91
SS	Vern Stephens, StL	.293-20-109
OF	Bob Johnson, Bos	.324-17-106
OF	Stan Spence, Was	.316-18-100
OF	Dick Wakefield, Det	.355-12-53
SP	Tex Hughson, Bos	18-5, 2.26
SP	Jack Kramer, StL	17-13, 2.49
SP	Hal Newhouser, Det	29-9, 2.22
SP	Dizzy Trout, Det	27-14, 2.12
RP	Joe Berry, Phi	1.94, 12 saves

1944 National League

Pos	Player, Team	Stats
C	Walker Cooper, StL	.317-13-72
1B	Phil Cavarretta, ChN	.321-5-82
2B	Pete Coscarart, Pit	.264-4-42
3B	Bob Elliott, Pit	.297-10-108
SS	Marty Marion, StL	.267-6-63
OF	Stan Musial, StL	.347-12-94
OF	Bill Nicholson, ChN	.287-33-122
OF	Dixie Walker, Bro	.357-13-91
SP	Mort Cooper, StL	22-7, 2.46
SP	Bill Voiselle, NYG	21-16, 3.02
SP	Bucky Walters, Cin	23-8, 2.40
SP	Ted Wilks, StL	17-4, 2.64
RP	Ace Adams, NYG	4.25, 13 saves

1945 American League

Pos	Player, Team	Stats
C	Frankie Hayes, Phi-Cle	.234-9-57
1B	Nick Etten, NYA	.285-18-111
2B	Snuffy Stirnweiss, NYA	.309-10-64
3B	Tony Cuccinello, ChA	.308-2-49
SS	Vern Stephens, StL	.289-24-89
OF	Roy Cullenbine, Cle-Det	.272-18-93
OF	Hank Greenberg, Det	.311-13-60
OF	Jeff Heath, Cle	.305-15-61
SP	Boo Ferriss, Bos	21-10, 2.96
SP	Dutch Leonard, Was	17-7, 2.13
SP	Hal Newhouser, Det	25-9, 1.81
SP	Roger Wolff, Was	20-10, 2.12
RP	Joe Berry, Phi	2.35, 5 saves

1945 National League

Pos	Player, Team	Stats
C	Bill Salkeld, Pit	.311-15-52
1B	Phil Cavarretta, ChN	.355-6-97
2B	Eddie Stanky, Bro	.258-1-39
3B	Whitey Kurowski, StL	.323-21-102
SS	Marty Marion, StL	.277-1-59
OF	Tommy Holmes, Bos	.352-28-117
OF	Goody Rosen, Bro	.325-12-75
OF	Dixie Walker, Bro	.300-8-124
SP	Red Barrett, Bos-StL	23-12, 3.00
SP	Hank Borowy, ChN	11-2, 2.13
SP	Claude Passeau, ChN	17-9, 2.46
SP	Hank Wyse, ChN	22-10, 2.68
RP	Andy Karl, Phi	2.99, 15 saves

1946 American League

Pos	Player, Team	Stats
C	Aaron Robinson, NYA	.297-16-64
1B	Hank Greenberg, Det	.277-44-127
2B	Bobby Doerr, Bos	.271-18-116
3B	George Kell, Phi-Det	.322-4-52
SS	Johnny Pesky, Bos	.335-2-55
OF	Roy Cullenbine, Det	.335-15-56
OF	Charlie Keller, NYA	.275-30-101
OF	Ted Williams, Bos	.342-38-123
SP	Spud Chandler, NYA	20-8, 2.10
SP	Bob Feller, Cle	26-15, 2.18
SP	Tex Hughson, Bos	20-11, 2.75
SP	Hal Newhouser, Det	26-9, 1.94
RP	Earl Caldwell, ChA	2.08, 8 saves

1946 National League

Pos	Player, Team	Stats
C	Andy Seminick, Phi	.264-12-52
1B	Stan Musial, StL	.365-16-103
2B	Eddie Stanky, Bro	.273-0-36
3B	Whitey Kurowski, StL	.301-14-89
SS	Pee Wee Reese, Bro	.284-5-60
OF	Phil Cavarretta, ChN	.294-8-78
OF	Enos Slaughter, StL	.300-18-130
OF	Dixie Walker, Bro	.319-9-116
SP	Joe Beggs, Cin	12-10, 2.32
SP	Kirby Higbe, Bro	17-8, 3.03
SP	Howie Pollet, StL	21-10, 2.10
SP	Johnny Sain, Bos	20-14, 2.21
RP	Hugh Casey, Bro	1.99, 5 saves

1947 American League

Pos	Player, Team	Stats
C	Aaron Robinson, NYA	.270-5-36
1B	George McQuinn, NYA	.304-13-80
2B	Joe Gordon, Cle	.272-29-93
3B	George Kell, Det	.320-5-93
SS	Lou Boudreau, Cle	.307-4-67
OF	Joe DiMaggio, NYA	.315-20-97
OF	Tommy Henrich, NYA	.287-16-98
OF	Ted Williams, Bos	.343-32-114
SP	Joe Dobson, Bos	18-8, 2.95
SP	Bob Feller, Cle	20-11, 2.68
SP	Phil Marchildon, Phi	19-9, 3.22
SP	Allie Reynolds, NYA	19-8, 3.20
RP	Joe Page, NYA	2.48, 17 saves

1947 National League

Pos	Player, Team	Stats
C	Walker Cooper, NYG	.305-35-122
1B	Johnny Mize, NYG	.302-51-138
2B	Bill Rigney, NYG	.267-17-59
3B	Bob Elliott, Bos	.317-22-113
SS	Pee Wee Reese, Bro	.284-12-73
OF	Ralph Kiner, Pit	.313-51-127
OF	Willard Marshall, NYG	.291-36-107
OF	Harry Walker, StL-Phi	.363-1-41
SP	Ewell Blackwell, Cin	22-8, 2.47
SP	Ralph Branca, Bro	21-12, 2.67
SP	Larry Jansen, NYG	21-5, 3.16
SP	Warren Spahn, Bos	21-10, 2.33
RP	Hugh Casey, Bro	3.99, 18 saves

1948 American League

Pos	Player, Team	Stats
C	Birdie Tebbetts, Bos	.280-5-68
1B	Ferris Fain, Phi	.281-7-88
2B	Bobby Doerr, Bos	.285-27-111
3B	Ken Keltner, Cle	.297-31-119
SS	Lou Boudreau, Cle	.355-18-106
OF	Joe DiMaggio, NYA	.320-39-155
OF	Tommy Henrich, NYA	.308-25-100
OF	Ted Williams, Bos	.369-25-127
SP	Gene Bearden, Cle	20-7, 2.43
SP	Bob Feller, Cle	19-15, 3.56
SP	Bob Lemon, Cle	20-14, 2.82
SP	Hal Newhouser, Det	21-12, 3.01
RP	Russ Christopher, Cle	2.90, 17 saves

1948 National League

Pos	Player, Team	Stats
C	Walker Cooper, NYG	.266-16-54
1B	Johnny Mize, NYG	.289-40-125
2B	Jackie Robinson, Bro	.296-12-85
3B	Sid Gordon, NYG	.299-30-107
SS	Pee Wee Reese, Bro	.274-9-75
OF	Ralph Kiner, Pit	.265-40-123
OF	Stan Musial, StL	.376-39-131
OF	Enos Slaughter, StL	.321-11-90
SP	Harry Brecheen, StL	20-7, 2.24
SP	Johnny Sain, Bos	24-15, 2.60
SP	Johnny Schmitz, ChN	18-13, 2.64
SP	Johnny Vander Meer, Cin	17-14, 3.41
RP	Ted Wilks, StL	2.62, 13 saves

1949 American League

Pos	Player, Team	Stats
C	Yogi Berra, NYA	.277-20-91
1B	Eddie Robinson, Was	.294-18-78
2B	Bobby Doerr, Bos	.309-18-109
3B	George Kell, Det	.343-3-59
SS	Vern Stephens, Bos	.290-39-159
OF	Tommy Henrich, NYA	.287-24-85
OF	Vic Wertz, Det	.304-20-133
OF	Ted Williams, Bos	.343-43-159
SP	Ellis Kinder, Bos	23-6, 3.36
SP	Bob Lemon, Cle	22-10, 2.99
SP	Mel Parnell, Bos	25-7, 2.77
SP	Virgil Trucks, Det	19-11, 2.81
RP	Joe Page, NYA	2.59, 27 saves

1949 National League

Pos	Player, Team	Stats
C	Roy Campanella, Bro	.287-22-82
1B	Gil Hodges, Bro	.285-23-115
2B	Jackie Robinson, Bro	.342-16-124
3B	Sid Gordon, NYG	.284-26-90
SS	Pee Wee Reese, Bro	.279-16-73
OF	Ralph Kiner, Pit	.310-54-127
OF	Stan Musial, StL	.338-36-123
OF	Enos Slaughter, StL	.336-13-96
SP	Russ Meyer, Phi	17-8, 3.08
SP	Don Newcombe, Bro	17-8, 3.17
SP	Howie Pollet, StL	20-9, 2.77
SP	Warren Spahn, Bos	21-14, 3.07
RP	Jim Konstanty, Phi	3.25, 7 saves

1950 American League

Pos	Player, Team	Stats
C	Yogi Berra, NYA	.322-28-124
1B	Walt Dropo, Bos	.322-34-144
2B	Bobby Doerr, Bos	.294-27-120
3B	Al Rosen, Cle	.287-37-116
SS	Phil Rizzuto, NYA	.324-7-66
OF	Joe DiMaggio, NYA	.301-32-122
OF	Larry Doby, Cle	.326-25-102
OF	Ted Williams, Bos	.317-28-97
SP	Art Houtteman, Det	19-12, 3.54
SP	Bob Lemon, Cle	23-11, 3.84
SP	Ed Lopat, NYA	18-8, 3.47
SP	Early Wynn, Cle	18-8, 3.20
RP	Tom Ferrick, StL-NYA	3.79, 11 saves

1950 National League

Pos	Player, Team	Stats
C	Roy Campanella, Bro	.281-31-89
1B	Earl Torgeson, Bos	.290-23-87
2B	Jackie Robinson, Bro	.328-14-81
3B	Bob Elliott, Bos	.305-24-107
SS	Al Dark, NYG	.279-16-67
OF	Ralph Kiner, Pit	.272-47-118
OF	Stan Musial, StL	.346-28-109
OF	Andy Pafko, ChN	.304-36-92
SP	Ewell Blackwell, Cin	17-15, 2.97
SP	Sal Maglie, NYG	18-4, 2.71
SP	Robin Roberts, Phi	20-11, 3.02
SP	Warren Spahn, Bos	21-17, 3.16
RP	Jim Konstanty, Phi	2.66, 22 saves

1951 American League

Pos	Player, Team	Stats
C	Yogi Berra, NYA	.294-27-88
1B	Ferris Fain, Phi	.344-6-57
2B	Nellie Fox, ChA	.313-4-55
3B	Eddie Yost, Was	.283-12-65
SS	Eddie Joost, Phi	.289-19-78
OF	Minnie Minoso, Cle-ChA	.326-10-76
OF	Ted Williams, Bos	.318-30-126
OF	Gus Zernial, ChA-Phi	.268-33-129
SP	Mike Garcia, Cle	20-13, 3.15
SP	Ned Garver, StL	20-12, 3.73
SP	Ed Lopat, NYA	21-9, 2.91
SP	Early Wynn, Cle	20-13, 3.02
RP	Ellis Kinder, Bos	2.55, 14 saves

1951 National League

Pos	Player, Team	Stats
C	Roy Campanella, Bro	.325-33-108
1B	Gil Hodges, Bro	.268-40-103
2B	Jackie Robinson, Bro	.338-19-88
3B	Puddin' Head Jones, Phi	.285-22-81
SS	Al Dark, NYG	.303-14-69
OF	Monte Irvin, NYG	.312-24-121
OF	Ralph Kiner, Pit	.309-42-109
OF	Stan Musial, StL	.355-32-108
SP	Larry Jansen, NYG	23-11, 3.04
SP	Sal Maglie, NYG	23-6, 2.93
SP	Preacher Roe, Bro	22-3, 3.04
SP	Warren Spahn, Bos	22-14, 2.98
RP	Ted Wilks, StL-Pit	2.86, 13 saves

1952 American League

Pos	Player, Team	Stats
C	Yogi Berra, NYA	.273-30-98
1B	Ferris Fain, Phi	.327-2-59
2B	Bobby Avila, Cle	.300-7-45
3B	Al Rosen, Cle	.302-28-105
SS	Eddie Joost, Phi	.244-20-75
OF	Larry Doby, Cle	.276-32-104
OF	Mickey Mantle, NYA	.311-23-87
OF	Vic Wertz, Det-StL	.277-23-70
SP	Mike Garcia, Cle	22-11, 2.37
SP	Bob Lemon, Cle	22-11, 2.50
SP	Allie Reynolds, NYA	20-8, 2.06
SP	Bobby Shantz, Phi	24-7, 2.48
RP	Satchel Paige, StL	3.07, 10 saves

1952 National League

Pos	Player, Team	Stats
C	Roy Campanella, Bro	.269-22-97
1B	Gil Hodges, Bro	.254-32-102
2B	Jackie Robinson, Bro	.308-19-75
3B	Bobby Thomson, NYG	.270-24-108
SS	Solly Hemus, StL	.268-15-52
OF	Ralph Kiner, Pit	.244-37-87
OF	Stan Musial, StL	.336-21-91
OF	Hank Sauer, ChN	.270-37-121
SP	Warren Hacker, ChN	15-9, 2.58
SP	Sal Maglie, NYG	18-8, 2.92
SP	Robin Roberts, Phi	28-7, 2.59
SP	Bob Rush, ChN	17-13, 2.70
RP	Joe Black, Bro	2.15, 15 saves

1953 American League

Pos	Player, Team	Stats
C	Yogi Berra, NYA	.296-27-108
1B	Mickey Vernon, Was	.337-15-115
2B	Billy Goodman, Bos	.313-2-41
3B	Al Rosen, Cle	.336-43-145
SS	Harvey Kuenn, Det	.308-2-48
OF	Mickey Mantle, NYA	.295-21-92
OF	Minnie Minoso, ChA	.313-15-104
OF	Gus Zernial, Phi	.284-42-108
SP	Ed Lopat, NYA	16-4, 2.42
SP	Mel Parnell, Bos	21-8, 3.06
SP	Bob Porterfield, Was	22-10, 3.35
SP	Virgil Trucks, StL-ChA	20-10, 2.93
RP	Ellis Kinder, Bos	1.85, 27 saves

1953 National League

Pos	Player, Team	Stats
C	Roy Campanella, Bro	.312-41-142
1B	Gil Hodges, Bro	.302-31-122
2B	Red Schoendienst, StL	.342-15-79
3B	Eddie Mathews, Mil	.302-47-135
SS	Al Dark, NYG	.300-23-88
OF	Carl Furillo, Bro	.344-21-92
OF	Stan Musial, StL	.337-30-113
OF	Duke Snider, Bro	.336-42-126
SP	Carl Erskine, Bro	20-6, 3.54
SP	Harvey Haddix, StL	20-9, 3.06
SP	Robin Roberts, Phi	23-16, 2.75
SP	Warren Spahn, Mil	23-7, 2.10
RP	Hoyt Wilhelm, NYG	3.04, 15 saves

1954 American League

Pos	Player, Team	Stats
C	Yogi Berra, NYA	.307-22-125
1B	Mickey Vernon, Was	.290-20-97
2B	Bobby Avila, Cle	.341-15-67
3B	Al Rosen, Cle	.300-24-102
SS	Chico Carrasquel, ChA	.255-12-62
OF	Mickey Mantle, NYA	.300-27-102
OF	Minnie Minoso, ChA	.320-19-116
OF	Ted Williams, Bos	.345-29-89
SP	Mike Garcia, Cle	19-8, 2.64
SP	Steve Gromek, Det	18-16, 2.74
SP	Bob Lemon, Cle	23-7, 2.72
SP	Early Wynn, Cle	23-11, 2.73
RP	Johnny Sain, NYA	3.16, 22 saves

1954 National League

Pos	Player, Team	Stats
C	Smoky Burgess, Phi	.368-4-46
1B	Ted Kluszewski, Cin	.326-49-141
2B	Red Schoendienst, StL	.315-5-79
3B	Eddie Mathews, Mil	.290-40-103
SS	Pee Wee Reese, Bro	.309-10-69
OF	Willie Mays, NYG	.345-41-110
OF	Stan Musial, StL	.330-35-126
OF	Duke Snider, Bro	.341-40-130
SP	Johnny Antonelli, NYG	21-7, 2.30
SP	Ruben Gomez, NYG	17-9, 2.88
SP	Robin Roberts, Phi	23-15, 2.97
SP	Warren Spahn, Mil	21-12, 3.14
RP	Marv Grissom, NYG	2.35, 19 saves

1955 American League

Pos	Player, Team	Stats
C	Yogi Berra, NYA	.272-27-108
1B	Vic Power, KCA	.319-19-76
2B	Nellie Fox, ChA	.311-6-59
3B	Ray Boone, Det	.284-20-116
SS	Harvey Kuenn, Det	.306-8-62
OF	Al Kaline, Det	.340-27-102
OF	Mickey Mantle, NYA	.306-37-99
OF	Ted Williams, Bos	.356-28-83
SP	Whitey Ford, NYA	18-7, 2.63
SP	Billy Pierce, ChA	15-10, 1.97
SP	Herb Score, Cle	16-10, 2.85
SP	Early Wynn, Cle	17-11, 2.82
RP	Ellis Kinder, Bos	2.84, 18 saves

1955 National League

Pos	Player, Team	Stats
C	Roy Campanella, Bro	.318-32-107
1B	Ted Kluszewski, Cin	.314-47-113
2B	Gene Baker, ChN	.268-11-52
3B	Eddie Mathews, Mil	.289-41-101
SS	Ernie Banks, ChN	.295-44-117
OF	Willie Mays, NYG	.319-51-127
OF	Wally Post, Cin	.309-40-109
OF	Duke Snider, Bro	.309-42-136
SP	Bob Friend, Pit	14-9, 2.83
SP	Don Newcombe, Bro	20-5, 3.20
SP	Robin Roberts, Phi	23-14, 3.28
SP	Warren Spahn, Mil	17-14, 3.26
RP	Clem Labine, Bro	3.24, 11 saves

1956 American League

Pos	Player, Team	Stats
C	Yogi Berra, NYA	.298-30-105
1B	Bill Skowron, NYA	.308-23-90
2B	Nellie Fox, ChA	.296-4-52
3B	Ray Boone, Det	.308-25-81
SS	Harvey Kuenn, Det	.332-12-88
OF	Mickey Mantle, NYA	.353-52-130
OF	Minnie Minoso, ChA	.316-21-88
OF	Ted Williams, Bos	.345-24-82
SP	Whitey Ford, NYA	19-6, 2.47
SP	Frank Lary, Det	21-13, 3.15
SP	Herb Score, Cle	20-9, 2.53
SP	Early Wynn, Cle	20-9, 2.72
RP	George Zuverink, Bal	4.16, 16 saves

1956 National League

Pos	Player, Team	Stats
C	Stan Lopata, Phi	.267-32-95
1B	Stan Musial, StL	.310-27-109
2B	Jim Gilliam, Bro	.300-6-43
3B	Eddie Mathews, Mil	.272-37-95
SS	Ernie Banks, ChN	.297-28-85
OF	Hank Aaron, Mil	.328-26-92
OF	Frank Robinson, Cin	.290-38-83
OF	Duke Snider, Bro	.292-43-101
SP	Johnny Antonelli, NYG	20-13, 2.86
SP	Lew Burdette, Mil	19-10, 2.70
SP	Don Newcombe, Bro	27-7, 3.06
SP	Warren Spahn, Mil	20-11, 2.78
RP	Clem Labine, Bro	3.35, 19 saves

1957 American League

Pos	Player, Team	Stats
C	Yogi Berra, NYA	.251-24-82
1B	Vic Wertz, Cle	.282-28-105
2B	Nellie Fox, ChA	.317-6-61
3B	Frank Malzone, Bos	.292-15-103
SS	Gil McDougald, NYA	.289-13-62
OF	Mickey Mantle, NYA	.365-34-94
OF	Roy Sievers, Was	.301-42-114
OF	Ted Williams, Bos	.388-38-87
SP	Jim Bunning, Det	20-8, 2.69
SP	Dick Donovan, ChA	16-6, 2.77
SP	Billy Pierce, ChA	20-12, 3.26
SP	Tom Sturdivant, NYA	16-6, 2.54
RP	Bob Grim, NYA	2.63, 19 saves

1957 National League

Pos	Player, Team	Stats
C	Ed Bailey, Cin	.261-20-48
1B	Stan Musial, StL	.351-29-102
2B	Red Schoendienst, NYG-Mil	.309-15-65
3B	Eddie Mathews, Mil	.292-32-94
SS	Ernie Banks, ChN	.285-43-102
OF	Hank Aaron, Mil	.322-44-132
OF	Willie Mays, NYG	.333-35-97
OF	Duke Snider, Bro	.274-40-92
SP	Bob Buhl, Mil	18-7, 2.74
SP	Don Drysdale, Bro	17-9, 2.69
SP	Jack Sanford, Phi	19-8, 3.08
SP	Warren Spahn, Mil	21-11, 2.69
RP	Turk Farrell, Phi	2.38, 10 saves

1958 American League

Pos	Player, Team	Stats
C	Sherm Lollar, ChA	.273-20-84
1B	Vic Power, KCA-Cle	.312-16-80
2B	Pete Runnels, Bos	.322-8-59
3B	Frank Malzone, Bos	.295-15-87
SS	Luis Aparicio, ChA	.266-2-40
OF	Jackie Jensen, Bos	.286-35-122
OF	Mickey Mantle, NYA	.304-42-97
OF	Ted Williams, Bos	.328-26-85
SP	Whitey Ford, NYA	14-7, 2.01
SP	Frank Lary, Det	16-15, 2.90
SP	Billy Pierce, ChA	17-11, 2.68
SP	Bob Turley, NYA	21-7, 2.97
RP	Dick Hyde, Was	1.75, 18 saves

1958 National League

Pos	Player, Team	Stats
C	Del Crandall, Mil	.272-18-63
1B	Orlando Cepeda, SF	.312-25-96
2B	Johnny Temple, Cin	.306-3-47
3B	Ken Boyer, StL	.307-23-90
SS	Ernie Banks, ChN	.313-47-129
OF	Hank Aaron, Mil	.326-30-95
OF	Richie Ashburn, Phi	.350-2-33
OF	Willie Mays, SF	.347-29-96
SP	Lew Burdette, Mil	20-10, 2.91
SP	Bob Friend, Pit	22-14, 3.68
SP	Robin Roberts, Phi	17-14, 3.24
SP	Warren Spahn, Mil	22-11, 3.07
RP	Roy Face, Pit	2.89, 20 saves

1959 American League

Pos	Player, Team	Stats
C	Sherm Lollar, ChA	.265-22-84
1B	Vic Power, Cle	.289-10-60
2B	Nellie Fox, ChA	.306-2-70
3B	Eddie Yost, Det	.278-21-61
SS	Luis Aparicio, ChA	.257-6-51
OF	Tito Francona, Cle	.363-20-79
OF	Al Kaline, Det	.327-27-94
OF	Mickey Mantle, NYA	.285-31-75
SP	Camilo Pascual, Was	17-10, 2.64
SP	Bob Shaw, ChA	18-6, 2.69
SP	Hoyt Wilhelm, Bal	15-11, 2.19
SP	Early Wynn, ChA	22-10, 3.17
RP	Gerry Staley, ChA	2.24, 14 saves

1959 National League

Pos	Player, Team	Stats
C	Del Crandall, Mil	.257-21-72
1B	Frank Robinson, Cin	.311-36-125
2B	Johnny Temple, Cin	.311-8-67
3B	Eddie Mathews, Mil	.306-46-114
SS	Ernie Banks, ChN	.304-45-143
OF	Hank Aaron, Mil	.355-39-123
OF	Willie Mays, SF	.313-34-104
OF	Vada Pinson, Cin	.316-20-84
SP	Johnny Antonelli, SF	19-10, 3.10
SP	Sam Jones, SF	21-15, 2.83
SP	Vern Law, Pit	18-9, 2.98
SP	Warren Spahn, Mil	21-15, 2.96
RP	Roy Face, Pit	2.70, 10 saves

1960 American League

Pos	Player, Team	Stats
C	John Romano, Cle	.272-16-52
1B	Roy Sievers, ChA	.295-28-93
2B	Pete Runnels, Bos	.320-2-35
3B	Brooks Robinson, Bal	.294-14-88
SS	Ron Hansen, Bal	.255-22-86
OF	Mickey Mantle, NYA	.275-40-94
OF	Roger Maris, NYA	.283-39-112
OF	Ted Williams, Bos	.316-29-72
SP	Art Ditmar, NYA	15-9, 3.06
SP	Chuck Estrada, Bal	18-11, 3.58
SP	Milt Pappas, Bal	15-11, 3.37
SP	Jim Perry, Cle	18-10, 3.62
RP	Mike Fornieles, Bos	2.64, 14 saves

1960 National League

Pos	Player, Team	Stats
C	Del Crandall, Mil	.294-19-77
1B	Frank Robinson, Cin	.297-31-83
2B	Bill Mazeroski, Pit	.273-11-64
3B	Eddie Mathews, Mil	.277-39-124
SS	Ernie Banks, ChN	.271-41-117
OF	Hank Aaron, Mil	.292-40-126
OF	Orlando Cepeda, SF	.297-24-96
OF	Willie Mays, SF	.319-29-103
SP	Ernie Broglio, StL	21-9, 2.74
SP	Bob Friend, Pit	18-12, 3.00
SP	Vern Law, Pit	20-9, 3.08
SP	Warren Spahn, Mil	21-10, 3.50
RP	Lindy McDaniel, StL	2.09, 26 saves

1961 American League

Pos	Player, Team	Stats
C	Elston Howard, NYA	.348-21-77
1B	Norm Cash, Det	.361-41-132
2B	Jerry Lumpe, KCA	.293-3-54
3B	Al Smith, ChA	.278-28-93
SS	Woodie Held, Cle	.267-23-78
OF	Rocky Colavito, Det	.290-45-140
OF	Mickey Mantle, NYA	.317-54-128
OF	Roger Maris, NYA	.269-61-142
SP	Jim Bunning, Det	17-11, 3.19
SP	Whitey Ford, NYA	25-4, 3.21
SP	Frank Lary, Det	23-9, 3.24
SP	Juan Pizarro, ChA	14-7, 3.05
RP	Luis Arroyo, NYA	2.19, 29 saves

1961 National League

Pos	Player, Team	Stats
C	John Roseboro, LA	.251-18-59
1B	Orlando Cepeda, SF	.311-46-142
2B	Bill Mazeroski, Pit	.265-13-59
3B	Ken Boyer, StL	.329-24-95
SS	Ernie Banks, ChN	.278-29-80
OF	Hank Aaron, Mil	.327-34-120
OF	Willie Mays, SF	.308-40-123
OF	Frank Robinson, Cin	.323-37-124
SP	Joey Jay, Cin	21-10, 3.53
SP	Sandy Koufax, LA	18-13, 3.52
SP	Jim O'Toole, Cin	19-9, 3.10
SP	Warren Spahn, Mil	21-13, 3.02
RP	Stu Miller, SF	2.66, 17 saves

1962 American League

Pos	Player, Team	Stats
C	John Romano, Cle	.261-25-81
1B	Norm Siebern, KCA	.308-25-117
2B	Billy Moran, LAA	.282-17-74
3B	Rich Rollins, Min	.298-16-96
SS	Tom Tresh, NYA	.286-20-93
OF	Rocky Colavito, Det	.273-37-112
OF	Harmon Killebrew, Min	.243-48-126
OF	Mickey Mantle, NYA	.321-30-89
SP	Hank Aguirre, Det	16-8, 2.21
SP	Whitey Ford, NYA	17-8, 2.90
SP	Camilo Pascual, Min	20-11, 3.32
SP	Ralph Terry, NYA	23-12, 3.19
RP	Dick Radatz, Bos	2.24, 24 saves

1962 National League

Pos	Player, Team	Stats
C	Smoky Burgess, Pit	.328-13-61
1B	Orlando Cepeda, SF	.306-35-114
2B	Bill Mazeroski, Pit	.271-14-81
3B	Eddie Mathews, Mil	.265-29-90
SS	Maury Wills, LA	.299-6-48
OF	Hank Aaron, Mil	.323-45-128
OF	Willie Mays, SF	.304-49-141
OF	Frank Robinson, Cin	.342-39-136
SP	Don Drysdale, LA	25-9, 2.83
SP	Sandy Koufax, LA	14-7, 2.54
SP	Bob Purkey, Cin	23-5, 2.81
SP	Jack Sanford, SF	24-7, 3.43
RP	Roy Face, Pit	1.88, 28 saves

1963 American League

Pos	Player, Team	Stats
C	Elston Howard, NYA	.287-28-85
1B	Dick Stuart, Bos	.261-42-118
2B	Jerry Lumpe, KCA	.271-5-59
3B	Pete Ward, ChA	.295-22-84
SS	Jim Fregosi, LAA	.287-9-50
OF	Bob Allison, Min	.271-35-91
OF	Al Kaline, Det	.312-27-101
OF	Harmon Killebrew, Min	.258-45-96
SP	Jim Bouton, NYA	21-7, 2.53
SP	Whitey Ford, NYA	24-7, 2.74
SP	Camilo Pascual, Min	21-9, 2.46
SP	Gary Peters, ChA	19-8, 2.33
RP	Dick Radatz, Bos	1.97, 25 saves

1963 National League

Pos	Player, Team	Stats
C	Ed Bailey, SF	.263-21-68
1B	Orlando Cepeda, SF	.316-34-97
2B	Tony Taylor, Phi	.281-5-49
3B	Eddie Mathews, Mil	.263-23-84
SS	Dick Groat, StL	.319-6-73
OF	Hank Aaron, Mil	.319-44-130
OF	Willie Mays, SF	.314-38-103
OF	Willie McCovey, SF	.280-44-102
SP	Dick Ellsworth, ChN	22-10, 2.11
SP	Sandy Koufax, LA	25-5, 1.88
SP	Jim Maloney, Cin	23-7, 2.77
SP	Juan Marichal, SF	25-8, 2.41
RP	Ron Perranoski, LA	1.67, 21 saves

1964 American League

Pos	Player, Team	Stats
C	Elston Howard, NYA	.313-15-84
1B	Bob Allison, Min	.287-32-86
2B	Bobby Richardson, NYA	.267-4-50
3B	Brooks Robinson, Bal	.317-28-118
SS	Jim Fregosi, LAA	.277-18-72
OF	Mickey Mantle, NYA	.303-35-111
OF	Tony Oliva, Min	.323-32-94
OF	Boog Powell, Bal	.290-39-99
SP	Dean Chance, LAA	20-9, 1.65
SP	Whitey Ford, NYA	17-6, 2.13
SP	Gary Peters, ChA	20-8, 2.50
SP	Juan Pizarro, ChA	19-9, 2.56
RP	Dick Radatz, Bos	2.29, 29 saves

Awards: STATS Retroactive All-Stars

1964 National League

Pos	Player, Team	Stats
C	Joe Torre, Mil	.321-20-109
1B	Orlando Cepeda, SF	.304-31-97
2B	Bill Mazeroski, Pit	.268-10-64
3B	Ron Santo, ChN	.313-30-114
SS	Denis Menke, Mil	.283-20-65
OF	Hank Aaron, Mil	.328-24-95
OF	Willie Mays, SF	.296-47-111
OF	Frank Robinson, Cin	.306-29-96
SP	Jim Bunning, Phi	19-8, 2.63
SP	Larry Jackson, ChN	24-11, 3.14
SP	Sandy Koufax, LA	19-5, 1.74
SP	Juan Marichal, SF	21-8, 2.48
RP	Al McBean, Pit	1.91, 22 saves

1965 American League

Pos	Player, Team	Stats
C	Earl Battey, Min	.297-6-60
1B	Norm Cash, Det	.266-30-82
2B	Felix Mantilla, Bos	.275-18-92
3B	Brooks Robinson, Bal	.297-18-80
SS	Zoilo Versalles, Min	.273-19-77
OF	Rocky Colavito, Cle	.287-26-108
OF	Tony Oliva, Min	.321-16-98
OF	Carl Yastrzemski, Bos	.312-20-72
SP	Mudcat Grant, Min	21-7, 3.30
SP	Sam McDowell, Cle	17-11, 2.18
SP	Sonny Siebert, Cle	16-8, 2.43
SP	Mel Stottlemyre, NYA	20-9, 2.63
RP	Stu Miller, Bal	1.89, 24 saves

1965 National League

Pos	Player, Team	Stats
C	Joe Torre, Mil	.291-27-80
1B	Willie McCovey, SF	.276-39-92
2B	Pete Rose, Cin	.312-11-81
3B	Deron Johnson, Cin	.287-32-130
SS	Maury Wills, LA	.286-0-33
OF	Hank Aaron, Mil	.318-32-89
OF	Willie Mays, SF	.317-52-112
OF	Billy Williams, ChN	.315-34-108
SP	Don Drysdale, LA	23-12, 2.77
SP	Sandy Koufax, LA	26-8, 2.04
SP	Jim Maloney, Cin	20-9, 2.54
SP	Juan Marichal, SF	22-13, 2.13
RP	Ted Abernathy, ChN	2.57, 31 saves

1966 American League

Pos	Player, Team	Stats
C	Bill Freehan, Det	.234-12-46
1B	Boog Powell, Bal	.287-34-109
2B	Bobby Knoop, Cal	.232-17-72
3B	Harmon Killebrew, Min	.281-39-110
SS	Dick McAuliffe, Det	.274-23-56
OF	Al Kaline, Det	.288-29-88
OF	Tony Oliva, Min	.307-25-87
OF	Frank Robinson, Bal	.316-49-122
SP	Jim Kaat, Min	25-13, 2.75
SP	Gary Peters, ChA	12-10, 1.98
SP	Sonny Siebert, Cle	16-8, 2.80
SP	Earl Wilson, Bos-Det	18-11, 3.07
RP	Jack Aker, KCA	1.99, 32 saves

1966 National League

Pos	Player, Team	Stats
C	Joe Torre, Atl	.315-36-101
1B	Willie McCovey, SF	.295-36-96
2B	Pete Rose, Cin	.313-16-70
3B	Dick Allen, Phi	.317-40-110
SS	Gene Alley, Pit	.299-7-43
OF	Hank Aaron, Atl	.279-44-127
OF	Roberto Clemente, Pit	.317-29-119
OF	Willie Mays, SF	.288-37-103
SP	Jim Bunning, Phi	19-14, 2.41
SP	Bob Gibson, StL	21-12, 2.44
SP	Sandy Koufax, LA	27-9, 1.73
SP	Juan Marichal, SF	25-6, 2.23
RP	Phil Regan, LA	1.62, 21 saves

1967 American League

Pos	Player, Team	Stats
C	Bill Freehan, Det	.282-20-74
1B	Harmon Killebrew, Min	.269-44-113
2B	Dick McAuliffe, Det	.239-22-65
3B	Brooks Robinson, Bal	.269-22-77
SS	Jim Fregosi, Cal	.290-9-56
OF	Al Kaline, Det	.308-25-78
OF	Frank Robinson, Bal	.311-30-94
OF	Carl Yastrzemski, Bos	.326-44-121
SP	Dean Chance, Min	20-14, 2.73
SP	Joe Horlen, ChA	19-7, 2.06
SP	Jim Lonborg, Bos	22-9, 3.16
SP	Gary Peters, ChA	16-11, 2.28
RP	Minnie Rojas, Cal	2.52, 27 saves

1967 National League

Pos	Player, Team	Stats
C	Tim McCarver, StL	.295-14-69
1B	Orlando Cepeda, StL	.325-25-111
2B	Joe Morgan, Hou	.275-6-42
3B	Ron Santo, ChN	.300-31-98
SS	Gene Alley, Pit	.287-6-55
OF	Hank Aaron, Atl	.307-39-109
OF	Roberto Clemente, Pit	.357-23-110
OF	Jimmy Wynn, Hou	.249-37-107
SP	Jim Bunning, Phi	17-15, 2.29
SP	Fergie Jenkins, ChN	20-13, 2.80
SP	Mike McCormick, SF	22-10, 2.85
SP	Gary Nolan, Cin	14-8, 2.58
RP	Ted Abernathy, Cin	1.27, 28 saves

1968 American League

Pos	Player, Team	Stats
C	Bill Freehan, Det	.263-25-84
1B	Norm Cash, Det	.263-25-63
2B	Dick McAuliffe, Det	.249-16-56
3B	Brooks Robinson, Bal	.253-17-75
SS	Bert Campaneris, Oak	.276-4-38
OF	Ken Harrelson, Bos	.275-35-109
OF	Frank Howard, Was	.274-44-106
OF	Carl Yastrzemski, Bos	.301-23-74
SP	Sam McDowell, Cle	15-14, 1.81
SP	Denny McLain, Det	31-6, 1.96
SP	Dave McNally, Bal	22-10, 1.95
SP	Luis Tiant, Cle	21-9, 1.60
RP	Wilbur Wood, ChA	1.87, 16 saves

1968 National League

Pos	Player, Team	Stats
C	Johnny Bench, Cin	.275-15-82
1B	Willie McCovey, SF	.293-36-105
2B	Glenn Beckert, ChN	.294-4-37
3B	Ron Santo, ChN	.246-26-98
SS	Don Kessinger, ChN	.240-1-32
OF	Hank Aaron, Atl	.287-29-86
OF	Dick Allen, Phi	.263-33-90
OF	Pete Rose, Cin	.335-10-49
SP	Steve Blass, Pit	18-6, 2.12
SP	Bob Gibson, StL	22-9, 1.12
SP	Jerry Koosman, NYN	19-12, 2.08
SP	Juan Marichal, SF	26-9, 2.43
RP	Phil Regan, LA -ChN	2.27, 25 saves

1969 American League

Pos	Player, Team	Stats
C	Bill Freehan, Det	.262-16-49
1B	Boog Powell, Bal	.304-37-121
2B	Rod Carew, Min	.332-8-56
3B	Harmon Killebrew, Min	.276-49-140
SS	Rico Petrocelli, Bos	.297-40-97
OF	Frank Howard, Was	.296-48-111
OF	Reggie Jackson, Oak	.275-47-118
OF	Frank Robinson, Bal	.308-32-100
SP	Mike Cuellar, Bal	23-11, 2.38
SP	Sam McDowell, Cle	18-14, 2.94
SP	Denny McLain, Det	24-9, 2.80
SP	Andy Messersmith, Cal	16-11, 2.52
RP	Ron Perranoski, Min	2.11, 31 saves

1969 National League

Pos	Player, Team	Stats
C	Johnny Bench, Cin	.293-26-90
1B	Willie McCovey, SF	.320-45-126
2B	Joe Morgan, Hou	.236-15-43
3B	Ron Santo, ChN	.289-29-123
SS	Denis Menke, Hou	.269-10-90
OF	Hank Aaron, Atl	.300-44-97
OF	Pete Rose, Cin	.348-16-82
OF	Jimmy Wynn, Hou	.269-33-87
SP	Bob Gibson, StL	20-13, 2.18
SP	Juan Marichal, SF	21-11, 2.10
SP	Phil Niekro, Atl	23-13, 2.56
SP	Tom Seaver, NYN	25-7, 2.21
RP	Wayne Granger, Cin	2.80, 27 saves

1970 American League

Pos	Player, Team	Stats
C	Ray Fosse, Cle	.307-18-61
1B	Carl Yastrzemski, Bos	.329-40-102
2B	Dave Johnson, Bal	.281-10-53
3B	Harmon Killebrew, Min	.271-41-113
SS	Jim Fregosi, Cal	.278-22-82
OF	Frank Howard, Was	.283-44-126
OF	Tony Oliva, Min	.325-23-107
OF	Roy White, NYA	.296-22-94
SP	Sam McDowell, Cle	20-12, 2.92
SP	Jim Palmer, Bal	20-10, 2.71
SP	Jim Perry, Min	24-12, 3.04
SP	Clyde Wright, Cal	22-12, 2.83
RP	Lindy McDaniel, NYA	2.01, 29 saves

1970 National League

Pos	Player, Team	Stats
C	Johnny Bench, Cin	.293-45-148
1B	Willie McCovey, SF	.289-39-126
2B	Joe Morgan, Hou	.268-8-52
3B	Tony Perez, Cin	.317-40-129
SS	Denis Menke, Hou	.304-13-92
OF	Rico Carty, Atl	.366-25-101
OF	Jim Hickman, ChN	.315-32-115
OF	Billy Williams, ChN	.322-42-129
SP	Bob Gibson, StL	23-7, 3.12
SP	Fergie Jenkins, ChN	22-16, 3.39
SP	Gaylord Perry, SF	23-13, 3.20
SP	Tom Seaver, NYN	18-12, 2.82
RP	Wayne Granger, Cin	2.66, 35 saves

1971 American League

Pos	Player, Team	Stats
C	Bill Freehan, Det	.277-21-71
1B	Norm Cash, Det	.283-32-91
2B	Dave Johnson, Bal	.282-18-72
3B	Graig Nettles, Cle	.261-28-86
SS	Leo Cardenas, Min	.264-18-75
OF	Bobby Murcer, NYA	.331-25-94
OF	Tony Oliva, Min	.337-22-81
OF	Frank Robinson, Bal	.281-28-99
SP	Vida Blue, Oak	24-8, 1.82
SP	Mickey Lolich, Det	25-14, 2.92
SP	Jim Palmer, Bal	20-9, 2.68
SP	Wilbur Wood, ChA	22-13, 1.91
RP	Ken Sanders, Mil	1.91, 31 saves

1971 National League

Pos	Player, Team	Stats
C	Earl Williams, Atl	.260-33-87
1B	Hank Aaron, Atl	.327-47-118
2B	Joe Morgan, Hou	.256-13-56
3B	Joe Torre, StL	.363-24-137
SS	Maury Wills, LA	.281-3-44
OF	Bobby Bonds, SF	.288-33-102
OF	Lou Brock, StL	.313-7-61
OF	Willie Stargell, Pit	.295-48-125
SP	Al Downing, LA	20-9, 2.68
SP	Fergie Jenkins, ChN	24-13, 2.77
SP	Tom Seaver, NYN	20-10, 1.76
SP	Don Wilson, Hou	16-10, 2.45
RP	Dave Giusti, Pit	2.93, 30 saves

1972 American League

Pos	Player, Team	Stats
C	Carlton Fisk, Bos	.293-22-61
1B	Dick Allen, ChA	.308-37-113
2B	Rod Carew, Min	.318-0-51
3B	Graig Nettles, Cle	.253-17-70
SS	Bert Campaneris, Oak	.240-8-32
OF	Carlos May, ChA	.308-12-68
OF	Bobby Murcer, NYA	.292-33-96
OF	Joe Rudi, Oak	.305-19-75
SP	Catfish Hunter, Oak	21-7, 2.04
SP	Jim Palmer, Bal	21-10, 2.07
SP	Gaylord Perry, Cle	24-16, 1.92
SP	Nolan Ryan, Cal	19-16, 2.28
RP	Sparky Lyle, NYA	1.92, 35 saves

1972 National League

Pos	Player, Team	Stats
C	Johnny Bench, Cin	.270-40-125
1B	Willie Stargell, Pit	.293-33-112
2B	Joe Morgan, Cin	.292-16-73
3B	Ron Santo, ChN	.302-17-74
SS	Chris Speier, SF	.269-15-71
OF	Cesar Cedeno, Hou	.320-22-82
OF	Billy Williams, ChN	.333-37-122
OF	Jimmy Wynn, Hou	.273-24-90
SP	Steve Carlton, Phi	27-10, 1.97
SP	Bob Gibson, StL	19-11, 2.46
SP	Tom Seaver, NYN	21-12, 2.92
SP	Don Sutton, LA	19-9, 2.08
RP	Clay Carroll, Cin	2.25, 37 saves

1973 American League

Pos	Player, Team	Stats
C	Thurman Munson, NYA	.301-20-74
1B	John Mayberry, KC	.278-26-100
2B	Rod Carew, Min	.350-6-62
3B	Sal Bando, Oak	.287-29-98
SS	Bert Campaneris, Oak	.250-4-46
OF	Reggie Jackson, Oak	.293-32-117
OF	Amos Otis, KC	.300-26-93
OF	Reggie Smith, Bos	.303-21-69
DH	Frank Robinson, Cal	.266-30-97
SP	Bert Blyleven, Min	20-17, 2.52
SP	Ken Holtzman, Oak	21-13, 2.97
SP	Jim Palmer, Bal	22-9, 2.40
SP	Nolan Ryan, Cal	21-16, 2.87
RP	John Hiller, Det	1.44, 38 saves

1973 National League

Pos	Player, Team	Stats
C	Joe Ferguson, LA	.263-25-88
1B	Tony Perez, Cin	.314-27-101
2B	Joe Morgan, Cin	.290-26-82
3B	Darrell Evans, Atl	.281-41-104
SS	Dave Concepcion, Cin	.287-8-46
OF	Hank Aaron, Atl	.301-40-96
OF	Pete Rose, Cin	.338-5-64
OF	Willie Stargell, Pit	.299-44-119
SP	Jack Billingham, Cin	19-10, 3.04
SP	Ron Bryant, SF	24-12, 3.53
SP	Tom Seaver, NYN	19-10, 2.08
SP	Don Sutton, LA	18-10, 2.42
RP	Mike Marshall, Mon	2.66, 31 saves

1974 American League

Pos	Player, Team	Stats
C	Thurman Munson, NYA	.261-13-60
1B	Dick Allen, ChA	.301-32-88
2B	Rod Carew, Min	.364-3-55
3B	Sal Bando, Oak	.243-22-103
SS	Toby Harrah, Tex	.260-21-74
OF	Jeff Burroughs, Tex	.301-25-118
OF	Reggie Jackson, Oak	.289-29-93
OF	Joe Rudi, Oak	.293-22-99
DH	Hal McRae, KC	.310-15-88
SP	Catfish Hunter, Oak	25-12, 2.49
SP	Fergie Jenkins, Tex	25-12, 2.82
SP	Gaylord Perry, Cle	21-13, 2.51
SP	Nolan Ryan, Cal	22-16, 2.89
RP	Tom Murphy, Mil	1.90, 20 saves

1974 National League

Pos	Player, Team	Stats
C	Johnny Bench, Cin	.280-33-129
1B	Steve Garvey, LA	.312-21-111
2B	Joe Morgan, Cin	.293-22-67
3B	Mike Schmidt, Phi	.282-36-116
SS	Dave Concepcion, Cin	.281-14-82
OF	Reggie Smith, StL	.309-23-100
OF	Willie Stargell, Pit	.301-25-96
OF	Jimmy Wynn, LA	.271-32-108
SP	Buzz Capra, Atl	16-8, 2.28
SP	Jon Matlack, NYN	13-15, 2.41
SP	Andy Messersmith, LA	20-6, 2.59
SP	Phil Niekro, Atl	20-13, 2.38
RP	Mike Marshall, LA	2.42, 21 saves

1975 American League

Pos	Player, Team	Stats
C	Gene Tenace, Oak	.255-29-87
1B	John Mayberry, KC	.291-34-106
2B	Rod Carew, Min	.359-14-80
3B	George Brett, KC	.308-11-89
SS	Toby Harrah, Tex	.293-20-93
OF	Bobby Bonds, NYA	.270-32-85
OF	Reggie Jackson, Oak	.253-36-104
OF	Fred Lynn, Bos	.331-21-105
DH	Willie Horton, Det	.275-25-92
SP	Vida Blue, Oak	22-11, 3.01
SP	Catfish Hunter, NYA	23-14, 2.58
SP	Jim Palmer, Bal	23-11, 2.09
SP	Frank Tanana, Cal	16-9, 2.62
RP	Goose Gossage, ChA	1.84, 26 saves

1975 National League

Pos	Player, Team	Stats
C	Johnny Bench, Cin	.283-28-110
1B	Willie Stargell, Pit	.295-22-90
2B	Joe Morgan, Cin	.327-17-94
3B	Mike Schmidt, Phi	.249-38-95
SS	Chris Speier, SF	.271-10-69
OF	George Foster, Cin	.300-23-78
OF	Greg Luzinski, Phi	.300-34-120
OF	Dave Parker, Pit	.308-25-101
SP	Randy Jones, SD	20-12, 2.24
SP	Andy Messersmith, LA	19-14, 2.29
SP	Jerry Reuss, Pit	18-11, 2.54
SP	Tom Seaver, NYN	22-9, 2.38
RP	Al Hrabosky, StL	1.66, 22 saves

1976 American League

Pos	Player, Team	Stats
C	Thurman Munson, NYA	.302-17-105
1B	Rod Carew, Min	.331-9-90
2B	Bobby Grich, Bal	.266-13-54
3B	George Brett, KC	.333-7-67
SS	Toby Harrah, Tex	.260-15-67
OF	Reggie Jackson, Bal	.277-27-91
OF	Fred Lynn, Bos	.314-10-65
OF	Rusty Staub, Det	.299-15-96
DH	Hal McRae, KC	.332-8-73
SP	Vida Blue, Oak	18-13, 2.35
SP	Mark Fidrych, Det	19-9, 2.34
SP	Jim Palmer, Bal	22-13, 2.51
SP	Frank Tanana, Cal	19-10, 2.43
RP	Rollie Fingers, Oak	2.47, 20 saves

1976 National League

Pos	Player, Team	Stats
C	Ted Simmons, StL	.291-5-75
1B	Bob Watson, Hou	.313-16-102
2B	Joe Morgan, Cin	.320-27-111
3B	Mike Schmidt, Phi	.262-38-107
SS	Dave Concepcion, Cin	.281-9-69
OF	George Foster, Cin	.306-29-121
OF	Ken Griffey Sr., Cin	.336-6-74
OF	Rick Monday, ChN	.272-32-77
SP	Steve Carlton, Phi	20-7, 3.13
SP	Randy Jones, SD	22-14, 2.74
SP	Jerry Koosman, NYN	21-10, 2.69
SP	J.R. Richard, Hou	20-15, 2.75
RP	Rawly Eastwick, Cin	2.09, 26 saves

1977 American League

Pos	Player, Team	Stats
C	Carlton Fisk, Bos	.315-26-102
1B	Rod Carew, Min	.388-14-100
2B	Don Money, Mil	.279-25-83
3B	George Brett, KC	.312-22-88
SS	Rick Burleson, Bos	.293-3-52
OF	Larry Hisle, Min	.302-28-119
OF	Reggie Jackson, NYA	.286-32-110
OF	Ken Singleton, Bal	.328-24-99
DH	Jim Rice, Bos	.320-39-114
SP	Dennis Leonard, KC	20-12, 3.04
SP	Jim Palmer, Bal	20-11, 2.91
SP	Nolan Ryan, Cal	19-16, 2.77
SP	Frank Tanana, Cal	15-9, 2.54
RP	Sparky Lyle, NYA	2.17, 26 saves

1977 National League

Pos	Player, Team	Stats
C	Ted Simmons, StL	.318-21-95
1B	Steve Garvey, LA	.297-33-115
2B	Joe Morgan, Cin	.288-22-78
3B	Mike Schmidt, Phi	.274-38-101
SS	Garry Templeton, StL	.322-8-79
OF	George Foster, Cin	.320-52-149
OF	Greg Luzinski, Phi	.309-39-130
OF	Reggie Smith, LA	.307-32-87
SP	John Candelaria, Pit	20-5, 2.34
SP	Steve Carlton, Phi	23-10, 2.64
SP	Rick Reuschel, ChN	20-10, 2.79
SP	Tom Seaver, NYN-Cin	21-6, 2.58
RP	Bruce Sutter, ChN	1.34, 31 saves

1978 American League

Pos	Player, Team	Stats
C	Carlton Fisk, Bos	.284-20-88
1B	Andre Thornton, Cle	.262-33-105
2B	Willie Randolph, NYA	.279-3-42
3B	Doug DeCinces, Bal	.286-28-80
SS	Roy Smalley, Min	.273-19-77
OF	Larry Hisle, Mil	.290-34-115
OF	Amos Otis, KC	.298-22-96
OF	Jim Rice, Bos	.315-46-139
DH	Don Baylor, Cal	.255-34-99
SP	Mike Caldwell, Mil	22-9, 2.36
SP	Dennis Eckersley, Bos	20-8, 2.99
SP	Ron Guidry, NYA	25-3, 1.74
SP	Jim Palmer, Bal	21-12, 2.46
RP	Goose Gossage, NYA	2.01, 27 saves

1978 National League

Pos	Player, Team	Stats
C	Ted Simmons, StL	.287-22-80
1B	Willie Stargell, Pit	.295-28-97
2B	Davey Lopes, LA	.278-17-58
3B	Ron Cey, LA	.270-23-84
SS	Dave Concepcion, Cin	.301-6-67
OF	George Foster, Cin	.281-40-120
OF	Dave Parker, Pit	.334-30-117
OF	Reggie Smith, LA	.295-29-93
SP	Vida Blue, SF	18-10, 2.79
SP	Burt Hooton, LA	19-10, 2.71
SP	Gaylord Perry, SD	21-6, 2.73
SP	J.R. Richard, Hou	18-11, 3.11
RP	Rollie Fingers, SD	2.52, 37 saves

1979 American League

Pos	Player, Team	Stats
C	Darrell Porter, KC	.291-20-112
1B	Cecil Cooper, Mil	.308-24-106
2B	Bobby Grich, Cal	.294-30-101
3B	George Brett, KC	.329-23-107
SS	Roy Smalley, Min	.271-24-95
OF	Don Baylor, Cal	.296-36-139
OF	Fred Lynn, Bos	.333-39-122
OF	Jim Rice, Bos	.325-39-130
DH	Willie Horton, Sea	.279-29-106
SP	Dennis Eckersley, Bos	17-10, 2.99
SP	Mike Flanagan, Bal	23-9, 3.08
SP	Ron Guidry, NYA	18-8, 2.78
SP	Tommy John, NYA	21-9, 2.96
RP	Jim Kern, Tex	1.57, 29 saves

1979 National League

Pos	Player, Team	Stats
C	Ted Simmons, StL	.283-26-87
1B	Keith Hernandez, StL	.344-11-105
2B	Davey Lopes, LA	.265-28-73
3B	Mike Schmidt, Phi	.253-45-114
SS	Garry Templeton, StL	.314-9-62
OF	Dave Kingman, ChN	.288-48-115
OF	Dave Parker, Pit	.310-25-94
OF	Dave Winfield, SD	.308-34-118
SP	Steve Carlton, Phi	18-11, 3.62
SP	Joe Niekro, Hou	21-11, 3.00
SP	Phil Niekro, Atl	21-20, 3.39
SP	J.R. Richard, Hou	18-13, 2.71
RP	Bruce Sutter, ChN	2.22, 37 saves

1980 American League

Pos	Player, Team	Stats
C	Lance Parrish, Det	.286-24-82
1B	Cecil Cooper, Mil	.352-25-122
2B	Willie Randolph, NYA	.294-7-46
3B	George Brett, KC	.390-24-118
SS	Robin Yount, Mil	.293-23-87
OF	Rickey Henderson, Oak	.303-9-53
OF	Reggie Jackson, NYA	.300-41-111
OF	Ben Oglivie, Mil	.304-41-118
DH	Hal McRae, KC	.297-14-83
SP	Larry Gura, KC	18-10, 2.95
SP	Tommy John, NYA	22-9, 3.43
SP	Mike Norris, Oak	22-9, 2.53
SP	Steve Stone, Bal	25-7, 3.23
RP	Goose Gossage, NYA	2.27, 33 saves

1980 National League

Pos	Player, Team	Stats
C	Ted Simmons, StL	.303-21-98
1B	Keith Hernandez, StL	.321-16-99
2B	Manny Trillo, Phi	.292-7-43
3B	Mike Schmidt, Phi	.286-48-121
SS	Garry Templeton, StL	.319-4-43
OF	Andre Dawson, Mon	.308-17-87
OF	Mike Easler, Pit	.338-21-74
OF	Dale Murphy, Atl	.281-33-89
SP	Jim Bibby, Pit	19-6, 3.32
SP	Steve Carlton, Phi	24-9, 2.34
SP	Jerry Reuss, LA	18-6, 2.51
SP	Steve Rogers, Mon	16-11, 2.98
RP	Tug McGraw, Phi	1.46, 20 saves

1981 American League

Pos	Player, Team	Stats
C	Lance Parrish, Det	.244-10-46
1B	Eddie Murray, Bal	.294-22-78
2B	Bobby Grich, Cal	.304-22-61
3B	Carney Lansford, Bos	.336-4-52
SS	Robin Yount, Mil	.273-10-49
OF	Dwight Evans, Bos	.296-22-71
OF	Rickey Henderson, Oak	.319-6-35
OF	Tom Paciorek, Sea	.326-14-66
DH	Greg Luzinski, ChA	.265-21-62
SP	Britt Burns, ChA	10-6, 2.64
SP	Ron Guidry, NYA	11-5, 2.76
SP	Steve McCatty, Oak	14-7, 2.33
SP	Jack Morris, Det	14-7, 3.05
RP	Rollie Fingers, Mil	1.04, 28 saves

1981 National League

Pos	Player, Team	Stats
C	Gary Carter, Mon	.251-16-68
1B	Keith Hernandez, StL	.306-8-48
2B	Ron Oester, Cin	.271-5-42
3B	Mike Schmidt, Phi	.316-31-91
SS	Dave Concepcion, Cin	.306-5-67
OF	Andre Dawson, Mon	.302-24-64
OF	George Foster, Cin	.295-22-90
OF	Tim Raines, Mon	.304-5-37
SP	Steve Carlton, Phi	13-4, 2.42
SP	Nolan Ryan, Hou	11-5, 1.69
SP	Tom Seaver, Cin	14-2, 2.54
SP	Fernando Valenzuela, LA	13-7, 2.48
RP	Rick Camp, Atl	1.78, 17 saves

1982 American League

Pos	Player, Team	Stats
C	Lance Parrish, Det	.284-32-87
1B	Eddie Murray, Bal	.316-32-110
2B	Bobby Grich, Cal	.261-19-65
3B	Doug DeCinces, Cal	.301-30-97
SS	Robin Yount, Mil	.331-29-114
OF	Dwight Evans, Bos	.292-32-98
OF	Reggie Jackson, Cal	.275-39-101
OF	Dave Winfield, NYA	.280-37-106
DH	Hal McRae, KC	.308-27-133
SP	Jim Palmer, Bal	15-5, 3.13
SP	Dave Stieb, Tor	17-14, 3.25
SP	Rick Sutcliffe, Cle	14-8, 2.96
SP	Pete Vuckovich, Mil	18-6, 3.34
RP	Bill Caudill, Sea	2.35, 26 saves

1982 National League

Pos	Player, Team	Stats
C	Gary Carter, Mon	.293-29-97
1B	Al Oliver, Mon	.331-22-109
2B	Joe Morgan, SF	.289-14-61
3B	Mike Schmidt, Phi	.280-35-87
SS	Ozzie Smith, StL	.248-2-43
OF	Leon Durham, ChN	.312-22-90
OF	Pedro Guerrero, LA	.304-32-100
OF	Dale Murphy, Atl	.281-36-109
SP	Steve Carlton, Phi	23-11, 3.10
SP	Joe Niekro, Hou	17-12, 2.47
SP	Steve Rogers, Mon	19-8, 2.40
SP	Fernando Valenzuela, LA	19-13, 2.87
RP	Bruce Sutter, StL	2.90, 36 saves

1983 American League

Pos	Player, Team	Stats
C	Carlton Fisk, ChA	.289-26-86
1B	Eddie Murray, Bal	.306-33-111
2B	Bobby Grich, Cal	.292-16-62
3B	Wade Boggs, Bos	.361-5-74
SS	Cal Ripken Jr., Bal	.318-27-102
OF	Rickey Henderson, Oak	.292-9-48
OF	Jim Rice, Bos	.305-39-126
OF	Dave Winfield, NYA	.283-32-116
DH	Greg Luzinski, ChA	.255-32-95
SP	Rich Dotson, ChA	22-7, 3.23
SP	LaMarr Hoyt, ChA	24-10, 3.66
SP	Jack Morris, Det	20-13, 3.34
SP	Dave Stieb, Tor	17-12, 3.04
RP	Dan Quisenberry, KC	1.94, 45 saves

1983 National League

Pos	Player, Team	Stats
C	Gary Carter, Mon	.270-17-79
1B	Darrell Evans, SF	.277-30-82
2B	Bill Doran, Hou	.271-8-39
3B	Mike Schmidt, Phi	.255-40-109
SS	Dickie Thon, Hou	.286-20-79
OF	Andre Dawson, Mon	.299-32-113
OF	Dale Murphy, Atl	.302-36-121
OF	Tim Raines, Mon	.298-11-71
SP	John Denny, Phi	19-6, 2.37
SP	Larry McWilliams, Pit	15-8, 3.25
SP	Nolan Ryan, Hou	14-9, 2.98
SP	Mario Soto, Cin	17-13, 2.70
RP	Lee Smith, ChN	1.65, 29 saves

1984 American League

Pos	Player, Team	Stats
C	Lance Parrish, Det	.237-33-98
1B	Eddie Murray, Bal	.306-29-110
2B	Lou Whitaker, Det	.289-13-56
3B	Buddy Bell, Tex	.315-11-83
SS	Cal Ripken Jr., Bal	.304-27-86
OF	Dwight Evans, Bos	.295-32-104
OF	Rickey Henderson, Oak	.293-16-58
OF	Dave Winfield, NYA	.340-19-100
DH	Mike Easler, Bos	.313-27-91
SP	Bert Blyleven, Cle	19-7, 2.87
SP	Mike Boddicker, Bal	20-11, 2.79
SP	Mark Langston, Sea	17-10, 3.40
SP	Dave Stieb, Tor	16-8, 2.83
RP	Willie Hernandez, Det	1.92, 32 saves

1984 National League

Pos	Player, Team	Stats
C	Gary Carter, Mon	.294-27-106
1B	Keith Hernandez, NYN	.311-15-94
2B	Ryne Sandberg, ChN	.314-19-84
3B	Mike Schmidt, Phi	.277-36-106
SS	Ozzie Smith, StL	.257-1-44
OF	Jose Cruz, Hou	.312-12-95
OF	Tony Gwynn, SD	.351-5-71
OF	Dale Murphy, Atl	.290-36-100
SP	Joaquin Andujar, StL	20-14, 3.34
SP	Dwight Gooden, NYN	17-9, 2.60
SP	Mario Soto, Cin	18-7, 3.53
SP	Rick Sutcliffe, ChN	16-1, 2.69
RP	Bruce Sutter, StL	1.54, 45 saves

1985 American League

Pos	Player, Team	Stats
C	Carlton Fisk, ChA	.238-37-107
1B	Don Mattingly, NYA	.324-35-145
2B	Lou Whitaker, Det	.279-21-73
3B	George Brett, KC	.335-30-112
SS	Cal Ripken Jr., Bal	.282-26-110
OF	Jesse Barfield, Tor	.289-27-84
OF	Kirk Gibson, Det	.287-29-97
OF	Rickey Henderson, NYA	.314-24-72
DH	Gorman Thomas, Sea	.215-32-87
SP	Ron Guidry, NYA	22-6, 3.27
SP	Jack Morris, Det	16-11, 3.33
SP	Bret Saberhagen, KC	20-6, 2.87
SP	Dave Stieb, Tor	14-13, 2.48
RP	Donnie Moore, Cal	1.92, 31 saves

1985 National League

Pos	Player, Team	Stats
C	Gary Carter, NYN	.281-32-100
1B	Mike Schmidt, Phi	.277-33-93
2B	Ryne Sandberg, ChN	.305-26-83
3B	Tim Wallach, Mon	.260-22-81
SS	Ozzie Smith, StL	.276-6-54
OF	Pedro Guerrero, LA	.320-33-87
OF	Willie McGee, StL	.353-10-82
OF	Dale Murphy, Atl	.300-37-111
SP	Dwight Gooden, NYN	24-4, 1.53
SP	Orel Hershiser, LA	19-3, 2.03
SP	John Tudor, StL	21-8, 1.93
SP	Fernando Valenzuela, LA	17-10, 2.45
RP	Jeff Reardon, Mon	3.18, 41 saves

1986 American League

Pos	Player, Team	Stats
C	Lance Parrish, Det	.257-22-62
1B	Don Mattingly, NYA	.352-31-113
2B	Tony Bernazard, Cle	.301-17-73
3B	Wade Boggs, Bos	.357-8-71
SS	Cal Ripken Jr., Bal	.282-25-81
OF	Jesse Barfield, Tor	.289-40-108
OF	Rickey Henderson, NYA	.263-28-74
OF	Kirby Puckett, Min	.328-31-96
DH	Larry Parrish, Tex	.276-28-94
SP	Roger Clemens, Bos	24-4, 2.48
SP	Teddy Higuera, Mil	20-11, 2.79
SP	Jack Morris, Det	21-8, 3.27
SP	Mike Witt, Cal	18-10, 2.84
RP	Dave Righetti, NYA	2.45, 46 saves

1986 National League

Pos	Player, Team	Stats
C	Gary Carter, NYN	.255-24-105
1B	Keith Hernandez, NYN	.310-13-83
2B	Steve Sax, LA	.332-6-56
3B	Mike Schmidt, Phi	.290-37-119
SS	Shawon Dunston, ChN	.250-17-68
OF	Eric Davis, Cin	.277-27-71
OF	Kevin McReynolds, SD	.288-26-96
OF	Tim Raines, Mon	.334-9-62
SP	Dwight Gooden, NYN	17-6, 2.84
SP	Bobby Ojeda, NYN	18-5, 2.57
SP	Mike Scott, Hou	18-10, 2.22
SP	Fernando Valenzuela, LA	21-11, 3.14
RP	Todd Worrell, StL	2.08, 36 saves

1987 American League

Pos	Player, Team	Stats
C	Matt Nokes, Det	.289-32-87
1B	Mark McGwire, Oak	.289-49-118
2B	Willie Randolph, NYA	.305-7-67
3B	Wade Boggs, Bos	.363-24-89
SS	Alan Trammell, Det	.343-28-105
OF	George Bell, Tor	.308-47-134
OF	Kirby Puckett, Min	.332-28-99
OF	Danny Tartabull, KC	.309-34-101
DH	Paul Molitor, Mil	.353-16-75
SP	Roger Clemens, Bos	20-9, 2.97
SP	Jimmy Key, Tor	17-8, 2.76
SP	Jack Morris, Det	18-11, 3.38
SP	Frank Viola, Min	17-10, 2.90
RP	Tom Henke, Tor	2.49, 34 saves

1987 National League

Pos	Player, Team	Stats
C	Benito Santiago, SD	.300-18-79
1B	Jack Clark, StL	.286-35-106
2B	Juan Samuel, Phi	.272-28-100
3B	Mike Schmidt, Phi	.293-35-113
SS	Ozzie Smith, StL	.303-0-75
OF	Eric Davis, Cin	.293-37-100
OF	Dale Murphy, Atl	.295-44-105
OF	Tim Raines, Mon	.330-18-68
SP	Orel Hershiser, LA	16-16, 3.06
SP	Nolan Ryan, Hou	8-16, 2.76
SP	Mike Scott, Hou	16-13, 3.23
SP	Rick Sutcliffe, ChN	18-10, 3.68
RP	Steve Bedrosian, Phi	2.83, 40 saves

1988 American League

Pos	Player, Team	Stats
C	Ernie Whitt, Tor	.251-16-70
1B	George Brett, KC	.306-24-103
2B	Julio Franco, Cle	.303-10-54
3B	Wade Boggs, Bos	.366-5-58
SS	Alan Trammell, Det	.311-15-69
OF	Jose Canseco, Oak	.307-42-124
OF	Mike Greenwell, Bos	.325-22-119
OF	Kirby Puckett, Min	.356-24-121
DH	Jack Clark, NYA	.242-27-93
SP	Roger Clemens, Bos	18-12, 2.93
SP	Mark Gubicza, KC	20-8, 2.70
SP	Teddy Higuera, Mil	16-9, 2.45
SP	Frank Viola, Min	24-7, 2.64
RP	Dennis Eckersley, Oak	2.35, 45 saves

1988 National League

Pos	Player, Team	Stats
C	Tony Pena, StL	.263-10-51
1B	Will Clark, SF	.282-29-109
2B	Ron Gant, Atl	.259-19-60
3B	Bobby Bonilla, Pit	.274-24-100
SS	Barry Larkin, Cin	.296-12-56
OF	Kirk Gibson, LA	.290-25-76
OF	Darryl Strawberry, NYN	.269-39-101
OF	Andy Van Slyke, Pit	.288-25-100
SP	David Cone, NYN	20-3, 2.22
SP	Orel Hershiser, LA	23-8, 2.26
SP	Danny Jackson, Cin	23-8, 2.73
SP	Greg Maddux, ChN	18-8, 3.18
RP	John Franco, Cin	1.57, 39 saves

1989 American League

Pos	Player, Team	Stats
C	Mickey Tettleton, Bal	.258-26-65
1B	Fred McGriff, Tor	.269-36-92
2B	Julio Franco, Tex	.316-13-92
3B	Wade Boggs, Bos	.330-3-54
SS	Cal Ripken Jr., Bal	.257-21-93
OF	Rickey Henderson, NYA-Oak	.274-12-57
OF	Ruben Sierra, Tex	.306-29-119
OF	Robin Yount, Mil	.318-21-103
DH	Harold Baines, ChA-Tex	.309-16-72
SP	Bert Blyleven, Cal	17-5, 2.73
SP	Roger Clemens, Bos	17-11, 3.13
SP	Mike Moore, Oak	19-11, 2.61
SP	Bret Saberhagen, KC	23-6, 2.16
RP	Dennis Eckersley, Oak	1.56, 33 saves

1989 National League

Pos	Player, Team	Stats
C	Craig Biggio, Hou	.257-13-60
1B	Will Clark, SF	.333-23-111
2B	Ryne Sandberg, ChN	.290-30-76
3B	Howard Johnson, NYN	.287-36-101
SS	Dickie Thon, Phi	.271-15-60
OF	Eric Davis, Cin	.281-34-101
OF	Kevin Mitchell, SF	.291-47-125
OF	Lonnie Smith, Atl	.315-21-79
SP	Sid Fernandez, NYN	14-5, 2.83
SP	Greg Maddux, ChN	19-12, 2.95
SP	Joe Magrane, StL	18-9, 2.91
SP	Mike Scott, Hou	20-10, 3.10
RP	Mark Davis, SD	1.85, 44 saves

1990 American League

Pos	Player, Team	Stats
C	Carlton Fisk, ChA	.285-18-65
1B	Cecil Fielder, Det	.277-51-132
2B	Julio Franco, Tex	.296-11-69
3B	Kelly Gruber, Tor	.274-31-118
SS	Alan Trammell, Det	.304-14-89
OF	Jose Canseco, Oak	.274-37-101
OF	Ken Griffey Jr., Sea	.300-22-80
OF	Rickey Henderson, Oak	.325-28-61
DH	Dave Parker, Mil	.289-21-92
SP	Roger Clemens, Bos	21-6, 1.93
SP	Chuck Finley, Cal	18-9, 2.40
SP	Dave Stewart, Oak	22-11, 2.56
SP	Bob Welch, Oak	27-6, 2.95
RP	Dennis Eckersley, Oak	0.61, 48 saves

1990 National League

Pos	Player, Team	Stats
C	Darren Daulton, Phi	.268-12-57
1B	Eddie Murray, LA	.330-26-95
2B	Ryne Sandberg, ChN	.306-40-100
3B	Matt Williams, SF	.277-33-122
SS	Barry Larkin, Cin	.301-7-67
OF	Barry Bonds, Pit	.301-33-114
OF	Ron Gant, Atl	.303-32-84
OF	Darryl Strawberry, NYN	.277-37-108
SP	Doug Drabek, Pit	22-6, 2.76
SP	Ramon Martinez, LA	20-6, 2.92
SP	Frank Viola, NYN	20-12, 2.67
SP	Ed Whitson, SD	14-9, 2.60
RP	Randy Myers, Cin	2.08, 31 saves

1991 American League

Pos	Player, Team	Stats
C	Mickey Tettleton, Det	.263-31-89
1B	Cecil Fielder, Det	.261-44-133
2B	Julio Franco, Tex	.341-15-78
3B	Wade Boggs, Bos	.332-8-51
SS	Cal Ripken Jr., Bal	.323-34-114
OF	Jose Canseco, Oak	.266-44-122
OF	Ken Griffey Jr., Sea	.327-22-100
OF	Danny Tartabull, KC	.316-31-100
DH	Frank Thomas, ChA	.318-32-109
SP	Jim Abbott, Cal	18-11, 2.89
SP	Roger Clemens, Bos	18-10, 2.62
SP	Scott Erickson, Min	20-8, 3.18
SP	Mark Langston, Cal	19-8, 3.00
RP	Bryan Harvey, Cal	1.60, 46 saves

1991 National League

Pos	Player, Team	Stats
C	Craig Biggio, Hou	.295-4-46
1B	Will Clark, SF	.301-29-116
2B	Ryne Sandberg, ChN	.291-26-100
3B	Terry Pendleton, Atl	.319-22-86
SS	Barry Larkin, Cin	.302-20-69
OF	Barry Bonds, Pit	.292-25-116
OF	Bobby Bonilla, Pit	.302-18-100
OF	Ron Gant, Atl	.251-32-105
SP	Tom Glavine, Atl	20-11, 2.55
SP	Dennis Martinez, Mon	14-11, 2.39
SP	Jose Rijo, Cin	15-6, 2.51
SP	John Smiley, Pit	20-8, 3.08
RP	Lee Smith, StL	2.34, 47 saves

1992 American League

Pos	Player, Team	Stats
C	Mickey Tettleton, Det	.238-32-83
1B	Frank Thomas, ChA	.323-24-115
2B	Roberto Alomar, Tor	.310-8-76
3B	Edgar Martinez, Sea	.343-18-73
SS	Travis Fryman, Det	.266-20-96
OF	Brady Anderson, Bal	.271-21-80
OF	Ken Griffey Jr., Sea	.308-27-103
OF	Kirby Puckett, Min	.329-19-110
DH	Dave Winfield, Tor	.290-26-108
SP	Kevin Appier, KC	15-8, 2.46
SP	Roger Clemens, Bos	18-11, 2.41
SP	Jack McDowell, ChA	20-10, 3.18
SP	Mike Mussina, Bal	18-5, 2.54
RP	Dennis Eckersley, Oak	1.91, 51 saves

1992 National League

Pos	Player, Team	Stats
C	Darren Daulton, Phi	.270-27-109
1B	Fred McGriff, SD	.286-35-104
2B	Ryne Sandberg, ChN	.304-26-87
3B	Gary Sheffield, SD	.330-33-100
SS	Barry Larkin, Cin	.304-12-78
OF	Barry Bonds, Pit	.311-34-103
OF	Ray Lankford, StL	.293-20-86
OF	Andy Van Slyke, Pit	.324-14-89
SP	Tom Glavine, Atl	20-8, 2.76
SP	Greg Maddux, ChN	20-11, 2.18
SP	Dennis Martinez, Mon	16-11, 2.47
SP	Bob Tewksbury, StL	16-5, 2.16
RP	Doug Jones, Hou	1.85, 36 saves

1993 American League

Pos	Player, Team	Stats
C	Chris Hoiles, Bal	.310-29-82
1B	John Olerud, Tor	.363-24-107
2B	Roberto Alomar, Tor	.326-17-93
3B	Robin Ventura, ChA	.262-22-94
SS	Travis Fryman, Det	.300-22-97
OF	Albert Belle, Cle	.290-38-129
OF	Juan Gonzalez, Tex	.310-46-118
OF	Ken Griffey Jr., Sea	.309-45-109
DH	Paul Molitor, Tor	.332-22-111
SP	Kevin Appier, KC	18-8, 2.56
SP	Randy Johnson, Sea	19-8, 3.24
SP	Jimmy Key, NYA	18-6, 3.00
SP	Jack McDowell, ChA	22-10, 3.37
RP	Duane Ward, Tor	2.13, 45 saves

1993 National League

Pos	Player, Team	Stats
C	Mike Piazza, LA	.318-35-112
1B	Andres Galarraga, Col	.370-22-98
2B	Robby Thompson, SF	.312-19-65
3B	Matt Williams, SF	.294-38-110
SS	Jeff Blauser, Atl	.305-15-73
OF	Barry Bonds, SF	.336-46-123
OF	Lenny Dykstra, Phi	.305-19-66
OF	Ron Gant, Atl	.274-36-117
SP	Tom Glavine, Atl	22-6, 3.20
SP	Greg Maddux, Atl	20-10, 2.36
SP	Jose Rijo, Cin	14-9, 2.48
SP	Bill Swift, SF	21-8, 2.82
RP	John Wetteland, Mon	1.37, 43 saves

1994 American League

Pos	Player, Team	Stats
C	Mike Stanley, NYA	.300-17-57
1B	Frank Thomas, ChA	.353-38-101
2B	Carlos Baerga, Cle	.314-19-80
3B	Wade Boggs, NYA	.342-11-55
SS	Cal Ripken Jr., Bal	.315-13-75
OF	Albert Belle, Cle	.357-36-101
OF	Ken Griffey Jr., Sea	.323-40-90
OF	Paul O'Neill, NYA	.359-21-83
DH	Chili Davis, Cal	.311-26-84
SP	Roger Clemens, Bos	9-7, 2.85
SP	David Cone, KC	16-5, 2.94
SP	Randy Johnson, Sea	13-6, 3.19
SP	Mike Mussina, Bal	16-5, 3.06
RP	Lee Smith, Bal	3.29, 33 saves

Awards: STATS Retroactive All-Stars

1994 National League

Pos	Player, Team	Stats
C	Mike Piazza, LA	.319-24-92
1B	Jeff Bagwell, Hou	.368-39-116
2B	Craig Biggio, Hou	.318-6-56
3B	Matt Williams, SF	.267-43-96
SS	Wil Cordero, Mon	.294-15-63
OF	Moises Alou, Mon	.339-22-78
OF	Barry Bonds, SF	.312-37-81
OF	Tony Gwynn, SD	.394-12-64
SP	Doug Drabek, Hou	12-6, 2.84
SP	Ken Hill, Mon	16-5, 3.32
SP	Greg Maddux, Atl	16-6, 1.56
SP	Bret Saberhagen, NYN	14-4, 2.74
RP	Doug Jones, Phi	2.17, 27 saves

1995 American League

Pos	Player, Team	Stats
C	Mike Stanley, NYA	.268-18-83
1B	Frank Thomas, ChA	.308-40-111
2B	Chuck Knoblauch, Min	.333-11-63
3B	Jim Thome, Cle	.314-25-73
SS	John Valentin, Bos	.298-27-102
OF	Albert Belle, Cle	.317-50-126
OF	Manny Ramirez, Cle	.308-31-107
OF	Tim Salmon, Cal	.330-34-105
DH	Edgar Martinez, Sea	.356-29-113
SP	David Cone, Tor-NYA	18-8, 3.57
SP	Randy Johnson, Sea	18-2, 2.48
SP	Mike Mussina, Bal	19-9, 3.29
SP	Tim Wakefield, Bos	16-8, 2.95
RP	Jose Mesa, Cle	1.13, 46 saves

1995 National League

Pos	Player, Team	Stats
C	Mike Piazza, LA	.346-32-93
1B	Mark Grace, ChN	.326-16-92
2B	Craig Biggio, Hou	.302-22-77
3B	Ken Caminiti, SD	.302-26-94
SS	Barry Larkin, Cin	.319-15-66
OF	Dante Bichette, Col	.340-40-128
OF	Barry Bonds, SF	.294-33-104
OF	Reggie Sanders, Cin	.306-28-99
SP	Tom Glavine, Atl	16-7, 3.08
SP	Greg Maddux, Atl	19-2, 1.63
SP	Hideo Nomo, LA	13-6, 2.54
SP	Pete Schourek, Cin	18-7, 3.22
RP	Tom Henke, StL	1.82, 36 saves

1996 American League

Pos	Player, Team	Stats
C	Ivan Rodriguez, Tex	.300-19-86
1B	Mark McGwire, Oak	.312-52-113
2B	Chuck Knoblauch, Min	.341-13-72
3B	Jim Thome, Cle	.311-38-116
SS	Alex Rodriguez, Sea	.358-36-123
OF	Albert Belle, Cle	.311-48-148
OF	Juan Gonzalez, Tex	.314-47-144
OF	Ken Griffey Jr., Sea	.303-49-140
DH	Edgar Martinez, Sea	.327-26-103
SP	Kevin Appier, KC	14-11, 3.62
SP	Alex Fernandez, ChA	16-10, 3.45
SP	Pat Hentgen, Tor	20-10, 3.22
SP	Charles Nagy, Cle	17-5, 3.41
RP	Roberto Hernandez, ChA	1.91, 38 saves

1996 National League

Pos	Player, Team	Stats
C	Mike Piazza, LA	.336-36-105
1B	Jeff Bagwell, Hou	.315-31-120
2B	Craig Biggio, Hou	.288-15-75
3B	Ken Caminiti, SD	.326-40-130
SS	Barry Larkin, Cin	.298-33-89
OF	Barry Bonds, SF	.308-42-129
OF	Ellis Burks, Col	.344-40-128
OF	Gary Sheffield, Fla	.314-42-120
SP	Kevin Brown, Fla	17-11, 1.89
SP	Al Leiter, Fla	16-12, 2.93
SP	Greg Maddux, Atl	15-11, 2.72
SP	John Smoltz, Atl	24-8, 2.94
RP	Trevor Hoffman, SD	2.25, 42 saves

1997 American League

Pos	Player, Team	Stats
C	Ivan Rodriguez, Tex	.313-20-77
1B	Frank Thomas, ChA	.347-35-125
2B	Chuck Knoblauch, Min	.291-9-58
3B	Matt Williams, Cle	.263-32-105
SS	Nomar Garciaparra, Bos	.306-30-98
OF	Ken Griffey Jr., Sea	.304-56-147
OF	David Justice, Cle	.329-33-101
OF	Bernie Williams, NYA	.328-21-100
DH	Edgar Martinez, Sea	.330-28-108
SP	Roger Clemens, Tor	21-7, 2.05
SP	Randy Johnson, Sea	20-4, 2.28
SP	Mike Mussina, Bal	15-8, 3.20
SP	Andy Pettitte, NYA	18-7, 2.88
RP	Randy Myers, Bal	1.51, 45 saves

1997 National League

Pos	Player, Team	Stats
C	Mike Piazza, LA	.362-40-124
1B	Jeff Bagwell, Hou	.286-43-135
2B	Craig Biggio, Hou	.309-22-81
3B	Ken Caminiti, SD	.290-26-90
SS	Jeff Blauser, Atl	.308-17-70
OF	Barry Bonds, SF	.291-40-101
OF	Tony Gwynn, SD	.372-17-119
OF	Larry Walker, Col	.366-49-130
SP	Darryl Kile, Hou	19-7, 2.57
SP	Greg Maddux, Atl	19-4, 2.20
SP	Pedro Martinez, Mon	17-8, 1.90
SP	Curt Schilling, Phi	17-11, 2.97
RP	Jeff Shaw, Cin	2.38, 42 saves

STATS Retroactive All-Star Selection Leaders

Total

1	Babe Ruth, of-sp	17
2	Hank Aaron, of-1b	16
	Ty Cobb, of	16
	Ted Williams, of	16
5	Eddie Collins, 2b	14
6	Rogers Hornsby, 2b-ss-3b	13
	Stan Musial, of-1b	13
	Mel Ott, of-3b	13
	Mike Schmidt, 3b-1b	13
	Warren Spahn, sp	13
	Honus Wagner, ss-of	13
12	Nap Lajoie, 2b-1b	12
	Mickey Mantle, of	12
	Willie Mays, of	12
15	Lefty Grove, sp	11
	Walter Johnson, sp	11
	Joe Morgan, 2b	11
	Frank Robinson, of-1b-dh	11
	Tris Speaker, of	11
	Cy Young, sp	11
21	Mickey Cochrane, c	10
	Joe DiMaggio, of	10
	Gabby Hartnett, c	10
	Christy Mathewson, sp	10
25	Eight tied with	9

Catcher

1	Mickey Cochrane	10
	Gabby Hartnett	10
3	Yogi Berra	9
4	Johnny Bench	6
	Roy Campanella	6
	Gary Carter	6
	Carlton Fisk	6
8	Jack Clements	5
	Buck Ewing	5
	Bill Freehan	5
	Ernie Lombardi	5
	Lance Parrish	5
	Mike Piazza	5
	Wally Schang	5
	Ted Simmons	5
16	Roger Bresnahan	4
	Walker Cooper	4
	Bill Dickey	4
	Frankie Hayes	4
	Chief Meyers	4
	Ossee Schreckengost	4
22	Nine tied with	3

First Base

1	Dan Brouthers	8
	Lou Gehrig	8
3	Johnny Mize	7
4	Cap Anson	6
	Orlando Cepeda	6
	Frank Chance	6
	Jimmie Foxx	6
	George Sisler	6
9	Keith Hernandez	5
	Ed Konetchy	5
	Willie McCovey	5
	Eddie Murray	5
13	Norm Cash	4
	Harry Davis	4
	Jack Fournier	4
	Gil Hodges	4
	Bill Terry	4
	Frank Thomas	4
19	12 tied with	3

Second Base

1	Eddie Collins	14
2	Nap Lajoie	11
	Joe Morgan	11
4	Rogers Hornsby	10
5	Charlie Gehringer	9
6	Larry Doyle	8
	Billy Herman	8
8	Cupid Childs	6
	Ryne Sandberg	6
10	Rod Carew	5
	Bobby Doerr	5
	Nellie Fox	5
	Joe Gordon	5
	Bobby Grich	5
	Jackie Robinson	5
16	Craig Biggio	4
	Julio Franco	4
	Frankie Frisch	4
	Bill Mazeroski	4
	Hardy Richardson	4
21	Six tied with	3

Third Base

1	Mike Schmidt	12
2	Eddie Mathews	9
3	Home Run Baker	8
4	Wade Boggs	7
5	George Brett	6
	Pie Traynor	6
7	Harlond Clift	5
	Brooks Robinson	5
	Ron Santo	5
10	Jimmy Collins	4
	Bob Elliott	4
	Heine Groh	4
	Stan Hack	4
	Bill Joyce	4
	Denny Lyons	4
	Al Rosen	4
	Matt Williams	4
18	11 tied with	3

Shortstop

1	Honus Wagner	11
2	Arky Vaughan	9
3	Joe Cronin	8
	Joe Sewell	8
5	Ernie Banks	7
	Cal Ripken Jr.	7
7	Barry Larkin	6
	Pee Wee Reese	6
9	Dave Concepcion	5
	George Davis	5
	Jack Glasscock	5
12	Dave Bancroft	4
	Ray Chapman	4
	Jim Fregosi	4
	Travis Jackson	4
	Ozzie Smith	4
17	17 tied with	3

Outfield

1	Ty Cobb	16
	Ted Williams	16
3	Hank Aaron	15
	Babe Ruth	15
5	Mickey Mantle	12
	Willie Mays	12
	Mel Ott	12
8	Tris Speaker	11
9	Joe DiMaggio	10
	Stan Musial	10
11	Barry Bonds	8
	Ed Delahanty	8
	Rickey Henderson	8
	Reggie Jackson	8
	Frank Robinson	8
	Al Simmons	8
17	Sam Crawford	7
	Ken Griffey Jr.	7
	Harry Heilmann	7
	Sherry Magee	7
21	11 tied with	6

Designated Hitter

1	Hal McRae	4
2	Edgar Martinez	3
3	Willie Horton	2
	Greg Luzinski	2
	Paul Molitor	2
6	Harold Baines	1
	Don Baylor	1
	Jack Clark	1
	Chili Davis	1
	Mike Easler	1
	Dave Parker	1
	Larry Parrish	1
	Jim Rice	1
	Frank Robinson	1
	Frank Thomas	1
	Gorman Thomas	1
	Dave Winfield	1

Pitcher

1	Warren Spahn	13
2	Lefty Grove	11
	Walter Johnson	11
	Cy Young	11
5	Christy Mathewson	10
6	Roger Clemens	9
	Jim Palmer	9
8	Pete Alexander	8
	Greg Maddux	8
	Tom Seaver	8
11	Steve Carlton	7
	Bob Feller	7
	Whitey Ford	7
	Carl Hubbell	7
	Kid Nichols	7
	Eddie Plank	7
	Nolan Ryan	7
18	Dennis Eckersley	6
	Sandy Koufax	6
	Juan Marichal	6
	Carl Mays	6
	Robin Roberts	6
	Early Wynn	6
24	16 tied with	5

Starting Pitcher

1	Warren Spahn	13
2	Lefty Grove	11
	Walter Johnson	11
	Cy Young	11
5	Christy Mathewson	10
6	Roger Clemens	9
	Jim Palmer	9
8	Pete Alexander	8
	Greg Maddux	8
	Tom Seaver	8
11	Steve Carlton	7
	Bob Feller	7
	Whitey Ford	7
	Carl Hubbell	7
	Kid Nichols	7
	Eddie Plank	7
	Nolan Ryan	7
18	Sandy Koufax	6
	Juan Marichal	6
	Carl Mays	6
	Robin Roberts	6
	Early Wynn	6
23	15 tied with	5

Relief Pitcher

1	Dennis Eckersley	4
	Firpo Marberry	4
	Johnny Murphy	4
	Bruce Sutter	4
5	Ace Adams	3
	Hugh Casey	3
	Roy Face	3
	Rollie Fingers	3
	Goose Gossage	3
	Ellis Kinder	3
	Dick Radatz	3
	Lee Smith	3
13	21 tied with	2

Consecutive

1	Hank Aaron, of	1956-1969	14
2	Ty Cobb, of	1907-1919	13
	Honus Wagner, ss-of	1900-1912	13
4	Mel Ott, of-3b	1931-1942	12
5	Mickey Mantle, of	1952-1962	11
6	Eddie Collins, 2b	1911-1920	10
	Rogers Hornsby, 2b	1920-1929	10
	Willie Mays, of	1957-1966	10
9	Yogi Berra, c	1949-1957	9
	Mickey Cochrane, c	1927-1935	9
	Joe Morgan, 2b	1969-1977	9
	Babe Ruth, of-sp	1916-1924	9
	Mike Schmidt, 3b-1b	1979-1987	9
	Warren Spahn, sp	1953-1961	9
15	Barry Bonds, of	1990-1997	8
	Nap Lajoie, 2b-1b	1897-1904	8
	Babe Ruth, of	1926-1933	8
	Joe Sewell, ss	1921-1928	8
19	Nine tied with		7

Greats

STATS All-Time Stars

A STATS panel of 15 voters chose a 25-man all-time all-star team. The first team consists of one player at each of the eight non-pitching positions, four starting pitchers and one relief pitcher. The second team of reserves has one player at each of the eight non-pitching positions, two starters and two relievers. A separate STATS panel also chose an all-time Gold Glove team of the top defenders ever to grace each position.

STATS Gold Gloves

In addition to picking an all-time Gold Glove team, we also chose Gold Glove teams for each league by decade. Because the National League played just four seasons in the 1870s, we combined that decade with the 1880s. Dan Ford, STATS' Negro Leagues expert, picked Gold Glove teams for the Negro Leagues' entire history as well as its three individual eras.

Games

We present summaries and detailed box scores for 90 of the most significant games in baseball history. We begin with the first major league game on April 22, 1876,
and end with the first regular-season interleague game on June 12, 1997. We consulted multiple sources for some of the box scores and believe them to be as complete and accurate as is possible. One of the most valuable sources was Retrosheet and especially David Smith. Their play-by-play information is available free of charge and is copyrighted by Retrosheet, which can be contacted at 20 Sunset Road, Newark, DE 19711.

Feats

We list every player who ever won the Triple Crown, threw a no-hitter, hit three or more home runs in a game, batted for the cycle or turned an unassisted triple play. Only no-hitters that meet baseball's revised standards (nine innings or longer, with no exceptions for hits allowed in extra innings) are included, with perfect games shown separately.

Abbreviations & Formulas

A complete list of team and statistical abbreviations are listed in the back of the book, along with an appendix explaining formulas and the availability of certain statistics.

STATS All-Time All-Star Team

Regulars

Pos	Player	Avg	HR	RBI	RC/27	LRC/27
C	Johnny Bench	.267	389	1376	5.47	4.07
1B	Lou Gehrig	.340	493	1995	10.30	5.13
2B	Rogers Hornsby	.358	301	1584	8.95	4.43
3B	Mike Schmidt	.267	548	1595	6.95	4.12
SS	Honus Wagner	.327	101	1732	7.63	4.23
LF	Ted Williams	.344	521	1839	11.48	4.54
CF	Ty Cobb	.366	117	1933	8.67	4.22
RF	Babe Ruth	.342	714	2210	11.72	4.84

Pos	Pitcher	W-L	SV	ERA	ERC	LERA
SP	Lefty Grove	300-141	55	3.06	3.12	4.41
SP	Walter Johnson	417-279	34	2.17	2.12	3.24
SP	Christy Mathewson	373-188	28	2.13	2.14	2.91
SP	Cy Young	511-316	17	2.63	2.51	3.61
RP	Dennis Eckersley	193-170	389	3.49	3.11	3.96

Reserves

Pos	Player	Avg	HR	RBI	RC/27	LRC/27
C	Josh Gibson			Negro Leagues		
1B	Jimmie Foxx	.325	534	1921	9.36	5.07
2B	Joe Morgan	.271	268	1133	6.64	4.11
3B	Eddie Mathews	.271	512	1453	6.93	4.25
SS	Cal Ripken Jr.	.276	370	1453	5.27	4.63
LF	Stan Musial	.331	475	1951	8.42	4.35
CF	Willie Mays	.302	660	1903	7.66	4.18
RF	Hank Aaron	.305	755	2297	7.22	4.15

Pos	Pitcher	W-L	SV	ERA	ERC	LERA
SP	Sandy Koufax	165-87	9	2.76	2.50	3.68
SP	Warren Spahn	363-245	28	3.09	3.03	3.88
RP	Rollie Fingers	114-118	341	2.90	2.78	3.69
RP	Hoyt Wilhelm	143-122	227	2.52	2.53	3.74

STATS All-Time Gold Glove Team

Pos	Player	Gold Gloves	Rng	LRng	FPct	LFPct
C	Roy Campanella	0	—	—	.988	.984
1B	Keith Hernandez	11	—	—	.994	.992
2B	Bill Mazeroski	8	5.57	4.70	.983	.976
3B	Brooks Robinson	16	3.10	2.74	.971	.953
SS	Ozzie Smith	13	5.03	4.12	.978	.965
OF	Roberto Clemente	12	2.08	1.85	.972	.976
OF	Willie Mays	12	2.56	1.88	.981	.977
OF	Tris Speaker	—	2.68	2.08	.970	.960
P	Pete Alexander	—	—	—	.985	.955

STATS Decade Gold Glove Teams

1876-89

	American Association	National League
P	Ed Stewart	Guy Hecker
C	Bill Holbert	Buck Ewing
1B	Charles Comiskey	Cap Anson
2B	Lou Bierbauer	Bid McPhee
3B	Frank Hankinson	Ned Williamson
SS	Henry Easterday	Jack Glasscock
OF	Jim McTamany	Pop Corkhill
OF	Harry Stovey	Jim Fogarty
OF	Curt Welch	Joe Horning

1890-99

		National League
P		Ted Breitenstein
C		Chief Zimmer
1B		Jake Beckley
2B		Bid McPhee
3B		Lave Cross
SS		George Davis
OF		Mike Griffin
OF		Bill Lange
OF		Tommy McCarthy

1900-09

	American League	National League
P	Ed Walsh	Christy Mathewson
C	Lou Criger	Johnny Kling
1B	Hal Chase	Fred Tenney
2B	Nap Lajoie	Johnny Evers
3B	Jimmy Collins	Art Devlin
SS	Bobby Wallace	Joe Tinker
OF	Jimmy Barnett	Fred Clarke
OF	Fielder Jones	Jimmy Sheckard
OF	Matty McIntyre	Roy Thomas

1910-19

	American League	National League
P	Walter Johnson	Pete Alexander
C	Ray Schalk	Jimmy Archer
1B	Stuffy McInnis	Ed Konetchy
2B	Eddie Collins	George Cutshaw
3B	Jimmy Austin	Heine Groh
SS	Everett Scott	Rabbit Maranville
OF	Harry Hooper	Max Carey
OF	Tris Speaker	Hi Myers
OF	Amos Strunk	Dode Paskert

1920-29

	American League	National League
P	Stan Coveleski	Pete Alexander
C	Muddy Ruel	Gabby Hartnett
1B	George Sisler	George Kelly
2B	Bucky Harris	Frankie Frisch
3B	Willie Kamm	Pie Traynor
SS	Joe Sewell	Dave Bancroft
OF	Bob Meusel	Max Carey
OF	Johnny Mostil	Taylor Douthit
OF	Tris Speaker	Edd Roush

1930-39

	American League	National League
P	Wes Ferrell	Bucky Walters
C	Rick Ferrell	Al Lopez
1B	Joe Kuhel	Bill Terry
2B	Charlie Gehringer	Billy Herman
3B	Harlond Clift	Pie Traynor
SS	Billy Rogell	Dick Bartell
OF	Earl Averill	Terry Moore
OF	Joe DiMaggio	Mel Ott
OF	Sammy West	Lloyd Waner

1940-49

	American League	National League
P	Fred Hutchinson	Curt Davis
C	Jim Hegan	Walker Cooper
1B	George McQuinn	Frank McCormick
2B	Joe Gordon	Red Schoendienst
3B	Ken Keltner	Whitey Kurowski
SS	Lou Boudreau	Marty Marion
OF	Dom DiMaggio	Vince DiMaggio
OF	Joe DiMaggio	Tommy Holmes
OF	Stan Spence	Terry Moore

1950-59

	American League	National League
P	Bob Lemon	Larry Jansen
C	Jim Hegan	Roy Campanella
1B	Mickey Vernon	Gil Hodges
2B	Nellie Fox	Red Schoendienst
3B	Frank Malzone	Puddin' Head Jones
SS	Luis Aparicio	Roy McMillan
OF	Jim Busby	Richie Ashburn
OF	Al Kaline	Willie Mays
OF	Jimmy Piersall	Duke Snider

1960-69

	American League	National League
P	Jim Kaat	Bob Gibson
C	Bill Freehan	Johnny Edwards
1B	Vic Power	Bill White
2B	Bobby Richardson	Bill Mazeroski
3B	Brooks Robinson	Ron Santo
SS	Luis Aparicio	Gene Alley
OF	Al Kaline	Roberto Clemente
OF	Jim Landis	Curt Flood
OF	Carl Yastrzemski	Willie Mays

1970-79

	American League	National League
P	Jim Palmer	Phil Niekro
C	Jim Sundberg	Johnny Bench
1B	George Scott	Keith Hernandez
2B	Bobby Grich	Joe Morgan
3B	Graig Nettles	Mike Schmidt
SS	Mark Belanger	Dave Concepcion
OF	Paul Blair	Cesar Cedeno
OF	Dwight Evans	Garry Maddox
OF	Amos Otis	Dave Parker

1980-89

	American League	National League
P	Ron Guidry	Rick Reuschel
C	Bob Boone	Gary Carter
1B	Don Mattingly	Keith Hernandez
2B	Frank White	Ryne Sandberg
3B	Gary Gaetti	Mike Schmidt
SS	Cal Ripken	Ozzie Smith
OF	Dwayne Murphy	Andre Dawson
OF	Kirby Puckett	Willie McGee
OF	Dave Winfield	Dale Murphy

1990-97

	American League	National League
P	Mark Langston	Greg Maddux
C	Ivan Rodriguez	Charles Johnson
1B	Don Mattingly	Mark Grace
2B	Roberto Alomar	Jose Lind
3B	Robin Ventura	Matt Williams
SS	Omar Vizquel	Barry Larkin
OF	Ken Griffey Jr.	Barry Bonds
OF	Kenny Lofton	Marquis Grissom
OF	Devon White	Larry Walker

STATS Negro League Gold Glove Teams

	All-Time Team		Pre-1920		1920-1932		1933-1950
P	Martin Dihigo	P	Jose Mendez	P	Martin Dihigo	P	Leon Day
C	Biz Mackey	C	Bruce Petway	C	Biz Mackey	C	Roy Campanella
1B	Showboat Thomas	1B	Ben Taylor	1B	George Giles	1B	Showboat Thomas
2B	Bingo DeMoss	2B	Bingo DeMoss	2B	Newt Allen	2B	Dick Seay
3B	Oliver Marcelle	3B	Bill Monroe	3B	Oliver Marcelle	3B	Ray Dandridge
SS	Pop Lloyd	SS	Pop Lloyd	SS	Dick Lundy	SS	Artie Wilson
OF	Oscar Charleston	OF	Pete Hill	OF	Oscar Charleston	OF	Gene Benson
OF	Jimmie Crutchfield	OF	Mike Moore	OF	Rap Dixon	OF	Jimmy Crutchfield
OF	Clint Thomas	OF	Cristobal Torriente	OF	Clint Thomas	OF	Henry Kimbro

Great Games

April 22, 1876

In the first major league game ever played, the visiting Boston Red Stockings defeat the Philadelphia Athletics with two unearned runs in the ninth inning. Joe Borden, pitching under the name Josephs, earns the win.

Boston Red Stockings	AB	R	H	RBI
George Wright, ss	4	2	1	—
Andy Leonard, 2b	4	0	2	—
Jim O'Rourke, cf	5	1	2	—
Tim Murnane, 1b	6	1	2	—
Harry Schafer, 3b	5	1	1	—
Tim McGinley, c	5	1	0	—
Jack Manning, rf	4	0	2	—
Bill Parks, lf	4	0	0	—
Joe Borden, p	3	0	0	—
Totals	40	6	10	—

Philadelphia Athletics	AB	R	H	RBI
Davy Force, ss	5	0	1	—
Dave Eggler, cf	5	0	1	—
Wes Fisler, 1b	5	1	3	—
Levi Meyerle, 2b-3b	5	1	2	—
Ezra Sutton, 3b-rf	5	0	0	—
William Coon, c	4	2	2	—
George Hall, lf	4	0	2	—
Bill Fouser, rf-2b	4	0	0	—
Lon Knight, p	4	1	1	—
Totals	41	5	12	—

	1 2 3	4 5 6	7 8 9		R	H	E
Bos	0 1 2	0 1 0	0 0 2		6	10	7
PhN	0 1 0	0 0 3	0 0 1		5	12	13

E—McGinley 3, Coon 3, Sutton 2, Fouser 2, Knight 2, Leonard, Schafer, Parks, Borden, Force, Eggler, Fisler, Meyerle. DP—Philadelphia 2. LOB—Boston 7, Philadelphia 9. 2B—Manning 2, Eggler. 3B—Meyerle.

Boston Red Stockings	IP	H	R	ER	BB	SO
Joe Borden (W)	9.0	12	5	2	2	—

Philadelphia Athletics	IP	H	R	ER	BB	SO
Lon Knight (L)	9.0	10	6	1	2	—

Time—2:05. Attendance—3,000. Umpire—McLean.

July 15, 1876

George Bradley of the St. Louis Brown Stockings throws the first no-hitter in major league history, beating the Hartford Dark Blues 2-0. It's his third shutout of Hartford in the three-game series.

St. Louis Brown Stockings	AB	R	H	RBI
Ned Cuthbert, lf	—	1	0	—
John Clapp, c	—	0	3	—
Mike McGeary, 2b	—	0	0	—
Lip Pike, cf	—	0	1	—
Joe Battin, 2b	—	0	0	—
Joe Blong, rf	—	1	1	—
George Bradley, p	—	0	1	—
Herman Dehlman, 1b	—	0	1	—
Dickey Pearce, ss	—	0	1	—
Totals	—	2	8	—

Hartford Dark Blues	AB	R	H	RBI
Jack Remsen, cf	—	0	0	0
Jack Burdock, 2b	—	0	0	0
Dick Higham, rf	—	0	0	0
Bob Ferguson, 3b	—	0	0	0
Tom Carey, ss	—	0	0	0
Tommy Bond, p	—	0	0	0
Tom York, lf	—	0	0	0
Everett Mills, 1b	—	0	0	0
Bill Harbidge, c	—	0	0	0
Totals	—	0	0	0

	1 2 3	4 5 6	7 8 9		R	H	E
StL	1 1 0	0 0 0	0 0 0		2	8	3
Har	0 0 0	0 0 0	0 0 0		0	0	4

E—Clapp 2, Harbidge 2, Pearce, York, Mills.

St. Louis Brown Stockings	IP	H	R	ER	BB	SO
George Bradley (W)	9.0	0	0	0	1	—

Hartford Dark Blues	IP	H	R	ER	BB	SO
Tommy Bond (L)	9.0	8	2	0	0	—

Time—2:00. Umpire—Daniels.

June 12, 1880

Worcester Brown Stockings ace Lee Richmond tosses the first perfect game in major league history, shutting down the Cleveland Blues 1-0. Worcester right fielder Lon Knight saves the gem by throwing a runner out at first.

Cleveland Blues	AB	R	H	RBI
Fred Dunlap, 2b	3	0	0	0
Frank Hankinson, 3b	3	0	0	0
Doc Kennedy, c	3	0	0	0
Bill Phillips, 1b	3	0	0	0
Orator Shaffer, rf	3	0	0	0
Jim McCormick, p	3	0	0	0
Barney Gilligan, cf	3	0	0	0
Jack Glasscock, ss	3	0	0	0
Ned Hanlon, lf	3	0	0	0
Totals	27	0	0	0

Worcester Brown Stockings	AB	R	H	RBI
George Wood, lf	4	0	0	—
Lee Richmond, p	3	0	1	—
Lon Knight, rf	3	0	0	—
Arthur Irwin, ss	3	1	2	—
Charlie Bennett, c	2	0	0	—
Art Whitney, 3b	3	0	0	—
Chub Sullivan, 1b	3	0	0	—
Fred Corey, cf	3	0	0	—
George Creamer, 2b	3	0	0	—
Totals	27	1	3	—

	1 2 3	4 5 6	7 8 9		R	H	E
Cle	0 0 0	0 0 0	0 0 0		0	0	2
Wor	0 0 0	0 1 0	0 0 x		1	3	0

E—Kennedy 2. DP—Cleveland 1. LOB—Cleveland 0, Worcester 3.

Cleveland Blues	IP	H	R	ER	BB	SO
Jim McCormick (L)	8.0	3	1	—	1	7

Worcester Brown Stockings	IP	H	R	ER	BB	SO
Lee Richmond (W)	9.0	0	0	0	0	5

Time—1:26. Umpire—Bradley.

June 17, 1880

Five days after the first perfect game in major league history, Monte Ward of the Providence Grays tosses the second in beating the Buffalo Bisons 5-0. The next National League perfecto won't come for another 84 years.

Providence Grays	AB	R	H	RBI
Paul Hines, cf	5	0	2	—
Joe Start, 1b	5	1	1	—
Mike Dorgan, rf	5	0	2	—
Emil Gross, c	5	0	0	—
Jack Farrell, 2b	4	3	3	—
Monte Ward, p	4	0	1	—
John Peters, ss	4	0	1	—
Tom York, lf	4	0	2	—
George Bradley, 3b	4	1	1	—
Totals	40	5	13	—

Buffalo Bisons	AB	R	H	RBI
Bill Crowley, rf-c	3	0	0	0
Hardy Richardson, 3b	3	0	0	0
Jack Rowe, c-rf	3	0	0	0
Oscar Walker, lf	3	0	0	0
Joe Hornung, 2b	3	0	0	0
Denny Mack, ss	3	0	0	0
Dude Esterbrook, 1b	3	0	0	0
Tom Poorman, cf	3	0	0	0
Pud Galvin, p	3	0	0	0
Totals	27	0	0	0

	1	2	3	4	5	6	7	8	9	R	H	E
Prv	0	1	0	1	0	0	1	1	1	5	13	0
Buf	0	0	0	0	0	0	0	0	0	0	0	7

E—Crowley 2, Galvin 2, Walker, Mack, Poorman. 2B—Farrell. 3B—Start, York, Bradley.

Providence Grays	IP	H	R	ER	BB	SO
Monte Ward (W)	9.0	0	0	0	0	2

Buffalo Bisons	IP	H	R	ER	BB	SO
Pud Galvin (L)	9.0	13	5	3	0	2

Umpire—Daniels.

September 6, 1883

The Chicago White Stockings enjoy the most prolific inning in major league history, scoring 18 times in the seventh. They score 14 runs before making an out, and shortstop Tom Burns strokes two doubles and a home run.

Detroit Wolverines	AB	R	H	RBI
George Wood, cf	4	2	3	—
Joe Farrell, 3b	5	0	1	—
Martin Powell, 1b	5	1	0	—
Ned Hanlon, 2b	4	2	0	—
Charlie Bennett, lf	5	1	1	—
Sadie Houck, ss	4	0	1	—
Sam Trott, c	3	0	1	—
Stump Wiedman, p-rf	4	0	0	—
Dick Burns, rf-p	4	0	1	—
Totals	38	6	8	—

Chicago White Stockings	AB	R	H	RBI
Abner Dalrymple, lf	6	3	2	—
George Gore, cf	7	2	3	—
King Kelly, c-2b	7	3	3	—
Cap Anson, 1b-c-p	6	3	4	—
Ned Williamson, 3b-p-c	6	3	3	—
Tom Burns, ss	6	4	4	—
Fred Pfeffer, 2b-3b	6	2	3	—
Fred Goldsmith, p-1b	6	3	3	—
Billy Sunday, rf	6	3	3	—
Totals	56	26	28	—

	1	2	3	4	5	6	7	8	9	R	H	E
Det	3	0	0	0	0	0	0	2	1	6	8	5
ChN	1	0	3	1	2	1	18	0	x	26	28	4

E—Farrell 2, DBurns 2, Dalrymple, Kelly, TBurns, Sunday, Wiedman. 2B—TBurns 3, Anson 2, Pfeffer 2, Goldsmith 2, Gore, Kelly, Williamson, Wood, Bennett, Houck, Trott. 3B—Gore. HR—TBurns.

Detroit Wolverines	IP	H	R	ER	BB	SO
Stump Wiedman	—	—	—	—	—	—
Dick Burns	—	—	—	—	—	—

Chicago White Stockings	IP	H	R	ER	BB	SO
Fred Goldsmith	—	—	—	—	—	—
Ned Williamson	—	—	—	—	—	—
Cap Anson	—	—	—	—	—	—

WP—Goldsmith, Williamson. Time—2:25. Umpire—Decker.

June 7, 1884

Providence's Charlie Sweeney becomes the first pitcher ever to strike out 19 batters in a nine-inning game. Hugh Daily will tie the record one month later, but it won't be surpassed for another 102 years.

Providence Grays	AB	R	H	RBI
Paul Hines, cf	4	0	1	—
Jack Farrell, 2b	4	1	1	—
Old Hoss Radbourn, 1b	4	0	1	—
Charlie Sweeney, p	4	0	1	—
Arthur Irwin, ss	3	1	1	—
Jerry Denny, 3b	3	0	1	—
Cliff Carroll, lf	3	0	0	—
Sandy Nava, c	3	0	0	—
Paul Radford, rf	3	0	0	—
Totals	31	2	6	—

Boston Red Stockings	AB	R	H	RBI
Joe Hornung, lf	4	0	0	—
Ezra Sutton, 3b	4	0	1	—
Jack Burdock, 2b	4	0	0	—
Jim Whitney, p	3	1	1	—
John Morrill, 1b	4	0	1	—
Jim Manning, cf	4	0	0	—
Bill Crowley, rf	4	0	1	—
Mike Hines, c	3	0	0	—
Sam Wise, ss	3	0	0	—
Totals	33	1	4	—

	1	2	3	4	5	6	7	8	9	R	H	E
Prv	0	0	0	0	1	1	0	0	0	2	6	4
Bos	0	0	0	0	0	0	1	0	0	1	4	4

E—MHines 2, Farrell, Sweeney, Radbourn, Carroll, Manning, Wise. 2B—Sutton, Crowley.

Providence Grays	IP	H	R	ER	BB	SO
Charlie Sweeney (W)	9.0	4	1	—	1	19

Boston Red Stockings	IP	H	R	ER	BB	SO
Jim Whitney (L)	9.0	6	2	—	0	10

Time—1:32. Umpire—Burns.

June 10, 1892

Baltimore Orioles catcher Wilbert Robinson becomes the first big leaguer to collect seven hits in a nine-inning game during a 25-4 rout of the St. Louis Browns. He sets another mark, since broken, with 11 RBI.

Baltimore Orioles	AB	R	H	RBI
Billy Shindle, 3b	7	2	2	—
George Van Haltren, rf	5	5	2	—
Jocko Halligan, 1b	5	3	2	—
George Shoch, ss	6	4	5	—
Curt Welch, cf	6	3	2	—
Joe Gunson, lf	5	4	2	—
John McGraw, 2b	6	3	3	—
Wilbert Robinson, c	7	1	7	11
Sadie McMahon, p	7	0	0	—
Totals	54	25	25	—

St. Louis Browns	AB	R	H	RBI
Jack Crooks, 2b	2	1	0	—
Cliff Carroll, lf	5	0	1	—
Perry Werden, 1b	4	1	1	—
Jack Glasscock, ss	4	1	1	—
Steve Brodie, cf	4	0	2	—
Bob Caruthers, rf	4	0	0	—
George Pinckney, 3b	4	0	1	—
Dick Buckley, c	4	0	0	—
Charlie Getzien, p	1	0	0	—
Joe Young, p	2	0	0	—
Frank Bird, c	1	0	0	—
Cub Stricker, 2b	3	0	1	—
Ted Breitenstein, p	2	1	0	—
Totals	40	4	7	—

	1	2	3	4	5	6	7	8	9	R	H	E
Bal	5	5	4	6	2	3	0	0	0	25	25	6
StL	1	0	0	0	0	2	1	0	0	4	7	8

E—Crooks 3, Shindle 2, Gunson 2, Carroll 2, Shoch, McGraw, Werden, Caruthers, Pinckney. 2B—Shindle, Shoch, Robinson, Glasscock. 3B—Shindle. SF—Halligan, McMahon, Werden, Glasscock, Brodie, Bird. SB—Welch, McGraw, Robinson.

Baltimore Orioles	IP	H	R	ER	BB	SO
Sadie McMahon (W)	9.0	7	4	—	1	3

St. Louis Browns	IP	H	R	ER	BB	SO
Charlie Getzien (L)	—	—	—	—	3	0
Joe Young	—	—	—	—	2	1
Ted Breitenstein	—	—	—	—	1	2

WP—Young. Time—1:50. Umpire—Hurst.

May 30, 1894

Boston Beaneaters second baseman Bobby Lowe becomes the first big leaguer ever to hit four homers in one game. He also ties another record by going deep twice in the third inning.

Cincinnati Reds	AB	R	H	RBI
Dummy Hoy, cf	6	1	1	0
Jack McCarthy, 1b	5	2	2	2
Arlie Latham, 3b	4	3	2	1
Bug Holliday, lf	4	3	2	5
Bid McPhee, 2b	5	0	2	0
Farmer Vaughn, c	5	1	2	4
Jim Canavan, rf	5	1	1	1
Germany Smith, ss	5	0	1	0
Elton Chamberlin, p	5	0	1	0
Totals	44	11	14	13

Boston Beaneaters	AB	R	H	RBI
Bobby Lowe, 2b	6	4	5	6
Herman Long, ss	3	5	2	1
Hugh Duffy, cf	5	0	1	1
Tommy McCarthy, lf	6	2	3	0
Billy Nash, 3b	4	3	3	1
Tommy Tucker, 1b	2	1	0	0
Jimmy Bannon, rf	4	2	2	2
Jack Ryan, c	5	2	2	2
Kid Nichols, p	5	1	1	4
Totals	40	20	19	17

	1	2	3	4	5	6	7	8	9	R	H	E
Cin	2	0	0	0	4	0	0	0	5	11	14	5
Bos	2	0	9	0	1	5	2	1	x	20	19	3

E—Latham 2, Long 2, Hoy, Vaughn, Smith, Lowe. LOB—Cincinnati 7, Boston 10. 2B—Latham 2, Smith, Chamberlin, Long, McCarthy. HR—Lowe 4, Holliday 2, Vaughn, Canavan, Long. SB—Nash 2, Hoy, Latham, Long, Duffy.

Cincinnati Reds	IP	H	R	ER	BB	SO
Elton Chamberlin (L)	8.0	19	20	18	8	3

Boston Beaneaters	IP	H	R	ER	BB	SO
Kid Nichols (W)	9.0	14	11	11	2	3

HBP—Long by Chamberlin, Tucker by Chamberlin. WP—Chamberlin, Nichols. Time—2:15. Attendance—8,000. Umpire—Swartwood.

July 13, 1896

Phillies first baseman Ed Delahanty ties the major league record with four homers and sets another (since broken) with 17 total bases. Still, Chicago's Adonis Terry goes the distance for the win.

Philadelphia Phillies	AB	R	H	RBI
Duff Cooley, lf	3	1	1	0
Billy Hulen, ss	4	1	1	0
Sam Mertes, cf	5	1	0	0
Ed Delahanty, 1b	5	4	5	7
Sam Thompson, rf	5	0	1	0
Bill Hallman, 2b	4	1	1	0
Jack Clements, c	2	0	0	0
Billy Nash, 3b	4	0	0	0
Ned Garvin, p	4	0	0	1
Totals	36	8	9	8

Chicago Colts	AB	R	H	RBI
Bill Everitt, 3b	3	1	2	0
Bill Dahlen, ss	2	2	0	0
Bill Lange, cf	4	2	2	5
Cap Anson, 1b	3	0	1	1
Jimmy Ryan, rf	4	1	1	0
George Decker, lf	4	1	1	0
Fred Pfeffer, 2b	4	0	2	2
Adonis Terry, p	4	1	2	0
Tim Donahue, c	3	1	0	0
Totals	31	9	11	8

	1	2	3	4	5	6	7	8	9	R	H	E
Phi	1	2	0	0	3	0	1	0	1	8	9	1
ChN	1	0	4	0	1	0	0	3	x	9	11	2

E—Nash, Ryan, Decker. DP—Philadelphia 1. LOB—Philadelphia 6, Chicago 4. 2B—Thompson, Lange, Decker, Terry. 3B—Lange, Pfeffer. HR—Delahanty 4.

Philadelphia Phillies	IP	H	R	ER	BB	SO
Ned Garvin (L)	8.0	11	9	8	4	4

Chicago Colts	IP	H	R	ER	BB	SO
Adonis Terry (W)	9.0	9	8	7	3	4

WP—Garvin. Time—2:15. Attendance—1,100. Umpire—Emslie.

June 29, 1897

The Chicago Colts set a record that has lasted for a century when they score 36 runs in one game. Chicago scores in each inning as shortstop Barry McCormick leads the way with six hits, including a triple and homer.

Chicago Colts	AB	R	H	RBI
Bill Everitt, 3b	7	3	2	—
Barry McCormick, ss	8	5	6	—
Bill Lange, cf	7	4	4	—
Cap Anson, 1b	4	4	1	—
Jimmy Ryan, rf	6	5	2	—
George Decker, lf	4	2	3	—
Walter Thornton, lf	2	2	2	—
Jim Connor, 2b	6	4	4	—
Nixey Callahan, p	7	4	5	—
Tim Donahue, c	6	3	3	—
Totals	57	36	32	—

Louisville Colonels	AB	R	H	RBI
Fred Clarke, lf	4	0	3	—
Tom McCreery, rf	4	1	0	—
Ollie Pickering, cf	5	1	2	—
General Stafford, ss	5	1	0	—
Perry Werden, 1b	5	1	3	—
Charlie Dexter, 3b	5	0	4	—
Dick Butler, c	5	0	0	—
Abbie Johnson, 2b	0	0	0	—
Tom Delahanty, 2b	3	1	1	—
Chick Fraser, p	0	0	0	—
Jim Jones, p	3	2	1	—
Totals	39	7	14	—

	1	2	3	4	5	6	7	8	9	R	H	E
ChN	3	5	7	1	2	1	2	7	8	36	32	1
Lou	0	0	1	0	5	0	1	0	0	7	14	9

E—Pickering 3, Butler 2, Delahanty 2, Thornton, Werden, Dexter. 2B—Callahan 2, Werden 2, Dexter 2, Everitt, Ryan, Decker, Donahue, Jones, Delahanty. 3B—McCormick, Lange, Connor. HR—McCormick, Ryan. SF—Everitt, McCreery. SB—McCormick 2, Lange 2, Connor, Callahan, Donahue.

Chicago Colts	IP	H	R	ER	BB	SO
Nixey Callahan (W)	9.0	14	7	6	2	4

Louisville Colonels	IP	H	R	ER	BB	SO
Chick Fraser (L)	—	—	—	—	5	—
Jim Jones	—	—	—	—	5	—

Time—2:15. Umpire—Sheridan.

April 24, 1901

Three rain postponements give the Chicago White Stockings the honor of hosting the first game in American League history. Roy Patterson defeats the Cleveland Blues 8-2, starting Chicago toward the first AL pennant.

Cleveland Blues	AB	R	H	RBI
Ollie Pickering, rf	4	0	1	1
Jack McCarthy, lf	4	0	2	0
Frank Genins, cf	4	0	0	0
Candy LaChance, 1b	4	1	1	0
Bill Bradley, 3b	4	0	0	0
Erve Beck, 2b	3	0	2	0
Bill Hallman, ss	3	1	0	0
Bob Wood, c	4	0	1	1
Bill Hoffer, p	4	0	0	0
Totals	34	2	7	2

Chicago White Stockings	AB	R	H	RBI
Dummy Hoy, cf	4	0	1	0
Fielder Jones, rf	2	2	1	0
Sam Mertes, lf	3	2	1	0
Frank Shugart, ss	1	2	0	1
Frank Isbell, 1b	3	1	2	3
Fred Hartman, 3b	4	0	1	2
Dave Brain, 2b	4	0	0	0
Billy Sullivan, c	4	1	2	0
Roy Patterson, p	4	0	0	0
Totals	29	8	8	6

	1	2	3	4	5	6	7	8	9	R	H	E
Cle	0	0	0	1	0	0	1	0	0	2	7	1
ChA	2	5	0	0	0	0	1	0	x	8	8	1

E—Hallman, Isbell. DP—Cleveland 1, Chicago 1. LOB—Cleveland 7, Chicago 5. 2B—Beck. SH—Hoy, Shugart. CS—Hoy.

Cleveland Blues	IP	H	R	ER	BB	SO
Bill Hoffer (L)	8.0	8	8	6	6	1

Chicago White Stockings	IP	H	R	ER	BB	SO
Roy Patterson (W)	9.0	7	2	1	2	0

WP—Hoffer. Time—1:30. Attendance—14,500. Umpire—Connolly.

May 5, 1904

Boston Pilgrims ace Cy Young tosses the first perfect game in American League history, outdueling Rube Waddell of the Philadelphia Athletics. The game is part of Young's major league-record streak of 23 hitless innings.

Philadelphia Athletics	AB	R	H	RBI
Topsy Hartsel, lf	1	0	0	0
Danny Hoffman, lf	2	0	0	0
Ollie Pickering, cf	3	0	0	0
Harry Davis, 1b	3	0	0	0
Lave Cross, 3b	3	0	0	0
Socks Seybold, rf	3	0	0	0
Danny Murphy, 2b	3	0	0	0
Monte Cross, ss	3	0	0	0
Ossee Schreckengost, c	3	0	0	0
Rube Waddell, p	3	0	0	0
Totals	27	0	0	0

Boston Pilgrims	AB	R	H	RBI
Patsy Dougherty, lf	4	0	1	—
Jimmy Collins, 3b	4	0	2	—
Chick Stahl, cf	4	1	1	—
Buck Freeman, rf	4	0	1	—
Freddy Parent, ss	4	0	2	—
Candy LaChance, 1b	3	0	1	—
Hobe Ferris, 2b	3	1	1	—
Lou Criger, c	3	1	1	—
Cy Young, p	3	0	0	—
Totals	32	3	10	—

	1	2	3	4	5	6	7	8	9	R	H	E
Phi	0	0	0	0	0	0	0	0	0	0	0	1
Bos	0	0	0	0	0	1	2	0	x	3	10	0

E—Davis. DP—Philadelphia 2. LOB—Philadelphia 0, Boston 5. 2B—Collins, Criger. 3B—Stahl, Freeman, Ferris. SF—LaChance.

Philadelphia Athletics	IP	H	R	ER	BB	SO
Rube Waddell (L)	8.0	10	3	—	—	6

Boston Pilgrims	IP	H	R	ER	BB	SO
Cy Young (W)	9.0	0	0	0	0	8

Time—1:23. Umpire—Dwyer.

September 23, 1908

The New York Giants apparently defeat the Cubs on Al Bridwell's RBI single in the ninth, but baserunner Fred Merkle is called out for not touching second base. In the chaos that ensues, the game is called and declared a tie. Chicago wins the makeup game on October 8 to win the pennant.

Chicago Cubs	AB	R	H	RBI
Jack Hayden, rf	4	0	0	0
Johnny Evers, 2b	4	0	1	0
Wildfire Schulte, lf	4	0	0	0
Frank Chance, 1b	4	0	1	0
Harry Steinfeldt, 3b	2	0	0	0
Solly Hofman, cf	3	0	1	0
Joe Tinker, ss	3	1	1	1
Johnny Kling, c	3	0	1	0
Jack Pfiester, p	3	0	0	0
Totals	30	1	5	1

New York Giants	AB	R	H	RBI
Buck Herzog, 2b	3	1	1	0
Roger Bresnahan, c	3	0	0	0
Mike Donlin, rf	4	0	1	1
Cy Seymour, cf	4	0	1	0
Art Devlin, 3b	4	0	2	0
Moose McCormick, lf	3	0	0	0
Fred Merkle, 1b	3	0	1	0
Al Bridwell, ss	4	0	0	0
Christy Mathewson, p	3	0	0	0
Totals	31	1	6	1

	1	2	3	4	5	6	7	8	9		R	H	E
ChN	0	0	0	1	0	0	0	0	0		1	5	3
NYG	0	0	0	0	1	0	0	0	0		1	6	0

E—Tinker 2, Steinfeldt. DP—Chicago 3, New York 1. LOB—Chicago 3, New York 7. HR—Tinker. SF—Bresnahan.

Chicago Cubs	IP	H	R	ER	BB	SO
Jack Pfiester	9.0	6	1	0	2	0

New York Giants	IP	H	R	ER	BB	SO
Christy Mathewson	9.0	5	1	1	0	9

HBP—McCormick by Pfiester. Time—1:30. Attendance—20,000. Umpires—HP, O'Day. Bases, Emslie.

September 26, 1908

Chicago's Ed Reulbach becomes the only pitcher ever to throw two shutouts in one day, blanking the Brooklyn Dodgers 5-0 and 3-0. The wins are part of a 44-inning scoreless streak for Reulbach.

Chicago Cubs	AB	R	H	RBI
Jack Hayden, rf	4	0	0	1
Johnny Evers, 2b	4	1	2	1
Wildfire Schulte, lf	4	0	0	0
Frank Chance, 1b	4	0	0	0
Harry Steinfeldt, 3b	4	1	3	1
Solly Hofman, cf	4	0	1	1
Joe Tinker, ss	4	1	1	0
Johnny Kling, c	4	2	3	1
Ed Reulbach, p	2	0	0	0
Totals	34	5	10	5

Brooklyn Dodgers	AB	R	H	RBI
Tom Catterson, lf	4	0	0	0
Harry Lumley, rf	4	0	0	0
John Hummel, 2b	4	0	1	0
Tim Jordan, 1b	3	0	0	0
Al Burch, cf	4	0	0	0
Tommy McMillan, ss	3	0	1	0
Tommy Sheehan, 3b	3	0	1	0
Joe Dunn, c	3	0	2	0
Kaiser Wilhelm, p	3	0	0	0
Totals	31	0	5	0

	1	2	3	4	5	6	7	8	9		R	H	E
ChN	0	0	0	0	1	0	1	2	1		5	10	0
Bro	0	0	0	0	0	0	0	0	0		0	5	4

E—McMillan 2, Hummel, Sheehan. LOB—Chicago 7, Brooklyn 5. 2B—Evers, Kling. SH—Hayden, Evers, Schulte, Reulbach. SB—Steinfeldt. CS—Steinfeldt, Burch.

Chicago Cubs	IP	H	R	ER	BB	SO
Ed Reulbach (W)	9.0	5	0	0	1	7

Brooklyn Dodgers	IP	H	R	ER	BB	SO
Kaiser Wilhelm (L)	9.0	10	5	4	1	5

Time—1:40. Umpires—HP, Owens. Bases, Emslie.

September 26, 1908

Chicago Cubs	AB	R	H	RBI
Jack Hayden, rf	4	1	1	0
Johnny Evers, 2b	4	0	1	0
Wildfire Schulte, lf	2	0	1	0
Frank Chance, 1b	4	0	0	0
Harry Steinfeldt, 3b	4	0	0	0
Solly Hofman, cf	3	0	0	0
Joe Tinker, ss	3	0	0	0
Johnny Kling, c	3	1	2	0
Ed Reulbach, p	1	1	0	1
Totals	28	3	5	1

Brooklyn Dodgers	AB	R	H	RBI
Tom Catterson, lf	4	0	1	0
Harry Lumley, rf	4	0	2	0
John Hummel, 2b	4	0	0	0
Tim Jordan, 1b	3	0	0	0
Al Burch, cf	3	0	0	0
Tommy McMillan, ss	3	0	0	0
Tommy Sheehan, 3b	3	0	0	0
Joe Dunn, c	3	0	0	0
Jim Pastorius, p	2	0	0	0
Harry Pattee, ph	1	0	0	0
Totals	30	0	3	0

	1	2	3	4	5	6	7	8	9		R	H	E
ChN	0	0	1	0	0	0	0	2	0		3	5	1
Bro	0	0	0	0	0	0	0	0	0		0	3	3

E—Reulbach, McMillan, Dunn 2. DP—Chicago 1, Brooklyn 1. LOB—Chicago 2, Brooklyn 3. SH—Reulbach. SB—Schulte. CS—Hayden, Schulte.

Chicago Cubs	IP	H	R	ER	BB	SO
Ed Reulbach (W)	9.0	3	0	0	1	4

Brooklyn Dodgers	IP	H	R	ER	BB	SO
Jim Pastorius (L)	9.0	5	3	1	3	2

WP—Reulbach, Pastorius. Time—1:12. Attendance—15,000. Umpires—HP, Emslie. Bases, Owens.

October 2, 1908

Cleveland Bronchos ace Addie Joss pitches the fourth perfect game in major league history, and Ed Walsh of the White Sox also shines in defeat. Walsh fans 15 and allows just four hits, but takes a 1-0 loss.

Chicago White Sox	AB	R	H	RBI
Ed Hahn, rf	3	0	0	0
Fielder Jones, cf	3	0	0	0
Frank Isbell, 1b	3	0	0	0
Patsy Dougherty, lf	3	0	0	0
George Davis, 2b	3	0	0	0
Freddy Parent, ss	3	0	0	0
Ossee Schreckengost, c	2	0	0	0
Al Shaw, c	0	0	0	0
Doc White, ph	1	0	0	0
Lee Tannehill, 3b	2	0	0	0
Jiggs Donahue, ph	1	0	0	0
Ed Walsh, p	2	0	0	0
John Anderson, ph	1	0	0	0
Totals	27	0	0	0

Cleveland Bronchos	AB	R	H	RBI
Wilbur Good, rf	4	0	0	0
Bill Bradley, 3b	4	0	0	0
Bill Hinchman, lf	3	0	0	0
Nap Lajoie, 2b	3	0	1	0
George Stovall, 1b	3	0	0	0
Nig Clarke, c	3	0	0	0
Joe Birmingham, cf	4	1	2	0
George Perring, ss	2	0	1	0
Addie Joss, p	3	0	0	0
Totals	29	1	4	0

	1	2	3	4	5	6	7	8	9		R	H	E
ChA	0	0	0	0	0	0	0	0	0		0	0	1
Cle	0	0	1	0	0	0	0	0	x		1	4	0

E—Isbell. LOB—Chicago 0, Cleveland 4. SB—Birmingham 2, Lajoie, Perring.

Chicago White Sox	IP	H	R	ER	BB	SO
Ed Walsh (L)	9.0	4	1	0	1	15

Cleveland Bronchos	IP	H	R	ER	BB	SO
Addie Joss (W)	9.0	0	0	0	0	3

WP—Walsh. Time—1:40. Umpires—HP, Connolly. Bases, O'Loughlin.

September 11, 1912

Philadelphia Athletics second baseman Eddie Collins becomes the first player in modern baseball history to steal six bases in one game. Eleven days later he repeats the feat, which isn't equalled for 79 years.

Philadelphia Athletics	AB	R	H	RBI
Eddie Murphy, rf	5	2	3	2
Harl Maggert, cf	5	1	1	0
Eddie Collins, 2b	5	2	3	1
Home Run Baker, 3b	3	0	0	0
Stuffy McInnis, 1b	4	1	1	0
Jimmy Walsh, lf	5	1	3	0
Jack Barry, ss	4	1	1	0
Ben Egan, c	3	1	2	1
Byron Houck, p	3	0	0	0
Stan Coveleski, p	0	0	0	0
Eddie Plank, p	0	0	0	0
Totals	37	9	14	4

Detroit Tigers	AB	R	H	RBI
Donie Bush, ss	1	1	0	0
Charlie Deal, 3b	1	1	1	1
Red Corriden, 3b-ss	4	1	2	0
Sam Crawford, rf	3	0	0	2
Ty Cobb, cf	4	0	2	0
Bobby Veach, lf	4	1	2	1
Baldy Louden, 2b	3	1	1	0
Eddie Onslow, 1b	4	1	1	0
Brad Kocher, c	4	0	1	1
Joe Lake, p	3	0	0	0
Davy Jones, ph	1	1	1	1
Totals	32	7	11	6

	1	2	3	4	5	6	7	8	9		R	H	E
Phi	0	1	1	4	1	0	1	1	0		9	14	2
Det	2	0	0	1	0	0	0	0	4		7	11	6

E—Egan, Houck, Bush, Corriden, Louden, Onslow, Kocher, Lake. DP—Philadelphia 1. LOB—Philadelphia 8, Detroit 6. 2B—Walsh, Louden, Kocher. SH—Houck. SF—Crawford 2, Veach. SB—Collins 6, Maggert 2, Cobb 2, Murphy, Baker, McInnis, Louden. CS—Baker, Cobb.

Philadelphia Athletics	IP	H	R	ER	BB	SO
Byron Houck (W)	8.1	10	5	5	3	2
Stan Coveleski	0.0	0	0	0	1	0
Eddie Plank	0.2	1	2	2	0	0

Detroit Tigers	IP	H	R	ER	BB	SO
Joe Lake (L)	9.0	14	9	5	6	4

Coveleski pitched to one batter in the 9th.

HBP—Cobb by Houck. WP—Houck, Plank. Time—2:32. Attendance—4,342. Umpires—HP, Connolly. Bases, Hart.

May 2, 1917

In the best pitchers' duel ever, Cincinnati's Fred Toney and Chicago's Hippo Vaughn both throw no-hitters for nine innings. The Reds get two hits and an unearned run in the top of the 10th when 1912 Olympic gold medalist Jim Thorpe drives in the game's lone run. Toney goes on to complete his gem.

Cincinnati Reds	AB	R	H	RBI
Heine Groh, 3b	1	0	0	0
Gus Getz, 3b	1	0	0	0
Larry Kopf, ss	4	1	1	0
Greasy Neale, cf	4	0	0	0
Hal Chase, 1b	4	0	0	0
Jim Thorpe, rf	4	0	1	1
Dave Shean, 2b	3	0	0	0
Manuel Cueto, lf	3	0	0	0
Emil Huhn, c	3	0	0	0
Fred Toney, p	3	0	0	0
Totals	30	1	2	1

Chicago Cubs	AB	R	H	RBI
Rollie Zeider, ss	4	0	0	0
Harry Wolter, rf	4	0	0	0
Larry Doyle, 2b	4	0	0	0
Fred Merkle, 1b	4	0	0	0
Cy Williams, cf	2	0	0	0
Les Mann, lf	3	0	0	0
Art Wilson, c	3	0	0	0
Charlie Deal, 3b	3	0	0	0
Hippo Vaughn, p	3	0	0	0
Totals	30	0	0	0

	1	2	3	4	5	6	7	8	9	10		R	H	E
Cin	0	0	0	0	0	0	0	0	0	1		1	2	0
ChN	0	0	0	0	0	0	0	0	0	0		0	0	1

E—Zeider, Williams. DP—Chicago 2. LOB—Cincinnati 1, Chicago 2. SB—Chase. CS—Neale.

Cincinnati Reds	IP	H	R	ER	BB	SO
Fred Toney (W)	10.0	0	0	0	2	3

Chicago Cubs	IP	H	R	ER	BB	SO
Hippo Vaughn (L)	10.0	2	1	0	2	10

Time—1:45. Attendance—2,500. Umpires—HP, Orth. Bases, Rigler.

May 1, 1920

The longest game in big league history ends in a 1-1 tie when darkness descends on Braves Field. Brooklyn's Leon Cadore and Boston's Joe Oeschger go the distance on the mound, while the Braves' Charlie Pick goes 0-for-11.

Brooklyn Dodgers	AB	R	H	RBI
Ivy Olson, 2b	10	0	1	1
Bernie Neis, rf	10	0	1	0
Jimmy Johnston, 3b	10	0	2	0
Zack Wheat, lf	9	0	2	0
Hi Myers, cf	2	0	1	0
Wally Hood, cf	6	0	1	0
Ed Konetchy, 1b	9	0	1	0
Chuck Ward, ss	10	0	0	0
Ernie Krueger, c	2	1	0	0
Rowdy Elliott, c	7	0	0	0
Leon Cadore, p	10	0	0	0
Totals	85	1	9	1

Boston Braves	AB	R	H	RBI
Ray Powell, cf	7	0	1	0
Charlie Pick, 2b	11	0	0	0
Les Mann, lf	10	0	2	0
Walton Cruise, rf	9	1	1	0
Walter Holke, 1b	10	0	2	0
Tony Boeckel, 3b	11	0	3	1
Rabbit Maranville, ss	10	0	3	0
Mickey O'Neil, c	2	0	0	0
Lloyd Christenbury, ph	1	0	1	0
Hank Gowdy, c	6	0	1	0
Joe Oeschger, p	9	0	1	0
Totals	86	1	15	1

	1	2	3	4	5	6	7	8	9	10	11	12	13	14	15
Bro	0	0	0	0	1	0	0	0	0	0	0	0	0	0	0
Bos	0	0	0	0	0	1	0	0	0	0	0	0	0	0	0

	16	17	18	19	20	21	22	23	24	25	26	R	H	E
Bro	0	0	0	0	0	0	0	0	0	0	0	1	9	2
Bos	0	0	0	0	0	0	0	0	0	0	0	1	15	2

E—Pick 2, Olson, Ward. DP—Brooklyn 1, Boston 1. LOB—Brooklyn 11, Boston 17. 2B—Maranville, Oeschger. 3B—Cruise. SH—Hood, Powell, Holke, O'Neil, Cruise, Oeschger. SB—Myers, Hood. CS—Myers, Boeckel.

Brooklyn Dodgers	IP	H	R	ER	BB	SO
Leon Cadore	26.0	15	1	1	5	7

Boston Braves	IP	H	R	ER	BB	SO
Joe Oeschger	26.0	9	1	1	4	7

WP—Oeschger. Time—3:50. Attendance—4,500. Umpires—HP, McCormick. Bases, Hart.

April 30, 1922

In the most unlikely perfect game in big league history, White Sox rookie Charlie Robertson befuddles the Tigers. Chicago center fielder Johnny Mostil plays his only game ever in left and makes two great catches. Robertson goes on to win only 49 games in his career, the fewest of any pitcher who ever authored a perfect game. He fails to post a winning record in any of his eight major league seasons.

Chicago White Sox	AB	R	H	RBI
Joe Mulligan, ss	4	0	1	—
Harvey McClellan, 3b	3	0	1	—
Eddie Collins, 2b	3	0	1	—
Harry Hooper, rf	3	1	0	—
Johnny Mostil, lf	4	1	1	—
Amos Strunk, cf	3	0	0	—
Earl Sheely, 1b	4	0	2	—
Ray Schalk, c	4	0	1	—
Charlie Robertson, p	4	0	0	—
Totals	32	2	7	—

Detroit Tigers	AB	R	H	RBI
Lu Blue, 1b	3	0	0	0
George Cutshaw, 2b	3	0	0	0
Ty Cobb, cf	3	0	0	0
Bobby Veach, lf	3	0	0	0
Harry Heilmann, rf	3	0	0	0
Bob Jones, 3b	3	0	0	0
Topper Rigney, ss	2	0	0	0
Danny Clark, ph	1	0	0	0
Clyde Manion, c	3	0	0	0
Herman Pillette, p	2	0	0	0
Johnny Bassler, ph	1	0	0	0
Totals	27	0	0	0

	1	2	3	4	5	6	7	8	9	R	H	E
ChA	0	2	0	0	0	0	0	0	0	2	7	0
Det	0	0	0	0	0	0	0	0	0	0	0	1

E—Blue. LOB—Chicago 8, Detroit 0. 2B—Mulligan, Sheely. SH—McClellan, Collins, Strunk.

Chicago White Sox	IP	H	R	ER	BB	SO
Charlie Robertson (W)	9.0	0	0	0	0	6

Detroit Tigers	IP	H	R	ER	BB	SO
Herman Pillette (L)	9.0	7	2	—	2	5

Time—1:55. Umpires—HP, Nallin. Bases, Evans.

August 25, 1922

In the highest scoring game in major league history, the Cubs outlast the Phillies 26-23. Chicago center fielder Cliff Heathcote becomes the first 20th-century player to reach base safely seven times in one game. The Cubs nearly blow a 26-9 lead when Philadelphia tallies 14 runs in the final two frames.

Philadelphia Phillies	AB	R	H	RBI
Russ Wrightstone, 3b	7	3	4	4
Frank Parkinson, 2b	4	1	2	2
Cy Williams, cf	3	1	0	0
Bevo LeBourveau, cf	4	2	3	2
Tilly Walker, rf	6	2	4	1
Johnny Mokan, lf	4	2	3	2
Art Fletcher, ss	3	1	0	0
Jimmy Smith, ss	4	2	1	2
Roy Leslie, 1b	1	1	0	1
Cliff Lee, 1b	4	4	3	0
Butch Henline, c	2	1	2	0
Frank Withrow, c	4	1	2	3
Jimmy Ring, p	2	0	1	1
Lefty Weinert, p	4	2	1	1
Goldie Rapp, ph	0	0	0	0
Totals	52	23	26	19

Chicago Cubs	AB	R	H	RBI
Cliff Heathcote, cf	5	5	5	4
Charlie Hollocher, ss	5	2	3	6
John Kelleher, ss	1	0	0	0
Zeb Terry, 2b	5	2	2	2
Bernie Friberg, 2b	1	0	1	0
Ray Grimes, 1b	4	2	2	2
Marty Callaghan, rf	7	3	2	1
Hack Miller, lf	5	3	4	6
Marty Krug, 3b	5	4	4	1
Bob O'Farrell, c	3	3	2	2
Gabby Hartnett, c	0	0	0	0
Tony Kaufmann, p	2	0	0	0
Turner Barber, ph	1	2	0	0
George Stueland, p	1	0	0	0
George Maisel, ph	1	0	0	0
Uel Eubanks, p	0	0	0	0
Ed Morris, p	0	0	0	0
Tiny Osborne, p	0	0	0	0
Totals	46	26	25	24

	1	2	3	4	5	6	7	8	9	R	H	E
Phi	0	3	2	1	3	0	0	8	6	23	26	4
ChN	1	10	0	14	0	1	0	0	x	26	25	5

E—Wrightstone, Williams, Walker, Lee, Heathcote, Hollocher, Callaghan, Krug, Hartnett. DP—Philadelphia 3. LOB—Philadelphia 16, Chicago 9. 2B—Heathcote 2, Krug 2, Parkinson, Walker, Mokan, Withrow, Hollocher, Terry, Friberg, Grimes. 3B—Wrightstone, Walker. HR—Miller 2, O'Farrell. SH—Parkinson, Walker, O'Farrell. SF—Leslie, Hollocher. SB—Weinert, Hollocher. CS—Williams.

Philadelphia Phillies	IP	H	R	ER	BB	SO
Jimmy Ring (L)	3.1	12	16	6	5	2
Lefty Weinert	4.2	14	10	5	5	2

Chicago Cubs	IP	H	R	ER	BB	SO
Tony Kaufmann (W)	4.0	9	6	3	3	0
George Stueland	3.0	7	3	3	2	1
Uel Eubanks	0.2	3	8	4	3	0
Ed Morris	0.1	4	4	4	1	1
Tiny Osborne	1.0	3	2	2	2	3

HBP—Grimes by Weinert. WP—Stueland. Time—3:01. Attendance—7,100. Umpires—HP, Hart. Bases, Rigler.

September 16, 1924

Cardinals first baseman Jim Bottomley becomes the first major league player ever to drive in 12 runs in a game. He collects six hits, including two home runs, in a 17-3 rout of the Brooklyn Dodgers.

St. Louis Cardinals	AB	R	H	RBI
Heinie Mueller, rf-1b	3	3	2	1
Taylor Douthit, cf	3	3	1	0
Rogers Hornsby, 2b	4	2	2	0
Ray Blades, 2b	0	1	0	0
Jim Bottomley, 1b	6	3	6	12
Jack Smith, rf	0	0	0	0
Chick Hafey, lf	6	1	2	0
Mike Gonzalez, c	4	1	1	1
Verne Clemons, c	2	0	0	0
Specs Toporcer, 3b	1	0	0	0
Jimmy Cooney, 3b	4	0	1	1
Tommy Thevenow, ss	5	0	0	0
Bill Sherdel, p	4	3	3	0
Flint Rhem, p	0	0	0	0
Totals	42	17	18	17

Brooklyn Dodgers	AB	R	H	RBI
Andy High, 2b	4	0	2	0
Johnny Mitchell, ss	4	0	1	0
Zack Wheat, lf	4	0	0	0
Jack Fournier, 1b	2	1	0	0
Dick Loftus, 1b	1	0	0	0
Eddie Brown, cf	4	0	1	0
Milt Stock, 3b	3	1	1	0
Tommy Griffith, rf	2	0	0	0
Hank DeBerry, c	3	0	1	1
Rube Ehrhardt, p	0	0	0	0
Bonnie Hollingsworth, p	1	0	0	0
Art Decatur, p	0	0	0	0
Jimmy Johnston, ph	1	0	1	0
Tex Wilson, p	0	0	0	0
Zack Taylor, ph	1	1	1	0
Jim Roberts, p	0	0	0	0
Charlie Hargreaves, ph	1	0	0	0
Totals	31	3	9	1

	1	2	3	4	5	6	7	8	9	R	H	E
StL	4	1	0	4	0	4	2	1	1	17	18	0
Bro	0	1	0	0	0	0	0	1	1	3	9	1

E—Fournier. DP—St. Louis 3. LOB—St. Louis 7, Brooklyn 6. 2B—Bottomley, Sherdel. 3B—Mueller, Hornsby, Hafey, Gonzalez. HR—Bottomley 2. SH—Douthit 2, Hornsby. SB—Douthit, Cooney.

St. Louis Cardinals	IP	H	R	ER	BB	SO
Bill Sherdel (W)	8.0	8	2	2	2	1
Flint Rhem	1.0	1	1	0	3	0

Brooklyn Dodgers	IP	H	R	ER	BB	SO
Rube Ehrhardt (L)	0.0	4	4	4	1	0
Bonnie Hollingsworth	3.0	2	3	3	3	2
Art Decatur	3.0	6	6	5	2	0
Tex Wilson	2.0	4	3	3	3	1
Jim Roberts	1.0	2	1	1	1	0

WP—Rhem, Decatur. Time—1:55. Attendance—3,000. Umpires—HP, Klem. Bases, Wilson.

September 30, 1927

Yankees right fielder Babe Ruth snaps a 2-2 tie in the eighth with his 60th home run of the season, breaking his own record. It will endure until 1961. In the ninth, Walter Johnson pinch-hits in his final playing appearance.

Washington Senators	AB	R	H	RBI
Sam Rice, rf	3	0	1	0
Bucky Harris, 2b	3	0	0	0
Babe Ganzel, cf	4	0	1	0
Goose Goslin, lf	4	1	1	0
Joe Judge, 1b	4	0	0	0
Muddy Ruel, c	2	1	1	0
Ossie Bluege, 3b	3	0	1	1
Grant Gillis, ss	4	0	0	0
Tom Zachary, p	2	0	0	0
Walter Johnson, ph	1	0	0	0
Totals	30	2	5	2

New York Yankees	AB	R	H	RBI
Earle Combs, cf	4	0	0	0
Mark Koenig, ss	4	1	1	0
Babe Ruth, rf	3	3	3	2
Lou Gehrig, 1b	4	0	2	0
Bob Meusel, lf	3	0	1	2
Tony Lazzeri, 2b	3	0	0	0
Joe Dugan, 3b	3	0	1	0
Benny Bengough, c	3	0	1	0
George Pipgras, p	2	0	0	0
Herb Pennock, p	1	0	0	0
Totals	30	4	9	4

	1	2	3	4	5	6	7	8	9	R	H	E
Was	0	0	0	2	0	0	0	0	0	2	5	0
NYA	0	0	0	1	0	1	0	2	x	4	9	1

E—Gehrig. DP—Washington 2. LOB—Washington 7, New York 4. 2B—Rice. 3B—Koenig. HR—Ruth. SF—Meusel. SB—Rice, Ruel, Bluege.

Washington Senators	IP	H	R	ER	BB	SO
Tom Zachary (L)	8.0	9	4	4	1	1

New York Yankees	IP	H	R	ER	BB	SO
George Pipgras	6.0	4	2	2	4	0
Herb Pennock (W)	3.0	1	0	0	1	0

HBP—Rice by Pipgras. Attendance—8,000. Umpires—HP, Dinneen. 1B, Connolly. 2B, Owens.

June 3, 1932

Yankees first baseman Lou Gehrig becomes the first American Leaguer and first modern player to swat four home runs in one game. The feat is overshadowed by the retirement of New York Giants manager John McGraw.

New York Yankees	AB	R	H	RBI
Earle Combs, cf	5	2	3	1
Jack Saltzgaver, 2b	4	1	1	1
Babe Ruth, lf	5	2	2	1
Myril Hoag, lf	0	1	0	0
Lou Gehrig, 1b	6	4	4	6
Ben Chapman, rf	5	3	2	1
Bill Dickey, c	4	2	2	1
Tony Lazzeri, 3b	6	3	5	6
Frankie Crosetti, ss	6	1	2	2
Johnny Allen, p	2	0	0	0
Gordon Rhodes, p	1	0	1	0
Jumbo Brown, p	1	0	0	0
Lefty Gomez, p	1	1	1	0
Totals	46	20	23	19

Philadelphia Athletics	AB	R	H	RBI
Max Bishop, 2b	4	2	2	0
Doc Cramer, cf	5	1	1	3
Oscar Roettger, ph	1	0	0	0
Bing Miller, lf	0	0	0	0
Mickey Cochrane, c	5	1	1	2
Dib Williams, ph	1	0	0	0
Al Simmons, lf-rf	4	2	0	0
Jimmie Foxx, 1b	3	3	2	1
Ed Coleman, rf	6	2	2	3
Eric McNair, ss	5	1	3	2
Jimmy Dykes, 3b	4	1	1	0
George Earnshaw, p	2	0	0	0
Mule Haas, ph	1	0	1	0
Roy Mahaffey, p	0	0	0	0
Rube Walberg, p	0	0	0	0
Lew Krausse, p	0	0	0	0
Ed Madjeski, ph	1	0	0	0
Eddie Rommel, p	0	0	0	0
Totals	42	13	13	11

	1	2	3	4	5	6	7	8	9	R	H	E
NYA	2	0	0	2	3	2	3	2	6	20	23	5
Phi	2	0	0	6	0	2	0	2	1	13	13	1

E—Crosetti 2, Ruth, Gehrig, Earnshaw, Allen. DP—Philadelphia 3. LOB—New York 6, Philadelphia 11. 2B—Ruth, Lazzeri, Coleman, McNair. 3B—Chapman, Lazzeri, Bishop, Cramer, Foxx. HR—Gehrig 4, Combs, Ruth, Lazzeri, Cochrane, Foxx. SH—Saltzgaver, Bishop. SB—Lazzeri. CS—Dickey.

New York Yankees	IP	H	R	ER	BB	SO
Johnny Allen	3.2	7	8	4	5	2
Gordon Rhodes	1.1	1	2	2	2	0
Jumbo Brown (W)	2.0	3	2	1	1	0
Lefty Gomez	2.0	2	1	1	0	1

Philadelphia Athletics	IP	H	R	ER	BB	SO
George Earnshaw	5.0	8	7	6	2	8
Roy Mahaffey (L)	1.0	6	4	4	0	0
Rube Walberg	1.0	2	1	1	1	0
Lew Krausse	1.0	4	2	2	0	0
Eddie Rommel	1.0	3	6	6	3	0

WP—Rhodes. Time—2:55. Attendance—5,000. Umpires—HP, Geisel. 1B, McGowan. 2B, Van Graflan.

July 10, 1932

Cleveland's Johnny Burnett becomes the only major leaguer ever to collect nine hits in one game, but the Indians lose 18-17 in 18 innings to Philadelphia. Eddie Rommel pitches 17 innings of relief to earn the win despite yielding a record 29 hits.

Philadelphia Athletics	AB	R	H	RBI
Mule Haas, rf	9	3	2	0
Doc Cramer, cf	8	2	2	1
Jimmy Dykes, 3b	10	2	3	4
Al Simmons, lf	9	4	5	2
Jimmie Foxx, 1b	9	4	6	8
Eric McNair, ss	10	0	2	1
Johnny Heving, c	4	0	0	0
Ed Madjeski, c	5	0	0	0
Dib Williams, 2b	8	1	2	0
Lew Krausse, p	1	0	0	0
Eddie Rommel, p	7	2	3	1
Totals	80	18	25	17

Cleveland Indians	AB	R	H	RBI
Dick Porter, rf	10	3	3	2
Johnny Burnett, ss	11	4	9	2
Earl Averill, cf	9	3	5	4
Joe Vosmik, lf	10	2	2	1
Eddie Morgan, 1b	11	1	5	4
Glenn Myatt, c	7	2	1	0
Bill Cissell, 2b	9	1	4	3
Willie Kamm, 3b	7	1	2	0
Clint Brown, p	4	0	2	0
Willis Hudlin, p	0	0	0	0
Wes Ferrell, p	5	0	0	0
Totals	83	17	33	16

	1	2	3	4	5	6	7	8	9	10	11	12	13	14	15
Phi	2	0	1	2	0	1	7	0	2	0	0	0	0	0	0
Cle	3	0	3	0	1	1	6	0	1	0	0	0	0	0	0

	16	17	18		R	H	E
Phi	2	0	1		18	25	0
Cle	2	0	0		17	33	5

E—Cissell 2, Rommel, Burnett, Morgan, Brown. DP—Philadelphia 2, Cleveland 2. LOB—Philadelphia 15, Cleveland 24. 2B—Burnett 2, Morgan 2, Haas, Dykes, Foxx, McNair, Porter, Vosmik, Myatt, Cissell, Kamm. HR—Foxx 3, Averill. SH—Kamm, Ferrell. SB—Cissell.

Philadelphia Athletics	IP	H	R	ER	BB	SO
Lew Krausse	1.0	4	3	3	1	0
Eddie Rommel (W)	17.0	29	14	13	9	7

Cleveland Indians	IP	H	R	ER	BB	SO
Clint Brown	6.2	13	8	7	1	3
Willis Hudlin	0.0	0	2	2	2	0
Wes Ferrell (L)	11.1	12	8	6	4	7

Hudlin pitched to two batters in the 7th.

WP—Rommel 2. Time—4:05. Attendance—10,000. Umpires—HP, Hildebrand. Bases, Owens.

May 24, 1935

The Reds host the first major league night game and defeat the Phillies 2-1. The game at Crosley Field begins with President Roosevelt flipping a switch at the White House that turns on the 600 lights at the ballpark.

Philadelphia Phillies	AB	R	H	RBI
Lou Chiozza, 2b	4	0	0	0
Ethan Allen, cf	4	0	1	0
Johnny Moore, rf	4	0	1	0
Dolph Camilli, 1b	4	0	1	0
Johnny Vergez, 3b	4	0	1	0
Al Todd, c	3	1	1	0
George Watkins, lf	3	0	0	0
Mickey Haslin, ss	3	0	1	0
Joe Bowman, p	2	0	0	1
Jimmie Wilson, ph	1	0	0	0
Jim Bivin, p	0	0	0	0
Totals	32	1	6	1

Cincinnati Reds	AB	R	H	RBI
Billy Myers, ss	3	1	1	0
Lew Riggs, 3b	4	0	0	0
Ival Goodman, rf	3	0	0	1
Joe Sullivan, 1b	3	1	2	0
Harlin Pool, lf	3	0	1	0
Gilly Campbell, c	3	0	0	1
Sammy Byrd, cf	3	0	0	0
Alex Kampouris, 2b	3	0	0	0
Paul Derringer, p	3	0	0	0
Totals	28	2	4	2

	1	2	3	4	5	6	7	8	9		R	H	E
Phi	0	0	0	0	1	0	0	0	0		1	6	0
Cin	1	0	0	1	0	0	0	0	x		2	4	0

DP—Cincinnati 1. LOB—Philadelphia 4, Cincinnati 3. 2B—Myers. SB—Vergez, Bowman, Myers.

Philadelphia Phillies	IP	H	R	ER	BB	SO
Joe Bowman (L)	7.0	4	2	2	1	1
Jim Bivin	1.0	0	0	0	0	1

Cincinnati Reds	IP	H	R	ER	BB	SO
Paul Derringer (W)	9.0	6	1	1	0	3

Time—1:55. Umpires—HP, Klem. 1B, Sears. 3B, Pinelli.

July 10, 1936

Phillies right fielder Chuck Klein becomes the first player in modern National League history to homer four times in a game, and he needs extra innings to do it. His 10th-inning shot off Bill Swift wins the game 9-6.

Philadelphia Phillies	AB	R	H	RBI
Ernie Sulik, cf	5	1	1	0
Johnny Moore, lf	5	1	1	0
Chuck Klein, rf	5	4	4	6
Dolph Camilli, 1b	4	2	1	0
Bill Atwood, c	4	0	1	0
Jimmie Wilson, c	0	1	0	0
Lou Chiozza, 3b	5	0	2	1
Leo Norris, ss	4	0	1	2
Chile Gomez, 2b	5	0	0	0
Claude Passeau, p	4	0	1	0
Bucky Walters, p	0	0	0	0
Totals	41	9	12	9

Pittsburgh Pirates	AB	R	H	RBI
Woody Jensen, lf	4	1	1	0
Lloyd Waner, cf	4	1	1	1
Paul Waner, rf	4	2	2	1
Arky Vaughan, ss	5	0	1	1
Gus Suhr, 1b	4	0	2	1
Bill Brubaker, 3b	5	0	0	0
Pep Young, 2b	3	0	1	0
Cookie Lavagetto, 2b	1	0	0	0
Al Todd, c	2	0	0	0
Tom Padden, c	2	1	0	0
Jim Weaver, p	1	0	0	0
Red Lucas, ph	1	0	0	0
Mace Brown, p	1	0	0	0
Fred Schulte, ph	1	0	1	1
Hal Finney, pr	0	0	0	0
Bill Swift, p	0	0	0	0
Totals	38	6	9	5

	1	2	3	4	5	6	7	8	9	10		R	H	E
Phi	4	0	0	0	1	0	1	0	0	3		9	12	2
Pit	0	0	0	1	0	3	0	0	2	0		6	9	4

E—Norris 2, Vaughan 2, LWaner, Young. DP—Philadelphia 3, Pittsburgh 1. LOB—Philadelphia 5, Pittsburgh 7. 2B—Camilli. 3B—Suhr. HR—Klein 4. SH—Atwood, Norris.

Philadelphia Phillies	IP	H	R	ER	BB	SO
Claude Passeau	8.2	8	6	4	2	1
Bucky Walters (W)	1.1	1	0	0	3	0

Pittsburgh Pirates	IP	H	R	ER	BB	SO
Jim Weaver	5.0	6	5	4	1	2
Mace Brown	4.0	2	1	1	0	1
Bill Swift (L)	1.0	4	3	2	0	0

Time—2:15. Attendance—2,500. Umpires—HP, Sears. 1B, Klem. 2B, Ballanfant.

June 11, 1938

In his first full season in the major leagues, Johnny Vander Meer no-hits the Boston Braves 3-0. His three strikeouts increase his National League-leading total to 56.

Boston Braves	AB	R	H	RBI
Gene Moore, rf	1	0	0	0
Elbie Fletcher, 1b	1	0	0	0
Ray Mueller, ph	1	0	0	0
Johnny Cooney, 1b-rf	3	0	0	0
Vince DiMaggio, cf	3	0	0	0
Tony Cuccinello, 2b	2	0	0	0
Bobby Reis, lf	3	0	0	0
Gil English, 3b	2	0	0	0
Johnny Riddle, c	3	0	0	0
Rabbit Warstler, ss	2	0	0	0
Bob Kahle, ph	1	0	0	0
Danny MacFayden, p	2	0	0	0
Harl Maggert, ph	1	0	0	0
Totals	25	0	0	0

Cincinnati Reds	AB	R	H	RBI
Lonny Frey, 2b	4	0	0	0
Wally Berger, lf	3	2	1	0
Ival Goodman, rf	3	0	0	1
Frank McCormick, 1b	4	0	1	0
Ernie Lombardi, c	4	1	2	2
Harry Craft, cf	3	0	0	0
Lew Riggs, 3b	3	0	1	0
Billy Myers, ss	3	0	0	0
Johnny Vander Meer, p	3	0	1	0
Totals	30	3	6	3

	1	2	3	4	5	6	7	8	9	R	H	E
Bos	0	0	0	0	0	0	0	0	0	0	0	1
Cin	0	0	0	1	0	2	0	0	x	3	6	0

E—Cuccinello. DP—Boston 1, Cincinnati 1. 3B—Berger, Riggs. HR—Lombardi.

Boston Braves	IP	H	R	ER	BB	SO
Danny MacFayden (L)	8.0	6	3	3	1	4

Cincinnati Reds	IP	H	R	ER	BB	SO
Johnny Vander Meer (W)	9.0	0	0	0	3	3

Umpires—HP, Magerkurth. 1B, Parker. 2B, Moran.

June 15, 1938

The first night game at Ebbets Field is unforgettable. Cincinnati's Johnny Vander Meer becomes the only big leaguer ever to throw consecutive no-hitters when he beats the Brooklyn Dodgers 6-0. He walks the bases loaded in the ninth before getting Leo Durocher to fly out to end the game.

Cincinnati Reds	AB	R	H	RBI
Lonny Frey, 2b	5	0	1	0
Wally Berger, lf	5	1	3	1
Ival Goodman, rf	3	2	1	0
Frank McCormick, 1b	5	1	1	3
Ernie Lombardi, c	3	1	0	0
Harry Craft, cf	5	0	3	1
Lew Riggs, 3b	4	0	1	1
Billy Myers, ss	4	0	0	0
Johnny Vander Meer, p	4	1	1	0
Totals	38	6	11	6

Brooklyn Dodgers	AB	R	H	RBI
Kiki Cuyler, rf	2	0	0	0
Pete Coscarart, 2b	2	0	0	0
Gibby Brack, ph	1	0	0	0
Johnny Hudson, 2b	1	0	0	0
Buddy Hassett, lf	4	0	0	0
Babe Phelps, c	3	0	0	0
Goody Rosen, pr	0	0	0	0
Cookie Lavagetto, 3b	2	0	0	0
Dolph Camilli, 1b	1	0	0	0
Ernie Koy, cf	4	0	0	0
Leo Durocher, ss	4	0	0	0
Max Butcher, p	0	0	0	0
Tot Pressnell, p	2	0	0	0
Luke Hamlin, p	0	0	0	0
Woody English, ph	1	0	0	0
Vito Tamulis, p	0	0	0	0
Totals	27	0	0	0

	1	2	3	4	5	6	7	8	9	R	H	E
Cin	0	0	4	0	0	0	1	1	0	6	11	0
Bro	0	0	0	0	0	0	0	0	0	0	0	2

E—Lavagetto 2. LOB—Cincinnati 9, Brooklyn 8. 2B—Berger. 3B—Berger. HR—McCormick. SB—Goodman.

Cincinnati Reds	IP	H	R	ER	BB	SO
Johnny Vander Meer (W)	9.0	0	0	0	8	7

Brooklyn Dodgers	IP	H	R	ER	BB	SO
Max Butcher (L)	2.2	5	4	4	3	1
Tot Pressnell	3.2	4	1	1	0	3
Luke Hamlin	1.2	2	1	1	1	3
Vito Tamulis	1.0	0	0	0	0	0

Time—2:22. Attendance—38,748. Umpires—HP, Stewart. 1B, Stark. 2B, Barr.

July 17, 1941

Yankees center fielder Joe DiMaggio's record 56-game hitting streak ends in a 4-3 win over the Indians. Two sterling plays by Indians third baseman Ken Keltner help stop DiMaggio, who hits into a double play in his last at-bat.

New York Yankees	AB	R	H	RBI
Johnny Sturm, 1b	4	0	1	0
Red Rolfe, 3b	4	1	2	1
Tommy Henrich, rf	3	0	1	1
Joe DiMaggio, cf	3	0	0	0
Joe Gordon, 2b	4	1	2	1
Buddy Rosar, c	4	0	0	0
Charlie Keller, lf	3	1	1	0
Phil Rizzuto, ss	4	0	0	0
Lefty Gomez, p	4	1	1	1
Johnny Murphy, p	0	0	0	0
Totals	33	4	8	4

Cleveland Indians	AB	R	H	RBI
Roy Weatherly, cf	5	0	1	0
Ken Keltner, 3b	3	0	1	0
Lou Boudreau, ss	3	0	0	0
Jeff Heath, rf	4	0	0	0
Gee Walker, lf	3	2	2	1
Oscar Grimes, 1b	3	1	1	0
Ray Mack, 2b	3	0	0	0
Larry Rosenthal, ph	1	0	1	2
Rollie Hemsley, c	3	0	1	0
Hal Trosky, ph	1	0	0	0
Al Smith, p	3	0	0	0
Jim Bagby Jr., p	0	0	0	0
Soup Campbell, ph	1	0	0	0
Totals	33	3	7	3

	1	2	3	4	5	6	7	8	9	R	H	E
NYA	1	0	0	0	0	0	1	2	0	4	8	0
Cle	0	0	0	1	0	0	0	0	2	3	7	0

DP—Cleveland 1. LOB—New York 5, Cleveland 7. 2B—Rolfe, Henrich. 3B—Keller, Rosenthal. HR—Gordon, Walker. SH—Boudreau.

New York Yankees	IP	H	R	ER	BB	SO
Lefty Gomez (W)	8.0	6	3	3	3	5
Johnny Murphy (S)	1.0	1	0	0	0	0

Cleveland Indians	IP	H	R	ER	BB	SO
Al Smith (L)	7.1	7	4	4	2	4
Jim Bagby Jr.	1.2	1	0	0	1	1

Gomez pitched to two batters in the 9th.

Time—2:03. Attendance—67,468. Umpires—HP, Summers. 1B, Rue. 2B, Stewart.

September 28, 1941

Red Sox left fielder Ted Williams enters the final day batting .3995, and refuses to sit out to protect his .400 average. He goes 6-for-8 in the doubleheader, raising his final mark to .406. The nightcap is called after eight innings because of darkness.

Boston Red Sox	AB	R	H	RBI
Dom DiMaggio, cf	5	1	3	0
Lou Finney, rf	4	1	0	0
Al Flair, 1b	5	2	1	2
Ted Williams, lf	5	2	4	2
Jim Tabor, 3b	4	2	2	1
Bobby Doerr, 2b	5	3	2	3
Skeeter Newsome, ss	3	0	1	1
Jimmie Foxx, ph	0	1	0	0
Tom Carey, ss	0	0	0	0
Frankie Pytlak, c	4	0	1	1
Dick Newsome, p	2	0	1	0
Charlie Wagner, p	3	0	1	1
Totals	40	12	16	11

Philadelphia Athletics	AB	R	H	RBI
Eddie Collins, rf	5	2	2	1
Elmer Valo, lf	5	3	2	2
Don Richmond, 3b	5	2	3	1
Bob Johnson, 1b	4	1	2	2
Sam Chapman, cf	5	0	2	1
Crash Davis, 2b	4	1	1	1
Pete Suder, ss	5	1	2	0
Frankie Hayes, c	3	0	0	0
Dick Fowler, p	2	0	0	0
Dee Miles, ph	1	1	1	1
Porter Vaughan, p	1	0	0	0
Tex Shirley, p	0	0	0	0
Benny McCoy, ph	1	0	0	0
Totals	41	11	15	9

	1	2	3	4	5	6	7	8	9	R	H	E
Bos	0	0	0	0	3	1	6	0	2	12	16	3
Phi	0	0	2	0	9	0	0	0	0	11	15	3

E—Davis 2, DiMaggio, Suder, Finney, Tabor. DP—Philadelphia 4. LOB—Boston 7, Philadelphia 9. 2B—Johnson, Tabor. 3B—Valo, Richmond, Flair, Doerr. HR—Williams, Tabor.

Boston Red Sox	IP	H	R	ER	BB	SO
Dick Newsome	4.2	13	—	—	3	5
Charlie Wagner (W)	4.1	2	—	—	2	0

Philadelphia Athletics	IP	H	R	ER	BB	SO
Dick Fowler	5.0	8	3	—	0	0
Porter Vaughan	1.2	5	—	—	3	0
Tex Shirley (L)	1.1	3	—	—	2	0

Umpires—HP, Quinn. 1B, Grieve. 2B, McGowan.

September 28, 1941

Boston Red Sox	AB	R	H	RBI
Dom DiMaggio, cf	4	0	1	0
Lou Finney, rf	2	0	0	0
Jimmie Foxx, rf	2	0	1	0
Al Flair, 1b	4	0	0	0
Ted Williams, lf	3	0	2	0
Jim Tabor, 3b	3	0	0	0
Tom Carey, 2b	3	0	1	0
Skeeter Newsome, ss	3	0	0	0
Johnny Peacock, c	2	0	0	0
Frankie Pytlak, c	1	1	1	1
Lefty Grove, p	0	0	0	0
Earl Johnson, p	2	0	0	0
Totals	29	1	6	1

Philadelphia Athletics	AB	R	H	RBI
Elmer Valo, lf	3	1	1	0
Felix Mackiewicz, cf	4	1	1	0
Dee Miles, rf	4	1	2	1
Curt Davis, 1b	3	1	0	0
Benny McCoy, 2b	3	1	2	0
Al Brancato, 3b	4	0	2	2
Pete Suder, ss	3	1	1	0
Hal Wagner, c	4	1	2	2
Fred Caligiuri, p	4	0	0	0
Totals	32	7	11	5

	1	2	3	4	5	6	7	8	R	H	E
Bos	0	0	0	0	0	0	0	1	1	6	1
Phi	3	1	0	1	1	0	1	0	7	11	0

E—DiMaggio. DP—Boston 1, Philadelphia 1. LOB—Boston 5, Philadelphia 5. 2B—Williams. 3B—Mackiewicz, Suder. HR—Pytlak, Wagner.

Boston Red Sox	IP	H	R	ER	BB	SO
Lefty Grove (L)	1.0	4	3	—	0	0
Earl Johnson	7.0	7	4	—	4	2

Philadelphia Athletics	IP	H	R	ER	BB	SO
Fred Caligiuri (W)	8.0	6	1	1	1	1

WP—Grove, Johnson. Attendance—10,268. Umpires—HP, Quinn. 1B, Grieve. 2B, McGowan.

October 1, 1946

In the opening game of the 1946 National League playoff, Howie Pollet goes the distance to give the Cardinals a 4-2 win and 1-0 lead. Catcher Joe Garagiola chips in with three hits and two RBI to lead the offense.

Brooklyn Dodgers	AB	R	H	RBI
Eddie Stanky, 2b	3	0	1	0
Cookie Lavagetto, 3b	3	0	0	0
Joe Medwick, lf	4	0	1	0
Joe Tepsic, pr	0	0	0	0
Dick Whitman, lf	0	0	0	0
Dixie Walker, rf	4	0	0	0
Carl Furillo, cf	4	0	0	0
Pee Wee Reese, ss	4	1	2	0
Bruce Edwards, c	4	0	2	0
Howie Schultz, 1b	3	1	2	2
Ralph Branca, p	1	0	0	0
Kirby Higbe, p	0	0	0	0
Stan Rojek, ph	0	0	0	0
Hal Gregg, p	0	0	0	0
Bob Ramazzotti, ph	1	0	0	0
Vic Lombardi, p	0	0	0	0
Rube Melton, p	0	0	0	0
Totals	31	2	8	2

St. Louis Cardinals	AB	R	H	RBI
Red Schoendienst, 2b	5	0	2	0
Terry Moore, cf	5	1	3	0
Stan Musial, 1b	4	2	1	0
Enos Slaughter, rf	4	0	2	0
Whitey Kurowski, 3b	2	1	0	1
Joe Garagiola, c	4	0	3	2
Harry Walker, lf	3	0	1	1
Marty Marion, ss	4	0	0	0
Howie Pollet, p	4	0	0	0
Totals	35	4	12	4

	1	2	3	4	5	6	7	8	9	R	H	E
Bro	0	0	1	0	0	0	1	0	0	2	8	0
StL	1	0	2	0	0	0	1	0	x	4	12	1

E—Pollet. DP—St. Louis 3. LOB—Brooklyn 6, St. Louis 11. 3B—Musial. HR—Schultz. SF—Schultz.

Brooklyn Dodgers	IP	H	R	ER	BB	SO
Ralph Branca (L)	2.2	6	3	3	2	3
Kirby Higbe	1.1	1	0	0	0	0
Hal Gregg	2.0	1	0	0	1	1
Vic Lombardi	0.1	1	1	1	0	0
Rube Melton	1.2	3	0	0	1	0

St. Louis Cardinals	IP	H	R	ER	BB	SO
Howie Pollet (W)	9.0	8	2	2	3	2

WP—Melton. Time—2:48. Attendance—26,012. Umpires—HP, Reardon. 1B, Pinelli. 2B, Goetz. 3B, Boggess.

October 3, 1946

The Cardinals complete a two-game sweep of the National League playoff with an 8-4 defeat of the Brooklyn Dodgers. St. Louis will go on to prevail in the World Series in seven games over the Red Sox.

St. Louis Cardinals	AB	R	H	RBI
Red Schoendienst, 2b	5	1	1	0
Terry Moore, cf	5	1	2	0
Stan Musial, 1b	4	1	1	0
Whitey Kurowski, 3b	2	2	1	2
Enos Slaughter, rf	3	1	1	2
Erv Dusak, lf	3	1	2	1
Harry Walker, ph-lf	1	0	0	0
Marty Marion, ss	3	0	1	2
Clyde Kluttz, c	5	1	2	0
Murry Dickson, p	5	0	2	1
Harry Brecheen, p	0	0	0	0
Totals	36	8	13	8

Brooklyn Dodgers	AB	R	H	RBI
Eddie Stanky, 2b	5	0	0	0
Dick Whitman, lf	4	0	0	0
Howie Schultz, ph	1	0	0	0
Augie Galan, 3b	4	2	2	0
Dixie Walker, rf	3	0	0	0
Ed Stevens, 1b	4	1	2	2
Carl Furillo, cf	4	1	1	1
Pee Wee Reese, ss	2	0	0	0
Bruce Edwards, c	2	0	1	1
Joe Hatten, p	1	0	0	0
Hank Behrman, p	0	0	0	0
Gene Hermanski, ph	1	0	0	0
Vic Lombardi, p	0	0	0	0
Kirby Higbe, p	0	0	0	0
Rube Melton, p	0	0	0	0
Joe Medwick, ph	1	0	0	0
Harry Taylor, p	0	0	0	0
Cookie Lavagetto, ph	0	0	0	0
Totals	32	4	6	4

	1	2	3	4	5	6	7	8	9	R	H	E
StL	0	2	0	0	3	0	1	2	0	8	13	0
Bro	1	0	0	0	0	0	0	0	3	4	6	0

DP—St. Louis 1, Brooklyn 1. LOB—St. Louis 11, Brooklyn 7. 2B—Moore, Musial, Galan. 3B—Slaughter, Dusak, Dickson, Stevens. SH—Schoendienst, Dusak, Marion.

St. Louis Cardinals	IP	H	R	ER	BB	SO
Murry Dickson (W)	8.1	5	4	4	5	3
Harry Brecheen	0.2	1	0	0	1	2

Brooklyn Dodgers	IP	H	R	ER	BB	SO
Joe Hatten (L)	4.2	7	5	5	3	0
Hank Behrman	0.1	1	0	0	0	0
Vic Lombardi	1.1	1	1	1	2	0
Kirby Higbe	1.0	3	2	2	2	1
Rube Melton	0.2	0	0	0	0	0
Harry Taylor	1.0	1	0	0	0	1

WP—Dickson. Time—2:44. Attendance—31,437. Umpires—HP, Pinelli. 1B, Goetz. 2B, Boggess. 3B, Reardon.

April 15, 1947

Jackie Robinson breaks baseball's color barrier when he debuts with the Brooklyn Dodgers. Playing at first base, he goes 0-for-3 but scores the winning run in the bottom of the seventh inning.

Boston Braves	AB	R	H	RBI
Dick Culler, ss	3	0	0	0
Tommy Holmes, ph	1	0	0	0
Sibby Sisti, ss	0	0	0	0
Johnny Hopp, cf	5	0	1	1
Mike McCormick, rf	4	0	3	0
Bob Elliott, 3b	2	0	1	0
Danny Litwhiler, lf	3	1	0	0
Bama Rowell, lf	1	0	0	0
Earl Torgeson, 1b	4	1	0	0
Phil Masi, c	3	0	0	0
Connie Ryan, 2b	4	1	3	2
Johnny Sain, p	1	0	0	0
Mort Cooper, p	0	0	0	0
Tommy Neill, ph	0	0	0	0
Walt Lanfranconi, p	0	0	0	0
Totals	31	3	8	3

Brooklyn Dodgers	AB	R	H	RBI
Eddie Stanky, 2b	3	1	0	0
Jackie Robinson, 1b	3	1	0	0
Howie Schultz, 1b	0	0	0	0
Pete Reiser, cf	2	3	2	2
Dixie Walker, rf	3	0	1	0
Tommy Tatum, rf	0	0	0	0
Arky Vaughan, ph	1	0	0	0
Carl Furillo, rf	0	0	0	0
Gene Hermanski, lf	4	0	1	1
Bruce Edwards, c	2	0	0	1
Marv Rackley, pr	0	0	0	0
Bobby Bragan, c	1	0	0	0
Spider Jorgensen, 3b	3	0	0	1
Pee Wee Reese, ss	3	0	1	0
Joe Hatten, p	2	0	1	0
Ed Stevens, ph	1	0	0	0
Hal Gregg, p	1	0	0	0
Hugh Casey, p	0	0	0	0
Totals	29	5	6	5

	1	2	3	4	5	6	7	8	9	R	H	E
Bos	0	0	0	0	1	2	0	0	0	3	8	1
Bro	0	0	0	1	0	1	3	0	x	5	6	1

E—Torgeson, Edwards. DP—Boston 1, Brooklyn 1. LOB—Boston 12, Brooklyn 7. 2B—Reiser, Reese. SH—Sain 2, Culler, Masi, Robinson.

Boston Braves	IP	H	R	ER	BB	SO
Johnny Sain (L)	6.0	6	5	4	5	1
Mort Cooper	1.0	0	0	0	0	0
Walt Lanfranconi	1.0	0	0	0	0	2

Brooklyn Dodgers	IP	H	R	ER	BB	SO
Joe Hatten	6.0	6	3	2	3	2
Hal Gregg (W)	2.1	2	0	0	2	2
Hugh Casey (S)	0.2	0	0	0	0	0

Sain pitched to three batters in the 7th.

HBP—Litwhiler by Hatten, Edwards by Sain, Neill by Gregg. WP—Hatten. Time—2:26. Attendance—25,623. Umpires—HP, Pinelli. 1B, Barlick. 2B, Gore.

July 18, 1948

White Sox left fielder Pat Seerey needs 11 innings to become the fifth big leaguer to hit four homers in one game. His final blow comes in the 11th off Lou Brissie and wins the game 12-11 for Chicago.

Chicago White Sox	AB	R	H	RBI
Don Kolloway, 2b	7	2	5	3
Tony Lupien, 1b	7	1	1	0
Luke Appling, 3b	7	1	3	1
Pat Seerey, lf	6	4	4	7
Aaron Robinson, c	6	0	3	0
Taffy Wright, rf	6	0	2	0
Dave Philley, cf	6	1	2	0
Cass Michaels, ss	6	3	4	0
Frank Papish, p	0	0	0	0
Glen Moulder, p	1	0	0	0
Ralph Hodgin, ph	1	0	0	0
Earl Caldwell, p	0	0	0	0
Floyd Baker, ph	1	0	0	1
Howie Judson, p	3	0	0	0
Marino Pieretti, p	0	0	0	0
Totals	57	12	24	12

Philadelphia Athletics	AB	R	H	RBI
Eddie Joost, ss	7	4	4	5
Barney McCosky, lf	2	2	1	1
Don White, cf	4	1	2	0
Lou Brissie, p	0	0	0	0
Sam Chapman, ph	1	0	0	0
Billy DeMars, pr	0	0	0	0
Ferris Fain, 1b	5	0	0	2
Hank Majeski, 3b	5	0	1	1
Elmer Valo, rf	3	0	1	0
Buddy Rosar, c	3	0	0	0
Mike Guerra, c	3	0	0	0
Pete Suder, 2b	5	2	1	0
Carl Scheib, p	1	1	0	0
Bob Savage, p	1	0	0	0
Charlie Harris, p	1	1	1	0
Joe Coleman, p	0	0	0	0
Ray Coleman, cf	2	0	1	0
Totals	42	11	12	9

	1	2	3	4	5	6	7	8	9	10	11	R	H	E
ChA	0	0	1	1	2	5	2	0	0	0	1	12	24	1
Phi	1	4	0	1	1	0	4	0	0	0	0	11	12	1

E—Michaels, Harris. DP—Chicago 1, Philadelphia 1. LOB—Chicago 15, Philadelphia 14. 2B—Joost 2, Kolloway, Robinson, Wright, Philley, Majeski. 3B—Kolloway. HR—Seerey 4, Joost. SH—White 2, McCosky. SB—Appling .

Chicago White Sox	IP	H	R	ER	BB	SO
Frank Papish	1.0	3	5	5	4	0
Glen Moulder	2.0	0	0	0	0	1
Earl Caldwell	2.0	4	2	2	1	1
Howie Judson (W)	5.2	5	4	4	7	2
Marino Pieretti (S)	0.1	0	0	0	0	0

Philadelphia Athletics	IP	H	R	ER	BB	SO
Carl Scheib	4.2	9	4	4	1	2
Bob Savage	1.0	5	5	5	1	0
Charlie Harris	1.2	4	2	1	0	0
Joe Coleman	1.2	2	0	0	1	1
Lou Brissie (L)	2.0	4	1	1	0	1

HBP—Valo by Papish. WP—Papish, Moulder, Savage. Balk—Judson. Time—3:44. Attendance—17,296. Umpires—HP, Hurley. 1B, Berry. 3B, Grieve.

October 4, 1948

The Indians beat the Red Sox 8-3 in a one-game playoff for the American League pennant, as player-manager Lou Boudreau hits two homers. Rookie knuckleballer Gene Bearden earns his 20th win for Cleveland on only one day's rest.

Cleveland Indians	AB	R	H	RBI
Dale Mitchell, lf	5	0	1	0
Allie Clark, 1b	2	0	0	0
Eddie Robinson, 1b	2	1	1	0
Lou Boudreau, ss	4	3	4	2
Joe Gordon, 2b	4	1	1	0
Ken Keltner, 3b	5	1	3	3
Larry Doby, cf	5	1	2	0
Bob Kennedy, rf	2	0	0	0
Jim Hegan, c	3	1	0	1
Gene Bearden, p	3	0	1	0
Totals	35	8	13	6

Boston Red Sox	AB	R	H	RBI
Dom DiMaggio, cf	4	0	0	0
Johnny Pesky, 3b	4	1	1	0
Ted Williams, lf	4	1	1	0
Vern Stephens, ss	4	0	1	1
Bobby Doerr, 2b	4	1	1	2
Stan Spence, rf	1	0	0	0
Billy Hitchcock, ph	0	0	0	0
Tom Wright, pr	0	0	0	0
Billy Goodman, 1b	3	0	0	0
Birdie Tebbetts, c	4	0	1	0
Denny Galehouse, p	0	0	0	0
Ellis Kinder, p	2	0	0	0
Totals	30	3	5	3

	1 2 3	4 5 6	7 8 9	R	H	E
Cle	1 0 0	4 1 0	0 1 1	8	13	1
Bos	1 0 0	0 0 2	0 0 0	3	5	1

E—Gordon, Williams. DP—Cleveland 2, Boston 2. LOB—Cleveland 7, Boston 5. 2B—Doby 2, Keltner, Pesky. HR—Boudreau 2, Keltner, Doerr. SH—Kennedy 2, Robinson. CS—Spence.

Cleveland Indians	IP	H	R	ER	BB	SO
Gene Bearden (W)	9.0	5	3	1	5	6

Boston Red Sox	IP	H	R	ER	BB	SO
Denny Galehouse (L)	3.0	5	4	4	1	1
Ellis Kinder	6.0	8	4	3	3	2

Galehouse pitched to three batters in the 4th.

Time—2:24. Attendance—33,957. Umpires—HP, McGowan. 1B, Summers. 2B, Rommel. 3B, Berry.

June 8, 1950

The Red Sox set modern records for runs and margin of victory as they crush the St. Louis Browns 29-4. Second baseman Bobby Doerr has three home runs and eight RBI for Boston, which beat the Browns 20-4 the day before.

St. Louis Browns	AB	R	H	RBI
Don Lenhardt, lf	4	2	2	0
Dick Kokos, rf	4	1	2	1
Sherm Lollar, c	3	0	1	0
Les Moss, c	1	0	0	0
Roy Sievers, cf	4	0	1	2
Hank Arft, 1b	3	0	1	1
Owen Friend, 2b	4	0	1	0
Tom Upton, ss	3	0	0	0
Leo Thomas, 3b	3	1	0	0
Cliff Fannin, p	0	0	0	0
Ned Garver, ph	1	0	0	0
Cuddles Marshall, p	1	0	0	0
Sid Schacht, p	2	0	0	0
Tom Ferrick, p	0	0	0	0
Totals	33	4	8	4

Boston Red Sox	AB	R	H	RBI
Clyde Vollmer, cf	7	1	1	2
Johnny Pesky, 3b	7	3	5	2
Ted Williams, lf	5	3	2	5
Vern Stephens, ss	6	4	3	3
Walt Dropo, 1b	6	5	4	7
Al Zarilla, rf	7	4	5	0
Bobby Doerr, 2b	6	4	4	8
Matt Batts, c	6	2	2	2
Chuck Stobbs, p	3	3	2	0
Totals	53	29	28	29

	1 2 3	4 5 6	7 8 9	R	H	E
StL	0 0 3	0 0 0	0 0 1	4	8	1
Bos	0 8 5	7 2 0	2 5 x	29	28	0

E—Kokos. DP—Boston 2. LOB—St. Louis 10, Boston 11. 2B—Zarilla 4, Pesky 2, Arft, Vollmer, Stephens, Batts. 3B—Stephens. HR—Doerr 3, Williams 2, Dropo 2.

St. Louis Browns	IP	H	R	ER	BB	SO
Cliff Fannin (L)	2.0	7	8	8	4	0
Cuddles Marshall	1.2	7	9	9	5	0
Sid Schacht	3.2	13	12	9	2	2
Tom Ferrick	0.2	1	0	0	0	0

Boston Red Sox	IP	H	R	ER	BB	SO
Chuck Stobbs (W)	9.0	8	4	4	7	5

HBP—Arft by Stobbs. Time—2:42. Attendance—5,105. Umpires—HP, Hubbard. 1B, Rommel. 3B, Paparella.

August 31, 1950

Brooklyn Dodgers first baseman Gil Hodges hits four homers in one game, the sixth player to do so. He's the first to hit four off four different pitchers, and his 17 total bases establish a new modern record (since broken).

Boston Braves	AB	R	H	RBI
Roy Hartsfield, 2b	5	0	1	0
Sam Jethroe, cf	5	0	0	0
Earl Torgeson, 1b	4	1	1	0
Bob Elliott, 3b	3	0	1	0
Walker Cooper, c	3	0	0	0
Del Crandall, c	1	1	0	0
Sid Gordon, lf	4	1	3	2
Willard Marshall, rf	4	0	2	1
Buddy Kerr, ss	3	0	0	0
Warren Spahn, p	1	0	0	0
Norm Roy, p	0	0	0	0
Mickey Haefner, p	0	0	0	0
Pete Reiser, ph	1	0	0	0
Bob Hall, p	0	0	0	0
Johnny Antonelli, p	1	0	0	0
Tommy Holmes, ph	1	0	0	0
Totals	36	3	8	3

Brooklyn Dodgers	AB	R	H	RBI
Tommy Brown, lf	4	0	1	2
Pee Wee Reese, ss	5	1	2	3
Duke Snider, cf	5	1	3	3
Jackie Robinson, 2b	5	1	1	0
Bobby Morgan, 3b	0	0	0	0
Carl Furillo, rf	5	4	2	0
Gil Hodges, 1b	6	5	5	9
Roy Campanella, c	4	2	2	0
Bruce Edwards, c	1	1	1	0
Billy Cox, 3b-2b	5	3	2	0
Carl Erskine, p	5	1	4	0
Totals	45	19	21	17

	1 2 3	4 5 6	7 8 9	R	H	E
Bos	0 1 0	0 0 0	0 2 0	3	8	4
Bro	0 3 7	0 0 4	3 2 x	19	21	1

E—Hartsfield 3, Crandall, Reese. LOB—Boston 9, Brooklyn 12. 2B—Marshall 2, Reese. HR—Hodges 4, Gordon, Snider. SH—Cox.

Boston Braves	IP	H	R	ER	BB	SO
Warren Spahn (L)	2.0	7	5	5	1	2
Norm Roy	0.1	3	3	3	0	0
Mickey Haefner	1.2	1	2	2	1	0
Bob Hall	1.2	6	4	4	3	1
Johnny Antonelli	2.1	4	5	4	2	2

Brooklyn Dodgers	IP	H	R	ER	BB	SO
Carl Erskine (W)	9.0	8	3	3	2	6

Spahn pitched to two batters in the 3rd.

HBP—Erskine by Antonelli. Time—3:03. Attendance—14,226. Umpires—HP, Conlan. 1B, Gore. 3B, Stewart.

October 1, 1951

Foreshadowing: Bobby Thomson homers off Ralph Branca to lead the New York Giants to a 3-1 win over the Brooklyn Dodgers to open the National League playoff. It's the first game ever broadcast live nationwide.

New York Giants	AB	R	H	RBI
Eddie Stanky, 2b	5	0	2	0
Al Dark, ss	4	0	1	0
Don Mueller, rf	5	0	0	0
Monte Irvin, lf	4	2	1	1
Whitey Lockman, 1b	4	0	1	0
Bobby Thomson, 3b	2	1	1	2
Willie Mays, cf	3	0	0	0
Wes Westrum, c	2	0	0	0
Jim Hearn, p	3	0	0	0
Totals	32	3	6	3

Brooklyn Dodgers	AB	R	H	RBI
Carl Furillo, rf	4	0	0	0
Pee Wee Reese, ss	3	0	1	0
Duke Snider, cf	4	0	1	0
Jackie Robinson, 2b	3	0	1	0
Roy Campanella, c	3	0	0	0
Andy Pafko, lf	3	1	1	1
Gil Hodges, 1b	2	0	0	0
Billy Cox, 3b	3	0	1	0
Ralph Branca, p	2	0	0	0
Jim Russell, ph	1	0	0	0
Bud Podbielan, p	0	0	0	0
Totals	28	1	5	1

```
      1 2 3  4 5 6  7 8 9      R H E
NYG   0 0 0  2 0 0  0 1 0      3 6 1
Bro   0 1 0  0 0 0  0 0 0      1 5 1
```

E—Dark, Snider. DP—New York 4. LOB—New York 10, Brooklyn 2. 2B—Dark. HR—Irvin, Pafko, Thomson. SH—Hearn, Thomson.

New York Giants	IP	H	R	ER	BB	SO
Jim Hearn (W)	9.0	5	1	1	2	5

Brooklyn Dodgers	IP	H	R	ER	BB	SO
Ralph Branca (L)	8.0	5	3	3	5	5
Bud Podbielan	1.0	1	0	0	0	0

HBP—Irvin by Branca. Time—2:39. Attendance—30,707. Umpires—HP, Stewart. 1B, Goetz. 2B, Jorda. 3B, Conlan.

October 2, 1951

Brooklyn Dodgers rookie Clem Labine squares the National League playoff at one game apiece with a 10-0 shutout of the New York Giants. Brooklyn backs Labine with four home runs.

Brooklyn Dodgers	AB	R	H	RBI
Carl Furillo, rf	5	0	0	0
Pee Wee Reese, ss	5	1	2	0
Duke Snider, cf	4	1	2	1
Jackie Robinson, 2b	5	1	3	3
Andy Pafko, lf	5	1	1	1
Gil Hodges, 1b	4	2	2	1
Billy Cox, 3b	3	2	0	0
Rube Walker, c	5	1	3	2
Clem Labine, p	4	1	0	0
Totals	40	10	13	8

New York Giants	AB	R	H	RBI
Eddie Stanky, 2b	5	0	1	0
Al Dark, ss	5	0	0	0
Don Mueller, rf	4	0	1	0
Monte Irvin, lf	4	0	1	0
Whitey Lockman, 1b	3	0	0	0
Bobby Thomson, 3b	4	0	1	0
Willie Mays, cf	4	0	1	0
Wes Westrum, c	3	0	0	0
Davey Williams, pr	0	0	0	0
Sheldon Jones, p	1	0	0	0
George Spencer, p	1	0	1	0
Bill Rigney, ph	0	0	0	0
Al Corwin, p	0	0	0	0
Hank Thompson, ph	1	0	0	0
Totals	35	0	6	0

```
      1 2 3  4 5 6  7 8 9      R H E
Bro   2 0 0  0 1 3  2 0 2     10 13 2
NYG   0 0 0  0 0 0  0 0 0      0 6 5
```

E—Spencer 2, Reese, Hodges, Thomson, Mays, Jones. DP—New York 1. LOB—Brooklyn 8, New York 11. 2B—Snider, Thomson. HR—Robinson, Pafko, Hodges, Walker. SH—Cox.

Brooklyn Dodgers	IP	H	R	ER	BB	SO
Clem Labine (W)	9.0	6	0	0	3	3

New York Giants	IP	H	R	ER	BB	SO
Sheldon Jones (L)	2.1	4	2	—	1	2
George Spencer	3.2	6	4	—	1	0
Al Corwin	3.0	3	4	—	2	2

Time—3:25. Attendance—38,609. Umpires—HP, Goetz. 1B, Jorda. 2B, Conlan. 3B, Stewart.

October 3, 1951

In the deciding game of the National League playoff, The Shot Heard 'Round The World gives the New York Giants the pennant. Bobby Thomson's three-run blow in the bottom of the ninth lives on as baseball's most dramatic homer.

Brooklyn Dodgers	AB	R	H	RBI
Carl Furillo, rf	5	0	0	0
Pee Wee Reese, ss	4	2	1	0
Duke Snider, cf	3	1	2	0
Jackie Robinson, 2b	2	1	1	1
Andy Pafko, lf	4	0	1	1
Gil Hodges, 1b	4	0	0	0
Billy Cox, 3b	4	0	2	1
Rube Walker, c	4	0	1	0
Don Newcombe, p	4	0	0	0
Ralph Branca, p	0	0	0	0
Totals	34	4	8	3

New York Giants	AB	R	H	RBI
Eddie Stanky, 2b	4	0	0	0
Al Dark, ss	4	1	1	0
Don Mueller, rf	4	0	1	0
Clint Hartung, pr	0	1	0	0
Monte Irvin, lf	4	1	1	0
Whitey Lockman, 1b	3	1	2	1
Bobby Thomson, 3b	4	1	3	4
Willie Mays, cf	3	0	0	0
Wes Westrum, c	0	0	0	0
Bill Rigney, ph	1	0	0	0
Ray Noble, c	0	0	0	0
Sal Maglie, p	2	0	0	0
Hank Thompson, ph	1	0	0	0
Larry Jansen, p	0	0	0	0
Totals	30	5	8	5

```
      1 2 3  4 5 6  7 8 9      R H E
Bro   1 0 0  0 0 0  0 3 0      4 8 0
NYG   0 0 0  0 0 0  1 0 4      5 8 0
```

One out when winning run scored.

DP—Brooklyn 2. LOB—Brooklyn 7, New York 3. 2B—Irvin, Lockman, Thomson. HR—Thomson. SH—Lockman.

Brooklyn Dodgers	IP	H	R	ER	BB	SO
Don Newcombe	8.1	7	4	4	2	2
Ralph Branca (L)	0.0	1	1	1	0	0

New York Giants	IP	H	R	ER	BB	SO
Sal Maglie	8.0	8	4	4	4	6
Larry Jansen (W)	1.0	0	0	0	0	0

Branca pitched to one batter in the 9th.

WP—Maglie. Time—2:28. Attendance—34,320. Umpires—HP, Jorda. 1B, Conlan. 2B, Stewart. 3B, Goetz.

June 18, 1953

The Red Sox set a modern record with a 17-run inning in the seventh frame of a 23-3 rout of Detroit. Boston left fielder Gene Stephens becomes the only modern player to collect three hits in one inning.

Detroit Tigers	AB	R	H	RBI
Harvey Kuenn, ss	4	0	1	0
Johnny Pesky, 2b	3	0	0	0
Ray Boone, 3b	3	1	0	0
Bob Nieman, rf	3	0	1	0
Jim Delsing, cf	3	1	1	1
Walt Dropo, 1b	4	1	3	2
Matt Batts, c	4	0	1	0
Don Lund, rf	4	0	0	0
Ned Garver, p	1	0	0	0
Steve Gromek, p	1	0	0	0
Dick Weik, p	0	0	0	0
Earl Harrist, p	0	0	0	0
Pat Mullin, ph	1	0	0	0
Totals	31	3	7	3

Boston Red Sox	AB	R	H	RBI
Billy Goodman, 2b	4	2	4	2
Ted Lepcio, 2b	1	2	1	0
Jimmy Piersall, rf	5	1	2	3
Al Zarilla, rf	1	1	1	0
Dick Gernert, 1b	5	2	2	4
Floyd Baker, 3b	3	0	1	0
Ellis Kinder, p	4	2	2	2
Sammy White, c	6	4	4	2
Gene Stephens, lf	6	3	3	3
Tom Umphlett, cf	5	2	3	3
Johnny Lipon, ss	4	3	2	3
Marv Grissom, p	1	0	0	0
Hersh Freeman, p	1	0	1	0
George Kell, 3b	4	1	1	0
Totals	50	23	27	22

	1	2	3	4	5	6	7	8	9	R	H	E
Det	0	0	0	2	0	1	0	0	0	3	7	5
Bos	0	3	0	0	0	2	17	1	x	23	27	0

E—Nieman 2, Kuenn, Pesky, Boone. DP—Boston 1. LOB—Detroit 6, Boston 13. 2B—Stephens, Kell. HR—Dropo, Gernert. SH—Goodman, Nieman. SB—Stephens.

Detroit Tigers	IP	H	R	ER	BB	SO
Ned Garver (L)	5.1	10	5	4	2	3
Steve Gromek	1.0	7	9	9	3	2
Dick Weik	0.1	3	4	4	1	0
Earl Harrist	1.1	7	5	5	3	1

Boston Red Sox	IP	H	R	ER	BB	SO
Marv Grissom	3.0	0	0	0	2	1
Hersh Freeman	2.0	2	2	2	1	0
Ellis Kinder (W)	4.0	5	1	1	1	1

WP—Weik. Time—3:03. Attendance—3,101. Umpires—HP, Hurley. 1B, Soar. 2B, Rommel. 3B, Berry.

July 31, 1954

Milwaukee Braves first baseman Joe Adcock becomes the seventh player to hit four home runs in one game, and does his predecessors one better. Adcock also adds a double, giving him an unmatched 18 total bases.

Milwaukee Braves	AB	R	H	RBI
Bill Bruton, cf	6	0	4	1
Danny O'Connell, 2b	5	0	0	0
Eddie Mathews, 3b	4	3	2	2
Hank Aaron, lf	5	2	2	0
Joe Adcock, 1b	5	5	5	7
Andy Pafko, rf	4	2	3	2
Jim Pendleton, rf	1	1	0	0
Johnny Logan, ss	2	1	1	1
Roy Smalley, ss	2	1	1	0
Del Crandall, c	4	0	0	0
Sam Calderone, c	1	0	1	0
Jim Wilson, p	1	0	0	0
Lew Burdette, p	3	0	0	0
Bob Buhl, p	0	0	0	0
Dave Jolly, p	1	0	0	0
Totals	44	15	19	13

Brooklyn Dodgers	AB	R	H	RBI
Jim Gilliam, 2b	4	1	4	0
Pee Wee Reese, ss	3	0	1	0
Don Zimmer, ss	1	0	0	0
Duke Snider, cf	4	0	1	1
George Shuba, lf	1	0	0	0
Gil Hodges, 1b	5	1	1	1
Sandy Amoros, lf-cf	5	2	3	0
Jackie Robinson, 3b	0	0	0	0
Don Hoak, 3b	2	1	1	2
Carl Furillo, rf	5	1	2	1
Rube Walker, c	5	1	1	2
Don Newcombe, p	0	0	0	0
Clem Labine, p	0	0	0	0
Walt Moryn, ph	1	0	0	0
Erv Palica, p	0	0	0	0
Pete Wojey, p	1	0	0	0
Johnny Podres, p	2	0	2	0
Totals	39	7	16	7

	1	2	3	4	5	6	7	8	9	R	H	E
Mil	1	3	2	0	3	0	3	0	3	15	19	0
Bro	1	0	0	0	0	1	0	4	1	7	16	1

E—Hoak. DP—Milwaukee 2, Brooklyn 1. LOB—Milwaukee 5, Brooklyn 10. 2B—Bruton 3, Aaron, Adcock, Pafko, Gilliam, Amoros. 3B—Amoros. HR—Adcock 4, Mathews 2, Pafko, Hodges, Hoak, Walker. SH—O'Connell. SF—Hoak.

Milwaukee Braves	IP	H	R	ER	BB	SO
Jim Wilson	1.0	5	1	1	0	0
Lew Burdette (W)	6.1	8	5	5	2	3
Bob Buhl	0.0	2	0	0	0	0
Dave Jolly	1.2	1	1	1	1	1

Brooklyn Dodgers	IP	H	R	ER	BB	SO
Don Newcombe (L)	1.0	4	4	4	0	0
Clem Labine	1.0	1	0	0	0	0
Erv Palica	2.1	5	5	5	2	1
Pete Wojey	2.2	4	3	3	0	3
Johnny Podres	2.0	5	3	1	0	1

HBP—Robinson by Wilson. WP—Podres. Time—2:53. Attendance—12,263. Umpires—HP, Boggess. 1B, Engeln. 2B, Stewart. 3B, Barlick.

April 23, 1955

The White Sox tie the modern record for runs in a game by tallying 29 on a day that 30-mph winds are gusting at Municipal Stadium. Chicago catcher Sherm Lollar gets two hits in an inning twice and bashes two home runs.

Chicago White Sox	AB	R	H	RBI
Chico Carrasquel, ss	6	5	5	0
Nellie Fox, 2b	5	2	1	1
Minnie Minoso, lf	6	5	4	5
George Kell, 3b	5	2	2	2
Stan Jok, 3b	1	1	0	1
Bob Nieman, rf	4	3	3	7
Ed McGhee, cf	1	1	0	0
Walt Dropo, 1b	7	3	3	3
Jim Rivera, cf-rf	7	1	3	2
Sherm Lollar, c	6	4	5	5
Jack Harshman, p	5	2	3	2
Harry Dorish, p	1	0	0	0
Totals	54	29	29	28

Kansas City Athletics	AB	R	H	RBI
Vic Power, 1b	5	1	1	1
Spook Jacobs, 2b	3	0	0	0
Jim Finigan, 3b	4	2	2	1
Gus Zernial, lf	4	0	0	0
Bill Renna, rf	3	1	2	4
Bill Wilson, cf	3	0	0	0
Joe DeMaestri, ss	3	0	0	0
Jack Littrell, ss	1	0	0	0
Joe Astroth, c	3	0	1	0
Eric MacKenzie, c	1	0	0	0
Bobby Shantz, p	0	0	0	0
Lee Wheat, p	0	0	0	0
Bill Stewart, ph	1	0	0	0
Bob Trice, p	0	0	0	0
Moe Burtschy, p	1	0	0	0
Bob Spicer, p	1	0	0	0
Ozzie Van Brabant, p	0	0	0	0
Elmer Valo, ph	1	0	0	0
Totals	34	6	6	6

	1	2	3	4	5	6	7	8	9	R	H	E
ChA	4	7	3	2	0	6	3	4	0	29	29	1
KCA	3	0	2	0	1	0	0	0	0	6	6	3

E—Kell, Finigan, Zernial, Wilson. LOB—Chicago 7, Kansas City 5. 2B—Rivera 2, Finigan 2, Minoso, Kell, Fox, Astroth. HR—Nieman 2, Lollar 2, Minoso, Dropo, Harshman, Power, Renna. SF—Jok, Fox. SB—Minoso.

Chicago White Sox	IP	H	R	ER	BB	SO
Jack Harshman (W)	7.0	6	6	5	3	7
Harry Dorish	2.0	0	0	0	1	2

Kansas City Athletics	IP	H	R	ER	BB	SO
Bobby Shantz (L)	1.2	7	9	8	1	0
Lee Wheat	0.1	3	2	2	1	0
Bob Trice	1.1	5	5	4	0	0
Moe Burtschy	2.1	7	6	6	1	1
Bob Spicer	1.2	4	5	5	2	2
Ozzie Van Brabant	1.2	3	2	2	1	1

HBP—Fox by Spicer. WP—Shantz. Time—3:08. Attendance—18,338. Umpires—HP, Rommel. 1B, Paparella. 2B, Honochick. 3B, Umont.

April 15, 1958

In the first big league game played on the West Coast, Ruben Gomez pitches the Giants to an 8-0 shutout win over the Dodgers. San Francisco shortstop Daryl Spencer hits the first West Coast home run.

Los Angeles Dodgers	AB	R	H	RBI
Gino Cimoli, cf	5	0	1	0
Pee Wee Reese, ss	3	0	0	0
Duke Snider, lf	2	0	0	0
Gil Hodges, 1b	4	0	0	0
Charlie Neal, 2b	4	0	2	0
Dick Gray, 3b	4	0	2	0
Carl Furillo, rf	3	0	0	0
Rube Walker, c	3	0	1	0
John Roseboro, pr-c	1	0	0	0
Don Drysdale, p	1	0	0	0
Don Bessent, p	1	0	0	0
Norm Larker, ph	1	0	0	0
Ron Negray, p	0	0	0	0
Jim Gilliam, ph	0	0	0	0
Totals	32	0	6	0

San Francisco Giants	AB	R	H	RBI
Jim Davenport, 3b	4	1	2	1
Jim King, lf	3	1	2	1
Willie Mays, cf	5	0	2	2
Willie Kirkland, rf	5	0	1	1
Orlando Cepeda, 1b	5	1	1	1
Daryl Spencer, ss	4	1	1	1
Danny O'Connell, 2b	2	1	0	0
Valmy Thomas, c	1	2	0	0
Ruben Gomez, p	4	1	2	1
Totals	33	8	11	8

	1	2	3	4	5	6	7	8	9		R	H	E
LA	0	0	0	0	0	0	0	0	0		0	6	1
SF	0	0	2	4	1	0	0	1	x		8	11	0

E—Hodges. DP—San Francisco 1. LOB—Los Angeles 11, San Francisco 9. HR—Cepeda, Spencer. SF—Davenport.

Los Angeles Dodgers	IP	H	R	ER	BB	SO
Don Drysdale (L)	3.2	5	6	6	3	1
Don Bessent	2.1	4	1	1	1	0
Ron Negray	2.0	2	1	1	3	1

San Francisco Giants	IP	H	R	ER	BB	SO
Ruben Gomez (W)	9.0	6	0	0	6	6

Balk—Negray. Time—2:29. Attendance—23,448. Umpires—HP, Conlan. 1B, Secory. 2B, Dixon. 3B, Venzon.

May 26, 1959

In the best single-game pitching performance ever, Pittsburgh's Harvey Haddix throws a perfect game for 12 innings against the Braves. He loses 1-0 in the 13th, and a rules revision years later denies him credit for an official perfect game.

Pittsburgh Pirates	AB	R	H	RBI
Dick Schofield, ss	6	0	3	0
Bill Virdon, cf	6	0	1	0
Smoky Burgess, c	5	0	0	0
Rocky Nelson, 1b	5	0	2	0
Bob Skinner, lf	5	0	1	0
Bill Mazeroski, 2b	5	0	1	0
Don Hoak, 3b	5	0	2	0
Roman Mejias, rf	3	0	1	0
Dick Stuart, ph	1	0	0	0
Joe Christopher, rf	1	0	0	0
Harvey Haddix, p	5	0	1	0
Totals	47	0	12	0

Milwaukee Braves	AB	R	H	RBI
Johnny O'Brien, 2b	3	0	0	0
Del Rice, ph	1	0	0	0
Felix Mantilla, 2b	1	1	0	0
Eddie Mathews, 3b	4	0	0	0
Hank Aaron, rf	4	0	0	0
Joe Adcock, 1b	5	0	1	1
Wes Covington, lf	4	0	0	0
Del Crandall, c	4	0	0	0
Andy Pafko, cf	4	0	0	0
Johnny Logan, ss	4	0	0	0
Lew Burdette, p	4	0	0	0
Totals	38	1	1	1

	1	2	3	4	5	6	7	8	9	10	11	12	13	R	H	E
Pit	0	0	0	0	0	0	0	0	0	0	0	0	0	0	12	1
Mil	0	0	0	0	0	0	0	0	0	0	0	0	1	1	1	0

Two outs when winning run scored.

E—Hoak. DP—Milwaukee 3. LOB—Pittsburgh 8, Milwaukee 1. 2B—Adcock. SH—Mathews.

Pittsburgh Pirates	IP	H	R	ER	BB	SO
Harvey Haddix (L)	12.2	1	1	1	1	8

Milwaukee Braves	IP	H	R	ER	BB	SO
Lew Burdette (W)	13.0	12	0	0	0	2

Time—2:54. Attendance—19,194. Umpires—HP, Smith. 1B, Dascoli. 2B, Secory. 3B, Dixon.

June 10, 1959

Indians right fielder Rocky Colavito joins Bobby Lowe and Lou Gehrig as the only players to homer in four consecutive at-bats in one game. Colavito is the eighth player with a four-homer game.

Cleveland Indians	AB	R	H	RBI
Woodie Held, ss	5	1	1	0
Vic Power, 1b	4	1	0	0
Tito Francona, cf	5	2	2	1
Rocky Colavito, rf	4	5	4	6
Minnie Minoso, lf	5	1	3	3
Puddin' Head Jones, 3b	3	0	0	0
George Strickland, 3b	2	0	1	0
Dick Brown, c	4	0	1	0
Billy Martin, 2b	3	1	1	1
Ray Webster, 2b	1	0	0	0
Gary Bell, p	3	0	0	0
Mike Garcia, p	1	0	0	0
Totals	40	11	13	11

Baltimore Orioles	AB	R	H	RBI
Albie Pearson, cf	3	1	2	0
Al Pilarcik, rf	5	1	1	2
Gene Woodling, lf	5	1	3	1
Gus Triandos, c	2	0	1	1
Joe Ginsberg, c	1	1	0	0
Bob Hale, 1b	3	0	0	0
George Zuverink, p	0	0	0	0
Bob Boyd, ph	1	0	0	0
Ernie Johnson, p	0	0	0	0
Bob Nieman, ph	1	1	1	0
Billy Klaus, 3b	5	0	2	4
Chico Carrasquel, ss	5	0	0	0
Billy Gardner, 2b	4	1	0	0
Jerry Walker, p	1	1	1	0
Arnie Portocarrero, p	1	0	0	0
Whitey Lockman, 1b	1	1	0	0
Totals	38	8	12	8

	1	2	3	4	5	6	7	8	9		R	H	E
Cle	3	1	2	0	1	3	0	0	1		11	13	0
Bal	1	2	0	0	0	0	4	0	1		8	12	0

LOB—Cleveland 5, Baltimore 8. 2B—Held, Francona, Brown, Nieman, Klaus. HR—Colavito 4, Minoso, Martin. SF—Triandos. SB—Minoso.

Cleveland Indians	IP	H	R	ER	BB	SO
Gary Bell (W)	6.1	8	7	7	4	3
Mike Garcia	2.2	4	1	1	0	3

Baltimore Orioles	IP	H	R	ER	BB	SO
Jerry Walker (L)	2.1	4	6	6	2	1
Arnie Portocarrero	3.1	7	4	4	1	3
George Zuverink	1.1	0	0	0	0	0
Ernie Johnson	2.0	2	1	1	0	0

Time—2:54. Attendance—15,883. Umpires—HP, Summers. 1B, McKinley. 2B, Soar. 3B, Chylak.

Rookie Larry Sherry wins the first game of the 1959 National League playoff by pitching 7.2 shutout innings of relief for the 3-2 victory.

Los Angeles Dodgers	AB	R	H	RBI
Jim Gilliam, 3b	4	0	0	0
Charlie Neal, 2b	5	1	3	0
Wally Moon, lf	4	1	1	0
Norm Larker, rf	4	0	3	1
Bob Lillis, pr	0	0	0	0
Ron Fairly, rf	0	0	0	0
Gil Hodges, 1b	3	0	1	1
Don Demeter, cf	4	0	1	0
John Roseboro, c	4	1	1	1
Maury Wills, ss	4	0	0	0
Danny McDevitt, p	1	0	0	0
Larry Sherry, p	2	0	0	0
Totals	35	3	10	3

Milwaukee Braves	AB	R	H	RBI
Bobby Avila, 2b	5	0	0	1
Eddie Mathews, 3b	4	0	0	0
Hank Aaron, rf	2	0	0	0
Joe Adcock, 1b	3	0	0	0
Andy Pafko, lf	2	0	0	0
Lee Maye, lf	2	0	1	0
Johnny Logan, ss	3	1	1	0
Del Crandall, c	4	1	2	0
Bill Bruton, cf	4	0	1	1
Carl Willey, p	2	0	0	0
Enos Slaughter, ph	1	0	0	0
Don McMahon, p	0	0	0	0
Frank Torre, ph	1	0	0	0
Totals	33	2	6	2

	1	2	3	4	5	6	7	8	9		R	H	E
LA	1	0	1	0	0	1	0	0	0		3	10	1
Mil	0	2	0	0	0	0	0	0	0		2	6	0

E—Wills. DP—Los Angeles 1, Milwaukee 2. LOB—Los Angeles 8, Milwaukee 8. HR—Roseboro.

Los Angeles Dodgers	IP	H	R	ER	BB	SO
Danny McDevitt	1.1	2	2	2	2	2
Larry Sherry (W)	7.2	4	0	0	2	4

Milwaukee Braves	IP	H	R	ER	BB	SO
Carl Willey (L)	6.0	8	3	3	2	3
Don McMahon	3.0	2	0	0	1	2

McDevitt pitched to three batters in the 2nd.

Time—2:40. Attendance—18,297. Umpires—HP, Conlan. 1B, Barlick. 2B, Boggess. 3B, Donatelli.

The Dodgers sweep the 1959 National League playoff in two games, scoring three runs in the bottom of the ninth to tie it before winning in the 12th on Milwaukee Braves second baseman Felix Mantilla's throwing error.

Milwaukee Braves	AB	R	H	RBI
Bill Bruton, cf	6	0	0	0
Eddie Mathews, 3b	4	2	2	1
Hank Aaron, rf	4	1	2	0
Frank Torre, 1b	3	0	1	2
Lee Maye, lf	2	0	0	0
Andy Pafko, lf	1	0	0	0
Enos Slaughter, ph	1	0	0	0
John DeMerit, lf	0	0	0	0
Al Spangler, lf	0	0	0	0
Johnny Logan, ss	3	1	2	0
Red Schoendienst, 2b	1	0	0	0
Mickey Vernon, ph	1	0	0	0
Chuck Cottier, 2b	0	0	0	0
Joe Adcock, ph	1	0	0	0
Bobby Avila, 2b	0	0	0	0
Del Crandall, c	6	1	1	0
Felix Mantilla, 2b-ss	5	0	1	1
Lew Burdette, p	4	0	1	0
Don McMahon, p	0	0	0	0
Warren Spahn, p	0	0	0	0
Joey Jay, p	1	0	0	0
Bob Rush, p	1	0	0	0
Totals	44	5	10	4

Los Angeles Dodgers	AB	R	H	RBI
Jim Gilliam, 3b	5	0	1	0
Charlie Neal, 2b	6	2	2	1
Wally Moon, rf-lf	6	1	3	1
Duke Snider, cf	4	0	1	0
Bob Lillis, pr	0	1	0	0
Stan Williams, p	2	0	0	0
Gil Hodges, 1b	5	2	2	0
Norm Larker, lf	4	0	2	2
Joe Pignatano, c	1	0	1	0
John Roseboro, c	3	0	0	0
Carl Furillo, rf	2	0	2	1
Maury Wills, ss	5	0	1	0
Don Drysdale, p	1	0	0	0
Johnny Podres, p	1	0	0	0
Chuck Churn, p	0	0	0	0
Don Demeter, ph	1	0	0	0
Sandy Koufax, p	0	0	0	0
Clem Labine, p	0	0	0	0
Chuck Essegian, ph	0	0	0	0
Ron Fairly, cf	2	0	0	0
Totals	48	6	15	5

	1	2	3	4	5	6	7	8	9	10	11	12	R	H	E
Mil	2	1	0	0	1	0	0	1	0	0	0	0	5	10	2
LA	1	0	0	1	0	0	0	0	3	0	0	1	6	15	2

Two outs when winning run scored.

E—Mantilla 2, Neal, Snider. DP—Milwaukee 1, Los Angeles 1. LOB—Milwaukee 13, Los Angeles 11. 2B—Aaron. 3B—Crandall, Neal. HR—Mathews, Neal. SF—Mantilla, Furillo.

Milwaukee Braves	IP	H	R	ER	BB	SO
Lew Burdette (L)	8.0	10	5	5	0	4
Don McMahon	0.0	1	0	0	0	0
Warren Spahn	0.1	1	0	0	0	0
Joey Jay	2.1	1	0	0	1	1
Bob Rush (L)	1.0	2	1	0	1	0

Los Angeles Dodgers	IP	H	R	ER	BB	SO
Don Drysdale	4.1	6	4	3	2	3
Johnny Podres	2.1	3	0	0	1	1
Chuck Churn	1.1	1	1	1	0	0
Sandy Koufax	0.2	0	0	0	3	1
Clem Labine	0.1	0	0	0	0	1
Stan Williams (W)	3.0	0	0	0	3	3

Burdette pitched to three batters in the 9th. McMahon pitched to one batter in the 9th.

HBP—Pignatano by Jay. WP—Podres. Time—4:06. Attendance—36,853. Umpires—HP, Barlick. 1B, Boggess. 2B, Donatelli. 3B, Conlan.

Giants center fielder Willie Mays is the ninth player to homer four times in a single game. His chance for an unprecedented fifth ends when he's stranded in the on-deck circle in the top of the ninth.

San Francisco Giants	AB	R	H	RBI
Chuck Hiller, 2b	6	2	3	1
Jim Davenport, 3b	4	3	1	1
Willie Mays, cf	5	4	4	8
Willie McCovey, 1b	3	0	0	0
Jim Marshall, 1b	0	0	0	0
Orlando Cepeda, lf	5	1	1	1
Matty Alou, lf	0	0	0	0
Felipe Alou, rf	4	1	1	1
Ed Bailey, c	4	0	0	0
Jose Pagan, ss	5	3	4	2
Billy Loes, p	3	0	0	0
Totals	39	14	14	14

Milwaukee Braves	AB	R	H	RBI
Roy McMillan, ss	4	1	1	0
Frank Bolling, 2b	4	1	2	0
Eddie Mathews, 3b	4	0	1	0
Hank Aaron, cf	4	2	2	4
Mel Roach, lf	4	0	1	0
Joe Adcock, 1b	4	0	0	0
Charlie Lau, c	3	0	1	0
Don McMahon, p	0	0	0	0
George Brunet, p	0	0	0	0
Lee Maye, ph	0	0	0	0
John DeMerit, rf	4	0	0	0
Lew Burdette, p	1	0	0	0
Carl Willey, p	0	0	0	0
Moe Drabowsky, p	0	0	0	0
Billy Martin, ph	1	0	0	0
Seth Morehead, p	0	0	0	0
Ken MacKenzie, p	0	0	0	0
Johnny Logan, ph	1	0	0	0
Hawk Taylor, c	0	0	0	0
Totals	34	4	8	4

	1	2	3	4	5	6	7	8	9		R	H	E
SF	1	0	3	3	0	4	0	3	0		14	14	0
Mil	3	0	0	0	0	1	0	0	0		4	8	1

E—Mathews. DP—San Francisco 1, Milwaukee 2. LOB—San Francisco 6, Milwaukee 4. 2B—Hiller 2. 3B—Davenport. HR—Mays 4, Pagan 2, Aaron 2, Cepeda, F.Alou. SH—Loes 2.

San Francisco Giants	IP	H	R	ER	BB	SO
Billy Loes (W)	9.0	8	4	4	1	3

Milwaukee Braves	IP	H	R	ER	BB	SO
Lew Burdette (L)	3.0	5	5	5	0	0
Carl Willey	1.0	3	2	2	0	0
Moe Drabowsky	1.0	0	0	0	1	0
Seth Morehead	1.0	2	4	4	1	1
Ken MacKenzie	1.0	0	0	0	0	1
Don McMahon	1.0	3	3	3	2	0
George Brunet	1.0	1	0	0	0	0

Burdette pitched to one batter in the 4th.

HBP—Davenport by Burdette, Bailey by MacKenzie. Time—2:40. Attendance—13,114. Umpires—HP, Pelekoudas. 1B, Forman. 2B, Conlan. 3B, Burkhart.

October 1, 1961

Yankees right fielder Roger Maris' pursuit of the single-season home run mark ends on the final day of the season. Maris blasts a fourth-inning pitch from Tracy Stallard for his 61st homer, surpassing Babe Ruth.

Boston Red Sox	AB	R	H	RBI
Chuck Schilling, 2b	4	0	1	0
Gary Geiger, cf	4	0	0	0
Carl Yastrzemski, lf	4	0	1	0
Frank Malzone, 3b	4	0	0	0
Lu Clinton, rf	4	0	0	0
Pete Runnels, 1b	3	0	0	0
Don Gile, 1b	0	0	0	0
Russ Nixon, c	3	0	2	0
Pumpsie Green, ss	2	0	0	0
Tracy Stallard, p	1	0	0	0
Jackie Jensen, ph	1	0	0	0
Chet Nichols, p	0	0	0	0
Totals	30	0	4	0

New York Yankees	AB	R	H	RBI
Bobby Richardson, 2b	4	0	0	0
Tony Kubek, ss	4	0	2	0
Roger Maris, cf	4	1	1	1
Yogi Berra, lf	2	0	0	0
Hector Lopez, lf-rf	1	0	0	0
Johnny Blanchard, rf-c	3	0	0	0
Elston Howard, c	2	0	0	0
Jack Reed, lf	1	0	1	0
Bill Skowron, 1b	2	0	0	0
Bob Hale, 1b	1	0	1	0
Clete Boyer, 3b	2	0	0	0
Bill Stafford, p	2	0	0	0
Hal Reniff, p	0	0	0	0
Tom Tresh, ph	1	0	0	0
Luis Arroyo, p	0	0	0	0
Totals	29	1	5	1

	1	2	3	4	5	6	7	8	9		R	H	E
Bos	0	0	0	0	0	0	0	0	0		0	4	0
NYA	0	0	0	1	0	0	0	0	x		1	5	0

LOB—Boston 5, New York 5. 3B—Nixon. HR—Maris. SH—Stallard. SB—Geiger.

Boston Red Sox	IP	H	R	ER	BB	SO
Tracy Stallard (L)	7.0	5	1	1	1	5
Chet Nichols	1.0	0	0	0	0	0

New York Yankees	IP	H	R	ER	BB	SO
Bill Stafford (W)	6.0	3	0	0	1	7
Hal Reniff	1.0	0	0	0	0	0
Luis Arroyo (S)	2.0	1	0	0	0	1

WP—Stallard. Time—1:57. Attendance—23,154. Umpires—HP, Kinnamon. 1B, Flaherty. 2B, Honochick. 3B, Salerno.

September 12, 1962

The only big league pitcher to exceed 20 strikeouts in one game is Tom Cheney of the Washington Senators, who fans 21 while going the distance for a 16-inning, 2-1 win over the Orioles.

Washington Senators	AB	R	H	RBI
John Kennedy, ss	6	0	1	0
Ron Stillwell, 2b	3	1	1	0
Jim King, ph	1	0	1	0
Chuck Cottier, 2b	2	0	0	0
Chuck Hinton, rf	7	0	1	0
Bud Zipfel, 1b	7	1	3	2
Ken Retzer, c	7	0	1	0
Claude Osteen, pr	0	0	0	0
Bob Schmidt, c	0	0	0	0
Joe Hicks, cf	5	0	1	0
Johnny Schaive, ph	1	0	0	0
Jimmy Piersall, cf	0	0	0	0
Don Lock, lf	7	0	1	0
Ed Brinkman, 3b	5	0	1	0
Tom Cheney, p	6	0	0	0
Totals	57	2	10	2

Baltimore Orioles	AB	R	H	RBI
Jerry Adair, ss	6	0	2	0
Russ Snyder, rf	7	0	2	0
Brooks Robinson, 3b	5	0	1	0
Jim Gentile, 1b	7	0	1	0
Boog Powell, lf	6	0	1	0
Dave Nicholson, cf	7	0	1	0
Hobie Landrith, c	6	0	0	0
Jackie Brandt, ph	1	0	0	0
Marv Breeding, 2b	6	1	1	0
Dick Williams, ph	1	0	0	0
Milt Pappas, p	2	0	0	0
Charlie Lau, ph	1	0	1	1
Dick Hall, p	3	0	0	0
Billy Hoeft, p	0	0	0	0
Wes Stock, p	0	0	0	0
Totals	58	1	10	1

	1	2	3	4	5	6	7	8	9	10	11	12	13	14	15
Was	1	0	0	0	0	0	0	0	0	0	0	0	0	0	0
Bal	0	0	0	0	0	0	1	0	0	0	0	0	0	0	0

	16		R	H	E
Was	1		2	10	0
Bal	0		1	10	2

E—Adair, Breeding. LOB—Washington 13, Baltimore 13. 2B—Hinton, Hicks, Adair, Snyder, Gentile, Breeding. HR—Zipfel. SH—Cheney. SB—Adair. CS—Kennedy.

Washington Senators	IP	H	R	ER	BB	SO
Tom Cheney (W)	16.0	10	1	1	4	21

Baltimore Orioles	IP	H	R	ER	BB	SO
Milt Pappas	7.0	4	1	1	3	4
Dick Hall (L)	8.1	5	1	1	1	4
Billy Hoeft	0.1	1	0	0	0	0
Wes Stock	0.1	0	0	0	1	0

WP—Cheney. Balk—Pappas. Time—3:59. Attendance—4,098. Umpires—HP, McKinley. 1B, Chylak. 2B, Umont. 3B, Stewart.

October 1, 1962

In the opening game of the National League playoff, Giants veteran Billy Pierce wins his 12th straight game at Candlestick Park with a three-hitter. San Francisco's Willie Mays homers twice to lead the big leagues with 49.

Los Angeles Dodgers	AB	R	H	RBI
Maury Wills, ss	4	0	0	0
Jim Gilliam, 2b	3	0	0	0
Tommy Davis, lf	4	0	0	0
Frank Howard, rf	4	0	0	0
Lee Walls, 1b	3	0	0	0
John Roseboro, c	3	0	0	0
Andy Carey, 3b	3	0	1	0
Willie Davis, cf	3	0	0	0
Sandy Koufax, p	0	0	0	0
Ed Roebuck, p	1	0	0	0
Ken McMullen, ph	1	0	1	0
Dick Tracewski, pr	0	0	0	0
Larry Sherry, p	0	0	0	0
Jack Smith, p	0	0	0	0
Doug Camilli, ph	1	0	1	0
Phil Ortega, p	0	0	0	0
Ron Perranoski, p	0	0	0	0
Totals	30	0	3	0

San Francisco Giants	AB	R	H	RBI
Harvey Kuenn, lf	5	0	0	0
Chuck Hiller, 2b	4	0	1	0
Felipe Alou, rf	4	1	1	0
Willie Mays, cf	3	3	3	3
Orlando Cepeda, 1b	4	1	1	1
Jim Davenport, 3b	3	2	2	1
Ed Bailey, c	2	1	1	0
Jose Pagan, ss	3	0	1	2
Billy Pierce, p	4	0	0	0
Totals	32	8	10	7

	1	2	3	4	5	6	7	8	9		R	H	E
LA	0	0	0	0	0	0	0	0	0		0	3	1
SF	2	1	0	0	0	2	0	3	x		8	10	0

E—Howard. DP—Los Angeles 1. LOB—Los Angeles 4, San Francisco 5. 2B—Camilli, Alou, Pagan. HR—Mays 2, Cepeda, Davenport. SH—Pagan. SB—Mays.

Los Angeles Dodgers	IP	H	R	ER	BB	SO
Sandy Koufax (L)	1.0	4	3	3	0	0
Ed Roebuck	4.0	1	0	0	0	2
Larry Sherry	0.1	3	2	2	1	0
Jack Smith	1.2	1	0	0	0	2
Phil Ortega	0.1	0	2	2	2	0
Ron Perranoski	0.2	1	1	0	1	0

San Francisco Giants	IP	H	R	ER	BB	SO
Billy Pierce (W)	9.0	3	0	0	1	6

Koufax pitched to two batters in the 2nd.

Time—2:39. Attendance—32,652. Umpires—HP, Conlan. 1B, Boggess. 2B, Donatelli. 3B, Landes.

October 2, 1962

The Dodgers even the National League playoff by pulling out an 8-7 win in the bottom of the ninth. First baseman Ron Fairly's sacrifice fly scores shortstop Maury Wills with the game-winner.

San Francisco Giants	AB	R	H	RBI
Chuck Hiller, 2b	3	1	1	1
Bob Nieman, ph	1	0	0	0
Ernie Bowman, 2b	1	0	0	0
Jim Davenport, 3b	6	1	2	1
Willie Mays, cf	5	0	1	0
Willie McCovey, lf	2	0	1	1
Stu Miller, p	0	0	0	0
Billy O'Dell, p	0	0	0	0
Don Larsen, p	0	0	0	0
Ed Bailey, ph	1	0	1	1
Carl Boles, pr	0	1	0	0
Bobby Bolin, p	0	0	0	0
Dick LeMay, p	0	0	0	0
Gaylord Perry, p	0	0	0	0
Mike McCormick, p	0	0	0	0
Orlando Cepeda, 1b	5	1	1	0
Felipe Alou, rf	4	0	2	1
Tom Haller, c	1	1	0	1
John Orsino, c	1	0	1	1
Jose Pagan, ss	5	1	3	0
Jack Sanford, p	3	1	0	0
Matty Alou, lf	0	0	0	0
Harvey Kuenn, ph	2	0	0	0
Totals	40	7	13	7

Los Angeles Dodgers	AB	R	H	RBI
Maury Wills, ss	4	1	0	0
Jim Gilliam, 2b-3b	3	1	0	0
Duke Snider, lf	3	1	1	0
Daryl Spencer, ph	0	0	0	0
Tommy Davis, 3b-cf	3	0	1	1
Wally Moon, 1b	2	1	1	0
Ron Fairly, 1b	1	0	1	1
Frank Howard, rf	3	1	1	1
John Roseboro, c	2	0	0	0
Doug Camilli, c	2	1	1	0
Willie Davis, cf	2	0	0	0
Andy Carey, ph	0	0	0	1
Larry Burright, 2b	0	1	0	0
Don Drysdale, p	2	0	0	0
Ed Roebuck, p	0	0	0	0
Lee Walls, ph	1	1	1	3
Ron Perranoski, p	0	0	0	0
Jack Smith, p	0	0	0	0
Stan Williams, p	1	0	0	0
Totals	29	8	7	7

	1	2	3	4	5	6	7	8	9	R	H	E
SF	0	1	0	0	4	0	2	0		7	13	1
LA	0	0	0	0	0	7	0	0	1	8	7	2

Two outs when winning run scored.

E—Haller, Howard, Drysdale. LOB—San Francisco 13, Los Angeles 7. 2B—Alou, Pagan, Snider, Walls. SH—Spencer. SF—Orsino, Davis, Fairly. SB—Wills.

San Francisco Giants	IP	H	R	ER	BB	SO
Jack Sanford	5.0	2	1	1	3	4
Stu Miller	0.1	2	3	3	1	0
Billy O'Dell	0.0	2	3	2	0	0
Don Larsen	1.2	1	0	0	0	1
Bobby Bolin (L)	1.0	0	1	1	2	2
Dick LeMay	0.0	0	0	0	1	0
Gaylord Perry	0.1	0	0	0	0	0
Mike McCormick	0.1	0	0	0	1	0

Los Angeles Dodgers	IP	H	R	ER	BB	SO
Don Drysdale	5.1	7	5	3	4	4
Ed Roebuck	0.2	1	0	0	0	0
Ron Perranoski	1.0	4	1	1	0	0
Jack Smith	0.1	1	1	0	0	0
Stan Williams (W)	1.2	0	0	0	1	2

Sanford pitched to one batter in the 6th. O'Dell pitched to three batters in the 6th. Perranoski pitched to two batters in the 8th. Bolin pitched to one batter in the 9th. LeMay pitched to one batter in the 9th.

HBP—Hiller by Drysdale, Carey by O'Dell. Time—4:18. Attendance—25,321. Umpires—HP, Barlick. 1B, Boggess. 2B, Donatelli. 3B, Conlan.

October 3, 1962

Shades of 1951: The Giants stun the Dodgers with a ninth-inning rally to win the third and deciding game of the National League playoff. Stan Williams walks Jim Davenport with the bases loaded to force home the go-ahead run.

San Francisco Giants	AB	R	H	RBI
Harvey Kuenn, lf	5	1	2	1
Chuck Hiller, 2b	3	0	1	0
Willie McCovey, ph	0	0	0	0
Ernie Bowman, pr	0	1	0	0
Felipe Alou, rf	4	1	1	0
Willie Mays, cf	3	1	1	1
Orlando Cepeda, 1b	4	0	1	1
Ed Bailey, c	4	0	2	0
Jim Davenport, 3b	4	0	1	1
Jose Pagan, ss	5	1	2	0
Juan Marichal, p	2	1	1	0
Don Larsen, p	0	0	0	0
Matty Alou, ph	1	0	1	0
Bob Nieman, ph	1	0	0	0
Billy Pierce, p	0	0	0	0
Totals	36	6	13	4

Los Angeles Dodgers	AB	R	H	RBI
Maury Wills, ss	5	1	4	0
Jim Gilliam, 2b-3b	5	0	0	0
Duke Snider, lf	3	2	2	0
Larry Burright, 2b	1	0	0	0
Lee Walls, ph	1	0	0	0
Tommy Davis, 3b-lf	3	1	2	2
Wally Moon, 1b	3	0	0	0
Ron Fairly, 1b-rf	0	0	0	0
Frank Howard, rf	4	0	0	1
Tim Harkness, 1b	0	0	0	0
John Roseboro, c	3	0	0	0
Willie Davis, cf	3	0	0	0
Johnny Podres, p	2	0	0	0
Ed Roebuck, p	2	0	0	0
Stan Williams, p	0	0	0	0
Ron Perranoski, p	0	0	0	0
Totals	35	4	8	3

	1	2	3	4	5	6	7	8	9	R	H	E
SF	0	0	2	0	0	0	0	0	4	6	13	3
LA	0	0	0	1	0	2	1	0	0	4	8	4

E—Bailey, Pagan, Marichal, Gilliam, Burright, Roseboro, Podres. DP—Los Angeles 3. LOB—San Francisco 12, Los Angeles 8. 2B—Hiller, Snider. HR—TDavis. SH—Hiller, Marichal, Fairly. SF—Cepeda. SB—Wills 3, TDavis.

San Francisco Giants	IP	H	R	ER	BB	SO
Juan Marichal	7.0	8	4	3	1	2
Don Larsen (W)	1.0	0	0	0	2	1
Billy Pierce	1.0	0	0	0	0	0

Los Angeles Dodgers	IP	H	R	ER	BB	SO
Johnny Podres	5.0	9	2	1	1	0
Ed Roebuck (L)	3.1	4	4	3	3	0
Stan Williams	0.1	0	0	0	2	0
Ron Perranoski	0.1	0	0	0	0	1

Podres pitched to three batters in the 6th. Marichal pitched to one batter in the 8th.

WP—Williams. Time—3:00. Attendance—45,693. Umpires—HP, Boggess. 1B, Donatelli. 2B, Conlan. 3B, Barlick.

June 21, 1964

Phillies ace Jim Bunning celebrates Fathers' Day by pitching the first regular-season perfect game in 42 years, a 6-0 gem against the Mets. Bunning is the first pitcher to win no-hitters in both leagues.

Philadelphia Phillies	AB	R	H	RBI
John Briggs, cf	4	1	0	0
John Herrnstein, 1b	4	0	0	0
Johnny Callison, rf	4	1	2	1
Dick Allen, 3b	3	0	1	1
Wes Covington, lf	2	0	0	0
Bobby Wine, ss	1	1	0	0
Tony Taylor, 2b	3	2	1	0
Cookie Rojas, ss-lf	3	0	1	0
Gus Triandos, c	4	1	2	2
Jim Bunning, p	4	0	1	2
Totals	32	6	8	6

New York Mets	AB	R	H	RBI
Jim Hickman, cf	3	0	0	0
Ron Hunt, 2b	3	0	0	0
Ed Kranepool, 1b	3	0	0	0
Joe Christopher, rf	3	0	0	0
Jesse Gonder, c	3	0	0	0
Hawk Taylor, lf	3	0	0	0
Charley Smith, ss	3	0	0	0
Amado Samuel, 3b	2	0	0	0
George Altman, ph	1	0	0	0
Tracy Stallard, p	1	0	0	0
Bill Wakefield, p	0	0	0	0
Rod Kanehl, ph	1	0	0	0
Tom Sturdivant, p	0	0	0	0
John Stephenson, ph	1	0	0	0
Totals	27	0	0	0

	1	2	3	4	5	6	7	8	9	R	H	E
Phi	1	1	0	0	0	4	0	0	0	6	8	0
NYN	0	0	0	0	0	0	0	0	0	0	0	0

LOB—Philadelphia 5, New York 0. 2B—Triandos, Bunning. HR—Callison. SH—Herrnstein, Rojas. CS—Rojas.

Philadelphia Phillies	IP	H	R	ER	BB	SO
Jim Bunning (W)	9.0	0	0	0	0	10

New York Mets	IP	H	R	ER	BB	SO
Tracy Stallard (L)	5.2	7	6	6	4	3
Bill Wakefield	0.1	0	0	0	0	0
Tom Sturdivant	3.0	1	0	0	0	3

WP—Stallard. Time—2:19. Attendance—32,026. Umpires—HP, Sudol. 1B, Pryor. 2B, Secory. 3B, Burkhart.

September 8, 1965

In a publicity stunt, Kansas City Athletics shortstop Bert Campaneris becomes the first player to play all nine positions in one game. He goes 0-for-3 and gives up one run in an inning on the mound.

California Angels	AB	R	H	RBI
Jose Cardenal, cf	6	0	0	1
Albie Pearson, lf	5	2	1	0
Jim Fregosi, ss	5	1	1	0
Joe Adcock, 1b	4	0	2	2
Marcelino Lopez, pr	0	0	0	0
Vic Power, 1b	0	0	0	0
Bobby Gene Smith, ph	1	0	0	0
Charlie Dees, 1b	1	0	0	0
Bobby Knoop, 2b	3	1	1	0
Ed Kirkpatrick, rf	5	0	2	0
Tom Egan, c	2	0	0	0
Bob Rodgers, c	2	1	0	0
Paul Schaal, 3b	5	0	1	0
Dean Chance, p	4	0	0	0
Bob Lee, p	1	0	0	0
Merritt Ranew, ph	1	0	0	0
Jim Coates, p	0	0	0	0
Totals	45	5	8	3

Kansas City Athletics	AB	R	H	RBI
Bert Campaneris, ss-2b-3b-lf-cf-rf-1b-p-c	3	1	0	0
Rene Lachemann, c	2	0	2	0
Jose Tartabull, lf-rf-lf	4	0	0	0
Wayne Causey, 2b-ss	5	1	2	0
Ed Charles, 3b-2b-3b	6	0	1	1
Jim Landis, cf-rf-cf	5	1	1	0
Billy Bryan, c	3	0	1	0
Aurelio Monteagudo, p	0	0	0	0
Ken Harrelson, ph	1	0	1	1
Fred Talbot, pr	0	0	0	0
John Wyatt, p	0	0	0	0
Tommie Reynolds, ph	1	0	0	0
John O'Donoghue, p	0	0	0	0
Diego Segui, p	0	0	0	0
Johnny Blanchard, ph	1	0	0	0
Randy Schwartz, 1b	2	0	0	0
Mike Hershberger, rf	0	0	0	0
Larry Stahl, rf	3	0	0	0
Lu Clinton, rf	1	0	0	0
Dick Green, 2b	4	0	1	1
Dick Joyce, p	2	0	0	0
Don Mossi, p	0	0	0	0
Jim Dickson, p	0	0	0	0
Santiago Rosario, 1b	3	0	0	0
Totals	46	3	9	3

	1	2	3	4	5	6	7	8	9	10	11	12	13	R	H	E
Cal	0	0	0	1	0	1	0	1	0	0	0	0	2	5	8	0
KCA	1	0	0	0	0	0	0	0	2	0	0	0	0	3	9	3

E—Causey, Campaneris, O'Donoghue. DP—Kansas City 1. LOB—California 12, Kansas City 10. 2B—Adcock, Charles, Bryan. SH—Kirkpatrick, Tartabull. SF—Cardenal. SB—Kirkpatrick, Tartabull, Campaneris. CS—Fregosi, Kirkpatrick.

California Angels	IP	H	R	ER	BB	SO
Dean Chance	8.1	5	3	3	2	6
Bob Lee (W)	3.2	4	0	0	2	2
Jim Coates (S)	1.0	0	0	0	0	0

Kansas City Athletics	IP	H	R	ER	BB	SO
Dick Joyce	6.0	5	2	1	1	2
Don Mossi	0.1	0	0	0	0	0
Jim Dickson	0.2	0	0	0	1	1
Bert Campaneris	1.0	1	1	1	2	1
Aurelio Monteagudo	1.0	1	0	0	1	1
John Wyatt	2.0	1	0	0	2	0
John O'Donoghue (L)	1.0	0	2	0	1	0
Diego Segui	1.0	0	0	0	1	0

Joyce pitched to one batter in the 7th. O'Donoghue pitched to three batters in the 13th.
HBP—Landis by Chance. WP—Dickson. Time—4:14. Attendance—21,576. Umpires—HP, Drummond. 1B, Kinnamon. 2B, Stevens. 3B, Napp.

September 9, 1965

Dodgers star Sandy Koufax pitches the seventh perfect game in major league history, his record fourth career no-hitter. Bob Hendley of the Cubs counters with a one-hitter, but takes the 1-0 loss.

Chicago Cubs	AB	R	H	RBI
Don Young, cf	3	0	0	0
Glenn Beckert, 2b	3	0	0	0
Billy Williams, rf	3	0	0	0
Ron Santo, 3b	3	0	0	0
Ernie Banks, 1b	3	0	0	0
Byron Browne, lf	3	0	0	0
Chris Krug, c	3	0	0	0
Don Kessinger, ss	2	0	0	0
Joey Amalfitano, ph	1	0	0	0
Bob Hendley, p	2	0	0	0
Harvey Kuenn, ph	1	0	0	0
Totals	27	0	0	0

Los Angeles Dodgers	AB	R	H	RBI
Maury Wills, ss	3	0	0	0
Jim Gilliam, 3b	3	0	0	0
John Kennedy, 3b	0	0	0	0
Tommy Davis, cf	3	0	0	0
Lou Johnson, lf	2	1	1	0
Ron Fairly, rf	2	0	0	0
Jim Lefebvre, 2b	3	0	0	0
Dick Tracewski, 2b	0	0	0	0
Wes Parker, 1b	3	0	0	0
Jeff Torborg, c	3	0	0	0
Sandy Koufax, p	2	0	0	0
Totals	24	1	1	0

	1	2	3	4	5	6	7	8	9	R	H	E
ChN	0	0	0	0	0	0	0	0	0	0	0	1
LA	0	0	0	0	1	0	0	0	x	1	1	0

E—Krug. LOB—Chicago 0, Los Angeles 1. 2B—Johnson. SH—Fairly. SB—Johnson.

Chicago Cubs	IP	H	R	ER	BB	SO
Bob Hendley (L)	8.0	1	1	0	1	3

Los Angeles Dodgers	IP	H	R	ER	BB	SO
Sandy Koufax (W)	9.0	0	0	0	0	14

Time—1:43. Attendance—29,139. Umpires—HP, Vargo. 1B, Pelekoudas. 2B, Jackowski. 3B, Pryor.

July 3, 1966

Atlanta's Tony Cloninger become the first pitcher and first National Leaguer to hit two grand slams in one game. His nine RBI also set a big league record for pitchers.

Atlanta Braves	AB	R	H	RBI
Felipe Alou, 1b	3	0	0	0
Mike de la Hoz, 3b	2	0	0	0
Mack Jones, cf	6	1	3	0
Hank Aaron, rf	4	2	1	1
Gary Geiger, rf	2	1	1	1
Rico Carty, lf	4	3	3	1
John Herrnstein, lf	1	0	0	0
Joe Torre, c	6	2	3	3
Frank Bolling, 2b	5	2	2	2
Woody Woodward, ss	6	2	4	0
Denis Menke, 3b-1b	3	2	0	0
Tony Cloninger, p	5	2	3	9
Totals	47	17	20	17

San Francisco Giants	AB	R	H	RBI
Jesus Alou, rf	4	0	1	0
Tom Haller, c-1b	3	1	1	1
Willie Mays, cf	1	1	0	0
Don Landrum, cf	2	0	0	0
Willie McCovey, 1b	1	0	0	0
Dick Dietz, c	3	0	0	0
Jim Ray Hart, 3b	3	0	1	0
Ozzie Virgil, 3b	1	0	0	0
Len Gabrielson, lf	4	0	1	1
Jim Davenport, ss	1	0	0	0
Don Mason, 2b	3	0	0	0
Hal Lanier, 2b-ss	4	0	2	0
Joe Gibbon, p	0	0	0	0
Bob Priddy, p	0	0	0	0
Ray Sadecki, p	3	1	1	1
Cap Peterson, ph	1	0	0	0
Totals	34	3	7	3

	1	2	3	4	5	6	7	8	9	R	H	E
Atl	7	1	0	5	1	0	0	1	2	17	20	1
SF	0	0	0	1	1	0	0	1	0	3	7	3

E—Cloninger, Hart, Gabrielson, Lanier. DP—Atlanta 1, San Francisco 1. LOB—Atlanta 8, San Francisco 6. 2B—Woodward 2, Jones, Geiger. HR—Cloninger 2, Aaron, Carty, Sadecki, Haller. SF—Bolling.

Atlanta Braves	IP	H	R	ER	BB	SO
Tony Cloninger (W)	9.0	7	3	3	2	5

San Francisco Giants	IP	H	R	ER	BB	SO
Joe Gibbon (L)	0.2	5	5	5	0	0
Bob Priddy	2.0	4	3	3	2	0
Ray Sadecki	6.1	11	9	5	2	4

WP—Cloninger, Sadecki. Time—2:42. Attendance—27,002. Umpires—HP, Harvey. 1B, Wendelstedt. 2B, Crawford. 3B, Vargo.

May 8, 1968

Oakland's Catfish Hunter tosses the fourth American League perfect game and eighth in big league history. He also strikes out 11 and goes 3-for-4 with three RBI.

Minnesota Twins	AB	R	H	RBI
Cesar Tovar, 3b	3	0	0	0
Rod Carew, 2b	3	0	0	0
Harmon Killebrew, 1b	3	0	0	0
Tony Oliva, rf	3	0	0	0
Ted Uhlaender, cf	3	0	0	0
Bob Allison, lf	3	0	0	0
Jackie Hernandez, ss	2	0	0	0
John Roseboro, ph	1	0	0	0
Bruce Look, c	3	0	0	0
Dave Boswell, p	2	0	0	0
Ron Perranoski, p	0	0	0	0
Rich Reese, ph	1	0	0	0
Totals	27	0	0	0

Oakland Athletics	AB	R	H	RBI
Bert Campaneris, ss	4	0	2	0
Reggie Jackson, rf	4	0	0	0
Sal Bando, 3b	3	0	1	0
Ray Webster, 1b	4	1	2	0
John Donaldson, 2b	3	0	0	0
Jim Pagliaroni, c	3	1	0	0
Rick Monday, cf	3	2	2	0
Joe Rudi, lf	3	0	0	0
Floyd Robinson, ph	0	0	0	0
Danny Cater, ph	0	0	0	1
Mike Hershberger, lf	0	0	0	0
Catfish Hunter, p	4	0	3	3
Totals	31	4	10	4

	1	2	3	4	5	6	7	8	9		R	H	E
Min	0	0	0	0	0	0	0	0	0		0	0	1
Oak	0	0	0	0	0	0	1	3	x		4	10	0

E—Boswell. DP—Minnesota 2. LOB—Minnesota 0, Oakland 9. 2B—Monday, Hunter. SB—Campaneris. CS—Monday.

Minnesota Twins	IP	H	R	ER	BB	SO
Dave Boswell (L)	7.2	9	4	4	4	6
Ron Perranoski	0.1	1	0	0	1	0

Oakland Athletics	IP	H	R	ER	BB	SO
Catfish Hunter (W)	9.0	0	0	0	0	11

HBP—Donaldson by Boswell. WP—Boswell 2. Time—2:28. Attendance—6,298. Umpires—HP, Neudecker. 1B, Napp. 2B, Salerno. 3B, Haller.

September 14, 1968

Tigers ace Denny McLain becomes the major leagues' first 30-game winner in 34 years when Detroit rallies for two runs in the bottom of the ninth. McLain finishes the year with 31 victories, a figure not approached since.

Oakland Athletics	AB	R	H	RBI
Bert Campaneris, ss	4	0	1	1
Rick Monday, cf	4	0	1	0
Danny Cater, 1b	4	1	2	0
Sal Bando, 3b	3	0	0	0
Reggie Jackson, rf	4	2	2	3
Dick Green, 2b	4	0	0	0
Joe Keough, lf	3	0	0	0
Jim Gosger, lf	0	0	0	0
Dave Duncan, c	2	1	0	0
Chuck Dobson, p	1	0	0	0
Jack Aker, p	0	0	0	0
Paul Lindblad, p	0	0	0	0
John Donaldson, ph	0	0	0	0
Diego Segui, p	1	0	0	0
Totals	30	4	6	4

Detroit Tigers	AB	R	H	RBI
Dick McAuliffe, 2b	5	0	1	0
Mickey Stanley, cf	5	1	2	0
Jim Northrup, rf	4	1	0	0
Willie Horton, lf	5	1	2	1
Norm Cash, 1b	4	1	2	3
Bill Freehan, c	3	0	1	0
Tommy Matchick, ss	4	0	1	0
Don Wert, 3b	2	0	0	0
Gates Brown, ph	1	0	0	0
Dick Tracewski, 3b	0	0	0	0
Denny McLain, p	1	0	0	0
Al Kaline, ph	0	1	0	0
Totals	34	5	9	4

	1	2	3	4	5	6	7	8	9		R	H	E
Oak	0	0	0	2	1	1	0	0	0		4	6	2
Det	0	0	0	3	0	0	0	0	2		5	9	1

One out when winning run scored.

E—Cater, Bando, Matchick. DP—Detroit 1. LOB—Oakland 2, Detroit 10. HR—Jackson 2, Cash. SH—Bando, Donaldson, McLain.

Oakland Athletics	IP	H	R	ER	BB	SO
Chuck Dobson	3.2	4	3	3	2	4
Jack Aker	0.0	0	0	0	1	0
Paul Lindblad	0.1	0	0	0	0	1
Diego Segui (L)	4.1	5	2	1	2	1

Detroit Tigers	IP	H	R	ER	BB	SO
Denny McLain (W)	9.0	6	4	4	1	10

Aker pitched to one batter in the 4th.

WP—Aker. Time—3:00. Attendance—33,688. Umpires—HP, Napp. 1B, Umont. 2B, Haller. 3B, Neudecker.

April 14, 1969

In the first big league game ever played in Canada, the Expos edge the Cardinals 8-7. Dan McGinn earns the victory with 5.1 innings of shutout relief and drives in the winning run with a seventh-inning single.

St. Louis Cardinals	AB	R	H	RBI
Lou Brock, lf	5	0	0	0
Curt Flood, cf	5	1	4	0
Vada Pinson, rf	5	1	1	1
Joe Torre, 1b	5	1	2	2
Mike Shannon, 3b	5	1	0	0
Tim McCarver, c	5	1	1	0
Julian Javier, 2b	3	1	2	0
Dal Maxvill, ss	4	1	2	4
Nelson Briles, p	2	0	0	0
Gary Waslewski, p	1	0	0	0
Phil Gagliano, ph	0	0	0	0
Joe Hoerner, p	0	0	0	0
Totals	40	7	12	7

Montreal Expos	AB	R	H	RBI
Don Bosch, cf	5	1	2	0
Maury Wills, ss	5	2	1	0
Rusty Staub, rf	4	2	2	0
Mack Jones, lf	4	1	2	5
Bob Bailey, 1b	4	0	1	0
John Bateman, c	2	0	0	0
Coco Laboy, 3b	3	2	1	0
Gary Sutherland, 2b	4	0	0	0
Larry Jaster, p	2	0	1	1
Dan McGinn, p	2	0	1	1
Totals	35	8	11	7

	1	2	3	4	5	6	7	8	9		R	H	E
StL	0	0	0	7	0	0	0	0	0		7	12	0
Mon	3	2	1	1	0	0	1	0	x		8	11	5

E—Bailey 2, Bosch, Wills, Bateman. LOB—St. Louis 8, Montreal 8. 2B—Flood, Torre, Staub, Bailey, Laboy. 3B—Jones. HR—Torre, Maxvill, Jones. SH—Javier.

St. Louis Cardinals	IP	H	R	ER	BB	SO
Nelson Briles	3.0	9	7	7	3	3
Gary Waslewski (L)	4.0	2	1	1	2	5
Joe Hoerner	1.0	0	0	0	0	1

Montreal Expos	IP	H	R	ER	BB	SO
Larry Jaster	3.2	9	7	2	0	1
Dan McGinn (W)	5.1	3	0	0	1	0

Briles pitched to two batters in the 4th.

WP—Waslewski. Balk—Jaster. Time—2:16. Attendance—29,184. Umpires—HP, Steiner. 1B, Engel. 2B, Stello. 3B, Donatelli.

June 21, 1970

Light-hitting Tigers shortstop Cesar Gutierrez becomes the first player in modern baseball history to stroke seven consecutive hits in one game. He batted just .235 for his career and .243 in 1970.

Detroit Tigers	AB	R	H	RBI
Mickey Stanley, cf	6	1	2	1
Cesar Gutierrez, ss	7	3	7	1
Al Kaline, 1b	6	1	1	2
Willie Horton, 1b	6	1	3	0
Jim Northrup, rf	5	2	2	5
Elliott Maddox, 3b	6	0	0	0
Ike Brown, 2b	3	0	0	0
Gates Brown, ph	1	1	1	0
Bill Freehan, c	1	0	0	0
Jim Price, c	1	0	0	0
Norm Cash, ph	1	0	0	0
John Hiller, p	0	0	0	0
Don Wert, p	1	0	1	0
Tom Timmermann, p	1	0	0	0
Mike Kilkenny, p	0	0	0	0
Daryl Patterson, p	2	0	0	0
Russ Nagelson, ph	1	0	0	0
Fred Scherman, p	0	0	0	0
Dick McAuliffe, 2b	3	0	0	0
Totals	51	9	17	9

Cleveland Indians	AB	R	H	RBI
Jack Heidemann, ss	5	1	1	1
Eddie Leon, 2b	5	1	1	0
Ted Uhlaender, cf	6	2	3	1
Ray Fosse, c	6	1	2	0
Tony Horton, 1b	5	1	4	5
Roy Foster, lf	4	0	0	0
Fred Lasher, p	0	0	0	0
Rich Rollins, ph	1	0	0	0
Dick Ellsworth, p	0	0	0	0
Lou Klimchock, ph	1	0	0	0
Phil Hennigan, p	0	0	0	0
Chuck Hinton, rf	6	1	3	1
Graig Nettles, 3b	3	1	3	0
Rick Austin, p	1	0	0	0
Dennis Higgins, p	1	0	0	0
Vada Pinson, rf	3	0	0	0
Totals	47	8	17	8

	1	2	3	4	5	6	7	8	9	10	11	12	R	H	E
Det	1	0	4	0	0	0	2	1	0	0	0	1	9	17	1
Cle	5	1	0	0	1	1	0	0	0	0	0	0	8	17	1

E—THorton. DP—Detroit 1, Cleveland 1. LOB—Detroit 13, Cleveland 11. 2B—Gutierrez, GBrown, Fosse, THorton. HR—Northrup 2, Stanley, Kaline, Uhlaender, THorton, Hinton. SH—Higgins. SF—Heidemann, THorton.

Detroit Tigers	IP	H	R	ER	BB	SO
Mike Kilkenny	0.2	5	5	5	1	2
Daryl Patterson	4.1	4	2	2	1	3
Fred Scherman	2.0	2	1	1	0	0
John Hiller	2.0	2	0	0	1	1
Tom Timmermann (W)	3.0	4	0	0	2	1

Cleveland Indians	IP	H	R	ER	BB	SO
Rick Austin	2.1	5	5	5	2	3
Dennis Higgins	4.2	4	2	2	2	5
Fred Lasher	2.0	3	1	1	1	1
Dick Ellsworth	2.0	3	0	0	1	0
Phil Hennigan (L)	1.0	2	1	1	1	0

WP—Scherman. Time—4:00. Attendance—23,904. Umpires—HP, Springstead. 1B, Barnett. 2B, Napp. 3B, Rice.

August 1, 1972

Padres first baseman Nate Colbert ties Stan Musial's 1954 record with five home runs in a doubleheader and sets another with 13 RBI for the day. As an 8 year old, Colbert was on hand to witness Musial's feat.

San Diego Padres	AB	R	H	RBI
Derrel Thomas, ss	5	0	1	0
Dave Roberts, 3b	2	2	0	0
Larry Stahl, lf	2	2	1	0
Jerry Morales, lf	2	0	0	0
Nate Colbert, 1b	5	3	4	5
Cito Gaston, rf	4	2	2	2
Enzo Hernandez, rf	1	0	0	0
Garry Jestadt, 2b	4	0	0	0
Johnny Jeter, cf	4	0	1	1
Joe Goddard, c	3	0	0	0
Clay Kirby, p	4	0	0	0
Totals	36	9	9	8

Atlanta Braves	AB	R	H	RBI
Dusty Baker, cf	4	0	0	0
George Stone, p	0	0	0	0
Ralph Garr, lf	3	0	1	0
Oscar Brown, lf	1	0	1	0
Hank Aaron, 1b	2	0	0	0
Paul Casanova, c	2	0	0	0
Earl Williams, c-1b	3	0	2	0
Mike Lum, rf	3	0	0	0
Darrell Evans, 3b	4	0	0	0
Felix Millan, 2b	4	0	1	0
Marty Perez, ss	2	0	1	0
Larvell Blanks, ss	2	0	1	0
Ron Schueler, p	0	0	0	0
Mike McQueen, p	2	0	0	0
Sonny Jackson, cf	1	0	0	0
Totals	33	0	7	0

	1	2	3	4	5	6	7	8	9		R	H	E
SD	3	0	4	0	0	0	2	0	0		9	9	1
Atl	0	0	0	0	0	0	0	0	0		0	7	0

E—Kirby. DP—San Diego 1. LOB—San Diego 6, Atlanta 8. 2B—Gaston, Williams, Perez, Blanks. 3B—Jeter. HR—Colbert 2, Gaston.

San Diego Padres	IP	H	R	ER	BB	SO
Clay Kirby (W)	9.0	7	0	0	2	7

Atlanta Braves	IP	H	R	ER	BB	SO
Ron Schueler (L)	2.0	3	6	6	4	1
Mike McQueen	5.0	6	3	3	2	4
George Stone	2.0	0	0	0	0	1

Schueler pitched to three batters in the 3rd.

WP—McQueen 2. Time—2:32. Umpires—HP, Donatelli. 1B, Landes. 2B, Davidson. 3B, Froemming.

August 1, 1972

San Diego Padres	AB	R	H	RBI
Derrel Thomas, ss	4	1	0	0
Dave Roberts, 3b	5	1	2	1
Larry Stahl, lf	3	4	2	0
Nate Colbert, 1b	4	4	3	8
Cito Gaston, rf	5	0	1	1
Curt Blefary, c	3	0	1	0
Johnny Jeter, cf	4	0	0	0
Fred Stanley, 2b	4	0	0	0
Ed Acosta, p	2	1	0	0
Mike Corkins, p	1	0	0	0
Mark Schaeffer, p	0	0	0	0
Al Severinsen, p	0	0	0	0
Totals	35	11	9	10

Atlanta Braves	AB	R	H	RBI
Dusty Baker, cf	4	0	2	2
Ralph Garr, lf	4	0	1	1
Hank Aaron, 1b	5	0	1	0
Earl Williams, c	3	0	0	0
Paul Casanova, c	2	0	0	0
Mike Lum, rf	4	2	3	0
Darrell Evans, 3b	4	2	2	2
Felix Millan, 2b	2	0	0	0
Larvell Blanks, 2b	2	1	1	0
Marty Perez, ss	3	1	2	1
Tom Kelley, p	0	0	0	0
Pat Jarvis, p	1	0	0	0
Sonny Jackson, ph	1	0	1	0
Jim Hardin, p	0	0	0	0
Oscar Brown, ph	1	1	1	0
Joe Hoerner, p	0	0	0	0
Gil Garrido, ph	1	0	0	0
Cecil Upshaw, p	0	0	0	0
Totals	37	7	14	6

	1	2	3	4	5	6	7	8	9		R	H	E
SD	2	5	0	0	0	0	2	0	2		11	9	0
Atl	0	0	0	1	0	0	4	2	0		7	14	3

E—Garr, Perez, Kelley. DP—San Diego 2, Atlanta 1. LOB—San Diego 3, Atlanta 8. 2B—Lum 2, Blefary, Evans. HR—Colbert 3, Evans. SF—Garr.

San Diego Padres	IP	H	R	ER	BB	SO
Ed Acosta (W)	6.0	9	5	5	2	3
Mike Corkins	1.2	3	2	2	2	1
Mark Schaeffer	0.1	0	0	0	0	0
Al Severinsen (S)	1.0	2	0	0	0	0

Atlanta Braves	IP	H	R	ER	BB	SO
Tom Kelley (L)	1.1	1	4	3	5	1
Pat Jarvis	3.2	4	3	3	1	3
Jim Hardin	2.0	2	2	2	0	1
Joe Hoerner	1.0	0	0	0	0	1
Cecil Upshaw	1.0	2	2	2	0	0

Acosta pitched to four batters in the 7th.

WP—Acosta, Corkins. Balk—Acosta. Time—2:52. Attendance—5,784. Umpires—HP, Landes. 1B, Davidson. 2B, Froemming. 3B, Donatelli.

April 6, 1973

Ron Blomberg of the Yankees makes history by becoming the first designated hitter ever in the major leagues. He walks with the bases loaded against Luis Tiant in the first inning of a 15-5 Red Sox win.

New York Yankees	AB	R	H	RBI
Horace Clarke, 2b	5	0	1	0
Roy White, lf	5	0	0	0
Matty Alou, rf	5	2	2	0
Bobby Murcer, cf	3	1	0	0
Graig Nettles, 3b	2	2	1	2
Ron Blomberg, dh	3	0	1	1
Felipe Alou, 1b	4	0	3	2
Thurman Munson, c	3	0	0	0
Gene Michael, ss	4	0	0	0
Totals	34	5	8	5

Boston Red Sox	AB	R	H	RBI
Tommy Harper, lf	6	1	3	1
Luis Aparicio, ss	6	0	1	1
Carl Yastrzemski, 1b	4	2	2	2
Reggie Smith, cf	5	2	2	0
Rick Miller, cf	0	0	0	0
Orlando Cepeda, dh	6	0	0	0
Rico Petrocelli, 3b	4	3	3	0
Carlton Fisk, c	4	4	3	6
Doug Griffin, 2b	5	3	4	2
Dwight Evans, rf	5	0	2	1
Totals	45	15	20	13

```
        1 2 3  4 5 6  7 8 9       R  H  E
NYA     3 0 1  0 1 0  0 0 0       5  8  2
Bos     1 4 3  4 0 3  0 0 x      15 20  0
```

E—Nettles, Michael. DP—Boston 1. LOB—New York 7, Boston 11. 2B—MAlou 2, FAlou, Harper, Smith, Fisk, Evans. HR—Fisk 2, Nettles, Yastrzemski. SF—Yastrzemski. SB—Yastrzemski, Griffin. CS—Clarke.

New York Yankees	IP	H	R	ER	BB	SO
Mel Stottlemyre (L)	2.2	8	8	6	0	1
Lindy McDaniel	2.1	7	4	4	1	2
Casey Cox	3.0	5	3	2	1	0

Boston Red Sox	IP	H	R	ER	BB	SO
Luis Tiant (W)	9.0	8	5	5	5	2

HBP—Smith by Cox, Fisk by Cox. Time—2:57. Attendance—32,882. Umpires—HP, Umont. 1B, Denkinger. 2B, Anthony. 3B, Deegan.

April 8, 1974

Move over, Babe: Braves left fielder Hank Aaron becomes the major leagues' all-time home run leader when he hits the 715th of his career, a fourth-inning shot to left-center off the Dodgers' Al Downing.

Los Angeles Dodgers	AB	R	H	RBI
Davey Lopes, 2b	2	1	0	0
Lee Lacy, 2b	1	0	0	0
Bill Buckner, lf	3	0	1	0
Jimmy Wynn, cf	4	0	1	2
Joe Ferguson, c	4	0	0	0
Willie Crawford, rf	4	1	1	0
Ron Cey, 3b	4	0	1	1
Steve Garvey, 1b	4	1	1	0
Bill Russell, ss	4	0	1	0
Al Downing, p	1	1	1	1
Mike Marshall, p	1	0	0	0
Von Joshua, ph	1	0	0	0
Charlie Hough, p	0	0	0	0
Manny Mota, ph	1	0	0	0
Totals	34	4	7	4

Atlanta Braves	AB	R	H	RBI
Ralph Garr, rf-lf	3	0	0	1
Mike Lum, 1b	5	0	0	1
Darrell Evans, 3b	4	1	0	0
Hank Aaron, lf	3	2	1	2
Rowland Office, cf	0	0	0	0
Dusty Baker, cf-rf	2	1	1	0
Dave Johnson, 2b	3	1	1	0
Leo Foster, 2b	0	0	0	0
Vic Correll, c	4	1	0	0
Craig Robinson, ss	0	0	0	0
Frank Tepedino, ph	0	0	0	1
Marty Perez, ss	2	1	1	0
Ron Reed, p	2	0	0	0
Johnny Oates, ph	1	0	0	1
Buzz Capra, p	0	0	0	0
Totals	29	7	4	6

```
        1 2 3  4 5 6  7 8 9       R  H  E
LA      0 0 3  0 0 1  0 0 0       4  7  6
Atl     0 1 0  4 0 2  0 0 x       7  4  0
```

E—Russell 2, Lopes, Buckner, Ferguson, Cey. LOB—Los Angeles 5, Atlanta 7. 2B—Russell, Wynn, Baker. HR—Aaron. SH—Garr. SF—Garr.

Los Angeles Dodgers	IP	H	R	ER	BB	SO
Al Downing (L)	3.0	2	5	2	4	2
Mike Marshall	3.0	2	2	1	1	1
Charlie Hough	2.0	0	0	0	2	1

Atlanta Braves	IP	H	R	ER	BB	SO
Ron Reed (W)	6.0	7	4	4	1	4
Buzz Capra (S)	3.0	0	0	0	1	6

Downing pitched to four batters in the 4th.

WP—Reed. Time—2:27. Attendance—53,775. Umpires—HP, Sudol. 1B, Weyer. 2B, Pulli. 3B, Davidson.

September 16, 1975

Pirates second baseman Rennie Stennett becomes the only modern player to collect seven hits in a nine-inning game. Pittsburgh's 22-0 rout of the Cubs is the most lopsided shutout in modern major league history.

Pittsburgh Pirates	AB	R	H	RBI
Rennie Stennett, 2b	7	5	7	2
Willie Randolph, 2b	0	0	0	0
Richie Hebner, 1b	7	3	2	3
Al Oliver, cf	4	2	1	1
Miguel Dilone, cf	1	0	0	0
Willie Stargell, 1b	4	2	3	3
Bob Robertson, 1b	3	1	1	0
Dave Parker, rf	4	3	2	5
Richie Zisk, lf	5	2	2	1
Manny Sanguillen, c	5	2	2	1
Ken Brett, p	1	0	0	0
Ramon Hernandez, p	0	0	0	0
Frank Taveras, ss	6	1	3	3
John Candelaria, p	5	1	1	2
Ed Ott, c	1	0	0	0
Totals	53	22	24	21

Chicago Cubs	AB	R	H	RBI
Don Kessinger, 3b	3	0	0	0
Ron Dunn, 3b	1	0	0	0
Jim Tyrone, lf	4	0	0	0
Jerry Morales, cf	3	0	0	0
Pete LaCock, rf	1	0	0	0
Jose Cardenal, rf	2	0	1	0
Vic Harris, cf	1	0	0	0
Andre Thornton, 1b	3	0	1	0
Paul Reuschel, p	0	0	0	0
Manny Trillo, 2b	2	0	0	0
Rob Sperring, 2b	1	0	0	0
George Mitterwald, c	3	0	0	0
Dave Rosello, ss	3	0	1	0
Rick Reuschel, p	0	0	0	0
Tom Dettore, p	1	0	0	0
Oscar Zamora, p	0	0	0	0
Tim Hosley, ph	1	0	0	0
Buddy Schultz, p	0	0	0	0
Champ Summers, p	1	0	0	0
Totals	30	0	3	0

```
        1 2 3  4 5 6  7 8 9       R  H  E
Pit     9 0 2  1 6 2  2 0 0      22 24  0
ChN     0 0 0  0 0 0  0 0 0       0  3  3
```

E—Dunn, Rosello, Dettore. LOB—Pittsburgh 12, Chicago 3. 2B—Stennett 2. 3B—Stennett. HR—Hebner, Parker. SF—Parker.

Pittsburgh Pirates	IP	H	R	ER	BB	SO
John Candelaria (W)	7.0	3	0	0	0	5
Ken Brett	1.0	0	0	0	0	2
Ramon Hernandez	1.0	0	0	0	0	0

Chicago Cubs	IP	H	R	ER	BB	SO
Rick Reuschel (L)	0.1	6	8	8	2	0
Tom Dettore	3.2	7	8	7	2	1
Oscar Zamora	1.0	4	2	2	0	2
Buddy Schultz	2.0	6	4	2	1	2
Paul Reuschel	2.0	1	0	0	1	0

HBP—Parker by Dettore. WP—Dettore. Time—2:35. Attendance—4,932. Umpires—HP, Wendelstedt. 1B, Engel. 2B, Rennert. 3B, Harvey.

September 28, 1975

In a major league first, four pitchers combine on a no-hitter. Oakland's Vida Blue, Glenn Abbott, Paul Lindblad and Rollie Fingers do the honors against the Angels, as the A's start tuning up for the postseason.

California Angels	AB	R	H	RBI
Jerry Remy, 2b	4	0	0	0
Dave Chalk, 3b	2	0	0	0
Mickey Rivers, ph	1	0	0	0
Lee Stanton, cf	3	0	0	0
John Balaz, rf	3	0	0	0
Bruce Bochte, 1b	3	0	0	0
Ron Jackson, lf	2	0	0	0
Morris Nettles, lf	1	0	0	0
Paul Dade, dh	1	0	0	0
Dan Briggs, dh	1	0	0	0
Bob Allietta, c	3	0	0	0
Ike Hampton, ss	2	0	0	0
Dave Collins, ph	1	0	0	0
Totals	27	0	0	0

Oakland Athletics	AB	R	H	RBI
Bill North, cf	4	0	1	0
Claudell Washington, lf	4	2	1	0
Gene Tenace, c-1b	3	1	0	0
Reggie Jackson, rf	4	2	2	3
Sal Bando, 3b	4	0	2	2
Billy Williams, ph	4	0	0	0
Joe Rudi, 1b	1	0	0	0
Jim Holt, 1b	1	0	0	0
Tommy Harper, ph	1	0	0	0
Ray Fosse, c	0	0	0	0
Bert Campaneris, ss	3	0	1	0
Don Hopkins, pr	0	0	0	0
Ted Martinez, 2b	1	0	0	0
Phil Garner, 2b	3	0	1	0
Dal Maxvill, ss	1	0	1	0
Totals	34	5	9	5

	1	2	3	4	5	6	7	8	9		R	H	E
Cal	0	0	0	0	0	0	0	0	0		0	0	1
Oak	2	0	1	0	0	0	2	0	x		5	9	1

E—Hampton, Campaneris. DP—Oakland 1. LOB—California 2, Oakland 8. 2B—Bando. HR—Jackson 2. SB—Stanton, Bando, Hopkins.

California Angels	IP	H	R	ER	BB	SO
Gary Ross (L)	5.0	6	3	3	1	4
Sid Monge	2.0	2	2	2	1	1
Joe Pactwa	1.0	1	0	0	1	0

Oakland Athletics	IP	H	R	ER	BB	SO
Vida Blue (W)	5.0	0	0	0	2	2
Glenn Abbott	1.0	0	0	0	0	0
Paul Lindblad	1.0	0	0	0	0	0
Rollie Fingers	2.0	0	0	0	0	2

Time—1:59. Attendance—22,131. Umpires—HP, Kunkel. 1B, Phillips. 2B, DiMuro.

April 17, 1976

Phillies third baseman Mike Schmidt hits four consecutive home runs, becoming the 10th player to hit four in one game. Philadelphia ties another record by overcoming an 11-run deficit to win.

Philadelphia Phillies	AB	R	H	RBI
Dave Cash, 2b	6	1	2	2
Larry Bowa, ss	6	3	3	1
Jay Johnstone, rf	5	2	4	2
Greg Luzinski, lf	5	0	1	1
Ollie Brown, lf	0	0	0	0
Dick Allen, 1b	5	2	1	2
Mike Schmidt, 3b	6	4	5	8
Garry Maddox, cf	5	2	2	1
Tug McGraw, p	0	0	0	0
Tim McCarver, ph	1	1	1	0
Tom Underwood, p	0	0	0	0
Jim Lonborg, p	0	0	0	0
Bob Boone, c	6	1	3	1
Steve Carlton, p	1	0	0	0
Ron Schueler, p	0	0	0	0
Gene Garber, p	0	0	0	0
Tom Hutton, ph	0	0	0	0
Ron Reed, p	0	0	0	0
Jerry Martin, ph	1	0	0	0
Wayne Twitchell, p	0	0	0	0
Bobby Tolan, cf	3	2	2	0
Totals	50	18	24	18

Chicago Cubs	AB	R	H	RBI
Rick Monday, cf	6	3	4	4
Jose Cardenal, lf	5	1	1	0
Champ Summers, lf	0	0	0	0
George Mitterwald, ph	1	0	0	0
Joe Wallis, lf	1	0	0	0
Bill Madlock, 3b	7	2	3	3
Jerry Morales, rf	5	2	1	0
Andre Thornton, 1b	4	3	1	1
Manny Trillo, 2b	5	0	2	3
Steve Swisher, c	6	1	3	4
Dave Rosello, ss	4	1	2	1
Mick Kelleher, ss	2	0	1	0
Rick Reuschel, p	1	2	0	0
Mike Garman, p	0	0	0	0
Darold Knowles, p	0	0	0	0
Paul Reuschel, p	0	0	0	0
Buddy Schultz, p	0	0	0	0
Mike Adams, ph	1	1	1	0
Totals	48	16	19	16

	1	2	3	4	5	6	7	8	9	10		R	H	E
Phi	0	1	0	1	2	0	3	5	3	3		18	24	0
ChN	0	7	5	1	0	0	0	0	2	1		16	19	0

DP—Philadelphia 1, Chicago 1. LOB—Philadelphia 8, Chicago 12. 2B—Boone, Cardenal, Madlock 2, Thornton, Adams. 3B—Bowa, Johnstone. HR—Schmidt 4, Monday 2, Maddox, Boone, Swisher. SH—Johnstone, RReuschel. SF—Cash, Luzinski.

Philadelphia Phillies	IP	H	R	ER	BB	SO
Steve Carlton	1.2	7	7	7	2	1
Ron Schueler	0.2	3	3	3	0	0
Gene Garber	0.2	2	2	2	1	1
Ron Reed	2.0	1	1	1	1	1
Wayne Twitchell	2.0	0	0	0	1	1
Tug McGraw (W)	2.0	4	2	2	1	2
Tom Underwood	0.2	2	1	1	0	1
Jim Lonborg (S)	0.1	0	0	0	0	0

Chicago Cubs	IP	H	R	ER	BB	SO
Rick Reuschel	7.0	14	7	7	1	4
Mike Garman	0.2	4	5	5	1	1
Darold Knowles (L)	1.1	3	4	4	1	0
Paul Reuschel	0.0	3	2	2	0	0
Buddy Schultz	1.0	0	0	0	0	0

Knowles pitched to two batters in the 10th. PReuschel pitched to two batters in the 10th.

HBP—RReuschel by Schueler, Thornton by Garber, Monday by Twitchell. Balk—Schultz. Time—3:42. Attendance—28,287. Umpires—HP, Olsen. 1B, Davidson. 2B, Rennert. 3B, Vargo.

October 2, 1978

Shortstop Bucky Dent's three-run homer in the seventh inning is the key blow as the Yankees defeat the Red Sox 5-4 in a one-game playoff for the American League East title. New York goes on to win the World Series.

New York Yankees	AB	R	H	RBI
Mickey Rivers, cf	2	1	1	0
Paul Blair, ph-cf	1	0	1	0
Thurman Munson, c	5	0	1	1
Lou Piniella, rf	4	0	1	0
Reggie Jackson, dh	4	1	1	1
Graig Nettles, 3b	4	0	0	0
Chris Chambliss, 1b	4	1	1	0
Roy White, lf	3	1	1	0
Gary Thomasson, lf	0	0	0	0
Brian Doyle, 2b	2	0	0	0
Jim Spencer, ph	1	0	0	0
Fred Stanley, 2b	1	0	0	0
Bucky Dent, ss	4	1	1	3
Totals	35	5	8	5

Boston Red Sox	AB	R	H	RBI
Rick Burleson, ss	4	1	1	0
Jerry Remy, 2b	4	1	2	0
Jim Rice, rf	5	0	1	1
Carl Yastrzemski, lf	5	2	2	2
Carlton Fisk, c	3	0	1	0
Fred Lynn, cf	4	0	1	1
Butch Hobson, dh	4	0	1	0
George Scott, 1b	4	0	2	0
Jack Brohamer, 3b	1	0	0	0
Bob Bailey, ph	1	0	0	0
Frank Duffy, 3b	0	0	0	0
Dwight Evans, ph	1	0	0	0
Totals	36	4	11	4

	1	2	3	4	5	6	7	8	9		R	H	E
NYA	0	0	0	0	0	0	4	1	0		5	8	0
Bos	0	1	0	0	0	1	0	2	0		4	11	0

LOB—New York 6, Boston 9. 2B—Rivers, Munson, Burleson, Remy, Scott. HR—Jackson, Dent, Yastrzemski. SH—Remy, Brohamer. SB—Rivers 2.

New York Yankees	IP	H	R	ER	BB	SO
Ron Guidry (W)	6.1	6	2	2	1	5
Goose Gossage (S)	2.2	5	2	2	1	2

Boston Red Sox	IP	H	R	ER	BB	SO
Mike Torrez (L)	6.2	5	4	4	3	4
Bob Stanley	0.1	2	1	1	0	0
Andy Hassler	1.2	1	0	0	0	2
Dick Drago	0.1	0	0	0	0	0

Time—2:52. Attendance—32,925. Umpires—HP, Denkinger. 1B, Evans. 2B, Clark. 3B, Palermo.

October 6, 1980

In a one-game playoff for the National League West title, Houston's Joe Niekro earns his 20th victory and the Astros' first-ever playoff berth by beating the Dodgers 7-1.

Houston Astros	AB	R	H	RBI
Terry Puhl, rf	5	2	1	0
Enos Cabell, 3b	4	2	2	0
Dave Bergman, 1b	0	0	0	0
Joe Morgan, 2b	2	1	0	0
Rafael Landestoy, 2b	2	0	0	0
Jose Cruz, lf	4	0	1	1
Cesar Cedeno, cf	4	1	1	1
Art Howe, 1b-3b	5	1	3	4
Alan Ashby, c	4	0	1	0
Craig Reynolds, ss	4	0	3	0
Joe Niekro, p	2	0	0	0
Totals	36	7	12	6

Los Angeles Dodgers	AB	R	H	RBI
Davey Lopes, 2b	4	0	0	0
Steve Howe, p	0	0	0	0
Jay Johnstone, rf	4	0	0	0
Dusty Baker, lf	4	1	1	0
Steve Garvey, 1b	4	0	0	0
Rick Monday, cf	3	0	1	1
Joe Ferguson, c	4	0	1	0
Mickey Hatcher, 3b	3	0	1	0
Gary Thomasson, ph	1	0	0	0
Derrel Thomas, ss	3	0	2	0
Dave Goltz, p	0	0	0	0
Rudy Law, ph	1	0	0	0
Rick Sutcliffe, p	0	0	0	0
Joe Beckwith, p	0	0	0	0
Bobby Castillo, p	0	0	0	0
Vic Davalillo, ph	1	0	0	0
Fernando Valenzuela, p	0	0	0	0
Jack Perconte, 2b	2	0	0	0
Totals	34	1	6	1

	1	2	3	4	5	6	7	8	9	R	H	E
Hou	2	0	2	3	0	0	0	0	0	7	12	1
LA	0	0	0	1	0	0	0	0	0	1	6	2

E—Cabell, Lopes, Ferguson. LOB—Houston 9, Los Angeles 8. 2B—Cabell, Reynolds. HR—Howe. SH—Niekro 2. SF—Cruz. SB—Puhl 2, Cabell, Cedeno.

Houston Astros	IP	H	R	ER	BB	SO
Joe Niekro (W)	9.0	6	1	0	2	6

Los Angeles Dodgers	IP	H	R	ER	BB	SO
Dave Goltz (L)	3.0	8	4	2	0	2
Rick Sutcliffe	0.1	1	3	3	2	0
Joe Beckwith	0.1	1	0	0	1	0
Bobby Castillo	1.1	1	0	0	1	2
Fernando Valenzuela	2.0	1	0	0	0	1
Steve Howe	2.0	0	0	0	0	0

Time—3:10. Attendance—51,127.

May 15, 1981

Cleveland's Len Barker tosses the ninth perfect game in major league history, vanquishing the Blue Jays 3-0. Just 7,290 fans attend the game at Municipal Stadium.

Toronto Blue Jays	AB	R	H	RBI
Alfredo Griffin, ss	3	0	0	0
Lloyd Moseby, ss	3	0	0	0
George Bell, lf	3	0	0	0
John Mayberry, 1b	3	0	0	0
Willie Upshaw, dh	3	0	0	0
Damaso Garcia, 2b	3	0	0	0
Rick Bosetti, cf	3	0	0	0
Danny Ainge, 3b	2	0	0	0
Al Woods, ph	1	0	0	0
Buck Martinez, c	2	0	0	0
Ernie Whitt, ph	1	0	0	0
Totals	27	0	0	0

Cleveland Indians	AB	R	H	RBI
Rick Manning, cf	4	1	1	0
Jorge Orta, rf	4	1	3	1
Mike Hargrove, 1b	4	1	1	0
Andre Thornton, dh	3	0	0	1
Ron Hassey, c	4	0	1	1
Toby Harrah, 3b	4	0	1	0
Joe Charboneau, lf	3	0	0	0
Duane Kuiper, 2b	3	0	0	0
Tom Veryzer, ss	3	0	0	0
Totals	32	3	7	3

	1	2	3	4	5	6	7	8	9	R	H	E
Tor	0	0	0	0	0	0	0	0	0	0	0	3
Cle	2	0	0	0	0	0	0	1	x	3	7	0

E—Griffin, Mayberry, Garcia. LOB—Toronto 0, Cleveland 6. HR—Orta. SF—Thornton. CS—Orta.

Toronto Blue Jays	IP	H	R	ER	BB	SO
Luis Leal (L)	8.0	7	3	1	0	5

Cleveland Indians	IP	H	R	ER	BB	SO
Len Barker (W)	9.0	0	0	0	0	11

Time—2:09. Attendance—7,290.

May 8, 1984

White Sox right fielder Harold Baines homers off the Brewers' Chuck Porter in the bottom of the 25th to end the longest game in American League history. It lasts 8:06 and isn't completed until May 9.

Milwaukee Brewers	AB	R	H	RBI
Randy Ready, 3b	8	1	1	0
Jim Sundberg, c	4	0	3	0
Ed Romero, pr	0	0	0	0
Bill Schroeder, c	4	0	2	0
Robin Yount, ss	10	1	3	1
Cecil Cooper, dh	11	1	2	0
Ted Simmons, 1b	7	2	1	0
Ben Oglivie, lf	10	1	2	4
Bobby Clark, cf	2	0	1	0
Rick Manning, cf	6	0	2	0
Charlie Moore, rf	2	0	0	0
Dion James, rf	2	0	0	0
Mark Brouhard, rf	4	0	1	0
Jim Gantner, 2b	10	0	2	0
Totals	80	6	20	5

Chicago White Sox	AB	R	H	RBI
Rudy Law, cf	11	1	4	1
Carlton Fisk, c	11	1	3	1
Greg Walker, 1b	4	1	2	0
Mike Squires, 1b	2	0	0	0
Marc Hill, 1b	4	0	2	0
Rich Dotson, pr	0	1	0	0
Ron Reed, p	1	0	0	0
Floyd Bannister, p	1	0	0	0
Tom Seaver, p	0	0	0	0
Greg Luzinski, dh	2	0	0	0
Dave Stegman, lf	8	0	1	0
Harold Baines, rf	10	1	2	1
Ron Kittle, lf	1	0	0	0
Tom Paciorek, lf-1b	9	1	5	3
Vance Law, 3b	10	0	1	0
Scott Fletcher, ss	3	0	0	0
Jerry Hairston, ph	1	0	0	0
Jerry Dybzinski, ss	6	0	2	0
Julio Cruz, 2b	11	1	1	1
Totals	95	7	23	7

	1	2	3	4	5	6	7	8	9	10	11	12	13	14	15
Mil	0	0	0	0	0	0	1	0	2	0	0	0	0	0	0
ChA	0	0	0	0	0	1	0	0	2	0	0	0	0	0	0

	16	17	18	19	20	21	22	23	24	25	R	H	E
Mil	0	0	0	0	0	3	0	0	0	0	6	20	3
ChA	0	0	0	0	0	3	0	0	0	1	7	23	1

One out when winning run scored.

E—Ready 2, James, Fisk. DP—Milwaukee 1, Chicago 6. LOB—Milwaukee 13, Chicago 24. 2B—Ready, Yount, Fisk, Hill, Cruz, Baines. HR—Oglivie, Baines. SH—Ready, Schroeder, Moore, VLaw, Dybzinski. SB—Yount, Manning, Walker. CS—Oglivie, Clark, James, Brouhard.

Milwaukee Brewers	IP	H	R	ER	BB	SO
Don Sutton	7.0	4	1	0	3	6
Peter Ladd	1.0	0	0	0	1	0
Rollie Fingers	2.0	2	2	0	0	2
Tom Tellmann	3.1	3	0	0	1	1
Rick Waits	3.2	3	0	0	0	3
Chuck Porter (L)	7.1	11	4	3	2	5

Chicago White Sox	IP	H	R	ER	BB	SO
Bob Fallon	6.0	1	1	1	3	4
Salome Barojas	0.0	2	0	0	0	0
Britt Burns	3.0	3	2	2	3	3
Al Jones	4.0	4	0	0	1	4
Juan Agosto	7.0	0	0	0	2	3
Ron Reed	2.2	3	3	3	2	3
Floyd Bannister	1.1	1	0	0	0	1
Tom Seaver (W)	1.0	1	0	0	0	0

Fallon pitched to one batter in the 7th. Barojas pitched to two batters in the 7th.

WP—Burns, Jones. Time—8:06. Attendance—14,754. Umpires—HP, Evans. 1B, Kosc. 2B, Hendry. 3B, Coble.

September 30, 1984

On the final day of the regular season, California's Mike Witt requires just 97 pitches for the 10th perfect game in big league history. He strikes out 10 in a 1-0 defeat of the Rangers.

California Angels	AB	R	H	RBI
Rob Wilfong, 2b	4	0	0	0
Daryl Sconiers, 1b	4	0	0	0
Bobby Grich, 1b	0	0	0	0
Fred Lynn, cf-rf	3	0	2	0
Doug DeCinces, 3b	4	1	2	0
Brian Downing, lf	4	0	0	0
Derrel Thomas, lf	0	0	0	0
Reggie Jackson, dh	4	0	0	1
Mike Brown, rf	3	0	3	0
Gary Pettis, cf	0	0	0	0
Bob Boone, c	3	0	0	0
Dick Schofield, ss	2	0	0	0
Totals	31	1	7	1

Texas Rangers	AB	R	H	RBI
Mickey Rivers, dh	3	0	0	0
Wayne Tolleson, 2b	3	0	0	0
Gary Ward, lf	3	0	0	0
Larry Parrish, 3b	3	0	0	0
Pete O'Brien, 1b	3	0	0	0
George Wright, cf	3	0	0	0
Tommy Dunbar, rf	3	0	0	0
Donnie Scott, c	2	0	0	0
Bobby Jones, ph	1	0	0	0
Curtis Wilkerson, ss	2	0	0	0
Marv Foley, ph	1	0	0	0
Totals	27	0	0	0

	1	2	3	4	5	6	7	8	9		R	H	E
Cal	0	0	0	0	0	0	1	0	0		1	7	0
Tex	0	0	0	0	0	0	0	0	0		0	0	0

DP—Texas 2. LOB—California 6, Texas 0. 2B—Brown. 3B—Brown. CS—Lynn, Pettis.

California Angels	IP	H	R	ER	BB	SO
Mike Witt (W)	9.0	0	0	0	0	10

Texas Rangers	IP	H	R	ER	BB	SO
Charlie Hough (L)	9.0	7	1	0	3	3

WP—Hough. Time—1:49. Attendance—8,375.

September 11, 1985

Reds player-manager Pete Rose lines a 2-1 pitch from the Padres' Eric Show into left-center, giving him the 4,192nd hit of his career to surpass Ty Cobb. Rose scores both runs in Cincinnati's 2-0 victory.

San Diego Padres	AB	R	H	RBI
Garry Templeton, ss	4	0	0	0
Jerry Royster, 2b	4	0	1	0
Tony Gwynn, rf	4	0	1	0
Steve Garvey, 1b	4	0	0	0
Carmelo Martinez, lf	3	0	0	0
Kevin McReynolds, cf	3	0	1	0
Bruce Bochy, c	3	0	1	0
Kurt Bevacqua, 3b	3	0	1	0
Eric Show, p	2	0	0	0
Gerry Davis, ph	1	0	0	0
Roy Lee Jackson, p	0	0	0	0
Gene Walter, p	0	0	0	0
Totals	31	0	5	0

Cincinnati Reds	AB	R	H	RBI
Eddie Milner, cf	5	0	0	0
Pete Rose, 1b	3	2	2	0
Dave Parker, rf	1	0	1	0
Nick Esasky, lf	3	0	0	2
Max Venable, lf	0	0	0	0
Buddy Bell, 1b	4	0	1	0
Dave Concepcion, ss	4	0	1	0
Bo Diaz, c	3	0	1	0
Gary Redus, pr	0	0	0	0
Dave Van Gorder, c	0	0	0	0
Ron Oester, 2b	3	0	1	0
Tom Browning, p	4	0	1	0
John Franco, p	0	0	0	0
Ted Power, p	0	0	0	0
Totals	30	2	8	2

	1	2	3	4	5	6	7	8	9		R	H	E
SD	0	0	0	0	0	0	0	0	0		0	5	1
Cin	0	0	1	0	0	0	1	0	x		2	8	0

E—Show. DP—San Diego 1, Cincinnati 1. LOB—San Diego 4, Cincinnati 11. 2B—Bell, Diaz, Browning. 3B—Rose. SF—Esasky. SB—Gwynn.

San Diego Padres	IP	H	R	ER	BB	SO
Eric Show (L)	7.0	7	2	2	5	1
Roy Lee Jackson	0.1	1	0	0	1	0
Gene Walter	0.2	0	0	0	0	2

Cincinnati Reds	IP	H	R	ER	BB	SO
Tom Browning (W)	8.1	5	0	0	0	6
John Franco	0.1	0	0	0	0	0
Ted Power (S)	0.1	0	0	0	0	0

Time—2:17. Attendance—47,237. Umpires—HP, Weyer. 1B, Montague. 2B, Brocklander. 3B, Rennert.

April 29, 1986

Boston's Roger Clemens becomes the first pitcher to strike out 20 in a nine-inning game, dominating the Mariners for a 3-1 victory. Clemens will win his first 14 decisions of the season.

Seattle Mariners	AB	R	H	RBI
Spike Owen, ss	4	0	1	0
Phil Bradley, lf	4	0	0	0
Ken Phelps, 1b	4	0	0	0
Gorman Thomas, dh	3	1	1	1
Jim Presley, 3b	3	0	0	0
Ivan Calderon, rf	3	0	0	0
Danny Tartabull, 2b	3	0	1	0
Dave Henderson, cf	3	0	0	0
Steve Yeager, c	2	0	0	0
Al Cowens, ph	1	0	0	0
Bob Kearney, c	0	0	0	0
Totals	30	1	3	1

Boston Red Sox	AB	R	H	RBI
Dwight Evans, rf	4	1	2	3
Wade Boggs, 3b	3	0	0	0
Bill Buckner, dh	4	0	2	0
Jim Rice, lf	4	0	1	0
Don Baylor, 1b	3	0	1	0
Dave Stapleton, 1b	0	0	0	0
Rich Gedman, c	4	0	1	0
Marty Barrett, 2b	3	0	0	0
Steve Lyons, cf	3	1	1	0
Glenn Hoffman, ss	2	0	0	0
Ed Romero, ss	0	1	0	0
Totals	30	3	8	3

	1	2	3	4	5	6	7	8	9		R	H	E
Sea	0	0	0	0	0	0	1	0	0		1	3	1
Bos	0	0	0	0	0	0	3	0	x		3	8	1

E—Tartabull, Baylor. DP—Seattle 1. LOB—Seattle 2, Boston 7. 2B—Buckner. HR—Thomas, Evans. CS—Rice, Evans.

Seattle Mariners	IP	H	R	ER	BB	SO
Mike Moore (L)	7.1	8	3	3	4	4
Matt Young	0.1	0	0	0	0	0
Karl Best	0.1	0	0	0	0	1

Boston Red Sox	IP	H	R	ER	BB	SO
Roger Clemens (W)	9.0	3	1	1	0	20

Time—2:39. Attendance—13,414. Umpires—HP, Voltaggio. 1B, Welke. 2B, Phillips. 3B, McCoy.

July 6, 1986

Braves first baseman Bob Horner becomes the 11th player in major league history to homer four times in one game. He joins Ed Delahanty as the only players to do so in a losing cause.

Montreal Expos	AB	R	H	RBI
Mitch Webster, lf	6	2	5	3
George Wright, cf	6	1	2	1
Andre Dawson, rf	6	1	2	2
Hubie Brooks, ss	5	0	2	0
Tim Wallach, 3b	2	1	0	0
Andres Galarraga, 1b	2	0	0	0
Wayne Krenchicki, 1b	1	0	1	0
Jeff Reardon, p	0	0	0	0
Mike Fitzgerald, c	3	3	1	2
Al Newman, 2b	4	3	2	2
Andy McGaffigan, p	2	0	1	1
Tim Burke, p	1	0	0	0
Rudy Law, 1b	1	0	0	0
Totals	39	11	16	11

Atlanta Braves	AB	R	H	RBI
Omar Moreno, rf	4	0	1	0
Ted Simmons, 3b	1	0	0	0
Ken Oberkfell, 3b-2b	5	1	4	1
Dale Murphy, cf	5	0	0	0
Bob Horner, 1b	5	4	4	6
Ken Griffey Sr., lf	5	0	2	1
Andres Thomas, ss	4	0	1	0
Ozzie Virgil, c	4	1	1	0
Glenn Hubbard, 2b	3	1	1	0
Chris Chambliss, ph	0	0	0	0
Gene Garber, p	0	0	0	0
Zane Smith, p	1	0	0	0
Jeff Dedmon, p	0	1	0	0
Billy Sample, ph	1	0	0	0
Paul Assenmacher, p	0	0	0	0
Rafael Ramirez, rf	1	0	0	0
Totals	39	8	14	8

	1	2	3	4	5	6	7	8	9	R	H	E
Mon	0	0	1	3	6	0	1	0	0	11	16	1
Atl	0	1	0	1	5	0	0	0	1	8	14	1

E—Wallach, Horner. DP—Montreal 2, Atlanta 1. LOB—Montreal 10, Atlanta 6. 2B—Webster, Wright, Dawson, Brooks, Krenchicki, Fitzgerald, Virgil, Hubbard. HR—Horner 4, Webster, Dawson, Newman. SH—Krenchicki, McGaffigan, Dedmon. SB—Webster, Griffey Sr. CS—Dawson.

Montreal Expos	IP	H	R	ER	BB	SO
Andy McGaffigan	4.2	8	7	4	0	2
Tim Burke (W)	2.2	4	0	0	1	1
Jeff Reardon	1.2	2	1	1	0	1

Atlanta Braves	IP	H	R	ER	BB	SO
Zane Smith (L)	4.0	9	8	8	2	3
Jeff Dedmon	2.0	4	2	2	1	2
Paul Assenmacher	2.0	2	1	1	2	1
Gene Garber	1.0	1	0	0	0	0

Smith pitched to four batters in the 5th.

HBP—Galarraga by Dedmon, Fitzgerald by Dedmon. Time—3:06. Attendance—18,153. Umpires—HP, Poncino. 1B, Gregg. 2B, Davis. 3B, Harvey.

September 16, 1988

Cincinnati's Tom Browning twirls the 11th perfect game in major league history, earning a 1-0 win over the Dodgers. In July 1989, Browning gets three outs away from an unprecedented second perfecto before yielding a hit.

Los Angeles Dodgers	AB	R	H	RBI
Alfredo Griffin, ss	3	0	0	0
Mickey Hatcher, 1b	3	0	0	0
Kirk Gibson, lf	3	0	0	0
Jose Gonzalez, lf	0	0	0	0
Mike Marshall, rf	3	0	0	0
John Shelby, cf	3	0	0	0
Jeff Hamilton, 3b	3	0	0	0
Rick Dempsey, c	3	0	0	0
Steve Sax, 2b	3	0	0	0
Tim Belcher, p	2	0	0	0
Tracy Woodson, ph	1	0	0	0
Totals	27	0	0	0

Cincinnati Reds	AB	R	H	RBI
Barry Larkin, ss	3	1	1	0
Chris Sabo, 3b	3	0	1	0
Kal Daniels, lf	3	0	0	0
Eric Davis, cf	2	0	0	0
Paul O'Neill, rf	3	0	0	0
Nick Esasky, 1b	3	0	0	0
Jeff Reed, c	3	0	0	0
Ron Oester, 2b	3	0	1	0
Tom Browning, p	3	0	0	0
Totals	26	1	3	0

	1	2	3	4	5	6	7	8	9	R	H	E
LA	0	0	0	0	0	0	0	0	0	0	0	1
Cin	0	0	0	0	0	1	0	0	x	1	3	0

E—Hamilton. LOB—Los Angeles 0, Cincinnati 2. 2B—Larkin.

Los Angeles Dodgers	IP	H	R	ER	BB	SO
Tim Belcher (L)	8.0	3	1	0	1	7

Cincinnati Reds	IP	H	R	ER	BB	SO
Tom Browning (W)	9.0	0	0	0	0	7

Time—1:51. Attendance—16,591. Umpires—HP, Quick. 1B, Hirschbeck. 2B, Kibler. 3B, Gregg.

September 28, 1988

Los Angeles' Orel Hershiser pitches 10 shutout innings against the Padres on the final day of the regular season to run his scoreless streak to 59 frames. That breaks the old mark of 58 set by Don Drysdale in 1968.

Los Angeles Dodgers	AB	R	H	RBI
Steve Sax, 2b	5	0	0	0
Mike Sharperson, 2b	2	0	0	0
Franklin Stubbs, 1b	5	0	0	0
Mickey Hatcher, 1b	1	1	1	0
Kirk Gibson, lf	5	0	1	0
Jesse Orosco, p	0	0	0	0
Tracy Woodson, 3b	2	0	1	0
John Shelby, cf	5	0	1	0
Chris Gwynn, lf	1	0	0	0
Mike Davis, rf	4	0	0	0
Jose Gonzalez, rf-lf-cf	3	0	0	0
Mike Scioscia, c	4	0	0	0
Rick Dempsey, c	3	0	0	0
Jeff Hamilton, 3b	5	0	0	0
Tim Crews, p	0	0	0	0
Danny Heep, ph	1	0	0	0
Ken Howell, p	0	0	0	0
Ricky Horton, p	0	0	0	0
Alfredo Griffin, ss	5	0	1	0
Orel Hershiser, p	3	0	1	0
Mike Devereaux, rf	2	0	0	0
Totals	56	1	6	0

San Diego Padres	AB	R	H	RBI
Roberto Alomar, 2b	7	0	1	0
Tim Flannery, 3b	4	0	1	0
Bip Roberts, 3b	1	0	0	0
Tony Gwynn, cf	5	0	0	0
Stan Jefferson, cf	1	0	0	0
Carmelo Martinez, 1b	5	1	0	0
Marvell Wynne, rf	5	0	2	0
Mark Parent, ph	1	1	1	2
Benito Santiago, c	5	0	0	0
Randy Ready, lf	6	0	0	0
Garry Templeton, ss	5	0	0	0
Andy Hawkins, p	3	0	0	0
Keith Moreland, ph	1	0	0	0
Mark Davis, p	0	0	0	0
Rob Nelson, ph	1	0	0	0
Lance McCullers, p	0	0	0	0
Chris Brown, ph	1	0	0	0
Dickie Thon, pr	0	0	0	0
Dave Leiper, p	0	0	0	0
Totals	50	2	5	2

	1	2	3	4	5	6	7	8	9	10	11	12	13	14	15
LA	0	0	0	0	0	0	0	0	0	0	0	0	0	0	0
SD	0	0	0	0	0	0	0	0	0	0	0	0	0	0	0

	16	R	H	E
LA	1	1	6	1
SD	2	2	5	2

Two outs when winning run scored.

E—Stubbs, Roberts, Templeton. DP—Los Angeles 1. LOB—Los Angeles 11, San Diego 10. 2B—Griffin. 3B—Woodson. HR—Parent. SH—Hershiser, Santiago. SB—Gonzalez, TGwynn, Thon.

Los Angeles Dodgers	IP	H	R	ER	BB	SO
Orel Hershiser	10.0	4	0	0	1	3
Jesse Orosco	1.0	0	0	0	4	0
Tim Crews	2.0	0	0	0	0	2
Ken Howell	2.2	0	1	1	3	3
Ricky Horton (L)	0.0	1	1	1	0	0

San Diego Padres	IP	H	R	ER	BB	SO
Andy Hawkins	10.0	4	0	0	2	6
Mark Davis	2.0	0	0	0	4	4
Lance McCullers	3.0	1	0	0	0	4
Dave Leiper (W)	1.0	1	1	0	0	0

Horton pitched to one batter in the 16th.

HBP—Griffin by Hawkins. Time—4:24. Attendance—22,596. Umpires—HP, West. 1B, Runge. 2B, Engel. 3B, Williams.

Greats: Games

Rangers icon Nolan Ryan throws the seventh no-hitter of his career (three more than second-place Sandy Koufax) at age 44. Ryan strikes out 16 Blue Jays in the process.

Toronto Blue Jays	AB	R	H	RBI
Devon White, cf	4	0	0	0
Roberto Alomar, 2b	4	0	0	0
Kelly Gruber, 3b	2	0	0	0
Joe Carter, lf	2	0	0	0
John Olerud, 1b	3	0	0	0
Mark Whiten, rf	3	0	0	0
Glenallen Hill, dh	3	0	0	0
Greg Myers, c	3	0	0	0
Manuel Lee, ss	3	0	0	0
Totals	27	0	0	0

Texas Rangers	AB	R	H	RBI
Gary Pettis, cf	4	1	1	0
Jack Daugherty, lf	4	0	1	0
Rafael Palmeiro, 1b	4	1	2	0
Ruben Sierra, rf	4	1	1	2
Julio Franco, 2b	4	0	0	0
Juan Gonzalez, dh	3	0	1	0
Mike Stanley, c	3	0	1	0
Steve Buechele, 3b	4	0	1	0
Jeff Huson, ss	2	0	0	0
Totals	32	3	8	2

	1	2	3	4	5	6	7	8	9		R	H	E
Tor	0	0	0	0	0	0	0	0	0		0	0	3
Tex	0	0	3	0	0	0	0	0	x		3	8	1

E—Gruber, Myers, Lee, Palmeiro. LOB—Toronto 2, Texas 8. 2B—Gonzalez, Stanley. HR—Sierra. SH—Huson. SB—Pettis. CS—Gonzalez.

Toronto Blue Jays	IP	H	R	ER	BB	SO
Jimmy Key (L)	6.0	5	3	3	1	5
Bob MacDonald	1.0	2	0	0	0	2
Willie Fraser	1.0	1	0	0	0	0

Texas Rangers	IP	H	R	ER	BB	SO
Nolan Ryan (W)	9.0	0	0	0	2	16

HBP—Gonzalez by Fraser. Time—2:25. Attendance—33,439. Umpires—HP, Tschida. 1B, Coble. 2B, Shulock. 3B, Johnson.

Athletics left fielder Rickey Henderson becomes baseball's all-time stolen base king with the 939th of his career. The record-breaker comes in the fourth inning, when he steals third base.

New York Yankees	AB	R	H	RBI
Roberto Kelly, cf	4	0	1	0
Steve Sax, 2b	3	1	1	1
Don Mattingly, dh	4	0	1	0
Kevin Maas, 1b	3	1	1	0
Mel Hall, rf	1	0	0	1
Jesse Barfield, rf	1	0	1	0
Matt Nokes, c	4	1	1	1
Hensley Meulens, lf	4	0	1	1
Randy Velarde, 3b	3	0	0	0
Jim Leyritz, ph	1	0	0	0
Alvaro Espinoza, ss	3	1	0	0
Totals	31	4	7	4

Oakland Athletics	AB	R	H	RBI
Rickey Henderson, lf	4	1	1	0
Dave Henderson, cf	4	2	2	1
Jose Canseco, rf	4	2	1	0
Harold Baines, dh	4	1	2	1
Lance Blankenship, dh	1	0	0	0
Terry Steinbach, c	5	0	0	0
Mark McGwire, 1b	1	1	0	1
Ernest Riles, 3b	5	0	4	4
Walt Weiss, ss	2	0	0	0
Mike Gallego, 2b	3	0	0	0
Totals	33	7	10	7

	1	2	3	4	5	6	7	8	9		R	H	E
NYA	1	0	0	1	1	1	0	0	0		4	7	2
Oak	0	0	3	2	0	1	0	1	x		7	10	0

E—Espinoza 2. LOB—New York 5, Oakland 12. 2B—Barfield, RHenderson, Canseco, Baines. 3B—Riles. HR—Nokes, RHenderson. SF—Hall, McGwire. SB—Sax, RHenderson, Canseco, Blankenship, Riles. CS—RHenderson 2, Kelly.

New York Yankees	IP	H	R	ER	BB	SO
Tim Leary (L)	3.2	6	5	3	7	5
Rich Monteleone	1.1	2	1	1	1	0
Greg Cadaret	1.0	1	0	0	1	0
Steve Farr	1.0	1	1	0	0	0
Lee Guetterman	1.0	0	0	0	0	0

Oakland Athletics	IP	H	R	ER	BB	SO
Mike Moore (W)	5.1	5	4	4	3	4
Curt Young	0.1	0	0	0	1	0
Steve Chitren	1.1	1	0	0	0	2
Joe Klink	0.2	0	0	0	0	2
Dennis Eckersley (S)	1.1	1	0	0	0	1

Monteleone pitched to one batter in the 6th. Farr pitched to one batter in the 8th.

WP—Moore. Time—3:24. Attendance—36,139. Umpires—HP, Merrill. 1B, McClelland. 2B, Denkinger. 3B, Cedarstrom.

Dennis Martinez pitches the 12th perfect game in big league history, and the first by a Latin American pitcher. Ron Hassey becomes the only man to catch two perfectos, having also teamed up with Len Barker in 1981.

Montreal Expos	AB	R	H	RBI
Delino DeShields, 2b	3	0	1	0
Marquis Grissom, cf	4	0	0	0
Dave Martinez, rf	4	1	0	0
Ivan Calderon, lf	3	0	0	0
Tim Wallach, 3b	4	0	0	0
Larry Walker, 1b	4	1	1	1
Ron Hassey, c	3	0	1	0
Spike Owen, c	3	0	0	0
Dennis Martinez, p	3	0	1	0
Totals	31	2	4	1

Los Angeles Dodgers	AB	R	H	RBI
Brett Butler, cf	3	0	0	0
Juan Samuel, 2b	3	0	0	0
Eddie Murray, 1b	3	0	0	0
Darryl Strawberry, rf	3	0	0	0
Kal Daniels, lf	3	0	0	0
Lenny Harris, 3b	3	0	0	0
Mike Scioscia, c	3	0	0	0
Alfredo Griffin, ss	2	0	0	0
Stan Javier, ph	1	0	0	0
Mike Morgan, p	2	0	0	0
Chris Gwynn, ph	1	0	0	0
Totals	27	0	0	0

	1	2	3	4	5	6	7	8	9		R	H	E
Mon	0	0	0	0	0	0	2	0	0		2	4	0
LA	0	0	0	0	0	0	0	0	0		0	0	2

E—Griffin 2. LOB—Montreal 4, Los Angeles 0. 3B—Walker. SH—Calderon. CS—Owen.

Montreal Expos	IP	H	R	ER	BB	SO
Dennis Martinez (W)	9.0	0	0	0	0	5

Los Angeles Dodgers	IP	H	R	ER	BB	SO
Mike Morgan (L)	9.0	4	2	0	1	5

WP—Morgan. Time—2:14. Attendance—45,560. Umpires—HP, Poncino. 1B, Froemming. 2B, DeMuth. 3B, Bonin.

September 7, 1993

Cardinals right fielder Mark Whiten ties major league records with four home runs and 12 RBI in a 15-2 rout of the Reds. He equals another mark with 13 RBI in a doubleheader, having driven in a run in the opener.

St. Louis Cardinals	AB	R	H	RBI
Geronimo Pena, 2b	3	1	1	1
Lonnie Maclin, lf	4	1	0	1
Bernard Gilkey, rf	5	1	1	0
Todd Zeile, 3b	2	3	1	0
Stan Royer, 3b	1	0	0	0
Gerald Perry, 1b	4	4	3	1
Mark Whiten, cf	5	4	4	12
Tom Pagnozzi, c	5	0	1	0
Tripp Cromer, ss	5	0	0	0
Bob Tewksbury, p	2	1	0	0
Totals	36	15	11	15

Cincinnati Reds	AB	R	H	RBI
Thomas Howard, lf	3	1	0	0
Rob Dibble, p	0	0	0	0
Jacob Brumfield, cf	4	1	2	0
Hal Morris, 1b	2	0	1	1
Jack Daugherty, rf	1	0	1	0
Chris Sabo, 3b	3	0	0	0
Gary Varsho, lf	1	0	0	0
Tim Costo, rf-3b	4	0	1	0
Juan Samuel, 2b	4	0	0	0
Dan Wilson, c	4	0	0	0
Jeff Branson, ss	4	0	1	0
Larry Luebbers, p	1	0	0	0
Greg Tubbs, ph	1	0	0	0
Brian Anderson, p	0	0	0	0
Chris Bushing, p	0	0	0	0
Brian Dorsett, 1b	2	0	1	0
Totals	34	2	7	1

	1	2	3	4	5	6	7	8	9		R	H	E
StL	4	0	0	0	1	3	4	1	2		15	11	2
Cin	2	0	0	0	0	0	0	0	0		2	7	0

E—Zeile, Pagnozzi. LOB—St. Louis 2, Cincinnati 7. 2B—Brumfield. HR—Whiten 4, Pena. SH—Pena. SF—Maclin, Morris. SB—Maclin, Brumfield.

St. Louis Cardinals	IP	H	R	ER	BB	SO
Bob Tewksbury (W)	9.0	7	2	2	1	4

Cincinnati Reds	IP	H	R	ER	BB	SO
Larry Luebbers (L)	5.0	2	5	5	4	3
Brian Anderson	1.2	6	7	2	2	2
Chris Bushing	0.1	0	0	0	0	1
Rob Dibble	2.0	3	3	3	0	5

WP—Luebbers. Time—2:17. Attendance—22,606. Umpires—HP, Marsh. 1B, Kellogg. 2B, Vanover. 3B, Wendelstedt.

July 28, 1994

Texas' Kenny Rogers becomes the first American League lefthander to throw a perfect game with a 4-0 gem against the California Angels. Rangers center fielder Rusty Greer saves it with a diving catch of a ninth-inning liner.

California Angels	AB	R	H	RBI
Chad Curtis, cf	3	0	0	0
Spike Owen, 3b	3	0	0	0
Jim Edmonds, lf	3	0	0	0
Chili Davis, dh	3	0	0	0
Bo Jackson, rf	3	0	0	0
J.T. Snow, 1b	3	0	0	0
Rex Hudler, 2b	3	0	0	0
Chris Turner, c	3	0	0	0
Gary DiSarcina, ss	3	0	0	0
Totals	27	0	0	0

Texas Rangers	AB	R	H	RBI
Butch Davis, rf	4	0	0	0
Ivan Rodriguez, c	3	1	1	1
Jose Canseco, dh	4	2	2	2
Will Clark, 1b	3	1	0	0
Juan Gonzalez, lf	4	0	2	0
Dean Palmer, 3b	4	0	1	1
Rusty Greer, cf	3	0	0	0
Manuel Lee, 2b	3	0	0	0
Esteban Beltre, ss	2	0	0	0
Totals	30	4	6	4

	1	2	3	4	5	6	7	8	9		R	H	E
Cal	0	0	0	0	0	0	0	0	0		0	0	0
Tex	2	0	2	0	0	0	0	0	x		4	6	0

LOB—California 0, Texas 5. HR—Canseco 2, Rodriguez.

California Angels	IP	H	R	ER	BB	SO
Andrew Lorraine (L)	6.2	6	4	4	2	4
Russ Springer	1.1	0	0	0	1	1

Texas Rangers	IP	H	R	ER	BB	SO
Kenny Rogers (W)	9.0	0	0	0	0	8

WP—Springer. Time—2:08. Attendance—46,581. Umpires—HP, Bean. 1B, Denkinger. 2B, Shulock. 3B, Tschida.

September 6, 1995

Orioles shortstop Cal Ripken Jr. breaks one of baseball's unbreakable records, passing Lou Gehrig by playing in his 2,131st consecutive game. Ripken homers in the fourth, one inning before the game becomes official.

California Angels	AB	R	H	RBI
Tony Phillips, 3b	4	0	0	0
Jim Edmonds, cf	3	1	1	0
Tim Salmon, rf	4	1	3	2
Chili Davis, dh	3	0	0	0
J.T. Snow, 1b	4	0	1	0
Garret Anderson, lf	4	0	0	0
Rex Hudler, 2b	2	0	0	0
Spike Owen, 2b	2	0	0	0
Jorge Fabregas, c	3	0	0	0
Damion Easley, ss	2	0	1	0
Orlando Palmeiro, ph	1	0	0	0
Rod Correia, ss	0	0	0	0
Totals	32	2	6	2

Baltimore Orioles	AB	R	H	RBI
Brady Anderson, cf	4	0	1	0
Manny Alexander, 2b	4	0	0	0
Rafael Palmeiro, 1b	4	2	3	2
Bobby Bonilla, rf	4	1	1	1
Jarvis Brown, rf	0	0	0	0
Cal Ripken Jr., ss	4	1	2	1
Harold Baines, dh	4	0	1	0
Chris Hoiles, c	4	0	1	0
Jeff Huson, 3b	4	0	0	0
Mark Smith, lf	2	0	0	0
Totals	34	4	9	4

	1	2	3	4	5	6	7	8	9		R	H	E
Cal	1	0	0	0	0	0	0	1	0		2	6	1
Bal	1	0	0	2	0	0	1	0	x		4	9	0

E—Phillips. DP—Baltimore 1. LOB—California 5, Baltimore 7. 2B—Salmon, Easley, Baines. 3B—Edmonds. HR—Palmeiro 2, Salmon, Bonilla, Ripken Jr..

California Angels	IP	H	R	ER	BB	SO
Shawn Boskie (L)	5.0	6	3	3	1	4
Mike Bielecki	1.0	1	0	0	0	2
Bob Patterson	0.2	1	1	1	0	1
Mike James	1.1	1	0	0	0	1

Baltimore Orioles	IP	H	R	ER	BB	SO
Mike Mussina (W)	7.2	5	2	2	2	7
Terry Clark	0.0	1	0	0	0	0
Jesse Orosco (S)	1.1	0	0	0	0	2

Clark pitched to one batter in the 8th.

Time—3:35. Attendance—46,272. Umpires—HP, Barron. 1B, Kosc. 2B, Morrison. 3B, Clark.

October 2, 1995

The Mariners cap a comeback from an 11-game deficit with two months to play by beating the Angels 9-1 in a one-game playoff for the American League West title. Randy Johnson improves to 18-2 with a dominating effort.

California Angels	AB	R	H	RBI
Tony Phillips, 3b	4	1	1	1
Gary DiSarcina, ss	3	0	0	0
Spike Owen, ph	1	0	0	0
Jim Edmonds, cf	3	0	0	0
Eduardo Perez, ph	1	0	0	0
Tim Salmon, rf	4	0	0	0
Chili Davis, dh	2	0	0	0
J.T. Snow, 1b	3	0	0	0
Garret Anderson, lf	2	0	0	0
Dave Gallagher, lf	1	0	0	0
Andy Allanson, c	2	0	0	0
Rene Gonzales, ph	1	0	1	0
Jorge Fabregas, c	0	0	0	0
Rex Hudler, 2b	3	0	1	0
Totals	30	1	3	1

Seattle Mariners	AB	R	H	RBI
Vince Coleman, lf	5	0	2	1
Luis Sojo, ss	3	1	2	3
Ken Griffey Jr., cf	3	0	0	0
Edgar Martinez, dh	3	1	2	0
Jay Buhner, rf	4	1	1	0
Mike Blowers, 3b	3	2	2	0
Tino Martinez, 1b	2	2	1	1
Dan Wilson, c	3	1	1	2
Joey Cora, 2b	2	1	1	1
Totals	28	9	12	8

	1	2	3	4	5	6	7	8	9	R	H	E
Cal	0	0	0	0	0	0	0	0	1	1	3	1
Sea	0	0	0	0	1	0	4	4	x	9	12	0

DP—California 4. LOB—California 3, Seattle 4. 2B—Gonzales, Sojo, Wilson. HR—Phillips. SH—Sojo, Martinez, Martinez, Wilson. SF—Cora. CS—Coleman.

California Angels	IP	H	R	ER	BB	SO
Mark Langston (L)	6.2	8	5	4	3	2
Bob Patterson	0.1	0	0	0	0	1
Mike James	0.0	2	3	3	1	0
Mark Holzemer	0.0	1	1	1	0	0
John Habyan	1.0	1	0	0	0	1

Seattle Mariners	IP	H	R	ER	BB	SO
Randy Johnson (W)	9.0	3	1	1	1	12

James pitched to three batters in the 8th. Holzemer pitched to one batter in the 8th.

HBP—Cora by Langston. Time—2:50. Attendance—52,356. Umpires—HP, Shulock. 1B, Evans. 2B, Young. 3B, Kosc.

September 18, 1996

Ten years after he first accomplished the feat, Roger Clemens matches his record of 20 strikeouts in one game. In one of his last appearances in a Boston uniform, he also ties Cy Young's team marks for wins (192) and shutouts (38).

Boston Red Sox	AB	R	H	RBI
Jeff Frye, 2b	4	0	0	0
Nomar Garciaparra, ss	3	0	0	0
Mo Vaughn, 1b	5	0	1	0
Jose Canseco, dh	5	0	1	0
John Valentin, 3b	4	1	1	0
Mike Greenwell, lf	4	1	2	0
Lee Tinsley, cf	0	0	0	0
Rudy Pemberton, rf	4	2	3	1
Bill Haselman, c	4	0	3	2
Darren Bragg, cf-lf	3	0	0	0
Totals	36	4	11	3

Detroit Tigers	AB	R	H	RBI
Bob Higginson, lf-cf	4	0	0	0
Alan Trammell, 2b	4	0	1	0
Ruben Sierra, dh	4	0	1	0
Tony Clark, 1b	4	0	0	0
Travis Fryman, ss	4	0	0	0
Melvin Nieves, rf	3	0	1	0
Phil Nevin, 3b	3	0	1	0
Brad Ausmus, c	3	0	1	0
Kimera Bartee, cf	2	0	0	0
Phil Hiatt, lf	1	0	0	0
Totals	32	0	5	0

	1	2	3	4	5	6	7	8	9	R	H	E
Bos	0	0	0	3	0	0	0	1	0	4	11	1
Det	0	0	0	0	0	0	0	0	0	0	4	1

E—Nieves. DP—Detroit 2. LOB—Boston 9, Detroit 5. 2B—Pemberton 2. SB—Garciaparra, Greenwell, Trammell, Ausmus.

Boston Red Sox	IP	H	R	ER	BB	SO
Roger Clemens (W)	9.0	5	0	0	0	20

Detroit Tigers	IP	H	R	ER	BB	SO
Justin Thompson (L)	4.0	6	3	3	2	3
C.J. Nitkowski	2.0	3	0	0	2	0
A.J. Sager	3.0	2	1	1	0	3

Nitkowski pitched to three batters in the 7th.

WP—Clemens. Time—2:56. Attendance—8,779. Umpires—HP, McClelland. 1B, Tschida. 2B, Shulock. 3B, Hickox.

June 12, 1997

In the first interleague regular-season game in major league history, the Giants defeat the Rangers 4-3. San Francisco right fielder Stan Javier hits the first interleague homer, while Mark Gardner earns the first interleague victory.

San Francisco Giants	AB	R	H	RBI
Darryl Hamilton, cf	4	0	1	0
Jose Vizcaino, ss	4	1	1	0
Jeff Kent, 2b	4	1	1	0
Barry Bonds, lf	3	1	1	0
Mark Lewis, 3b	4	0	1	1
Bill Mueller, 3b	0	0	0	0
Glenallen Hill, dh	3	0	0	1
Stan Javier, rf	4	1	3	2
J.T. Snow, 1b	3	0	1	0
Marcus Jensen, c	4	0	0	0
Totals	33	4	9	4

Texas Rangers	AB	R	H	RBI
Warren Newson, rf	5	0	0	0
Ivan Rodriguez, c	4	0	0	0
Rusty Greer, lf	4	0	3	0
Juan Gonzalez, dh	4	0	1	0
Will Clark, 1b	3	1	1	0
Dean Palmer, 3b	4	0	0	0
Mark McLemore, 2b	4	1	1	1
Damon Buford, cf	3	1	0	0
Domingo Cedeno, ph	1	0	0	0
Billy Ripken, ss	3	0	2	2
Lee Stevens, ph	1	0	0	0
Totals	36	3	8	3

	1	2	3	4	5	6	7	8	9	R	H	E
SF	0	0	1	0	0	0	3	0	0	4	9	1
Tex	0	1	0	0	0	2	0	0	0	3	8	0

E—Kent. DP—Texas 1. LOB—San Francisco 5, Texas 7. 2B—Bonds, Javier, Greer. 3B—McLemore. HR—Javier. SF—Hill. SB—Greer, Buford. CS—Snow.

San Francisco Giants	IP	H	R	ER	BB	SO
Mark Gardner (W)	8.0	8	3	2	1	4
Rod Beck (S)	1.0	0	0	0	0	0

Detroit Tigers	IP	H	R	ER	BB	SO
Darren Oliver (L)	7.2	8	4	4	1	2
Xavier Hernandez	1.1	1	0	0	0	1

HBP—Bonds by Oliver. Time—2:23. Attendance—46,507. Umpires—HP, McKean. 1B, Hendry. 2B, Joyce. 3B, Hickox.

Great Feats

Triple Crowns

Player	Team	Lg	Year	Avg	HR	RBI
Paul Hines	Providence Grays	NL	1878	.358	4	50
Tip O'Neill	St. Louis Browns	AA	1887	.435	14	123
Hugh Duffy	Boston Beaneaters	NL	1894	.440	18	145
Nap Lajoie	Philadelphia Athletics	AL	1901	.426	14	125
Ty Cobb	Detroit Tigers	AL	1909	.377	9	107
Rogers Hornsby	St. Louis Cardinals	NL	1922	.401	42	152
Rogers Hornsby	St. Louis Cardinals	NL	1925	.403	39	143
Jimmie Foxx	Philadelphia Athletics	AL	1933	.356	48	163
Chuck Klein	Philadelphia Phillies	NL	1933	.368	28	120
Lou Gehrig	New York Yankees	AL	1934	.363	49	165
Joe Medwick	St. Louis Cardinals	NL	1937	.374	31	154
Ted Williams	Boston Red Sox	AL	1942	.356	36	137
Ted Williams	Boston Red Sox	AL	1947	.343	32	114
Mickey Mantle	New York Yankees	AL	1956	.353	52	130
Frank Robinson	Baltimore Orioles	AL	1966	.316	49	122
Carl Yastrzemski	Boston Red Sox	AL	1967	.326	44	121

Perfect Games

Player(s)	Team	Lg	Date	Opponent	Result
Lee Richmond	Worcester Brown Stockings	NL	June 12, 1880	Cleveland Blues	W 1-0
Monte Ward	Providence Grays	NL	June 17, 1880	Buffalo Bisons	W 5-0
Cy Young	Boston Pilgrims	AL	May 5, 1904	Philadelphia Athletics	W 3-0
Addie Joss	Cleveland Bronchos	AL	October 2, 1908	Chicago White Sox	W 1-0
Charlie Robertson	Chicago White Sox	AL	April 30, 1922	Detroit Tigers	W 2-0
Jim Bunning	Philadelphia Phillies	NL	June 21, 1964 (first game)	New York Mets	W 6-0
Sandy Koufax	Los Angeles Dodgers	NL	September 9, 1965	Chicago Cubs	W 1-0
Catfish Hunter	Oakland Athletics	AL	May 8, 1968	Minnesota Twins	W 4-0
Len Barker	Cleveland Indians	AL	May 15, 1981	Toronto Blue Jays	W 3-0
Mike Witt	California Angels	AL	September 30, 1984	Texas Rangers	W 1-0
Tom Browning	Cincinnati Reds	NL	September 16, 1988	Los Angeles Dodgers	W 1-0
Dennis Martinez	Montreal Expos	NL	July 28, 1991	Los Angeles Dodgers	W 2-0
Kenny Rogers	Texas Rangers	AL	July 28, 1994	California Angels	W 4-0

No-Hitters

Player(s)	Team	Lg	Date	Opponent	Result
George Bradley	St. Louis Brown Stockings	NL	July 15, 1876	Hartford Dark Blues	W 2-0
Larry Corcoran	Chicago White Stockings	NL	August 19, 1880	Boston Red Stockings	W 6-0
Pud Galvin	Buffalo Bisons	NL	August 20, 1880	Worcester Brown Stockings	W 1-0
Tony Mullane	Louisville Eclipse	AA	September 11, 1882	Cincinnati Reds	W 2-0
Guy Hecker	Louisville Eclipse	AA	September 19, 1882	Pittsburgh Alleghenys	W 3-1
Larry Corcoran	Chicago White Stockings	NL	September 20, 1882	Worcester Brown Stockings	W 5-0
Old Hoss Radbourn	Providence Grays	NL	July 25, 1883	Cleveland Blues	W 8-0
One Arm Daily	Cleveland Blues	NL	September 13, 1883	Philadelphia Phillies	W 1-0
Al Atkinson	Philadelphia Athletics	AA	May 24, 1884	Pittsburgh Alleghenys	W 10-1
Ed Morris	Columbus Colts	AA	May 29, 1884	Pittsburgh Alleghenys	W 5-0
Frank Mountain	Columbus Colts	AA	June 5, 1884	Washington DC	W 12-0
Larry Corcoran	Chicago White Stockings	NL	June 27, 1884	Providence Grays	W 6-0
Pud Galvin	Buffalo Bisons	NL	August 4, 1884	Detroit Wolverines	W 18-0
Dick Burns	Cincinnati Outlaw Reds	UA	August 26, 1884	Kansas City Unions	W 3-1
Ed Cushman	Milwaukee Grays	UA	September 28, 1884	Washington Nationals	W 5-0
Sam Kimber	Brooklyn Bridegrooms	AA	October 4, 1884	Toledo Blue Stockings	N 0-0 (10)
John Clarkson	Chicago White Stockings	NL	July 27, 1885	Providence Grays	W 4-0
Charlie Ferguson	Philadelphia Phillies	NL	August 29, 1885	Providence Grays	W 1-0
Al Atkinson	Philadelphia Athletics	AA	May 1, 1886	New York Metropolitans	W 3-2
Adonis Terry	Brooklyn Bridegrooms	AA	July 24, 1886	St. Louis Browns	W 1-0
Matt Kilroy	Baltimore Orioles	AA	October 6, 1886	Pittsburgh Alleghenys	W 6-0
Adonis Terry	Brooklyn Bridegrooms	AA	May 27, 1888	Louisville Colonels	W 4-0
Henry Porter	Kansas City Blues	AA	June 6, 1888	Baltimore Orioles	W 4-0
Ed Seward	Philadelphia Athletics	AA	July 26, 1888	Cincinnati Reds	W 12-2

Player(s)	Team	Lg	Date	Opponent	Result
Gus Weyhing	Philadelphia Athletics	AA	July 31, 1888	Kansas City Blues	W 4-0
Cannonball Titcomb	Rochester Hop Bitters	AA	September 15, 1890	Syracuse Stars	W 7-0
Tom Lovett	Brooklyn Bridegrooms	NL	June 22, 1891	New York Giants	W 4-0
Amos Rusie	New York Giants	NL	July 31, 1891	Brooklyn Bridegrooms	W 6-0
Ted Breitenstein (first major league start)	St. Louis Browns	AA	October 4, 1891 (first game)	Louisville Colonels	W 8-0
Jack Stivetts	Boston Beaneaters	NL	August 6, 1892	Brooklyn Bridegrooms	W 11-0
Ben Sanders	Louisville Colonels	NL	August 22, 1892	Baltimore Orioles	W 6-2
Bumpus Jones (first major league game)	Cincinnati Reds	NL	October 15, 1892	Pittsburgh Pirates	W 7-1
Bill Hawke (first no-hitter at 60 feet, 6 inches)	Baltimore Orioles	NL	August 16, 1893	Washington Senators	W 5-0
Cy Young	Cleveland Spiders	NL	September 18, 1897 (first game)	Cincinnati Reds	W 6-0
Ted Breitenstein	Cincinnati Reds	NL	April 22, 1898	Pittsburgh Pirates	W 11-0
Jim Hughes	Baltimore Orioles	NL	April 22, 1898	Boston Beaneaters	W 8-0
Red Donahue	Philadelphia Phillies	NL	July 8, 1898	Boston Beaneaters	W 5-0
Walter Thornton	Chicago Orphans	NL	August 21, 1898 (second game)	Brooklyn Bridegrooms	W 2-0
Deacon Phillippe	Louisville Colonels	NL	May 25, 1899	New York Giants	W 7-0
Vic Willis	Boston Beaneaters	NL	August 7, 1899	Washington Senators	W 7-1
Noodles Hahn	Cincinnati Reds	NL	July 12, 1900	Philadelphia Phillies	W 4-0
Christy Mathewson	New York Giants	NL	July 15, 1901	St. Louis Cardinals	W 5-0
Nixey Callahan	Chicago White Sox	AL	September 20, 1902 (first game)	Detroit Tigers	W 3-0
Chick Fraser	Philadelphia Phillies	NL	September 18, 1903 (second game)	Chicago Cubs	W 10-0
Jesse Tannehill	Boston Pilgrims	AL	August 17, 1904	Chicago White Sox	W 6-0
Christy Mathewson	New York Giants	NL	June 13, 1905	Chicago Cubs	W 1-0
Weldon Henley	Philadelphia Athletics	AL	July 22, 1905 (first game)	St. Louis Browns	W 6-0
Frank Smith	Chicago White Sox	AL	September 6, 1905 (second game)	Detroit Tigers	W 15-0
Bill Dinneen	Boston Pilgrims	AL	September 27, 1905 (first game)	Chicago White Sox	W 2-0
Johnny Lush	Philadelphia Phillies	NL	May 1, 1906	Brooklyn Dodgers	W 6-0
Mal Eason	Brooklyn Dodgers	NL	July 20, 1906	St. Louis Cardinals	W 2-0
Big Jeff Pfeffer	Boston Beaneaters	NL	May 8, 1907	Cincinnati Reds	W 6-0
Nick Maddox	Pittsburgh Pirates	NL	September 20, 1907	Brooklyn Dodgers	W 2-1
Cy Young	Boston Pilgrims	AL	June 30, 1908	New York Highlanders	W 8-0
Hooks Wiltse	New York Giants	NL	July 4, 1908 (first game)	Philadelphia Phillies	W 1-0 (10)
Nap Rucker	Brooklyn Dodgers	NL	September 5, 1908 (second game)	Boston Beaneaters	W 6-0
Bob Rhoads	Cleveland Bronchos	AL	September 18, 1908	Boston Pilgrims	W 2-1
Frank Smith	Chicago White Sox	AL	September 20, 1908	Philadelphia Athletics	W 1-0
Addie Joss	Cleveland Bronchos	AL	April 20, 1910	Chicago White Sox	W 1-0
Chief Bender	Philadelphia Athletics	AL	May 12, 1910	Cleveland Bronchos	W 4-0
Joe Wood	Boston Red Sox	AL	July 29, 1911 (first game)	St. Louis Browns	W 5-0
Ed Walsh	Chicago White Sox	AL	August 27, 1911	Boston Red Sox	W 5-0
George Mullin	Detroit Tigers	AL	July 4, 1912 (second game)	St. Louis Browns	W 7-0
Earl Hamilton	St. Louis Browns	AL	August 30, 1912	Detroit Tigers	W 5-1
Jeff Tesreau	New York Giants	NL	September 6, 1912 (first game)	Philadelphia Phillies	W 3-0
Joe Benz	Chicago White Sox	AL	May 31, 1914	Cleveland Bronchos	W 6-1
Iron Davis	Boston Braves	NL	September 9, 1914 (second game)	Philadelphia Phillies	W 7-0
Rube Marquard	New York Giants	NL	April 15, 1915	Brooklyn Dodgers	W 2-0
Jimmy Lavender	Chicago Cubs	NL	August 31, 1915 (first game)	New York Giants	W 2-0
Tom Hughes	Boston Braves	NL	June 16, 1916	Pittsburgh Pirates	W 2-0
Rube Foster	Boston Red Sox	AL	June 21, 1916	New York Yankees	W 2-0
Joe Bush	Philadelphia Athletics	AL	August 26, 1916	Cleveland Indians	W 5-0
Dutch Leonard	Boston Red Sox	AL	August 30, 1916	St. Louis Browns	W 4-0
Eddie Cicotte	Chicago White Sox	AL	April 14, 1917	St. Louis Browns	W 11-0
George Mogridge	New York Yankees	AL	April 24, 1917	Boston Red Sox	W 2-1
Fred Toney	Cincinnati Reds	NL	May 2, 1917	Chicago Cubs	W 1-0 (10)
Ernie Koob	St. Louis Browns	AL	May 5, 1917	Chicago White Sox	W 1-0
Bob Groom	St. Louis Browns	AL	May 6, 1917 (second game)	Chicago White Sox	W 3-0
Babe Ruth (0), Ernie Shore (9)	Boston Red Sox	AL	June 23, 1917 (first game)	Washington Senators	W 4-0
Dutch Leonard	Boston Red Sox	AL	June 3, 1918	Detroit Tigers	W 5-0
Hod Eller	Cincinnati Reds	NL	May 11, 1919	St. Louis Cardinals	W 6-0
Ray Caldwell	Cleveland Indians	AL	September 10, 1919 (first game)	New York Yankees	W 3-0
Walter Johnson	Washington Senators	AL	July 1, 1920	Boston Red Sox	W 1-0
Jesse Barnes	New York Giants	NL	May 7, 1922	Philadelphia Phillies	W 6-0
Sad Sam Jones	New York Yankees	AL	September 4, 1923	Philadelphia Athletics	W 2-0
Howard Ehmke	Boston Red Sox	AL	September 7, 1923	Philadelphia Athletics	W 4-0
Jesse Haines	St. Louis Cardinals	NL	July 17, 1924	Boston Braves	W 5-0

Greats: Feats

Player(s)	Team	Lg	Date	Opponent	Result
Dazzy Vance	Brooklyn Dodgers	NL	September 13, 1925 (first game)	Philadelphia Phillies	W 10-1
Ted Lyons	Chicago White Sox	AL	August 21, 1926	Boston Red Sox	W 6-0
Carl Hubbell	New York Giants	NL	May 8, 1929	Pittsburgh Pirates	W 11-0
Wes Ferrell	Cleveland Indians	AL	April 29, 1931	St. Louis Browns	W 9-0
Bobby Burke	Washington Senators	AL	August 8, 1931	Boston Red Sox	W 5-0
Paul Dean	St. Louis Cardinals	NL	September 21, 1934 (second game)	Brooklyn Dodgers	W 3-0
Vern Kennedy	Chicago White Sox	AL	August 31, 1935	Cleveland Indians	W 5-0
Bill Dietrich	Chicago White Sox	AL	June 1, 1937	St. Louis Browns	W 8-0
Johnny Vander Meer	Cincinnati Reds	NL	June 11, 1938	Boston Braves	W 3-0
Johnny Vander Meer (consecutive)	Cincinnati Reds	NL	June 15, 1938	Brooklyn Dodgers	W 6-0
Monte Pearson	New York Yankees	AL	August 27, 1938 (second game)	Cleveland Indians	W 13-0
Bob Feller (Opening Day)	Cleveland Indians	AL	April 16, 1940	Chicago White Sox	W 1-0
Tex Carleton	Brooklyn Dodgers	NL	April 30, 1940	Cincinnati Reds	W 3-0
Lon Warneke	St. Louis Cardinals	NL	August 30, 1941	Cincinnati Reds	W 2-0
Jim Tobin	Boston Braves	NL	April 27, 1944	Brooklyn Dodgers	W 2-0
Clyde Shoun	Cincinnati Reds	NL	May 15, 1944	Boston Braves	W 1-0
Dick Fowler	Philadelphia Athletics	AL	September 9, 1945 (second game)	St. Louis Browns	W 1-0
Ed Head	Brooklyn Dodgers	NL	April 23, 1946	Boston Braves	W 5-0
Bob Feller	Cleveland Indians	AL	April 30, 1946	New York Yankees	W 1-0
Ewell Blackwell	Cincinnati Reds	NL	June 18, 1947	Boston Braves	W 6-0
Don Black	Cleveland Indians	AL	July 10, 1947 (first game)	Philadelphia Athletics	W 3-0
Bill McCahan	Philadelphia Athletics	AL	September 3, 1947	Washington Senators	W 3-0
Bob Lemon	Cleveland Indians	AL	June 30, 1948	Detroit Tigers	W 2-0
Rex Barney	Brooklyn Dodgers	NL	September 9, 1948	New York Giants	W 2-0
Vern Bickford	Boston Braves	NL	August 11, 1950	Brooklyn Dodgers	W 7-0
Cliff Chambers	Pittsburgh Pirates	NL	May 6, 1951 (second game)	Boston Braves	W 3-0
Bob Feller	Cleveland Indians	AL	July 1, 1951 (first game)	Detroit Tigers	W 2-1
Allie Reynolds	New York Yankees	AL	July 12, 1951	Cleveland Indians	W 1-0
Allie Reynolds	New York Yankees	AL	September 28, 1951 (first game)	Boston Red Sox	W 8-0
Virgil Trucks	Detroit Tigers	AL	May 15, 1952	Washington Senators	W 1-0
Carl Erskine	Brooklyn Dodgers	NL	June 19, 1952	Chicago Cubs	W 5-0
Virgil Trucks	Detroit Tigers	AL	August 25, 1952	New York Yankees	W 1-0
Bobo Holloman (first major league start)	St. Louis Browns	AL	May 6, 1953	Philadelphia Athletics	W 6-0
Jim Wilson	Milwaukee Braves	NL	June 12, 1954	Philadelphia Phillies	W 2-0
Sam Jones	Chicago Cubs	NL	May 12, 1955	Pittsburgh Pirates	W 4-0
Carl Erskine	Brooklyn Dodgers	NL	May 12, 1956	New York Giants	W 3-0
Mel Parnell	Boston Red Sox	AL	July 14, 1956	Chicago White Sox	W 4-0
Sal Maglie	Brooklyn Dodgers	NL	September 25, 1956	Philadelphia Phillies	W 5-0
Bob Keegan	Chicago White Sox	AL	August 20, 1957 (second game)	Washington Senators	W 6-0
Jim Bunning	Detroit Tigers	AL	July 20, 1958 (first game)	Boston Red Sox	W 3-0
Hoyt Wilhelm	Baltimore Orioles	AL	September 20, 1958	New York Yankees	W 1-0
Don Cardwell	Chicago Cubs	NL	May 15, 1960 (second game)	St. Louis Cardinals	W 4-0
Lew Burdette	Milwaukee Braves	NL	August 18, 1960	Philadelphia Phillies	W 1-0
Warren Spahn	Milwaukee Braves	NL	September 16, 1960	Philadelphia Phillies	W 4-0
Warren Spahn	Milwaukee Braves	NL	April 28, 1961	San Francisco Giants	W 1-0
Bo Belinsky	Los Angeles Angels	AL	May 5, 1962	Baltimore Orioles	W 2-0
Earl Wilson	Boston Red Sox	AL	June 26, 1962	Los Angeles Angels	W 2-0
Sandy Koufax	Los Angeles Dodgers	NL	June 30, 1962	New York Mets	W 5-0
Bill Monbouquette	Boston Red Sox	AL	August 1, 1962	Chicago White Sox	W 1-0
Jack Kralick	Minnesota Twins	AL	August 26, 1962	Kansas City Athletics	W 1-0
Sandy Koufax	Los Angeles Dodgers	NL	May 11, 1963	San Francisco Giants	W 8-0
Don Nottebart	Houston Colt .45s	NL	May 17, 1963	Philadelphia Phillies	W 4-1
Juan Marichal	San Francisco Giants	NL	June 15, 1963	Houston Colt .45s	W 1-0
Ken Johnson	Houston Colt .45s	NL	April 23, 1964	Cincinnati Reds	L 0-1
Sandy Koufax	Los Angeles Dodgers	NL	June 4, 1964	Philadelphia Phillies	W 3-0
Jim Maloney	Cincinnati Reds	NL	August 19, 1965 (first game)	Chicago Cubs	W 1-0 (10)
Dave Morehead	Boston Red Sox	AL	September 16, 1965	Cleveland Indians	W 2-0
Sonny Siebert	Cleveland Indians	AL	June 10, 1966	Washington Senators	W 2-0
Steve Barber (8.2), Stu Miller (0.1)	Baltimore Orioles	AL	April 30, 1967 (first game)	Detroit Tigers	L 1-2
Don Wilson	Houston Astros	NL	June 18, 1967	Atlanta Braves	W 2-0
Dean Chance	Minnesota Twins	AL	August 25, 1967 (second game)	Cleveland Indians	W 2-1
Joe Horlen	Chicago White Sox	AL	September 10, 1967 (first game)	Detroit Tigers	W 6-0
Tom Phoebus	Baltimore Orioles	AL	April 27, 1968	Boston Red Sox	W 6-0

Player(s)	Team	Lg	Date	Opponent	Result
George Culver	Cincinnati Reds	NL	July 29, 1968 (second game)	Philadelphia Phillies	W 6-1
Gaylord Perry	San Francisco Giants	NL	September 17, 1968	St. Louis Cardinals	W 1-0
Ray Washburn	St. Louis Cardinals	NL	September 18, 1968	San Francisco Giants	W 2-0
Bill Stoneman	Montreal Expos	NL	April 17, 1969	Philadelphia Phillies	W 7-0
Jim Maloney	Cincinnati Reds	NL	April 30, 1969	Houston Astros	W 10-0
Don Wilson	Houston Astros	NL	May 1, 1969	Cincinnati Reds	W 4-0
Jim Palmer	Baltimore Orioles	AL	August 13, 1969	Oakland Athletics	W 8-0
Ken Holtzman	Chicago Cubs	NL	August 19, 1969	Atlanta Braves	W 3-0
Bob Moose	Pittsburgh Pirates	NL	September 20, 1969	New York Mets	W 4-0
Dock Ellis	Pittsburgh Pirates	NL	June 12, 1970 (first game)	San Diego Padres	W 2-0
Clyde Wright	California Angels	AL	July 3, 1970	Oakland Athletics	W 4-0
Bill Singer	Los Angeles Dodgers	NL	July 20, 1970	Philadelphia Phillies	W 5-0
Vida Blue	Oakland Athletics	AL	September 21, 1970	Minnesota Twins	W 6-0
Ken Holtzman	Chicago Cubs	NL	June 3, 1971	Cincinnati Reds	W 1-0
Rick Wise	Philadelphia Phillies	NL	June 23, 1971	Cincinnati Reds	W 4-0
Bob Gibson	St. Louis Cardinals	NL	August 14, 1971	Pittsburgh Pirates	W 11-0
Burt Hooton	Chicago Cubs	NL	April 16, 1972	Philadelphia Phillies	W 4-0
Milt Pappas	Chicago Cubs	NL	September 2, 1972	San Diego Padres	W 8-0
Bill Stoneman	Montreal Expos	NL	October 2, 1972 (first game)	New York Mets	W 7-0
Steve Busby	Kansas City Royals	AL	April 27, 1973	Detroit Tigers	W 3-0
Nolan Ryan	California Angels	AL	May 15, 1973	Kansas City Royals	W 3-0
Nolan Ryan	California Angels	AL	July 15, 1973	Detroit Tigers	W 6-0
Jim Bibby	Texas Rangers	AL	July 30, 1973	Oakland Athletics	W 6-0
Phil Niekro	Atlanta Braves	NL	August 5, 1973	San Diego Padres	W 9-0
Steve Busby	Kansas City Royals	AL	June 19, 1974	Milwaukee Brewers	W 2-0
Dick Bosman	Cleveland Indians	AL	July 19, 1974	Oakland Athletics	W 4-0
Nolan Ryan	California Angels	AL	September 28, 1974	Minnesota Twins	W 4-0
Nolan Ryan	California Angels	AL	June 1, 1975	Baltimore Orioles	W 1-0
Ed Halicki	San Francisco Giants	NL	August 24, 1975 (second game)	New York Mets	W 6-0
Vida Blue (5), Glenn Abbott (1), Paul Lindblad (1), Rollie Fingers (2)	Oakland Athletics	AL	September 28, 1975	California Angels	W 5-0
Larry Dierker	Houston Astros	NL	July 9, 1976	Montreal Expos	W 6-0
Blue Moon Odom (5), Francisco Barrios (4)	Chicago White Sox	AL	July 28, 1976	Oakland Athletics	W 2-1
John Candelaria	Pittsburgh Pirates	NL	August 9, 1976	Los Angeles Dodgers	W 2-0
John Montefusco	San Francisco Giants	NL	September 29, 1976	Atlanta Braves	W 9-0
Jim Colborn	Kansas City Royals	AL	May 14, 1977	Texas Rangers	W 6-0
Dennis Eckersley	Cleveland Indians	AL	May 20, 1977	California Angels	W 1-0
Bert Blyleven	Texas Rangers	AL	September 22, 1977	California Angels	W 6-0
Bob Forsch	St. Louis Cardinals	NL	April 16, 1978	Philadelphia Phillies	W 5-0
Tom Seaver	Cincinnati Reds	NL	June 16, 1978	St. Louis Cardinals	W 4-0
Ken Forsch	Houston Astros	NL	April 7, 1979	Atlanta Braves	W 6-0
Jerry Reuss	Los Angeles Dodgers	NL	June 27, 1980	San Francisco Giants	W 8-0
Charlie Lea	Montreal Expos	NL	May 10, 1981 (second game)	San Francisco Giants	W 4-0
Nolan Ryan	Houston Astros	NL	September 26, 1981	Los Angeles Dodgers	W 5-0
Dave Righetti	New York Yankees	AL	July 4, 1983	Boston Red Sox	W 4-0
Bob Forsch	St. Louis Cardinals	NL	September 26, 1983	Montreal Expos	W 3-0
Mike Warren	Oakland Athletics	AL	September 29, 1983	Chicago White Sox	W 3-0
Jack Morris	Detroit Tigers	AL	April 7, 1984	Chicago White Sox	W 4-0
Joe Cowley	Chicago White Sox	AL	September 19, 1986	California Angels	W 7-1
Mike Scott	Houston Astros	NL	September 25, 1986	San Francisco Giants	W 2-0
Juan Nieves	Milwaukee Brewers	AL	April 15, 1987	Baltimore Orioles	W 7-0
Mark Langston (7), Mike Witt (2)	California Angels	AL	April 11, 1990	Seattle Mariners	W 1-0
Randy Johnson	Seattle Mariners	AL	June 2, 1990	Detroit Tigers	W 2-0
Nolan Ryan	Texas Rangers	AL	June 11, 1990	Oakland Athletics	W 5-0
Dave Stewart	Oakland Athletics	AL	June 29, 1990	Toronto Blue Jays	W 5-0
Fernando Valenzuela	Los Angeles Dodgers	NL	June 29, 1990	St. Louis Cardinals	W 6-0
Terry Mulholland	Philadelphia Phillies	NL	August 15, 1990	San Francisco Giants	W 6-0
Dave Stieb	Toronto Blue Jays	AL	September 2, 1990	Cleveland Indians	W 3-0
Nolan Ryan	Texas Rangers	AL	May 1, 1991	Toronto Blue Jays	W 3-0
Tommy Greene	Philadelphia Phillies	NL	May 23, 1991	Montreal Expos	W 2-0
Bob Milacki (6), Mike Flanagan (1), Mark Williamson (1), Gregg Olson (1)	Baltimore Orioles	AL	July 13, 1991	Oakland Athletics	W 2-0
Wilson Alvarez	Chicago White Sox	AL	August 11, 1991	Baltimore Orioles	W 7-0
Bret Saberhagen	Kansas City Royals	AL	August 26, 1991	Chicago White Sox	W 7-0

Greats: Feats

Player(s)	Team	Lg	Date	Opponent	Result
Kent Mercker (6), Mark Wohlers (2), Alejandro Pena (1)	Atlanta Braves	NL	September 11, 1991	San Diego Padres	W 1-0
Kevin Gross	Los Angeles Dodgers	NL	August 17, 1992	San Francisco Giants	W 2-0
Chris Bosio	Seattle Mariners	AL	April 22, 1993	Boston Red Sox	W 2-0
Jim Abbott	New York Yankees	AL	September 4, 1993	Cleveland Indians	W 4-0
Darryl Kile	Houston Astros	NL	September 8, 1993	New York Mets	W 7-1
Kent Mercker	Atlanta Braves	NL	April 8, 1994	Los Angeles Dodgers	W 6-0
Scott Erickson	Minnesota Twins	AL	April 27, 1994	Milwaukee Brewers	W 6-0
Ramon Martinez	Los Angeles Dodgers	NL	July 14, 1995	Florida Marlins	W 7-0
Al Leiter	Florida Marlins	NL	May 11, 1996	Colorado Rockies	W 11-0
Dwight Gooden	New York Yankees	AL	May 14, 1996	Seattle Mariners	W 2-0
Hideo Nomo	Los Angeles Dodgers	NL	September 17, 1996	Colorado Rockies	W 9-0
Kevin Brown	Florida Marlins	NL	June 10, 1997	San Francisco Giants	W 9-0
Francisco Cordova (9), Ricardo Rincon (1)	Pittsburgh Pirates	NL	July 12, 1997	Houston Astros	W 3-0 (10)

Four-Homer Games

Player	Team	Lg	Date
Bobby Lowe	Boston Beaneaters	NL	May 30, 1894 (second game)
Ed Delahanty	Philadelphia Phillies	NL	July 13, 1896
Lou Gehrig	New York Yankees	AL	June 3, 1932
Chuck Klein	Philadelphia Phillies	NL	July 10, 1936 (10 innings)
Pat Seerey	Chicago White Sox	AL	July 18, 1948 (first game, 11 innings)
Gil Hodges	Brooklyn Dodgers	NL	August 31, 1950
Joe Adcock	Milwaukee Braves	NL	July 31, 1954
Rocky Colavito	Cleveland Indians	AL	June 10, 1959
Willie Mays	San Francisco Giants	NL	April 30, 1961
Mike Schmidt	Philadelphia Phillies	NL	April 17, 1976 (10 innings)
Bob Horner	Atlanta Braves	NL	July 6, 1986
Mark Whiten	St. Louis Cardinals	NL	September 7, 1993

Three-Homer Games

Player	Team	Lg	Date
Ned Williamson	Chicago White Stockings	NL	May 30, 1884 (second game)
Cap Anson	Chicago White Stockings	NL	August 6, 1884
Jack Manning	Philadelphia Phillies	NL	October 9, 1884
Guy Hecker	Louisville Colonels	AA	August 15, 1886 (second game)
Dan Brouthers	Detroit Wolverines	NL	September 10, 1886
Roger Connor	New York Giants	NL	May 9, 1888
Frank Shugart	St. Louis Browns	NL	May 10, 1894
Bill Joyce	Washington Senators	NL	August 20, 1894
Tom McCreery	Louisville Colonels	NL	July 12, 1897
Jake Beckley	Cincinnati Reds	NL	September 26, 1897 (first game)
Ken Williams	St. Louis Browns	AL	April 22, 1922
Butch Henline	Philadelphia Phillies	NL	September 15, 1922
Cy Williams	Philadelphia Phillies	NL	May 11, 1923
George Kelly	New York Giants	NL	September 17, 1923
George Kelly	New York Giants	NL	June 14, 1924
Joe Hauser	Philadelphia Athletics	AL	August 2, 1924
Ty Cobb	Detroit Tigers	AL	May 5, 1925
Mickey Cochrane	Philadelphia Athletics	AL	May 21, 1925
Goose Goslin	Washington Senators	AL	June 19, 1925 (12 innings)
Jack Fournier	Brooklyn Dodgers	NL	July 13, 1926
Tony Lazzeri	New York Yankees	AL	June 8, 1927
Lou Gehrig	New York Yankees	AL	June 23, 1927
Les Bell	Boston Braves	NL	June 2, 1928
George Harper	St. Louis Cardinals	NL	September 20, 1928 (first game)
Lou Gehrig	New York Yankees	AL	May 4, 1929
Babe Ruth	New York Yankees	AL	May 21, 1930 (first game)
Lou Gehrig	New York Yankees	AL	May 22, 1930 (second game)
Carl Reynolds	Chicago White Sox	AL	July 2, 1930 (second game)
Hack Wilson	Chicago Cubs	NL	July 26, 1930
Goose Goslin	St. Louis Browns	AL	August 19, 1930
Mel Ott	New York Giants	NL	August 31, 1930 (second game)

Player	Team	Lg	Date
Earl Averill	Cleveland Indians	AL	September 17, 1930 (first game)
Rogers Hornsby	Chicago Cubs	NL	April 24, 1931
George Watkins	St. Louis Cardinals	NL	June 24, 1931 (second game)
Goose Goslin	St. Louis Browns	AL	June 23, 1932
Ben Chapman	New York Yankees	AL	July 9, 1932 (second game)
Jimmie Foxx	Philadelphia Athletics	AL	July 10, 1932 (18 innings)
Al Simmons	Philadelphia Athletics	AL	July 15, 1932
Bill Terry	New York Giants	NL	August 13, 1932 (first game)
Jimmie Foxx	Philadelphia Athletics	AL	June 8, 1933
Babe Herman	Chicago Cubs	NL	July 20, 1933
Hal Trosky	Cleveland Indians	AL	May 30, 1934 (second game)
Hal Lee	Boston Braves	NL	July 6, 1934
Ed Coleman	Philadelphia Athletics	AL	August 17, 1934 (first game)
Babe Ruth	Boston Braves	NL	May 25, 1935
Mike Higgins	Philadelphia Athletics	AL	June 27, 1935
Moose Solters	St. Louis Browns	AL	July 7, 1935
Tony Lazzeri	New York Yankees	AL	May 24, 1936
Johnny Moore	Philadelphia Phillies	NL	July 22, 1936
Alex Kampouris	Cincinnati Reds	NL	May 9, 1937
Joe DiMaggio	New York Yankees	AL	June 13, 1937 (second game, 11 innings)
Hal Trosky	Cleveland Indians	AL	July 5, 1937 (first game)
Johnny Mize	St. Louis Cardinals	NL	July 13, 1938
Johnny Mize	St. Louis Cardinals	NL	July 20, 1938 (second game)
Merv Connors	Chicago White Sox	AL	September 17, 1938 (second game)
Ken Keltner	Cleveland Indians	AL	May 25, 1939
Jim Tabor	Boston Red Sox	AL	July 4, 1939 (second game)
Hank Leiber	Chicago Cubs	NL	July 4, 1939 (first game)
Bill Dickey	New York Yankees	AL	July 26, 1939
Johnny Mize	St. Louis Cardinals	NL	May 13, 1940 (14 innings)
Mike Higgins	Detroit Tigers	AL	May 20, 1940
Charlie Keller	New York Yankees	AL	July 28, 1940 (first game)
Johnny Mize	St. Louis Cardinals	NL	September 8, 1940 (first game)
Rudy York	Detroit Tigers	AL	September 1, 1941 (first game)
Jim Tobin	Boston Braves	NL	May 13, 1942
Clyde McCullough	Chicago Cubs	NL	July 26, 1942 (first game)
Bill Nicholson	Chicago Cubs	NL	July 23, 1944 (first game)
Pat Seerey	Cleveland Indians	AL	July 13, 1945
Ted Williams	Boston Red Sox	AL	July 14, 1946 (first game)
Sam Chapman	Philadelphia Athletics	AL	August 15, 1946
Johnny Mize	New York Giants	NL	April 24, 1947
Willard Marshall	New York Giants	NL	July 18, 1947
Ralph Kiner	Pittsburgh Pirates	NL	August 16, 1947
Ralph Kiner	Pittsburgh Pirates	NL	September 11, 1947 (second game)
Joe DiMaggio	New York Yankees	AL	May 23, 1948 (first game)
Ralph Kiner	Pittsburgh Pirates	NL	July 5, 1948 (first game)
Gene Hermanski	Brooklyn Dodgers	NL	August 5, 1948
Andy Seminick	Philadelphia Phillies	NL	June 2, 1949
Pat Mullin	Detroit Tigers	AL	June 26, 1949 (second game)
Walker Cooper	Cincinnati Reds	NL	July 6, 1949
Bob Elliott	Boston Braves	NL	September 24, 1949
Duke Snider	Brooklyn Dodgers	NL	May 30, 1950 (second game)
Bobby Doerr	Boston Red Sox	AL	June 8, 1950
Wes Westrum	New York Giants	NL	June 24, 1950
Larry Doby	Cleveland Indians	AL	August 2, 1950
Andy Pafko	Chicago Cubs	NL	August 2, 1950 (second game)
Roy Campanella	Brooklyn Dodgers	NL	August 26, 1950
Hank Sauer	Chicago Cubs	NL	August 28, 1950 (first game)
Joe DiMaggio	New York Yankees	AL	September 10, 1950
Johnny Mize	New York Yankees	AL	September 15, 1950
Tommy Brown	Brooklyn Dodgers	NL	September 18, 1950
Gus Zernial	Chicago White Sox	AL	October 1, 1950 (second game)
Bobby Avila	Cleveland Indians	AL	June 20, 1951
Ralph Kiner	Pittsburgh Pirates	NL	July 18, 1951

Greats: Feats

Player	Team	Lg	Date
Clyde Vollmer	Boston Red Sox	AL	July 26, 1951
Del Wilber	Philadelphia Phillies	NL	August 27, 1951 (second game)
Don Mueller	New York Giants	NL	September 1, 1951
Al Rosen	Cleveland Indians	AL	April 29, 1952
Hank Sauer	Chicago Cubs	NL	June 11, 1952
Eddie Mathews	Boston Braves	NL	September 27, 1952
Dusty Rhodes	New York Giants	NL	August 26, 1953
Jim Pendleton	Milwaukee Braves	NL	August 30, 1953 (first game)
Stan Musial	St. Louis Cardinals	NL	May 2, 1954 (first game)
Hank Thompson	New York Giants	NL	June 3, 1954
Bill Glynn	Cleveland Indians	AL	July 5, 1954 (first game)
Dusty Rhodes	New York Giants	NL	July 28, 1954
Al Kaline	Detroit Tigers	AL	April 17, 1955
Mickey Mantle	New York Yankees	AL	May 13, 1955
Norm Zauchin	Boston Red Sox	AL	May 27, 1955
Duke Snider	Brooklyn Dodgers	NL	June 1, 1955
Gus Bell	Cincinnati Reds	NL	July 21, 1955
Del Ennis	Philadelphia Phillies	NL	July 23, 1955
Smoky Burgess	Cincinnati Reds	NL	July 29, 1955
Ernie Banks	Chicago Cubs	NL	August 4, 1955
Gus Bell	Cincinnati Reds	NL	May 29, 1956
Ed Bailey	Cincinnati Reds	NL	June 24, 1956 (first game)
Ted Kluszewski	Cincinnati Reds	NL	July 1, 1956 (first game, 10 innings)
Bob Thurman	Cincinnati Reds	NL	August 18, 1956
Jim Lemon	Washington Senators	AL	August 31, 1956
Ted Williams	Boston Red Sox	AL	May 8, 1957
Ted Williams	Boston Red Sox	AL	June 13, 1957
Ernie Banks	Chicago Cubs	NL	September 14, 1957 (second game)
Lee Walls	Chicago Cubs	NL	April 24, 1958
Roman Mejias	Pittsburgh Pirates	NL	May 4, 1958 (first game)
Walt Moryn	Chicago Cubs	NL	May 30, 1958 (second game)
Hector Lopez	Kansas City Athletics	AL	June 26, 1958
Frank Thomas	Pittsburgh Pirates	NL	August 16, 1958
Preston Ward	Kansas City Athletics	AL	September 9, 1958
Don Demeter	Los Angeles Dodgers	NL	April 21, 1959 (11 innings)
Charlie Maxwell	Detroit Tigers	AL	May 3, 1959 (second game)
Hank Aaron	Milwaukee Braves	NL	June 21, 1959
Bob Cerv	Kansas City Athletics	AL	August 20, 1959
Frank Robinson	Cincinnati Reds	NL	August 22, 1959
Dick Stuart	Pittsburgh Pirates	NL	June 30, 1960 (second game)
Willie Mays	San Francisco Giants	NL	June 29, 1961 (10 innings)
Bill White	St. Louis Cardinals	NL	July 5, 1961
Willie Kirkland	Cleveland Indians	AL	July 9, 1961 (second game)
Rocky Colavito	Detroit Tigers	AL	August 27, 1961 (second game)
Lee Thomas	Los Angeles Angels	AL	September 5, 1961 (second game)
Don Demeter	Philadelphia Phillies	NL	September 12, 1961
Ernie Banks	Chicago Cubs	NL	May 29, 1962
Rocky Colavito	Detroit Tigers	AL	July 5, 1962
Stan Musial	St. Louis Cardinals	NL	July 8, 1962
Steve Boros	Detroit Tigers	AL	August 6, 1962
Don Leppert	Washington Senators	AL	April 11, 1963
Bob Allison	Minnesota Twins	AL	May 17, 1963
Willie Mays	San Francisco Giants	NL	June 2, 1963
Ernie Banks	Chicago Cubs	NL	June 9, 1963
Boog Powell	Baltimore Orioles	AL	August 10, 1963
Harmon Killebrew	Minnesota Twins	AL	September 21, 1963 (first game)
Willie McCovey	San Francisco Giants	NL	September 22, 1963
Willie McCovey	San Francisco Giants	NL	April 22, 1964
Jim King	Washington Senators	AL	June 8, 1964
Boog Powell	Baltimore Orioles	AL	June 27, 1964
Manny Jimenez	Kansas City Athletics	AL	July 4, 1964
Johnny Callison	Philadelphia Phillies	NL	September 27, 1964
Tom Tresh	New York Yankees	AL	June 6, 1965 (second game)

Player	Team	Lg	Date
Johnny Callison	Philadelphia Phillies	NL	June 6, 1965 (second game)
Willie Stargell	Pittsburgh Pirates	NL	June 24, 1965
Jim Hickman	New York Mets	NL	September 3, 1965
Gene Oliver	Atlanta Braves	NL	July 30, 1966 (second game)
Art Shamsky	Cincinnati Reds	NL	August 12, 1966 (13 innings)
Boog Powell	Baltimore Orioles	AL	August 15, 1966
Willie McCovey	San Francisco Giants	NL	September 17, 1966 (10 innings)
Roberto Clemente	Pittsburgh Pirates	NL	May 15, 1967 (10 innings)
Tom McCraw	Chicago White Sox	AL	May 24, 1967
Curt Blefary	Baltimore Orioles	AL	June 6, 1967 (first game)
Adolfo Phillips	Chicago Cubs	NL	June 11, 1967 (second game)
Jimmy Wynn	Houston Astros	NL	June 15, 1967
Willie Stargell	Pittsburgh Pirates	NL	May 22, 1968
Ken Harrelson	Boston Red Sox	AL	June 14, 1968
Billy Williams	Chicago Cubs	NL	September 10, 1968
Dick Allen	Philadelphia Phillies	NL	September 29, 1968
Mike Epstein	Washington Senators	AL	May 16, 1969
Joe Lahoud	Boston Red Sox	AL	June 11, 1969
Bill Melton	Chicago White Sox	AL	June 24, 1969 (second game)
Reggie Jackson	Oakland Athletics	AL	July 2, 1969
Bob Tillman	Atlanta Braves	NL	July 30, 1969 (first game)
Roberto Clemente	Pittsburgh Pirates	NL	August 13, 1969
Paul Blair	Baltimore Orioles	AL	April 29, 1970
Tony Horton	Cleveland Indians	AL	May 24, 1970 (second game)
Rico Carty	Atlanta Braves	NL	May 31, 1970
Willie Horton	Detroit Tigers	AL	June 9, 1970
Bobby Murcer	New York Yankees	AL	June 24, 1970 (second game)
Mike Lum	Atlanta Braves	NL	July 3, 1970 (first game)
Johnny Bench	Cincinnati Reds	NL	July 26, 1970
Orlando Cepeda	Atlanta Braves	NL	July 26, 1970 (first game)
Willie Stargell	Pittsburgh Pirates	NL	April 10, 1971 (12 innings)
Willie Stargell	Pittsburgh Pirates	NL	April 21, 1971
Deron Johnson	Philadelphia Phillies	NL	July 11, 1971
Bill Freehan	Detroit Tigers	AL	August 9, 1971
Rick Monday	Chicago Cubs	NL	May 16, 1972
Nate Colbert	San Diego Padres	NL	August 1, 1972 (second game)
Johnny Bench	Cincinnati Reds	NL	May 9, 1973
George Hendrick	Cleveland Indians	AL	June 19, 1973
Lee May	Houston Astros	NL	June 21, 1973
Tony Oliva	Minnesota Twins	AL	July 3, 1973
Lee Stanton	California Angels	AL	July 10, 1973 (10 innings)
Bobby Murcer	New York Yankees	AL	July 13, 1973
George Mitterwald	Chicago Cubs	NL	April 17, 1974
Jimmy Wynn	Los Angeles Dodgers	NL	May 11, 1974
Bobby Grich	Baltimore Orioles	AL	June 18, 1974
Davey Lopes	Los Angeles Dodgers	NL	August 20, 1974
Fred Lynn	Boston Red Sox	AL	June 18, 1975
John Mayberry	Kansas City Royals	AL	July 1, 1975
Don Baylor	Baltimore Orioles	AL	July 2, 1975
Tony Solaita	Kansas City Royals	AL	September 7, 1975 (11 innings)
Carl Yastrzemski	Boston Red Sox	AL	May 19, 1976
Reggie Smith	St. Louis Cardinals	NL	May 22, 1976
Dave Kingman	New York Mets	NL	June 4, 1976
Bill Robinson	Pittsburgh Pirates	NL	June 5, 1976 (15 innings)
Gary Matthews	San Francisco Giants	NL	September 25, 1976
Gary Carter	Montreal Expos	NL	April 20, 1977
Willie Horton	Texas Rangers	AL	May 15, 1977
Larry Parrish	Montreal Expos	NL	May 29, 1977
John Mayberry	Kansas City Royals	AL	June 1, 1977
Cliff Johnson	New York Yankees	AL	June 30, 1977
George Foster	Cincinnati Reds	NL	July 14, 1977
Jim Rice	Boston Red Sox	AL	August 29, 1977
Pete Rose	Cincinnati Reds	NL	April 29, 1978

Greats: Feats

Player	Team	Lg	Date
Dave Kingman	Chicago Cubs	NL	May 14, 1978
Larry Parrish	Montreal Expos	NL	July 30, 1978
Dave Kingman	Chicago Cubs	NL	May 17, 1979
Dale Murphy	Atlanta Braves	NL	May 18, 1979
Al Oliver	Texas Rangers	AL	May 23, 1979
Mike Schmidt	Philadelphia Phillies	NL	July 7, 1979
Ben Oglivie	Milwaukee Brewers	AL	July 8, 1979 (first game)
Claudell Washington	Chicago White Sox	AL	July 14, 1979
George Brett	Kansas City Royals	AL	July 22, 1979
Cecil Cooper	Milwaukee Brewers	AL	July 27, 1979
Dave Kingman	Chicago Cubs	NL	July 28, 1979
Eddie Murray	Baltimore Orioles	AL	August 29, 1979 (second game)
Carney Lansford	California Angels	AL	September 1, 1979
Larry Parrish	Montreal Expos	NL	April 25, 1980
Otto Velez	Toronto Blue Jays	AL	May 4, 1980 (first game, 10 innings)
Johnny Bench	Cincinnati Reds	NL	May 29, 1980
Freddie Patek	California Angels	AL	June 20, 1980
Claudell Washington	New York Mets	NL	June 22, 1980
Al Oliver	Texas Rangers	AL	August 17, 1980 (second game)
Eddie Murray	Baltimore Orioles	AL	September 14, 1980 (13 innings)
Jeff Burroughs	Seattle Mariners	AL	August 14, 1981 (second game)
Paul Molitor	Milwaukee Brewers	AL	May 12, 1982
Larry Herndon	Detroit Tigers	AL	May 18, 1982
Ben Oglivie	Milwaukee Brewers	AL	June 20, 1982
Harold Baines	Chicago White Sox	AL	July 7, 1982
Doug DeCinces	California Angels	AL	August 3, 1982
Doug DeCinces	California Angels	AL	August 8, 1982
George Brett	Kansas City Royals	AL	April 20, 1983
Ben Oglivie	Milwaukee Brewers	AL	May 14, 1983
Darrell Evans	San Francisco Giants	NL	June 15, 1983
Dan Ford	Baltimore Orioles	AL	July 20, 1983
Jim Rice	Boston Red Sox	AL	August 29, 1983 (second game)
Dave Kingman	Oakland Athletics	AL	April 16, 1984
Harold Baines	Chicago White Sox	AL	September 17, 1984
Gorman Thomas	Seattle Mariners	AL	April 11, 1985
Larry Parrish	Texas Rangers	AL	April 29, 1985
Darryl Strawberry	New York Mets	NL	August 5, 1985
Eddie Murray	Baltimore Orioles	AL	August 26, 1985
Gary Carter	New York Mets	NL	September 3, 1985
Andre Dawson	Montreal Expos	NL	September 24, 1985
Lee Lacy	Baltimore Orioles	AL	June 8, 1986
Juan Beniquez	Baltimore Orioles	AL	June 12, 1986
Ken Griffey Sr.	Atlanta Braves	NL	July 22, 1986 (11 innings)
Joe Carter	Cleveland Indians	AL	August 29, 1986
Jim Presley	Seattle Mariners	AL	September 1, 1986
Eric Davis	Cincinnati Reds	NL	September 10, 1986
Reggie Jackson	California Angels	AL	September 18, 1986
Eric Davis	Cincinnati Reds	NL	May 3, 1987
Tim Wallach	Montreal Expos	NL	May 4, 1987
Cory Snyder	Cleveland Indians	AL	May 21, 1987
Joe Carter	Cleveland Indians	AL	May 28, 1987
Mike Schmidt	Philadelphia Phillies	NL	June 14, 1987
Mark McGwire	Oakland Athletics	AL	June 27, 1987
Bill Madlock	Detroit Tigers	AL	June 28, 1987 (11 innings)
Brook Jacoby	Cleveland Indians	AL	July 3, 1987
Dale Sveum	Milwaukee Brewers	AL	July 17, 1987
Andre Dawson	Chicago Cubs	NL	August 1, 1987
Glenn Davis	Houston Astros	NL	September 10, 1987
Mickey Brantley	Seattle Mariners	AL	September 14, 1987
Ernie Whitt	Toronto Blue Jays	AL	September 14, 1987
Darnell Coles	Pittsburgh Pirates	NL	September 30, 1987 (second game)
Wally Joyner	California Angels	AL	October 3, 1987
George Bell	Toronto Blue Jays	AL	April 4, 1988

Greats: Feats

Player	Team	Lg	Date
Jose Canseco	Oakland Athletics	AL	July 3, 1988
Joe Carter	Cleveland Indians	AL	June 24, 1989
Joe Carter	Cleveland Indians	AL	July 19, 1989
Von Hayes	Philadelphia Phillies	NL	August 29, 1989
Cecil Fielder	Detroit Tigers	AL	May 6, 1990
Kevin Mitchell	San Francisco Giants	NL	May 25, 1990
Jeff Treadway	Atlanta Braves	NL	May 26, 1990
Glenn Davis	Houston Astros	NL	June 1, 1990
Cecil Fielder	Detroit Tigers	AL	June 6, 1990
Randy Milligan	Baltimore Orioles	AL	June 9, 1990
Bo Jackson	Kansas City Royals	AL	July 17, 1990
Tom Brunansky	Boston Red Sox	AL	September 29, 1990
Dave Winfield	California Angels	AL	April 13, 1991
Harold Baines	Oakland Athletics	AL	May 7, 1991
Barry Larkin	Cincinnati Reds	NL	June 28, 1991
Danny Tartabull	Kansas City Royals	AL	July 6, 1991
Jack Clark	Boston Red Sox	AL	July 31, 1991
Dave Henderson	Oakland Athletics	AL	August 3, 1991
Juan Gonzalez	Texas Rangers	AL	June 7, 1992
Jeff Blauser	Atlanta Braves	NL	July 12, 1992 (10 innings)
Albert Belle	Cleveland Indians	AL	September 6, 1992
Carlos Baerga	Cleveland Indians	AL	June 17, 1993
Joe Carter	Toronto Blue Jays	AL	August 23, 1993
Juan Gonzalez	Texas Rangers	AL	August 28, 1993
Karl Rhodes	Chicago Cubs	NL	April 4, 1994
Cory Snyder	Los Angeles Dodgers	NL	April 17, 1994
Tim Raines	Chicago White Sox	AL	April 18, 1994
Jose Canseco	Texas Rangers	AL	June 13, 1994
Jeff Bagwell	Houston Astros	NL	June 24, 1994
Darnell Coles	Toronto Blue Jays	AL	July 5, 1994
Jim Thome	Cleveland Indians	AL	July 22, 1994
Barry Bonds	San Francisco Giants	NL	August 2, 1994
John Valentin	Boston Red Sox	AL	June 2, 1995
Mark McGwire	Oakland Athletics	AL	June 11, 1995
Andres Galarraga	Colorado Rockies	NL	June 25, 1995
Mike Stanley	New York Yankees	AL	August 10, 1995 (first game)
Reggie Sanders	Cincinnati Reds	NL	August 15, 1995
Paul O'Neill	New York Yankees	AL	August 31, 1995
Albert Belle	Cleveland Indians	AL	September 19, 1995
Dan Wilson	Seattle Mariners	AL	April 11, 1996
Cecil Fielder	Detroit Tigers	AL	April 16, 1996
Ernie Young	Oakland Athletics	AL	May 10, 1996
Geronimo Berroa	Oakland Athletics	AL	May 22, 1996
Ken Griffey Jr.	Seattle Mariners	AL	May 24, 1996
Cal Ripken Jr.	Baltimore Orioles	AL	May 28, 1996
Sammy Sosa	Chicago Cubs	NL	June 5, 1996
Mike Piazza	Los Angeles Dodgers	NL	June 29, 1996
Edgar Martinez	Seattle Mariners	AL	July 6, 1996
Darryl Strawberry	New York Yankees	AL	August 6, 1996
Geronimo Berroa	Oakland Athletics	AL	August 12, 1996
Benito Santiago	Philadelphia Phillies	NL	September 15, 1996
Frank Thomas	Chicago White Sox	AL	September 15, 1996
Mo Vaughn	Boston Red Sox	AL	September 24, 1996
Willie Greene	Cincinnati Reds	NL	September 24, 1996
Tino Martinez	New York Yankees	AL	April 2, 1997
Larry Walker	Colorado Rockies	NL	April 5, 1997
Ken Griffey Jr.	Seattle Mariners	AL	April 25, 1997
Matt Williams	Cleveland Indians	AL	April 25, 1997
Roberto Alomar	Baltimore Orioles	AL	April 26, 1997
Steve Finley	San Diego Padres	NL	May 19, 1997
Mo Vaughn	Boston Red Sox	AL	May 30, 1997
Steve Finley	San Diego Padres	NL	June 23, 1997
Bob Higginson	Detroit Tigers	AL	June 30, 1997

Greats: Feats

Player	Team	Lg	Date
Bobby Estalella	Philadelphia Phillies	NL	September 4, 1997
Ivan Rodriguez	Texas Rangers	AL	September 11, 1997

Cycles

Player	Team	Lg	Date
Curry Foley	Buffalo Bisons	NL	May 25, 1882
Lon Knight	Philadelphia Athletics	AA	July 30, 1883
John Reilly	Cincinnati Reds	AA	September 12, 1883
John Reilly	Cincinnati Reds	AA	September 19, 1883
Jim O'Rourke	Buffalo Bisons	NL	June 16, 1884
Dave Orr	New York Metropolitans	AA	June 12, 1885
George Wood	Detroit Wolverines	NL	June 13, 1885
Henry Larkin	Philadelphia Athletics	AA	June 16, 1885
Mox McQuery	Detroit Wolverines	NL	September 28, 1885
Fred Dunlap	St. Louis Maroons	NL	May 24, 1886
Pete Browning	Louisville Colonels	AA	August 8, 1886
Jack Rowe	Detroit Wolverines	NL	August 21, 1886
Jim McGarr	Philadelphia Athletics	AA	September 23, 1886
Tip O'Neill	St. Louis Browns	AA	April 30, 1887
Fred Carroll	Pittsburgh Alleghenys	NL	May 2, 1887
Tip O'Neill	St. Louis Browns	AA	May 7, 1887
Dave Orr	New York Metropolitans	AA	August 10, 1887
Bid McPhee	Cincinnati Reds	AA	August 26, 1887
Harry Stovey	Philadelphia Athletics	AA	May 15, 1888
Sam Barkley	Kansas City Blues	AA	June 13, 1888
Jimmy Ryan	Chicago White Stockings	NL	July 28, 1888
Mike Tiernan	New York Giants	NL	August 25, 1888
Pete Browning	Louisville Colonels	AA	June 7, 1889
Jack Glasscock	Indianapolis Hoosiers	NL	August 8, 1889
Larry Twitchell	Cleveland Spiders	NL	August 15, 1889
Bill Van Dyke	Toledo Maumees	AA	July 5, 1890
Jumbo Davis	Brooklyn Gladiators	AA	July 18, 1890
Roger Connor	New York Giants	PL	July 21, 1890
Tom Burns	Brooklyn Bridegrooms	NL	August 1, 1890 (second game)
John Reilly	Cincinnati Reds	NL	August 6, 1890
Farmer Weaver	Louisville Colonels	AA	August 12, 1890
Jimmy Ryan	Chicago Colts	NL	July 1, 1891
Abner Dalrymple	Milwaukee Brewers	AA	September 12, 1891
Lave Cross	Philadelphia Phillies	NL	April 24, 1894
Bill Hassamaer	Washington Senators	NL	June 13, 1894
Sam Thompson	Philadelphia Phillies	NL	August 17, 1894
Tom Parrott	Cincinnati Reds	NL	September 28, 1894
Tommy Dowd	St. Louis Browns	NL	August 16, 1895
Ed Cartwright	Washington Senators	NL	September 30, 1895 (first game)
Herman Long	Boston Beaneaters	NL	May 9, 1896
Bill Joyce	Washington Senators	NL	May 30, 1896 (first game)
Harry Davis	Philadelphia Athletics	AL	July 10, 1901
Fred Clarke	Pittsburgh Pirates	NL	July 23, 1901
Nap Lajoie	Philadelphia Athletics	AL	July 30, 1901
Fred Clarke	Pittsburgh Pirates	NL	May 7, 1903
Patsy Dougherty	Boston Pilgrims	AL	July 29, 1903
Bill Bradley	Cleveland Bronchos	AL	September 24, 1903
Duff Cooley	Boston Beaneaters	NL	June 20, 1904 (second game)
Sam Mertes	New York Giants	NL	October 4, 1904 (first game)
Johnny Bates	Boston Beaneaters	NL	April 26, 1907
Otis Clymer	Washington Senators	AL	October 2, 1908
Chief Wilson	Pittsburgh Pirates	NL	July 3, 1910
Danny Murphy	Philadelphia Athletics	AL	August 25, 1910
Bill Collins	Boston Beaneaters	NL	October 6, 1910
Home Run Baker	Philadelphia Athletics	AL	July 3, 1911 (second game)
Mike Mitchell	Cincinnati Reds	NL	August 19, 1911 (second game)
Tris Speaker	Boston Red Sox	AL	June 9, 1912
Chief Meyers	New York Giants	NL	June 10, 1912

Greats: Feats

Player	Team	Lg	Date
Bert Daniels	New York Highlanders	AL	July 25, 1912
Honus Wagner	Pittsburgh Pirates	NL	August 22, 1912 (second game)
Heine Groh	Cincinnati Reds	NL	July 5, 1915 (second game)
Cliff Heathcote	St. Louis Cardinals	NL	June 13, 1918 (19 innings)
George Sisler	St. Louis Browns	AL	August 8, 1920 (second game)
Bobby Veach	Detroit Tigers	AL	September 17, 1920 (12 innings)
George Burns	New York Giants	NL	September 17, 1920 (10 innings)
Bob Meusel	New York Yankees	AL	May 7, 1921
Dave Bancroft	New York Giants	NL	June 1, 1921 (second game)
George Sisler	St. Louis Browns	AL	August 13, 1921 (10 innings)
Dave Robertson	Pittsburgh Pirates	NL	August 30, 1921
Ross Youngs	New York Giants	NL	April 29, 1922
Jimmy Johnston	Brooklyn Dodgers	NL	May 25, 1922 (first game)
Ray Schalk	Chicago White Sox	AL	June 27, 1922
Bob Meusel	New York Yankees	AL	July 3, 1922
Pie Traynor	Pittsburgh Pirates	NL	July 7, 1923
Baby Doll Jacobson	St. Louis Browns	AL	April 17, 1924
Goose Goslin	Washington Senators	AL	August 28, 1924
Kiki Cuyler	Pittsburgh Pirates	NL	June 4, 1925
Max Carey	Pittsburgh Pirates	NL	June 20, 1925
Roy Carlyle	Boston Red Sox	AL	July 21, 1925 (first game)
Bob Fothergill	Detroit Tigers	AL	September 26, 1926 (first game)
Jim Bottomley	St. Louis Cardinals	NL	July 15, 1927
Cy Williams	Philadelphia Phillies	NL	August 5, 1927
Bill Terry	New York Giants	NL	May 29, 1928
Bob Meusel	New York Yankees	AL	July 26, 1928 (first game, 12 innings)
Mel Ott	New York Giants	NL	May 16, 1929 (second game)
Ski Melillo	St. Louis Browns	AL	May 23, 1929 (second game)
Joe Cronin	Washington Senators	AL	September 2, 1929 (first game)
Freddy Lindstrom	New York Giants	NL	May 8, 1930
Hack Wilson	Chicago Cubs	NL	June 23, 1930
Chick Hafey	St. Louis Cardinals	NL	August 21, 1930
Babe Herman	Brooklyn Dodgers	NL	May 18, 1931
Chuck Klein	Philadelphia Phillies	NL	July 1, 1931
Babe Herman	Brooklyn Dodgers	NL	July 24, 1931
Tony Lazzeri	New York Yankees	AL	June 3, 1932
Mickey Cochrane	Philadelphia Athletics	AL	July 22, 1932
Pepper Martin	St. Louis Cardinals	NL	May 5, 1933
Chuck Klein	Philadelphia Phillies	NL	May 26, 1933 (14 innings)
Arky Vaughan	Pittsburgh Pirates	NL	June 24, 1933
Mickey Cochrane	Philadelphia Athletics	AL	August 2, 1933
Mike Higgins	Philadelphia Athletics	AL	August 6, 1933
Jimmie Foxx	Philadelphia Athletics	AL	August 14, 1933
Earl Averill	Cleveland Indians	AL	August 17, 1933
Babe Herman	Chicago Cubs	NL	September 30, 1933
Doc Cramer	Philadelphia Athletics	AL	June 10, 1934
Lou Gehrig	New York Yankees	AL	June 25, 1934
Moose Solters	Boston Red Sox	AL	August 19, 1934 (first game)
Joe Medwick	St. Louis Cardinals	NL	June 29, 1935
Sam Leslie	New York Giants	NL	May 24, 1936
Gee Walker	Detroit Tigers	AL	April 20, 1937
Joe DiMaggio	New York Yankees	AL	July 9, 1937
Lou Gehrig	New York Yankees	AL	August 1, 1937
Odell Hale	Cleveland Indians	AL	July 12, 1938
Sam Chapman	Philadelphia Athletics	AL	May 5, 1939
Charlie Gehringer	Detroit Tigers	AL	May 27, 1939
Arky Vaughan	Pittsburgh Pirates	NL	July 19, 1939
Harry Craft	Cincinnati Reds	NL	June 8, 1940
Harry Danning	New York Giants	NL	June 15, 1940
Johnny Mize	St. Louis Cardinals	NL	July 13, 1940 (first game)
Buddy Rosar	New York Yankees	AL	July 19, 1940
Joe Cronin	Boston Red Sox	AL	August 2, 1940
Joe Gordon	New York Yankees	AL	September 8, 1940
George McQuinn	St. Louis Browns	AL	July 19, 1941 (first game)

Greats: Feats

Player	Team	Lg	Date
Leon Culberson	Boston Red Sox	AL	July 3, 1943
Bobby Doerr	Boston Red Sox	AL	May 17, 1944 (second game)
Bob Johnson	Boston Red Sox	AL	July 6, 1944
Dixie Walker	Brooklyn Dodgers	NL	September 2, 1944
Bob Elliott	Pittsburgh Pirates	NL	July 15, 1945 (second game)
Bill Salkeld	Pittsburgh Pirates	NL	August 4, 1945
Mickey Vernon	Washington Senators	AL	May 19, 1946 (second game)
Ted Williams	Boston Red Sox	AL	July 21, 1946 (second game)
Bobby Doerr	Boston Red Sox	AL	May 13, 1947
Vic Wertz	Detroit Tigers	AL	September 14, 1947 (first game)
Joe DiMaggio	New York Yankees	AL	May 20, 1948
Wally Westlake	Pittsburgh Pirates	NL	July 30, 1948
Jackie Robinson	Brooklyn Dodgers	NL	August 29, 1948 (first game)
Wally Westlake	Pittsburgh Pirates	NL	June 14, 1949
Gil Hodges	Brooklyn Dodgers	NL	June 25, 1949
Stan Musial	St. Louis Cardinals	NL	July 24, 1949
George Kell	Detroit Tigers	AL	June 2, 1950 (second game)
Ralph Kiner	Pittsburgh Pirates	NL	June 25, 1950
Roy Smalley	Chicago Cubs	NL	June 28, 1950
Elmer Valo	Philadelphia Athletics	AL	August 2, 1950
Hoot Evers	Detroit Tigers	AL	September 7, 1950 (10 innings)
Gus Bell	Pittsburgh Pirates	NL	June 4, 1951
Larry Doby	Cleveland Indians	AL	June 4, 1952
Don Mueller	New York Giants	NL	July 11, 1954 (first game)
Lee Walls	Chicago Cubs	NL	July 2, 1957 (10 innings)
Mickey Mantle	New York Yankees	AL	July 23, 1957
Frank Robinson	Cincinnati Reds	NL	May 2, 1959
Brooks Robinson	Baltimore Orioles	AL	July 15, 1960
Bill White	St. Louis Cardinals	NL	August 14, 1960 (first game)
Ken Boyer	St. Louis Cardinals	NL	September 14, 1961 (second game, 11 innings)
Lu Clinton	Boston Red Sox	AL	July 13, 1962 (15 innings)
Johnny Callison	Philadelphia Phillies	NL	June 27, 1963
Jim Hickman	New York Mets	NL	August 7, 1963
Jim King	Washington Senators	AL	May 26, 1964
Ken Boyer	St. Louis Cardinals	NL	June 16, 1964
Willie Stargell	Pittsburgh Pirates	NL	July 22, 1964
Jim Fregosi	Los Angeles Angels	AL	July 28, 1964
Carl Yastrzemski	Boston Red Sox	AL	May 14, 1965 (10 innings)
Billy Williams	Chicago Cubs	NL	July 17, 1966 (second game)
Randy Hundley	Chicago Cubs	NL	August 11, 1966 (first game, 11 innings)
Jim Fregosi	California Angels	AL	May 20, 1968 (11 innings)
Wes Parker	Los Angeles Dodgers	NL	May 7, 1970 (10 innings)
Rod Carew	Minnesota Twins	AL	May 20, 1970
Tony Horton	Cleveland Indians	AL	July 2, 1970
Tommie Agee	New York Mets	NL	July 6, 1970
Jim Ray Hart	San Francisco Giants	NL	July 8, 1970
Freddie Patek	Kansas City Royals	AL	July 9, 1971
Dave Kingman	San Francisco Giants	NL	April 16, 1972
Cesar Cedeno	Houston Astros	NL	August 2, 1972
Bobby Murcer	New York Yankees	AL	August 29, 1972 (first game, 11 innings)
Cesar Tovar	Minnesota Twins	AL	September 19, 1972
Joe Torre	St. Louis Cardinals	NL	June 27, 1973
Richie Zisk	Pittsburgh Pirates	NL	June 9, 1974
Lou Brock	St. Louis Cardinals	NL	May 27, 1975
Tim Foli	Montreal Expos	NL	April 21, 1976
Larry Hisle	Minnesota Twins	AL	June 4, 1976 (10 innings)
Mike Phillips	New York Mets	NL	June 25, 1976
Lyman Bostock	Minnesota Twins	AL	July 24, 1976
Cesar Cedeno	Houston Astros	NL	August 9, 1976
Mike Hegan	Milwaukee Brewers	AL	September 3, 1976
Bob Watson	Houston Astros	NL	June 24, 1977 (11 innings)
John Mayberry	Kansas City Royals	AL	August 5, 1977
Jack Brohamer	Chicago White Sox	AL	September 24, 1977
Andre Thornton	Cleveland Indians	AL	April 22, 1978

Greats: Feats

Player	Team	Lg	Date
Chris Speier	Montreal Expos	NL	July 20, 1978
Mike Cubbage	Minnesota Twins	AL	July 27, 1978
George Brett	Kansas City Royals	AL	May 28, 1979 (16 innings)
Dan Ford	California Angels	AL	August 10, 1979 (14 innings)
Bob Watson	Boston Red Sox	AL	September 15, 1979
Frank White	Kansas City Royals	AL	September 26, 1979
Ivan DeJesus	Chicago Cubs	NL	April 22, 1980
Fred Lynn	Boston Red Sox	AL	May 13, 1980
Mike Easler	Pittsburgh Pirates	NL	June 12, 1980
Gary Ward	Minnesota Twins	AL	September 18, 1980 (first game)
Charlie Moore	Milwaukee Brewers	AL	October 1, 1980
Frank White	Kansas City Royals	AL	August 3, 1982
Cal Ripken Jr.	Baltimore Orioles	AL	May 6, 1984
Carlton Fisk	Chicago White Sox	AL	May 16, 1984
Willie McGee	St. Louis Cardinals	NL	June 23, 1984 (11 innings)
Dwight Evans	Boston Red Sox	AL	June 28, 1984 (11 innings)
Jeffrey Leonard	San Francisco Giants	NL	June 27, 1985
Keith Hernandez	New York Mets	NL	July 4, 1985 (19 innings)
Oddibe McDowell	Texas Rangers	AL	July 23, 1985
Rich Gedman	Boston Red Sox	AL	September 18, 1985
Tony Phillips	Oakland Athletics	AL	May 16, 1986
Kirby Puckett	Minnesota Twins	AL	August 1, 1986
Andre Dawson	Chicago Cubs	NL	April 29, 1987
Candy Maldonado	San Francisco Giants	NL	May 4, 1987
Tim Raines	Montreal Expos	NL	August 16, 1987
Albert Hall	St. Louis Cardinals	NL	September 23, 1987
Robin Yount	Milwaukee Brewers	AL	June 12, 1988
Chris Speier	San Francisco Giants	NL	July 9, 1988
Mike Greenwell	Boston Red Sox	AL	September 14, 1988
Kelly Gruber	Toronto Blue Jays	AL	April 16, 1989
Eric Davis	Cincinnati Reds	NL	June 2, 1989
Kevin McReynolds	New York Mets	NL	August 1, 1989
Gary Redus	Pittsburgh Pirates	NL	August 25, 1989
George Brett	Kansas City Royals	AL	July 25, 1990
Robby Thompson	San Francisco Giants	NL	April 22, 1991
Paul Molitor	Milwaukee Brewers	AL	May 15, 1991
Ray Lankford	St. Louis Cardinals	NL	September 15, 1991
Andujar Cedeno	Houston Astros	NL	August 25, 1992
Mark Grace	Chicago Cubs	NL	May 9, 1993
Jay Buhner	Seattle Mariners	AL	June 23, 1993 (14 innings)
Travis Fryman	Detroit Tigers	AL	July 28, 1993
Scott Cooper	Boston Red Sox	AL	April 12, 1994
Rondell White	Montreal Expos	NL	June 11, 1995 (13 innings)
Gregg Jefferies	Philadelphia Phillies	NL	August 25, 1995
Tony Fernandez	New York Yankees	AL	September 3, 1995 (10 innings)
John Mabry	St. Louis Cardinals	NL	May 18, 1996
John Valentin	Boston Red Sox	AL	June 6, 1996
Alex Ochoa	New York Mets	NL	July 3, 1996
Alex Rodriguez	Seattle Mariners	AL	June 5, 1997
John Olerud	New York Mets	NL	September 11, 1997

Unassisted Triple Plays

Player	Team	Lg	Date	Opponent	Batter
Paul Hines, of	Providence Grays	NL	May 8, 1878	Boston Red Stockings	Jack Burdock
Neal Ball, ss	Cleveland Bronchos	AL	July 19, 1909	Boston Red Sox	Amby McConnell
George Burns, 1b	Boston Red Sox	AL	September 14, 1923	Cleveland Indians	Frank Brower
Ernie Padgett, ss	Boston Braves	NL	October 6, 1923	Philadelphia Phillies	Walter Holke
Glenn Wright, ss	Pittsburgh Pirates	NL	May 7, 1925	St. Louis Cardinals	Jim Bottomley
Jimmy Cooney, ss	Chicago Cubs	NL	May 30, 1927	Pittsburgh Pirates	Paul Waner
Johnny Neun, 1b	Detroit Tigers	AL	May 31, 1927	Cleveland Indians	Homer Summa
Ron Hansen, ss	Washington Senators	AL	July 29, 1968	Cleveland Indians	Joe Azcue
Mickey Morandini, 2b	Philadelphia Phillies	NL	September 23, 1992	Pittsburgh Pirates	Jeff King
John Valentin, ss	Boston Red Sox	AL	July 15, 1994	Seattle Mariners	Marc Newfield

Ballparks

Register

For each ballpark a team has played in, we list the years the team played there; a home/road breakdown of the team's won-lost record as well as the runs and home runs by the team and its opponents; and a calculation of each ballpark's effect on scoring and homers. If a ballpark was used by more than one team, we also present the totals for all of the teams that played there.

Leaders

We list the top 20 ballparks, over the course of their lifetime as well as during a single season, in terms of highest and lowest run and home run indexes. Minimums are 10 seasons for the lifetime leaders and 20 home and 20 road games for the season leaders.

Abbreviations & Formulas

A complete list of team and statistical abbreviations are listed in the back of the book, along with an appendix explaining formulas and the availability of certain statistics.

Ballpark Register

Ballpark	Team	Years	Lg	W	L	Pct	R	OR	HR	OHR	W	L	Pct	R	OR	HR	OHR	R	HR
				Home							**Road**							**Park Index**	
Anaheim Stadium/Edison International Field	Ana	1997	AL	46	36	.561	444	419	87	123	38	42	.475	385	375	74	79	111	134
Oriole Park IV	Bal	1901-1902	AL	72	56	.563	821	736	26	29	46	97	.322	654	862	31	22	115	116
Memorial Stadium	Bal	1954-1991	AL	1687	1310	.563	12262	11306	2490	2254	1515	1502	.502	13015	12634	2804	2475	92	90
Oriole Park at Camden Yards	Bal	1992-1997	AL	244	207	.541	2251	2093	555	501	250	203	.552	2294	2029	515	429	101	112
Huntington Avenue Grounds	Bos	1901-1911	AL	465	357	.566	3507	3075	216	168	385	424	.476	3217	3201	109	125	101	162
Fenway Park I	Bos	1912-1933	AL	834	821	.504	6818	7274	178	359	679	983	.409	6745	8007	478	557	96	52
Fenway Park II	Bos	1934-1997	AL	2929	2075	.585	26249	23334	4548	4025	2332	2663	.467	21758	22113	3988	3793	113	110
Dodger Stadium	Cal	1965	AL	46	34	.575	265	254	36	35	29	53	.354	262	315	56	56	92	65
Anaheim Stadium/Edison International Field	Cal	1966-1996	AL	1258	1199	.512	9955	10131	1916	2113	1107	1330	.454	10084	10933	1904	2023	94	102
White Sox Park/Comiskey Park I	ChA	1910-1990	AL	3345	2917	.534	26768	26375	2810	3465	2872	3416	.457	26920	27823	3352	3990	97	86
Comiskey Park II	ChA	1991-1997	AL	302	229	.569	2574	2314	480	495	265	270	.495	2763	2604	551	535	92	90
South Side Park III	ChA	1901-1909	AL	433	235	.648	2811	1987	31	32	311	340	.478	2598	2659	73	115	89	33
League Park I (Cle)	Cle	1901-1909	AL	384	281	.577	2846	2375	65	57	313	351	.471	2614	2767	107	89	97	62
League Park II (Cle)	Cle	1910-1931	AL	905	761	.543	8152	7758	287	304	782	884	.469	7374	7576	415	441	106	69
League Park II (Cle) & Municipal Stadium (Cle)/Cleveland Stadium (shared)	Cle	1932-1946	AL	667	495	.574	5485	4939	558	418	532	598	.471	5300	5495	710	592	94	73
Municipal Stadium (Cle)/Cleveland Stadium	Cle	1947-1993	AL	1975	1736	.532	15906	15850	3252	3217	1711	1998	.461	15948	16332	2968	2927	98	110
Jacobs Field	Cle	1994-1997	AL	184	100	.648	1648	1316	384	268	167	128	.566	1691	1437	428	315	98	91
Bennett Park	Det	1901-1911	AL	483	327	.596	3727	3284	105	94	375	438	.461	3199	3364	99	106	107	97
Navin Field	Det	1912-1937	AL	1088	891	.550	10244	9711	631	727	940	1031	.477	9838	9787	751	709	101	93
Briggs Stadium/Tiger Stadium	Det	1938-1997	AL	2605	2107	.553	22194	20997	4730	4581	2210	2482	.471	20506	20694	3776	3598	104	126
Municipal Stadium (KC)	KCA	1955-1967	AL	452	575	.440	4267	5037	767	1086	377	649	.367	3837	4947	713	995	106	108
Municipal Stadium (KC)	KC	1969-1972	AL	159	159	.500	1211	1227	137	175	136	185	.424	1169	1277	216	268	101	65
Royals Stadium/Kauffman Stadium	KC	1973-1997	AL	1110	848	.567	9077	8350	1234	1310	930	1034	.474	8408	8601	1644	1676	103	77
Wrigley Field (LA)	LAA	1961	AL	46	36	.561	447	421	122	126	24	55	.304	297	363	67	54	127	197
Dodger Stadium	LAA	1962-1964	AL	124	119	.510	851	900	106	125	114	128	.471	1008	1017	228	213	86	52
Lloyd Street Grounds	Mil	1901	AL	32	37	.464	342	373	15	14	16	52	.235	299	455	11	18	93	99
County Stadium	Mil	1970-1997	AL	1146	1052	.521	9743	9707	1716	1817	990	1217	.449	9821	10045	1948	2057	98	89
Metropolitan Stadium	Min	1961-1981	AL	910	759	.545	7698	7026	1424	1443	809	853	.487	6929	6680	1325	1270	108	110
Hubert H. Humphrey Metrodome	Min	1982-1997	AL	672	597	.530	6190	6292	1075	1399	528	728	.420	5408	6063	1067	1315	108	103
Hilltop Park	NYA	1903-1912	AL	400	344	.538	3299	3270	134	116	334	415	.446	2702	3082	58	109	114	151
Polo Grounds V	NYA	1913-1922	AL	416	336	.553	3312	2922	333	292	358	377	.487	3054	2939	189	119	102	198
Yankee Stadium I	NYA	1923-1973	AL	2553	1410	.644	19607	14741	3655	2408	2168	1790	.548	20696	17497	3531	2427	90	102
Shea Stadium	NYA	1974-1975	AL	90	69	.566	638	571	92	106	82	81	.503	714	640	119	102	92	92
Yankee Stadium II	NYA	1976-1997	AL	1014	699	.592	8129	7158	1665	1478	865	857	.502	8285	7851	1704	1486	95	99
Oakland-Alameda Coliseum	Oak	1968-1997	AL	1311	1056	.554	9983	9501	2106	1942	1112	1252	.470	10844	11038	2283	2204	89	90
Columbia Park	Phi	1901-1908	AL	383	189	.670	2758	2120	128	64	256	321	.444	2228	2406	107	75	106	106
Shibe Park/Connie Mack Stadium	Phi	1909-1954	AL	1763	1707	.508	16091	16918	1806	1900	1484	2031	.422	15436	17179	1461	1533	103	125
Kingdome	Sea	1977-1997	AL	790	845	.483	7494	7931	1700	1741	679	964	.413	6975	7980	1384	1432	104	123
Sicks Stadium	Sea	1969	AL	34	47	.420	329	399	74	93	30	51	.370	310	400	51	79	103	128
Sportsman's Park II	StL	1902-1908	AL	275	243	.531	1906	1793	61	73	215	300	.417	1849	2087	56	71	93	105
Sportsman's Park III/Busch Stadium I	StL	1909-1953	AL	1615	1796	.473	15888	17694	1680	2000	1309	2126	.381	13903	17169	1217	1463	109	138
Arlington Stadium	Tex	1972-1993	AL	906	844	.518	7528	7641	1323	1391	759	984	.435	7439	7954	1445	1408	98	95
The Ballpark at Arlington	Tex	1994-1997	AL	161	136	.542	1631	1552	351	317	132	153	.463	1408	1487	319	329	106	99
Exhibition Stadium	Tor	1977-1988	AL	480	462	.510	4243	4319	798	914	414	529	.439	3890	4147	810	803	107	106
Exhibition Stadium & SkyDome (shared)	Tor	1989	AL	46	35	.568	330	308	64	50	43	38	.531	401	343	78	49	86	92
SkyDome	Tor	1990-1997	AL	330	287	.535	2876	2830	628	612	299	315	.487	2830	2736	573	536	102	111
American League Park I	Was	1901-1903	AL	100	103	.493	1015	1065	68	98	65	138	.320	811	1187	29	47	104	218
American League Park II	Was	1904-1910	AL	224	297	.430	1709	2048	31	32	157	380	.292	1671	2418	65	71	95	48
Griffith Stadium	Was	1911-1960	AL	1999	1828	.522	16761	16989	860	1165	1678	2118	.442	17093	18484	1733	2218	94	51
Griffith Stadium	Was	1961	AL	33	46	.418	288	366	34	53	28	54	.341	330	410	85	78	92	55
RFK Stadium	Was	1962-1971	AL	363	441	.451	2906	3356	616	715	316	491	.392	2928	3580	652	735	97	96
Atlanta-Fulton County Stadium	Atl	1966-1996	NL	1265	1166	.520	10802	10928	2385	2232	1123	1327	.458	9548	10012	1908	1547	112	135
Ted Turner Field	Atl	1997	NL	50	31	.617	378	302	76	55	51	30	.630	413	279	98	56	98	85
Oriole Park III	Bal	1892-1899	NL	378	168	.692	4106	2775	72	54	266	279	.488	3392	3254	114	158	103	46
South End Grounds II & III & Congress Street Grounds (shared)	Bos	1894	NL	44	19	.698	672	519	77	70	39	30	.565	550	483	26	19	126	358
South End Grounds III	Bos	1895-1914	NL	763	699	.522	7175	6934	440	465	571	887	.392	5832	6996	182	297	110	188
Fenway Park I & Braves Field (shared)	Bos	1915	NL	49	27	.645	280	263	3	5	34	42	.447	302	282	14	18	93	25
Braves Field	Bos	1916-1952	NL	1362	1403	.493	10715	11559	889	996	1154	1697	.405	11909	13816	1268	1615	89	67
South End Grounds I	Bos	1876-1887	NL	342	201	.630	3403	2396	127	58	256	285	.473	2953	3149	117	145	95	70
South End Grounds II	Bos	1888-1893	NL	281	126	.690	2829	1893	169	142	223	182	.551	2146	2045	112	120	112	133
Washington Park II	Bro	1890	NL	58	16	.784	547	303	27	9	28	27	.509	337	318	16	18	96	79
Eastern Park	Bro	1891-1897	NL	293	182	.617	3026	2567	117	117	188	281	.401	2831	3282	114	145	90	89
Washington Park III	Bro	1898-1912	NL	554	556	.499	4460	4647	171	155	436	662	.397	4314	5092	181	206	96	83
Ebbets Field	Bro	1913-1957	NL	1974	1632	.576	16255	14838	1958	1931	1683	1750	.490	15474	15118	1752	1785	102	110
Riverside Grounds	Buf	1879-1883	NL	123	87	.586	1278	1068	12	12	89	125	.416	997	1285	31	38	105	35
Olympic Park I	Buf	1884-1885	NL	56	56	.500	674	717	36	33	46	65	.414	521	669	26	44	116	98
West Side Park & South Side Park II (shared)	ChN	1891	NL	43	22	.662	467	343	39	30	39	31	.557	366	387	21	23	116	169
South Side Park II	ChN	1892-1893	NL	75	65	.536	830	749	29	24	51	82	.383	634	860	29	37	100	76
West Side Grounds	ChN	1894-1915	NL	1008	633	.614	8152	6881	333	247	816	750	.521	7402	6967	361	260	100	89
Weeghman Park/Wrigley Field (Chi)	ChN	1916-1997	NL	3413	2978	.534	29063	28448	4836	4717	2828	3501	.447	26174	27627	4098	4036	106	116
23rd Street Grounds	ChN	1876-1877	NL	42	18	.700	558	299	3	9	36	29	.554	432	333	5	8	121	67
Lake Front Park I	ChN	1878-1882	NL	150	56	.728	1443	875	21	16	104	81	.562	1056	916	16	28	106	76
Lake Front Park II	ChN	1883-1884	NL	75	30	.714	908	566	142	72	46	59	.438	605	621	13	32	120	476

Ballpark	Team	Years	Lg	Home W	L	Pct	R	OR	HR	OHR	Road W	L	Pct	R	OR	HR	OHR	Park Index R	HR
West Side Park	ChN	1885-1890	NL	267	123	.685	2931	1994	318	230	209	162	.563	2069	1916	92	86	118	293
Avenue Grounds	Cin	1876-1879	NL	64	65	.496	681	766	18	11	40	93	.301	666	1043	5	15	87	149
Bank Street Grounds	Cin	1880	NL	14	25	.359	163	216	5	8	7	34	.171	131	256	2	2	103	342
League Park I (Cin)	Cin	1890-1893	NL	158	123	.562	1630	1378	86	84	122	144	.459	1294	1590	54	74	99	126
League Park II (Cin)	Cin	1894-1901	NL	349	217	.617	3532	3113	100	108	214	319	.402	2778	3224	142	182	104	60
Palace of the Fans	Cin	1902-1911	NL	410	355	.536	3436	3108	85	62	326	412	.442	2848	2993	120	119	108	59
Redland Field/Crosley Field	Cin	1912-1969	NL	2441	2043	.544	19346	18722	2313	2155	1961	2484	.441	18426	19751	2477	2654	99	86
Riverfront Stadium/Cinergy Field	Cin	1970-1997	NL	1248	954	.567	9949	9189	1921	1855	1122	1080	.510	9556	9140	1833	1695	102	107
National League Park I	Cle	1879-1884	NL	132	139	.487	1226	1310	17	23	110	160	.407	1209	1471	45	58	94	39
National League Park II	Cle	1889-1890	NL	63	72	.467	710	696	21	21	42	88	.323	570	855	25	48	95	55
League Park I (Cle)	Cle	1891-1899	NL	361	198	.646	3822	2958	56	68	272	406	.401	3566	4263	164	234	105	38
Mile High Stadium	Col	1993-1994	NL	64	74	.464	806	907	136	168	56	85	.397	525	698	131	133	143	118
Coors Field	Col	1995-1997	NL	146	88	.624	1688	1550	407	350	97	137	.415	981	1105	253	204	155	166
Recreation Park (Det)	Det	1881-1888	NL	248	179	.581	2602	2146	153	95	178	258	.408	2245	2621	111	124	100	108
Joe Robbie Stadium/Pro Player Stadium	Fla	1993-1997	NL	201	172	.539	1602	1632	294	311	153	218	.412	1548	1713	324	327	99	92
Hartford Ball Club Grounds	Har	1876	NL	23	9	.719	220	107	0	0	24	12	.667	209	154	2	2	101	0
Union Grounds (Bro)	Har	1877	NL	19	8	.704	167	92	2	1	12	19	.387	174	219	2	1	76	115
Colt Stadium	Hou	1962-1964	NL	117	125	.483	750	898	98	119	79	163	.326	801	1087	139	194	87	65
Astrodome	Hou	1965-1997	NL	1459	1152	.559	10313	9598	1300	1358	1126	1483	.432	10797	11664	1962	2166	89	64
South Street Park	Ind	1878	NL	10	17	.370	106	115	1	1	14	19	.424	187	213	2	2	68	61
Seventh Street Park II	Ind	1887	NL	24	39	.381	349	456	19	28	13	50	.206	278	507	14	32	103	102
Seventh Street Park III	Ind	1888-1889	NL	63	71	.470	823	780	77	94	46	89	.341	595	842	19	43	112	278
Association Park	KCN	1886	NL	19	42	.311	301	456	9	4	11	49	.183	193	420	10	23	121	39
Los Angeles Memorial Coliseum	LA	1958-1961	NL	172	137	.557	1474	1430	346	397	158	151	.511	1296	1291	257	254	112	145
Dodger Stadium	LA	1962-1997	NL	1644	1208	.576	11069	9641	1927	1756	1435	1419	.503	12237	11471	2301	2035	87	85
Eclipse Park I	Lou	1892	NL	37	31	.544	309	286	7	3	26	58	.310	340	518	11	23	86	36
Eclipse Park II	Lou	1893-1899	NL	202	233	.464	2422	2727	130	136	154	361	.299	2604	3770	114	134	96	127
Louisville Baseball Park	Lou	1876-1877	NL	36	25	.590	368	326	13	6	29	36	.446	251	307	2	1	133	675
County Stadium	Mil	1953-1965	NL	602	414	.593	4408	3694	998	776	544	476	.533	4977	4424	1232	951	87	82
Milwaukee Base-Ball Grounds	Mil	1878	NL	7	18	.280	127	177	1	0	8	27	.229	129	209	1	3	126	35
Parc Jarry	Mon	1969-1976	NL	285	356	.445	2519	2927	461	519	269	378	.416	2347	2792	382	442	107	120
Stade Olympique	Mon	1977-1997	NL	900	722	.555	6805	6332	1107	1142	800	854	.484	6828	6748	1355	1311	99	86
Polo Grounds III	NYG	1889-1890	NL	84	42	.667	874	583	26	17	62	69	.473	769	820	51	35	95	52
Polo Grounds IV	NYG	1891-1910	NL	876	564	.608	7662	6329	375	227	686	736	.482	7031	7160	227	255	97	134
Hilltop Park & Polo Grounds V (shared)	NYG	1911	NL	49	25	.662	357	267	25	15	50	29	.633	399	275	16	18	99	126
Polo Grounds V	NYG	1912-1957	NL	2058	1440	.588	16553	14167	3124	2511	1782	1720	.509	16554	15254	1744	1583	97	170
Polo Grounds I	NYG	1883-1888	NL	234	113	.674	2111	1418	87	46	186	160	.538	1973	1905	100	89	91	70
Polo Grounds V	NYN	1962-1963	NL	56	105	.348	611	891	154	213	35	126	.217	507	831	81	141	112	165
Shea Stadium	NYN	1964-1997	NL	1367	1316	.510	10356	10393	1873	1997	1197	1491	.445	10791	11294	1952	2012	94	98
Union Grounds (Bro)	NYM	1876	NL	13	20	.394	143	207	2	7	8	15	.348	117	205	0	1	76	627
Jefferson Street Grounds	PhN	1876	NL	10	24	.294	259	309	4	0	4	21	.160	119	225	3	2	121	59
Recreation Park (Phi)	Phi	1883-1886	NL	102	117	.466	1115	1286	21	21	81	134	.377	1013	1435	42	84	96	33
Philadelphia Baseball Grounds	Phi	1887-1894	NL	352	200	.638	3889	2735	185	117	231	276	.456	2871	3201	136	157	100	95
Baker Bowl	Phi	1895-1937	NL	1607	1577	.505	16007	16788	1612	1392	1288	1913	.402	13361	15590	910	998	114	158
Baker Bowl & Shibe Park/ Connie Mack Stadium (shared)	Phi	1938	NL	26	48	.351	286	439	23	40	19	57	.250	264	401	17	36	112	122
Shibe Park/Connie Mack Stadium	Phi	1939-1970	NL	1185	1302	.476	9715	10746	1533	1691	1043	1459	.417	9832	11428	1681	1935	97	90
Veterans Stadium	Phi	1971-1997	NL	1164	965	.547	9529	9061	1753	1631	938	1179	.443	8518	9248	1543	1610	104	107
Recreation Park (Pit)	Pit	1887-1890	NL	122	117	.510	1229	1138	15	12	83	204	.289	1249	2230	81	144	82	14
Exposition Park III (Pit)	Pit	1891-1908	NL	813	502	.618	7058	5714	227	103	641	604	.515	6376	6196	244	245	96	64
Exposition Park III (Pit) & Forbes Field (shared)	Pit	1909	NL	56	21	.727	354	237	10	6	54	21	.720	345	210	15	6	104	74
Forbes Field	Pit	1910-1969	NL	2537	2092	.548	21014	19839	1839	1923	2108	2487	.459	19674	20108	2518	2919	102	69
Forbes Field & Three Rivers Stadium (shared)	Pit	1970	NL	50	32	.610	356	315	43	41	39	41	.488	373	349	87	65	91	54
Three Rivers Stadium	Pit	1971-1997	NL	1178	945	.555	9396	8667	1582	1542	1008	1105	.477	8961	8925	1597	1626	101	96
Messer Street Grounds	Prv	1878-1885	NL	244	115	.680	2033	1363	44	28	194	163	.543	2004	1765	54	66	90	60
San Diego Stadium/Jack Murphy Stadium/ Qualcomm Stadium	SD	1969-1997	NL	1117	1171	.488	8662	9312	1546	1819	950	1333	.416	9073	10429	1557	1825	92	99
Seals Stadium	SF	1958-1959	NL	86	68	.558	702	625	165	151	77	77	.500	730	686	172	154	94	97
Candlestick Park/3Com Park	SF	1960-1997	NL	1677	1334	.557	12814	12022	2599	2324	1407	1599	.468	12884	13121	2642	2439	95	97
Grand Avenue Park	StL	1876-1877	NL	44	16	.733	327	182	1	2	29	35	.453	344	365	2	3	77	64
Sportsman's Park I	StL	1892	NL	37	36	.507	379	380	32	32	19	58	.247	324	542	13	15	92	241
Robison Field	StL	1893-1919	NL	885	1063	.454	8222	9494	383	417	691	1268	.353	7719	10291	277	457	99	110
Robison Field & Sportsman's Park III/ Busch Stadium I (shared)	StL	1920	NL	38	38	.500	330	332	10	10	37	41	.474	345	350	22	20	98	49
Sportsman's Park III/Busch Stadium I	StL	1921-1966	NL	2138	1429	.599	18013	15501	2347	2320	1813	1730	.512	16336	15178	2226	2268	106	103
Busch Stadium II	StL	1967-1997	NL	1327	1122	.542	10297	9793	1257	1486	1183	1254	.485	10065	10061	1489	1866	99	81
Union Grounds (StL)	StL	1885-1886	NL	50	67	.427	503	575	19	14	29	84	.257	435	731	19	35	89	59
Star Park I	Syr	1879	NL	11	22	.333	115	200	1	2	11	26	.297	160	257	4	2	85	56
Putnam Grounds	Try	1879	NL	12	27	.308	191	263	3	6	7	29	.194	130	281	1	7	102	104
Haymakers Grounds	Try	1880-1881	NL	44	39	.530	426	453	9	15	36	48	.429	365	413	1	4	114	486
Troy Ball Club Grounds	Try	1882	NL	22	20	.524	238	217	7	2	13	28	.317	192	305	5	11	89	55
Swampoodle Grounds	WaN	1886-1889	NL	96	141	.405	1136	1362	71	66	67	196	.255	1023	1865	54	102	96	97
Boundary Field	Was	1892-1899	NL	264	270	.494	3413	3347	222	139	146	427	.255	2805	4359	116	184	101	129
Agricultural County Fair Grounds	Wor	1880-1882	NL	55	69	.444	703	777	21	25	35	90	.280	498	737	10	20	121	155
Newington Park	Bal	1882	AA	9	25	.265	138	225	2	7	10	29	.256	134	287	2	8	99	103
Oriole Park I	Bal	1883-1889	AA	232	170	.577	2572	2148	71	39	152	295	.340	2103	3102	61	92	101	80
Oriole Park II	Bal	1890	AA	8	11	.421	117	115	1	0	7	8	.467	65	77	1	3	129	20

Ballparks: Register

Ballpark	Team	Years	Lg	Home							Road							Park Index	
				W	L	Pct	R	OR	HR	OHR	W	L	Pct	R	OR	HR	OHR	R	HR
Oriole Park III	Bal	1891	AA	44	24	.647	481	354	13	8	27	40	.403	367	442	17	25	102	49
Congress Street Grounds	Bos	1891	AA	51	17	.750	518	299	37	22	42	25	.627	507	379	15	20	91	166
Washington Park I	Bro	1884-1888	AA	191	131	.593	2067	1674	63	53	126	179	.413	1535	1943	33	53	102	128
Washington Park II	Bro	1889	AA	50	18	.735	488	297	28	19	43	26	.623	510	417	19	14	86	145
Ridgewood Park	Brk	1890	AA	15	22	.405	220	252	4	3	11	50	.180	272	481	9	18	103	43
Pendleton Park	Cin	1891	AA	24	20	.545	290	282	21	9	19	37	.339	250	354	7	11	121	212
Bank Street Grounds	Cin	1882-1883	AA	68	24	.739	648	293	29	18	48	38	.558	498	388	10	6	99	275
League Park I (Cin)	Cin	1884-1889	AA	262	144	.645	2796	1947	165	93	171	190	.474	2012	2148	63	65	101	179
National League Park II	Cle	1887-1888	AA	56	65	.463	749	807	10	19	33	109	.232	632	1132	16	53	104	49
Recreation Park I (Col)	Col	1883-1884	AA	56	45	.554	480	490	28	22	45	59	.433	579	628	27	16	83	120
Recreation Park II (Col)	CoC	1889-1891	AA	117	84	.582	1169	859	26	27	83	125	.399	1148	1454	46	55	81	54
Seventh Street Park I	Ind	1884	AA	16	39	.291	244	377	13	15	13	39	.250	219	378	7	15	98	120
Association Park	KC	1888-1889	AA	58	69	.457	853	910	23	27	40	102	.282	578	1014	14	56	124	80
Association Park	KC	1888-1889	AA	58	69	.457	853	910	23	27	40	102	.282	578	1014	14	56	124	80
Exposition Park (KC)	KC	1889	AA	35	35	.500	523	518	8	17	20	47	.299	329	512	10	34	118	54
Eclipse Park I	Lou	1882-1891	AA	357	240	.598	3709	2955	83	66	217	397	.353	3057	4055	91	138	96	67
Borchert Field	Mil	1891	AA	16	5	.762	172	82	11	5	5	10	.333	56	74	2	1	140	381
Polo Grounds II	NY	1883	AA	30	17	.638	273	189	3	4	24	25	.490	225	216	3	8	109	66
Metropolitan Park & Polo Grounds I (shared)	NY	1884	AA	42	9	.824	370	179	11	4	33	23	.589	364	244	11	11	99	75
Polo Grounds I	NY	1885	AA	28	24	.538	262	212	10	5	16	40	.286	265	476	11	31	69	38
St. George Cricket Grounds	NY	1886-1887	AA	55	67	.451	658	750	20	19	42	104	.288	715	1108	19	43	92	75
Forepaugh Park	Phi	1891	AA	43	26	.623	465	366	29	9	30	40	.429	354	427	26	26	108	74
Oakdale Park	Phi	1882	AA	21	18	.538	236	220	3	11	20	16	.556	166	166	2	2	127	323
Jefferson Street Grounds	Phi	1883-1890	AA	322	189	.630	3689	2780	122	70	197	275	.417	2559	3164	102	109	104	84
Exposition Park I (Pit)	Pit	1882	AA	17	18	.486	185	172	12	3	22	21	.512	237	241	6	1	92	263
Exposition Park I & II (Pit) (shared)	Pit	1883	AA	18	31	.367	292	321	10	3	13	36	.265	231	405	3	18	96	62
Recreation Park (Pit)	Pit	1884-1886	AA	101	86	.540	990	864	6	10	65	104	.385	774	1043	17	39	92	26
Virginia Base-Ball Park	Ric	1884	AA	5	15	.250	96	142	3	8	7	15	.318	98	153	4	6	104	121
Culver Field I	Roc	1890	AA	40	22	.645	348	252	13	4	23	41	.359	361	458	18	15	76	53
Sportsman's Park I	STL	1882-1891	AA	458	178	.720	4739	2929	214	145	322	254	.559	3182	2972	91	75	113	196
Star Park II	Syr	1890	AA	30	30	.500	321	320	2	4	25	42	.373	373	501	12	24	82	19
League Park (Tol)	Tol	1884	AA	28	25	.528	270	267	3	2	18	33	.353	193	305	5	10	104	32
Speranza Park	Tol	1890	AA	40	27	.597	422	316	17	11	28	37	.431	316	374	7	12	104	143
Athletic Park (Was)	WaD	1884	AA	10	20	.333	137	181	3	4	2	31	.061	111	300	3	17	85	39
Boundary Field	Was	1891	AA	28	40	.412	389	519	13	18	16	51	.239	300	547	6	26	106	95
Columbia Park	Alt	1884	UA	6	12	.333	73	156	0	2	0	7	.000	17	60	2	1	116	26
Belair Lot	Bal	1884	UA	29	21	.580	372	312	12	16	29	26	.527	304	318	5	8	121	237
Dartmouth Grounds	Bos	1884	UA	34	23	.596	346	260	7	5	24	28	.462	290	297	12	12	94	46
South Side Park I	Chi	1884	UA	20	14	.588	177	159	2	2	14	25	.359	183	252	8	9	89	27
Bank Street Grounds	Cin	1884	UA	35	17	.673	382	239	18	12	34	19	.642	325	241	8	5	112	235
Athletic Park (KC)	KC	1884	UA	11	23	.324	150	205	3	6	5	40	.111	159	414	3	8	82	108
Wright Street Grounds	Mil	1884	UA	8	4	.667	53	34	0	1	0	0	—	0	0	0	0	—	—
Keystone Park	Phi	1884	UA	13	21	.382	223	249	4	1	8	25	.242	192	296	3	6	94	54
Exposition Park I (Pit)	Pit	1884	UA	1	4	.200	22	29	0	1	6	7	.462	56	42	0	0	135	—
Union Grounds (StL)	StL	1884	UA	50	6	.893	461	179	10	4	44	13	.772	426	250	22	5	96	53
unknown	STP	1884	UA	0	0	—	0	0	0	0	2	6	.250	24	57	0	1	—	—
Capitol Grounds	Was	1884	UA	36	27	.571	382	318	4	10	11	38	.224	192	362	0	6	98	181
Union Street Park	Wil	1884	UA	1	6	.143	16	46	1	4	1	10	.091	19	68	1	0	112	786
Congress Street Grounds	Bos	1890	PL	48	21	.696	602	383	42	38	33	27	.550	386	384	12	11	111	302
Eastern Park	Bro	1890	PL	46	19	.708	564	410	20	7	30	37	.448	398	480	14	19	114	84
Olympic Park II	Buf	1890	PL	23	42	.354	425	498	7	20	13	54	.194	367	698	13	47	89	46
South Side Park II	Chi	1890	PL	46	23	.667	504	345	18	12	29	39	.426	381	425	13	15	104	106
Brotherhood Park	Cle	1890	PL	31	30	.508	416	403	10	15	24	45	.348	433	623	17	30	88	60
Polo Grounds IV	NY	1890	PL	47	19	.712	628	404	35	21	27	38	.415	389	477	31	16	117	117
Forepaugh Park	Phi	1890	PL	35	30	.538	482	418	20	15	33	33	.500	465	434	29	18	102	76
Exposition Park III (Pit)	Pit	1890	PL	37	28	.569	435	356	21	15	23	40	.365	398	535	14	17	82	113
Oriole Park V	Bal	1914-1915	FL	77	77	.500	649	717	54	51	54	100	.351	546	671	14	35	112	214
Washington Park III	Bro	1914-1915	FL	81	72	.529	673	659	46	24	66	87	.431	636	691	32	34	100	106
Federal League Park (Buf)	Buf	1914-1915	FL	84	69	.549	635	624	41	39	70	80	.467	559	612	36	41	105	102
Weeghman Park/Wrigley Field (Chi)	Chi	1914-1915	FL	85	66	.563	558	460	52	29	88	67	.568	703	595	50	47	81	86
Federal League Park (Ind)	Ind	1914	FL	53	23	.697	439	339	14	8	35	42	.455	323	283	19	21	130	56
Gordon And Koppel Field	KC	1914-1915	FL	84	68	.553	596	555	43	40	64	88	.421	595	679	24	26	90	166
Harrison Park	New	1915	FL	40	39	.506	267	271	4	2	40	33	.548	318	291	13	13	82	21
Exposition Park III (Pit)	Pit	1914-1915	FL	82	68	.547	589	576	15	20	68	85	.444	608	646	39	55	95	38
Federal League Park (StL)	STL	1914-1915	FL	74	78	.487	638	648	24	38	75	78	.490	561	576	25	22	114	133

Multiteam Ballparks

Ballpark	Years	Lg	Home							Road							Park Index	
			W	L	Pct	R	OR	HR	OHR	W	L	Pct	R	OR	HR	OHR	R	HR
Anaheim Stadium/Edison International Field	1966-1997	AL	1304	1235	.514	10399	10550	2003	2236	1145	1372	.455	10669	11308	1978	2102	94	103
Association Park	1886-1889	NL,AA	77	111	.410	1154	1366	32	31	51	151	.252	771	1434	24	79	123	66
Bank Street Grounds	1880-1884	NL,UA,AA	117	66	.639	1193	748	52	38	89	91	.494	954	885	20	13	104	268
Boundary Field	1891-1899	NL,AA	292	310	.485	3802	3866	235	157	162	478	.253	3105	4906	122	210	102	126
Columbia Park	1884-1908	AL,UA	389	201	.659	2831	2276	128	66	256	328	.438	2245	2466	109	76	107	104
Congress Street Grounds	1890-1891	PL,AA	99	38	.723	1120	682	79	60	75	52	.591	893	763	27	31	101	222
County Stadium	1953-1997	AL,NL	1748	1466	.544	14151	13401	2714	2593	1534	1693	.475	14798	14469	3180	3008	95	86
Dodger Stadium	1962-1997	AL,NL	1814	1361	.571	12185	10795	2069	1916	1578	1600	.497	13507	12803	2585	2304	87	82
Eastern Park	1890-1897	NL,PL	339	201	.628	3590	2977	137	124	218	318	.407	3229	3762	128	164	93	89
Eclipse Park I	1882-1892	NL,AA	394	271	.592	4018	3241	90	69	243	455	.348	3397	4573	102	161	96	63
Exposition Park I (Pit)	1882-1884	UA,AA	18	22	.450	207	201	12	4	28	28	.500	293	283	6	1	99	320
Exposition Park III (Pit)	1890-1915	NL,FL,PL	932	598	.609	8082	6646	263	138	732	729	.501	7382	7377	297	317	95	62
Forepaugh Park	1890-1891	PL,AA	78	56	.582	947	784	49	24	63	73	.463	819	861	55	44	105	75
Griffith Stadium	1911-1961	AL	2032	1874	.520	17049	17355	894	1218	1706	2172	.440	17423	18894	1818	2296	94	51
Jefferson Street Grounds	1876-1890	NL,AA	332	213	.609	3948	3089	126	70	201	296	.404	2678	3389	105	111	106	83
League Park I (Cin)	1884-1893	NL,AA	420	267	.611	4426	3325	251	177	293	334	.467	3306	3738	117	139	100	153
League Park I (Cle)	1891-1909	AL,NL	745	479	.609	6668	5333	121	125	585	757	.436	6180	7030	271	323	100	45
Municipal Stadium (KC)	1955-1972	AL	611	734	.454	5478	6264	904	1261	513	834	.381	5006	6224	929	1263	105	99
National League Park II	1887-1890	NL,AA	119	137	.465	1459	1503	31	40	75	197	.276	1202	1987	41	101	99	53
Oriole Park III	1891-1899	NL,AA	422	192	.687	4587	3129	85	62	293	319	.479	3759	3696	131	183	103	47
Polo Grounds I	1883-1888	NL,AA	262	137	.657	2373	1630	97	51	202	200	.502	2238	2381	111	120	87	65
Polo Grounds IV	1890-1910	NL,PL	923	583	.613	8290	6733	410	299	713	774	.479	7420	7637	258	271	99	132
Polo Grounds V	1912-1963	AL,NL	2530	1881	.574	20476	17980	3611	3016	2175	2223	.495	20115	19024	2014	1843	98	171
Recreation Park (Pit)	1884-1890	NL,AA	223	203	.523	2219	2002	21	22	148	308	.325	2023	3273	98	183	85	16
Shea Stadium	1964-1997	AL,NL	1457	1385	.513	10994	10964	1965	2103	1279	1572	.449	11505	11934	2071	2114	94	98
Shibe Park/Connie Mack Stadium	1909-1970	AL,NL	2948	3009	.495	25806	27664	3339	3591	2527	3490	.420	25268	28607	3142	3468	100	106
South Side Park II	1890-1893	NL,PL	121	88	.579	1334	1094	47	36	80	121	.398	1015	1285	42	52	102	85
Sportsman's Park I	1882-1892	NL,AA	495	214	.698	5118	3309	246	177	341	312	.522	3506	3514	104	90	111	201
Sportsman's Park III/Busch Stadium I	1909-1966	AL,NL	3753	3225	.538	33901	33195	4027	4320	3122	3856	.447	30239	32347	3443	3731	107	116
Union Grounds (Bro)	1876-1877	NL	32	28	.533	310	299	4	8	20	34	.370	291	424	2	2	77	270
Union Grounds (StL)	1884-1886	NL,UA	100	73	.578	964	754	29	18	73	97	.429	861	981	41	40	92	57
Washington Park II	1889-1890	NL,AA	108	34	.761	1035	600	55	28	71	53	.573	847	735	35	32	90	108
Washington Park III	1898-1915	NL,FL	635	628	.503	5133	5306	217	179	502	749	.401	4950	5783	213	240	96	87
Weeghman Park/Wrigley Field (Chi)	1914-1997	NL,FL	3498	3044	.535	29621	28908	4888	4746	2916	3568	.450	26877	28222	4148	4083	105	116

Ballpark Leaders— Lifetime

Highest Run Index
(minimum 10 seasons)

1 Hilltop Park	New York (AL)	1903-1912	114
2 Baker Bowl	Philadelphia (NL)	1895-1937	114
3 Fenway Park II	Boston (AL)	1934-1997	113
4 Atlanta-Fulton County Stadium	Atlanta (NL)	1966-1996	112
5 Sportsman's Park I	St. Louis (AA/NL)	1882-1892	111
6 South End Grounds III	Boston (NL)	1895-1914	110
7 Palace of the Fans	Cincinnati (NL)	1902-1911	108
8 Metropolitan Stadium	Minnesota (AL)	1961-1981	108
9 Hubert H. Humphrey Metrodome	Minnesota (AL)	1982-1997	108
10 Bennett Park	Detroit (AL)	1901-1911	107
11 Sportsman's Park III/Busch Stadium I	St. Louis (AL/NL)	1909-1966	107
12 Exhibition Stadium	Toronto (AL)	1977-1988	107
13 League Park II	Cleveland (AL)	1910-1931	106
14 Weeghman Park/Wrigley Field	Chicago (FL/NL)	1914-1997	105
15 Municipal Stadium	Kansas City (AL)	1955-1972	105
16 Briggs Stadium/Tiger Stadium	Detroit (AL)	1938-1997	104
17 Veterans Stadium	Philadelphia (NL)	1971-1997	104
18 Kingdome	Seattle (AL)	1977-1997	104
19 Royals Stadium/Kauffman Stadium	Kansas City (AL)	1973-1997	103
20 Riverfront Stadium/Cinergy Field	Cincinnati (NL)	1970-1997	102

Lowest Run Index
(minimum 10 seasons)

1 Dodger Stadium	Los Angeles (NL/AL)	1962-1997	87
2 Astrodome	Houston (NL)	1965-1997	89
3 Oakland-Alameda Coliseum	Oakland (AL)	1968-1997	89
4 Braves Field	Boston (NL)	1916-1952	89
5 Yankee Stadium I	New York (AL)	1923-1973	90
6 San Diego Stadium/Jack Murphy Stadium/Qualcomm Stadium	San Diego (NL)	1969-1997	92
7 Memorial Stadium	Baltimore (AL)	1954-1991	92
8 League Park II & Municipal Stadium/ Cleveland Stadium (shared)	Cleveland (AL)	1932-1946	94
9 Shea Stadium	New York (NL/AL)	1964-1997	94
10 Griffith Stadium	Washington (AL)	1911-1961	94
11 Anaheim Stadium/ Edison International Field	Anaheim (AL)	1966-1997	94
12 County Stadium	Milwaukee (NL/AL)	1953-1997	95
13 South End Grounds I	Boston (NL)	1876-1887	95
14 Yankee Stadium II	New York (AL)	1976-1997	95
15 Exposition Park III	Pittsburgh (PL/NL/FL)	1890-1915	95
16 Candlestick Park/3Com Park	San Francisco (NL)	1960-1997	95
17 Eclipse Park I	Louisville (AA/NL)	1882-1892	96
18 Fenway Park I	Boston (AL)	1912-1933	96
19 Washington Park III	Brooklyn (NL/FL)	1898-1915	96
20 RFK Stadium	Washington (AL)	1962-1971	97

Highest Home Run Index
(minimum 10 seasons)

1 Sportsman's Park I	St. Louis (AA/NL)	1882-1892	201
2 South End Grounds III	Boston (NL)	1895-1914	188
3 Polo Grounds V	New York (NL/AL)	1912-1963	171
4 Huntington Avenue Grounds	Boston (AL)	1901-1911	162
5 Baker Bowl	Philadelphia (NL)	1895-1937	158
6 League Park I	Cincinnati (AA/NL)	1884-1893	153
7 Hilltop Park	New York (AL)	1903-1912	151
8 Atlanta-Fulton County Stadium	Atlanta (NL)	1966-1996	135
9 Polo Grounds IV	New York (PL/NL)	1890-1910	132
10 Briggs Stadium/Tiger Stadium	Detroit (AL)	1938-1997	126
11 Kingdome	Seattle (AL)	1977-1997	123
12 Sportsman's Park III/Busch Stadium I	St. Louis (AL/NL)	1909-1966	116
13 Weeghman Park/Wrigley Field	Chicago (FL/NL)	1914-1997	116
14 Ebbets Field	Brooklyn (NL)	1913-1957	110
15 Metropolitan Stadium	Minnesota (AL)	1961-1981	110
16 Fenway Park II	Boston (AL)	1934-1997	110
17 Municipal Stadium/Cleveland Stadium	Cleveland (AL)	1947-1993	110
18 Robison Field	St. Louis (NL)	1893-1919	110
19 Riverfront Stadium/Cinergy Field	Cincinnati (NL)	1970-1997	107
20 Veterans Stadium	Philadelphia (NL)	1971-1997	107

Lowest Home Run Index
(minimum 10 seasons)

1 League Park I	Cleveland (NL/AL)	1891-1909	45
2 Griffith Stadium	Washington (AL)	1911-1961	51
3 Fenway Park I	Boston (AL)	1912-1933	52
4 Palace of the Fans	Cincinnati (NL)	1902-1911	59
5 Exposition Park III	Pittsburgh (PL/NL/FL)	1890-1915	62
6 Eclipse Park I	Louisville (AA/NL)	1882-1892	63
7 Astrodome	Houston (NL)	1965-1997	64
8 Braves Field	Boston (NL)	1916-1952	67
9 Forbes Field	Pittsburgh (NL)	1910-1969	69
10 League Park II	Cleveland (AL)	1910-1931	69
11 South End Grounds I	Boston (NL)	1876-1887	70
12 League Park II & Municipal Stadium/ Cleveland Stadium (shared)	Cleveland (AL)	1932-1946	73
13 Royals Stadium/Kauffman Stadium	Kansas City (AL)	1973-1997	77
14 Busch Stadium II	St. Louis (NL)	1967-1997	81
15 Dodger Stadium	Los Angeles (NL/AL)	1962-1997	82
16 White Sox Park/Comiskey Park I	Chicago (AL)	1910-1990	86
17 Stade Olympique	Montreal (NL)	1977-1997	86
18 County Stadium	Milwaukee (NL/AL)	1953-1997	86
19 Redland Field/Crosley Field	Cincinnati (NL)	1912-1969	86
20 Washington Park III	Brooklyn (NL/FL)	1898-1915	87

Ballpark Leaders— Single Season

Highest Run Index
(minimum 20 home and 20 road games)

1 Coors Field	Colorado (NL)	1996	172
2 Louisville Baseball Park	Louisville (NL)	1877	165
3 Coors Field	Colorado (NL)	1995	164
4 Fenway Park II	Boston (AL)	1955	156
5 Baker Bowl	Philadelphia (NL)	1933	153
6 Mile High Stadium	Colorado (NL)	1993	152
7 South End Grounds III	Boston (NL)	1900	148
8 23rd Street Grounds	Chicago (NL)	1876	145
9 Baker Bowl	Philadephia (NL)	1925	144
10 Baker Bowl	Philadelphia (NL)	1923	144
11 Weeghman Park/Wrigley Field	Chicago (NL)	1970	143
12 Baker Bowl	Philadelphia (NL)	1922	141
13 Weeghman Park/Wrigley Field	Chicago (NL)	1985	140
14 Sportsman's Park I	St. Louis (AA)	1890	139
15 Weeghman Park/Wrigley Field	Chicago (NL)	1916	138
16 Sportsman's Park III/Busch Stadium I	St. Louis (AL)	1933	138
17 Hilltop Park	New York (AL)	1906	138
18 Palace of the Fans	Cincinnati (NL)	1906	137
19 Baker Bowl	Philadelphia (NL)	1935	137
20 Fenway Park II	Boston (AL)	1977	137

Lowest Run Index
(minimum 20 home and 20 road games)

1 Grand Avenue Park	St. Louis (NL)	1876	58
2 South Street Park	Indianapolis (NL)	1878	68
3 Braves Field	Boston (NL)	1934	68
4 Polo Grounds I	New York (AA)	1885	69
5 Braves Field	Boston (NL)	1938	69
6 County Stadium	Milwaukee (NL)	1958	69
7 Astrodome	Houston (NL)	1981	69
8 Braves Field	Boston (NL)	1926	70
9 Oakland-Alameda Coliseum	Oakland (AL)	1973	70
10 Yankee Stadium I	New York (AL)	1939	70
11 Weeghman Park/Wrigley Field	Chicago (FL)	1914	70
12 Eclipse Park I	Louisville (AA)	1884	71
13 Astrodome	Houston (NL)	1976	71
14 Dodger Stadium	Los Angeles (AL)	1964	71
15 Braves Field	Boston (NL)	1950	72
16 Braves Field	Boston (NL)	1937	72
17 League Park II & Municipal Stadium/ Cleveland Stadium (shared)	Cleveland (AL)	1946	73
18 Polo Grounds I	New York (NL)	1886	73
19 Dodger Stadium	Los Angeles (NL)	1967	73
20 Polo Grounds I	New York (NL)	1888	74

Highest Home Run Index
(minimum 20 home and 20 road games)

1 Louisville Baseball Park	Louisville (NL)	1876	Infinite
2 Lake Front Park II	Chicago (NL)	1884	704
3 Union Grounds (Bro)	New York (NL)	1876	627
4 Haymakers Grounds	Troy (NL)	1880	563
5 Sportsman's Park I	St. Louis (AA)	1890	537
6 Hilltop Park	New York (AL)	1904	529
7 Avenue Grounds	Cincinnati (NL)	1878	491
8 Polo Grounds I	New York (NL)	1883	456
9 Polo Grounds IV	New York (NL)	1905	451
10 Bank Street Grounds	Cincinnati (AA)	1883	448
11 West Side Park	Chicago (NL)	1887	440
12 Polo Grounds V	New York (AL)	1915	438
13 Haymakers Grounds	Troy (NL)	1881	433
14 West Side Park	Chicago (NL)	1885	420
15 Polo Grounds V	New York (AL)	1917	416
16 Baker Bowl	Philadephia (NL)	1920	416
17 League Park I	Cincinnati (AA)	1884	402
18 Polo Grounds IV	New York (NL)	1907	395
19 South End Grounds III	Boston (NL)	1902	394
20 South End Grounds III	Boston (NL)	1895	382

Lowest Home Run Index
(minimum 20 home and 20 road games)

1 Hartford Ball Club Grounds	Hartford (NL)	1876	0
Eclipse Park I	Louisville (AA)	1882	0
3 Recreation Park	Pittsburgh (NL)	1888	3
4 Recreation Park	Philadelphia (NL)	1884	4
5 Recreation Park	Philadelphia (NL)	1883	5
6 South Side Park III	Chicago (AL)	1904	8
7 Lake Front Park I	Chicago (NL)	1880	9
8 Fenway Park I	Boston (AL)	1916	9
9 Recreation Park	Pittsburgh (NL)	1889	10
10 Redland Field/Crosley Field	Cincinnati (NL)	1924	10
11 Riverside Grounds	Buffalo (NL)	1881	11
12 South End Grounds I	Boston (NL)	1877	11
13 Griffith Stadium	Washington (AL)	1945	11
14 League Park I	Cleveland (AL)	1909	12
15 League Park I	Cincinnati (NL)	1898	13
16 Redland Field/Crosley Field	Cincinnati (NL)	1921	14
17 Redland Field/Crosley Field	Cincinnati (NL)	1931	14
18 Fenway Park I	Boston (AL)	1913	15
19 Redland Field/Crosley Field	Cincinnati (NL)	1923	15
20 Oriole Park I	Baltimore (AA)	1886	16

Situational Statistics

Data

STATS has been compiling pitch-by-pitch data since 1987. The data from 1984-1986 was compiled by Project Scoresheet. The Project Scoresheet splits do not add up to a player's overall totals in all cases, but the differences are minor. We believe that it was more illuminating to add three years to our situational statistic database rather than ignore it because, for instance, Darryl Strawberry's splits total one more strikeout than his actual total. Where the discrepancies do occur, the splits and the totals almost always are within one unit of each other.

Hitting

For every batter with 1,000 career plate appearances since 1984, we show his overall plate appearances, batting average, on-base percentage and slugging percentage and also show how he performed: in home/road games, against lefthanded/righthanded pitchers, with runners in scoring position, in late & close situations (seventh inning or later, and the batting team is ahead by one run, tied or has the potential tying run on base, at the plate or on deck), and against groundball/flyball pitchers. A groundball pitcher is defined as one who has a groundball/flyball ratio greater than 1.50, while a flyball pitcher has a groundball/flyball ratio less than 1.00.

Pitching

For every pitcher with 250 career innings pitched since 1984, we show his overall innings pitched, won-lost record and ERA, and also break it down for home and road games. We also list his opponents' plate appearances, batting average, on-base percentage and slugging percentage: by lefthanded/righthanded hitters, with runners in scoring position, in late & close situations (see definition above), with the bases empty and with runners on base.

Abbreviations & Formulas

A complete list of team and statistical abbreviations are listed in the back of the book, along with an appendix explaining formulas and the availability of certain statistics.

Situational Batting Splits—1984-1997

Batter	PA	Avg	OBP	Slg		PA	Avg	OBP	Slg		PA	Avg	OBP	Slg		PA	Avg	OBP	Slg		PA	Avg	OBP	Slg
		Total					**Home/Road**					**vs. Left/Right**					**Scoring Position/Late & Close**					**vs. Groundball/Flyball Pitcher**		
Kurt Abbott (1993-1997)					H	709	.276	.332	.477	L	439	.279	.319	.449	SP	360	.261	.336	.448	GB	367	.258	.328	.426
Bats Right	1528	.256	.307	.427	R	819	.239	.285	.385	R	1089	.246	.302	.418	LC	278	.251	.315	.395	FB	239	.240	.297	.415
Luis Aguayo (1984-1989)					H	500	.246	.321	.419	L	445	.231	.304	.386	SP	244	.222	.305	.315	GB	373	.227	.291	.373
Bats Right	1032	.233	.304	.392	R	528	.222	.287	.367	R	583	.235	.303	.397	LC	153	.271	.358	.368	FB	398	.236	.320	.394
Mike Aldrete (1986-1996)					H	1212	.247	.355	.358	L	319	.236	.315	.330	SP	678	.287	.408	.405	GB	853	.260	.348	.357
Bats Left	2498	.263	.356	.377	R	1282	.278	.357	.395	R	2175	.267	.362	.384	LC	435	.227	.331	.311	FB	620	.295	.381	.443
Edgardo Alfonzo (1995-1997)					H	671	.293	.347	.389	L	367	.317	.372	.457	SP	342	.332	.368	.498	GB	324	.302	.359	.402
Bats Right	1362	.288	.342	.392	R	691	.284	.336	.396	R	995	.278	.330	.369	LC	275	.298	.373	.377	FB	168	.237	.298	.283
Luis Alicea (1988-1997)					H	1370	.250	.342	.373	L	666	.265	.338	.349	SP	743	.252	.372	.386	GB	835	.252	.322	.353
Bats Both	2800	.255	.347	.367	R	1430	.260	.352	.363	R	2134	.252	.350	.373	LC	578	.251	.353	.378	FB	465	.254	.369	.385
Andy Allanson (1986-1995)					H	794	.232	.280	.300	L	545	.245	.286	.301	SP	430	.232	.289	.314	GB	447	.263	.310	.337
Bats Right	1634	.240	.283	.310	R	828	.248	.287	.320	R	1077	.238	.282	.315	LC	212	.294	.338	.397	FB	545	.232	.272	.317
Roberto Alomar (1988-1997)					H	3063	.316	.385	.461	L	1867	.263	.334	.398	SP	1526	.303	.376	.438	GB	1770	.289	.351	.403
Bats Both	6232	.304	.372	.440	R	3169	.292	.360	.420	R	4365	.321	.389	.458	LC	963	.304	.383	.420	FB	1275	.311	.379	.446
Sandy Alomar Jr. (1988-1997)					H	1321	.281	.326	.417	L	690	.284	.325	.410	SP	780	.277	.332	.416	GB	679	.268	.317	.358
Bats Right	2724	.280	.320	.426	R	1403	.279	.315	.435	R	2034	.278	.319	.432	LC	501	.304	.342	.451	FB	545	.264	.304	.437
Moises Alou (1990-1997)					H	1421	.298	.364	.515	L	797	.314	.375	.520	SP	974	.317	.397	.519	GB	820	.268	.326	.417
Bats Right	3007	.292	.354	.489	R	1586	.287	.344	.467	R	2210	.284	.346	.478	LC	497	.271	.348	.419	FB	523	.257	.312	.477
Rich Amaral (1991-1997)					H	767	.271	.349	.344	L	784	.298	.359	.400	SP	399	.272	.341	.356	GB	324	.290	.370	.362
Bats Right	1650	.278	.345	.356	R	883	.284	.342	.365	R	866	.259	.333	.314	LC	260	.267	.332	.333	FB	299	.192	.264	.263
Brady Anderson (1988-1997)					H	2582	.245	.346	.404	L	1546	.231	.343	.368	SP	1222	.260	.387	.403	GB	1268	.300	.398	.468
Bats Left	5251	.261	.361	.435	R	2669	.276	.376	.465	R	3705	.273	.369	.462	LC	760	.258	.360	.391	FB	1065	.210	.318	.344
Dave Anderson (1984-1992)					H	1044	.251	.321	.313	L	823	.245	.323	.325	SP	510	.208	.289	.251	GB	840	.250	.321	.327
Bats Right	2156	.246	.316	.321	R	1099	.243	.310	.329	R	1320	.247	.311	.319	LC	394	.266	.339	.354	FB	819	.237	.314	.315
Garret Anderson (1994-1997)					H	872	.314	.346	.449	L	537	.283	.293	.387	SP	501	.280	.327	.400	GB	336	.296	.338	.427
Bats Left	1717	.301	.331	.430	R	845	.288	.316	.410	R	1180	.309	.348	.449	LC	271	.315	.343	.446	FB	305	.307	.328	.448
Eric Anthony (1989-1997)					H	1029	.245	.316	.405	L	583	.220	.286	.345	SP	602	.226	.324	.353	GB	706	.226	.296	.374
Bats Left	2244	.231	.305	.397	R	1215	.219	.296	.390	R	1661	.235	.312	.415	LC	401	.229	.313	.386	FB	462	.233	.316	.462
Alex Arias (1992-1997)					H	497	.295	.363	.367	L	318	.264	.341	.325	SP	323	.260	.340	.330	GB	296	.247	.341	.318
Bats Right	1125	.268	.339	.343	R	628	.246	.321	.324	R	807	.269	.339	.350	LC	246	.231	.321	.293	FB	201	.228	.279	.288
Tony Armas (1984-1989)					H	1114	.266	.307	.473	L	787	.278	.318	.475	SP	597	.274	.323	.451	GB	881	.256	.299	.467
Bats Right	2230	.263	.297	.475	R	1116	.261	.287	.477	R	1443	.255	.286	.475	LC	336	.211	.244	.385	FB	999	.268	.296	.493
Alan Ashby (1984-1989)					H	772	.267	.341	.368	L	500	.245	.303	.322	SP	433	.266	.361	.389	GB	632	.252	.329	.384
Bats Both	1575	.262	.341	.393	R	791	.258	.341	.418	R	1063	.271	.359	.428	LC	237	.233	.328	.386	FB	636	.282	.361	.427
Brad Ausmus (1993-1997)					H	895	.265	.331	.378	L	436	.238	.304	.358	SP	470	.223	.309	.327	GB	478	.231	.287	.346
Bats Right	1807	.257	.320	.362	R	912	.249	.308	.345	R	1371	.263	.324	.363	LC	337	.222	.290	.338	FB	257	.223	.300	.300
Wally Backman (1984-1993)					H	1550	.288	.361	.348	L	462	.171	.264	.210	SP	699	.271	.353	.329	GB	1216	.275	.344	.338
Bats Both	3199	.276	.345	.337	R	1616	.264	.330	.326	R	2704	.293	.359	.358	LC	469	.271	.351	.325	FB	1137	.278	.350	.336
Carlos Baerga (1990-1997)					H	2154	.315	.349	.446	L	1291	.293	.329	.415	SP	1323	.294	.349	.435	GB	1043	.277	.315	.390
Bats Both	4499	.296	.335	.438	R	2345	.278	.322	.431	R	3208	.297	.337	.447	LC	768	.285	.343	.388	FB	937	.287	.331	.419
Jeff Bagwell (1991-1997)					H	2173	.302	.414	.540	L	1248	.321	.439	.573	SP	1401	.298	.436	.493	GB	1240	.295	.390	.487
Bats Right	4410	.304	.409	.536	R	2237	.306	.404	.532	R	3162	.297	.397	.521	LC	736	.303	.447	.547	FB	755	.275	.397	.536
Mark Bailey (1984-1992)					H	556	.247	.362	.372	L	405	.235	.348	.339	SP	323	.211	.381	.291	GB	535	.219	.335	.332
Bats Both	1126	.220	.337	.337	R	568	.194	.312	.303	R	719	.212	.330	.336	LC	195	.230	.349	.352	FB	539	.228	.349	.357
Harold Baines (1984-1997)					H	3758	.295	.372	.478	L	1938	.276	.326	.418	SP	2191	.293	.385	.470	GB	2400	.312	.374	.473
Bats Left	7727	.296	.367	.472	R	3967	.296	.363	.467	R	5787	.303	.381	.491	LC	1078	.292	.382	.493	FB	2395	.287	.362	.460
Steve Balboni (1984-1993)					H	1580	.224	.286	.438	L	1208	.232	.315	.468	SP	882	.233	.297	.426	GB	1181	.249	.309	.482
Bats Right	3223	.230	.295	.457	R	1643	.236	.302	.474	R	2015	.229	.283	.450	LC	483	.249	.317	.469	FB	1336	.224	.295	.453
Chris Bando (1984-1989)					H	497	.244	.312	.342	L	338	.241	.281	.324	SP	289	.230	.323	.301	GB	446	.236	.305	.313
Bats Both	1066	.227	.298	.330	R	554	.213	.286	.320	R	713	.220	.307	.334	LC	148	.223	.297	.323	FB	498	.227	.302	.358
Bret Barberie (1991-1996)					H	807	.259	.357	.353	L	476	.254	.333	.341	SP	413	.254	.364	.332	GB	556	.291	.385	.360
Bats Both	1660	.271	.356	.363	R	853	.281	.355	.373	R	1184	.277	.365	.372	LC	340	.276	.348	.370	FB	339	.303	.390	.384
Jesse Barfield (1984-1992)					H	2202	.262	.344	.480	L	1579	.275	.375	.493	SP	1218	.242	.359	.432	GB	1558	.266	.346	.462
Bats Right	4428	.258	.342	.468	R	2225	.255	.340	.456	R	2848	.249	.324	.455	LC	638	.227	.330	.395	FB	1610	.270	.352	.519
Marty Barrett (1984-1991)					H	1832	.286	.349	.371	L	1108	.294	.359	.379	SP	950	.290	.361	.381	GB	1383	.293	.353	.359
Bats Right	3767	.280	.339	.350	R	1901	.274	.330	.329	R	2625	.274	.331	.337	LC	468	.280	.352	.359	FB	1472	.284	.343	.365
Kevin Bass (1984-1995)					H	2501	.276	.335	.413	L	1862	.281	.320	.475	SP	1366	.292	.369	.438	GB	1912	.268	.320	.393
Bats Both	5050	.273	.328	.417	R	2542	.271	.321	.422	R	3181	.269	.332	.382	LC	861	.284	.341	.415	FB	1650	.281	.328	.446
Don Baylor (1984-1988)					H	1212	.235	.339	.403	L	933	.253	.356	.421	SP	785	.261	.382	.442	GB	1097	.237	.341	.393
Bats Right	2589	.241	.342	.426	R	1375	.246	.344	.447	R	1654	.234	.334	.429	LC	345	.256	.328	.503	FB	1190	.246	.345	.476
Rich Becker (1993-1997)					H	822	.282	.360	.401	L	312	.171	.254	.207	SP	454	.259	.355	.401	GB	425	.277	.344	.377
Bats Both	1678	.267	.349	.379	R	856	.253	.338	.358	R	1366	.289	.370	.418	LC	250	.239	.318	.344	FB	256	.274	.379	.361
Buddy Bell (1984-1989)					H	1447	.278	.356	.424	L	863	.271	.351	.423	SP	830	.272	.366	.426	GB	1269	.265	.345	.388
Bats Right	2959	.269	.345	.404	R	1505	.260	.334	.385	R	2089	.268	.342	.396	LC	400	.259	.328	.375	FB	1294	.272	.343	.427
Derek Bell (1991-1997)					H	1498	.273	.339	.421	L	776	.294	.343	.447	SP	983	.260	.338	.387	GB	779	.239	.292	.362
Bats Right	3000	.282	.335	.425	R	1502	.291	.332	.428	R	2224	.278	.332	.417	LC	525	.261	.323	.374	FB	507	.290	.358	.493

Situational Statistics: Hitting

	Total				Home/Road					vs. Left/Right					Scoring Position/Late & Close					vs. Groundball/Flyball Pitcher				
Batter	PA	Avg	OBP	Slg		PA	Avg	OBP	Slg		PA	Avg	OBP	Slg		PA	Avg	OBP	Slg		PA	Avg	OBP	Slg
George Bell (1984-1993)					H	3090	.282	.324	.470	L	1899	.286	.330	.511	SP	1882	.287	.326	.479	GB	2078	.280	.313	.463
Bats Right	6306	.279	.318	.473	R	3210	.277	.312	.477	R	4401	.276	.313	.457	LC	901	.274	.317	.459	FB	2237	.290	.334	.520
Jay Bell (1986-1997)					H	2898	.268	.345	.404	L	1841	.300	.380	.451	SP	1407	.282	.360	.419	GB	1847	.271	.336	.390
Bats Right	5836	.268	.339	.403	R	2938	.268	.333	.402	R	3995	.254	.320	.381	LC	945	.267	.345	.371	FB	1122	.245	.317	.398
Albert Belle (1989-1997)					H	2248	.299	.370	.572	L	1204	.302	.389	.583	SP	1380	.293	.387	.593	GB	1038	.289	.369	.521
Bats Right	4626	.292	.364	.566	R	2378	.285	.358	.560	R	3422	.288	.355	.560	LC	725	.274	.359	.517	FB	954	.293	.355	.623
Rafael Belliard (1984-1997)					H	1168	.207	.261	.244	L	706	.232	.276	.268	SP	622	.224	.286	.273	GB	893	.210	.262	.231
Bats Right	2501	.220	.271	.259	R	1322	.232	.279	.273	R	1784	.216	.268	.256	LC	279	.232	.292	.276	FB	638	.203	.256	.242
Bruce Benedict (1984-1989)					H	701	.230	.309	.279	L	402	.210	.291	.278	SP	307	.223	.339	.283	GB	602	.232	.315	.279
Bats Right	1322	.213	.293	.262	R	611	.194	.275	.244	R	910	.215	.294	.256	LC	173	.178	.241	.210	FB	524	.184	.269	.245
Juan Beniquez (1984-1988)					H	781	.323	.376	.446	L	698	.334	.384	.484	SP	394	.303	.353	.443	GB	666	.299	.355	.402
Bats Right	1583	.301	.356	.417	R	786	.280	.336	.387	R	869	.274	.334	.362	LC	237	.321	.371	.391	FB	794	.308	.359	.430
Todd Benzinger (1987-1995)					H	1533	.268	.314	.406	L	1069	.269	.303	.374	SP	944	.231	.297	.364	GB	1053	.287	.327	.442
Bats Both	3106	.257	.301	.386	R	1573	.246	.288	.366	R	2037	.250	.300	.392	LC	539	.239	.297	.363	FB	750	.257	.303	.400
Dave Bergman (1984-1992)					H	1110	.242	.336	.365	L	201	.201	.267	.257	SP	579	.246	.352	.332	GB	799	.251	.351	.348
Bats Left	2276	.259	.346	.368	R	1161	.274	.355	.370	R	2070	.265	.353	.379	LC	379	.233	.316	.342	FB	703	.243	.321	.363
Tony Bernazard (1984-1991)					H	1100	.282	.354	.406	L	640	.269	.359	.392	SP	599	.239	.347	.328	GB	1042	.273	.338	.398
Bats Both	2297	.263	.336	.389	R	1178	.246	.319	.373	R	1638	.261	.326	.387	LC	263	.227	.316	.323	FB	1061	.269	.347	.399
Geronimo Berroa (1989-1997)					H	1231	.281	.346	.451	L	809	.307	.381	.482	SP	689	.278	.354	.429	GB	577	.280	.350	.447
Bats Right	2500	.283	.352	.468	R	1269	.285	.359	.485	R	1691	.272	.339	.462	LC	400	.261	.345	.403	FB	473	.277	.340	.444
Sean Berry (1990-1997)					H	916	.266	.333	.417	L	534	.261	.333	.424	SP	636	.264	.340	.444	GB	522	.268	.317	.389
Bats Right	2015	.275	.336	.460	R	1099	.283	.338	.495	R	1481	.281	.337	.473	LC	332	.228	.279	.361	FB	312	.231	.309	.436
Damon Berryhill (1987-1997)					H	1114	.269	.317	.429	L	589	.261	.300	.367	SP	638	.258	.318	.377	GB	771	.248	.288	.364
Bats Both	2208	.240	.288	.368	R	1094	.211	.258	.307	R	1619	.233	.284	.368	LC	440	.235	.286	.355	FB	460	.234	.291	.353
Dante Bichette (1988-1997)					H	2231	.329	.364	.580	L	1274	.297	.335	.534	SP	1285	.299	.332	.513	GB	1212	.294	.319	.474
Bats Right	4451	.295	.329	.498	R	2220	.262	.295	.416	R	3177	.295	.327	.483	LC	679	.295	.328	.510	FB	845	.321	.351	.535
Craig Biggio (1988-1997)					H	2947	.287	.381	.419	L	1730	.288	.394	.426	SP	1435	.292	.399	.412	GB	1766	.302	.390	.431
Bats Right	5949	.288	.377	.426	R	3002	.289	.373	.432	R	4219	.288	.370	.426	LC	1025	.266	.365	.390	FB	1137	.259	.351	.397
Lance Blankenship (1988-1993)					H	636	.220	.357	.301	L	444	.205	.345	.264	SP	352	.211	.356	.244	GB	339	.244	.370	.320
Bats Right	1292	.222	.350	.299	R	656	.224	.344	.298	R	848	.231	.353	.317	LC	220	.214	.377	.280	FB	303	.253	.369	.341
Jeff Blauser (1987-1997)					H	2240	.268	.363	.414	L	1430	.282	.375	.458	SP	1106	.276	.386	.410	GB	1411	.285	.363	.420
Bats Right	4598	.268	.355	.415	R	2358	.267	.348	.416	R	3168	.261	.346	.396	LC	748	.260	.341	.430	FB	933	.240	.337	.400
Mike Blowers (1989-1997)					H	1026	.263	.352	.449	L	779	.310	.385	.523	SP	579	.288	.373	.478	GB	457	.258	.319	.390
Bats Right	2080	.262	.335	.423	R	1054	.260	.319	.400	R	1301	.233	.306	.364	LC	321	.244	.317	.428	FB	414	.253	.320	.435
Bruce Bochte (1984-1986)					H	721	.277	.365	.373	L	237	.256	.321	.335	SP	371	.290	.385	.375	GB	734	.273	.342	.361
Bats Left	1480	.272	.352	.373	R	755	.267	.339	.373	R	1239	.275	.358	.381	LC	230	.285	.378	.350	FB	742	.270	.361	.386
Wade Boggs (1984-1997)					H	4408	.358	.450	.496	L	2604	.300	.378	.394	SP	2204	.327	.459	.432	GB	2734	.336	.422	.455
Bats Left	8857	.328	.418	.444	R	4434	.300	.387	.394	R	6238	.340	.435	.466	LC	1177	.307	.411	.376	FB	2677	.327	.417	.445
Barry Bonds (1986-1997)					H	3597	.285	.409	.546	L	2556	.285	.390	.532	SP	1963	.295	.474	.540	GB	2412	.295	.394	.533
Bats Left	7403	.288	.408	.551	R	3804	.291	.407	.556	R	4845	.290	.418	.561	LC	1146	.276	.418	.503	FB	1627	.258	.385	.519
Bobby Bonilla (1986-1997)					H	3504	.280	.357	.465	L	2548	.283	.345	.475	SP	2131	.287	.390	.481	GB	2360	.275	.345	.441
Bats Both	7259	.285	.362	.486	R	3750	.290	.367	.505	R	4706	.286	.371	.492	LC	1158	.260	.372	.449	FB	1627	.273	.369	.480
Bob Boone (1984-1990)					H	1443	.245	.313	.301	L	968	.244	.313	.295	SP	824	.260	.322	.322	GB	1122	.256	.310	.324
Bats Right	2948	.245	.306	.313	R	1471	.245	.300	.325	R	1946	.245	.303	.321	LC	411	.281	.341	.357	FB	1176	.232	.301	.310
Bret Boone (1992-1997)					H	1227	.257	.316	.411	L	620	.237	.305	.398	SP	688	.250	.311	.386	GB	633	.248	.308	.342
Bats Right	2501	.253	.307	.398	R	1274	.250	.298	.386	R	1881	.259	.308	.398	LC	405	.239	.296	.346	FB	386	.254	.296	.482
Pat Borders (1988-1997)					H	1469	.258	.295	.395	L	1222	.264	.306	.398	SP	804	.230	.286	.331	GB	693	.250	.283	.357
Bats Right	3039	.257	.291	.386	R	1570	.255	.288	.378	R	1817	.252	.281	.378	LC	561	.263	.303	.386	FB	642	.252	.286	.397
Mike Bordick (1990-1997)					H	1713	.254	.319	.333	L	999	.248	.312	.316	SP	920	.259	.331	.329	GB	874	.271	.342	.339
Bats Right	3550	.254	.318	.327	R	1837	.255	.317	.322	R	2551	.257	.320	.331	LC	533	.242	.329	.293	FB	661	.223	.298	.310
Daryl Boston (1984-1994)					H	1434	.250	.315	.395	L	381	.236	.285	.336	SP	682	.240	.322	.418	GB	1045	.272	.323	.422
Bats Left	2901	.249	.312	.410	R	1463	.248	.308	.426	R	2516	.251	.316	.422	LC	457	.214	.304	.349	FB	812	.217	.283	.371
Phil Bradley (1984-1990)					H	2077	.295	.379	.452	L	1269	.281	.363	.459	SP	1036	.264	.378	.374	GB	1633	.286	.366	.430
Bats Right	4178	.287	.370	.424	R	2079	.278	.360	.395	R	2887	.289	.373	.408	LC	522	.278	.355	.400	FB	1443	.289	.380	.432
Scott Bradley (1984-1992)					H	863	.269	.319	.385	L	195	.188	.225	.244	SP	489	.261	.312	.371	GB	595	.236	.289	.301
Bats Left	1801	.257	.302	.343	R	936	.246	.286	.304	R	1604	.266	.311	.355	LC	262	.266	.322	.386	FB	491	.289	.326	.401
Darren Bragg (1994-1997)					H	645	.267	.350	.404	L	260	.227	.336	.305	SP	353	.239	.382	.403	GB	263	.259	.336	.390
Bats Left	1276	.254	.346	.385	R	631	.241	.342	.365	R	1016	.261	.349	.405	LC	204	.281	.390	.419	FB	210	.239	.333	.417
Glenn Braggs (1986-1992)					H	1301	.257	.326	.414	L	995	.277	.351	.445	SP	715	.262	.336	.379	GB	802	.279	.338	.432
Bats Right	2609	.257	.322	.405	R	1306	.257	.317	.395	R	1612	.246	.303	.380	LC	346	.267	.340	.378	FB	710	.250	.316	.402
Jeff Branson (1992-1997)					H	707	.259	.303	.418	L	257	.230	.291	.336	SP	406	.215	.318	.319	GB	498	.236	.283	.345
Bats Left	1576	.249	.305	.380	R	869	.241	.307	.349	R	1319	.253	.308	.389	LC	296	.231	.283	.337	FB	274	.227	.271	.344
Mickey Brantley (1986-1989)					H	592	.269	.309	.475	L	386	.220	.259	.382	SP	286	.287	.322	.457	GB	363	.252	.287	.386
Bats Right	1222	.259	.300	.407	R	629	.250	.291	.344	R	835	.278	.318	.419	LC	127	.280	.320	.466	FB	380	.259	.308	.446
Sid Bream (1984-1994)					H	1663	.267	.337	.432	L	790	.233	.276	.376	SP	1042	.269	.368	.403	GB	1327	.273	.345	.417
Bats Left	3518	.264	.336	.420	R	1850	.261	.335	.410	R	2723	.273	.353	.434	LC	537	.240	.333	.387	FB	1078	.250	.325	.437
Bob Brenly (1984-1989)					H	1186	.245	.329	.396	L	756	.231	.317	.400	SP	657	.237	.333	.434	GB	1026	.279	.370	.467
Bats Right	2425	.246	.328	.409	R	1219	.246	.328	.421	R	1649	.252	.334	.413	LC	429	.223	.300	.349	FB	1071	.227	.307	.380
George Brett (1984-1993)					H	2893	.297	.372	.468	L	1910	.270	.330	.422	SP	1675	.295	.416	.445	GB	1756	.314	.395	.480
Bats Left	5762	.293	.369	.471	R	2868	.289	.365	.475	R	3851	.305	.388	.497	LC	849	.268	.370	.426	FB	1973	.296	.377	.502

Situational Statistics: Hitting 2523

Batter	Total PA	Avg	OBP	Slg	Home/Road	PA	Avg	OBP	Slg	vs. Left/Right	PA	Avg	OBP	Slg	Scoring Position/Late & Close	PA	Avg	OBP	Slg	vs. Groundball/Flyball Pitcher	PA	Avg	OBP	Slg
Greg Briley (1988-1993)					H	799	.232	.294	.335	L	162	.243	.300	.351	SP	373	.232	.288	.337	GB	479	.248	.303	.353
Bats Left	1670	.253	.310	.372	R	871	.272	.324	.404	R	1508	.254	.311	.374	LC	302	.253	.297	.359	FB	353	.269	.320	.427
Greg Brock (1984-1991)					H	1531	.256	.339	.388	L	770	.237	.304	.356	SP	930	.264	.373	.411	GB	1047	.251	.337	.402
Bats Left	3134	.253	.338	.401	R	1601	.249	.337	.413	R	2362	.258	.349	.416	LC	386	.193	.292	.261	FB	1188	.241	.330	.412
Rico Brogna (1992-1997)					H	712	.286	.338	.492	L	315	.218	.259	.299	SP	422	.275	.339	.445	GB	364	.297	.364	.511
Bats Left	1498	.274	.322	.468	R	786	.263	.307	.446	R	1183	.289	.338	.513	LC	262	.298	.352	.550	FB	237	.279	.326	.475
Tom Brookens (1984-1990)					H	1171	.242	.300	.361	L	1123	.262	.325	.405	SP	614	.250	.296	.347	GB	859	.249	.288	.359
Bats Right	2428	.245	.299	.366	R	1235	.249	.299	.371	R	1283	.231	.277	.333	LC	292	.272	.321	.392	FB	954	.245	.297	.398
Hubie Brooks (1984-1994)					H	2384	.280	.331	.429	L	1603	.290	.347	.469	SP	1469	.279	.347	.436	GB	1951	.292	.343	.439
Bats Right	4876	.270	.317	.422	R	2492	.260	.303	.415	R	3273	.260	.302	.399	LC	814	.280	.332	.429	FB	1560	.259	.304	.409
Scott Brosius (1991-1997)					H	1072	.260	.326	.459	L	665	.234	.312	.399	SP	594	.239	.312	.372	GB	543	.270	.316	.439
Bats Right	2227	.248	.315	.416	R	1155	.238	.304	.376	R	1562	.255	.316	.423	LC	341	.270	.359	.446	FB	410	.245	.303	.418
Chris Brown (1984-1989)					H	866	.276	.346	.385	L	533	.256	.320	.396	SP	436	.308	.390	.436	GB	719	.284	.344	.425
Bats Right	1690	.269	.333	.392	R	823	.263	.319	.399	R	1156	.276	.339	.390	LC	270	.331	.401	.432	FB	744	.278	.349	.381
Jerry Browne (1986-1995)					H	1875	.297	.374	.374	L	978	.278	.353	.365	SP	885	.269	.369	.347	GB	1040	.295	.374	.378
Bats Both	3707	.271	.351	.351	R	1831	.245	.326	.328	R	2728	.269	.350	.346	LC	567	.286	.372	.369	FB	908	.264	.343	.331
Jacob Brumfield (1992-1997)					H	717	.264	.329	.416	L	603	.277	.319	.421	SP	361	.282	.365	.449	GB	386	.254	.322	.366
Bats Right	1535	.259	.320	.398	R	818	.254	.312	.382	R	932	.246	.320	.382	LC	285	.243	.319	.390	FB	219	.226	.289	.379
Tom Brunansky (1984-1994)					H	2943	.261	.338	.459	L	1951	.244	.329	.446	SP	1760	.237	.331	.405	GB	2221	.258	.340	.436
Bats Right	5972	.245	.325	.429	R	3028	.231	.312	.401	R	4020	.246	.322	.422	LC	900	.245	.340	.420	FB	2008	.245	.317	.439
Bill Buckner (1984-1990)					H	1468	.273	.310	.385	L	806	.265	.297	.361	SP	852	.289	.339	.426	GB	1236	.289	.322	.407
Bats Left	2958	.272	.307	.391	R	1486	.272	.305	.397	R	2148	.275	.311	.402	LC	410	.335	.389	.434	FB	1295	.256	.295	.392
Steve Buechele (1985-1995)					H	2383	.249	.321	.389	L	1542	.272	.351	.458	SP	1277	.257	.341	.375	GB	1581	.237	.304	.358
Bats Right	4790	.245	.316	.394	R	2398	.242	.311	.399	R	3239	.233	.299	.364	LC	743	.235	.306	.341	FB	1315	.242	.314	.420
Jay Buhner (1987-1997)					H	2367	.256	.370	.499	L	1382	.275	.378	.529	SP	1451	.274	.390	.512	GB	1159	.278	.361	.499
Bats Right	4815	.257	.357	.499	R	2448	.259	.345	.498	R	3433	.250	.349	.486	LC	774	.247	.361	.438	FB	960	.225	.335	.462
Ellis Burks (1987-1997)					H	2619	.315	.382	.548	L	1488	.307	.380	.509	SP	1513	.287	.364	.497	GB	1384	.296	.355	.479
Bats Right	5318	.290	.356	.498	R	2699	.266	.331	.451	R	3830	.283	.347	.494	LC	725	.265	.348	.439	FB	1194	.273	.336	.488
Jeromy Burnitz (1993-1997)					H	636	.279	.379	.552	L	248	.244	.331	.392	SP	349	.249	.333	.458	GB	306	.286	.386	.515
Bats Left	1297	.266	.367	.491	R	661	.253	.356	.432	R	1049	.271	.376	.516	LC	237	.277	.396	.523	FB	237	.261	.370	.513
Randy Bush (1984-1993)					H	1438	.258	.356	.441	L	95	.159	.245	.256	SP	815	.250	.370	.418	GB	1022	.247	.321	.402
Bats Left	2935	.251	.337	.412	R	1496	.245	.318	.385	R	2839	.254	.340	.417	LC	458	.254	.356	.401	FB	978	.245	.341	.420
Brett Butler (1984-1997)					H	4150	.306	.397	.383	L	2808	.295	.386	.362	SP	1747	.288	.394	.368	GB	3007	.292	.376	.365
Bats Left	8519	.294	.382	.381	R	4334	.283	.368	.379	R	5676	.294	.381	.390	LC	1312	.289	.383	.356	FB	2456	.299	.388	.404
Enos Cabell (1984-1986)					H	580	.270	.314	.362	L	608	.304	.354	.400	SP	307	.255	.322	.332	GB	562	.282	.331	.367
Bats Right	1129	.283	.325	.370	R	542	.298	.338	.378	R	514	.259	.292	.335	LC	223	.271	.318	.338	FB	560	.285	.320	.374
Ivan Calderon (1984-1993)					H	1740	.272	.336	.438	L	1221	.292	.362	.495	SP	979	.275	.338	.447	GB	1095	.281	.338	.444
Bats Right	3672	.272	.333	.442	R	1931	.272	.330	.445	R	2450	.262	.318	.415	LC	520	.274	.342	.420	FB	1029	.253	.317	.424
Ken Caminiti (1987-1997)					H	2768	.287	.350	.457	L	1942	.295	.349	.477	SP	1718	.290	.387	.465	GB	1683	.276	.337	.429
Bats Both	5605	.275	.343	.437	R	2837	.263	.337	.417	R	3663	.264	.340	.415	LC	923	.250	.331	.381	FB	1090	.257	.333	.436
Casey Candaele (1986-1997)					H	1090	.251	.316	.338	L	759	.285	.340	.376	SP	495	.236	.307	.313	GB	724	.265	.307	.335
Bats Both	2132	.250	.308	.332	R	1042	.248	.299	.326	R	1373	.230	.289	.307	LC	379	.264	.336	.348	FB	543	.218	.291	.304
John Cangelosi (1985-1997)					H	1135	.264	.390	.348	L	726	.233	.350	.349	SP	460	.252	.393	.325	GB	691	.250	.368	.327
Bats Both	2218	.250	.371	.320	R	1076	.235	.351	.290	R	1485	.258	.382	.305	LC	487	.226	.356	.282	FB	660	.249	.381	.319
Jose Canseco (1985-1997)					H	3025	.274	.363	.516	L	1579	.285	.372	.560	SP	1859	.293	.377	.534	GB	1839	.269	.345	.493
Bats Right	6262	.269	.353	.516	R	3237	.265	.344	.517	R	4683	.264	.346	.502	LC	882	.270	.363	.507	FB	1705	.269	.342	.518
Chuck Carr (1990-1997)					H	935	.274	.331	.354	L	597	.249	.306	.354	SP	434	.253	.339	.328	GB	528	.249	.307	.316
Bats Both	1914	.254	.316	.332	R	979	.235	.302	.311	R	1317	.256	.321	.322	LC	324	.287	.357	.371	FB	335	.280	.331	.397
Mark Carreon (1987-1996)					H	1084	.261	.320	.408	L	892	.268	.314	.430	SP	640	.286	.346	.415	GB	602	.300	.338	.461
Bats Right	2191	.277	.327	.438	R	1106	.292	.334	.467	R	1298	.283	.336	.444	LC	420	.278	.333	.423	FB	458	.232	.282	.389
Gary Carter (1984-1992)					H	1969	.251	.327	.404	L	1588	.268	.352	.438	SP	1246	.271	.364	.415	GB	1646	.266	.337	.407
Bats Right	3994	.254	.326	.416	R	2025	.257	.325	.427	R	2406	.245	.309	.402	LC	625	.258	.327	.382	FB	1498	.249	.326	.445
Joe Carter (1984-1997)					H	4312	.261	.310	.477	L	2393	.277	.321	.486	SP	2676	.271	.338	.467	GB	2536	.265	.308	.449
Bats Right	8684	.260	.307	.466	R	4368	.258	.304	.455	R	6287	.253	.302	.458	LC	1268	.238	.293	.396	FB	2373	.261	.310	.484
Vinny Castilla (1991-1997)					H	1262	.340	.378	.612	L	575	.329	.373	.582	SP	622	.295	.365	.489	GB	611	.294	.338	.514
Bats Right	2434	.299	.339	.525	R	1172	.255	.298	.431	R	1859	.290	.329	.507	LC	339	.299	.341	.510	FB	398	.293	.343	.529
Carmelo Castillo (1984-1991)					H	703	.292	.336	.498	L	954	.266	.314	.455	SP	388	.237	.280	.377	GB	457	.262	.303	.450
Bats Right	1470	.255	.299	.428	R	766	.223	.266	.364	R	515	.236	.271	.379	LC	190	.269	.310	.411	FB	667	.257	.315	.438
Andujar Cedeno (1990-1996)					H	1145	.241	.305	.383	L	665	.268	.320	.402	SP	614	.250	.330	.381	GB	697	.224	.273	.347
Bats Right	2238	.236	.292	.366	R	1093	.232	.278	.348	R	1573	.223	.280	.350	LC	357	.242	.300	.383	FB	367	.222	.292	.402
Domingo Cedeno (1993-1997)					H	491	.266	.317	.379	L	256	.246	.275	.325	SP	258	.264	.299	.352	GB	274	.286	.307	.386
Bats Both	1064	.258	.304	.354	R	573	.250	.294	.332	R	808	.262	.314	.363	LC	190	.244	.304	.369	FB	181	.229	.313	.325
Rick Cerone (1984-1992)					H	1121	.261	.319	.361	L	858	.267	.320	.358	SP	545	.244	.346	.316	GB	729	.216	.275	.288
Bats Right	2119	.251	.316	.342	R	991	.240	.313	.319	R	1254	.240	.314	.330	LC	302	.234	.304	.305	FB	755	.263	.328	.370
Ron Cey (1984-1987)					H	814	.242	.344	.443	L	493	.254	.371	.500	SP	433	.263	.388	.512	GB	718	.239	.334	.421
Bats Right	1578	.242	.335	.438	R	763	.241	.326	.433	R	1084	.237	.319	.412	LC	258	.235	.333	.394	FB	821	.245	.336	.456
Wes Chamberlain (1990-1995)					H	764	.272	.310	.426	L	555	.290	.344	.495	SP	377	.239	.304	.400	GB	495	.251	.294	.442
Bats Right	1352	.255	.299	.424	R	588	.232	.283	.421	R	797	.231	.267	.376	LC	225	.223	.267	.327	FB	263	.246	.293	.430
Archi Cianfrocco (1992-1997)					H	672	.245	.299	.388	L	440	.259	.312	.395	SP	367	.290	.352	.462	GB	416	.211	.267	.332
Bats Right	1317	.248	.298	.389	R	645	.252	.296	.390	R	877	.243	.290	.385	LC	246	.244	.300	.364	FB	208	.253	.300	.469

	Total					Home/Road					vs. Left/Right					Scoring Position/Late & Close					vs. Groundball/Flyball Pitcher			
Batter	PA	Avg	OBP	Slg		PA	Avg	OBP	Slg		PA	Avg	OBP	Slg		PA	Avg	OBP	Slg		PA	Avg	OBP	Slg
Jeff Cirillo (1994-1997)					H	925	.290	.371	.439	L	553	.285	.370	.440	SP	466	.313	.385	.483	GB	383	.293	.376	.447
Bats Right	1827	.295	.372	.453	R	902	.300	.373	.467	R	1274	.299	.372	.459	LC	296	.306	.395	.476	FB	318	.229	.322	.327
Dave Clark (1986-1997)					H	1020	.274	.348	.454	L	167	.259	.343	.378	SP	626	.268	.364	.404	GB	654	.291	.364	.440
Bats Left	2065	.268	.341	.418	R	1043	.262	.334	.384	R	1896	.269	.341	.422	LC	449	.256	.327	.387	FB	452	.239	.313	.387
Jack Clark (1984-1992)					H	2036	.257	.396	.475	L	1366	.298	.470	.535	SP	1353	.263	.437	.489	GB	1457	.270	.407	.478
Bats Right	4179	.258	.402	.478	R	2140	.259	.408	.480	R	2810	.241	.369	.452	LC	642	.242	.381	.435	FB	1359	.255	.389	.490
Jerald Clark (1988-1995)					H	869	.266	.316	.449	L	561	.241	.282	.401	SP	448	.262	.308	.431	GB	608	.272	.312	.411
Bats Right	1728	.257	.301	.408	R	859	.249	.285	.368	R	1167	.265	.310	.412	LC	298	.235	.259	.377	FB	333	.247	.284	.426
Tony Clark (1995-1997)					H	607	.257	.346	.512	L	325	.259	.323	.469	SP	322	.284	.394	.591	GB	250	.278	.372	.491
Bats Both	1201	.263	.342	.491	R	594	.269	.338	.470	R	876	.265	.349	.499	LC	183	.232	.350	.361	FB	204	.262	.309	.475
Will Clark (1986-1997)					H	3478	.311	.389	.515	L	2349	.291	.349	.446	SP	1999	.305	.407	.500	GB	2204	.311	.389	.489
Bats Left	6846	.302	.381	.493	R	3359	.293	.372	.470	R	4488	.308	.397	.518	LC	1000	.288	.385	.477	FB	1627	.304	.372	.509
Royce Clayton (1991-1997)					H	1541	.261	.313	.368	L	801	.248	.296	.364	SP	859	.240	.303	.336	GB	940	.245	.290	.329
Bats Right	3116	.257	.306	.356	R	1575	.253	.300	.345	R	2315	.260	.310	.354	LC	540	.220	.275	.273	FB	437	.223	.273	.321
Greg Colbrunn (1992-1997)					H	936	.285	.324	.433	L	611	.280	.308	.432	SP	559	.288	.341	.442	GB	486	.247	.283	.379
Bats Right	1914	.279	.316	.432	R	978	.274	.308	.430	R	1303	.279	.320	.431	LC	325	.273	.322	.387	FB	340	.290	.338	.443
Alex Cole (1990-1996)					H	1026	.286	.374	.373	L	309	.253	.362	.327	SP	434	.264	.354	.333	GB	655	.290	.366	.361
Bats Left	2012	.280	.360	.351	R	986	.274	.345	.329	R	1703	.285	.359	.355	LC	310	.269	.346	.317	FB	407	.240	.330	.291
Vince Coleman (1985-1997)					H	2991	.280	.342	.377	L	2067	.253	.312	.367	SP	1230	.255	.319	.347	GB	2231	.276	.333	.344
Bats Both	5970	.264	.324	.345	R	2971	.247	.305	.312	R	3895	.269	.330	.333	LC	860	.236	.302	.302	FB	1765	.239	.305	.331
Darnell Coles (1984-1997)					H	1517	.254	.322	.405	L	1235	.241	.306	.387	SP	831	.239	.302	.350	GB	970	.224	.292	.336
Bats Right	3124	.244	.306	.382	R	1596	.234	.291	.359	R	1878	.246	.306	.378	LC	477	.233	.303	.337	FB	976	.236	.302	.396
Dave Collins (1984-1990)					H	898	.248	.314	.339	L	486	.252	.301	.338	SP	418	.297	.375	.384	GB	798	.268	.335	.358
Bats Both	1867	.270	.334	.354	R	949	.290	.353	.369	R	1361	.276	.346	.360	LC	375	.269	.358	.316	FB	867	.265	.330	.353
Dave Concepcion (1984-1988)					H	1030	.259	.324	.334	L	791	.282	.346	.376	SP	555	.249	.344	.293	GB	964	.258	.324	.336
Bats Right	2093	.256	.317	.329	R	1047	.253	.310	.323	R	1286	.239	.298	.299	LC	342	.217	.279	.307	FB	956	.247	.303	.311
Jeff Conine (1990-1997)					H	1458	.299	.366	.464	L	782	.316	.387	.523	SP	893	.289	.380	.440	GB	781	.329	.385	.476
Bats Right	2973	.290	.358	.462	R	1515	.280	.351	.460	R	2191	.280	.348	.440	LC	517	.258	.342	.411	FB	514	.221	.296	.341
Cecil Cooper (1984-1987)					H	1015	.271	.312	.393	L	697	.298	.341	.413	SP	595	.301	.355	.447	GB	1018	.278	.319	.400
Bats Left	2168	.273	.311	.403	R	1151	.274	.309	.411	R	1469	.262	.296	.398	LC	290	.306	.348	.381	FB	1056	.270	.303	.407
Scott Cooper (1990-1997)					H	1010	.292	.362	.424	L	474	.236	.311	.340	SP	537	.266	.362	.373	GB	415	.310	.354	.445
Bats Left	2032	.265	.337	.386	R	1022	.239	.313	.348	R	1558	.274	.345	.400	LC	380	.232	.322	.317	FB	500	.266	.343	.376
Joey Cora (1987-1997)					H	1721	.282	.356	.369	L	738	.279	.342	.350	SP	830	.273	.339	.348	GB	911	.264	.327	.331
Bats Both	3584	.277	.346	.369	R	1863	.273	.337	.369	R	2846	.277	.347	.373	LC	501	.255	.333	.314	FB	768	.310	.384	.420
Wil Cordero (1992-1997)					H	1178	.272	.326	.434	L	713	.297	.357	.444	SP	673	.272	.357	.427	GB	697	.278	.331	.377
Bats Right	2511	.279	.333	.426	R	1333	.286	.339	.419	R	1798	.273	.323	.419	LC	415	.288	.348	.435	FB	413	.314	.362	.484
Marty Cordova (1995-1997)					H	803	.282	.358	.485	L	401	.284	.362	.491	SP	494	.272	.337	.454	GB	405	.319	.373	.519
Bats Right	1632	.282	.348	.469	R	829	.281	.338	.455	R	1231	.281	.343	.463	LC	226	.269	.336	.468	FB	232	.228	.315	.460
Henry Cotto (1984-1993)					H	1138	.263	.307	.374	L	1241	.275	.312	.382	SP	565	.243	.303	.327	GB	611	.281	.318	.388
Bats Right	2334	.261	.299	.370	R	1191	.260	.292	.367	R	1088	.246	.285	.356	LC	376	.245	.297	.327	FB	684	.259	.301	.350
Al Cowens (1984-1986)					H	532	.268	.312	.427	L	360	.263	.317	.459	SP	323	.285	.325	.426	GB	502	.254	.293	.397
Bats Right	1133	.265	.303	.426	R	599	.261	.295	.426	R	771	.265	.297	.412	LC	210	.278	.324	.428	FB	629	.274	.312	.450
Jose Cruz (1984-1988)					H	1135	.284	.354	.397	L	829	.278	.322	.403	SP	649	.321	.405	.494	GB	1023	.281	.341	.421
Bats Left	2304	.284	.349	.420	R	1167	.284	.344	.442	R	1473	.287	.363	.431	LC	330	.265	.361	.352	FB	1107	.296	.363	.428
Chad Curtis (1992-1997)					H	1617	.269	.352	.396	L	917	.307	.394	.473	SP	798	.254	.324	.348	GB	749	.267	.354	.379
Bats Right	3349	.267	.346	.402	R	1732	.266	.339	.407	R	2432	.252	.327	.376	LC	503	.255	.344	.360	FB	698	.264	.324	.398
Milt Cuyler (1990-1996)					H	789	.230	.311	.296	L	450	.239	.304	.298	SP	398	.220	.281	.342	GB	443	.217	.287	.271
Bats Both	1560	.236	.303	.322	R	771	.242	.295	.347	R	1110	.235	.303	.331	LC	213	.219	.291	.332	FB	319	.252	.322	.390
Johnny Damon (1995-1997)					H	637	.276	.324	.391	L	328	.235	.298	.304	SP	313	.276	.332	.407	GB	266	.260	.284	.386
Bats Left	1296	.274	.325	.387	R	659	.273	.326	.382	R	968	.287	.334	.413	LC	227	.200	.260	.239	FB	214	.270	.322	.378
Kal Daniels (1986-1992)					H	1351	.289	.382	.497	L	842	.247	.343	.363	SP	734	.286	.416	.493	GB	969	.300	.402	.476
Bats Left	2739	.285	.382	.479	R	1387	.281	.382	.461	R	1896	.302	.399	.530	LC	377	.253	.363	.388	FB	667	.248	.354	.452
Doug Dascenzo (1988-1996)					H	700	.243	.301	.313	L	581	.261	.298	.317	SP	314	.232	.294	.251	GB	481	.267	.318	.324
Bats Both	1362	.234	.293	.297	R	662	.225	.285	.281	R	781	.213	.290	.282	LC	271	.265	.336	.322	FB	329	.169	.232	.217
Darren Daulton (1985-1997)					H	2135	.253	.370	.446	L	1175	.232	.339	.394	SP	1300	.259	.389	.433	GB	1462	.281	.377	.496
Bats Left	4336	.245	.357	.427	R	2197	.238	.344	.409	R	3157	.250	.364	.439	LC	740	.227	.331	.344	FB	924	.193	.321	.346
Alvin Davis (1984-1992)					H	2498	.294	.398	.503	L	1510	.267	.366	.403	SP	1429	.287	.417	.463	GB	1754	.299	.401	.457
Bats Left	5010	.280	.380	.450	R	2510	.267	.362	.398	R	3498	.286	.386	.471	LC	673	.257	.374	.413	FB	1775	.268	.370	.466
Chili Davis (1984-1997)					H	4048	.280	.371	.465	L	2374	.271	.340	.459	SP	2331	.291	.413	.491	GB	2233	.286	.365	.453
Bats Both	8054	.279	.368	.463	R	4001	.278	.364	.461	R	5675	.283	.379	.465	LC	1233	.261	.374	.424	FB	2431	.271	.357	.451
Eric Davis (1984-1997)					H	2383	.265	.370	.479	L	1594	.269	.373	.498	SP	1438	.279	.401	.509	GB	1784	.279	.370	.485
Bats Right	4952	.263	.357	.483	R	2567	.262	.345	.487	R	3356	.261	.349	.476	LC	756	.257	.356	.461	FB	1267	.255	.354	.506
Glenn Davis (1984-1993)					H	2072	.279	.347	.470	L	1382	.257	.341	.498	SP	1219	.252	.359	.419	GB	1535	.265	.336	.459
Bats Right	4189	.259	.332	.467	R	2113	.240	.318	.464	R	2803	.261	.328	.452	LC	608	.241	.322	.410	FB	1337	.262	.339	.485
Jody Davis (1984-1990)					H	1348	.245	.317	.415	L	800	.230	.303	.381	SP	772	.219	.305	.359	GB	1216	.255	.322	.411
Bats Right	2761	.236	.303	.390	R	1406	.227	.289	.366	R	1954	.238	.303	.393	LC	418	.192	.281	.286	FB	1122	.214	.276	.377
Mike Davis (1984-1989)					H	1248	.250	.314	.418	L	606	.254	.305	.437	SP	631	.239	.302	.382	GB	1156	.277	.330	.468
Bats Left	2608	.256	.312	.423	R	1351	.261	.310	.427	R	1993	.256	.314	.418	LC	359	.240	.293	.410	FB	1076	.238	.300	.387
Andre Dawson (1984-1996)					H	3115	.286	.332	.495	L	1940	.298	.340	.529	SP	1943	.288	.359	.495	GB	2279	.268	.312	.450
Bats Right	6330	.274	.318	.478	R	3211	.264	.304	.461	R	4386	.264	.308	.455	LC	1049	.261	.315	.420	FB	1993	.270	.314	.488

Situational Statistics: Hitting 2525

Batter	Total PA	Total Avg	Total OBP	Total Slg		Home/Road PA	Home/Road Avg	Home/Road OBP	Home/Road Slg		vs. Left/Right PA	vs. Left/Right Avg	vs. Left/Right OBP	vs. Left/Right Slg		Scoring Position/Late & Close PA	Scoring Position/Late & Close Avg	Scoring Position/Late & Close OBP	Scoring Position/Late & Close Slg		vs. Groundball/Flyball Pitcher PA	vs. Groundball/Flyball Pitcher Avg	vs. Groundball/Flyball Pitcher OBP	vs. Groundball/Flyball Pitcher Slg
Doug DeCinces (1984-1987)					H	1105	.263	.344	.451	L	746	.279	.373	.480	SP	683	.251	.338	.432	GB	984	.281	.347	.471
Bats Right	2211	.252	.326	.431	R	1099	.240	.308	.411	R	1458	.238	.302	.408	LC	278	.273	.327	.419	FB	1082	.224	.307	.395
Rob Deer (1984-1996)					H	2185	.217	.329	.446	L	1353	.259	.373	.549	SP	1265	.222	.350	.433	GB	1346	.237	.341	.466
Bats Right	4513	.220	.324	.442	R	2325	.222	.319	.440	R	3157	.204	.303	.398	LC	633	.208	.306	.423	FB	1358	.213	.320	.453
Carlos Delgado (1993-1997)					H	731	.266	.364	.514	L	302	.210	.278	.395	SP	390	.262	.354	.536	GB	329	.251	.356	.437
Bats Left	1418	.253	.342	.486	R	687	.240	.319	.456	R	1116	.265	.359	.511	LC	231	.215	.307	.420	FB	228	.235	.325	.425
Rick Dempsey (1984-1992)					H	978	.224	.327	.366	L	1007	.241	.345	.405	SP	553	.230	.331	.354	GB	856	.254	.351	.386
Bats Right	2069	.221	.322	.363	R	1075	.218	.317	.359	R	1046	.203	.299	.323	LC	334	.218	.313	.343	FB	880	.194	.286	.343
Bob Dernier (1984-1989)					H	991	.267	.322	.355	L	840	.284	.348	.384	SP	416	.241	.323	.302	GB	941	.277	.338	.359
Bats Right	2088	.257	.319	.339	R	1074	.248	.317	.324	R	1225	.239	.300	.309	LC	289	.240	.303	.313	FB	924	.240	.306	.314
Delino DeShields (1990-1997)					H	2160	.274	.362	.368	L	1385	.261	.351	.357	SP	1017	.274	.378	.383	GB	1382	.261	.340	.357
Bats Left	4560	.268	.352	.368	R	2400	.262	.343	.369	R	3175	.270	.352	.373	LC	819	.267	.356	.356	FB	842	.250	.340	.361
Mike Devereaux (1987-1997)					H	1953	.246	.307	.405	L	1426	.274	.331	.439	SP	1072	.263	.313	.415	GB	1016	.249	.312	.381
Bats Right	4086	.254	.307	.401	R	2133	.260	.308	.398	R	2660	.243	.295	.381	LC	667	.225	.280	.349	FB	823	.231	.282	.374
Bo Diaz (1984-1989)					H	869	.267	.309	.427	L	568	.272	.322	.399	SP	493	.273	.334	.397	GB	764	.261	.307	.362
Bats Right	1860	.250	.291	.372	R	986	.236	.275	.324	R	1287	.241	.277	.360	LC	238	.244	.287	.385	FB	739	.247	.289	.378
Gary DiSarcina (1989-1997)					H	1586	.252	.282	.328	L	846	.245	.271	.328	SP	792	.250	.297	.331	GB	661	.263	.299	.343
Bats Right	3097	.253	.287	.336	R	1511	.256	.292	.345	R	2251	.257	.293	.340	LC	526	.208	.256	.265	FB	660	.216	.262	.283
Bill Doran (1984-1993)					H	2534	.270	.367	.385	L	1780	.272	.371	.387	SP	1238	.259	.370	.350	GB	2044	.258	.340	.354
Bats Both	5191	.265	.353	.376	R	2643	.261	.339	.367	R	3397	.262	.344	.370	LC	764	.232	.331	.330	FB	1813	.264	.358	.385
Brian Downing (1984-1992)					H	2478	.270	.381	.453	L	1757	.278	.399	.475	SP	1304	.263	.387	.425	GB	1669	.294	.391	.481
Bats Right	5031	.270	.376	.448	R	2541	.269	.372	.444	R	3262	.265	.364	.434	LC	715	.276	.378	.460	FB	1890	.256	.374	.437
Dan Driessen (1984-1987)					H	571	.255	.345	.412	L	207	.229	.290	.309	SP	348	.201	.330	.288	GB	496	.240	.315	.369
Bats Left	1116	.253	.333	.392	R	543	.252	.320	.371	R	907	.259	.343	.412	LC	199	.291	.382	.448	FB	586	.263	.350	.415
Mariano Duncan (1985-1997)					H	2360	.270	.305	.394	L	1856	.297	.328	.443	SP	1253	.280	.303	.413	GB	1770	.258	.292	.347
Bats Both	4998	.267	.300	.388	R	2620	.264	.295	.383	R	3124	.249	.284	.355	LC	729	.264	.295	.370	FB	1373	.263	.299	.401
Shawon Dunston (1985-1997)					H	2588	.283	.311	.428	L	1450	.272	.295	.437	SP	1290	.271	.308	.407	GB	1797	.284	.311	.423
Bats Right	5223	.270	.298	.412	R	2630	.258	.286	.396	R	3768	.270	.299	.402	LC	849	.274	.306	.397	FB	1343	.242	.269	.391
Leon Durham (1984-1989)					H	1247	.299	.381	.554	L	497	.251	.320	.389	SP	656	.247	.393	.431	GB	1022	.293	.376	.507
Bats Left	2364	.269	.351	.475	R	1117	.237	.318	.387	R	1867	.274	.359	.498	LC	321	.265	.374	.467	FB	1092	.255	.341	.455
Ray Durham (1995-1997)					H	910	.251	.320	.348	L	550	.269	.320	.401	SP	477	.252	.331	.356	GB	438	.276	.346	.379
Bats Both	1867	.268	.334	.390	R	957	.284	.347	.430	R	1317	.268	.339	.386	LC	316	.241	.326	.307	FB	343	.252	.293	.397
Jim Dwyer (1984-1990)					H	661	.243	.356	.371	L	34	.294	.294	.412	SP	379	.255	.357	.425	GB	507	.275	.357	.411
Bats Left	1401	.265	.363	.413	R	733	.283	.369	.449	R	1360	.264	.364	.413	LC	218	.257	.362	.447	FB	556	.251	.357	.430
Lenny Dykstra (1985-1996)					H	2597	.290	.384	.440	L	1565	.275	.375	.376	SP	1084	.280	.403	.391	GB	1905	.270	.356	.381
Bats Left	5282	.285	.375	.419	R	2674	.280	.366	.398	R	3706	.289	.375	.436	LC	777	.296	.405	.408	FB	1316	.297	.393	.464
Mike Easler (1984-1987)					H	1071	.308	.367	.472	L	538	.244	.301	.358	SP	601	.281	.358	.429	GB	1019	.294	.357	.442
Bats Left	2144	.291	.351	.448	R	1070	.274	.335	.424	R	1603	.307	.367	.478	LC	293	.279	.345	.438	FB	1039	.294	.349	.468
Damion Easley (1992-1997)					H	935	.244	.328	.373	L	579	.256	.318	.413	SP	518	.233	.331	.367	GB	399	.213	.298	.299
Bats Right	1938	.251	.330	.381	R	1003	.257	.333	.388	R	1359	.249	.336	.367	LC	283	.285	.381	.404	FB	388	.251	.310	.403
Jim Edmonds (1993-1997)					H	1055	.301	.371	.522	L	576	.261	.332	.411	SP	575	.276	.353	.429	GB	424	.272	.349	.444
Bats Left	2059	.290	.358	.503	R	1004	.278	.344	.483	R	1483	.301	.368	.539	LC	301	.218	.303	.338	FB	382	.282	.344	.520
Jim Eisenreich (1984-1997)					H	1978	.301	.354	.431	L	796	.276	.321	.354	SP	1210	.284	.351	.390	GB	1174	.300	.349	.398
Bats Left	4064	.294	.344	.411	R	2086	.287	.334	.392	R	3268	.298	.349	.424	LC	772	.261	.317	.351	FB	887	.274	.324	.418
Kevin Elster (1986-1997)					H	1305	.220	.288	.350	L	932	.253	.321	.365	SP	749	.238	.324	.369	GB	818	.251	.306	.382
Bats Right	2630	.227	.294	.373	R	1325	.234	.300	.394	R	1698	.213	.280	.377	LC	417	.181	.259	.266	FB	501	.213	.281	.364
Nick Esasky (1984-1990)					H	1386	.249	.324	.444	L	923	.254	.353	.466	SP	791	.263	.369	.492	GB	1084	.255	.339	.433
Bats Right	2729	.249	.329	.445	R	1336	.248	.335	.446	R	1799	.246	.317	.435	LC	415	.240	.320	.441	FB	972	.223	.312	.418
Alvaro Espinoza (1985-1997)					H	1297	.249	.275	.321	L	922	.298	.324	.384	SP	636	.262	.288	.324	GB	645	.224	.253	.289
Bats Right	2659	.254	.279	.331	R	1357	.260	.283	.339	R	1732	.231	.255	.302	LC	415	.249	.278	.320	FB	588	.261	.278	.337
Cecil Espy (1987-1993)					H	655	.269	.315	.367	L	302	.243	.296	.338	SP	340	.255	.299	.342	GB	385	.249	.311	.312
Bats Both	1373	.243	.301	.320	R	718	.219	.288	.277	R	1071	.244	.302	.315	LC	296	.210	.301	.254	FB	377	.223	.285	.291
Darrell Evans (1984-1989)					H	1524	.237	.353	.455	L	745	.231	.328	.386	SP	857	.258	.392	.455	GB	1252	.217	.326	.406
Bats Left	3132	.235	.351	.440	R	1607	.232	.350	.425	R	2386	.236	.359	.457	LC	412	.237	.330	.440	FB	1308	.244	.370	.464
Dwight Evans (1984-1991)					H	2357	.287	.390	.491	L	1404	.300	.422	.498	SP	1389	.296	.410	.495	GB	1764	.289	.397	.455
Bats Right	4905	.279	.385	.478	R	2544	.271	.379	.465	R	3497	.271	.369	.470	LC	700	.279	.372	.500	FB	1873	.257	.362	.487
Carl Everett (1993-1997)					H	536	.291	.375	.513	L	290	.207	.279	.352	SP	306	.260	.364	.407	GB	271	.214	.275	.278
Bats Both	1111	.245	.319	.393	R	575	.205	.267	.287	R	821	.259	.333	.408	LC	236	.237	.318	.367	FB	176	.280	.351	.414
Jorge Fabregas (1994-1997)					H	519	.249	.301	.300	L	150	.277	.311	.343	SP	296	.285	.320	.354	GB	231	.273	.291	.323
Bats Left	1047	.267	.304	.331	R	528	.283	.307	.360	R	897	.265	.302	.329	LC	148	.267	.301	.363	FB	203	.326	.376	.424
Mike Felder (1985-1994)					H	1210	.248	.306	.321	L	729	.269	.317	.344	SP	574	.241	.305	.329	GB	788	.259	.305	.319
Bats Both	2497	.249	.301	.322	R	1285	.251	.297	.323	R	1766	.241	.294	.313	LC	471	.223	.290	.294	FB	653	.245	.300	.351
Junior Felix (1989-1994)					H	1143	.261	.324	.409	L	659	.244	.289	.422	SP	633	.262	.321	.396	GB	630	.282	.329	.438
Bats Both	2340	.264	.317	.413	R	1197	.266	.310	.417	R	1681	.271	.328	.409	LC	367	.220	.275	.352	FB	577	.243	.304	.400
Felix Fermin (1987-1996)					H	1485	.263	.310	.316	L	947	.275	.324	.324	SP	784	.248	.303	.292	GB	843	.240	.282	.279
Bats Right	3072	.259	.305	.303	R	1587	.256	.300	.291	R	2125	.252	.297	.294	LC	464	.275	.336	.326	FB	661	.251	.313	.298
Tony Fernandez (1984-1997)					H	3672	.284	.344	.395	L	2427	.279	.338	.378	SP	1773	.309	.377	.431	GB	2414	.280	.329	.375
Bats Both	7494	.282	.338	.392	R	3809	.281	.333	.389	R	5054	.284	.338	.398	LC	1096	.306	.362	.407	FB	2129	.287	.344	.398
Cecil Fielder (1985-1997)					H	2666	.264	.356	.516	L	1694	.278	.385	.551	SP	1666	.266	.380	.481	GB	1440	.256	.328	.413
Bats Right	5463	.256	.347	.489	R	2797	.249	.338	.463	R	3769	.247	.330	.462	LC	758	.232	.336	.355	FB	1285	.237	.325	.509

Batter	Total PA	Avg	OBP	Slg	Home/Road	PA	Avg	OBP	Slg	vs. Left/Right	PA	Avg	OBP	Slg	Scoring Position/Late & Close	PA	Avg	OBP	Slg	vs. Groundball/Flyball Pitcher	PA	Avg	OBP	Slg
Steve Finley (1989-1997)					H	2467	.268	.324	.391	L	1495	.260	.309	.360	SP	1204	.273	.338	.426	GB	1457	.275	.335	.389
Bats Left	5064	.279	.332	.422	R	2597	.289	.341	.452	R	3569	.286	.342	.448	LC	815	.289	.342	.424	FB	901	.270	.314	.457
Carlton Fisk (1984-1993)					H	1992	.247	.321	.418	L	1426	.259	.326	.455	SP	1122	.257	.349	.414	GB	1438	.247	.316	.392
Bats Right	4025	.251	.321	.439	R	2030	.254	.322	.459	R	2596	.247	.319	.429	LC	625	.265	.338	.467	FB	1410	.249	.314	.478
Mike Fitzgerald (1984-1992)					H	1287	.228	.309	.327	L	1031	.242	.336	.344	SP	756	.266	.382	.374	GB	1089	.229	.311	.316
Bats Right	2644	.236	.321	.347	R	1347	.245	.333	.367	R	1603	.233	.312	.349	LC	515	.226	.304	.319	FB	916	.242	.323	.371
John Flaherty (1992-1997)					H	704	.255	.298	.406	L	336	.246	.310	.339	SP	388	.257	.309	.363	GB	337	.294	.342	.424
Bats Right	1449	.258	.298	.389	R	745	.261	.299	.372	R	1113	.262	.295	.403	LC	201	.243	.292	.326	FB	258	.260	.276	.427
Tim Flannery (1984-1989)					H	776	.269	.375	.321	L	192	.170	.253	.228	SP	380	.293	.358	.360	GB	714	.270	.362	.322
Bats Left	1710	.264	.361	.323	R	926	.260	.348	.325	R	1510	.276	.374	.336	LC	295	.240	.328	.295	FB	735	.273	.372	.349
Darrin Fletcher (1989-1997)					H	1083	.271	.327	.437	L	370	.249	.312	.393	SP	735	.241	.323	.392	GB	699	.291	.341	.436
Bats Left	2344	.263	.317	.414	R	1261	.255	.309	.394	R	1974	.265	.318	.418	LC	399	.272	.351	.396	FB	403	.266	.323	.447
Scott Fletcher (1984-1995)					H	2753	.276	.348	.355	L	1884	.277	.346	.361	SP	1387	.292	.365	.370	GB	1656	.275	.334	.340
Bats Right	5598	.264	.334	.341	R	2815	.252	.320	.328	R	3684	.257	.328	.331	LC	757	.235	.312	.285	FB	1887	.276	.349	.364
Tom Foley (1984-1995)					H	1388	.246	.304	.360	L	302	.233	.268	.280	SP	725	.244	.327	.373	GB	1165	.239	.293	.336
Bats Left	2875	.246	.303	.347	R	1484	.245	.302	.334	R	2570	.247	.307	.355	LC	580	.236	.301	.334	FB	887	.244	.303	.331
George Foster (1984-1986)					H	685	.247	.311	.434	L	557	.262	.320	.461	SP	411	.252	.321	.401	GB	685	.252	.315	.415
Bats Right	1409	.258	.312	.443	R	724	.268	.314	.451	R	852	.255	.308	.431	LC	253	.203	.265	.264	FB	724	.263	.309	.469
Julio Franco (1984-1997)					H	3720	.324	.393	.448	L	2032	.318	.392	.480	SP	2077	.312	.391	.438	GB	2401	.301	.362	.403
Bats Right	7482	.303	.371	.421	R	3760	.282	.349	.395	R	5448	.297	.363	.399	LC	1030	.285	.359	.398	FB	2331	.298	.362	.419
Terry Francona (1984-1990)					H	638	.270	.295	.350	L	129	.285	.310	.325	SP	324	.287	.344	.339	GB	487	.275	.309	.334
Bats Left	1341	.272	.298	.354	R	699	.275	.300	.357	R	1208	.271	.297	.357	LC	216	.285	.298	.367	FB	545	.273	.295	.388
Jeff Frye (1992-1997)					H	851	.306	.376	.411	L	510	.296	.367	.419	SP	418	.281	.342	.386	GB	372	.313	.395	.388
Bats Right	1755	.293	.358	.399	R	904	.281	.341	.387	R	1245	.291	.354	.391	LC	268	.256	.331	.344	FB	369	.272	.308	.387
Travis Fryman (1990-1997)					H	2305	.270	.341	.445	L	1192	.272	.339	.456	SP	1399	.288	.349	.441	GB	1187	.276	.328	.421
Bats Right	4792	.274	.334	.444	R	2487	.277	.328	.444	R	3600	.274	.333	.441	LC	653	.255	.314	.418	FB	1031	.272	.337	.436
Gary Gaetti (1984-1997)					H	3847	.272	.321	.457	L	2148	.253	.316	.435	SP	2180	.265	.326	.451	GB	2427	.257	.309	.412
Bats Right	7765	.258	.309	.435	R	3912	.245	.298	.414	R	5611	.260	.306	.435	LC	1169	.256	.306	.447	FB	2274	.259	.313	.453
Greg Gagne (1984-1997)					H	3021	.255	.309	.379	L	1730	.263	.312	.407	SP	1582	.257	.319	.385	GB	1711	.249	.298	.360
Bats Right	6180	.255	.303	.383	R	3140	.254	.297	.388	R	4431	.251	.299	.374	LC	875	.248	.298	.343	FB	1594	.252	.294	.415
Andres Galarraga (1985-1997)					H	3308	.308	.364	.535	L	1922	.302	.353	.548	SP	1990	.291	.369	.497	GB	2250	.290	.344	.491
Bats Right	6637	.288	.342	.496	R	3328	.269	.320	.457	R	4714	.283	.337	.475	LC	1040	.262	.330	.445	FB	1469	.260	.323	.466
Dave Gallagher (1987-1995)					H	1145	.268	.336	.351	L	1138	.264	.329	.341	SP	595	.262	.342	.331	GB	641	.288	.344	.387
Bats Right	2343	.271	.331	.353	R	1198	.274	.327	.355	R	1205	.277	.334	.365	LC	442	.233	.309	.297	FB	479	.252	.329	.339
Mike Gallego (1985-1997)					H	1658	.248	.334	.338	L	1086	.266	.345	.376	SP	839	.221	.311	.290	GB	910	.247	.322	.319
Bats Right	3379	.239	.320	.328	R	1717	.230	.306	.318	R	2289	.226	.308	.305	LC	455	.246	.321	.341	FB	797	.215	.313	.320
Ron Gant (1987-1997)					H	2482	.263	.340	.485	L	1487	.255	.344	.462	SP	1414	.265	.359	.463	GB	1605	.258	.329	.455
Bats Right	5101	.258	.333	.469	R	2619	.254	.327	.455	R	3614	.259	.329	.472	LC	820	.242	.317	.428	FB	1083	.236	.323	.458
Jim Gantner (1984-1992)					H	2112	.269	.316	.336	L	1208	.271	.320	.309	SP	1067	.248	.312	.314	GB	1502	.275	.316	.337
Bats Left	4319	.271	.315	.343	R	2184	.274	.314	.350	R	3088	.271	.313	.356	LC	696	.280	.333	.357	FB	1523	.269	.315	.351
Carlos Garcia (1990-1997)					H	1195	.277	.318	.389	L	636	.278	.315	.403	SP	535	.242	.315	.344	GB	642	.295	.333	.412
Bats Right	2307	.269	.309	.379	R	1112	.260	.300	.367	R	1671	.265	.307	.369	LC	373	.241	.311	.337	FB	374	.251	.298	.361
Damaso Garcia (1984-1989)					H	980	.280	.310	.383	L	750	.299	.327	.401	SP	429	.274	.310	.359	GB	947	.266	.289	.361
Bats Right	2024	.276	.303	.369	R	1034	.273	.296	.356	R	1264	.263	.288	.350	LC	334	.262	.292	.338	FB	1005	.288	.319	.381
Phil Garner (1984-1988)					H	782	.273	.339	.362	L	833	.280	.344	.416	SP	417	.263	.338	.411	GB	716	.240	.307	.349
Bats Right	1571	.258	.324	.382	R	783	.244	.308	.402	R	732	.234	.301	.343	LC	255	.278	.345	.445	FB	757	.284	.344	.420
Steve Garvey (1984-1987)					H	990	.269	.305	.407	L	664	.289	.325	.468	SP	579	.284	.320	.416	GB	1023	.263	.294	.374
Bats Right	2014	.272	.301	.399	R	1022	.274	.297	.391	R	1348	.263	.289	.365	LC	357	.262	.300	.325	FB	955	.280	.308	.428
Brent Gates (1993-1997)					H	907	.272	.332	.362	L	513	.257	.318	.358	SP	529	.252	.316	.346	GB	420	.283	.316	.361
Bats Both	1902	.269	.328	.367	R	995	.267	.324	.372	R	1389	.274	.331	.371	LC	304	.250	.306	.347	FB	390	.302	.358	.428
Rich Gedman (1984-1992)					H	1344	.260	.322	.420	L	487	.221	.272	.342	SP	714	.236	.325	.382	GB	1077	.276	.331	.438
Bats Left	2697	.246	.304	.400	R	1347	.232	.286	.381	R	2204	.251	.311	.414	LC	431	.234	.302	.384	FB	1064	.225	.280	.396
Jason Giambi (1995-1997)					H	686	.299	.387	.505	L	313	.267	.353	.419	SP	380	.293	.382	.524	GB	335	.309	.373	.500
Bats Left	1396	.287	.359	.475	R	710	.275	.333	.448	R	1083	.292	.361	.491	LC	207	.274	.379	.446	FB	201	.271	.343	.448
Kirk Gibson (1984-1995)					H	2627	.269	.356	.472	L	1522	.245	.328	.414	SP	1405	.272	.379	.484	GB	1931	.281	.365	.492
Bats Left	5354	.268	.356	.469	R	2720	.266	.356	.467	R	3825	.277	.367	.491	LC	758	.248	.351	.439	FB	1842	.265	.355	.480
Bernard Gilkey (1990-1997)					H	1784	.270	.345	.419	L	1091	.302	.379	.468	SP	947	.317	.410	.497	GB	1063	.286	.353	.435
Bats Right	3660	.283	.358	.452	R	1876	.295	.371	.484	R	2569	.275	.349	.446	LC	648	.281	.374	.466	FB	590	.262	.346	.422
Joe Girardi (1989-1997)					H	1532	.290	.338	.376	L	938	.279	.323	.355	SP	829	.300	.366	.377	GB	904	.279	.324	.351
Bats Right	3085	.272	.319	.351	R	1553	.254	.301	.327	R	2147	.268	.317	.349	LC	517	.284	.325	.338	FB	592	.267	.307	.349
Dan Gladden (1984-1993)					H	2392	.280	.341	.404	L	1516	.282	.343	.410	SP	1119	.264	.314	.381	GB	1604	.296	.358	.408
Bats Right	4890	.271	.325	.383	R	2475	.262	.310	.363	R	3351	.265	.317	.371	LC	703	.261	.329	.382	FB	1558	.254	.310	.365
Chris Gomez (1993-1997)					H	1001	.242	.321	.346	L	515	.274	.367	.380	SP	541	.272	.350	.368	GB	478	.249	.326	.318
Bats Right	2076	.247	.324	.346	R	1075	.252	.326	.347	R	1561	.239	.309	.336	LC	304	.215	.310	.258	FB	369	.213	.305	.346
Leo Gomez (1990-1996)					H	1114	.241	.340	.432	L	633	.258	.355	.436	SP	569	.232	.329	.384	GB	590	.266	.344	.436
Bats Right	2240	.243	.336	.417	R	1126	.246	.332	.402	R	1607	.238	.329	.410	LC	357	.240	.324	.409	FB	435	.157	.265	.281
Rene Gonzales (1984-1997)					H	862	.246	.326	.345	L	589	.256	.347	.354	SP	420	.256	.361	.342	GB	471	.220	.290	.273
Bats Right	1756	.239	.315	.320	R	894	.232	.303	.296	R	1167	.231	.298	.303	LC	276	.235	.330	.299	FB	437	.256	.322	.360
Alex Gonzalez (1994-1997)					H	830	.227	.293	.368	L	467	.256	.329	.411	SP	396	.225	.294	.336	GB	317	.214	.290	.354
Bats Right	1549	.235	.304	.386	R	719	.245	.316	.407	R	1082	.226	.293	.375	LC	250	.210	.275	.370	FB	232	.245	.327	.365

Situational Statistics: Hitting 2527

Batter	Total PA	Avg	OBP	Slg	Home/Road	PA	Avg	OBP	Slg	vs. Left/Right	PA	Avg	OBP	Slg	Scoring Position/Late & Close	PA	Avg	OBP	Slg	vs. Groundball/Flyball Pitcher	PA	Avg	OBP	Slg
Juan Gonzalez (1989-1997)					H	1956	.292	.347	.561	L	1043	.305	.360	.604	SP	1274	.289	.360	.539	GB	917	.297	.336	.556
Bats Right	3985	.285	.334	.557	R	2029	.278	.321	.554	R	2942	.279	.325	.541	LC	616	.256	.320	.508	FB	845	.258	.308	.524
Luis Gonzalez (1990-1997)					H	1835	.274	.346	.422	L	907	.258	.332	.385	SP	1129	.279	.376	.435	GB	1069	.278	.343	.450
Bats Left	3752	.268	.342	.425	R	1917	.263	.337	.428	R	2845	.272	.344	.438	LC	615	.272	.355	.390	FB	668	.282	.376	.475
Tom Goodwin (1991-1997)					H	883	.269	.321	.321	L	505	.281	.336	.339	SP	435	.256	.314	.319	GB	412	.308	.341	.371
Bats Left	1865	.273	.328	.337	R	982	.277	.333	.351	R	1360	.270	.325	.336	LC	287	.261	.319	.327	FB	329	.231	.299	.307
Mark Grace (1988-1997)					H	3201	.324	.400	.442	L	1971	.297	.359	.415	SP	1682	.313	.406	.432	GB	2004	.303	.376	.419
Bats Left	6227	.310	.384	.440	R	3026	.295	.367	.438	R	4256	.316	.395	.452	LC	1049	.325	.423	.438	FB	1223	.298	.373	.424
Craig Grebeck (1990-1997)					H	744	.267	.351	.366	L	719	.250	.324	.354	SP	375	.265	.377	.352	GB	377	.268	.344	.335
Bats Right	1507	.253	.337	.351	R	763	.239	.323	.336	R	788	.256	.348	.348	LC	249	.221	.299	.298	FB	333	.290	.365	.442
Shawn Green (1993-1997)					H	665	.262	.319	.451	L	225	.262	.317	.340	SP	357	.256	.331	.390	GB	327	.302	.355	.537
Bats Left	1381	.278	.330	.463	R	716	.293	.339	.473	R	1156	.281	.332	.486	LC	230	.274	.322	.512	FB	219	.232	.301	.384
Willie Greene (1992-1997)					H	579	.244	.339	.454	L	232	.169	.286	.272	SP	356	.246	.366	.488	GB	286	.233	.318	.364
Bats Left	1126	.243	.333	.446	R	547	.241	.326	.438	R	894	.261	.345	.490	LC	166	.181	.315	.283	FB	155	.227	.290	.433
Mike Greenwell (1985-1996)					H	2564	.312	.379	.490	L	1517	.293	.338	.421	SP	1557	.299	.382	.452	GB	1248	.314	.369	.460
Bats Left	5166	.303	.368	.463	R	2602	.294	.357	.437	R	3649	.307	.380	.481	LC	725	.301	.378	.424	FB	1263	.282	.353	.472
Rusty Greer (1994-1997)					H	1060	.324	.407	.519	L	574	.297	.370	.480	SP	649	.287	.389	.465	GB	469	.281	.370	.416
Bats Left	2116	.312	.392	.500	R	1056	.300	.377	.481	R	1542	.318	.400	.507	LC	305	.300	.384	.512	FB	408	.296	.373	.511
Bobby Grich (1984-1986)					H	667	.266	.358	.419	L	526	.270	.365	.444	SP	328	.237	.366	.342	GB	635	.236	.337	.382
Bats Right	1369	.254	.355	.408	R	678	.242	.353	.397	R	819	.243	.349	.384	LC	214	.260	.332	.370	FB	710	.269	.372	.431
Ken Griffey Jr. (1989-1997)					H	2564	.315	.398	.600	L	1663	.299	.364	.543	SP	1500	.302	.415	.555	GB	1268	.323	.395	.572
Bats Left	5262	.302	.381	.562	R	2698	.291	.365	.526	R	3599	.304	.389	.571	LC	809	.277	.384	.500	FB	1095	.296	.368	.571
Ken Griffey Sr. (1984-1991)					H	1336	.287	.349	.453	L	528	.259	.298	.379	SP	784	.255	.339	.384	GB	1109	.262	.327	.401
Bats Left	2692	.281	.340	.425	R	1352	.275	.331	.398	R	2160	.287	.350	.437	LC	435	.291	.338	.386	FB	1026	.301	.347	.461
Alfredo Griffin (1984-1993)					H	2074	.236	.273	.283	L	1458	.253	.292	.301	SP	1079	.255	.294	.322	GB	1671	.270	.301	.325
Bats Both	4330	.248	.284	.308	R	2224	.259	.294	.331	R	2840	.245	.280	.311	LC	626	.235	.269	.292	FB	1550	.243	.278	.307
Marquis Grissom (1989-1997)					H	2297	.279	.331	.413	L	1512	.276	.332	.441	SP	1205	.277	.345	.416	GB	1490	.280	.336	.375
Bats Right	4876	.279	.330	.413	R	2579	.278	.329	.413	R	3364	.280	.329	.400	LC	793	.276	.328	.389	FB	897	.261	.314	.409
Kelly Gruber (1984-1993)					H	1694	.263	.309	.440	L	1072	.266	.308	.443	SP	954	.277	.328	.469	GB	1004	.250	.303	.404
Bats Right	3442	.259	.307	.432	R	1746	.255	.305	.425	R	2368	.256	.306	.427	LC	488	.257	.300	.406	FB	925	.262	.308	.460
Mark Grudzielanek (1995-1997)					H	795	.308	.343	.430	L	369	.280	.309	.366	SP	390	.251	.314	.303	GB	367	.249	.290	.339
Bats Right	1677	.282	.319	.378	R	882	.258	.298	.331	R	1308	.282	.322	.381	LC	266	.297	.350	.397	FB	235	.329	.355	.418
Pedro Guerrero (1984-1992)					H	2121	.300	.369	.443	L	1385	.299	.378	.454	SP	1269	.310	.406	.474	GB	1561	.303	.377	.448
Bats Right	4141	.299	.371	.465	R	2018	.298	.372	.488	R	2754	.299	.366	.470	LC	559	.273	.360	.423	FB	1401	.295	.372	.499
Ozzie Guillen (1985-1997)					H	3137	.271	.295	.349	L	1853	.241	.259	.289	SP	1644	.287	.308	.380	GB	1960	.270	.289	.337
Bats Left	6451	.265	.286	.339	R	3294	.259	.278	.330	R	4578	.275	.297	.359	LC	1123	.271	.303	.340	FB	1812	.261	.279	.337
Jackie Gutierrez (1984-1988)					H	502	.237	.263	.296	L	317	.242	.263	.308	SP	265	.172	.189	.188	GB	501	.230	.250	.277
Bats Right	1012	.237	.260	.285	R	487	.236	.257	.274	R	672	.234	.259	.274	LC	119	.214	.261	.214	FB	458	.245	.273	.291
Ricky Gutierrez (1993-1997)					H	755	.260	.335	.327	L	490	.274	.339	.363	SP	425	.234	.326	.272	GB	397	.273	.332	.350
Bats Right	1554	.259	.330	.333	R	799	.258	.325	.339	R	1064	.252	.326	.319	LC	296	.262	.343	.320	FB	252	.229	.311	.287
Chris Gwynn (1987-1996)					H	494	.267	.314	.351	L	94	.190	.236	.274	SP	292	.256	.317	.372	GB	269	.253	.294	.327
Bats Left	1100	.261	.308	.369	R	606	.257	.304	.384	R	1006	.268	.315	.378	LC	259	.237	.302	.364	FB	252	.258	.306	.403
Tony Gwynn (1984-1997)					H	4163	.349	.402	.472	L	3007	.325	.372	.426	SP	2070	.353	.442	.494	GB	3093	.339	.386	.450
Bats Left	8486	.342	.393	.460	R	4314	.335	.385	.449	R	5470	.351	.404	.480	LC	1349	.361	.424	.482	FB	2289	.336	.391	.460
Mel Hall (1984-1996)					H	1994	.276	.315	.432	L	670	.237	.286	.335	SP	1144	.281	.332	.425	GB	1350	.285	.330	.439
Bats Left	4017	.276	.315	.434	R	2024	.277	.314	.435	R	3348	.284	.320	.453	LC	570	.274	.316	.458	FB	1296	.269	.313	.418
Bob Hamelin (1993-1997)					H	672	.244	.360	.465	L	207	.235	.362	.394	SP	391	.212	.350	.401	GB	308	.212	.337	.365
Bats Left	1341	.250	.359	.472	R	669	.255	.359	.478	R	1134	.252	.359	.485	LC	193	.279	.415	.597	FB	299	.246	.368	.496
Darryl Hamilton (1988-1997)					H	1814	.296	.370	.388	L	938	.249	.317	.309	SP	919	.299	.370	.385	GB	879	.277	.330	.351
Bats Left	3677	.288	.351	.381	R	1863	.280	.333	.374	R	2739	.301	.363	.405	LC	546	.298	.372	.389	FB	704	.290	.359	.398
Jeff Hamilton (1986-1991)					H	610	.246	.274	.381	L	525	.214	.247	.293	SP	323	.242	.305	.359	GB	443	.251	.290	.358
Bats Right	1273	.234	.263	.349	R	663	.223	.253	.320	R	748	.248	.274	.389	LC	257	.211	.250	.329	FB	344	.212	.247	.335
Jeffrey Hammonds (1993-1997)					H	633	.270	.320	.440	L	433	.255	.309	.430	SP	332	.252	.324	.418	GB	285	.275	.339	.431
Bats Right	1291	.263	.314	.444	R	658	.256	.308	.448	R	858	.267	.317	.451	LC	212	.238	.297	.392	FB	192	.240	.270	.394
Dave Hansen (1990-1997)					H	538	.268	.349	.316	L	89	.200	.258	.263	SP	311	.261	.375	.332	GB	329	.254	.354	.306
Bats Left	1133	.267	.353	.357	R	595	.266	.357	.394	R	1044	.273	.361	.365	LC	271	.262	.351	.363	FB	250	.292	.348	.447
Brian Harper (1984-1995)					H	1550	.308	.345	.422	L	995	.290	.331	.427	SP	925	.302	.345	.404	GB	894	.308	.335	.418
Bats Right	3201	.299	.334	.418	R	1649	.291	.323	.415	R	2204	.303	.335	.415	LC	533	.312	.347	.436	FB	774	.274	.311	.381
Terry Harper (1984-1987)					H	522	.269	.340	.410	L	510	.237	.299	.373	SP	291	.246	.330	.365	GB	516	.262	.335	.402
Bats Right	1095	.249	.315	.379	R	571	.230	.292	.351	R	583	.259	.329	.385	LC	178	.314	.388	.478	FB	525	.241	.300	.365
Toby Harrah (1984-1986)					H	559	.246	.383	.355	L	482	.262	.400	.392	SP	294	.287	.405	.422	GB	531	.267	.409	.381
Bats Right	1161	.240	.374	.357	R	597	.235	.365	.359	R	674	.224	.355	.333	LC	209	.250	.373	.355	FB	625	.218	.344	.338
Lenny Harris (1988-1997)					H	1377	.269	.317	.328	L	393	.247	.304	.302	SP	644	.290	.340	.379	GB	878	.271	.301	.341
Bats Left	2832	.273	.323	.346	R	1455	.277	.330	.362	R	2439	.277	.326	.353	LC	542	.254	.321	.286	FB	567	.282	.351	.338
Ron Hassey (1984-1991)					H	1030	.263	.334	.377	L	321	.194	.267	.229	SP	569	.249	.333	.347	GB	808	.267	.332	.382
Bats Left	2142	.260	.334	.385	R	1111	.258	.333	.393	R	1820	.272	.345	.413	LC	334	.262	.327	.369	FB	772	.284	.367	.444
Billy Hatcher (1984-1995)					H	2360	.266	.318	.361	L	1690	.259	.302	.352	SP	1152	.267	.323	.362	GB	1550	.267	.313	.357
Bats Right	4752	.264	.312	.364	R	2384	.262	.306	.367	R	3054	.267	.318	.370	LC	686	.282	.329	.384	FB	1274	.270	.315	.387
Mickey Hatcher (1984-1990)					H	1180	.289	.322	.397	L	1027	.305	.343	.417	SP	638	.290	.337	.384	GB	1025	.292	.325	.384
Bats Right	2332	.285	.320	.378	R	1148	.280	.319	.357	R	1301	.269	.303	.348	LC	331	.287	.335	.377	FB	1013	.279	.319	.373

	Total					Home/Road					vs. Left/Right					Scoring Position/Late & Close					vs. Groundball/Flyball Pitcher			
Batter	PA	Avg	OBP	Slg		PA	Avg	OBP	Slg		PA	Avg	OBP	Slg		PA	Avg	OBP	Slg		PA	Avg	OBP	Slg
Charlie Hayes (1988-1997)					H	2303	.272	.322	.424	L	1376	.281	.327	.440	SP	1270	.269	.328	.408	GB	1430	.258	.300	.359
Bats Right	4606	.265	.313	.406	R	2303	.259	.303	.388	R	3230	.259	.307	.391	LC	772	.271	.324	.422	FB	883	.243	.282	.373
Von Hayes (1984-1992)					H	2360	.268	.367	.450	L	1432	.230	.317	.345	SP	1398	.263	.377	.402	GB	1932	.269	.354	.412
Bats Left	4946	.270	.361	.424	R	2583	.271	.355	.401	R	3511	.286	.379	.457	LC	746	.254	.350	.389	FB	1772	.277	.366	.448
Mike Heath (1984-1991)					H	1362	.249	.300	.404	L	1273	.272	.320	.428	SP	731	.255	.330	.376	GB	1002	.246	.306	.370
Bats Right	2834	.253	.304	.385	R	1459	.256	.307	.367	R	1548	.237	.291	.350	LC	470	.215	.274	.345	FB	1095	.263	.311	.407
Danny Heep (1984-1991)					H	723	.267	.349	.345	L	137	.219	.321	.263	SP	430	.282	.366	.401	GB	559	.261	.342	.333
Bats Left	1491	.260	.335	.354	R	766	.254	.322	.363	R	1352	.264	.336	.363	LC	286	.250	.353	.354	FB	610	.263	.342	.373
Dave Henderson (1984-1994)					H	2380	.267	.327	.449	L	1432	.293	.353	.508	SP	1281	.262	.328	.393	GB	1512	.268	.326	.426
Bats Right	4649	.260	.323	.437	R	2264	.253	.318	.425	R	3212	.245	.309	.406	LC	698	.251	.304	.421	FB	1507	.258	.322	.438
Rickey Henderson (1984-1997)					H	3871	.281	.410	.437	L	2364	.292	.424	.491	SP	1705	.255	.417	.388	GB	2513	.291	.402	.461
Bats Right	7969	.283	.408	.443	R	4097	.286	.407	.449	R	5604	.280	.401	.424	LC	1123	.293	.427	.457	FB	2273	.287	.414	.478
George Hendrick (1984-1988)					H	724	.246	.299	.360	L	715	.258	.311	.404	SP	447	.274	.333	.408	GB	565	.252	.308	.365
Bats Right	1435	.254	.306	.389	R	706	.263	.313	.419	R	715	.250	.301	.375	LC	236	.222	.285	.307	FB	748	.260	.307	.417
Jose Hernandez (1991-1997)					H	528	.236	.291	.383	L	323	.236	.275	.401	SP	276	.233	.293	.318	GB	265	.243	.268	.418
Bats Right	1087	.242	.286	.401	R	559	.247	.282	.417	R	764	.244	.291	.401	LC	223	.228	.287	.389	FB	171	.192	.254	.314
Keith Hernandez (1984-1990)					H	1590	.299	.394	.414	L	1320	.287	.361	.392	SP	1047	.282	.396	.430	GB	1461	.296	.376	.414
Bats Left	3440	.292	.379	.420	R	1850	.285	.365	.426	R	2120	.294	.390	.438	LC	492	.287	.388	.393	FB	1406	.293	.390	.430
Larry Herndon (1984-1988)					H	836	.269	.329	.423	L	1015	.286	.353	.447	SP	450	.232	.307	.334	GB	694	.255	.311	.380
Bats Right	1696	.264	.323	.402	R	856	.259	.318	.380	R	677	.232	.279	.337	LC	235	.261	.340	.362	FB	819	.265	.325	.405
Tom Herr (1984-1991)					H	2175	.269	.350	.347	L	1590	.286	.359	.369	SP	1239	.262	.348	.339	GB	1757	.292	.359	.366
Bats Both	4470	.269	.348	.349	R	2272	.270	.345	.352	R	2857	.260	.341	.338	LC	655	.235	.311	.311	FB	1611	.248	.331	.335
Bob Higginson (1995-1997)					H	796	.294	.385	.549	L	335	.265	.355	.431	SP	419	.304	.410	.538	GB	362	.268	.350	.481
Bats Left	1624	.284	.372	.501	R	828	.274	.359	.456	R	1289	.288	.376	.518	LC	236	.251	.350	.443	FB	293	.262	.348	.457
Donnie Hill (1984-1992)					H	1123	.251	.308	.318	L	674	.242	.311	.334	SP	643	.269	.336	.365	GB	845	.277	.321	.349
Bats Both	2382	.257	.310	.342	R	1235	.262	.313	.365	R	1684	.263	.310	.346	LC	316	.264	.339	.336	FB	899	.247	.301	.341
Glenallen Hill (1989-1997)					H	1420	.257	.311	.438	L	994	.277	.329	.505	SP	835	.277	.350	.431	GB	753	.316	.360	.526
Bats Right	2946	.263	.315	.459	R	1526	.268	.319	.479	R	1952	.256	.308	.436	LC	513	.239	.288	.397	FB	527	.212	.268	.410
Chris Hoiles (1989-1997)					H	1489	.272	.382	.482	L	872	.277	.380	.531	SP	759	.261	.391	.444	GB	722	.316	.419	.581
Bats Right	3021	.262	.367	.467	R	1532	.252	.353	.452	R	2149	.256	.362	.440	LC	482	.226	.340	.422	FB	536	.200	.325	.351
Dave Hollins (1990-1997)					H	1663	.266	.371	.448	L	1100	.310	.388	.539	SP	1041	.257	.380	.407	GB	1009	.254	.343	.405
Bats Both	3364	.265	.366	.429	R	1701	.263	.360	.411	R	2264	.241	.355	.374	LC	548	.237	.333	.392	FB	565	.257	.358	.451
Sam Horn (1987-1995)					H	610	.250	.351	.478	L	86	.158	.256	.342	SP	334	.232	.329	.444	GB	363	.246	.336	.476
Bats Left	1185	.240	.328	.468	R	575	.230	.304	.458	R	1099	.247	.334	.478	LC	173	.221	.324	.362	FB	271	.253	.354	.498
Bob Horner (1984-1988)					H	759	.282	.350	.498	L	479	.299	.372	.500	SP	446	.268	.372	.455	GB	703	.286	.360	.466
Bats Right	1497	.268	.338	.459	R	738	.254	.325	.420	R	1018	.254	.322	.440	LC	265	.274	.362	.475	FB	693	.260	.323	.483
Dave Howard (1991-1997)					H	844	.242	.306	.316	L	531	.221	.277	.299	SP	437	.231	.298	.327	GB	353	.245	.304	.315
Bats Both	1586	.229	.289	.302	R	742	.214	.270	.286	R	1055	.233	.295	.303	LC	273	.225	.290	.292	FB	329	.179	.245	.234
Thomas Howard (1990-1997)					H	1107	.265	.315	.381	L	431	.226	.282	.293	SP	566	.268	.332	.380	GB	592	.294	.337	.412
Bats Both	2261	.267	.313	.381	R	1154	.270	.312	.382	R	1830	.277	.321	.402	LC	468	.281	.330	.376	FB	416	.266	.294	.411
Jack Howell (1985-1997)					H	1414	.236	.314	.410	L	612	.179	.250	.293	SP	735	.224	.331	.369	GB	782	.279	.348	.486
Bats Left	2899	.239	.317	.423	R	1478	.242	.320	.435	R	2280	.255	.335	.458	LC	425	.235	.314	.401	FB	895	.218	.300	.396
Kent Hrbek (1984-1994)					H	2987	.295	.383	.517	L	1545	.266	.344	.412	SP	1735	.270	.388	.456	GB	2033	.286	.376	.465
Bats Left	5891	.280	.368	.481	R	2903	.264	.353	.444	R	4345	.285	.377	.506	LC	802	.299	.393	.436	FB	1940	.297	.380	.522
Glenn Hubbard (1984-1989)					H	1238	.247	.351	.358	L	749	.242	.349	.334	SP	628	.242	.374	.342	GB	998	.254	.349	.358
Bats Right	2489	.240	.339	.342	R	1235	.233	.326	.327	R	1724	.239	.334	.346	LC	301	.191	.300	.254	FB	1023	.232	.336	.336
Rex Hudler (1984-1997)					H	884	.264	.303	.439	L	1053	.274	.307	.457	SP	417	.248	.304	.406	GB	551	.252	.293	.408
Bats Right	1844	.264	.298	.428	R	954	.264	.293	.418	R	785	.251	.285	.389	LC	343	.230	.256	.382	FB	420	.234	.269	.361
Tim Hulett (1984-1995)					H	1103	.255	.309	.380	L	881	.256	.307	.401	SP	578	.249	.301	.353	GB	756	.254	.291	.342
Bats Right	2312	.249	.298	.371	R	1198	.243	.288	.363	R	1420	.244	.293	.352	LC	341	.215	.254	.300	FB	883	.253	.296	.426
David Hulse (1992-1996)					H	692	.290	.328	.369	L	242	.229	.300	.308	SP	333	.268	.322	.333	GB	326	.239	.272	.289
Bats Left	1370	.266	.307	.337	R	678	.241	.285	.303	R	1128	.273	.309	.343	LC	200	.261	.321	.356	FB	307	.275	.329	.344
Todd Hundley (1990-1997)					H	1317	.245	.328	.438	L	661	.212	.313	.356	SP	795	.253	.372	.474	GB	832	.268	.345	.439
Bats Both	2762	.244	.326	.447	R	1445	.244	.325	.454	R	2101	.254	.330	.474	LC	563	.224	.322	.386	FB	444	.207	.283	.396
Brian Hunter (1991-1996)					H	605	.264	.316	.454	L	627	.252	.305	.453	SP	373	.245	.290	.414	GB	383	.231	.280	.422
Bats Right	1236	.237	.288	.434	R	631	.212	.261	.416	R	609	.222	.270	.415	LC	218	.234	.301	.505	FB	257	.221	.284	.455
Brian Hunter (1994-1997)					H	817	.282	.334	.361	L	406	.268	.315	.362	SP	384	.253	.301	.322	GB	361	.323	.367	.410
Bats Right	1666	.278	.323	.364	R	849	.274	.313	.367	R	1260	.281	.326	.365	LC	265	.284	.311	.370	FB	286	.250	.292	.323
Butch Huskey (1993-1997)					H	566	.289	.315	.445	L	312	.289	.337	.467	SP	299	.253	.295	.345	GB	242	.309	.347	.439
Bats Right	1096	.269	.308	.444	R	530	.247	.300	.442	R	784	.261	.296	.435	LC	186	.273	.303	.443	FB	156	.254	.295	.401
Jeff Huson (1988-1997)					H	814	.223	.300	.268	L	197	.219	.289	.278	SP	400	.228	.320	.289	GB	473	.215	.280	.272
Bats Left	1684	.233	.307	.296	R	870	.243	.314	.323	R	1487	.235	.309	.299	LC	300	.210	.303	.242	FB	350	.234	.312	.280
Pete Incaviglia (1986-1997)					H	2307	.257	.325	.472	L	1626	.275	.341	.511	SP	1328	.232	.306	.414	GB	1448	.258	.319	.482
Bats Right	4645	.247	.311	.450	R	2339	.239	.297	.430	R	3020	.233	.294	.419	LC	693	.209	.270	.349	FB	1269	.232	.310	.408
Garth Iorg (1984-1987)					H	604	.261	.300	.364	L	734	.263	.306	.376	SP	348	.294	.350	.417	GB	506	.259	.308	.334
Bats Right	1262	.253	.294	.352	R	653	.245	.289	.341	R	523	.238	.277	.320	LC	163	.316	.362	.434	FB	655	.253	.284	.375
Bo Jackson (1986-1994)					H	1297	.272	.330	.515	L	868	.252	.321	.480	SP	754	.253	.335	.503	GB	657	.263	.317	.434
Bats Right	2626	.250	.309	.474	R	1329	.228	.289	.435	R	1758	.249	.304	.471	LC	344	.262	.320	.467	FB	704	.230	.294	.461
Darrin Jackson (1985-1997)					H	1182	.274	.310	.437	L	991	.262	.302	.438	SP	672	.259	.319	.423	GB	761	.253	.291	.395
Bats Right	2447	.257	.295	.404	R	1265	.242	.281	.374	R	1456	.254	.291	.381	LC	415	.241	.283	.380	FB	545	.230	.275	.415

Situational Statistics: Hitting 2529

Batter	Total					Home/Road					vs. Left/Right					Scoring Position/Late & Close					vs. Groundball/Flyball Pitcher			
	PA	Avg	OBP	Slg		PA	Avg	OBP	Slg		PA	Avg	OBP	Slg		PA	Avg	OBP	Slg		PA	Avg	OBP	Slg
Reggie Jackson (1984-1987)					H	971	.230	.337	.443	L	427	.233	.319	.405	SP	538	.227	.355	.420	GB	915	.251	.352	.443
Bats Left	2016	.234	.336	.427	R	1044	.239	.335	.413	R	1588	.235	.341	.433	LC	262	.190	.313	.253	FB	993	.218	.322	.411
Brook Jacoby (1984-1992)					H	2434	.265	.336	.417	L	1433	.276	.347	.417	SP	1283	.258	.352	.367	GB	1813	.274	.333	.396
Bats Right	5008	.271	.335	.406	R	2570	.275	.333	.397	R	3571	.268	.330	.402	LC	715	.254	.309	.356	FB	1789	.272	.341	.425
John Jaha (1992-1997)					H	1086	.267	.354	.433	L	596	.287	.374	.495	SP	640	.275	.378	.484	GB	520	.305	.385	.496
Bats Right	2257	.274	.360	.476	R	1171	.281	.366	.516	R	1661	.270	.355	.469	LC	351	.289	.386	.480	FB	416	.286	.359	.530
Chris James (1986-1995)					H	1576	.271	.318	.433	L	1258	.271	.321	.463	SP	958	.249	.308	.382	GB	1143	.273	.317	.418
Bats Right	3294	.261	.307	.413	R	1717	.252	.297	.396	R	2035	.255	.299	.383	LC	509	.241	.300	.354	FB	739	.268	.325	.450
Dion James (1984-1996)					H	1479	.295	.373	.409	L	368	.248	.357	.340	SP	724	.266	.371	.367	GB	1007	.276	.361	.380
Bats Left	3052	.290	.365	.394	R	1568	.285	.357	.380	R	2679	.295	.366	.401	LC	442	.233	.335	.279	FB	871	.278	.363	.360
Stan Javier (1984-1997)					H	1937	.265	.349	.347	L	1392	.258	.328	.355	SP	1073	.251	.339	.336	GB	1077	.274	.342	.368
Bats Both	4104	.263	.337	.356	R	2167	.260	.326	.364	R	2712	.265	.341	.357	LC	726	.238	.323	.314	FB	919	.233	.309	.339
Gregg Jefferies (1987-1997)					H	2488	.311	.375	.462	L	1524	.296	.340	.445	SP	1327	.291	.369	.403	GB	1497	.307	.365	.440
Bats Both	5095	.291	.349	.428	R	2607	.273	.325	.397	R	3571	.290	.353	.421	LC	832	.286	.359	.390	FB	1044	.269	.334	.388
Reggie Jefferson (1991-1997)					H	921	.312	.354	.495	L	356	.214	.285	.285	SP	499	.300	.366	.480	GB	380	.300	.348	.429
Bats Both	1862	.302	.347	.475	R	941	.292	.340	.455	R	1506	.323	.362	.519	LC	303	.258	.321	.376	FB	389	.298	.348	.494
Steve Jeltz (1984-1990)					H	1012	.211	.302	.280	L	566	.207	.313	.269	SP	508	.219	.333	.294	GB	821	.215	.313	.269
Bats Both	2031	.210	.308	.267	R	1010	.209	.314	.254	R	1456	.211	.306	.266	LC	288	.187	.313	.226	FB	705	.214	.320	.277
Derek Jeter (1995-1997)					H	718	.289	.362	.390	L	389	.316	.386	.426	SP	391	.248	.352	.331	GB	319	.254	.337	.337
Bats Right	1453	.300	.368	.415	R	735	.311	.373	.440	R	1064	.294	.361	.411	LC	220	.269	.364	.398	FB	229	.365	.415	.591
Charles Johnson (1994-1997)					H	675	.235	.326	.381	L	303	.267	.360	.439	SP	360	.213	.333	.371	GB	269	.222	.312	.350
Bats Right	1303	.241	.331	.412	R	628	.247	.336	.445	R	1000	.233	.322	.404	LC	216	.263	.348	.430	FB	209	.285	.349	.473
Cliff Johnson (1984-1986)					H	597	.276	.369	.459	L	477	.313	.417	.509	SP	358	.302	.394	.450	GB	541	.267	.362	.430
Bats Right	1226	.272	.360	.450	R	628	.267	.352	.442	R	748	.247	.324	.415	LC	232	.317	.392	.468	FB	684	.275	.358	.466
Howard Johnson (1984-1995)					H	2651	.242	.336	.434	L	1672	.230	.323	.405	SP	1487	.261	.388	.457	GB	2023	.252	.336	.451
Bats Both	5468	.247	.339	.448	R	2810	.252	.341	.462	R	3789	.255	.345	.467	LC	883	.234	.337	.423	FB	1510	.238	.334	.423
Lance Johnson (1987-1997)					H	2473	.285	.326	.375	L	1427	.284	.323	.351	SP	1193	.303	.353	.423	GB	1349	.292	.330	.362
Bats Left	5061	.294	.334	.392	R	2588	.302	.342	.408	R	3634	.298	.338	.408	LC	851	.272	.326	.356	FB	1065	.281	.319	.393
Chipper Jones (1993-1997)					H	996	.311	.392	.525	L	566	.276	.359	.398	SP	541	.311	.391	.483	GB	475	.266	.331	.447
Bats Both	1978	.292	.374	.489	R	982	.272	.356	.452	R	1412	.298	.380	.526	LC	314	.280	.375	.478	FB	280	.289	.373	.459
Ruppert Jones (1984-1987)					H	645	.257	.360	.476	L	130	.200	.285	.400	SP	355	.237	.349	.447	GB	586	.259	.340	.464
Bats Left	1377	.242	.333	.451	R	716	.229	.309	.429	R	1231	.247	.338	.456	LC	187	.237	.374	.401	FB	695	.230	.330	.436
Tracy Jones (1986-1991)					H	696	.271	.342	.384	L	758	.298	.361	.419	SP	399	.287	.359	.396	GB	501	.288	.344	.396
Bats Right	1434	.273	.329	.388	R	738	.275	.317	.391	R	676	.247	.292	.354	LC	223	.266	.342	.333	FB	407	.265	.318	.388
Brian Jordan (1992-1997)					H	994	.303	.347	.481	L	494	.294	.350	.511	SP	567	.304	.369	.492	GB	563	.264	.306	.406
Bats Right	1889	.283	.330	.455	R	895	.261	.310	.425	R	1395	.279	.322	.435	LC	324	.262	.321	.409	FB	303	.283	.330	.477
Ricky Jordan (1988-1996)					H	1087	.289	.309	.430	L	892	.310	.345	.473	SP	657	.271	.314	.404	GB	755	.288	.319	.399
Bats Right	2221	.281	.308	.424	R	1134	.274	.307	.419	R	1329	.263	.283	.393	LC	424	.273	.316	.390	FB	481	.286	.308	.473
Felix Jose (1988-1995)					H	1351	.275	.334	.405	L	811	.300	.350	.430	SP	719	.294	.359	.427	GB	709	.293	.341	.392
Bats Both	2675	.280	.333	.407	R	1324	.285	.333	.410	R	1864	.272	.326	.397	LC	460	.295	.354	.446	FB	594	.280	.340	.447
Wally Joyner (1986-1997)					H	3332	.289	.358	.438	L	2139	.259	.316	.369	SP	1967	.308	.399	.463	GB	1736	.312	.378	.462
Bats Left	6814	.292	.363	.447	R	3472	.295	.368	.456	R	4665	.307	.384	.484	LC	995	.297	.374	.442	FB	1874	.291	.363	.465
David Justice (1989-1997)					H	1925	.296	.388	.552	L	1255	.294	.376	.509	SP	1159	.307	.438	.550	GB	1181	.297	.389	.532
Bats Left	3931	.283	.380	.513	R	2006	.270	.374	.475	R	2676	.278	.382	.515	LC	577	.277	.365	.507	FB	773	.267	.378	.475
Ron Karkovice (1986-1997)					H	1408	.212	.275	.349	L	1025	.227	.301	.392	SP	835	.200	.302	.341	GB	782	.214	.284	.364
Bats Right	2948	.221	.289	.383	R	1539	.229	.302	.414	R	1922	.218	.283	.378	LC	426	.213	.261	.360	FB	698	.199	.267	.353
Eric Karros (1991-1997)					H	1773	.264	.324	.446	L	969	.282	.343	.452	SP	1079	.264	.335	.443	GB	996	.265	.317	.399
Bats Right	3700	.264	.319	.455	R	1927	.264	.314	.463	R	2731	.258	.311	.456	LC	633	.232	.311	.424	FB	655	.257	.321	.457
Bob Kearney (1984-1987)					H	527	.261	.298	.404	L	357	.201	.234	.334	SP	265	.244	.270	.341	GB	469	.242	.280	.362
Bats Right	1067	.231	.265	.348	R	517	.201	.231	.289	R	687	.247	.281	.353	LC	162	.244	.265	.308	FB	571	.222	.253	.335
Pat Kelly (1991-1997)					H	985	.243	.306	.352	L	648	.266	.313	.383	SP	525	.213	.287	.290	GB	468	.222	.270	.296
Bats Right	1937	.251	.309	.365	R	952	.259	.312	.379	R	1289	.243	.307	.356	LC	271	.240	.306	.367	FB	424	.272	.335	.441
Roberto Kelly (1987-1997)					H	2266	.287	.337	.417	L	1466	.307	.363	.457	SP	1156	.292	.347	.418	GB	1360	.302	.345	.442
Bats Right	4627	.288	.336	.422	R	2359	.289	.336	.426	R	3159	.279	.324	.405	LC	733	.282	.331	.437	FB	932	.289	.343	.447
Jason Kendall (1996-1997)					H	511	.307	.382	.438	L	207	.296	.373	.441	SP	271	.276	.372	.353	GB	219	.270	.361	.349
Bats Right	1043	.297	.382	.419	R	532	.287	.382	.400	R	836	.297	.384	.413	LC	176	.359	.454	.528	FB	174	.308	.374	.481
Terry Kennedy (1984-1991)					H	1674	.242	.297	.366	L	746	.217	.254	.334	SP	880	.253	.339	.374	GB	1390	.275	.324	.395
Bats Left	3363	.251	.302	.361	R	1685	.260	.308	.357	R	2613	.260	.316	.369	LC	497	.262	.335	.350	FB	1234	.227	.281	.332
Jeff Kent (1992-1997)					H	1474	.272	.328	.462	L	837	.268	.333	.403	SP	902	.273	.345	.462	GB	826	.278	.328	.475
Bats Right	2981	.269	.324	.455	R	1507	.266	.321	.449	R	2144	.270	.321	.475	LC	521	.263	.313	.458	FB	456	.238	.286	.371
Jeff King (1989-1997)					H	2117	.259	.324	.424	L	1444	.263	.340	.450	SP	1273	.264	.342	.407	GB	1256	.254	.315	.389
Bats Right	4181	.255	.323	.422	R	2064	.251	.322	.421	R	2737	.251	.314	.408	LC	712	.220	.294	.346	FB	764	.248	.316	.455
Mike Kingery (1986-1996)					H	1133	.270	.337	.413	L	252	.245	.321	.306	SP	596	.258	.326	.358	GB	730	.279	.334	.405
Bats Left	2282	.268	.330	.391	R	1143	.267	.323	.371	R	2024	.271	.331	.402	LC	349	.246	.325	.355	FB	540	.243	.301	.374
Dave Kingman (1984-1986)					H	943	.235	.295	.436	L	597	.245	.317	.488	SP	516	.257	.316	.461	GB	902	.256	.315	.470
Bats Right	1883	.239	.296	.450	R	938	.242	.296	.465	R	1284	.236	.286	.433	LC	278	.230	.299	.456	FB	979	.223	.278	.432
Wayne Kirby (1991-1997)					H	613	.253	.319	.348	L	224	.233	.294	.297	SP	348	.259	.317	.362	GB	285	.294	.358	.389
Bats Left	1292	.254	.312	.347	R	679	.254	.305	.346	R	1068	.258	.315	.358	LC	250	.240	.318	.318	FB	253	.203	.267	.326
Ron Kittle (1984-1991)					H	1180	.228	.300	.450	L	1036	.234	.318	.474	SP	605	.221	.279	.380	GB	816	.233	.305	.438
Bats Right	2411	.236	.304	.467	R	1231	.243	.308	.483	R	1375	.237	.294	.462	LC	337	.215	.294	.362	FB	1124	.228	.291	.459

Batter	Total PA	Avg	OBP	Slg		H/R PA	Avg	OBP	Slg		L/R PA	Avg	OBP	Slg		SP PA	Avg	OBP	Slg		GB/FB PA	Avg	OBP	Slg
Ryan Klesko (1992-1997)					H	910	.291	.361	.549	L	393	.222	.302	.357	SP	491	.275	.376	.529	GB	474	.300	.369	.567
Bats Left	1822	.279	.358	.538	R	912	.268	.355	.526	R	1429	.295	.373	.587	LC	277	.208	.319	.335	FB	254	.257	.356	.528
Ray Knight (1984-1988)					H	1053	.247	.298	.374	L	940	.268	.307	.415	SP	565	.280	.333	.396	GB	887	.247	.301	.341
Bats Right	2165	.252	.301	.355	R	1109	.256	.304	.337	R	1222	.239	.296	.308	LC	278	.240	.274	.342	FB	954	.264	.303	.366
Chuck Knoblauch (1991-1997)					H	2329	.316	.401	.419	L	1080	.310	.384	.432	SP	1035	.315	.408	.415	GB	1133	.317	.399	.422
Bats Right	4573	.304	.391	.416	R	2244	.291	.380	.412	R	3493	.302	.393	.411	LC	634	.254	.351	.339	FB	860	.307	.388	.422
Brad Komminsk (1984-1991)					H	548	.216	.303	.356	L	470	.200	.269	.311	SP	289	.239	.324	.377	GB	433	.214	.294	.320
Bats Right	1078	.218	.301	.338	R	527	.220	.298	.320	R	605	.233	.325	.359	LC	189	.195	.287	.274	FB	440	.230	.312	.353
Chad Kreuter (1988-1997)					H	802	.236	.338	.370	L	478	.206	.305	.358	SP	433	.208	.313	.325	GB	362	.230	.325	.301
Bats Both	1636	.236	.325	.362	R	834	.235	.313	.355	R	1158	.248	.333	.364	LC	261	.217	.323	.290	FB	344	.242	.321	.414
John Kruk (1986-1995)					H	2265	.302	.405	.456	L	1442	.271	.353	.369	SP	1401	.280	.408	.416	GB	1674	.299	.393	.426
Bats Left	4603	.300	.397	.446	R	2336	.298	.389	.436	R	3159	.314	.416	.482	LC	703	.294	.409	.413	FB	1065	.315	.411	.476
Lee Lacy (1984-1987)					H	930	.302	.356	.417	L	711	.295	.354	.459	SP	436	.290	.354	.404	GB	851	.289	.337	.397
Bats Right	1890	.292	.343	.417	R	943	.281	.331	.418	R	1162	.289	.337	.392	LC	257	.295	.354	.419	FB	926	.298	.351	.443
Steve Lake (1984-1993)					H	501	.239	.267	.330	L	619	.250	.280	.345	SP	284	.258	.317	.306	GB	409	.215	.247	.298
Bats Right	1109	.236	.267	.328	R	602	.233	.267	.326	R	484	.218	.250	.305	LC	143	.210	.254	.260	FB	360	.260	.287	.374
Ken Landreaux (1984-1987)					H	746	.253	.309	.347	L	203	.238	.303	.337	SP	377	.218	.281	.308	GB	662	.279	.329	.403
Bats Left	1518	.253	.301	.376	R	766	.252	.293	.404	R	1309	.255	.300	.382	LC	230	.250	.287	.407	FB	794	.232	.278	.348
Ray Lankford (1990-1997)					H	2059	.287	.371	.497	L	1259	.250	.331	.396	SP	1165	.288	.404	.512	GB	1180	.295	.378	.461
Bats Left	4167	.272	.361	.470	R	2108	.258	.352	.444	R	2908	.282	.374	.503	LC	735	.250	.339	.419	FB	757	.256	.338	.462
Carney Lansford (1984-1992)					H	2257	.291	.346	.408	L	1390	.297	.355	.411	SP	1248	.284	.361	.403	GB	1705	.283	.334	.401
Bats Right	4718	.287	.342	.399	R	2454	.284	.339	.391	R	3321	.283	.337	.394	LC	624	.243	.312	.346	FB	1669	.281	.338	.406
Mike Lansing (1993-1997)					H	1395	.275	.336	.402	L	664	.282	.339	.403	SP	718	.293	.375	.459	GB	741	.295	.343	.418
Bats Right	2828	.276	.333	.405	R	1433	.278	.330	.408	R	2164	.275	.331	.406	LC	451	.266	.333	.365	FB	425	.272	.325	.376
Barry Larkin (1986-1997)					H	3033	.300	.382	.458	L	1709	.322	.409	.529	SP	1545	.309	.408	.455	GB	1992	.291	.363	.415
Bats Right	5894	.299	.373	.452	R	2861	.298	.362	.446	R	4185	.290	.358	.422	LC	856	.305	.391	.427	FB	1215	.278	.351	.434
Gene Larkin (1987-1993)					H	1346	.277	.357	.394	L	784	.293	.366	.398	SP	801	.247	.345	.364	GB	746	.279	.359	.374
Bats Both	2670	.266	.348	.374	R	1324	.255	.339	.354	R	1886	.255	.341	.364	LC	400	.274	.357	.369	FB	667	.254	.345	.394
Tim Laudner (1984-1989)					H	821	.223	.295	.419	L	697	.263	.337	.482	SP	487	.214	.291	.366	GB	614	.239	.288	.390
Bats Right	1694	.225	.290	.396	R	867	.226	.286	.375	R	991	.199	.257	.338	LC	199	.179	.253	.307	FB	630	.210	.285	.405
Mike LaValliere (1984-1995)					H	1421	.276	.362	.340	L	492	.237	.326	.321	SP	860	.279	.393	.381	GB	1053	.263	.344	.323
Bats Left	2871	.268	.351	.338	R	1440	.260	.340	.336	R	2369	.274	.356	.341	LC	398	.246	.358	.348	FB	772	.265	.351	.362
Rudy Law (1984-1986)					H	625	.264	.330	.393	L	179	.211	.240	.257	SP	270	.322	.389	.469	GB	628	.243	.291	.337
Bats Left	1302	.256	.315	.366	R	665	.248	.301	.341	R	1111	.264	.327	.384	LC	192	.264	.313	.393	FB	662	.269	.337	.394
Vance Law (1984-1991)					H	1599	.266	.343	.401	L	1074	.266	.348	.418	SP	918	.257	.348	.365	GB	1330	.263	.333	.381
Bats Right	3280	.258	.332	.386	R	1665	.250	.321	.371	R	2190	.254	.324	.370	LC	465	.259	.328	.340	FB	1235	.247	.331	.386
Rick Leach (1984-1990)					H	693	.275	.337	.391	L	91	.220	.297	.280	SP	376	.296	.372	.384	GB	421	.281	.338	.365
Bats Left	1316	.282	.348	.384	R	623	.291	.361	.376	R	1225	.287	.352	.392	LC	206	.275	.353	.360	FB	483	.283	.354	.410
Manuel Lee (1985-1995)					H	1431	.253	.313	.324	L	985	.272	.318	.364	SP	752	.277	.315	.368	GB	772	.237	.287	.295
Bats Both	2960	.255	.305	.323	R	1526	.256	.299	.323	R	1972	.246	.299	.303	LC	486	.230	.295	.265	FB	771	.257	.314	.326
Scott Leius (1990-1996)					H	803	.253	.326	.361	L	575	.275	.367	.370	SP	476	.226	.303	.316	GB	424	.247	.318	.378
Bats Right	1598	.249	.323	.364	R	795	.244	.320	.366	R	1023	.235	.299	.360	LC	231	.209	.279	.291	FB	318	.237	.326	.356
Mark Lemke (1988-1997)					H	1792	.263	.327	.346	L	1068	.262	.332	.387	SP	915	.254	.351	.336	GB	1091	.249	.327	.320
Bats Both	3564	.248	.319	.327	R	1772	.232	.311	.306	R	2496	.242	.314	.300	LC	633	.244	.316	.333	FB	669	.268	.334	.376
Chet Lemon (1984-1990)					H	1701	.262	.351	.444	L	1302	.305	.384	.519	SP	913	.276	.374	.446	GB	1302	.271	.346	.422
Bats Right	3591	.264	.346	.431	R	1884	.265	.343	.419	R	2283	.240	.325	.380	LC	522	.245	.340	.389	FB	1371	.244	.334	.424
Jeffrey Leonard (1984-1990)					H	1786	.262	.306	.411	L	1149	.299	.336	.496	SP	1100	.256	.306	.398	GB	1253	.285	.324	.426
Bats Right	3711	.263	.305	.409	R	1923	.264	.304	.408	R	2560	.247	.292	.371	LC	553	.236	.291	.343	FB	1366	.252	.295	.416
Darren Lewis (1990-1997)					H	1421	.234	.311	.294	L	875	.237	.306	.303	SP	634	.276	.346	.354	GB	861	.247	.314	.312
Bats Right	2870	.247	.321	.314	R	1449	.260	.331	.333	R	1995	.251	.327	.319	LC	455	.248	.329	.301	FB	470	.246	.324	.305
Mark Lewis (1991-1997)					H	1033	.265	.311	.382	L	667	.305	.354	.437	SP	518	.280	.341	.381	GB	487	.268	.333	.366
Bats Right	2076	.270	.318	.383	R	1043	.276	.324	.383	R	1409	.254	.300	.358	LC	362	.247	.306	.349	FB	400	.276	.328	.404
Jim Leyritz (1990-1997)					H	1092	.279	.374	.398	L	988	.276	.387	.427	SP	648	.273	.378	.427	GB	510	.266	.352	.405
Bats Right	2270	.269	.364	.416	R	1178	.259	.356	.434	R	1282	.263	.347	.409	LC	345	.275	.364	.388	FB	420	.261	.364	.384
Jose Lind (1987-1995)					H	2039	.262	.302	.332	L	1396	.255	.305	.332	SP	1069	.269	.325	.342	GB	1295	.253	.296	.309
Bats Right	4001	.254	.295	.316	R	1962	.246	.287	.299	R	2605	.254	.289	.307	LC	692	.256	.293	.308	FB	871	.246	.285	.312
Nelson Liriano (1987-1997)					H	1205	.262	.332	.377	L	546	.233	.308	.329	SP	654	.288	.356	.417	GB	683	.269	.338	.340
Bats Both	2470	.262	.326	.368	R	1265	.261	.320	.360	R	1924	.270	.331	.379	LC	472	.239	.311	.332	FB	515	.283	.352	.406
Pat Listach (1992-1997)					H	988	.246	.313	.293	L	660	.283	.338	.374	SP	492	.252	.315	.309	GB	453	.242	.296	.291
Bats Both	1991	.251	.316	.309	R	1003	.255	.320	.325	R	1331	.234	.306	.276	LC	317	.257	.317	.307	FB	415	.246	.320	.287
Scott Livingstone (1991-1997)					H	731	.268	.310	.349	L	144	.292	.336	.415	SP	408	.279	.316	.354	GB	363	.251	.283	.338
Bats Left	1528	.287	.323	.377	R	797	.304	.335	.404	R	1384	.286	.322	.374	LC	268	.289	.325	.390	FB	361	.276	.313	.369
Kenny Lofton (1991-1997)					H	1871	.321	.393	.449	L	1179	.313	.386	.406	SP	783	.327	.402	.442	GB	748	.310	.381	.433
Bats Left	3739	.316	.384	.431	R	1868	.311	.374	.413	R	2560	.317	.383	.442	LC	588	.275	.355	.344	FB	765	.305	.380	.429
Steve Lombardozzi (1985-1990)					H	719	.233	.311	.374	L	410	.250	.321	.365	SP	351	.223	.347	.379	GB	535	.261	.331	.387
Bats Right	1437	.233	.307	.347	R	705	.232	.302	.321	R	1014	.226	.301	.340	LC	111	.235	.299	.347	FB	583	.201	.274	.312
Javy Lopez (1992-1997)					H	814	.288	.334	.465	L	435	.286	.339	.441	SP	449	.273	.356	.425	GB	446	.317	.356	.518
Bats Right	1678	.288	.335	.486	R	864	.288	.335	.506	R	1243	.289	.333	.502	LC	328	.284	.349	.459	FB	228	.262	.294	.425
Fred Lynn (1984-1990)					H	1509	.251	.331	.468	L	786	.224	.301	.388	SP	758	.244	.347	.442	GB	1269	.286	.365	.491
Bats Left	3063	.259	.338	.454	R	1552	.267	.344	.441	R	2275	.272	.350	.477	LC	436	.242	.346	.406	FB	1125	.236	.311	.421

Situational Statistics: Hitting

Batter	Total PA	Avg	OBP	Slg	Home/Road	PA	Avg	OBP	Slg	vs. Left/Right	PA	Avg	OBP	Slg	Scoring Position/Late & Close	PA	Avg	OBP	Slg	vs. Groundball/Flyball Pitcher	PA	Avg	OBP	Slg
Steve Lyons (1985-1993)					H	1190	.241	.291	.326	L	456	.239	.281	.320	SP	635	.266	.312	.366	GB	800	.271	.316	.359
Bats Left	2388	.252	.301	.340	R	1192	.263	.311	.355	R	1926	.255	.306	.345	LC	419	.251	.313	.324	FB	788	.227	.286	.310
Kevin Maas (1990-1995)					H	695	.210	.315	.419	L	372	.210	.306	.361	SP	372	.197	.347	.345	GB	423	.228	.310	.357
Bats Left	1448	.230	.329	.422	R	753	.248	.343	.425	R	1076	.237	.337	.444	LC	266	.215	.320	.408	FB	324	.219	.306	.413
John Mabry (1994-1997)					H	733	.287	.344	.404	L	314	.314	.350	.427	SP	397	.296	.404	.399	GB	337	.313	.369	.404
Bats Left	1468	.296	.347	.406	R	735	.304	.349	.408	R	1154	.291	.345	.400	LC	265	.309	.383	.400	FB	219	.252	.306	.396
Mike Macfarlane (1987-1997)					H	1734	.270	.342	.465	L	1210	.249	.313	.437	SP	1010	.238	.333	.409	GB	797	.273	.350	.445
Bats Right	3562	.253	.327	.436	R	1828	.236	.312	.409	R	2352	.255	.333	.436	LC	621	.236	.317	.411	FB	826	.226	.294	.435
Shane Mack (1987-1997)					H	1422	.304	.372	.480	L	957	.320	.379	.519	SP	764	.299	.381	.476	GB	754	.308	.370	.447
Bats Right	2987	.300	.366	.457	R	1565	.297	.361	.437	R	2030	.291	.360	.428	LC	419	.265	.326	.388	FB	663	.291	.362	.484
Bill Madlock (1984-1987)					H	916	.273	.341	.388	L	657	.282	.345	.439	SP	513	.282	.368	.348	GB	832	.282	.340	.378
Bats Right	1878	.268	.330	.392	R	958	.263	.320	.397	R	1217	.261	.322	.368	LC	270	.234	.300	.307	FB	925	.260	.329	.398
Dave Magadan (1986-1997)					H	2064	.299	.406	.390	L	1086	.267	.351	.321	SP	1170	.289	.408	.375	GB	1286	.281	.396	.355
Bats Left	4232	.290	.393	.379	R	2168	.281	.381	.368	R	3146	.298	.407	.400	LC	721	.261	.377	.324	FB	848	.266	.374	.356
Candy Maldonado (1984-1995)					H	2143	.240	.302	.407	L	1821	.267	.341	.433	SP	1330	.260	.356	.435	GB	1616	.260	.320	.412
Bats Right	4505	.255	.324	.428	R	2359	.269	.343	.446	R	2681	.248	.312	.424	LC	715	.231	.293	.377	FB	1346	.255	.323	.427
Fred Manrique (1984-1991)					H	696	.270	.319	.387	L	581	.272	.315	.384	SP	344	.308	.353	.427	GB	385	.230	.278	.303
Bats Right	1430	.257	.294	.364	R	734	.245	.271	.344	R	849	.246	.279	.351	LC	186	.224	.277	.327	FB	411	.233	.270	.351
Kirt Manwaring (1987-1997)					H	1370	.256	.308	.335	L	945	.254	.312	.328	SP	757	.255	.330	.316	GB	872	.258	.309	.337
Bats Right	2848	.243	.305	.311	R	1477	.230	.302	.289	R	1902	.237	.301	.303	LC	447	.215	.277	.271	FB	484	.225	.293	.280
Mike Marshall (1984-1991)					H	1623	.271	.316	.461	L	1109	.258	.324	.455	SP	900	.272	.330	.461	GB	1301	.281	.329	.456
Bats Right	3253	.270	.317	.450	R	1627	.268	.318	.438	R	2141	.275	.314	.447	LC	479	.231	.282	.375	FB	1219	.247	.300	.450
Al Martin (1992-1997)					H	1254	.297	.357	.503	L	496	.224	.299	.333	SP	662	.258	.358	.404	GB	724	.274	.333	.395
Bats Left	2511	.288	.352	.460	R	1257	.280	.347	.417	R	2015	.304	.364	.491	LC	408	.267	.362	.385	FB	390	.276	.347	.443
Carlos Martinez (1988-1995)					H	760	.267	.304	.363	L	673	.266	.299	.372	SP	436	.243	.285	.338	GB	341	.254	.290	.329
Bats Right	1586	.258	.293	.359	R	826	.250	.283	.355	R	913	.252	.288	.350	LC	234	.208	.243	.306	FB	355	.227	.266	.299
Carmelo Martinez (1984-1991)					H	1611	.242	.343	.419	L	1321	.254	.364	.426	SP	966	.244	.347	.406	GB	1436	.246	.344	.399
Bats Right	3262	.245	.338	.405	R	1648	.248	.334	.391	R	1938	.239	.320	.391	LC	560	.227	.315	.365	FB	1137	.248	.336	.418
Dave Martinez (1986-1997)					H	2313	.262	.327	.373	L	672	.246	.323	.346	SP	1185	.272	.364	.381	GB	1576	.277	.335	.380
Bats Left	4767	.276	.339	.396	R	2459	.289	.350	.418	R	4100	.281	.341	.404	LC	735	.243	.322	.334	FB	1040	.258	.329	.400
Edgar Martinez (1987-1997)					H	2179	.321	.431	.531	L	1257	.331	.441	.517	SP	1280	.297	.440	.479	GB	1155	.318	.421	.495
Bats Right	4589	.317	.423	.513	R	2410	.314	.415	.498	R	3332	.312	.416	.512	LC	704	.339	.486	.513	FB	903	.322	.416	.559
Tino Martinez (1990-1997)					H	1659	.267	.347	.469	L	1091	.272	.335	.466	SP	1052	.289	.384	.530	GB	791	.280	.352	.449
Bats Left	3495	.276	.347	.488	R	1836	.284	.347	.504	R	2404	.278	.353	.497	LC	595	.307	.382	.544	FB	706	.269	.326	.472
Gary Matthews (1984-1987)					H	737	.272	.384	.463	L	482	.298	.390	.455	SP	467	.257	.364	.407	GB	715	.260	.369	.435
Bats Right	1583	.264	.375	.424	R	845	.256	.368	.391	R	1100	.248	.369	.410	LC	199	.244	.357	.384	FB	796	.268	.386	.428
Don Mattingly (1984-1995)					H	3553	.314	.364	.500	L	2617	.298	.345	.451	SP	2093	.317	.393	.480	GB	2405	.315	.360	.491
Bats Left	7404	.309	.360	.475	R	3839	.304	.356	.451	R	4775	.315	.368	.487	LC	1040	.311	.381	.489	FB	2408	.322	.375	.505
Derrick May (1990-1997)					H	1098	.278	.332	.394	L	313	.261	.292	.386	SP	655	.286	.355	.440	GB	687	.282	.327	.381
Bats Left	2141	.274	.322	.398	R	1043	.269	.312	.401	R	1828	.276	.328	.400	LC	377	.265	.312	.410	FB	398	.248	.278	.349
Brent Mayne (1990-1997)					H	839	.282	.343	.369	L	200	.203	.250	.232	SP	413	.276	.347	.370	GB	400	.256	.314	.339
Bats Left	1631	.255	.315	.337	R	792	.229	.285	.303	R	1431	.263	.324	.351	LC	300	.266	.328	.331	FB	406	.249	.305	.357
Lee Mazzilli (1984-1989)					H	535	.272	.400	.394	L	223	.215	.309	.282	SP	322	.231	.394	.293	GB	435	.219	.345	.292
Bats Both	1091	.238	.362	.344	R	554	.206	.325	.298	R	866	.244	.375	.362	LC	289	.235	.356	.298	FB	485	.254	.384	.370
Lloyd McClendon (1987-1994)					H	653	.233	.311	.365	L	913	.263	.341	.395	SP	420	.226	.312	.323	GB	469	.250	.344	.374
Bats Right	1375	.244	.325	.381	R	722	.254	.337	.396	R	462	.206	.292	.353	LC	288	.238	.320	.302	FB	304	.212	.276	.387
Oddibe McDowell (1985-1994)					H	1548	.266	.334	.408	L	737	.222	.307	.322	SP	660	.267	.356	.412	GB	1153	.266	.326	.403
Bats Left	3172	.253	.323	.395	R	1616	.240	.313	.383	R	2427	.262	.328	.417	LC	423	.263	.336	.389	FB	1132	.232	.313	.371
Willie McGee (1984-1997)					H	3187	.308	.345	.414	L	2173	.295	.326	.433	SP	1830	.294	.354	.407	GB	2468	.303	.342	.408
Bats Both	6542	.299	.340	.407	R	3354	.291	.334	.400	R	4368	.301	.346	.393	LC	1082	.297	.340	.389	FB	1801	.300	.339	.435
Fred McGriff (1986-1997)					H	3252	.278	.380	.512	L	2202	.270	.350	.456	SP	1883	.266	.403	.465	GB	1926	.289	.390	.530
Bats Left	6650	.285	.381	.521	R	3398	.292	.381	.530	R	4448	.292	.395	.555	LC	974	.276	.392	.475	FB	1326	.267	.363	.511
Mark McGwire (1986-1997)					H	2726	.254	.383	.543	L	1537	.271	.403	.589	SP	1561	.282	.426	.568	GB	1534	.286	.401	.581
Bats Right	5633	.260	.382	.556	R	2907	.266	.380	.568	R	4096	.256	.373	.544	LC	749	.253	.411	.503	FB	1337	.222	.348	.493
Mark McLemore (1986-1997)					H	1930	.263	.345	.344	L	1070	.237	.314	.292	SP	1037	.257	.356	.331	GB	941	.258	.338	.323
Bats Both	3889	.258	.338	.334	R	1958	.254	.332	.323	R	2818	.266	.347	.349	LC	565	.257	.339	.324	FB	907	.257	.334	.351
Brian McRae (1990-1997)					H	2325	.278	.341	.410	L	1303	.297	.336	.424	SP	1058	.264	.347	.379	GB	1068	.269	.325	.382
Bats Both	4620	.265	.327	.391	R	2295	.252	.313	.372	R	3317	.252	.323	.377	LC	770	.261	.337	.390	FB	958	.244	.303	.368
Hal McRae (1984-1987)					H	547	.282	.351	.423	L	547	.284	.362	.462	SP	322	.288	.360	.402	GB	458	.299	.362	.427
Bats Right	1066	.273	.341	.413	R	517	.264	.331	.403	R	517	.263	.319	.363	LC	190	.300	.389	.431	FB	590	.252	.322	.396
Kevin McReynolds (1984-1994)					H	2894	.269	.330	.454	L	2020	.278	.353	.476	SP	1670	.280	.363	.453	GB	2228	.277	.335	.448
Bats Right	5884	.267	.329	.450	R	2980	.264	.328	.446	R	3854	.261	.317	.437	LC	961	.261	.320	.444	FB	1826	.252	.313	.433
Bobby Meacham (1984-1988)					H	687	.244	.316	.320	L	550	.253	.318	.334	SP	415	.226	.309	.269	GB	694	.230	.302	.284
Bats Both	1535	.236	.313	.309	R	807	.230	.311	.300	R	944	.227	.311	.294	LC	185	.220	.297	.280	FB	666	.243	.331	.323
Pat Meares (1993-1997)					H	1052	.260	.291	.363	L	562	.243	.281	.357	SP	559	.272	.308	.422	GB	489	.271	.315	.365
Bats Right	2077	.267	.303	.384	R	1025	.273	.315	.406	R	1515	.275	.311	.394	LC	260	.319	.352	.458	FB	327	.254	.290	.388
Bob Melvin (1985-1994)					H	971	.219	.248	.318	L	883	.284	.325	.410	SP	618	.240	.282	.334	GB	633	.225	.263	.312
Bats Right	2095	.233	.268	.337	R	1119	.246	.285	.353	R	1207	.196	.225	.283	LC	313	.204	.244	.254	FB	662	.225	.257	.334
Orlando Merced (1990-1997)					H	1669	.285	.375	.437	L	802	.243	.327	.371	SP	981	.301	.398	.477	GB	1033	.256	.329	.345
Bats Both	3400	.281	.363	.426	R	1731	.277	.351	.416	R	2598	.292	.374	.443	LC	594	.267	.372	.420	FB	615	.255	.350	.422

	Total				Home/Road					vs. Left/Right					Scoring Position/Late & Close					vs. Groundball/Flyball Pitcher				
Batter	PA	Avg	OBP	Slg		PA	Avg	OBP	Slg		PA	Avg	OBP	Slg		PA	Avg	OBP	Slg		PA	Avg	OBP	Slg
Matt Mieske (1993-1997)					H	659	.254	.314	.412	L	514	.305	.362	.582	SP	397	.256	.314	.429	GB	267	.250	.302	.373
Bats Right	1334	.260	.317	.436	R	675	.266	.319	.459	R	820	.232	.288	.346	LC	207	.237	.288	.395	FB	263	.252	.304	.433
Keith Miller (1987-1995)					H	743	.256	.326	.333	L	626	.258	.317	.350	SP	308	.263	.330	.333	GB	424	.272	.334	.330
Bats Right	1468	.262	.323	.351	R	725	.267	.321	.370	R	842	.264	.328	.353	LC	248	.272	.348	.332	FB	384	.248	.300	.327
Orlando Miller (1994-1997)					H	497	.231	.267	.355	L	223	.220	.276	.366	SP	287	.247	.331	.352	GB	242	.252	.288	.350
Bats Right	1017	.259	.305	.402	R	520	.286	.340	.448	R	794	.270	.313	.412	LC	180	.273	.310	.418	FB	173	.263	.304	.413
Randy Milligan (1987-1994)					H	1300	.250	.400	.415	L	933	.275	.409	.462	SP	705	.262	.394	.397	GB	749	.253	.377	.372
Bats Right	2594	.261	.391	.420	R	1294	.272	.381	.424	R	1661	.253	.380	.396	LC	440	.243	.389	.397	FB	551	.277	.425	.501
Eddie Milner (1984-1988)					H	804	.257	.340	.403	L	257	.211	.296	.259	SP	358	.235	.341	.336	GB	733	.270	.337	.376
Bats Left	1673	.248	.327	.373	R	862	.239	.316	.345	R	1409	.254	.333	.394	LC	239	.242	.339	.377	FB	828	.225	.313	.364
Kevin Mitchell (1984-1997)					H	2318	.298	.374	.536	L	1483	.308	.389	.574	SP	1424	.279	.390	.483	GB	1508	.303	.366	.552
Bats Right	4560	.286	.363	.525	R	2242	.273	.351	.514	R	3077	.275	.350	.502	LC	659	.258	.353	.466	FB	1171	.273	.358	.511
Paul Molitor (1984-1997)					H	3991	.326	.391	.483	L	2152	.329	.403	.493	SP	2114	.345	.429	.480	GB	2278	.309	.374	.435
Bats Right	8178	.314	.380	.464	R	4177	.303	.369	.446	R	6016	.309	.371	.454	LC	1086	.308	.387	.442	FB	2099	.313	.376	.482
Raul Mondesi (1993-1997)					H	1184	.300	.337	.513	L	596	.273	.322	.470	SP	623	.289	.354	.524	GB	604	.304	.333	.470
Bats Right	2468	.299	.339	.511	R	1284	.298	.341	.510	R	1872	.307	.344	.524	LC	420	.302	.337	.488	FB	412	.281	.318	.558
Mickey Morandini (1990-1997)					H	1744	.269	.335	.367	L	779	.231	.308	.302	SP	813	.274	.366	.374	GB	1074	.261	.324	.366
Bats Left	3488	.268	.335	.364	R	1744	.268	.335	.361	R	2709	.279	.342	.382	LC	574	.249	.330	.333	FB	588	.263	.318	.358
Keith Moreland (1984-1989)					H	1721	.289	.344	.446	L	1030	.288	.359	.418	SP	1068	.269	.326	.397	GB	1444	.273	.331	.391
Bats Right	3492	.277	.330	.404	R	1765	.265	.316	.363	R	2456	.272	.317	.398	LC	487	.267	.328	.382	FB	1344	.292	.345	.445
Hal Morris (1988-1997)					H	1763	.317	.369	.476	L	885	.247	.304	.310	SP	1026	.285	.367	.384	GB	1111	.303	.351	.426
Bats Left	3611	.305	.361	.445	R	1848	.294	.354	.414	R	2726	.324	.380	.488	LC	587	.285	.341	.418	FB	681	.282	.336	.420
Jim Morrison (1984-1988)					H	928	.268	.320	.429	L	766	.263	.317	.405	SP	519	.264	.313	.392	GB	781	.269	.323	.416
Bats Right	1864	.258	.303	.411	R	933	.247	.286	.395	R	1095	.254	.293	.417	LC	283	.229	.279	.374	FB	845	.258	.301	.438
Lloyd Moseby (1984-1991)					H	2262	.254	.347	.428	L	1488	.240	.319	.359	SP	1190	.258	.354	.422	GB	1696	.270	.349	.435
Bats Left	4595	.257	.340	.418	R	2327	.259	.333	.408	R	3101	.265	.350	.446	LC	639	.248	.337	.368	FB	1743	.249	.342	.423
John Moses (1984-1992)					H	835	.241	.309	.330	L	400	.253	.319	.318	SP	397	.270	.334	.331	GB	605	.254	.304	.318
Bats Both	1719	.256	.314	.334	R	877	.271	.319	.337	R	1312	.257	.313	.339	LC	231	.258	.314	.311	FB	593	.257	.318	.343
Darryl Motley (1984-1987)					H	579	.240	.278	.394	L	474	.267	.306	.461	SP	292	.244	.281	.440	GB	538	.233	.279	.345
Bats Right	1213	.245	.281	.410	R	632	.249	.285	.424	R	737	.230	.266	.377	LC	212	.186	.222	.276	FB	672	.254	.284	.460
James Mouton (1994-1997)					H	583	.267	.332	.363	L	490	.313	.378	.429	SP	341	.222	.305	.300	GB	270	.273	.330	.376
Bats Right	1223	.249	.321	.338	R	640	.233	.312	.316	R	733	.206	.283	.277	LC	219	.199	.291	.290	FB	192	.216	.270	.301
Rance Mulliniks (1984-1992)					H	1279	.290	.372	.446	L	141	.263	.370	.381	SP	723	.310	.418	.453	GB	1096	.289	.373	.425
Bats Left	2690	.285	.369	.426	R	1408	.281	.366	.408	R	2546	.286	.369	.428	LC	359	.271	.378	.395	FB	967	.285	.370	.451
Jerry Mumphrey (1984-1988)					H	888	.304	.372	.431	L	426	.234	.308	.274	SP	558	.293	.380	.396	GB	809	.296	.351	.422
Bats Both	1832	.291	.351	.412	R	942	.279	.331	.395	R	1404	.308	.364	.453	LC	319	.256	.329	.306	FB	875	.278	.344	.378
Pedro Munoz (1990-1996)					H	882	.276	.326	.456	L	598	.286	.338	.494	SP	508	.279	.320	.459	GB	459	.285	.315	.435
Bats Right	1832	.273	.315	.444	R	950	.271	.306	.433	R	1234	.267	.304	.421	LC	238	.286	.335	.456	FB	358	.261	.291	.449
Dale Murphy (1984-1993)					H	2739	.276	.369	.488	L	1770	.289	.401	.518	SP	1539	.270	.396	.497	GB	2164	.259	.342	.426
Bats Right	5446	.261	.345	.466	R	2708	.246	.320	.444	R	3677	.248	.318	.442	LC	855	.241	.337	.428	FB	1924	.272	.361	.519
Dwayne Murphy (1984-1989)					H	1114	.232	.352	.376	L	655	.216	.304	.359	SP	623	.239	.365	.372	GB	1037	.250	.352	.395
Bats Left	2306	.243	.352	.415	R	1177	.253	.353	.450	R	1636	.254	.372	.438	LC	322	.212	.330	.361	FB	1026	.241	.354	.443
Eddie Murray (1984-1997)					H	4092	.283	.362	.458	L	2747	.260	.328	.412	SP	2287	.296	.401	.512	GB	2811	.286	.360	.448
Bats Both	8362	.282	.356	.459	R	4270	.281	.351	.460	R	5615	.293	.370	.483	LC	1241	.267	.360	.461	FB	2514	.280	.367	.486
Greg Myers (1987-1997)					H	1022	.271	.319	.420	L	256	.267	.311	.358	SP	604	.238	.294	.350	GB	516	.255	.293	.390
Bats Left	2048	.255	.300	.383	R	1026	.238	.282	.347	R	1792	.253	.299	.387	LC	312	.277	.321	.408	FB	385	.261	.298	.420
Tim Naehring (1990-1997)					H	1051	.295	.387	.443	L	631	.277	.376	.418	SP	604	.293	.398	.449	GB	428	.266	.345	.371
Bats Right	2162	.282	.365	.420	R	1111	.269	.344	.398	R	1531	.283	.360	.421	LC	336	.247	.327	.389	FB	414	.246	.337	.383
Graig Nettles (1984-1988)					H	821	.241	.341	.423	L	316	.186	.259	.329	SP	512	.236	.342	.389	GB	813	.261	.355	.429
Bats Left	1685	.230	.323	.389	R	864	.219	.306	.357	R	1369	.240	.337	.403	LC	291	.232	.333	.432	FB	780	.207	.303	.360
Al Newman (1985-1992)					H	1201	.230	.320	.270	L	719	.252	.337	.323	SP	607	.221	.278	.278	GB	696	.211	.292	.242
Bats Both	2409	.226	.304	.266	R	1204	.222	.289	.263	R	1686	.215	.290	.243	LC	344	.229	.299	.266	FB	664	.193	.282	.231
Warren Newson (1991-1997)					H	593	.238	.365	.388	L	81	.197	.395	.213	SP	316	.225	.392	.299	GB	335	.224	.345	.313
Bats Left	1171	.251	.376	.405	R	578	.265	.388	.422	R	1090	.255	.375	.418	LC	235	.305	.415	.406	FB	218	.264	.399	.528
Melvin Nieves (1992-1997)					H	606	.212	.286	.387	L	323	.223	.292	.438	SP	309	.232	.311	.453	GB	294	.235	.307	.470
Bats Both	1245	.229	.306	.449	R	639	.246	.326	.509	R	922	.231	.311	.453	LC	214	.253	.319	.443	FB	196	.147	.240	.265
Dave Nilsson (1992-1997)					H	1187	.299	.370	.448	L	613	.243	.292	.351	SP	752	.269	.358	.420	GB	503	.294	.363	.437
Bats Left	2402	.282	.351	.449	R	1215	.266	.333	.451	R	1789	.296	.371	.485	LC	363	.272	.336	.416	FB	475	.260	.333	.413
Otis Nixon (1984-1997)					H	2579	.270	.350	.314	L	1715	.268	.331	.325	SP	1093	.257	.326	.307	GB	1527	.257	.328	.292
Bats Both	5109	.269	.343	.315	R	2521	.269	.336	.315	R	3385	.270	.350	.309	LC	829	.289	.367	.331	FB	1150	.260	.342	.316
Matt Nokes (1985-1995)					H	1396	.262	.317	.474	L	458	.222	.276	.418	SP	845	.241	.312	.407	GB	876	.260	.306	.421
Bats Left	2997	.254	.308	.441	R	1601	.247	.301	.413	R	2539	.260	.314	.445	LC	410	.250	.321	.420	FB	735	.241	.307	.460
Charlie O'Brien (1985-1997)					H	1064	.224	.313	.377	L	930	.226	.300	.360	SP	593	.232	.336	.390	GB	602	.223	.308	.345
Bats Right	2279	.222	.308	.357	R	1214	.220	.302	.339	R	1348	.219	.313	.354	LC	346	.235	.298	.399	FB	405	.226	.318	.383
Pete O'Brien (1984-1993)					H	2684	.271	.347	.421	L	1552	.246	.311	.345	SP	1526	.264	.363	.412	GB	1866	.270	.342	.414
Bats Left	5506	.264	.339	.414	R	2818	.258	.332	.408	R	3950	.272	.350	.442	LC	838	.248	.337	.390	FB	1907	.273	.356	.460
Troy O'Leary (1993-1997)					H	845	.317	.375	.507	L	305	.230	.304	.316	SP	467	.314	.411	.531	GB	361	.265	.324	.391
Bats Left	1653	.290	.346	.459	R	808	.263	.315	.409	R	1348	.303	.355	.490	LC	276	.267	.360	.404	FB	314	.259	.322	.399
Paul O'Neill (1985-1997)					H	2849	.301	.383	.502	L	1722	.239	.310	.381	SP	1781	.298	.407	.471	GB	1669	.296	.377	.445
Bats Left	5791	.287	.369	.473	R	2942	.274	.356	.445	R	4069	.308	.394	.513	LC	861	.277	.382	.438	FB	1238	.276	.358	.507

Situational Statistics: Hitting 2533

Batter	Total PA	Avg	OBP	Slg		Home/Road PA	Avg	OBP	Slg		vs. Left/Right PA	Avg	OBP	Slg		Scoring Position/Late & Close PA	Avg	OBP	Slg		vs. Groundball/Flyball Pitcher PA	Avg	OBP	Slg
Ken Oberkfell (1984-1992)					H	1517	.274	.351	.353	L	669	.249	.307	.322	SP	781	.245	.355	.355	GB	1182	.262	.322	.334
Bats Left	3051	.267	.341	.348	R	1526	.260	.330	.344	R	2374	.273	.350	.356	LC	503	.229	.320	.278	FB	1174	.274	.371	.361
Ron Oester (1984-1990)					H	1355	.271	.335	.356	L	696	.228	.286	.278	SP	676	.246	.364	.316	GB	1220	.264	.329	.347
Bats Both	2703	.264	.323	.342	R	1334	.257	.311	.329	R	1993	.277	.337	.365	LC	463	.299	.352	.372	FB	1112	.263	.314	.344
Jose Offerman (1990-1997)					H	1703	.283	.368	.366	L	1104	.272	.344	.360	SP	814	.274	.379	.361	GB	902	.292	.372	.366
Bats Both	3413	.271	.354	.353	R	1710	.259	.339	.339	R	2309	.270	.358	.349	LC	592	.246	.337	.287	FB	643	.248	.334	.322
Ben Oglivie (1984-1986)					H	604	.288	.341	.431	L	316	.234	.285	.337	SP	357	.305	.373	.444	GB	644	.299	.359	.415
Bats Left	1287	.277	.337	.402	R	677	.267	.334	.376	R	965	.292	.354	.425	LC	222	.286	.387	.439	FB	637	.255	.316	.390
John Olerud (1989-1997)					H	2148	.294	.400	.472	L	1089	.268	.381	.406	SP	1254	.295	.438	.459	GB	1092	.298	.399	.443
Bats Left	4319	.293	.396	.474	R	2171	.293	.391	.475	R	3230	.302	.401	.496	LC	720	.295	.398	.462	FB	816	.291	.390	.524
Joe Oliver (1989-1997)					H	1492	.247	.304	.400	L	1091	.279	.340	.438	SP	882	.260	.338	.424	GB	976	.255	.295	.388
Bats Right	3017	.250	.302	.394	R	1525	.252	.301	.388	R	1926	.233	.281	.369	LC	499	.240	.293	.348	FB	569	.207	.273	.375
Greg Olson (1989-1993)					H	686	.258	.320	.369	L	511	.278	.329	.415	SP	370	.228	.331	.319	GB	445	.223	.291	.320
Bats Right	1433	.242	.317	.342	R	747	.228	.315	.317	R	922	.222	.311	.300	LC	257	.202	.298	.298	FB	363	.285	.373	.440
Jose Oquendo (1984-1995)					H	1636	.270	.364	.337	L	1199	.258	.342	.350	SP	854	.272	.380	.362	GB	1250	.282	.369	.348
Bats Both	3384	.261	.355	.325	R	1743	.253	.346	.314	R	2180	.263	.361	.311	LC	582	.275	.377	.331	FB	859	.251	.345	.331
Joe Orsulak (1984-1997)					H	2243	.281	.336	.383	L	704	.236	.281	.278	SP	1120	.260	.343	.361	GB	1489	.257	.310	.337
Bats Left	4702	.273	.325	.374	R	2441	.267	.314	.366	R	3980	.280	.332	.391	LC	880	.263	.326	.356	FB	1213	.281	.336	.392
Jorge Orta (1984-1987)					H	581	.275	.324	.411	L	55	.235	.291	.235	SP	360	.249	.311	.404	GB	556	.296	.349	.432
Bats Left	1182	.277	.324	.419	R	598	.280	.324	.426	R	1124	.279	.326	.428	LC	182	.319	.374	.488	FB	599	.265	.307	.409
Junior Ortiz (1984-1994)					H	911	.277	.337	.325	L	767	.263	.317	.320	SP	507	.292	.360	.349	GB	614	.234	.292	.275
Bats Right	1855	.257	.309	.309	R	942	.239	.282	.295	R	1086	.253	.304	.301	LC	245	.248	.288	.301	FB	493	.285	.333	.352
Spike Owen (1984-1995)					H	2539	.249	.328	.352	L	1730	.273	.339	.401	SP	1308	.258	.361	.342	GB	1821	.232	.313	.316
Bats Both	5276	.249	.328	.346	R	2713	.249	.327	.340	R	3522	.237	.323	.318	LC	823	.248	.336	.342	FB	1805	.250	.326	.361
Mike Pagliarulo (1984-1995)					H	2052	.242	.312	.407	L	823	.218	.290	.337	SP	1119	.242	.329	.402	GB	1490	.240	.300	.403
Bats Left	4317	.241	.306	.407	R	2261	.241	.300	.407	R	3490	.247	.309	.423	LC	592	.239	.308	.346	FB	1447	.239	.310	.448
Tom Pagnozzi (1987-1997)					H	1428	.257	.311	.367	L	972	.263	.316	.379	SP	858	.247	.312	.336	GB	979	.252	.300	.348
Bats Right	2964	.255	.300	.363	R	1536	.254	.290	.359	R	1992	.251	.292	.355	LC	571	.200	.254	.276	FB	570	.219	.276	.306
Rafael Palmeiro (1986-1997)					H	3360	.293	.370	.503	L	2096	.284	.342	.471	SP	1889	.276	.388	.459	GB	1806	.291	.356	.467
Bats Left	6881	.294	.364	.496	R	3521	.295	.358	.491	R	4785	.298	.373	.508	LC	978	.273	.345	.479	FB	1423	.307	.388	.538
Dean Palmer (1989-1997)					H	1638	.242	.322	.442	L	842	.270	.347	.518	SP	883	.219	.301	.398	GB	727	.249	.331	.465
Bats Right	3282	.249	.321	.471	R	1644	.255	.320	.499	R	2440	.241	.312	.454	LC	501	.246	.325	.492	FB	709	.231	.311	.479
Craig Paquette (1993-1997)					H	703	.248	.281	.455	L	542	.244	.290	.427	SP	419	.229	.257	.432	GB	292	.230	.256	.335
Bats Right	1492	.232	.263	.405	R	789	.217	.247	.362	R	950	.225	.248	.394	LC	223	.248	.266	.395	FB	248	.240	.256	.421
Mark Parent (1986-1997)					H	607	.219	.272	.390	L	475	.234	.308	.430	SP	339	.189	.266	.320	GB	398	.192	.235	.310
Bats Right	1302	.213	.267	.383	R	695	.208	.262	.377	R	827	.202	.243	.357	LC	204	.211	.265	.362	FB	263	.197	.270	.441
Dave Parker (1984-1991)					H	2394	.278	.330	.455	L	1413	.262	.289	.420	SP	1451	.288	.363	.473	GB	1869	.273	.320	.431
Bats Left	4917	.273	.324	.445	R	2523	.269	.317	.436	R	3504	.278	.337	.456	LC	704	.258	.328	.430	FB	1739	.276	.331	.467
Lance Parrish (1984-1995)					H	2347	.254	.317	.433	L	1491	.263	.338	.440	SP	1350	.239	.316	.390	GB	1634	.252	.317	.421
Bats Right	4726	.242	.309	.420	R	2373	.231	.301	.407	R	3229	.233	.296	.411	LC	731	.206	.283	.328	FB	1609	.241	.306	.447
Larry Parrish (1984-1988)					H	1367	.270	.330	.462	L	802	.265	.335	.494	SP	713	.314	.381	.532	GB	1078	.285	.335	.477
Bats Right	2624	.262	.322	.455	R	1257	.255	.313	.448	R	1822	.261	.316	.438	LC	328	.235	.317	.419	FB	1132	.237	.307	.437
Dan Pasqua (1985-1994)					H	1461	.259	.352	.455	L	435	.188	.272	.316	SP	845	.228	.337	.406	GB	941	.259	.342	.433
Bats Left	3000	.244	.330	.438	R	1538	.229	.310	.422	R	2564	.253	.340	.459	LC	442	.218	.323	.399	FB	908	.228	.320	.445
Bill Pecota (1986-1994)					H	814	.249	.331	.349	L	636	.277	.347	.394	SP	454	.245	.357	.334	GB	579	.255	.323	.337
Bats Right	1729	.249	.323	.354	R	915	.249	.316	.357	R	1093	.232	.309	.330	LC	275	.246	.326	.298	FB	425	.250	.315	.384
Geronimo Pena (1990-1996)					H	576	.267	.356	.439	L	436	.313	.385	.513	SP	299	.259	.346	.424	GB	347	.260	.338	.359
Bats Both	1170	.262	.345	.427	R	594	.258	.334	.415	R	734	.233	.321	.376	LC	232	.221	.302	.342	FB	231	.277	.371	.477
Tony Pena (1984-1997)					H	2841	.247	.306	.340	L	1789	.288	.337	.412	SP	1601	.249	.312	.334	GB	1934	.266	.317	.361
Bats Right	5726	.250	.304	.348	R	2874	.253	.301	.356	R	3926	.232	.289	.319	LC	947	.242	.297	.325	FB	1842	.249	.306	.361
Terry Pendleton (1984-1997)					H	3710	.278	.322	.417	L	2313	.287	.324	.400	SP	2195	.289	.348	.422	GB	2641	.281	.327	.390
Bats Both	7383	.270	.316	.393	R	3664	.263	.310	.369	R	5061	.262	.313	.390	LC	1135	.257	.319	.360	FB	2055	.252	.302	.379
Jack Perconte (1984-1986)					H	671	.282	.358	.342	L	359	.283	.365	.321	SP	269	.271	.342	.314	GB	580	.266	.324	.324
Bats Left	1316	.277	.346	.337	R	630	.272	.333	.331	R	942	.275	.339	.343	LC	186	.297	.403	.361	FB	721	.286	.363	.347
Gerald Perry (1984-1995)					H	1758	.270	.339	.379	L	906	.251	.298	.358	SP	1033	.266	.362	.385	GB	1224	.259	.323	.356
Bats Left	3482	.263	.332	.374	R	1720	.257	.324	.369	R	2572	.268	.343	.380	LC	650	.248	.353	.359	FB	1102	.261	.334	.384
Geno Petralli (1984-1993)					H	968	.247	.334	.320	L	174	.193	.279	.207	SP	546	.263	.370	.367	GB	607	.327	.390	.425
Bats Both	2077	.266	.342	.359	R	1106	.281	.350	.393	R	1900	.272	.348	.373	LC	337	.241	.341	.329	FB	644	.230	.316	.310
Gary Pettis (1984-1992)					H	1964	.234	.336	.305	L	1338	.240	.324	.306	SP	902	.242	.338	.323	GB	1456	.246	.332	.325
Bats Both	4139	.234	.332	.305	R	2148	.234	.329	.305	R	2774	.232	.336	.304	LC	532	.227	.323	.285	FB	1518	.236	.343	.297
Ken Phelps (1984-1990)					H	1067	.246	.383	.517	L	229	.204	.345	.370	SP	588	.217	.406	.461	GB	839	.235	.372	.476
Bats Left	2107	.241	.382	.488	R	1039	.236	.380	.459	R	1877	.246	.386	.502	LC	294	.197	.350	.437	FB	847	.235	.373	.485
Tony Phillips (1984-1997)					H	3820	.263	.378	.380	L	2340	.290	.410	.424	SP	1769	.283	.393	.412	GB	2201	.276	.379	.384
Bats Both	7761	.269	.379	.393	R	3922	.276	.379	.405	R	5402	.261	.365	.379	LC	1075	.260	.390	.384	FB	2156	.272	.376	.416
Mike Piazza (1992-1997)					H	1394	.316	.379	.541	L	645	.348	.411	.617	SP	820	.346	.433	.588	GB	721	.295	.352	.440
Bats Right	2856	.334	.398	.576	R	1462	.351	.416	.610	R	2211	.330	.394	.564	LC	481	.291	.378	.502	FB	465	.362	.430	.672
Phil Plantier (1990-1997)					H	1075	.239	.325	.418	L	449	.193	.281	.361	SP	652	.236	.347	.435	GB	613	.264	.340	.467
Bats Left	2166	.243	.332	.439	R	1091	.246	.339	.460	R	1717	.256	.345	.459	LC	401	.211	.309	.379	FB	380	.250	.335	.497
Luis Polonia (1987-1996)					H	2266	.286	.341	.364	L	808	.248	.294	.303	SP	1038	.311	.360	.392	GB	1267	.276	.326	.348
Bats Left	4558	.292	.342	.370	R	2292	.297	.344	.375	R	3750	.301	.353	.384	LC	606	.281	.329	.343	FB	1075	.303	.351	.389

2534 Situational Statistics: Hitting

	Total					Home/Road					vs. Left/Right					Scoring Position/Late & Close					vs. Groundball/Flyball Pitcher			
Batter	PA	Avg	OBP	Slg		PA	Avg	OBP	Slg		PA	Avg	OBP	Slg		PA	Avg	OBP	Slg		PA	Avg	OBP	Slg
Darrell Porter (1984-1987)					H	517	.249	.360	.429	L	167	.246	.335	.437	SP	345	.239	.383	.422	GB	469	.213	.318	.345
Bats Left	1118	.235	.344	.412	R	601	.224	.331	.398	R	951	.234	.346	.407	LC	172	.215	.314	.356	FB	601	.256	.366	.462
Jim Presley (1984-1991)					H	1974	.260	.303	.441	L	1157	.277	.322	.444	SP	1042	.253	.318	.417	GB	1370	.253	.301	.401
Bats Right	3818	.247	.290	.420	R	1841	.232	.276	.397	R	2658	.234	.276	.409	LC	508	.212	.261	.374	FB	1441	.252	.293	.460
Kirby Puckett (1984-1995)					H	4007	.344	.388	.521	L	2065	.336	.380	.525	SP	2140	.322	.383	.496	GB	2523	.313	.358	.449
Bats Right	7831	.318	.360	.477	R	3813	.291	.331	.430	R	5755	.312	.353	.459	LC	1043	.314	.366	.454	FB	2377	.312	.352	.481
Terry Puhl (1984-1991)					H	918	.282	.360	.379	L	358	.263	.323	.331	SP	457	.282	.372	.396	GB	771	.281	.358	.387
Bats Left	1814	.280	.356	.387	R	882	.277	.353	.396	R	1442	.284	.365	.401	LC	341	.306	.418	.381	FB	700	.288	.355	.401
Luis Quinones (1986-1992)					H	469	.240	.297	.360	L	368	.219	.282	.380	SP	279	.266	.331	.392	GB	378	.212	.269	.293
Bats Both	1068	.228	.285	.343	R	595	.218	.276	.330	R	696	.233	.287	.324	LC	219	.225	.263	.335	FB	304	.174	.236	.279
Rey Quinones (1986-1989)					H	802	.256	.306	.390	L	501	.253	.299	.406	SP	427	.278	.324	.382	GB	545	.251	.286	.354
Bats Right	1668	.243	.287	.357	R	861	.232	.269	.326	R	1162	.239	.282	.336	LC	195	.149	.229	.247	FB	592	.246	.301	.373
Carlos Quintana (1988-1993)					H	742	.284	.361	.347	L	542	.319	.394	.417	SP	430	.269	.352	.356	GB	411	.263	.334	.326
Bats Right	1557	.276	.350	.362	R	815	.269	.339	.375	R	1015	.254	.326	.333	LC	236	.322	.374	.384	FB	367	.276	.352	.408
Jamie Quirk (1984-1992)					H	770	.237	.312	.350	L	138	.298	.341	.347	SP	390	.258	.347	.358	GB	552	.262	.325	.362
Bats Left	1536	.237	.308	.348	R	766	.238	.304	.345	R	1398	.231	.305	.348	LC	228	.253	.338	.340	FB	428	.187	.265	.321
Tim Raines (1984-1997)					H	3769	.302	.394	.442	L	2232	.295	.377	.413	SP	1875	.307	.445	.430	GB	2779	.301	.385	.436
Bats Both	7749	.298	.388	.436	R	3973	.295	.384	.431	R	5510	.300	.393	.446	LC	1278	.305	.406	.418	FB	2326	.308	.406	.445
Manny Ramirez (1993-1997)					H	1117	.294	.389	.541	L	649	.347	.435	.594	SP	653	.288	.391	.494	GB	430	.295	.377	.546
Bats Right	2260	.304	.393	.546	R	1143	.314	.398	.552	R	1611	.288	.377	.527	LC	316	.273	.417	.514	FB	408	.284	.381	.556
Rafael Ramirez (1984-1992)					H	1923	.256	.296	.333	L	1419	.264	.298	.347	SP	1022	.250	.297	.326	GB	1632	.264	.291	.338
Bats Right	4034	.255	.286	.334	R	2097	.254	.278	.334	R	2601	.250	.280	.327	LC	765	.254	.297	.326	FB	1450	.245	.281	.333
Domingo Ramos (1984-1990)					H	515	.239	.293	.299	L	394	.249	.331	.292	SP	240	.214	.293	.267	GB	426	.242	.289	.285
Bats Right	1026	.239	.302	.293	R	505	.239	.311	.288	R	626	.233	.284	.294	LC	173	.145	.210	.158	FB	363	.227	.306	.280
Willie Randolph (1984-1992)					H	2376	.281	.383	.352	L	1617	.310	.407	.398	SP	1190	.268	.393	.343	GB	1881	.277	.375	.330
Bats Right	4806	.279	.376	.347	R	2410	.277	.370	.341	R	3169	.264	.361	.320	LC	702	.269	.361	.333	FB	1656	.283	.381	.370
Johnny Ray (1984-1990)					H	2077	.281	.332	.381	L	1367	.272	.316	.343	SP	1166	.293	.343	.401	GB	1482	.320	.362	.420
Bats Both	4229	.293	.338	.392	R	2138	.305	.344	.402	R	2848	.303	.348	.415	LC	657	.251	.307	.346	FB	1649	.285	.339	.396
Randy Ready (1984-1995)					H	1210	.255	.362	.377	L	1283	.270	.374	.415	SP	657	.264	.374	.353	GB	916	.263	.355	.380
Bats Right	2445	.257	.356	.382	R	1229	.258	.351	.386	R	1156	.242	.337	.345	LC	417	.241	.359	.325	FB	672	.233	.339	.348
Jeff Reboulet (1992-1997)					H	670	.252	.334	.327	L	531	.255	.338	.357	SP	373	.277	.380	.380	GB	301	.269	.354	.304
Bats Right	1438	.246	.330	.325	R	768	.241	.326	.323	R	907	.241	.325	.306	LC	206	.287	.366	.368	FB	258	.210	.307	.269
Gary Redus (1984-1994)					H	1773	.266	.357	.422	L	1746	.264	.358	.424	SP	749	.240	.334	.410	GB	1283	.265	.340	.416
Bats Right	3446	.254	.342	.407	R	1666	.241	.326	.391	R	1693	.244	.326	.390	LC	544	.254	.346	.385	FB	1226	.239	.340	.396
Jeff Reed (1984-1997)					H	1328	.255	.333	.385	L	299	.215	.302	.331	SP	691	.233	.358	.326	GB	893	.262	.332	.355
Bats Left	2680	.248	.324	.354	R	1348	.241	.315	.324	R	2377	.252	.326	.357	LC	417	.222	.308	.315	FB	600	.226	.296	.337
Jody Reed (1987-1997)					H	2652	.276	.359	.365	L	1421	.275	.364	.349	SP	1334	.275	.394	.343	GB	1368	.273	.350	.348
Bats Right	5248	.270	.349	.350	R	2596	.264	.340	.336	R	3827	.268	.344	.351	LC	877	.259	.344	.313	FB	1083	.274	.356	.367
Kevin Reimer (1988-1993)					H	772	.264	.332	.471	L	271	.222	.303	.314	SP	451	.235	.322	.389	GB	405	.307	.358	.476
Bats Left	1606	.258	.320	.430	R	834	.254	.309	.392	R	1335	.266	.324	.452	LC	286	.283	.357	.442	FB	388	.221	.279	.430
Edgar Renteria (1996-1997)					H	563	.281	.348	.364	L	224	.253	.320	.343	SP	257	.294	.345	.357	GB	202	.328	.364	.387
Bats Right	1162	.290	.340	.365	R	599	.298	.333	.365	R	938	.299	.345	.369	LC	182	.282	.365	.365	FB	190	.276	.302	.337
Craig Reynolds (1984-1989)					H	1029	.254	.295	.330	L	326	.220	.252	.275	SP	519	.244	.298	.344	GB	868	.263	.293	.375
Bats Left	2095	.253	.288	.349	R	1046	.252	.281	.368	R	1749	.259	.295	.364	LC	320	.246	.297	.341	FB	924	.248	.282	.338
Harold Reynolds (1984-1994)					H	2677	.260	.333	.353	L	1462	.266	.320	.338	SP	1167	.278	.344	.373	GB	1518	.262	.328	.346
Bats Both	5335	.259	.328	.342	R	2647	.257	.324	.330	R	3862	.256	.331	.343	LC	730	.275	.344	.351	FB	1428	.239	.317	.317
R.J. Reynolds (1984-1990)					H	1238	.270	.330	.403	L	716	.284	.333	.364	SP	708	.264	.331	.362	GB	903	.294	.347	.418
Bats Both	2451	.267	.323	.382	R	1196	.264	.315	.361	R	1718	.260	.318	.390	LC	474	.273	.328	.363	FB	976	.256	.308	.370
Jim Rice (1984-1989)					H	1597	.307	.364	.487	L	915	.300	.373	.485	SP	1049	.307	.378	.479	GB	1259	.292	.346	.427
Bats Right	3238	.285	.344	.449	R	1641	.263	.324	.411	R	2323	.279	.332	.435	LC	415	.244	.311	.399	FB	1450	.287	.350	.476
Ernest Riles (1985-1993)					H	1357	.275	.348	.403	L	481	.211	.278	.297	SP	753	.250	.330	.371	GB	1108	.261	.328	.353
Bats Left	2811	.254	.319	.365	R	1442	.236	.293	.330	R	2318	.263	.328	.379	LC	447	.253	.329	.384	FB	956	.256	.320	.378
Billy Ripken (1987-1997)					H	1441	.257	.306	.326	L	1058	.272	.315	.340	SP	711	.261	.300	.312	GB	750	.221	.271	.274
Bats Right	2934	.246	.294	.318	R	1493	.236	.282	.310	R	1876	.232	.281	.305	LC	330	.271	.328	.330	FB	652	.279	.323	.372
Cal Ripken Jr. (1984-1997)					H	4674	.263	.338	.432	L	2773	.285	.358	.472	SP	2598	.283	.380	.461	GB	2912	.274	.344	.409
Bats Right	9594	.274	.344	.445	R	4920	.285	.350	.457	R	6821	.270	.339	.434	LC	1319	.284	.360	.456	FB	2739	.262	.332	.451
Luis Rivera (1986-1997)					H	1171	.237	.292	.346	L	788	.236	.286	.352	SP	662	.213	.281	.302	GB	701	.250	.297	.359
Bats Right	2355	.232	.290	.335	R	1183	.228	.289	.324	R	1566	.230	.292	.326	LC	382	.209	.262	.295	FB	586	.197	.253	.285
Bip Roberts (1986-1997)					H	2107	.295	.354	.387	L	1440	.276	.328	.365	SP	920	.304	.361	.422	GB	1443	.302	.360	.386
Bats Both	4298	.296	.359	.383	R	2189	.297	.363	.380	R	2856	.307	.374	.392	LC	711	.286	.369	.351	FB	838	.298	.364	.410
Alex Rodriguez (1994-1997)					H	723	.332	.383	.584	L	408	.314	.373	.568	SP	390	.310	.362	.526	GB	365	.348	.409	.523
Bats Right	1523	.314	.366	.534	R	800	.298	.351	.488	R	1115	.315	.364	.522	LC	223	.310	.374	.523	FB	214	.279	.319	.478
Henry Rodriguez (1992-1997)					H	996	.262	.314	.486	L	341	.229	.290	.419	SP	539	.276	.336	.521	GB	508	.234	.283	.419
Bats Left	1923	.253	.303	.461	R	927	.244	.291	.433	R	1582	.258	.306	.469	LC	341	.230	.301	.401	FB	291	.264	.311	.468
Ivan Rodriguez (1991-1997)					H	1751	.293	.331	.451	L	929	.296	.342	.460	SP	925	.280	.343	.394	GB	783	.265	.300	.384
Bats Right	3516	.290	.330	.439	R	1765	.288	.330	.428	R	2587	.289	.326	.432	LC	558	.302	.360	.386	FB	718	.254	.304	.411
Gary Roenicke (1984-1988)					H	552	.250	.370	.467	L	767	.235	.356	.422	SP	314	.243	.357	.455	GB	481	.231	.339	.406
Bats Right	1141	.228	.345	.398	R	584	.207	.322	.333	R	369	.213	.322	.349	LC	156	.185	.353	.258	FB	561	.222	.349	.387
Ed Romero (1984-1990)					H	724	.242	.295	.296	L	557	.224	.290	.283	SP	398	.255	.301	.295	GB	610	.248	.300	.305
Bats Right	1555	.242	.295	.289	R	813	.241	.295	.283	R	980	.251	.298	.293	LC	201	.269	.337	.326	FB	655	.228	.294	.277

Situational Statistics: Hitting 2535

Batter	Total PA	Total Avg	Total OBP	Total Slg	Home/Road	PA	Avg	OBP	Slg	vs. Left/Right	PA	Avg	OBP	Slg	Scoring Position/Late & Close	PA	Avg	OBP	Slg	vs. Groundball/Flyball Pitcher	PA	Avg	OBP	Slg
Pete Rose (1984-1986)					H	585	.260	.368	.310	L	184	.261	.353	.311	SP	332	.300	.449	.383	GB	562	.244	.351	.285
Bats Both	1194	.262	.364	.314	R	604	.264	.361	.317	R	1005	.262	.366	.315	LC	198	.308	.409	.367	FB	627	.278	.376	.340
Jerry Royster (1984-1988)					H	568	.249	.321	.370	L	719	.264	.335	.394	SP	271	.287	.371	.359	GB	572	.260	.325	.365
Bats Right	1168	.245	.316	.358	R	589	.242	.312	.347	R	438	.215	.286	.299	LC	187	.199	.297	.286	FB	481	.233	.321	.348
John Russell (1984-1993)					H	599	.251	.306	.419	L	563	.223	.290	.348	SP	306	.234	.302	.377	GB	502	.263	.317	.434
Bats Right	1189	.225	.282	.371	R	589	.200	.258	.322	R	625	.227	.276	.391	LC	214	.219	.257	.323	FB	471	.210	.274	.375
Chris Sabo (1988-1996)					H	1850	.276	.337	.474	L	1227	.298	.370	.499	SP	997	.261	.345	.439	GB	1292	.294	.347	.471
Bats Right	3714	.268	.326	.445	R	1864	.260	.316	.418	R	2487	.253	.305	.420	LC	579	.250	.316	.415	FB	736	.235	.304	.395
Mark Salas (1984-1991)					H	728	.254	.305	.427	L	121	.241	.308	.324	SP	362	.226	.293	.414	GB	536	.269	.307	.403
Bats Left	1410	.247	.300	.389	R	676	.239	.293	.347	R	1283	.247	.299	.394	LC	220	.216	.283	.322	FB	522	.234	.292	.382
Luis Salazar (1984-1992)					H	1312	.259	.293	.394	L	1292	.274	.303	.436	SP	706	.255	.305	.383	GB	936	.255	.292	.366
Bats Right	2699	.254	.287	.380	R	1376	.248	.281	.367	R	1396	.234	.271	.328	LC	462	.291	.336	.406	FB	864	.247	.278	.381
Tim Salmon (1992-1997)					H	1570	.283	.383	.530	L	826	.278	.413	.526	SP	931	.301	.430	.538	GB	620	.321	.402	.528
Bats Right	3151	.293	.392	.527	R	1581	.303	.402	.524	R	2325	.298	.385	.528	LC	486	.290	.393	.494	FB	648	.260	.378	.519
Juan Samuel (1984-1997)					H	3180	.263	.326	.437	L	2327	.262	.320	.430	SP	1657	.269	.338	.447	GB	2359	.259	.314	.401
Bats Right	6534	.260	.315	.421	R	3351	.257	.305	.405	R	4204	.259	.313	.415	LC	961	.258	.318	.394	FB	2098	.257	.307	.437
Rey Sanchez (1991-1997)					H	1003	.265	.300	.324	L	575	.270	.307	.338	SP	496	.258	.333	.341	GB	642	.235	.273	.285
Bats Right	2145	.266	.306	.330	R	1142	.266	.311	.335	R	1570	.264	.305	.327	LC	378	.284	.325	.329	FB	345	.272	.319	.351
Ryne Sandberg (1984-1997)					H	3990	.299	.361	.502	L	2208	.302	.376	.485	SP	1932	.289	.372	.453	GB	2914	.301	.361	.469
Bats Right	7890	.288	.349	.468	R	3890	.277	.337	.433	R	5672	.283	.339	.461	LC	1210	.275	.344	.424	FB	2355	.284	.341	.462
Deion Sanders (1989-1997)					H	1091	.274	.332	.396	L	493	.236	.292	.334	SP	480	.270	.349	.382	GB	674	.282	.334	.417
Bats Left	2242	.266	.322	.398	R	1151	.259	.313	.400	R	1749	.275	.331	.416	LC	356	.255	.334	.384	FB	392	.285	.344	.470
Reggie Sanders (1991-1997)					H	1369	.270	.360	.484	L	739	.313	.392	.564	SP	838	.265	.384	.460	GB	848	.300	.381	.509
Bats Right	2747	.271	.354	.488	R	1378	.273	.348	.491	R	2008	.256	.340	.460	LC	426	.257	.344	.449	FB	433	.244	.333	.450
Rafael Santana (1984-1990)					H	1049	.230	.279	.287	L	787	.260	.316	.327	SP	546	.220	.297	.297	GB	807	.256	.297	.327
Bats Right	2166	.246	.294	.307	R	1111	.262	.308	.326	R	1373	.239	.282	.296	LC	262	.253	.296	.273	FB	936	.249	.301	.306
F.P. Santangelo (1995-1997)					H	518	.305	.416	.483	L	231	.278	.388	.380	SP	253	.255	.371	.398	GB	244	.262	.375	.366
Bats Both	1020	.268	.375	.392	R	502	.231	.333	.304	R	789	.265	.371	.396	LC	180	.226	.335	.295	FB	156	.187	.284	.261
Benito Santiago (1986-1997)					H	2605	.266	.307	.417	L	1476	.295	.341	.479	SP	1440	.249	.305	.421	GB	1710	.260	.301	.406
Bats Right	5145	.261	.304	.418	R	2540	.256	.301	.419	R	3669	.247	.290	.393	LC	823	.248	.294	.394	FB	1124	.263	.302	.452
Mackey Sasser (1987-1995)					H	651	.264	.299	.383	L	156	.199	.227	.274	SP	376	.276	.326	.427	GB	385	.306	.328	.418
Bats Left	1267	.267	.296	.377	R	616	.270	.294	.370	R	1111	.276	.306	.391	LC	276	.217	.254	.315	FB	286	.253	.269	.374
Steve Sax (1984-1994)					H	3000	.274	.330	.349	L	1999	.292	.349	.385	SP	1374	.283	.353	.366	GB	2115	.269	.326	.334
Bats Right	6114	.281	.334	.359	R	3103	.287	.338	.368	R	4104	.275	.327	.346	LC	860	.302	.354	.377	FB	2028	.290	.347	.379
Mike Schmidt (1984-1989)					H	1515	.293	.395	.533	L	876	.306	.418	.539	SP	1037	.288	.412	.523	GB	1307	.290	.382	.534
Bats Right	3170	.274	.373	.512	R	1655	.258	.352	.493	R	2294	.263	.355	.502	LC	433	.267	.381	.479	FB	1370	.270	.378	.522
Dick Schofield (1984-1996)					H	2391	.225	.302	.303	L	1620	.240	.326	.334	SP	1160	.231	.331	.331	GB	1583	.248	.316	.329
Bats Right	4866	.230	.308	.315	R	2441	.236	.313	.326	R	3212	.226	.299	.305	LC	674	.219	.301	.287	FB	1597	.205	.282	.301
Bill Schroeder (1984-1990)					H	623	.240	.282	.381	L	512	.259	.292	.472	SP	319	.211	.263	.450	GB	525	.246	.290	.422
Bats Right	1277	.244	.285	.430	R	646	.248	.288	.477	R	757	.234	.280	.400	LC	159	.207	.259	.324	FB	473	.239	.279	.464
Rick Schu (1984-1996)					H	822	.243	.309	.385	L	771	.266	.319	.450	SP	405	.186	.279	.271	GB	640	.273	.330	.442
Bats Right	1729	.246	.310	.384	R	903	.249	.310	.383	R	954	.229	.303	.329	LC	262	.199	.272	.246	FB	599	.206	.281	.323
Mike Scioscia (1984-1992)					H	1967	.267	.354	.345	L	971	.232	.310	.311	SP	1035	.255	.370	.327	GB	1571	.279	.364	.366
Bats Left	4111	.261	.348	.364	R	2125	.256	.342	.382	R	3121	.270	.360	.381	LC	651	.249	.353	.324	FB	1388	.251	.353	.377
David Segui (1990-1997)					H	1490	.285	.355	.431	L	899	.281	.348	.422	SP	818	.281	.374	.401	GB	728	.280	.338	.393
Bats Both	2980	.279	.350	.419	R	1490	.274	.344	.407	R	2081	.279	.350	.418	LC	521	.238	.320	.349	FB	499	.272	.336	.441
Kevin Seitzer (1986-1997)					H	3009	.300	.385	.415	L	1787	.299	.388	.424	SP	1591	.302	.413	.418	GB	1593	.296	.367	.389
Bats Right	6062	.295	.375	.404	R	3053	.290	.366	.394	R	4275	.294	.370	.396	LC	806	.290	.365	.387	FB	1446	.298	.376	.419
Scott Servais (1991-1997)					H	1035	.242	.297	.380	L	700	.271	.335	.430	SP	573	.245	.321	.358	GB	543	.261	.328	.401
Bats Right	2063	.247	.307	.384	R	1028	.252	.317	.388	R	1363	.234	.293	.361	LC	361	.254	.313	.390	FB	350	.263	.314	.448
Mike Sharperson (1987-1995)					H	666	.292	.360	.369	L	820	.303	.370	.398	SP	390	.254	.354	.308	GB	431	.323	.400	.390
Bats Right	1383	.280	.355	.364	R	717	.269	.350	.359	R	563	.246	.333	.314	LC	273	.255	.335	.364	FB	354	.232	.297	.286
Danny Sheaffer (1987-1997)					H	495	.244	.300	.349	L	336	.235	.297	.321	SP	300	.255	.336	.343	GB	253	.215	.259	.291
Bats Right	1032	.232	.278	.323	R	537	.220	.259	.301	R	696	.230	.270	.325	LC	168	.293	.346	.408	FB	180	.244	.281	.363
Larry Sheets (1984-1993)					H	1243	.263	.317	.441	L	398	.232	.302	.355	SP	615	.277	.335	.462	GB	885	.261	.313	.407
Bats Left	2502	.266	.321	.437	R	1256	.269	.324	.432	R	2101	.272	.324	.452	LC	303	.255	.330	.395	FB	829	.288	.339	.499
Gary Sheffield (1988-1997)					H	2148	.300	.408	.521	L	1140	.299	.393	.509	SP	1182	.293	.422	.527	GB	1197	.282	.374	.481
Bats Right	4336	.286	.386	.495	R	2188	.274	.364	.469	R	3196	.282	.383	.490	LC	672	.311	.429	.490	FB	806	.277	.366	.470
John Shelby (1984-1991)					H	1425	.228	.267	.339	L	1068	.231	.268	.367	SP	695	.245	.299	.359	GB	1117	.230	.277	.357
Bats Both	2940	.236	.279	.363	R	1499	.243	.290	.386	R	1856	.239	.285	.361	LC	439	.213	.259	.328	FB	1024	.238	.276	.374
Pat Sheridan (1984-1991)					H	1104	.253	.322	.385	L	260	.198	.251	.283	SP	616	.253	.337	.368	GB	885	.244	.308	.336
Bats Left	2344	.250	.320	.369	R	1229	.247	.319	.355	R	2073	.256	.329	.380	LC	288	.267	.331	.372	FB	906	.271	.347	.414
Craig Shipley (1986-1997)					H	602	.255	.285	.350	L	514	.285	.313	.373	SP	319	.269	.311	.381	GB	394	.253	.281	.323
Bats Right	1271	.272	.302	.372	R	668	.287	.317	.392	R	756	.264	.294	.372	LC	262	.291	.320	.402	FB	211	.282	.294	.388
Ruben Sierra (1986-1997)					H	3370	.268	.316	.462	L	2205	.296	.337	.482	SP	2040	.282	.338	.482	GB	1842	.282	.321	.446
Bats Both	6932	.269	.318	.451	R	3561	.271	.320	.441	R	4726	.257	.309	.437	LC	990	.261	.330	.425	FB	1818	.273	.325	.469
Ted Simmons (1984-1988)					H	759	.238	.294	.337	L	581	.251	.306	.402	SP	499	.279	.359	.432	GB	719	.240	.307	.333
Bats Both	1591	.248	.312	.357	R	830	.257	.329	.375	R	1008	.246	.315	.330	LC	319	.201	.273	.324	FB	756	.258	.321	.380
Joel Skinner (1984-1991)					H	738	.217	.260	.285	L	511	.233	.280	.294	SP	343	.234	.290	.343	GB	484	.226	.275	.296
Bats Right	1540	.228	.269	.311	R	799	.238	.278	.335	R	1026	.225	.264	.320	LC	177	.245	.293	.344	FB	562	.222	.263	.322

Batter	Total PA	Total Avg	Total OBP	Total Slg		Home/Road PA	Avg	OBP	Slg		vs. Left/Right PA	Avg	OBP	Slg		Scoring Position/Late & Close PA	Avg	OBP	Slg		vs. Groundball/Flyball Pitcher PA	Avg	OBP	Slg
Don Slaught (1984-1997)					H	2059	.292	.347	.428	L	1657	.300	.358	.448	SP	1102	.272	.340	.353	GB	1394	.288	.343	.415
Bats Right	4087	.281	.338	.414	R	2015	.271	.329	.399	R	2417	.268	.324	.390	LC	699	.295	.354	.416	FB	1261	.269	.324	.417
Roy Smalley (1984-1987)					H	842	.251	.342	.424	L	270	.181	.274	.295	SP	424	.233	.366	.330	GB	774	.267	.349	.425
Bats Both	1715	.247	.335	.403	R	870	.243	.329	.382	R	1442	.260	.347	.423	LC	241	.182	.282	.273	FB	820	.225	.322	.390
Dwight Smith (1989-1996)					H	970	.285	.349	.439	L	144	.218	.303	.347	SP	505	.281	.344	.399	GB	712	.297	.343	.439
Bats Left	1988	.275	.333	.422	R	1018	.266	.318	.407	R	1844	.279	.336	.428	LC	408	.245	.305	.359	FB	417	.252	.325	.389
Lonnie Smith (1984-1994)					H	2044	.287	.379	.428	L	1543	.293	.381	.444	SP	976	.266	.380	.372	GB	1693	.292	.374	.427
Bats Right	4161	.275	.366	.411	R	2112	.264	.354	.394	R	2613	.265	.358	.391	LC	664	.242	.365	.358	FB	1458	.242	.344	.373
Ozzie Smith (1984-1996)					H	3543	.287	.368	.362	L	2469	.275	.356	.369	SP	1882	.270	.369	.336	GB	2610	.282	.353	.345
Bats Both	7049	.276	.354	.347	R	3475	.265	.339	.332	R	4549	.276	.353	.336	LC	1107	.267	.352	.345	FB	2015	.264	.352	.343
J.T. Snow (1992-1997)					H	1338	.277	.360	.457	L	751	.219	.299	.318	SP	754	.266	.374	.471	GB	542	.317	.379	.488
Bats Both	2640	.263	.344	.432	R	1302	.248	.328	.406	R	1889	.280	.362	.477	LC	415	.241	.354	.344	FB	477	.244	.333	.396
Cory Snyder (1986-1994)					H	1903	.242	.291	.407	L	1336	.258	.307	.448	SP	1049	.237	.297	.378	GB	1253	.260	.298	.417
Bats Right	3933	.247	.291	.425	R	2029	.251	.291	.441	R	2596	.241	.282	.413	LC	601	.223	.271	.374	FB	1077	.232	.277	.423
Luis Sojo (1990-1997)					H	1010	.247	.291	.334	L	647	.264	.313	.368	SP	538	.276	.311	.388	GB	505	.267	.296	.363
Bats Right	2076	.265	.302	.356	R	1066	.281	.313	.377	R	1429	.265	.297	.351	LC	315	.262	.315	.355	FB	421	.269	.297	.386
Paul Sorrento (1989-1997)					H	1507	.286	.370	.515	L	406	.212	.289	.374	SP	880	.252	.358	.440	GB	718	.278	.353	.441
Bats Left	3047	.264	.344	.472	R	1540	.243	.318	.431	R	2641	.272	.352	.487	LC	506	.266	.340	.465	FB	606	.240	.320	.441
Sammy Sosa (1989-1997)					H	2169	.266	.322	.511	L	1306	.274	.337	.506	SP	1223	.258	.322	.478	GB	1240	.281	.335	.502
Bats Right	4374	.257	.308	.469	R	2205	.249	.295	.427	R	3068	.251	.296	.453	LC	743	.237	.293	.406	FB	819	.242	.289	.424
Chris Speier (1984-1989)					H	612	.235	.317	.368	L	404	.250	.334	.392	SP	308	.250	.337	.402	GB	475	.237	.305	.366
Bats Right	1234	.235	.310	.361	R	575	.237	.305	.363	R	783	.229	.299	.352	LC	219	.264	.366	.401	FB	503	.235	.319	.345
Bill Spiers (1989-1997)					H	1228	.290	.352	.383	L	491	.221	.295	.290	SP	684	.296	.358	.416	GB	654	.261	.326	.360
Bats Left	2551	.262	.326	.359	R	1323	.237	.303	.337	R	2060	.272	.334	.375	LC	505	.272	.336	.393	FB	468	.251	.317	.376
Ed Sprague (1991-1997)					H	1542	.246	.317	.417	L	895	.266	.335	.454	SP	865	.220	.306	.363	GB	658	.282	.338	.426
Bats Right	3108	.246	.317	.411	R	1566	.245	.318	.405	R	2213	.238	.310	.394	LC	464	.232	.322	.374	FB	524	.231	.301	.393
Scott Stahoviak (1993-1997)					H	581	.273	.349	.424	L	71	.237	.357	.339	SP	320	.251	.350	.416	GB	291	.240	.338	.368
Bats Left	1134	.259	.339	.413	R	553	.244	.328	.401	R	1063	.260	.338	.418	LC	155	.226	.331	.338	FB	188	.228	.309	.371
Mike Stanley (1986-1997)					H	1778	.293	.390	.483	L	1579	.284	.390	.483	SP	1000	.288	.399	.480	GB	835	.274	.356	.421
Bats Right	3553	.273	.370	.456	R	1776	.253	.350	.428	R	1975	.264	.354	.434	LC	510	.274	.381	.391	FB	802	.249	.355	.452
Terry Steinbach (1986-1997)					H	2430	.274	.328	.417	L	1528	.298	.355	.475	SP	1338	.277	.341	.448	GB	1388	.269	.314	.399
Bats Right	5060	.272	.325	.423	R	2630	.270	.323	.429	R	3532	.261	.313	.400	LC	735	.233	.295	.339	FB	1133	.269	.318	.437
Lee Stevens (1990-1997)					H	636	.267	.308	.434	L	225	.221	.283	.333	SP	320	.277	.339	.475	GB	288	.255	.307	.384
Bats Left	1226	.254	.306	.420	R	590	.240	.304	.404	R	1001	.261	.312	.439	LC	189	.250	.317	.417	FB	283	.277	.343	.486
Kurt Stillwell (1986-1996)					H	1704	.246	.309	.350	L	917	.237	.309	.319	SP	887	.267	.338	.376	GB	1106	.260	.321	.350
Bats Both	3478	.249	.311	.349	R	1770	.253	.313	.349	R	2557	.254	.312	.360	LC	555	.213	.294	.261	FB	907	.223	.286	.320
Kevin Stocker (1993-1997)					H	1057	.269	.360	.366	L	494	.288	.361	.370	SP	589	.226	.370	.319	GB	538	.242	.343	.339
Bats Both	2121	.262	.347	.350	R	1064	.256	.333	.335	R	1627	.254	.342	.344	LC	386	.289	.378	.379	FB	339	.243	.313	.320
Jeff Stone (1984-1990)					H	497	.295	.343	.406	L	152	.285	.355	.394	SP	212	.236	.280	.349	GB	378	.280	.318	.367
Bats Left	1018	.275	.325	.369	R	516	.256	.309	.334	R	861	.274	.320	.365	LC	147	.243	.295	.338	FB	524	.285	.338	.386
Doug Strange (1989-1997)					H	966	.253	.324	.370	L	372	.217	.264	.258	SP	519	.258	.343	.396	GB	429	.239	.319	.357
Bats Both	1868	.240	.304	.351	R	901	.227	.283	.332	R	1495	.246	.314	.375	LC	393	.254	.315	.382	FB	349	.252	.303	.374
Darryl Strawberry (1984-1997)					H	2570	.267	.360	.528	L	1999	.238	.317	.444	SP	1632	.264	.396	.499	GB	2033	.265	.362	.489
Bats Left	5442	.259	.357	.501	R	2870	.251	.354	.478	R	3441	.272	.380	.537	LC	808	.220	.337	.391	FB	1679	.253	.349	.539
Franklin Stubbs (1984-1995)					H	1429	.225	.298	.379	L	609	.227	.256	.358	SP	810	.223	.333	.416	GB	988	.254	.304	.447
Bats Left	2899	.232	.303	.404	R	1463	.240	.307	.428	R	2283	.234	.315	.417	LC	482	.238	.324	.401	FB	867	.203	.281	.356
Jim Sundberg (1984-1989)					H	863	.211	.285	.316	L	592	.245	.328	.426	SP	445	.253	.339	.384	GB	699	.227	.294	.320
Bats Right	1797	.234	.313	.359	R	922	.255	.339	.400	R	1193	.228	.305	.326	LC	278	.280	.333	.400	FB	870	.239	.323	.388
B.J. Surhoff (1987-1997)					H	2696	.280	.338	.413	L	1431	.288	.337	.405	SP	1509	.307	.364	.453	GB	1413	.291	.340	.412
Bats Left	5489	.277	.328	.400	R	2793	.274	.319	.387	R	4058	.273	.325	.398	LC	851	.247	.310	.338	FB	1164	.276	.332	.390
Dale Sveum (1986-1997)					H	1315	.231	.297	.353	L	859	.246	.315	.402	SP	742	.257	.316	.426	GB	750	.270	.334	.411
Bats Both	2666	.239	.301	.382	R	1346	.247	.305	.409	R	1802	.236	.294	.372	LC	405	.268	.323	.367	FB	792	.239	.298	.388
Pat Tabler (1984-1992)					H	1787	.303	.364	.412	L	1403	.308	.370	.413	SP	1099	.313	.385	.429	GB	1332	.274	.333	.351
Bats Right	3661	.284	.345	.379	R	1868	.266	.327	.347	R	2252	.270	.329	.358	LC	489	.257	.331	.360	FB	1376	.284	.342	.398
Danny Tartabull (1984-1997)					H	2768	.270	.363	.483	L	1808	.285	.413	.515	SP	1750	.277	.392	.500	GB	1638	.281	.361	.455
Bats Right	5842	.273	.368	.496	R	3072	.275	.373	.508	R	4032	.267	.348	.488	LC	828	.269	.366	.466	FB	1627	.266	.369	.532
Eddie Taubensee (1991-1997)					H	889	.261	.325	.423	L	251	.245	.304	.406	SP	525	.257	.349	.386	GB	590	.252	.304	.388
Bats Left	1807	.264	.321	.422	R	918	.267	.318	.421	R	1556	.267	.324	.425	LC	325	.232	.307	.363	FB	306	.295	.348	.516
Garry Templeton (1984-1991)					H	2027	.245	.292	.348	L	1275	.264	.305	.349	SP	1025	.249	.351	.353	GB	1680	.259	.307	.346
Bats Both	4003	.249	.293	.336	R	1970	.254	.294	.323	R	2722	.242	.287	.330	LC	694	.256	.306	.332	FB	1413	.237	.282	.325
Mickey Tettleton (1984-1997)					H	2883	.255	.385	.487	L	1714	.241	.352	.458	SP	1601	.226	.403	.428	GB	1584	.266	.381	.478
Bats Both	5745	.241	.369	.449	R	2849	.227	.352	.411	R	4018	.241	.376	.445	LC	818	.257	.366	.462	FB	1490	.216	.342	.435
Tim Teufel (1984-1993)					H	1665	.251	.333	.396	L	1671	.265	.354	.427	SP	932	.242	.344	.386	GB	1433	.245	.331	.374
Bats Right	3481	.252	.336	.400	R	1803	.253	.339	.404	R	1797	.240	.320	.375	LC	576	.231	.331	.349	FB	1236	.274	.356	.440
Andres Thomas (1985-1990)					H	1056	.232	.256	.317	L	739	.234	.258	.352	SP	577	.256	.287	.331	GB	824	.257	.276	.346
Bats Right	2185	.234	.255	.334	R	1126	.237	.254	.350	R	1443	.235	.253	.325	LC	347	.246	.269	.339	FB	660	.209	.235	.294
Frank Thomas (1990-1997)					H	2313	.332	.460	.613	L	1248	.370	.487	.725	SP	1445	.337	.476	.580	GB	1257	.342	.466	.577
Bats Right	4790	.330	.452	.600	R	2477	.328	.445	.589	R	3542	.316	.440	.557	LC	770	.296	.440	.515	FB	1011	.312	.427	.596
Gorman Thomas (1984-1986)					H	520	.187	.313	.379	L	343	.185	.338	.409	SP	347	.163	.323	.330	GB	497	.190	.314	.361
Bats Right	1094	.198	.324	.395	R	569	.209	.334	.409	R	746	.204	.318	.388	LC	180	.137	.256	.261	FB	592	.205	.333	.423

Situational Statistics: Hitting 2537

	Total					Home/Road					vs. Left/Right					Scoring Position/Late & Close					vs. Groundball/Flyball Pitcher			
Batter	**PA**	**Avg**	**OBP**	**Slg**		**PA**	**Avg**	**OBP**	**Slg**		**PA**	**Avg**	**OBP**	**Slg**		**PA**	**Avg**	**OBP**	**Slg**		**PA**	**Avg**	**OBP**	**Slg**
Jim Thome (1991-1997)					H	1327	.283	.409	.534	L	655	.244	.341	.396	SP	736	.267	.402	.498	GB	536	.271	.379	.512
Bats Left	2616	.288	.408	.541	R	1289	.293	.408	.549	R	1961	.303	.431	.593	LC	401	.266	.378	.515	FB	493	.259	.379	.521
Jason Thompson (1984-1986)					H	624	.226	.357	.360	L	302	.245	.351	.315	SP	360	.293	.447	.437	GB	577	.238	.366	.381
Bats Left	1195	.246	.365	.379	R	570	.267	.372	.398	R	892	.246	.369	.401	LC	231	.223	.372	.288	FB	617	.253	.363	.376
Milt Thompson (1984-1996)					H	2085	.280	.343	.394	L	765	.220	.268	.283	SP	1013	.281	.374	.378	GB	1498	.297	.353	.387
Bats Left	4155	.274	.335	.372	R	2064	.267	.328	.350	R	3384	.286	.351	.393	LC	744	.273	.351	.361	FB	1111	.261	.320	.354
Robby Thompson (1986-1996)					H	2591	.266	.346	.432	L	1635	.296	.365	.467	SP	1246	.242	.339	.360	GB	1869	.259	.326	.385
Bats Right	5235	.257	.329	.403	R	2626	.249	.313	.376	R	3582	.240	.313	.374	LC	786	.246	.310	.364	FB	1234	.246	.313	.389
Ryan Thompson (1992-1996)					H	561	.219	.282	.366	L	326	.246	.302	.392	SP	296	.215	.304	.360	GB	346	.246	.284	.388
Bats Right	1129	.240	.301	.418	R	568	.262	.319	.469	R	803	.238	.300	.429	LC	201	.251	.335	.404	FB	165	.229	.305	.403
Dickie Thon (1984-1993)					H	1560	.251	.306	.344	L	1485	.267	.332	.375	SP	814	.276	.345	.389	GB	1196	.247	.306	.320
Bats Right	3193	.257	.311	.359	R	1631	.262	.315	.374	R	1706	.249	.292	.346	LC	558	.257	.311	.341	FB	879	.269	.328	.422
Andre Thornton (1984-1987)					H	890	.274	.357	.482	L	581	.241	.351	.420	SP	517	.257	.354	.452	GB	849	.257	.338	.421
Bats Right	1776	.241	.330	.418	R	885	.208	.303	.353	R	1194	.241	.320	.417	LC	256	.274	.383	.500	FB	894	.229	.324	.423
Wayne Tolleson (1984-1990)					H	976	.245	.317	.296	L	612	.259	.331	.332	SP	430	.224	.314	.284	GB	796	.238	.300	.291
Bats Both	1990	.242	.310	.295	R	982	.239	.304	.294	R	1346	.234	.301	.279	LC	272	.249	.310	.314	FB	884	.265	.330	.323
Alan Trammell (1984-1996)					H	3031	.293	.361	.435	L	2008	.298	.368	.471	SP	1635	.291	.366	.418	GB	2011	.300	.358	.441
Bats Right	6052	.288	.352	.433	R	2992	.283	.344	.430	R	4015	.283	.344	.414	LC	849	.268	.346	.359	FB	2039	.281	.350	.437
Jeff Treadway (1987-1995)					H	1114	.273	.324	.364	L	366	.233	.290	.296	SP	550	.301	.362	.411	GB	784	.282	.321	.360
Bats Left	2318	.281	.326	.383	R	1204	.289	.328	.400	R	1952	.290	.333	.399	LC	410	.266	.319	.359	FB	522	.285	.339	.399
Alex Trevino (1984-1990)					H	642	.234	.299	.350	L	623	.237	.320	.350	SP	387	.213	.309	.320	GB	598	.257	.322	.388
Bats Right	1327	.245	.312	.366	R	677	.255	.325	.382	R	696	.251	.305	.380	LC	267	.279	.332	.413	FB	471	.230	.296	.340
Manny Trillo (1984-1989)					H	733	.247	.302	.343	L	524	.257	.316	.334	SP	392	.237	.314	.285	GB	689	.268	.324	.353
Bats Right	1577	.253	.310	.336	R	827	.259	.317	.329	R	1036	.252	.307	.337	LC	254	.229	.289	.286	FB	720	.219	.279	.288
Michael Tucker (1995-1997)					H	557	.266	.340	.398	L	227	.260	.326	.377	SP	290	.264	.335	.400	GB	266	.296	.350	.432
Bats Left	1145	.271	.344	.433	R	588	.276	.348	.467	R	918	.274	.349	.448	LC	167	.221	.319	.393	FB	177	.268	.362	.451
Willie Upshaw (1984-1988)					H	1436	.258	.342	.404	L	842	.241	.302	.375	SP	838	.242	.340	.368	GB	1229	.270	.345	.413
Bats Left	2994	.259	.337	.408	R	1550	.260	.332	.412	R	2144	.266	.350	.422	LC	401	.231	.318	.353	FB	1327	.259	.337	.428
Jose Uribe (1984-1993)					H	1616	.243	.304	.317	L	1039	.252	.306	.336	SP	843	.255	.365	.330	GB	1303	.273	.325	.359
Bats Both	3369	.241	.300	.314	R	1744	.239	.296	.312	R	2321	.236	.297	.304	LC	498	.221	.302	.279	FB	1115	.223	.287	.297
John Valentin (1992-1997)					H	1515	.314	.403	.513	L	770	.296	.401	.485	SP	843	.304	.401	.470	GB	608	.316	.385	.485
Bats Right	2977	.296	.375	.479	R	1462	.279	.347	.445	R	2207	.296	.366	.477	LC	460	.317	.390	.514	FB	592	.276	.346	.431
Jose Valentin (1992-1997)					H	973	.237	.320	.412	L	492	.217	.288	.282	SP	562	.262	.338	.478	GB	426	.258	.304	.481
Bats Both	1958	.245	.319	.429	R	985	.253	.318	.446	R	1466	.255	.329	.478	LC	308	.195	.299	.327	FB	385	.241	.338	.386
Dave Valle (1984-1996)					H	1609	.237	.309	.365	L	1080	.265	.336	.436	SP	857	.260	.329	.406	GB	835	.267	.336	.405
Bats Right	3147	.237	.314	.373	R	1537	.237	.320	.381	R	2066	.222	.303	.339	LC	452	.224	.302	.332	FB	841	.231	.311	.391
Andy Van Slyke (1984-1995)					H	3019	.267	.344	.439	L	1936	.237	.306	.361	SP	1727	.272	.367	.427	GB	2319	.275	.356	.423
Bats Left	6131	.274	.348	.444	R	3102	.281	.353	.449	R	4185	.291	.368	.483	LC	992	.250	.332	.379	FB	1781	.253	.334	.453
John VanderWal (1991-1997)					H	448	.276	.364	.430	L	97	.182	.247	.205	SP	323	.281	.372	.467	GB	333	.245	.321	.413
Bats Left	1064	.244	.324	.390	R	616	.221	.295	.362	R	967	.250	.332	.409	LC	264	.202	.303	.298	FB	183	.214	.317	.302
Greg Vaughn (1989-1997)					H	2077	.251	.343	.475	L	1159	.247	.359	.464	SP	1301	.258	.364	.452	GB	1059	.231	.316	.398
Bats Right	4316	.242	.332	.453	R	2239	.233	.321	.432	R	3157	.240	.322	.449	LC	667	.204	.305	.334	FB	880	.243	.332	.486
Mo Vaughn (1991-1997)					H	1938	.324	.421	.574	L	1122	.286	.375	.516	SP	1128	.318	.447	.578	GB	727	.297	.392	.505
Bats Left	3771	.298	.393	.532	R	1833	.271	.363	.490	R	2649	.304	.400	.539	LC	562	.261	.370	.438	FB	767	.272	.356	.487
Randy Velarde (1987-1997)					H	1346	.284	.358	.401	L	996	.286	.363	.431	SP	709	.274	.379	.397	GB	696	.270	.328	.367
Bats Right	2788	.269	.342	.400	R	1442	.254	.327	.398	R	1792	.259	.330	.382	LC	427	.260	.341	.371	FB	580	.243	.326	.374
Robin Ventura (1989-1997)					H	2228	.286	.378	.441	L	1389	.258	.343	.396	SP	1415	.293	.408	.454	GB	1206	.257	.346	.379
Bats Left	4636	.276	.367	.441	R	2408	.266	.357	.441	R	3247	.283	.377	.460	LC	759	.265	.343	.392	FB	1025	.279	.372	.481
Quilvio Veras (1995-1997)					H	703	.261	.375	.347	L	355	.235	.345	.319	SP	320	.232	.372	.301	GB	325	.236	.332	.293
Bats Both	1477	.261	.372	.347	R	774	.262	.369	.346	R	1122	.270	.380	.355	LC	227	.274	.386	.366	FB	216	.219	.341	.320
Fernando Vina (1993-1997)					H	775	.280	.342	.369	L	298	.248	.318	.305	SP	341	.277	.354	.382	GB	379	.280	.339	.335
Bats Left	1491	.270	.334	.365	R	716	.260	.326	.360	R	1193	.276	.338	.379	LC	256	.245	.336	.282	FB	270	.311	.372	.426
Ozzie Virgil (1984-1990)					H	1120	.272	.355	.463	L	670	.247	.341	.406	SP	631	.242	.350	.355	GB	911	.235	.320	.375
Bats Right	2282	.246	.330	.420	R	1158	.222	.305	.378	R	1608	.246	.325	.426	LC	363	.260	.355	.322	FB	1020	.251	.336	.435
Jose Vizcaino (1989-1997)					H	1687	.271	.323	.329	L	871	.282	.331	.319	SP	808	.292	.344	.356	GB	995	.261	.300	.310
Bats Both	3382	.273	.321	.345	R	1695	.275	.320	.360	R	2511	.270	.318	.354	LC	603	.284	.336	.340	FB	552	.286	.333	.371
Omar Vizquel (1989-1997)					H	2243	.274	.332	.351	L	1244	.239	.293	.319	SP	1188	.261	.312	.332	GB	994	.261	.329	.318
Bats Both	4564	.265	.326	.335	R	2321	.256	.320	.320	R	3320	.275	.338	.341	LC	723	.277	.335	.352	FB	876	.282	.335	.364
Matt Walbeck (1993-1997)					H	578	.242	.288	.316	L	328	.272	.306	.346	SP	318	.272	.310	.393	GB	324	.241	.299	.299
Bats Both	1190	.235	.277	.310	R	612	.230	.267	.304	R	862	.221	.266	.296	LC	208	.232	.271	.325	FB	223	.248	.275	.374
Chico Walker (1984-1993)					H	609	.252	.312	.316	L	352	.272	.308	.373	SP	324	.231	.326	.341	GB	442	.272	.308	.358
Bats Both	1262	.245	.304	.329	R	653	.239	.296	.340	R	910	.234	.302	.311	LC	324	.218	.297	.275	FB	337	.213	.306	.282
Greg Walker (1984-1990)					H	1405	.258	.332	.458	L	805	.225	.290	.373	SP	758	.268	.358	.474	GB	1069	.273	.341	.478
Bats Left	2818	.258	.324	.447	R	1414	.259	.316	.436	R	2014	.272	.338	.477	LC	338	.231	.286	.375	FB	1200	.260	.319	.445
Larry Walker (1989-1997)					H	2035	.319	.392	.591	L	1296	.285	.357	.486	SP	1269	.284	.392	.467	GB	1199	.301	.362	.513
Bats Left	4220	.297	.374	.542	R	2185	.277	.357	.496	R	2924	.303	.381	.568	LC	695	.273	.373	.477	FB	788	.297	.379	.560
Tim Wallach (1984-1996)					H	3544	.259	.323	.404	L	2195	.258	.318	.429	SP	2187	.258	.348	.413	GB	2781	.267	.326	.425
Bats Right	7373	.256	.315	.412	R	3829	.253	.308	.419	R	5178	.256	.314	.404	LC	1284	.239	.320	.367	FB	2108	.247	.307	.403
Denny Walling (1984-1992)					H	965	.279	.336	.385	L	224	.214	.264	.257	SP	585	.259	.342	.375	GB	843	.276	.326	.369
Bats Left	1968	.272	.330	.395	R	1003	.266	.324	.405	R	1744	.280	.338	.413	LC	356	.248	.315	.320	FB	756	.271	.339	.441

2538 Situational Statistics: Hitting

	Total					Home/Road					vs. Left/Right					Scoring Position/Late & Close					vs. Groundball/Flyball Pitcher			
Batter	PA	Avg	OBP	Slg		PA	Avg	OBP	Slg		PA	Avg	OBP	Slg		PA	Avg	OBP	Slg		PA	Avg	OBP	Slg
Jerome Walton (1989-1997)					H	829	.278	.335	.396	L	733	.277	.349	.390	SP	371	.256	.318	.358	GB	594	.242	.300	.320
Bats Right	1725	.268	.332	.375	R	896	.258	.329	.355	R	992	.261	.319	.364	LC	302	.203	.274	.284	FB	387	.234	.323	.331
Gary Ward (1984-1990)					H	1524	.292	.345	.438	L	1255	.276	.336	.439	SP	834	.278	.352	.419	GB	1225	.297	.339	.426
Bats Right	3211	.271	.326	.406	R	1685	.253	.308	.378	R	1954	.268	.319	.385	LC	444	.275	.333	.393	FB	1346	.257	.319	.395
Turner Ward (1990-1997)					H	561	.261	.345	.433	L	291	.246	.322	.375	SP	368	.265	.354	.401	GB	290	.259	.309	.384
Bats Both	1255	.253	.338	.394	R	694	.247	.332	.361	R	964	.256	.343	.399	LC	227	.276	.360	.443	FB	247	.213	.302	.341
Claudell Washington (1984-1990)					H	1297	.291	.348	.459	L	489	.291	.345	.408	SP	633	.270	.350	.382	GB	1005	.272	.334	.413
Bats Left	2611	.276	.333	.432	R	1313	.261	.318	.406	R	2121	.273	.330	.438	LC	401	.256	.318	.394	FB	1025	.285	.346	.469
Lenny Webster (1989-1997)					H	590	.243	.305	.353	L	398	.273	.369	.422	SP	323	.231	.325	.321	GB	279	.266	.345	.406
Bats Right	1140	.254	.332	.379	R	550	.267	.361	.408	R	742	.245	.313	.357	LC	188	.255	.332	.345	FB	168	.252	.345	.442
Mitch Webster (1984-1995)					H	1841	.256	.327	.381	L	1431	.286	.334	.442	SP	958	.253	.341	.384	GB	1410	.289	.350	.428
Bats Both	3839	.263	.330	.401	R	1968	.271	.333	.420	R	2378	.250	.328	.376	LC	721	.237	.320	.365	FB	1193	.247	.320	.400
Walt Weiss (1987-1997)					H	2298	.260	.355	.323	L	1113	.240	.325	.290	SP	1113	.225	.335	.281	GB	1267	.256	.343	.309
Bats Both	4538	.258	.350	.325	R	2240	.256	.346	.327	R	3425	.264	.359	.337	LC	721	.253	.360	.296	FB	903	.266	.356	.343
Lou Whitaker (1984-1995)					H	3191	.275	.375	.470	L	1527	.222	.312	.328	SP	1563	.266	.369	.450	GB	2183	.284	.368	.460
Bats Left	6554	.274	.365	.447	R	3354	.273	.356	.427	R	5018	.289	.381	.484	LC	929	.254	.363	.407	FB	2169	.274	.366	.438
Devon White (1985-1997)					H	3143	.262	.316	.422	L	1826	.260	.312	.420	SP	1470	.257	.326	.396	GB	1555	.272	.321	.412
Bats Both	6327	.260	.315	.415	R	3184	.259	.314	.408	R	4501	.261	.316	.412	LC	904	.255	.333	.387	FB	1506	.243	.294	.388
Frank White (1984-1990)					H	1840	.256	.302	.392	L	1040	.260	.310	.394	SP	991	.254	.306	.385	GB	1306	.273	.316	.412
Bats Right	3649	.252	.296	.393	R	1798	.247	.290	.393	R	2598	.248	.291	.392	LC	508	.241	.284	.377	FB	1478	.236	.285	.388
Rondell White (1993-1997)					H	807	.297	.362	.456	L	452	.323	.372	.531	SP	474	.247	.333	.375	GB	419	.246	.303	.365
Bats Right	1714	.283	.336	.459	R	907	.271	.313	.462	R	1262	.268	.323	.433	LC	271	.250	.307	.464	FB	260	.294	.367	.576
Mark Whiten (1990-1997)					H	1524	.254	.338	.413	L	931	.256	.336	.423	SP	913	.258	.366	.417	GB	944	.245	.320	.370
Bats Both	3226	.258	.339	.415	R	1702	.261	.340	.417	R	2295	.259	.340	.412	LC	607	.232	.334	.387	FB	600	.257	.359	.447
Ernie Whitt (1984-1991)					H	1438	.239	.337	.420	L	358	.232	.312	.340	SP	830	.239	.342	.406	GB	1143	.260	.336	.423
Bats Left	2938	.250	.329	.417	R	1497	.260	.322	.415	R	2577	.253	.332	.428	LC	417	.266	.342	.392	FB	1086	.240	.324	.431
Alan Wiggins (1984-1987)					H	797	.246	.324	.304	L	562	.283	.344	.354	SP	290	.263	.332	.324	GB	790	.250	.321	.292
Bats Both	1679	.252	.324	.305	R	856	.258	.325	.306	R	1091	.236	.314	.279	LC	181	.253	.343	.285	FB	741	.266	.338	.332
Curtis Wilkerson (1984-1993)					H	1247	.254	.296	.322	L	589	.236	.293	.299	SP	643	.231	.286	.301	GB	1008	.257	.297	.296
Bats Both	2614	.246	.287	.306	R	1349	.238	.279	.292	R	2007	.249	.286	.308	LC	433	.271	.311	.341	FB	993	.233	.278	.306
Rick Wilkins (1991-1997)					H	1145	.217	.299	.351	L	403	.193	.286	.305	SP	672	.229	.372	.378	GB	725	.242	.330	.394
Bats Left	2331	.246	.335	.416	R	1186	.276	.371	.480	R	1928	.258	.346	.439	LC	425	.227	.335	.377	FB	430	.227	.334	.403
Bernie Williams (1991-1997)					H	1738	.295	.378	.462	L	1197	.320	.403	.553	SP	1004	.304	.385	.465	GB	867	.290	.376	.402
Bats Both	3650	.292	.374	.464	R	1912	.289	.371	.466	R	2453	.278	.360	.422	LC	545	.263	.345	.381	FB	700	.271	.359	.462
Eddie Williams (1986-1997)					H	548	.257	.331	.405	L	461	.265	.332	.418	SP	363	.249	.337	.380	GB	320	.279	.359	.370
Bats Right	1250	.254	.322	.405	R	702	.252	.315	.404	R	789	.248	.316	.397	LC	199	.232	.292	.345	FB	228	.255	.319	.402
Gerald Williams (1992-1997)					H	652	.257	.299	.407	L	573	.272	.325	.475	SP	378	.216	.271	.329	GB	237	.299	.331	.442
Bats Right	1355	.250	.291	.399	R	703	.243	.284	.392	R	782	.234	.266	.345	LC	206	.250	.272	.362	FB	248	.276	.332	.484
Kenny Williams (1986-1991)					H	609	.228	.281	.347	L	645	.235	.283	.377	SP	315	.210	.265	.313	GB	370	.216	.266	.352
Bats Right	1253	.218	.269	.339	R	644	.209	.257	.331	R	608	.200	.255	.297	LC	158	.169	.237	.261	FB	356	.216	.266	.337
Matt Williams (1987-1997)					H	2521	.266	.317	.502	L	1459	.272	.327	.565	SP	1516	.264	.334	.481	GB	1619	.264	.311	.460
Bats Right	5133	.264	.312	.497	R	2612	.261	.307	.493	R	3674	.261	.306	.471	LC	766	.240	.301	.411	FB	951	.250	.299	.488
Dan Wilson (1992-1997)					H	978	.261	.320	.408	L	505	.276	.325	.452	SP	542	.311	.365	.450	GB	497	.251	.301	.359
Bats Right	1962	.267	.317	.403	R	984	.273	.314	.397	R	1457	.263	.314	.385	LC	307	.305	.353	.489	FB	349	.282	.340	.456
Glenn Wilson (1984-1993)					H	1737	.271	.320	.406	L	1207	.272	.313	.405	SP	989	.264	.302	.399	GB	1408	.271	.310	.377
Bats Right	3593	.261	.304	.391	R	1855	.252	.289	.377	R	2385	.256	.300	.384	LC	561	.267	.319	.379	FB	1385	.250	.298	.400
Mookie Wilson (1984-1991)					H	1744	.267	.308	.378	L	1499	.268	.314	.394	SP	876	.265	.316	.374	GB	1403	.289	.332	.412
Bats Both	3633	.274	.316	.395	R	1885	.281	.324	.412	R	2130	.279	.318	.396	LC	603	.268	.323	.402	FB	1245	.270	.316	.394
Willie Wilson (1984-1994)					H	2491	.283	.328	.378	L	1517	.275	.307	.368	SP	1067	.273	.323	.367	GB	1724	.285	.326	.379
Bats Both	4969	.272	.316	.365	R	2470	.261	.304	.352	R	3444	.270	.320	.363	LC	694	.270	.317	.334	FB	1795	.275	.320	.375
Dave Winfield (1984-1995)					H	2965	.282	.358	.473	L	1932	.294	.386	.520	SP	1815	.292	.382	.487	GB	2052	.289	.360	.455
Bats Right	6145	.281	.352	.471	R	3178	.281	.345	.468	R	4211	.276	.336	.449	LC	829	.267	.335	.426	FB	2073	.283	.352	.501
Herm Winningham (1984-1992)					H	1060	.231	.296	.309	L	258	.233	.253	.329	SP	486	.253	.338	.348	GB	782	.218	.278	.293
Bats Left	2069	.239	.296	.334	R	1007	.248	.297	.359	R	1809	.240	.302	.334	LC	356	.264	.311	.368	FB	702	.236	.289	.355
Craig Worthington (1988-1996)					H	717	.243	.339	.363	L	487	.251	.364	.361	SP	391	.235	.326	.271	GB	383	.259	.338	.372
Bats Right	1423	.230	.322	.351	R	706	.218	.305	.339	R	936	.220	.300	.346	LC	223	.216	.313	.384	FB	257	.182	.278	.280
George Wright (1984-1986)					H	485	.197	.241	.303	L	321	.186	.240	.271	SP	248	.203	.266	.258	GB	551	.229	.269	.334
Bats Both	1045	.214	.257	.310	R	552	.228	.270	.317	R	716	.226	.264	.328	LC	217	.240	.276	.324	FB	486	.196	.243	.284
Butch Wynegar (1984-1988)					H	643	.229	.333	.312	L	449	.251	.355	.381	SP	345	.223	.368	.341	GB	575	.244	.346	.294
Bats Both	1280	.238	.342	.331	R	632	.247	.352	.349	R	826	.231	.335	.303	LC	235	.240	.340	.343	FB	638	.238	.347	.373
Marvell Wynne (1984-1990)					H	1229	.260	.305	.380	L	549	.258	.314	.356	SP	578	.274	.337	.389	GB	1075	.254	.296	.345
Bats Left	2522	.247	.294	.351	R	1280	.235	.283	.323	R	1960	.244	.288	.350	LC	468	.246	.293	.356	FB	1010	.235	.289	.342
Eric Yelding (1989-1993)					H	524	.235	.286	.270	L	452	.280	.326	.329	SP	241	.241	.277	.296	GB	369	.254	.293	.306
Bats Right	1085	.244	.292	.294	R	561	.252	.298	.316	R	633	.218	.268	.269	LC	189	.265	.320	.277	FB	195	.205	.258	.233
Eric Young (1992-1997)					H	1392	.331	.417	.465	L	776	.298	.373	.432	SP	661	.299	.386	.384	GB	711	.263	.345	.352
Bats Right	2769	.292	.372	.402	R	1377	.254	.326	.341	R	1993	.289	.371	.391	LC	389	.325	.420	.409	FB	435	.306	.397	.442
Gerald Young (1987-1994)					H	1077	.254	.333	.314	L	724	.267	.340	.334	SP	434	.285	.393	.369	GB	741	.237	.320	.290
Bats Both	2083	.246	.329	.304	R	1006	.237	.325	.292	R	1359	.234	.323	.287	LC	367	.236	.309	.296	FB	523	.245	.330	.294
Kevin Young (1992-1997)					H	706	.248	.306	.447	L	485	.256	.311	.435	SP	397	.234	.299	.389	GB	333	.261	.308	.380
Bats Right	1351	.252	.303	.413	R	645	.257	.299	.378	R	866	.250	.298	.401	LC	260	.257	.307	.438	FB	213	.233	.278	.430

Situational Statistics: Hitting 2539

Batter	PA	Avg	OBP	Slg		PA	Avg	OBP	Slg		PA	Avg	OBP	Slg		PA	Avg	OBP	Slg		PA	Avg	OBP	Slg
		Total					**Home/Road**					**vs. Left/Right**					**Scoring Position/Late & Close**					**vs. Groundball/Flyball Pitcher**			
Mike Young (1984-1989)					H	995	.258	.356	.452	L	757	.251	.331	.406	SP	531	.240	.343	.392	GB	921	.249	.334	.435
Bats Both	2071	.249	.340	.417	R	1071	.240	.325	.386	R	1309	.247	.345	.424	LC	324	.222	.336	.378	FB	922	.258	.352	.418
Joel Youngblood (1984-1989)					H	658	.249	.320	.341	L	557	.251	.323	.338	SP	388	.283	.376	.382	GB	598	.253	.317	.335
Bats Right	1366	.253	.325	.355	R	702	.256	.330	.368	R	803	.254	.326	.366	LC	318	.269	.351	.358	FB	619	.259	.349	.383
Robin Yount (1984-1993)					H	3141	.288	.359	.447	L	1793	.284	.367	.427	SP	1774	.299	.381	.443	GB	2035	.299	.369	.430
Bats Right	6330	.287	.356	.434	R	3182	.285	.354	.422	R	4530	.288	.352	.437	LC	835	.287	.365	.405	FB	2070	.281	.344	.429
Todd Zeile (1989-1997)					H	2285	.272	.351	.434	L	1367	.271	.358	.429	SP	1468	.252	.367	.390	GB	1392	.252	.339	.387
Bats Right	4788	.264	.346	.421	R	2503	.256	.340	.410	R	3421	.261	.341	.418	LC	844	.239	.329	.347	FB	881	.242	.323	.400

Situational Statistics: Hitting

Situational Pitching Splits—1984-1997

Pitcher	IP	W-L	ERA	H/R	IP	W-L	ERA	L/R	PA	Avg	OBP	Slg	SP/LC	PA	Avg	OBP	Slg	NO/RO	PA	Avg	OBP	Slg
Don Aase (1984-1990)				H	200.1	18-8	3.10	L	774	.233	.323	.353	SP	510	.284	.381	.443	NO	730	.221	.301	.325
Throws Right	360.2	25-20	3.52	R	160.1	7-12	4.04	R	744	.250	.327	.376	LC	780	.239	.322	.346	RO	788	.261	.347	.402
Jim Abbott (1989-1996)				H	769.1	35-52	4.18	L	1100	.302	.363	.447	SP	1665	.270	.344	.393	NO	3759	.268	.333	.386
Throws Left	1560.1	80-100	4.11	R	791.0	45-48	4.04	R	5583	.268	.332	.383	LC	523	.316	.364	.469	RO	2924	.281	.342	.404
Jim Acker (1984-1992)				H	422.0	15-18	3.82	L	1660	.288	.357	.406	SP	1020	.269	.353	.407	NO	1836	.257	.319	.380
Throws Right	806.2	28-48	3.93	R	384.2	14-30	4.09	R	1764	.247	.310	.385	LC	651	.281	.352	.373	RO	1588	.278	.348	.413
Juan Agosto (1984-1993)				H	313.2	24-14	3.50	L	882	.229	.314	.298	SP	820	.301	.401	.414	NO	1216	.260	.326	.338
Throws Left	577.0	38-31	3.95	R	262.1	14-17	4.49	R	1619	.292	.363	.400	LC	836	.251	.333	.323	RO	1285	.280	.365	.391
Rick Aguilera (1985-1997)				H	545.1	36-28	3.40	L	2329	.251	.308	.373	SP	1244	.244	.323	.386	NO	2552	.251	.297	.385
Throws Right	1101.2	72-66	3.50	R	556.1	36-38	3.62	R	2265	.253	.302	.409	LC	1443	.235	.296	.352	RO	2042	.252	.316	.398
Scott Aldred (1990-1997)				H	192.2	7-16	7.38	L	355	.317	.370	.528	SP	490	.302	.397	.525	NO	949	.298	.366	.498
Throws Left	391.1	15-33	6.44	R	198.2	8-17	5.53	R	1428	.295	.375	.501	LC	84	.299	.405	.522	RO	834	.302	.383	.516
Doyle Alexander (1984-1989)				H	805.1	49-31	3.26	L	3023	.273	.324	.431	SP	1255	.256	.316	.382	NO	3538	.265	.306	.414
Throws Right	1408.2	79-64	3.74	R	603.1	30-33	4.39	R	2856	.256	.291	.394	LC	530	.275	.317	.453	RO	2341	.264	.312	.410
Neil Allen (1984-1989)				H	228.2	10-8	3.98	L	960	.270	.343	.410	SP	566	.288	.379	.408	NO	1143	.250	.304	.381
Throws Right	485.0	23-24	4.19	R	256.1	13-16	4.39	R	1113	.262	.325	.378	LC	303	.216	.321	.317	RO	930	.287	.370	.409
Wilson Alvarez (1989-1997)				H	541.0	35-26	3.91	L	819	.262	.352	.357	SP	1133	.248	.346	.388	NO	2694	.251	.343	.375
Throws Left	1130.1	71-54	3.83	R	589.1	36-28	3.76	R	4048	.242	.332	.380	LC	351	.267	.386	.407	RO	2173	.239	.325	.379
Larry Andersen (1984-1994)				H	404.0	22-12	2.12	L	1587	.272	.342	.359	SP	1040	.246	.322	.319	NO	1674	.246	.297	.337
Throws Right	785.0	36-35	2.82	R	381.0	14-24	3.57	R	1672	.218	.264	.298	LC	1296	.247	.311	.316	RO	1585	.241	.307	.314
Allan Anderson (1986-1991)				H	411.0	23-27	4.77	L	621	.288	.346	.393	SP	822	.281	.335	.392	NO	2005	.275	.323	.429
Throws Left	818.2	49-54	4.11	R	407.2	26-27	3.44	R	2851	.281	.325	.433	LC	199	.250	.311	.350	RO	1467	.293	.337	.421
Brian Anderson (1993-1997)				H	180.0	11-9	4.75	L	257	.313	.340	.539	SP	313	.307	.346	.511	NO	783	.291	.340	.519
Throws Left	312.0	20-16	5.25	R	132.0	9-7	5.93	R	1076	.287	.336	.486	LC	39	.429	.459	.771	RO	550	.294	.333	.464
Joaquin Andujar (1984-1988)				H	459.1	27-30	3.74	L	1701	.266	.331	.397	SP	822	.251	.331	.420	NO	2021	.245	.302	.360
Throws Right	825.2	58-43	3.72	R	366.1	31-13	3.69	R	1717	.236	.293	.362	LC	362	.225	.338	.345	RO	1397	.259	.325	.409
Kevin Appier (1989-1997)				H	810.2	49-40	3.29	L	3610	.254	.331	.382	SP	1635	.230	.299	.324	NO	4007	.235	.302	.350
Throws Right	1665.1	104-78	3.30	R	854.2	55-38	3.31	R	3297	.220	.272	.311	LC	718	.225	.294	.340	RO	2900	.241	.303	.343
Luis Aquino (1986-1995)				H	318.0	16-12	3.25	L	1407	.271	.336	.394	SP	778	.267	.345	.405	NO	1578	.259	.314	.361
Throws Right	678.1	31-32	3.68	R	360.1	15-20	4.05	R	1495	.264	.322	.373	LC	384	.284	.370	.405	RO	1324	.278	.346	.411
Jack Armstrong (1988-1994)				H	386.2	24-35	5.07	L	1874	.276	.360	.448	SP	861	.271	.350	.430	NO	1987	.249	.321	.401
Throws Right	786.2	40-65	4.58	R	400.0	16-30	4.10	R	1576	.253	.305	.405	LC	162	.259	.321	.350	RO	1463	.289	.354	.466
Rene Arocha (1993-1997)				H	177.0	11-8	3.61	L	648	.297	.344	.436	SP	401	.289	.360	.453	NO	786	.279	.312	.437
Throws Right	331.0	18-17	4.11	R	154.0	7-9	4.68	R	756	.269	.309	.452	LC	314	.255	.319	.415	RO	618	.287	.343	.455
Andy Ashby (1991-1997)				H	452.0	21-21	3.66	L	1948	.277	.338	.413	SP	1007	.270	.350	.407	NO	2215	.261	.313	.395
Throws Right	910.1	41-55	4.18	R	458.1	20-34	4.69	R	1931	.256	.312	.396	LC	265	.234	.278	.344	RO	1664	.275	.341	.419
Paul Assenmacher (1986-1997)				H	421.0	39-20	3.40	L	1179	.224	.283	.312	SP	1083	.240	.344	.334	NO	1620	.251	.304	.380
Throws Left	775.2	57-38	3.35	R	354.2	18-18	3.32	R	2100	.257	.330	.386	LC	1565	.240	.312	.335	RO	1659	.239	.323	.336
Pedro Astacio (1992-1997)				H	470.0	27-21	3.24	L	1900	.260	.323	.408	SP	909	.231	.313	.361	NO	2263	.267	.324	.397
Throws Right	935.1	53-48	3.71	R	465.1	26-27	4.20	R	2026	.249	.307	.365	LC	368	.241	.296	.349	RO	1663	.236	.301	.370
Keith Atherton (1984-1989)				H	256.0	18-9	3.48	L	988	.276	.356	.468	SP	670	.262	.353	.454	NO	1049	.253	.312	.416
Throws Right	498.0	31-36	4.16	R	242.0	14-27	4.87	R	1153	.243	.299	.398	LC	602	.259	.336	.455	RO	1092	.264	.339	.443
Don August (1988-1991)				H	211.0	21-12	3.88	L	1000	.294	.356	.421	SP	467	.269	.333	.461	NO	1079	.288	.341	.402
Throws Right	440.0	34-30	4.64	R	229.0	13-18	5.34	R	926	.272	.328	.403	LC	96	.346	.418	.590	RO	847	.278	.345	.427
Steve Avery (1990-1997)				H	657.0	41-29	3.79	L	971	.236	.310	.327	SP	1327	.278	.347	.408	NO	3330	.243	.298	.365
Throws Left	1319.0	78-69	4.02	R	662.0	37-40	4.24	R	4595	.265	.319	.403	LC	410	.253	.313	.322	RO	2236	.289	.347	.429
Bobby Ayala (1992-1997)				H	222.1	23-13	4.74	L	962	.264	.346	.419	SP	552	.273	.360	.440	NO	944	.245	.323	.390
Throws Right	418.2	35-27	4.58	R	196.1	12-14	4.40	R	859	.252	.329	.407	LC	758	.243	.320	.378	RO	877	.274	.354	.441
Scott Bailes (1986-1997)				H	325.1	24-21	4.59	L	743	.268	.328	.363	SP	768	.295	.376	.452	NO	1460	.277	.336	.428
Throws Left	639.1	38-44	4.86	R	314.0	14-24	5.25	R	2074	.282	.348	.454	LC	390	.284	.363	.379	RO	1357	.280	.350	.432
Roger Bailey (1995-1997)				H	176.1	12-5	5.82	L	738	.302	.392	.483	SP	455	.249	.357	.397	NO	846	.296	.363	.483
Throws Right	356.0	18-19	4.90	R	179.2	6-14	4.01	R	842	.270	.337	.441	LC	123	.283	.405	.424	RO	734	.270	.364	.431
Doug Bair (1984-1990)				H	164.0	7-5	3.18	L	628	.257	.337	.379	SP	418	.242	.338	.369	NO	648	.250	.315	.394
Throws Right	308.1	13-9	3.88	R	144.1	6-4	4.68	R	677	.240	.305	.398	LC	275	.163	.247	.271	RO	657	.246	.326	.384
James Baldwin (1995-1997)				H	200.2	11-11	4.71	L	883	.280	.358	.429	SP	421	.279	.355	.470	NO	955	.267	.326	.423
Throws Right	383.2	23-22	5.18	R	183.0	12-11	5.70	R	796	.257	.313	.450	LC	111	.350	.409	.770	RO	724	.270	.350	.461
Jeff Ballard (1987-1994)				H	386.0	17-29	4.38	L	644	.285	.342	.413	SP	808	.312	.395	.502	NO	1924	.296	.337	.445
Throws Left	773.1	41-53	4.71	R	387.1	24-26	5.14	R	2713	.301	.350	.468	LC	215	.268	.322	.389	RO	1433	.301	.364	.475
Scott Bankhead (1986-1995)				H	450.0	30-22	4.42	L	1921	.260	.317	.422	SP	917	.262	.348	.419	NO	2270	.242	.293	.406
Throws Right	901.0	57-48	4.18	R	451.0	27-26	3.93	R	1888	.247	.305	.413	LC	396	.234	.327	.377	RO	1539	.272	.339	.436
Willie Banks (1991-1997)				H	279.1	17-19	4.29	L	1131	.286	.352	.420	SP	592	.275	.369	.438	NO	1215	.275	.356	.409
Throws Right	502.2	29-35	4.94	R	223.1	12-16	5.76	R	1117	.266	.364	.412	LC	147	.280	.371	.432	RO	1033	.278	.360	.425
Floyd Bannister (1984-1992)				H	566.0	29-28	3.93	L	879	.251	.315	.404	SP	1154	.238	.317	.409	NO	2903	.253	.308	.418
Throws Left	1149.1	67-65	4.34	R	583.1	38-37	4.78	R	4006	.258	.319	.427	LC	235	.312	.397	.441	RO	1982	.263	.333	.432
Brian Barnes (1990-1994)				H	202.0	7-11	3.39	L	365	.269	.383	.441	SP	474	.242	.345	.376	NO	980	.230	.317	.350
Throws Left	406.1	14-22	3.94	R	204.1	7-11	4.49	R	1389	.235	.321	.359	LC	160	.185	.284	.230	RO	774	.257	.355	.409

Pitcher	IP	W-L	ERA		IP	W-L	ERA		PA	Avg	OBP	Slg		PA	Avg	OBP	Slg		PA	Avg	OBP	Slg
		Total				Home/Road				vs. Left/Right					Scoring Position/Late & Close					None On/Runners On		
Jose Bautista (1988-1997)				H	381.1	20-20	4.20	L	1326	.278	.335	.457	SP	756	.292	.356	.477	NO	1677	.264	.306	.417
Throws Right	685.2	32-42	4.62	R	304.1	12-22	5.15	R	1599	.270	.309	.446	LC	481	.264	.326	.409	RO	1248	.286	.341	.500
Jim Beattie (1984-1986)				H	145.2	9-11	4.10	L	705	.295	.362	.443	SP	382	.298	.366	.419	NO	787	.268	.334	.427
Throws Right	321.2	17-28	4.59	R	176.0	8-17	4.70	R	633	.282	.335	.408	LC	112	.250	.304	.375	RO	611	.305	.370	.426
Rod Beck (1991-1997)				H	246.2	15-15	2.96	L	944	.223	.269	.343	SP	471	.237	.298	.381	NO	1032	.234	.270	.357
Throws Right	463.0	21-28	2.97	R	216.1	6-13	3.00	R	922	.246	.283	.387	LC	1116	.243	.289	.383	RO	834	.235	.284	.375
Steve Bedrosian (1984-1995)				H	458.1	31-28	3.46	L	1999	.256	.347	.417	SP	1196	.222	.334	.337	NO	2027	.233	.304	.370
Throws Right	909.1	58-61	3.46	R	451.0	27-33	3.51	R	1859	.220	.287	.317	LC	1179	.225	.317	.360	RO	1831	.245	.334	.365
Tim Belcher (1987-1997)				H	1069.0	74-51	3.77	L	4729	.262	.333	.382	SP	2041	.261	.337	.416	NO	5012	.241	.303	.369
Throws Right	2035.2	122-113	3.93	R	966.2	48-62	4.11	R	3904	.243	.301	.392	LC	729	.270	.338	.393	RO	3621	.272	.340	.412
Stan Belinda (1989-1997)				H	279.2	15-10	3.67	L	1017	.236	.325	.383	SP	737	.234	.333	.412	NO	1174	.209	.287	.336
Throws Right	534.2	33-25	3.85	R	255.0	18-15	4.06	R	1242	.220	.297	.356	LC	1261	.214	.295	.337	RO	1085	.248	.334	.405
Alan Benes (1995-1997)				H	178.2	11-10	3.12	L	742	.290	.375	.452	SP	375	.269	.359	.387	NO	893	.236	.327	.389
Throws Right	368.2	23-21	4.17	R	190.0	12-11	5.16	R	840	.215	.289	.339	LC	141	.267	.377	.457	RO	689	.268	.334	.395
Andy Benes (1989-1997)				H	854.2	52-43	3.82	L	3824	.251	.321	.379	SP	1685	.239	.326	.356	NO	4198	.238	.295	.373
Throws Right	1705.1	104-94	3.64	R	850.2	52-51	3.46	R	3320	.235	.290	.372	LC	590	.253	.328	.370	RO	2946	.252	.323	.379
Jason Bere (1993-1997)				H	238.2	17-11	4.68	L	1102	.256	.389	.378	SP	559	.256	.373	.398	NO	1123	.239	.362	.380
Throws Right	467.1	36-25	4.99	R	228.2	19-14	5.31	R	1000	.228	.318	.389	LC	104	.295	.380	.409	RO	979	.245	.347	.387
Juan Berenguer (1984-1992)				H	482.2	35-20	3.82	L	1928	.266	.362	.419	SP	1072	.239	.343	.376	NO	2079	.227	.316	.345
Throws Right	897.1	55-40	3.82	R	414.2	20-20	3.82	R	1909	.204	.287	.308	LC	751	.219	.325	.345	RO	1758	.245	.335	.385
Sean Bergman (1993-1997)				H	201.0	7-16	4.97	L	911	.299	.379	.479	SP	537	.317	.406	.477	NO	958	.305	.367	.474
Throws Right	405.0	18-27	5.22	R	204.0	11-11	5.47	R	923	.298	.352	.450	LC	93	.329	.427	.487	RO	876	.291	.363	.453
Mike Bielecki (1984-1997)				H	631.2	37-38	4.05	L	2872	.264	.333	.400	SP	1389	.272	.367	.398	NO	2986	.262	.325	.403
Throws Right	1231.0	70-73	4.18	R	599.1	33-35	4.32	R	2445	.260	.332	.404	LC	487	.230	.333	.354	RO	2331	.263	.342	.400
Mike Birkbeck (1986-1995)				H	141.0	8-10	4.72	L	585	.267	.321	.369	SP	319	.286	.380	.405	NO	657	.304	.346	.442
Throws Right	270.1	12-19	4.86	R	129.1	4-9	5.01	R	611	.322	.380	.482	LC	30	.250	.276	.286	RO	539	.282	.357	.405
Tim Birtsas (1985-1990)				H	182.2	7-6	3.70	L	392	.233	.305	.381	SP	393	.249	.367	.388	NO	776	.270	.357	.439
Throws Left	328.2	14-14	4.08	R	146.0	7-8	4.56	R	1055	.271	.367	.431	LC	59	.313	.441	.521	RO	671	.248	.342	.390
Bud Black (1984-1995)				H	945.0	62-49	3.56	L	1545	.238	.293	.360	SP	1712	.248	.327	.384	NO	4504	.250	.299	.384
Throws Left	1802.2	107-103	3.81	R	857.2	45-54	4.08	R	5997	.255	.313	.396	LC	712	.243	.312	.377	RO	3038	.254	.324	.396
Willie Blair (1990-1997)				H	363.2	20-20	4.60	L	1621	.279	.345	.424	SP	888	.286	.367	.487	NO	1895	.264	.320	.385
Throws Right	784.0	41-49	4.60	R	420.1	21-29	4.60	R	1805	.279	.331	.435	LC	420	.317	.382	.488	RO	1531	.298	.359	.489
Vida Blue (1985-1986)				H	174.2	12-8	3.66	L	181	.210	.293	.346	SP	274	.247	.321	.379	NO	699	.251	.365	.449
Throws Left	287.2	18-18	3.82	R	113.0	6-10	4.06	R	1038	.245	.344	.411	LC	74	.239	.297	.552	RO	520	.224	.298	.340
Bert Blyleven (1984-1992)				H	975.0	64-40	3.75	L	4094	.253	.306	.387	SP	1718	.270	.333	.413	NO	4464	.250	.298	.394
Throws Right	1792.2	111-90	3.85	R	817.2	47-50	3.97	R	3359	.261	.310	.413	LC	481	.251	.312	.379	RO	2989	.266	.321	.406
Mike Boddicker (1984-1993)				H	971.0	61-56	3.78	L	4344	.272	.335	.402	SP	2032	.243	.320	.365	NO	4623	.263	.327	.393
Throws Right	1906.0	117-107	3.89	R	935.0	56-51	4.00	R	3761	.249	.319	.373	LC	582	.201	.285	.303	RO	3482	.260	.328	.382
Joe Boever (1985-1996)				H	418.1	24-20	3.49	L	1636	.255	.346	.365	SP	1062	.258	.376	.400	NO	1593	.267	.328	.402
Throws Right	754.1	34-45	3.93	R	327.2	9-25	4.39	R	1622	.266	.333	.415	LC	1161	.256	.348	.374	RO	1668	.250	.347	.371
Brian Bohanon (1990-1997)				H	237.1	11-12	5.65	L	508	.282	.352	.393	SP	654	.268	.352	.402	NO	1156	.284	.355	.420
Throws Left	493.0	18-19	5.35	R	255.2	7-7	5.07	R	1728	.288	.361	.451	LC	173	.320	.398	.533	RO	1080	.290	.363	.458
Tom Bolton (1987-1994)				H	278.0	18-12	4.24	L	640	.267	.342	.373	SP	697	.286	.386	.411	NO	1241	.283	.351	.399
Throws Left	540.1	31-34	4.56	R	262.1	13-22	5.15	R	1786	.296	.371	.428	LC	223	.346	.434	.511	RO	1185	.295	.377	.429
Ricky Bones (1991-1997)				H	505.1	28-32	4.68	L	2312	.283	.339	.445	SP	1071	.269	.346	.429	NO	2654	.274	.331	.459
Throws Right	1040.0	55-70	4.91	R	534.2	27-38	5.12	R	2244	.279	.345	.463	LC	242	.235	.288	.434	RO	1902	.292	.357	.446
Greg Booker (1984-1990)				H	118.2	3-3	3.72	L	492	.304	.375	.438	SP	375	.267	.341	.376	NO	537	.259	.341	.362
Throws Right	252.1	5-6	3.71	R	133.2	2-3	3.70	R	602	.242	.319	.328	LC	52	.381	.480	.667	RO	557	.280	.347	.393
Rich Bordi (1984-1988)				H	208.2	13-9	3.49	L	634	.289	.352	.430	SP	392	.270	.330	.388	NO	744	.249	.310	.391
Throws Right	329.0	20-16	4.16	R	120.1	7-7	5.31	R	765	.229	.281	.361	LC	281	.294	.374	.403	RO	655	.264	.317	.392
Chris Bosio (1986-1996)				H	897.1	52-46	3.80	L	3822	.273	.326	.400	SP	1746	.259	.317	.396	NO	4154	.255	.305	.380
Throws Right	1710.0	94-93	3.96	R	812.2	42-47	4.23	R	3402	.255	.304	.386	LC	535	.259	.309	.361	RO	3070	.277	.329	.413
Shawn Boskie (1990-1997)				H	437.1	25-29	5.06	L	2026	.281	.358	.465	SP	946	.277	.347	.472	NO	2092	.286	.346	.474
Throws Right	852.2	48-60	5.06	R	415.1	23-31	5.05	R	1738	.285	.327	.472	LC	278	.280	.373	.500	RO	1672	.278	.341	.460
Kent Bottenfield (1992-1997)				H	180.1	6-7	4.69	L	704	.292	.368	.435	SP	494	.258	.340	.390	NO	828	.273	.347	.441
Throws Right	364.0	14-21	4.20	R	183.2	8-14	3.72	R	881	.260	.330	.436	LC	212	.285	.376	.480	RO	757	.275	.348	.429
Ryan Bowen (1991-1995)				H	182.1	9-16	5.23	L	789	.292	.384	.421	SP	446	.235	.344	.349	NO	779	.292	.384	.453
Throws Right	326.0	17-28	5.30	R	143.2	8-12	5.39	R	695	.260	.354	.418	LC	84	.232	.346	.362	RO	705	.260	.354	.381
Oil Can Boyd (1984-1991)				H	678.2	42-35	3.93	L	2935	.253	.299	.382	SP	1196	.254	.304	.427	NO	3216	.266	.317	.424
Throws Right	1282.2	74-68	4.09	R	604.0	32-33	4.28	R	2430	.281	.329	.480	LC	417	.300	.345	.434	RO	2149	.265	.306	.429
Jeff Brantley (1988-1997)				H	355.2	22-14	2.94	L	1600	.241	.336	.358	SP	849	.199	.310	.285	NO	1642	.238	.312	.386
Throws Right	723.2	40-31	3.06	R	368.0	18-17	3.18	R	1445	.225	.289	.357	LC	1396	.223	.315	.334	RO	1403	.227	.316	.321
Doug Brocail (1992-1997)				H	180.2	9-7	3.84	L	743	.307	.381	.470	SP	445	.279	.371	.436	NO	884	.260	.318	.423
Throws Right	367.2	14-26	4.33	R	187.0	5-19	4.81	R	872	.256	.311	.413	LC	256	.263	.341	.429	RO	731	.304	.374	.460
Kevin Brown (1986-1997)				H	998.0	68-40	2.95	L	4145	.259	.324	.359	SP	1941	.255	.331	.358	NO	4638	.250	.307	.343
Throws Right	1921.1	121-92	3.42	R	923.1	53-52	3.93	R	3930	.253	.309	.345	LC	847	.267	.331	.401	RO	3437	.265	.330	.364
Tom Browning (1984-1995)				H	945.0	63-46	4.21	L	1424	.246	.313	.388	SP	1716	.273	.344	.428	NO	4843	.260	.305	.416
Throws Left	1920.2	123-90	3.94	R	975.2	60-44	3.68	R	6613	.265	.309	.424	LC	524	.236	.282	.344	RO	3194	.266	.317	.420
Jim Bullinger (1992-1997)				H	324.1	16-20	4.72	L	1354	.255	.356	.402	SP	808	.273	.387	.417	NO	1508	.260	.338	.389
Throws Right	636.1	34-40	4.96	R	312.0	18-20	5.22	R	1473	.270	.345	.407	LC	316	.225	.334	.336	RO	1319	.267	.364	.424

Situational Statistics: Pitching

Pitcher	IP	W-L	ERA		IP	W-L	ERA		PA	Avg	OBP	Slg		PA	Avg	OBP	Slg		PA	Avg	OBP	Slg
		Total			Home/Road				vs. Left/Right					Scoring Position/Late & Close					None On/Runners On			
Dave Burba (1990-1997)				H	421.1	26-26	3.70	L	1428	.277	.365	.425	SP	886	.252	.371	.384	NO	1788	.243	.314	.387
Throws Right	746.1	49-45	4.26	R	325.0	23-19	4.98	R	1814	.228	.310	.369	LC	422	.201	.320	.332	RO	1454	.258	.360	.402
Tim Burke (1985-1992)				H	342.0	28-12	2.55	L	1450	.268	.335	.378	SP	953	.230	.335	.319	NO	1489	.241	.283	.358
Throws Right	699.1	49-33	2.72	R	357.1	22-21	2.87	R	1441	.212	.268	.312	LC	1324	.236	.308	.338	RO	1402	.238	.321	.329
John Burkett (1987-1997)				H	810.0	48-37	4.04	L	3646	.279	.326	.404	SP	1594	.285	.347	.424	NO	3899	.264	.308	.384
Throws Right	1597.2	101-80	4.03	R	787.2	53-43	4.02	R	3118	.269	.314	.402	LC	506	.286	.335	.415	RO	2865	.288	.338	.430
Britt Burns (1984-1985)				H	184.1	13-12	4.15	L	262	.239	.286	.350	SP	344	.254	.346	.426	NO	856	.245	.298	.359
Throws Left	344.0	22-23	4.32	R	159.2	9-11	4.51	R	1192	.259	.328	.394	LC	144	.239	.285	.388	RO	598	.271	.353	.427
Todd Burns (1988-1993)				H	249.1	13-6	2.53	L	902	.227	.302	.348	SP	523	.250	.329	.374	NO	1125	.248	.317	.396
Throws Right	489.2	21-23	3.47	R	240.1	8-17	4.46	R	1143	.252	.312	.401	LC	403	.263	.350	.431	RO	920	.232	.296	.355
Ray Burris (1984-1987)				H	289.2	20-13	3.70	L	1077	.257	.326	.421	SP	507	.259	.369	.426	NO	1223	.262	.320	.439
Throws Right	487.0	28-30	4.27	R	197.1	8-17	5.20	R	1017	.276	.345	.438	LC	177	.236	.316	.369	RO	871	.273	.357	.415
John Butcher (1984-1986)				H	274.2	14-16	4.95	L	1343	.300	.339	.464	SP	597	.298	.345	.455	NO	1382	.281	.320	.428
Throws Right	553.1	25-33	4.70	R	278.2	11-17	4.46	R	1037	.285	.329	.418	LC	193	.289	.332	.444	RO	998	.313	.355	.466
Greg Cadaret (1987-1997)				H	365.2	22-12	3.54	L	880	.246	.337	.325	SP	950	.269	.379	.385	NO	1483	.258	.351	.379
Throws Left	679.2	37-30	3.97	R	314.0	15-18	4.47	R	2123	.268	.368	.400	LC	595	.263	.379	.344	RO	1520	.265	.366	.376
Rick Camp (1984-1985)				H	148.1	6-7	3.70	L	586	.263	.352	.331	SP	348	.241	.345	.303	NO	622	.266	.347	.405
Throws Right	276.1	12-12	3.58	R	128.0	6-5	3.45	R	591	.244	.320	.379	LC	155	.269	.355	.328	RO	555	.240	.323	.299
John Candelaria (1984-1993)				H	494.0	34-30	3.95	L	736	.209	.247	.292	SP	912	.254	.303	.437	NO	2192	.254	.304	.404
Throws Left	912.0	67-53	3.66	R	418.0	33-23	3.32	R	3030	.270	.313	.445	LC	670	.243	.303	.388	RO	1574	.264	.309	.432
Tom Candiotti (1984-1997)				H	1251.0	76-64	3.41	L	5173	.253	.318	.363	SP	2581	.242	.330	.358	NO	5841	.252	.306	.376
Throws Right	2397.0	132-138	3.54	R	1146.0	56-74	3.69	R	4955	.250	.307	.379	LC	865	.243	.310	.352	RO	4287	.251	.322	.363
Steve Carlton (1984-1988)				H	335.1	13-20	4.56	L	407	.255	.320	.366	SP	775	.271	.372	.431	NO	1601	.260	.331	.410
Throws Left	659.1	29-44	4.64	R	324.0	16-24	4.75	R	2472	.269	.350	.427	LC	133	.288	.361	.398	RO	1278	.277	.364	.430
Don Carman (1984-1992)				H	472.2	34-22	3.94	L	796	.244	.304	.403	SP	997	.260	.376	.404	NO	2251	.240	.303	.413
Throws Left	920.2	53-54	4.12	R	448.0	19-33	4.40	R	3127	.246	.326	.404	LC	593	.211	.304	.283	RO	1672	.253	.346	.391
Cris Carpenter (1988-1996)				H	210.1	10-9	4.11	L	841	.287	.351	.445	SP	576	.249	.327	.389	NO	908	.242	.289	.367
Throws Right	414.1	27-22	3.91	R	204.0	17-13	3.71	R	913	.223	.275	.346	LC	587	.272	.343	.448	RO	846	.267	.337	.423
Hector Carrasco (1994-1997)				H	156.2	6-9	3.39	L	569	.257	.346	.381	SP	405	.246	.368	.360	NO	674	.220	.316	.310
Throws Right	304.0	13-24	3.76	R	147.1	7-15	4.15	R	772	.216	.323	.287	LC	596	.249	.354	.339	RO	667	.249	.350	.347
Chuck Cary (1985-1993)				H	229.0	9-9	3.54	L	393	.264	.338	.406	SP	458	.295	.384	.534	NO	1015	.230	.300	.384
Throws Left	410.1	14-26	4.17	R	181.1	5-17	5.01	R	1357	.246	.314	.418	LC	153	.240	.375	.312	RO	735	.279	.347	.462
Frank Castillo (1991-1997)				H	555.1	29-34	3.97	L	2193	.261	.333	.398	SP	1047	.283	.376	.435	NO	2625	.257	.301	.412
Throws Right	1036.0	53-65	4.39	R	480.2	24-31	4.87	R	2254	.276	.317	.447	LC	287	.294	.349	.417	RO	1822	.288	.361	.441
Tony Castillo (1988-1997)				H	247.1	12-14	4.37	L	634	.249	.291	.363	SP	689	.278	.348	.394	NO	1036	.270	.322	.406
Throws Left	499.2	27-21	3.71	R	252.1	15-7	3.07	R	1513	.280	.346	.409	LC	729	.259	.324	.397	RO	1111	.272	.336	.384
John Cerutti (1985-1991)				H	405.1	21-19	4.24	L	765	.235	.287	.392	SP	843	.252	.327	.407	NO	2137	.274	.332	.446
Throws Left	861.0	49-43	3.94	R	455.2	28-24	3.89	R	2899	.280	.342	.452	LC	301	.257	.312	.429	RO	1527	.266	.330	.430
Norm Charlton (1988-1997)				H	375.0	23-21	3.60	L	780	.225	.328	.310	SP	924	.245	.345	.368	NO	1693	.221	.300	.325
Throws Left	750.0	43-48	3.50	R	375.0	20-27	3.41	R	2392	.240	.319	.359	LC	1301	.229	.321	.346	RO	1479	.255	.345	.376
Jim Clancy (1984-1991)				H	562.0	35-37	4.69	L	2969	.277	.342	.412	SP	1326	.288	.354	.451	NO	3249	.252	.313	.396
Throws Right	1318.0	74-86	4.40	R	756.0	39-49	4.19	R	2638	.249	.303	.406	LC	412	.299	.363	.427	RO	2358	.280	.338	.429
Mark Clark (1991-1997)				H	463.2	28-24	3.80	L	1911	.287	.340	.452	SP	926	.250	.329	.393	NO	2267	.273	.318	.435
Throws Right	914.1	59-45	4.07	R	450.2	31-21	4.33	R	1965	.256	.303	.402	LC	249	.250	.297	.368	RO	1609	.267	.326	.413
Mark Clear (1984-1990)				H	153.2	13-4	3.22	L	666	.209	.377	.292	SP	576	.202	.351	.299	NO	578	.225	.363	.335
Throws Right	311.1	23-16	3.58	R	157.2	10-12	3.94	R	739	.222	.336	.334	LC	430	.204	.351	.277	RO	827	.209	.350	.301
Roger Clemens (1984-1997)				H	1528.0	105-59	3.03	L	6791	.235	.303	.333	SP	2819	.213	.295	.302	NO	7413	.226	.285	.331
Throws Right	3040.0	213-118	2.97	R	1512.0	108-59	2.97	R	5629	.219	.275	.332	LC	1212	.210	.278	.313	RO	5007	.229	.298	.335
Pat Clements (1985-1992)				H	201.0	8-3	2.60	L	531	.231	.319	.323	SP	499	.300	.405	.378	NO	737	.263	.327	.352
Throws Left	360.1	17-11	3.77	R	159.1	9-8	5.25	R	1004	.293	.368	.386	LC	321	.310	.401	.388	RO	798	.281	.374	.377
Jamie Cocanower (1984-1986)				H	163.1	9-13	3.64	L	765	.285	.391	.384	SP	423	.261	.359	.349	NO	777	.273	.382	.374
Throws Right	335.2	14-25	4.18	R	172.1	5-12	4.80	R	733	.263	.353	.349	LC	136	.211	.324	.325	RO	721	.275	.362	.359
Chris Codiroli (1984-1990)				H	210.1	16-12	4.32	L	1023	.270	.346	.432	SP	527	.289	.389	.431	NO	1111	.271	.336	.440
Throws Right	448.0	25-33	5.08	R	237.2	9-21	5.68	R	972	.277	.344	.432	LC	140	.282	.357	.411	RO	884	.276	.358	.421
Pat Combs (1989-1992)				H	136.0	7-4	3.44	L	246	.245	.353	.377	SP	363	.247	.319	.372	NO	717	.249	.340	.341
Throws Left	305.0	17-17	4.22	R	169.0	10-13	4.85	R	1095	.259	.338	.373	LC	80	.160	.203	.213	RO	624	.265	.340	.411
David Cone (1986-1997)				H	1073.2	72-40	3.24	L	5104	.234	.317	.359	SP	2238	.203	.304	.312	NO	5338	.223	.295	.342
Throws Right	2189.0	148-86	3.13	R	1115.1	76-46	3.13	R	3955	.210	.276	.317	LC	885	.231	.309	.354	RO	3721	.222	.305	.337
Tim Conroy (1984-1987)				H	154.2	4-12	5.12	L	287	.230	.339	.354	SP	319	.258	.370	.431	NO	678	.255	.354	.369
Throws Left	274.1	9-20	5.18	R	119.2	5-8	5.49	R	941	.273	.365	.439	LC	79	.279	.367	.515	RO	550	.273	.366	.485
Dennis Cook (1988-1997)				H	411.1	24-15	3.46	L	812	.250	.315	.406	SP	837	.256	.353	.423	NO	1844	.245	.297	.406
Throws Left	752.0	38-32	3.93	R	340.2	14-17	4.49	R	2375	.253	.323	.425	LC	463	.246	.338	.359	RO	1343	.264	.354	.441
Steve Cooke (1992-1997)				H	278.0	13-19	4.50	L	436	.286	.369	.436	SP	632	.284	.370	.430	NO	1312	.276	.333	.445
Throws Left	543.2	25-36	4.34	R	265.2	12-17	4.17	R	1924	.275	.334	.443	LC	195	.244	.284	.389	RO	1048	.278	.349	.437
Francisco Cordova (1996-1997)				H	149.0	8-11	3.93	L	540	.317	.370	.471	SP	281	.284	.354	.440	NO	689	.243	.286	.363
Throws Right	277.2	15-15	3.79	R	128.2	7-4	3.64	R	618	.212	.257	.325	LC	191	.275	.312	.449	RO	469	.288	.346	.439
Rheal Cormier (1991-1997)				H	366.0	25-19	3.98	L	609	.246	.284	.337	SP	732	.252	.306	.395	NO	1761	.269	.309	.399
Throws Left	714.2	38-39	4.18	R	348.2	13-20	4.39	R	2403	.285	.326	.441	LC	255	.300	.343	.391	RO	1251	.289	.329	.452
Edwin Correa (1985-1987)				H	120.2	9-7	5.07	L	637	.230	.334	.325	SP	378	.224	.354	.360	NO	694	.234	.350	.365
Throws Right	282.2	16-19	5.16	R	162.0	7-12	5.33	R	635	.259	.385	.458	LC	60	.154	.267	.231	RO	578	.256	.371	.420

Situational Statistics: Pitching

Pitcher	Total IP	W-L	ERA	H/R	IP	W-L	ERA	L/R	PA	Avg	OBP	Slg	SP/LC	PA	Avg	OBP	Slg	NO/RO	PA	Avg	OBP	Slg
Jim Corsi (1988-1997)				H	183.0	15-9	3.44	L	728	.270	.344	.374	SP	469	.249	.338	.340	NO	808	.253	.328	.330
Throws Right	378.0	18-19	3.26	R	195.0	3-10	3.09	R	864	.241	.313	.324	LC	599	.272	.361	.396	RO	784	.256	.327	.365
Joe Cowley (1984-1987)				H	217.1	17-11	3.23	L	1020	.010	.351	.405	SP	433	.194	.335	.325	NO	1070	.238	.320	.421
Throws Right	417.0	32-23	4.17	R	199.2	15-12	5.41	R	775	.219	.298	.393	LC	167	.213	.293	.360	RO	728	.222	.341	.366
Danny Cox (1984-1995)				H	666.0	39-31	3.35	L	2557	.277	.343	.418	SP	1287	.259	.328	.387	NO	2923	.258	.320	.387
Throws Right	1215.0	71-69	3.67	R	549.0	32-38	4.05	R	2525	.247	.301	.358	LC	606	.241	.311	.325	RO	2159	.267	.325	.389
Steve Crawford (1984-1991)				H	240.2	19-6	4.71	L	955	.320	.386	.463	SP	685	.294	.372	.437	NO	975	.270	.318	.391
Throws Right	463.2	27-18	4.15	R	223.0	10-12	3.55	R	1050	.257	.307	.377	LC	473	.276	.348	.353	RO	1030	.302	.370	.444
Tim Crews (1987-1992)				H	215.1	7-7	3.55	L	898	.284	.335	.413	SP	526	.267	.372	.433	NO	972	.263	.286	.361
Throws Right	423.2	11-13	3.44	R	208.1	4-6	3.37	R	899	.257	.297	.376	LC	370	.258	.320	.390	RO	825	.280	.352	.439
Chuck Crim (1987-1994)				H	359.1	27-20	3.86	L	1273	.274	.335	.394	SP	896	.282	.372	.406	NO	1542	.261	.302	.397
Throws Right	696.1	47-43	3.83	R	337.0	20-23	3.79	R	1696	.270	.320	.395	LC	932	.275	.336	.393	RO	1427	.285	.354	.392
Ron Darling (1984-1995)				H	1204.1	75-55	3.52	L	5203	.254	.323	.386	SP	2419	.247	.337	.381	NO	5745	.251	.317	.390
Throws Right	2325.0	135-113	3.89	R	1120.2	60-60	4.29	R	4650	.250	.322	.400	LC	703	.230	.315	.340	RO	4108	.254	.330	.397
Danny Darwin (1984-1997)				H	1111.0	56-64	3.73	L	4936	.284	.339	.449	SP	2327	.250	.313	.383	NO	5504	.254	.301	.413
Throws Right	2253.2	118-134	3.83	R	1142.2	62-70	3.93	R	4511	.230	.272	.363	LC	1148	.243	.300	.361	RO	3943	.263	.316	.400
Mark Davis (1984-1997)				H	492.0	28-32	3.86	L	1030	.221	.299	.332	SP	1267	.254	.355	.392	NO	2158	.243	.321	.380
Throws Left	984.0	44-76	4.10	R	492.0	16-45	4.35	R	3203	.259	.344	.408	LC	1136	.233	.327	.342	RO	2075	.257	.346	.400
Ron Davis (1984-1988)				H	129.2	9-6	5.21	L	575	.289	.382	.481	SP	469	.280	.388	.454	NO	488	.270	.340	.451
Throws Right	260.0	12-26	5.40	R	130.1	3-20	6.01	R	596	.274	.352	.441	LC	561	.276	.369	.469	RO	683	.291	.386	.468
Storm Davis (1984-1994)				H	790.0	50-44	3.95	L	3228	.269	.350	.387	SP	1700	.277	.362	.391	NO	3489	.263	.327	.389
Throws Right	1479.2	92-85	4.12	R	689.2	43-41	4.33	R	3138	.265	.321	.383	LC	662	.273	.349	.405	RO	2877	.272	.347	.380
Bill Dawley (1984-1989)				H	206.2	9-12	3.88	L	678	.265	.340	.395	SP	514	.261	.366	.423	NO	851	.251	.300	.389
Throws Right	391.0	21-24	3.54	R	184.1	13-13	3.27	R	942	.247	.305	.389	LC	480	.230	.315	.316	RO	769	.258	.342	.394
Ken Dayley (1984-1993)				H	208.1	13-13	3.20	L	542	.267	.332	.351	SP	555	.287	.392	.389	NO	824	.233	.297	.340
Throws Left	397.2	23-31	3.30	R	189.1	10-18	3.66	R	1147	.252	.327	.370	LC	673	.272	.339	.367	RO	865	.281	.359	.387
Jeff Dedmon (1984-1988)				H	206.2	10-6	3.44	L	781	.259	.357	.377	SP	607	.256	.379	.367	NO	792	.260	.330	.357
Throws Right	390.0	20-16	3.74	R	183.1	10-10	4.07	R	895	.258	.331	.356	LC	399	.264	.356	.345	RO	884	.256	.356	.374
Jose DeJesus (1988-1994)				H	169.1	8-11	4.09	L	897	.217	.356	.298	SP	430	.229	.348	.328	NO	805	.222	.347	.325
Throws Right	349.0	20-19	3.84	R	179.2	12-8	3.61	R	616	.239	.332	.379	LC	114	.235	.295	.333	RO	708	.231	.346	.340
Jose DeLeon (1984-1995)				H	938.0	40-60	3.76	L	3994	.258	.351	.390	SP	1923	.233	.324	.355	NO	4342	.217	.307	.344
Throws Right	1789.1	79-116	3.82	R	851.1	39-57	4.00	R	3534	.191	.268	.305	LC	670	.233	.325	.376	RO	3186	.239	.320	.358
Rich DeLucia (1990-1997)				H	276.0	24-16	4.70	L	1041	.284	.383	.466	SP	623	.261	.364	.432	NO	1313	.244	.312	.419
Throws Right	543.0	36-44	4.62	R	267.0	12-28	4.55	R	1313	.231	.295	.402	LC	561	.261	.370	.460	RO	1041	.268	.362	.444
John Denny (1984-1986)				H	300.1	13-20	3.69	L	1221	.275	.336	.398	SP	573	.231	.318	.350	NO	1344	.259	.311	.379
Throws Right	556.1	29-31	3.56	R	256.0	16-11	3.41	R	1094	.245	.294	.360	LC	206	.266	.330	.424	RO	971	.263	.323	.381
Jim Deshaies (1984-1995)				H	773.2	47-37	3.85	L	1084	.277	.368	.430	SP	1498	.247	.331	.389	NO	3831	.247	.315	.406
Throws Left	1525.0	84-95	4.14	R	751.1	37-58	4.65	R	5344	.246	.310	.407	LC	346	.225	.287	.318	RO	2597	.258	.327	.418
Rob Dibble (1988-1995)				H	238.0	12-10	3.10	L	1031	.194	.318	.284	SP	733	.184	.292	.268	NO	981	.196	.291	.289
Throws Right	477.0	27-25	2.98	R	239.0	15-15	2.86	R	948	.200	.275	.294	LC	1079	.219	.311	.320	RO	998	.198	.304	.289
Frank DiPino (1984-1993)				H	306.2	19-17	3.43	L	817	.234	.288	.315	SP	812	.275	.358	.384	NO	1278	.248	.315	.360
Throws Left	598.0	30-32	3.88	R	291.1	12-15	4.36	R	1736	.274	.347	.420	LC	751	.266	.346	.381	RO	1275	.274	.343	.413
Jerry Dipoto (1993-1997)				H	169.0	11-4	3.73	L	648	.292	.379	.372	SP	533	.294	.392	.372	NO	632	.301	.364	.407
Throws Right	323.2	20-15	4.12	R	154.2	9-11	4.54	R	794	.286	.353	.383	LC	579	.288	.371	.355	RO	810	.278	.365	.353
Ken Dixon (1984-1987)				H	265.0	12-20	5.13	L	1069	.248	.322	.436	SP	511	.256	.344	.432	NO	1236	.248	.306	.457
Throws Right	482.1	26-28	4.66	R	217.1	14-8	4.10	R	1000	.264	.318	.468	LC	146	.260	.336	.405	RO	833	.268	.341	.445
John Doherty (1992-1996)				H	283.1	19-14	4.99	L	1121	.302	.349	.438	SP	592	.323	.403	.481	NO	1251	.283	.320	.403
Throws Right	521.1	32-31	4.87	R	238.0	13-17	4.73	R	1137	.290	.340	.404	LC	290	.327	.370	.477	RO	1007	.314	.375	.445
John Dopson (1985-1994)				H	410.2	17-22	3.88	L	1538	.269	.334	.386	SP	790	.263	.340	.384	NO	1803	.268	.330	.404
Throws Right	725.1	30-47	4.27	R	314.2	13-25	4.78	R	1587	.266	.327	.418	LC	168	.338	.394	.538	RO	1322	.267	.331	.399
Rich Dotson (1984-1990)				H	556.2	31-39	4.28	L	2387	.259	.329	.424	SP	1076	.268	.347	.413	NO	2646	.257	.325	.416
Throws Right	1057.1	55-73	4.59	R	500.2	24-35	4.96	R	2201	.277	.343	.424	LC	301	.271	.340	.416	RO	1942	.283	.349	.435
Kelly Downs (1986-1993)				H	479.0	32-19	3.51	L	2197	.261	.332	.365	SP	1112	.235	.332	.355	NO	2277	.246	.311	.344
Throws Right	963.2	57-53	3.86	R	484.2	25-34	4.20	R	1921	.237	.308	.358	LC	283	.215	.307	.260	RO	1841	.255	.334	.386
Doug Drabek (1986-1997)				H	1261.1	80-57	3.23	L	5356	.264	.323	.395	SP	2342	.246	.324	.379	NO	6021	.247	.296	.373
Throws Right	2426.1	149-123	3.58	R	1165.0	70-66	3.96	R	4673	.240	.285	.370	LC	845	.218	.288	.312	RO	4008	.261	.319	.399
Dave Dravecky (1984-1989)				H	385.1	22-21	3.15	L	447	.198	.261	.272	SP	709	.226	.304	.338	NO	1905	.250	.305	.367
Throws Left	774.0	45-44	3.10	R	388.2	23-23	3.10	R	2705	.252	.310	.379	LC	294	.270	.330	.468	RO	1247	.236	.300	.361
Mike Dunne (1987-1992)				H	258.0	14-14	3.49	L	1101	.278	.371	.391	SP	586	.253	.358	.340	NO	1129	.259	.338	.386
Throws Right	474.1	25-30	4.08	R	216.1	11-16	4.78	R	980	.244	.313	.352	LC	61	.255	.410	.362	RO	952	.264	.350	.355
Dennis Eckersley (1984-1997)				H	661.1	52-36	3.24	L	2746	.267	.304	.411	SP	1364	.236	.293	.371	NO	3150	.243	.268	.372
Throws Right	1345.1	73-72	3.27	R	684.0	23-36	3.30	R	2647	.213	.240	.338	LC	1802	.223	.259	.356	RO	2243	.235	.280	.379
Tom Edens (1987-1995)				H	145.0	12-5	4.66	L	555	.271	.336	.382	SP	426	.266	.360	.373	NO	689	.273	.334	.404
Throws Right	312.1	19-12	3.86	R	167.1	7-7	3.17	R	786	.263	.339	.384	LC	262	.241	.331	.313	RO	652	.259	.341	.359
Mark Eichhorn (1986-1996)				H	441.1	26-20	2.83	L	1534	.285	.351	.398	SP	1266	.239	.335	.337	NO	1738	.245	.285	.342
Throws Right	847.2	48-40	2.89	R	406.1	22-20	2.95	R	1987	.222	.280	.311	LC	1175	.238	.309	.311	RO	1783	.253	.336	.356
Cal Eldred (1991-1997)				H	462.1	34-18	3.50	L	1918	.241	.322	.384	SP	896	.230	.325	.370	NO	2155	.251	.318	.404
Throws Right	863.2	58-49	4.16	R	401.1	24-31	4.91	R	1757	.250	.317	.417	LC	298	.272	.314	.456	RO	1520	.237	.322	.393
Scott Erickson (1990-1997)				H	798.1	55-39	4.15	L	3599	.291	.353	.421	SP	1700	.284	.354	.427	NO	3671	.270	.336	.400
Throws Right	1532.0	99-83	4.24	R	733.2	44-44	4.33	R	2981	.256	.321	.380	LC	474	.288	.357	.435	RO	2909	.283	.342	.407

Pitcher	IP	W-L	ERA		IP	W-L	ERA		PA	Avg	OBP	Slg		PA	Avg	OBP	Slg		PA	Avg	OBP	Slg
		Total				Home/Road				vs. Left/Right				Scoring Position/Late & Close					None On/Runners On			
Shawn Estes (1995-1997)				H	147.2	12-5	2.99	L	243	.245	.368	.300	SP	311	.220	.336	.282	NO	695	.213	.308	.303
Throws Left	288.1	22-13	3.50	R	140.2	10-8	4.03	R	987	.225	.317	.324	LC	70	.153	.265	.203	RO	535	.250	.352	.342
Steve Farr (1984-1994)				H	442.1	32-17	3.05	L	1659	.251	.340	.367	SP	1016	.234	.336	.344	NO	1820	.250	.321	.380
Throws Right	824.1	48-45	3.25	R	382.0	16-28	3.51	R	1822	.239	.306	.367	LC	1031	.244	.329	.333	RO	1661	.238	.324	.352
John Farrell (1987-1996)				H	331.0	18-22	4.62	L	1666	.273	.347	.408	SP	763	.271	.345	.412	NO	1725	.261	.327	.407
Throws Right	698.2	36-46	4.56	R	367.2	18-24	4.60	R	1374	.266	.323	.419	LC	163	.322	.361	.470	RO	1315	.283	.349	.422
Jeff Fassero (1991-1997)				H	541.2	39-29	3.49	L	847	.226	.285	.299	SP	1199	.247	.328	.350	NO	2601	.239	.293	.352
Throws Left	1084.1	74-57	3.29	R	542.2	35-28	3.08	R	3739	.249	.310	.372	LC	693	.226	.299	.310	RO	1985	.254	.321	.367
Alex Fernandez (1990-1997)				H	778.1	50-36	3.63	L	3264	.262	.321	.413	SP	1435	.247	.324	.352	NO	3893	.247	.302	.397
Throws Right	1567.0	96-75	3.76	R	788.2	46-39	3.88	R	3294	.243	.302	.375	LC	576	.236	.287	.352	RO	2665	.262	.326	.390
Sid Fernandez (1984-1997)				H	973.1	67-39	2.71	L	1202	.211	.288	.322	SP	1601	.211	.301	.338	NO	4728	.206	.279	.342
Throws Left	1860.2	114-95	3.35	R	887.1	48-56	4.05	R	6415	.209	.285	.355	LC	435	.260	.317	.444	RO	2889	.215	.296	.363
Mike Fetters (1989-1997)				H	218.0	11-10	2.97	L	893	.283	.358	.405	SP	619	.259	.349	.365	NO	923	.259	.343	.367
Throws Right	450.0	16-25	3.38	R	232.0	5-15	3.76	R	1040	.245	.333	.333	LC	872	.256	.355	.362	RO	1010	.266	.345	.367
Tom Filer (1985-1992)				H	126.2	11-9	3.69	L	561	.255	.325	.398	SP	242	.254	.331	.448	NO	655	.256	.311	.371
Throws Right	266.2	21-15	4.05	R	140.0	10-6	4.37	R	549	.273	.325	.386	LC	33	.296	.387	.333	RO	455	.277	.345	.424
Pete Filson (1984-1990)				H	180.1	9-7	3.99	L	384	.244	.307	.388	SP	306	.233	.337	.342	NO	701	.273	.334	.456
Throws Right	289.1	11-15	4.23	R	109.0	2-8	4.62	R	877	.266	.338	.447	LC	212	.226	.302	.332	RO	560	.242	.323	.393
Chuck Finley (1986-1997)				H	1195.2	80-54	3.30	L	1482	.265	.343	.358	SP	2300	.257	.343	.373	NO	5434	.254	.329	.392
Throws Left	2238.1	142-120	3.69	R	1042.2	63-66	4.15	R	8023	.253	.327	.387	LC	913	.254	.331	.364	RO	4071	.255	.330	.369
Brian Fisher (1985-1992)				H	323.2	16-20	4.84	L	1378	.284	.371	.432	SP	791	.243	.329	.407	NO	1506	.262	.324	.404
Throws Right	640.0	36-34	4.39	R	316.1	20-15	4.24	R	1372	.238	.289	.394	LC	457	.240	.332	.361	RO	1244	.258	.337	.424
Mike Flanagan (1984-1992)				H	562.1	33-27	3.73	L	942	.234	.294	.309	SP	1151	.264	.325	.386	NO	2792	.270	.342	.408
Throws Left	1164.2	55-69	4.06	R	602.1	23-42	4.38	R	4032	.279	.341	.429	LC	435	.248	.329	.351	RO	2182	.271	.319	.404
Dave Fleming (1991-1995)				H	272.2	16-11	4.26	L	471	.252	.322	.404	SP	719	.260	.349	.389	NO	1491	.282	.343	.448
Throws Left	610.1	38-32	4.67	R	337.2	22-21	5.01	R	2220	.285	.354	.437	LC	171	.292	.355	.461	RO	1200	.276	.355	.409
Ray Fontenot (1984-1986)				H	212.1	8-14	4.28	L	325	.241	.308	.357	SP	437	.304	.364	.486	NO	937	.285	.345	.410
Throws Left	396.1	17-24	4.20	R	184.0	9-10	4.11	R	1356	.304	.356	.445	LC	249	.317	.398	.458	RO	744	.300	.349	.451
Bob Forsch (1984-1989)				H	429.1	26-19	3.65	L	1786	.265	.328	.372	SP	849	.298	.371	.426	NO	2109	.264	.313	.402
Throws Right	842.0	50-41	4.19	R	412.2	24-23	4.78	R	1787	.280	.327	.433	LC	241	.244	.314	.376	RO	1464	.284	.349	.405
Tony Fossas (1988-1997)				H	206.2	10-9	2.70	L	726	.206	.275	.285	SP	644	.247	.343	.344	NO	758	.263	.330	.403
Throws Left	392.0	16-21	3.70	R	185.1	6-12	4.81	R	996	.304	.381	.469	LC	577	.254	.344	.380	RO	964	.262	.342	.380
Kevin Foster (1993-1997)				H	254.1	19-9	3.82	L	999	.273	.345	.458	SP	492	.253	.346	.401	NO	1264	.257	.327	.466
Throws Right	488.2	32-29	4.71	R	234.1	13-20	5.68	R	1104	.239	.319	.442	LC	126	.316	.365	.544	RO	839	.252	.338	.422
John Franco (1984-1997)				H	509.0	48-23	2.46	L	824	.234	.295	.294	SP	1190	.237	.343	.312	NO	1978	.246	.304	.334
Throws Left	936.0	77-60	2.57	R	427.0	29-37	2.82	R	3090	.248	.320	.338	LC	2422	.243	.317	.325	RO	1936	.245	.326	.323
Willie Fraser (1986-1995)				H	316.2	17-19	4.35	L	1353	.258	.333	.456	SP	738	.287	.368	.461	NO	1602	.235	.306	.401
Throws Right	657.0	38-40	4.47	R	340.1	21-22	4.68	R	1471	.251	.314	.393	LC	410	.279	.346	.417	RO	1222	.280	.345	.453
George Frazier (1984-1987)				H	179.2	15-8	4.66	L	767	.265	.360	.397	SP	508	.264	.386	.416	NO	779	.248	.341	.368
Throws Right	343.2	24-23	4.98	R	164.0	10-15	5.32	R	763	.268	.358	.410	LC	423	.264	.352	.410	RO	751	.287	.377	.443
Marvin Freeman (1986-1996)				H	304.2	17-12	5.29	L	1237	.291	.376	.442	SP	757	.267	.354	.370	NO	1397	.263	.341	.410
Throws Right	593.2	35-28	4.64	R	289.0	18-16	3.96	R	1367	.249	.316	.379	LC	277	.238	.320	.340	RO	1207	.275	.349	.407
Steve Frey (1989-1996)				H	155.0	9-7	2.79	L	462	.249	.339	.400	SP	461	.237	.349	.320	NO	622	.265	.352	.436
Throws Left	304.0	18-15	3.76	R	149.0	9-8	4.77	R	873	.269	.358	.395	LC	573	.242	.351	.344	RO	713	.261	.351	.360
Todd Frohwirth (1987-1996)				H	238.0	14-4	3.21	L	678	.285	.376	.398	SP	626	.260	.367	.371	NO	857	.238	.302	.318
Throws Right	417.2	20-19	3.60	R	179.2	6-15	4.11	R	1098	.229	.298	.311	LC	575	.232	.331	.296	RO	919	.262	.353	.369
Gene Garber (1984-1988)				H	217.2	16-16	3.80	L	810	.252	.306	.358	SP	562	.254	.342	.350	NO	844	.270	.303	.382
Throws Right	397.2	22-31	3.35	R	180.0	8-15	2.90	R	854	.278	.327	.384	LC	594	.262	.317	.362	RO	820	.260	.331	.375
Ramon Garcia (1991-1997)				H	158.1	7-8	4.66	L	643	.282	.354	.469	SP	314	.300	.384	.455	NO	769	.265	.325	.452
Throws Right	312.2	17-16	4.84	R	154.1	10-8	5.02	R	680	.258	.317	.432	LC	190	.287	.364	.451	RO	554	.277	.350	.446
Mike Gardiner (1990-1995)				H	190.1	8-12	5.11	L	811	.273	.335	.422	SP	487	.271	.364	.420	NO	930	.251	.313	.401
Throws Right	393.2	17-27	5.21	R	203.1	9-15	5.31	R	927	.271	.343	.439	LC	188	.286	.362	.440	RO	808	.298	.370	.468
Mark Gardner (1989-1997)				H	605.0	34-27	4.09	L	2625	.269	.343	.420	SP	1244	.273	.364	.437	NO	2947	.249	.310	.404
Throws Right	1173.0	65-64	4.37	R	568.0	31-37	4.67	R	2384	.252	.314	.422	LC	338	.296	.371	.478	RO	2062	.279	.357	.447
Wes Gardner (1984-1991)				H	232.0	10-10	4.07	L	987	.292	.385	.437	SP	565	.269	.355	.399	NO	1105	.249	.332	.394
Throws Right	466.1	18-30	4.90	R	234.1	8-20	5.72	R	1068	.242	.307	.395	LC	154	.336	.441	.531	RO	950	.284	.360	.440
Scott Garrelts (1984-1991)				H	481.1	39-29	2.97	L	1991	.250	.332	.353	SP	1068	.233	.347	.352	NO	2144	.224	.293	.325
Throws Right	921.2	67-51	3.30	R	440.1	28-22	3.70	R	1847	.211	.287	.325	LC	811	.220	.314	.283	RO	1694	.241	.333	.359
Paul Gibson (1988-1996)				H	297.1	14-10	3.36	L	746	.278	.338	.429	SP	749	.270	.364	.398	NO	1219	.268	.339	.409
Throws Right	556.2	22-24	4.07	R	259.1	8-14	4.89	R	1677	.263	.342	.402	LC	497	.271	.335	.424	RO	1204	.267	.343	.412
Tom Glavine (1987-1997)				H	1067.2	75-46	3.35	L	1733	.262	.334	.351	SP	2221	.243	.353	.341	NO	5312	.247	.295	.358
Throws Left	2196.2	153-99	3.40	R	1129.0	79-53	3.45	R	7483	.247	.307	.359	LC	830	.254	.307	.353	RO	3904	.254	.335	.356
Jerry Don Gleaton (1984-1992)				H	174.2	4-6	4.02	L	469	.254	.315	.356	SP	478	.229	.334	.336	NO	683	.276	.351	.402
Throws Left	340.2	11-15	3.96	R	166.0	7-9	3.90	R	969	.255	.344	.379	LC	324	.252	.348	.380	RO	755	.234	.319	.342
Dwight Gooden (1984-1997)				H	1310.2	102-45	2.91	L	5629	.237	.305	.334	SP	2615	.230	.303	.324	NO	5855	.239	.304	.346
Throws Right	2446.2	177-97	3.31	R	1136.0	75-53	3.79	R	4477	.241	.298	.353	LC	968	.216	.277	.289	RO	4251	.239	.299	.337
Tom Gordon (1988-1997)				H	834.1	47-45	3.90	L	3500	.262	.351	.367	SP	1858	.249	.351	.379	NO	3653	.245	.326	.369
Throws Right	1548.0	97-90	4.21	R	713.2	50-45	4.57	R	3243	.231	.316	.372	LC	821	.245	.334	.361	RO	3090	.249	.344	.370
Goose Gossage (1984-1994)				H	273.0	26-13	2.84	L	1120	.247	.327	.357	SP	733	.261	.348	.379	NO	1211	.221	.292	.324
Throws Right	573.0	43-34	3.35	R	300.0	17-21	3.81	R	1261	.236	.299	.361	LC	1227	.234	.313	.334	RO	1170	.262	.333	.397

Situational Statistics: Pitching

Pitcher	IP	W-L	ERA		IP	W-L	ERA		PA	Avg	OBP	Slg		PA	Avg	OBP	Slg		PA	Avg	OBP	Slg
	Total			**Home/Road**				**vs. Left/Right**					**Scoring Position/Late & Close**					**None On/Runners On**				
Jim Gott (1984-1995)				H	420.2	24-22	3.02	L	1721	.249	.338	.364	SP	1024	.240	.344	.341	NO	1834	.239	.308	.345
Throws Right	807.1	42-50	3.58	R	386.2	18-28	4.19	R	1717	.247	.308	.347	LC	1070	.266	.348	.370	RO	1604	.260	.341	.368
Joe Grahe (1990-1995)				H	195.1	11-14	4.88	L	747	.0?0	.000	.151	SP	521	.287	.391	.439	NO	823	.268	.338	.362
Throws Right	367.2	21-26	4.46	R	172.1	10-12	3.97	R	912	.252	.340	.350	LC	457	.254	.337	.358	RO	836	.302	.390	.435
Mark Grant (1984-1993)				H	306.0	11-14	4.59	L	1416	.274	.343	.403	SP	748	.258	.350	.408	NO	1495	.270	.329	.407
Throws Right	638.2	22-32	4.31	R	332.2	11-18	4.09	R	1325	.280	.338	.461	LC	245	.290	.377	.448	RO	1246	.286	.355	.462
Tommy Greene (1989-1997)				H	344.1	23-10	3.61	L	1426	.275	.356	.417	SP	667	.254	.328	.401	NO	1551	.244	.314	.383
Throws Right	628.0	38-25	4.14	R	283.2	15-15	4.79	R	1264	.220	.273	.357	LC	141	.252	.312	.378	RO	1139	.255	.322	.395
Jason Grimsley (1989-1996)				H	219.0	9-9	5.30	L	1014	.275	.372	.396	SP	621	.256	.401	.392	NO	990	.273	.362	.396
Throws Right	426.0	18-25	5.39	R	207.0	9-16	5.48	R	951	.272	.388	.417	LC	92	.350	.411	.538	RO	975	.274	.398	.418
Buddy Groom (1992-1997)				H	152.0	1-5	6.45	L	483	.280	.347	.395	SP	434	.305	.403	.458	NO	686	.287	.348	.450
Throws Left	305.0	9-15	5.31	R	153.0	8-10	4.18	R	903	.315	.389	.484	LC	260	.323	.390	.498	RO	700	.320	.399	.456
Kevin Gross (1984-1997)				H	1209.1	76-70	3.83	L	5699	.272	.357	.408	SP	2738	.266	.352	.379	NO	5764	.263	.332	.408
Throws Right	2391.2	138-152	4.14	R	1182.1	62-83	4.45	R	4645	.254	.310	.375	LC	876	.287	.358	.374	RO	4580	.265	.340	.373
Cecilio Guante (1984-1990)				H	254.0	17-8	3.19	L	822	.239	.343	.403	SP	610	.210	.305	.341	NO	1046	.222	.299	.387
Throws Right	467.2	27-28	3.52	R	213.2	10-20	3.92	R	1140	.220	.282	.373	LC	659	.222	.316	.345	RO	916	.235	.317	.382
Eddie Guardado (1993-1997)				H	150.2	7-12	5.08	L	432	.244	.285	.382	SP	397	.329	.386	.541	NO	771	.264	.335	.466
Throws Left	322.2	13-28	5.47	R	172.0	6-16	5.81	R	999	.298	.378	.515	LC	319	.254	.332	.460	RO	660	.302	.368	.480
Mark Gubicza (1984-1997)				H	1251.1	75-71	3.68	L	5010	.265	.335	.379	SP	2441	.267	.334	.392	NO	5360	.256	.322	.372
Throws Right	2224.1	132-136	3.96	R	973.0	57-65	4.32	R	4468	.262	.318	.378	LC	778	.262	.345	.366	RO	4118	.274	.334	.388
Lee Guetterman (1984-1996)				H	360.2	27-16	4.54	L	810	.246	.315	.329	SP	898	.268	.354	.403	NO	1408	.278	.325	.392
Throws Left	658.1	38-36	4.33	R	297.2	11-20	4.08	R	2022	.296	.350	.436	LC	773	.284	.344	.426	RO	1424	.285	.355	.419
Ron Guidry (1984-1988)				H	436.0	30-17	3.24	L	617	.259	.291	.400	SP	754	.246	.286	.409	NO	2031	.264	.306	.423
Throws Left	820.2	48-40	3.85	R	384.2	18-23	4.54	R	2783	.263	.302	.428	LC	275	.307	.335	.452	RO	1369	.259	.292	.422
Bill Gullickson (1984-1994)				H	971.1	69-46	4.00	L	3987	.287	.332	.454	SP	1758	.268	.324	.423	NO	4480	.275	.313	.441
Throws Right	1781.2	116-96	4.18	R	810.1	47-50	4.45	R	3508	.267	.300	.430	LC	556	.272	.322	.382	RO	3015	.281	.324	.444
Mark Guthrie (1989-1997)				H	309.0	15-17	3.79	L	749	.275	.325	.379	SP	803	.269	.349	.397	NO	1486	.285	.341	.423
Throws Right	651.2	32-36	4.07	R	342.2	17-19	4.33	R	2050	.273	.338	.420	LC	747	.273	.335	.430	RO	1313	.259	.328	.391
Jose Guzman (1985-1994)				H	635.2	44-39	4.05	L	2616	.259	.329	.401	SP	1280	.236	.325	.350	NO	3061	.253	.321	.398
Throws Right	1224.1	80-74	4.05	R	588.2	37-36	4.10	R	2619	.253	.324	.393	LC	345	.265	.337	.356	RO	2174	.260	.336	.396
Juan Guzman (1991-1997)				H	535.1	33-21	4.02	L	2364	.254	.339	.348	SP	1160	.238	.331	.361	NO	2601	.232	.315	.340
Throws Right	1070.2	70-50	4.03	R	535.1	37-29	4.03	R	2213	.226	.305	.369	LC	327	.264	.350	.387	RO	1976	.251	.332	.383
Moose Haas (1984-1987)				H	249.1	16-9	3.32	L	1035	.270	.315	.385	SP	388	.297	.358	.450	NO	1178	.262	.289	.397
Throws Right	464.0	26-23	3.90	R	214.2	10-15	4.57	R	885	.267	.290	.434	LC	167	.292	.341	.455	RO	742	.280	.328	.425
John Habyan (1985-1996)				H	280.2	20-10	3.66	L	984	.277	.337	.423	SP	718	.266	.363	.415	NO	1182	.261	.308	.397
Throws Right	532.1	26-24	3.85	R	251.2	6-15	4.33	R	1276	.256	.320	.399	LC	619	.288	.347	.404	RO	1078	.270	.349	.425
Joey Hamilton (1994-1997)				H	375.2	22-18	3.43	L	1439	.268	.334	.402	SP	723	.256	.335	.357	NO	1746	.252	.314	.384
Throws Right	717.1	42-31	3.70	R	341.2	20-13	4.00	R	1597	.244	.311	.353	LC	273	.272	.353	.353	RO	1290	.260	.332	.365
Atlee Hammaker (1984-1995)				H	384.1	23-17	3.33	L	537	.214	.277	.288	SP	688	.277	.355	.394	NO	1717	.245	.292	.378
Throws Left	692.1	36-47	3.80	R	308.0	15-30	4.38	R	2371	.264	.318	.395	LC	279	.273	.349	.384	RO	1191	.270	.337	.372
Chris Hammond (1990-1997)				H	406.1	25-22	3.96	L	793	.264	.331	.405	SP	903	.298	.377	.437	NO	2042	.251	.313	.369
Throws Left	830.0	46-53	4.51	R	423.2	21-31	5.03	R	2797	.278	.343	.415	LC	243	.298	.361	.482	RO	1548	.310	.377	.474
Mike Hampton (1993-1997)				H	310.0	23-13	3.40	L	552	.298	.351	.439	SP	680	.260	.342	.396	NO	1374	.264	.321	.376
Throws Left	592.1	37-32	3.80	R	282.1	14-19	4.24	R	1997	.258	.322	.375	LC	206	.254	.312	.344	RO	1175	.269	.337	.404
Chris Haney (1991-1997)				H	337.1	16-25	5.07	L	541	.256	.325	.365	SP	740	.291	.358	.424	NO	1572	.274	.331	.419
Throws Left	651.0	32-44	4.82	R	313.2	16-19	4.56	R	2304	.288	.344	.448	LC	173	.244	.282	.344	RO	1273	.292	.351	.449
Erik Hanson (1988-1997)				H	733.2	39-37	4.07	L	3291	.238	.294	.348	SP	1526	.270	.336	.412	NO	3729	.249	.305	.372
Throws Right	1506.1	89-81	4.08	R	772.2	50-44	4.09	R	3096	.293	.350	.441	LC	495	.245	.306	.385	RO	2658	.287	.344	.423
Mike Harkey (1988-1997)				H	361.2	18-19	4.16	L	1558	.278	.345	.441	SP	714	.274	.362	.412	NO	1645	.280	.331	.449
Throws Right	656.0	36-36	4.49	R	294.1	18-17	4.89	R	1294	.285	.336	.438	LC	156	.292	.380	.485	RO	1207	.283	.355	.425
Pete Harnisch (1988-1997)				H	768.2	45-34	3.41	L	3151	.260	.339	.405	SP	1470	.240	.331	.376	NO	3426	.237	.306	.383
Throws Right	1385.1	72-77	3.88	R	616.2	27-43	4.48	R	2760	.224	.287	.363	LC	390	.212	.294	.344	RO	2485	.252	.326	.389
Greg Harris (1984-1995)				H	657.2	38-36	3.79	L	2627	.234	.322	.340	SP	1635	.238	.344	.345	NO	2928	.229	.312	.351
Throws Right	1306.0	69-79	3.55	R	648.1	31-43	3.30	R	2949	.247	.329	.385	LC	1495	.229	.322	.333	RO	2648	.254	.341	.380
Greg Harris (1988-1995)				H	473.2	25-30	3.59	L	2166	.266	.327	.413	SP	996	.242	.348	.370	NO	2247	.253	.301	.395
Throws Right	909.1	45-64	3.98	R	435.2	20-34	4.40	R	1700	.241	.305	.392	LC	705	.218	.300	.296	RO	1619	.259	.340	.417
Mike Hartley (1989-1995)				H	168.1	12-5	3.64	L	681	.234	.329	.337	SP	447	.229	.335	.384	NO	723	.231	.317	.340
Throws Right	318.2	19-13	3.70	R	150.1	7-8	3.77	R	692	.249	.327	.404	LC	297	.242	.361	.346	RO	650	.254	.340	.408
Bryan Harvey (1987-1995)				H	209.2	11-11	2.40	L	824	.175	.258	.257	SP	519	.165	.279	.261	NO	772	.208	.267	.308
Throws Right	387.0	17-25	2.49	R	177.1	6-14	2.59	R	758	.225	.286	.325	LC	977	.198	.268	.288	RO	810	.189	.276	.270
Andy Hawkins (1984-1991)				H	777.0	42-46	3.93	L	3064	.293	.375	.441	SP	1416	.289	.375	.442	NO	3418	.262	.324	.406
Throws Right	1375.0	77-79	4.34	R	598.0	35-33	4.92	R	2834	.240	.293	.378	LC	438	.272	.366	.427	RO	2480	.274	.352	.415
Neal Heaton (1984-1993)				H	690.1	37-39	3.83	L	1154	.263	.320	.403	SP	1414	.272	.348	.421	NO	3250	.274	.331	.426
Throws Left	1326.2	69-87	4.38	R	636.1	32-48	4.96	R	4529	.277	.339	.431	LC	462	.281	.358	.432	RO	2433	.275	.342	.424
Tom Henke (1984-1995)				H	382.2	25-12	2.35	L	1568	.210	.281	.330	SP	900	.215	.306	.360	NO	1642	.204	.252	.303
Throws Right	758.0	39-42	2.68	R	375.1	14-30	3.02	R	1489	.209	.264	.321	LC	1615	.215	.278	.346	RO	1415	.216	.297	.355
Mike Henneman (1987-1996)				H	377.2	39-14	3.03	L	1441	.266	.350	.378	SP	972	.237	.335	.347	NO	1542	.244	.300	.339
Throws Right	732.2	57-42	3.21	R	355.0	19-28	3.40	R	1671	.234	.290	.326	LC	1601	.253	.332	.351	RO	1570	.254	.336	.362
Butch Henry (1992-1997)				H	277.0	12-14	3.64	L	540	.293	.338	.424	SP	590	.257	.319	.396	NO	1423	.283	.318	.425
Throws Left	587.0	31-33	3.77	R	310.0	19-19	3.89	R	1939	.276	.314	.417	LC	230	.286	.329	.429	RO	1056	.275	.321	.409

Situational Statistics: Pitching

Pitcher	Total IP	W-L	ERA		Home/Road IP	W-L	ERA		vs. PA	Avg	OBP	Slg		Scoring Position/Late & Close PA	Avg	OBP	Slg		None On/Runners On PA	Avg	OBP	Slg
Doug Henry (1991-1997)				H	215.2	13-10	3.80	L	784	.235	.335	.360	SP	523	.271	.387	.427	NO	911	.234	.301	.359
Throws Right	400.0	18-31	4.07	R	184.1	5-21	4.39	R	966	.260	.329	.403	LC	901	.263	.346	.400	RO	839	.267	.365	.415
Dwayne Henry (1984-1995)				H	180.1	12-7	4.29	L	710	.236	.370	.384	SP	509	.279	.402	.414	NO	731	.208	.321	.331
Throws Right	334.2	14-15	4.65	R	154.1	2-8	5.07	R	786	.244	.340	.366	LC	424	.239	.351	.360	RO	765	.275	.386	.418
Pat Hentgen (1991-1997)				H	635.0	38-31	3.86	L	2603	.266	.334	.405	SP	1191	.247	.323	.379	NO	2828	.258	.324	.410
Throws Right	1179.0	82-53	3.88	R	544.0	44-22	3.90	R	2408	.245	.310	.394	LC	511	.245	.306	.400	RO	2183	.253	.321	.386
Gil Heredia (1991-1996)				H	192.2	9-10	4.25	L	807	.275	.313	.370	SP	454	.325	.386	.446	NO	978	.260	.291	.373
Throws Right	402.2	19-21	4.34	R	210.0	10-11	4.41	R	906	.294	.336	.435	LC	196	.264	.308	.390	RO	735	.322	.371	.449
Roberto Hernandez (1991-1997)				H	223.0	18-9	2.22	L	909	.214	.301	.295	SP	566	.230	.323	.346	NO	906	.214	.292	.306
Throws Right	437.1	34-26	2.84	R	214.1	16-17	3.49	R	924	.236	.300	.352	LC	1230	.227	.303	.331	RO	927	.236	.308	.342
Willie Hernandez (1984-1989)				H	240.2	23-16	3.07	L	578	.197	.242	.272	SP	539	.250	.335	.378	NO	1043	.212	.261	.347
Throws Left	483.2	36-31	2.98	R	243.0	13-15	2.96	R	1389	.238	.302	.392	LC	937	.217	.268	.344	RO	924	.243	.311	.368
Xavier Hernandez (1989-1997)				H	298.0	19-14	3.59	L	1183	.254	.346	.399	SP	792	.244	.334	.366	NO	1370	.246	.315	.383
Throws Right	613.0	34-29	3.93	R	315.0	15-15	4.26	R	1453	.242	.298	.376	LC	934	.242	.316	.362	RO	1266	.249	.324	.390
Orel Hershiser (1984-1997)				H	1393.1	94-54	2.87	L	6105	.262	.329	.378	SP	2768	.239	.330	.349	NO	6583	.242	.294	.357
Throws Right	2716.2	179-123	3.25	R	1323.1	85-69	3.66	R	5188	.226	.278	.330	LC	939	.238	.321	.351	RO	4710	.251	.322	.354
Joe Hesketh (1984-1994)				H	482.1	32-20	3.60	L	825	.234	.308	.330	SP	1092	.237	.329	.358	NO	2279	.262	.327	.401
Throws Left	961.2	60-47	3.78	R	479.1	28-27	3.96	R	3275	.266	.333	.416	LC	466	.251	.340	.356	RO	1821	.256	.329	.396
Greg Hibbard (1989-1994)				H	512.2	30-24	3.76	L	626	.250	.312	.369	SP	958	.291	.349	.441	NO	2446	.267	.321	.386
Throws Left	990.0	57-50	4.05	R	477.1	27-26	4.37	R	3579	.280	.330	.409	LC	328	.250	.310	.345	RO	1759	.287	.336	.430
Bryan Hickerson (1991-1995)				H	199.2	12-9	4.37	L	454	.259	.318	.353	SP	445	.285	.353	.427	NO	979	.286	.342	.462
Throws Left	404.1	21-21	4.72	R	204.2	9-12	5.06	R	1303	.295	.354	.475	LC	332	.241	.304	.337	RO	778	.286	.348	.419
Teddy Higuera (1985-1994)				H	731.1	55-26	3.38	L	969	.237	.281	.350	SP	1234	.272	.330	.406	NO	3433	.230	.295	.362
Throws Left	1380.0	94-64	3.61	R	648.2	40-38	3.87	R	4771	.245	.308	.379	LC	531	.251	.310	.314	RO	2307	.263	.316	.391
Ken Hill (1988-1997)				H	783.2	43-42	3.92	L	3858	.254	.336	.370	SP	1873	.245	.329	.364	NO	3945	.251	.327	.379
Throws Right	1652.2	99-83	3.76	R	869.0	56-41	3.62	R	3198	.249	.312	.380	LC	477	.305	.381	.474	RO	3111	.253	.323	.368
Shawn Hillegas (1987-1993)				H	274.0	15-15	4.01	L	1139	.290	.377	.425	SP	620	.267	.357	.413	NO	1238	.254	.330	.402
Throws Right	515.1	24-38	4.61	R	241.1	9-23	5.37	R	1126	.238	.310	.391	LC	335	.268	.362	.386	RO	1027	.277	.360	.414
Sterling Hitchcock (1992-1997)				H	309.0	19-18	4.75	L	525	.270	.337	.437	SP	667	.294	.363	.475	NO	1524	.278	.346	.439
Throws Left	619.1	39-35	5.07	R	310.1	20-17	5.39	R	2193	.283	.350	.450	LC	172	.262	.327	.336	RO	1194	.283	.349	.459
Guy Hoffman (1986-1988)				H	135.2	9-5	4.11	L	223	.286	.376	.407	SP	277	.284	.377	.484	NO	642	.266	.316	.415
Throws Left	265.1	15-12	4.27	R	129.2	6-7	4.44	R	898	.268	.318	.449	LC	42	.308	.333	.333	RO	479	.278	.348	.479
Trevor Hoffman (1993-1997)				H	180.1	22-7	2.65	L	736	.193	.279	.308	SP	436	.185	.297	.337	NO	823	.193	.249	.330
Throws Right	368.2	30-23	3.03	R	188.1	8-16	3.39	R	768	.214	.266	.383	LC	1062	.199	.271	.319	RO	681	.218	.301	.369
Brian Holman (1988-1991)				H	372.2	20-24	3.45	L	1509	.276	.354	.392	SP	724	.236	.329	.334	NO	1619	.260	.324	.369
Throws Right	676.2	37-45	3.71	R	304.0	17-21	4.03	R	1389	.250	.310	.357	LC	206	.280	.343	.376	RO	1279	.268	.344	.383
Darren Holmes (1990-1997)				H	248.0	19-11	4.72	L	952	.267	.343	.386	SP	651	.257	.358	.404	NO	1002	.264	.316	.388
Throws Right	464.0	28-22	4.33	R	216.0	9-11	3.88	R	1083	.268	.330	.418	LC	794	.270	.344	.404	RO	1033	.271	.356	.420
Brian Holton (1985-1990)				H	202.0	9-9	2.94	L	769	.280	.350	.393	SP	511	.247	.335	.370	NO	811	.300	.346	.435
Throws Right	370.2	20-19	3.62	R	168.2	11-10	4.43	R	826	.276	.320	.414	LC	150	.326	.384	.492	RO	784	.254	.321	.370
Rick Honeycutt (1984-1997)				H	573.2	31-32	2.86	L	1188	.216	.264	.314	SP	1176	.274	.365	.395	NO	2536	.243	.293	.344
Throws Left	1094.0	51-68	3.41	R	520.1	20-36	4.05	R	3405	.266	.329	.383	LC	1127	.213	.286	.286	RO	2057	.267	.337	.393
Ricky Horton (1984-1990)				H	338.1	16-12	3.38	L	771	.252	.310	.323	SP	786	.275	.348	.380	NO	1555	.267	.320	.405
Throws Left	673.1	32-27	3.76	R	335.0	16-15	4.14	R	2073	.280	.339	.437	LC	376	.275	.356	.377	RO	1289	.280	.346	.408
Charlie Hough (1984-1994)				H	1172.0	71-66	4.02	L	4905	.238	.319	.363	SP	2498	.233	.343	.350	NO	6031	.232	.307	.382
Throws Right	2378.1	132-141	3.89	R	1206.1	62-76	3.84	R	5230	.234	.318	.393	LC	925	.238	.319	.346	RO	4104	.242	.336	.374
Steve Howe (1985-1996)				H	152.0	15-6	3.85	L	406	.245	.276	.321	SP	402	.315	.377	.437	NO	620	.235	.279	.344
Throws Left	299.1	24-17	3.91	R	147.1	9-11	3.97	R	862	.280	.334	.410	LC	518	.254	.304	.361	RO	648	.302	.351	.418
Jay Howell (1984-1994)				H	385.2	36-20	2.33	L	1507	.234	.303	.328	SP	846	.257	.337	.337	NO	1556	.225	.280	.331
Throws Right	709.0	53-45	2.83	R	323.1	17-25	3.42	R	1426	.236	.292	.336	LC	1618	.240	.303	.323	RO	1377	.247	.318	.333
Ken Howell (1984-1990)				H	313.2	17-23	3.84	L	1418	.258	.346	.365	SP	669	.266	.360	.428	NO	1411	.232	.314	.322
Throws Right	613.1	38-48	3.95	R	299.2	21-25	4.05	R	1156	.213	.288	.338	LC	799	.238	.327	.348	RO	1163	.244	.328	.391
LaMarr Hoyt (1984-1986)				H	326.0	23-17	4.36	L	1346	.279	.327	.445	SP	552	.282	.351	.464	NO	1562	.251	.284	.407
Throws Right	605.0	37-37	4.30	R	279.0	14-20	4.23	R	1144	.253	.284	.412	LC	235	.231	.277	.376	RO	928	.296	.347	.470
Charles Hudson (1984-1989)				H	372.1	17-24	4.30	L	1827	.266	.338	.402	SP	854	.278	.349	.415	NO	2096	.244	.313	.397
Throws Right	838.1	42-52	4.29	R	466.0	25-28	4.35	R	1755	.254	.310	.418	LC	224	.307	.361	.477	RO	1486	.283	.341	.428
Mark Huismann (1984-1991)				H	148.2	6-5	3.81	L	543	.297	.336	.458	SP	339	.241	.285	.375	NO	578	.277	.324	.462
Throws Right	265.2	11-10	4.27	R	117.0	5-5	4.85	R	579	.239	.286	.411	LC	203	.247	.320	.401	RO	544	.256	.296	.402
Tom Hume (1984-1987)				H	197.0	7-7	4.02	L	761	.288	.384	.429	SP	519	.262	.356	.413	NO	834	.275	.336	.415
Throws Right	371.2	13-23	4.33	R	174.2	6-16	4.69	R	851	.257	.307	.403	LC	347	.269	.352	.387	RO	778	.266	.351	.414
Bruce Hurst (1984-1994)				H	1104.2	74-43	3.63	L	1426	.259	.319	.398	SP	1811	.257	.310	.385	NO	5030	.253	.313	.392
Throws Left	2035.1	126-92	3.71	R	930.2	55-49	3.81	R	7075	.257	.310	.394	LC	695	.269	.320	.403	RO	3471	.264	.310	.398
Jeff Innis (1987-1993)				H	187.2	6-11	2.59	L	642	.290	.372	.407	SP	488	.223	.335	.289	NO	777	.262	.308	.383
Throws Right	360.0	10-20	3.05	R	172.1	4-9	3.55	R	865	.227	.279	.314	LC	506	.279	.360	.396	RO	730	.242	.332	.315
Jason Isringhausen (1995-1997)				H	180.1	12-9	3.49	L	604	.316	.385	.402	SP	368	.278	.380	.336	NO	710	.257	.320	.352
Throws Right	294.1	17-18	4.43	R	114.0	5-9	5.92	R	692	.249	.327	.360	LC	96	.241	.319	.277	RO	586	.312	.397	.415
Danny Jackson (1984-1997)				H	1063.0	63-54	3.73	L	1540	.269	.342	.364	SP	2386	.272	.341	.391	NO	4840	.254	.328	.363
Throws Left	2053.2	111-130	4.00	R	990.0	48-76	4.31	R	7340	.265	.334	.382	LC	585	.283	.339	.423	RO	4040	.279	.344	.399
Mike Jackson (1986-1997)				H	446.0	29-22	3.15	L	1647	.253	.354	.389	SP	1152	.221	.341	.350	NO	1895	.215	.291	.335
Throws Right	885.0	49-56	3.33	R	439.0	20-34	3.51	R	2055	.190	.265	.307	LC	1590	.213	.299	.328	RO	1807	.220	.318	.351

Situational Statistics: Pitching

Pitcher		Total				Home/Road				vs. Left/Right					Scoring Position/Late & Close					None On/Runners On			
	IP	W-L	ERA		IP	W-L	ERA		PA	Avg	OBP	Slg		PA	Avg	OBP	Slg		PA	Avg	OBP	Slg
Jason Jacome (1994-1997)				H	122.2	7-7	4.70	L	265	.281	.355	.489	SP	315	.323	.417	.538	NO	598	.320	.361	.491
Throws Left	256.0	10-17	5.17	R	133.1	3-10	5.60	R	875	.312	.368	.489	LC	95	.341	.419	.622	RO	542	.287	.370	.486
Bob James (1984-1987)				H	170.1	14-10	3.70	I	662	.255	.329	.394	SP	494	.231	.302	.368	NO	633	.234	.303	.382
Throws Right	318.1	23-23	3.59	R	148.0	9-13	3.47	R	688	.238	.294	.373	LC	665	.235	.293	.348	NO	717	.257	.318	.384
Kevin Jarvis (1994-1997)				H	140.1	7-6	6.03	L	560	.317	.380	.559	SP	395	.298	.366	.450	NO	704	.304	.362	.532
Throws Right	285.0	12-18	6.38	R	144.2	5-12	6.72	R	754	.303	.359	.468	LC	35	.167	.286	.367	RO	610	.315	.375	.476
Mike Jeffcoat (1984-1994)				H	238.2	14-6	3.92	L	572	.273	.316	.383	SP	538	.308	.368	.483	NO	1086	.291	.334	.418
Throws Left	467.1	24-23	4.45	R	228.2	10-17	5.00	R	1467	.302	.354	.467	LC	373	.340	.390	.512	RO	953	.298	.354	.475
Tommy John (1984-1989)				H	336.0	13-22	4.69	L	634	.282	.339	.388	SP	859	.272	.357	.373	NO	1841	.317	.355	.444
Throws Left	766.0	40-47	4.46	R	430.0	27-25	4.35	R	2701	.310	.356	.432	LC	169	.344	.381	.446	RO	1494	.289	.350	.396
Dave Johnson (1987-1993)				H	193.0	11-14	4.80	L	804	.335	.385	.551	SP	365	.277	.330	.409	NO	942	.301	.345	.508
Throws Right	368.0	22-25	5.11	R	175.0	11-11	5.45	R	802	.262	.308	.435	LC	76	.304	.368	.551	RO	664	.294	.349	.469
Joe Johnson (1985-1987)				H	163.1	8-11	4.30	L	743	.290	.342	.426	SP	353	.291	.365	.434	NO	821	.272	.323	.403
Throws Right	327.1	20-18	4.48	R	164.0	12-7	4.66	R	660	.282	.337	.413	LC	75	.273	.347	.318	RO	582	.306	.364	.445
Randy Johnson (1988-1997)				H	909.1	66-29	2.99	L	746	.197	.278	.288	SP	1816	.208	.313	.319	NO	4240	.208	.308	.330
Throws Left	1734.0	124-68	3.37	R	824.2	58-39	3.80	R	6542	.212	.315	.335	LC	684	.201	.300	.307	RO	3048	.215	.317	.331
Barry Jones (1986-1993)				H	229.1	20-13	3.65	L	825	.287	.370	.401	SP	633	.283	.372	.421	NO	903	.234	.308	.330
Throws Right	433.0	33-33	3.66	R	203.2	13-20	3.67	R	1023	.239	.313	.349	LC	896	.276	.352	.382	RO	945	.287	.369	.417
Bobby Jones (1993-1997)				H	397.2	19-20	3.73	L	1669	.256	.319	.397	SP	788	.256	.335	.396	NO	1979	.264	.318	.397
Throws Right	806.1	51-38	3.86	R	408.2	32-18	3.99	R	1752	.275	.322	.420	LC	277	.221	.279	.313	RO	1442	.269	.323	.426
Doug Jones (1986-1997)				H	452.0	38-34	3.37	L	1862	.255	.300	.357	SP	1114	.260	.318	.374	NO	1782	.258	.295	.350
Throws Right	863.0	56-66	3.08	R	411.0	19-32	2.82	R	1756	.261	.302	.352	LC	1843	.268	.310	.373	RO	1836	.258	.307	.360
Jimmy Jones (1986-1993)				H	405.2	22-19	3.73	L	1810	.289	.349	.425	SP	807	.311	.377	.463	NO	1858	.258	.313	.379
Throws Right	755.0	43-39	4.46	R	349.1	21-21	5.31	R	1449	.257	.307	.388	LC	138	.219	.265	.320	RO	1401	.298	.355	.450
Todd Jones (1993-1997)				H	165.0	12-10	2.78	L	664	.262	.353	.376	SP	477	.207	.347	.303	NO	702	.247	.326	.354
Throws Right	337.0	23-16	3.23	R	172.0	11-6	3.66	R	780	.208	.300	.303	LC	851	.234	.331	.335	RO	742	.218	.322	.319
Jeff Juden (1991-1997)				H	188.2	12-6	4.10	L	676	.285	.384	.452	SP	445	.219	.343	.334	NO	842	.253	.335	.417
Throws Right	349.0	19-17	4.36	R	160.1	7-11	4.66	R	844	.219	.296	.364	LC	140	.248	.317	.400	RO	678	.241	.336	.382
Scott Kamieniecki (1991-1997)				H	427.2	27-18	4.10	L	1715	.272	.351	.418	SP	901	.267	.365	.405	NO	1978	.266	.333	.410
Throws Right	806.2	46-45	4.26	R	379.0	19-27	4.44	R	1771	.263	.338	.410	LC	211	.289	.386	.439	RO	1508	.269	.359	.420
Scott Karl (1995-1997)				H	262.0	15-15	4.64	L	410	.234	.312	.357	SP	582	.270	.351	.412	NO	1305	.272	.333	.444
Throws Left	524.2	29-29	4.55	R	262.2	14-14	4.45	R	1882	.287	.348	.460	LC	88	.325	.386	.538	RO	987	.286	.355	.438
Kurt Kepshire (1984-1986)				H	133.2	9-8	4.58	L	558	.288	.357	.439	SP	260	.299	.392	.393	NO	698	.241	.309	.364
Throws Right	270.1	16-15	4.16	R	136.2	7-7	3.75	R	592	.229	.309	.323	LC	87	.375	.425	.563	RO	452	.285	.367	.404
Jimmy Key (1984-1997)				H	1301.2	86-66	3.64	L	1814	.233	.282	.334	SP	2229	.248	.320	.390	NO	6247	.252	.295	.383
Throws Left	2512.1	180-114	3.49	R	1210.2	94-48	3.32	R	8557	.260	.307	.404	LC	736	.275	.324	.394	RO	4124	.261	.315	.406
Darryl Kile (1991-1997)				H	617.1	35-34	3.51	L	2743	.260	.355	.383	SP	1458	.229	.332	.324	NO	2774	.253	.346	.384
Throws Right	1200.0	71-65	3.79	R	582.2	36-31	4.08	R	2498	.240	.325	.355	LC	411	.245	.319	.396	RO	2467	.249	.335	.353
Paul Kilgus (1987-1993)				H	287.1	10-17	4.32	L	502	.235	.309	.378	SP	559	.276	.352	.451	NO	1321	.252	.321	.368
Throws Left	545.1	21-34	4.19	R	258.0	11-18	4.12	R	1846	.266	.329	.396	LC	194	.246	.326	.359	RO	1027	.269	.330	.425
Eric King (1986-1992)				H	430.2	24-26	4.08	L	1835	.246	.323	.378	SP	899	.243	.322	.337	NO	2080	.241	.316	.363
Throws Right	863.1	52-45	3.97	R	432.2	28-19	3.99	R	1847	.252	.321	.351	LC	215	.241	.322	.380	RO	1602	.259	.330	.367
Bob Kipper (1985-1992)				H	294.0	13-20	4.47	L	599	.240	.294	.342	SP	599	.255	.338	.445	NO	1385	.236	.309	.401
Throws Left	562.0	27-37	4.34	R	268.0	14-17	4.20	R	1802	.250	.325	.451	LC	434	.220	.313	.346	RO	1016	.263	.329	.453
Bob Knepper (1984-1990)				H	686.2	39-37	3.67	L	760	.259	.292	.394	SP	1330	.252	.332	.383	NO	3168	.267	.314	.410
Throws Left	1294.2	79-72	3.86	R	608.0	40-35	4.07	R	4685	.270	.326	.415	LC	281	.263	.314	.398	RO	2277	.270	.332	.415
Mark Knudson (1985-1993)				H	235.2	12-15	5.16	L	1022	.285	.330	.431	SP	506	.289	.344	.436	NO	1187	.299	.338	.456
Throws Right	482.0	24-29	4.72	R	246.1	13-15	4.53	R	1082	.295	.338	.460	LC	126	.350	.384	.496	RO	917	.279	.329	.433
Jerry Koosman (1984-1985)				H	160.0	11-8	3.38	L	212	.250	.292	.295	SP	338	.249	.320	.382	NO	777	.274	.324	.387
Throws Left	323.1	20-19	3.67	R	163.1	9-11	3.97	R	1153	.274	.327	.404	LC	82	.333	.366	.507	RO	588	.265	.318	.385
Bill Krueger (1984-1995)				H	553.0	32-28	4.18	L	957	.281	.344	.397	SP	1315	.285	.376	.412	NO	2559	.280	.341	.413
Throws Left	1084.2	61-60	4.42	R	531.2	29-32	4.69	R	3821	.283	.352	.414	LC	355	.257	.317	.342	RO	2219	.286	.360	.407
Mike Krukow (1984-1989)				H	520.2	31-19	3.13	L	2197	.273	.332	.427	SP	1020	.226	.310	.354	NO	2410	.252	.297	.398
Throws Right	969.2	55-45	3.82	R	449.0	24-26	4.63	R	1865	.231	.278	.366	LC	337	.218	.277	.322	RO	1652	.257	.321	.400
Mike LaCoss (1984-1991)				H	499.2	34-24	3.24	L	2200	.259	.344	.352	SP	1085	.278	.376	.389	NO	2223	.249	.314	.334
Throws Right	937.2	55-55	3.88	R	438.0	21-33	4.60	R	1791	.264	.327	.363	LC	371	.230	.332	.338	RO	1768	.278	.365	.387
Dennis Lamp (1984-1992)				H	381.1	25-13	4.04	L	1395	.300	.368	.390	SP	1041	.305	.371	.436	NO	1602	.253	.303	.346
Throws Right	741.0	43-34	4.07	R	359.2	18-21	4.10	R	1768	.259	.299	.380	LC	645	.299	.365	.409	RO	1561	.303	.358	.426
Les Lancaster (1987-1993)				H	377.1	23-13	4.29	L	1498	.281	.360	.399	SP	891	.280	.355	.438	NO	1594	.259	.317	.374
Throws Right	703.2	41-28	4.05	R	326.1	19-15	3.78	R	1534	.251	.299	.382	LC	654	.284	.358	.384	RO	1438	.272	.343	.409
Bill Landrum (1986-1993)				H	179.1	10-6	3.76	L	748	.253	.322	.342	SP	487	.277	.371	.368	NO	761	.267	.311	.362
Throws Right	361.1	18-15	3.39	R	182.0	8-9	3.02	R	767	.275	.328	.375	LC	520	.243	.313	.309	RO	754	.262	.339	.354
Mark Langston (1984-1997)				H	1435.2	88-72	3.99	L	1772	.203	.279	.300	SP	2708	.267	.337	.412	NO	6942	.231	.320	.370
Throws Left	2819.2	174-150	3.88	R	1384.0	86-79	3.82	R	10115	.250	.330	.397	LC	1136	.247	.326	.374	RO	4945	.259	.325	.400
Dave LaPoint (1984-1991)				H	587.0	33-28	3.51	L	755	.277	.326	.397	SP	1190	.280	.358	.393	NO	2729	.274	.332	.414
Throws Left	1117.0	57-74	4.09	R	530.0	24-46	4.74	R	4084	.277	.340	.406	LC	308	.287	.356	.434	RO	2110	.281	.345	.392
Bill Laskey (1984-1988)				H	196.2	5-17	4.48	L	933	.290	.345	.433	SP	473	.278	.333	.407	NO	1010	.263	.316	.406
Throws Right	407.2	16-31	4.59	R	211.0	11-14	4.69	R	813	.268	.314	.425	LC	110	.262	.309	.359	RO	736	.304	.351	.463
Charlie Lea (1984-1988)				H	189.2	10-10	3.37	L	753	.298	.365	.477	SP	386	.199	.255	.277	NO	852	.279	.349	.445
Throws Right	355.1	22-18	3.70	R	165.2	12-8	4.07	R	746	.230	.282	.352	LC	129	.270	.341	.383	RO	647	.243	.289	.372

Situational Statistics: Pitching

Pitcher	IP	W-L	ERA		IP	W-L	ERA		PA	Avg	OBP	Slg		PA	Avg	OBP	Slg		PA	Avg	OBP	Slg
		Total			Home/Road				vs. Left/Right					Scoring Position/Late & Close					None On/Runners On			
Terry Leach (1985-1993)				H	281.0	12-2	2.98	L	1133	.291	.348	.408	SP	779	.252	.318	.344	NO	1401	.258	.301	.375
Throws Right	619.1	35-25	3.11	R	338.1	23-23	3.38	R	1457	.238	.283	.331	LC	457	.302	.369	.393	RO	1189	.264	.324	.351
Luis Leal (1984-1985)				H	155.2	8-7	4.34	L	642	.273	.344	.441	SP	285	.278	.337	.453	NO	736	.264	.329	.426
Throws Right	289.2	16-14	4.32	R	134.0	8-7	4.30	R	604	.265	.315	.444	LC	72	.388	.417	.761	RO	510	.277	.331	.466
Tim Leary (1984-1994)				H	714.2	36-51	4.22	L	3246	.283	.352	.428	SP	1643	.260	.354	.388	NO	3610	.266	.325	.411
Throws Right	1478.2	77-104	4.38	R	764.0	41-53	4.52	R	3124	.262	.323	.392	LC	480	.280	.362	.390	RO	2760	.282	.354	.409
Craig Lefferts (1984-1994)				H	515.0	33-30	2.99	L	1052	.231	.275	.331	SP	1232	.244	.319	.360	NO	2328	.264	.305	.409
Throws Left	1056.2	55-68	3.45	R	541.2	23-38	3.89	R	3315	.267	.319	.413	LC	1475	.246	.299	.345	RO	2039	.252	.312	.372
Charlie Leibrandt (1984-1993)				H	932.1	60-45	3.53	L	1610	.269	.313	.367	SP	2030	.250	.324	.367	NO	4885	.266	.306	.386
Throws Right	1992.1	124-102	3.60	R	1059.2	64-57	3.66	R	6756	.263	.313	.390	LC	604	.246	.305	.341	RO	3481	.261	.323	.385
Dave Leiper (1984-1996)				H	145.0	6-4	2.79	L	469	.234	.315	.383	SP	409	.261	.364	.390	NO	580	.273	.329	.393
Throws Left	278.0	12-8	3.98	R	133.0	6-4	5.35	R	741	.287	.352	.413	LC	209	.253	.348	.397	RO	630	.260	.345	.410
Al Leiter (1987-1997)				H	475.2	36-18	3.24	L	700	.234	.313	.342	SP	989	.250	.369	.344	NO	2106	.231	.341	.359
Throws Left	888.2	60-53	4.01	R	413.0	24-35	4.90	R	3190	.238	.354	.358	LC	201	.266	.401	.373	RO	1784	.245	.353	.351
Mark Leiter (1990-1997)				H	560.1	27-33	4.79	L	2150	.282	.361	.467	SP	1229	.287	.373	.435	NO	2593	.262	.324	.446
Throws Right	1058.1	56-67	4.69	R	498.0	29-34	4.57	R	2471	.259	.315	.419	LC	400	.238	.314	.386	RO	2028	.281	.353	.434
Curt Leskanic (1993-1997)				H	156.2	12-3	4.83	L	615	.267	.352	.452	SP	385	.271	.344	.437	NO	705	.243	.311	.360
Throws Right	309.1	19-14	5.00	R	152.2	7-11	5.19	R	731	.259	.321	.389	LC	447	.243	.321	.404	RO	641	.285	.363	.485
Richie Lewis (1992-1997)				H	161.2	10-8	5.07	L	579	.267	.382	.445	SP	500	.221	.363	.389	NO	625	.249	.344	.447
Throws Right	288.2	14-15	4.71	R	127.0	4-7	4.25	R	746	.246	.347	.444	LC	373	.247	.388	.415	RO	700	.261	.380	.442
Jon Lieber (1994-1997)				H	279.1	17-15	4.54	L	1093	.309	.355	.499	SP	535	.296	.345	.467	NO	1243	.286	.324	.456
Throws Right	511.2	30-33	4.45	R	232.1	13-18	4.34	R	1093	.253	.287	.385	LC	177	.286	.335	.497	RO	943	.275	.317	.421
Derek Lilliquist (1989-1996)				H	253.0	13-17	3.81	L	492	.267	.313	.417	SP	567	.279	.345	.424	NO	1142	.266	.311	.424
Throws Left	483.2	25-34	4.13	R	230.2	12-17	4.49	R	1588	.288	.336	.445	LC	436	.273	.337	.403	RO	938	.305	.354	.457
Felipe Lira (1995-1997)				H	254.1	12-19	4.18	L	1098	.276	.348	.453	SP	508	.256	.352	.412	NO	1116	.267	.335	.428
Throws Right	451.2	20-38	5.20	R	197.1	8-19	6.52	R	903	.276	.344	.451	LC	167	.315	.390	.490	RO	885	.289	.361	.485
Esteban Loaiza (1995-1997)				H	193.1	7-15	5.35	L	898	.286	.355	.407	SP	509	.297	.369	.394	NO	1014	.286	.335	.466
Throws Right	421.2	21-23	4.65	R	228.1	14-8	4.06	R	951	.297	.339	.487	LC	79	.328	.410	.537	RO	835	.299	.361	.425
Tim Lollar (1984-1986)				H	201.2	11-9	3.79	L	377	.234	.326	.348	SP	456	.241	.338	.378	NO	932	.241	.358	.373
Throws Left	388.2	21-23	4.52	R	187.0	10-14	5.29	R	1325	.252	.362	.415	LC	84	.328	.452	.716	RO	770	.257	.348	.432
Bill Long (1985-1991)				H	232.0	10-15	4.85	L	1108	.297	.349	.477	SP	580	.275	.341	.455	NO	1251	.277	.321	.433
Throws Right	518.2	27-27	4.37	R	286.2	17-13	4.14	R	1108	.265	.308	.424	LC	232	.265	.320	.355	RO	965	.286	.338	.473
Aurelio Lopez (1984-1987)				H	185.0	9-5	3.79	L	705	.226	.309	.358	SP	388	.276	.345	.446	NO	797	.221	.284	.370
Throws Right	340.0	18-12	3.71	R	155.0	9-7	3.60	R	706	.243	.301	.411	LC	489	.221	.305	.363	RO	614	.254	.333	.406
Ed Lynch (1984-1987)				H	280.2	16-15	3.88	L	1154	.311	.351	.479	SP	550	.285	.338	.445	NO	1260	.284	.323	.442
Throws Right	526.2	28-30	4.15	R	246.0	12-15	4.46	R	1077	.258	.298	.395	LC	142	.235	.282	.348	RO	971	.287	.328	.433
Greg Maddux (1986-1997)				H	1299.0	86-50	2.82	L	5673	.246	.304	.335	SP	2486	.237	.312	.333	NO	6271	.231	.274	.313
Throws Right	2598.1	184-108	2.81	R	1299.1	98-58	2.79	R	4856	.228	.267	.316	LC	1188	.235	.292	.315	RO	4258	.248	.305	.348
Mike Maddux (1986-1997)				H	354.2	24-11	3.65	L	1560	.271	.339	.390	SP	921	.260	.347	.390	NO	1637	.254	.307	.360
Throws Right	719.0	33-30	4.02	R	364.1	9-19	4.37	R	1506	.258	.311	.373	LC	576	.279	.352	.386	RO	1429	.278	.347	.408
Mike Magnante (1991-1997)				H	197.2	8-6	2.64	L	472	.274	.354	.375	SP	482	.280	.360	.443	NO	823	.275	.337	.386
Throws Left	373.0	13-19	4.13	R	175.1	5-13	5.80	R	1142	.285	.339	.416	LC	347	.314	.375	.412	RO	791	.289	.351	.423
Joe Magrane (1987-1996)				H	560.1	25-32	3.73	L	792	.257	.342	.364	SP	1226	.251	.334	.367	NO	2676	.253	.319	.369
Throws Left	1096.2	57-67	3.81	R	536.1	32-35	3.89	R	3893	.260	.324	.383	LC	316	.279	.336	.382	RO	2009	.269	.338	.396
Rick Mahler (1984-1991)				H	782.1	42-37	4.10	L	3728	.288	.340	.416	SP	1724	.284	.365	.417	NO	3930	.266	.308	.391
Throws Right	1593.2	79-95	4.02	R	811.1	38-58	3.94	R	3030	.262	.318	.386	LC	473	.265	.339	.371	RO	2828	.292	.362	.420
Pat Mahomes (1992-1997)				H	199.2	9-15	6.67	L	900	.302	.387	.528	SP	468	.288	.369	.509	NO	933	.286	.379	.498
Throws Right	389.0	21-28	5.88	R	189.1	12-13	5.04	R	840	.265	.349	.479	LC	200	.277	.369	.457	RO	807	.282	.356	.511
Dennis Martinez (1984-1997)				H	1205.2	69-57	3.49	L	5727	.246	.302	.368	SP	2475	.231	.318	.355	NO	6132	.252	.296	.387
Throws Right	2462.0	152-114	3.53	R	1256.1	83-57	3.57	R	4499	.253	.306	.397	LC	871	.243	.294	.368	RO	4094	.243	.315	.371
Pedro Martinez (1992-1997)				H	453.0	34-21	2.78	L	1953	.223	.294	.342	SP	803	.212	.306	.317	NO	2252	.208	.278	.332
Throws Right	912.1	65-39	3.00	R	459.1	31-18	3.21	R	1738	.200	.276	.322	LC	551	.198	.274	.293	RO	1439	.220	.298	.334
Ramon Martinez (1988-1997)				H	881.2	61-41	3.45	L	3611	.246	.344	.373	SP	1674	.223	.317	.321	NO	3974	.235	.310	.367
Throws Right	1630.0	116-74	3.48	R	748.1	55-33	3.52	R	3295	.228	.283	.342	LC	563	.210	.285	.297	RO	2932	.241	.322	.345
Mike Mason (1984-1988)				H	273.1	13-15	4.81	L	519	.279	.353	.410	SP	607	.271	.343	.386	NO	1375	.268	.341	.422
Throws Left	572.0	28-35	4.48	R	298.2	15-20	4.28	R	1957	.267	.335	.413	LC	145	.268	.379	.382	RO	1101	.272	.336	.399
Roger Mason (1984-1994)				H	228.2	14-12	3.38	L	867	.264	.346	.387	SP	495	.257	.353	.387	NO	960	.245	.310	.387
Throws Right	416.1	22-35	4.02	R	187.2	8-23	4.80	R	895	.233	.295	.380	LC	620	.257	.331	.395	RO	802	.251	.332	.380
Greg Mathews (1986-1992)				H	242.1	13-13	3.71	L	407	.251	.325	.393	SP	526	.261	.353	.408	NO	1269	.254	.322	.398
Throws Left	514.0	28-33	4.08	R	271.2	15-21	4.51	R	1742	.258	.329	.400	LC	93	.195	.280	.293	RO	880	.260	.337	.400
Terry Mathews (1991-1997)				H	175.2	6-11	4.25	L	611	.299	.381	.495	SP	442	.277	.375	.438	NO	829	.268	.333	.421
Throws Right	362.1	20-19	4.12	R	186.2	14-8	4.00	R	946	.240	.310	.370	LC	559	.280	.372	.458	RO	728	.257	.344	.415
Kirk McCaskill (1985-1996)				H	876.1	58-46	3.65	L	3706	.276	.343	.410	SP	1794	.280	.349	.422	NO	4175	.250	.323	.369
Throws Right	1729.0	106-108	4.12	R	852.2	48-62	4.60	R	3691	.251	.322	.368	LC	835	.261	.332	.402	RO	3222	.282	.345	.417
Steve McCatty (1984-1985)				H	133.1	5-9	3.92	L	596	.287	.371	.458	SP	307	.280	.345	.421	NO	627	.288	.364	.441
Throws Right	265.1	12-18	5.02	R	132.0	7-9	6.14	R	571	.289	.345	.433	LC	68	.246	.309	.344	RO	540	.289	.352	.450
Bob McClure (1984-1993)				H	275.2	21-10	3.75	L	785	.223	.292	.349	SP	687	.271	.364	.418	NO	1175	.263	.315	.388
Throws Left	539.0	32-24	3.86	R	263.1	11-14	3.96	R	1521	.289	.354	.432	LC	581	.263	.344	.369	RO	1131	.271	.352	.423
Lance McCullers (1985-1992)				H	289.0	16-11	2.99	L	1074	.230	.341	.322	SP	698	.223	.345	.347	NO	1160	.221	.302	.344
Throws Right	526.1	28-31	3.25	R	237.1	13-20	3.56	R	1132	.217	.289	.381	LC	584	.221	.334	.338	RO	1046	.225	.328	.363

Situational Statistics: Pitching

Pitcher	IP	W-L	ERA	H/R	IP	W-L	ERA	L/R	PA	Avg	OBP	Slg	SP/LC	PA	Avg	OBP	Slg	NO/RO	PA	Avg	OBP	Slg
		Total				**Home/Road**				**vs. Left/Right**				**Scoring Position/Late & Close**					**None On/Runners On**			
Ben McDonald (1989-1997)				H	692.0	39-34	3.73	L	2833	.234	.304	.366	SP	1232	.246	.336	.375	NO	3304	.231	.290	.367
Throws Right	1291.1	78-70	3.91	R	599.1	39-36	4.11	R	2575	.254	.312	.400	LC	400	.240	.295	.391	RO	2104	.264	.336	.407
Jack McDowell (1987-1997)				H	948.2	64-42	3.84	L	3942	.257	.320	.387	SP	1812	.243	.316	.373	NO	4387	.254	.314	.382
Throws Right	1794.0	122-80	3.76	R	845.1	58-38	3.67	R	3597	.249	.309	.380	LC	789	.239	.290	.358	RO	3152	.253	.316	.385
Roger McDowell (1985-1996)				H	505.2	40-30	2.92	L	2239	.276	.365	.369	SP	1498	.260	.368	.352	NO	2166	.261	.318	.336
Throws Right	1050.0	70-70	3.30	R	544.1	30-40	3.69	R	2265	.251	.303	.327	LC	2123	.265	.342	.348	RO	2338	.266	.349	.358
Chuck McElroy (1989-1997)				H	266.0	13-10	3.32	L	723	.243	.319	.363	SP	636	.276	.377	.401	NO	1024	.236	.313	.354
Throws Left	478.2	24-22	3.53	R	212.2	11-12	3.81	R	1339	.255	.340	.367	LC	779	.258	.351	.379	RO	1038	.267	.352	.378
Andy McGaffigan (1984-1991)				H	333.1	17-10	3.16	L	1520	.241	.321	.335	SP	796	.261	.348	.365	NO	1570	.240	.305	.341
Throws Right	684.0	34-24	3.25	R	350.2	17-14	3.41	R	1348	.251	.307	.359	LC	446	.240	.323	.310	RO	1298	.253	.326	.355
Scott McGregor (1984-1988)				H	360.2	24-24	4.07	L	619	.245	.288	.445	SP	672	.289	.345	.460	NO	1775	.283	.334	.445
Throws Left	706.0	42-51	4.81	R	345.1	18-28	5.58	R	2431	.296	.350	.457	LC	240	.290	.338	.424	RO	1275	.290	.343	.469
Greg McMichael (1993-1997)				H	203.2	13-11	2.96	L	793	.247	.303	.350	SP	497	.210	.310	.277	NO	907	.233	.283	.338
Throws Right	405.1	25-24	2.91	R	201.2	12-13	2.86	R	889	.224	.291	.320	LC	1003	.253	.326	.371	RO	775	.238	.313	.330
Craig McMurtry (1984-1995)				H	241.1	5-21	5.00	L	914	.306	.414	.457	SP	627	.280	.377	.423	NO	1006	.277	.366	.409
Throws Right	443.0	13-33	4.59	R	201.2	8-12	4.11	R	1045	.234	.313	.360	LC	232	.297	.397	.438	RO	953	.256	.354	.397
Larry McWilliams (1984-1990)				H	391.1	17-29	4.16	L	568	.243	.317	.386	SP	924	.266	.358	.418	NO	1884	.260	.326	.383
Throws Left	794.0	32-54	4.09	R	402.2	15-25	4.05	R	2863	.272	.342	.401	LC	320	.258	.340	.366	RO	1547	.275	.354	.419
Rusty Meacham (1991-1996)				H	170.0	12-5	4.98	L	553	.295	.347	.457	SP	404	.280	.329	.429	NO	664	.265	.307	.404
Throws Right	303.0	22-14	4.19	R	133.0	10-9	3.18	R	756	.270	.313	.416	LC	440	.272	.303	.400	RO	645	.298	.347	.465
Kent Mercker (1989-1997)				H	369.1	23-18	4.14	L	687	.236	.327	.336	SP	808	.234	.330	.375	NO	1760	.239	.325	.387
Throws Left	730.0	43-42	3.91	R	360.2	20-24	3.67	R	2456	.243	.327	.397	LC	506	.228	.335	.348	RO	1383	.245	.329	.379
Jose Mesa (1987-1997)				H	436.1	21-31	3.94	L	1872	.285	.354	.379	SP	968	.280	.356	.405	NO	2044	.263	.334	.384
Throws Right	862.2	43-56	4.28	R	426.1	22-26	4.71	R	1861	.257	.325	.399	LC	896	.253	.322	.335	RO	1689	.282	.346	.395
Danny Miceli (1993-1997)				H	132.2	7-8	4.21	L	466	.298	.391	.529	SP	379	.298	.388	.505	NO	593	.242	.325	.419
Throws Right	259.0	11-17	5.28	R	126.1	4-9	6.41	R	699	.252	.326	.416	LC	395	.271	.358	.426	RO	572	.301	.380	.507
Bob Milacki (1988-1996)				H	392.1	18-22	4.50	L	1721	.259	.329	.385	SP	791	.287	.354	.425	NO	1981	.259	.328	.406
Throws Right	795.2	39-47	4.38	R	403.1	21-25	4.26	R	1703	.273	.333	.437	LC	259	.214	.313	.364	RO	1443	.276	.334	.417
Alan Mills (1990-1997)				H	209.1	15-11	3.61	L	762	.281	.387	.410	SP	634	.214	.355	.354	NO	910	.255	.351	.421
Throws Right	423.1	28-22	3.93	R	214.0	13-11	4.25	R	1101	.215	.324	.386	LC	625	.250	.375	.417	RO	953	.229	.349	.369
Michael Mimbs (1995-1997)				H	153.0	7-13	5.29	L	257	.273	.361	.405	SP	322	.271	.382	.470	NO	617	.274	.355	.398
Throws Left	264.2	12-19	5.03	R	111.2	5-6	4.67	R	940	.269	.363	.426	LC	73	.190	.282	.254	RO	580	.265	.371	.449
Greg Minton (1984-1990)				H	273.0	14-13	3.00	L	1100	.271	.355	.355	SP	845	.253	.361	.323	NO	1185	.242	.312	.339
Throws Right	573.1	28-30	3.23	R	300.1	14-17	3.45	R	1339	.243	.322	.325	LC	997	.246	.337	.333	RO	1254	.270	.361	.338
Paul Mirabella (1984-1990)				H	113.1	3-5	3.89	L	393	.223	.320	.277	SP	365	.271	.371	.399	NO	530	.268	.321	.392
Throws Left	251.2	10-10	3.83	R	138.1	7-5	3.77	R	710	.283	.347	.435	LC	171	.303	.385	.428	RO	573	.257	.352	.368
Angel Miranda (1993-1997)				H	192.2	8-11	4.16	L	362	.280	.386	.405	SP	448	.242	.369	.360	NO	869	.253	.336	.420
Throws Left	363.1	17-21	4.46	R	170.2	9-10	4.80	R	1246	.254	.347	.433	LC	203	.253	.369	.446	RO	739	.268	.379	.436
Dave Mlicki (1992-1997)				H	240.0	13-14	3.34	L	988	.273	.349	.439	SP	549	.231	.334	.377	NO	1149	.274	.334	.436
Throws Right	479.1	23-28	3.98	R	239.1	10-14	4.63	R	1098	.251	.317	.393	LC	265	.293	.370	.427	RO	937	.244	.330	.387
Mike Mohler (1993-1997)				H	133.0	2-11	4.74	L	389	.273	.361	.400	SP	394	.263	.373	.435	NO	575	.259	.358	.392
Throws Left	273.0	9-21	4.65	R	140.0	7-10	4.56	R	829	.263	.369	.426	LC	334	.281	.377	.416	RO	643	.273	.375	.443
Dale Mohorcic (1986-1990)				H	177.1	11-5	3.65	L	661	.305	.351	.445	SP	524	.266	.340	.387	NO	723	.279	.326	.400
Throws Right	363.2	16-21	3.49	R	186.1	5-16	3.48	R	875	.247	.309	.364	LC	314	.296	.360	.432	RO	813	.266	.327	.399
Rich Monteleone (1987-1996)				H	173.0	10-7	3.80	L	647	.273	.337	.439	SP	421	.291	.369	.450	NO	813	.244	.293	.413
Throws Right	353.1	24-17	3.87	R	180.1	14-10	3.94	R	852	.243	.297	.399	LC	384	.268	.339	.434	RO	686	.270	.340	.422
Jeff Montgomery (1987-1997)				H	403.1	33-20	2.66	L	1591	.252	.322	.378	SP	941	.225	.308	.310	NO	1646	.234	.295	.364
Throws Right	761.1	43-43	2.91	R	358.0	11-23	3.19	R	1562	.212	.274	.320	LC	1905	.244	.309	.359	RO	1507	.230	.303	.331
Donnie Moore (1984-1988)				H	155.1	15-9	2.55	L	656	.227	.284	.307	SP	370	.259	.325	.407	NO	615	.251	.296	.353
Throws Right	299.2	23-22	2.79	R	144.1	8-13	3.06	R	575	.286	.325	.430	LC	693	.235	.280	.347	RO	616	.259	.311	.377
Mike Moore (1984-1995)				H	1306.1	80-65	3.92	L	5935	.263	.337	.389	SP	2706	.270	.356	.407	NO	6345	.254	.321	.394
Throws Right	2559.1	148-154	4.32	R	1253.0	68-89	4.73	R	5044	.262	.327	.417	LC	770	.260	.324	.398	RO	4634	.274	.348	.412
Mike Morgan (1985-1997)				H	1063.2	51-66	3.59	L	4546	.271	.337	.398	SP	2182	.261	.344	.386	NO	4987	.259	.310	.383
Throws Right	2052.0	108-140	3.93	R	989.0	57-74	4.32	R	4104	.259	.308	.385	LC	531	.275	.331	.386	RO	3663	.275	.342	.405
Jack Morris (1984-1994)				H	1228.1	85-55	4.08	L	5452	.257	.328	.397	SP	2533	.255	.336	.391	NO	6078	.241	.309	.380
Throws Right	2466.2	166-122	4.02	R	1238.1	81-67	3.97	R	4998	.240	.303	.371	LC	980	.246	.305	.364	RO	4372	.259	.326	.391
Jamie Moyer (1986-1997)				H	775.1	44-40	4.40	L	1195	.282	.349	.440	SP	1502	.275	.350	.420	NO	3639	.267	.321	.411
Throws Left	1466.0	89-84	4.36	R	690.2	45-44	4.33	R	5111	.272	.328	.418	LC	292	.286	.348	.462	RO	2667	.284	.348	.438
Terry Mulholland (1986-1997)				H	860.2	48-42	3.87	L	1288	.253	.300	.382	SP	1706	.297	.351	.447	NO	4157	.265	.306	.407
Throws Left	1707.2	87-102	4.29	R	847.0	39-60	4.72	R	5954	.277	.322	.425	LC	626	.295	.322	.485	RO	3085	.283	.335	.432
Mike Munoz (1989-1997)				H	145.0	10-3	5.46	L	494	.265	.333	.403	SP	420	.279	.391	.401	NO	554	.292	.356	.458
Throws Left	266.1	14-16	5.24	R	121.1	4-13	4.97	R	704	.295	.386	.436	LC	396	.290	.366	.431	RO	644	.274	.372	.388
Rob Murphy (1985-1995)				H	324.2	15-17	3.38	L	852	.238	.293	.326	SP	819	.273	.367	.377	NO	1358	.245	.306	.380
Throws Left	623.1	32-38	3.64	R	298.2	17-21	4.07	R	1804	.262	.339	.406	LC	865	.270	.348	.385	RO	1298	.265	.343	.379
Mike Mussina (1991-1997)				H	692.0	51-25	3.71	L	2883	.231	.283	.339	SP	1114	.245	.292	.390	NO	3447	.243	.290	.385
Throws Right	1362.1	105-49	3.50	R	670.1	54-24	3.29	R	2654	.262	.301	.446	LC	487	.227	.287	.361	RO	2090	.252	.294	.401
Randy Myers (1985-1997)				H	427.1	21-19	2.97	L	820	.201	.310	.312	SP	1062	.221	.318	.327	NO	1721	.235	.316	.356
Throws Loft	828.0	40-56	3.08	R	400.2	19-37	3.21	R	2670	.239	.314	.349	LC	2015	.231	.314	.342	RO	1769	.226	.311	.325
Chris Nabholz (1990-1995)				H	324.1	18-19	3.33	L	472	.241	.329	.063	SP	629	.257	.349	.377	NO	1465	.237	.326	.352
Throws Left	611.2	37-35	3.94	R	287.1	19-16	4.64	R	2116	.240	.326	.354	LC	200	.213	.328	.284	RO	1123	.246	.328	.361

Situational Statistics: Pitching

Pitcher	Total			Home/Road				vs. Left/Right					Scoring Position/Late & Close					None On/Runners On				
	IP	W-L	ERA		IP	W-L	ERA		PA	Avg	OBP	Slg		PA	Avg	OBP	Slg		PA	Avg	OBP	Slg
Charles Nagy (1990-1997)				H	725.1	50-28	3.51	L	2932	.273	.330	.390	SP	1468	.262	.332	.385	NO	3248	.285	.331	.422
Throws Right	1354.0	89-65	3.93	R	628.2	39-37	4.41	R	2831	.272	.322	.411	LC	451	.271	.327	.401	RO	2515	.256	.320	.371
Jaime Navarro (1989-1997)				H	817.0	50-42	4.10	L	3532	.287	.343	.417	SP	1861	.276	.340	.395	NO	4144	.266	.318	.388
Throws Right	1689.2	100-91	4.31	R	872.2	50-49	4.51	R	3765	.268	.319	.390	LC	606	.285	.331	.431	RO	3153	.293	.348	.423
Denny Neagle (1991-1997)				H	471.1	32-14	3.84	L	787	.253	.314	.411	SP	962	.270	.347	.412	NO	2475	.252	.299	.400
Throws Left	989.0	65-44	3.83	R	517.2	33-30	3.82	R	3365	.260	.310	.405	LC	443	.249	.316	.404	RO	1677	.269	.329	.416
Gene Nelson (1984-1993)				H	442.0	26-24	3.67	L	1696	.265	.335	.409	SP	1068	.244	.330	.365	NO	2014	.257	.319	.414
Throws Right	886.0	44-51	3.90	R	444.0	18-27	4.14	R	2061	.243	.306	.395	LC	844	.244	.331	.375	RO	1743	.249	.320	.386
Jeff Nelson (1992-1997)				H	212.2	12-9	3.22	L	665	.277	.391	.437	SP	655	.227	.365	.344	NO	844	.225	.305	.339
Throws Right	415.0	20-24	3.32	R	202.1	8-15	3.43	R	1114	.206	.296	.297	LC	702	.252	.361	.365	RO	935	.239	.357	.356
Robb Nen (1993-1997)				H	192.0	15-8	3.52	L	677	.225	.309	.331	SP	472	.230	.313	.331	NO	698	.249	.331	.405
Throws Right	336.2	21-17	3.61	R	144.2	6-9	3.73	R	760	.261	.333	.420	LC	766	.228	.295	.347	RO	739	.239	.313	.352
Rod Nichols (1988-1995)				H	226.2	5-16	4.37	L	848	.302	.357	.444	SP	458	.280	.336	.421	NO	984	.279	.331	.398
Throws Right	412.2	11-31	4.43	R	186.0	6-15	4.50	R	943	.266	.315	.399	LC	212	.251	.293	.421	RO	807	.287	.339	.448
Tom Niedenfuer (1984-1990)				H	261.1	12-16	3.62	L	985	.281	.364	.455	SP	635	.242	.330	.366	NO	981	.263	.321	.430
Throws Right	462.2	22-38	3.64	R	201.1	10-22	3.67	R	969	.233	.277	.352	LC	856	.267	.336	.387	RO	973	.249	.321	.373
Joe Niekro (1984-1988)				H	356.2	18-23	4.01	L	1656	.272	.361	.408	SP	868	.264	.369	.365	NO	1906	.246	.319	.373
Throws Right	758.0	44-49	4.13	R	401.1	27-26	4.24	R	1626	.241	.306	.357	LC	165	.287	.382	.497	RO	1376	.271	.355	.395
Phil Niekro (1984-1987)				H	366.1	24-20	4.45	L	1878	.279	.361	.427	SP	880	.265	.372	.395	NO	1923	.275	.345	.440
Throws Right	784.2	50-44	4.27	R	418.1	26-24	4.30	R	1568	.261	.332	.413	LC	230	.271	.365	.452	RO	1523	.265	.351	.395
Juan Nieves (1986-1988)				H	199.2	10-12	5.81	L	389	.227	.312	.327	SP	519	.288	.351	.432	NO	1211	.250	.334	.387
Throws Left	490.2	32-25	4.71	R	291.0	22-14	4.24	R	1767	.274	.350	.421	LC	108	.219	.296	.302	RO	945	.286	.354	.427
Al Nipper (1984-1990)				H	392.0	21-20	3.83	L	1798	.275	.343	.423	SP	871	.260	.336	.429	NO	1932	.272	.338	.437
Throws Right	781.2	45-49	4.57	R	389.2	24-29	5.31	R	1626	.266	.334	.447	LC	232	.274	.310	.397	RO	1492	.270	.340	.431
Dickie Noles (1984-1990)				H	176.1	8-9	5.10	L	808	.312	.387	.455	SP	478	.308	.386	.459	NO	784	.255	.330	.376
Throws Right	343.1	15-20	5.01	R	167.0	7-11	4.90	R	726	.241	.314	.358	LC	190	.290	.368	.414	RO	750	.303	.375	.444
Hideo Nomo (1995-1997)				H	343.0	23-15	2.73	L	1220	.225	.301	.347	SP	658	.209	.325	.336	NO	1563	.211	.283	.335
Throws Right	627.0	43-29	3.34	R	284.0	20-14	4.09	R	1396	.208	.294	.345	LC	184	.178	.291	.306	RO	1053	.224	.319	.364
Edwin Nunez (1984-1994)				H	289.1	15-14	4.04	L	1148	.263	.343	.424	SP	830	.285	.365	.441	NO	1242	.248	.317	.398
Throws Right	580.0	27-30	4.16	R	290.2	12-16	4.33	R	1390	.267	.333	.410	LC	834	.281	.356	.454	RO	1296	.282	.357	.435
Randy O'Neal (1984-1990)				H	191.2	7-9	4.37	L	953	.261	.329	.394	SP	506	.263	.343	.363	NO	1070	.263	.314	.430
Throws Right	440.2	17-19	4.35	R	249.0	10-10	4.34	R	928	.284	.333	.447	LC	126	.357	.392	.504	RO	811	.285	.353	.407
Chad Ogea (1994-1997)				H	207.2	15-8	3.99	L	908	.270	.329	.423	SP	431	.237	.304	.377	NO	988	.263	.321	.424
Throws Right	395.2	26-19	4.44	R	188.0	11-11	4.93	R	786	.259	.318	.423	LC	72	.254	.347	.397	RO	706	.267	.327	.422
Bobby Ojeda (1984-1994)				H	786.2	46-38	3.32	L	1242	.226	.282	.327	SP	1615	.251	.331	.352	NO	3681	.261	.318	.387
Throws Left	1540.0	92-82	3.47	R	753.1	46-44	3.63	R	5220	.261	.324	.381	LC	571	.263	.343	.359	RO	2781	.244	.314	.348
Steve Olin (1989-1992)				H	121.2	5-6	4.44	L	494	.319	.386	.408	SP	372	.268	.361	.331	NO	559	.256	.309	.326
Throws Right	273.0	16-19	3.10	R	151.1	11-13	2.02	R	661	.221	.283	.302	LC	494	.249	.331	.333	RO	596	.269	.344	.368
Omar Olivares (1990-1997)				H	506.2	23-26	4.32	L	2281	.280	.366	.436	SP	1082	.261	.341	.397	NO	2339	.269	.354	.411
Throws Right	985.0	43-49	4.46	R	478.1	20-23	4.61	R	1993	.260	.327	.382	LC	395	.263	.348	.409	RO	1935	.273	.341	.409
Darren Oliver (1993-1997)				H	269.0	21-9	4.18	L	389	.228	.336	.356	SP	587	.246	.359	.376	NO	1152	.274	.347	.440
Throws Left	477.1	35-20	4.28	R	208.1	14-11	4.41	R	1737	.275	.357	.433	LC	175	.218	.345	.296	RO	974	.257	.361	.392
Gregg Olson (1988-1997)				H	243.2	18-6	2.88	L	1028	.206	.295	.280	SP	764	.245	.370	.333	NO	1010	.233	.308	.324
Throws Right	500.1	28-29	3.20	R	256.2	10-23	3.51	R	1122	.267	.362	.361	LC	1162	.235	.335	.313	RO	1140	.242	.348	.319
Steve Ontiveros (1985-1995)				H	341.0	16-19	3.19	L	1502	.247	.312	.366	SP	677	.238	.305	.338	NO	1543	.246	.306	.369
Throws Right	656.1	33-30	3.62	R	315.1	17-11	4.08	R	1240	.246	.298	.366	LC	395	.198	.267	.297	RO	1199	.246	.305	.362
Jesse Orosco (1984-1997)				H	440.2	29-30	3.06	L	1080	.207	.279	.283	SP	1209	.197	.307	.293	NO	1703	.229	.311	.350
Throws Left	855.2	62-52	3.12	R	415.0	33-22	3.19	R	2511	.223	.316	.352	LC	1816	.206	.297	.313	RO	1888	.209	.300	.313
Donovan Osborne (1992-1997)				H	369.2	25-12	3.19	L	526	.263	.312	.412	SP	692	.285	.344	.404	NO	1836	.249	.296	.403
Throws Left	727.0	41-38	3.84	R	357.1	16-26	4.51	R	2521	.263	.314	.414	LC	210	.260	.292	.448	RO	1211	.285	.340	.431
Dave Otto (1987-1994)				H	170.1	4-10	4.39	L	302	.317	.384	.376	SP	402	.302	.379	.470	NO	743	.307	.363	.444
Throws Left	318.1	10-22	5.06	R	148.0	6-12	5.96	R	1103	.298	.363	.463	LC	146	.344	.397	.563	RO	662	.297	.372	.444
Vicente Palacios (1987-1995)				H	189.2	9-8	4.22	L	734	.253	.332	.384	SP	388	.294	.375	.484	NO	874	.224	.306	.339
Throws Right	361.1	17-19	4.36	R	171.2	8-11	4.67	R	796	.250	.326	.407	LC	183	.224	.326	.353	RO	656	.290	.361	.475
Donn Pall (1988-1997)				H	237.0	13-8	3.91	L	846	.269	.325	.389	SP	596	.266	.342	.384	NO	1037	.254	.303	.382
Throws Right	472.0	24-22	3.53	R	235.0	11-14	3.14	R	1152	.260	.315	.395	LC	623	.270	.340	.384	RO	961	.275	.337	.404
David Palmer (1984-1989)				H	386.1	20-25	3.96	L	1718	.264	.350	.364	SP	885	.270	.373	.364	NO	1814	.245	.321	.349
Throws Right	749.1	40-46	4.18	R	363.0	20-22	4.66	R	1512	.250	.322	.365	LC	157	.369	.401	.463	RO	1416	.274	.357	.384
Chan Ho Park (1994-1997)				H	161.1	10-6	2.73	L	640	.242	.356	.372	SP	291	.236	.350	.335	NO	757	.203	.305	.339
Throws Right	308.2	19-13	3.59	R	147.1	9-7	4.52	R	668	.184	.263	.307	LC	105	.213	.295	.351	RO	551	.224	.315	.336
Jeff Parrett (1986-1996)				H	392.0	29-20	3.86	L	1497	.255	.355	.367	SP	1013	.254	.362	.385	NO	1592	.247	.321	.378
Throws Right	724.2	56-43	3.80	R	332.2	27-23	3.73	R	1629	.244	.313	.392	LC	979	.268	.356	.392	RO	1534	.252	.346	.383
Bob Patterson (1985-1997)				H	331.2	24-18	3.99	L	842	.212	.267	.318	SP	743	.275	.342	.460	NO	1291	.248	.296	.399
Throws Left	597.0	38-39	3.96	R	265.1	14-21	3.93	R	1643	.282	.331	.458	LC	847	.244	.306	.379	RO	1194	.270	.324	.426
Ken Patterson (1988-1994)				H	161.1	6-4	4.02	L	427	.261	.355	.378	SP	435	.238	.352	.401	NO	696	.266	.351	.422
Throws Left	317.2	14-8	3.88	R	156.1	8-4	3.74	R	945	.242	.334	.412	LC	184	.278	.395	.465	RO	676	.227	.329	.379
Roger Pavlik (1992-1997)				H	374.0	28-18	4.76	L	1724	.254	.338	.385	SP	795	.266	.361	.414	NO	1834	.258	.333	.417
Throws Right	729.0	46-38	4.59	R	355.0	18-20	4.41	R	1460	.271	.355	.446	LC	247	.270	.350	.428	RO	1350	.267	.364	.407
Alejandro Pena (1984-1996)				H	391.2	19-21	3.06	L	1711	.239	.310	.338	SP	882	.243	.326	.348	NO	1914	.238	.290	.350
Throws Right	819.2	43-40	3.12	R	428.0	24-19	3.18	R	1684	.247	.288	.368	LC	1028	.225	.287	.330	RO	1481	.250	.311	.357

Situational Statistics: Pitching

Pitcher	IP	W-L	ERA		IP	W-L	ERA		PA	Avg	OBP	Slg		PA	Avg	OBP	Slg		PA	Avg	OBP	Slg
	Total				**Home/Road**				**vs. Left/Right**				**Scoring Position/Late & Close**					**None On/Runners On**				
Carlos Perez (1995-1997)				H	195.2	16-8	3.63	L	266	.193	.247	.279	SP	343	.255	.295	.455	NO	868	.249	.300	.401
Throws Left	348.0	22-21	3.80	R	152.1	6-13	4.02	R	1183	.273	.313	.454	LC	102	.226	.270	.312	RO	581	.273	.304	.454
Melido Perez (1987-1995)				H	618.1	33-35	4.32	L	2926	.250	.327	.392	SP	1373	.266	.339	.407	NO	3340	.238	.312	.382
Throws Right	1354.2	78-85	4.17	R	736.1	45-50	4.03	R	2826	.246	.316	.393	LC	539	.253	.322	.381	RO	2412	.262	.334	.407
Mike Perez (1990-1997)				H	179.1	18-10	3.26	L	620	.284	.360	.380	SP	439	.260	.356	.374	NO	766	.257	.311	.376
Throws Right	346.0	24-16	3.56	R	166.2	6-6	3.89	R	855	.239	.295	.359	LC	690	.265	.334	.389	RO	709	.258	.336	.358
Pascual Perez (1984-1991)				H	452.2	24-28	3.22	L	1897	.248	.309	.388	SP	784	.241	.333	.369	NO	2140	.233	.278	.355
Throws Right	851.1	46-48	3.41	R	398.2	22-20	3.68	R	1585	.229	.276	.339	LC	234	.273	.336	.392	RO	1342	.249	.321	.385
Pat Perry (1985-1990)				H	122.0	7-4	4.35	L	305	.262	.297	.376	SP	289	.270	.360	.399	NO	629	.201	.269	.335
Throws Left	263.0	12-10	3.46	R	141.0	5-6	2.68	R	778	.210	.297	.347	LC	173	.206	.326	.312	RO	454	.261	.336	.386
Mark Petkovsek (1991-1997)				H	194.0	16-4	3.66	L	669	.288	.340	.438	SP	433	.322	.393	.505	NO	865	.255	.312	.413
Throws Right	363.2	24-16	4.70	R	169.2	8-12	5.89	R	889	.273	.338	.445	LC	248	.266	.352	.397	RO	693	.311	.373	.480
Dan Petry (1984-1991)				H	622.0	33-37	4.17	L	2532	.256	.335	.402	SP	1251	.261	.339	.416	NO	2864	.249	.324	.388
Throws Right	1164.2	65-61	4.22	R	542.2	32-24	4.31	R	2472	.260	.330	.415	LC	377	.227	.309	.331	RO	2140	.271	.344	.437
Andy Pettitte (1995-1997)				H	339.0	27-10	2.84	L	495	.307	.343	.387	SP	620	.277	.341	.383	NO	1545	.255	.312	.377
Throws Left	636.1	51-24	3.58	R	297.1	24-14	4.42	R	2165	.256	.318	.378	LC	188	.318	.351	.426	RO	1115	.281	.337	.384
Hipolito Pichardo (1992-1997)				H	284.0	20-15	4.44	L	1163	.297	.359	.418	SP	709	.285	.370	.387	NO	1248	.278	.340	.401
Throws Right	557.1	35-31	4.34	R	273.1	15-16	4.25	R	1271	.262	.332	.371	LC	592	.286	.369	.385	RO	1186	.279	.351	.385
Jeff Pico (1988-1990)				H	168.1	7-4	4.22	L	670	.326	.393	.459	SP	374	.315	.394	.478	NO	671	.258	.313	.349
Throws Right	295.1	13-12	4.24	R	127.0	6-8	4.25	R	617	.237	.284	.339	LC	116	.243	.313	.379	RO	616	.311	.371	.460
Dan Plesac (1986-1997)				H	399.2	21-24	3.96	L	931	.226	.286	.357	SP	1045	.265	.334	.412	NO	1720	.237	.303	.354
Throws Left	822.2	45-54	3.54	R	423.0	24-30	3.19	R	2535	.253	.319	.379	LC	1340	.278	.346	.417	RO	1746	.255	.317	.392
Eric Plunk (1986-1997)				H	477.1	42-17	3.94	L	2042	.251	.357	.378	SP	1386	.219	.340	.333	NO	2239	.237	.339	.376
Throws Right	1003.0	64-51	3.69	R	525.2	22-34	3.46	R	2327	.216	.317	.347	LC	1183	.238	.334	.384	RO	2130	.227	.334	.345
Jim Poole (1990-1997)				H	157.1	10-3	3.15	L	499	.244	.302	.371	SP	412	.253	.362	.383	NO	557	.245	.307	.389
Throws Left	276.1	18-8	3.87	R	119.1	8-5	4.83	R	690	.254	.349	.403	LC	363	.195	.286	.326	RO	632	.255	.350	.389
Mark Portugal (1985-1997)				H	769.2	50-34	3.27	L	3327	.242	.315	.368	SP	1499	.254	.327	.396	NO	3646	.258	.324	.388
Throws Right	1509.2	92-78	3.83	R	740.0	42-44	4.50	R	3023	.268	.325	.412	LC	471	.272	.325	.408	RO	2704	.250	.313	.390
Dennis Powell (1985-1993)				H	148.1	3-9	5.04	L	448	.228	.288	.345	SP	444	.275	.372	.372	NO	757	.284	.363	.431
Throws Left	339.2	11-22	4.95	R	191.1	8-13	4.89	R	1045	.302	.390	.453	LC	238	.315	.400	.435	RO	736	.273	.356	.406
Ted Power (1984-1993)				H	504.1	31-23	3.80	L	2034	.272	.350	.404	SP	1297	.258	.340	.386	NO	2181	.259	.316	.380
Throws Right	1001.0	61-59	3.86	R	496.2	30-36	4.11	R	2218	.250	.303	.369	LC	1092	.264	.338	.365	RO	2071	.262	.335	.392
Joe Price (1984-1990)				H	284.2	12-11	3.13	L	524	.248	.297	.375	SP	576	.256	.344	.390	NO	1223	.248	.312	.382
Throws Left	524.1	19-35	4.10	R	239.2	7-24	5.26	R	1728	.256	.328	.412	LC	263	.260	.335	.392	RO	1029	.262	.332	.430
Ariel Prieto (1995-1997)				H	148.0	11-8	4.26	L	769	.274	.375	.406	SP	396	.263	.370	.403	NO	730	.283	.368	.432
Throws Right	308.2	14-21	4.67	R	160.2	3-13	5.04	R	624	.299	.370	.456	LC	63	.268	.328	.482	RO	663	.288	.377	.425
Tim Pugh (1992-1997)				H	214.0	12-11	4.75	L	879	.292	.367	.452	SP	479	.312	.389	.475	NO	1018	.280	.340	.434
Throws Right	416.2	25-28	4.97	R	202.2	13-17	5.20	R	970	.290	.345	.433	LC	106	.301	.375	.376	RO	831	.306	.375	.452
Charlie Puleo (1984-1989)				H	134.1	7-4	3.68	L	666	.280	.365	.463	SP	375	.287	.378	.446	NO	708	.235	.306	.368
Throws Right	305.0	14-18	4.01	R	170.2	8-14	4.27	R	650	.223	.288	.311	LC	123	.243	.355	.369	RO	608	.273	.351	.412
Paul Quantrill (1992-1997)				H	345.1	17-24	4.12	L	1278	.312	.371	.510	SP	808	.263	.341	.413	NO	1512	.308	.346	.479
Throws Right	642.0	33-51	4.12	R	296.2	16-27	4.13	R	1531	.284	.325	.406	LC	532	.341	.397	.496	RO	1297	.283	.346	.418
Dan Quisenberry (1984-1990)				H	266.2	19-9	3.07	L	1118	.298	.337	.405	SP	704	.295	.350	.400	NO	1154	.267	.284	.359
Throws Right	537.0	26-23	3.03	R	270.1	8-14	3.00	R	1109	.263	.280	.355	LC	984	.279	.310	.361	RO	1073	.295	.335	.403
Scott Radinsky (1990-1997)				H	203.2	16-9	2.87	L	554	.226	.279	.337	SP	587	.227	.321	.324	NO	768	.271	.333	.383
Throws Left	390.1	34-18	3.34	R	186.2	18-9	3.86	R	1133	.260	.346	.356	LC	856	.228	.313	.320	RO	919	.228	.316	.319
Brad Radke (1995-1997)				H	363.2	23-20	4.06	L	1492	.272	.316	.461	SP	556	.288	.325	.500	NO	1713	.244	.289	.426
Throws Right	652.2	42-40	4.48	R	289.0	19-20	5.01	R	1242	.249	.288	.439	LC	177	.241	.278	.410	RO	1021	.292	.328	.496
Pat Rapp (1992-1997)				H	351.1	21-20	4.20	L	1513	.288	.380	.411	SP	869	.250	.355	.342	NO	1628	.289	.369	.437
Throws Right	708.2	38-47	4.31	R	357.1	17-27	4.41	R	1608	.268	.349	.403	LC	127	.311	.423	.641	RO	1493	.264	.359	.371
Dennis Rasmussen (1984-1995)				H	657.1	47-34	3.96	L	1043	.257	.314	.395	SP	1318	.268	.340	.436	NO	3667	.246	.313	.398
Throws Left	1447.0	91-77	4.17	R	789.2	46-43	4.34	R	5088	.257	.323	.413	LC	345	.280	.356	.387	RO	2464	.274	.333	.428
Shane Rawley (1984-1989)				H	553.2	33-33	4.42	L	680	.282	.335	.417	SP	1175	.248	.333	.378	NO	2670	.278	.338	.422
Throws Left	1091.1	66-63	4.15	R	537.2	33-30	3.87	R	4029	.271	.337	.413	LC	267	.242	.299	.383	RO	2039	.266	.335	.403
Jeff Reardon (1984-1994)				H	378.0	35-31	3.55	L	1565	.262	.326	.406	SP	946	.249	.324	.394	NO	1589	.231	.276	.367
Throws Right	730.0	47-55	3.55	R	352.0	12-24	3.55	R	1458	.221	.266	.351	LC	1749	.243	.301	.374	RO	1434	.256	.320	.393
Jerry Reed (1985-1990)				H	220.1	11-8	2.86	L	801	.280	.349	.426	SP	564	.256	.352	.389	NO	944	.250	.299	.391
Throws Right	429.0	18-17	3.73	R	208.2	7-9	4.66	R	1019	.238	.297	.371	LC	245	.311	.400	.529	RO	876	.263	.343	.399
Rick Reed (1988-1997)				H	224.0	13-11	3.42	L	996	.236	.285	.375	SP	440	.285	.334	.431	NO	1201	.245	.280	.385
Throws Right	474.2	22-24	3.87	R	250.2	9-13	4.27	R	966	.289	.317	.437	LC	117	.252	.284	.405	RO	761	.291	.334	.442
Steve Reed (1992-1997)				H	205.2	15-10	4.38	L	625	.285	.367	.471	SP	449	.273	.351	.435	NO	881	.240	.301	.401
Throws Right	385.1	26-18	3.62	R	179.2	11-8	2.76	R	976	.218	.276	.368	LC	653	.228	.304	.406	RO	720	.250	.325	.415
Rick Reuschel (1984-1991)				H	650.0	47-28	3.10	L	2891	.278	.323	.392	SP	1260	.255	.320	.351	NO	3105	.254	.293	.372
Throws Right	1280.0	80-65	3.31	R	630.0	33-37	3.59	R	2418	.239	.283	.352	LC	389	.288	.344	.407	RO	2204	.270	.322	.376
Jerry Reuss (1984-1990)				H	459.0	24-25	3.88	L	553	.287	.328	.427	SP	844	.301	.355	.452	NO	2061	.272	.314	.394
Throws Left	835.2	47-51	4.21	R	376.2	23-26	4.61	R	3006	.284	.329	.411	LC	183	.271	.324	.392	RO	1498	.303	.350	.441
Carlos Reyes (1994-1997)				H	183.0	4-7	4.38	L	792	.286	.361	.435	SP	441	.267	.370	.487	NO	807	.285	.354	.451
Throws Right	346.2	14-23	4.93	R	163.2	10-16	5.55	R	760	.268	.347	.471	LC	213	.269	.350	.396	RO	745	.269	.355	.453
Shane Reynolds (1992-1997)				H	376.1	23-14	3.30	L	1586	.260	.307	.370	SP	790	.256	.309	.373	NO	1838	.268	.305	.402
Throws Right	769.2	44-39	3.72	R	393.1	21-25	4.12	R	1648	.267	.302	.414	LC	258	.274	.303	.371	RO	1396	.259	.304	.380

Situational Statistics: Pitching

Pitcher	Total IP	W-L	ERA		H/R IP	W-L	ERA		PA	Avg	OBP	Slg		PA	Avg	OBP	Slg		PA	Avg	OBP	Slg
										vs. Left/Right					Scoring Position/Late & Close					None On/Runners On		
Armando Reynoso (1991-1997)				H	311.1	21-13	4.71	L	1269	.292	.358	.477	SP	729	.270	.364	.419	NO	1536	.283	.339	.471
Throws Right	625.1	39-35	4.69	R	314.0	18-22	4.67	R	1461	.286	.347	.458	LC	110	.219	.303	.427	RO	1194	.297	.370	.462
Rick Rhoden (1984-1989)				H	662.0	43-35	3.32	L	2675	.267	.327	.377	SP	1194	.254	.348	.387	NO	2932	.264	.310	.391
Throws Right	1180.2	69-64	3.63	R	518.2	27-29	4.03	R	2266	.256	.309	.399	LC	355	.283	.345	.382	RO	2009	.258	.331	.381
Arthur Rhodes (1991-1997)				H	248.2	18-16	5.57	L	421	.224	.303	.365	SP	550	.246	.335	.395	NO	1195	.240	.328	.396
Throws Left	492.1	36-28	5.01	R	243.2	18-12	4.43	R	1710	.259	.345	.431	LC	266	.210	.285	.319	RO	936	.267	.348	.446
Dave Righetti (1984-1995)				H	448.0	30-22	2.77	L	930	.245	.322	.366	SP	1177	.255	.338	.359	NO	1849	.241	.315	.349
Throws Left	881.0	49-56	3.57	R	433.0	19-34	4.36	R	2850	.259	.332	.363	LC	1856	.239	.317	.333	RO	1931	.270	.343	.379
Jose Rijo (1984-1995)				H	876.0	55-39	3.20	L	4075	.258	.338	.385	SP	1887	.234	.323	.308	NO	4308	.244	.302	.377
Throws Right	1786.0	111-87	3.16	R	910.0	56-48	3.14	R	3351	.220	.269	.322	LC	603	.249	.319	.376	RO	3118	.236	.314	.326
Kevin Ritz (1989-1997)				H	366.1	22-18	5.48	L	1556	.302	.399	.450	SP	1001	.291	.404	.462	NO	1771	.278	.352	.398
Throws Right	744.1	45-54	5.28	R	378.0	23-36	5.10	R	1814	.273	.344	.402	LC	90	.250	.367	.461	RO	1599	.295	.389	.454
Ben Rivera (1992-1994)				H	158.1	11-7	4.32	L	723	.274	.354	.414	SP	396	.231	.338	.357	NO	753	.255	.336	.399
Throws Right	318.1	23-17	4.52	R	160.0	12-10	4.73	R	682	.240	.332	.384	LC	65	.241	.323	.414	RO	652	.261	.352	.400
Rich Robertson (1993-1997)				H	227.1	9-19	5.62	L	417	.274	.387	.380	SP	525	.276	.381	.458	NO	962	.281	.372	.435
Throws Left	409.2	17-30	5.25	R	182.1	8-11	4.79	R	1450	.284	.371	.450	LC	81	.333	.429	.545	RO	905	.282	.377	.435
Don Robinson (1984-1992)				H	511.1	37-16	3.03	L	2437	.253	.319	.374	SP	1228	.259	.337	.395	NO	2646	.246	.295	.375
Throws Right	1107.1	63-64	3.62	R	596.0	26-48	4.18	R	2187	.252	.295	.392	LC	867	.223	.298	.315	RO	1978	.263	.325	.393
Jeff Robinson (1984-1992)				H	430.1	17-24	3.37	L	1934	.267	.328	.392	SP	1165	.244	.349	.362	NO	2091	.254	.310	.382
Throws Right	901.1	46-57	3.79	R	471.0	29-33	4.18	R	1909	.248	.326	.370	LC	805	.247	.316	.354	RO	1752	.263	.348	.381
Jeff Robinson (1987-1992)				H	407.0	26-17	4.05	L	1566	.251	.344	.423	SP	735	.271	.370	.445	NO	1804	.234	.322	.378
Throws Right	708.2	47-40	4.79	R	301.2	21-23	5.79	R	1529	.249	.333	.387	LC	154	.210	.270	.341	RO	1291	.274	.363	.445
Ron Robinson (1984-1992)				H	379.0	20-20	3.78	L	1724	.290	.354	.417	SP	872	.264	.338	.383	NO	1930	.259	.312	.390
Throws Right	800.0	48-39	3.63	R	421.0	28-21	3.66	R	1668	.243	.291	.367	LC	428	.279	.348	.396	RO	1462	.278	.338	.396
Frank Rodriguez (1995-1997)				H	239.0	10-11	4.07	L	1028	.275	.361	.414	SP	518	.308	.375	.475	NO	1074	.256	.342	.422
Throws Right	454.2	21-28	5.17	R	215.2	11-17	6.38	R	962	.270	.334	.432	LC	166	.273	.370	.439	RO	916	.293	.355	.424
Rich Rodriguez (1990-1997)				H	216.1	12-7	3.37	L	601	.249	.329	.363	SP	546	.257	.365	.369	NO	915	.244	.310	.372
Throws Left	422.0	19-17	3.20	R	205.2	7-10	3.02	R	1170	.253	.323	.382	LC	578	.238	.327	.356	RO	856	.260	.341	.380
Kenny Rogers (1989-1997)				H	676.2	55-32	4.02	L	996	.223	.305	.347	SP	1465	.277	.370	.429	NO	3020	.247	.312	.383
Throws Left	1267.1	88-66	4.20	R	590.2	33-34	4.40	R	4507	.268	.339	.411	LC	929	.250	.329	.369	RO	2483	.277	.358	.422
Mel Rojas (1990-1997)				H	290.0	17-14	3.54	L	1309	.227	.308	.359	SP	769	.221	.314	.344	NO	1260	.243	.316	.380
Throws Right	595.0	29-29	3.27	R	305.0	12-15	3.01	R	1180	.227	.295	.342	LC	1371	.223	.302	.331	RO	1229	.210	.287	.319
Ron Romanick (1984-1986)				H	297.2	16-16	4.02	L	1224	.278	.324	.427	SP	511	.268	.317	.405	NO	1307	.284	.336	.439
Throws Right	531.0	31-29	4.24	R	233.1	15-13	4.51	R	1035	.281	.340	.431	LC	190	.320	.347	.475	RO	952	.272	.326	.415
Jose Rosado (1996-1997)				H	158.0	10-9	3.82	L	250	.271	.341	.452	SP	298	.237	.293	.336	NO	758	.268	.330	.437
Throws Left	310.0	17-18	4.18	R	152.0	7-9	4.56	R	1072	.256	.311	.389	LC	103	.233	.307	.344	RO	564	.246	.298	.351
Kirk Rueter (1993-1997)				H	270.2	19-13	3.89	L	390	.262	.308	.354	SP	459	.275	.341	.417	NO	1268	.270	.310	.396
Throws Left	518.0	39-20	3.72	R	247.1	20-7	3.53	R	1764	.270	.314	.405	LC	94	.182	.234	.295	RO	886	.267	.317	.395
Bruce Ruffin (1986-1997)				H	672.0	40-36	4.14	L	1177	.255	.354	.343	SP	1532	.281	.370	.409	NO	2924	.271	.342	.390
Throws Left	1268.0	60-82	4.19	R	596.0	22-46	4.36	R	4390	.280	.347	.408	LC	799	.245	.341	.344	RO	2643	.280	.356	.400
Vern Ruhle (1984-1986)				H	118.2	2-7	4.85	L	538	.271	.318	.369	SP	282	.321	.379	.455	NO	643	.253	.292	.360
Throws Right	263.0	4-22	4.38	R	144.1	2-15	3.99	R	583	.298	.340	.428	LC	159	.234	.314	.291	RO	478	.331	.379	.456
Jeff Russell (1984-1996)				H	513.0	22-28	3.82	L	2109	.278	.351	.402	SP	1342	.270	.351	.395	NO	2282	.239	.306	.346
Throws Right	1031.1	52-68	3.80	R	518.1	30-40	3.85	R	2293	.237	.302	.354	LC	1402	.233	.307	.339	RO	2120	.276	.346	.411
Nolan Ryan (1984-1993)				H	1075.0	67-46	3.03	L	3978	.207	.296	.303	SP	1995	.217	.318	.324	NO	4617	.191	.275	.294
Throws Right	1865.2	105-97	3.36	R	790.2	38-51	3.81	R	3732	.206	.287	.328	LC	584	.206	.270	.316	RO	3093	.231	.317	.349
Bret Saberhagen (1984-1997)				H	1124.2	66-45	3.12	L	4835	.239	.283	.371	SP	1922	.259	.309	.399	NO	5582	.247	.283	.372
Throws Right	2253.2	141-101	3.30	R	1129.0	76-56	3.50	R	4297	.262	.294	.382	LC	875	.233	.271	.359	RO	3550	.255	.296	.384
Bill Sampen (1990-1994)				H	140.1	12-8	3.33	L	658	.285	.371	.406	SP	420	.262	.356	.398	NO	664	.274	.358	.400
Throws Right	299.1	25-21	3.73	R	159.0	13-13	4.08	R	657	.264	.340	.378	LC	403	.301	.388	.399	RO	651	.274	.352	.383
Scott Sanders (1993-1997)				H	288.0	16-19	4.66	L	1103	.279	.371	.458	SP	555	.281	.352	.458	NO	1369	.219	.297	.361
Throws Right	537.0	27-35	4.54	R	249.0	11-16	4.41	R	1216	.219	.270	.360	LC	153	.285	.362	.377	RO	950	.288	.349	.471
Scott Sanderson (1984-1996)				H	790.2	50-46	4.12	L	3747	.270	.317	.440	SP	1614	.265	.321	.423	NO	4198	.268	.306	.437
Throws Right	1678.2	107-96	4.11	R	888.0	57-50	4.14	R	3293	.268	.301	.431	LC	332	.257	.307	.365	RO	2842	.270	.316	.433
Bob Scanlan (1991-1996)				H	247.2	11-19	5.20	L	1045	.276	.348	.407	SP	647	.281	.356	.399	NO	1081	.265	.338	.384
Throws Right	482.1	20-33	4.46	R	234.2	9-14	3.68	R	1055	.279	.342	.402	LC	583	.276	.328	.381	RO	1019	.292	.352	.427
Dan Schatzeder (1984-1991)				H	315.0	15-14	3.17	L	644	.273	.318	.355	SP	658	.288	.354	.425	NO	1324	.250	.316	.392
Throws Left	569.1	27-26	3.73	R	254.1	12-12	4.42	R	1765	.261	.328	.425	LC	357	.222	.301	.330	RO	1085	.282	.336	.423
Curt Schilling (1988-1997)				H	648.2	34-35	3.25	L	2536	.236	.296	.373	SP	1150	.246	.319	.367	NO	3070	.221	.270	.342
Throws Right	1242.2	69-63	3.38	R	594.0	35-28	3.53	R	2556	.234	.282	.348	LC	710	.251	.314	.394	RO	2022	.257	.318	.390
Calvin Schiraldi (1984-1991)				H	265.0	15-18	4.31	L	1278	.264	.359	.417	SP	669	.256	.344	.423	NO	1288	.241	.329	.353
Throws Right	553.1	32-39	4.28	R	288.1	17-21	4.25	R	1129	.232	.305	.371	LC	285	.221	.308	.361	RO	1119	.257	.339	.445
Dave Schmidt (1984-1992)				H	362.0	22-18	4.00	L	1482	.283	.328	.435	SP	879	.273	.339	.409	NO	1638	.282	.319	.443
Throws Right	714.1	47-45	4.02	R	352.1	25-27	4.04	R	1546	.270	.316	.401	LC	646	.273	.327	.359	RO	1390	.269	.326	.386
Jason Schmidt (1995-1997)				H	170.2	11-11	5.43	L	646	.288	.386	.462	SP	382	.290	.386	.429	NO	726	.274	.351	.422
Throws Right	309.0	17-17	5.04	R	138.1	6-6	4.55	R	743	.262	.327	.404	LC	74	.180	.301	.295	RO	663	.273	.359	.404
Mike Schooler (1988-1993)				H	150.2	7-14	3.29	L	600	.262	.344	.390	SP	411	.295	.359	.436	NO	606	.227	.294	.329
Throws Right	291.2	15-29	3.49	R	141.0	8-15	3.70	R	653	.245	.289	.340	LC	629	.272	.336	.402	RO	647	.277	.337	.398
Pete Schourek (1991-1997)				H	421.2	34-21	3.84	L	714	.295	.356	.444	SP	835	.297	.377	.430	NO	1909	.242	.300	.386
Throws Left	774.1	50-46	4.44	R	352.2	16-25	5.16	R	2618	.257	.321	.410	LC	253	.242	.303	.401	RO	1423	.300	.367	.463

Situational Statistics: Pitching

Pitcher	Total IP	W-L	ERA		Home/Road IP	W-L	ERA		vs. Left/Right PA	Avg	OBP	Slg		Scoring Position/Late & Close PA	Avg	OBP	Slg		None On/Runners On PA	Avg	OBP	Slg
Ken Schrom (1984-1987)				H	397.2	23-25	4.98	L	1541	.300	.351	.485	SP	661	.281	.335	.447	NO	1691	.275	.328	.473
Throws Right	657.1	34-43	5.09	R	259.2	11-18	5.34	R	1293	.257	.314	.444	LC	154	.261	.325	.391	RO	1143	.290	.343	.456
Don Schulze (1984-1989)				H	195.2	8-13	4.60	L	764	.337	.383	.486	SP	379	.325	.381	.525	NO	789	.299	.346	.427
Throws Right	324.2	15-24	5.41	R	129.0	7-11	6.63	R	682	.271	.324	.430	LC	91	.225	.319	.450	RO	657	.314	.366	.501
Mike Scott (1984-1991)				H	838.2	59-32	2.55	L	3415	.230	.294	.340	SP	1550	.220	.300	.327	NO	3910	.215	.267	.337
Throws Right	1559.0	100-75	3.26	R	720.1	43-43	4.09	R	2938	.218	.270	.357	LC	467	.173	.260	.260	RO	2443	.242	.308	.367
Tim Scott (1991-1997)				H	166.1	14-6	3.25	L	639	.222	.329	.340	SP	461	.259	.364	.368	NO	690	.252	.332	.372
Throws Right	314.0	24-13	4.13	R	147.2	10-7	5.12	R	736	.286	.348	.425	LC	541	.255	.353	.377	RO	685	.262	.345	.401
Scott Scudder (1989-1993)				H	194.0	10-17	5.15	L	969	.268	.360	.398	SP	483	.249	.372	.373	NO	937	.264	.352	.405
Throws Right	386.1	21-34	4.80	R	192.1	11-17	4.45	R	770	.263	.355	.435	LC	145	.323	.406	.444	RO	802	.268	.365	.427
Ray Searage (1984-1990)				H	130.0	8-7	3.60	L	374	.263	.342	.367	SP	360	.269	.374	.379	NO	513	.245	.320	.364
Throws Left	251.0	10-13	3.48	R	121.0	2-6	3.35	R	704	.241	.326	.365	LC	287	.241	.336	.322	RO	565	.252	.343	.368
Tom Seaver (1984-1986)				H	310.2	17-17	4.14	L	1414	.246	.307	.385	SP	647	.235	.312	.356	NO	1645	.243	.292	.385
Throws Right	651.2	38-35	3.69	R	341.0	21-18	3.27	R	1294	.252	.300	.386	LC	332	.262	.325	.385	RO	1063	.259	.322	.385
Bob Sebra (1985-1990)				H	188.1	7-10	4.16	L	894	.280	.363	.446	SP	500	.247	.334	.358	NO	891	.273	.338	.422
Throws Right	366.2	15-29	4.71	R	178.1	8-19	5.30	R	729	.272	.326	.407	LC	75	.213	.319	.361	RO	732	.280	.357	.436
Aaron Sele (1993-1997)				H	324.2	21-19	4.38	L	1471	.301	.384	.464	SP	734	.263	.347	.367	NO	1470	.273	.359	.429
Throws Right	622.0	38-33	4.41	R	297.1	17-14	4.45	R	1306	.242	.316	.349	LC	121	.287	.387	.475	RO	1307	.272	.344	.386
Jeff Sellers (1985-1988)				H	163.0	7-9	4.97	L	805	.301	.385	.420	SP	386	.312	.393	.464	NO	802	.267	.363	.397
Throws Right	330.1	13-22	4.96	R	167.1	6-13	4.95	R	668	.265	.346	.431	LC	39	.294	.385	.618	RO	671	.306	.372	.459
Jeff Shaw (1990-1997)				H	306.2	13-17	3.73	L	1080	.275	.336	.405	SP	692	.234	.316	.326	NO	1273	.262	.311	.442
Throws Right	563.0	23-33	3.77	R	256.1	10-16	3.83	R	1294	.249	.300	.407	LC	720	.243	.311	.380	RO	1101	.259	.324	.362
Bob Shirley (1984-1987)				H	224.1	8-6	3.57	L	448	.223	.270	.328	SP	424	.248	.295	.380	NO	847	.246	.307	.370
Throws Left	370.0	9-12	3.96	R	145.2	1-6	4.76	R	1104	.287	.348	.441	LC	210	.236	.290	.319	RO	705	.296	.348	.454
Eric Show (1984-1991)				H	646.2	37-34	3.62	L	2915	.270	.351	.417	SP	1251	.247	.341	.388	NO	3218	.251	.310	.397
Throws Right	1281.1	75-68	3.71	R	634.2	38-34	3.80	R	2455	.223	.280	.354	LC	375	.255	.331	.382	RO	2152	.244	.332	.373
Doug Sisk (1984-1991)				H	201.0	6-7	3.36	L	840	.285	.386	.361	SP	600	.296	.382	.393	NO	855	.255	.342	.310
Throws Right	410.1	17-15	3.58	R	209.1	11-8	3.83	R	964	.270	.345	.342	LC	526	.258	.371	.296	RO	949	.297	.384	.389
Jim Slaton (1984-1986)				H	232.0	9-11	4.15	L	952	.294	.366	.455	SP	453	.263	.347	.430	NO	1035	.288	.352	.460
Throws Right	424.2	17-26	4.79	R	192.2	8-15	5.56	R	898	.287	.336	.473	LC	152	.285	.375	.431	RO	815	.293	.351	.469
Heathcliff Slocumb (1991-1997)				H	217.0	10-10	3.86	L	916	.276	.380	.342	SP	699	.258	.362	.341	NO	874	.249	.334	.306
Throws Right	432.2	21-26	3.79	R	215.2	11-16	3.71	R	1028	.248	.333	.328	LC	1040	.257	.370	.330	RO	1070	.271	.372	.360
John Smiley (1986-1997)				H	920.0	64-52	3.64	L	1338	.248	.309	.389	SP	1836	.284	.339	.436	NO	4701	.247	.297	.379
Throws Left	1907.2	126-103	3.80	R	987.2	63-51	3.95	R	6562	.257	.304	.395	LC	570	.209	.261	.331	RO	3199	.269	.317	.417
Bryn Smith (1984-1993)				H	814.2	52-34	3.28	L	3517	.264	.310	.370	SP	1536	.255	.310	.398	NO	3782	.247	.292	.355
Throws Right	1543.2	99-79	3.60	R	729.0	47-45	3.99	R	2861	.238	.285	.372	LC	338	.293	.333	.462	RO	2596	.262	.310	.396
Dave Smith (1984-1992)				H	264.0	25-20	2.63	L	992	.236	.305	.318	SP	650	.221	.309	.334	NO	1014	.223	.287	.293
Throws Right	495.2	33-40	2.60	R	231.2	8-20	2.56	R	1020	.222	.281	.316	LC	1104	.240	.309	.353	RO	998	.234	.299	.342
Lee Smith (1984-1997)				H	535.0	40-36	3.33	L	2269	.244	.324	.362	SP	1335	.219	.307	.327	NO	2060	.244	.302	.364
Throws Right	980.2	60-71	3.18	R	445.2	21-35	3.05	R	1834	.233	.284	.347	LC	2580	.241	.307	.366	RO	2043	.234	.310	.346
Pete Smith (1987-1997)				H	500.2	23-38	4.57	L	2206	.283	.359	.422	SP	996	.271	.343	.409	NO	2362	.258	.325	.407
Throws Right	937.1	42-66	4.46	R	436.2	19-28	4.33	R	1820	.241	.296	.405	LC	272	.261	.322	.357	RO	1664	.273	.340	.425
Roy Smith (1984-1991)				H	332.0	20-13	4.17	L	1361	.306	.365	.475	SP	650	.288	.351	.439	NO	1536	.288	.342	.435
Throws Right	618.1	30-31	4.60	R	286.1	10-18	5.09	R	1336	.272	.320	.423	LC	148	.331	.406	.449	RO	1161	.291	.343	.467
Zane Smith (1984-1996)				H	1033.1	54-50	3.48	L	1255	.232	.273	.305	SP	2054	.290	.363	.430	NO	4591	.265	.315	.370
Throws Left	1919.1	100-115	3.74	R	886.0	46-66	4.24	R	6792	.278	.335	.398	LC	707	.250	.308	.322	RO	3456	.279	.341	.403
Mike Smithson (1984-1989)				H	548.2	38-26	4.58	L	2675	.294	.342	.486	SP	1113	.282	.341	.461	NO	2747	.271	.326	.432
Throws Right	1086.1	63-68	4.70	R	537.2	25-42	4.84	R	2007	.257	.318	.390	LC	286	.305	.360	.502	RO	1935	.288	.340	.465
John Smoltz (1988-1997)				H	1050.2	61-51	3.50	L	4651	.255	.329	.371	SP	2010	.231	.325	.364	NO	5036	.225	.284	.338
Throws Right	2060.1	129-102	3.40	R	1009.2	68-51	3.29	R	3869	.207	.257	.333	LC	853	.258	.312	.401	RO	3484	.244	.315	.378
Lary Sorensen (1984-1988)				H	162.1	4-15	5.05	L	706	.319	.369	.487	SP	403	.318	.377	.453	NO	782	.290	.327	.418
Throws Right	330.0	12-24	4.72	R	167.2	8-11	4.99	R	745	.288	.325	.399	LC	143	.391	.427	.579	RO	669	.319	.369	.469
Mario Soto (1984-1988)				H	343.2	21-18	4.35	L	1557	.234	.323	.393	SP	738	.230	.329	.396	NO	1802	.225	.290	.365
Throws Right	717.2	41-41	3.93	R	374.0	20-23	3.54	R	1406	.228	.284	.376	LC	340	.224	.312	.331	RO	1161	.242	.327	.417
Steve Sparks (1995-1996)				H	129.1	4-8	6.54	L	722	.279	.358	.434	SP	355	.284	.373	.467	NO	704	.285	.364	.455
Throws Right	290.2	13-18	5.23	R	161.1	9-10	4.18	R	559	.284	.363	.470	LC	96	.302	.362	.477	RO	577	.275	.357	.444
Dennis Springer (1995-1997)				H	158.2	7-9	5.50	L	667	.259	.331	.477	SP	324	.261	.359	.460	NO	810	.254	.328	.471
Throws Right	311.2	14-18	5.26	R	153.0	7-9	5.00	R	686	.263	.341	.467	LC	95	.235	.333	.481	RO	543	.273	.348	.474
Russ Springer (1992-1997)				H	184.1	7-8	5.18	L	718	.284	.373	.462	SP	463	.285	.368	.533	NO	810	.253	.337	.373
Throws Right	352.0	10-23	5.34	R	167.2	3-15	5.53	R	861	.266	.335	.448	LC	306	.287	.387	.504	RO	769	.296	.368	.541
Randy St. Claire (1984-1994)				H	128.1	5-4	5.19	L	503	.256	.327	.367	SP	326	.259	.361	.406	NO	571	.258	.312	.400
Throws Right	252.1	12-6	4.14	R	124.0	7-3	3.27	R	579	.264	.323	.424	LC	158	.277	.365	.416	RO	511	.263	.341	.395
Bob Stanley (1984-1989)				H	309.0	20-18	4.05	L	1282	.304	.368	.432	SP	865	.296	.361	.426	NO	1282	.274	.314	.393
Throws Right	610.1	36-43	4.04	R	301.1	17-25	4.03	R	1339	.273	.305	.391	LC	831	.257	.315	.374	RO	1339	.303	.357	.429
Mike Stanton (1989-1997)				H	231.0	17-10	3.16	L	653	.213	.293	.285	SP	605	.264	.352	.379	NO	964	.240	.307	.357
Throws Left	456.0	29-26	3.69	R	225.0	12-16	4.24	R	1282	.265	.338	.399	LC	1057	.249	.322	.359	RO	971	.255	.339	.364
Dave Stewart (1984-1995)				H	1214.1	73-49	3.51	L	5098	.256	.334	.390	SP	2513	.239	.321	.367	NO	5644	.247	.317	.390
Throws Right	2303.0	145-114	4.07	R	1088.2	72-65	4.70	R	4768	.247	.313	.397	LC	741	.243	.324	.365	RO	4222	.259	.335	.397
Sammy Stewart (1984-1987)				H	178.1	13-5	3.18	L	630	.255	.383	.362	SP	467	.250	.362	.362	NO	642	.246	.340	.379
Throws Right	313.1	20-14	3.85	R	135.0	8-9	4.73	R	730	.241	.316	.388	LC	425	.240	.325	.348	RO	718	.250	.354	.374

Situational Statistics: Pitching

Pitcher	Total IP	W-L	ERA		Home/Road IP	W-L	ERA		vs. Left/Right PA	Avg	OBP	Slg		Scoring Position/Late & Close PA	Avg	OBP	Slg		None On/Runners On PA	Avg	OBP	Slg
Dave Stieb (1984-1993)				H	852.1	59-41	3.57	L	3817	.244	.323	.364	SP	1619	.251	.319	.355	NO	4210	.223	.310	.350
Throws Right	1723.0	110-76	3.42	R	870.2	51-35	3.34	R	3356	.227	.304	.342	LC	572	.263	.335	.407	RO	2963	.254	.320	.358
Tim Stoddard (1984-1989)				H	216.1	16-10	3.74	L	754	.256	.355	.409	SP	601	.256	.373	.374	NO	908	.246	.319	.398
Throws Right	415.2	22-21	4.16	R	199.1	6-11	4.61	R	1040	.241	.322	.379	LC	389	.252	.355	.399	RO	886	.249	.353	.384
Todd Stottlemyre (1988-1997)				H	896.1	54-48	4.26	L	3834	.283	.357	.430	SP	1935	.266	.354	.422	NO	4259	.263	.325	.401
Throws Right	1753.0	109-97	4.29	R	856.2	55-49	4.32	R	3712	.240	.303	.379	LC	544	.270	.338	.378	RO	3287	.261	.338	.410
Rick Sutcliffe (1984-1994)				H	924.2	58-45	4.08	L	4240	.266	.338	.402	SP	1983	.263	.367	.413	NO	4522	.258	.317	.388
Throws Right	1832.2	118-99	4.19	R	908.0	60-54	4.31	R	3616	.263	.325	.396	LC	539	.261	.318	.369	RO	3334	.275	.354	.416
Bruce Sutter (1984-1988)				H	143.2	7-11	3.70	L	567	.238	.293	.332	SP	318	.273	.344	.417	NO	604	.254	.303	.387
Throws Right	275.0	15-18	3.21	R	131.1	8-7	2.67	R	553	.277	.321	.442	LC	766	.262	.311	.379	RO	516	.262	.312	.387
Don Sutton (1984-1988)				H	504.2	30-27	3.64	L	2006	.251	.305	.385	SP	814	.241	.300	.397	NO	2371	.251	.296	.398
Throws Right	924.2	58-50	3.99	R	420.0	28-23	4.41	R	1866	.266	.301	.432	LC	159	.309	.340	.513	RO	1501	.270	.315	.425
Russ Swan (1989-1994)				H	118.0	5-12	5.64	L	322	.214	.288	.246	SP	370	.275	.358	.427	NO	591	.267	.343	.388
Throws Left	266.2	14-22	4.83	R	148.2	9-10	4.18	R	861	.298	.378	.480	LC	354	.246	.321	.359	RO	592	.284	.364	.446
Bill Swift (1985-1997)				H	743.2	44-31	3.49	L	3226	.296	.361	.420	SP	1577	.273	.350	.384	NO	3398	.260	.319	.355
Throws Right	1455.0	83-69	3.76	R	711.1	39-38	4.05	R	2918	.243	.293	.325	LC	708	.247	.300	.329	RO	2746	.283	.341	.399
Greg Swindell (1986-1997)				H	998.2	58-49	3.51	L	1453	.267	.301	.390	SP	1795	.275	.324	.422	NO	4771	.265	.301	.409
Throws Left	1915.2	110-102	3.88	R	917.0	52-53	4.29	R	6524	.272	.310	.426	LC	774	.271	.310	.411	RO	3206	.281	.320	.437
Frank Tanana (1984-1993)				H	1066.2	64-62	4.23	L	1472	.249	.301	.375	SP	2081	.256	.350	.388	NO	5218	.262	.313	.421
Throws Left	2078.0	120-121	4.08	R	1011.1	58-59	3.92	R	7410	.267	.329	.426	LC	552	.273	.361	.442	RO	3664	.268	.340	.411
Kevin Tapani (1989-1997)				H	808.2	61-34	3.72	L	3520	.270	.311	.430	SP	1585	.271	.325	.404	NO	3884	.263	.305	.415
Throws Right	1546.0	101-78	4.13	R	737.1	40-44	4.59	R	2986	.268	.314	.408	LC	499	.266	.325	.424	RO	2622	.279	.324	.428
Julian Tavarez (1993-1997)				H	142.0	12-5	3.93	L	570	.311	.371	.469	SP	378	.277	.342	.431	NO	645	.294	.346	.433
Throws Right	292.2	22-16	4.31	R	150.2	10-11	4.66	R	697	.267	.315	.399	LC	453	.243	.307	.351	RO	622	.278	.334	.426
Kent Tekulve (1984-1989)				H	274.0	15-17	3.58	L	964	.282	.354	.386	SP	758	.219	.328	.317	NO	1060	.262	.294	.361
Throws Right	510.2	27-38	3.24	R	236.2	12-21	2.89	R	1176	.235	.278	.320	LC	857	.283	.344	.389	RO	1080	.249	.331	.335
Dave Telgheder (1993-1997)				H	132.1	9-9	5.37	L	670	.317	.369	.527	SP	349	.279	.347	.429	NO	718	.307	.364	.543
Throws Right	291.2	15-18	5.34	R	159.1	6-9	5.31	R	627	.285	.339	.473	LC	84	.250	.305	.408	RO	579	.294	.344	.446
Walt Terrell (1984-1992)				H	895.2	61-42	3.80	L	4081	.275	.340	.405	SP	1877	.285	.360	.414	NO	4445	.266	.331	.410
Throws Right	1832.0	103-113	4.27	R	936.1	45-71	4.73	R	3805	.275	.338	.420	LC	616	.282	.343	.459	RO	3441	.288	.350	.416
Scott Terry (1986-1991)				H	277.2	17-12	3.08	L	1052	.266	.337	.389	SP	601	.268	.362	.416	NO	1157	.236	.294	.334
Throws Right	499.1	24-28	3.73	R	221.2	7-16	4.55	R	1065	.251	.306	.367	LC	356	.281	.357	.376	RO	960	.287	.355	.435
Bob Tewksbury (1986-1997)				H	824.0	51-39	3.47	L	3682	.284	.314	.402	SP	1719	.293	.331	.428	NO	4038	.280	.306	.406
Throws Right	1658.2	103-89	3.84	R	834.2	52-50	4.21	R	3302	.289	.317	.424	LC	459	.253	.286	.348	RO	2946	.297	.329	.421
Bobby Thigpen (1986-1994)				H	301.0	21-16	3.47	L	1168	.264	.348	.374	SP	778	.247	.334	.374	NO	1137	.256	.334	.375
Throws Right	568.2	31-36	3.43	R	267.2	10-20	3.40	R	1279	.241	.314	.367	LC	1129	.239	.327	.353	RO	1310	.248	.327	.366
Justin Thompson (1996-1997)				H	161.1	11-8	3.35	L	192	.213	.283	.345	SP	255	.278	.351	.378	NO	707	.229	.290	.360
Throws Left	282.1	16-17	3.35	R	121.0	5-9	3.35	R	966	.246	.309	.371	LC	100	.217	.270	.467	RO	451	.260	.327	.378
Mark Thompson (1994-1997)				H	128.2	7-8	6.99	L	544	.318	.399	.523	SP	366	.304	.384	.502	NO	610	.322	.390	.546
Throws Right	259.1	15-18	5.97	R	130.2	8-10	4.96	R	654	.298	.372	.512	LC	50	.342	.468	.474	RO	588	.290	.378	.485
Mark Thurmond (1984-1990)				H	366.2	19-22	3.63	L	717	.246	.306	.344	SP	822	.268	.362	.387	NO	1694	.275	.313	.398
Throws Left	722.1	33-43	3.85	R	355.2	14-21	4.07	R	2347	.292	.343	.422	LC	313	.215	.281	.362	RO	1370	.290	.361	.412
Jay Tibbs (1984-1990)				H	480.0	20-29	3.98	L	1941	.277	.344	.405	SP	876	.297	.364	.420	NO	2133	.250	.317	.372
Throws Right	862.2	39-54	4.20	R	382.2	19-25	4.49	R	1713	.260	.320	.383	LC	220	.261	.362	.340	RO	1521	.297	.355	.427
Mike Timlin (1991-1997)				H	227.1	17-9	3.17	L	852	.284	.361	.392	SP	553	.269	.380	.356	NO	924	.221	.282	.307
Throws Right	419.0	26-24	3.63	R	191.2	9-15	4.18	R	940	.222	.295	.303	LC	782	.272	.349	.387	RO	868	.287	.375	.390
Fred Toliver (1984-1993)				H	127.0	5-5	5.03	L	582	.278	.366	.394	SP	358	.253	.352	.401	NO	609	.277	.361	.403
Throws Right	270.1	10-16	4.73	R	143.1	5-11	4.65	R	610	.281	.363	.414	LC	64	.346	.460	.538	RO	583	.283	.368	.404
Randy Tomlin (1990-1994)				H	319.0	16-16	3.05	L	473	.240	.296	.336	SP	579	.280	.330	.401	NO	1391	.263	.311	.383
Throws Left	580.1	30-31	3.43	R	261.1	14-15	3.89	R	1926	.274	.316	.406	LC	186	.257	.315	.413	RO	1008	.275	.314	.405
Salomon Torres (1993-1997)				H	146.2	5-15	6.26	L	691	.301	.394	.460	SP	342	.285	.378	.455	NO	691	.264	.353	.410
Throws Right	283.2	11-25	5.71	R	137.0	6-10	5.12	R	606	.255	.340	.431	LC	51	.348	.412	.522	RO	606	.298	.388	.491
Steve Trachsel (1993-1997)				H	401.0	19-25	3.93	L	1384	.241	.307	.404	SP	758	.214	.311	.329	NO	1817	.276	.334	.487
Throws Right	732.2	37-43	3.98	R	331.2	18-18	4.04	R	1751	.275	.338	.466	LC	221	.289	.356	.503	RO	1318	.237	.312	.367
Mike Trombley (1992-1997)				H	230.0	9-9	4.85	L	940	.287	.369	.475	SP	610	.266	.349	.406	NO	1041	.261	.324	.447
Throws Right	457.2	22-20	4.66	R	227.2	13-11	4.47	R	1062	.249	.304	.409	LC	321	.227	.292	.346	RO	961	.273	.347	.431
Steve Trout (1984-1989)				H	391.1	24-16	4.09	L	492	.286	.356	.349	SP	847	.283	.369	.367	NO	1625	.287	.359	.391
Throws Left	699.1	41-38	4.38	R	308.0	17-22	4.73	R	2546	.292	.366	.394	LC	131	.281	.374	.377	RO	1413	.295	.370	.381
John Tudor (1984-1990)				H	625.0	43-15	2.35	L	775	.225	.263	.334	SP	956	.224	.301	.326	NO	2930	.239	.276	.350
Throws Left	1160.1	78-40	2.66	R	535.1	35-25	3.03	R	3859	.243	.288	.359	LC	481	.270	.322	.367	RO	1704	.241	.299	.346
Lee Tunnell (1984-1989)				H	158.2	8-10	4.54	L	591	.293	.381	.396	SP	363	.291	.401	.439	NO	685	.271	.340	.368
Throws Right	287.0	10-21	4.61	R	128.1	3-11	4.70	R	678	.271	.339	.416	LC	127	.279	.370	.405	RO	584	.294	.380	.456
Tom Urbani (1993-1996)				H	136.1	4-11	5.48	L	257	.258	.331	.418	SP	302	.277	.326	.443	NO	643	.303	.356	.495
Throws Left	260.1	10-17	4.98	R	124.0	6-6	4.43	R	904	.315	.364	.499	LC	77	.303	.387	.439	RO	518	.302	.357	.464
Ismael Valdes (1994-1997)				H	334.1	20-13	2.42	L	1260	.245	.298	.377	SP	631	.229	.304	.351	NO	1606	.240	.279	.359
Throws Right	647.2	41-30	3.03	R	313.1	21-17	3.68	R	1399	.229	.272	.342	LC	343	.233	.278	.351	RO	1053	.232	.294	.358
Sergio Valdez (1986-1995)				H	158.0	7-9	4.90	L	646	.277	.348	.455	SP	348	.285	.365	.426	NO	750	.260	.319	.444
Throws Right	302.2	12-20	5.06	R	144.2	5-11	5.23	R	679	.282	.333	.460	LC	127	.278	.336	.452	RO	575	.306	.369	.477
Fernando Valenzuela (1984-1997)				H	1124.0	62-57	3.44	L	1630	.265	.328	.387	SP	2407	.247	.334	.348	NO	5242	.240	.313	.361
Throws Left	2178.0	124-123	3.73	R	1054.0	62-66	4.05	R	7655	.250	.326	.374	LC	731	.245	.324	.322	RO	4043	.270	.343	.397

Situational Statistics: Pitching

Pitcher	Total				Home/Road				vs. Left/Right					Scoring Position/Late & Close					None On/Runners On			
	IP	W-L	ERA		IP	W-L	ERA		PA	Avg	OBP	Slg		PA	Avg	OBP	Slg		PA	Avg	OBP	Slg
Julio Valera (1990-1996)				H	172.2	10-8	3.60	L	652	.321	.383	.456	SP	391	.274	.359	.398	NO	746	.289	.343	.431
Throws Right	317.1	15-20	4.85	R	144.2	5-12	6.35	R	740	.261	.322	.403	LC	154	.306	.372	.425	RO	646	.289	.360	.424
Todd Van Poppel (1991-1996)				H	230.0	9-17	5.75	L	1101	.284	.402	.520	SP	532	.341	.429	.633	NO	1085	.236	.347	.409
Throws Right	443.0	20-33	6.22	R	213.0	11-16	6.72	R	905	.252	.331	.411	LC	130	.227	.287	.378	RO	921	.308	.397	.541
Ed Vande Berg (1984-1988)				H	189.2	8-9	4.56	L	561	.258	.329	.339	SP	568	.288	.363	.425	NO	777	.315	.366	.478
Throws Left	378.2	14-20	4.33	R	189.0	6-11	4.33	R	1118	.327	.379	.502	LC	282	.350	.444	.509	RO	902	.294	.359	.422
William VanLandingham (1994-1997)				H	267.0	14-14	4.21	L	941	.280	.349	.409	SP	551	.273	.381	.424	NO	1190	.238	.314	.370
Throws Right	477.1	27-26	4.54	R	210.1	13-12	4.96	R	1158	.237	.328	.385	LC	126	.259	.328	.352	RO	909	.283	.368	.432
Dave Veres (1994-1997)				H	130.2	10-2	3.31	L	504	.275	.367	.424	SP	386	.211	.303	.297	NO	636	.279	.329	.443
Throws Right	284.0	16-10	3.07	R	153.1	6-8	2.88	R	714	.250	.293	.364	LC	513	.257	.327	.363	RO	582	.238	.319	.322
Frank Viola (1984-1996)				H	1251.1	87-54	3.38	L	1821	.255	.305	.380	SP	2262	.256	.316	.383	NO	6154	.254	.308	.382
Throws Left	2500.1	165-125	3.51	R	1249.0	79-71	3.63	R	8610	.256	.310	.384	LC	830	.234	.287	.336	RO	4277	.258	.312	.384
Paul Wagner (1992-1997)				H	274.2	17-22	4.55	L	1104	.290	.366	.404	SP	683	.273	.358	.424	NO	1251	.281	.352	.427
Throws Right	538.2	27-40	4.59	R	264.0	10-18	4.64	R	1254	.260	.330	.414	LC	198	.322	.360	.439	RO	1107	.266	.342	.388
Tim Wakefield (1992-1997)				H	415.1	28-21	3.81	L	1774	.260	.343	.406	SP	925	.241	.324	.398	NO	2020	.256	.341	.414
Throws Right	828.2	56-48	4.15	R	413.1	28-27	4.49	R	1827	.258	.337	.429	LC	381	.229	.311	.377	RO	1581	.264	.338	.422
Bob Walk (1984-1993)				H	660.1	46-30	3.67	L	3038	.269	.338	.397	SP	1401	.264	.344	.412	NO	3200	.250	.311	.368
Throws Right	1303.0	82-61	3.83	R	642.2	36-31	4.01	R	2481	.246	.304	.371	LC	404	.281	.350	.404	RO	2319	.271	.339	.410
Duane Ward (1986-1995)				H	344.0	19-20	3.17	L	1296	.235	.341	.343	SP	882	.249	.343	.343	NO	1431	.213	.288	.294
Throws Right	666.2	32-37	3.28	R	322.2	13-17	3.43	R	1485	.222	.284	.284	LC	1314	.216	.299	.301	RO	1350	.245	.335	.330
John Wasdin (1995-1997)				H	147.2	9-7	4.81	L	610	.291	.365	.520	SP	292	.304	.360	.595	NO	687	.240	.310	.389
Throws Right	273.1	13-14	5.17	R	125.2	4-7	5.59	R	568	.238	.279	.403	LC	130	.319	.378	.558	RO	491	.299	.343	.566
Allen Watson (1993-1997)				H	349.0	20-20	4.93	L	522	.227	.312	.370	SP	746	.292	.354	.490	NO	1753	.267	.344	.447
Throws Left	700.2	39-45	4.91	R	351.2	19-25	4.89	R	2538	.289	.354	.489	LC	151	.276	.342	.449	RO	1307	.295	.351	.500
Dave Weathers (1991-1997)				H	190.0	10-12	6.11	L	903	.330	.410	.472	SP	573	.308	.421	.422	NO	927	.293	.364	.429
Throws Right	403.1	18-27	5.67	R	213.1	8-15	5.27	R	968	.284	.365	.412	LC	117	.330	.468	.455	RO	944	.320	.410	.455
Bill Wegman (1985-1995)				H	823.1	46-38	3.74	L	3187	.266	.308	.413	SP	1375	.280	.323	.427	NO	3758	.266	.311	.426
Throws Right	1482.2	81-90	4.16	R	659.1	35-52	4.68	R	3063	.277	.323	.449	LC	490	.298	.351	.470	RO	2492	.279	.322	.437
Bob Welch (1984-1994)				H	1113.1	81-46	3.20	L	4667	.254	.320	.374	SP	2121	.259	.345	.380	NO	5208	.255	.308	.392
Throws Right	2104.2	145-99	3.63	R	991.1	64-54	4.12	R	4195	.253	.314	.399	LC	628	.239	.294	.355	RO	3654	.251	.330	.376
Bob Wells (1994-1997)				H	133.0	7-5	5.28	L	592	.299	.374	.495	SP	337	.291	.364	.493	NO	683	.282	.347	.467
Throws Right	283.2	20-10	5.43	R	150.2	13-5	5.56	R	682	.274	.331	.488	LC	106	.316	.369	.537	RO	591	.290	.355	.520
David Wells (1987-1997)				H	849.1	59-34	3.38	L	1301	.258	.302	.381	SP	1614	.254	.330	.413	NO	3977	.262	.305	.407
Throws Left	1631.0	106-85	4.02	R	781.2	47-51	4.71	R	5508	.262	.311	.426	LC	868	.278	.327	.440	RO	2832	.260	.315	.433
Turk Wendell (1993-1997)				H	133.0	8-7	4.06	L	473	.299	.394	.454	SP	339	.288	.409	.479	NO	573	.249	.330	.376
Throws Right	253.0	11-14	4.45	R	120.0	3-7	4.88	R	655	.220	.317	.369	LC	378	.219	.341	.358	RO	555	.258	.370	.437
Don Wengert (1995-1997)				H	168.2	7-11	5.71	L	746	.315	.380	.523	SP	432	.270	.349	.413	NO	776	.303	.353	.519
Throws Right	325.0	13-23	5.57	R	156.1	6-12	5.41	R	720	.304	.354	.492	LC	122	.379	.462	.495	RO	690	.317	.383	.493
David West (1988-1996)				H	265.2	14-19	5.18	L	451	.209	.341	.327	SP	698	.256	.355	.423	NO	1371	.224	.316	.354
Throws Left	567.1	31-38	4.58	R	301.2	17-19	4.06	R	2051	.249	.338	.412	LC	319	.230	.359	.344	RO	1131	.266	.366	.452
John Wetteland (1989-1997)				H	277.2	24-16	2.92	L	1307	.211	.287	.324	SP	671	.232	.314	.354	NO	1279	.198	.266	.311
Throws Right	577.0	35-35	2.81	R	299.1	11-19	2.71	R	1039	.202	.265	.322	LC	1362	.213	.286	.345	RO	1067	.219	.291	.338
Wally Whitehurst (1989-1996)				H	237.0	10-19	3.53	L	1050	.278	.337	.413	SP	547	.273	.352	.399	NO	1165	.274	.312	.399
Throws Right	487.2	20-37	4.02	R	250.2	10-18	4.49	R	1025	.276	.313	.408	LC	218	.283	.333	.384	RO	910	.282	.343	.428
Matt Whiteside (1992-1997)				H	181.0	9-4	3.83	L	542	.302	.361	.420	SP	446	.254	.351	.333	NO	692	.269	.324	.394
Throws Right	320.0	14-10	4.61	R	139.0	5-6	5.63	R	847	.266	.331	.393	LC	447	.270	.329	.361	RO	697	.293	.361	.414
Ed Whitson (1984-1991)				H	729.1	44-38	3.68	L	3288	.276	.326	.410	SP	1247	.276	.327	.414	NO	3485	.258	.307	.386
Throws Right	1405.2	87-75	3.86	R	676.1	43-37	4.09	R	2572	.250	.291	.395	LC	310	.253	.302	.384	RO	2375	.274	.316	.429
Bob Wickman (1992-1997)				H	261.2	24-5	3.78	L	1017	.282	.370	.403	SP	731	.243	.348	.379	NO	1150	.273	.350	.391
Throws Right	531.2	41-20	3.91	R	270.0	17-15	4.03	R	1292	.250	.323	.365	LC	782	.262	.340	.362	RO	1159	.254	.337	.373
Milt Wilcox (1984-1986)				H	150.2	11-9	3.40	L	672	.287	.357	.428	SP	301	.316	.392	.476	NO	706	.274	.334	.436
Throws Right	288.1	18-19	4.40	R	137.2	7-10	5.49	R	571	.264	.324	.427	LC	45	.279	.311	.558	RO	537	.281	.352	.415
Brian Williams (1991-1997)				H	239.0	10-13	4.93	L	1120	.313	.405	.468	SP	679	.292	.387	.437	NO	1110	.274	.371	.404
Throws Right	485.2	23-36	5.34	R	246.2	13-23	5.73	R	1109	.252	.344	.390	LC	282	.297	.408	.454	RO	1119	.292	.379	.455
Frank Williams (1984-1989)				H	247.0	8-7	2.73	L	879	.277	.378	.371	SP	634	.245	.366	.343	NO	1031	.249	.327	.335
Throws Right	471.2	24-14	3.00	R	224.2	16-7	3.28	R	1123	.215	.299	.296	LC	398	.246	.356	.323	RO	971	.233	.342	.320
Mike Williams (1992-1997)				H	210.2	8-10	4.96	L	812	.258	.340	.448	SP	476	.284	.369	.467	NO	949	.281	.337	.456
Throws Right	398.2	13-27	4.92	R	188.0	5-17	4.88	R	921	.291	.345	.448	LC	150	.295	.400	.443	RO	784	.270	.350	.438
Mitch Williams (1986-1997)				H	353.1	28-25	3.87	L	819	.213	.347	.306	SP	1136	.208	.358	.315	NO	1364	.216	.371	.315
Throws Left	691.1	45-58	3.63	R	338.0	18-33	3.38	R	2300	.220	.374	.341	LC	1491	.220	.364	.323	RO	1755	.220	.364	.345
Woody Williams (1993-1997)				H	223.2	11-13	4.23	L	932	.255	.347	.394	SP	451	.250	.356	.399	NO	962	.259	.326	.445
Throws Right	403.2	18-25	4.21	R	180.0	7-12	4.20	R	813	.255	.314	.447	LC	236	.227	.322	.374	RO	783	.251	.338	.385
Mark Williamson (1987-1994)				H	356.2	28-16	3.18	L	1265	.254	.312	.373	SP	891	.281	.368	.411	NO	1515	.245	.292	.372
Throws Right	689.2	46-35	3.86	R	333.0	19-19	4.65	R	1662	.275	.332	.416	LC	741	.271	.344	.411	RO	1412	.290	.357	.427
Carl Willis (1984-1995)				H	209.2	15-9	4.64	L	669	.285	.344	.420	SP	541	.292	.362	.419	NO	810	.275	.315	.394
Throws Right	390.0	22-16	4.25	R	180.1	7-7	3.79	R	991	.275	.317	.405	LC	521	.271	.326	.383	RO	850	.283	.340	.428
Frank Wills (1984-1991)				H	234.2	12-12	4.45	L	838	.272	.366	.418	SP	519	.266	.353	.445	NO	898	.257	.331	.407
Throws Right	401.0	20-25	5.14	R	166.1	8-13	6.11	R	902	.257	.318	.418	LC	235	.305	.368	.452	RO	842	.272	.353	.431
Steve Wilson (1988-1993)				H	170.2	8-10	4.96	L	454	.252	.320	.365	SP	426	.265	.347	.380	NO	792	.260	.319	.390
Throws Left	345.1	13-18	4.40	R	174.2	5-8	3.86	R	1040	.267	.331	.422	LC	214	.311	.389	.433	RO	702	.265	.337	.422

Situational Statistics: Pitching

Pitcher	Total IP	W-L	ERA		Home/Road IP	W-L	ERA		vs. Left/Right PA	Avg	OBP	Slg		Scoring Position/Late & Close PA	Avg	OBP	Slg		None On/Runners On PA	Avg	OBP	Slg
Trevor Wilson (1988-1995)				H	414.0	24-22	3.24	L	604	.211	.294	.285	SP	701	.269	.351	.437	NO	1709	.240	.329	.343
Throws Left	720.1	41-46	3.87	R	306.1	17-24	4.73	R	2427	.259	.338	.390	LC	225	.218	.304	.280	RO	1322	.261	.330	.405
Jim Winn (1984-1988)				H	131.0	5-3	4.81	L	590	.285	.380	.405	SP	419	.281	.398	.365	NO	656	.261	.338	.405
Throws Right	297.1	12-17	4.57	R	166.1	7-14	4.60	R	714	.262	.346	.377	LC	107	.333	.430	.522	RO	648	.285	.384	.372
Bobby Witt (1986-1997)				H	1100.2	65-58	4.23	L	4799	.269	.370	.407	SP	2515	.250	.350	.383	NO	5102	.252	.350	.379
Throws Right	2109.1	124-131	4.63	R	1008.2	59-73	5.08	R	4570	.248	.336	.372	LC	601	.242	.329	.346	RO	4267	.266	.358	.402
Mike Witt (1984-1993)				H	851.1	51-44	3.41	L	3783	.259	.320	.383	SP	1549	.258	.325	.387	NO	4072	.247	.306	.368
Throws Right	1645.2	94-87	3.81	R	794.1	43-43	4.24	R	3144	.248	.307	.380	LC	663	.242	.306	.361	RO	2855	.265	.327	.403
Mark Wohlers (1991-1997)				H	197.1	21-15	3.83	L	754	.238	.340	.331	SP	527	.229	.340	.300	NO	789	.221	.299	.311
Throws Right	365.1	31-21	3.33	R	168.0	10-6	2.73	R	802	.227	.293	.311	LC	965	.238	.324	.322	RO	767	.244	.334	.331
Bob Wolcott (1995-1997)				H	148.0	6-10	5.53	L	674	.340	.402	.613	SP	312	.265	.332	.489	NO	706	.319	.377	.557
Throws Right	286.0	15-18	5.66	R	138.0	9-8	5.80	R	613	.263	.317	.452	LC	39	.297	.333	.432	RO	581	.283	.343	.508
Tim Worrell (1993-1997)				H	217.2	11-17	4.47	L	738	.280	.361	.407	SP	459	.262	.348	.386	NO	845	.237	.307	.388
Throws Right	356.0	16-23	4.30	R	138.1	5-6	4.03	R	820	.240	.306	.394	LC	290	.218	.316	.343	RO	713	.286	.363	.415
Todd Worrell (1985-1997)				H	360.2	30-26	2.92	L	1428	.230	.306	.374	SP	955	.223	.316	.328	NO	1460	.242	.297	.385
Throws Right	693.2	50-52	3.09	R	333.0	21-26	3.32	R	1458	.240	.296	.354	LC	1690	.228	.297	.346	RO	1426	.229	.306	.340
Rich Yett (1985-1990)				H	198.1	13-8	4.72	L	973	.281	.351	.425	SP	479	.272	.366	.436	NO	1019	.264	.340	.438
Throws Right	414.1	22-24	4.95	R	216.0	9-16	5.17	R	867	.265	.350	.461	LC	120	.315	.370	.454	RO	821	.285	.365	.446
Floyd Youmans (1985-1989)				H	271.0	12-21	4.15	L	1280	.233	.340	.354	SP	609	.210	.317	.325	NO	1332	.207	.312	.331
Throws Right	539.0	30-34	3.74	R	268.0	18-13	3.32	R	1003	.201	.285	.336	LC	154	.240	.353	.419	RO	951	.234	.323	.367
Anthony Young (1991-1996)				H	247.0	8-28	4.26	L	973	.302	.372	.456	SP	544	.269	.350	.405	NO	1083	.258	.319	.386
Throws Right	460.0	15-48	3.89	R	213.0	7-20	3.46	R	1004	.236	.295	.357	LC	380	.279	.361	.424	RO	894	.282	.352	.430
Curt Young (1984-1993)				H	578.2	32-24	3.83	L	944	.243	.291	.332	SP	1050	.263	.335	.417	NO	2774	.257	.316	.421
Throws Left	1098.0	69-52	4.21	R	519.1	37-28	4.64	R	3728	.269	.333	.447	LC	243	.208	.298	.325	RO	1898	.274	.337	.427
Matt Young (1984-1993)				H	549.2	30-37	3.88	L	829	.232	.322	.298	SP	1281	.283	.379	.401	NO	2270	.263	.345	.381
Throws Left	986.0	44-80	4.64	R	436.1	15-43	5.63	R	3544	.279	.363	.404	LC	491	.299	.377	.419	RO	2103	.279	.366	.388

Managers

Register

For every manager of a major league game, we provide his season-by-season and career totals in eight regular-season and six postseason categories. This includes fill-in managers in case of illness, such as when Gene Tenace subbed for Cito Gaston with the 1991 Blue Jays.

Leaders

We list the top 50 managers in eight career categories. The minimum to qualify for winning percentage leadership is 1,000 games.

Strategic Statistics

STATS has been tracking a number of manager statistics since 1988, and all of the ones included in this book since 1991. We present 15 offensive, seven defensive, nine lineup and 11 pitching statistics for every man who has managed a major league game since 1991, and the same statistics on a seasonal basis (per 162 games) for every man who has managed 162 or more games during that time.

Most of these statistics' definitions simply can be derived from their name. Some of the more complicated ones are:

Offense Stolen Bases/Out Percentage—The percentage of stolen base attempts with that number of outs.

Sacrifice Bunts/Success Percentage—The percentage of sacrifice bunts resulting in a sacrifice or hit.

Hit & Run/Success Percentage—The percentage of hit-and-runs resulting in baserunner advancement and no double play.

Defense

Intentional Walks/Percent of Situations—The percentage of times an intentional walk is issued with runners on base, first base open and anyone but the pitcher at the plate.

Defensive Subs/Totals—Straight defensive substitutions with the team leading by no more than four runs.

Lineups

Starting Lineup/Lineups Used—Based on batting order, all nine hitters in the American League and the first eight in the National League.

Substitutes/Percentage of Pinch-Hitters with Platoon Advantage—The percentage of times the manager uses a lefthanded pinch-hitter against a righthanded pitcher or a righthanded pinch- hitter against a lefthanded pitcher. Switch-hitters always are considered to have the platoon advantage.

Pitching

Starters/Slow Hooks—The number of times a starting pitcher worked more than nine innings, allowed seven or more runs, or totaled 13 or more combined innings pitched plus runs allowed.

Starters/Quick Hooks—The numbers of times a starting pitcher was removed after working less than six innings and givein up three or less runs.

Superlatives

Mat Olkin rated managers and provided analysis in five categories: the best handler of rookie pitchers, the best handler of young players, the best at taking over a team in midseason, the best at generating the greatest immediate improvement and the team with the most future managers.

Abbreviations & Formulas

A complete list of team and statistical abbreviations are listed in the back of the book, along with an appendix explaining formulas and the availability of certain statistics.

Bill Adair

Born: 2/10/1913 in Mobile, Alabama; MLB Career: Did Not Play

REGULAR SEASON							Index			Playoffs			World Series		
Year Tm	Lg	G	W	L	Pct	Standing	EW	+/-	Pt	W	L	Pct	W	L	Pct
1970 ChA	AL	10	4	6	.400	6W 6W 6W	5	-1	0						

Joe Adcock

Born: 10/30/1927 in Coushatta, Louisiana; MLB Career: 17 years, 1959 G (.277-336-1122)

REGULAR SEASON							Index			Playoffs			World Series		
Year Tm	Lg	G	W	L	Pct	Standing	EW	+/-	Pt	W	L	Pct	W	L	Pct
1967 Cle	AL	162	75	87	.463	8	82	-7	0						

Bob Addy

Born: Unknown in Rochester, New York; Died: 4/9/1910; MLB Career: 2 years, 89 G (.279-0-47)

REGULAR SEASON							Index			Playoffs			World Series		
Year Tm	Lg	G	W	L	Pct	Standing	EW	+/-	Pt	W	L	Pct	W	L	Pct
1877 Cin	NL	24	5	19	.208	6 6 6			0						

Bob Allen

Born: 7/10/1867 in Marion, Ohio; Died: 5/4/1943; MLB Career: 1 year, 3 G (0-1, 6.75)

REGULAR SEASON							Index			Playoffs			World Series		
Year Tm	Lg	G	W	L	Pct	Standing	EW	+/-	Pt	W	L	Pct	W	L	Pct
1890 Phi	NL	35	25	10	.714	3 2 3			0						
1900 Cin	NL	144	62	77	.446	7	70	-8	0						
2 Years		179	87	87	.500	— — —	70	-8	0						

Felipe Alou

Born: 5/12/1935 in Haina, Dominican Republic; MLB Career: 17 years, 2082 G (.286-206-852)

REGULAR SEASON							Index			Playoffs			World Series		
Year Tm	Lg	G	W	L	Pct	Standing	EW	+/-	Pt	W	L	Pct	W	L	Pct
1992 Mon	NL	125	70	55	.560	4E 2E	59	11	1						
1993 Mon	NL	163	94	68	.580	2E	87	7	2						
1994 Mon	NL	114	74	40	.649	1E	63	11	3						
1995 Mon	NL	144	66	78	.458	5E	85	-19	0						
1996 Mon	NL	162	88	74	.543	2E	82	6	1						
1997 Mon	NL	162	78	84	.481	4E	86	-8	0						
6 Years		870	470	399	.541	— — —	462	8	7						

Walter Alston

Born: 12/1/1911 in Venice, Ohio; Died: 10/1/1984; MLB Career: 1 year, 1 G (.000-0-0)

REGULAR SEASON							Index			Playoffs			World Series		
Year Tm	Lg	G	W	L	Pct	Standing	EW	+/-	Pt	W	L	Pct	W	L	Pct
1954 Bro	NL	154	92	62	.597	2	96	-4	2						
1955 Bro	NL	154	98	55	.641	1	90	8	5				4	3	.571
1956 Bro	NL	154	93	61	.604	1	93	0	4				3	4	.429
1957 Bro	NL	154	84	70	.545	3	90	-6	1						
1958 LA	NL	154	71	83	.461	7	85	-14	0						
1959 LA	NL	156	88	68	.564	1	78	10	5				4	2	.667
1960 LA	NL	154	82	72	.532	4	82	0	1						
1961 LA	NL	154	89	65	.578	2	80	9	2						
1962 LA	NL	165	102	63	.618	2	96	6	3						
1963 LA	NL	163	99	63	.611	1	95	4	5				4	0	1.000
1964 LA	NL	164	80	82	.494	6	95	-15	0						
1965 LA	NL	162	97	65	.599	1	85	12	5				4	3	.571
1966 LA	NL	162	95	67	.586	1	91	4	4				0	4	.000
1967 LA	NL	162	73	89	.451	8	90	-17	0						
1968 LA	NL	162	76	86	.469	7	81	-5	0						
1969 LA	NL	162	85	77	.525	4W	83	2	1						
1970 LA	NL	161	87	74	.540	2W	82	5	1						
1971 LA	NL	162	89	73	.549	2W	85	4	1						
1972 LA	NL	155	85	70	.548	3W	83	2	1						
1973 LA	NL	162	95	66	.590	2W	86	9	2						
1974 LA	NL	162	102	60	.630	1W	90	12	5	3	1	.750	1	4	.200
1975 LA	NL	162	88	74	.543	2W	94	-6	1						
1976 LA	NL	158	90	68	.570	2W 2W	87	3	1						
23 Years		3658	2040	1613	.558	— — —	2017	23	50	3	1	.750	20	20	.500

Joe Altobelli

Born: 5/26/1932 in Detroit, Michigan; MLB Career: 3 years, 166 G (.210-5-28)

REGULAR SEASON							Index			Playoffs			World Series		
Year Tm	Lg	G	W	L	Pct	Standing	EW	+/-	Pt	W	L	Pct	W	L	Pct
1977 SF	NL	162	75	87	.463	4W	76	-1	0						
1978 SF	NL	162	89	73	.549	3W	77	12	1						
1979 SF	NL	140	61	79	.436	4W 4W	72	-11	0						
1983 Bal	AL	162	98	64	.605	1E	91	7	5	3	1	.750	4	1	.800
1984 Bal	AL	162	85	77	.525	5E	92	-7	1						
1985 Bal	AL	55	29	26	.527	4E 4E	29	0	0						
1991 ChN	NL	1	0	1	.000	4E 5E 4E	0	0	0						
3 AL Years		379	212	167	.559	— — —	212	0	6	3	1	.750	4	1	.800
4 NL Years		465	225	240	.484	— — —	225	0	1						
7 Years		844	437	407	.518	— — —	437	0	7	3	1	.750	4	1	.800

Joey Amalfitano

Born: 1/23/1934 in San Pedro, California; MLB Career: 10 years, 643 G (.244-9-123)

REGULAR SEASON							Index			Playoffs			World Series		
Year Tm	Lg	G	W	L	Pct	Standing	EW	+/-	Pt	W	L	Pct	W	L	Pct
1979 ChN	NL	7	2	5	.286	5E 6E	3	-1	0						
1980 ChN	NL	72	25	47	.347	6E 6E	36	-11	0						
1981 ChN	NL	54	15	37	.288	6E	23	-8	0						
ChN	NL	52	23	28	.451	5E	22	1	0						
3 Years		185	65	117	.357	— — —	84	-19	0						

Sparky Anderson

Born: 2/22/1934 in Bridgewater, South Dakota; MLB Career: 1 year, 152 G (.218-0-34)

REGULAR SEASON							Index			Playoffs			World Series		
Year Tm	Lg	G	W	L	Pct	Standing	EW	+/-	Pt	W	L	Pct	W	L	Pct
1970 Cin	NL	162	102	60	.630	1W	87	15	5	3	0	1.000	1	4	.200
1971 Cin	NL	162	79	83	.488	4W	94	-15	0						
1972 Cin	NL	154	95	59	.617	1W	80	15	4	3	2	.600	3	4	.429
1973 Cin	NL	162	99	63	.611	1W	93	6	3	2	3	.400			
1974 Cin	NL	163	98	64	.605	2W	92	6	2						
1975 Cin	NL	162	108	54	.667	1W	94	14	6	3	0	1.000	4	3	.571
1976 Cin	NL	162	102	60	.630	1W	99	3	6	3	0	1.000	4	0	1.000
1977 Cin	NL	162	88	74	.543	2W	97	-9	1						
1978 Cin	NL	161	92	69	.571	2W	90	2	2						
1979 Det	AL	106	56	50	.528	5E 5E	54	2	1						
1980 Det	AL	163	84	78	.519	4E	83	1	1						
1981 Det	AL	57	31	26	.544	4E	30	1	0						
Det	AL	52	29	23	.558	2E	27	2	1						
1982 Det	AL	162	83	79	.512	4E	85	-2	1						
1983 Det	AL	162	92	70	.568	2E	83	9	2						
1984 Det	AL	162	104	58	.642	1E	88	16	6	3	0	1.000	4	1	.800
1985 Det	AL	161	84	77	.522	3E	94	-10	1						
1986 Det	AL	162	87	75	.537	3E	87	0	1						
1987 Det	AL	162	98	64	.605	1E	87	11	3	1	4	.200			
1988 Det	AL	162	88	74	.543	2E	91	-3	1						
1989 Det	AL	162	59	103	.364	7E	87	-28	0						
1990 Det	AL	162	79	83	.488	3E	73	6	0						
1991 Det	AL	162	84	78	.519	2E	78	6	1						
1992 Det	AL	162	75	87	.463	6E	80	-5	0						
1993 Det	AL	162	85	77	.525	3E	78	7	1						
1994 Det	AL	115	53	62	.461	5E	59	-6	0						
1995 Det	AL	144	60	84	.417	4E	69	-9	0						
17 AL Years		2580	1331	1248	.516	— — —	1333	-2	20	4	4	.500	4	1	.800
9 NL Years		1450	863	586	.596	— — —	826	37	29	14	5	.737	12	11	.522
26 Years		4030	2194	1834	.545	— — —	2159	35	49	18	9	.667	16	12	.571

Cap Anson

Born: 4/11/1852 in Marshalltown, Iowa; Died: 4/14/1922; MLB Career: 22 years, 2276 G (.329-97-1879)

REGULAR SEASON							Index			Playoffs			World Series		
Year Tm	Lg	G	W	L	Pct	Standing	EW	+/-	Pt	W	L	Pct	W	L	Pct
1879 ChN	NL	64	41	21	.661	2 4			1						
1880 ChN	NL	86	67	17	.798	1			4						
1881 ChN	NL	84	56	28	.667	1			4						
1882 ChN	NL	84	55	29	.655	1			4						
1883 ChN	NL	98	59	39	.602	2			2						
1884 ChN	NL	113	62	50	.554	4			1						
1885 ChN	NL	113	87	25	.777	1			4				3	3	.500
1886 ChN	NL	126	90	34	.726	1			4				2	4	.333
1887 ChN	NL	127	71	50	.587	3			2						
1888 ChN	NL	136	77	58	.570	2			1						
1889 ChN	NL	136	67	65	.508	3			1						
1890 ChN	NL	139	84	53	.613	2			2						
1891 ChN	NL	137	82	53	.607	2			2						
1892 ChN	NL	71	31	39	.443	8			0						
ChN	NL	76	39	37	.513	7			0						
1893 ChN	NL	128	56	71	.441	9			0						
1894 ChN	NL	137	57	75	.432	8			0						
1895 ChN	NL	133	72	58	.554	4			1						
1896 ChN	NL	132	71	57	.555	5			1						
1897 ChN	NL	138	59	73	.447	9			0						
1898 NYG	NL	22	9	13	.409	6 7 7			0						
20 Years		2280	1292	945	.578	— — —			34				5	7	.417

Luke Appling

Born: 4/2/1907 in High Point, North Carolina; Died: 1/3/1991; MLB Career: 20 years, 2422 G (.310-45-1116)

REGULAR SEASON							Index			Playoffs			World Series		
Year Tm	Lg	G	W	L	Pct	Standing	EW	+/-	Pt	W	L	Pct	W	L	Pct
1967 KCA	AL	40	10	30	.250	10 10	18	-8	0						

Bill Armour

Born: 9/3/1869 in Homestead, Pennsylvania; Died: 12/2/1922; MLB Career: Did Not Play

REGULAR SEASON							Index			Playoffs			World Series		
Year Tm	Lg	G	W	L	Pct	Standing	EW	+/-	Pt	W	L	Pct	W	L	Pct
1902 Cle	AL	137	69	67	.507	5	61	8	1						
1903 Cle	AL	140	77	63	.550	3	69	8	1						
1904 Cle	AL	154	86	65	.570	4	78	8	2						
1905 Det	AL	154	79	74	.516	3	67	12	1						
1906 Det	AL	151	71	78	.477	6	74	-3	0						
5 Years		736	382	347	.524	— — —	349	33	5						

Ken Aspromonte

Born: 9/22/1931 in Brooklyn, New York; MLB Career: 7 years, 475 G (.249-19-124)

REGULAR SEASON							Index			Playoffs			World Series		
Year Tm	Lg	G	W	L	Pct	Standing	EW	+/-	Pt	W	L	Pct	W	L	Pct
1972 Cle	AL	156	72	84	.462	5E	65	7	0						
1973 Cle	AL	162	71	91	.438	6E	75	-4	0						

REGULAR SEASON							Index			Playoffs			World Series		
Year Tm	Lg	G	W	L	Pct	Standing	EW	+/-	Pt	W	L	Pct	W	L	Pct
1974 Cle	AL	162	77	85	.475	**4E**	73	4	0						
3 Years		480	220	260	.458	— — —	213	7	0						

Jimmy Austin

Born: 12/8/1879 in Swanswea, Wales; Died: 3/6/1965; MLB Career: 18 years, 1580 G (.246-13-390)

REGULAR SEASON							Index			Playoffs			World Series		
Year Tm	Lg	G	W	L	Pct	Standing	EW	+/-	Pt	W	L	Pct	W	L	Pct
1913 StL	AL	8	2	6	.250	7 **8** 8	3	-1	0						
1918 StL	AL	16	7	9	.438	5 **6** 5	7	0	0						
1923 StL	AL	51	22	29	.431	3 **5**	28	-6	0						
3 Years		75	31	44	.413	— — —	38	-7	0						

Del Baker

Born: 5/3/1892 in Sherwood, Oregon; Died: 9/11/1973; MLB Career: 3 years, 172 G (.209-0-22)

REGULAR SEASON							Index			Playoffs			World Series		
Year Tm	Lg	G	W	L	Pct	Standing	EW	+/-	Pt	W	L	Pct	W	L	Pct
1933 Det	AL	2	2	0	1.000	5 **5**	1	1	0						
1936 Det	AL	34	18	16	.529	3 **4** 2	20	-2	0						
1937 Det	AL	54	34	20	.630	3 **3** 2	30	4	0						
1938 Det	AL	57	37	19	.661	5 **4**	31	6	1						
1939 Det	AL	155	81	73	.526	**5**	83	-2	1						
1940 Det	AL	155	90	64	.584	**1**	81	9	4				3	4	.429
1941 Det	AL	155	75	79	.487	**4**	85	-10	0						
1942 Det	AL	156	73	81	.474	**5**	78	-5	0						
1960 Bos	AL	7	2	5	.286	8 **8** 7	3	-1	0						
9 Years		775	412	357	.536	— — —	412	0	6				3	4	.429

Dusty Baker

Born: 6/15/1949 in Riverside, California; MLB Career: 19 years, 2039 G (.278-242-1013)

REGULAR SEASON							Index			Playoffs			World Series		
Year Tm	Lg	G	W	L	Pct	Standing	EW	+/-	Pt	W	L	Pct	W	L	Pct
1993 SF	NL	162	103	59	.636	**2W**	79	24	3						
1994 SF	NL	115	55	60	.478	**2W**	65	-10	0						
1995 SF	NL	144	67	77	.465	**4W**	73	-6	0						
1996 SF	NL	162	68	94	.420	**4W**	81	-13	0						
1997 SF	NL	162	90	72	.556	**1W**	73	17	2	0	3	.000			
5 Years		745	383	362	.514	— — —	371	12	5	0	3	.000			

George Bamberger

Born: 8/1/1925 in Staten Island, New York; MLB Career: 3 years, 11 G (0-0, 9.42)

REGULAR SEASON							Index			Playoffs			World Series		
Year Tm	Lg	G	W	L	Pct	Standing	EW	+/-	Pt	W	L	Pct	W	L	Pct
1978 Mil	AL	162	93	69	.574	**3E**	72	21	2						
1979 Mil	AL	161	95	66	.590	**2E**	84	11	2						
1980 Mil	AL	92	47	45	.511	2E **4E** 3E	50	-3	0						
1982 NYN	NL	162	65	97	.401	**6E**	70	-5	0						
1983 NYN	NL	46	16	30	.348	**6E** 6E	20	-4	0						
1985 Mil	AL	161	71	90	.441	**6E**	76	-5	0						
1986 Mil	AL	152	71	81	.467	**6E** 6E	71	0	0						
5 AL Years		728	377	351	.518	— — —	353	24	4						
2 NL Years		208	81	127	.389	— — —	90	-9	0						
7 Years		936	458	478	.489	— — —	443	15	4						

Dave Bancroft

Born: 4/20/1891 in Superior, Wisconsin; Died: 10/9/1972; MLB Career: 16 years, 1913 G (.279-32-591)

REGULAR SEASON							Index			Playoffs			World Series		
Year Tm	Lg	G	W	L	Pct	Standing	EW	+/-	Pt	W	L	Pct	W	L	Pct
1924 Bos	NL	66	27	38	.415	**6** 8	27	0	0						
Bos	NL	50	15	35	.300	8 **8**	20	-5	0						
1925 Bos	NL	153	70	83	.458	**5**	59	11	0						
1926 Bos	NL	153	66	86	.434	**7**	67	-1	0						
1927 Bos	NL	155	60	94	.390	**7**	68	-8	0						
4 Years		577	238	336	.415	— — —	241	-3	0						

Frank Bancroft

Born: 5/9/1846 in Lancaster, Massachusetts; Died: 3/30/1921; MLB Career: Did Not Play

REGULAR SEASON							Index			Playoffs			World Series		
Year Tm	Lg	G	W	L	Pct	Standing	EW	+/-	Pt	W	L	Pct	W	L	Pct
1880 Wor	NL	85	40	43	.482	**5**			0						
1881 Det	NL	84	41	43	.488	**4**			0						
1882 Det	NL	86	42	41	.506	**6**			1						
1883 Cle	NL	100	55	42	.567	**4**			1						
1884 Prv	NL	114	84	28	.750	**1**			5				3	0	1.000
1885 Prv	NL	110	53	57	.482	**4**			0						
1887 Phi	AA	55	26	29	.473	**5**			0						
1889 Ind	NL	68	25	43	.368	**7** 7			0						
1902 Cin	NL	16	9	7	.563	7 **5** 4	7	2	0						
8 NL Years		663	349	304	.534	— — —	7	2	7				3	0	1.000
1 AA Year		55	26	29	.473	— — —			0						
9 Years		718	375	333	.530	— — —	7	2	7				3	0	1.000

Sam Barkley

Born: 5/24/1858 in Wheeling, West Virginia; Died: 4/20/1912; MLB Career: 6 years, 582 G (.258-10-231)

REGULAR SEASON							Index			Playoffs			World Series		
Year Tm	Lg	G	W	L	Pct	Standing	EW	+/-	Pt	W	L	Pct	W	L	Pct
1888 KC	AA	57	21	36	.368	8 **8** 8			0						

Billy Barnie

Born: 1/26/1853 in New York, New York; Died: 7/15/1900; MLB Career: 2 years, 19 G (.180-0-0)

REGULAR SEASON							Index			Playoffs			World Series		
Year Tm	Lg	G	W	L	Pct	Standing	EW	+/-	Pt	W	L	Pct	W	L	Pct
1883 Bal	AA	96	28	68	.292	**8**			0						
1884 Bal	AA	108	63	43	.594	**6**			2						
1885 Bal	AA	110	41	68	.376	**8**			0						
1886 Bal	AA	139	48	83	.366	**8**			0						
1887 Bal	AA	141	77	58	.570	**3**			1						
1888 Bal	AA	138	57	80	.416	**5**			0						
1889 Bal	AA	139	70	65	.519	**5**			1						
1890 Bal	AA	38	15	19	.441	**6**			0						
1891 Bal	AA	139	71	64	.526	**4**			1						
1892 Was	NL	2	0	2	.000	**11** 7			0						
1893 Lou	NL	126	50	75	.400	**11** 11			0						
1894 Lou	NL	131	36	94	.277	**11** 11			0						
1897 Bro	NL	136	61	71	.462	**11** 11			0						
1898 Bro	NL	35	15	20	.429	**9** 10			0						
5 NL Years		430	162	262	.382	— — —			0						
9 AA Years		1048	470	548	.462	— — —			5						
14 Years		1478	632	810	.438	— — —			5						

Ed Barrow

Born: 5/10/1868 in Springfield, Illinois; Died: 12/15/1953; MLB Career: Did Not Play

REGULAR SEASON							Index			Playoffs			World Series		
Year Tm	Lg	G	W	L	Pct	Standing	EW	+/-	Pt	W	L	Pct	W	L	Pct
1903 Det	AL	137	65	71	.478	**5**	61	4	0						
1904 Det	AL	84	32	46	.410	**7** 7	38	-6	0						
1918 Bos	AL	126	75	51	.595	**1**	73	2	5				4	2	.667
1919 Bos	AL	138	66	71	.482	**6**	78	-12	0						
1920 Bos	AL	154	72	81	.471	**5**	79	-7	0						
5 Years		639	310	320	.492	— — —	329	-19	5				4	2	.667

Jack Barry

Born: 4/26/1887 in Meriden, Connecticut; Died: 4/23/1961; MLB Career: 11 years, 1223 G (.243-10-429)

REGULAR SEASON							Index			Playoffs			World Series		
Year Tm	Lg	G	W	L	Pct	Standing	EW	+/-	Pt	W	L	Pct	W	L	Pct
1917 Bos	AL	157	90	62	.592	**2**	88	2	2						

Joe Battin

Born: 11/11/1851 in Philadelphia, Pennsylvania; Died: 12/10/1937; MLB Career: 6 years, 360 G (.218-3-81)

REGULAR SEASON							Index			Playoffs			World Series		
Year Tm	Lg	G	W	L	Pct	Standing	EW	+/-	Pt	W	L	Pct	W	L	Pct
1883 Pit	AA	13	2	11	.154	7 **7**			0						
1884 Pit	UA	6	1	5	.167	**8** 11			0						
Pit	AA	13	6	7	.462	9 **10** 11			0						
1 UA Year		6	1	5	.167	— — —			0						
2 AA Years		26	8	18	.308	— — —			0						
2 Years		32	9	23	.281	— — —			0						

Hank Bauer

Born: 7/31/1922 in East St. Louis, Illinois; MLB Career: 14 years, 1544 G (.277-164-703)

REGULAR SEASON							Index			Playoffs			World Series		
Year Tm	Lg	G	W	L	Pct	Standing	EW	+/-	Pt	W	L	Pct	W	L	Pct
1961 KCA	AL	102	35	67	.343	8 **9**	46	-11	0						
1962 KCA	AL	162	72	90	.444	**9**	68	4	0						
1964 Bal	AL	163	97	65	.599	**3**	85	12	2						
1965 Bal	AL	162	94	68	.580	**3**	89	5	2						
1966 Bal	AL	160	97	63	.606	**1**	89	8	5				4	0	1.000
1967 Bal	AL	161	76	85	.472	**6**	93	-17	0						
1968 Bal	AL	80	43	37	.538	**3** 2	41	2	0						
1969 Oak	AL	149	80	69	.537	**2W** 2W	75	5	0						
8 Years		1139	594	544	.522	— — —	586	8	9				4	0	1.000

Don Baylor

Born: 6/28/1949 in Austin, Texas; MLB Career: 19 years, 2292 G (.260-338-1276)

REGULAR SEASON							Index			Playoffs			World Series		
Year Tm	Lg	G	W	L	Pct	Standing	EW	+/-	Pt	W	L	Pct	W	L	Pct
1993 Col	NL	162	67	95	.414	**6W**	61	6	0						
1994 Col	NL	117	53	64	.453	**3W**	48	5	0						
1995 Col	NL	144	77	67	.535	**2W**	64	13	1	1	3	.250			
1996 Col	NL	162	83	79	.512	**3W**	81	2	1						
1997 Col	NL	162	83	79	.512	**3W**	82	1	1						
5 Years		747	363	384	.486	— — —	336	27	3	1	3	.250			

Buddy Bell

Born: 8/27/1951 in Pittsburgh, Pennsylvania; MLB Career: 18 years, 2405 G (.279-201-1106)

REGULAR SEASON							Index			Playoffs			World Series		
Year Tm	Lg	G	W	L	Pct	Standing	EW	+/-	Pt	W	L	Pct	W	L	Pct
1996 Det	AL	162	53	109	.327	**5E**	74	-21	0						
1997 Det	AL	162	79	83	.488	**3E**	64	15	0						
2 Years		324	132	192	.407	— — —	138	-6	0						

Vern Benson

Born: 9/19/1924 in Granite Quarry, North Carolina; MLB Career: 5 years, 55 G (.202-3-12)

REGULAR SEASON							Index			Playoffs			World Series		
Year Tm	Lg	G	W	L	Pct	Standing	EW	+/-	Pt	W	L	Pct	W	L	Pct
1977 Atl	NL	1	1	0	1.000	6W **6W** 6W	0	1	0						

Yogi Berra

Born: 5/12/1925 in St. Louis, Missouri; MLB Career: 19 years, 2120 G (.285-358-1430)

REGULAR SEASON							Index			Playoffs			World Series		
Year Tm	Lg	G	W	L	Pct	Standing	EW	+/-	Pt	W	L	Pct	W	L	Pct
1964 NYA	AL	164	99	63	.611	1	98	1	4				3	4	.429
1972 NYN	NL	156	83	73	.532	3E	82	1	1						
1973 NYN	NL	161	82	79	.509	1E	84	-2	3	3	2	.600	3	4	.429
1974 NYN	NL	162	71	91	.438	5E	83	-12	0						
1975 NYN	NL	109	56	53	.514	3E	52	4	0						
1984 NYA	AL	162	87	75	.537	3E	87	0	1						
1985 NYA	AL	16	6	10	.375	7E 2E	8	-2	0						
3 AL Years		342	192	148	.565	— — —	193	-1	5				3	4	.429
4 NL Years		588	292	296	.497	— — —	301	-9	4	3	2	.600	3	4	.429
7 Years		930	484	444	.522	— — —	494	-10	9	3	2	.600	6	8	.429

Terry Bevington

Born: 7/7/1956 in Akron, Ohio; MLB Career: Did Not Play

REGULAR SEASON							Index			Playoffs			World Series		
Year Tm	Lg	G	W	L	Pct	Standing	EW	+/-	Pt	W	L	Pct	W	L	Pct
1995 ChA	AL	114	57	56	.504	4C 3C	63	-6	1						
1996 ChA	AL	162	85	77	.525	2C	82	3	1						
1997 ChA	AL	161	80	81	.497	2C	83	-3	0						
3 Years		437	222	214	.509	— — —	228	-6	2						

Hugo Bezdek

Born: 4/1/1883 in Prague, Austria-Hungary; Died: 9/19/1952; MLB Career: Did Not Play

REGULAR SEASON							Index			Playoffs			World Series		
Year Tm	Lg	G	W	L	Pct	Standing	EW	+/-	Pt	W	L	Pct	W	L	Pct
1917 Pit	NL	91	30	59	.337	8 8	40	-10	1						
1918 Pit	NL	126	65	60	.520	4	50	15	1						
1919 Pit	NL	139	71	68	.511	4	66	5	1						
3 Years		356	166	187	.470	— — —	156	10	2						

Bickerson

Born: Unknown; MLB Career: Did Not Play

REGULAR SEASON							Index			Playoffs			World Series		
Year Tm	Lg	G	W	L	Pct	Standing	EW	+/-	Pt	W	L	Pct	W	L	Pct
1884 WaD	AA	1	0	1	.000	13 13			0						

Joe Birmingham

Born: 8/6/1884 in Elmira, New York; Died: 4/24/1946; MLB Career: 9 years, 772 G (.254-7-265)

REGULAR SEASON							Index			Playoffs			World Series		
Year Tm	Lg	G	W	L	Pct	Standing	EW	+/-	Pt	W	L	Pct	W	L	Pct
1912 Cle	AL	28	21	7	.750	6 5	14	7	0						
1913 Cle	AL	155	86	66	.566	3	75	11	2						
1914 Cle	AL	157	51	102	.333	8	82	-31	0						
1915 Cle	AL	28	12	16	.429	6 7	12	0	0						
4 Years		368	170	191	.471	— — —	183	-13	2						

Del Bissonette

Born: 9/6/1899 in Winthrop, Maine; Died: 6/9/1972; MLB Career: 5 years, 604 G (.305-66-391)

REGULAR SEASON							Index			Playoffs			World Series		
Year Tm	Lg	G	W	L	Pct	Standing	EW	+/-	Pt	W	L	Pct	W	L	Pct
1945 Bos	NL	60	25	34	.424	7 6	26	-1	0						

Lena Blackburne

Born: 10/23/1886 in Clifton Heights, Pennsylvania; Died: 2/29/1968; MLB Career: 8 years, 548 G (.214-4-139)

REGULAR SEASON							Index			Playoffs			World Series		
Year Tm	Lg	G	W	L	Pct	Standing	EW	+/-	Pt	W	L	Pct	W	L	Pct
1928 ChA	AL	80	40	40	.500	6 5	39	1	0						
1929 ChA	AL	152	59	93	.388	7	73	-14	0						
2 Years		232	99	133	.427	— — —	112	-13	0						

Ray Blades

Born: 8/6/1896 in Mount Vernon, Illinois; Died: 5/18/1979; MLB Career: 10 years, 767 G (.301-50-340)

REGULAR SEASON							Index			Playoffs			World Series		
Year Tm	Lg	G	W	L	Pct	Standing	EW	+/-	Pt	W	L	Pct	W	L	Pct
1939 StL	NL	155	92	61	.601	2	76	16	2						
1940 StL	NL	39	14	24	.368	6 3	21	-7	0						
1948 Bro	NL	1	1	0	1.000	5 5 3	1	0	0						
3 Years		195	107	85	.557	— — —	98	9	2						

Walter Blair

Born: 10/13/1883 in Landrus, Pennsylvania; Died: 8/20/1948; MLB Career: 7 years, 442 G (.217-3-106)

REGULAR SEASON							Index			Playoffs			World Series		
Year Tm	Lg	G	W	L	Pct	Standing	EW	+/-	Pt	W	L	Pct	W	L	Pct
1915 Buf	FL	2	1	1	.500	8 8 6	1	0	0						

Ossie Bluege

Born: 10/24/1900 in Chicago, Illinois; Died: 10/14/1985; MLB Career: 18 years, 1867 G (.272-43-848)

REGULAR SEASON							Index			Playoffs			World Series		
Year Tm	Lg	G	W	L	Pct	Standing	EW	+/-	Pt	W	L	Pct	W	L	Pct
1943 Was	AL	153	84	69	.549	2	67	17	1						
1944 Was	AL	154	64	90	.416	8	78	-14	0						
1945 Was	AL	156	87	67	.565	2	70	17	2						
1946 Was	AL	155	76	78	.494	4	81	-5	0						
1947 Was	AL	154	64	90	.416	7	76	-12	0						
5 Years		772	375	394	.488	— — —	372	3	3						

Bruce Bochy

Born: 4/16/1955 in Landes De Bussac, France; MLB Career: 9 years, 358 G (.239-26-93)

REGULAR SEASON							Index			Playoffs			World Series		
Year Tm	Lg	G	W	L	Pct	Standing	EW	+/-	Pt	W	L	Pct	W	L	Pct
1995 SD	NL	144	70	74	.486	3W	64	6	0						
1996 SD	NL	162	91	71	.562	1W	76	15	3	0	3	.000			
1997 SD	NL	162	76	86	.469	4W	84	-8	0						
3 Years		468	237	231	.506	— — —	224	13	3	0	3	.000			

John Boles

Born: 8/19/1948 in Chicago, Illinois; MLB Career: Did Not Play

REGULAR SEASON							Index			Playoffs			World Series		
Year Tm	Lg	G	W	L	Pct	Standing	EW	+/-	Pt	W	L	Pct	W	L	Pct
1996 Fla	NL	75	40	35	.533	4E 3E	35	5	1						

Tommy Bond

Born: 4/2/1856 in Granard, Ireland; Died: 1/24/1941; MLB Career: 8 years, 361 G (193-115, 2.25)

REGULAR SEASON							Index			Playoffs			World Series		
Year Tm	Lg	G	W	L	Pct	Standing	EW	+/-	Pt	W	L	Pct	W	L	Pct
1882 Wor	NL	6	2	4	.333	8 8 8			0						

Bob Boone

Born: 11/19/1947 in San Diego, California; MLB Career: 19 years, 2264 G (.254-105-826)

REGULAR SEASON							Index			Playoffs			World Series		
Year Tm	Lg	G	W	L	Pct	Standing	EW	+/-	Pt	W	L	Pct	W	L	Pct
1995 KC	AL	144	70	74	.486	2C	75	-5	0						
1996 KC	AL	161	75	86	.466	5C	81	-6	0						
1997 KC	AL	82	36	46	.439	4C 5C	40	-4	0						
3 Years		387	181	206	.468	— — —	196	-15	0						

Steve Boros

Born: 9/3/1936 in Flint, Michigan; MLB Career: 7 years, 422 G (.245-26-149)

REGULAR SEASON							Index			Playoffs			World Series		
Year Tm	Lg	G	W	L	Pct	Standing	EW	+/-	Pt	W	L	Pct	W	L	Pct
1983 Oak	AL	162	74	88	.457	4W	76	-2	0						
1984 Oak	AL	44	20	24	.455	4W 4W	21	-1	0						
1986 SD	NL	162	74	88	.457	4W	83	-9	0						
2 AL Years		206	94	112	.456	— — —	97	-3	0						
1 NL Year		162	74	88	.457	— — —	83	-9	0						
3 Years		368	168	200	.457	— — —	180	-12	0						

Jim Bottomley

Born: 4/23/1900 in Oglesby, Illinois; Died: 12/11/1959; MLB Career: 16 years, 1991 G (.310-219-1422)

REGULAR SEASON							Index			Playoffs			World Series		
Year Tm	Lg	G	W	L	Pct	Standing	EW	+/-	Pt	W	L	Pct	W	L	Pct
1937 StL	AL	78	21	56	.273	7 8	32	-11	0						

Lou Boudreau

Born: 7/17/1917 in Harvey, Illinois; MLB Career: 15 years, 1646 G (.295-68-789)

REGULAR SEASON							Index			Playoffs			World Series		
Year Tm	Lg	G	W	L	Pct	Standing	EW	+/-	Pt	W	L	Pct	W	L	Pct
1942 Cle	AL	156	75	79	.487	4	79	-4	0						
1943 Cle	AL	153	82	71	.536	3	77	5	1						
1944 Cle	AL	155	72	82	.468	5	79	-7	0						
1945 Cle	AL	147	73	72	.503	5	71	2	1						
1946 Cle	AL	156	68	86	.442	6	77	-9	0						
1947 Cle	AL	157	80	74	.519	4	72	8	1						
1948 Cle	AL	156	97	58	.626	1	78	19	5				4	2	.667
1949 Cle	AL	154	89	65	.578	3	86	3	2						
1950 Cle	AL	155	92	62	.597	4	86	6	2						
1952 Bos	AL	154	76	78	.494	6	87	-11	0						
1953 Bos	AL	153	84	69	.549	4	79	5	1						
1954 Bos	AL	156	69	85	.448	4	82	-13	0						
1955 KCA	AL	155	63	91	.409	6	62	1	0						
1956 KCA	AL	154	52	102	.338	8	65	-13	0						
1957 KCA	AL	104	36	67	.350	8 7	40	-4	0						
1960 ChN	NL	139	54	83	.394	8 7	65	-11	0						
15 AL Years		2265	1108	1141	.493	— — —	1120	-12	13				4	2	.667
1 NL Year		139	54	83	.394	— — —	65	-11	0						
16 Years		2404	1162	1224	.487	— — —	1185	-23	13				4	2	.667

Larry Bowa

Born: 12/6/1945 in Sacramento, California; MLB Career: 16 years, 2247 G (.260-15-525)

REGULAR SEASON							Index			Playoffs			World Series		
Year Tm	Lg	G	W	L	Pct	Standing	EW	+/-	Pt	W	L	Pct	W	L	Pct
1987 SD	NL	162	65	97	.401	6W	79	-14	0						
1988 SD	NL	46	16	30	.348	5W 3W	21	-5	0						
2 Years		208	81	127	.389	— — —	100	-19	0						

Frank Bowerman

Born: 12/5/1868 in Romeo, Michigan; Died: 11/30/1948; MLB Career: 15 years, 1045 G (.251-13-392)

		REGULAR SEASON					Index			Playoffs			World Series		
Year Tm	Lg	G	W	L	Pct	Standing	EW	+/-	Pt	W	L	Pct	W	L	Pct
1909 Bos	NL	76	22	54	.289	8 8	32	-10	0						

Ken Boyer

Born: 5/20/1931 in Liberty, Missouri; Died: 9/7/1982; MLB Career: 15 years, 2034 G (.287-282-1141)

		REGULAR SEASON					Index			Playoffs			World Series		
Year Tm	Lg	G	W	L	Pct	Standing	EW	+/-	Pt	W	L	Pct	W	L	Pct
1978 StL	NL	143	62	81	.434	6E 5E	72	-10	0						
1979 StL	NL	163	86	76	.531	3E	74	12	1						
1980 StL	NL	51	18	33	.353	6E 4E	26	-8	0						
3 Years		357	166	190	.466	— — —	172	-6	1						

Bill Bradley

Born: 2/13/1878 in Cleveland, Ohio; Died: 3/11/1954; MLB Career: 14 years, 1460 G (.271-34-552)

		REGULAR SEASON					Index			Playoffs			World Series		
Year Tm	Lg	G	W	L	Pct	Standing	EW	+/-	Pt	W	L	Pct	W	L	Pct
1905 Cle	AL	41	20	21	.488	1 2 5	22	-2	0						
1914 Bro	FL	157	77	77	.500	5	77	0	0						
1 AL Year		41	20	21	.488	— — —	22	-2	0						
1 FL Year		157	77	77	.500		77	0	0						
2 Years		198	97	98	.497	— — —	99	-2	0						

Bobby Bragan

Born: 10/30/1917 in Birmingham, Alabama; MLB Career: 7 years, 597 G (.240-15-172)

		REGULAR SEASON					Index			Playoffs			World Series		
Year Tm	Lg	G	W	L	Pct	Standing	EW	+/-	Pt	W	L	Pct	W	L	Pct
1956 Pit	NL	157	66	88	.429	7	62	4	0						
1957 Pit	NL	104	36	67	.350	8 7	44	-8	0						
1958 Cle	AL	67	31	36	.463	5 4	35	-4	0						
1963 Mil	NL	163	84	78	.519	6	88	4	1						
1964 Mil	NL	162	88	74	.543	5	85	3	1						
1965 Mil	NL	162	86	76	.531	5	86	0	1						
1966 Atl	NL	112	52	59	.468	5 5	58	-6	0						
1 AL Year		67	31	36	.463	— — —	35	-4	0						
6 NL Years		860	412	442	.482	— — —	423	-11	3						
7 Years		927	443	478	.481	— — —	458	-15	3						

Roger Bresnahan

Born: 6/11/1879 in Toledo, Ohio; Died: 12/4/1944; MLB Career: 17 years, 1446 G (.279-26-530)

		REGULAR SEASON					Index			Playoffs			World Series		
Year Tm	Lg	G	W	L	Pct	Standing	EW	+/-	Pt	W	L	Pct	W	L	Pct
1909 StL	NL	154	54	98	.355	7	56	-2	0						
1910 StL	NL	153	63	90	.412	7	59	4	0						
1911 StL	NL	158	75	74	.503	5	62	13	1						
1912 StL	NL	153	63	90	.412	6	72	-9	0						
1915 ChN	NL	157	73	80	.477	4	80	-7	0						
5 Years		775	328	432	.432	— — —	329	-1	1						

Dave Bristol

Born: 6/23/1933 in Macon, Georgia; MLB Career: Did Not Play

		REGULAR SEASON					Index			Playoffs			World Series		
Year Tm	Lg	G	W	L	Pct	Standing	EW	+/-	Pt	W	L	Pct	W	L	Pct
1966 Cin	NL	77	39	38	.506	8 7	41	-2	1						
1967 Cin	NL	162	87	75	.537	4	81	6	1						
1968 Cin	NL	163	83	79	.512	4	85	-2	1						
1969 Cin	NL	163	89	73	.549	3W	86	3	1						
1970 Mil	AL	163	65	97	.401	5W	66	-1	0						
1971 Mil	AL	161	69	92	.429	6W	67	2	0						
1972 Mil	AL	30	10	20	.333	6E 6E	13	-3	0						
1976 Atl	NL	162	70	92	.432	6W	75	-5	0						
1977 Atl	NL	29	8	21	.276	6W 6W	13	-5	0						
Atl	NL	131	52	79	.397	6W 6W	60	-8	0						
1979 SF	NL	22	10	12	.455	4W 4W	11	-1	0						
1980 SF	NL	161	75	86	.466	5W	76	-1	0						
3 AL Years		354	144	209	.408	— — —	146	-2	0						
8 NL Years		1070	513	555	.480	— — —	528	-15	4						
11 Years		1424	657	764	.462	— — —	674	-17	4						

Freeman Brown

Born: 1/31/1845 in Hubbardston, Massachusetts; Died: 12/27/1916; MLB Career: Did Not Play

		REGULAR SEASON					Index			Playoffs			World Series		
Year Tm	Lg	G	W	L	Pct	Standing	EW	+/-	Pt	W	L	Pct	W	L	Pct
1882 Wor	NL	41	9	32	.220	8 8			0						

Three Finger Brown

Born: 10/19/1876 in Nyesville, Indiana; Died: 2/14/1948; MLB Career: 14 years, 493 G (239-129, 2.06)

		REGULAR SEASON					Index			Playoffs			World Series		
Year Tm	Lg	G	W	L	Pct	Standing	EW	+/-	Pt	W	L	Pct	W	L	Pct
1914 STL	FL	114	50	63	.442	7 8	57	-7	0						

Tom Brown

Born: 9/21/1860 in Liverpool, England; Died: 10/25/1927; MLB Career: 17 years, 1786 G (.265-64-671)

		REGULAR SEASON					Index			Playoffs			World Series		
Year Tm	Lg	G	W	L	Pct	Standing	EW	+/-	Pt	W	L	Pct	W	L	Pct
1897 Was	NL	99	52	46	.531	11 6			1						
1898 Was	NL	38	12	26	.316	11 11			0						
2 Years		137	64	72	.471	— — —			1						

Earle Brucker

Born: 5/6/1901 in Albany, New York; Died: 5/8/1981; MLB Career: 5 years, 241 G (.290-12-105)

		REGULAR SEASON					Index			Playoffs			World Series		
Year Tm	Lg	G	W	L	Pct	Standing	EW	+/-	Pt	W	L	Pct	W	L	Pct
1952 Cin	NL	5	3	2	.600	7 7 6	2	1	0						

Al Buckenberger

Born: 1/31/1861 in Detroit, Michigan; Died: 7/1/1917; MLB Career: Did Not Play

		REGULAR SEASON					Index			Playoffs			World Series		
Year Tm	Lg	G	W	L	Pct	Standing	EW	+/-	Pt	W	L	Pct	W	L	Pct
1889 CoC	AA	140	60	78	.435	6			0						
1890 CoC	AA	80	39	41	.488	5 2			0						
1892 Pit	NL	29	15	14	.517	7 6			0						
Pit	NL	66	38	27	.585	2			1						
1893 Pit	NL	131	81	48	.628	2			2						
1894 Pit	NL	110	53	55	.491	7 7			0						
1895 StL	NL	50	16	34	.320	11 11			0						
1902 Bos	NL	142	73	64	.533	3	68	5	1						
1903 Bos	NL	140	58	80	.420	6	71	-13	0						
1904 Bos	NL	155	55	98	.359	7	71	-16	0						
7 NL Years		823	389	420	.481	— — —	210	-24	4						
2 AA Years		220	99	119	.454	— — —			0						
9 Years		1043	488	539	.475	— — —	210	-24	4						

Charlie Buffinton

Born: 6/14/1861 in Fall River, Massachusetts; Died: 9/23/1907; MLB Career: 11 years, 586 G (233-152, 2.96)

		REGULAR SEASON					Index			Playoffs			World Series		
Year Tm	Lg	G	W	L	Pct	Standing	EW	+/-	Pt	W	L	Pct	W	L	Pct
1890 Phi	PL	116	61	54	.530	5 5			1						

Jack Burdock

Born: Unknown in Brooklyn, New York; Died: 3/26/1942; MLB Career: 14 years, 960 G (.244-15-390)

		REGULAR SEASON					Index			Playoffs			World Series		
Year Tm	Lg	G	W	L	Pct	Standing	EW	+/-	Pt	W	L	Pct	W	L	Pct
1883 Bos	NL	54	30	24	.556	4 1			0						

Jimmy Burke

Born: 10/12/1874 in St. Louis, Missouri; Died: 3/26/1942; MLB Career: 7 years, 548 G (.244-1-187)

		REGULAR SEASON					Index			Playoffs			World Series		
Year Tm	Lg	G	W	L	Pct	Standing	EW	+/-	Pt	W	L	Pct	W	L	Pct
1905 StL	NL	90	34	56	.378	7 6 6	42	-8	0						
1918 StL	AL	61	29	31	.483	6 5	25	4	0						
1919 StL	AL	140	67	72	.482	5	66	1	0						
1920 StL	AL	154	76	77	.497	4	72	4	0						
3 AL Years		355	172	180	.489	— — —	163	9	0						
1 NL Year		90	34	56	.378	— — —	42	-8	0						
4 Years		445	206	236	.466	— — —	205	1	0						

Watch Burnham

Born: 5/20/1860 in Albion, Michigan; Died: 11/18/1902; MLB Career: Did Not Play

		REGULAR SEASON					Index			Playoffs			World Series		
Year Tm	Lg	G	W	L	Pct	Standing	EW	+/-	Pt	W	L	Pct	W	L	Pct
1887 Ind	NL	28	6	22	.214	8 8			0						

Tom Burns

Born: 3/30/1857 in Honesdale, Pennsylvania; Died: 3/19/1902; MLB Career: 13 years, 1251 G (.264-39-683)

		REGULAR SEASON					Index			Playoffs			World Series		
Year Tm	Lg	G	W	L	Pct	Standing	EW	+/-	Pt	W	L	Pct	W	L	Pct
1892 Pit	NL	48	22	25	.468	7 6			0						
Pit	NL	13	5	7	.417	10 4			0						
1898 ChN	NL	152	85	65	.567	4			2						
1899 ChN	NL	152	75	73	.507	8			1						
3 Years		365	187	170	.524	— — —			3						

Bill Burwell

Born: 3/27/1895 in Jarbalo, Kansas; Died: 6/11/1973; MLB Career: 3 years, 72 G (9-8, 4.37)

		REGULAR SEASON					Index			Playoffs			World Series		
Year Tm	Lg	G	W	L	Pct	Standing	EW	+/-	Pt	W	L	Pct	W	L	Pct
1947 Pit	NL	1	1	0	1.000	8 7	0	1	0						

Donie Bush

Born: 10/8/1887 in Indianapolis, Indiana; Died: 3/28/1972; MLB Career: 16 years, 1946 G (.250-9-436)

		REGULAR SEASON					Index			Playoffs			World Series		
Year Tm	Lg	G	W	L	Pct	Standing	EW	+/-	Pt	W	L	Pct	W	L	Pct
1923 Was	AL	155	75	78	.490	4	72	3	0						
1927 Pit	NL	156	94	60	.610	1	85	9	4				0	4	.000
1928 Pit	NL	152	85	67	.559	4	88	-3	1						
1929 Pit	NL	119	67	51	.568	2 2	65	2	0						

REGULAR SEASON							Index			Playoffs			World Series		
Year Tm	Lg	G	W	L	Pct	Standing	EW	+/-	Pt	W	L	Pct	W	L	Pct
1930 ChA	AL	154	62	92	.403	7	67	-5	0						
1931 ChA	AL	156	56	97	.366	8	66	-10	0						
1933 Cin	NL	153	58	94	.382	8	63	-5	0						
3 AL Years		465	193	267	.420	— — —	205	-12	0						
4 NL Years		580	304	272	.528	— — —	301	3	5				0	4	.000
7 Years		1045	497	539	.480	— — —	506	-9	5				0	4	.000

Ormond Butler

Born: 11/18/1854 in West Virginia; Died: 9/12/1915; MLB Career: Did Not Play

REGULAR SEASON							Index			Playoffs			World Series		
Year Tm	Lg	G	W	L	Pct	Standing	EW	+/-	Pt	W	L	Pct	W	L	Pct
1883 Pit	AA	53	17	36	.321	6 7 7			0						

Charlie Byrne

Born: Unknown in New York, New York; Died: 1/4/1898; MLB Career: Did Not Play

REGULAR SEASON							Index			Playoffs			World Series		
Year Tm	Lg	G	W	L	Pct	Standing	EW	+/-	Pt	W	L	Pct	W	L	Pct
1885 Bro	AA	75	38	37	.507	7 5			1						
1886 Bro	AA	141	76	61	.555	3			1						
1887 Bro	AA	138	60	74	.448	6			0						
3 Years		354	174	172	.503	— — —			2						

Nixey Callahan

Born: 3/18/1874 in Fitchburg, Massachusetts; Died: 10/4/1934; MLB Career: 13 years, 923 G (.273-11-394)

REGULAR SEASON							Index			Playoffs			World Series		
Year Tm	Lg	G	W	L	Pct	Standing	EW	+/-	Pt	W	L	Pct	W	L	Pct
1903 ChA	AL	138	60	77	.438	7	74	-14	0						
1904 ChA	AL	42	23	18	.561	4 3	20	3	0						
1912 ChA	AL	158	78	76	.506	4	77	1	1						
1913 ChA	AL	153	78	74	.513	5	76	2	1						
1914 ChA	AL	157	70	84	.455	6	78	-8	0						
1916 Pit	NL	157	65	89	.422	6	74	-9	0						
1917 Pit	NL	61	20	40	.333	8 8	27	-7	0						
5 AL Years		648	309	329	.484	— — —	325	-16	2						
2 NL Years		218	85	129	.397	— — —	101	-16	0						
7 Years		866	394	458	.462	— — —	426	-32	2						

Count Campau

Born: 10/17/1863 in Detroit, Michigan; Died: 4/3/1938; MLB Career: 3 years, 147 G (.267-10-93)

REGULAR SEASON							Index			Playoffs			World Series		
Year Tm	Lg	G	W	L	Pct	Standing	EW	+/-	Pt	W	L	Pct	W	L	Pct
1890 STL	AA	42	26	14	.650	5 2 3			0						

Joe Cantillon

Born: 8/19/1861 in Janesville, Wisconsin; Died: 1/31/1930; MLB Career: Did Not Play

REGULAR SEASON							Index			Playoffs			World Series		
Year Tm	Lg	G	W	L	Pct	Standing	EW	+/-	Pt	W	L	Pct	W	L	Pct
1907 Was	AL	154	49	102	.325	8	59	-10	0						
1908 Was	AL	155	67	85	.441	7	59	8	0						
1909 Was	AL	156	42	110	.276	8	66	-24	0						
3 Years		465	158	297	.347	— — —	184	-26	0						

Max Carey

Born: 1/11/1890 in Terre Haute, Indiana; Died: 5/30/1976; MLB Career: 20 years, 2476 G (.285-70-800)

REGULAR SEASON							Index			Playoffs			World Series		
Year Tm	Lg	G	W	L	Pct	Standing	EW	+/-	Pt	W	L	Pct	W	L	Pct
1932 Bro	NL	154	81	73	.526	3	79	2	1						
1933 Bro	NL	157	65	88	.425	6	80	-15	0						
2 Years		311	146	161	.476	— — —	159	-13	1						

Bill Carrigan

Born: 10/22/1883 in Lewiston, Maine; Died: 7/8/1969; MLB Career: 10 years, 706 G (.257-6-235)

REGULAR SEASON							Index			Playoffs			World Series		
Year Tm	Lg	G	W	L	Pct	Standing	EW	+/-	Pt	W	L	Pct	W	L	Pct
1913 Bos	AL	70	40	30	.571	5 4	42	-2	1						
1914 Bos	AL	159	91	62	.595	2	82	9	2						
1915 Bos	AL	155	101	50	.669	1	87	14	6				4	1	.800
1916 Bos	AL	156	91	63	.591	1	92	-1	5				4	1	.800
1927 Bos	AL	154	51	103	.331	8	57	-6	0						
1928 Bos	AL	154	57	96	.373	8	56	1	0						
1929 Bos	AL	155	58	96	.377	8	60	-2	0						
7 Years		1003	489	500	.494	— — —	476	13	14				8	2	.800

Bob Caruthers

Born: 1/5/1864 in Memphis, Tennessee; Died: 8/5/1911; MLB Career: 10 years, 705 G (218-99, 2.83)

REGULAR SEASON							Index			Playoffs			World Series		
Year Tm	Lg	G	W	L	Pct	Standing	EW	+/-	Pt	W	L	Pct	W	L	Pct
1892 StL	NL	50	16	32	.333	12 11			0						

Phil Cavarretta

Born: 7/19/1916 in Chicago, Illinois; MLB Career: 22 years, 2030 G (.293-95-920)

REGULAR SEASON							Index			Playoffs			World Series		
Year Tm	Lg	G	W	L	Pct	Standing	EW	+/-	Pt	W	L	Pct	W	L	Pct
1951 ChN	NL	74	27	47	.365	7 8	32	-5	0						
1952 ChN	NL	155	77	77	.500	5	66	11	0						
1953 ChN	NL	155	65	89	.422	7	74	-9	0						
3 Years		384	169	213	.442	— — —	172	-3	0						

Ollie Caylor

Born: 12/14/1849 in Dayton, Ohio; Died: 10/19/1897; MLB Career: Did Not Play

REGULAR SEASON							Index			Playoffs			World Series		
Year Tm	Lg	G	W	L	Pct	Standing	EW	+/-	Pt	W	L	Pct	W	L	Pct
1885 Cin	AA	112	63	49	.563	2			1						
1886 Cin	AA	141	65	73	.471	5			0						
1887 NY	AA	100	35	60	.368	7 7			0						
3 Years		353	163	182	.472	— — —			1						

Frank Chance

Born: 9/9/1877 in Fresno, California; Died: 9/15/1924; MLB Career: 17 years, 1286 G (.296-20-596)

REGULAR SEASON							Index			Playoffs			World Series		
Year Tm	Lg	G	W	L	Pct	Standing	EW	+/-	Pt	W	L	Pct	W	L	Pct
1905 ChN	NL	90	55	33	.625	4 3	50	5	2						
1906 ChN	NL	155	116	36	.763	1	88	28	5				2	4	.333
1907 ChN	NL	155	107	45	.704	1	100	7	6				4	0	1.000
1908 ChN	NL	158	99	55	.643	1	100	-1	5				4	1	.800
1909 ChN	NL	155	104	49	.680	2	96	8	3						
1910 ChN	NL	154	104	50	.675	1	97	7	5				1	4	.200
1911 ChN	NL	158	92	62	.597	2	97	-5	2						
1912 ChN	NL	153	91	59	.607	3	89	2	2						
1913 NYA	AL	153	57	94	.377	7	64	-7	0						
1914 NYA	AL	137	60	74	.448	7 6	56	4	0						
1923 Bos	AL	154	61	91	.401	8	67	-6	0						
3 AL Years		444	178	259	.407	— — —	187	-9	0						
8 NL Years		1178	768	389	.664	— — —	717	51	30				11	9	.550
11 Years		1622	946	648	.593	— — —	904	42	30				11	9	.550

Ben Chapman

Born: 12/25/1908 in Nashville, Tennessee; Died: 7/7/1993; MLB Career: 15 years, 1717 G (.302-90-977)

REGULAR SEASON							Index			Playoffs			World Series		
Year Tm	Lg	G	W	L	Pct	Standing	EW	+/-	Pt	W	L	Pct	W	L	Pct
1945 Phi	NL	85	28	57	.329	8 8	35	-7	0						
1946 Phi	NL	155	69	85	.448	5	58	11	0						
1947 Phi	NL	155	62	92	.403	7	67	-5	0						
1948 Phi	NL	79	37	42	.468	7 6	33	4	0						
4 Years		474	196	276	.415	— — —	193	3	0						

Jack Chapman

Born: 5/8/1843 in Brooklyn, New York; Died: 6/10/1916; MLB Career: 1 year, 17 G (.239-0-5)

REGULAR SEASON							Index			Playoffs			World Series		
Year Tm	Lg	G	W	L	Pct	Standing	EW	+/-	Pt	W	L	Pct	W	L	Pct
1876 Lou	NL	69	30	36	.455	5			0						
1877 Lou	NL	61	35	25	.583	2			1						
1878 Mil	NL	61	15	45	.250	6			0						
1882 Wor	NL	37	7	30	.189	8 8			0						
1883 Det	NL	101	40	58	.408	7			0						
1884 Det	NL	114	28	84	.250	8			0						
1885 Buf	NL	88	31	57	.352	7 6			0						
1889 Lou	AA	7	1	6	.143	8 8			0						
1890 Lou	AA	136	88	44	.667	1			4				3	3	.500
1891 Lou	AA	139	54	83	.394	7			0						
1892 Lou	NL	54	21	33	.389	10 11			0						
8 NL Years		585	207	368	.360	— — —			1						
3 AA Years		282	143	133	.518	— — —			4				3	3	.500
11 Years		867	350	501	.411	— — —			5				3	3	.500

Hal Chase

Born: 2/13/1883 in Los Gatos, California; Died: 5/18/1947; MLB Career: 15 years, 1917 G (.291-57-941)

REGULAR SEASON							Index			Playoffs			World Series		
Year Tm	Lg	G	W	L	Pct	Standing	EW	+/-	Pt	W	L	Pct	W	L	Pct
1910 NYA	AL	14	10	4	.714	3 2	7	3	0						
1911 NYA	AL	153	76	76	.500	6	79	-3	0						
2 Years		167	86	80	.518	— — —	86	0	0						

John Clapp

Born: 7/17/1851 in Ithaca, New York; Died: 12/18/1904; MLB Career: 7 years, 425 G (.283-2-178)

REGULAR SEASON							Index			Playoffs			World Series		
Year Tm	Lg	G	W	L	Pct	Standing	EW	+/-	Pt	W	L	Pct	W	L	Pct
1878 Ind	NL	63	24	36	.400	5			0						
1879 Buf	NL	79	46	32	.590	3			1						
1880 Cin	NL	83	21	59	.263	8			0						
1881 Cle	NL	74	32	41	.438	7 7			0						
1883 NYG	NL	98	46	50	.479	6			0						
5 Years		397	169	218	.437	— — —			1						

Fred Clarke

Born: 10/3/1872 in Winterset, Iowa; Died: 8/14/1960; MLB Career: 21 years, 2242 G (.312-67-1015)

REGULAR SEASON							Index			Playoffs			World Series		
Year Tm	Lg	G	W	L	Pct	Standing	EW	+/-	Pt	W	L	Pct	W	L	Pct
1897 Lou	NL	92	35	54	.393	9 11			0						
1898 Lou	NL	154	70	81	.464	9			0						
1899 Lou	NL	156	75	77	.493	9			0						
1900 Pit	NL	140	79	60	.568	2	70	9	1				1	3	.250

Year Tm	Lg	G	W	L	Pct	Standing	EW	+/-	Pt	W	L	Pct	W	L	Pct
		REGULAR SEASON					**Index**			**Playoffs**			**World Series**		
1901 Pit	NL	140	90	49	.647	1	74	16	4						
1902 Pit	NL	142	103	36	.741	1	81	22	5						
1903 Pit	NL	141	91	49	.650	1	91	0	4				3	5	.375
1904 Pit	NL	156	87	66	.569	4	95	-8	2						
1905 Pit	NL	155	96	57	.627	2	89	7	2						
1906 Pit	NL	154	93	60	.608	3	90	3	2						
1907 Pit	NL	157	91	63	.591	2	89	2	2						
1908 Pit	NL	155	98	56	.636	2	89	9	2						
1909 Pit	NL	154	110	42	.724	1	90	20	6				4	3	.571
1910 Pit	NL	154	86	67	.562	3	98	-12	1						
1911 Pit	NL	156	85	69	.552	3	89	-4	1						
1912 Pit	NL	153	93	58	.616	5	85	8	2						
1913 Pit	NL	155	78	71	.523	4	85	-7	1						
1914 Pit	NL	158	69	85	.448	7	82	-13	0						
1915 Pit	NL	157	73	81	.474	5	76	-3	0						
19 Years		2829	1602	1181	.576	— — —	1373	49	35				8	11	.421

Jack Clements

Born: 6/24/1864 in Philadelphia, Pennsylvania; Died: 5/23/1941; MLB Career: 17 years, 1157 G (.286-77-687)

Year Tm	Lg	G	W	L	Pct	Standing	EW	+/-	Pt	W	L	Pct	W	L	Pct
1890 Phi	NL	19	13	6	.684	1 2 3			0						

Ty Cobb

Born: 12/18/1886 in Narrows, Georgia; Died: 7/17/1961; MLB Career: 24 years, 3034 G (.366-117-1933)

Year Tm	Lg	G	W	L	Pct	Standing	EW	+/-	Pt	W	L	Pct	W	L	Pct
1921 Det	AL	154	71	82	.464	6	69	2	0						
1922 Det	AL	155	79	75	.513	3	73	6	1						
1923 Det	AL	155	83	71	.539	2	75	8	1						
1924 Det	AL	156	86	68	.558	3	80	6	1						
1925 Det	AL	156	81	73	.526	4	83	-2	1						
1926 Det	AL	157	79	75	.513	6	81	-2	1						
6 Years		933	479	444	.519	— — —	461	18	5						

Mickey Cochrane

Born: 4/6/1903 in Bridgewater, Massachusetts; Died: 6/28/1962; MLB Career: 13 years, 1482 G (.320-119-832)

Year Tm	Lg	G	W	L	Pct	Standing	EW	+/-	Pt	W	L	Pct	W	L	Pct
1934 Det	AL	154	101	53	.656	1	74	27	5				3	4	.429
1935 Det	AL	152	93	58	.616	1	87	6	5				4	2	.667
1936 Det	AL	53	29	24	.547		30	-1	0						
Det	AL	67	36	31	.537	4 2	39	-3	1						
1937 Det	AL	29	16	13	.552	3 2	16	0	0						
Det	AL	72	39	32	.549	3 2	39	0	1						
1938 Det	AL	98	47	51	.480	5 4	55	-8	0						
5 Years		625	361	262	.579	— — —	340	21	12				7	6	.538

Andy Cohen

Born: 10/25/1904 in Baltimore, Maryland; Died: 10/29/1988; MLB Career: 3 years, 262 G (.281-14-114)

Year Tm	Lg	G	W	L	Pct	Standing	EW	+/-	Pt	W	L	Pct	W	L	Pct
1960 Phi	NL	1	1	0	1.000	8 4 8	0	1	0						

Bob Coleman

Born: 9/26/1890 in Huntingburg, Indiana; Died: 7/16/1959; MLB Career: 3 years, 116 G (.241-1-27)

Year Tm	Lg	G	W	L	Pct	Standing	EW	+/-	Pt	W	L	Pct	W	L	Pct
1943 Bos	NL	46	21	25	.457	6 6	20	1	0						
1944 Bos	NL	155	65	89	.422	6	69	-4	0						
1945 Bos	NL	94	42	51	.452	7 6	41	1	0						
3 Years		295	128	165	.437	— — —	130	-2	0						

Jerry Coleman

Born: 9/14/1924 in San Jose, California; MLB Career: 9 years, 723 G (.263-16-217)

Year Tm	Lg	G	W	L	Pct	Standing	EW	+/-	Pt	W	L	Pct	W	L	Pct
1980 SD	NL	163	73	89	.451	6W	74	-1	0						

Eddie Collins

Born: 5/2/1887 in Millerton, New York; Died: 3/25/1951; MLB Career: 25 years, 2826 G (.333-47-1300)

Year Tm	Lg	G	W	L	Pct	Standing	EW	+/-	Pt	W	L	Pct	W	L	Pct
1924 ChA	AL	27	14	13	.519	6 6 8	12	2	0						
1925 ChA	AL	154	79	75	.513	5	71	8	1						
1926 ChA	AL	155	81	72	.529	5	75	6	1						
3 Years		336	174	160	.521	— — —	158	16	2						

Jimmy Collins

Born: 1/16/1870 in Buffalo, New York; Died: 3/6/1943; MLB Career: 14 years, 1728 G (.294-65-983)

Year Tm	Lg	G	W	L	Pct	Standing	EW	+/-	Pt	W	L	Pct	W	L	Pct
1901 Bos	AL	138	79	57	.581	2	68	11	2						
1902 Bos	AL	138	77	60	.562	3	74	3	1						
1903 Bos	AL	141	91	47	.659	1	75	16	5				5	3	.625
1904 Bos	AL	157	95	59	.617	1	92	3	4						
1905 Bos	AL	153	78	74	.513	4	89	-11	1						
1906 Bos	AL	115	35	79	.307	8 8	62	-27	0						
6 Years		842	455	376	.548	— — —	460	-5	13				5	3	.625

Shano Collins

Born: 12/4/1885 in Charlestown, Massachusetts; Died: 9/10/1955; MLB Career: 16 years, 1799 G (.264-22-705)

Year Tm	Lg	G	W	L	Pct	Standing	EW	+/-	Pt	W	L	Pct	W	L	Pct
1931 Bos	AL	153	62	90	.408	6	59	3	0						
1932 Bos	AL	55	11	44	.200	8 8	23	-12	0						
2 Years		208	73	134	.353	— — —	82	-9	0						

Terry Collins

Born: 5/27/1949 in Midland, Michigan; MLB Career: Did Not Play

Year Tm	Lg	G	W	L	Pct	Standing	EW	+/-	Pt	W	L	Pct	W	L	Pct
1994 Hou	NL	115	66	49	.574	2C	59	7	1						
1995 Hou	NL	144	76	68	.528	2C	78	-2	1						
1996 Hou	NL	162	82	80	.506	2C	85	-3	1						
1997 Ana	AL	162	84	78	.519	2W	75	9	1						
1 AL Year		162	84	78	.519	— — —	75	9	1						
3 NL Years		421	224	197	.532	— — —	222	2	3						
4 Years		583	308	275	.528	— — —	297	11	4						

Charlie Comiskey

Born: 8/15/1859 in Chicago, Illinois; Died: 10/26/1931; MLB Career: 13 years, 1390 G (.264-29-735)

Year Tm	Lg	G	W	L	Pct	Standing	EW	+/-	Pt	W	L	Pct	W	L	Pct
1883 STL	AA	19	12	7	.632	2 2			0						
1884 STL	AA	25	16	7	.696	5 4			0						
1885 STL	AA	112	79	33	.705	1			4				3	3	.500
1886 STL	AA	139	93	46	.669	1			5				4	2	.667
1887 STL	AA	138	95	40	.704	1			4				5	10	.333
1888 STL	AA	137	92	43	.681	1			4				4	6	.400
1889 STL	AA	141	90	45	.667	2			4						
1890 Chi	PL	138	75	62	.547	4			1						
1891 STL	AA	139	85	51	.625	2			2						
1892 Cin	NL	77	44	31	.587	4			0						
Cin	NL	78	38	37	.507	8			1						
1893 Cin	NL	131	65	63	.508	6			1						
1894 Cin	NL	134	55	75	.423	10			1						
3 NL Years		420	202	206	.495	— — —			2						
1 PL Year		138	75	62	.547	— — —			1						
8 AA Years		850	562	272	.674	— — —			21				16	21	.432
12 Years		1408	839	540	.608	— — —			24				16	21	.432

Roger Connor

Born: 7/1/1857 in Waterbury, Connecticut; Died: 1/4/1931; MLB Career: 18 years, 1997 G (.317-138-1322)

Year Tm	Lg	G	W	L	Pct	Standing	EW	+/-	Pt	W	L	Pct	W	L	Pct
1896 StL	NL	46	8	37	.178	11 11 11			0						

Dusty Cooke

Born: 6/23/1907 in Swepsonville, North Carolina; Died: 11/21/1987; MLB Career: 8 years, 608 G (.280-24-229)

Year Tm	Lg	G	W	L	Pct	Standing	EW	+/-	Pt	W	L	Pct	W	L	Pct
1948 Phi	NL	13	6	6	.500	7 6 6	5	1	0						

Jack Coombs

Born: 11/18/1882 in LeGrand, Iowa; Died: 4/15/1957; MLB Career: 14 years, 460 G (158-110, 2.78)

Year Tm	Lg	G	W	L	Pct	Standing	EW	+/-	Pt	W	L	Pct	W	L	Pct
1919 Phi	NL	63	18	44	.290	8 8	31	-13	0						

Johnny Cooney

Born: 3/18/1901 in Cranston, Rhode Island; Died: 7/8/1986; MLB Career: 20 years, 1172 G (.286-2-219)

Year Tm	Lg	G	W	L	Pct	Standing	EW	+/-	Pt	W	L	Pct	W	L	Pct
1949 Bos	NL	46	20	25	.444	4 4	25	-5	0						

Pat Corrales

Born: 3/20/1941 in Los Angeles, California; MLB Career: 9 years, 300 G (.216-4-54)

Year Tm	Lg	G	W	L	Pct	Standing	EW	+/-	Pt	W	L	Pct	W	L	Pct
1978 Tex	AL	1	1	0	1.000	2W 2W	1	0	0						
1979 Tex	AL	162	83	79	.512	3W	86	-3	1						
1980 Tex	AL	163	76	85	.472	4W	84	-8	0						
1982 Phi	NL	162	89	73	.549	2E	86	3	1						
1983 Phi	NL	86	43	42	.506	1E 1E	46	-3	0						
Cle	AL	62	30	32	.484	7E 7E	30	0	0						
1984 Cle	AL	163	75	87	.463	6E	75	0	0						
1985 Cle	AL	162	60	102	.370	7E	76	-16	0						
1986 Cle	AL	163	84	78	.519	5E	68	16	1						
1987 Cle	AL	87	31	56	.356	7E 7E	42	-11	0						
8 AL Years		963	440	519	.459	— — —	462	-22	2						
2 NL Years		248	132	115	.534	— — —	132	0	2						
9 Years		1211	572	634	.474	— — —	594	-22	3						

Red Corriden

Born: 9/4/1887 in Logansport, Indiana; Died: 9/28/1959; MLB Career: 5 years, 223 G (.205-6-47)

REGULAR SEASON							Index			Playoffs			World Series		
Year Tm	Lg	G	W	L	Pct	Standing	EW	+/-	Pt	W	L	Pct	W	L	Pct
1950 ChA	AL	125	52	72	.419	8 6	53	-1	0						

Chuck Cottier

Born: 1/8/1936 in Delta, Colorado; MLB Career: 9 years, 580 G (.220-19-127)

REGULAR SEASON							Index			Playoffs			World Series		
Year Tm	Lg	G	W	L	Pct	Standing	EW	+/-	Pt	W	L	Pct	W	L	Pct
1984 Sea	AL	27	15	12	.556	7W 6W	11	4	0						
1985 Sea	AL	162	74	88	.457	6W	74	0	0						
1986 Sea	AL	28	9	19	.321	6W 7W	13	-4	0						
3 Years		217	98	119	.452	— — —	98	0	0						

Bobby Cox

Born: 5/21/1941 in Tulsa, Oklahoma; MLB Career: 2 years, 220 G (.225-9-58)

REGULAR SEASON							Index			Playoffs			World Series		
Year Tm	Lg	G	W	L	Pct	Standing	EW	+/-	Pt	W	L	Pct	W	L	Pct
1978 Atl	NL	162	69	93	.426	6W	68	1	0						
1979 Atl	NL	160	66	94	.413	6W	70	-4	0						
1980 Atl	NL	161	81	80	.503	4W	69	12	1						
1981 Atl	NL	55	25	29	.463	4W	26	-1	0						
Atl	NL	52	25	27	.481	5W	25	0	0						
1982 Tor	AL	162	78	84	.481	6E	65	13	0						
1983 Tor	AL	162	89	73	.549	4E	76	13	1						
1984 Tor	AL	163	89	73	.549	2E	83	6	1						
1985 Tor	AL	161	99	62	.615	1E	85	14	3	3	4	.429			
1990 Atl	NL	97	40	57	.412	6W 6W	41	-1	0						
1991 Atl	NL	162	94	68	.580	1W	68	26	4	4	3	.571	3	4	.429
1992 Atl	NL	162	98	64	.605	1W	83	15	4	4	3	.571	2	4	.333
1993 Atl	NL	162	104	58	.642	1W	93	11	4	2	4	.333			
1994 Atl	NL	114	68	46	.596	2E	70	-2	2						
1995 Atl	NL	144	90	54	.625	1E	84	6	5	7	1	.875	4	2	.667
1996 Atl	NL	162	96	66	.593	1E	96	0	4	7	3	.700	2	4	.333
1997 Atl	NL	162	101	61	.623	1E	93	8	4	5	4	.556			
4 AL Years		648	355	292	.549	— — —	309	46	5	3	4	.429			
12 NL Years		1755	957	797	.546	— — —	886	71	28	29	18	.617	11	14	.440
16 Years		2403	1312	1089	.546	— — —	1195	117	33	32	22	.593	11	14	.440

Harry Craft

Born: 4/19/1915 in Ellisville, Mississippi; Died: 8/3/1995; MLB Career: 6 years, 566 G (.253-44-267)

REGULAR SEASON							Index			Playoffs			World Series		
Year Tm	Lg	G	W	L	Pct	Standing	EW	+/-	Pt	W	L	Pct	W	L	Pct
1957 KCA	AL	50	23	27	.460	8 7	19	4	0						
1958 KCA	AL	156	73	81	.474	7	63	10	0						
1959 KCA	AL	154	66	88	.429	7	70	-4	0						
1961 ChN	NL	12	4	8	.333	6 7 7	5	-1	0						
ChN	NL	6	3	1	.750	7 7 7	2	1	0						
1962 Hou	NL	162	64	96	.400	8	60	4	0						
1963 Hou	NL	162	66	96	.407	9	66	0	0						
1964 Hou	NL	149	61	88	.409	9 9	63	-2	0						
3 AL Years		360	162	196	.453	— — —	152	10	0						
4 NL Years		491	198	289	.407	— — —	196	2	0						
7 Years		851	360	485	.426	— — —	348	12	0						

Roger Craig

Born: 2/17/1930 in Durham, North Carolina; MLB Career: 12 years, 368 G (74-98, 3.83)

REGULAR SEASON							Index			Playoffs			World Series		
Year Tm	Lg	G	W	L	Pct	Standing	EW	+/-	Pt	W	L	Pct	W	L	Pct
1978 SD	NL	162	84	78	.519	4W	73	11	1						
1979 SD	NL	161	68	93	.422	5W	80	-12	0						
1985 SF	NL	18	6	12	.333	6W 6W	8	-2	0						
1986 SF	NL	162	83	79	.512	3W	69	14	1						
1987 SF	NL	162	90	72	.556	1W	78	12	2	3	4	.429			
1988 SF	NL	162	83	79	.512	4W	83	0	1						
1989 SF	NL	162	92	70	.568	1W	83	9	4	4	1	.800	0	4	.000
1990 SF	NL	162	85	77	.525	3W	88	-3	1						
1991 SF	NL	162	75	87	.463	4W	85	-10	0						
1992 SF	NL	162	72	90	.444	5W	80	-8	0						
10 Years		1475	738	737	.500	— — —	727	11	10	7	5	.583	0	4	.000

Del Crandall

Born: 3/5/1930 in Ontario, California; MLB Career: 16 years, 1573 G (.254-179-657)

REGULAR SEASON							Index			Playoffs			World Series		
Year Tm	Lg	G	W	L	Pct	Standing	EW	+/-	Pt	W	L	Pct	W	L	Pct
1972 Mil	AL	124	54	70	.435	6E 6E	54	0	0						
1973 Mil	AL	162	74	88	.457	5E	71	3	0						
1974 Mil	AL	162	76	86	.469	5E	74	2	0						
1975 Mil	AL	161	67	94	.416	5E 5E	76	-9	0						
1983 Sea	AL	89	34	55	.382	7W 7W	41	-7	0						
1984 Sea	AL	135	59	76	.437	7W 6W	57	2	0						
6 Years		833	364	469	.437	— — —	373	-9	0						

Sam Crane

Born: 1/2/1854 in Springfield, Massachusetts; Died: 6/26/1925; MLB Career: 7 years, 373 G (.203-3-45)

REGULAR SEASON							Index			Playoffs			World Series		
Year Tm	Lg	G	W	L	Pct	Standing	EW	+/-	Pt	W	L	Pct	W	L	Pct
1880 Buf	NL	85	24	58	.293	7			0						
1884 Cin	UA	70	49	21	.700	5 3			2						
1 NL Year		85	24	58	.293	— — —			0						
1 UA Year		70	49	21	.700	— — —			2						
2 Years		155	73	79	.480	— — —			2						

Gavvy Cravath

Born: 3/23/1881 in Escondido, California; Died: 5/23/1963; MLB Career: 11 years, 1221 G (.287-119-719)

REGULAR SEASON							Index			Playoffs			World Series		
Year Tm	Lg	G	W	L	Pct	Standing	EW	+/-	Pt	W	L	Pct	W	L	Pct
1919 Phi	NL	75	29	46	.387	8 8	37	-8	0						
1920 Phi	NL	153	62	91	.405	8	65	-3	0						
2 Years		228	91	137	.399	— — —	102	-11	0						

Bill Craver

Born: 6/1/1844 in Troy, New York; Died: 6/17/1901; MLB Career: 2 years, 113 G (.244-0-51)

REGULAR SEASON							Index			Playoffs			World Series		
Year Tm	Lg	G	W	L	Pct	Standing	EW	+/-	Pt	W	L	Pct	W	L	Pct
1876 NYM	NL	57	21	35	.375	6			0						

George Creamer

Born: Unknown in Philadelphia, Pennsylvania; Died: 6/27/1886; MLB Career: 7 years, 500 G (.215-1-99)

REGULAR SEASON							Index			Playoffs			World Series		
Year Tm	Lg	G	W	L	Pct	Standing	EW	+/-	Pt	W	L	Pct	W	L	Pct
1884 Pit	AA	8	0	8	.000	12 12 11			0						

Joe Cronin

Born: 10/12/1906 in San Francisco, California; Died: 9/7/1984; MLB Career: 20 years, 2124 G (.301-170-1424)

REGULAR SEASON							Index			Playoffs			World Series		
Year Tm	Lg	G	W	L	Pct	Standing	EW	+/-	Pt	W	L	Pct	W	L	Pct
1933 Was	AL	153	99	53	.651	1	88	11	4				1	4	.200
1934 Was	AL	155	66	86	.434	7	91	-25	0						
1935 Bos	AL	154	78	75	.510	4	71	7	1						
1936 Bos	AL	155	74	80	.481	6	76	-2	0						
1937 Bos	AL	154	80	72	.526	5	75	5	1						
1938 Bos	AL	150	88	61	.591	2	76	12	2						
1939 Bos	AL	152	89	62	.589	2	82	7	2						
1940 Bos	AL	154	82	72	.532	4	86	-4	1						
1941 Bos	AL	154	84	70	.545	2	83	1	1						
1942 Bos	AL	152	93	59	.612	2	82	11	2						
1943 Bos	AL	155	68	84	.447	7	86	-18	0						
1944 Bos	AL	156	77	77	.500	4	76	1	0						
1945 Bos	AL	157	71	83	.461	7	78	-7	0						
1946 Bos	AL	156	104	50	.675	1	73	31	5				3	4	.429
1947 Bos	AL	157	83	71	.539	3	90	-7	1						
15 Years		2314	1236	1055	.540	— — —	1213	23	20				4	8	.333

Jack Crooks

Born: 11/9/1865 in St. Paul, Minnesota; Died: 2/2/1918; MLB Career: 8 years, 794 G (.240-21-313)

REGULAR SEASON							Index			Playoffs			World Series		
Year Tm	Lg	G	W	L	Pct	Standing	EW	+/-	Pt	W	L	Pct	W	L	Pct
1892 StL	NL	47	24	22	.522	11 9			0						
StL	NL	15	3	11	.214	12 11			0						
1 Year		62	27	33	.450	— — —			0						

Lave Cross

Born: 5/12/1866 in Milwaukee, Wisconsin; Died: 9/6/1927; MLB Career: 21 years, 2275 G (.292-47-1371)

REGULAR SEASON							Index			Playoffs			World Series		
Year Tm	Lg	G	W	L	Pct	Standing	EW	+/-	Pt	W	L	Pct	W	L	Pct
1899 Cle	NL	38	8	30	.211	12 12			0						

Mike Cubbage

Born: 7/21/1950 in Charlottesville, Virginia; MLB Career: 8 years, 703 G (.258-34-251)

REGULAR SEASON							Index			Playoffs			World Series		
Year Tm	Lg	G	W	L	Pct	Standing	EW	+/-	Pt	W	L	Pct	W	L	Pct
1991 NYN	NL	7	3	4	.429	3E 5E	4	-1	0						

Ed Curtis

Born: Unknown; MLB Career: Did Not Play

REGULAR SEASON							Index			Playoffs			World Series		
Year Tm	Lg	G	W	L	Pct	Standing	EW	+/-	Pt	W	L	Pct	W	L	Pct
1884 Alt	UA	25	6	19	.240	11			0						

Charlie Cushman

Born: 5/25/1850 in New York, New York; Died: 6/29/1909; MLB Career: Did Not Play

REGULAR SEASON							Index			Playoffs			World Series		
Year Tm	Lg	G	W	L	Pct	Standing	EW	+/-	Pt	W	L	Pct	W	L	Pct
1891 Mil	AA	36	21	15	.583	3			0						

Ned Cuthbert

Born: 6/20/1845 in Philadelphia, Pennsylvania; Died: 2/6/1905; MLB Career: 5 years, 200 G (.219-0-27)

REGULAR SEASON							Index			Playoffs			World Series		
Year Tm	Lg	G	W	L	Pct	Standing	EW	+/-	Pt	W	L	Pct	W	L	Pct
1882 STL	AA	80	37	43	.463	**5**			0						

Bill Dahlen

Born: 1/5/1870 in Nelliston, New York; Died: 12/5/1950; MLB Career: 21 years, 2443 G (.272-84-1233)

REGULAR SEASON							Index			Playoffs			World Series		
Year Tm	Lg	G	W	L	Pct	Standing	EW	+/-	Pt	W	L	Pct	W	L	Pct
1910 Bro	NL	156	64	90	.416	**6**	62	2	0						
1911 Bro	NL	154	64	86	.427	**7**	63	1	0						
1912 Bro	NL	153	58	95	.379	**7**	67	-9	0						
1913 Bro	NL	152	65	84	.436	**6**	62	3	0						
4 Years		615	251	355	.414	— — —	254	-3	0						

Alvin Dark

Born: 1/7/1922 in Comanche, Oklahoma; MLB Career: 14 years, 1828 G (.289-126-757)

REGULAR SEASON							Index			Playoffs			World Series		
Year Tm	Lg	G	W	L	Pct	Standing	EW	+/-	Pt	W	L	Pct	W	L	Pct
1961 SF	NL	155	85	69	.552	**3**	79	6	1						
1962 SF	NL	165	103	62	.624	**1**	93	10	5				3	4	.429
1963 SF	NL	162	88	74	.543	**3**	95	-7	1						
1964 SF	NL	162	90	72	.556	**4**	89	1	1						
1966 KCA	AL	160	74	86	.463	**7**	65	9	0						
1967 KCA	AL	121	52	69	.430	**10** 10	54	-2	0						
1968 Cle	AL	162	86	75	.534	**3**	78	8	1						
1969 Cle	AL	161	62	99	.385	**6E**	86	-24	0						
1970 Cle	AL	162	76	86	.469	**5E**	73	3	0						
1971 Cle	AL	103	42	61	.408	**6E** 6E	50	-8	0						
1974 Oak	AL	162	90	72	.556	**1W**	92	-2	4	3	1	.750	4	1	.800
1975 Oak	AL	162	98	64	.605	**1W**	89	9	3	0	3	.000			
1977 SD	NL	113	48	65	.425	5W **5W**	51	-3	0						
8 AL Years		1193	580	612	.487	— — —	587	-7	8	3	4	.429	4	1	.800
5 NL Years		757	414	342	.548	— — —	407	7	8				3	4	.429
13 Years		1950	994	954	.510	— — —	994	0	16	3	4	.429	7	5	.583

Jim Davenport

Born: 8/17/1933 in Siluria, Alabama; MLB Career: 13 years, 1501 G (.258-77-456)

REGULAR SEASON							Index			Playoffs			World Series		
Year Tm	Lg	G	W	L	Pct	Standing	EW	+/-	Pt	W	L	Pct	W	L	Pct
1985 SF	NL	144	56	88	.389	**6W** 6W	66	-10	0						

Mordecai Davidson

Born: 11/30/1846 in Port Washington, Ohio; Died: 9/6/1940; MLB Career: Did Not Play

REGULAR SEASON							Index			Playoffs			World Series		
Year Tm	Lg	G	W	L	Pct	Standing	EW	+/-	Pt	W	L	Pct	W	L	Pct
1888 Lou	AA	3	1	2	.333	8 **8** 7			0						
Lou	AA	90	34	52	.395	8 **7**			0						
1 Year		93	35	54	.393	— — —			0						

George Davis

Born: 7/19/1873 in Philadelphia, Pennsylvania; Died: 8/11/1947; MLB Career: 20 years, 2368 G (.295-73-1437)

REGULAR SEASON							Index			Playoffs			World Series		
Year Tm	Lg	G	W	L	Pct	Standing	EW	+/-	Pt	W	L	Pct	W	L	Pct
1895 NYG	NL	33	16	17	.485	**8** 9			0						
1900 NYG	NL	78	39	37	.513	8 **8**	38	1	1						
1901 NYG	NL	141	52	85	.380	**7**	64	-12	0						
3 Years		252	107	139	.435	— — —	102	-11	1						

Harry Davis

Born: 7/19/1873 in Philadelphia, Pennsylvania; Died: 8/11/1947; MLB Career: 22 years, 1755 G (.276-75-952)

REGULAR SEASON							Index			Playoffs			World Series		
Year Tm	Lg	G	W	L	Pct	Standing	EW	+/-	Pt	W	L	Pct	W	L	Pct
1912 Cle	AL	127	54	71	.432	**6** 5	63	-9	0						

Spud Davis

Born: 12/20/1904 in Birmingham, Alabama; Died: 8/14/1984; MLB Career: 16 years, 1458 G (.308-77-647)

REGULAR SEASON							Index			Playoffs			World Series		
Year Tm	Lg	G	W	L	Pct	Standing	EW	+/-	Pt	W	L	Pct	W	L	Pct
1946 Pit	NL	3	1	2	.333	7 **7**	2	-1	0						

John Day

Born: 9/23/1847 in Colchester, Connecticut; Died: 1/25/1925; MLB Career: Did Not Play

REGULAR SEASON							Index			Playoffs			World Series		
Year Tm	Lg	G	W	L	Pct	Standing	EW	+/-	Pt	W	L	Pct	W	L	Pct
1899 NYG	NL	66	29	35	.453	**9** 10			0						

Bucky Dent

Born: 11/25/1951 in Savannah, Georgia; MLB Career: 12 years, 1392 G (.247-40-423)

REGULAR SEASON							Index			Playoffs			World Series		
Year Tm	Lg	G	W	L	Pct	Standing	EW	+/-	Pt	W	L	Pct	W	L	Pct
1989 NYA	AL	40	18	22	.450	6E **5E**	21	-3	0						
1990 NYA	AL	49	18	31	.367	**7E** 7E	24	-6	0						
2 Years		89	36	53	.404	— — —	45	-9	0						

Bill Dickey

Born: 6/6/1907 in Bastrop, Louisiana; Died: 11/12/1993; MLB Career: 17 years, 1789 G (.313-202-1209)

REGULAR SEASON							Index			Playoffs			World Series		
Year Tm	Lg	G	W	L	Pct	Standing	EW	+/-	Pt	W	L	Pct	W	L	Pct
1946 NYA	AL	105	57	48	.543	2 **3** 3	57	0	0						

Harry Diddlebock

Born: 6/27/1854 in Philadelphia, Pennsylvania; Died: 2/5/1900; MLB Career: Did Not Play

REGULAR SEASON							Index			Playoffs			World Series		
Year Tm	Lg	G	W	L	Pct	Standing	EW	+/-	Pt	W	L	Pct	W	L	Pct
1896 StL	NL	17	7	10	.412	**10** 11			0						

Larry Dierker

Born: 9/22/1946 in Hollywood, California; MLB Career: 14 years, 357 G (139-123, 3.31)

REGULAR SEASON							Index			Playoffs			World Series		
Year Tm	Lg	G	W	L	Pct	Standing	EW	+/-	Pt	W	L	Pct	W	L	Pct
1997 Hou	NL	162	84	78	.519	**1C**	83	1	2	0	3	.000			

Larry Doby

Born: 12/13/1923 in Camden, South Carolina; MLB Career: 13 years, 1533 G (.283-253-970)

REGULAR SEASON							Index			Playoffs			World Series		
Year Tm	Lg	G	W	L	Pct	Standing	EW	+/-	Pt	W	L	Pct	W	L	Pct
1978 ChA	AL	87	37	50	.425	5W **5W**	45	-8	0						

Patsy Donovan

Born: 3/16/1865 in Queenstown, Ireland; Died: 12/25/1953; MLB Career: 17 years, 1821 G (.301-16-736)

REGULAR SEASON							Index			Playoffs			World Series		
Year Tm	Lg	G	W	L	Pct	Standing	EW	+/-	Pt	W	L	Pct	W	L	Pct
1897 Pit	NL	135	60	71	.458	**8**			0						
1899 Pit	NL	131	69	58	.543	10 **7**			1						
1901 StL	NL	142	76	64	.543	**4**	68	8	1						
1902 StL	NL	140	56	78	.418	**6**	69	-13	0						
1903 StL	NL	139	43	94	.314	**8**	63	-20	0						
1904 Was	AL	139	37	97	.276	8 **8**	53	-16	0						
1906 Bro	NL	153	66	86	.434	**5**	59	7	0						
1907 Bro	NL	153	65	83	.439	**5**	63	2	0						
1908 Bro	NL	154	53	101	.344	**7**	68	-15	0						
1910 Bos	AL	158	81	72	.529	**4**	81	0	1						
1911 Bos	AL	153	78	75	.510	**5**	80	-2	1						
3 AL Years		450	196	244	.445	— — —	214	-18	2						
8 NL Years		1147	488	635	.435	— — —	390	-31	2						
11 Years		1597	684	879	.438	— — —	604	-49	4						

Wild Bill Donovan

Born: 10/13/1876 in Lawrence, Massachusetts; Died: 12/9/1923; MLB Career: 18 years, 461 G (186-139, 2.69)

REGULAR SEASON							Index			Playoffs			World Series		
Year Tm	Lg	G	W	L	Pct	Standing	EW	+/-	Pt	W	L	Pct	W	L	Pct
1915 NYA	AL	154	69	83	.454	**5**	67	2	0						
1916 NYA	AL	156	80	74	.519	**4**	70	10	1						
1917 NYA	AL	155	71	82	.464	**6**	76	-5	0						
1921 Phi	NL	87	25	62	.287	**8** 8	37	-12	0						
3 AL Years		465	220	239	.479	— — —	213	7	1						
1 NL Year		87	25	62	.287	— — —	37	-12	0						
4 Years		552	245	301	.449	— — —	250	-5	1						

Red Dooin

Born: 6/12/1879 in Cincinnati, Ohio; Died: 5/12/1952; MLB Career: 15 years, 1286 G (.240-10-344)

REGULAR SEASON							Index			Playoffs			World Series		
Year Tm	Lg	G	W	L	Pct	Standing	EW	+/-	Pt	W	L	Pct	W	L	Pct
1910 Phi	NL	157	78	75	.510	**4**	77	1	1						
1911 Phi	NL	153	79	73	.520	**4**	77	2	1						
1912 Phi	NL	152	73	79	.480	**5**	77	-4	0						
1913 Phi	NL	159	88	63	.583	**2**	75	13	2						
1914 Phi	NL	154	74	80	.481	**6**	83	-9	0						
5 Years		775	392	370	.514	— — —	389	3	4						

Mike Dorgan

Born: 10/2/1853 in Middletown, Connecticut; Died: 4/26/1909; MLB Career: 10 years, 715 G (.274-4-346)

REGULAR SEASON							Index			Playoffs			World Series		
Year Tm	Lg	G	W	L	Pct	Standing	EW	+/-	Pt	W	L	Pct	W	L	Pct
1879 Syr	NL	43	17	26	.395	**6** 7			0						
1880 Prv	NL	39	26	12	.684	3 **2**			0						
1881 Wor	NL	56	24	32	.429	**7** 8			0						
3 Years		138	67	70	.489	— — —			0						

Tommy Dowd

Born: 4/20/1869 in Holyoke, Massachusetts; Died: 7/2/1933; MLB Career: 10 years, 1320 G (.271-24-501)

REGULAR SEASON							Index			Playoffs			World Series		
Year Tm	Lg	G	W	L	Pct	Standing	EW	+/-	Pt	W	L	Pct	W	L	Pct
1896 StL	NL	63	25	38	.397	11 **11**			0						
1897 StL	NL	29	6	22	.214	**12** 12			0						
2 Years		92	31	60	.341	— — —			0						

Jack Doyle

Born: 10/25/1869 in Killorglin, Ireland; Died: 12/31/1958; MLB Career: 17 years, 1564 G (.299-26-968)

REGULAR SEASON							Index			Playoffs			World Series		
Year Tm	Lg	G	W	L	Pct	Standing	EW	+/-	Pt	W	L	Pct	W	L	Pct
1895 NYG	NL	64	32	31	.508	8 **9** 9			0						
1898 Was	NL	17	8	9	.471	11 **10** 11			0						
2 Years		81	40	40	.500	— — —			0						

Chuck Dressen

Born: 9/20/1898 in Decatur, Illinois; Died: 8/10/1966; MLB Career: 8 years, 646 G (.272-11-221)

REGULAR SEASON							Index			Playoffs			World Series		
Year Tm	Lg	G	W	L	Pct	Standing	EW	+/-	Pt	W	L	Pct	W	L	Pct
1934 Cin	NL	60	21	39	.350	8 **8**	25	-4	0						
1935 Cin	NL	154	68	85	.444	**6**	60	8	0						
1936 Cin	NL	154	74	80	.481	**5**	67	7	0						
1937 Cin	NL	130	51	78	.395	**8** 8	60	-9	0						
1951 Bro	NL	158	97	60	.618	**2**	88	9	2						
1952 Bro	NL	155	96	57	.627	**1**	90	6	4				3	4	.429
1953 Bro	NL	155	105	49	.682	**1**	91	14	5				2	4	.333
1955 Was	AL	154	53	101	.344	**8**	72	-19	0						
1956 Was	AL	155	59	95	.383	**7**	64	-5	0						
1957 Was	AL	20	4	16	.200	**8** 8	8	-4	0						
1960 Mil	NL	154	88	66	.571	**2**	85	3	2						
1961 Mil	NL	130	71	58	.550	**3** 4	72	-1	0						
1963 Det	AL	102	55	47	.539	9 **5**	54	1	1						
1964 Det	AL	163	85	77	.525	**4**	83	2	1						
1965 Det	AL	120	65	55	.542	3 **4**	62	3	1						
1966 Det	AL	26	16	10	.615	**3** 3	14	2	0						
7 AL Years		740	337	401	.457	— — —	357	-20	3						
9 NL Years		1250	671	572	.540	— — —	638	33	13				5	8	.385
16 Years		1990	1008	973	.509	— — —	995	13	16				5	8	.385

Hugh Duffy

Born: 11/26/1866 in Cranston, Rhode Island; Died: 10/19/1954; MLB Career: 17 years, 1737 G (.324-106-1302)

REGULAR SEASON							Index			Playoffs			World Series		
Year Tm	Lg	G	W	L	Pct	Standing	EW	+/-	Pt	W	L	Pct	W	L	Pct
1901 Mil	AL	139	48	89	.350	**8**	69	-21	0						
1904 Phi	NL	155	52	100	.342	**8**	66	-14	0						
1905 Phi	NL	155	83	69	.546	**4**	60	23	1						
1906 Phi	NL	154	71	82	.464	**4**	75	-4	0						
1910 ChA	AL	156	68	85	.444	**6**	80	-12	0						
1911 ChA	AL	154	77	74	.510	**4**	73	4	1						
1921 Bos	AL	154	75	79	.487	**5**	76	-1	0						
1922 Bos	AL	154	61	93	.396	**8**	75	-14	0						
5 AL Years		757	329	420	.439	— — —	373	-44	1						
3 NL Years		464	206	251	.451	— — —	201	5	1						
8 Years		1221	535	671	.444	— — —	574	-39	2						

Fred Dunlap

Born: 5/21/1859 in Philadelphia, Pennsylvania; Died: 12/1/1902; MLB Career: 12 years, 965 G (.292-41-366)

REGULAR SEASON							Index			Playoffs			World Series		
Year Tm	Lg	G	W	L	Pct	Standing	EW	+/-	Pt	W	L	Pct	W	L	Pct
1882 Cle	NL	80	42	36	.538	8 **5**			1						
1884 STL	UA	83	66	16	.805	1 **1**			4						
1885 StL	NL	50	21	29	.420	**5** 8			0						
StL	NL	22	9	11	.450	8 **8**			0						
1889 Pit	NL	17	7	10	.412	7 **7** 5			0						
3 NL Years		169	79	86	.479	— — —			1						
1 UA Year		83	66	16	.805	— — —			4						
4 Years		252	145	102	.587	— — —			5						

Leo Durocher

Born: 7/27/1905 in West Springfield, Mass.; Died: 10/7/1991; MLB Career: 17 years, 1637 G (.247-24-567)

REGULAR SEASON							Index			Playoffs			World Series		
Year Tm	Lg	G	W	L	Pct	Standing	EW	+/-	Pt	W	L	Pct	W	L	Pct
1939 Bro	NL	157	84	69	.549	**3**	71	13	1						
1940 Bro	NL	156	88	65	.575	**2**	78	10	2						
1941 Bro	NL	157	100	54	.649	**1**	83	17	5				1	4	.200
1942 Bro	NL	155	104	50	.675	**2**	91	13	3						
1943 Bro	NL	153	81	72	.529	**3**	94	-13	1						
1944 Bro	NL	155	63	91	.409	**7**	86	-23	0						
1945 Bro	NL	155	87	67	.565	**3**	74	13	2						
1946 Bro	NL	157	96	60	.615	**2**	82	14	2						
1948 Bro	NL	73	35	37	.486	**5** 3	42	-7	0						
NYG	NL	79	41	38	.519	4 **5**	40	1	1						
1949 NYG	NL	156	73	81	.474	**5**	76	-3	0						
1950 NYG	NL	154	86	68	.558	**3**	76	10	1						
1951 NYG	NL	157	98	59	.624	**1**	83	15	4				2	4	.333
1952 NYG	NL	154	92	62	.597	**2**	87	5	2						
1953 NYG	NL	155	70	84	.455	**5**	88	-18	0						
1954 NYG	NL	154	97	57	.630	**1**	78	19	5				4	0	1.000
1955 NYG	NL	154	80	74	.519	**3**	88	-8	1						
1966 ChN	NL	162	59	103	.364	**10**	76	-17	0						
1967 ChN	NL	162	87	74	.540	**3**	68	19	1						
1968 ChN	NL	163	84	78	.519	**3**	80	4	1						
1969 ChN	NL	163	92	70	.568	**2E**	85	7	2						
1970 ChN	NL	162	84	78	.519	**2E**	89	-5	1						
1971 ChN	NL	162	83	79	.512	**3E**	85	-2	1						
1972 ChN	NL	91	46	44	.511	**4E** 2E	47	-1	0						
Hou	NL	31	16	15	.516	2W **2W**	15	1	0						
1973 Hou	NL	162	82	80	.506	**4W**	84	-2	1						
24 Years		3739	2008	1709	.540	— — —	1946	62	37				7	8	.467

Frank Dwyer

Born: 3/25/1868 in Lee, Massachusetts; Died: 2/4/1943; MLB Career: 12 years, 393 G (176-152, 3.84)

REGULAR SEASON							Index			Playoffs			World Series		
Year Tm	Lg	G	W	L	Pct	Standing	EW	+/-	Pt	W	L	Pct	W	L	Pct
1902 Det	AL	137	52	83	.385	**7**	71	-19	0						

Eddie Dyer

Born: 10/11/1900 in Morgan City, Louisiana; Died: 4/20/1964; MLB Career: 6 years, 129 G (15-15, 4.75)

REGULAR SEASON							Index			Playoffs			World Series		
Year Tm	Lg	G	W	L	Pct	Standing	EW	+/-	Pt	W	L	Pct	W	L	Pct
1946 StL	NL	156	98	58	.628	**1**	94	4	5				4	3	.571
1947 StL	NL	156	89	65	.578	**2**	93	-4	2						
1948 StL	NL	155	85	69	.552	**2**	88	-3	1						
1949 StL	NL	157	96	58	.623	**2**	85	11	2						
1950 StL	NL	153	78	75	.510	**5**	88	-10	1						
5 Years		777	446	325	.578	— — —	448	-2	11				4	3	.571

Jimmy Dykes

Born: 11/10/1896 in Philadelphia, Pa.; Died: 6/15/1976; MLB Career: 22 years, 2282 G (.280-108-1071)

REGULAR SEASON							Index			Playoffs			World Series		
Year Tm	Lg	G	W	L	Pct	Standing	EW	+/-	Pt	W	L	Pct	W	L	Pct
1934 ChA	AL	138	49	88	.358	8 **8**	60	-11	0						
1935 ChA	AL	153	74	78	.487	**5**	60	14	0						
1936 ChA	AL	153	81	70	.536	**3**	71	10	1						
1937 ChA	AL	154	86	68	.558	**3**	77	9	1						
1938 ChA	AL	149	65	83	.439	**6**	79	-14	0						
1939 ChA	AL	155	85	69	.552	**4**	74	11	1						
1940 ChA	AL	155	82	72	.532	**4**	81	1	1						
1941 ChA	AL	156	77	77	.500	**3**	79	-2	0						
1942 ChA	AL	148	66	82	.446	**6**	76	-10	0						
1943 ChA	AL	155	82	72	.532	**4**	74	8	1						
1944 ChA	AL	154	71	83	.461	**7**	79	-8	0						
1945 ChA	AL	150	71	78	.477	**6**	71	0	0						
1946 ChA	AL	30	10	20	.333	**7** 5	15	-5	0						
1951 Phi	AL	154	70	84	.455	**6**	66	4	0						
1952 Phi	AL	155	79	75	.513	**4**	71	8	1						
1953 Phi	AL	157	59	95	.383	**7**	74	-15	0						
1954 Bal	AL	154	54	100	.351	**7**	61	-7	0						
1958 Cin	NL	41	24	17	.585	7 **4**	21	3	0						
1959 Det	AL	137	74	63	.540	8 **4**	69	5	1						
1960 Det	AL	96	44	52	.458	**6** 6	48	-4	0						
Cle	AL	58	26	32	.448	4 **4**	31	-5	0						
1961 Cle	AL	160	77	83	.481	**5** 5	86	-9	0						
21 AL Years		2921	1382	1524	.476	— — —	1402	-20	7						
1 NL Year		41	24	17	.585	— — —	21	3	0						
21 Years		2962	1406	1541	.477	— — —	1423	-17	7						

Charlie Ebbets

Born: 10/29/1859 in New York, New York; Died: 4/18/1925; MLB Career: Did Not Play

REGULAR SEASON							Index			Playoffs			World Series		
Year Tm	Lg	G	W	L	Pct	Standing	EW	+/-	Pt	W	L	Pct	W	L	Pct
1898 Bro	NL	110	38	68	.358	9 **10**			0						

Doc Edwards

Born: 12/10/1936 in Red Jacket, West Virginia; MLB Career: 5 years, 317 G (.238-15-87)

REGULAR SEASON							Index			Playoffs			World Series		
Year Tm	Lg	G	W	L	Pct	Standing	EW	+/-	Pt	W	L	Pct	W	L	Pct
1987 Cle	AL	75	30	45	.400	7E **7E**	37	-7	0						
1988 Cle	AL	162	78	84	.481	**6E**	69	9	0						
1989 Cle	AL	143	65	78	.455	**6E** 6E	68	-3	0						
3 Years		380	173	207	.455	— — —	174	-1	0						

Kid Elberfeld

Born: 4/13/1875 in Pomeroy, Ohio; Died: 1/13/1944; MLB Career: 14 years, 1292 G (.271-10-535)

REGULAR SEASON							Index			Playoffs			World Series		
Year Tm	Lg	G	W	L	Pct	Standing	EW	+/-	Pt	W	L	Pct	W	L	Pct
1908 NYA	AL	98	27	71	.276	6 **8**	49	-22	0						

Lee Elia

Born: 7/16/1937 in Philadelphia, Pennsylvania; MLB Career: 2 years, 95 G (.203-3-25)

REGULAR SEASON							Index			Playoffs			World Series		
Year Tm	Lg	G	W	L	Pct	Standing	EW	+/-	Pt	W	L	Pct	W	L	Pct
1982 ChN	NL	162	73	89	.451	**5E**	70	3	0						
1983 ChN	NL	123	54	69	.439	**5E** 5E	55	-1	0						
1987 Phi	NL	101	51	50	.505	5E **4E**	52	-1	1						
1988 Phi	NL	153	60	92	.395	**6E** 6E	75	-15	0						
4 Years		539	238	300	.442	— — —	252	-14	1						

Joe Ellick

Born: 4/3/1854 in Cincinnati, Ohio; Died: 4/21/1923; MLB Career: 3 years, 109 G (.217-0-1)

REGULAR SEASON							Index			Playoffs			World Series		
Year Tm	Lg	G	W	L	Pct	Standing	EW	+/-	Pt	W	L	Pct	W	L	Pct
1884 Pit	UA	13	6	6	.500	**8** 8			0						

Bob Elliott

Born: 11/26/1916 in San Francisco, California; Died: 5/4/1966; MLB Career: 15 years, 1978 G (.289-170-1195)

REGULAR SEASON							Index			Playoffs			World Series		
Year Tm	Lg	G	W	L	Pct	Standing	EW	+/-	Pt	W	L	Pct	W	L	Pct
1960 KCA	AL	155	58	96	.377	8	69	-11	0						

Jewel Ens

Born: 8/24/1889 in St. Louis, Missouri; Died: 1/17/1950; MLB Career: 4 years, 67 G (.290-1-24)

REGULAR SEASON							Index			Playoffs			World Series		
Year Tm	Lg	G	W	L	Pct	Standing	EW	+/-	Pt	W	L	Pct	W	L	Pct
1929 Pit	NL	35	21	14	.600	2 2	19	2	0						
1930 Pit	NL	154	80	74	.519	5	86	-6	1						
1931 Pit	NL	155	75	79	.487	5	81	-6	0						
3 Years		344	176	167	.513	— —	186	-10	1						

Cal Ermer

Born: 11/10/1923 in Baltimore, Maryland; MLB Career: 1 year, 1 G (.000-0-0)

REGULAR SEASON							Index			Playoffs			World Series		
Year Tm	Lg	G	W	L	Pct	Standing	EW	+/-	Pt	W	L	Pct	W	L	Pct
1967 Min	AL	114	66	46	.589	6 2	60	6	2						
1968 Min	AL	162	79	83	.488	7	90	-11	0						
2 Years		276	145	129	.529	— —	150	-5	2						

Jim Essian

Born: 1/2/1951 in Detroit, Michigan; MLB Career: 12 years, 710 G (.244-33-207)

REGULAR SEASON							Index			Playoffs			World Series		
Year Tm	Lg	G	W	L	Pct	Standing	EW	+/-	Pt	W	L	Pct	W	L	Pct
1991 ChN	NL	122	59	63	.484	5E 4E	60	-1	0						

Dude Esterbrook

Born: 6/9/1857 in Staten Island, New York; Died: 4/30/1901; MLB Career: 11 years, 701 G (.261-6-210)

REGULAR SEASON							Index			Playoffs			World Series		
Year Tm	Lg	G	W	L	Pct	Standing	EW	+/-	Pt	W	L	Pct	W	L	Pct
1889 Lou	AA	10	2	8	.200	8 8			0						

Johnny Evers

Born: 7/21/1881 in Troy, New York; Died: 3/28/1947; MLB Career: 18 years, 1784 G (.270-12-538)

REGULAR SEASON							Index			Playoffs			World Series		
Year Tm	Lg	G	W	L	Pct	Standing	EW	+/-	Pt	W	L	Pct	W	L	Pct
1913 ChN	NL	155	88	65	.575	3	90	-2	2						
1921 ChN	NL	96	41	55	.427	6 7	49	-8	0						
1924 ChA	AL	21	10	11	.476	6 8	10	0	0						
ChA	AL	103	41	61	.402	6 8	47	-6	0						
1 AL Year		124	51	72	.415	— —	57	-6	0						
2 NL Years		251	129	120	.518	— —	139	-10	2						
3 Years		375	180	192	.484	— —	196	-16	2						

Buck Ewing

Born: 10/17/1859 in Hoagland, Ohio; Died: 10/20/1906; MLB Career: 18 years, 1315 G (.303-71-883)

REGULAR SEASON							Index			Playoffs			World Series		
Year Tm	Lg	G	W	L	Pct	Standing	EW	+/-	Pt	W	L	Pct	W	L	Pct
1890 NY	PL	132	74	57	.565	3			1						
1895 Cin	NL	132	66	64	.508	8			1						
1896 Cin	NL	128	77	50	.606	3			2						
1897 Cin	NL	134	76	56	.576	4			2						
1898 Cin	NL	157	92	60	.605	3			2						
1899 Cin	NL	157	83	67	.553	6			1						
1900 NYG	NL	63	21	41	.339	8 8	31	-10	0						
6 NL Years		771	415	338	.551	— —	31	-10	8						
1 PL Year		132	74	57	.565	— —			1						
7 Years		903	489	395	.553	— —	31	-10	9						

Jay Faatz

Born: 10/24/1860 in Weedsport, New York; Died: 4/10/1923; MLB Career: 4 years, 298 G (.241-3-105)

REGULAR SEASON							Index			Playoffs			World Series		
Year Tm	Lg	G	W	L	Pct	Standing	EW	+/-	Pt	W	L	Pct	W	L	Pct
1890 Buf	PL	34	9	24	.273	8 8			0						

Bibb Falk

Born: 1/27/1899 in Austin, Texas; Died: 6/8/1989; MLB Career: 12 years, 1354 G (.314-69-785)

REGULAR SEASON							Index			Playoffs			World Series		
Year Tm	Lg	G	W	L	Pct	Standing	EW	+/-	Pt	W	L	Pct	W	L	Pct
1933 Cle	AL	1	1	0	1.000	5 5 4	1	0	0						

Jim Fanning

Born: 9/14/1927 in Chicago, Illinois; MLB Career: 4 years, 64 G (.170-0-5)

REGULAR SEASON							Index			Playoffs			World Series		
Year Tm	Lg	G	W	L	Pct	Standing	EW	+/-	Pt	W	L	Pct	W	L	Pct
1981 Mon	NL	27	16	11	.593	6E 1E	15	1	1	5	5	.500			
1982 Mon	NL	162	86	76	.531	3E	88	-2	1						
1984 Mon	NL	30	14	16	.467	5E 5E	15	-1	0						
3 Years		219	116	103	.530	— —	118	-2	2	5	5	.500			

Jack Farrell

Born: 7/5/1857 in Newark, New Jersey; Died: 2/10/1914; MLB Career: 11 years, 884 G (.243-23-370)

REGULAR SEASON							Index			Playoffs			World Series		
Year Tm	Lg	G	W	L	Pct	Standing	EW	+/-	Pt	W	L	Pct	W	L	Pct
1881 Prv	NL	51	24	27	.471	4 2			0						

Kerby Farrell

Born: 9/3/1913 in Leapwood, Tennessee; Died: 12/17/1975; MLB Career: 2 years, 188 G (.262-0-55)

REGULAR SEASON							Index			Playoffs			World Series		
Year Tm	Lg	G	W	L	Pct	Standing	EW	+/-	Pt	W	L	Pct	W	L	Pct
1957 Cle	AL	153	76	77	.497	6	88	-12	0						

John Felske

Born: 5/30/1942 in Chicago, Illinois; MLB Career: 3 years, 54 G (.135-1-9)

REGULAR SEASON							Index			Playoffs			World Series		
Year Tm	Lg	G	W	L	Pct	Standing	EW	+/-	Pt	W	L	Pct	W	L	Pct
1985 Phi	NL	162	75	87	.463	5E	83	-8	0						
1986 Phi	NL	161	86	75	.534	2E	79	7	1						
1987 Phi	NL	61	29	32	.475	5E 4E	31	-2	0						
3 Years		384	190	194	.495	— —	193	-3	1						

Bob Ferguson

Born: 1/31/1845 in Brooklyn, New York; Died: 5/3/1894; MLB Career: 9 years, 562 G (.271-1-226)

REGULAR SEASON							Index			Playoffs			World Series		
Year Tm	Lg	G	W	L	Pct	Standing	EW	+/-	Pt	W	L	Pct	W	L	Pct
1876 Har	NL	69	47	21	.691	3			2						
1877 Har	NL	60	31	27	.534	3			1						
1878 ChN	NL	61	30	30	.500	4			0						
1879 Try	NL	30	7	22	.241	8 8			0						
1880 Try	NL	83	41	42	.494	4			0						
1881 Try	NL	85	39	45	.464	5			0						
1882 Try	NL	85	35	48	.422	7			0						
1883 Phi	NL	17	4	13	.235	8 8			0						
1884 Pit	AA	42	11	31	.262	10 12 11			0						
1886 NY	AA	120	48	70	.407	8 7			0						
1887 NY	AA	30	6	24	.200	8 7			0						
8 NL Years		490	234	248	.485	— — —			3						
3 AA Years		192	65	125	.342	— — —			0						
11 Years		682	299	373	.445	— — —			3						

Mike Ferraro

Born: 8/14/1944 in Kingston, New York; MLB Career: 4 years, 162 G (.232-2-30)

REGULAR SEASON							Index			Playoffs			World Series		
Year Tm	Lg	G	W	L	Pct	Standing	EW	+/-	Pt	W	L	Pct	W	L	Pct
1983 Cle	AL	100	40	60	.400	7E 7E	49	-9	0						
1986 KC	AL	74	36	38	.486	4W 3W	39	-3	0						
2 Years		174	76	98	.437	— —	88	-12	0						

Wally Fessenden

Born: 10/5/1860 in Windham, New Hampshire; MLB Career: Did Not Play

REGULAR SEASON							Index			Playoffs			World Series		
Year Tm	Lg	G	W	L	Pct	Standing	EW	+/-	Pt	W	L	Pct	W	L	Pct
1890 Syr	AA	11	4	7	.364	7 6 6			0						

Freddie Fitzsimmons

Born: 7/26/1901 in Mishawaka, Indiana; MLB Career: 19 years, 513 G (217-146, 3.51)

REGULAR SEASON							Index			Playoffs			World Series		
Year Tm	Lg	G	W	L	Pct	Standing	EW	+/-	Pt	W	L	Pct	W	L	Pct
1943 Phi	NL	65	26	38	.406	5 7	22	4	0						
1944 Phi	NL	154	61	92	.399	8	62	-1	0						
1945 Phi	NL	69	18	51	.261	8 8	28	-10	0						
3 Years		288	105	181	.367	— —	112	-7	0						

Art Fletcher

Born: 1/5/1885 in Collinsville, Illinois; Died: 2/6/1950; MLB Career: 13 years, 1533 G (.277-32-675)

REGULAR SEASON							Index			Playoffs			World Series		
Year Tm	Lg	G	W	L	Pct	Standing	EW	+/-	Pt	W	L	Pct	W	L	Pct
1923 Phi	NL	155	50	104	.325	8	62	-12	0						
1924 Phi	NL	152	55	96	.364	7	57	-2	0						
1925 Phi	NL	153	68	85	.444	6	60	8	0						
1926 Phi	NL	152	58	93	.384	8	65	-7	0						
1929 NYA	AL	11	6	5	.545	2 2	7	-1	0						
1 AL Year		11	6	5	.545	— —	7	-1	0						
4 NL Years		612	231	378	.379	— —	244	-13	0						
5 Years		623	237	383	.382	— —	251	-14	0						

Silver Flint

Born: 8/3/1855 in Philadelphia, Pennsylvania; Died: 1/14/1892; MLB Career: 12 years, 743 G (.239-21-294)

REGULAR SEASON							Index			Playoffs			World Series		
Year Tm	Lg	G	W	L	Pct	Standing	EW	+/-	Pt	W	L	Pct	W	L	Pct
1879 ChN	NL	19	5	12	.294	2 4			0						

Jim Fogarty

Born: 2/12/1864 in San Francisco, California; Died: 5/20/1891; MLB Career: 7 years, 751 G (.246-20-320)

		REGULAR SEASON					Index			Playoffs			World Series		
Year Tm	Lg	G	W	L	Pct	Standing	EW	+/-	Pt	W	L	Pct	W	L	Pct
1890 Phi	PL	16	7	9	.438	5 5			0						

Horace Fogel

Born: 3/2/1861 in Macungie, Pennsylvania; Died: 11/15/1928; MLB Career: Did Not Play

		REGULAR SEASON					Index			Playoffs			World Series		
Year Tm	Lg	G	W	L	Pct	Standing	EW	+/-	Pt	W	L	Pct	W	L	Pct
1887 Ind	NL	70	20	49	.290	8 8			0						
1902 NYG	NL	44	18	23	.439	4 8	18	0	0						
2 Years		114	38	72	.345	— — —	18	0	0						

Lee Fohl

Born: 11/28/1870 in Pittsburgh, Pennsylvania; Died: 10/30/1965; MLB Career: 2 years, 5 G (.294-0-3)

		REGULAR SEASON					Index			Playoffs			World Series		
Year Tm	Lg	G	W	L	Pct	Standing	EW	+/-	Pt	W	L	Pct	W	L	Pct
1915 Cle	AL	127	45	79	.363	6 7	53	-8	0						
1916 Cle	AL	157	77	77	.500	6	65	12	0						
1917 Cle	AL	156	88	66	.571	3	71	17	2						
1918 Cle	AL	129	73	54	.575	2	66	7	1						
1919 Cle	AL	78	44	34	.564	3 2	42	2	0						
1921 StL	AL	154	81	73	.526	3	76	5	1						
1922 StL	AL	154	93	61	.604	2	79	14	2						
1923 StL	AL	103	52	49	.515	3 5	56	-4	0						
1924 Bos	AL	157	67	87	.435	7	67	0	0						
1925 Bos	AL	152	47	105	.309	8	67	-20	0						
1926 Bos	AL	154	46	107	.301	8	59	-13	0						
11 Years		1521	713	792	.474	— — —	701	12	6						

Lew Fonseca

Born: 1/21/1899 in Oakland, California; Died: 11/26/1989; MLB Career: 12 years, 937 G (.316-31-485)

		REGULAR SEASON					Index			Playoffs			World Series		
Year Tm	Lg	G	W	L	Pct	Standing	EW	+/-	Pt	W	L	Pct	W	L	Pct
1932 ChA	AL	152	49	102	.325	7	61	-12	0						
1933 ChA	AL	151	67	83	.447	6	57	10	0						
1934 ChA	AL	15	4	11	.267	8 8	7	-3	0						
3 Years		318	120	196	.380	— — —	125	-5	0						

Dave Foutz

Born: 9/7/1856 in Carroll County, Maryland; Died: 3/5/1897; MLB Career: 13 years, 1135 G (.276-31-749)

		REGULAR SEASON					Index			Playoffs			World Series		
Year Tm	Lg	G	W	L	Pct	Standing	EW	+/-	Pt	W	L	Pct	W	L	Pct
1893 Bro	NL	130	65	63	.508	6			1						
1894 Bro	NL	135	70	61	.534	5			1						
1895 Bro	NL	134	71	60	.542	5			1						
1896 Bro	NL	133	58	73	.443	9			0						
4 Years		532	264	257	.507	— — —			3						

Charlie Fox

Born: 10/7/1921 in New York, New York; MLB Career: 1 year, 3 G (.429-0-1)

		REGULAR SEASON					Index			Playoffs			World Series		
Year Tm	Lg	G	W	L	Pct	Standing	EW	+/-	Pt	W	L	Pct	W	L	Pct
1970 SF	NL	120	67	53	.558	4W 3W	66	1	1						
1971 SF	NL	162	90	72	.556	1W	87	3	2	1	3	.250			
1972 SF	NL	155	69	86	.445	5W	84	-15	0						
1973 SF	NL	162	88	74	.543	3W	78	10	1						
1974 SF	NL	76	34	42	.447	5W 5W	40	-6	0						
1976 Mon	NL	34	12	22	.353	6E 5E	16	-4	0						
1983 ChN	NL	39	17	22	.436	5E 5E	18	-1	0						
7 Years		748	377	371	.504	— — —	389	-12	4	1	3	.250			

Terry Francona

Born: 4/22/1959 in Aberdeen, South Dakota; MLB Career: 10 years, 708 G (.274-16-143)

		REGULAR SEASON					Index			Playoffs			World Series		
Year Tm	Lg	G	W	L	Pct	Standing	EW	+/-	Pt	W	L	Pct	W	L	Pct
1997 Phi	NL	162	68	94	.420	5E	73	-5	0						

Herman Franks

Born: 1/4/1914 in Price, Utah; MLB Career: 6 years, 188 G (.199-3-43)

		REGULAR SEASON					Index			Playoffs			World Series		
Year Tm	Lg	G	W	L	Pct	Standing	EW	+/-	Pt	W	L	Pct	W	L	Pct
1965 SF	NL	163	95	67	.586	2	89	6	2						
1966 SF	NL	161	93	68	.578	2	89	4	2						
1967 SF	NL	162	91	71	.562	2	90	1	2						
1968 SF	NL	163	88	74	.543	2	89	-1	1						
1977 ChN	NL	162	81	81	.500	4E	75	6	0						
1978 ChN	NL	162	79	83	.488	3E	80	-1	0						
1979 ChN	NL	155	78	77	.503	5E 5E	76	2	0						
7 Years		1128	605	521	.537	— — —	588	17	7						

George Frazer

Born: 1/7/1861 in Syracuse, New York; Died: 2/5/1913; MLB Career: Did Not Play

		REGULAR SEASON					Index			Playoffs			World Series		
Year Tm	Lg	G	W	L	Pct	Standing	EW	+/-	Pt	W	L	Pct	W	L	Pct
1890 Syr	AA	71	31	40	.437	7 6			0						
Syr	AA	46	20	25	.444	6 6			0						
1 Year		117	51	65	.440	— — —			0						

Joe Frazier

Born: 1/7/1861 in Liberty, North Carolina; MLB Career: 4 years, 217 G (.241-10-45)

		REGULAR SEASON					Index			Playoffs			World Series		
Year Tm	Lg	G	W	L	Pct	Standing	EW	+/-	Pt	W	L	Pct	W	L	Pct
1976 NYN	NL	162	86	76	.531	3E	80	6	1						
1977 NYN	NL	45	15	30	.333	6E 6E	23	-8	0						
2 Years		207	101	106	.488	— — —	103	-2	1						

Jim Fregosi

Born: 4/4/1942 in San Francisco, California; MLB Career: 18 years, 1902 G (.265-151-706)

		REGULAR SEASON					Index			Playoffs			World Series		
Year Tm	Lg	G	W	L	Pct	Standing	EW	+/-	Pt	W	L	Pct	W	L	Pct
1978 Cal	AL	117	62	55	.530	3W 2W	56	6	1						
1979 Cal	AL	162	88	74	.543	1W	84	4	2	1	3	.250			
1980 Cal	AL	160	65	95	.406	6W	83	-18	0						
1981 Cal	AL	47	22	25	.468	4W 4W	22	0	0						
1986 ChA	AL	96	45	51	.469	5W 5W	50	-5	0						
1987 ChA	AL	162	77	85	.475	5W	76	1	0						
1988 ChA	AL	161	71	90	.441	5W	78	-7	0						
1991 Phi	NL	149	74	75	.497	6E 3E	69	5	0						
1992 Phi	NL	162	70	92	.432	6E	77	-7	0						
1993 Phi	NL	162	97	65	.599	1E	78	19	4	4	2	.667	2	4	.333
1994 Phi	NL	115	54	61	.470	4E	63	-9	0						
1995 Phi	NL	144	69	75	.479	2E	72	-3	0						
1996 Phi	NL	162	67	95	.414	5E	81	-14	0						
7 AL Years		905	430	475	.475	— — —	449	-19	3	1	3	.250			
6 NL Years		894	431	463	.482	— — —	440	-9	4	4	2	.667	2	4	.333
13 Years		1799	861	938	.479	— — —	889	-28	7	5	5	.500	2	4	.333

Jim Frey

Born: 5/26/1931 in Cleveland, Ohio; MLB Career: Did Not Play

		REGULAR SEASON					Index			Playoffs			World Series		
Year Tm	Lg	G	W	L	Pct	Standing	EW	+/-	Pt	W	L	Pct	W	L	Pct
1980 KC	AL	162	97	65	.599	1W	87	10	4	3	0	1.000	2	4	.333
1981 KC	AL	50	20	30	.400	5W	28	-8	0						
KC	AL	20	10	10	.500	2W 1W	11	-1	0						
1984 ChN	NL	161	96	65	.596	1E	72	24	3	2	3	.400			
1985 ChN	NL	162	77	84	.478	4E	86	-9	0						
1986 ChN	NL	56	23	33	.411	5E 5E	28	-5	0						
2 AL Years		232	127	105	.547	— — —	126	1	4	3	0	1.000	2	4	.333
3 NL Years		379	196	182	.519	— — —	186	10	3	2	3	.400			
5 Years		611	323	287	.530	— — —	312	11	7	5	3	.625	2	4	.333

Frank Frisch

Born: 9/9/1898 in Bronx, New York; Died: 3/12/1973; MLB Career: 19 years, 2311 G (.316-105-1244)

		REGULAR SEASON					Index			Playoffs			World Series		
Year Tm	Lg	G	W	L	Pct	Standing	EW	+/-	Pt	W	L	Pct	W	L	Pct
1933 StL	NL	63	36	26	.581	5 5	32	4	1						
1934 StL	NL	154	95	58	.621	1	82	13	5				4	3	.571
1935 StL	NL	154	96	58	.623	2	86	10	2						
1936 StL	NL	155	87	67	.565	2	90	-3	2						
1937 StL	NL	157	81	73	.526	4	87	-6	1						
1938 StL	NL	139	63	72	.467	6 6	72	-9	0						
1940 Pit	NL	156	78	76	.506	4	75	3	1						
1941 Pit	NL	156	81	73	.526	4	78	3	1						
1942 Pit	NL	151	66	81	.449	5	75	-9	0						
1943 Pit	NL	157	80	74	.519	4	74	6	1						
1944 Pit	NL	158	90	63	.588	2	78	12	2						
1945 Pit	NL	155	82	72	.532	4	83	-1	1						
1946 Pit	NL	152	62	89	.411	7 7	80	-18	0						
1949 ChN	NL	104	42	62	.404	8 8	47	-5	0						
1950 ChN	NL	154	64	89	.418	7	66	-2	0						
1951 ChN	NL	81	35	45	.438	7 8	35	0	0						
16 Years		2246	1138	1078	.514	— — —	1140	-2	17				4	3	.571

Judge Fuchs

Born: 4/17/1878 in Hamburg, Germany; Died: 12/5/1961; MLB Career: Did Not Play

		REGULAR SEASON					Index			Playoffs			World Series		
Year Tm	Lg	G	W	L	Pct	Standing	EW	+/-	Pt	W	L	Pct	W	L	Pct
1929 Bos	NL	154	56	98	.364	8	60	-4	0						

John Gaffney

Born: 6/29/1855 in Roxbury, Massachusetts; Died: 8/8/1913; MLB Career: Did Not Play

		REGULAR SEASON					Index			Playoffs			World Series		
Year Tm	Lg	G	W	L	Pct	Standing	EW	+/-	Pt	W	L	Pct	W	L	Pct
1886 WaN	NL	43	15	25	.375	8 8			0						
1887 WaN	NL	126	46	76	.377	7			0						
2 Years		169	61	101	.377	— — —			0						

Pud Galvin

Born: 12/25/1856 in St. Louis, Missouri; Died: 3/7/1902; MLB Career: 14 years, 718 G (360-308, 2.87)

REGULAR SEASON							Index			Playoffs			World Series		
Year Tm	Lg	G	W	L	Pct	Standing	EW	+/-	Pt	W	L	Pct	W	L	Pct
1885 Buf	NL	24	7	17	.292	**7** 6			0						

John Ganzel

Born: 4/7/1874 in Kalamazoo, Michigan; Died: 1/14/1959; MLB Career: 7 years, 747 G (.251-18-336)

REGULAR SEASON							Index			Playoffs			World Series		
Year Tm	Lg	G	W	L	Pct	Standing	EW	+/-	Pt	W	L	Pct	W	L	Pct
1908 Cin	NL	155	73	81	.474	**5**	71	2	0						
1915 Bro	FL	35	17	18	.486	7 **7**	18	-1	0						
1 NL Year		155	73	81	.474	— — —	71	2	0						
1 FL Year		35	17	18	.486	— — —	18	-1	0						
2 Years		190	90	99	.476	— — —	89	1	0						

Dave Garcia

Born: 9/15/1920 in East St. Louis, Illinois; MLB Career: Did Not Play

REGULAR SEASON							Index			Playoffs			World Series		
Year Tm	Lg	G	W	L	Pct	Standing	EW	+/-	Pt	W	L	Pct	W	L	Pct
1977 Cal	AL	81	35	46	.432	5W **5W**	40	-5	0						
1978 Cal	AL	45	25	20	.556	**3W** 2W	21	4	0						
1979 Cle	AL	66	38	28	.576	6E **6E**	31	7	1						
1980 Cle	AL	160	79	81	.494	**6E**	78	1	0						
1981 Cle	AL	50	26	24	.520	**6E**	24	2	0						
Cle	AL	53	26	27	.491	**5E**	26	0	0						
1982 Cle	AL	162	78	84	.481	**6E**	81	-3	0						
6 Years		617	307	310	.498	— — —	301	6	1						

Billy Gardner

Born: 7/19/1927 in Waterford, Connecticut; MLB Career: 10 years, 1034 G (.237-41-271)

REGULAR SEASON							Index			Playoffs			World Series		
Year Tm	Lg	G	W	L	Pct	Standing	EW	+/-	Pt	W	L	Pct	W	L	Pct
1981 Min	AL	20	6	14	.300	5W **7W**	10	-4	0						
Min	AL	53	24	29	.453	**4W**	26	-2	0						
1982 Min	AL	162	60	102	.370	**7W**	73	-13	0						
1983 Min	AL	162	70	92	.432	**5W**	68	2	0						
1984 Min	AL	162	81	81	.500	**2W**	71	10	0						
1985 Min	AL	62	27	35	.435	**6W** 4W	29	-2	0						
1987 KC	AL	126	62	64	.492	**4W** 2W	62	0	0						
6 Years		747	330	417	.442	— — —	339	-9	0						

Phil Garner

Born: 4/30/1949 in Jefferson City, Tennessee; MLB Career: 16 years, 1860 G (.260-109-738)

REGULAR SEASON							Index			Playoffs			World Series		
Year Tm	Lg	G	W	L	Pct	Standing	EW	+/-	Pt	W	L	Pct	W	L	Pct
1992 Mil	AL	162	92	70	.568	**2E**	81	11	2						
1993 Mil	AL	162	69	93	.426	**7E**	86	-17	0						
1994 Mil	AL	115	53	62	.461	**5C**	54	-1	0						
1995 Mil	AL	144	65	79	.451	**4C**	69	-4	0						
1996 Mil	AL	162	80	82	.494	**3C**	75	5	0						
1997 Mil	AL	161	78	83	.484	**3C**	78	0	0						
6 Years		906	437	469	.482	— — —	443	-6	2						

Cito Gaston

Born: 3/17/1944 in San Antonio, Texas; MLB Career: 11 years, 1026 G (.256-91-387)

REGULAR SEASON							Index			Playoffs			World Series		
Year Tm	Lg	G	W	L	Pct	Standing	EW	+/-	Pt	W	L	Pct	W	L	Pct
1989 Tor	AL	126	77	49	.611	6E **1E**	67	10	3	1	4	.200			
1990 Tor	AL	162	86	76	.531	**2E**	88	-2	1						
1991 Tor	AL	120	66	54	.550	**1E** 1E	63	3	0						
Tor	AL	9	6	3	.667	1E **1E**	5	1	2	1	4	.200			
1992 Tor	AL	162	96	66	.593	**1E**	88	8	5	4	2	.667	4	2	.667
1993 Tor	AL	162	95	67	.586	**1E**	90	5	5	4	2	.667	4	2	.667
1994 Tor	AL	115	55	60	.478	**3E**	65	-10	0						
1995 Tor	AL	144	56	88	.389	**5E**	75	-19	0						
1996 Tor	AL	162	74	88	.457	**4E**	74	0	0						
1997 Tor	AL	157	72	85	.459	**5E** 5E	73	-1	0						
9 Years		1319	683	636	.518	— — —	688	-5	16	10	12	.455	8	4	.667

Joe Gerhardt

Born: 2/14/1855 in Washington, D.C.; Died: 3/11/1922; MLB Career: 12 years, 986 G (.227-7-307)

REGULAR SEASON							Index			Playoffs			World Series		
Year Tm	Lg	G	W	L	Pct	Standing	EW	+/-	Pt	W	L	Pct	W	L	Pct
1883 Lou	AA	98	52	45	.536	**5**			1						
1890 STL	AA	38	20	16	.556	2 **3**			0						
2 Years		136	72	61	.541	— — —			1						

Doc Gessler

Born: 12/23/1880 in Greensburgh, Pennsylvania; Died: 12/25/1924; MLB Career: 8 years, 880 G (.281-14-363)

REGULAR SEASON							Index			Playoffs			World Series		
Year Tm	Lg	G	W	L	Pct	Standing	EW	+/-	Pt	W	L	Pct	W	L	Pct
1914 Pit	FL	11	3	8	.273	**8** 7	6	-3	0						

George Gibson

Born: 7/22/1880 in London, Ontario; Died: 1/25/1967; MLB Career: 14 years, 1213 G (.236-15-345)

REGULAR SEASON							Index			Playoffs			World Series		
Year Tm	Lg	G	W	L	Pct	Standing	EW	+/-	Pt	W	L	Pct	W	L	Pct
1920 Pit	NL	155	79	75	.513	**4**	75	4	1						
1921 Pit	NL	154	90	63	.588	**2**	78	12	2						
1922 Pit	NL	65	32	33	.492	**5** 3	36	-4	0						
1925 ChN	NL	26	12	14	.462	8 **8**	14	-2	0						
1932 Pit	NL	154	86	68	.558	**2**	78	8	1						
1933 Pit	NL	154	87	67	.565	**2**	82	5	2						
1934 Pit	NL	51	27	24	.529	**4** 5	27	0	0						
7 Years		759	413	344	.546	— — —	390	23	6						

Jim Gifford

Born: 10/18/1845 in Warren, New York; Died: 12/19/1901; MLB Career: Did Not Play

REGULAR SEASON							Index			Playoffs			World Series		
Year Tm	Lg	G	W	L	Pct	Standing	EW	+/-	Pt	W	L	Pct	W	L	Pct
1884 Ind	AA	87	25	60	.294	**10** 11			0						
1885 NY	AA	108	44	64	.407	**7**			0						
1886 NY	AA	17	5	12	.294	**8** 7			0						
3 Years		212	74	136	.352	— — —			0						

Jack Glasscock

Born: 7/22/1859 in Wheeling, West Virginia; Died: 2/24/1947; MLB Career: 17 years, 1736 G (.290-27-825)

REGULAR SEASON							Index			Playoffs			World Series		
Year Tm	Lg	G	W	L	Pct	Standing	EW	+/-	Pt	W	L	Pct	W	L	Pct
1889 Ind	NL	67	34	32	.515	7 **7**			1						
1892 StL	NL	4	1	3	.250	**10** 9			0						
2 Years		71	35	35	.500	— — —			1						

Kid Gleason

Born: 10/26/1866 in Camden, New Jersey; Died: 1/2/1933; MLB Career: 22 years, 1966 G (.261-15-823)

REGULAR SEASON							Index			Playoffs			World Series		
Year Tm	Lg	G	W	L	Pct	Standing	EW	+/-	Pt	W	L	Pct	W	L	Pct
1919 ChA	AL	140	88	52	.629	**1**	72	16	4				3	5	.375
1920 ChA	AL	154	96	58	.623	**2**	89	7	2						
1921 ChA	AL	154	62	92	.403	**7**	89	-27	0						
1922 ChA	AL	155	77	77	.500	**5**	74	3	0						
1923 ChA	AL	156	69	85	.448	**7**	77	-8	0						
5 Years		759	392	364	.519	— — —	401	-9	6				3	5	.375

Preston Gomez

Born: 4/20/1923 in Central Preston, Cuba; MLB Career: 1 year, 8 G (.286-0-2)

REGULAR SEASON							Index			Playoffs			World Series		
Year Tm	Lg	G	W	L	Pct	Standing	EW	+/-	Pt	W	L	Pct	W	L	Pct
1969 SD	NL	162	52	110	.321	**6W**	61	-9	0						
1970 SD	NL	162	63	99	.389	**6W**	60	3	0						
1971 SD	NL	161	61	100	.379	**6W**	65	-4	0						
1972 SD	NL	11	4	7	.364	**4W** 6W	4	0	0						
1974 Hou	NL	162	81	81	.500	**4W**	82	-1	0						
1975 Hou	NL	127	47	80	.370	**6W** 6W	64	-17	0						
1980 ChN	NL	90	39	51	.433	**6E** 6E	45	-6	0						
7 Years		875	347	528	.397	— — —	381	-34	0						

Mike Gonzalez

Born: 9/24/1890 in Havana, Cuba; Died: 2/19/1977; MLB Career: 17 years, 1042 G (.253-13-263)

REGULAR SEASON							Index			Playoffs			World Series		
Year Tm	Lg	G	W	L	Pct	Standing	EW	+/-	Pt	W	L	Pct	W	L	Pct
1938 StL	NL	17	8	8	.500	6 **6**	9	-1	0						
1940 StL	NL	6	1	5	.167	6 **7** 3	3	-2	0						
2 Years		23	9	13	.409	— — —	12	-3	0						

Joe Gordon

Born: 2/18/1915 in Los Angeles, California; Died: 4/14/1978; MLB Career: 11 years, 1566 G (.268-253-975)

REGULAR SEASON							Index			Playoffs			World Series		
Year Tm	Lg	G	W	L	Pct	Standing	EW	+/-	Pt	W	L	Pct	W	L	Pct
1958 Cle	AL	86	46	40	.535	5 **4**	45	1	1						
1959 Cle	AL	154	89	65	.578	**2**	79	10	2						
1960 Cle	AL	95	49	46	.516	**4** 4	51	-2	0						
Det	AL	57	26	31	.456	6 **6**	28	-2	0						
1961 KCA	AL	60	26	33	.441	**8** 9	27	-1	0						
1969 KC	AL	163	69	93	.426	**4W**	61	8	0						
5 Years		615	305	308	.498	— — —	291	14	3						

George Gore

Born: 5/3/1857 in Saccarappa, Maine; Died: 9/16/1933; MLB Career: 14 years, 1310 G (.301-46-618)

REGULAR SEASON							Index			Playoffs			World Series		
Year Tm	Lg	G	W	L	Pct	Standing	EW	+/-	Pt	W	L	Pct	W	L	Pct
1892 StL	NL	16	6	9	.400	12 **12** 11			0						

John Goryl

Born: 10/21/1933 in Cumberland, Rhode Island; MLB Career: 6 years, 276 G (.225-16-48)

REGULAR SEASON							Index			Playoffs			World Series		
Year Tm	Lg	G	W	L	Pct	Standing	EW	+/-	Pt	W	L	Pct	W	L	Pct
1980 Min	AL	36	23	13	.639	6W **3W**	18	5	0						
1981 Min	AL	37	11	25	.306	**5W** 7W	17	-6	0						
2 Years		73	34	38	.472	— — —	35	-1	0						

Charlie Gould

Born: 8/21/1847 in Cincinnati, Ohio; Died: 4/10/1917; MLB Career: 2 years, 85 G (.258-0-24)

Year	Tm	Lg	G	W	L	Pct	Standing	EW	+/-	Pt	W	L	Pct	W	L	Pct
								Index			**Playoffs**			**World Series**		
1876 Cin	NL		65	9	56	.138	8			0						

Hank Gowdy

Born: 8/24/1889 in Columbus, Ohio; Died: 8/1/1966; MLB Career: 17 years, 1050 G (.270-21-322)

Year	Tm	Lg	G	W	L	Pct	Standing	EW	+/-	Pt	W	L	Pct	W	L	Pct
1946 Cin	NL		4	3	1	.750	6 6	2	1	0						

Mase Graffen

Born: Unknown in Philadelphia, Pennsylvania; Died: 11/18/1883; MLB Career: Did Not Play

Year	Tm	Lg	G	W	L	Pct	Standing	EW	+/-	Pt	W	L	Pct	W	L	Pct
1876 StL	NL		56	39	17	.696	2 2			1						

Alex Grammas

Born: 4/3/1926 in Birmingham, Alabama; MLB Career: 10 years, 913 G (.247-12-163)

Year	Tm	Lg	G	W	L	Pct	Standing	EW	+/-	Pt	W	L	Pct	W	L	Pct
1969 Pit	NL		5	4	1	.800	3E 3E	3	1	0						
1976 Mil	AL		161	66	95	.410	6E	73	-7	0						
1977 Mil	AL		162	67	95	.414	6E	74	-7	0						
2 AL Years			323	133	190	.412	— — —	147	-14	0						
1 NL Year			5	4	1	.800		3	1	0						
3 Years			328	137	191	.418	— — —	150	-13	0						

Dallas Green

Born: 8/4/1934 in Newport, Delaware; MLB Career: 8 years, 199 G (20-22, 4.26)

Year	Tm	Lg	G	W	L	Pct	Standing	EW	+/-	Pt	W	L	Pct	W	L	Pct
1979 Phi	NL		30	19	11	.633	5E 4E	17	2	0						
1980 Phi	NL		162	91	71	.562	1E	86	5	5	3	2	.600	4	2	.667
1981 Phi	NL		55	34	21	.618	1E	30	4	0						
Phi	NL		52	25	27	.481	3E	28	-3	1	2	3	.400			
1989 NYA	AL		121	56	65	.463	6E 5E	64	-8	0						
1993 NYN	NL		124	46	78	.371	7E 7E	61	-15	0						
1994 NYN	NL		113	55	58	.487	3E	48	7	0						
1995 NYN	NL		144	69	75	.479	2E	68	1	0						
1996 NYN	NL		131	59	72	.450	4E 4E	62	-3	0						
1 AL Year			121	56	65	.463		64	-8	0						
7 NL Years			811	398	413	.491	— — —	400	-2	6	5	5	.500	4	2	.667
8 Years			932	454	478	.487	— — —	464	-10	6	5	5	.500	4	2	.667

Mike Griffin

Born: 3/20/1865 in Utica, New York; Died: 4/10/1908; MLB Career: 12 years, 1511 G (.296-42-719)

Year	Tm	Lg	G	W	L	Pct	Standing	EW	+/-	Pt	W	L	Pct	W	L	Pct
1898 Bro	NL		4	1	3	.250	9 9 10			0						

Sandy Griffin

Born: 10/24/1858 in Fayetteville, New York; Died: 6/4/1926; MLB Career: 4 years, 166 G (.275-5-78)

Year	Tm	Lg	G	W	L	Pct	Standing	EW	+/-	Pt	W	L	Pct	W	L	Pct
1891 Was	AA		6	2	4	.333	9 9			0						

Clark Griffith

Born: 11/20/1869 in Clear Creek, Missouri; Died: 10/27/1955; MLB Career: 21 years, 485 G (237-146, 3.31)

Year	Tm	Lg	G	W	L	Pct	Standing	EW	+/-	Pt	W	L	Pct	W	L	Pct
1901 ChA	AL		137	83	53	.610	1	68	15	4						
1902 ChA	AL		138	74	60	.552	4	74	0	1						
1903 NYA	AL		136	72	62	.537	4	58	14	1						
1904 NYA	AL		155	92	59	.609	2	76	16	2						
1905 NYA	AL		152	71	78	.477	6	81	-10	0						
1906 NYA	AL		155	90	61	.596	2	76	14	0						
1907 NYA	AL		152	70	78	.473	5	83	-13	0						
1908 NYA	AL		57	24	32	.429	6 8	28	-4	0						
1909 Cin	NL		157	77	76	.503	4	72	5	1						
1910 Cin	NL		156	75	79	.487	5	75	0	0						
1911 Cin	NL		159	70	83	.458	6	75	-5	0						
1912 Was	AL		154	91	61	.599	2	64	27	2						
1913 Was	AL		155	90	64	.584	2	82	8	2						
1914 Was	AL		158	81	73	.526	3	84	-3	1						
1915 Was	AL		155	85	68	.556	4	82	3	1						
1916 Was	AL		159	76	77	.497	7	83	-7	0						
1917 Was	AL		158	74	79	.484	5	78	-4	0						
1918 Was	AL		130	72	56	.563	3	64	8	0						
1919 Was	AL		142	56	84	.400	7	74	-18	0						
1920 Was	AL		153	68	84	.447	6	69	-1	0						
17 AL Years			2446	1269	1129	.529	— — —	1224	45	17						
3 NL Years			472	222	238	.483	— — —	222	0	1						
20 Years			2918	1491	1367	.522	— — —	1446	45	18						

Burleigh Grimes

Born: 8/18/1893 in Emerald, Wisconsin; Died: 12/6/1985; MLB Career: 19 years, 632 G (270-212, 3.52)

Year	Tm	Lg	G	W	L	Pct	Standing	EW	+/-	Pt	W	L	Pct	W	L	Pct
1937 Bro	NL		155	62	91	.405	6	70	-8	0						
1938 Bro	NL		151	69	80	.463	7	65	4	0						
2 Years			306	131	171	.434	— — —	135	-4	0						

Charlie Grimm

Born: 8/28/1898 in St. Louis, Missouri; Died: 11/15/1983; MLB Career: 20 years, 2166 G (.290-79-1078)

Year	Tm	Lg	G	W	L	Pct	Standing	EW	+/-	Pt	W	L	Pct	W	L	Pct
1932 ChN	NL		55	37	18	.673	2 1	30	7	3				0	4	.000
1933 ChN	NL		154	86	68	.558	3	86	0	1						
1934 ChN	NL		152	86	65	.570	3	82	4	2						
1935 ChN	NL		154	100	54	.649	1	85	15	5				2	4	.333
1936 ChN	NL		154	87	67	.565	2	91	-4	2						
1937 ChN	NL		154	93	61	.604	2	86	7	2						
1938 ChN	NL		81	45	36	.556	3 1	47	-2	0						
1944 ChN	NL		146	74	69	.517	8 4	68	6	1						
1945 ChN	NL		155	98	56	.636	1	75	23	6				3	4	.429
1946 ChN	NL		155	82	71	.536	3	86	-4	0						
1947 ChN	NL		155	69	85	.448	6	82	-13	0						
1948 ChN	NL		155	64	90	.416	8	76	-12	0						
1949 ChN	NL		50	19	31	.380	8 8	23	-4	0						
1952 Bos	NL		120	51	67	.432	6 7	59	-8	0						
1953 Mil	NL		159	92	62	.597	2	71	21	2						
1954 Mil	NL		154	89	65	.578	3	83	6	2						
1955 Mil	NL		154	85	69	.552	2	83	2	1						
1956 Mil	NL		46	24	22	.522	5 2	25	-1	0						
1960 ChN	NL		17	6	11	.353	8 7	8	-2	0						
19 Years			2370	1287	1067	.547	— — —	1246	41	26				5	12	.294

Heine Groh

Born: 9/18/1889 in Rochester, New York; Died: 8/22/1968; MLB Career: 16 years, 1676 G (.292-26-566)

Year	Tm	Lg	G	W	L	Pct	Standing	EW	+/-	Pt	W	L	Pct	W	L	Pct
1918 Cin	NL		10	7	3	.700	4 3	5	2	0						

Don Gutteridge

Born: 6/19/1912 in Pittsburg, Kansas; MLB Career: 12 years, 1151 G (.256-39-391)

Year	Tm	Lg	G	W	L	Pct	Standing	EW	+/-	Pt	W	L	Pct	W	L	Pct
1969 ChA	AL		145	60	85	.414	4W 5W	71	-11	0						
1970 ChA	AL		136	49	87	.360	6W 6W	63	-14	0						
2 Years			281	109	172	.388	— — —	134	-25	0						

Eddie Haas

Born: 5/26/1935 in Paducah, Kentucky; MLB Career: 3 years, 55 G (.243-1-10)

Year	Tm	Lg	G	W	L	Pct	Standing	EW	+/-	Pt	W	L	Pct	W	L	Pct
1985 Atl	NL		121	50	71	.413	5W 5W	62	-12	0						

Stan Hack

Born: 12/6/1909 in Sacramento, California; Died: 12/15/1979; MLB Career: 16 years, 1938 G (.301-57-642)

Year	Tm	Lg	G	W	L	Pct	Standing	EW	+/-	Pt	W	L	Pct	W	L	Pct
1954 ChN	NL		154	64	90	.416	7	69	-5	0						
1955 ChN	NL		154	72	81	.471	6	69	3	0						
1956 ChN	NL		157	60	94	.390	8	72	-12	0						
1958 StL	NL		10	3	7	.300	5 5	5	-2	0						
4 Years			475	199	272	.423	— — —	215	-16	0						

Charlie Hackett

Born: Unknown in Holyoke, Massachusetts; Died: 8/1/1898; MLB Career: Did Not Play

Year	Tm	Lg	G	W	L	Pct	Standing	EW	+/-	Pt	W	L	Pct	W	L	Pct
1884 Cle	NL		113	35	77	.313	7			0						
1885 Bro	AA		37	15	22	.405	7 5			0						
1 NL Year			113	35	77	.313	— — —			0						
1 AA Year			37	15	22	.405	— — —			0						
2 Years			150	50	99	.336	— — —			0						

Bill Hallman

Born: 3/31/1867 in Pittsburgh, Pennsylvania; Died: 9/11/1920; MLB Career: 14 years, 1503 G (.272-21-769)

Year	Tm	Lg	G	W	L	Pct	Standing	EW	+/-	Pt	W	L	Pct	W	L	Pct
1897 StL	NL		50	13	36	.265	12 12 12			0						

Fred Haney

Born: 4/25/1898 in Albuquerque, New Mexico; Died: 11/9/1977; MLB Career: 7 years, 622 G (.275-8-228)

Year	Tm	Lg	G	W	L	Pct	Standing	EW	+/-	Pt	W	L	Pct	W	L	Pct
1939 StL	AL		156	43	111	.279	8	60	-17	0						
1940 StL	AL		156	67	87	.435	8	53	14	0						
1941 StL	AL		44	15	29	.341	7 6	19	-4	0						
1953 Pit	NL		154	50	104	.325	8	55	-5	0						

Year Tm	Lg	G	W	L	Pct	Standing		EW	+/-	Pt	W	L	Pct	W	L	Pct
1954 Pit	NL	154	53	101	.344		8	58	-5	0						
1955 Pit	NL	154	60	94	.390		8	57	3	0						
1956 Mil	NL	109	68	40	.630	5	2	59	9	2						
1957 Mil	NL	155	95	59	.617		1	87	8	5				4	3	.571
1958 Mil	NL	154	92	62	.597		1	89	3	4				3	4	.429
1959 Mil	NL	157	86	70	.551		2	90	-4	1						
3 AL Years		356	125	227	.355	—	— —	132	-7	0						
7 NL Years		1037	504	533	.487	—	— —	495	9	12				7	7	.500
10 Years		1393	629	757	.454	—	— —	627	2	12				7	7	.500

Ned Hanlon

Born: 8/22/1857 in Montville, Connecticut; Died: 4/14/1937; MLB Career: 13 years, 1267 G (.260-30-517)

Year Tm	Lg	G	W	L	Pct	Standing		EW	+/-	Pt	W	L	Pct	W	L	Pct
1889 Pit	NL	46	26	18	.591	7	5			0						
1890 Pit	PL	131	60	68	.469		6			0						
1891 Pit	NL	78	31	47	.397	8	8			0						
1892 Bal	NL	56	17	39	.304	12	12			0						
Bal	NL	77	26	46	.361		10			0						
1893 Bal	NL	130	60	70	.462		8			0						
1894 Bal	NL	129	89	39	.695		1			4				0	4	.000
1895 Bal	NL	132	87	43	.669		1			4				1	4	.200
1896 Bal	NL	132	90	39	.698		1			5				4	0	1.000
1897 Bal	NL	136	90	40	.692		2			5				4	1	.800
1898 Bal	NL	154	96	53	.644		2			2						
1899 Bro	NL	150	101	47	.682		1			5						
1900 Bro	NL	142	82	54	.603		1	68	14	5				3	1	.750
1901 Bro	NL	137	79	57	.581		3	75	4	2						
1902 Bro	NL	141	75	63	.543		2	76	-1	1						
1903 Bro	NL	139	70	66	.515		5	74	-4	1						
1904 Bro	NL	154	56	97	.366		6	80	-24	0						
1905 Bro	NL	155	48	104	.316		8	67	-19	0						
1906 Cin	NL	155	64	87	.424		6	79	-15	0						
1907 Cin	NL	156	66	87	.431		6	72	-6	0						
18 NL Years		2399	1253	1096	.533	—	— —	591	-51	34				12	10	.545
1 PL Year		131	60	68	.469	—	— —			0						
19 Years		2530	1313	1164	.530	—	— —	591	-51	34				12	10	.545

Mel Harder

Born: 10/15/1909 in Beemer, Nebraska; MLB Career: 20 years, 584 G (223-186, 3.80)

Year Tm	Lg	G	W	L	Pct	Standing		EW	+/-	Pt	W	L	Pct	W	L	Pct
1961 Cle	AL	1	1	0	1.000	5	5	1	1	0						
1962 Cle	AL	2	2	0	1.000	6	6	1	1	0						
2 Years		3	3	0	1.000	—	— —	2	1	0						

Mike Hargrove

Born: 10/26/1949 in Perryton, Texas; MLB Career: 12 years, 1666 G (.290-80-686)

Year Tm	Lg	G	W	L	Pct	Standing		EW	+/-	Pt	W	L	Pct	W	L	Pct
1991 Cle	AL	85	32	53	.376	7E	7E	41	-9	0						
1992 Cle	AL	162	76	86	.469		4E	68	8	0						
1993 Cle	AL	162	76	86	.469		6E	75	1	0						
1994 Cle	AL	113	66	47	.584		2C	52	14	1						
1995 Cle	AL	144	100	44	.694		1C	76	24	5	7	2	.778	2	4	.333
1996 Cle	AL	161	99	62	.615		1C	96	3	3	1	3	.250			
1997 Cle	AL	161	86	75	.534		1C	95	-9	3	7	4	.636	3	4	.429
7 Years		988	535	453	.541	—	— —	503	32	12	15	9	.625	5	8	.385

Toby Harrah

Born: 10/26/1948 in Sissonville, West Virginia; MLB Career: 17 years, 2155 G (.264-195-918)

Year Tm	Lg	G	W	L	Pct	Standing		EW	+/-	Pt	W	L	Pct	W	L	Pct
1992 Tex	AL	76	32	44	.421	3W	4W	39	-7	0						

Bud Harrelson

Born: 6/6/1944 in Niles, California; MLB Career: 16 years, 1533 G (.236-7-267)

Year Tm	Lg	G	W	L	Pct	Standing		EW	+/-	Pt	W	L	Pct	W	L	Pct
1990 NYN	NL	120	71	49	.592	4E	2E	65	6	2						
1991 NYN	NL	154	74	80	.481	3E	5E	85	-11	0						
2 Years		274	145	129	.529	—	— —	150	-5	2						

Bucky Harris

Born: 11/8/1896 in Port Jervis, New York; Died: 11/8/1977; MLB Career: 12 years, 1264 G (.274-9-506)

Year Tm	Lg	G	W	L	Pct	Standing		EW	+/-	Pt	W	L	Pct	W	L	Pct
1924 Was	AL	156	92	62	.597		1	76	16	5				4	3	.571
1925 Was	AL	152	96	55	.636		1	82	14	4				3	4	.429
1926 Was	AL	152	81	69	.540		4	87	-6	1						
1927 Was	AL	157	85	69	.552		3	85	0	1						
1928 Was	AL	155	75	79	.487		4	84	-9	0						
1929 Det	AL	155	70	84	.455		6	73	-3	0						
1930 Det	AL	154	75	79	.487		5	73	2	0						
1931 Det	AL	154	61	93	.396		7	74	-13	0						
1932 Det	AL	153	76	75	.503		5	67	9	1						
1933 Det	AL	153	73	79	.480	5	5	74	-1	0						
1934 Bos	AL	153	76	76	.500		4	64	12	0						
1935 Was	AL	154	67	86	.438		6	76	-9	0						
1936 Was	AL	153	82	71	.536		4	73	9	1						
1937 Was	AL	158	73	80	.477		6	77	-4	0						
1938 Was	AL	152	75	76	.497		5	73	2	0						
1939 Was	AL	153	65	87	.428		6	76	-11	0						
1940 Was	AL	154	64	90	.416		7	71	-7	0						
1941 Was	AL	156	70	84	.455		6	69	1	0						
1942 Was	AL	151	62	89	.411		7	69	-7	0						
1943 Phi	NL	92	38	52	.422	5	7	31	7	0						
1947 NYA	AL	155	97	57	.630		1	83	14	5				4	3	.571
1948 NYA	AL	154	94	60	.610		3	89	5	2						
1950 Was	AL	154	67	87	.435		5	59	8	0						
1951 Was	AL	154	62	92	.403		7	66	-4	0						
1952 Was	AL	157	78	76	.506		5	65	13	1						
1953 Was	AL	152	76	76	.500		5	73	3	0						
1954 Was	AL	155	66	88	.429		6	75	-9	0						
1955 Det	AL	154	79	75	.513		5	67	12	1						
1956 Det	AL	155	82	72	.532		5	75	7	1						
28 AL Years		4316	2119	2166	.495	—	— —	2075	44	23				11	10	.524
1 NL Year		92	38	52	.422	—	— —	31	7	0						
29 Years		4408	2157	2218	.493	—	— —	2106	51	23				11	10	.524

Lum Harris

Born: 1/17/1915 in New Castle, Alabama; Died: 11/11/1996; MLB Career: 6 years, 151 G (35-63, 4.16)

Year Tm	Lg	G	W	L	Pct	Standing		EW	+/-	Pt	W	L	Pct	W	L	Pct
1961 Bal	AL	27	17	10	.630	3	3	15	2	0						
1964 Hou	NL	13	5	8	.385	9	9	5	0	0						
1965 Hou	NL	162	65	97	.401		9	70	-5	0						
1968 Atl	NL	163	81	81	.500		5	80	1	0						
1969 Atl	NL	162	93	69	.574		1W	85	8	3	0	3	.000			
1970 Atl	NL	162	76	86	.469		5W	88	-12	0						
1971 Atl	NL	162	82	80	.506		3W	81	1	1						
1972 Atl	NL	105	47	57	.452	5W	4W	53	-6	0						
1 AL Year		27	17	10	.630	—	— —	15	2	0						
7 NL Years		929	449	478	.484	—	— —	462	-13	4	0	3	.000			
8 Years		956	466	488	.488	—	— —	477	-11	4	0	3	.000			

Jim Hart

Born: 7/10/1855 in Fairview, Pennsylvania; Died: 7/18/1919; MLB Career: Did Not Play

Year Tm	Lg	G	W	L	Pct	Standing		EW	+/-	Pt	W	L	Pct	W	L	Pct
1885 Lou	AA	112	53	59	.473		5			0						
1886 Lou	AA	138	66	70	.485		4			0						
1889 Bos	NL	133	83	45	.648		2			2						
1 NL Year		133	83	45	.648	—	— —			2						
2 AA Years		250	119	129	.480	—	— —			0						
3 Years		383	202	174	.537	—	— —			2						

John Hart

Born: 7/21/1948 in Tampa, Florida; MLB Career: Did Not Play

Year Tm	Lg	G	W	L	Pct	Standing		EW	+/-	Pt	W	L	Pct	W	L	Pct
1989 Cle	AL	19	8	11	.421	6E	6E	9	-1	0						

Gabby Hartnett

Born: 12/20/1900 in Woonsocket, R.I.; Died: 12/20/1972; MLB Career: 20 years, 1990 G (.297-236-1179)

Year Tm	Lg	G	W	L	Pct	Standing		EW	+/-	Pt	W	L	Pct	W	L	Pct
1938 ChN	NL	73	44	27	.620	3	1	41	3	3				0	4	.000
1939 ChN	NL	156	84	70	.545		4	87	-3	1						
1940 ChN	NL	154	75	79	.487		5	84	-9	0						
3 Years		383	203	176	.536	—	— —	212	-9	4				0	4	.000

Roy Hartsfield

Born: 10/25/1925 in Chattahoochee, Georgia; MLB Career: 3 years, 265 G (.273-13-59)

Year Tm	Lg	G	W	L	Pct	Standing		EW	+/-	Pt	W	L	Pct	W	L	Pct
1977 Tor	AL	161	54	107	.335		7E	60	-6	0						
1978 Tor	AL	161	59	102	.366		7E	61	-2	0						
1979 Tor	AL	162	53	109	.327		7E	63	-10	0						
3 Years		484	166	318	.343	—	— —	184	-18	0						

Grady Hatton

Born: 10/7/1922 in Beaumont, Texas; MLB Career: 12 years, 1312 G (.254-91-533)

Year Tm	Lg	G	W	L	Pct	Standing		EW	+/-	Pt	W	L	Pct	W	L	Pct
1966 Hou	NL	163	72	90	.444		8	69	3	0						
1967 Hou	NL	162	69	93	.426		9	73	-4	0						
1968 Hou	NL	61	23	38	.377	10	10	27	-4	0						
3 Years		386	164	221	.426	—	— —	169	-5	0						

Guy Hecker

Born: 4/3/1856 in Youngsville, Pennsylvania; Died: 12/3/1938; MLB Career: 9 years, 703 G (173-146, 2.92)

Year Tm	Lg	G	W	L	Pct	Standing		EW	+/-	Pt	W	L	Pct	W	L	Pct
1890 Pit	NL	138	23	113	.169		8			0						

Don Heffner

Born: 2/8/1911 in Rouzerville, Pennsylvania; Died: 8/1/1989; MLB Career: 11 years, 743 G (.241-6-248)

		REGULAR SEASON					Index			Playoffs			World Series		
Year Tm	Lg	G	W	L	Pct	Standing	EW	+/-	Pt	W	L	Pct	W	L	Pct
1966 Cin	NL	83	37	46	.446	8 7	45	-8	0						

Louie Heilbroner

Born: 7/4/1861 in Fort Wayne, Indiana; Died: 12/21/1933; MLB Career: Did Not Play

		REGULAR SEASON					Index			Playoffs			World Series		
Year Tm	Lg	G	W	L	Pct	Standing	EW	+/-	Pt	W	L	Pct	W	L	Pct
1900 StL	NL	50	23	25	.479	7 5	24	-1	0						

Tommy Helms

Born: 5/5/1941 in Charlotte, North Carolina; MLB Career: 14 years, 1435 G (.269-34-477)

		REGULAR SEASON					Index			Playoffs			World Series		
Year Tm	Lg	G	W	L	Pct	Standing	EW	+/-	Pt	W	L	Pct	W	L	Pct
1988 Cin	NL	27	12	15	.444	4W 4W 2W	14	-2	0						
1989 Cin	NL	37	16	21	.432	4W 5W	19	-3	0						
2 Years		64	28	36	.438		33	-5	0						

Solly Hemus

Born: 4/17/1923 in Phoenix, Arizona; MLB Career: 11 years, 961 G (.273-51-263)

		REGULAR SEASON					Index			Playoffs			World Series		
Year Tm	Lg	G	W	L	Pct	Standing	EW	+/-	Pt	W	L	Pct	W	L	Pct
1959 StL	NL	154	71	83	.461	7	76	-5	0						
1960 StL	NL	155	86	68	.558	3	75	11	1						
1961 StL	NL	75	33	41	.446	6 5	39	-6	0						
3 Years		384	190	192	.497		190	0	1						

Bill Henderson

Born: Unknown; MLB Career: Did Not Play

		REGULAR SEASON					Index			Playoffs			World Series		
Year Tm	Lg	G	W	L	Pct	Standing	EW	+/-	Pt	W	L	Pct	W	L	Pct
1884 Bal	UA	106	58	47	.552	4			1						

Jack Hendricks

Born: 4/9/1875 in Joliet, Illinois; Died: 5/13/1943; MLB Career: 2 years, 42 G (.207-0-4)

		REGULAR SEASON					Index			Playoffs			World Series		
Year Tm	Lg	G	W	L	Pct	Standing	EW	+/-	Pt	W	L	Pct	W	L	Pct
1918 StL	NL	133	51	78	.395	8	65	-14	0						
1924 Cin	NL	153	83	70	.542	4	84	-1	1						
1925 Cin	NL	153	80	73	.523	3	83	-3	1						
1926 Cin	NL	157	87	67	.565	2	81	6	2						
1927 Cin	NL	153	75	78	.490	5	83	-8	0						
1928 Cin	NL	153	78	74	.513	5	77	1	1						
1929 Cin	NL	155	66	88	.429	7	79	-13	0						
7 Years		1057	520	528	.496	— — —	552	-32	5						

Ed Hengle

Born: Unknown in Chicago, Illinois; Died: 11/4/1927; MLB Career: Did Not Play

		REGULAR SEASON					Index			Playoffs			World Series		
Year Tm	Lg	G	W	L	Pct	Standing	EW	+/-	Pt	W	L	Pct	W	L	Pct
1884 Chi	UA	74	34	39	.466	6			0						

Billy Herman

Born: 7/7/1909 in New Albany, Indiana; Died: 9/5/1992; MLB Career: 15 years, 1922 G (.304-47-839)

		REGULAR SEASON					Index			Playoffs			World Series		
Year Tm	Lg	G	W	L	Pct	Standing	EW	+/-	Pt	W	L	Pct	W	L	Pct
1947 Pit	NL	155	61	92	.399	8 7	72	-11	0						
1964 Bos	AL	2	2	0	1.000	8 8	1	1	0						
1965 Bos	AL	162	62	100	.383	9	75	-13	0						
1966 Bos	AL	146	64	82	.438	10 9	63	1	0						
3 AL Years		310	128	182	.413	— — —	139	-11	0						
1 NL Year		155	61	92	.399		72	-11	0						
4 Years		465	189	274	.408	— — —	211	-22	0						

Buck Herzog

Born: 7/9/1885 in Baltimore, Maryland; Died: 9/4/1953; MLB Career: 13 years, 1493 G (.259-20-445)

		REGULAR SEASON					Index			Playoffs			World Series		
Year Tm	Lg	G	W	L	Pct	Standing	EW	+/-	Pt	W	L	Pct	W	L	Pct
1914 Cin	NL	157	60	94	.390	8	70	-10	0						
1915 Cin	NL	160	71	83	.461	7	67	4	0						
1916 Cin	NL	84	34	49	.410	8 7	38	-4	0						
3 Years		401	165	226	.422	— — —	175	-10	0						

Whitey Herzog

Born: 11/9/1931 in New Athens, Illinois; MLB Career: 8 years, 634 G (.257-25-172)

		REGULAR SEASON					Index			Playoffs			World Series		
Year Tm	Lg	G	W	L	Pct	Standing	EW	+/-	Pt	W	L	Pct	W	L	Pct
1973 Tex	AL	138	47	91	.341	6W 6W	56	-9	0						
1974 Cal	AL	4	2	2	.500	6W 6W 6W	2	0	0						
1975 KC	AL	66	41	25	.621	2W 2W	32	9	1						
1976 KC	AL	162	90	72	.556	1W	86	4	2	2	3	.400			
1977 KC	AL	162	102	60	.630	1W	90	12	4	2	3	.400			
1978 KC	AL	162	92	70	.568	1W	95	-3	3	1	3	.250			
1979 KC	AL	162	85	77	.525	2W	91	-6	1						
1980 StL	NL	73	38	35	.521	6E 5E 4E	37	1	0						
1981 StL	NL	51	30	20	.600	2E	24	6	0						
StL	NL	52	29	23	.558	2E	24	5	1						
1982 StL	NL	162	92	70	.568	1E	86	6	5	3	0	1.000	4	3	.571
1983 StL	NL	162	79	83	.488	4E	87	-8	0						
1984 StL	NL	162	84	78	.519	3E	82	2	1						
1985 StL	NL	162	101	61	.623	1E	84	17	5	4	2	.667	3	4	.429
1986 StL	NL	161	79	82	.491	3E	91	-12	0						
1987 StL	NL	162	95	67	.586	1E	83	12	4	4	3	.571	3	4	.429
1988 StL	NL	162	76	86	.469	5E	90	-14	0						
1989 StL	NL	164	86	76	.531	3E	80	6	1						
1990 StL	NL	80	33	47	.413	6E 6E	42	-9	0						
7 AL Years		856	459	397	.536	— — —	452	7	11	5	9	.357			
11 NL Years		1553	822	728	.530	— — —	810	12	17	11	5	.688	10	11	.476
18 Years		2409	1281	1125	.532	— — —	1262	19	28	16	14	.533	10	11	.476

Walter Hewett

Born: Unknown in Washington, D.C.; Died: 10/7/1944; MLB Career: Did Not Play

		REGULAR SEASON					Index			Playoffs			World Series		
Year Tm	Lg	G	W	L	Pct	Standing	EW	+/-	Pt	W	L	Pct	W	L	Pct
1888 WaN	NL	40	10	29	.256	8 8			0						

Pinky Higgins

Born: 5/27/1909 in Red Oak, Texas; Died: 3/21/1969; MLB Career: 14 years, 1802 G (.292-140-1075)

		REGULAR SEASON					Index			Playoffs			World Series		
Year Tm	Lg	G	W	L	Pct	Standing	EW	+/-	Pt	W	L	Pct	W	L	Pct
1955 Bos	AL	154	84	70	.545	4	74	10	1						
1956 Bos	AL	155	84	70	.545	4	80	4	1						
1957 Bos	AL	154	82	72	.532	3	80	2	1						
1958 Bos	AL	155	79	75	.513	3	81	-2	1						
1959 Bos	AL	73	31	42	.425	8 5	38	-7	0						
1960 Bos	AL	105	48	57	.457	8 7	52	-4	0						
1961 Bos	AL	163	76	86	.469	6	80	-4	0						
1962 Bos	AL	160	76	84	.475	8	77	-1	0						
8 Years		1119	560	556	.502	— —	562	-2	4						

Vedie Himsl

Born: 4/2/1917 in Plevna, Montana; MLB Career: Did Not Play

		REGULAR SEASON					Index			Playoffs			World Series		
Year Tm	Lg	G	W	L	Pct	Standing	EW	+/-	Pt	W	L	Pct	W	L	Pct
1961 ChN	NL	11	5	6	.455	6 7	5	0	0						
ChN	NL	17	5	12	.294	7 7 7	7	-2	0						
ChN	NL	4	0	3	.000	7 7 7	1	-1	0						
1 Year		32	10	21	.323	— — —	13	-3	0						

Billy Hitchcock

Born: 7/31/1916 in Inverness, Alabama; MLB Career: 9 years, 703 G (.243-5-257)

		REGULAR SEASON					Index			Playoffs			World Series		
Year Tm	Lg	G	W	L	Pct	Standing	EW	+/-	Pt	W	L	Pct	W	L	Pct
1960 Det	AL	1	1	0	1.000	6 6 6	0	1	0						
1962 Bal	AL	162	77	85	.475	7	91	-14	0						
1963 Bal	AL	162	86	76	.531	4	83	3	1						
1966 Atl	NL	51	33	18	.647	5 5	27	6	0						
1967 Atl	NL	159	77	82	.484	7 7	83	-6	0						
3 AL Years		325	164	161	.505	— — —	174	-10	1						
2 NL Years		210	110	100	.524	— — —	110	0	0						
5 Years		535	274	261	.512	— — —	284	-10	1						

Butch Hobson

Born: 8/17/1951 in Tuscaloosa, Alabama; MLB Career: 8 years, 738 G (.248-98-397)

		REGULAR SEASON					Index			Playoffs			World Series		
Year Tm	Lg	G	W	L	Pct	Standing	EW	+/-	Pt	W	L	Pct	W	L	Pct
1992 Bos	AL	162	73	89	.451	7E	84	-11	0						
1993 Bos	AL	162	80	82	.494	5E	78	2	0						
1994 Bos	AL	115	54	61	.470	4E	57	-3	0						
3 Years		439	207	232	.472	— — —	219	-12	0						

Gil Hodges

Born: 4/4/1924 in Princeton, Indiana; Died: 4/2/1972; MLB Career: 18 years, 2071 G (.273-370-1274)

		REGULAR SEASON					Index			Playoffs			World Series		
Year Tm	Lg	G	W	L	Pct	Standing	EW	+/-	Pt	W	L	Pct	W	L	Pct
1963 Was	AL	121	42	79	.347	10 10	48	-6	0						
1964 Was	AL	162	62	100	.383	9	63	-1	0						
1965 Was	AL	162	70	92	.432	8	66	4	0						
1966 Was	AL	159	71	88	.447	8	69	2	0						
1967 Was	AL	161	76	85	.472	6	72	4	0						
1968 NYN	NL	163	73	89	.451	9	65	8	0						
1969 NYN	NL	162	100	62	.617	1E	77	23	6	3	0	1.000	4	1	.800

REGULAR SEASON							Index			Playoffs			World Series		
Year Tm	Lg	G	W	L	Pct	Standing	EW	+/-	Pt	W	L	Pct	W	L	Pct
1970 NYN	NL	162	83	79	.512	3E	88	-5	1						
1971 NYN	NL	162	83	79	.512	3E	84	-1	1						
5 AL Years		765	321	444	.420	— — —	318	3	0						
4 NL Years		649	339	309	.523	— — —	314	25	8	3	0	1.000	4	1	.800
9 Years		1414	660	753	.467	— — —	632	28	8	3	0	1.000	4	1	.800

Fred Hoey

Born: Unknown in New York, New York; Died: 12/7/1933; MLB Career: Did Not Play

REGULAR SEASON							Index			Playoffs			World Series		
Year Tm	Lg	G	W	L	Pct	Standing	EW	+/-	Pt	W	L	Pct	W	L	Pct
1899 NYG	NL	87	31	55	.360	9 10			0						

Bill Holbert

Born: 3/14/1855 in Baltimore, Maryland; Died: 3/20/1935; MLB Career: 12 years, 623 G (.208-0-144)

REGULAR SEASON							Index			Playoffs			World Series		
Year Tm	Lg	G	W	L	Pct	Standing	EW	+/-	Pt	W	L	Pct	W	L	Pct
1879 Syr	NL	1	0	1	.000	6 6 7			0						

Holly Hollingshead

Born: 1/17/1853 in Washington, D.C.; Died: 10/6/1926; MLB Career: Did Not Play

REGULAR SEASON							Index			Playoffs			World Series		
Year Tm	Lg	G	W	L	Pct	Standing	EW	+/-	Pt	W	L	Pct	W	L	Pct
1884 WaD	AA	62	12	50	.194	13 13			0						

Tommy Holmes

Born: 3/29/1917 in Brooklyn, New York; MLB Career: 11 years, 1320 G (.302-88-581)

REGULAR SEASON							Index			Playoffs			World Series		
Year Tm	Lg	G	W	L	Pct	Standing	EW	+/-	Pt	W	L	Pct	W	L	Pct
1951 Bos	NL	95	48	47	.505	5 4	50	-2	1						
1952 Bos	NL	35	13	22	.371	6 7	18	-5	0						
2 Years		130	61	69	.469	— — —	68	-7	1						

Rogers Hornsby

Born: 4/27/1896 in Winters, Texas; Died: 1/5/1963; MLB Career: 23 years, 2259 G (.358-301-1584)

REGULAR SEASON							Index			Playoffs			World Series		
Year Tm	Lg	G	W	L	Pct	Standing	EW	+/-	Pt	W	L	Pct	W	L	Pct
1925 StL	NL	115	64	51	.557	8 4	54	10	1						
1926 StL	NL	156	89	65	.578	1	76	13	5				4	3	.571
1927 NYG	NL	33	22	10	.688	4 3	17	5	0						
1928 Bos	NL	122	39	83	.320	7 7	53	-14	0						
1930 ChN	NL	4	4	0	1.000	2 2	2	2	0						
1931 ChN	NL	156	84	70	.545	3	88	-4	1						
1932 ChN	NL	99	53	46	.535	2 1	55	-2	0						
1933 StL	AL	54	19	33	.365	8 8	22	-3	0						
1934 StL	AL	154	67	85	.441	6	62	5	0						
1935 StL	AL	155	65	87	.428	7	67	-2	0						
1936 StL	AL	155	57	95	.375	7	67	-10	0						
1937 StL	AL	78	25	52	.325	7 8	32	-7	0						
1952 StL	AL	53	22	29	.431	8 7	20	2	0						
Cin	NL	51	27	24	.529	7 6	23	4	0						
1953 Cin	NL	147	64	82	.438	6 6	67	-3	0						
6 AL Years		649	255	381	.401	— — —	270	-15	0						
9 NL Years		883	446	431	.509	— — —	435	11	7				4	3	.571
14 Years		1532	701	812	.463	— — —	705	-4	7				4	3	.571

Ralph Houk

Born: 8/9/1919 in Lawrence, Kansas; Died: 8/9/1919; MLB Career: 8 years, 91 G (.272-0-20)

REGULAR SEASON							Index			Playoffs			World Series		
Year Tm	Lg	G	W	L	Pct	Standing	EW	+/-	Pt	W	L	Pct	W	L	Pct
1961 NYA	AL	163	109	53	.673	1	100	9	6				4	1	.800
1962 NYA	AL	162	96	66	.593	1	100	-4	5				4	3	.571
1963 NYA	AL	161	104	57	.646	1	95	9	5				0	4	.000
1966 NYA	AL	140	66	73	.475	10 10	72	-6	0						
1967 NYA	AL	163	72	90	.444	9	78	-6	0						
1968 NYA	AL	164	83	79	.512	5	75	8	1						
1969 NYA	AL	162	80	81	.497	5E	83	-3	0						
1970 NYA	AL	163	93	69	.574	2E	81	12	2						
1971 NYA	AL	162	82	80	.506	4E	88	-6	1						
1972 NYA	AL	155	79	76	.510	4E	79	0	1						
1973 NYA	AL	162	80	82	.494	4E	83	-3	0						
1974 Det	AL	162	72	90	.444	6E	85	-13	0						
1975 Det	AL	159	57	102	.358	6E	77	-20	0						
1976 Det	AL	161	74	87	.460	5E	69	5	0						
1977 Det	AL	162	74	88	.457	4E	77	-3	0						
1978 Det	AL	162	86	76	.531	5E	75	11	1						
1981 Bos	AL	56	30	26	.536	5E	30	0	0						
Bos	AL	52	29	23	.558	2E	28	1	1						
1982 Bos	AL	162	89	73	.549	3E	86	3	1						
1983 Bos	AL	162	78	84	.481	6E	86	-8	0						
1984 Bos	AL	162	86	76	.531	4E	81	5	1						
20 Years		3157	1619	1531	.514	— — —	1628	-9	25				8	8	.500

Frank Howard

Born: 8/8/1936 in Columbus, Ohio; MLB Career: 16 years, 1895 G (.273-382-1119)

REGULAR SEASON							Index			Playoffs			World Series		
Year Tm	Lg	G	W	L	Pct	Standing	EW	+/-	Pt	W	L	Pct	W	L	Pct
1981 SD	NL	56	23	33	.411	6W	26	-3	0						
SD	NL	54	18	36	.333	6W	25	-7	0						
1983 NYN	NL	116	52	64	.448	6E 6E	50	2	0						
2 Years		226	93	133	.412	— — —	101	-8	0						

Art Howe

Born: 12/15/1946 in Pittsburgh, Pennsylvania; MLB Career: 11 years, 891 G (.260-43-293)

REGULAR SEASON							Index			Playoffs			World Series		
Year Tm	Lg	G	W	L	Pct	Standing	EW	+/-	Pt	W	L	Pct	W	L	Pct
1989 Hou	NL	162	86	76	.531	3W	83	3	1						
1990 Hou	NL	162	75	87	.463	4W	83	-8	0						
1991 Hou	NL	162	65	97	.401	6W	79	-14	0						
1992 Hou	NL	162	81	81	.500	4W	73	8	0						
1993 Hou	NL	162	85	77	.525	3W	81	4	1						
1996 Oak	AL	162	78	84	.481	3W	76	2	0						
1997 Oak	AL	162	65	97	.401	4W	78	-13	0						
2 AL Years		324	143	181	.441	— — —	154	-11	0						
5 NL Years		810	392	418	.484	— — —	399	-7	2						
7 Years		1134	535	599	.472	— — —	553	-18	2						

Dan Howley

Born: 10/16/1885 in Weymouth, Massachusetts; Died: 3/10/1944; MLB Career: 1 year, 26 G (.125-0-2)

REGULAR SEASON							Index			Playoffs			World Series		
Year Tm	Lg	G	W	L	Pct	Standing	EW	+/-	Pt	W	L	Pct	W	L	Pct
1927 StL	AL	155	59	94	.386	7	69	-10	0						
1928 StL	AL	154	82	72	.532	3	67	15	1						
1929 StL	AL	154	79	73	.520	4	74	5	1						
1930 Cin	NL	154	59	95	.383	7	72	-13	0						
1931 Cin	NL	154	58	96	.377	8	67	-9	0						
1932 Cin	NL	155	60	94	.390	8	64	-4	0						
3 AL Years		463	220	239	.479	— — —	210	10	2						
3 NL Years		463	177	285	.383	— — —	203	-26	0						
6 Years		926	397	524	.431	— — —	413	-16	2						

Dick Howser

Born: 5/14/1936 in Miami, Florida; Died: 6/17/1987; MLB Career: 8 years, 789 G (.248-16-165)

REGULAR SEASON							Index			Playoffs			World Series		
Year Tm	Lg	G	W	L	Pct	Standing	EW	+/-	Pt	W	L	Pct	W	L	Pct
1978 NYA	AL	1	0	1	.000	3E 3E 1E	1	-1	0						
1980 NYA	AL	162	103	59	.636	1E	90	13	4	0	3	.000			
1981 KC	AL	33	20	13	.606	2W 1W	19	1	2	0	3	.000			
1982 KC	AL	162	90	72	.556	2W	83	7	1						
1983 KC	AL	163	79	83	.488	2W	88	-9	0						
1984 KC	AL	162	84	78	.519	1W	81	3	2	0	3	.000			
1985 KC	AL	162	91	71	.562	1W	83	8	5	4	3	.571	4	3	.571
1986 KC	AL	88	40	48	.455	4W 3W	47	-7	0						
8 Years		933	507	425	.544	— — —	492	15	14	4	12	.250	4	3	.571

George Huff

Born: 6/11/1872 in Champaign, Illinois; Died: 10/1/1936; MLB Career: Did Not Play

REGULAR SEASON							Index			Playoffs			World Series		
Year Tm	Lg	G	W	L	Pct	Standing	EW	+/-	Pt	W	L	Pct	W	L	Pct
1907 Bos	AL	8	2	6	.250	4 6 7	3	-1	0						

Miller Huggins

Born: 3/27/1879 in Cincinnati, Ohio; Died: 9/25/1929; MLB Career: 13 years, 1586 G (.265-9-318)

REGULAR SEASON							Index			Playoffs			World Series		
Year Tm	Lg	G	W	L	Pct	Standing	EW	+/-	Pt	W	L	Pct	W	L	Pct
1913 StL	NL	153	51	99	.340	8	67	-16	0						
1914 StL	NL	157	81	72	.529	3	63	18	1						
1915 StL	NL	157	72	81	.471	6	74	-2	0						
1916 StL	NL	153	60	93	.392	7	72	-12	0						
1917 StL	NL	154	82	70	.539	3	68	14	1						
1918 NYA	AL	126	60	63	.488	4	59	1	0						
1919 NYA	AL	141	80	59	.576	3	68	12	2						
1920 NYA	AL	154	95	59	.617	3	82	13	2						
1921 NYA	AL	153	98	55	.641	1	87	11	4				3	5	.375
1922 NYA	AL	154	94	60	.610	1	92	2	4				0	4	.000
1923 NYA	AL	152	98	54	.645	1	89	9	5				4	2	.667
1924 NYA	AL	153	89	63	.586	2	92	-3	2						
1925 NYA	AL	156	69	85	.448	7	88	-19	0						
1926 NYA	AL	155	91	63	.591	1	77	14	4				3	4	.429
1927 NYA	AL	155	110	44	.714	1	85	25	6				4	0	1.000
1928 NYA	AL	154	101	53	.656	1	94	7	6				4	0	1.000
1929 NYA	AL	143	82	61	.573	2 2	88	-6	1						
12 AL Years		1796	1067	719	.597	— — —	1001	66	36				18	15	.545
5 NL Years		774	346	415	.455	— — —	344	2	2						
17 Years		2570	1413	1134	.555	— — —	1345	68	38				18	15	.545

Billy Hunter

Born: 6/4/1928 in Punxsutawney, Pennsylvania; MLB Career: 6 years, 630 G (.219-16-144)

Year Tm	Lg	G	W	L	Pct	Standing		EW	+/-	Pt	W	L	Pct	W	L	Pct
												REGULAR SEASON / Index / Playoffs / World Series				
1977 Tex	AL	93	60	33	.645	4W	2W	47	13	2						
1978 Tex	AL	161	86	75	.534	2W	2W	87	-1	0						
2 Years		254	146	108	.575			134	12	2						

Tim Hurst

Born: 6/30/1865 in Ashland, Pennsylvania; Died: 6/4/1915; MLB Career: Did Not Play

Year Tm	Lg	G	W	L	Pct	Standing	EW	+/-	Pt	W	L	Pct	W	L	Pct
1898 StL	NL	154	39	111	.260	12			0						

Fred Hutchinson

Born: 8/12/1919 in Seattle, Washington; Died: 11/12/1964; MLB Career: 11 years, 354 G (95-71, 3.73)

Year Tm	Lg	G	W	L	Pct	Standing		EW	+/-	Pt	W	L	Pct	W	L	Pct
1952 Det	AL	83	27	55	.329	8	8	42	-15	0						
1953 Det	AL	158	60	94	.390		6	65	-5	0						
1954 Det	AL	157	68	86	.442		5	65	3	0						
1956 StL	NL	156	76	78	.494		4	73	3	0						
1957 StL	NL	154	87	67	.565		2	75	12	2						
1958 StL	NL	144	69	75	.479	5	5	76	-7	0						
1959 Cin	NL	74	39	35	.527	7	5	38	1	1						
1960 Cin	NL	154	67	87	.435		6	76	-9	0						
1961 Cin	NL	154	93	61	.604		1	72	21	4				1	4	.200
1962 Cin	NL	162	98	64	.605		3	93	5	2						
1963 Cin	NL	162	86	76	.531		5	92	-6	1						
1964 Cin	NL	100	54	45	.545	3	2	54	0	0						
Cin	NL	10	6	4	.600	4	3 2	6	1	1						
3 AL Years		398	155	235	.397	—	— —	172	-17	0						
9 NL Years		1270	675	592	.533	—	— —	654	21	10				1	4	.200
12 Years		1668	830	827	.501			826	4	10				1	4	.200

Arthur Irwin

Born: 2/14/1858 in Toronto, Canada; Died: 7/16/1921; MLB Career: 13 years, 1010 G (.241-5-396)

Year Tm	Lg	G	W	L	Pct	Standing		EW	+/-	Pt	W	L	Pct	W	L	Pct
1889 WaN	NL	76	28	45	.384	8	8			0						
1891 Bos	AA	139	93	42	.689		1			4						
1892 Was	NL	74	35	39	.473	11	7			0						
Was	NL	34	11	21	.344		11 12			0						
1894 Phi	NL	132	71	57	.555		4			1						
1895 Phi	NL	133	78	53	.595		3			2						
1896 NYG	NL	90	36	53	.404		10 7			0						
1898 Was	NL	30	10	19	.345	11	11			0						
1899 Was	NL	155	54	98	.355		11			0						
7 NL Years		724	323	385	.456	—	— —			3						
1 AA Year		139	93	42	.689	—	— —			4						
8 Years		863	416	427	.493	—	— —			7						

Hughie Jennings

Born: 4/2/1869 in Pittston, Pennsylvania; Died: 2/1/1928; MLB Career: 17 years, 1285 G (.311-18-840)

Year Tm	Lg	G	W	L	Pct	Standing		EW	+/-	Pt	W	L	Pct	W	L	Pct
1907 Det	AL	153	92	58	.613		1	72	20	4				0	4	.000
1908 Det	AL	154	90	63	.588		1	85	5	4				1	4	.200
1909 Det	AL	158	98	54	.645		1	84	14	4				3	4	.429
1910 Det	AL	155	86	68	.558		3	92	-6	1						
1911 Det	AL	154	89	65	.578		2	86	3	2						
1912 Det	AL	154	69	84	.451		6	86	-17	0						
1913 Det	AL	153	66	87	.431		6	75	-9	0						
1914 Det	AL	157	80	73	.523		4	72	8	1						
1915 Det	AL	156	100	54	.649		2	76	24	3						
1916 Det	AL	155	87	67	.565		3	88	-1	2						
1917 Det	AL	155	78	75	.510		4	85	-7	1						
1918 Det	AL	128	55	71	.437		7	67	-12	0						
1919 Det	AL	140	80	60	.571		4	67	13	2						
1920 Det	AL	155	61	93	.396		7	81	-20	0						
1924 NYG	NL	44	32	12	.727	3	1 1	26	6	1						
1925 NYG	NL	32	21	11	.656	1	1 2	19	2	0						
14 AL Years		2127	1131	972	.538	—	— —	1116	15	24				4	12	.250
2 NL Years		76	53	23	.697	—	— —	45	8	1						
16 Years		2203	1184	995	.543	—	— —	1161	23	25				4	12	.250

Darrell Johnson

Born: 8/25/1928 in Horace, Nebraska; MLB Career: 6 years, 134 G (.234-2-28)

Year Tm	Lg	G	W	L	Pct	Standing		EW	+/-	Pt	W	L	Pct	W	L	Pct
1974 Bos	AL	162	84	78	.519		3E	86	-2	1						
1975 Bos	AL	160	95	65	.594		1E	83	12	4	3	0	1.000	3	4	.429
1976 Bos	AL	86	41	45	.477	3E	3E	48	-7	0						
1977 Sea	AL	162	64	98	.395		6W	61	3	0						
1978 Sea	AL	160	56	104	.350		7W	65	-9	0						
1979 Sea	AL	162	67	95	.414		6W	63	4	0						
1980 Sea	AL	105	39	65	.375	7W	7W	44	-5	0						
1982 Tex	AL	66	26	40	.394	6W	6W	34	-8	0						
8 Years		1063	472	590	.444			484	-12	5	3	0	1.000	3	4	.429

Davey Johnson

Born: 1/30/1943 in Orlando, Florida; MLB Career: 13 years, 1435 G (.261-136-609)

Year Tm	Lg	G	W	L	Pct	Standing		EW	+/-	Pt	W	L	Pct	W	L	Pct
1984 NYN	NL	162	90	72	.556		2E	71	19	1						
1985 NYN	NL	162	98	64	.605		2E	82	16	2						
1986 NYN	NL	162	108	54	.667		1E	89	19	6	4	2	.667	4	3	.571
1987 NYN	NL	162	92	70	.568		2E	98	-6	2						
1988 NYN	NL	160	100	60	.625		1E	91	9	4	3	4	.429			
1989 NYN	NL	162	87	75	.537		2E	96	-9	1						
1990 NYN	NL	42	20	22	.476	4E	2E	23	-3	0						
1993 Cin	NL	118	53	65	.449	5W	5W	66	-13	0						
1994 Cin	NL	115	66	48	.579		1C	55	11	2						
1995 Cin	NL	144	85	59	.590		1C	78	7	3	3	4	.429			
1996 Bal	AL	163	88	74	.543		2E	82	6	1	4	5	.444			
1997 Bal	AL	162	98	64	.605		1E	85	13	3	5	5	.500			
2 AL Years		325	186	138	.574	—	— —	167	19	4	9	10	.474			
10 NL Years		1389	799	589	.576	—	— —	749	50	21	10	10	.500	4	3	.571
12 Years		1714	985	727	.575	—	— —	916	69	25	19	20	.487	4	3	.571

Roy Johnson

Born: 10/1/1895 in Madill, Oklahoma; Died: 1/10/1986; MLB Career: 1 year, 10 G (1-5, 3.42)

Year Tm	Lg	G	W	L	Pct	Standing		EW	+/-	Pt	W	L	Pct	W	L	Pct
1944 ChN	NL	1	0	1	.000	8	8 4	0	0	0						

Walter Johnson

Born: 11/6/1887 in Humboldt, Kansas; Died: 12/10/1946; MLB Career: 21 years, 928 G (417-279, 2.17)

Year Tm	Lg	G	W	L	Pct	Standing		EW	+/-	Pt	W	L	Pct	W	L	Pct
1929 Was	AL	153	71	81	.467		5	77	-6	0						
1930 Was	AL	154	94	60	.610		2	75	19	2						
1931 Was	AL	156	92	62	.597		3	85	7	2						
1932 Was	AL	154	93	61	.604		3	86	7	2						
1933 Cle	AL	99	48	51	.485	5	4	53	-5	0						
1934 Cle	AL	154	85	69	.552		3	78	7	1						
1935 Cle	AL	96	46	48	.489	5	3	50	-4	0						
7 Years		966	529	432	.550			504	25	7						

Fielder Jones

Born: 8/13/1871 in Shinglehouse, Pennsylvania; Died: 3/13/1934; MLB Career: 15 years, 1788 G (.285-21-631)

Year Tm	Lg	G	W	L	Pct	Standing		EW	+/-	Pt	W	L	Pct	W	L	Pct
1904 ChA	AL	114	66	47	.584	4	3	55	11	1						
1905 ChA	AL	158	92	60	.605		2	82	10	2						
1906 ChA	AL	154	93	58	.616		1	84	9	5				4	2	.667
1907 ChA	AL	157	87	64	.576		3	88	-1	2						
1908 ChA	AL	156	88	64	.579		3	86	2	2						
1914 StL	FL	40	12	26	.316	7	8	19	-7	0						
1915 StL	FL	159	87	67	.565		2	70	17	2						
1916 StL	AL	158	79	75	.513		5	67	12	1						
1917 StL	AL	155	57	97	.370		7	76	-19	0						
1918 StL	AL	46	22	24	.478	5	5	19	3	0						
8 AL Years		1098	584	489	.544	—	— —	557	27	13				4	2	.667
2 FL Years		199	99	93	.516	—	— —	89	10	2						
10 Years		1297	683	582	.540	—	— —	646	37	15				4	2	.667

Eddie Joost

Born: 6/5/1916 in San Francisco, California; MLB Career: 17 years, 1574 G (.239-134-601)

Year Tm	Lg	G	W	L	Pct	Standing	EW	+/-	Pt	W	L	Pct	W	L	Pct
1954 Phi	AL	156	51	103	.331	8	67	-16	0						

Mike Jorgensen

Born: 8/16/1948 in Passaic, New Jersey; MLB Career: 17 years, 1633 G (.243-95-426)

Year Tm	Lg	G	W	L	Pct	Standing		EW	+/-	Pt	W	L	Pct	W	L	Pct
1995 StL	NL	96	42	54	.438	4C	4C	48	-6	0						

Bill Joyce

Born: 9/21/1865 in St. Louis, Missouri; Died: 5/8/1941; MLB Career: 8 years, 904 G (.294-70-607)

Year Tm	Lg	G	W	L	Pct	Standing		EW	+/-	Pt	W	L	Pct	W	L	Pct
1896 NYG	NL	43	28	14	.667	10	7			0						
1897 NYG	NL	138	83	48	.634		3			2						
1898 NYG	NL	43	22	21	.512	6	7			0						
NYG	NL	92	46	39	.541	7	7			1						
3 Years		316	179	122	.595	—	— —			3						

Billy Jurges

Born: 5/9/1908 in Bronx, New York; Died: 3/3/1997; MLB Career: 17 years, 1816 G (.258-43-656)

Year Tm	Lg	G	W	L	Pct	Standing		EW	+/-	Pt	W	L	Pct	W	L	Pct
1959 Bos	AL	80	44	36	.550	8	5	41	3	1						
1960 Bos	AL	42	15	27	.357	8	7	21	-6	0						
2 Years		122	59	63	.484			62	-3	1						

Eddie Kasko

Born: 6/27/1932 in Linden, New Jersey; MLB Career: 10 years, 1077 G (.264-22-261)

Year Tm	Lg	G	W	L	Pct	Standing	EW	+/-	Pt	W	L	Pct	W	L	Pct
1970 Bos	AL	162	87	75	.537	3E	87	0	1						
1971 Bos	AL	162	85	77	.525	3E	86	-1	1						
1972 Bos	AL	155	85	70	.548	2E	81	4	1						
1973 Bos	AL	161	88	73	.547	2E 2E	86	2	0						
4 Years		640	345	295	.539	— — —	340	5	3						

Johnny Keane

Born: 11/3/1911 in St. Louis, Missouri; Died: 1/6/1967; MLB Career: Did Not Play

Year Tm	Lg	G	W	L	Pct	Standing	EW	+/-	Pt	W	L	Pct	W	L	Pct
1961 StL	NL	80	47	33	.588	6 5	42	5	1						
1962 StL	NL	163	84	78	.519	6	88	-4	1						
1963 StL	NL	162	93	69	.574	2	86	7	2						
1964 StL	NL	162	93	69	.574	1	89	4	5				4	3	.571
1965 NYA	AL	162	77	85	.475	6	95	-18	0						
1966 NYA	AL	20	4	16	.200	10 10	10	-6	0						
2 AL Years		182	81	101	.445		105	-24	0						
4 NL Years		567	317	249	.560	— — —	305	12	9				4	3	.571
6 Years		749	398	350	.532	— — —	410	-12	9				4	3	.571

Joe Kelley

Born: 12/9/1871 in Cambridge, Massachusetts; Died: 8/14/1943; MLB Career: 17 years, 1842 G (.317-65-1194)

Year Tm	Lg	G	W	L	Pct	Standing	EW	+/-	Pt	W	L	Pct	W	L	Pct
1902 Cin	NL	60	34	26	.567	5 4	26	8	1						
1903 Cin	NL	141	74	65	.532	4	66	8	1						
1904 Cin	NL	157	88	65	.575	3	77	11	2						
1905 Cin	NL	155	79	74	.516	5	83	-4	1						
1908 Bos	NL	156	63	91	.409	8	62	1	0						
5 Years		669	338	321	.513	— — —	314	24	5						

Honest John Kelly

Born: 10/31/1856 in New York, New York; Died: 3/27/1926; MLB Career: Did Not Play

Year Tm	Lg	G	W	L	Pct	Standing	EW	+/-	Pt	W	L	Pct	W	L	Pct
1887 Lou	AA	139	76	60	.559	4			1						
1888 Lou	AA	39	10	29	.256	8 7			0						
2 Years		178	86	89	.491	— — —			1						

King Kelly

Born: 12/31/1857 in Troy, New York; Died: 11/8/1894; MLB Career: 16 years, 1455 G (.308-69-950)

Year Tm	Lg	G	W	L	Pct	Standing	EW	+/-	Pt	W	L	Pct	W	L	Pct
1887 Bos	NL	94	49	43	.533	5 5			0						
1890 Bos	PL	133	81	48	.628	1			4						
1891 Cin	AA	102	43	57	.430	7			0						
1 NL Year		94	49	43	.533	— — —			0						
1 PL Year		133	81	48	.628				4						
1 AA Year		102	43	57	.430				0						
3 Years		329	173	148	.539	— — —			4						

Tom Kelly

Born: 8/15/1950 in Graceville, Minnesota; MLB Career: 1 year, 49 G (.181-1-11)

Year Tm	Lg	G	W	L	Pct	Standing	EW	+/-	Pt	W	L	Pct	W	L	Pct
1986 Min	AL	23	12	11	.522	7W 6W	11	1	0						
1987 Min	AL	162	85	77	.525	1W	76	9	4	4	1	.800	4	3	.571
1988 Min	AL	162	91	71	.562	2W	81	10	2						
1989 Min	AL	162	80	82	.494	5W	85	-5	0						
1990 Min	AL	162	74	88	.457	7W	82	-8	0						
1991 Min	AL	162	95	67	.586	1W	79	16	5	4	1	.800	4	3	.571
1992 Min	AL	162	90	72	.556	2W	87	3	1						
1993 Min	AL	162	71	91	.438	5W	86	-15	0						
1994 Min	AL	113	53	60	.469	4C	55	-2	0						
1995 Min	AL	144	56	88	.389	5C	70	-14	0						
1996 Min	AL	162	78	84	.481	4C	70	8	0						
1997 Min	AL	162	68	94	.420	4C	77	-9	0						
12 Years		1738	853	885	.491	— — —	859	-6	12	8	2	.800	8	6	.571

Bob Kennedy

Born: 8/18/1920 in Chicago, Illinois; MLB Career: 16 years, 1483 G (.254-63-514)

Year Tm	Lg	G	W	L	Pct	Standing	EW	+/-	Pt	W	L	Pct	W	L	Pct
1963 ChN	NL	162	82	80	.506	7	67	15	1						
1964 ChN	NL	162	76	86	.469	8	78	-2	0						
1965 ChN	NL	58	24	32	.429	9 8	26	-2	0						
1968 Oak	AL	163	82	80	.506	6	68	14	1						
1 AL Year		163	82	80	.506	— — —	68	14	1						
3 NL Years		382	182	198	.479	— — —	171	11	1						
4 Years		545	264	278	.487	— — —	239	25	2						

Jim Kennedy

Born: Unknown in New York, New York; Died: 4/20/1904; MLB Career: Did Not Play

Year Tm	Lg	G	W	L	Pct	Standing	EW	+/-	Pt	W	L	Pct	W	L	Pct
1890 Brk	AA	100	26	72	.265	9			0						

Kevin Kennedy

Born: 5/26/1954 in Los Angeles, California; MLB Career: Did Not Play

Year Tm	Lg	G	W	L	Pct	Standing	EW	+/-	Pt	W	L	Pct	W	L	Pct
1993 Tex	AL	162	86	76	.531	2W	80	6	1						
1994 Tex	AL	114	52	62	.456	1W	59	-7	2						
1995 Bos	AL	144	86	58	.597	1E	69	17	3	0	3	.000			
1996 Bos	AL	162	85	77	.525	3E	88	-3	1						
4 Years		582	309	273	.531	— — —	296	13	7	0	3	.000			

John Kerins

Born: 7/15/1858 in Indianapolis, Indiana; Died: 9/8/1919; MLB Career: 7 years, 557 G (.252-20-217)

Year Tm	Lg	G	W	L	Pct	Standing	EW	+/-	Pt	W	L	Pct	W	L	Pct
1888 Lou	AA	7	3	4	.429	8 8 7			0						
1890 StL	AA	17	9	8	.529	4 4 3			0						
2 Years		24	12	12	.500	— — —			0						

Don Kessinger

Born: 7/17/1942 in Forrest City, Arkansas; MLB Career: 16 years, 2078 G (.252-14-527)

Year Tm	Lg	G	W	L	Pct	Standing	EW	+/-	Pt	W	L	Pct	W	L	Pct
1979 ChA	AL	106	46	60	.434	5W 5W	50	-4	0						

Bill Killefer

Born: 10/10/1887 in Bloomingdale, Michigan; Died: 7/3/1960; MLB Career: 13 years, 1035 G (.238-4-240)

Year Tm	Lg	G	W	L	Pct	Standing	EW	+/-	Pt	W	L	Pct	W	L	Pct
1921 ChN	NL	57	23	34	.404	6 7	29	-6	0						
1922 ChN	NL	156	80	74	.519	5	71	9	1						
1923 ChN	NL	154	83	71	.539	4	77	6	1						
1924 ChN	NL	154	81	72	.529	5	78	3	1						
1925 ChN	NL	75	33	42	.440	7 8	39	-6	0						
1930 StL	AL	154	64	90	.416	6	77	-13	0						
1931 StL	AL	154	63	91	.409	5	71	-8	0						
1932 StL	AL	154	63	91	.409	6	69	-6	0						
1933 StL	AL	91	34	57	.374	8 8	39	-5	0						
4 AL Years		553	224	329	.405	— — —	256	-32	0						
5 NL Years		596	300	293	.506	— — —	294	6	3						
9 Years		1149	524	622	.457	— — —	550	-26	3						

Clyde King

Born: 5/23/1925 in Goldsboro, North Carolina; MLB Career: 7 years, 201 G (32-25, 4.14)

Year Tm	Lg	G	W	L	Pct	Standing	EW	+/-	Pt	W	L	Pct	W	L	Pct
1969 SF	NL	162	90	72	.556	2W	91	-1	1						
1970 SF	NL	42	19	23	.452	4W 3W	23	-4	0						
1974 Atl	NL	64	38	25	.603	4W 3W	30	8	1						
1975 Atl	NL	134	58	76	.433	5W 5W	69	-11	0						
1982 NYA	AL	62	29	33	.468	5E 5E	34	-5	0						
1 AL Year		62	29	33	.468	— — —	34	-5	0						
4 NL Years		402	205	196	.511	— — —	213	-8	2						
5 Years		464	234	229	.505	— — —	247	-13	2						

Mal Kittridge

Born: 10/12/1869 in Clinton, Massachusetts; Died: 6/23/1928; MLB Career: 16 years, 1214 G (.219-17-390)

Year Tm	Lg	G	W	L	Pct	Standing	EW	+/-	Pt	W	L	Pct	W	L	Pct
1904 Was	AL	18	1	16	.059	8 8	7	-6	0						

Lou Klein

Born: 10/22/1918 in New Orleans, Louisiana; Died: 6/20/1976; MLB Career: 5 years, 305 G (.259-16-101)

Year Tm	Lg	G	W	L	Pct	Standing	EW	+/-	Pt	W	L	Pct	W	L	Pct
1961 ChN	NL	11	5	6	.455	7 7 7	5	0	0						
1962 ChN	NL	30	12	18	.400	9 9 9	14	-2	0						
1965 ChN	NL	106	48	58	.453	9 8	50	-2	0						
3 Years		147	65	82	.442	— — —	69	-4	0						

Johnny Kling

Born: 2/25/1875 in Kansas City, Missouri; Died: 1/31/1947; MLB Career: 13 years, 1260 G (.272-20-513)

Year Tm	Lg	G	W	L	Pct	Standing	EW	+/-	Pt	W	L	Pct	W	L	Pct
1912 Bos	NL	155	52	101	.340	8	54	-2	0						

Otto Knabe

Born: 6/12/1884 in Carrick, Pennsylvania; Died: 5/17/1961; MLB Career: 11 years, 1279 G (.247-8-365)

Year Tm	Lg	G	W	L	Pct	Standing		EW	+/-	Pt	W	L	Pct	W	L	Pct
						REGULAR SEASON		Index			Playoffs			World Series		
1914 Bal	FL	160	84	70	.545		3	77	7	1						
1915 Bal	FL	155	47	107	.305		8	81	-34	0						
2 Years		315	131	177	.425	—	—	158	-27	1						

Lon Knight

Born: 6/16/1853 in Philadelphia, Pennsylvania; Died: 4/23/1932; MLB Career: 7 years, 532 G (.245-3-143)

Year Tm	Lg	G	W	L	Pct	Standing		EW	+/-	Pt	W	L	Pct	W	L	Pct
1883 Phi	AA	98	66	32	.673		1			4						
1884 Phi	AA	108	61	46	.570		7			1						
2 Years		206	127	78	.620	—	—			5						

Ray Knight

Born: 12/28/1952 in Albany, Georgia; MLB Career: 13 years, 1495 G (.271-84-595)

Year Tm	Lg	G	W	L	Pct	Standing		EW	+/-	Pt	W	L	Pct	W	L	Pct
1996 Cin	NL	162	81	81	.500		3C	88	-7	0						
1997 Cin	NL	96	42	54	.438	4C	3C	50	-8	0						
2 Years		258	123	135	.477			138	-15	0						

Bobby Knoop

Born: 10/18/1938 in Sioux City, Iowa; MLB Career: 9 years, 1153 G (.236-56-331)

Year Tm	Lg	G	W	L	Pct	Standing			EW	+/-	Pt	W	L	Pct	W	L	Pct
1994 Cal	AL	2	1	1	.500	3W	2W	4W	1	0	0						

Jack Krol

Born: 7/5/1936 in Chicago, Illinois; Died: 5/30/1994; MLB Career: Did Not Play

Year Tm	Lg	G	W	L	Pct	Standing			EW	+/-	Pt	W	L	Pct	W	L	Pct
1978 StL	NL	2	1	1	.500	6E	6E	5E	1	0	0						
1980 StL	NL	1	0	1	.000	6E	6E	4E	1	-1	0						
2 Years		3	1	2	.333	—	—		2	-1	0						

Karl Kuehl

Born: 9/5/1937 in Monterey Park, California; MLB Career: Did Not Play

Year Tm	Lg	G	W	L	Pct	Standing		EW	+/-	Pt	W	L	Pct	W	L	Pct
1976 Mon	NL	128	43	85	.336	6E	6E	61	-18	0						

Harvey Kuenn

Born: 12/4/1930 in West Allis, Wisconsin; Died: 2/28/1988; MLB Career: 15 years, 1833 G (.303-87-671)

Year Tm	Lg	G	W	L	Pct	Standing		EW	+/-	Pt	W	L	Pct	W	L	Pct
1975 Mil	AL	1	1	0	1.000	5E	5E	0	1	0						
1982 Mil	AL	116	72	43	.626	5E	1E	63	9	4	3	2	.600	3	4	.429
1983 Mil	AL	162	87	75	.537		5E	90	-3	1						
3 Years		279	160	118	.576			153	7	5	3	2	.600	3	4	.429

Joe Kuhel

Born: 6/25/1906 in Cleveland, Ohio; Died: 2/26/1984; MLB Career: 18 years, 2104 G (.277-131-1049)

Year Tm	Lg	G	W	L	Pct	Standing	EW	+/-	Pt	W	L	Pct	W	L	Pct
1948 Was	AL	154	56	97	.366	7	71	-15	0						
1949 Was	AL	154	50	104	.325	8	65	-15	0						
2 Years		308	106	201	.345		136	-30	0						

Tony La Russa

Born: 10/4/1944 in Tampa, Florida; MLB Career: 6 years, 132 G (.199-0-7)

Year Tm	Lg	G	W	L	Pct	Standing		EW	+/-	Pt	W	L	Pct	W	L	Pct
1979 ChA	AL	54	27	27	.500	5W	5W	25	2	0						
1980 ChA	AL	162	70	90	.438		5W	76	-6	0						
1981 ChA	AL	53	31	22	.585		3W	24	7	0						
ChA	AL	53	23	30	.434		6W	24	-1	0						
1982 ChA	AL	162	87	75	.537		3W	79	8	1						
1983 ChA	AL	162	99	63	.611		1W	83	16	3	1	3	.250			
1984 ChA	AL	162	74	88	.457		5W	91	-17	0						
1985 ChA	AL	163	85	77	.525		3W	81	4	1						
1986 ChA	AL	64	26	38	.406	6W	5W	33	-7	0						
Oak	AL	79	45	34	.570	7W	3W	38	7	1						
1987 Oak	AL	162	81	81	.500		3W	78	3	0						
1988 Oak	AL	162	104	58	.642		1W	80	24	5	4	0	1.000	1	4	.200
1989 Oak	AL	162	99	63	.611		1W	92	7	5	4	1	.800	4	0	1.000
1990 Oak	AL	162	103	59	.636		1W	93	10	5	4	0	1.000	0	4	.000
1991 Oak	AL	162	84	78	.519		4W	97	-13	1						
1992 Oak	AL	162	96	66	.593		1W	88	8	3	2	4	.333			
1993 Oak	AL	162	68	94	.420		7W	92	-24	0						
1994 Oak	AL	114	51	63	.447		2W	54	-3	0						
1995 Oak	AL	144	67	77	.465		4W	69	-2	0						
1996 StL	NL	162	88	74	.543		1C	76	12	5	6	4	.600			
1997 StL	NL	162	73	89	.451		4C	83	-10	0						
18 AL Years		2506	1320	1183	.527	—	—	1297	23	26	15	8	.652	5	8	.385

Year Tm	Lg	G	W	L	Pct	Standing		EW	+/-	Pt	W	L	Pct	W	L	Pct
2 NL Years		324	161	163	.497	—	—	159	2	2	6	4	.600			
19 Years		2830	1481	1346	.524	—	—	1456	25	28	21	12	.636	5	8	.385

Marcel Lachemann

Born: 6/13/1941 in Los Angeles, California; MLB Career: 3 years, 70 G (7-4, 3.44)

Year Tm	Lg	G	W	L	Pct	Standing		EW	+/-	Pt	W	L	Pct	W	L	Pct
1994 Cal	AL	74	30	44	.405	2W	4W	34	-4	0						
1995 Cal	AL	145	78	67	.538		2W	64	14	1						
1996 Cal	AL	117	53	64	.453		4W 4W	59	-6	0						
3 Years		336	161	175	.479			157	4	1						

Rene Lachemann

Born: 5/4/1945 in Los Angeles, California; MLB Career: 3 years, 118 G (.210-9-33)

Year Tm	Lg	G	W	L	Pct	Standing		EW	+/-	Pt	W	L	Pct	W	L	Pct
1981 Sea	AL	33	15	18	.455	7W	6W	13	2	0						
Sea	AL	52	23	29	.442		5W	20	3	0						
1982 Sea	AL	162	76	86	.469		4W	69	7	0						
1983 Sea	AL	73	26	47	.356	7W	7W	33	-7	0						
1984 Mil	AL	161	67	94	.416		7E	86	-19	0						
1993 Fla	NL	162	64	98	.395		6E	61	3	0						
1994 Fla	NL	115	51	64	.443		5E	46	5	0						
1995 Fla	NL	143	67	76	.469		4E	62	5	0						
1996 Fla	NL	86	39	47	.453	4E	3E	40	-1	0						
4 AL Years		481	207	274	.430	—	—	221	-14	0						
4 NL Years		506	221	285	.437	—	—	209	12	0						
8 Years		987	428	559	.434	—	—	430	-2	0						

Nap Lajoie

Born: 9/5/1874 in Woonsocket, Rhode Island; Died: 2/7/1959; MLB Career: 21 years, 2480 G (.338-82-1599)

Year Tm	Lg	G	W	L	Pct	Standing		EW	+/-	Pt	W	L	Pct	W	L	Pct
1905 Cle	AL	58	37	21	.638	1	5	31	6	0						
Cle	AL	56	19	36	.345	2	5	30	-11	0						
1906 Cle	AL	157	89	64	.582		3	78	11	2						
1907 Cle	AL	158	85	67	.559		4	83	2	1						
1908 Cle	AL	157	90	64	.584		2	83	7	2						
1909 Cle	AL	114	57	57	.500	6	6	64	-7	0						
5 Years		700	377	309	.550	—	— —	369	8	5						

Fred Lake

Born: 10/16/1866 in Nova Scotia, Canada; Died: 11/24/1931; MLB Career: 5 years, 48 G (.232-1-16)

Year Tm	Lg	G	W	L	Pct	Standing		EW	+/-	Pt	W	L	Pct	W	L	Pct
1908 Bos	AL	40	22	17	.564	6	5	17	5	0						
1909 Bos	AL	152	88	63	.583		3	69	19	2						
1910 Bos	NL	157	53	100	.346		8	57	-4	0						
2 AL Years		192	110	80	.579	—	—	86	24	2						
1 NL Year		157	53	100	.346	—	—	57	-4	0						
3 Years		349	163	180	.475	—	—	143	20	2						

Gene Lamont

Born: 12/25/1946 in Rockford, Illinois; MLB Career: 5 years, 87 G (.233-4-14)

Year Tm	Lg	G	W	L	Pct	Standing		EW	+/-	Pt	W	L	Pct	W	L	Pct
1992 ChA	AL	162	86	76	.531		3W	84	2	1						
1993 ChA	AL	162	94	68	.580		1W	86	8	3	2	4	.333			
1994 ChA	AL	113	67	46	.593		1C	62	5	3						
1995 ChA	AL	31	11	20	.355	4C	3C	17	-6	0						
1997 Pit	NL	162	79	83	.488		2C	74	5	0						
4 AL Years		468	258	210	.551	—	—	249	9	7	2	4	.333			
1 NL Year		162	79	83	.488	—	—	74	5	0						
5 Years		630	337	293	.535	—	—	323	14	7	2	4	.333			

Hal Lanier

Born: 7/4/1942 in Denton, North Carolina; MLB Career: 10 years, 1196 G (.228-8-273)

Year Tm	Lg	G	W	L	Pct	Standing		EW	+/-	Pt	W	L	Pct	W	L	Pct
1986 Hou	NL	162	96	66	.593		1W	82	14	3	2	4	.333			
1987 Hou	NL	162	76	86	.469		3W	89	-13	0						
1988 Hou	NL	162	82	80	.506		5W	81	1	1						
3 Years		486	254	232	.523	—	—	252	2	4	2	4	.333			

Henry Larkin

Born: 1/12/1860 in Reading, Pennsylvania; Died: 1/31/1942; MLB Career: 10 years, 1184 G (.303-53-799)

Year Tm	Lg	G	W	L	Pct	Standing		EW	+/-	Pt	W	L	Pct	W	L	Pct
1890 Cle	PL	79	34	45	.430	7	7			0						

Tom Lasorda

Born: 9/22/1927 in Norristown, Pennsylvania; MLB Career: 3 years, 27 G (0-4, 6.48)

Year Tm	Lg	G	W	L	Pct	Standing		EW	+/-	Pt	W	L	Pct	W	L	Pct
1976 LA	NL	4	2	2	.500	2W	2W	2	0	0						
1977 LA	NL	162	98	64	.605		1W	90	8	4	3	1	.750	2	4	.333

Year Tm	Lg	G	W	L	Pct	Standing	EW	+/-	Pt	W	L	Pct	W	L	Pct
1978 LA	NL	162	95	67	.586	1W	92	3	4	3	1	.750	2	4	.333
1979 LA	NL	162	79	83	.488	3W	92	-13	0						
1980 LA	NL	163	92	71	.564	2W	84	8	2						
1981 LA	NL	57	36	21	.632	1W	31	5	0						
LA	NL	53	27	26	.509	4W	29	-2	4	6	4	.600	4	2	.667
1982 LA	NL	162	88	74	.543	2W	87	1	1						
1983 LA	NL	163	91	71	.562	1W	87	4	3	1	3	.250			
1984 LA	NL	162	79	83	.488	4W	88	-9	0						
1985 LA	NL	162	95	67	.586	1W	82	13	3	2	4	.333			
1986 LA	NL	162	73	89	.451	5W	89	-16	0						
1987 LA	NL	162	73	89	.451	4W	79	-6	0						
1988 LA	NL	162	94	67	.584	1W	77	17	5	4	3	.571	4	1	.800
1989 LA	NL	160	77	83	.481	2W	85	-8	0						
1990 LA	NL	162	86	76	.531	2W	80	6	1						
1991 LA	NL	162	93	69	.574	2W	85	8	2						
1992 LA	NL	162	63	99	.389	6W	87	-24	0						
1993 LA	NL	162	81	81	.500	4W	77	4	0						
1994 LA	NL	114	58	56	.509	1W	57	1	2						
1995 LA	NL	144	78	66	.542	1W	71	7	2	0	3	.000			
1996 LA	NL	76	41	35	.539	1W 2W	40	1	0						
21 Years		3040	1599	1439	.526	— — —	1591	8	33	19	19	.500	12	11	.522

Arlie Latham

Born: 3/15/1860 in West Lebanon, N.H.; Died: 11/29/1952; MLB Career: 17 years, 1627 G (.269-27-562)

Year Tm	Lg	G	W	L	Pct	Standing	EW	+/-	Pt	W	L	Pct	W	L	Pct
1896 StL	NL	3	0	3	.000	10 10 11			0						

Juice Latham

Born: 9/6/1852 in Utica, New York; Died: 5/26/1914; MLB Career: 4 years, 298 G (.248-0-60)

Year Tm	Lg	G	W	L	Pct	Standing	EW	+/-	Pt	W	L	Pct	W	L	Pct
1882 Phi	AA	75	41	34	.547	2			1						

Cookie Lavagetto

Born: 12/1/1912 in Oakland, California; Died: 8/10/1990; MLB Career: 10 years, 1043 G (.269-40-486)

Year Tm	Lg	G	W	L	Pct	Standing	EW	+/-	Pt	W	L	Pct	W	L	Pct
1957 Was	AL	134	51	83	.381	8 8	55	-4	0						
1958 Was	AL	156	61	93	.396	8	61	0	0						
1959 Was	AL	154	63	91	.409	8	64	-1	0						
1960 Was	AL	154	73	81	.474	5	65	8	0						
1961 Min	AL	49	19	30	.388	8 7	24	-5	0						
Min	AL	10	4	6	.400	9 9 7	5	-1	0						
5 Years		657	271	384	.414	— — —	274	-3	0						

Bob Leadley

Born: 1/1/1858 in Brooklyn, New York; MLB Career: Did Not Play

Year Tm	Lg	G	W	L	Pct	Standing	EW	+/-	Pt	W	L	Pct	W	L	Pct
1888 Det	NL	40	19	19	.500	3 5			0						
1890 Cle	NL	58	23	33	.411	7 7			0						
1891 Cle	NL	68	34	34	.500	6 5			0						
3 Years		166	76	86	.469				0						

Jim Lefebvre

Born: 1/7/1942 in Inglewood, California; MLB Career: 8 years, 922 G (.251-74-404)

Year Tm	Lg	G	W	L	Pct	Standing	EW	+/-	Pt	W	L	Pct	W	L	Pct
1989 Sea	AL	162	73	89	.451	6W	73	0	0						
1990 Sea	AL	162	77	85	.475	5W	75	2	0						
1991 Sea	AL	162	83	79	.512	5W	76	7	1						
1992 ChN	NL	162	78	84	.481	4E	80	-2	0						
1993 ChN	NL	163	84	78	.519	4E	82	2	1						
3 AL Years		486	233	253	.479	— — —	224	9	1						
2 NL Years		325	162	162	.500	— — —	162	0	1						
5 Years		811	395	415	.488	— — —	386	9	2						

Bob Lemon

Born: 9/22/1920 in San Bernardino, California; MLB Career: 15 years, 615 G (207-128, 3.23)

Year Tm	Lg	G	W	L	Pct	Standing	EW	+/-	Pt	W	L	Pct	W	L	Pct
1970 KC	AL	110	46	64	.418	5W 4W	46	0	0						
1971 KC	AL	161	85	76	.528	2W	68	17	1						
1972 KC	AL	154	76	78	.494	4W	76	0	0						
1977 ChA	AL	162	90	72	.556	3W	75	15	1						
1978 ChA	AL	74	34	40	.459	5W 5W	38	-4	0						
NYA	AL	68	48	20	.706	3E 1E	40	8	5	3	1	.750	4	2	.667
1979 NYA	AL	65	34	31	.523	4E 4E	39	-5	0						
1981 NYA	AL	25	11	14	.440	5E 6E	15	-4	3	6	2	.750	2	4	.333
1982 NYA	AL	14	6	8	.429	4E 5E	8	-2	0						
8 Years		833	430	403	.516	— — —	405	25	10	9	3	.750	6	6	.500

Jim Lemon

Born: 3/23/1928 in Covington, Virginia; MLB Career: 12 years, 1010 G (.262-164-529)

Year Tm	Lg	G	W	L	Pct	Standing	EW	+/-	Pt	W	L	Pct	W	L	Pct
1968 Was	AL	161	65	96	.404	10	76	-11	0						

Jim Leyland

Born: 12/15/1944 in Toledo, Ohio; MLB Career: Did Not Play

Year Tm	Lg	G	W	L	Pct	Standing	EW	+/-	Pt	W	L	Pct	W	L	Pct
1986 Pit	NL	162	64	98	.395	6E	69	-5	0						
1987 Pit	NL	162	80	82	.494	4E	69	11	0						
1988 Pit	NL	160	85	75	.531	2E	74	11	1						
1989 Pit	NL	164	74	88	.457	5E	81	-7	0						
1990 Pit	NL	162	95	67	.586	1E	78	17	3	2	4	.333			
1991 Pit	NL	162	98	64	.605	1E	88	10	3	3	4	.429			
1992 Pit	NL	162	96	66	.593	1E	90	6	3	3	4	.429			
1993 Pit	NL	162	75	87	.463	5E	96	-21	0						
1994 Pit	NL	114	53	61	.465	3C	59	-6	0						
1995 Pit	NL	144	58	86	.403	5C	72	-14	0						
1996 Pit	NL	162	73	89	.451	5C	72	1	0						
1997 Fla	NL	162	92	70	.568	2E	79	13	5	7	2	.778	4	3	.571
12 Years		1878	943	933	.503	— — —	927	16	15	15	14	.517	4	3	.571

Nick Leyva

Born: 8/16/1953 in Ontario, California; MLB Career: Did Not Play

Year Tm	Lg	G	W	L	Pct	Standing	EW	+/-	Pt	W	L	Pct	W	L	Pct
1989 Phi	NL	163	67	95	.414	6E	74	-7	0						
1990 Phi	NL	162	77	85	.475	4E	72	5	0						
1991 Phi	NL	13	4	9	.308	6E 3E	6	-2	0						
3 Years		338	148	189	.439	— — —	152	-4	0						

Bob Lillis

Born: 6/2/1930 in Altadena, California; MLB Career: 10 years, 817 G (.236-3-137)

Year Tm	Lg	G	W	L	Pct	Standing	EW	+/-	Pt	W	L	Pct	W	L	Pct
1982 Hou	NL	51	28	23	.549	5W 5W	28	0	0						
1983 Hou	NL	162	85	77	.525	3W	81	4	1						
1984 Hou	NL	162	80	82	.494	2W	83	-3	0						
1985 Hou	NL	162	83	79	.512	3W	81	2	1						
4 Years		537	276	261	.514	— — —	273	3	2						

Johnny Lipon

Born: 11/10/1922 in Martins Ferry, Ohio; MLB Career: 9 years, 758 G (.259-10-266)

Year Tm	Lg	G	W	L	Pct	Standing	EW	+/-	Pt	W	L	Pct	W	L	Pct
1971 Cle	AL	59	18	41	.305	6E 6E	28	-10	0						

Hans Lobert

Born: 10/18/1881 in Wilmington, Delaware; Died: 9/14/1968; MLB Career: 14 years, 1317 G (.274-32-482)

Year Tm	Lg	G	W	L	Pct	Standing	EW	+/-	Pt	W	L	Pct	W	L	Pct
1938 Phi	NL	2	0	2	.000	8 8	1	-1	0						
1942 Phi	NL	151	42	109	.278	8	52	-10	0						
2 Years		153	42	111	.275	— — —	53	-11	0						

Whitey Lockman

Born: 7/25/1926 in Lowell, North Carolina; MLB Career: 15 years, 1666 G (.279-114-563)

Year Tm	Lg	G	W	L	Pct	Standing	EW	+/-	Pt	W	L	Pct	W	L	Pct
1972 ChN	NL	65	39	26	.600	4E 2E	34	5	1						
1973 ChN	NL	161	77	84	.478	5E	85	-8	0						
1974 ChN	NL	93	41	52	.441	5E 6E	46	-5	0						
3 Years		319	157	162	.492	— — —	165	-8	1						

Tom Loftus

Born: 11/15/1856 in St. Louis, Missouri; Died: 4/16/1910; MLB Career: 2 years, 9 G (.182-0-0)

Year Tm	Lg	G	W	L	Pct	Standing	EW	+/-	Pt	W	L	Pct	W	L	Pct
1884 Mil	UA	12	8	4	.667	2			0						
1888 Cle	AA	71	30	38	.441	7 6			0						
1889 Cle	NL	136	61	72	.459	6			0						
1890 Cin	NL	134	77	55	.583	4			2						
1891 Cin	NL	138	56	81	.409	7			0						
1900 ChN	NL	146	65	75	.464	5	70	-5	0						
1901 ChN	NL	140	53	86	.381	6	67	-14	0						
1902 Was	AL	138	61	75	.449	6	65	-4	0						
1903 Was	AL	140	43	94	.314	8	64	-21	0						
2 AL Years		278	104	169	.381	— — —	129	-25	0						
5 NL Years		694	312	369	.458	— — —	137	-19	2						
1 UA Year		12	8	4	.667	— — —			0						
1 AA Year		71	30	38	.441	— — —			0						
9 Years		1055	454	580	.439	— — —	266	-44	2						

Ed Lopat

Born: 6/21/1918 in New York, New York; Died: 6/15/1992; MLB Career: 12 years, 357 G (166-112, 3.21)

Year Tm	Lg		REGULAR SEASON					Index			Playoffs			World Series		
		G	W	L	Pct	Standing		EW	+/-	Pt	W	L	Pct	W	L	Pct
1963 KCA	AL	162	73	89	.451	8		73	0	0						
1964 KCA	AL	52	17	35	.327	10	10	24	-7	0						
2 Years		214	90	124	.421	—	—	97	-7	0						

Al Lopez

Born: 8/20/1908 in Tampa, Florida; MLB Career: 19 years, 1950 G (.261-51-652)

Year Tm	Lg	G	W	L	Pct	Standing		EW	+/-	Pt	W	L	Pct	W	L	Pct
1951 Cle	AL	155	93	61	.604	2		88	5	2						
1952 Cle	AL	155	93	61	.604	2		88	5	2						
1953 Cle	AL	155	92	62	.597	2		89	3	2						
1954 Cle	AL	156	111	43	.721	1		89	22	5				0	4	.000
1955 Cle	AL	154	93	61	.604	2		98	-5	2						
1956 Cle	AL	155	88	66	.571	2		91	-3	2						
1957 ChA	AL	155	90	64	.584	2		85	5	2						
1958 ChA	AL	155	82	72	.532	2		86	-4	1						
1959 ChA	AL	156	94	60	.610	1		82	12	4				2	4	.333
1960 ChA	AL	154	87	67	.565	3		88	-1	2						
1961 ChA	AL	163	86	76	.531	4		94	-8	1						
1962 ChA	AL	162	85	77	.525	5		89	-4	1						
1963 ChA	AL	162	94	68	.580	2		86	8	2						
1964 ChA	AL	162	98	64	.605	2		89	9	2						
1965 ChA	AL	162	95	67	.586	2		92	3	2						
1968 ChA	AL	11	6	5	.545	9	9 8	6	0	0						
ChA		36	15	21	.417	9	8	19	-4	0						
1969 ChA	AL	17	8	9	.471	4W	5W	8	0	0						
17 Years		2425	1410	1004	.584	—	—	1367	43	32				2	8	.200

Harry Lord

Born: 3/8/1882 in Porter, Maine; Died: 8/9/1948; MLB Career: 9 years, 972 G (.278-14-294)

Year Tm	Lg	G	W	L	Pct	Standing		EW	+/-	Pt	W	L	Pct	W	L	Pct
1915 Buf	FL	110	60	49	.550	8	6	56	4	1						

Bobby Lowe

Born: 7/10/1868 in Pittsburgh, Pennsylvania; Died: 12/8/1951; MLB Career: 18 years, 1820 G (.273-71-984)

Year Tm	Lg	G	W	L	Pct	Standing		EW	+/-	Pt	W	L	Pct	W	L	Pct
1904 Det	AL	78	30	44	.405	7	7	36	-6	0						

Frank Lucchesi

Born: 4/24/1927 in San Francisco, California; MLB Career: Did Not Play

Year Tm	Lg	G	W	L	Pct	Standing		EW	+/-	Pt	W	L	Pct	W	L	Pct
1970 Phi	NL	161	73	88	.453		5E	72	1	0						
1971 Phi	NL	162	67	95	.414		6E	75	-8	0						
1972 Phi	NL	76	26	50	.342	6E	6E	33	-7	0						
1975 Tex	AL	67	35	32	.522	4W	3W	32	3	1						
1976 Tex	AL	162	76	86	.469		5W	77	-1	0						
1977 Tex	AL	62	31	31	.500	4W	2W	31	0	0						
1987 ChN	NL	25	8	17	.320	5E	6E	12	-4	0						
3 AL Years		291	142	149	.488	—	—	140	2	1						
4 NL Years		424	174	250	.410	—	—	192	-18	0						
7 Years		715	316	399	.442	—	—	332	-16	1						

Harry Lumley

Born: 9/29/1880 in Forest City, Pennsylvania; Died: 5/22/1938; MLB Career: 7 years, 730 G (.274-38-305)

Year Tm	Lg	G	W	L	Pct	Standing		EW	+/-	Pt	W	L	Pct	W	L	Pct
1909 Bro	NL	155	55	98	.359	6		62	-7	0						

Ted Lyons

Born: 12/28/1900 in Lake Charles, Louisiana; Died: 7/25/1986; MLB Career: 21 years, 705 G (260-230, 3.67)

Year Tm	Lg	G	W	L	Pct	Standing		EW	+/-	Pt	W	L	Pct	W	L	Pct
1946 ChA	AL	125	64	60	.516	7	5	60	4	1						
1947 ChA	AL	155	70	84	.455	6		74	-4	0						
1948 ChA	AL	154	51	101	.336	8		72	-21	0						
3 Years		434	185	245	.430	—	—	206	-21	1						

Connie Mack

Born: 12/22/1862 in East Brookfield, Massachusetts; Died: 2/8/1956; MLB Career: 11 years, 723 G (.245-5-265)

Year Tm	Lg	G	W	L	Pct	Standing		EW	+/-	Pt	W	L	Pct	W	L	Pct
1894 Pit	NL	23	12	10	.545	7	7			0						
1895 Pit	NL	135	71	61	.538	7				1						
1896 Pit	NL	131	66	63	.512	6				1						
1901 Phi	AL	137	74	62	.544	4		68	6	1						
1902 Phi	AL	137	83	53	.610	1		71	12	4						
1903 Phi	AL	137	75	60	.556	2		76	-1	0						
1904 Phi	AL	155	81	70	.536	5		82	-1	1						
1905 Phi	AL	152	92	56	.622	1		80	12	4				1	4	.200
1906 Phi	AL	149	78	67	.538	4		83	-5	0						
1907 Phi	AL	150	88	57	.607	2		78	10	2						
1908 Phi	AL	157	68	85	.444	6		88	-20	0						
1909 Phi	AL	153	95	58	.621	2		75	20	2						
1910 Phi	AL	155	102	48	.680	1		85	17	6				4	1	.800
1911 Phi	AL	152	101	50	.669	1		90	11	6				4	2	.667
1912 Phi	AL	153	90	62	.592	3		95	-5	2						
1913 Phi	AL	153	96	57	.627	1		90	6	5				4	1	.800
1914 Phi	AL	158	99	53	.651	1		91	8	4				0	4	.000
1915 Phi	AL	154	43	109	.283	8		92	-49	0						
1916 Phi	AL	154	36	117	.235	8		65	-29	0						
1917 Phi	AL	154	55	98	.359	8		55	0	0						
1918 Phi	AL	130	52	76	.406	8		47	5	0						
1919 Phi	AL	140	36	104	.257	8		56	-20	0						
1920 Phi	AL	156	48	106	.312	8		54	-6	0						
1921 Phi	AL	155	53	100	.346	8		56	-3	0						
1922 Phi	AL	155	65	89	.422	7		57	8	0						
1923 Phi	AL	153	69	83	.454	6		64	5	0						
1924 Phi	AL	152	71	81	.467	5		68	3	0						
1925 Phi	AL	153	88	64	.579	2		71	17	2						
1926 Phi	AL	150	83	67	.553	3		79	4	1						
1927 Phi	AL	155	91	63	.591	2		82	9	2						
1928 Phi	AL	153	98	55	.641	2		86	12	2						
1929 Phi	AL	151	104	46	.693	1		88	16	6				4	1	.800
1930 Phi	AL	154	102	52	.662	1		96	6	6				4	2	.667
1931 Phi	AL	153	107	45	.704	1		95	12	5				3	4	.429
1932 Phi	AL	154	94	60	.610	2		99	-5	2						
1933 Phi	AL	152	79	72	.523	3		91	-12	1						
1934 Phi	AL	153	68	82	.453	5		83	-15	0						
1935 Phi	AL	149	58	91	.389	8		74	-16	0						
1936 Phi	AL	154	53	100	.346	8		68	-15	0						
1937 Phi	AL	120	39	80	.328	7	7	48	-9	0						
1938 Phi	AL	154	53	99	.349	8		60	-7	0						
1939 Phi	AL	62	25	37	.403	6	7	24	1	0						
1940 Phi	AL	154	54	100	.351	8		61	-7	0						
1941 Phi	AL	154	64	90	.416	8		60	4	0						
1942 Phi	AL	154	55	99	.357	8		65	-10	0						
1943 Phi	AL	155	49	105	.318	8		62	-13	0						
1944 Phi	AL	155	72	82	.468	5		59	13	0						
1945 Phi	AL	153	52	98	.347	8		66	-14	0						
1946 Phi	AL	155	49	105	.318	8		61	-12	0						
1947 Phi	AL	156	78	76	.506	5		59	19	1						
1948 Phi	AL	154	84	70	.545	4		71	13	1						
1949 Phi	AL	154	81	73	.526	5		77	4	1						
1950 Phi	AL	154	52	102	.338	8		80	-28	0						
50 AL Years		7466	3582	3814	.484	—	—	3631	-49	69				24	19	.558
3 NL Years		289	149	134	.527	—	—			2						
53 Years		7755	3731	3948	.486	—	—	3631	-49	71				24	19	.558

Denny Mack

Born: Unknown in Easton, Pennsylvania; Died: 4/10/1888; MLB Career: 4 years, 197 G (.197-1-10)

Year Tm	Lg	G	W	L	Pct	Standing		EW	+/-	Pt	W	L	Pct	W	L	Pct
1882 Lou	AA	80	42	38	.525	3				1						

Earle Mack

Born: 2/1/1890 in Spencer, Massachusetts; Died: 2/4/1967; MLB Career: 3 years, 5 G (.125-0-1)

Year Tm	Lg	G	W	L	Pct	Standing		EW	+/-	Pt	W	L	Pct	W	L	Pct
1937 Phi	AL	34	15	17	.469	6	7	13	2	0						
1939 Phi	AL	91	30	60	.333	6	7	35	-5	0						
2 Years		125	45	77	.369	—	—	48	-3	0						

Jimmy Macullar

Born: 1/16/1855 in Boston, Massachusetts; Died: 4/8/1924; MLB Career: 6 years, 449 G (.207-7-87)

Year Tm	Lg	G	W	L	Pct	Standing		EW	+/-	Pt	W	L	Pct	W	L	Pct
1879 Syr	NL	27	5	21	.192	7				0						

Lee Magee

Born: 6/4/1889 in Cincinnati, Ohio; Died: 3/14/1966; MLB Career: 9 years, 1015 G (.276-12-277)

Year Tm	Lg	G	W	L	Pct	Standing		EW	+/-	Pt	W	L	Pct	W	L	Pct
1915 Bro	FL	118	53	64	.453	7	7	59	-6	0						

Fergy Malone

Born: Unknown in Ireland; Died: 1/1/1905; MLB Career: 2 years, 23 G (.230-0-6)

Year Tm	Lg	G	W	L	Pct	Standing		EW	+/-	Pt	W	L	Pct	W	L	Pct
1884 Phi	UA	67	21	46	.313	9				0						

Jack Manning

Born: 12/20/1853 in Braintree, Massachusetts; Died: 8/15/1929; MLB Career: 9 years, 682 G (.257-13-275)

Year Tm	Lg	G	W	L	Pct	Standing		EW	+/-	Pt	W	L	Pct	W	L	Pct
1877 Cin	NL	20	7	12	.368	6	6			0						

Jimmy Manning

Born: 1/31/1862 in Fall River, Massachusetts; Died: 10/22/1929; MLB Career: 5 years, 364 G (.215-8-149)

REGULAR SEASON							Index			Playoffs			World Series		
Year Tm	Lg	G	W	L	Pct	Standing	EW	+/-	Pt	W	L	Pct	W	L	Pct
1901 Was	AL	137	61	72	.459	6	67	-6	0						

Rabbit Maranville

Born: 11/11/1891 in Springfield, Massachusetts; Died: 1/5/1954; MLB Career: 23 years, 2670 G (.258-28-884)

REGULAR SEASON							Index			Playoffs			World Series		
Year Tm	Lg	G	W	L	Pct	Standing	EW	+/-	Pt	W	L	Pct	W	L	Pct
1925 ChN	NL	53	23	30	.434	7 **8** 8	28	-5	0						

Marty Marion

Born: 12/1/1917 in Richburgh, South Carolina; MLB Career: 13 years, 1572 G (.263-36-624)

REGULAR SEASON							Index			Playoffs			World Series		
Year Tm	Lg	G	W	L	Pct	Standing	EW	+/-	Pt	W	L	Pct	W	L	Pct
1951 StL	NL	155	81	73	.526	3	81	0	1						
1952 StL	AL	106	42	61	.408	8 **7**	40	2	0						
1953 StL	AL	154	54	100	.351	8	65	-11	0						
1954 ChA	AL	9	3	6	.333	3 **3**	5	-2	0						
1955 ChA	AL	155	91	63	.591	3	88	3	2						
1956 ChA	AL	154	85	69	.552	3	88	-3	1						
5 AL Years		578	275	299	.479	— — —	286	-11	3						
1 NL Year		155	81	73	.526	— — —	81	0	1						
6 Years		733	356	372	.489	— — —	367	-11	4						

Jim Marshall

Born: 5/25/1931 in Danville, Illinois; MLB Career: 5 years, 410 G (.242-29-106)

REGULAR SEASON							Index			Playoffs			World Series		
Year Tm	Lg	G	W	L	Pct	Standing	EW	+/-	Pt	W	L	Pct	W	L	Pct
1974 ChN	NL	69	25	44	.362	5E **6E**	34	-9	0						
1975 ChN	NL	162	75	87	.463	6E	74	1	0						
1976 ChN	NL	162	75	87	.463	4E	76	-1	0						
1979 Oak	AL	162	54	108	.333	7W	75	-21	0						
1 AL Year		162	54	108	.333	— — —	75	-21	0						
3 NL Years		393	175	218	.445	— — —	184	-9	0						
4 Years		555	229	326	.413	— — —	259	-30	0						

Billy Martin

Born: 5/16/1928 in Berkeley, California; Died: 12/25/1989; MLB Career: 11 years, 1021 G (.257-64-333)

REGULAR SEASON							Index			Playoffs			World Series		
Year Tm	Lg	G	W	L	Pct	Standing	EW	+/-	Pt	W	L	Pct	W	L	Pct
1969 Min	AL	162	97	65	.599	1W	86	11	3	0	3	.000			
1971 Det	AL	162	91	71	.562	2E	85	6	2						
1972 Det	AL	156	86	70	.551	1E	84	2	2	2	3	.400			
1973 Det	AL	134	71	63	.530	**3E** 3E	71	0	0						
Tex	AL	23	9	14	.391	6W **6W**	9	0	0						
1974 Tex	AL	161	84	76	.525	2W	63	21	1						
1975 Tex	AL	95	44	51	.463	**4W** 3W	45	-1	0						
NYA	AL	56	30	26	.536	3E **3E**	29	1	1						
1976 NYA	AL	159	97	62	.610	1E	82	15	4	3	2	.600	0	4	.000
1977 NYA	AL	162	100	62	.617	1E	95	5	6	3	2	.600	4	2	.667
1978 NYA	AL	94	52	42	.553	**3E** 1E	55	-3	0						
1979 NYA	AL	95	55	40	.579	4E **4E**	56	-1	1						
1980 Oak	AL	162	83	79	.512	2W	64	19	1						
1981 Oak	AL	60	37	23	.617	1W	28	9	0						
Oak	AL	49	27	22	.551	2W	23	4	3	3	3	.500			
1982 Oak	AL	162	68	94	.420	5W	83	-15	0						
1983 NYA	AL	162	91	71	.562	3E	84	7	2						
1985 NYA	AL	145	91	54	.628	7E **2E**	76	15	2						
1988 NYA	AL	68	40	28	.588	**2E** 5E	37	3	0						
16 Years		2267	1253	1013	.553	— — —	1155	98	28	11	13	.458	4	6	.400

Marty Martinez

Born: 8/23/1941 in Havana, Cuba; MLB Career: 7 years, 436 G (.243-0-57)

REGULAR SEASON							Index			Playoffs			World Series		
Year Tm	Lg	G	W	L	Pct	Standing	EW	+/-	Pt	W	L	Pct	W	L	Pct
1986 Sea	AL	1	0	1	.000	6W **6W** 7W	0	0	0						

Charlie Mason

Born: 6/25/1853 in New Orleans, Louisiana; Died: 10/21/1936; MLB Career: 1 year, 1 G (.500-0-0)

REGULAR SEASON							Index			Playoffs			World Series		
Year Tm	Lg	G	W	L	Pct	Standing	EW	+/-	Pt	W	L	Pct	W	L	Pct
1887 Phi	AA	82	38	40	.487	5 **5**			0						

Eddie Mathews

Born: 10/13/1931 in Texarkana, Texas; MLB Career: 17 years, 2391 G (.271-512-1453)

REGULAR SEASON							Index			Playoffs			World Series		
Year Tm	Lg	G	W	L	Pct	Standing	EW	+/-	Pt	W	L	Pct	W	L	Pct
1972 Atl	NL	50	23	27	.460	5W **4W**	25	-2	0						
1973 Atl	NL	162	76	85	.472	5W	76	0	0						
1974 Atl	NL	99	50	49	.505	**4W** 3W	48	2	0						
3 Years		311	149	161	.481	— — —	149	0	0						

Christy Mathewson

Born: 8/12/1880 in Factoryville, Pennsylvania; Died: 10/7/1925; MLB Career: 17 years, 646 G (373-188, 2.13)

REGULAR SEASON							Index			Playoffs			World Series		
Year Tm	Lg	G	W	L	Pct	Standing	EW	+/-	Pt	W	L	Pct	W	L	Pct
1916 Cin	NL	69	25	43	.368	8 **7**	31	-6	0						
1917 Cin	NL	157	78	76	.506	4	66	12	1						
1918 Cin	NL	120	61	57	.517	**4** 3	57	4	0						
3 Years		346	164	176	.482	— — —	154	10	1						

Bobby Mattick

Born: 12/5/1915 in Sioux City, Iowa; MLB Career: 5 years, 206 G (.233-0-64)

REGULAR SEASON							Index			Playoffs			World Series		
Year Tm	Lg	G	W	L	Pct	Standing	EW	+/-	Pt	W	L	Pct	W	L	Pct
1980 Tor	AL	162	67	95	.414	7E	61	6	0						
1981 Tor	AL	58	16	42	.276	7E	24	-8	0						
Tor	AL	48	21	27	.438	7E	20	1	0						
2 Years		268	104	164	.388	— — —	105	-1	0						

Gene Mauch

Born: 11/18/1925 in Salina, Kansas; MLB Career: 9 years, 304 G (.239-5-62)

REGULAR SEASON							Index			Playoffs			World Series		
Year Tm	Lg	G	W	L	Pct	Standing	EW	+/-	Pt	W	L	Pct	W	L	Pct
1960 Phi	NL	152	58	94	.382	4 **8**	69	-11	0						
1961 Phi	NL	155	47	107	.305	8	65	-18	0						
1962 Phi	NL	161	81	80	.503	7	65	16	1						
1963 Phi	NL	162	87	75	.537	4	77	10	1						
1964 Phi	NL	162	92	70	.568	2	81	11	2						
1965 Phi	NL	162	85	76	.528	6	87	-2	1						
1966 Phi	NL	162	87	75	.537	4	85	2	1						
1967 Phi	NL	162	82	80	.506	5	86	-4	1						
1968 Phi	NL	54	27	27	.500	**6** 8	28	-1	0						
1969 Mon	NL	162	52	110	.321	6E	61	-9	0						
1970 Mon	NL	162	73	89	.451	6E	60	13	0						
1971 Mon	NL	162	71	90	.441	5E	70	1	0						
1972 Mon	NL	156	70	86	.449	5E	69	1	0						
1973 Mon	NL	162	79	83	.488	4E	75	4	0						
1974 Mon	NL	161	79	82	.491	4E	77	2	0						
1975 Mon	NL	162	75	87	.463	5E	79	-4	0						
1976 Min	AL	162	85	77	.525	3W	79	6	1						
1977 Min	AL	161	84	77	.522	4W	85	-1	1						
1978 Min	AL	162	73	89	.451	4W	84	-11	0						
1979 Min	AL	162	82	80	.506	4W	79	3	1						
1980 Min	AL	125	54	71	.432	**6W** 3W	62	-8	0						
1981 Cal	AL	13	9	4	.692	4W **4W**	6	3	0						
Cal	AL	50	20	30	.400	7W	23	-3	0						
1982 Cal	AL	162	93	69	.574	1W	77	16	3	2	3	.400			
1985 Cal	AL	162	90	72	.556	2W	81	9	1						
1986 Cal	AL	162	92	70	.568	1W	84	8	3	3	4	.429			
1987 Cal	AL	162	75	87	.463	6W	88	-13	0						
10 AL Years		1483	757	726	.510	— — —	748	9	10	5	7	.417			
16 NL Years		2459	1145	1311	.466	— — —	1134	11	7						
26 Years		3942	1902	2037	.483	— — —	1882	20	17	5	7	.417			

Jimmy McAleer

Born: 7/10/1864 in Youngstown, Ohio; Died: 12/29/1931; MLB Career: 13 years, 1020 G (.253-12-469)

REGULAR SEASON							Index			Playoffs			World Series		
Year Tm	Lg	G	W	L	Pct	Standing	EW	+/-	Pt	W	L	Pct	W	L	Pct
1901 Cle	AL	138	54	82	.397	7	69	-15	0						
1902 StL	AL	140	78	58	.574	2	58	20	2						
1903 StL	AL	139	65	74	.468	6	72	-7	0						
1904 StL	AL	156	65	87	.428	6	72	-7	0						
1905 StL	AL	156	54	99	.353	8	72	-18	0						
1906 StL	AL	154	76	73	.510	5	61	15	1						
1907 StL	AL	155	69	83	.454	6	73	-4	0						
1908 StL	AL	155	83	69	.546	4	70	13	1						
1909 StL	AL	154	61	89	.407	7	78	-17	0						
1910 Was	AL	157	66	85	.437	7	54	12	0						
1911 Was	AL	154	64	90	.416	7	67	-3	0						
11 Years		1658	735	889	.453	— — —	746	-11	4						

George McBride

Born: 11/20/1880 in Milwaukee, Wisconsin; Died: 7/2/1973; MLB Career: 16 years, 1659 G (.218-7-447)

REGULAR SEASON							Index			Playoffs			World Series		
Year Tm	Lg	G	W	L	Pct	Standing	EW	+/-	Pt	W	L	Pct	W	L	Pct
1921 Was	AL	154	80	73	.523	4	72	8	1						

Jack McCallister

Born: 1/19/1879 in Marietta, Ohio; Died: 10/18/1946; MLB Career: Did Not Play

REGULAR SEASON							Index			Playoffs			World Series		
Year Tm	Lg	G	W	L	Pct	Standing	EW	+/-	Pt	W	L	Pct	W	L	Pct
1927 Cle	AL	153	66	87	.431	6	80	-14	0						

Joe McCarthy

Born: 4/21/1887 in Philadelphia, Pennsylvania; Died: 1/13/1978; MLB Career: 2 years, 16 G (.231-0-2)

REGULAR SEASON							Index			Playoffs			World Series		
Year Tm	Lg	G	W	L	Pct	Standing	EW	+/-	Pt	W	L	Pct	W	L	Pct
1926 ChN	NL	155	82	72	.532	4	74	8	1						
1927 ChN	NL	153	85	68	.556	4	78	7	1						
1928 ChN	NL	154	91	63	.591	3	81	10	2						

REGULAR SEASON							Index			Playoffs			World Series		
Year Tm	Lg	G	W	L	Pct	Standing	EW	+/-	Pt	W	L	Pct	W	L	Pct
1929 ChN	NL	156	98	54	.645	1	85	13	4				1	4	.200
1930 ChN	NL	152	86	64	.573	2 2	89	-3	1						
1931 NYA	AL	155	94	59	.614	2	85	9	2						
1932 NYA	AL	156	107	47	.695	1	88	19	6				4	0	1.000
1933 NYA	AL	152	91	59	.607	2	93	-2	2						
1934 NYA	AL	154	94	60	.610	2	91	3	2						
1935 NYA	AL	149	89	60	.597	2	88	1	2						
1936 NYA	AL	155	102	51	.667	1	88	14	6				4	2	.667
1937 NYA	AL	157	102	52	.662	1	94	8	6				4	1	.800
1938 NYA	AL	157	99	53	.651	1	93	6	5				4	0	1.000
1939 NYA	AL	152	106	45	.702	1	93	13	6				4	0	1.000
1940 NYA	AL	155	88	66	.571	3	98	-10	2						
1941 NYA	AL	156	101	53	.656	1	89	12	6				4	1	.800
1942 NYA	AL	154	103	51	.669	1	94	9	5				1	4	.200
1943 NYA	AL	155	98	56	.636	1	94	4	5				4	1	.800
1944 NYA	AL	154	83	71	.539	3	94	-11	1						
1945 NYA	AL	152	81	71	.533	4	85	-4	1						
1946 NYA	AL	35	22	13	.629	2 3	19	3	0						
1948 Bos	AL	155	96	59	.619	2	83	13	2						
1949 Bos	AL	155	96	58	.623	2	90	6	2						
1950 Bos	AL	59	31	28	.525	4 3	34	-3	0						
19 AL Years		2717	1683	1012	.624	— — —	1593	90	61				29	9	.763
5 NL Years		770	442	321	.579	— — —	407	35	9				1	4	.200
24 Years		3487	2125	1333	.615	— — —	2000	125	70				30	13	.698

Tommy McCarthy

Born: 7/24/1863 in Louisville, Kentucky; Died: 8/5/1922; MLB Career: 13 years, 1275 G (.292-44-735)

REGULAR SEASON							Index			Playoffs			World Series		
Year Tm	Lg	G	W	L	Pct	Standing	EW	+/-	Pt	W	L	Pct	W	L	Pct
1890 STL	AA	22	11	11	.500	4 3			0						
STL	AA	5	4	1	.800	2 2 3			0						
1 Year		27	15	12	.556	— — —			0						

John McCloskey

Born: 4/4/1862 in Louisville, Kentucky; Died: 11/17/1940; MLB Career: 2 years, 12 G (3-2, 3.60)

REGULAR SEASON							Index			Playoffs			World Series		
Year Tm	Lg	G	W	L	Pct	Standing	EW	+/-	Pt	W	L	Pct	W	L	Pct
1895 Lou	NL	133	35	96	.267	12			0						
1896 Lou	NL	19	2	17	.105	12 12			0						
1906 StL	NL	154	52	98	.347	7	62	-10	0						
1907 StL	NL	155	52	101	.340	8	62	-10	0						
1908 StL	NL	154	49	105	.318	8	59	-10	0						
5 Years		615	190	417	.313	— — —	183	-30	0						

Jim McCormick

Born: 11/3/1856 in Glasgow, Scotland; Died: 3/10/1918; MLB Career: 10 years, 534 G (265-214, 2.43)

REGULAR SEASON							Index			Playoffs			World Series		
Year Tm	Lg	G	W	L	Pct	Standing	EW	+/-	Pt	W	L	Pct	W	L	Pct
1879 Cle	NL	82	27	55	.329	6			0						
1880 Cle	NL	85	47	37	.560	3			1						
1882 Cle	NL	4	0	4	.000	8 5			0						
3 Years		171	74	96	.435	— — —			1						

Mel McGaha

Born: 9/26/1926 in Bastrop, Louisiana; MLB Career: Did Not Play

REGULAR SEASON							Index			Playoffs			World Series		
Year Tm	Lg	G	W	L	Pct	Standing	EW	+/-	Pt	W	L	Pct	W	L	Pct
1962 Cle	AL	160	78	82	.488	6 6	82	-4	0						
1964 KCA	AL	111	40	70	.364	10 10	50	-10	0						
1965 KCA	AL	26	5	21	.192	10 10	11	-6	0						
3 Years		297	123	173	.416	— — —	143	-20	0						

Mike McGeary

Born: Unknown in Philadelphia, Pennsylvania; MLB Career: 6 years, 297 G (.243-0-99)

REGULAR SEASON							Index			Playoffs			World Series		
Year Tm	Lg	G	W	L	Pct	Standing	EW	+/-	Pt	W	L	Pct	W	L	Pct
1880 Prv	NL	16	8	7	.533	4 2			0						
1881 Cle	NL	11	4	7	.364	7 7			0						
2 Years		27	12	14	.462	— — —			0						

John McGraw

Born: 4/7/1873 in Truxton, New York; Died: 2/25/1934; MLB Career: 16 years, 1099 G (.334-13-462)

REGULAR SEASON							Index			Playoffs			World Series		
Year Tm	Lg	G	W	L	Pct	Standing	EW	+/-	Pt	W	L	Pct	W	L	Pct
1899 Bal	NL	152	86	62	.581	4			2						
1901 Bal	AL	135	68	65	.511	5	67	1	1						
1902 Bal	AL	58	26	31	.456	7 8	29	-3	0						
NYG	NL	65	25	38	.397	8 8	27	-2	0						
1903 NYG	NL	142	84	55	.604	2	56	28	2						
1904 NYG	NL	158	106	47	.693	1	79	27	5						
1905 NYG	NL	155	105	48	.686	1	91	14	6				4	1	.800
1906 NYG	NL	153	96	56	.632	2	96	0	2						
1907 NYG	NL	155	82	71	.536	4	94	-12	1						
1908 NYG	NL	157	98	56	.636	2	86	12	2						
1909 NYG	NL	158	92	61	.601	3	90	2	2						
1910 NYG	NL	155	91	63	.591	2	88	3	2						
1911 NYG	NL	154	99	54	.647	1	88	11	4				2	4	.333
1912 NYG	NL	154	103	48	.682	1	90	13	5				3	4	.429

REGULAR SEASON							Index			Playoffs			World Series		
Year Tm	Lg	G	W	L	Pct	Standing	EW	+/-	Pt	W	L	Pct	W	L	Pct
1913 NYG	NL	156	101	51	.664	1	94	7	5				1	4	.200
1914 NYG	NL	156	84	70	.545	2	96	-12	1						
1915 NYG	NL	155	69	83	.454	8	86	-17	0						
1916 NYG	NL	155	86	66	.566	4	76	10	2						
1917 NYG	NL	158	98	56	.636	1	82	16	4				2	4	.333
1918 NYG	NL	124	71	53	.573	2	71	0	1						
1919 NYG	NL	140	87	53	.621	2	79	8	2						
1920 NYG	NL	155	86	68	.558	2	90	-4	1						
1921 NYG	NL	153	94	59	.614	1	84	10	5				5	3	.625
1922 NYG	NL	156	93	61	.604	1	89	4	5				4	0	1.000
1923 NYG	NL	153	95	58	.621	1	88	7	4				2	4	.333
1924 NYG	NL	29	16	13	.552	3 1	17	-1	0						
NYG	NL	81	45	35	.563	1 1	47	-2	3				3	4	.429
1925 NYG	NL	14	10	4	.714	1 2	8	2	0						
NYG	NL	106	55	51	.519	1 2	62	-7	1						
1926 NYG	NL	151	74	77	.490	5	85	-11	0						
1927 NYG	NL	122	70	52	.574	4 3	63	7	0						
1928 NYG	NL	155	93	61	.604	2	86	7	2						
1929 NYG	NL	152	84	67	.556	3	85	-1	1						
1930 NYG	NL	154	87	67	.565	3	85	2	2						
1931 NYG	NL	153	87	65	.572	2	84	3	2						
1932 NYG	NL	40	17	23	.425	8 6	22	-5	0						
2 AL Years		193	94	96	.495	— — —	96	-2	1						
32 NL Years		4576	2669	1852	.590	— — —	2464	119	74				26	28	.481
33 Years		4769	2763	1948	.586	— — —	2560	117	75				26	28	.481

Deacon McGuire

Born: 11/18/1863 in Youngstown, Ohio; Died: 10/31/1936; MLB Career: 26 years, 1781 G (.278-45-840)

REGULAR SEASON							Index			Playoffs			World Series		
Year Tm	Lg	G	W	L	Pct	Standing	EW	+/-	Pt	W	L	Pct	W	L	Pct
1898 Was	NL	70	21	47	.309	10 11 11			0						
1907 Bos	AL	112	45	61	.425	8 7	45	0	0						
1908 Bos	AL	115	53	62	.461	6 5	49	4	0						
1909 Cle	AL	41	14	25	.359	6 6	22	-8	0						
1910 Cle	AL	161	71	81	.467	5	76	-5	0						
1911 Cle	AL	17	6	11	.353	7 3	8	-2	0						
5 AL Years		446	189	240	.441	— — —	200	-11	0						
1 NL Year		70	21	47	.309	— — —			0						
6 Years		516	210	287	.423	— — —	200	-11	0						

Bill McGunnigle

Born: 1/1/1855 in Boston, Massachusetts; Died: 3/9/1899; MLB Career: 3 years, 56 G (.173-0-6)

REGULAR SEASON							Index			Playoffs			World Series		
Year Tm	Lg	G	W	L	Pct	Standing	EW	+/-	Pt	W	L	Pct	W	L	Pct
1888 Bro	AA	143	88	52	.629	2			2						
1889 Bro	AA	140	93	44	.679	1			4				3	6	.333
1890 Bro	NL	129	86	43	.667	1			4				3	3	.500
1891 Pit	NL	59	24	33	.421	8 8			0						
1896 Lou	NL	115	36	76	.321	12 12			0						
3 NL Years		303	146	152	.490	— — —			4				3	3	.500
2 AA Years		283	181	96	.653	— — —			6				3	6	.333
5 Years		586	327	248	.569	— — —			10				6	9	.400

Stuffy McInnis

Born: 9/19/1890 in Gloucester, Massachusetts; Died: 2/16/1960; MLB Career: 19 years, 2128 G (.308-20-1060)

REGULAR SEASON							Index			Playoffs			World Series		
Year Tm	Lg	G	W	L	Pct	Standing	EW	+/-	Pt	W	L	Pct	W	L	Pct
1927 Phi	NL	155	51	103	.331	8	64	-13	0						

Bill McKechnie

Born: 8/7/1886 in Wilkinsburg, Pennsylvania; Died: 10/29/1965; MLB Career: 11 years, 845 G (.251-8-240)

REGULAR SEASON							Index			Playoffs			World Series		
Year Tm	Lg	G	W	L	Pct	Standing	EW	+/-	Pt	W	L	Pct	W	L	Pct
1915 New	FL	102	54	45	.545	6 5	53	1	1						
1922 Pit	NL	90	53	36	.596	5 3	49	4	1						
1923 Pit	NL	154	87	67	.565	3	83	4	1						
1924 Pit	NL	153	90	63	.588	3	84	6	2						
1925 Pit	NL	153	95	58	.621	1	85	10	5				4	3	.571
1926 Pit	NL	157	84	69	.549	3	89	-5	1						
1928 StL	NL	154	95	59	.617	1	86	9	4				0	4	.000
1929 StL	NL	63	34	29	.540	4 4	37	-3	1						
1930 Bos	NL	154	70	84	.455	6	61	9	0						
1931 Bos	NL	156	64	90	.416	7	68	-4	0						
1932 Bos	NL	155	77	77	.500	5	67	10	0						
1933 Bos	NL	156	83	71	.539	4	75	8	1						
1934 Bos	NL	152	78	73	.517	4	77	1	1						
1935 Bos	NL	153	38	115	.248	8	79	-41	0						
1936 Bos	NL	157	71	83	.461	6	59	12	0						
1937 Bos	NL	152	79	73	.520	5	69	10	1						
1938 Cin	NL	151	82	68	.547	4	63	19	1						
1939 Cin	NL	156	97	57	.630	1	78	19	4				0	4	.000
1940 Cin	NL	155	100	53	.654	1	85	15	6				4	3	.571
1941 Cin	NL	154	88	66	.571	3	92	-4	2						
1942 Cin	NL	154	76	76	.500	4	87	-11	0						
1943 Cin	NL	155	87	67	.565	2	81	6	2						
1944 Cin	NL	155	89	65	.578	3	83	6	2						
1945 Cin	NL	154	61	93	.396	7	84	-23	0						
1946 Cin	NL	152	64	86	.427	6 6	70	-6	0						
24 NL Years		3545	1842	1678	.523	— — —	1791	51	36				8	14	.364
1 FL Year		102	54	45	.545	— — —	53	1	1						
25 Years		3647	1896	1723	.524	— — —	1844	52	37				8	14	.364

Jack McKeon

Born: 11/23/1930 in South Amboy, New Jersey; MLB Career: Did Not Play

		REGULAR SEASON					Index			Playoffs			World Series		
Year Tm	Lg	G	W	L	Pct	Standing	EW	+/-	Pt	W	L	Pct	W	L	Pct
1973 KC	AL	162	88	74	.543	2W	79	9	1						
1974 KC	AL	162	77	85	.475	5W	85	-8	0						
1975 KC	AL	96	50	46	.521	2W 2W	47	3	0						
1977 Oak	AL	53	26	27	.491	7W 7W	30	-4	0						
1978 Oak	AL	123	45	78	.366	6W 6W	58	-13	0						
1988 SD	NL	115	67	48	.583	5W 3W	51	16	1						
1989 SD	NL	162	89	73	.549	2W	79	10	1						
1990 SD	NL	80	37	43	.463	4W 4W	41	-4	0						
1997 Cin	NL	66	34	32	.515	4C 3C	34	0	1						
5 AL Years		596	286	310	.480	— — —	299	-13	1						
4 NL Years		423	227	196	.537		205	22	3						
9 Years		1019	513	506	.503	— — —	504	9	4						

Alex McKinnon

Born: 8/14/1856 in Boston, Massachusetts; Died: 7/24/1887; MLB Career: 4 years, 386 G (.296-14-219)

		REGULAR SEASON					Index			Playoffs			World Series		
Year Tm	Lg	G	W	L	Pct	Standing	EW	+/-	Pt	W	L	Pct	W	L	Pct
1885 StL	NL	39	6	32	.158	5 8 8			0						

Denny McKnight

Born: Unknown in Pittsburgh, Pennsylvania; Died: 5/5/1900; MLB Career: Did Not Play

		REGULAR SEASON					Index			Playoffs			World Series		
Year Tm	Lg	G	W	L	Pct	Standing	EW	+/-	Pt	W	L	Pct	W	L	Pct
1884 Pit	AA	12	4	8	.333	9 11			0						

George McManus

Born: Unknown; Died: 10/2/1918; MLB Career: Did Not Play

		REGULAR SEASON					Index			Playoffs			World Series		
Year Tm	Lg	G	W	L	Pct	Standing	EW	+/-	Pt	W	L	Pct	W	L	Pct
1876 StL	NL	8	6	2	.750	2 2			0						
1877 StL	NL	60	28	32	.467	4			0						
2 Years		68	34	34	.500	— — —			0						

Marty McManus

Born: 3/14/1900 in Chicago, Illinois; Died: 2/18/1966; MLB Career: 15 years, 1831 G (.289-120-996)

		REGULAR SEASON					Index			Playoffs			World Series		
Year Tm	Lg	G	W	L	Pct	Standing	EW	+/-	Pt	W	L	Pct	W	L	Pct
1932 Bos	AL	99	32	67	.323	8 8	41	-9	0						
1933 Bos	AL	149	63	86	.423	7	53	10	0						
2 Years		248	95	153	.383	— — —	94	1	0						

Roy McMillan

Born: 3/4/1900 in Bonham, Texas; MLB Career: 16 years, 2093 G (.243-68-594)

		REGULAR SEASON					Index			Playoffs			World Series		
Year Tm	Lg	G	W	L	Pct	Standing	EW	+/-	Pt	W	L	Pct	W	L	Pct
1972 Mil	AL	2	1	1	.500	6E 6E 6E	1	0	0						
1975 NYN	NL	53	26	27	.491	3E 3E	25	1	0						
1 AL Year		2	1	1	.500	— — —	1	0	0						
1 NL Year		53	26	27	.491		25	1	0						
2 Years		55	27	28	.491	— — —	26	1	0						

John McNamara

Born: 6/4/1932 in Sacramento, California; MLB Career: Did Not Play

		REGULAR SEASON					Index			Playoffs			World Series		
Year Tm	Lg	G	W	L	Pct	Standing	EW	+/-	Pt	W	L	Pct	W	L	Pct
1969 Oak	AL	13	8	5	.615	2W 2W	7	1	0						
1970 Oak	AL	162	89	73	.549	2W	83	6	1						
1974 SD	NL	162	60	102	.370	6W	66	-6	0						
1975 SD	NL	162	71	91	.438	4W	65	6	0						
1976 SD	NL	162	73	89	.451	5W	71	2	0						
1977 SD	NL	48	20	28	.417	5W 5W	22	-2	0						
1979 Cin	NL	161	90	71	.559	1W	90	0	2	0	3	.000			
1980 Cin	NL	163	89	73	.549	3W	88	1	1						
1981 Cin	NL	56	35	21	.625	2W	31	4	0						
Cin	NL	52	31	21	.596	2W	28	3	2						
1982 Cin	NL	92	34	58	.370	6W 6W	52	-18	0						
1983 Cal	AL	162	70	92	.432	5W	85	-15	0						
1984 Cal	AL	162	81	81	.500	2W	76	5	0						
1985 Bos	AL	163	81	81	.500	5E	84	-3	0						
1986 Bos	AL	161	95	66	.590	1E	81	14	4	4	3	.571	3	4	.429
1987 Bos	AL	162	78	84	.481	5E	89	-11	0						
1988 Bos	AL	85	43	42	.506	4E 1E	43	0	1						
1990 Cle	AL	162	77	85	.475	4E	74	3	0						
1991 Cle	AL	77	25	52	.325	7E 7E	37	-12	0						
1996 Cal	AL	44	17	27	.386	4W 4W	22	-5	0						
11 AL Years		1353	664	688	.491	— — —	681	-17	5	4	3	.571	3	4	.429
8 NL Years		1058	503	554	.476	— — —	513	-10	5	0	3	.000			
19 Years		2411	1167	1242	.484	— — —	1194	-27	10	4	6	.400	3	4	.429

Bid McPhee

Born: 11/1/1859 in Massena, New York; Died: 1/3/1943; MLB Career: 18 years, 2135 G (.271-53-961)

		REGULAR SEASON					Index			Playoffs			World Series		
Year Tm	Lg	G	W	L	Pct	Standing	EW	+/-	Pt	W	L	Pct	W	L	Pct
1901 Cin	NL	142	52	87	.374	8	66	-14	0						
1902 Cin	NL	65	27	37	.422	7 4	28	-1	0						
2 Years		207	79	124	.389	— — —	94	-15	0						

Hal McRae

Born: 7/10/1945 in Avon Park, Florida; MLB Career: 19 years, 2084 G (.290-191-1097)

		REGULAR SEASON					Index			Playoffs			World Series		
Year Tm	Lg	G	W	L	Pct	Standing	EW	+/-	Pt	W	L	Pct	W	L	Pct
1991 KC	AL	124	66	58	.532	7W 6W	61	5	1						
1992 KC	AL	162	72	90	.444	5W	82	-10	0						
1993 KC	AL	162	84	78	.519	3W	76	8	0						
1994 KC	AL	115	64	51	.557	3C	58	6	1						
4 Years		563	286	277	.508	— — —	277	9	3						

Cal McVey

Born: 8/30/1850 in Montrose, Iowa; Died: 8/20/1926; MLB Career: 4 years, 265 G (.328-3-169)

		REGULAR SEASON					Index			Playoffs			World Series		
Year Tm	Lg	G	W	L	Pct	Standing	EW	+/-	Pt	W	L	Pct	W	L	Pct
1878 Cin	NL	61	37	23	.617	2			1						
1879 Cin	NL	63	34	28	.548	5 5			1						
2 Years		124	71	51	.582	— — —			2						

Sam Mele

Born: 1/21/1923 in Astoria, New York; MLB Career: 10 years, 1046 G (.267-80-544)

		REGULAR SEASON					Index			Playoffs			World Series		
Year Tm	Lg	G	W	L	Pct	Standing	EW	+/-	Pt	W	L	Pct	W	L	Pct
1961 Min	AL	7	2	5	.286	8 9 7	3	-1	0						
Min	AL	95	45	49	.479	9 7	46	-1	0						
1962 Min	AL	163	91	71	.562	2	75	16	2						
1963 Min	AL	161	91	70	.565	3	85	6	2						
1964 Min	AL	163	79	83	.488	6	86	-7	0						
1965 Min	AL	162	102	60	.630	1	83	19	5				3	4	.429
1966 Min	AL	162	89	73	.549	2	93	-4	1						
1967 Min	AL	50	25	25	.500	6 2	27	-2	0						
7 Years		963	524	436	.546	— — —	498	26	10				3	4	.429

Oscar Melillo

Born: 8/4/1899 in Chicago, Illinois; Died: 11/14/1963; MLB Career: 12 years, 1377 G (.260-22-548)

		REGULAR SEASON					Index			Playoffs			World Series		
Year Tm	Lg	G	W	L	Pct	Standing	EW	+/-	Pt	W	L	Pct	W	L	Pct
1938 StL	AL	10	2	7	.222	7 7	3	-1	0						

Stump Merrill

Born: 2/25/1944 in Brunswick, Maine; MLB Career: Did Not Play

		REGULAR SEASON					Index			Playoffs			World Series		
Year Tm	Lg	G	W	L	Pct	Standing	EW	+/-	Pt	W	L	Pct	W	L	Pct
1990 NYA	AL	113	49	64	.434	7E 7E	55	-6	0						
1991 NYA	AL	162	71	91	.438	5E	74	-3	0						
2 Years		275	120	155	.436	— — —	129	-9	0						

Charlie Metro

Born: 4/28/1919 in Nanty Glo, Pennsylvania; MLB Career: 3 years, 171 G (.193-3-23)

		REGULAR SEASON					Index			Playoffs			World Series		
Year Tm	Lg	G	W	L	Pct	Standing	EW	+/-	Pt	W	L	Pct	W	L	Pct
1962 ChN	NL	112	43	69	.384	9 9	53	-10	0						
1970 KC	AL	52	19	33	.365	5W 4W	22	-3	0						
1 AL Year		52	19	33	.365	— — —	22	-3	0						
1 NL Year		112	43	69	.384	— — —	53	-10	0						
2 Years		164	62	102	.378	— — —	75	-13	0						

Billy Meyer

Born: 1/14/1892 in Knoxville, Tennessee; Died: 3/31/1957; MLB Career: 3 years, 113 G (.236-1-21)

		REGULAR SEASON					Index			Playoffs			World Series		
Year Tm	Lg	G	W	L	Pct	Standing	EW	+/-	Pt	W	L	Pct	W	L	Pct
1948 Pit	NL	156	83	71	.539	4	68	15	1						
1949 Pit	NL	154	71	83	.461	6	76	-5	0						
1950 Pit	NL	154	57	96	.373	8	72	-15	0						
1951 Pit	NL	155	64	90	.416	7	67	-3	0						
1952 Pit	NL	155	42	112	.273	8	67	-25	0						
5 Years		774	317	452	.412	— — —	350	-33	1						

Gene Michael

Born: 6/2/1938 in Kent, Ohio; MLB Career: 10 years, 973 G (.229-15-226)

		REGULAR SEASON					Index			Playoffs			World Series		
Year Tm	Lg	G	W	L	Pct	Standing	EW	+/-	Pt	W	L	Pct	W	L	Pct
1981 NYA	AL	56	34	22	.607	1E	33	1	0						
NYA	AL	26	14	12	.538	5E 6E	16	-2	0						
1982 NYA	AL	86	44	42	.512	4E 5E 5E	47	-3	0						
1986 ChN	NL	102	46	56	.451	5E	50	-4	0						
1987 ChN	NL	136	68	68	.500	5E 6E	65	3	0						
2 AL Years		168	92	76	.548	— — —	96	-4	0						
2 NL Years		238	114	124	.479	— — —	115	-1	0						
4 Years		406	206	200	.507	— — —	211	-5	0						

Clyde Milan

Born: 3/25/1887 in Linden, Tennessee; Died: 3/3/1953; MLB Career: 16 years, 1981 G (.285-17-617)

Year Tm	Lg	G	W	L	Pct	Standing	EW	+/-	Pt	W	L	Pct	W	L	Pct
1922 Was	AL	154	69	85	.448	6	76	-7	0						

Doggie Miller

Born: 8/15/1864 in Brooklyn, New York; Died: 4/6/1909; MLB Career: 13 years, 1317 G (.267-33-567)

Year Tm	Lg	G	W	L	Pct	Standing	EW	+/-	Pt	W	L	Pct	W	L	Pct
1894 StL	NL	133	56	76	.424	9			0						

Ray Miller

Born: 4/30/1945 in Takoma Park, Maryland; MLB Career: 1 year, 25 G (.167-0-2)

Year Tm	Lg	G	W	L	Pct	Standing	EW	+/-	Pt	W	L	Pct	W	L	Pct
1985 Min	AL	100	50	50	.500	6W 4W	48	2	0						
1986 Min	AL	139	59	80	.424	7W 6W	67	-8	0						
2 Years		239	109	130	.456	— — —	115	-6	0						

Buster Mills

Born: 9/16/1908 in Ranger, Texas; Died: 12/1/1991; MLB Career: 7 years, 415 G (.287-14-163)

Year Tm	Lg	G	W	L	Pct	Standing	EW	+/-	Pt	W	L	Pct	W	L	Pct
1953 Cin	NL	8	4	4	.500	6 6	4	0							

Fred Mitchell

Born: 6/5/1878 in Cambridge, Massachusetts; Died: 10/13/1970; MLB Career: 7 years, 201 G (31-49, 4.10)

Year Tm	Lg	G	W	L	Pct	Standing	EW	+/-	Pt	W	L	Pct	W	L	Pct
1917 ChN	NL	157	74	80	.481	5	72	2	0						
1918 ChN	NL	131	84	45	.651	1	62	22	4				2	4	.333
1919 ChN	NL	140	75	65	.536	3	78	-3	1						
1920 ChN	NL	154	75	79	.487	5	82	-7	0						
1921 Bos	NL	153	79	74	.516	4	66	13	1						
1922 Bos	NL	154	53	100	.346	8	74	-21	0						
1923 Bos	NL	155	54	100	.351	7	64	-10	0						
7 Years		1044	494	543	.476	— — —	498	-4	6				2	4	.333

Jackie Moore

Born: 2/19/1939 in Jay, Florida; MLB Career: 1 year, 21 G (.094-0-2)

Year Tm	Lg	G	W	L	Pct	Standing	EW	+/-	Pt	W	L	Pct	W	L	Pct
1984 Oak	AL	118	57	61	.483	4W 4W	56	1	0						
1985 Oak	AL	162	77	85	.475	4W	77	0	0						
1986 Oak	AL	73	29	44	.397	6W 3W	35	-6	0						
3 Years		353	163	190	.462	— — —	168	-5	0						

Terry Moore

Born: 5/27/1912 in Vernon, Alabama; Died: 3/29/1995; MLB Career: 11 years, 1298 G (.280-80-513)

Year Tm	Lg	G	W	L	Pct	Standing	EW	+/-	Pt	W	L	Pct	W	L	Pct
1954 Phi	NL	77	35	42	.455	3 4	40	-5	0						

Pat Moran

Born: 2/7/1876 in Fitchburg, Massachusetts; Died: 3/7/1924; MLB Career: 14 years, 818 G (.235-18-262)

Year Tm	Lg	G	W	L	Pct	Standing	EW	+/-	Pt	W	L	Pct	W	L	Pct
1915 Phi	NL	153	90	62	.592	1	76	14	4				1	4	.200
1916 Phi	NL	154	91	62	.595	2	85	6	2						
1917 Phi	NL	155	87	65	.572	2	85	2	2						
1918 Phi	NL	125	55	68	.447	6	69	-14	0						
1919 Cin	NL	140	96	44	.686	1	70	26	5				5	3	.625
1920 Cin	NL	154	82	71	.536	3	91	-9	1						
1921 Cin	NL	153	70	83	.458	6	83	-13	0						
1922 Cin	NL	156	86	68	.558	2	78	8	1						
1923 Cin	NL	154	91	63	.591	2	81	10	2						
9 Years		1344	748	586	.561	— — —	718	30	17				6	7	.462

Joe Morgan

Born: 11/19/1930 in Walpole, Massachusetts; MLB Career: 4 years, 88 G (.193-2-10)

Year Tm	Lg	G	W	L	Pct	Standing	EW	+/-	Pt	W	L	Pct	W	L	Pct
1988 Bos	AL	77	46	31	.597	4E 1E	39	7	2	0	4	.000			
1989 Bos	AL	162	83	79	.512	3E	86	-3	1						
1990 Bos	AL	162	88	74	.543	1E	83	5	2	0	4	.000			
1991 Bos	AL	162	84	78	.519	2E	86	-2	1						
4 Years		563	301	262	.535	— — —	294	7	6	0	8	.000			

George Moriarty

Born: 7/7/1884 in Chicago, Illinois; Died: 4/8/1964; MLB Career: 13 years, 1073 G (.251-5-376)

Year Tm	Lg	G	W	L	Pct	Standing	EW	+/-	Pt	W	L	Pct	W	L	Pct
1927 Det	AL	156	82	71	.536	4	79	3	1						
1928 Det	AL	154	68	86	.442	6	81	-13	0						
2 Years		310	150	157	.489	— — —	160	-10	1						

John Morrill

Born: 2/19/1855 in Boston, Massachusetts; Died: 4/2/1932; MLB Career: 15 years, 1265 G (.260-43-643)

Year Tm	Lg	G	W	L	Pct	Standing	EW	+/-	Pt	W	L	Pct	W	L	Pct
1882 Bos	NL	85	45	39	.536	3				1					
1883 Bos	NL	44	33	11	.750	4 1				4					
1884 Bos	NL	116	73	38	.658	2				2					
1885 Bos	NL	113	46	66	.411	5				0					
1886 Bos	NL	118	56	61	.479	5				5					
1887 Bos	NL	32	12	17	.414	5 5				0					
1888 Bos	NL	137	70	64	.522	4				1					
1889 WaN	NL	51	13	38	.255	8 8				0					
8 Years		696	348	334	.510	— — —				8					

Charlie Morton

Born: 10/12/1854 in Kingsville, Ohio; Died: 12/9/1921; MLB Career: 3 years, 88 G (.194-0-3)

Year Tm	Lg	G	W	L	Pct	Standing	EW	+/-	Pt	W	L	Pct	W	L	Pct
1884 Tol	AA	110	46	58	.442	8				0					
1885 Det	NL	38	7	31	.184	7 6				0					
1890 Tol	AA	134	68	64	.515	4				1					
1 NL Year		38	7	31	.184	— — —				0					
2 AA Years		244	114	122	.483	— — —				1					
3 Years		282	121	153	.442	— — —				1					

Felix Moses

Born: Unknown in Richmond, Virginia; MLB Career: Did Not Play

Year Tm	Lg	G	W	L	Pct	Standing	EW	+/-	Pt	W	L	Pct	W	L	Pct
1884 Ric	AA	46	12	30	.286	10				0					

Les Moss

Born: 5/14/1925 in Tulsa, Oklahoma; MLB Career: 13 years, 824 G (.247-63-276)

Year Tm	Lg	G	W	L	Pct	Standing	EW	+/-	Pt	W	L	Pct	W	L	Pct
1968 ChA	AL	2	0	2	.000	9 9 8	1	-1	0						
ChA	AL	34	12	22	.353	9 9 8	18	-6	0						
1979 Det	AL	53	27	26	.509	5E 5E	27	0	0						
2 Years		89	39	50	.438	— — —	46	-7	0						

Tim Murnane

Born: 6/4/1852 in Naugatuck, Connecticut; Died: 2/7/1917; MLB Career: 4 years, 229 G (.258-3-63)

Year Tm	Lg	G	W	L	Pct	Standing	EW	+/-	Pt	W	L	Pct	W	L	Pct
1884 Bos	UA	111	58	51	.532	5				1					

Billy Murray

Born: 4/13/1864 in Peabody, Massachusetts; Died: 3/25/1937; MLB Career: Did Not Play

Year Tm	Lg	G	W	L	Pct	Standing	EW	+/-	Pt	W	L	Pct	W	L	Pct
1907 Phi	NL	149	83	64	.565	3	69	14	1						
1908 Phi	NL	155	83	71	.539	4	82	1	1						
1909 Phi	NL	154	74	79	.484	5	80	-6	0						
3 Years		458	240	214	.529	— — —	231	9	2						

Danny Murtaugh

Born: 10/8/1917 in Chester, Pennsylvania; Died: 12/2/1976; MLB Career: 9 years, 767 G (.254-8-219)

Year Tm	Lg	G	W	L	Pct	Standing	EW	+/-	Pt	W	L	Pct	W	L	Pct
1957 Pit	NL	51	26	25	.510	8 7	22	4	0						
1958 Pit	NL	154	84	70	.545	2	66	18	1						
1959 Pit	NL	155	78	76	.506	4	77	1	1						
1960 Pit	NL	155	95	59	.617	1	77	18	5				4	3	.571
1961 Pit	NL	154	75	79	.487	6	87	-12	0						
1962 Pit	NL	161	93	68	.578	4	87	6	2						
1963 Pit	NL	162	74	88	.457	8	91	-17	0						
1964 Pit	NL	162	80	82	.494	6	80	0	0						
1967 Pit	NL	79	39	39	.500	6 6	42	-3	0						
1970 Pit	NL	162	89	73	.549	1E	85	4	2	0	3	.000			
1971 Pit	NL	162	97	65	.599	1E	87	10	5	3	1	.750	4	3	.571
1973 Pit	NL	26	13	13	.500	2E 3E	15	-2	0						
1974 Pit	NL	162	88	74	.543	1E	85	3	2	1	3	.250			
1975 Pit	NL	161	92	69	.571	1E	86	6	3	0	3	.000			
1976 Pit	NL	162	92	70	.568	2E	88	4	2						
15 Years		2068	1115	950	.540	— — —	1075	40	23	4	10	.286	8	6	.571

Tony Muser

Born: 8/1/1947 in Van Nuys, California; MLB Career: 9 years, 663 G (.259-7-117)

Year Tm	Lg	G	W	L	Pct	Standing	EW	+/-	Pt	W	L	Pct	W	L	Pct
1997 KC	AL	79	31	48	.392	4C 5C	38	-7	0						

Jim Mutrie

Born: 6/13/1851 in Chelsea, Massachusetts; Died: 1/24/1938; MLB Career: Did Not Play

Year Tm	Lg	G	W	L	Pct	Standing	EW	+/-	Pt	W	L	Pct	W	L	Pct
1883 NY	AA	97	54	42	.563	4			1						
1884 NY	AA	112	75	32	.701	1			4				0	3	.000
1885 NYG	NL	112	85	27	.759	2			2						
1886 NYG	NL	124	75	44	.630	3			2						
1887 NYG	NL	129	68	55	.553	4			1						
1888 NYG	NL	138	84	47	.641	1			5				6	4	.600
1889 NYG	NL	131	83	43	.659	1			5				6	3	.667
1890 NYG	NL	135	63	68	.481	6			0						
1891 NYG	NL	136	71	61	.538	3			1						
7 NL Years		905	529	345	.605	— —			16				12	7	.632
2 AA Years		209	129	74	.635				5				0	3	.000
9 Years		1114	658	419	.611	— —			21				12	10	.545

George Myatt

Born: 6/14/1914 in Denver, Colorado; MLB Career: 7 years, 407 G (.283-4-99)

Year Tm	Lg	G	W	L	Pct	Standing	EW	+/-	Pt	W	L	Pct	W	L	Pct
1968 Phi	NL	1	1	0	1.000	6 5 8	1	0	0						
1969 Phi	NL	54	19	35	.352	5E 5E	28	-9	0						
2 Years		55	20	35	.364		29	-9	0						

Henry Myers

Born: Unknown in Philadelphia, Pennsylvania; Died: 4/18/1895; MLB Career: 3 years, 76 G (.174-0-0)

Year Tm	Lg	G	W	L	Pct	Standing	EW	+/-	Pt	W	L	Pct	W	L	Pct
1882 Bal	AA	74	19	54	.260	6			0						

Billy Nash

Born: 6/24/1865 in Richmond, Virginia; Died: 11/15/1929; MLB Career: 15 years, 1549 G (.275-60-977)

Year Tm	Lg	G	W	L	Pct	Standing	EW	+/-	Pt	W	L	Pct	W	L	Pct
1896 Phi	NL	130	62	68	.477	8			0						

Johnny Neun

Born: 10/28/1900 in Baltimore, Maryland; Died: 3/28/1990; MLB Career: 6 years, 432 G (.289-2-85)

Year Tm	Lg	G	W	L	Pct	Standing	EW	+/-	Pt	W	L	Pct	W	L	Pct
1946 NYA	AL	14	8	6	.571	3 3	8	0	0						
1947 Cin	NL	154	73	81	.474	5	72	1	0						
1948 Cin	NL	100	44	56	.440	7 7	47	-3	0						
1 AL Year		14	8	6	.571		8	0	0						
2 NL Years		254	117	137	.461	— —	119	-2	0						
3 Years		268	125	143	.466	— —	127	-2	0						

Jeff Newman

Born: 9/11/1948 in Fort Worth, Texas; MLB Career: 9 years, 735 G (.224-63-233)

Year Tm	Lg	G	W	L	Pct	Standing	EW	+/-	Pt	W	L	Pct	W	L	Pct
1986 Oak	AL	10	2	8	.200	6W 7W 3W	5	-3	0						

Kid Nichols

Born: 9/14/1869 in Madison, Wisconsin; Died: 4/11/1953; MLB Career: 15 years, 650 G (361-208, 2.95)

Year Tm	Lg	G	W	L	Pct	Standing	EW	+/-	Pt	W	L	Pct	W	L	Pct
1904 StL	NL	155	75	79	.487	5	62	13	0						
1905 StL	NL	14	5	9	.357	7 6	6	-1	0						
2 Years		169	80	88	.476	— —	68	12	0						

Hugh Nicol

Born: 1/1/1858 in Campsie, Scotland; Died: 6/27/1921; MLB Career: 10 years, 888 G (.235-5-233)

Year Tm	Lg	G	W	L	Pct	Standing	EW	+/-	Pt	W	L	Pct	W	L	Pct
1897 StL	NL	40	8	32	.200	12 12 12			0						

Russ Nixon

Born: 2/19/1935 in Cleves, Ohio; MLB Career: 10 years, 888 G (.235-5-233)

Year Tm	Lg	G	W	L	Pct	Standing	EW	+/-	Pt	W	L	Pct	W	L	Pct
1982 Cin	NL	70	27	43	.386	6W 6W	39	-12	0						
1983 Cin	NL	162	74	88	.457	6W	73	1	0						
1988 Atl	NL	121	42	79	.347	6W 6W	54	-12	0						
1989 Atl	NL	161	63	97	.394	6W	65	-2	0						
1990 Atl	NL	65	25	40	.385	6W 6W	27	-2	0						
5 Years		579	231	347	.400	— —	258	-27	0						

Bill Norman

Born: 7/16/1910 in St. Louis, Missouri; Died: 4/21/1962; MLB Career: 2 years, 37 G (.204-0-8)

Year Tm	Lg	G	W	L	Pct	Standing	EW	+/-	Pt	W	L	Pct	W	L	Pct
1958 Det	AL	105	56	49	.533	5 5	53	3	1						
1959 Det	AL	17	2	15	.118	8 4	9	-7	0						
2 Years		122	58	64	.475	— —	62	-4	1						

Rebel Oakes

Born: 12/17/1883 in Lisbon, Louisiana; Died: 3/1/1948; MLB Career: 7 years, 986 G (.279-15-397)

Year Tm	Lg	G	W	L	Pct	Standing	EW	+/-	Pt	W	L	Pct	W	L	Pct
1914 Pit	FL	143	61	78	.439	8 7	70	-9	0						
1915 Pit	FL	156	86	67	.562	3	71	15	1						
2 Years		299	147	145	.503	— —	141	6	1						

Johnny Oates

Born: 1/21/1946 in Sylva, North Carolina; MLB Career: 11 years, 593 G (.250-14-126)

Year Tm	Lg	G	W	L	Pct	Standing	EW	+/-	Pt	W	L	Pct	W	L	Pct
1991 Bal	AL	125	54	71	.432	7E 6E	59	-5	0						
1992 Bal	AL	162	89	73	.549	3E	74	15	1						
1993 Bal	AL	162	85	77	.525	3E	83	2	1						
1994 Bal	AL	112	63	49	.563	2E	57	6	1						
1995 Tex	AL	144	74	70	.514	3W	69	5	1						
1996 Tex	AL	163	90	72	.556	1W	82	8	2	1	3	.250			
1997 Tex	AL	162	77	85	.475	3W	85	-8	0						
7 Years		1030	532	497	.517	— —	509	23	6	1	3	.250			

Jack O'Connor

Born: 6/2/1869 in St. Louis, Missouri; Died: 11/14/1937; MLB Career: 21 years, 1451 G (.263-19-738)

Year Tm	Lg	G	W	L	Pct	Standing	EW	+/-	Pt	W	L	Pct	W	L	Pct
1910 StL	AL	158	47	107	.305	8	70	-23	0						

Hank O'Day

Born: 7/8/1862 in Chicago, Illinois; Died: 7/2/1935; MLB Career: 7 years, 232 G (73-110, 3.74)

Year Tm	Lg	G	W	L	Pct	Standing	EW	+/-	Pt	W	L	Pct	W	L	Pct
1912 Cin	NL	155	75	78	.490	4	73	2	0						
1914 ChN	NL	156	78	76	.506	4	87	-9	1						
2 Years		311	153	154	.498	— —	160	-7	1						

Bob O'Farrell

Born: 10/19/1896 in Waukegan, Illinois; Died: 2/20/1988; MLB Career: 21 years, 1492 G (.273-51-549)

Year Tm	Lg	G	W	L	Pct	Standing	EW	+/-	Pt	W	L	Pct	W	L	Pct
1927 StL	NL	153	92	61	.601	2	81	11	2						
1934 Cin	NL	91	30	60	.333	8 8	37	-7	0						
2 Years		244	122	121	.502	— —	118	4	2						

Dan O'Leary

Born: 10/22/1856 in Detroit, Michigan; Died: 6/24/1922; MLB Career: 5 years, 45 G (.243-1-5)

Year Tm	Lg	G	W	L	Pct	Standing	EW	+/-	Pt	W	L	Pct	W	L	Pct
1884 Cin	UA	35	20	15	.571	5 3			0						

Steve O'Neill

Born: 7/6/1891 in Minooka, Pennsylvania; Died: 1/26/1962; MLB Career: 17 years, 1586 G (.263-13-537)

Year Tm	Lg	G	W	L	Pct	Standing	EW	+/-	Pt	W	L	Pct	W	L	Pct
1935 Cle	AL	60	36	23	.610	5 3	32	4	1						
1936 Cle	AL	157	80	74	.519	5	81	-1	1						
1937 Cle	AL	156	83	71	.539	4	80	3	1						
1943 Det	AL	155	78	76	.506	5	76	2	1						
1944 Det	AL	156	88	66	.571	2	77	11	2						
1945 Det	AL	155	88	65	.575	1	82	6	5				4	3	.571
1946 Det	AL	155	92	62	.597	2	84	8	2						
1947 Det	AL	158	85	69	.552	2	87	-2	1						
1948 Det	AL	154	78	76	.506	5	84	-6	1						
1950 Bos	AL	95	63	32	.663	4 3	55	8	2						
1951 Bos	AL	154	87	67	.565	3	90	-3	2						
1952 Phi	NL	91	59	32	.648	6 4	46	13	2						
1953 Phi	NL	156	83	71	.539	3	83	0	1						
1954 Phi	NL	77	40	37	.519	3 4	40	0	0						
11 AL Years		1555	858	681	.558	— —	828	30	19				4	3	.571
3 NL Years		324	182	140	.565	— —	169	13	3						
14 Years		1879	1040	821	.559	— —	997	43	22				4	3	.571

Jack Onslow

Born: 10/13/1888 in Scottdale, Pennsylvania; Died: 12/22/1960; MLB Career: 2 years, 40 G (.169-0-4)

Year Tm	Lg	G	W	L	Pct	Standing	EW	+/-	Pt	W	L	Pct	W	L	Pct
1949 ChA	AL	154	63	91	.409	6	63	0	0						
1950 ChA	AL	31	8	22	.267	8 6	13	-5	0						
2 Years		185	71	113	.386	— —	76	-5	0						

Jim O'Rourke

Born: 9/1/1850 in Bridgeport, Connecticut; Died: 1/8/1919; MLB Career: 19 years, 1774 G (.310-51-1010)

Year Tm	Lg	G	W	L	Pct	Standing	EW	+/-	Pt	W	L	Pct	W	L	Pct
1881 Buf	NL	83	45	38	.542	3			1						
1882 Buf	NL	84	45	39	.536	3			1						
1883 Buf	NL	98	52	45	.536	5			1						
1884 Buf	NL	114	64	47	.577	3			1						

		REGULAR SEASON					Index			Playoffs			World Series		
Year Tm	Lg	G	W	L	Pct	Standing	EW	+/-	Pt	W	L	Pct	W	L	Pct
1893 Was	NL	130	40	89	.310	12			0						
5 Years		509	246	258	.488	— —			4						

Dave Orr

Born: 9/29/1859 in New York, New York; Died: 6/3/1915; MLB Career: 8 years, 791 G (.342-37-504)

		REGULAR SEASON					Index			Playoffs			World Series		
Year Tm	Lg	G	W	L	Pct	Standing	EW	+/-	Pt	W	L	Pct	W	L	Pct
1887 NY	AA	8	3	5	.375	8 7 7			0						

Mel Ott

Born: 3/2/1909 in Gretna, Louisiana; Died: 11/21/1958; MLB Career: 22 years, 2730 G (.304-511-1860)

		REGULAR SEASON					Index			Playoffs			World Series		
Year Tm	Lg	G	W	L	Pct	Standing	EW	+/-	Pt	W	L	Pct	W	L	Pct
1942 NYG	NL	154	85	67	.559	3	74	11	1						
1943 NYG	NL	156	55	98	.359	8	80	-25	0						
1944 NYG	NL	155	67	87	.435	5	67	0	0						
1945 NYG	NL	154	78	74	.513	5	69	9	1						
1946 NYG	NL	154	61	93	.396	8	74	-13	0						
1947 NYG	NL	155	81	73	.526	4	68	13	1						
1948 NYG	NL	76	37	38	.493	4 5	38	-1	0						
7 Years		1004	464	530	.467	— — —	470	-6	3						

Paul Owens

Born: 2/7/1924 in Salamanca, New York; MLB Career: Did Not Play

		REGULAR SEASON					Index			Playoffs			World Series		
Year Tm	Lg	G	W	L	Pct	Standing	EW	+/-	Pt	W	L	Pct	W	L	Pct
1972 Phi	NL	80	33	47	.413	6E 6E	35	-2	0						
1983 Phi	NL	77	47	30	.610	1E 1E	41	6	3	3	1	.750	1	4	.200
1984 Phi	NL	162	81	81	.500	4E	87	-6	0						
3 Years		319	161	158	.505	— — —	163	-2	3	3	1	.750	1	4	.200

Danny Ozark

Born: 11/24/1923 in Buffalo, New York; MLB Career: Did Not Play

		REGULAR SEASON					Index			Playoffs			World Series		
Year Tm	Lg	G	W	L	Pct	Standing	EW	+/-	Pt	W	L	Pct	W	L	Pct
1973 Phi	NL	162	71	91	.438	6E	69	2	0						
1974 Phi	NL	162	80	82	.494	3E	72	8	0						
1975 Phi	NL	162	86	76	.531	2E	77	9	1						
1976 Phi	NL	162	101	61	.623	1E	82	19	4	0	3	.000			
1977 Phi	NL	162	101	61	.623	1E	92	9	4	1	3	.250			
1978 Phi	NL	162	90	72	.556	1E	94	-4	2	1	3	.250			
1979 Phi	NL	133	65	67	.492	5E 4E	74	-9	0						
1984 SF	NL	56	24	32	.429	6W 6W	28	-4	0						
8 Years		1161	618	542	.533	— — —	588	30	11	2	9	.182			

Salty Parker

Born: 7/8/1913 in East St. Louis, Illinois; Died: 7/27/1992; MLB Career: 1 year, 11 G (.280-0-4)

		REGULAR SEASON					Index			Playoffs			World Series		
Year Tm	Lg	G	W	L	Pct	Standing	EW	+/-	Pt	W	L	Pct	W	L	Pct
1967 NYN	NL	11	4	7	.364	10 10	5	-1	0						
1972 Hou	NL	1	1	0	1.000	3W 2W 2W	0	1	0						
2 Years		12	5	7	.417	— — —	5	0	0						

Roger Peckinpaugh

Born: 2/5/1891 in Wooster, Ohio; Died: 11/17/1977; MLB Career: 17 years, 2012 G (.259-48-739)

		REGULAR SEASON					Index			Playoffs			World Series		
Year Tm	Lg	G	W	L	Pct	Standing	EW	+/-	Pt	W	L	Pct	W	L	Pct
1914 NYA	AL	20	10	10	.500	7 6	8	2	0						
1928 Cle	AL	155	62	92	.403	7	72	-10	0						
1929 Cle	AL	152	81	71	.533	3	69	12	1						
1930 Cle	AL	154	81	73	.526	4	76	5	1						
1931 Cle	AL	155	78	76	.506	4	78	0	1						
1932 Cle	AL	153	87	65	.572	4	78	9	2						
1933 Cle	AL	51	26	25	.510	5 4	28	-2	0						
1941 Cle	AL	155	75	79	.487	4	86	-11	0						
8 Years		995	500	491	.505	— — —	495	5	5						

Tony Perez

Born: 5/14/1942 in Camaguey, Cuba; MLB Career: 23 years, 2777 G (.279-379-1652)

		REGULAR SEASON					Index			Playoffs			World Series		
Year Tm	Lg	G	W	L	Pct	Standing	EW	+/-	Pt	W	L	Pct	W	L	Pct
1993 Cin	NL	44	20	24	.455	5W 5W	24	-4	0						

Johnny Pesky

Born: 9/27/1919 in Portland, Oregon; MLB Career: 10 years, 1270 G (.307-17-404)

		REGULAR SEASON					Index			Playoffs			World Series		
Year Tm	Lg	G	W	L	Pct	Standing	EW	+/-	Pt	W	L	Pct	W	L	Pct
1963 Bos	AL	161	76	85	.472	7	77	-1	0						
1964 Bos	AL	160	70	90	.438	8 8	77	-7	0						
1980 Bos	AL	5	1	4	.200	4E 4E	3	-2	0						
3 Years		326	147	179	.451	— — —	157	-10	0						

Fred Pfeffer

Born: 3/17/1860 in Louisville, Kentucky; Died: 4/10/1932; MLB Career: 16 years, 1670 G (.255-94-1019)

		REGULAR SEASON					Index			Playoffs			World Series		
Year Tm	Lg	G	W	L	Pct	Standing	EW	+/-	Pt	W	L	Pct	W	L	Pct
1892 Lou	NL	23	9	14	.391	10 11			0						
Lou	NL	77	33	42	.440	9			0						
1 Year		100	42	56	.429	— —			0						

Lew Phelan

Born: Unknown; MLB Career: Did Not Play

		REGULAR SEASON					Index			Playoffs			World Series		
Year Tm	Lg	G	W	L	Pct	Standing	EW	+/-	Pt	W	L	Pct	W	L	Pct
1895 StL	NL	45	11	30	.268	11 11			0						

Bill Phillips

Born: 11/9/1868 in Allenport, Pennsylvania; Died: 10/25/1941; MLB Career: 7 years, 191 G (70-76, 4.09)

		REGULAR SEASON					Index			Playoffs			World Series		
Year Tm	Lg	G	W	L	Pct	Standing	EW	+/-	Pt	W	L	Pct	W	L	Pct
1914 Ind	FL	157	88	65	.575	1	77	11	4						
1915 New	FL	53	26	27	.491	6 5	28	-2	0						
2 Years		210	114	92	.553	— — —	105	9	4						

Horace Phillips

Born: 5/14/1853 in Salem, Ohio; MLB Career: Did Not Play

		REGULAR SEASON					Index			Playoffs			World Series		
Year Tm	Lg	G	W	L	Pct	Standing	EW	+/-	Pt	W	L	Pct	W	L	Pct
1879 Try	NL	47	12	34	.261	8 8			0						
1883 Col	AA	97	32	65	.330	6			0						
1884 Pit	AA	35	9	24	.273	12 11			0						
1885 Pit	AA	111	56	55	.505	3			1						
1886 Pit	AA	140	80	57	.584	2			2						
1887 Pit	NL	125	55	69	.444	6			0						
1888 Pit	NL	139	66	68	.493	6			0						
1889 Pit	NL	71	28	43	.394	7 5			0						
4 NL Years		382	161	214	.429	— — —			0						
4 AA Years		383	177	201	.468	— — —			3						
8 Years		765	338	415	.449	— — —			3						

Lefty Phillips

Born: 5/16/1919 in Los Angeles, California; Died: 6/10/1972; MLB Career: Did Not Play

		REGULAR SEASON					Index			Playoffs			World Series		
Year Tm	Lg	G	W	L	Pct	Standing	EW	+/-	Pt	W	L	Pct	W	L	Pct
1969 Cal	AL	124	60	63	.488	6W 3W	59	1	0						
1970 Cal	AL	162	86	76	.531	3W	76	10	1						
1971 Cal	AL	162	76	86	.469	4W	82	-6	0						
3 Years		448	222	225	.497	— — —	217	5	1						

Lip Pike

Born: 5/25/1845 in New York, New York; Died: 10/10/1893; MLB Career: 5 years, 163 G (.304-5-88)

		REGULAR SEASON					Index			Playoffs			World Series		
Year Tm	Lg	G	W	L	Pct	Standing	EW	+/-	Pt	W	L	Pct	W	L	Pct
1877 Cin	NL	14	3	11	.214	6 6			0						

Lou Piniella

Born: 8/28/1943 in Tampa, Florida; MLB Career: 18 years, 1747 G (.291-102-766)

		REGULAR SEASON					Index			Playoffs			World Series		
Year Tm	Lg	G	W	L	Pct	Standing	EW	+/-	Pt	W	L	Pct	W	L	Pct
1986 NYA	AL	162	90	72	.556	2E	91	-1	1						
1987 NYA	AL	162	89	73	.549	4E	88	1	1						
1988 NYA	AL	93	45	48	.484	2E 5E	51	-6	0						
1990 Cin	NL	162	91	71	.562	1W	79	12	5	4	2	.667	4	0	1.000
1991 Cin	NL	162	74	88	.457	5W	86	-12	0						
1992 Cin	NL	162	90	72	.556	2W	78	12	1						
1993 Sea	AL	162	82	80	.506	4W	72	10	1						
1994 Sea	AL	112	49	63	.438	3W	55	-6	0						
1995 Sea	AL	145	79	66	.545	1W	66	13	2	5	6	.455			
1996 Sea	AL	161	85	76	.528	2W	83	2	1						
1997 Sea	AL	162	90	72	.556	1W	83	7	2	1	3	.250			
8 AL Years		1159	609	550	.525	— — —	589	20	8	6	9	.400			
3 NL Years		486	255	231	.525	— — —	243	12	6	4	2	.667	4	0	1.000
11 Years		1645	864	781	.525	— — —	832	32	14	10	11	.476	4	0	1.000

Bill Plummer

Born: 3/21/1947 in Oakland, California; MLB Career: 10 years, 367 G (.188-14-82)

		REGULAR SEASON					Index			Playoffs			World Series		
Year Tm	Lg	G	W	L	Pct	Standing	EW	+/-	Pt	W	L	Pct	W	L	Pct
1992 Sea	AL	162	64	98	.395	7W	81	-17	0						

Eddie Popowski

Born: 8/20/1913 in Sayreville, New Jersey; MLB Career: Did Not Play

		REGULAR SEASON					Index			Playoffs			World Series		
Year Tm	Lg	G	W	L	Pct	Standing	EW	+/-	Pt	W	L	Pct	W	L	Pct
1969 Bos	AL	9	5	4	.556	3E 3E	5	0	0						
1973 Bos	AL	1	1	0	1.000	2E 2E	1	0	0						
2 Years		10	6	4	.600	— — —	6	0	0						

Matt Porter

Born: 1/1/1859 in New York; MLB Career: 1 year, 3 G (.083-0-0)

Year Tm	Lg	G	W	L	Pct	Standing	EW	+/-	Pt	W	L	Pct	W	L	Pct
						REGULAR SEASON	Index			Playoffs			World Series		
1884 KC	UA	16	3	13	.188	12 **12** 12			0						

Pat Powers

Born: 6/27/1860 in Trenton, New Jersey; Died: 8/29/1925; MLB Career: Did Not Play

Year Tm	Lg	G	W	L	Pct	Standing	EW	+/-	Pt	W	L	Pct	W	L	Pct
1890 Roc	AA	133	63	63	.500	5			0						
1892 NYG	NL	74	31	43	.419	10			0						
NYG	NL	79	40	37	.519	6			0						
1 NL Year		153	71	80	.470	— — —			0						
1 AA Year		133	63	63	.500	— — —			0						
2 Years		286	134	143	.484	— — —			0						

Al Pratt

Born: 11/19/1947 in Pittsburgh, Pennsylvania; Died: 11/21/1937; MLB Career: Did Not Play

Year Tm	Lg	G	W	L	Pct	Standing	EW	+/-	Pt	W	L	Pct	W	L	Pct
1882 Pit	AA	79	39	39	.500	4			0						
1883 Pit	AA	32	12	20	.375	6 7			0						
2 Years		111	51	59	.464	— — —			0						

Jim Price

Born: 1/1/1847 in New York, New York; Died: 10/6/1931; MLB Career: 5 years, 261 G (.214-18-71)

Year Tm	Lg	G	W	L	Pct	Standing	EW	+/-	Pt	W	L	Pct	W	L	Pct
1884 NYG	NL	100	56	42	.571	4 4			0						

Doc Prothro

Born: 7/16/1893 in Memphis, Tennessee; Died: 10/14/1971; MLB Career: 5 years, 180 G (.318-0-81)

Year Tm	Lg	G	W	L	Pct	Standing	EW	+/-	Pt	W	L	Pct	W	L	Pct
1939 Phi	NL	152	45	106	.298	8	56	-11	0						
1940 Phi	NL	153	50	103	.327	8	55	-5	0						
1941 Phi	NL	155	43	111	.279	8	56	-13	0						
3 Years		460	138	320	.301	— — —	167	-29	0						

Blondie Purcell

Born: 3/16/1854 in Memphis, Tennessee; Died: 2/20/1912; MLB Career: 12 years, 1097 G (.267-13-495)

Year Tm	Lg	G	W	L	Pct	Standing	EW	+/-	Pt	W	L	Pct	W	L	Pct
1883 Phi	NL	82	13	68	.160	8 **8**			0						

Mel Queen

Born: 3/26/1942 in Johnson City, New York; MLB Career: 9 years, 269 G (20-17, 3.14)

Year Tm	Lg	G	W	L	Pct	Standing	EW	+/-	Pt	W	L	Pct	W	L	Pct
1997 Tor	AL	5	4	1	.800	5E **5E**	2	2	0						

Frank Quilici

Born: 3/11/1939 in Chicago, Illinois; MLB Career: 5 years, 405 G (.214-5-53)

Year Tm	Lg	G	W	L	Pct	Standing	EW	+/-	Pt	W	L	Pct	W	L	Pct
1972 Min	AL	84	41	43	.488	3W **3W**	43	-2	0						
1973 Min	AL	162	81	81	.500	3W	82	-1	0						
1974 Min	AL	163	82	80	.506	3W	80	2	1						
1975 Min	AL	159	76	83	.478	4W	80	-4	0						
4 Years		568	280	287	.494	— — —	285	-5	1						

Joe Quinn

Born: 12/25/1864 in Sydney, Australia; Died: 11/12/1940; MLB Career: 17 years, 1768 G (.261-29-794)

Year Tm	Lg	G	W	L	Pct	Standing	EW	+/-	Pt	W	L	Pct	W	L	Pct
1895 StL	NL	40	11	28	.282	11 **11** 11			0						
1899 Cle	NL	116	12	104	.103	12 **12**			0						
2 Years		156	23	132	.148	— — —			0						

Doug Rader

Born: 7/30/1944 in Chicago, Illinois; MLB Career: 11 years, 1465 G (.251-155-722)

Year Tm	Lg	G	W	L	Pct	Standing	EW	+/-	Pt	W	L	Pct	W	L	Pct
1983 Tex	AL	163	77	85	.475	3W	72	5	0						
1984 Tex	AL	161	69	92	.429	7W	77	-8	0						
1985 Tex	AL	32	9	23	.281	7W 7W	14	-5	0						
1986 ChA	AL	2	1	1	.500	6W **5W** 5W	1	0	0						
1989 Cal	AL	162	91	71	.562	3W	79	12	2						
1990 Cal	AL	162	80	82	.494	4W	85	-5	0						
1991 Cal	AL	124	61	63	.492	7W 7W	62	-1	0						
7 Years		806	388	417	.482	— — —	390	-2	2						

Vern Rapp

Born: 5/11/1928 in St. Louis, Missouri; MLB Career: Did Not Play

Year Tm	Lg	G	W	L	Pct	Standing	EW	+/-	Pt	W	L	Pct	W	L	Pct
1977 StL	NL	162	83	79	.512	3E	77	6	1						
1978 StL	NL	17	6	11	.353	6E 5E	9	-3	0						
1984 Cin	NL	121	51	70	.421	5W 5W	57	-6	0						
3 Years		300	140	160	.467	— — —	143	-3	1						

Al Reach

Born: 5/25/1840 in London, England; Died: 1/14/1928; MLB Career: Did Not Play

Year Tm	Lg	G	W	L	Pct	Standing	EW	+/-	Pt	W	L	Pct	W	L	Pct
1890 Phi	NL	11	4	7	.364	2 3 3			0						

Phil Regan

Born: 4/6/1937 in Otsego, Michigan; MLB Career: 13 years, 553 G (96-81, 3.84)

Year Tm	Lg	G	W	L	Pct	Standing	EW	+/-	Pt	W	L	Pct	W	L	Pct
1995 Bal	AL	144	71	73	.493	3E	77	-6	0						

Del Rice

Born: 10/27/1922 in Portsmouth, Ohio; Died: 1/26/1983; MLB Career: 17 years, 1309 G (.237-79-441)

Year Tm	Lg	G	W	L	Pct	Standing	EW	+/-	Pt	W	L	Pct	W	L	Pct
1972 Cal	AL	155	75	80	.484	5W	74	1	0						

Paul Richards

Born: 11/21/1908 in Waxahachie, Texas; Died: 5/4/1986; MLB Career: 8 years, 523 G (.227-15-155)

Year Tm	Lg	G	W	L	Pct	Standing	EW	+/-	Pt	W	L	Pct	W	L	Pct
1951 ChA	AL	155	81	73	.526	4	64	17	1						
1952 ChA	AL	156	81	73	.526	3	75	6	1						
1953 ChA	AL	156	89	65	.578	3	77	12	2						
1954 ChA	AL	146	91	54	.628	3 3	79	12	1						
1955 Bal	AL	156	57	97	.370	7	61	-4	0						
1956 Bal	AL	154	69	85	.448	6	61	8	0						
1957 Bal	AL	154	76	76	.500	5	67	9	0						
1958 Bal	AL	154	74	79	.484	6	73	1	0						
1959 Bal	AL	155	74	80	.481	6	75	-1	0						
1960 Bal	AL	154	89	65	.578	2	75	14	2						
1961 Bal	AL	136	78	57	.578	3 3	77	1	1						
1976 ChA	AL	161	64	97	.398	6W	77	-13	0						
12 Years		1837	923	901	.506	— — —	861	62	8						

Danny Richardson

Born: 1/25/1863 in Elmira, New York; Died: 9/12/1926; MLB Career: 11 years, 1131 G (.254-32-558)

Year Tm	Lg	G	W	L	Pct	Standing	EW	+/-	Pt	W	L	Pct	W	L	Pct
1892 Was	NL	43	12	31	.279	11 **12**			0						

Branch Rickey

Born: 12/20/1881 in Flat, Ohio; Died: 12/9/1965; MLB Career: 4 years, 120 G (.239-3-39)

Year Tm	Lg	G	W	L	Pct	Standing	EW	+/-	Pt	W	L	Pct	W	L	Pct
1913 StL	AL	12	5	6	.455	8 8	4	1	0						
1914 StL	AL	159	71	82	.464	5	60	11	0						
1915 StL	AL	159	63	91	.409	6	69	-6	0						
1919 StL	NL	138	54	83	.394	7	60	-6	0						
1920 StL	NL	155	75	79	.487	5	68	7	0						
1921 StL	NL	154	87	66	.569	3	72	15	2						
1922 StL	NL	154	85	69	.552	3	80	5	1						
1923 StL	NL	154	79	74	.516	5	82	-3	1						
1924 StL	NL	154	65	89	.422	6	81	-16	0						
1925 StL	NL	38	13	25	.342	8 4	18	-5	0						
3 AL Years		330	139	179	.437	— — —	133	6	0						
7 NL Years		947	458	485	.486	— — —	461	-3	4						
10 Years		1277	597	664	.473	— — —	594	3	4						

Greg Riddoch

Born: 7/15/1945 in Greeley, Colorado; MLB Career: Did Not Play

Year Tm	Lg	G	W	L	Pct	Standing	EW	+/-	Pt	W	L	Pct	W	L	Pct
1990 SD	NL	82	38	44	.463	4W **4W**	42	-4	0						
1991 SD	NL	162	84	78	.519	3W	79	5	1						
1992 SD	NL	150	78	72	.520	3W **3W**	77	1	0						
3 Years		394	200	194	.508	— — —	198	2	1						

Jim Riggleman

Born: 11/9/1952 in Fort Dix, New Jersey; MLB Career: Did Not Play

Year Tm	Lg	G	W	L	Pct	Standing	EW	+/-	Pt	W	L	Pct	W	L	Pct
1992 SD	NL	12	4	8	.333	3W **3W**	6	-2	0						
1993 SD	NL	162	61	101	.377	7W	84	-23	0						
1994 SD	NL	117	47	70	.402	4W	52	-5	0						
1995 ChN	NL	144	73	71	.507	3C	69	4	1						
1996 ChN	NL	162	76	86	.469	4C	81	-5	0						

REGULAR SEASON							Index			Playoffs			World Series		
Year Tm	Lg	G	W	L	Pct	Standing	EW	+/-	Pt	W	L	Pct	W	L	Pct
1997 ChN	NL	162	68	94	.420	5C	78	-10	0						
6 Years		759	329	430	.433	— — —	370	-41	1						

Bill Rigney

Born: 1/29/1918 in Alameda, California; MLB Career: 8 years, 654 G (.259-41-212)

REGULAR SEASON							Index			Playoffs			World Series		
Year Tm	Lg	G	W	L	Pct	Standing	EW	+/-	Pt	W	L	Pct	W	L	Pct
1956 NYG	NL	154	67	87	.435	6	80	-13	0						
1957 NYG	NL	154	69	85	.448	6	75	-6	0						
1958 SF	NL	154	80	74	.519	3	72	8	1						
1959 SF	NL	154	83	71	.539	3	76	7	1						
1960 SF	NL	58	33	25	.569	2 5	30	3	0						
1961 LAA	AL	162	70	91	.435	8	60	10	0						
1962 LAA	AL	162	86	76	.531	3	69	17	1						
1963 LAA	AL	161	70	91	.435	9	78	-8	0						
1964 LAA	AL	162	82	80	.506	5	75	7	1						
1965 Cal	AL	162	75	87	.463	7	81	-6	0						
1966 Cal	AL	162	80	82	.494	6	77	3	0						
1967 Cal	AL	161	84	77	.522	5	79	5	1						
1968 Cal	AL	162	67	95	.414	8	82	-15	0						
1969 Cal	AL	39	11	28	.282	6W 3W	19	-8	0						
1970 Min	AL	162	98	64	.605	1W	91	7	3	0	3	.000			
1971 Min	AL	160	74	86	.463	5W	91	-17	0						
1972 Min	AL	70	36	34	.514	3W 3W	35	1	0						
1976 SF	NL	162	74	88	.457	4W	80	-6	0						
12 AL Years		1725	833	891	.483	— — —	837	-4	6	0	3	.000			
6 NL Years		836	406	430	.486	— — —	413	-7	2						
18 Years		2561	1239	1321	.484	— — —	1250	-11	8	0	3	.000			

Cal Ripken

Born: 12/17/1935 in Aberdeen, Maryland; MLB Career: Did Not Play

REGULAR SEASON							Index			Playoffs			World Series		
Year Tm	Lg	G	W	L	Pct	Standing	EW	+/-	Pt	W	L	Pct	W	L	Pct
1985 Bal	AL	1	1	0	1.000	4E 4E 4E	1	0	0						
1987 Bal	AL	162	67	95	.414	6E	78	-11	0						
1988 Bal	AL	6	0	6	.000	6E 7E	3	-3	0						
3 Years		169	68	101	.402	— — —	82	-14	0						

Frank Robinson

Born: 8/31/1935 in Beaumont, Texas; MLB Career: 21 years, 2808 G (.294-586-1812)

REGULAR SEASON							Index			Playoffs			World Series		
Year Tm	Lg	G	W	L	Pct	Standing	EW	+/-	Pt	W	L	Pct	W	L	Pct
1975 Cle	AL	159	79	80	.497	4E	76	3	0						
1976 Cle	AL	159	81	78	.509	4E	78	3	1						
1977 Cle	AL	57	26	31	.456	6E 5E	30	-4	0						
1981 SF	NL	59	27	32	.458	5W	28	-1	0						
SF	NL	52	29	23	.558	3W	25	4	1						
1982 SF	NL	162	87	75	.537	3W	79	8	1						
1983 SF	NL	162	79	83	.488	5W	83	-4	0						
1984 SF	NL	106	42	64	.396	6W 6W	53	-11	0						
1988 Bal	AL	155	54	101	.348	6E 7E	70	-16	0						
1989 Bal	AL	162	87	75	.537	2E	65	22	1						
1990 Bal	AL	161	76	85	.472	5E	78	-2	0						
1991 Bal	AL	37	13	24	.351	7E 6E	17	-4	0						
7 AL Years		890	416	474	.467	— — —	414	2	2						
4 NL Years		541	264	277	.488	— — —	268	-4	2						
11 Years		1431	680	751	.475	— — —	682	-2	4						

Wilbert Robinson

Born: 6/29/1863 in Bolton, Massachusetts; Died: 8/8/1934; MLB Career: 17 years, 1371 G (.273-18-722)

REGULAR SEASON							Index			Playoffs			World Series		
Year Tm	Lg	G	W	L	Pct	Standing	EW	+/-	Pt	W	L	Pct	W	L	Pct
1902 Bal	AL	83	24	57	.296	7 8	41	-17	0						
1914 Bro	NL	154	75	79	.487	5	68	7	0						
1915 Bro	NL	154	80	72	.526	3	72	8	1						
1916 Bro	NL	156	94	60	.610	1	78	16	4				1	4	.200
1917 Bro	NL	156	70	81	.464	7	84	-14	0						
1918 Bro	NL	127	57	69	.452	5	63	-6	0						
1919 Bro	NL	141	69	71	.493	5	68	1	0						
1920 Bro	NL	155	93	61	.604	1	75	18	4				2	5	.286
1921 Bro	NL	152	77	75	.507	5	83	-6	1						
1922 Bro	NL	155	76	78	.494	6	79	-3	0						
1923 Bro	NL	155	76	78	.494	6	79	-3	0						
1924 Bro	NL	154	92	62	.597	2	76	16	2						
1925 Bro	NL	153	68	85	.444	6	84	-16	0						
1926 Bro	NL	155	71	82	.464	6	74	-3	0						
1927 Bro	NL	154	65	88	.425	6	75	-10	0						
1928 Bro	NL	155	77	76	.503	6	69	8	1						
1929 Bro	NL	153	70	83	.458	6	75	-5	0						
1930 Bro	NL	154	86	68	.558	4	72	14	1						
1931 Bro	NL	153	79	73	.520	4	80	-1	1						
1 AL Year		83	24	57	.296	— — —	41	-17	0						
18 NL Years		2736	1375	1341	.506	— — —	1354	21	15				3	9	.250
19 Years		2819	1399	1398	.500	— — —	1395	4	15				3	9	.250

Matt Robison

Born: 3/30/1859 in Pittsburgh, Pennsylvania; Died: 3/24/1911; MLB Career: Did Not Play

REGULAR SEASON							Index			Playoffs			World Series		
Year Tm	Lg	G	W	L	Pct	Standing	EW	+/-	Pt	W	L	Pct	W	L	Pct
1905 StL	NL	50	19	31	.380	6 6	23	-4	0						

Buck Rodgers

Born: 8/16/1938 in Delaware, Ohio; MLB Career: 9 years, 932 G (.232-31-288)

REGULAR SEASON							Index			Playoffs			World Series		
Year Tm	Lg	G	W	L	Pct	Standing	EW	+/-	Pt	W	L	Pct	W	L	Pct
1980 Mil	AL	47	26	21	.553	2E 3E	26	0	0						
Mil	AL	23	13	10	.565	4E 3E	12	1	1						
1981 Mil	AL	56	31	25	.554	3E	30	1	0						
Mil	AL	53	31	22	.585	1E	29	2	1	2	3	.400			
1982 Mil	AL	47	23	24	.489	5E 1E	26	-3	0						
1985 Mon	NL	161	84	77	.522	3E	80	4	1						
1986 Mon	NL	161	78	83	.484	4E	82	-4	0						
1987 Mon	NL	162	91	71	.562	3E	80	11	2						
1988 Mon	NL	163	81	81	.500	3E	86	-5	0						
1989 Mon	NL	162	81	81	.500	4E	82	-1	0						
1990 Mon	NL	162	85	77	.525	3E	82	3	1						
1991 Mon	NL	49	20	29	.408	6E 6E	25	-5	0						
Cal	AL	38	20	18	.526	7W 7W	19	1	0						
1992 Cal	AL	39	19	20	.487	5W 5W	20	-1	0						
Cal	AL	34	14	20	.412	5W 5W	17	-3	0						
1993 Cal	AL	162	71	91	.438	5W	76	-5	0						
1994 Cal	AL	39	16	23	.410	3W 4W	18	-2	0						
7 AL Years		538	264	274	.491	— — —	273	-9	2	2	3	.400			
7 NL Years		1020	520	499	.510	— — —	517	3	4						
13 Years		1558	784	773	.504	— — —	790	-6	6	2	3	.400			

Jim Rogers

Born: 4/9/1872 in Hartford, Connecticut; Died: 1/21/1900; MLB Career: 2 years, 151 G (.236-3-90)

REGULAR SEASON							Index			Playoffs			World Series		
Year Tm	Lg	G	W	L	Pct	Standing	EW	+/-	Pt	W	L	Pct	W	L	Pct
1897 Lou	NL	44	17	24	.415	9 11			0						

Cookie Rojas

Born: 3/6/1939 in Havana, Cuba; MLB Career: 16 years, 1822 G (.263-54-593)

REGULAR SEASON							Index			Playoffs			World Series		
Year Tm	Lg	G	W	L	Pct	Standing	EW	+/-	Pt	W	L	Pct	W	L	Pct
1988 Cal	AL	154	75	79	.487	4W 4W	77	-2	0						
1996 Fla	NL	1	1	0	1.000	4E 4E 3E	0	1	0						
1 AL Year		154	75	79	.487	— — —	77	-2	0						
1 NL Year		1	1	0	1.000	— — —			0						
2 Years		155	76	79	.490	— — —	77	-1	0						

Red Rolfe

Born: 10/17/1908 in Penacook, New Hampshire; Died: 7/8/1969; MLB Career: 10 years, 1175 G (.289-69-497)

REGULAR SEASON							Index			Playoffs			World Series		
Year Tm	Lg	G	W	L	Pct	Standing	EW	+/-	Pt	W	L	Pct	W	L	Pct
1949 Det	AL	155	87	67	.565	4	80	7	2						
1950 Det	AL	157	95	59	.617	2	83	12	2						
1951 Det	AL	154	73	81	.474	5	87	-14	0						
1952 Det	AL	73	23	49	.319	8 8	37	-14	0						
4 Years		539	278	256	.521	— — —	287	-9	4						

Pete Rose

Born: 4/14/1941 in Cincinnati, Ohio; MLB Career: 24 years, 3562 G (.303-160-1314)

REGULAR SEASON							Index			Playoffs			World Series		
Year Tm	Lg	G	W	L	Pct	Standing	EW	+/-	Pt	W	L	Pct	W	L	Pct
1984 Cin	NL	41	19	22	.463	5W 5W	19	0	0						
1985 Cin	NL	162	89	72	.553	2W	72	17	1						
1986 Cin	NL	162	86	76	.531	2W	83	3	1						
1987 Cin	NL	162	84	78	.519	2W	83	1	1						
1988 Cin	NL	23	11	12	.478	4W 2W	12	-1	0						
Cin	NL	111	64	47	.577	4W 2W	58	6	1						
1989 Cin	NL	125	59	66	.472	4W 5W	66	-7	0						
6 Years		786	412	373	.525	— — —	393	19	4						

Chief Roseman

Born: 4/4/1856 in Brooklyn, New York; Died: 4/4/1938; MLB Career: 7 years, 681 G (.263-17-223)

REGULAR SEASON							Index			Playoffs			World Series		
Year Tm	Lg	G	W	L	Pct	Standing	EW	+/-	Pt	W	L	Pct	W	L	Pct
1890 STL	AA	15	7	8	.467	4 5 3			0						

Dave Rowe

Born: 10/9/1854 in Harrisburg, Pennsylvania; Died: 12/9/1930; MLB Career: 7 years, 347 G (.263-8-90)

REGULAR SEASON							Index			Playoffs			World Series		
Year Tm	Lg	G	W	L	Pct	Standing	EW	+/-	Pt	W	L	Pct	W	L	Pct
1886 KCN	NL	126	30	91	.248	7			0						
1888 KC	AA	50	14	36	.280	8 8			0						
1 NL Year		126	30	91	.248	— — —			0						
1 AA Year		50	14	36	.280	— — —			0						
2 Years		176	44	127	.257	— — —			0						

Jack Rowe

Born: 12/8/1856 in Hamburg, Pennsylvania; Died: 4/25/1911; MLB Career: 12 years, 1044 G (.286-28-644)

		REGULAR SEASON					Index			Playoffs			World Series		
Year Tm	Lg	G	W	L	Pct	Standing	EW	+/-	Pt	W	L	Pct	W	L	Pct
1890 Buf	PL	81	22	58	.275	8 8			0						
Buf	PL	19	5	14	.263	8 8			0						
1 Year		100	27	72	.273	— — —			0						

Pants Rowland

Born: 2/12/1879 in Platteville, Wisconsin; Died: 3/17/1969; MLB Career: Did Not Play

		REGULAR SEASON					Index			Playoffs			World Series		
Year Tm	Lg	G	W	L	Pct	Standing	EW	+/-	Pt	W	L	Pct	W	L	Pct
1915 ChA	AL	156	93	61	.604	3	74	19	2						
1916 ChA	AL	155	89	65	.578	2	84	5	2						
1917 ChA	AL	156	100	54	.649	1	84	16	6				4	2	.667
1918 ChA	AL	124	57	67	.460	6	75	-18	0						
4 Years		591	339	247	.578	— — —	317	22	10				4	2	.667

Dick Rudolph

Born: 8/25/1887 in New York, New York; Died: 10/20/1949; MLB Career: 13 years, 285 G (121-108, 2.66)

		REGULAR SEASON					Index			Playoffs			World Series		
Year Tm	Lg	G	W	L	Pct	Standing	EW	+/-	Pt	W	L	Pct	W	L	Pct
1924 Bos	NL	38	11	27	.289	6 8 8	16	-5	0						

Muddy Ruel

Born: 2/20/1896 in St. Louis, Missouri; Died: 11/13/1963; MLB Career: 19 years, 1470 G (.275-4-532)

		REGULAR SEASON					Index			Playoffs			World Series		
Year Tm	Lg	G	W	L	Pct	Standing	EW	+/-	Pt	W	L	Pct	W	L	Pct
1947 StL	AL	154	59	95	.383	8	74	-15	0						

Tom Runnells

Born: 4/17/1955 in Greeley, Colorado; MLB Career: 2 years, 40 G (.174-0-0)

		REGULAR SEASON					Index			Playoffs			World Series		
Year Tm	Lg	G	W	L	Pct	Standing	EW	+/-	Pt	W	L	Pct	W	L	Pct
1991 Mon	NL	112	51	61	.455	6E 6E	57	-6	0						
1992 Mon	NL	37	17	20	.459	4E 2E	18	-1	0						
2 Years		149	68	81	.456	— — —	75	-7	0						

Pete Runnels

Born: 1/28/1928 in Lufkin, Texas; Died: 5/20/1991; MLB Career: 14 years, 1799 G (.291-49-630)

		REGULAR SEASON					Index			Playoffs			World Series		
Year Tm	Lg	G	W	L	Pct	Standing	EW	+/-	Pt	W	L	Pct	W	L	Pct
1966 Bos	AL	16	8	8	.500	10 9	7	1	0						

Bill Russell

Born: 10/21/1948 in Pittsburg, Kansas; MLB Career: 18 years, 2181 G (.263-46-627)

		REGULAR SEASON					Index			Playoffs			World Series		
Year Tm	Lg	G	W	L	Pct	Standing	EW	+/-	Pt	W	L	Pct	W	L	Pct
1996 LA	NL	86	49	37	.570	1W 2W	45	4	1	0	3	.000			
1997 LA	NL	162	88	74	.543	2W	87	1	1						
2 Years		248	137	111	.552	— — —	132	5	2	0	3	.000			

Connie Ryan

Born: 2/27/1920 in New Orleans, Louisiana; Died: 1/3/1996; MLB Career: 12 years, 1184 G (.248-56-381)

		REGULAR SEASON					Index			Playoffs			World Series		
Year Tm	Lg	G	W	L	Pct	Standing	EW	+/-	Pt	W	L	Pct	W	L	Pct
1975 Atl	NL	27	9	18	.333	5W 5W	14	-5	0						
1977 Tex	AL	6	2	4	.333	2W 4W 2W	3	-1	0						
1 AL Year		6	2	4	.333	— — —	3	-1	0						
1 NL Year		27	9	18	.333	— — —	14	-5	0						
2 Years		33	11	22	.333	— — —	17	-6	0						

Eddie Sawyer

Born: 9/10/1910 in Westerly, Rhode Island; Died: 9/22/1997; MLB Career: Did Not Play

		REGULAR SEASON					Index			Playoffs			World Series		
Year Tm	Lg	G	W	L	Pct	Standing	EW	+/-	Pt	W	L	Pct	W	L	Pct
1948 Phi	NL	63	23	40	.365	6 6	26	-3	0						
1949 Phi	NL	154	81	73	.526	3	69	12	1						
1950 Phi	NL	157	91	63	.591	1	76	15	4				0	4	.000
1951 Phi	NL	154	73	81	.474	5	83	-10	0						
1952 Phi	NL	63	28	35	.444	6 4	32	-4	0						
1958 Phi	NL	70	30	40	.429	7 8	35	-5	0						
1959 Phi	NL	155	64	90	.416	8	72	-8	0						
1960 Phi	NL	1	0	1	.000	8 8	0	0	0						
8 Years		817	390	423	.480	— — —	393	-3	5				0	4	.000

Mike Scanlon

Born: Unknown in Cork, Ireland; Died: 1/18/1929; MLB Career: Did Not Play

		REGULAR SEASON					Index			Playoffs			World Series		
Year Tm	Lg	G	W	L	Pct	Standing	EW	+/-	Pt	W	L	Pct	W	L	Pct
1884 Was	UA	114	47	65	.420	7			0						
1886 WaN	NL	82	13	67	.163	8 8			0						
1 NL Year		82	13	67	.163	— — —			0						
1 UA Year		114	47	65	.420	— — —			0						
2 Years		196	60	132	.313	— — —			0						

Bob Schaefer

Born: 5/22/1944 in Putnam, Connecticut; MLB Career: Did Not Play

		REGULAR SEASON					Index			Playoffs			World Series		
Year Tm	Lg	G	W	L	Pct	Standing	EW	+/-	Pt	W	L	Pct	W	L	Pct
1991 KC	AL	1	1	0	1.000	7W 7W 6W	0	1	0						

Ray Schalk

Born: 8/12/1892 in Harvel, Illinois; Died: 5/19/1970; MLB Career: 18 years, 1760 G (.253-11-594)

		REGULAR SEASON					Index			Playoffs			World Series		
Year Tm	Lg	G	W	L	Pct	Standing	EW	+/-	Pt	W	L	Pct	W	L	Pct
1927 ChA	AL	153	70	83	.458	5	78	-8	0						
1928 ChA	AL	75	32	42	.432	6 5	36	-4	0						
2 Years		228	102	125	.449	— — —	114	-12	0						

Bob Scheffing

Born: 8/11/1913 in Overland, Missouri; Died: 10/26/1985; MLB Career: 8 years, 517 G (.263-20-187)

		REGULAR SEASON					Index			Playoffs			World Series		
Year Tm	Lg	G	W	L	Pct	Standing	EW	+/-	Pt	W	L	Pct	W	L	Pct
1957 ChN	NL	156	62	92	.403	7	66	-4	0						
1958 ChN	NL	154	72	82	.468	5	67	5	0						
1959 ChN	NL	155	74	80	.481	5	71	3	0						
1961 Det	AL	163	101	61	.623	2	83	18	3						
1962 Det	AL	161	85	76	.528	4	92	-7	1						
1963 Det	AL	60	24	36	.400	9 5	32	-8	0						
3 AL Years		384	210	173	.548	— — —	207	3	4						
3 NL Years		465	208	254	.450	— — —	204	4	0						
6 Years		849	418	427	.495	— — —	411	7	4						

Harry Schlafly

Born: 9/20/1878 in Port Washington, Ohio; Died: 6/27/1919; MLB Career: 4 years, 208 G (.240-5-58)

		REGULAR SEASON					Index			Playoffs			World Series		
Year Tm	Lg	G	W	L	Pct	Standing	EW	+/-	Pt	W	L	Pct	W	L	Pct
1914 Buf	FL	156	80	71	.530	4	76	4	1						
1915 Buf	FL	41	13	28	.317	8 6	21	-8	0						
2 Years		197	93	99	.484	— — —	97	-4	1						

Gus Schmelz

Born: 9/26/1850 in Columbus, Ohio; Died: 10/14/1925; MLB Career: Did Not Play

		REGULAR SEASON					Index			Playoffs			World Series		
Year Tm	Lg	G	W	L	Pct	Standing	EW	+/-	Pt	W	L	Pct	W	L	Pct
1884 Col	AA	110	69	39	.639	2			2						
1886 StL	NL	126	43	79	.352	6			0						
1887 Cin	AA	136	81	54	.600	2			2						
1888 Cin	AA	137	80	54	.597	4			2						
1889 Cin	AA	141	76	63	.547	4			1						
1890 Cle	NL	78	21	55	.276	7 7			0						
CoC	AA	57	38	13	.745	5 2 2			1						
1891 CoC	AA	138	61	76	.445	6			0						
1894 Was	NL	132	45	87	.341	11			0						
1895 Was	NL	133	43	85	.336	10			0						
1896 Was	NL	133	58	73	.443	9			0						
1897 Was	NL	36	9	25	.265	11 6			0						
6 NL Years		638	219	404	.352	— — —			0						
6 AA Years		719	405	299	.575	— — —			8						
11 Years		1357	624	703	.470	— — —			8						

Red Schoendienst

Born: 2/2/1923 in Germantown, Illinois; MLB Career: 19 years, 2216 G (.289-84-773)

		REGULAR SEASON					Index			Playoffs			World Series		
Year Tm	Lg	G	W	L	Pct	Standing	EW	+/-	Pt	W	L	Pct	W	L	Pct
1965 StL	NL	162	80	81	.497	7	88	-8	0						
1966 StL	NL	162	83	79	.512	6	84	-1	1						
1967 StL	NL	161	101	60	.627	1	83	18	6				4	3	.571
1968 StL	NL	162	97	65	.599	1	91	6	4				3	4	.429
1969 StL	NL	162	87	75	.537	4E	97	-10	1						
1970 StL	NL	162	76	86	.469	4E	90	-14	0						
1971 StL	NL	163	90	72	.556	2E	82	8	1						
1972 StL	NL	156	75	81	.481	4E	82	-7	0						
1973 StL	NL	162	81	81	.500	2E	80	1	0						
1974 StL	NL	161	86	75	.534	2E	81	5	1						
1975 StL	NL	163	82	80	.506	3E	83	-1	1						
1976 StL	NL	162	72	90	.444	5E	82	-10	0						
1980 StL	NL	37	18	19	.486	5E 4E	19	-1	0						
1990 StL	NL	24	13	11	.542	6E 6E 6E	13	0	0						
14 Years		1999	1041	955	.522	— — —	1055	-14	15				7	7	.500

Joe Schultz

Born: 8/29/1918 in Chicago, Illinois; Died: 1/10/1996; MLB Career: 9 years, 240 G (.259-1-46)

		REGULAR SEASON					Index			Playoffs			World Series		
Year Tm	Lg	G	W	L	Pct	Standing	EW	+/-	Pt	W	L	Pct	W	L	Pct
1969 Sea	AL	163	64	98	.395	6W	61	3	0						
1973 Det	AL	28	14	14	.500	3E 3E	15	-1	0						
2 Years		191	78	112	.411	— — —	76	2	0						

Frank Selee

Born: 10/26/1859 in Amherst, New Hampshire; Died: 7/5/1909; MLB Career: Did Not Play

Year Tm	Lg	G	W	L	Pct	Standing	EW	+/-	Pt	W	L	Pct	W	L	Pct
						REGULAR SEASON		Index		Playoffs			World Series		
1890 Bos	NL	134	76	57	.571	5			1						
1891 Bos	NL	140	87	51	.630	1			4						
1892 Bos	NL	75	52	22	.703	1			0						
Bos		77	50	26	.658	2			6				5	0	1.000
1893 Bos	NL	131	86	43	.667	1			4						
1894 Bos	NL	133	83	49	.629	3			2						
1895 Bos	NL	133	71	60	.542	5			1						
1896 Bos	NL	132	74	57	.565	4			1						
1897 Bos	NL	135	93	39	.705	1			4				1	4	.200
1898 Bos	NL	152	102	47	.685	1			5						
1899 Bos	NL	153	95	57	.625	2			2						
1900 Bos	NL	142	66	72	.478	4	69	-3	0						
1901 Bos	NL	140	69	69	.500	5	68	1	0						
1902 ChN	NL	143	68	69	.496	5	60	8	0						
1903 ChN	NL	139	82	56	.594	3	66	16	2						
1904 ChN	NL	156	93	60	.608	2	81	12	2						
1905 ChN	NL	65	37	28	.569	4 3	37	0	0						
16 Years		2180	1284	862	.598	— — —	381	34	34				6	4	.600

Luke Sewell

Born: 1/5/1901 in Titus, Texas; Died: 5/14/1987; MLB Career: 20 years, 1630 G (.259-20-696)

Year Tm	Lg	G	W	L	Pct	Standing	EW	+/-	Pt	W	L	Pct	W	L	Pct
1941 StL	AL	113	55	55	.500	7 6	47	8	0						
1942 StL	AL	151	82	69	.543	3	67	15	1						
1943 StL	AL	153	72	80	.474	6	77	-5	0						
1944 StL	AL	154	89	65	.578	1	75	14	4				2	4	.333
1945 StL	AL	154	81	70	.536	3	82	-1	1						
1946 StL	AL	125	53	71	.427	7 7	65	-12	0						
1949 Cin	NL	3	1	2	.333	7 7	1	0	0						
1950 Cin	NL	153	66	87	.431	6	67	-1	0						
1951 Cin	NL	155	68	86	.442	6	68	0	0						
1952 Cin	NL	98	39	59	.398	7 6	44	-5	0						
6 AL Years		850	432	410	.513	— — —	413	19	6				2	4	.333
4 NL Years		409	174	234	.426	— — —	180	-6	0						
10 Years		1259	606	644	.485	— — —	593	13	6				2	4	.333

Dan Shannon

Born: 3/23/1865 in Bridgeport, Connecticut; Died: 10/25/1913; MLB Career: 3 years, 242 G (.233-8-111)

Year Tm	Lg	G	W	L	Pct	Standing	EW	+/-	Pt	W	L	Pct	W	L	Pct
1889 Lou	AA	58	10	46	.179	8 8			0						
1891 Was	AA	51	15	34	.306	7 9 9			0						
2 Years		109	25	80	.238	— — —			0						

Bill Sharsig

Born: Unknown in Philadelphia, Pennsylvania; Died: 2/1/1902; MLB Career: Did Not Play

Year Tm	Lg	G	W	L	Pct	Standing	EW	+/-	Pt	W	L	Pct	W	L	Pct
1886 Phi	AA	41	22	17	.564	6 6			0						
1888 Phi	AA	137	81	52	.609	3			2						
1889 Phi	AA	138	75	58	.564	3			1						
1890 Phi	AA	132	54	78	.409	8			0						
1891 Phi	AA	18	6	11	.353	7 5			0						
5 Years		466	238	216	.524	— — —			3						

Bob Shawkey

Born: 12/4/1890 in Sigel, Pennsylvania; Died: 12/31/1980; MLB Career: 15 years, 488 G (196-150, 3.09)

Year Tm	Lg	G	W	L	Pct	Standing	EW	+/-	Pt	W	L	Pct	W	L	Pct
1930 NYA	AL	154	86	68	.558	3	90	-4	1						

Tom Sheehan

Born: 3/31/1894 in Grand Ridge, Illinois; Died: 10/29/1982; MLB Career: 6 years, 150 G (17-39, 4.00)

Year Tm	Lg	G	W	L	Pct	Standing	EW	+/-	Pt	W	L	Pct	W	L	Pct
1960 SF	NL	98	46	50	.479	2 5	49	-3	0						

Larry Shepard

Born: 4/3/1919 in Lakewood, Ohio; MLB Career: Did Not Play

Year Tm	Lg	G	W	L	Pct	Standing	EW	+/-	Pt	W	L	Pct	W	L	Pct
1968 Pit	NL	163	80	82	.494	6	84	-4	0						
1969 Pit	NL	157	84	73	.535	3E 3E	83	1	0						
2 Years		320	164	155	.514	— — —	167	-3	0						

Norm Sherry

Born: 7/16/1931 in New York, New York; MLB Career: 5 years, 194 G (.215-18-69)

Year Tm	Lg	G	W	L	Pct	Standing	EW	+/-	Pt	W	L	Pct	W	L	Pct
1976 Cal	AL	66	37	29	.561	4W 4W	30	7	1						
1977 Cal	AL	81	39	42	.481	5W 5W	40	-1	0						
2 Years		147	76	71	.517	— — —	70	6	1						

Bill Shettsline

Born: 10/25/1863 in Philadelphia, Pennsylvania; Died: 2/22/1933; MLB Career: Did Not Play

Year Tm	Lg	G	W	L	Pct	Standing	EW	+/-	Pt	W	L	Pct	W	L	Pct
1898 Phi	NL	104	59	44	.573	8 6			1						
1899 Phi	NL	154	94	58	.618	3			2						
1900 Phi	NL	141	75	63	.543	3	69	6	1						
1901 Phi	NL	140	83	57	.593	2	73	10	2						
1902 Phi	NL	138	56	81	.409	7	76	-20	0						
5 Years		677	367	303	.548	— — —	218	-4	6						

Burt Shotton

Born: 10/18/1884 in Brownhelm, Ohio; Died: 7/29/1962; MLB Career: 14 years, 1387 G (.271-9-290)

Year Tm	Lg	G	W	L	Pct	Standing	EW	+/-	Pt	W	L	Pct	W	L	Pct
1928 Phi	NL	152	43	109	.283	8	60	-17	0						
1929 Phi	NL	154	71	82	.464	5	54	17	0						
1930 Phi	NL	156	52	102	.338	8	67	-15	0						
1931 Phi	NL	155	66	88	.429	6	60	6	0						
1932 Phi	NL	154	78	76	.506	4	68	10	1						
1933 Phi	NL	152	60	92	.395	7	72	-12	0						
1934 Cin	NL	1	1	0	1.000	8 8	0	1	0						
1947 Bro	NL	153	92	60	.605	1 1	84	8	4				3	4	.429
1948 Bro	NL	81	48	33	.593	5 3	47	1	1						
1949 Bro	NL	156	97	57	.630	1	85	12	4				1	4	.200
1950 Bro	NL	155	89	65	.578	2	90	-1	2						
11 Years		1469	697	764	.477	— — —	687	10	12				4	8	.333

Buck Showalter

Born: 5/23/1956 in DeFuniak, Florida; MLB Career: Did Not Play

Year Tm	Lg	G	W	L	Pct	Standing	EW	+/-	Pt	W	L	Pct	W	L	Pct
1992 NYA	AL	162	76	86	.469	4E	73	3	0						
1993 NYA	AL	162	88	74	.543	2E	76	12	1						
1994 NYA	AL	113	70	43	.619	1E	58	12	3						
1995 NYA	AL	144	79	65	.549	2E	80	-1	1				2	3	.400
4 Years		581	313	268	.539	— — —	287	26	5				2	3	.400

Ken Silvestri

Born: 5/3/1916 in Chicago, Illinois; Died: 3/31/1992; MLB Career: 8 years, 102 G (.217-5-25)

Year Tm	Lg	G	W	L	Pct	Standing	EW	+/-	Pt	W	L	Pct	W	L	Pct
1967 Atl	NL	3	0	3	.000	7 7	2	-2	0						

Joe Simmons

Born: 6/13/1845 in New York, New York; MLB Career: Did Not Play

Year Tm	Lg	G	W	L	Pct	Standing	EW	+/-	Pt	W	L	Pct	W	L	Pct
1884 Wil	UA	18	2	16	.111	13			0						

Lew Simmons

Born: 8/27/1838 in New Castle, Pennsylvania; Died: 9/2/1911; MLB Career: Did Not Play

Year Tm	Lg	G	W	L	Pct	Standing	EW	+/-	Pt	W	L	Pct	W	L	Pct
1886 Phi	AA	98	41	55	.427	6 6			0						

Dick Sisler

Born: 11/2/1920 in St. Louis, Missouri; MLB Career: 8 years, 799 G (.276-55-360)

Year Tm	Lg	G	W	L	Pct	Standing	EW	+/-	Pt	W	L	Pct	W	L	Pct
1964 Cin	NL	6	3	3	.500	3 4 2	3	0	0						
Cin	NL	47	29	18	.617	3 2	26	3	0						
1965 Cin	NL	162	89	73	.549	4	89	0	1						
2 Years		215	121	94	.563	— — —	118	3	1						

George Sisler

Born: 3/24/1893 in Manchester, Ohio; Died: 3/26/1973; MLB Career: 15 years, 2055 G (.340-102-1175)

Year Tm	Lg	G	W	L	Pct	Standing	EW	+/-	Pt	W	L	Pct	W	L	Pct
1924 StL	AL	153	74	78	.487	4	77	-3	0						
1925 StL	AL	154	82	71	.536	3	77	5	1						
1926 StL	AL	155	62	92	.403	7	79	-17	0						
3 Years		462	218	241	.475	— — —	233	-15	0						

Frank Skaff

Born: 9/30/1913 in LaCrosse, Wisconsin; Died: 4/12/1988; MLB Career: 2 years, 38 G (.320-1-11)

Year Tm	Lg	G	W	L	Pct	Standing	EW	+/-	Pt	W	L	Pct	W	L	Pct
1966 Det	AL	79	40	39	.506	3 3	42	-2	1						

Bob Skinner

Born: 10/3/1931 in La Jolla, California; MLB Career: 12 years, 1381 G (.277-103-531)

Year Tm	Lg	G	W	L	Pct	Standing	EW	+/-	Pt	W	L	Pct	W	L	Pct
1968 Phi	NL	107	48	59	.449	5 8	55	-7	0						
1969 Phi	NL	108	44	64	.407	5E 5E	55	-11	0						

REGULAR SEASON							Index			Playoffs			World Series		
Year Tm	Lg	G	W	L	Pct	Standing	EW	+/-	Pt	W	L	Pct	W	L	Pct
1977 SD	NL	1	1	0	1.000	5W 5W 5W	0	1	0						
3 Years		216	93	123	.431	— — —	110	-17	0						

Jack Slattery

Born: 1/6/1878 in South Boston, Massachusetts; Died: 7/17/1949; MLB Career: 4 years, 103 G (.212-0-27)

REGULAR SEASON							Index			Playoffs			World Series		
Year Tm	Lg	G	W	L	Pct	Standing	EW	+/-	Pt	W	L	Pct	W	L	Pct
1928 Bos	NL	31	11	20	.355	7 7	13	-2	0						

Harry Smith

Born: 10/31/1874 in Yorkshire, England; Died: 2/17/1933; MLB Career: 10 years, 343 G (.213-2-89)

REGULAR SEASON							Index			Playoffs			World Series		
Year Tm	Lg	G	W	L	Pct	Standing	EW	+/-	Pt	W	L	Pct	W	L	Pct
1909 Bos	NL	79	23	54	.299	8 8	32	-9	0						

Heinie Smith

Born: 10/24/1871 in Pittsburgh, Pennsylvania; Died: 6/25/1939; MLB Career: 6 years, 311 G (.238-3-91)

REGULAR SEASON							Index			Playoffs			World Series		
Year Tm	Lg	G	W	L	Pct	Standing	EW	+/-	Pt	W	L	Pct	W	L	Pct
1902 NYG	NL	32	5	27	.156	4 8 8	14	-9	0						

Mayo Smith

Born: 1/17/1915 in New London, Missouri; Died: 11/24/1977; MLB Career: 1 year, 73 G (.212-0-11)

REGULAR SEASON							Index			Playoffs			World Series		
Year Tm	Lg	G	W	L	Pct	Standing	EW	+/-	Pt	W	L	Pct	W	L	Pct
1955 Phi	NL	154	77	77	.500	4	78	-1	0						
1956 Phi	NL	154	71	83	.461	5	77	-6	0						
1957 Phi	NL	156	77	77	.500	5	74	3	0						
1958 Phi	NL	84	39	45	.464	7 8	42	-3	0						
1959 Cin	NL	80	35	45	.438	7 5	41	-6	0						
1967 Det	AL	163	91	71	.562	2	86	5	2						
1968 Det	AL	164	103	59	.636	1	88	15	6				4	3	.571
1969 Det	AL	162	90	72	.556	2E	99	-9	1						
1970 Det	AL	162	79	83	.488	4E	91	-12	0						
4 AL Years		651	363	285	.560	— — —	364	-1	9				4	3	.571
5 NL Years		628	299	327	.478	— — —	312	-13	0						
9 Years		1279	662	612	.520	— — —	676	-14	9				4	3	.571

Jimmy Snyder

Born: 8/15/1932 in Dearborn, Michigan; MLB Career: 3 years, 41 G (.140-1-10)

REGULAR SEASON							Index			Playoffs			World Series		
Year Tm	Lg	G	W	L	Pct	Standing	EW	+/-	Pt	W	L	Pct	W	L	Pct
1988 Sea	AL	105	45	60	.429	6W 7W	50	-5	0						

Pop Snyder

Born: 10/6/1854 in Washington, D.C.; Died: 10/29/1924; MLB Career: 15 years, 797 G (.236-7-266)

REGULAR SEASON							Index			Playoffs			World Series		
Year Tm	Lg	G	W	L	Pct	Standing	EW	+/-	Pt	W	L	Pct	W	L	Pct
1882 Cin	AA	80	55	25	.688	1			4						
1883 Cin	AA	98	61	37	.622	3			2						
1884 Cin	AA	40	24	14	.632	5 5			0						
1891 Was	AA	70	23	46	.333	6 7 9			0						
4 Years		288	163	122	.572	— — —			6						

Allen Sothoron

Born: 4/27/1893 in Bradford, Ohio; Died: 6/17/1939; MLB Career: 11 years, 265 G (91-100, 3.31)

REGULAR SEASON							Index			Playoffs			World Series		
Year Tm	Lg	G	W	L	Pct	Standing	EW	+/-	Pt	W	L	Pct	W	L	Pct
1933 StL	AL	8	2	6	.250	8 8 8	3	-1	0						

Billy Southworth

Born: 3/9/1893 in Harvard, Nebraska; Died: 11/15/1969; MLB Career: 13 years, 1192 G (.297-52-561)

REGULAR SEASON							Index			Playoffs			World Series		
Year Tm	Lg	G	W	L	Pct	Standing	EW	+/-	Pt	W	L	Pct	W	L	Pct
1929 StL	NL	90	43	45	.489	4 4	51	-8	0						
1940 StL	NL	111	69	40	.633	7 3	60	9	2						
1941 StL	NL	155	97	56	.634	2	82	15	2						
1942 StL	NL	156	106	48	.688	1	90	16	6				4	1	.800
1943 StL	NL	157	105	49	.682	1	95	10	5				1	4	.200
1944 StL	NL	157	105	49	.682	1	97	8	6				4	2	.667
1945 StL	NL	155	95	59	.617	2	98	-3	2						
1946 Bos	NL	154	81	72	.529	4	69	12	1						
1947 Bos	NL	154	86	68	.558	3	77	9	1						
1948 Bos	NL	154	91	62	.595	1	80	11	4				2	4	.333
1949 Bos	NL	111	55	54	.505	4 4	61	-6	0						
1950 Bos	NL	156	83	71	.539	4	79	4	1						
1951 Bos	NL	60	28	31	.475	5 4	31	-3	0						
13 Years		1770	1044	704	.597	— — —	970	74	30				11	11	.500

Al Spalding

Born: 9/2/1850 in Byron, Illinois; Died: 9/9/1915; MLB Career: 3 years, 127 G (48-12, 1.78)

REGULAR SEASON							Index			Playoffs			World Series		
Year Tm	Lg	G	W	L	Pct	Standing	EW	+/-	Pt	W	L	Pct	W	L	Pct
1876 ChN	NL	66	52	14	.788	1			4						
1877 ChN	NL	60	26	33	.441	5			0						
2 Years		126	78	47	.624	— — —			4						

Tris Speaker

Born: 4/4/1888 in Hubbard, Texas; Died: 12/8/1958; MLB Career: 22 years, 2789 G (.345-117-1537)

REGULAR SEASON							Index			Playoffs			World Series		
Year Tm	Lg	G	W	L	Pct	Standing	EW	+/-	Pt	W	L	Pct	W	L	Pct
1919 Cle	AL	61	40	21	.656	3 2	33	7	1						
1920 Cle	AL	154	98	56	.636	1	88	10	5				5	2	.714
1921 Cle	AL	154	94	60	.610	2	91	3	2						
1922 Cle	AL	155	78	76	.506	4	90	-12	1						
1923 Cle	AL	153	82	71	.536	3	82	0	1						
1924 Cle	AL	153	67	86	.438	6	81	-14	0						
1925 Cle	AL	155	70	84	.455	6	73	-3	0						
1926 Cle	AL	154	88	66	.571	2	73	15	2						
8 Years		1139	617	520	.543	— — —	611	6	12				5	2	.714

Harry Spence

Born: 2/22/1856 in New York, New York; Died: 5/17/1908; MLB Career: Did Not Play

REGULAR SEASON							Index			Playoffs			World Series		
Year Tm	Lg	G	W	L	Pct	Standing	EW	+/-	Pt	W	L	Pct	W	L	Pct
1888 Ind	NL	136	50	85	.370	7			0						

Chick Stahl

Born: 1/10/1873 in Avila, Indiana; Died: 3/28/1907; MLB Career: 10 years, 1304 G (.305-36-622)

REGULAR SEASON							Index			Playoffs			World Series		
Year Tm	Lg	G	W	L	Pct	Standing	EW	+/-	Pt	W	L	Pct	W	L	Pct
1906 Bos	AL	40	14	26	.350	8 8	22	-8	0						

Jake Stahl

Born: 4/13/1879 in Elkhart, Illinois; Died: 9/18/1922; MLB Career: 9 years, 981 G (.260-31-437)

REGULAR SEASON							Index			Playoffs			World Series		
Year Tm	Lg	G	W	L	Pct	Standing	EW	+/-	Pt	W	L	Pct	W	L	Pct
1905 Was	AL	154	64	87	.424	7	52	12	0						
1906 Was	AL	151	55	95	.367	7	61	-6	0						
1912 Bos	AL	154	105	47	.691	1	79	26	6				4	3	.571
1913 Bos	AL	81	39	41	.488	5 4	48	-9	0						
4 Years		540	263	270	.493	— — —	240	23	6				4	3	.571

George Stallings

Born: 11/17/1867 in Augusta, Georgia; Died: 5/13/1929; MLB Career: 3 years, 7 G (.100-0-0)

REGULAR SEASON							Index			Playoffs			World Series		
Year Tm	Lg	G	W	L	Pct	Standing	EW	+/-	Pt	W	L	Pct	W	L	Pct
1897 Phi	NL	134	55	77	.417	10			0						
1898 Phi	NL	46	19	27	.413	8 6			0						
1901 Det	AL	136	74	61	.548	3	68	6	1						
1909 NYA	AL	153	74	77	.490	5	64	10	0						
1910 NYA	AL	142	78	59	.569	3 2	64	14	0						
1913 Bos	NL	154	69	82	.457	5	57	12	0						
1914 Bos	NL	158	94	59	.614	1	66	28	5				4	0	1.000
1915 Bos	NL	157	83	69	.546	2	81	2	1						
1916 Bos	NL	158	89	63	.586	3	81	8	2						
1917 Bos	NL	158	72	81	.471	6	86	-14	0						
1918 Bos	NL	124	53	71	.427	7	62	-9	0						
1919 Bos	NL	140	57	82	.410	6	66	-9	0						
1920 Bos	NL	153	62	90	.408	7	68	-6	0						
3 AL Years		431	226	197	.534	— — —	196	30	1						
10 NL Years		1382	653	701	.482	— — —	567	12	8				4	0	1.000
13 Years		1813	879	898	.495	— — —	763	42	9				4	0	1.000

Eddie Stanky

Born: 9/3/1916 in Philadelphia, Pennsylvania; MLB Career: 11 years, 1259 G (.268-29-364)

REGULAR SEASON							Index			Playoffs			World Series		
Year Tm	Lg	G	W	L	Pct	Standing	EW	+/-	Pt	W	L	Pct	W	L	Pct
1952 StL	NL	154	88	66	.571	3	82	6	2						
1953 StL	NL	157	83	71	.539	3	83	0	1						
1954 StL	NL	154	72	82	.468	6	82	-10	0						
1955 StL	NL	36	17	19	.472	5 7	18	-1	0						
1966 ChA	AL	163	83	79	.512	4	92	-9	1						
1967 ChA	AL	162	89	73	.549	4	86	3	1						
1968 ChA	AL	79	34	45	.430	9 8	42	-8	0						
1977 Tex	AL	1	1	0	1.000	4W 2W 2W	1	0	0						
4 AL Years		405	207	197	.512	— — —	221	-14	2						
4 NL Years		501	260	238	.522	— — —	265	-5	3						
8 Years		906	467	435	.518	— — —	486	-19	5						

Casey Stengel

Born: 7/30/1890 in Kansas City, Missouri; Died: 9/29/1975; MLB Career: 14 years, 1277 G (.284-60-535)

REGULAR SEASON							Index			Playoffs			World Series		
Year Tm	Lg	G	W	L	Pct	Standing	EW	+/-	Pt	W	L	Pct	W	L	Pct
1934 Bro	NL	153	71	81	.467	6	71	0	0						
1935 Bro	NL	154	70	83	.458	5	73	-3	0						
1936 Bro	NL	156	67	87	.435	7	72	-5	0						
1938 Bos	NL	153	77	75	.507	5	72	5	1						
1939 Bos	NL	152	63	88	.417	7	76	-13	0						
1940 Bos	NL	152	65	87	.428	7	70	-5	0						
1941 Bos	NL	156	62	92	.403	7	70	-8	0						
1942 Bos	NL	150	59	89	.399	7	64	-5	0						
1943 Bos	NL	107	47	60	.439	6 6	46	1	0						
1949 NYA	AL	155	97	57	.630	1	89	8	5				4	1	.800
1950 NYA	AL	155	98	56	.636	1	92	6	5				4	0	1.000
1951 NYA	AL	154	98	56	.636	1	92	6	5				4	2	.667

Year Tm Lg	G	W	L	Pct	Standing	EW	+/-	Pt	W	L	Pct	W	L	Pct
1952 NYA AL	154	95	59	.617	1	93	2	5				4	3	.571
1953 NYA AL	151	99	52	.656	1	90	9	5				4	2	.667
1954 NYA AL	155	103	51	.669	2	94	9	3						
1955 NYA AL	154	96	58	.623	1	95	1	4				3	4	.429
1956 NYA AL	154	97	57	.630	1	93	4	5				4	3	.571
1957 NYA AL	154	98	56	.636	1	93	5	4				3	4	.429
1958 NYA AL	155	92	62	.597	1	92	0	5				4	3	.571
1959 NYA AL	155	79	75	.513	3	90	-11	1						
1960 NYA AL	155	97	57	.630	1	83	14	4				3	4	.429
1962 NYN NL	161	40	120	.250	10	60	-20	0						
1963 NYN NL	162	51	111	.315	10	54	-3	0						
1964 NYN NL	163	53	109	.327	10	58	-5	0						
1965 NYN NL	96	31	64	.326	10 10	34	-3	0						
12 AL Years	1851	1149	696	.623	— — —	1096	53	51				37	26	.587
13 NL Years	1915	756	1146	.397		820	-64	1						
25 Years	3766	1905	1842	.508	— — —	1916	-11	52				37	26	.587

George Stovall

Born: 11/23/1878 in Independence, Missouri; Died: 11/5/1951; MLB Career: 12 years, 1414 G (.265-15-564)

Year Tm Lg	G	W	L	Pct	Standing	EW	+/-	Pt	W	L	Pct	W	L	Pct
1911 Cle AL	139	74	62	.544	7 3	67	7	1						
1912 StL AL	117	41	74	.357	8 7	42	-1	0						
1913 StL AL	135	50	84	.373	7 8	50	0	0						
1914 KC FL	154	67	84	.444	6	76	-9	0						
1915 KC FL	153	81	72	.529	4	72	9	1						
3 AL Years	391	165	220	.429	— — —	159	6	1						
2 FL Years	307	148	156	.487	— — —	148	0	1						
5 Years	698	313	376	.454	— — —	307	6	2						

Harry Stovey

Born: 12/20/1856 in Philadelphia, Pennsylvania; Died: 9/20/1937; MLB Career: 14 years, 1486 G (.288-122-760)

Year Tm Lg	G	W	L	Pct	Standing	EW	+/-	Pt	W	L	Pct	W	L	Pct
1881 Wor NL	27	8	18	.308	7 8			0						
1885 Phi AA	113	55	57	.491	4			0						
1 NL Year	27	8	18	.308	— — —			0						
1 AA Year	113	55	57	.491	— — —			0						
2 Years	140	63	75	.457				0						

Gabby Street

Born: 9/30/1882 in Huntsville, Alabama; Died: 2/6/1951; MLB Career: 8 years, 503 G (.208-2-105)

Year Tm Lg	G	W	L	Pct	Standing	EW	+/-	Pt	W	L	Pct	W	L	Pct
1929 StL NL	1	1	0	1.000	4 4	1	0	0						
1930 StL NL	154	92	62	.597	1	82	10	4				2	4	.333
1931 StL NL	154	101	53	.656	1	87	14	6				4	3	.571
1932 StL NL	156	72	82	.468	6	91	-19	0						
1933 StL NL	91	46	45	.505	5 5	47	-1	0						
1938 StL AL	146	53	90	.371	7 7	54	-1	0						
1 AL Year	146	53	90	.371		54	-1	0						
5 NL Years	556	312	242	.563	— — —	308	4	10				6	7	.462
6 Years	702	365	332	.524		362	3	10				6	7	.462

Cub Stricker

Born: 6/8/1859 in Philadelphia, Pennsylvania; Died: 11/19/1937; MLB Career: 11 years, 1196 G (.239-12-371)

Year Tm Lg	G	W	L	Pct	Standing	EW	+/-	Pt	W	L	Pct	W	L	Pct
1892 StL NL	23	6	17	.261	10 11 9			0						

George Strickland

Born: 1/10/1926 in New Orleans, Louisiana; MLB Career: 10 years, 971 G (.224-36-284)

Year Tm Lg	G	W	L	Pct	Standing	EW	+/-	Pt	W	L	Pct	W	L	Pct
1964 Cle AL	73	33	39	.458	8 6	35	-2	0						
1966 Cle AL	39	15	24	.385	5 5	20	-5	0						
2 Years	112	48	63	.432	— — —	55	-7	0						

Moose Stubing

Born: 3/31/1938 in Bronx, New York; MLB Career: 1 year, 5 G (.000-0-0)

Year Tm Lg	G	W	L	Pct	Standing	EW	+/-	Pt	W	L	Pct	W	L	Pct
1988 Cal AL	8	0	8	.000	4W 4W	4	-4	0						

Clyde Sukeforth

Born: 11/30/1901 in Washington, Maine; MLB Career: 10 years, 486 G (.264-2-96)

Year Tm Lg	G	W	L	Pct	Standing	EW	+/-	Pt	W	L	Pct	W	L	Pct
1947 Bro NL	2	2	0	1.000	1 1	1	1	0						

Billy Sullivan

Born: 2/1/1875 in Oakland, Wisconsin; Died: 1/28/1965; MLB Career: 16 years, 1146 G (.212-21-378)

Year Tm Lg	G	W	L	Pct	Standing	EW	+/-	Pt	W	L	Pct	W	L	Pct
1909 ChA AL	159	78	74	.513	4	86	-8	1						

Haywood Sullivan

Born: 12/15/1930 in Donalsonville, Georgia; MLB Career: 7 years, 312 G (.226-13-87)

Year Tm Lg	G	W	L	Pct	Standing	EW	+/-	Pt	W	L	Pct	W	L	Pct
1965 KCA AL	136	54	82	.397	10 10	56	-2	0						

Pat Sullivan

Born: Unknown; Died: 5/22/1898; MLB Career: 1 year, 31 G (.193-0-0)

Year Tm Lg	G	W	L	Pct	Standing	EW	+/-	Pt	W	L	Pct	W	L	Pct
1890 CoC AA	3	2	1	.667	2 2			0						

Ted Sullivan

Born: Unknown in County Clare, Ireland; Died: 7/5/1929; MLB Career: 1 year, 3 G (.333-0-0)

Year Tm Lg	G	W	L	Pct	Standing	EW	+/-	Pt	W	L	Pct	W	L	Pct
1883 StL AA	79	53	26	.671	2 2			1						
1884 StL UA	31	28	3	.903	1 1			1						
KC UA	62	13	46	.220	12 12			0						
1888 WaN NL	96	38	57	.400	8 8			0						
1 NL Year	96	38	57	.400	— — —			0						
2 UA Years	93	41	49	.456	— — —			1						
1 AA Year	79	53	26	.671	— — —			1						
3 Years	268	132	132	.500	— — —			2						

Bob Swift

Born: 3/6/1915 in Salina, Kansas; Died: 10/17/1966; MLB Career: 14 years, 1001 G (.231-14-238)

Year Tm Lg	G	W	L	Pct	Standing	EW	+/-	Pt	W	L	Pct	W	L	Pct
1965 Det AL	42	24	18	.571	3 4	22	2	0						
1966 Det AL	57	32	25	.561	3 3 3	30	2	0						
2 Years	99	56	43	.566	— — —	52	4	0						

Chuck Tanner

Born: 7/4/1929 in New Castle, Pennsylvania; MLB Career: 8 years, 396 G (.261-21-105)

Year Tm Lg	G	W	L	Pct	Standing	EW	+/-	Pt	W	L	Pct	W	L	Pct
1970 ChA AL	16	3	13	.188	6W 6W	7	-4	0						
1971 ChA AL	162	79	83	.488	3W	66	13	0						
1972 ChA AL	154	87	67	.565	2W	71	16	2						
1973 ChA AL	162	77	85	.475	5W	83	-6	0						
1974 ChA AL	163	80	80	.500	4W	79	1	0						
1975 ChA AL	161	75	86	.466	5W	81	-6	0						
1976 Oak AL	161	87	74	.540	2W	92	-5	1						
1977 Pit NL	162	96	66	.593	2E	89	7	2						
1978 Pit NL	161	88	73	.547	2E	91	-3	1						
1979 Pit NL	163	98	64	.605	1E	88	10	5	3	0	1.000	4	3	.571
1980 Pit NL	162	83	79	.512	3E	92	-9	1						
1981 Pit NL	49	25	23	.521	4E	25	0	0						
Pit NL	54	21	33	.389	6E	28	-7	0						
1982 Pit NL	162	84	78	.519	4E	81	3	1						
1983 Pit NL	162	84	78	.519	2E	82	2	1						
1984 Pit NL	162	75	87	.463	6E	82	-7	0						
1985 Pit NL	161	57	104	.354	6E	78	-21	0						
1986 Atl NL	161	72	89	.447	6W	74	-2	0						
1987 Atl NL	161	69	92	.429	5W	74	-5	0						
1988 Atl NL	39	12	27	.308	6W 6W	17	-5	0						
7 AL Years	979	488	488	.500	— — —	479	9	3						
12 NL Years	1759	864	893	.492	— — —	901	-37	11	3	0	1.000	4	3	.571
19 Years	2738	1352	1381	.495	— — —	1380	-28	14	3	0	1.000	4	3	.571

El Tappe

Born: 5/21/1927 in Quincy, Illinois; MLB Career: 6 years, 145 G (.207-0-17)

Year Tm Lg	G	W	L	Pct	Standing	EW	+/-	Pt	W	L	Pct	W	L	Pct
1961 ChN NL	2	2	0	1.000	7 7	1	1	0						
ChN NL	79	35	43	.449	7 7 7	34	1	0						
ChN NL	16	5	11	.313	7 7	7	-2	0						
1962 ChN NL	20	4	16	.200	9 9	9	-5	0						
2 Years	117	46	70	.397	— — —	51	-5	0						

George Taylor

Born: 11/22/1853 in New York, New York; MLB Career: Did Not Play

Year Tm Lg	G	W	L	Pct	Standing	EW	+/-	Pt	W	L	Pct	W	L	Pct
1884 Bro AA	109	40	64	.385	9			0						

Zack Taylor

Born: 7/27/1898 in Yulee, Florida; Died: 9/19/1974; MLB Career: 16 years, 918 G (.261-9-311)

Year Tm Lg	G	W	L	Pct	Standing	EW	+/-	Pt	W	L	Pct	W	L	Pct
1946 StL AL	31	13	17	.433	7 7	16	-3	0						
1948 StL AL	155	59	94	.386	6	67	-8	0						
1949 StL AL	155	53	101	.344	7	65	-12	0						
1950 StL AL	154	58	96	.377	7	61	-3	0						
1951 StL AL	154	52	102	.338	8	62	-10	0						
5 Years	649	235	410	.364	— — —	271	-36	0						

Birdie Tebbetts

Born: 11/10/1912 in Burlington, Vermont; MLB Career: 14 years, 1162 G (.270-38-469)

Year Tm	Lg	G	W	L	Pct	Standing		EW	+/-	Pt	W	L	Pct	W	L	Pct
1954 Cin	NL	154	74	80	.481		5	70	4	0						
1955 Cin	NL	154	75	79	.487		5	73	2	0						
1956 Cin	NL	155	91	63	.591		3	75	16	2						
1957 Cin	NL	154	80	74	.519		4	83	-3	1						
1958 Cin	NL	113	52	61	.460	7	4	59	-7	0						
1961 Mil	NL	25	12	13	.480	3	4	14	-2	0						
1962 Mil	NL	162	86	76	.531		5	92	-6	1						
1963 Cle	AL	162	79	83	.488		5	81	-2	0						
1964 Cle	AL	91	46	44	.511	8	6	44	2	1						
1965 Cle	AL	162	87	75	.537		5	80	7	1						
1966 Cle	AL	123	66	57	.537	5	5	63	3	0						
4 AL Years		538	278	259	.518	—	—	268	10	2						
7 NL Years		917	470	446	.513	—	—	466	4	4						
11 Years		1455	748	705	.515	—	—	734	14	6						

Patsy Tebeau

Born: 12/5/1864 in St. Louis, Missouri; Died: 5/15/1918; MLB Career: 13 years, 1167 G (.280-27-735)

Year Tm	Lg	G	W	L	Pct	Standing		EW	+/-	Pt	W	L	Pct	W	L	Pct
1890 Cle	PL	52	21	30	.412	7	7			0						
1891 Cle	NL	73	31	40	.437	6	5			0						
1892 Cle	NL	74	40	33	.548		5			0						
Cle	NL	79	53	23	.697		1			2				0	5	.000
1893 Cle	NL	129	73	55	.570		3			1						
1894 Cle	NL	130	68	61	.527		6			1						
1895 Cle	NL	132	84	46	.646		2			5				4	1	.800
1896 Cle	NL	135	80	48	.625		2			2				0	4	.000
1897 Cle	NL	132	69	62	.527		5			1						
1898 Cle	NL	156	81	68	.544		5			1						
1899 StL	NL	155	84	67	.556		5			1						
1900 StL	NL	92	42	50	.457	7	5	46	-4	0						
10 NL Years		1287	705	553	.560	—	—	46	-4	14				4	10	.286
1 PL Year		52	21	30	.412	—	—			0						
11 Years		1339	726	583	.555	—	—	46	-4	14				4	10	.286

Gene Tenace

Born: 10/10/1946 in Russellton, Pennsylvania; MLB Career: 15 years, 1555 G (.241-201-674)

Year Tm	Lg	G	W	L	Pct	Standing			EW	+/-	Pt	W	L	Pct	W	L	Pct
1991 Tor	AL	33	19	14	.576	1E	1E	1E	17	2	0						

Fred Tenney

Born: 11/26/1871 in Georgetown, Massachusetts; Died: 4/3/1952; MLB Career: 17 years, 1994 G (.294-22-688)

Year Tm	Lg	G	W	L	Pct	Standing	EW	+/-	Pt	W	L	Pct	W	L	Pct
1905 Bos	NL	156	51	103	.331	7	65	-14	0						
1906 Bos	NL	152	49	102	.325	8	58	-9	0						
1907 Bos	NL	152	58	90	.392	7	55	3	0						
1911 Bos	NL	156	44	107	.291	8	58	-14	0						
4 Years		616	202	402	.334	— —	236	-34	0						

Bill Terry

Born: 10/30/1896 in Atlanta, Georgia; Died: 1/9/1989; MLB Career: 14 years, 1721 G (.341-154-1078)

Year Tm	Lg	G	W	L	Pct	Standing		EW	+/-	Pt	W	L	Pct	W	L	Pct
1932 NYG	NL	114	55	59	.482	8	6	63	-8	0						
1933 NYG	NL	156	91	61	.599		1	76	15	5				4	1	.800
1934 NYG	NL	153	93	60	.608		2	85	8	2						
1935 NYG	NL	156	91	62	.595		3	86	5	2						
1936 NYG	NL	154	92	62	.597		1	88	4	4				2	4	.333
1937 NYG	NL	152	95	57	.625		1	87	8	4				1	4	.200
1938 NYG	NL	152	83	67	.553		3	88	-5	1						
1939 NYG	NL	151	77	74	.510		5	84	-7	1						
1940 NYG	NL	152	72	80	.474		6	80	-8	0						
1941 NYG	NL	156	74	79	.484		5	76	-2	0						
10 Years		1496	823	661	.555	— —	813	10	19				7	9	.438

Fred Thomas

Born: Unknown in Indiana; MLB Career: Did Not Play

Year Tm	Lg	G	W	L	Pct	Standing	EW	+/-	Pt	W	L	Pct	W	L	Pct
1887 Ind	NL	29	11	18	.379	8 8 8			0						

Andrew Thompson

Born: Unknown in Illinois; MLB Career: Did Not Play

Year Tm	Lg	G	W	L	Pct	Standing	EW	+/-	Pt	W	L	Pct	W	L	Pct
1884 STP	UA	9	2	6	.250	10			0						

Jack Tighe

Born: 8/9/1913 in Kearny, New Jersey; MLB Career: Did Not Play

Year Tm	Lg	G	W	L	Pct	Standing	EW	+/-	Pt	W	L	Pct	W	L	Pct
1957 Det	AL	154	78	76	.506	4	79	-1	1						

Year Tm	Lg	G	W	L	Pct	Standing		EW	+/-	Pt	W	L	Pct	W	L	Pct
1958 Det	AL	49	21	28	.429	5	5	25	-4	0						
2 Years		203	99	104	.488	—	—	104	-5	1						

Joe Tinker

Born: 7/27/1880 in Muscotah, Kansas; Died: 7/27/1948; MLB Career: 15 years, 1803 G (.262-31-782)

Year Tm	Lg	G	W	L	Pct	Standing	EW	+/-	Pt	W	L	Pct	W	L	Pct
1913 Cin	NL	156	64	89	.418	7	75	-11	0						
1914 Chi	FL	158	87	67	.565	2	77	10	2						
1915 Chi	FL	156	86	66	.566	1	81	5	4						
1916 ChN	NL	156	67	86	.438	5	76	-9	0						
2 NL Years		312	131	175	.428	— —	151	-20	0						
2 FL Years		314	173	133	.565	— —	158	15	6						
4 Years		626	304	308	.497	— —	309	-5	6						

Jeff Torborg

Born: 11/26/1941 in Plainfield, New Jersey; MLB Career: 10 years, 574 G (.214-8-101)

Year Tm	Lg	G	W	L	Pct	Standing		EW	+/-	Pt	W	L	Pct	W	L	Pct
1977 Cle	AL	104	45	59	.433	6E	5E	54	-9	0						
1978 Cle	AL	159	69	90	.434		6E	76	-7	0						
1979 Cle	AL	95	43	52	.453	6E	6E	44	-1	0						
1989 ChA	AL	161	69	92	.429		7W	74	-5	0						
1990 ChA	AL	162	94	68	.580		2W	74	20	2						
1991 ChA	AL	162	87	75	.537		2W	85	2	1						
1992 NYN	NL	162	72	90	.444		5E	81	-9	0						
1993 NYN	NL	38	13	25	.342	7E	7E	19	-6	0						
6 AL Years		843	407	436	.483	—	—	407	0	3						
2 NL Years		200	85	115	.425	—	—	100	-15	0						
8 Years		1043	492	551	.472	—	—	507	-15	3						

Joe Torre

Born: 7/18/1940 in Brooklyn, New York; MLB Career: 18 years, 2209 G (.297-252-1185)

Year Tm	Lg	G	W	L	Pct	Standing		EW	+/-	Pt	W	L	Pct	W	L	Pct
1977 NYN	NL	117	49	68	.419	6E	6E	59	-10	0						
1978 NYN	NL	162	66	96	.407		6E	73	-7	0						
1979 NYN	NL	163	63	99	.389		6E	72	-9	0						
1980 NYN	NL	162	67	95	.414		5E	68	-1	0						
1981 NYN	NL	52	17	34	.333		5E	22	-5	0						
NYN	NL	53	24	28	.462		4E	22	2	0						
1982 Atl	NL	162	89	73	.549		1W	77	12	2				0	3	.000
1983 Atl	NL	162	88	74	.543		2W	85	3	1						
1984 Atl	NL	162	80	82	.494		2W	85	-5	0						
1990 StL	NL	58	24	34	.414	6E	6E	30	-6	0						
1991 StL	NL	162	84	78	.519		2E	76	8	1						
1992 StL	NL	162	83	79	.512		3E	82	1	1						
1993 StL	NL	162	87	75	.537		3E	84	3	1						
1994 StL	NL	115	53	61	.465		3C	61	-8	0						
1995 StL	NL	47	20	27	.426	4C	4C	23	-3	0						
1996 NYA	AL	162	92	70	.568		1E	88	4	3				7	2	.778	4	2	.667
1997 NYA	AL	162	96	66	.593		2E	90	6	2				2	3	.400
2 AL Years		324	188	136	.580	—	—	178	10	7				9	5	.643	4	2	.667
14 NL Years		1901	894	1003	.471	—	—	919	-25	6				0	3	.000
16 Years		2225	1082	1139	.487	—	—	1097	-15	13				9	8	.529	4	2	.667

Dick Tracewski

Born: 2/3/1935 in Eynon, Pennsylvania; MLB Career: 8 years, 614 G (.213-8-91)

Year Tm	Lg	G	W	L	Pct	Standing			EW	+/-	Pt	W	L	Pct	W	L	Pct
1979 Det	AL	2	2	0	1.000	5E	5E	5E	1	1	0						

Pie Traynor

Born: 11/11/1899 in Framingham, Mass.; Died: 3/16/1972; MLB Career: 17 years, 1941 G (.320-58-1273)

Year Tm	Lg	G	W	L	Pct	Standing		EW	+/-	Pt	W	L	Pct	W	L	Pct
1934 Pit	NL	100	47	52	.475	4	5	53	-6	0						
1935 Pit	NL	153	86	67	.562		4	78	8	1						
1936 Pit	NL	156	84	70	.545		4	83	1	1						
1937 Pit	NL	154	86	68	.558		3	82	4	1						
1938 Pit	NL	152	86	64	.573		2	81	5	2						
1939 Pit	NL	153	68	85	.444		6	84	-16	0						
6 Years		868	457	406	.530	—	—	461	-4	5						

Tom Trebelhorn

Born: 1/27/1948 in Portland, Oregon; MLB Career: Did Not Play

Year Tm	Lg	G	W	L	Pct	Standing		EW	+/-	Pt	W	L	Pct	W	L	Pct
1986 Mil	AL	9	6	3	.667	6E	6E	4	2	0						
1987 Mil	AL	162	91	71	.562		3E	76	15	2						
1988 Mil	AL	162	87	75	.537		3E	84	3	1						
1989 Mil	AL	162	81	81	.500		4E	85	-4	0						
1990 Mil	AL	162	74	88	.457		6E	83	-9	0						
1991 Mil	AL	162	83	79	.512		4E	78	5	1						
1994 ChN	NL	113	49	64	.434		5C	58	-9	0						
6 AL Years		819	422	397	.515	—	—	410	12	4						
1 NL Year		113	49	64	.434	—	—	58	-9	0						
7 Years		932	471	461	.505	—	—	468	3	4						

Sam Trott

Born: Unknown in Washington, D.C.; Died: 6/5/1925; MLB Career: 8 years, 360 G (.250-3-123)

		REGULAR SEASON					Index			Playoffs			World Series		
Year Tm	Lg	G	W	L	Pct	Standing	EW	+/-	Pt	W	L	Pct	W	L	Pct
1891 Was	AA	12	4	7	.364	6 9			0						

Ted Turner

Born: 11/19/1938 in Cincinnati, Ohio; MLB Career: Did Not Play

		REGULAR SEASON					Index			Playoffs			World Series		
Year Tm	Lg	G	W	L	Pct	Standing	EW	+/-	Pt	W	L	Pct	W	L	Pct
1977 Atl	NL	1	0	1	.000	6W 6W 6W	0	0	0						

Bob Unglaub

Born: 7/31/1881 in Baltimore, Maryland; Died: 11/29/1916; MLB Career: 6 years, 595 G (.258-5-216)

		REGULAR SEASON					Index			Playoffs			World Series		
Year Tm	Lg	G	W	L	Pct	Standing	EW	+/-	Pt	W	L	Pct	W	L	Pct
1907 Bos	AL	29	9	20	.310	6 8 7	12	-3	0						

Bobby Valentine

Born: 5/13/1950 in Stamford, Connecticut; MLB Career: 10 years, 639 G (.260-12-157)

		REGULAR SEASON					Index			Playoffs			World Series		
Year Tm	Lg	G	W	L	Pct	Standing	EW	+/-	Pt	W	L	Pct	W	L	Pct
1985 Tex	AL	129	53	76	.411	7W 7W	58	-5	0						
1986 Tex	AL	162	87	75	.537	2W	70	17	1						
1987 Tex	AL	162	75	87	.463	6W	80	-5	0						
1988 Tex	AL	161	70	91	.435	6W	76	-6	0						
1989 Tex	AL	162	83	79	.512	4W	76	7	1						
1990 Tex	AL	162	83	79	.512	3W	80	3	1						
1991 Tex	AL	162	85	77	.525	3W	81	4	1						
1992 Tex	AL	86	45	41	.523	3W 4W	44	1	0						
1996 NYN	NL	31	12	19	.387	4E 4E	15	-3	0						
1997 NYN	NL	162	88	74	.543	3E	75	13	1						
8 AL Years		1186	581	605	.490	— — —	565	16	4						
2 NL Years		193	100	93	.518		90	10	1						
10 Years		1379	681	698	.494	— — —	655	26	5						

George Van Haltren

Born: 3/30/1866 in St. Louis, Missouri; Died: 9/29/1945; MLB Career: 17 years, 1984 G (.316-69-1014)

		REGULAR SEASON					Index			Playoffs			World Series		
Year Tm	Lg	G	W	L	Pct	Standing	EW	+/-	Pt	W	L	Pct	W	L	Pct
1892 Bal	NL	11	1	10	.091	12 12			0						

Mickey Vernon

Born: 4/22/1918 in Marcus Hook, Pennsylvania; MLB Career: 20 years, 2409 G (.286-172-1311)

		REGULAR SEASON					Index			Playoffs			World Series		
Year Tm	Lg	G	W	L	Pct	Standing	EW	+/-	Pt	W	L	Pct	W	L	Pct
1961 Was	AL	161	61	100	.379	9	60	1	0						
1962 Was	AL	162	60	101	.373	10	64	-4	0						
1963 Was	AL	40	14	26	.350	10 10	16	-2	0						
3 Years		363	135	227	.373	— — —	140	-5	0						

Bill Virdon

Born: 6/9/1931 in Hazel Park, Michigan; MLB Career: 12 years, 1583 G (.267-91-502)

		REGULAR SEASON					Index			Playoffs			World Series		
Year Tm	Lg	G	W	L	Pct	Standing	EW	+/-	Pt	W	L	Pct	W	L	Pct
1972 Pit	NL	155	96	59	.619	1E	87	9	3	2	3	.400			
1973 Pit	NL	136	67	69	.493	2E 3E	79	-12	0						
1974 NYA	AL	162	89	73	.549	2E	81	8	1						
1975 NYA	AL	104	53	51	.510	3E 3E	55	-2	0						
Hou	NL	35	17	17	.500	6W 6W	17	0	0						
1976 Hou	NL	162	80	82	.494	3W	73	7	0						
1977 Hou	NL	162	81	81	.500	3W	78	3	0						
1978 Hou	NL	162	74	88	.457	5W	79	-5	0						
1979 Hou	NL	162	89	73	.549	2W	77	12	1						
1980 Hou	NL	163	93	70	.571	1W	85	8	3	2	3	.400			
1981 Hou	NL	57	28	29	.491	3W	31	-3	0						
Hou	NL	53	33	20	.623	1W	29	4	1	2	3	.400			
1982 Hou	NL	111	49	62	.441	5W 5W	60	-11	0						
1983 Mon	NL	163	82	80	.506	3E	86	-4	1						
1984 Mon	NL	131	64	67	.489	5E 5E	67	-3	0						
2 AL Years		266	142	124	.534	— — —	136	6	1						
12 NL Years		1652	853	797	.517		848	5	9	6	9	.400			
13 Years		1918	995	921	.519	— — —	984	11	10	6	9	.400			

Ossie Vitt

Born: 1/4/1890 in San Francisco, California; Died: 1/31/1963; MLB Career: 10 years, 1062 G (.238-4-294)

		REGULAR SEASON					Index			Playoffs			World Series		
Year Tm	Lg	G	W	L	Pct	Standing	EW	+/-	Pt	W	L	Pct	W	L	Pct
1938 Cle	AL	153	86	66	.566	3	80	6	2						
1939 Cle	AL	154	87	67	.565	3	83	4	2						
1940 Cle	AL	155	89	65	.578	2	84	5	2						
3 Years		462	262	198	.570	— — —	247	15	6						

Chris Von Der Ahe

Born: 10/7/1851 in Hille, Prussia; Died: 6/5/1913; MLB Career: Did Not Play

		REGULAR SEASON					Index			Playoffs			World Series		
Year Tm	Lg	G	W	L	Pct	Standing	EW	+/-	Pt	W	L	Pct	W	L	Pct
1895 StL	NL	1	1	0	1.000	11 11 11			0						
1896 StL	NL	2	0	2	.000	10 11 11			0						
1897 StL	NL	14	2	12	.143	12 12			0						
3 Years		17	3	14	.176	— — —			0						

John Vukovich

Born: 7/31/1947 in Sacramento, California; MLB Career: 10 years, 277 G (.161-6-44)

		REGULAR SEASON					Index			Playoffs			World Series		
Year Tm	Lg	G	W	L	Pct	Standing	EW	+/-	Pt	W	L	Pct	W	L	Pct
1986 ChN	NL	2	1	1	.500	5E 5E 5E	1	0							
1988 Phi	NL	9	5	4	.556	6E 6E	4	1	0						
2 Years		11	6	5	.545	— — —	5	1	0						

Heinie Wagner

Born: 9/23/1880 in New York, New York; Died: 3/20/1943; MLB Career: 12 years, 983 G (.250-10-343)

		REGULAR SEASON					Index			Playoffs			World Series		
Year Tm	Lg	G	W	L	Pct	Standing	EW	+/-	Pt	W	L	Pct	W	L	Pct
1930 Bos	AL	154	52	102	.338	8	62	-10	0						

Honus Wagner

Born: 2/24/1874 in Chartiers, Pennsylvania; Died: 12/6/1955; MLB Career: 21 years, 2792 G (.327-101-1732)

		REGULAR SEASON					Index			Playoffs			World Series		
Year Tm	Lg	G	W	L	Pct	Standing	EW	+/-	Pt	W	L	Pct	W	L	Pct
1917 Pit	NL	5	1	4	.200	8 8 8	2	-1	0						

Harry Walker

Born: 10/22/1916 in Pascagoula, Mississippi; MLB Career: 11 years, 807 G (.296-10-214)

		REGULAR SEASON					Index			Playoffs			World Series		
Year Tm	Lg	G	W	L	Pct	Standing	EW	+/-	Pt	W	L	Pct	W	L	Pct
1955 StL	NL	118	51	67	.432	5 7	59	-8	0						
1965 Pit	NL	163	90	72	.556	3	81	9	1						
1966 Pit	NL	162	92	70	.568	3	85	7	2						
1967 Pit	NL	84	42	42	.500	6 6	45	-3	0						
1968 Hou	NL	101	49	52	.485	10 10	45	4	0						
1969 Hou	NL	162	81	81	.500	5W	78	3	0						
1970 Hou	NL	162	79	83	.488	4W	79	0	0						
1971 Hou	NL	162	79	83	.488	4W	80	-1	0						
1972 Hou	NL	121	67	54	.554	3W 2W	67	1	0						
9 Years		1235	630	604	.511	— — —	612	18	3						

Bobby Wallace

Born: 11/4/1873 in Pittsburgh, Pennsylvania; Died: 11/3/1960; MLB Career: 25 years, 2383 G (.268-34-1121)

		REGULAR SEASON					Index			Playoffs			World Series		
Year Tm	Lg	G	W	L	Pct	Standing	EW	+/-	Pt	W	L	Pct	W	L	Pct
1911 StL	AL	152	45	107	.296	8	60	-15	0						
1912 StL	AL	40	12	27	.308	8 7	14	-2	0						
1937 Cin	NL	25	5	20	.200	8 8	12	-7	0						
2 AL Years		192	57	134	.298	— — —	74	-17	0						
1 NL Year		25	5	20	.200	— — —	12	-7	0						
3 Years		217	62	154	.287	— — —	86	-24	0						

Ed Walsh

Born: 5/14/1881 in Plains, Pennsylvania; Died: 5/26/1959; MLB Career: 14 years, 461 G (195-126, 1.81)

		REGULAR SEASON					Index			Playoffs			World Series		
Year Tm	Lg	G	W	L	Pct	Standing	EW	+/-	Pt	W	L	Pct	W	L	Pct
1924 ChA	AL	3	1	2	.333	6 6 8	1	0	0						

Mike Walsh

Born: 4/29/1850 in Ireland ; Died: 2/2/1929; MLB Career: Did Not Play

		REGULAR SEASON					Index			Playoffs			World Series		
Year Tm	Lg	G	W	L	Pct	Standing	EW	+/-	Pt	W	L	Pct	W	L	Pct
1884 Lou	AA	110	68	40	.630	3			2						

Bucky Walters

Born: 4/19/1909 in Philadelphia, Pennsylvania; Died: 4/20/1991; MLB Career: 19 years, 715 G (198-160, 3.30)

		REGULAR SEASON					Index			Playoffs			World Series		
Year Tm	Lg	G	W	L	Pct	Standing	EW	+/-	Pt	W	L	Pct	W	L	Pct
1948 Cin	NL	53	20	33	.377	7 7	25	-5	0						
1949 Cin	NL	153	61	90	.404	7 7	68	-7	0						
2 Years		206	81	123	.397	— — —	93	-12	0						

John Waltz

Born: Unknown; MLB Career: Did Not Play

		REGULAR SEASON					Index			Playoffs			World Series		
Year Tm	Lg	G	W	L	Pct	Standing	EW	+/-	Pt	W	L	Pct	W	L	Pct
1892 Bal	NL	8	2	6	.250	12 12 12			0						

Monte Ward

Born: 3/3/1860 in Bellefonte, Pennsylvania; Died: 3/4/1925; MLB Career: 17 years, 1825 G (164-102, 2.10)

Year	Tm	Lg	G	W	L	Pct	Standing	EW	+/-	Pt	W	L	Pct	W	L	Pct
							REGULAR SEASON		**Index**			**Playoffs**			**World Series**	
1880	Prv	NL	32	18	13	.581	4 **3** 2			0						
1884	NYG	NL	16	6	8	.429	4 **4**			0						
1890	Bro	PL	133	76	56	.576	**2**			2						
1891	Bro	NL	137	61	76	.445	**6**			0						
1892	Bro	NL	78	51	26	.662	**2**			0						
	Bro	NL	80	44	33	.571	**3**			2						
1893	NYG	NL	136	68	64	.515	**5**			1						
1894	NYG	NL	139	88	44	.667	**2**			5				4	0	1.000
6 NL Years			618	336	264	.560	— — —			8				4	0	1.000
1 PL Year			133	76	56	.576	— — —			2						
7 Years			751	412	320	.563	— — —			10				4	0	1.000

John Wathan

Born: 10/4/1949 in Cedar Rapids, Iowa; MLB Career: 10 years, 860 G (.262-21-261)

Year	Tm	Lg	G	W	L	Pct	Standing	EW	+/-	Pt	W	L	Pct	W	L	Pct
1987	KC	AL	38	21	15	.583	4W **2W**	18	3	0						
1988	KC	AL	163	84	77	.522	**3W**	82	2	1						
1989	KC	AL	164	92	70	.568	**2W**	82	10	2						
1990	KC	AL	163	75	86	.466	**6W**	87	-12	0						
1991	KC	AL	39	15	22	.405	**7W** 6W	18	-3	0						
1992	Cal	AL	91	39	50	.438	5W **5W** 5W	45	-6	0						
6 Years			658	326	320	.505		332	-6	3						

Bill Watkins

Born: 5/5/1858 in Brantford, Ontario, Canada; Died: 6/9/1937; MLB Career: 1 year, 34 G (.205-0-0)

Year	Tm	Lg	G	W	L	Pct	Standing	EW	+/-	Pt	W	L	Pct	W	L	Pct
1884	Ind	AA	23	4	18	.182	10 **11**			0						
1885	Det	NL	70	34	36	.486	7 **6**			0						
1886	Det	NL	126	87	36	.707	**2**			2						
1887	Det	NL	127	79	45	.637	**1**			5				10	5	.667
1888	Det	NL	94	49	44	.527	3 **5**			0						
	KC	AA	25	8	17	.320	8 **8**			0						
1889	KC	AA	139	55	82	.401	**7**			0						
1893	StL	NL	135	57	75	.432	**10**			0						
1898	Pit	NL	152	72	76	.486	**8**			0						
1899	Pit	NL	24	7	15	.318	**10** 7			0						
7 NL Years			728	385	327	.541	— — —			7				10	5	.667
3 AA Years			187	67	117	.364	— — —			0						
9 Years			915	452	444	.504	— — —			7				10	5	.667

Harvey Watkins

Born: Unknown; MLB Career: Did Not Play

Year	Tm	Lg	G	W	L	Pct	Standing	EW	+/-	Pt	W	L	Pct	W	L	Pct
1895	NYG	NL	35	18	17	.514	9 **9**			0						

Earl Weaver

Born: 8/14/1930 in St. Louis, Missouri; MLB Career: Did Not Play

Year	Tm	Lg	G	W	L	Pct	Standing	EW	+/-	Pt	W	L	Pct	W	L	Pct
1968	Bal	AL	82	48	34	.585	3 **2**	42	6	1						
1969	Bal	AL	162	109	53	.673	**1E**	92	17	5	3	0	1.000	1	4	.200
1970	Bal	AL	162	108	54	.667	**1E**	97	11	6	3	0	1.000	4	1	.800
1971	Bal	AL	158	101	57	.639	**1E**	98	3	5	3	0	1.000	3	4	.429
1972	Bal	AL	154	80	74	.519	**3E**	94	-14	1						
1973	Bal	AL	162	97	65	.599	**1E**	89	8	3	2	3	.400			
1974	Bal	AL	162	91	71	.562	**1E**	92	-1	3	1	3	.250			
1975	Bal	AL	159	90	69	.566	**2E**	87	3	2						
1976	Bal	AL	162	88	74	.543	**2E**	90	-2	1						
1977	Bal	AL	161	97	64	.602	**2E**	91	6	2						
1978	Bal	AL	161	90	71	.559	**4E**	92	-2	1						
1979	Bal	AL	159	102	57	.642	**1E**	88	14	5	3	1	.750	3	4	.429
1980	Bal	AL	162	100	62	.617	**2E**	96	4	3						
1981	Bal	AL	54	31	23	.574	**2E**	32	-1	0						
	Bal	AL	51	28	23	.549	**4E**	30	-2	1						
1982	Bal	AL	163	94	68	.580	**2E**	91	3	2						
1985	Bal	AL	105	53	52	.505	4E **4E**	56	-3	1						
1986	Bal	AL	162	73	89	.451	**7E**	85	-12	0						
17 Years			2541	1480	1060	.583	— — —	1442	38	42	15	7	.682	11	13	.458

Wes Westrum

Born: 11/28/1922 in Clearbrook, Minnesota; MLB Career: 11 years, 919 G (.217-96-315)

Year	Tm	Lg	G	W	L	Pct	Standing	EW	+/-	Pt	W	L	Pct	W	L	Pct
1965	NYN	NL	68	19	48	.284	10 **10**	24	-5	0						
1966	NYN	NL	161	66	95	.410	**9**	58	8	0						
1967	NYN	NL	151	57	94	.377	**10** 10	62	-5	0						
1974	SF	NL	86	38	48	.442	5W **5W**	45	-7	0						
1975	SF	NL	161	80	81	.497	**3W**	76	4	0						
5 Years			627	260	366	.415	— — —	265	-5	0						

Harry Wheeler

Born: 3/3/1858 in Versailles, Indiana; Died: 10/9/1900; MLB Career: 6 years, 257 G (.228-2-3)

Year	Tm	Lg	G	W	L	Pct	Standing	EW	+/-	Pt	W	L	Pct	W	L	Pct
1884	KC	UA	4	0	4	.000	**12** 12			0						

Deacon White

Born: 12/7/1847 in Caton, New York; Died: 7/7/1939; MLB Career: 15 years, 1299 G (.303-18-756)

Year	Tm	Lg	G	W	L	Pct	Standing	EW	+/-	Pt	W	L	Pct	W	L	Pct
1879	Cin	NL	18	9	9	.500	5 **5**			0						

Jo-Jo White

Born: 6/1/1909 in Red Oak, Georgia; Died: 10/9/1986; MLB Career: 9 years, 878 G (.256-8-229)

Year	Tm	Lg	G	W	L	Pct	Standing	EW	+/-	Pt	W	L	Pct	W	L	Pct
1960	Cle	AL	1	1	0	1.000	4 **4** 4	1	0	0						

Will White

Born: 10/11/1854 in Caton, New York; Died: 8/31/1911; MLB Career: 10 years, 403 G (229-166, 2.28)

Year	Tm	Lg	G	W	L	Pct	Standing	EW	+/-	Pt	W	L	Pct	W	L	Pct
1884	Cin	AA	72	44	27	.620	5 **5**			0						

Del Wilber

Born: 2/24/1919 in Lincoln Park, Michigan; MLB Career: 8 years, 299 G (.242-19-115)

Year	Tm	Lg	G	W	L	Pct	Standing	EW	+/-	Pt	W	L	Pct	W	L	Pct
1973	Tex	AL	1	1	0	1.000	6W **6W** 6W	0	1	0						

Kaiser Wilhelm

Born: 1/26/1874 in Wooster, Ohio; Died: 5/22/1936; MLB Career: 9 years, 223 G (56-105, 3.44)

Year	Tm	Lg	G	W	L	Pct	Standing	EW	+/-	Pt	W	L	Pct	W	L	Pct
1921	Phi	NL	67	26	41	.388	8 **8**	29	-3	0						
1922	Phi	NL	154	57	96	.373	**7**	59	-2	0						
2 Years			221	83	137	.377	— — —	88	-5	0						

Dick Williams

Born: 5/7/1929 in St. Louis, Missouri; MLB Career: 13 years, 1023 G (.260-70-331)

Year	Tm	Lg	G	W	L	Pct	Standing	EW	+/-	Pt	W	L	Pct	W	L	Pct
1967	Bos	AL	162	92	70	.568	**1**	73	19	4				3	4	.429
1968	Bos	AL	162	86	76	.531	**4**	83	3	1						
1969	Bos	AL	153	82	71	.536	3E **3E**	83	-1	0						
1971	Oak	AL	161	101	60	.627	**1W**	86	15	4	0	3	.000			
1972	Oak	AL	155	93	62	.600	**1W**	89	4	5	3	2	.600	4	3	.571
1973	Oak	AL	162	94	68	.580	**1W**	93	1	5	3	2	.600	4	3	.571
1974	Cal	AL	84	36	48	.429	6W **6W**	41	-5	0						
1975	Cal	AL	161	72	89	.447	**6W**	73	-1	0						
1976	Cal	AL	96	39	57	.406	4W **4W**	44	-5	0						
1977	Mon	NL	162	75	87	.463	**5E**	67	8	0						
1978	Mon	NL	162	76	86	.469	**4E**	74	2	0						
1979	Mon	NL	160	95	65	.594	**2E**	74	21	2						
1980	Mon	NL	162	90	72	.556	**2E**	87	3	1						
1981	Mon	NL	55	30	25	.545	**3E**	30	0	0						
	Mon	NL	26	14	12	.538	**6E** 1E	14	0	0						
1982	SD	NL	162	81	81	.500	**4W**	70	11	0						
1983	SD	NL	163	81	81	.500	**4W**	78	3	0						
1984	SD	NL	162	92	70	.568	**1W**	79	13	4	3	2	.600	1	4	.200
1985	SD	NL	162	83	79	.512	**3W**	87	-4	1						
1986	Sea	AL	133	58	75	.436	6W **7W**	61	-3	0						
1987	Sea	AL	162	78	84	.481	**4W**	72	6	0						
1988	Sea	AL	56	23	33	.411	**6W** 7W	27	-4	0						
12 AL Years			1647	854	793	.519	— — —	825	29	19	6	7	.462	11	10	.524
9 NL Years			1376	717	658	.521	— — —	660	57	8	3	2	.600	1	4	.200
21 Years			3023	1571	1451	.520	— — —	1485	86	27	9	9	.500	12	14	.462

Jimmy Williams

Born: 1/3/1848 in Columbus, Ohio; Died: 10/24/1918; MLB Career: Did Not Play

Year	Tm	Lg	G	W	L	Pct	Standing	EW	+/-	Pt	W	L	Pct	W	L	Pct
1884	STL	AA	85	51	33	.607	5 **4**			0						
1887	Cle	AA	133	39	92	.298	**8**			0						
1888	Cle	AA	64	20	44	.313	7 **6**			0						
3 Years			282	110	169	.394	— — —			0						

Jimy Williams

Born: 10/4/1943 in Santa Maria, California; MLB Career: 2 years, 14 G (.231-0-1)

Year	Tm	Lg	G	W	L	Pct	Standing	EW	+/-	Pt	W	L	Pct	W	L	Pct
1986	Tor	AL	163	86	76	.531	**4E**	92	-6	1						
1987	Tor	AL	162	96	66	.593	**2E**	87	9	2						
1988	Tor	AL	162	87	75	.537	**3E**	91	-4	1						
1989	Tor	AL	36	12	24	.333	**6E** 1E	19	-7	0						
1997	Bos	AL	162	78	84	.481	**4E**	84	-6	0						
5 Years			685	359	325	.525	— — —	373	-14	4						

Ted Williams

Born: 8/30/1918 in San Diego, California; MLB Career: 19 years, 2292 G (.344-521-1839)

Year Tm	Lg	REGULAR SEASON G	W	L	Pct	Standing	Index EW	+/-	Pt	Playoffs W	L	Pct	World Series W	L	Pct
1969 Was	AL	162	86	76	.531	4E	76	10	1						
1970 Was	AL	162	70	92	.432	6E	82	-12	0						
1971 Was	AL	159	63	96	.396	5E	74	-11	0						
1972 Tex	AL	154	54	100	.351	6W	68	-14	0						
4 Years		637	273	364	.429	— — —	300	-27	1						

Maury Wills

Born: 10/2/1932 in Washington, D.C.; MLB Career: 14 years, 1942 G (.281-20-458)

Year Tm	Lg	REGULAR SEASON G	W	L	Pct	Standing	Index EW	+/-	Pt	Playoffs W	L	Pct	World Series W	L	Pct
1980 Sea	AL	58	20	38	.345	7W 7W	25	-5	0						
1981 Sea	AL	25	6	18	.250	7W 6W	9	-3	0						
2 Years		83	26	56	.317	— — —	34	-8	0						

Jimmie Wilson

Born: 7/23/1900 in Philadelphia, Pennsylvania; Died: 5/31/1947; MLB Career: 18 years, 1525 G (.284-32-621)

Year Tm	Lg	REGULAR SEASON G	W	L	Pct	Standing	Index EW	+/-	Pt	Playoffs W	L	Pct	World Series W	L	Pct
1934 Phi	NL	149	56	93	.376	7	65	-9	0						
1935 Phi	NL	156	64	89	.418	7	65	-1	0						
1936 Phi	NL	154	54	100	.351	8	66	-12	0						
1937 Phi	NL	155	61	92	.399	7	61	0	0						
1938 Phi	NL	149	45	103	.304	8 8	62	-17	0						
1941 ChN	NL	155	70	84	.455	6	79	-9	0						
1942 ChN	NL	155	68	86	.442	6	74	-6	0						
1943 ChN	NL	154	74	79	.484	5	71	3	0						
1944 ChN	NL	10	1	9	.100	8 4	5	-4	0						
9 Years		1237	493	735	.401	— — —	548	-55	0						

Bobby Wine

Born: 9/17/1938 in New York, New York; MLB Career: 12 years, 1164 G (.215-30-268)

Year Tm	Lg	REGULAR SEASON G	W	L	Pct	Standing	Index EW	+/-	Pt	Playoffs W	L	Pct	World Series W	L	Pct
1985 Atl	NL	41	16	25	.390	5W 5W	21	-5	0						

Ivy Wingo

Born: 7/8/1890 in Gainesville, Georgia; Died: 3/1/1941; MLB Career: 17 years, 1327 G (.260-25-455)

Year Tm	Lg	REGULAR SEASON G	W	L	Pct	Standing	Index EW	+/-	Pt	Playoffs W	L	Pct	World Series W	L	Pct
1916 Cin	NL	2	1	1	.500	8 8 7	1	0	0						

Bobby Winkles

Born: 3/11/1930 in Tuckerman, Arkansas; MLB Career: Did Not Play

Year Tm	Lg	REGULAR SEASON G	W	L	Pct	Standing	Index EW	+/-	Pt	Playoffs W	L	Pct	World Series W	L	Pct
1973 Cal	AL	162	79	83	.488	4W	80	-1	0						
1974 Cal	AL	75	30	44	.405	6W 6W	36	-6	0						
1977 Oak	AL	108	37	71	.343	7W 7W	61	-24	0						
1978 Oak	AL	39	24	15	.615	6W 6W	18	6	0						
4 Years		384	170	213	.444	— — —	195	-25	0						

Chicken Wolf

Born: 5/12/1862 in Louisville, Kentucky; Died: 5/16/1903; MLB Career: 11 years, 1198 G (.290-18-520)

Year Tm	Lg	REGULAR SEASON G	W	L	Pct	Standing	Index EW	+/-	Pt	Playoffs W	L	Pct	World Series W	L	Pct
1889 Lou	AA	65	14	51	.215	8 8 8			0						

Harry Wolverton

Born: 12/6/1873 in Mount Vernon, Ohio; Died: 2/4/1937; MLB Career: 9 years, 782 G (.278-7-352)

Year Tm	Lg	REGULAR SEASON G	W	L	Pct	Standing	Index EW	+/-	Pt	Playoffs W	L	Pct	World Series W	L	Pct
1912 NYA	AL	153	50	102	.329	8	77	-27	0						

George Wood

Born: 11/9/1858 in Boston, Massachusetts; Died: 4/4/1924; MLB Career: 13 years, 1280 G (.273-68-601)

Year Tm	Lg	REGULAR SEASON G	W	L	Pct	Standing	Index EW	+/-	Pt	Playoffs W	L	Pct	World Series W	L	Pct
1891 Phi	AA	125	67	55	.549	7 5			1						

Al Wright

Born: 3/30/1842 in Cedar Grove, New Jersey; Died: 4/20/1905; MLB Career: Did Not Play

Year Tm	Lg	REGULAR SEASON G	W	L	Pct	Standing	Index EW	+/-	Pt	Playoffs W	L	Pct	World Series W	L	Pct
1876 PhN	NL	60	14	45	.237	7			0						

George Wright

Born: 1/28/1847 in Yonkers, New York; Died: 8/21/1937; MLB Career: 7 years, 329 G (.256-2-132)

Year Tm	Lg	REGULAR SEASON G	W	L	Pct	Standing	Index EW	+/-	Pt	Playoffs W	L	Pct	World Series W	L	Pct
1879 Prv	NL	85	59	25	.702	1			4						

Harry Wright

Born: 1/10/1835 in Sheffield, England; Died: 10/3/1895; MLB Career: 2 years, 2 G (.000-0-0)

Year Tm	Lg	REGULAR SEASON G	W	L	Pct	Standing	Index EW	+/-	Pt	Playoffs W	L	Pct	World Series W	L	Pct
1876 Bos	NL	70	39	31	.557	4			1						
1877 Bos	NL	61	42	18	.700	1			4						
1878 Bos	NL	60	41	19	.683	1			4						
1879 Bos	NL	84	54	30	.643	2			2						
1880 Bos	NL	86	40	44	.476	6			0						
1881 Bos	NL	83	38	45	.458	6			0						
1882 Prv	NL	84	52	32	.619	2			2						
1883 Prv	NL	98	58	40	.592	3			1						
1884 Phi	NL	113	39	73	.348	6			0						
1885 Phi	NL	111	56	54	.509	3			1						
1886 Phi	NL	119	71	43	.623	4			2						
1887 Phi	NL	128	75	48	.610	2			2						
1888 Phi	NL	132	69	61	.531	3			1						
1889 Phi	NL	130	63	64	.496	4			0						
1890 Phi	NL	22	14	8	.636	1	3		0						
Phi	NL	46	22	23	.489	2	3		1						
1891 Phi	NL	138	68	69	.496	4			0						
1892 Phi	NL	77	46	30	.605	3			0						
Phi	NL	78	41	36	.532	5			1						
1893 Phi	NL	133	72	57	.558	4			1						
18 Years		1853	1000	825	.548	— — —			23						

Rudy York

Born: 8/17/1913 in Ragland, Alabama; Died: 2/5/1970; MLB Career: 13 years, 1603 G (.275-277-1152)

Year Tm	Lg	REGULAR SEASON G	W	L	Pct	Standing	Index EW	+/-	Pt	Playoffs W	L	Pct	World Series W	L	Pct
1959 Bos	AL	1	0	1	.000	8 8 5	1	-1	0						

Tom York

Born: 7/13/1851 in Brooklyn, New York; Died: 2/17/1936; MLB Career: 10 years, 690 G (.271-10-315)

Year Tm	Lg	REGULAR SEASON G	W	L	Pct	Standing	Index EW	+/-	Pt	Playoffs W	L	Pct	World Series W	L	Pct
1878 Prv	NL	62	33	27	.550	3			1						
1881 Prv	NL	34	23	10	.697	4 2			1						
2 Years		96	56	37	.602	— — —			1						

Eddie Yost

Born: 10/13/1926 in Brooklyn, New York; MLB Career: 18 years, 2109 G (.254-139-683)

Year Tm	Lg	REGULAR SEASON G	W	L	Pct	Standing	Index EW	+/-	Pt	Playoffs W	L	Pct	World Series W	L	Pct
1963 Was	AL	1	0	1	.000	10 10 10	0	0	0						

Cy Young

Born: 3/29/1867 in Gilmore, Ohio; Died: 11/4/1955; MLB Career: 22 years, 918 G (511-316, 2.63)

Year Tm	Lg	REGULAR SEASON G	W	L	Pct	Standing	Index EW	+/-	Pt	Playoffs W	L	Pct	World Series W	L	Pct
1907 Bos	AL	6	3	3	.500	4 7	3	0	0						

Chief Zimmer

Born: 11/23/1860 in Marietta, Ohio; Died: 8/22/1949; MLB Career: 19 years, 1280 G (.269-26-625)

Year Tm	Lg	REGULAR SEASON G	W	L	Pct	Standing	Index EW	+/-	Pt	Playoffs W	L	Pct	World Series W	L	Pct
1903 Phi	NL	139	49	86	.363	7	64	-15	0						

Don Zimmer

Born: 1/17/1931 in Cincinnati, Ohio; MLB Career: 12 years, 1095 G (.235-91-352)

Year Tm	Lg	REGULAR SEASON G	W	L	Pct	Standing	Index EW	+/-	Pt	Playoffs W	L	Pct	World Series W	L	Pct
1972 SD	NL	142	54	88	.380	4W 6W	57	-3	0						
1973 SD	NL	162	60	102	.370	6W	67	-7	0						
1976 Bos	AL	76	42	34	.553	3E 3E	42	0	1						
1977 Bos	AL	161	97	64	.602	2E	87	10	2						
1978 Bos	AL	163	99	64	.607	2E	93	6	2						
1979 Bos	AL	160	91	69	.569	3E	92	-1	2						
1980 Bos	AL	155	82	73	.529	4E 4E	87	-5	0						
1981 Tex	AL	55	33	22	.600	2W	27	6	0						
Tex	AL	50	24	26	.480	3W	25	-1	1						
1982 Tex	AL	96	38	58	.396	6W 6W	49	-11	0						
1988 ChN	NL	163	77	85	.475	4E	77	0	0						
1989 ChN	NL	162	93	69	.574	1E	77	16	3	1	4	.200			
1990 ChN	NL	162	77	85	.475	4E	86	-9	0						
1991 ChN	NL	37	18	19	.486	4E 4E	18	0	0						
7 AL Years		916	506	410	.552	— — —	502	4	8						
6 NL Years		828	379	448	.458	— — —	382	-3	3	1	4	.200			
13 Years		1744	885	858	.508	— — —	884	1	11	1	4	.200			

Manager Leaders—Career

Games

1	Connie Mack	7,755
2	John McGraw	4,769
3	Bucky Harris	4,408
4	Sparky Anderson	4,030
5	Gene Mauch	3,942
6	Casey Stengel	3,766
7	Leo Durocher	3,739
8	Walter Alston	3,658
9	Bill McKechnie	3,647
10	Joe McCarthy	3,487
11	Ralph Houk	3,157
12	Tom Lasorda	3,040
13	Dick Williams	3,023
14	Jimmy Dykes	2,962
15	Clark Griffith	2,918
16	Tony La Russa	2,830
17	Fred Clarke	2,829
18	Wilbert Robinson	2,819
19	Chuck Tanner	2,738
20	Miller Huggins	2,570
21	Bill Rigney	2,561
22	Earl Weaver	2,541
23	Ned Hanlon	2,530
24	Al Lopez	2,425
25	John McNamara	2,411
26	Whitey Herzog	2,409
27	Lou Boudreau	2,404
28	Bobby Cox	2,403
29	Charlie Grimm	2,370
30	Joe Cronin	2,314
31	Cap Anson	2,280
32	Billy Martin	2,267
33	Frank Frisch	2,246
34	Joe Torre	2,225
35	Hughie Jennings	2,203
36	Frank Selee	2,180
37	Danny Murtaugh	2,068
38	Red Schoendienst	1,999
39	Chuck Dressen	1,990
40	Alvin Dark	1,950
41	Bill Virdon	1,918
42	Steve O'Neill	1,879
43	Jim Leyland	1,878
44	Harry Wright	1,853
45	Paul Richards	1,837
46	George Stallings	1,813
47	Jim Fregosi	1,799
48	Billy Southworth	1,770
49	Don Zimmer	1,744
50	Tom Kelly	1,738

Wins

1	Connie Mack	3,731
2	John McGraw	2,763
3	Sparky Anderson	2,194
4	Bucky Harris	2,157
5	Joe McCarthy	2,125
6	Walter Alston	2,040
7	Leo Durocher	2,008
8	Casey Stengel	1,905
9	Gene Mauch	1,902
10	Bill McKechnie	1,896
11	Ralph Houk	1,619
12	Fred Clarke	1,602
13	Tom Lasorda	1,599
14	Dick Williams	1,571
15	Clark Griffith	1,491
16	Tony La Russa	1,481
17	Earl Weaver	1,480
18	Miller Huggins	1,413
19	Al Lopez	1,410
20	Jimmy Dykes	1,406
21	Wilbert Robinson	1,399
22	Chuck Tanner	1,352
23	Ned Hanlon	1,313
24	Bobby Cox	1,312
25	Cap Anson	1,292
26	Charlie Grimm	1,287
27	Frank Selee	1,284
28	Whitey Herzog	1,281
29	Billy Martin	1,253
30	Bill Rigney	1,239
31	Joe Cronin	1,236
32	Hughie Jennings	1,184
33	John McNamara	1,167
34	Lou Boudreau	1,162
35	Frank Frisch	1,138
36	Danny Murtaugh	1,115
37	Joe Torre	1,082
38	Billy Southworth	1,044
39	Red Schoendienst	1,041
40	Steve O'Neill	1,040
41	Chuck Dressen	1,008
42	Harry Wright	1,000
43	Bill Virdon	995
44	Alvin Dark	994
45	Davey Johnson	985
46	Frank Chance	946
47	Jim Leyland	943
48	Paul Richards	923
49	Don Zimmer	885
50	George Stallings	879

Losses

1	Connie Mack	3,948
2	Bucky Harris	2,218
3	Gene Mauch	2,037
4	John McGraw	1,948
5	Casey Stengel	1,842
6	Sparky Anderson	1,834
7	Bill McKechnie	1,723
8	Leo Durocher	1,709
9	Walter Alston	1,613
10	Jimmy Dykes	1,541
11	Ralph Houk	1,531
12	Dick Williams	1,451
13	Tom Lasorda	1,439
14	Wilbert Robinson	1,398
15	Chuck Tanner	1,381
16	Clark Griffith	1,367
17	Tony La Russa	1,346
18	Joe McCarthy	1,333
19	Bill Rigney	1,321
20	John McNamara	1,242
21	Lou Boudreau	1,224
22	Fred Clarke	1,181
23	Ned Hanlon	1,164
24	Joe Torre	1,139
25	Miller Huggins	1,134
26	Whitey Herzog	1,125
27	Bobby Cox	1,089
28	Frank Frisch	1,078
29	Charlie Grimm	1,067
30	Earl Weaver	1,060
31	Joe Cronin	1,055
32	Billy Martin	1,013
33	Al Lopez	1,004
34	Hughie Jennings	995
35	Chuck Dressen	973
36	Red Schoendienst	955
37	Alvin Dark	954
38	Danny Murtaugh	950
39	Cap Anson	945
40	Jim Fregosi	938
41	Jim Leyland	933
42	Bill Virdon	921
43	Paul Richards	901
44	George Stallings	898
45	Jimmy McAleer	889
46	Tom Kelly	885
47	Patsy Donovan	879
48	Frank Selee	862
49	Don Zimmer	858
50	Fred Hutchinson	827

Winning Percentage
(minimum 1,000 Games)

1	Joe McCarthy	.615
2	Jim Mutrie	.611
3	Charlie Comiskey	.608
4	Frank Selee	.598
5	Billy Southworth	.597
6	Frank Chance	.593
7	John McGraw	.586
8	Al Lopez	.584
9	Earl Weaver	.583
10	Cap Anson	.578
11	Fred Clarke	.576
12	Davey Johnson	.575
13	Pat Moran	.561
14	Steve O'Neill	.559
15	Walter Alston	.558
16	Miller Huggins	.555
17	Patsy Tebeau	.555
18	Bill Terry	.555
19	Billy Martin	.553
20	Harry Wright	.548
21	Charlie Grimm	.547
22	Bobby Cox	.546
23	Sparky Anderson	.545
24	Hughie Jennings	.543
25	Tris Speaker	.543
26	Leo Durocher	.540
27	Danny Murtaugh	.540
28	Fielder Jones	.540
29	Joe Cronin	.540
30	Herman Franks	.537
31	Danny Ozark	.533
32	Whitey Herzog	.532
33	Ned Hanlon	.530
34	Tom Lasorda	.526
35	Lou Piniella	.525
36	Bill McKechnie	.524
37	Tony La Russa	.524
38	Hank Bauer	.522
39	Clark Griffith	.522
40	Red Schoendienst	.522
41	Dick Williams	.520
42	Mayo Smith	.520
43	Bill Virdon	.519
44	Cito Gaston	.518
45	Johnny Oates	.517
46	Birdie Tebbetts	.515
47	Ralph Houk	.514
48	Frank Frisch	.514
49	Harry Walker	.511
50	Alvin Dark	.510

+/-

1	Joe McCarthy	125
2	Bobby Cox	117
	John McGraw	117
4	Billy Martin	98
5	Dick Williams	86
6	Billy Southworth	74
7	Davey Johnson	69
8	Miller Huggins	68
9	Leo Durocher	62
	Paul Richards	62
11	Bill McKechnie	52
12	Bucky Harris	51
13	Fred Clarke	49
14	Clark Griffith	45
15	Al Lopez	43
	Steve O'Neill	43
17	Frank Chance	42
	George Stallings	42
19	Charlie Grimm	41
20	Danny Murtaugh	40
21	Earl Weaver	38
22	Fielder Jones	37
23	Sparky Anderson	35
24	Frank Selee	34
25	Bill Armour	33
26	Mike Hargrove	32
	Lou Piniella	32
28	Pat Moran	30
	Danny Ozark	30
30	Gil Hodges	28
31	Don Baylor	27
32	Sam Mele	26
	Buck Showalter	26
	Bobby Valentine	26
35	Walter Johnson	25
	Bob Kennedy	25
	Tony La Russa	25
	Bob Lemon	25
39	Joe Kelley	24
40	Walter Alston	23
	Joe Cronin	23
	George Gibson	23
	Hughie Jennings	23
	Johnny Oates	23
	Jake Stahl	23
46	Pants Rowland	22
47	Mickey Cochrane	21
48	Fred Lake	20
	Gene Mauch	20
50	Two tied with	19

Points

1	John McGraw	75
2	Connie Mack	71
3	Joe McCarthy	70
4	Casey Stengel	52
5	Walter Alston	50
6	Sparky Anderson	49
7	Earl Weaver	42
8	Miller Huggins	38
9	Leo Durocher	37
	Bill McKechnie	37
11	Fred Clarke	35
12	Cap Anson	34
	Ned Hanlon	34
	Frank Selee	34
15	Bobby Cox	33
	Tom Lasorda	33
17	Al Lopez	32
18	Frank Chance	30
	Billy Southworth	30
20	Whitey Herzog	28
	Tony La Russa	28
	Billy Martin	28
23	Dick Williams	27
24	Charlie Grimm	26
25	Ralph Houk	25
	Hughie Jennings	25
	Davey Johnson	25
28	Charlie Comiskey	24
29	Bucky Harris	23
	Danny Murtaugh	23
	Harry Wright	23
32	Steve O'Neill	22
33	Jim Mutrie	21
34	Joe Cronin	20
35	Bill Terry	19
36	Clark Griffith	18
37	Frank Frisch	17
	Gene Mauch	17
	Pat Moran	17
40	Alvin Dark	16
	Chuck Dressen	16
	Cito Gaston	16
43	Fielder Jones	15
	Jim Leyland	15
	Wilbert Robinson	15
	Red Schoendienst	15
47	Five tied with	14

World Series Won

1	Joe McCarthy	7
	Casey Stengel	7
3	Connie Mack	5
4	Walter Alston	4
5	Sparky Anderson	3
	Ned Hanlon	3
	Miller Huggins	3
	John McGraw	3
9	Bill Carrigan	2
	Frank Chance	2
	Cito Gaston	2
	Bucky Harris	2
	Ralph Houk	2
	Tom Kelly	2
	Tom Lasorda	2
	Bill McKechnie	2
	Danny Murtaugh	2
	Jim Mutrie	2
	Billy Southworth	2
	Dick Williams	2
21	45 tied with	1

League Titles

1	John McGraw	10
	Casey Stengel	10
3	Connie Mack	9
	Joe McCarthy	9
5	Walter Alston	7
6	Miller Huggins	6
7	Sparky Anderson	5
	Cap Anson	5
9	Frank Chance	4
	Fred Clarke	4
	Charlie Comiskey	4
	Bobby Cox	4
	Ned Hanlon	4
	Tom Lasorda	4
	Bill McKechnie	4
	Frank Selee	4
	Billy Southworth	4
	Earl Weaver	4
	Dick Williams	4
20	Leo Durocher	3
	Charlie Grimm	3
	Bucky Harris	3
	Whitey Herzog	3
	Ralph Houk	3
	Hughie Jennings	3
	Tony La Russa	3
	Jim Mutrie	3
	Bill Terry	3
29	Yogi Berra	2
	Bill Carrigan	2
	Mickey Cochrane	2
	Jimmy Collins	2
	Joe Cronin	2
	Alvin Dark	2
	Chuck Dressen	2
	Cito Gaston	2
	Fred Haney	2
	Mike Hargrove	2
	Tom Kelly	2
	Bob Lemon	2
	Al Lopez	2
	Billy Martin	2
	Bill McGunnigle	2
	Pat Moran	2
	Danny Murtaugh	2
	Wilbert Robinson	2
	Red Schoendienst	2
	Burt Shotton	2
	Gabby Street	2
	Harry Wright	2

Strategic Statistics—1991-1997

Offense

				Stolen Bases								Sacrifice Bunts			Hit & Run	
				Ptchout	2nd	3rd	Home	Double	-----Out Percentage-----				Suc.			Suc.
	G	Att	SB%	Rn Mvg	SB-CS	SB-CS	SB-CS	Steals	0	1	2	Att	%	Sqz	Att	%
Alou, Felipe	870	1082	75.2	36	701-229	103-30	10-10	36	22.1	39.6	38.3	530	83.4	52	569	38.3
Anderson, Sparky	745	622	64.0	28	338-186	60-33	0-5	28	19.5	44.7	35.9	230	79.1	9	388	35.1
Baker, Dusty	745	859	70.5	35	533-219	73-27	0-7	14	25.5	37.0	37.5	501	83.0	19	680	36.6
Baylor, Don	747	1033	67.8	52	567-272	124-43	9-18	37	20.3	40.7	39.0	463	82.3	32	635	40.8
Bell, Buddy	324	370	67.0	9	209-106	38-10	1-6	11	18.4	36.2	45.4	107	86.0	4	205	34.6
Bevington, Terry	437	419	69.9	14	253-113	39-9	1-4	7	18.4	36.5	45.1	198	84.3	18	261	35.6
Bochy, Bruce	468	534	69.9	11	300-133	71-24	2-5	21	19.9	35.6	44.6	222	82.0	21	356	39.9
Boles, John	75	90	78.9	2	62-17	8-1	1-1	3	36.7	28.9	34.4	26	57.7	1	57	40.4
Boone, Bob	386	579	68.6	26	329-144	52-28	16-11	20	18.7	33.2	48.2	233	79.8	14	309	37.5
Collins, Terry	583	845	71.7	33	506-202	99-31	1-5	39	19.8	38.0	42.2	332	85.8	19	462	38.1
Cox, Bobby	1068	1087	67.0	55	647-311	80-38	1-11	12	23.6	35.5	40.8	696	81.0	43	524	38.7
Craig, Roger	324	328	63.1	24	185-110	20-6	2-5	8	26.2	37.5	36.3	228	86.4	25	282	39.0
Cubbage, Mike	7	8	87.5	0	5-1	2-0	0-0	0	0.0	12.5	87.5	3	100.0	0	3	0.0
Dierker, Larry	162	245	69.8	3	142-61	29-12	0-0	10	19.6	40.0	40.4	96	80.2	7	131	27.5
Essian, Jim	122	149	65.1	5	83-45	14-6	0-1	3	28.9	32.9	38.3	81	84.0	6	103	44.7
Francona, Terry	162	148	62.2	5	79-48	11-6	2-2	4	18.2	31.1	50.7	91	93.4	3	90	27.8
Fregosi, Jim	894	733	75.4	17	475-166	75-11	3-3	18	18.3	38.2	43.5	491	80.0	25	337	32.3
Garner, Phil	906	1150	66.3	53	666-322	88-40	9-27	38	17.1	34.5	48.3	410	79.5	47	669	39.8
Gaston, Cito	1029	1074	75.8	34	667-231	148-25	1-3	30	23.0	33.5	43.5	379	79.4	22	472	33.3
Green, Dallas	511	356	61.2	16	184-122	33-12	1-4	9	23.6	32.9	43.5	348	85.6	20	312	42.9
Hargrove, Mike	988	1251	71.1	60	733-295	147-47	10-19	52	22.9	37.0	40.1	359	85.5	32	554	37.2
Harrah, Toby	76	42	54.8	5	21-17	2-1	0-1	0	33.3	28.6	38.1	37	91.9	2	61	41.0
Harrelson, Bud	153	212	67.9	10	124-63	16-4	4-1	9	19.3	35.4	45.3	88	72.7	1	86	32.6
Hobson, Butch	439	322	61.5	15	172-109	22-9	4-6	5	17.7	41.3	41.0	230	84.8	13	241	40.7
Howe, Art	810	749	66.2	28	436-220	56-21	4-12	18	16.7	42.1	41.3	433	79.2	17	477	38.2
Johnson, Davey	702	778	70.6	34	446-195	99-33	5-2	28	21.6	40.2	38.2	328	80.2	7	370	34.9
Jorgensen, Mike	96	83	60.2	5	42-29	7-2	1-2	2	19.3	30.1	50.6	37	78.4	1	47	42.6
Kelly, Tom	1067	1199	67.2	48	736-344	63-28	7-21	29	17.5	33.6	48.9	281	81.9	15	737	37.7
Kennedy, Kevin	582	575	67.0	16	356-164	27-19	2-7	8	19.3	36.0	44.7	250	82.8	9	328	36.0
Knight, Ray	257	407	73.7	20	234-88	64-9	2-9	16	21.1	36.6	42.3	162	77.2	15	204	40.2
Knoop, Bobby	1	1	100.0	0	1-0	0-0	0-0	0	100.0	0.0	0.0	0	-	0	0	-
La Russa, Tony	1068	1326	71.0	51	763-316	171-51	7-17	65	24.4	34.6	41.0	491	84.7	20	857	38.2
Lachemann, Marcel	335	231	58.0	11	118-85	14-9	2-3	3	19.5	38.4	42.0	139	74.1	9	208	39.9
Lachemann, Rene	505	503	67.8	23	296-141	45-19	0-2	14	32.8	37.6	29.6	286	74.5	18	243	38.7
Lamont, Gene	629	727	72.9	32	463-169	64-20	3-9	12	20.1	33.4	46.5	344	83.4	32	391	32.2
Lasorda, Tom	829	979	68.2	55	565-271	102-29	1-12	29	23.0	37.9	39.1	612	81.4	43	641	40.7
Lefebvre, Jim	487	412	66.5	33	251-125	23-12	0-1	9	25.0	31.6	43.4	273	80.2	16	342	37.1
Leyland, Jim	1068	1045	67.4	36	613-288	82-43	10-10	33	22.0	36.0	42.0	640	81.6	33	664	36.0
Leyva, Nick	12	14	78.6	0	9-3	2-0	0-0	2	0.0	64.3	35.7	5	80.0	0	8	37.5
McKeon, Jack	66	84	72.6	3	50-16	9-5	2-2	5	20.2	35.7	44.0	42	78.6	0	29	41.4
McNamara, John	120	95	58.9	6	51-36	5-3	0-0	2	32.6	30.5	36.8	69	75.4	0	86	32.6
McRae, Hal	563	731	64.0	49	411-228	58-27	1-8	18	19.2	39.9	40.9	242	76.4	17	437	36.6
Merrill, Stump	162	145	75.2	6	89-31	18-2	2-3	6	23.4	35.2	41.4	54	77.8	2	98	39.8
Morgan, Joe	162	98	60.2	3	52-35	7-3	0-1	1	23.5	42.9	33.7	61	85.2	3	50	28.0
Muser, Tony	79	70	68.6	2	44-16	4-5	0-1	1	15.7	30.0	54.3	30	90.0	3	46	30.4
Oates, Johnny	1030	753	67.3	33	444-226	60-18	3-2	12	20.3	39.3	40.4	346	85.0	18	529	35.3
Perez, Tony	43	56	73.2	3	33-14	8-1	0-0	2	26.8	42.9	30.4	26	76.9	1	35	40.0
Piniella, Lou	1066	1007	67.2	51	556-275	121-49	0-6	38	20.3	40.8	38.9	528	79.5	22	630	41.1
Plummer, Bill	162	155	64.5	8	85-45	15-6	0-4	5	16.8	40.0	43.2	75	81.3	4	91	39.6
Queen, Mel	5	7	42.9	1	2-4	1-0	0-0	0	14.3	28.6	57.1	1	100.0	0	3	33.3
Rader, Doug	123	98	68.4	6	49-29	18-2	0-0	4	19.4	27.6	53.1	60	85.0	3	69	39.1
Regan, Phil	144	137	67.2	8	84-41	8-4	0-0	3	18.2	34.3	47.4	54	77.8	0	70	38.6
Riddoch, Greg	311	273	59.0	13	137-94	23-13	1-4	3	23.8	34.1	42.1	196	83.7	21	186	39.8
Riggleman, Jim	759	738	69.0	25	432-190	73-19	4-17	20	19.6	33.5	46.9	472	82.6	37	515	40.8
Robinson, Frank	36	31	61.3	0	16-10	3-2	0-0	1	29.0	48.4	22.6	16	81.3	2	22	36.4
Rodgers, Buck	358	605	60.0	48	308-195	56-34	0-14	10	21.8	36.4	41.8	167	83.8	11	376	40.4
Runnells, Tom	148	268	71.6	20	161-63	30-10	1-3	5	21.3	38.4	40.3	82	84.1	3	127	31.5
Russell, Bill	248	279	70.3	22	174-71	22-6	0-6	10	21.1	35.5	43.4	174	86.2	18	206	41.7
Showalter, Buck	582	364	61.0	15	193-122	28-17	1-3	8	16.8	38.5	44.8	132	84.1	7	227	37.9
Tenace, Gene	32	39	82.1	2	25-7	7-0	0-0	1	20.5	43.6	35.9	14	85.7	0	19	26.3
Torborg, Jeff	361	432	67.8	26	266-120	26-8	1-11	11	22.0	31.3	46.8	227	82.4	17	250	35.6
Torre, Joe	971	1325	65.1	94	776-413	84-39	4-11	30	22.4	35.4	42.2	437	79.6	29	840	43.2
Trebelhorn, Tom	275	296	59.1	14	158-102	14-15	3-5	13	17.6	40.9	41.6	155	77.4	12	186	39.2
Valentine, Bobby	440	424	62.3	21	226-126	38-21	1-14	11	16.3	39.2	44.6	218	78.4	22	310	41.9
Wathan, John	124	168	64.9	11	91-54	16-2	2-3	4	19.0	37.5	43.5	56	80.4	2	129	40.3
Williams, Jimy	162	116	58.6	4	60-42	8-4	0-2	3	25.0	36.2	38.8	30	80.0	2	85	44.7
Zimmer, Don	36	35	68.6	3	22-8	2-1	0-2	1	17.1	48.6	34.3	21	76.2	1	39	41.0

Defense

	G	Pitchout			Non-PO CS%	Intentional BB		Defensive Subs
		Total	Runners Moving	CS%		IBB	% of Situations	Total
Alou, Felipe	870	243	79	41.8	22.1	155	3.9	290
Anderson, Sparky	745	440	93	45.2	32.2	310	10.0	100
Baker, Dusty	745	439	86	60.5	35.6	176	6.4	172
Baylor, Don	747	352	76	48.7	29.3	122	3.7	164
Bell, Buddy	324	45	9	66.7	28.2	64	4.8	47
Bevington, Terry	437	142	36	44.4	31.9	99	5.3	120
Bochy, Bruce	468	161	42	47.6	30.2	92	4.8	115
Boles, John	75	12	2	0.0	27.3	10	3.9	28
Boone, Bob	386	100	18	61.1	30.2	65	4.4	71
Collins, Terry	583	176	49	40.8	31.9	134	5.3	166
Cox, Bobby	1068	355	75	48.0	26.8	286	6.4	454
Craig, Roger	324	233	65	60.0	37.8	95	7.6	113
Cubbage, Mike	7	2	1	100.0	25.0	1	2.3	3
Dierker, Larry	162	35	7	85.7	35.9	25	4.1	44
Essian, Jim	122	77	23	47.8	31.2	33	5.7	78
Francona, Terry	162	30	6	66.7	33.5	31	4.8	52
Fregosi, Jim	894	200	61	36.1	28.0	181	4.8	225
Garner, Phil	906	250	52	50.0	27.6	144	3.9	222
Gaston, Cito	1029	417	105	38.1	32.9	156	3.7	129
Green, Dallas	511	161	38	50.0	24.7	142	6.6	130
Hargrove, Mike	988	435	90	57.8	30.3	186	4.3	246
Harrah, Toby	76	37	8	75.0	44.8	7	2.1	19
Harrelson, Bud	153	51	17	52.9	34.1	28	4.0	60
Hobson, Butch	439	253	49	51.0	27.8	127	6.8	94
Howe, Art	810	319	96	41.7	26.3	202	5.9	264
Johnson, Davey	702	162	44	50.0	24.9	117	4.2	215
Jorgensen, Mike	96	13	6	66.7	30.4	14	3.5	19
Kelly, Tom	1067	217	57	36.8	30.3	138	3.0	162
Kennedy, Kevin	582	80	19	47.4	32.0	90	3.7	139
Knight, Ray	257	49	15	26.7	25.4	81	7.4	84
Knoop, Bobby	1	0	0	-	-	0	0.0	0
La Russa, Tony	1068	429	119	58.0	33.8	199	4.6	217
Lachemann, Marcel	335	102	26	50.0	27.1	49	3.6	51
Lachemann, Rene	505	75	19	42.1	39.7	134	6.5	128
Lamont, Gene	629	382	81	55.6	34.9	137	5.5	144
Lasorda, Tom	829	226	59	52.5	27.0	266	7.5	278
Lefebvre, Jim	487	211	42	83.3	35.1	143	7.0	140
Leyland, Jim	1068	406	98	53.1	30.0	246	5.2	267
Leyva, Nick	12	9	3	33.3	7.7	9	11.5	2
McKeon, Jack	66	18	2	50.0	24.3	12	4.4	21
McNamara, John	120	29	6	83.3	28.3	27	5.5	30
McRae, Hal	563	276	63	42.9	31.9	108	4.3	141
Merrill, Stump	162	62	13	46.2	25.7	22	3.2	28
Morgan, Joe	162	52	10	60.0	33.6	48	7.0	43
Muser, Tony	79	20	5	40.0	44.2	12	4.1	17
Oates, Johnny	1030	170	38	50.0	36.7	192	4.9	193
Perez, Tony	43	25	6	66.7	23.5	6	3.8	13
Piniella, Lou	1066	386	78	64.1	33.2	251	5.9	231
Plummer, Bill	162	66	12	50.0	29.5	33	4.6	38
Queen, Mel	5	1	0	-	50.0	0	0.0	0
Rader, Doug	123	15	4	25.0	45.6	13	3.0	6
Regan, Phil	144	36	7	14.3	31.9	28	5.4	29
Riddoch, Greg	311	127	31	54.8	33.1	69	5.8	59
Riggleman, Jim	759	331	89	49.4	28.2	222	6.9	276
Robinson, Frank	36	17	4	0.0	40.0	7	5.2	7
Rodgers, Buck	358	245	54	40.7	34.3	62	4.1	63
Runnells, Tom	148	90	22	59.1	28.2	32	4.2	34
Russell, Bill	248	75	17	70.6	25.4	53	5.0	55
Showalter, Buck	582	142	38	52.6	26.7	107	4.5	80
Tenace, Gene	32	15	5	60.0	30.8	12	10.2	5
Torborg, Jeff	361	213	61	54.1	30.9	74	4.8	113
Torre, Joe	971	330	70	60.0	29.6	193	4.7	224
Trebelhorn, Tom	275	69	13	38.5	32.6	47	4.2	43
Valentine, Bobby	440	94	19	52.6	34.5	86	4.4	134
Wathan, John	124	35	10	40.0	39.8	16	3.2	10
Williams, Jimy	162	108	29	27.6	23.1	40	5.1	17
Zimmer, Don	36	11	4	25.0	23.5	15	8.8	14

Lineups

	Starting Lineup			Substitutes					
	G	Lineups Used	% LHB vs. RHSP	% RHB vs. LHSP	PH	% PH Platoon	PH Avg	PH HR	PR	PR SB-CS
Alou, Felipe	870	680	44.9	81.0	1222	74.8	.229	17	175	11-5
Anderson, Sparky	745	525	53.0	98.2	598	84.8	.245	14	205	16-5
Baker, Dusty	745	498	46.3	79.2	1116	73.7	.215	15	93	2-1
Baylor, Don	747	480	32.9	93.0	1290	72.9	.247	28	125	9-6
Bell, Buddy	324	244	44.5	93.7	286	75.5	.181	7	48	5-3
Bevington, Terry	437	298	62.4	81.0	374	75.4	.218	4	128	15-6
Bochy, Bruce	468	321	51.2	77.4	842	70.5	.239	21	85	7-5
Boles, John	75	50	36.2	97.2	132	48.5	.260	3	13	0-0
Boone, Bob	386	339	68.9	80.5	474	84.0	.247	10	130	4-8
Collins, Terry	583	408	39.6	87.2	830	80.4	.250	22	122	10-5
Cox, Bobby	1068	503	60.7	76.4	1735	73.0	.227	34	331	22-14
Craig, Roger	324	247	46.7	85.1	574	75.6	.216	7	75	3-0
Cubbage, Mike	7	7	74.1	80.6	17	100.0	.200	0	2	0-0
Dierker, Larry	162	131	30.9	88.3	264	73.5	.223	2	35	3-1
Essian, Jim	122	81	43.6	86.5	197	86.3	.226	4	56	11-4
Francona, Terry	162	98	61.5	77.8	288	76.7	.184	3	19	3-0
Fregosi, Jim	894	589	62.5	74.3	1398	69.4	.239	23	93	3-2
Garner, Phil	906	710	51.0	80.4	630	76.7	.215	8	246	22-14
Gaston, Cito	1029	529	49.1	91.0	519	78.2	.196	6	173	5-5
Green, Dallas	511	324	56.3	89.3	892	86.4	.254	12	94	2-1
Hargrove, Mike	988	605	56.8	81.0	767	83.1	.221	20	148	13-7
Harrah, Toby	76	69	50.1	85.2	111	79.3	.149	1	17	2-2
Harrelson, Bud	153	118	62.0	86.7	247	84.2	.210	8	37	9-1
Hobson, Butch	439	367	41.6	74.5	383	76.8	.228	4	151	10-4
Howe, Art	810	564	49.2	81.7	1213	82.0	.223	16	226	14-3
Johnson, Davey	702	487	48.7	77.8	824	80.8	.240	12	142	9-4
Jorgensen, Mike	96	84	46.5	71.8	151	72.8	.236	2	8	0-0
Kelly, Tom	1067	843	38.2	92.9	1187	87.4	.279	20	259	18-9
Kennedy, Kevin	582	425	50.7	77.8	453	73.1	.261	7	142	4-3
Knight, Ray	257	233	54.3	75.6	517	74.7	.217	12	38	7-1
Knoop, Bobby	1	1	44.4	-	1	100.0	.000	0	0	0-0
La Russa, Tony	1068	904	41.9	91.2	1175	80.8	.237	20	223	19-10
Lachemann, Marcel	335	229	58.8	82.1	308	86.0	.239	10	39	1-0
Lachemann, Rene	505	343	44.2	94.4	771	67.6	.205	2	59	5-2
Lamont, Gene	629	358	52.5	79.1	571	79.5	.233	8	157	8-1
Lasorda, Tom	829	473	51.1	78.1	1646	87.0	.229	27	217	16-8
Lefebvre, Jim	487	325	58.4	81.7	724	81.6	.259	10	101	4-5
Leyland, Jim	1068	709	50.3	79.2	1853	77.2	.250	36	153	5-3
Leyva, Nick	12	7	57.8	50.0	20	90.0	.250	0	1	0-0
McKeon, Jack	66	53	37.8	77.0	110	74.5	.196	1	18	0-2
McNamara, John	120	100	46.6	91.2	98	83.7	.268	0	24	1-1
McRae, Hal	563	417	62.1	84.2	511	68.9	.257	5	116	8-4
Merrill, Stump	162	106	52.4	76.6	139	86.3	.265	4	24	1-1
Morgan, Joe	162	106	35.5	79.5	114	78.1	.240	1	42	1-1
Muser, Tony	79	71	45.9	91.6	75	82.7	.180	1	30	2-1
Oates, Johnny	1030	644	48.6	83.3	738	80.2	.221	15	282	15-8
Perez, Tony	43	19	18.5	96.6	56	87.5	.152	1	14	1-2
Piniella, Lou	1066	767	48.9	84.3	1248	83.3	.244	27	219	28-6
Plummer, Bill	162	120	55.7	84.4	175	82.9	.234	4	26	1-0
Queen, Mel	5	4	33.3	88.9	3	66.7	.000	0	1	0-0
Rader, Doug	123	89	48.0	73.7	62	83.9	.278	2	14	0-0
Regan, Phil	144	104	63.5	71.2	154	83.8	.308	2	51	6-3
Riddoch, Greg	311	197	52.5	74.6	496	77.2	.187	5	38	0-1
Riggleman, Jim	759	524	43.0	81.9	1337	76.2	.233	23	148	6-0
Robinson, Frank	36	34	31.2	94.4	52	86.5	.239	1	10	0-0
Rodgers, Buck	358	283	47.4	90.7	342	78.4	.251	7	86	4-8
Runnells, Tom	148	124	55.2	75.1	222	84.7	.219	3	19	2-2
Russell, Bill	248	139	27.9	92.4	421	81.2	.204	8	71	3-1
Showalter, Buck	582	397	59.7	80.8	489	81.6	.249	14	125	3-2
Tenace, Gene	32	27	59.9	96.3	46	82.6	.275	1	10	2-0
Torborg, Jeff	361	293	67.8	81.7	604	84.4	.204	10	152	11-6
Torre, Joe	971	698	57.2	82.4	1254	79.6	.246	21	277	17-13
Trebelhorn, Tom	275	189	47.7	79.8	279	76.3	.256	4	52	2-1
Valentine, Bobby	440	366	52.8	87.3	741	81.2	.239	17	130	8-3
Wathan, John	124	102	46.3	83.3	129	84.5	.223	2	20	0-0
Williams, Jimy	162	97	49.5	75.7	123	75.6	.291	5	48	3-4
Zimmer, Don	36	18	31.7	87.5	45	75.6	.286	3	7	1-1

Pitching

		Starters						Relievers				
	G	Slow Hooks	Quick Hooks	>120 Pitches	>140 Pitches	3 Days Rest	Rel	Mid-Inning Change	Save >1 IP	1st Batter Platoon Pct	1-Batter App	3 Pitchers (≤2 runs)
Alou, Felipe	870	29	158	53	1	6	2135	894	127	52.9	151	134
Anderson, Sparky	745	63	93	73	8	41	1668	889	76	60.4	142	66
Baker, Dusty	745	43	83	42	1	19	1989	855	41	59.7	149	122
Baylor, Don	747	84	105	35	2	6	2112	752	45	57.4	161	83
Bell, Buddy	324	34	41	38	0	1	843	468	19	64.5	82	37
Bevington, Terry	437	48	61	82	5	5	1065	561	27	62.7	131	47
Bochy, Bruce	468	32	64	30	0	14	1174	448	26	55.9	69	69
Boles, John	75	5	9	4	0	0	200	74	5	58.5	10	15
Boone, Bob	386	41	43	50	2	45	802	430	33	63.0	71	41
Collins, Terry	583	41	44	42	3	39	1433	624	30	61.8	134	65
Cox, Bobby	1068	44	124	127	2	63	2401	769	60	55.4	179	186
Craig, Roger	324	16	59	12	1	19	720	256	32	50.8	30	45
Cubbage, Mike	7	0	1	1	1	0	14	2	0	42.9	0	0
Dierker, Larry	162	5	12	13	0	5	354	136	8	48.3	21	19
Essian, Jim	122	6	18	7	0	16	273	122	14	50.9	16	11
Francona, Terry	162	15	14	22	0	1	409	141	9	58.6	23	15
Fregosi, Jim	894	35	104	100	5	6	1931	640	54	56.0	102	91
Garner, Phil	906	119	113	86	9	22	2015	1045	38	58.8	153	121
Gaston, Cito	1029	141	88	173	4	12	2002	706	54	56.4	133	139
Green, Dallas	511	56	28	45	4	17	1017	325	39	55.6	74	34
Hargrove, Mike	988	92	114	91	1	14	2317	1175	55	62.4	247	129
Harrah, Toby	76	5	3	13	0	0	170	87	6	62.4	17	6
Harrelson, Bud	153	10	13	23	3	3	296	109	10	52.7	20	16
Hobson, Butch	439	26	50	69	7	13	1025	593	21	64.9	145	54
Howe, Art	810	59	105	51	1	21	2011	945	82	60.3	174	106
Johnson, Davey	702	60	81	39	0	32	1648	699	57	59.0	103	89
Jorgensen, Mike	96	8	8	1	0	1	231	74	6	63.6	17	13
Kelly, Tom	1067	78	99	81	3	41	2355	1248	84	59.0	204	113
Kennedy, Kevin	582	75	59	102	9	27	1439	785	36	61.3	140	59
Knight, Ray	257	15	43	10	1	4	686	227	19	61.4	41	45
Knoop, Bobby	1	1	0	0	0	0	3	1	0	66.7	0	0
La Russa, Tony	1068	92	150	134	8	57	2699	1323	70	62.9	256	174
Lachemann, Marcel	335	53	25	52	4	10	814	446	19	60.5	72	34
Lachemann, Rene	505	24	56	39	2	1	1320	560	37	62.1	122	73
Lamont, Gene	629	35	39	107	4	10	1391	631	59	63.4	125	89
Lasorda, Tom	829	50	66	134	5	15	1863	737	58	59.7	211	124
Lefebvre, Jim	487	19	54	47	3	12	1177	560	44	59.1	98	69
Leyland, Jim	1068	62	150	84	4	44	2593	987	69	62.0	195	154
Leyva, Nick	12	0	4	1	0	0	31	17	1	54.8	4	2
McKeon, Jack	66	2	14	5	0	0	161	57	3	59.6	8	9
McNamara, John	120	13	7	25	1	1	226	134	10	60.2	28	12
McRae, Hal	563	44	91	89	2	0	1126	519	63	60.1	92	73
Merrill, Stump	162	11	25	3	0	1	377	190	8	54.9	19	23
Morgan, Joe	162	12	21	16	3	4	328	205	15	63.7	19	22
Muser, Tony	79	11	9	4	0	0	219	94	1	67.1	17	14
Oates, Johnny	1030	97	109	139	10	23	2184	1346	58	65.8	263	108
Perez, Tony	43	2	3	3	0	0	94	24	2	50.0	6	7
Piniella, Lou	1066	83	128	148	24	54	2435	1203	106	59.9	168	140
Plummer, Bill	162	15	18	34	6	5	372	215	12	60.8	47	18
Queen, Mel	5	0	1	1	1	0	14	8	0	71.4	2	2
Rader, Doug	123	8	4	25	1	14	224	116	16	61.6	13	16
Regan, Phil	144	3	16	27	1	2	336	212	5	68.8	49	24
Riddoch, Greg	311	14	28	21	2	0	665	256	37	50.7	37	38
Riggleman, Jim	759	38	85	35	0	18	1995	889	55	60.8	185	100
Robinson, Frank	36	3	2	5	0	3	77	45	1	57.1	4	5
Rodgers, Buck	358	37	39	60	6	4	734	356	46	62.7	48	47
Runnells, Tom	148	5	19	14	0	0	327	142	22	59.0	27	24
Russell, Bill	248	12	23	24	0	4	617	212	6	56.1	45	44
Showalter, Buck	582	53	41	90	5	5	1183	617	34	65.0	106	61
Tenace, Gene	32	1	2	2	0	3	78	41	2	70.5	4	3
Torborg, Jeff	361	25	42	58	4	6	743	364	18	55.5	55	56
Torre, Joe	971	51	110	64	3	34	2470	991	59	57.2	225	183
Trebelhorn, Tom	275	18	42	27	0	3	627	292	22	56.1	50	25
Valentine, Bobby	440	36	47	37	0	7	1025	442	45	59.2	68	49
Wathan, John	124	16	12	24	0	0	217	123	17	59.7	16	6
Williams, Jimy	162	13	17	13	1	4	417	180	11	60.0	27	23
Zimmer, Don	36	1	3	1	0	0	81	40	2	65.4	2	4

Strategic Statistics Per 162 Games—1991-1997

Offense

				Stolen Bases					Out Percentage			Sacrifice Bunts			Hit & Run	
	G	Att	SB%	Ptchout Rn Mvg	2nd SB-CS	3rd SB-CS	Home SB-CS	Double Steals	0	1	2	Att	Suc. %	Sqz	Att	Suc. %
Alou, Felipe	870	201	75.2	7	131-43	19-6	2-2	7	22.1	39.6	38.3	99	83.4	10	106	38.3
Anderson, Sparky	745	135	64.0	6	73-40	13-7	0-1	6	19.5	44.7	35.9	50	79.1	2	84	35.1
Baker, Dusty	745	187	70.5	8	116-48	16-6	0-2	3	25.5	37.0	37.5	109	83.0	4	148	36.6
Baylor, Don	747	224	67.8	11	123-59	27-9	2-4	8	20.3	40.7	39.0	100	82.3	7	138	40.8
Bell, Buddy	324	185	67.0	5	105-53	19-5	1-3	6	18.4	36.2	45.4	54	86.0	2	103	34.6
Bevington, Terry	437	155	69.9	5	94-42	14-3	0-1	3	18.4	36.5	45.1	73	84.3	7	97	35.6
Bochy, Bruce	468	185	69.9	4	104-46	25-8	1-2	7	19.9	35.6	44.6	77	82.0	7	123	39.9
Boone, Bob	386	243	68.6	11	138-60	22-12	7-5	8	18.7	33.2	48.2	98	79.8	6	130	37.5
Collins, Terry	583	235	71.7	9	141-56	28-9	0-1	11	19.8	38.0	42.2	92	85.8	5	128	38.1
Cox, Bobby	1068	165	67.0	8	98-47	12-6	0-2	2	23.6	35.5	40.8	106	81.0	7	79	38.7
Craig, Roger	324	164	63.1	12	93-55	10-3	1-3	4	26.2	37.5	36.3	114	86.4	13	141	39.0
Dierker, Larry	162	245	69.8	3	142-61	29-12	0-0	10	19.6	40.0	40.4	96	80.2	7	131	27.5
Francona, Terry	162	148	62.2	5	79-48	11-6	2-2	4	18.2	31.1	50.7	91	93.4	3	90	27.8
Fregosi, Jim	894	133	75.4	3	86-30	14-2	1-1	3	18.3	38.2	43.5	89	80.0	5	61	32.3
Garner, Phil	906	206	66.3	9	119-58	16-7	2-5	7	17.1	34.5	48.3	73	79.5	8	120	39.8
Gaston, Cito	1029	169	75.8	5	105-36	23-4	0-0	5	23.0	33.5	43.5	60	79.4	3	74	33.3
Green, Dallas	511	113	61.2	5	58-39	10-4	0-1	3	23.6	32.9	43.5	110	85.6	6	99	42.9
Hargrove, Mike	988	205	71.1	10	120-48	24-8	2-3	9	22.9	37.0	40.1	59	85.5	5	91	37.2
Hobson, Butch	439	119	61.5	6	63-40	8-3	1-2	2	17.7	41.3	41.0	85	84.8	5	89	40.7
Howe, Art	810	150	66.2	6	87-44	11-4	1-2	4	16.7	42.1	41.3	87	79.2	3	95	38.2
Johnson, Davey	702	180	70.6	8	103-45	23-8	1-0	6	21.6	40.2	38.2	76	80.2	2	85	34.9
Kelly, Tom	1067	182	67.2	7	112-52	10-4	1-3	4	17.5	33.6	48.9	43	81.9	2	112	37.7
Kennedy, Kevin	582	160	67.0	4	99-46	8-5	1-2	2	19.3	36.0	44.7	70	82.8	3	91	36.0
Knight, Ray	257	257	73.7	13	148-55	40-6	1-6	10	21.1	36.6	42.3	102	77.2	9	129	40.2
La Russa, Tony	1068	201	71.0	8	116-48	26-8	1-3	10	24.4	34.6	41.0	74	84.7	3	130	38.2
Lachemann, Marcel	335	112	58.0	5	57-41	7-4	1-1	1	19.5	38.5	42.0	67	74.1	4	101	39.9
Lachemann, Rene	505	161	67.8	7	95-45	14-6	0-1	4	32.8	37.6	29.6	92	74.5	6	78	38.7
Lamont, Gene	629	187	72.9	8	119-44	16-5	1-2	3	20.1	33.4	46.5	89	83.4	8	101	32.2
Lasorda, Tom	829	191	68.2	11	110-53	20-6	0-2	6	23.0	37.9	39.1	120	81.4	8	125	40.7
Lefebvre, Jim	487	137	66.5	11	83-42	8-4	0-0	3	25.0	31.6	43.4	91	80.2	5	114	37.1
Leyland, Jim	1068	159	67.4	5	93-44	12-7	2-2	5	22.0	36.0	42.0	97	81.6	5	101	36.0
McRae, Hal	563	210	64.0	14	118-66	17-8	0-2	5	19.2	39.9	40.9	70	76.4	5	126	36.6
Merrill, Stump	162	145	75.2	6	89-31	18-2	2-3	6	23.4	35.2	41.4	54	77.8	2	98	39.8
Morgan, Joe	162	98	60.2	3	52-35	7-3	0-1	1	23.5	42.9	33.7	61	85.2	3	50	28.0
Oates, Johnny	1030	118	67.3	5	70-36	9-3	0-0	2	20.3	39.3	40.4	54	85.0	3	83	35.3
Piniella, Lou	1066	153	67.2	8	84-42	18-7	0-1	6	20.3	40.8	38.9	80	79.5	3	96	41.1
Plummer, Bill	162	155	64.5	8	85-45	15-6	0-4	5	16.8	40.0	43.2	75	81.3	4	91	39.6
Riddoch, Greg	311	142	59.0	7	71-49	12-7	1-2	2	23.8	34.1	42.1	102	83.7	11	97	39.8
Riggleman, Jim	759	158	69.0	5	92-41	16-4	1-4	4	19.6	33.5	46.9	101	82.6	8	110	40.8
Rodgers, Buck	358	274	60.0	22	139-88	25-15	0-6	5	21.8	36.4	41.8	76	83.8	5	170	40.4
Russell, Bill	248	182	70.3	14	114-46	14-4	0-4	7	21.1	35.5	43.4	114	86.2	12	135	41.7
Showalter, Buck	582	101	61.0	4	54-34	8-5	0-1	2	16.8	38.5	44.8	37	84.1	2	63	37.9
Torborg, Jeff	361	194	67.8	12	119-54	12-4	0-5	5	22.0	31.3	46.8	102	82.4	8	112	35.6
Torre, Joe	971	221	65.1	16	129-69	14-7	1-2	5	22.4	35.4	42.2	73	79.6	5	140	43.2
Trebelhorn, Tom	275	174	59.1	8	93-60	8-9	2-3	8	17.6	40.9	41.6	91	77.4	7	110	39.2
Valentine, Bobby	440	156	62.3	8	83-46	14-8	0-5	4	16.3	39.2	44.6	80	78.4	8	114	41.9
Williams, Jimy	162	116	58.6	4	60-42	8-4	0-2	3	25.0	36.2	38.8	30	80.0	2	85	44.7

Defense

	G	Pitchout			Non-PO CS%	Intentional BB		Defensive Subs
		Total	Runners Moving	CS%		IBB	% of Situations	Total
Alou, Felipe	870	45	15	41.8	22.1	29	3.9	54
Anderson, Sparky	745	96	20	45.2	32.2	67	10.0	22
Baker, Dusty	745	95	19	60.5	35.6	38	6.4	37
Baylor, Don	747	76	16	48.7	29.3	26	3.7	36
Bell, Buddy	324	23	5	66.7	28.2	32	4.8	24
Bevington, Terry	437	53	13	44.4	31.9	37	5.3	44
Bochy, Bruce	468	56	15	47.6	30.2	32	4.8	40
Boone, Bob	386	42	8	61.1	30.2	27	4.4	30
Collins, Terry	583	49	14	40.8	31.9	37	5.3	46
Cox, Bobby	1068	54	11	48.0	26.8	43	6.4	69
Craig, Roger	324	117	33	60.0	37.8	48	7.6	57
Dierker, Larry	162	35	7	85.7	35.9	25	4.1	44
Francona, Terry	162	30	6	66.7	33.5	31	4.8	52
Fregosi, Jim	894	36	11	36.1	28.0	33	4.8	41
Garner, Phil	906	45	9	50.0	27.6	26	3.9	40
Gaston, Cito	1029	66	17	38.1	32.9	25	3.7	20
Green, Dallas	511	51	12	50.0	24.7	45	6.6	41
Hargrove, Mike	988	71	15	57.8	30.3	30	4.3	40
Hobson, Butch	439	93	18	51.0	27.8	47	6.8	35
Howe, Art	810	64	19	41.7	26.3	40	5.9	53
Johnson, Davey	702	37	10	50.0	24.9	27	4.2	50
Kelly, Tom	1067	33	9	36.8	30.3	21	3.0	25
Kennedy, Kevin	582	22	5	47.4	32.0	25	3.7	39
Knight, Ray	257	31	9	26.7	25.4	51	7.4	53
La Russa, Tony	1068	65	18	58.0	33.8	30	4.6	33
Lachemann, Marcel	335	49	13	50.0	27.1	24	3.6	25
Lachemann, Rene	505	24	6	42.1	39.7	43	6.5	41
Lamont, Gene	629	98	21	55.6	34.9	35	5.5	37
Lasorda, Tom	829	44	12	52.5	27.0	52	7.5	54
Lefebvre, Jim	487	70	14	83.3	35.1	48	7.0	47
Leyland, Jim	1068	62	15	53.1	30.0	37	5.2	41
McRae, Hal	563	79	18	42.9	31.9	31	4.3	41
Merrill, Stump	162	62	13	46.2	25.7	22	3.2	28
Morgan, Joe	162	52	10	60.0	33.6	48	7.0	43
Oates, Johnny	1030	27	6	50.0	36.7	30	4.9	30
Piniella, Lou	1066	59	12	64.1	33.2	38	5.9	35
Plummer, Bill	162	66	12	50.0	29.5	33	4.6	38
Riddoch, Greg	311	66	16	54.8	33.1	36	5.8	31
Riggleman, Jim	759	71	19	49.4	28.2	47	6.9	59
Rodgers, Buck	358	111	24	40.7	34.3	28	4.1	29
Russell, Bill	248	49	11	70.6	25.4	35	5.0	36
Showalter, Buck	582	40	11	52.6	26.7	30	4.5	22
Torborg, Jeff	361	96	27	54.1	30.9	33	4.8	51
Torre, Joe	971	55	12	60.0	29.6	32	4.7	37
Trebelhorn, Tom	275	41	8	38.5	32.6	28	4.2	25
Valentine, Bobby	440	35	7	52.6	34.5	32	4.4	49
Williams, Jimy	162	108	29	27.6	23.1	40	5.1	17

Lineups

		Starting Lineup			Substitutes					
	G	Lineups Used	% LHB vs. RHSP	% RHB vs. LHSP	PH	% PH Platoon	PH Avg	PH HR	PR	PR SB-CS
Alou, Felipe	870	127	44.9	81.0	228	74.8	.229	3	33	2-1
Anderson, Sparky	745	114	53.0	98.2	130	84.8	.245	3	45	3-1
Baker, Dusty	745	108	46.3	79.2	243	73.7	.215	3	20	0-0
Baylor, Don	747	104	32.9	93.0	280	72.9	.247	6	27	2-1
Bell, Buddy	324	122	44.5	93.7	143	75.5	.181	4	24	3-2
Bevington, Terry	437	110	62.4	81.0	139	75.4	.218	1	47	6-2
Bochy, Bruce	468	111	51.2	77.4	291	70.5	.239	7	29	2-2
Boone, Bob	386	142	68.9	80.5	199	84.0	.247	4	55	2-3
Collins, Terry	583	113	39.6	87.2	231	80.4	.250	6	34	3-1
Cox, Bobby	1068	76	60.7	76.4	263	73.0	.227	5	50	3-2
Craig, Roger	324	124	46.7	85.1	287	75.6	.216	4	38	2-0
Dierker, Larry	162	131	30.9	88.3	264	73.5	.223	2	35	3-1
Francona, Terry	162	98	61.5	77.8	288	76.7	.184	3	19	3-0
Fregosi, Jim	894	107	62.5	74.3	253	69.4	.239	4	17	1-0
Garner, Phil	906	127	51.0	80.4	113	76.7	.215	1	44	4-3
Gaston, Cito	1029	83	49.1	91.0	82	78.2	.196	1	27	1-1
Green, Dallas	511	103	56.3	89.3	283	86.4	.254	4	30	1-0
Hargrove, Mike	988	99	56.8	81.0	126	83.1	.221	3	24	2-1
Hobson, Butch	439	135	41.6	74.5	141	76.8	.228	1	56	4-1
Howe, Art	810	113	49.2	81.7	243	82.0	.223	3	45	3-1
Johnson, Davey	702	112	48.7	77.8	190	80.8	.240	3	33	2-1
Kelly, Tom	1067	128	38.2	92.9	180	87.4	.279	3	39	3-1
Kennedy, Kevin	582	118	50.7	77.8	126	73.1	.261	2	40	1-1
Knight, Ray	257	147	54.3	75.6	326	74.7	.217	8	24	4-1
La Russa, Tony	1068	137	41.9	91.2	178	80.8	.237	3	34	3-2
Lachemann, Marcel	335	111	58.8	82.1	149	86.0	.239	5	19	0-0
Lachemann, Rene	505	110	44.2	94.4	247	67.6	.205	1	19	2-1
Lamont, Gene	629	92	52.5	79.1	147	79.5	.233	2	40	2-0
Lasorda, Tom	829	92	51.1	78.1	322	87.0	.229	5	42	3-2
Lefebvre, Jim	487	108	58.4	81.7	241	81.6	.259	3	34	1-2
Leyland, Jim	1068	108	50.3	79.2	281	77.2	.250	5	23	1-0
McRae, Hal	563	120	62.1	84.2	147	68.9	.257	1	33	2-1
Merrill, Stump	162	106	52.4	76.6	139	86.3	.265	4	24	1-1
Morgan, Joe	162	106	35.5	79.5	114	78.1	.240	1	42	1-1
Oates, Johnny	1030	101	48.6	83.3	116	80.2	.221	2	44	2-1
Piniella, Lou	1066	117	48.9	84.3	190	83.3	.244	4	33	4-1
Plummer, Bill	162	120	55.7	84.4	175	82.9	.234	4	26	1-0
Riddoch, Greg	311	103	52.5	74.6	258	77.2	.187	3	20	0-1
Riggleman, Jim	759	112	43.0	81.9	285	76.2	.233	5	32	1-0
Rodgers, Buck	358	128	47.4	90.7	155	78.4	.251	3	39	2-4
Russell, Bill	248	91	27.9	92.4	275	81.2	.204	5	46	2-1
Showalter, Buck	582	111	59.7	80.8	136	81.6	.249	4	35	1-1
Torborg, Jeff	361	131	67.8	81.7	271	84.4	.204	4	68	5-3
Torre, Joe	971	116	57.2	82.4	209	79.6	.246	4	46	3-2
Trebelhorn, Tom	275	111	47.7	79.8	164	76.3	.256	2	31	1-1
Valentine, Bobby	440	135	52.8	87.3	273	81.2	.239	6	48	3-1
Williams, Jimy	162	97	49.5	75.7	123	75.6	.291	5	48	3-4

Pitching

| | Starters | | | | | | Relievers | | | | |
	G	Slow Hooks	Quick Hooks	>120 Pitches	>140 Pitches	3 Days Rest	Rel	Mid-Inning Change	Save >1 IP	1st Batter Platoon Pct	1-Batter App	3 Pitchers (≤ 2 runs)
Alou, Felipe	870	5	29	10	0	1	398	166	24	52.9	28	25
Anderson, Sparky	745	14	20	16	2	9	363	193	17	60.4	31	14
Baker, Dusty	745	9	18	9	0	4	433	186	9	59.7	32	27
Baylor, Don	747	18	23	8	0	1	458	163	10	57.4	35	18
Bell, Buddy	324	17	21	19	0	1	422	234	10	64.5	41	19
Bevington, Terry	437	18	23	30	2	2	395	208	10	62.7	49	17
Bochy, Bruce	468	11	22	10	0	5	406	155	9	55.9	24	24
Boone, Bob	386	17	18	21	1	19	337	180	14	63.0	30	17
Collins, Terry	583	11	12	12	1	11	398	173	8	61.8	37	18
Cox, Bobby	1068	7	19	19	0	10	364	117	9	55.4	27	28
Craig, Roger	324	8	30	6	1	10	360	128	16	50.8	15	23
Dierker, Larry	162	5	12	13	0	5	354	136	8	48.3	21	19
Francona, Terry	162	15	14	22	0	1	409	141	9	58.6	23	15
Fregosi, Jim	894	6	19	18	1	1	350	116	10	56.0	18	16
Garner, Phil	906	21	20	15	2	4	360	187	7	58.8	27	22
Gaston, Cito	1029	22	14	27	1	2	315	111	9	56.4	21	22
Green, Dallas	511	18	9	14	1	5	322	103	12	55.6	23	11
Hargrove, Mike	988	15	19	15	0	2	380	193	9	62.4	41	21
Hobson, Butch	439	10	18	25	3	5	378	219	8	64.9	54	20
Howe, Art	810	12	21	10	0	4	402	189	16	60.3	35	21
Johnson, Davey	702	14	19	9	0	7	380	161	13	59.0	24	21
Kelly, Tom	1067	12	15	12	0	6	358	189	13	59.0	31	17
Kennedy, Kevin	582	21	16	28	3	8	401	219	10	61.3	39	16
Knight, Ray	257	9	27	6	1	3	432	143	12	61.4	26	28
La Russa, Tony	1068	14	23	20	1	9	409	201	11	62.9	39	26
Lachemann, Marcel	335	26	12	25	2	5	394	216	9	60.5	35	16
Lachemann, Rene	505	8	18	13	1	0	423	180	12	62.1	39	23
Lamont, Gene	629	9	10	28	1	3	358	163	15	63.4	32	23
Lasorda, Tom	829	10	13	26	1	3	364	144	11	59.7	41	24
Lefebvre, Jim	487	6	18	16	1	4	392	186	15	59.1	33	23
Leyland, Jim	1068	9	23	13	1	7	393	150	10	62.0	30	23
McRae, Hal	563	13	26	26	1	0	324	149	18	60.1	26	21
Merrill, Stump	162	11	25	3	0	1	377	190	8	54.9	19	23
Morgan, Joe	162	12	21	16	3	4	328	205	15	63.7	19	22
Oates, Johnny	1030	15	17	22	2	4	344	212	9	65.8	41	17
Piniella, Lou	1066	13	19	22	4	8	370	183	16	59.9	26	21
Plummer, Bill	162	15	18	34	6	5	372	215	12	60.8	47	18
Riddoch, Greg	311	7	15	11	1	0	346	133	19	50.7	19	20
Riggleman, Jim	759	8	18	7	0	4	426	190	12	60.8	39	21
Rodgers, Buck	358	17	18	27	3	2	332	161	21	62.7	22	21
Russell, Bill	248	8	15	16	0	3	403	138	4	56.1	29	29
Showalter, Buck	582	15	11	25	1	1	329	172	9	65.0	30	17
Torborg, Jeff	361	11	19	26	2	3	333	163	8	55.5	25	25
Torre, Joe	971	9	18	11	1	6	412	165	10	57.2	38	31
Trebelhorn, Tom	275	11	25	16	0	2	369	172	13	56.1	29	15
Valentine, Bobby	440	13	17	14	0	3	377	163	17	59.2	25	18
Williams, Jimy	162	13	17	13	1	4	417	180	11	60.0	27	23

Managerial Superlatives

The best handler of rookie pitchers: Gene Mauch

Mauch managed in the majors for 26 years. In almost every one of those seasons, at least one rookie pitcher—and sometimes two or three—made a significant contribution. Mauch simply had a knack for identifying pitchers with little or no major league experience who could help his club. Here are the best performances turned in by his rookie starters and relievers:

Starters						Relievers					
Pitcher	Year	GS	W-L	ERA		Pitcher	Year	G	W-L	ERA	Sv
Art Mahaffey	1960	12	7-3	2.31		Chris Short	1960	42	6-9	3.94	3
Dennis Bennett	1962	24	9-9	3.81		Jack Baldschun	1961	65	5-3	3.88	3
Ray Culp	1963	30	14-11	2.97		Gary Wagner	1965	59	7-7	3.00	7
Carl Morton	1970	37	18-11	3.60		Dan McGinn	1969	74	7-10	3.94	6
Ernie McAnally	1971	25	11-12	3.90		Dale Murray	1974	32	1-1	1.03	10
Balor Moore	1972	22	9-9	3.47		Doug Corbett	1980	73	8-6	1.98	23
Steve Rogers	1973	17	10-5	1.54		Luis Sanchez	1982	46	7-4	3.21	5
Dennis Blair	1974	22	11-7	3.27		Stew Cliburn	1985	44	9-3	2.09	6
Dan Warthen	1975	18	8-6	3.11		DeWayne Buice	1987	57	6-7	3.39	17
Roger Erickson	1978	37	14-13	3.96							
Mike Witt	1981	21	8-9	3.28							
Willie Fraser	1987	23	10-10	3.92							

Although Mauch was a deft handler of rookies, he was decidedly less successful with more experienced pitchers—including those who had performed so well for him as rookies. Although some of Mauch's rookies went on to have fine careers, a surprisingly high number of them did not. In fact, roughly half of the pitchers on the above list never were able to duplicate the success they enjoyed as rookies. Even Steve Rogers, who enjoyed the best career of the rookies listed above, never approached the spectacular 1.54 ERA he posted in his rookie year. One could say the same of Dale Murray, who pitched respectably for more than a decade but never approached his rookie ERA of 1.03 again. Chris Short, Jack Baldschun and Mike Witt were the only ones who were able to make significant improvements over their rookie numbers.

The best handler of young players: Dick Williams

Consider this remarkable fact: At least one rookie or first-time regular made an impact on every single Williams-managed team, with the exception of two: the 1968 Red Sox and the 1985 Padres. Both of the exceptions were defending league champions.

Here are some of the players brought to the majors by Williams:

- When Williams took over the 1967 Red Sox, the only lineup changes he made were to add rookie 2B Mike Andrews and CF Reggie Smith, who began the year at second base before an early shift to the outfield. The Sox went from ninth place to the World Series.

- With the 1971 Athletics, he added starting pitcher Vida Blue, who won the American League MVP Award. Oakland won its first AL West title.

- The following season, he replaced departed CF Rick Monday with rookie Bill North. North scored 98 runs and batted .285 with 53 stolen bases, and the A's won their first World Series championship.

- When the A's traded away 1B Mike Epstein after the '72 season, Williams gave Epstein's job to Gene Tenace. The former backup catcher homered 24 times and drew 101 walks, and the A's won their second consecutive World Series.

- Williams' first full season as the Angels' manager came in 1975. That year, he broke in 1B Bruce Bochte, 2B Jerry Remy and OF Dave Collins.

- Taking over the '77 Expos, Williams gave jobs to OF Andre Dawson and OF Warren Cromartie. He also made Gary Carter the full-time catcher. Carter had spent the previous two seasons backing up Barry Foote and playing the outfield.

- Over the next three years, he introduced starting pitchers David Palmer, Scott Sanderson, Bill Gullickson and Charlie Lea.

- In 1981, Williams took minor league second baseman Tim Raines and made him the Expos' left fielder. Williams was fired late in the 1981 season, only days before the Expos attained their first and only playoff berth.

- Moving on to the Padres, Williams oversaw the introduction and development of a significant number of young players who went on to form the core of the pennant-winning 1984 club. The rookies included outfielders Tony Gwynn, Kevin McReynolds and Carmelo Martinez. Williams pulled a reverse Tim Raines move with Alan Wiggins, shifting him from the outfield to second base. He also groomed pitchers Tim Lollar, Eric Show, Dave Dravecky, Mark Thurmond, Andy Hawkins and Gary Lucas.

- The '86 Mariners possessed highly touted rookie Danny Tartabull, who'd played shortstop in the minors the year before. Williams tried him at second for a month before moving him to the outfield and installing another rookie, Harold Reynolds, at second.

Simply put, Williams' appraisals of his young hitters' abilities were virtually flawless. When he decided that a youngster could play, he was almost always correct, and when he decided a guy couldn't play, he was usually right too. During his 21-year managerial career, only two players later developed into useful players after Williams had passed them over: George Hendrick and Tony Bernazard. Williams clearly missed on Hendrick, keeping him on the bench in favor of Angel Mangual in 1972. Rookie second baseman Tony Bernazard was given 183 at-bats in 1980, but failed to unseat Rodney Scott, who was a personal favorite of Williams.

The manager who was best at taking over a team in midseason: Steve O'Neill

No manager in history can match Steve O'Neill's record for reinvigorating floundering clubs in midseason. During his 14-year managerial career, he took over three clubs in midyear. None of the three clubs were more than two games over .500 when O'Neill took over, but each of the three teams played well over .600 ball under O'Neill:

Team	Year	W-L Before	Pct	W-L Under O'Neill	Pct	+/−
Indians	1935	46-48	.489	36-23	.610	+.121
Red Sox	1950	32-30	.516	62-30	.674	+.158
Phillies	1952	28-35	.444	59-32	.648	+.204

The '35 Indians were the AL preseason favorites, but got off to a sluggish start under manager Walter Johnson. The press and public turned against Johnson when he released some popular veterans and the team continued to slump. Johnson stepped down on August 5. O'Neill took over and brought the team up from fifth to third place by the end of the season.

Like the '35 Indians, the 1950 Red Sox were the consensus pick to win the division, but stumbled from the gate. Manager Joe McCarthy stepped down in late June with the club in fourth place, two games over .500. Just days later, Ted Williams broke his elbow in the All-Star Game and was lost for over two months. Even without Williams, the Red Sox won more than two-thirds of their games under O'Neill, and finished with 94 wins and the third-best record in the majors.

The 1952 Phillies were little over a year removed from the pennant-winning "Whiz Kids" club of 1950. Manager Eddie Sawyer was fired in June with the club mired in sixth place. O'Neill brought them up to fourth behind the red-hot pitching of Robin Roberts, who won 17 of his last 18 decisions to finish with a career-high 28 victories.

The most curious thing of all is that O'Neill didn't turn his clubs around by making sweeping changes. On all three clubs, he used virtually the same starting lineup and pitching rotation that his predecessor had. One last note: O'Neill was replaced in midseason only once—in 1954, his final year as a manager. The Phillies were 40-37 when they gave O'Neill the axe. Terry Moore piloted the club the rest of the way and compiled a 35-42 mark.

The manager who generated the greatest immediate improvement: Billy Martin

Martin was hired nine times during his managerial career, and all nine times his new club showed immediate improvement under his command. In most cases, the turnaround was staggering.

The first club he managed at the big league level was the 1969 Twins. They had posted a losing record the year before, but Martin improved them by 18 games and led them to the AL West title.

His next club was the 1971 Tigers. They improved by 12 games and took the AL East crown the following year.

Then came the 1973-74 Rangers. He took them over in late '73 when the club stood at 48-91. He went 9-14 with them the rest of the way, and led them to an 84-78, second-place finish in '74, an improvement of 28 games.

His first term as the Yankees skipper began in midseason of 1975, when New York's record was 53-51. The club went 30-26 for the remainder of the season, and won the division with a 97-62 record in '76. This time, Martin's team showed a 14.5-game improvement.

Martin was fired in the middle of the '78 season and was rehired in June the following year. With the club languishing at 34-31 when he took over, Martin led them to a 55-40 mark the rest of the way. Over a full season, that would project to a nine-game improvement.

Martin's next assignment probably was his toughest: the 1980 A's. He came through like a champion, though, turning a 54-108 club into an 83-game winner in one year. The 29-game improvement topped his Texas mark by one game.

His final three stints were spent with the Yankees, and he brought them immediate improvement each time. In 1983, the club improved by 12 games; in 1985, he took over the club after it lost 10 of its first 16 games, but still produced a 10.5-game improvement; and in 1988, he was fired for the last time with the club at 40-28. If the Yanks had maintained that pace over the rest of the season, it would have represented a 6.5-game improvement over the previous season. Without Martin, they actually finished with 85 wins, a 4.5-game decline.

Since World War II, only eight clubs have finished over .500 after losing 100 games or more the previous season. Martin was responsible for turning around two of those eight clubs, the '74 Rangers and the '80 A's. That's impressive enough by itself, but it's also significant to note that Martin used a different approach each time.

With the Rangers, Martin promoted three young players from the minors and installed them in the lineup. Each of them had excellent rookie seasons: Mike Hargrove, Lenny Randle and Jim Sundberg. He also rebuilt the starting rotation, moving Jackie Brown in from the bullpen to join Ferguson Jenkins and Steve Hargan, who arrived via trades.

But in 1980, Martin inherited a last-place club and simply decided to stand pat. Other than bringing in a new double-play combo, he didn't replace a single position player or member of the starting rotation. But under Martin, the outfield of Rickey Henderson, Dwayne Murphy and Tony Armas suddenly developed into the finest young outfield in baseball, and starters Mike Norris, Matt Keough, Rick Langford and Steve McCatty matured into winners overnight.

Of course, Martin's clubs' inability to sustain their success raises legitimate objections. But if the assignment was to win, and to win *now,* Martin was the man.

The team with the most future managers: the 1956 St. Louis Cardinals

In hindsight, the 1956 Cardinals' clubhouse must have featured nonstop strategy sessions. No less than nine future managers graced the St. Louis roster that season, an all-time record.

Three of the '56 Cardinals went on to manage more than 1,900 major league games: Alvin Dark, Red Schoendienst and Bill Virdon. Schoendienst was one of three members of the club who later managed the Cardinals, along with Ken Boyer and Solly Hemus. Other future skippers on the team included Joe Frazier (Mets), Alex Grammas (Brewers), Grady Hatton (Astros) and Whitey Lockman (Cubs).

Schoendienst was the only one of the nine to capture a World Series championship, piloting the Cardinals to a seven-game victory over the Red Sox in the 1967 World Series. Schoendienst's Redbirds won another pennant the following season. Dark managed the Giants to a pennant in 1962 and did the same with the neighboring Athletics 12 years later. Bill Virdon won a pair of division titles. The first came with the Pirates in 1972 in his first year as a manager, and the other came in 1980 with the Astros.

All together, the nine managers accumulated 7,874 games and 56 seasons of managerial experience. All that potential had little apparent impact in 1956. The Cardinals finished fourth in the National League that year, two games below .500.

—Mat Olkin

Managers: Superlatives

Amateur Draft

First-Round Picks

For each year since baseball's amateur draft began in 1965, we list each first-round pick, his order and team of selection, and his position, school, hometown and major league career statistics. If he did not reach the majors, we indicate the highest level of the minors that he reached. Jim Callis wrote recaps of each year's draft as well.

Analysis

Jim Callis also provided some highlights from the first 32 years of the draft. Included are a detailed listing of No. 1 overall picks, draftees who went straight to the major leagues, the evolution of the bonus record, two-time first-round picks and the lowest-drafted players to reach the majors. He also ranks the best and worst drafts of all time, and picks all-star teams based on draft status. David Rawnsley's draft database was helpful in compiling some of these lists.

Abbreviations & Formulas

A complete list of team and statistical abbreviations are listed in the back of the book, along with an appendix explaining formulas and the availability of certain statistics.

1965

Rick Reichardt is the father of baseball's amateur draft. He didn't create the concept, but he was as responsible as anyone for its creation. A college football and baseball star at Wisconsin, Reichardt signed with the Los Angeles Angels for the then-astronomical sum of $205,000 on June 24, 1964. He smashed the previous bonus record of $175,000 set by Bob Bailey three years earlier, and Kansas City Athletics owner Charlie Finley offered double what the Angels paid Reichardt. All told, the 20 big league clubs would spend $7 million to sign amateur talent in 1964, more than the total salaries of all major league players.

On January 15, 1964, a number of concerns had led the owners to unanimously authorize commissioner Ford Frick and league presidents Joe Cronin and Warren Giles to develop a proposal for an amateur draft. Spiraling bonus payments not only were costing teams more money than they wanted to spend, but also were sucking the life out of the minor leagues. With big league clubs putting most of their player-development money into signing talent rather than maintaining affiliates, the minors had shrunk from 460 teams to 121 over the past 15 years. There also was little competitive balance. The Dodgers and the Yankees were among the most aggressive teams in paying for amateurs, giving them a significant edge. New York had won 13 pennants in the previous 15 years and would win again in 1964, while Los Angeles was coming off a World Series championship and had won six pennants in 12 seasons. Baseball had tried a number of measures to try to curb spending, but none had worked. "We'd pass a bonus rule," former Tigers GM Joe Campbell said, "and by the time we got out of the room we'd already figured out how to skin the cat."

Less than two months after the Reichardt signing, the owners gathered in Chicago to hear the draft proposal and vote on it. Approval by both leagues was needed at the Aug. 10-11 meeting, and overwhelming support was expected. Though the National League backed the draft by an 8-2 vote, the American League was against it by the same margin. The biggest concern was that a draft could cost baseball its antitrust status. Thanks to lobbying, however, the draft was approved 13-7 at the Winter Meetings, which began Nov. 30 in Houston. It became official Dec. 2 when the National Association, the governing body of the minors, ratified the draft. Not until Andy Benes, the top pick in the 1988 draft, signed for $235,000 would Reichardt's bonus record be broken.

The Kansas City Athletics had the first pick in the first draft and surprised no one by taking Rick Monday, an All-America outfielder from Arizona State. Monday signed for $104,000, barely half of what Reichardt received the year before, and would spend 19 years in the majors. The A's had a solid effort, also signing Arizona State third baseman Sal Bando (sixth round) and Lucasville, Ohio, high school shortstop Gene Tenace (11th), who would play on their 1972-74 World Series champions, and drafting a total of 10 future big leaguers. The Mets, picking second, struck out with Billings, Mont., prep lefthander Les Rohr, but scored nine rounds later when they grabbed Alvin, Texas, high school righthander Nolan Ryan. Binger, Okla., prep catcher Johnny Bench lasted until the Reds took him in the second round.

Pick	Team	Player	Pos	School	Hometown	Major League Career
1	Kansas City Athletics	Rick Monday	of	Arizona State	Santa Monica, CA	1986 G (.264-241-775)
2	New York Mets	Les Rohr	lhp	West HS	Billings, MT	6 G (2-3, 3.70)
3	Washington Senators	Joe Coleman	rhp	Natick HS	Natick, MA	484 G (142-135, 3.70)
4	Houston Colt .45s	Alex Barrett	ss	Atwater HS	Winton, CA	Peaked in Triple-A
5	Boston Red Sox	Billy Conigliaro	of	Swampscott HS	Swampscott, MA	347 G (.256-40-128)
6	Chicago Cubs	Rick James	rhp	Coffee HS	Florence, AL	3 G (13.50, 0 saves)
7	Cleveland Indians	Ray Fosse	c	Marion HS	Marion, IL	924 G (.256-61-324)
8	Los Angeles Dodgers	John Wyatt	ss	Bakersfield HS	Bakersfield, CA	435 G (3.47, 103 saves)
9	Minnesota Twins	*Eddie Leon	ss	Arizona	Tucson, AZ	601 G (.236-24-159)
10	Pittsburgh Pirates	Doug Dickerson	of	Ensley HS	Birmingham, AL	Peaked in Class-A
11	California Angels	Jim Spencer	1b	Andover HS	Glen Burnie, MD	1553 G (.250-146-599)
12	Milwaukee Braves	Dick Grant	1b	Watertown HS	Watertown, MA	Peaked in Double-A
13	Detroit Tigers	Gene Lamont	c	Hiawatha HS	Kirkland, IL	87 G (.233-4-14)
14	San Francisco Giants	Al Gallagher	3b	Santa Clara	Daly City, CA	442 G (.263-11-130)
15	Baltimore Orioles	Scott McDonald	rhp	Marquette HS	Yakima, WA	Peaked in Double-A
16	Cincinnati Reds	Bernie Carbo	3b	Livonia HS	Garden City, MI	1010 G (.264-96-358)
17	Chicago White Sox	Ken Plesha	c	Notre Dame	McCook, IL	Peaked in Double-A
18	Philadelphia Phillies	*Mike Adamson	rhp	Point Loma HS	San Diego, CA	11 G (7.46, 0 saves)
19	New York Yankees	Bill Burbach	rhp	Wahlert HS	Dickeyville, WI	37 G (6-11, 4.48)
20	St. Louis Cardinals	Joe DiFabio	rhp	Delta State	Cranford, NJ	Peaked in Triple-A

* Did not sign.

1966

The Mets narrowed their choices for the first pick down to Lancaster, Calif., high school catcher Steve Chilcott and yet another outfielder from Arizona State. To New York's eternal regret, it chose Chilcott because of its need for catching, leaving the Kansas City Athletics to take Reggie Jackson. Chilcott is the only No. 1 choice to have completed his career without reaching the big leagues, peaking in Triple-A after a series of injuries. Jackson would go lead his teams to 11 division titles, six pennants and five World Series championships en route to the Hall of Fame. The Mets did get a fine consolation prize when they were awarded the rights to Southern Cal righthander Tom Seaver in a special lottery. The Braves had taken Seaver in the secondary phase of the January draft and signed him for $40,000, but the contract was voided because Seaver's team had begun its college schedule.

Pick	Team	Player	Pos	School	Hometown	Major League Career
1	New York Mets	Steve Chilcott	c	Antelope Valley HS	Lancaster, CA	Peaked in Triple-A
2	Kansas City Athletics	Reggie Jackson	of	Arizona State	Wyncote, PA	2820 G (.262-563-1702)
3	Houston Astros	Wayne Twitchell	rhp	Wilson HS	Portland, OR	282 G (3.98, 2 saves)
4	Boston Red Sox	Ken Brett	lhp-of	El Segundo HS	El Segundo, CA	349 G (83-85, 3.93)
5	Chicago Cubs	Dean Burk	rhp	Highland HS	Highland, IL	Peaked in Triple-A
6	Washington Senators	Tom Grieve	of	Pittsfield HS	Pittsfield, MA	670 G (.249-65-254)
7	St. Louis Cardinals	Leron Lee	of	Grant HS	Sacramento, CA	614 G (.250-31-152)
8	California Angels	Jim DeNeff	ss	Indiana	Holland, MI	Peaked in Triple-A
9	Philadelphia Phillies	Mike Biko	rhp	Samuel HS	Dallas, TX	Peaked in Class-A
10	New York Yankees	Jim Lyttle	of	Florida State	Harrison, OH	391 G (.248-9-70)
11	Atlanta Braves	Al Santorini	rhp	Union HS	Union, NJ	127 G (17-38, 4.29)
12	Cleveland Indians	*John Curtis	lhp	Central HS	Smithtown, NY	438 G (3.96, 11 saves)
13	Cincinnati Reds	Gary Nolan	rhp	Oroville HS	Oroville, CA	250 G (110-70, 3.08)
14	Detroit Tigers	*Rick Konik	1b	St. Andrew's HS	Detroit, MI	Never played pro ball
15	Pittsburgh Pirates	Richie Hebner	ss	Norwood HS	Norwood, MA	1908 G (.276-203-890)
16	Baltimore Orioles	Ted Parks	ss	California	Berkeley, CA	Peaked in Triple-A
17	San Francisco Giants	Bob Reynolds	rhp	Ingraham HS	Seattle, WA	140 G (3.15, 21 saves)
18	Chicago White Sox	Carlos May	of	Parker HS	Birmingham, AL	1165 G (.274-90-536)
19	Los Angeles Dodgers	Larry Hutton	rhp	Greenfield HS	Greenfield, IN	Peaked in Double-A
20	Minnesota Twins	Bob Jones	3b	No school	Dawson, GA	Peaked in Class-A

* Did not sign.

1967

The Yankees had the top pick in the draft, showing just how far the once-proud franchise had fallen. They selected Atlanta high school first baseman Ron Blomberg for his power and for his projected appeal to the Jewish fan base in New York. Blomberg would hit .293 in the majors, but never became more than a platoon player and is best remembered as the first designated hitter in American League history. Both the Cardinals and Orioles did well with their first two selections. St. Louis landed Southfield, Mich., high school catcher Ted Simmons and Overland, Mo., prep lefthander Jerry Reuss, while Baltimore grabbed Long Beach high school shortstop Bobby Grich and Austin, Texas, prep outfielder Don Baylor. Another astute pick was Mansfield, La., high school southpaw Vida Blue, a second-round choice of the Athletics. Southern Cal righthander Mike Adamson, the Orioles' top pick in the June secondary phase, became the first draftee to debut in the big leagues. He never won a game in the majors.

Pick	Team	Player	Pos	School	Hometown	Major League Career
1	New York Yankees	Ron Blomberg	1b	Druid Hills HS	Atlanta, GA	461 G (.293-52-224)
2	Chicago Cubs	Terry Hughes	ss	Dorman HS	Spartanburg, SC	54 G (.209-1-7)
3	Boston Red Sox	Mike Garman	rhp	Caldwell HS	Caldwell, ID	303 G (3.63, 42 saves)
4	New York Mets	Jon Matlack	lhp	Henderson HS	West Chester, PA	361 G (125-126, 3.18)
5	Washington Senators	John Jones	c	Loretto HS	St. Joseph, TN	Peaked in Class-A
6	Houston Astros	John Mayberry	1b	Northwestern HS	Detroit, MI	1620 G (.253-255-879)
7	Kansas City Athletics	Brian Bickerton	lhp	Santana HS	Santee, CA	Peaked in Triple-A
8	Cincinnati Reds	Wayne Simpson	rhp	Centennial HS	Los Angeles, CA	122 G (36-31, 4.37)
9	California Angels	Mike Nunn	c	Smith HS	Greensboro, NC	Peaked in Triple-A
10	St. Louis Cardinals	Ted Simmons	c	Southfield HS	Southfield, MI	2456 G (.285-248-1389)
11	Cleveland Indians	Jack Heidemann	ss	Brenham HS	Brenham, TX	426 G (.211-9-75)
12	Atlanta Braves	Andrew Finlay	of	Burbank HS	Sacramento, CA	Peaked in Double-A
13	Chicago White Sox	Dan Haynes	3b	Headland HS	East Point, GA	Peaked in Triple-A
14	Philadelphia Phillies	Phil Meyer	lhp	Pius X HS	Downey, CA	Peaked in Triple-A
15	Detroit Tigers	Jim Foor	lhp	McCluer HS	Ferguson, MO	13 G (12.00, 0 saves)
16	Pittsburgh Pirates	Joe Grigas	of	Coyle HS	Brockton, MA	Peaked in Class-A
17	Minnesota Twins	Steve Brye	3b-of	St. Elizabeth HS	Oakland, CA	697 G (.258-30-193)
18	San Francisco Giants	Dave Rader	c	South HS	Bakersfield, CA	846 G (.257-30-235)
19	Baltimore Orioles	Bobby Grich	ss	Wilson HS	Long Beach, CA	2008 G (.266-224-864)
20	Los Angeles Dodgers	Don Denbow	3b	Southern Methodist	Dallas, TX	Peaked in Class-A

1968

The Dodgers had the best June draft ever. They signed Stamford, Conn., high school outfielder Bobby Valentine (first round);

Vallejo, Calif., prep first baseman Bill Buckner (second); Houston outfielder Tom Paciorek (fifth); Pacific outfielder Joe Ferguson (eighth); and Birmingham righthander Doyle Alexander (ninth) in the regular phase; and Michigan State third baseman Steve Garvey (first) and Washington State third baseman Ron Cey (third) in the secondary phase. As a bonus, they also landed Washburn outfielder Davey Lopes (second) and Michigan lefthander Geoff Zahn (fifth) in the January draft. The Mets weren't as fortunate when they used the No. 1 choice on Canoga Park, Calif., high school shortstop Tim Foli, who had a lengthy big league career but never lived up to their offensive projections. The crosstown Yankees did much better three picks later with Kent State catcher Thurman Munson.

Pick	Team	Player	Pos	School	Hometown	Major League Career
1	New York Mets	Tim Foli	ss	Notre Dame HS	Canoga Park, CA	1696 G (.251-25-501)
2	Oakland Athletics	*Pete Broberg	rhp	Palm Beach HS	Palm Beach, FL	206 G (41-71, 4.56)
3	Houston Astros	Marty Cott	c	Hutchinson Tech HS	Buffalo, NY	Peaked in Triple-A
4	New York Yankees	Thurman Munson	c	Kent State	Canton, OH	1423 G (.292-113-701)
5	Los Angeles Dodgers	Bobby Valentine	of	Rippowam HS	Stamford, CT	639 G (.260-12-157)
6	Cleveland Indians	Robert Weaver	ss	Paxon HS	Jacksonville, FL	Peaked in Double-A
7	Atlanta Braves	Curtis Moore	of	Denison HS	Denison, TX	Peaked in Triple-A
8	Washington Senators	Donnie Castle	lhp-of	Coldwater HS	Coldwater, MS	4 G (.308-0-2)
9	Pittsburgh Pirates	Dick Sharon	of	Sequoia HS	Redwood City, CA	242 G (.218-13-46)
10	Baltimore Orioles	Junior Kennedy	ss	Arvin HS	Arvin, CA	447 G (.248-4-95)
11	Philadelphia Phillies	Greg Luzinski	1b	Notre Dame HS	Prospect Hts, IL	1821 G (.276-307-1128)
12	California Angels	Lloyd Allen	rhp	Selma HS	Selma, CA	159 G (4.69, 22 saves)
13	Cincinnati Reds	Tim Grant	rhp	Riverview HS	Boykins, VA	Peaked in Class-A
14	Chicago White Sox	Rich McKinney	ss	Ohio	Troy, OH	341 G (.225-20-100)
15	Chicago Cubs	Ralph Rickey	of	Oklahoma	Oklahoma City, OK	Peaked in Triple-A
16	Minnesota Twins	Alex Rowell	of	Luther College	North Chicago, IL	Peaked in Double-A
17	San Francisco Giants	Gary Matthews	of	San Fernando HS	Pacoima, CA	2033 G (.281-234-978)
18	Detroit Tigers	Robert Robinson	of	Thomas Dale HS	Chester, VA	Peaked in Class-A
19	St. Louis Cardinals	James Hairston	of	Roth HS	Dayton, OH	Peaked in Class-A
20	Boston Red Sox	Tom Maggard	of-c	John Glenn HS	Norwalk, CA	Peaked in Triple-A

* Did not sign.

1969

The Washington Senators used the top choice on Long Beach high school outfielder Jeff Burroughs, whom Senators manager Ted Williams called the best 18-year-old hitter he ever had seen. It was a good year for outfielders. The best major leaguer turned out to be Northridge, Calif., high schooler Dwight Evans, Boston's fifth-round pick, and the Reds (Donora, Pa., prepster Ken Griffey, 29th round) and Royals (Los Angeles high schooler Al Cowens, 75th) got late-round steals. The Seattle Pilots spent the only first-round pick in team history on Charleston, S.C., prepster Gorman Thomas.

Pick	Team	Player	Pos	School	Hometown	Major League Career
1	Washington Senators	Jeff Burroughs	of	Wilson HS	Long Beach, CA	1689 G (.261-240-882)
2	Houston Astros	J.R. Richard	rhp	Lincoln HS	Ruston, LA	238 G (107-71, 3.15)
3	Chicago White Sox	Ted Nicholson	3b	Oak Park HS	Laurel, MS	Peaked in Class-A
4	New York Mets	Randy Sterling	rhp	Key West HS	Key West, FL	3 G (1-1, 4.82)
5	California Angels	*Alan Bannister	ss	Kennedy HS	Buena Park, CA	972 G (.270-19-288)
6	Philadelphia Phillies	Mike Anderson	1b	Timmonsville HS	Timmonsville, SC	721 G (.246-28-134)
7	Minnesota Twins	Paul Ray Powell	of	Arizona State	Eloy, AZ	30 G (.167-1-2)
8	Los Angeles Dodgers	Terry McDermott	c	St. Agnes HS	West Hempstead, NY	9 G (.130-0-0)
9	Oakland Athletics	Don Stanhouse	rhp-ss	DuQuoin HS	DuQuoin, IL	294 G (3.84, 64 saves)
10	Pittsburgh Pirates	Bob May	rhp	Merritt Island HS	Merritt Island, FL	Peaked in Class-A
11	New York Yankees	Charlie Spikes	3b-of	Central Memorial HS	Bogalusa, LA	670 G (.246-65-256)
12	Atlanta Braves	Gene Holbert	c	Palmyra HS	Campbelltown, PA	Peaked in Double-A
13	Boston Red Sox	Noel Jenke	of	Minnesota	Owatonna, MN	Peaked in Triple-A
14	Cincinnati Reds	Don Gullett	lhp	McKell HS	Lynn, KY	266 G (109-50, 3.11)
15	Cleveland Indians	Alvin McGrew	of	Parker HS	Fairfield, AL	Peaked in Triple-A
16	Chicago Cubs	Roger Metzger	ss	St. Edward's	San Antonio, TX	1219 G (.231-5-254)
17	Baltimore Orioles	Don Hood	lhp	Southside HS	Florence, SC	297 G (3.79, 6 saves)
18	San Francisco Giants	Mike Phillips	ss	McArthur HS	Irving, TX	712 G (.240-11-145)
19	Detroit Tigers	Lenny Baxley	1b	Enterprise HS	Redding, CA	Peaked in Class-A
20	St. Louis Cardinals	Charles Minott	lhp	Royal Oak HS	Covina, CA	Peaked in Class-A
21	Seattle Pilots	Gorman Thomas	ss	James Island HS	Charleston, SC	1435 G (.225-268-782)
22	Montreal Expos	Balor Moore	lhp	Deer Park HS	Deer Park, TX	180 G (28-48, 4.52)
23	Kansas City Royals	*John Simmons	ss	Childersburg HS	Childersburg, AL	Never played pro ball
24	San Diego Padres	Randy Elliott	1b	Camarillo HS	Camarillo, CA	114 G (.215-8-35)

* Did not sign.

Amateur Draft: First-Round Picks

1970

High school catchers went with three of the first four picks, as the Padres took Mike Ivie of Decatur, Ga., with the No. 1 selection. While he spent 11 years in the majors, Ivie developed a throwing phobia and spent just nine games behind the plate. Years later, many veteran scouts still considered him the best young catcher ever. The Expos didn't get much out of Smithfield, N.C., prep backstop Barry Foote with the third selection, but the Brewers did well with Oklahoma City high school catcher Darrell Porter at No. 4. The White Sox found a pair of top-notch relievers in Santee, Calif., high schooler Terry Forster (second round) and Colorado Springs prepster Rich Gossage (ninth), while the Pirates found Cincinnati high school catcher Dave Parker in the 14th round. Stanford righthander Steve Dunning, whom the Indians took with the No. 2 pick, became the first player selected in the June regular phase to debut in the majors. He won his first start but finished with a career record of 23-41.

Pick	Team	Player	Pos	School	Hometown	Major League Career
1	San Diego Padres	Mike Ivie	c	Walker HS	Decatur, GA	857 G (.269-81-411)
2	Cleveland Indians	Steve Dunning	rhp	Stanford	San Diego, CA	136 G (23-41, 4.56)
3	Montreal Expos	Barry Foote	c	Selma HS	Smithfield, NC	687 G (.230-57-230)
4	Milwaukee Brewers	Darrell Porter	c	Southeast HS	Oklahoma City, OK	1782 G (.247-188-826)
5	Philadelphia Phillies	Mike Martin	lhp	Olympia HS	Columbia, SC	Peaked in Triple-A
6	Chicago White Sox	Lee Richard	ss	Southern	Port Arthur, TX	239 G (.209-2-29)
7	Houston Astros	*Randy Scarbery	rhp	Roosevelt HS	Fresno, CA	60 G (4.50, 6 saves)
8	Kansas City Royals	Rex Goodson	c	Pine Tree HS	Longview, TX	Peaked in Double-A
9	Los Angeles Dodgers	Jim Haller	rhp	Creighton Prep HS	Omaha, NE	Peaked in Triple-A
10	California Angels	Paul Dade	3b-of	Nathan Hale HS	Seattle, WA	439 G (.270-10-107)
11	St. Louis Cardinals	Jim Browning	rhp	Emma Sansom HS	Gadsden, AL	Peaked in Double-A
12	New York Yankees	Dave Cheadle	lhp	Asheville HS	Asheville, NC	2 G (18.00, 0 saves)
13	Pittsburgh Pirates	John Bedard	rhp	Tech HS	Springfield, MA	Peaked in Triple-A
14	Washington Senators	Charles Maxwell	3b-ss	Zane Trace HS	Kingston, OH	Peaked in Triple-A
15	Cincinnati Reds	Gary Polczynski	ss	Nathan Hale HS	West Allis, WI	Peaked in Double-A
16	Boston Red Sox	*Jimmy Hacker	ss	Temple HS	Temple, TX	Peaked in Double-A
17	San Francisco Giants	John D'Acquisto	rhp	St. Augustine HS	San Diego, CA	266 G (4.56, 15 saves)
18	Oakland Athletics	Dan Ford	of	Fremont HS	Los Angeles, CA	1153 G (.270-121-566)
19	Chicago Cubs	Gene Hiser	of	Maryland	Baltimore, MD	206 G (.202-1-18)
20	Detroit Tigers	Terry Mappin	c	Durrett HS	Louisville, KY	Peaked in Double-A
21	Atlanta Braves	Ron Broaddus	rhp	Brazosport HS	Freeport, TX	Peaked in Class-A
22	Minnesota Twins	Bob Gorinski	ss	Mount Pleasant HS	Calumet, PA	54 G (.195-3-22)
23	New York Mets	*George Ambrow	ss	Poly HS	Long Beach, CA	Never played pro ball
24	Baltimore Orioles	James West	c	Vashon HS	St. Louis, MO	Peaked in Class-A

* Did not sign.

1971

The 1971 draft featured more than its share of talent, though teams were slow to recognize it. The White Sox started off by choosing Peoria, Ill., high school catcher Danny Goodwin, who became the first No. 1 pick in draft history not to sign. He opted to attend Southern University instead. The fourth pick, Huntsville, Ala., prep shortstop Condredge Holloway, didn't sign either, going on to star as a Tennessee and Canadian Football League quarterback. The best player taken in the first half of the first round was Islip, N.Y., prep shortstop Tom Veryzer, who went 11th to the Tigers. Four future All-Stars would go in the second half of the initial round—Detroit high school lefthander Frank Tanana (Angels); Anderson, S.C., prep outfielder Jim Rice (Red Sox); Boynton Beach, Fla., high school righthander Rick Rhoden (Dodgers); and Houston prep shortstop Craig Reynolds (Pirates)—but that was merely a prelude. Arguably the two best third basemen ever, El Segundo, Calif., high schooler George Brett and Ohio's Mike Schmidt, were consecutive second-round picks by the Royals and Phillies, respectively. Future Cy Young Award winner Ron Guidry was a third-round choice out of Southwestern Louisiana by the Yankees, while future MVP Keith Hernandez lasted until the Cardinals took him in the 42nd round out of a Millbrae, Calif., high school. It was also the final year in which collegians who had been drafted previously were subject to the secondary phase of the June draft. Dartmouth righthander Pete Broberg (Washington Senators), Texas righthander Burt Hooton (Cubs) and Michigan State outfielder Rob Ellis (Brewers), the first three picks in that segment of the draft, all went straight to the big leagues.

Pick	Team	Player	Pos	School	Hometown	Major League Career
1	Chicago White Sox	*Danny Goodwin	c	Central HS	Peoria, IL	252 G (.236-13-81)
2	San Diego Padres	Jay Franklin	rhp	James Madison HS	Vienna, VA	3 G (6.35, 0 saves)
3	Milwaukee Brewers	Tom Bianco	ss	Sewanhaka HS	Elmont, NY	18 G (.176-0-0)
4	Montreal Expos	*Condredge Holloway	ss	Robert E. Lee HS	Huntsville, AL	Never played pro ball
5	Kansas City Royals	Roy Branch	rhp	Beaumont HS	St. Louis, MO	2 G (0-1, 7.94)
6	Philadelphia Phillies	Roy Thomas	rhp	Lompoc HS	Lompoc, CA	182 G (3.82, 7 saves)
7	Washington Senators	Roger Quiroga	rhp	Ball HS	Galveston, TX	Peaked in Class-A
8	St. Louis Cardinals	Ed Kurpiel	1b-lhp	Archbishop Molloy HS	Hollis, NY	Peaked in Triple-A
9	Cleveland Indians	David Sloan	rhp	Santa Clara HS	Santa Clara, CA	Peaked in Double-A

Pick	Team	Player	Pos	School	Hometown	Major League Career
10	Atlanta Braves	Taylor Duncan	ss	Grant HS	Sacramento, CA	112 G (.260-3-39)
11	Detroit Tigers	Tom Veryzer	ss	Islip HS	Islip, NY	996 G (.241-14-231)
12	Houston Astros	Neil Rasmussen	ss	Arcadia HS	Arcadia, CA	Peaked in Double-A
13	California Angels	Frank Tanana	lhp	Catholic Central HS	Detroit, MI	638 G (240-236, 3.66)
14	New York Mets	Rich Puig	2b	Hillsborough HS	Tampa, FL	4 G (.000-0-0)
15	Boston Red Sox	Jim Rice	of	Hannah HS	Anderson, SC	2089 G (.298-382-1451)
16	Chicago Cubs	Jeff Wehmeier	rhp	Brebeuf HS	Indianapolis, IN	Peaked in Class-A
17	Oakland Athletics	Sugar Bear Daniels	rhp	MacKenzie HS	Detroit, MI	Peaked in Class-A
18	San Francisco Giants	Frank Riccelli	lhp	Christian Brothers HS	Syracuse, NY	17 G (4.39, 0 saves)
19	New York Yankees	Terry Whitfield	of	Palo Verde HS	Blythe, CA	730 G (.281-33-179)
20	Los Angeles Dodgers	Rick Rhoden	rhp	Atlantic HS	Boynton Beach, FL	413 G (151-125, 3.59)
21	Minnesota Twins	Dale Soderholm	ss	Coral Park HS	Miami, FL	Peaked in Triple-A
22	Pittsburgh Pirates	Craig Reynolds	ss	Regan HS	Houston, TX	1491 G (.256-42-377)
23	Baltimore Orioles	Randy Stein	rhp	Ganesha HS	Pomona, CA	65 G (5.72, 1 saves)
24	Cincinnati Reds	*Mike Miley	ss	East Jefferson HS	New Orleans, LA	84 G (.176-4-30)

* Did not sign.

1972

Third baseman Dave Roberts became the first No. 1 pick to debut in the majors, going from the University of Oregon to the Padres. His career got off to a promising start, but he lost his power stroke after a back injury in 1974. In another first, Rancho Cordova (Calif.) High became the first high school to produce two first-rounders in the same year, with outfielder Mike Ondina (White Sox) and shortstop Jerry Manuel (Tigers). The Expos were desperate for a catcher and struck out with the fifth pick, Memphis high schooler Bobby Goodman, but bounced back by taking two more in the next two rounds: Los Angeles prepster Ellis Valentine, who became a strong-armed right fielder, and Fullerton, Calif., high schooler Gary Carter.

Pick	Team	Player	Pos	School	Hometown	Major League Career
1	San Diego Padres	Dave Roberts	3b	Oregon	Corvallis, OR	709 G (.239-49-208)
2	Cleveland Indians	Rick Manning	ss	LaSalle HS	Niagara Falls, NY	1555 G (.257-56-458)
3	Philadelphia Phillies	Larry Christenson	rhp	Marysville HS	Marysville, WA	243 G (83-71, 3.79)
4	Texas Rangers	Roy Howell	3b	Lompoc HS	Lompoc, CA	1112 G (.261-80-454)
5	Montreal Expos	Bobby Goodman	c	Bishop Byrne HS	Memphis, TN	Peaked in Triple-A
6	Milwaukee Brewers	Danny Thomas	1b	Southern Illinois	East Carondelet, IL	54 G (.274-6-26)
7	Cincinnati Reds	Larry Payne	rhp	Huntsville HS	Bedias, TX	Peaked in Triple-A
8	Minnesota Twins	*Dick Ruthven	rhp	Fresno State	Fremont, CA	355 G (123-127, 4.14)
9	Houston Astros	Steve Englishbey	of	South Houston HS	Houston, TX	Peaked in Double-A
10	California Angels	Dave Chalk	3b	Texas	Dallas, TX	903 G (.252-15-243)
11	Atlanta Braves	Preston Hanna	rhp	Escambia HS	Pensacola, FL	156 G (4.61, 1 saves)
12	Chicago White Sox	Mike Ondina	of	Rancho Cordova HS	Rancho Cordova, CA	Peaked in Triple-A
13	New York Mets	Richard Bengston	c	Richwoods HS	Peoria, IL	Peaked in Double-A
14	New York Yankees	Scott McGregor	lhp	El Segundo HS	El Segundo, CA	356 G (138-108, 3.99)
15	Chicago Cubs	Brian Vernoy	lhp	LaQuinta HS	Westminster, CA	Peaked in Class-A
16	Boston Red Sox	Joel Bishop	ss	McClatchy HS	Sacramento, CA	Peaked in Class-A
17	Los Angeles Dodgers	John Harbin	ss	Newberry	Greenville, SC	Peaked in Class-A
18	Kansas City Royals	Jamie Quirk	ss	St. Paul HS	Whittier, CA	984 G (.240-43-247)
19	San Francisco Giants	Rob Dressler	rhp	Madison HS	Portland, OR	82 G (11-23, 4.17)
20	Detroit Tigers	Jerry Manuel	ss	Rancho Cordova HS	Rancho Cordova, CA	96 G (.150-3-13)
21	St. Louis Cardinals	Dan Larson	rhp	Alhambra HS	Alhambra, CA	78 G (10-25, 4.40)
22	Oakland Athletics	Chet Lemon	ss	Fremont HS	Los Angeles, CA	1988 G (.273-215-884)
23	Pittsburgh Pirates	Dwayne Peltier	ss	Servite HS	Anaheim, CA	Peaked in Double-A
24	Baltimore Orioles	Ken Thomas	c	Clear Fork HS	Bellville, OH	Peaked in Class-A

* Did not sign.

1973

For the second year in a row, the top draft choice immediately joined his big league club. Houston high school lefthander David Clyde joined the Rangers at age 18, giving the team a much-needed boost in attendance. While he spared Texas from bankruptcy, Clyde's career was irreparably harmed. That wasn't the case with the No. 4 pick, who also went straight to the majors with the Padres. University of Minnesota outfielder Dave Winfield never looked back. He wasn't even the first future Hall of Famer selected in the 1973 draft, as the Brewers took Woodland Hills, Calif., high school shortstop Robin Yount with the pick before Winfield. A third first-rounder, Arizona State lefthander Eddie Bane, also debuted in the big leagues with the Twins but had little success. Future MVP Fred Lynn lasted until the Red Sox grabbed him late in the second round because scouts believed he had

Amateur Draft: First-Round Picks

tailed off as a Southern Cal junior. One round later, the Orioles took Los Angeles high school catcher Eddie Murray, and they added Massachusetts lefthander Mike Flanagan in the seventh.

Pick	Team	Player	Pos	School	Hometown	Major League Career
1	Texas Rangers	David Clyde	lhp	Westchester HS	Houston, TX	84 G (18-33, 4.63)
2	Philadelphia Phillies	John Stearns	c	Colorado	Denver, CO	810 G (.260-46-312)
3	Milwaukee Brewers	Robin Yount	ss	Taft HS	Woodland Hills, CA	2856 G (.285-251-1406)
4	San Diego Padres	Dave Winfield	rhp-of	Minnesota	St. Paul, MN	2973 G (.283-465-1833)
5	Cleveland Indians	Glenn Tufts	1b	Raynham HS	Bridgewater, MS	Peaked in Double-A
6	San Francisco Giants	Johnnie LeMaster	ss	Paintsville HS	Paintsville, KY	1039 G (.222-22-229)
7	California Angels	Billy Taylor	of	Windsor Forest HS	Savannah, GA	Peaked in Class-A
8	Montreal Expos	Gary Roenicke	ss	Edgewood HS	West Covina, CA	1064 G (.247-121-410)
9	Kansas City Royals	Lew Olsen	rhp	San Ramon HS	Alamo, CA	Peaked in Triple-A
10	Atlanta Braves	Pat Rockett	ss	Robert E. Lee HS	San Antonio, TX	152 G (.214-1-28)
11	Minnesota Twins	Eddie Bane	lhp	Arizona State	Westminster, CA	44 G (7-13, 4.66)
12	St. Louis Cardinals	Joe Edelen	3b-rhp	Gracemont HS	Gracemont, OK	27 G (6.75, 0 saves)
13	Oakland Athletics	Doug Heinhold	rhp	Stroman HS	Victoria, TX	Peaked in Triple-A
14	New York Mets	Lee Mazzilli	of	Lincoln HS	Brooklyn, NY	1475 G (.259-93-460)
15	Baltimore Orioles	Mike Parrott	rhp	Camarillo HS	Camarillo, CA	119 G (19-39, 4.87)
16	Chicago Cubs	Jerry Tabb	1b	Tulsa	Altus, OK	74 G (.226-6-20)
17	Boston Red Sox	Ted Cox	ss	Midwest City HS	Midwest City, OK	272 G (.245-10-79)
18	Los Angeles Dodgers	Ted Farr	c	Shadle Park HS	Spokane, WA	Peaked in Triple-A
19	Detroit Tigers	Charles Bates	1b	Cal State Los Angeles	Los Angeles, CA	Peaked in Double-A
20	Houston Astros	Calvin Portley	ss	Longview HS	Longview, TX	Peaked in Double-A
21	Chicago White Sox	Steve Swisher	c	Ohio	Parkersburg, WV	509 G (.216-20-124)
22	Cincinnati Reds	Charles Kessler	of	Claremont HS	Claremont, CA	Peaked in Double-A
23	Oakland Athletics	Randy Scarbery	rhp	Southern California	Fresno, CA	60 G (4.50, 6 saves)
24	Pittsburgh Pirates	Steve Nicosia	c	North Miami Beach HS	North Miami Beach, FL	358 G (.248-11-88)

1974

The first round of the 1974 draft was rife with football overtones. The Angels took quarterback Mike Miley of Orange Bowl champion Louisiana State with the 10th pick, and Maryland running back recruit Willie Wilson might have gone earlier if teams hadn't been frightened by his gridiron commitment. He went 18th to the Royals. UCLA lost a pair of prized recruits who went in different directions in baseball: running back/outfielder Kevin Drake (Astros) and linebacker/catcher Lance Parrish (Tigers). The Orioles took California quarterback/first baseman Steve Bartkowski in the 19th round, but he didn't sign and went on to be the top choice in the 1975 National Football League draft. The No. 1 selection was Brown shortstop Bill Almon, who had a journeyman career. Four picks later, the Braves chose a Portland, Ore., high school catcher who would win two Most Valuable Player Awards: Dale Murphy.

Pick	Team	Player	Pos	School	Hometown	Major League Career
1	San Diego Padres	Bill Almon	ss	Brown	Warwick, RI	1236 G (.254-36-296)
2	Texas Rangers	Tommy Boggs	rhp	Lanier HS	Austin, TX	114 G (20-44, 4.22)
3	Philadelphia Phillies	Lonnie Smith	of	Centennial HS	Compton, CA	1613 G (.288-98-533)
4	Cleveland Indians	Tom Brennan	rhp	Lewis	Oaklawn, IL	64 G (4.40, 2 saves)
5	Atlanta Braves	Dale Murphy	c	Wilson HS	Portland, OR	2180 G (.265-398-1266)
6	Milwaukee Brewers	Butch Edge	rhp	El Camino HS	Sacramento, CA	9 G (3-4, 5.23)
7	Chicago Cubs	Scot Thompson	of	Knox HS	Renfrew, PA	626 G (.262-5-110)
8	Chicago White Sox	Larry Monroe	rhp	Forest View HS	Mount Prospect, IL	8 G (4.15, 0 saves)
9	Montreal Expos	Ron Sorey	3b	Stebbins HS	Dayton, OH	Peaked in Class-A
10	California Angels	Mike Miley	ss	Louisiana State	Metairie, LA	84 G (.176-4-30)
11	Pittsburgh Pirates	Rod Scurry	lhp	Proctor Hug HS	Sparks, NV	332 G (3.24, 39 saves)
12	New York Yankees	Dennis Sherrill	ss	South Miami HS	Miami, FL	5 G (.200-0-0)
13	St. Louis Cardinals	Garry Templeton	ss	Valley HS	Santa Ana, CA	2079 G (.271-70-728)
14	Minnesota Twins	Ted Shipley	ss	Vanderbilt	Chattanooga, TN	Peaked in Double-A
15	Houston Astros	Kevin Drake	of	Cabrillo HS	Lompoc, CA	Peaked in Triple-A
16	Detroit Tigers	Lance Parrish	3b	Walnut HS	Diamond Bar, CA	1988 G (.252-324-1070)
17	New York Mets	Cliff Speck	rhp	Beaverton HS	Beaverton, OR	13 G (4.13, 0 saves)
18	Kansas City Royals	Willie Wilson	of	Summit HS	Summit, NJ	2154 G (.285-41-585)
19	San Francisco Giants	Terry Lee	2b	San Luis Obispo HS	San Luis Obispo, CA	Peaked in Triple-A
20	Boston Red Sox	Eddie Ford	ss	South Carolina	Great Neck, NY	Peaked in Triple-A
21	Los Angeles Dodgers	Rick Sutcliffe	rhp	Van Horn HS	Kansas City, MO	457 G (171-139, 4.08)
22	Oakland Athletics	*Jerry Johnson	c	McCallum HS	Austin, TX	Peaked in Class-A
23	Cincinnati Reds	Steve Reed	rhp	Fort Wayne HS	Fort Wayne, IN	Peaked in Triple-A
24	Baltimore Orioles	Rich Dauer	3b	Southern California	Colton, CA	1140 G (.257-43-372)

* Did not sign.

1975

The first round in 1975 was the weakest in draft history. The Angels made Southern University catcher Danny Goodwin the only player taken with the top choice twice, and he rewarded them with a brief and disappointing big league career. Still, Goodwin was the only one of the first five picks to even reach the majors, a level that just 12 of 24 first-rounders attained. While Seton Hall catcher Rick Cerone was the only first-round choice to have a career of note, going seventh to the Indians, there were some later-round finds. The best came when the Expos took Andre Dawson in the 11th round after he spent his college career in the obscurity of Florida A&M. All-time saves leader Lee Smith was a second-round selection of the Cubs out of Northwestern State, while future batting champion Carney Lansford was a third-round pick of the Angels out of a Santa Clara, Calif., high school. Lansford's brothers Phil (Indians, 1978) and Joey (Padres, 1979) would be first-round picks in later years.

Pick	Team	Player	Pos	School	Hometown	Major League Career
1	California Angels	Danny Goodwin	c	Southern	Peoria, IL	252 G (.236-13-81)
2	San Diego Padres	Mike Lentz	lhp	Juanita HS	Kirkland, WA	Peaked in Double-A
3	Detroit Tigers	Les Filkins	of	George Washington HS	Chicago, IL	Peaked in Triple-A
4	Chicago Cubs	Brian Rosinski	of	Evanston HS	Evanston, IL	Peaked in Triple-A
5	Milwaukee Brewers	Rich O'Keefe	lhp	Yorktown Heights HS	Yorktown Heights, NY	Peaked in Triple-A
6	New York Mets	Butch Benton	c	Godby HS	Tallahassee, FL	51 G (.162-0-10)
7	Cleveland Indians	Rick Cerone	c	Seton Hall	Newark, NJ	1329 G (.245-59-436)
8	San Francisco Giants	Ted Barnicle	lhp	Jacksonville State	Sudbury, MA	Peaked in Triple-A
9	Kansas City Royals	Clint Hurdle	of	Merritt Island	Merritt Island, FL	515 G (.259-32-193)
10	Montreal Expos	Art Miles	ss	Crockett HS	Austin, TX	Peaked in Class-A
11	Chicago White Sox	Chris Knapp	rhp	Central Michigan	St. Joseph, MI	122 G (36-32, 4.99)
12	Philadelphia Phillies	Sam Welborn	rhp	Wichita Falls HS	Wichita Falls, TX	Peaked in Triple-A
13	Minnesota Twins	Rick Sofield	ss	Morristown HS	Morristown, NJ	207 G (.243-9-66)
14	Houston Astros	Bo McLaughlin	rhp	David Lipscomb	Amelia, OH	156 G (4.49, 9 saves)
15	Boston Red Sox	Otis Foster	1b	High Point	High Point, NC	Peaked in Triple-A
16	St. Louis Cardinals	David Johnson	lhp	Gaylord HS	Gaylord, MI	Peaked in Double-A
17	Texas Rangers	Jim Gideon	rhp	Texas	Houston, TX	1 G (0-0, 7.94)
18	Atlanta Braves	Donald Young	c	Dos Pueblos HS	Goleta, CA	Peaked in Class-A
19	New York Yankees	Jim McDonald	1b	Verbum Dei HS	Los Angeles, CA	Peaked in Triple-A
20	Pittsburgh Pirates	Dale Berra	ss	Montclair HS	Montclair, NJ	853 G (.236-49-278)
21	Oakland Athletics	Bruce Robinson	c	Stanford	LaJolla, CA	38 G (.228-0-10)
22	Cincinnati Reds	Tony Moretto	of	Harrison HS	Evansville, IN	Peaked in Double-A
23	Baltimore Orioles	Dave Ford	rhp	Lincoln West HS	Cleveland, OH	51 G (4.02, 3 saves)
24	Los Angeles Dodgers	Mark Bradley	ss	Elizabethtown HS	Elizabethtown, KY	90 G (.204-3-5)

1976

Arizona State lefthander Floyd Bannister went to the Astros with the first pick, a fitting choice in a draft deep in southpaws and Sun Devils. Four of the first five choices were lefthanders, though none of the others enjoyed close to Bannister's success. A record 13 Sun Devils were selected, and six besides Bannister would reach the majors: Ken Landreaux (first round, Angels), Mike Colbern (second, White Sox), Gary Allenson (ninth, Red Sox), Gary Rajsich (11th, Astros), Ricky Peters (12th, Braves) and Ken Phelps (15th, Royals). The Tigers took Kokomo, Ind., high school lefthander Pat Underwood with the No. 2 selection, but rallied to land San Diego high school shortstop Alan Trammell (second); Placentia, Calif., prep righthander Dan Petry (fourth); and Brigham Young righthander Jack Morris (fifth) in subsequent rounds. The Red Sox also did well with Georgia Southern lefthander John Tudor (third round) in January, and St. George, Utah, high school lefthander Bruce Hurst (first) and Tampa prep shortstop Wade Boggs (seventh) in June. The Athletics got a steal in the fourth round, where they found Oakland high school outfielder Rickey Henderson.

Pick	Team	Player	Pos	School	Hometown	Major League Career
1	Houston Astros	Floyd Bannister	lhp	Arizona State	Seattle, WA	431 G (134-143, 4.06)
2	Detroit Tigers	Pat Underwood	lhp	Kokomo HS	Kokomo, IN	113 G (4.43, 8 saves)
3	Atlanta Braves	Ken Smith	3b	East HS	Youngstown, OH	83 G (.268-1-5)
4	Milwaukee Brewers	*Bill Bordley	lhp	Bishop Montgomery HS	Rolling Hills Estates, CA	8 G (2-3, 4.70)
5	San Diego Padres	Bob Owchinko	lhp	Eastern Michigan	Detroit, MI	275 G (4.28, 7 saves)
6	California Angels	Ken Landreaux	of	Arizona State	Compton, CA	1264 G (.268-91-479)
7	Chicago Cubs	Herm Segelke	rhp	El Camino HS	South Sacramento, CA	3 G (8.31, 0 saves)
8	Chicago White Sox	Steve Trout	lhp	Thornwood HS	South Holland, IL	301 G (88-92, 4.18)
9	Montreal Expos	Bob James	rhp	Verdugo Hills HS	Sunland, CA	279 G (3.80, 73 saves)
10	Minnesota Twins	*Jamie Allen	3b-rhp	Davis HS	Yakima, WA	86 G (.223-4-21)
11	San Francisco Giants	Mark Kuecker	ss	Brenham HS	Brenham, TX	Peaked in Triple-A
12	Texas Rangers	Billy Simpson	of	Lakewood HS	Lakewood, CA	Peaked in Class-A
13	New York Mets	Tom Thurberg	of-rhp	South Weymouth HS	South Weymouth, MA	Peaked in Triple-A
14	Cleveland Indians	Tim Glass	c	South HS	Springfield, OH	Peaked in Double-A

Pick	Team	Player	Pos	School	Hometown	Major League Career
15	St. Louis Cardinals	Leon Durham	1b	Woodward HS	Cincinnati, OH	1067 G (.277-147-530)
16	New York Yankees	Pat Tabler	of	McNicholas HS	Cincinnati, OH	1202 G (.282-47-512)
17	Philadelphia Phillies	Jeff Kraus	ss	Colerain HS	Cincinnati, OH	Peaked in Double-A
18	Kansas City Royals	Ben Grzybek	rhp	Hialeah HS	Hialeah, FL	Peaked in Double-A
19	Los Angeles Dodgers	Mike Scioscia	c	Springfield HS	Morton, PA	1441 G (.259-68-446)
20	Baltimore Orioles	Dallas Williams	of	Lincoln HS	Brooklyn, NY	20 G (.079-0-1)
21	Pittsburgh Pirates	Jim Parke	rhp	Henry Ford II HS	Sterling Heights, MI	Peaked in Class-A
22	Boston Red Sox	Bruce Hurst	lhp	Dixie HS	St. George, UT	379 G (145-113, 3.92)
23	Cincinnati Reds	Mark King	rhp	Owensboro HS	Owensboro, KY	Peaked in Class-A
24	Oakland Athletics	*Mike Sullivan	rhp	Garfield HS	Woodbridge, VA	Peaked in Double-A

* Did not sign.

1977

Orland Park, Ill., high school righthander Bill Gullickson seemed like a logical No. 1 choice for the nearby White Sox, but Chicago owner Bill Veeck surprisingly went for St. Michaels, Md., prep outfielder Harold Baines. Veeck had begun scouting Baines in Little League six years earlier and, more importantly for the cash-strapped owner, was able to sign him for $40,000, by far the lowest bonus ever for the top draft pick. Gullickson went second to the Expos, while the Brewers opted for University of Minnesota shortstop Paul Molitor with the third choice. A slick-fielding shortstop from Cal Poly San Luis Obispo lasted until the fourth round because of his questionable bat, but the Padres had no qualms with Ozzie Smith. Besides Gullickson, Montreal also did well with Vanderbilt righthander Scott Sanderson (third round) and Sanford, Fla., high school outfielder Tim Raines (fifth).

Pick	Team	Player	Pos	School	Hometown	Major League Career
1	Chicago White Sox	Harold Baines	1b-of	St. Michaels HS	St. Michaels, MD	2463 G (.290-339-1423)
2	Montreal Expos	Bill Gullickson	rhp	Joliet Catholic HS	Orland Park, IL	398 G (162-136, 3.93)
3	Milwaukee Brewers	Paul Molitor	ss	Minnesota	St. Paul, MN	2557 G (.308-230-1238)
4	Atlanta Braves	Tim Cole	lhp	Saugerties HS	Saugerties, NY	Peaked in Triple-A
5	Detroit Tigers	Kevin Richards	rhp	Roosevelt HS	Wyandotte, MI	Peaked in Double-A
6	St. Louis Cardinals	Terry Kennedy	c	Florida State	Mesa, AZ	1491 G (.264-113-628)
7	California Angels	Richard Dotson	rhp	Anderson HS	Cincinnati, OH	305 G (111-113, 4.23)
8	San Diego Padres	Brian Greer	of	Sonora HS	Brea, CA	5 G (.000-0-0)
9	Texas Rangers	David Hibner	ss	Howell HS	Howell, MI	Peaked in Class-A
10	San Francisco Giants	Craig Landis	ss	Vintage HS	Napa, CA	Peaked in Triple-A
11	Cleveland Indians	Bruce Compton	of	Norman HS	Norman, OK	Peaked in Class-A
12	Chicago Cubs	Randy Martz	rhp	South Carolina	Elizabethville, PA	68 G (17-19, 3.78)
13	Boston Red Sox	Andrew Madden	rhp	New Hartford HS	New Hartford, NY	Peaked in Class-A
14	Houston Astros	Ricky Adams	ss	Montclair HS	Montclair, CA	120 G (.215-4-16)
15	Minnesota Twins	Paul Croft	of	Morristown HS	Morristown, NJ	Peaked in Double-A
16	New York Mets	Wally Backman	ss	Aloha HS	Beaverton, OR	1102 G (.275-10-240)
17	Oakland Athletics	Craig Harris	rhp	Buena HS	Sierra Vista, AZ	Peaked in Double-A
18	Pittsburgh Pirates	Anthony Nicely	of	Meadowdale HS	Dayton, OH	Peaked in Class-A
19	Baltimore Orioles	Drungo Hazewood	of	Sacramento HS	Sacramento, CA	6 G (.000-0-0)
20	Los Angeles Dodgers	Bob Welch	rhp	Eastern Michigan	Ferndale, MI	506 G (211-146, 3.47)
21	Kansas City Royals	Mike Jones	lhp	Sutherland HS	Pittsford, NY	71 G (4.43, 0 saves)
22	Philadelphia Phillies	Scott Munninghoff	rhp	Purcell HS	Cincinnati, OH	4 G (4.50, 0 saves)
23	New York Yankees	Steve Taylor	rhp	Delaware	Newark, DE	Peaked in Triple-A
24	Cincinnati Reds	Tad Venger	3b	Hart HS	Newhall, CA	Peaked in Class-A
25	Toronto Blue Jays	Tom Goffena	ss	Sidney HS	Sidney, OH	Peaked in Class-A
26	Seattle Mariners	Dave Henderson	of	Dos Palos HS	Dos Palos, CA	1538 G (.258-197-708)

1978

No. 1 pick Bob Horner, a third baseman from Arizona State, joined the Braves immediately and became the only draftee ever to win a Rookie of the Year Award in the same year in which he was picked. Horner homered in his first game off of Bert Blyleven and went deep 23 times in 89 games, but he actually was second on Atlanta's list. The Braves coveted Michigan State outfielder/wide receiver Kirk Gibson, but didn't think they could steer him away from football. The Tigers gambled that they could with the 12th pick, and succeeded with a $150,000 bonus that ranked second in draft history to Horner's $175,000. Gibson, as well as Aberdeen, Md., high school third baseman Cal Ripken Jr. (Orioles, second round) and Spokane, Wash., prep infielder Ryne Sandberg (Phillies, 20th), eventually would win MVP Awards. Shortstop Hubie Brooks, Horner's double-play partner with the Sun Devils, went third to the Mets, the only time a pair of college teammates have gone that high in a single draft. Besides Horner, three high school draftees went straight to the majors. Athletics pitchers Tim Conroy and Mike Morgan (both first-rounders) and Blue Jays catcher Brian Milner (seventh) didn't fare nearly as well. For the first time, compensation picks were awarded to clubs that lost major league free agents. The first such choice went to the Yankees, who used the 18th pick (via Texas for Ron Blomberg) on Fresno high school shortstop Rex Hudler.

Pick	Team	Player	Pos	School	Hometown	Major League Career
1	Atlanta Braves	Bob Horner	3b	Arizona State	Glendale, AZ	1020 G (.277-218-685)
2	Toronto Blue Jays	Lloyd Moseby	1b	Oakland HS	Oakland, CA	1588 G (.257-169-737)
3	New York Mets	Hubie Brooks	ss	Arizona State	Tempe, AZ	1645 G (.269-149-824)
4	Oakland Athletics	Mike Morgan	rhp	Valley HS	Las Vegas, NV	420 G (117-167, 4.07)
5	San Diego Padres	Andy Hawkins	rhp	Midway HS	Waco, TX	280 G (84-91, 4.22)
6	Seattle Mariners	Tito Nanni	of-1b	Chestnut Hill Academy	Philadelphia, PA	Peaked in Triple-A
7	San Francisco Giants	Bob Cummings	c	Brother Rice HS	Chicago, IL	Peaked in Double-A
8	Milwaukee Brewers	Nick Hernandez	c	Hialeah HS	Hialeah, FL	Peaked in Class-A
9	Montreal Expos	Glenn Franklin	ss	Chipola (FL) JC	St. Louis, MO	Peaked in Triple-A
10	Cleveland Indians	Phil Lansford	ss	Wilcox HS	Santa Clara, CA	Peaked in Double-A
11	Houston Astros	Rod Boxberger	rhp	Southern California	Santa Ana, CA	Peaked in Double-A
12	Detroit Tigers	Kirk Gibson	of	Michigan State	Waterford, MI	1635 G (.268-255-870)
13	Chicago Cubs	Bill Hayes	c	Indiana State	North Platte, NE	5 G (.222-0-0)
14	California Angels	Tom Brunansky	of	West Covina HS	West Covina, CA	1800 G (.245-271-919)
15	St. Louis Cardinals	Robert Hicks	1b	Tate HS	Pensacola, FL	Peaked in Double-A
16	Minnesota Twins	Lenny Faedo	ss	Jefferson HS	Tampa, FL	174 G (.251-5-52)
17	Cincinnati Reds	Nick Esasky	ss	Carol City HS	Carol City, FL	810 G (.250-122-427)
18	New York Yankees	Rex Hudler	ss	Bullard HS	Fresno, CA	749 G (.264-56-167)
19	Pittsburgh Pirates	Brad Garnett	1b	DeSoto HS	DeSoto, TX	Peaked in Class-A
20	Oakland Athletics	Tim Conroy	lhp	Gateway HS	Monroeville, PA	135 G (18-32, 4.69)
21	Pittsburgh Pirates	Gerry Aubin	of	Dougherty HS	Albany, GA	Peaked in Class-A
22	Baltimore Orioles	Robert Boyce	3b	Deer Park HS	Cincinnati, OH	Peaked in Class-A
23	Philadelphia Phillies	Rip Rollins	1b-rhp	Alleghany HS	Sparta, NC	Peaked in Class-A
24	New York Yankees	Matt Winters	of	Williamsville HS	Williamsville, NY	42 G (.234-2-9)
25	Kansas City Royals	Buddy Biancalana	ss	Redwood HS	Greenbrae, CA	311 G (.205-6-30)
26	New York Yankees	Brian Ryder	rhp	Shrewsbury HS	Shrewsbury, MA	Peaked in Triple-A

1979

Of all the top picks who reached the majors, none had a worse career than Harrisburg, Pa., high school outfielder Al Chambers. The Mariners envisioned him as a slugger, but he hit just two homers in 57 big league games. Chambers, a top-rated defensive-end prospect who had been headed to Arizona State, was an appropriate first pick in a draft with several familiar football names. Two of the top quarterbacks in NFL history were chosen, Dan Marino (fourth, Royals) and John Elway (19th, Royals)--as were future NFL first-round picks Curt Warner (32nd, Phillies) and Jack Thompson (34th, Mariners). Jay Schroeder, the third pick in the baseball draft, signed with Toronto and split his time between playing baseball and quarterbacking UCLA until joining the Washington Redskins full-time in 1984. The two best players in the draft weren't taken until long afterward. Bowling Green righthander Orel Hershiser went in the 17th round to the Dodgers, while Evansville, Ind., high school first baseman Don Mattingly lasted until the Yankees selected him two rounds later. Michigan became the first school to produce three first-rounders in the same year: outfielder Rick Leach (No. 13, Tigers), lefthander Steve Howe (No. 16, Dodgers) and righthander Steve Perry (No. 25, Dodgers).

Pick	Team	Player	Pos	School	Hometown	Major League Career
1	Seattle Mariners	Al Chambers	of	John Harris HS	Harrisburg, PA	57 G (.208-2-11)
2	New York Mets	Tim Leary	rhp	UCLA	Santa Monica, CA	292 G (78-105, 4.36)
3	Toronto Blue Jays	Jay Schroeder	c	Palisades HS	Pacific Palisades, CA	Peaked in Class-A
4	Atlanta Braves	Brad Komminsk	of	Shawnee HS	Lima, OH	376 G (.218-23-105)
5	Oakland Athletics	*Juan Bustabad	ss	Miami Lakes HS	Hialeah, FL	Peaked in Triple-A
6	St. Louis Cardinals	Andy Van Slyke	of	New Hartford HS	New Hartford, NY	1658 G (.274-164-792)
7	Cleveland Indians	Jon Bohnet	lhp	Hogan HS	Vallejo, CA	3 G (0-0, 6.94)
8	Houston Astros	John Mizerock	c	Punxsutawney HS	Punxsutawney, PA	103 G (.186-2-24)
9	Chicago White Sox	*Steve Buechele	ss	Servite HS	Fullerton, CA	1334 G (.245-137-547)
10	Montreal Expos	Tim Wallach	1b	Cal State Fullerton	Tustin, CA	2212 G (.257-260-1125)
11	Minnesota Twins	Kevin Brandt	of	Nekoosa HS	Nekoosa, WI	Peaked in Class-A
12	Chicago Cubs	Jon Perlman	rhp	Baylor	Carthage, TX	26 G (6.35, 0 saves)
13	Detroit Tigers	Rick Leach	of	Michigan	Flint, MI	799 G (.268-18-183)
14	San Diego Padres	Joe Lansford	1b	Wilcox HS	San Jose, CA	25 G (.200-1-5)
15	San Francisco Giants	Scott Garrelts	rhp	Buckley-Loda HS	Buckley, IL	352 G (3.29, 48 saves)
16	Los Angeles Dodgers	Steve Howe	lhp	Michigan	Clarkston, MI	497 G (3.03, 91 saves)
17	Texas Rangers	Jerry Don Gleaton	lhp	Texas	Brownwood, TX	307 G (4.25, 26 saves)
18	San Francisco Giants	*Rick Luecken	rhp	Spring-Woods HS	Houston, TX	56 G (5.10, 2 saves)
19	Chicago White Sox	Rick Seilheimer	c	Brenham HS	Brenham, TX	21 G (.212-1-3)
20	Cincinnati Reds	Dan Lamar	c	Bellaire HS	Houston, TX	Peaked in Class-A
21	Kansas City Royals	Atlee Hammaker	lhp	East Tennessee State	Alexandria, VA	249 G (59-67, 3.66)

Amateur Draft: First-Round Picks

Pick	Team	Player	Pos	School	Hometown	Major League Career
22	Cincinnati Reds	Mike Sullivan	rhp	Clemson	Woodbridge, VA	Peaked in Double-A
23	Detroit Tigers	Chris Baker	of	Livonia Franklin HS	Dearborn Hts, MI	Peaked in Class-A
24	San Diego Padres	Bob Geren	c	Clairemont HS	San Diego, CA	307 G (.233-22-76)
25	Los Angeles Dodgers	Steve Perry	rhp	Michigan	Ann Arbor, MI	Peaked in Triple-A
26	Oakland Athletics	*Mike Stenhouse	of	Harvard	Cranston, RI	207 G (.190-9-40)

* Did not sign.

1980

The Mets, who blew previous No. 1 picks on Steve Chilcott and Tim Foli, did it right this time. They selected Los Angeles high school outfielder Darryl Strawberry, who would win the National League Rookie of the Year Award three years later and help lead the franchise back to prominence. One of the highest-rated prospects became embroiled in controversy. Baton Rouge prep shortstop Billy Cannon Jr. was coveted by the Yankees, who didn't have a pick in the first two rounds. Shortly before the draft, his father Billy Sr. (the former Heisman Trophy winner) sent telegrams informing each team that his son wouldn't sign for less than $250,000. That scared off everyone but the Yankees, who took Cannon in the third round. Four clubs filed a grievance accusing New York owner George Steinbrenner of conspiring with the Cannons, and commissioner Bowie Kuhn voided the choice. The Indians won Cannon's rights in a special lottery, but were unwilling to match Steinbrenner's offer. Cannon went to Texas A&M and later became a first-round pick of the NFL's Dallas Cowboys.

Pick	Team	Player	Pos	School	Hometown	Major League Career
1	New York Mets	Darryl Strawberry	of	Crenshaw HS	Los Angeles, CA	1458 G (.259-308-937)
2	Toronto Blue Jays	Garry Harris	ss	Hoover HS	San Diego, CA	Peaked in Double-A
3	Atlanta Braves	Ken Dayley	lhp	Portland	The Dalles, OR	385 G (3.64, 39 saves)
4	Oakland Athletics	Mike King	lhp	Morningside	Soux City, IA	Peaked in Triple-A
5	San Diego Padres	Jeff Pyburn	of	Georgia	Athens, GA	Peaked in Triple-A
6	Seattle Mariners	Darnell Coles	ss	Eisenhower HS	Rialto, CA	957 G (.245-75-368)
7	San Francisco Giants	Jessie Reid	1b	Lynwood HS	Lynwood, CA	8 G (.100-1-1)
8	Chicago White Sox	Cecil Espy	of	Point Loma HS	San Diego, CA	546 G (.244-7-108)
9	Los Angeles Dodgers	Ross Jones	ss	Miami	Hialeah, FL	67 G (.221-0-11)
10	Cleveland Indians	Kelly Gruber	ss	Westlake HS	Austin, TX	939 G (.259-117-443)
11	Chicago Cubs	Don Schulze	rhp	Lake Park HS	Roselle, IL	76 G (15-25, 5.47)
12	Minnesota Twins	Jeff Reed	c	West HS	Joliet, IL	928 G (.248-45-231)
13	Philadelphia Phillies	Lebo Powell	c	Pine Forest HS	Pensacola, FL	Peaked in Class-A
14	Texas Rangers	Tim Maki	rhp	Carrol HS	Humtertown, IN	Peaked in Class-A
15	St. Louis Cardinals	Don Collins	rhp	Ferguson HS	Newport News, VA	Peaked in Class-A
16	Kansas City Royals	Frank Wills	rhp	Tulane	New Orleans, LA	154 G (5.06, 6 saves)
17	California Angels	Dennis Rasmussen	lhp	Creighton	Lakewood, CO	256 G (91-77, 4.15)
18	Detroit Tigers	Glenn Wilson	3b	Sam Houston State	Channelview, TX	1201 G (.265-98-521)
19	Cincinnati Reds	Ron Robinson	rhp-ss	Woodlake HS	Woodlake, CA	232 G (3.63, 19 saves)
20	Pittsburgh Pirates	Rich Renteria	ss	South Gate HS	South Gate, CA	184 G (.237-4-41)
21	Atlanta Braves	Jim Acker	rhp	Texas	Freer, TX	467 G (3.97, 30 saves)
22	Montreal Expos	Terry Francona	of	Arizona	New Brighton, PA	708 G (.274-16-143)
23	New York Mets	Billy Beane	of	Mount Carmel HS	Rancho Bernardo, CA	148 G (.219-3-29)
24	New York Mets	John Gibbons	c	MacArthur HS	San Antonio, TX	18 G (.220-1-2)
25	Milwaukee Brewers	Dion James	of	McClatchy HS	Sacramento, CA	917 G (.288-32-266)
26	Baltimore Orioles	Jeff Williams	of	Princeton HS	Cincinnati, OH	Peaked in Triple-A

1981

Rising bonuses were making money a more important consideration when choosing players, and an agent helped the Mariners decide on the top choice. Yale righthander Ron Darling had one and Oral Roberts righthander Mike Moore didn't, so Seattle went with Moore, who reached the majors in 1982 and had a solid career. The Mariners also did well with their next two choices, San Jose State lefthander Mark Langston (second round) and Missouri outfielder Phil Bradley (third). Darling, who fared a bit better than Moore, lasted until the Rangers chose him ninth . Wichita State outfielder Joe Carter was the second choice, going to the Cubs. A San Diego State point guard was drafted on the same day by the NBA's San Diego Clippers as well as the Padres (third round). Tony Gwynn decided to play baseball and immediately led the Northwest League in hitting, foreshadowing the eight National League batting titles he would win. The Yankees used their first pick (second round) on Stanford quarterback John Elway, who signed for $150,000. Elway used his baseball leverage to force the Baltimore Colts to trade him to the Denver Broncos after he was the first selection in the 1983 NFL draft.

Pick	Team	Player	Pos	School	Hometown	Major League Career
1	Seattle Mariners	Mike Moore	rhp	Oral Roberts	Eakly, OK	450 G (161-176, 4.39)
2	Chicago Cubs	Joe Carter	of	Wichita State	Oklahoma City, OK	2063 G (.259-378-1382)
3	California Angels	Dick Schofield	ss	Griffin HS	Springfield, IL	1368 G (.230-56-353)
4	New York Mets	Terry Blocker	of	Tennessee State	Columbia, SC	110 G (.205-2-11)
5	Toronto Blue Jays	Matt Williams	rhp	Rice	Clute, TX	10 G (3-2, 5.29)
6	San Diego Padres	Kevin McReynolds	of	Arkansas	Little Rock, AR	1502 G (.265-211-807)
7	Chicago White Sox	Darryl Boston	of	Woodward HS	Cincinnati, OH	1058 G (.249-83-278)
8	St. Louis Cardinals	Bobby Meacham	ss	San Diego State	Westminster, CA	457 G (.236-8-114)
9	Texas Rangers	Ron Darling	rhp	Yale	Millbury, MA	382 G (136-116, 3.87)
10	San Francisco Giants	Mark Grant	rhp	Catholic HS	Joliet, IL	233 G (4.31, 8 saves)
11	Minnesota Twins	Mike Sodders	3b	Arizona State	Westminster, CA	Peaked in Triple-A
12	Atlanta Braves	Jay Roberts	of	Centralia HS	Centralia, WA	Peaked in Class-A
13	Cleveland Indians	George Alpert	of	Livingston HS	Livingston, NJ	Peaked in Class-A
14	Pittsburgh Pirates	Jim Winn	rhp	John Brown	Clever, MO	161 G (4.67, 10 saves)
15	Oakland Athletics	Tim Pyznarski	3b-of	Eastern Illinois	Chicago Ridge, IL	15 G (.238-0-0)
16	Chicago Cubs	Vance Lovelace	lhp	Hillsborough HS	Tampa, FL	9 G (5.79, 0 saves)
17	Detroit Tigers	Ricky Barlow	rhp	Woodville HS	Woodville, TX	Peaked in Triple-A
18	Montreal Expos	Darren Dilks	lhp	Oklahoma State	Ontario, CA	Peaked in Triple-A
19	Boston Red Sox	Steve Lyons	of-ss	Oregon State	Corvallis, OR	853 G (.252-19-196)
20	Philadelphia Phillies	Johnny Abrego	rhp	Mission HS	San Jose, CA	6 G (1-1, 6.38)
21	Toronto Blue Jays	John Cerutti	lhp	Amherst	Albany, NY	229 G (49-43, 3.94)
22	Los Angeles Dodgers	Dave Anderson	ss	Memphis State	Memphis, TN	873 G (.242-19-143)
23	Kansas City Royals	Dave Leeper	of	Southern California	Orange, CA	19 G (.075-0-4)
24	Texas Rangers	Al Lachowicz	rhp	Pittsburgh	McKees Rocks, PA	2 G (0-1, 2.25)
25	Boston Red Sox	Kevin Burrell	c	Poway HS	Poway, CA	Peaked in Triple-A
26	San Diego Padres	Frank Castro	c	Miami	Hialeah, FL	Peaked in Double-A

1982

The Cubs used the top selection on Brooklyn high school shortstop Shawon Dunston, who would earn two All-Star berths with Chicago. The biggest winners were the Mets, who had the best pitching draft ever. They gambled the fifth choice on prep righthander Dwight Gooden, who was considered the third-best mound prospect in Tampa, and also signed Fontana, Calif., high schooler Floyd Youmans (second round); Bowling Green's Roger McDowell (third); Eastern Michigan's Mickey Weston (12th); Central Arkansas' Wes Gardner (22nd); and Clark (Wash.) Community College's Randy Myers (first round, secondary phase). Future MVPs Terry Pendleton (seventh round, Cardinals, out of Fresno State) and Jose Canseco (15th, Athletics, from of a Miami high school) and two-time Cy Young Award winner Bret Saberhagen (19th, Royals, out of a Northridge, Calif., high school) all lasted until the later rounds.

Pick	Team	Player	Pos	School	Hometown	Major League Career
1	Chicago Cubs	Shawon Dunston	ss	Thomas Jefferson HS	Brooklyn, NY	1354 G (.270-117-530)
2	Toronto Blue Jays	Augie Schmidt	ss	New Orleans	Kenosha, WI	Peaked in Triple-A
3	San Diego Padres	Jimmy Jones	rhp	Thomas Jefferson HS	Dallas, TX	153 G (43-39, 4.46)
4	Minnesota Twins	Bryan Oelkers	lhp	Wichita State	St. Louis, MO	45 G (6.01, 1 saves)
5	New York Mets	Dwight Gooden	rhp	Hillsborough HS	Tampa, FL	354 G (177-97, 3.31)
6	Seattle Mariners	Spike Owen	ss	Texas	Cleburne, TX	1544 G (.246-46-439)
7	Pittsburgh Pirates	Sam Khalifa	ss	Sahuaro HS	Tucson, AZ	164 G (.219-2-37)
8	California Angels	Bob Kipper	lhp	Central Catholic HS	Aurora, IL	271 G (4.34, 11 saves)
9	Atlanta Braves	Duane Ward	rhp	Farmington HS	Farmington, NM	462 G (3.28, 121 saves)
10	Kansas City Royals	John Morris	of	Seton Hall	Bellmore, NY	402 G (.236-8-63)
11	San Francisco Giants	Steve Stanicek	1B	Nebraska	Park Forest, IL	13 G (.188-0-1)
12	Cleveland Indians	Mark Snyder	rhp	Beardon HS	Knoxville, TN	Peaked in Class-A
13	Philadelphia Phillies	John Russell	c-of	Oklahoma	Norman, OK	448 G (.225-34-129)
14	Chicago White Sox	Ron Karkovice	c	Boone HS	Orlando, FL	939 G (.221-96-335)
15	Houston Astros	Steve Swain	of	Grossmont HS	El Cajon, CA	Peaked in Class-A
16	Boston Red Sox	Sam Horn	1b	Morse HS	San Diego, CA	389 G (.240-62-179)
17	Chicago Cubs	Tony Woods	ss	Whittier	Oakland, CA	Peaked in Triple-A
18	Boston Red Sox	Rob Parkins	rhp	Cerritos HS	Cerritos, CA	Peaked in Class-A
19	Los Angeles Dodgers	Franklin Stubbs	1b	Virginia Tech	Hamlet, NC	945 G (.232-104-348)
20	Detroit Tigers	Rich Monteleone	rhp	Tampa Catholic HS	Tampa, FL	210 G (3.87, 0 saves)
21	St. Louis Cardinals	Todd Worrell	rhp	Biola College	Arcadia, CA	617 G (3.09, 256 saves)
22	Cincinnati Reds	Scott Jones	lhp	South HS	Hinsdale, IL	Peaked in Class-A
23	Cincinnati Reds	Billy Hawley	rhp	Brookland Cayce HS	West Columbia, SC	Peaked in Double-A
24	Baltimore Orioles	Joe Kucharski	rhp	South Carolina	Clinton, MD	Peaked in Triple-A
25	Milwaukee Brewers	Dale Sveum	ss	Pinole Valley HS	Pinole, CA	783 G (.239-66-324)
26	Boston Red Sox	Jeff Ledbetter	1b-of	Florida State	Clearwater, FL	Peaked in Double-A

1983

Mount Vernon Nazarene's Tim Belcher was an obscure Ohio college righthander six weeks before the 1983 draft, but finished strong and went first to the Twins. Minnesota took a hardline stance in contract negotiations, however, and Belcher joined Danny Goodwin as the only No. 1 choices not to sign. Belcher went first again in the January 1984 draft and signed with the Yankees, who lost him to the Athletics through a loophole in the rules governing the free-agent compensation pool. The Twins also couldn't come to terms with second-round choice Billy Swift, and got him suspended for a third of the following season at Maine when they informed the NCAA that Swift had used an agent. In one of the weaker draft pools ever, 18 teams passed on a righthander considered the No. 3 pitcher on College World Series champion Texas. The Red Sox took Roger Clemens over the other Longhorns, and he won his first of four Cy Young Awards three years later.

Pick	Team	Player	Pos	School	Hometown	Major League Career
1	Minnesota Twins	*Tim Belcher	rhp	Mount Vernon Nazarene	Sparta, OH	327 G (122-113, 3.93)
2	Cincinnati Reds	Kurt Stillwell	ss	Thousand Oaks HS	Thousand Oaks, CA	998 G (.249-34-310)
3	Texas Rangers	Jeff Kunkel	ss	Rider	Leonardo, NJ	357 G (.221-18-73)
4	New York Mets	Eddie Williams	3b	Hoover HS	San Diego, CA	378 G (.254-39-147)
5	Oakland Athletics	Stan Hilton	rhp	Baylor	Hurst, TX	Peaked in Triple-A
6	Chicago Cubs	Jackie Davidson	rhp	Everman HS	Everman, TX	Peaked in Triple-A
7	Seattle Mariners	Darrel Akerfelds	rhp	Mesa	Lakewood, CO.	125 G (5.08, 3 saves)
8	Houston Astros	Robbie Wine	c	Oklahoma State	Norristown, PA	23 G (.146-0-0)
9	Toronto Blue Jays	Matt Stark	c	Los Altos HS	Hacienda Hts, CA	13 G (.179-0-3)
10	San Diego Padres	Ray Hayward	lhp	Oklahoma	Enid, OK	19 G (4-8, 6.75)
11	Cleveland Indians	Dave Clark	of	Jackson State	Tupelo, MO	812 G (.268-62-280)
12	Pittsburgh Pirates	Ron DeLucchi	of	Campolinda HS	Moraga, CA	Peaked in Class-A
13	Chicago White Sox	Joel Davis	rhp	Sandalwood HS	Jacksonville, FL	49 G (8-14, 4.91)
14	Montreal Expos	Rich Stoll	rhp	Michigan	Attica, IN	Peaked in Triple-A
15	Detroit Tigers	Wayne Dotson	rhp	Estacado HS	Lubbock, TX	Peaked in Class-A
16	Montreal Expos	Brian Holman	rhp	North HS	Wichita, KS	109 G (37-45, 3.71)
17	Seattle Mariners	Terry Bell	c	Old Dominion	Kettering, OH	9 G (.000-0-0)
18	Los Angeles Dodgers	Erik Sonberg	lhp	Wichita State	Tulsa, OK	Peaked in Triple-A
19	Boston Red Sox	Roger Clemens	rhp	Texas	Katy, TX	417 G (213-118, 2.97)
20	New York Mets	Stan Jefferson	of	Bethune-Cookman	Bronx, NY	296 G (.216-16-67)
21	Kansas City Royals	Gary Thurman	of	North Central HS	Indianapolis, IN	424 G (.243-2-64)
22	Philadelphia Phillies	Ricky Jordan	1b	Grant HS	Sacramento, CA	677 G (.281-55-304)
23	California Angels	Mark Doran	of	Wisconsin	South Holland, IL	Peaked in Triple-A
24	St. Louis Cardinals	Jim Lindeman	3b	Bradley	Des Plaines, IA	351 G (.244-21-89)
25	Baltimore Orioles	Wayne Wilson	rhp	Redondo Beach HS	Redondo Beach, CA	Peaked in Class-A
26	Milwaukee Brewers	Dan Plesac	lhp	North Carolina State	Crown Point, IN	680 G (3.54, 149 saves)

* Did not sign.

1984

The U.S. Olympic team had a profound effect on the 1984 draft, as 13 of the 20 players from the silver-medal team were first-round choices. Five more would join them as first-rounders a year later. The Mets couldn't determine Southern Cal first baseman Mark McGwire's bonus demands, so they opted for Mechanicsburg, Pa., high school outfielder Shawn Abner instead. Abner became one of the biggest busts among No. 1 picks, while McGwire broke into the majors with a rookie-record 49 homers three years later. New York wasn't alone in overlooking McGwire, as eight other teams declined to choose him because of concerns about his signability and long swing. The Athletics finally took him with the 10th pick. The Cubs bypassed McGwire in the first round, but found an even better player in the second when they took a skinny high school righthander from Las Vegas. Greg Maddux blossomed into arguably the best pitcher in baseball history.

Pick	Team	Player	Pos	School	Hometown	Major League Career
1	New York Mets	Shawn Abner	of	Mechanicsburg HS	Mechanicsburg, PA	392 G (.227-11-71)
2	Seattle Mariners	Billy Swift	rhp	Maine	South Portland, ME	374 G (83-69, 3.76)
3	Chicago Cubs	Drew Hall	lhp	Morehead State	Rush, KY	125 G (5.21, 5 saves)
4	Cleveland Indians	Cory Snyder	ss	Brigham Young	Canyon Country, CA	1068 G (.247-149-488)
5	Cincinnati Reds	Pat Pacillo	rhp	Seton Hall	Rutherford, NJ	18 G (5.90, 0 saves)
6	California Angels	Erik Pappas	c	Mount Carmel HS	Chicago, IL	104 G (.242-1-35)
7	St. Louis Cardinals	Mike Dunne	rhp	Bradley	Bartonville, IL	85 G (25-30, 4.08)
8	Minnesota Twins	Jay Bell	ss	Gonzalez Tate HS	Pensacola, FL	1375 G (.268-104-553)
9	San Francisco Giants	Alan Cockrell	of	Tennessee	Knoxville, TN	Peaked in Triple-A
10	Oakland Athletics	Mark McGwire	1b	Southern California	Claremont, CA	1380 G (.260-387-983)
11	San Diego Padres	Shane Mack	of	UCLA	Cerritos, CA	854 G (.300-74-369)
12	Texas Rangers	Oddibe McDowell	of	Arizona State	Hollywood, FL	830 G (.253-74-266)
13	Montreal Expos	Bob Caffrey	c	Cal State Fullerton	Fullerton, CA	Peaked in Double-A
14	Boston Red Sox	John Marzano	c	Temple	Philadelphia, PA	251 G (.242-7-60)

Pick	Team	Player	Pos	School	Hometown	Major League Career
15	Pittsburgh Pirates	Kevin Andersh	lhp	New Mexico	Albuquerque, NM	Peaked in Double-A
16	Kansas City Royals	Scott Bankhead	rhp	North Carolina	Reidsville, NC	267 G (4.18, 1 saves)
17	Houston Astros	Don August	rhp	Chapman	Mission Viejo, CA	88 G (34-30, 4.64)
18	Milwaukee Brewers	Isaiah Clark	ss	Crockett HS	Crockett, TX	Peaked in Double-A
19	Atlanta Braves	Drew Denson	1b-of	Purcell Marion HS	Cincinnati, OH	16 G (.244-0-5)
20	Chicago White Sox	Tony Menendez	rhp	American HS	Carol City, FL	23 G (4.97, 0 saves)
21	Philadelphia Phillies	Pete Smith	rhp	Burlington HS	Burlington, MA	194 G (42-66, 4.46)
22	New York Yankees	Jeff Pries	rhp	UCLA	Newport Beach, CA	Peaked in Triple-A
23	Los Angeles Dodgers	Dennis Livingston	lhp	Oklahoma State	North Reading, MA	Peaked in Triple-A
24	San Francisco Giants	Terry Mulholland	lhp	Marietta	Uniontown, PA	303 G (87-102, 4.29)
25	Baltimore Orioles	John Hoover	rhp	Fresno State	Fresno, CA	2 G (11.57, 0 saves)
26	Chicago White Sox	Tom Hartley	of	Hudson Bay HS	Vancouver, WA	Peaked in Class-A

1985

The 1985 draft immediately was hailed as the best talent pool ever, and that assessment hasn't changed. Nineteen first-round picks reached the major leagues, and six became All-Stars. North Carolina catcher B.J. Surhoff went No. 1 to the Brewers, one of five 1984 U.S. Olympians to go in the first round. As steady as he became, he was surpassed by such stars as Mississippi State first baseman Will Clark (No. 2, Giants), Michigan shortstop Barry Larkin (No. 4, Reds), Arizona State outfielder Barry Bonds (No. 6, Pirates) and Mississippi State outfielder Rafael Palmeiro (No. 22, Cubs). Oklahoma State slugger Pete Incaviglia told the Expos he wouldn't sign with them, and they were forced to trade him to the Rangers after gambling on him with the eighth selection. Incaviglia immediately joined Texas' big league club the next year without spending a day in the minors. Afterward, Major League Baseball passed a rule forbidding teams from trading draftees until one year after their selection. There was talent later in the draft as well, as the Tigers landed Lansing, Mich., high school righthander John Smoltz with a 22nd-round pick and the Cubs found San Diego State first baseman Mark Grace two rounds later.

Pick	Team	Player	Pos	School	Hometown	Major League Career
1	Milwaukee Brewers	B.J. Surhoff	ss-c	North Carolina	Rye, NY	1392 G (.277-96-694)
2	San Francisco Giants	Will Clark	1b	Mississippi State	New Orleans, LA	1620 G (.302-230-1004)
3	Texas Rangers	Bobby Witt	rhp	Oklahoma	Canton, MA	346 G (124-131, 4.63)
4	Cincinnati Reds	Barry Larkin	ss	Michigan	Cincinnati, OH	1401 G (.299-139-646)
5	Chicago White Sox	Kurt Brown	c	Glendora HS	Glendora, CA	Peaked in Triple-A
6	Pittsburgh Pirates	Barry Bonds	of	Arizona State	San Carlos, CA	1742 G (.288-374-1094)
7	Seattle Mariners	Mike Campbell	rhp	Hawaii	Seattle, WA	51 G (12-19, 5.86)
8	Montreal Expos	Pete Incaviglia	of	Oklahoma State	Pebble Beach, CA	1264 G (.247-206-653)
9	Cleveland Indians	Mike Poehl	rhp	Texas	Houston, TX	Peaked in Double-A
10	Los Angeles Dodgers	Chris Gwynn	of	San Diego State	Long Beach, CA	599 G (.261-17-118)
11	Oakland Athletics	Walt Weiss	ss	North Carolina	Suffern, NY	1209 G (.258-23-312)
12	Houston Astros	Cameron Drew	of	New Haven	Yardville, NJ	7 G (.188-0-1)
13	Minnesota Twins	Jeff Bumgarner	rhp	Hanford HS	Richland, WA	Peaked in Triple-A
14	Atlanta Braves	Tommy Greene	rhp	Whiteville HS	Whiteville, NC	119 G (38-25, 4.14)
15	California Angels	Willie Fraser	rhp	Concordia	Newburgh, NY	239 G (4.47, 7 saves)
16	Philadelphia Phillies	Trey McCall	c	Abingdon HS	Abingdon, VA	Peaked in Class-A
17	Kansas City Royals	Brian McRae	ss	Manatee HS	Blue Springs, FL	1061 G (.265-70-405)
18	St. Louis Cardinals	Joe Magrane	lhp	Arizona	Morehead, KY	190 G (57-67, 3.81)
19	California Angels	Mike Cook	rhp	South Carolina	Charleston, SC	41 G (5.55, 0 saves)
20	New York Mets	Gregg Jefferies	ss	Serra HS	Millbrae, CA	1210 G (.291-109-573)
21	Boston Red Sox	Dan Gabriele	rhp	Western HS	Walled Lake, MI	Peaked in Double-A
22	Chicago Cubs	Rafael Palmeiro	of	Mississippi State	Miami, FL	1620 G (.294-271-958)
23	San Diego Padres	Joey Cora	ss	Vanderbilt	Caguas, PR	964 G (.277-24-262)
24	Chicago Cubs	Dave Masters	rhp	California	Honolulu, HI	Peaked in Triple-A
25	Toronto Blue Jays	Greg David	of	Barron Collier HS	Naples, FL	Peaked in Double-A
26	Detroit Tigers	Randy Nosek	rhp	Chillicothe HS	Chillicothe, MO	5 G (1-3, 10.22)

1986

The 1986 draft crop will be best remembered for Bo Jackson. The Heisman Trophy winner had been taken No. 1 in the NFL draft by the Tampa Bay Buccaneers, then stunned the sports world by signing with the Royals as a fourth-round pick. Every other team believed he would play football, but Kansas City did its homework and confirmed the Auburn outfielder's interest in baseball on the day of the draft. A month later he signed a three-year, $1.066 million contract that included a $100,000 signing bonus. Jackson reached the majors for good that September, though his career was more style than substance before it ended prematurely

Amateur Draft: First-Round Picks

due to complications from a hip injury suffered with the NFL's Los Angeles Raiders. As he did in both sports, Jackson overshadowed the rest of the draft. The first 13 players drafted, starting with Arkansas third baseman Jeff King by the Pirates, reached the majors, and most enjoyed extensive careers. Among them were Texas lefthander Greg Swindell (No. 2, Indians), Nevada-Las Vegas shortstop Matt Williams (No. 3, Giants), Georgia Tech righthander Kevin Brown (No. 4, Rangers) and Tampa high school outfielder Gary Sheffield (No. 6, Brewers).

Pick	Team	Player	Pos	School	Hometown	Major League Career
1	Pittsburgh Pirates	Jeff King	3b	Arkansas	Colorado Springs, CO	1049 G (.255-127-605)
2	Cleveland Indians	Greg Swindell	lhp	Texas	Houston, TX	358 G (110-102, 3.88)
3	San Francisco Giants	Matt Williams	ss	Nevada-Las Vegas	Carson City, NV	1271 G (.264-279-837)
4	Texas Rangers	Kevin Brown	rhp	Georgia Tech	McIntyre, GA	278 G (121-92, 3.42)
5	Atlanta Braves	Kent Mercker	lhp	Dublin HS	Dublin, OH	285 G (3.91, 19 saves)
6	Milwaukee Brewers	Gary Sheffield	ss	Hillsborough HS	Tampa, FL	1026 G (.286-180-621)
7	Philadelphia Phillies	Brad Brink	rhp	Southern California	Modesto, CA	14 G (0-4, 3.56)
8	Seattle Mariners	Patrick Lennon	ss	Whiteville HS	Whiteville, NC	80 G (.269-1-16)
9	Chicago Cubs	Derrick May	of	Newark HS	Newark, DE	686 G (.274-43-283)
10	Minnesota Twins	Derek Parks	c	Montclair HS	Upland, CA	45 G (.200-1-10)
11	San Diego Padres	Thomas Howard	of	Ball State	Germantown, OH	784 G (.267-30-204)
12	Oakland Athletics	Scott Hemond	c	South Florida	Dunedin, FL	298 G (.217-12-58)
13	Houston Astros	Ryan Bowen	rhp	Hanford HS	Hanford, CA	64 G (17-28, 5.30)
14	Boston Red Sox	*Greg McMurtry	of	Brockton HS	Brockton, MA	Never played pro ball
15	Montreal Expos	Kevin Dean	of	Hogan HS	Vallejo, CA	Peaked in Triple-A
16	California Angels	Roberto Hernandez	rhp	South Carolina-Aiken	New York City, NY	373 G (2.84, 165 saves)
17	Cincinnati Reds	Scott Scudder	rhp	Prairiland HS	Blossom, TX	96 G (21-34, 4.80)
18	Detroit Tigers	Phil Clark	c	Crockett HS	Crockett, TX	264 G (.276-17-65)
19	Los Angeles Dodgers	Mike White	of	Loudon HS	Loudon, TN	Peaked in Triple-A
20	Chicago White Sox	Grady Hall	lhp	Northwestern	Findlay, OH	Peaked in Triple-A
21	New York Mets	Lee May	of	Purcell Marion HS	Cincinnati, OH	Peaked in Triple-A
22	California Angels	Lee Stevens	of	Lawrence HS	Lawrence, KS	355 G (.254-38-164)
23	St. Louis Cardinals	Luis Alicea	2b	Florida State	Guaynabo, PR	826 G (.255-27-254)
24	Kansas City Royals	Tony Clements	ss	Don Lugo HS	Chino, CA	Peaked in Double-A
25	California Angels	Terry Carr	of	Bennett HS	Salisbury, MD	Peaked in Class-A
26	Toronto Blue Jays	Earl Sanders	rhp	Jackson State	Moss Point, MS	Peaked in Double-A

* Did not sign.

1987

The Mariners had the top pick for the third time in nine years, and this time they hit the jackpot. Scouting director Roger Jongewaard, the Mets scout who convinced New York to draft Darryl Strawberry with the first selection in 1980, persuaded Seattle owner George Argyros to let him draft a Cincinnati high school outfielder rather than a more polished college player. The outfielder was Ken Griffey Jr., the best No. 1 pick ever. Griffey would join the Mariners for good two years later at age 19. Another outfielder with big-time power lasted until the second round because of repeated discipline problems, but the Indians were ultimately happy with Louisiana State's Albert Belle. Twenty of 26 first-rounders would play in the big leagues, including Stanford righthander Jack McDowell (No. 5 , White Sox), Antelope Valley (Calif.) Junior College righthander Kevin Appier (No. 9, Royals) and Seton Hall catcher Craig Biggio (No. 22, Astros).

Pick	Team	Player	Pos	School	Hometown	Major League Career
1	Seattle Mariners	Ken Griffey Jr.	of	Moeller HS	Cincinnati, OH	1214 G (.302-294-872)
2	Pittsburgh Pirates	Mark Merchant	of	Oviedo HS	Oviedo, FL	Peaked in Triple-A
3	Minnesota Twins	Willie Banks	rhp	St. Anthony's HS	Jersey City, NJ	105 G (29-35, 4.94)
4	Chicago Cubs	Mike Harkey	rhp	Cal State Fullerton	Diamond Bar, CA	131 G (36-36, 4.49)
5	Chicago White Sox	Jack McDowell	rhp	Stanford	Van Nuys, CA	259 G (122-80, 3.76)
6	Atlanta Braves	Derek Lilliquist	lhp	Georgia	Sarasota, FL	262 G (4.13, 17 saves)
7	Baltimore Orioles	Chris Myers	lhp	Plant HS	Tampa, FL	Peaked in Triple-A
8	Los Angeles Dodgers	Dan Opperman	rhp	Valley HS	Las Vegas, NV	Peaked in Triple-A
9	Kansas City Royals	Kevin Appier	rhp	Antelope Valley (CA) JC	Lancaster, CA	256 G (104-78, 3.30)
10	San Diego Padres	Kevin Garner	rhp-of	Texas	Midland, MI	Peaked in Triple-A
11	Oakland Athletics	Lee Tinsley	of	Shelby County HS	Shelbyville, KY	361 G (.241-13-79)
12	Montreal Expos	Delino DeShields	ss-2b	Seaford HS	Seaford, DE	1058 G (.268-49-350)
13	Milwaukee Brewers	Bill Spiers	ss	Clemson	Cameron, SC	874 G (.262-26-263)
14	St. Louis Cardinals	Cris Carpenter	rhp	Georgia	Gainesville, GA	291 G (3.91, 7 saves)
15	Baltimore Orioles	*Brad DuVall	rhp	Virginia Tech	Silver Spring, MD	Peaked in Class-A
16	San Francisco Giants	Mike Remlinger	lhp	Dartmouth	Plymouth, MA	113 G (4.51, 2 saves)
17	Toronto Blue Jays	Alex Sanchez	rhp	UCLA	Antioch, CA	4 G (0-1, 10.03)
18	Cincinnati Reds	Jack Armstrong	rhp	Oklahoma	Neptune, NJ	152 G (40-65, 4.58)
19	Texas Rangers	Brian Bohanon	lhp	North Shore HS	Houston, TX	178 G (5.35, 2 saves)
20	Detroit Tigers	Bill Henderson	c	Westminster Christian HS	Miami, FL	Peaked in Class-A
21	Detroit Tigers	Steve Pegues	of	Pontotoc HS	Pontotoc, MS	100 G (.266-6-18)

Pick	Team	Player	Pos	School	Hometown	Major League Career
22	Houston Astros	Craig Biggio	c	Seton Hall	Kings Park, NY	1379 G (.288-116-545)
23	Texas Rangers	Bill Haselman	c	UCLA	Saratoga, CA	319 G (.246-25-110)
24	New York Mets	Chris Donnels	3b	Loyola Marymount	Torrance, CA	283 G (.238-7-53)
25	California Angels	John Orton	c	Cal Poly San Luis Obispo	Santa Cruz, CA	156 G (.200-4-29)
26	Boston Red Sox	Reggie Harris	rhp	Waynesboro HS	Waynesboro, VA	72 G (5.07, 0 saves)

* Did not sign.

1988

Twenty-four years after Rick Reichardt signed for $204,000 and led to the creation of the draft, his bonus standard finally was topped. Evansville righthander Andy Benes, one of nine U.S. Olympians drafted in the first round, signed with the Padres for $235,000 as the top choice. In less than a year, he was established in San Diego's rotation. Michigan lefthander Jim Abbott, picked ninth by the Angels, won the Olympic gold-medal game in 1988 and then went straight to California without spending a day in the minors. His 12 big league victories in 1989 were the most ever by a first-year professional. One of the top players to come out of the draft had played little baseball at Arizona, where he was a star guard on the basketball team. The Astros grabbed outfielder Kenny Lofton in the 17th round, then sent him to Cleveland in an ill-advised trade three years later. Another two-sport star went 13 rounds later to the Yankees. Florida State outfielder Deion Sanders signed and had his moments in baseball, but became better known as an All-Pro cornerback in the NFL. An even better late-round selection, and perhaps the best ever, came when the Dodgers spent their 62nd-round and final pick on Miami-Dade North Community College first baseman Mike Piazza.

Pick	Team	Player	Pos	School	Hometown	Major League Career
1	San Diego Padres	Andy Benes	rhp	Evansville	Evansville, IN	261 G (104-94, 3.64)
2	Cleveland Indians	Mark Lewis	ss	Hamilton HS	Hamilton, OH	584 G (.270-31-200)
3	Atlanta Braves	Steve Avery	lhp	Kennedy HS	Taylor, MI	225 G (78-69, 4.02)
4	Baltimore Orioles	Gregg Olson	rhp	Auburn	Omaha, NE	456 G (3.20, 173 saves)
5	Los Angeles Dodgers	Bill Bene	rhp	Cal State Los Angeles	Long Beach, CA	Peaked in Triple-A
6	Texas Rangers	Monty Fariss	ss	Oklahoma State	Leedey, OK	104 G (.217-4-29)
7	Houston Astros	Willie Ansley	of	Plainview HS	Plainview, TX	Peaked in Triple-A
8	California Angels	Jim Abbott	lhp	Michigan	Flint, MI	238 G (80-100, 4.11)
9	Chicago Cubs	Ty Griffin	2b	Georgia Tech	Tampa, FL	Peaked in Double-A
10	Chicago White Sox	Robin Ventura	3b	Oklahoma State	Santa Maria, CA	1093 G (.276-150-650)
11	Philadelphia Phillies	Pat Combs	lhp	Baylor	Houston, TX	56 G (17-17, 4.22)
12	Boston Red Sox	Tom Fischer	lhp	Wisconsin	West Bend, WI	Peaked in Triple-A
13	Pittsburgh Pirates	Austin Manahan	ss	Horizon HS	Phoenix, AZ	Peaked in Double-A
14	Seattle Mariners	Tino Martinez	1b	Tampa	Tampa, FL	856 G (.276-157-570)
15	San Francisco Giants	Royce Clayton	ss	St. Bernard HS	Playa del Rey, CA	789 G (.257-33-280)
16	Oakland Athletics	Stan Royer	3b	Eastern Illinois	Charleston, IL	89 G (.250-4-21)
17	Cleveland Indians	Charles Nagy	rhp	Connecticut	Fairfield, CT	202 G (89-65, 3.93)
18	Kansas City Royals	Hugh Walker	of	Jacksonville HS	Jacksonville, AR	Peaked in Double-A
19	Montreal Expos	Dave Wainhouse	rhp	Washington State	Mercer Island, WA	47 G (7.78, 0 saves)
20	Minnesota Twins	Johnny Ard	rhp	Manatee (FL) JC	Hemingway, SC	Peaked in Triple-A
21	New York Mets	Dave Proctor	rhp	Allen County (KS) CC	Topeka, KS	Peaked in Double-A
22	St. Louis Cardinals	John Ericks	rhp	Illinois	Tinley Park, IL	57 G (4.78, 14 saves)
23	St. Louis Cardinals	Brad DuVall	rhp	Virginia Tech	Silver Spring, MD	Peaked in Class-A
24	Milwaukee Brewers	*Alex Fernandez	rhp	Pace HS	Miami, FL	231 G (96-75, 3.76)
25	Toronto Blue Jays	Ed Sprague	3b	Stanford	Stockton, CA	783 G (.246-96-367)
26	Detroit Tigers	Rico Brogna	1b	Watertown HS	Watertown, CT	385 G (.274-57-210)

* Did not sign.

1989

Benes' Olympic roommate, Louisiana State righthander Ben McDonald, had been pegged as 1989's top pick the year before. The twist was that the Orioles were in first place when they made McDonald the No. 1 choice, the only time that happened in draft history. McDonald held out for most of the summer before signing a three-year package worth $825,000 (including a $350,000 bonus), then joined Baltimore in September. Washington State first baseman John Olerud might have given McDonald a run for the top spot had he not been sidelined by a potentially fatal aneurysm near the base of his brain in January. He told teams he intended to return to college, but the Blue Jays drafted him in the third round and signed him for a package similar to McDonald's, including a record $575,000 bonus. Olerud never played a day in the minors and was starting for Toronto by 1990. While both McDonald and Olerud had solid careers, the prize of the draft turned out to be Auburn first baseman Frank Thomas, selected seventh by the White Sox. The Red Sox snagged a pair of future MVPs in Seton Hall first baseman Mo Vaughn (first round) and Hartford third baseman Jeff Bagwell (fourth). The Twins also had a strong draft, landing Texas A&M shortstop Chuck Knoblauch (first round), Minnesota lefthander Denny Neagle (third), Arizona righthander Scott Erickson (fourth) and Orange Coast (Calif.) Junior College outfielder Marty Cordova (10th). Fresno State matched Michigan's 1979 standard with three first-rounders: outfielder Steve Hosey (No. 14 , Giants), shortstop Eddie Zosky (No. 19, Blue Jays) and outfielder Tom Goodwin (No. 22, Dodgers).

Pick	Team	Player	Pos	School	Hometown	Major League Career
1	Baltimore Orioles	Ben McDonald	rhp	Louisiana State	Denham Springs, LA	211 G (78-70, 3.91)
2	Atlanta Braves	Tyler Houston	c	Valley HS	Las Vegas, NV	151 G (.284-5-55)
3	Seattle Mariners	Roger Salkeld	rhp	Saugus HS	Saugus, CA	45 G (10-10, 5.61)
4	Philadelphia Phillies	Jeff Jackson	of	Simeon HS	Chicago, IL	Peaked in Double-A
5	Texas Rangers	Donald Harris	of	Texas Tech	Lubbock, TX	82 G (.205-2-11)
6	St. Louis Cardinals	Paul Coleman	of	Frankston HS	Frankston, TX	Peaked in Double-A
7	Chicago White Sox	Frank Thomas	1b	Auburn	Columbus, GA	1076 G (.330-257-854)
8	Chicago Cubs	Earl Cunningham	of	Lancaster HS	Lancaster, SC	Peaked in Class-A
9	California Angels	Kyle Abbott	lhp	Long Beach State	Mission Viejo, CA	57 G (5.20, 0 saves)
10	Montreal Expos	*Charles Johnson	c	Westwood HS	Fort Pierce, FL	345 G (.241-44-143)
11	Cleveland Indians	*Calvin Murray	3b	White HS	Dallas, TX	Peaked in Triple-A
12	Houston Astros	Jeff Juden	rhp	Salem HS	Salem, MA	113 G (4.36, 0 saves)
13	Kansas City Royals	Brent Mayne	c	Cal State Fullerton	Costa Mesa, CA	554 G (.255-15-147)
14	San Francisco Giants	Steve Hosey	of	Fresno State	Inglewood, CA	24 G (.259-1-7)
15	Los Angeles Dodgers	Kiki Jones	rhp	Hillsborough HS	Tampa, FL	Peaked in Double-A
16	Boston Red Sox	Greg Blosser	of	Sarasota HS	Sarasota, FL	22 G (.077-0-2)
17	Milwaukee Brewers	Cal Eldred	rhp	Iowa	Urbana, IA	131 G (58-49, 4.16)
18	Pittsburgh Pirates	Willie Greene	ss	Jones County HS	Gray, GA	334 G (.243-49-175)
19	Toronto Blue Jays	Eddie Zosky	ss	Fresno State	Whittier, CA	32 G (.179-0-3)
20	Cincinnati Reds	Scott Bryant	of-rhp	Texas	San Antonio, TX	Peaked in Triple-A
21	Detroit Tigers	Greg Gohr	rhp	Santa Clara	Campbell, CA	66 G (6.21, 1 saves)
22	Los Angeles Dodgers	Tom Goodwin	of	Fresno State	Fresno, CA	531 G (.273-7-106)
23	Boston Red Sox	Maurice Vaughn	1b	Seton Hall	Norwalk, CT	892 G (.298-190-637)
24	New York Mets	Alan Zinter	c	Arizona	El Paso, TX	Peaked in Triple-A
25	Minnesota Twins	Chuck Knoblauch	ss	Texas A&M	Houston, TX	1013 G (.304-43-391)
26	Seattle Mariners	*Scott Burrell	rhp	Hamden HS	Hamden, CT	Peaked in Double-A

* Did not sign.

1990

The most coveted prospect was Arlington, Texas, righthander Todd Van Poppel, who insisted he wanted to pitch for the University of Texas. Convinced they couldn't sign him, the Braves settled on a Jacksonville prep shortstop with the top pick. Van Poppel went 14th to the Athletics, who wooed him with a $1.2 million contract, including a $500,000 bonus. When the Braves' shortstop hit .229 in the Gulf Coast League, they were second-guessed. Ultimately, Chipper Jones would prove to be a much better player than Van Poppel. A record 21 first-rounders eventually reached the majors, including righthander Alex Fernandez (No. 4 , White Sox) and lefthander Lance Dickson (No. 23, Cubs) later in 1990.

Pick	Team	Player	Pos	School	Hometown	Major League Career
1	Atlanta Braves	Chipper Jones	ss	Bolles HS	Pearson, FL	462 G (.292-74-307)
2	Detroit Tigers	Tony Clark	of	Christian HS	El Cajon, CA	286 G (.263-62-200)
3	Philadelphia Phillies	Mike Lieberthal	c	Westlake HS	Westlake Village, CA	224 G (.250-28-109)
4	Chicago White Sox	Alex Fernandez	rhp	Miami-Dade CC South	Miami, FL	231 G (96-75, 3.76)
5	Pittsburgh Pirates	Kurt Miller	rhp	West HS	Bakersfield, CA	37 G (7.45, 0 saves)
6	Seattle Mariners	Mark Newfield	1b	Marina HS	Huntington Beach, CA	262 G (.252-19-107)
7	Cincinnati Reds	Dan Wilson	c	Minnesota	Barrington, IL	542 G (.267-45-246)
8	Cleveland Indians	Tim Costo	ss	Iowa	Glen Ellyn, IL	43 G (.224-3-14)
9	Los Angeles Dodgers	Ron Walden	lhp	Blanchard HS	Blanchard, OK	Peaked in Class-A
10	New York Yankees	Carl Everett	of	Hillsborough HS	Tampa, FL	349 G (.245-29-133)
11	Montreal Expos	Shane Andrews	3b	Carlsbad HS	Carlsbad, NM	229 G (.220-31-104)
12	Minnesota Twins	Todd Ritchie	rhp	Duncanville HS	Duncanville, TX	42 G (4.58, 0 saves)
13	St. Louis Cardinals	Donovan Osborne	lhp	Nevada-Las Vegas	Carson City, NV	123 G (41-38, 3.84)
14	Oakland Athletics	Todd Van Poppel	rhp	Martin HS	Arlington, TX	113 G (20-33, 6.22)
15	San Francisco Giants	Adam Hyzdu	of	Moeller HS	Cincinnati, OH	Peaked in Triple-A
16	Texas Rangers	Dan Smith	lhp	Creighton	Apple Valley, MN	17 G (4.66, 0 saves)
17	New York Mets	Jeromy Burnitz	of	Oklahoma State	Conroe, TX	387 G (.266-52-178)
18	St. Louis Cardinals	Aaron Holbert	ss	Jordan HS	Long Beach, CA	1 G (.000-0-0)
19	San Francisco Giants	Eric Christopherson	c	San Diego State	Huntington Beach, CA	Peaked in Triple-A
20	Baltimore Orioles	Mike Mussina	rhp	Stanford	Montoursville, PA	194 G (105-49, 3.50)
21	Houston Astros	Tom Nevers	ss	Edina HS	Edina, MN	Peaked in Triple-A
22	Toronto Blue Jays	Steve Karsay	rhp	Christ the King HS	Queens, NY	36 G (7-16, 4.94)
23	Chicago Cubs	Lance Dickson	lhp	Arizona	La Mesa, CA	3 G (0-3, 7.24)
24	Montreal Expos	Rondell White	of	Jones County HS	Gray, GA	432 G (.283-51-208)
25	San Diego Padres	Robbie Beckett	lhp	McCallum HS	Austin, TX	7 G (11.57, 0 saves)
26	Oakland Athletics	Don Peters	rhp	St. Francis	Crestwood, IL	Peaked in Double-A

Amateur Draft: First-Round Picks

1991

Bonuses were rising rapidly, and after 1991 there would be no turning back. Hours before No. 1 pick Brien Taylor would have attended classes at Louisburg (N.C.) Junior College, the Yankees gave the Beaufort, N.C., high school lefthander a stunning $1.55 million bonus. Taylor had two strong minor league seasons before injuring his left shoulder in a fight after the 1993 season, and he never was the same again. He's in danger of becoming the only top selection to not reach Triple-A. Fourteen other first-round choices received $300,000 or more, with Tustin, Calif., prep outfielder Shawn Green getting $700,000 from the Blue Jays as the 16th pick. The best player in the draft proved to be Indians outfielder Manny Ramirez, the 13th choice.

Pick	Team	Player	Pos	School	Hometown	Major League Career
1	New York Mets	Brien Taylor	lhp	East Carteret HS	Beaufort, NC	Peaked in Double-A
2	Atlanta Braves	Mike Kelly	of	Arizona State	Los Alamitos, CA	219 G (.241-12-52)
3	Minnesota Twins	David McCarty	1b	Stanford	Houston, TX	270 G (.224-9-63)
4	St. Louis Cardinals	Dmitri Young	3b	Rio Mesa HS	Oxnard, CA	126 G (.257-5-36)
5	Milwaukee Brewers	*Kenny Henderson	rhp	Ringgold HS	Ringgold, GA	Peaked in Class-A
6	Houston Astros	*John Burke	rhp	Florida	Littleton, CO	28 G (6.75, 0 saves)
7	Kansas City Royals	Joe Vitiello	1b-of	Alabama	Stoneham, MA	189 G (.244-20-79)
8	San Diego Padres	Joey Hamilton	rhp	Georgia Southern	Statesboro, GA	112 G (42-31, 3.70)
9	Baltimore Orioles	Mark Smith	of	Southern California	Arcadia, CA	138 G (.259-16-62)
10	Philadelphia Phillies	Tyler Green	rhp	Wichita State	Denver, CO	43 G (12-13, 5.25)
11	Seattle Mariners	Sean Estes	lhp	Minden HS	Douglas, NV	46 G (22-13, 3.50)
12	Chicago Cubs	Doug Glanville	of	Pennsylvania	Teaneck, NJ	195 G (.291-5-45)
13	Cleveland Indians	Manny Ramirez	of	George Washington HS	New York, NY	552 G (.304-109-372)
14	Montreal Expos	Cliff Floyd	1b	Thornwood HS	South Holland, IL	317 G (.247-18-96)
15	Milwaukee Brewers	Tyrone Hill	lhp	Yucaipa HS	Yucaipa, CA	Peaked in Class-A
16	Toronto Blue Jays	Shawn Green	of	Tustin HS	Tustin, CA	405 G (.278-42-153)
17	California Angels	Eduardo Perez	1b	Florida State	Santruce, PR	243 G (.234-29-110)
18	New York Mets	Al Shirley	of	George Washington HS	Danville, VA	Peaked in Double-A
19	Texas Rangers	Benji Gil	ss	Castle Park HS	Chula Vista, CA	267 G (.215-14-80)
20	Cincinnati Reds	Calvin Reese	ss	Lower Richland HS	Hopkins, SC	128 G (.219-4-26)
21	St. Louis Cardinals	Allen Watson	lhp	New York Tech	Middle Village, NY	123 G (39-45, 4.91)
22	St. Louis Cardinals	Brian Barber	rhp	Dr. Phillips HS	Orlando, FL	10 G (2-1, 6.12)
23	Boston Red Sox	Aaron Sele	rhp	Washington State	Poulsbo, WA	108 G (38-33, 4.41)
24	Pittsburgh Pirates	Jon Farrell	c-of	Florida CC	Jacksonville, FL	Peaked in Double-A
25	Chicago White Sox	Scott Ruffcorn	rhp	Baylor	Austin, TX	30 G (8.57, 0 saves)
26	Oakland Athletics	Brent Gates	ss	Minnesota	Grandville, MI	468 G (.269-19-199)

* Did not sign.

1992

The extent to which money now mattered was reinforced when the first three teams passed on Stanford outfielder Jeffrey Hammonds, the consensus top prospect. Hammonds got $975,000 as the No. 4 choice by the Orioles, while Cal State Fullerton third baseman Phil Nevin received $700,000 as the top pick by the Astros. Neither player has panned out as expected, with Nevin a particular disappointment. The first high school player chosen was Kalamazoo, Mich., shortstop Derek Jeter, who went sixth to the Yankees and has been the draft's best player. Catchers drafted in the first round rarely fare well, but the Pirates and Marlins found exceptions with Torrance, Calif., prepster Jason Kendall (No. 23) and Miami's Charles Johnson (No. 28), respectively. Nevin, Hammonds and Johnson were three of 11 U.S. Olympians taken in the first round.

Pick	Team	Player	Pos	School	Hometown	Major League Career
1	Houston Astros	Phil Nevin	3b	Cal State Fullerton	Placentia, CA	178 G (.231-19-67)
2	Cleveland Indians	Paul Shuey	rhp	North Carolina	Raleigh, NC	103 G (4.78, 11 saves)
3	Montreal Expos	B.J. Wallace	lhp	Mississippi State	Monroeville, AL	Peaked in Double-A
4	Baltimore Orioles	Jeffrey Hammonds	of	Stanford	Scotch Plains, NJ	347 G (.263-45-155)
5	Cincinnati Reds	Chad Mottola	of	Central Florida	Pembroke Pines, FL	35 G (.215-3-6)
6	New York Yankees	Derek Jeter	of	Central HS	Kalamazoo, MI	331 G (.300-20-155)
7	San Francisco Giants	Calvin Murray	of	Texas	Dallas, TX	Peaked in Triple-A
8	California Angels	Pete Janicki	rhp	UCLA	Placentia, CA	Peaked in Triple-A
9	New York Mets	Preston Wilson	of	Bamberg-Ehrhardt HS	Bamberg, SC	Peaked in Double-A
10	Kansas City Royals	Michael Tucker	ss	Longwood	Chase City, VA	308 G (.271-30-126)
11	Chicago Cubs	Derek Wallace	rhp	Pepperdine	Oxnard, CA	19 G (4.01, 3 saves)
12	Milwaukee Brewers	Kenny Felder	of	Florida State	Niceville, FL	Peaked in Triple-A
13	Philadelphia Phillies	Chad McConnell	of	Creighton	Sioux Falls, SD	Peaked in Triple-A
14	Seattle Mariners	Ron Villone	lhp	Massachusetts	Bergenfield, NJ	132 G (4.09, 3 saves)
15	St. Louis Cardinals	Sean Lowe	rhp	Arizona State	Mesquite, TX	Peaked in Triple-A
16	Detroit Tigers	Rick Greene	rhp	Louisiana State	Miami, FL	Peaked in Triple-A
17	Kansas City Royals	Jim Pittsley	rhp	DuBois Area HS	DuBois, PA	22 G (5-8, 5.70)

Amateur Draft: First-Round Picks

Pick	Team	Player	Pos	School	Hometown	Major League Career
18	New York Mets	Chris Roberts	lhp	Florida State	Middleburg, FL	Peaked in Triple-A
19	Toronto Blue Jays	Shannon Stewart	of	Southridge HS	Miami, FL	63 G (.265-0-25)
20	Oakland Athletics	Benji Grigsby	rhp	San Diego State	Lafayette, LA	Peaked in Triple-A
21	Atlanta Braves	Jamie Arnold	rhp	Osceola HS	Kissimmee, FL	Peaked in Double-A
22	Texas Rangers	Rick Helling	rhp	Stanford	Fargo, ND	64 G (11-16, 4.85)
23	Pittsburgh Pirates	Jason Kendall	c	Torrance HS	Torrance, CA	274 G (.297-11-91)
24	Chicago White Sox	Eddie Pearson	1b	Bishop State (AL) JC	Mobile, AL	Peaked in Triple-A
25	Toronto Blue Jays	Todd Steverson	of	Arizona State	Inglewood, CA	31 G (.256-2-6)
26	Minnesota Twins	Dan Serafini	lhp	Serra HS	San Mateo, CA	7 G (2-2, 4.40)
27	Colorado Rockies	John Burke	rhp	Florida	Englewood, CO	28 G (6.75, 0 saves)
28	Florida Marlins	Charles Johnson	c	Miami	Fort Pierce, FL	345 G (.241-44-143)

1993

Six years after landing the best No. 1 pick ever in Ken Griffey Jr., the Mariners grabbed the second-best in high school shortstop Alex Rodriguez. He held out most of the summer before signing for $1 million, and reached Seattle at the end of his first pro season in 1994. Wichita State righthander Darren Dreifort, who was picked second by the Dodgers, signed shortly after Rodriguez for $1.3 million and went straight to Los Angeles when he made his pro debut in 1994. All in all, it was not a particularly deep draft. Five years later, Rodriguez and Dreifort were the only top-10 choices with much of an upside.

Pick	Team	Player	Pos	School	Hometown	Major League Career
1	Seattle Mariners	Alex Rodriguez	ss	Westminster Christian HS	Miami, FL	352 G (.314-64-228)
2	Los Angeles Dodgers	Darren Dreifort	rhp	Wichita State	Wichita, KS	94 G (4.12, 10 saves)
3	California Angels	Brian Anderson	lhp	Wright State	Geneva, OH	58 G (20-16, 5.25)
4	Philadelphia Phillies	Wayne Gomes	rhp	Old Dominion	Hampton, VA	37 G (5.27, 0 saves)
5	Kansas City Royals	Jeff Granger	lhp	Texas A&M	Orange, TX	27 G (9.09, 0 saves)
6	San Francisco Giants	Steve Soderstrom	rhp	Fresno State	Turlock, CA	3 G (2-0, 5.27)
7	Boston Red Sox	Trot Nixon	of	New Hanover HS	Wilmington, NC	2 G (.500-0-0)
8	New York Mets	Kirk Presley	rhp	Tupelo HS	Tupelo, MS	Peaked in Class-A
9	Detroit Tigers	Matt Brunson	ss	Cherry Creek HS	Englewood, CO	Peaked in Class-A
10	Chicago Cubs	Brooks Kieschnick	1b-of	Texas	Corpus Christi, TX	64 G (.235-5-18)
11	Cleveland Indians	Daron Kirkreit	rhp	California-Riverside	Norco, CA	Peaked in Triple-A
12	Houston Astros	Billy Wagner	lhp	Ferrum	Tazewell, VA	100 G (2.66, 32 saves)
13	New York Yankees	Matt Drews	rhp	Sarasota HS	Sarasota, FL	Peaked in Triple-A
14	San Diego Padres	Derrek Lee	1b	El Camino HS	Sacramento, CA	22 G (.259-1-4)
15	Toronto Blue Jays	Chris Carpenter	rhp	Trinity HS	Manchester, NH	14 G (3-7, 5.09)
16	St. Louis Cardinals	Alan Benes	rhp	Creighton	Lake Forest, IL	60 G (23-21, 4.17)
17	Chicago White Sox	Scott Christman	lhp	Oregon State	Tualatin, OR	Peaked in Double-A
18	Montreal Expos	Chris Schwab	of	Cretin-Derham HS	Eagan, MN	Peaked in Class-A
19	Baltimore Orioles	Jay Powell	rhp	Mississippi State	Collinsville, MS	150 G (3.73, 4 saves)
20	Minnesota Twins	Torii Hunter	of	Pine Bluff HS	Pine Bluff, AR	1 G (--0-0)
21	Minnesota Twins	*Jason Varitek	c	Georgia Tech	Altamonte Springs, FL	1 G (1.000-0-0)
22	Pittsburgh Pirates	Charles Peterson	of	Laurens HS	Laurens, SC	Peaked in Double-A
23	Milwaukee Brewers	Jeff D'Amico	rhp	Northeast HS	St. Petersburg, FL	40 G (15-13, 4.99)
24	Chicago Cubs	Jon Ratliff	rhp	LeMoyne	Clay, NY	Peaked in Triple-A
25	Oakland Athletics	John Wasdin	rhp	Florida State	Tallahassee, FL	83 G (5.17, 0 saves)
26	Milwaukee Brewers	Kelly Wunsch	lhp	Texas A&M	Houston, TX	Peaked in Class-A
27	Florida Marlins	Marc Valdes	rhp	Florida	Tampa, FL	62 G (4.18, 2 saves)
28	Colorado Rockies	Jamey Wright	rhp	Westmoore HS	Oklahoma City, OK	42 G (12-16, 5.75)

* Did not sign.

1994

Florida State righthander Paul Wilson tied Brien Taylor's bonus mark of $1.55 million as the top choice by the Mets, and a few weeks later No. 5 pick Josh Booty topped them both. A Shreveport, La., high school shortstop who was also the nation's top high school quarterback, Booty gave up the gridiron for $1.6 million from the Marlins. Unlike in 1993, big money didn't buy results. Wilson made New York's Opening Day rotation in 1996, but hurt his shoulder and has yet to recover. Booty never has made consistent contact, though he has surfaced briefly in Florida. Arlington, Texas, prep outfielder Ben Grieve went second to the Athletics, making him and father Tom (the No. 6 pick in 1966 by the Washington Senators) the first father-son duo each selected in the first round. By 1998, Grieve, Georgia Tech shortstop Nomar Garciaparra (No. 12 , Red Sox) and Scottsdale, Ariz., high school catcher Paul Konerko (No. 13, Dodgers) were considered the class of this draft. Garciaparra's college teammate, catcher Jason Varitek, was taken 14th by the Mariners after not signing as a Twins first-rounder the year before. Varitek turned pro with

Amateur Draft: First-Round Picks

the independent St. Paul Saints before agreeing to a $650,000 bonus with Seattle in 1995. Prep catcher Ramon Castro became the first Puerto Rican taken in the first round since that nation's players became eligible for the draft in 1989, going 17th to the Astros.

Pick	Team	Player	Pos	School	Hometown	Major League Career
1	New York Mets	Paul Wilson	rhp	Florida State	Orlando, FL	26 G (5-12, 5.38)
2	Oakland Athletics	Ben Grieve	of	Martin HS	Arlington, TX	24 G (.312-3-24)
3	San Diego Padres	Dustin Hermanson	rhp	Kent	Springfield, OH	66 G (4.51, 0 saves)
4	Milwaukee Brewers	Antone Williamson	3b	Arizona State	Torrance, CA	24 G (.204-0-6)
5	Florida Marlins	Josh Booty	ss	Evangel Christian HS	Shreveport, LA	6 G (.571-0-1)
6	California Angels	McKay Christensen	of	Clovis West HS	Fresno, CA	Peaked in Class-A
7	Colorado Rockies	Doug Million	lhp	Sarasota HS	Sarasota, FL	Peaked in Double-A
8	Minnesota Twins	Todd Walker	2b	Louisiana State	Bossier City, LA	77 G (.244-3-22)
9	Cincinnati Reds	C.J. Nitkowski	lhp	St. John's	Suffern, NY	31 G (4-10, 7.21)
10	Cleveland Indians	Jaret Wright	rhp	Katella HS	Anaheim, CA	16 G (8-3, 4.38)
11	Pittsburgh Pirates	Mark Farris	ss	Angleton HS	Angleton, TX	Peaked in Class-A
12	Boston Red Sox	Nomar Garciaparra	ss	Georgia Tech	Whittier, CA	177 G (.298-34-114)
13	Los Angeles Dodgers	Paul Konerko	c	Chapparal HS	Scottsdale, AZ	6 G (.143-0-0)
14	Seattle Mariners	Jason Varitek	c	Georgia Tech	Altamonte Springs, FL	1 G (1.000-0-0)
15	Chicago Cubs	Jayson Peterson	rhp	East HS	Denver, CO	Peaked in Class-A
16	Kansas City Royals	Matt Smith	lhp-1b	Grants Pass HS	Grants Pass, OR	Peaked in Double-A
17	Houston Astros	Ramon Castro	c	Rivera HS	Vega Baja, PR	Peaked in Class-A
18	Detroit Tigers	Cade Gaspar	rhp	Pepperdine	Mission Viejo, CA	Peaked in Class-A
19	St. Louis Cardinals	Bret Wagner	lhp	Wake Forest	New Cumberland, PA	Peaked in Double-A
20	New York Mets	Terrence Long	1b	Stanhope Elmore HS	Millbrook, AL	Peaked in Class-A
21	Montreal Expos	Hiram Bocachica	ss	Rexville HS	Bayamon, PR	Peaked in Double-A
22	San Francisco Giants	Dante Powell	of	Cal State Fullerton	Long Beach, CA	27 G (.308-1-3)
23	Philadelphia Phillies	Carlton Loewer	rhp	Mississippi State	Eunice, LA	Peaked in Triple-A
24	New York Yankees	Brian Buchanan	1b-of	Virginia	Clifton, VA	Peaked in Triple-A
25	Houston Astros	Scott Elarton	rhp	Lamar HS	Lamar, CO	Peaked in Triple-A
26	Chicago White Sox	Mark Johnson	c	Warner Robins HS	Warner Robins, GA	Peaked in Class-A
27	Atlanta Braves	Jacob Shumate	rhp	Hartsville HS	Hartsville, SC	Peaked in Class-A
28	Toronto Blue Jays	Kevin Witt	ss	Bishop Kenny HS	Jacksonville, FL	Peaked in Double-A

1995

Nebraska outfielder Darin Erstad didn't break any bonus records, getting $1.575 million from the Angels as the No. 1 pick, but he was in Anaheim for good less than a year after he signed. Three years later, he was an All-Star. Tennessee first baseman Todd Helton (No. 8, Rockies) was the only other player holding down an everyday job in the majors. Grand Prairie, Texas, high school righthander Kerry Wood, the No. 4 choice by the Cubs, was one of the most talked-about pitching phenoms in years when he made his Chicago debut at age 20 in 1998. Interestingly, the biggest buzz at the time of the draft was for righthander Ariel Prieto, a Cuban defector who was eligible for the draft because he had sought political asylum in the United States. Taken fifth by the Athletics and given a $1.2 million bonus, he went straight to Oakland but has enjoyed little success.

Pick	Team	Player	Pos	School	Hometown	Major League Career
1	California Angels	Darin Erstad	of	Nebraska	Jamestown, ND	196 G (.295-20-97)
2	San Diego Padres	Ben Davis	c	Malvern Prep HS	Malvern, PA	Peaked in Class-A
3	Seattle Mariners	Jose Cruz Jr.	of	Rice	Houston, TX	104 G (.248-26-68)
4	Chicago Cubs	Kerry Wood	rhp	Grand Prairie HS	Grand Prairie, TX	Peaked in Triple-A
5	Oakland Athletics	Ariel Prieto	rhp	Palm Springs (Western League)	Marianao, Cuba	57 G (14-21, 4.67)
6	Florida Marlins	Jaime Jones	of	Rancho Bernardo HS	San Diego, CA	Peaked in Class-A
7	Texas Rangers	Jonathan Johnson	rhp	Florida State	Ocala, FL	Peaked in Triple-A
8	Colorado Rockies	Todd Helton	1b-lhp	Tennessee	Knoxville, TN	35 G (.280-5-11)
9	Milwaukee Brewers	Geoff Jenkins	of	Southern California	Rancho Cordova, CA	Peaked in Triple-A
10	Pittsburgh Pirates	Chad Hermansen	ss	Green Valley HS	Henderson, NV	Peaked in Double-A
11	Detroit Tigers	Mike Drumright	rhp	Wichita State	Valley Center, KS	Peaked in Triple-A
12	St. Louis Cardinals	Matt Morris	rhp	Seton Hall	Montgomery, NY	33 G (12-9, 3.19)
13	Minnesota Twins	Mark Redman	lhp	Oklahoma	Del Mar, CA	Peaked in Triple-A
14	Philadelphia Phillies	Reggie Taylor	of	Newberry HS	Newberry, SC	Peaked in Class-A
15	Boston Red Sox	Andy Yount	rhp	Kingwood HS	Kingwood, TX	Peaked in Class-A
16	San Francisco Giants	Joe Fontenot	rhp	Acadiana HS	Lafayette, LA	Peaked in Double-A
17	Toronto Blue Jays	Roy Halladay	rhp	West HS	Arvada, CO	Peaked in Triple-A
18	New York Mets	Ryan Jaroncyk	ss	Orange Glen HS	Escondido, CA	Peaked in Class-A
19	Kansas City Royals	Juan LeBron	of	Huyke HS	Arroyo, PR	Peaked in Class-A
20	Los Angeles Dodgers	David Yocum	lhp	Florida State	Miami, FL	Peaked in Class-A
21	Baltimore Orioles	Alvie Shepherd	rhp-1b	Nebraska	Bellwood, IL	Peaked in Double-A
22	Houston Astros	Tony McKnight	rhp	Arkansas HS	Texarkana, AR	Peaked in Double-A
23	Cleveland Indians	David Miller	1b	Clemson	Philadelphia, PA	Peaked in Double-A
24	Boston Red Sox	Corey Jenkins	of	Dreher HS	Columbia, SC	Peaked in Class-A

Amateur Draft: First-Round Picks

Pick	Team	Player	Pos	School	Hometown	Major League Career
25	Chicago White Sox	Jeff Liefer	3b	Long Beach State	Upland, CA	Peaked in Double-A
26	Atlanta Braves	*Chad Hutchinson	rhp	Torrey Pines HS	Encinitas, CA	Never played pro ball
27	New York Yankees	Shea Morenz	of	Texas	San Angelo, TX	Peaked in Class-A
28	Montreal Expos	Michael Barrett	ss	Pace HS	Atlanta, GA	Peaked in Class-A

* Did not sign.

1996

This will be remembered as the year that all hell broke loose with the draft, thanks to a little-known rule that required teams to make a formal contract offer to all picks within 15 days of their selection. Sarasota, Fla., high school lefthander Bobby Seay was the first to file a grievance over not receiving such an offer, and the White Sox relinquished their rights to the 12th overall choice rather than pursue a hearing. Five weeks later, the second (San Diego State first baseman Travis Lee, Twins), fifth (Orange, Texas, prep righthander John Patterson) and seventh (Waynesboro, Pa., high school righthander Matt White) picks were declared free agents after filing similar complaints. Two new expansion teams gobbled up all four players for the staggering total of $29.275 million. White, the last of the group to sign, received a record $10.2 million from the Devil Rays, who also landed Seay for $3 million. The Diamondbacks inked Lee for $10 million and Patterson for $6.075 million. Two years later, Lee would be Arizona's first baseman when it played its first major league game. The four free agents' bonuses dwarfed that of No. 1 pick Kris Benson, a Clemson righthander who got $2 million from the Pirates. Fellow Clemson righthander Billy Koch went fourth to the Blue Jays, making them the highest-selected pair of pitchers from the same college in draft history. They were two of the nine U.S. Olympians taken in the first round.

Pick	Team	Player	Pos	School	Hometown	Major League Career
1	Pittsburgh Pirates	Kris Benson	rhp	Clemson	Kennesaw, GA	Peaked in Double-A
2	Minnesota Twins	Travis Lee	1b	San Diego State	Olympia, WA	Peaked in Triple-A
3	St. Louis Cardinals	Braden Looper	rhp	Wichita State	Mangum, OK	Peaked in Double-A
4	Toronto Blue Jays	Bill Koch	rhp	Clemson	West Babylon, NY	Peaked in Class-A
5	Montreal Expos	John Patterson	rhp	West Orange Stark HS	Orange, TX	Peaked in Class-A
6	Detroit Tigers	Seth Greisinger	rhp	Virginia	Falls Church, VA	Peaked in Double-A
7	San Francisco Giants	Matt White	rhp	Waynesboro Area HS	Waynesboro, PA	Peaked in Class-A
8	Milwaukee Brewers	Chad Green	of	Kentucky	Mentor, OH	Peaked in Class-A
9	Florida Marlins	Mark Kotsay	of	Cal State Fullerton	Santa Fe Springs, CA	14 G (.192-0-4)
10	Oakland Athletics	Eric Chavez	3b	Mount Carmel HS	San Diego, CA	Peaked in Double-A
11	Philadelphia Phillies	Adam Eaton	rhp	Snohomish HS	Snohomish, WA	Peaked in Class-A
12	Chicago White Sox	Bobby Seay	lhp	Sarasota HS	Sarasota, FL	Peaked in Class-A
13	New York Mets	Robert Stratton	of	San Marcos HS	Santa Barbara, CA	Peaked in Rookie League
14	Kansas City Royals	Dermal Brown	of	Marlboro Central HS	Marlboro, NY	Peaked in Class-A
15	San Diego Padres	Matt Halloran	ss	Chancellor HS	Fredericksburg, VA	Peaked in Class-A
16	Toronto Blue Jays	Joe Lawrence	ss	Barbe HS	Lake Charles, LA	Peaked in Class-A
17	Chicago Cubs	Todd Noel	rhp	North Vermillion HS	Maurice, LA	Peaked in Rookie League
18	Texas Rangers	R.A. Dickey	rhp	Tennessee	Nashville, TN	Peaked in Class-A
19	Houston Astros	Mark Johnson	rhp	Hawaii	Lebanon, OH	Peaked in Class-A
20	New York Yankees	Eric Milton	lhp	Maryland	Bellefonte, PA	Peaked in Double-A
21	Colorado Rockies	Jake Westbrook	rhp	Madison County HS	Danielsville, GA	Peaked in Class-A
22	Seattle Mariners	Gilbert Meche	rhp	Acadiana HS	Lafayette, LA	Peaked in Class-A
23	Los Angeles Dodgers	Damian Rolls	3b	Schlagel HS	Kansas City, KS	Peaked in Class-A
24	Texas Rangers	Sam Marsonek	rhp	Jesuit HS	Tampa, FL	Peaked in Class-A
25	Cincinnati Reds	John Oliver	of	Lake-Lehman HS	Lehman, PA	Peaked in Rookie League
26	Boston Red Sox	Josh Garrett	rhp	South Spencer HS	Richland, IN	Peaked in Class-A
27	Atlanta Braves	A.J. Zapp	1b	Center Grove HS	Greenwood, IN	Peaked in Rookie League
28	Cleveland Indians	Danny Peoples	1b	Texas	Round Rock, TX	Peaked in Class-A
29	Tampa Bay Devil Rays	Paul Wilder	of	Cary HS	Cary, NC	Peaked in Rookie League
30	Arizona Diamondbacks	Nick Bierbrodt	lhp	Millikan HS	Long Beach, CA	Peaked in Class-A

1997

Signability mattered more than ever, as several players considered for the top choice lasted well after the Tigers selected Rice righthander Matt Anderson. Westland, Mich., high school lefthander Ryan Anderson went to the Mariners with the 19th pick and signed for $2.175 million. Englewood, Colo., prep outfielder Darnell McDonald, also a top running-back prospect, dropped to 26th and inked with the Orioles for $1.9 million. Port St. Lucie, Fla., lefthander Rick Ankiel, the best high school pitching prospect, slid into the second round but joined the Cardinals for $2.5 million. Ironically, all three players signed well before Anderson, who finally agreed to a $2.505 million bonus. The consensus top prospect was Florida State outfielder J.D. Drew, who went second to the Phillies. Like Jason Varitek, Drew turned pro with the independent St. Paul Saints. He filed a grievance seeking to become a free agent, but lost. Hahira, Ga., prep righthander Tim Drew, J.D.'s brother, was picked 28th by the Indians, making them the first siblings to go in the first round of the same draft. The Padres took Stetson shortstop Kevin Nicholson one pick before Tim Drew, making him the first Canadian selected in the first round since they became eligible for the draft in 1991. Chesapeake (Va.) Great Bridge High became the second high school to produce two first-rounders in the same draft, as shortstop Michael Cuddyer went ninth to the Twins and lefthander John Curtice went eight picks later to the Red Sox.

Pick	Team	Player	Pos	School	Hometown	Major League Career
1	Detroit Tigers	Matt Anderson	rhp	Rice	Louisville, KY	Did not debut in 1997
2	Philadelphia Phillies	*J.D. Drew	of	Florida State	Hahira, GA	Never played pro ball
3	Anaheim Angels	Troy Glaus	3b	UCLA	Carlsbad, CA	Did not debut in 1997
4	San Francisco Giants	Jason Grilli	rhp	Seton Hall	Baldwinsville, NY	Did not debut in 1997
5	Toronto Blue Jays	Vernon Wells	of	Bowie HS	Arlington, TX	Peaked in Class-A
6	New York Mets	Geoff Goetz	lhp	Jesuit HS	Tampa, FL	Peaked in Rookie League
7	Kansas City Royals	Dan Reichert	rhp	Pacific	Turlock, CA	Peaked in Class-A
8	Pittsburgh Pirates	J.J. Davis	1b-rhp	Baldwin Park HS	Pomona, CA	Peaked in Class-A
9	Minnesota Twins	Michael Cuddyer	ss	Great Bridge HS	Chesapeake, VA	Did not debut in 1997
10	Chicago Cubs	Jon Garland	rhp	Kennedy HS	Granada Hills, CA	Peaked in Rookie League
11	Oakland Athletics	Chris Enochs	rhp	West Virginia	Newell, WV	Peaked in Class-A
12	Florida Marlins	Aaron Akin	rhp	Cowley County (KS) CC	Manhattan, KS	Peaked in Rookie League
13	Milwaukee Brewers	Kyle Peterson	rhp	Stanford	Elkhorn, NE	Peaked in Rookie League
14	Cincinnati Reds	Brandon Larson	ss	Louisiana State	San Antonio, TX	Peaked in Double-A
15	Chicago White Sox	Jason Dellaero	ss	South Florida	Brewster, NY	Peaked in Class-A
16	Houston Astros	Lance Berkman	1b	Rice	New Braunfels, TX	Peaked in Class-A
17	Boston Red Sox	John Curtice	lhp	Great Bridge HS	Chesapeake, VA	Peaked in Rookie League
18	Colorado Rockies	Mark Mangum	rhp	Kingwood HS	Kingwood, TX	Peaked in Rookie League
19	Seattle Mariners	Ryan Anderson	lhp	Divine Child HS	Westland, MI	Did not debut in 1997
20	St. Louis Cardinals	Adam Kennedy	ss	Cal State Northridge	Riverside, CA	Peaked in Class-A
21	Oakland Athletics	Eric DuBose	lhp	Mississippi State	Gilbertown, AL	Peaked in Class-A
22	Baltimore Orioles	Jason Werth	c	Glenwood HS	Chatham, IL	Peaked in Rookie League
23	Montreal Expos	Donnie Bridges	rhp	Oak Grove HS	Hattiesburg, MS	Peaked in Rookie League
24	New York Yankees	*Tyrell Godwin	of	East Bladen HS	Elizabethtown, NC	Never played pro ball
25	Los Angeles Dodgers	Glenn Davis	1b	Vanderbilt	Aston, PA	Peaked in Class-A
26	Baltimore Orioles	Darnell McDonald	of	Cherry Creek HS	Englewood, CO	Did not debut in 1997
27	San Diego Padres	Kevin Nicholson	ss	Stetson	Surrey, BC	Peaked in Class-A
28	Cleveland Indians	Tim Drew	rhp	Lowndes County HS	Hahira, GA	Peaked in Class-A
29	Atlanta Braves	Troy Cameron	ss	St. Thomas Aquinas HS	Ft Lauderdale, FL	Peaked in Rookie League
30	Arizona Diamondbacks	Jack Cust	1b	Immaculata HS	Flemington, NJ	Peaked in Rookie League
31	Tampa Bay Devil Rays	Jason Standridge	rhp	Hewitt Trussville HS	Trussville, AL	Peaked in Rookie League

* Did not sign.

Amateur Draft: First-Round Picks

No. 1 Overall Draft Picks, 1965-1997

Year	Player, Pos., School	Team	Bonus	Debut	Career (Through 1997)
1965	Rick Monday, of, Arizona State	Athletics	$104,000	Sept. 3, 1966	1986 G (.264-241-775)
1966	Steve Chilcott, c, Antelope Valley HS (Lancaster, CA)	Mets	$75,000	None	Peaked in Triple-A
1967	Ron Blomberg, 1b, Druid Hills HS (Atlanta)	Yankees	$75,000	Sept. 10, 1969	461 G (.293-52- 224)
1968	Tim Foli, ss, Notre Dame HS (Canoga Park, CA)	Mets	$75,000	Sept. 11, 1970	1696 G (.251- 25-501)
1969	Jeff Burroughs, of, Wilson HS (Long Beach)	Senators	$88,000	July 20, 1970	1689 G (.261- 240-882)
1970	Mike Ivie, c, Walker HS (Decatur, GA)	Padres	$80,000	Sept. 4, 1971	857 G (.269-81-411)
1971	Danny Goodwin, c, Central HS (Peoria, IL)	White Sox	Did not sign	Sept. 3, 1975	252 G (.236- 13-81)
1972	Dave Roberts, 3b, Oregon	Padres	$60,000	June 7, 1972	709 G (.239-49-208)
1973	David Clyde, lhp, Westchester HS (Houston)	Rangers	$125,000	June 27, 1973	84 G (18-33, 4.63)
1974	Bill Almon, ss, Brown	Padres	$90,000	Sept. 2, 1974	1236 G (.254-36-296)
1975	Danny Goodwin, c, Southern	Angels	$125,000	Sept. 3, 1975	252 G (.236-13-81)
1976	Floyd Bannister, lhp, Arizona State	Astros	$100,000	April 19, 1977	431 G (134-143, 4.06)
1977	Harold Baines, of, St. Michaels (MD) HS	White Sox	$40,000	April 10, 1980	2463 G (.290- 339-1423)
1978	Bob Horner, 3b, Arizona State	Braves	$175,000	June 16, 1978	1020 G (.277-218-685)
1979	Al Chambers, of, Harris HS (Harrisburg, PA)	Mariners	$60,000	July 23, 1983	57 G (.208-2-11)
1980	Darryl Strawberry, of, Crenshaw HS (Los Angeles)	Mets	$152,500	May 6, 1983	1458 G (.259- 308-937)
1981	Mike Moore, rhp, Oral Roberts	Mariners	$100,000	April 11, 1982	450 G (161-176, 4.39)
1982	Shawon Dunston, ss, Jefferson HS (New York)	Cubs	$100,000	April 9, 1985	1354 G (.270- 117-530)
1983	Tim Belcher, rhp, Mount Vernon Nazarene	Twins	Did not sign	Sept. 6, 1987	327 G (122-113, 3.93)
1984	Shawn Abner, of, Mechanicsburg (PA) HS	Mets	$150,000	Sept. 8, 1987	392 G (.227-11-71)
1985	B.J. Surhoff, c, North Carolina	Brewers	$150,000	April 8, 1987	1392 G (.277-96-694)
1986	Jeff King, 3b, Arkansas	Pirates	$160,000	June 2, 1989	1049 G (.255-127-605)
1987	Ken Griffey Jr., of, Moeller HS (Cincinnati)	Mariners	$169,000	April 3, 1989	1214 G (.302- 294-872)
1988	Andy Benes, rhp, Evansville	Padres	$235,000	Aug. 11, 1989	261 G (104-94, 3.64)
1989	Ben McDonald, rhp, Louisiana State	Orioles	$350,000	Sept. 6, 1989	211 G (78-70, 3.91)
1990	Chipper Jones, ss, Bolles HS (Pearson, FL)	Braves	$275,000	Sept. 11, 1993	462 G (.292-74- 307)
1991	Brien Taylor, lhp, East Carteret HS (Beaufort, NC)	Yankees	$1,550,000	None	Peaked in Double-A
1992	Phil Nevin, 3b, Cal State Fullerton	Astros	$700,000	June 11, 1995	178 G (.231-19-67)
1993	Alex Rodriguez, ss, Westminster Christian HS (Miami)	Mariners	$1,000,000	July 8, 1994	352 G (.314-64-228)
1994	Paul Wilson, rhp, Florida State	Mets	$1,550,000	April 4, 1996	26 G (5-12, 5.38)
1995	Darin Erstad, of, Nebraska	Angels	$1,575,000	June 14, 1996	196 G (.295-20-97)
1996	Kris Benson, rhp, Clemson	Pirates	$2,000,000	None	Peaked in Double-A
1997	Matt Anderson, rhp, Rice	Tigers	$2,505,000	None	Did not debut in 1997

Draft Picks Who Went Straight To The Majors

Year	Player, Pos., School	Team	Round	Age	Debut	Career (Through 1997)
1967	Mike Adamson, rhp, Southern California	Orioles	1*	19	July 1, 1967	11 G (7.46, 0 saves)
1970	Steve Dunning, rhp, Stanford	Indians	1	21	June 14, 1970	136 G (23-41, 4.56)
1971	Burt Hooton, rhp, Texas	Cubs	1*	21	June 17, 1971	480 G (151-136, 3.38)
	Rob Ellis, of, Michigan State	Brewers	1*	20	June 18, 1971	64 G (.229-0-10)
	Pete Broberg, rhp, Dartmouth	Senators	1*	21	June 20, 1971	206 G (41-71, 4.56)
1972	Dave Roberts, 3b, Oregon	Padres	1	21	June 7, 1972	709 G (.239-49-208)
1973	Dick Ruthven, rhp, Fresno State	Phillies	1#	22	April 17, 1973	355 G (123-127, 4.14)
	Dave Winfield, of, Minnesota	Padres	1	21	June 19, 1973	2973 G (.283-465-1833)
	David Clyde, lhp, Westchester HS (Houston)	Rangers	1	18	June 27, 1973	84 G (18-33, 4.63)
	Eddie Bane, lhp, Arizona State	Twins	1	21	July 4, 1973	44 G (7-13, 4.66)
1978	Mike Morgan, rhp, Valley HS (Las Vegas)	Athletics	1	18	June 11, 1978	420 G (117-167, 4.07)
	Bob Horner, 3b, Arizona State	Braves	1	20	June 16, 1978	1020 G (.277-218-685)
	Tim Conroy, lhp, Gateway HS (Monroeville, PA)	Athletics	1	18	June 23, 1978	135 G (18-32, 4.69)
	Brian Milner, c, Southwest HS (Fort Worth)	Blue Jays	7	18	June 23, 1978	2 G (.444-0-2)
1985	Pete Incaviglia, of, Oklahoma State	Rangers+	1	22	April 8, 1986	1264 G (.247-206-653)
1988	Jim Abbott, lhp, Michigan	Angels	1	21	April 8, 1989	238 G (80-100, 4.11)
1989	John Olerud, 1b, Washington State	Blue Jays	3	21	Sept. 3, 1989	1074 G (.293-131-573)
1993	Darren Dreifort, rhp, Wichita State	Dodgers	1	21	April 7, 1994	94 G (4.12, 10 saves)
1995	Ariel Prieto, rhp, Palm Springs (Western League)	Athletics	1	25	July 2, 1995	57 G (14-21, 4.67)

*June secondary phase. #January draft. +Drafted by Expos.

Evolution Of The Bonus Record

Year	Player, Pos., School	Team	Round	Bonus	Career (Through 1997)
1964	Rick Reichardt, of, Wisconsin	Angels	N/A	$205,000	997 G (.261-116-445)
1988	Andy Benes, rhp, Evansville	Padres	1	$235,000	261 G (104-94, 3.64)
1989	Tyler Houston, c, Valley HS (Las Vegas)	Braves	1	$241,000	151 G (.284-5-55)
	Ben McDonald, rhp, Louisiana State	Orioles	1	$350,000	211 G (78-70, 3.91)
	John Olerud, 1b, Washington State	Blue Jays	3	$575,000	1074 G (.293-131-573)
1991	Mike Kelly, of, Arizona State	Braves	1	$575,000	219 G (.241-12-52)
	Brien Taylor, lhp, East Carteret HS (Beaufort, NC)	Yankees	1	$1,550,000	Peaked in Double-A
1994	Paul Wilson, rhp, Florida State	Mets	1	$1,550,000	26 G (5-12, 5.38)
	Josh Booty, ss, Evangel HS (Shreveport)	Marlins	1	$1,600,000	6 G (.571-0-1)
1996	Kris Benson, rhp, Clemson	Pirates	1	$2,000,000	Peaked in Double-A
	Travis Lee, 1b, San Diego State	Diamondbacks*	1	$10,000,000	Peaked in Triple-A
	Matt White, rhp, Waynesboro (Pa.) HS	Devil Rays#	1	$10,200,000	Peaked in Class-A

*Drafted by Twins, signed as free agent. #Drafted by Giants, signed as free agent.

Two-Time First-Round Picks, June Regular Phase

Player, Pos.	Year	Team	School	Year	Team	School	Career (Through 1997)
Randy Scarbery, rhp	1970	Astros	Roosevelt HS (Fresno)	1973	Athletics	Southern California	60 G (4.50, 6 saves)
Mike Miley, ss	1971	Reds	East Jefferson HS (New Orleans)	1974	Angels	Louisiana State	84 G (.176-4-30)
Danny Goodwin, c	1971	White Sox	Central HS (Peoria, IL)	1975	Angels	Southern	252 G (.236-13- 81)
Mike Sullivan, lhp	1976	Athletics	Garfield HS (Woodbridge, VA)	1979	Reds	Clemson	Peaked in Double-A
Brad DuVall, rhp	1987	Orioles	Virginia Tech	1988	Cardinals	Virginia Tech	Peaked in Class-A
Alex Fernandez, rhp	1988	Brewers	Pace HS (Miami)	1990	White Sox	Miami-Dade CC South	231 G (96-75, 3.76)
Charles Johnson, c	1989	Expos	Westwood HS (Fort Pierce, FL)	1992	Marlins	Miami	345 G (.241- 44-143)
Calvin Murray, of	1989	Indians	White HS (Dallas)	1992	Giants	Texas	Peaked in Triple-A
John Burke, rhp	1991	Astros	Florida	1992	Rockies	Florida	28 G (6.75, 0 saves)
Jason Varitek, rhp	1993	Twins	Georgia Tech	1994	Mariners	Georgia Tech	1 G (1.000-0-0)

Lowest-Drafted Players To Reach Majors

Round	Player, Pos., School	Year	Team	Career (Through 1997)
75	Al Cowens, ss, Centennial HS (Los Angeles)	1969	Royals	1584 G (.270-108-717)
71	Tony Scott, of, Withrow HS (Cincinnati)	1969	Expos	991 G (.249-17-253)
70	Jose Santiago, rhp, Loaiza, P.R.	1994	Royals	4 G (1.93, 0 saves)
67	Roger Hambright, rhp, Columbia River HS (Vancouver, WA)	1967	Yankees	18 G (4.39, 2 saves)
63	Bruce Ellingsen, lhp, Lakewood (CA) HS	1967	Dodgers	16 G (3.21, 0 saves)
62	Mike Piazza, c, Miami-Dade North CC	1988	Dodgers	689 G (.334-168-533)
58	Jeff Conine, 3b-1b, UCLA	1987	Royals	755 G (.290-98-433)
	Jeff Patterson, rhp, Cypress (CA) JC	1988	Phillies	3 G (2.70, 0 saves)
	Shannon Penn, ss, Lakeland (OH) CC	1988	Rangers	9 G (.174-0-1)
54	Rusty Torres, of, New York Vocational HS (Jamaica, NY)	1966	Yankees	654 G (.212-35-126)
	Todd Williams, rhp, Onondaga (NY) CC	1990	Dodgers	16 G (5.12, 0 saves)

Best Drafts

1. Dodgers, 1968. In unquestionably the best draft ever, Los Angeles assembled the foundation for a team that would contend for most of the next two decades. Six picks would become All-Stars: Bill Buckner (second round), Tom Paciorek (fifth) and Doyle Alexander (ninth) from the June regular phase; Davey Lopes, a second-rounder in the January secondary phase; and Steve Garvey (first round) and Ron Cey (third) from the June secondary phase. Bobby Valentine (first round, June regular), Joe Ferguson (eighth, June regular) and Geoff Zahn (fifth, January secondary) also enjoyed lengthy major league careers, and two others reached the bigs.

2. Tigers, 1976. Like the 1968 Dodgers, Detroit found quality and quantity. Alan Trammell (second round), Dan Petry (fourth) and Jack Morris (fifth) formed the heart of the Tigers' 1984 World Series champions, and January first-rounder Steve Kemp also had a successful career. Just imagine if Detroit had signed its seventh-round choice, Ozzie Smith.

3. Reds, 1965. Cincinnati signed three big leaguers in the first draft. First-rounder Bernie Carbo was the worst of the lot. Second-rounder Johnny Bench can state his case to being the best catcher in baseball history, and sixth-rounder Hal McRae played in three All-Star Games.

4. Twins, 1989. Minnesota drafted two Rookies of the Year in Chuck Knoblauch (first round) and Marty Cordova (10th), and two 20-game winners in Denny Neagle (third) and Scott Erickson (fourth). Four other players made it to the majors, including 52nd-rounder Denny Hocking.

5. Red Sox, 1989. Boston is the only team to draft two eventual MVPs, snagging Mo Vaughn in the first round and Jeff Bagwell three rounds later. The Red Sox' first six selections became big leaguers, though only Vaughn made much of an impact in Beantown.

6. Athletics, 1965. Kansas City exercised the first-ever draft pick on Rick Monday, a wise choice. Sixth-rounder Sal Bando and 11th-rounder Gene Tenace helped the A's win three consecutive World Series in the mid-1970s.

7. Red Sox, 1976. Five-time batting champion Wade Boggs was a steal in the seventh round, and Boston also landed a pair of quality lefthanders in John Tudor (third round, January secondary) and Bruce Hurst (first round, June).

8. Royals, 1971. One pick after Philadelphia took Mike Schmidt in the second round, Kansas City chose George Brett. John Wathan (first round, January), Mark Littell (12th round, June) and Steve Busby (second round, June secondary delayed) also had significant careers.

9. Mets, 1982. New York's draft has lost some of its luster as Dwight Gooden's star has dimmed, but no draft can match this one's pitching depth. Floyd Youmans (second round), Roger McDowell (third), Mickey Weston (12th), Wes Gardner (22nd) and Randy Myers (first, June secondary) all pitched in the majors, with McDowell and Myers having long careers as quality relievers. Despite failing to sign eighth-rounder Rafael Palmeiro, the Mets rode this draft for the rest of the 1980s.

10. Red Sox, 1968. Boston selected four All-Stars in the June regular phase, believed to be a record: Lynn McGlothen (third round), Cecil Cooper (sixth), Ben Oglivie (11th) and Bill Lee (22nd). John Curtis, a first-rounder in the June secondary phase, pitched 15 years in the big leagues.

11. Royals, 1982. Kansas City found three impact players in Danny Jackson (first round, January secondary), Bret Saberhagen (19th, June) and Cecil Fielder (fourth, June secondary). The only downside was the Royals' failure to sign fourth-rounder Will Clark.

12. Dodgers, 1966. Los Angeles didn't match the star quality of its 1968 crop, but still signed eight major leaguers. Among them were All-Stars Charlie Hough (eighth round), Bill Russell (ninth) and Billy Grabarkewitz (12th) and 1969 National League Rookie of the Year Ted Sizemore (15th).

13. Reds, 1983. Cincinnati didn't draft a superstar, but did find six players who had lengthy big league careers: Kurt Stillwell (first round), Chris Sabo (second), Joe Oliver (second), Lenny Harris (fifth), Jeff Montgomery (ninth) and Rob Dibble (first, June secondary).

14. Cardinals, 1971. St. Louis scored a coup with 42nd-rounder Keith Hernandez, who scared teams by sitting out his high school senior season after an argument with his coach. Larry Herndon (third round), Jerry Mumphrey (fourth) and Jim Dwyer (11th) all played extensively in the majors.

15. Giants, 1970. San Francisco succeeded with all four of its first-round picks: Randy Moffitt (January regular), Chris Speier (January secondary), John D'Acquisto (June regular) and Dave Kingman (June secondary). Butch Metzger (second round, June regular) was co-1976 NL Rookie of the Year, while Jim Barr (third, June secondary) had a solid career.

Worst Drafts

1. Braves, 1981. Atlanta went 0-for-34 in the four different drafts, failing to find a big leaguer. Jay Roberts was the biggest reach in the first round of the June draft and hit .187 in the minors before quitting to play college football. Only one June draftee reached Triple-A.

2. Dodgers, 1992. Los Angeles didn't have a true first-round pick, but had two supplemental first-rounders and spent more than $1 million to sign Ryan Luzinski. Six years later, none of the Dodgers' choices had played in the majors—and none figured to.

3. Blue Jays, 1980. Picking first, the Mets took Darryl Strawberry. Picking second, Toronto took Garry Harris and considered him a much better prospect. Harris never made it past Double-A, and the Blue Jays didn't net any major leaguers afterward. The only big leaguer they took was January second-rounder Roger Samuels, who didn't sign.

4. Twins, 1983. Minnesota had no problem identifying talent, but stingy owner Calvin Griffith wouldn't pay the going rate to sign it. The Twins became only the second team to fail to sign the top overall June pick when negotiations with Tim Belcher turned nasty. Second-rounder Billy Swift also didn't come to terms, nor did the first overall choice in the June secondary phase, Oddibe McDowell. Nobody else drafted by Minnesota made it to the majors.

5. Athletics, 1979. When owner Charlie Finley was gutting the Oakland franchise, he all but abandoned scouting and player development. The A's became the first team to fail to sign two first-round picks in the same draft, missing out on Juan Bustabad (who never got past Triple-A) and Mike Stenhouse. Oakland failed to sign nine of its 12 picks in the first 10 rounds, and got only one big leaguer: 27th-rounder Bert Bradley, who appeared in six games.

Strangest Draft

Expos, 1968. So you want to be a scouting director? That's the position a Montreal politician found himself in when the city was awarded a National League franchise shortly before the draft. Despite little time to prepare and no scouting help, the politician managed to make 15 picks. Only six signed, and none made a name for himself.

Best First-Round Picks

C—Ted Simmons, Cardinals (1967). Simmons was only the third catcher picked in 1967. The other two never reached the majors, while Simba was named to eight All-Star teams.

1B—Frank Thomas, White Sox (1989). Chicago took some heat for spending 1989's seventh pick on a one-dimensional player. That one dimension, however, made Thomas baseball's best all-around hitter since Ted Williams.

2B—Craig Biggio, Astros (1987). Drafted as a catcher, Biggio reached Houston for good in 1988. He moved to second base in 1992, and has missed just one All-Star Game since.

3B—Robin Ventura, White Sox (1988). Like Thomas, Ventura was considered a hitter who could do little else, which is why he lasted until the 10th pick in 1988 after a prolific college career that included a 58-game hitting streak. Ventura hit as expected, and also made himself into a Gold Glove third baseman.

SS—Robin Yount, Brewers (1973). The first high school position player taken in the 1973 draft, Yount needed only a half-season in the minors before taking over at shortstop for Milwaukee. He went on to collect 3,142 hits and two Most Valuable Player Awards.

OF—Barry Bonds, Pirates (1985). Bonds wouldn't have made this list if he hadn't decided to go to Arizona State because the Giants wouldn't give him an extra $5,000 as a second-round pick in 1982. He since has established himself as perhaps the best all-around left fielder in baseball history.

OF—Ken Griffey Jr., Mariners (1987). Seattle owner George Argyros wanted to draft Mike Harkey with the top pick in 1987. Scouting director Roger Jongewaard argued for Griffey. Fortunately for Mariners fans, Jongewaard won out and Argyros sold the club.

OF—Reggie Jackson, Athletics (1966). Jackson was considered for the No. 1 choice in 1966, but the Mets misfired on high school catcher Steve Chilcott. He never reached the majors, while Jackson hit 563 homers in the regular season and a record 18 in the postseason.

LHP—Frank Tanana, Angels (1971). Tanana looked like a potential Hall of Famer at the end of the 1978 season, when he owned a career 84-61 record at age 25. Arm injuries robbed him of his fastball, but he reinvented himself as a finesse pitcher and won 240 games over 21 seasons.

RHP—Roger Clemens, Red Sox (1983). Clemens was considered the No. 3 pitcher on Texas' College World Series champions, and 10 pitchers went before him in the 1983 draft. The only one of the 10 to make a significant big league impact was Tim Belcher, while Clemens has won four Cy Young Awards.

RP—Todd Worrell, Cardinals (1982). Most first-round pitchers are projected as starters, but St. Louis found a top closer at tiny Biola College in California. Worrell was the Cards' relief ace in the 1985 World Series, and saved a rookie-record 36 games the following year.

Biggest First-Round Busts

C—Ken Thomas, Orioles (1972). Thomas went two rounds ahead of Gary Carter in 1972, but batted just .148 in a pro career that ended a year later.

1B—Rip Rollins, Phillies (1978). Rollins had two-way potential as a first baseman and righthanded pitcher, but it carried him nowhere. He never made it higher than Class-A before getting released in 1981.

2B—Ty Griffin, Cubs (1988). Only six players have been drafted in the first round as second basemen, and five of them reached the majors. The sixth was Griffin, a U.S. Olympic hero whose power and speed disappeared in the pros.

3B—Ted Nicholson, White Sox (1969). The third choice in the 1969 draft behind Jeff Burroughs and J.R. Richard, Nicholson didn't come close to matching their accomplishments. A military commitment kept him away from baseball for two years, and he never surfaced above Class-A before he was finished in 1973.

SS—John Harbin, Dodgers (1972). Harbin tore up his knee in his first spring training, ending his career after one half-season. The quick end to his career eventually caused Harbin to lapse into a severe depression, and he killed himself in 1983.

OF—Kevin Brandt, Twins (1979). Nobody projected Brandt as a first-rounder except the Twins, who signed him for less than $30,000. They cut him 13 months later, the quickest release ever given a first-round choice, after he hit .155 in 47 games.

OF—Tom Hartley, White Sox (1984). Often compared to Dale Murphy, Hartley hit .218 with two homers in 162 minor league games, none above Class A. He quit after getting traded to the Brewers in a deal for Ray Searage midway through the 1986 season.

OF—Billy Simpson, Rangers (1976). Some clubs considered Simpson the best position player in the 1976 draft, but Texas released him following the 1978 season. He was out of baseball after 1979, and later was sentenced to a 10-year prison term for his involvement in a drug-smuggling ring.

LHP—Ron Walden, Dodgers (1990). Walden injured his elbow four games into his pro career, missed the next two seasons and made three more appearance in 1993 before giving up for good.

RHP—Brad DuVall, Cardinals (1988). One of 10 players to get selected in the first round of two June regular drafts, DuVall won only seven games before injuries ended his career in low Class-A ball in 1990.

Best Picks, Rounds 2-10

C—Johnny Bench, Reds (1965, second round). Arguably the greatest catcher ever, Bench was the first drafted player to make the Hall of Fame. His signing bonus? A bargain $8,000.

1B—Eddie Murray, Orioles (1973, third). Murray was one of three 1973 draftees to reach 3,000 hits. The others were Robin Yount and Dave Winfield, who went in the top four picks.

2B—Lou Whitaker, Tigers (1975, fifth). Not only did Detroit land the supremely underrated Whitaker in the fifth round in 1975, they found longtime first baseman Jason Thompson with their previous pick.

3B—Mike Schmidt, Phillies (1971, second). An All-America shortstop at Ohio, Schmidt became the best third baseman in baseball history. With the pick right before him, the Royals selected George Brett.

SS—Cal Ripken Jr., Orioles (1978, second). Ripken would win two American League MVP Awards and break Lou Gehrig's consecutive-games record, but he wasn't even the first third baseman drafted by Baltimore in 1978. The Orioles used their first-round choice on Robert Boyce, who never made it out of Class A.

OF—Dwight Evans, Red Sox (1969, fifth). Evans was the third outfielder taken by Boston in 1969, behind three-sport star Noel Jenke (first round) and Rick Miller (second). One of the best all-around right fielders of his era, Evans has an outside chance at making the Hall of Fame.

OF—Tony Gwynn, Padres (1981, third). Gwynn was drafted by two San Diego teams, the Padres and the NBA's Clippers, on the same day. He obviously made the right choice, winning eight batting titles and nearing 3,000 hits as this book went to press.

OF—Rickey Henderson, Athletics (1976, fourth). Owner Charlie Finley was pinching pennies, so Oakland didn't even sign its first two draft picks in 1976. They recovered by finding baseball's stolen-base king in the fourth round.

LHP—Ron Guidry, Yankees (1971, third). One of the best pennant races ever wouldn't have happened if New York hadn't drafted Guidry out of Southwestern Louisiana. He won one Cy Young Award and back-to-back World Series rings.

RHP—Greg Maddux, Cubs (1984, second). With apologies to Nolan Ryan, a Mets 10th-rounder in 1965, Maddux has been better. Chicago did a nice job of projecting a 5-foot-11, 155-pound high schooler with an average fastball.

RP—Lee Smith, Cubs (1975, second). Just one of Chicago's 29 selections in 1975 reached the majors, but the Cubs hit on a good one. Smith became baseball's career saves leader.

Best Picks, Rounds 11-20

C—Gene Tenace, Athletics (1965, 11th round). Tenace, an underappreciated player who was part of three World Series champions, was the icing on a Kansas City draft that also included Rick Monday (first round) and Sal Bando (sixth).

1B—Don Mattingly, Yankees (1979, 19th). Despite setting a national high school record for career RBI, Mattingly was viewed as a one-tool player. He eventually developed power and improved his fielding, making six All-Star teams and winning nine Gold Gloves.

2B—Ryne Sandberg, Phillies (1978, 20th). Sandberg would have been a significantly higher pick had he not been headed to Washington State to play quarterback. Philadelphia ruined its coup by letting him get away to the Cubs, for whom he set a big league record for career homers by a second baseman.

3B—Buddy Bell, Indians (1969, 16th). His son Mike would be a supplemental first-round pick of the Rangers 24 years later, but Buddy was an oversight in the 1969 draft. He was a big league starter at 20 and made five All-Star teams.

SS—Fred Patek, Pirates (1965, 12th). Premium middle infielders aren't found in the lower rounds of the draft. Patek is the only shortstop taken after the 10th round to enjoy an extensive career.

OF—Jose Canseco, Athletics (1982, 15th). An awkward third baseman in high school, Canseco didn't even merit a report from the Major League Scouting Bureau. Oakland didn't realize he had 40-40 potential, so it let him slide until the 15th round because no one else knew about him.

OF—Andre Dawson, Expos (1975, 11th). Tiny Florida A&M has produced more than its share of big leaguers, including Vince Coleman, Marquis Grissom and Hal McRae. The Rattlers' prize alumnus is Dawson, whom Montreal drafted primarily for his defense.

OF—Dave Parker, Pirates (1970, 14th). Parker had football scholarship offers from Michigan and Ohio State, but tore up his knee as a senior. Colleges backed away and so did pro teams, who didn't realize he'd rebound to win two batting titles and an MVP Award.

LHP—John Smiley, Pirates (1983, 12th). Like shortstops, most lefthanders with ability go early in the draft. One who didn't was Smiley, who made two all-star teams and won 126 games before breaking his left arm in 1997.

RHP—Orel Hershiser, Dodgers (1979, 17th). Mattingly wasn't the only star who fell through the cracks in 1979. Hershiser was overlooked because he was skinny and didn't throw hard, but nine years later threw a record 59 consecutive scoreless innings and carried Los Angeles to the World Series title.

RP—Gene Garber, Pirates (1965, 12th). Garber was the 387th player taken in the first draft, but only eight players ever pitched more games in the majors. Pittsburgh deserves a lot of credit for finding both Garber and Patek in the 12th round in 1965.

Best Picks, Rounds 21+

C—Mike Piazza, Dodgers (1988, 62nd round). Piazza didn't look like he had a remote chance into developing into the best-hitting catcher ever when he played at Miami and Miami-Dade North CC. Los Angeles took him only as a favor to manager Tom Lasorda, a Piazza family friend.

1B—Keith Hernandez, Cardinals (1971, 42nd). Hernandez lasted until the 783rd pick in 1971 because he didn't play baseball as a high school senior after getting into an argument with his coach. He still signed for $50,000, first-round money at the time, and developed into a perennial All-Star.

2B—Eric Young, Dodgers (1989, 43rd). Young played two sports at Rutgers, but his lack of size made more of an impression on scouts than his speed. Los Angeles let Young go in the expansion draft, and didn't reap any rewards from its astute pick until it reacquired him in 1997.

3B—Vance Law, Pirates (1978, 39th). Law spent only 55 games in Pittsburgh, but did play in two Championship Series and one All-Star Game during an 11-year career.

SS—Al Cowens, Royals (1969, 75th). This is cheating a bit, but Cowens was drafted as a shortstop before enjoying a productive 13 years in the majors as an outfielder. As for pure shortstops, the eminently mediocre David Howard (Royals, 1986, 32nd round) is the best.

OF—Dusty Baker, Braves (1967, 26th). Atlanta found two longtime big league outfielders in 1967, grabbing Ralph Garr in the third round and Baker 23 rounds later. Despite his lowly draft status, Baker was the first high school player in the 1967 draft to reach the majors, where he stayed for 19 seasons.

Amateur Draft: Analysis

OF—Brett Butler, Braves (1979, 23rd). Atlanta was more excited about first-round choice Brad Komminsk, who was billed as better than Dale Murphy, but Butler turned out to be the solid outfielder the Braves were looking for. His 558 stolen bases rank 23rd on the all-time list.

OF—Ken Griffey Sr., Reds (1969, 29th). Eighteen years before his son went first in the 1987 draft, Griffey Sr. was the sixth outfielder taken by Cincinnati. He went on to play in three All-Star Games and was a vital cog in the Big Red Machine.

LHP—Paul Splittorff, Royals (1968, 25th). The 1969 expansion teams were allowed to participate in the draft a year before they began play, and Kansas City made the most of the opportunity. The Royals found Splittorff at tiny Morningside College, and he became the winningest pitcher in franchise history with 166 victories.

RHP—John Smoltz, Tigers (1985, 22nd). Smoltz would have been a higher pick, but teams were convinced that he wanted to attend Michigan State. Detroit signed him days before he left for college, then used him to acquire Doyle Alexander for the stretch drive in 1987. While the Tigers won the American League East that year, Smoltz has won a Cy Young Award and has a record-tying 10 postseason victories.

RP—Robb Nen, Rangers (1987, 32nd). Nen threw hard and had some name recognition as the son of former big leaguer Dick Nen, but he was so raw that he lasted well into the 1987 draft. It took Robb six years to establish himself as a big leaguer, but once he did he became one of baseball's better closers.

Best Non-Drafted Free Agents

C—Brian Downing, White Sox (1969). Chicago didn't sign an impact player in the 1969 drafts, but found one in Downing, who enjoyed a 17-year major league career.

1B—Andre Thornton, Phillies (1967). Philadelphia didn't draft a big leaguer in the June regular phase. They also squandered their signing of Thornton, who hit 253 big league homers but never played a game for the Phillies.

2B—Frank White, Royals (1970). One of the slickest-fielding second basemen ever, White also was the most prominent graduate of Kansas City's baseball academy.

3B—Bobby Bonilla, Pirates (1981). Pittsburgh made up for not signing a big league hitter in the 1981 drafts by landing Bonilla. When they lost him to the White Sox in the 1985 major league Rule 5 draft, the Pirates traded Jose DeLeon to get him back.

SS—Toby Harrah, Phillies (1966). As with Thornton, Philadelphia made little use of a fine scouting find. After his first season in the Phillies system, Harrah was lost to the Washington Senators in the minor league draft. He made All-Star teams as both a shortstop and a third baseman.

OF—Bernard Gilkey, Cardinals (1984). Not only did St. Louis draft Lance Johnson in 1984, but it also signed local product Gilkey, who had been headed to Drake to play basketball.

OF—Kevin Mitchell, Mets (1980). Joe McIlvaine had a lot of success as New York's scouting director, and it began with his first free-agent signing. Mitchell helped the Mets win the 1986 World Series, and was named National League MVP three years later with the Giants.

OF—Claudell Washington, Athletics (1972). Oakland's signing of Washington was just one of many nondrafted free agent success stories in 1972. Others included Tippy Martinez (Yankees), John Montefusco (Giants), Larry Parrish (Expos) and Gary Ward (Twins).

LHP—Bob Ojeda, Red Sox (1978). Ojeda won 115 games in 15 years and pitched in two postseasons. Then again, he was the key player Boston used to acquire Calvin Schiraldi in a trade with the Mets, so maybe the Red Sox would have been better off not signing him.

RHP—Danny Darwin, Rangers (1976). Not getting drafted didn't stop Darwin from making the majors two years later. Twenty years after that, he still was taking a regular turn in the Giants' rotation.

RP—Bruce Sutter, Cubs (1971). One of baseball's most dominant relievers ever, Sutter was drafted out of high school by the Washington Senators in 1970 but was neglected a year later. Other longtime closers who were nondrafted free agents include Dan Quisenberry (Royals, 1975), Jeff Reardon (Mets, 1977) and Kent Tekulve (Pirates, 1969).

—Jim Callis

Umpires

Register

Every full-time umpire employed by a major league is listed, along with the total years and the span of his career by league.

Strike Register

We provide the same information as in the Register for all men who filled in during the umpire strikes of 1976, 1978, 1979, 1984, 1991 and 1995.

Abbreviations & Formulas

A complete list of team and statistical abbreviations are listed in the back of the book, along with an appendix explaining formulas and the availability of certain statistics.

Name	Years	Span	League
John Adams	1	1903	AL
Ollie Anderson	1	1914	FL
Ed Andrews	3	1895, 1898-1899	NL
Merlyn Anthony	7	1969-1975	AL
Emmett Ashford	5	1966-1970	AL
Nick Avants	3	1969-1971	AL
Bill Baker	1	1957	NL
Lee Ballanfant	22	1936-1957	NL
Al Barlick	28	1940-1943, 1946-1955, 1958-1971	NL
Ron Barnes	7	1990-1994, 1996-1997	NL
Ross Barnes	1	1890	PL
Larry Barnett	30	1968-1997	AL
Billy Barnie	1	1892	NL
George Barnum	1	1890	AA
George Barr	19	1931-1949	NL
Ted Barrett	4	1994-1997	AL
Mark Barron	6	1992-1997	NL
Dan Barry	1	1928	AL
Steve Basil	7	1936-1942	AL
Joe Battin	1	1891	NL
Al Bauers	1	1887	AA
George Bausewine	1	1905	NL
Ed Bean	1	1994	AL
William Becannon	1	1883	AA
Frank Behle	1	1901	NL
Wally Bell	6	1992-1997	NL
Charlie Berry	21	1942-1962	AL
William Betts	4	1894-1896, 1899	NL
		1901	AL
Edwin Betz	1	1961	NL
Dusty Boggess	18	1944-1948, 1950-1962	NL
Charles Boles	1	1877	NL
Tommy Bond	2	1883, 1885	NL
Greg Bonin	12	1986-1997	NL
Jim Boyer	7	1944-1950	AL
Foghorn Bradley	5	1879-1883	NL
	1	1886	AA
Jackson Brady	1	1887	NL
Kitty Bransfield	1	1917	NL
George Bredburg	1	1877	NL
Nick Bremigan	15	1974-1988	AL
Bill Brennan	6	1909-1913, 1921	NL
	2	1914-1915	FL
Jack Brennan	1	1884	AA
	1	1899	NL
Joe Brinkman	25	1973-1997	AL
Fred Brocklander	12	1979-1990	NL
Tom Brown	4	1898-1899, 1901-1902	NL
C.B. Bucknor	2	1996-1997	NL
Joshua Bunce	1	1877	NL
Ken Burkhart	17	1957-1973	NL
George Burnham	3	1883, 1889, 1895	NL
John Burns	1	1884	NL
Oyster Burns	1	1899	NL
Tom Burns	1	1892	NL
L.W. Burtis	2	1876-1877	NL
Garnet Bush	2	1911-1912	NL
	1	1914	FL
Ormond Butler	1	1883	AA
Bill Byron	7	1913-1919	NL
Edward Callahan	1	1881	NL
Bick Campbell	4	1928-1931	AL
	2	1939-1940	NL
Joe Cantillon	1	1901	AL
	1	1902	NL
Tom Carey	1	1882	AA
Bill Carpenter	4	1897, 1904, 1906-1907	NL
	1	1904	AL
Sam Carrigan	5	1961-1965	AL
Bob Caruthers	2	1902-1903	AL
Gary Cederstrom	1	1997	AL
Jack Chapman	1	1880	NL
Ollie Chill	7	1914-1916, 1919-1922	AL
Harry Chipman	2	1883, 1885	NL
Nestor Chylak	25	1954-1978	AL
Al Clark	22	1976-1997	AL
Bob Clarke	2	1930-1931	NL
Jim Clinton	1	1886	AA
Drew Coble	15	1983-1997	AL
George Cockill	1	1915	NL
Harry Colgan	1	1901	NL
James Colliflower	1	1910	AL
Nick Colosi	15	1968-1982	NL
Ed Conahan	1	1896	NL
Fred Cone	1	1877	NL
Jocko Conlan	24	1941-1964	NL
Terence Connell	2	1884, 1890	AA
John Connelly	2	1885, 1887	AA
William Connelly	1	1884	AA
John Connolly	1	1886	NL
Tommy Connolly	3	1898-1900	NL
	31	1901-1931	AL
Tom Connor	2	1905-1906	AL
John Conway	1	1906	NL
Terry Cooney	18	1975-1992	AL
Eric Cooper	2	1996-1997	AL
Tommy Corcoran	1	1915	FL
Derryl Cousins	19	1979-1997	AL
Terry Craft	9	1989-1997	AL
Robert Crandall	1	1877	NL
Alexander Crawford	1	1884	UA
Jerry Crawford	22	1976-1997	NL
Shag Crawford	20	1956-1975	NL
John Cross	1	1878	NL
Monte Cross	1	1914	FL
Fieldin Culbreth	5	1993-1997	AL
Bert Cunningham	1	1901	NL
Wes Curry	4	1885-1886, 1889, 1898	NL
	2	1887, 1890	AA
Stephen Cusack	1	1909	NL
	1	1914	FL
Charley Cushman	2	1885, 1898	NL
Ned Cuthbert	1	1901	AA
Phil Cuzzi	3	1991-1993	NL
John Dailey	1	1882	NL
	1	1884	AA
Jerry Dale	16	1970-1985	NL
Charles Daniels	6	1876, 1878-1880, 1887-1888	NL
	4	1883-1885, 1889	AA
Kerwin Danley	7	1991-1997	NL
Gary Darling	10	1988-1997	NL
Frank Dascoli	15	1948-1962	NL
Bob Davidson	15	1983-1997	NL
Satch Davidson	16	1969-1984	NL
Gerry Davis	13	1985-1997	NL
Jumbo Davis	1	1891	AA
Stewart Decker	4	1883-1885, 1888	NL
Bill Deegan	11	1970-1980	AL
Vic Delmore	4	1956-1959	NL
Dana DeMuth	12	1986-1997	NL
Don Denkinger	30	1968-1997	AL
Doll Derr	1	1923	NL
Dan Devinney	1	1877	NL
	1	1884	AA
	1	1884	UA
Frank Dezelan	6	1966-1968, 1969-1971	NL
Lazaro Diaz	1	1995	AL
Lou DiMuro	18	1963-1980	AL
Ray DiMuro	2	1996-1997	AL
Bill Dinneen	29	1909-1937	AL
Hal Dixon	7	1953-1959	NL
Augie Donatelli	24	1950-1973	NL
Charles Donnelly	2	1931-1932	NL
	2	1934-1935	AL
Michael Donohue	1	1930	NL
Herm Doscher	3	1880-1881, 1887	NL
	2	1888, 1890	AA
Jack Doyle	1	1911	NL
Walter Doyle	1	1963	AL
Bruce Dreckman	2	1996-1997	NL
Cal Drummond	10	1960-1969	AL
Ducharme	2	1876-1877	NL
Jim Duffy	5	1951-1955	AL
Tom Dunn	8	1939-1946	NL
Joseph Dunnigan	2	1881-1882	NL
Patrick Dutton	1	1884	UA
Frank Dwyer	2	1899, 1901	NL
	1	1904	AL
John Dyler	1	1884	AA
John Eagan	2	1878, 1886	NL
Mal Eason	8	1902, 1910-1916	NL
Rip Egan	9	1903, 1907-1914	AL
Clarence Eldridge	2	1914-1915	AL
Joe Ellick	1	1886	NL
Bob Emslie	1	1890	AA
	34	1891-1924	NL
Bob Engel	26	1965-1990	NL
Bill Engeln	5	1952-1956	NL
Billy Evans	22	1906-1927	AL
Jim Evans	27	1971-1997	AL
Mike Everitt	2	1996-1997	AL
Bob Ferguson	3	1879, 1884-1885	NL
	5	1886-1889, 1891	AA
	1	1890	PL
Charles Ferguson	1	1913	AL
Wally Fessenden	2	1889-1890	NL
Steve Fields	4	1979-1982	NL
William E. Finneran	1	1915	FL
William F. Finneran	3	1911-1912, 1924	NL
Red Flaherty	21	1953-1973	AL
Dale Ford	23	1975-1997	AL
Al Forman	5	1961-1965	NL
Mark Foster	2	1996-1997	AL
Edward Fountain	1	1879	NL
Art Frantz	9	1969-1977	AL
Ralph Frary	1	1911	NL
Bill Friel	1	1920	AL
Bruce Froemming	27	1971-1997	NL
Grover Froese	2	1952-1953	AL
Chick Fulmer	1	1886	NL
Bill Furlong	4	1878-1879, 1883-1884	NL
Lee Fyfe	1	1920	NL
Louis Fyfe	1	1915	FL
John Gaffney	9	1884-1886, 1891-1894, 1899-1900	NL
	2	1888-1889	AA
	1	1890	PL
Jim Galvin	1	1895	NL
Rich Garcia	23	1975-1997	AL
Harry Geisel	18	1925-1942	AL
Brian Gibbons	4	1994-1997	NL
Thomas Gillean	2	1879-1880	NL
Bill Gleason	1	1891	AA
E. Goeckel	1	1914	FL
Larry Goetz	22	1936-1957	NL
Russ Goetz	16	1968-1983	AL
Fred Goldsmith	2	1888-1889	AA
Artie Gore	10	1947-1956	NL
Brian Gorman	7	1991-1997	NL
Tom Gorman	26	1951-1976	NL
Eric Gregg	20	1977-1991, 1993-1997	NL
Bill Grieve	18	1938-1955	AL
E.A. Griffith	1	1884	AA
Augie Guglielmo	1	1952	NL
Tom Gunning	1	1887	NL
	1	1890	PL
Bill Guthrie	3	1913-1915	NL
	6	1922, 1928-1932	AL
Bill Haller	21	1961, 1963-1982	AL
Tom Hallion	12	1986-1997	NL
Lannie Harris	7	1979-1985	NL
Pete Harrison	5	1916-1920	NL
Bertie Hart	2	1912-1913	NL
Bill Hart	1	1901	AL
	2	1914-1915	NL
Bob Hart	10	1920-1929	NL
Doug Harvey	31	1962-1992	NL
John Haskell	1	1901	AL
James Hassett	1	1903	AL
Charlie Hautz	2	1876, 1879	NL
	1	1882	AA
Gerald Hayes	2	1925-1926	AL
Hardie Henderson	2	1895-1896	NL
Ted Hendry	20	1978-1997	AL
Ed Hengle	1	1887	NL
Moxie Hengle	1	1884	UA
Butch Henline	4	1945-1948	NL
Jeff Henrichs	1	1993	AL
Angel Hernandez	7	1991-1997	NL
George Heuble	1	1876	NL
John Heydler	1	1898	NL
Ed Hickox	8	1990-1997	AL
Dick Higham	2	1881-1882	NL
George Hildebrand	23	1912-1934	AL
John Hirschbeck	14	1984-1997	AL
Mark Hirschbeck	10	1988-1997	NL
Willard Hoagland	1	1894	NL
A.D. Hodges	1	1876	NL
Bill Hohn	11	1987-1997	NL
Bill Holbert	1	1890	PL
Sam Holbrook	2	1996-1997	AL
John Holland	1	1884	AA
	1	1884	UA
	1	1887	NL
Willard Holland	1	1889	AA
Bug Holliday	1	1903	NL
Ducky Holmes	1	1921	NL
	2	1923-1924	AL
Jim Honochick	25	1949-1973	AL
Michael Hooper	1	1884	UA
Joe Hornung	2	1893, 1896	NL
Harry Howell	1	1915	FL
Cal Hubbard	16	1936-1951	AL
John Hunt	3	1895, 1898-1899	NL
Dan Hurley	1	1887	AA
Eddie Hurley	19	1947-1965	AL
Tim Hurst	9	1891-1897, 1900, 1903	NL
	5	1905-1909	AL
Arthur Irwin	1	1902	NL
Bill Jackowski	17	1952-1968	NL
W.W. Jeffers	1	1881	NL
Al Jennings	1	1884	UA
	1	1887	AA
Fred Jevne	1	1895	NL
Mark Johnson	18	1980-1997	AL
Steamboat Johnson	1	1914	NL
Charles Johnston	2	1936-1937	AL
Jim Johnstone	1	1902	AL
	10	1903-1912	NL
	1	1915	FL
Charley Jones	1	1890	PL
	1	1891	AA
Red Jones	6	1944-1949	AL

Name	Years	Span	League
Lou Jorda	18	1927-1931, 1940-1952	NL
Bill Jordan	1	1884	UA
Jim Joyce	9	1989-1997	AL
Joseph Julian	1	1878	NL
Ken Kaiser	21	1977-1997	AL
Stephen Kane	2	1909-1910	NL
Stephen Karie	1	1914	FL
Tim Keefe	3	1894-1896	NL
Jeff Kellogg	7	1991-1997	NL
John Kelly	3	1882, 1888, 1897	NL
	4	1883-1886	AA
Thomas Kelly	1	1905	AL
Charles Kennedy	1	1904	NL
John Kenney	1	1877	NL
John Kerin	2	1909-1910	AL
Jack Kerins	3	1889-1891	AA
John Kibler	27	1963-1989	NL
Charles King	1	1904	AL
Bill Kinnamon	10	1960-1969	AL
Bill Klem	37	1905-1941	NL
Lon Knight	1	1887	AA
	1	1889	NL
	1	1890	PL
Lou Kolls	8	1933-1940	AL
Greg Kosc	22	1976-1997	AL
Bill Kunkel	17	1968-1984	AL
Bud Lally	1	1896	NL
Stan Landes	18	1955-1972	NL
Frank Lane	1	1883	NL
Joseph Langden	1	1915	FL
Arlie Latham	2	1899, 1902	NL
John Lawler	1	1884	AA
Jerry Layne	9	1989-1997	NL
Henry Leach	1	1890	PL
Tom Leppart	3	1984-1986	AL
Stephen Libby	1	1880	NL
Frederick Lincoln	2	1914, 1917	NL
Joe Linsalata	2	1961-1962	AL
Billy Long	1	1895	NL
Bob Long	1	1992	NL
Ron Luciano	13	1968-1980	AL
Tom Lynch	12	1888-1899	NL
Denny Mack	1	1886	AA
Jimmy Macullar	1	1891	AA
	1	1892	NL
Sherry Magee	1	1928	NL
George Magerkurth	19	1929-1947	NL
John Magner	1	1883	AA
Michael Mahoney	1	1891	AA
	1	1892	NL
Fergy Malone	1	1884	NL
George Maloney	15	1969-1983	AL
Al Manassau	1	1899	NL
	1	1901	AL
	1	1914	FL
Blake Mapledoram	1	1884	UA
Firpo Marberry	1	1935	AL
Randy Marsh	15	1983-1997	NL
Bobby Mathews	1	1880	NL
	1	1891	AA
John Matthews	1	1890	PL
Charles McCafferty	2	1921, 1923	NL
Harry McCaffrey	1	1884	UA
Jack McCarthy	1	1905	AL
Tim McClelland	14	1984-1997	AL
Barry McCormick	2	1914-1915	FL
	1	1917	AL
	11	1919-1929	NL
Larry McCoy	28	1970-1997	AL
Sandy McDermott	2	1890, 1897	NL
James McDonald	2	1895, 1899	NL
Harvey McElwee	1	1877	NL
Horace McFarland	2	1896-1897	NL
Chippy McGarr	1	1899	NL
Bill McGowan	30	1925-1954	AL
Edward McGreevy	2	1912-1913	AL
Ted McGrew	4	1930-1931, 1933-1934	NL
Jim McKean	24	1974-1997	AL
Bill McKinley	20	1946-1965	AL
Edward McLaughlin	1	1929	NL
Michael McLaughlin	1	1893	NL
Peter McLaughlin	5	1924-1928	NL
Thomas McLaughlin	1	1891	NL
Billy McLean	7	1876, 1878-1880, 1882-1884	NL
	1	1885	AA
Robert McNichol	1	1883	AA
Jack McQuaid	3	1886-1888	AA
	6	1889-1894	NL
John McSherry	26	1971-1996	NL
Chuck Meriwether	10	1988-1997	AL
Durwood Merrill	21	1977-1997	AL
George Miller	1	1879	NL
Charles Mitchell	1	1892	NL
Ed Montague	22	1976-1997	NL
Augie Moran	4	1903-1904, 1910, 1918	NL
Charlie Moran	23	1917-1939	NL
Hank Morgenweck	4	1972-1975	AL
George Moriarty	22	1917-1926, 1929-1940	AL
Dan Morrison	19	1979-1997	AL
Charlie Morton	1	1886	AA
Dominic Mullaney	1	1915	AL
John Mullin	1	1909	NL
	2	1911-1912	AL
	1	1915	FL
Dick Nallin	18	1915-1932	AL
Larry Napp	24	1951-1974	AL
Billy Nash	1	1901	NL
Paul Nauert	3	1995-1997	NL
Jerry Neudecker	21	1965-1985	AL
Frank O'Brien	1	1890	AA
Joe O'Brien	2	1912, 1914	AL
	1	1915	FL
Arthur O'Connor	1	1914	NL
Hank O'Day	29	1895, 1897-1911, 1915-1927	NL
Jake O'Donnell	4	1968-1971	AL
O'Hara	1	1915	NL
Silk O'Loughlin	17	1902-1918	AL
Brian O'Nora	6	1992-1997	AL
Jim O'Rourke	1	1894	NL
John O'Sullivan	1	1922	NL
Albert Odlin	1	1883	NL
Jim Odom	10	1965-1974	AL
Andy Olsen	14	1968-1981	NL
Al Orth	6	1912-1917	NL
Red Ormsby	19	1923-1941	AL
Brick Owens	3	1908, 1912-1913	NL
	22	1916-1937	AL
Steve Palermo	15	1977-1991	AL
Dave Pallone	10	1979-1988	NL
Joe Paparella	20	1946-1965	AL
George Parker	3	1936-1938	NL
Harley Parker	1	1911	AL
Dallas Parks	5	1979-1983	AL
Art Passarella	11	1941-1942, 1945-1953	AL
Dicky Pearce	2	1878, 1882	NL
Frank Pears	2	1897, 1905	NL
Chris Pelekoudas	16	1960-1975	NL
Jimmy Peoples	1	1890	AA
Bull Perrine	4	1909-1912	AL
Cy Pfirman	15	1922-1936	NL
Dave Phillips	27	1971-1997	AL
Gracie Pierce	2	1886-1887	NL
	1	1890	PL
Lip Pike	1	1889	AA
Babe Pinelli	22	1935-1956	NL
George Pipgras	9	1938-1946	AL
Larry Poncino	10	1986-1988, 1991-1997	NL
Scott Potter	5	1991-1995	NL
Jack Powell	3	1923-1924, 1933	NL
Charles Power	1	1902	NL
Phil Powers	8	1879, 1881, 1886-1891	NL
Al Pratt	1	1879	NL
	1	1883	AA
Tom Pratt	1	1886	NL
Paul Pryor	21	1961-1981	NL
Frank Pulli	26	1972-1997	NL
Joe Quest	2	1886-1887	NL
Jim Quick	22	1976-1997	NL
Ernie Quigley	25	1913-1937	NL
A.J. Quinn	1	1886	AA
Joe Quinn	1	1882	NL
John Quinn	8	1935-1942	AL
Quisser	1	1914	FL
Ed Rapuano	8	1990-1997	NL
Beans Reardon	24	1926-1949	NL
Rick Reed	14	1984-1997	AL
Mike Reilly	20	1978-1997	AL
Charlie Reliford	9	1989-1997	NL
Dutch Rennert	20	1973-1992	NL
John Rice	19	1955-1973	AL
Rich Rieker	6	1992-1997	NL
Cy Rigler	29	1906-1922, 1924-1935	NL
William Riley	1	1880	NL
	1	1882	AA
Steve Rippley	13	1985-1997	NL
Scotty Robb	5	1948-1952	NL
	2	1952-1953	AL
Lenny Roberts	3	1953-1955	NL
Armando Rodriguez	2	1974-1975	AL
Rocky Roe	19	1979-1997	AL
Eddie Rommel	22	1938-1959	AL
Robert Ross	1	1882	AA
Pants Rowland	5	1923-1927	AL
John Rudderham	1	1908	NL
Joe Rue	10	1938-1947	AL
Ed Runge	17	1954-1970	AL
Paul Runge	25	1973-1997	NL
Walter Ryan	1	1946	NL
Al Salerno	8	1961-1968	AL
Harry Schwarts	3	1960-1962	AL
Dale Scott	12	1986-1997	AL
Jim Scott	2	1930-1931	NL
Ziggy Sears	12	1934-1945	NL
Frank Secory	19	1952-1970	NL
Paul Sentelle	2	1922-1923	NL
Ed Seward	1	1893	NL
George Seward	3	1876-1878	NL
	1	1884	AA
Spike Shannon	2	1914-1915	FL
Jack Sheridan	1	1890	PL
	3	1892, 1896-1897	NL
	14	1901-1914	AL
John Shulock	19	1979-1997	AL
Joe Simmons	1	1882	AA
Al Smith	6	1960-1965	AL
Billy Smith	2	1898-1899	NL
Pop Smith	1	1881	NL
	1	1882	AA
Vinnie Smith	9	1957-1965	NL
Pop Snyder	1	1890	PL
	1	1891	AA
	6	1892-1893, 1898-1901	NL
Hank Soar	24	1950-1973	AL
Benjamin Sommer	1	1883	AA
Fred Spenn	2	1979-1980	AL
Marty Springstead	22	1965-1986	AL
Jack Stafford	1	1907	AL
Billy Stage	1	1894	NL
Calvin Stambough	2	1877-1878	NL
Dolly Stark	12	1928-1935, 1937-1939, 1942	NL
Ecky Stearns	1	1884	UA
Mel Steiner	12	1961-1972	NL
Harry Steinfeldt	1	1905	NL
Dick Stello	19	1969-1987	NL
Paul Sternburg	1	1909	NL
Johnny Stevens	24	1948-1971	AL
Bill Stewart	22	1933-1954	NL
Bob Stewart	12	1959-1970	AL
Ernest Stewart	5	1941-1945	AL
M.J. Stockdale	1	1915	NL
Otis Stocksdale	1	1915	FL
George Strief	1	1890	NL
Ed Sudol	21	1957-1977	NL
Dave Sullivan	2	1882, 1885	NL
Jerry Sullivan	1	1887	NL
T.P. Sullivan	1	1880	NL
Ted Sullivan	1	1887	AA
James Summer	1	1877	NL
Bill Summers	27	1933-1959	AL
Ed Swartwood	4	1894, 1898-1900	NL
Jim Sweeney	3	1924-1926	NL
Frank Tabacchi	4	1956-1959	AL
Terry Tata	25	1973-1997	NL
Walter Taylor	1	1890	AA
Adonis Terry	1	1900	NL
Otis Tilden	1	1880	NL
Steve Toole	1	1890	AA
Dick Tremblay	1	1971	NL
Harry Truby	1	1909	NL
Tim Tschida	12	1986-1997	AL
William Tunnison	2	1885-1886	AA
Frank Umont	20	1954-1973	AL
Bill Valentine	6	1963-1968	AL
John Valentine	4	1884-1887	AA
	2	1887-1888	NL
Eugene Van Court	1	1884	NL
Roy Van Graflan	7	1927-1933	AL
Charles Van Sickle	1	1914	FL
Larry Vanover	6	1991, 1993-1997	NL
Ed Vargo	24	1960-1983	NL
Tony Venzon	15	1957-1971	NL
Vic Voltaggio	20	1977-1996	AL
William Walker	2	1876-1877	NL
Bobby Wallace	2	1915-1916	AL
Ed Walsh	1	1922	AL
Frank Walsh	3	1961-1963	NL
Mike Walsh	3	1876, 1878, 1880	NL
	4	1882-1883, 1885-1886	AA
Bennie Walton	1	1996	AL
Lon Warneke	7	1949-1955	NL
Al Warner	3	1898-1900	NL
Hal Weafer	5	1943-1947	AL
Tim Welke	13	1985-1997	AL
Harry Wendelstedt	32	1966-1997	NL
Joe West	21	1976, 1978-1997	NL
Frederick Westervelt	2	1911-1912	AL
	1	1915	FL
	1	1922	NL
Lee Weyer	27	1961, 1963-1988	NL
Gideon White	1	1878	NL
Dan Wickham	3	1990-1992	NL
Stump Wiedman	1	1896	NL
Charles Wilbur	1	1879	NL
Kaiser Wilhelm	1	1915	FL
Art Williams	6	1972-1977	NL
Bill Williams	25	1963-1987	NL
Charlie Williams	16	1978, 1983-1997	NL
Frank Wilson	2	1921-1922	AL
	7	1922-1928	NL
John Wilson	1	1887	NL
Mark Winans	1	1994	AL
Mike Winters	8	1990-1997	NL
Sam Wise	2	1889, 1893	NL
George Wood	1	1898	NL
Tom York	1	1886	NL
	1	1886	AA
Ben Young	1	1886	NL
Joseph Young	1	1879	NL
Larry Young	13	1985-1997	AL
Thomas Zacharias	1	1890	NL
Chief Zimmer	1	1904	NL

Strike Umpire Register

Name	Years	Span	League
Andy Anderson	2	1978-1979	NL
Bill Andress	1	1979	NL
Mark Arata	1	1991	AL
John Baird	1	1979	NL
Frank Ballino	2	1991, 1995	NL
Mike Barston	1	1979	NL
Jack Baswell	1	1979	NL
Bob Beck	1	1979	NL
Joe Bendekovits	1	1979	NL
Charlie Berry	1	1970	AL
Ralph Betcher	1	1976	NL
Larry Bialorucko	1	1995	AL
Jon Bible	1	1984	AL
Homer Bishop	1	1979	AL
Fred Blandford	1	1970	NL
Matt Bohn	1	1995	AL
Steve Bonga	1	1979	AL
Terry Bovey	3	1979, 1984, 1995	NL
Mike Briscese	1	1979	AL
Bud Brown	1	1979	AL
Doug Brown	1	1979	AL
Jeff Brown	2	1978-1979	AL
Randy Bruns	1	1991	NL
John Camp	1	1979	AL
Frank Campagna	2	1979, 1984	NL
Bob Campbell	1	1979	AL
Joe Carcao	1	1995	AL
Dick Cavenaugh	2	1979, 1984	NL
Dick Clegg	1	1979	AL
Bob Clement	2	1978-1979	AL
Al Cohen	1	1976	NL
Craig Compton	1	1995	AL
Alan Contant	2	1978-1979	AL
Doug Cossey	3	1978-1979, 1984	AL
Emilien Cote	1	1979	NL
Randy Cristal	1	1984	AL
Jim Cuneo	2	1978-1979	NL
	1	1979	AL
Davidson	1	1995	NL
Dale Davidson	1	1979	AL
Bill Davis	1	1995	NL
Bill Deegan	3	1970, 1984, 1995	AL
Pete DeFlesco	1	1991	AL
Shan Deniston	1	1978	NL
Richard Denny	1	1984	AL
Roger Dierking	1	1979	NL
Roy Dreke	1	1979	AL
Al Dresser	1	1995	AL
Joe Driscoll	1	1978	AL
Robert Duncan	1	1995	AL
Jim Dunne	2	1978-1979	AL
Harold Easley	1	1979	AL
Larry Edwards	1	1978	NL
George Eshelman	1	1979	AL
Jeff Evans	1	1991	AL
Mike Farmer	1	1979	AL
Harry Farnsworth	1	1979	AL
Dick Feaser	1	1979	AL
Jerry Fick	2	1978-1979	NL
Frank Fisher	2	1979, 1984	NL
Mike Fitzpatrick	1	1979	AL
Tom Fleming	1	1979	NL
John Floras	1	1991	NL
Bill Follmer	1	1979	NL
Wade Ford	1	1995	NL
Al Forman	2	1978-1979	AL
Wheeler Fowler	1	1978	NL
Bob Freels	1	1979	NL
Todd Freese	1	1995	AL
Lester Fuchs	2	1978-1979	AL
Larry Gallagher	1	1979	AL
Jim Garman	1	1995	NL
Ed George	1	1979	AL
Bob Giard	1	1978	AL
Tony Gisondi	1	1991	NL
Scott Graham	2	1991, 1995	NL
John Grimsley	1	1970	NL
Scott Grinder	1	1976	NL
Roger Grooms	1	1979	NL
George Grygiel	1	1970	NL
Elmer Guckert	1	1976	NL
Dave Gustafson	1	1978	AL
Merrill Hadry	1	1979	NL
	1	1979	AL
Bill Hafner	1	1979	AL
Ray Hamil	1	1979	NL
Howard Hansen	2	1978-1979	NL
Bob Hantak	1	1979	NL
Vance Harris	1	1995	NL
	1	1995	AL
Randy Harvey	2	1991, 1995	AL
Dick Heitzer	1	1979	AL
Jeff Henrichs	1	1995	AL
Bill Henry	1	1979	NL
	1	1979	AL
Bob Hernandez	1	1995	NL
John Higgins	2	1991, 1995	AL
Mike Holoka	2	1991, 1995	NL
Bob Homolka	1	1995	NL
Mike Huber	1	1995	AL
Rick Humphrey	1	1995	NL
Ron Hutson	1	1979	NL
Bill Ivory	1	1979	AL
Charles Jackson	1	1979	AL
Dick Jackson	1	1995	NL
Johnny James	2	1978-1979	AL
Don January	2	1991, 1995	NL
Ron Jeffers	1	1979	NL
Jeff Jenkins	1	1995	NL
Bob Jones	1	1995	NL
Bob Jones	2	1979, 1984	AL
Jim Jones	1	1979	NL
Harold Jordan	1	1984	AL
Howard Jumper	1	1979	NL
Al Kaplan	1	1995	AL
Joe Kavulich	2	1978-1979	AL
Wayne Keister	2	1978-1979	AL
Gene Kelly	1	1979	AL
Shawn Kimball	1	1991	AL
Ken Kirby	1	1979	AL
Gus Klein	2	1991, 1995	AL
Jim Knauss	1	1991	AL
Jim Lambeth	1	1995	NL
Richard LaPierre	1	1979	AL
Bill Laude	2	1978-1979	AL
Jacques Lauzon	1	1979	NL
Bill Lawson	1	1979	NL
Richie Lazar	2	1978-1979	AL
Jay Levet	1	1979	AL
Jerry Loeber	1	1979	NL
	1	1979	AL
Phil Lospitalier	1	1979	NL
	1	1979	AL
Dale Luker	1	1995	AL
Charlie Lupo	2	1978-1979	NL
	1	1979	AL
Fred Mabbot	1	1979	AL
John Mackin	1	1979	AL
Bob Maher	2	1979, 1984	NL
Terry Mann	1	1995	AL
Jimmy Marino	1	1979	AL
Bruce Martine	1	1991	NL
Danny Mason	1	1995	AL
Boyd Mauer	2	1978-1979	NL
	1	1979	AL
Scott McDougall	1	1991	AL
Jim McNally	1	1979	AL
Dave Melton	1	1978	NL
Clarence Merritt	1	1979	AL
Bud Miller	1	1979	NL
Gale Miller	1	1979	AL
Jack Miller	1	1979	AL
Greg Mills	1	1979	NL
Hank Morgenweck	1	1970	NL
Bob Moyer	1	1979	NL
Joe Mrvos	1	1979	NL
Jim Mulcahy	1	1979	AL
Ed Murray	1	1991	AL
Joe Myers	1	1979	NL
Pete Negri	1	1979	NL
Bob Nelson	3	1979, 1991, 1995	NL
Dick Nelson	1	1979	AL
Ed Norris	2	1978-1979	NL
Carl Nothnagel	1	1984	AL
Les Novack	1	1979	AL
Jim O'Brien	1	1979	AL
Tim O'Connor	2	1978-1979	AL
Tom O'Connor	1	1979	AL
Mike O'Dell	1	1984	AL
Ed Oliger	1	1979	NL
Jim Pacheco	1	1995	NL
Joe Padilla	1	1995	NL
Rich Panas	2	1978-1979	AL
Dallas Parks	2	1991, 1995	AL
Tony Patch	2	1978-1979	NL
	1	1979	AL
Jim Paylor	1	1995	AL
Dave Perez	1	1979	AL
Ray Perez	1	1979	NL
Jerry Phipps	2	1978-1979	AL
Mike Pilato	1	1995	AL
Joe Pomponi	2	1979, 1984	NL
Lester Pratt	1	1979	AL
Al Purduski	1	1979	AL
Jim Rains	2	1978-1979	NL
Larry Randall	2	1978-1979	NL
Bruce Ravan	1	1995	AL
Tom Ravashiere	1	1979	AL
Dennis Riccio	1	1979	NL
Len Riccio	1	1979	NL
	1	1979	AL
Bob Rice	1	1979	AL
Mike Riggers	1	1995	NL
Bill Robinson	2	1978-1979	AL
Gus Rodriguez	1	1995	NL
Bob Roesner	2	1978-1979	AL
Bill Rosenberry	1	1995	NL
Roy Roth	2	1978-1979	NL
	1	1979	AL
Hank Rountree	2	1978-1979	NL
	1	1991	AL
Dick Runchey	6	1979-1984	AL
Sy Ryberg	1	1995	NL
Darold Satchell	1	1970	AL
Joe Sawchuk	2	1978-1979	AL
Fred Schaff	1	1995	NL
Cliff Schaller	2	1978-1979	NL
Jim Schaly	1	1995	AL
Al Scheel	1	1979	AL
Don Schirmer	1	1979	AL
John Schleyer	1	1979	NL
Joe Schratz	1	1979	NL
Bobby Schroeder	2	1978-1979	NL
Don Schulte	1	1979	AL
Hank Schwarz	1	1995	AL
Jim Scott	2	1978-1979	NL
Mick Sharkey	2	1978-1979	NL
Bob Sharp	1	1979	AL
Duane Shaw	1	1979	AL
Jim Shewmake	1	1978	AL
Harold Siroka	1	1979	NL
	1	1979	AL
Don Slattery	1	1979	NL
	1	1979	AL
Dave Slickenmeyer	2	1979, 1984	NL
	3	1979, 1991, 1995	AL
Harry Smail	1	1979	NL
John Spange	1	1991	NL
Fred Spenn	1	1991	AL
Michel Spinelli	1	1979	NL
Bill Sprincz	2	1978-1979	AL
Jack Stansell	1	1979	NL
Johnny Stevens	1	1970	AL
John Stewart	2	1979, 1984	NL
Murray Strey	2	1978-1979	NL
George Sweeney	1	1979	AL
Charles Swenson	1	1979	AL
Frank Sylvester	1	1995	NL
Joe Bob Taylor	1	1979	AL
Tom Telford	1	1979	NL
Russ Terlop	1	1979	NL
Ted Theilander	1	1979	NL
Mike Thompson	2	1978-1979	AL
Hank Tillman	2	1978-1979	NL
	1	1979	AL
Vic Travis	1	1995	AL
Les Treitel	2	1978-1979	NL
Dick Tremblay	1	1979	NL
Harry Trimmer	1	1979	AL
Leo Turner	1	1978	AL
George Ulrich	1	1995	AL
Woody Urchak	2	1978-1979	AL
Jim Uremovich	2	1991, 1995	NL
Dick Urlage	2	1979, 1991	NL
Larry Walding	1	1995	AL
Jim Waller	1	1979	NL
Whaley	1	1995	NL
Dale Williams	2	1978-1979	NL
	1	1979	AL
Bob Willman	2	1991, 1995	NL
Marvin Wright	1	1995	AL
Dave Yeast	1	1995	NL
Larry Zirbel	2	1979, 1984	AL
Dick Zivic	1	1984	AL
Rico Zuccaro	2	1978-1979	AL

Team & League Abbreviations

American League (AL), 1901-

Abbr.	First	Last	Team
Ana	1997		Anaheim
Bal	1901	1902	Baltimore (replaced by New York)
	1954		Baltimore
Bos	1901		Boston
Cal	1965	1996	California (changed to Anaheim)
ChA	1901		Chicago
Cle	1901		Cleveland
Det	1901		Detroit
KCA	1955	1967	Kansas City (transferred to Oakland)
KC	1969		Kansas City
LAA	1961	1964	Los Angeles (transferred to California)
Mil	1901	1901	Milwaukee (replaced by St. Louis)
	1970		Milwaukee
Min	1961		Minnesota
NYA	1903		New York
Oak	1968		Oakland
Phi	1901	1954	Philadelphia (transferred to Kansas City)
Sea	1969	1969	Seattle (transferred to Milwaukee)
Sea	1977		Seattle
STL	1902	1953	St. Louis (transferred to Baltimore)
Tex	1972		Texas
Tor	1977		Toronto
Was	1901	1960	Washington (transferred to Minnesota)
	1961	1971	Washington (transferred to Texas)

National League (NL), 1876-

Abbr.	First	Last	Team
Atl	1966		Atlanta
Bal	1892	1899	Baltimore
Bos	1876	1952	Boston (transferred to Milwaukee)
Bro	1890	1957	Brooklyn (transferred to Los Angeles)
Buf	1879	1885	Buffalo
ChN	1876		Chicago
Cin	1876	1880	Cincinnati
	1890		Cincinnati
Cle	1879	1884	Cleveland
	1889	1899	Cleveland
Col	1993		Colorado
Det	1881	1888	Detroit
Fla	1993		Florida
Har	1876	1877	Hartford (played in Brooklyn in 1877)
Hou	1962		Houston
Ind	1878	1878	Indianapolis
	1887	1889	Indianapolis
KCN	1886	1886	Kansas City
LA	1958		Los Angeles
Lou	1876	1877	Louisville
	1892	1899	Louisville
Mil	1878	1878	Milwaukee
	1953	1965	Milwaukee (transferred to Atlanta)
Mon	1969		Montreal
NYM	1876	1876	New York (played in Brooklyn)
NYG	1883	1957	New York (transferred to San Francisco)
NYN	1962		New York
PhN	1876	1876	Philadelphia
Phi	1883		Philadelphia
Pit	1887		Pittsburgh
Prv	1878	1885	Providence
SD	1969		San Diego
SF	1958		San Francisco
StL	1876	1877	St. Louis
	1885	1886	St. Louis
	1892		St. Louis
Syr	1879	1879	Syracuse
Try	1879	1882	Troy
WaN	1886	1889	Washington
Was	1892	1899	Washington
Wor	1880	1882	Worcester

American Association (AA), 1882-91

Abbr.	First	Last	Team
Bal	1882	1891	Baltimore (transferred to National League)
Bos	1891	1891	Boston
Bro	1884	1890	Brooklyn (transferred to National League)
Cin	1882	1889	Cincinnati (transferred to National League)
	1891	1891	Cincinnati
Cle	1887	1888	Cleveland (transferred to National League)
Col	1883	1884	Columbus
CoC	1889	1891	Columbus
Ind	1884	1884	Indianapolis
KC	1888	1889	Kansas City
Lou	1882	1891	Louisville (transferred to National League)
Mil	1891	1891	Milwaukee
NY	1883	1887	New York
Phi	1882	1891	Philadelphia
Pit	1882	1886	Pittsburgh (transferred to National League)
Ric	1884	1884	Richmond
Roc	1890	1890	Rochester
STL	1882	1891	St. Louis (transferred to National League)
Syr	1890	1890	Syracuse
Tol	1884	1884	Toledo
Tol	1890	1890	Toledo
WaD	1884	1884	Washington
Was	1891	1891	Washington (transferred to National League)

Federal League (FL), 1914-15

Abbr.	First	Last	Team
Bal	1914	1915	Baltimore
Bro	1914	1915	Brooklyn
Buf	1914	1915	Buffalo
Chi	1914	1915	Chicago
Ind	1914	1914	Indianapolis (transferred to Newark)
KC	1914	1915	Kansas City
New	1915	1915	Newark
Pit	1914	1915	Pittsburgh
STL	1914	1915	St. Louis

Players' League (PL), 1890

Abbr.	First	Last	Team
Bos	1890	1890	Boston
Bro	1890	1890	Brooklyn
Buf	1890	1890	Buffalo
Chi	1890	1890	Chicago
Cle	1890	1890	Cleveland
NY	1890	1890	New York
Phi	1890	1890	Philadelphia
Pit	1890	1890	Pittsburgh

Union Association (UA), 1884

Abbr.	First	Last	Team
Alt	1884	1884	Altoona
Bal	1884	1884	Baltimore
Bos	1884	1884	Boston
Chi	1884	1884	Chicago
Cin	1884	1884	Cincinnati
KC	1884	1884	Kansas City
Mil	1884	1884	Milwaukee
Phi	1884	1884	Philadelphia
Pit	1884	1884	Pittsburgh
STL	1884	1884	St. Louis
STP	1884	1884	St. Paul
Was	1884	1884	Washington
Wil	1884	1884	Wilmington

Statistical Abbreviations

The following abbreviations appear throughout this register. Please refer to the Appendix and "The Evolution of Baseball Statistics" for more detailed explanations of terms and formulas.

Hitting Categories

2B	Doubles
3B	Triples
AB	At-Bats
Avg	Batting Average
BB	Bases on Balls
CS	Caught Stealing (1914 AL only; 1915 AL and NL; 1916 AL and NL for players with 20 or more SB; 1920-25, 1951-present NL; 1920-present AL with some data for 1927 missing)
G	Games played
GDP	Grounded into Double Play
H	Hits
HBP	Hit By Pitcher (1887 to present; 1884-91 AA only)
HR	Home Runs
IBB	Intentional Bases on Balls (1955 to present)
LOB	Left On Base
LRC/27	League Runs Created per 27 Outs
OBP	On-Base Percentage
PA	Plate Appearances
Pos	Position
R	Runs
RBI	Runs Batted In
RC	Runs Created
RC/27	Runs Created per 27 Outs
RQ	Relativity Quotient
S	Sacrifice Hits
SB	Stolen Bases (1886 to present)
SB%	Stolen-Base Percentage
SF	Sacrifice Flies (1954 to present)
SH	Sacrifice Hits (Not available for batters 1882-88 AA, 1884 UA, 1897-1909 NL, 1901-12 AL and 1914-15 FL)
SLG	Slugging Percentage
SO	Strikeouts
TB	Total Bases
TBB	Total Bases on Balls

Pitching Categories

BB	Bases on Balls allowed
BB/9	Bases on Balls per 9 innings
BFP	Batters Facing Pitcher
Bk	Balks
CG	Complete Games
ER	Earned Runs allowed
ERA	Earned Run Average
ERC	Component ERA
G	Games pitched
GF	Games Finished
GS	Games Started
H	Hits allowed
H/9	Hits per 9 innings
HB	Hit Batsmen
Hld	Holds
HR	Home Runs allowed
IBB	Intentional Bases on Balls allowed
IP	Innings Pitched
K	Strikeouts
L	Losses
LERA	League ERA
OAvg	Opponents' Batting Average
OHR	Opponent Home Runs
OOBP	Opponents' On-Base Percentage
Op	Save Opportunities
OR	Opponent Runs
Pct	Winning Percentage
Pos	Position
R	Runs allowed
Rel	Relievers used
RQ	Relativity Quotient
SF	Sacrifice Flies allowed
SH	Sacrifice Hits allowed
ShO	Shutouts
SO	Strikeouts
SO/9	Strikeouts per 9 innings
Sv	Saves
TBB	Total Bases on Balls allowed
W	Wins
WP	Wild Pitches

Fielding Categories

A	Assists
DP	Double Plays
E	Errors
FPct	Fielding Percentage
G	Games played
LFPct	League Fielding Percentage at that position
LRng	League Range Factor at that position
PB	Passed Balls
PO	Putouts
Rng	Range Factor
TC	Total Chances

Team Categories

DIF	Days In First place
G	Games
GB	Games Behind
L	Losses
Lg	League
Pct	Winning Percentage
W	Wins

Positional Categories

1B	First Baseman
2B	Second Baseman
3B	Third Baseman
C	Catcher
CF	Center Fielder
DH	Designated Hitter
LF	Left Fielder
LHP	Lefthanded Pitcher
OF	Outfielder
P	Pitcher
PH	Pinch-Hitter
PR	Pinch-Runner
RF	Right Fielder
RHP	Righthander Pitcher
RP	Relief Pitcher
SS	Shortstop

Managerial Categories

+/-	Wins minus Expected Wins
% LHB vs. RHSP	Percentage of Lefthanded Batters against Righthanded Starting Pitchers
% PH Platoon	Percentage of Pinch-Hitters with Platoon Advantage
% RHB vs. LHSP	Percentage of Righthanded Batters against Lefthanded Starting Pitchers
1-Batter App	One-Batter relief Appearances
Att	Attempts
CS%	Caught-Stealing Percentage
EW	Expected Wins
Non-PO CS%	Non-Pitchout Caught-Stealing Percentage
PH	Pinch-Hitters
PH Avg	Pinch-Hit Batting Average
PH HR	Pinch-Hit Home Runs
Pitchout Rn Mvg	Pitchouts with Runners Moving
PR	Pinch-Runners
PR SB-CS	Pinch-Runner Stolen Bases-Caught Stealing
Pt	Manager Points
Sqz	Squeeze plays
Suc %	Success Percentage

Awards Categories

1st Pl	First Place votes
C	Cy Young
M	Most Valuable Player
Pct	Percentage of possible votes received
Pts	Points
RY	Rookie of the Year
Share	Awards Share

Box Score Categories

(BS)	Blown Save
(H)	Hold
(L)	Loss
(S)	Save
(W)	Win

Appendix

This Appendix lists the formulas and definitions for statistical categories listed in the career register, along with notes on what stats are incomplete, what year a particular stat became official, etc. For an overview of the historical evolution of baseball statistics, please see Neil Munro's article, "The Evolution of Baseball Statistics." For more information on Runs Created and Component ERA, please see the articles by Bill James.

Age. Ages are calculated as of July 1 each year, roughly the midpoint of a baseball season.

Assists per 162 Games/Innings. Assists multiplied by 162 and divided by Games (or Innings Pitched).

Award Shares (Share). Introduced by Bill James in his "Historical Baseball Abstract," this statistic measures the support a player received in award voting. His awards share each year is the percentage of possible points; a player receiving half of the points would get a share of .50. His shares for each year can be totaled to see how he fared over the course of his career. For example, Stan Musial is the all-time leader in MVP shares with 6.97

Baserunners per Nine Innings (Baserunners/9). (Hits Allowed + Walks Allowed + Hit Batsmen) * 9/Innings Pitched.

Bases on Balls (BB). In baseball's early years, the number of balls required for a batter to be awarded a base on balls varied until the present-day four was adopted in 1889 (see "The Evolution of Baseball Statistics"). In 1887 walks were considered the same as hits, but Major League Baseball changed the 1887 figures retroactively and this book does not count 1887 walks as hits.

Bases on Balls per Nine Innings (BB/9). Bases on Balls multiplied by nine and divided by Innings Pitched.

Batting Average (Avg). At-Bats divided by Hits.

Batters Facing Pitcher (BFP). The American League compiled opponents' at-bats for the seasons 1908-1973, the NL for 1903-1911. The NL adopted batters facing pitcher in 1912, the AL in 1974; BFP is the sum of opponents' at-bats, walks, hit batters, sacrifice hits, sacrifice flies and the number of times batters reached base on interference or obstruction. BFP can only be compiled for the pre-1974 AL and pre-1912 NL with complete accuracy when all the necessary components are available. We have compiled BFP for those years we had all the component elements; in years where we had all the components except times opponents reached base on interference or obstruction, we compiled BFP working on the assumption that the times reaching base on interference was zero, which is almost always the case. Neil Munro has also compiled BFP for a few famous pitchers such as Kid Nichols and Cy Young through newspaper research.

Catcher's Interference. Batters have been awarded first base for catcher's interference since about 1905, but the number of occurrences has been very rare (see note on Batters Facing Pitcher) and the record-keeping inconsistent until recent years. Our data for this stat is incomplete before the 1950s, but complete since then.

Caught Stealing (CS). The number of times a runner was caught stealing was first recorded in the 1920 season by both the AL and NL, but after 1925, the NL stopped recording CS data until 1951. The AL has kept CS for every season since 1920 except 1927. Caught-stealing data for some earlier years has been compiled by various researchers; we have complete CS data for 1915 NL and FL, 1914 AL only and 1916 for players with 20 or more stolen bases. We also have some incomplete data for the seasons from 1912 to 1919, the 1927 AL and for some Brooklyn Dodger and New York Giant players of the 1940s.

Component ERA (ERC). The steps in producing a pitcher's Component ERA are as follows:

1) Subtract the pitcher's Home Runs Allowed from his Hits Allowed,
2) Multiply that by 1.255,
3) Multiply his Home Runs allowed by four, and
4) Add those two [(1) + (3)] together.
5) Multiply all of that by .89.
6) Add his Walks and Hit Batsmen, and
7) Multiply that by .475, then
8) Add those two [(5) + (7)] together.

That makes:

$$(((H - HR) * 1.255) + (HR * 4)) * .89 + ((BB + HB) * .475)$$

For those pitchers for whom there is intentional walk data, use this formula instead:

$$(((H - HR) * 1.255) + (HR * 4)) * .89 + ((BB + HB - IBB) * .56)$$

9) Call that "PTB" for "Pitcher's Total Base Estimate"
10) Figure his baserunners allowed (Hits + Walks + Hit Batsmen)
11) Multiply that by his PTB
12) Divide by his Batters Facing Pitcher
13) Multiply by 9
14) Divide by Innings Pitched, and
15) Subtract 0.56.

The result will be the pitcher's ERC.

NOTE: If the result after step 14 is less than 2.24, modify step 15 by multiplying by 0.75 rather than subtracting 0.56.

When BFP is not known, use this formula to estimate it: (IP * 2.9) + H + BB + HBP (when known)

Days In First (DIF). The number of days a team spent in first place in a season. In the case of ties, both teams are credited with a day in first. Bob Tiemann was an especially valuable source for this information, especially for teams from the 1800s.

Double Plays (DP). Double plays for fielders have been recorded officially since 1922, but we have filled in the preceding years thanks to the research of Information Concepts, Inc. (ICI) and others.

Earned Run Average (ERA). Earned Runs multiplied by nine divided by Innings Pitched. First compiled officially in 1912 (1913 in the AL), but research by ICI and others has enabled us to compile ERAs for all pitchers in major league history.

Errors (E). Data for errors is complete back to 1876. However, prior to 1889, pitchers were often charged with errors on hit batsmen and wild pitches, and catchers were charged with errors on passed balls.

Expected Wins (EW). Introduced by Bill James in "The Bill James Guide To Baseball Managers," this statistic is used to compare managers. A team's expected winning percentage for a season can be calculated by taking:

1) 50 percent of the team's Winning Percentage from the previous season,
2) 25 percent of a .500 Winning Percentage (based on the premise that all teams have a pronounced tendency to drift toward .500),
3) 12.5 percent of the team's Winning Percentage from two seasons ago, and
4) 12.5 percent of the team's Winning Percentage from three seasons ago.

Multiplying a team's expected winning percentage by the number of games under one manager produces the skipper's expected wins. How well the team fared compared to expectations is related as **+/-**. The all-time leader in +/- is Joe McCarthy with 125.

For expansion teams, figure that all three of their previous seasons had .333 winning percentages. This will produce projected expansion winning percentages of .375, which is remarkably close to how those teams actually performed. However, this will make the expected winning percentage for that league well below .500, so the other teams in the league will have to be adjusted upward for both the expansion year and the subsequent season. Bill doesn't consider this statistic valid for 19th-century managers, so we don't apply it to them in this book.

Fielding Percentage (FPct). (Putouts plus Assists) divided by (Putouts plus Assists plus Errors).

Games Behind (GB). The number of games a team finished out of first place. This is calculated by subtracting the team's wins from the first-place club's total, subtract-

ing the first-place club's losses from the team's total, and then taking the average of those two figures.

Grounded into Double Play (GDP). The number of times a batter grounded into a double play has been kept since 1939 by both leagues; in the seasons 1933-1938, the National League kept **Hit into Double Play (HDP)**, which included line and flyball DPs.

Hit Batsmen (HB)/Hit By Pitch (HBP). An official stat since 1917 in the NL and 1920 in the AL. However, HBP had the modern definition (the batter is awarded first when hit by a pitch and not charged with an at-bat) beginning in 1884 in the American Association and 1887 in the NL; this book contains complete data for all seasons back to 1901 (AL), 1887 (NL) and 1884 (AA). In the 19th century, a batter was awarded a walk, not an HBP, if he was hit by a pitch on what would have been ball four. For the year 1888-1896, HB data is missing where HBP data exists.

Hits per Nine Innings (H/9). Hits multiplied by nine divided by Innings Pitched.

Holds (Hld). A hold is credited any time a relief pitcher enters a game with a save opportunity (see definition), records at least one out and leaves the game never having relinquished the lead. STATS has compiled regular-season hold data since 1989 and has applied this definition to postseason games in this book.

Intentional Walk (IBB). Compiled officially since 1955; some data is available for noteworthy players in seasons prior to then.

Innings Pitched (IP). Available since 1876, with thirds of innings incomplete prior to 1920. This book uses thirds of innings where available and computes ERAs on that basis, even though the major league custom from 1920 through 1981 was to round off the thirds before compiling the ERA.

Isolated Power. Slugging Percentage minus Batting Average.

Manager Points (Pt). This is another statistic developed by Bill James in "The Bill James Guide To Baseball Managers." It recognizes six types of accomplishment in a season:

1) Posting a winning record
2) Winning the division
3) Winning the league
4) Winning the World Series
5) Finishing 20 games over .500
6) Winning 100 games

Bill consideres the first four categories basic levels, which are scored 1, 2, 3 and 4. A manager winning a World Series gets four points, while a manager winning his league but not the World Series gets three. A manager who wins his division but not his league gets two, while one who finishes over .500 without winning the division gets one. A manager gets one point extra if he finishes 20 games above .500, and a second additional point if he reaches 100 victories. Thus a perfect season in which a manager won the World Series as well as 100 regular-season games would count as six points. The all-time leader in manager points is John McGraw with 75.

For the purposes of this book, the postseason competitions between National League teams in the last decade of the 19th century were considered World Series, not league championships. Also a skipper had to manager at least 54 games and finish the season with his team to get credit for the four basic levels.

On-Base Percentage (OBP). (Hits plus Walks plus Hit By Pitch) divided by (At-Bats plus Walks plus Hit By Pitch plus Sacrifice Flies). SF are available only since 1954, so for years prior to 1954, the formula is (H + BB + HBP)/(AB + BB + HBP).

On-Base plus Slugging Percentage (OBP+Slugging). A very quick yet very effective way of measuring a hitter's productivity by combining the two stats which measure his most important skills. The formula is exactly what its name suggests.

Opponents' Batting Average (OAvg). Hits Allowed divided by Opponents' At-Bats. For years in which Opponents' At-Bats were not known, we estimated them using this formula:

Hits Allowed + (Innings Pitched * [(League At-Bats - League Hits)/League Innings Pitched]

Opponents' On-Base Percentage (OOBP). The same formula as On-Base Percentage, using whichever opponents' statistics are available for a given year. If Opponents' At-Bats are unknown, derive an estimate by using the formula detailed in Opponents' Batting Average above.

Park Index. This index compares a park's effect on a statistic, compared to the league's ballparks as a whole. In this book, we calculate the index for runs and home runs. To calculate a run index:

1) Add Runs in home games to Opponent Runs in home games,
2) Divide that by home games.
3) Add Runs in road games to Opponent Runs in road games,
4) Divided that by road games.
5) Divided (2) by (4), and
6) Multiply by 100.

An index for any statistic can be calculated in this manner. A neutral park will have an index of 100. The greater the index is over 100, the more favorable the park is for that statistic. The lower the index is under 100, the less favorable it is.

Passed Balls (PB). Passed balls have been recorded by the NL since the 1880s and by the AL since 1925. The data for years prior to this has been fully compiled through the work of various researchers and is complete.

Range Factor (Rng). (Putouts plus Assists) divided by Games.

Relativity Quotient (RQ). This statistic measures how a hitter or pitcher compares to the players of his era. For hitters, the formula is Runs Created per 27 Outs divided by League Runs Created per 27 Outs. For pitchers, it's Component ERA divided by League ERA. In both cases, the result is multiplied by 100 and a 100 RQ indicates an average player.

Rookie. For the purposes of this book, a player's rookie season is considered the year in which he exceeds 130 at-bats or 50 innings pitched for his career. This is in keeping with the modern rookie guidelines.

Run Batted In (RBI). An official stat since 1920; seasons prior to that were compiled by various historians and ICI.

Runs Created (RC). The Runs Created estimates in this book are based on 24 Technical Runs Created Formulas. Baseball history can be divided into 24 Historical Data Groups (HDGs), the statistics available in each group being a little bit different. There are four relevant statistics which are universally available since 1876: at-bats, hits, walks and total bases. Everything else is missing for at least some seasons. The 24 HDGs, and the formulas which apply to each group, are as follows:

HDG1

| Data Available: | Basic 4 plus SO |
| Applicable Leagues: | National League, 1876-1885 |

Formula:
A Factor	H + W
B Factor	(TB * 1.2) + (W * .26) + ((AB - SO) * .116)
C Factor	AB + W

HDG2

Data Available:	Basic 4 only
Applicable Leagues:	American Association, 1882-1883
	Union Association, 1884

Formula:
A Factor	H + W + (AB * .015)
B Factor	(TB * 1.26) + (W * .26) + (AB * .116)
C Factor	AB + W

HDG3

| Data Available: | Basic 4 plus HBP |
| Applicable Leagues: | American Association, 1884-1885 |

Formula:
A Factor	(H + W + HBP) * 1.184
B Factor	(TB * 1.184) + (W + HBP)
C Factor	AB + W + HBP

HDG4

Data Available:	Basic 4 plus SO, pSB
Applicable Leagues:	National League, 1884-1885

Formula:

A Factor	H + W
B Factor	(TB * 1.21) + (W * .28) + ((AB - SO) * .05) + (SB * .69)
C Factor	AB + W

HDG5

Data Available:	Basic 4 plus HBP, pSB
Applicable Leagues:	American Association, 1886-1888 and 1890

Formula:

A Factor	H + W + HBP
B Factor	TB + ((W+HBP) * .26) + (AB * .158) + (SB * .05)
C Factor	AB + W + HBP

HDG6

Data Available:	Basic 4 plus SO, HBP, pSB
Applicable Leagues:	National League, 1887-1893
	American Association, 1889 and 1891
	Players League, 1890

Formula:

A Factor	H + W + HBP
B Factor	(TB * 1.1)+((W + HBP) * .34) + ((AB - SO) * .04) + (SB * .7)
C Factor	AB + W + HBP

HDG7

Data Available:	Basic 4 plus SO, HBP, pSB, SH
Applicable Leagues:	National League, 1894-1896

Formula:

A Factor	H + W + HBP
B Factor	TB + ((W + HBP) * .26) + ((AB - SO) * .045) + (SB * .65) + (SH * .45)
C Factor	AB + W + HBP + SH

HDG8

Data Available:	Basic 4 plus pSB, HBP, SH
Applicable Leagues:	National League, 1897

Formula:

A Factor	H + W + HBP
B Factor	(TB * 1.09) + (W * .24) + (SB * .5) + (SH * .6)
C Factor	AB + W + HBP + SH

HDG9

Data Available:	Basic 4 plus SB, HB, SH
Applicable Leagues:	National League, 1898-1907
	American League, 1901-1907

Formula:

A Factor	(H + W + HBP) * 1.15
B Factor	(.828 * (TB + SB)) + (.32 * (BB + TB - H))
C Factor	AB + W + HBP + SH

HDG10

Data Available:	Basic 4 plus SB, HBP and SHv1
Applicable Leagues:	National League, 1908-1909
	American League, 1908-1912
	Federal League, 1914-1915

Formula:

A Factor	H + W + HBP
B Factor	TB + ((W + HBP) * .24) + (SB * .55) + (SH * .38)
C Factor	AB + W + HBP + SH

HDG11

Data Available:	Basic 4 plus SB, HBP, SHv1, SO
Applicable Leagues:	National League, 1910-1914 and 1916-1919
	American League, 1913 and 1916-1919

Formula:

A Factor	H + W + HBP
B Factor	TB + ((W + HBP) * .26) + (SB * .05) + (SH * .5) - (.05 * SO)
C Factor	AB + W + HBP + SH

HDG12

Data Available:	Basic 4 plus HBP, SHv1, SO, SB, CS
Applicable Leagues:	Both Leagues, 1915 and 1920-1925
	American League, 1914

Formula:

A Factor	H + W + HBP - CS
B Factor	(TB * .98) + ((W + HBP) * .25) + ((SB + SH) * .46)
C Factor	AB + W + HBP + SH

HDG13

Data Available:	Basic 4 plus HBP, SHv2, SO, SB, CS
Applicable Leagues:	American League, 1926-1930

Formula:

A Factor	H + W + HBP - CS
B Factor	TB + ((W + HBP) * .22) + (SB * .5) + (SH * .36) - (.06 * SO)
C Factor	AB + W + HBP + SH

HDG14

Data Available:	Basic 4 plus HBP, SHv2, SO, SB
Applicable Leagues:	National League, 1926-1930

Formula:

A Factor	H + W + HBP
B Factor	(TB * .97) + ((W + HBP) * .22) + (SB * .05) + (SH * .36) - (.06 * SO)
C Factor	AB + W + HBP + SH

HDG15

Data Available:	Basic 4 plus HBP, SH, SO, SB, CS
Applicable Leagues:	American League, 1931-1938

Formula:

A Factor	H + W + HBP - CS
B Factor	TB + ((W + HBP) * .23) + ((SB + SH) * .5) - (.06 * SO)
C Factor	AB + W + HBP + SH

HDG16

Data Available:	Basic 4 plus HBP, SH, SO, SB
Applicable Leagues:	National League, 1931-1932

Formula:

A Factor	H + W + HBP
B Factor	(TB * .96) + ((W + HBP) * .23) + (SB * .05) + (SH * .5) - (.06 * SO)
C Factor	AB + W + HBP + SH

HDG17

Data Available:	Basic 4 plus HBP, SH, SO, SB, HDP
Applicable Leagues:	National League, 1933-1938

Formula:

A Factor	H + W + HBP - HDP
B Factor	(TB * 1.03) + ((W + HBP) * .26) + (SB * .05) + (SH * .5) - (.03 * SO)
C Factor	AB + W + HBP + SH

HDG18

Data Available:	Basic 4 plus HBP, SHv1, SO, SB, CS, GDP
Applicable Leagues:	American League, 1939

Formula:

A Factor	H + W + HBP - CS - GDP
B Factor	(TB * 1.04) + ((W + HBP) * .26) + (SB * .62) + (SH * .5) - (.03 * SO)
C Factor	AB + W + HBP + SH

HDG19

Data Available:	Basic 4 plus HBP, SHv1, SO, SB, GDP
Applicable Leagues:	National League, 1939

Formula:

A Factor	H + W + HBP - GDP
B Factor	TB + ((W + HBP) * .26) + (SB * .05) + (SH * .5) - (.03 * SO)
C Factor	AB + W + HBP + SH

HDG20

Data Available:	Basic 4 plus HBP, SH, SO, SB, CS, GDP
Applicable Leagues:	American League, 1940-1953 National League, 1951-1953

Formula:

A Factor	H + W + HBP - GDP - CS
B Factor	(TB * 1.025) + ((W + HBP) * .26) + (SB * .62) + (SH * .5) - (.03 * SO)
C Factor	AB + W + HBP + SH

HDG21

Data Available:	Basic 4 plus HBP, SH, SO, SB, GDP
Applicable Leagues:	National League, 1940-1950

Formula:

A Factor	H + W + HBP - GDP
B Factor	(TB * 1.02) + ((W + HBP) * .26) + (SB * .05) + (SH * .5) - (.03 * SO)
C Factor	AB + W + HBP + SH

HDG22

Data Available:	Basic 4 plus HBP, SH, SO, SB, CS, GDP, SF (All current data except IBB and Situational Stats)
Applicable Leagues:	Both Leagues, 1954

Formula:

A Factor	H + W + HBP - GDP - CS
B Factor	(TB * .98) + ((W + HBP) * .26) + (SB * .62) + ((SH + SF) * .5) - (.03 * SO)
C Factor	AB + W + HBP + SH + SF

HDG23

Data Available:	Basic 4 plus HBP, SH, SO, SB, CS, GDP, SF, IBB
Applicable Leagues:	Both Leagues, 1955-1958

Formula:

A Factor	H + W + HBP - GDP - CS
B Factor	TB + ((W + HBP - IBB) * .29) + (SB * .64) + ((SH + SF) * .53) - (.03 * SO)
C Factor	AB + W + HBP + SH + SF

HDG24

Data Available:	Same as HDG23, plus Home Runs with Men on Base and Batting Average with Runners in Scoring Position (All current data except Situational Stats)
Applicable Leagues:	Both Leagues, 1988-1997

Formula:

A Factor	H + W + HBP - GDP - CS
B Factor	TB + ((W + HBP - IBB) * .24) + (SB * .62) + ((SH + SF) * .5) - (.03 * SO)
C Factor	AB + W + HBP + SH + SF

Subsequently adjusted by Home Runs with Men on Base and Batting Average with Runners in Scoring Position

We figure each player's Runs Created as if he was operating in a context of eight other players of average skill.

Each player's Runs Created formula has an A factor, a B factor and a C factor, which are combined, for a team, as (A * B)/C. But for an individual, the formula is:

$$\frac{(A + (2.4 * C)) * (B + (3 * C))}{9 * C} \quad \text{Minus } .9 * C$$

Ken Griffey Jr. in 1997 had 185 hits, 76 walks, 8 hit by pitches, 4 caught stealing and 12 grounded into double plays, which makes an A factor of 253.

He had 393 total bases, 53 *unintentional* walks (76 - 23), 15 stolen bases, no sac hits, 12 sac flies and 121 strike-outs, which creates a B factor of 419.31.

He had 704 plate appearances, which are the C factor.

Thus, by the old formula, he would have 151 runs created—actually, 150.6895313:

253 * 419.31/ 704 = 150.6895313

However, instead of this, we add 2.4 * 704 to his A factor, which makes an A factor of 1942.6.

We add 3 * 704 to his B factor, which makes a B factor of 2531.31.

We multiply his C factor by 9, which makes a C factor of 6336.

Working this through, we have 776.0926146 runs created:

$$1942.6 * 2531.31 / 6336 = 776.0926146$$

From which we subtract .9 multiplied by his C factor, which is 633.6:

$$776.0926146 - 633.6 = 142.4926146$$

Which we round off to 142 Runs Created.

This process is run for all players from all 24 HDGs, regardless of what the A, B and C formulas are for that HDG.

For HDG24, which Griffey is in, we then adjust the Runs Created by his batting average with men in scoring position and his home runs with men on base—*after* we have figured it in this way. Griffey hit 27 homers with men on base, whereas we would have expected him, proportional to his at bats, to have 25.88; that increases his Runs Created by 1.12. He also hit .336 with runners in scoring position; that moves him up by another four and a half runs. When all is said and done, he winds up with 148 Runs Created for the season.

Runs Created per 27 Outs (RC/27). The name of this statistic is actually a misnomer. Bill James has revised the formula to use the actual league average of outs per game, rather than 27 outs. The new formula is:

Runs Created * (3 * League Outs/League Team Games)/Outs Made

The results estimates how many runs per game a team of nine Mickey Mantles would have produced in 1956, to use one example.

Sacrifice Hits (SH) and Sacrifice Flies (SF). Compiled since 1889. At first a batter was given a sacrifice almost any time he advanced a teammate on the basepaths by making an out, and from 1889-1893, the batter was charged with an at-bat on the sacrifice play. Beginning in 1894, the rule evolved as follows:

1894-1907	SH	Batter credited with a sacrifice hit for advancing a runner with a bunt only, and not charged with a time at-bat.
1908-1925	SHv1	Same as 1894-1907 and current sacrifice hit rule, but the batter was also given credit for a sacrifice hit if he hit a fly ball which allowed a baserunner to score.
1926-1930	SHv2	Same as 1908-1925, but the batter was also given a sacrifice hit for advancing ANY baserunner with a fly ball, not just a runner who scored.
1931-1938	SH	Same as 1894-1907 which is the same as the current sacrifice hit rule.
1939	SHv1	Same as 1908-1925.
1940-1953	SH	Same as 1894-1907 and 1931-1938.
1954-	SH	Sacrifice hit rules remained the same, but a new category, sacrifice flies, was added for fly ball outs on which a baserunner scored (no time at-bat charged).

The abbreviations above are used in the Historical Data Groups for the Technical Runs Created Formulas.

Saves (Sv). Saves were unofficial prior to 1969. For years prior to 1973, a save was credited to any relief pitcher who finished a game which his team won, unless he was credited with the win. For 1973-1974, a reliever was credited with a save when he finished a game his team won (unless he was credited with the win) *and* met the following conditions: he needed either to have worked at least the final three innings of a game which his team won or entered the game with the potential tying or winning run on base or at the plate.

From 1975 to date, a relief pitcher has been credited with a save if he met all three of the following condtions:

1) He was the finishing pitcher in a game won by his club.
2) He was not the winning pitcher.
3) He qualified under one of the following conditions:
    a) He entered the game with a lead of no more than three runs and pitched at least one inning.
    b) He entered the game, regardless of the count, with the potential tying run either on base, at bat or on deck.
    c) He pitched effectively, in the opinion of the Official Scorer, for at least three innings.

If he enters a game with the potential to earn a save, then he is credited with a **Save Opportunity (Op).**

Secondary Average. A measure of the extra bases gained by a player. The formula is:

(Total Bases - Hits + Walks + Stolen Bases)/At-Bats

Situational Batting/Pitching Statistics. STATS has been compiling pitch-by-pitch data since 1987. The data from 1984-1986 was compiled by Project Scoresheet. The Project Scoresheet splits do not add up to a player's overall totals in all cases, but the differences are minor. We believe that it was more illuminating to add three years to our situational statistic database rather than ignore it because, for instance, Darryl Strawberry's splits total one more strikeout than his actual total. Where the discrepancies do occur, the splits and the totals almost always are within one unit of each other.

Slugging Percentage. Total Bases divided by At-Bats.

Stolen Base Percentage (SB%). Stolen Bases divided by Stolen Base Attempts.

Stolen Bases (SB). First recorded in 1886. From 1886-1897, a player was also awarded a stolen base if he advanced an extra base on a hit or out by a teammate, as in the case of a runner going from first to third on a single. The 1886-1897 stolen bases are abbreviated as pSB in the Historical Data Groups for the Technical Runs Created Formulas.

Strikeouts (SO, K). The number of strikes needed to record a strikeout, as well as rules on called strikes and foul balls, varied in the early years of the game (see "The Evolution of Baseball Statistics"). Batter strikeouts are not available for the NL 1897-1909, the AL 1901-1912, the AA 1882-1888, the UA 1884 and the FL 1914-1915.

Strikeouts per Nine Innings (SO/9). Strikeouts multiplied by nine and divided by Innings Pitched.

Walks per Plate Appearance (Walks/PA). Walks divided by Plate Appearances.

Wild Pitches (WP). First compiled officially by the NL in 1903 and the AL in 1908. Research by STATS and others has produced complete data for most seasons back to 1881, with the following exceptions: 1882-1891 AA, 1890 PL and 1884 UA. In some of these years, data is available for a few notable pitchers. Prior to 1887 and to some extent for a few years after that, pitchers were charged with an error when they threw a wild pitch.

Wins (W) and Losses (L) for pitchers. Compiled officially since 1920, but data has been completed for all years back to 1876 through the work of ICI and a number of researchers, most notably Frank Williams.

Winning Percentage (Pct.). Wins divided by (Wins plus Losses).

About Jim Callis

Associate Editor Jim Callis joined STATS, Inc. in September 1997. He has served as associate editor of the *STATS Scouting Notebook 1998* and the *STATS Minor League Scouting Notebook*, as well as co-authoring the company's first fantasy baseball magazine, the *STATS Fantasy Insider 1998 Baseball Edition*. He also was an assistant editor on this book's companion volume, the *STATS All-Time Major League Handbook*.

Prior to arriving at STATS, Jim worked at *Baseball America* for nine years, including four as managing editor. While at *Baseball America*, he established himself as the nation's leading authority on amateur and college baseball, winning USA Baseball's 1995 media award for increasing the awareness of college and amateur baseball. He also worked extensively on evaluating prospects and the amateur draft. Jim lives in Winnetka, IL with his wife Ann and sons A.J. and Ryan.

About STATS, Inc.

STATS, Inc. is the nation's leading independent sports information and statistical analysis company, providing detailed sports services for a wide array of commercial clients.

As one of the fastest-growing sports companies—in 1994, we ranked 144th on the "Inc. 500" list of fastest-growing privately held firms—STATS provides the most up-to-the-minute sports information to professional teams, print and broadcast media, software developers and interactive service providers around the country. Some of our major clients are ESPN, the Associated Press, Fox Sports, Electronic Arts, MSNBC, SONY and Topps. Much of the information we provide is available to the public via STATS On-Line. With a computer and a modem, you can follow live action in the four major professional sports, as well as NCAA football and basketball.

STATS Publishing, a division of STATS, Inc., produces 12 annual books, including the *Major League Handbook*, *The Scouting Notebook*, the *Pro Football Handbook*, the *Pro Basketball Handbook* and the *Hockey Handbook*, as well as the *STATS Fantasy Insider* magazines. These publications deliver STATS' expertise to fans, scouts, general managers and media around the country.

In addition, STATS offers the most innovative and fun fantasy sports games and support products around, from *Bill James Fantasy Baseball* and *Bill James Classic Baseball* to *STATS Fantasy Football* and *STATS Fantasy Hoops*. Check out the latest STATS and Bill James fantasy game, *Stock Market Baseball*, and our immensely popular Fantasy Portfolios.

Information technology has grown by leaps and bounds in the last decade, and STATS will continue to be at the forefront as a supplier of the most up-to-date, in-depth sports information available. For those of you on the information superhighway, you can always catch STATS in our area on America Online or at our Internet site.

For more information on our products, or on joining our reporter network, contact us on:

America On-Line — (Keyword: STATS)

Internet — www.stats.com

Toll Free in the USA at 1-800-63-STATS (1-800-637-8287)

Outside the USA at 1-847-676-3383

Or write:

STATS, Inc.
8131 Monticello Ave.
Skokie, IL 60076-3300